The MILLION WORD Crossword Dictionary

Stanley Newman and Daniel Stark

HarperResource
An Imprint of HarperCollins*Publishers*

HarperCollins books may be purchased for educational, business, or sales promotional use. For information please write: Special Markets Department, HarperCollins Publishers Inc., 10 East 53rd Street, New York, NY 10022.

First HarperResource paperpack edition published 2005.

Text design and typography by Daniel Stark

The Library of Congress has cataloged the hardcover as follows:

Newman, Stanley, 1952–
The million word crossword dictionary/Stanley Newman and Daniel Stark—1st ed.
p. cm.
ISBN 0-06-051756-5
1. Crossword puzzles—Glossaries, vocabularies, etc. I. Stark, Daniel. II. Title.

GV1507.C7N45 2005
793.73'2'03—dc22 2003056769

ISBN 0-06-051757-3 (pbk)

05 06 07 08 09 ❖/QW 10 9 8 7 6 5 4 3 2

"*The Million Word Crossword Dictionary*, compiled by my colleagues Stanley Newman and Daniel Stark, has been created to break solving impasses. . . . The result is the largest, most up-to-date, and most useful crossword dictionary available."

—Will Shortz, *New York Times* crossword editor

"[T]he most comprehensive, accurate, and useful book I have ever seen in my 35 years of creating and solving crossword puzzles. . . . This one book will replace them all: dictionaries, atlases, thesauruses, almanacs, crossword puzzle dictionaries, and Internet search engines. . . . [It] is destined to be not just another crossword dictionary, but *the* crossword dictionary."

—Wayne Robert Williams, *Chicago Tribune* crossword editor

"This book is . . . a dozen or more of your favorite references all rolled into one. Besides the most comprehensive list of synonyms I've ever seen, there are famous names, TV shows, movies, drama, music—nary a stone unturned. A must for the crossword aficionado."

—Rich Norris, *Los Angeles Times* crossword editor

"[A] cornucopia of cruciverbal lore from two savvy veterans of the crossword trade. We especially love the generous servings of popular-culture knowledge."

—Emily Cox and Henry Rathvon, *Boston Globe* and *Atlantic Monthly* crossword creators

"[C]rossword puzzles have evolved enormously over the past 40 years, yet most crossword dictionaries have remained mired in the past. . . . Long overdue but well worth the wait, this is the only crossword dictionary you'll ever need."

—Merl Reagle, *San Francisco Chronicle* crossword creator

"Newman and Stark . . . know what should (and shouldn't) be in a 21st-century crossword dictionary. . . . This is the book you want."

—Fred Piscop, *Washington Post Magazine* crossword editor

"You'll find 40 entries here under 'comprehensive.' I'd say that pretty well sums it up."

—Mike Shenk, *Wall Street Journal* crossword editor

Books by Daniel Stark (Author/Editor)

The Crossword Answer Book (with Stanley Newman)
Square One Crossword Dictionary (with Stanley Newman)
Random House Mega Crossword Omnibus
Crosswords Challenge (with Roslyn Stark)
Large-Print Crosswords Challenge (with Roslyn Stark)
The Ultimate Crosswords Omnibus (with Roslyn Stark)
The Ultimate Large-Print Crosswords Omnibus (with Roslyn Stark)

Books by Stanley Newman (Author/Editor)

The Ultimate Crossword Book
Bull's Eye Crosswords
The Crossworder's Own Puzzle Book
The Expert's Book of Crosswords
Random House Masterpiece Crosswords
Random House UltraHard Crosswords
Random House Cryptic Crosswords
Random House Sunday Crosswords
Random House Monster Sunday Crossword Omnibus
Sport Magazine Crosswords
Random House Monster Crossword Omnibus
Random House UltraHard Crossword Omnibus
Random House Vacation Crosswords
Random House Sunday Crossword Omnibus
Random House By the Fireside Crosswords
Random House Golf Crosswords
Random House More Vacation Crosswords
10,000 Answers: The Ultimate Trivia Encyclopedia (with Hal Fittipaldi)
Random House Mammoth Crossword Omnibus
Random House Bedtime Crosswords
Stanley Newman's Coffee Time Word Games
Random House Back to the Beach Crosswords
Stanley Newman's Sunday Crosswords
Stanley Newman's Movie Mania Crosswords
Random House Cabin Fever Crosswords
Stanley Newman's Literary Crosswords
Random House Spring Training Crosswords
Stanley Newman's Sitcom Crosswords
Random House Summer Vacation Crosswords
Stanley Newman's Ultimate Trivia Crosswords
Stanley Newman's Cartoon Crosswords

INTRODUCTION

For almost as long as there have been crossword puzzles, there have been crossword dictionaries. Within just a few months of the fad for crosswords starting in 1924, books appeared to help solvers with their emus, okapis, esnes, and other strange but common denizens of Crosswordland.

No matter how carefully crosswords are constructed, some words do show up in them much more frequently than in everyday speech and writing. In fact, many crosswords contain words that even a well-rounded person may never encounter outside a puzzle context.

If you run into a puzzle that has too many answers you don't know, or if the answers to two unknowable clues cross, you may need help to finish.

The Million Word Crossword Dictionary, compiled by my colleagues Stanley Newman and Daniel Stark, has been created to break solving impasses. Two years in the making, and designed from the ground up, it contains more than 250,000 clues and 1,000,000+ answers, specifically chosen to help with crosswords of the kind found in newspapers, books, and magazines today.

All the classic clues are here: "Celebes ox" (ANOA), "Arrow poison" (INEE), "Sea eagle" (ERN or ERNE), "Eskimo knife" (ULU), and other obscurities from the depths of the unabridged dictionary.

The volume also contains tens of thousands of names from modern culture that frequently crop up in puzzles now: "Singer DiFranco" (ANI), "Golfer Ernie" (ELS), "Sarah McLachlan hit" (ADIA), "Peter Fonda title role" (ULEE), and so on.

Of special help are lists of Oscar winners, Nobelists, Wimbledon champions, popes, makes of autos, dogs in TV shows, and dozens of other fact-based categories useful to puzzlers.

The book even contains more than 75,000 fill-in-the-blank clues like "__ minute" (IN A) and "__ point" (TO THE), based on phrases you know but may not be able to complete on the spot.

The result is the largest, most up-to-date, and most useful crossword dictionary available.

Is it cheating to use a book like this?

Well, say you're stuck in the middle of a puzzle. You can give up . . . or you can get an answer or two, allowing you to proceed and finish the puzzle on your own. In a situation like this, it makes sense to get help. Using a reference book is educational besides.

Whatever "rules" you follow, it's ultimately your puzzle. Solve it any way you like!

Will Shortz
Crossword Editor
The *New York Times*

How to Use
The Million Word Crossword Dictionary

Generally speaking, you'll find the clue you're looking for under the clue's most important word. For example, "Artist's need" would be under "artist." Clues are indexed under multiple words if they have more than one "important" word.

Headwords

"Headwords" are the main boldface clues that introduce each set of answers. Answers that follow headwords are generally listed alphabetically by word length. Sub-headwords, those indented in boldface under a headword, should be read with the headword preceding it. For example, the headword "circle" has the sub-headword "portion," which should be read "circle portion" (answer ARC). In sub-headwords that contain a tilde (~), the tilde takes the place of the headword in the reading. For example: the sub-headword "flattened ~" under "circle" should be read "flattened circle" (answers OVAL and ELLIPSE).

Alphabetization of Headwords

Headwords are alphabetized on a letter-by-letter basis. Solid words precede hyphenated words or words with spaces, and lowercase letters precede capital letters. Headwords followed by a "fill-in-the-blank" follow the same stand-alone headword.

Leading articles (A, The, An) in titles are ignored in alphabetization.

Multiword personal names are listed "last name first."

Fill-in-the-blank clues that start with the fill-in are alphabetized in full. Alphabetization for other fill-in-the-blank clues ends at the fill-in, so "Fort __, IN" precedes "Fort Apache."

To make clues that start with numbers easy to find, they are sorted numerically at the beginning of the initial letter, considering how the number is spoken. So "400" is at the beginning of F, and "2001" is at the beginning of T.

Inflected Forms

Most clues that are nouns are listed in the singular form. Most clues that are verbs are listed in the infinitive form. There are exceptions for inflected answers that don't follow normal American spelling rules.

Clues that involve a country or nationality are listed under the name of the country ("Denmark" or "Mexico") rather than the nationality ("Danish" or "Mexican").

Foreign Words

Clues for common foreign words are listed under both the language and the English meaning. Crossword clues for foreign words often use references to foreign places and names, such as "Here, to Henri," so hundreds of names and places with language cross-references are listed herein. For example, you will find "*see also* French" under "Henri."

Clues by Example

Clues like "Man, for one" (ISLE) and "Sycamore, e.g." (TREE) are crossword staples. So, unlike other crossword dictionaries, you will not only find the "specific" listed under the "generic" (SYCAMORE under "tree") but also the other way around (TREE under "sycamore").

"Starters" and "Enders"

Clues like "Back starter" (HORSE), "Novel ender" (ETTE), and "Type of dance" (BARN) require another word or prefix/suffix to be added to a clue word. When the answer forms a solid word with the clue, it is indexed as a "starter" if added at the beginning, and "ender" if added at the end. If the answer is hyphenated or has more than one word, it is indexed as a fill-in-the-blank. Thus, HORSE will be found under "Back starter." And BARN will be found under "__ dance."

Abbreviations and Acronyms

The many common crossword abbreviations and acronyms in this book can be readily identified as such, either by a period at the end or their rendering in all uppercase letters. When looking up clues that contain abbreviations, be sure to check both the abbreviated word ("dr.") and its unabbreviated form ("doctor").

Answer Words

For the sake of clarity and accuracy, answer words (as well as clue words) are given with the appropriate capitalization, diacritical marks, and spacing for multiple words.

Other Things to Keep in Mind

A word in parentheses at the end of a clue, such as "File (by)" (MARCH), is added to the answer word to give the indicated meaning—"File by" means "march by."

The clue you're looking for will often be found under a related nearby entry, so be sure to look nearby if necessary.

Miscellaneous Conventions

Some longer titles have been truncated, indicated by an ellipsis (...).

A country's monetary units may be current or previous.

The listings of celebrity marriages represent both current and previous relationships.

Lists of a person's works (films, books, songs, etc.) give the best-known works and are generally not exhaustive. Similarly, listings for films include the top-billed cast only, and exclude a director credit if not well-known. These listings are presented alphabetically and omit letter counts.

Word lengths are often omitted from "credit" answers, such as the singer of a song or author of a book.

Within film credits, "AA" after the year indicates the actor or director received an Academy Award for that film.

Within song credits, both the composer and lyricist are called "composer."

Titles can be inferred as such from their capitalization and/or context, and lack the usual italics or quotation marks.

Headwords that are the full name of a person often include as answers the person's occupation and nationality, if not American.

Frequently Asked Questions

Q: Why will this book be so much more useful to me than any other crossword dictionary?

A:
- It is the only crossword dictionary based on the actual clues and answers in today's puzzles.
- It has more than twice as many answers as any other crossword dictionary.
- It is the only crossword dictionary compiled entirely by crossword professionals.
- It will have the answer you're looking for more than twice as often as any other crossword dictionary.

Q: Where did the material in this book come from?

A: The heart of *The Million Word Crossword Dictionary* is hundreds of thousands of clues and answers from actual crosswords. They were selected by the authors one by one, from an archive of more than 2,000,000 clues that have appeared in America's most popular crosswords over the past 10 years. These entries were then supplemented by clues and answers that, based on the authors' extensive experience in the crossword field, are most likely to be needed by puzzlers.

Q: What are these additional clues and answers, and where did they come from?

A: Additional synonym-type clues were gleaned from dozens of current dictionaries and thesauruses. Factual clues were obtained from hundreds of authoritative reference books and Web sites. Every factual subject area that appears in today's crosswords is comprehensively covered. These include academic subjects such as science, literature, and geography; popular culture including films, music, and celebrities; and contemporary life such as slang, politics, and brand names. Thus, *The Million Word Crossword Dictionary* is the only book that fully reflects the diversity of contemporary crosswords. No other reference book of any kind includes all of these: members of the British Commonwealth, songs of George Gershwin, characters in *Aïda*, films of Brad Pitt, colors of Crayola crayons, and the names of Santa's reindeer.

Q: Why are there so few answer words more than 10 letters long?

A: With only occasional exceptions, "synonym" answers of 11 letters or more have been omitted because more than 95 percent of all "synonym" crossword answers are 10 letters or less. This has made possible the inclusion of many more shorter synonyms that are far more likely to be answers to puzzle clues.

Q: Are there really more than 1,000,000 answers in this book?

A: Yes, there are exactly 1,004,429 answers in this book, as counted by our computer. If you'd like to check our addition, each non-boldface entry after a boldface "clue" counts as one answer (multiple-word answers, such as "work out" and "Mr. Ed," count as one answer).

Write to Us!

In our ongoing effort to keep this book the most useful and up-to-date crossword dictionary, we hope to hear from you. Please write us if you have questions, comments, quibbles, or suggestions for new material to include. We would especially appreciate your sending along any "new" clues and/or answers you encounter in your crossword solving, so we can consider including them in future editions. (See below for more info on that.) Writing to us constitutes consent to publish your material without compensation.

Concerning quibbles: Thousands of person-hours have gone into the preparation, proofreading, and fact-checking of the material in this book, but it is possible that a few errors have gotten through. If you think you have found one, please let us know. But, before you write, we ask that you check standard reference sources (such as unabridged dictionaries, almanacs, etc.) to be as sure as you can be that what you have found actually is an error. Since we will need verification in order to make any correction, we ask that you include with your correspondence the source(s) you consulted.

Wanted—Puzzle Patrollers. Reward!

Professional lexicographers, whose job it is to compile "real" dictionaries, depend on contributors to send them examples of how words are used in contemporary writing. For this reason, we are establishing the first-ever such system for crossword dictionaries: "Stan and Dan's Puzzle Patrol."

Please send us any "new" answer words, clues, celebrity names, fill-in-the-blanks, etc. that you encounter in your crossword-solving, so we can consider using them in future editions. (Factual clues only, please. Wordplay clues are beyond the scope of this book.) Each submission should include the puzzle's source (newspaper, magazine, or Web site address) and date, along with your name, street address, and e-mail address (if any).

We will thank our 25 most prolific Puzzle Patrollers (the first senders of 50 or more original entries that we will print in subsequent editions of the book) with a free copy of the next edition of *The Million Word Crossword Dictionary*.

How to Contact Us:

We can be reached in both low-tech and high-tech fashion.

Regular mail: Stanley Newman and Daniel Stark, P.O. Box 69, Massapequa Park, NY 11762. Please enclose a self-addressed, stamped envelope if you'd like a reply.

E-mail: MillionXword@aol.com

Acknowledgments

The suggestions, encouragement, and assistance of many people have made this book possible. The authors would especially like to thank:

- Joseph Vallely, our literary agent, who edited our proposal and skillfully guided it to the right publisher
- Toni Sciarra, our HarperCollins editor, who concurred with our assessment that puzzle fans sorely needed an up-to-date crossword dictionary
- Jon Delfin and Nancy Schuster, who proofread the manuscript
- Adam Cohen and Lisa Marie Marselle, who assisted in the gathering of entries
- Our puzzle colleagues Emily Cox and Henry Rathvon, Rich Norris, Fred Piscop, Merl Reagle, Mike Shenk, and Wayne Robert Williams, for their kind comments, which are excerpted on the back cover
- Will Shortz, for his many helpful suggestions and thoughtful Introduction
- And Roslyn Stark, for her invaluable assistance in many areas over the two years this book has been in preparation

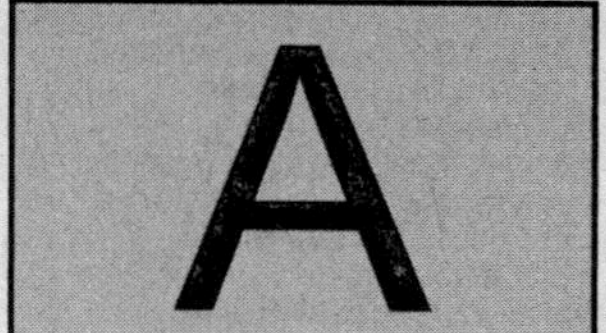

a: 3 per
in code: 4 able, alfa
in French: 3 une
in German: 3 ein 4 eine
in Spanish: 3 una, uno
a ___: 3 bit, quo 5 leg up, tempo, tergo, to zed 6 little, priori, trifle
a ___ a dozen: 4 dime
a ___ and a day: 4 year
a ___'clock scholar: 4 ten o
a ___ cry: 3 far
a ___ dozen: 5 dime a
a ___ for one's money: 3 run
a ___ for sore eyes: 5 sight
a ___ in one's bonnet: 3 bee
a ___ in one's cap: 7 feather
a ___ in one's ear: 4 flea
a ___ in one's own time: 6 legend
a ___ in the bucket: 4 drop
a ___ lease on life: 3 new
a ___ nut to crack: 4 hard 5 tough
a ___ of: 6 couple
a ___ of another color: 5 horse
a ___ of fate: 5 twist
a ___ of one's mind: 5 piece
a ___ of the action: 5 piece
a ___ one's bonnet: 5 bee in
a ___ on one's escutcheon: 4 blot
a ___ order: 4 tall
a ___ pass: 6 pretty
a ___ row to hoe: 5 tough
a ___ situation: 5 no-win
a ___ unto oneself: 3 law
a ___ up: 3 leg
à ___: 3 bas 4 fond, gogo, jour, pied 5 point, terre 6 cheval, gauche, propos 7 bientôt, l'étuvée
A: 4 mark, type 5 grade, vowel, width 6 letter 8 Martinez 9 blood type
in communications: 4 alfa
in phonetic alphabet: 5 Alpha
list: 5 elite
major: 3 key
minor: 3 key
A ___: 3 one, to Z 4 list, star, Team 5 level 6 supply 7 battery, horizon
A ___ apple: 4 as in
A ___ of Honey: 5 Taste
A ___ one: 6 number
A, ___ adorable...: 5 you're
A-___: 4 axes, axis, bomb, line 5 frame
A-___, A-Tasket: 6 Tisket
___ A: 4 Q and, Type 6 Cygnus, Linear, radium 7 Project, vitamin
'A' ___ Alibi: 5 Is for
___-A: 5 Retin
AA: 5 width 7 battery
candidate: 5 toper
like ~ shoes: 3 nar.
part of ~: 4 Anon.
A.A.: 4 Fair 5 Milne
affiliate: 6 Al-Anon
AAA: 5 width 7 battery 8 top-rated 9 top-drawer, topflight
class ~ baseball: 6 minors
giveaway: 3 map
job: 3 tow
opposite: 3 EEE
suggestion: 3 hwy., rte. 5 route 7 highway
Aachen: 4 city, town
locale: 7 Germany
Aage: 4 Bohr
aah partner: 3 ooh
Aaker: 3 Lee
Aalborg: 4 port
locale: 7 Denmark, Jutland
Aaliyah
last name: Haughton
song: At Your Best (1994)
Back & Forth (1994)
The One I Gave My Heart to (1997)
Try Again (2000)
Aalto: 5 Alvar
Aames: 6 Willie
AAM firer: 3 MiG
A and E alternative: 3 BET, CMT, MTV, PAX, TBS, TLC, TNN, TNT, USA 4 ESPN, HGTV 5 C-SPAN, Style 6 Noggin, Tech TV, TV Land 7 Court TV, Ovation, SoapNet 8 Lifetime
___ A and M: 5 Texas
Aar: 5 river
city on the ~: 4 Bern 5 Berne
aardvark: 6 animal, mammal
feature: 5 snout
food: 3 ant
home: 6 Africa
young: 3 pup
aardwolf: 6 mammal
prey: 6 insect
Aare: 5 river
city on the ~: 4 Bern 5 Berne
Aargau: 6 canton
Aaron: 4 Burr, Hank, Klug 5 Tommy 6 Sorkin, Tommie 7 Copland, Neville 8 Caroline, Lipstadt, Spelling
brother of ~: 5 Moses
daughter: 4 Tori
idol: 4 calf
parent of ~: 5 Amram 8 Jochebed
sister of ~: 6 Miriam
son of ~: 3 Eli 5 Abihu, Amram, Nadab 7 Eleazar, Ithamar
wife of ~: 8 Elisheba
Aaron, Hank: 5 Brave 7 slugger 10 outfielder
weapon: 3 bat
Aaron Loves Angela (1975 film)
cast: Irene Cara, Moses Gunn, Kevin Hooks
director: Gordon Parks
Aaron's ___: 3 rod 5 beard
Aaron, Tommy: 6 golfer
AARP
member: 2 sr. 3 snr.
part of ~: 3 Ret. 4 Amer. 5 Assoc. 7 Persons, Retired 8 American
___ A. Arthur: 7 Chester
ab: 6 muscle
neighbor: 3 pec
ab ___: 3 ovo 4 esse 5 extra, intra 6 initio 7 aeterno, origine
Ab: 5 month 6 Hebrew
month after: 4 Elul
AB: 4 type 9 blood type
A.B.: 4 Dick 7 Guthrie
aba: 4 robe 6 fabric 7 garment
Aba: 4 city, town
locale: 7 Nigeria
Aba ___ Honeymoon, The: 4 Daba
ABA
member: 3 att. 4 atty. 6 lawyer
part of ~: 3 Bar 4 Amer., Assn. 8 American
title: 3 esq.
___ Ababa: 5 Addis
abaca: 4 hemp, rope 5 fiber
aback: 8 confused, off-guard, unawares 9 surprised, thrown off 10 by surprise
take ~: 4 faze, stun 5 shake 7 astound, nonplus, stagger, startle 8 astonish, bowl over, surprise 9 discomfit, dumbfound, give a turn 10 disconcert
taken ~: 7 fuddled
abacus: 10 calculator
unit: 4 bead
use an ~: 3 add
user: 5 adder
Abadan: 4 port
locale: 4 Iran
___ a bad example: 3 set
Abadi: 4 font 8 typeface
___ a bad moon rising: 4 I see
abaft: 4 back 6 astern 8 backward 9 to the rear
not ~: 7 forward
___ a ball: 4 have
___ a Ball: 4 I Had
abalone: 5 shell 7 mollusk 8 seashell
eater: 5 otter
product: 5 nacre
shell: 5 ormer
___-à-banc: 4 char
abandon: 4 cede, drop, duck, dump, élan, fail, jilt, kick, quit, sell, shed 5 break, chuck, ditch, forgo, leave, let go, scrap, scrub, sever, verve, waive, yield 6 betray, bow out, cop out, desert, disown, forego, give up, maroon, opt out, reject, resign, strand, vacate 7 bail out, discard, forfeit, forsake, freedom, impulse, let down, let go of, license, pull out, scuttle, ship out 8 abdicate, cut loose, forswear, get rid of, give up on, hand over, jettison, lay aside, lewdness, part with, renounce, run out on, throw out, wildness, withdraw 9 back out of, cast aside, dispose of, disregard, foreswear, frivolity, looseness, lubricity, repudiate, skip out on, surrender, take a walk, throw away, throw over, walk out on 10 chicken out, exuberance, fly the coop, go away from, relinquish, storm out of, wantonness
Abandon ___!: 4 ship
abandoned: 4 left, lone, lorn, lost 5 alone, empty, loose, stray 6 lonely, rakish, vacant, wicked 7 lustful, outcast, run-down, shunned 8 cast away, derelict, deserted, desolate, forsaken, helpless, isolated, passed up, stranded, untended 9 cast aside, corrupted, debauched, discarded, dissolute, forgotten, left alone, neglected, ownerless, shameless, sidelined 10 dissipated, eliminated, friendless, high and dry, licentious, profligate, unattended, unoccupied
abandonment: 6 waiver 8 apostasy 10 abdication
Abandon Ship (1957 film)
cast: Tyrone Power, Mai Zetterling
director: Richard Sale
___ a bang out of: 3 get
___ a barrel: 4 over
à bas: 8 down with
abase: 5 lower, shame 6 demean, humble, insult, reduce 7 corrupt, cut down, deflate, degrade, depress, put down, run down, vitiate 8 belittle, bring low, cast down, dishonor, take down 9 bring down, devaluate, disparage, downgrade, humiliate 10 put to shame
oneself: 5 crawl 6 grovel
abased: 4 vile
abasement: 8 dishonor 10 degeneracy, depression
abaser: 5 bully
abash: 4 faze 5 shame, shock 6 dismay, humble, rattle, ruffle 7 chagrin, fluster, mortify 8 confound 9 discomfit, embarrass, humiliate 10 demoralize, discompose, disconcert, disgruntle, dishearten
abashed: 5 fazed 6 afraid, bugged, shamed 7 anxious, ashamed, crushed, fuddled, humbled, nervous, panicky, rattled 8 confused, hesitant, in a tizzy, sheepish, timorous 9 awestruck, chagrined, diffident, flinching, ill at ease, mortified 10 bewildered, confounded, humiliated, taken aback
abashment: 3 awe 5 shame 6 dismay 7 chagrin, shyness 8 vexation 9 confusion
Abasolo: 4 city, town
locale: 6 Mexico 10 Guanajuato
abat-___: 4 jour
abate: 3 die, ebb 4 cool, ease, fade, fall, flag, lull, sink, slow, wane 5 allay, drain, let up, lower, quash, quell, relax, remit, slack, taper 6 dampen, deaden, ease up, go down, lessen, modify, recede, reduce, slow up, soften, subdue, weaken 7 abolish, cut down, decline, die down, drop off, dwindle, ease off, mollify, relieve, slacken, subside, tail off 8 abrogate, blow over, decrease, diminish, fade away, head away, level off, mitigate, moderate, palliate, peter out, slack off, taper off 9 attenuate, quiet down 10 invalidate, slacken off
abatement: 3 ebb 4 curb, fall 5 check, letup 6 easing, fading, relief, waning 7 anodyne, control, cutback, decline, falloff 8 decrease, discount, markdown, quashing, quelling, stoppage, write-off 9 abolition, allowance, annulment, deduction, lessening, reduction, remission, restraint, softening, tempering, weakening 10 arrestment, diminution, limitation, mitigation, moderation, palliation, prevention, repression, subsidence
___ a bath: 4 draw, take
___ a Battlefield: 6 Love Is
Abaya: 4 lake
locale: 8 Ethiopia
abba-___: 5 dabba
Abba: 4 Eban
ABBA (pop group)
homeland: Sweden
song: Chiquitita (1979)
Dancing Queen (1977)
Fernando (1976)
I Do, I Do, I Do, I Do, I Do (1976)
Knowing Me, Knowing You (1977)
Mamma Mia (1976)
SOS (1975)
Take a Chance on Me (1978)
Waterloo (1974)
The Winner Takes It All (1980)
Abbado, Claudio: 9 conductor
abbé: 4 monk 5 friar, padre, prior, title 6 cleric, curate, divine, pastor, priest 7 Prévost 8 celibate, minister, monastic 9 clergyman 10 monastical
Abbe: 4 Lane 9 Cleveland
abbess: 3 nun 4 rank 5 title 7 Héloïse 9 religious
Abbess, The author: Athol Fugard
abbey: 6 church, friary, priory, temple 7 convent, nunnery 8 cloister, ministry 9 monastery 10 tabernacle
dweller: 3 nun 4 monk 5 friar, prior
Abbey: 5 Edwin 6 Edward
Abbey ___: 4 Road 7 Theatre
___ Abbey: 7 Tintern
Abbey, Edward: 11 illustrator
Abbey Road Studios owner: 3 EMI
Abbie: 7 Hoffman
Abbie an' ___: 5 Slats
abbot: 3 Dom 4 abbé, monk, rank 5 title 6 cleric 8 minister 9 churchman, religious
headwear: 5 miter
subordinate: 5 prior
Abbotsford: 4 city, town
locale: 6 Canada
Abbott: 3 Bud 6 George, Philip 7 Gregory 8 Berenice
Abbott and Costello: 3 duo 4 pair, team
Abbott and Costello Meet Frankenstein (1948 film)
cast: Bud Abbott, Lon Chaney Jr., Lou Costello, Bela Lugosi
director: Charles Barton

Abbott, Berenice: 12 photographer
Abbott, George: 8 director
film: Damn Yankees (1958)
The Pajama Game (1957)
Too Many Girls (1940)
abbreviate: 4 clip, pare, trim 5 prune, slash 6 cut off, cut out, digest, narrow, recede, reduce, shrink 7 abridge, compact, curtail, cut back, cut down, shorten 8 abstract, boil down, compress, condense, contract, diminish, minimize, restrict, truncate 9 capsulize, stop short, summarize, telescope
abbreviated: 3 cut 5 short 7 partial, sketchy 9 condensed 10 compressed, unfinished
version: 4 mini
abbreviation: 3 cut 6 digest, sketch 7 outline, summary 8 abstract, clipping, synopsis
Abby: 6 Dalton 8 Van Buren
sister: 3 Ann
__ Abby: 4 Dear
ABC: 3 net 7 network
a.m. show: 3 GMA
follower: 3 DEF 4 DEFG 5 DEFGH
HQ: 3 NYC
part of ~: 4 Amer.
rival of ~: 3 CBS, Fox, NBC, UPN 5 The WB
telephone ~: 3 two
watchdog: 3 FCC
__ ABC: 6 easy as
ABC (1970 song) artist: Jackson 5
ABC of Relativity, The author: Bertrand Russell
ABCs: 6 basics, letter 8 alphabet 9 rudiments 10 essentials, foundation
ABC's __ World of Sports: 4 Wide
__ Abdel Nasser: 5 Gamal
abdicate: 4 cede, drop, quit 5 bag it, demit, forgo, leave, yield 6 abjure, depart, forego, give up, opt out, resign, retire, secede, vacate 7 abandon, bail out 8 abnegate, renounce, step down, withdraw 9 go to sleep, quitclaim, surrender 10 relinquish
abdication: 6 ceding, waiver 7 cession 8 retiring, transfer, yielding 9 demission, deserting, desertion, disowning, rejection, resigning, surrender 10 abnegation, renouncing, retirement, transferal
abdomen: 3 gut, pot 5 belly, tummy 6 middle, paunch 7 midriff, stomach 10 midsection
combining form: 4 celi- 5 celio-, coeli-, ventr- 6 coelio-, ventri-, ventro-
crustacean ~: 5 pleon
muscle: 6 rectus
muscles: 5 recti
of the ~: 6 celiac 7 coeliac
terminus: 5 groin
abdominal exercise: 5 sit-up
abdominous: 3 fat 5 obese, plump, pudgy, round, tubby 6 chubby, portly, rotund 7 paunchy 9 corpulent 10 big-bellied, overweight, potbellied, well-padded
abduct: 4 take 5 seize, steal 6 collar, kidnap, ravish, snatch 7 capture 8 carry off, grab away, shanghai, take away 9 carry away 10 run off with, spirit away
combining form: 3 -nap
abduction: 7 seizure
abductor: 9 kidnapper
Abdul Abulbul __: 4 Amir
Abdul-Jabbar, Kareem
alma mater: 4 UCLA
milieu: 5 court
org.: 3 NBA
sport: 10 basketball
Abdul, Paula
song: Blowing Kisses in the Wind (1991)
Cold Hearted (1989)
Forever Your Girl (1989)
Opposites Attract (1990)
The Promise of a New Day (1991)
Rush, Rush (1991)
Straight Up (1988)
The Way That You Love Me (1989)
spouse: Emilio Estevez
Abe: 4 Kobo 5 Beame 6 Attell, Fortas, Pollin, Vigoda 7 Burrows, Lincoln, Simpson 10 Saperstein
boy: 3 Tad
like ~: 6 honest
Mary, to ~: 4 wife
parent: 3 Tom 5 Nancy
wife: 4 Mary
__ a bead on: 3 get 4 draw
abeam: 6 across
Abebe: 6 Bikila
abecedarian: 4 tiro, tyro 6 novice 7 learner 8 beginner, neophyte 10 tenderfoot
phrase: 4 as in
abecedary: 7 primary 10 elementary
__ à Becket: 6 Thomas
abed: 5 not up 6 laid up 7 retired 8 sleeping, snoozing, tucked in 9 in the sack, sacked out 10 sawing logs, slumbering
maybe: 3 ill
not ~: 5 astir
__-abed: 3 lie
__-A-Bed: 4 Hide
__ a bee: 6 busy as
a bee in one's __: 6 bonnet
__ a beet: 5 red as
Abe Family, The author: Mori Ögai
Abe Kobo: 6 writer 8 Japanese 10 playwright
Abel: 3 Bob 4 Alan, Elie 5 Gance 6 Jeanne, Rudolf, Tasman, Walter 7 Ferrara 8 Magwitch
brother of ~: 4 Cain, Seth
love: 4 Rima
nephew of ~: 4 Enos
parent of: 3 Eve 4 Adam
Abelard: 5 Peter
Abel composer: 4 Arne
abele: 4 tree 6 poplar
abelia: 5 shrub
relative: 5 elder 8 snowball
Abe Lincoln in Illinois: 4 film, play
author: Robert E. Sherwood
cast: Ruth Gordon, Gene Lockhart, Raymond Massey
character: 3 Ann 4 Gale, Seth
studio: 3 RKO
__ a bell: 4 ring
Abel, Rudolf: 3 spy
Abenaki: 6 Indian 7 Amerind
Aberdeen: 4 city, port, town
locale: 8 Maryland, Scotland
river: 3 Dee
Aberdeen __: 5 Angus 7 terrier
Aberdeen __ Ground: 7 Proving
aberrance: 5 quirk
aberrant: 3 odd 4 eery 5 eerie, flaky, weird 6 atypic, flakey, freaky, morbid, quirky, way-out 7 bizarre, deviant, offbase, offbeat, strange, unalike, unusual 8 abnormal, atypical, freakish, peculiar, uncommon 9 anomalous, different, divergent, eccentric, fantastic, grotesque, irregular, monstrous, not normal, out of line, unnatural 10 nonuniform, unorthodox
aberrate: 7 deviate
aberration: 3 pip 4 blip, warp 5 freak, lapse, mania, quirk 6 oddity 7 anomaly, mistake, veering 8 delusion 9 deformity, departure, deviation, diversion, variation, wandering, weirdness 10 difference, distortion, divergence
ab esse: 6 absent
abet: 3 aid 4 back, help 5 egg on 6 assist, excite, foment, foster, incite, lead on, spur on, urge on 7 advance, collude, forward, support 8 embolden, imbolden 9 encourage, instigate, lend a hand, stimulate, subsidize
__ a bet: 5 place
__ a bet!: 5 Not on
abetment: 3 aid 4 help 6 assist 10 assistance
abettor: 4 ally 5 agent 6 helper 8 henchman 9 accessory, assistant 10 accomplice
abeyance: 4 lull 5 pause 6 recess 7 latency, waiting 8 deferral, dormancy, reprieve, stoppage 9 remission 10 inactivity, quiescence, suspension
be in ~: 4 pend 5 await
hold in ~: 8 postpone
in ~: 5 on ice 6 latent 10 unrealized
abeyant: 6 latent, put off, tabled 7 dormant, resting, shelved, waiting 8 deferred, inactive, set aside 9 postponed, quiescent, suspended
abhor: 4 hate, loth 5 loath, scorn 6 detest, loathe 7 deplore, despise, disdain, dislike, hold low 8 execrate 9 abominate, can't stand 10 look down on, recoil from
old-style: 5 spise
abhorred: 7 unloved
abhorrence: 4 hate 5 odium 6 enmity, hatred, horror, malice 7 disgust 8 aversion, distaste, loathing 9 antipathy, hostility, repulsion, revulsion 10 execration, ill feeling, repellence
abhorrent: 4 base, foul, grim, poor 5 awful, lousy, nasty, woful 6 crumby, crummy, dismal, horrid, odious, rotten, woeful 7 accurst, baleful, baneful, beastly, doleful, ghastly, hateful, heinous, satanic, vicious 8 accursed, dreadful, God-awful, grievous, horrible, shameful, stinking, terrible, wretched 9 appalling, atrocious, defective, execrable, frightful, insidious, loathsome, miserable, offensive, repellant, repellent, repugnant, repulsive, revolting, satanical 10 abominable, despicable, detestable, disastrous, forbidding, horrendous, petrifying
Abib, month before: 4 Adar
abide: 2 go 4 bear, last, live, lump, stay, take, wait 5 brook, dwell, exist, lodge, sit by, stand, stick, tarry 6 accept, endure, hang in, hold on, inhere, keep on, linger, remain, reside, settle, suffer, take it 7 consent, persist, sojourn, stomach, sustain, swallow, undergo 8 continue, kill time, stand for, tolerate 9 persevere, put up with, withstand 10 hang around, stay a while, wait around
apt rhyme for ~: 6 reside
by: 4 heed, mind, obey 5 bow to 6 accept, adhere, bend to, follow, fulfil, hold to, redeem 7 agree to, conform, consent, defer to, fulfill, observe, respect, stand by, stick to 8 adhere to, carry out, listen to, submit to 9 conform to, discharge, persist in, stick with 10 comply with, keep in step, toe the line
abiding: 4 fast, firm 5 fixed 6 stable, steady 7 chronic, durable, endless, eternal, lasting, undying 8 constant, enduring, timeless, unending 9 ceaseless, chronical, perennial, permanent, perpetual, steadfast, unabating, unceasing 10 changeless, continuing, habituated, inveterate, persistent, unchanging, unwavering
__-abiding: 3 law
Abidjan: 4 city, port, town 7 capital
capital east of ~: 5 Accra, Akkra
locale: 10 Ivory Coast
à bientôt: 8 au revoir
Abie's Irish Rose star: 3 Dru
abigail: 4 maid
Abigail: 5 Adams 8 Fillmore, Van Buren
sib: 3 Ann
Abigail Adams, __ Smith: 3 née
__ a Big Boy Now: 5 You're
Abiko: 4 city, town
locale: 5 Japan
Abilene: 4 city, town
locale: 5 Texas 6 Kansas
Abilene Town (1946 film)
cast: Edgar Buchanan, Ann Dvorak, Randolph Scott
ability: 4 bent, gift, head 5 craft, flair, knack, might, power, reach, savvy, sense, skill, touch 6 talent 7 command, faculty, finesse, freedom, know-how, mastery, prowess, stature 8 aptitude, artistry, capacity, deftness, facility, hang of it, strength 9 adeptness, dexterity, endowment, expertise, handiness, ingenuity, intellect, knowledge, potential 10 adroitness, competence, efficiency, expertness, green thumb, right stuff
has no ~ to: 6 cannot
having the ~ for: 9 capable of
natural ~: 5 knack 6 genius 8 instinct 9 endowment
__ a bill of goods: 4 sell
__-A-Billy: 4 Rock
__ a bird,...: 3 It's
__ a bite: 4 grab
abject: 3 low 4 base 5 sorry 6 broody, humble, menial, sordid 7 fawning, forlorn, hangdog, ignoble, outcast, pitiful, servile 8 degraded, dejected, hopeless, penitent, pitiable, wretched 9 groveling, miserable, prostrate, worthless 10 deplorable, despicable, humiliated, submissive
abjectly, act: 6 cringe
abjectness: 10 depression, woefulness
abjuration: 8 apostasy
abjure: 3 ban, bar, nix 4 veto 5 debar, forgo 6 disown, eschew, forbid, forego, recall, recant, reject 7 abstain, disavow, forsake, retract 8 abdicate, disallow, disclaim, forswear, keep from, prohibit, renounce, swear off, withdraw 9 foreswear, proscribe, repudiate 10 contravene
ablactate: 4 wean
__ a blank: 4 draw
__ a blanket: 5 pig in
ablare: 4 loud 10 trumpeting
ablate: 4 melt 5 erode 8 vaporize 9 dissipate
ablative: 4 case
ablaze: 3 lit 5 afire, aglow, angry, fiery, light, shiny 6 aflame, alight, bright, flashy, fuming, heated, on fire, raging 7 aroused, beaming, blazing, burning, fervent, flaming, flaring, fulgent, furious, glowing, ignited, lambent, lighted, radiant, shining, zealous 8 dazzling, flashing, frenzied, gleaming, incensed, in flames, luminous, lustrous, vehement 9 brilliant, refulgent, sparkling
be ~: 4 burn
set ~: 3 lit 5 light 6 ignite
able: 3 apt, fit 4 deft, good, keen 5 adept, can-do, handy, hardy, quick, savvy, sharp, smart 6 adroit, artful, clever, expert, facile, gifted, strong, up to it 7 knowing, skilled, trained 8 adequate,

dextrous, equipped, powerful, prepared, skillful **9** competent, dexterous, effective, efficient, empowered, masterful, permitted, practiced, promising, qualified, versatile **10** proficient
become ~: **5** learn
be ~ to: **3** can **6** afford
facetiously: **3** ept
follower: **5** baker
isn't ~ to: **4** can't
is ~ to: **3** can
able __: **6** seaman
able-__ seaman: **6** bodied
Able __ ere...: **4** was I
Able, Baker, __: **7** Charlie
able-bodied: **3** fit **4** hale, iron, well, wiry **5** beefy, burly, hardy, hefty, hunky, husky, lusty, stout, tough, whole **6** brawny, hearty, mighty, potent, robust, rugged, sinewy, steely, stocky, strong, sturdy, virile **7** doughty, healthy **8** athletic, forceful, indurate, muscular, powerful, puissant, stalwart, vigorous **9** Atlantean, Herculean, strapping, well-built **10** red-blooded
Able to __ tall buildings...: **4** leap
Able was I __...: **3** ere **4** ere I
__ a blind eye: **4** turn
__-a-block: **5** chock
abloom: **8** in flower **9** flowering **10** blossoming
ablush: **3** red **4** pink **8** reddened
ablution: **4** bath, wash **6** shower **7** washing **8** lavation **9** cleansing, showering
Islamic ~: **4** wudu
ably: **4** well **6** deftly **7** capably, rightly **8** adroitly, laudably, worthily **10** skillfully
ABM: **6** weapon
part of ~: **4** Anti **7** Missile **9** Ballistic
user: **4** USAF
Abnaki: **6** Indian **7** Amerind
abnegate: **6** disown, recant, refute **7** abstain **8** abdicate, disclaim, keep from, renounce **10** relinquish
abnegating: **5** sober
abnegation: **6** denial **7** refusal **8** eschewal **9** rejection, sacrifice, surrender **10** abdication, abstinence, self-denial, temperance
Abner: **5** Yokum **9** Doubleday
creator: **4** Capp **6** Al Capp
father of ~: **3** Ner
friend: **3** Lum
__ Abner: **3** Li'l
abnormal: **3** odd **5** gross, queer, weird **6** atypic, morbid, off-key, screwy, way-out **7** bizarre, curious, deviant, oddball, off-base, strange, unusual **8** aberrant, atypical, freakish, isolated, peculiar, uncommon **9** anomalous, deviating, divergent, eccentric, fantastic, heterodox, irregular, malformed, out of line, shapeless, unnatural **10** unexpected, unorthodox
combining form: **4** anom- **5** anomo-
prefix: **3** mal- **4** para-
abnormality: **4** flaw **6** oddity **7** anomaly **8** deviance **9** variation
abnormally: **5** oddly **10** especially
aboard: **2** on **6** loaded, on base, on deck **7** en route, on a ship **8** embarked **9** consigned, in transit, traveling
come ~: **4** join **6** embark, jump on **9** affiliate
go ~: **6** embark **7** emplane, entrain, set sail, ship out **9** leave port
put ~: **4** lade, load
ship: **4** asea **5** at sea
__ aboard!: **3** All
__ a board: **6** flat as
abode: **3** pad **4** base, co-op, digs, farm, flat, home, iglu, nest, seat, tipi **5** cabin, condo, house, igloo, lodge, manor, place, shack, tepee **6** teepee **7** address, château, domicil, habitat, housing, lodging, mansion **8** domicile, dwelling, fireside, log cabin, quarters **9** apartment, motor home, residence
animal ~: **3** den **4** lair
bird ~: **4** aery, eyry, nest **5** aerie, eyrie
fowl ~: **4** coop **5** roost
humble ~: **3** hut **5** hovel, shack **6** shanty
Indian ~: **4** tent, tipi **5** hogan, tepee **6** teepee, wigwam
see also home, house
aboil: **7** cooking **8** seething, steaming **9** simmering
abolish: **3** end, nix, rid, zap **4** kill, undo, void **5** abate, annul, erase, quash, scrub **6** cancel, finish, negate, repeal, revoke, vacate **7** call off, destroy, expunge, inhibit, nullify, rescind, root out, squelch, subvert, vitiate, wipe out **8** abrogate, dissolve, overturn, prohibit, set aside, stamp out, suppress **9** eradicate, extirpate, liquidate, overthrow, repudiate, supersede, terminate **10** annihilate, do away with, extinguish, invalidate, obliterate, put an end to
abolition: **9** abatement, annulment, overthrow **10** abrogation, rescinding, rescission, revocation, subversion, withdrawal
abolla: **5** cloak
aboma: **5** snake **6** animal **7** reptile
relative: **3** asp, boa **5** adder, cobra, krait, mamba, racer, viper **6** dhaman, python, taipan **7** markhor, rattler **8** anaconda, moccasin, ringhals **9** boomslang, coachwhip **10** bushmaster, copperhead, sidewinder
A-bomb scientist: **4** Urey **5** Fermi
abominable: **3** bad **4** base, foul, grim, poor, vile **5** awful, curst, gross, hairy, lousy, seamy, woful **6** crumby, crummy, cursed, dismal, grisly, horrid, odious, rotten, wicked, woeful **7** accurst, baleful, baneful, beastly, doleful, ghastly, hateful, heinous, hellish, hideous, satanic, squalid **8** accursed, dreadful, God-awful, grievous, gruesome, horrible, inferior, shameful, shocking, stinking, terrible, wretched **9** abhorrent, appalling, atrocious, defective, execrable, frightful, insidious, invidious, loathsome, miserable, nefarious, obnoxious, offensive, repellant, repellent, repugnant, repulsive, revolting, satanical **10** despicable, detestable, disastrous, disgusting, horrendous, petrifying
snowman: **4** yeti
Abominable __: **7** Snowman
Abominable Dr. Phibes, The (1971 film)
cast: Joseph Cotten, Vincent Price
abominate: **4** hate **5** abhor **6** detest, loathe **7** despise, disgust, dislike, hold low **8** execrate **10** recoil from
abomination: **4** hate **5** crime, odium, wrong **6** hatred **7** disgust, offense **8** enormity, iniquity **9** revulsion
__ a bone: **5** dry as
__ a bone to pick: **4** have
__ a book: **4** like **5** crack
__-a-Boom: **5** Chick
aboriginal: **3** old **5** early, first **6** native **7** ancient, endemic, primary **8** primeval **9** endemical, primaeval, primitive, unevolved **10** indigenous, primordial
aborigine: **6** native **7** bushman **8** indigene, original **10** inhabitant
Antilles: **5** Carib
Australia: **4** Mara
call: **5** cooee
hatchet: **4** mogo
India: **4** Gond
Japan: **4** Ainu
New Zealand: **5** Maori
Panama: **4** Cuna
Sri Lanka: **5** Vedda **6** Veddah
weapon: **5** spear, waddy **6** waddie
abort: **3** end **5** cease, check, scrub **6** arrest, cancel **8** cut short **9** terminate **10** contravene
abortive: **4** vain **7** useless **9** premature
Abou Ben Adhem: **4** poem
author: Leigh Hunt
abound: **4** flow, teem **5** crawl, crowd, swarm, swell **6** infest, rich in, thrive **7** prevail, run riot **8** flourish, overflow **9** luxuriate
abounding: **4** full, rich, rife **5** alive, flush, leafy, thick **6** filled, heaped, plenty **7** copious, profuse, replete **8** infested, prodigal, prolific **9** plentiful
about: **3** say **4** as to, back, in re **5** anent, circa **6** active, almost, around, moving, nearby, nearly, toward **7** apropos, close to, roughly, towards **8** backward, in motion, relative, stirring, well-nigh **9** apropos of, as regards, generally, regarding, somewhere **10** as concerns, concerning, give or take, relating to
prefix: **4** peri-
starter: **3** gad, lay, run **4** here, turn, walk **5** knock, round, roust, there
suffix: **3** -ish
about-__: **4** face
__ about: **3** gad, get, put, see, set **4** cast, come, just, kick, muck, nose, on or **5** knock, noise, up and
About __: **4** a Boy, Adam **5** a Girl
About __ Leslie: **3** Mrs.
About __ Night ...: **4** Last
About a Boy (2002 film)
cast: Toni Colette, Hugh Grant, Rachel Weisz
About Adam (2001 film)
cast: Kate Hudson, Frances O'Connor, Stuart Townsend
About a Girl (1994 song) artist: Nirvana
About a Quarter to Nine composer: **5** Dubin **6** Warren
__ About Bob?: **4** What
__ About Eve: **3** All
about-face: **4** turn **5** shift, U-turn **6** change, switch **7** reverse, setback **8** apostasy, flip-flop, reversal, variance **9** inversion, one-eighty, vice versa **10** alteration, conversion
do an ~: **9** back-pedal
About Last Night ... (1986 film)
cast: James Belushi, Rob Lowe, Demi Moore, Elizabeth Perkins
director: Edward Zwick
About Mrs. Leslie (1954 film)
cast: Shirley Booth, Robert Ryan
director: Daniel Mann
abouts starter: **5** there
__ about that: **3** how
__ about the bush: **4** beat
__ about the gills: **5** green
__ about time!: **3** It's
__ about town: **3** man **5** woman
__ About You: **3** How, Mad
above: **3** o'er **4** atop, high, over **5** aloft, on top, upper **6** beyond, on high, upward **7** aloft of, north of, on top of, skyward, topping **8** hovering, in heaven, more than, overhead, superior, upraised, upstairs **9** aforesaid, exceeding, foregoing, upwards of **10** better than, heavenward, larger than, superior to, surpassing, up in the sky
ender: **5** board **6** ground
in German: **4** über
prefix: **3** epi-, sur- **5** hyper-, super-, supra-
above __: **3** all **5** it all, water **6** stairs
above __ beyond: **3** and
__ above: **4** a cut
Above and Beyond (1952 film)
cast: Eleanor Parker, Robert Taylor, James Whitmore
aboveboard: **4** fair, just, open, true **5** frank, legal, legit, licit, moral, overt, right **6** candid, honest, lawful, openly, square **7** sincere, up-front, upright **8** straight, truthful **9** guileless, high-toned, sincerely, veracious **10** believable, forthright, from the hip, virtuously
above it __: **3** all
above-mentioned: **5** prior
Above Suspicion (1943 film)
cast: Joan Crawford, Fred MacMurray, Conrad Veidt
director: Richard Thorpe
above the __: **3** law **4** line
Above the Law (1988 film)
cast: Pam Grier, Steven Seagal, Sharon Stone
ab ovo: **3** new
__ a bow: **4** take
__ a boy!: **3** It's
__-a-brac: **4** bric
abracadabra: **3** gas, hex, rot **4** blah, bosh, bull, bunk, guff, jazz, jive, pooh, tosh **5** bilge, fudge, hokum, hooey, magic, prate, spell, stuff, trash, tripe **6** bunkum, bushwa, drivel, footle, gabble, gammon, gibber, havers, hot air, humbug, jabber, jargon, kibosh, piffle **7** baloney, blarney, blather, blether, boloney, bushwah, eyewash, flannel, flubdub, fustian, garbage, hogwash, inanity, rubbish, sorcery, twaddle **8** buncombe, claptrap, falderal, falderol, flimflam, flummery, folderal, folderol, nonsense, slipslop, tommyrot, trumpery **9** banana oil, gibberish, kidstakes, moonshine, poppycock, rigmarole **10** applesauce, balderdash, bilge water, codswallop, double-talk, flapdoodle, galimatias, Jabberwock, mumbo jumbo, rigamarole, taradiddle
Abracadabra (1982 song) artist: Steve Miller Band
abrade: **3** bug, irk, rub **4** file, gall, rasp, sand, skin, wear **5** annoy, chafe, erode, grate, graze, grind, scour, scrub, scuff **6** scrape **7** flatten, roughen, rub down, wear off **8** irritate, wear away, wear down **9** excoriate, sandpaper, scrape off, stone-wash
abraded: **3** raw
abrading: **7** erosive
Abraham: **6** Cowley **7** Lincoln
brother of ~: **5** Haran, Nahor
father of ~: **5** Terah
grandfather of ~: **5** Nahor
grandson of ~: **4** Esau **5** Jacob
half-sister of ~: **5** Sarah
nephew of ~: **3** Lot **4** Hazo **5** Gaham, Tebah **6** Kemuel, Maacah, Tahash **7** Pildash
partner: **6** Straus
son of ~: **5** Isaac, Medan, Shuah **6** Midian, Zimrah **7** Ishmael
wife of ~: **5** Sarah, Sarai **7** Keturah
Abraham, F. Murray: **5** actor
film: Amadeus (1984, AA)
Finding Forrester (2000)
Last Action Hero (1993)
Mighty Aphrodite (1995)
The Name of the Rose (1986)
Abraham, Martin and John (1968 song) artist: Dion

Abrahams: 3 Jim 5 Peter
Abraham's ___: 5 bosom
Abrahams, Jim: 8 director
film: Airplane! (1980)
Big Business (1988)
Hot Shots! (1991)
Jane Austen's Mafia! (1998)
Ruthless People (1986)
Abrahams, Peter: 6 writer 12 South African
abrasion: 4 sore, wear 5 chafe, scuff, wound 6 injury, lesion, scrape 7 erosion, grating, rubbing, scratch 8 friction
abrasive: 4 grit, sand 5 emery, harsh, nasty, rough, sharp, spiky 6 biting, gritty 7 caustic, cutting, erosive, galling, hateful, hurtful 8 annoying, cleanser, grinding, scratchy, scuffing 9 polishing, smoothing 10 hard to take, irritating, scratching, sharpening, unpleasant
mineral: 5 emery 6 garnet
use an ~: 5 scour
abreaction: 9 catharsis
___ a Break: 5 Gimme
abreast: 4 near 5 equal, level 6 au fait, beside, in line, versed 7 in touch 8 familiar, informed, opposite, up-to-date 9 au courant, laterally 10 acquainted, side by side
keep ~ of: 6 follow 7 monitor
of: 2 by 6 beside
of things: 6 versed 8 up-to-date
abri: 6 dugout 7 shelter
abridge: 3 cut 4 chop, clip, pare, snip, trim 5 elide, limit, prune, slash 6 censor, digest, lessen, narrow, recede, reduce, shrink 7 compact, curtail, scissor, shorten 8 abstract, boil down, compress, condense, contract, decrease, diminish, downsize, restrict, simplify, truncate 9 capsulize, summarize, telescope 10 abbreviate, blue-pencil
perhaps: 4 edit
abridged: 3 cut 5 short 7 capsule, concise, partial, reduced, sketchy 9 condensed 10 compressed, synopsized, unfinished
not ~: 5 uncut
abridgment: 4 lack 5 brief 6 digest, précis 7 epitome, pandect, summary 8 synopsis 10 compendium
abroach: 5 astir
abroad: 4 away 7 oversea, touring 8 in Europe, overseas 9 elsewhere, not at home, traveling
bring from ~: 6 import
go ~: 4 tour 6 travel 8 sightsee, vacation
move ~: 8 emigrate
sell ~: 6 export
abrogate: 3 end, nix 4 do in, undo, void 5 abate, annul, quash, scrub 6 cancel, negate, recant, reject, renege, repeal, revoke, vacate 7 abolish, nullify, rescind, retract, torpedo, vitiate 8 dissolve, knock out 9 discharge, finish off 10 invalidate, neutralize, put an end to
abrogation: 9 abolition, annulment, desertion
abrupt: 4 curt, rude 5 bluff, blunt, brief, brusk, crude, frank, gruff, hasty, jerky, quick, rough, sharp, short, swift, terse 6 candid, crusty, direct, snappy, snippy, sudden 7 brusque, hurried, offhand, rushing, uncivil 8 headlong, impolite, pell-mell, snippety, tactless 9 impatient, impetuous, impulsive, outspoken 10 indelicate, surprising, unexpected, unforeseen, ungracious
abruptly: 4 bang, wham 5 sharp 8 pell-mell, suddenly, unawares
Abruzzi commune: 4 Atri
Abruzzi e ___: 6 Molise
Absalom
father of ~: 5 David
sister of ~: 5 Tamar
Absalom, Absalom! author: William Faulkner
Absalom and Achitophel: 4 poem
author: John Dryden
Absalom My ___: 3 Son
Absaroka ___: 5 Range
abscind: 5 sever
abscond: 2 go 3 fly, get, run 4 bolt, flee, jump, quit, slip 5 break, eloin, elope, leave, scram, split 6 beat it, decamp, defect, depart, desert, eloign, escape, go AWOL, run off, vanish 7 duck out, go south, make off, pull out, ride off, run away, skip out, take off, vamoose 8 clear out, fugitate, hightail, light out, run for it 9 cut and run, disappear, skedaddle, sneak away, steal away 10 fly the coop, hightail it, make a break
absconder: 4 AWOL 6 coward, dodger 7 escapee, runaway 8 defector, deserter, recreant, renegade, swindler
Abse, Dannie: 5 Welsh 6 writer
absence: 4 AWOL, lack, need, void, want 5 hooky 6 dearth, drouth, hookey, no-show 7 drought, paucity, truancy, vacancy, vacuity 8 exiguity, omission, sparsity, truantry 9 privation 10 deficiency, inadequacy
leave of ~: 4 rest 5 break, leave, R and R 7 holiday, respite, time off 8 furlough, vacation 10 sabbatical
of order: 4 mess, riot 5 havoc, snarl 6 bedlam, mayhem, tumult, uproar 7 anarchy, clutter, discord, turmoil 8 disarray, shambles 9 confusion 10 unruliness
prefix: 3 dis-, non-
Absence of Malice (1981 film)
cast: Bob Balaban, Sally Field, Paul Newman
director: Sydney Pollack
absent: 3 off, out 4 away, AWOL, bare, gone 5 blank, empty, minus 6 astray, devoid, hollow, no-show, vacant 7 lacking, missing, not here, omitted, vacuous, wanting, without 8 listless, not there, vanished 9 elsewhere, not around 10 not in class, on vacation, part of AWOL
be ~ from: 4 skip
in Latin: 6 ab esse
not ~: 4 here
oneself: 5 leave 6 retire 8 withdraw
absent ___ leave: 7 without
absent-___: 6 minded
absente ___: 3 reo
absentee: 6 truant
absentee ___: 4 vote 5 voter 6 ballot
absently: 8 dreamily, musingly, sloppily 10 carelessly, heedlessly
absent-minded: 4 lost 5 moony 6 dreamy, remote, spacey, vacant 7 bemused, faraway, mooning 8 careless, distrait, dreaming, heedless
Absent-Minded Professor, The (1961 film)
cast: Fred MacMurray, Nancy Olson, Keenan Wynn
dog: 7 Charlie
absent without ___: 5 leave
absinthe: 5 drink 8 beverage
relative: 6 pastis
Absinthe Drinker artist: 5 Manet
Absolut competitor: 5 Stoli
absolute: 4 flat, free, full, pure, rank, sure 5 clean, exact, final, fixed, ideal, plumb, rigid, sheer, stark, total, utter, whole 6 actual, all-out, direct, entire, simple, strict, utmost 7 certain, decided, factual, flat-out, genuine, perfect, plenary, precise, supreme 8 accurate, almighty, complete, decisive, definite, despotic, emphatic, explicit, flawless, implicit, inerrant, infinite, outright, positive, profound, thorough, ultimate, unflawed 9 arbitrary, axiomatic, downright, faultless, out-and-out, sovereign, unfailing, unlimited 10 autocratic, autonomous, conclusive, consummate, definitive, despotical, impeccable, inarguable, infallible, monocratic, peremptory, preeminent, tyrannical, unabridged, unarguable, undeniable
not ~ in law: 4 nisi
ruler: 4 tsar 6 despot, tyrant
absolute ___: 4 zero 5 music, pitch, scale, space, value 7 alcohol, ceiling, maximum, minimum, monarch
absolutely: 2 ay, da, ja, sí 3 aye, oui, yea, yep, yes, yup 4 amen, fine, flat, just, okay, sí sí, sure, very, yeah 5 good-o, natch, plumb, quite, right, roger, stark, truly, uh-huh 6 agreed, and how, gladly, good-oh, indeed, just so, purely, rather, really, righto, simply, surely, wholly, you bet, yowzah 7 exactly, for sure, go ahead, indeedy, mais oui, quite so, ten-four, totally, utterly 8 all right, as you say, entirely, for a fact, of course, thumbs up, very well 9 be my guest, certainly, darn right, decidedly, doubtless, expressly, hands down, naturally, no mistake, on the nose, perfectly, precisely, sure thing, you betcha, you said it 10 altogether, by all means, completely, decisively, definitely, far and away, on the money, positively, sure as heck, sure as hell, sure enough, that's right, thoroughly, to the limit
Absolutely!: 3 yep 4 amen 6 I agree, you bet
in Spanish: 4 si si
Absolutely Fabulous
character: 5 Edina, Patsy
Absolute Power (1997 film)
cast: Clint Eastwood, Gene Hackman, Ed Harris, Laura Linney
director: Clint Eastwood
Absolute Strangers author: Robert Anderson
Absolute, the: 4 Lord
Absolute Torch and Twang singer: 4 Lang
absolution: 6 pardon 7 amnesty, release 9 acquittal, exemption
absolutism: 7 tyranny 9 autocracy
absolve: 4 free 5 clear, remit, spare 6 acquit, bleach, excuse, exempt, let off, pardon, purify, redeem, spring, wink at 7 blink at, forgive, release, relieve, set free 8 go easy on, liberate, sanctify, sanitize 9 discharge, exculpate, exonerate, vindicate, whitewash
absolved: 6 exempt
absonant: 7 raucous
absorb: 3 eat, get, sop 4 blot, hold, soak 5 co-opt, drink, grasp, learn, mop up, rivet, sense, sopup 6 arrest, devour, digest, engage, engulf, follow, imbibe, ingest, ingulf, obsess, occupy, osmose, retain, soak in, soak up, suck in, suck up, take in 7 concern, consume, drink in, engross, enthral, get into, immerse, inthral, involve, swallow 8 enthrall, interest, inthrall, sponge up 9 apprehend, captivate, entertain, fascinate, latch onto, preoccupy, swallow up 10 assimilate, comprehend, monopolize, understand
facts: 4 cram 6 soak up, take in 7 drink in 8 memorize
absorbed: 4 deep, lost, rapt 5 fixed 6 enrapt, intent 7 focused, pensive 8 held fast 9 undivided, wrapped up 10 thoughtful
by: 4 into
___-absorbed: 4 self
absorbent: 6 porous, spongy 7 thirsty 8 bibulous 9 permeable, pregnable, retentive 10 penetrable
cloth: 5 terry, towel 6 diaper
absorbent ___: 6 cotton
absorber: 6 shield
___ absorber: 5 shock
absorbing: 8 readable 9 arresting, consuming 10 engrossing, impressive, intriguing
absorption: 6 intake 8 interest 9 attention, digestion, immersion, ingestion, reception, retention 10 engagement, exhaustion, intentness, saturation
absorption ___: 4 band, edge 5 limit 6 nebula
absquatulate: 3 run 4 flee
abstain: 4 curb, fast, shun 5 avoid, cease, evade, forgo, spurn 6 abjure, desist, eschew, forego, pass up, refuse, resist, sit out 7 decline, forbear, refrain 8 abnegate, fence-sit, keep from, leave off, renounce, withhold 9 constrain, do without
from: 4 duck, omit, shun 5 avoid, dodge, forgo, shirk 6 bypass, eschew, forego 7 forbear 8 renounce 10 circumvent
abstainer: 10 nondrinker, teetotaler
abstaining: 5 sober 6 frugal 7 ascetic, austere, sparing 8 moderate 9 continent, temperate 10 moderating, restrained
abstemious: 5 sober 6 frugal 7 ascetic, austere, sparing 8 moderate, ungiving 9 continent, temperate 10 moderating, restrained
abstinence: 8 chastity, eschewal, sobriety 9 austerity, avoidance, frugality, restraint, soberness 10 abnegation, asceticism, continence, moderation, refraining, self-denial, temperance
org.: 4 WCTU
abstinent: 5 sober 6 frugal 7 ascetic, austere, sparing 8 moderate 9 continent, temperate 10 moderating, restrained
abstract: 4 deep, lift, pure 5 brief, ideal 6 digest, précis, résumé, review, unreal 7 abridge, complex, epitome, outline, shorten, summary 8 abstruse, academic, compress, condense, synopsis 9 capsulize, difficult, imaginary, recondite, summarize, synopsize, telescope 10 abbreviate, compendium, conspectus, impersonal, indefinite, intangible, literature
of only ~ interest: 4 moot
painter: 4 Klee 7 Picasso 8 Mondrian, Paul Klee 9 Kandinsky
abstract ___: 3 art 4 noun 5 music, space 6 number 7 algebra
abstracted: 4 lost 6 remote, vacant 7 pensive 8 listless 9 condensed, forgetful 10 compressed, synopsized
abstraction: 3 art 4 idea 7 concept
abstract of ___: 5 title
abstruse: 4 dark, deep 5 heavy, muddy, vague 6 arcane, hidden, mystic, occult, opaque, subtle 7 complex, cryptic, learned, obscure, unclear 8 abstract, esoteric, involved, mystical, nebulous, pedantic, profound, puzzling 9 confusing, cryptical, enigmatic, intricate, recondite, technical 10 indistinct, intangible, mysterious, pedantical, perplexing

absurd: 3 mad 4 daft, luny, rich, tall 5 balmy, batty, campy, crazy, daffy, dippy, dotty, droll, flaky, funny, goofy, goony, inane, kooky, loony, nutty, sappy, silly, wacky 6 flakey, freaky, kookie, looney, screwy, whacky 7 asinine, comical, fatuous, foolish, idiotic, tomfool, unsound 8 cockeyed, specious, unlikely 9 fantastic, fatuitous, grotesque, idiotical, illogical, laughable, ludicrous, pointless, priceless, senseless, unearthly, untenable 10 groundless, impossible, incredible, irrational, off-the-wall, ridiculous, unfeasible
Absurd ___ Singular: 6 Person
absurdity: 4 joke 5 farce, folly 6 bêtise, lunacy 7 baloney, boloney, fatuity, inanity 8 nonsense 9 craziness, goofiness, silliness, stupidity 10 applesauce, flapdoodle
  seeming ~: 7 paradox
Absurd Person Singular author: Alan Ayckbourn
abt.: 6 approx.
Abt ___: 6 Vogler
ABT locale: 3 NYC
Abt Vogler author: Robert Browning
Abu: 5 Nidal
Abu ___: 5 Dhabi 6 Simbel
Abu-___: 4 Bakr
Abu Dhabi: 4 city, town 7 capital
  denizen: 4 Arab
  leader: 4 amir, emir 5 ameer, emeer
  locale: 3 UAE 4 Asia 7 Mideast 10 Middle East
___ a bug...: 6 Snug as
___ a bug in one's ear: 3 put
Abuja: 4 city, town 7 capital
  locale: 7 Nigeria
  predecessor: 5 Lagos
Abukir: 3 bay
___ Abulbul Amir: 5 Abdul
abundance: 3 lot, sea 4 heap, many, mine, much 5 flood, hoard, ocean, store 6 argosy, bounty, myriad, plenty, riches, wealth 7 fortune 8 lushness, mountain, opulence, opulency, plethora, quantity 9 affluence, ampleness, amplitude, fecundity, fertility, frequency, greatness, plenitude, profusion 10 efficiency, exuberance, prosperity
  in ~: 6 galore
Abundance author: Beth Henley
abundant: 4 full, lush, many, much, rich, rife 5 ample, flush, great, heavy, large, leafy, thick 6 a lot of, divers, enough, filled, gobs of, heaped, lavish, lots of, myriad, plenty, umteen, untold 7 a host of, a slew of, copious, eco-rich, fertile, heaps of, liberal, no end of, piles of, profuse, replete, scads of, teeming, umpteen 8 a bunch of, affluent, an army of, fruitful, generous, handsome, infested, manifold, numerous, oodles of, princely, prodigal, prolific, scores of, umpsteen 9 a passel of, bounteous, bountiful, capacious, countless, exuberant, luxuriant, plenteous, plentiful, quite a few, unsparing 10 voluminous, zillions of
  be ~: 4 teem
  not ~: 4 rare
  source: 10 cornucopia
  with: 9 rolling in
  (with): 5 lousy
abundantly: 4 much, well 6 enough, vastly 7 greatly, largely 10 adequately, handsomely, incredibly
aburst: 8 erupting
abuse: 3 dig, hit, mar, rag 4 barb, bash, beat, flak, gibe, harm, hurt, jeer, jibe, lash, mall, maul, mock, ride, slam, slap, slur, snub, zing 5 decry, flack, knock, libel, roast, scold, scorn, smear, spurn, taint, taunt, trash, wrong 6 assail, attack, bang up, berate, damage, defame, defile, deride, dump on, heckle, hosing, impugn, injure, injury, insult, malign, misuse, molest, offend, play on, punish, rebuff, revile, slight, tirade, vilify 7 affront, asperse, assault, beating, calumny, catcall, chew out, corrupt, degrade, disdain, exploit, lambast, mauling, mockery, obloquy, offense, oppress, outrage, overtax, profane, put down, railing, rank out, rip into, rough up, run down, slander, torment, torture, traduce, upbraid, violate 8 aggrieve, backbite, badmouth, belittle, berating, breakage, contempt, denounce, derision, derogate, diatribe, ill-treat, inequity, keep down, lambaste, maltreat, misapply, mistreat, play upon, reproach, ridicule, sail into, scolding, vilipend 9 aspersion, blaspheme, castigate, cheap shot, contumely, denigrate, deprecate, desecrate, discredit, disparage, dissipate, excoriate, humiliate, injustice, insolence, invective, lash out at, maligning, manhandle, misemploy, mishandle, mismanage, persecute, profanity, victimize, violation 10 assailment, backbiting, calumniate, debasement, defamation, defilement, disrespect, excruciate, impairment, impugnment, imputation, kick around, knock about, oppression, opprobrium, overburden, punishment, revilement, roughhouse, tormenting, upbraiding, vituperate, wrongdoing
  verbal ~: 3 rap 6 outcry 9 criticism
abuser: 5 bully 6 sadist
abusive: 4 foul, rude 5 harsh, nasty 7 profane 8 insolent, libelous 9 injurious, insulting, offensive, sarcastic, truculent 10 defamatory, scurrilous
abut: 4 join, meet 5 end at, touch, verge 6 adjoin, border, lean on 7 bolster, touch on 8 border on, finish at, neighbor 9 juxtapose, touch upon
abutilon: 5 shrub
  relative: 4 ocra, okra, okro 5 urena 6 mallow
abutment: 5 joint 7 support 8 end piece 10 contiguity
abutting: 4 near, next 6 beside 8 adjacent 10 contiguity, contiguous, juxtaposed
___ a button: 6 cute as
abuzz: 4 busy 7 humming
___-a-bye: 4 rock
abysmal: 3 bad 4 base, deep 5 awful 7 yawning 8 profound, terrible, unending 9 boundless, cavernous, plumbless 10 bottomless, fathomless, unknowable
abyss: 3 pit 4 gulf, hell, hole, rift, void, well 5 chasm, depth, gorge 6 cavity, depths, ravine 7 crevice, vacuity 8 low point, nihility 9 black hole 10 underworld
  the ~: 5 Hades
abyssal: 4 deep 10 bottomless
Abyssinia: 8 Ethiopia, farewell
  city: 5 Harar
  cry: 5 miaou
  monkey: 6 grivet
  peak: 5 Amara
  prince: 3 ras
Abyssinian: 3 cat 5 felid 6 feline
  word from an ~: 3 mew 4 meow 5 miaou, miaow, miaul
Abyssinian ___: 3 cat 4 gold, well 6 banana, Church
Abyss, The (1989 film)
  cast: Michael Biehn, Ed Harris, Mary Elizabeth Mastrantonio
  director: James Cameron
Abzug: 5 Bella
Ac: 4 elem. 7 element 8 actinium
  89 for ~: 4 at. no.
Ac-___-tchu-ate the Positive: 4 cent
AC: 6 cooler 9 appliance
  part of ~: 3 air
  place: 2 rm.
  power: 4 elec.
  time: 3 Aug., Jul.
  unit: 3 BTU
  see also air conditioner
acacia: 4 tree 5 plant, shrub 6 flower, locust 7 shittah 9 gum arabic
  Hawaiian ~: 3 koa
  relative: 6 mimosa
  tree: 3 koa 5 babul
___ acacia: 3 gum 4 rose 5 black, false, sweet
acad.: 3 sch. 4 coll., inst.
  award: 3 deg.
academe: 6 lector 8 lecturer
academes: 8 literati 9 longhairs
academese: 6 patois
academic: 4 moot 5 pupil, tutor 6 formal, lector 7 bookish, erudite, learned, scholar, student 8 abstract, highbrow, lecturer, notional, pedantic, studious, unproved 9 pedagogic, professor, recondite, scholarly 10 collegiate, pedantical, scholastic
  climber: 3 ivy
  locale: 6 school 7 college 10 university
  rookie: 5 frosh 8 freshman
  specialty: 5 major
  stat: 3 GPA
  work: 5 study
  year part: 3 sem. 4 term 8 semester
  see also college, school
academic ___: 4 gown, rank, year 5 dress 7 costume, freedom
___ academic: 3 it's
Academic Festival composer: 6 Brahms
academician: 6 artist, fellow, savant 7 scholar 9 scientist
academics: 7 faculty 9 lecturers
academism: 9 formality
academy: 3 sch. 5 lycée 6 circle, league, lyceum, school 7 council 8 alliance, brainery, seminary 9 institute 10 federation, foundation, fraternity, halls of ivy, prep school
  freshman: 4 pleb 5 plebe
  in French: 5 école
  member: 6 fellow
  student: 5 cadet
___ academy: 5 naval
___ Academy: 5 Dream, Royal 6 French
Academy Awards
  see Oscar
Academy founder: 5 Plato
Acadia: 4 park
  locale: 5 Maine
Acadian: 5 Cajan, Cajun
Acadia University
  location: 6 Canada 9 Wolfville 10 Nova Scotia
Acajete: 4 city, town
  locale: 6 Mexico, Puebla
acajou: 3 nut 4 tree 6 cashew
  relative: 4 neem 6 carapa, sapele 7 avodire 8 andiroba, crabwood, mahogany
___-a-cake: 3 pat
Acala: 4 city, town
  locale: 6 Mexico 7 Chiapas
Acamar: 4 star
Acámbaro: 4 city, town
  locale: 6 Mexico 10 Guanajuato
___ a Camera: 3 I Am
___ a candle to: 4 hold
acanthoid: 5 spiny
Acapulco: 4 city, port, town
  locale: 6 Mexico 8 Guerrero
  see also Spanish
___ Acapulco: 5 Fun in
___-a-car: 4 rent
acarid: 3 bug 4 mite, tick
acarus: 3 bug 4 mite, tick
___ a case for: 4 make
___-a-cat: 3 one, two 4 four 5 three
Acatic: 4 city, town
  locale: 6 Mexico 7 Jalisco
Acatlán: 4 city, town
  locale: 6 Mexico, Puebla
Acatzingo: 4 city, town
  locale: 6 Mexico, Puebla
Acayucan: 4 city, town
  locale: 6 Mexico 8 Veracruz
ACC
  school: 3 FSU, U. Va. 4 Duke 7 Clemson 8 Maryland, Virginia 10 Wake Forest 11 Georgia Tech
Accad, Evelyne: 4 poet 8 Lebanese
Accadian: 8 language
accede: 2 OK 3 let 4 okay 5 admit, agree, allow, grant, yield 6 accept, accord, assent, cave in, comply, concur, fess up, give in, permit, say yes 7 approve, concede, consent, go along, succeed 8 cry uncle 9 acquiesce, cooperate 10 come around, get crowned
  to: 3 let 5 brook 6 accept, permit 8 assent to, sanction, tolerate 9 approve of, authorize, put up with
accelerando undoer: 6 a tempo
accelerate: 3 gun, rev 4 rush 5 build, drive, hurry, impel, raise, rev up, spirt, spurt 6 fire up, hasten, jack up, open up, step up 7 advance, forward, further, quicken, speed up 8 expedite 9 fast-track, stimulate 10 burn rubber, make tracks, peel rubber
accelerated: 4 fast 5 quick, rapid 6 speedy
acceleration: 5 speed, spirt, spurt, surge 8 rapidity, velocity
  unit of ~: 3 gal
accelerator: 3 gas 5 pedal
  item: 4 atom
  opposite: 5 brake
___ accelerator: 6 linear
accent: 4 beat, burr, tone 5 acute, drawl, grave, twang 6 brogue, play up, rhythm, speech, stress, timbre, weight 7 cadence, cadency, point up 8 contrast, emphasis, language, localism, locution, tonality 9 emphasize, highlight, intensify, punctuate, spotlight, underline 10 decoration, inflection, intonation, modulation, underscore
  kind of ~: 4 burr 5 acute, drawl, grave 6 brogue
  lacking ~: 6 atonic
  lack of ~: 5 atony 6 atonia
accent ___: 4 mark
___ accent: 4 word 5 acute, tonic 6 agogic 7 graphic, primary
Accent: 3 car 4 auto 7 Hyundai 10 automobile
Ac-cent-___-ate the Positive: 4 tchu
accented: 8 emphatic
  in music: 3 sfz. 8 marcando 9 sforzando
Ac-cent-tchu-ate the Positive composer: 5 Arlen 6 Mercer
accentuate: 6 play up, stress 7 feature, point up 8 heighten, overplay, reassert 9 emphasize, highlight, intensify, italicize, punctuate, spotlight, underline 10 strengthen, underscore
accentuation: 8 emphasis
accept: 2 OK 3 buy, get, let, use 4 avow, bear, gain, heed, hold, like, mind,

obey, okay, pass, pick, take 5 abide, admit, adopt, agree, allow, bow to, brook, defer, elect, enrol, favor, go for, grant, let in, say OK, serve, stand, trust, yield 6 accede, affirm, assent, assume, bank on, bend to, comply, credit, endure, enroll, fess up, follow, fulfil, grow on, join in, listen, look to, obtain, pardon, permit, ratify, relish, rely on, say yes, secure, suffer, tackle, take on 7 abide by, acquire, agree to, approve, believe, concede, conform, consent, count on, defer to, embrace, fulfill, observe, receive, respect, sign for, stomach, swallow, welcome, yield to 8 accede to, adhere to, assent to, carry out, deal with, depend on, grow upon, hold with, live with, sanction, shoulder, stand for, submit to, take part, tolerate 9 acquiesce, approbate, approve of, authorize, believe in, count upon, partake of, put up with, recognize, reconcile, sign off on 10 capitulate, concur with, give the nod, set store by, toe the line, understand

don't ~: 8 turn down 10 disbelieve

eagerly: 5 eat up, lap up 6 jump at, leap at

acceptable: 2 OK 3 A-OK 4 fair, fine, good, nice, okay, okeh, okey, so-so, tidy 5 great, legit, licit, moral, noble, valid 6 decent, enough, kasher, kosher, likely, proper 7 correct, ethical, livable, right on, up to par 8 adequate, all right, eligible, laudable, liveable, passable, pleasant, pleasing, splendid, standard, suitable, superior 9 admirable, agreeable, allowable, copacetic, desirable, excellent, hunky-dory, in the swim, on the ball, on the beam, palatable, reputable, tolerable, up to grade, up to snuff, wonderful 10 admissible, believable, beneficial, convenient, convincing, creditable, delightful, fairly good, infallible, in the rules, peachy keen, reasonable, sufficient

be ~: 4 suit 5 serve

is ~: 4 goes

least ~: 5 worst

Acceptable Risk author: Robin Cook

acceptably: 4 well 6 enough

acceptance: 2 OK 3 nod 4 okay, okeh, okey 5 usage, vogue 6 assent, belief 7 passage, receipt 8 adoption 9 accedence, accession, acquiring, admission, agreement, belonging, enrolment, fosterage, reception 10 assumption, compliance, concession, enrollment, green light, permission

exclamation: 3 def, rad 4 cool, fine, good, neat, nice, phat 5 dandy, ducky, neato, super 6 dreamy, far-out, gnarly, groovy, peachy, terrif, wicked 7 amazing, awesome, stellar 8 terrific 9 bodacious, fantastic, hunky-dory, marvelous 10 out of sight, peachy-keen, super-duper

propose for ~: 5 offer

__ acceptance: 4 bank 5 trade 7 banker's

acceptant: 9 receptive

accepted: 3 Ok'd, rcd. 4 recd. 5 known, legit, let in, liked, sound, usual 6 chosen, common, kasher, kosher, normal, proper 7 current, general, in vogue, popular, regular, welcome 8 habitual, orthodox, standard 9 canonical, customary, unanimous, universal, unwritten 10 accustomed, legitimate, understood

be ~: 4 rate 5 fit in, get in

by: 6 in with

accepting: 9 credulous 10 assumption, falling for

callers: 2 in 6 at home

acceptor: 5 taker

access: 2 in 3 get, tap, way 4 door, gate, path, ramp, road 5 enter, entry, get at, get to, route, spirt, spurt 6 avenue, course, entrée, obtain 7 get into, ingress, passage 8 approach, entrance, entryway, outburst 9 admission, gangplank, influence, penetrate 10 admittance, connection, passageway

ending: 3 ory

gain ~: 5 get in

garden ~: 7 postern

give ~ to: 5 admit

means of ~: 4 door, ramp 6 avenue, entrée

provide ~ to: 5 let at, let in

right of ~: 7 ingress 10 admittance

access __: 4 code, road, time 5 point 6 charge, method

__-access: 6 direct, random, serial

__ access highway: 7 limited

accessibility: 9 handiness

accessible: 4 easy, near, open 5 handy, ready 6 at hand, public, usable 7 exposed, getable, obvious, popular, useable 8 exoteric, passable, possible, sociable 9 available, easy to use, operative, reachable, receptive, unblocked, unguarded 10 attainable, convenient, employable, hospitable, obtainable, up for grabs

accession: 6 assent 7 arrival, receipt 8 addition, kingship 9 accedence, accretion, admission, agreement, enrolment, extension, increment, induction, reception 10 acceptance, assumption, attainment, enrollment, investment, succession, taking over

accessories: 3 rig 4 gear 5 stuff

accessory: 3 aid 4 aide, tool 5 add-on, extra, minor, plant, shill, stall 6 device, helper, ringer 7 abetter, abettor, adjunct, fitting, fixture, insider, partner 8 henchman, ornament 9 adornment, ancillary, appendage, appliance, assistant, associate, attendant, auxiliary, colleague, component, conducive, extension 10 accomplice, attachment, collateral, decoration, supplement

auto ~: 5 alarm

accessory __: 4 cell 5 fruit, nerve 7 pigment

accessory __ the fact: 5 after 6 before

__-access TV: 6 public

accident: 3 hap 4 blow, loss, luck 5 crash, event, fluke, smash, wreck 6 chance, hazard, mishap, pileup 7 crack-up, setback, smashup, stack-up, tragedy, wrack-up 8 calamity, casualty, disaster, fortuity 9 collision, happening, rear-ender 10 misfortune, occurrence

investigation agcy.: 4 NTSB

like some ~s: 5 freak

opposite: 6 design

sound: 5 splat

accident-__: 5 prone

accidental: 5 happy 6 casual, chance, random 9 haphazard, unplanned, unwitting 10 contingent, extraneous, fortuitous, incidental, unexpected, unforeseen, unintended

accidentally: 8 by chance, unawares

Accidental Man, An author: Iris Murdoch

Accidental Tourist, The: 4 film 5 novel

author: Anne Tyler

cast: Geena Davis, William Hurt, Kathleen Turner

composer: 8 Williams

director: Lawrence Kasdan

dog: 6 Edward

Accident author: Danielle Steel

Accident, The author: Elie Wiesel

accipiter: 4 hawk

acclaim: 4 clap, fame, hail, laud, rave, tout 5 cheer, éclat, exalt, extol, honor, kudos 6 credit, eulogy, extoll, homage, honors, praise, renown, salute 7 applaud, approve, commend, flatter, glorify, laurels, lionize, ovation, plaudit, tribute 8 accolade, applause, approval, cheering, clapping, encomium, eulogize, flattery, good word, plaudits 9 celebrate, laudation, panegyric, recommend 10 compliment, exaltation, panegyrize, popularity

attain ~: 7 succeed

Acclaim: 3 car 4 auto 8 Plymouth 10 automobile

acclaimed: 5 noted 6 famous 8 laureate, renowned 9 well-known 10 celebrated

acclamation: 5 cheer, éclat, honor 6 eulogy, praise 7 big hand, ovation, tribute 8 applause, encomium, plaudits 9 standing O

exclamation: 4 hail 5 hallo 6 hurrah, huzzah

acclamatory: 9 laudatory

acclimate: 5 adapt, enure, inure 6 harden, season 7 conform, toughen 8 accustom, indurate 9 get used to, habituate

acclimated: 5 hardy 8 seasoned

get ~: 6 attune

acclimatize: 5 adapt, enure, inure 6 adjust, harden, orient 8 accustom

acclivitous: 5 steep 6 uphill

acclivity: 4 bank, hill, rise 5 grade 6 ascent, glacis 7 hillock, incline, upgrade 8 gradient, hillside 9 elevation 10 high ground

accolade: 4 kudo 5 award, brava, bravo, honor, huzza, kudos, prize 6 eulogy, homage, huzzah, praise, reward, salute 7 acclaim, big hand, laurels, plaudit, tribute 8 approval, encomium, flattery, good word 9 extolment, laudation, panegyric 10 decoration, exaltation

accommodate: 3 aid, fit 4 help, hold, lend, loan, rent, seat, suit, take 5 adapt, board, defer, favor, fit in, house, humor, lodge, put up, serve, shape, stoop 6 adjust, assist, attune, comply, harbor, oblige, pamper, please, settle, supply, tailor, take in 7 conform, contain, embrace, furnish, gratify, harbour, include, indulge, provide, quarter, receive, shelter, support, sustain, welcome 8 accustom

accommodating: 4 easy, kind 5 civil, handy 6 aidful, decent, polite 7 helpful, patient, willing 8 flexible, friendly, generous, gracious, obliging, yielding 9 compliant

one: 5 sport

accommodation: 3 inn 4 room 5 berth, favor 7 fitting, lodging 8 courtesy, kindness, quarters

accommodation __: 4 bill, line 5 paper, train 6 collar, ladder

accommodations: 3 inn, pad 4 digs, roof 5 board, hotel, house, motel, rooms, suite 6 billet 7 housing, lodging, shelter 8 quarters

deluxe ~: 5 suite

accompanied by: 4 with

accompaniment: 7 adjunct

accompanist: 6 escort

accompany: 3 see, tag 4 join, show, take 5 bring, guard, guide, usher 6 attend, convoy, escort, follow, go with, shadow, squire 7 coexist, conduct, consort, go along, stick to 8 chaperon, join with 9 associate, chaperone, come along, look after, occur with 10 appear with, go together, happen with, show around, supplement

to a seat: 3 ush

accompanying: 4 with 7 related

accomplice: 3 aid 4 aide, ally, tool 5 crony, plant, shill, stall 6 cohort, helper, jackal 7 abetter, abettor, insider, partner 8 henchman 9 accessory, assistant, associate, auxiliary, colleague, companion

be an ~: 4 abet

unwitting ~: 4 pawn

accompli, fait: 4 fact 5 given 7 reality 9 actuality, certainty

accomplish: 2 do 3 get, win 4 gain, work 5 carry, reach, sew up 6 attain, commit, effect, finish, fulfil, manage, obtain 7 achieve, execute, fulfill, perfect, perform, produce, pull off, realize, satisfy, succeed, work out 8 bring off, carry out, complete, conclude, generate, make good, progress 9 discharge, go forward, hammer out 10 bring about, complement, consummate, do the trick, effectuate, get through, make good on, put through, take care of

fail to ~: 4 miss

old-style: 5 doeth

perfectly: 3 ace 4 nail

accomplished: 4 able, deft, done, good, over 5 adept, savvy, sharp, slick 6 adroit, au fait, brainy, expert, gifted, learnt, nimble, versed 7 capable, learned, skilled, trained 8 dextrous, graceful, lettered, masterly, polished, seasoned, skillful, talented 9 competent, dexterous, efficient, masterful, practiced, qualified, versatile, virtuosic 10 proficient

accomplishment: 3 act 4 coup, deed, feat, gain, work 5 doing, skill 6 action, effort, record, stroke 7 ability, exploit, success, triumph 8 fruition

cry: 4 ta-da 5 ta-dah 6 I did it

accord: 4 deal, give, pact 5 admit, agree, amity, endow, grant, peace, truce, union, unity 6 accede, affirm, assent, concur, confer, impart, render, square, tender, treaty, unison 7 comport, concede, concert, concord, entente, harmony, keeping, present, rapport 8 alliance, decision, sympathy 9 acquiesce, agreement, communion, concordat, congruity, consensus, good vibes, harmonize, reconcile, unanimity, vouchsafe 10 compromise, congruence, friendship, settlement, solidarity

be in ~: 4 jibe

bring into ~: 6 attune

in ~: 5 as one, at one 6 united 8 together 9 agreeable, unanimous 10 harmonious, like-minded

of one's own ~: 6 at will, freely, gladly 7 happily, readily 8 by choice 9 agreeably, voluntary, willingly

one in ~: 6 agreer

Accord: 3 car 4 auto 5 Honda 10 automobile

accordance: 9 agreement, congruity, propriety

in ~ (with): 5 along

accordant: 7 regular 8 amicable 9 congruous, consonant, unanimous 10 compatible, consistent, harmonious, true to type

according: 4 akin 7 regular, similar, uniform 8 relevant 9 accordant, agreeable, analogous, congenial, congru-

ous, consonant, unanimous **10** coincident, comparable, compatible, concordant, consistent, harmonious
to: **3** a la, per **5** as per
to Hoyle: **5** legal, legit, licit, valid **6** kosher **8** bona fide, orthodox **9** allowable **10** admissible, authorized, meticulous, on the level, scrupulous
accordingly: **4** duly, ergo, then, thus **5** fitly, hence **7** equally **8** suitably **9** therefore
according to __: **5** Hoyle
__ According to Garp, The: **5** World
according to law in Latin: **6** ex lege
__ According to St. John: **7** Passion
accordion: **8** keyboard **10** instrument
accordion __: **5** pleat
accordion-__: **4** fold
accost: **4** face, hail, meet, talk **5** annoy, greet **6** bother, harass, waylay **7** address, run into **8** approach, confront **9** challenge **10** buttonhole
account: **3** log, rpt., tab **4** bill, book, news, tale, word **5** annal, books, diary, score, story, tally, worth **6** behalf, client, detail, ledger, legend, litany, memoir, notice, reason, reckon, regard, report, sketch **7** adjudge, history, journal, lowdown, reading, recital, rundown, version **8** keep tabs, portrait, register **9** chronicle, inventory, liability, narration, narrative, rationale, reckoning, statement **10** play-by-play
abbr.: **3** bal., int., NSF
bank ~: **6** escrow **7** savings
book: **6** ledger
call to ~: **3** rag **5** blame, scold **6** rebuke **7** reprove **9** reprehend, reprimand **10** take to task
entry: **4** item **5** debit **6** credit
exec: **3** rep **8** salesman
fictional ~: **5** novel
for: **5** solve **6** recite **7** explain **9** attribute, elucidate **10** illuminate
give an ~ of: **4** tell **6** relate **7** narrate, recount
keep ~: **3** log **4** file, list **5** tally **6** report **7** archive, catalog, itemize, jot down, journal, monitor, put down, set down **8** mark down, register, tabulate **9** chronicle, inventory, write down
long ~: **4** saga **6** litany
of no ~: **7** trivial
on ~ of: **5** due to **7** because **9** therefore
on that ~: **4** thus
put on ~: **6** charge
receivable: **3** IOU
take into ~: **4** heed, note **5** cover **7** conside, respect **8** allow for, consider
take no ~ of: **8** override, overrule
take ~ of: **6** reckon
taking that into ~: **6** even so
third-party ~: **6** escrow
total: **7** balance
turn to ~: **3** use **7** utilize
account __: **3** for **4** book **7** current, payable
__ account: **3** NOW **4** bank, cash, long, on no, open, wrap **5** joint, Keogh, share, short, sweep, trust **6** charge, income, margin **7** banking, capital, control, current, drawing, expense, savings, trustee
accountability: **5** blame **9** liability
accountable: **6** liable **7** at fault, obliged, subject **8** culpable, indebted **10** chargeable
hold ~: **5** blame **6** accuse
accountant: **3** CPA **7** actuary, analyst, auditor **8** examiner **10** bookkeeper, calculator
at times: **5** adder
concern: **3** net **4** item **5** audit, books, costs, debit, taxes **6** credit, income, ledger, return **9** deduction, exemption
__ accountant: **4** cost **6** public
accounted for: **4** here **5** there **6** on hand **7** present
accounting: **8** auditing
abbr.: **3** ROA, YTD **4** FIFO, LIFO
period: **2** yr. **3** qtr. **4** year **7** quarter
accounting __: **5** clerk **6** period **7** machine
__ accounting: **4** cost
__ Accounting Office: **7** General
__ account of: **4** take
accounts
check the ~: **5** audit
falsify ~: **3** pad
settle ~: **3** pay **5** pay up, repay **6** avenge
accounts __: **7** current, payable **10** receivable
__ accounts: **5** at all
accouter: **3** arm, fit, rig **4** deck, garb, gear, trap **5** adorn, dress, equip, fit up, habit, rig up **6** attire, bedeck, clothe, fit out, gear up, invest, outfit, rig out, supply **7** apparel, bedrape, deck out, furnish, provide, turn out **8** decorate, munition, ornament **9** caparison, provision
anew: **5** refit
accouterment: **4** garb **5** dress **7** apparel, clothes, fitting **8** trapping
accouterments: **3** kit, rig **4** garb, gear, tack **5** dress, stuff **6** attire, livery, outfit, tackle **7** apparel, baggage, clothes, effects, fixings, harness, rigging, vesture **8** equipage, fittings, fixtures **9** caparison, trappings, trimmings
Accra: **4** city, port, town **7** capital
locale: **5** Ghana
accredit: **2** OK **4** okay **5** refer **6** assign, charge, enable, impute, ratify **7** appoint, approve, ascribe, certify, empower, endorse, entrust, indorse, intrust, license **8** delegate, relegate, sanction, vouch for **9** attribute, authorize, chalk up to, recognize **10** commission
accredited: **5** valid **8** official
accrete: **4** grow
accretion: **4** gain **7** buildup **8** addition, increase **9** accession, increment
accrual: **4** gain **6** growth, return **7** buildup **8** addition, amassing, increase **9** increment
accrue: **3** add **4** grow **5** add up, amass, build, yield **6** gather, result **7** build up, collect, enlarge, mount up **8** hold on to, increase **10** accumulate
accrued __: **6** income **7** expense, revenue **8** interest
acct.: **3** CPA
bank ~ datum: **3** SSN
entry: **2** cr. **3** int.
insurer: **4** FDIC **5** FSLIC
kind of ~: **2** CD **3** IRA, sav.
see also account, accountant, accounting
acct. __: **4** exec.
__ acct.: **4** svgs.
acctg.
see accounting
acculturate: **8** accustom **9** acclimate
accumbent: **10** horizontal
accumulate: **4** cull, gain, grow, heap, hold, keep, mass, pile, save **5** add to, amass, cache, glean, hoard, lay by, lay up, mount, put by, run up, stack, store, swell **6** accrue, bundle, garner, gather, heap up, pile up, rack up, retain, save up **7** acquire, collect, compile, harvest, procure, put away, round up, scare up, stack up, store up **8** assemble, gather up, hang onto, hold onto, increase, load up on, maintain, multiply, put aside, salt away **9** aggregate, collocate, stockpile **10** amalgamate, centralize
slowly: **5** glean
accumulation: **3** set **4** gain, heap, help, hunk, mass, pile **5** batch, cache, chunk, drift, group, hoard, stack, stock, store, trove **6** bundle, growth, pileup, supply **7** backlog, buildup, deposit **8** addition, assembly, increase, lodgment, quantity **9** congeries, reservoir
accumulator: **5** piler **7** pack rat
accuracy: **5** right, truth **6** verity **7** clarity **8** fidelity, sureness, veracity **9** certainty, closeness, exactness, precision **10** exactitude, factuality, perfection
accurate: **2** OK, so **4** good, just, okay, okeh, okey, true **5** exact, right, solid, sound, valid **6** deadly, direct, trusty **7** careful, certain, correct, factual, genuine, literal, perfect, pointed, precise **8** absolute, concrete, definite, detailed, faithful, flawless, inerrant, on the dot, rigorous, straight, truthful, unerring, verified **9** authentic, errorless, faultless, on the nose, veracious **10** conclusive, definitive, impeccable, infallible, methodical, meticulous, on the money, particular, scrupulous, systematic, unarguable, undeniable, undoubtful, unmistaken
prefix: **4** docu-
accurately: **4** to a T, well **5** right, sharp, smack **6** aright **7** rightly **8** verbatim **9** correctly, just right, precisely
accursed: **4** base, foul, grim, poor, vile **5** awful, hexed, lousy, woful **6** crumby, crummy, dismal, doomed, horrid, odious, rotten, woeful **7** baleful, baneful, beastly, doleful, done for, ghastly, hateful, heinous, hellish **8** devilish, dreadful, God-awful, grievous, horrible, ill-fated, inferior, infernal, luckless, shameful, stinking, terrible, wretched **9** abhorrent, appalling, atrocious, bedeviled, condemned, defective, execrable, frightful, insidious, loathsome, miserable, offensive, revolting **10** abominable, despicable, detestable, disastrous, horrendous
accusation: **4** slur **5** blame **6** charge **7** lawsuit **9** complaint, invective **10** allegation, imputation, indictment
false ~: **4** slur **5** smear **6** bad rap, bum rap **7** calumny
response: **6** denial
accusatory: **10** censorious
accuse: **3** sue, tax **4** book, cite **5** blame, brand, fault **6** allege, attack, charge, delate, impute, indict, malign **7** arraign, asperse, censure, charges, impeach, slander **8** confront, denounce **9** attribute, implicate, inculpate, prosecute **10** villainize, vituperate
falsely: **6** defame **7** asperse **8** backbite **10** calumniate
accused: **8** litigant
need: **4** bail
Accused, The (1948 film)
cast: Wendell Corey, Robert Cummings, Sam Jaffe, Loretta Young
Accused, The (1988 film)
cast: Jodie Foster, Kelly McGillis
director: Jonathan Kaplan
accuser: **8** informer, litigant **9** informant
accustom: **5** adapt, enure, inure, train **6** adjust, harden, orient, season **7** break in **8** acquaint, indurate **9** acclimate, condition, get used to, habituate, reconcile
accustomed: **4** wont **5** prone, typic, usual **6** common, normal **7** grooved, regular, routine, trained, typical **8** accepted, everyday, familiar, habitual, ordinary, orthodox, prepared **9** confirmed, customary, prevalent, settled in **10** acquainted, habituated, in the habit, inveterate, prevailing
get ~: **5** adapt
get ~ to: **6** grow on **8** grow upon
grow ~: **5** inure **6** adjust, harden, orient **7** conform **9** acclimate, reconcile **10** assimilate, come around
(to): **4** used **5** given
ace: **3** one, pro, top **4** A-one, best, card, deft, good, sole, star, whiz **5** adept, brain, crack, excel, flier, flyer, great, pilot, super **6** au fait, bullet, dollar, expert, facile, fly boy, genius, master, superb, talent, tiptop, wizard **7** aviator, egghead, hotshot, old hand, one-spot, prodigy, skilled, thinker, war hero **8** dextrous, Einstein, highbrow, masterly, peerless, polished, skillful, superior, talented, virtuoso **9** brilliant, excellent, first-rate, hole in one, honor card, marvelous, masterful, matchless, practiced, top-drawer, topflight, wonderful **10** A number one, mastermind, proficient, remarkable, specialist, super-duper
emulate an ~: **3** fly **6** aviate
plus one: **5** deuce
ace __ hole: **5** in the
ace-__: **4** high
Ace: **3** car **4** auto, Jane **6** Parker, Willys **7** bandage, Frehley, Goodman, Ventura **8** Drummond **10** automobile
alternative: **5** Curad **7** Band-Aid
Ace __: **7** bandage
acedia: **5** sloth **6** apathy, torpor **7** inertia, languor **8** idleness, laziness, otiosity **9** faineance, indolence, torpidity **10** difference, stagnation
ace in the __: **4** hole
Acela Express offerer: **6** Amtrak
Ace of Base
homeland: Sweden
song: All That She Wants (1993)
Cruel Summer (1998)
Don't Turn Around (1994)
The Sign (1994)
acerb: **4** sour, tart **5** harsh **6** biting, bitter **7** caustic, mordant **8** incisive, vinegary **9** acidulous, corrosive, sarcastic
acerbate: **8** embitter, imbitter
acerbic: **3** dry **4** acid, sour, tart **5** acrid, harsh, sharp, spiky **6** acidic, biting, bitter **7** caustic, cutting **8** incisive **9** acidulous, corrosive, sarcastic, trenchant
acerbity: **6** rancor **7** acidity, sarcasm **8** acrimony, asperity, mordancy, rudeness, sourness, tartness **9** ill temper **10** bitterness, irritation, unkindness
acerola: **4** tree **5** fruit
acerous: **8** hornless
aces: **3** def, rad **4** A-one, boss, braw, cool, dece, fine, gear, good, keen, neat, nice, phat, tuff **5** dandy, ducky, grand, great, marvy, neato, nobby, prime, slick, super, swell **6** bang on, bang-up, bonzer, bosker, choice, divine, dreamy, far-out, gnarly, groovy, lovely, peachy, slap-up, spot on, superb, terrif, tiptop, unreal, whizzo, wicked **7** amazing, awesome, capital, corking, perfect, ripping, skookum, stellar, sublime **8** dazzling, especial, eximious, fabulous, five-star, four-star, frabjous, glorious, heavenly, jim-dandy, slam-bang, smashing, splendid, standout, sterling, stickout, superior, terrific, top-level, topnotch,

very good, wondrous 9 bodacious, Endsville, excellent, exemplary, exquisite, first-rate, high-grade, hunky-dory, marvelous, sollicker, top-flight, unrivaled, wonderful 10 first-class, hotsy-totsy, jack-a-dandy, out of sight, peachy-keen, phenomenal, remarkable, stupendous, super-duper, unrivalled
___ Aces: 4 Easy
Aces High (1977 film)
cast: Malcolm McDowell, Christopher Plummer
director: Jack Gold
acetal: 7 solvent 8 vinegary
acetaminophen: 5 amide 9 analgesic
acetate: 4 salt 5 ester
___ acetate: 4 amyl, lead 5 butyl, ethyl, vinyl 6 anisyl, benzyl, bornyl, methyl, nickel, phenyl 7 chromic, isoamyl, linalyl
acetic: 4 acid, sour 5 tangy 8 vinegary 10 astringent
acetic ___: 4 acid 5 ether
acetol: 6 ketone
acetous: 4 acid, sour 5 tangy 8 vinegary 10 astringent
acetum: 7 vinegar
acetyl ender: 7 choline
acetylene
starter: 3 oxy
use an ~ torch: 4 weld
acetylsalicylic ___: 4 acid
Ace Ventura: Pet Detective (1994 film)
cast: Jim Carrey, Courteney Cox, Tone Loc, Sean Young
director: Tom Shadyac
acey-___: 5 deucy
___ a chance: 5 stand
___ a chance!: 3 Not
___ a Chance on Love: 6 Taking
Ach du ___!: 6 lieber
ache: 3 ail, yen 4 hurt, long, lust, mope, pain, pang, pine, sigh, stab, want 5 angst, cramp, crick, dolor, grief, mourn, smart, spasm, throb, throe, yearn 6 desire, grieve, misery, sorrow, strain, suffer, twinge 7 anguish, anxiety, craving, feel bad, lumbago 8 distress, migraine, pounding, smarting, soreness, yearning 9 complaint, hankering, suffering, throbbing 10 discomfort
for: 4 pity, want 5 covet, crave 6 desire
(for): 4 feel, long, pant, pine 5 yearn 6 hanker, starve
starter: 3 ear 4 back, head 5 belly, heart, tooth 7 stomach
Achebe, Chinua: 6 writer 8 Nigerian
achene: 9 buttercup
Achernar: 4 star
aches and pains: 3 woe
Acheson: 4 Dean
Achetes' friend: 5 Eneas 6 Aeneas
Achieva: 3 car 4 auto, Olds 10 automobile, Oldsmobile
achievable: 6 doable, likely, viable 8 credible, feasible, possible, workable 9 available, plausible, potential, practical 10 attainable, imaginable
achieve: 2 do 3 get, win 4 earn, find, gain, make, work 5 close, enact, reach, score, solve 6 attain, commit, effect, finish, fulfil, manage, obtain, rack up, secure, settle, wind up 7 acquire, compass, deliver, execute, fulfill, get done, make out, perfect, perform, pull off, realize, resolve, succeed, triumph, work out 8 bring off, carry out, complete, conclude, generate, progress 9 actualize, discharge, go forward, negotiate 10 accomplish, bring about, consummate, put through, see through
achieved: 4 done 8 complete
achievement: 3 act 4 coup, deed, feat, gain 5 doing, level, stunt 6 action, effort, output, record 7 exploit, success, triumph, victory 8 conquest, progress 9 milestone
cry: 4 ta-da 5 ta-dah 6 presto
heroic ~: 4 coup, deed 7 exploit, triumph, victory 8 conquest
symbol of ~: 5 award
achievement ___: 3 age 4 test
achiever: 4 doer 6 dynamo
Achille ___: 5 Lauro
Achilles: 4 hero 5 Greek
epic: 5 Iliad
friend of ~: 4 Aias, Ajax
heel: 8 weakness
horse: 7 Xanthus
parent of ~: 6 Peleus, Thetis
slayer of ~: 5 Paris
victim of ~: 4 Tros 5 Mydon, Mynes, Tenes 6 Aenius, Cycnus, Dryops, Eetion, Hector, Lycaon, Memnon, Mentes, Mestor, Mnesus, Mulius 7 Rhigmus, Troilus 8 Antandre, Dardanus, Demoleon, Demuchus, Echeclus, Hicetaon, Iphition, Lampetus, Laogonus, Menoetes, Orythaon, Pisidice, Polemusa, Thaulius, Thrasius 9 Antibrote, Areithous, Astypylus, Deucalion, Harmothoe, Hipponous, Hippothoe, Polydorus, Thersites, Trambelus 10 Alacathous, Hippodamas, Hypsipylus, Lepetymnus, Ophelestes
weak spot: 4 heel
wife of ~: 8 Deidamia
Achilles ___: 4 heel, jerk 6 reflex, tendon
aching: 4 hurt, pain, sore 6 in pain, tender 7 hurtful, painful 10 in distress
___ aching back!: 4 Oh my
Achird: 4 star
achkan: 4 coat 6 jacket
achoo cause: 4 cold 7 allergy 8 hay fever
___ à chou: 4 pâte
achromatic: 5 white 7 neutral 9 colorless
achromatic ___: 4 lens 5 prism
achromatize: 4 fade 6 bleach
acht: 5 eight 6 German
a quarter of ~: 4 zwei
follower: 4 neun
preceder: 6 sieben
Achtung Baby producer: 3 Eno
achy: 4 sore 7 bruised, hurting, painful 9 throbbing
achy-breaky: 5 dance
Achy Breaky Heart singer: 5 Cyrus
acid: 3 HCl 4 sour, tart 5 folic, harsh, sharp, spiky 6 acetic, biting, bitter, formic, lemony, oxalic 7 acerbic, caustic, cutting, mordant, nucleic, prussic, pungent, sarcasm, vinegar, vitriol 8 incisive, stinging, vinegary, vitamin C 9 sarcastic, splenetic, trenchant, vitriolic 10 aqua fortis
amino ~: 3 leu. 4 dopa 6 lysine
antiseptic ~: 5 boric 7 boracic
combining form: 3 oxy-
derivative: 6 acetyl
dye: 5 eosin 6 eosine
essential ~: 5 amino
fatty ~: 3 DHA 5 oleic
nutritive ~: 5 folic 8 Vitamin C
opposite: 4 base 6 alkali
plus alcohol product: 5 ester
salt: 5 ester
solution: 4 bath
suffix: 3 -oic 4 -olic, -onic
test: 5 proof, trial
work with ~: 4 etch
acid ___: 3 dye 4 bath, cell, drop, dust, rain, rock, salt, soil, test 5 house, value 6 number, rocker, tongue 7 radical
acid-___: 4 fast 6 loving, washed 7 forming, tongued
___ acid: 4 bile, thio 5 amino, boric, Caro's, fatty, folic, humic, iodic, Lewis, malic, mixed, mucic, oleic, usnic, xenic, xylic 6 acetic, adipic, agaric, bromic, capric, chinic, cholic, citric, cyanic, decoic, erucic, formic, gallic, kainic, lactic, lauric, maleic, niobic, nitric, oxalic, oxygen, pectic, phytic, picric, quinic, sorbic, sylvic, tannic, tiglic, toluic 7 abietic, acrylic, alginic, arsenic, behenic, benzoic, boletic, butyric, caproic, cerinic, cerotic, cetylic, chloric, chromic, decylic, ellagic, ferulic, folinic, fumaric, hydroxy, linolic, malonic, nitrous, nucleic, pimelic, pyruvic, racemic, sebacic, selenic, silicic, stannic, stearic, suberic, terebic, thionic, titanic, valeric, vanadic, xanthic
___ Acidalium: 4 Mare
acid house: 5 dance
acidic: 4 sour, tart 5 low pH, sharp 7 acerbic 8 vinegary
acidify: 4 clot, sour, turn 5 spoil 6 curdle, go sour 7 thicken
acidity: 8 acerbity, pungency, sourness, tartness 9 acridness 10 bitterness, causticity
measure: 2 pH
acidophilus ___: 4 milk
acid rain watchdog org.: 3 EPA
acid-tongued: 5 acerb
acidulate: 8 embitter, imbitter
acidulous: 4 sour, tart 5 acerb, sharp 6 bitter 7 acerbic 9 sarcastic
acid-washed fabric: 5 denim
acinus: 3 pit, sac 5 berry 8 drupelet
ack-ack: 3 gun 9 artillery
Ackerman: 6 Bettye
acknowledge: 3 nod, own 4 avow, hail, sign 5 abide, admit, agree, allow, grant, greet, let on, nod to, react, thank, yield 6 accede, accept, answer, avouch, credit, fess up, notice, ratify, salute, uphold 7 abide by, approve, certify, concede, confess, declare, defer to, endorse, indorse, mention, own up to, profess, respond, support 8 attest to, face up to 9 recognize
refuse to ~: 6 disown
acknowledged: 5 known 8 orthodox
universally ~: 5 given 7 evident, granted, obvious 8 manifest 9 axiomatic 10 understood
acknowledgment: 3 nod 4 hail 5 reply, toast 6 answer, assent, avowal, credit, letter, notice, salute, thanks 7 apology, receipt, tribute 8 applause, greeting, reaction, response 9 reception, statement
acle: 4 tree, wood
___ a clean breast of: 4 make
___ à clef: 5 roman
ACLU
concern: 3 rts. 6 rights
part of ~: 3 Civ. 4 Amer. 5 Civil, Union 8 American 9 Liberties
acme: 3 top 4 apex, head, peak, pink 5 crest, crown, spire 6 climax, height, heyday, heydey, summit, tiptop, vertex, zenith 8 capstone, high spot, meridian, pinnacle 9 high point
at the ~ of: 4 atop
___ a cog: 4 slip
___ a coin: 4 flip
___ a cold...: 4 Feed
acolyte: 4 aide 6 helper 8 follower 9 assistant, attendant
spot: 5 altar
acomia: 8 baldness
___ a common proof...: 3 'tis
___ a complaint: 5 lodge
Aconcagua: 4 peak 5 mount 8 mountain
locale: 5 Andes 9 Argentina
aconite: 5 plant 6 flower
___ a consummation devoutly...: 3 'tis
___-A-Cop: 4 Rent
acorn: 3 nut 4 seed 5 hazel
cap: 6 cupule
coating: 5 testa
producer: 3 oak 6 bur oak
acorn ___: 4 tube, worm 5 chair, clock, spoon, sugar 6 squash
___ a corner: 4 turn
acorn squash: 6 veggie 9 vegetable
___ a course: 3 lay
acoustic: 5 audio, aural, music 6 audile, phonic 7 sensory 8 auditory 9 sensorial
insulation: 5 kapok
organ: 3 ear
pro: 5 tuner
unit: 3 bel 4 sone 5 sabin
see also sound
acoustic ___: 3 ohm 4 mass, mine 5 nerve 6 guitar 7 coupler, feature, torpedo
acoustical ___: 4 tile 5 cloud
acoustics: 7 science
study: 5 sound
ACP member: 2 dr., MD
acquaint: 4 post, tell, warn 6 advise, ground, inform 7 mention, present 8 accustom, instruct 9 enlighten 10 put on guard
with: 8 advise of
acquaintance: 3 ken 4 mate 5 grasp 6 friend 7 contact 8 intimacy, neighbor
___ acquaintance: 7 nodding
acquaintances: 4 kith
acquainted: 5 aware, privy 6 wise to 7 abreast, advised, clued in 8 familiar 9 cognizant, conscious 10 accustomed, conversant
be ~ with: 4 know
get ~ with: 4 meet
with: 6 used to 8 versed in
acquiesce: 3 bow, nod 4 obey 5 adapt, agree, allow, bow to, yield 6 accede, accept, accord, adjust, assent, cave in, comply, concur, give in, permit, relent, submit, suffer 7 approve, conform, consent, go along 8 cut a deal, play ball, say uncle 9 reconcile, subscribe 10 come across, come around, condescend
acquiescence: 6 assent 7 consent 8 approval 9 surrender
acquiescent: 4 meek 6 docile 7 passive 8 amenable, lamblike, resigned, yielding 9 compliant, tractable
acquire: 3 bag, buy, cop, get, win 4 earn, find, gain, grab, have, land, snag, take 5 amass, annex, catch, incur 6 accept, assume, attain, come by, corral, gather, line up, lock up, obtain, pick up, rack up, secure, take on, wangle 7 achieve, bring in, capture, collect, garners, inherit, possess, preempt, procure, realize, receive, scare up, succeed 8 come into, invest in, purchase, scrape up 9 get hold of, latch onto 10 accumulate, fall heir to, get hands on, monopolize
again: 5 rebuy, reget, rewin
information: 4 read 5 study 6 absorb, pick up 7 find out
acquired
not ~: 6 inbred
acquisition: 3 buy 4 gain, gift 5 award, bonus, grant, prize 6 income, profit, return, reward, wealth 7 benefit, receipt 8 addition, dividend, donation, earnings, learning, proceeds, purchase, recovery, winnings 9 reception
acquisitive: 4 avid 6 grabby, greedy

7 hoggish, lustful 8 covetous, desirous, grasping 9 mercenary

acquisitiveness: 4 lust 5 greed 6 hunger 7 avarice, avidity, craving 8 cupidity, rapacity, voracity

acquit: 3 act 4 free 5 clear, let go 6 behave, deport, excuse, let off, pardon, redeem, unhand 7 absolve, comport, conduct, deliver, forgive, perform, release 8 liberate 9 discharge, exculpate, exonerate, vindicate 10 disculpate

oneself: 6 behave

acquittal: 6 pardon 7 release 9 clearance, discharge, dismissal, exemption, releasing 10 absolution, liberation, observance

acquittance: 6 refund 7 release

acquitted: 10 off the hook, vindicated

___ a crab: 5 catch

___ a crack at it: 4 take

acre: 4 unit 7 measure

anagram: 4 care, race

ender: 3 age

one-quarter ~: 4 rood

starter: 4 wise

acre-___: 4 foot, inch

Acre: 4 city, port, town

locale: 6 Israel

acreage: 3 lot 4 area, land, plot 5 field, ranch 6 estate, parcel 7 expanse, grounds 8 property 9 farmstead 10 real estate

acres: 4 land, lots 5 scads, tract 6 estate 8 plottage, property

___ Acres: 5 Green

acrid: 4 rank, sour, tart 5 harsh, sharp 6 bitter 7 acerbic, caustic, pungent 8 alkaline 9 corrosive 10 astringent

acridity: 10 bitterness

acrimonious: 3 ill 4 acid, sour 5 angry, cross, irate, nasty, sharp, testy 6 biting, bitter, heated, ireful, morose 7 acerbic, caustic, cutting, mordant, peevish, pungent 8 captious, churlish, petulant, scathing, spiteful, virulent, wrathful 9 sarcastic, splenetic, stringent

acrimony: 4 fury 5 anger, odium, spite, venom, wrath 6 enmity, hatred, malice, rancor, spleen 7 ill will, sarcasm 8 acerbity, asperity, mordancy, rudeness, tartness 9 animosity, antipathy, harshness, nastiness, virulence 10 bitterness, grumpiness, irritation, resentment, unkindness

acrobat: 7 gymnast, tumbler, vaulter 9 aerialist, trapezist

feat: 5 nip-up, split, stunt

security: 3 net

wear: 6 tights

workplace: 4 ring 6 circus

___ Acrobat: 5 Adobe

acrobatics: 5 sport

acrophobe fear: 7 heights

acropolis: 4 fort 7 citadel 8 fortress

Acropolis

goddess: 6 Athena, Athene

locale: 6 Athens, Greece

___ a cropper: 4 come

across: 4 over, thru 6 beyond, facing 7 athwart, through 8 spanning 9 astraddle 10 side to side, straddling, traversing

an ocean: 6 abroad 7 far away, foreign

come ~: 4 find, meet 5 dig up, spend 6 locate, strike 7 stumble 8 chance on 9 acquiesce, encounter, light upon 10 capitulate, chance upon, happen upon

come ~ with: 3 pay

cut ~: 8 go beyond, traverse 9 intersect, rise above, transcend

distance ~: 5 width 7 breadth

get ~: 5 speak 6 convey, effect 7 explain 8 convince, spell out 9 bring home, elucidate, make clear 10 illustrate

go ~: 4 ford 5 reach 6 bridge 7 connect, stretch 8 pass over, traverse 10 extend over

nautically: 5 abeam 7 athwart

old-style: 4 thro

prefix: 3 dia- 5 trans-

reach ~: 4 span 5 cover 6 bridge 8 traverse

run ~: 4 find, meet 5 hit on 7 hit upon 8 bump into, chance on, come upon 9 encounter, stumble on 10 chance upon

stumble ~: 5 hit on 6 strike

the way from: 3 opp. 8 opposite

___ across: 3 cut, get, put, run 4 come

Across 110th Street (1972 film)

cast: Tony Franciosa, Yaphet Kotto, Anthony Quinn

across-the-board: 5 total 7 blanket, general 8 complete, sweeping

___ Across the Sea: 5 Hands

___ Across the Table: 5 Hands

___ a crowd: 6 three's

acrylic: 5 Orlon, paint

acrylic ___: 4 acid 5 ester, fiber, resin

act: 2 do 3 job, law 4 deed, feat, move, play, pose, sham, show, step 5 bylaw, doing, edict, emote, feign, front, labor, put on, serve, shtik, stunt 6 acquit, affect, appear, assume, behave, facade, fake it, shtick 7 charade, conduct, display, exploit, get busy, ham it up, hop to it, measure, perform, portray, posture, pretend, respond, routine, show off, statute 8 function, judgment, maneuver, pretense, rehearse, simulate 9 dramatize, make a move, ordinance, play a part, take steps 10 false front, make a scene, masquerade, perpetrate, put on a show, resolution, simulation

catch in the ~: 8 surprise

clean up one's ~: 6 reform 7 rectify

ender: 3 ion, ive 4 gong

failure to ~ in law: 6 laches

for: 2 do 5 serve, speak 6 fill in 8 pinch-hit 9 represent 10 substitute

formal ~: 4 rite 6 ritual 8 ceremony

get in the ~: 7 partake

hypocritical: 7 deceive, mislead 8 simulate 9 dissemble, misinform

injurious ~: 4 tort 9 violation

in the ~: 9 red-handed

introducer: 2 MC 5 emcee

junta ~: 4 fiat 5 order 6 decree, dictum 7 command, dictate, mandate 9 directive, manifesto 10 injunction

last ~: 3 end 6 climax, ending, finale, finish, windup 10 conclusion, denouement

like: 3 ape 4 copy 5 mimic 6 mirror 7 imitate 8 simulate

on: 4 head, obey 5 alter 6 affect, change, follow, modify 7 respond, yield to 9 conform to, influence, transform 10 comply with, take care of

out: 7 express 9 dramatize, pantomime

portion: 5 scene

properly: 6 behave

put on an ~: 4 fake 6 fake it 7 pretend 8 simulate 9 dissemble, misinform

quickly: 4 leap

read the riot ~ to: 3 hit 4 flay, flog, slam 5 blast, chide, scold 6 berate, rebuke 7 bawl out, censure, chasten, chew out, condemn, lecture, reprove, upbraid 8 admonish, chastise, denounce, lambaste, reproach, sail into, tear into, threaten 9 castigate, criticize, dress down, excoriate, reprehend, reprimand 10 come down on, discipline, take to task, vituperate

starter: 5 inter, trans 7 counter

suffix: 3 -ure

together: 6 club up

toward: 5 treat

unlawful ~: 4 tort 5 crime, heist, theft, wrong 6 felony, holdup, murder 7 larceny, misdeed, offense, treason 8 atrocity, burglary, delictum, thievery 9 violation 10 infraction

unwise ~: 5 taboo

up: 7 carry on 8 be bratty, be unruly 9 misbehave 10 make a scene

upon: 4 head, obey 5 alter 6 affect, change, follow, modify 7 yield to 9 conform to, influence, transform 10 comply with

vainly: 5 groom, preen 7 deck out, dress up, spiff up

act ___: 3 out 4 call, drop 5 a part, of God, of war 7 curtain, warning

act ___ hunch: 3 on a

___ act: 4 riot, test 5 class 6 circus, public, reflex, ripper, speech 7 novelty, special

___-act: 4 play

Act: 9 mouthwash

alternative: 4 Plax 5 Scope 6 Signal 7 Lavoris 9 Listerine 10 Fluorigard

Act ___: 3 One

___ Act: 3 Tea 4 Riot 5 Hatch, Stamp, Sugar 6 Canada, Reform, Sister, Wagner 7 Kinkaid, Morrill

acta: 4 proc. 5 deeds

Actaeon: 6 hunter

___'acte: 4 entr

Acte author: Lawrence Durrell

___-acter: 3 one

ACTH part: 6 adreno, tropic 7 cortico, hormone

Actifed alternative: 5 Afrin 6 Contac, Nyquil, Tavist 7 Comtrex, Dayquil, Dristan, Sinutab, Sudafed 8 Benadryl, Dimetapp, Drixoral, TheraFlu 9 Coricidin, Triaminic 10 Robitussin

acting: 4 mime 6 deputy, pro tem 7 interim, mimicry 8 pretense 9 depiction, dramatics, imitation, portrayal, surrogate, temporary, tentative 10 pro tempore, stagecraft

as one: 6 allied

award: 4 Emmy, Obie, Tony 5 Oscar

for: 10 in behalf of, on behalf of

group: 4 cast 6 troupe 8 ensemble

job: 4 role

up: 6 errant

___-acting: 4 long 6 direct, double, single

actinium: 7 element

action: 3 job, vim 4 case, deed, feat, fray, move, plot, rush, step, stir, suit 5 claim, doing, fight, sport, trial, vigor 6 battle, bustle, combat, effect, effort, energy, flurry, hoopla, motion, spirit 7 agility, exploit, gesture, lawsuit, measure, process, service, turmoil 8 activity, alacrity, conflict, exercise, exertion, goings-on, industry, maneuver, measures, movement, practice, response, skirmish, vitality, vivacity 9 animation, commotion, execution, happening, operation, procedure, shootouts 10 engagement, enterprise, excitement, initiative, litigation, liveliness, locomotion, proceeding

combining form: 3 cin-, kin- 4 cino-, kine-, kino-

starter: 5 inter, trans

suffix: 3 -ism 4 -ence

action ___: 4 line 5 grant 6 replay 7 painter

___ action: 3 job 4 knee 5 class, lever 6 covert, direct, police, reflex, rising, social 7 falling

___-action: 4 bolt, live, pump 5 after, cross, slide 6 double, single 7 delayed

___ Action, A: 5 Civil

actionable: 7 illegal 8 unlawful

wrong: 4 tort

___ Action Hero: 4 Last

Action in the North Atlantic (1943 film)

cast: Humphrey Bogart, Alan Hale, Raymond Massey

director: Lloyd Bacon

Action Man, Britain's: 5 GI Joe

___-action photography: 4 stop

actions: 8 behavior 10 deportment

___-action suit: 5 class

Actium: 6 battle

activate: 3 jog 4 stir 5 begin, impel, liven, pep up, put on, rouse, spark, start 6 awaken, call up, enable, engage, kindle, prompt, propel, pump up, turn on, vivify 7 animate, enliven, juice up, liven up, quicken, trigger 8 energize, initiate, mobilize, switch on, vitalize 9 intermesh, stimulate 10 predispose

activated ___: 4 mine 6 carbon, sludge 7 alumina

___-activated: 5 voice

activated by combining form: 5 -ergic

activation: 4 spur 9 awakening

active: 4 bold, busy, go-go, live, spry 5 about, agile, alert, alive, astir, brisk, fresh, jazzy, peppy, perky, quick, ready, voice 6 at work, daring, feisty, frisky, in play, lively, living, moving, nimble, on duty, speedy, strong 7 animate, dynamic, engaged, flowing, healthy, in force, on the go, pushing, roaring, rocking, rolling, running, serving, working, zealous 8 animated, bustling, diligent, employed, forceful, in effect, involved, occupied, spirited, swarming, tireless, vigorous, youthful 9 assiduous, effective, energetic, enlivened, laborious, on the move, operating, sprightly, streaming, strenuous, vivacious 10 aggressive, unflagging, up and about

become ~: 4 stir

combining form: 7 -kinetic

not ~: 4 idle, retd. 5 inert 7 retired

one: 4 doer

starter: 4 over 5 radio, retro

active ___: 3 sun 4 duty, mass, site, wear 5 layer 6 reason 7 service

activist: 4 doer 7 fanatic 8 militant

concern: 5 cause

___ activist: 6 animal

activity: 3 ado, job 4 life, task, to-do, work 5 hobby, labor, stunt 6 action, bustle, energy, hoopla, hustle, motion 7 pastime, project, pursuit, venture 8 endeavor, exercise, exertion, function, industry, interest, movement 9 animation, avocation, operation 10 discipline, enterprise, excitement, liveliness, occupation

combining form: 7 -kinesis

___ activity: 5 solar 7 optical

act of ___: 3 God, war 5 faith

Act of Murder, An (1948 film)

cast: Florence Eldridge, Fredric March, Edmond O'Brien

Act of the Heart, The (1970 film)

cast: Genevieve Bujold, Donald Sutherland

Act of Violence (1949 film)

cast: Van Heflin, Janet Leigh, Robert Ryan

director: Fred Zinnemann

act on a ___: 5 hunch

Act One author: Moss Hart

Actopan: 4 city, town
locale: 6 Mexico 7 Hidalgo
actor: 3 ham 4 fake, lead, star 5 mimic, party 6 artist, emoter, mummer, player 7 trouper 8 imposter, impostor, thespian 9 performer 10 leading man, understudy
blunder: 5 fluff
concern: 5 lines 6 script 7 billing
direction: 4 exit 5 enter
goal: 4 part, role
workplace: 3 set 5 stage
actors: 4 cast 6 troupe 7 company
org.: 3 AEA, SAG 5 AFTRA
Actors' __: 6 Equity
__ Actors Guild: 6 Screen
actress: 3 ham 4 diva, lead, star 5 actor 6 artist, emoter, player 7 ingénue, starlet, trouper 8 thespian, virtuoso 9 performer 10 prima donna
actresses: 4 cast 6 troupe 7 company
acts: 4 does 9 res gestae
group of ~: 5 revue 6 review
Acts: 4 book
follower: 6 Romans
preceder: 4 John
Acts __ Apostles: 5 of the
Acts of Faith author: 5 Segal
act the __: 4 fool
actual: 2 so 4 just, live, real, true, very 5 exact, right 6 living 7 certain, correct, de facto, genuine, literal, sincere 8 absolute, bona fide, concrete, definite, existent, existing, explicit, material, physical, positive, tangible, truthful, verified 9 authentic, confirmed, happening, veritable 10 definitive, historical, true-to-life, undeniable, unimagined, unmistaken
not ~: 9 imaginary
actuality: 4 fact 5 being, right, truth 6 entity, gospel, verity 7 de facto, reality 9 existence, real world, substance 10 attainment, brass tacks, experience, phenomenon
in ~: 5 truly 6 really 7 de facto
actualization: 8 fruition
actualize: 5 begin 6 create, effect 7 achieve, develop, realize 9 implement
actualized: 9 fulfilled
not ~: 6 latent
actually: 4 just 5 quite, truly 6 indeed, in fact, really 7 de facto, in truth 8 in effect 9 in reality, literally
in Latin: 6 in esse 7 ex facto
actuary: 10 accountant
concern: 3 age 4 rate
actuate: 4 move, spur 5 cause, drive, egg on, impel, key up, rouse 6 arouse, bestir, effect, fire up, incite, induce, kindle, propel, turn on 7 animate, inspire, quicken 8 energize, mobilize, motivate, touch off 9 instigate, stimulate
actuation: 4 spur 7 impulse
Act your __!: 3 age
acuate: 5 sharp 7 pointed 9 sharpened
Acuautla: 4 city, town
locale: 6 Mexico
Acubens: 4 star
__ a cucumber: 6 cool as
Acuff: 3 Roy
acuity: 3 wit 5 depth, sense 8 eagle eye, keenness 9 intellect, sharpness, vigilance
mental ~: 6 brains
__ acuity: 6 visual
ACU locale: 3 Tex. 5 Texas
acumen: 3 wit 4 wits 5 depth, grasp, guile 6 brains, genius, reason, sanity, smarts, wisdom 7 cunning, finesse, insight 8 judgment, keenness, sagacity 9 awareness, ingenuity, intellect, intuition, mentality, reasoning, sharpness, smartness 10 astuteness, brilliance, cleverness, horse sense, perception, shrewdness
acuminate: 4 hone, whet 5 sharp 7 sharpen
acuminous: 5 sharp
Acuña: 4 city, town
locale: 6 Mexico 8 Coahuila
Acura: 3 car 4 auto 5 Honda 10 automobile
model: 3 MDX, NSX, RSX, SLX, TSX 5 Vigor 6 Legend 7 Integra
__ a customer: 5 one to
acute: 4 dire, fine, keen, sore 5 canny, grave, quick, ready, sharp, smart, vital 6 accent, astute, clever, severe, shrewd, shrill, strong, sudden, urgent 7 crucial, cutting, exigent, intense, pungent, racking, raucous, serious, violent 8 critical, decisive, deep-felt, exigeant, incisive, keen-eyed, lynx-eyed, piercing, pressing, profound, vigilant 9 astucious, desperate, exquisite, important, intuitive, sagacious 10 discerning, imperative, insightful, perceptive, pronounced
combining form: 3 oxy-
make ~: 7 sharpen
acute __: 5 angle 6 accent
acute-__: 4 care
acutely: 4 very 5 sharp 6 keenly, vastly 8 severely 9 extremely
acuteness: 3 wit 4 wits 7 gravity 9 extremity, intensity
ACV: 10 hovercraft
ad: 4 bill, plug 5 blurb, flier, flyer, pitch, promo 6 come-on 7 leaflet 8 circular 9 billboard, publicity
agency account: 6 client
answer an: 5 apply
award: 4 Clio
business: 6 agency
classified ~ abbr.: 3 EEO, EOE
directive: 3 buy 6 act now
free media ~: 3 PSA
infinitum: 4 ever 5 no end 7 forever
Internet ~: 6 banner
lib: 6 freely 7 offhand 9 improvise 10 off the cuff
name: 5 brand
personal ~ abbr.: 3 SWF, SWM
place the same ~: 5 rerun
publisher ~: 5 blurb
realty ~ abbr.: 3 EIK, fpl., rms. 4 bdrm., bsmt.
rem: 7 germane 8 directly, material, relevant 9 pertinent 10 to the point
sign: 4 neon
space: 6 linage 7 lineage
spiel: 4 hype
target: 5 buyer
teaser ~: 5 promo
two-page ~: 6 spread
word: 3 new 4 free, sale
ad __: 3 fin, hoc, inf., int., loc., rem, val. 4 init., quem 5 infin., litem, vitam, vivum 6 damnum, hocery, patres, verbum 7 feminam, gloriam, hockery, hominem, initium, interim, libitum, nauseam, valorem
ad __ per aspera: 5 astra
ad-__: 3 lib 6 libbed, libber
ad-__ committee: 3 hoc
__ ad: 4 want 7 display
A.D.: 4 Hope
coiner: 4 Bede 5 Baeda
part: 4 Anno 6 Domini
Ada: 4 city, town 5 Maris, Rehan 8 Comstock, Huxtable, Lovelace
locale: 4 Okla. 8 Oklahoma
Ada (1961 film)
cast: Susan Hayward, Dean Martin
director: Daniel Mann
ADA: 8 language
alternative: 3 APL, SQL 4 Alef, html, Icon, Java, LISP, Logo, Orca, Perl 5 Algol, Basic, Cecil, COBOL, Dylan, SISAL 6 Delphi, Eiffel, Erlang, Oberon, Pascal, Prolog, Sather, Scheme, Snobol 7 Fortran
member: 3 DDS, DMD
Ada author: Vladimir Nabokov
adage: 3 saw 5 axiom, maxim, moral, motto 6 byword, dictum, saying, truism 7 bromide, precept, proverb 8 aphorism, apothegm 10 apophthegm
like an ~: 5 pithy
start: 4 if at 6 no news
adages: 4 lore
adagio: 4 slow 5 music, tempo 6 slowly
faster than ~: 7 andante
slower than ~: 5 largo, lento
Adagio for Strings composer: 6 Barber
adagio non __: 6 troppo
Adah
father of ~: 4 Elon
husband of: 4 Esau
son of ~: 7 Eliphaz
Adair: 3 Red 7 Deborah
__-a-Dale: 4 Alan 5 Allan
Adam: 3 Ant 4 Bede, Rich, Wade, West 5 Arkin, Smith 6 Powell, Robert 7 Adolphe, Baldwin, Sandler 9 Dalgliesh 10 Cartwright, Mickiewicz
brother of ~: 3 Joe 4 Hoss 9 Little Joe
first wife: 6 Lilith
grandson of ~: 4 Enos 5 Enoch
habitation: 4 Eden
mate: 3 Eve
son of: 4 Abel, Cain, Seth
to Ben: 3 son
Adam __: 4 Bede
Adam, Adolphe ballet: Giselle
Adam and Eve __ raft!: 3 on a
Adam and Eve painter: 5 Durer
adamant: 4 firm, iron 5 fixed, flint, rigid, stony, tough 6 steely, stoney, wilful 7 hard-set, piggish, willful 8 obdurate, resolute, stubborn 9 hard-nosed, immovable, impliable, insistent, obstinate, pigheaded, steadfast, tenacious, unbending 10 determined, hard-bitten, headstrong, inexorable, inflexible, relentless, set in stone, unshakable, unswayable, unyielding
be ~: 6 insist
adamantine: 4 firm, hard 5 stern 6 steely 7 lithoid 8 indurate 9 lithoidal 10 inexorable, inflexible
Adam at 6 A.M. (1970 film)
cast: Joe Don Baker, Michael Douglas
Adam Bede author: George Eliot
character: 4 Rann, Seth 5 Burge, Dinah, Hetty 6 Arthur, Bartle, Hester, Irwine, Joshua, Martin, Massey, Morris, Poyser, Rachel, Sorrel 7 Lisbeth, Mattias 8 Jonathan
Adam Clayton __: 6 Powell
Adam had 'em poet: Ogden Nash
Adams: 3 Doc, Don, Sam 4 Edie, Joey, John, Maud, Nick, peak 5 Ansel, Bryan, Cindy, Gerry, Henry, Julie, Mason, mount, Oleta 6 Brooke, Hannah, Samuel 7 Abigail, Richard 8 mountain
locale: 8 Cascades 10 Washington
Adam's __: 3 ale, cup, Rib 5 apple 6 Bridge
__ Adams: 5 Alice, Patch, Sarah
Adam's ale: 5 water
Adams, Ansel: 12 photographer
milieu: 8 Yosemite 10 California
Adams, Brooke: 7 actress
film: Cuba (1979)
Days of Heaven (1978)
The Dead Zone (1983)
Invasion of the Body Snatchers (1978)
Key Exchange (1985)
Adams, Bryan
homeland: Canada
song: All for Love (1993)
Can't Stop This Thing We Started (1991)
Have You Ever Really Loved a Woman? (1995)
Heat of the Night (1987)
Heaven (1985)
I Do It for You (1991)
I Finally Found Someone (1996)
Please Forgive Me (1993)
Run to You (1984)
Straight From the Heart (1983)
Summer of '69 (1985)
Adams, Edie: 6 singer 7 actress
film: The Best Man (1964)
It's a Mad Mad Mad Mad World (1963)
Lover Come Back (1961)
Love With the Proper Stranger (1963)
Under the Yum Yum Tree (1963)
spouse: Ernie Kovacs
Adams, Gerry
land: 4 Eire
org.: 3 IRA
Adams, Hannah: 6 author, writer
Adams, Henry: 6 author, writer
Adams, John: 9 president
alma mater: 7 Harvard
excellent instrument: 3 pen
former occupation: 6 lawyer
home: 6 Quincy
opponent: 9 Jefferson
V.P.: 9 Jefferson
wife: 7 Abigail
Adams, John Quincy: 9 president
alma mater: 7 Harvard
former occupation: 6 lawyer
mother: 7 Abigail
opponent: 4 Clay 7 Jackson 8 Crawford
V.P.: 7 Calhoun
wife: 6 Louisa
Adams, Julie: 7 actress
film: Creature From the Black Lagoon (1954)
Four Girls in Town (1956)
The Lawless Breed (1952)
The Man From the Alamo (1953)
Tickle Me (1965)
Adams, Maud: 7 actress
film: The Man With the Golden Gun (1974)
Octopussy (1983)
Rollerball (1975)
Adam's-needle: 5 yucca
Adams, Nick: 5 actor
film: The Hook (1963)
No Time for Sergeants (1958)
TV: The Rebel
Adams, Oleta song: Get Here (1991)
Adamson: 3 Joy
pet: 4 Elsa 7 lioness
Adam's Rib (1949 film)
cast: Tom Ewell, Katharine Hepburn, Judy Holliday, Spencer Tracy, David Wayne
director: George Cukor
Adam 12 (NBC drama)
cast: Kent McCord (Jim Reed)
Martin Milner (Pete Malloy)
org.: LAPD
producer: Jack Webb
Adana: 4 city, town
locale: 6 Turkey
__ a Dancer: 3 I Am
__ a Dancing Mood: 4 I'm in
__-a-dandy: 4 jack
adapt: 2 do 3 fit 4 edit, gear, suit, tune 5 alter, enure, inure, shape 6 adjust,

attune, change, harden, make do, modify, orient, revise, square, tailor 7 conform, convert, fashion, make fit, prepare, qualify, remodel, restyle 8 accustom, go native, regulate 9 acclimate, acquiesce, condition, get used to, reconcile 10 assimilate, come around

(to): 7 get used

adaptable: 5 fluid 6 docile, lissom, mobile, supple, usable 7 lissome, pliable, useable 8 flexible, obedient 9 all-around, alterable, compliant, easygoing, malleable, resilient, revocable, tractable, versatile 10 adjustable, changeable, compatible, convenient, modifiable

adaptation: 7 version 9 agreement, allowance, refitting, reworking, variation 10 adjustment, alteration, compliance, conversion, remodeling

Adaptation (2002 film)

cast: Nicolas Cage, Meryl Streep, Tilda Swinton

director: Spike Jonze

Adar: 5 month 6 Hebrew

holiday: 5 Purim

predecessor: 6 Shevat

successor: 5 Nisan

___ a dare!: 5 Not on

___ a dark and stormy...: 5 It was

___ a Dark Shadow: 4 Cast

___ a darn: 4 give

ad astra ___ aspera: 3 per

Adatara: 7 volcano

locale: 4 Asia 5 Japan 6 Honshu

___ a date: 3 set

___ a date!: 3 It's

...a date which will live in ___: 6 infamy

___-A-Day: 3 One

___ a day..., An: 5 apple

...___ a day in June?: 6 rare as

___ a day's work: 5 all in

ADC: 4 asst.

part of ~: 4 aide, camp

Adcock: 3 Joe 5 Fleur

Adcock, Fleur: 4 poet

add: 3 say, sum, tag, tot 4 go on, lace, tack 5 affix, annex, count, dub in, put in, put on, sum up, tag on, tally, total, tot up 6 accrue, adjoin, append, appose, chip in, edge in, extend, figure, fold in, foot up, hook on, insert, number, reckon, slap on, stir in, suffix, tack on, take on, toss in, tote up 7 amplify, compound, augment, bring to, compute, count up, enlarge, include, overdub, stick on, subjoin, thicken, throw in 8 figure in, increase, multiply, tabulate 9 calculate, enumerate, interject, introduce, keep score 10 complement, contribute, count heads, supplement

a lane to: 7 broaden

fuel to fire: 4 spur 5 rouse 6 whip up, work up 7 agitate 9 stimulate

liquor to: 5 spike 7 fortify

on: 5 affix, annex 6 append, attach, expand

(on): 3 tag 5 build

to: 4 grow, hike, rise 5 boost, build, raise, swell, widen 6 append, enrich, expand, extend, step up 7 amplify, augment, broaden, build up, enhance, enlarge, magnify, spice up 8 compound, escalate, expand on, heighten, increase, lengthen 9 aggravate, branch out, increment, intensify, reinforce, spread out 10 accumulate, aggrandize, complement, exacerbate, exaggerate, expand upon, strengthen, supplement

to the payroll: 4 hire 6 employ, engage, sign on, take on 7 bring on

up: 3 sum 4 tote 5 count, prove, tally, total 6 accrue, amount, figure, reckon 9 aggregate, enumerate, keep score, make sense 10 count heads

up again: 5 retot

up to: 4 make, mean 5 equal, spell 6 number, reveal 7 contain, express, signify 8 comprise, indicate 9 aggregate

up (to): 6 amount

value to: 6 better 7 build up, elevate, enhance, fortify 8 decorate 9 embellish 10 supplement

water to: 4 thin 6 weaken

zest to: 5 pep up 6 excite, perk up, spur on, stir up, vivify 7 animate 8 energize, vitalize 10 exhilarate, invigorate

zing to: 5 spice 6 pepper

add ___: 4 up to

Adda: 5 river

locale: 5 Italy

Addams: 4 Jane 5 Gomez 7 Charles, Pugsley 8 Morticia 9 Wednesday

Addams Family, The (1991 film)

cast: Anjelica Huston, Raul Julia, Christopher Lloyd, Christina Ricci

director: Barry Sonnenfeld

Addams Family, The (ABC sitcom)

cast: John Astin (Gomez Addams)
Ted Cassidy (Lurch/Thing)
Jackie Coogan (Uncle Fester)
Carolyn Jones (Morticia Addams)
Lisa Loring (Wednesday Addams)
Blossom Rock (Grandmama)
Felix Silla (Cousin Itt)
Ken Weatherwax (Pugsley Addams)

dance: 5 tango

lion: 8 Kitty Kat

nickname: 4 Tish

Addams Family Values (1993 film)

cast: Joan Cusack, Anjelica Huston, Raul Julia, Christopher Lloyd, Christina Ricci

director: Barry Sonnenfeld

Addams Groove (1991 song) artist: M.C. Hammer

Addams, Jane: 8 Nobelist

addax: 8 antelope

relative: 3 gnu, kob 4 guib, kudu, oryx, puku, topi 5 bongo, chiru, eland, goral, korin, nyala, oribi, saiga, serow 6 chammy, dik-dik, duiker, impala, koodoo, lechwe, nilgai, rhebok, shammy, shamoy 7 blaubok, blesbok, chamois, defassa, gazelle, gemsbok, gerenuk, grysbok, nylghai, nylghau, sassaby 8 blesbuck, bontebok, bushbuck, gemsbuck, reedbuck, steenbok, steinbok 9 blackbuck, pronghorn, sitatunga, springbok, waterbuck 10 hartebeest, wildebeest

added: 3 new 5 extra, fresh, other, ran up 7 another, further, updated 9 aggregate 10 additional

something ~: 6 augend

to: 4 plus

added ___: 4 line 5 entry, value

___-added: 5 value

___ added attraction: 5 extra

___-added tax: 5 value

addendum: 2 PS 4 supp. 5 annex, extra, rider 7 adjunct, codicil 8 appendix 9 appendage, extension 10 attachment, postscript, supplement

insurance ~: 9 amendment

second: 3 pps

third: 4 ppps

adder: 5 snake 6 animal, summer 7 reptile, serpent 9 milk snake

relative: 3 asp, boa 5 aboma, cobra, krait, mamba, racer, viper 6 dhaman, python, taipan 7 markhor, rattler 8 anaconda, moccasin, ringhals 9 boomslang, coachwhip 10 bushmaster, copperhead, sidewinder

___ adder: 4 milk, puff 7 chicken, spotted

Adderley, Cannonball

genre: 4 jazz

instrument: alto sax, sax

real first name: Julian

adder's-tongue: 4 fern 5 plant

addict: 3 fan, nut 4 buff 5 fiend, freak, hound 6 zealot 7 devotee, fanatic, habitué 8 follower 10 aficionado, chocoholic, enthusiast

combining form: 5 -holic 6 -aholic

Addicted to Love (1986 song) artist: Robert Palmer

addiction: 5 habit 9 obsession 10 dependance, dependence, sweet tooth

Addiction, The (1995 film)

cast: Annabella Sciorra, Lili Taylor, Christopher Walken

director: Abel Ferrara

Addie: 4 Joss

adding ___: 7 machine

adding device: 6 abacus 10 calculator

Adding Machine, The author: Elmer Rice

Addis Ababa: 4 city, town 7 capital

locale: 3 Eth. 8 Ethiopia

Addison: 4 city, town

locale: 8 Illinois

partner: 6 Steele

addition: 3 ell 4 gain, hike, plus, wing 5 annex, bonus, boost, extra, raise, rider 6 lean-to 7 accrual, adjunct, codicil, summing 8 appendix, counting, dividend, figuring, increase, totaling 9 accession, accretion, appendage, expansion, extension, increment, reckoning, summation 10 arithmetic, attachment, elongation, postscript, supplement, tabulating

column: 4 ones, tens 8 hundreds

house ~: 3 ell 5 annex

in ~: 3 and, too, yet 4 also, else, more, over, plus 5 again 6 as well, at that 7 besides 8 likewise, moreover

injury ~: 6 insult

in ~ (prefix): 3 sur-

in ~ to: 3 and 6 beyond 9 apart from, aside from

problem: 3 sum

additional: 3 aux., new 4 else, more, plus, supp. 5 extra, fresh, other, spare 6 longer, second 7 affixed, further 8 appended, optional 9 ancillary, auxiliary, increased 10 extraneous

in ads: 4 xtra

ones: 6 others

prefix: 3 sur-

additionally: 3 and, too, yet 4 also, else, over, then 5 again 7 besides, further 8 likewise, moreover 9 on the side

additive: 10 supplement

additive ___: 5 color, group 7 inverse, primary, process

___ additive: 4 food

addle: 5 cloud, floor, mix up, spoil, throw 6 baffle, bemuse, go sour, muddle, puzzle, rattle 7 confuse, flummox, fluster, nonplus, perplex, shake up, stupefy, unhinge 8 befuddle, bewilder, confound, scramble 9 disorient, inebriate, unbalance 10 discompose, disconcert, intoxicate

ender: 5 pated

addled: 4 asea, hazy 5 at sea, dizzy, tipsy 6 punchy, shaken 7 fuddled, mixed up, out of it, rattled, unglued 9 befuddled, slaphappy 10 bewildered

addlepate: 3 ass, oaf, sap 4 boob, clod, dodo, dolt, dope, fool, jerk, twit 5 chump, clown, cluck, dummy, dunce, joker, looby, ninny, patsy 6 dimwit, lummox, nitwit, sucker, turkey 7 buffoon, bumbler, dingbat, dullard, fathead, half-wit, jackass, pinhead, saphead 8 bonehead, dumbbell, dummkopf, lunkhead, meathead, numskull 9 birdbrain, blockhead, harebrain, lamebrain, numbskull, simpleton 10 dunderhead, muttonhead, nincompoop

addlepated: 4 daft, dumb 5 goosy, inane, silly 6 absurd, goosey, simple 7 asinine, fatuous, foolish, idiotic 8 mindless 9 fatuitous, idiotical, laughable, senseless 10 ridiculous, sophomoric, weak-minded

add-on: 4 plus 5 rider 9 accessory, extension, surcharge 10 peripheral, supplement

address: 3 aim, woo 4 call, home, talk 5 abode, hallo, hillo, house, hullo, label, level, orate, route, see to, speak, spiel, title 6 accost, direct, halloa, halloo, hallow, have at, hilloa, hulloo, preach, recite, salute, sermon, speech, take up 7 bespeak, consign, discuss, domicil, focus on, lecture, lodging, monolog, oration, pep talk 8 attend to, domicile, dwelling, engage in, inscribe, location, rhetoric 9 chalk talk, discourse, have a go at, honorific, monologue, readiness, residence, sermonize, touch base, undertake 10 apostrophe, plug away at, recitation, salutation, take care of

abbr.: 2 rd., st. 3 ave., hts., rte. 4 blvd.

change one's ~: 4 move

courteous ~: 3 sir 4 ma'am 5 madam

familiar ~: 3 bub, mac 5 deary, kiddo 6 dearie

location: 3 env. 8 envelope

make an ~: 5 orate

nonspecific ~: 3 GPO

palindromic ~: 3 bub 4 ma'am

part: 3 zip 4 city 5 PO box, state 7 zip code

phrase: 6 care of

preceder: 4 name

___ address: 6 direct 7 keynote

addressee: 6 tenant 8 occupant 10 inhabitant

___-address system: 6 public

adduce: 4 cite, show 5 quote 6 affirm, impute, reason 7 mention 8 point out 10 illustrate

ade: 5 drink 6 cooler 8 beverage 9 soft drink

starter: 4 lime 5 block, lemon, stock 6 cannon, orange

___ a deaf ear: 4 turn

___ a deal: 3 cut

___ a deal!: 3 It's

___-a-Dee-Doo-Dah: 3 Zip

___, a deer: 3 doe

Ade, George: 6 author, writer

nickname: Aesop of Indiana

work: Artie
The College Widow
The County Chairman
Doc Horne
Fables in Slang
Forty Modern Fables
Hand-Made Fables
Modern Fables
The Old Time Saloon
Peggy from Paris
Pink Marsh
The Sultan of Sulu

Adela: 5 Turin 7 St. Johns 8 Nicolson

Adelaide: 4 city, port, town 7 Manning

locale: 9 Australia

river: 7 Torrens

Adelaide's Lament composer: 7 Loesser
Adele: 4 Mara 7 Astaire, Jergens, Simpson, Wiseman
to Fred: 3 sis
Adélie __: 4 Land 5 Coast 7 penguin
Adelina: 5 Patti
__ Adeline: 5 Sweet
Adelle: 5 Davis
Aden: 4 city, port, town
locale: 5 Yemen
Adenauer: 6 Konrad 7 Der Alte
see also German
adenoidal: 5 nasal
Adeodatus: 4 pope 7 pontiff
adept: 3 ace, apt 4 able, deft, good, whiz 5 crack, great, handy, quick, ready, savvy, sharp, slick, smart 6 adroit, artful, au fait, clever, expert, facile, habile, master, nimble, smooth, wizard 7 capable, hotshot, maestro, old hand, skilled, veteran 8 delicate, dextrous, masterly, skillful, talented, topnotch, virtuoso 9 dexterous, efficient, masterful, on the ball, on the beam, practiced, qualified, top-drawer, top-flight 10 past master, proficient, specialist, well-versed
adeptly: 4 neat, well 7 rightly 8 laudably
adeptness: 5 craft, skill 7 ability, finesse, mastery, sleight 9 dexterity 10 efficiency, expertness, nimbleness
adequacy: 7 fitness, utility 8 capacity 10 capability, competence, efficiency
words of ~: 6 it'll do
adequate: 2 OK 3 fit 4 able, fair, good, okay, okeh; okey, so-so, tidy 6 decent, enough, up to it 7 capable, livable 8 all right, liveable, middling, passable, suitable 9 competent, effective, efficient, qualified, requisite, tolerable, unnotable, up to grade 10 acceptable, fairly good, sufficient
be ~: 2 do 5 serve 7 satisfy, suffice
informally: 4 enuf
more than ~: 5 ample
not ~: 4 puny 5 scant
adequately: 4 so-so, well 7 rightly 9 copiously, fittingly, tolerably 10 abundantly, acceptably, fairly well, well enough
Adeste __: 7 Fideles
Adhara: 4 star
adhere: 4 bond, glue, hold, join 5 cling, paste, stick 6 attach, be true, cement, cleave, fasten, hang on 7 abide by, be loyal, conform 8 hold fast 9 stick fast 10 toe the line
to: 4 heed, keep, meet, mind, obey 6 accept, follow, fulfil, redeem 7 abide by, fulfill, observe, respect 8 belong to, carry out 9 agree with 10 comply with
adherence: 7 loyalty 8 cohesion, devotion, sticking, traction 9 coherence, constancy, fixedness, stability 10 allegiance, dedication, observance
adherent: 3 fan, nut 5 pupil 6 backer, helper 7 devotee, sponsor 8 advocate, believer, disciple, follower, henchman, loyalist, partisan 9 sectarian, supporter, worshiper 10 aficionado, enthusiast
suffix: 3 -ist, -ite 5 -arian
adherents: 6 school 9 following
adhesive: 3 gum 4 glue 5 epoxy, gluey, gooey, gummy, paste, putty, tacky 6 cement, clingy, sticky 7 stickum, viscose, viscous 8 clinging, fixative, mucilage
pane ~: 5 putty
philatelist's ~: 5 hinge
adhesive __: 4 tape 6 factor 7 bandage, binding, plaster
ad-hoc: 9 impromptu, temporary 10 improvised, pro tempore
coalition: 4 bloc
Adia (1998 song) artist: Sarah McLachlan
Adidas: 6 sneaks 8 sneakers
rival: 3 Ked 4 Avia, Nike 6 Reebok 8 Converse
__ a diet: 4 go on
adieu: 3 bye 4 exit, ta-ta 5 leave 6 bye-bye, so long 7 goodbye, parting 8 farewell, Godspeed, sayonara 9 departure
bid ~: 6 depart
in Hawaiian: 5 aloha
in Italian: 4 ciao
in Latin: 3 ave 4 vale
in Spanish: 5 adios
__ a Difference a Day Makes: 4 What
Adige: 5 river
city on the ~: 5 Trent 6 Trento, Verona
locale: 5 Italy
a dime a __: 5 dozen
__ a dim view: 4 take
adios: 3 bye 4 ta-ta 6 bye-bye, so long 7 goodbye 8 au revoir, farewell, Godspeed, sayonara
in French: 5 adieu
in Hawaiian: 5 aloha
in Italian: 4 ciao
in Latin: 3 ave 4 vale
adipose: 4 oily 5 beefy, fatty, fubsy, obese, plump, pudgy, pursy, stout 6 chubby, fleshy, portly, pyknic, rotund, stocky, zaftig, zoftig 7 paunchy 8 roly-poly 9 corpulent 10 overweight
__-à-dire: 4 c'est
Adirondack: 6 Indian 7 Amerind
Adirondack __: 5 chair
Adirondacks: 3 mts. 4 mtns. 5 range 9 mountains
locale: 7 New York
mountain: 5 Marcy
__ a disadvantage: 5 put at
__ a distance: 4 from
adit: 4 ramp 5 entry 6 portal, tunnel 7 ingress 8 entrance
adjacency: 8 nearness 10 contiguity
adjacent: 4 near, next, nigh 5 close, handy 6 at hand, beside, nearby 7 close by 8 abutting, imminent, next-door, touching 9 alongside, bordering, immediate, impending, proximate 10 contiguous, convenient, juxtaposed
lie ~ to: 4 abut, join, meet 5 touch, verge 6 adjoin 8 border on, neighbor
to: 4 near 6 beside
(to): 4 next
Adjani, Isabelle: 7 actress
film: The Driver (1978)
Ishtar (1987)
Nosferatu the Vampyre (1979)
Queen Margot (1994)
The Tenant (1976)
adjective: 4 word 8 modifier 9 attribute, qualifier 10 identifier
modifier: 3 adv. 6 adverb
suffix: 3 -ant, -ary, -ate, ent, -ern, -ese, est, -eth, -ful, -ial, -ian, -ier, ile, ine, -ior, ish, -ive, -oid, -ory, -ose, -ous, -tic, -ule 4 -able, -eous, -etic, -fold, -free, -ible, -ical, -ious, -less, -like, -long, -most, -otic, -some, -tory, -ward 5 -ative, -atory, -esque, -istic, -itive, -orial, -proof, -tious, -ulent, -ulous, -urous, -wards 6 -aceous, -escent, -itious, -worthy
adjective __: 6 clause, phrase 7 pronoun
__ adjective: 6 proper, verbal
adjoin: 3 add 4 abut, link, meet 5 affix, annex, touch, unite, verge 6 append, attach, border, couple 7 connect 8 border on, neighbor 9 juxtapose
adjoining: 4 near, next 6 beside, nearby 8 next-door 9 impinging 10 approximal, connecting, contiguous, convenient, juxtaposed
adjourn: 3 end 4 halt, quit, stay, stop 5 cease, close, delay 6 finish, put off, recess, shelve, wind up, wrap up 7 break up, hold off, suspend 8 conclude, dissolve, pack it in, postpone 9 terminate 10 call it a day
adjournment: 3 end 5 close, delay 7 respite
adjt.: 4 asst.
see also adjutant
adjudge: 4 rate 6 decide, regard 7 account, referee 8 appraise, sentence 9 arbitrate
__ adjudicata: 3 res
adjudicate: 3 try 4 hear, rule 6 decide, settle, umpire 7 mediate, referee 9 arbitrate, determine, negotiate
adjudication: 6 ruling 7 verdict 8 decision
adjudicator: 6 umpire 7 arbiter, referee 10 peacemaker
adjunct: 5 extra 6 helper 7 fitting 8 addendum, addition, appendix, henchman, offshoot 9 accessory, appendage, assistant, associate, auxiliary, extension 10 attachment, elongation, supplement
adjuration: 4 oath
adjure: 3 beg 4 pray, urge 5 order 6 attest, enjoin 7 beseech, command, entreat, implore, require, swear in 8 obligate 10 supplicate
adjust: 3 fit, fix, pay, set 4 gear, suit, true, tune 5 adapt, align, aline, alter, fix up, focus, reset, scale, tweak 6 attune, change, doctor, harden, modify, orient, refund, repair, settle, square, tailor, tune up 7 arrange, balance, conform, correct, fashion, improve, prepare, realign, rectify, redress, restyle, sharpen 8 accustom, fine-tune, modulate, regulate, set right 9 acquiesce, calibrate, get over it, habituate, negotiate, reconcile 10 assimilate, coordinate, fiddle with, straighten, tinker with
adjustable: 7 movable, pliable 8 flexible, moveable 9 adaptable, versatile
adjustable-__ mortgage: 4 rate
adjusted: 5 ready 8 prepared
adjusted __ income: 5 gross
__-adjusted: 4 well
__-adjusting: 4 self
adjustment: 5 tweak 6 change, fixing, payoff, repair 7 fitting, revisal, setting, shaping 8 revision 9 agreement, allotment, allowance, balancing, refitting, reshaping 10 adaptation, alteration, compromise, concession, correction, regulation, settlement
adjustments, make: 5 adapt
adjutant: 4 aide, asst. 6 helper 9 auxiliary
adjutant __: 4 bird 5 stork 7 general
Adlai: 9 Stevenson
opponent: 3 Ike
running mate: 5 Estes
Adlai __ Stevenson: 5 Ewing
Adler: 3 Lou 4 Kurt 5 Irene, Larry, Peter, Polly 6 Alfred, Luther, Stella 8 Mortimer
Adler, Kurt: 9 conductor
Adler, Larry forte: 9 harmonica
Adler, Mortimer: 11 philosopher
Adler, Peter: 9 conductor
ad lib: 4 quip 6 devise, fake it, freely, make up, wing it 7 offhand 9 extempore, impromptu, improvise, play by ear, unplanned, whipped up 10 improvised, informally, off-the-cuff, unprepared
comedy: 6 improv
ad litteram: 7 exactly
Adlon: 5 Percy
adm.
employer: 3 USN
see also admiral
__ Adm.: 4 Rear
admeasure: 9 apportion
Admeto composer: 6 Handel
admin.: 3 mgr., mgt. 4 mgmt.
admin. __: 4 asst.
administer: 3 run, use 4 boss, deal, give, head, keep, rule, tend 5 apply, issue, offer, serve 6 direct, govern, handle, impose, manage, supply, tender 7 conduct, control, deliver, dole out, execute, furnish, inflict, mete out, oversee, preside, proffer, provide 8 carry out, disburse, dispense 9 apportion, authorize, supervise 10 contribute, distribute, measure out, ride herd on, run the show
administration: 3 ins 4 rule, term 5 board, power, reign 6 agency, bureau, policy, record, regime, tenure 7 cabinet, command, conduct, control, running 8 advisors, handling, top brass
__ administration: 6 public
administrative __: 3 law 5 leave 6 county 9 assistant
administrator: 3 CEO 4 boss, dean, exec, head, prin. 5 chair, chief 6 honcho, leader, tycoon, warden 7 curator, manager, officer 8 director, executor, governor, official, overseer 9 principal
admirable: 4 fine, good, keen, neat, nice, okay 5 grand, great, legit, moral, noble, super 6 lovely, peachy, proper, superb, worthy 7 ethical 8 all right, laudable, pleasant, pleasing, splendid, superior 9 agreeable, beautiful, copacetic, deserving, estimable, excellent, exemplary, exquisite, hunky-dory, praisable, reputable, wonderful 10 acceptable, attractive, beneficial, creditable, out of sight, super-duper
act: 4 feat
name meaning ~: 7 Miranda
Admirable Crichton, The author: James M. Barrie
admirably: 4 well 7 rightly 8 laudably, worthily
admiral: 4 rank
answer to an ~: 3 aye 6 aye aye 9 aye aye sir
org.: 3 USN
subordinate: 4 capt. 7 captain
white ~: 3 bug 6 insect
WWI German ~: 4 Spee
WWII: 6 Halsey, Nimitz
see also navy
__ admiral: 3 red 4 rear 5 fleet, white
__-admiral: 4 vice
Admiral __ Fleet: 5 of the
Admiral alternative: 5 Amana, Norge 6 Bendix, Maytag, Tappan 7 Jenn-Air, Kenmore 8 Hotpoint 9 Magic Chef, Whirlpool 10 Frigidaire, Kelvinator, KitchenAid
Admiral Benbow __: 3 Inn
admiralty __: 3 law 5 brass, cloth, metal 6 bronze
Admiralty __: 4 mile 5 Inlet, Range 7 Islands
Admiralty Range locale: 9 Antartica
__ admirari: 3 nil
admiration: 4 love 5 favor, honor 6 esteem, homage, praise, regard, wonder 7 respect, valuing, worship 8 approval, idolatry 9 adoration, affection, amazement, deference, marveling, obeisance, reverence

10 compliment, estimation, popularity, veneration, wonderment
exclamation: 6 good-oh, touché
___ Admiration Society: 6 Mutual
admire: 4 laud, like, look, love, ogle 5 adore, go for, honor 6 esteem, praise, regard, revere 7 cherish, glorify, idolize, respect, worship 8 hand it to, look up to, venerate 9 care about 10 appreciate
oneself: 5 preen
admired: 7 beloved
one: 4 hero, idol
admirer: 3 fan, nut 4 beau, buff 5 freak, hound, liker, lover, swain, wooer 6 patron, rooter, suitor 7 booster, devotee, fancier, groupie 8 disciple, follower, partisan 9 boyfriend, inamorato, supporter 10 enthusiast, girlfriend, sweetheart
group: 4 cult
admiring: 6 loving 7 valuing 10 respectful
greatly ~: 5 in awe
admissibility: 7 fitness
admissible: 2 OK 4 good, okay 5 jural, legal, licit, right 6 lawful 7 allowed 8 passable 9 allowable, permitted, pertinent, tolerable, tolerated, warranted 10 acceptable, applicable, concedable, in the rules, legitimate, reasonable
admission: 4 pass 5 entry 6 access, assent, avowal, entrée, ticket 7 ingress, receipt 8 entrance 9 accession, affidavit, allowance, assertion, enrolment, reception, statement, testimony 10 acceptance, concession, confession, deposition, disclosure, divulgence, enrollment, initiation, permission, profession, revelation, unbosoming
gain ~: 5 get in
price of ~: 4 fare
refuse ~: 5 block 6 forbid 7 exclude, keep out 9 freeze out
requirement: 6 ticket
select for ~: 3 tap
admission ___: 3 fee
___ admission: 4 free 7 general
___ admissions: 4 open
admit: 2 OK 3 own 4 avow, fess, okay, take 5 adopt, agree, allow, enrol, go for, grant, house, let in, let on, own up, see in 6 accede, accept, accord, affirm, assent, avouch, comply, enroll, expose, fess up, induct, listen, open up, reveal, take in 7 concede, confess, confide, confirm, declare, divulge, embrace, include, lay bare, own up to, profess, receive, shelter, welcome 8 disclose, face up to, initiate, proclaim, stand for 9 come clean, make known, put up with, recognize, sign off on 10 concur with, give the nod
defeat: 4 quit 5 yield
guilt: 9 apologize, beg pardon 10 make amends
to: 5 let on
admit ___: 3 one
admittance: 5 entry 6 access, entrée 7 ingress, passage 8 entrance 9 inclusion
refuse ~ to: 7 exclude
admitted: 5 known, let in 10 undisputed
be ~: 5 get in
admittedly: 6 indeed, really
admix: 5 alloy, blend 6 mingle 7 blend in, combine 8 compound 9 commingle, interlard 10 amalgamate
admixed: 6 impure
admixture: 5 blend 6 fusion 7 mélange 8 blending 10 sprinkling
admonish: 3 rag, rap 4 warn 5 chide, scold 6 advise, berate, exhort, preach, punish, rebuke 7 caution, censure, counsel, lecture, reprove, tell off, upbraid 8 forewarn, threaten 9 criticize, reprimand
admonisher comment: 3 tsk 6 tsk tsk
admonition: 5 alert 6 caveat, homily, lesson, notice, rebuke 7 caution, censure, warning 8 berating, reminder, reproval 10 correction, injunction, upbraiding
mom's ~: 4 don't 6 be good, be nice
theater ~: 3 shh 4 hush
Adnan: 4 Etel 9 Khashoggi
Adnan, Etel: 4 poet 8 Lebanese
adnate: 8 attached
ado: 4 flap, fuss, spat, stir, tiff 5 furor, hoo-ha, melee, scene 6 bother, bustle, clamor, dustup, flurry, fracas, hoopla, hubbub, racket, ruckus, rumpus, tumult, uproar 7 big deal, blether, clutter, fanfare, travail, trouble, turmoil 8 activity, brouhaha, busyness, foofaraw, rowdydow, squabble 9 commotion, confusion, hue and cry, whoop-de-do 10 difficulty, excitement, hullabaloo, hurly-burly
without further ~: 3 now, PDQ 6 at once 8 promptly, right now 9 forthwith, right away
Ado ___: 5 Annie
___ Ado About Nothing: 4 Much
Ado Annie
what ~ couldn't do: 5 say no
adobe: 4 clay 5 brick
ingredient: 5 straw
Adobe ___: 7 Acrobat, Systems
adobo: 4 stew
adodo: 6 rattle 10 percussion
origin: 4 Togo
___: a Dog: 3 Lad
___ a dog's life: 4 lead
adolescence: 5 teens, youth 7 boyhood, puberty 8 girlhood 10 immaturity
adolescent: 3 kid 4 girl, teen 5 child, minor, young, youth 6 boyish 7 girlish, puerile, teenage 8 immature, juvenile, teenager, youthful 9 beardless, halfgrown, pubescent, stripling, youngster
affliction: 4 acne
mustache: 4 wisp
no longer ~: 5 adult, of age 6 mature 7 grown up
Adolf: 7 Windaus 9 Butenandt, von Baeyer
___, a dollar..., A: 6 dillar
Adolph: 4 Ochs, Rupp 5 Green, Zukor 6 Caesar
Adolphe: 3 Sax 4 Adam 6 Menjou
___ Adolphus: 8 Gustavus
Adonai: 3 God 4 Lord 5 Jahve, Jahwe, Yahve, Yahwe 6 Jahveh, Jahweh, Yahveh, Yahweh 8 Almighty
Adonais: 4 poem 5 elegy
author: 7 Shelley
honoree: 5 Keats
last word of ~: 3 are
Adonis: 6 beauty
daughter of ~: 5 Beroe
lover of ~: 9 Aphrodite
parent of ~: 6 Myrrha 7 Cinyras
slayer of ~: 4 boar
son of ~: 6 Golgos
___-a-doodle-doo!: 4 Cock
___-a-dope: 4 rope
adopt: 3 use 4 okay, pass, pick, take 5 admit, allow, co-opt, go for 6 accept, assent, assume, borrow, choose, comply, follow, listen, prefer, take in, take on, take up 7 approve, embrace, espouse, include, observe, welcome 8 stand for, take over 9 put up with, recognize, sign off on 10 concur with, give the nod, legitimize, settle upon
adoptee: 4 ward
shelter ~: 3 cat, dog 5 stray
adoption: 8 approval, espousal 9 fosterage, selection 10 acceptance, assumption, employment
org.: 4 SPCA
adorable: 4 cute, dear 6 comely, dreamy, lovely, pretty 7 angelic, darling, lovable, winning, winsome 8 alluring, charming, fetching, gorgeous, handsome, heavenly, loveable, pleasing, precious, stunning 9 angelical, appealing, covetable, delicious, desirable 10 attractive, delectable, delightful
___ adorable..., A: 5 you're
adoration: 4 love 5 ardor, honor 6 esteem, homage, praise, prayer 7 passion, worship 8 devotion, idolatry 9 extolment, hankering, puppy love, reverence 10 admiration, attachment, estimation, exaltation, veneration
adore: 3 dig 4 laud, like, love 5 deify, enjoy, exalt, fancy, go for, honor, prize, swain 6 admire, dote on, praise, revere 7 adulate, care for, cherish, glorify, idolize, worship 8 dote upon, enshrine, fawn over, flip over, hold dear, inshrine, look up to, sanctify, treasure, venerate 9 care about, delight in
nonstandardly: 3 luv
adored: 3 pet 7 beloved 8 precious
one: 4 idol
Adorée: 5 Renee
adorer: 3 fan 5 swain 9 inamorata, inamorato
poem: 3 ode
adoring: 4 fond 6 devout, loving 7 valuing 8 enamored
one: 5 doter
adorn: 4 deck, gild, trim 5 array, color, grace 6 bedeck, doll up, emboss, enrich, purfle 7 bedizen, bejewel, deck out, dress up, encrust, enhance, festoon, flatter, furbish, garnish, gussy up, incrust, varnish 8 accouter, accoutre, beautify, decorate, emblazon, ornament, prettify, spruce up 9 bespangle, caparison, embellish, glamorize
adorned: 5 fancy 6 frilly 9 gussied up
culinarily: 5 garni
not ~: 5 plain, stark
adornment: 4 trim 5 dodad, floss, frill 6 choker, doodad, finery, geegaw, gewgaw 7 dingbat, garnish, gilding, jewelry 8 fretwork, frippery, froufrou, ornament, trimming 9 accessory, fandangle 10 decoration, embroidery
helmet ~: 7 feather
lobe ~: 4 hoop 7 earring
adornments: 9 trappings
___ a doubt: 6 beyond 7 without
Adoum, Jorge: 6 writer 9 Ecuadoran
adoze: 7 napping
___ a dozen: 5 a dime
Adrastea: 4 moon
planet: 7 Jupiter
Adrastos' domain: 5 Argos
adread: 7 terrify
___ a dream: 5 I have
adrenal ___: 5 gland 6 cortex 7 medulla
adrenaline catalyst: 4 fear
Adrian: 4 city, Lyne, Paul, pope, town, Zmed 5 Boult, Edgar 6 Balboa, Pasdar 7 Dantley, pontiff
locale: 8 Michigan
Adrian, Edgar: 8 Nobelist 12 physiologist
Adriatic: 3 sea
country: 3 Alb. 5 Italy 6 Bosnia 7 Albania, Croatia
gulf: 6 Venice 7 Trieste 8 Quarnero
locale: 5 Italy
peninsula: 6 Istria
river to the ~: 4 Drin 5 Adige, Piave 7 Livenza, Rubicon
town: 4 Bari, Fano 11 Zadar. Ancona
wind: 4 bora
Adrien: 5 Arpel, Brody
Adrienne: 4 Rich 7 Barbeau
adrift: 4 lost 5 amiss, at sea, loose, wrong 6 astray, erring 7 aimless 8 castaway, floating, goalless, unmoored 10 unanchored, unattached
go ~: 3 err
___ adrift: 4 cast
adrip: 3 wet 7 leaking
adroit: 3 apt 4 able, deft, foxy, good, neat, spry 5 adept, canny, crack, great, handy, nifty, quick, ready, savvy, sharp, slick 6 artful, astute, au fait, clever, expert, facile, gifted, habile, nimble 7 capable, cunning, politic, skilled, trained 8 dextrous, graceful, masterly, seasoned, skillful, talented 9 astucious, competent, dexterous, efficient, ingenious, inventive, masterful, versatile 10 proficient
starter: 3 mal
adroitly: 4 ably, neat 7 handily 10 swimmingly
adroitness: 3 art 4 ease 5 craft, knack 7 ability, faculty, finesse, know-how, mastery, sleight 8 facility 9 dexterity, handiness, readiness, smartness 10 cleverness, nimbleness
adroop: 7 sagging
a drop in the ___: 6 bucket
ads: 8 junk mail 9 promotion
___ ads: 4 want
adsuki: 4 bean
___-a-dub: 3 rub
adulate: 5 adore, honor 6 praise 7 flatter, lionize, worship 8 fawn over, gush over, kowtow to
adulated one: 4 idol
adulation: 5 honor 6 homage, praise 7 worship 8 flattery 10 compliment, sycophancy
adulator: 5 toady 6 fawner, yes man 7 flunkey 8 bootlick, courtier, truckler 9 flatterer, sycophant, toadeater
adulatory: 4 oily 6 honied 7 buttery, candied, fawning, glowing, honeyed, servile, slavish 8 obeisant, toadyish, unctuous 9 laudatory 10 obsequious
adult: 3 big, man 4 ripe 5 grown, imago, of age, woman 6 mature, X-rated 7 grownup, naughty, ripened 8 full-size 9 developed, full-grown 10 fully grown
education subj.: 3 ESL
to be: 3 kid 4 teen
___ adult: 5 young
Adult Education (1984 song) artist: Hall and Oates
adulterate: 3 cut, mar, mix 4 thin 5 alloy, alter, blend, spike, sully, taint 6 debase, defile, dilute, impair, poison, weaken 7 cheapen, corrupt, degrade, devalue, pollute, vitiate 8 denature, intermix 9 attenuate, commingle, devaluate, transfuse, water down 10 amalgamate, depreciate, infiltrate
adulterated: 4 sham 6 doctor, impure, watery 7 corrupt 8 maculate
adulteration: 3 mix 7 mixture 8 impurity
adulthood: 8 majority, maturity 9 voting age
reach ~: 6 grow up, mature
adumbrate: 3 dim 4 blur, hide, hint, mark, mean, veil, warn 5 bedim, chart, cloud, cover, draft, gloom, image, paint, shade, trace 6 darken, denote, emblem, muddle, opaque, shadow, sketch, typify 7 becloud, conceal, confuse, diagram, eclipse, explain,

obscure, outline, portend, portray, predict, presage, suggest **8** describe, forecast, foreshow, foretell, indicate, overcast, prophesy, rough out **9** cloud over, delineate, obfuscate, prefigure, represent, symbolize, tell about **10** allegorize, foreshadow, overshadow, silhouette
adumbration: **6** sketch
advance: **2** go **3** put **4** abet, bump, come, gain, grow, hype, lead, leap, lend, lift, loan, make, move, near, pass, plug, pose, push, rise, send, step, walk **5** boost, drive, early, exalt, go far, lobby, march, prior, raise, speed, trust **6** better, bump up, course, credit, evolve, feeler, foster, growth, hasten, inroad, look up, mature, motion, move up, propel, push on, submit, thrive, uplift **7** assault, deposit, develop, earlier, elevate, enlarge, forward, furnish, further, go ahead, go forth, headway, impetus, improve, magnify, make for, nurture, press on, proceed, produce, proffer, promote, propose, prosper, provide, suggest, support, upgrade **8** advocate, approach, ballyhoo, escalate, get ahead, go places, go toward, increase, leapfrog, movement, overture, progress, retainer, threaten **9** allowance, cultivate, encourage, go forward, hold forth, promotion, push ahead, recommend, volunteer **10** accelerate, beforehand, betterment, forge ahead, front money, gain ground, lay forward, move onward, prepayment, put forward
after a catch: **5** tag up
cash ~: **4** loan
get an ~: **3** owe
go in ~: **5** usher **6** herald **7** precede, presage **8** antecede, run ahead **10** anticipate, come before
in ~: **3** ere **5** ahead, early, first, prior **6** before **7** betimes, forward **9** preceding **10** beforehand, previously
info: **3** tip **4** omen
in ~ of: **5** until
oneself: **5** climb
person: **5** scout
rudely: **5** elbow
showing: **6** prevue **7** preview
advance __: **3** fee, man **5** guard **6** notice, person
advanced: **3** new **4** late **5** ahead, front **7** extreme, forward, liberal, radical **8** up-to-date **10** avant-garde, precocious
degree: **3** Ed.D., Ed.M., MBA, Ph.D. **4** D.Lit.
in age: **7** elderly
it may be ~: **5** money
more ~: **6** senior **7** ahead of **8** superior
advanced __: **6** credit, degree
advancement: **3** aid **4** gain, rise, step **8** progress **9** promotion
advances, make: **3** woo
advancing: **7** en route, forward, ongoing **8** oncoming, thriving, underway **9** on the move **10** aggressive, cumulative, on the march
not ~: **5** mired, stuck **8** moribund
advantage: **3** aid, use **4** boon, edge, good, jump, lead, luck, odds, perc, perk, plus, sake **5** asset, avail, break, leg up, merit, start **6** beauty, behoof, profit, virtue **7** benefit, vantage **8** blessing, handicap, interest, leverage, purchase **9** allowance, dominance, influence, landslide, privilege, seniority, supremacy, upper hand **10** ascendance, ascendancy, ascendence, ascendency, expediency, percentage, precedence, preference
at an ~: **5** ahead, one up
show to ~: **7** flatter
take ~: **5** avail
take ~ of: **3** use **4** milk **5** abuse, cozen, wrong **6** impose, play on, prey on **7** deceive, exploit, put upon, utilize **8** hoodwink, play upon **9** victimize
take ~ of again: **5** reuse
without ~: **7** useless
__ advantage of: **4** take
advantageous: **4** good **5** handy, happy, lucky, utile **6** aidful, benign, usable, useful **7** gainful, healthy, helpful, hopeful, useable **8** enviable, fruitful, positive, remedial, salutary, valuable **9** effectual, favorable, lucrative, opportune, rewarding **10** productive, profitable, propitious, worthwhile
most ~: **7** optimum
advantageously: **4** well
more ~: **6** better
advantageousness: **7** utility
advent: **4** dawn **5** onset, start **6** coming, outset **7** arrival, kickoff, leadoff **8** entrance, exordium **9** beginning, inception **10** appearance
Advent __: **6** Sunday
adventitious: **5** lucky **6** random
adventure: **4** dare, deed, feat, lark, risk, saga, yarn **5** geste, jaunt, novel, peril, quest, story **6** hazard, thrill, travel **7** episode, exploit, journey, romance, venture **8** incident, long shot **9** happening **10** enterprise, excitement, experience, occurrence
ender: **4** some
grand ~: **4** epic, tale, yarn **5** story **6** legend **9** chronicle
in search of ~: **6** errant
story: **4** epic, gest, saga, tale **5** conte, geste
adventure __: **4** tale **5** story **6** travel
adventurer: **5** rover, scout **6** risker **7** gambler, voyager **8** explorer, traveler, wanderer, wayfarer **9** charlatan, daredevil, journeyer, mercenary **10** speculator
Adventurer: **3** car **4** auto **6** DeSoto **10** automobile
Adventurers, The author: Harold Robbins
Adventures __ Juan: **5** of Don
Adventures __ Tin Tin, The: **5** of Rin
Adventures in Paradise (ABC drama) cast: Gardner McKay (Adam Troy)
__ Adventures in Wonderland: **6** Alice's
Adventures of Augie March, The author: Saul Bellow
Adventures of Baron Munchausen, The (1989 film)
cast: Eric Idle, John Neville, Sarah Polley
director: Terry Gilliam
Adventures of Bullwhip Griffin, The (1967 film)
cast: Roddy McDowall, Suzanne Pleshette
Adventures of Don Juan (1949 film) cast: Errol Flynn, Viveca Lindfors
Adventures of Elmo in Grouchland, The (1999 film)
cast: Mandy Patinkin, Vanessa Williams
Adventures of Ford Fairlane, The star: **4** Clay
Adventures of Huckleberry Finn (1985 film)
cast: Jim Dale, Patrick Day, Frederic Forrest
director: Peter H. Hunt
Adventures of Huckleberry Finn, The (1960 film)
cast: Eddie Hodges, Archie Moore, Tony Randall
director: Michael Curtiz
Adventures of Mark Twain, The (1944 film)
cast: Donald Crisp, Fredric March, Alexis Smith
director: Irving Rapper
Adventures of Martin Eden, The (1942 film)
cast: Glenn Ford, Claire Trevor
director: Sidney Salkow
Adventures of Ozzie and Harriet, The (ABC sitcom)
cast: Don DeFore (Thorny Thornberry)
David Nelson
Harriet Nelson
Kris Nelson
Ozzie Nelson
Ricky Nelson
Adventures of Rin Tin Tin, The (ABC western) cast: Lee Aaker (Rusty)
Adventures of Robin Hood, The (1938 film)
cast: Olivia de Havilland, Errol Flynn, Claude Rains, Basil Rathbone
director: Michael Curtiz
Adventures of Rocky and Bullwinkle, The (2000 film)
cast: Jason Alexander, Robert De Niro, Rene Russo
director: Des McAnuff
Adventures of Sebastian Cole, The (1999 film)
cast: Margaret Colin, Clark Gregg, Adrian Grenier, Aleska Palladino
Adventures of Sherlock Holmes, The (1939 film)
cast: Nigel Bruce, Ida Lupino, Basil Rathbone
director: Alfred Werker
Adventures of Superman, The (TV sci-fi)
cast: Phyllis Coates (Lois Lane)
John Hamilton (Perry White)
Jack Larson (Jimmy Olsen)
Noel Neill (Lois Lane)
George Reeves (Superman/Clark Kent)
Robert Shayne (Inspector Henderson)
Adventures of Wild Bill Hickok, The (TV western)
cast: Andy Devine (Jingles)
Guy Madison (Wild Bill Hickok)
adventuresome: **6** daring **8** reckless
Adventuress, The (1946 film)
cast: Trevor Howard, Deborah Kerr
adventuring, go: **5** sally
adventurous: **4** bold, game, rash **5** brace, brave, gutsy, nervy, risky **6** awless, daring, gritty, heroic, plucky, spunky **7** aweless, dashing, defiant, doughty, gallant, staunch, valiant **8** fearless, heroical, intrepid, reckless, resolute, romantic, stalwart, unafraid, valorous **9** audacious, daredevil, dauntless, dreadless, undaunted, unfearful **10** courageous
be ~: **4** dare
not ~: **5** staid
one: **5** darer
adventurousness: **8** audacity
adverb: **3** too **4** very, word **6** hardly, likely, poorly, rudely, softly **7** quickly **8** modifier, politely, probably **9** qualifier
archaic ~: **4** erst
poetic: **3** e'en, e'er, o'er, oft, yon **4** enow, ne'er **5** anear
suffix: **4** -ably, -ally, -ibly, -ward, -ways, -wise **5** -fully, -wards **6** -ically
adverb __: **6** clause
adversary: **3** foe, opp. **5** enemy, rival **6** foeman **7** opposer **8** attacked, opponent **9** ill-wisher **10** antagonist, competitor, contestant, opposition
Adversary in the House author: Irving Stone
adversary of the fortunate, The: **4** envy
adverse: **3** bad, ill **5** onery, toxic **6** malign, ornery, tragic **7** baleful, baneful, counter, harmful, hostile, opposed, ruinous **8** contrary, damaging, inimical, negative, opposite, tragical, untoward **9** dangerous, injurious, reluctant, resistive **10** calamitous, disastrous
prefix: **7** counter-
to: **7** athwart
__ Adverse: **7** Anthony
adversely: **3** ill
affect ~: **4** hurt
adversity: **3** woe **4** harm **5** trial **6** crunch, misery, mishap **7** bad luck, reverse, tragedy, travail, trouble, undoing **8** bad break, calamity, disaster, distress, hard luck, hardship, pressure **9** deep water, extremity, hard times, mischance, situation, suffering, tough luck **10** affliction, can of worms, difficulty, hard knocks, misfortune
overcome ~: **3** win **4** beat **6** attain, manage **7** achieve, conquer, make out, prevail, pull off, realize, succeed, triumph **8** struggle **9** withstand **10** accomplish
advert: **3** see **4** heed, mark, mind, view **5** imply, refer, see to, watch **6** hint at, look at, notice, regard, remark **7** mention, observe, refer to, suggest **8** allude to, attend to, glance at, indicate, intimate, listen to **9** insinuate, look after, touch upon **10** commercial, take care of, take heed of, take note of
advertent: **7** heedful **9** attentive
advertise: **4** hawk, hype, plug, puff, push, tout **5** boost, pitch **6** flaunt, herald, market, regard, spread **7** display, exhibit, promote, show off **8** announce, ballyhoo, proclaim **9** broadcast, make known, publicize **10** promulgate
advertisement: **4** bill, plug **5** blurb, flyer **6** poster **7** display, leaflet **8** handbill **9** publicity
Advertiser: **5** paper **9** newspaper
locale: **8** Honolulu
advertising: **4** hype **5** promo **6** hoopla **8** ballyhoo, hard sell **9** publicity
arrangement: **5** tie-in
award: **4** Clio
circular: **6** insert
lure: **6** coupon
pitch: **5** try it
selling point: **6** status **7** benefit, feature
sign: **4** neon
trademark: **4** logo
watchdog: **3** FTC
advertising __: **3** man **6** agency **7** account
advice: **3** aid, tip **4** help, info, word **5** input, steer **6** caveat, earful, sermon, tipoff **7** caution, counsel, pointer, tidings, warning **8** guidance **10** directions, dissuasion, persuasion, suggestion
bad ~: **8** bum steer
follow, as ~: **4** heed, obey
give unwanted ~: **6** kibitz, meddle
in Britain: **4** rede
name: **3** Ann **4** Abby **7** Landers **8** Van Buren
piece of ~: **3** tip **4** don't, MYOB
seek the ~ of: **6** look to **7** consult
take ~: **4** heed **5** act on **6** listen
advice and __: **7** consent

Advice fo' Chillun cartoonist: 4 Capp
Advil: 9 analgesic 10 painkiller
alternative: 3 APF 4 Cope 5 Aleve, Bayer 6 Anacin, Datril, Motrin 7 Ecotrin, Tylenol 8 Bufferin, Excedrin, St. Joseph, Vanquish 9 Ascriptin
target: 4 ache, pain
advisable: 3 apt, fit 4 well, wise 5 sound 6 seemly 7 fitting, politic, prudent 8 sensible, suitable 9 desirable, expedient, judicious, suggested 10 reasonable
advise: 3 tip 4 post, tell, tout, urge, warn 5 alert, brief, coach, guide, teach 6 clue in, direct, exhort, fill in, inform, notify, preach, report, tip off 7 apprise, apprize, caution, commend, counsel, let in on, preside, propose, put on to, suggest 8 acquaint, admonish, advocate, dissuade, forewarn, instruct, persuade, point out 9 encourage, make known, prescribe, recommend 10 keep posted
against: 8 dissuade
in Britain: 4 rede
of: 6 impart, inform, notify, relate, report 7 apprise, apprize, let in on 9 enlighten, make known
Advise and Consent
author: Allen Drury
cast: Henry Fonda, Charles Laughton, Don Murray
director: Otto Preminger
advised: 10 acquainted, considered
be ~: 4 hear
___-advised: 3 ill 4 well
advisedly: 9 carefully, prudently 10 cautiously, discreetly
advisement: 9 direction
take under ~: 8 consider
advisor: 4 aide 5 coach, guide, tutor 6 expert, helped, lawyer, mentor, oracle, priest 7 counsel, teacher 8 attorney 9 authority, confidant, counselor 10 consultant, Dutch uncle, instructor
chief ~: 5 elder
female ~: 6 egeria
financial ~: 3 CPA 10 accountant
legal ~: 3 att. 4 atty. 6 lawyer 8 attorney
personal ~: 4 guru 5 rabbi, rebbe
advisory: 5 alert 6 notice
group: 5 board, panel 7 cabinet
___ advisory: 7 weather
ad vitam: 7 for life
advocacy: 3 aid 6 urging 7 backing, defense, support 8 espousal 9 promotion 10 assistance
advocate: 4 back, plug, tout, urge 5 agent, boost, favor, urger 6 advise, backer, defend, friend, lawyer, praise, uphold, votary 7 advance, apostle, bolster, booster, counsel, espouse, further, nurture, paladin, pleader, promote, push for, root for, sponsor, suggest, support 8 adherent, argue for, attorney, champion, crusader, defender, endorser, exponent, plead for, press for, promoter, proposer, propound, reformer, speak for, stand for, stump for 9 barrister, counselor, encourage, expounder, paraclete, proponent, recommend, subscribe, supporter 10 campaigner, go to bat for
combining form: 4 -crat 5 -arian, -ocrat
org.: 3 ABA
suffix: 3 -ist, -ite 5 -arian
___ advocate: 5 judge 6 devil's
___ advocate general: 5 judge
adytum: 6 shrine
adz: 4 tool
relative: 2 ax 3 axe
adze: 4 tool 8 smoother
Adzharistan capital: 6 Batumi
adzuki: 4 bean 6 legume
A.E.: 7 Housman, van Vogt 8 Hotchner
AEC
part of ~: 4 Comm. 6 Atomic, Energy
successor: 3 NRC
aedes kin: 5 culex
aedile: 5 Roman
garb: 4 toga
Aeetes
daughter of ~: 5 Medea
sister of ~: 5 Aeaea, Circe, Kirke
A.E.F. author: Carl Sandburg
A.E.F. conflict: 3 WWI
Aegean: 3 sea 7 islands
ancient ~ region: 5 Ionia
gulf: 5 Izmir, Saros 7 Argolis, Saronic 8 Salonika
island: 3 Cos, Ios, Kea, Kos, Zea 4 Keos, Milo 5 Chios, Crete, Delos, Khios, Melos, Milos, Samos 6 Candia, Icaria, Lemnos, Lesbos, Patmos, Rhodes, Rhodos, Skiros, Skyros 7 Mykonos 8 Cyclades
locale: 6 Greece
river to the ~: 6 Struma 7 Maritsa
Aegeus
son of ~: 7 Theseus
wife of ~: 5 Medea
Aegina: 4 gulf
aegis: 3 aid 4 care 5 favor, guard 6 escrow, shield 7 backing, custody, keeping, support 8 auspices, security, umbrella 9 oversight, patronage, safeguard 10 protection
Aegle: 5 nymph 8 asteroid
aeiou: 6 vowels
Aelfric: 5 abbot 6 writer
Aello: 5 Harpy
Aeneas: 4 hero
brother of ~: 4 Eryx 5 Lyrus
companion: 7 Achates
daughter of ~: 7 Aemilia
friend of ~: 7 Achates
home: 4 Troy
lover of ~: 4 Dido, Roma 6 Codone 7 Lavinia 8 Dexithea, Eurydice 9 Anthemone
mother-in-law: 5 Amata
parent of ~: 5 Venus 8 Anchises 9 Aphrodite
son of ~: 5 Etias 7 Silvius 8 Ascanius
wife of ~: 4 Dido 6 Creusa
Aeneid, The: 4 epic, epos, poem 8 epic poem
author: 6 Vergil, Virgil
character: 4 Anna, Dido, Opis 5 Amata, Anius, Aruns, Eneas, Nisus 6 Aeneas, Creusa, Nautes, Pallas, Turnus 7 Acestes, Camilla, Celaeno, Evander, Latinus, Lavinia 8 Anchises, Ascanius, Euryalus 9 Palinurus
site: 4 Troy 5 Egean 6 Aegean
starter: 4 Arma
Aeolian ___: 4 harp, lyre, mode 7 Islands
Aeolus
father of ~: 8 Poseidon
mother of ~: 4 Arne
son of ~: 6 Boreas 8 Sisyphus
aeon: 3 age 6 period
A&E, part of: 4 arts
aequo animo: 8 serenely
aer-: 4 atmo-
Aer ___: 6 Lingus
aerate: 4 foam 5 froth 6 bubble, purify, refine 7 freshen, inflate 9 oxygenate, oxygenize, ventilate
aerator, soil: 4 root, worm
aerial: 4 high, pass 5 aloft, lofty 6 flying, volant 7 antenna 8 elevated, ethereal, in the sky, overhead 9 dreamlike, from above, TV antenna 10 rabbit ears
maneuver: 4 loop, spin
support: 4 mast
view provider: 5 blimp 7 airship, balloon 8 aircraft, zeppelin 9 dirigible
aerial ___: 4 mine 5 photo 6 ladder, mosaic, survey, tanker 7 railway, tramway
aerialist: 7 acrobat, gymnast, vaulter
like an ~: 5 agile
safeguard: 3 net
aerie: 4 nest 5 perch 6 refuge 7 retreat 8 fortress, hideaway 9 sanctuary
resident: 4 hawk 5 eagle 6 condor, eaglet
aeriform: 4 fumy 5 gassy
aerify: 8 vaporize
Aerio: 3 car 4 auto 6 Suzuki 10 automobile
Aer Lingus land: 4 Eire, Erin 7 Ireland
aero-: 4 atmo-
Aero: 3 car 4 auto 6 Willys 10 automobile
aerobatic maneuver: 4 loop, spin
aerobe: 4 germ 9 bacterium
aerobic ___: 7 dancing
aerobicize: 7 work out
aerobics: 5 drill, sport 7 workout 8 exercise
aftereffect: 4 ache
center: 3 gym, spa
command: 6 exhale
measure: 5 pulse
outpouring: 5 sweat
prefix: 3 oxy-
___ aerobics: 4 step
aerodynamic: 5 sleek
aerodynamics: 8 aviation
Aero-Falcon: 3 car 4 auto 6 Willys 10 automobile
Aero-Lark: 3 car 4 auto 6 Willys 10 automobile
aeronaut: 5 flier, flyer, pilot 6 fly boy 7 aviator
aeronautics: 7 science 8 aviation
org.: 3 NAA
study: 6 flight
___ Aeronautics Board: 5 Civil
Aerope's son: 8 Menelaus 9 Agamemnon
aerophobe fear: 6 drafts
Aerosmith
leader: Steven Tyler
song: Angel (1988)
Dream On (1976)
I Don't Want to Miss a Thing (1998)
Janie's Got a Gun (1989)
Love in an Elevator (1989)
Walk This Way (1976)
What It Takes (1990)
aerosol: 9 vaporizer
aerosol ___: 3 can 4 bomb 5 spray
Aerospatiale product: 3 jet, SST 5 plane
Aerostar: 3 van 4 Ford
aery: 9 pneumatic
Aeschylus: 4 poet 5 Greek 10 playwright
work: Agamemnon
Eumenides
Libation Bearers
Oresteia
The Persians
Prometheus Bound
Seven Against Thebes
The Suppliant Women
Aesir: 4 gods 5 Norse
VIP: 4 Odin 5 Othin
Aesop: 8 fabulist
character: 3 ant, dog, fox 4 bear, crow, dove, fawn, frog, hare, lamb, lion, mole, swan, wolf 5 crane, eagle, mouse, raven, snake, stork 6 pigeon 7 cat. Mule 8 Hercules, tortoise
lesson: 5 moral
like ~'s grapes: 4 sour
AES opponent: 3 DDE
aesthete: 8 longhair
passion: 4 arts
aesthetes: 8 literati 9 longhairs 10 illuminati
aesthetic: 7 refined 8 artistic, creative, graceful, tasteful 10 artistical
putting on ~ airs: 4 arty 5 artsy
aestheticism: 5 taste 7 culture
Aetna: 5 nymph
competitor: 7 MetLife 8 Allstate 9 State Farm
offering: 3 HMO
parent of ~: 4 Gaea 6 Uranus
A.F. ___: 3 of L.
___ a face: 4 make
___ à fait: 4 tout
___ a Falling Star: 5 Catch
afar: 3 off 6 way off, yonder 7 distant 8 outlying
not ~: 4 near
a far ___: 3 cry
Afar home: 6 Africa, Jibuti 7 Eritrea 8 Djibouti, Ethiopia
___ a fashion: 5 after
___ a fast one: 4 pull
... ___ a fat pig: 5 to buy
AFB: 5 Altus, Beale, Dover, Dyess, Minot, Moody, Vance 6 Arnold, Brooks, Cannon, Hickam, Nellis, Offutt, Robins, Travis 7 Andrews, Bolling, Buckley, Edwards, Keesler, Kessler, Langley, Maxwell, Patrick 8 Columbus, Holloman, Kirtland, Lackland, Laughlin, Peterson, Sheppard 9 Barksdale, Ellsworth, Fairchild 10 Charleston, Goodfellow, Vandenberg
nautical counterpart: 3 NAS
AFC
division: 4 East, West
part: 4 Amer., Conf. 8 American, Football 10 Conference
team: 4 Jets 5 Bills, Colts 6 Browns, Chiefs, Ravens, Texans, Titans 7 Bengals, Broncos, Jaguars, Raiders 8 Chargers, Dolphins, Patriots, Steelers
afeard: 6 scared, trepid 10 frightened
a feather in one's ___: 3 cap
___ A Feeling: 4 What
___ a Few Dollars More: 3 For
affability: 4 ease 7 amenity 9 geniality 10 cordiality, fellowship, good nature
affable: 4 easy, kind, nice, warm 5 bland, close, suave 6 benign, breezy, chummy, clubby, genial, gentle, hearty, jovial, kindly, polite, urbane 7 amiable, cordial 8 amicable, familiar, friendly, gracious, intimate, likeable, obliging, outgoing, pleasant, sociable 9 congenial, convivial, courteous, expansive 10 benevolent, buddy-buddy, gregarious, neighborly, personable, solicitous
affair: 2 do 4 duty, fest, fete, gala 5 event, party, thing, topic 6 dinner, formal, matter, soiree 7 benefit, concern, episode, mission, project, romance, shindig 8 business, function, incident, intrigue, luncheon, occasion 9 festivity, gathering, happening, operation, reception 10 assignment, enterprise, occurrence, proceeding
fancy ~: 2 do 4 ball, bash, gala 7 banquet, shindig 8 function, wingding
of honor: 4 duel
___ Affair: 3 XYZ 4 Love 6 Family 7 Holiday
___ Affair, A: 6 Family 7 Foreign

affaire d'honneur: 4 duel
affaires __: 5 d'état
Affair of the Heart (1983 song) artist: Rick Springfield
affairs: 7 matters 8 dealings
foreign ~: 9 diplomacy 10 statecraft
state of ~: 9 situation
__ affairs: 6 public 7 foreign
Affairs of Cellini (1934 film)
cast: Constance Bennett, Fredric March
director: Gregory La Cava
Affairs of Dobie Gillis, The (1953 film)
cast: Hans Conried, Debbie Reynolds, Bobby Van
director: Don Weis
Affair to Remember (195 film), An
cast: Cary Grant, Deborah Kerr
director: Leo McCarey
affect: 3 act, get 4 fake, move, pose, stir, sway, tint 5 act on, alter, feign, get to, lobby, put on, reach, set on, touch, upset 6 assume, bear on, change, fake it, grow on, impact, matter, modify, sicken, take on 7 act upon, disturb, impinge, impress, inspire, involve, pertain, perturb, pretend 8 bear upon, come over, contrive, distress, grow upon, impact on, interest, persuade, simulate 9 determine, influence, penetrate, transform 10 predispose
adversely: 4 hurt
personally: 7 concern
strongly: 4 stir
affectation: 3 act, air 4 airs, mask, pomp, pose, sham 5 front, put-on, quirk 6 facade, vanity 7 display 8 pretense 9 mannerism 10 pretension
exclamation: 6 la-de-da, la-di-da 8 lah-di-dah
affected: 3 coy 4 arty, camp, fake 5 apish, artsy, campy, false, hammy, phony, stagy 6 chichi, coyish, cutesy, demure, forced, formal, la-de-da, la-di-da, phoney, stagey 7 assumed, awkward, cutesie, feigned, labored, mincing, pompous, prudish, stilted, studied, touched 8 lah-di-dah, mannered, overcome, overdone, pedantic, schmalzy, shmaltzy, spurious 9 conceited, contrived, grandiose, high-toned, impressed, insincere, pretended, schmaltzy, unnatural 10 artificial, factitious, pedantical, theatrical
be ~ by: 4 feel
easily ~: 9 sensitive
manner: 4 airs
not ~: 6 immune
affectedness: 4 camp
affecting: 4 near 7 pitiful 8 dramatic, pathetic, poignant, touching 9 emotional, sorrowful 10 impressive, pathetical
affection: 4 care, love 5 amore, ardor, crush 6 desire, liking, regard 7 feeling, passion 8 devotion, fondness, interest, intimacy, kindness 9 appetence, closeness, hankering, puppy love, sentiment 10 admiration, attachment, endearment, friendship, propensity, solicitude, tenderness
evoke ~: 6 endear
have ~ for: 4 love
lavish ~: 4 dote
show of ~: 3 hug 4 kiss 6 caress 7 embrace
term of ~: 3 luv, pet 4 baby, dear, love 5 angel, chéri, cooky, cutey, cutie, deary, ducky, honey, lovey, sugar, sweet 6 cookie, dearie, sweets 7 beloved, dearest, sweetie, tootsie 8 chou-chou, cutie pie, precious, snookums, sugar pie, sweetums 10 honeybunch, sweetheart, sweetie pie, turtledove
affectionate: 4 dear, fond, kind, soft, warm 5 close, kissy, mushy, sweet 6 caring, chummy, clubby, doting, filial, genial, kindly, loving, tender 7 affable, amatory, amiable, amorous, cordial, devoted, gushing 8 amicable, friendly, intimate, outgoing, parental, sociable 9 amatorial, convivial, fraternal 10 benevolent, buddy-buddy, neighborly, solicitous
sound: 3 coo
affective: 7 piteous 9 emotional, intuitive 10 perceptual
Affenpinscher: 3 dog 5 canid, pooch 6 canine
afferent: 7 sensory 9 sensorial
affiance: 3 vow 6 engage 7 promise
affiancing: 9 betrothal
affiche: 6 poster
affidavit: 5 paper, proof 8 evidence 9 admission, agreement, statement, testimony 10 deposition
give an ~: 5 swear, vouch 6 attest
affiliate: 3 arm 4 ally, band, join 5 align, aline, unite 6 branch, hook up, member, team up 7 chapter, combine, connect, partner 8 division, offshoot, unionize 9 associate 10 amalgamate, come aboard, go partners
affiliated: 4 akin 6 allied, joined, united 7 cognate, related 8 familial, hooked up, in league 9 ancestral, bracketed, connected
be ~: 6 belong
affiliation: 3 tie 4 bond 5 union 6 hookup, league 7 cahoots, merging 8 alliance, relation
affine: 5 in-law 9 kinswoman
affinity: 6 liking 7 analogy, empathy, kinship, rapport 8 fondness, intimacy, likeness, penchant, relation, sympathy, velleity 9 appetence, belonging, closeness, communion, community, good vibes 10 attachment, attraction, connection, friendship, partiality, proclivity, propensity, similarity
affinity __: 4 card 5 group
affirm: 3 say, vow 4 aver, avow, hold 5 admit, posit, prove, state, swear, utter, vouch 6 accept, accord, adduce, allege, assert, assure, attest, avouch, depone, insist, ratify, uphold 7 believe, certify, confess, confirm, contend, declare, endorse, indorse, profess, protest, ratifie, testify 8 attest to, maintain, make sure, proclaim, validate, vouch for 9 enunciate, guarantee, predicate, pronounce 10 asseverate
affirmation: 2 OK 3 vow 4 oath, okay, okeh, okey 5 claim 6 assent, avowal 8 averment, evidence 9 statement, testimony
terse ~: 3 I do
affirmative: 2 ay, da, ja, sí 3 aye, nod, oui, yea, yep, yes, yup 4 fine, okay, sure, yeah 5 good-o, natch, quite, right, roger, uh-huh 6 agreed, gladly, good-oh, indeed, just so, rather, righto, surely, you bet, yowzah 7 exactly, go ahead, indeedy, mais oui, quite so, ten-four 8 all right, as you say, of course, positive, thumbs up, very well 9 be my guest, certainly, darn right, naturally, precisely, sure thing, you betcha, you said it 10 absolutely, by all means, definitely, positively, sure enough, that's right
astronaut ~: 3 A-OK
beatnik ~: 4 I dig
emphatic ~: 6 yes yes
gesture: 3 nod
oater ~: 3 yep, yup 10 darn tootin'
pilot ~: 5 roger
sailor ~: 3 aye
affirmative __: 4 flag 6 action
Affirmed rival: 6 Alydar
affix: 3 add, pin, set, tag 4 bind, glue, join, tack 5 add on, annex, paste, put on, rivet, sew on, stick, tag on, tie on 6 adjoin, append, attach, fasten, glue on, hook on, iron on, slap on, staple, tack on 7 appends, stick on, subjoin 9 thumbtack
one's name: 4 sign
afflatus: 4 fire 6 genius 10 revelation
Affleck, Ben: 5 actor
colleague: Matt Damon
film: Armageddon (1998)
The Boiler Room (2000)
Bounce (2000)
Changing Lanes (2002)
Dogma (1999)
Good Will Hunting (1997)
Pearl Harbor (2001)
The Sum of All Fears (2002)
afflict: 3 ail, irk, try, vex 4 hurt, rack, rend 5 annoy, beset, harry, visit, worry 6 bother, burden, grieve, harass, pester, plague, sicken 7 agonize, disturb, oppress, scourge, torment, torture, trouble 8 aggrieve, distress, keep down 9 force upon, persecute
suddenly: 5 seize
afflicted: 3 ill 4 sick, sore 5 ailed, woful 6 ailing, infirm, laid up, sickly, unwell, woeful 7 unhappy, unsound 8 diseased, dolorous, wretched 9 aggrieved, bedridden, miserable, sorrowful 10 distressed, indisposed
be ~ with: 3 get 4 have 8 contract
affliction: 3 ill, woe 4 bane, care, hurt, load 5 curse, grief, trial 6 blight, burden, injury, malady, misery, ordeal, plague, rebuke, regret, sorrow 7 disease, illness, scourge, torment, trouble, undoing 8 calamity, disorder, distress, hardship, sickness 9 adversity, annoyance, complaint, grievance, ill health, infirmity, suffering 10 difficulty, heartbreak, misfortune, unwellness, woefulness
Affliction (1998 film)
cast: James Coburn, Willem Dafoe, Nick Nolte, Sissy Spacek
director: Paul Schrader
afflictive: 7 hurtful 10 calamitous, deplorable, lamentable
affluence: 4 ease 5 funds, means, money, purse 6 luxury, plenty, riches, wealth 7 fortune 8 good life, opulence, opulency 9 abundance, substance, well-being 10 exuberance, prosperity
affluent: 4 full, rich 5 flush 6 loaded, monied 7 copious, moneyed, opulent, upscale, wealthy, well-off 8 abundant, in clover, thriving, well-to-do 9 bountiful, doing well, fortunate, luxurious, plenteous, well-fixed 10 in the dough, in the money, privileged, propertied, prosperous, upper-class, well-heeled
the ~: 5 haves
afflux: 6 inflow
afford: 4 bear, give, lend 5 allow, grant, incur, offer, spare, yield 6 bestow, impart, manage, pay for, render, supply 7 furnish, produce, provide, radiate, sustain
affordable: 7 low-cost 10 reasonable
not: 4 dear, high 5 steep 6 costly
affray: 3 row 5 brawl, clash, fight, melee 6 barney, combat, fracas, rumpus, strife, tumult 7 contest, quarrel, scuffle 10 donnybrook, free-for-all
affright: 5 dread 6 dismay 7 horrify, startle 9 give a turn
affront: 3 dig 4 barb, gibe, jeer, jibe, mock, slam, slap, slur, snub 5 abuse, anger, annoy, decry, libel, pique, scorn, sneer, spurn, taunt, wrong 6 defame, deride, dump on, heckle, impugn, injury, insult, malign, offend, rebuff, slight, vilify 7 aggress, asperse, calumny, catcall, degrade, disdain, mockery, obloquy, offense, outrage, provoke, put-down, rank out, slander, traduce 8 belittle, brickbat, contempt, defiance, denounce, derision, irritate, ridicule, vexation, vilipend 9 aspersion, cheap shot, contumely, criticize, denigrate, discredit, disparage, grievance, humiliate, indignity 10 calumniate, defamation, disrespect, impugnment, opprobrium
affronted: 4 hurt, sore
be ~: 4 mind
Affton: 4 city, town
locale: 8 Missouri
afghan: 5 shawl, throw 7 blanket 8 coverlet, coverlid
material: 4 wool
Afghan: 3 dog 5 canid, pooch 6 canine, Kaffir 8 language, Turkoman
neighbor: 5 Irani
Afghanistan: 6 nation 7 country
airline: 6 Ariana
capital: 5 Kabul
city: 5 Herat, Kabul 8 Kandahar
continent: 4 Asia
goat: 7 markhor 8 markhoor
language: 6 Pashto, Pushto, Pushtu
money: 3 pul 7 afghani
mountain: 9 Hindu Kush
neighbor: 4 Iran 5 China 8 Pakistan 10 Tajikistan, Uzbekistan
river: 5 Farah
aficionado: 3 fan, nut 4 buff 5 fiend, freak, lover 6 addict, rooter 7 devotee, fanatic, groupie 8 adherent, follower 10 enthusiast
__ a fiddle: 5 fit as
afield: 4 away, awry 5 amiss, wrong 6 astray 7 off base 8 straying 9 off course 10 far and wide, off the mark, ungrounded
__ afield: 3 far
__ Afield: 6 Sports
__ a finger: 4 lift
afire: 3 lit 4 avid 5 fiery, het up 6 ablaze, ardent, flambé, red-hot 7 blazing, burning, excited, flaming, flaring, zealous 8 in flames 9 combusted
like a house ~: 6 wildly 8 fiercely 9 furiously 10 vigorously
set ~: 6 ignite, kindle
__ Afire: 6 Hearts
__ a fire under: 5 build, light, start
__ a fit: 5 throw
AFL: 5 union
chapter: 3 lcl. 5 local
members: 5 labor
partner: 3 CIO
part of ~: 3 Fed. 4 Amer. 5 Labor 8 American 10 Federation
aflame: 3 lit 5 eager, fiery, wired 6 ablaze, on fire, red-hot 7 blazing, burning, excited, fired up, flaring, lighted 8 juiced up 9 burning up
set ~: 6 ignite, kindle
AFL-CIO: 5 union
constituent: 3 UAW
afloat: 4 asea 5 at sea, awash 7 buoyant, solvent 8 swimming 9 out of debt 10 on the water, waterborne
keep ~: 4 swim 7 survive
set ~: 6 launch
aflutter: 4 agog
AFM member: 6 oboist 7 cellist, flutist, violist 8 flautist, musician 9 violinist 10 bassoonist

___ a Fool Believes: 4 What
afoot: 5 astir 7 going on, walking 8 in motion, stirring, underway 9 happening, in process, on the move 10 in progress, in the works
it may be ~: 4 game
set ~: 8 motivate
afore: 3 ere 6 erenow 7 earlier, in front
ender: 4 said, time 7 thought 9 mentioned
___ a for effort: 5 get an
aforementioned: 4 prec., prev., said, same, such 5 above, prior 8 previous 9 foregoing, preceding
aforesaid: 4 prec., prev., said, same, such 5 above, prior 8 previous 9 foregoing, preceding
___ aforethought: 6 malice
afoul: 5 amiss 7 tangled
run ~ of: 3 irk 4 rile
___ afoul of: 3 run 4 fall
___ a fox: 5 sly as
___ A. Fox: 6 Vivica
Afr.: 4 cont.
former ~ nation: 4 Rhod.
nation: 3 Ang., Eth., Mor.
neighbor: 3 Eur.
see also Africa
afraid: 4 loth 5 cowed, funky, loath, pavid, timid 6 gun-shy, scared, trepid, uneasy, yellow 7 abashed, alarmed, anxious, chicken, daunted, fearful, nervous, panicky, spooked, uneager, worried 8 cowardly, hesitant, recreant, startled, timorous 9 nerveless, petrified, regretful, reluctant, terrified, tremulous, unwilling 10 distressed, frightened, indisposed
be ~ of: 4 fear
___ afraid: 5 Be not
___ Afraid of Virginia Woolf?: 4 Who's
A-frame: 4 roof 6 chalet 8 ski lodge
feature: 4 eave
site: 3 lot
afresh: 3 new 4 anew, over 5 again, newly 6 de novo, lately, of late 8 once more, recently, repeated 9 once again, over again 10 from the top
Africa: 9 continent
ancient ~ land: 5 Nubia
ancient ~ town: 4 Zama
antelope: 3 gnu, kob 4 kudu, oryx, pala, puku, topi, tora 5 ariel, bongo, eland, nyala, oribi 6 dik-dik, duiker, impala, koodoo 7 gazelle
assn.: 3 OAU
beast: 3 asp, gnu, kob 4 croc, ibex, kudu, lion, oryx, pala, puku, topi, tora 5 ariel, bongo, camel, chita, civet, cobra, eland, hyena, hyrax, mamba, nyala, okapi, oribi, rhino, xerus, zoril 6 aoudad, cheeta, chetah, dassie, dik-dik, duiker, fennec, hyaena, impala, jackal, koodoo, quagga, serval 7 caracal, cheetah, gazelle, leopard, zorilla, zorille 9 crocodile
bird: 4 coly 6 bishop, drongo, lanner, turaco, whidah, whydah 7 courser, finfoot, marabou, ostrich 8 marabout, oxpecker, whinchat, woodchat 9 francolin, hammerkop 10 hammerhead
board game: 3 bao
bovine: 4 Kuri, Tuli 5 Barka, N'dama, Nguni 6 Ankole 7 Mashona
canine: 6 fennec, jackal
cape: 5 Verde
capital: 4 Lomé 5 Abuja, Accra, Akkra, Cairo, Dakar, Rabat, Tunis 6 Asmara, Bamako, Bangui, Bissau, Dodoma, Harare, Kigali, Luanda, Lusaka, Malabo, Maputo, Maseru, Niamey 7 Abidjan, Algiers, Conakry, Kampala, Mbabane, Nairobi, Tripoli, Yaoundé 8 Cape Town, Djibouti, Freetown, Gaborone, Khartoum, Kinshasa, Lilongwe, Monrovia, Pretoria, Windhoek 9 Bujumbura, Mogadishu, Porto-Novo 10 Addis Ababa, Libreville, Nouakchott 11 Brazzaville, Ouagadougou
cattle enclosure: 5 craal, kraal
council: 6 indaba
country: 4 Chad, Mali, Togo 5 Benin, Congo, Egypt, Gabon, Ghana, Kenya, Libya, Niger, Sudan 6 Angola, Gambia, Malawi, Uganda, Zambia 7 Algeria, Eritrea, Lesotho, Morocco, Namibia, Nigeria, Senegal, Somalia, Tunisia 8 Botswana, Cameroon, Ethiopia, Tanzania, Zimbabwe 9 Swaziland 10 Ivory Coast, Madagascar, Mauritania, Mozambique 11 Burkina Faso, Côte d'Ivoire, Sierra Leone, South Africa 12 Guinea-Bissau
dance: 4 juba
delta: 4 Nile
desert: 5 Namib 6 Libyan, Nubian, Sahara 7 Arabian 8 Kalahari
easternmost point of ~: 5 Hafun
equine: 5 zebra 6 quagga
evergreen: 4 akee
explorer: 4 Park 7 Johnson, Stanley 11 Livingstone
feline: 4 lion 5 chita, civet 6 cheeta, chetah, serval 7 caracal, cheetah, leopard
fish: 5 bolti 6 anabas, bichir 7 tilapia 8 characin 10 coelacanth
fly: 6 tsetse, tzetze 8 glossina
fox: 6 fennec
game warden: 6 askari
garment: 4 bubu, izar 5 kanzu, pagne 6 boubou, kaross 7 dashiki 9 djellabah
goat: 4 ibex
grass: 4 teff 6 kikuyu, napier 7 esparto
grassland: 4 veld 5 veldt
gulf: 6 Guinea
Iron Age pottery: 5 Urewe
it's n. of ~: 5 Medit.
knife: 5 panga
lake: 4 Chad, Tana 5 Mweru, Ngami, Nyasa, Tsana
language: 3 Ebo, Ibo, Kwa, Tiv 4 Eboe, Igbo, Lozi, Zulu 5 Bantu 7 Kirundi
largest city: 5 Cairo
lily: 4 aloe 5 plant 6 flower
menace: 4 croc 6 tsetse, tzetze 8 glossina
mountain: 4 Batu, Guna, Meru 5 Elgon, Gughe, Kenya 7 Toubkal 9 Ras Dashan 11 Kilimanjaro
music: 3 rai
musical instrument: 5 mbira
people: 3 Ebo, Edo, Ewe, Fan, Fon, Ibo, Ijo, Luo, Tiv, Yao 4 Afar, Akan, Beja, Cewa, Eboe, Efik, Fang, Fula, Hutu, Igbo, Ijaw, Lozi, Luba, Nama, Nuer, Riff, Tusi, Xosa, Yedo 5 Bantu, Bemba, Chaga, Chewa, Dinka, Dogon, Fante, Galla, Gbari, Gwari, Hausa, Kamba, Lunda, Makua, Masai, Mende, Mongo, Mossi, Nandi, Ngoni, Nguni, Oromo, Rundi, Shilh, Shona, Sotho, Swazi, Temne, Tigré, Tussi, Tutsi, Wolof, Xhosa, Yeddo, Zande 6 Amhara, Asante, Azande, Basuto, Chagga, Dorobo, Fulani, Haussa, Herero, Ibibio, Kanuri, Kikuyu, Kpelle, Maasai, Mbundu, Nubian, Nyanja, Pangwe, Senufo, Sidamo, Somali, Sukuma, Tswana, Tuareg, Watusi, Yoruba 7 Ashanti, Bambara, Danakil, Makonde, Malinka, Malinke, Mashona, Ndebele, Pahouin, Shilluk, Songhai, Turkana, Watutsi 8 Khoekhoe, Khoikhoi, Mandingo, Mandinka, Matabele, Nyamwezi 9 Ovimbundu, Wandorobo
plain: 4 veld 5 veldt
primate: 5 chimp, drill, potto 6 baboon, chacma, galago, guenon, vervet 7 colobus, gorilla, guereza 8 bush baby, mandrill, mangabey, talapoin 10 Barbary ape, chimpanzee
rebel org.: 5 SWAPO
region: 5 Sahel 6 Gezira
river: 4 Bomu, Geba, Juba, Nile, Tana, Uele, Vaal 5 Benin, Benue, Chari, Congo, Kafue, Kasai, Mbomu, Niger, Shari, Tsana, Volta, Zaire 6 Atbara, Kagera, Molopo, Orange, Rovuma, Ruvuma, Shashi, Ubangi 7 Aruwimi, Calabar, Limpopo, Lualaba, Luapula, Mangoky, Senegal, Zambezi 8 Blue Nile, Okavango
rodent: 4 jird 5 gundi, xerus 6 gerbil, jerboa 7 mole rat
rope material: 4 riem
sanctuary: 6 casbah
sea: 3 Red
sheep: 6 aoudad
shrub: 4 aloe 5 aalii, buchu
skunk: 5 zoril 7 zorilla, zorille
snake: 3 asp 5 cobra, mamba 8 ringhals 9 boomslang
spiritual power: 4 ngai
squirrel: 5 xerus
tableland: 5 karoo
tree: 4 kola, shea 5 babul, limba 6 baobab, gaboon, obeche, sapele 7 almique, assagai, assegai, avodire, yohimbe 8 alamiqui, sandarac 9 bloodwood
village: 4 stad
volcano: 3 Oku 4 Fogo 7 Erta-Ale 8 Karthala 10 Nyiragongo
waterfall: 8 Victoria
weapon: 5 panga
weasel: 5 ratel
wind: 6 samiel
___ Africa: 4 West 5 North, Out of 6 German, Inside
Africa (1982 song) artist: Toto
African ___: 4 gray, lily 5 daisy, grape, Plate 6 millet, violet
African Queen, The: 4 film 5 novel
author: C.S. Forester
cast: Humphrey Bogart, Katharine Hepburn, Robert Morley
director: John Huston
screenwriter: 4 Agee
Africa Screams (1949 film)
cast: Bud Abbott, Max Baer, Hillary Brooke, Lou Costello
Afrikaans: 4 Taal 8 language
Afrikaner: 4 Boer
Afrin alternative: 6 Contac, Nyquil, Tavist 7 Actifed, Comtrex, Dayquil, Dristan, Sinutab, Sudafed 8 Benadryl, Dimetapp, Drixoral, TheraFlu 9 Coricidin, Triaminic 10 Robitussin
Afrique du ___: 3 Sud
Afrique, part of: 5 Tchad
Afro: 4 coif 6 hairdo 8 coiffure 9 hairstyle
like an ~: 5 bushy
Afro-___: 3 pop 5 Asian, Cuban 7 Asiatic
Afro-American festival: 6 Kwanza
aft: 4 back, rear 5 arear, stern 6 astern, behind 8 backward, rearward, tailward 9 at the back, backwards, in the rear, sternward, to the rear
aft.: 2 p.m.
AFT: 5 union
part of ~: 3 Fed. 4 Amer. 8 American, Teachers 10 Federation
rival: 3 NEA
after: 4 anon, back, post, soon, then 5 later 6 behind, in a bit, in time 7 by and by, chasing, ensuing, later on, seeking, someday 8 in a while, pursuing, rearmost, sometime 9 following, hereafter, in honor of, in quest of 10 before long, eventually, gunning for, in search of, subsequent, succeeding
ender: 4 care, clap, damp, deck, glow, life, math, most, noon, time, word, work 5 image, piece, shock, taste, world 6 burner, effect 7 thought
in French: 5 après
prefix: 3 epi- 4 meta-, post- 5 infra-
starter: 4 here 5 there 6 herein 7 therein
after ___: 3 all 4 mast 5 a sort
after-___: 3 run, tax 5 hours, shave 6 action, dinner, market
___ after: 3 get, run, see 4 look, take 7 inquire
___-after: 6 sought
After
author: Robert Anderson
After ___ Gone: 5 You've
after a ___: 4 sort 7 fashion
After All (1989 song)
artist: Cher, Peter Cetera
after-bath wear: 4 robe
After Dark, My Sweet (1990 film)
cast: Bruce Dern, Jason Patric, Rachel Ward
after-dinner ___: 4 mint
after-dinner drink: 4 port 6 brandy, cognac
aftereffect: 4 scar 6 result, upshot 7 fallout, outcome 9 outgrowth
afterglow: 6 luster 8 twilight
After Henry author: Joan Didion
after-hours joint: 9 nightclub, nightspot 10 supper club
aftermath: 4 wake 5 rowen 6 effect, impact, result, sequel, upshot 7 fallout, outcome, product 8 backwash, residual 9 remainder
workout ~: 4 ache 5 cramp 8 soreness
___ After Midnight: 6 Walkin'
aftermost: 4 hind, last
afternoon: 2 p.m.
early ~: 3 one, two 5 one p.m., two p.m.
gathering: 3 tea
late ~: 4 five, four 6 five p.m., four p.m. 8 twilight
meal: 5 lunch
prayers: 5 nones
ritual: 3 nap 6 siesta
___ afternoon: 4 good
Afternoon Delight (1976 song) artist: Starland Vocal Band
Afternoon of ___, The: 5 a Faun
after-school
org.: 3 PTA
treat: 4 Oreo 5 cooky 6 cookie
aftershave: 6 bay rum, lotion
name: 4 Afta, Brut 8 Gillette, Old Spice 9 Aqua Velva 10 Skin Bracer
powder: 4 talc
aftershock: 5 quake 6 tremor
After Such Pleasures author: Dorothy Parker
after the ___: 4 fact
After the ___: 4 Fall 5 Lovin'
___ After, The: 7 Morning
After the Bath artist: 5 Degas, Peale
After the Fall: 4 play 5 drama
author: Arthur Miller
character: 3 Dan, Lou 5 Elsie, Holga, Lucas 6 Felice, Louise, Maggie 7 Quentin

After the Last Race author: Dean Koontz
After the Love Has Gone (1979 song) artist: Earth, Wind & Fire
After the Lovin' (1976 song) artist: Engelbert Humperdinck
After the Rain (1990 song) artist: Nelson
After the Rehearsal star: 4 Olin
After the Thin Man (1936 film)
cast: Myrna Loy, William Powell, James Stewart
director: W.S. Van Dyke
...after they've __ Paree: 4 seen
afterthought: 6 epilog, review 10 retrospect
afterward: 4 anon, next, soon, then 5 later 6 in a bit, in time, not now 7 by and by, later on, someday 8 in a while, sometime 9 following, hereafter, thereupon 10 before long, eventually
immediately ~: 6 hereon
in Latin: 7 post hoc
afterword: 6 epilog 8 epilogue 10 postscript
__ Afton: 5 Sweet
Afton Water author: Robert Burns
AFTRA cousin: 3 SAG
aftward: 4 back 5 arear 6 astern, behind 9 at the back, in the rear, to the rear
afuché: 6 shaker 10 percussion
__ a Fugitive From a Chain Gang: 3 I am
__ a fuse: 4 blow
Ag: 4 elem. 6 silver 7 element
47 for ~: 4 at. no.
Aga __: 4 Khan
Agadez: 4 city, town
locale: 5 Niger
Agadir: 4 city, port, town
locale: 7 Morocco
again: 4 also, anew, over, then 5 ditto, twice 6 afresh, de novo, encore 7 besides, further 8 moreover, once more 9 thereupon 10 from the top, in addition, repeatedly
come ~: 7 revisit
do ~: 6 repeat 7 iterate, run over 8 practice 9 reiterate
happen ~: 6 repeat, return
make usable ~: 5 renew 9 refurbish
now and ~: 7 at times 9 sometimes
obtain ~: 4 find 6 ransom, recoup, redeem, regain, retake 7 get back, reclaim, win back 8 reoccupy, retrieve, take back 9 bring back, reacquire, recapture, repossess
prefix: 3 ana-
time and ~: 4 a lot, much 5 often 9 quite a bit, regularly
working ~: 7 rebuilt
__ again: 4 come, over, then
__ again!: 5 Guess
__-again: 4 born
Again!: 6 encore
__ Again: 3 Try 4 Dead, Do It 5 Hello, Never 7 Breathe, Goodbye
Again (1993 song) artist: Janet Jackson
against: 3 con 4 anti, loth 5 loath 6 contra, facing, versus 7 athwart, counter, opposed, vis-à-vis 8 opposing, opposite 9 counter to, opposed to 10 regardless, unfriendly
prefix: 3 cat- 4 anti-, cata-, cath- 6 contra-
__ against: 3 run
...against __ of troubles: 4 a sea
Against All Odds (1984 song) artist: Phil Collins
__ Against Thebes: 5 Seven
...__ against the dying of the light: 4 rage
__ against the tide: 4 swim
Against the Wind (1948 film)
cast: Robert Beatty, Simone Signoret
Against the Wind (1980 song) artist: Bob Seger
__ against time: 4 race 5 a race
Aga Khan's son: 3 Aly
agama: 6 animal 7 reptile
Agamemnon: 8 asteroid
brother of ~: 8 Menelaus
daughter of ~: 7 Electra 9 Iphigenia
lover of ~: 9 Cassandra
parent of ~: 6 Aerope, Atreus
sister-in-law of ~: 5 Helen
sister of ~: 8 Anaxibia
son of ~: 6 Pelops 7 Orestes 9 Teledamus
wife of ~: 12 Clytemnestra
Agamemnon author: Aeschylus
agamid: 6 animal 7 reptile
Agana: 4 city, town
locale: 4 Guam
agape: 4 open 5 in awe 6 aghast, amazed, jolted 7 staring, yawning 8 wide-eyed, wide open 9 astounded, awestruck, stupefied, surprised 10 astonished, bewildered, dumbstruck, slack-jawed, spellbound
Agapitus: 4 pope 7 pontiff
Agar: 4 John 7 Herbert
agaric: 6 fungus 8 mushroom
agarita: 5 shrub
relative: 7 mahonia 8 algerita, barberry
Agar, John: 5 actor
film: Fort Apache (1948)
Sands of Iwo Jima (1949)
She Wore a Yellow Ribbon (1949)
Tarantula (1955)
spouse: Shirley Temple
__ a gasket: 4 blow
agasp: 6 bushed 7 shocked, stunned 8 startled 10 breathless
Agassi, Andre: 7 netster 9 tennis pro
milieu: 5 court
rival: 5 Chang, Stich
spouse: Steffi Graf, Brooke Shields
Agassiz: 4 lake 5 Louis
agate: 4 type 6 marble 7 mineral 10 chalcedony
origin: 4 lava
Agatha: 5 saint 8 Christie
colleague: 3 Rex 4 Erle 6 Ellery 8 Dashiell
Agatha (1979 film)
cast: Timothy Dalton, Dustin Hoffman, Vanessa Redgrave
director: Michael Apted
Agatho: 4 pope 7 pontiff
agave: 5 plant, sisal, yucca 6 flower 9 amaryllis, succulent
fiber: 5 istle, ixtle, sisal
root: 5 amole
Agawam: 4 city, town
locale: 4 Mass.
agaze: 7 staring
agba: 4 tree
agcy.: 3 org.
Agde: 4 city, town
locale: 6 France
age: 3 eon, era 4 aeon, gray, grey, grow, span, time 5 cycle, epoch, get on, ripen, years 6 mature, mellow, period, season 7 develop 8 long time 9 antiquate, fossilize, grow older, obsolesce 10 generation
a coon's ~: 5 years
act one's ~: 6 behave
awkward ~: 5 teens, youth
come of ~: 6 grow up, mature
counter: 6 candle
ender: 4 less
group: 10 generation
important ~: 3 era 5 epoch
in a way: 4 rust
in this day and ~: 3 now 5 today
of ~: 5 adult 6 mature 7 grown-up 9 full-grown
of an ~: 4 eral
of the same ~: 6 coeval
one under legal ~: 5 minor 6 infant
proof of ~: 2 ID
starter: 3 dam, man, out, pot, tow 4 acre, band, bond, cart, coin, cord, cork, dock, flow, foot, garb, haul, herb, leaf, leak, line, link, mess, mile, mill, mint, moor, over, pack, pass, peer, pill, port, post, root, seep, sign, sink, soil, stow, till, vent, volt, watt, word, yard 5 baron, block, break, cover, drain, dress, drift, equip, float, floor, front, fruit, graft, grill, layer, lever, pilot, pound, rough, sabot, short, spill, spoil, steer, under, vicar, wharf, wreck 6 anchor, append, broker, cellar, cooper, hermit, orphan, parent, parson, patron, person, pilfer, porter, report, shrink, vassal 7 baronet, brigand, percent, pilgrim
tender ~: 4 teen 5 youth 6 cradle 7 infancy, puberty 8 minority 9 childhood, juniority 10 immaturity, juvenility, schooldays
this day and ~: 3 now 4 here
under legal ~: 8 juvenile 10 adolescent
voting ~: 8 majority 9 adulthood
age __ beauty: 6 before
age-__: 3 old
__ age: 3 ice 4 dog's 5 coon's, legal 6 golden, heroic, mental, middle, school, silver 7 awkward, nuclear
__ Age: 3 Ice, New 4 Iron, Jazz 5 Space, Stone 6 Atomic, Bronze, Copper 15 Gilded. Victorian
aged: 4 ripe 6 mature, mellow 7 ancient, antique, elderly, wizened 8 grizzled 9 geriatric, getting on, up in years, venerable 10 antiquated, gray-haired
__-aged: 6 middle
agee: 4 awry 7 crooked 8 cockeyed
Agee: 3 Jon 5 James 6 Tommie
Agee, James: 6 writer
work: A Death in the Family
Letters to Father Flye
Let Us Now Praise Famous Men
The Morning Watch
Agee, Tommie sport: 8 baseball
ageless: 6 eterne 7 eternal 10 immemorial
Agen: 4 city, town
locale: 6 France
agency: 4 firm 5 means, organ, power 6 bureau, factor, medium, office 7 channel, company, machine, vehicle 8 auspices 9 expedient, franchise, implement, influence, machinery, mechanism 10 commission, department, expediency, instrument
worker: 4 temp 5 clerk 6 typist
__ agency: 4 news, wire 6 credit, Indian, ticket, travel 9 insurance
agenda: 4 card, list, plan, sked 5 slate, table 6 docket, lineup, roster 7 listing, program 8 calendar, schedule, time line, to-do list 9 ax to grind, checklist, procedure, timetable
component: 4 item
guide's ~: 4 tour
__ agenda: 6 hidden
Agendas author: George Sand
__ Agenda, The: 6 Icarus
Agenor
daughter of ~: 6 Europa
father of ~: 8 Poseidon
son of ~: 6 Cadmus
agent: 3 Fed, rep, spy 4 G-man, mole, narc, nark, pawn, T-man, tool 5 cause, envoy, fixer, force, means, organ, party, proxy, spook 6 broker, deputy, factor, jobber, lawyer, legate, medium, origin, seller, shamus 7 abetter, abettor, channel, employe, handler, officer, stand-in, steward, vehicle 8 advocate, assignee, attorney, catalyst, delegate, emissary, employee, executor, factotum, minister, official, promoter 9 appointee, deal maker, detective, go-between, implement, messenger, middleman, negotiant, operative, surrogate 10 ambassador, connection, instrument, interceder, mouthpiece, negotiator, substitute
appoint an ~: 6 depute
be an ~ of: 6 act for 9 represent
client: 5 actor 6 artist, author, singer, writer
cut: 5 tenth 7 percent 10 percentage
double ~: 3 spy 4 mole 8 turncoat
org.: 3 CIA, FBI, KGB
press ~: 5 flack 8 promoter
quest: 4 role
__ agent: 3 FBI, IRS 4 free, land, play, road 5 house, press 6 county, double, estate, fiscal, Indian, secret, ticket, travel 7 booking, freight, revenue, special, station, wetting
Agent 8 3/4 (1965 film)
cast: Dirk Bogarde, Sylva Koscina
Agent 86: 5 Smart
Ageo: 4 city, town
locale: 5 Japan
age of __: 7 consent
Age of __: 6 Reason
Age of Anxiety, The
author: W.H. Auden
composer: 9 Bernstein
Age of Aquarius show: 4 Hair
Age of Innocence, The: 4 film 5 novel
author: Edith Wharton
cast: Daniel Day Lewis, Michelle Pfeiffer, Winona Ryder
character: 3 Ned 5 Ellen
director: Martin Scorsese
Age of Napoleon, The author: Will Durant
Age of Reason, The author: Thomas Paine
Age of Scandal, The author: T.H. White
age-old: 7 ancient 9 venerable
ager: 3 sun 7 ripener
starter: 4 teen
__ ager: 6 golden
Ager: 6 Milton
__ Ager: 3 New
ageratum: 5 plant 6 flower
ages: 3 eon 4 aeon 7 forever 8 eternity, long time 9 millennia
ago: 4 once, yore
from ~ past: 3 old 7 ancient
__ Ages: 4 Dark 5 Three 6 Middle
Agfa rival: 4 Fuji 5 Kodak
aggie: 3 mib, taw 6 marble
Aggies: 9 Utah State
agglomerate: 4 clot 8 assemble
agglomeration: 4 heap, load, lump, mass, pile 5 bunch, hoard, stack 6 jumble 7 cluster 9 congeries
agglutinant: 8 adhesive
agglutinate: 4 clot 5 clump
aggrandize: 5 add to, boast, boost, build, ensky, exalt 6 beef up, enrich, expand, extend, jack up, praise 7 augment, enlarge, ennoble, glorify, inflate, lionize, magnify, promote 8 heighten, increase, multiply 9 embroider, intensify
aggrandizement: 6 growth 8 increase
aggravate: 3 bug, get, irk, nag, vex 4 gall, rile, roil, sink, slip 5 add to, anger, annoy, decay, get to, grate, peeve, pique, slide, tease, upset

6 bother, deepen, needle, nettle, pester, pick on, put out, rankle, worsen 7 enflame, inflame, magnify, provoke 8 compound, distress, embitter, imbitter, irritate 9 displease, infuriate, intensify 10 complicate, degenerate, exacerbate, exaggerate, exasperate, retrogress

aggravated: 5 angry 6 ireful

aggravated __: 7 assault

aggravating: 5 pesky, pesty 6 trying 7 irksome 9 vexatious

aggravation: 4 bane, care, pain 5 anger, worry 6 bother, hassle, tsuris 7 tsouris 8 distress, headache, pet peeve, vexation 9 annoyance

aggregate: 3 all, lot, mix, sum 4 bulk, heap, lump, mass, mixt, pile 5 added, add up, amass, gross, group, mixed, total, whole 6 amount, entire, gather, heaped, number 7 add up to, amassed, collect, combine 8 assemble, compound, ensemble, entirety, hold on to, integral, quantity, totality 9 assembled, collected, composite, corporate, gathering 10 accumulate, assemblage, collection, collective, complement, constitute, cumulation, cumulative, everything

aggregation: 4 band, heap, mass 5 array, batch, group, hoard, stack, swarm 7 company 8 assembly 9 congeries, multitude

aggress: 5 begin, start 6 attack, foment, incite 7 affront, assault, besiege, provoke 8 commence, initiate

aggression: 5 fight, onset 6 attack 7 offense 9 hostility, incursion, offensive, onslaught, pugnacity 10 antagonism, assailment, blitzkrieg

aggressive: 4 go-go 5 macho, pushy, type A 6 active, strong 7 defiant, dynamic, forward, hawkish, martial, rampant, warlike 8 fighting, militant, military, ravaging, ructious 9 advancing, ambitious, assertive, assertory, attacking, bellicose, bumptious, combative, imperious, intruding, intrusive, masterful, offensive, predatory, rapacious, strenuous, truculent 10 disruptive, disturbing, jingoistic, peremptory, pugnacious

not ~: 5 timid, type B

one: 5 Rambo, tiger

aggressiveness: 5 moxie 8 gumption

aggressor: 3 foe 5 enemy 6 raider 7 fighter, invader 8 attacker, intruder, provoker 9 assailant

aggrieve: 3 vex 4 harm, hurt, miff, pain, rack 5 abuse, harry, worry, wrong 6 bruise, damage, harass, ill-use, injure, misuse, offend, plague 7 afflict, agonize, oppress, outrage, torment, torture, trouble 8 bullyrag, distress, ill-treat, keep down, maltreat, mistreat 9 mishandle, persecute

aggrieved: 4 hurt, sore 5 woful 6 harmed, pained, peeved, woeful 7 injured, unhappy, wronged 9 afflicted, depressed, disturbed, oppressed 10 persecuted

aghast: 4 agog 5 agape 6 amazed, scared 7 alarmed, shocked, shook up, stunned 8 appalled, dismayed, frighted 9 astounded, awestruck, horrified, mortified, terrified 10 astonished, frightened, speechless

leave ~: 8 surprise

__ a Gift: 3 it's

agile: 3 fit, yar 4 deft, spry, wiry, yare 5 brisk, fleet, light, lithe, quick, smart 6 active, dapper, limber, lissom, lively, nimble, speedy, supple 7 catlike, lambent, lissome, springy 8 athletic, dextrous, graceful 9 dexterous, lightsome, lithesome, sprightly 10 surefooted

not ~: 6 clumsy

agility: 5 speed 6 action 8 legerity 9 dexterity, lightness 10 liveliness, nimbleness

agin: 7 opposed

not ~: 3 fer

Agincourt: 6 battle

aging: 7 ancient, elderly, wizened 8 grizzled 9 geriatric, getting on, senescent, up in years

__ a girl!: 3 It's

__ a Girl in My Soup: 6 There's

__ a girl, just...: 5 I want

__ a Girl Marries: 4 When

agita: 9 heartburn

agitate: 3 bug, get, jar, jog, vex 4 beat, flap, move, rile, rock, roil, stir, toss 5 alarm, anger, annoy, churn, egg on, get to, psych, rouse, shake, shock, swirl, upset 6 arouse, bother, dismay, excite, foment, incite, jiggle, kindle, ruffle, whip up, work up 7 concuss, disrupt, disturb, enflame, fluster, inflame, perturb, shake up, startle, trouble, unhinge, unnerve 8 convulse, disquiet, distress, exercise, unsettle, unstring 9 impassion 10 cause a riot, discompose, disconcert, exasperate

agitated: 3 hot, mad 5 antsy, fazed, het up, irate, itchy, jumpy, manic, tense, upset 6 hectic, jangly, uneasy, yeasty 7 anxious, foaming, frantic, jittery, keyed up, nervous, restive, uptight 8 feverish, fluttery, frenetic, frenzied, restless, skittish, troubled, unstrung 9 concerned, excitable, ill at ease, turbulent, unsettled 10 high-strung, infuriated

be ~: 4 stew 6 simmer

state: 4 snit

agitation: 4 flap, fuss, to-do 5 anger, furor, tizzy, upset 6 clamor, dismay, frenzy, lather, motion, racket, tumult, unrest 7 emotion, ferment, turmoil 8 movement, upheaval 9 commotion, confusion, sensation 10 combustion, convulsion, ebullience, excitement, impatience

agitato: 9 excitedly

agitator: 5 rebel, riler 7 hellion, heretic, inciter 8 fomenter, frondeur, inflamer 9 anarchist, demagogue, disrupter, dissident, extremist, firebrand, insurgent 10 instigator, malcontent

Aglaia: 5 Grace

colleague: 6 Thalia 10 Euphrosyne

Aglaope: 5 Siren

aglare: 7 blazing, shining, staring 8 blinding

__ a Glass, Darkly: 7 Through

Aglaura: 4 poem

author: 8 Suckling

agleam: 3 lit 5 shiny 6 bright 7 radiant, shining 9 sparkling

aglet target: 6 eyelet

agley: 4 awry

aglow: 3 lit, red 4 warm 5 happy, light, lit up, shiny 6 ablaze, bright, flashy 7 beaming, blazing, burning, fulgent, lambent, radiant, shining 8 dazzling, gleaming, luminous, lustrous 9 brilliant, exuberant, refulgent, sparkling 10 shimmering

agnail: 7 whitlow

agnate: 7 kindred, kinsman, related 8 paternal, relative 10 equivalent

Agnes: 5 saint 7 de Mille 9 Moorehead

in Spanish: 4 Ines, Inez

to Cecil B.: 5 niece

Agnes __: 4 Grey 5 of God

__ Agnes' Eve: 5 Saint

Agnes Grey author: Anne Brontë

Agnes of God (1985 film)

cast: Anne Bancroft, Jane Fonda, Meg Tilly

director: Norman Jewison

Agnew: 5 Spiro

plea, for short: 4 nolo

agnolotti: 5 pasta

alternative: 4 orzo, ziti 5 penne 6 noodle 7 lasagna, lasagne, pastina, ravioli 8 bucatini, couscous, farfalle, linguine, linguini, macaroni, rigatoni 9 angelhair, cavatelli, manicotti, spaghetti 10 cannelloni, fettuccini, tortellini, vermicelli

agnomen: 4 name 9 sobriquet

Agnon, Shmuel: 6 Hebrew, writer 8 Nobelist

agnostic: 5 pagan 7 doubter, impious, infidel 8 doubtful

Agnus __: 3 Dei

ago: 3 ere 4 back, past 5 since 6 before, gone by, lapsed 7 earlier, history 8 formerly, long gone, until now 9 before now, in the past 10 back in time, heretofore

a while ~: 4 once 6 before 7 earlier 9 at one time, in the past 10 beforehand

in German: 3 von

in Scottish: 4 syne

long ~: 4 once, past, then, yore 5 of old 6 erenow 8 formerly 9 in the past 10 previously

not long ~: 5 newly 6 lately, of late 8 latterly, recently 9 yesterday

__ ago: 4 long

__ Ago and Far Away: 4 Long

__ a go at: 4 have

agog: 4 awed, keen 5 eager, het up, in awe 6 aghast, amazed, ardent 7 anxious, bug-eyed, excited, in shock, psyched, shook up, stunned 8 atwitter, in a tizzy, thrilled, wide-eyed, worked up 9 awestruck, ebullient, expectant, stirred up 10 astonished, bewildered, breathless, enthralled, fascinated, slack-jawed

Agon: 6 ballet

composer: 10 Stravinsky

__ Agonistes: 6 Samson

agonize: 4 fret, stew 5 brood, mourn, sweat, worry 6 grieve, harrow, sorrow, squirm, suffer, writhe 7 afflict, bedevil, torment 8 aggrieve, distress 10 excruciate

agonizing: 5 sharp, woful 6 fierce, woeful 7 intense, painful 8 grievous, piercing 9 harrowing, torturing 10 disturbing, tormenting

agony: 3 woe 4 pain 5 dolor, grief 6 misery, ordeal, sorrow, throes, trauma 7 anguish, torment, torture, travail 8 distress 9 heartache, martyrdom, suffering 10 bitterness, heartbreak

agony __: 6 column

Agony and the Ecstasy, The author: Irving Stone

__ a Good Day: 3 It's

__ a good example: 3 set

__ a good mind to: 4 have

... a good night!: 5 to all

__ a good word: 5 put in

__ a go of it: 4 make

agora: 5 money

modern ~: 4 mall

site: 6 Athens, Greece

agoraphobe fear: 6 crowds

agosto: 3 mes 6 August 7 Spanish

Agoura Hills: 4 city, town

locale: 10 California

agouti: 6 animal, mammal, rodent

relative: 3 rat 4 cavy, degu, jird, paca, vole 5 coypu, gundi, mouse, xerus 6 beaver, gerbil, gopher, jerboa, marmot, murine 7 hamster, lemming, muskrat, visacha 8 chipmunk, cricetid, dormouse, squirrel, tuco-tuco 9 chickaree, groundhog, guinea pig, porcupine, woodchuck 10 chinchilla, prairie dog

agouti cousin: 4 paca

A.G. part of: 3 Att., Gen. 4 Atty. 7 General 8 Attorney

Agra: 4 city, town

attire: 4 sari 5 saree

locale: 5 India

river: 5 Jumna 6 Yamuna

__ a grain of salt: 4 with

__ a Grand Night for Singing: 3 It's

__ a Grand Old Flag: 5 You're

__ a Grand Old Name: 5 Mary's

agrarian: 5 rural 6 rustic 7 bucolic, country 8 pastoral 9 bucolical

__ a Grecian Urn: 5 Ode on

agree: 2 go 3 fit, nod 4 gibe, gybe, heed, jibe, mesh, mind 5 admit, allow, chime, defer, get on, match, say OK, tally, yield 6 accede, accept, accord, adhere, assent, belong, cohere, comply, concur, decide, follow, fulfil, listen, permit, say yes, settle, square 7 approve, chime in, comport, concede, conform, consent, fulfill, go along, observe, promise, resolve, respect 8 coincide, cut a deal, get along, hit it off, parallel, play ball 9 acquiesce, cooperate, harmonize, negotiate, recognize, shake on it, stipulate, subscribe 10 condescend, coordinate, correspond, go together, sympathize, toe the line

don't ~: 4 balk 5 demur 6 resist

don't ~ to: 3 nix 4 veto

silently: 3 nod

to: 2 OK 4 obey, okay, okeh, okey 5 allow, grant 6 accept 7 abide by 8 carry out 10 keep in step

(to): 3 bow 4 bend

to do: 6 take on 9 undertake

with: 4 suit 7 support

(with): 4 side 6 square

agreeable: 4 fine, good, nice, okay, open 5 dandy, great, legit, moral, nifty, noble, ready, suave, sweet, swell 6 genial, gentle, lovely, peachy, proper, smooth 7 amiable, cordial, dutiful, easeful, ethical, fitting, likable, lovable, lyrical, melodic, musical, welcome, willing 8 all right, amenable, becoming, gracious, in accord, laudable, likeable, loveable, obedient, pleasant, pleasing, resigned, splendid, superior, yielding 9 according, admirable, approving, befitting, compliant, complying, congenial, congruent, congruous, consonant, delicious, desirable, enjoyable, excellent, favorable, hunky-dory, in keeping, palatable, reputable, temperate, tractable, unextreme, wonderful 10 acceptable, attractive, beneficial, compatible, concurring, consenting, consistent, convenient, creditable, delectable, delightful, gratifying, harmonious, infallible, permissive, personable, responsive, satisfying, submissive

to: 5 up for

agreeably: 7 happily 9 favorably, in keeping, willingly 10 charmingly, cheerfully, graciously, obligingly, peacefully, pleasantly, pleasingly

agreed: 2 ay, da, ja, sí 3 aye, oui, set, yea, yep, yes, yup 4 amen, fine, okay, sure, yeah 5 good-o, jibed, natch, quite, right, roger, uh-huh 6 gladly, good-oh, indeed, just so, rather, righto,

surely, united, you bet, yowzah **7** exactly, go ahead, indeedy, mais oui, quite so, ten-four **8** all right, as you say, of course, thumbs up, very well **9** be my guest, certainly, darn right, naturally, precisely, sure thing, you betcha, you said it **10** absolutely, by all means, definitely, positively, sure enough, that's right
not ~ to, as demands: **5** unmet
to: **3** OK'd **4** OK'ed
upon: **5** given, joint **6** mutual, united **9** concerted, unanimous, undivided **10** collective, concurrent
agreeing: **5** as one, at one **9** accordant, according, unanimous **10** like-minded
agreement: **2** OK **4** bond, deal, mise, okay, pact, sync **5** lease, peace, terms, truce, unity **6** accord, assent, avowal, pledge, treaty, unison **7** bargain, charter, compact, concert, concord, entente, harmony, promise, proviso, rapport **8** alliance, approval, contract, covenant, decision, likeness, protocol, symmetry, sympathy **9** accession, affidavit, assenting, coherence, communion, community, congruity, endorsing, good vibes, guarantee, indenture, mediation, orthodoxy, provision, ratifying, unanimity, verifying **10** acceptance, accordance, adaptation, adjustment, bargaining, compliance, complicity, compromise, concession, conclusion, concurring, conditions, conformity, congruence, consonance, friendship, permission, proportion, settlement, similarity
bring into ~: **5** align, aline **6** attune
bring to ~: **7** mediate
come to an ~: **6** settle
component: **4** term
cowboy ~: **3** yep, yup
emphatic ~: **6** yes yes
formal ~: **4** pact **6** accord, treaty **7** charter, compact, concord **8** contract, protocol **9** concordat **10** convention
ham's ~: **5** roger, wilco
in ~: **3** one **5** as one, at one **6** jibing, united **9** unanimous **10** like-minded
nonverbal ~: **3** nod
not in ~: **6** at odds
slangy ~: **3** yep, yup **4** yeah **5** uh-huh
word of ~: **2** ay **3** aye, yes **4** amen
words of ~: **4** I too **5** as am I, me too, so am I, so do I
agricultural: **5** rural **6** rustic **7** bucolic **9** bucolical
business: **4** farm
club: **5** four H
agricultural __: **3** ant **5** agent
agriculturalist: **6** farmer **7** granger
agriculture: **7** farming, science, tillage
association: **6** grange
goddess: **5** Ceres **7** Demeter
study: **7** farming
Agri Dagi: **6** Ararat
Agrippa: **5** Roman
son of ~: **4** Nero
wife of ~: **5** Julia
see also Latin
__ Agrippa: **5** Herod
Agrippina's
agrology: **7** science
study: **4** soil
agronomic: **5** rural
agronomist: **6** farmer, grower
agronomy: **7** farming
Agronsky: **6** Martin
aground: **7** beached **8** marooned, stranded **9** foundered **10** high and dry
run ~: **4** fail **5** wreck **8** stranded
where ships run ~: **4** reef
agt.: **3** rep **4** G-man, T-man
agua: **5** water **7** Spanish
desire for: **3** sed
Agua Dulce: **4** city, town
locale: **6** Mexico **8** Veracruz
Agua Prieta: **4** city, town
locale: **6** Mexico, Sonora
Aguascalientes: **4** city, town
locale: **6** Mexico
ague: **5** chill, fever
cousin: **3** flu
Aguilera, Christina
song: Come on Over (2000)
Genie in a Bottle (1999)
I Turn to You (2000)
Lady Marmalade (2000)
What a Girl Wants (1999)
Agulhas: **4** cape
locale: South Africa
__ a gun: **5** son of
agush: **8** spouting
Agutter, Jenny: **7** actress
film: An American Werewolf in London (1981)
Amy (1981)
Silas Marner (1985)
Ah __: **3** Sin
Ah!: **3** oho **4** I see, sigh **5** got it **6** I get it
Aha!: **4** I see **5** got it **6** I get it
A-HA
homeland: Norway
song: Take on Me (1985)
Ahab
father of ~: **4** Omri
foe: **5** whale
god: **4** Baal
wife of ~: **7** Jezebel
Ahab, the Arab (1962 song) artist: Ray Stevens
__ a hair: **4** turn
__ a hand: **4** lend
__ a hand in: **4** have
__ a handle on: **3** get **4** have
__ a hang: **4** care, give
__ a Hap-Hap-Happy Day: **3** It's
__ a Happy Face: **5** Put on
__ a happy note: **5** end on
__ a hasty retreat: **4** beat
Ahasuerus, wife of: **6** Esther
__ a hatter: **5** mad as
à haute __: **4** voix
ahead: **3** ldg. **5** early, first, forth, on top, prior **6** before, onward **7** already, earlier, forward, in front, leading, onwards, winning **8** advanced, in the van, oncoming **9** at the fore, in advance, in the lead **10** beforehand, out in front, previously
barely ~: **5** one up, up one
be ~: **4** lead
forge ~: **4** lead **5** march **7** advance, recover **8** continue, progress **9** go forward
get ~: **3** win **4** grow **5** go far **6** make it, pan out, thrive **7** advance, luck out, make out, prevail, prosper, triumph, work out **8** flourish, go places, grow rich, hit it big, make good, progress **9** go forward **10** gain ground
get ~ of: **4** lead **5** one-up **9** forestall
go ~: **2** ay, da, ja, sí **3** aye, oui, yea, yep, yes, yup **4** fine, lead, okay, pass, sure, yeah **5** begin, good-o, natch, quite, right, roger, start, uh-huh **6** agreed, gladly, good-oh, indeed, just so, rather, righto, set off, set out, surely, you bet, yowzah **7** advance, exactly, indeedy, lead off, mais oui, proceed, quite so, ten-four **8** all right, as you say, of course, set forth, thumbs up, very well **9** be my guest, certainly, darn right, naturally, precisely, sure thing, you betcha, you said it **10** absolutely, by all means, definitely, positively, sure enough, that's right
go ~ of: **4** lead **7** precede, presage **8** antecede **9** introduce
go ~ with: **5** act on **6** follow
keep a step ~ of: **5** outdo
look ~: **4** plan **7** prepare
of: **3** ere **4** up on **6** before, beyond **7** beating, prior to **9** in advance, preceding **10** outranking, superior to, surpassing
of its time: **3** new
of time: **5** early **7** betimes **9** in advance **10** beforehand
one who's ~: **3** ldr. **6** leader
plunge ~: **3** ram **4** race
run ~: **4** lead **5** scout **7** precede **8** antecede, go before **10** show the way, trail-blaze
shoot ~: **4** pass **5** outdo **8** progress **9** go forward
__ ahead: **3** get **4** plan
ahead of __: **4** time
__ a heart: **4** have
__ A. Heinlein: **6** Robert
Ahem!: **3** pst **4** psst **8** excuse me
Aherne, Brian: **5** actor
film: Beloved Enemy (1936)
Captain Fury (1939)
The Great Garrick (1937)
Hired Wife (1940)
Juarez (1939)
Merrily We Live (1938)
A Night to Remember (1943)
Rosie! (1967)
Skylark (1941)
Smart Woman (1948)
Sylvia Scarlett (1935)
Vigil in the Night (1940)
What Every Woman Knows (1934)
spouse: Joan Fontaine
__ a high note: **5** end on
__ a high standard: **3** set
__ a hike: **4** take
Ahmad: **6** Rashad
Ah, me!: **4** alas **5** alack
Ahmet: **7** Ertegun
Ahn: **6** Philip
Ahna: **5** Capri
ahold: **4** grip **5** grasp
__ ahold of: **3** get
__ a Hold of Me: **3** Got
__ a hole in one's pocket: **4** burn
Ahome: **4** city, town
locale: **6** Mexico **7** Sinaloa
__ a hoot: **4** care, give
__ a hornet: **5** mad as
ahorse: **6** riding
__ a Horseman: **5** Comes
__ a Hot Tin Roof: **5** Cat on
__ a house: **5** big as
ahoy: **8** greeting
Ah Sin author: Bret Harte
Ahtna: **6** Indian **7** Amerind
ahum: **7** buzzing
Ahura __: **5** Mazda
Ahvaz: **4** city, town
locale: **4** Iran
Ah, Wilderness!: **4** film, play
author: Eugene O'Neill
cast: Lionel Barrymore, Wallace Beery, Aline MacMahon
character: **3** Nat, Sid **4** Lily **5** Belle, Essie, Norah **6** Muriel
Ah, Wilderness were Paradise __!: **4** Enow
Ah, yes!: **4** I see **6** so I see
ai: **5** sloth **6** mammal
AI: Artificial Intelligence (2001 film)
cast: Jude Law, Frances O'Connor, Haley Joel Osment
director: Steven Spielberg
Aichinger, Ilse: **6** writer **8** Austrian
aichmophobe fear: **7** needles
aid: **4** abet, back, boon, egis, help, lift **5** aegis, a hand, boost, favor, guide, serve, speed **6** advice, assist, buck up, prop up, relief, remedy, rescue, succor, uphold **7** backing, bailout, benefit, bolster, charity, comfort, forward, further, help out, largess, pitch in, promote, redress, relieve, service, stand by, stick by, subsidy, support, sustain, welfare **8** advocacy, altruism, donation, guidance, kindness, largesse, recourse, sympathy, tide over **9** accessory, advantage, auxiliary, cooperate, encourage, intercede, lend a hand, patronage, subsidize **10** accomplice, ameliorate, assistance, facilitate, go to bat for, stick up for, sustenance
financial ~: **5** grant **6** credit **7** alimony, backing, pension, subsidy, support **8** donation **9** allowance, endowment, patronage **10** assistance, fellowship, honorarium
first ~ job: **4** gash **6** lesion **8** fracture
in wrongdoing: **7** collude
visual ~: **3** map **4** grid, plan, plot **5** chart, graph, table **6** sketch **7** diagram **9** blueprint, floor plan
aid __: **7** station
__ aid: **5** first, legal, state **6** mutual, visual **7** foreign, hearing
__ Aid: **4** Rite **6** Ladies
__-Aid: **4** Band, Kool
Aida: **8** Turturro
Aïda: **5** opera, slave
character: **6** Ramfis **7** Amneris, Radames **8** Amonasro
composer: **5** Verdi
goddess: **4** Isis
opener: **4** Act I
piece: **4** aria
setting: **4** tomb **5** Egypt **6** Thebes **7** Memphis
where ~ premiered: **5** Cairo
Aidan: **5** Quinn, saint
aid and __: **4** abet
aide: **3** ADC **4** asst., hand, page, secy. **5** gofer **6** cohort, deputy, flunky, gopher, helper, second **7** acolyte, adviser, advisor, attaché, flunkey, orderly, staffer **8** adjutant, factotum, henchman, minister, sidekick **9** accessory, assistant, attendant, companion, gal Friday, man Friday, secretary, underling **10** accomplice, apprentice, girl Friday, lieutenant
in baseball: **6** batboy
aide-__: **7** mémoire
__ aide: **6** nurse's **8** teacher's
aide-de-camp: **4** adjt., asst. **8** adjutant **9** assistant
British ~: **6** batman
aides: **4** help **5** staff
aidful: **6** benign, useful **7** helpful **8** flexible, obliging, positive, remedial, salutary **9** effectual, favorable, of service **10** productive, worthwhile
__-aid kit: **5** first
aidman: **5** medic
Aidoo, Ama Ata: **6** writer **8** Ghanaian
__-Aids: **4** Band
__ Aid Society: **5** Legal
Aiea: **4** city, town
locale: **4** Oahu **6** Hawaii
Aiello, Danny: **5** actor
film: City Hall (1996)
Dinner Rush (2001)
Do the Right Thing (1989)
Fort Apache, The Bronx (1981)
Moonstruck (1987)
The Purple Rose of Cairo (1985)
Aigi, Gennady: **4** poet **7** Chuvash
aigret: **5** plume

aiguille: 4 peak
Aiken: 4 city, town **6** Conrad
locale: 4 S. Car.
Aiken, Conrad: 4 poet **6** author, writer
work: Blue Voyage
Brownstone Eclogues
The Charnel Rose
Great Circle
House of Dust
The Jig of Forslin
The Kid
aikido: 5 sport
Aikman, Troy: 2 QB
sport: 8 football
ail: 4 ache, hurt, pain **5** annoy, upset, worry **6** bother, sicken, suffer **7** afflict, disturb, feel bad, perturb, trouble **8** distress, languish
ailanthus: 4 tree
Aileen: 7 Pringle
aileron: 4 flap, wing
Ailey: 5 Alvin
ailing: 3 bad, ill, low **4** sick, weak **6** infirm, laid up, poorly, sickly, unwell **7** invalid, not well, run-down, unsound **8** below par, diseased, under par **9** afflicted, bedridden, miserable, unhealthy **10** indisposed, out of sorts
perhaps: 4 abed
ailment: 3 bug, flu **6** malady **7** disease, illness **8** disorder, sickness, syndrome **9** complaint, condition, ill health, infirmity **10** unwellness
modern ~: 6 stress
suffix: 4 -itis
ailurophobe fear: 4 cats
aim: 3 end, set, try **4** goal, mean, plan, sake, seek, want, will, wish **5** angle, drift, essay, level, point, sight **6** aspire, design, desire, direct, intend, intent, motive, object, reason, scheme, strive, target **7** address, attempt, meaning, mission, propose, purport, purpose, thought **8** ambition, bearings, endeavor, zero in on **9** draw a bead, intention, objective **10** aspiration
at: 5 shoot, train **6** gun for, target **8** aspire to, shoot for **9** strive for
for: 6 pursue
(for): 3 try **4** head **5** angle, labor, steer **6** strive
high: 5 dream **6** aspire
improver: 5 scope, sight
(to): 4 mean **6** aspire, intend, strive
Aim: 10 toothpaste
alternative: 5 Crest, Gleem, Topol **7** Close-Up, Colgate, Viadent **9** Aquafresh, Mentadent, Pepsodent, Rembrandt, Sensodyne **10** Pearl Drops, Ultra Brite **11** Tom's of Maine
aimara: 4 fish
Aimee: 4 Mann **5** Anouk **9** McPherson
Aimee __ McPherson: 6 Semple
Aimée, Anouk: 7 actress
film: 8 1/2 (1963)
Festival in Cannes (2002)
Justine (1969)
La Dolce Vita (1960)
Lola (1961)
A Man and a Woman (1966)
aimless: 4 idle **5** unled **6** adrift, casual, chance, errant, random **7** erratic, flighty, wayward **8** drifting, feckless, headless, unguided, vagabond **9** desultory, excursive, haphazard, hit-or-miss, irregular, pointless, unplanned, wandering **10** capricious, disjointed, incohesive, indecisive, undirected, unintended, willy-nilly
Ain: 4 star
ain't: 6 are not
Ain't __ a Shame: 4 That
Ain't __ Fun: 5 We Got
Ain't __ Proud to Beg: 3 Too
Ain't __ Sweet?: 3 She
Ain't __ truth?: 5 it the
Ain't 2 Proud 2 Beg (1992 song) artist: TLC
__ ain't broke...: 4 If it
Ain't it the truth!: 4 amen
Ain't No Mountain High Enough (song) artist: Diana Ross, Tammi Terrell
Ain't No Sunshine (1971 song) artist: Bill Withers
Ain't Nothing Like the Real Thing (1968 song)
artist: Marvin Gaye, Tammi Terrell
Ain't No Way to Treat a Lady (1975 song) artist: Helen Reddy
Ain't No Woman (1973 song) artist: Four Tops
Ain't! response: 5 Am too, Are so
Ain't She Sweet? composer: 4 Ager
__ ain't so!: 5 Say it
Ain't That a Shame (1955 song)
artist: Fats Domino, Pat Boone
Ain't That Loving You Baby (1964 song) artist: Elvis Presley
Ain't That Peculiar (1965 song) artist: Marvin Gaye
Ain't Too Proud to Beg (song) artist: Rolling Stones, Temptations
Ain't We __ Fun?: 3 Got
Ainu: 5 Asian **8** language
aioli: 8 dressing
air: 3 gas **4** aria, aura, cast, face, feel, look, mask, mien, mood, odor, pose, puff, show, song, tell, tone, tune, vent, wind **5** carol, carry, ditty, draft, music, ozone, speak, state, style, utter, voice, whiff **6** aspect, breeze, chanty, expose, flavor, manner, melody, oxygen, parade, report, reveal, shanty, spirit, strain **7** bearing, chantey, declare, display, divulge, exhibit, express, feeling, freshen, lay bare, publish, quality, refresh, shantey **8** ambiance, ambience, attitude, carriage, demeanor, disclose, presence, proclaim, televise **9** broadcast, character, circulate, leitmotif, make known, mannerism, oxygenate, publicize, put on view, semblance, talk about, ventilate **10** appearance, atmosphere, deportment, exhalation, impression, make public
anew: 5 rerun
arrive by ~: 5 fly in
be in the ~: 8 threaten
be up in the ~: 4 pend
breath of ~: 4 wind
bubble: 4 bleb
build castles in the ~: 9 speculate
castle in the ~: 5 dream **6** revery **7** fantasy, reverie **8** daydream **9** pipe dream
chambers: 5 plena
combining form: 3 atm- **4** atmo- **6** pneumo- **7** pneumat- **8** pneumato-
come up for ~: 4 vent **6** emerge
component: 5 argon, xenon **6** oxygen **8** nitrogen
current: 4 wind **5** draft **6** stream
dead ~: 5 quiet **7** silence
duct: 4 flue, vent
ender: 3 man, men, way **4** boat, crew, date, drop, fare, flow, foil, glow, head, lift, line, mail, park, play, port, ship, sick, time **5** borne, brush, burst, craft, field, frame, liner, plane, power, screw, space, strip, tight, waves **6** mobile, worthy **7** freight
fight for ~: 4 gasp
fill with ~: 4 pump
float through the ~: 4 blow, waft
force: 8 military, soldiers
fresh ~: 5 ozone **7** outside **8** outdoors
full of hot ~: 5 gassy, windy, wrong **7** verbose **9** talkative
get some ~: 6 inhale
go by ~: 3 fly **6** fly out
go on the ~: 6 report **7** network **8** announce, televise, transmit **9** advertise, broadcast, publicize **10** make public
hero: 3 ace **5** pilot **7** aviator
homophone: 3 ere
hot ~: 3 gas, rot **4** blah, bosh, bull, bunk, guff, jazz, jive, pooh, talk, tosh **5** bilge, fudge, hokum, hooey, mouth, prate, stuff, trash, tripe **6** bunkum, bushwa, drivel, footle, gabble, gammon, gibber, havers, humbug, jabber, jargon, kibosh, piffle **7** baloney, blarney, blather, blether, bluster, boloney, bombast, bushwah, eyewash, flannel, flubdub, fustian, garbage, hogwash, inanity, malarky, rubbish, twaddle **8** babbling, buncombe, claptrap, falderal, falderol, fast talk, flimflam, flummery, folderal, folderol, malarkey, nonsense, rhetoric, slipslop, tommyrot, trumpery **9** banana oil, gasconade, gibberish, kidstakes, loquacity, moonshine, poppycock, rigmarole **10** applesauce, balderdash, bilge water, codswallop, double-talk, flapdoodle, galimatias, Jabberwock, mumbo jumbo, rigamarole, taradiddle
in the ~: 5 aloft **6** flying, volant **8** imminent
like morning ~: 5 brisk
mass: 5 front
monitoring org.: 3 EPA
move on a puff of ~: 4 waft
navigate in ~: 6 aviate
navigation system: 5 loran
nip in the ~: 4 bite, cold **5** chill
open ~: 6 nature **7** outside **8** outdoors
organ: 4 gill, lung
out: 4 vent **7** freshen **8** talk over **9** ventilate
passage: 4 flue **5** naris **6** intake **7** nostril
pollution: 4 haze, smog **5** smaze
resistance: 4 drag
rifle: 5 BB gun
route: 4 lane
sac: 8 alveolus
sign: 5 Libra **6** Gemini **8** Aquarius
something in the ~: 4 odor
starter: 3 mid
stir the ~: 3 fan
strike: 4 raid
take ~: 6 inhale **7** breathe
take off the ~: 6 cancel
test the ~: 5 smell, sniff
to a poet: 5 ether **6** aether
traffic controller's place: 5 tower
traveler's bane: 4 wait
unlike desert ~: 5 humid
up in the ~: 4 high, iffy, open **5** aloft, angry, shaky, unset, vexed **6** chancy, unsure **7** pending **9** ambiguous, perturbed, suspended, uncertain, undecided, unsettled **10** indefinite, undecdided, unresolved
walking on ~: 4 glad, high **5** happy, merry **6** blithe, cheery, elated, jovial, joyful, joyous, upbeat **7** gleeful, pleased, tickled **8** blissful, cheerful, ecstatic, euphoric, exultant, jubilant, mirthful, thrilled **9** delighted, overjoyed, rapturous, rejoicing, rhapsodic
walk on ~: 5 exult
air __: 3 arm, bag, bed, bus, dam, gap, gas, gun, log, map, sac, tee, war **4** ball, base, bell, cell, cock, crew, door, duct, fare, hole, horn, kiss, lane, lift, lock, mail, mass, mile, plot, plug, pump, raid, shed, sign, sock, taxi, time, trap, well, wood **5** alert, blast, brake, brick, cargo, coach, cover, drill, fleet, force, gauge, hoist, lance, layer, meter, plant, power, rifle, route, scoop, shaft, space, speed, stack, train, twist, valve, varié **6** casing, castle, hammer, harbor, jacket, letter, piracy, pirate, pistol, pocket, potato, rights, shower, sleeve, splint, spring, stream, strike, switch, system **7** attaché, battery, bladder, carrier, cavalry, chamber, cleaner, command, curtain, cushion, express, freight, harbour, marshal, passage, service, sprayer, station, traffic, turbine, vesicle, waybill
air-__: 3 dry **4** cool, core, ship **5** bound, dried, lance, slake, spray **6** logged, minded **7** breathe, twisted
air-__ control: 7 traffic
air-__ shelter: 4 raid
__ air: 3 hot **4** dead, free, open **5** fresh, in the, light, plein, tidal, upper **6** liquid
__-air: 3 off **4** open
Air __: 5 Corps, Force, India, Medal **6** France, Jordan, Police, Supply **7** America
Air __ Breathe, The: 5 That I
Air __: Golden Receiver: 3 Bud
Air __ One: 5 Force
__ Air: 3 Bel, Con
Air America (1990 film)
cast: Robert Downey Jr., Mel Gibson, Nancy Travis
director: Roger Spottiswoode
Air and Angels author: John Donne
__-air balloon: 3 hot
airborne: 6 flying, volant
Airbus: 3 jet **5** plane
air-condition: 4 cool **5** chill
air-conditioned: 4 cool
Air-Conditioned Nightmare, The
author: Henry Miller
air conditioner: 5 Rheem, Trane **6** Lennox **7** Carrier, Fedders **9** Friedrich
feature: 3 fan
measure: 3 BTU
outlet: 4 vent
aircraft: 3 jet, SST, UFO **4** giro, STOL, VTOL **5** blimp, liner, plane **6** copter, glider **7** balloon, chopper **8** autogiro, autogyro, zeppelin **9** dirigible **10** helicopter
carrier: 4 ship **7** warship **8** man-of-war
company: 4 Lear **5** Piper **6** Airbus, Boeing, Cessna **10** Beechcraft, Gulfstream
detecting grp.: 5 NORAD
door: 5 hatch
Russian ~: 3 MiG
safety device: 6 deicer
US detection ~: 5 AWACS
walkway: 5 aisle
see also airplane
aircraft __: 7 carrier
aircraft-accident investigator: 4 NTSB
Airdrie: 4 city, town
locale: 8 Scotland
Aire: 5 river
city on the ~: 5 Leeds
locale: 7 England
Airedale: 3 dog **5** pooch **6** canine **7** terrier
__ Aires: 6 Buenos
airflow: 6 breeze
airfoil: 3 fin **4** wing
Air Force
arm: 3 SAC **5** NORAD
join the ~: 6 enlist

member: 5 pilot 6 fly boy
missile: 4 Thor
NCO: 4 TSgt.
officer: 2 lt. 3 col., gen., maj. 4 capt. 5 lieut., major 7 captain, colonel, general
refusal: 5 no sir
unit: 4 wing
woman: 3 WAF
Air Force (1943 film)
cast: John Garfield, Gig Young
director: Howard Hawks
Air Force __: 3 One 5 Cross
Air Force Academy
athletes: 7 Falcons
freshman: 6 doolie
locale: 8 Colorado
Air Force Base: 5 Altus, Beale, Dover, Dyess, Minot, Moody, Vance 6 Arnold, Brooks, Cannon, Hickam, Nellis, Offutt, Robins, Travis 7 Andrews, Bolling, Buckley, Edwards, Keesler, Kessler, Langley, Maxwell, Patrick 8 Columbus, Holloman, Kirtland, Lackland, Laughlin, Peterson, Sheppard 9 Barksdale, Ellsworth, Fairchild 10 Charleston, Goodfellow, Vandenberg
Air Force One: 3 jet
Air Force One (1997 film)
cast: Glenn Close, Harrison Ford, Gary Oldman, Dean Stockwell
director: Wolfgang Petersen
Airframe author: Michael Crichton
Air France
alternative: 3 KLM, SAS 6 Iberia, Sabena 9 Lufthansa
destination: 4 Orly 5 Paris 8 de Gaulle
former plane: 3 SST
air freshener: 5 Glade 6 Wizard 7 Airwick, Renuzit 8 Stick-Ups
asset: 5 scent
form: 5 spray
scent: 4 pine 5 lilac
target: 4 odor
air-gun ammo: 3 BBs
airhead: 3 nit 4 ditz, dodo, dolt, simp 5 dummy, dunce 7 dullard 8 dumbbell
airheaded: 7 vacuous 9 forgetful
airiness: 8 delicacy 9 joviality, lightness 10 liveliness
airing: 4 on TV, ride 6 junket, stroll 7 saunter 8 exposure 9 broadcast 10 discussion, exhibition
Air Jordans maker: 4 Nike
airless: 5 fuggy, musty 6 stuffy 10 oppressive, sweltering
airline: 3 ANA, KLM, LAN, SAS, TWA 4 El Al 5 Aloha, Delta, MALEV, Pan Am, US Air, Varig 6 Ariana, Iberia, QANTAS, Sabena, United 7 Jet Blue, Olympic 8 Aeroflot, Alitalia, American 9 Lufthansa, Southwest, US Airways 11 America West, Continental
Afghanistan: 6 Ariana
Australia: 6 QANTAS
Belgium: 6 Sabena
Brazil: 5 Varig
bygone ~: 3 TWA 4 BOAC 5 Ozark 7 Braniff, Eastern 8 National
Chile: 3 LAN
employee: 5 agent, pilot 7 steward 8 mechanic
European ~: 3 KLM, SAS 5 MALEV 6 Iberia, Sabena 7 Olympic 8 Aeroflot, Alitalia, Luftansa
former name: 5 USAir
Germany: 9 Lufthansa
Greece: 7 Olympic
Holland: 3 KLM
Hungary: 5 MALEV
Israel: 4 El Al
Italy: 8 Alitalia
Japan: 3 ANA
patron: 5 flier, flyer
regulating org.: 3 FAA
Russia: 8 Aeroflot
transfer point: 3 hub
airliner: 3 jet 5 plane
Airmail (1932 film)
cast: Ralph Bellamy, Pat O'Brien
director: John Ford
airman: 2 GI 4 rank 5 flier, flyer, pilot 6 fly boy, Yeager 7 aviator, recruit 9 Lindbergh
Air Music composer: 5 Rorem
Air National __: 5 Guard
__ Air Patrol: 5 Civil
airplane: 3 jet 5 craft, liner
access: 4 ramp
engine: 5 turbo 6 fanjet
flap: 6 elevon
fuel: 5 avgas
maker: 4 Lear 5 Piper 6 Airbus, Boeing, Cessna 10 Beechcraft, Gulfstream
maneuver: 4 loop
model ~: 3 toy
needing little runway: 4 STOL
part: 4 flap, nose, wing 5 aisle, strut 7 aileron, cockpit 9 propeller
ride: 6 flight
'60s spy ~: 4 U two
speed indicator: 4 Mach
tracker: 5 radar
WWI ~: 4 Spad
see also aircraft
Airplane! (1980 film)
cast: Lloyd Bridges, Peter Graves, Julie Hagerty, Robert Hays, Leslie Nielsen, Robert Stack
director: Jim Abrahams, David Zucker, Jerry Zucker
dog: 6 Scraps
air-pollution measure: 3 ppm
airport
annoyance: 5 delay
area: 4 gate 5 apron 6 lounge, runway 7 Customs
Atlanta: 10 Hartsfield
booth leaser: 4 Avis 5 Alamo, Hertz 6 Budget, Dollar
Boston: 5 Logan
Calcutta: 6 Dum Dum
California: 3 LAX, SFO
Caracas: 7 Bolívár
Chicago: 5 O'Hare 6 Midway
closer: 3 fog
control center: 5 tower
corridor: 4 ramp
do winter ~ work: 5 deice
event: 7 takeoff
Florence: 8 Vespucci
fluid: 6 deicer
Genoa: 8 Columbus
Havana: 5 Martí
Houston: 5 Hobby 10 George Bush
info: 3 arr., ETA, ETD 5 delay 7 arrival 9 departure
Israel: 3 Lod
Istanbul: 7 Ataturk
Las Vegas: 8 McCarran
major ~: 3 hub
Mexico City: 6 Juárez
monitor: 3 FAA
Montreal: 7 Mirabel
Nairobi: 8 Kenyatta
Nebraska ~ code: 3 OMA
Newfoundland: 6 Gander
New York: 7 Kennedy 9 La Guardia
NYC: 3 JFK, LGA
Oklahoma City: 10 Will Rogers
Paris: 4 Orly 8 de Gaulle
Phoenix: 9 Sky Harbor
Pisa: 7 Galileo
Rio de Janeiro: 5 Galea
Rome: 7 da Vinci
San Diego: 9 Lindbergh
service: 3 ATC
St. Louis: 7 Lambert
strand at an ~: 5 ice in
Tel Aviv: 9 Ben-Gurion
Toronto: 7 Pearson
vehicle: 3 bus, cab 4 limo 6 jitney 7 shuttle
Venice: 9 Marco Polo
Washington ~: 6 Dulles, Reagan 8 National
airport __: 4 code
Airport (1970 film)
cast: Jacqueline Bisset, Helen Hayes, Van Heflin, George Kennedy, Burt Lancaster, Dean Martin, Jean Seberg
director: George Seaton
Airport '77 (1977 film)
cast: Lee Grant, George Kennedy, Jack Lemmon, James Stewart, Brenda Vaccaro
air pressure measure: 6 atm. PSI
air-race marker: 5 pylon
air-raid __: 6 warden 7 shelter
air-raid warning: 5 alert
airs: 5 pride 6 vanity 7 hauteur 8 pretense, snobbery 9 arrogance, pomposity 10 false front, pretension, snootiness
one with ~: 4 snob
put on ~: 4 pose 5 mince, strut 6 fake it 7 swagger
putting on ~: 8 snobbish
__ airs: 5 put on
Airs Above the Ground author: Mary Stewart
airship: 5 blimp, craft 7 balloon 9 dirigible
like a ~: 5 rigid
airshow maneuver: 4 loop 5 flyby
airspeed unit: 4 Mach
airstrip: 6 runway
Air Supply
homeland: Australia
song: All out of Love (1980)
Even the Nights Are Better (1982)
Every Woman in the World (1980)
Here I Am (1981)
Lost in Love (1980)
Making Love out of Nothing at All (1983)
The One That You Love (1981)
Sweet Dreams (1982)
Air That I Breathe, The (1974 song)
artist: Hollies
airtight: 4 shut 5 tight 6 closed, sealed 9 leakproof
it may be ~: 4 case 5 alibi
make ~: 4 calk, seal 5 caulk 6 enseal
air-to-__: 6 ground 7 surface
air-traffic __: 7 control
airway: 4 flue, lane, vent 5 route 7 sky path 8 corridor, windpipe
Airwick alternative: 5 Glade 6 Wizard 7 Renuzit 8 Stick-Ups
Airwolf dog: 3 Tet
airy: 4 open 5 fresh, light, lofty, sheer, windy 6 breezy, fluffy, jaunty, jovial, rakish 7 buoyant, utopian 8 carefree, ethereal, gossamer, graceful, spacious 9 lightsome, spiritual, sprightly 10 diaphanous, immaterial, nonchalant, unbothered, unfeasible, unphysical, ventilated
airy-__: 5 fairy
__ Airy: 5 Mount
'A' Is for Alibi author: Sue Grafton
aisle: 3 row 4 lane, path, walk 5 alley 7 gangway, hallway, passage, walkway 8 corridor 10 passageway
lead down the ~: 3 ush 4 seat 5 guide, usher 6 escort, show in 7 conduct 9 accompany
walk down the ~: 3 wed 5 marry 10 get hitched, tie the knot
aisle __: 4 seat 6 sitter
aisles, roll in the: 4 howl, roar 5 laugh 6 guffaw 7 break up, crack up 8 convulse
Aisne: 5 river 10 department
capital of ~: 4 Laon
River locale: 6 France
tributary: 4 Aire
ait: 4 eyot, isle 5 islet
in French: 3 île
aitch preceder: 3 gee
Aix-en-Provence: 3 spa 4 city, town
locale: 6 France
Aix-les-Bains: 3 spa 6 resort
A.J.: 4 Foyt 6 Cronin, Langer
Ajaccio: 4 city, port, town
locale: 6 France
Ajalpán: 4 city, town
locale: 6 Mexico, Puebla
ajar: 4 open 10 discordant
not ~: 4 shut 6 closed
Ajax: 4 city, hero, town 8 cleanser 9 detergent
alternative: 3 Joy 4 Bab-O, Dawn 5 Comet 6 Bon Ami 7 Cascade 8 Sunlight 9 Palmolive, Soft Scrub 10 Electrasol
father of ~: 7 Telamon
foe: 4 dirt 5 grime
friend of ~: 8 Achilles
locale: 6 Canada 7 Ontario
parent of ~: 7 Telamon 8 Periboea
son of ~: 8 Philaeus 9 Eurysaces
wife of ~: 8 Tecmessa
Ajax author: Sophocles
aji: 6 pepper
Ajijic: 4 city, town
locale: 6 Mexico 7 Jalisco
__ a Job: 3 Get
...__ a jolly good fellow: 3 he's
AK
native: 3 Esk.
once: 3 ter. 4 terr.
see also Alaska
AKA: 5 alias
business ~: 3 DBA
indicator: 9 pseudonym
part of ~: 4 also 5 known
Akaka: 5 falls 9 waterfall
locale: 6 Hawaii
Akan: 7 volcano
locale: 4 Asia 5 Japan 8 Hokkaido
Akashi: 4 city, town
locale: 5 Japan 6 Honshu
__ akbar: 5 Allah
AKC
part of ~: 4 Amer., Club 6 Kennel
reject: 3 mut 4 mutt
akee: 4 tree 5 fruit
relative: 5 genip 6 lichee, litchi, longan, lungan 7 genipap, leechee 9 soapberry
Akeem: 8 Olajuwon
Akela org.: 3 BSA
__ à Kempis: 6 Thomas
Akerlof, George: 8 Nobelist 9 economist
Akers: 5 Karen
AK-47 relative: 3 Uzi
Akhmadulina, Bella: 4 poet 7 Russian
Akhmatova, Anna: 4 poet 7 Russian
__ a Kick Out of You: 4 I Get
Akihito son: 3 Aya
Akiko Yosano: 4 poet 8 Japanese
Akim: 8 Tamiroff
akimbo: 4 bent 7 angular 8 angulose, angulous
akin: 4 like, near, such 5 alike, level 6 allied, on a par 7 cognate, kindred, related, similar 8 parallel 9 analogous, bracketed, connected, consonant 10 affiliated, comparable, equivalent, resembling

__ a kind: 5 one of, two of
__ a Kind of Hush: 6 There's
Akins: 3 Zoë 6 Claude
Akins, Claude TV role: 4 Lobo
Akio: 6 Morita
Akira: 8 Kurosawa
Akita: 3 dog, pet 4 city, port, town 5 canid, pooch 6 canine
locale: 5 Hondo, Japan 6 Honshu
__ a kite: 5 go fly
__ A. Knopf: 6 Alfred
Akron: 4 city, town
athletes: 4 Zips
conference: 3 MAC
county: 6 Summit
locale: 4 Ohio
product: 4 tire
Aksakov, Sergei: 6 writer 7 Russian
Ak-Sar-Ben Coliseum site: 5 Omaha
Aksyonov, Vasily: 6 writer 7 Russian
akule: 4 fish
al __: 4 fine 5 dente 6 fresco
Al: 4 Capp, elem., Gore, Hirt 5 Green, Hodge, Lewis, Lopez, Purdy, Roker, Unser 6 Capone, Jolson, Kaline, Oerter, Pacino, Wilson 7 element, Franken, Hibbler, Jarreau, Martino, McGuire, Schacht, Simmons, Stewart 8 aluminum, Molinaro, Neuharth, Sharpton 9 aluminium, Geiberger 10 Hirschfeld
13 for ~: 4 at. no.
veep before ~: 3 Dan
Al __: 6 Aaraaf
Al __, Iraq: 6 Basrah
Al-__: 4 Anon
AL
award: 3 MVP
cap letters: 3 SOX
team: 5 Bosox, The A's, Twins, Yanks 6 Angels, Chisox, Red Sox, Royals, Tigers 7 Indians, Orioles, Rangers, Yankees 8 Blue Jays, Mariners, White Sox 9 Athletics 10 Buccaneers
see also Alabama, baseball
ala: 4 wing
à la __: 4 king, mode 5 carte 6 broche, maison, vapeur 7 rigueur
à la __ heure: 5 bonne
Ala.
see Alabama
Al Aaraaf author: Edgar Allan Poe
Alabama: 4 band 5 river, state
bay: 6 Mobile
city: 5 Selma 6 Auburn, Dothan, Emelle, Hoover, Mobile, Smiths 7 Cullman, Decatur, Gadsden, Madison, Opelika 8 Anniston, Bessemer, Florence, Homewood, Prichard 9 Alabaster 10 Birmingham, Enterprise, Huntsville, Montgomery, Phenix City, Prattville, Tuscaloosa
city on the ~: 10 Montgomery
conference: 3 SEC
Indian: 5 Creek
neighbor: 7 Florida, Georgia 9 Tennessee 11 Mississippi
rival: 6 Auburn
school: 6 Auburn 9 Troy State
state flower: 8 camellia
state game bird: 10 wild turkey
state mineral: 8 hematite
state nut: 5 pecan
state rock: 6 marble
state saltwater fish: 6 tarpon
Alabamy __: 5 Bound
alabaster: 5 milky, white 7 mineral, niveous 9 yellowish
Alabaster: 4 city, town
locale: 7 Alabama
Alacant: 4 city, town
locale: 5 Spain
alack partner: 4 alas
alacrity: 4 zeal 5 haste, hurry, speed 6 action, fervor 8 celerity, dispatch, rapidity, velocity 9 briskness, eagerness, fleetness, quickness, readiness, swiftness 10 enthusiasm, expedition, liveliness, promptness
Ala Dagh: 5 range
locale: 4 Asia 6 Turkey
Aladdin: 4 Arab, hero
discovery: 4 lamp
Aladdin (1992 film)
role: 3 Abu, Ali 4 Iago 5 genie, Jafar, Rajah 7 Jasmine
voice cast: Gilbert Gottfried, Robin Williams
__ a Lady: 4 She's
__ alai: 3 jai
Alai: 5 range
locale: 4 Asia 11 Kirghyzstan
Alaid: 7 volcano
locale: 4 Asia 6 Russia
Alain: 5 Delon, Locke, Prost 6 Lesage 7 Lombard, Resnais 8 Chartier 9 Grandbois
in English: 4 Alan
Alain __-Grillet: 5 Robbe
Alaina: 4 Reed 8 Reed-Hall
Alain und __: 5 Elise
__ à la king: 7 chicken
Alamance County college: 4 Elon
__ a lamb: 6 meek as
Alameda: 4 city, town
locale: 10 California
__ Alamitos, CA: 3 Los
alamo: 4 tree 10 cottonwood
Alamo: 4 city, town 6 battle 9 car rental 10 auto rental
alternative: 4 Avis 5 Hertz 6 Budget, Dollar 7 Thrifty 8 National 10 Enterprise
defender: 5 Bowie, Texan 6 Travis 8 Crockett
locale: 3 Tex. 5 Texas 6 Mexico 8 Veracruz 10 San Antonio
à la mode: 3 new
__ à la mode: 3 pie
Alamogordo: 4 city, town
county: 5 Otero
detonation: 5 A bomb, A test
locale: 9 New Mexico
__ Alamos, NM: 3 Los
Alamo, The (1960 film): 5 oater
cast: Laurence Harvey, John Wayne, Richard Widmark
composer: 7 Tiomkin
director: John Wayne
Alan: 4 Abel, Alda, Bean, Dale, Hale, King, Ladd, O'Day, Opie, Page, Raph, Reed, Ruck, Sues 5 Arkin, Ashby, Bates, Freed, Paton, Young 6 Ameche, Clarke, Heeger, Metter, Napier, Osmond, Pakula, Parker, Seeger, Thicke, Turing 7 Bergman, Bridges, Cumming, Hodgkin, Jackson, Jardine, Marshal, Mowbray, Myerson, Parsons, Rachins, Rickman, Rudolph, Seymour, Shepard, Simpson 8 Cranston, Crosland, Osbiston, Sillitoe, Trammell 9 Ayckbourn, Greenspan, Hovhaness, Moorehead, Rosenberg 10 Dershowitz, MacDiarmid
in French: 5 Alain
Alan __ Foster: 4 Dean
Alan __ Lerner: 3 Jay
Alan __ Project: 7 Parsons
Alan-__: 5 a-dale
Alan Alexander __: 5 Milne
Åland __: 7 Islands
Alan Dean __: 6 Foster
Ala. neighbor: 3 Fla. 4 Miss, Tenn.
Alanis: 10 Morissette
Alan J. __: 6 Pakula
Alan Jay __: 6 Lerner
Alannah: 5 Myles
alar: 6 winged 8 axillary, winglike 10 wing-shaped
__-Al-Arab: 5 Shatt
Alarcón, Pedro de: 6 writer 7 Spanish
A la Recherche du Temps __: 5 Perdu
alarm: 4 bell, call, care, fear 5 alert, chill, clock, daunt, dread, pager, panic, scare, shake, siren, spook, upset 6 arouse, beeper, buzzer, caveat, dismay, fright, horror, Mayday, signal, terror, tocsin, unease, war cry 7 agitate, anxiety, concern, disturb, horrify, perturb, petrify, red flag, shake up, startle, terrify, unnerve, warning 8 cold feet, disquiet, distress, frighten, high sign, surprise, unstring 9 give a turn, give pause, hue and cry, terrorize, trepidity 10 discomfort, intimidate, scare stiff, waker-upper
activate the ~: 3 set
button: 5 reset 6 snooze
cause for ~: 5 alert, peril 6 danger
cry of ~: 2 oy 3 eek 4 yipe 5 yikes, yipes
ender: 3 ist
heed the ~: 4 rise, stir 5 arise, awake, get up 6 awaken, bestir, wake up
show ~: 5 cower
sound the ~: 4 warn 6 arouse
time, perhaps: 3 six 5 seven, six a.m. 7 seven a.m.
view with ~: 4 fear 5 dread, panic 6 dismay
alarm __: 4 bell 5 clock
__ alarm: 4 fire 5 false, smoke, still 6 silent 7 burglar
alarmable: 8 skittish 9 excitable
alarmed: 5 jumpy, timid 6 afraid, aghast, scared, trepid, uneasy 7 anxious, chicken, daunted, fearful, nervous, panicky 8 cowardly, fearsome, hesitant, timorous
be ~ about: 4 fear
easily ~: 5 timid
alarming: 4 dire 5 awful, dread, scary 6 unsafe 7 dreaded 8 dreadful, menacing 9 dangerous, frightful, harrowing, ill-omened
Alarms and Diversions author: James Thurber
alarum: 7 warning 10 call to arms
alas: 3 tsk, woe 4 ah me, oh no 5 alack, sadly 6 dear me, lament, tsk tsk
in German: 3 ach
partner: 5 alack
Alas! __ Yorick...: 4 poor
Alaska: 4 gulf, peak 5 mount, state 8 mountain
art form: 5 totem
bay: 7 Prudhoe
cape: 4 Nome
city: 4 Nome 5 Homer, Kenai, Sitka 6 Barrow, Bethel, Haines, Juneau, Kodiak, Seward, Valdez 7 Skagway, Wasilla 9 Anchorage, Fairbanks, Ketchikan
craft: 5 kayak, umiak
first governor: 4 Egan
glacier: 4 Muir
Indian: 3 Han 4 Eyak 5 Ahtna, Haida 6 Ahtena, Tanana 7 Chilcat, Chilkat, Koyukon, Kutchin, Tanaina, Tlingit
island: 3 Rat 4 Adak, Atka, Attu 6 Kodiak 8 Unalaska 9 Aleutians
jacket: 5 parka
mountain: 5 Baird 6 Brooks 8 McKinley 9 Aleutians
national park: 6 Denali, Katmai 9 Lake Clark 10 Glacier Bay
native: 3 Esk. 5 Aleut, Inuit 6 Eskimo, Innuit, Inupik 8 Aleutian
native language: 5 Aleut, Haida 7 Tlingit 8 Aleutian
neighbor: 5 Yukon 6 Canada, Russia 7 Siberia
peninsula: 5 Kenai
port: 4 Nome 9 Ketchikan
river: 5 Yukon
sea: 6 Bering 8 Beaufort
state fish: 10 king salmon
state gem: 4 jade
state land mammal: 5 moose
state mineral: 4 gold
state sport: 10 dog mushing
vehicle: 4 sled
volcano: 6 Katmai, Pavlof 7 Gareloi, Iliamna, Redoubt 8 Wrangell
Alaska __: 3 cod 4 crab, time 5 cedar, Range 7 Current, Highway, pollock
Alaska-__ time: 6 Hawaii
__ Alaska: 5 baked
Alaska king __: 4 crab
Alaskan: 5 Aleut 6 Eskimo 8 Aleutian
Alaskan __ crab: 4 king
Alaskan Highway, river near the: 5 Liard
Alaskan king __: 4 crab
Alaskan Malamute: 3 dog 5 canid 6 canine
__-Alaska Pipeline: 5 Trans
Alaska Standard __: 4 Time
Alas! poor __: 6 Yorick
Al-Assad: 5 Hafez
Alastair: 3 Sim
Alastor author: Percy Bysshe Shelley
__ à la suisse: 4 eggs
alate: 6 winged
__ a Latin From Manhattan: 4 She's
Alauda: 8 asteroid
Alava: 4 cape
a law __ oneself: 4 unto
alb: 7 garment 8 vestment
coverer: 5 orale
partner: 5 amice, orale
Al B. __: 4 Sure
__ alba: 5 terra
Alba: 7 Jessica
to Goya: 5 model
albacore: 4 fish, tuna 5 tunny
kin: 6 bonito
Alban: 4 Berg 5 saint
Albanese, Licia: 6 singer 7 soprano
specialty: 5 opera
Albania: 6 nation 7 country
bay: 6 Valona
capital: 6 Tirana, Tiranë
former president: 4 Alia
from ~: 6 Balkan
guerrilla: 6 klepht
lake: 7 Scutari
money: 3 lek 6 qindar, qintar
mountain: 5 Korab
neighbor: 6 Greece 9 Macedonia 10 Yugoslavia
Nobelist in Peace: 6 Teresa
port: 5 Vlore 6 Durres
river: 4 Drin
Albanian: 8 language
Albano: 4 lake
locale: 5 Italy
Albany: 4 city, town
canal: 4 Erie
college near ~: 5 Siena
father-in-law: 4 Lear
locale: 6 Oregon 7 Georgia, New York
river: 6 Hudson
Albariño: 4 wine 5 white
origin: 5 Spain
albatross: 4 bird, load 5 goony 6 burden, gooney 9 hindrance, mallemuck, millstone, mollymawk, mollymoke
abode: 4 nest
albedo: 4 rind
Albee, Edward: 6 writer 10 playwright
work: All Over
The American Dream

Box
Counting the Ways
The Death of Bessie Smith
A Delicate Balance
Fam and Yam
Finding the Sun
Fragments
The Lady From Dubuque
Listening
The Man Who Had Three Arms
Marriage Play
The Sandbox
Seascape
Three Tall Women
Tiny Alice
Who's Afraid of Virginia Woolf?
The Zoo Story
albeit: **3** tho **5** altho **6** even if, though **7** thought **8** although **10** even though
Albemarle __: **5** Sound
Alben: **7** Barkley
Albéniz: **5** Isaac **8** composer
piano opus: **6** Iberia
Alberes: **3** cow **4** bull **6** bovine, cattle
Albert: **3** Lee **4** band, Carl, Kahn, King, lake, Marv, pope **5** Belle, Camus, Eddie, Sabin **6** Brooks, Claude, Dekker, Edward, Finney, Lasker, Lutuli, Morris, Pujols **7** Hackett, Hammond, Luthuli, Moravia, Paulsen, pontiff, Terhune **8** Einstein **9** Michelson **10** Schweitzer
locale: **5** Congo **6** Uganda
Victoria, to ~: **4** wife **6** cousin **8** relative
Albert __: **7** Herring
__ Albert: **3** Fat
Alberta: **6** Hunter **8** province
city: **4** Olds **5** Banff, Hanna, Leduc, Taber **6** Onoway **7** Calgary, Red Deer **8** Edmonton, St. Albert **10** Lethbridge, Strathcona
hockey player: **5** Oiler
lake: **6** Louise **9** Athabasca
locale: **6** Canada
mountain: **8** Columbia
native: **4** Cree
waterfall: **7** Panther
__ Albert coat: **6** Prince
Albert, Eddie: **5** actor
film: Attack! (1956)
Birch Interval (1977)
Captain Newman, M.D. (1963)
Escape to Witch Mountain (1975)
The Heartbreak Kid (1972)
The Longest Day (1962)
The Longest Yard (1974)
McQ (1974)
Oklahoma! (1955)
Roman Holiday (1953)
spouse: Margo
TV: Green Acres, Switch
Albert Herring composer: **7** Britten
Alberti: **4** Leon **6** Rafael
Alberti __: **4** bass
Alberti, Leon: **6** writer **7** Italian
Alberti, Rafael: **4** poet **7** Spanish **10** playwright
Albert Lea: **4** city, town
locale: **9** Minnesota
Albert, Morris song: Feelings (1975)
Alberto: **5** Tomba **6** Vitale **10** Giacometti
Alberto-__: **6** Culver
Alberto VO5
rival: **5** Prell
Albertson, Jack: **5** actor
film: Kissin' Cousins (1964)
The Poseidon Adventure (1972)
The Subject Was Roses (1968, AA)
Willy Wonka and the Chocolate Factory (1971)
TV: Chico and the Man
Albertus Magnus: **5** saint **11** philosopher
Albertville
gear: **3** ski **4** skee
locale: **4** Alps **6** France
albescent: **3** wan **4** pale **5** ashen, milky, white **6** chalky, pallid, sallow **8** blanched, bleached **9** bloodless
Albi: **4** city, town
locale: **6** France
Albine author: Emile Zola
Albion: **7** Britain, England
neighbor: **4** Eire, Erin **7** Ireland
Albireo: **4** star
albizzia: **4** tree **5** shrub
alboka: **4** wind **8** hornpipe **10** instrument
Alborada: **4** city, town
locale: **6** Mexico
Alborak: **5** horse **6** equine
Ålborg: **4** city, port, town
locale: **7** Denmark
Albrecht: **5** Dürer **6** Kossel
Albright: **4** Lola **6** Tenley **9** Madeleine
Albright, Lola: **7** actress
film: Kid Galahad (1962)
Lord Love a Duck (1966)
TV: Peter Gunn
Albright, Tenley: **6** skater
album: **2** LP **4** book **6** volume **9** anthology, blank book, portfolio, scrapbook **10** collection, memory book
cover: **5** liner
item: **5** photo
like some ~ s: **4** mono **6** stereo
place in a stamp ~: **5** mount
selection: **5** track
__ album: **5** stamp **6** record
albumen __: **5** paper, plate
__ albumin: **5** serum
__ Album, The: **3** Inn **5** White
Albuquerque: **4** city, town
athletes: **5** Lobos
locale: **9** New Mexico
newspaper: **7** Journal, Tribune
river: **9** Rio Grande
school: **3** UNM
alc.: **3** liq.
ALC: **8** division
team: **5** Twins **6** Chisox, Royals, Tigers **7** Indians **8** White Sox
Alcaeus: **4** poet **5** Greek
Alcan Highway site: **5** Yukon **6** Alaska
Alcatraz: **6** island
Birdman of ~: **5** lifer **6** Stroud
alcazar: **6** palace
alces: **5** moose
Alcestis author: Euripides
alchemist
element: **3** air **4** fire **5** earth, water
liquid: **6** elixir
mercury: **5** azoth
Alchemist, The author: Ben Jonson
Alchiba: **4** star
Alcina composer: **6** Handel
Alcoa: **4** city, town
competitor: **8** Reynolds
locale: **9** Tennessee
alcohol: **4** grog, kava **5** booze, drink, sauce **6** hootch, liquor, red-eye, rotgut, whisky **7** liqueur, spirits, whiskey **8** vermouth **9** aqua vitae, firewater, hard stuff, inebriant, moonshine **10** intoxicant
acid + ~ product: **5** ester
awareness org.: **4** MADD
burner: **4** etna
ender: **5** meter
high in ~: **4** hard
not partaking of ~: **5** sober
rose-scented ~: **5** nerol
solution: **5** tinct. **8** tincture
solvent: **6** acetal
__ alcohol: **4** amyl, wood **5** allyl, butyl, cetyl, decyl, ethyl, grain, nonyl, octyl, oleyl, vinyl **6** anisic, anisyl, benzyl, bornyl, lauryl, methyl, propyl **7** caustic, cetylic, decatyl, rubbing
alcoholic: **4** hard **9** distilled, fermented, inebriant **10** spirituous
beverage: **3** ale, gin, rum, rye **4** beer, grog, mead, ouzo, port, sake, saki, wine **5** booze, hooch, lager, stout, toddy, vodka **6** brandy, bubbly, cassis, liquor, redeye, scotch, whisky **7** bourbon, liqueur, sloe gin, tequila, whiskey **8** aperitif, cocktail, Drambuie, Galliano, highball, nightcap, potation **9** applejack, Champagne, firewater, hard cider, moonshine
Alcor: **4** star
Alcott: **3** Amy **7** Bronson
Alcott, Amy: **6** golfer
milieu: **5** links **6** course
org.: **4** LPGA
Alcott, Bronson: **11** philosopher
Alcott, Louisa May: **6** author, writer
character: **3** Amy, Meg **5** March
work: Eight Cousins
Flower Fables
Hospital Sketches
The Inheritance
Jo's Boys
Little Men
Little Women
alcove: **3** bay **4** apse, cell, nook, room **5** arbor, booth, bower, inlet, niche **6** carrel, corner, cranny, grotto, recess **7** carrell, chamber, cubicle **8** anteroom **9** cubbyhole
vaulted ~: **6** recess
Alcyone: **4** star **6** Pleiad
father of ~: **5** Atlas
ald.: **3** pol.
Alda: **4** Alan **6** Robert **7** Frances
Alda, Alan: **5** actor **8** director
colleague: **4** Farr, Swit **6** Morgan, Rogers **7** Farrell **9** Stevenson
film: Betsy's Wedding (1990)
California Suite (1978)
Canadian Bacon (1995)
Crimes and Misdemeanors (1989)
Everyone Says I Love You (1996)
The Four Seasons (1981)
Manhattan Murder Mystery (1993)
The Mephisto Waltz (1971)
Murder at 1600 (1997)
A New Life (1988)
The Object of My Affection (1998)
Paper Lion (1968)
Same Time, Next Year (1978)
The Seduction of Joe Tynan (1979)
Sweet Liberty (1986)
TV: MASH
Aldabra __: **7** Islands
Alda, Frances: **6** singer **7** soprano
specialty: **5** opera
Aldama: **4** city, town
locale: **6** Mexico **10** Tamaulipas
Aldebaran: **4** star **5** K star
__ aldehyde: **5** butyl **6** anisic, lauric, lauryl, propyl **7** acrylic, benzoic, dodecyl, pyruvic
Alden: **4** John **6** Nowlan
al dente: **4** firm
__ al dente: **5** pasta
alder: **4** tree **5** birch, shrub
ender: **3** man, men
in Scottish: **3** arn
relative: **5** birch, hazel **8** hornbeam
__ alder: **3** red **5** black, white, witch
Alder, Kurt: **7** chemist **8** Nobelist
Aldine: **4** font **8** typeface
Aldiss, Brian: **6** writer **7** British
Aldo: **3** Ray **4** Moro **5** Gucci **7** Fabrizi, Gabrizi, Leopold **8** Mannucci
in English: **6** Donald
Aldous: **6** Huxley
Aldrich: **4** Ames **6** Robert
Aldrich __, The: **6** Family
Aldrich Family, The: **9** radio show
Aldrich, Robert: **8** director
film: 4 for Texas (1963)
... All the Marbles (1981)
Attack! (1956)
The Big Knife (1955)
The Dirty Dozen (1967)
Emperor of the North (1973)
Flight of the Phoenix (1966)
The Frisco Kid (1979)
The Grissom Gang (1971)
Hush ... Hush, Sweet Charlotte (1965)
Kiss Me Deadly (1955)
The Last Sunset (1961)
The Longest Yard (1974)
Too Late the Hero (1970)
Ulzana's Raid (1972)
Vera Cruz (1954)
What Ever Happened to Baby Jane? (1962)
Aldridge: **3** Ira
Aldrin, Buzz: **5** Edwin **8** explorer
alma mater: **3** MIT
craft: **5** Eagle
Aldus: **4** font **8** Manutius, typeface
ale: **3** nog **4** brew, grog, suds **5** draft, drink, quaff **6** bitter, porter **7** draught **8** beverage, Guinness **10** malt liquor
Adam's ~: **5** water
cousin: **4** beer **5** lager, stout
ender: **4** wife **5** house
ginger ~: **4** soda **5** mixer **9** soft drink
head: **4** foam
holder: **3** mug **4** toby **5** stein **7** growler
how ~ may be offered: **5** on tap
ingredient: **4** hops, malt
measure: **2** pt. **4** pint
source: **3** pub **7** brewery
tasting of ~: **5** malty
__ ale: **4** pale **5** Adam's, draft **6** ginger
ALE: **8** division
team: **6** Red Sox **7** Orioles, Yankees **8** Blue Jays **9** Devil Rays
__ alea est: **5** lacta, Jacta
Alec: **5** Waugh **6** Wilder **7** Baldwin, McCowen **8** Guinness **9** Templeton
Alec Douglas-__: **4** Home
aleck, smart: **8** quipster, wiseacre
Alecto: **4** Fury **6** Erinys
colleague: **7** Megaera **9** Tisiphone
alee: **8** downwind **9** protected
__-a-leekie: **4** cock
Alef: **8** language
alternative: **3** ADA, APL, SQL **4** html, Icon, Java, LISP, Logo, Orca, Perl **5** Algol, Basic, Cecil, COBOL, Dylan, SISAL **6** Delphi, Eiffel, Erlang, Oberon, Pascal, Prolog, Sather, Scheme, Snobol **7** Fortran
__ a left: **4** hang
__ a leg: **5** break, shake
alegras: **5** dance
alegre: **7** festivo
__ Alegre, Brazil: **5** Porto
Alegría, Ciro: **6** writer **8** Peruvian
Alegría, Claribel: **6** writer **10** Salvadoran
__ a leg up: **3** get **4** give
alehouse: **3** bar, pub **6** saloon, tavern **7** barroom **8** taphouse
fixture: **3** tap
order: **5** draft
aleichem __: **6** shalom
__ aleichem: **6** shalom
Aleichem, Shalom: **6** writer **7** Yiddish **8** humorist
Aleixandre, Vicente: **6** writer **8** Nobelist
Alejandro: **3** Rey **4** Peña
in English: **9** Alexander
Alekhine, Alexander forte: **5** chess
Aleksandr: **4** Blok, Grin **6** Kuprin **7** Borodin, Fadayev, Pushkin **8** Glazunov **9** Prokhorov
Aleksei: **7** Kosygin
Alemán, Mateo: **6** writer **7** Spanish

Alembert, Jean Le Rond d': 6 French 11 philosopher
alembic: 5 cruet, still 6 beaker, carafe, retort 7 arcanum, refiner 8 crucible, purifier 9 converter, distiller
locale: 3 lab
Alencar, José de: 6 writer 9 Brazilian
Alençon: 4 city, lace, town
department: 4 Orne
locale: 6 France
...___ a lender be: 3 nor
aleph: 6 Hebrew, letter
successor: 3 bes, bet 4 beth
aleph-___: 4 null, zero
Aleppo: 4 city, town
archeological site near ~: 4 Ebla
Aleppo ___: 4 gall, pine 5 grass
alerce: 4 tree 9 evergreen
Alero: 3 car 4 auto, Olds 10 automobile, Oldsmobile
alert: 3 APB 4 flag, live, spry, warn, wary, wise 5 alarm, alive, awake, aware, fresh, peppy, perky, quick, ready, scare, sharp, siren, smart 6 active, advise, arouse, awaken, bright, inform, intent, lively, living, nimble, notify, prompt, signal, tip off, tocsin, with it 7 all ears, careful, caution, heads-up, heedful, mindful, on guard, wakeful, warning 8 advisory, cautious, forewarn, high sign, keen-eyed, spirited, vigilant, watchful, wide-eyed 9 Argus-eyed, attentive, conscious, expectant, observant, on the ball, receptive, sharp-eyed, sprightly, vivacious, wide awake 10 admonition, call to arms, insightful, keen-witted, on one's toes, on the stick, perceptive, put on guard
became ~: 5 sat up
be ~ to: 4 heed
keep ~: 6 beware 7 look out
military ~ status: 6 DEFCON
on the ~: 7 wakeful 8 vigilant
ozone ~ prompter: 3 fog 4 murk, smog 5 brume, vapor 9 fogginess
___ alert: 3 air, red 4 blue 5 on the, white 6 ground, yellow
___ Alert: 5 First
alertness: 4 care, heed 7 caution 9 assiduity, awareness, diligence, vigilance 10 enterprise, weather eye
Alès: 4 city, town
locale: 6 France
alesan: 5 beige
Aleshkovsky, Yuz: 6 writer 7 Russian
Alesia locale: 4 Gaul
Alessandro: 5 Volta 7 Manzoni
see also Italian
Aleta's son: 3 Arn
Aletheia: 8 asteroid
___ a Letter to My Love: 5 I Sent
Aleut: 6 Eskimo 7 Alaskan
abode: 4 iglu 5 igloo
carving: 5 totem
craft: 5 kayak, umiak
language: 5 Inuit 6 Innuit, Inupik
outerwear: 5 parka
Aleutian ___: 5 Range 7 Current, Islands
Aleutians: 4 isle 5 range 6 island
island: 3 Rat 4 Adak, Atka, Attu 8 Unalaska
locale: 6 Alaska
volcano: 6 Katmai
wind: 8 williwaw
Aleve: 9 analgesic 10 painkiller
alternative: 3 APF 4 Cope 5 Advil, Bayer 6 Anacin, Datril, Motrin 7 Ecotrin, Tylenol 8 Bufferin, Excedrin, St. Joseph, Vanquish 9 Ascriptin
alewife: 4 fish
Alex: 3 Cox 4 Cord 5 Haley, March, Rocco, Segal 6 Désert, Karras, Proyas, Rieger, Trebek, Winter 7 Comfort, English, Raymond 8 Van Halen 10 Delvecchio
alexander: 5 drink 8 beverage, cocktail
___ alexander: 6 brandy
Alexander: 3 Ben 4 Haig, Hall, Jane, Knox, pope, Todd, tsar 5 Jason, Korda, Lebed, Shana 6 Calder, Müller, Nevski, Nevsky, Parkes, Siddig 7 Fleming, Godunov, pontiff, Scourby 8 Alekhine, Glazunov, Hamilton, Smallens 9 Mackenzie, Woollcott 10 Cartwright
group: 4 band
in Russian: 5 Sacha
in Spanish: 9 Alejandro
Alexander ___: 6 Nevski, Nevsky 7 Severus
Alexander Graham ___: 4 Bell
Alexander, Grover Cleveland: 6 hurler 7 pitcher
Alexander, Jane: 7 actress
film: Brubaker (1980)
City Heat (1984)
The Great White Hope (1970)
Kramer vs. Kramer (1979)
The New Centurions (1972)
Testament (1983)
Alexander, Jason: 5 actor
film: The Adventures of Rocky and Bullwinkle (2000)
White Palace (1990)
TV: Seinfeld
Alexander Nevsky (1938 film) director: Sergei Eisenstein
Alexander Nevsky composer: 9 Prokofiev
Alexander of ___: 5 Tunis
___ Alexanderplatz: 6 Berlin
Alexander's Bridge author: Willa Cather
Alexander's Ragtime Band (1938 film)
cast: Don Ameche, Alice Faye, Tyrone Power
director: Henry King
Alexander's Ragtime Band composer: Irving Berlin
Alexander the Great (1956 film)
cast: Claire Bloom, Richard Burton, Fredric March
director: Robert Rossen
Alexander the Great horse: 10 Bucephalus
Alexandra: 4 Paul 8 Danilova 9 David-Neel
Alexandre: 5 Dumas, Hardy 6 Eiffel
see also French
Alexandria: 4 city, port, town
ancient ~ lighthouse: 6 Pharos
locale: 5 Egypt 8 Virginia 9 Louisiana
river: 4 Nile
Alexandria ___: 5 senna 7 Quartet
Alexandria Quartet
author: Lawrence Durrell
book: 4 Clea 7 Justine 9 Balthazar 10 Mountolive
alexandrite: 3 gem 8 gemstone
Alexei: 7 Kosygin
see also Russian
Alexis: 3 Kim 4 czar, tsar 5 Smith 6 Carrel 8 Arquette
see also Russian
Aléxis: 5 Léger
Alexsandr: 6 Yashin 8 Scriabin
Alf: 6 Landon 7 Kjellin
ALF: 2 ET 5 alien
ALF (NBC sitcom)
cast: Paul Fusco (ALF/Gordon Shumway)
cat: 5 Lucky
food: cats
home planet: Melmac
alfalfa: 3 hay 6 clover, lucern 7 fodders, lucerne
Alfalfa friend: 5 Darla, Porky 6 Spanky 9 Buckwheat
Alfa Romeo: 3 car 4 auto 10 automobile
model: 3 GTV 6 Milano, Spider
Alferov, Zhores: 8 Nobelist 9 physicist
Alfie (1966 film)
cast: Michael Caine, Millicent Martin, Shelley Winters
character: 3 Flo 4 Perc, Ruby 5 Carla, Gilda, Lacey, Lofty 6 Siddie
director: Lewis Gilbert
Alfie (1967 song) artist: Dionne Warwick
Alfieri, Vittorio: 6 writer 7 Italian
alfiona: 4 fish
Alfirk: 4 star
Alfonse: 6 Capone, D'Amato
Alfonso: 3 rey 4 king 7 Spanish
queen: 3 Ena
Alfre: 7 Woodard
Alfred: 4 king, Lunt 5 Adler, Binet, Drake, Fried, Green, Jarry, Kazin, Knopf, Krupp, Nobel, Noyes, Ryder, Sloan 6 Austin, Bester, Cortot, Döblin, Fuller, Gilman, Kinsey, Molina, Neuman, Newman, Piscop, Werker, Werner 7 Brendel, Dreyfus, Hershey, Kastler, Wegener 8 de Musset, Tennyson 9 Hitchcock, Stieglitz, Whitehead
composer: 4 Arne
poet: 3 Pye
Alfred ___ Birney: 5 Earle
Alfredo: 5 sauce 6 Oriani 7 Casella
alternative: 5 pesto 8 marinara
Alfred the ___: 5 Great
alfresco: 7 outdoor, outside
dining ~: 6 picnic
locale: 5 patio
not ~: 6 indoor, inside 7 indoors
Alfvén, Hannes: 8 Nobelist 9 physicist
alga: 4 kelp 5 plant 6 diatom, nostoc 7 seaweed 9 spirogyra, stonewort
and fungus: 6 lichen
___ alga: 5 brown 6 marine
algae: 4 kelp, scum 5 dulse, sloke 6 diatom 7 seaweed 9 spirogyra
combining form: 4 phyc- 5 phyco-
genus: 6 chorda
Japanese ~: 4 nori
___ algae: 3 red 5 green
algebra: 4 math
___ algebra: 6 linear 7 Boolean
Algeciras: 4 city, port, town
locale: 5 Spain
Algedi: 4 star
Algenib: 4 star
Algenubi: 4 star
Alger: 4 Hiss 7 Horatio
Alger, Horatio: 6 author, writer
work: Frank's Campaign
Luck and Pluck
Ragged Dick
Tattered Tom
The Young Miner
Algeria: 6 nation 7 country
capital: 7 Algiers
cavalryman: 5 spahi 6 spahee
city: 4 Oran 5 Batna, Blida, Saida, Setif 6 Annaba 7 Algiers
desert: 6 Sahara
governor: 3 dey
group: 4 OPEC 10 Arab League
it's n. of ~: 5 Medit.
money: 5 dinar
mountains: 5 Atlas
music: 3 rai
neighbor: 4 Mali 5 Libya, Niger 7 Morocco, Tunisia 10 Mauritania
people: 6 Tuareg
port: 4 Oran 6 Skikda 7 Algiers
writer: 6 Djebar
Algerian: 5 Orani
algerine: 6 fabric 8 material
algerita: 5 shrub
relative: 7 agarita, mahonia 8 barberry
Algernon: 9 Blackwood, Swinburne
algid: 3 icy 4 cold, cool 6 chilly 7 ice-cold
Algieba: 4 star
Algiers: 4 city, port, town 7 capital
area: 6 Casbah, Kasbah
locale: 7 Algeria
Algiers (1938 film)
cast: Charles Boyer, Hedy Lamarr
director: John Cromwell
Algol: 4 star 8 language
alternative: 3 ADA, APL, SQL 4 Alef, html, Icon, Java, LISP, Logo, Orca, Perl 5 Basic, Cecil, COBOL, Dylan, SISAL 6 Delphi, Eiffel, Erlang, Oberon, Pascal, Prolog, Sather, Scheme, Snobol 7 Fortran
Algonquian: 4 Cree 8 language
Indian: 5 Miami 6 Ottawa 7 Arapaho 8 Arapahoe, Illinois 9 Blackfoot
Algonquin: 4 city, town 6 Indian
locale: 8 Illinois
transport: 5 canoe
tribe: 5 Unami
Algonquin Round Table
member: 3 wit 5 Broun 6 Parker 8 Benchley, Woolcott
algophobe fear: 4 pain
Algorab: 4 star
Algren, Nelson: 6 author, writer
work: The Last Carousel
The Man With the Golden Arm
The Neon Wilderness
Never Come Morning
Notes From a Sea Diary
Somebody in Boots
A Walk on the Wild Side
Who Lost an American?
algum: 4 tree
Alhambra: 4 city, town
locale: 10 California
Alhena: 4 star
Ali: 5 Ahmed, Laila 6 Landry, Larter 7 MacGraw, Mahomet, Tatyana 8 Mohammed, Muhammad
carried one in '96: 5 torch
defeat, a la ~: 4 whup
faith: 5 Islam
formerly: 4 Clay
stat: 3 KOs
stung like one: 3 bee
see also boxing
Ali (2001 film)
cast: Jamie Foxx, Will Smith, Mario Van Peebles, Jon Voight
director: Michael Mann
Ali ___: 4 Baba 5 Pasha
Ali ___ and the Forty Thieves: 4 Baba
___ alia: 5 inter
alia, et: 9 and others
cousin: 3 etc.
alias: 3 aka, nom 4 name 5 pseud. 6 anonym, handle 7 moniker, pen name 8 monicker, nickname 9 false name, pseudonym, stage name 10 nom de plume
common ~: 5 Jones, Smith
Alias Jesse James (1952 film)
cast: Rhonda Fleming, Bob Hope
director: Norman Z. McLeod
Alias Nick Beal (1943 film)
cast: Ray Milland, Audrey Totter
director: John Farrow
Ali Baba: 4 Arab, hero
brother: 6 Cassim
command: 10 open sesame
locale: 4 cave
alibi: 4 plea, yarn 5 cover, story 6 excuse 7 defense, pretext, voucher
Alibi ___: 3 Ike
___ Alibi: 3 Her
Alibi Ike (1935 film)
cast: Joe E. Brown, Olivia de Havilland
director: Ray Enright

alible: 10 nourishing
Alicante: 4 city, port, town
locale: 5 Spain
Alice: 4 blue, city, Faye, town 5 Brady, Krige, Munro 6 Cooper, Marble, Toklas, Walker, Waters 7 grayish, Kramden 8 Ghostley 9 Childress, Longworth, Roosevelt
chronicler: 4 Arlo
husband: 5 Ralph
locale: 5 Texas
relative: 4 anil, cyan, navy, Nile, teal 5 azure, slate 6 cobalt, indigo, raisin, violet 7 peacock 8 cerulean, sapphire 9 turquoise 10 aquamarine, periwinkle
Alice (1990 film)
cast: Alec Baldwin, Blythe Danner, Judy Davis, Mia Farrow
director: Woody Allen
Alice (CBS sitcom)
cast: Polly Holliday (Flo Castleberry) Beth Howland (Vera Gorman) Linda Lavin (Alice Hyatt) Philip McKeon (Tommy Hyatt) Martha Raye (Carrie Sharples) Vic Tayback (Mel Sharples) Celia Weston (Jolene Hunnicutt)
setting: Mel's, diner, Phoenix, Arizona
spinoff: 3 Flo
Alice ___: 4 blue 5 Adams 7 Springs
Alice ___ Gown: 4 Blue
Alice ___ Miller: 4 Duer
___ Alice: 4 Tiny
Alice Adams: 4 film 5 novel
author: Booth Tarkington
cast: Katharine Hepburn, Fred MacMurray, Fred Stone
director: George Stevens
Alice Doesn't Live Here Anymore (1974 film)
cast: Ellen Burstyn, Kris Kristofferson
director: Martin Scorsese
Alice in Wonderland cat: 5 Dinah
Alice's Adventures in Wonderland
author: Lewis Carroll
character: 3 Two 4 Bill, Cook, Crab, Dodo, Duck, Five, King 5 Dinah, Elsie, Knave, Lacie, Lorry, Puppy, Queen, Seven 6 Eaglet, Lizard, Pigeon, Rabbit, Tillie 7 Duchess, Gryphon, William 8 Baby Crab, Dormouse, Flamingo, Hedgehog 9 Mad Hatter, March Hare 10 Mock Turtle 11 Caterpillar, Cheshire Cat, Fish Footman, Frog Footman
Alice's Restaurant: 4 film, song
artist: Arlo Guthrie
cast: James Broderick, Arlo Guthrie, Pat Quinn
director: Arthur Penn
Alicia: 3 Ana 4 Witt 6 Alonso 7 Bridges, Markova 10 de Larrocha
Alida: 5 Valli
___ a lid on it!: 3 Put
alien: 3 ALF, odd 4 Mork, Yoda 5 outer, Sarek, Spock 6 exotic, Klaatu, remote 7 foreign, invader, Klingon, Martian, offbeat, outside, oversea, refugee, Romulan, Starman, strange, unknown, unusual 8 contrary, emigrant, intruder, newcomer, offshore, outsider, overseas, stranger, uncommon, Venusian 9 auslander, different, extrinsic, foreigner, immigrant, nonnative, outlander, peregrine, unheard-of 10 noncitizen, outlandish, unfamiliar
combining form: 3 xen- 4 xeno-
investigation: 5 X file
search org.: 4 SETI
spacecraft: 3 UFO 6 saucer
subj.: 3 ESL
___ alien: 5 enemy 7 illegal
Alien (1979 film)
cast: John Hurt, Tom Skerritt, Sigourney Weaver
cat: 6 Jonesy
character: 5 Brett 6 Dallas, Ripley 7 Lambert
director: Ridley Scott
alienate: 4 sour 6 divide, offend, sicken 7 disgust, fend off, hold off, repulse, strange, turn off 8 disunite, drive off, embitter, imbitter, separate, turn away 9 disaffect 10 antagonize, set against
alienated: 6 bitter 8 factious 10 antisocial, friendless, rebellious, unfriendly
alienation: 4 rift 5 anomy, break, split 6 anomie, breach, enmity 9 defection, sundering 10 remoteness, separation, withdrawal
alieni ___: 5 juris 7 generis
Alienist, The author: 4 Carr 9 Caleb Carr
Aliens (1986 film)
cast: Michael Biehn, Carrie Henn, Sigourney Weaver
character: 4 Newt 5 Ellen, Hicks 6 Dwayne, Ripley
director: James Cameron
___-a-lievio: 4 ring
___ a life!: 3 Get
alif follower: 2 ba
Ali-Foreman fight site: 5 Zaire
Alighieri: 5 Dante
alight: 4 land 5 light, perch, roost 6 ablaze, arrive, debark, get off, hop off, settle 7 descend, flaming, get down, jump off, step off 8 come down, dismount 9 disembark, touch down
set ~: 6 ignite, kindle
upon: 9 encounter
align: 3 fix, set 4 ally, even, rank 5 array, order, range, reset 6 adjust, even up, line up, orient, square, true up 7 arrange, marshal 8 regulate 9 affiliate, associate, calibrate, collimate, cooperate 10 coordinate, join up with, straighten
the crosshairs: 3 aim 5 aim at
(with): 4 side
aligned: 4 true 5 level 6 in a row 7 abreast 8 parallel, straight
___ alignment: 5 wheel
aligoté: 4 wine 5 white
origin: 6 France
alii: 6 others
et ~ cousin: 3 etc.
___ alii: 5 inter
alike: 4 akin, both, same, such 5 equal, level 6 allied, evenly, on a par 7 cognate, equally, kindred, related, similar, the same, uniform 8 in common, parallel 9 analogous, identical, similarly, uniformly 10 comparable, comparably, equivalent, synonymous, the same way
look ~: 5 match
make ~: 6 equate
not ~: 9 different 10 dissimilar
think ~: 5 agree
___-alike: 4 look
alikeness: 10 similarity
___ a limb: 5 out on
aliment: 4 chow, diet, eats, fare, feed, food, grub, keep, meal, meat 5 board, bread, manna 6 fooder, forage, living, repast, viands 7 commons, edibles, nurture, rations, victual, vittles 8 eatables, victuals 9 foodstuff, nutriment, provender, refection 10 livelihood, provisions, sustenance
alimentary: 7 dietary 9 digestive, nutritive 10 comestible, digestible, nourishing, nutritious, sustaining
canal part: 5 ileum
alimentary ___: 5 canal
alimentation: 6 living 7 support 10 livelihood
alimony: 7 payment, subsidy, support
recipients: 4 exes
Ali, Muhammad: 3 pug 5 boxer
milieu: 4 ring
aline: 4 true 6 adjust 10 straighten
___ a line: 4 drop
Aline: 8 MacMahon, Saarinen
A-line: 5 dress, skirt 7 skimmer
creator: 4 Dior
alined: 6 in a row
___ a line in the sand: 4 draw
___ a lineman for the county: 3 I Am
___-a-liner: 5 penny
___-a-ling: 4 ding, ting
___ alios: 5 inter
Alioth: 4 star
Alioto: 6 Joseph
aliped: 3 bat
Alison: 5 Doody, Lurie, Moyet 6 Krauss 7 Arngrim, La Placa 8 Steadman 9 Skipworth
Alison's House author: Susan Glaspell
Aliso Viejo: 4 city, town
locale: 10 California
alist: 6 tilted 7 heeling, leaning, listing, tilting 8 inclined 9 careening
Alistair: 5 Cooke 7 MacLean
alit: 6 got off, landed 7 set down, settled 8 debussed, deplaned 9 descended 10 came to rest, dismounted
Ali, Tatyana song: Daydreamin' (1998)
___ a little: 3 not 4 just
___ a Little Bit of Luck: 4 With
___ a Little Help...: 4 With
___ a Little Prayer: 4 I Say
___ a Little Tenderness: 3 Try
alive: 4 rife, spry 5 alert, awake, brisk, quick, vital 6 active, extant, feisty, mortal, upbeat, viable, with us 7 animate, dynamic, growing, replete, running, teeming, vibrant, wakeful, working, zestful 8 animated, bustling, existent, existing, spirited, stirring, swarming, vigorous 9 abounding, breathing, cognizant, conscious, energetic, observant, operative, sprightly, vivacious 10 responsive, subsisting
act ~: 6 perk up
and kicking: 4 well 5 sound
combining form: 4 vivi-
keep ~: 7 sustain
remain ~: 5 exist 6 manage 7 subsist, survive
skin ~: 4 flay 6 review, vilify 9 criticize
to: 7 aware of 9 mindful of
(with): 4 rife 7 profuse, replete, teeming 8 thronged 9 abounding
___ alive!: 3 It's 4 Look 5 Sakes
Alive: 4 book, film
author: Piers Paul Read
cast: Ethan Hawke, Vincent Spano
director: Frank Marshall
setting: 5 Andes
Alive!
band: 4 Kiss
___ Alive: 6 Stayin'
alive and ___: 4 well 7 kicking
___ a living!: 3 It's
Alka-___: 7 Seltzer
Al Kab: 4 star
Alkaid: 4 star
alkali: 3 KOH, lye 4 base, lime, NaOH 6 potash 7 antacid 9 hydroxide
measure: 2 pH
opposite: 4 acid
alkali ___: 4 blue, flat, rock, soil 5 grass, metal
alkaline: 5 acrid, basic, salty 6 bitter 7 caustic
not ~: 6 acidic
alkaloid: 6 curara, curare
Alka-Seltzer: 7 antacid
alternative: 4 Tums 6 Maalox, Pepcid, Riopan, Zantac 7 Gelusil, Lactaid, Mylanta, Rolaids 8 Gaviscon 11 Pepto-Bismol
sound: 4 fizz, plop
alkene: 6 olefin 7 olefine
Alkes: 4 star
all: 3 sum 4 full, just, only 5 every, fully, gross, quite, total, whole 6 entire, in toto, purely, solely, wholly 7 bar none, pronoun, totally, utterly 8 complete, entirely, entirety, everyone, the works 9 aggregate, everybody 10 completely, everything, lion's share, nothing but
combining form: 3 omn-, pan- 4 omni-, pano-, pant- 5 panta-, panto-
ender: 4 heal, over, seed 5 spice
in music: 5 tutti
in Spanish: 4 toda, todo
name meaning ~: 4 Ella
starter: 4 hold 5 carry, catch
the time, to a poet: 3 e'er
together: 6 at once 7 en masse
wound up: 5 tense
all ___: 3 but, set, wet 4 ears, eyes, gone, hail, over, told 5 along, clear, fours, in all, right, there 6 thumbs
all ___ and a yard wide: 4 wool
all ___ and bothered: 3 hot
all ___ day's work: 3 in a
all ___ good: 5 to the
all ___ out: 3 get
all ___ sudden: 3 of a
all ___ the line: 5 along
all ___ with: 4 over
all-___: 3 day, out 4 heal, pass, star, time, year 5 clear, fired, in-one, night, right, round, State 6 around 7 nighter, purpose, weather
all-___ bulletin: 6 points
all-___ vehicle: 7 terrain
___ all: 4 bare 5 above, after, not at
___-all: 3 end, you 4 cure, heal, know
All: 9 detergent
alternative: 3 Biz, Era, Fab, Yes 4 Bold, Dash, Gain, Surf, Tide, Wisk 5 Cheer, Dreft, Purex 6 Calgon, Dynamo, Oxydol 7 Octagon 9 Ivory Snow
All ___: 4 of Me, Over, Star 5 Alone, at Sea, I Know, I Need, of You 6 My Sons, Saints
All ___!: 4 rise, stop 6 aboard
All ___ Airways: 6 Nippon
All ___ Am I: 5 Alone
All ___ and Heaven Too: 4 This
All ___ are off!: 4 bets
All ___ Day: 5 Fools', Souls' 6 Saints'
All ___ day's work: 3 in a
All ___ down: 4 fall
All ___ Dream of You: 5 I Do Is
All ___ Eve: 5 About 7 Hallows'
All ___ Family: 5 in the
All ___ for Christmas...: 5 I Want
All ___ Glitters: 4 That
All ___ is a tall ship...: 4 I ask
All ___ Is Dream of You: 3 I Do
All ___ Jazz: 4 That
All ___ Long: 5 Night 6 Summer
All ___ Need Is Love: 3 You
All ___ Need Is You: 5 I Ever
All ___ on the Western Front: 5 Quiet
All ___ that's going...: 6 ashore
All ___ the Watchtower: 5 Along
All ___ to Do Is Dream: 5 I Have
All ___ Up: 5 Shook
All ___ were the borogoves: 5 mimsy
All ___ Years Ago: 5 Those
All-___: 3 Pro 4 Bran
All-___ Game: 4 Star
___ All: 5 After, Armor
All 4 Love (1991 song) artist: Color Me Badd

alla ___: **5** breve, prima **6** marcia
Alla: **8** Nazimova
All About ___: **3** Eve **4** Soul
All About Eve (1950 film)
cast: Anne Baxter, Bette Davis, Celeste Holm, George Sanders
character: **4** Bill **5** Karen, Margo **6** DeWitt **7** Addison, Sampson **8** Channing, Richards **10** Harrington
director: Joseph L. Mankiewicz
All About My Mother (1999 film)
cast: Penélope Cruz, Marisa Peredes, Cecilia Roth, Antonia San Juan
director: Pedro Almodóvar
alla breve: **7** cut time
...___ all a good night: **5** and to
Allah: **3** God **4** Lord
worship of ~: **5** Islam
Allahabad's river: **6** Ganges
Allais, Maurice: **8** Nobelist **9** economist
All Alone Am I (1962 song) artist: Brenda Lee
All Alone composer: Irving Berlin
all along the ___: **4** line
All American Boy, The (1958 song) artist: Bobby Bare
Allan: **4** Dwan **5** Arbus, Jones **6** Nevins **7** Cormack, Sherman **8** Gurganus **9** Pinkerton
Allan-___: **5** a-Dale
___ Allan Poe: **5** Edgar
Allan Quatermain author: H. Rider Haggard
Allante: **3** car **4** auto **8** Cadillac **10** automobile
all-around: **6** global **7** general **8** sweeping **9** adaptable, inclusive, versatile
All Around the Town author: Mary Higgins Clark
All Around the World (1990 song) artist: Lisa Stansfield
___ alla Scala: **6** Teatro
all at ___: **3** sea **4** once
allay: **4** calm, cool, ease, lull **5** abate, blunt, quell, quiet, slake **6** dampen, lessen, pacify, quench, reduce, settle, smooth, soften, solace, soothe, temper **7** appease, assuage, compose, lighten, mollify, relieve **8** decrease, mitigate, moderate, palliate **9** alleviate, put to rest, untrouble **10** propitiate
one's fears: **6** assure
___-all book: **4** tell
All-Bran: **6** cereal
alternative: **3** Kix **4** Life, Trix **5** Kashi, Quisp, Total **6** Kaboom, Muesli, Oreo O's, Pablum, Smacks **7** Crispix, Harmony, Hunny B's, Mueslix, Oat Bran, Pokemon **8** Boo Berry, Cheerios, Corn Chex, Corn Pops, Fiber One, Rice Chex, Special K, Uncle Sam, Wheaties **9** Alpha Bits, Apple Zaps, Grape Nuts, Honey Comb, Just Right, Wheat Chex **10** Apple Jacks, Bran Flakes, Cap'n Crunch, Cocoa Puffs, Froot Loops, Mini-Wheats, Nutri-Grain, Puffed Rice, Quaker Oats, Smart Start **11** Cocoa Blasts, Cookie Crisp, Golden Crisp, Lucky Charms, Puffed Wheat, Sweet Crunch, Waffle Crisp
Allbritton: **6** Louise
All by Myself composer: Irving Berlin
All by Myself (song) artist: Eric Carmen
artist: Celine Dion
all-consuming: **7** intense
All Creatures ___ and Small: **5** Great
All Cried Out (1986 song) artist: Lisa Lisa and Cult Jam
all-day ___: **6** sucker
All Day and All of the Night (1965 song) artist: Kinks
All Dogs Go to Heaven
dog: **3** Flo **5** Itchy **6** Killer **7** Carface, Charlie
___ allé: **3** pas
allegation: **5** claim, story **6** charge **9** assertion, statement **10** accusation, contention, deposition, indictment, profession
allege: **3** say **4** aver, avow, hold **5** claim, state **6** accuse, affirm, assert, attest, avouch, charge **7** charges, contend, declare, pretend, profess, purport, testify **8** maintain **10** asseverate
alleged: **7** nominal, reputed **8** putative, reported, so-called **9** pretended **10** ostensible
reason: **5** alibi, bluff, cover, guise **6** excuse **7** cover-up **8** pretense **10** cover story
allegedly: **8** so-called **10** apparently
Alleghenies: **5** range **9** mountains
Allegheny: **5** river
city on the ~: **5** Olean **10** Pittsburgh
ex-name: **5** USAir
locale: **4** Penn. **7** New York
Allegheny Moon (1956 song) artist: Patti Page
Allegheny Uprising (1939 film)
cast: Claire Trevor, John Wayne
director: William A. Seiter
allegiance: **3** tie **4** love **5** faith **6** fealty, homage **7** loyalty **8** devotion, fidelity **9** adherence, constancy, deference, fixedness, obedience **10** conformity, dedication, obligation
owe ~: **6** adhere, belong
allegiant: **4** true **5** loyal **6** ardent, steady **7** devoted, dutiful, staunch **8** constant, faithful, true-blue, yeomanly **9** dedicated, steadfast
allegorical: **8** mythical, symbolic **9** legendary
allegorize: **9** adumbrate **10** illustrate
allegory: **4** myth **5** fable, story **7** parable **8** metaphor **10** fairy story
relative: **6** apolog **8** apologue
Allegory of Love, The author: C.S. Lewis
Allegret: **4** Marc
allegro: **5** tempo
faster than ~: **6** presto
slower than ~: **8** moderato
allegro ___: **5** assai
___ allegro: **5** molto
Allegro: **7** musical
songwriter: **7** Rodgers **11** Hammerstein
allegro con ___: **4** brio
allele: **4** gene
alleluia: **4** pean **5** paean **10** hallelujah
allemande: **5** dance, sauce
ingredient: **4** yolk
all-embracing: **3** big **4** vast **6** cosmic **7** general, overall **8** catholic, cosmical, sweeping, thorough **9** universal
Allen: **3** Mel, Rex, Tim **4** Fred, Funt, Joan, Lane, Tate **5** Byron, Drury, Ethan, Irwin, Karen, Lewis, Nancy, Peter, Steve, Woody **6** Curnow, Debbie, Du Mont, George, Gracie, Hervey, Ludden, Marcus **7** Barbara, Iverson, Jenkins **8** Garfield, Ginsberg **9** Elizabeth, Steverino
Keaton, to ~: **6** costar
partner: **5** Burns, Rossi
successor: **4** Paar
to Burns: **4** foil, wife
Allen ___: **5** screw **6** wrench
___ Allen belt: **3** Van
Allenby: **6** Edmund
conquest of 1918: **6** Beirut **8** Beyrouth
all-encompassing: **6** global **7** generic **8** sweeping **9** generical, unlimited
Allende: **4** city, town **6** Isabel **8** Salvador
locale: **6** Mexico **8** Coahuila, Veracruz **9** Nuevo León **10** Guanajuato
Allende, Isabel: **6** writer **7** Chilean
work: City of the Beasts
Daughter of Fortune
Eva Luna
The House of the Spirits
The Infinite Plan
Mothers and Sons
Of Love and Shadows
Paula
Portrait in Sepia
Allen, Ethan brother: **3** Ira
Allen, Fred: **3** wit **8** comedian
feuder with ~: Jack Benny
milieu: **5** radio
spouse: Portland Hoffa
Allen, George: **5** coach
sport: **8** football
Allen, Gracie: **5** comic **7** actress **10** comedienne
film: The Big Broadcast (1932)
College Swing (1938)
A Damsel in Distress (1937)
Six of a Kind (1934)
milieu: **5** radio
spouse: George Burns
Allen, Joan: **7** actress
film: Face/Off (1997)
The Ice Storm (1997)
In Country (1989)
Manhunter (1986)
Nixon (1995)
Pleasantville (1998)
Searching for Bobby Fischer (1993)
Tucker: The Man and His Dream (1988)
Allen, Karen: **7** actress
film: The Glass Menagerie (1987)
Raiders of the Lost Ark (1981)
Scrooged (1988)
Shoot the Moon (1982)
Split Image (1982)
The Wanderers (1979)
Allen, Nancy: **7** actress
film: Blow Out (1981)
Dressed to Kill (1980)
I Wanna Hold Your Hand (1978)
RoboCop (1987)
spouse: Brian De Palma
Allen Park: **4** city, town
locale: **8** Michigan
Allen, Peter spouse: Liza Minnelli
Allen, Steve spouse: Jayne Meadows
Allen, Tim: **5** actor
film: Big Trouble (2002)
Galaxy Quest (1999)
Joe Somebody (2001)
The Santa Clause (1994)
film (voice): Toy Story (1995)
movie character: **5** Santa
TV: Home Improvement
Allentown: **4** city
city near ~: **6** Easton **9** Bethlehem
locale: **4** Penn.
river: **6** Lehigh
Allentown (1982 song) artist: Billy Joel
Allen, Woody: **5** actor **8** director
film: Alice (1990)
Annie Hall (1977, AA)
Another Woman (1988)
Bananas (1971)
Broadway Danny Rose (1984)
Bullets Over Broadway (1994)
Casino Royale (1967)
Celebrity (1998)
Crimes and Misdemeanors (1989)
The Curse of the Jade Scorpion (2001)
Everyone Says I Love You (1996)
The Front (1976)
Hannah and Her Sisters (1986)
Hollywood Ending (2002)
Husbands and Wives (1992)
Interiors (1978)
Love and Death (1975)
Manhattan (1979)
Manhattan Murder Mystery (1993)
A Midsummer Night's Sex Comedy (1982)
Mighty Aphrodite (1995)
Play It Again, Sam (1972)
The Purple Rose of Cairo (1985)
Radio Days (1987)
Shadows and Fog (1992)
Sleeper (1973)
Small Time Crooks (2000)
Stardust Memories (1980)
Sweet and Lowdown (1999)
Take the Money and Run (1969)
What's Up, Tiger Lily? (1966)
Zelig (1983)
film (voice): Antz (1998)
spouse: Louise Lasser
allergen dispenser: **6** anther
___-allergenic: **4** hypo
allergic: **6** averse
reaction: **4** itch, rash **6** asthma
allergy: **8** aversion, hay fever **9** antipathy
medication: **5** Afrin **6** Contac, Nyquil, Tavist **7** Actifed, Comtrex, Dayquil, Dristan, Sinutab, Sudafed **8** Benadryl, Dimetapp, Drixoral, TheraFlu **9** Coricidin, Triaminic **10** Robitussin
sound: **5** achoo **6** ahchoo, hachoo **7** kerchoo
alleviate: **4** calm, cure, ease, help **5** allay, loose, quell, salve **6** deaden, defuse, defuze, lessen, loosen, pacify, quench, remedy, smooth, soften, solace, soothe **7** appease, assuage, lighten, mollify, relieve, sweeten **8** mitigate, moderate, palliate **9** soft-pedal, untrouble **10** ameliorate
alleviation: **6** relief, solace **7** anodyne **9** abatement
alleviative: **8** curative
all-expenses-___: **4** paid
alley: **4** mews, path, road, walk **5** aisle, track **6** street **7** back way, passage, pathway **8** corridor, cul-de-sac **10** back street, passageway
blind ~: **7** dead end, impasse **8** cul-de-sac
bowling ~: **4** lane
button: **5** reset
challenge: **5** split
ender: **3** way
haunt an ~: **5** prowl
org.: **3** PBA
player: **6** bowler, kegler **7** kegeler
score: **5** spare **6** strike
target: **3** pin
see also bowling
alley ___: **3** cat **5** light
alley-___: **3** oop
___ alley: **5** blind, shaft **7** bowling
___-alley: **4** back
Alley: **5** Mills **7** Kirstie
Alley ___: **3** Cat, Oop
Alley Cat (1962 song) artist: Bent Fabric
Alley, Kirstie: **7** actress
film: Drop Dead Gorgeous (1999)
Look Who's Talking (1989)
role: **4** Howe
spouse: Parker Stevenson
TV: Cheers
Alley-Oop (1960 song) artist: Hollywood Argyles
Alley Oop kingdom: **3** Moo
All Fall Down (1962 film)
cast: Warren Beatty, Karl Malden, Eva Marie Saint
director: John Frankenheimer
All Fall Down subject: **4** Iran

__ All Fears, The: 5 Sum of
__ All Flesh, The: 5 Way of
__ all, folks!: 5 That's
All Fools' __: 3 Day
All for Love (1993 song)
artist: Bryan Adams, Rod Stewart, Sting
All for Love poet: 6 Dryden
All for one and one for all: 5 motto
All for You (2001 song) artist: Janet Jackson
all fours: 4 game 8 card game
variety: 5 cinch
all get __: 3 out
All God's Chillun Got Wings author: Eugene O'Neill
All gone!: 4 poof
Allgood: 4 Sara
Allhallows __: 3 Eve
All Hallows' Eve author: Charles Williams
__ all hang out: 5 let it
alliance: 3 tie 4 bloc, bond, club, pact, ring 5 junto, trust, union, unity 6 accord, league, treaty 7 academy, compact, entente, society 8 marriage, relation 9 agreement, anschluss, coalition, matrimony 10 federation, fellowship, friendship
former ~: 3 PAU, UAR 5 SEATO
global ~: 3 OAS 4 NATO
political ~: 4 bloc 5 junta
WWII ~: 4 Axis
Alliance: 4 city, town
locale: 4 Ohio
Alliance __ Progress: 3 for
__ Alliance: 4 Dual, Holy 6 Little, Triple
All I ask is __ ship: 5 a tall
Allie: 5 Light 7 Sherman 8 Reynolds
friend: 4 Kate
__ & Allie: 4 Kate
allied: 3 wed 4 akin 5 alike 6 joined, linked, united 7 cognate, kindred, related, similar, unified 8 combined, friendly, hooked up, in league, parallel, relative 9 analogous, bracketed, connected, corporate, in cahoots 10 affiliated, associated, comparable, equivalent
Allied: 5 mover
rival: 6 Global, United
Allier: 5 river
city on the ~: 5 Vichy
locale: 6 France
Allies opponent: 4 Axis
All I Ever Need Is You (1971 song)
artist: Sonny and Cher
alligator: 5 dance 6 animal, lizard 7 leather, reptile
female: 3 cow
home: 5 swamp
label: 4 Izod
male: 4 bull
on a shirt: 4 logo
relative: 4 croc 6 caiman, cayman 9 crocodile
young: 9 hatchling
alligator __: 3 gar 4 clip, pear, weed 5 clamp, shear 6 lizard, wrench 7 snapper
Alligator __: 5 Alley
alligator pear: 5 fruit 7 avocado
All I gotta do __ naturally: 5 is act
All I Have to Do Is Dream (1958 song)
artist: Everly Brothers
All I Have to Give (1999 song) artist: Backstreet Boys
All I Know (1973 song) artist: Art Garfunkel
all-important: 5 vital 8 critical 9 necessary 10 portentous
all in __ time: 4 good
all in __ work: 5 a day's
all-in-__: 3 one
all-inclusive: 3 big 4 a to z, full, vast, wide 5 broad, roomy, total, uncut, whole 6 entire, global 7 blanket, general, plenary 8 catholic, complete, detailed, far-flung, finished, spacious, sweeping, thorough, umbrella 9 capacious, expansive, extensive, universal, unreduced, wholesale 10 exhaustive, unabridged, widespread
category: 4 misc.
All I Need (song) artist: Jack Wagner, Temptations
all in good __: 4 time
all-in-one: 6 entire
__ all intents and purposes: 3 for
All in the Family (CBS sitcom)
cast: Carroll O'Connor (Archie Bunker)
Rob Reiner (Mike Meathead Stivic)
Jean Stapleton (Edith Dingbat Bunker)
Sally Struthers (Gloria Bunker Stivic)
producer: Lear
setting: Queens, New York
spinoff: The Jeffersons, Maude
__ All in the Game: 3 It's
__ all in this together!: 4 We're
Allison: 3 Roe 4 Fran, Mose 5 Bobby 6 Anders
on Peyton Place: 3 Mia
Allison, Bobby: 9 auto racer
milieu: 5 track
Allison, Mose: 7 pianist
genre: 4 jazz
allium: 4 leek 5 bulbs, chive, onion 6 garlic 7 shallot
All I Wanna Do (1998 film)
cast: Rachael Leigh Cook, Kirsten Dunst, Gaby Hoffmann, Lynn Redgrave
All I Wanna Do (1994 song) artist: Sheryl Crow
all kidding __: 5 aside
all-knowing: 4 wise 10 omniscient
__ All Laughed: 4 They
Allman: 5 Duane, Gregg
Allman Brothers Band
song: Midnight Rider (1975)
Ramblin Man (1973)
Allman, Gregg spouse: Cher
All My __: 4 Sons
All My __ Live in Texas: 3 Ex's
All My Children (ABC): 4 soap 9 soap opera
actress: 4 Ripa 5 Lucci
role: 4 Kane, Opal 5 Erica
All My Friends Are Going to Be Strangers author: Larry McMurtry
All My Life (1990 song) artist: Linda Ronstadt
All My Sons: 4 film, play
author: Arthur Miller
cast: Burt Lancaster, Edward G. Robinson
character: 3 Joe, Sue 4 Anne, Bert, Kate 5 Lydia
director: Irving Reis
all-nighter: 5 binge, event
pull an ~: 4 cram
All Night Long (1981 film)
cast: Gene Hackman, Diane Ladd, Barbra Streisand
All Night Long (song)
artist: Faith Evans, Joe Walsh, Lionel Richie, Puff Daddy
allocate: 3 set 4 mete 5 allot, allow, divvy, grant, spend, split 6 assign, assort, budget, devote, divide, parcel, ration 7 divvy up, earmark, mete out, portion 8 dispense, regulate, set aside 9 apportion, designate 10 distribute, measure out
allocation: 4 dole 5 grant, quota, share 6 budget, ration 7 portion 9 allotment, allowance 10 assignment
allocution: 6 speech 7 lecture
__ All Odds: 7 Against
all of a __: 6 sudden
All of Me (1984 film)
cast: Steve Martin, Lily Tomlin
director: Carl Reiner
dog: 3 Bix
All of You (1984 song) artist: Diana Ross
all-or-__: 4 none 7 nothing
All or Nothing (1990 song) artist: Milli Vanilli
allosaur: 5 biped 7 reptile
allot: 3 set 4 deal, dole, mete 5 allow, divvy, grant, leave, share, split 6 assign, bestow, devote, divide, parcel, ration, render 7 carve up, dole out, give out, hand out, mete out, portion, prorate, station 8 allocate, dedicate, dispense, divide up, set aside 9 apportion, parcel out 10 distribute, measure out, proportion
allotment: 3 cut, lot 4 dole, part, time 5 grant, piece, quota, share, slice 6 ration 7 measure, portion 8 dividend, quantity 9 allowance 10 adjustment, allocation, assignment
all-out: 4 firm, full 5 total, utter 6 utmost 7 maximum, optimum, supreme 8 absolute, complete, emphatic, forceful, full-bore, resolute, sweeping, thorough, to the max, whole-hog 9 full-blown, full-dress, full-scale, intensive, last-ditch, unlimited 10 conclusive, exhaustive, soup to nuts, unswerving, unwavering
All out of Love (1980 song) artist: Air Supply
all over __: 4 with
all-over: 9 universal 10 ubiquitous
__ all over: 4 fall
__ All Over: 4 Glad
All Over author: Edward Albee
__ All Over Now: 3 It's
allow: 2 go, OK 3 let, own 4 avow, bear, give, lend, loan, mete, okay 5 admit, adopt, agree, allot, brook, go for, grant, leave, let on, spare, spell, stand, yield 6 accede, afford, assent, comply, deduct, enable, fess up, impart, permit, suffer 7 agree to, approve, concede, confess, empower, entitle, include, intitle, let pass, license, provide, support, welcome 8 allocate, assent to, legalize, sanction, set aside, stand for, submit to, tolerate 9 acquiesce, apportion, approve of, authorize, be game for, give leave, put up with, recognize, sign off on 10 concur with, give the nod
for: 6 offset 7 forgive, include 8 consider
(for): 4 plan
to enter: 5 admit, greet, let in 6 accept 7 embrace, receive, welcome
to go: 4 free 5 loose 6 acquit, let off, pardon, parole 7 cashier, dismiss, release, set free 8 liberate 9 exonerate, muster out, terminate
to pass: 5 let by
to use: 4 lend
allowable: 2 OK 3 apt 4 good, okay 5 jural, legal, legit, licit 6 kasher, kosher, lawful, proper, venial 8 all right, optional, suitable 9 excusable, legalized 10 acceptable, admissible, approvable, forgivable, in the rules, legitimate
allowance: 3 cut, pay 4 dole, gift, odds, room 5 grant, leave, quota, share, slice, start 6 margin, ration, rebate, refund 7 advance, pension, percent, stipend, subsidy, support 8 headroom 9 abatement, admission, advantage, allotment, clearance, deduction, endowment, endurance, exception, insurance, reduction 10 adaptation, adjustment, allocation, commission, concession, confession, fellowship, honorarium, indulgence, percentage, recompense, remittance, sufferance, toleration, unbosoming
make ~ for: 7 include 8 overlook
scale ~: 4 tare, tret
time ~: 5 grace
allowed: 5 legal, legit, licit 6 kasher, kosher, lawful, proper 8 rightful 9 by the book, permitted 10 admissible, sanctioned
is not ~ to: 5 mayn't
allowing: 6 though 7 lenient
alloy: 3 mix 5 admix, blend, brass, Invar, metal, Monel, steel 6 alnico, bronze, latten, mingle, oreide, ormolu, oroide, pewter, solder, tambac, tombac 7 amalgam, combine, Elinvar, Everdur, Inconel, mixture, Mumetal, nitinol, platina, pollute, tinfoil 8 bismanol, calamine, cast iron, electrum, gunmetal, intermix, kamacite, Manganin, Nichrome, pot metal 9 barberite, bell metal, composite, duralumin, Dutch foil, Dutch gold, Dutch leaf, magnalium, pinchbeck, Platinite, platinoid, type metal, Vitallium, white gold 10 adulterate, amalgamate, constantan, Dutch metal, gold bronze, misch metal, mosaic gold, soft solder, superalloy, terne metal, Wood's metal
aluminum ~: 6 alnico 9 duralumin, magnalium
antimony ~: 9 type metal
bismuth ~: 8 bismanol 10 Wood's metal
brasslike ~: 6 latten
cadmium ~: 10 Wood's metal
carbon ~: 5 steel 8 cast iron
cerium ~: 10 misch metal
chromium ~: 7 Elinvar, Inconel 8 Nichrome 9 Vitallium
cobalt ~: 6 alnico 9 Vitallium 10 superalloy
component: 5 metal
copper ~: 5 brass, Monel 6 bronze, latten, oreide, ormolu, oroide, tambac, tombac 7 Everdur, Mumetal 8 gunmetal, Manganin, pot metal 9 barberite, bell metal, duralumin, Dutch foil, Dutch gold, Dutch leaf, pinchbeck, platinoid 10 constantan, Dutch metal, gold bronze, mosaic gold
gold ~: 8 electrum
heat-resistant ~: 6 cermet 7 ceramal
iridium ~: 7 platina
iron ~: 5 Invar, Monel, steel 7 Elinvar, Inconel, Mumetal 8 kamacite, Nichrome 9 Platinite 10 superalloy
lanthanum ~: 10 misch metal
lead ~: 5 terne 6 pewter 7 tinfoil 8 calamine, pot metal 9 type metal 10 gold bronze, soft solder, terne metal, Wood's metal
magnesium ~: 9 magnalium
magnetic ~: 6 alnico
manganese ~: 5 Monel 7 Everdur 8 bismanol, Manganin
mercury ~: 7 amalgam
molybdenum ~: 9 Vitallium
nickel ~: 5 Invar, Monel 6 alnico 7 Elinvar, Inconel, Mumetal, nitinol 8 electrum, kamacite, Manganin, Nichrome 9 barberite, Platinite, platinoid, white gold 10 constantan, superalloy
osmium ~: 7 platina

palladium ~: 7 platina 9 white gold
platinum ~: 7 platina 9 white gold
silicon ~: 7 Everdur 9 barberite
silver ~: 7 amalgam 8 electrum
tin ~: 5 terne 6 bronze, oreide, oroide, pewter 8 calamine, gunmetal 9 barberite, bell metal, type metal 10 gold bronze, soft solder, terne metal, Wood's metal
titanium ~: 7 nitinol
zinc ~: 5 brass 6 latten, oreide, ormolu, oroide, tambac, tombac 8 calamine, gunmetal 9 Dutch foil, Dutch gold, Dutch leaf, pinchbeck, platinoid, white gold 10 Dutch metal, gold bronze, mosaic gold
alloyed: 4 mixt 5 mixed 6 impure
alloys science: 10 metallurgy
all-points bulletin: 7 dragnet
all-powerful: 6 divine 10 omnipotent
All praise to __: 5 Allah
All-Pro: 4 star 10 footballer
all-purpose: 6 useful 9 versatile
__ all question: 6 beyond
All Quiet on the Western Front: 4 film 5 novel
author: Erich Maria Remarque
cast: Lew Ayres, Louis Wolheim, John Wray
character: 3 Kat 4 Erna, Leer 6 Müller
director: Lewis Milestone
all right: 4 okay 5 roger
All Right Now (1970 song) artist: Free
All Said and Done author: Simone de Beauvoir
All Saints' __: 3 Day
All sales __: 5 final
all-seeing: 8 lynx-eyed 10 omniscient
All She Wants to Do is Dance (1985 song) artist: Don Henley
__ all she wrote: 5 That's
All Shook Up (1957 song) artist: Elvis Presley
All Souls' __: 3 Day
allspice: 4 tree 7 pimento
all-sports
channel: 4 ESPN
first ~ radio station: 4 WFAN
All-Star Games, like: 6 annual
Allstate: 9 insurance
owner: 5 Sears
rival: 5 Aetna 7 MetLife 8 Hartford 9 State Farm, Travelers
All Summer Long author: Robert Anderson
all sweetness, name meaning: 6 Pamela
All's Well That Ends Well
author: William Shakespeare
character: 5 Lafeu 6 Helena 7 Bertram, Lavache, Rinaldo 8 Marianna, Parolles, Violenta
All systems go: 3 A-OK
all-terrain __: 4 bike 7 vehicle
all-terrain vehicle: 4 jeep
__ All That: 4 She's
All that glitters __ gold: 5 is not
All That Glitters author: Thomas Tryon
All That Heaven Allows (1955 film)
cast: Rock Hudson, Jane Wyman
director: Douglas Sirk
All That Jazz (1979 film)
cast: Jessica Lange, Ann Reinking, Roy Scheider
director: Bob Fosse
All That She Wants (1993 song) artist: Ace of Base
all the __: 4 rage, same
All the Best People author: Sloan Wilson
All the King's Men: 4 film 5 novel
author: Robert Penn Warren
cast: Broderick Crawford, Joanne Dru, John Ireland, Mercedes McCambridge
director: Robert Rossen
All the Man That I Need (1991 song) artist: Whitney Houston
... All the Marbles (1981 film)
cast: Peter Falk, Vicki Frederick, Laurene Landon
director: Robert Aldrich
All the news that's fit to print coiner: 4 Ochs
All the perfumes of __: 6 Arabia
All the President's Men (1976 film)
cast: Martin Balsam, Dustin Hoffman, Hal Holbrook, Robert Redford, Jason Robards, Jack Warden
director: Alan J. Pakula
All the Pretty Horses (2000 film)
cast: Penélope Cruz, Matt Damon, Henry Thomas
director: Billy Bob Thornton
All the Right Moves (1983 film)
cast: Tom Cruise, Craig T. Nelson, Lea Thompson
All the Things You Are composer: 4 Kern 11 Hammerstein
All the Way (1957 song) artist: Frank Sinatra
composer: 4 Cahn 9 Van Heusen
All the Way Home (1963 film)
cast: Aline MacMahon, Robert Preston, Jean Simmons
director: Alex Segal
__ All the Way Home: 4 I Ran
__ all the world: 3 for
All the world's __: 6 a stage
All the Young Men (1960 film)
cast: James Darren, Alan Ladd, Sidney Poitier
All Things Considered network: 3 NPR
All This and Heaven Too (1940 film)
cast: Charles Boyer, Bette Davis, Jeffrey Lynn
director: Anatole Litvak
All This Time (song) artist: Sting, Tiffany
All Those Years Ago (1981 song) artist: George Harrison
All Through the Night (1942 film)
cast: Humphrey Bogart, Conrad Veidt, Kaaren Verne
dog: 6 Hansel
All Through the Night (1984 song) artist: Cyndi Lauper
__ all together: 5 get it, put it
all to the __: 4 good
__ All True: 3 It's
allude: 5 refer, touch
to: 4 cite, hint, mean 5 imply, quote 6 advert, hint at, impute 7 mention, purport, suggest, touch on 8 intimate 9 insinuate, touch upon
alluded to: 5 tacit 7 implied 9 intimated
allure: 4 bait, coax, draw, hook, lure, pull 5 charm, decoy, grace, shill, spell, tempt 6 appeal, beauty, beckon, engage, entice, entrap, glamor, lead on, pull in 7 attract, beguile, bewitch, charism, enchant, glamour, win over 8 appeal to, charisma, entrance, interest, inveigle 9 captivate, enrapture, fascinate, infatuate, magnetism 10 attraction, come hither, enticement, loveliness, sultriness, temptation
Allure competitor: 4 Elle 5 Vogue
allurement: 4 bait, lure 5 charm, decoy, snare 6 appeal, come-on 7 baiting, teasing 9 appetence, incentive 10 attraction, enticement, invitation
Allure song: All Cried Out (1997)
alluring: 4 cute, foxy, glam, sexy 5 bonny, siren 6 bonnie, comely, lovely, pretty 7 darling, lovable, winning, winsome 8 adorable, charming, enticing, fetching, gorgeous, handsome, heavenly, inviting, loveable, magnetic, pleasing, striking, stunning, tempting 9 beautiful, beguiling, glamorous, ravishing 10 attractive, bewitching, magnetical, persuasive
woman: 5 houri, siren
allusion: 4 hint 7 mention 8 innuendo 9 inference, reference 10 imputation, intimation, suggestion
alluvial: 5 silty
alluvial __: 3 fan 4 cone 5 plain
alluvium: 4 ooze, silt 5 drift, earth 7 deposit
__ All We Know: 3 For
all-wise: 10 omniscient
all wool __ yard wide: 4 and a
ally: 3 pal 4 chum, mate 5 align, aline, amigo, buddy, crony, unite 6 backer, cohort, friend, helper, league 7 abetter, abettor, comrade, conjoin, connect, partner 8 co-worker, henchman, partisan, sidekick, unionize 9 affiliate, associate, auxiliary, bedfellow, colleague, companion, confidant, supporter 10 accomplice, close ranks, compatriot, well-wisher
opposite: 3 foe 5 enemy
Ally: 6 McBeal, Sheedy, Walker
Allyce: 7 Beasley
__, All Ye Faithful: 5 O Come
Ally McBeal (Fox drama)
cast: Lisa Nicole Carson (Renee Raddick)
Calista Flockhart (Ally McBeal)
Greg Germann (Richard Fish)
Jane Krakowski (Elaine Bassell)
Peter MacNicol (John Cage)
Courtney Thorne-Smith (Georgia Thomas)
all-you-can-eat place: 6 buffet
All You Need Is Love (1967 song)
artist: Beatles
Allyson, June: 7 actress
film: Executive Suite (1954)
The Glenn Miller Story (1954)
Good News (1947)
The McConnell Story (1955)
The Opposite Sex (1956)
Remains to Be Seen (1953)
The Stratton Story (1949)
Two Girls and a Sailor (1944)
Two Sisters From Boston (1946)
Woman's World (1954)
spouse: Dick Powell
Alma: 4 city, town 5 Gluck 6 Kruger, Mahler
locale: 6 Canada, Québec
Alma-Ata: 4 city, town
locale: 10 Kazakhstan
Almaaz: 4 star
Almach: 4 star
alma mater: 6 school 7 college 9 old school 10 university
souvenir: 2 yb. 8 yearbook
visitor: 4 alum, grad 6 alumna 7 alumnus 8 graduate
almanac: 4 book 6 record
feature: 5 atlas, facts, index
almandine: 3 gem 8 gemstone
Almay: 6 makeup
alternative: 4 Avon 6 Revlon 7 Lancome, Mary Kay 8 Clinique 9 Cover Girl, Max Factor 10 Maybelline 11 Estée Lauder, Merle Norman
almighty: 5 maker 6 deific, divine 7 eternal, godlike, supreme 8 absolute, heavenly, immortal, infinite, puissant 10 invincible, omnipotent, omniscient
almighty __: 6 dollar
Almighty: 3 God 7 Creator
almique: 4 tree
relative: 4 shea 6 balata 9 sapodilla
Almodóvar: 5 Pedro
almon: 4 tree
almond: 3 nut, tan 4 tree 5 beige, brown, color
combining form: 7 amygdal- 8 amygdalo-
relative: 4 buff, pear, plum, rose 5 apple, camel, peach 6 cherry, medlar, quince 7 apricot, caramel 8 hawthorn, oiticica 10 blackthorn
almond __: 3 oil 4 bark, cake, meal, milk 5 paste
almond-__: 4 eyed 6 shaped
__ almond: 5 burnt, earth, sweet 6 bitter, Indian, Jordan
Almond Joy: 5 candy 9 chocolate
alternative: 4 Mars, Twix 5 Clark, Heath 6 Kit Kat, Mounds, PayDay, Reese's, Zagnut 7 Krackel, Oh Henry 8 Baby Ruth, Hershey's, Milky Way, Snickers 9 Mr. Goodbar 10 NutRageous
almost: 4 most, near, nigh 5 about, close, quasi 6 barely, nearly, toward 7 close to, halfway, short of, towards 8 as good as, in effect, narrowly, not quite, well-nigh 9 just about, virtually
combining form: 3 pen- 4 pene-
never: 6 rarely, seldom 8 not often 10 hardly ever, now and then
prefix: 4 para-
there: 4 near 6 nearby
up: 4 next
Almost Famous (2000 film)
cast: Billy Crudup, Kate Hudson, Jason Lee, Frances McDormand
director: Cameron Crowe
Almost Like Being in Love composer: 5 Loewe 6 Lerner
Almqvist, Carl: 6 writer 7 Swedish
alms: 4 dole, gift 5 grant 6 income 7 charity, handout, largess 8 donation, largesse, offering 9 baksheesh 10 liberality
ask ~: 3 beg
dispense ~: 4 dole
seeker: 6 beggar
almuce: 4 cape
almug: 4 tree
Al Nair: 4 star
Alnasl: 4 star
alnico: 5 alloy
component: 6 cobalt, nickel 8 aluminum
Alnilam: 4 star
Alnitak: 4 star
Al Niyat: 4 star
__ a load of: 3 get
__ a loaf...: 4 Half
aloe: 4 lily 5 plant, shrub 9 emollient, succulent
aloe __: 4 vera
__ aloe: 5 false 6 golden
__ aloes: 6 bitter
aloft: 4 atop, high, over 5 above, risen 6 aerial, flying, high, on high, upward 7 sky-high, skyward, soaring 8 at the top, in flight, in heaven, in the air, overhead, skywards, to heaven 9 on the wing 10 up in the air, up in the sky
bear ~: 4 lift 5 hoist 7 upheave
combining form: 4 hyps- 5 hypsi-, hypso-
gone ~: 6 arisen
of: 5 above
aloha: 5 hello 7 goodbye 8 Hawaiian
gift: 3 lei
in French: 5 adieu
in Hebrew: 6 shalom
in Italian: 4 ciao
in Latin: 3 ave 4 vale
in Spanish: 5 adios
aloha __: 5 shirt
Aloha: 4 city, town
locale: 6 Oregon

Aloha __: 4 Bowl
Aloha Oe instrument: 3 uke
Aloha State: 6 Hawaii
Alomar, Roberto sport: 8 baseball
alone: 4 sole, solo, stag 5 apart, aside, per se, solus, unled, unwed 6 remote, single, singly, solely, unique 7 forlorn, unaided 8 by itself, dateless, desolate, detached, eremitic, forsaken, hermitic, isolated, marooned, peerless, secluded, separate, set apart, singular, solitary, unhelped 9 abandoned, by oneself, matchless, on one's own, privately, separated, unequaled, unmatched, unrivaled 10 friendless, individual, personally, separately, solitarily, unassisted, unattached, unattended, unequalled, unescorted, unexcelled, unrivalled
  combining form: 3 mon- 4 mono-, soli-
  in Latin: 5 solus
  leave ~: 5 let be 6 lay off, resist 7 neglect
  left ~: 9 abandoned
  living ~: 5 unwed 8 isolated, solitary 9 by oneself, on one's own, separated, unmarried 10 spouseless, unattached
  on stage: 4 sola 5 solus
  prefix: 7 mono- mon-
  that ~: 5 per se 6 itself
__ alone: 3 let 4 go it 5 leave
__-alone: 5 stand
__ Alone: 3 All, One 4 Home
Alone (1987 song) artist: Heart
Alone Again (Naturally) (1972 song) artist: Gilbert O'Sullivan
__ Alone Am I: 3 All
Alone at Last (1960 song) artist: Jackie Wilson
Alone author: Edgar Allan Poe
__ a Lonely Number: 5 One Is
aloneness: 7 privacy 8 solitude 9 seclusion
Aloneness author: Gwendolyn Brooks
along: 3 too, via, yet 4 also 5 forth 6 as well, beside, onward 7 besides, forward, onwards 8 likewise 10 lengthways, lengthwise
  ender: 4 side 5 shore
  starter: 3 tag
along __ the ride: 3 for
__ along: 3 all, get, run, tag 4 come, inch, pass, play 6 follow, string
__-along: 4 sing, take
Along __ a spider...: 4 came
Along Came Jones (1945 film): 5 oater
  cast: Gary Cooper, William Demarest, Loretta Young
  director: Stuart Heisler
Along Came Jones (1959 song) artist: Coasters
Along Comes Mary (1966 song) artist: Association
along for the __: 4 ride
along in __: 5 years
__ Along Little Dogie: 3 Git
__ a long shot: 5 not by
alongside: 4 near, next, with 6 next to 7 close by, equal to 8 adjacent, parallel 10 parallel to
  lie ~: 5 skirt
  place ~: 6 appose
  prefix: 4 para-
__ along the line: 3 all
__ Along the Mohawk: 5 Drums
__ Along the Watchtower: 3 All
__ a Long Way to Tipperary: 3 It's
__ along with: 3 tag
__ Along With Mitch: 4 Sing
Alonso, Alicia: 6 dancer 8 danseuse 9 ballerina
  specialty: 5 dance 6 ballet
Alonso, Maria Conchita: 7 actress
  film: Colors (1988)
    Moscow on the Hudson (1984)
    The Running Man (1987)
Alonzo: 3 cat 8 Mourning
__ Alonzo Stagg: 4 Amos
aloof: 3 icy, shy 4 cold, cool 5 stiff, stoic 6 chilly, formal, frigid, modest, offish, remote, snooty 7 bashful, distant, glacial, haughty, ice-cold, neutral, offhand, removed, stoical, stuck up 8 contrary, detached, reserved, reticent, retiring, snobbish, solitary, taciturn, unbiased 9 apathetic, diffident, impassive, incurious, reclusive, unbending, unstirred, withdrawn 10 above it all, antisocial, insociable, nonchalant, phlegmatic, unaffected, unagitated, unamicable, unfriendly, unsociable
  stand ~ from: 4 shun
aloofness: 5 chill 6 apathy 7 reserve 9 arrogance 10 detachment, neutrality
  with ~: 5 icily
alop: 4 awry 5 askew 6 droopy, tilted, uneven 7 crooked 10 unbalanced
__ à l'orange: 4 duck
__ alors!: 3 Zut
__ a lot: 3 not
Alou: 5 Jesús, Matty 6 Felipe, Moises
  sport: 8 baseball
aloud: 6 orally, spoken, voiced 7 audible, audibly, noisily, vocally 8 hearable, verbally, viva voce
  wonder ~: 7 request
Alouette word: 4 tête
__ a Lovely Day Today: 3 It's
alow: 5 under 6 inside
__ a low profile: 4 keep
Aloysius: 5 saint
Alp: 3 mtn. 4 peak, Zupo 5 Eiger 6 Arslan, Castor, Ecrins 7 Bernina, Pilatus 8 Jungfrau, mountain 9 Mont Blanc, Monte Rosa, Taschhorn, Weisshorn 10 Matterhorn, Piz Bernina
  ender: 3 ine
alpaca: 4 wool 6 animal, fabric, mammal 8 ruminant
  habitat: 4 Peru 5 Andes
  herder, once: 5 Incan
  relative: 5 camel, llama 6 vicuna 7 guanaco 8 Bactrian 9 dromedary
alpe: 4 mont
alpenhorn: 4 wind 10 instrument
alpenstock: 5 staff
Alpert and the Tijuana Brass, Herb
  song: Casino Royale (1967)
    The Lonely Bull (1962)
    Mame (1966)
    Spanish Flea (1966)
    A Taste of Honey (1965)
    Tijuana Taxi (1966)
Alpert, Herb: 9 trumpeter
  instrument: 4 horn
  song: Diamonds (1987)
    Rise (1979)
    This Guy's in Love With You (1968)
__-Alpes: 6 Basses, Hautes
alpha: 5 Greek 6 letter
  ender: 7 numeric
  follower: 4 beta
  opposite: 5 omega
alpha __: 3 ray 4 iron, male, test 5 brass, decay, helix 6 rhythm 7 blocker
Alpha __: 4 Bits 6 Crucis
Alpha __ Majoris: 5 Ursae
Alpha __ Minoris: 5 Ursae
alpha and __: 5 omega
alphabet: 4 ABCs, soup 7 letters
  beginning: 3 ABC 4 ABCD 5 ABCDE
  British ~ ender: 3 zed
  ender: 3 zee
Koran: 5 Kufic
Korean: 6 Hangul
old Irish ~: 4 ogam 5 ogham
phonetic: 3 IPA
quartet: 4 ABCD, BCDE, CDEF, DEFG, EFGH, FGHI, GHIJ, HIJK, IJKL, JKLM, KLMN, LMNO, MNOP, NOPQ, OPQR, PQRS, QRST, RSTU, STUV, TUVW, UVWX, VWXY, WXYZ
quintet: 5 ABCDE, BCDEF, CDEFG, DEFGH, EFGHI, FGHIJ, GHIJK, HIJKL, IJKLM, JKLMN, KLMNO, LMNOP, MNOPQ, NOPQR, OPQRS, PQRST, QRSTU, RSTUV, STUVW, TUVWX, UVWXY, VWXYZ 6 vowels
soup letter: 6 noodle
trio: 3 ABC, BCD, CDE, DEF, EFG, FGH, GHI, HIJ, IJK, JKL, KLM, LMN, MNO, NOP, OPQ, PQR, RST, STU, TUV, UVW, VWX, WXY, XYZ
unit: 6 letter
written right-to-left: 6 Arabic, Hebrew
alphabet (phonetic):
  A - Alpha
  B - Bravo
  C - Charlie
  D - Delta
  E - Echo
  F - Foxtrot
  G - Golf
  H - Hotel
  I - India
  J - Juliet
  K - Kilo
  L - Lima
  M - Mike
  N - November
  O - Oscar
  P - Papa
  Q - Quebec
  R - Romeo
  S - Sierra
  T - Tango
  U - Uniform
  V - Victor
  W - Whiskey
  X - X-ray
  Y - Yankee
  Z - Zulu
alphabet __: 4 code, soup
__ alphabet: 5 Latin, Morse, Roman 6 manual
alphabetical: 4 A to Z 7 indexed, ordered
  guide: 5 index
alphabetical __: 5 order
Alphabetical Order author: Michael Frayn
alphabetize: 4 file, sort 5 index, order 6 assort 8 classify, tabulate 10 pigeonhole
alphabetizers
  word ~ ignore: 3 the
alphabets: 5 pasta
Alphabet Song start: 3 ABC 4 ABCD 5 ABCDE
Alphabet St. (1988 song) artist: Prince
Alphabet, The artist: 4 Erté
Alpha Bits: 6 cereal
  competitor: 3 Kix 4 Life, Trix 5 Kashi, Quisp, Total 6 Kaboom, Muesli, Oreo O's, Pablum, Smacks 7 All-Bran, Crispix, Harmony, Hunny B's, Mueslix, Oat Bran, Pokemon 8 Boo Berry, Cheerios, Corn Chex, Corn Pops, Fiber One, Rice Chex, Special K, Uncle Sam, Wheaties 9 Apple Zaps, Grape Nuts, Honey Comb, Just Right, Wheat Chex 10 Apple Jacks, Bran Flakes, Cap'n Crunch, Cocoa Puffs, Froot Loops, Mini-Wheats, Nutri-Grain, Puffed Rice, Quaker Oats, Smart Start 11 Cocoa Blasts, Cookie Crisp, Golden Crisp, Lucky Charms, Puffed Wheat, Sweet Crunch, Waffle Crisp
Alpha Centauri: 4 star
Alphard: 4 star
Alpharetta: 4 city, town
  locale: 7 Georgia
Alphecca: 4 star
Alphonse: 6 Daudet
  friend: 6 Gaston
alpine: 4 high, tall 5 Swiss 8 elevated, towering
alpine __: 3 fir 6 garden, tundra 7 bistort
Alpine
  abode: 6 chalet
  archer: 4 Tell
  capital: 4 Bern 5 Berne 6 Vienna
  comeback: 4 echo
  enthusiast: 5 skier
  feature: 5 arete
  gear: 3 ski 4 skee
  locale: 5 Tirol, Tyrol 6 Europe, France 7 Austria
  music: 5 yodel, yodle
  outfit: 6 dirndl
  resort: 6 Gstaad
  river: 3 Aar 4 Aare 5 Isère
  snowfield: 4 firn
  surface: 4 snow
  tool: 5 ice ax, piton
  wind: 4 bise, bora, fohn 5 foehn
Alpine __: 4 ibex 6 azalea, skiing 7 currant
Alpo: 7 dog food
  alternative: 4 Iams 5 Nutro, Rival 6 Purina 8 Eukanuba 10 Ken-L Ration
Alps: 3 mts. 5 range 8 Pennines
  locale: 6 Europe, France 7 Austria 9 Australia
  mountain: 4 Zupo 5 Eiger 6 Arslan, Castor, Ecrins 7 Bernina, Pilatus 8 Jungfrau 9 Mont Blanc, Monte Rosa, Taschhorn, Weisshorn 10 Matterhorn, Piz Bernina
  river: 5 Rhone
__ Alps: 5 Savoy, Swiss 6 Carnic, French, Julian 7 Bernese, Bernina, Cottian, Dinaric, Italian, Pennine 8 Maritime
already: 4 once 5 by now 6 by then 8 formerly 9 at present, before now 10 beforehand, by that time, heretofore, previously
  enough ~: 4 OK OK
Already?: 6 so soon
Alrescha: 4 star
Alright (1990 song) artist: Janet Jackson
Alsatian: 3 dog 5 canid, pooch 6 canine
Alshain: 4 star
__ al-Sheikh: 5 Sharm
alsike: 6 clover
also: 3 and, too, yet 4 more, plus 5 again, along, ditto 6 as well, either, to boot 7 besides, further 8 likewise, moreover 9 along with, including, similarly, what's more 10 conjointly, in addition
  called: 5 alias
  not: 3 nor
also-__: 3 ran
Alsop: 6 Joseph 7 Stewart
also-ran: 5 loser 7 failure 9 nonwinner
__ Also Rises, The: 3 Sun
__ also serve...: 4 They
Also Sprach Zarathustra (1973 song) artist: Deodato
Also Sprach Zarathustra composer: 7 Strauss
Alston: 6 Dodger, Walter 7 manager
alt: 4 high
alt.: 3 hgt. 4 elev. 6 height
Alt: 3 key 5 Carol

emulate ~: **4** pose **5** model
Alta: **4** city, town **6** resort **9** ski resort
locale: **4** Utah **7** Rockies
Alta.: **4** prov.
neighbor: **3** NWT **4** Mont., Sask.
Altadena: **4** city, town
locale: **10** California
Altai: **5** range
locale: **4** Asia
___-Altaic: **4** Ural
Altair: **4** star
constellation: **6** Aquila
Altamira: **4** cave, city, town
locale: **6** Mexico **10** Tamaulipas
Altamirano: **4** city, town
locale: **6** Mexico **8** Guerrero
Altamont: **4** city, town
locale: **6** Oregon
Altamonte Springs: **4** city, town
locale: **7** Florida
altar: **6** shrine **9** sanctuary
act: **3** vow
activity: **4** rite **7** wedding
area: **4** bema
cloth: **6** dossal, dossel
compartment: **7** loculus
constellation: **3** Ara
exchange: **3** I do
item: **4** icon, ikon **5** eikon **6** ancona **7** reredos
leave at the ~: **4** jilt
locale: **6** church
neighbor: **4** apse
path to the ~: **5** aisle
plate: **5** paten
robe: **3** alb
stone: **5** mensa
altar ___: **3** boy **4** call, card, girl, rail, slab, wine **5** board, bread, cloth, stand, stone
___ altar: **4** high **6** double
Al Tarf: **4** star
Alt, Carol spouse: Ron Greschner
___-ALT-DEL: **4** CTRL
Altdorf canton: **3** Uri
___ Alte: **3** Der
___-Altenburg: **4** Saxe
alte, opposite of: **4** neue
Altepexi: **4** city, town
locale: **6** Mexico, Puebla
alter: **3** fit **4** edit, hoke, spay, turn, vary **5** act on, adapt, amend, color, let in, lobby, morph, resew, shift **6** adjust, affect, change, divert, doctor, juggle, modify, mutate, neuter, recast, reform, remold, revamp, revise, tailor, take up, tamper **7** act upon, convert, correct, distort, inflect, permute, qualify, remodel, replace, reshape, restyle **8** disguise, fine-tune, impact on, innovate, make over, override, overrule, redirect, renovate **9** diversify, influence, rearrange, refashion, sterilize, transform, translate, transmute, transpose **10** adulterate, blue-pencil, fiddle with, reposition
again: **5** refit, rehem
ego: **3** pal **4** ally, chum, mate **5** buddy, crony **6** backer, cohort, friend **7** comrade, consort, partner **8** intimate, playmate, sidekick, soulmate **9** associate, companion, confidant **10** bosom buddy, compatriot
alter ___: **3** ego **4** idem
alteration: **4** flux **5** shift **6** change, switch **7** revisal, veering **8** mutation, revision, variance **9** about-face, amendment, deviation, diversion, refitting, reshaping, variation **10** adaptation, adjustment, conversion, correction, difference, divergence, emendation, innovation, remodeling, switchover
___ alteration: **7** author's
altercate: **3** row **4** spat, tiff **5** brawl, fight **6** bicker **7** quarrel, quibble **9** have words
altercation: **3** row **4** feud, flap, fuss, spat, tiff **5** brawl, clash, fight, melee, run-in, scene, set-to **6** barney, blowup, fracas, hassle, rumble, rumpus, strife **7** contest, dispute, quarrel, wrangle **8** argument, skirmish, squabble
altered: **3** new **5** let in **7** unalike **9** different
altered ___: **5** chord, state
Altered ___: **6** States
Altered States (1980 film)
cast: Bob Balaban, Blair Brown, William Hurt
director: Ken Russell
Altered States author: Paddy Chayefsky
alter ego, fictional: **4** Hyde, Kent
Alterman, Nathan: **4** poet **6** Hebrew
alternate: **3** sub, var. **4** turn, vary **5** other, proxy **6** backup, change, double, fill-in, rotate, seesaw **7** librate, stagger, stand-in, variant **8** periodic **9** change off, come and go, different, fill in for, fluctuate, oscillate, recurrent, secondary, surrogate, take turns, temporary, vacillate **10** equivalent, every other, reciprocal, substitute, understudy
route: **6** bypass, detour
alternate ___: **4** host **5** angle **7** plumage
alternately: **6** rather **7** by turns, instead
alternating ___: **5** group, light **6** series **7** current, voltage
alternating current pioneer: **5** Tesla
alternative: **3** way **4** pick **5** other, plan B **6** acting, choice, option, second **7** variant **8** loophole, recourse **9** variation
combining form: **6** allelo-
word: **3** syn. **7** synonym
alternative ___: **6** energy, school **7** society
alternatively: **4** else **6** rather **7** instead **9** otherwise
alternatives: **6** others
Althea: **6** Gibson
Althing locale: **4** Icel. **7** Iceland
although: **2** if **3** yet **5** while **6** albeit, even if, though, whilst **7** despite **9** in spite of **10** regardless
alti-: **4** high
Altima: **3** car **4** auto **6** Nissan **10** automobile
Altiplano: **7** plateau
beast: **5** llama
locale: **4** Peru **5** Andes **7** Bolivia **9** Argentina
altitude: **2** ht. **3** hgt. **4** elev. **5** level **6** height **8** eminence **9** elevation, loftiness
combining form: **4** hyps- **5** hypsi-, hypso-
gain ~: **4** rise, soar **5** climb **6** ascend
sickness: **4** puna
altitudinous: **4** high, tall **5** lofty **7** soaring **8** elevated, towering, uplifted
Altman: **6** Robert, Sidney
Altman, Robert: **8** director
film: 3 Women (1977)
Brewster McCloud (1970)
Cookie's Fortune (1999)
Countdown (1968)
Gosford Park (2001)
Images (1972)
MASH (1970)
McCabe & Mrs. Miller (1971)
Nashville (1975)
A Perfect Couple (1979)
The Player (1992)
Popeye (1980)
Secret Honor (1984)
Short Cuts (1993)
Streamers (1983)
Thieves Like Us (1974)
Vincent & Theo (1990)
Altman, Sidney: **7** chemist **8** Nobelist
alto: **5** range, voice **6** singer **7** caroler **8** vocalist **9** chorister
instrument: **5** viola
alto ___: **3** sax **4** clef, horn **5** flute
Altoaquirre, Manuel: **4** poet **7** Spanish
___ Alto, CA: **4** Palo
altocumulus: **5** cloud
altogether: **5** fully, in sum, quite, sheer, stark **6** bodily, in toto, purely, wholly **7** en masse, totally, utterly **8** as a whole, entirely **9** generally, perfectly **10** absolutely, by and large, completely, conjointly, on the whole, thoroughly
in the ~: **4** bare, nude **5** naked
altohorn: **4** wind **10** instrument
Altoids alternative: **5** Certs **6** Binaca, Mentos, Tic Tac **7** Clorets, Dentyne
Alto Lucero: **4** city, town
locale: **6** Mexico **8** Veracruz
Alton: **4** city, town
locale: **8** Illinois
Altoona: **4** city, town
locale: **4** Penn.
___ Altos, CA: **3** Los
altostratus: **5** cloud
altruism: **3** aid **7** charity **8** goodwill, kindness **9** tolerance **10** knighthood
altruist: **5** donor **7** grantor **10** benefactor
altruistic: **3** big **4** good, kind **5** human **6** decent, gentle, humane, kindly, tender **7** clement, largess, lenient, liberal, sparing **8** all heart, generous, gracious, largesse, merciful, princely **9** brotherly, good scout, unselfish, unsparing **10** benevolent, bighearted, charitable, munificent, openhanded, unstinting
Altus: **4** city, town
locale: **8** Oklahoma
___-a-luck: **5** chuck
aludel: **6** bottle, vessel
Aludra: **4** star
___-a-lug: **4** chug
Aluko, Timothy: **6** writer **8** Nigerian
___-A-Lula: **5** Be-Bop
alum: **4** grad **6** emetic, reuner **7** styptic **8** graduate **10** astringent
___ alum: **5** roche **6** chrome, potash **7** ammonia
aluminum: **5** metal **7** element
alloy: **6** alnico **9** duralumin, magnalium
boat: **5** canoe
company: **5** Alcoa **8** Reynolds
foil alternative: **5** Saran
sheet: **4** foil
source: **3** ore **7** bauxite
yarn: **5** lurex
aluminum ___: **4** soap **5** brass, oxide, plant **6** borate, bronze **7** acetate, carbide, hydrate, nitrate, sulfate
alumna: **4** male **6** female, reuner **8** graduate
bio word: **3** née
alumni do, what: **5** reune
alumnus: **4** grad, male **6** reuner **8** graduate
next year's ~: **2** sr. **3** snr. **6** senior
Alva: **5** Luigi **6** Myrdal
Alvar: **5** Aalto
Alvarado: **4** city, town **5** Trini
locale: **6** Mexico **8** Veracruz
Alvarado, Trini: **7** actress
film: The Babe (1992)
Little Women (1994)
Rich Kids (1979)
Sweet Lorraine (1987)
Alvarez, Luis: **8** Nobelist **9** physicist
alveolus: **6** air sac
Alverstone: **4** peak **5** mount **8** mountain
locale: **5** Yukon **6** Canada
Alvin: **3** Lee **4** city, town, York **5** Ailey **7** Toffler **8** chipmunk
brother of ~: **5** Simon **8** Theodore
locale: **5** Texas
Alvino: **3** Rey
Alvin's Harmonica (1959 song) artist: David Seville and the Chipmunks
Alvy: **5** Moore
ALW: **8** division
team: **6** Angels **7** Rangers **8** Mariners **9** Athletics
alway: **2** ay **3** aye, e'er
opposite: **4** ne'er
always: **3** e'er **4** ever **7** forever **8** evermore, for keeps **9** eternally **10** constantly, enduringly, inevitably, invariably, unendingly
in music: **6** sempre
not ~: **7** at times
there: **6** trusty **9** unfailing
Always: **4** song **5** waltz
composer: Irving Berlin
Always (1985 film)
cast: Joanna Frank, Henry Jaglom, Patrice Townsend
director: Henry Jaglom
Always (1989 film)
cast: Richard Dreyfuss, John Goodman, Holly Hunter
director: Steven Spielberg
Always ___ to You in My Fashion: **4** True
Always a Reckoning author: **6** Carter
___ Always a Woman: **4** She's **6** There's
Always Be My Baby (1996 song) artist: Mariah Carey
___ Always Fair Weather: **3** It's
___ always liked you best!: **3** Mom
___ Always Love You: **3** I'll **5** I Will
Always on My Mind (song) artist: Pet Shop Boys, Willie Nelson
___ Always Rings Twice, The: **7** Postman
___ always say...: **3** As I
___ Always Something: **3** It's
Always (song) artist: Atlantic Starr, Bon Jovi
always the same (Lat.): **10** semper idem
Always True to You in My Fashion
composer: **6** Porter
Alworth, Lance sport: **8** football
Aly: **4** Khan
dad: **3** Aga
Alya: **4** star
___ Al Yankovic: **5** Weird
Alysheba: **5** horse
Alyssa: **6** Milano
alyssum
sweet ~: **5** plant **6** flower
Alzado: **4** Lyle
Alzira composer: **5** Verdi
a.m.: **4** morn **7** morning **8** forenoon
broadcaster: **3** sta., stn. **7** station
early ~: **3** one, two **4** four **5** three **7** wee hour
part: **4** ante **8** meridiam
when ~ meets p.m.: **4** noon **6** midday
___-am: **3** pro
Am: **3** cat **4** elem. **7** element **9** americium
95 for ~: **4** at. no.
Am ___: **5** I Blue
Am ___ believe...: **3** I to
Am ___ brother's keeper?: **3** I my
Am ___ to see you!: **5** I glad
Am ___ understand...: **3** I to
___ Am: **5** Here I, What I
AM: **4** band **5** radio
part: **9** amplitude **10** modulation
AMA: **3** org.
member: **2** dr., GP, MD **3** doc **6** doctor
part: **3** Med. **4** Amer., Assn. **5** Assoc. **7** Medical **8** American

Ama Dablam: 4 peak 5 mount 8 mountain
locale: 4 Asia 5 Nepal 9 Himalayas
amadavat: 4 bird
Amadeus: 4 film, play
author: Peter Shaffer
cast: F. Murray Abraham, Elizabeth Berridge, Tom Hulce
choreographer: Twyla Tharp
director: Milos Forman
___ Amadeus Mozart: 8 Wolfgang
Amadi, Elechi: 6 writer 8 Nigerian
amadinda: 9 xylophone 10 instrument, percussion
origin: 5 Ghana
Amadis of ___: 4 Gaul
___ a Mad Mad Mad Mad World: 3 It's
Amado, Jorge: 6 writer 9 Brazilian
work: Doña Flor and Her Two Husbands
The Golden Harvest
Sea of Death
Showdown
The War of the Saints
Amadora: 4 city, town
locale: 8 Portugal
amadou: 6 tinder
Amagasaki: 4 port
locale: 5 Japan
amah: 9 governess, nursemaid
Amahl and the Night Visitors: 5 opera
composer: 7 Menotti
amain: 8 headlong 10 at full tilt, vigorously
___ a Male War Bride: 4 I Was
amalgam: 3 mix 5 alloy, blend, union 6 hybrid 7 filling, mixture 8 compound 9 coalition, composite, immixture, synthesis
component: 6 silver 7 mercury
amalgamate: 3 mix 4 fuse, join, meld, pool 5 admix, alloy, blend, merge, unify, unite 6 commix, embody, harden, hook up, imbody, league, team up 7 combine 8 coalesce 9 affiliate, associate, commingle, integrate 10 accumulate, adulterate, centralize, synthesize
amalgamated: 4 mixt 5 mixed 6 united
amalgamation: 3 mix 5 union 6 merger 8 compound
Amalrik, Andrei: 6 writer 7 Russian
Amalthea: 4 moon 5 nymph, sibyl
planet: 7 Jupiter
...a man ___ mouse?: 3 or a
Amana: 4 city, town 9 appliance
alternative: 5 Norge 6 Bendix, Maytag, Tappan 7 Admiral, Jenn-Air, Kenmore 8 Hotpoint 9 Magic Chef, Whirlpool 10 Frigidaire, Kelvinator, KitchenAid
locale: 4 Iowa
Amand: 5 saint
Amanda: 4 Pays, Peet 5 Blake, Cross 6 Bearse 7 Donohoe, Plummer
son: 5 Spock
Amanda (1986 song) artist: Boston
___ amandine: 4 sole
___ à manger: 5 salle
amanita: 6 fungus
unlike: 6 edible
___ a Man Loves a Woman: 4 When
___ a man's heart..., The: 5 way to
Amantium ___: 4 Irae
amanuensis: 5 clerk 6 copier, scribe 7 copyist 9 scrivener, secretary
...___ a man with...: 4 I met
amaranth: 3 azo, dye, red 5 plant 6 flower, purply 8 purplish
relative: 4 rose, ruby, rust, wine 5 brick, coral, grape, poppy, rusty, sandy 6 cerise, cherry, claret, garnet, maroon 7 carmine, crimson, fuchsia, magenta, pimento, scarlet, sultana, vermeil 8 cardinal, dubonnet, geranium, rubicund 9 carnation, cranberry, vermilion 10 strawberry
amaranthine: 6 purple 7 endless 8 unending
___ a March hare: 5 mad as
___ a march on: 5 steal
Amarcord (1974 film) director: Federico Fellini
amaretto flavor: 6 almond
Amarillo: 4 city, town
locale: 5 Texas
___ Amarna: 3 Tel 5 Tel el
Amarone: 3 red 4 wine
origin: 5 Italy
amaryllis: 5 agave, plant 6 flower
family plant: 4 aloe
___, amas, amat: 3 amo
___, amas, I love a lass: 3 amo
Amasis: 4 font 8 typeface
amass: 4 cull, heap, hold, keep, lump, pile, save 5 cache, glean, hoard, lay by, lay up, put by, run up, stack, stock, store 6 accrue, corral, garner, gather, heap up, load up, pile up, rake in, retain, roll up, save up 7 acquire, build up, collect, compile, deposit, harvest, lay away, put away, round up, scare up, store up 8 assemble, gather up, hang onto, hold onto, maintain, put aside, salt away, scrape up, set aside, stow away 9 aggregate, stockpile 10 accumulate
amasser: 7 pack rat
amassment: 4 heap 5 array, hoard 6 pileup 7 accrual 10 collection, cumulation
amateur: 3 lay 4 tiro, tyro 5 unfit 6 layman, novice, simple 7 dabbler 8 beginner, putterer 9 greenhorn, layperson, untrained 10 apprentice, dilettante, uninitiate
lose ~ status: 5 go pro
mag: 4 zine
opposite: 3 pro
radio operator: 3 ham
sports org.: 3 AAU 4 NCAA
amateur ___: 4 hour 5 night 6 status
amateurish: 5 crude, inept, rough 6 coarse 7 awkward 8 fumbling, homemade, inexpert 9 inelegant, makeshift, primitive, unrefined 10 dilettante, unpolished, unskillful
Amateurs, The author: David Halberstam
Amati: 6 Nicolò, violin
kin: 5 Strad
amatol: 9 explosive
ingredient: 3 TNT
___ Amatoria: 3 Ars
amatory: 4 fond 6 ardent, doting, erotic, loving, tender 7 fervent 8 romantic 10 passionate
writing: 3 ode
amaze: 3 awe, wow 4 jolt, stun 5 floor, shock 6 baffle, boggle, dazzle 7 astound, impress, perplex, petrify, stagger, startle, stupefy 8 astonish, bewilder, blow away, bowl over, confound, surprise 9 dumbfound, overwhelm
amazed: 4 agog 5 agape, in awe 6 aghast, jolted 9 awestruck 10 dumbstruck, speechless, spellbound
amazement: 3 awe 6 marvel, wonder 8 surprise 9 confusion 10 admiration, perplexity, wonderment
show ~: 4 gape
word of ~: 3 gee
amazing: 3 def, ooh, rad, wow 4 aces, A-one, boss, braw, cool, dece, fine, gear, keen, neat, nice, phat, tuff 5 dandy, ducky, grand, great, marvy, neato, nobby, prime, slick, super, swell 6 bang on, bang-up, bonzer, bosker, choice, divine, dreamy, far-out, gnarly, groovy, lovely, peachy, slap-up, spot on, superb, terrif, tiptop, unreal, whizzo, wicked 7 awesome, capital, corking, perfect, ripping, skookum, stellar, sublime, unusual 8 dazzling, especial, eximious, fabulous, five-star, four-star, frabjous, glorious, heavenly, jim-dandy, slam-bang, smashing, splendid, standout, sterling, stickout, stunning, superior, terrific, top-level, topnotch, very good, wondrous 9 bodacious, Endsville, excellent, exemplary, exquisite, first-rate, high-grade, hunky-dory, marvelous, sol-licker, top-flight, unrivaled, wonderful 10 first-class, hotsy-totsy, incredible, jack-a-dandy, miraculous, out of sight, peachy-keen, phenomenal, prodigious, remarkable, stupendous, super-duper, tremendous, unexpected, unrivalled
Amazing ___, The: 5 Randi 7 Kreskin
Amazing!: 3 ooh, wow
Amazing Doctor Clitterhouse, The (1938 film)
cast: Edward G. Robinson, Claire Trevor
director: Anatole Litvak
Amazing Grace: 4 hymn
ending: 4 I see
Amazon: 4 Lyce, Thoe 5 Aella, Agave, giant, Harpe, Marpe, river, woman 6 Clonie, female, Glauce, Myrina, Ocyale, Otrere, Phoebe, Xanthe 7 Alcibie, Alcippe, Antiope, Asteria, Bremusa, Celaeno, Clymene, Derinoe, Eriboea, Euryale, Evandre, Menippe, Prothoe 8 Antandre, Antioche, Deianira, Dioxippe, Iphinome, Laomache, Molpadia, Polemusa, Polydora, Tecmessa 9 Antianira, Antibrote, Harmothoe, Hippolyta, Hippolyte, Hippothoe, Philippis 10 bookseller, Thermodosa
father: 4 Ares
feeder: 3 Ica 5 Negro, Purus, Xingu 6 Japura
how the ~ flows: 4 east
language: 4 Tupi
monkey: 4 titi
mouth: 4 Pará
origin: 4 Peru
people: 4 Tupi
port: 4 Pará 5 Belém
River locale: 4 Peru 6 Brazil
river to the ~: 4 Juru, Napo 5 Japur, Negro, Purús, Xingú 6 Javari, Javary 7 Madeira, Taoajós 8 Putumayo
rodent: 6 agouti
Amazon ___: 3 ant 5 stone 6 parrot
Amazon.com offering: 4 book 5 novel
amazonite: 3 gem 7 mineral
ambassador: 5 agent, envoy 6 consul, deputy, legate 8 delegate, diplomat, emissary, minister 9 messenger 10 peacemaker
address: 3 exc. 10 excellency
asset: 4 tact
place: 3 emb. 7 embassy 9 consulate
Ambassador: 3 AMC, car 4 auto, Nash 7 Rambler 10 automobile
ambassador at ___: 5 large
ambassadors: 8 legation 10 delegation
ambassadorship often: 4 plum
Ambassadors, The author: Henry James
Ambassador, The (1984 film)
cast: Ellen Burstyn, Rock Hudson, Robert Mitchum
director: J. Lee Thompson
ambatch: 4 tree
Ambato: 4 city, town
locale: 7 Ecuador
amber: 5 brown, color, resin 6 fossil, yellow 7 old gold 9 yellowish
combining form: 6 succin- 7 succino-
ender: 4 jack
nectar: 4 beer, brew, suds 5 lager 7 brewski
relative: 3 bay, dun, tan 4 bole, ecru, fawn, foxy, nude, seal 5 beige, camel, cocoa, hazel, khaki, mocha, sepia, tawny, umber 6 auburn, bister, bistre, bronze, coffee, copper, ginger, russet, sienna, sorrel, suntan, walnut 7 biscuit, caramel, dogwood 8 chestnut, cinnamon, mahogany 9 butternut, chocolate
Amber ___: 7 Islands
___ Amber: 7 Forever
ambergris source: 5 whale
amberjack: 4 fish
ambience: 3 air 4 aura, feel, mood, tone 6 medium, milieu 7 setting 10 atmosphere, local color
ambient: 9 embracing, enclosing 10 encircling, enveloping
ambient ___: 5 noise
ambiguity: 5 doubt 9 obscurity, vagueness 10 equivocacy
ambiguous: 4 iffy, open 5 mirky, murky, vague 6 chancy, unsure 7 dubious, evasive 8 doubtful, nebulous, oracular, puzzling, tortuous 9 deceptive, enigmatic, equivocal, imprecise, tenebrous, uncertain, unsettled 10 borderline, indefinite, indistinct, inexplicit, misleading, unexplicit, unresolved, unspecific, up for grabs, up in the air
thing: 6 enigma
ambit: 5 orbit, range, reach, scope, sweep 6 bounds, extent, radius, sphere 7 circuit, compass 8 boundary 9 dimension, perimeter
ambition: 3 aim 4 goal, hope, plan, push, will, wish 5 dream, drive, quest, vigor 6 desire, intent, target 7 avidity, craving, longing, passion, purpose 8 initiate, yearning 9 eagerness, objective 10 aspiration, enterprise, enthusiasm, get up and go, initiative, pretension
devoid of ~: 4 lazy
excessive ~: 5 greed
have ~: 6 aspire
lack of ~: 5 sloth
one without ~: 5 idler
ambitious: 4 avid, bold, hard 5 eager, grand, lofty, pushy 6 ardent, hungry, intent 7 arduous, wishful, zealous 8 aspiring, desirous 9 demanding, designing, difficult, elaborate, energetic, grandiose, strenuous, visionary 10 aggressive, determined, formidable, impressive, purposeful
ambivalence: 7 dubiety 9 dubiosity
ambivalent: 5 timid 6 fickle 8 hesitant, wavering 9 debatable, equivocal, faltering, uncertain, undecided 10 borderline, irresolute, of two minds, unexplicit, unresolved, weak-willed, wishy-washy
amble: 3 lag 4 gait, idle, laze, loaf, poke, roam, rove, walk 5 dally, drift, mosey, stall, tarry 6 canter, dawdle, linger, loiter, ramble, sashay, stroll, wander 7 meander, saunter 8 lollygag, straggle 9 promenade 10 dillydally
ambler: 10 pedestrian
Ambler, Eric: 6 author, writer 7 British
work: The Care of Time
Epitaph for a Spy
Journey Into Fear

The Mask of Dimitrios
A Passage of Arms
Ambling Alp, The: Primo Carnera
amblygonite: 3 ore
ambo: 6 pulpit 7 lectern
Ambon: 4 city, town
locale: 9 Indonesia
___ Amboy, NJ: 5 Perth
Ambrose: 5 saint 6 Bierce 7 Stephen
ambrosia: 7 dessert 8 delicacy
Ambrosia
song: Biggest Part of Me (1980)
How Much I Feel (1978)
ambrosial: 5 balmy, godly, sweet, tasty 6 divine, savory, toothy 7 elysian, scented 8 aromatic, empyreal, empyrean, ethereal, fragrant, heavenly, luscious, perfumed, supernal, tasteful 9 celestial, delicious, flavorful, nectarous, palatable, toothsome 10 delectable, delightful
Ambrym: 7 volcano
locale: 4 Asia 7 Vanuatu
ambulance: 7 vehicle 9 transport
destination: 2 ER
driver: 3 EMS, EMT 5 medic
equipment: 6 litter
sound: 5 siren
ambulance ___: 6 chaser
ambulate: 4 foot, hoof, pace, roam, rove, step, trek, walk 5 range, tread 6 ramble, stroll, travel 7 saunter 8 gad about 9 gallivant, promenade
ambulatory: 5 astir 7 walking
ambulophobe fear: 7 walking
ambuscade: 4 trap
ambush: 3 mug 4 jump, trap 5 seize, sneak, stalk, trick 6 assail, attack, entrap, lay for, pounce, recess, refuge, waylay 7 assault 8 surprise 9 blindside, bushwhack, intercept
lie in ~: 4 lurk, wait 5 sculk, skulk
Ambushers, The (1968 film)
cast: Senta Berger, Dean Martin, Janice Rule
director: Henry Levin
AMC: 3 car 4 auto 7 channel 10 automobile
alternative: 3 HBO, IFC, SHO, TMC 4 Flix 5 Bravo, Starz 6 Encore 7 Cinemax 8 Showtime, Sundance
car: 5 Eagle, Pacer, Rebel 6 Hornet, Marlin, Spirit 7 Concord, Gremlin, Javelin, Matador, Rambler 10 Ambassador
offering: 4 film 5 movie
series radio station: 4 WENN
AMD rival: 5 Intel
___-a-Me: 5 Botch
ameba
see amoeba
Ameca: 4 city, town
locale: 6 Mexico 7 Jalisco
Amecameca: 4 city, town
locale: 6 Mexico
Ameche: 3 Don 4 Alan
Ameche, Don: 5 actor
film: Alexander's Ragtime Band (1938)
Cocoon (1985, AA)
Corrina, Corrina (1994)
Down Argentine Way (1940)
Heaven Can Wait (1943)
In Old Chicago (1938)
The Magnificent Dope (1942)
Midnight (1939)
Moon Over Miami (1941)
One in a Million (1936)
Sleep My Love (1948)
Something to Shout About (1943)
The Story of Alexander Graham Bell (1939)
The Three Musketeers (1939)
Trading Places (1983)
Wing and a Prayer (1944)
You Can't Have Everything (1937)
Amédée author: Eugène Ionesco
Amedeo: 8 Avogadro 10 Modigliani
see also Italian
Amelia: 7 Bloomer, Earhart, Peabody
emulate ~: 3 fly 6 aviate
Amelia author: Henry Fielding
ameliorate: 3 aid 4 ease, help, lift 5 amend, fix up, quiet 6 better, enrich, look up, pacify, polish, reform, remedy 7 correct, enhance, improve, lighten, mollify, relieve, shape up, sharpen, upgrade 8 mitigate, spruce up 9 alleviate 10 recuperate
amelioration: 6 relief
Amelita: 10 Galli-Curci
amen: 3 yea, yep, yes 5 truly 6 be it so, I agree, I'll say, indeed, it is so, so be it, so true, verily 7 right on 8 for a fact 10 absolutely, positively
amen ___: 6 corner
Amen (NBC sitcom)
cast: Clifton Davis (Reverend Reuben Gregory)
Jester Hairston (Rolly Forbes)
Sherman Hemsley (Deacon Ernest Frye)
Anna Maria Horsford (Thelma Frye)
Roz Ryan (Amelia Hetebrink)
amenability: 9 liability
amenable: 4 easy, game, open, tame 6 docile, liable, polite 7 dutiful, pliable, willing 8 gracious, resigned, yielding 9 agreeable, compliant, receptive, tractable 10 hospitable, open-minded, submissive
Amen Corner, The author: James Baldwin
amend: 3 fix 4 edit 5 alter 6 better, change, modify, reform, repair, revise, update 7 correct, enhance, improve, rectify, redress, touch up 8 rephrase 10 ameliorate
amendment: 5 rider 6 change, clause, reform 7 codicil, redress, revisal 8 revision 10 alteration, attachment, betterment, correction, suggestion, supplement
letters: 3 ERA
subject: 5 right
amends: 7 payment, redress 8 requital 9 atonement, expiation 10 recompense, reparation
make ~: 3 pay 5 atone, repay 6 redeem, reform, refund 7 appease, expiate, redress, requite 8 atone for 9 apologize, indemnify 10 compensate, recompense
Amenhotep god: 4 Aten, Aton
amenities: 8 protocol 9 etiquette, propriety
amenity: 5 charm, frill 6 luxury 7 comfort 8 courtesy, facility, kindness 9 geniality, gentility 10 affability, amiability, cordiality, politeness, refinement
Amen-Ra, wife of: 3 Mut
ament: 6 catkin
Amer.
Central ~ country: 3 Nic., Pan. 4 Guat.
counterpart: 4 Natl.
Hist. subj.: 3 WWI 4 WWII
news org.: 4 USIA
northern ~: 3 Esk.
propaganda source: 4 USIA
S. ~ country: 3 Arg., Col., Uru. 4 Ecua. 5 Venez.
Amerada ___: 4 Hess
amerce: 4 fine 5 mulct 6 punish 8 penalize
amercement: 4 fine 5 mulct
America: 4 song 5 The US 6 anthem
song: A Horse With No Name (1972)
I Need You (1972)
Lonely People (1975)
Sister Golden Hair (1975)
Tin Man (1974)
Ventura Highway (1972)
You Can Do Magic (1982)
word: 3 'tis 4 thee
America ___: 6 Online 7 Firster
___ America: 3 Air 4 Miss 5 Latin, Men of, North, South 6 Little, Middle 7 British, Central, Spanish
America (1981 song) artist: Neil Diamond
America, America (1963 film) director: Elia Kazan
___ America Cruises: 7 Holland
American: 3 car 4 auto, Yank 6 cheese 7 airline, Rambler 10 automobile
alternative: 3 DAL, UAL 5 Delta 6 United 7 Jet Blue 9 Southwest 11 America West, Continental
early ~: 8 colonial
flag color: 3 red 4 blue 5 white
former rival: 3 TWA 5 Pan-Am 7 Eastern
former ~ territory: 6 Dakota, Hawaii, Oregon
majority: 5 women
American ___: 3 elk, elm, ivy, Pie, rig 4 aloe, bond, plan, star 5 bison, Breed, chair, cloth, dream, eagle, Falls, Heart, holly, lotus, Movie, Music, Notes, organ, party, sable, Samoa, senna, Storm, twist, Woman 6 Beauty, blight, cheese, copper, cotton, Empire, Flyers, Gothic, Indian, ipecac, League, Legion, linden, marten 7 bittern, buffalo, cowslip, English, Express, kestrel, Madness, Spanish
American ___, An: 5 Dream 7 Tragedy
American ___ Award: 4 Book
American ___ Exchange: 5 Stock
American ___ Language: 4 Sign
___ American: 3 Pan 5 Asian, Early, Latin, South 6 native 7 Central, General, Spanish
___-American: 3 all 4 Afro, Arab, Euro 5 Anglo, Italo 6 Franco, Middle 7 African, Mexican
Americana author: Don DeLillo
American Appetites author: Joyce Carol Oates
Americana set: 3 enc. 4 ency. 5 encyc.
American Bandstand (ABC music)
fan: 4 teen
host: Dick Clark
American Beauty: 4 rose 5 plant 6 flower
American Beauty (1999 film)
cast: Annette Bening, Thora Birch, Kevin Spacey, Mena Suvari
director: Sam Mendes
American Bobtail: 3 cat 5 felid 6 feline
American Buffalo: 4 film, play
author: David Mamet
cast: Dennis Franz, Dustin Hoffman, Sean Nelson
American Century, The author: 5 Evans
___ American Cousin: 3 Our
American Crisis, The writer: 5 Paine
American Curl: 3 cat 5 felid 6 feline
American Dream, An (1980 song)
artist: Nitty Gritty Dirt Band
American Dream, An author: Norman Mailer
American Dream, The author: Edward Albee
American Dynasty, An subject: 5 Fords
American Express, use: 3 owe 6 charge
American Flyer rival: 6 Lionel
American Flyers (1985 film)
cast: Rae Dawn Chong, Kevin Costner, David Grant
director: John Badham
dog: 5 Eddie
American Fork: 4 city, town
locale: 4 Utah
___ American Games: 3 Pan
American Gigolo actor: 4 Gere
American Gothic: 8 painting
artist: Grant Wood
American Graffiti (1973 film)
cast: Richard Dreyfuss, Ron Howard, Paul LeMat, Cindy Williams
director: George Lucas
drive-in: 4 Mel's
American Hall of Fame site: 3 NYU
American Heart (1993 film)
cast: Jeff Bridges, Edward Furlong, Lucinda Jenney
director: Martin Bell
___-American Highway: 3 Pan
American History X (1998 film)
cast: Fairuza Balk, Beverly D'Angelo, Edward Furlong, Edward Norton
director: Tony Kaye
American Hot Wax (1978 film)
cast: Fran Drescher, Jay Leno, Tim McIntire
American in Paris, An (1951 film)
cast: Leslie Caron, Gene Kelly, Oscar Levant
director: Vincente Minnelli
American in Paris, An composer: 8 Gershwin
Americanization of Emily, The (1964 film)
cast: Julie Andrews, James Coburn, Melvyn Douglas, James Garner
director: Arthur Hiller
American Kennel Club
reject: 3 mut 4 mutt
American League
division: 4 East, West 7 Central
team: 5 Bosox, The A's, Twins, Yanks 6 Angels, Chisox, Red Sox, Royals, Tigers 7 Indians, Orioles, Rangers, Yankees 8 Blue Jays, Mariners, White Sox 9 Athletics 10 Buccaneers
three-time ~ batting champ: Tony Oliva
American Legion
member: 3 vet 7 veteran
relative: 3 VFW
American Madness (1932 film)
cast: Walter Huston, Pat O'Brien
director: Frank Capra
American Music (1982 song) artist: Pointer Sisters
American Notes author: Charles Dickens
American Pie (1999 film)
cast: Jason Biggs, Shannon Elizabeth, Alyson Hannigan, Chris Klein
director: Paul Weitz
American Pie (1971 song) artist: Don McLean
car: 5 Chevy
place: 5 levee
American pit ___ terrier: 4 bull
American Popular Songs author: 4 Ewen
American President, The (1995 film)
cast: Annette Bening, Michael Douglas, Richard Dreyfuss, Michael J. Fox, Martin Sheen
director: Rob Reiner
American Psycho: 4 film 5 novel
author: Bret Easton Ellis
cast: Christian Bale, Willem Dafoe, Jared Leto, Reese Witherspoon
director: Mary Harron
American Revolution: 3 war
supporter: 4 Tory, Whig

American Rhapsody, An (2001 film)
cast: Tony Goldwyn, Nastassja Kinski
Americans (1974 song) artist: Byron MacGregor
American Samoa capital: 8 Pago Pago
American Scoundrel author: Thomas Keneally
American Shorthair: 3 cat **5** felid **6** feline
American Storm (1986 song) artist: Bob Seger
__-American Symphony: 4 Afro
American Tail, An character: 5 mouse **6** Fievel
__ American, The: 4 Ugly
American, The author: Henry James
American Tragedy, An
author: Theodore Dreiser
character: 3 Asa **4** Esta, Myra **5** Alden, Bella, Titus **6** Elvira, Hester
__ American Union: 3 Pan
American University
locale: 6 Beirut **7** Lebanon **8** Beyrouth
__-American War: 7 Spanish
American Way of Death, The author: Jessica Mitford
American Werewolf in London, An (1981 film)
cast: Jenny Agutter, Griffin Dunne, David Naughton
director: John Landis
American Wirehair: 3 cat **5** felid **6** feline
American Woman (1970 song) artist: Guess Who
Americar: 3 car **4** auto **6** Willys **10** automobile
America's Cup: 6 trophy
contender: 5 sloop, yacht
__ America Singing: 5 I Hear
America's longest-lasting car: 3 Reo
America's Most Wanted (Fox)
host: John Walsh
info: 5 alias
America's Sweethearts (2001 film)
cast: Billy Crystal, John Cusack, Julia Roberts, Catherine Zeta-Jones
director: Joe Roth
__ America, The: 5 Other
America the Beautiful
ender: 3 sea
pronoun: 4 thee
writer: 5 Bates
America/The Fall of Babylon (1924 film) director: D.W. Griffith
America West: 7 airline
alternative: 5 Delta **6** United **7** Jet Blue **8** American **9** Southwest **11** Continental
americium: 7 element
Amerigo: 4 font **8** typeface, Vespucci
Amerika author: Franz Kafka
Amerind: 3 Fox, Han, Kaw, Oto, Sac, Ute **4** Cree, Crow, Cuna, Erie, Eyak, Hopi, Inca, Iowa, Maya, Otoe, Pima, Pomo, Sauk, Seri, Taos, Tewa, Tiwa, Tupi, Yana, Yuma, Zuni **5** Ahtna, Brulé, Caddo, Carib, Creek, Haida, Huron, Kansa, Kaska, Kiowa, Lenca, Lipan, Maidu, Makah, Miami, Miwok, Modoc, Omaha, Osage, Otomi, Piute, Ponca, Sioux, Taino, Teton, Unami, Washo, Wintu, Yaqui **6** Abnaki, Ahtena, Apache, Arawak, Aymara, Cayuga, Cayuse, Dakota, Galibi, Jivaro, Kechua, Laguna, Lengua, Lumbee, Mandan, Micmac, Mohave, Mohawk, Mojave, Munsee, Navaho, Navajo, Nootka, Oglala, Ojibwa, Oneida, Ottawa, Paiute, Papago, Patwin, Pawnee, Pequot, Plains, Pueblo, Quapaw, Salish, Santee, Seneca, Tanana, Toltec, Wintun, Yahgan, Yakima, Yokuts **7** Abenaki, Arapaho, Arikara, Atakapa, Bannock, Chibcha, Chilcat, Chilkat, Chinook, Choctaw, Chumash, Guarani, Huastec, Kechuan, Klamath, Koyukon, Kutchin, Kutenai, Mahican, Mazatec, Miskito, Mohegan, Mohican, Naskapi, Nipmuck, Ojibway, Quechua, Quichua, San Blas, Shawnee, Takelma, Tanaina, Tlingit, Washita, Wichita, Wyandot, Yankton, Yavapai, Yucatec, Zapotec **8** Arapahoe, Cahuilla, Caingang, Cherokee, Cheyenne, Chippewa, Comanche, Delaware, Hunkpapa, Illinois, Iroquois, Kickapoo, Kwakiutl, Malecite, Maricopa, Mikasuki, Missouri, Muskogee, Nez Percé, Onondaga, Ouachita, Puyallup, Quechuan, Sahaptin, Seminole, Squamish, Tarascan, Wabanaki, Wahpeton **9** Blackfoot, Chickasaw, Havasupai, Jicarilla, Karankawa, Menominee, Mescalero, Nanticoke, Penobscot, Saulteaux, Suquamish, Tehuelche, Tsimshian, Tuscarora, Wahpekute, Wampanoag, Winnebago, Wyandotte **10** Adirondack, Araucanian, Assiniboin, Athabaskan, Bellabella, Bellacoola, Chiricahua, Miniconjou, Potawatomi, Tarahumara
Ames: 2 Ed **3** Joe, Vic **4** city, Gene, Leon, town **5** Nancy **6** Jessie **7** Aldrich
athletes: 8 Cyclones
locale: 4 Iowa
school: 3 ISU
Ames, Aldrich ex-employer: 3 CIA
Ames Brothers: 2 Ed **3** Joe, Vic **4** Gene
real last name: Urick
song: It Only Hurts for a Little While (1956)
Melodie d'Amour (1957)
My Bonnie Lassie (1955)
The Naughty Lady of Shady Lane (1954)
Rag Mop (1950)
Tammy (1957)
You You You (1953)
Ames, Ed song: My Cup Runneth Over (1967)
amethyst: 3 gem **5** color **6** purple **8** gemstone
month: 8 February
relative: 4 plum, puce **5** lilac, mauve **6** dahlia, damson, orchid **7** heather, petunia **8** burgundy, eggplant, lavender, mulberry **9** raspberry **10** heliotrope
Amethyst Ring, The author: 5 O'Dell
AMEX: 3 ASE, mkt.
alternative: 3 OTC **4** NYSE **6** NASDAQ
buy: 5 stock
number: 5 quote
overseer: 3 SEC
unit: 3 shr., stk. **5** share
AMF competitor: 4 Voit **9** Brunswick
AM/FM regulator: 3 FCC
Amhara home: 6 Africa **8** Ethiopia
Amherst: 4 city, town
athletes: 9 Minutemen
school: 4 Mass. **5** U Mass.
__ ami: 3 bon, mon
Ami: 6 Dolenz
Am I __?: 4 Blue
amia: 4 fish **6** bowfin **7** grindle
amiability: 7 amenity **8** kindness **9** geniality **10** cordiality, friendship, good nature
amiable: 4 calm, cool, easy, kind, mild, nice, soft, warm **5** close, quiet, sweet, type B **6** benign, chummy, clubby, genial, gentle, jovial, kindly, lovely, loving, low-key, mellow, placid, polite, sedate, serene **7** affable, cordial, equable, lenient, likable, lovable, pacific, relaxed **8** charming, composed, engaging, fireside, friendly, gracious, intimate, laid-back, likeable, loveable, obliging, outgoing, peaceful, pleasant, pleasing, sociable, tranquil **9** agreeable, collected, convivial, easy-going, peaceable, quiescent, temperate, unexcited, unruffled **10** benevolent, buddy-buddy, neighborly, personable, solicitous, unagitated, untroubled
look: 4 grin **5** smile
not ~: 5 type B
amiably, act: 6 be nice
Am I Blue author: Beth Henley
ami, bon: 2 jo **3** pet **4** baby, dear, love **5** amour, angel, chéri, cooky, cutey, cutie, deary, ducky, flame, honey, leman, lover, lovey, novio, sugar, sweet **6** cookie, dautie, dearie, steady, sweets **7** beloved, dearest, dear one, pigsney, schatzi, squeeze, sweetie, tootsie **8** chou-chou, cutie pie, dowsabel, intimate, lovebird, macushla, paramour, precious, snookums, sugar pie, sweetums, truelove **9** boyfriend, dreamboat, inamorato, petit chou, valentine **10** heartthrob, honeybunch, mavourneen, sweetheart, sweetie pie, turtledove
amicable: 4 calm, cool, kind **5** close, quiet, sweet **6** chummy, clubby, genial, kindly, low-key, mellow, placid, polite, sedate, serene **7** affable, cordial, equable, pacific, relaxed, stoical **8** composed, familiar, friendly, gracious, intimate, laid-back, likeable, outgoing, peaceful, sociable, tranquil **9** accordant, collected, congenial, convivial, courteous, easy-going, favorable, peaceable, quiescent, temperate, unexcited, unruffled **10** benevolent, buddy-buddy, harmonious, hospitable, neighborly, personable, solicitous, unagitated, untroubled
Amica composer: 8 Mascagni
amice: 4 cape
Amichai, Yehuda: 6 writer **7** Israeli
__ A. Michener: 5 James
amici __: 6 curiae
Amick: 7 Mädchen
amicus __: 6 curiae
amid: 5 among, 'twixt **6** during, in with, mongst **7** amongst, between, betwixt **9** in-between
__ __ a Midnight Clear: 4 Upon
amidst: 2 in **5** among, 'twixt **6** during, mongst **7** amongst, between **10** in the hub of
amie, bonne: 2 jo **3** pet **4** baby, dear, jill, love **5** amour, angel, cooky, cutey, cutie, deary, ducky, flame, honey, leman, lover, lovey, novia, sugar, sweet **6** chérie, cookie, dautie, dearie, steady, sweets **7** beloved, dearest, dear one, pigsney, schatzi, squeeze, sweetie, tootsie **8** chou-chou, cutie pie, dowsabel, dulcinea, ladylove, lovebird, macushla, paramour, precious, snookums, sugar pie, sweetums, truelove **9** dreamboat, inamorata, petit chou, valentine **10** girlfriend, heartthrob, honeybunch, mavourneen, sweetheart, sweetie pie, turtledove
Amiel, Jon: 8 director
film: Copycat (1995)
Entrapment (1999)
Queen of Hearts (1989)
Sommersby (1993)
Amiens: 4 city, town
locale: 6 France
river: 5 Somme
amigo: 3 pal **4** ally, chum **5** buddy, crony **6** cohort, friend **7** comrade **8** compadre, sidekick **9** associate, colleague, compañero, confidant **10** compatriot, well-wisher
Amigo: 3 SUV **5** Isuzu
__, amigos!: 5 Adios
__ Amigos!: 5 Three
Amilcare: 10 Ponchielli
__ a Mile in My Shoes: 4 Walk
__ a million: 5 one in **6** thanks
__ a million years!: 5 Not in
Am I my brother's __?: 6 keeper
Amin: 3 Idi **5** exile **7** Gemayel
__ Amin Dada: 3 Idi
Amindivi __: 7 Islands
amino acid: 3 leu. **4** dopa **6** lysine
suffix: 3 ine
__-aminobenzoic acid: 4 para
Aminta author: Torquato Tasso
__ a minute: 4 wait **5** a mile
amir: 5 Osman **6** Othman **9** potentate
Amir: 8 Williams
__ a Miracle: 3 It's
__ Amiri Baraka: 5 Imamu
__ amis: 3 mes
Amis: 4 Suzy **6** Martin **8** Kingsley
Amish: 4 sect
Amis, Kingsley: 6 author, writer **7** British
work: Ending Up
The Folks That Live on the Hill
Girl, 20
The Green Man
How's Your Glass?
I Like It Here
I Want It Now
Jake's Thing
Lucky Jim
The Old Devils
The Russian Girl
Stanley and the Women
Take a Girl Like You
That Uncertain Feeling
Amis, Martin: 6 writer **7** British
work: London Fields
Money
The Rachel Papers
Success
Time's Arrow
amiss: 3 bad **4** awry **5** afoul, badly, wrong **6** adrift, astray, faulty, flooey, flooie, rotten **7** off base, wrongly **8** cockeyed, erringly, faultily, not right **9** defective, deficient, foolishly, imperfect **10** improperly, mistakenly, off the mark, out of joint, out of order, out of place, out of whack, unsuitably
go ~: 3 err
Amis, Suzy: 7 actress
film: The Ballad of Little Jo (1993)
Nadja (1994)
Rocket Gibraltar (1988)
Watch It (1993)
spouse: James Cameron
Amistad (1997 film)
cast: Morgan Freeman, Nigel Hawthorne, Anthony Hopkins, Matthew McConaughey
composer: John Williams
director: Steven Spielberg
role: 5 Adams, slave **6** Cinque
Amittai, son of: 5 Jonah
amity: 4 love **5** peace, unity **6** accord, comity **7** concord, harmony **8** goodwill **10** cordiality, fellowship, friendship
Amityville Horror, The: 4 book, film
author: Jay Anson
cast: James Brolin, Margot Kidder, Rod Steiger
dog: 5 Harry
Amman: 4 city, town **7** capital
locale: 6 Jordan
ammo
see ammunition
ammonia
compound: 5 amide, imide, imine
derivative: 5 amine

__ ammoniac: **3** gum, sal
ammonite: **5** shell **6** fossil **8** seashell
ammonium __: **4** alum, salt **7** acetate, cyanate, lactate, nitrate, sulfate
ammunition: **3** BBs **4** fuel, shot **5** bombs, shots, slugs **6** beebee, bullet, rounds, shells **7** bullets, missile **8** grenades, materiel, missiles, ordnance **9** armaments, cartridge, explosive, gunpowder, munitions, torpedoes **10** cannonball, cartridges, explosives
air-gun ~: **3** BBs **6** beebee
blowgun ~: **4** dart
holder: **7** arsenal **8** magazine
kiddie ~: **3** cap, pea
material: **5** niter
military: **4** ordn. **8** ordnance
oater ~: **5** blank
prankster's ~: **3** egg **6** tomato
provide ~: **3** arm
put ~ in: **4** load
round of ~: **5** salvo
slanderer's ~: **3** mud
starter pistol's ~: **5** blank
unit: **3** rnd. **5** round
Amne Machin: **4** peak **5** mount **8** mountain
locale: **4** Asia **5** China
amnemonic: **9** forgetful
Amneris' slave: **4** Aïda
amnesty: **5** truce **6** pardon **9** remission **10** absolution
Amnesty Intl. concern: **3** MIA
Am not answer: **5** are so **6** are too
amo, __, amat: **4** amas
Amo, __, I love a lass: **4** amas
Amoco: **3** gas **8** gasoline
rival: **4** Gulf, Hess **5** Exxon, Getty, Shell **7** Chevron
amoeba: **4** cell **5** monad **6** animal **7** microbe **9** protozoan **10** animalcule
emulate an ~: **6** divide
amok: **4** loco **6** crazed, wildly **7** berserk, flipped, haywire **8** frenzied **9** rampaging **10** on a rampage
__ amok: **3** run
amole: **4** root **8** manfreda **9** soap plant
source: **5** yucca
Amonasro's daughter: **4** Aïda
among: **3** mid **4** amid, with **5** 'twixt **6** amidst, in with **7** between, betwixt **9** in-between
in French: **5** entre
in Spanish: **5** entre
prefix: **5** inter-
Among My Souvenirs (1959 song) artist: Connie Francis
among other persons: **10** inter alios
among other things: **9** inter alia
amongst: **4** amid **5** 'tween **6** amidst
Among the Cannibals author: Jules Verne
__ Among the Ruins: **4** Love
__ a monkey's uncle!: **5** I'll be
Amon-Ra's wife: **3** Mut
__ a Moon Out Tonight: **6** There's
amor __: **7** patriae
Amor: **3** god **4** Eros **5** Cupid **6** cherub **7** love god
amoral: **3** bad **5** wrong **6** wicked **9** libertine, qualmless, unethical **10** licentious, nonethical
amore: **4** love **9** affection
__ amore: **3** con
Amore: **7** cat food
alternative: **6** Figaro, Purina **7** Whiskas **8** Friskies **10** Chef's Blend, Fancy Feast
__ Amore: **5** That's
Amores poet: **4** Ovid
amoretto: **4** Eros **6** cherub
amorous: **4** fond, warm **6** doting, in love, loving, tender **7** hugging, kissing **8** romantic **10** lovey-dovey, passionate
amorousness: **4** love
amorphous: **5** baggy, vague **6** blobby **8** formless, inchoate, nebulous, unformed, unshaped **9** irregular, shapeless
mass: **4** blob, glob
Amory, Cleveland: **6** author, critic, writer
Amos: **2** Oz **4** city, John, Otis, Tori, town **5** Jones, McCoy, Rusie, Stagg, Wally **6** Alcott, Tupper
book after: **4** Obad. **7** Obadiah
book before ~: **4** Joel
locale: **6** Canada, Québec
partner: **4** Andy
Amos __: **5** 'n' Andy
Amos __ Stagg: **6** Alonzo
__ Amos: **6** Famous
Amos & Andrew actor: **4** Cage
Amos Bronson __: **6** Alcott
Amos, John: **5** actor
film: Coming to America (1988) The World's Greatest Athlete (1973)
TV: Good Times, Roots
Amos Moses (1971 song) artist: Jerry Reed
Amos 'n' Andy: **9** radio show
Amos, Tori real first names: Mary Ellen
__ a Most Unusual Day: **3** It's
amount: **3** qty., sum, tab **4** cost, deal, size, span **5** add up, batch, order, price, reach, shade, total, value **6** charge, degree, extent, number, outlay, output, supply, volume **7** add up to, expense, measure, quantum **8** price tag, quantity **9** aggregate, magnitude **10** complement
determine the ~ of: **6** assess
end ~: **3** net
excessive ~: **5** spate
full ~: **3** all **4** body **5** total, whole **8** entirety, the works, totality **9** aggregate
greatest ~: **7** maximum
indefinite ~: **3** any **4** some
large ~: **3** sea **4** lots, mint, much, scad, slew, tons **5** ocean **6** bagful, oodles, plenty
least ~: **3** jot **4** iota, whit **7** minimum **9** scintilla
measured ~: **4** dose
necessary ~: **5** quota
outstanding ~: **4** debt, levy **6** arrear **7** arrears
prescribed ~: **4** dose
red-ink ~: **4** debt **5** debit **7** deficit
small ~: **3** bit, dot, fig, tad **4** atom, dash, drab, dram, drib, drop, hoot, iota, lick, mite, song, whit **5** grain, minim, pinch, skosh, speck, touch, trace **6** little, trifle **7** modicum **8** pittance
smaller ~: **4** less
small in ~: **5** light **6** little
taken in: **4** gate
to: **4** cost, make **5** equal, reach, spell, total
(to): **4** come
vitamin ~: **4** pill **6** tablet
worthless ~: **3** fig, sou **6** diddly
amour: **2** jo **3** pet **4** baby, dear, jill, love **5** angel, chéri, cooky, cutey, cutie, deary, ducky, flame, honey, leman, lover, lovey, novia, novio, sugar, sweet **6** bon ami, chérie, cookie, dautie, dearie, steady, sweets **7** beloved, dearest, dear one, liaison, passion, pigsney, romance, schatzi, squeeze, sweetie, tootsie **8** chou-chou, cutie pie, dowsabel, dulcinea, ladylove, lovebird, macushla, paramour, precious, snookums, sugar pie, sweetums, truelove **9** bonne amie, boyfriend, dreamboat, inamorata, inamorato, petit chou, valentine **10** girlfriend, heartthrob, honeybunch, mavourneen, sweetheart, sweetie pie, turtledove
amour-propre: **3** ego **5** pride **7** conceit **10** self-esteem
__, a mouse!: **3** Eek
__ a move on: **3** get **4** make
Amozoc: **4** city, town
locale: **6** Mexico, Puebla
Amoz, son of: **6** Isaiah
__-amp: **3** pre
AMPAS trophy: **5** Oscar
Ampato: **4** peak **5** mount **8** mountain
locale: **4** Peru **5** Andes
amp attachment: **4** mike
ampere: **4** unit **7** measure
Ampère, André: **9** physicist, scientist
ampersand: **3** and, sym. **6** symbol
amphibian: **3** eft, olm **4** frog, hyla, newt, toad **5** ranid **6** anuran, mud eel, peeper **7** axolotl, crapaud, tadpole **8** mudpuppy **10** salamander
order: **5** anura
utterance: **5** croak
amphibious
fish: **6** anabas
vehicle: **6** amtrac **7** amtrack
amphigoric: **5** inane, silly
amphigory: **8** flummery
Amphion: **7** centaur **8** Argonaut
father of ~: **4** Zeus
instrument: **4** lyre
wife of ~: **5** Niobe
amphitheater: **4** bowl, hall, oval, ring **5** arena, field **6** lyceum **7** stadium, theater, theatre **8** coliseum **9** colosseum
natural ~: **3** cwm
section: **4** tier
amphitheaters, Roman: **6** arenae
Amphitrite: **6** Nereid **8** asteroid
husband of ~: **8** Poseidon
mother of ~: **6** Triton
amphora: **3** jar, pot, urn **5** crock **6** flagon, vessel **9** container **10** jardiniere
handle: **4** ansa
ample: **3** big **4** full, much, tidy, vast, wide **5** broad, great, heavy, hefty, large, roomy, stout **6** decent, enough, goodly, lavish, plenty, portly **7** copious, liberal, profuse, sizable **8** abundant, generous, handsome, prodigal, sizeable, spacious **9** bounteous, bountiful, capacious, expansive, extensive, good-sized, luxuriant, plenteous, plentiful, unsparing **10** commodious, munificent, overweight, sufficient, voluminous
amount: **8** plethora
amplified beam: **5** laser
amplifier, wave: **5** maser
amplify: **3** add, pad, wax **4** grow **5** add to, boost, swell **6** beef up, expand, hike up, overdo, ramble **7** augment, build up, develop, enhance, enlarge, inflate, magnify **8** escalate, heighten, increase, lengthen **9** elaborate, expatiate **10** exaggerate, make much of
amplitude: **4** mass, size **5** scope, width **6** extent, volume **7** bigness, breadth, fulness **8** capacity, hugeness, loudness, vastness, wideness **9** abundance, broadness, greatness, immensity, largeness, magnitude, plenitude, roominess **10** dimensions
amply: **4** very, well **6** enough, galore, vastly
ampule: **4** bulb, hypo, vial **5** phial
Amram
daughter of ~: **6** Miriam
son of ~: **5** Aaron, Moses
Amrita author: Ruth Prawer Jhabvala
Amscray!: **3** git **4** scat, shoo **5** scoot, scram **6** beat it, begone, get out
Amstel: **4** Beck, beer **5** Dutch
alternative: **5** Becks, Coors, Pabst **6** Corona, Miller, Molson **7** Schlitz **8** Heineken, Michelob **9** Lowenbrau **10** Ballantine
city on the ~: **9** Amsterdam
Amsterdam: **4** city, port, town **5** Morey **7** capital
locale: **7** Holland, New York **11** Netherlands
neighbor: **3** Ede
river: **6** Amstel
see also Dutch
__ Amsterdam: **3** New **5** Nieuw
amt.: **3** num., qty.
comparable ~: **5** equiv.
largest ~: **3** max.
least ~: **3** min.
see also amount
Am too! response: **5** are so **6** are not
Amtrak: **2** RR **3** rwy. **7** railway **8** railroad
advisory: **3** ETD
bullet train: **5** Acela
car: **5** diner **7** sleeper
overseer: **4** NTSB
stop: **3** sta., stn. **7** station
track: **4** rail
worker: **4** engr. **8** engineer **9** conductor
see also train
amuck: **6** crazed
run ~: **4** rage, riot **7** rampage **8** have a fit
Amu Darya: **4** Oxus **5** river
outlet: **7** Aral Sea
amugis: **4** tree
amulet: **4** ankh, juju, mojo **5** charm, jewel, spell **6** fetich, fetish, grigri, scarab **7** periapt **8** greegree, grisgris, talisman **9** horseshoe
word: **7** abraxas
Amundsen: **3** sea **4** gulf **5** Norse, Roald
locale: **10** Antarctica
Amundsen, Roald: **8** explorer **9** Norwegian
contemporary: **5** Peary
quest: **4** Pole **9** South Pole
Amur: **5** river
locale: **6** Russia **9** Manchuria
river to the ~: **6** Ussuri **7** Songhua
amuse: **3** get **5** cheer **6** divert, occupy, please, regale, tickle **7** beguile, crack up, delight, disport, satisfy **8** interest **9** entertain, knock dead, make merry, titillate **10** tickle pink
oneself: **4** play
to the max: **4** slay
amused, look: **4** grin **5** smile
amusement: **3** fun, rec **4** game, play **5** cheer, humor, mirth, party, sport, treat **6** frolic, laughs **7** delight, disport, jollies, pastime **8** laughter, pleasure **9** avocation, diversion, enjoyment, festivity, funniness, merriment **10** recreation, regalement, relaxation, risibility
center: **6** arcade
exclamation: **4** ha-ha **5** te-hee **6** haw-haw, tee-hee
expression of ~: **5** laugh **8** laughter
amusement __: **3** tax **4** park
amusement park
feature: **4** maze, ride, whip **5** flume, slide **6** Dodgem **8** carousel **10** water slide
shout: **4** whee
amusing: **3** fun **4** nice, rich **5** comic, droll, funny, kicky, light, merry, silly, witty **6** har-har, jocose **7** comical, jocular, waggish **8** farcical, humorous, pleasant, readable **9** facetious, laughable, priceless, quizzical, whimsical **10** delightful
sort: **3** wag, wit **5** comic **6** gagman **7** gagster **8** comedian

Amy: 3 Ray, Tan 5 Grant, March 6 Alcott, Carter, Irving, Locane, Lowell, Wright 7 Madigan, Yasbeck 8 Clampitt, Van Dyken 9 Brenneman 10 Heckerling, Vanderbilt
sister of ~: 4 Beth
Amy (1981 film)
cast: Jenny Agutter, Barry Newman
director: Vincent McEveety
amyl ___: 7 acetate, alcohol, nitrite, sulfide
___ a Mystery: 5 I Love
An: 4 Wang
ana: 10 compendium, miscellany
Ana: 6 Alicia
ANA: 3 org. 7 airline
member: 2 RN 3 LPN
Anabaptist sect: 5 Amish
anabas: 4 fish 7 gourami
Anabasis author: Xenophon
anableps: 4 fish
anabolic ___: 7 steroid
___ Ana, CA: 5 Santa
anachronistic: 8 obsolete, outdated, outmoded 9 out-of-date
Anacin: 7 aspirin 9 analgesic 10 painkiller
alternative: 3 APF 4 Cope 5 Advil, Aleve, Bayer 6 Datril, Motrin 7 Ecotrin, Tylenol 8 Bufferin, Excedrin, St. Joseph, Vanquish 9 Ascriptin
Anacletus: 4 pope 7 pontiff
anaconda: 3 boa 4 game 5 snake 6 animal 7 reptile 8 card game
relative: 3 asp 5 aboma, adder, cobra, krait, mamba, racer, viper 6 dhaman, python, taipan 7 markhor, rattler 8 moccasin, ringhals 9 boomslang, coachwhip 10 bushmaster, copperhead, sidewinder
Anacostia: 5 river
city on the ~: 10 Washington
Anacreon: 4 poet 5 Greek
birthplace: 4 Teos
subject: 4 wine
___ an act: 5 put on
anadem: 6 wreath 7 coronet 9 headpiece
Anadir: 3 mts. 4 mtns. 5 range 9 mountains
locale: 4 Asia 6 Russia 7 Siberia
anaglyph: 5 cameo
Anagnostakis, Manolis: 4 poet 5 Greek
anagogic: 6 mystic 8 mystical
anagrams: 4 game 8 word game
Anaheim: 4 city, town
county: 6 Orange
locale: 10 California
team: 6 Angels
town near ~: 4 Brea
Anaheim ___ and Cucamonga: 5 Azusa
Anáhuac: 4 city, town
locale: 6 Mexico 8 Veracruz 9 Chihuahua, Nuevo León
Anaïs: 3 Nin
see also French
Anakin's child: 4 Leia, Luke
analects: 6 pieces 7 sayings 8 excerpts, extracts, passages 9 anthology, citations 10 quotations, selections
analeptic: 9 stimulant 10 comforting
analgesic: 3 APF 4 balm, Cope 5 Advil, Aleve, Bayer 6 Anacin, Datril, Motrin 7 anodyne, aspirin, Ecotrin, soother, Tylenol 8 Bufferin, Excedrin, St. Joseph, Vanquish 9 Ascriptin 10 anesthetic, painkiller
need an ~: 4 ache
target: 4 pain
analog: 8 parallel
not ~: 7 digital
analog ___: 5 clock, watch
analogize: 6 relate
analogous: 4 akin, like, same, such 5 alike 6 allied, on a par 7 cognate, kindred, related, similar, uniform 8 matching, parallel, relative 9 consonant 10 comparable, equivalent, homogenous, homologous, resembling
analogy: 8 affinity, likeness, likening, metaphor, parallel, sameness 9 semblance 10 comparison, similarity
make an ~: 5 liken
phrase: 4 is to
analysis: 4 test, view 5 assay, audit, check, study, trial 6 review, survey 7 opinion, profile, remarks, summary, therapy 8 critique, exegesis, judgment, research, scrutiny 9 breakdown, criticism, reasoning, treatment, voice-over 10 commentary, dissection, evaluation, inspection
financial ~ tool: 5 chart
kind of ~: 4 qual.
mental ~: 6 reason
___ analysis: 3 ego, job 5 dream, error, final 6 factor, market, tensor, vector 7 complex, content, Fourier, network, systems, thermal
analyst: 6 critic, shrink 8 examiner 9 columnist, evaluator, therapist 10 accountant
concern: 2 id 3 ego
___ analyst: 3 lay 4 news 7 systems
analytical: 5 sound 6 cogent 7 logical, tenable 8 cerebral, coherent, methodic, rational, sensible, thinking 9 heuristic, inquiring, pragmatic 10 consistent, reasonable
analytical ___: 5 entry 6 cubism 7 balance
analyze: 4 sift, test, x-ray 5 assay, audit, check, prove, study, think, weigh 6 decode, detail, digest, peruse, review 7 compare, dissect, examine, explain 8 construe, decipher, evaluate, factor in, identify 9 criticize, enter into, figure out, interpret, pick apart 10 brainstorm
grammatically: 5 parse
mentally: 6 reason
verse: 4 scan
Analyze ___: 4 That, This
___ analyzer: 6 breath 7 circuit
Analyze This (1999 film)
cast: Billy Crystal, Robert De Niro, Lisa Kudrow
director: Harold Ramis
___ a Name: 4 I Got
___ a name for oneself: 4 make
___ an American Band: 4 We're
anamnesis: 6 memory, recall
Anand, Mulk Raj: 6 Indian, writer
Ananias, emulate: 3 lie
Ananke: 4 moon
planet: 7 Jupiter
anapest: 4 foot
kin: 4 iamb 6 dactyl 7 spondee
relative: 4 iamb 6 dactyl 7 pyrrhic, spondee, trochee
Anápolis: 4 city, town
locale: 6 Brazil
anarchic: 7 chaotic, lawless, radical, riotous 8 confused 9 insurgent 10 disorderly, tumultuous, ungoverned
anarchist: 5 rebel, Sacco 7 leftist, radical 8 agitator, ultraist, Vanzetti 9 insurgent, terrorist 10 malcontent
anarchy: 4 mess 5 chaos 6 bedlam, mayhem, tumult, unrest, uproar 7 ferment, license, mob rule, turmoil 8 civil war, disarray, disorder, nihilism, shambles, upheaval 9 confusion, mobocracy 10 revolution, turbulence
___ an arm and a leg: 4 cost
___ an arrow...: 5 I shot
Anastasia
father: 4 czar, tsar, tzar
see also Russian
Anastasia (1956 film)
cast: Ingrid Bergman, Yul Brynner, Helen Hayes, Akim Tamiroff
director: Anatole Litvak
Anastasius: 4 pope 7 pontiff
anat.: 3 sci.
anathema: 4 bane, tabu 5 taboo 6 pariah 7 bugbear 10 not allowed
anathematize: 5 blast 7 condemn 8 denounce 9 imprecate
Anatole: 6 France, Litvak
Anatolian: 4 Turk
Anatoly: 6 Karpov 8 Dobrynin
anatomical: 7 organic 8 corporal 9 corporeal
canal: 4 iter 5 lumen
cavities: 4 vasa 5 antra
cavity: 5 lumen, sinus 6 antrum
dividers: 5 septa
fold: 5 plica
foot: 3 pes
hinge: 4 knee
hooked ~ part: 5 uncus
loop: 4 ansa
pouch: 3 sac
ring: 6 areola, areole
sac: 5 bursa
tissue: 4 tela
tissues: 5 telae
vessel: 3 vas
wrinkle: 4 ruga
anatomist: 4 Gray 5 Galen
anatomize: 7 dissect
anatomy: 4 body, form 5 build, frame 6 figure, makeup 7 science 9 structure
back, in ~: 6 dorsum
branch of ~: 7 myology
external, in ~: 5 ectal
inner, in ~: 5 ental
knee, in ~: 4 genu
of the back, in ~: 5 notal
study: 9 structure
___ anatomy: 5 gross
___ Anatomy: 5 Gray's
Anatomy Lesson, The author: Philip Roth
Anatomy of a Murder (1959 film)
cast: Eve Arden, Ben Gazzara, Arthur O'Connell, Lee Remick, James Stewart
director: Otto Preminger
dog: 5 Muffy
___ Ana winds: 5 Santa
Anaxagoras: 5 Greek 11 philosopher
Anaximander: 5 Greek 11 philosopher
Ancaster: 4 city, town
locale: 6 Canada 7 Ontario
ancestor: 4 sire 6 father, mother, origin, parent 9 precursor, prototype 10 forefather, forerunner, progenitor
ancestors: 5 roots 7 kinfolk 8 kinfolks, kinsfolk 9 forebears
ancestral: 6 lineal, racial 7 genetic 8 familial, primeval 9 genetical, inherited, primaeval 10 affiliated, congenital, connatural, derivative, hereditary
image: 5 totem
ancestry: 4 line 5 birth, blood, class, roots, stock 6 origin, strain 7 descent, kinfolk, lineage 8 heredity, heritage, kinfolks, kinsfolk, pedigree 9 etymology, forebears, genealogy 10 derivation, extraction
Anchises' son: 5 Eneas 6 Aeneas
anchor: 3 fix, set, tie 4 dock, host, moor 5 bower, imbed, kedge, plant, rivet 6 Brokaw, fasten, Lehrer, Rather, secure 7 Huntley, lookout, MacNeil 8 Brinkley, Cronkite, entrench, foothold, hold down, Jennings, mainstay, reporter 9 stabilize 10 newscaster
a ship: 5 lay to
botanical ~: 4 root
domain: 3 sea 4 news
drop ~: 4 land 6 arrive 8 get there
ender: 3 age, man, men 5 woman, women 6 person
hole for an ~ cable: 5 hawse
lift ~: 4 sail 7 set sail 8 shove off
mountain-climber's ~: 5 belay
overseer: 4 bo's'n 5 bosun
position: 4 desk 5 apeak, apeek
race: 5 relay
remain at ~: 4 ride 5 lie to
rope: 6 hawser
sound: 5 clank
anchor ___: 3 bed, ice 4 ball, bell, bend, bolt, buoy, deck, knot, ring, shot, span 5 light, plant, store, watch 6 pocket
___ anchor: 3 ice, sea 4 back, rail 5 bower, drift, kedge, screw, sheet
anchorage: 3 bay 4 dock, pier, port, quay 5 basin, berth, haven, jetty, wharf 6 asylum, harbor, refuge 7 harbour, landing, mooring, shelter 9 harborage, sanctuary
Anchorage: 4 city, town
locale: 6 Alaska
newspaper: 4 News
anchored: 4 firm 6 secure, stable 8 embedded, immobile 10 stationary
anchoress: 3 nun 7 eremite, recluse
anchoret
see anchorite
anchorite: 4 monk 5 loner 6 hermit 7 eremite, isolato, recluse 8 solitary 9 religious 10 troglodyte
abode: 4 cell
like an ~: 4 lone
Anchors Aweigh: 4 song
group: 3 USN 4 Navy
Anchors Aweigh (1945 film)
cast: Kathryn Grayson, Gene Kelly, Frank Sinatra
director: George Sidney
anchovies: 4 fish
how ~ are packed: 5 in oil
like ~: 5 salty
sauce: 4 alec
anchovy ___: 4 pear 5 pizza
Anchurus, father of: 5 Midas
ancien ___: 6 régime
ancient: 3 old 4 aged 5 aging, early, hoary, of old, olden, passé 6 ageing, age-old, bygone, creaky, former, native 7 antique, archaic, elderly, wizened 8 grizzled, Noachian, obsolete, primeval 9 geriatric, getting on, primaeval, primitive, senescent, unevolved, up in years, venerable, vestigial 10 aboriginal, antiquated, immemorial, primordial
combining form: 4 pale- 5 palae-, paleo- 6 archeo-, palaeo-, palaio- 7 archaeo-
ancient ___: 6 regime 7 history
Ancient Evenings setting: 5 Egypt
Ancient Mariner's cry: 5 asail
Ancient of ___: 4 Days
Ancient Wonders, one of the: 6 Pharos 7 pyramid 8 Colossus
ancillary: 4 side 5 extra, minor 9 accessory, appendage, attendant, attending, auxiliary, dependant, dependent, satellite, secondary 10 additional, coincident, collateral, incidental, subsidiary
combining form: 3 par- 4 para-
Ancohuma: 4 peak 5 mount 8 mountain
locale: 5 Andes 7 Bolivia
Ancona: 4 city, port, town
locale: 5 Italy
town near ~: 4 Lesi

ANC, part of: 3 Afr., Nat. 4 Cong., Natl. 7 African 8 Congress, National
and: 4 also, more, plus 7 besides, further 8 as well as, moreover 9 along with, ampersand, connector, including, what's more 10 connective, in addition
and __: 3 how 4 so on
and __ some: 4 then
...and __ far: 5 yet so
...and __ grow on!: 5 one to
...and __ in the morning: 5 see me
...and __ my cap: 3 I in
...and __ need to know: 5 all ye
...and __ the child: 5 spoil
...and __ well: 4 all's 5 all is
And __ bed: 4 so to
And __ goes: 4 so it
And __ grow on: 5 one to
And __ Her: 5 I Love
And __ I wrote...: 4 then
And __ off!: 6 they're
And __ the opposite shore...: 3 I on
And __ There Were None: 4 Then
And __ to every purpose...: 5 a time
And __ word from...: 4 now a
And __ wrote...: 5 then I
__ and aah: 3 ooh
__ and Abélard: 7 Héloise
__ and abet: 3 aid
__ and abetting: 6 aiding
__ and Abner: 3 Lum
__ and a bone...: 4 a rag
...and a bottle of __: 3 rum
__ and above: 4 over
__ and Accepted Masons: 4 Free
__ and a day: 5 a year 7 forever
__ and Aeneas: 4 Dido
__ and aft: 4 fore
__ and after: 6 before
__ and again: 3 now 4 ever, time
__ and age: 3 day
__ and a half: 4 time
__ and alack: 4 alas
__ and Ale: 5 Cakes
__ and a leg: 5 an arm
__ and Alexander: 5 Fanny
__ and all: 3 one 5 still, warts
__ and Allen: 5 Burns
And all ye __ to know: 4 need
Andaman: 3 sea
locale: 8 Malaysia, Thailand 9 Indonesia
Andaman __: 3 Sea 7 Islands
__ and anon: 4 ever
andante: 5 music, tempo 6 slowly
faster than ~: 8 moderato
slower than ~: 5 largo, lento 6 adagio
...and a partridge in a __ tree: 4 pear
__ and a Peck, A: 6 Bushel
__ and a Prayer: 4 Wing
__ and a promise: 4 lick
__ and asked: 3 bid
__ and assigns: 5 heirs
...and a time to __: 3 sew 4 heal, lose
__ and away: 3 far, out
__ and Away: 3 Far 4 Up Up
And away __!: 4 we go
__ and a Woman: 4 A Man
__ and axle: 5 wheel
__ and balances: 6 checks
__-and-ball foot: 4 claw
__ and Barbuda: 7 Antigua
__ and Bars: 5 Stars
__ and battery: 7 assault
__ and bear it: 4 grin
__ and bees: 5 birds
__ and bells: 3 cap
...and bells on her __: 4 toes
__ and Bess: 5 Porgy
__ and between: 7 betwixt
__ and beyond: 5 above
__ and Bill: 3 Min
__ and bit: 5 brace
__ and blood: 5 flesh
__-and-blue: 5 black
__ and blues: 6 rhythm
__ and board: 3 bed 4 room
__ and bobtail: 6 ragtag, tagrag
__ and bolts: 4 nuts
__ and bones: 4 skin
__ and Bones: 6 Sticks
__ and bothered: 3 hot
__ and bounds: 5 butts, leaps, metes
__ and Bows: 7 Buttons
__ and Bradstreet: 3 Dun
__-and-break: 4 make
__ and breakfast: 3 bed
__ and bred: 4 born
__-and-brimstone: 4 fire
__-and-buggy: 5 horse
__ and bugle corps: 4 drum
__-and-bull story: 4 cock
__ and burn: 5 crash, slash
__-and-bust: 4 boom
__ and butter: 5 bread
__ and caboodle: 3 kit
__ and Caicos Islands: 5 Turks
__ and call: 4 beck
__ and carry: 4 cash
__ and center: 5 front
__-and-cents: 7 dollars
__ and chain: 4 ball
__ and Cher: 5 Sonny
__ and Child: 7 Madonna
...and children of all __!: 4 ages
__ and Child Reunion: 6 Mother
__ and chips: 4 fish
__ and Chloe: 7 Daphnis
__ and Chocolate: 5 Bread
__ and Chong: 6 Cheech
__ and choose: 4 pick
__ and Circumstance: 4 Pomp
__ and circuses: 5 bread
__ and Civilization: 4 Eros
__ and Clark: 4 Lois 5 Lewis
__-and-claw foot: 4 ball
__ and clear: 4 free, loud
__ and Cleopatra: 6 Antony, Caesar
__ and Clover: 7 Crimson
__ and Clyde: 6 Bonnie
__ and Coca-Cola: 3 Rum
__ and Coke: 3 rum
__ and con: 3 pro
__ and conquer: 6 divide
__ and cons: 4 pros
__ and consent: 6 advice
and Consent: 4 film 5 novel
__ and Consent: 6 Advise
__ and coo: 4 bill
__ and Costello: 6 Abbott
__-and-cover: 3 cut
__ and crafts: 4 arts
__ and cranny: 4 nook
__ and cream: 7 peaches
__ and Cressida: 7 Troilus
__ and Crofts: 5 Seals
__ and crossbones: 5 skull
__-and-crosses: 7 noughts
__ and cry: 3 hue
__-and-dagger: 5 cloak
__ and dance: 4 song
__ and dandy: 4 fine
__ and dangerous: 5 armed
__ and Daniel Webster, The: 5 Devil
__ and dart: 3 egg
__ and Dave: 3 Sam
__ and Day: 5 Night
__ and deal: 5 wheel
__ and Death: 4 Love
__ and Decker: 5 Black
__ and Delilah: 6 Samson
__ and Deliver: 5 Stand
__ and desist: 5 cease
__ and die: 4 tool
__-and-dime: 4 five 6 nickel
__ and dine: 4 wine
__ and dip: 4 chip
__-and-dirty: 4 down 5 quick
__ and Dolls: 4 Guys
__ and don'ts: 3 do's
__ and doom: 5 gloom
__ and downs: 3 ups
__ and drabs: 5 dribs
__ and drakes: 5 ducks
__-and-dried: 3 cut
__ and Driver: 3 Car
__ and Drug Administration: 4 Food
__ and dry: 4 high
Andean: 4 Inca 5 lofty 7 Chilean 8 Peruvian
see also Andes
Andean __: 4 deer 6 condor
__ and early: 6 bright
__ and easy: 4 free
...and eat __: 5 it too
__ and effect: 5 cause
__-and-egg: 7 chicken
__-and-egg man: 6 butter
__ and eggs: 3 ham 5 bacon, steak
__ and Ellice Islands: 7 Gilbert
__ and end-all: 5 be-all
__ and ends: 4 odds
__ and error: 5 trial
Anders: 5 Luana 7 Allison, Celsius 8 Ångström
Andersen, Hans Christian: 4 Dane 6 Danish, writer
work: The Little Mermaid
The Princess and the Pea
The Snow Queen
The Tinderbox
The Ugly Duckling
Anderson: 3 Ian 4 Bill, Brad, Carl, city, Jack, Loni, Lynn, town 5 Daryl, Eddie, Harry, Leroy, Louie 6 Judith, Marian, Melody, Pamela, Philip, Robert, Sparky 7 Barbara, Gillian, Herbert, Lindsay, Maxwell, Michael, Richard 8 Sherwood
locale: 7 Indiana
Anderson, Carl: 8 Nobelist 9 physicist
Anderson, Judith: 4 Dame 7 actress
film: Laura (1944)
Pursued (1947)
Rebecca (1940)
Specter of the Rose (1946)
The Ten Commandments (1956)
Anderson, Leroy: 8 composer
work: Belle of the Ball
Blue Tango
Bugler's Holiday
Fiddle-Faddle
Jazz Pizzicato
The Phantom Regiment
Plink, Plank, Plunk!
Sandpaper Ballet
Sleigh Ride
The Syncopated Clock
A Trumpeter's Lullaby
The Typewriter
The Waltzing Cat
Anderson, Lindsay: 8 director
film: if ... (1968)
O Lucky Man! (1973)
This Sporting Life (1963)
The Whales of August (1987)
Anderson, Loni spouse: Burt Reynolds
Anderson, Lynn song: Rose Garden (1970)
Anderson, Marian: 4 alto 6 singer 9 contralto
specialty: 5 opera
Anderson, Maxwell: 6 author, writer
work: Anne of the Thousand Days
The Bad Seed
Barefoot in Athens
The Buccaneer
Candle in the Wind
Elizabeth the Queen
The Eve of St. Mark
First Flight
Gods of the Lightning
Joan of Lorraine
Key Largo
Knickerbocker Holiday
Lost in the Stars
Mary of Scotland
Night Over Taos
Storm Operation
Valley Forge
What Price Glory?
Winterset
Anderson, Michael: 8 director
film: 1984 (1956)
Around the World in Eighty Days (1956)
Chase a Crooked Shadow (1958)
The Dam Busters (1955)
Operation Crossbow (1965)
The Quiller Memorandum (1966)
Shake Hands With the Devil (1959)
__ Anderson My Jo: 4 John
Anderson, Pamela spouse: Tommy Lee
Anderson, Philip: 8 Nobelist 9 physicist
Anderson, Robert: 6 author 10 playwright
work: Absolute Strangers
After
All Summer Long
Getting Up and Going Home
I Never Sang for My Father
The Last Act Is a Solo
Tea and Sympathy
A Wreath and a Curse
You Know I Can't Hear You When the Water's Running
Anderson, Sherwood: 6 author, writer
work: Horses and Men
Marching Man
The Triumph of the Egg
Winesburg, Ohio
Anderson Tapes, The: 4 film 5 novel
author: Lawrence Sanders
cast: Martin Balsam, Dyan Cannon, Sean Connery
director: Sidney Lumet
Andersson: 4 Arne, Bibi
Andersson, Bibi: 7 actress
film: Duel at Diablo (1966)
The Girls (1968)
I Never Promised You a Rose Garden (1977)
The Passion of Anna (1969)
Persona (1966)
Scenes From a Marriage (1973)
The Seventh Seal (1957)
Wild Strawberries (1957)
Andes: 3 mts. 4 mtns. 5 range 9 mountains
ancient ~ dweller: 4 Inca 5 Incan
animal: 4 pudu 5 llama 6 alpaca, vicuna
capital: 4 Lima 5 Quito 6 Bogotá 8 Santiago
city: 4 Cali 5 Cusco, Cuzco
country: 4 Ecua., Peru 5 Chile 8 Colombia
explorer: 4 Peck
flyer: 6 condor
Indian: 6 Aymara
mountain: 4 Ruiz, Solo, Toro 5 Cachi, Chani, Cusco, Cuzco, Galan, Laudo, Negro, Pular, Quela 6 Ampato, Bonete, Juncal, Pissis, Sajama 7 Huandoy, Illampu, Palermo, San Juan 8 Ancohuma, Coropuna, El Condor, El Muerto, Famatina, Illimani, Polleras, Solimana, Tortolas, Yerupaja 9 Aconcagua, Antofalla, Condoriri, Huascarán, Incahuasi, Marmolejo, Pumasillo, Salcantay, Tupungato 10 Chimborazo, Mercedario, Nacimiento, Parinacota, Tres Cruces

native language: 6 Kechua 7 Kechuan, Quechua, Quichua 8 Quechuan
shrub: 4 coca 8 cinchona
tuber: 3 oca, oka
__ and Eve: 4 Adam
__ and every: 4 each
__ and Ewell: 5 Epsom
__ and excursions: 7 alarums
__ and eye: 4 hook
__ and fall: 4 rise 7 decline
__ and famous: 4 rich
__ and far: 4 near
__ and far between: 3 few
__ and farewell: 4 Hail
__ and fast: 4 hard
__ and fauna: 5 flora
__ and feather: 3 tar
__ and feathers: 4 fuss, plug
__ and feel: 4 look
__ and female: 4 male
__ and field: 5 track
__ and file: 4 rank
__ and fill: 3 cut 4 back
__ and flowers: 6 hearts
__ and Fog: 7 Shadows
__ and foot: 4 hand
__ and for all: 4 once
__ and foremost: 5 first
__ and Forever: 3 Now
__ and forth: 4 back
__ and fortune: 4 fame
__ and found: 4 lost
__-and-four: 5 coach
__ and Fruity: 4 Good
__ and Futuna Islands: 6 Wallis
__ and Future King, The: 4 Once
__ and Galatea: 4 Acis
__ and games: 3 fun
__ and Garfunkel: 5 Simon
__ and Get It: 4 Come
...__ and gimble...: 4 gyre
And giving __, up...: 4 a nod
__ and Glory: 4 Hope 5 Power
__ and glove: 4 hand
__ and go: 4 come 5 touch
__-and-go: 4 stop 5 get-up
__-and-go-seek: 4 hide
__ and gown: 3 cap
__ and grill: 3 bar
__ and groan: 4 moan
__-and-groove joint: 6 tongue
__ and Gus: 6 Tillie
__-and-guts: 5 blood
__ and Hammer: 3 Arm
__ and Hardy: 6 Laurel
__ and Harriet: 5 Ozzie
And hast thou __ the Jabberwock?: 5 slain
__ and haw: 3 hem
__ and hearty: 4 hale
__ and Herb: 7 Peaches
__ and hers: 3 his
__ and Her Sisters: 6 Hannah
__ and Herzegovina: 6 Bosnia
__ and His Brothers: 6 Joseph
__ and his money...: 5 A fool
__ and hiss: 3 boo
__ and Hobbes: 6 Calvin
__ and holler: 4 hoot
__ and Honey: 4 Milk
__ and Hopin': 6 Wishin'
__ and hounds: 4 hare
And how!: 6 I'll say, you bet
__ and Howard: 6 Melvin
__ and Howell: 4 Bell
...__ and hungry look: 5 a lean
__ and Hyde: 6 Jekyll
__ and I: 3 You
__ and Ice: 4 Fire
Andie: 9 MacDowell
And I Love Her (1964 song) artist: Beatles
And I Love You So (1973 song) artist: Perry Como
__ and improved: 3 new
__ and Indians: 7 cowboys
__ and Indian War: 6 French
__ and Innocent: 5 Sweet, Young
...and into __ martini: 4 a dry
andiron: 7 firedog
__ and Isolde: 7 Tristan
__ and Issas: 5 Afars
__ and I, The: 3 Egg 4 King 5 Klone
__ and Ives: 7 Currier
__ and Ivory: 5 Ebony
__ and Janis: 4 Arlo
__ and Jeff: 4 Mutt
__ and Jeremy: 4 Chad
__ and jerk: 5 clean
__ and Jerry: 3 Tom
__ and jetsam: 7 flotsam
__ and Jill: 4 Jack
And Jill came tumbling __: 5 after
__ and Jim: 5 Jules
__ and Joan: 5 Darby 6 Bobbin
__ and Johnny: 5 Santo 7 Frankie
__ and joy: 5 pride 7 comfort
__ and Judy: 5 Punch
__ and Juliet: 5 Romeo
... And Justice for All (1979 film)
cast: John Forsythe, Al Pacino, Lee Strasberg, Jack Warden
director: Norman Jewison
__ and kicking: 5 alive
__ and kin: 4 kith
__ and labor: 5 parts
__ and ladder: 4 hook
__ and Ladders: 6 Chutes
__-and-ladies: 5 lords
__ and last: 5 first
...__ and lasting peace: 5 a just
__ and Leander: 4 Hero
__ and learn: 4 live
__ and left: 5 right
__ and Let Die: 4 Live
__ and letters: 4 arts
__ and Lisa: 5 David
__ and Livingstone: 7 Stanley
__ and loan: 7 savings
__ and Lomb: 6 Bausch
__ and loss: 6 profit
__ and Lovers: 4 Sons 7 Friends
__ and low: 4 high
__ and Lowdown: 5 Sweet
__ and Ludmilla: 7 Russlan
__ and Mabel: 4 Cain, Mack
__ and Magog: 3 Gog
__ and main: 5 might
And make it snappy!: 3 PDQ 6 pronto
__ and Mammon: 3 God
__ and Marge: 4 Myrt
__ and Marian: 5 Robin
__ and Marie: 5 Donny
__ and Marriage: 4 Love
__ and Martin: 5 Rowan
__ and Mary: 7 William
__-and-match: 3 mix
__ and Maude: 6 Harold
__ and Me: 3 You 5 Molly, Roger
__ and mean: 4 lean
__ and means: 4 ways
__ and Meek: 3 Eek
__ and mehitabel: 5 archy
__ and mighty: 4 high
__ and Mike: 3 Pat
__ and mild: 4 meek
And miles to go before I __: 5 sleep
__ and minds: 6 hearts
__ and mirrors: 5 smoke
__ and Misdemeanors: 6 Crimes
__-and-miss: 3 hit
__ and Models: 7 Artists
__ and Moe: 4 Izzy
and more: 3 etc.
__ and mortar: 6 bricks, clicks
__ and motion study: 4 time
__ and mouse: 3 cat
__ and Mrs. Muir, The: 5 Ghost
__ and My Gal: 5 For Me
__ and nail: 5 tooth
__ and Nancy: 3 Sid
__ and near: 3 far
__ and needles: 4 pins
__ and Noble: 6 Barnes
...and not __ to drink: 5 a drop
...__ and not heard: 4 seen
__ and Nothingness: 5 Being
__ and now: 4 here
And Now for Something Completely Different (1972 film)
cast: Graham Chapman, John Cleese, Terry Gilliam, Eric Idle, Terry Jones, Michael Palin
__ and Old Lace: 7 Arsenic
__ and Oman: 6 Muscat
__ and omega: 5 alpha
__ and on: 3 off
__ and onions: 5 liver
__ and only: 3 one
__ and Only: 5 My One
__ and order: 3 law
Andorra: 4 city, town 6 nation 7 capital, country
locale: 6 Europe
neighbor: 5 Spain 6 France
and others: 4 et al.
__ and Other Strangers: 6 Lovers
andouille: 4 meat
__ and Our Gang: 6 Spanky
__ and out: 4 down, over
__-and-outer: 4 down
__ and outs: 3 ins
Andover: 4 city, town 6 school 10 prep school
address: 3 sir
attendee: 5 pupil
locale: 4 Mass. 9 Minnesota
__ and pains: 5 aches
__ and papa: 4 mama
__ and parcel: 4 part
__ and paste: 3 cut
__ and Peace: 3 War
__ and peck: 4 hunt
__ and penates: 5 lares
__ and pepper: 4 salt
__ and Perrins: 3 Lea
__ and pieces: 4 bits
__-and-pinion: 4 rack
__ and Pins: 7 Needles
__ and play: 4 plug
__ and Plenty: 4 Good
__ and Pluck: 4 Luck
__ and polish: 4 spit
__ and Pollux: 6 Castor
__ and pony show: 3 dog
__-and-pop: 3 mom
__ and potatoes: 4 meat
__ and Prejudice: 5 Pride
__ and Present Danger: 5 Clear
And pretty maids all in __: 4 a row
__ and proper: 3 due 4 prim
__ and puff: 4 huff
__ and Punishment: 5 Crime
__-and-putt: 5 pitch
__ and Pythias: 5 Damon
__ and quarter: 4 draw
__ and quiet: 5 peace
__ and rabbet: 6 square
Andrade, Mario: 4 poet 9 Brazilian
__ and Rain: 4 Fire
__ and rat: 3 cat
__ and rave: 4 rant
Andre: 6 Agassi, Dawson, de Toth 8 Braugher
André: 4 Gide 5 Lwoff, Watts 6 Agassi, Ampère, Breton, Dawson, Derain, Norton, Previn 7 Citroën, Maginot, Malraux, Maurois 8 Cournand, Eglevsky 9 de Chénier
ex: 3 Mia
in English: 6 Andrew
see also French
Andrea: 5 Doria, Leeds 7 McArdle 8 del Sarto, Mantegna, Mitchell, Palladio 10 Marcovicci
in English: 6 Andrew
Andrea __: 5 Doria
Andrea __ Robbia: 5 Della
Andrea del Sarto: 4 poem 6 artist 7 Italian, painter
author: Robert Browning
Andrea Doria: 4 boat, ship 5 liner
__ and ready: 4 good
__-and-ready: 5 rough
Andreanof island: 4 Atka
Andreas: 8 Gryphius, Marggraf, Vesalius
in English: 6 Andrew
__ Andreas Fault: 3 San
Andre de __: 4 Toth
__ and reel: 3 rod 4 bead
Andrei: 4 Bely 7 Amalrik, Gromyko 8 Sakharov
see also Russian
Andres: 9 Galarraga
Andrés: 5 Bello 7 Segovia
Andress, Ursula: 7 actress
film: 4 for Texas (1963)
Casino Royale (1967)
Dr. No (1962)
Fun in Acapulco (1963)
She (1965)
spouse: John Derek
Andre the __: 5 Giant
Andretti, Mario: 9 auto racer
milieu: 5 track
__-andrew: 5 merry
Andrew: 3 Ure 4 Gold, Lang, Shue 5 Cuomo, Davis, saint, Wyeth, Young 6 Huxley, Marton, Mellon, Motion, Tobias 7 Bergman, Fleming, Greeley, Jackson, Johnson, Marvell, Schally, Stevens, Windsor 8 Burnside, Carnegie, McCarthy, McLaglen 10 Duke of York
brother of ~: 6 Edward 7 Charles
ex: 5 Sarah 6 Fergie
in French: 5 André
in German: 7 Andreas
in Italian: 6 Andrea
sister: 4 Anne
Andrew __ Clay: 4 Dice
Andrew __ Webber: 5 Lloyd
Andrews: 3 AFB 4 Dana, Tige 5 Julie, Patty 6 Maxene 7 LaVerne
Andrews __: 7 Sisters
Andrews, Dana: 5 actor
film: The Best Years of Our Lives (1946)
Boomerang! (1947)
Canyon Passage (1946)
Curse of the Demon (1957)
The Frogmen (1951)
The Iron Curtain (1948)
I Want You (1951)
Kit Carson (1940)
Laura (1944)
My Foolish Heart (1949)
The Ox-Bow Incident (1943)
The Purple Heart (1944)
State Fair (1945)
Three Hours to Kill (1954)
A Walk in the Sun (1945)
Where the Sidewalk Ends (1950)
While the City Sleeps (1956)
Wing and a Prayer (1944)
Andrews, Julie: 4 Dame 6 singer 7 actress
film: 10 (1979)
The Americanization of Emily (1964)
Darling Lili (1970)
Hawaii (1966)
Mary Poppins (1964, AA)
The Princess Diaries (2001)
S.O.B. (1981)

The Sound of Music (1965)
Star! (1968)
The Tamarind Seed (1974)
That's Life! (1986)
Thoroughly Modern Millie (1967)
Torn Curtain (1966)
Victor/Victoria (1982)
spouse: Blake Edwards
Andrews Sisters: 4 trio
members: Patty, Maxene, LaVerne
song: Bei Mir Bist du Schoen (1938)
Boogie Woogie Bugle Boy (1941)
Rum and Coca-Cola (1945)
Andreyev, Leonid: 6 writer **7** Russian
Andric, Ivo: 6 writer **7** Bosnian **8** Nobelist
__-and-ride: 4 kiss, park
__ and robbers: 4 cops
Androcles: 5 Roman, slave
friend: 4 lion
Androcles and the Lion: 4 film, play
author: George Bernard Shaw
cast: Jean Simmons, Alan Young
director: Chester Erskine
locale: 5 arena
android
model: 5 human
relative: 5 robot
Star Trek ~: 4 Data
__ and roll: 4 rock
Andromache author: Euripides
Andromache, husband of: 6 Hector
Andromaque author: Jean Racine
Andromeda
daughter of ~: 10 Gorgophone
husband of ~: 7 Perseus
parent of ~: 7 Cepheus **10** Cassiopeia
son of ~: 6 Heleus, Mestor, Perses **7** Alcaeus, Cynurus **9** Electyron, Sthenelus
Andromeda __: 6 galaxy, strain
Andromeda Strain, The author: Michael Crichton
Andronicus: 5 saint
__ Andronicus: 5 Titus
androphobe fear: 3 men
Andropov: 4 Yuri
__ and Roses: 5 Bread, Tears
Andros locale: 7 Bahamas
__ and ruin: 5 wrack
__ and run: 3 cut, eat, hit
__-and-run: 5 pitch
__ and running: 3 off
Andrzej: 5 Wajda
ands
no ifs ~ or buts: 7 exactly **10** absolutely, definitely, positively
__ and saddles: 5 boots
__ and Sade: 3 Vic
__-and-salt: 6 pepper
__ and Sand: 5 Blood
...__ and sane Fourth: 5 a safe
__ and Satires: 4 Odes
__ and saucer: 3 cup
__ and sciences: 4 arts
__ and scrape: 3 bow
__ and Sedition Acts: 5 Alien
__ and see: 4 wait
__-and-seek: 4 hide
__ and Sensibility: 5 Sense
__-and-serve: 5 brown
__ and shaker: 5 mover
__ and Sheba: 7 Solomon
__ and shine: 4 rise
__-and-shoot: 5 point
__ and shoulders: 4 head
__ and Shout: 5 Twist
__ and shovel: 4 pick
__-and-shut: 4 open
__ and sickle: 6 hammer
__ and sign in please: 5 Enter
__ and Sing!: 5 Awake
__ and Sixpence, The: 4 Moon
__ and skittles: 4 beer
__ and Smell the Roses: 4 Stop
__ and Smoke: 6 Summer
and so __: 5 forth, to bed **6** it goes
__ and soda: 6 scotch
and so forth: 3 etc.
__ and Son: 6 Dombey **7** Sanford
__, ands, or buts: 5 no ifs
And so to bed writer: 5 Pepys
__ and soul: 4 body **5** heart
__ and sound: 4 safe
__-and-sour: 5 sweet
__-and-span: 4 spic **5** spick
__-and-spoke: 3 hub
__ and spoon race: 3 egg
__ and square: 4 fair
__ and squeak: 6 bubble
__ and Stacey: 3 Ned
__-and-stick: 4 peel **6** carrot
And Still __: 5 I Rise
__ and Stimpy: 3 Ren
__ and Stream: 5 Field
__ and Stress: 5 Storm
__ and Stripes: 5 Stars
__ and substance: 3 sum
__-and-suiter: 5 cloak
__ and sway: 5 swing
__ and sweet: 5 short
__ and switch: 4 bait
__ and Sympathy: 3 Tea
__ and Taboo: 5 Totem
__ and tackle: 5 block
__ and take: 3 put **4** give
__ and take notice: 5 sit up
__ and tan: 5 black
__ and tear: 4 wear
__ and tell: 4 kiss, show
__-and-ten: 4 five
__ and tenon: 7 mortise
__ and terminer: 4 oyer
__ and that: 4 this
And that __ hay!: 4 ain't
And That Reminds Me (1957 song)
artist: Della Reese
And that's the way __: 4 it is
And the __ Played On: 4 Band
And the __ Sing: 6 Angels
__ and the Americans: 3 Jay
__ and the Arrow, The: 5 Flame
__ and the Art of Motorcycle Maintenance: 3 Zen
__ and the Bandit: 6 Smokey
And the Band Played On actor: 4 Alda, Gere **6** Modine
__ and the Beast: 6 Beauty
__ and the Beautiful, The: 3 Bad **4** Bold
__ and the Bees, The: 5 Birds
__ and the Belmonts: 4 Dion
__ and the Black, The: 3 Red
__ and the Blowfish: 6 Hootie
__ and the Brightest, The: 4 Best
__ and the Canary, The: 3 Cat
__ and the Cruisers: 5 Eddie
__ and the Dead, The: 5 Naked, Quick
__ and the Detectives: 4 Emil
__ and the Dominos: 5 Derek
__ and the Dragon: 3 Bel
__ and the Dreamers: 7 Freddie
__ and the Ecstasy, The: 5 Agony
__ and the Family Stone: 3 Sly
__ and the Fatman: 4 Jake
__ and the Fiddle, The: 3 Cat
__ and the Furious, The: 4 Fast
__ and the Fury, The: 5 Sound
__ and the Gang: 4 Kool
__ and the Giant Peach: 5 James
__ and the Glory, The: 5 Power
__ and the Hound, The: 3 Fox
__ and the Id, The: 3 Ego
__ and the Jets: 6 Bennie
__ and the Juniors: 5 Danny
__ and the King of Siam: 4 Anna
__ and the Limelites: 4 Shep
And the Lord set __ upon Cain...: 5 a mark
__ and the Man: 4 Arms **5** Chico
__ and the Mighty, The: 4 High
__ and the Minor, The: 5 Major
and then __: 4 some **6** I wrote
__ and then: 3 now **5** there
__ and the Night Visitors: 5 Amahl
And Then There Were None: 4 film **5** novel
cast: Barry Fitzgerald, Louis Hayward, Walter Huston
director: René Clair
writer: Agatha Christie
__ and the Pacemakers: 5 Gerry
__ and the Papas, The: 5 Mamas
__ and the Pauper, The: 6 Prince
__ and the Paycock: 4 Juno
__ and the Pebble, The: 4 Clod
__ and the Pendulum, The: 3 Pit
__ and the Pirates: 5 Terry
__ and the Pussycats: 5 Josie
__ and the Pussycat, The: 3 Owl
__ and there: 4 here, then
And thereby hangs __: 5 a tale
__ and the Restless, The: 5 Young
__ and the Romantics: 4 Ruby
__ and the Rose, The: 4 Ring **5** Sword **7** Slipper
__ and the Seven Hoods: 5 Robin
__ and the short of it, the: 4 long
__ and the Single Girl: 3 Sex
__ and the Swan: 4 Leda
__ and the Tramp: 4 Lady
__ and the Wolf: 5 Peter
__ and thin: 5 thick
__ and think: 4 stop
And This __ Beloved: 4 Is My
__ and Thisbe: 7 Pyramus
__ and thither: 6 hither
__ and thread: 6 needle
__ and Thummim: 4 Urim
__ and tide: 4 time
__ and tie: 4 suit
__ and Tina Turner: 3 Ike
__ and tired: 4 sick
__ and tittle: 3 jot
...and to __ good night!: 4 all a
__-and-toe: 4 heel
__ and tongs: 6 hammer
__ and tonic: 3 gin
__ and Tonto: 5 Harry
And to Think That I Saw It on Mulberry Street author: Dr. Seuss
__ and Tragedy: 7 Triumph
__ and trouble: 4 toil
__ and true: 5 tried
__ and tuck: 3 nip
__ and tucker: 3 bib
__-and-tumble: 5 rough
__ and turf: 4 surf
__ and turn: 4 toss
__ and Turnin': 6 Tossin'
__-and-turn indicator: 4 bank
__ and verse: 7 chapter
__ and vigor: 3 vim
__ and vinegar: 3 oil
__ and void: 4 null
__-and-wear: 4 wash
__ and weave: 3 bob
__ and well: 5 alive
And we'll have __ good time: 5 a real
__ and Wesson: 5 Smith
__ and western: 7 country
And When I Die (1969 song) artist: Blood, Sweat & Tears
__ and wherefores: 4 whys
__ and whey: 5 curds
__ and whistles: 5 bells
__ and white: 5 black
__ and wide: 3 far
__ and wife: 3 man
__ and Winding Road, The: 4 Long
__ and Wine: 5 Bread
__ and wing: 4 buck
__ and wiser: 5 older
__ and woof: 4 warp
__-and-woolly: 4 wild
Andy: 3 Kim **4** Bean, Capp, Dick, doll, Gibb, Gump **5** Clyde, Hardy **6** Devine, Garcia, Rooney, Warhol **7** Kaufman, rag doll, Russell, Tennant **8** Bathgate, Griffith, Pettitte, Van Slyke, Williams **10** Granatelli, Robustelli
aunt: 3 Bee
partner: 4 Amos
__ Andy: 5 Amos 'n', Handy **7** Raggedy
__ and yang: 3 yin
__, and ye shall...: 3 Ask
...and yet so __: 3 far
Andy Griffith Show, The (CBS sitcom)
cast: Frances Bavier (Aunt Bee Taylor)
Elinor Donahue (Ellie Walker)
Andy Griffith (Andy Taylor)
Ronny Howard (Opie Taylor)
Don Knotts (Barney Fife)
George Lindsey (Goober Pyle)
Hal Smith (Otis Campbell)
dog: 8 Gulliver
setting: Mayberry, N. Car.
__ and yon: 6 hither **7** thither
__ and Zooey: 6 Franny
anear: 4 nigh **5** close
__ an ear: 4 bend, give, lend
__ an ear to the ground: 4 have, keep
anecdotal knowledge: 3 ana **4** lore **5** myths, tales **6** fables **7** legends, sayings **10** traditions
anecdote: 4 tale, yarn **5** story **9** narration, narrative
anecdotist: 8 narrator **9** raconteur
__ a neck: 5 win by
__ an egg: 3 lay
anelace: 5 sword
__ Ane Langdon: 3 Sue
anemia: 6 pallor **7** fatigue, frailty, wanness **8** debility, paleness, puniness, weakness **9** fragility, tiredness **10** enervation, exhaustion, feebleness, insipidity, pallidness
anemic: 3 wan **4** pale, puny, weak **5** frail, pasty, wimpy **6** atonic, effete, feeble, flimsy, infirm, sallow **7** fragile, wimpish **8** delicate, helpless, listless, pithless **9** faltering, powerless **10** exsanguine, vulnerable
anemometer: 5 gauge
reading: 3 vel. **8** velocity
spinner: 4 gust, wind
anemone: 5 plant **6** flower
sea ~: 5 polyp **6** animal
__ anemone: 3 rue, sea **4** wood **5** clown, poppy
__ an end to: 3 put
anent: 2 re **4** as to, in re **5** about **9** as regards, regarding **10** concerning
__ an era, the: 5 end of
anesthetic: 3 gas **4** drug, numb **5** ether **6** ethane, opiate **7** anodyne, dulling, numbing **8** deadened, hypnotic, narcotic, sedative **9** analgesic, deadening, soporific **10** painkiller
__ anesthetic: 5 local
anesthetize: 4 numb **6** benumb, deaden
anesthetized: 4 numb **5** under **9** unfeeling
anet: 4 dill
Aneto: 4 peak **5** mount **8** mountain
locale: 5 Spain **6** Europe **8** Pyrenees
anew: 4 over **5** again, fresh, newly **6** afresh, de novo, lately **7** freshly **8** once more, recently **9** once again, over again **10** from the top
in Latin: 6 de nova
__ a New Day: 4 Many
__ an eye on: 4 keep
__ an eye to: 4 with
Anfinsen, Christian: 7 chemist **8** Nobelist

anfractuous: **4** mazy **5** curvy, snaky **6** coiled, curved, curvey, volute **7** crooked, sinuous, turning, twisted, winding **8** flexuous, tortuous **10** convoluted, meandering, serpentine
Ang: **3** Lee
Angara: **5** river
  city on the ~: **6** Bratsk
  locale: **6** Russia
ange feature: **4** aile
angel: **2** jo **3** gem, pet **4** baby, dear, jill, love **5** amour, chéri, cooky, cutey, cutie, deary, donor, dream, ducky, flame, honey, jewel, leman, lover, lovey, money, novia, novio, saint, sugar, sweet, Uriel **6** Azrael, backer, bon ami, chérie, cherub, cookie, dautie, dearie, Moroni, patron, seraph, steady, sweets, vision **7** beloved, darling, dearest, dear one, Gabriel, grantor, Israfil, Lucifer, Michael, paragon, pigsney, Raphael, schatzi, sponsor, squeeze, sweetie, tootsie **8** chou-chou, cutie pie, dowsabel, dulcinea, guardian, ladylove, lovebird, macushla, paramour, precious, snookums, sugar pie, sweetums, treasure, truelove **9** bonne amie, boyfriend, dreamboat, inamorata, inamorato, petit chou, supporter, valentine **10** benefactor, girlfriend, heartthrob, honeybunch, mavourneen, sweetheart, sweetie pie, turtledove, underwrite
  accessory: **4** halo, harp
  be an ~: **4** give
  ender: **4** fish
  fallen ~: **5** devil, Satan **6** Belial, diablo **7** evil one, Lucifer **9** Beelzebub
  guardian ~: **6** savior **7** saviour
  hair: **5** pasta
  in Persian mythology: **3** mah
  little ~: **4** baby **5** child
  nightmare: **4** flop **6** turkey
  place: **6** heaven
  theater ~: **6** backer, patron
angel ___: **3** bed **4** cake, hair **5** light, shark
angel ___ cake: **4** food
Angel: **5** falls **7** Cordero, Vanessa **9** waterfall
  rival: **3** Cub, Met, Red **4** Expo, Twin **5** Astro, Brave, Giant, Padre, Rocky, Royal, Tiger **6** Brewer, Dodger, Indian, Marlin, Oriole, Philly, Pirate, Ranger, Red Sox, Yankee **7** Blue Jay, Mariner **8** Athletic, Cardinal, Devil Ray, White Sox
Angel ___: **4** Baby, Eyes **5** Falls
Angel ___ Morning: **5** of the
Angel ___ Shoulder: **4** on My
___ Angel: **4** Blue, I'm No, Teen **5** Black, Earth, Hell's **6** Fallen, Johnny, Street
Angela: **5** Davis **6** Merici **7** Bassett **8** Baddeley, Lansbury **10** Cartwright
  Broadway role for ~: **4** Mame
Angel and the Badman (1947 film)
  cast: Harry Carey, Gail Russell, John Wayne
Angela's Ashes: **4** book, film
  author: Frank McCourt
  cast: Joe Breen, Robert Carlyle, Ciaran Owens, Emily Watson
  director: Alan Parker
  sequel: **3** 'Tis
Angel at My Table, An (1990 film)
  cast: Karen Fergusson, Kerry Fox, Alexia Keogh
  director: Jane Campion
Angel Baby (1961 film)
  cast: George Hamilton, Salome Jens
___ Angeles, CA: **3** Los
Angeles, Victoria de los: **6** singer **7** soprano
  specialty: **5** opera
Angel Eyes (2001 film)
  cast: Sonia Braga, Jim Caviezel, Terrence Howard, Jennifer Lopez
  director: Luis Mandoki
Angel Eyes (1989 song) artist: Jeff Healey Band
angelfish: **3** pet
angel food ___: **4** cake
angelhair: **5** pasta
  alternative: **4** orzo, ziti **5** penne **6** noodle **7** lasagna, lasagne, pastina, ravioli **8** bucatini, couscous, farfalle, linguine, linguini, macaroni, rigatoni **9** agnolotti, cavatelli, manicotti, spaghetti **10** cannelloni, fettuccini, tortellini, vermicelli
Angelia (1989 song) artist: Richard Marx
angelic: **4** holy **5** godly, pious, sweet **6** devout, divine **7** lovable, saintly **8** adorable, beatific, cherubic, ethereal, heavenly, innocent, loveable, seraphic, supernal **9** beautiful, celestial, righteous **10** seraphical
  glow: **4** aura
  provide an ~ aura: **6** enhalo
angelica: **4** herb
Angelico, Fra: **6** artist **7** painter
  homeland: **5** Italy
Angelina: **5** Jolie
  father: **3** Jon
Angeli, Pier: **7** actress
  film: The Angry Silence (1960)
    Somebody Up There Likes Me (1956)
    The Story of Three Loves (1953)
  spouse: Vic Damone
Angélique composer: **5** Ibert
Angell: **5** Roger **6** Norman
Angel Levine, The (1970 film)
  cast: Harry Belafonte, Ida Kaminska, Zero Mostel
  director: Jan Kadar
Angell, Norman: **8** Nobelist
Angeln: **3** cow **4** bull **6** bovine, cattle
Angelo: **6** Dundee, Maggio
Angel of Light author: Joyce Carol Oates
Angel of the Battlefield: **6** Barton
Angel of the Morning (song) artist: Juice Newton, Merrillee Rush and the Turnabouts
Angel of the Odd, The author: Edgar Allan Poe
Angelo, My Love (1983 film) director: Robert Duvall
Angel on My Shoulder (1946 film)
  cast: Anne Baxter, Paul Muni, Claude Rains
  director: Archie Mayo
___ Angelo, TX: **3** San
Angelou, Maya: **4** poet
  work: Gather Together in My Name
    The Heart of a Woman
    How Sheba Sings the Song
    I Know Why the Caged Bird Sings
    I Shall Not Be Moved
    Lessons in Living
    Life Doesn't Frighten Me
    Shaker, Why Don't You Sing
    A Song Flung up to Heaven
    Still I Rise
    Wouldn't Take Nothing for My Journey Now
angel's ___: **4** hair **7** trumpet
Angels: **3** ten **4** team
  home: **7** Anaheim **10** California
  org.: **3** ALW, MLB
  sport: **8** baseball
___ Angels: **5** Hell's
Angels & Insects (1995 film)
  cast: Patsy Kensit, Kristin Scott Thomas
  director: Philip Haas
Angels in the Outfield (1951 film)
  cast: Paul Douglas, Janet Leigh, Keenan Wynn
Angels in the Outfield (1994 film)
  cast: Tony Danza, William Dear, Brenda Fricker, Danny Glover
Angel (song) artist: Aerosmith, Madonna, Sarah McLachlan
Angels Over Broadway (1940 film)
  cast: Douglas Fairbanks Jr., Rita Hayworth, Thomas Mitchell
  director: Ben Hecht
Angels song: My Boyfriend's Back (1963)
Angels With Dirty Faces (1938 film)
  cast: Humphrey Bogart, James Cagney, Pat O'Brien
  director: Michael Curtiz
___ Angel, The: **4** Blue, Dark, Lost
Angel, The artist: **4** Erté
angelus: **4** bell **10** church bell
  pair on an ~: **4** alae
anger: **3** get, ire, sin, vex **4** bait, boil, burn, fury, gall, heat, miff, rage, rile, roil **5** annoy, get to, peeve, pique, shock, steam, venom, wrath **6** arouse, burn up, choler, dander, enmity, enrage, fire up, get mad, madden, nettle, offend, rankle, ruffle, spleen, stir up, tee off, temper, tirade **7** affront, agitate, dudgeon, emotion, enflame, hackles, incense, inflame, offense, outrage, passion, perturb, provoke, steam up, tick off, umbrage **8** acrimony, embitter, imbitter, irritate, rankling, vexation **9** aggravate, agitation, animosity, displease, distemper, hostility, infuriate, petulance, surliness **10** antagonism, antagonize, conniption, exasperate, irritation, resentment, run afoul of, unkindness
  display of ~: **5** scene
  express, as ~: **4** vent
  inclination to ~: **4** bile
  internalize ~: **4** fret, fume, stew **5** chafe **6** seethe
  symbol of ~: **4** fist
  unleash one's ~: **4** rail, rant, rave, yell **5** erupt, freak, storm **6** blow up, scream **7** bluster, bristle, explode, rampage **8** boil over, have a fit, run amuck **9** blow a fuse, fulminate, go berserk **10** hit the roof, kick up a row
angered: **3** hot, mad **4** ired, sore, ugly, warm **5** cross, het up, huffy, irate, livid, moody, riled, sharp, upset, vexed, wroth **6** ablaze, fierce, fuming, heated, ireful, miffed, peeved, piqued, raging, red-hot, stormy **7** boiling, burnt up, enraged, furious, hostile, steamed, teed off **8** choleric, fighting, frowning, incensed, inflamed, lowering, maddened, outraged, spiteful, up in arms, vehement, worked up, wrathful **9** indignant, irascible, irritated, resentful, seeing red, splenetic, ticked off **10** infuriated, up in the air
  easily ~: **5** testy
Angers: **4** city, town
  locale: **6** France
Angie: **6** Harmon **8** Everhart **9** Dickinson
Angie (1994 film)
  cast: Geena Davis, James Gandolfini, Stephen Rea
  director: Martha Coolidge
Angie (1973 song) artist: Rolling Stones
Angie Baby (1974 song) artist: Helen Reddy
angioplasty target: **6** artery
angiosperm: **5** plant
angklung: **4** bell **10** instrument, percussion
  origin: **4** Bali
Angkor ___: **3** Vat, Wat **4** Thom
___ anglais: **3** cor **6** jardin
___ anglaise: **5** crème
angle: **3** aim, bow **4** bend, bias, fish, hook, ruse, side, tilt **5** crook, light, phase, pitch, slant, slope, stand, troll **6** corner, dogleg, recess, scheme **7** flexure, outlook, purpose **8** flection, maneuver, position, strategy **9** intention, viewpoint **10** motivation, standpoint
  at an ~: **5** atilt, bevel **6** aslant **9** crossways, crosswise, on the bias, slantways, slantwise **10** diagonally
  be at an ~: **4** lean, tilt
  botanist's ~: **4** axil
  brace: **4** L bar
  carpenter's ~: **5** bevel
  combining form: **4** goni- **5** gonio-
  ender: **4** worm
  (for): **3** aim, try
  kind of ~: **5** acute, right **6** obtuse, reflex
  off: **4** skew, veer **5** slant
  on an ~: **6** aslant, aslope
  projecting ~: **4** cant
  reporter ~: **5** focus **9** viewpoint **10** standpoint
  right ~: **3** ell
  sharp ~: **3** zag, zig
  starter: **3** tri **4** pent, rect
  writer's ~: **5** focus, slant
angle ___: **3** bar **4** iron, shot **5** board, cleat, of dip, of lag, of yaw, plate **6** collar **7** bracket
___ angle: **4** face, hour, seat **5** acute, Bragg, drift, glide, phase, plane, polar, right, round, shelf, solid **6** danger, facial, obtuse, reflex **7** central, oblique
Angle
  counterpart: **5** Saxon
angled: **4** bent **5** bevel **6** skewed **7** crooked **8** diagonal
___-angle lens: **4** wide
angle of ___: **3** dip, lag, yaw **4** lead, roll, view **5** climb, pitch, slide, stall **6** attack, repose
angler: **5** eeler **6** fisher **7** trawler, troller **8** piscator **9** fisherman
  see also fisherman
angles
  at right ~: **4** orth., perp. **5** plumb **10** orthogonal
  at right ~ to the keel: **5** abeam
  without ~: **6** agonic
Anglet: **4** city, town
  locale: **6** France
___ Anglia: **4** East
Anglican
  clergyman: **5** vicar
  headdress: **5** mitre
Anglican ___: **5** chant **6** Church
angling
  see fishing
Anglo-___: **5** Irish, Latin, Saxon **6** French, Gallic, Indian, Norman
Anglophobe fear: **7** England
Anglo-Saxon
  bailiff: **5** reeve
  council: **5** witan
  freeman: **5** ceorl
  kingdom: **5** Essex
  letter: **3** edh **4** wynn, yogh
  lord: **5** thane, thegn
  money: **3** ora **5** sceat **7** sceatta
  tax: **4** geld
  worker: **4** esne
Angola: **6** nation **7** country
  capital: **6** Luanda
  desert: **5** Namib
  language: **6** Mbundu
  money: **4** lwei
  neighbor: **5** Congo **6** Zambia **7** Namibia
  people: **5** Lunda **6** Herero, Mbundu

9 Ovimbundu
rebel org.: 5 UNITA
Angora: 3 cat **4** goat, wool **5** felid **6** fabric, feline, rabbit
relative: 4 geep, ibex, tahr, thar **7** markhor **8** markhoor
today: 6 Ankara
angry: 3 hot, mad **4** ired, sore, ugly, warm **5** cross, het up, huffy, irate, livid, moody, riled, sharp, upset, vexed, wroth **6** ablaze, fierce, fuming, galled, heated, ireful, miffed, peeved, piqued, raging, red-hot, stormy **7** boiling, burnt up, enraged, furious, hostile, steamed, teed off **8** choleric, fighting, frowning, hopped up, incensed, inflamed, lowering, maddened, outraged, reddened, spiteful, up in arms, vehement, volcanic, white-hot, worked up, wrathful **9** indignant, irascible, irritated, resentful, seeing red, splenetic, ticked off, wrought up **10** hopping mad, infuriated, up in the air
be ~: 4 burn **6** seethe, simmer **7** bristle
be ~ about: 6 resent
become ~: 6 get mad
be quietly ~: 4 fume
get ~: 4 fume, snap **6** rear up, see red
look: 5 frown, glare, scowl
looking ~: 6 aglare
make ~: 3 ire **4** rile **5** frost, peeve **6** burn up, enrage, fire up, madden **9** infuriate
mood: 4 huff, snit
one: 5 rager
reaction: 4 rise
retort: 5 my eye
with: 5 mad at **6** down on
angry ___ man: 5 young
___ Angry Man, The: 4 Last
___ Angry Men: 5 Seven **6** Twelve
Angry Silence, The (1960 film)
cast: Pier Angeli, Sir Richard Attenborough
Angry Young Men, The author: 4 Amis
angst: 3 woe **4** ache, fear **5** blues, dread, worry **7** anxiety, malaise **8** disquiet **10** inquietude, uneasiness
angstrom ___: 4 unit
Ångström, Anders: 7 Swedish **9** physicist **10** astronomer
anguilliform creature: 3 eel
anguish: 3 woe **4** ache, care, fret, hell, pain **5** agony, dolor, gloom, grief, worry, wound **6** harrow, misery, ordeal, regret, sorrow, trauma **7** despair, remorse, sadness, torment, torture, travail **8** distress, hangover, the blues **9** dejection, heartache, suffering **10** bitterness, depression, desolation, heartbreak, heavy heart, loneliness, melancholy
cry of ~: 4 oh no
anguished: 5 woful **6** tragic, woeful **8** dolorous, tragical
be ~: 4 ache
angular: 4 bent, lean **5** bowed, gaunt, lanky **6** akimbo, meager, skewed, zigzag **7** crooked, scrawny, v-shaped, winding **8** cockeyed
combining form: 3 -gon
cut: 5 notch
lead-in: 3 tri **4** equi, rect
letter: 3 ell
Angus: 3 cow **4** bull, Scot **5** steer, Young **6** bovine, cattle, Wilson
___ Angus: 3 Red **5** Black
Anheuser Busch rival: 5 Coors, Pabst, Stroh **8** Heineken
anhinga: 4 bird **6** darter **9** snakebird
Anhui: 7 Chinese **8** province
city: 6 Bengbu
former capital of ~: 6 Anqing
anhydrate: 3 dry **5** parch **9** dehydrate, desiccate, evaporate, exsiccate **10** devitalize
anhydrous: 3 dry **4** arid **5** unwet
ani: 6 cuckoo **8** tickbird **9** blackbird
Ani: 8 DiFranco, Kavafian
___ a nice day!: 4 Have
Anicetus: 4 pope **7** pontiff
anigh, not: 4 afar
___ a Nightingale: 5 Ode to
anil: 3 dye **4** blue **5** shrub **6** indigo
relative: 4 cyan, navy, Nile, teal **5** Alice, azure, slate **6** cobalt, raisin, violet **7** peacock **8** cerulean, sapphire **9** turquoise **10** aquamarine, periwinkle
anile: 6 infirm **9** doddering
aniline ___: 3 dye, oil **5** black
aniline source: 6 indigo
anima: 4 soul **6** psyche
___ anima: 3 con
animadversion: 4 flak, slam **5** flack, knock, swipe **6** rebuke **7** censure **8** reproach **9** criticism, invective, stricture
animal: 2 ox **3** ant, ape, asp, ass, auk, ayu, bat, bee, bot, bug, cat, cod, cow, dab, dog, dor, eel, elk, emu, ern, ewe, fly, fox, fry, gar, ged, gnu, hen, ide, ihi, jay, kea, koi, man, mew, moa, nit, orf, owl, pie, pig, ram, rat, ray, roc, sey, sow, tai, tit, tui, yak **4** anoa, barb, bass, bear, bird, blay, boar, boce, boga, bret, brit, buck, bull, calf, carp, cero, char, chat, chub, chum, coho, colt, coot, crab, crow, cusk, dace, deer, dodo, dory, dove, drum, duck, dupe, emeu, erne, fawn, flea, foal, frog, fugu, game, gnat, goat, goby, grub, guan, gull, hake, hare, hart, hawk, hiku, huia, huss, ibis, jack, jocu, kagu, kaka, kite, kiwi, knot, kudu, lamb, lark, lice, lija, ling, lion, loon, loro, lory, lynx, mado, mapo, mare, masu, mean, meat, merl, mero, mina, mink, mite, mola, mole, moth, mule, myna, nene, opah, orfe, oryx, parr, pega, pest, peto, pike, pogy, pony, pout, puma, pupa, quab, raad, rail, rhea, rook, rudd, ruff, sama, scad, seal, sesi, shad, shag, skil, skua, smew, sole, sora, spet, stag, swan, teal, tern, tick, tine, toad, tody, tope, tuna, ulua, unau, wasp, wild, wolf, wren, zebu **5** akule, aphid, aphis, beast, being, betta, biped, bison, bleak, bolti, booby, borer, brant, bream, brill, bruin, brute, burro, buteo, camel, chimp, chiro, chopa, cimex, cisco, civet, coati, cobia, colin, coney, cooty, crake, crane, dance, danio, dingo, drone, eagle, egret, eider, eland, elver, emmet, feral, filly, finch, galah, goony, goose, grebe, grope, grunt, guasa, guppy, harsh, heron, hilsa, horse, hound, hyena, imago, jager, junco, jurel, koala, koloa, krill, larva, lemur, llama, loach, lotte, louse, macaw, manta, mavis, merle, midge, minah, moose, moray, mouse, murre, mynah, nasty, noddy, okapi, otter, ousel, ouzel, oxeye, panda, pargo, perch, pewee, pewit, pipit, pitta, plane, porgy, potoo, prawn, quail, raven, roach, robin, sable, saker, sargo, saury, scaup, scrod, serin, shama, shark, sheep, skate, skunk, sloth, smelt, smolt, snake, snipe, snook, solan, sprat, steed, steer, stilt, stint, stoat, stork, swift, swine, tapir, tench, tetra, tiger, torsk, trout, tunny, twite, vireo, vixen, wahoo, whale, yager, zebra **6** agouti, aimara, alpaca, anabas, avocet, baboon, badger, barbel, barbet, beaver, becard, bedbug, beetle, beluga, beshow, bichir, bigeye, bishop, blenny, bonaci, bonito, bonxie, botfly, bowfin, brolga, brutal, bulbul, burbot, canary, caplin, caribe, chafer, chebec, chigoe, chinch, chough, chukar, cicada, cocoon, condor, congér, conure, cootie, cougar, coyote, cuchia, cuckoo, cunner, curlew, darter, dayfly, dipper, donkey, drongo, dunlin, earthy, earwig, equine, ermine, falcon, feline, ferret, fierce, fulmar, gadfly, gander, gannet, gerbil, godwit, gooney, gopher, grilse, groper, grouse, gunnel, hapuku, heifer, hilsah, hoopoe, hornet, iguana, impala, inanga, insect, Io moth, isopod, jabiru, jacana, jackal, jaeger, jaguar, kakapo, kitten, koodoo, lanner, larvae, linnet, lizard, locust, looper, louvar, maggot, magpie, maigre, mammal, mantid, mantis, marlin, marmot, marten, martin, mayfly, medaka, merlin, minnow, monkey, motmot, mud hen, mullet, musk ox, mussel, nonnat, ocelot, onager, oriole, osprey, parrot, parula, peewit, petrel, phoebe, pigeon, piraña, plaice, plakat, plover, pollan, possum, pouter, puffer, puffin, puneca, python, quezal, rabbit, remora, rodent, roller, roughy, saithe, salele, salema, salmon, saurel, savage, savola, scarab, schrod, scoter, sea mew, sennet, shiner, shrike, shrimp, simian, siskin, sucker, suslik, takahe, tandan, tarpon, tautog, testar, tetard, thrips, thrush, tiñosa, tityra, tomcod, tomtit, toucan, towhee, trogon, turaco, turbot, turkey, tussah, unkind, verdin, vermin, vicuna, walrus, wanton, wapiti, weasel, weever, weevil, whidah, whydah, wigeon, willet, wombat, wrasse, zander **7** alewife, alfiona, anchovy, anhinga, ant lion, axolotl, babbler, bacalao, barbudo, barn owl, beastly, billbug, bittern, bloater, blowfly, bluefin, bluejay, brutish, buffalo, bunting, bustard, buzzard, cabezon, callous, capelin, cariama, caribou, catbird, catfish, cavalla, cheetah, chicken, chigger, codfish, corbina, corvina, cotinga, courser, crappie, creeper, cricket, critter, crittur, croaker, decapod, dogfish, dottrel, dovekey, dovekie, echidna, eelpout, elaenia, elepaio, escolar, fantail, finfoot, finspot, firefly, flycast, gadwall, garlopa, garpike, gazelle, gemsbok, giraffe, gorilla, goshawk, gourami, grackle, gray jay, graylag, graysby, greylag, gribble, grindle, grouper, grunion, guanaco, gudgeon, gurnard, gwyniad, haddock, halcyon, halibut, hamster, harrier, helleri, hen hawk, herring, hexapod, hoatzin, hurtful, inconnu, jacamar, jackass, jackdaw, katydid, kestrel, kinglet, ladybug, lamprey, lapwing, leopard, limpkin, lingcod, lobster, mallard, manakin, marabou, margate, mojarra, mollusc, mollusk, mooneye, mudlark, mustang, nibbler, no-see-um, oldwife, opaleye, opossum, ortolan, ostrich, panther, peacock, peafowl, pelican, penguin, phoenix, pigfoot, piranha, pismire, pochard, polecat, pollack, pollock, pomfret, pompano, quetzal, redpoll, redwing, reptile, ronquil, sandbug, sand dab, sardine, sawfish, scalare, scooter, sculpin, sea bass, seagull, seriema, serpent, skimmer, skylark, snapper, sockeye, souslik, sparrow, sterlet, swallow, sweeper, tanager, tattler, termite, tilapia, tinamou, titlark, torpedo, touraco, unicorn, untamed, varment, varmint, viceroy, vicious, vulture, wagtail, walleye, waxbill, waxwing, whapuku, whiting, widgeon, wolf-eel, wryneck **8** aardvark, albacore, amadavat, amphipod, anableps, anaconda, antelope, arapaima, armyworm, avadavat, barbaric, barnacle, baysmelt, bee-eater, bellbird, bigmouth, blackcap, bloodfin, blowfish, bluebill, bluebird, bluefish, bluegill, bluehead, boatbill, bobolink, bobwhite, brisling, bullhead, bullneck, cabrilla, caracara, cardinal, characin, chimaera, chipmunk, cirriped, cockatoo, conenose, coturnix, crawfish, crayfish, creature, crevalle, curassow, dabchick, didapper, dormouse, dotterel, dragonet, eagle owl, elephant, fiendish, firebrat, fish hawk, flamingo, flathead, flounder, fruit fly, gambusia, garganey, gilthead, glowworm, goldfish, grayback, grayling, grosbeak, guacharo, halfbeak, halfmoon, hawfinch, hedgehog, hemipode, hiwi hiwi, hoactzin, honeybee, hornbill, housefly, inhumane, John Dory, kangaroo, killdeer, kinkajou, kiskadee, lacewing, landrail, longspur, lorikeet, lungfish, mackerel, macruran, manacode, mandrill, manta ray, marabout, marmoset, mealybug, medregal, megapode, menhaden, mole crab, mongoose, moorfowl, mosquito, muckworm, mulloway, murrelet, nannygai, nightjar, notornis, nuthatch, organism, oxpecker, palometa, parakeet, paraquet, paroquet, parroket, pearleye, peetweet, pheasant, pilchard, pitiless, platypus, porpoise, redshank, redstart, reduviid, reindeer, ringdove, ruthless, sadistic, scorpion, screamer, sea bream, sea eagle, sea horse, sea otter, sea raven, shelduck, shoebill, shoveler, silkworm, skipjack, snowbird, squirrel, stallion, starling, stingray, stinkbug, sturgeon, terrapin, thrasher, titmouse, tommycod, topsmelt, tortoise, tragopan, trembler, tremblor, trevally, troupial, tubenose, vengeful, water hen, wheatear, whimbrel, whinchat, whistler, white ant, white-eye, woodchat, woodcock, woodlark, woodworm, wrymouth **9** albatross, alligator, amberjack, amphibian, angelfish, argentine, arthropod, bandicoot, barbarian, barracuda, barreleye, beach flea, beastlike, blackbird, blue shark, broadbill, bullfinch, bumblebee, butterfly, cassowary, chaffinch, chameleon, chickadee, cockateel, cockatiel, cockroach, cormorant, corn borer, crocodile, crossbill, currawong, cutthroat, damselfly, dobsonfly, doodlebug, dorbeetle, Dover sole, dowitcher, dragonfly, dromedary, earthworm, eelblenny, feel about, ferocious, fieldfare, flinthead, francolin, frogmouth, gallinule, gerfalcon, goldeneye, goldfinch, grassquit, greenling, grenadier, groundhog, guillemot, guinea pig, gyrfalcon, hammerkop, jellyfish, kittiwake, lake trout, mallemuck, marsupial, martinico, merciless, merganser, millipede, mollymawk, mollymoke, monstrous, mudminnow, neon tetra, nighthawk, orangutan, ossifrage, pachyderm, pardalote, parrakeet, parroquet, partridge, peregrine, phalarope, pikeperch, porcupine, primitive, ptarmigan, quadruped, razorbill, redbreast, red mullet, sand lance, sandpiper, saturniid, schnapper, sea urchin, seedeater, sharpbill, sheep tick, sheldrake, shellfish, spikedace,

spoonbill, sprigtail, stonechat, surfperch, swordfish, swordtail, tarantula, thickhead, threadfin, topminnow, truculent, trumpeter, tubesnout, turnstone, whitebait, whitefish, wolverine, woodborer, woodchuck, wood louse, yellowfin, zebrafish 10 Beanie Baby, bitterling, blanquillo, bluebottle, brook trout, brown trout, budgerigar, budgerygah, calicoback, chiffchaff, chimpanzee, chinchilla, coelacanth, crustacean, deathwatch, demoiselle, dickcissel, digger wasp, flycatcher, froghopper, goatsucker, greenfinch, greenshank, hammerhead, honeyeater, kingfisher, kookaburra, licentious, nutcracker, pear thrips, pikeblenny, prairie dog, pratincole, red snapper, rhinoceros, rose chafer, salamander, sanderling, sandroller, sea anemone, shearwater, sheathbill, sicklebill, silverside, spittlebug, squaretail, tiger shark, treehopper, troutperch, turtledove, vindictive, whale shark, white cloud, white shark, woodpecker, woolly bear, yellow jack, yellowlegs, yellowtail, zoological
  category: 4 bird, fish 5 breed 6 insect, mammal 7 reptile 9 amphibian, marsupial
  combining form: 2 zo- 3 zoo- 4 -zoon
  doc: 3 DVM, vet
  feed: 4 bran 6 fodder, forage
  prehistoric ~: 4 T-rex 7 aurochs, mammoth 8 allosaur, dinosaur, dire wolf, eohippus, sauropod, smilodon, stegodon, theropod 9 dinothere, iguanodon, pterosaur, stegosaur, supersaur 10 brontosaur, diplodocus, megalosaur, titanosaur 11 brachiosaur, ichthyosaur, pterodactyl, titanothere, triceratops, tyrannosaur
  protection org.: 4 PETA, SPCA 5 ASPCA
  sound: 4 bark, roar 5 bleat, chirp, growl 6 squawk
  see also beast
animal ___: 4 park, pole 5 black, faith 6 rights, starch, warden 7 cracker, kingdom, shelter, spirits
___ animal: 4 moss, pack 5 draft, party
Animal ___: 4 Farm 7 Factory
Animal Crackers: 4 film, play
  author: George S. Kaufman
  cast: Margaret Dumont, Chico Marx, Groucho Marx, Harpo Marx, Zeppo Marx
animalcule: 5 ameba 6 amoeba
animal descriptions, science of: 9 zoography
Animal Factory (2000 film)
  cast: Tom Arnold, Willem Dafoe, Edward Furlong, Mickey Rourke
  director: Steve Buscemi
Animal Farm: 5 fable, novel
  author: George Orwell
  beast: 3 pig
  dog: 6 Jessie 7 Pincher 8 Bluebell
  pig: 8 Napoleon, Old Major, Snowball, Squealer
Animal House
  see National Lampoon's Animal House
Animal Kingdom, The (1932 film)
  cast: Ann Harding, Leslie Howard, Myrna Loy
Animal Planet: 7 station
  alternative: 3 BET, CMT, MTV, PAX, TBS, TLC, TNN, TNT, USA 4 ESPN, HGTV 5 A and E, C-SPAN, Style 6 Noggin, Tech TV, TV Land 7 Court TV, Ovation, SoapNet 8 Lifetime
animals: 5 fauna, stock 9 livestock
  combining form: 3 -zoa
  science of ~: 7 zoology
Animals
  leader: Eric Burdon
  song: The House of the Rising Sun (1964)
    San Franciscan Nights (1967)
    See See Rider (1966)
___ Animal, The: 4 Male
Animaniacs
  character: 5 Wakko 7 Buttons
___ Animas, CO: 3 Las
animate: 4 fire, live, spur 5 alive, drive, flush, light, liven, pep up, rouse, spark 6 active, arouse, awaken, excite, incite, infuse, kindle, lively, living, mortal, pump up, thrill, turn on, vivify 7 actuate, dynamic, enliven, inspire, juice up, liven up, organic, quicken 8 activate, energize, enspirit, inspirit, spirited, vitalize 9 breathing, encourage, energetic, galvanize, impassion, inebriate, sprightly, stimulate, vivacious 10 exhilarate, intoxicate, strengthen
animated: 3 gay 4 busy, keen, live, pert, spry, warm 5 alive, astir, brisk, eager, jazzy, light, peppy, perky, vivid, zingy, zippy 6 active, at work, fervid, hearty, hectic, jaunty, lively, living, yeasty 7 buoyant, dashing, dynamic, excited, fervent, hyped-up, rocking, rousing, vibrant, working, zestful, zinging 8 bustling, grooving, inspired, spirited 9 assiduous, ebullient, energetic, exuberant, sprightly, vivacious 10 keen-witted
  character: 4 toon
animated ___: 3 oat 7 cartoon
animation: 3 pep, vim, zip 4 brio, dash, élan, fire, life, snap, soul, zeal, zest, zing 5 oomph, spark, verve, vigor 6 action, bounce, energy, esprit, fervor, gaiety, gayety, spirit 7 cartoon, sparkle 8 activity, buoyance, buoyancy, movement, vitality, vivacity 9 briskness, élan vital, existence, life force 10 ebullience, enthusiasm, exaltation, excitement, exuberance, liveliness
  collectible: 3 cel 4 cell
animato: 5 tempo 6 lively
animosity: 4 hate 5 anger, odium, spite, venom 6 enmity, grudge, hatred, malice, rancor, strife 7 discord, dislike, ill will 8 acrimony, aversion, bad blood, conflict, friction 9 antipathy, hostility, malignity, nastiness, prejudice, virulence 10 antagonism, bitterness, ill feeling, resentment, unkindness
animus: 4 hate, mind, will 5 odium 6 enmity, grudge, hatred, malice, rancor, spirit, temper 7 dislike, ill will, purpose 8 bad blood 9 antipathy, hostility, intention, malignity, surliness 10 antagonism, ill feeling, resentment
anise: 4 herb, seed 5 drink, spice 8 beverage
  flavored drink: 4 ouzo 6 pastis
anise ___: 3 oil 4 seed 6 hyssop 7 camphor
___ anise: 4 star 5 oil of 7 Chinese
anisette: 5 drink 8 beverage
Anissa: 5 Jones
Aniston, Jennifer: 7 actress
  film: The Object of My Affection (1998)
    Rock Star (2001)
  spouse: Brad Pitt
  TV: Friends
Anita: 4 Hill, Kerr, Loos, O'Day, Ward 5 Baker, Desai 6 Bryant, Ekberg, Louise, Morris 8 Brookner, Gillette
___ Anita: 5 Santa
Anitra: 4 Ford
Anitra's Dance composer: 5 Grieg
Anjanette: 5 Comer
Anjelica: 6 Huston
Anjo: 4 city, town
  locale: 5 Japan
Anjou: 4 city, pear, town
  kin: 4 Bosc 6 Comice, Seckel 8 Bartlett
  locale: 6 Canada, Québec
Ankaa: 4 star
Anka, Paul
  homeland: Canada
  song: Dance on Little Girl (1961)
    Diana (1957)
    Eso Beso (1962)
    Having My Baby (1974)
    I Don't Like to Sleep Alone (1975)
    It's Time to Cry (1959)
    Lonely Boy (1959)
    My Home Town (1960)
    One Man Woman/One Woman Man (1974)
    Puppy Love (1960)
    Put Your Head on My Shoulder (1959)
    Times of Your Life (1975)
    You Are My Destiny (1958)
Ankara: 4 city, town 6 Angora 7 capital
  locale: 6 Turkey
Ankeny: 4 city, town
  locale: 4 Iowa
Ankers: 6 Evelyn
ankh shape: 3 tau
ankle: 4 hock 5 joint, talus 6 tarsus 10 astragalus
  animal ~: 4 hock
  bones: 4 tali 5 tarsi
  combining form: 4 tali- 5 tarso-
  counterpart: 5 wrist
  cover: 4 spat
  ender: 4 bone
  hurt an ~: 5 twist
  sore ~ treatment: 6 ice bag 7 ice pack
ankle ___: 4 jerk
ankle-___: 4 deep
anklet: 4 hose, sock 6 bangle 7 hosiery, jewelry 8 ornament
  alternative: 6 argyle
  feature: 3 toe 4 heel 5 clasp 7 elastic
Ankole: 3 cow 4 bull 6 bovine, cattle
ankylosaur feature: 5 armor
Ann: 3 Lee 4 cape, Rule, Todd 5 Blyth, Doran 6 Darrow, Dvorak, Meyers, Miller, Petrie, Turkel, Wilson 7 Beattie, Compton, Harding, Jillian, Landers, rag doll, Sothern 8 Jellicoe, Magnuson, Reinking, Richards, Rutledge, Sheridan 9 Radcliffe 10 Dusenberry, Rutherford, Wedgeworth
  in Russian: 4 Nina
  to Abby: 4 twin
Ann ___: 5 Arbor, Marie 7 Vickers
Ann-___: 7 Margret
___ Ann: 4 Cape 5 Edith 7 Barbara
Anna: 3 Lee 4 Held, Sten 5 Freud, Moffo 6 Neagle, Paquin, Sewell 7 Comnena, Magnani, Pavlova 8 Chlumsky, Christie, Ivanovna, Quindlen 9 Akhmatova, Leonowens 10 Kournikova
Anna ___: 6 Bolena
Anna ___ Alberghetti: 5 Maria
Anna ___ Horsford: 5 Maria
Anna ___ Wong: 3 May
___ Anna: 5 Santa
Anna and the King (1999 film)
  cast: Tom Felton, Jodie Foster, Bai Ling, Chow Yun-Fat
  director: Andy Tennant
Anna and the King of Siam (1946 film)
  cast: Lee J. Cobb, Linda Darnell, Irene Dunne, Rex Harrison, Gale Sondergaard
  director: John Cromwell
Anna author: Robert Burns
Annaba: 4 city, town
  locale: 7 Algeria
Annabel ___: 3 Lee
Annabella: 7 Sciorra
Annabel Lee: 4 poem
  author: Edgar Allan Poe
Annabeth: 4 Gish
Anna Bolena composer: 9 Donizetti
Anna Christie (1930 film)
  cast: Charles Bickford, Marie Dressler, Greta Garbo
  character: 3 Mat 4 Owen 5 Burke, Chris 6 Marthy
Anna Karenina: 4 film 5 novel
  author: Leo Tolstoy
  cast: Freddie Bartholomew, Greta Garbo, Fredric March
  character: 5 Darya, Levin, Tanya 6 Alexei, Alexey, Grisha, Stepan
  director: Clarence Brown
Annakin, Ken: 8 director
  film: The Longest Day (1962)
    Quartet (1949)
    The Story of Robin Hood and His Merrie Men (1952)
    Swiss Family Robinson (1960)
    The Sword and the Rose (1953)
    Third Man on the Mountain (1959)
    Those Magnificent Men in Their Flying Machines (1965)
    Trio (1950)
    Underworld Informers (1965)
    Value for Money (1955)
annal: 7 account
Annales author: Tacitus
annalist: 6 scribe 9 historian 10 chronicler
annals: 5 files 6 record 7 archive, history 8 register 9 chronicle, recountal
Anna Maria ___: 8 Horsford
Anna May ___: 4 Wong
Annamese land measure: 3 mau
Annandale: 4 city, town
  locale: 8 Virginia
Annan, Kofi: 8 diplomat, Nobelist
Annapolis: 4 city, town
  freshman: 4 pleb 5 plebe
  locale: 8 Maryland
  org.: 3 USN 4 Navy, USNA
  river: 6 Severn
  student: 3 mid 5 middy 10 midshipman
Annapurna: 4 peak 5 mount 8 mountain
  locale: 4 Asia 5 Nepal
Ann Arbor: 4 city, town
  athletes: 10 Wolverines
  locale: 4 Mich. 8 Michigan
annatto: 3 dye 4 tree
Ann B. ___: 5 Davis
Anne: 4 peak, Rice 5 Frank, Heche, Klein, Meara, mount, saint, Tyler 6 Archer, Baxter, Boleyn, Brontë, Hébert, Murray, Ramsey, Revere, Sexton 7 Francis, Jackson, Nichols, Seymour, Shirley, Wheeler 8 Bancroft, Collette, Hathaway, Jeffreys, mountain, Sullivan 9 Lindbergh, McCaffrey, Parillaud 10 Bradstreet
  locale: 10 Antarctica
  sister of ~: 5 Emily 9 Charlotte
  to Margaret: 5 niece
Anne-___ Mutter: 6 Sophie
anneal: 4 gird, tone 5 build, shore, steel 6 beef up, firm up, harden, prop up, temper, tone up 7 bolster, brace up, build up, burgeon, develop, empower, enhance, fortify, shore up, stiffen, toughen 8 bourgeon, buttress, energize, indurate, vitalize 9 intensify, reinforce 10 invigorate, strengthen
annealed: 5 stiff
annealing oven: 4 lehr
Annecy: 4 city, town
  locale: 6 France

Anne de Beaupré: 3 Ste.
__-Anne Down: 6 Lesley
annelid: 4 worm
Annenberg: 6 Walter
Anne of __: 6 Cleves, France 7 Austria, Bohemia, Denmark
Anne of Green Gables (1985 film)
author: Lucy Maud Montgomery
cast: Colleen Dewhurst, Richard Farnsworth, Megan Follows
character: 3 Ira, Pye 5 Allan, Diana, Josie, Lynde, Moody 6 Minnie, Rachel, Stearn 7 Marilla
loc.: 3 PEI 6 Canada
Anne of the Thousand Days: 4 film, play
author: Maxwell Anderson
cast: Genevieve Bujold, Richard Burton, Irene Papas
director: Charles Jarrott
__ Anne Porter: 9 Katherine
__ Anne's lace: 5 Queen
Anne-Sophie: 6 Mutter
Annette: 6 Bening, O'Toole 9 Funicello
Annette author: Erskine Caldwell
annex: 3 add, arm, ell, get 4 gain, link, tack, wing 5 add on, affix, seize, usurp 6 adjoin, append, assume, attach, branch, fasten, hook up, lean-to, obtain, secure, tack on, take on 7 acquire, connect, hitch on, procure 8 addendum, addition, appendix 9 appendage, extension 10 attachment, commandeer, elongation, supplement
annexation: 4 gain 7 seizure 9 increment 10 attachment
__ Ann Garner: 5 Peggy
__ Ann Grau: 7 Shirley
__ Ann Hurd: 4 Gale
Annie: 5 Potts 6 Lennox, Oakley 7 Dillard, musical 9 Leibovitz
to Warbucks: 4 ward
Annie (1982 film): 7 musical
cast: Carol Burnett, Tim Curry, Albert Finney, Edward Herrmann, Geoffrey Holder, Bernadette Peters, Aileen Quinn, Ann Reinking
composer: 7 Charnin, Strouse
role: 3 FDR 4 Lily 5 Grace, Healy, Sandy 6 Oliver, Pepper, Punjab 7 Farrell, Rooster 8 Hannigan, Warbucks 9 Roosevelt
Annie __: 4 Hall 5 Allen 6 Laurie
__ Annie: 3 Ado, For 5 Apple 7 Six-Pack
Annie Allen author: Gwendolyn Brooks
Annie Get Your Gun (1950 film): 7 musical
cast: Betty Hutton, Howard Keel
composer: Irving Berlin
director: George Sidney
Annie Hall (1977 film)
cast: Woody Allen, Diane Keaton, Tony Roberts
director: Woody Allen
Annie Oakley: 7 freebee, freebie 8 marksman
like an ~: 4 free
Annie Oakley (1935 film)
cast: Melvyn Douglas, Preston Foster, Barbara Stanwyck
director: George Stevens
Annie's Song (1974 song) artist: John Denver
annihilate: 4 do in, ruin, slay 5 blast, crush, erase, quash, smash 6 defeat, devour, negate, ravage, rub out, squash, uproot 7 abolish, blot out, destroy, expunge, wipe out 8 decimate, demolish, massacre, suppress 9 dismantle, eliminate, eradicate, extirpate, finish off, liquidate 10 extinguish, invalidate, obliterate
annihilation: 4 doom 5 waste 6 defeat, finish
Annika: 9 Sorenstam
Anniston: 4 city, town
locale: 7 Alabama
anniversaries:
1st - Paper
2nd - Cotton
3rd - Leather
4th - Linen, Silk
5th - Wood
6th - Iron
7th - Wool, Copper
8th - Bronze
9th - Pottery, China
10th - Tin, Aluminum
11th - Steel
12th - Silk
13th - Lace
14th - Ivory
15th - Crystal
20th - China
25th - Silver
30th - Pearl
35th - Coral, Jade
40th - Ruby
45th - Sapphire
50th - Gold
55th - Emerald
60th - Diamond
anniversary: 4 date 5 event 7 holiday
item: 4 cake
__ anniversary: 7 wedding
__ Anniversary: 4 On an
Anniversary Party, The (2001 film)
cast: Jane Adams, Jennifer Beals, Phoebe Cates, Alan Cumming, Kevin Kline, Jennifer Jason Leigh, Gwyneth Paltrow
director: Alan Cumming, Jennifer Jason Leigh
Ann-Margret: 7 actress, Swedish
film: Bye Bye Birdie (1963)
Carnal Knowledge (1971)
The Cheap Detective (1978)
The Cincinnati Kid (1965)
Grumpier Old Men (1995)
Grumpy Old Men (1993)
Murderers' Row (1966)
A New Life (1988)
The Outside Man (1973)
State Fair (1962)
Tommy (1975)
Twice in a Lifetime (1985)
Viva Las Vegas (1964)
spouse: Roger Smith
__ Ann Miller: 8 Penelope
__ Ann Mobley: 4 Mary
anno __: 5 mundi, regni 6 Domini 7 Hejirae
annona: 4 tree 5 fruit, shrub
tree: 5 papaw 6 pawpaw 7 soursop
annotate: 4 edit, mark, note 5 gloss 7 explain 8 footnote 9 interpret
annotation: 4 note 5 gloss 7 comment 8 footnote 10 commentary, definition, exposition
annotator: 6 editor
announce: 3 say 4 call, page, tell 5 break, state, utter, voice 6 herald, impart, report, reveal, unfold 7 declare, deliver, divulge, precede, signify, trumpet 8 antecede, disclose, indicate, proclaim 9 advertise, broadcast, make known, pronounce, publicize 10 make public, promulgate
announced: 6 spoken
announcement: 2 ad 3 cry 4 call, memo, news, word 6 notice, report 7 message, release 8 bulletin, handbill 9 publicity, statement, utterance 10 communiqué
announcer: 5 crier, sayer 6 deejay, herald 8 reporter 10 disc jockey, disk jockey, forerunner, journalist, newscaster, proclaimer, telecaster
in horse racing: 6 caller
annoy: 3 ail, bug, eat, get, ire, irk, nag, rag, try, vex 4 bait, fret, gall, goad, miff, poke, ride, rile, roil, tire 5 anger, beset, chafe, eat at, egg on, get at, get to, grate, grind, harry, hound, peeve, pique, spite, tease, tweak, upset, weary, worry 6 abrade, accost, badger, bother, burn up, harass, hassle, heckle, hector, madden, needle, nettle, noodge, offend, pester, plague, pother, put out, rankle, ruffle, tee off 7 afflict, affront, agitate, bedevil, disturb, enflame, henpeck, inflame, perturb, provoke, tick off, torment, trouble 8 disquiet, exercise, irritate 9 aggravate, beleaguer, displease 10 antagonize, discompose, disconcert, disgruntle, exasperate
annoyance: 3 bur, rub 4 drag, pain, pest 5 gripe, peeve, pique, thorn, worry 6 bother, burden, gadfly, hassle, regret, riding, vexing 7 bugging, chagrin, dogging, nagging, offense, problem, teasing, trouble, umbrage 8 bullying, headache, hounding, irritant, nettling, nuisance, ruffling, taunting, vexation 9 bothering, commotion, complaint, grievance, harassing, pestering 10 affliction, difficulty, discomfort, discontent, disturbing, harassment, impatience, incitement, irritating, irritation, resentment
exclamation: 3 bah, duh, fie, tsk 4 heck, rats, umph 6 tsk tsk
neck ~: 4 kink, pain 5 spasm 6 twinge
annoyed: 4 ired, sore 5 cross, huffy, irate, testy, tired, upset 6 galled, ireful 9 indignant, irritable, irritated, resentful
state: 4 snit 5 pique
with: 5 mad at
annoying: 4 sore 5 nasty, pesky, pesty 6 odious, trying 7 grating, hateful, irksome, naughty, prickly, tedious 8 a bit much, abrasive, tiresome, worrying 9 invidious, obnoxious, offensive, troubling, vexatious, worrisome 10 bothersome, in one's hair, irritating, nettlesome, unpleasant
one: 3 nag 4 pain, pest 5 vexer 6 gadfly
succeed in ~: 5 get to
__ Ann Seton: 9 Elizabeth
annual: 4 corn 5 beans, plant 6 flower, yearly, zinnia 8 larkspur, marigold, periodic, yearbook 9 once-a-year
division: 5 month
visitor: 5 Santa
annual __: 4 ring, wage 6 report
annually: 4 yrly. 6 yearly 8 per annum
annual-ring tissue: 6 cambia
annuit __: 7 coeptis
annuity: 6 income 7 payment, pension, revenue
alternative: 3 IRA 5 Keogh
__ annuity: 4 bank, life 5 group 6 refund
__ annuity mortgage: 7 reverse
annul: 3 nix 4 kill, lift, undo, void 5 erase, quash 6 cancel, delete, negate, recall, recant, repeal, revoke 7 abolish, disavow, redress, rescind, reverse, scratch 8 abrogate, dissolve, override, overrule, overturn, renounce, set aside 9 discharge, liquidate, repudiate, supersede, terminate 10 contravene, counteract, invalidate, neutralize
annular __: 4 gear, ring 5 clock 7 eclipse
annulet: 4 ring
annulment: 6 recall, repeal 7 undoing 9 abatement, abolition, discharge, vitiation 10 abrogation, rescinding, rescission, retraction, revocation
annum, per: 6 yearly
annunciate: 9 broadcast
Annunzio: 9 Mantovani
__ Annus: 6 Magnus
Ann Vickers author: Sinclair Lewis
__ Ann Warren: 6 Lesley
__ Ann Womack: 3 Lee
ano-: 2 up
año: 4 year 7 Spanish
starter: 5 enero
año __: 5 nuevo
anoa: 5 bovid 6 animal, bovine, mammal
home: 3 zoo 7 Celebes 8 Sulawesi
relative: 3 yak 4 arna, gaur, urus, zebu 5 bison, gayal, takin 6 mithan, muskox 7 aurochs, banteng, banting, beefalo, buffalo, carabao, cattalo, kouprey, tamarao, tamarau, timarau
anode: 8 terminal 9 electrode
like some ~ s: 3 neg., pos. 8 negative, positive
anode __: 3 ray 4 glow
anodize: 5 plate
anodyne: 4 balm 5 letup, opium, poppy, salve 6 easing, opiate 7 comfort, relieve, respite 8 easement, laudanum, lenitive, mandrake, morphine, narcotic, nepenthe, sedative, soothing 9 abatement, analgesic, assuasive, calmative, demulcent, relieving, remission, softening 10 anesthetic, mitigation, painkiller, palliation, palliative
target: 4 pain
anoint: 3 oil 4 name 5 anele, apply, bless 6 choose, hallow, ordain 7 promote 8 coronate, dedicate, sanctify 9 designate, embrocate, lubricate 10 consecrate
anointed: 6 divine
anole: 6 animal 7 reptile 9 chameleon
anomalous: 3 odd 4 eery 5 eerie, queer, weird 6 atypic, freaky, off-key, quirky, unique 7 bizarre, deviant, offbeat, strange, unusual 8 aberrant, abnormal, atypical, freakish, isolated, peculiar, uncommon 9 dissonant, divergent, eccentric, fantastic, irregular, shapeless, unnatural, untypical 10 prodigious, unfamiliar, unorthodox
anomaly: 3 dev. 5 freak, quirk 6 oddity 7 paradox 8 mutation, original 9 curiosity, deviation, exception 10 aberration, difference, phenomenon
anomie: 10 alienation
anon: 3 now 4 soon, then 5 after, later 6 at once, in a bit, in time, not now, pronto 7 betimes, by and by, erelong, in a wink, later on, shortly, someday 8 directly, hereupon, in a jiffy, in a while, in no time, promptly, right now, right off, sometime 9 afterward, any day now, any minute, any second, forthwith, hereafter, in a moment, instantly, presently, right away, thereupon 10 afterwards, any time now, before long, eventually, in good time, this moment
companion: 4 ever
ever and ~: 3 oft
__ año nuevo!: 5 Feliz
anonym: 5 alias 7 pen name 9 pseudonym 10 nom de plume
anonymity opposite: 4 fame
anonymous: 7 Jane Doe, John Doe, unfamed, unknown 8 nameless 9 incognito, unclaimed 10 innominate, Richard Roe, unattested, uncredited
no longer ~: 5 named
one, maybe: 6 author
anorak: 4 coat 5 parka 6 jacket 7 cover-up 9 ski jacket 10 winter coat
__ a nose: 5 win by
another: 4 more 5 added, other

6 second 10 substitute
at ~ time: 4 anon 5 later
from ~ country: 5 alien 7 foreign, oversea 8 offshore, overseas
have ~ opinion: 4 vary 7 deviate, dissent, diverge 8 disagree
in Spanish: 4 otra, otro
one after ~: 7 by turns
one time or ~: 7 someday
one way or ~: 7 somehow
send to ~: 4 pass 5 refer
take ~ look: 5 audit, check, weigh 6 assess, go over, rehash, survey 7 analyze, examine, inspect, revisit 8 appraise, critique, evaluate, reassess 9 reexamine, think over 10 reconsider, reevaluate, run through, scrutinize
time: 4 anew, anon, soon, then 5 after, again 6 in a bit, in time 7 by and by, later on, someday 8 in a while, sometime 9 afterward, hereafter 10 before long, eventually
to ~ place: 4 away
___ another: 3 one
Another ___: 3 Day, You 4 Time 5 Night, Woman, World 7 Country
Another Brick in the Wall (1980 song) artist: Pink Floyd
Another card!: 5 hit me
Another Country author: James Baldwin
___ Another Day: 3 Die 4 Just
Another Day (1971 song) artist: Paul McCartney
Another Day in Paradise (1998 film) cast: Melanie Griffith, Natasha Gregson Wagner, James Woods
Another Day in Paradise (1989 song) artist: Phil Collins
Another Green World composer: 3 Eno
Another Language (1933 film) cast: Helen Hayes, Robert Montgomery
Another One Bites the Dust (1980 song) artist: Queen
Another Op'nin', Another Show composer: 6 Porter
Another Part of the Forest (1948 film) cast: Dan Duryea, Fredric March
Another Sad Love Song (1993 song) artist: Toni Braxton
Another Saturday Night (song) artist: Cat Stevens, Sam Cooke
Another Somebody Done... (1975 song) artist: B.J. Thomas
Another Thin Man (1939 film)
cast: Myrna Loy, William Powell
director: W.S. Van Dyke
Another Time, Another Place (1958 song) artist: Patti Page
Another Time author: W.H. Auden
Another Woman (1988 film)
cast: Mia Farrow, Ian Holm, Gena Rowlands
director: Woody Allen
Another World (NBC): 4 soap 9 soap opera
Another year ___...: 5 older
Another You author: Ann Beattie
Anouilh, Jean: 6 French 10 playwright
work: Antigone
The Ermine
The Lark
Ring Around the Moon
Thieves' Carnival
Anouk: 5 Aimee
ans.: 4 resp., soln. 5 reply 6 retort
evoker: 4 ques.
see also answer
Ansan: 4 city, town
locale: 10 South Korea
Ansara, Michael: 5 actor
film: And Now Miguel (1966)
Harum Scarum (1965)
spouse: Barbara Eden
TV: Broken Arrow
ansate ___: 5 cross
anschluss: 4 bloc 6 league 7 combine 8 alliance 9 coalition 10 federation
Ansel: 5 Adams
Anselm: 5 saint 11 philosopher
anser: 4 duck 5 goose
Anser: 4 star
anserine: 5 silly
bird: 5 goose
Ansermet, Ernest: 9 conductor
Ansgar: 5 saint
Anshan: 4 city, town
locale: 5 China
Anson: 3 Cap 8 Williams
Ansonia: 4 city, town
locale: 4 Conn.
Anspach, Susan: 7 actress
film: The Big Fix (1978)
Blume in Love (1973)
Five Easy Pieces (1970)
Anspaugh, David: 8 director
film: Hoosiers (1986)
Moonlight and Valentino (1995)
Rudy (1993)
answer: 3 key, pay, say 4 echo, meet, resp., RSVP, suit 5 field, rebut, reply, serve, solve 6 letter, oracle, recite, refute, rejoin, result, retort, ripost 7 clarify, counter, defense, dispute, explain, hit back, resolve, respond, riposte, satisfy, suffice, verdict 8 comeback, disprove, feedback, reaction, rebuttal, response, solution, talk back 9 deduction, rejoinder, respond to, retaliate, write back 10 refutation
a charge: 5 plead, rebut
affirmative ~: 3 yes
again: 5 resay
back: 4 sass 5 react 8 get fresh
don't take no for an ~: 6 be firm, insist 7 persist, protest 8 speak out 9 stand firm
evasive ~: 5 parry
find the ~: 5 solve
for: 7 sponsor 9 guarantee, undertake
(for): 3 pay
get the same ~: 5 agree
indefinite ~: 5 maybe 7 perhaps 8 possibly, probably 9 it could be, it might be, perchance 10 imaginably
kind of ~: 5 yes/no
negative ~: 3 nay
quiz ~: 4 true 5 false
answer ___: 3 key 4 back 5 print, sheet
answerability: 5 blame, guilt 9 liability
answerable: 6 liable 7 subject 8 blamable, governed, indebted 9 blameable, obligated 10 chargeable
Answered Prayers author: Danielle Steel
answering ___: 7 machine, pennant, service
answering machine
option: 5 erase
sound: 4 tone
unit: 3 msg. 7 message
answers, try to get: 3 ask 4 pump, quiz 5 grill, query 7 canvass, consult, inquire, request
ant: 3 bug 4 army, pest 5 emmet, kelep, queen 6 insect, worker 7 pismire 8 micraner 9 carpenter
combining form: 6 myrmec- 7 myrmeco-
cow: 5 aphid
ender: 4 hill 5 eater
group: 6 colony
home: 4 hill
morsel: 5 crumb
of an ~: 6 formic
white ~ genus: 6 termes
worker ~: 6 ergate
ant ___: 3 cow, egg 4 bear, farm, hill, lion
ant.: 3 opp.
opposite: 3 syn.
___ ant: 3 red 4 army, bull, fire 5 honey, slave, thief, white 6 Amazon, driver, jumper, velvet, worker 7 bulldog, parasol, Pharaoh
Ant: 4 Adam
anta: 4 pier 8 pilaster
antacid: 4 Tums 6 alkali, bicarb, Maalox, Pepcid, Riopan, Zantac 7 Gelusil, Lactaid, Mylanta, Rolaids 8 Gaviscon 11 Alka-Seltzer, Pepto-Bismol
target: 5 agita
Ant, Adam real name: Stuart Goddard
antagonism: 4 feud, hate 5 anger 6 animus, enmity, hatred, rancor 7 discord, dislike, ill will 8 aversion, conflict, friction 9 animosity, antipathy, hostility 10 aggression, antithesis, contention, difference, dissension, dissonance, opposition, oppugnancy, resistance
antagonist: 3 foe 4 part 5 enemy, rival 7 fighter, opposer 8 opponent 9 adversary, assailant, contender, disputant, ill-wisher, oppugnant 10 competitor, contestant
prefix: 4 anti-
antagonistic: 3 ill 4 cold, cool, mean 5 aloof, nasty, enemy, rival, surly 6 at odds, averse, bitter, chilly, down on, ornery 7 adverse, counter, glacial, hateful, hostile, opposed, warlike 8 clashing, contrary, inimical, negative, opposing, opposite, rivaling, spiteful, venomous, virulent 9 bellicose, competing, malicious, truculent 10 antithetic, malevolent, pugnacious, unfriendly
antagonize: 3 vex 5 anger, annoy, repel, shock 6 insult, offend, oppose, resist 8 alienate, estrange, irritate 9 disaffect, displease 10 counteract, neutralize
antagonized: 3 hot, mad 4 ired, sore 5 angry, cross, huffy, irate, livid, riled, wroth 6 fuming, ireful, raging, raving, red-hot 7 furious, ranting 8 choleric, wrathful 9 indignant, resentful, splenetic
Antal: 6 Dorati
Antananarivo: 4 city, town 7 capital
locale: 10 Madagascar
Antarctic ___: 4 Zone 5 Ocean, Plate 6 Circle
Antarctica: 9 continent
bay: 6 Whales
bird: 4 skua 7 penguin
cape: 5 Adare
coast: 6 Adelie
covering: 6 icecap
explorer: 4 Byrd, Ross 6 Mawson 8 Amundsen 10 Shackleton
ice shelf: 5 Amery
like ~: 6 frigid
mountain: 4 Anne, Mohl, Wade 5 Astor, Coman, Falla, Minto, Press, Shear, Shinn, Tyree 6 Erebus, Kaplan, Lister, Sabine, Sidley, Wexler 7 Epperly, Gardner, Lysaght, Markham, Odishaw, Ostenso, Sellery
of ~: 5 polar
sea: 4 Ross 7 Weddell 8 Amundsen
volcano: 6 Erebus
Antares: 4 star 5 M star 8 red giant
ante: 3 bet, fee 5 pay up, put in, put up, stake, wager 6 chip in, kick in, pony up 7 cough up 8 entry fee, shell out
again: 5 rebet
destination: 3 pot
follower: 4 deal
lowest ~: 4 cent, chip 5 penny
meridiem: 7 morning
penny ~: 5 minor
relative: 3 pre-
up: 3 pay 4 give 5 pay in, spend 6 chip in, kick in 8 disburse, shell out 9 subscribe 10 contribute, recompense, remunerate
up the ~: 5 raise, rebid
___ ante: 4 vide 5 penny
anteater: 6 animal, mammal 7 echidna 8 aardvark, pangolin
feature: 5 snout
___ anteater: 5 giant, scaly, silky, spiny 6 banded 7 two-toed
antebellum: 6 prewar
antecede: 4 head, lead 6 head up, herald 7 outrank, predate, presage, usher in 8 announce, foreshow, go before, outstrip, proclaim 9 come first, go ahead of, introduce 10 anticipate, come before
antecedence: 8 priority
antecedent: 5 basis, cause, prior 6 origin, reason, source 8 occasion, previous 9 beginning, foregoing, precedent, preceding, precursor, prototype 10 forebearer, forefather, forerunner, hypothesis, precursory, progenitor
antecedents: 5 roots
antecessor: 10 forerunner
antechamber: 5 foyer, lobby 9 vestibule
antedate: 7 precede
antediluvian: 3 old 4 aged 5 hoary 7 ancient, antique 8 medieval, obsolete, outmoded, primeval 9 mediaeval, primaeval 10 antiquated
antelope: 3 gnu, goa, kob 4 guib, kudu, oryx, puku, topi 5 addax, bongo, bovid, chiru, eland, goral, korin, nyala, oribi, saiga, sasin, serow 6 animal, chammy, dik-dik, duiker, impala, koodoo, lechwe, mammal, nilgai, rhebok, shammy, shamoy 7 blaubok, blesbok, chamois, defassa, gazelle, gemsbok, gerenuk, grysbok, nylghai, nylghau, sassaby 8 blesbuck, bontebok, bushbuck, gemsbuck, reedbuck, steenbok, steinbok 9 blackbuck, pronghorn, sitatunga, springbok, waterbuck 10 hartebeest, wildebeest
Asian goat ~: 5 serow
female: 3 cow, doe, ewe
foot: 4 hoof
gait: 4 stot
male: 4 bull
playmate: 4 deer
young: 3 kid 4 calf
___ antelope: 4 goat 5 sable 7 Tibetan
antenna: 4 ears 5 organ 6 aerial, feeler 10 rabbit ears
alternative: 4 dish 5 cable 7 cable TV
owner: 6 insect
pole: 4 mast
range: 3 UHF, VHF
tip: 6 arista
___ antenna: 3 UHF 4 beam, dish, Yagi 6 Adcock, dipole
anterior: 3 bow 4 past 5 front, prior 6 former 7 forward 8 forepart, previous 9 foregoing, preceding
prefix: 3 pro-
Antero: 4 peak 5 mount 8 mountain
locale: 7 Rockies, Sawatch 8 Colorado
anteroom: 4 hall 5 foyer, lobby 6 alcove, parlor 7 ingress, narthex 8 entrance 9 vestibule
Anteros
brother of ~: 4 Eros
mother of ~: 9 Aphrodite
Anterus: 4 pope 7 pontiff
anthem: 4 hymn, pean, song 5 music,

paean 8 canticle
author: 3 Key
Civil War: 5 Dixie
ender: 5 brave
preposition: 3 o'er
start: 4 o say 5 oh say
anthemion: 9 arabesque
anthill: 4 nest 5 mound
anthologize: 4 cull 5 amass 6 garner, gather, muster 7 arrange, collect, compile, marshal 8 assemble, organize 10 accumulate
anthology: 5 album 7 omnibus 8 analecta, analects, treasury 9 selection 10 collection, compendium, cumulation, miscellany
Anthony: 3 Ray 4 Earl, Eden, Hope, Mann, Marc, Page, West 5 Clark, Geary, Heald, Price, Quinn, Zerbe 6 Eisley, Fokker, Harvey, Joseph, Newley, Powell, Quayle 7 Asquith, Burgess, Edwards, Hopkins, Kennedy, Perkins, Shaffer, van Dyck 8 LaPaglia, Trollope 9 Franciosa, Minghella 10 Montgomery
in German: 5 Anton
in Spanish: 7 Antonio
Anthony __: 6 dollar 7 Adverse, of Padua
Anthony __ Hall: 7 Michael
__ Anthony: 6 Little
Anthony Adverse: 4 film 5 novel
author: Hervey Allen
cast: Olivia de Havilland, Fredric March, Donald Woods
director: Mervyn LeRoy
Anthony, Earl: 6 bowler
milieu: 5 alley
org: 3 PBA
Anthony Michael __: 4 Hall
Anthony of Padua: 5 saint
__ Anthony Ray: 4 Gene
Anthony, Saint cross: 3 tau
Anthony, Susan B.: 6 dollar 8 feminist 10 suffragist
Anthony the Abbot: 5 saint
anthracite: 4 coal
deposit: 4 seam
kin: 7 lignite 10 bituminous
anthropoid: 3 ape 6 monkey
anthropologist: 4 Mead 6 Frazer, Leakey 10 Malinowski
prefix: 5 paleo-
anthropology: 7 science
branch of ~: 9 ethnology
prefix with ~: 5 paleo
study: 6 humans
anti: 3 con, foe, opp. 7 against, opposed, opposer 8 naysayer, negative, opponent, opposing 9 counter to
opposite: 3 pro
vote: 2 no 3 nay
anti-: 6 contra-
anti-__ bar: 4 roll, sway
Anti-__ League: 6 Saloon
antiaircraft fire: 4 flak 5 flack 6 ack ack
anti-apartheid org.: 3 ANC
antiar: 4 tree, upas
relative: 3 fig 4 upas 5 ficus, ramon 6 fustic 8 mulberry 10 breadfruit
antiballistic __: 7 missile
Antibes neighbor: 4 Nice
antibiotic: 4 drug 5 sulfa 8 medicine 9 antitoxin 10 antiseptic, medication
combining form: 5 -mycin
predecessor: 5 sulfa
source: 4 mold
antibody: 6 ligand
in tears: 3 IGA
target: 5 toxin
antic: 4 dido, jape, joke, lark, romp 5 caper, funny, prank, trick 6 frolic 7 foolery, hotfoot 8 clowning, escapade, mischief, sporting, sportive 9 grotesque, ludicrous 10 buffoonery, frolicsome, hanky-panky, ridiculous, shenanigan, tomfoolery
Antic Hay author: Aldous Huxley
anticipate: 3 see 4 hope, look, mean, wait 5 await, parry, sense 6 expect, plan on 7 count on, foresee, hope for, look for, obviate, precede, predict, preempt, prepare, prevent, wait for 8 antecede, envisage, envision, forecast, foretell, theorize, watch for 9 apprehend, calculate, count upon, entertain, forestall, foretaste, intercept, prevision, see coming, visualize 10 bargain for, conjecture, have a hunch, jump the gun, prepare for
anticipating: 5 ready 7 hopeful
anticipation: 4 hope 7 inkling, thought 8 optimism, prospect, suspense 9 foretaste 10 precaution
Anticipation (1972 song) artist: Carly Simon
anticipatory: 5 early
shout: 4 TGIF
anticlimax: 6 bathos 7 decline, letdown 8 comedown
anticrime acronym: 4 RICO
antics: 5 sport 7 foolery 8 jocosity 9 horseplay 10 tomfoolery
anti-discrimination org.: 4 EEOC 5 NAACP
antidotal: 8 curative 10 corrective
antidote: 4 cure 6 remedy 8 medicine 10 medication
target: 5 toxin
antidrug
advice: 5 say no
cop: 4 narc, nark 5 narco
org.: 3 DEA
anti-DWI org.: 4 MADD, SADD
Antietam: 6 battle
general: 3 Lee
locale: 8 Maryland
antifreeze: 6 glycol
use ~: 5 deice
anti-fur org.: 4 PETA
Antigone
author: Jean Anouilh, Sophocles
brother of ~: 8 Eteocles 9 Polynices
husband of ~: 6 Haemon
parent of ~: 7 Jocasta, Oedipus
sister of ~: 6 Ismene
son of ~: 5 Maeon
uncle of ~: 5 Creon
Antigua: 3 isl. 4 isle 6 island
Antigua and Barbuda: 6 nation 7 country
capital: 7 St. John's
org.: 3 OAS
antiknock
fluid: 5 ethyl
number: 6 octane
Antilles: 4 isls. 5 isles 7 islands
Indian: 5 Carib 6 Arawak
island: 4 Cuba, Saba 5 Aruba 7 St. Croix 8 Dominica, St. Thomas 10 Hispaniola, Martinique
jaunt: 6 cruise
language: 5 Carib
__ Antilles: 6 Lesser 7 Greater
antilock __: 5 brake
antimacassar: 4 tidy 5 doily 6 doyley
make a ~: 3 tat
antimonopoly org.: 3 FTC
antimony: 5 metal 7 element
combining form: 4 stib- 5 stibi-, stibo- 6 stibio-
ore: 8 stibnite
antimony __: 6 yellow 7 hydride, sulfate, sulfide
anti-narcotics org.: 3 DEA
anti-nuke org.: 4 SANE
Antioch: 4 city, town
locale: 4 Ohio 10 California
__ Antipas: 5 Herod
antipasto: 9 appetizer 10 finger food
ingredient: 5 olive
antipathetic: 6 averse, down on 7 opposed 8 clashing, opposing
be ~ toward: 6 detest
antipathy: 4 hate 5 odium, spite 6 animus, enmity, grudge, hatred, malice, rancor 7 allergy, discord, disdain, disgust, dislike, ill will 8 acrimony, aversion, bad blood, contempt, distaste, loathing 9 animosity, avoidance, hostility, prejudice, repulsion, revulsion 10 abhorrence, antagonism, opposition, repellence, repellency, repugnance, unkindness
antiphon: 5 reply 8 response
Antiphus
brother of ~: 5 Paris 6 Hector
parent of ~: 5 Priam 6 Hecuba 7 Priamus
sister of ~: 9 Cassandra
antipodal: 4 last 5 polar 7 counter 8 converse, opposite
antipode: 7 reverse 8 converse, opposite
antipodean: 5 polar 8 opposite 10 antithetic
Antipodes: 4 isls. 5 isles 7 islands
locale: 10 New Zealand
antipole: 8 converse
antipollution org.: 3 EPA
anti-prohibitionist: 3 Wet
__ Antiqua: 3 Ars
antiquark + quark: 5 meson
Antiquary, The author: Walter Scott
antiquate: 3 age 6 retire 7 outdate, outmode, replace 8 archaize 9 supersede
antiquated: 3 obs., old, out 4 aged 5 dated, dowdy, fusty, hoary, moldy, mossy, musty, olden, passé, stale 6 old hat, quaint 7 ancient, archaic, fogyish 8 decrepit, medieval, obsolete, outdated, outmoded, out of use, timeworn, unusable 9 hackneyed, mediaeval, out-of-date 10 old-fangled, out of style
term: 8 archaism 10 archaicism
antique: 3 old 4 aged 5 curio, hoary, passé, relic 6 quaint 7 ancient 8 heirloom, obsolete, outdated, outmoded, valuable 9 out-of-date
store adjective: 4 olde
__ antique: 4 verd
antiques
love of ~: 5 vertu, virtu
work with ~: 7 restore
Antiques Roadshow network: 3 PBS
antiquing medium: 4 ager
antiquity: 3 eld 4 past, yore 5 relic 9 days of old, hoariness, olden days 10 archaicism, days of yore
anti-racketeering org.: 3 FBI
anti-roll __: 3 bar
Anti-Sartre author: Colin Wilson
antiseptic: 4 pure 5 clean, iodin, iodol 6 iodine 7 sterile 8 cleanser, fumigant, germfree, hygienic, pristine, purifier, sanitary 9 boric acid, germicide, medicated, purifying 10 antibiotic, germicidal, immaculate, preventive, sterilized, sterilizer, unpolluted
pioneer: 6 Lister
antisocial: 5 aloof 6 remote 7 ascetic, recluse 8 eremitic, hermitic, reserved, solitary, taciturn 9 alienated, reclusive, withdrawn 10 hermitlike, unfriendly, unsociable
one: 4 nerd 5 loner
Antisthenes: 11 philosopher
antisubmarine weapon: 4 Y gun
antithesis: 4 foil 7 inverse, reverse 8 converse, flip side, negation, opposite 9 inversion, other side 10 antagonism, difference, opposition
antithetic: 7 counter, inverse, opposed, reverse, unalike 8 contrary, converse, opposite 9 different 10 antipodean, contrasted, poles apart
antithetical: 5 polar 7 counter, opposed, reverse 8 contrary, converse, opposing, opposite
antitoxin: 5 serum 7 vaccine 8 medicine 9 antiserum, antivenin 10 antibiotic, medication, preventive
like an ~: 6 serous
antitoxins: 4 sera
Antitrust (2001 film)
cast: Rachael Leigh Cook, Claire Forlani, Ryan Phillippe, Tim Robbins
__ Antitrust Act: 7 Clayton, Sherman
antitrust org.: 3 FTC
antivenins: 4 sera
antler: 4 horn 7 hatrack
budding ~: 4 knob
part: 4 tine 5 prong
wearer: 3 elk 4 deer, hart, stag 5 moose 8 reindeer
__ antler: 3 bay, bes, bez 4 brow 5 crown, royal 6 rusine
antlers: 4 rack
remove ~: 6 dehorn
Antofagasta: 4 city, port, town
locale: 5 Chile
Antofalla: 4 peak 5 mount 8 mountain
locale: 5 Andes 9 Argentina
Antoine: 6 Le Nain 7 Watteau 9 Becquerel, Lavoisier
see also French
Antoine de __-Exupéry: 5 Saint
Antoinette: 5 Bower, Marie, Perry
see also French
Anton: 5 Dolin, Karas, Susan 6 Cermak, Dvorák, Webern 7 Arensky, Chekhov 8 Bruckner, Walbrook 10 Rubinstein
in English: 7 Anthony
Antonia: 4 Bird 6 Fraser
Antonin: 6 Dvorák, Scalia
Antoninus __: 4 Pius
Antonio: 3 Lou 5 Gaudí, Moniz 6 Sabáto, Scotto 7 Salieri, Vivaldi 8 Banderas 9 Correggio 10 Stradivari
in English: 7 Anthony
in Evita: 3 Che
Antonio __ Jobim: 6 Carlos
__ Antonio, TX: 3 San
__ Antonius: 6 Marcus
Antony: 4 Marc, Mark 5 Roman, saint 6 Hewish
attendant: 4 Eros
foe: 6 Brutus
friend: 4 Cleo 6 Caesar 9 Cleopatra
see also Latin
__ Antony: 4 Marc, Mark
Antony and Cleopatra
author: William Shakespeare
character: 4 Eros, Iras 5 Menas, Philo 6 Alexas, Gallus, Pompey, Scarus, Silius, Taurus 7 Agrippa, Mardian, Octavia, Thyreus 8 Canidius, Charmian, Dercetas, Octavius 9 Cleopatra 10 Marc Antony
antonym: 3 opp. 8 opposite
antonymous: 7 opposed 8 opposing 10 dissimilar
antre: 4 cave 6 cavern, grotto
Antron: 5 fiber, nylon 8 material
antrum: 6 cavity
ants in one's __: 5 pants
ant-sized: 3 wee 4 tiny 5 small, teeny
ants, of: 6 formic
antsy: 4 edgy 5 eager, itchy, jumpy, tense 6 on edge, uneasy 7 anxious, fidgety, jittery, keyed up, nervous, restive, uptight, zealous 8 agitated, restless, skittish, troubled 9 con-

cerned, excitable, ill at ease, impatient, overeager, unsettled **10** high-strung
be ~: **6** fidget
Antwerp: **4** city, port, town
locale: **7** Belgium
river: **7** Schelde, Scheldt
Antz (1998 film)
director: Eric Darnell
voice cast: Woody Allen, Gene Hackman, Sylvester Stallone, Sharon Stone
Anubis father: **6** Osiris
A number __: **3** one
anuran: **4** frog, toad **9** amphibian
anvil: **4** bone **5** incus
site: **3** ear
sound: **5** clang
user: **5** smith
anvil __: **3** top **5** cloud
Anvil __: **6** Chorus
Anwar: **5** Sadat **9** Gabrielle
anxiety: **3** woe **4** ache, care, fear, pain **5** agita, alarm, angst, qualm, worry **6** dismay, misery, nerves, phobia, strain, stress, terror, unease, unrest **7** concern, fidgets, jitters, malaise, scruple, tension, turmoil, willies **8** disquiet, distress, suspense **9** misgiving, tightness, trepidity **10** difficulty, foreboding, impatience, inquietude, insecurity, solicitude
__ Anxiety: **4** High
__ Anxiety, The: **5** Age of
anxious: **4** agog, avid, edgy, keen **5** antsy, eager, hyper, itchy, jumpy, nervy, tense, wired, worry **6** afraid, gung-ho, loving, pacing, queasy, queazy, scared, uneasy **7** abashed, alarmed, fearful, gulping, jittery, keyed up, longing, nervous, panicky, restive, uptight, worried **8** agitated, desirous, fluttery, hesitant, hopped up, in a state, in a tizzy, restless, skittish, troubled **9** concerned, excitable, expectant, ill at ease, impatient, unsettled **10** breathless, disquieted, distressed, frightened, high-strung, inspirited, solicitous
be ~: **5** sweat, worry
make ~: **3** nag **5** alarm
any: **4** a bit, part, some **5** at all, aught, ought **7** a little, even one, pronoun **8** whatever **9** whichever
and every: **3** all
at ~ cost: **10** regardless
at ~ point: **8** even once
at ~ rate: **3** yet **5** still **6** anyhow, anyway **7** at least **10** all the same, regardless
at ~ time: **4** ever **8** even once
day: **4** anon, soon **7** shortly **8** sometime **10** imminently
ender: **3** how, one, way **4** body, more, time, ways, wise **5** place, thing, where
hardly ~: **3** few **5** light, scant **6** little, meager, paltry **7** limited **8** one or two
in ~ way: **5** at all
not ~: **4** nary, none, zero
not at ~ time: **5** never
not, in law: **3** nul
not in ~ way: **5** no how
old way: **5** about **6** remiss **8** reckless **9** haphazard **10** incautious
on ~ occasion: **6** always **10** at all times, invariably
to ~ extent: **3** any **4** ever
any __ can play: **6** number
any __ in a storm: **4** port
any __ now: **3** day
any __ you slice it: **3** way
Any __?: **5** ideas **6** takers
Any __ Way You Can: **5** Which
Anya: **5** Seton
Anyama: **4** city, town
locale: **10** Ivory Coast
anybody: **5** whoso
not ~: **5** no one
anybody's game: **5** close **10** nip and tuck, up for grabs
any day __: **3** now
... __ any drop to drink: **3** nor
Any Given Sunday (1999 film)
cast: Cameron Diaz, Al Pacino, Dennis Quaid, James Woods
director: Oliver Stone
anyhow: **10** all the same, carelessly, in any event, regardless
Anyidoho, Kofi: **4** poet **8** Ghanaian
any number can __: **4** play
Any Old Iron author: Anthony Burgess
anyone: **5** whoso **7** whoever **8** somebody **9** whosoever
but us: **6** others
not ~: **4** none **5** no one
not with ~: **5** alone
__, anyone?: **6** Tennis
Anyone home?: **6** yoo-hoo
Anyone Who Had a Heart (1964 song)
artist: Dionne Warwick
Any Place I Hang My Hat Is Home
composer: **5** Arlen **6** Mercer
any port __ storm: **3** in a
anything: **8** whatever
before ~ else: **5** first **6** maiden, mainly, virgin **7** chiefly, initial, leading, leadoff, opening, pioneer, premier, to start **8** above all, earliest, foremost, original, virginal **9** in advance, inaugural, initially, primarily, primitive, prototype **10** originally
like ~: **4** a lot **7** acutely, awfully **8** terribly, very much
not ~: **4** none
anything __: **3** but
Anything __?: **4** else
__ Anything: **4** I'd Do
Anything for Billy author: Larry McMurtry
Anything for You (1988 song) artist: Gloria Estefan
Anything Goes (1936 film): **7** musical
cast: Bing Crosby, Ida Lupino, Ethel Merman, Charlie Ruggles
character: **4** Hope, Ling, Reno **5** Ching **6** Elisha **7** Sweeney
composer: Cole Porter
director: Lewis Milestone
Anything You Can Do...: **4** duet, song
composer: Irving Berlin
anytime: **6** at will **7** someday
any time __: **5** at all
Anytime (1998 song) artist: Brian McKnight
Any Time, Any Place (1994 song)
artist: Janet Jackson
anyway: **5** at all **7** somehow **8** after all **10** all the same, in any event, regardless
any way you __ it: **5** slice
Any Way You Want Me (1956 song)
artist: Elvis Presley
Any Wednesday (1966 film)
cast: Jane Fonda, Jason Robards
anywhere: **7** all over
__ anywhere for your smile...: **4** I'd go
Any Which Way You Can (1980 film)
beast: **5** Clyde, orang
cast: Clint Eastwood, Geoffrey Lewis, Sondra Locke
director: Buddy Van Horn
Any Woman's Blues author: Erica Jong
Anzac: **6** Aussie **7** soldier
Anzio: **4** city, town **6** battle
locale: **5** Italy
Aoide: **4** Muse
A-OK: **4** fine **5** dandy **7** perfect **9** copacetic, excellent, hunky-dory **10** acceptable, impeccable
Aoki, Isao: **6** golfer
milieu: **5** links **6** course
org.: **3** PGA
AOL: **3** ISP
access ~: **5** log in **6** dial up
competitor: **3** MSN **5** Web TV
customer: **4** user
exchange: **2** IM **5** E-mail
Aomori: **4** city, port, town
locale: **5** Japan
__ a one: **3** not **4** nary
A-one: **3** ace, def, rad, top **4** aces, best, boss, braw, cool, dece, fine, gear, keen, neat, nice, phat, tuff **5** dandy, ducky, grand, great, marvy, neato, nobby, prime, slick, super, swell **6** bang on, bang-up, bonzer, bosker, choice, divine, dreamy, far-out, gnarly, groovy, lovely, peachy, slap-up, spot on, superb, terrif, tiptop, unreal, whizzo, wicked **7** amazing, awesome, capital, corking, optimum, perfect, ripping, skookum, stellar, sublime **8** dazzling, especial, eximious, fabulous, five-star, four-star, frabjous, glorious, heavenly, jim-dandy, slam-bang, smashing, splendid, standout, sterling, stickout, superior, terrific, top-level, topnotch, very good, wondrous **9** bodacious, Endsville, excellent, exemplary, exquisite, fantastic, first-rate, high-class, high-grade, hunky-dory, marvelous, sollicker, topflight, unrivaled, wonderful **10** first-class, hotsy-totsy, jack-a-dandy, out of sight, peachy-keen, phenomenal, remarkable, stupendous, super-duper, unrivalled
aorta: **5** trunk **6** artery
aortic __: **4** arch **5** valve
aoudad: **5** sheep **6** animal
relative: **4** geep **5** argal, shapu, urial **6** argali, bharal, merino **7** bighorn, burrhel, mouflon **8** cimarron, moufflon
Août: **4** mois **5** month **6** August, French
AP
archive item: **5** photo
former ~ equipment: **3** TTY
part: **5** Assoc., Press **10** Associated
rival: **3** UPI **7** Reuters
A.P.: **8** Giannini
apa: **4** tree
Apa: **5** river
locale: **6** Brazil **8** Paraguay
apace: **3** PDQ **4** ASAP, fast **5** swift **6** presto **7** fleetly, hastily, quickly, rapidly, swiftly **8** in a flash, in a jiffy, in no time, pell mell, speedily **9** forthwith, hurriedly, instantly, like a shot, posthaste **10** in high gear
with: **9** alongside
Apache: **5** tribe **6** archer, Indian **7** Amerind, Cochise **8** Geronimo
__ Apache: **4** Fort
Apache (1961 song) artist: Jorgen Ingmann
Apache Junction: **4** city, town
locale: **7** Arizona
Apalachee: **3** bay
locale: **3** Fla. **7** Florida
__ a pall over: **4** cast
Apan: **4** city, town
locale: **6** Mexico **7** Hidalgo
apara: **9** armadillo
__ a Parade: **5** I Love
Aparajito (1956 film) director: Satyajit Ray
Aparicio, Luis: **9** shortstop
Aparri: **4** city, port, town
locale: **5** Luzon
apart: **3** off, sep. **4** away **5** alone, aside, in two, loose, per se, split **6** cut off, lonely, remote, singly **7** asunder, distant, divided, split up, strange **8** broken up, by itself, detached, discrete, distinct, divorced, excluded, in pieces, isolated, separate, sundered **9** by oneself, different, in reserve, separated **10** disjointed, disjointly, out of touch, segregated, separately
combining form: **4** dich- **5** dicho-
come ~: **4** open, snap, tear **5** burst, panic, ravel, split **7** unweave **8** fragment, separate **9** break down
cut ~: **5** sever **8** separate
drive ~: **8** alienate, separate **9** disaffect
fall ~: **3** rot **6** go awry **8** collapse, disunite **9** break down, decompose
falling ~: **5** shaky **7** rickety, run-down **8** decrepit **9** crumbling **10** ramshackle, tumbledown
far ~: **3** few **4** rare **6** meager, scarce, seldom, sparse **7** limited, unusual **8** isolated, sporadic, uncommon **9** irregular, scattered, spasmodic, uncrowded **10** infrequent, occasional, sporadical, unfrequent
from: **3** bar **6** beyond, except **7** besides, outside **9** except for, excluding, other than **10** beyond that, leaving out
(from): **5** aside
keep ~: **6** enisle **7** isolate, seclude **8** separate
pick ~: **3** pan **5** probe, roast, study, trash **6** assess, review **7** analyze, examine, run down **8** evaluate **9** criticize, cut to bits, find fault **10** scrutinize
poles ~: **5** split **6** at odds, unlike **7** unalike, unequal **9** different, disparate, divergent **10** antithetic, dissimilar
prefix: **3** dis-
pull ~: **4** rend, tear, undo **5** split **7** split up **9** find fault
set ~: **4** part, save **5** alone, lay by, lay up, sever, split, store **6** cut off, detach, devote, divide, enisle, unlink **7** disjoin, earmark, isolate, lay away, put away, reserve, rope off, split up, store up **8** break off, dedicate, disunite, reserved, sanctify, separate, uncouple **9** preferred, segregate, sequester **10** disconnect, pigeonhole
stand ~: **6** differ
take ~: **4** ruin, undo **5** level, spoil, unrig, unrip, wreck **6** detach, tinker **7** destroy, dissect **8** demolish, tear down **9** devastate, dismantle, knock down **10** demoralize, disconnect
tear ~: **4** rive **5** rip up **6** avulse, rebuke
torn ~ old-style: **4** reft
__ apart: **3** set **4** fall, pick, pull, take **5** poles **6** worlds
apartment: **3** eff., pad **4** co-op, flat, home, loft, room, unit **5** abode, house, place, suite **6** duplex, walk-up **7** domicil, habitat, housing, lodging, shelter, vacancy **8** domicile, lodgment, quarters **9** penthouse, residence **10** efficiency
converted ~: **4** loft
dweller: **3** res. **6** lessee, renter, tenant **8** occupant, resident
feature: **2** AC, rm. **3** EIK **4** bdrm., room **6** closet **7** bedroom, kitchen **8** bathroom **10** dining room, living room
get an ~: **4** rent
heater: **5** steam
in England: **4** flat
invite to one's ~: **5** ask in, ask up
like some ~ s: **5** unlet

location, maybe: 4 bsmt.
manager: 4 supt. 5 super
number: 4 one A, one B, one C, one D, one E, one F, one G, six A, six B, six C, six D, six E, six F, six G, two A, two B, two C, two D, two E, two F, two G 5 five A, five B, five C, five D, five E, five F, five G, four A, four B, four C, four D, four E, four F, four G 6 three A, three B, three C, three D, three E, three F, three G
owned ~: 4 co-op 5 condo
owner: 6 lessor 8 landlord
pest: 3 ant 5 roach
prohibition: 6 no pets
sign: 5 to let
apartment __: 5 hotel, house
__ apartment: 4 co-op 6 duplex, garden, studio, walk-in, walk-up
Apartment for Peggy (1948 film)
cast: Jeanne Crain, William Holden
director: George Seaton
Apartment, The (1960 film)
cast: Jack Lemmon, Shirley MacLaine, Fred MacMurray
director: Billy Wilder
Apartment Zero (1988 film)
cast: Hart Bochner, Dora Bryan, Colin Firth
Apaseo el Alto: 4 city, town
locale: 6 Mexico 10 Guanajuato
Apaseo el Grande: 4 city, town
locale: 6 Mexico 10 Guanajuato
apathetic: 4 blah, cool, lazy, logy, numb 5 aloof, blasé, musty, stoic, tepid 6 otiose, stolid, torpid 7 languid, passive, stoical, unmoved, warmish 8 dallying, detached, indolent, listless, lukewarm, slothful, sluggish, uncaring 9 impassive, lethargic, negligent, shiftless, unfeeling, untouched 10 insensible, neglectful, nonchalant, phlegmatic, spiritless, unagitated, world-weary
be ~: 4 mope
one: 5 moper
apathy: 5 ennui 6 acedia, stupor, torpor 7 boredom, inertia, languor, laxness 8 coolness, doldrums, dullness, laziness, lethargy, loginess 9 aloofness, disregard, indolence, inertness, lassitude
apatite to Mohs: 4 five
Apatlaco: 4 city, town
locale: 6 Mexico 7 Morelos
Apatzingán: 4 city, town
locale: 6 Mexico 9 Michoacán
Apaxco: 4 city, town
locale: 6 Mexico
APB: 5 alert 7 dragnet
broadcaster: 2 PD
datum: 3 AKA
part of ~: 3 all 6 points 8 bulletin
APC riders: 5 troop
ape: 2 do 3 lug 4 boor, copy, echo, goon, hood, lout, luny, mime, mock, sham 5 biped, Bonzo, brute, chimp, jocko, loony, mimer, mimic, Muggs, orang 6 baboon, galoot, gibbon, looney, lummox, mammal, mirror, parody, parrot, pongid, simian 7 act like, bananas, bruiser, Cheetah, copycat, emulate, galloot, gorilla, hoodlum, imitate, primate, siamang 8 imitator, King Kong, lunkhead, make like, simulate, talk like 9 orangutan, pantomime 10 caricature, chimpanzee, follow suit, orangutang
big ~: 6 galoot, lummox 7 galloot 8 lumberer
combining form: 6 pithec- 7 pitheco-
dog ~: 6 baboon
go ~: 4 flip, rage, rave 5 crack, freak 6 lose it 8 freak out
naked ~: 3 man 5 being, human
relative: 4 saki, titi 5 drill, lemur, loris, magot, potto, shrew 6 aye-aye, Bandar, galago, gelada, grivet, guenon, howler, langur, macaco, monkey, rhesus, uakari, vervet 7 colobus, gorilla, guereza, hoolock, macaque, sapajou, tamarin, tarsier 8 bush baby, capuchin, mandrill, mangabey, marmoset, talapoin
__ ape: 3 dog 5 great 6 lesser 7 Barbary
apeak: 8 vertical
Ape in Me, The author: Cornelia Otis Skinner
apeman: 6 Tarzan
Apennines: 5 peaks, range 9 mountains
locale: 5 Italy 6 Europe
peak: 5 Amaro 9 Monte Como
religious center: 6 Assisi
__ a penny...: 5 In for
aper: 4 mime 5 mimer, mimic 6 copier, Little, parrot 7 copycat 8 emulator, imitator 10 Rich Little
aperçu: 5 sight 6 digest, glance, précis 7 glimpse, outline, summary
__ a perfumed sea...: 3 o'er
apéritif: 3 kir 4 ouzo 5 drink 7 liqueur 8 beverage, libation 9 appetizer
flavoring: 5 anise
aperitive: 10 appetizing
aperture: 3 gap 4 hole, leak, pore, rift, slit, slot, vent 5 crack, mouth, space 6 louver, outlet 7 ingress, keyhole, opening, pinhole 10 interspace, interstice
camera lens ~: 5 f-stop, t-stop
leaf ~: 5 stoma
violin ~: 5 f hole
aperture __: 4 card, mask, stop 5 ratio
apery: 7 mimicry 9 imitation
__ Ape, The: 5 Naked
apex: 3 tip, top 4 acme, cusp, head, noon, peak 5 crest, crown, point, ridge, spire 6 apogee, climax, height, summit, tipoff, tiptop, vertex, zenith 7 maximum 8 high spot, meridian, pinnacle 9 crescendo, high point
at the ~ of: 4 atop
APF: 9 analgesic 10 painkiller
alternative: 4 Cope 5 Advil, Aleve, Bayer 6 Anacin, Datril, Motrin 7 Ecotrin, Tylenol 8 Bufferin, Excedrin, St. Joseph, Vanquish 9 Ascriptin
Apgar: 8 Virginia
Apgar __: 5 score
aphid: 3 bug 4 pest 6 ant cow, insect
milker: 3 ant
__ aphid: 3 pea 4 bean, rose 6 woolly 7 cabbage, spinach
aphis: 3 bug 4 pest 5 louse 6 insect
aphonic: 3 mum 6 silent 8 nonvocal 10 speechless
aphorism: 3 saw 4 rule 5 adage, axiom, gnome, maxim, moral, motto, truth 6 byword, dictum, phrase, saying, truism 7 epigram, precept, proverb 8 apothegm, laconism 10 apophthegm
Hindu ~: 5 sutra
mysterious ~: 4 rune
aphoristic: 5 terse 6 gnomic 9 axiomatic 10 of few words
Aphrodite
animal sacred to ~: 3 ram 4 dove, goat, hare, swan 7 sparrow, swallow
daughter of ~: 5 Beroe 8 Harmonia
epithet: 5 Areia 6 Acraea, Morpho, Pontia, Praxis, Scotia, Urania 7 Asteria, Doritis, Erycina, Euploia, Limenia 8 Despoena, Melaenis, Nymphaea, Pandemos, Pasiphae 9 Migonitis
equivalent: 5 Venus
girdle of ~: 6 cestus
lover of ~: 4 Ares 5 Butes 6 Adonis, Hermes 8 Anchises, Dionysus, Phaethon 10 Hephaestus
parent of ~: 4 Zeus 5 Dione
plant sacred to ~: 4 rose 5 apple, poppy 6 myrtle
son of ~: 4 Eros, Eryx 5 Eneas, Lyrus 6 Aeneas, Deimos, Phobus 8 Astynous
__ Aphrodite: 6 Mighty
Aphrodite in Aulis author: George Moore
Aphrodite sculptor: 4 Erté
Api: 4 peak 5 mount 8 mountain
locale: 4 Asia 5 Nepal 9 Himalayas
Apia: 4 city, town 7 capital
locale: 5 Samoa, Upolu
apian defense: 5 sting
__ a Piano: 5 I Love
apiarist: 9 beekeeper
apiary: 4 hive 7 beehive
resident: 3 bee
apical: 5 sharp 8 loftiest 9 uppermost
apiculture concern: 4 bees, hive 5 honey
apiculus: 5 thorn
__-à-pie: 3 cap
apiece: 3 per 4 a pop, each 6 for one, singly 7 per unit 8 one by one 9 per capita, per person 10 separately
a piece of one's __: 4 mind
a piece of the __: 6 action
à pied: 6 on foot
__ a pin: 6 neat as
apiphobe fear: 4 bees
apis: 3 bee
apish: 5 silly 9 emulative, imitative
__-à-pistons: 6 cornet
Apizaco: 4 city, town
locale: 6 Mexico 8 Tlaxcala
APL: 8 language
alternative: 3 ADA, SQL 4 Alef, html, Icon, Java, LISP, Logo, Orca, Perl 5 Algol, Basic, Cecil, COBOL, Dylan, SISAL 6 Delphi, Eiffel, Erlang, Oberon, Pascal, Prolog, Sather, Scheme, Snobol 7 Fortran
__ a Place: 5 I Know
__, a plan..., A: 3 man
__ a play for: 4 make
__ a plea: 3 cop
aplenty: 4 enow, lots, much 6 galore 7 liberal, profuse
aplite: 7 granite
aplomb: 4 cool, ease 5 poise, style 7 balance 8 calmness 9 assurance, composure, sang-froid, stability 10 confidence, equanimity, sedateness, steadiness
APO
addressee: 2 GI 3 PFC, pvt., sgt.
apocalypse: 4 doom
Apocalypse __: 3 Now
Apocalypse, Horseman of the: 3 War 5 Death 6 Famine 10 Pestilence
Apocalypse Now (1979 film)
cast: Marlon Brando, Robert Duvall, Martin Sheen
director: Francis Ford Coppola
role: 5 Hicks, Kurtz 7 Kilgore, Willard
setting: 3 Nam 7 Vietnam
Apocalypse Postponed author: Umberto Eco
Apocalypse Watch, The author: Robert Ludlum
apocalyptic: 5 vatic 7 fatidic, ominous, vatical 8 oracular 9 prophetic 10 predictive, revelatory
Apocrypha book: 3 Esd., Tob. 4 Macc. 5 Tobit 6 Baruch, Esdras, Judith, Sirach 7 Azariah, Susanna 8 Manasseh 9 Maccabees
apocryphal: 6 untrue 8 spurious 9 equivocal, imaginary, legendary, ungenuine 10 fictitious, inaccurate, unverified
apod: 3 eel 4 worm 5 ameba, snail, snake 6 amoeba
lack: 4 foot
Apodaca: 4 city, town
locale: 6 Mexico 9 Nuevo León
apodal: 8 footless
Apodes member: 3 eel
apodictic: 9 axiomatic 10 infallible
apogee: 3 top 4 apex, head, peak 5 bound, crest, limit, spire 6 climax, height, summit, tip-top, vertex, zenith 7 maximum 8 meridian, pinnacle 9 extremity 10 outer limit
__ a point: 7 stretch
__ a poke: 5 pig in
Apollo: 3 car, god 4 auto, font, hunk, seer 5 Buick, Creed 6 beauty 8 asteroid, Olympian, typeface 10 automobile
animal sacred to ~: 4 hawk, swan, wolf 5 mouse, raven, snake
astronaut: 4 Bean, Duke 5 Evans, Haise, Irwin, Roosa, Scott, Young 6 Aldrin, Anders, Borman, Cernan, Conrad, Eisele, Gordon, Lovell, Worden 7 Collins, Schirra, Schmitt, Shepard, Swigert 8 McDivitt, Mitchell, Stafford 9 Armstrong, Mattingly 10 Cunningham 11 Schweickart
attendant: 5 Erato
daughter of ~: 6 Phoebe, Scylla 7 Eriopis, Hilaira 9 Parthenos
destination: 4 moon
epithet of ~: 6 Actius, Delius, Loxias 7 Acesius, Acritas, Agraeus, Agyieus, Carneus, Patrous, Phoebus, Pythian 8 Ecbasion, Embasius, Grynaeus, Ismenius 9 Parnopius, Smintheus 10 Archegetes
instrument: 4 lyre
lover of ~: 4 Aria, Urea 5 Hyrie, Manto, Melia, Rhoeo, Thero 6 Acalle, Chione, Creusa, Cyrene, Dryope, Evadne, Hecate, Hecuba, Hekate, Othris, Phthia, Rhetia, Sinope, Stilbe, Syllis, Urania 7 Aethusa, Arsinoe, Corycia 8 Calliope, Chryseis, Psamathe 10 Chrysorthe, Parthenope
opponent: 5 Rocky
org.: 4 NASA
parent of ~: 4 Leto, Zeus 7 Jupiter
shrine: 6 Delphi, oracle
son of ~: 3 Hap, Ion 4 Apis, Hapi 5 Anius, Dorus, Iamus, Idmon, Ileus, Linus, Oncus, Syrus, Tenes 6 Cycnus, Galeus, Mopsus 7 Chaeron, Chryses, Coronus, Delphus, Lycorus, Miletus, Tenerus, Troilus 8 Eleuther, Laodocus, Lapithus, Melaneus, Pythaeus 9 Amphissus, Aristaeus, Asclepius, Centaurus, Lycomedes, Philammon, Philander, Zeuxippus 10 Amphiaraus, Phylacides, Polypoetes, Trophonius
twin of ~: 5 Diana 7 Artemis
vehicle: 3 LEM
victim of ~: 6 Tityus
__ Apollo: 6 Johnny
Apollo 13 (1995 film)
cast: Kevin Bacon, Tom Hanks, Ed Harris, Bill Paxton, Kathleen Quinlan, Gary Sinise
director: Ron Howard
role: 5 Haise 6 Lovell 7 Swigert 9 Mattingly
subject: 4 NASA
__ Apollo Forte: 4 Nick
Apollo in Masagète: 6 ballet
composer: 10 Stravinsky
Apollonia: 5 saint

Apollonian: 6 serene
Apollonius of Rhodes: 4 poet
Apollo Theater site: 3 NYC 6 Harlem 7 New York 9 Manhattan
apolog: 5 fable
apologetic: 5 sorry 6 rueful 8 contrite, penitent 9 expiatory, regretful, repentant 10 remorseful
apologia: 6 reason
Apologia pro vita __: 3 sua
Apologies!: 5 sorry 7 I'm sorry 8 mea culpa
apologist: 5 urger 6 arguer 7 pleader 8 champion, defender, seconder 9 justifier, proponent, supporter
apologize: 6 regret 9 beg pardon, make up for 10 make amends
for: 6 defend
to: 10 make up with
apologue: 5 fable
apology: 4 plea 5 sorry 6 reason, regret 7 defense 8 mea culpa 10 reparation
accept one's ~: 7 forgive
in Italian: 5 scusa
response: 5 it's OK
Apology author: Plato
__-a-poo: 4 cock
Apopa: 4 city, town
locale: 10 El Salvador
Apopka: 4 city, town
locale: 7 Florida
aport: 9 to the left
__-à-porter: 4 prêt
__ a positive note: 5 end on
apostasy: 8 flip-flop, reversal 9 about-face, defection, desertion, forsaking, one-eighty, rebellion, sundering, turnabout 10 abjuration, changeover, copping out, recidivism, switcheroo, switchover, withdrawal
apostate: 3 rat 7 impious, sceptic, skeptic, traitor 8 betrayer, defector, deserter, disloyal, forsaker, recreant, renegade, turncoat
apostatize: 5 lapse 6 recant
apostle: 4 John, Paul 5 envoy, James, Judas, Peter, Simon, urger 6 Andrew, Philip, Thomas 7 Matthew 8 advocate, believer, champion, disciple, follower, preacher 9 expounder, proponent, supporter, Thaddaeus 10 missionary, Simon Peter
apostle __: 4 bird 5 plant
Apostle __: 5 spoon 7 pitcher
__ Apostle: 4 Holy 7 John the
Apostle of California: 5 Serra
Apostle of the Slavs: 5 Cyril
Apostles' __: 5 Creed
Apostles, The composer: 5 Elgar
Apostle, The (1997 film)
cast: Robert Duvall, Farrah Fawcett, Miranda Richardson, Billy Bob Thornton
director: Robert Duvall
Apostle, The author: Sholem Asch
apostolic: 8 clerical
apostolic __: 3 age 5 vicar
__ apostolic: 5 vicar 7 prefect
Apostolic __: 3 See 6 Church, Father
apostrophe: 4 mark 6 speech 7 address, oration 10 digression, discursion, salutation
apothecaries' __: 6 weight 7 measure
apothecary: 4 phar. 5 pharm. 8 druggist, pharmacy 9 drugstore 10 pharmacist
measure: 3 scr. 4 dram 7 scruple
apothecary __: 3 jar
apothegm: 3 saw 5 adage, axiom, motto 6 dictum 7 proverb 8 aphorism, laconism
apothegmatic: 9 axiomatic
apotheosis: 5 ideal 7 epitome, paragon 8 cynosure 9 elevation, extolment 10 embodiment, exaltation
apotheosize: 8 enshrine, inshrine
__ a pound: 5 in for
__ a powder: 4 take
__ app: 6 killer
appal: 4 faze, stun 5 daunt, shock 6 dismay, revolt 7 disgust, horrify, mortify, outrage, petrify, terrify, unnerve 8 frighten, gross out 9 terrorize 10 disconcert, dishearten, scandalize, scare stiff
Appalachia composer: 6 Delius
Appalachian __: 3 tea 5 Trail 6 Spring
Appalachians: 5 range 9 mountains
locale: 3 Ala. 4 N. Car., Penn., S. Car., Tenn. 5 Maine 6 Canada 7 Alabama, Georgia, New York, Vermont 8 Virginia 9 Tennessee
peak: 6 Rogers 8 Katahdin, Mitchell
Appalachian Spring: 6 ballet
composer: 7 Copland
Appalachian Trail start: 5 Maine
appall: 4 faze, stun 5 daunt, shock 6 dismay, revolt 7 disgust, horrify, mortify, outrage, petrify, terrify, unnerve 8 frighten, gross out 9 terrorize 10 disconcert, dishearten, scandalize, scare stiff
appalled: 6 aghast 9 awestruck
appalling: 3 bad 4 dire, foul, grim, poor, ugly, vile 5 awful, gross, lousy, lurid, woful 6 crumby, crummy, dismal, grisly, horrid, odious, rotten, tragic, unholy, woeful 7 accurst, baleful, baneful, beastly, doleful, fearful, ghastly, hideous, ungodly 8 accursed, dreadful, God-awful, grievous, gruesome, horrible, horrific, inferior, shameful, shocking, stinking, terrible, terrific, tragical, wretched 9 abhorrent, atrocious, defective, dismaying, execrable, frightful, harrowing, insidious, loathsome, miserable, monstrous, offensive, repellant, revolting, unnerving, unsightly 10 abominable, astounding, despicable, detestable, disastrous, formidable, horrendous, horrifying, petrifying, terrifying, unpleasant
Appaloosa: 5 horse 6 equine
apparatus: 3 kit, rig 4 gear, tool 5 gizmo, means, thing 6 device, engine, gadget, outfit, tackle 7 machine 8 workings 9 appliance, doohickey, equipment, hierarchy, implement, invention, machinery, mechanism, structure 10 instrument
provide with ~: 5 equip
apparel: 4 duds, garb, gear, togs, vest, wear 5 array, dress, getup, habit, robes 6 attire, livery, outfit, things 7 clothes, costume, garment, raiment, threads 8 accouter, accoutre, clothing, garments, wardrobe 9 trappings 10 habiliment, Sunday best
put on ~: 3 don 6 clothe
see also clothing
__ apparel: 7 wearing
apparent: 4 easy, open, over 5 clear, gross, overt, plain, quasi, vivid 6 cogent, in view, likely, marked, patent, public 7 evident, exposed, express, glaring, nominal, obvious, outward, seeming, surface, visible 8 clear-cut, distinct, explicit, illusive, illusory, manifest, palpable, possible, probable, supposed, unhidden, unveiled 9 barefaced, big as life, graspable, plausible, prominent 10 noticeable, observable, ostensible, pronounced, spelled out, unshrouded
become ~: 4 dawn
apparent __: 4 time, wind 7 horizon
__ apparent: 4 heir
apparently: 8 probably 9 allegedly, at a glance, doubtless, evidently, expressly, obviously, outwardly, plausibly, reputably, seemingly 10 manifestly, most likely, officially, ostensibly, reasonably, speciously, supposedly
__ apparent reason: 5 for no
apparition: 5 ghost, shade 6 fantom, spirit, wraith 7 eidolon, fantasy, phantom, specter 8 bogeyman, delusion, illusion, presence, revenant
apparitional: 7 ghostly
A&P part: 3 Atl., Pac. 7 Pacific 8 Atlantic
Appassionata Sonata composer: 9 Beethoven
appeal: 3 ask, beg, sue 4 call, plea, pray, pull, suit 5 apply, argue, charm, drive, plead, savor, tempt 6 allure, beauty, demand, desire, engage, entice, glamor, please, prayer, speech 7 attract, beseech, charism, enchant, entreat, glamour, implore, request, solicit 8 charisma, entreaty, litigate, petition, proposal, recourse, telethon 9 captivate, fascinate, go to court, impetrate, importune, magnetism 10 allurement, attraction, fund-raiser, invitation, invocation, recitation, supplicate
lose ~: 4 pall
make an ~: 3 ask 4 pray
to: 3 sue 4 draw, hook, lure, urge 5 plead, press, tempt 6 allure, entice, invoke, pull in 7 attract, entreat 8 interest
urgent ~: 4 suit 6 orison, prayer 8 entreaty, petition
appeal __: 4 play
__ appeal: 3 eye, sex 4 curb, mass, snob
appealing: 4 cute, nice 5 sweet 6 pretty 7 likable, lovable 8 adorable, charming, inviting, loveable, readable 9 beautiful 10 appetizing, attractive, enchanting
find ~: 4 like
make more ~: 5 sugar
appeals-court ruling: 6 denial
appear: 3 act, pop 4 come, form, look, loom, peep, peer, rise, seem, show 5 arise, begin, break, occur, pop in, pop up 6 arrive, attend, blow in, come up, crop up, drop in, emerge, fade in, grow up, happen, loom up, result, roll in, show up, spring, turn up 7 check in, clock in, punch in, surface, turn out 8 breeze in, look as if, look like, spring up 10 burst forth
again: 5 recur
as: 7 perform 9 represent
gradually: 5 set in 6 fade in
imminent: 4 loom
like: 8 resemble
suddenly: 5 bob up, pop up
to be: 4 seem 5 sound
with: 9 accompany
appearance: 3 air 4 aura, cast, face, form, look, mask, mien, rise, role, show, side, view 5 debut, dress, front, guise, image, phase, shape, sight 6 advent, aspect, coming, facade, facies, format, manner, veneer, vision 7 arrival, bearing, outside 8 attitude, carriage, demeanor, entrance, epiphany, features, likeness, presence, pretense 9 character, condition, emergence, semblance, showing up, turning up, unveiling 10 attendance, complexion, deportment, exhibition, impression, phenomenon, reflection
assumed ~: 5 guise
brief ~: 5 cameo
combining form: 5 -phany
enhance one's ~: 5 primp
external ~: 4 look, mask, mien, pose, role 5 cover, front, guise 6 aspect, facade, outfit 7 posture 8 demeanor, likeness 9 semblance
false ~: 4 sham 5 guise 10 camouflage
first ~: 4 rise 5 debut 7 baptism, kickoff 8 premiere 9 coming out 10 initiation
in ~: 9 outwardly
make an ~: 4 come, show 5 arise, enter, visit 6 attend, show up, turn up 7 turn out
outward ~: 3 air 4 face, look, mask, mien, pose 5 cloak, cover, front, guise, shape 6 aspect, facade, manner, veneer 7 bearing 8 demeanor, disguise, exterior 9 semblance 10 camouflage, false front, impression, masquerade
appearing combining form: 4 phen- 5 pheno-
appease: 3 lay 4 calm, sate 5 allay, quell, quiet, slake 6 pacify, smooth, soften, soothe, subdue 7 assuage, compose, content, gratify, mollify, placate, relieve, satisfy, sweeten 8 mitigate, moderate 9 alleviate, reconcile, untrouble 10 conciliate, make amends
Appelfeld, Aharon: 6 writer 7 Israeli
appellant: 8 litigant 9 applicant
appellation: 4 name, term 5 label, title 6 handle 7 epithet, moniker 8 monicker, nickname
appellative: 5 title
append: 3 add, tag 4 join, tack 5 add on, add to, affix, annex, tag on 6 adjoin, attach, fasten, tack on 7 conjoin, include 10 supplement
appendage: 3 arm, tab, toe 4 limb, tail, wing 5 annex, digit 6 finger, member 7 adjunct 8 addendum, addition, offshoot 9 accessory, ancillary, auxiliary, extension, extremity 10 attachment, elongation, projection, supplement
legislative ~: 7 proviso 9 amendment
appendix: 5 annex, table 7 adjunct, codicil 8 addendum, addition 9 extension 10 attachment, elongation, postscript, supplement, tabulation
neighbor: 5 index
appertain: 5 apply, refer 6 belong, relate 8 belong to 9 touch upon
to: 7 concern
appetence: 4 bias, lure, lust, need, want, wish 5 drive 6 desire, hunger, liking, thirst 7 craving, leaning, longing, passion 8 affinity, instinct, penchant, tendency, yearning 9 affection, magnetism 10 allurement, attraction, partiality, propensity
__ appétit!: 3 Bon
appetite: 3 yen 4 itch, lust, urge, will, zest 5 gusto, taste 6 desire, hunger, liking, relish, thirst 7 craving, longing, passion, stomach 8 fondness, penchant, voracity, weakness, yearning 9 esurience, hankering 10 love of life, proclivity
arouser: 5 aroma
build an ~: 4 whet
combining form: 6 -orexia
in French: 4 faim
in psychology: 6 orexis
voracious ~: 3 maw
whet the ~: 5 tempt
appetizer: 3 lox 4 Brie, Edam, pâté, pupu, whet 5 tapas 6 canapé, celery, dim sum, fondue, nachos, radish, rumaki 7 bean dip, ceviche, egg roll, fajitas, gravlax, saltine 8 caponata, cocktail, crabcake, crab puff, crudités, drumette, empanada, escargot, fruit cup, party mix 9 antipasto, guacamole, macédoine 10 black olive, breadstick,

deviled egg, finger food, green olive, potato skin
avocado ~: 9 guacamole
bar mitzvah ~: 5 knish
chicken ~: 8 drumette
Chinese ~: 4 pupu 6 dim sum
eggplant ~: 8 caponata
fish ~: 3 lox 7 ceviche, gravlax
follower: 6 entrée
French ~: 9 macédoine
Japanese ~: 6 rumaki
liver ~: 4 pâté 6 rumaki
Mexican ~: 6 nachos 7 fajitas
Spanish ~: 5 tapas
appetizing: 5 sapid, spicy, tasty, yummy 6 delish, divine, savory, spicey, toothy 8 luscious, tempting 9 aperitive, appealing, delicious, flavorful, nectarous, palatable, succulent, sweetened, toothsome 10 delectable, flavorsome
___ Appia: 3 Via
Appian Way terminus: 4 Rome 5 Capua
applaud: 4 clap, hail, laud 5 cheer, exalt, extol, honor 6 extoll, praise, salute 7 acclaim, commend, flatter, glorify, root for 8 eulogize, hand it to 9 approve of, encourage, recommend 10 compliment, panegyrize
applauder: 5 toady 6 claque
applause: 4 hand 5 éclat, kudos 6 praise 7 acclaim, big hand, ovation, tribute 8 plaudits 9 standing O
acknowledge ~: 3 bow
burst of ~: 4 hand 5 round
response: 6 encore
Applause: 7 musical
character: 3 Eve 4 Bert, Buzz 5 Duane, Karen, Margo
composer: 5 Adams 7 Strouse
writer: 5 Green 6 Comden
apple: 3 Mac, pie 4 crab, Gala, Lodi, pome, Rome, tree 5 fruit, Mutsu 6 Empire, Ida Red, medlar, pippin, russet, sphere 7 Baldwin, Bramley, costard, Freedom, Liberty, Spartan, Wealthy, Winesap 8 Cortland, Jonathan, McIntosh 9 Delicious, Macintosh 10 Rome Beauty
acid: 5 malic
center: 4 core
cider girl: 3 Ida
color: 3 red 5 green 6 yellow
combining form: 4 pomi-
custard ~: 5 papaw 6 pawpaw
drink: 5 cider, juice 9 hard cider
eater: 3 Eve 4 Adam
ender: 4 jack 5 sauce
European ~ tree: 4 sorb
family: 4 rose
gadget: 5 corer, parer
in ~ pie order: 4 neat, tidy
invader: 4 worm
juice brand: 5 Mott's
like an ~: 5 round 6 crispy 7 crunchy 8 spheroid 9 spherical
of discord contender: 4 Hera
of one's eye: 3 pet 5 pearl 7 darling 8 favorite
quantity: 4 peck 6 bushel
relative: 4 pear, plum 5 peach 6 almond, cherry, medlar, quince 7 apricot 8 hawthorn, oiticica 10 blackthorn
search for ~ s: 3 bob
seed: 3 pip
skin: 4 peel
spray: 4 Alar
spread: 3 jam 5 jelly
starter: 4 crab, pine
targeter: 4 Tell
tosser of myth: 4 Eris
apple ___: 3 bee, pie 5 dowdy, green, grunt 6 brandy, butter, sucker 7 blossom
apple ___..., An: 4 a day
apple ___ la mode: 4 pie à
apple-___: 6 polish
apple-___ order: 3 pie
___ apple: 3 bad, may, oak 4 bake, crab, lady, love, rose, snow, sorb, star 5 Adam's, baked, blade, candy, cedar, hedge, sugar, taffy, thorn 6 balsam, bitter, cashew, mammee, potato 7 custard, Mexican
___-apple: 3 kei 4 cran, pond
Apple: 3 Mac 4 Imac 5 Fiona 8 computer 10 Mackintosh
alternative: 2 PC 3 IBM
Apple ___: 4 Isle 5 Jacks
___ Apple: 3 Big
apple brown ___: 5 Betty
___ apple every day...: 5 Eat an
Apple, Fiona real last name: Maggart
Applegate, Christina: 7 actress
film: The Big Hit (1998)
Jane Austen's Mafia! (1998)
The Sweetest Thing (2002)
spouse: Johnathon Schaech
TV: Married...With Children
applejack: 5 drink 8 beverage
ingredient: 5 cider 6 brandy
Apple Jacks: 6 cereal
competitor: 3 Kix 4 Life, Trix 5 Kashi, Quisp, Total 6 Kaboom, Muesli, Oreo O's, Pablum, Smacks 7 All-Bran, Crispix, Harmony, Hunny B's, Mueslix, Oat Bran, Pokemon 8 Boo Berry, Cheerios, Corn Chex, Corn Pops, Fiber One, Rice Chex, Special K, Uncle Sam, Wheaties 9 Alpha Bits, Apple Zaps, Grape Nuts, Honey Comb, Just Right, Wheat Chex 10 Bran Flakes, Cap'n Crunch, Cocoa Puffs, Froot Loops, Mini-Wheats, Nutri-Grain, Puffed Rice, Quaker Oats, Smart Start 11 Cocoa Blasts, Cookie Crisp, Golden Crisp, Lucky Charms, Puffed Wheat, Sweet Crunch, Waffle Crisp
apple of ___: 4 Peru 7 discord
apple of one's ___: 3 eye
apple-pie ___: 5 order 7 à la mode
apple-polish: 4 fawn 5 toady 6 cajole, grovel 7 adulate 8 fawn over, play up to
apple-polisher: 5 toady 6 fawner, flunky 7 flunkey 8 adulator, kowtower
apples and oranges: 6 unlike
applesauce: 3 gas, pap, rot 4 blah, bosh, bull, bunk, guff, jazz, jive, pooh, tosh 5 bilge, fudge, hokum, hooey, prate, stuff, trash, tripe 6 bunkum, bushwa, drivel, footle, gabble, gammon, gibber, havers, hot air, humbug, jabber, jargon, kibosh, piffle 7 baloney, blarney, blather, blether, boloney, bushwah, eyewash, flannel, flubdub, fustian, garbage, hogwash, inanity, malarky, rubbish, twaddle 8 buncombe, claptrap, falderal, falderol, fast talk, flimflam, flummery, folderal, folderol, malarkey, nonsense, slipslop, tommyrot, trumpery 9 absurdity, banana oil, gibberish, goofiness, kidstakes, moonshine, poppycock, rigmarole 10 balderdash, bilge water, codswallop, double-talk, flapdoodle, galimatias, Jabberwock, mumbo jumbo, rigamarole, taradiddle
brand: 5 Mott's
Appleseed: 6 Johnny
Apples, Peaches, Pumpkin Pie (1967 song) artist: Jay and the Techniques
apple strudel: 6 pastry 7 dessert
applet: 7 program 8 software
Appleton: 4 city, town 6 Edward
locale: 4 Wisc. 9 Wisconsin
Appleton, Edward: 8 Nobelist 9 physicist
Apple Valley: 4 city, town
locale: 9 Minnesota 10 California
Apple Zaps: 6 cereal
competitor: 3 Kix 4 Life, Trix 5 Kashi, Quisp, Total 6 Kaboom, Muesli, Oreo O's, Pablum, Smacks 7 All-Bran, Crispix, Harmony, Hunny B's, Mueslix, Oat Bran, Pokemon 8 Boo Berry, Cheerios, Corn Chex, Corn Pops, Fiber One, Rice Chex, Special K, Uncle Sam, Wheaties 9 Alpha Bits, Grape Nuts, Honey Comb, Just Right, Wheat Chex 10 Apple Jacks, Bran Flakes, Cap'n Crunch, Cocoa Puffs, Froot Loops, Mini-Wheats, Nutri-Grain, Puffed Rice, Quaker Oats, Smart Start 11 Cocoa Blasts, Cookie Crisp, Golden Crisp, Lucky Charms, Puffed Wheat, Sweet Crunch, Waffle Crisp
appliance: 4 tool, unit 6 device, gadget 7 fixture, machine 9 accessory, apparatus, furniture, implement, mechanism 10 employment, instrument
brand: 5 Amana, Norge, Oster 6 Bendix, Maytag, Tappan 7 Admiral, Jenn-Air, Kenmore 8 Hotpoint 9 Magic Chef, Whirlpool 10 Frigidaire, Kelvinator, KitchenAid
button: 5 reset
household ~: 2 TV 3 fan, vac, VCR 4 iron, oven 5 drier, dryer, grill, mixer, radio, range, stove, TV set, waxer 6 fridge, juicer, vacuum, washer 7 blender, freezer 8 barbecue 9 compactor, DVD player, microwave 10 clock radio, dishwasher, television
ID: 2 SN
letters: 4 ACDC
part: 4 cord, plug
applicability: 7 fitness, service, utility
applicable: 3 apt, fit 4 meet 5 utile, valid 6 proper, usable, useful, viable 7 apropos, fitting, germane, helpful, on point, useable 8 apposite, material, on target, relative, relevant, suitable, workable 9 available, befitting, connected, on the nose, pertinent 10 admissible, associable, felicitous, to the point
be ~ to: 7 concern
applicant: 6 seeker 7 entrant, hopeful 8 aspirant, claimant 9 appellant, candidate, job-hunter, postulant, suppliant 10 petitioner
accept an ~: 4 hire
application: 3 use 4 form, suit 5 claim, usage, value 6 appeal, demand, effort, praxis 7 purpose, request 8 entreaty, exercise, function, hard work, petition, practice
abbr.: 3 NMI
find a new ~ for: 5 reuse
job ~ entry: 3 sex 4 name 7 address, hobbies 9 reference 10 experience
lack of ~: 6 disuse
submitter: 5 filer
wrong ~: 6 misuse
application ___: 7 program
applicator: 4 swab, swob, wand
Appling, Luke: 8 White Sox 9 shortstop
appliqué: 4 lace 5 patch 6 iron-on 10 decoration
apply: 3 fit, rub, set, use 4 give, hold 5 exert, lay on, put on, refer, rub on, smear, spend, wield 6 anoint, appeal, belong, devote, direct, employ, engage, invoke, relate, resort 7 enforce, enquire, execute, exploit, harness, inflict, inquire, pertain, request, smear on, utilize 8 dedicate, dispense, exercise, petition, practice, put in for, put to use, spread on 9 appertain, embrocate, implement, put to work 10 administer, be relevant
again: 5 reuse
as lotion: 5 smear
(for): 3 sue, try 5 put in
gently: 3 dab
lace: 4 edge 5 adorn 6 bedeck 7 dress up 8 decorate, ornament, pretty up 9 embellish
lipstick: 4 tint 5 color, paint
logic: 3 see 4 muse 5 guess, infer, judge, study, weigh 6 assume, deduce, gather, ideate, ponder, reason, reckon 7 analyze, examine, presume, reflect, sort out, surmise, suspect 8 appraise, cogitate, conceive, conclude, consider, estimate, evaluate, mull over, perceive, ruminate, theorize 9 cerebrate, determine, figure out, speculate 10 conjecture, deliberate
oneself: 4 work 5 labor, lay to, study 6 hustle, pursue
oneself to: 7 address
to: 7 concern
(to): 6 matter, relate
unguent: 3 oil 5 bless 6 ordain 8 sanctify 9 lubricate 10 consecrate
wrongly: 6 misuse
apply for ___: 5 a loan
appoggiatura: 4 note
appoint: 3 rig, tap 4 make, name 5 equip, place 6 assign, choose, engage, enlist, instal, outfit, select, settle, supply 7 furnish, install, provide, station, turn out 8 accredit, delegate, deputize, nominate, schedule 9 designate, prescribe 10 commission, constitute, settle upon
appointed: 3 set
finely ~: 4 posh
time: 4 hour 5 H-hour 8 zero hour
___-appointed: 4 self, well
appointee: 5 agent, envoy, proxy 6 deputy, factor, legate 7 nominee, officer 8 delegate, emissary, mediator, selectee 9 assistant, candidate, go-between, middleman, surrogate 10 commissary
appointment: 3 gig 4 date, gear, post 5 berth, tryst, visit 6 billet, choice, naming, office, outfit 7 fixture, meeting, session 8 election, position, trapping 9 situation
book slot: 4 date, hour
make an ~: 4 name 6 select
Appointment in London (1953 film)
cast: Dirk Bogarde, Ian Hunter
director: Philip Leacock
Appointment in Samarra author: John O'Hara
appointments: 3 rig 4 gear, tack 5 decor, stuff 6 outfit, tackle 7 harness, rigging, turnout 8 fittings, fixtures, schedule 9 apparatus, caparison, equipment, trappings 10 habilments, outfitting
Appointment With Danger (1951 film)
cast: Phyllis Calvert, Alan Ladd
director: Lewis Allen
Appomattox: 4 city, town 5 river
figure: 3 Lee 5 Grant
locale: 8 Virginia
monogram: 3 REL, USG
part of an ~ signature: 4 E. Lee
apportion: 4 deal, mete 5 allot, allow, cut up, divvy, share, split 6 assign, bestow, budget, devote, divide, ration 7 divvy up, dole out, give out, mete

out, portion, prorate, split up 8 allocate, dedicate, dispense, divide up 9 admeasure, designate, parcel out, partition 10 administer, distribute, measure out
apportioned: 8 separate
apportionment: 4 dole 5 quota, share 6 ration
apportune: 8 apposite
apposite: 3 apt, fit, pat 4 meet 6 cogent, proper, seemly, suited, timely 7 apropos, fitting, germane, well put 8 becoming, material, relative, relevant, suitable 9 apportune, befitting, pertinent 10 applicable, convenient, felicitous, seasonable, to the point, well-suited
not ~: 5 unapt
appositeness: 7 fitness
appraisal: 5 price, value 6 rating, review 8 estimate, judgment 9 criticism, reckoning, valuation 10 assessment, estimation, evaluation
appraise: 3 eye, see 4 rate 5 assay, audit, gauge, judge, price, set at, think, value, weigh 6 assess, figure, reckon, review, size up, survey 7 adjudge, examine, inspect, measure, valuate 8 check out, estimate, evaluate, factor in, keep tabs, look over
the situation: 6 ponder
appraiser: 5 rater 6 lister
appreciable: 3 any 5 large 6 goodly, marked 7 evident, healthy, obvious, sizable 8 clear-cut, definite, manifest, material, sizeable, tangible
amount: 4 much
effect: 4 dent, mark 10 impression
appreciate: 3 dig, get, see 4 boom, gain, grok, grow, know, like, rise 5 enjoy, grasp, prize, savor, savvy, sense 6 admire, esteem, fathom, follow, praise, relish 7 cherish, realize, respect, welcome 8 conceive, flip over, increase, perceive, relate to, treasure 9 apprehend, care about, delight in, get high on, recognize 10 comprehend, freak out on, give thanks, understand
I ~ it: 5 danke, merci 6 gracis, thanks 8 thank you
appreciated: 7 welcome 8 valuable
appreciation: 3 ear 4 gain, love, rise 5 grasp, sense, taste 6 growth, liking, praise, regard, thanks 7 empathy, premium, thought, tribute
exclamation: 2 ah 3 gee, ooh, wow 5 great, huzza 6 hoorah, hooray, hurrah, hurray, huzzah, thanks
informal ~: 5 thanx
show ~: 4 clap 5 thank
token of ~: 4 gift
__-appreciation mortgage: 6 shared
appreciative: 5 proud 6 loving 7 mindful, obliged, pleased 8 admiring, grateful, indebted, thankful
like ~ fans: 5 aroar
apprehend: 3 bag, get, nab 4 bust, grab, hear, know, nail, take 5 catch, grasp, pinch, run in, seize, sense 6 absorb, arrest, collar, detain, fathom, follow, intuit, pick up, pull in, take in 7 capture, cognize, discern, realize, receive 8 perceive 9 extradite, recognize, track down 10 anticipate, appreciate, comprehend, understand
apprehended: 6 in jail 10 behind bars
apprehensible: 5 lucid 8 knowable, luminous
apprehension: 3 ken 4 care, fear 5 alarm, doubt, dread, grasp, qualm, worry 6 arrest, dismay, fright, phobia, reason 7 anxiety, booking, capture, concern, seizure, tension 8 disquiet, suspense 9 collaring, detention, misgiving 10 foreboding, misgivings, perception, uneasiness
expression: 4 oh-oh, uh-oh, yipe 5 yikes, yipes 7 omigosh
apprehensive: 3 shy 4 wary 5 chary, jumpy, leery, tense, timid 6 afraid, on edge, scared, trepid, uneasy, unsure 7 abashed, alarmed, anxious, chicken, daunted, dubious, fearful, guarded, jittery, nervous, spooked, uptight, worried 8 cautious, cowardly, doubtful, doubting, fearsome, hesitant, timorous 9 skeptical, uncertain 10 frightened, suspicious
be ~: 5 worry 8 mistrust
be ~ about: 4 fear
apprehensively: 6 in fear
apprehensiveness: 4 fear 5 qualm 9 misgiving
apprentice: 3 cub 4 aide, hand, tiro, tyro 5 labor, learn, newie, pupil 6 greeny, helper, intern, novice, rookie 7 amateur, employe, interne, learner, recruit, student 8 beginner, employee, henchman, neophyte, newcomer 9 assistant, fledgling, greenhorn, novitiate 10 tenderfoot
apprenticed: 5 bound
Apprenticeship of Duddy Kravitz, The: 4 film 5 novel
author: Mordecai Richter
cast: Richard Dreyfuss, Jack Warden
director: Ted Kotcheff
setting: 6 Canada, Quebec 8 Montreal
apprise: 4 tell, warn 5 brief 6 advise, fill in, inform, notify, tip off 8 advise of, forewarn, instruct 9 enlighten 10 put on guard
apprised: 3 hep, hip 4 wise 5 aware, privy, savvy 6 versed, with it 7 knowing, mindful 9 cognizant, in the know
be ~ of: 3 see 5 learn
of: 4 in on 7 privy to
approach: 3 way 4 come, meet, mode, near, path, plan, tack 5 light, means, reach, rival, slant, stalk, start, style, verge 6 access, accost, avenue, come at, course, embark, gain on, go near, go up to, loom up, manner, method, policy, talk to 7 advance, apply to, contact, ingress, solicit, speak to, tactics 8 attitude, commence, draw near, go toward, overture, set about, sound out, strategy, threaten 9 belly up to, catch up to, close in on, creep up on, procedure, technique, treatment, undertake, verge upon 10 converge on, draw near to, get a hold of, move toward
a deadline: 5 laten
eagerly: 5 run to
furtively: 5 sidle
intrusively: 6 accost
journalist ~: 5 angle, pitch, slant, twist 7 opinion 9 viewpoint
quickly: 5 run to
way of ~: 6 access, avenue
approach __: 4 shot 5 light
approachable: 4 open 7 affable 8 gracious, outgoing, sociable 9 receptive
approaching: 4 near, nigh 5 close 6 almost, at hand, coming, in view, nearly, toward 7 brewing, in store, looming, pending, towards 8 imminent, in the air, oncoming, on the way 9 impending, in the wind
the hour: 5 ten of, ten to
approbate: 5 favor 6 accept
approbation: 5 favor 6 praise, regard 7 acclaim, respect
approbative: 9 laudatory
appropriate: 3 apt, cop, due, fit, nip, rob 4 good, grab, just, lift, loot, meet, take 5 allot, annex, co-opt, filch, right, seize, steal, swipe, usurp 6 assign, assume, borrow, budget, decent, devote, fitted, pilfer, pocket, proper, rip off, seemly, snatch, timely, useful 7 condign, correct, earmark, fitting, germane, in order, preempt, procure, ransack, receive, require, reserve, utilize 8 allocate, apposite, becoming, decorous, dedicate, deserved, disburse, eligible, glom on to, relative, relevant, rightful, set apart, set aside, suitable 9 allowable, opportune 10 commandeer
be ~: 4 suit 5 apply, befit 6 beseem
more ~: 6 better
not ~: 5 inapt, unapt
to: 3 for
appropriately: 4 well 5 right 6 aright
appropriateness: 7 fitness 9 congruity, propriety
appropriation: 4 grab 5 grant, theft 6 taking 7 funding, seizure, stipend, subsidy 8 adoption, stealing
approval: 2 OK 4 okay 5 favor, leave 6 assent, credit, esteem, praise, regard, the nod 7 acclaim, consent, go-ahead, license, support 8 accolade, adoption, blessing, plaudits, sanction 9 agreement, clearance 10 admiration, green light, permission, popularity
enthusiastic ~: 6 yes yes
exclamation: 2 ah, ay 3 aah, aye, boy, olé, rah, yay, yea, yes 4 amen, good, yeah 5 brava, bravo, goody, great, zowie 6 by Jove, encore, goodie, good-oh, hoorah, hooray, hurrah, hurray, rather, whizzo 7 attaboy, by jingo 8 all right, attagirl
gesture of ~: 3 nod 5 V sign
give a stamp of ~: 2 OK 4 pass 5 bless 7 approve, certify, confirm, consent, endorse, license 8 sanction, validate 9 authorize, sign off on
legal ~: 3 lic. 7 license
seal of ~: 6 cachet 8 sanction
show ~: 4 buoy, clap, yell 5 cheer, elate, huzza, liven, pep up, shout, whoop 6 buck up, hoorah, hooray, hurrah, hurray, huzzah, perk up, praise, revive, scream, uplift 7 acclaim, applaud, elevate, enliven, gladden, hearten, root for, support 8 enspirit, inspirit, reassure 9 encourage 10 brighten up, exhilarate, strengthen
silent ~: 3 nod
approve: 2 OK 3 let, nod 4 back, hail, laud, like, okay, pass 5 adopt, agree, allow, bless, favor, stamp 6 accede, accept, assent, comply, concur, permit, praise, ratify, second, uphold 7 acclaim, certify, commend, confirm, consent, endorse, go along, indorse, support, sustain 8 accede to, accredit, legalize, sanction, validate 9 acquiesce, authorize, get behind, give leave, recognize, recommend, sign off on, subscribe 10 underwrite
don't ~: 3 nix 4 veto
of: 3 let 5 allow, brook, favor 6 accept, permit 7 applaud 8 accede to, assent to, sanction, stand for, tolerate 9 authorize, put up with
approved: 2 OK 3 Ok'd 4 okay 5 liked, tried 7 popular, regular 8 official, orthodox, standard 9 canonical, preferred
approving: 5 OK'ing 9 agreeable, favorable, laudatory 10 permissive
approx.: 3 abt., est.
approximal: 9 adjoining 10 contiguous
approximate: 4 near, rude 5 alike, close, loose, rival, rough, round 6 nearby, reckon 7 general, inexact, similar, verge on 8 adjacent, approach, border on, come near, relative, resemble 9 adumbrate, imprecise, uncertain
approximately: 3 say 4 or so 5 about, circa 6 almost, around, nearly 7 close to, loosely, roughly 9 somewhere 10 more or less
suffix: 3 -ish
approximation: 5 guess 8 estimate 9 guesswork 10 conjecture, estimation
appt.: 3 mtg.
appurtenance: 5 annex, extra 7 adjunct, ancilla, apanage 8 appanage 9 accessory, appendage, auxiliary 10 subsidiary
appurtenances: 3 rig 5 stuff
appurtenant: 7 adjunct 8 relative 9 accessory, auxiliary, belonging 10 subsidiary
to: 6 part of
Apr.: 2 mo.
agency: 3 IRS
busy ~ worker: 3 CPA
it starts in ~: 3 DST
predecessor: 3 Mar.
APR
part: 4 rate 6 annual 10 percentage
__ a Prayer: 4 Like
__-a Preacher Man: 5 Son-of
__ a precedent: 3 set
après __ le déluge: 3 moi
après-__: 3 ski 4 midi
après-midi: 6 French 9 afternoon
follower: 4 nuit, soir
après-ski beverage: 5 cocoa, toddy
Apres un __: 4 Rêve
apricot: 4 pink, tree 5 color, drupe, fruit 6 orange, yellow 7 pinkish 9 yellowish
family: 4 rose
Japanese ~: 3 ume
Korean ~: 4 ansu
relative: 4 buff, corn, gold, lime, nude, pear, plum, rust, sand 5 apple, blond, brass, coral, cream, flaxy, lemon, maize, melon, ocher, ochre, peach, rusty, straw 6 almond, blonde, canary, chammy, cherry, citron, crocus, damask, flaxen, medlar, quince, salmon, shammy, shamoy 7 chamois, citrine, jasmine, mustard, nankeen, old gold, saffron, xanthic 8 daffodil, flamingo, hawthorn, oiticica, primrose 9 carnation, champagne, goldenrod, jessamine 10 blackthorn
spread: 6 lekvar
April: 5 month 7 Stevens
birthstone: 7 diamond
concern: 3 tax 5 taxes 9 tax return
fifth: 5 nones
follower: 3 May
fool: 3 gag 5 prank
forecast: 4 rain
preceder: 5 March
sign: 3 Ram 4 Bull 5 Aries 6 Taurus
victim: 4 fool
April __: 4 fool, Love 7 Morning, Showers
April __ Day: 5 Fools'
April 5: 5 nones
April is the cruellest month poet: 5 Eliot
April Love (1957 song) artist: Pat Boone
composer: 4 Fain 7 Webster
April Morning author: Howard Fast
April Showers (1922 song) artist: Al Jolson
a priori: 9 deductive
__ a profit: 4 turn
apron: 5 smock 7 garment 8 pinafore 9 forestage 10 proscenium, protection

part: 3 bib 7 strings
wearer: 4 chef, cook, maid
apron ___: 5 piece 6 string
apropos: 3 apt, fit, pat 5 about 6 proper, timely, toward 7 fitting, germane, on point, towards, well-put 8 apposite, material, relative, relevant, suitable 9 opportune, pertinent, well-timed 10 applicable, felicitous, to the point
of: 4 as to, in re
apse: 6 chevet, concha, recess
path to an ~: 5 aisle
table: 5 altar
___ apso: 5 Lhasa
apt: 3 fit, pat 4 able, deft, good, just, meet 5 adept, given, happy, prone, quick, ready, right, savvy, sharp, smart 6 adroit, astute, bright, clever, cogent, decent, expert, gifted, liable, likely, proper, seemly, timely 7 apropos, capable, fitting, germane, skilled, subject, tending, well-put 8 apposite, dextrous, disposed, inclined, on target, probable, relevant, rightful, skillful, suitable 9 advisable, allowable, astucious, befitting, dexterous, efficient, ingenious, on the mark, opportune, pertinent, promising, qualified, sagacious 10 applicable, felicitous, precocious, proficient, to the point
be ~ (to): 4 tend
(to): 5 prone 7 of a mind, tending 8 disposed, inclined
apt.
see apartment
Apted, Michael: 8 director
film: 28 Up (1985)
35 Up (1991)
Agatha (1979)
Bring On the Night (1985)
Class Action (1991)
Coal Miner's Daughter (1980)
Continental Divide (1981)
Enigma (2001)
Enough (2002)
Gorillas in the Mist (1988)
Gorky Park (1983)
Incident at Oglala (1992)
Moving the Mountain (1994)
Nell (1994)
Stardust (1975)
Stronger Than the Sun (1980)
Thunderheart (1992)
The World Is Not Enough (1999)
apterous, not: 5 alary 6 winged
apteryx: 3 moa 4 kiwi
aptitude: 4 bent, gift, head, turn 5 craft, flair, knack, sense, skill 6 smarts, talent 7 ability, faculty, fitness, know-how, leaning, promise 8 capacity, facility, instinct 9 endowment, intellect, potential, smartness 10 capability, cleverness, competence, proclivity, proficient, propensity, right stuff
aptitude ___: 4 test
Aptiva maker: 3 IBM
aptly: 5 right 6 aright
aptness: 4 gift, tact 5 flair, knack 7 faculty, fitness 9 dexterity, expertise, readiness
___ a puddy tat!: 4 I taw
Apuleius, Lucius: 5 Roman 11 philosopher
a punta ___: 5 d'arco
Apure: 5 river
locale: 9 Venezuela
Aqaba: 4 city, gulf, port, town
Gulf of ~ port: 4 Elat 5 Eilat, Elath
Gulf of ~ strait: 5 Tiran
aqua: 5 water 6 liquid 8 greenish, sea green 9 blue-green, Nile green, turquoise
vitae: 3 rye 5 booze, drink, sauce, vodka 6 brandy, liquor, scotch, whisky 7 alcohol, bourbon, liqueur, potable, spirits, whiskey 8 beverage 9 firewater, inebriant, moonshine 10 intoxicant
aqua ___: 4 pura 5 regia, vitae 6 fortis 7 ammonia
Aqua ___: 5 Velva
Aqua-___: 4 Lung
aquaculture: 7 science
Aquafina: 5 water
alternative: 4 Naya 5 Evian 7 Perrier 9 Arrowhead
aqua fortis: 4 acid
Aquafresh: 10 toothpaste
alternative: 3 Aim 5 Crest, Gleem, Topol 7 Close-Up, Colgate, Viadent 9 Mentadent, Pepsodent, Rembrandt, Sensodyne 10 Pearl Drops, Ultra Brite 11 Tom's of Maine
aquake: 5 shaky
Aqua-Lung device: 5 scuba
aquamarine: 3 gem 4 blue 5 beryl, color, green 8 gemstone, greenish
mineral: 5 beryl
month: 5 March
relative: 3 pea 4 anil, cyan, jade, navy, Nile, sage, teal 5 Alice, azure, breen, olive, slate, virid 6 cobalt, indigo, myrtle, raisin, reseda, violet 7 avocado, celadon, emerald, peacock, verdant 8 cerulean, sapphire 9 pistachio, turquoise 10 chartreuse, periwinkle
aquanaut: 5 diver
gear: 5 scuba
aquarelle: 8 painting
Aquarian ___: 3 Age
___ Aquarids: 3 Eta 5 Delta
aquarium: 4 tank
accessory: 6 filter
dweller: 3 eel, orf 4 barb, orfe 5 danio, guppy, platy, skate, tetra 6 medaka 7 gourami, helleri, scalare 8 bloodfin, goldfish 9 neon tetra, swordtail
freshen a ~: 6 aerate
Aquarium artist: 4 Erté
Aquarius: 4 sign
month: 3 Feb., Jan. 7 January 8 February
predecessor: 9 Capricorn
successor: 6 Pisces
tote: 4 ewer 5 water
___ Aquarius: 5 Age of
Aquarius/Let the Sunshine In (1969 song) artist: Fifth Dimension
Aquarius show: 4 Hair
___ a Quarter to Nine: 5 About
aquatic: 5 naval 6 marine 7 oceanic 8 maritime, natatory, nautical
bird: 4 gull, swan, tern 5 grebe 6 jaçana
mammal: 4 seal 5 hippo, otary, otter 6 desman, dugong
nymph: 5 naiad
organism: 4 alga
plant: 5 lotus 6 elodea 8 duckweed 9 arrowhead, water lily
rodent: 5 coypu 7 muskrat
worm: 5 leech
Aqua Velva: 6 lotion 10 aftershave
competitor: 4 Brut 8 Gillette, Old Spice 10 Skin Bracer
aquavit: 5 drink 6 liquor 7 alcohol 8 beverage
aqueduct: 4 pipe 5 canal 6 course 7 channel, conduit 8 pipeline
contents: 5 water
Aqueduct transaction: 3 bet 5 wager
aqueous: 3 wet 5 fluid 6 liquid, serous, watery 7 hydrous 9 waterlike
material: 6 liquid
aqueous ___: 5 humor 7 ammonia
aquifer feature: 4 pore
Aquila: 5 Eagle
aquiline: 5 Roman 6 beaked, curved, hooked 9 eagle-like, prominent 10 protruding
Aquinas, Thomas: 5 saint 7 Italian 11 philosopher
Aquino: 4 Cory 5 Ninoy 7 Benigno, Corazon
Aquitaine: 5 duchy
locale: 6 France
Aquitaine Progression, The author: Robert Ludlum
aquiver: 5 shaky 7 vibrant 9 jellylike
Ar: 4 elem. 5 argon 7 element
18 for ~: 4 at. no.
AR
see Arkansas
ara: 4 bird 5 macaw
Ara: 9 Berberian 10 Parseghian
Ara ___: 5 Pacis
Arab: 4 amir, emir 5 ameer, emeer, horse, Iraki, Iraqi, Omani, Saudi, sheik, steed 6 Beduin, equine, Qatari, Semite, shaikh, sheikh, Shi'ite, Syrian, Yemeni 7 Bedouin, Kuwaiti, Saracen 8 Egyptian, Lebanese 9 Damascene, Jordanian
animal: 5 camel 9 dromedary
bazaar: 3 suk, suq 4 souk
boat: 3 dau, dow 4 dhow
demon: 5 afrit 6 afreet
garment: 3 aba 4 abba, haik 5 haick 7 burnous 8 burnoose
grp.: 3 PLO
headband cord: 4 agal
lute: 3 oud
name part: 3 ibn
noble: 3 aga 4 agha, amir, emir 5 ameer, emeer, sheik 6 shaikh, sheikh
of song: 4 Ahab
prename: 3 Ali
street ~: 4 waif 6 urchin
tea: 3 qat
Arab ___: 6 League, Legion
Arabella: 5 opera
composer: 7 Strauss
___ Arab Emirates: 6 United
arabesque: 5 motif 6 linear, spiral 8 position 9 anthemion, sinuosity 10 decoration, embroidery, undulation
Arabesque (1966 film)
cast: Sophia Loren, Gregory Peck
director: Stanley Donen
Arabia: 9 peninsula
coffee: 5 mocha
desert: 5 Nafud, Nefud
gazelle: 5 ariel
gulf: 4 Aden
nation: 4 Oman 5 Dubai, Katar, Qatar, Yemen 6 Koweit, Kuwait 8 Abu Dhabi
old ~ sultanate: 4 Nejd
peninsula: 4 Aden
port: 4 Aden
primate: 6 baboon
sea: 3 Red 7 Arabian
shrub: 3 kat, qat 4 khat 5 retem
stopover: 5 serai
___ Arabia: 5 Saudi, South
Arabian: 5 horse, steed 6 equine
Arabian ___: 3 Sea 4 Gulf 5 camel 6 coffee, Desert 7 jasmine
Arabian Nights
bird: 3 roc
character: 3 Ali 5 Ahmed, genie 7 Ali Baba
locale: 7 Baghdad
ruler: 5 calif, kalif 6 caliph, kaliph, khalif
Arabian Sea
gulf: 4 Oman
river to the ~: 5 Indus 7 Narbada 8 Nerbudda
territory: 3 Goa
___ arabic: 3 gum
Arabic: 3 Sem. 7 Semitic 8 language
father, in ~: 3 abu
first ~ letter: 4 alif
glottal stop: 5 hamza
letter: 2 ba, fa, ha, ra, ta, ya, za 3 ain, dad, dal, jim, kaf, kha, lam, mim, qaf, sad, sin, tha, waw 4 alif, dhal, shin 5 ghain
master, in ~: 5 saheb, sahib
name of Egypt: 4 Misr
wise men: 5 ulama, ulema
Arabic ___: 7 numeral
arabica: 6 coffee
arable: 5 loamy 7 fertile 8 farmable, plowable, tillable 10 cultivable, productive
area: 5 field
Arab League: 8 alliance
headquarters: 5 Cairo, Tunis
member: 4 Irak, Iraq, Oman 5 Egypt, Katar, Libya, Qatar, Sudan, Yemen 6 Jibuti, Jordan, Koweit, Kuwait 7 Algeria, Bahrain, Bahrein, Comoros, Lebanon, Morocco, Somalia 8 Djibouti 9 Palestine 10 Mauritania
___ Arab Republic: 6 Syrian, United
Arab Republic of ___: 5 Egypt
Arab Song artist: 4 Klee
Aracaju: 4 city, town
locale: 6 Brazil
Arachne home: 5 Lydia
arachnid: 4 mite
creation: 3 web 6 cobweb
arachnophobe fear: 7 spiders
Arachnophobia (1990 film)
cast: Jeff Daniels, John Goodman, Harley Jane Kozak
director: Frank Marshall
Arad: 4 city, town
locale: 7 Romania, Rumania 8 Roumania
Arafat: 4 Arab 5 Yasir 6 Yasser 8 Nobelist
birthplace: 5 Cairo, Egypt
grp.: 3 PLO
Arafura: 3 sea
locale: 9 Australia, New Guinea
strait off the ~: 6 Torres
Aragats: 4 peak 5 mount 8 mountain
locale: 6 Europe 7 Armenia
Aragón: 5 river 7 kingdom
locale: 5 Spain
river through ~: 4 Ebro
Aragon, Louis: 6 French, writer
___ a Rag Picker: 3 He's
Araguaya: 5 river
locale: 6 Brazil
___ a rail: 6 thin as
Araldo composer: 5 Verdi
Aral locale: 6 Russia
Aral Sea: 4 lake
river to the ~: 8 Amu Darya, Syr Darya
Aram: 7 Avakian, Saroyan
father of ~: 4 Shem
grandfather of ~: 4 Noah
Aramaic: 8 language
Aramis colleague: 5 Athos 7 Porthos 9 d'Artagnan
Aran: 4 isls. 5 isles 7 islands
locale: 7 Ireland
Arandas: 4 city, town
locale: 6 Mexico 7 Jalisco
Aran Islands, The author: 5 Synge
Arapaho: 5 tribe 6 Indian 7 Amerind 8 language
abode: 4 tipi 5 tepee 6 teepee
enemy: 3 Ute
arapaima: 4 fish
arara: 4 bird 5 macaw
Ararat: 4 peak 5 mount 8 Agri Dagi, mountain

locale: 4 Asia 6 Turkey
visitor: 3 ark, Ham 4 Noah, Shem 7 Japheth
araroba: 4 tree
relative: 3 koa 5 carob 6 cassia, cercis, locust, padauk, padouk, redbud 7 mesquit 8 mesquite, tamarind 9 poinciana
__ a rat: 5 smell
Araucana: 4 fowl 7 chicken
relative: 6 Bantam, Brahma, Houdan, Sussex 7 Cornish, Dorking, Leghorn 8 Langshan, Shanghai 9 Dominique, Orpington, Wyandotte
Araucanian: 6 Indian 7 Amerind
Arawak: 5 Taino 6 Indian 7 Amerind 8 language
Arbela: 6 battle
Arber, Werner: 8 Nobelist
Arbil: 4 city, town
locale: 4 Irak, Iraq
arbiter: 3 ref, ump 5 judge 6 critic, umpire 7 referee 8 mediator 9 authority, evaluator, go-between 10 interceder
arbitrageur concern: 3 stk. 4 risk 5 hedge, stock
arbitrarily: 8 at random
arbitrary: 5 bossy 6 biased, chance, fickle, lordly, random, unfair, unjust, wilful 7 erratic, offhand, partial, willful 8 absolute, despotic, dogmatic, one-sided, partisan 9 downright, frivolous, haphazard, imperious, tyrannous, vagarious, whimsical 10 autocratic, capricious, despotical, dogmatical, fortuitous, high-handed, irrational, monocratic, peremptory, prejudiced, subjective, tyrannical, unbalanced, undisputed
arbitrate: 5 judge 6 decide, settle, strike 7 adjudge, mediate, referee 9 determine, intercede, interpose, intervene, make a deal, negotiate, reconcile 10 adjudicate, compromise, conciliate
arbitration: 7 verdict 8 judgment 9 mediation
arbitrator: 3 ref, ump 5 judge 6 umpire 7 referee 8 mediator 9 go-between 10 interceder, peacemaker
agcy.: 4 NLRB
arbor: 5 bower 6 ramada, recess 7 pergola, trellis
arbor __: 5 vitae
Arbor Day month: 5 April
arboreal: 5 shady 6 ramose, silvan, sylvan, wooded 8 branched, dendroid, forested, ramiform, treelike 9 dendritic 10 branchlike, dendriform, tree-shaped
fluid: 3 sap
home: 4 nest
lizard: 5 anole 6 iguana
mammal: 5 koala, lemur, sloth
rodent: 8 squirrel
arboretum specimen: 4 tree
__ Arbor, MI: 3 Ann
arborvitae: 4 tree 5 thuja, thuya 9 evergreen
relative: 7 cypress, juniper 8 sandarac
Arbuckle: 3 Jon 5 Fatty 6 Roscoe
Arbuckle, Jon pet: 4 Odie 8 Garfield
Arbus: 5 Allan, Diane
Arbus, Diane: 12 photographer
arbutus: 4 tree 5 plant, shrub 6 flower 9 evergreen
relative: 5 erica, heath, salal 6 azalea, kalmia, sorrel 7 madrone, rhodora 8 cassiope, cowberry 9 blueberry, deerberry
Arbutus: 4 city, town
locale: 8 Maryland
arc: 3 bow, lob 4 bend, loop, turn, weld 5 curve, spark, sweep, twist 7 azimuth, flexure, rainbow 8 crescent, half-moon, parabola 9 curvature, hyperbola, sinuosity 10 semicircle
arc __: 3 cos, cot, csc, sec, sin, tan 4 lamp, sine 5 light 6 cosine, secant, second 7 furnace, tangent, welding
__ arc: 5 xenon 6 carbon, island, Jordan, Lowitz, reflex, simple 7 diurnal, mercury
__ Arc: 6 Joan of
arcade: 4 mall, stoa 6 loggia 7 gallery, ingress, portico 8 cloister 9 colonnade, peristyle 10 passageway
habitué: 4 teen 5 gamer
infraction: 4 tilt
like ~ games: 6 coin-op
pioneering ~ game: 4 Pong
price, once: 5 penny
arcade __: 4 game
__ arcade: 5 penny
Arcade: 4 city, town
locale: 10 California
Arcadia: 4 city, Eden, town 6 heaven, utopia 8 paradise
locale: 10 California
Arcadia author: Philip Sidney
Arcadian: 5 rural 6 rustic 7 bucolic, country 8 pastoral 9 bucolical
ancient ~ city: 4 Alea
arcana: 5 tarot 7 secrets 9 mysteries
arcane: 4 dark, deep 5 vague 6 exotic, hidden, mystic, occult, secret 7 cryptic, obscure, unclear 8 abstruse, esoteric, mystical, nebulous, oracular, puzzling, uncommon 9 confusing, cryptical, enigmatic, recherché, recondite 10 cabalistic, indistinct, mysterious, perplexing, unknowable
arcanum: 6 cabala, elixir, engima, kabala, secret 7 alembic, cabbala, kabbala, mystery, nostrum, panacea 9 conundrum
Arcaro, Eddie: 6 jockey
milieu: 5 track
prop: 4 crop
arced: 5 curvy 6 curvey 9 bow-shaped
Arcelia: 4 city, town
locale: 6 Mexico 8 Guerrero
arch: 3 bow, coy, sly 4 bend, cagy, camp, flex, foxy, hump, loop, main, ogee, span, wily 5 cagey, canny, chief, curve, embow, hunch, major, vault 6 artful, bridge, crafty, instep, ironic, portal 7 cunning, knowing, leading, primary, roguish, waggish 8 foremost, greatest 9 curvature, principal, quizzical, sinuosity 10 consummate, preeminent, serpentine
architectural ~: 4 ogee 5 ogive
end: 8 abutment
over: 4 span 6 bridge
(over): 4 hang
site: 3 St. L. 4 foot 5 Paris 7 St. Louis
slightly: 6 camber
support: 4 pier 6 insole
type of ~: 6 lancet
arch __: 3 dam 4 beam, head 5 board, brace 7 support
__ arch: 3 pot 4 bell, drop, flat, gill, jack, ogee, rood, skew 5 Roman, round, Tudor 6 aortic, braced, corbel, French, Gothic, lancet 7 Moorish, pointed, trefoil, trimmer
Arch: 6 Oboler
__ Arch: 7 Gateway
archaeologist: 5 Evans 6 Carter, digger, Petrie 7 Woolley 8 Breasted 10 Schliemann
British ~: 5 Evans 6 Petrie 7 Woolley
datum: 3 age
Egyptian ~ site: 5 Luxor 6 Amarna, Karnak
find: 4 abri, ansa, bone, idol, ruin 5 mound, relic, ruins, shard, sherd, stela, stele 6 fossil 8 artifact
German ~: 10 Schliemann
Hindu ~ site: 6 Ellora
Kenya ~ site: 7 Olduvai
Maya ~ site: 5 Copan
prefix: 5 paleo-
site: 3 dig
Switzerland ~ site: 4 Biel
Syria ~ site: 4 Ebla
archaeology: 7 science
__ archaeology: 3 new 6 marine 7 salvage
archaic: 3 obs., old, out 5 dated, fusty, olden, passé 6 bygone, old hat 7 ancient, extinct, fogyish 8 obsolete, outdated, outmoded, out of use, time-worn 9 out of date, primitive 10 antiquated, out of style
archaism: 5 relic 9 throwback
archaize: 9 antiquate
archangel: 5 Uriel 7 Gabriel, Lucifer, Michael, Raphael
Archangel: 4 port
locale: 6 Russia
archbishop: 4 rank 6 cleric, priest 7 prelate 8 minister
archdeacon: 6 cleric
archduchess: 4 lady 5 noble
archduke: 5 noble
Archduke __: 4 Trio
arched: 5 round 6 convex
ceiling: 5 vault
combining form: 3 tox- 4 toxi-, toxo-
recess: 4 apse
archeologist
see archaeologist
archer: 4 Amor, Eros, Tell 5 Cupid 6 Apache, bowman, Indian 9 Robin Hood 10 longbowman
mythical ~: 4 Amor, Eros 5 Cupid
need: 3 bow 5 arrow 6 quiver
shield: 5 pavis 6 pavise
skill: 3 aim
supplier: 6 bowyer
Archer: 3 Lew 4 Anne, sign 6 George, Martin 7 Jeffery
month: 3 Dec., Nov. 8 December, November
predecessor: 8 Scorpion
successor: 4 Goat
Archer, Anne: 7 actress
film: The Art of War (2000)
Clear and Present Danger (1994)
Fatal Attraction (1987)
Patriot Games (1992)
mother: Lord`$. Marjorie
Archerd: 4 Army
Archer, George: 6 golfer
Archer, Miles partner: 5 Spade 8 Sam Spade
Archers of St. George artist: 4 Hals
archery: 5 sport
sound: 5 twang
wood: 3 yew
Arches National Park
city near ~: 4 Moab
locale: 4 Utah
archetypal: 5 ideal, model 8 original 9 inceptive
archetype: 5 ideal, model 6 avatar 7 epitome, example, paragon, pattern 8 exemplar, original, paradigm, standard 9 criterion, prototype 10 embodiment, progenitor, touchstone
archfiend: 4 ogre 5 beast, brute, demon, devil, ghoul 6 bad guy, daemon, daimon, diablo 7 evil one, incubus, monster, villain
Archibald: 3 Cox 4 Hill, Nate, Tiny 8 MacLeish
Archibald, Nate
milieu: 5 court
org.: 3 NBA
sport: 10 basketball
Archie: 4 Bell, Mayo, teen 5 Moore, strip 6 Bunker 7 Andrews, Griffin, Manning
daughter: 6 Gloria
friend: 5 Betty, Moose 7 Jughead 8 Veronica
to Mike: 5 in-law
Archie Bunker's Place actress: 5 Meara
Archies
song: Jingle Jangle (1969)
Sugar, Sugar (1969)
Archimedes: 5 Greek 9 physicist
forte: 4 math
tool for ~: 5 lever
archipelago: 4 isls. 5 isles 7 islands
Asian: 5 Malay
Baltic: 5 Aland
Indian Ocean ~: 7 Comoros
Pacific: 4 Fiji
__ Archipelago: 3 Low 4 Sulu 5 Colón, Malay 6 Arctic, Chagos 7 Paumotu, Tuamotu
__ Archipelago, The: 5 Gulag
Archipiélago de __: 5 Colón
architect: 3 Lin, Pei 4 Adam, Nash, Wren 5 Bacon, Hoban, I.M. Pei, maker, Pelli, White 6 artist, Morris, parent, Scopas, Wright 7 builder, creator, founder, Gilbert, Gropius, Johnson, Latrobe, Maya Lin, Olmsted, planner 8 Bulfinch, designer, Saarinen 9 fashioner 10 mastermind, originator, prime mover
British ~: 4 Nash, Wren 6 Morris
detail: 4 spec
glass pyramid ~: 3 Pei 5 I.M. Pei
Greek ~: 6 Scopas
John Hancock Building ~: 3 Pei 5 I.M. Pei
Kennedy Library: 3 Pei 5 I.M. Pei
measure: 4 sq. ft. 10 square feet
Mile High Center ~: 3 Pei 5 I.M. Pei
neoclassical ~: 4 Adam
org.: 3 AIA
architectural
addition: 3 ell
adornments: 5 putti
arch: 5 ogive
brace: 5 strut
convexity: 7 entasis
crossbeam: 5 trave
decoration: 6 frieze
deg.: 3 MFA
detail: 4 dado, ogee
do ~ work: 6 design
drawing: 4 plan 5 epure
drop: 5 gutta
Gothic ~ feature: 5 gable
moldings: 4 tori
order: 5 Doric, Ionic 10 Corinthian
pier: 4 anta
rib: 6 lierne
school: 7 Bauhaus
style: 5 Tudor 6 Gothic
support: 5 ancon 6 lintel
vault feature: 5 groin
architecture: 5 shape 6 design, make-up 7 science 8 building 9 structure
first name in ~: 4 Eero, Ieoh
archival: 10 historical
archive: 4 list 5 files 6 annals, museum, record 7 catalog, dossier, records 8 treasury 9 catalogue 10 chronicles, depository
archives: 6 record 8 register 9 reference
archivist: 6 keeper 9 historian
Arch of __: 5 Titus 7 Triumph
Arch of Triumph (1948 film)
cast: Ingrid Bergman, Charles Boyer, Charles Laughton
director: Lewis Milestone
archon: 5 ruler
Archway alternative: 7 Keebler, Nabisco 8 Sunshine 9 Mrs. Fields 10 Famous Amos, Peak Freans

Archy friend: 9 Mehitabel
arc-lamp gas: 5 xenon
arco: 3 bow
arc-shaped mark: 5 paren.
arctic: 3 icy 4 cold, cool, wind 5 chill, gelid, nippy, north, polar 6 biting, chilly, frigid, frosty, frozen, wintry 7 glacial, ice-cold, numbing, shivery, wintery 8 freezing
bird: 4 skua, tern 5 brant 6 fulmar 9 gerfalcon, gyrfalcon
bovine: 6 muskox
coat: 5 parka 6 anorak
dweller: 3 Esk. 4 Lapp 5 Inuit 6 Eskimo, Innuit, Inupik
dwelling: 4 iglu 5 igloo
explorer: 3 Rae 4 Ross 5 Davys 7 Barents
explorer's base: 4 Etah
finger: 5 fiord
hazard: 4 berg, cold, floe
hill: 5 pingo
island: 6 Baffin
leave stranded in the ~: 5 ice in
mammal: 6 walrus 9 polar bear
of the ~: 5 polar
position: 4 N. Lat.
sea: 4 Kara 7 Barents
sight: 6 aurora, icecap
surface: 3 ice
trout: 4 char
vehicle: 4 sled 5 kayak, umiak
Arctic __: 3 fox 4 char, seal, tern, Zone 5 daisy, Ocean 6 Circle 7 Current
Arctic Ocean
bay: 6 Baffin
island: 7 Wrangel
river to the ~: 6 Kolyma 7 Pechora 9 Mackenzie 10 Coppermine
Arcturus: 4 star 5 K star
constellation: 6 Boötes
arcus: 5 cloud
Arden: 3 Eve 4 city, Dale, John, town 5 Enoch 6 forest 9 Elizabeth
locale: 10 California
rival: 6 Lauder
ardency: 4 zeal 6 fervor 10 enthusiasm
Arden, Eve: 7 actress
film: Anatomy of a Murder (1959)
The Dark at the Top of the Stairs (1960)
Grease (1978)
The Lady Wants Mink (1953)
The Voice of the Turtle (1947)
TV: Our Miss Brooks
Arden, John: 7 British 10 playwright
Ardennes waterway: 4 Oise
ardent: 3 hot 4 agog, avid, fast, keen, true, warm 5 afire, eager, fiery, loyal, ready 6 devout, fervid, fierce, gung-ho, hearty, loving, rah-rah, red-hot, steady, torrid 7 amatory, burning, devoted, earnest, fervent, flaming, glowing, intense, longing, staunch, zealous 8 constant, desirous, faithful, resolute, romantic, spirited, vehement, vigorous 9 allegiant, amatorial, ambitious, emotional, exuberant, heartfelt, steadfast, strenuous 10 hot-blooded, passionate, solicitous
ardently: 4 hard 5 madly 6 keenly 8 heartily 9 fervently, like crazy
Ardmore: 4 city, town
locale: 8 Oklahoma
Ardolino, Emile: 8 director
film: Chances Are (1989)
Dirty Dancing (1987)
Sister Act (1992)
ardor: 4 élan, fire, heat, love, soul, zeal, zest, zing 5 flame, gusto, oomph, verve 6 desire, energy, fervor, spirit 7 avidity, emotion, loyalty, passion 8 devotion, fervency, keenness, lyricism, vitality 9 adoration, affection, eagerness, inner fire, intensity, puppy love 10 enthusiasm, exuberance, fierceness, liveliness
in Tin Pan Alley: 4 pash
arduous: 4 hard 5 harsh, heavy, rocky, rough, steep, stiff, tight, tough 6 rugged, severe, taxing, thorny, trying, uphill 7 hard-won, labored, onerous, operose, painful, serious 8 grueling, tiresome, toilsome 9 ambitious, demanding, difficult, herculean, laborious, murderous, punishing, strenuous 10 burdensome, enervating, exhausting, formidable, oppressive
arduously: 4 hard 8 mightily
are: 5 exist 7 breathe
in French: 4 êtes
in Spanish: 4 esta
not: 4 ain't
Are __ Bromide?: 4 You a
Are __ Lonesome Tonight?: 3 You
Are __ pair?: 3 we a
__ Are: 3 You 7 Chances
area: 3 lot 4 beat, belt, 'hood, land, site, size, turf, ward, zone 5 field, patch, place, range, scope, sheet, space, sweep, tract 6 domain, extent, locale, métier, milieu, parcel, region, sector, sphere, square 7 acreage, breadth, compass, environ, expanse, grounds, purlieu, purview, quarter, section, stretch, surface, terrain 8 confines, district, dominion, environs, locality, location, plottage, precinct, province, purlieus, vicinage, vicinity 9 bailiwick, enclosure, incidence, largeness, specialty, territory 10 department, discipline, floor space
ender: 3 way
in baseball: 5 mound 7 bullpen, infield 8 backstop, outfield
in basketball: 5 court 8 foul line
in bowling: 5 alley 6 gutter 7 channel 8 foul line
in boxing: 4 ring 5 apron, ropes 8 ringside
in football: 7 end zone 8 midfield, sideline
in French: 4 aire
in golf: 5 apron, green, rough 6 fringe 7 fairway
in horse racing: 7 paddock
in ice hockey: 4 cage, rink 6 crease 7 red line 8 blue line
in tennis: 5 court 8 baseline
unit: 4 acre, sq. ft., sq. in., sq. mi. 7 hectare 10 square foot, square inch, square mile, square yard
area __: 3 rug 4 code 5 study 7 bombing
__ area: 4 fire, gray, rest 5 focal, relic 6 acting, Broca's, dollar, fringe, graded 7 culture, penalty, special, staging
__ are a few of my favorite...: 5 these
__ a real nowhere man: 3 He's
__ area network: 4 wide 5 local
arear: 3 aft 6 astern
areas: 4 loca, loci
__ a Rebel: 3 He's
areca: 4 palm, tree
__ are called...: 4 Many
__ are for kids!: 4 Trix
__ Are Funny: 6 People
... are getting fat, the: 5 geese
__ are Heard, The: 5 Muses
__ Are Love: 3 You
__ are lovely..., The: 5 woods
__ Are My Destiny: 3 You
__ Are My Lucky Star: 3 You
__ Are My Sunshine: 3 You
arena: 3 gym 4 bowl, dome, rink 5 field, realm, scene, space, stage 6 domain, region, sector, sphere 7 ice rink, stadium, theater, theatre 8 bullring, coliseum, province 9 colosseum, palaestra, territory 10 hippodrome
accommodation: 4 seat
section: 4 loge, tier 5 level 10 grandstand
arena __: 7 theater, theatre 8 football
Arenal: 7 volcano
locale: 9 Costa Rica
__ Arenas, Chile: 5 Punta
Arenas, Reinaldo: 5 Cuban 6 writer
Arendt: 6 Hannah
arenose: 5 sandy
__ Are Not Alone: 3 You
Are not! response: 4 am so 5 am too
Aren't __?: 5 We All
Areopagitica author: John Milton
Arequipa: 4 city, town
locale: 4 Peru
__ are red...: 5 Roses
__ Are Ringing: 5 Bells
Ares: 3 god 6 war god
animal sacred to ~: 3 dog 4 boar 7 vulture
daughter of ~: 4 Lyce, Nike, Thoe 5 Aella, Agave, Harpe, Marpe 6 Amazon, Clonie, Glauce, Myrina, Ocyale, Otrere, Phoebe, Xanthe 7 Alcibie, Alcippe, Antiope, Asteria, Bremusa, Celaeno, Clymene, Derinoe, Eriboea, Euryale, Evandre, Menippe, Prothoe 8 Antandre, Antioche, Deianira, Dioxippe, Harmonia, Iphinome, Laomache, Molpadia, Polemusa, Polydora, Tecmessa 9 Antianira, Antibrote, Harmothoe, Hippolyte, Hippothoe, Melanippe, Philippis 10 Thermodosa
epithet of ~: 8 Aphneius, Enyalius, Theritas
equivalent: 4 Mars
lover of ~: 3 Eos 4 Ilia 5 Dotis 6 Aerope, Chryse, Cyrene, Pyrene, Tirine 7 Althaea, Harpina, Pelopia, Sterope, Triteia 8 Aglaurus, Astyoche, Atalanta, Atalante, Demonice, Harmonia 9 Aphrodite 10 Protogenia
parent of ~: 4 Enyo, Hera, Zeus
sister of ~: 4 Eris, Hebe
son of ~: 5 Alcon, Dryas, Molus, Nisus, Pylus, Remus 6 Cycnus, Deimos, Evenus, Oxylus, Phobus, Tereus 7 Oeagrus, Romulus 8 Diomedes, Ialmenus, Meleager, Oenomaus, Phlegyas, Porthaon, Thestius 9 Licymnius 10 Melanippus
twin of ~: 4 Eris
__ Are So Beautiful: 3 You
arête: 4 crag 5 ledge, ridge
Aretha: 8 Franklin
music: 4 soul
__ Are There: 3 You
__ Are the Sunshine of My Life: 3 You
__ are the times...: 5 These
arethusa: 5 plant 6 flower
Arethusa: 5 nymph 6 Nereid
father of ~: 5 Atlas
Aretino, Pietro: 6 writer 7 Italian
__ a retreat: 4 beat
Are we __?: 5 a pair
Are we having fun __?: 3 yet
Are we there __?: 3 yet
Are You a Bromide? author: Gelett Burgess
Are you a man __ mouse?: 3 or a
Are you calling me __?: 5 a liar
Are you for __?: 4 real
Are You Lonesome Tonight? (song)
artist: Donny Osmond, Elvis Presley
Are You Really Mine (1958 song)
artist: Jimmie Rodgers
Are You Sincere (1958 song) artist: Andy Williams
Are you sure?: 6 really
arf: 4 bark, woof 6 bowwow
sayer: 5 Sandy
ar follower: 3 ess
Arg.
locale: 5 S. Amer.
neighbor: 3 Bol., Uru.
see also Argentina
argal: 5 sheep
relative: 4 geep 5 shapu, urial 6 aoudad, bharal, merino 7 bighorn, burrhel, mouflon 8 cimarron, moufflon
argala: 5 stork
argali: 5 sheep
relative: 4 geep 5 shapu, urial 6 aoudad, bharal, merino 7 bighorn, burrhel, mouflon 8 cimarron, moufflon
argent: 5 metal, white 6 silver 7 silvery
relative: 4 bone, milk, snow 5 cream, ivory, milky 6 oyster, silver 8 eggshell
Argent author: Emile Zola
Argentina: 6 nation 7 country
bird: 7 cariama, seriema
city: 5 Jujuy, Lanus, Moron, Salta, Tigre 6 Paraná 7 Córdoba, La Plata, Quilmes, Rosario 9 La Matanza, San Isidro 10 Avellaneda, Corrientes
dance: 5 tango
desert: 10 Patagonian
dictator: 5 Perón
gulf: 8 San Jorge 9 San Matias
Indian: 9 Tehuelche
money: 4 peso 7 austral
mountain: 4 Solo, Toro 5 Cachi, Chani, Galan, Laudo, Negro, Quela 6 Bonete, Juncal, Pissis 7 Palermo, San Juan 8 El Condor, El Muerto, Famatina, Polleras, Tortolas 9 Aconcagua, Antofalla, Incahuasi, Marmolejo, Tupungato 10 Mercedario, Nacimiento, Tres Cruces
musical set in ~: 5 Evita
neighbor: 5 Chile 6 Brazil 7 Bolivia, Uruguay 8 Paraguay
Nobelist in Chemistry: 6 Leloir
Nobelist in Medicine: 7 Houssay
Nobelist in Peace: 5 Lamas 8 Esquivel
org.: 3 OAS
plain: 5 campo, pampa
poet: 6 Storni
port: 7 La Plata
river: 5 Negro
stateman: 9 Sarmiento
tennis pro: 5 Vilas
waterfall: 6 Iguaçu 7 Iguassú
wind: 7 pampero
writer: 6 Borges, Gálvez, Sábato 8 Cortázar 9 Güiraldes, Sarmiento
see also Spanish
argentine: 4 fish
argentite: 3 ore 7 mineral
arghool: 4 oboe, wind 10 instrument
origin: 7 Mideast
argil: 4 clay
Argo: 4 boat, ship
captain: 5 Jason
Argolis: 4 gulf
ancient city near ~: 4 Alea
argon: 3 gas 7 element 8 noble gas
like ~: 5 inert
argonaut: 5 shell 8 seashell
Argonaut: 4 Idas 5 Areus, Argus, Butes, Hylas, Idmon, Jason, Zetes 6 Augeas, Calais, Castor, Echion, Erytus, Mopsus, Oileus, Peleus, Phlias, Talaus, Tiphys 7 Acastus, Admetus, Amphion, Ancaeus, Canthus, Cepheus, Clytius, Coronus, Erginus, Iphitus, Laocoon, Laokoon, Lynceus, Orpheus, Telamon 8 Asterion, Asterius, Eribotes, Euphemus, Eurytion,

Heracles, Iphiclus, Leodocus, Meleager, Nauplius, Phalerus, Taenarus **9** Eurydamas, Menoetius **10** Aethalides, Amphidamas, Polydeuces **11** Palaemenius
patron: **4** Hera
Argonautica: **4** epic
character: **5** Medea
Argonne Forest river: **5** Aisne
Argos, king of: **8** Adrastos
argosy: **4** boat, brig **5** fleet **6** armada, carack, trader **7** carrack, galleon **8** flotilla, schooner **9** abundance, plenitude **10** brigantine
argot: **4** cant, talk **5** idiom, lingo, slang **6** jargon, patois, patter, tongue **7** dialect **8** language, parlance, shoptalk **10** vernacular
arguable: **4** moot **7** dubious, tenable **9** debatable **10** disputable, reasonable
argue: **4** spat, talk, tiff **5** brawl, claim, clash, fight, plead, scrap **6** appeal, assert, attest, bicker, debate, dicker, differ, evince, haggle, niggle, oppose, reason **7** contend, contest, dispute, dissent, explain, face off, mix it up, protest, quarrel, quibble, suggest, testify, wrangle **8** conflict, disagree, hash over, have at it, indicate, maintain, squabble, vocalize **9** establish, fight over, have words, lock horns, take issue, thrash out **10** controvert, deliberate
against: **5** rebut **6** refute
back: **5** rebut
for: **4** urge **7** justify **8** advocate
into: **7** win over **8** persuade **9** influence, prevail on
Arguedas, José Maria: **6** writer **8** Peruvian
arguer: **6** lawyer **8** attorney, polemist **9** apologist, disputant
argument: **3** row **4** beef, feud, flap, fuss, plea, spat, text, tiff **5** brawl, claim, clash, fight, issue, point, proof, run-in, scrap, set-to, theme, topic **6** barney, blowup, breach, debate, hassle, jangle, matter, reason, ruckus, rumpus, strife, theory, thesis **7** discord, dispute, dissent, lawsuit, polemic, premise, quarrel, rhubarb, wrangle **8** conflict, disunity, polemics, question, skirmish, squabble, variance **9** assertion, bickering, encounter, imbroglio, reasoning **10** bone to pick, contention, difference, war of words
closer: **3** QED
side: **3** con, for, pro **7** against
starter: **7** counter
argumentation: **5** logic **6** reason
argumentative: **5** onery **6** ornery **7** hostile **8** fighting, forensic **9** bellicose, litigious **10** pugnacious
arguments
hear ~: **5** judge
like some ~: **5** sound **6** heated
Argun: **5** river
locale: **5** China **6** Russia
Argus: **3** dog **5** giant
Argus-eyed: **5** alert
argyle: **4** hose, sock **7** hosiery
Argyle: **4** city, town
locale: **6** Canada **10** Nova Scotia
Arhus: **4** city, town
locale: **7** Denmark
Ari: **6** Meyers **7** Onassis
Jackie, to ~: **4** wife
aria: **3** air **4** solo, song, tune **5** music **6** melody
ace: **4** diva
aria da __: **4** capo
Ariadne
brother of ~: **7** Catreus, Glaucus **9** Androgeus
father of ~: **5** Minos
lover of ~: **7** Oenarus, Theseus **8** Dionysus
sister of ~: **7** Phaedra **9** Acacallis
son of ~: **5** Thoas **6** Phlias **7** Ceramus **8** Oenopion **9** Eurymedon, Staphylus **10** Peparethus
Ariadne __ Naxos: **3** auf
Arial: **4** font **8** typeface
Ariana: **4** city, town
locale: **7** Tunisia
-arian cousin: **3** -ist, -ite, -nik **4** -ster
Arianna composer: **6** Handel
Arias: **5** Jimmy, Oscar
__ Arias Sanchez: **5** Oscar
Arica: **4** city, port, town
locale: **5** Chile
arid: **3** dry **4** bare, drab, dull, flat, sere **5** baked, dusty, stale, unwet, vapid **6** barren, boring, desert, dreary, jejune, torrid **7** bone-dry, dried up, humdrum, insipid, parched, parches, sapless, tedious, thirsty **8** dried out, droughty, lifeless, pedantic, rainless **9** anhydrous, colorless, juiceless, ponderous, unfertile, waterless, wearisome **10** dehydrated, desertlike, lackluster, pedantical, spiritless, unanimated, uninspired
area: **6** desert
combining form: **3** xer- **4** xero-
plateau: **4** puna
__ a ride: **3** bum **5** thumb
aridity: **5** waste **6** desert **7** dryness **8** jejunity **9** sterility **10** insipidity
Arie: **8** Luyendyk
ariel: **7** gazelle **8** antelope
relative: **3** gnu, kob **4** guib, kudu, oryx, puku, topi **5** addax, bongo, chiru, eland, goral, korin, nyala, oribi, saiga, serow **6** chammy, dik-dik, duiker, impala, koodoo, lechwe, nilgai, rhebok, shammy, shamoy **7** blaubok, blesbok, chamois, defassa, gemsbok, gerenuk, grysbok, nylghai, nylghau, sassaby **8** blesbuck, bontebok, bushbuck, gemsbuck, reedbuck, steenbok, steinbok **9** blackbuck, pronghorn, sitatunga, springbok, waterbuck **10** hartebeest, wildebeest
Ariel: **4** moon **6** Durant, Sharon **7** Dorfman
planet: **6** Uranus
Ariel author: André Maurois, Sylvia Plath
Aries: **3** car, ram **4** auto, sign **5** Dodge **7** sky sign **8** fire sign **10** automobile
month: **3** Apr., Mar. **5** April, March
predecessor: **6** Pisces
successor: **6** Taurus
arietta: **4** solo **5** music
arigato: **6** thanks **8** Japanese
aright: **2** OK **4** duly, okay, okeh, okey, well **5** aptly, fitly, truly **6** justly **7** exactly, in order **8** properly, suitably, worthily **9** correctly **10** accurately
__ a right: **4** hang
Arikara: **3** Ree **5** tribe **6** Indian **7** Amerind
aril: **4** husk **8** pericarp **10** integument
Ario: **4** city, town
locale: **6** Mexico **9** Michoacán
Arion: **5** horse
father of ~: **8** Poseidon
lifesaver: **4** lyre
mother of ~: **4** Gaea **7** Demeter
ariose: **7** melodic, musical, tuneful **8** songlike
Ariosto, Lodovico: **4** poet **7** Italian
patron: **4** Este
work: Orlando Furioso
arise: **4** go up, leap, lift, rise, soar, stem, wake **5** awake, begin, bob up, climb, ensue, get up, occur, pop up, rebel, stand, start, surge, waken **6** appear, ascend, awaken, come up, crop up, emerge, grow up, happen, loom up, move up, result, spring, wake up **7** develop, emanate, proceed, roll out, stand up, surface, turn out **8** commence, escalate, flow from, spring up **9** come about, grow out of, originate, transpire **10** come to mind, hit the deck
(from): **4** flow, stem **5** ensue, issue **6** derive, follow, result **7** emanate, proceed
unexpectedly: **5** bob up, pop up
arisen: **2** up **6** sprung **8** out of bed **10** on one's feet
not ~: **4** abed
arista: **3** awn **5** beard **7** bristle
Aristarchus: **5** Greek **10** astronomer
home: **5** Samos
Aristide: **6** Briand **7** Maillol **9** Boucicaut
realm: **5** Haiti
see also French
Aristippus of Cyrene: **11** philosopher
aristo: **3** nob **5** elite **9** patrician **10** upper class, upper crust
Aristocats, The (1970 film) director: Wolfgang Reitherman
dog: **8** Napoleon **9** Lafayette
aristocracy: **5** elite **6** gentry **7** peerage, society **8** nobility
aristocrat: **4** dame, lord, peer **5** baron, noble **8** nobleman **9** authority, blueblood, patrician **10** noblewoman
aristocratic: **5** aloof, elite, noble, royal **7** courtly, elegant, haughty, refined **8** highborn, ladylike, snobbish, wellborn, well-bred **9** patrician **10** upperclass
Ariston, son of: **5** Plato
Aristophanes: **5** Greek **10** playwright
work: The Birds
The Clouds
The Frogs
The Knights
Plutus
Aristos, The author: John Fowles
Aristotelian __: **5** logic
Aristotle: **5** Greek **7** Onassis **11** philosopher
teacher: **5** Plato
arithmetic: **4** math **8** addition, figuring **9** reckoning **10** estimation
device: **6** abacus **10** calculator
do ~: **3** add, sum **6** cipher, divide, figure **8** multiply, subtract
figure: **3** sum **6** addend **7** divisor, minuend, product **8** dividend, quotient **10** difference, subtrahend
sign: **4** plus **5** minus
term: **3** LCD
arithmetic __: **4** mean **6** series
__ a River: **5** Cry Me
Arizona: **5** state
city: **4** Mesa, Yuma **5** Tempe, Tubac **6** Bisbee, Peoria, Sedona, Tucson **7** Gilbert, Kingman, Nogales, Phoenix, Sun City, Winslow **8** Avondale, Carefree, Chandler, Glendale, Goodyear, Prescott, Surprise **9** Flagstaff, Oro Valley **10** Casa Grande, Scottsdale
conference: **6** Pac-Ten
county: **4** Yuma
desert: **7** Sonoran **10** Chihuahuan
elevation: **4** mesa
fish: **9** spikedace
Indian: **4** Hopi, Pima, Tewa, Yuma **5** Piute **6** Mohave, Mojave, Navaho, Navajo, Paiute, Papago, Pueblo **7** Yavapai **8** Maricopa **9** Havasupai
much of ~: **6** desert
national park: **7** Saguaro
neighbor: **3** Cal., Nev. **4** Colo., N. Mex., Utah **5** Calif. **6** Mexico, Nevada **8** Colorado **9** New Mexico **10** California
observatory: **6** Lowell
once: **3** ter. **4** terr. **9** territory
pro team: **6** D-Backs **9** Cardinals
river: **4** Gila, Salt
state amphibian: **8** tree frog
state bird: **10** cactus wren
state fish: **5** trout
state gemstone: **9** turquoise
state mammal: **8** ringtail
state neckwear: **7** bola tie
state tree: **9** palo verde
__ Arizona: **3** USS **5** In Old **7** Raising
Arizona (1970 song) artist: Mark Lindsay
Arizona Ames author: Zane Grey
Arizona Clan author: Zane Grey
Arizona Republic: **5** paper **9** newspaper
locale: **7** Phoenix
Arizona State
athletes: **9** Sun Devils
conference: **6** Pac-Ten
locale: **5** Tempe
ark: **4** boat **5** barge **6** asylum **8** flatboat
builder: **4** Noah
group: **3** duo, two **4** pair
landing site: **6** Ararat
passenger: **3** Ham **4** Shem **7** Japheth
scroll in an ~: **4** Tora **5** Torah
Ark __ Covenant: **5** of the
Ark.
see Arkansas
__ Ark: **4** Holy **5** Noah's **7** Joan Van
Arkansas: **5** river, state
city: **4** Mena **6** Benton, Conway, Rogers **8** El Dorado, Sherwood **9** Fort Smith, Jonesboro, Paragould, Pine Bluff, Texarkana **10** Hot Springs, Little Rock, Springdale
city on the ~: **4** Mena **5** Tulsa **10** Little Rock
conference: **3** SEC
mountains: **6** Ozarks
national forest: **5** Ozark
national park: **10** Hot Springs
neighbor: **5** Texas **8** Missouri, Oklahoma **9** Louisiana, Tennessee
River locale: **6** Kansas **8** Colorado, Oklahoma
river to the ~: **8** Canadian, Cimarron
state beverage: **4** milk
state gem: **7** diamond
state insect: **8** honeybee
state instrument: **6** fiddle
state mineral: **7** bauxite
state tree: **4** pine
Arkansas State athletes: **7** Indians
Arkhangelsk: **4** city, port, town
see also Russian
Arkin, Adam: **5** actor
father: **4** Alan
film: Full Moon High (1981)
Halloween H20: 20 Years Later (1998)
Personal Foul (1987)
With Friends Like These ... (1999)
TV: Chicago Hope
Arkin, Alan: **5** actor
film: Catch-22 (1970)
Glengarry Glen Ross (1992)
Grosse Pointe Blank (1997)
Havana (1990)
Indian Summer (1993)
The In-Laws (1979)
Jakob the Liar (1999)
Last of the Red Hot Lovers (1972)
Little Murders (1971)
Popi (1969)
The Rocketeer (1991)
The Seven-Per-Cent Solution (1976)
Slums of Beverly Hills (1998)

Thirteen Conversations About One Thing (2001)
Wait Until Dark (1967)
Ark. neighbor: 3 Tex. 4 Miss, Okla., Tenn.
Arky: 7 Vaughan
Arledge: 5 Roone
Arleen: 6 Sorkin
Arlen: 6 Harold 7 Michael, Richard, Specter
Arlene: 4 Dahl 7 Francis
Arlen, Harold: 8 composer
collaborator: 7 Harburg, Koehler
song: Ac-cent-tchu-ate the Positive
Any Place I Hang My Hat Is Home
Between the Devil and the Deep Blue Sea
Blues in the Night
Come Rain or Come Shine
Get Happy
If I Only Had a Brain
I Gotta Right to Sing the Blues
I Love a Parade
It's Only a Paper Moon
I've Got the World on a String
Let's Fall in Love
Lydia, the Tattooed Lady
The Man That Got Away
One for My Baby
Over the Rainbow
Stormy Weather
That Old Black Magic
This Time the Dream's on Me
We're Off to See the Wizard
Arlen, Michael: 6 author, writer 7 British
work: The Green Hat
Arles: 4 city, town
locale: 6 France
neighbor: 5 Nîmes
river: 5 Rhone
Arli$$ (HBO sitcom) cast: Robert Wuhl (Arliss Michaels)
Arlington: 4 city, town
locale: 5 Texas 8 Virginia
Arlington ___, IL: 3 Hts.
Arlington Heights: 4 city, town
locale: 8 Illinois
___ Arlington Robinson: 5 Edwin
Arliss: 6 George, Howard
Arliss, George: 5 actor
film: Disraeli (1929, AA)
House of Rothschild (1934)
The Last Gentleman (1934)
The Working Man (1933)
Arlo: 7 Guthrie
to Woody: 3 son
arm: 3 bay, fit, rig 4 cove, limb, load, unit, wing 5 annex, bough, crank, equip, power, rifle 6 branch, cannon, member, musket, outfit, supply, weapon 7 estuary, fortify, officer, prepare, shotgun 8 accouter, accoutre, division, embattle, howitzer, offshoot, revolver, tentacle 9 affiliate, appendage, extension, extremity, flint-lock 10 department, militarize, six-shooter
an ~ and a leg: 4 high 5 pricy, steep 6 costly, pricey 7 ruinous 9 expensive 10 exorbitant
band: 8 bracelet
bone: 4 ulna 6 radius 7 humerus
bones: 5 radii
builder: 6 chin-up
combining form: 6 brachi- 7 brachio-
ender: 3 ory, pit 4 hole, load, rest 5 chair
good right ~: 8 backbone, linchpin, mainstay
in French: 4 bras
joint: 5 elbow, wrist
muscle: 6 biceps 7 triceps
of an ~ bone: 5 ulnar
opposite: 3 leg
put the ~ on: 5 run in 9 shake down
shot in the ~: 4 lift 5 boost, tonic 8 pick-me-up, stimulus 9 stimulant
starter: 4 fire, fore, side, tone, yard
strong ~: 5 might 9 authority
twist one's ~: 4 make 5 force 6 coerce, compel, lean on 8 browbeat, bulldoze, pressure 10 bear down on
arm ___: 7 twister 9 wrestling
arm-___: 5 twist 7 wrestle
___ arm: 3 air 4 side, tone 5 small, upper 6 pickup, rocker, spiral
___-arm: 5 stiff 6 strong
armada: 4 navy 5 boats, fleet, ships 6 argosy 8 flotilla, sea power, warships
___ Armada: 7 Spanish
armadas, of: 5 naval
armadillo: 4 peba, tatu 5 apara, tatou 6 animal, mammal, peludo 7 tatuasu
like an ~: 5 scaly
plate: 5 scute
plates: 5 scuta
protection: 5 armor
Armageddon (1998 film)
cast: Ben Affleck, Billy Bob Thornton, Liv Tyler, Bruce Willis
director: Michael Bay
Armageddon author: Leon Uris
Armageddon It (1988 song) artist: Def Leppard
Armageddon nation: 3 Gog 5 Magog
Armah, Ayi Kwei: 6 writer 8 Ghanaian
armament: 6 shield 8 ordnance
armaments: 8 materiel, ordnance 9 munitions 10 ammunition, protection
Armand: 6 Hammer 7 Assante 8 Salacrou
Arm and ___: 6 Hammer
___ Armand, The: 7 Vampire
Armani: 7 Giorgio 8 designer
rival: 5 Blass, Klein 6 Lauren 7 Versace
Armatrading: 4 Joan
Arma virumque ___: 4 cano
armed: 6 girded, loaded 7 packing 8 carrying, equipped, supplied 9 fitted out, fortified, outfitted 10 accoutered
conflict: 6 battle, hot war
service: 3 USA, USN 4 army, navy, USAF, USMC 7 marines 8 air force, military
armed ___: 6 forces 7 robbery
___-armed bandit: 3 one
armed to the ___: 5 teeth
Armen: 3 Kay
Armendariz, Pedro: 5 actor
film: 3 Godfathers (1948)
Fort Apache (1948)
From Russia With Love (1963)
The Fugitive (1947)
The Littlest Outlaw (1955)
Original Sin (2001)
The Pearl (1948)
Tulsa (1949)
We Were Strangers (1949)
Armenia: 6 nation 7 country
capital: 7 Yerevan
city: 6 Erevan, Erivan, Gyumri 7 Yerevan 8 Vanadzor
mountain: 7 Aragats
neighbor: 4 Iran 6 Turkey 7 Georgia 10 Azerbaijan
once: 3 SSR
Armenian: 8 language
Armería: 4 city, town
locale: 6 Colima, Mexico
armet: 6 helmet
armful: 3 lot 4 load 6 plenty
Arm & Hammer: 9 detergent 10 baking soda, toothpaste
detergent alternative: 3 All, Biz, Era, Fab, Yes 4 Bold, Dash, Gain, Surf, Tide, Wisk 5 Cheer, Dreft, Purex 6 Calgon, Dynamo, Oxydol 7 Octagon 9 Ivory Snow
toothpaste alternative: 3 Aim 5 Crest, Gleem, Topol 7 Close-Up, Colgate, Viadent 9 Aquafresh, Mentadent, Pepsodent, Rembrandt, Sensodyne 10 Pearl Drops, Ultra Brite 11 Tom's of Maine
Armies of the Night, The author: Norman Mailer
armistice: 5 peace, truce 6 treaty 9 ceasefire, white flag 10 suspension
Armistice ___: 3 Day
armless
combining form: 5 anopi- 6 anoplo-
couch: 5 divan
garment: 4 vest
statue: 5 Venus
armlet: 4 cove 6 bangle 7 jewelry 8 bracelet
___ arm of the law: 4 long
armoire alternative: 6 closet
armor: 5 guard 6 shield, tuille 7 panoply 8 chamfron, plastron 9 brassardo, nosepiece, safeguard 10 protection
breaker: 4 mace
chink in one's ~: 8 weakness
cover with ~: 5 plate
defect: 5 chink
elbow ~: 6 couter
equine ~: 4 bard 5 barde
leather ~: 6 lorica
leg ~: 6 greave
part: 5 fauld, visor, vizor
piece: 5 culet 6 helmet
plate: 4 tace 5 tasse
shin ~: 6 greave
shirt: 7 hauberk
thigh ~: 5 cuish 6 cuisse
throat ~: 6 gorget
wearer: 6 knight
armor ___: 5 plate 7 plating
armor-___: 4 clad 6 plated
___ armor: 4 soft 5 plate 6 Gothic, parade
Armor ___: 3 All
armored ___: 3 car 4 rope 5 cable, scale
armored-car job: 5 heist
armored personnel ___: 7 carrier
armory: 5 depot 7 arsenal 8 magazine
supply: 4 ammo
Armour: 5 Tommy 6 hot dog 7 Richard
alternative: 5 Kahn's 8 Ball Park 10 Oscar Mayer
Armour, Tommy: 6 golfer
milieu: 5 links 6 course
org.: 3 PGA
armpit: 6 axilla
arms: 4 guns, ordn. 6 rifles, sabers, swords 7 pistols, weapons 8 bayonets, materiel, ordnance, shotguns, weaponry 9 artillery, firepower, munitions
call to ~: 5 alert, rally 6 alarum 7 recruit 8 mobilize
clash of ~: 3 war 7 warfare
coat of ~: 4 seal 6 emblem 7 insigne 8 insignia
hold in one's ~: 6 cradle
lay down ~: 5 yield 6 submit
position: 6 akimbo
take in one's ~: 3 hug
take up ~: 3 war 4 rise 5 arise, rebel 6 revolt
up in ~: 4 ired 5 angry, irate 6 roused 7 excited, furious, keyed-up 8 incensed, militant 9 indignant, wrought up
with ~ held low, in ballet: 5 en bas
with open ~: 6 warmly 8 friendly 9 cordially 10 graciously
arms ___: 4 race 6 akimbo 7 control
arm's
at ~ length: 5 aloof
keep at ~ length: 6 rebuff 7 neglect, ward off
arm's-___: 6 length
___ arms: 4 port, up in 5 order 7 present
___-arms: 5 man-at
Arms and the man ___: 5 I sing
Arms and the Man: 4 play
author: George Bernard Shaw
Arms of the One Who Loves You, The (1998 song) artist: Xscape
armstand: 4 dive
Armstrong: 2 R.G. 4 Bess, Neil, Otis 5 Edwin, Henry, Louis 6 Robert
___ Armstrong Custer: 6 George
Armstrong, Louis: 9 trumpeter
genre: 4 jazz
nickname: 4 Pops 7 Satchmo
song: Hello, Dolly! (1964)
What a Wonderful World (1988)
Armstrong, Neil: 9 astronaut
program: 6 Apollo
transport: 3 LEM 5 Eagle
Armstrong, Robert: 5 actor
film: King Kong (1933)
Mighty Joe Young (1949)
The Paleface (1948)
The Son of Kong (1933)
arm-twist: 4 coax 6 coerce
arm-twisting: 6 duress
armure: 4 silk 6 fabric
army: 3 ant, mob 4 host 5 array, corps, crowd, flock, force, horde, squad, swarm, troop 6 cohort, detail, legion, myriad, scores, throng, troops 7 brigade, cavalry, legions, platoon 8 division, infantry, military, regiment, soldiers 9 battalion, multitude 10 detachment
address: 3 sir
an ~ of: 6 divers, myriad, umteen, untold 7 copious, profuse, umpteen 8 abundant, manifold, numerous, umpsteen 9 bountiful, countless, quite a few
athletes: 6 Cadets
bed: 3 cot
British ~ orderly: 6 batman
coll. ~ program: 4 ROTC
command: 5 march 6 at ease 8 left face 9 about face, attention, right face
competitor: 4 Navy
cops: 3 MPs
doc: 5 medic
E-2: 3 pvt.
E-6: 4 SSgt.
E-7: 3 SFC
food: 3 MRE 4 chow, mess
glitch: 5 snafu
group: 3 rgt., trp. 4 regt., unit 5 troop 7 brigade 8 infantry, regiment 12 division unit
helicopter: 6 Apache
housing for singles: 3 BOQ
instructional facility (abbr.): 3 OTC, OTS
job: 5 recon
join the ~: 5 serve 6 enlist
leaders: 5 brass
magazine: 4 Yank
mail addr.: 3 APO, FPO
medal: 3 DSC
member: 3 ant
moving ~: 6 convoy
need: 4 ammo
officer: 3 col., gen., maj. 4 capt. 5 lieut., major 7 captain, colonel, general
post: 4 base, fort
rank: 3 Col., gen., maj., NCO, PFC, SFC, sgt. 4 SSgt. 5 lieut., lt. col. 7 private 8 corporal, sergeant
refusal: 5 no sir
Roman ~: 6 legion
rookie: 3 rct. 7 recruit

shelter: 8 barracks
stay in the ~: 4 reup
training site: 3 OCS, OTS
truant: 4 AWOL
vehicle: 4 jeep, tank 6 amtrac 7 amtrack
wear: 3 ODs 5 khaki 6 khakis
woman: 3 WAC 4 WAAC
WWI ~: 3 AEF
see also GI, military
army __: 3 ant 4 brat 5 corps 7 cutworm
army-__ store: 4 navy
Army: 4 USMA 7 Archerd 9 West Point
__ Army: 3 Red 4 Blue 5 Bonus 6 Arnie's 7 Regular
army battle, name meaning: 6 Harvey
__ army knife: 5 Swiss
army-navy __: 5 store
__ Army of the Republic: 5 Grand
__ Army Plaza: 5 Grand
Arn
domain: 3 Orr
father: Prince Valiant:
mother: 5 Aleta
arna: 5 bovid 6 bovine
relative: 3 yak 4 anoa, gaur, urus, zebu 5 bison, gayal, takin 6 mithan, muskox 7 aurochs, banteng, banting, beefalo, buffalo, carabao, cattalo, kouprey, tamarao, tamarau, timarau
Arna: 8 Bontemps
Arnage: 3 car 4 auto 7 Bentley 10 automobile
Arnaz: 4 Desi 5 Lucie
Arnaz, Desi spouse: Lucille Ball
Arnaz, Lucie spouse: Laurence Luckinbill
Arndt, Felix tune: 4 Nola
Arne: 5 nymph 6 Thomas 7 Carlson 8 Nordheim, Tiselius 9 Andersson
parent of ~: 4 Thea 6 Aeolus
Arneb: 4 star
Arneis: 4 wine 5 white
origin: 5 Italy
Arness: 5 James
costar: 5 Blake, Stone 6 Weaver
Arne, Thomas: 7 British 8 composer
alma mater: 4 Eton
work: Abel
Alfred
Artaxerxes
Britannia
Caractacus
Comus
Dido and Aeneas
Eliza
The Judgment of Paris
Judith
Olimpiade
Opera of Operas
Rosamund
Rule Britannia
Zara
Arngrim: 6 Alison
Arnhem: 4 city, town
locale: 7 Holland
neighbor: 3 Ede
Arnhem __: 4 Land
arnica: 4 balm, weed 5 plant 6 flower
Arnie: 6 Herber, Palmer
Arnie's __: 4 Army
Arnim, Bettina von: 6 German, writer
Arno: 3 Sig 4 Holz 5 Peter, river 7 Penzias
city on the ~: 4 Pisa 8 Florence
River locale: 5 Italy
Arnold: 3 Bax, Hap, Tom 4 city, Eddy, Jack, Moss, town 5 Stang, Zweig 6 Edward, Palmer, Wesker 7 Bennett, Matthew, Toynbee 8 Benedict 9 Rothstein 10 Schoenberg
locale: 8 Maryland, Missouri
mother-in-law: 6 Eunice
Arnold __ Schwarzenegger: 5 Alois
Arnold, Benedict: 7 traitor 8 recreant, turncoat
Arnold, Eddy song: Make the World Go Away (1965)
Arnold, Edward: 5 actor
film: Come and Get It (1936)
Crime and Punishment (1935)
The Devil and Daniel Webster (1941)
Diamond Jim (1935)
Easy Living (1937)
The Glass Key (1935)
Idiot's Delight (1939)
I'm No Angel (1933)
Johnny Apollo (1940)
Johnny Eager (1941)
Meet John Doe (1941)
Mrs. Parkington (1944)
Nothing but the Truth (1941)
The Toast of New York (1937)
Unholy Partners (1941)
Arnold, Jack: 8 director
film: Creature From the Black Lagoon (1954)
The Glass Web (1953)
The Incredible Shrinking Man (1957)
It Came From Outer Space (1953)
The Mouse That Roared (1959)
No Name on the Bullet (1959)
Tarantula (1955)
Arnold, Matthew: 4 poet 7 British
work: Dover Beach
Empedocles on Etna
The Scholar-Gipsy
Thyrsis
Arnoldson, Klas: 8 Nobelist
Arnold, Tom spouse: Roseanne
aroar: 4 loud 5 noisy 8 shouting 9 bellowing, clamorous 10 boisterous, thundering, tumultuous
__ a Rock: 3 I Am 4 Like
aroid: 4 taro 9 calla lily, wake-robin 10 cuckoopint
__ a Rolling Stone: 4 Like
aroma: 4 nose, odor, tang, waft 5 scent, smell, spice, whiff 6 breath 7 bouquet, incense, perfume 9 emanation, fragrance, redolence 10 atmosphere
faint ~: 5 sniff, whiff
in Britain: 5 odour
aromatic: 5 balmy, spicy, sweet 6 spicey 7 odorous, pungent, scented 8 fragrant, perfumed, redolent 9 ambrosial
compound: 5 ester
flavoring: 5 anise
herb: 4 mint, nard, sage 5 myrrh, tansy, thyme 6 fennel, hyssop
hydrocarbon: 5 arene
oil: 6 bay rum
ointment: 4 balm 6 balsam
radical: 4 aryl
root: 5 orris
seed: 5 cumin
tree: 4 pine 5 cedar 8 bayberry, rosewood
__ A. Romero: 6 George
__-A-Roni: 4 Rice
Aron's love: 4 Abra
Aroostook: 5 river
locale: 5 Maine
arose: 5 got up 6 went up 7 stood up 9 levitated
__ a Rose: 4 Only
around: 4 near 5 about, circa, round 6 in town, living, nearby 7 all over, close by, roughly 9 in the area, somewhere 10 more or less
combining form: 4 peri- 6 circum-
prefix: 3 epi-
starter: 3 run 4 turn, wrap
__ around: 3 bat, bum, end, get, pal, sit 4 been, come, fool, hang, kick, loaf, mess, muck, nose, push, shop, talk, toss 5 bring, crowd, horse, knock, stick, up and
__-around: 3 all 4 roll
__ Around: 4 I Get, Jump, Shop 5 I'll Be
__-around money: 7 walking
around the __: 4 bend 5 clock
__ Around the Clock: 4 Rock
__ around the collar: 4 ring
__ Around the Corner, The: 4 Shop
Around the Fish painter: 4 Klee
... __ around the neck: 4 a hug
__-around-the-rosey: 4 ring
Around the Way Girl (1991 song)
artist: LL Cool J
Around the World (1957 song) artist: Mantovani
Around the World in Eighty Days: 4 film 5 novel
author: Jules Verne
cast: Cantinflas, Shirley MacLaine, Robert Morley, David Niven
director: Michael Anderson
hero: 4 Fogg 7 Phileas
Around the World in 72 Days writer: 3 Bly
__ around to: 3 get
__ Around Us, The: 3 Sea
arouse: 3 get, jog 4 fire, goad, poke, spur, stir, wake, whet 5 alarm, alert, anger, awake, drive, evoke, flush, hop up, impel, liven, pique, rally, rouse, spark, start, waken 6 awaken, bestir, buck up, elicit, entice, excite, fillip, fire up, foment, foster, heat up, hype up, incite, kindle, recall, rile up, stir up, thrill, turn on, wake up, whip up, work up 7 actuate, agitate, animate, disturb, enflame, enliven, fortify, hearten, impress, inflame, inspire, provoke, quicken 8 embolden, engender, enkindle, enspirit, imbolden, inspirit, interest, motivate, psyche up, summon up, vitalize 9 electrify, enhearten, galvanize, impassion, instigate, recollect, stimulate, titillate 10 get excited, intoxicate
aroused: 6 ablaze 7 violent 8 inspired 10 passionate
arow: 7 in a line, lined up 8 queued up
Arp: 4 Hans, Jean
contemporary: 6 Calder
genre: 4 Dada
Arpel: 6 Adrien
Arp, Hans: 6 artist 7 painter 8 sculptor
homeland: 6 France
Arp, Jean: 6 artist 7 painter 8 sculptor
homeland: 6 France
Arquette: 5 Cliff, David 6 Alexis 7 Rosanna 8 Patricia
Arquette, David spouse: Courteney Cox
Arquette, Patricia spouse: Nicolas Cage
Arquette, Rosanna: 7 actress
film: Baby It's You (1982)
Big Bad Love (2002)
Black Rainbow (1991)
Desperately Seeking Susan (1985)
I'm Losing You (1999)
Silverado (1985)
The Whole Nine Yards (2000)
arr.
opposite: 3 dep.
Arrabal, Fernando: 6 writer 7 Spanish
arraign: 3 tax 6 accuse, charge, indict 9 inculpate, prosecute
arraignment: 5 trial 7 lawsuit
offering: 4 bail, plea
Arraignment of Paris, The author: 5 Peele
Arran: 3 isl. 4 isle 6 island
locale: 8 Scotland
arrange: 2 do 3 fix, lay, set 4 do up, edit, file, form, pose, rank, sort 5 align, aline, drape, fix up, frame, group, index, order, place, ready, set up, stack, stage 6 adjust, assort, codify, deploy, design, devise, direct, divide, format, get set, lay out, line up, settle, spread, tailor, tidy up, wangle 7 compile, display, dispose, iron out, marshal, prepare, work out 8 classify, contrive, engineer, graduate, organize, position, regulate, schedule, spruce up, tabulate 9 establish, make plans, make ready, methodize, negotiate, reconcile 10 pigeonhole
for: 4 book
arranged: 3 set 5 ready 6 packed 7 regular 8 prepared
carefully ~: 4 neat, tidy
arrangement: 3 set, sys. 4 deal, form, syst. 5 array, order, setup 6 design, format, layout, lineup, scheme, series, system 7 display, pattern 8 contract, covenant, grouping, ordering, sequence 9 provision, rendition, structure
combining form: 3 tax- 4 -nomy, taxi-, taxo-, -taxy 5 -taxis
flower ~: 4 posy 5 spray 7 nosegay
arrangements: 5 plans 10 groundwork, provisions
make ~: 4 plan
arrant: 4 rank 5 sheer, utter 6 brazen 7 blatant, extreme, glaring 8 flagrant, impudent, outright, thorough 9 barefaced, downright, itinerant, notorious, out-and-out, shameless
arras: 7 drapery 8 tapestry
spot: 4 wall
Arras: 4 city, town
locale: 6 France
Arrau, Claudio: 7 Chilean, pianist
array: 3 lot, rig, set 4 army, deck, duds, garb, gear, host, rank, show, sort, trim, vest 5 adorn, align, aline, batch, bunch, crowd, drape, dress, equip, field, getup, order, range, stock 6 attire, bedeck, bundle, clothe, dude up, finery, fit out, format, lineup, matrix, muster, outfit, parade, series, spread, suit up, tog out 7 apparel, battery, bedrape, clothes, cluster, deck out, display, dispose, dress up, exhibit, furnish, marshal, panoply, pattern, threads, variety 8 beautify, clothing, decorate, ensemble, garments, glad rags, organize, ornament, sequence, showcase 9 amassment, cavalcade, embellish, glamorize, methodize 10 assortment, collection, cumulation, exhibition, procession, Sunday best
__ array: 4 gate 5 logic 6 phased 7 antenna
arrayed: 4 clad
arrears: 4 debt 6 red ink 7 deficit 8 lateness 9 liability, shortfall 10 obligation
be in ~: 3 owe
in ~: 3 due 6 behind, unpaid 9 unsettled
arrest: 3 bag, fix, get, nab, nip 4 book, bust, cuff, grab, grip, halt, hold, hook, jail, nail, raid, slow, snag, stay, stem, stop, take 5 abate, abort, block, catch, check, pinch, rivet, run in, seize, snare, stall 6 absorb, collar, detain, engage, freeze, haul in, hinder, pick up, pull in, retard, stanch 7 capture, control, custody, engross, inhibit, jailing, prevent, refrain, round up, staunch, suspend 8 blockage, hold back, imprison, interest, intermit, obstruct, paralyse, paralyze, restrain, restrict, shut down, slowdown, stalling, stoppage, suppress, transfix 9 apprehend, cessation, detention, extradite,

fascinate, frustrate, intercept, interrupt, restraint, stalemate 10 constraint, internment, prevention, put a stop to, suspension
don't ~: 5 let go
under ~: 6 in jail
___ arrest: 5 false, house
arrested: 5 ran in 6 in jail
Arrested Development offering: 3 rap
arresting: 5 lofty 6 marked 7 salient, unusual 8 dazzling, exciting, magnetic, striking, stunning 9 absorbing, prominent 10 commanding, impressive, magnetical, noteworthy, noticeable, remarkable
Arrhenius, Svante: 7 chemist, Swedish 8 Nobelist 9 physicist
Arriaga: 4 city, town
locale: 6 Mexico 7 Chiapas
Arrid: 9 deodorant
alternative: 3 Ban 4 Sure 5 Tussy 6 Degree, Secret 7 Dry Idea, Mitchum 10 Right Guard, Soft and Dri, Speed Stick
arrière-___: 3 ban 5 garde 6 pensée
___ 'Arris Goes to Paris: 3 Mrs.
arrival: 4 mail 6 advent, coming, influx, parcel 7 package, receipt 8 delivery, entrance, shipment 9 accession, passenger 10 appearance, homecoming
recent ~: 6 infant 8 newcomer
Arrival, The (1996 film)
cast: Lindsay Crouse, Charlie Sheen, Ron Silver
arrive: 4 come, go in, land, show 5 debut, enter, get in, light, pop in, reach, set in, visit 6 alight, appear, blow in, drop in, edge in, fall in, happen, make it, mature, pull in, pull up, roll in, roll up, show up, sign in, spring, thrive, turn up, walk in 7 barge in, check in, clock in, deplane, fetch up, hit town, prosper, punch in, succeed, turn out, weigh in 8 breeze in, dismount, get there, go ashore, hit it big, make good 9 disembark, make it big, touch down 10 drop anchor
at: 3 fix, hit 4 find 5 get to, infer, reach 6 attain, derive
at, as a solution: 5 hit on
back: 6 return
by air: 5 fly in
unexpectedly: 5 pop in
arrivederci: 3 bye 4 ta-ta 5 aloha 6 bye-bye, so long 7 goodbye, Italian 8 farewell
Arrivederci, ___: 4 Roma
arrived, recently: 3 new 6 just in
Arrivi, Francesco: 10 playwright 11 Puerto Rican
arriving: 3 due
arriviste: 5 yahoo 7 parvenu, upstart, wannabe 9 vulgarian
arrogance: 3 ego 4 airs, gall 5 brass, cheek, crust, nerve, pride, scorn 6 hubris, hutzpa, hybris, vanity 7 bluster, chutzpa, conceit, disdain, egotism, hauteur, hutzpah, license, swagger 8 audacity, chutzpah 9 aloofness, assurance, insolence, loftiness, pomposity 10 assumption, effrontery, pretension
arrogant: 3 big 4 smug, vain 5 bossy, cocky, lofty, proud 6 cheeky, lordly, snooty 7 fustian, haughty, pompous, stuck-up 8 assuming, boastful, cavalier, cocksure, dogmatic, gloating, snobbish, superior 9 audacious, bigheaded, conceited, egotistic, hubristic, imperious, sarcastic 10 autocratic, bigtalking, disdainful, dogmatical, hoitytoity, swaggering
one: 6 egoist
arrogate: 4 take 5 claim, seize, usurp 6 assume 7 preempt, receive 10 commandeer, confiscate, plagiarize
arrogation: 10 usurpation
arrow: 4 bolt 6 cursor, marker, weapon 7 missile, pointer, Sagitta 10 projectile, street sign
combining form: 3 tox- 4 toxi-, toxo-
crossbow ~: 4 bolt
desktop ~: 6 cursor
ender: 4 head, root
group: 5 sheaf
launcher: 3 bow
like an ~: 6 linear, unbent 7 unbowed 8 straight 10 unswerving
maker: 5 brave 6 Indian 8 fletcher
notch: 4 nock
part: 5 notch, shaft
poison: 4 inee, upas 5 urare 6 antiar, curara, curare
straight as an ~: 8 orthodox
Arrow: 5 shirt
competitor: 4 Izod 8 Hathaway 9 Van Heusen
___ Arrow: 5 Time's 6 Broken, Pierce
arrowhead: 5 plant 6 flower
makings: 5 flint
part: 4 barb
shape an ~: 4 knap
Arrowhead: 5 water
alternative: 4 Naya 5 Evian 7 Perrier 8 Aquafina
Arrow, Kenneth: 8 Nobelist 9 economist
Arrowrock Dam river: 5 Boise
___ arrows: 4 love 6 Cupid's
Arrowsmith author: Sinclair Lewis
character: 3 Fox 5 Leora, Tozer 6 Martin 8 Madeline
arrowsmith, name meaning: 8 Fletcher
arrows' partner: 6 slings
arroyo: 4 wadi, wady 5 cañon, gorge, gulch, gully 6 canyon, coulee, gulley, ravine, valley 7 channel
arroz con ___: 5 pollo
ars ___ artis: 6 gratia
ars ___, vita brevis: 5 longa
Ars ___: 4 Nova 7 Antiqua, Poetica
Ars Amatoria poet: 4 Ovid
arsenal: 5 store 6 armory 8 magazine 9 stockpile 10 depository, repository, storehouse
stock: 4 ammo, arms, guns 8 ordnance
Arsene Lupin (1932 film)
cast: John Barrymore, Lionel Barrymore
arsenic: 5 metal 7 element
ore: 7 realgar
Arsenic and Old Lace (1944 film)
cast: Cary Grant, Priscilla Lane, Raymond Massey
director: Frank Capra
role: 4 Abby 5 Gibbs, O'Hara, Teddy 6 Elaine, Martha, Rooney 8 Brewster, Mortimer
Arsenio: 4 Hall
buddy: 5 Eddie
ars gratia ___: 5 artis
arsis: 6 upbeat
Arslan: 3 Alp
ars longa, ___ brevis: 4 vita
arson: 5 crime 6 felony 8 torching, torch job 9 pyromania
arsonist: 5 felon, match, torch 7 firebug 10 incendiary, pyromaniac
Ars Poetica author: Horace
art: 3 oil 4 oils, wile 5 busts, craft, dance, guile, knack, mural, skill, trick, wiles 6 ballet, canvas, deceit, medium, mobile, murals, poetry, sketch 7 carving, collage, cunning, etching, finesse, gouache, ikebana, know-how, mastery, picture, pottery, science, slyness, theater, theatre 8 canvases, facility, juggling, ornament, painting, pictures, portrait, trickery, wiliness 9 canniness, composing, dexterity, duplicity, expertise, ingenuity, landscape, paintings, sculpture, showpiece, technique 10 adroitness, astuteness, caricature, cleverness, craftiness, creativity, livelihood, profession, sculptures, virtuosity, watercolor
black ~: 5 magic 7 sorcery 10 necromancy, witchcraft
combining form: 4 -urgy 6 techno-
deg.: 3 BFA, MFA
ender: 3 ist 4 work
figure: 4 nude
gallery: 5 salon
gum: 6 eraser
hardly fine ~: 6 kitsch
in Italian: 4 arte
in Latin: 3 ars
love of fine ~: 5 vertu, virtu
martial ~: 4 judo 5 kendo, taebo, wushu 6 aikido, karate, kung fu, t'ai chi 7 jujitsu 9 tae kwon do
medium: 3 ink 4 oils 10 watercolor
movement prefix: 3 neo
pens: 5 styli
performance ~: 4 mime
print: 4 lith. 5 litho 10 lithograph
stand: 5 easel
state of the ~: 6 latest
studio: 4 loft 7 atelier
style: 4 Dada, Deco 5 genre 6 Ashcan, Cubism 7 Nouveau
suffix: 4 -ship
work of ~: 5 litho, mural, print 6 fresco 7 drawing, etching 8 painting, pastiche 10 lithograph
work with ~: 6 curate 7 restore
art ___: 4 deco, film, form, rock, song 5 glass, house, salon, union 6 editor, lining, runner 7 nouveau, theater, theatre
art ___ art's sake: 3 for
___ art: 3 pop 4 body, cave, clip, fine, folk, junk, land, line 5 black, earth, found, tramp, video 6 gentle 7 concept, kinetic, minimal, optical, plastic
Art: 4 Wall 5 Shell, Tatum, Ulene 6 Blakey, Carney, Pepper, Rooney, Sansom 7 Donovan, Fleming, Shamsky, Stevens 8 Buchwald 9 Garfunkel 10 Linkletter
Art ___: 4 Deco 7 Nouveau
Art ___, The: 5 of War
Art ___ Trophy: 4 Ross
Artaxerxes composer: 4 Arne
Artaxerxes' foe: 5 Cyrus
art-class wear: 5 smock
Art Deco artist: 4 Erté
Arte: 7 Johnson
Artemis
animal sacred to ~: 3 dog 4 bear, boar, hind
companion: 4 Aura 5 Maera
epithet of ~: 5 Delia 6 Ariste, Lyceia, Orthia, Peitho, Savior 7 Eurippa, Heireia, Laphria, Limnaea, Pyronia 8 Aeginaea, Agrotera, Calliste, Caryatis, Cedratis, Daphnaea, Elaphios, Limnatis 9 Coryphaea, Lygodesma
equivalent: 5 Diana
parent of ~: 4 Leto, Zeus
temple of ~ site: 5 Ionia
tree sacred to ~: 3 fir 6 laurel
twin of ~: 6 Apollo
victim: 5 Orion
Artemus: 4 Ward
arterial, not: 6 venous
artery: 3 hwy., way 4 duct, line, road 5 aorta, canal, route, track 6 avenue, course, street 7 channel, conduit, freeway, highway, passage, pathway 8 corridor 9 auto route, boulevard, heart line
clogger: 3 fat
major ~: 3 hwy. 5 aorta 7 highway
of a major ~: 6 aortal, aortic
opposite: 4 vein
___ artery: 5 iliac, renal, ulnar 7 carotid, femoral
artesian ___: 4 well
art for art's ___: 4 sake
artful: 3 coy, sly 4 able, arch, foxy, glib, wily 5 adept, canny, sharp, slick 6 adroit, clever, crafty, shrewd, smooth, subtle, tricky 7 cunning, devious, furtive, knavish, politic 8 dextrous, guileful, masterly, scheming, skillful 9 deceitful, designing, dexterous, ingenious, insidious 10 diplomatic, serpentine
deception: 4 ploy 5 guile
artfulness: 5 guile, wiles 7 finesse, knavery 9 diplomacy
arthropod: 6 insect, spider 10 crustacean
Arthur: 3 Bea 4 Ashe, Hill, Jean, king, Lake, Penn, Zura 5 Brown, Evans, Franz, Freed, Kopit, Krock, Lewis, Lubin, Lyman 6 Conley, Hailey, Hallam, Harden, Hiller, Miller, Murray 7 Balfour, Compton, Fiedler, Godfrey, Kennedy, Nielsen, Rimbaud 8 Ferrante, Goldberg, Honegger, Koestler, Kornberg, Laurents, Mitchell, O'Connell, Schawlow, Sullivan, Treacher 9 Eddington, Henderson 10 Rubinstein, Schnitzler
in Italian: 6 Arturo
in Spanish: 6 Arturo
Arthur (1981 film)
cast: Sir John Gielgud, Liza Minnelli, Dudley Moore
Arthur ___ Doyle: 5 Conan
Arthur ___ Sulzberger: 4 Hays, Ochs
Arthur Ashe Stadium inits.: 4 USTA
Arthur, Bea: 7 actress
film: Lovers and Other Strangers (1970)
TV: The Golden Girls, Maude
___ Arthur Blair: 4 Eric
Arthur C. ___: 6 Clarke
Arthur, Chester A.: 9 president
alma mater: 5 Union
former occupation: 6 lawyer
home: 7 New York, Vermont
middle name: 4 Alan
wife: 5 Ellen
Arthur Conan ___: 5 Doyle
Arthur, Jean: 7 actress
film: The Devil and Miss Jones (1941)
Diamond Jim (1935)
Easy Living (1937)
The Ex-Mrs. Bradford (1936)
A Foreign Affair (1948)
History Is Made at Night (1937)
If You Could Only Cook (1935)
A Lady Takes a Chance (1943)
The More the Merrier (1943)
Mr. Deeds Goes to Town (1936)
Mr. Smith Goes to Washington (1939)
Only Angels Have Wings (1939)
Party Wire (1935)
The Plainsman (1936)
Shane (1953)
The Talk of the Town (1942)
Too Many Husbands (1940)
The Whole Town's Talking (1935)
You Can't Take It With You (1938)
Arthur, King
foster brother: 3 Kay
knight: 3 Kay, Tor 4 Bors, Eric 5 Driam, Ector, Floll, Lucan, Yvain, Ywain 6 Acolon, Brunor, Ewaine, Gareth, Gawain, Hector, knight, Lanval, Lavain, Manier, Morolt,

Ryence, Sagrid, Torres **7** Belvour, Bersunt, Caradoc, Dinadam, Dodynas, Gaheris, Galahad, Grislet, Ladynas, Lionell, Marhaus, Mordred, Pelleas, Peredur, Tristan, Wigamor **8** Agravain, Beaumans, Bevidere, Galohalt, Lancelot, Meliadus, Palamede, Percival, Tristram, Turquine, Wigalois **9** Ballamore, Brandiles, Launcelot, Pellinore
lady: **4** Enid **6** Elaine **9** Guinevere
nephew: **6** Gareth, Gawain
paradise: **6** Avalon
sister: **4** Anne
sword holder: **5** stone
time of ~: **4** yore
Arthur Rex author: Thomas Berger
__ Arthur, TX: **4** Port
artichoke: **5** plant, tuber **6** flower, veggie **9** vegetable
morsel: **5** heart
__ artichoke: **5** globe **7** Chinese
article: **3** the **4** item, unit, ware, word **5** essay, piece, prose, story, thing **6** clause, column, entity, object, report, review **7** feature, write-up, writing **8** doctrine **9** commodity, editorial, narrative, provision, something **10** commentary, literature
legal ~: **7** codicil, proviso **9** amendment
length: **6** linage **7** lineage
newspaper ~: **4** item, Op-Ed **5** piece **6** column **9** editorial
topper: **6** byline
unusual ~: **5** relic **7** bibelot, whatnot **9** objet d'art **10** knickknack
article of __: **5** faith **6** belief
articles: **5** wares
of faith: **5** canon, creed, dogma **6** belief, tenets **8** doctrine, ideology, religion **9** teachings **10** persuasion, principles
touch up ~: **4** edit
articulate: **3** say **4** glib, oral, talk **5** clear, lucid, speak, state, utter, vocal, voice **6** fluent, intone, spoken **7** breathe, express **8** coherent, distinct, eloquent, set forth **9** emphasize, enunciate, pronounce, talkative, verbalize **10** coherently, expressive, well-spoken
articulated: **5** vocal
articulateness: **8** literacy
articulation: **4** form, link **6** accent, speech **7** clarity, diction **8** language, locution **9** statement, utterance
Artie: **4** Shaw **7** Shapiro **8** Auerbach
author: **3** Ade
ex: **3** Ava **4** Lana
artifact: **5** relic **6** eolith
place: **6** museum
to an archaeologist: **4** find
artifice: **3** con **4** hoax, ploy, ruse, scam, sham, trap, wile **5** craft, dodge, feint, fraud, guile, shift, trick **6** deceit, device, dupery, gambit, humbug, racket, tactic **7** finesse, gimmick, sleight, snow job, swindle **8** intrigue, maneuver, pretense, strategy, trickery **9** chicanery, deception, duplicity, expedient, imposture, stratagem **10** craftiness, imposition, subterfuge
artificer: **5** maker **7** artisan, builder, creator, deviser **8** designer, inventer, inventor **9** contriver, craftsman **10** originator
artificial: **4** camp, fake, faux, mock, sham **5** bogus, campy, faked, false, phony, put-on, stiff **6** ersatz, forced, forged, hollow, la-de-da, la-di-da, phoney, pseudo, unreal **7** assumed, feigned, labored, mincing, plastic, stilted **8** affected, lah-di-dah, mannered, specious, spurious **9** contrived, fantastic, imitation, insincere, pretended, simulated, synthetic, unnatural **10** fabricated, factitious, fictitious, fraudulent, substitute, theatrical
artificial __: **3** aid **4** gene, life, turf **5** blood, heart **6** person **7** gravity, horizon, reality
artificial intelligence: **7** science
study: **8** learning **9** computers
artificiality: **4** camp
artillery: **4** arms **7** battery, big guns, cannons, weapons **8** bazookas, materiel, ordnance, weaponry **9** munitions
burst: **5** salvo **9** cannonade
need: **4** ammo
__ artillery: **5** coast, field, heavy, light **6** medium
artiodactyl: **4** deer
Artis: **7** Gilmore
artisan: **4** hand **6** joiner, master, worker **9** artificer, carpenter, craftsman **10** journeyman
league: **4** gild **5** guild
name meaning ~: **5** Faber
artist: **3** Arp **4** Dalí, diva, Dufy, Goya, Gris, Hals, Kent, Klee, Lely, Miró, Reni, Sert, whiz, Wood **5** actor, Bosch, Corot, Degas, Dürer, Ensor, Ernst, Homer, Johns, Kahlo, Klimt, Léger, Manet, Monet, Moore, Moses, Munch, Peale, Rodin, Shahn, Sloan, Steen, Wyeth **6** Benton, Braque, Calder, Copley, drawer, Eakins, etcher, expert, French, Giotto, Hassam, Hopper, imager, Ingres, Inness, Leutze, Man Ray, master, player, Renoir, Rivera, Rothko, Rubens, Seurat, singer, Stuart, Tanguy, Tissot, Titian, Warhol **7** actress, Bonheur, Borglum, Bruegel, Cassatt, Cellini, Cezanne, Chagall, creator, da Vinci, Duchamp, El Greco, Gauguin, Hans Arp, Hogarth, Holbein, Indiana, Jean Arp, jeweler, Matisse, N.C. Wyeth, Noguchi, O'Keeffe, painter, Picasso, Pisarro, Pollock, Raphael, Sargent, Tiepolo, Utrillo, van Dyck, van Eyck, van Gogh, Vermeer **8** Angelico, Ben Shahn, composer, del Sarto, Dubuffet, Jan Steen, Jean Miró, José Sert, Juan Gris, Magritte, Max Ernst, Mondrian, musician, Paul Klee, Reynolds, Rockwell, sculptor, Ter Borch, virtuoso, Whistler **9** architect, Constable, de Kooning, Delacroix, Donatello, Frans Hals, Grant Wood, Guido Reni, Jean Corot, John Sloan, Kandinsky, performer, Peter Lely, Raoul Dufy, Rembrandt, Remington, Velázquez **10** Botticelli, Edgar Degas, Frida Kahlo, Henry Moore, James Ensor, Jamie Wyeth, Jan van Eyck, Jan Vermeer, Jean Ingres, Modigliani, prima donna, Tintoretto, Yves Tanguy **11** Rosa Bonheur **12** Gainsborough, Michelangelo
abstract ~: **3** Arp **4** Klee **7** Picasso **8** Mondrian, Paul Klee **9** Kandinsky **10** Botticelli
Austrian: **5** Klimt
Baroque: **6** Rubens **9** Velázquez
Belgian: **8** Magritte
British: **5** Moore **7** Hogarth **8** Reynolds **9** Constable **10** Henry Moore **12** Gainsborough
bunco ~: **4** liar **5** cheat, quack, rogue, shark, sneak, taker **6** bad guy, bilker, conman, robber **7** grifter, hustler, scammer **8** swindler **9** defrauder, hypocrite
cel ~: **5** inker
Cubist: **6** Braque **7** Picasso
Dada: **3** Arp, Ray **6** Man Ray **7** Duchamp, Hans Arp, Jean Arp
Dutch: **4** Hals, Lely **5** Steen **7** van Gogh, Vermeer **8** Jan Steen, Mondrian, Ter Borch **9** de Kooning, Frans Hals, Peter Lely, Rembrandt **10** Jan Vermeer
escape ~: **8** magician
Fauvist: **4** Dufy **7** Matisse **9** Raoul Dufy
Flemish: **5** Bosch **6** Rubens **7** Bruegel, van Eyck **10** Jan van Eyck
French: **3** Arp **4** Dufy **5** Corot, Léger, Manet, Monet, Rodin **6** Braque, Ingres, Renoir, Seurat, Tanguy, Tissot **7** Bonheur, Cézanne, Duchamp, Gauguin, Hans Arp, Jean Arp, Matisse, Utrillo **8** Dubuffet **9** Delacroix, Jean Corot, Raoul Dufy **10** Jean Ingres, Yves Tanguy
German: **5** Dürer **7** Holbein
gum: **6** eraser
headgear: **5** beret
Impressionist: **5** Monet **6** Renoir **7** Cassatt, Utrillo
Italian: **4** Reni **6** Giotto, Titian **7** Cellini, da Vinci, Mexican, Raphael, Tiepolo **8** Angelico, del Sarto **9** Donatello, Guido Reni **10** Botticelli, Modigliani, Tintoretto **12** Michelangelo
like a con ~: **5** shady
like some ~ models: **5** naked
Mexican: **5** Kahlo **6** Rivera **10** Frida Kahlo
mobile ~: **6** Calder
need: **5** chalk, light, paint, smock **6** canvas, eraser
Norwegian: **5** Munch
paste: **5** gesso
performance ~: **5** mimer
place: **4** loft **6** colony, garret
pop ~: **6** Warhol **7** Indiana **10** Andy Warhol
prefix: **3** neo-
Renaissance: **5** Dürer **6** TItian **7** Raphael **8** Angelico, del Sarto **9** Donatello **10** Botticelli
rep: **5** agent
Russian: **7** Chagall **9** Kandinsky
Spanish: **4** Dalí, Gris, Miró, Sert **7** El Greco, Picasso, Pisarro **8** Joan Miró, José Sert, Juan Gris **9** Velázquez
subject: **4** anat. **7** anatomy
Surrealist: **4** Dalí **6** Tanguy **10** Yves Tanguy
Swiss: **4** Klee **8** Paul Klee
__ artist: **3** con **4** body, junk **6** escape **7** trapeze
artiste: **6** master, singer **8** musician, virtuoso
artistic: **7** elegant, stylish **8** creative, cultural, esthetic, graceful, talented, tasteful **9** aesthetic, ingenious, inventive, uplifting **10** expressive
be ~: **6** create
expression: **5** style
judgment: **5** taste
merit: **5** vertu, virtu
skill: **5** craft
style: **5** genre, idiom
theme: **5** motif
work: **4** opus
artistry: **5** craft, flair, skill, style, touch **6** beauty, genius, talent **7** ability, finesse, mastery **9** dexterity, technique **10** brilliance, creativity, expertness, virtuosity
Artists and Models (1955 film)
cast: Jerry Lewis, Dean Martin
director: Frank Tashlin
Artists and Models Abroad (1938 film)
cast: Joan Bennett, Jack Benny
director: Mitchell Leisen
Artists in Crime author: Ngaio Marsh
artless: **4** naif, open **5** frank, fresh, inept, naive **6** honest, simple **7** genuine, natural, sincere **8** innocent, lamblike **9** childlike, guileless, ingenuous, outspoken, primitive, unguarded, unworldly **10** unaffected
one: **4** lamb, naif
artlessness: **7** naiveté
Art of Love, The author: Ovid
Art of Loving, The author: Erich Fromm
Art of the Deal, The author: **5** Trump
Art of the Fugue composer: **4** Bach
Art of War, The (2000 film)
cast: Anne Archer, Marie Matiko, Wesley Snipes
director: Christian Duguay
Artoo __: **5** Detoo
Art Ross Trophy org.: **3** NHL
arts: **10** humanities
fed. ~ sponsor: **3** NEA
one of the ~: **5** dance, drama
__ arts: **4** fine **5** beaux **6** visual **7** graphic, liberal, martial
arts and __: **6** crafts **7** letters
artsy: **5** showy **6** too-too **8** affected, bohemian, mannered
artsy-__: **7** craftsy
Artur: **8** Schnabel **9** Rodzinski **10** Rubinstein
Arturo: **9** de Cordova, Toscanini
in English: **6** Arthur
arty: **5** showy **6** chichi **8** affected, bohemian, overdone **10** avant-garde
arty-__: **6** crafty
Aru: **4** isls. **5** isles **7** islands
locale: **9** Indonesia
Aruba: **3** isl. **4** isle **6** island, resort
capital: **10** Oranjestad
__ a rug: **3** cut
arugula: **6** veggie **9** vegetable
arum: **5** calla **9** calla lily **10** cuckoopint
Arum: **3** Bob
Arundel author: Kenneth Roberts
a run for one's __: **5** money
ARU part: **4** unit **5** audio **8** response
Aruwimi: **5** river
locale: **5** Congo
Arvada: **4** city, town
locale: **8** Colorado
Aryan: **6** Nordic **9** Caucasian
__-Aryan: **4** Indo
Arye: **5** Gross
as: **3** qua
as __: **3** for, one, yet **4** such, well **5** a rule, far as, of now, usual **6** though **7** regards
as __ as: **3** far **4** good, long, much, well
as __ as ABC: **4** easy **6** simple
as __ as a fiddle: **3** fit
as __ as life: **3** big
as __ as one's word: **4** good
as __ as rain: **5** right
as __ get-out: **3** all
as __ man: **3** one
as __ possible: **6** soon as
as __ resort: **5** a last
as __ to: **4** told
__ as: **4** such **5** as far, so far
As: **4** elem. **7** arsenic, element
33 for ~: **4** at. no.
As __ and breathe!: **5** I live
As __ as It Gets: **4** Good
As __ care!: **3** if I
As __ didn't know!: **3** If I
As __ Dying: **4** I Lay
As __ Goes By: **4** Time
As __ going to St. Ives: **4** I was
As __ It: **4** I See
As __ Like It: **3** You
As __ my witness: **5** God is
As __ Never Said Goodbye: **4** If We
As __ on TV: **4** seen
As __ saying...: **4** I was

As ___, so shall...: 5 ye sow
A's: 3 ten 4 team
get straight ~: 5 excel
home: 7 Oakland 10 California
A.S.: 5 Byatt
A6 manufacturer: 4 Audi
as a ___: 4 rule 5 whole
as a ___ of fact: 6 matter
Asa: 4 Gray 7 Candler
___ as a bat: 5 blind
___ as ABC: 4 easy 6 simple
___ as a bear: 6 hungry
___ as a beaver: 4 busy
___ as a bee: 4 busy
___ as a beet: 3 red
___ as a bell: 5 clear, sound
___ as a bird: 4 free
___ as a board: 4 flat 5 stiff
___ as a bone: 3 dry
___ as a brick: 5 thick
___ as a button: 4 cute
___ as a church mouse: 4 poor
___ as a clam: 5 happy
ASA cousin: 3 ISO
___ as a cucumber: 4 cool
___ as a daisy: 5 fresh
...as a day in ___: 4 June
___ as a dog: 4 sick
___ as a dollar: 5 sound
___ as a doornail: 4 dead
___ as a drum: 5 tight
___ as a feather: 5 light
___ as a fiddle: 3 fit
___ as a fox: 3 sly
___ as a fruitcake: 5 nutty
___ as a ghost: 4 pale 5 white
___ as a goose: 5 loose, silly
___ as a hatter: 3 mad
___ as a hornet: 3 mad
___ as a horse: 7 healthy
___ as a house: 3 big
___ as a jaybird: 5 naked
___ as a judge: 5 sober
Asaka: 4 city, town
locale: 5 Japan
___ as a kite: 4 high
___ as a lamb: 6 gentle
___ as a lark: 5 happy
___ as a loon: 5 crazy
Asama: 7 volcano
locale: 4 Asia 5 Japan 6 Honshu
___ as a March hare: 3 mad
as a matter of ___: 4 fact
___ as a mouse: 5 quiet
as an ___: 7 example
asana practicer: 4 yogi 5 yogin
___ as an oak: 6 mighty
___ as an owl: 4 wise
___ as an ox: 4 dumb 6 strong
à ___ santé: 5 votre
Asante home: 5 Ghana 6 Africa
ASAP: 3 now, PDQ 4 stat 5 apace, quick 6 pronto 7 quickly 8 chop-chop, directly, right now, right off 9 forthwith, posthaste, right away
part of ~: 6 as soon, soon as 8 possible
___ as a pancake: 4 flat
___ as a peacock: 5 proud
___ as a picture: 6 pretty
___ as a pin: 4 neat
___ as a pistol: 3 hot
___ as a rail: 4 thin
___ as a reed: 4 thin
___ as a rock: 4 hard 5 solid
___ as a seal upon thine heart: 5 Set me
___ as a sheet: 5 white
___ as a skunk: 5 drunk
___ as a Stranger: 3 Not
___ as a tack: 5 sharp
___ as a team: 4 work
___ as a three-dollar bill: 5 phony
___ as a wet hen: 3 mad
___ as a whip: 5 smart
___ as a whistle: 5 clean
...as a wild bull in ___: 4 a net
___ as a wink: 5 quick
asbestos: 7 mineral
as big as ___: 4 life
ASCAP
alternative: 3 BMI
part of ~: 3 Soc. 4 Amer. 7 Authors, Society 8 American 9 Composers 10 Publishers
ascend: 3 fly 4 go up, leap, lift, rise, soar, upgo 5 arise, climb, mount, scale, slope 6 move up, shinny 7 clamber, lift off, shinney, take off 8 escalate 9 succeed to
ascendancy: 4 rule 5 power, reign 7 command, control, mastery, primacy, success, triumph, victory 8 dominion, kingship, leverage 9 advantage, authority, dominance, influence, supremacy 10 domination
ascendant: 9 sovereign 10 forebearer
ascendency: 8 priority
Ascender: 3 SUV 5 Isuzu
ascending: 6 uphill 9 acclivous
ascension: 10 incipience
Ascension: 3 isl. 4 isle 6 island
Ascension ___: 3 Day
Ascension Oratorio composer: 4 Bach
ascent: 4 rise, upgo 5 climb, slope, way up 6 glacis 7 incline, liftoff, takeoff, upgrade 9 acclivity, elevation 10 flight path
Ascent ___, The: 5 of Man
Ascent of F6, The author: W.H. Auden
ascertain: 3 see 4 find, hear, tell 5 check, gauge, glean, infer, judge, learn, prove 6 define, detect, verify 7 certify, confirm, discern, find out, unearth 8 discover, smell out 9 check up on, determine, establish, ferret out, get hold of, get to know, get word of 10 get down pat
ascertainable: 8 knowable 9 definable
ascetic: 4 monk 5 faker, fakir, faqir, sober, stern 6 faquir, hermit, severe 7 austere, recluse, Spartan 9 abstinent, reclusive, religious 10 abstaining, abstemious, antisocial
ancient ~: 6 Essene
Asian ~: 4 Sufi, yogi 5 faker, fakir, faqir, sadhu, yogin 6 faquir
asceticism: 9 austerity 10 abstinence
Asch, Sholem: 6 author, writer
work: The Apostle
East River
Mary
Moses
The Nazarene
The Prophet
ascorbic acid: 7 vitamin 8 vitamin C
ascot: 3 tie 5 scarf 6 cravat 7 necktie 8 neckwear 10 four-in-hand
ascribe: 3 lay 4 name 6 credit, impute, relate 7 project, qualify 8 accredit 9 attribute, chalk up to, insinuate
Ascriptin: 9 analgesic 10 painkiller
alternative: 3 APF 4 Cope 5 Advil, Aleve, Bayer 6 Anacin, Datril, Motrin 7 Ecotrin, Tylenol 8 Bufferin, Excedrin, St. Joseph, Vanquish
___ as day: 5 plain
___ as directed: 3 use
___ as dust: 3 dry
asea: 4 lost 6 addled, afloat, in a fog, unsure 7 at a loss, baffled, bemused, in a daze, muddled, puzzled, sailing, stumped 8 clueless, confused, cruising, drifting, floating, offshore, voyaging, yachting 9 befuddled, flummoxed, perplexed, uncertain, under sail 10 bewildered, nonplussed
not ~: 6 ashore
ASEAN kin: 5 SEATO
___ a seat: 4 have, take
___ a secret: 4 in on
aseptic: 5 clean 7 sterile 8 germ-free, hygienic, pristine, sanitary 10 immaculate
___ A session: 4 Q and
as fit ___ fiddle: 3 as a
Asgard dweller: 4 Odin, Thin, Thor 5 Aesir
___ as gold: 4 good
...as good as ___: 5 a mile
As Good as It Gets (1997 film)
cast: Cuba Gooding Jr., Helen Hunt, Greg Kinnear, Jack Nicholson
director: James L. Brooks
dog: 7 Verdell
as good as one's ___: 4 word
ash: 4 gray, grey, tree 5 ember, rowan 6 blonde, cinder, dottel, dottle 7 cinders 8 hardwood 9 shade tree 10 incinerate, silver-gray
ender: 3 can 4 cake, tray
family: 5 olive
holder: 4 dump, tray 8 landfill
relative: 4 dove, drab 5 beige, dusty, merle, pearl, putty, slate, taupe 6 silver 7 grizzly 8 charcoal, gunmetal, platinum
volcanic ~ formation: 4 maar
ash ___: 3 can 4 fall, flow, gray, grey, heap 5 blond, color 6 blonde
___ ash: 3 fly, tin 4 bone, soda 5 white 7 prickly
Ash: 7 Mary Kay
ashake: 9 trembling, tremulous
ashamed: 5 sorry 7 abashed, bashful, debased, humbled 8 blushing, penitent, sheepish 9 regretful 10 remorseful
be ~: 3 rue 6 repent
make ~: 5 abash
Ashanti: 8 language
capital of ~: 6 Kumasi
home: 5 Ghana 6 Africa
A-sharp alias: 5 B flat
Ashbery, John: 4 poet
Ashburn, Richie: 7 Phillie 10 outfielder
___-Ashbury: 6 Haight
Ashby: 3 Hal 4 Alan
Ashby, Hal: 8 director
film: Being There (1979)
Bound for Glory (1976)
Coming Home (1978)
Harold and Maude (1972)
The Landlord (1970)
The Last Detail (1973)
Shampoo (1975)
ashcan: 4 dump 6 barrel
target: 3 sub
Ashcan ___: 6 school
Ashcroft, Peggy: 4 Dame 7 actress
Oscar: A Passage to India
Ashdod: 4 city, town
locale: 6 Israel
Ashe, Arthur: 7 netster 9 tennis pro
milieu: 5 court
Asheboro: 4 city, town
locale: 4 N. Car.
ashen: 3 wan 4 gray, grey, pale 5 livid, lurid, pasty, white 6 chalky, pallid, peaked, sallow 7 ghastly, greyish, whitish 8 blanched 9 albescent, bloodless, cinereous, colorless, gray-faced, terrified, whey-faced 10 cinderlike, pasty-faced
___ as hen's teeth: 4 rare 6 scarce
Asher
brother of ~: 3 Dan, Gad 4 Levi 5 Judah 6 Joseph, Reuben, Simeon 7 Zebulun 8 Benjamin, Issachar, Naphtali
parent of ~: 5 Jacob 6 Zilpah
sister of ~: 5 Dinah
son of ~: 5 Imnah, Ishvi 6 Beriah, Ishvah
ashes: 5 ruins 6 relics 7 remains 8 leavings, vestiges
reduce to ~: 4 burn
sackcloth and ~: 7 penance
___ Ashes: 7 Angela's
Ashe Stadium need: 3 net
Ashes to Ashes author: 4 Hoag
Asheville: 4 city, town
locale: 4 N. Car.
sch.: 3 UNC
Ashford: 4 Nick 6 Evelyn 8 Nickolas
Ashford and Simpson song: Solid (1985)
Ashford, Evelyn: 6 runner 8 sprinter
Ashford, Nickolas spouse: Valerie Simpson
Ashikaga: 4 city, town
locale: 5 Japan
ashine: 7 glowing 8 gleaming 10 glimmering, glistening
___ a shine to: 4 take
Ashkenazy, Vladimir: 7 pianist, Russian
Ashkhabad: 4 city, town 7 capital
locale: Turkmenistan
Ashland: 4 city, town
locale: 4 Ohio 6 Oregon 8 Kentucky 10 California
Ashley: 4 Judd 5 Laura, Olsen 7 Montagu 9 Elizabeth
rival: 5 Rhett
Ashley, Elizabeth
spouse: James Farentino, George Peppard
ashore: 6 in port, landed, on land 7 on leave 8 grounded, stranded 9 on liberty
cast ~: 6 maroon
go ~: 4 land 6 arrive, debark 9 disembark
not ~: 4 asea 5 at sea
___ a shot: 4 like
___ a shot at: 4 have, take
ashram: 6 temple
Ashtabula: 4 city, town
lake: 4 Erie
locale: 4 Ohio
Ashton-under-___: 4 Lyne
Ashton-Warner, Sylvia: 6 writer
Ash Wednesday: 4 poem
author: T.S. Eliot
Ash Wednesday season: 4 Lent
ashy: 3 wan 4 gray, grey, pale 5 livid, pasty 6 pallid 7 cindery, ghastly, grayish, greyish, whitish 9 cinderous, colorless, pale-faced, whey-faced 10 pasty-faced
residue: 4 calx
As I ___...: 5 see it
As I ___ saying...: 3 was
Asia: 4 cont. 6 Orient 9 continent
antelope: 3 goa 5 saiga
archipelago: 5 Malay
bean: 3 soy, urd
bird: 4 lory, ruff, smew 5 shama 6 argala, chukar, drongo, lanner 7 courser, dottrel, finfoot, marabou, ostrich 8 amadavat, avadavat, dotterel, eagle owl, leafbird, lorikeet, marabout, megapode, tragopan 9 cormorant, francolin, friarbird, frogmouth, ossifrage 10 greenfinch, honeyeater, weaverbird
border part: 5 Urals
bovine: 3 yak 4 anoa, zebu
buy from ~: 6 import
canine: 5 dhole 6 corsac, jackal
capital: 4 Baku, Dili, Doha, Malé, Sana 5 Amman, Dacca, Dhaka, Hanoi, Kabul, Sanaa, Seoul, Tokyo 6 Ankara, Bagdad, Beirut, Manama, Muscat, Riyadh, Taipei, Tehran, Yangon 7 Baghdad, Bangkok, Beijing, Bishkek, Colombo, Jakarta,

Rangoon, Teheran, Thimphu **8** Abu Dhabi, Beyrouth, Damascus, Djakarta, Dushanbe, Katmandu, New Delhi, Tashkent **9** Islamabad, Jerusalem, Phnom Penh, Pyongyang, Ulan Bator, Vientiane **10** Kuwait City **11** Kuala Lumpur, Ulaanbaatar
cereal grass: **4** ragi **5** raggy **6** raggee
country: **3** Isr., Leb., Nam, Pak., Syr. **4** Irak, Iran, Iraq, Laos, Oman **5** China, India, Japan, Korea, Nepal, Qatar, Syria, Tibet, Yemen **6** Brunei, Israel, Taiwan, Thibet, Turkey, Xizang **7** Lebanon, Myanmar, Sitsang, Vietnam **8** Cambodia, Malaysia, Maldives, Mongolia, Pakistan, Sri Lanka, Thailand **9** Indonesia, Kirghizia, New Guinea **10** Kazakhstan, North Korea, South Korea, Uzbekistan **11** Philippines
country of old: **4** Siam **5** Burma
cuisine: **3** Tai **4** Thai **5** Hunan **7** Chinese **8** Szechuan
deer: **4** sika **6** thamin **7** muntjac, muntjak
desert: **4** Gobi, Tahr, Thar, Tuhr **6** Syrian **7** Arabian, Kara Kum **8** Kyzyl Kum **9** Dasht-e Lut, Great Salt
divided ~ nation: **5** Korea
equine: **6** onager
feline: **4** lion **5** chita, civet, ounce, tiger **6** cheeta, chetah **7** cheetah, leopard
fish: **5** betta, loach, tench **6** anabas **7** gourami, sterlet
fruit: **6** durian, loquat **7** bilimbi **8** tamarind
goat: **4** ibex
goat antelope: **5** goral, serow
herb: **5** orach **6** orache
island: **4** Java **5** Macao, Macau
island chain: **6** Kurile
kingdom: **6** Bhutan
language: **3** Lao, Tai **4** Shan, Thai **5** Malay **7** Kirghiz **8** Scythian
language group: **5** Indic
mountain: **3** Api **4** Alai, Jaja, Mana **5** Altai, Horeb, Kabru, Kamet, Sinai **6** Ararat, Cho Oyu, Gilead, Hermon, Kangto, Kungur, Lhotse, Makalu, Nunkun, Nuptse, Pisgah, Trisul **7** Everest, Manaslu, Pyramid, Trikora, Trisuli **8** Anapurna, Baruntse, Chamlang, Changtzu, Dunagiri, Pauhunri, Stanovoi, Tent Peak **9** Ama Dablam, Annapurna, Badrinath, Broad Peak, Istoro Nal, Kanjut Sar, Lenin Peak, Nanda Devi, Nepal Peak, Rakaposhi, Sia Kangri, Tirich Mir **10** Amne Machin, Chomo Lhari, Dhaulagiri, Gasherbrum, Himalchuli, Kula Kangri, Masherbrum, Minya Konka, Muztagh Ata
onetime ~ kingdom: **4** Anam **5** Annam
palm: **4** nipa **5** areca, betel
peninsula: **5** Malay **6** Arabia
people: **4** Kurd **5** Tajik **6** Tadjik **7** Tadzhik
place-name suffix: **4** -stan
primate: **6** gibbon, langur **7** macaque
river: **3** Fly, Han, Qom, Qum, Red **4** Amur, Kura, Lena, Liao, Oxus, Yalu, Yüen **5** Argun, Atrak, Atrek, Indus, Jumna, Kabul, Karun, Murat, Ouémé, Tarim, Tobol, Tumen **6** Angara, Chenab, Cydnus, Gambia, Ganges, Irtish, Irtysh, Jhelum, Jordan, Khabur, Kolyma, Mekong, Orkhon, Seyhan, Sutlej, Tigris, Ussuri, Yamuna, Yarmuk, Yellow **7** Cauvery, Helmand, Hooghly, Huang He, Karkheh, Krishna, Narbada, Orontes, Salween, Selenga, Songhua, Xi Jiang, Yangtze, Yenisei **8** Amu Darya, Chindwin, Godavari, Granicus, Menderes, Nerbudda, Syr Darya **9** Euphrates, Irrawaddy **10** Chao Phraya
rodent: **4** jird **6** gerbil, jerboa, suslik **7** hamster, souslik
sea: **4** Aral **7** Caspian
sheep: **5** argal, shapu, urial **6** argali **7** Karakul
shrub: **4** gumi **5** henna, ramee, ramie **6** aucuba, kerria **7** skimmia **8** camellia, caragana **9** firethorn
snake: **5** krait **6** dhaman
tree: **4** toon **5** henna **6** cassia, durian, lichee, litchi, padauk, padouk **7** champac, leechee, zelkova **8** caragana, champaca **9** candlenut
volcano: **3** Aso, Usu **4** Akan, Fuji, Gaua, Nasu, Taal **5** Alaid, Asama, Azuma, Kelut, Manam, Mayon, Raung, Unzen, Yasur **6** Ambrym, Bagana, Bandai, Chokai, Dukono, Lopevi, Merapi, Ontake, Oshima, Rabaul, Semeru, Slamet, Tiatia, Ulawun **7** Adatara, Bulusan, Canlaon, Kerinci, Langila **8** Gamalama, Karymsky, Pinatubo **9** Tolbachik
weasel: **8** kolinsky
weight: **4** tael **5** picul
weights: **5** artal
Asia Minor
ancient city: **4** Myra, Teos **5** Iasus, Lydia, Troia **6** Cnidus, Sardis
ancient country: **5** Lycia **6** Pontus
ancient district: **5** Caria
ancient language: **8** Phrygian
ancient region: **5** Troad, Troas **6** Aeolia, Aeolis
capital: **6** Angora, Ankara
peak: **5** Mt. Ida
region: **5** Ionia
Asia Minor (1961 song) artist: Kokomo
Asian: **3** Tai **4** Kurd, Sikh, Thai, Turk **5** Iraki, Iraqi, Tamil **6** Indian, Korean, Mongol **7** Bornean, Burmese, Chinese, Laotian, Tibetan **8** Balinese, Japanese, Lebanese, Thibetan **9** Bhutanese, Cambodian, Dravidian, Pakistani, Taiwanese **10** Vietnamese
ancient ~: **4** Mede, Pers. **7** Persian
Asian ___: **3** flu **4** pear
Asian Princess sculptor: **4** Erté
___ as ice: **4** cold
aside: **2** by **3** off **4** away, near **5** alone, apart **6** nearby **9** by oneself, in private, in reserve, privately **10** digression, discursion, separately
all joking ~: **9** seriously, sincerely
brush ~: **7** neglect **9** disregard
cast ~: **4** cede, drop, dump, jilt, sell, shed, shun, veto **5** chuck, ditch, forgo, spurn, yield **6** bounce, forego, give up, pass on, rebuff, reject **7** abandon, discard, disdain, dismiss, exclude, forfeit, forsake **8** disallow, forswear, get rid of, hand over, jettison, leave out, part with, throw out, turn down **9** abandoned, blackball, dispose of, foreswear, repudiate, surrender, throw away **10** relinquish
from: **6** except **7** besides **9** except for, excluding, other than **10** beyond that, leaving out, regardless
held ~: **9** in reserve
leap ~: **4** duck **5** avoid
push ~: **5** elbow, shunt **8** shoulder
put ~: **4** drop, hold, keep, save **5** allow, amass, annul, cache, defer, delay, lay by, lay in, lay up, on ice, quash, shunt, store, table, waive **6** cancel, devote, ignore, refuse, reject, repeal, revoke, shelve **7** abandon, abeyant, abolish, deposit, discard, earmark, lay away, rescind, reserve, rope off, store up, suspend **8** allocate, file away, hold on to, laid away, override, overrule, overturn, postpone, renounce, reserved, salt away, stow away **9** designate, disregard, in reserve, pay no mind, stockpile, supersede **10** pigeonhole, relinquish
step ~: **6** resign **9** stand down
turn ~: **4** skew, veer **5** avert, avoid, parry, shunt **6** divert, swerve **7** deflect, prevent, ward off **10** discourage
___ aside: **3** lay, put, set **4** cast, step
As if!: **3** hah
As If I Didn't Know (1961 song) artist: Adam Wade
a sight for ___ eyes: **4** sore
___ as I know: **5** as far
As I Lay Dying author: **8** Faulkner
character: **4** Anse, Cora, Darl, Lafe, Tull **5** Addie
As I Lay Me Down (1995 song) artist: Sophie B. Hawkins
___ a silly question...: **3** Ask
Asimov, Isaac: **6** author, writer
genre: sci-fi
work: The Caves of Steel
The Currents of Space
Foundation
In Joy Still Felt
In Memory Yet Green
Inside the Atom
I, Robot
The Naked Sun
The Stars Like Dust
___ a Simple Melody: **4** Play
asinine: **4** daft, dumb **5** goosy, inane, silly **6** absurd, goosey, simple **7** fatuous, foolish, idiotic **8** mindless **9** fatuitous, idiotical, laughable, senseless **10** ridiculous, sophomoric, weak-minded
asininity: **6** lunacy **7** fatuity
___ asinorum: **4** pons
___ a Sin to Tell a Lie: **3** It's
as it ___: **4** were **6** stands **7** happens
___ as it is: **4** such
___ as it seems: **7** strange
As I was going to St. ___...: **4** Ives
ask: **3** beg, bid, inq. **4** pose, pray, pump, quiz, seek, urge **5** grill, plead, probe, put to, query **6** appeal, call on, charge, invite, summon **7** beseech, canvass, consult, enquire, entreat, implore, inquire, propose, put it to, request, require, solicit **8** call upon, petition, question **9** catechize, impetrate, interview
a toughie: **5** stump **6** baffle, puzzle, stymie **7** confuse, mystify, nonplus, perplex **8** bewilder, confound **9** dumbfound
desperately: **3** beg **5** plead
for: **3** bid **6** desire, incite, induce **7** bespeak, bring on, inspire, provoke, request, solicit **9** encourage, instigate **10** bring about
(for): **4** call **6** clamor
forgiveness: **5** atone
out: **4** date
pardon: **9** apologize
too much: **5** snoop **6** impose
ask ___: **3** for, out **5** for it
ask ___ trouble: **3** for
Ask ___ what your country...: **3** not
askance: **6** canted **7** asquint, charily **8** cockeyed
look ~: **6** squint
askant: **7** athwart **9** obliquely
Ask Any Girl (1959 film)
cast: Shirley MacLaine, David Niven
director: Charles Walters
___ Asked for It: **3** You
asked for, name meaning: **4** Saul
asked for, not: **5** unbid
___ asked you?: **3** Who
asker: **9** requester, solicitor **10** suppliant
___ a Sketch: **4** Etch
askew: **3** off, wry **4** alop, awry, bent **5** atilt, bandy, wrong **6** aslant, canted, flooey, zigzag **7** athwart, crooked, oblique, slanted, twisted **8** cockeyed, diagonal, lopsided **9** off-center, out of line, to one side **10** diagonally, topsy-turvy
in Scottish: **4** agee
ask for ___: **7** trouble
Ask for it ___: **6** by name
asking: **7** enquiry, inquiry **10** invitation
for the ~: **4** free **6** gratis **7** as a gift **8** costless **9** on the cuff **10** on the house
asking ___: **3** bid **5** price
Ask Me (1964 song) artist: Elvis Presley
Ask me if ___!: **5** I care
___ Ask of You: **4** All I
Ask Your Mama author: Langston Hughes
aslant: **3** wry **5** askew **6** tilted **7** crooked, leaning, oblique, sideway, sloping **8** cockeyed, inclined, sideways, sidewise **9** at an angle, crossways, crosswise, obliquely, on an angle, on the bias **10** diagonally
asleep: **3** lax, out **4** abed, idle, lazy, numb **5** inert, tired, under **6** dozing, draggy, torpid **7** dormant, napping, nodding, passive, resting **8** dreaming, inactive, indolent, lifeless, slothful, sluggish, snoozing **9** gone to bed, lethargic, sacked out, sedentary, somnolent, zonked out **10** disengaged, in la-la land, sawing logs, slumbering
at the switch: **6** remiss **9** negligent
fall ~: **3** nap, nod **4** doze, rest **5** droop **6** catnap, drowse, snooze **7** drop off **8** drift off
half ~: **6** drowsy
___-asleep: **4** half
Asleep ___ Deep: **5** in the
asleep at the ___: **6** switch
___ as life: **3** big
As Long ___ Needs Me: **4** As He
As Long as the Grass Shall Grow author: Oliver La Farge
As Long As You Love Me (1997 song) artist: Backstreet Boys
aslope: **6** tilted **7** sideway, slanted **8** inclined, sideways, sidewise **9** on an angle **10** diagonally
ASL, part of: **4** Amer., Lang., Sign **8** American, Language
___ a Small Hotel: **6** There's
___ a Small World: **3** It's
Asmara: **4** city, town **7** capital
locale: **7** Eritrea
___ as Methuselah: **3** old
___ a smile: **5** crack
Asmodée author: François Mauriac
___ as molasses: **4** slow
___ as mud: **5** clear
___ a snag: **3** hit
___ as nails: **4** hard **5** tough
___-a-snee: **5** snick
Asner: **2** Ed **5** Jules **6** Edward
Asner, Edward: **5** actor
film: Daniel (1983)
Fort Apache, The Bronx (1981)
Gus (1976)

JFK (1991)
TV: Lou Grant, The Mary Tyler Moore Show, Roots
Asnières-__-Seine: 3 sur
Aso: 7 volcano
locale: 4 Asia **5** Japan **6** Kyushu
__ as 1,2,3: 4 easy
asocial one: 5 loner
as of __: 3 now
as one __: 3 man **6** person
__ a song: 3 for
__ a Song: 4 Sing **7** Without
__ a Song Comin' On: 5 I Feel
__ a Song Go...: 4 I Let
__ a Song in My Heart: 4 With
__ à son goût: 6 chacun
asonia: 6 tin ear
asor: 4 lyre
__ a soul: 4 nary
__ a sour note: 5 end on
asp: 5 snake, viper **6** animal, uraeus **7** reptile, serpent **8** ophidian
cousin: 5 cobra, mamba
home: 4 Nile
relative: 3 boa **5** aboma, adder, cobra, krait, racer **6** dhaman, python, taipan **7** markhor, rattler **8** anaconda, moccasin, ringhals **9** boomslang, coachwhip **10** bushmaster, copperhead, sidewinder
victim: 4 Cleo **9** Cleopatra
weapon: 4 fang **5** venom
__ a spade a spade: 4 call
asparagus: 4 fern **6** veggie **9** vegetable
shoot: 5 spear
asparagus __: 3 pea **4** bean, fern **6** beetle
asparagus-like plant: 3 udo
ASPCA: 3 org.
cousin: 4 PETA
document: 10 lic.. license
offering: 7 shelter
part of ~: 3 Soc. **4** Amer. **7** Animals, Cruelty, Society **8** American **10** Prevention
aspect: 3 air **4** aura, face, item, look, mask, mien, part, role, side, view **5** facet, guise, light, phase, slant, thing **6** detail, manner, nature, regard, visage **7** bearing, element, feature, outlook, quality **8** attitude, demeanor, position, qualitie **9** attribute, character, dimension, semblance, viewpoint **10** appearance, complexion, deportment
aspect __: 5 ratio
Aspects of Love: 7 musical
songwriter: 11 Lloyd Webber
aspen: 4 tree
emulate an ~: 5 quake
Aspen: 3 car **4** auto, city, town **5** Dodge **6** resort **9** ski resort **10** automobile
enjoy ~: 3 ski **4** skee
feature: 4 J-bar, snow, T-bar **5** slope
locale: 8 Colorado
visitor: 5 skier
Aspen Hill: 4 city, town
locale: 8 Maryland
asperity: 4 fury **5** rigor, wrath **6** temper **8** acerbity, acrimony, meanness **9** crossness, harshness **10** crabbiness, unkindness
Aspern Papers, The author: Henry James
asperse: 4 gibe, jeer, jibe, mock, slam, slur, snub **5** abuse, decry, libel, scorn, smear, spurn, sully, taint, taunt **6** accuse, attack, defame, deride, dump on, heckle, impugn, malign, offend, rebuff, slight, vilify **7** affront, blacken, censure, degrade, disdain, put down, rank out, run down, slander, spatter, traduce **8** backbite, badmouth, belittle, denounce, derogate, reproach, ridicule, sprinkle, vilipend **9** denigrate, deprecate, discredit, disparage, fling dirt, humiliate **10** besprinkle, calumniate, depreciate, disrespect, speak ill of, stigmatize, throw mud on
asperser: 8 vilifier **9** detractor
aspersion: 3 dig, lie **4** barb, gibe, jibe, slam, slap, slur, snub **5** abuse, libel, scorn, smear, taunt **6** insult, rebuff, slight **7** affront, calumny, catcall, disdain, mockery, obloquy, offense, put-down, sarcasm, slander **8** contempt, derision, innuendo, ridicule **9** cheap shot, contumely, criticism, invective **10** backbiting, defamation, detraction, disrespect, impugnment, imputation, muckraking, opprobrium, reflection
aspersive: 8 libelous **10** detractive
asphalt: 3 tar **5** pitch
lay ~: 4 pave
asphalt __: 4 rock **5** paper **6** jungle
Asphalt Jungle, The (1950 film)
cast: Louis Calhern, Jean Hagen, Sterling Hayden, Marilyn Monroe
director: John Huston
asphodel: 5 plant **6** flower
aspic: 5 gelée, jelly
shaper: 4 mold
aspidistra: 5 plant **6** flower
__ as pie: 4 easy, nice
aspin: 8 whirling
Aspin: 3 Les
aspirant: 7 entrant **9** applicant, candidate, job-hunter
aspirate: 4 sigh
aspiration: 3 aim, end **4** goal, hope, plan, wish **5** dream **6** desire **7** longing, purpose, thought **8** ambition, yearning **9** direction, eagerness, hankering, objective **10** inhalation, right stuff
aspire: 3 aim, try **4** hope, lift, long, mean, seek, soar, want, wish **5** dream **6** hope to, intend, long to, pursue, seek to, strive, wish to **7** aim high, dream to, propose, yearn to **8** desire to **10** have in view
to: 5 aim at, covet **6** desire, try for **7** hope for **8** shoot for
(to): 3 aim **4** long
Aspire: 3 car **4** auto, Ford **10** automobile
aspirin: 9 analgesic **10** painkiller
brand: 5 Bayer **6** Anacin **8** Bufferin, St. Joseph
like ~: 3 OTC
open, as an ~ bottle: 5 uncap
target: 4 ache, pain
unit: 4 pill
aspiring: 5 eager **7** hopeful, wishful, would-be **8** desirous **9** ambitious
aspish: 5 snaky **8** venomous, viperous
__ as pitch: 5 black
__ as Punch: 7 pleased
asquint: 4 awry **5** askey, slyly **6** askant **7** askance, sideway **8** sidelong, sideways, sidewise **9** furtively, obliquely
Asquith: 7 Anthony, Herbert
Asquith, Anthony: 8 director
film: The Browning Version (1951)
Court Martial (1955)
The Demi-Paradise (1943)
Doctor's Dilemma (1958)
Pygmalion (1938)
The V.I.P.s (1963)
The Way to the Stars (1945)
The Winslow Boy (1948)
The Woman in Question (1950)
The Yellow Rolls-Royce (1964)
as right as __: 4 rain
ass: 3 oaf, sap **4** boob, clod, dodo, dolt, dope, fool, jerk, twit **5** burro, chump, clown, cluck, dummy, dunce, genet, idiot, jenny, joker, kiang, looby, ninny, patsy **6** brayer, dimwit, donkey, equine, jennet, lummox, nitwit, onager, sucker, turkey **7** buffoon, bumbler, dingbat, dullard, fathead, half-wit, pinhead, saphead **8** bonehead, dumbbell, dummkopf, lunkhead, meathead, numskull **9** birdbrain, blockhead, harebrain, lamebrain, numbskull, simpleton **10** dunderhead, muttonhead, nincompoop
emulate an ~: 4 bray
relative: 5 horse, kiang, zebra **6** quagga **8** chigetai **9** dziggetai
starter: 4 jack
Assad nation: 5 Syria
assai: 4 palm, very **9** extremely
assail: 3 ply **4** bash, go at, pelt **5** abuse, beset, blast, fly at, sally, set at, set on, storm **6** ambush, attach, attack, berate, engage, fall on, have at, hit out, impugn, invade, malign, oppose, oppugn, rail at, resist, revile, strike, vilify, waylay **7** assault, besiege, bombard, censure, falls on, go after, lambast, lay into, rip into, set upon, slander **8** fall upon, lace into, lambaste, pounce on, strike at, tear into **9** beleaguer, criticize, descend on, excoriate, haul off on, intrude on, lash out at, light into **10** villainize
the ramparts: 6 attack, charge
assailable: 6 liable **8** vincible
assailant: 3 foe, for **5** enemy **6** mugger **7** fighter, invader **8** attacker, opponent **9** aggressor, ill-wisher **10** antagonist
assailment: 5 abuse **6** attack **10** aggression, impugnment
Assam
product: 3 tea
silkworm: 3 eri **4** eria
Assante: 6 Armand
assassin: 6 killer
Assassination Bureau, The (1969 film)
cast: Oliver Reed, Diana Rigg, Telly Savalas
Assassins (1995 film)
cast: Antonio Banderas, Julianne Moore, Sylvester Stallone
director: Richard Donner
Assateague: 3 isl. **4** isle **6** island
locale: 8 Maryland, Virginia
__ as satin: 6 smooth
assault: 3 mug **4** bash, raid, rush **5** abuse, blast, blitz, fight, fly at, foray, force, onset, sally, set on, storm **6** ambush, assail, attack, batter, battle, change, charge, engage, fall on, felony, invade, oppose, sortie, strike **7** advance, aggress, barrage, bombard, lay into, offense, set upon, violate **8** fall upon, gang up on, invasion, lace into, violence **9** broadside, bushwhack, cannonade, haul off on, incursion, intrude on, light into, offensive, onslaught, violation **10** ambushment, impugnment
blunt an ~: 4 stem
the ear: 6 deafen
the nostrils: 4 reek
verbal ~: 5 salvo, shout **7** barrage, ovation **8** outburst **9** explosion
assault __: 4 boat **5** rifle **6** jacket
assault and __: 7 battery
Assault on Precinct 13 (1976 film)
director: John Carpenter
assay: 4 test **5** prove, study, trial **6** assess, regard, size up, survey, try out **7** analyze, examine, explore, venture **8** analysis, appraise, check out, endeavor, estimate, evaluate **10** scrutinize
assay __: 3 cup, ton **6** groove, office
assayer: 6 tester
concern: 3 ore
cup: 5 cupel
As seen __!: 4 on TV
assegai: 4 tree **5** spear **7** javelin
relative: 6 kapuka **7** dogwood
assemblage: 3 mob, set **4** band, gang, herd, pile, unit **5** batch, bunch, crowd, group, rally **6** huddle, throng **7** cluster, company **8** audience, ensemble, junction, juncture **9** aggregate, concourse, congeries, gathering, listeners **10** attendance, collection, concursion, confluence, convention, cumulation
assemble: 3 sit **4** band, call, form, herd, join, leap, make, mass, meet, mold **5** amass, build, bunch, erect, flock, focus, forge, frame, group, merge, model, piece, put up, rally, set up, shape, troop, unite **6** corral, create, gang up, garner, gather, hook up, huddle, muster, summon **7** collate, collect, compile, convene, convoke, fashion, marshal, prepare, produce, reunite, round up, scare up, turn out **8** contrive, converge, hold on to, mobilize, scrape up **9** aggregate, construct, establish, fabricate, forgather **10** accumulate, close ranks, congregate
again: 5 resit
something to ~: 3 kit
assembled: 6 united **7** grouped **9** aggregate **10** collective
assembler: 6 framer **10** fabricator
assemblies, full: 5 plena
assembly: 3 set **4** band, bevy, body, unit **5** bunch, crowd, flock, forum, group, rally, salon, synod, troop, union, whole **6** caucus, confab, hookup, huddle, muster, throng **7** chamber, cluster, company, council, joining, meeting, reunion, session, turnout, viewers **8** audience, building, conclave, congress, ecclesia, visitors **9** concourse, gathering, listeners, multitude, symposium, witnesses **10** collection, conference, convention
combining form: 4 -fest
instruction: 4 step
room: 3 aud. **10** auditorium
assembly __: 4 line, time **5** plant **7** routine
__ Assembly: 7 General
assembly-line
innovator: 4 Ford
worker: 5 robot
assent: 2 OK **3** nod, yes **4** okay, okeh, okey **5** admit, adopt, agree, allow, go for, leave, say OK, yield **6** accede, accept, accord, comply, concur, give in, say yes **7** approve, consent, go-ahead, go along, include, welcome **8** approval, sanction, stand for, thumbs-up, very well **9** accession, acquiesce, admission, agreement, recognize, sign off on **10** acceptance, compliance, concession, concur with, green light, permission, submission
nautical ~: 3 aye **6** aye aye **9** aye aye sir
silent ~: 3 nod
slangy ~: 3 yeh, yep, yup **4** yeah **5** uh-huh **6** righto
to: 3 let **5** allow, brook **6** accept, permit **8** sanction, tolerate **9** approve of, authorize, put up with
word of ~: 3 yea, yes **4** amen **5** right **6** rather
assenter: 5 sheep, toady **6** yes man **7** Babbitt
assert: 3 own, say, vow **4** aver, avow, cite, hold, show **5** argue, claim, posit, press, speak, state, swear, utter, voice, vouch **6** affirm, allege, attest, avouch, depone, insist, submit **7** comment, confess, contend, declare, express, profess, protest, purport,

speak up, testify, warrant **8** insist on, maintain, point out, proclaim, propound, put forth, speak out **9** emphasize, postulate, predicate, pronounce **10** asseverate, put forward
assertion: **4** oath **5** claim, posit, say-so **6** avowal, remark **7** premise **8** argument **9** admission, assurance, statement, stressing, utterance **10** allegation, confession, contention, expression, insistence, profession
without proof (Lat.): **9** ipse dixit
assertive: **4** firm, sure **5** bossy, macho, pushy **7** assured, certain, decided, forward **8** decisive, emphatic, forceful, militant **9** confident, demanding, insistent, presuming **10** aggressive, commanding, peremptory
not ~: **5** timid
too ~: **5** bossy, pushy
Asser, Tobias: **8** Nobelist
assertory: **10** aggressive
assess: **3** fix, peg, set, tax **4** levy, rate, test **5** assay, check, gauge, guess, judge, value, weigh **6** figure, impose, reckon, regard, review, size up, survey **7** compute, eyeball, measure, valuate **8** appraise, check out, estimate, evaluate, factor in, judgment, keep tabs **9** criticize, determine, pick apart
too highly: **8** overrate
assessed ___: **5** value
assessment: **3** fee, tax **4** dues, duty, fine, levy, toll, view **5** price, value **6** charge, rating, tariff, towage **7** opinion **8** estimate, exaction, judgment, usage fee **9** appraisal, criticism, reckoning, valuation **10** estimation, evaluation
amount: **5** ratal
assessor: **5** rater **6** lister **9** inspector
asset: **4** bond, boon, cash, help, plus, tact **5** charm, poise, stock, value **6** beauty, brains, credit, virtue, wealth **7** benefit, capital, holding, service **8** blessing, deftness, good name, good will, resource, strength, valuable **9** advantage, commodity, integrity, inventory **10** investment
financial ~: **2** CD **4** bond, cash **5** money, stock **7** capital, savings **10** investment, real estate
in Italian: **4** bene
negotiator ~: **8** delicacy **9** diplomacy
personal ~: **4** pull **5** charm, magic **6** allure, appeal, glamor **7** charism, glamour **8** charisma, mystique, presence **9** magnetism
___ asset: **5** fixed **6** liquid **7** capital, working
assets: **4** cash **5** funds, goods, means, money, stock, worth **6** equity, estate, riches, wealth **7** capital, chattel, effects, reserve, savings **8** bankroll, holdings, property, reserves **9** principal, resources **10** belongings
aplenty: **6** riches
___ assets: **3** net **5** quick **6** frozen **7** current
___ asset value: **3** net
asseverate: **3** say **4** aver, avow **5** swear, utter, vouch **6** affirm, allege, assert, assure, attest, avouch **7** certify, protest **8** attest to, maintain
asseveration: **3** vow **4** oath **5** claim **6** avowal, pledge **8** averment **9** assurance, utterance
___ as she goes!: **6** Steady
___ as shootin': **4** sure
assibilate: **4** lisp
assiduity: **4** care, zeal **8** industry, keenness, tenacity **9** alertness, attention, briskness, diligence **10** intentness
assiduous: **4** busy, spry **5** astir, fussy, perky **6** active, at work, lively **7** careful, dynamic, finicky, prudent, working **8** animated, bustling, cautious, diligent, exacting, finiking, finnicky, rigorous, sedulous, studious, thorough **9** attentive, energetic, engrossed, judicious, laborious, motivated, observant, sprightly, unfailing **10** fastidious, meticulous, particular, persistent, scrupulous, unflagging
assiduously: **4** hard
assign: **3** put, set, tap **4** cede, deal, give, mete, name, post, rank, send **5** allot, elect, order, place, share **6** assort, choose, commit, devote, enlist, heap on, impute, ration, select **7** appoint, dole out, earmark, empower, entrust, give out, hand out, intrust, mete out, pass out, qualify, specify, station **8** accredit, allocate, dedicate, delegate, deputize, dispense, instruct, nominate, relegate, separate, transfer, turn over **9** apportion, authorize, designate, prescribe **10** commission, distribute, settle upon
assignation: **4** date **5** tryst **7** meeting **10** rendezvous
Assignation, The author: Edgar Allan Poe
assigned ___: **4** risk **7** counsel
assignee: **5** agent
assignment: **3** job **4** duty, post, task, text, work **5** chore, drill, paper, quota, stint **6** affair, charge, errand, lesson, ration **7** mission, project **8** homework, transfer **9** allotment, selection **10** allocation, ascription, commission, delegation, department, employment, hypothesis, nomination, transferal
enviable ~: **4** plum
on ~: **4** busy
work ~: **5** chore, stint **6** errand **7** project **8** activity
Assignment to Kill actor: **5** O'Neal
___ as silk: **6** smooth
assimilate: **5** adapt, co-opt, sop up **6** absorb, adjust, digest, draw in, embody, gather, imbody, ingest, mingle, osmose, soak up, suck up, take in **7** blend in, conform, drink in, swallow **8** go native, intermix **9** integrate, swallow up **10** comprehend, correspond, homogenize, homologize, understand
as simple as ___: **3** ABC
Assiniboin: **6** Indian **7** Amerind
Assisi: **4** city, town **10** embroidery
locale: **5** Italy
assist: **3** aid **4** abet, back, hand, help, lift, tide **5** boost, favor, leg up, serve **6** back up, chip in, second, squire, succor, uphold, wait on **7** backing, bail out, benefit, bolster, further, help out, pitch in, promote, relieve, support, sustain, work for **8** abetment, expedite, stump for, tide over, wait upon **9** be good for, cooperate, court stat, encourage, give a hand, lend a hand **10** facilitate, give a boost, give a leg up, go to bat for, rally round
to a cockney: **3** 'elp
with: **2** go **4** join **5** coact **6** team up **7** connive, go along **8** conspire, take part **9** cooperate, synergize **10** join forces
___ assist: **5** power
assistance: **3** aid **4** hand, help, lift, serv. **5** boost, leg up **6** relief, succor **7** backing, comfort, offices, redress, service, subsidy, support **8** abetment, advocacy, donation, guidance, kindness **9** patronage **10** sustenance
Cockney: **3** 'elp
deserving ~: **5** needy
exclamation: **4** help
of ~: **6** aidful, useful
without ~: **4** solo **5** alone
___ assistance: **6** public
assistant: **4** aide, mate, temp **5** gofer **6** backup, cohort, deputy, flunky, gopher, helper, second **7** abetter, abettor, acolyte, adjunct, employe, flunkey, partner, teacher **8** employee, henchman, minister **9** accessory, appointee, associate, attendant, auxiliary, coadjutor, colleague, companion, gal Friday, man Friday, secretary, supporter **10** accomplice, apprentice, benefactor, coadjutant, cooperator, girl Friday, substitute
Cockney ~: **5** 'elper
graduate ~: **7** teacher **10** instructor
legal ~: **10** amanuensis
remedial ~: **5** coach **7** trainer
assistants: **4** help **5** staff
Assistant, The author: Bernard Malamud
assists: **4** stat
assize: **3** law **4** rule **7** inquest
assn.: **2** gp. **3** grp., org., soc.
assoc.: **2** gp. **3** grp., org., soc.
associate: **3** bro, mix, pal **4** ally, chum, link, mate, peer, yoke **5** align, aline, amigo, buddy, crony, group, unite **6** cohort, couple, degree, equate, fellow, friend, hobnob, league, member, mingle, relate **7** adjunct, comrade, conjoin, consort, partner **8** co-worker, intimate, roommate, sidekick, workmate **9** accessory, accompany, affiliate, assistant, attribute, auxiliary, colleague, companion, confidant, correlate, implicate, integrate, pal around, socialize, truck with **10** accomplice, amalgamate, compatriot, connection, cooperator, fraternize, go partners, hang around, join up with, well-wisher
with: **3** mix, see **4** know **5** tie to **6** hobnob, mingle **8** befriend **9** accompany, socialize **10** fraternize
(with): **5** get in, swing **6** attach, line up, take up
with riffraff: **4** slum
associated: **6** allied, joined, mutual, united **7** cognate, related **8** in league, relative **9** attendant, bracketed, connected
be ~ with: **8** belong to
one ~ with (suffix): **3** -eer
Associated ___: **5** Press
Associate of ___: **4** Arts **7** Science
associates: **6** cohort **9** entourage, personnel
associate's ___: **6** degree
association: **3** set, tie **4** band, bond, clan, club, crew, gild, link, ring **5** bunch, crowd, group, guild, order, troop, union **6** circle, clique, league, outfit **7** company, contact, linkage, pairing, society **8** alliance, assembly, congress, marriage, relation **9** syndicate
in close ~: **10** hand in hand
___ association: **4** free, word **5** block, press, trade **6** alumni **7** benefit, stellar
Association
song: Along Comes Mary (1966)
Cherish (1966)
Everything That Touches You (1968)
Never My Love (1967)
Windy (1967)
assoil: **6** pardon
___ as Solomon: **4** wise
Assommoir author: Emile Zola
assort: **4** cull, rank, rate, sift, sort, type, vary **5** class, grade, group, order, range **6** assign, divide, lay out **7** arrange, catalog, collate **8** allocate, classify, separate, tabulate **9** catalogue, match with **10** categorize, distribute, pigeonhole
assortative ___: **6** mating
assorted: **3** var. **4** misc., mixt **5** mixed **6** divers, hybrid, motley, sundry, varied **7** diverse, several, unalike, various **8** manifold, multiple **9** different
assortment: **3** lot, mix, set **4** hash, olio, pile **5** array, batch, bunch, group, range **6** bundle, choice, jumble, medley **7** mélange, mixture, package, variety **8** mishmash, mixed bag, pastiche **9** diversity, potpourri, selection **10** collection, cumulation, hodgepodge, miscellany
asst.: **3** ADC, dep. **4** adjt., secy.
asst. ___: **4** prof.
___ asst.: **5** admin.
assuage: **4** calm, cool, ease **5** allay, quell, quiet, quite, salve, slake, still **6** lessen, pacify, quench, remedy, smooth, soften, solace, soothe, temper **7** appease, comfort, compose, console, lighten, mollify, placate, qualify, relieve, satisfy, sweeten **8** mitigate, moderate, palliate **9** alleviate, reconcile, untrouble **10** conciliate, propitiate
assuagement: **4** balm **7** anodyne
assuasive: **3** lax **4** easy, kind, mild, soft **5** loose **6** easing, gentle, kindly **7** anodyne, clement, lenient, ruthful, sparing **8** flexible, laid-back, merciful, placable, tolerant **9** compliant, easygoing, forgiving, indulgent **10** forbearing, permissive, unexacting
assumably: **6** likely **8** probably
assume: **3** act **4** deem, fake, hold, seem, take **5** adopt, annex, begin, bluff, endue, feign, grant, indue, infer, mimic, posit, put on, seize, swipe, think, trust, usurp **6** accept, affect, bank on, borrow, deduce, gather, look to, reckon, rely on, snatch, take on, take up **7** acquire, believe, count on, imagine, imitate, preempt, presume, pretend, receive, succeed, suppose, surmise, suspect **8** arrogate, conclude, depend on, shoulder, simulate, take over, theorize **9** calculate, count upon, enter upon, postulate, speculate, undertake **10** commandeer, confiscate, conjecture, embark upon, presuppose, set about to, understand
one can ~: **8** probably
the form of: **6** become **8** turn into
assumed: **4** fake, sham **5** bogus, false, given, phony, put-on, tacit **6** ersatz, forged, made-up, phoney, pseudo, unreal **7** feigned, reputed **8** affected, putative, spurious, unproved, unspoken, unvoiced **9** axiomatic, imaginary, imitation, pretended, synthetic, unnatural **10** artificial, fictitious, fraudulent, understood
appearance: **5** guise
as fact: **5** given **9** axiomatic **10** postulated, understood
identity: **5** cover
name: **5** alias **6** anonym
assuming: **4** bold, rude **5** given, pushy **7** forward, haughty **8** arrogant **9** conceited, egotistic, given that, imperious, providing
that: **4** if so **8** as long as
assumption: **5** basis, guess, hunch, posit **6** belief, taking, theory **7** opinion, premise, seizure, surmise, theorem, thought **8** adoption, takeover **9** accepting, accession, arrogance, cockiness,

deduction, embracing, inference, insolence, postulate, suspicion **10** acceptance, arrogation, conjecture, expectancy, hypothesis, usurpation
logical ~: **5** axiom, given, lemma
assurance: **3** vow **4** oath, pawn, seal, sign, word **5** nerve, poise **6** aplomb, pledge, safety **7** bravery, courage, promise **8** audacity, boldness, chutzpah, coolness, firmness, optimism, reliance, security, warranty **9** arrogance, assertion, certainty, certitude, composure, guarantee, impudence, insurance, stability, statement, sure thing **10** collateral, commitment, confidence, conviction, effrontery, engagement, equanimity, expectancy, profession, protection, sedateness
assure: **3** vow **4** aver, avow, seal **5** cinch, sew up, swear, vouch **6** affirm, attest, avouch, clinch, lock up, pledge, secure, settle **7** certify, comfort, confirm, hearten, promise, protect, satisfy, warrant **8** attest to, convince, keep safe, nail down, persuade, put on ice, vouch for **9** guarantee **10** asseverate, underwrite
assured: **3** set **4** bold, cool **5** gutsy, on ice **6** brazen, poised, sealed **7** certain, decided, settled **8** clear-cut, composed, decisive, definite, fearless, in the bag, positive, sanguine **9** assertive, audacious, automatic, confident, presuming **10** conclusive, courageous, inevitable, unagitated, undisputed
__-assured: **4** self
assuredly: **3** yes **5** truly **6** really **8** for a fact, of course **9** certainly, doubtless **10** positively
Assyria
city: **6** Arbela, Kalakh **7** Nineveh
foe: **4** Mede
language: **8** Accadian, Akkadian
Asta: **3** dog **5** pooch **6** canine **7** terrier
owner: **4** Nick, Nora **7** Charles
__ a stab at: **4** take
Astaire: **4** Fred **5** Adele
Astaire and Rogers: **3** duo **4** pair, team
Astaire, Fred: **5** actor **6** dancer
film: The Band Wagon (1953)
The Barkleys of Broadway (1949)
Blue Skies (1946)
Broadway Melody of 1940 (1940)
Carefree (1938)
Daddy Long Legs (1955)
A Damsel in Distress (1937)
Easter Parade (1948)
Finian's Rainbow (1968)
Flying Down to Rio (1933)
Follow the Fleet (1936)
Funny Face (1957)
The Gay Divorcee (1934)
Ghost Story (1981)
Holiday Inn (1942)
On the Beach (1959)
The Pleasure of His Company (1961)
Roberta (1935)
Royal Wedding (1951)
Shall We Dance (1937)
Silk Stockings (1957)
The Sky's the Limit (1943)
The Story of Vernon & Irene Castle (1939)
Swing Time (1936)
Three Little Words (1950)
Top Hat (1935)
The Towering Inferno (1974)
You'll Never Get Rich (1941)
You Were Never Lovelier (1942)
Ziegfeld Follies (1946)
hometown: **5** Omaha
like ~: **5** suave
prop: **4** cane **6** top hat
sister: **5** Adele
spouse: Robyn Smith
Astana: **4** city, town
locale: **10** Kazakhstan
__ a stand: **4** take
astare: **6** gaping, gazing **7** gawking, glaring **8** goggling, open-eyed **10** goggle-eyed
astart: **8** suddenly
astatine: **7** element, halogen
compound: **6** halide
asteam: **7** boiling **8** vaporous
As Tears Go By (1966 song) artist: Rolling Stones
aster: **5** plant **6** flower **8** starwort
ending: **3** oid
__ aster: **4** tree **5** beach, China **6** golden **7** Italian
asterisk: **4** star
neighbor: **3** PRS **4** OPER **9** ampersand **10** paren. eight
Asterius' wife: **6** Europa
astern: **3** aft **4** back, rear **5** abaft **6** behind **7** aftward **8** backward, rearward **9** backwards, to the rear
asteroid: **3** Ida **4** Eros, Hebe, Iris, Juno **5** Aegle, Ceres, Doris, Elpis, Freia, Hilda, Irene, Palma, Vesta **6** Alauda, Apollo, Aurora, Bertha, Chiron, Cybebe, Cybele, Daphne, Davida, Egeria, Europa, Gaspra, Hygiea, Icarus, Nereus, Pallas, Prokne, Psyche, Rodari, Shipka, Sylvia **7** Camilla, Diotima, Elektra, Eugenia, Eunomia, Nemesis, Siegena **8** Aletheia, Bamberga, Hermione, Kalliope, Lachesis, Mathilde, Pretoria **9** Agamemnon, Herculina, Patientia **10** Amphitrite, Euphrosyne, Geographos, Interamnia, Winchester
fourth-largest ~: **4** Juno
largest ~: **5** Ceres
region: **4** belt
second-largest ~: **6** Pallas
third-largest ~: **5** Vesta
as the __ flies: **4** crow
__ as the day is long: **6** honest
__ as the driven snow: **4** pure
__ as the eye can see: **5** as far
__ as the hills: **3** old
Asther: **4** Nils
As the World Turns: **4** soap **9** soap opera
As Thousands Cheer: **7** musical
composer: Irving Berlin
Asti: **4** city, town
locale: **5** Italy
product: **4** vino
river: **6** Tanaro
__ a stick at: **5** shake
__ a stiff upper lip: **4** keep
As Time Goes By: **4** song, tune
requester: **4** Ilsa
singer: **3** Sam
Astin: **4** John, Sean **9** Mackenzie
Astin, John spouse: Patty Duke
__ a stink: **4** make **5** raise
__ a stinker?: **5** Ain't I
astir: **2** up **4** busy, spry **5** afoot, perky **6** active, at work, lively, moving, roused **7** abroach, buzzing, dynamic, excited, wakeful, walking, working **8** animated, bustling, in motion, out of bed, stirring, underway, waking up **9** assiduous, energetic, on the move, sprightly **10** ambulatory, busy as a bee, up and about
set ~: **8** motivate
Astley, Rick
homeland: England
song: Cry for Help (1991)
It Would Take a Strong Strong Man (1988)
Never Gonna Give You Up (1988)
She Wants to Dance With Me (1989)
Together Forever (1988)
Astolat, lily maid of: **6** Elaine
Aston, Francis: **7** chemist **8** Nobelist
astonish: **3** awe **4** daze, jolt, stun **5** amaze, floor, shock, throw **6** boggle, dazzle **7** astound, nonplus, perplex, petrify, stagger, startle, stupefy **8** bewilder, blow away, bowl over, confound, surprise **9** dumbfound, knock over, overwhelm, take aback
astonished: **4** agog **5** agape **6** aghast **10** bewildered
astonishing: **7** awesome, strange, uncanny, unusual **8** striking **9** marvelous, wonderful **10** prodigious, stupendous
astonishingly: **4** very
astonishment: **3** awe **5** shock **6** wonder **8** surprise
exclamation: **3** wow **4** jeez, whew **5** zowie **6** by Jove, crikey, cripes **7** by jingo, caramba, holy cow **8** holy moly
show ~: **4** gape, gasp
astoop: **4** bent **8** bent over
Astor: **4** Mary, peak **5** mount, Nancy **6** Brooke **8** mountain **9** John Jacob
concern: **3** fur **4** pelt
locale: **10** Antarctica
__ Astoria: **7** Waldorf
Astoria author: Edgar Allan Poe
Astoria locale: **3** Ore. **6** Oregon
Astor, Mary: **7** actress
film: Claudia and David (1946)
Dodsworth (1936)
Don Juan (1926)
The Great Lie (1941, AA)
Holiday (1930)
The Hurricane (1937)
Hush ... Hush, Sweet Charlotte (1965)
Jennie Gerhardt (1933)
The Kennel Murder Case (1933)
The Little Giant (1933)
The Maltese Falcon (1941)
Meet Me in St. Louis (1944)
Red Dust (1932)
There's Always a Woman (1938)
Two Arabian Knights (1927)
Upperworld (1934)
The World Changes (1933)
astound: **3** wow **4** daze, jolt, stun **5** amaze, floor, shock **6** baffle, boggle **7** nonplus, perplex, petrify, stagger, startle, stupefy **8** astonish, bewilder, blow away, bowl over, surprise **9** dumbfound, knock over, overwhelm, take aback
astounded: **5** agape **6** aghast **9** awestruck **10** bewildered, breathless, speechless
astounding: **7** strange, uncanny **8** fabulous **9** appalling, marvelous, wonderful **10** incredible, prodigious
Astra: **3** car **4** auto, Opel **10** automobile
astraddle: **2** on **6** across **7** astride **9** pickaback, piggyback **10** indecisive
astragalus: **4** bone **5** ankle
__ a straight face: **4** keep
astrakhan: **3** fur **5** cloth **6** fabric
astral: **6** sphery, starry **7** stellar **8** heavenly, sidereal, starlike **9** celestial, unworldly **10** of the stars, star-shaped
astral __: **4** body
__ a Stranger: **5** Not as
astraphobe fear: **7** thunder **9** lightning
astray: **3** off **4** awry, lost, wide **5** amiss, wrong **6** absent, adrift, afield, erring **7** in error, missing, roaming **8** errantly **9** far afield, off course, wandering **10** off the beam, off the mark, off the path
go ~: **3** err, sin **4** fail **6** derail, ramble, wander **9** backslide, misbehave
gone ~: **4** lost **7** mislaid, missing **9** misplaced
lead ~: **4** ruin **5** tempt **6** outwit **7** deprave, mislead **8** outsmart **9** misinform
Astre: **3** car **4** auto **7** Pontiac **10** automobile
astride: **4** atop **7** athwart **9** astraddle
get ~: **5** mount
astringency: **7** acidity
astringent: **4** alum, sour, tart **5** acrid, harsh, sharp, stern **6** acetic, biting, bitter, severe **7** cutting, pungent
astro-: **4** star
Astro: **3** dog, van **5** Chevy **9** Chevrolet
rival: **3** Cub, Met, Red **4** Expo, Twin **5** Angel, Brave, Giant, Padre, Rocky, Royal, Tiger **6** Brewer, Dodger, Indian, Marlin, Oriole, Philly, Pirate, Ranger, Red Sox, Yankee **7** Blue Jay, Mariner **8** Athletic, Cardinal, Devil Ray, White Sox
astrobiology: **7** science
astrochemistry: **7** science
astrogeology: **7** science
astrologer: **5** magus **7** diviner, prophet
concern: **3** zod. **4** cusp, moon, sign **6** zodiac **9** horoscope
astrologers: **4** magi
astrological sign: **3** Leo, Ram **4** Bull, Crab, Goat, Lion **5** Aries, Libra, Twins, Virgo **6** Archer, Cancer, Fishes, Gemini, Maiden, Pisces, Scales, Taurus **7** Balance, Scorpio **8** Aquarius, Scorpion **9** Capricorn **11** Sagittarius, Water Bearer
astron.: **3** sci.
astronaut: **8** spaceman **9** cosmonaut, rocketeer **10** moonwalker
affirmative: **3** A-OK
Apollo: **4** Bean, Duke **5** Evans, Haise, Irwin, Roosa, Scott, Young **6** Aldrin, Anders, Borman, Cernan, Conrad, Eisele, Gordon, Lovell, Worden **7** Collins, Schirra, Schmitt, Shepard, Swigert **8** McDivitt, Mitchell, Stafford **9** Armstrong, Mattingly **10** Cunningham **11** Schweickart
concern: **6** G force **7** reentry
drink: **4** Tang
excursion: **3** EVA
Gemini: **5** Scott, White, Young **6** Aldrin, Borman, Cernan, Conrad, Cooper, Gordon, Lovell **7** Collins, Grissom, Schirra **8** McDivitt, Stafford **9** Armstrong
Mercury: **5** Glenn **6** Cooper **7** Grissom, Schirra, Shepard, Slayton **9** Carpenter
milieu: **4** moon **5** ether, space **6** aether **10** outer space
org.: **4** NASA
rotate, to an ~: **3** yaw
vehicle: **3** LEM
wear: **5** G-suit **6** helmet
astronautics: **7** science
astronomer: **4** Ryle **5** Brahe, Sagan **6** Draper, Halley, Hubble, Kepler, Piazzi, Sitter **7** Celsius, Galilei, Huggins, Huygens, Laplace, Ptolemy **8** Ångström, Herschel, Lagrange, Tombaugh **9** Eddington **10** Copernicus, Hipparchus **11** Aristarchus, Omar Khayyám **12** Eratosthenes, Schiaparelli
British ~: **4** Ryle **6** Halley **7** Huggins **8** Herschel **9** Eddington
Danish ~: **5** Brahe **10** Tycho Brahe
Dutch ~: **6** Sitter **7** Huygens
Egyptian ~: **7** Ptolemy
French ~: **7** Laplace **8** Lagrange
German ~: **6** Kepler

Greek ~: **10** Hipparchus **11** Aristarchus **12** Eratosthenes
Italian ~: **6** Piazzi **7** Galilei **12** Schiaparelli
Persian ~: **4** Omar
Polish ~: **10** Copernicus
Swedish ~: **7** Celsius **8** Ångström
astronomical: **4** vast **8** enormous
adjective: **5** lunar, solar
difference: **5** epact
instrument: **6** gnomon **9** telescope
shadow: **5** umbra
unit: **4** year
astronomical __: **4** unit, year **5** clock
astronomy: **7** science **9** uranology **10** astrometry, selenology, stargazing
high point in ~: **6** apogee
study: **5** stars
__ astronomy: **4** x-ray **5** radar, radio **7** optical
Astrophel
author: Algernon Swinburne, Edmund Spenser
Astrophel and Stella: **4** poem
author: Philip Sidney
astrophysics: **7** science
study: **5** stars **9** radiation
Astros: **4** nine, team
home: **5** Texas **7** Houston
org.: **3** MLB, NLC
sport: **8** baseball
Astroturf
alternative: **3** sod **5** grass
component: **5** nylon, vinyl
Astrud: **8** Gilberto
Asturias, Miguel: **6** writer **8** Nobelist **10** Guatemalan
astute: **3** apt, hip, sly **4** foxy, keen, sage, wily, wise **5** acute, canny, quick, ready, savvy, sharp, smart **6** adroit, brainy, bright, clever, crafty, shrewd, subtle **7** cunning, knowing **8** sensible **9** brilliant, farseeing, ingenious, in the know, inventive, judicious, on the ball, realistic, sagacious **10** discerning, insightful, longheaded, perceptive, thoughtful
astuteness: **3** art, wit **4** wits **5** depth **6** acumen, genius, vision, wisdom **8** judgment, keenness **9** smartness **10** cleverness, horse sense
ASU conference: **6** Pac-Ten
__ a sudden: **5** all of
Asunción: **4** city, port, town **7** capital
locale: **8** Paraguay
see also Spanish
asunder: **4** torn **5** apart, in two, loose, riven, split **6** ripped **7** divided **8** separate **9** disjoined, separated **10** into pieces
prefix: **3** dis-
put ~: **3** cut, hew, rip **4** chop, part, rend **5** sever, slash, split **6** cleave, divide **7** disjoin **8** dissever, disunite, separate
As Usual (1963 song) artist: Brenda Lee
Aswan: **3** dam **4** city, town
locale: **5** Egypt
river: **4** Nile
Aswan High __: **3** Dam
aswarm: **7** buzzing, teeming
__ a swath: **3** cut
__ as we speak: **4** even
aswim: **5** dizzy **8** floating
aswirl: **7** eddying, turning **8** twisting
aswoon: **8** fainting **10** blacked out
asylum: **3** ark **4** nest **5** cover, haven, oasis **6** harbor, refuge, safety **7** harbour, retreat, shelter **8** hideaway **9** anchorage, safe house, sanctuary
seeker: **5** alien **6** émigré
Asylum (1972 film)
cast: Barbara Parkins, Sylvia Syms
asymmetric: **6** skewed, uneven **7** crooked, unequal **8** cockeyed, lopsided
asymmetry: **9** deformity **10** contortion, difference, distortion
__ a Symphony: **5** I Hear
as you __: **4** were
__ as you are: **4** come
__-as-you-go: **3** pay
As You Like It
character: **4** Adam **5** Celia, Corin, Phebe **6** Amiens, Audrey, Jaques, Le Beau, Oliver **7** Charles, Orlando, Silvius, William **8** Rosalind **9** Frederick **10** Duke Senior, Touchstone
setting: **5** Arden
As You Like It author: Shakespeare
As you wish: **6** so be it
Asyut: **4** city, town
locale: **5** Egypt
at: **2** by, on **4** when
at __: **3** all, bat, one, sea, war **4** best, cost, ease, hand, heel, home, last, most, odds, once, rest, risk, that, will, work **5** a blow, a clip, a loss, an end, a word, fault, heart, issue, large, least, peace, sight, stake, times, worst **6** bottom, length, random **7** liberty, present
at __ and sevens: **5** sixes
at __ cost: **3** any
at __ ebb: **3** low
at __ end: **4** wit's
at __ ends: **5** loose
at __ for words: **5** a loss
at __ glance: **5** first
at __ juncture: **4** this
at __ last: **4** long
at __ length: **4** arm's
at __-purposes: **5** cross
at __ rate: **3** any
at __ sight: **5** first
at __ tilt: **4** full
at __ time: **3** one **4** this
at __ turn: **5** every
__ at: **3** aim, eat, fly, get, has, set **4** come, gnaw, have, hint, keep, pick, play, rail, tear, wink **5** drive, laugh, scoff, snipe, swear **6** arrive, nibble, sneeze
__ a T: **4** do to **5** fit to
At: **4** elem. **7** element **8** astatine
85 for ~: **4** at. no.
At __!: **4** ease
At __ Last Love: **4** Long
AT: **2** PC **3** IBM
at a __: **4** blow, clip, loss, word **5** price **6** gallop, glance **7** premium, venture
at a __ date: **5** later
at a __ for words: **4** loss
at a __ notice: **7** moment's
at a __ pace: **6** snail's
__-Ata: **4** Alma
Atacama Desert locale: **5** Chile
__ a tad: **4** just
__ at a disadvantage: **3** put
__ at a glance: **4** tell
__ at a gnat: **6** strain
Atahualpa: **4** Inca
Atakapa: **6** Indian **7** Amerind
Atalanta: **6** hunter
fruit: **5** apple
like ~: **5** fleet
lover of ~: **4** Ares
Atalanta composer: **6** Handel
Atalanta in Calydon: **4** poem
author: Algernon Swinburne
at a later __: **4** date
__ a tale told by an idiot: **4** It is
atamasco: **4** lily
at a moment's __: **6** notice
__ a tangent: **5** off on
at any __: **4** cost, rate
__ At Any Speed: **6** Unsafe
atap: **4** nipa, palm **6** thatch
ataraxy: **10** equanimity
Atari
early ~ game: **4** Pong
rival: **6** Coleco
at arm's __: **6** length
__-at-arms: **3** man **6** master
Atascadero: **4** city, town
locale: **10** California
Atascocita: **4** city, town
locale: **5** Texas
at a snail's __: **4** pace
__-a-tat: **3** rat
__ at a time: **3** one, two
Atatürk: **5** Kemal
colleague: **5** Inonu
atavism: **9** reversion, throwback **10** recurrence
atavistic: **9** primitive
Atbara: **5** river
locale: **5** Sudan **8** Ethiopia
at bat: **4** stat
has an ~: **4** is up
successful ~: **3** hit
__ at Bay: **4** Bech
__ at Campobello: **7** Sunrise
At Close Range (1986 film)
cast: Christopher Penn, Sean Penn, Christopher Walken
director: James Foley
__ at Diablo: **4** Duel
ate: **5** dined **6** eroded, noshed, supped **7** snacked
ate __: **4** crow
A-team: **7** varsity
A-Team, The (NBC adventure)
cast: Dirk Benedict (Templeton "Face" Peck)
Mr. T (B.A. Baracus)
George Peppard (Hannibal Smith)
__ at ease: **3** ill
__ a Teen-age Werewolf: **4** I Was
__ at Eight: **6** Dinner
atelier: **3** den **4** loft **6** garret, studio **8** workroom, workshop
item: **5** easel
occupant: **6** artist
__ at 'em!: **5** Up and
Atempa: **4** city, town
locale: **6** Mexico, Oaxaca
__ a temperature: **3** run
Atenco: **4** city, town
locale: **6** Mexico
Ate, parent of: **4** Eris, Zeus
a tergo: **9** in the back
__ à terre: **6** ventre
__-à-terre: **4** pied
Ates: **6** Roscoe
A-test site: **6** Bikini
at every __: **4** turn
ATF
department: **8** Treasury
part: **7** Alcohol, Tobacco **8** Firearms
at first __: **5** sight **6** glance
__ at First Bite: **4** Love
at first glance in Latin: **10** prima facie
__ at first sight: **4** love
At First Sight (1998 film)
cast: Val Kilmer, Kelly McGillis, Mira Sorvino, Steven Weber
director: Irwin Winkler
at full __: **4** tilt
at full length in Latin: **9** in extenso
Athabasca: **4** lake
locale: **6** Canada **7** Alberta
Athabaskan: **6** Indian **7** Amerind
Athamas
brother of ~: **8** Sisyphus
wife of ~: **3** Ino
Athanasius: **5** saint
__ at hand: **4** near **5** close
at hand, not: **4** afar
__ at Heart: **5** Young
At Heaven's Gate author: Robert Penn Warren
__-at-heel: **4** down
atheism: **8** nihilism **9** disbelief, nonbelief
atheist: **5** pagan **6** denier **7** infidel, sceptic, skeptic
atheistic: **7** godless, impious, profane **9** heretical
athel: **4** tree **9** evergreen
Athena: **7** goddess **8** Olympian
animal sacred to ~: **7** rooster, serpent **8** sea eagle
epithet of ~: **4** Alea, Nike **5** Xenia **6** Ergane, Hippia, Leitis, Pallas, Polias, Saitis, Sciras **7** Aeantis, Agoraea, Cissaea, Paeonia, Pronaea, Pronaus, Salpinx **8** Aethyria, Anemotis, Apaturia, Larisaea, Sthenias, Zosteria **9** Celeuthea, Oxyderces, Parthenos, Promachus
equivalent: **7** Minerva
lover of ~: **10** Hephaestus
parent of ~: **4** Zeus **5** Metis **8** Poseidon
shield: **4** egis **5** aegis
symbol: **3** owl
__ Athena: **6** Pallas
Athena artist: **4** Erté
athenaeum: **7** library
Athenian: **5** Attic
see also Greek
Athens: **4** city, town **5** polis **7** capital
athletes: **7** Bobcats **8** Bulldogs
locale: **4** Ohio **6** Greece **7** Georgia
of America: **6** Boston
region: **6** Attica
rival: **5** Argos **6** Sparta, Thebes
school: **3** U. Ga. **4** Ohio **5** Ohio U **7** Georgia
see also Greek
Atherton: **7** William
athirst: **3** dry **4** avid, keen **5** eager **7** craving, longing, orectic, parched, wishful **8** desirous
athlete: **3** end **4** jock **5** boxer, guard **6** bowler, goalie, golfer, jockey, player, runner, tackle **7** catcher, forward, gymnast, hurdler, pitcher **8** fullback, halfback **9** shortstop, sportsman **10** competitor, marathoner, outfielder
assignment: **6** locker
contract clause: **5** no-cut
energy source: **4** carb
__ Athlete Dying Young: **4** To an
athlete's foot: **5** tinea
foot: **5** tinea
like ~ foot: **5** itchy
athletic: **3** fir **4** hale, iron, team, wiry **5** agile, beefy, burly, hardy, hefty, hunky, husky, lusty, stout, tough **6** brawny, hearty, mighty, potent, robust, rugged, sinewy, steely, stocky, strong, sturdy, virile **7** doughty, healthy **8** forceful, indurate, muscular, powerful, puissant, sporting, stalwart, vigorous **9** Atlantean, Herculean, strapping, well-built **10** able-bodied, red-blooded
activity: **5** sport
award: **6** letter
club: **3** gym
event: **4** bout, game, meet **5** match
field: **5** arena **7** stadium
group: **3** sqd. **4** team **5** squad
old ~ contest: **4** agon
shirt: **6** jersey
trial: **4** heat
athletic __: **4** shoe
Athletic
Hall of Famer: **6** Bender
rival: **3** Cub, Met, Red **4** Expo, Twin **5** Angel, Astro, Brave, Giant, Padre, Rocky, Royal, Tiger **6** Brewer, Dodger, Indian, Marlin, Oriole, Philly, Pirate, Ranger, Red Sox, Yankee **7** Blue Jay, Mariner **8** Cardinal, Devil Ray, White Sox

athletics: 5 games, races, sport 6 sports 7 contest 9 exercises 10 recreation
Athletics: 3 ten 4 team
- **home:** 7 Oakland 10 California
- **org.:** 3 ALW, MLB
- **sport:** 8 baseball

Athol: 6 Fugard
at-home: 5 party
__-at-home: 4 stay
Athos' companion: 6 Aramis 7 Porthos 9 d'Artagnan
...a thousand __ no!: 5 times
__ a Thousand Faces: 5 Man of
__, a thousand times...: 4 No no
athrob: 7 beating, pulsing 8 pounding 9 pulsating
athwart: 4 awry 5 askew 6 across, askant, versus 7 against, astride, sideway 8 sidelong, sideways, sidewise 9 adverse to, counter to, crossways, crosswise, obliquely, on the bias, opposed to 10 contrary to, contrawise, crisscross, perversely
__ a tie: 5 end in
__ a Tightrope: 5 Man on
__ a tight ship: 3 run
atilt: 5 askew 6 canted 7 leaning, listing 8 cockeyed, inclined, jousting, lopsided, off plumb, slanting 9 at an angle, off-center 10 out of whack
__ a time: 4 many 5 one at, two at
atip: 9 expectant
A-Tisket, A-Tasket
- **singer:** Ella Fitzgerald

__ at it: 4 keep
Atitlán: 4 lake
- **locale:** 9 Guatemala

__ at Joe's: 3 Eat
__ Atkins: 5 Tommy
Atkins, Chet: 9 guitarist
Atkins diet no-no: 5 sugar
Atkinson: 5 Rowan 6 Brooks
Atlanta: 4 city, town
- **city near ~:** 5 Macon
- **county:** 6 Fulton
- **for Delta Airlines:** 3 hub
- **former ~ arena:** 4 Omni
- **health agcy.:** 3 CDC
- **locale:** 7 Georgia
- **network:** 3 CNN
- **pro team:** 5 Hawks 6 Braves 7 Falcons 9 Thrashers
- **school:** 3 GIT 5 Emory 6 Emory U.
- **zone:** 3 EDT, EST

Atlantean: 4 hale, iron, wiry 5 beefy, burly, hardy, hefty, hunky, husky, lusty, stout, tough 6 brawny, hearty, mighty, potent, robust, rugged, sinewy, steely, stocky, sturdy, virile 7 doughty 8 athletic, forceful, indurate, muscular, powerful, puissant, stalwart, vigorous 9 Herculean, strapping, well-built 10 able-bodied, red-blooded
Atlantic: 5 ocean 6 avenue
- **bay:** 4 Faxa, Vigo 5 Fundy 6 Biscay, Walvis 7 Setúbal, Walfish 8 Biscayne, Delaware 9 Frobisher, Penobscot 10 Chesapeake
- **cape:** 3 Cod
- **desert on the ~:** 6 Sahara
- **fish:** 3 cod, sey 4 cero, cusk, hake, jack, mapo 5 lotte, porgy, saury, snook 6 gunnel, saithe, tarpon, tautog, tomcod 7 cavalla, croaker, graysby, haddock, halibut, herring, margate, pollack, pollock, pomfret, torpedo, whiting 8 mackerel, sea raven, wrymouth 9 amberjack
- **flier:** 3 ern 4 erne 5 Lindy 9 Lindbergh
- **gulf:** 6 Guinea, Mexico 8 San Jorge 9 San Matias
- **island:** 4 Icel. 7 Bermuda, Iceland
- **on the ~:** 4 asea 5 at sea
- **river to the ~:** 4 Miño 5 Congo, Douro, Loire, Minho, Tagus, Zaire 6 Amazon, Gambia, Orange, Pee Dee, Santee, Thjórs 7 Orinoco, Shannon 8 Demerara, Hamilton, Kennebec, Parnaiba, Savannah 9 Merrimack
- **state:** 3 Del., Fla. 4 Mass., N. Car., S. Car. 5 Maine 7 Florida, Georgia, New York 8 Delaware, Maryland, Virginia 9 New Jersey 11 Rhode Island

Atlantic __: 4 City, Pact, time 5 Ocean, Starr 6 puffin, ridley, salmon 7 Charter, croaker
Atlantic City: 4 town
- **attraction:** 4 surf 5 beach 6 casino, dealer 7 pit boss 8 croupier, employee 9 boardwalk
- **game:** 4 faro, keno 5 craps, poker 8 baccarat, roulette
- **locale:** 9 New Jersey
- **treat:** 5 taffy

Atlantic City (1981 film)
- **cast:** Burt Lancaster, Kate Reid, Susan Sarandon
- **director:** Louis Malle

Atlantic Coast Conference
- **school:** 3 FSU 4 Duke 7 Clemson 8 Maryland, Virginia 10 Wake Forest 11 Georgia Tech

__-Atlantique: 5 Loire
Atlantis: 3 isl. 4 isle 6 island 7 shuttle
- **org.:** 4 NASA

Atlantis (1969 song) artist: Donovan
Atlantis: The Lost Empire (2001 film)
- **voice cast:** Michael J. Fox, James Garner, Leonard Nimoy

atlas: 3 map 4 book 7 telamon
- **abbr.:** 3 Atl., isl., lat., mtn., mts., Pac., riv., str., ter., tpk. 4 isth., terr.
- **alternative:** 5 globe
- **amend an ~:** 5 remap
- **blowup:** 5 inset
- **datum:** 4 area
- **dot:** 3 isl. 4 isle, town 5 islet 6 island
- **line:** 4 road 5 route
- **section:** 4 Asia
- **unit:** 3 map 4 sq. mi. 10 square mile

__ atlas: 4 road 7 dialect
Atlas: 4 ICBM, moon, star 5 giant, he-man, range, Titan 7 Charles, missile
- **brother of ~:** 9 Menoetius 10 Epimetheus, Prometheus
- **daughter of ~:** 4 Maia 5 Aegle, Maera, Phaeo, Phyto 6 Cleeia, Eudore, Merope, Pedile, Polyxo, Thyone 7 Alcyone, Calypso, Celaeno, Coronis, Electra, Erythia, Halcyon, Sterope, Taygete 8 Ambrosia, Arethusa, Erytheis, Halcyone, Hesperia, Phaesyla
- **lover of ~:** 7 Pleione 8 Hesperis
- **mountains locale:** 3 Afr. 6 Africa, Sahara 7 Algeria, Morocco, Tunisia
- **parent of ~:** 7 Clymene, Iapetus
- **planet:** 6 Saturn
- **rocket:** 5 Agena
- **son of ~:** 4 Hyas

Atlas Shrugged author: Ayn Rand
- **character:** 3 Ben, Dan 4 Dick, Galt, Hank, Mort, Owen, Paul 5 Balph, Boyle, Dagny, Eddie, Ellis, Liddy, Mouch, Mowen, Nealy, Orren, Simon, Wyatt 6 Conway, Eubank, Halley, Larkin, Ragnar, Robert, Wesley 7 Bertram, Kellogg, Lillian, Reardon, Richard, Scudder, Stadler, Taggart, Willers 8 d'Anconia, McNamara 9 Francisco, Pritchett

Atlautla: 4 city, town
- **locale:** 6 Mexico

Atli: 3 Hun
Atlixco: 4 city, town
- **locale:** 6 Mexico, Puebla

at long __: 4 last
At Long Last Love composer: 6 Porter
at loose __: 4 ends
at low __: 3 ebb
ATM
- **action:** 5 swipe
- **button:** 5 enter 6 cancel
- **code:** 3 PIN
- **device:** 3 CRT
- **maker:** 3 NCR
- **part:** 6 keypad, teller 7 machine 9 automatic

atman: 4 self
atmo- kin: 3 aer- 4 aero-
Atmos: 5 clock
atmosphere: 3 air, sky 4 aura, feel, mood 5 aroma, clime, sense 6 milieu, spirit 7 climate, heavens 8 ambiance, ambience, empyrean, envelope 9 character, semblance, undertone 10 background, impression, local color
- **combining form:** 3 aer- 4 aeri-, aero-
- **part of the ~:** 4 neon 5 argon, ozone 6 oxygen 8 nitrogen
- **unhealthful ~:** 9 pollution
- **upper ~:** 3 sky 5 ether 6 aether

atmospheric: 4 airy 5 light 6 aerial
atmospheric __: 4 tide 6 engine, window 7 braking
At My Front Door (1955 song) artist: Pat Boone
__ at Nite: 4 Nick
at no __: 4 cost, time 7 expense
at no extra __: 4 cost 6 charge
__ at nothing: 4 stop
a to __: 3 zed
atoll: 4 reef, Wake 6 Bikini, island 8 Eniwetok
- **feature:** 5 coral 6 lagoon
- **like an ~:** 5 reefy

__ a toll on: 4 take
atom: 3 bit, dot, jot 4 iota, mite, mote, whit 5 crumb, grain, scrap, shred, speck, trace 6 morsel 7 modicum, smidgen, smidgin 8 particle, smidgeon 9 scintilla
- **charged ~:** 3 ion 5 anion 6 cation
- **ender:** 3 ism
- **exciter:** 5 maser
- **group of ~ s:** 3 mol. 8 molecule
- **ID:** 4 at. no.
- **smashing:** 7 fission
- **with a valence of one:** 5 monad

atom __: 4 bomb 7 smasher
atomic: 3 wee 4 puny, tiny 5 bitty, least, small, teeny 6 little, minute, peewee, petite, teensy 7 nuclear, trivial 9 itsy-bitsy, itty-bitty, miniature, pint-sized 10 diminutive, teeny-weeny, vest-pocket
- **clock device:** 5 maser
- **energy org.:** 3 NRC
- **experiment:** 5 A-test, N-test
- **particle:** 4 beta, muon
- **reaction:** 6 fusion 7 fission

atomic __: 4 bomb, mass, pile 5 clock, power 6 energy, number, theory, volume, weight 7 orbital, reactor
Atomic __: 3 Age
Atomic __ Commission: 6 Energy
__ Atomic Dustbin: 4 Ned's
Atomic Leda artist: 4 Dalí
atomize: 5 grind, spray 9 granulate, pulverize
atomizer: 9 vaporizer
- **output:** 4 mist 5 scent, spray 7 perfume

atomlike: 3 wee 4 puny, tiny 5 small
Atoms for __: 5 Peace
atonal: 7 keyless, raucous, unkeyed 9 dissonant, unmelodic 10 discordant
__ at once: 3 all
atone: 3 pay 5 purge 6 make up, purify, repent 7 satisfy 9 indemnify, make right, reconcile 10 compensate, make amends
- **for:** 6 redeem 7 expiate 8 make good, outweigh, set right 9 make right 10 recompense

at one __: 4 time
at one __ swoop: 4 fell
atonement: 6 amends 7 penance, redress 8 offering 9 expiation 10 recompense, redemption, reparation
__ Atonement: 5 Day of
atoner: 4 ruer
at one's __: 5 elbow, mercy 7 leisure
at one's __ and call: 4 beck
at one's __ end: 4 wit's
__ at one's door: 3 lay
__ at one's word: 4 take
atonic: 4 puny, weak 5 frail, wimpy 6 anemic, effete, feeble, flabby, flimsy 7 anaemic, fragile, wimpish 8 delicate, helpless, pithless 9 faltering, out of tune, powerless 10 unaccented, unstressed, vulnerable
atony: 8 weakness 10 flabbiness
atop: 3 o'er 4 over, upon 5 above, aloft 6 upward 7 astride 8 overhead 9 resting on, sitting on 10 straddling
- **rest ~:** 5 lie on

__ a torch: 5 carry
Atotonilco el Alto: 4 city, town
- **locale:** 6 Mexico 7 Jalisco

__ at Oxford: 5 A Yank
atoxic: 6 benign
Atoyac: 4 city, town
- **locale:** 6 Mexico 8 Guerrero

__ A to Z: 4 from
At Play in the Fields of the Lord: 4 film 5 novel
- **author:** Peter Matthiessen
- **cast:** Kathy Bates, Tom Berenger, Aidan Quinn
- **director:** Hector Babenco

__ at Pooh Corner, The: 5 House
__ atque vale: 3 ave
__ a trail: 5 blaze
__ a trap: 3 set
Atrek: 5 river
- **locale:** 4 Iran

atremble: 5 jumpy
__ at Rest: 6 Rabbit
Atreus son: 8 Menelaus 9 Agamemnon
atrip: 6 aweigh 7 hoisted
atrium: 5 court, lobby 9 courtyard
atrocious: 3 bad 4 foul, grim, poor 5 awful, lousy, woful 6 crumby, crummy, dismal, horrid, odious, rotten, savage, wicked, woeful 7 accurst, baleful, baneful, beastly, doleful, fearful, ghastly, heinous, hellish, ill-done, ungodly, vicious 8 accursed, barbaric, dreadful, fiendish, flagrant, God-awful, grievous, horrible, inferior, shameful, shocking, stinking, terrible, wretched 9 abhorrent, appalling, barbarous, defective, desperate, egregious, execrable, frightful, insidious, loathsome, miserable, monstrous, nefarious, offensive, repulsive, revolting 10 abominable, despicable, detestable, diabolical, disastrous, disgusting, horrendous, horrifying, outrageous, petrifying, scandalous, villainous
atrocity: 3 sin 4 evil 5 crime 6 infamy 7 outrage 8 enormity 10 corruption, inhumanity, wickedness
atrophy: 5 decay, waste 6 wither 8 emaciate
Atropos: 4 Fate
- **colleague:** 6 Clotho 8 Lachesis
- **mother of ~:** 6 Themis

__ at Sea: 3 All 4 Saps 5 Dames, Souls 7 Pilgrim
At Seventeen (1975 song) artist: Janis Ian

AT&SF: 2 RR 8 railroad
stop: 3 sta., stn. 7 station
at sixes and ___: 6 sevens
___ at straws: 5 grasp
Atsugi: 4 city, town
locale: 5 Japan
att.: 3 LL.B., LL.D., rep. 4 lwyr.
Att. ___: 3 Gen.
AT&T
competitor: 3 GTE, MCI 6 Nextel 7 T-Mobile, Verizon
employee: 4 oper. 8 operator
part of ~: 3 Tel. 4 Amer., Tele 8 American 9 Telegraph, Telephone
spin-off: 5 NYNEX
Atta ___: 5 Troll
___ Atta Annan: 4 Kofi
attach: 3 fix, pin, tie 4 bind, glue, join, lace, link, nail, tack, weld, yoke 5 add on, affix, annex, cling, hitch, pin on, river, rivet, sew on, stick, tie on, unite 6 adhere, adjoin, append, assail, cement, cleave, clip on, cohere, couple, enroot, fasten, hook on, hook up, impute, iron on, secure, slap on, staple, tack on, take on 7 combine, conjoin, connect, garnish, hitch on, latch on, stick on 8 hook onto 9 thumbtack
weight to: 6 accept 7 presume
attaché: 3 bag 4 aide 5 envoy 6 consul, legate 8 diplomat 9 briefcase
case: 3 bag 9 portfolio
attaché ___: 4 case
attached: 4 fast 5 loyal 6 adnate, loving
be ~ to: 4 love
no strings ~: 8 optional
attachment: 3 tie 4 bond, lien, link, love 5 annex, extra, rider 6 liking, regard, Velcro 7 adapter, adaptor, adjunct, fitting, loyalty, passion, romance 8 addendum, addition, affinity, appendix, coupling, devotion, fastener, fondness, junction, juncture, vinculum 9 accessory, adoration, affection, amendment, appendage, auxiliary, belonging, coherence, connector, constancy, extension, fastening, fixedness, hankering, puppy love 10 annexation, attraction, connection, elongation, endearment, friendship, high regard, partiality, supplement, tenderness
attack: 3 fit, mob, mug, ply, rip, sic, war 4 bash, bomb, bout, claw, fire, flay, go at, lash, raid, rush, slam, tilt, turn 5 abuse, beset, blast, blitz, blows, fight, fly at, foray, go for, lay to, libel, onset, run at, sally, salvo, set at, set on, siege, spasm, spell, stone, storm, swoop 6 accuse, ambush, assail, battle, charge, claw at, combat, dump on, engage, fall on, have at, hit out, impugn, invade, jump on, larrup, oppose, oppugn, pounce, prey on, rail at, sortie, strike, tackle, take up, vilify, volley, wallop, waylay 7 aggress, asperse, assault, barrage, battery, besiege, bombard, calumny, charges, contest, descent, go after, lambast, lay into, mugging, offense, rip into, set upon, slander 8 backbite, campaign, deal with, denounce, dive into, fall upon, fire upon, gang up on, invasion, lambaste, outbreak, outburst, skirmish, tear into, violence 9 broadside, criticism, criticize, encounter, excoriate, fustigate, haul off on, incursion, intrude on, intrusion, irruption, lash out at, light into, offensive, onslaught, pitch into, start in on 10 aggression, ambushment, assailment, impugnment, lay siege to, plunge into, pounce upon
like a hawk: 7 descend, plummet 9 sweep down
open to ~: 9 unguarded 10 vulnerable
starter: 7 counter
succumb to ~: 4 fall
surprise ~: 4 raid 5 foray 6 ambush 10 ambushment
time: 4 D-Day 5 H-Hour
unfair ~: 9 cheap shot
unlikely to ~: 4 tame
verbally: 4 bash, belt, damn, slur 5 abuse, smear 6 defame, deride, impugn, insult, malign, scathe, vilify 7 potshot, run down, slander 8 badmouth, belittle, lace into, lambaste, reproach, throw mud 9 castigate, criticize, disparage, shoot down
word: 3 sic
attack ___: 3 dog
___ attack: 4 Shaq 5 panic, sneak
Attack!: 5 sic 'em
Attack! (1956 film)
cast: Eddie Albert, Lee Marvin, Jack Palance
director: Robert Aldrich
attackable: 8 vincible
attacker: 3 foe 5 enemy 6 critic, mugger, raider 7 invader 8 vilifier 9 aggressor, assailant, assaulter, combatant, ill-wisher
___ Attacks!: 4 Mars
attain: 3 get, hit, win 4 earn, find, gain 5 get to, grasp, learn, reach 6 come by, come to, fulfil, obtain, rack up, secure 7 achieve, acquire, compass, fulfill, procure, realize 8 arrive at, bring off, glom onto 10 accomplish
fail to ~: 4 miss
attainable: 6 doable, likely, viable 7 in reach 8 credible, feasible, possible, workable 9 available, no problem, plausible, potential, practical, reachable, securable 10 accessible, achievable, imaginable, obtainable, procurable, realizable
attainment: 4 feat, gain 7 mastery, success, triumph 8 fruition 9 accession, actuality, obtaining 10 background, completion, succeeding
attaint: 8 disgrace, dishonor
attar: 7 essence, perfume 9 fragrance
attar of ___: 5 roses
Atta Troll: 4 poem
author: Heinrich Heine
Attell: 3 Abe
attempt: 2 go 3 aim, bid, try 4 seek, shot, stab 5 crack, essay, fling, trial, whack, whirl 6 chance, effort, header, intend, pursue, strive, tackle, take on, tryout 7 pursuit, venture 8 endeavor, struggle 9 give it a go, undertake 10 enterprise, experiment, make a run at
again: 5 retry
boldly ~: 4 dare
brief ~: 4 stab 5 whirl
failed ~: 4 miss
Attenborough, Richard: 3 Sir 5 actor 8 director
film: 10 Rillington Place (1971)
The Angry Silence (1960)
The Bliss of Mrs. Blossom (1968)
Brighton Rock (1947)
Chaplin (1992)
A Chorus Line (1985)
Cry Freedom (1987)
Doctor Dolittle (1967)
Flight of the Phoenix (1966)
Gandhi (1982, AA)
The Great Escape (1963)
Jurassic Park (1993)
Private's Progress (1956)
The Sand Pebbles (1966)
Séance on a Wet Afternoon (1964)
A Severed Head (1971)
Shadowlands (1993)
Young Winston (1972)
attend: 3 see, tag 4 be at, go to, hark, heed, look, mark, mind, show, tend 5 guard, guide, nurse, pop up, see to, serve, sit in, visit, watch 6 appear, come to, drop in, escort, listen, look to, make it, notice, occupy, regard, show up, squire, take in, turn up, wait on 7 care for, cater to, check in, clock in, go to see, hearken, hear out, pay heed, punch in, sit with, turn out, witness 8 chaperon, don't skip, get there, listen to, wait upon 9 accompany, be present, chaperone, give ear to, look after 10 minister to, result from, take care of
again: 5 resee
don't: 6 ignore 8 stay away
to: 4 mind 5 nurse, serve 6 advert, wait on 7 address 8 see about, wait upon 10 take care of
attendance: 4 draw, gate 5 crowd 7 turnout 8 audience, presence 9 attending, box office, gathering, observers, onlookers, witnesses 10 appearance, assemblage, spectators
book notation: 6 absent 7 absence
in ~: 4 here 5 there 6 on hand 7 present
attendant: 4 aide, hand, page 5 guide, usher, valet 6 coeval, convoy, escort, helper, keeper, lackey, server 7 acolyte, janitor, lacquey, orderly, servant 8 chaperon, courtier, follower, guardian, henchman, incident, retainer, servitor, watchdog 9 accessory, ancillary, assistant, attending, auxiliary, chaperone, companion, custodian, following, secretary 10 associated, baby sitter, coincident, collateral, consequent, incidental, understudy, waitperson
___ attendant: 5 cabin 6 flight
attendants: 4 help 5 court, suite 7 retinue 9 entourage, hangers-on, retainers
attended: 5 was at
attendee: 4 goer 6 viewer 9 spectator
attendees: 5 crowd 7 turnout 8 audience 9 listeners
attending: 4 here 6 with us 7 present 9 ancillary, attendant 10 attendance, coincident
attention: 3 ear, TLC 4 care, heed, look, mind 5 study 6 notice, regard 7 caution, concern, thought 8 emphasis, scrutiny 9 assiduity, awareness, deference, diligence, immersion, precision, publicity, spotlight, treatment, vigilance 10 absorption, discretion, importance, indulgence, intentness, solicitude
at ~: 5 erect
attract ~: 8 stand out
attracting ~: 5 showy
call ~ to: 4 note 6 accent, advert, play up, stress 7 feature, mention, point up 8 point out 9 highlight, punctuate, spotlight, underline 10 underscore
center of ~: 5 focus 8 cynosure
direct one's ~: 3 fix
don't pay ~: 3 nap
exclamation: 3 hey, say 4 ahem, ahoy, ecce, help, yo-ho 5 hello 6 behold, yoo-hoo
hold one's ~: 5 rivet 6 absorb, arrest, engage 7 bewitch, engross 8 enthrall, transfix 9 captivate, enrapture, fascinate, preoccupy
hold the ~ of: 4 grab, grip, lure 5 catch, rivet, tempt 6 absorb, divert, engage, entice, occupy 7 attract, engross, impress, involve 8 enthrall 9 entertain, fascinate, tantalize, titillate
lavisher of ~: 5 doter
needing immediate ~: 4 dire 5 acute 6 urgent 7 crucial, exigent, serious 8 critical, pressing 9 desperate, important 10 compelling, imperative
one paying ~: 5 noter
opposite: 6 at ease
pay ~: 4 hark, heed, mark 5 sit up, watch 6 harken, listen, regard 7 hearken, look out, observe, respect
paying ~: 5 alert
pay no ~ to: 4 snub 6 ignore 7 disobey, neglect, tune out 8 overlook, sneeze at
pay ~ to: 4 hear, heed, mind, note 5 court, study 6 advert, attend, notice
public ~: 9 spotlight
shower ~: 4 dote
snap to ~: 6 salute
stop paying ~: 5 drift
to detail: 4 care 9 diligence
watchful ~: 5 vigil
attention ___: 4 line, span
attention-___: 7 getting
___ attention: 3 pay 5 pay no
attention-getter: 2 yo 3 hey, pst 4 ahem, psst, yo-ho 5 gavel 6 halloo, hey you
attention-getting: 5 lurid 6 catchy
attentions: 9 deference, gallantry 10 compliment, politeness
attentive: 4 kind, rapt, wary 5 alert, awake, aware, fussy, glued 6 enrapt, intent, loving, polite 7 all ears, all eyes, careful, devoted, finicky, focused, gallant, heedful, mindful, prudent, wakeful 8 cautious, diligent, exacting, finiking, finnicky, friendly, gracious, obliging, on the job, rigorous, sensible, studious, thorough, vigilant, watchful 9 assiduous, concerned, conscious, courteous, judicious, listening, observant, on the ball, regardful, wide-awake 10 enthralled, fascinated, fastidious, interested, meticulous, on one's toes, particular, respectful, scrupulous, solicitous, thoughtful
be ~: 5 watch 6 listen
one: 6 heeder
attentiveness: 4 heed 7 thought 9 vigilance
attenuate: 3 sag, sap 4 fade, flag, slim, thin, tire, wane 5 abate, blunt 6 dilute, impair, lessen, reduce, shrink, slight, soften, weaken 7 deplete, exhaust, fatigue, lighten, vitiate 8 contract, enervate, enfeeble, minimize, mitigate, undercut 9 constrict, dissipate, extenuate, undermine 10 adulterate, debilitate, devitalize
attenuated: 4 thin 5 lanky 6 narrow 7 tenuous 9 emaciated
attenuation: 9 abatement
attest: 4 aver, avow, mean, seal 5 argue, prove, quote, swear, vouch 6 adjure, affirm, allege, assert, assure, avouch, depone, depose, ratify, uphold, verify 7 bear out, certify, confess, confirm, declare, protest, stand by, testify, warrant, witness 8 indicate, maintain, manifest, validate, vouch for 9 guarantee 10 asseverate
to: 4 aver 5 vouch 6 affirm, assure, avouch, back up, depose, ensure, insure 7 endorse, indorse, stand by, swear to, testify, warrant, witness 8 vouch for 9 guarantee 10 asseverate
attestation: 3 vow 4 oath 5 proof 8 evidence
at the ___: 5 ready, wheel 6 latest

at the __ minute: 4 last
at the __ of: 4 hand
at the __ of a hat: 4 drop
at the __ of one's lungs: 3 top
at the __ of one's rope: 3 end
at the __ time: 4 same
At the __: 3 Hop 4 Copa
At The Ball artist: 4 Erté
__ at the Bat: 5 Casey
__ at the bit: 5 champ
At the Circus (1939 film)
 cast: Margaret Dumont, Chico Marx, Groucho Marx, Harpo Marx
At the Copa girl: 4 Lola
at the drop of __: 4 a hat
__ at the elbows: 3 out
at the end of one's __: 4 rope
__ at the Gates: 5 Enemy
__ at the heels: 3 out 4 down
At the Hop (1957 song) artist: Danny and the Juniors
at the last __: 6 minute
__ at the mouth: 4 down
__ at the office!: 5 I gave
__ at the Opera, A: 5 Night
at the outset in Latin: 8 in limine
__ at the Races: 4 A Day
at the same __: 4 time
__ at the Savoy: 7 Stompin'
At the sound of the ___: 4 tone
__ at the Stars: 4 I Aim
__ at the switch: 6 asleep
__ at the Top: 4 Room
at the top of one's __: 5 lungs
At the Zoo (1967 song) artist: Simon and Garfunkel
at this __: 4 time 6 moment 8 juncture
at this __ in time: 5 point
At This Moment (1986 song) artist: Billy Vera
attic: 4 loft 6 garret 7 mansard 9 storeroom
 end: 5 gable
 like some ~ s: 5 dusty, musty
 view: 4 eave
 window: 6 dormer
attic __: 3 wit 4 salt
Attic: 5 Greek 8 Athenian 9 classical
 dialect: 5 Ionic
Attica
 district: 4 deme
 locale: 6 Greece
Atticism: 3 saw
Attila: 3 Hun 6 József
Attila composer: 5 Verdi
Attila the __: 3 Hun
attire: 3 rig, tux 4 deck, duds, garb, gear, rags, suit, togs, tuck, wear 5 array, drape, dress, getup, guise, habit, robes 6 clothe, doll up, dude up, enrobe, finery, fit out, invest, livery, outfit, rig out, suit up, things, tog out 7 apparel, bedrape, clothes, costume, deck out, dress up, garment, raiment, regalia, threads, toggery, uniform 8 accouter, accoutre, clothing, ensemble, garments, vestment, wardrobe 9 trappings 10 canonicals, Sunday best
 don ~: 5 dress
 formal ~: 3 tux 4 gown, tuck 5 tails 6 finery 8 black tie, white tie
 night ~: 3 PJs 6 kimono, nighty 7 jammies, nightie, pajamas 8 negligee
 see also clothes, clothing
attired: 4 clad
 well ~: 6 dapper
attitude: 3 air 4 bent, bias, mien, mood, pose, side, tone, vein, view 5 light, slant, stand, state, thing 6 aspect, belief, esprit, manner, morale, spirit, stance 7 bearing, conduct, feeling, leaning, mindset, opinion, outlook, posture 8 approach, carriage, demeanor, position, reaction 9 character, mentality, sentiment, viewpoint 10 appearance, proclivity, standpoint
 strike an ~: 4 pose
attitudes, group: 5 ethos, mores
attitudinize: 4 camp, pose 7 show off 8 camp it up 9 put on airs 10 put on an act
Attleboro: 4 city, town
 locale: 4 Mass.
Attlee, Clement: 2 P.M. 7 British
 predecessor: 9 Churchill
 successor: 9 Churchill
__ at Toko-Ri, The: 7 Bridges
attorney: 5 agent 6 arguer, jurist, lawyer, legist 7 adviser, advisor, counsel 8 advocate 9 barrister, counselor, go-between 10 legal eagle, mouthpiece
 be ~ for: 9 represent
 concern: 3 law
 degree: 2 JD 3 LL.B., LL.M.
 hire an ~: 6 retain
 income: 3 fee 8 retainer
 org.: 3 ABA
 title: 3 esq. 7 esquire
 to-be exam: 4 LSAT
 see also lawyer, legal
attorney __: 5 at law 7 general
attorney general
 first female ~: 4 Reno
 Reagan ~: 5 Meese
attract: 3 wow 4 bait, draw, hook, lure, pull 5 charm, tempt 6 allure, appeal, beckon, center, draw in, endear, engage, entice, invite, pull in, rope in 7 beguile, bewitch, enchant, enthral, inthral 8 appeal to, enthrall, entrance, interest, inthrall, intrigue 9 captivate, enrapture, fascinate, magnetize
 attention: 8 stand out
attractant: 4 lure
attracted: 10 fascinated, interested
 be ~ to: 4 like
attracting attention: 5 showy
attraction: 4 bait, draw, lure, pull 5 charm, savor 6 allure, appeal, beauty, come-on, glamor, liking 7 glamour 8 affinity, interest, velleity 9 appetence, chemistry, magnetism, obsession 10 allurement, attachment, come hither, endearment, enticement, friendship, inducement, invitation, temptation
 center of ~: 5 focus, Mecca
 kitchen ~: 4 odor 5 scent, smell, whiff 9 fragrance, redolence
__ attraction: 5 added
__ Attraction: 5 Fatal
attractive: 4 cute, fair, foxy, nice, sexy 5 bonny, sweet 6 bonnie, comely, dainty, lovely, pretty 7 likable, lovable, popular, winning, winsome 8 adorable, alluring, engaging, enticing, fetching, gorgeous, handsome, inviting, likeable, loveable, magnetic, pleasing, striking, stunning 9 admirable, agreeable, appealing, beautiful, beckoning, covetable, desirable, excellent, exquisite, glamorous, palatable, ravishing 10 bewitching, delightful, enchanting, magnetical, well-formed
 find ~: 4 like
 one: 4 hunk 6 looker
attractively, more: 6 better
attractiveness: 5 charm, grace 6 appeal, beauty
attributable: 5 owing
attribute: 3 lay, owe 5 blame, facet, quirk, trace, trait 6 accuse, aspect, credit, impute, symbol 7 ascribe, connect, earmark, feature, qualify, quality 8 accredit, property 9 adjective, associate, chalk up to, character, endowment, reference 10 account for, indication, speciality
 to: 4 cite 5 pin on
 (to): 6 credit
attribution: 5 blame 6 credit
attrit: 5 erode 6 weaken 8 wear down
attrition: 4 wear 7 erosion 9 penitence, weakening 10 contrition, repentance
attritive: 7 erosive
Attu: 3 isl. 4 isle 6 island
 52° 56', for ~: 4 N. Lat.
 island group: 4 Near
 resident: 5 Aleut 8 Aleutian
Attucks: 7 Crispus
attune: 5 adapt 6 adjust, tailor 7 balance, blend in 9 get used to, harmonize, reconcile 10 coordinate
attuned, perfectly: 5 at one
__ at twice the price: 5 cheap
atty. __: 3 gen.
__ atty.: 4 dist., pros.
___ a tuffet: 5 sat on
atumpan: 4 drum
 origin: 5 Ghana
ATV: 3 ute 9 dune buggy
 part of ~: 3 all 7 terrain, vehicle
Atwater: 4 city, town
 locale: 10 California
'at, where to 'ang one's: 3 'ome
__ at will: 4 fire
Atwill, Lionel: 5 actor
 film: Captain Blood (1935)
  The Devil Is a Woman (1935)
  The Man Who Reclaimed His Head (1934)
  The Murder Man (1935)
  Murders in the Zoo (1933)
  Pardon My Sarong (1942)
  Sherlock Holmes and the Secret Weapon (1942)
  The Three Musketeers (1939)
__ at windmills: 4 tilt
atwist: 9 contorted
At Wit's End name: 4 Erma
atwitter: 4 agog
Atwood, Margaret: 6 author, writer 8 Canadian
 work: Bodily Harm
  Cat's Eye
  The Circle Game
  The Handmaid's Tale
  Lady Oracle
  Life Before Man
  Power Politics
  The Robber Bride
__ at Work: 3 Men
atychiphobe fear: 7 failure
At Your Best (1994 song) artist: Aaliyah
atypical: 3 odd 4 eery 5 eerie, queer, weird 6 freaky, quirky 7 bizarre, deviant, oddball, offbeat, strange, unalike, unusual 8 aberrant, abnormal, freakish, isolated, peculiar, singular, uncommon 9 anomalous, different, divergent, eccentric, fantastic, irregular, unnatural 10 unorthodox
 of: 6 unlike
au __: 3 jus, vol 4 fait, fond, lait, pair 6 gratin, poivre, revoir 7 courant, naturel
Au: 4 elem., gold 7 element
 79 for ~: 4 at. no.
Au __, Les Enfants: 6 Revoir
aubade: 5 music
Aube: 5 river
 locale: 6 France
auberge: 3 inn 5 hotel, lodge 8 rest stop 10 guesthouse
aubergine: 6 veggie 8 eggplant 9 vegetable
Auberjonois, Rene: 5 actor
 film: Eyes of Laura Mars (1978)
  The Feud (1989)
  Images (1972)
  McCabe & Mrs. Miller (1971)
 TV: Star Trek: Deep Space Nine
Aubigné, Agrippa d': 6 French, writer
Aub, Max: 6 writer 7 Spanish
Aubrac: 3 cow 4 bull 6 bovine, cattle
Aubrey: 5 Menen 9 Beardsley
auburn: 4 rust 5 brown, color 7 reddish 9 hair color, yellowish
 relative: 3 bay, dun, tan 4 bole, ecru, fawn, foxy, nude, seal 5 amber, beige, camel, cocoa, hazel, khaki, mocha, sepia, tawny, umber 6 bister, bistre, bronze, coffee, copper, ginger, russet, sienna, sorrel, suntan, walnut 7 biscuit, caramel, dogwood 8 chestnut, cinnamon, mahogany 9 butternut, chocolate
Auburn: 4 city, town
 athletes: 6 Tigers
 conference: 3 SEC
 locale: 5 Maine 6 Auburn 7 Alabama, New York 10 Washington
Auburn Hills: 4 city, town
 locale: 8 Michigan
auburn locks, one with: 5 Annie
Auburon: 5 Waugh
Aubusson: 6 carpet
Auch: 4 city, town
 locale: 6 France
Auchincloss, Louis: 6 author, writer
 work: Diary of a Yuppie
  The House of Five Talents
  I Come as a Thief
  Portrait in Brownstone
  The Rector of Justin
Auckland: 4 city, port, town
 locale: 10 New Zealand
au contraire: 2 no 3 nah, naw, nay, nix, non 4 nein, nope, nyet, uh-uh 5 I won't, ixnay, never, no how, not so, no way 6 no deal, noways, nowise 7 I refuse 8 forget it, I will not, negative, negatory 9 by no means, fat chance, I think not 10 count me out, not a chance, thumbs down
au courant: 3 hot, new 5 aware, newsy 6 posted, versed, wise to 7 abreast, updated 8 familiar, informed, up-to-date 9 cognizant, conscious, in fashion, observant 10 conversant
 not ~: 5 passé
A.U.C., part of: 4 anno 5 urbis 8 conditae
auction: 4 sale, sell 5 put up 7 sell-off 9 vendition
 action: 3 bid 5 offer, rebid
 caveat: 4 as is
 ender: 3 eer 4 sold
 hammer: 5 gavel
 ID: 5 lot no.
 Internet ~ site: 4 eBay
 off: 4 sell, vend 6 peddle, unload 9 dispose of, liquidate
 signal: 3 bid, nod
 try to buy at ~: 5 bid on
 unit: 3 lot
 victor: 5 buyer
 word: 4 gone, once 5 going, twice
auction __: 5 block, pitch 6 bridge 8 pinochle
__ auction: 5 Dutch 6 silent
auctioneer: 2 MC 5 emcee 6 seller
audacious: 4 bold, game, pert, rash, rude 5 brash, brave, gutsy, nervy, saucy 6 awless, brassy, brazen, cheeky, daring, gritty, heroic, plucky, spunky 7 assured, aweless, defiant, doughty, forward, gallant, glaring, staunch, valiant 8 arrogant, fearless, heroical, impudent, insolent, intrepid, reckless, resolute, spirited, stalwart, unafraid, valorous 9 barefaced, dare-

devil, dauntless, desperate, dreadless, foolhardy, shameless, uncareful, undaunted, unfearful, unfearing **10** courageous, undismayed, ungoverned
be ~: **4** dare
audacity: **4** gall, guts, sass **5** brass, cheek, crust, moxie, nerve, sauce, spunk, valor **6** daring, hubris, hybris, mettle **7** bravery, courage, hauteur, license **8** boldness, chutzpah, defiance, rashness, rudeness, temerity **9** arrogance, assurance, cockiness, gallantry, hardiness, impudence, insolence **10** effrontery, enterprise, feistiness
have the ~: **7** presume
Auden, W.H.: **4** poet **6** writer **7** British
work: The Age of Anxiety
Another Time
The Ascent of F6
City Without Walls
The Double Man
Homage to Clio
Musée des Beaux Arts
Night Mail
On the Frontier
The Orators
Audi: **3** car **4** auto **7** Quattro **10** automobile
rival: **3** BMW **4** Saab
audial: **4** otic
audible: **5** aloud, clear, plain **7** sensory **8** definite, distinct **9** sensorial **10** detectable
barely ~: **5** faint **7** muffled
something ~: **5** sound
audibly: **5** aloud
overwhelm ~: **5** drown **8** drown out
Audie: **6** Murphy
audience: **3** ear **5** crowd, house **6** public **7** gallery, hearers, hearing, meeting, turnout, viewers **8** assembly **9** attendees, gathering, listeners, observers, onlookers, playgoers, showgoers, witnesses **10** assemblage, attendance, moviegoers, spectators
before an ~: **4** live
be in the ~: **6** attend
give ~ to: **4** hear **6** listen
praise: **5** brava, bravo **6** cheers, encore **7** ovation **8** applause **9** standing O
reading to an ~: **10** recitation
audience __: **4** room **5** share
audile: **8** acoustic **10** acoustical
audio: **5** sound **8** acoustic **10** acoustical
add in ~: **3** dub, mix
alter the ~: **5** remix
component: **5** tuner **8** CD player **9** turntable
ender: **4** gram, tape **5** meter, phile **6** metric, typist, visual **8** cassette
partner: **5** video
problem: **4** echo
receiver: **3** ear **4** hi-fi **6** stereo **7** boombox
audio __: **4** book, disk
audio-__: **6** visual **7** lingual
__ audiodisk: **7** digital
__ audiotape: **7** digital
audiotape name: **3** TDK **4** Sony **6** Maxell **7** Memorex
audiovisual: **7** sensory **9** sensorial
audiovisual __: **3** aid
audit: **4** view **5** check **6** go over, listen, review, survey, verify **7** analyze, enquiry, examine, inquiry, inspect, monitor, sit in on **8** analysis, appraise, checking, listen in, look into, scrutiny **9** go through **10** inspection, scrutinize
ace: **3** CPA **4** acct. **10** accountant
a course: **5** sit in
ending: **3** ory
org.: **3** IRS
audit __: **5** trail
__ audit: **4** cash **6** energy
auditing: **10** accounting
audition: **4** read, test **5** trial **6** tryout **7** hearing, reading
attendee: **5** actor
objective: **4** part, role
tape: **4** demo
auditor: **3** CPA **7** monitor **8** examiner **9** inspector **10** accountant, bookkeeper
concern: **3** acc. **4** acct. **7** account
federal: **3** GAO
auditorium: **4** hall, room **5** odeon, odeum **6** lyceum **7** theater, theatre **9** music hall, playhouse **10** movie house, opera house
sign: **4** Exit
auditory: **4** otic **7** sensory **8** acoustic **9** sensorial **10** acoustical
auditory __: **5** canal, nerve **7** aphasia, vesicle
Audra: **7** Lindley
Audrey: **6** Totter **7** Hepburn, Landers, Meadows
to Jayne: **3** sis
Audubon, of interest to: **5** avian
Audubon Society member: **6** birder
Auel, Jean: **6** author, writer
work: The Clan of the Cave Bear
The Mammoth Hunters
The Plains of Passage
The Shelters of Stone
The Valley of Horses
Auer: **6** Mischa **7** Leopold
Auerbach: **3** Red **5** Artie
Auerbach, Red: **5** coach
milieu: **5** court
org.: **3** NBA
sport: **10** basketball
Auer, Leopold: **9** Hungarian, violinist
Auer, Mischa: **5** actor
film: Hellzapoppin' (1941)
The Rage of Paris (1938)
Spring Parade (1940)
au fait: **3** ace **4** able, deft **5** adept, slick, smart **6** adroit, expert, nimble, posted, proper, versed **7** abreast, capable, skilled, trained **8** decorous, dextrous, graceful, informed, masterly, seasoned, skillful **9** competent, dexterous, efficient, masterful, qualified **10** conversant, proficient, well-versed
__-au-feu: **3** pot
au fond: **6** wholly **7** in depth, totally **8** from A to Z, in detail, whole hog **9** to the full **10** completely, thoroughly, to the limit
auf Wiedersehen: **3** bye **4** ta-ta **5** later, see ya **6** bye-bye, so long **7** goodbye **8** farewell, sayonara
Aug.: **2** mo.
follower: **3** Sep. **4** Sept
hrs.: **3** DST
preceder: **3** Jul.
see also August
Augean: **9** difficult **10** unpleasant
Augean __: **7** stables
auger: **3** bit **4** tool **5** borer, drill **10** jackhammer
combining form: **6** trypan- **7** trypano-
product: **4** hole
auger __: **3** bit
Auger: **8** Claudine
aught: **3** any, nil **4** none, zero **6** cipher **7** nothing
augment: **3** add, eke, pad, wax **4** feed, grow, hike, incr., rise **5** add to, bloat, boost, build, mount, raise, swell, widen **6** beef up, dilate, expand, extend, jack up, step up **7** amplify, broaden, build up, burgeon, develop, enhance, enlarge, improve, inflate, magnify, recruit, scale up **8** bourgeon, escalate, heighten, increase, lengthen, multiply **9** increment, intensify, reinforce, spread out **10** aggrandize, strengthen, supplement
augmentation: **4** gain, hike, rise **5** boost, raise **6** growth, upping **7** buildup **8** addendum, addition, increase
augmented: **6** bigger, longer
Augsburg: **4** city, town
locale: **7** Germany
river: **4** Lech
augur: **4** bode, mean, omen, seer, sign **5** sibyl **6** auspex, herald, oracle **7** aruspex, betoken, diviner, portend, predict, presage, promise, prophet **8** forecast, foreshow, foretell, haruspex, indicate, prophesy, threaten **9** foretoken, harbinger, predictor **10** forecaster, foreshadow, soothsayer
augury: **4** omen, sign **5** hunch **6** oracle **7** portent, warning **8** forecast, prophecy **9** foretoken, harbinger **10** divination, foreboding, forerunner, indication, prediction
august: **5** grand, great, lofty, noble, proud, regal, royal **6** lordly, proper, solemn **7** awesome, courtly, elegant, eminent, exalted, stately **8** baronial, decorous, glorious, highbred, highbrow, imposing, kinglike, majestic **9** dignified, grandiose, honorable, venerable **10** ceremonial, impressive, majestical
August: **5** month **6** Möbius, Wilson **8** Weismann **10** Strindberg
birthstone: **7** peridot
fifth: **5** nones
like Kansas in ~: **5** corny
period: **7** dog days
sign: **3** Leo **4** Lion **5** Virgo **6** Virgin
Augusta: **4** city, peak, town **5** mount **8** mountain
county: **8** Kennebec
locale: **5** Maine **7** Georgia
river: **8** Kennebec
Auguste: **5** Comte, Rodin **7** Piccard **9** Beernaert, Escoffier
see also French
__-Auguste Renoir: **6** Pierre
August 5: **5** nones
August 15, 1945: **5** V-J Day
Augustine: **5** saint **11** philosopher
augustness: **8** grandeur
Augusto: **8** Pinochet
Augustus: **5** Roman **6** Caesar
wife of: **5** Livia
see also Latin
Augustus Saint-__: **7** Gaudens
__ au Haut: **4** Isle
aujourd'hui: **5** today **6** French
auk: **4** bird **5** murre **6** puffin **7** dovekey, dovekie **9** razorbill
__ au lait: **4** café
Aulby, Mike: **6** bowler
milieu: **5** alley
org.: **3** PBA
auld lang syne: **4** past, yore **9** yesterday
Auld Lang Syne: **4** poem
author: Robert Burns
writer: **5** Burns
auld sod, the: **4** Eire, Erin **7** Ireland
Auletta: **3** Ken
aulos: **4** wind
origin: **6** Greece
Aumont, Jean-Pierre: **5** actor
film: The Cross of Lorraine (1943)
Day for Night (1973)
The Horse Without a Head (1963)
Lili (1953)
au naturel: **3** raw **4** bare, nude **5** naked **9** unattired
aunt: **3** kin, rel. **5** woman **6** female **7** kinsman **8** relative **9** kinswoman
fictional: **2** Em **3** Bee **4** Mame **5** Polly
in French: **5** tante
in Spanish: **3** tía
kid: **3** coz **6** cousin
of song: **5** Rhody
's husband: **3** unc, unk **5** uncle
sis: **3** Mom
__-aunt: **5** great
Aunt __ Cope Book: **5** Erma's
Aunt Helen author: T.S. Eliot
Auntie Em's home: **3** Kan. **6** Kansas
Auntie Mame: **4** film **5** novel
author: Patrick Dennis
cast: Peggy Cass, Fred Clark, Rosalind Russell, Forrest Tucker
character: **3** Ito **4** Vera **5** Agnes, Gooch, Norah **6** Osbert, Pegeen
director: Morton Da Costa
Aunt March creator: **6** Alcott
Aunt Millie's: **10** pasta sauce
alternative: **4** Ragu **5** Prego **6** Prince **8** Classico **10** Newman's Own
Aunt Polly creator: **5** Twain
au pair: **4** maid **5** nanny **6** nannie **8** domestic **9** launderer, nursemaid
__ au poivre: **5** steak
__-au-Prince: **4** Port
aura: **3** air **4** feel, halo, mien, mood, tone, vibe **5** scent, sense, vibes **6** aspect, nimbus **7** charism, essence, feeling, quality **8** ambiance, ambience, charisma, gloriole, mystique, presence **9** character, emanation, radiation, semblance **10** appearance, atmosphere, suggestion
Aura __: **3** Lee
Aura author: Carlos Fuentes
aural: **4** otic **7** sensory **8** acoustic **9** sensorial **10** acoustical
auras: **5** nimbi
aureate: **4** gild **5** flaxy **6** flaxen, golden, ornate
Aurelian: **5** Roman **6** Caesar
__ Aurelius: **6** Marcus
aureole: **4** halo **6** circle, corona, nimbus **8** gloriole, radiance, radiancy **10** effulgence
au revoir: **3** bye **4** ciao, ta-ta **5** adieu, adios, aloha, later, see ya **6** bye-bye, so long **7** goodbye **8** farewell, sayonara
in Hawaiian: **5** aloha
in Italian: **4** ciao
in Latin: **3** ave **4** vale
in Spanish: **5** adios
Au Revoir, Les Enfants (1987 film)
director: Louis Malle
__ au rhum: **4** baba
auric: **6** golden
Auric: **10** Goldfinger
auricle: **3** ear **5** pinna
auricomous: **5** blond **6** blonde
auricular: **4** otic
problem: **6** earwax **7** cerumen
auriculate: **5** eared
aurify: **4** gild
Auriga: **10** Charioteer
Auriol: **4** font **8** typeface
aurochs: **2** ox **4** urus **5** bovid **6** animal, bovine
relative: **3** yak **4** anoa, arna, gaur, zebu **5** bison, gayal, takin **6** mithan, muskox **7** banteng, banting, beefalo, buffalo, carabao, cattalo, kouprey, tamarao, tamarau, timarau
aurophobe fear: **4** gold
aurora: **4** dawn **5** light **7** morning, sky show, sunrise **8** daybreak, daylight
locale: **3** sky
aurora __: **7** polaris **8** borealis **9** australis
Aurora: **3** car **4** auto, city, Olds, town **8** asteroid, Greenway **10** automobile, Oldsmobile
brother of ~: **3** Sol

equivalent: 3 Eos
locale: 6 Canada 7 Ontario 8 Colorado, Illinois
realm: 4 dawn
Aurora artist: 4 Reni
auroral: 4 eoan
Aurora Leigh author: Elizabeth Barrett Browning
aurous: 6 golden
Aus.
locale: 3 Eur.
neighbor: 3 Ger. 5 Switz.
see also Austria
auslander: 5 alien
Auslese: 4 wine
origin: 7 Germany
auspex: 4 seer 5 augur, sibyl 6 herald, oracle 7 diviner, prophet 9 predictor 10 soothsayer
auspice: 4 omen, sign 7 presage 8 foreshow 10 indication
auspices: 4 care, egis 5 aegis 6 agency, charge 7 backing, custody, keeping, support 8 wardship 9 authority, patronage 10 protection
auspicious: 4 good, ripe, rosy 5 blest, lucky 6 bright, golden, timely 7 blessed, charmed, favored, hopeful, on a roll 8 oracular 9 favorable, fortunate, on a streak, opportune, promising, well-timed 10 felicitous, fortuitous, indicative, propitious, prosperous
auspiciously: 4 well
Aussie: 3 emu 4 emeu 5 dingo, koala 6 sheila 7 swagman 8 jackeroo 9 Paul Hogan
see also Australia
Aust.
see Australia, Austria
__ Austen: 6 Godwin
Austen, Jane: 6 author, writer 7 British
work: Emma
Mansfield Park
Northanger Abbey
Persuasion
Pride and Prejudice
Sense and Sensibility
austere: 4 bare, firm, grim, hard 5 bleak, bossy, cruel, harsh, picky, plain, rigid, rough, sharp, sober, stark, stern, stiff, stoic, tough 6 barren, Lenten, rustic, severe, simple, solemn, strict 7 ascetic, Spartan 8 despotic, exacting, hard-line, pitiless, rigorous 9 barebones, cheerless, demanding, draconian, primitive, stringent, unadorned, unbending, unsparing 10 abstemious, despotical, inflexible, iron-fisted, no-nonsense, oppressive, tenebrific, tyrannical
austerely: 4 hard
austerity: 5 rigor 6 thrift 8 bareness, chastity, dourness, eschewal, hardship, iron hand, stoicism 9 exactness, formality, harshness, plainness, rusticism, solemnity, spareness, starkness, sternness, stiffness 10 abstinence, asceticism, barrenness, chasteness, continence, inclemency, puritanism, refraining, self-denial, simplicity, Spartanism, strictness, stringency, temperance
Austerlitz: 6 battle
Auster, Paul: 4 poet 6 author, writer
Austin: 4 city, Teri, town 5 Patti, Steve, Tracy 6 Alfred, Powers 7 Roberts, Stephen 9 Pendleton
county: 6 Travis
locale: 3 Tex. 4 Minn. 5 Texas 9 Minnesota
river: 8 Colorado
Austin __: 4 Peay 5 friar
Austin, Alfred: 4 poet
Austin, Patti song: Baby, Come to Me (1982)
Austin Powers in Goldmember (2002 film)
cast: Michael Caine, Seth Green, Beyoncé Knowles, Mike Myers, Verne Troyer, Robert Wagner, Michael York
director: Jay Roach
Austin Powers: International Man of Mystery (1997 film)
cast: Mike Myers, Mimi Rogers, Verne Troyer, Robert Wagner, Michael York
cat: Mr. Bigglesworth
director: Jay Roach
Austin Powers: The Spy Who Shagged Me (1999 film)
cast: Heather Graham, Elizabeth Hurley, Rob Lowe, Mike Myers, Verne Troyer, Robert Wagner, Michael York
director: Jay Roach
Austintown: 4 city
locale: 4 Ohio
Austin, Tracy: 7 netster 9 tennis pro
milieu: 5 court
austral: 4 wind 5 money 8 southern
__ Australe: 4 Mare
Australia: 4 cont., isle 6 island, nation 7 country 9 continent
airline: 6 QANTAS
bay: 6 Botany 10 Port Philip
bird: 3 emu, iao 4 emeu, koel, lory 5 galah 6 brolga, drongo 7 mudlark 8 cockatoo, lorikeet, lyrebird, megapode 9 bowerbird, cassowary, cockateel, cockatiel, currawong, friarbird, frogmouth, pardalote, riflebird 10 budgerigar, budgerygah, honeyeater, kookaburra
bovine: 10 Murray Grey
buddy: 4 mate
canine: 5 dingo
capital: 8 Canberra
city: 5 Perth 6 Cairns, Darwin, Hobart, Sydney 7 Geelong 8 Adelaide, Brisbane, Canberra 9 Melbourne, Newcastle 10 Townsville, Wollongong
college: 3 uni
desert: 6 Gibson 7 Simpson 10 Great Sandy, Sturt Stony
egg: 4 goog
explorer: 6 Mawson 8 Flinders 9 Vancouver
fish: 4 mado 6 groper, roughy, tandan 8 mulloway, nannygai, trevally 9 schnapper
golfer: 6 Norman 9 Stevenson 10 Baker-Finch
hello: 4 g'day
horse: 4 moke 5 neddy, waler
island: 4 Tasm. 5 Adele 8 Tasmania
island near ~: 7 Norfolk
journalist: 7 Slessor
jumper: 3 'roo 4 euro 7 wallaby 8 kangaroo, wallaroo
lake: 4 Eyre 7 Torrens
marsupial: 4 euro, tait 5 bilby, koala 6 jerboa, numbat, wombat 7 opossum, wallaby 8 kangaroo, wallaroo 9 bandicoot, phalanger
mineral: 4 opal
money: 4 cent 5 penny 6 dollar
moth: 6 bogong
mountain: 9 Kosciusko
national blossom: 6 acacia
native: 3 abo 4 Mara 5 Maori 9 aborigine
Nobelist in Chemistry: 9 Cornforth
Nobelist in Literature: 5 White
Nobelist in Medicine: 6 Burnet, Eccles 7 Doherty
pilots: 4 RAAF
playwright: 6 Palmer, Porter 7 Seymour, Stewart
poet: 4 Hope, Stow 6 Palmer, Porter, Wright 7 Brennan, Slessor, Stewart
port: 6 Darwin, Sydney 7 Geelong 8 Adelaide, Brisbane 9 Melbourne, Newcastle
reptile: 6 goanna, moloch, taipan
river: 5 Tamar 6 Murray 7 Darling, Durwent 9 Macquarie
rock: 5 Ayers
rock band: 4 ACDC, INXS
sea: 5 Coral, Timor 6 Tasman 7 Arafura
shout: 5 cooee
shrub: 5 aalii, hakea, mulga 6 pituri 7 banksia, geebung, logania 8 myoporum
soldier: 5 Anzac
soprano: 5 Melba 10 Sutherland
state: 3 NSW, Tas. 4 Tasm. 8 Tasmania, Victoria 10 Queensland 13 New South Wales
strait off ~: 6 Torres
swag: 5 bluey
swamp monster: 6 bunyip
swimmer: 5 Gould 6 Fraser
tennis pro: 4 Hoad 5 Court, Laver 6 Fraser, Rafter, Stolle 7 Emerson 8 Newcombe, Rosewall 9 Goolagong
tree: 5 bunya, hakea, karri, mulga 6 jarrah, pituri, wandoo 7 banksia, cajeput, geebung 8 beefwood, coolabah 10 eucalyptus
tree-dweller: 5 koala
waterfall: 5 Tully
writer: 4 Stow, West 5 Stead, White 6 Furphy, Jolley, Palmer, Porter 7 Herbert, Manning, Travers 8 Franklin, Keneally 9 Moorehead 10 McCullough
Australia __: 3 Day 7 Current
__ Australia: 5 South 6 Inside 7 Western
Australian __: 4 Alps, pine 5 crawl 6 ballot, kelpie 7 doubles, terrier
Australian Open game: 6 tennis
__-Australian Plate: 4 Indo
__ australis: 6 aurora
Australopithecas descendant: 5 human
Austria: 6 nation 7 country
ancient ~ town: 4 Enns
botanist: 6 Mendel
capital: 4 Wien 6 Vienna
city: 4 Graz, Linz, Wien 6 Vienna 8 Salzburg 9 Innsbruck
composer: 4 Berg, Wolf 6 Mozart
conductor: 4 Böhm, Graf 5 Adler, Krips, Rudel 6 Krauss, Mahler 7 Karajan, Kleiber 9 Leinsdorf
dance: 5 waltz 7 ländler
horse: 10 Lippizaner
language: 6 German
legislature: 9 Bundesrat
money: 5 krone 8 groschen, kreutzer 9 schilling
mountains: 4 Alps 5 Alpen 10 Carnic Alps
neighbor: 5 Italy 7 Germany, Hungary 8 Slovakia, Slovenia
Nobelist in Chemistry: 5 Pregl
Nobelist in Economics: 8 von Hayek
Nobelist in Medicine: 6 Bárány, Kandel 13 Wagner-Jauregg
Nobelist in Peace: 5 Fried 10 von Suttner
Nobelist in Physics: 4 Hess 11 Schrödinger
painter: 5 Klimt 7 Schiele
physicist: 5 Pauli 7 Doppler, Meitner
pianist: 7 Brendel 8 Schnabel
playwright: 10 Schnitzler 11 Grillparzer
poet: 7 Bachman
psychiatrist: 5 Adler, Freud
region: 5 Tirol, Tyrol
river: 3 Mur 4 Enns, Raab, Raba
scientist: 5 Pauli 6 Mendel 7 Doppler, Meitner
sharpshooter: 5 yager
skier: 7 Klammer
soprano: 4 Popp
violinist: 8 Kreisler
waterfall: 7 Gastein 8 Krimmler
western boundary: 5 Rhine
wine: 7 heurige
writer: 5 Broch, Freud, Kafka, Kraus, Musil, Zweig 6 Handke, Lorenz, Werfel 7 Stifter 8 Bernhard 9 Aichinger 10 Wassermann
see also German
Austria-__: 7 Hungary
Austrian __, The: 3 Oak
Austronesian language: 5 Malay, Maori
Ausuble: 5 river
locale: 7 New York
autarch: 6 despot
autarchy: 7 freedom, liberty
aut Caesar, aut __: 5 nihil
auteur: 8 director 9 filmmaker
authentic: 4 good, just, real, true 5 legit, pucka, pukka, right, valid 6 actual, dinkum, kasher, kosher, trusty 7 certain, factual, genuine, literal 8 accurate, bona fide, credible, faithful, original, straight, verified 9 realistic, veritable 10 believable, convincing, creditable, dependable, historical, legitimate, true-to-life, undoubtful, unimagined
authenticate: 5 prove 6 attest, ratify, verify 7 bear out, certify, confirm, witness 8 validate, vouch for
authenticated: 5 valid 7 genuine 8 official
authentication: 4 seal 5 proof 8 hallmark
authenticity: 4 fact 5 right, truth 7 reality
author: 3 pen 4 poet 5 ghost, write 6 byline, create, origin, parent, scribe, source, writer 7 compose, creator, produce 8 composer, essayist, inventer, inventor, novelist, reporter 9 columnist, wordsmith 10 biographer, journalist, librettist, playwright
concern: 4 plot
correspondent: 6 editor
submission: 2 ms. 10 manuscript
unknown: 4 anon. 9 anonymous
work: 4 book, play 5 novel 6 column 7 article
Author! Author! (1982 film)
cast: Dyan Cannon, Al Pacino, Tuesday Weld
director: Arthur Hiller
authoritarian: 4 firm, hard, tsar 5 bossy, cruel, harsh, picky, rigid, stern, tough 6 despot, severe, strict, tyrant 7 austere, Spartan 8 absolute, autocrat, despotic, dictator, dogmatic, exacting, hard-line, rigorous 9 demanding, draconian, stringent, unbending, unsparing 10 despotical, dogmatical, inflexible, iron-fisted, no-nonsense, oppressive, tyrannical
authoritarianism: 7 tyranny
authoritative: 4 true 5 legal, legit, sound, valid 6 lawful, proven 7 certain, factual 8 accurate, approved, decisive, imperial, masterly, official, oracular, orthodox, powerful, reliable, verified 9 canonical 10 peremptory
order: 4 fiat 5 edict, ukase 6 decree
source: 5 bible
authority: 3 law 4 boss, czar, dean, exec, guru, rank, rule, sage, sway, tsar, tzar 5 basis, bible, clout, force, judge, maven, mavin, might, power,

right, say-so, title **6** bigwig, credit, critic, domain, expert, master, pundit, savant, source, top dog, weight, wizard **7** adviser, advisor, arbiter, big shot, captain, command, control, kingpin, license, potence, potency, regency, scholar **8** auspices, dominion, eminence, higher-up, kingship, leverage, prestige, validity **9** big cheese, dominance, evaluator, executive, franchise, influence, precedent, privilege, professor, strong arm, supremacy, upper hand **10** aristocrat, ascendance, ascendancy, ascendence, ascendency, commission, domination, executives, foundation, government, leadership, legitimacy, management, permission, power elite, powerhouse, specialist
be in ~: **6** govern **7** preside
challenge ~: **5** rebel
give ~ to: **4** name **6** assign, charge, commit, depute, invest, ordain **7** appoint, consign, empower, entrust, intrust, license **8** accredit, delegate, deputize, hand over, relegate, turn over **9** authorize, designate **10** commission
state with ~: **4** aver **6** attest
symbol of ~: **4** mace **5** staff
to act for another: **5** proxy
authority __: **4** file **6** figure **7** control
__ authority: **4** port
__ Authority: **6** Sports
Authority Song (1984 song) artist: John Cougar Mellencamp
authorization: **2** OK **4** okay, seal **5** leave, order **6** assent, permit, signal, ticket **7** go-ahead, liberty, license, mandate, warrant **8** approval, passport, sanction **9** privilege
authorize: **2** OK **3** let **4** okay, sign, tell, vest **5** allow, brook, grant, order **6** accept, assign, commit, enable, invest, permit, ratify **7** approve, certify, empower, endorse, entitle, indorse, intitle, license, qualify, warrant **8** accede to, accredit, assent to, delegate, deputize, legalize, sanction, tolerate, validate **9** approve of, designate, establish, give leave, put up with **10** administer, commission, constitute, say the word
authorized: **3** Ok'd **5** jural, legal, legit, licit **6** kasher, kosher, lawful, proper, vested **7** allowed **8** official, rightful **9** by the book, canonical, permitted **10** legitimate, sanctioned
Authorized __: **7** Version
authors: **4** game **8** card game
authorship: **6** source
Autlán: **4** city, town
locale: **6** Mexico **7** Jalisco
auto
see automobile, car
auto __: **4** lift **5** court **6** racing
auto-: **4** self
auto-__: **4** da-fé, dial **5** focus **6** dialer
autobahn: **4** pike **7** highway
auto: **3** BMW **4** Audi, Opel
unit: **2** km. **9** kilometer
autobiography: **4** life **5** story **6** memoir **7** memoirs
Autobiography of Alice B. Toklas, The
author: Gertrude Stein
Autobiography of Malcolm X, The
author: Alex Haley
autocade: **6** parade
autochthon: **6** native **10** inhabitant
autochthonous: **6** native **8** original **10** aboriginal, indigenous
auto-club service: **3** tow
autocracy: **7** fascism, tyranny **8** iron hand **9** despotism, monocracy **10** absolutism, oppression
autocrat: **4** czar, tsar, tzar **6** despot, tyrant **7** monarch **8** dictator, overlord **9** sovereign
autocratic: **5** royal, stern **6** kingly **8** absolute, arrogant, despotic, imperial, kinglike **9** arbitrary, imperious, tyrannous **10** commanding, despotical, imperative, iron-willed, monocratic, peremptory, tyrannical
Autocrat of the Breakfast-Table, The
author: Oliver Wendell Holmes
autogiro: **8** aircraft
capability: **4** STOL
autograph: **3** pen, sig **4** name, sign **5** write **7** endorse, indorse, writing **8** inscribe, longhand **9** handwrite, signature, subscribe
hound target: **4** star **5** celeb **9** celebrity
site: **4** cast **5** album
autographed: **3** sgd. **6** signed
autoharp: **6** string, zither **10** instrument
automaker
see automobile
automated: **9** automatic, motorized **10** electrical, electronic, industrial, mechanical, mechanized, programmed
automated __ machine: **6** teller
automatic: **3** gun, Uzi **4** mech. **5** Luger **6** reflex, weapon **7** assured, certain, firearm, regular, robotic **8** electric, habitual, knee-jerk, mindless **9** automated, impulsive, intuitive, motorized **10** electrical, electronic, inevitable, mechanical, mechanized, self-moving, unthinking
automatic __: **5** drive, pilot, rifle **6** dialer, pistol, redial, teller **7** writing
automatic __ processing: **4** data
Automatic (1984 song) artist: Pointer Sisters
automaton: **5** droid, golem, robot **7** android, machine
automobile: **3** AMC, Bug, car, Fox, FTO, Geo, GTO, GTX, Kia, LTD, Reo, XJS, XKE, XKR **4** Audi, Colt, Dart, Echo, Ford, Fury, Golf, heap, Lada, Lynx, Nash, Neon, Nova, Olds, Omni, Opel, Vega, Vibe **5** Acura, Aerio, Alero, Aries, Aspen, Astre, buggy, Buick, Caddy, Camry, Capri, Chevy, Ciera, Civic, Cobra, Comet, coupe, crate, Delta, Dodge, Eagle, Edsel, Essex, Excel, Fiero, Focus, Honda, Isuzu, Jetta, Laser, Le Car, Magna, Mazda, Metro, Miata, Monza, Omega, Pacer, Paseo, Pinto, Prizm, Probe, Ranch, Rebel, Regal, Rolls, Royal, Sable, sedan, Sigma, Storm, Supra, Targa, T-Bird, Tempo, Topaz, Viper **6** Accent, Accord, Altima, Apollo, Aspire, Aurora, Avalon, Beetle, Bel Air, Bobcat, Breeze, Bronco, Cabrio, Calais, Camaro, Catera, Celica, Cirrus, Cordia, Cougar, Custom, Daewoo, Del Sol, DeLuxe, DeSoto, Duster, Escort, Esteem, Falcon, Fiesta, Futura, Galant, Hornet, hot rod, Hudson, Impala, Jaguar, jalopy, Kadett, Kaiser, Kissel, Laguna, Lancer, landau, Legend, LeMans, Lumina, Malibu, Marlin, Matrix, Maxima, Meteor, Mirada, Mirage, Model A, Model B, Model T, Monaco, Nissan, Passat, Pierce, Polara, Precis, Pulsar, Rabbit, Reatta, Royale, Safari, Saturn, Scoupe, Seneca, Sentra, Shadow, Sierra, Solara, Sonata, Spirit, Spyder, Stanza, Subaru, Suzuki, Taurus, Tercel, Torino, Toyota, Tracer, Tredia, Volare, wheels, Willys, Zephyr **7** Acclaim, Achieva, Allante, Avenger, Bentley, Beretta, Boxster, Caprice, Carrera, Century, Charger, Checker, Citroen, clunker, compact, Concord, Contour, Cordoba, Corolla, Coronet, Corsica, Corvair, Cutlass, DeVille, Dynasty, Eclipse, Elantra, Electra, Ferrari, Festiva, Firenza, flivver, Galaxie, Grabber, Granada, Gremlin, hardtop, Horizon, Hyundai, Integra, Javelin, La Salle, LeBaron, LeSabre, Lincoln, machine, Marquis, Matador, Maxwell, Mercury, Monarch, Montego, Mustang, Newport, Packard, phaeton, Phantom, Phoenix, Pioneer, Pontiac, Porsche, Prelude, Protege, Prowler, Quattro, Rambler, Reliant, Renault, Riviera, Sebring, Seville, Skyhawk, Skylark, Starion, Stealth, Stratus, St. Regis, Sunbird, Sunfire, Swinger, Tempest, Tiburon, Torpedo, Town Car, Trans Am, Valiant, vehicle, Ventura, Voyager, Wildcat **8** Biscayne, Cadillac, Camargue, Catalina, Cavalier, Chevelle, Chrysler, Cimarron, Citation, Concorde, Concours, Conquest, Corniche, Corvette, Cressida, Daihatsu, Dauphine, Diamante, Diplomat, dragster, Eldorado, Fairlane, Fairmont, Firebird, Gran Fury, Imperial, Intrepid, Intrigue, Marauder, Maverick, Medalist, Millenia, Monterey, motor car, Mystique, Parklane, Plymouth, roadster, runabout, Starfire, Sting Ray, Suburban, Sundance, Toronado **9** Alfa Romeo, Barracuda, Belvedere, cabriolet, Celebrity, Chevrolet, Evolution, Fleetwood, Grand Prix, hatchback, Hupmobile, limousine, Medallion, Montclair, New Yorker, PT Cruiser, Satellite, sports car, tin lizzie, transport, two-seater **10** Ambassador, Bonneville, Challenger, Duesenberg, gas guzzler, Mitsubishi, Monte Carlo, Oldsmobile, Park Avenue, rattletrap, Road Runner, Rolls Royce, Silver Dawn, Silver Spur, Studebaker, subcompact, Volkswagen **11** Eighty-Eight, Fifth Avenue, Lamborghini, Ninety-Eight, Silver Cloud, Silver Ghost, Thunderbird **12** Coupe de Ville, Sedan de Ville, Silver Seraph, Silver Shadow, Silver Spirit, Silver Wraith
ad stat: **3** mpg
antique ~: **3** Reo **4** Aero, Cord, Nash **5** Edsel, Essex, Stutz
body: **7** chassis
brand: **4** make
British ~: **2** MG **5** Rolls **6** Austin, Jaguar **10** Rolls-Royce
British ~ part: **4** boot, tyre **6** bonnet
certain ~ worker: **5** robot
club: **3** AAA
defective ~: **4** heap **5** crate, lemon
document: **5** title
emporium: **6** car lot
family ~: **5** sedan
fancy: **4** limo **5** Caddy, Rolls **7** Bentley, Lincoln **8** Cadillac **10** Rolls-Royce
fast ~: **5** racer **6** hot rod
financing letters: **3** APR **4** GMAC
fuel: **3** gas **8** gasoline
gauge: **3** odo **4** tach **8** odometer **10** tachometer
German: **3** BMW **4** Audi, Opel
grille protector: **3** bra
ID: **3** VIN **5** plate
inspection evidence: **5** decal
Japanese ~: **6** Accord, Datsun, Nissan
job: **3** LOG, lub **4** lube
mishap: **4** dent, ding
motor: **4** V-six **5** V-four **6** V-eight
option: **2** AC **3** air, bra **5** alarm, lease, phone **7** nose bra, ski rack
part: **3** cam **4** axle, carb, horn, tire **5** break, grill, strut, wheel, wiper **6** aerial, engine, fender, filter, gas cap, grille, heater, hubcap **7** nose bra **10** carburetor
parts brand: **4** Fram, Napa
problem: **5** no oil
race: **4** Indy **5** rally **6** enduro, Le Mans
race area: **3** pit
racer: **4** Foyt **5** Jones, Mears, Petty, Rahal, Sneva, Unser **6** A.J. Foyt **7** Allison, Al Unser, Garlits, Jarrett **8** Andretti, Luyendyk, Oldfield, Tom Sneva **9** Breedlove, Earnhardt, Muldowney, Rick Mears **10** Bobby Rahal, Don Garlits, Fittipaldi, Yarborough
racing org.: **4** NHRA
renter: **4** Avis **5** Alamo, Hertz **6** Budget, Dollar **7** Thrifty **8** National **10** Enterprise
route: **6** artery
Russian ~: **3** Zil **4** Lada
safety advocate: **5** Nader
safety device: **6** airbag
shelter: **6** garage
sound: **4** beep, honk, toot
supercharger: **5** turbo
Swedish: **4** Saab **5** Volvo
testing org.: **3** EPA
theft deterrent: **4** club
track: **3** rut
trim: **6** chrome
see also car
autonomous: **4** free **8** absolute, separate **9** sovereign, voluntary **10** democratic, self-ruling
autonomy: **7** freedom, liberty
Autopan: **4** city, town
locale: **6** Mexico
auto racing: **5** sport
autostrada: **7** highway, Italian
autosuggestion popularizer: **4** Coué
Autry: **4** Gene
film: **5** oater
autumn: **4** fall **6** season
beverage: **5** cider
bloom: **3** mum **5** aster
fruit: **4** pear
like ~ leaves: **3** dry **4** sere **7** parched **9** shriveled
like ~ weather: **5** crisp
month: **3** Dec., Nov., Oct., Sep. **4** Sept. **7** October **8** December, November **9** September
sign: **5** Libra **7** Scorpio **11** Sagittarius
toiler: **5** raker
tool: **4** rake
Autumn __: **4** Tale **6** Leaves, Sequel, Sonata
Autumn __ York: **5** in New
__ Autumn: **3** 'Tis **5** Ode to
autumnal __: **5** point **7** equinox
Autumn Leaves (1955 song) artist: Roger Williams
Autumn Poem writer: **5** Dario
Autumn Sequel author: Louis MacNeice
Autumn Sonata (1978 film)
cast: Ingrid Bergman, Lena Nyman, Liv Ullmann
director: Ingmar Bergman
setting: **6** Sweden
autunite: **3** ore
__ au vin: **3** coq
aux.: **4** add'l.
auxiliary: **3** aid **4** ally, side **5** extra, other **6** helper **7** adjunct **8** adjutant **9** accessory, ancillary, appendage, assistant, associate, attendant, colleague, companion, secondary, supporter **10** accomplice, attachment, collateral,

subsidiary, substitute, supporting
verb: 3 are 4 been 5 would
auxiliary ___: 4 note, tone, verb 6 memory, rafter 7 storage
___ Auxiliary: 6 Ladies
Av: 5 month 6 Hebrew
predecessor: 6 Tammuz
successor: 4 Elul
AV
part: 5 audio 6 visual
Ava: 7 Gardner
ex: 5 Artie, Frank 6 Mickey
___ a vacation!: 5 I need
avadavat: 4 bird
avail: 2 do 3 use 4 gain, good 5 serve, worth 6 look to, profit 7 benefit, promote, purpose, satisfy, service, succeed, suffice, utility 8 efficacy, put to use 9 advantage, make use of 10 usefulness
of some ~: 5 utile
oneself of: 3 use 6 resort 7 consume, embrace, exploit, utilize
to no ~: 4 vain 6 futile, in vain, otiose, vainly 8 bootless 9 fruitless, uselessly 10 for nothing
___ avail: 4 to no
availability: 7 opening
available: 4 free, open 5 handy, on tap, ready, to let 6 at hand, at home, on hand, usable, vacant 7 for sale, untaken, useable 8 optional, possible, prepared 9 derivable, getatable, reachable, ready to go, securable 10 accessible, achievable, applicable, attainable, convenient, disposable, obtainable, procurable, realizable, unoccupied, up for grabs
make ~: 4 rent 5 offer 6 afford, free up, render 7 provide
no longer ~: 5 taken
not generally ~: 4 rare
availing: 5 utile
Avakian, Aram: 8 director
film: 11 Harrowhouse (1974)
Cops and Robbers (1973)
End of the Road (1970)
avalanche: 4 rush 5 flood 6 deluge, onrush 7 barrage, cascade, torrent 9 earthfall, landslide, snowslide 10 inundation
research center site: 5 Davos
Avalanche: 3 six, van 4 team 5 Chevy 9 Chevrolet
home: 8 Colorado
milieu: 3 ice 4 rink
org.: 3 NHL
rival: 4 Blue, King, Star, Wild 5 Bruin, Devil, Flame, Flyer, Oiler, Sabre, Shark 6 Canuck, Coyote, Ranger 7 Capital, Panther, Penguin, Red Wing, Senator 8 Canadien, Islander, Predator, Thrasher 9 Blackhawk, Hurricane, Lightning, Maple Leaf 10 Blue Jacket, Mighty Duck
sport: 6 hockey
Avalon: 3 car 4 auto, isle 6 Toyota 7 Frankie 10 automobile
Avalon (1990 film)
cast: Armin Mueller-Stahl, Elizabeth Perkins, Aidan Quinn
director: Barry Levinson
dog: 4 Nemo
Avalon, Frankie: 5 actor 6 singer
film: Back to the Beach (1987)
Beach Blanket Bingo (1965)
Beach Party (1963)
Bikini Beach (1964)
Muscle Beach Party (1964)
film partner: Annette Funicello
real last name: Avallone
song: Bobby Sox to Stockings (1959)
A Boy Without a Girl (1959)
DeDe Dinah (1958)
Ginger Bread (1958)
Just Ask Your Heart (1959)
Venus (1959)
Why (1959)
avant-garde: 3 odd 4 arty 5 artsy, novel 6 exotic, far-out, modern 7 liberal, new wave, oddball, pioneer, radical 8 advanced, original, up-to-date, vanguard 9 inventive 10 innovative, pioneering
Avant Garde: 4 font 8 typeface
Avanti: 3 car 4 auto 10 automobile, Studebaker
Avanti! (1972 film)
cast: Jack Lemmon, Juliet Mills, Clive Revill
director: Billy Wilder
avarice: 3 sin 5 greed 8 cupidity, rapacity 9 esurience, gold fever 10 grabbiness
avaricious: 5 tight 6 grabby, greedy, sordid, stingy 7 hoggish, lustful, miserly, selfish, sparing 8 covetous, grasping, ravenous, ungiving 9 mercenary, penurious, rapacious 10 economical, skinflinty
one: 5 miser
avast: 4 halt, stop 5 cease
avatar: 7 Krishna 9 archetype 10 embodiment
Avaunt!: 4 away 5 hence 6 begone
avdp.: 2 wt.
ave: 4 bead, hail 5 Latin 7 welcome
ave.: 2 st. 3 rte. 4 blvd.
Ave ___: 5 Maria
___ Ave.: 3 Lex., Mad. 4 Park, Penn. 5 Fifth 7 Madison
ave atque ___: 4 vale
avec: 4 with 6 French
opposite: 4 sans
avec ___: 7 plaisir
avec ___ permission: 5 votre
Avedon, Richard: 12 photographer
Aveeno: 6 lotion
alternative: 4 Keri 5 Curel, Nivea 7 Eucerin, Jergens, Pacquin 9 Lubriderm
Avellaneda: 4 city, town
locale: 9 Argentina
avena: 3 oat
avenaceous: 4 oaty 5 oaten
avenge: 5 repay, right 6 punish 7 get even, pay back, redress, requite, revenge 9 pay in kind, retaliate, retribute, vindicate 10 get back for, get even for
___ a vengeance: 4 with
avenged, be: 9 get back at
Avenger: 3 car 4 auto 5 Dodge 10 automobile
avenger of unrequited love: 7 Anteros, Anterus
Avengers, The (1998 film)
cast: Jim Broadbent, Sean Connery, Ralph Fiennes, Uma Thurman
director: Jeremiah Chechik
Avengers, The (ABC drama)
cast: Patrick Macnee (John Steed)
Diana Rigg (Emma Peel)
Linda Thorson (Tara King)
avenging: 10 vindictive
Avenir: 4 font 8 typeface
Aventura: 4 city, town
locale: 7 Florida
avenue: 3 way 4 path, road 5 byway, drive, means, paseo, route 6 access, artery, course, medium, outlet, street 7 channel, ingress, passage, pathway 8 approach 9 boulevard, concourse
___ Avenue: 4 Park 5 Fifth, On the 6 Acacia, Wabash 7 Madison, Seventh 8 Atlantic, Michigan 9 Lexington
aver: 4 avow, hold 5 claim, opine, swear 6 affirm, allege, assert, assure, attest, avouch, insist 7 certify, confess, confirm, contend, declare, express, profess, swear to 8 attest to, maintain, proclaim 9 guarantee, predicate 10 asseverate, insist upon
average: 3 par 4 fair, mean, norm, so-so 5 lowly, typic, usual 6 common, median, medium, middle, modest, normal 7 typical 8 everyday, mediocre, middling, moderate, ordinary, passable, standard 9 customary, tolerable, unnotable 10 fairly good, mainstream, reasonable, stereotype
below ~: 4 poor
better than ~: 5 C plus
financial ~: 3 Dow
grade: 3 cee
guy: 3 Joe 7 Joe Blow 9 Joe Doakes
on ~: 7 usually 9 generally, typically
(out): 4 even 7 balance
___ average: 4 on an 6 moving 7 batting, general
___ averages: 5 law of
___ averaging: 6 dollar
Averback: 2 Hy
Averell: 8 Harriman
Averill, Earl: 6 Pirate 10 outfielder
averment: 4 oath 5 claim
Averno: 4 lake
locale: 5 Italy
Avernus: 5 Hades
Averroës: 11 philosopher
averse: 3 shy 4 loth 5 balky, loath 7 hostile, opposed, uneager 8 allergic, contrary, hesitant, inimical, opposing 9 reluctant, shrinking, unwilling 10 indisposed, uninclined
be ~ to: 6 loathe 7 dislike
to: 3 con 6 down on 8 opposing 10 at odds with
to work: 4 idle 6 otiose, torpid 7 laggard, languid, passive 8 indolent, slothful 9 do-nothing, lethargic, sedentary, shiftless 10 languourous
aversion: 4 hate 5 dread, odium 6 enmity, hatred, horror, phobia, rancor 7 allergy, disdain, disgust, dislike, ill will 8 contempt, disfavor, distaste, loathing 9 animosity, antipathy, hostility, prejudice, repulsion, revulsion 10 abhorrence, antagonism, opposition, reluctance, repellence, repugnance
exclamation: 3 ack, ick, ugh 4 yuck 5 yecch
avert: 4 foil, veer 5 shunt 6 escape, thwart 7 deflect, fend off, head off, inhibit, obviate, prevent, rule out, ward off 8 forefend, preclude, sidestep, stave off, turn away 9 forestall, frustrate, sidetrack, turn aside 10 circumvent
Avery: 3 Tex, Val 5 James 6 Brooks 8 Brundage 9 Schreiber
to Murphy: 3 son
___ a Very Good Year: 5 It Was
___ aves: 5 rarae
aves have them: 4 alae
___-Avesta: 4 Zend
avg.: 3 std.
bigger than ~: 3 lge.
size: 3 med.
avgolemono: 4 soup
avian: 8 birdlike
Avia rival: 4 Nike 6 Etonic, Reebok
aviary: 4 cage 6 volary 7 dovecot 8 birdcage, dovecote 9 birdhouse, enclosure
sound: 5 cheep, chirp, tweet
aviate: 3 fly 4 go up, soar 5 pilot 7 take off 8 navigate, take wing 9 barnstorm, hit the sky
aviation: 6 flight, flying 8 piloting 10 volitation
combining form: 3 aer- 4 aero-
concern: 3 fog 4 fuel, wind 7 weather 8 airspeed, headwind, tailwind
marker: 5 pylon
science of ~: 8 avionics
watchdog agcy.: 3 CAB
aviator: 3 ace 5 flier, flyer, pilot 6 airman, fly boy 7 war hero 8 aeronaut
Aviator: 3 SUV 4 Linc 7 Lincoln
aviatrix: 3 ace 5 flier, flyer, pilot, woman 8 aeronaut
for short: 3 WAF
Avicenna: 7 Persian 11 philosopher
avid: 3 mad 4 keen, wild 5 afire, eager, itchy 6 ardent, fervid, greedy, gung-ho, hearty, on edge, red-hot 7 anxious, athirst, earnest, emotive, fired up, glowing, intense, longing, lustful, thirsty, wishful, zealous 8 desirous, effusive, grasping, inspired, spirited, wild-eyed 9 ambitious, dedicated, fanatical, voracious 10 all fired up, cupidinous, insatiable, inspirited, inveterate, passionate, raring to go, solicitous
avidity: 4 lust, zeal 5 ardor, greed 6 desire 8 ambition, cupidity, yearning 9 eagerness 10 enthusiasm
avidly: 4 hard 6 keenly 8 heartily
avifauna: 5 birds, ornis
Avignon: 4 city, town
locale: 6 France
river: 5 Rhone
Avila saint: 6 Teresa
Avildsen, John G.: 8 director
film: The Karate Kid (1984)
Lean on Me (1989)
Neighbors (1981)
Rocky (1976, AA)
Save the Tiger (1973)
___ avion: 3 par
avionics: 7 science
study: 8 aviation
aviophobe fear: 6 flying
Avior: 4 star
___ a Virgin: 4 Like
avis: 4 bird 5 Latin
pair: 4 alae
rara ~: 3 gem 6 oddity, wonder 7 oddball
___ avis: 4 rara
Avis: 9 car rental 10 auto rental
alternative: 5 Alamo, Hertz 6 Budget, Dollar 7 Thrifty 8 National 10 Enterprise
aviso: 4 boat 10 communiqué
Avison, Margaret: 4 poet 8 Canadian
___ Aviv: 3 Tel
Avnet, Jon: 8 director
film: Fried Green Tomatoes (1991)
Up Close & Personal (1996)
avocado: 4 tree 5 color, fruit, green 6 veggie 9 vegetable
appetizer: 9 guacamole
color relative: 3 pea 4 cyan, jade, sage 5 beryl, breen, olive, virid 6 myrtle, reseda 7 camphor, celadon, emerald, verdant 8 cinnamon 9 pistachio, sassafras, turquoise 10 aquamarine, chartreuse
family: 6 laurel
avocation: 5 field, hobby 7 pastime, pursuit 8 activity, interest, sideline 9 amusement, diversion 10 employment, occupation, recreation
avocet: 4 bird 5 wader 9 shorebird
avodire: 4 tree
relative: 4 neem 6 acajou, carapa, sapele 8 andiroba, crabwood, mahogany
Avogadro, Amedeo: 7 chemist, Italian 9 physicist
Avogadro's ___: 3 law 6 number

avoid: **4** duck, fear, jump, lose, omit, shun, skip **5** dodge, elude, evade, hedge, parry, shake, shirk, skirt, spare **6** beware, bypass, escape, eschew, ignore **7** abstain, boycott, dislike, fend off, forbear, prevent, quibble, refrain, shy from, ward off **8** flee from, get out of, hide from, keep from, shake off, sidestep **9** get around, go without, leap aside, ostracize, pussyfoot, turn aside **10** circumvent, escape from, get clear of, recoil from, shrink from, work around
thing to ~: **4** no-no **9** tabu. taboo
work: **4** idle, laze, loaf **5** dog it, shirk, slack **6** dawdle **7** goof off **8** lollygag, malinger, slack off **9** bum around, pussyfoot **10** featherbed, mess around
avoidance: **6** escape **7** evasion, veering **9** absention, antipathy, departure, desertion, restraint, runaround **10** abstinence, prevention
avoiding others: **3** shy **5** timid
avoirdupois: **4** heft **6** weight
à __ voix: **5** haute
Avon: **5** river **6** makeup
alternative: **5** Almay **6** Revlon **7** Lancome, Mary Kay **8** Clinique **9** Cover Girl, Max Factor **10** Maybelline **11** Estée Lauder, Merle Norman
city on the ~: **4** Bath
feeder: **4** Leam **5** Leame
River locale: **7** England
Avondale: **4** city, town
locale: **7** Arizona
Avonlea: **4** city, town
locale: **6** Canada
A votre santé: **5** toast **6** French
avouch: **4** aver, avow **5** admit **6** affirm, allege, assert, assure, attest, depone, depose **7** certify, confess, declare, profess, protest, testify **8** attest to **9** guarantee **10** asseverate
avouchment: **4** oath
__ à vous: **4** tout
avow: **3** own **4** aver, hold **5** admit, allow, claim, grant, let on, state, swear, vouch **6** accept, affirm, allege, assert, attest, avouch, fess up, insist, pledge **7** certify, concede, confess, confirm, contend, declare, own up to, profess, promise, protest, swear to **8** maintain, proclaim, speak out **9** recognize **10** asseverate
avowal: **4** oath **5** claim **6** pledge **7** promise **9** admission, agreement, assertion, statement, testimony **10** confession, profession, unbosoming
avowed: **5** known, sworn **10** ostensible
avower: **8** deponent
avril: **4** mois **5** month **6** French
follower: **3** mai
preceder: **4** mars
a vuestra __: **5** salud
avulse: **7** extract
avulsion: **10** extraction
avuncular: **4** kind **10** protective
aw-__: **6** shucks
A&W: **8** root beer **9** soft drink
alternative: **3** TAB **4** Nehi **5** Fanta **6** Fresca, Sprite **8** Diet Rite, Dr Pepper **9** Canada Dry **10** Mello Yello, Royal Crown **11** Mountain Dew
rival: **4** Dad's
AWACS: **5** plane **8** airplane
device: **5** radar
mission: **5** recon
await: **4** bide, look, pend, wait **6** expect, impend **7** expects, look for, stand by, stay for **8** sit up for, watch for **10** anticipate, hang out for
judgment: **6** dangle **8** hang fire
awake: **4** rise, stir **5** alert, alive, arise, aware, get up, risen, rouse **6** arouse, come to, living, revive, roused **7** enliven, heedful, on guard **8** stirring, vigilant, watchful **9** attentive, cognizant, conscious, impassion, observant, on the ball, up and at 'em **10** come around, on the stick, responsive, up and about
__-awake: **4** wide
Awake and Sing! author: Clifford Odets
awaken: **4** rise, spur, stir, whet **5** alert, arise, get up, rally, rouse, roust **6** arouse, bestir, come to, excite, kindle, recall, revive, stir up **7** animate, enliven, quicken, realize, roll out **8** activate, summon up **9** galvanize, impassion, recollect
awakening: **5** birth **7** arousal, revival **8** kindling **9** animating, evocative **10** activation, enlivening, incitement, stirring up
time: **2** a.m. **4** morn **7** morning
__ awakening: **4** rude
Awakenings (1990 film)
cast: Robert De Niro, Julie Kavner, Robin Williams
director: Penny Marshall
Awakening, The character: **4** Edna
__ a walk: **4** take
award: **3** MVP **4** Clio, gift, give, Hugo, Obie, Tony **5** Edgar, endow, grant, honor, medal, Oscar, prize, purse, stake **6** bestow, confer, donate, extend, Grammy, plaque, reward, trophy **7** hand out, jackpot, laurels, present, tribute **8** accolade, bestowal, citation, gold star **9** conferral, endowment **10** confer upon, decoration
advertising ~: **4** Clio
British: **3** MBE, OBE
British military ~: **3** DFM, DSO
computer-game ~: **5** Arkie
dance ~: **6** Bessie
film ~: **5** Oscar
French film ~: **5** César
jury ~: **5** costs **7** damages, penalty **9** indemnity **10** reparation
military ~: **3** DFC, DSM
music ~: **6** Grammy
mystery writers' ~: **5** Edgar
rock-video ~: **3** Ava
science-fiction ~: **4** Hugo
sports ~: **3** MVP **6** letter
theater ~: **4** Obie, Tony
TV ~: **4** Emmy
university ~: **7** diploma, master's **9** doctorate, sheepskin
__ Award: **7** Academy, Newbery
awarded, be: **3** win
award-winning: **5** prize
aware: **3** hep, hip **4** onto, wise **5** alert, awake, privy, savvy **6** posted, wise to, with it **7** heads-up, heedful, knowing, mindful, tactful, tuned in **8** apprised, familiar, informed, lynx-eyed, sensible, sentient, vigilant, watchful **9** attentive, au courant, cognizant, conscious, in the know, observant, on the ball, on the beam, plugged in, regardful, wide-awake **10** acquainted, conversant, on the stick, perceptive, responsive, thoughtful
be ~ of: **3** see **4** know **5** sense **6** intuit **7** cognize, realize **8** perceive **9** recognize **10** appreciate, understand
make ~: **4** warn **5** alert, cue in **9** enlighten
of: **4** in on, onto **5** hep to, hip to **7** alive to, privy to
__-aware: **4** well
awareness: **3** ken, wit **4** wits **5** grasp, light, sense **6** acumen, memory **7** feeling, insight **8** judgment, keenness **9** alertness, aliveness, attention, knowledge, sensation, sentience **10** cognizance, experience, observance, perception, weather eye
__-awareness: **4** self
awash: **3** big **4** full, rife **6** afloat, imbued, packed **7** brimful, crowded, flooded, replete, swamped **8** brimfull, brimming, floating
away: **3** fro, off, out **4** gone **5** apart, aside, forth, hence **6** abroad, absent, avaunt, far-off, loiter, remote, yonder **7** distant, missing, outside **8** departed, vanished **9** elsewhere, far afield, on the road **10** on vacation, out of range
combining form: **3** apo-
in Italian: **3** via
starter: **3** cut, far, fly, get, lay, run **4** cast, fade, give, hide, roll, stow, take, that, this, walk, well **5** break, throw **8** straight
__ away: **3** eat, get, lay, put, run **4** back, blow, draw, fall, fire, fool, give, hide, pack, pull, salt, slip, sock, stow, tear, tuck, turn **5** carry, clear, laugh, right, swept, throw **6** fiddle, square **7** explain
__ away!: **5** Bombs
Away __ Manger: **3** in a
__ Away: **3** Run **4** Cast, Fade, Look, Move, Slip **5** Drift, So Far, Steal, Swept **7** Walking
__-away camp: **5** sleep
__ away from: **3** shy **4** take, walk
Away in a Manger: **4** noel **5** carol
__-Away Places: **3** Far
__ Away Renee: **4** Walk
__ away with: **3** get, run **4** make
__ a way with: **4** have
__-away zone: **3** tow
Aw, c'mon!: **6** please
awe: **3** cow, wow **4** stun **5** amaze, dread, floor, scare, shock **6** dazzle, marvel, terror, wonder **7** impress, respect, startle, terrify, worship **8** astonish, blow away, bowl over, frighten, knock out, overcome, surprise, transfix **9** abashment, amazement, disbelief, dumbfound, overpower, overwhelm, reverence, terrorize **10** intimidate, scare stiff, veneration, wonderment
ender: **4** some **6** struck **8** stricken
exclamation: **3** boy, gee, ooh **4** gosh **5** golly, hello **6** jiminy **7** jeepers
hold in ~: **6** revere
in ~: **4** agog, rapt **5** agape **6** amazed **7** stunned **9** bedazzled, blown away **10** bowled over, dumbstruck, spellbound
stand in ~: **6** marvel
aweary: **5** all in, tired, wiped **6** bushed, pooped **9** exhausted
aweather opposite: **4** alee
awed: **4** agog, rapt **10** speechless
aweigh: **5** atrip
__ Aweigh: **7** Anchors
awe-inspiring: **5** grand, weird **6** solemn **7** unusual **8** terrible **9** wonderful
aweless: **4** bold, flip, game, pert, rude **5** fresh, gutsy, nervy, sassy, saucy **6** brazen, cheeky, daring, gritty, heroic, plucky, snippy, spunky **7** defiant, doughty, gallant, staunch, uncivil, valiant **8** fearless, flippant, heroical, impolite, impudent, insolent, intrepid, resolute, snippety, stalwart, unafraid, valorous **9** audacious, dauntless, dreadless, out of line, undaunted, unfearful, unfearing **10** courageous, irreverent
awesome: **3** def, rad **4** aces, A-one, boss, braw, cool, dece, fine, gear, keen, neat, nice, phat, tuff **5** dandy, ducky, grand, great, marvy, neato, nobby, prime, slick, super, swell **6** august, bang on, bang-up, bonzer, bosker, choice, divine, dreamy, far-out, gnarly, groovy, lovely, peachy, slap-up, spot on, superb, terrif, tiptop, unreal, whizzo, wicked **7** amazing, capital, corking, perfect, ripping, skookum, stellar, sublime, unusual **8** daunting, dazzling, especial, eximious, fabulous, five-star, four-star, frabjous, glorious, heavenly, imposing, jim-dandy, majestic, slam-bang, smashing, splendid, standout, sterling, stickout, striking, stunning, superior, terrible, terrific, top-level, topnotch, very good, wondrous **9** bodacious, Endsville, excellent, exemplary, exquisite, fantastic, first-rate, high-grade, hunky-dory, marvelous, sollicker, top-flight, unrivaled, wonderful, wunderbar **10** first-class, formidable, hotsy-totsy, impressive, incredible, jack-a-dandy, majestical, miraculous, monumental, out of sight, peachy-keen, petrifying, phenomenal, remarkable, stupendous, super-duper, tremendous, unrivalled
Awesome!: **3** ooh, rad, wow
awesomeness: **8** grandeur
awestruck: **4** agog, rapt **5** agape, blank, cowed **6** aghast, amazed, solemn **7** abashed, daunted, humbled, stunned **8** appalled, dismayed, reverent **9** astounded **10** bewildered
be ~: **6** wonder
look ~: **4** gape, gawk, gaze **5** stare **6** goggle, marvel
__ a wet hen: **5** mad as
awful: **3** bad **4** dire, foul, grim, poor, ugly **5** dread, gross, lousy, nasty, weird, woful **6** crumby, crummy, dismal, grisly, horrid, no-good, odious, putrid, rotten, tragic, unholy, wicked, woeful **7** accurst, baleful, baneful, beastly, doleful, fearful, ghastly, hateful, heinous, hideous, ill-done, the pits, ungodly **8** accursed, alarming, dreadful, flagrant, grievous, gruesome, horrible, horrific, inferior, shameful, shocking, stinking, terrible, terrific, tragical, wretched **9** abhorrent, appalling, atrocious, defective, execrable, fifth-rate, frightful, insidious, loathsome, miserable, monstrous, offensive, repellant, revolting, unsightly **10** abominable, deplorable, despicable, detestable, disastrous, disgusting, formidable, horrendous, lamentable, petrifying, tremendous, unpleasant
be ~: **5** stink
feel ~: **3** ail
feel ~ about: **3** rue **6** regret
feeling ~: **3** ill
find ~: **4** hate **5** abhor **6** detest, loathe
most ~: **5** worst
something ~: **5** loser
__-awful: **3** God
awfully: **3** too **4** much, very **6** hugely **8** terribly **9** extremely, immensely, unusually
Awful Truth, The (1937 film)
cast: Ralph Bellamy, Irene Dunne, Cary Grant
director: Leo McCarey
__ a whack at: **4** have, take
awhile: **7** shortly **8** for a time **9** for a spell
awhirl: **5** giddy **8** rotating, spinning
__ a wide swath: **3** cut
awkward: **5** bulky, gawky, inapt, inept, messy, unapt, wrong **6** clumsy, gangly, gauche, klutzy, oafish, sloppy, sticky, thorny, trying, uneasy, wooden **7** boorish, gawkish, halting, labored,

lumpish, strange, unadept, uncouth **8** affected, bumbling, bungling, cloddish, delicate, fumbling, gangling, improper, inexpert, lubberly, strained, tactless, ticklish, ungainly, unpoised, unsubtle, untimely, unwieldy **9** all thumbs, graceless, ill at ease, inelegant, lumbering, maladroit, ponderous, stumbling, unskilled, unwieldly **10** amateurish, blundering, cumbersome, galumphing, leadfooted, left-handed, outlandish, unbecoming, unpolished, unskillful
age: **5** teens, youth
one: **5** klutz **6** galoot, lubber
situation: **6** plight
awkward __: **3** age
Awkward Age, The author: Henry James
awl: **4** tool **5** punch **6** gimlet
awn: **5** beard **6** arista **7** bristle
awning: **5** cover, shade **6** canopy, screen **7** marquee, shelter **8** covering, sunshade
AWOL: **4** gone **6** absent, no show **7** missing **8** deserter
go ~: **4** flee **7** abscond
part of ~: **3** out **4** with **5** leave **6** absent **7** without
pursuer: **2** MP, SP
__ a Woman: **4** Born, I Got, She's
__ a Wonderful Life: **3** It's
__ a Wonderful World: **3** It's **4** What
Awoonor, Kofi: **6** writer **8** Ghanaian
awry: **3** off **4** agee, agly, ajee, alop **5** agley, amiss, askew, badly, bandy, wrong **6** afield, astray, canted, faulty, flooey, flooie, skewed, zigzag **7** asquint, athwart, crooked, twisted **8** cockeyed, lopsided **9** off-center, off course **10** off the mark, out of whack
go ~: **3** err **9** break down, fall apart
something gone ~: **5** snafu
Aw, shucks!: **5** pshaw
Awwa: **4** star
ax: **3** can, cut, hew **4** boot, chop, drop, dump, fell, fire, hack, oust, sack, tool **5** hewer, let go, slash **6** bounce, cancel, cleave, hack up, lay off **7** cashier, chopper, cleaver, cut down, destroy, dismiss, drum out, hack off, hatchet, kick out, release, scissor, turn out **8** chop down, furlough, get rid of, hack down, pink-slip, throw out, tomahawk **9** discharge, eliminate, get rid off, terminate
grind an ~: **4** edge, file, hone **5** strop **7** sharpen
handle: **4** haft **5** helve
prehistoric ~ head: **4** Celt
relative: **3** adz **4** adze **5** vouge
starter: **4** pick, pole **5** broad
to grind: **9** grievance
use an ~: **3** hew **4** chop, fell **7** cut down
__ ax: **3** ice **4** hand, meat **5** tooth **6** curtal, curtle, double **7** jedding
Ax: **7** Emanuel
axatse: **6** rattle **10** percussion
origin: **6** Africa
axe
see ax
Axe-Helve, The author: Robert Frost
axel: **4** leap
do an ~: **5** skate
where to do an ~: **3** ice **4** rink
__ axel: **6** double, triple
Axel: **5** Foley **6** Schulz **7** Paulsen **8** Stordahl, Theorell
__ Axel Karlfeldt: **4** Erik
Axelrod: **6** George, Julius
Axelrod, Julius: **8** Nobelist
Axel's Castle author: Edmund Wilson
axeman: **5** hewer **10** lumberjack
Ax, Emanuel: **7** pianist
axenic: **7** sterile **8** germfree
axes
standard ~: **5** X and Y
where ~ cross: **5** graph **6** origin
axilla: **6** armpit
axillary: **4** alar **5** alary
axiom: **3** law, saw **4** rule **5** adage, given, maxim, moral, motto, truth **6** byword, dictum, saying, truism **7** precept, proverb, theorem **8** aphorism, apothegm, doctrine, standard **9** postulate, principle **10** apophthegm, principium
Axiom: **3** SUV **5** Isuzu
axiomatic: **5** given, pithy, terse **6** gnomic **7** assumed, certain, evident, granted, obvious **8** absolute, gnomical, manifest **9** apodictic **10** aphoristic, proverbial, understood, undoubtful
axis: **4** deer, line, stem **5** pivot, shaft, stalk **7** fulcrum, spindle
central ~: **5** spine
combining form: **3** axi-, axo-
extremity: **4** pole
having no ~ extremities: **6** apolar
relative: **3** elk, roe **4** pudu, shou, sika **5** moose **6** chital, guemal, hangul, huemul, sambar, sambur, thamin, wapiti **7** brocket, caribou, muntjac, muntjak, sambhar, sambhur **8** reindeer **9** barasingh
__ axis: **4** real **5** major, minor, optic, polar, screw **7** neutral, radical
Axis __: **5** Sally
Axl: **4** Rose
axle: **3** rod **4** pole **5** pivot, shaft **7** spindle **8** auto part
cover: **6** hubcap
end: **3** hub
holder: **5** U-bolt
axle __: **6** grease
axolotl: **4** newt **7** Mexican **9** amphibian **10** salamander
axon site: **5** nerve
Axton: **4** Hoyt
Axxess: **3** van **6** Nissan
Ay, __ the rub: **6** there's
ayah: **4** maid **5** nurse **9** governess
Ayako: **7** Okamoto
Ayatollah: **5** title **6** cleric
land: **4** Iran
language: **5** Farsi
preceder: **4** shah
subject: **5** Irani
title: **4** imam **5** imaum
Ayckbourn, Alan: **7** British **10** playwright
work: Absurd Person Singular
Bedroom Farce
How the Other Half Loves
Intimate Exchanges
Invisible Friends
Making Tracks
Relatively Speaking
Standing Room Only
Time and Time Again
Time of My Life
Way Upstream
Woman in Mind
aye: **2** da, ja, sí **3** e'er, for, oui, pro, yea, yep, yes, yup **4** fine, okay, sure, vote, yeah **5** alway, good-o, natch, quite, right, roger, truly, uh-huh **6** agreed, backer, gladly, good-oh, indeed, just so, rather, righto, surely, you bet, yowzah **7** exactly, go ahead, indeedy, in favor, mais oui, quite so, ten-four, vote for, yes vote **8** all right, as you say, of course, thumbs up, very well **9** be my guest, certainly, darn right, naturally, precisely, proponent, supporter, sure thing, you betcha, you said it **10** absolutely, by all means, definitely, positively, sure enough, that's right
opposite: **3** nay
voting ~: **3** for
__-a-year man: **6** dollar
aye-aye: **5** lemur **6** mammal **7** primate
relative: **3** ape **4** saki, titi **5** chimp, drill, jocko, lemur, loris, magot, orang, potto, shrew **6** baboon, Bandar, galago, gelada, gibbon, grivet, guenon, howler, langur, macaco, monkey, rhesus, uakari, vervet **7** colobus, gorilla, guereza, hoolock, macaque, sapajou, siamang, tamarin, tarsier **8** bush baby, capuchin, mandrill, mangabey, marmoset, talapoin **9** orangutan **10** Barbary ape, chimpanzee, orangutang
__ a Yellow Ribbon...: **3** Tie
ayem: **4** morn **7** morning
Ayers __: **4** Rock
Ayesha author: H. Rider Haggard
Ayesha, Haggard's: **3** She
ayin: **6** Hebrew, letter
predecessor: **6** samech, samekh
successor: **2** pe **3** peh
Aykroyd, Dan: **5** actor **8** comedian
film: 1941 (1979)
The Blues Brothers (1980)
Blues Brothers 2000 (1998)
Chaplin (1992)
Coneheads (1993)
The Curse of the Jade Scorpion (2001)
Diamonds (1999)
Doctor Detroit (1983)
Dragnet (1987)
Driving Miss Daisy (1989)
Ghostbusters (1984)
Ghostbusters II (1989)
The Great Outdoors (1988)
Grosse Pointe Blank (1997)
My Fellow Americans (1996)
My Girl (1991)
My Stepmother Is an Alien (1988)
Neighbors (1981)
Sgt. Bilko (1996)
Sneakers (1992)
Spies Like Us (1985)
Trading Places (1983)
spouse: Donna Dixon
TV: Saturday Night Live
Aylmer: **4** city, town
locale: **6** Canada, Québec
Aymara: **6** Indian **7** Amerind **8** language
Aymé, Marcel: **6** author, French, writer
Ayn: **4** Rand
Ayotlán: **4** city, town
locale: **6** Mexico **7** Jalisco
Ayr: **4** city, port, town
locale: **8** Scotland
Ayres: **3** Lew **8** Mitchell
Ayres, Lew: **5** actor
film: All Quiet on the Western Front (1930)
The Capture (1950)
The Dark Mirror (1946)
Donovan's Brain (1953)
Johnny Belinda (1948)
The Last Train From Madrid (1937)
Night World (1932)
State Fair (1933)
spouse: Ginger Rogers
Ayrshire: **3** cow **4** bull **6** bovine, cattle
Ay, there's the __: **3** rub
AZ
see Arizona
azalea: **5** plant, shrub **6** flower **10** ornamental
relative: **5** heath, salal **6** kalmia **7** arbutus, rhodora **8** cassiope, cowberry **9** blueberry, deerberry
__ azalea: **5** flame, swamp **6** Alpine
Azande home: **5** Congo, Sudan **6** Africa
Azaria, Hank: **5** actor
film: Cradle Will Rock (1999)
Godzilla (1998)
Homegrown (1998)
Mystery Men (1999)
spouse: Helen Hunt
TV: The Simpsons
Azcatepec: **4** city, town
locale: **6** Mexico
Azerbaijan: **6** nation **7** country
bovine: **5** Kurdi **6** Sarabi
capital: **4** Baku
location: **4** Asia
mountains: **8** Caucasus
neighbor: **4** Iran **6** Russia, Turkey **7** Armenia, Georgia
once: **3** SSR
azimuth: **3** arc
Azinger, Paul: **6** golfer
milieu: **5** links **6** course
org.: **3** PGA
Aziyad author: **4** Loti
Aznavour: **7** Charles
azo: **3** dye **8** amaranth
Azores: **4** isls. **5** isles **7** islands
essentially: **4** lava
island: **4** Pico **5** Corvo, Faial, Fayal **6** Flores **8** Graciosa, Sao Jorge, Terceira **9** Sao Miguel **10** Santa Maria
loc.: **3** Atl. **8** Atlantic
Azov: **3** sea
feeder: **5** Kuban
locale: **6** Russia
Azrael: **5** angel
Azrael author: Longfellow
Aztec: **5** Nahua **8** language
foe: **6** Cortés
spear-thrower: **6** atlatl
__-Aztecan: **3** Uto
Azuela, Mariano: **6** author, writer **7** Mexican
Azuma: **7** volcano
locale: **4** Asia **5** Japan **6** Honshu
azure: **3** sky **4** blue **5** color, lapis, skyey **6** cobalt, heaven, purply **7** sky blue **8** cerulean, deep-blue, empyrean, purplish **9** firmament **10** cobalt blue
relative: **4** anil, cyan, navy, Nile, teal **5** Alice, slate **6** indigo, raisin, violet **7** peacock **8** sapphire **9** turquoise **10** aquamarine, periwinkle
Azure: **3** car **4** auto **7** Bentley **10** automobile
azurite: **3** gem, ore **7** mineral **8** gemstone
Azusa: **4** city, town
locale: **10** California

B

b __: 4 and w 5 quark
B: 4 elem., mark, type 5 boron, grade, width 6 letter 7 element
  and B: 3 inn 7 lodging
  5 for ~: 4 at. no.
  flat: 3 key 6 A sharp
  in phonetic alphabet: 5 Bravo
  neighbor: 6 A sharp
  plus: 5 grade
  sharp: 6 C alias
  team: 6 scrubs
  type ~: 7 amiable, patient 8 laid-back 9 easygoing
  vitamin: 6 biotin, folate
B __: 4 and B, and O, cell, star 5 meson, movie 6 school 7 battery, complex, horizon, picture, vitamin
B __ boy: 4 as in
B-__: 4 axes, axis, girl, Rock
__ B: 3 Jon, Mel 4 B and, R and, Type 6 Linear, radium, Stevie 7 vitamin
'B' __ Burglar: 5 Is for
__-B: 4 Oral
ba: 6 Arabic, letter
  preceder: 4 alif
Ba: 4 elem. 6 barium 7 element
  56 for ~: 4 at. no.
B.A.: 6 degree
  institute: 7 college 10 university
  part of ~: 4 arts 8 bachelor
B-1: 6 bomber
B-29: 6 bomber
B-52: 6 bomber
baa: 4 blat, bray 5 bleat
  relative: 3 moo
Baa Baa Black Sheep dog: 8 Meatball
__ b-a-a-d boy!: 3 I'm a
baal: 4 idol 8 false god
Baal author: Bertolt Brecht
baba: 4 cake 6 pastry 7 rum cake
Baba __: 4 Wawa
__ Baba and the 40 Thieves: 3 Ali
baba au rhum: 4 cake 6 pastry
baba ghanouj: 5 salad
Babaloo singer: 4 Desi 5 Arnaz
babassu: 3 oil 4 palm
Babbage: 7 Charles
Babbitt: 5 Bruce, sheep, toady 6 yes man 8 assenter, emulator, orthodox 10 conformist
  author: Sinclair Lewis
  character: 3 Ted 4 Myra 5 Doane, Tanis, Zilla 6 Eunice, Seneca, Verona
Babbitt metal: 5 alloy
  component: 3 tin 6 copper 8 antimony
babble: 3 jaw, yak, yap 4 chat, gush, rave, talk 5 bleat, noise, prate, run on, sound 6 cackle, drivel, footle, gabble, gibber, gossip, gurgle, humbug, jabber, jargon, mumble, murmur, patter, ramble, rattle, tattle, uproar, wander 7 blather, blether, chatter, maunder, prattle 8 nonsense, rattle on 9 gibberish, go on and on, jabbering, loquacity
  starter: 6 psycho
babbler: 4 bird 6 gossip, magpie
babbling: 3 gab 4 blab 5 noise, noisy, prate, wordy 6 drivel, hot air 7 blather, blether, chatter, gabbing, palaver, prating, prattle, unterse 8 chit-chat, nonsense 9 garrulity, garrulous, gibberish, jabbering, prattling, small talk 10 chattering, loquacious
Babcock: 7 Barbara
babe: 3 hon, tot 4 naif 5 bairn, child 6 infant, rug rat 7 neonate, newborn 8 innocent 9 greenhorn, little one
  in the woods: 4 fawn, lamb, naif 6 victim
  like a ~ in the woods: 4 naif 5 naïve 9 unworldly
babe __ woods: 5 in the
Babe: 3 pig 4 Ruth 6 Herman, Phelps 8 Zaharias 9 Didrikson
Babe __ Zaharias: 9 Didrikson
Babe (1979 song) artist: Styx
Babe (1995 film) director: Chris Noonan
  character: 4 Esme
  dog: 3 Fly, Rex
babel: 3 din 6 hubbub, jangle, racket, tumult, uproar 8 shambles 9 cacophony, gibberish 10 hullabaloo
Babel: 5 Isaak, tower
Babel, Isaak: 6 writer 7 Russian
Babel Tower author: A.S. Byatt
Babenco, Hector: 8 director
  film: At Play in the Fields of the Lord (1991)
    Ironweed (1987)
    Kiss of the Spider Woman (1985)
    Pixote (1981)
Babes in Arms: 7 musical
  songwriter: 4 Hart 7 Rodgers
Babes in Toyland (1934 film)
  cast: Oliver Hardy, Stan Laurel
Babe, The (1992 film)
  cast: Trini Alvarado, John Goodman, Kelly McGillis
  director: Arthur Hiller
Babette: 7 Deutsch
Babette's Feast (1987 film)
  cast: Stephane Audran, Jean-Philippe Lafont, Gudmar Wivesson
  director: Gabriel Axel
babies: 5 young
  kiss ~: 3 run 4 gush 5 stump 6 hustle 8 campaign, politick
babies'-__: 6 breath
__ Babies: 6 Beanie
Babilonia, Tai: 6 skater
babirusa: 5 swine
babka: 4 cake 6 Slavic
Bab-O: 8 cleanser
  alternative: 4 Ajax 5 Comet 6 Bon Ami 9 Soft Scrub
baboon: 3 ape 4 boor 5 jocko 6 animal, dimwit, dog ape, gelada, monkey, simian 7 primate 8 mandrill
  relative: 4 saki, titi 5 chimp, drill, lemur, loris, magot, orang, potto, shrew 6 aye-aye, Bandar, galago, gibbon, grivet, guenon, howler, langur, macaco, monkey, rhesus, uakari, vervet 7 colobus, gorilla, guereza, hoolock, macaque, sapajou, siamang, tamarin, tarsier 8 bush baby, capuchin, mangabey, marmoset, talapoin 9 orangutan 10 Barbary ape, chimpanzee, orangutang
babu: 3 sir
babul: 4 tree 6 acacia
babushka: 4 nana 5 scarf 8 kerchief
Babuyan __: 7 Islands
baby: 2 jo 3 kid, pet, tot, wee 4 dear, dote, jill, love, puny, tiny 5 amour, angel, bairn, bitty, chéri, child, cooky, cutey, cutie, deary, ducky, flame, honey, humor, leman, lover, lovey, minor, novia, novio, nurse, small, spoil, sugar, sweet, teeny, young 6 bantam, bon ami, chérie, cherub, coddle, cookie, cosset, coward, dautie, dearie, dote on, infant, little, midget, minute, nipper, pamper, peewee, petite, rug rat, steady, sweets, teensy 7 bambino, beloved, cater to, crawler, darling, dearest, dear one, indulge, newborn, papoose, pigsney, preemie, project, schatzi, squeeze, sweetie, toddler, tootsie 8 chou-chou, cutie pie, dote upon, dowsabel, dulcinea, dumpling, immature, juvenile, ladylove, lovebird, macushla, nonvoter, paramour, precious, snookums, sugar pie, sweetums, truelove, weakling 9 bonne amie, boyfriend, dreamboat, inamorata, inamorato, itsy-bitsy, itty-bitty, little one, miniature, offspring, petit chou, pint-sized, spoon-feed, undersize, valentine, youngster 10 diminutive, girlfriend, heartthrob, honeybunch, mavourneen, sweetheart, sweetie pie, teeny-weeny, turtledove, vest-pocket
  act like a ~: 3 cry 4 bawl, pule
  admonition: 4 no no
  bed: 4 crib 6 cradle
  boomer offspring: 4 Gen-X
  bouncer: 4 knee
  boy's clothes color: 4 blue
  bringer: 5 stork
  caretaker: 4 nana
  carriage: 4 pram 5 buggy
  comfort for ~: 6 bottle
  cover: 3 bib
  cry: 3 goo, wah 4 dada, mama 5 daddy, mamma, mommy
  digestion aid: 4 burp
  ender: 3 ish, sit
  girl's clothes color: 4 pink
  grand: 5 piano
  in French: 4 bébé
  in Italian: 5 bimbo
  in Spanish: 4 bebé, nena
  kisser: 3 pol
  like ~ food: 5 bland
  like ~ hair: 5 silky
  meal: 3 pap 6 din-din
  mind the ~: 3 sit
  often: 5 crier
  seat: 3 lap
  shoe: 6 bootee, bootie
  sitter: 5 nanny 8 watchdog 9 attendant, caregiver, caretaker
  soothe a ~: 4 rock
  soother: 4 talc 7 lullaby
  sound: 3 coo 4 mewl
  starter: 3 cry 5 grand
  start on ~ food: 4 wean
  talk: 4 lisp 6 goo-goo
  wear: 6 bonnet, diaper
baby __: 4 beef, blue, bond, book, boom, bust, doll, face, food, spot, step, talk 5 blues, buggy, coach, grand, split, teeth, tooth 6 boomer, buster, sitter
baby __ ribs: 4 back
baby-__: 3 sat, sit 5 faced, proof, tears 7 sitting
baby-__-eyes: 4 blue
__ baby: 3 tar 4 bush 5 bonus, notch 6 bottle
__-baby: 3 cry
Baby __: 4 Baby, Bell, Boom, Doll, Face, Jane, Love, Talk 5 LeRoy 7 Workout
Baby __ Back: 3 Got 4 Come
Baby __ Nelson: 4 Face
__ Baby: 3 Cry, Tar 4 Abie, Baby, Be My, Do It, Ruby 5 Angel, Angie, Beach, Be-Bop, Dream 6 Pretty 7 Goodbye
Baby and Child Care author: 5 Spock
Baby Baby (1991 song) artist: Amy Grant
Baby-Baby-Baby (1992 song) artist: TLC
Baby, Baby Don't Cry (1969 song) artist: Miracles
Baby Bell, former: 5 NYNEX
baby-blue-eyes: 5 plant 6 flower
Baby Boom (1987 film)
  cast: Diane Keaton, Harold Ramis, Sam Shepard
  director: Charles Shyer
Baby Boomer kid: 3 X-er
Baby, Come to Me (1982 song) artist: James Ingram, Patti Austin
Baby Doc country: 5 Haiti
babydoll: 5 sugar
Baby Doll (1956 film)
  cast: Carroll Baker, Karl Malden, Eli Wallach
  director: Elia Kazan
Baby Don't Forget My Number (1989 song) artist: Milli Vanilli
Baby Don't Get Hooked on Me (1972 song) artist: Mac Davis
Baby Don't Go (1965 song) artist: Sonny and Cher
baby-faced: 4 cute
baby-food name: 6 Gerber
Baby Got Back (1992 song) artist: Sir Mix-a-Lot
Baby Hold On (1978 song) artist: Eddie Money
babyhood: 6 cradle 7 infancy
Baby I Love You (song) artist: Andy Kim, Aretha Franklin
Baby I'm-a Want You (song) artist: Bread
Baby I'm Yours (song) artist: Barbara Lewis, Shai
Baby I Need Your Loving (song) artist: Four Tops, Johnny Rivers
babying: 10 indulgence
babyish: 6 infant, little 7 kiddish, puerile 8 immature, juvenile 9 infantile
Baby, It's Cold Qutside singer: 4 Ella
Baby It's You (1982 film)
  cast: Rosanna Arquette, Joanna Merlin, Vincent Spano
  director: John Sayles
Baby It's You (song) artist: Shirelles, Smith
Baby Jane (1983 song) artist: Rod Stewart
Babylonia
  battle site: 6 Cunaxa
  city of ancient ~: 5 Accad, Akkad
  language: 8 Accadian, Akkadian
  neighbor: 4 Elam
  region: 5 Sumer
  sun god: 3 Utu
  today: 4 Irak, Iraq
  underworld: 5 Aralu 6 Arallu
Baby Love (song) artist: Regina, Supremes
...Baby One More Time (1998 song) artist: Britney Spears
Baby Ruth: 3 bar 5 candy 9 chocolate
  alternative: 4 Mars, Twix 5 Clark, Heath 6 Kit Kat, Mounds, PayDay, Reese's, Zagnut 7 Krackel, Oh Henry 8 Hershey's, Milky Way, Snickers 9 Almond Joy, Mr. Goodbar 10 NutRageous
baby's __: 5 tears 6 breath
baby-sit: 4 mind, tend 5 guard, watch 7 oversee 9 look after 10 take care of
Baby (song) artist: Brandy, Brook Benton
Baby, Take __: 4 a Bow
Baby Talk (1959 song) artist: Jan & Dean
__-Baby, The: 3 Tar
Baby The Rain Must Fall (1965 film)
  cast: Steve McQueen, Lee Remick
  director: Robert Mulligan
Baby, What a Big Surprise (1977 song) artist: Chicago
Baby Workout (1963 song) artist: Jackie Wilson
Baby You're a Rich Man (1967 song) artist: Beatles

Baby (You've Got What It Takes) (1960 song) artist: Dinah Washington
bacalao: 4 fish
Bacall, Lauren: 7 actress
film: The Big Sleep (1946)
Confidential Agent (1945)
Dark Passage (1947)
Designing Woman (1957)
Diamonds (1999)
Flame Over India (1959)
Harper (1966)
How to Marry a Millionaire (1953)
Key Largo (1948)
The Mirror Has Two Faces (1996)
Murder on the Orient Express (1974)
My Fellow Americans (1996)
Sex and the Single Girl (1964)
The Shootist (1976)
To Have and Have Not (1944)
Written on the Wind (1956)
Young Man With a Horn (1950)
spouse: Humphrey Bogart, Jason Robards
Bacardi: 3 rum 5 drink 8 beverage
Bacau: 4 city, town
locale: 7 Romania, Rumania 8 Roumania
baccalaureate: 6 degree 8 graduate
baccalaureate __: 6 sermon
baccanal: 5 menad 6 maenad 7 reveler 8 bacchant, carouser 9 bacchante, frolicker, party-goer, wassailer 10 merrymaker
baccarat: 4 game 8 card game
cry ~: 5 banco
play ~: 3 bet
table item: 4 shoe
Bacchae author: Euripides
bacchanalia: 4 bash 5 binge, feast, party, revel, spree 6 frolic, revels 7 revelry 8 carnival, carousal, Dionysia, festival, partying, reveling 10 saturnalia
bacchanalian: 3 gay, mad 4 wild 5 merry 6 jocund, wanton 7 bacchic, festive, riotous 8 frenetic, frenzied, sportive 9 abandoned, Dionysian, dissolute 10 dissipated, licentious
cry: 4 evoe
bacchante: 5 menad 8 baccanal
Bacchus: 3 god 5 Roman
attendant: 5 satyr
equivalent: 8 Dionysus
parent of ~: 4 Zeus 6 Semele
Bach: 3 P.D.Q. 4 Jean 7 Barbara, Richard 9 Catherine
Bacharach, Burt: 8 composer
collaborator: 5 David, Sager
song: Alfie
Anyone Who Had a Heart
Baby, It's You
Blue on Blue
Close to You
Don't Make Me Over
Do You Know the Way to San Jose?
A House Is Not a Home
I'll Never Fall in Love Again
I Say a Little Prayer
The Look of Love
Make It Easy on Yourself
Message to Michael
One Less Bell to Answer
Raindrops Keep Fallin' on My Head
This Guy's in Love With You
Walk on By
Wishin' and Hopin'
spouse: Angie Dickinson, Carole Bayer Sager
Bachaur: 3 cow 4 bull 6 bovine, cattle
Bach, Barbara spouse: Ringo Starr
bachelor: 4 male 5 unwed 6 single 8 graduate 9 unmarried
home: 3 pad
lack: 4 wife
last words of a ~: 3 I do
party: 4 stag
bachelor __: 4 girl 5 chest, party 6 of arts
Bachelor __: 5 Party 6 Father, Mother
Bachelor and the Bobby-Soxer, The (1947 film)
cast: Cary Grant, Myrna Loy, Shirley Temple
director: Irving Reis
bachelor-at-__: 4 arms
Bachelor Father (CBS/NBC/ABC sitcom)
cast: Noreen Corcoran (Kelly Gregg)
John Forsythe (Bentley Gregg)
Sammee Tong (Peter Tong)
dog: Jasper
Bachelor Mother (1939 film)
cast: Charles Coburn, David Niven, Ginger Rogers
director: Garson Kanin
Bachelor of __: 4 Arts 7 Science
Bachelor Party (1984 film)
cast: George Grizzard, Tom Hanks, Tawny Kitaen, Adrian Zmed
director: Neal Israel
Bachelor Party, The (1957 film)
cast: E.G. Marshall, Don Murray
director: Delbert Mann
bachelor's __: 6 button, degree
bachelor's-button: 5 plant 6 flower
Bachelor, The (1993 film)
cast: Keith Carradine, Miranda Richardson
Bach, Johann Sebastian: 6 German 8 composer
contemporary: 6 Handel
instrument: 5 organ
work: The Art of Fugue
Ascension Oratorio
Brandenburg Concertos
Christmas Oratorio
Easter Oratorio
English Suites
French Suites
Passion According to St. John
Passion According to St. Matthew
Twelve Little Preludes
The Well-Tempered Clavier
Bachman, Ingeborg: 4 poet 8 Austrian
Bachman-Turner Overdrive song: You Ain't Seen Nothing Yet (1974)
Bach, P.D.Q.
work: The Art of the Ground Round
Breakfast Antiphonies
Canine Cantata
Fanfare for Fred
Fanfare for the Common Cold
Four Curmudgeonly Canons
Four Folk Song Upsettings
Fuga Meshuga
'Goldbrick' Variations
Hansel & Gretel & Ted & Alice
'Howdy' Symphony
Iphegenia in Brooklyn
Last Tango in Bayreuth
Lip My Reeds
Missa Hilarious
No-No Nonette
Octoot
Oedipus Tex
Rounds for Squares
Royal Firewater Musick
Schleptet
The Seasonings
The Short-Tempered Clavier
Three Teeny Preludes
'Unbegun' Symphony
Uptown Hoedown
Bach's Mass __ Minor: 3 in B
Bach's Partita __ Minor: 3 in E
bacillus: 3 bug 4 germ 7 microbe 9 bacterium
shape: 3 rod
back: 3 aft, ago, aid, fro 4 abet, fund, hind, rear 5 abaft, about, after, bet on, boost, favor, set up, spine, stake, stern, vouch 6 assist, astern, dorsal, dorsum, foster, recede, second, uphold 7 approve, confirm, endorse, espouse, finance, forward, indorse, nurture, promote, reverse, sponsor, support, sustain, tail end, warrant 8 advocate, bankroll, champion, hindmost, returned, sanction, side with, stand for 9 encourage, get behind, patronize, recommend, subscribe, subsidize 10 go to bat for, rally round, stick up for, strengthen, underwrite
a borrower: 6 cosign
and forth: 6 fickle 7 by turns 8 to and fro, wavering 9 tentative, uncertain, undecided 10 indecisive
answer ~: 4 sass 5 react, rebut
at the ~: 3 aft 6 astern
a while ~: 4 once
bat ~ and forth: 4 mull 6 debate
beat ~: 5 repel
behind one's ~: 5 slyly 7 falsely 8 secretly, sneakily 9 deviously, furtively 10 disloyally
be on the ~ burner: 4 pend
biter: 4 flea
bone: 6 sacrum
bounce ~: 4 echo 5 carom, rally, react 6 carrom, return, revive 7 rebound, recover 8 ricochet 9 boomerang 10 recuperate
bring ~: 6 revive 7 recover, restore 9 reinstate
bring ~ to snuff: 5 rehab
bug ~: 5 notum
buy ~: 6 redeem, unpawn 10 repurchase
call ~: 6 recall, recant
chair ~: 5 splat
change ~: 6 revert
choke ~: 6 stifle
combining form: 3 not- 4 dors-, noto- 5 dorsi-, dorso- 7 opistho-
come ~: 5 reply 6 return 7 revisit
come ~ to mind: 5 recur
come ~ to school: 5 reune
country: 4 wild 5 wilds
cut ~: 4 clip, pare, slow, snip, thin, trim 5 limit, lower, prune, shave, shear, skimp, slash 6 lessen, reduce 7 curtail, shorten 8 conserve, downsize, lessened 9 condensed 10 abbreviate, compressed, synopsized
door: 7 postern
double ~: 4 turn 6 return 7 reverse
down: 5 blink, yield 6 recant
draw ~: 5 quail, start, wince 6 cringe, flinch, recede, recoil, retire, shrink 7 retreat 8 withdraw 9 sequester
ender: 3 bit, hoe, lit, log, saw, set 4 ache, beat, bite, bone, date, door, drop, fire, hand, lash, list, pack, rest, room, rush, side, slap, slid, spin, stab, stay, stop, ward, wash, yard 5 bench, biter, board, cloth, court, cross, field, light, pedal, shore, slide, space, stage, stair, swept, sword, track, water, woods 6 ground, handed, logged, packer, stairs, stitch, stroke 7 breaker, country, scatter, stabber, stretch, swimmer 8 breaking, pressure, woodsman
fall ~: 3 ebb 5 lapse, trail 6 recede, retire 7 regress, relapse, retreat 8 withdraw 9 retrocede 10 lose ground, recidivate
fall ~ on: 3 use 6 employ, look to, resort, take to 7 count on 8 call upon, resort to, retire to 9 count upon, make use of, retreat to 10 withdraw to
fight ~: 5 react, rebel, reply 6 mutiny, resist 7 respond
financially: 4 fund 5 stake
fire ~: 5 rebut, reply 6 answer, retort 7 counter, respond 9 rejoinder
flat on one's ~: 6 beaten, laid up 7 forlorn 8 helpless 9 abandoned, destitute, powerless 10 friendless
flow ~: 3 ebb 4 fade, wane 5 abate 6 recede 7 dwindle, subside 8 slack off 9 retrocede
force ~: 5 repel 6 defeat, put off, rebuff 7 fend off, repulse, ward off 8 drive off, turn back 9 drive away
from way ~: 5 of old 6 age-old 7 veteran
from work: 4 home
get ~: 6 recoup, redeem, regain 7 reclaim, recover, salvage 8 retrieve 9 reacquire, recapture
get ~ at: 5 react, repay 6 avenge 7 revenge 9 pay in kind, retaliate
get ~ in shape: 5 rally
get one's ~ up: 3 irk 4 rile 5 peeve, upset
get ~ on one's feet: 7 rebound, recover
get ~ to: 5 reply 7 respond
get ~ together: 9 reconcile 10 conciliate
give ~: 5 repay 6 refund, return 7 reflect, replace, restore
go ~: 4 turn 6 recede, return, revert 7 regress, retreat, revisit 9 weasel out
go ~ and forth: 3 wag 4 jolt, pace, reel, rock, roll, sway, toss, yo-yo 5 hedge, hover, lurch, pitch, shake, shift, swing, waver 6 careen, dither, jiggle, jounce, seesaw, teeter, waffle, wobble 7 vibrate 8 fence-sit, hesitate, straddle 9 alternate, fluctuate, hem and haw, oscillate, pussyfoot, vacillate
go ~ on: 3 lie 4 deny 5 belie, renig 6 betray, cop out, recant, renege 7 disavow, forsake, retract 9 play false, repudiate
go ~ on one's word: 5 unsay 6 renege 7 back off, retract 8 back down, take back 9 back-pedal, weasel out, worm out of
hang ~: 3 lag 4 poke 5 trail 6 boggle, falter, loiter, shrink 8 hesitate
hanging ~: 3 shy 5 balky, chary 7 fearful 8 wavering 9 reluctant, skeptical, tentative 10 wishy-washy
hark ~: 6 recall 8 look back 9 recollect, reminisce
held ~: 6 pent-up 8 reined in 9 in reserve
hit ~: 5 react, reply 6 answer, resist 7 counter, revenge 9 retaliate
hold ~: 3 dam 4 curb, halt, hide, save, slow, stay, stem, stop 5 check, demur, deter, leash, sit on, stint, tarry 6 arrest, bridle, detain, hinder, impede, refuse, rein in, slow up 7 confine, contain, control, inhibit, prevent, prolong, repulse, reserve, trammel 8 handicap, hesitate, restrain, slow down, stave off, suppress, withhold 9 constrain, keep at bay 10 discourage, keep a lid on, keep in line
in ~: 7 lagging 8 trailing
in anatomy: 6 dorsum
in French: 3 dos
in ~ of: 6 behind 7 ensuing 9 follow-

ing **10** succeeding
in time: 3 ago **4** once, then
keep ~: **5** check, dam up, delay, flunk **6** detain **7** forbear, reserve **8** withhold
keep nothing ~: **5** level **9** come clean
kept ~: **9** in reserve
kick ~: **3** pay **5** relax **7** rebound
kicking ~: **6** at ease **7** content, relaxed **8** carefree
knock ~: **4** gulp **5** drink **6** guzzle
laid ~: **4** calm **5** Type B **6** serene **10** unbothered
lay ~: **4** lull **5** relax, slack **6** relent **7** slacken **9** lighten up
look ~: **4** muse **5** brood **6** ponder, recall, regret, review **7** reflect **8** dredge up, mull over, remember, ruminate **9** recollect, reminisce
lower ~: **6** lumbar
money ~: **6** rebate, refund
muscle, in the gym: **3** lat
number: **7** vintage **8** obsolete, outdated, outmoded **9** out-of-date **10** antiquated
of a book: **5** spine
of a 45: **5** B-side
off: **4** stop **5** cease, let up, wince **6** ease up, recant, relent **7** forbear, refrain, retreat **8** keep from, withdraw **9** lighten up
of the ~ in anatomy: **5** notal
of the neck: **4** nape **5** nucha, nuque
one of the ~ forty: **4** acre
out: **5** leave **6** recant, renege **8** withdraw
out of: **7** abandon, scuttle **8** give up on
part: **5** small, stern
pat oneself on the ~: **4** brag, crow
pat on the ~: **4** hail, kudo, laud **5** exalt, extol, honor, kudos **6** credit, extoll, homage, praise, salute **7** acclaim, applaud, commend, flatter, glorify, plaudit, tribute **8** accolade, approval, encomium, flattery, good word **9** laudation, panegyric, patronize **10** compliment, exaltation, panegyrize
pay ~: **3** fix **6** avenge, punish, refund, render, return **7** get even, revenge **8** make good, square up **9** indemnify, reimburse, retaliate **10** recompense
play ~: **6** repeat **7** recount **9** reiterate
pull ~: **5** quail **6** recoil, retire **7** retract, retreat **8** hesitate, withdraw
pulling ~: **10** evacuation
put ~: **6** return **7** replace, restore **8** postpone
put on a ~ burner: **5** table **6** shelve **7** suspend **8** postpone
put ~ on one's feet: **4** heal, mend **5** treat
put ~ to zero: **5** reset
read ~: **6** repeat
roll ~: **5** lower, skimp **6** deduct, lessen, reduce, return **7** regress, tail off **8** decrease, downsize **10** underspend
rub: **7** massage
scrubber: **5** loofa, luffa **6** loofah
send ~: **6** return
set ~: **4** mire, slow **5** delay **6** detain, hang up, hinder, hold up, impede, retard, slow up **7** bog down, reverse **8** slow down **9** depressed
settle ~: **5** relax **9** lose speed
shift ~ and forth: **5** waver
sit ~: **4** rest **5** relax **6** unwind **9** lose speed
slip ~: **7** relapse **10** recidivate
snap ~: **6** bounce, recoil, resile **7** rebound, recover
stab in the ~: **4** sell **5** cross **6** betray **7** sell out **9** duplicity, treachery
starter: **3** cut, die, fat, fin, hog, net, out, pay, run, set, tie **4** bare, blow, call, come, draw, fall, fast, feed, full, give, half, hard, hump, kick, moss, play, plow, pull, push, roll, seat, sell, skew, sway, tail, wing **5** camel, crook, flare, flash, green, hatch, horse, hunch, lease, notch, paper, piggy, quill, razor, ridge, rough, shell, spill, sweep, thorn, throw, touch, whale **6** calico, canvas, corner, hackle, narrow, piggie, saddle, silver, switch, turtle **7** flanker, leather, quarter, stickle
street: **5** alley
strike ~: **6** resist **9** retaliate
take ~: **5** rewin, unsay **6** recall, recant, regain, return, revoke **7** disavow, forgive, reclaim, recover, retract **8** disclaim, exchange, withdraw **9** back-pedal, recapture, repossess, repudiate
take a ~ seat (to): **5** defer
talk: **3** jaw, lip **4** echo, guff, sass **5** cheek, mouth, reply, sauce **8** defiance, reaction, response **9** impudence, insolence, wisemouth **10** smartmouth
talk ~: **4** sass **5** react **6** answer **7** respond **8** mouth off
the wrong horse: **4** fail, lose
think ~: **6** recall, relive **8** remember **9** reminisce
throw ~: **6** revert **7** reflect, regress
throw ~ and forth: **5** bandy
tooth: **5** molar
toss ~: **5** drink **6** imbibe
toward the ~: **3** aft **6** astern
turn ~: **5** repel, spurn **6** rebuff, thwart **7** regress, relapse, repulse **8** stave off
turn one's ~ on: **4** shun **5** scorn **6** desert, disown, ignore, refuse, reject **7** abandon, forsake, neglect **8** overlook, renounce **9** disregard, repudiate **10** apostatize, leave alone
up: **5** prone, prove **6** assist, defend, second, uphold **7** further, support **8** attest to **9** reinforce
when: **4** once, past, yore **8** formerly **9** at one time **10** previously
win ~: **6** recoup, redeem, regain **7** recover, restore **8** retrieve **9** reacquire
with one's ~ to the wall: **4** dire **5** grave **6** hard up **7** drastic, frantic **8** frenzied, hopeless **9** desperate, in the soup **10** despairing, up the creek
write ~: **5** reply **6** answer **9** respond to

back __: **3** hoe, lot, off, out, run **4** away, dive, door, down, gear, nine, road, room, seat, talk, vent, yard **5** and to, bacon, bench, float, focus, forty, order, score, shaft, staff **6** anchor, burner, matter, number, office, stairs, street **7** channel, country, molding
back-__: **4** load **5** alley, check, cloth, pedal, story, trail **6** mutate, paddle **7** patting
back-__ driver: **4** seat
__ back: **3** bow, cut, get, jig, lay, set **4** call, come, fall, flat, give, hang, hark, hold, hoop, keep, kick, loop, lyre, plow, pull, roll, seat, snap, take, talk, turn **5** choke, heart, knock, roach, shell, throw, water **6** answer, center, corner, hollow, shield, window **7** channel, flanker, gondola, running, Watteau
__-back: **3** arc **4** laid **6** bounce
Back __: **3** Bay **5** at One **6** Street
Back __!: **4** at ya
Back __ USSR: **5** in the
__ Back: **3** Get **5** Stand **7** Looking, Welcome
backache pill maker: **4** Doan
back and __: **4** fill **5** forth
back-and-forth: **6** banter
__ back at: **3** get
Back Bay locale: **6** Boston
backbeat, provide the: **4** drum
back-bending dance: **5** limbo
backbite: **4** slur **5** abuse, belie, decry, libel, smear, sully **6** attack, defame, engage, impugn, malign, revile, smirch, vilify **7** asperse, cry down, run down, slander, traduce **8** badmouth, belittle, besmirch, mistreat, throw mud **9** criticize, denigrate, deprecate, disparage, fling dirt, fustigate **10** calumniate
backbiting: **5** abuse, catty **6** gossip, malice **7** calumny, obloquy, slander, vicious **8** libelous **9** aspersion, cattiness, dishonest, invective **10** defamation, detraction, impugnment, muckraking
backboard: **4** goal
attachment: **4** hoop
shot off the ~: **5** lay up
backbone: **4** base, grit, guts, will **5** basis, chine, heart, nerve, pluck, ridge, spine, spunk, valor **6** mettle, spirit **7** bravery, courage, essence, reserve, stamina **8** decision, firmness, mainstay, tenacity **9** fortitude, stability, toughness, vertebrae, willpower **10** confidence, foundation, moral fiber, resolution
boat ~: **4** keel
lacking ~: **5** timid
backbreaking: **4** hard **5** heavy, tough **6** taxing **7** arduous, onerous, weighty **8** grueling, toilsome **9** herculean, laborious **10** exhausting
__-back chair: **4** slat **5** press, spoon, wheel **6** barrel, ladder
backcomb: **5** tease
backcountry: **4** bush **8** frontier
Back Country, The author: Gary Snyder
backdoor: **6** secret
backdoor __: **4** play
Back Door to Heaven (1939 film)
cast: Stuart Erwin, Wallace Ford, Aline MacMahon
Backdraft (1991 film)
cast: William Baldwin, Robert De Niro, Rebecca De Mornay, Kurt Russell, Donald Sutherland
crime: **5** arson
director: Ron Howard
gear: **5** hoses
special effect: **4** fire
backdrop: **5** scene, scrim **7** scenery, setting
in westerns: **4** mesa **5** cañon **6** canyon
__-backed: **3** hog **5** razor **6** saddle
backer: **3** aye **4** ally **5** angel, donor, giver **6** friend, helper, patron, votary **7** grantor, sponsor **8** adherent, advocate, champion, defender, endorser, exponent, financer, investor, partisan **9** financier, guarantor, proponent, supporter **10** benefactor, well-wisher
favorite sign: **3** SRO
starter: **4** line
backfire: **4** bomb, fail, flop **5** react **6** recoil **7** explode, go kaput, rebound, wash out **8** reaction **9** boomerang, explosion
sound: **4** bang
backflow: **3** ebb **4** eddy
backflow __: **5** valve
Back & Forth (1994 song) artist: Aaliyah
backgammon: **4** game **8** card game
cube: **3** die
impossibility: **3** tie
piece: **5** stone
background: **5** scene, stock **6** milieu, record **7** history, setting **8** literacy, training **9** education, framework, grounding, seasoning, tradition **10** atmosphere, attainment, experience, groundwork, local color, upbringing
in heraldry: **5** field
in the ~: **6** unseen **8** offstage, retiring **9** backstage, unnoticed **10** out of sight
background __: **5** music
Background to Danger (1943 film)
cast: Sydney Greenstreet, George Raft
director: Raoul Walsh
backhanded: **9** insincere, sarcastic
compliment: **5** taunt **7** affront
backhoe: **6** digger **9** excavator
Back Home Again (1974 song) artist: John Denver
__ Back in Anger: **4** Look
Back in Black artist: **4** AC/DC
backing: **3** aid **4** egis, help **5** aegis, favor, funds, grant, means **6** assist, behind, lining **7** subsidy, support **8** advocacy, auspices, blessing, sanction **9** insurance, patronage, resources **10** assistance, investment
mirror ~: **4** foil, tain
picture ~: **3** mat
screw ~: **6** cap nut
stamp ~: **3** gum **4** glue
stop ~: **6** defund
Back in Love Again (1977 song)
artist: L.T.D.
Back in My Arms Again (1965 song)
artist: Supremes
Back in the High Live Again (1987 song) artist: Steve Winwood
Back in the Saddle: **5** oater
Back In The Saddle Again singer: **5** Autry
__ Back in Town: **5** Lulu's
__ Back, Kotter: **7** Welcome
backlash: **4** kick **8** reaction
backless
seat: **5** stool
slipper: **4** mule
sofa: **5** divan
__ Back, Little Sheba: **4** Come
backlog: **5** stock, store **6** excess, supply **8** reserves **9** inventory, reservoir, stockpile
back-number: **6** bygone, former **7** onetime, vintage **8** obsolete, outdated **9** out-of-date
Back Off Boogaloo (1972 song) artist: Ringo Starr
__ back on: **3** cut **4** fall
Back on the Chain Gang (1983 song)
artist: Pretenders
backpack: **3** bag **4** hike **6** kitbag **7** holdall, tote bag **8** knapsack, rucksack
contents: **4** gear
backpacker: **5** hiker, toter
accessory: **4** tent
snack: **4** gorp
stuff: **4** gear
backpacking: **5** sport
back-pedal: **5** unsay **6** cop out, recant, renege **7** disavow, rescind, retract, retreat, reverse **8** flip-flop, withdraw
back-pedaler's words: **5** I mean
__-back position: **4** fall

__ back ribs: 4 baby
backroom denizen: 3 pol
backrub, need a: 4 ache
backscratcher: 9 sycophant
  target: 4 itch
backseat driver: 3 nag 6 critic 7 adviser, advisor 8 busybody
backslapper: 5 toady 6 yes man 8 adulator 9 sycophant
backslide: 3 sin 4 fail, fall, sink, slip, turn 5 lapse 6 revert 7 decline, regress, relapse 8 go astray 10 apostatize, degenerate
backsliding: 5 lapse 7 decline 8 apostasy, reaction
backspace: 5 erase
backspace __: 3 key
backspin a tennis ball: 5 slice
backstabber: 5 Judas, viper 7 traitor
Back Stabbers (1972 song) artist: O'Jays
Backstage at the Kirov director: 4 Hart
backstage section: 4 wing
backstop: 4 cage
Back Street (1941 film)
  cast: Charles Boyer, Margaret Sullavan
Back Street author: 5 Hurst
Backstreet Boys
  hometown: Orlando
  members: Carter, Dorough, Littrell, McLean, Richardson
  song: All I Have to Give (1999)
    As Long As You Love Me (1997)
    The Call (2001)
    Drowning (2001)
    Everybody (1998)
    I Want It That Way (1999)
    Larger Than Life (1999)
    More Than That (2001)
    The One (2000)
    Quit Playing Games (1997)
    Shape Of My Heart (2000)
    Show Me the Meaning of Being Lonely (2000)
backstroke: 4 swim
backtalk: 3 jaw, lip 4 echo, guff, sass 5 cheek 7 comment
  prone to ~: 5 fresh
__ Back the Clock: 4 Turn
back the wrong __: 5 horse
back-to-__: 6 basics
back-to-back: 10 successive
Back to Bataan (1945 film)
  cast: Beulah Bondi, Anthony Quinn, John Wayne
  director: Edward Dmytryk
__ Back to Me: 4 Come
Back to Methuselah
  author: George Bernard Shaw
  character: 3 Eve, Lua, Zoo 4 Acis, Adam, Cain 5 Chloe, Enoch, Zozim 7 Ecrasia
back-to-school
  month: 3 Sep. 4 Sept. 9 September
Back to School (1986 film)
  cast: Rodney Dangerfield, Sally Kellerman, Burt Young
  name: 5 Melon
Back to the Beach (1987 film)
  cast: Frankie Avalon, Annette Funicello, Lori Loughlin
Back to the Future (1985 film)
  cast: Michael J. Fox, Christopher Lloyd, Lea Thompson
  character: 4 Biff
  director: Robert Zemeckis
  dog: 8 Einstein 10 Copernicus
  event: 5 dance
  medium: 4 time
Back to the Future Part II (1989 film)
  cast: Michael J. Fox, Christopher Lloyd, Elisabeth Shue, Lea Thompson
  director: Robert Zemeckis
Back to the Future Part III (1990 film)
  cast: Michael J. Fox, Christopher Lloyd, Mary Steenburgen, Lea Thompson
  director: Robert Zemeckis
  role: 5 Clara
backtrack: 6 recant 7 retreat
Backtrack (1989 film)
  cast: Jodie Foster, Dennis Hopper, Dean Stockwell
  director: Dennis Hopper
backtracking: 9 turnabout
backup: 3 sub 4 copy 5 extra, spare 6 deputy, helper, logjam 7 stand-in 8 henchman 9 alternate, assistant, secondary, surrogate 10 subsidiary, substitute, understudy
  make a ~: 4 save
  performer, perhaps: 5 sysop
  prez ~: 2 VP 4 veep 6 veepee
  strategy: 5 plan B
backup __: 5 light
Backus, Jim: 5 actor
  film: Rebel Without a Cause (1955)
    The Wheeler Dealers (1963)
  TV: Gilligan's Island
  voice: Mr. Magoo
backward: 3 aft, fro, shy 4 slow 5 abaft, about 6 astern, behind, simple 7 lumpish 8 inverted 9 inside out, reluctant 10 retrograde, upside-down
  bend over ~: 6 strive 8 struggle
  go ~: 7 reverse 8 flip-flop
  lean ~: 4 arch, flex
  prefix: 3 ana- 5 retro-
Backward Glance, A author: Edith Wharton
backwash: 4 wake 6 result 9 aftermath
backwater: 3 bog 4 bush, hick, naif, pond, rude, slow, snye 5 bayou, marsh, naive, swamp, wilds, woods 6 simple 7 boorish, outback, uncouth 8 ignorant, salt pond 9 backwoods, boondocks, unlearned, unrefined 10 uncultured, unpolished
  in Canada: 4 snye
  Louisiana ~: 5 bayou
Back When We Were Grownups
  author: Anne Tyler
backwoods: 4 bush 5 rural 6 forest, inland, Podunk, rustic, sticks 7 boonies, country 8 frontier, outlying 9 backwater, boondocks, isolation 10 hinterland, provincial, timberland
  person: 5 yokel
  turndown: 3 naw
backyard: 4 lawn
  deck: 5 patio
  device: 6 hot tub
  planting: 5 shrub
  seat: 5 swing
  structure: 4 shed 6 feeder
  swing part: 4 tire
Backyards artist: 5 Sloan
Baclanova, Olga: 6 dancer 7 Russian
Bacolod: 4 city, town
  locale: 11 Philippines
bacon: 3 pay 4 meat, wage 5 wages 6 salary 10 sustenance
  bring home the ~: 4 earn
  cook ~: 3 fry
  cut of ~: 4 slab
  ingredient: 4 pork
  like ~: 6 crispy
  on the hoof: 3 pig 5 swine
  partner: 5 liver
  portion: 5 slice, strip 6 rasher
  save one's ~: 5 spare
__ bacon: 4 back 5 white
Bacon: 5 Henry, Kevin, Lloyd, Roger 7 Francis
  product: 5 essay
Bacon, Francis: 7 British 11 philosopher
Bacon, Henry: 9 architect
Baconian __: 6 method, theory
Bacon, Kevin: 5 actor
  film: Apollo 13 (1995)
    Diner (1982)
    A Few Good Men (1992)
    Flatliners (1990)
    Footloose (1984)
    Friday the 13th (1980)
    He Said, She Said (1991)
    JFK (1991)
    My Dog Skip (2000)
    The River Wild (1994)
    She's Having a Baby (1988)
    Sleepers (1996)
    Stir of Echoes (1999)
    Wild Things (1998)
  spouse: Kyra Sedgwick
Bacon, Lloyd: 8 director
  film: 42nd Street (1933)
    Action in the North Atlantic (1943)
    Boy Meets Girl (1938)
    Brother Orchid (1940)
    A Child Is Born (1940)
    Footlight Parade (1933)
    The Frogmen (1951)
    Invisible Stripes (1939)
    It Happens Every Spring (1949)
    Knute Rockne, All American (1940)
    Larceny, Inc. (1942)
    Marked Woman (1937)
    Navy Blues (1941)
    The Oklahoma Kid (1939)
    Picture Snatcher (1933)
    A Slight Case of Murder (1938)
    Son of a Sailor (1933)
    The Sullivans (1944)
    Sunday Dinner for a Soldier (1944)
    Walking My Baby Back Home (1953)
    You Said a Mouthful (1932)
    You Were Meant for Me (1948)
Bacon, Roger: 7 British 11 philosopher
Bacoor: 4 city, town
  locale: 11 Philippines
bacteria: 4 bugs 5 cocci, germs, staph, strep 7 bacilli 8 microbes 9 pathogens
  destroyer: 5 phage
  fighter: 5 sulfa
  remover: 5 lymph
  spherical ~: 5 cocci, staph
__ bacteria: 4 true 5 slime 6 purple, sulfur 7 gliding, nitrous
bactericide: 9 germicide
bacteriologist: 4 Koch 7 Fleming
  medium: 4 agar 8 agar-agar
  wire: 4 oese
bacterium: 3 bug 4 germ 6 aerobe 7 microbe 8 bacillus, pathogen
Bactria: 6 nation 7 country
  capital of ancient ~: 5 Balkh
  today: 4 Iran
Bactrian: 5 camel
  feature: 4 hump
  relative: 5 llama 6 alpaca, vicuna 7 guanaco 9 dromedary
baculite: 5 shell 8 seashell
bad: 3 ill, low, off, sad 4 base, evil, fake, grim, icky, mean, poor, rank, sick, sour, vile 5 amiss, awful, cruel, error, grave, harsh, junky, lousy, moldy, nasty, sorry, woful, wrong 6 ailing, amoral, cheesy, crumby, crummy, faulty, gloomy, grungy, putrid, rancid, rotten, severe, sinful, sordid, spoilt, unruly, unwell, vulgar, wicked, woeful 7 adverse, beastly, brutish, corrupt, decayed, demonic, harmful, heinous, hurtful, ill-done, immoral, invalid, lawless, naughty, noisome, painful, ruinous, serious, spoiled, unsound, vicious 8 acting up, criminal, daemonic, damaging, demoniac, depraved, diabolic, disloyal, dreadful, indocile, inedible, infamous, inferior, inhumane, overripe, sinister, slipshod, stinking, terrible 9 appalling, atrocious, corrupted, dangerous, defective, deficient, demonical, erroneous, falsified, imperfect, inclement, incorrect, injurious, miserable, nefarious, third-rate, troubling, unhealthy 10 abominable, delinquent, detestable, diabolical, disastrous, fallacious, ill-behaved, inadequate, inexpiable, iniquitous, lamentable, malodorous, pernicious, treasonous, unpleasant, unreliable, villainous, virtueless
  as ~ as it gets: 5 worst
  as weather: 5 nasty
  be ~: 5 act up 9 misbehave
  blood: 4 feud 5 spite, venom 6 animus, enmity, grudge, hatred, malice, rancor 7 ill will 8 conflict, friction 9 animosity, antipathy, hostility, nastiness 10 ill feeling
  boy: 3 imp 4 brat 10 holy terror
  break: 8 hard luck 10 ill fortune, rotten luck
  bringer of ~ luck: 4 jinx
  bring ~ luck: 4 jinx 5 curse
  combining form: 3 cac-, dys-, mal- 4 caco-
  deed: 3 sin 5 crime, wrong
  don't be ~: 6 behave
  dream: 9 nightmare
  end: 7 undoing 8 calamity, disaster, downfall 9 cataclysm, ruination 10 extinction
  ender: 5 lands, mouth
  experience: 6 bummer 9 nightmare
  faith: 5 fraud 6 deceit, dupery 8 betrayal, quackery 9 deception, duplicity, treachery 10 dishonesty, disloyalty
  feel ~: 3 ail 4 ache
  form: 8 improper, unseemly 9 graceless 10 indecorous, indelicacy, indelicate, out of order, unsuitable
  get the ~ guy: 3 nab
  give a ~ name: 7 asperse, slander 8 backbite
  give a ~ time to: 3 vex 6 harass
  go ~: 3 rot 4 sour, turn 5 decay, spoil
  gone ~: 3 off 4 rank 6 rancid, rotten, turned 7 curdled 8 vinegary
  guy: 3 cad, dog, rat 4 heel, toad 5 brute, churl, creep, crook, enemy, fraud, heavy, knave, louse, nasty, phony, rogue, snake 6 con man, outlaw, rascal, rotter, wretch 7 bounder, brigand, caitiff, dastard, lowlife, monster, ruffian, sharpie, shyster, stinker, villain, wastrel 8 blighter, chiseler, criminal, evildoer, hooligan, offender, spalpeen, swindler 9 archfiend, con artist, desperado, libertine, reprobate, scoundrel 10 blackguard, black sheep, malefactor, mountebank, profligate, scapegrace
  habit: 4 vice 6 foible
  hat: 3 cad 5 knave, scamp, skunk 6 rascal 8 picaroon, recreant, scalawag 9 reprobate, scoundrel 10 blackguard, ne'er-do-well, scapegrace
  have a ~ time: 6 suffer
  having a ~ odor: 4 foul, rank 5 fetid, musty, reeky 6 putrid, rancid, rotten, stinky, strong 7 noisome, reeking 8 mephitic, stinking 10 malodorous
  health: 7 illness
  in ~: 9 on the outs 10 out of favor
  in a ~ mood: 4 mean, sour, ugly

5 cross, gruff, huffy, nasty, onery, short, surly, testy **6** crabby, grouty, grumpy, ireful, morose, ornery, touchy **7** bearish, bristly, peevish, prickly, waspish **8** choleric, grumpish, petulant **9** crotchety, truculent
in a ~ way: 3 ill **4** illy, sick
in ~ shape: 5 ratty **6** shoddy **7** pitiful, run-down **8** untended
in ~ taste: 4 lewd **8** unseemly
judge as ~: 3 pan, rap **4** bash, damn, flay, slam **5** blame, blast, decry, knock, roast, trash **6** assail, berate, impugn, oppugn, rail at **7** censure, condemn, run down **8** belittle, denounce, talk down **9** cut to bits, disparage, excoriate, find fault, frown upon, skin alive **10** come down on, disapprove
like ~ news: 4 glum **5** bleak **6** gloomy **7** ghastly, serious, unhappy **9** cheerless **10** lamentable
lot: 7 rotters **8** stinkers, villains **10** no-goodniks, scoundrels
luck: 4 blow, jinx, loss, pity **6** downer, hoodoo **7** reverse, setback, tragedy, undoing **8** distress **9** adversity, mischance **10** hard knocks, infelicity, misfortune
luck, old-style: 5 unhap
mark: 2 ef **5** stain
mood: 4 funk, huff, sulk, tiff **6** temper **8** ill humor **9** surliness **10** grumpiness
move: 5 error, folly **7** misstep **9** indecorum
news: 5 rogue, worry **6** downer, misery, sorrow **7** problem, trouble **9** liability, reckoning, scoundrel **10** misfortune, unpleasant
not ~: 2 OK **4** fair, okay, okeh, okey, so-so **9** tolerable, unnotable **10** fairly good
not so ~: 6 better
not too ~: 8 passable **9** excusable
off: 4 poor **5** broke, needy **6** hard up, in need, in want **7** pinched **8** bankrupt, beggarly, indigent, strapped **9** destitute, insolvent, moneyless, penniless, penurious **10** down and out, pauperized, straitened
period: 5 slump
prefix: 3 dys-, mal-, mis-
react to a ~ joke: 4 moan **6** flinch **7** grimace **9** make a face
regardless: 5 no-win
review: 3 pan
scene: 4 mess **6** downer **10** unpleasant
service result: 5 no tip
sign: 4 omen
smell: 4 reek **5** stink
taste: 9 indecorum **10** indelicacy
temper: 4 bile, snit **8** asperity
thing: 4 bane **6** bummer
times: 5 slump **9** recession **10** depression
treatment: 5 abuse
very ~: 5 awful, lousy **6** tragic **8** tragical, wretched **10** outrageous, unbearable
vibes: 5 doubt, qualm, smell **6** augury, signal, threat **7** warning **8** distrust, mistrust, wariness **9** chariness, harbinger, misgiving **10** foreboding, indication, prediction
write a ~ check: 6 bounce
bad __: 3 egg, hop, man, off, rap **4** news **5** actor, apple, blood, faith, paper, vibes **6** breath
bad __ day: 4 hair
bad-__: 5 mouth
__ bad: 3 not **5** not so
__ bad!: 3 Too
Bad __: 3 Axe, Boy, Ems **4** Boys, Girl, Love, Luck, Time, to Me **5** Blood, Girls, Lands, Taste **7** Company, English, Homburg, Manners
Bad __, The: 4 Seed **5** Place
Bad!: 3 tsk **6** tsk tsk
Bad (1987 song) artist: Michael Jackson
Bad and the Beautiful, The (1952 film) cast: Kirk Douglas, Dick Powell, Lana Turner
director: Vincente Minnelli
__ Bad Apple: 3 One
Bad, Bad Leroy Brown (1973 song) artist: Jim Croce
Bad Behaviour star: 3 Rea
Bad Blood (1975 song) artist: Neil Sedaka
__ bad boy!: 3 I'm a
__ Bad Boy: 5 Peck's
Bad Boy (1986 song) artist: Gloria Estefan
Bad Boys (1983 film)
cast: Esai Morales, Sean Penn, Reni Santoni
Bad Case of Loving You (1979 song) artist: Robert Palmer
bad-check
letters: 3 NSF
writer: 5 kiter
Bad Company
song: Can't Get Enough (1974)
Feel Like Makin' Love (1975)
Bad Company (1972 film)
cast: Jeff Bridges, Jim Davis
director: Robert Benton
Bad Day at Black Rock (1955 film)
cast: Walter Brennan, Anne Francis, Dean Jagger, Robert Ryan, Spencer Tracy
director: John Sturges
Baddeley: 6 Angela **8** Hermione
baddie: 7 villain **8** evil sort **9** no-goodnik
fairy-tale ~: 4 ogre **5** giant
bade: 7 offered, ordered **8** beckoned, directed **9** commanded
Bad Ems: 3 spa **4** city, town
locale: 7 Germany
Baden: 3 spa **4** city, town
locale: 7 Germany
Badenov: 5 Boris
Baden-Powell: 6 Robert
__ Bader Ginsburg: 4 Ruth
__ bad example: 4 set a
badge: 2 ID **3** pin, tag **4** mark, pass, sign **5** award, brand, ID tag, medal, token **6** cordon, device, emblem, ensign, riband, shield, symbol, ticket **7** insigne, laurels, officer **8** hallmark, heraldry, insignia **9** medallion **10** decoration
employee ~: 6 ID card
material: 3 tin
merit ~ org.: 3 BSA
of authority: 6 ensign
wearer: 6 deputy **7** marshal, sheriff
__ badge: 4 film **5** merit **6** rating
__ Badge of Courage, The: 3 Red
badger: 3 bug, nag, ply, rag, vex **4** bait, goad, haze, ride, roil **5** annoy, bully, harry, hound, nudge, tease **6** animal, bother, harass, hassle, heckle, hector, needle, noodge, pester, pick at, pick on, plague, pursue, put out, weasel **7** bedevil, disturb, henpeck, torment **8** browbeat, insist on **9** importune, persecute
female: 3 sow
group: 4 cete
male: 4 boar
name meaning ~: 5 Brock
relative: 4 mink **5** fitch, otter, ratel, sable, skunk, stoat, tayra **6** ermine, ferret, marten **7** foumart, polecat **8** carcajou, foulmart, kolinsky, muishond **9** wolverine
young: 3 cub, kit
badger __: 4 game **5** plane, skunk
__ badger: 5 honey **6** ferret
badgering: 10 harassment
Badger State: 3 Wis. **4** Wisc. **9** Wisconsin
Badge 714 holder: 6 Friday
Bad Girls (1979 song) artist: Donna Summer
bad hair __: 3 day
Badham, John: 8 director
film: American Flyers (1985)
The Bingo Long Traveling All-Stars & Motor Kings (1976)
Bird on a Wire (1990)
Saturday Night Fever (1977)
Short Circuit (1986)
Stakeout (1987)
WarGames (1983)
Whose Life Is It Anyway? (1981)
Bad Henry: 5 Aaron
badinage: 3 rag, wit **4** jest, quip, talk **5** humor, roast **6** banter, joking **7** jesting, joshing, kidding, ribbing, teasing **8** quiddity, raillery, repartee, wordplay **10** jocoseness, persiflage
__ Bad John: 3 Big
Badlanders, The (1958 film)
cast: Ernest Borgnine, Katy Jurado, Alan Ladd
director: Delmer Daves
badlands: 5 waste, wilds **10** wilderness
Badlands: 4 park
locale: 11 South Dakota
sight: 5 bison
__ bad light: 3 in a
Bad Love author: Jonathan Kellerman
bad-luck bringer: 4 jinx **5** Jonah
badly: 3 ill **4** awry **5** amiss, wrong **6** poorly, ragged **8** severely, terribly, very much **9** seriously **10** malapropos
in French: 3 mal
prefix: 3 mal-
bad-mannered: 4 rude **5** rough **7** boorish, loutish **8** impolite, inurbane **10** ungracious
Bad Manners (1998 film)
cast: Bonnie Bedelia, Saul Rubinek, David Strathairn
Badman's Territory (1946 film)
cast: Ann Richards, Randolph Scott
Bad Medicine (1988 song) artist: Bon Jovi
Bad Men of Missouri (1941 film)
cast: Dennis Morgan, Jane Wyman
director: Ray Enright
badminton: 4 game **5** sport
call: 3 let
former name for ~: 5 poona
need: 3 net
stroke: 3 lob
target: 6 birdie
Bad Moon Rising (1969 song) artist: Creedence Clearwater Revival
start: 4 I see
badmouth: 3 dis, pan, rap, rip **4** slam **5** abuse, decry, knock, libel, rip on, roast, smear **6** defame, demean, dump on, malign, vilify **7** asperse, blacken, put down, run down, slander, traduce **8** backbite, belittle, tear down, throw mud **9** blaspheme, criticize, denigrate, deprecate, disparage, fustigate **10** calumniate, villainize
bad-natured: 9 malicious **10** evil-minded
badness: 3 ill **4** evil
Bad News Bears, The (1976 film)
cast: Walter Matthau, Vic Morrow, Tatum O'Neal
director: Michael Ritchie
Bad Place, The author: Dean Koontz
Badrinath: 4 peak **5** mount **8** mountain
locale: 4 Asia **5** India **9** Himalayas
Bad Seed, The author: Maxwell Anderson
bad-smelling: 4 foul **6** rotten
bad-tasting: 4 sour **8** unsavory
bad-tempered: 4 mean, ugly **5** gruff, nasty, onery, short, surly, testy **6** crabby, grouty, grumpy, ireful, ornery, touchy **7** bearish, bristly, peevish, prickly, waspish **8** choleric, grumpish, petulant **9** crotchety, truculent
Bad Time (1975 song) artist: Grand Funk
Badu, Erykah: 6 singer
Baedeker: 4 Karl **8** handbook
alternative: 5 Fodor
Baekeland: 3 Leo
bael: 4 tree **5** fruit **6** citrus
Baer: 3 Max **4** Bugs **5** Buddy **6** Parley
Baer, Max: 5 boxer
milieu: 4 ring
Baeza, Braulio: 6 jockey
milieu: 5 track
Baez, Joan: 6 singer **9** protester
Baez, Joan song: The Night They Drove Old Dixie Down (1971)
baff a golf ball: 4 loft
Baffin: 3 bay **4** isle **6** island **7** William
Baffin Bay sight: 4 berg
Baffin Island locale: 6 Canada
Baffin, William: 7 British **8** explorer
baffle: 4 daze, foil, lose, stun **5** addle, amaze, elude, floor, stick, stimy, stump, stymy, throw **6** hamper, muddle, outwit, puzzle, rattle, retard, stymie, thwart **7** astound, buffalo, confuse, mystify, nonplus, perplex, prevent **8** befuddle, bewilder, confound, outsmart **9** discomfit, dumbfound **10** disconcert
ender: 3 gab
baffled: 4 asea **5** at sea, stuck **7** at a loss, puzzled **9** flummoxed
bafflement: 10 difficulty
baffler: 6 enigma
baffling: 4 dark **5** tough **6** knotty, thorny **7** elusive, elusory **8** puzzling **9** difficult, insoluble **10** mysterious
question: 5 poser
Bafoussam: 4 city, town
locale: 8 Cameroon
bag: 3 get, job, nab, net, sag, win **4** base, case, gain, haul, hook, land, nail, poke, sack, take, trap **5** catch, hobby, pouch, purse, score, seize, shoot, snare, thing **6** arrest, collar, duffel, duffle, entrap, pocket, secure, valise **7** acquire, attaché, bladder, capture, carry-on, ensnare, holdall, insnare, luggage, satchel **8** backpack, carryall, knapsack, reticule, rucksack, suitcase **9** apprehend, briefcase, container, extradite, gunnysack, haversack, intumesce, portfolio, specialty **10** pocketbook
baseball ~: 4 base **5** rosen
brand: 4 Glad
carrier: 5 caddy, toter **6** caddie
ender: 3 man, men, wig **4** pipe, worm **5** piper
half in the ~: 5 tipsy
in the ~: 4 sure **5** on ice **6** secure **7** assured, certain, decided, settled **8** definite, positive, resolved **10** conclusive, determined, guaranteed, inevitable
it: 4 quit **5** leave **8** abdicate
job: 7 break-in
let the cat out of the ~: 3 air **4** bare, blab, leak, tell **5** admit, blurt, spill **6** betray, expose, gossip, reveal, squeal, tattle **7** divulge, let slip

8 disclose, give away 9 make known
material: 6 burlap
mixed ~: 3 mix 4 olio, stew 6 medley 7 mélange, mixture, variety 9 diversity, potpourri 10 assortment, hodgepodge, miscellany, salmagundi
of bones: 3 nag
old-fashioned ~: 4 grip
one left holding the ~: 4 dupe, goat 5 chump, patsy 6 sucker, victim 7 cat's-paw, fall guy 9 scapegoat
shoulder ~: 5 purse 9 haversack
small ~: 4 poke
starter: 3 gas, rag 4 bean, feed, flea, hand, mail, nose, sand, wind 5 money 6 carpet, litter, saddle, school
traveling ~: 3 kit 4 grip
bag __: 3 job 5 table
__ bag: 3 air, ice, kit, sea, tea 4 belt, book, bota, burn, club, feed, golf, grab, nose, poly, roll, tote, wine 5 brown, dilly, ditty, doggy, green, in the, mixed, mummy, paper 6 Boston, bowser, clutch, crocus, croker, doggie, duffel, duffle, flight, Lister, pounce, sponge, string, vanity, Ziploc 7 bowling, Douglas, evening, garment, musette, weekend
__-bag: 5 brown, gunny 6 tucker
bagana: 4 lyre 6 string
origin: 8 Ethiopia
Bagana: 7 volcano
locale: 4 Asia
bagatelle: 3 toy 4 game, gaud 5 dodad 6 bauble, doodad, geegaw, gewgaw, trifle 7 fribble, trinket 8 gimcrack, kickshaw, nicknack 9 brummagem 10 knickknack
__ bagatelle!: 5 A mere
Bagdad: 4 city, town
locale: 4 Irak, Iraq
Bagdad Cafe (1988 film)
cast: Jack Palance, CCH Pounder, Marianne Sägebrecht
director: Percy Adlon
Bagdasarian: 4 Ross
bagel: 4 roll 5 bread 8 hard roll
alternative: 5 bialy
companion: 3 lox
feature: 4 hole
ingredient: 6 gluten
look-alike: 5 donut
shape: 5 torus
shop: 4 deli
topping: 4 salt 5 onion, poppy
bagful: 4 haul, heap
baggage: 4 case, gear 5 cargo, trunk 6 things 7 luggage 8 carry-ons, equipage 9 equipment, hindrance, liability, suitcases
excess ~: 4 load 6 weight 9 unwelcome
handler: 4 cart 5 toter 6 porter
baggage __: 3 car 7 handler
__ baggage: 6 excess 7 carry-on
bagged out: 10 disheveled
__-bagger: 3 one, two 4 four 5 brown, three
bagger starter: 4 sand 6 carpet
Baggie: 7 plastic
baggy: 4 limp, wide 5 loose, slack 6 droopy, flabby, floppy 7 flaccid, hanging, sagging 8 dangling, drooping 9 amorphous, oversized, shapeless 10 ill-fitting
Baghdad: 4 city, town 7 capital
bigwig: 5 calif, kalif 6 caliph, kaliph, khalif
locale: 4 Irak, Iraq
river: 6 Tigris
baglike structure: 3 sac
bagnio: 9 bathhouse
Bagnold: 4 Enid
bag of __: 4 wind 5 bones 6 tricks
Bag of Bones author: Stephen King
bagpipe: 4 wind 6 biniou 7 musette
key: 5 B flat
origin: 8 Scotland
play the ~: 5 skirl
sound: 5 drone
bagpiper garment: 4 kilt
Bagpipers, The author: George Sand
bags'
three ~ contents, in rhyme: 4 wool
baguette: 3 gem 5 bread, jewel
like a ~: 6 crusty
surface: 5 facet
Bagwell, Jeff sport: 8 baseball
Bah!: 3 fie 4 pfui, pooh 5 pshaw
in German: 3 ach
__-Bah: 4 Pooh
Baha'i
origin: 4 Iran
preceder: 4 Babi
Bahama __: 5 grass 7 Islands
__ Bahama: 5 Grand
Bahamas: 4 isls. 5 isles 6 nation 7 country, islands
group: 6 Indies
island: 3 Cat 4 Long 5 Abaco, Exuma 6 Andros, Bimini, Inagua 7 Acklins, Crooked 9 Eleuthera, Mayaguana
locale: 3 BWI 10 West Indies
money: 4 cent 6 dollar
org.: 3 OAS
Bahia: 5 grass
Bahrain: 4 isle 6 island, nation 7 country
capital: 6 Manama
group: 10 Arab League
money: 4 fils 5 dinar
native: 4 Arab
VIP: 4 amir, emir 5 ameer, emeer, sheik 6 shaikh, sheikh
baht: 4 coin 5 money
Baie: 4 city, town
locale: 6 Canada, Québec
Baikal: 4 lake
locale: 6 Russia 7 Siberia
bail: 4 bond, flee 5 chuck, scoop 6 dipper, pledge, surety 7 draw off, warrant 8 drain off, fugitate, security, warranty 10 break loose, collateral
jump ~: 3 fly 6 run out 7 skip out 10 fly the coop
out: 3 aid 4 bolt, free, help, jump, quit, save 5 eject, leave, spare 6 assist, desert, escape, get out, give up, rescue, resign 7 abandon, make off, release, relieve 8 abdicate, liberate, run for it, withdraw 9 extricate, give a hand
bail __: 3 out 4 bond
__ bail: 4 jump, skip
Bailamos (1999 song) artist: Enrique Iglesias
bailer: 4 pail 5 scoop 6 dipper, trough
bailey: 4 wall
Bailey: 3 Lee 4 F. Lee, Jack 5 Pearl 6 Philip 7 Mildred, Raymond
partner: 6 Barnum
__ Bailey: 3 Old 6 Beetle
Bailey, Beetle: 2 GI 4 toon 7 private, soldier
barracks-mate: 4 Zero
superior: 5 sarge
Bailey, F. Lee: 6 lawyer 8 attorney
org.: 3 ABA
Bailey, Pearl: 6 singer
middle name: 3 Mae
spouse: Louis Bellson
bailiff: 5 jurat 6 deputy 7 marshal, sheriff 9 constable 10 magistrate
Anglo-Saxon ~: 5 reeve
cry: 4 oyes, oyez 6 hear ye
obey the ~: 4 rise
bailing, in need of: 5 leaky
bailiwick: 3 job 4 area, turf 5 field, place 6 domain, locale, region, sphere 7 purview 8 dominion, locality, province 10 department
bailout: 3 aid 6 escape, rescue
PC ~: 3 ESC
bain-__: 5 marie
Bain: 6 Conrad 7 Barbara
Bain, Barbara spouse: Martin Landau
Bainbridge: 5 Beryl 6 Merril
Bainbridge, Beryl: 6 writer 7 British
Bain de __: 6 Soleil
Baines, Harold sport: 8 baseball
Bainter, Fay: 7 actress
film: Daughters Courageous (1939)
Jezebel (1938, AA)
Journey for Margaret (1942)
June Bride (1948)
Make Way for Tomorrow (1937)
Quality Street (1937)
The Secret Life of Walter Mitty (1947)
Woman of the Year (1942)
Young Tom Edison (1940)
Baio: 5 Jimmy, Scott
Baird: 3 Bil 4 Cora 5 range
locale: 6 Alaska
bairn: 3 lad 4 babe, baby 5 child, kiddy 6 infant, lassie
like a ~: 3 sma, wee
bait: 3 irk, nag, rag 4 chum, draw, gall, lure, mock, ride, roil, trap, twit, worm 5 anger, annoy, beset, decoy, get on, hound, shill, snare, tease, tempt, worms, worry 6 allure, badger, bother, chivvy, come-on, entice, harass, heckle, incite, lead on, minnow, needle, pick on 7 attract, bedevil, beguile, enflame, minnows, mislead, provoke, torment 8 inveigle, irritate, ridicule 9 beleaguer, fascinate, incentive, make fun of, persecute, tantalize 10 allurement, attraction, enticement, inducement, temptation
and switch: 8 trickery
dangle ~: 3 dap
fish ~: 4 chub, dace, lure, worm 6 minnow
mousetrap ~: 6 cheese
take the ~: 4 bite 5 react
__ bait: 5 spoon 6 ground, sucker
bait and __: 6 switch
Bait, The author: John Donne
Baiul, Oksana: 6 skater
milieu: 3 ice 4 rink
baiza: 5 money
locale: 4 Oman
baize: 6 fabric
Baja: 6 desert
creature: 6 iguana
locale: 6 Mexico
neighbor: 3 USA
Baja California
city: 6 La Joya, Tecate 7 Tijuana 8 Ensenada, Mexicali, Rosarito, Tia Juana
Baja California Sur
city: 5 La Paz 6 Loreto 8 Los Cabos
Bajer, Fredrik: 8 Nobelist
bake: 4 burn, cook, heat, warm 5 roast, shirr 6 scorch 7 swelter 8 barbecue, escallop
ender: 4 shop, ware
pottery: 4 fire
sale: 7 benefit 10 fund-raiser
starter: 4 clam
bake __: 4 sale 5 apple
Bake-__: 3 Off
baked: 3 dry 4 arid
dessert: 5 crisp
goody: 5 knish
ham insert: 5 clove
starter: 3 sun
baked __: 3 ham 4 meat, ziti 5 apple, beans, goods 6 Alaska, potato
__-baked: 4 half 5 slack
...baked __ pie: 3 in a
baked Alaska: 7 dessert
alternative: 5 bombe 6 frappe 9 milk shake 10 peach Melba
ingredient: 8 ice cream
__ baked beans: 6 Boston
baked-potato garnish: 5 chive
baker: 4 chef, cook
creation: 3 bun, pie 4 cake, loaf, roll 5 bread, cooky, donut, scone 6 cookie, éclair, muffin, pastry 8 doughnut
device: 4 oven
ingredient: 3 egg 5 flour, spice, sugar, yeast
like a ~ hands: 6 floury
measure: 5 dozen
name meaning ~: 4 Beck 6 Baxter, Becker
product: 4 cake, roll 5 bread
tool: 4 peel 5 sieve
Baker: 4 Chet, diva, Ward 5 Anita, Diane, Dusty, Dylan, Frank, James, Kathy, Kenny 6 George, LaVern, Samuel 7 Carroll, Russell, Stanley 8 Diedrich 9 Josephine
word before ~: 4 Able
Baker __: 4 Lake 6 Island, Street
__ Baker: 6 Joe Don 7 Home Run
Baker, Anita
song: Giving You the Best That I Got (1988)
Sweet Love (1986)
Baker, Carroll: 7 actress
film: Baby Doll (1956)
Cheyenne Autumn (1964)
The Game (1997)
Giant (1956)
How the West Was Won (1962)
Ironweed (1987)
__, Baker, Charlie: 4 Able
Baker, Diane: 7 actress
film: The Horse in the Gray Flannel Suit (1968)
Marnie (1964)
Mirage (1965)
The Net (1995)
__ Baker Eddy: 4 Mary
Baker-Finch, Ian: 6 golfer
milieu: 5 links 6 course
org.: 3 PGA
Baker, Janet: 4 Dame
Baker, Joe Don: 5 actor
film: Adam at 6 A.M. (1970)
Charley Varrick (1973)
Fletch (1985)
GoldenEye (1995)
The Living Daylights (1987)
Baker, Kathy: 7 actress
film: Clean and Sober (1988)
Jacknife (1989)
The Right Stuff (1983)
Things You Can Tell Just by Looking at Her (2001)
TV: Boston Public, Picket Fences
Baker, LaVern
song: I Cried a Tear (1958)
Tweedlee Dee (1955)
Baker, Russell specialty: 5 essay
baker's __: 5 dozen, yeast
Baker, Samuel: 3 Sir 8 explorer
Bakersfield: 4 city, town
city near ~: 6 Delano
locale: 10 California
Baker's Hawk (1976 film)
cast: Burl Ives, Clint Walker
Baker Street (1978 song) artist: Gerry Rafferty
baker's yeast: 6 fungus
bakery: 4 shop 5 store 9 sweet shop

10 patisserie
call: 4 next
fixture: 4 oven
item: 3 bun, pie, rye 4 loaf, roll, tart 5 bread, cooky, donut, scone 6 cookie, éclair, pastry
lure: 4 odor 5 aroma
machine: 6 glazer
worker: 4 icer
bake sale sponsor: 3 PTA
baking: 3 hot 6 sultry 8 in the sun 10 sweltering
ingredient: 3 egg 5 flour, spice, sugar, yeast
pan: 3 tin 5 sheet
potato: 5 Idaho
baking ___: 4 soda 5 sheet 6 powder
baking-dish name: 5 Pyrex
baking powder: 6 leaven
ingredient: 4 alum
Bakker, Jim: 10 evangelist
Bakker, Tammy Faye: 10 evangelist
baklava: 6 pastry
___-Bakr: 3 Abu
baksheesh: 4 alms
Bakshi: 5 Ralph
Bakst: 4 Leon
Baku: 4 city, port, town 7 capital
locale: 10 Azerbaijan
Bakula: 5 Scott
Bakunin: 7 Mikhail
bal ___: 6 masqué
Bal ___: 7 Harbour
Balaam: 7 diviner
beast: 3 ass
father: 4 Beor
Balaban, Bob: 5 actor
film: Absence of Malice (1981)
Altered States (1980)
Gosford Park (2001)
Jakob the Liar (1999)
The Last Good Time (1994)
balaclava: 3 cap, hat
Baladi: 3 cow 4 bull 6 bovine, cattle
balafon: 9 xylophone 10 percussion
origin: 5 Ghana
Balaklava: 6 battle
locale: 6 Crimea 7 Ukraine
balalaika: 4 lute 6 string
origin: 6 Russia
play the ~: 5 strum
Balancán: 4 city, town
locale: 6 Mexico 7 Tabasco
balance: 3 par, tie 4 even, mean, rest, wits 5 level, perch, poise, reset, scale, weigh 6 adjust, aplomb, attune, equate, even up, offset, parity, redeem, refund, sanity, square, stasis, steady, teeter, wisdom 7 compare, isonomy, nullify, recover, redress, remnant, residue, surplus 8 consider, equality, equalize, evaluate, evenness, modulate, outweigh, regulate, residual, symmetry 9 composure, equipoise, liability, make up for, reimburse, remainder, stability, stabilize 10 compensate, counteract, equanimity, moderation, neutralize, proportion, recompense, sedateness
beam: 5 event
center: 3 ear
combining form: 5 stato-
due: 7 arrears
heavenly ~: 5 Libra
in the ~: 6 at risk 7 pending
lose ~: 4 fall, reel, slip, trip 5 lurch, slide 6 sprawl, teeter, topple, totter, tumble, wobble 7 stagger, stumble
out: 6 cancel 7 average
starter: 7 counter
throw off ~: 5 upset 7 fluster, stagger
balance ___: 3 lug 4 beam 5 shaft, sheet, staff, wheel 6 spring 7 control
___ balance: 4 bank, head, hull 5 Jolly, trade, trial 6 occult 7 current, torsion
Balance: 4 sign 5 Libra
month: 3 Oct., Sep. 4 Sept. 7 October 9 September
predecessor: 6 Virgin
successor: 8 Scorpion
balanced: 4 even, fair, just, sane 5 equal, level 6 square, stable 7 regular, uniform 8 moderate, rational, unbiased 9 equitable, impartial, objective, uncolored 10 evenhanded, harmonious
precariously ~: 5 tippy
balanced ___: 4 diet, fund, line, step 5 valve 6 rudder, ticket
___-balanced diet: 4 well
balance of ___: 5 power, trade 6 nature, terror
balance sheet
check: 5 audit
guru: 3 CPA
item: 4 debt 5 asset
word: 4 loss
Balanchine, George: 6 dancer 7 danseur
specialty: 6 ballet
balancing: 7 redress 9 measuring 10 adjustment, comparison
balas: 3 gem 4 ruby 8 gemstone
balata: 4 tree
family: 9 sapodilla
relative: 4 shea 7 almique 8 alamiqui
Balaton: 4 lake
locale: 7 Hungary
Balbo: 5 Italo, pilot 7 aviator
balboa: 5 money
Balboa, Vasco Núñez de: 7 Spanish 8 explorer
balbriggan: 6 fabric 8 material
balche: 4 tree
Balch, Emily: 8 Nobelist
balcony: 5 porch 6 loggia, piazza 7 gallery, portico, terrace, veranda 8 platform, verandah 10 balustrade
area: 4 loge
church ~: 4 loft
Balcony, The: 4 play 8 painting
author: 5 Genet
painter: 5 Manet
bald: 5 naked, stark 6 barren 8 glabrate, glabrous, hairless 9 treadless, unadorned, uncovered
baby: 6 eaglet
ender: 4 head, pate
head: 4 dome
name meaning ~: 6 Calvin
starter: 3 pie 4 skew
bald ___: 5 eagle 7 cypress
bald-___ lie: 5 faced
baldachin: 6 canopy
bald cypress: 4 tree 7 redwood, sequoia
bald eagle: 4 bird 6 raptor
look-alike: 3 ern 4 erne
Balder: 3 god 5 Norse
brother: 4 Thor
parent of ~: 4 Odin 5 Othin 6 Frigga
balderdash: 3 gas, rot 4 blah, bosh, bull, bunk, guff, jazz, jive, pooh, tosh, wind 5 bilge, fudge, hokum, hooey, prate, stuff, trash, tripe 6 bunkum, bushwa, drivel, footle, gabble, gammon, gibber, havers, hot air, humbug, jabber, jargon, kibosh, piffle 7 baloney, blarney, blather, blether, boloney, bushwah, eyewash, flannel, flubdub, fustian, garbage, hogwash, inanity, malarky, rubbish, twaddle 8 buncombe, claptrap, falderal, falderol, fast talk, flimflam, flummery, folderal, folderol, malarkey, nonsense, rhetoric, slipslop, tommyrot, trumpery 9 banana oil, bombastic, gibberish, goofiness, kidstakes, moonshine, poppycock, rigmarole 10 applesauce, bilge water, codswallop, double-talk, flapdoodle, galimatias, Jabberwock, mumbo jumbo, rigamarole, taradiddle
Balderdash!: 5 pshaw
bald-faced: 4 bare
bald-faced ___: 3 lie
baldness: 6 acomia 8 alopecia
Baldr
see Balder
baldric: 4 belt
Baldridge: 7 Letitia, Malcolm
Bald Soprano, The author: Eugène Ionesco
Baldwin: 4 Adam, Alec, city, town 5 apple, Billy, James, piano 6 Daniel 7 Stanley, Stephen, William
locale: 7 New York
relative: 4 crab, Gala, Lodi, Rome 5 Mutsu 6 Empire, Ida Red, medlar, Pippin, russet 7 Bramley, costard, Freedom, Liberty, Spartan, Wealthy, Winesap 8 Cortland, Jonathan, McIntosh 10 Rome Beauty
Baldwin, Alec: 5 actor
film: Alice (1990)
Beetlejuice (1988)
Ghosts of Mississippi (1996)
Glengarry Glen Ross (1992)
The Hunt for Red October (1990)
The Juror (1996)
Malice (1993)
Married to the Mob (1988)
The Marrying Man (1991)
Mercury Rising (1998)
Outside Providence (1999)
Prelude to a Kiss (1992)
The Shadow (1994)
She's Having a Baby (1988)
State and Main (2000)
Talk Radio (1988)
Working Girl (1988)
spouse: Kim Basinger
Baldwin, James: 6 author, writer
work: The Amen Corner
Another Country
Blues for Mister Charlie
The Fire Next Time
Giovanni's Room
Go Tell It on the Mountain
If Beale Street Could Talk
Just Above My Head
Nobody Knows My Name
Notes of a Native Son
Tell Me How Long the Train's Been Gone
Baldwin Park: 4 city, town
locale: 10 California
Baldwin, Stanley successor: 11 Chamberlain
Baldwin, William spouse: Chynna Phillips
bale: 4 bind, pack 5 bunch 6 bundle, parcel 7 package
binder: 5 twine
contents: 3 hay
Bale: 9 Christian
Balearic Islands
city: 5 Mahon, Palma
island: 5 Ibiza, Iviza 7 Majorca, Minorca
Baled Hay writer: 3 Nye
baleen: 9 whalebone
baleen ___: 5 whale
baleful: 4 dire, evil, foul, grim, poor 5 awful, fatal, lousy, toxic, woful 6 crumby, crummy, dismal, horrid, lethal, malign, nocent, odious, rotten, woeful 7 accurst, adverse, baneful, beastly, doleful, fearful, ghastly, harmful, ominous, ruinous 8 accursed, damaging, dreadful, God-awful, grievous, horrible, inferior, menacing, negative, shameful, sinister, stinking, terrible, venomous, wretched 9 abhorrent, appalling, atrocious, dangerous, defective, execrable, frightful, ill-omened, injurious, insidious, loathsome, malicious, miserable, offensive, poisonous, revolting 10 abominable, calamitous, despicable, detestable, disastrous, horrendous, malevolent, pernicious
baler: 7 machine 8 farmhand
material: 3 hay
Balfour, Arthur: 2 P.M. 7 British
Bal Harbour: 4 city, town
locale: 7 Florida
Bali: 3 isl. 4 isle 6 island
island near ~: 6 Lombok
Bali Ha'i: 4 isle
composer: 7 Rodgers 11 Hammerstein
Balikpapan: 4 city, port, town
locale: 6 Borneo 9 Indonesia
Balin: 3 Ina 5 Marty
Balinese: 3 cat 5 Asian, felid 6 feline 8 language
dance: 7 djanger
Balint: 6 Eszter
balk: 4 flub 5 check, demur, stimy, stymy 6 flinch, recoil, refuse, resist, retard, stymie, thwart, timber 7 decline, dissent, letdown, nonplus, perplex, prevent, scruple 8 hesitate 9 frustrate, stop short 10 put up a fuss
as a horse: 5 reest
caller: 3 ump 6 umpire
ender: 4 line
Balk: 7 Fairuza
Balkan: 5 range 9 peninsula
capital: 5 Sofia 6 Athens, Skopje, Sofiya, Tirana, Zagreb 8 Belgrade, Sarajevo 9 Bucharest
locale: 6 Europe
nation: 6 Bosnia, Greece, Serbia 7 Albania, Croatia, Romania 8 Bulgaria, Roumania 9 Macedonia 10 Montenegro
native: 4 Slav 5 Greek 7 Bosnian, Serbian 8 Albanian, Croatian, Romanian 9 Bulgarian 10 Macedonian
river: 4 Drin 6 Danube
skirt: 10 fustanella
Balkan ___: 3 War 5 frame 6 States
Balk, Fairuza: 7 actress
film: American History X (1998)
The Craft (1996)
Tollbooth (1994)
The Waterboy (1998)
Balkhash: 4 lake
locale: 10 Kazakhstan
balky: 5 onery, rigid 6 averse, gun-shy, mulish, ornery, unruly 7 piggish, restive 8 contrary, hesitant, negative, obdurate, perverse, stubborn 9 obstinate, pigheaded, reluctant, resistive, unbending 10 hard-bitten, inflexible, refractory
beast: 3 ass 4 mule 5 burro
ball: 2 do 3 orb, wad 4 fest, fete, gala, lump, prom, shot 5 blast, dance, globe, party, spree 6 formal, sphere 7 globule, pigskin, shindig 9 festivity, great time, horsehide, reception 10 recreation
AAA ~: 6 minors
advance on a fly ~: 5 tag up
and chain: 6 burden
attendee: 3 deb 5 belle
attire: 4 gown
balancer: 4 seal
behind the eight ~: 6 in a fix, in a jam 7 trapped
black billiard ~: 5 eight
caller: 3 ump 6 umpire

carrier: 4 back
celestial ice ~: 5 comet
club: 4 team
club VIP: 2 GM 3 mgr. 5 owner 7 manager
combining form: 5 spher- 6 sphaer-, sphero- 7 sphaero-
cricket ~: 6 googly
drop the ~: 3 err 4 miss, slip 6 bumble, bungle, falter, fumble 7 blunder 8 misjudge
ender: 4 game, park, room 6 flower 7 carrier
fast ~: 4 heat 5 smoke
follower: 3 oon
game: 5 bocce, bocci, lotto, rugby 6 squash 7 jai alai 9 situation
get the ~ rolling: 4 open 5 begin, cause, start 6 launch, tackle 8 commence 10 lead the way
give up the ~: 4 punt
have a ~: 4 play 5 caper, enjoy, party, revel 6 cavort, frolic, gambol, prance 7 carouse, roister, rollick 9 celebrate, make merry
high ~: 3 lob 5 pop up
hit the ~ hard: 5 drive
indoor ~: 4 Nerf
in jai alai: 6 pelota
kind of ~ game: 5 no-hit, no-run 7 shutout
make into a ~: 5 wad up
mirrored ~ locale: 5 disco
musket ~: 4 slug
of cotton: 3 wad
of fire: 3 sun 6 dynamo 7 hustler 8 tireless 9 ambitious, energetic
of yarn: 4 clew 5 skein
on the ~: 5 adept, alert, awake, aware, quick, ready, sharp, smart 6 astute, prompt, up to it 7 capable, mindful 8 vigilant, watchful 9 astucious, attentive, competent, effective, observant, wide-awake 10 acceptable
play ~: 5 agree 6 comply 9 acquiesce, cooperate
rubber ~: 3 toy
run with the ~: 7 perform
simple ~ game: 5 catch
starter: 3 air, cue, eye, gum, low, odd, pin 4 base, bean, corn, fast, fire, foot, fork, goof, hair, hand, hard, heel, high, meat, moth, puff, push, snow, soft, sour, spit 5 black, broom, curve, screw, stick, stink, stoop 6 basket, butter, button, cannon, ground, paddle, sinker, tether, volley 7 knuckle, racquet
use a crystal ~: 4 gaze
well-hit ~: 5 drive, liner
whole ~ of wax: 3 all 5 total 8 entirety, sum total 9 aggregate 10 everything

ball __: 3 boy, cap, ice 4 clay, club, cock, fern, foot, game, girl, hawk, mill, park 5 joint, of wax, valve 7 bearing, carrier, control, turning
ball-__ hammer: 4 peen
__ ball: 3 air, cue, fly, ink, tar, tea 4 bean, coal, curb, dust, fair, foul, golf, jump, mast, Nerf, nine, play 5 beach, carom, curve, dodge, have a, matzo, on the, stoop, witch 6 anchor, cannon, gopher, ground, masked, matzah, matzoh, object, passed, rabbit, rubber, tennis 7 bowling, camphor, crystal, knuckle
__ ball!: 4 Play
__-ball: 3 low 4 best
Ball: 4 Hugo 5 Kenny 6 Ernest 7 Lucille
Ball __: 5 State
__ Ball: 6 Rubber, Wiffle
__-Ball: 4 Skee
ballad: 3 lay 4 poem, song 5 carol, ditty, music, verse 8 serenade
ender: 3 eer
German ~: 4 lied
subject: 4 love
ballad __: 5 opera 6 stanza
ballade: 4 poem, song
ending: 5 envoi
balladist: 4 poet
balladmonger: 4 bard
Ballad of __ Hayes, The: 3 Ira
Ballad of Cable Hogue, The (1970 film)
cast: Jason Robards, Stella Stevens, David Warner
director: Sam Peckinpah
Ballad of Davy Crockett (1955 song)
artist: Bill Hayes, Fess Parker, Tennessee Ernie Ford
Ballad of East and West, The: 4 poem
author: Rudyard Kipling
Ballad of John and Yoko, The (1969 song) artist: Beatles
Ballad of Little Jo, The (1993 film)
cast: Suzy Amis, Bo Hopkins, Ian McKellen
Ballad of Reading Gaol, The author: Oscar Wilde
Ballad of the Green Berets, The (1966 song) artist: Barry Sadler
Ballad of the Sad Cafe, The author: Carson McCullers
__ Ballads: 3 Bab 7 Lyrical
Ballads and Other Poems author: Henry Wadsworth Longfellow
ball and __: 4 ring 5 chain
ball-and-__ foot: 4 claw
ball-and-__ joint: 6 socket
Ballantine: 3 ale, Ian 4 beer, Carl
alternative: 5 Becks, Coors, Pabst 6 Amstel, Corona, Miller, Molson 7 Schlitz 8 Heineken, Michelob 9 Lowenbrau
Ballard: 4 Hank, Kaye 8 Florence
ballast: 6 weight 10 stabilizer
ballerina: 6 dancer, étoile
asset: 3 toe
costume: 4 tutu
painter: 5 Degas
prop: 3 bar 5 barre
step: 3 pas
__ ballerina: 5 prima
Ballerina Girl (1987 song) artist: Lionel Richie
Ballesteros, Seve: 6 golfer
milieu: 5 links 6 course
org.: 3 PGA
ballet: 3 art 5 dance 8 Swan Lake
barre: 4 rail
bend: 4 plie
darting ~ movement: 6 élancé
duet: 6 adagio
glide: 6 chassé
held, in ~: 5 tendu
move: 3 pas 4 jete, leap, lift
movement: 6 frappé
pivot: 3 toe
pose: 9 arabesque
position: 6 à terre, écarté, en haut
rail: 3 bar 5 barre
Russian ~: 5 Kirov
step: 5 coupe, pique, tombé
turn: 6 chaine
wear: 5 tutut 6 tights
with arms held low, in ~: 5 en bas
ballet __: 5 blanc, suite 6 master 7 slipper
__ ballet: 5 water
Ballet __: 5 Russe
__ Ballet: 5 At the 7 Bolshoi, Spandau
Ballet Class, The painter: 5 Degas
ballet dancer
American ~: 5 Tharp 6 Duncan 7 Bujones, Farrell 8 d'Amboise, Eglevsky, Mitchell, Villella 9 Tallchief 10 Balanchine
British ~: 5 Dolin 7 Fonteyn, Markova
Cuban ~: 6 Alonso
Danish ~: 5 Bruhn 7 Martins
French ~: 6 Béjart
German ~: 5 Jooss
Irish ~: 8 De Valois
Russian ~: 5 Lifar 7 Massine, Nureyev, Pavlova, Ulanova 8 Danilova, Nijinsky 11 Baryshnikov, Youskevitch
Scottish ~: 7 Shearer
Ballet Rehearsal artist: 5 Degas
ballfield protector: 4 tarp
__-ball foursome: 4 best
ballgame
anybody's ~: 10 up for grabs
arbiter: 3 ump 6 umpire
division: 6 inning
fare: 6 hot dog
opener: 6 anthem
stat: 2 AB, BA, BB, HR, SB 3 ERA
see also ballpark, baseball
Ball, Hugo movement: 4 Dada
ballistic
go ~: 4 rant, vent 5 freak 6 lose it
missile: 4 ICBM, MIRV, Thor
ballistic __: 4 wind 6 camera 7 missile
Ball, Lucille: 7 actress 10 comedienne
film: Best Foot Forward (1943)
The Dark Corner (1946)
DuBarry Was a Lady (1943)
Easy Living (1949)
Easy to Wed (1946)
The Facts of Life (1960)
Fancy Pants (1950)
Five Came Back (1939)
Room Service (1938)
Too Many Girls (1940)
Valley of the Sun (1942)
Without Love (1945)
Yours, Mine and Ours (1968)
Ziegfeld Follies (1946)
spouse: Desi Arnaz
TV: Here's Lucy, I Love Lucy, The Lucy Show
__-ball match: 4 four 5 three
ballo: 5 dance
ball of __: 3 wax 4 fire
Ball of Confusion (1970 song) artist: Temptations
Ball of Fire (1941 film)
cast: Gary Cooper, Oscar Homolka, Barbara Stanwyck
director: Howard Hawks
ballon: 5 grace 9 lightness
ballonné: 4 leap
balloon: 3 toy 4 blot, grow, rise 5 blimp, bloat, bulge, swell 6 billow, blow up, dilate, expand, puff up, pump up 7 airship, distend, enlarge, inflate, mount up 8 aircraft, zeppelin 9 billow out, dirigible
atmospheric ~: 5 sonde
filler: 3 air, gas 6 helium, hot air
go by ~: 6 aviate
lead ~: 3 dud 4 flop 6 fiasco 7 failure
material: 5 Mylar
sound: 3 pop
trial ~: 4 poll, test 6 feeler 7 enquiry, inquiry
balloon __: 4 sail, seat, tire, vine 5 chuck, clock, frame, shade 6 flower 7 barrage, payment
__ balloon: 4 fire, free, lead 5 pilot, trial 7 barrage, weather
Balloon Hoax, The author: Edgar Allan Poe
ballooning: 5 sport
go ~: 4 rise, soar 7 lift off
balloonlike: 5 round
balloons, like some: 3 LTA
ballot: 4 poll, vote 6 voting 9 franchise 10 plebiscite, referendum
cast a ~: 3 x'ed 4 vote 6 choose
month: 3 Nov. 8 November
ballot __: 3 box
__ ballot: 5 short 6 secret 7 Indiana
balloting: 6 voting 8 election
__ Ballou: 3 Cat
ballpark: 8 vicinity
aide: 6 bat boy
antic: 4 wave
area: 5 seats 6 dugout, stands 7 bullpen, infield 8 outfield 9 bleachers 10 scoreboard
display: 6 banner
entertainment: 5 organ
fare: 5 frank, weeny 6 hotdog
figure: 8 estimate 9 appraisal 10 assessment
in the ~: 4 near 5 close 6 almost, around, nearby, nearly 13 approximately
level: 4 tier
official: 3 ump 5 usher 6 umpire
see also ballgame, baseball
Ball Park: 6 hot dog
alternative: 5 Kahn's 6 Armour 10 Oscar Mayer
ball-peen __: 6 hammer
ballplayer: 6 hitter 7 athlete, catcher, pitcher
ballpoint: 3 pen
ancestor: 5 quill
maker: 3 Bic 6 Parker 9 PaperMate
point: 3 nib
use a ~: 5 write
ballroom: 4 hall
dance: 5 conga, mambo, rumba, samba, tango, waltz 6 cha-cha, rhumba 7 beguine, fox trot, lambada, one-step, peabody, two-step 8 habanera 9 bossa nova, polonaise 10 Charleston
glide: 6 chassé
ballroom __: 5 dance 7 dancing
balls
base on ~: 4 walk
four ~: 4 walk
ball-shaped: 5 round 8 globular
__ Balls of Fire: 5 Great
Ball State: 6 school 10 university
athletes: 9 Cardinals
conference: 3 MAC
locale: 6 Muncie 7 Indiana
Ballston __, NY: 3 Spa
Balluet, Paul: 6 French 8 Nobelist
Ballwin: 4 city, town
locale: 8 Missouri
ballyhoo: 3 row 4 hype, tout 6 herald, hoopla, hype up, talk up 7 advance, clatter, fanfare, puffery 9 advertise, commotion, promotion, publicity
balm: 4 aloe, calm, herb, lull, save 5 cream, salve 6 arnica, lotion, potion, relief, remedy, solace, soothe 7 anodyne, comfort, perfume, soother, unction, unguent 8 easement, lenitive, liniment, medicine, ointment, poultice 9 analgesic, demulcent, emollient, fragrance 10 medication, mitigation, palliative
of Gilead: 5 resin 6 balsam
__ balm: 3 bee 5 horse, lemon
balmacaan: 4 coat 6 jacket 8 overcoat
balminess: 8 calmness 9 fragrancy, redolence
balm of __: 6 Gilead
balmoral: 3 cap, hat, tam 4 shoe 8 footwear
Balmoral Castle river: 3 Dee
balmy: 4 daft, fair, mild, warm, zany 5 bland, dotty, goosy, inane, sweet, wacky 6 absurd, gentle, whacky 7 clement, foolish, scented, summery 8 aromatic, fragrant, perfumed, pleas-

ant, soothing, tropical **9** ambrosial, eccentric, soporific, temperate, unextreme **10** refreshing
balon: **5** grace **9** lightness
baloney: **3** gas, rot **4** blah, bosh, bull, bunk, guff, jazz, jive, pooh, tosh, wind **5** bilge, fudge, hokum, hooey, prate, story, stuff, trash, tripe **6** bunkum, bushwa, drivel, footle, gabble, gammon, gibber, havers, hot air, humbug, jabber, jargon, kibosh, piffle **7** blarney, blather, blether, bushwah, eyewash, flannel, flubdub, fustian, garbage, hogwash, inanity, malarky, rubbish, twaddle **8** buncombe, claptrap, falderal, falderol, fast talk, flimflam, flummery, folderal, folderol, malarkey, nonsense, slipslop, tommyrot, trumpery **9** absurdity, banana oil, gibberish, goofiness, kidstakes, moonshine, poppycock, rigmarole **10** applesauce, balderdash, bilge water, codswallop, double-talk, flapdoodle, galimatias, Jabberwock, mumbo jumbo, rigamarole, taradiddle
full of ~: **6** all wet
___-baloney: **5** phony
Baloney!: **3** hah **5** my eye, nerts, nertz, pshaw
balsa: **4** tree, wood **8** corkwood
balsam: **3** fir **4** tolu, tree **9** evergreen
ender: **4** root
balsam ___: **3** fir **4** pear **5** apple, of fir **6** capivi, family, poplar
___ balsam: **4** Peru **5** black, Mecca **6** Canada, Indian
balsamic: **9** emollient
balsamic ___: **7** vinegar
Balsam, Martin: **5** actor
film: 12 Angry Men (1957)
All the President's Men (1976)
The Anderson Tapes (1972)
Catch-22 (1970)
Little Big Man (1970)
Murder on the Orient Express (1974)
Psycho (1960)
Summer Wishes, Winter Dreams (1973)
The Taking of Pelham One Two Three (1974)
A Thousand Clowns (1965, AA)
Tora! Tora! Tora! (1970)
balsam of ___: **3** fir **4** Peru, tolu
Balt: **7** Latvian **8** Estonian **10** Lithuanian
Balthazar: **5** Getty
and others: **4** Magi
colleague: **6** Caspar **8** Melchior
like ~: **4** wise
Balthazar author: Lawrence Durrell
Baltic: **3** sea
capital: **4** Riga **5** Vilna **7** Tallinn, Vilnius
country: **6** Latvia **7** Estonia **9** Lithuania
feeder: **4** Oder, Odra **5** Memel, Neman, Peene **6** Niemen **7** Vistula
gulf: **4** Riga **6** Danzig **7** Bothnia, Finland
island: **4** Aero **5** Oland
locale: **6** Europe
port: **4** Kiel **6** Gdansk
Baltic ___: **3** Sea **6** States
Baltic Sea
archipelago: **5** Aland
feeder: **5** Dvina
Baltimore: **4** city, port, town **5** David
locale: **8** Maryland
newspaper: **3** Sun
pro team: **6** Ravens **7** Orioles
river: **8** Patapsco
Baltimore ___: **4** chop **6** Canyon, heater, oriole **7** clipper
___ Baltimore cake: **4** Lady, Lord
Baltimore, David: **8** Nobelist
___ Baltimore, The: **4** Hot I
Balto-___: **6** Slavic
Balto (1995 film) director: Simon Wells
Baltoro Kangri: **2** mt. **3** mtn. **4** peak **5** mount **8** mountain
locale: **4** Asia **7** Kashmir **8** Cashmere **9** Himalayas
Baluchistan: **6** desert
baluster: **3** leg, rod **4** pole, post **5** spoke **7** spindle, upright **8** vertical
baluster ___: **4** stem **7** measure
balustrade: **4** rail **6** wallop **7** balcony, railing
Balzac, Honoré de: **6** French, writer
work: The Black Sheep
The Country Doctor
Cousin Bette
Cousin Pons
The Human Comedy
Le Père Goriot
A Shady Business
Bam!: **3** pow
Bama group: **3** SEC
Bamako: **4** city, town **7** capital
locale: **4** Mali
Bambara home: **4** Mali **6** Africa
Bambara, Toni: **6** writer
Bamberga: **8** asteroid
Bambi: **4** deer **5** novel
author: Felix Salten
Bambi (1942 film) director: David Hand
character: **3** Ena **4** Gobo **5** Bambi, Karus, Ronno **6** Faline, Flower, Marena, Nettla
bambino: **4** baby **5** child, kiddy **6** infant **9** offspring
watcher: **5** mamma
Bambino, The: **4** Ruth
bamboo: **4** cane, reed **5** grass
eater: **5** panda
shoot: **6** veggie **9** vegetable
swordplay: **5** kendo
bamboo ___: **4** ware **5** shoot **6** shoots **7** turning
___ bamboo: **6** sacred **7** Mexican
Bamboo ___: **7** Curtain
Bamboo artist: **4** Erté
bamboozle: **3** con **4** bilk, dupe, fool, gull, have, hoax, nick, snow, take **5** cheat, cozen, trick **6** delude, fleece, outwit, puzzle, suck in, take in **7** deceive, defraud, mystify, swindle, two-time **8** flimflam, hoodwink, outsmart, pettifog **9** disinform, four-flush, victimize **10** run a game on
bamboozlement: **3** con **5** fraud **6** fakery
bamboozler: **6** conman
Bamenda: **4** city, town
locale: **8** Cameroon
Bamm Bamm: **6** Rubble
parent of: **5** Betty **6** Barney
ban: **3** bar, nix **4** tabu, veto **5** debar, estop, expel, money **6** abjure, censor, enjoin, except, forbid, ice out, outlaw, reject **7** boycott, embargo, exclude, keep out, refusal, rule out, shut out **8** disallow, outlawry, prohibit, restrict, sanction, throw out **9** blackball, exclusion, interdict, ostracize, proscribe, restraint **10** censorship, do away with, injunction
___ ban: **4** test
Ban: **9** deodorant
alternative: **4** Sure **5** Arrid, Tussy **6** Degree, Secret **7** Dry Idea, Mitchum **10** Right Guard, Soft and Dri, Speed Stick
Ban-___: **3** Lon
banal: **4** blah, flat **5** bland, campy, corny, hokey, musty, stale, stock, trite **6** common, jejune **7** humdrum, insipid, mundane, prosaic, tedious **8** ordinary, plebeian, trifling **9** hackneyed, innocuous, played out, prosaical **10** pedestrian, threadbare, uninspired, warmed-over
banality: **6** tedium **8** flatness **10** insipidity
banana: **4** tree **5** fruit **8** ice cream **9** Cavendish **10** Martinique
alternative: **5** lemon, mocha, peach **6** coffee, Jamoca, toffee **7** caramel, coconut, vanilla **8** cinnamon, hazelnut **9** bubblegum, chocolate, pineapple, pistachio, raspberry, rocky road, rum raisin **10** blackberry, cheesecake, Neapolitan, peppermint, strawberry
bunch: **4** hand
buy: **5** bunch
covering: **4** peel
family plant: **5** abaca
oil: **3** gas, rot **4** blah, bosh, bull, bunk, guff, jazz, jive, pooh, tosh **5** bilge, ester, fudge, hokum, hooey, prate, stuff, trash, tripe **6** bunkum, bushwa, drivel, footle, gabble, gammon, gibber, havers, hot air, humbug, jabber, jargon, kibosh, piffle **7** baloney, blarney, blather, blether, boloney, bushwah, eyewash, flannel, flubdub, fustian, garbage, hogwash, inanity, rubbish, twaddle **8** buncombe, claptrap, falderal, falderol, fast talk, flimflam, flummery, folderal, folderol, nonsense, slipslop, tommyrot, trumpery **9** gibberish, goofiness, kidstakes, moonshine, poppycock, rigmarole **10** applesauce, balderdash, bilge water, codswallop, double-talk, flapdoodle, galimatias, Jabberwock, mumbo jumbo, rigamarole, taradiddle
peel mishap: **4** slip
top ~: **5** comic **8** comedian, kingfish **9** commander
banana ___: **3** oil **4** seat **5** shrub, split **6** spider
___ banana: **3** top **5** dwarf **6** second **7** Chinese
Banana ___ Song, The: **4** Boat
___ Banana: **3** Top
Banana Boat Song, The: **4** Day-o
bananahead: **3** ass, lug, nit, oaf, sap **4** boob, clod, dolt, dope, fool, gowk, lunk **5** chump, clown, cluck, dummy, dunce, joker, klutz, looby, ninny, patsy, schmo **6** dimwit, lubber, lummox, nitwit, schmoe, sucker, turkey **7** buffoon, bungler, dingbat, dullard, half-wit, jackass **8** dumbbell, numskull **9** birdbrain, harebrain, ignoramus, lamebrain, numbskull, simpleton **10** nincompoop
Bananarama
song: Cruel Summer (1984)
I Heard a Rumour (1987)
Venus (1986)
bananas: **3** ape, mad **4** bats, gaga, loco **5** batty **7** bonkers, tetched **8** nonsense **10** freaked out, moonstruck
drive ~: **3** irk **4** rile **5** annoy, upset **6** harass **7** torment
go ~: **4** rave **6** lose it
go ~ over: **5** eat up
Bananas (1971 film)
cast: Woody Allen, Louise Lasser, Carlos Montalban
director: Woody Allen
banana split: **7** dessert
alternative: **5** bombe **6** frappe **9** milk shake **10** peach Melba
holder: **4** boat
ingredient: **8** ice cream
banausic: **8** temporal **10** monotonous, pedestrian
Banbury: **4** city, town
locale: **7** England
Banbury ___: **3** bun **4** cake, tart
banc: **4** seat
___-banc: **5** char-à
Bancroft: **4** Anne **6** George
Bancroft, Anne: **7** actress
film: 84 Charing Cross Road (1987)
Agnes of God (1985)
The Elephant Man (1980)
Garbo Talks (1984)
G.I. Jane (1997)
Gorilla at Large (1954)
The Graduate (1967)
Great Expectations (1998)
How to Make an American Quilt (1995)
Keeping the Faith (2000)
The Miracle Worker (1962, AA)
Nightfall (1956)
The Prisoner of Second Avenue (1975)
The Pumpkin Eater (1964)
The Raid (1954)
The Turning Point (1977)
Walk the Proud Land (1956)
Young Winston (1972)
spouse: Mel Brooks
Bancroft, George: **5** actor
film: Blood Money (1933)
The Docks of New York (1928)
Each Dawn I Die (1939)
Mr. Deeds Goes to Town (1936)
The Rainbow Trail (1925)
Whistling in Dixie (1942)
Young Tom Edison (1940)
band: **3** set, tie **4** belt, bevy, body, clan, club, crew, gang, gird, girt, hoop, join, lace, line, pack, ring, tape, team, zone **5** bunch, chain, combo, corps, covey, girth, group, junto, layer, merge, party, range, squad, strap, strip, troop, unite **6** circle, clique, fasten, gather, girdle, league, outfit, ribbon, streak, stripe, troupe **7** binding, brigade, caravan, cluster, combine, company, coterie, faction, jewelry, shackle **8** assemble, assembly, cincture, encircle, ensemble, federate, ligature **9** affiliate, gathering, orchestra, shortwave **10** assemblage, collection
acknowledge the ~: **4** clap
alternative: **2** DJ **6** deejay
arm ~: **8** bracelet
bartender's ~: **6** garter
be in a ~: **4** play
biceps ~: **6** armlet
booster: **3** amp
combining form: **3** zon- **4** zono-
dance ~: **5** combo
ender: **3** age, box **5** shell, stand, wagon, width **6** leader, master
engagement: **3** gig
grouping: **3** set
hair ~: **6** fascia
heraldic ~: **4** orle **5** fesse
hillbilly ~ instrument: **3** jug
horizontal ~: **6** fascia
instrument: **3** sax **4** drum, horn, oboe, tuba **5** brass, bugle **8** clarinet
marching ~ hat: **5** shako
marching ~ need: **4** drum
mourning ~: **5** crape
narrow ~: **4** rein **5** leash
number: **4** song, tune
of a sort: **4** trio **5** nonet, octet **6** septet, sestet **7** octette, quartet, quintet
of color: **7** rainbow
of color, in zoology: **5** vitta
one-man ~: **4** solo
ornamental ~: **4** sash **5** patte **6** armlet, frieze **8** bracelet
radio ~: **2** AM, FM
sheriff's ~: **5** posse

spectrum ~: 3 red 4 blue 5 green 6 indigo, orange, violet, yellow
starter: 3 hat 4 head, neck, nose, side, wave 5 belly, broad, sweat, train, waist, watch, wrist
to beat the ~: 7 like mad
together: 5 group, merge, troop, unite
TV ~: 3 UHF, VHF
waist ~: 3 obi 4 sash
wedding ~: 4 ring
band __: 3 saw 4 mill 5 brake, razor, shell
__ band: 3 big, ear, gum, jug 4 bird, file, jazz, mast, side, wave 5 brake, brass, dance, guard, spasm, steel 6 dentil, energy, garage, guttae, Möbius, one-man, rhythm, rubber, spider 7 falling, futtock, wedding
Band __ On, The: 6 Played
Band-__: 3 Aid
Banda: 3 sea
locale: 7 Celebes 8 Sulawesi
bandage: 3 Ace, tie 4 tape, wrap 5 Curad, dress, spica, truss 6 swathe 8 dressing, ligature
applier: 5 medic
material: 5 gauze
nature's ~: 4 scab
Bandai: 7 volcano
locale: 4 Asia 5 Japan 6 Honshu
Band-Aid: 7 stopgap 8 dressing, solution 9 makeshift, temporary
alternative: 3 Ace 5 Curad
bandanna: 5 scarf 8 kerchief, neckwear
Bandar: 7 primate
relative: 3 ape 4 saki, titi 5 chimp, drill, jocko, lemur, loris, magot, orang, potto, shrew 6 aye-aye, baboon, galago, gelada, gibbon, grivet, guenon, howler, langur, macaco, monkey, rhesus, uakari, vervet 7 colobus, gorilla, guereza, hoolock, macaque, sapajou, siamang, tamarin, tarsier 8 bush baby, capuchin, mandrill, mangabey, marmoset, talapoin 9 orangutan 10 Barbary ape, chimpanzee, orangutang
bandeau: 3 bra
Bandeira, Manuel: 4 poet 9 Brazilian
bandelet: 4 ring
__ Band Era: 3 Big
Banderas, Antonio: 5 actor
film: The 13th Warrior (1999)
Assassins (1995)
Crazy in Alabama (1999)
Evita (1996)
Frida (2002)
Interview With the Vampire: The Vampire Chronicles (1994)
The Mask of Zorro (1998)
Original Sin (2001)
Play It to the Bone (1999)
Spy Kids (2001)
role: 3 Che
spouse: Melanie Griffith
banderilla item: 4 barb
banderillero adversary: 6 el toro
banderole: 4 flag 6 ensign 7 pennant 8 standard
bandicoot: 6 animal, mammal 9 marsupial
relative: 4 euro 5 bilbi, bilby, koala 6 numbat, wombat 7 bettong, dasyure, opossum, wallaby 8 kangaroo, wallaroo 9 phalanger
Bandido (1956 film)
cast: Robert Mitchum, Zachary Scott
banding: 4 lace
bandit: 4 thug 5 crook, thief 6 outlaw, pirate, raider, robber 7 brigand, ravager, rustler 8 criminal, gangster, hijacker, hooligan, marauder, opponent, pillager 9 buccaneer, desperado, masked man, plunderer, purloiner, Robin Hood 10 highwayman
Asian ~: 6 dacoit, dakoit
casino ~ feature: 3 arm
furry ~: 4 coon 7 raccoon
Bandit Queen, The: Belle Starr
banditry: 5 theft 8 thievery
Bandits (2001 film)
cast: Cate Blanchett, Billy Bob Thornton, Bruce Willis
director: Barry Levinson
__ Bandits: 4 Time
bandleader's cue: 5 hit it
__ Band music: 3 Big
Band of __: 6 Renown
Band of Gold (song) artist: Don Cherry, Freda Payne
bandoleer: 4 belt
Bandolero! (1968 film)
cast: George Kennedy, Dean Martin, James Stewart, Raquel Welch
director: Andrew V. McLaglen
Band on the Run (1974 song) artist: Paul McCartney
bandore: 4 lute 6 string
Bando, Sal sport: 8 baseball
bandshell: 8 pavilion
bandstand: 5 kiosk
equipment: 3 amp
Bandung: 4 city, town
locale: 9 Indonesia
bandwagon
get on the ~: 4 back 5 boost 7 espouse, promote, sponsor, support 8 advocate, champion
jumper's phrase: 5 me too
Band Wagon, The (1953 film)
cast: Fred Astaire, Jack Buchanan, Cyd Charisse, Nanette Fabray, Oscar Levant
director: Vincente Minnelli
studio: 3 MGM
bandy: 4 awry, bent, game, pass, swap, swop, toss 5 askew, bowed, rally, throw, trade 6 barter, curved 7 crooked, shuffle, twisted 8 exchange 9 bowlegged, toss about
words: 3 rap 4 spar 5 argue
bandy-__: 6 legged
Bandy: 3 Moe
bane: 4 pest, ruin 5 curse, trial 6 blight, misery, plague, poison 7 bugaboo, bugbear, nemesis, scourge, undoing 8 anathema, calamity, disaster, distress, downfall, headache, nuisance 9 bête noire, detriment, nightmare, ruination 10 affliction
ender: 5 berry
starter: 3 bug, cow, dog, hen 4 flea, rats 5 wolfs
baneful: 4 evil, foul, grim, poor 5 awful, fatal, lousy, toxic, woful 6 crumby, crummy, dismal, horrid, malign, nocent, odious, rotten, woeful 7 accurst, adverse, baleful, beastly, doleful, ghastly, harmful, hurtful, malefic, nocuous, noisome, noxious, ominous, ruinous 8 accursed, damaging, dreadful, God-awful, grievous, horrible, inferior, negative, shameful, sinister, stinking, terrible, venomous, virulent, wretched 9 abhorrent, appalling, atrocious, dangerous, defective, execrable, frightful, injurious, insidious, loathsome, miserable, offensive, pestilent, poisonous, revolting, unhealthy 10 abominable, calamitous, despicable, detestable, disastrous, horrendous, pernicious
Banff: 4 city, lake, town 6 resort
lake: 6 Louise
locale: 4 Alta. 6 Canada 7 Alberta
bang: 3 hit, jar, pop, tip 4 beat, blow, boom, jolt, kick, shot, slam, slap, sock, thud, wham 5 blast, burst, crack, crash, knock, noise, pound, salvo, smack, smash, sound, thump, whack 6 hammer, impact, pummel, rattle, report, strike, thrill, tipoff, wallop 7 clatter 8 abruptly, bludgeon, suddenly 9 discharge, explosion, fisticuff, violently 10 detonation
big ~ creator: 5 nitro
ender: 4 tail
into: 3 hit, ram 4 jolt 5 knock 6 impact, jostle, justle
on: 3 def, rad 4 aces, A-one, boss, braw, cool, dece, fine, gear, keen, neat, nice, phat, tuff 5 dandy, ducky, grand, great, marvy, neato, nobby, prime, slick, super, swell 6 bonzer, bosker, choice, divine, dreamy, far-out, gnarly, groovy, lovely, peachy, slap-up, spot on, superb, terrif, tiptop, unreal, whizzo, wicked 7 amazing, awesome, capital, corking, perfect, ripping, skookum, stellar, sublime 8 dazzling, especial, eximious, fabulous, five-star, four-star, frabjous, glorious, heavenly, jim-dandy, smashing, splendid, standout, sterling, stickout, superior, terrific, top-level, topnotch, very good, wondrous 9 bodacious, excellent, exemplary, exquisite, first-rate, high-grade, hunky-dory, marvelous, sollicker, top-flight, wonderful 10 first-class, hotsy-totsy, jack-a-dandy, out of sight, peachy-keen, phenomenal, remarkable, stupendous, super-duper
out: 5 write
up: 3 bar, mar 4 dent, mall, maul 5 abuse, wreck 6 bruise, damage 7 lay into 8 work over 9 manhandle 10 knock about
__-bang: 4 slam, slap, whiz 5 whizz
Bang a Gong (1972 song) artist: T. Rex
Bangalore: 4 city, town
locale: 5 India
Bang and Blame (1995 song) artist: R.E.M.
Bang Bang (1966 song) artist: Cher
banger: 7 sausage
Bang, Herman: 6 Danish, writer
Bangkok: 4 city, port, town 7 capital
locale: 8 Thailand
Bangladesh: 6 nation 7 country
bay: 6 Bengal
capital: 5 Dacca, Dhaka
city: 5 Tongi 6 Khulna 7 Saidpur 8 Rajshahi
continent: 4 Asia
language: 7 Bengali
money: 4 pice, taka 5 paisa 6 poisha
neighbor: 5 Burma, India
bangle: 5 charm, jewel 6 anklet, armlet, geegaw, gewgaw 7 circlet, jewelry, trinket 8 bracelet, ornament, wristlet
Bangles
song: Eternal Flame (1989)
Hazy Shade of Winter (1987)
In Your Room (1988)
Manic Monday (1986)
Walk Like an Egyptian (1986)
Bangor: 4 city, town
college: 4 Beal
locale: 5 Maine
neighbor: 5 Orono
__ bang out of: 4 get a
bangs: 4 coif 6 hairdo 8 coiffure
bangtail: 5 horse, mount
Bang the Drum Slowly (1973 film)
cast: Robert De Niro, Vincent Gardenia, Michael Moriarty
__ Bang Theory: 3 Big
Bangui: 4 city, port, town 7 capital
locale: 22 Central African Republic
river: 6 Ubangi
bang-up: 3 def, rad 4 aces, A-one, boss, braw, cool, dece, fine, gear, keen, neat, nice, phat, tuff 5 dandy, ducky, grand, great, marvy, neato, nobby, prime, slick, super, swell 6 bonzer, bosker, choice, divine, dreamy, far-out, gnarly, groovy, lovely, peachy, slap-up, spot on, superb, terrif, tiptop, unreal, whizzo, wicked 7 amazing, awesome, capital, corking, perfect, ripping, skookum, stellar, sublime 8 dazzling, especial, eximious, fabulous, five-star, four-star, frabjous, glorious, heavenly, jim-dandy, slam-bang, smashing, splendid, standout, sterling, stickout, superior, terrific, top-level, topnotch, very good, wondrous 9 bodacious, Endsville, excellent, exemplary, exquisite, first-rate, high-grade, hunky-dory, marvelous, sollicker, top-flight, wonderful 10 first-class, hotsy-totsy, jack-a-dandy, out of sight, peachy-keen, phenomenal, remarkable, stupendous, super-duper
do a ~ job: 5 excel
Bangweulu: 4 lake
locale: 6 Zambia
bani
100 ~: 3 leu, ley
Bani-Sadr: 5 Irani
banish: 4 oust 5 eject, evict, exile, expel, purge 6 deport, dispel, outlaw, remove 7 cast out, discard, dismiss, isolate, kick out 8 displace, get rid of, relegate, send away 9 drive away, eradicate, ostracize, proscribe, transport 10 expatriate
from a flat: 5 evict
banishment: 5 exile 9 dismissal, expulsion
banister: 4 post, rail 7 railing, support 8 handrail
go down the ~: 5 slide
post: 5 newel
Banja Luka: 4 city, town
locale: 10 Yugoslavia
Banjarmasin: 4 city, port, town
locale: 6 Borneo 9 Indonesia
banjo
ancestor: 4 lute
cousin: 3 uke 6 guitar 7 ukelele
key changer: 4 capo
perch: 4 knee
play the ~: 4 pick 5 plunk, strum, twang
banjo __: 5 clock
Banjo Eyes: Eddie Cantor
banjoist: 6 Seeger 7 Scruggs
Banjo on My Knee (1936 film)
cast: Joel McCrea, Barbara Stanwyck
__ Banjos: 7 Dueling
Banjul: 4 city, town 7 capital
locale: 6 Gambia
bank: 3 dam, pot 4 dike, pile, pool, reef, save, tier 5 carom, coast, drift, mound, shelf, shore, slope, stack, store 6 branch, carrom, depend, glacis, lender, lienor, pile up 7 jackpot 8 salt away, treasury 9 acclivity 10 depository
account: 6 escrow 7 savings
acct. datum: 3 SSN
breaker: 3 run
canal ~: 4 berm 5 berme
claim: 4 lien 8 mortgage
contents: 3 fog 4 cash 5 money
customer: 5 saver 6 lienee 9 depositor
deal: 4 loan, mtge. 8 mortgage
deposit: 5 pay-in
deposit abuser: 5 kiter

employee: 5 guard 6 teller 7 cashier
ender: 4 book, card, note, roll
feature: 4 safe 5 vault
figure: 3 int., IRT
job: 5 heist 7 robbery
like some ~ checking: 5 no-fee
modern ~ teller: 3 ATM
money in the ~: 5 asset 7 deposit, savings
offering: 2 CD 3 IRA 4 loan 6 credit
officer: 5 treas. 9 treasurer
on: 4 lean, rely 5 count, trust 6 accept, assume, credit, depend, expect, look to, reckon 7 believe, presume, swear by 8 be sure of, gamble on 9 calculate 10 set store by
org.: 3 FRS, IMF 4 SBLI 5 FSLIC
patron: 3 acc. 4 acct. 7 account
posting: 4 rate 6 CD rate
river ~: 5 shore
robber's nemesis: 5 alarm 6 camera
sight: 4 line 5 queue
stack: 4 ones, tens 5 fives 8 hundreds, twenties
stamp: 3 NSF
starter: 4 data, sand, snow 5 piggy, river
statement entry: 3 bal., dep., int. 5 debit 7 balance, deposit 8 interest
statement period: 5 month
takeback: 4 repo
teller's call: 4 next
total: 7 balance
up: 5 stack
visit a blood ~: 6 donate
bank ___: 3 box 4 barn, bill, card, loan, note, rate, shot 5 check, clerk, draft, heist, money, night, paper 7 account, annuity, balance, deposit, holiday, swallow
___ bank: 3 fog, job 4 data, food, land, soil 5 blood, piggy, spoil, state 6 memory 7 central, reserve, savings, wildcat
Bank: 5 Frank
Bank ___: 3 One 4 Shot 5 Leumi
Bank ___, The: 4 Dick
___ Bank: 4 Left, West 5 Grand, Right, World 6 Dogger 7 Georges
bankable: 10 marketable
Bank Dick, The (1940 film)
cast: W.C. Fields, Una Merkel, Cora Witherspoon
director: Edward Cline
banker: 6 dealer, lender 8 croupier, investor 9 financier, treasurer
byword: 4 save
Banker author: Dick Francis
bankers' ___: 5 hours
Bankhead, Tallulah: 7 actress
banking: 7 finance 9 economics
see also bank
banknote: 4 bill, buck 5 money 6 dollar, tenner 7 sawbuck, smacker 8 currency, frogskin, simoleon 9 greenback
banknotes: 3 oof 4 cash, gelt, jack, kail, kale, loot, peag, pelf 5 bread, dough, funds, lucre, money, moola, mopus, pesos, rhino, sewan 6 dinero, do-re-mi, mammon, mazuma, moolah, seawan, silver, specie, wampum, wealth 7 cabbage, capital, lettuce, ooftish, scratch, shekels 8 cold cash, currency, hard cash 9 long green 10 green stuff
___ Bank Observatory: 7 Jodrell
bankroll: 3 wad 4 back, fund 5 funds, means, money, purse, stake 6 assets, invest 7 finance, sponsor, support, sustain 8 hard cash 9 resources, subsidize 10 underwrite
bankroller: 6 backer, patron 9 financier
bankrupt: 4 poor, ruin, sink 5 break, broke, drain, needy 6 bad off, busted, hard up, ill off, in need, in want, pauper, reduce, ruined 7 deplete, pinched 8 badly off, beggarly, depleted, deprived, indigent, straiten, strapped 9 destitute, insolvent, moneyless, penniless, penurious, tapped out 10 down and out, impoverish, pauperized, straitened
go ~: 4 bust, fail, fold, sink
bankruptcy: 4 ruin 7 default, failure, poverty 8 collapse 9 indigence, overdraft, pauperism, privation, recession, ruination 10 depression, exhaustion, insolvency, nonpayment
Banks: 4 Tyra 5 Ernie 6 Joseph
Banks ___: 6 Island
___ Banks: 5 Grand, Outer
Banks, Ernie: 3 Cub 9 shortstop
Bank Shot (1974 film)
cast: Sorrell Booke, Joanna Cassidy, George C. Scott
director: Gower Champion
banksia: 4 tree 5 shrub
family: 6 protea
Banks, Joseph: 7 British 8 botanist
___ Banks, NC: 5 Outer
Banks o'Doon, The author: Robert Burns
bank statement entry: 5 debit
period: 5 month
Banks, Tyra: 5 model
Banky: 5 Vilma
banned: 4 tabu 5 taboo 7 illegal, illicit 8 criminal, improper, outlawed, unlawful, verboten, wrongful 9 felonious, forbidden 10 not allowed, prohibited
act: 4 no-no, tabu 5 taboo
chemical: 3 PCB
fruit spray: 4 Alar
pesticide: 3 DDT
Banneker, Benjamin: 10 astronomer
Bannen: 3 Ian
banner: 4 flag, sign 5 title, Web ad 6 burgee, emblem, ensign, poster 7 pennant, stellar 8 gonfalon, headline, standard, streamer 9 red-letter 10 successful
church ~: 7 labarum
puller: 5 blimp 9 dirigible
roll up a ~: 4 furl
banner ___: 3 day 4 line 5 cloud
___ banner: 4 snow 5 cloud
Banner: 4 John
Star-Spangled ~: 4 flag
Banning: 4 city, town
locale: 10 California
Banning (1967 film)
cast: Anjanette Comer, Robert Wagner
Bannister: 5 miler, Roger
distance for ~: 4 mile
emulate ~: 3 run 4 race
bannock: 5 bread
Bannock: 6 Indian 7 Amerind
Bannockburn: 6 battle
locale: 8 Scotland
banon: 6 cheese
___ Banos, CA: 3 Los
banque payment: 5 rente
banquet: 3 sup 4 fete, meal 5 feast, party 6 dinner, repast, spread 9 festivity, reception
attend a ~: 3 eat 4 dine 5 feast
course: 4 fish, meat, soup 5 salad 6 entrée 7 dessert 9 appetizer
delicacy: 4 paté 6 caviar 7 caviare
give a ~ for: 4 fete 5 honor
need: 2 MC 5 china, emcee
platform: 4 dais
provide a ~: 5 cater
banquet ___: 4 room
banshee: 5 ghost
lament: 4 wail
like a ~: 6 Gaelic
bant: 4 diet 6 reduce
bantam: 3 hen, wee 4 baby, fowl, puny, tiny 5 bitty, saucy, small, teeny 6 little, midget, minute, peewee, petite, teensy 7 chicken, rooster, stunted 9 itsy-bitsy, itty-bitty, miniature, pint-sized, undersize 10 diminutive, teeny-weeny, vest-pocket
ender: 6 weight
Bantam: 4 fowl 7 chicken
relative: 6 Brahma, Houdan, Sussex 7 Cornish, Dorking, Leghorn 8 Araucana, Langshan, Shanghai 9 Dominique, Orpington, Wyandotte
bantamweight, like a: 4 wiry
banteng: 5 bovid 6 bovine
relative: 3 yak 4 anoa, arna, gaur, urus, zebu 5 bison, gayal, takin 6 mithan, muskox 7 aurochs, beefalo, buffalo, carabao, cattalo, kouprey, tamarao, tamarau, timarau
banter: 3 kid, rib, wit 4 jeer, jest, jive, joke, josh, mock, quip, razz, talk 5 chaff, humor, taunt, tease 6 deride, joking 7 jesting, joshing, kidding, ribbing, sarcasm, teasing 8 badinage, chitchat, fast talk, raillery, repartee, ridicule, wordplay 9 make fun of, small talk, table talk, witty talk 10 jocoseness, joke around, persiflage
banterer: 3 wag, wit
bantering: 9 quizzical
___ B. Anthony: 5 Susan
banting: 5 bovid 6 bovine
relative: 3 yak 4 anoa, arna, gaur, urus, zebu 5 bison, gayal, takin 6 mithan, muskox 7 aurochs, beefalo, buffalo, carabao, cattalo, kouprey, tamarao, tamarau, timarau
Banting, Frederick: 3 Sir 8 Canadian, Nobelist
___-ban treaty: 4 test
Bantu: 4 Zulu 5 tribe 7 Swahili 8 language, Matabele
home: 6 Africa
language: 3 Yao 4 Lozi, Luba, Xosa, Zulu 5 Makua, Mongo, Shona, Sotho, Swazi, Xhosa 6 Kikuyu
people: 4 Goma, Luba, Zulu
territory: 5 Venda 6 Ciskei
banyan: 3 fig 4 coat, tree 5 ficus, shirt 6 jacket 8 mulberry
banzai: 5 huzza 6 hoorah, hooray, hurrah, hurray, huzzah
Bao ___: 3 Dai
baobab: 4 tree
family: 6 bombax
relative: 6 durian
baptism: 4 rite 5 debut 6 ritual 9 launching, sacrament 10 initiation
area: 4 font 5 laver
baptism of ___: 4 fire
Baptist: 4 sect 8 religion 10 Protestant
baptize: 3 dub 4 call, name, term 5 bless, title 7 convert, entitle, immerse, intitle 8 christen, sprinkle
bar: 3 ban, but, dam, nix, pub, rod 4 bolt, boom, cake, deny, dike, dive, halt, line, lock, pole, rail, reef, rung, save, seal, shut, slab, snag, stop, tabu, veto 5 block, close, court, crank, debar, estop, expel, haunt, ingot, latch, ledge, lever, limit, shaft, spoke, stick, strip, table 6 abjure, bang up, bistro, cookie, enjoin, except, forbid, hinder, hurdle, impede, lounge, oppose, outlaw, reject, saloon, secure, streak, stripe, tavern 7 besides, boycott, embargo, exclude, hangout, inhibit, keep out, lock out, measure, prevent, railing, rule out, shut off, shut out, suspend, taproom, without 8 alehouse, blockade, blockage, disallow, estoppel, gin joint, leave out, obstacle, obstruct, omitting, preclude, prohibit, restrain, taphouse 9 apart from, constrain, deterrent, except for, excluding, exclusion, foreclose, freeze out, hindrance, honky-tonk, interdict, judiciary, nightclub, ostracize, other than, outside of, proscribe, restraint, roadblock 10 constraint, crosspiece, disqualify, impediment, limitation, restaurant
bill: 3 tab
candy ~: 5 snack
car ~: 4 axle 5 strut
car with a ~: 4 limo
chart: 5 graph
chaser: 4 soda
cheap ~: 4 dive 5 joint
code: 3 UPC
companion: 5 grill
container: 3 mug 5 glass, stein 8 schooner
dance under a ~: 5 limbo
ender: 3 fly, hop, man, men 4 bell, girl, keep, king, maid, room, ware 5 berry, guest, stool 6 keeper, tender
for draft animals: 4 yoke
horizontal ~: 5 event 7 railing
hostess: 5 B-girl
ice: 5 rocks
j ~: 6 ski tow 7 ski lift
legally: 5 estop
member: 3 att. 8 attorney 9 barrister 10 atty.. lawyer
member's abbr.: 3 esq., LL.B.
metal ~: 5 ingot
millstone ~: 4 rynd
mixer: 4 soda 5 water 7 bitters
mouthful: 3 sip 4 swig
none: 3 all
of gold: 5 ingot
of soap: 4 cake
order: 3 ale, rum, rye 4 beer, flip, neat, pint, shot, sour 5 Bronx, draft, drink, lager, round, sling, usual, vodka 6 bishop, brandy, chaser, Cognac, double, eggnog, Gibson, gimlet, mai tai, mimosa, posset, rickey, rob roy, scotch, whisky, zombie 7 Collins, martini, negroni, sidecar, stinger, whiskey 8 cocktail, coco loco, daiquiri, highball, Jack Rose, pink lady, salty dog, vermouth 9 alexander, Manhattan, margarita, moosemilk 10 Bloody Mary, golden fizz, horse's neck, Moscow mule, piña colada, rock and rye, silver fizz
pivoted ~: 4 pawl
pry ~: 5 jimmy, lever 7 crowbar
pull: 3 tap
read ~ codes: 4 scan
rectangular ~: 6 billet
request: 5 glass
rocks: 3 ice
sand ~: 4 reef 5 shoal
seat: 5 stool
selection: 5 salad
shot: 3 tot 5 snort
sign: 5 on tap
snack: 4 nuts 5 sushi 7 peanuts, popcorn
sound: 3 hic
starter: 4 crow, draw, sand, side 5 cross 6 handle
supply: 3 ale, ice 4 beer 6 liquor
toothed ~: 5 ratch
wheel ~: 4 axle
work at the ~: 3 mix 4 tend 5 serve
bar ___: 3 car, pin, pit 4 cart, code, exam, foot, girl, line, none, tack 5 chart, clamp, ditch, gemel, graph,

joist, syrup **6** magnet, mizvah **7** mitsvah, mitzvah
bar-__: **4** b-que **5** le-duc
__ bar: **3** bus, pry, tie, tow, wet **4** cash, claw, fern, gill, grab, high, Mars, milk, muck, open, roll, sand, sash, sway, toll, wine, wing **5** angle, inner, joint, outer, panic, piano, pinch, salad, sissy, slice, snack, space, utter **6** boring, cutter, dating, double, public, sickle, sports **7** azimuth, bay-head, capstan, quarter, reverse, ripping, singles, torsion
Bar __: **6** Harbor
__ Bar: **4** Dove
Barabbas (1962 film)
cast: Silvana Mangano, Anthony Quinn
Barabbas author: Pär Lagerkvist
Baracus, B.A. group: **5** A-Team
Barada: **5** river
city on the: **8** Damascus
locale: **5** Syria
__ barada nikto: **6** Klaatu
Baraka, Imamu Amiri: **6** writer
real name: **10** LeRoi Jones
Barak, Ehud: **2** P.M. **7** Israeli
predecessor: **9** Netanyahu
successor: **6** Sharon
bar and __: **5** grill
Baranof Island city: **5** Sitka
Baranski: **9** Christine
Bárány, Robert: **8** Austrian, Nobelist
barasingh: **4** deer
relative: **3** elk, roe **4** axis, pudu, shou, sika **5** moose **6** chital, guemal, hangul, huemul, sambar, sambur, thamin, wapiti **7** brocket, caribou, muntjac, muntjak, sambhar, sambhur **8** reindeer
barathea: **6** fabric **8** material
Bara, Theda: **5** siren **7** actress
contemporary: **5** Negri
Bar at the Folies-Bergère, A painter: **5** Manet
barb: **3** cut, dig **4** fish, gibe, hook, jibe, quip, slam, slap, slur, snub, spur **5** abuse, horse, libel, point, scorn, spike, taunt, thorn **6** equine, insult, needle, rebuff, ripost, slight, zinger **7** affront, calumny, catcall, disdain, mockery, obloquy, offense, potshot, prickle, put-down, riposte, slander, stinger **8** contempt, critique, derision, ridicule **9** aspersion, cheap shot, contumely **10** defamation, disrespect, opprobrium
combining form: **3** onc- **4** onch-, onci-, onco- **5** oncho-
feather ~: **4** herl
bar-b-__: **3** que
Barbados: **3** isl. **4** isle **6** island, nation **7** country
capital: **10** Bridgetown
export: **4** aloe
locale: **3** BWI **10** West Indies
money: **4** cent **6** dollar
org.: **3** OAS
__ barbara: **3** vox
Barbara: **3** Pym **4** Bach, Bain, Bush, Eden, Hale, Heck, Luna, Lynn, Rush **5** Allen, Boxer, Lewis, major, Mason, saint, Trent **6** Barrie, Bosson, Feldon, George, Harris, Hutton, Jordan, McNair **7** Babcock, Britton, Carrera, Hershey, Parkins, Tuchman, Walters **8** Anderson, Cartland, Hepworth, Mandrell, Michaels, Stanwyck **9** Bel Geddes **10** Kingsolver, McClintock
Barbara __ Bradford: **6** Taylor
__ Barbara: **5** Major, Santa
Barbara Ann (song) artist: Beach Boys, Regents
Barbara Bush, __ Pierce: **3** née
Barbara Frietchie: **4** poem
author: John Greenleaf Whittier
Barbara Mc__: **4** Nair
Barbara Taylor __: **8** Bradford
Barbarella (1968 film)
cast: Jane Fonda, John Phillip Law, Milo O'Shea
director: Roger Vadim
barbarian: **3** hun, pig **4** boor, Goth, ogre, wild **5** beast, brute, crude, cruel, fiend **6** animal, brutal, coarse, savage, vandal, vulgar **7** bestial, boorish, heathen, inhuman, lowbrow, monster, uncivil, vicious **8** inhumane, ruthless **9** graceless, hellhound, ignoramus, merciless, primitive **10** philistine, troglodyte, uncultured
behave like a ~: **4** sack **6** invade **7** overrun, plunder
6th-century ~: **4** Avar
barbaric: **4** mean, wild **5** crude, cruel, feral, harsh, nasty **6** animal, brutal, coarse, fierce, Gothic, savage, unholy, unkind, vulgar, wanton **7** beastly, bestial, boorish, callous, hellish, hurtful, inhuman, lawless, loutish, lowbrow, uncivil, uncouth, ungodly, vicious **8** fiendish, inhumane, pitiless, ruthless, sadistic, vengeful **9** atrocious, cutthroat, ferocious, graceless, heartless, merciless, monstrous, primitive, truculent, unpitying **10** outlandish, outrageous, uncultured, vindictive
barbarism: **7** cruelty, outrage **8** ferocity **9** brutality, crudeness, vulgarity **10** coarseness, corruption, inhumanity, savageness
Barbarosa (1982 film)
cast: Gary Busey, Willie Nelson, Isela Vega
director: Fred Schepisi
Barbary
beast: **3** ape
pirate's vessel: **5** zebec **6** zebeck **7** chebeck
sheep: **6** aoudad
Barbary __: **3** ape, fig **5** Coast, sheep **6** States
Barbary ape: **5** magot **7** primate
relative: **4** saki, titi **5** chimp, drill, jocko, lemur, loris, orang, potto, shrew **6** aye-aye, baboon, Bandar, galago, gelada, gibbon, grivet, guenon, howler, langur, macaco, monkey, rhesus, uakari, vervet **7** colobus, gorilla, guereza, hoolock, macaque, sapajou, siamang, tamarin, tarsier **8** bush baby, capuchin, mandrill, mangabey, marmoset, talapoin **9** orangutan **10** chimpanzee, orangutang
Barbary Coast (1935 film)
cast: Miriam Hopkins, Joel McCrea, Edward G. Robinson
director: Howard Hawks
Barbary Coast city: **5** Tunis
Barbary State
former ~: **5** Tunis **7** Algiers
barbasco: **4** tree **5** shrub
barbate: **7** bearded
barbe: **5** scarf
Barbeau: **8** Adrienne
barbecue: **4** bake, cook, meal, meat, sear **5** broil, grill, party, roast **6** picnic **7** broiler, cookout, roaster **10** rotisserie
fare: **4** brat, ribs, slaw **5** kabab, kabob, kebab, kebob, patty, salad, steak **6** hot dog, pattie **8** coleslaw **9** bratwurst, hamburger
garb: **5** apron
leftover: **3** ash **5** ember
like ~ sauce: **5** tangy, zesty
need: **4** coal **5** ember **6** butane **8** charcoal
part: **5** grill **6** ashpit, grille
rocks: **4** lava
rod: **4** spit
southwestern ~: **5** asado
spot: **4** deck, yard **5** patio **8** backyard
barbecue __: **5** sauce
barbed: **5** sharp, spiny **6** thorny **7** cutting, pointed, prickly **8** spiteful
barbed-wire
barricade: **6** abatis
item: **5** fence
barbel: **4** fish
barbell: **6** weight
material: **4** iron
unit: **2** lb. **5** pound
use a ~: **4** jerk, lift
barber: **4** trim **5** shave **6** Figaro, shaver **7** stylist **10** hair cutter
belt: **5** strop
call: **4** next
challenge: **3** mop
ender: **4** shop
job: **3** cut **4** snip, trim **5** shave
mishap: **4** nick
name meaning ~: **7** Scherer
pole color: **3** red **5** white
shout: **4** next
sign: **4** pole
sound: **4** snip
sweepings: **4** hair
symbol: **4** pole
tool: **5** razor **6** shears **8** scissors
barber __: **4** pole **5** chair **7** college
Barber: **3** Red **4** Tiki **5** Chris **6** Samuel
Barbera: **3** red **4** wine **6** Joseph
origin: **5** Italy
__-Barbera: **5** Hanna
barberite: **5** alloy
component: **3** tin **6** copper, nickel **7** silicon
Barber of Seville, The: **5** opera
composer: **7** Rossini
role: **5** Berta **6** Figaro, Rosina **7** Bartolo, Basilio **8** Almaviva, Fiorello **10** Don Basilio
setting: **5** Spain
barberry: **5** fruit, shrub
family shrub: **7** agarita, mahonia **8** algerita
barber's __: **4** itch **5** chair
Barber, Samuel
work: Adagio for Strings
Capricorn Concerto
A Hand of Bridge
Toccata Festiva
Vanessa
barbershop quartet member: **4** bass **5** tenor **8** baritone
Barber, Tiki sport: **8** football
Barberton: **4** city, town
locale: **4** Ohio
barbet: **4** bird
Barbet: **9** Schroeder
Barbi: **6** Benton
Barbie: **4** doll
boyfriend: **3** Ken
dog: **4** Wags **6** Beauty, Ginger
friend: **5** Midge
rival: **3** Jem
Barbie __: **4** doll, Girl
Barbie Girl (1997 song) artist: Aqua
Barbie Girl artist: **4** Aqua
Barbirolli, John: **3** Sir **7** British **9** conductor
Barbizon __: **6** School
Barbra: **9** Streisand
barbs
throw ~ at: **3** dis **4** zing **6** insult, offend
barbudo: **4** fish
barbule: **5** thorn
barca: **4** boat **5** skiff
barcarole: **4** song
Barcelona: **4** city, port, town
city near ~: **6** Lérida
locale: **5** Spain **6** España
Barchester Towers author: Anthony Trollope
bard: **4** poet, scop **5** odist, rimer **6** rhymer **8** minstrel, poetizer **9** poetaster, rhymester, sonneteer, versifier
ametrical ~: **4** Nash
old-style: **4** scop
Scandinavian ~: **5** scald, skald
work: **4** epic, poem, rime, tale **5** rhyme, verse **6** ballad
see also poet
Bard
see Shakespeare
Bardeen, John: **8** Nobelist **9** physicist
bardic: **7** of poets
Bard of __: **4** Avon
Bardolino: **3** red **4** wine **7** red wine
origin: **5** Italy
Bardot, Brigitte: **6** French **7** actress
spouse: Roger Vadim
bare: **4** arid, nude, open, poor, show, skin, void **5** basic, blank, bleak, clear, empty, naked, plain, scant, shorn, spare, stark, strip **6** absent, barren, denude, desert, devoid, divest, expose, meager, modest, peeled, reveal, scanty, scarce, shabby, simple, unclad, unmask, unveil, used up, vacant **7** austere, denuded, display, divulge, drained, exhibit, exposed, publish, slender, sold out, sterile, tell all, uncover, unrobed, vacated, vacuous **8** depleted, deserted, desolate, disclose, disrobed, divested, in the raw, knowable, leafless, lifeless, stripped, unclothe, undraped **9** au naturel, baldfaced, come clean, evacuated, exhausted, in the buff, make known, publicize, put on view, unadorned, unattired, unclothed, uncovered, undressed **10** make public, unshielded
combining form: **4** gymn-, nudi-, psil- **5** gymno-, psilo-
ender: **4** back, foot **5** faced **6** footed, handed, headed, legged
facts: **7** outline
fix some ~ spots: **5** resod
lay ~: **3** air **4** blab, leak, skin, tell **5** admit, strip **6** denude, expose, relate, reveal, show up, unfold, unmask, unveil **7** breathe, confess, divulge, exhibit, let slip, publish, uncloak, uncover **8** blurt out, disclose, unburden **9** broadcast, make known **10** make public
on top: **4** bald
peak: **3** tor **4** crag **5** spire **6** needle
rocky slope: **4** scar
starter: **6** thread
the teeth: **4** gnar **5** gnarl, growl, snarl
bare __: **5** bones
bare-__: **4** root **5** bones **7** knuckle
Bare: **5** Bobby
bare-bones: **5** stark **6** barren, severe **7** austere, Spartan **9** unadorned
bare-faced: **4** bold, open **5** brash **6** arrant, brassy, brazen **7** blatant, forward, glaring, obvious **8** apparent, flagrant, immodest, impudent, insolent, manifest, palpable, unsubtle **9** audacious, shameless, unabashed
barefoot: **6** unshod **8** shoeless
go ~: **3** pad
not ~: **4** shod
Barefoot Boy, The: **4** poem
author: John Greenleaf Whittier
Barefoot Contessa, The (1954 film)
cast: Humphrey Bogart, Ava Gardner, Edmond O'Brien

director: Joseph L. Mankiewicz
Barefoot in Athens author: Maxwell Anderson
Barefoot in the Park: 4 film, play
author: Neil Simon
cast: Charles Boyer, Jane Fonda, Mildred Natwick, Robert Redford
director: Gene Saks
barege: 6 fabric 8 material
barehanded: 7 unarmed 8 ungloved 10 vulnerable, weaponless
bareheaded: 7 hatless
barely: 4 just, only 6 almost, hardly, little, simply 7 by a hair, by a nose 8 narrowly, scarcely 10 by a whisker
Barenaked Ladies
song: It's All Been Done (1999)
One Week (1998)
Pinch Me (2000)
Barenboim, Daniel: 9 conductor
bareness: 9 austerity 10 desolation
Barents: 3 sea 6 Willem
locale: 6 Arctic
Barents, Willem: 5 Dutch 8 explorer
bare one's __: 5 teeth
barest: 5 least 7 minimal, minimum
Baretta (ABC drama)
cast: Robert Blake (Tony Baretta)
cockatoo: Fred
barfly: 3 sot 4 lush 5 toper 7 tippler
Barfly (1987 film)
cast: Faye Dunaway, Alice Krige, Mickey Rourke
director: Barbet Schroeder
bargain: 3 buy, low 4 deal, find, pact, sale, swap, swop 5 cheap, steal, value 6 dicker, haggle, higgle, pledge 7 cut-rate, good buy, low-cost, promise, traffic 8 closeout, contract, discount, good deal, markdown, moderate, purchase 9 agreement, low-priced, negotiate, reduction, stipulate 10 compromise, do business, economical, reasonable
at a ~: 5 cheap 6 on sale 7 reduced
caveat: 3 irr. 5 irreg.
for: 4 plan 5 incur 6 reckon 9 undertake 10 anticipate
hunter delight: 4 sale 7 auction 8 yard sale 9 clearance 10 garage sale
in the ~: 3 too 4 also 5 extra
terrific ~: 3 buy 4 deal 5 steal
with: 6 haggle 9 negotiate
bargain __: 3 for 7 counter
__-bargain: 4 plea
bargain-basement: 4 poor 5 cheap, tatty 6 budget, cheesy, shlock 7 schlock 8 inferior 9 low-priced, third-rate 10 reasonable, second-rate
bargain-hunt: 4 shop
bargaining chip: 8 leverage
barge: 3 ark, hoy 4 boat, dory, scow, ship 5 craft 6 lumber, vessel 7 intrude, lighter 8 flatboat 9 interrupt
canal of song: 4 Erie
helper: 3 tug 7 tugboat
in: 5 burst, enter 6 arrive, meddle, muscle 7 intrude, obtrude 9 intercede, interfere, interpose, interrupt, intervene, push aside
into: 3 ram 7 collide, rear-end
like a ~: 5 in tow
locale: 4 lake, Nile 5 canal, river 6 harbor
Barge Canal alias: 4 Erie
bargeman, name meaning: 6 Keeler
barger: 8 deckhand
barghest: 7 gremlin
__-bargle: 5 argle
__-bargy: 4 argy
Bar Harbor: 4 city, town 6 resort
locale: 5 Maine
park near: 6 Acadia
barhop: 8 pub-crawl 9 do the town
Bari: 4 city, Lynn, port, town
locale: 5 Italy 6 Apulia
Bari, Lynn: 7 actress
film: The Falcon Takes Over (1942)
Kit Carson (1940)
The Magnificent Dope (1942)
Margie (1946)
Nocturne (1946)
Baring: 4 Earl 7 Francis
barite: 3 ore 4 spar
baritone: 4 deep, male 5 range, voice 6 Duncan, Milnes, Warren 7 Merrill, Tibbett 8 vocalist
aria: 5 eri tu
fiddle: 5 cello
in Marouf: 3 Ali
voice above ~: 5 tenor
voice under ~: 4 bass
barium: 5 metal 7 element
barium __: 4 x-ray 5 oxide 6 yellow 7 bromate, dioxide, hydrate, sulfate, sulfide
bark: 3 arf, bay, cry, rap, rub, yap, yip 4 bawl, boat, case, coat, howl, husk, peel, rind, roar, skin, snap, woof, yell, yelp 5 candy, craft, crust, growl, shell, shout, snarl, sound, speak 6 bellow, bowwow, casing, cortex, mutter, scrape, vessel 7 grumble, kyoodle 10 integument
boat: 5 canoe
combining form: 6 phello-
comic-strip ~: 3 arf 4 woof
for tanning: 5 sumac 6 sumach
high-pitched ~: 3 yap, yip 4 yelp
mulberry ~: 4 tapa
place: 4 bole, tree 5 trunk
starter: 3 tan 4 nine, shag, soap 5 shell
up the wrong tree: 3 err 7 blunder 8 misjudge
bark __: 5 cloth, louse 6 beetle
__ bark: 5 china, sassy 6 almond, cassia 7 jackass, Jesuit's, pereira, quillai, Winter's
Barka: 3 cow 4 bull 6 bovine, cattle
barkentine: 4 boat
barker: 3 dog 4 seal 5 carny 6 carney 8 huckster, pitchman
baby ~: 3 pup 5 puppy
come-on: 5 spiel
partner: 5 shill
Barker: 2 Ma, MC 3 Bob, Lex 5 Clive, emcee
Barker, Lex
spouse: Arlene Dahl, Lana Turner
Barkin, Ellen: 7 actress
film: The Big Easy (1987)
Daniel (1983)
Desert Bloom (1986)
Diner (1982)
Drop Dead Gorgeous (1999)
The Fan (1996)
Sea of Love (1989)
This Boy's Life (1993)
spouse: Gabriel Byrne
barking __: 4 deer, frog
barking up the wrong tree: 6 all wet 8 mistaken
Barkla, Charles: 8 Nobelist 9 physicist
Barkley: 4 Iran 5 Alben 7 Charles
Barkleys of Broadway, The (1949 film)
cast: Fred Astaire, Ginger Rogers
barks
animal that ~: 3 dog 4 deer, seal
like some tree ~: 5 mossy, rough 6 smooth
Bark Tree, The author: Raymond Queneau
bar-le-__: 3 duc
barley: 4 feed 5 grain
bristle: 3 awn
ender: 4 corn
product: 4 beer, malt
barley __: 4 coal, corn, sack 5 candy, sugar, water 6 stripe
__ barley: 5 pearl 6 winter
__ Barleycorn: 4 John
Barlow, Joel: 5 poetr
barm: 6 leaven
Barmeno: 4 font 8 typeface
bar mitzvah: 4 rite
appetizer: 5 knish
dance: 4 hora
official: 5 rabbi, rebbe
reading: 4 Tora 5 Torah
barmy: 4 luny 5 foamy, loony, spumy 6 frothy, looney, yeasty 10 fermenting
barn: 7 theater, theatre
area: 4 loft 5 stall 6 haymow
baby: 3 kid 4 calf, colt, foal, lamb 5 owlet
bellow: 3 low, moo
cow ~: 5 dairy
dance: 4 reel
dweller: 3 cow, ewe, owl, ram 4 goat 5 horse
ender: 4 yard 5 storm 6 burner
handful: 3 hay 5 straw, udder
locale: 4 farm
loft: 6 haymow
neighbor: 4 silo
storage unit: 4 bale
symbol: 7 hex sign
topper: 4 vane
barn __: 3 owl 5 dance, grass 7 raising, swallow
Barnabas: 5 saint
Barnaby __: 5 Jones, Rudge
Barnaby Jones (CBS drama)
cast: Buddy Ebsen (Barnaby Jones)
Lee Meriwether (Betty Jones)
Mark Shera (J.R. Jones)
Barnaby Rudge
author: Charles Dickens
character: 3 Ned 4 Emma
barnacle: 10 crustacean
barnacle __: 5 goose
__ barnacle: 4 rock 5 acorn, goose
Barnard: 4 coll. 6 Hughes 7 college 10 Christiaan
grad: 5 woman 6 alumna
locale: 7 New York
barnburner: 5 event 7 success
Barnes: 5 Clive, Djuna 6 Binnie, Joanna, Julian, Norman 9 Priscilla
& Noble competitor: 6 Amazon 7 Borders
Barnes, Binnie: 7 actress
film: Diamond Jim (1935)
It's in the Bag! (1945)
The Last of the Mohicans (1936)
The Private Life of Henry VIII (1933)
Small Town Girl (1936)
This Thing Called Love (1941)
Three Smart Girls (1936)
Wife, Husband and Friend (1939)
Barnes, Djuna: 6 writer
Barnes, Julian: 6 author, writer 7 British
Barnet: 6 Miguel 7 Charlie
Barnet, Charlie: 11 saxophonist
genre: 4 jazz
Barnet, Miguel: 5 Cuban 6 writer
barney: 3 row 4 fray, spat, tiff 5 brawl, error, fight, melee, scrap 6 affray, dustup, engine, tussle 7 blunder, dispute, mistake, quarrel, rhubarb, scuffle, wrangle 8 argument, squabble 9 brannigan 10 donnybrook, free-for-all, locomotive, prizefight
Barney: 3 Lem, Rex 4 Fife 6 Kessel, Miller, Rubble 8 Oldfield
buddy: 4 Fred
partner: 5 Smith
Barney Google kid: 5 Tater
Barney Miller (ABC sitcom)
cast: Max Gail (Det. Stanley Wojo Wojohowicz)
Ron Glass (Det. Ron Harris)
Hal Linden (Capt. Barney Miller)
Gregory Sierra (Det. Sgt. Chano Amenguale)
Jack Soo (Det. Nick Yemana)
Abe Vigoda (Det. Sgt. Phil Fish)
Barnstable: 4 city, town
locale: 4 Mass.
barnstorm: 3 fly 4 tour 6 aviate, travel 8 campaign
barnstormer: 5 flier, flyer 7 aviator 8 traveler
feat: 4 dive, loop 8 nosedive
Barnum: 2 P.T. 7 Phineas
attraction: 3 Eng 4 Lind 5 Chang, Thumb 6 circus 8 Tom Thumb 9 Jenny Lind
Barnum of Wall Street, The: 4 Fisk
barnyard: 4 farm
animal: 3 cow, ewe, hen, hog, pig, ram, sow 4 duck, goat 5 goose, horse, sheep 6 rabbit
baby: 3 kid, pig 4 calf, colt, foal, lamb 5 chick 6 piglet 7 gosling 8 duckling
bird: 3 hen 4 duck, fowl 5 drake, goose, layer 6 gander 7 chicken, rooster
cry: 3 baa, low, maa, moo 4 bray, honk, oink 5 bleat, neigh, quack 6 squawk, whinny 7 whinney
enclosure: 3 pen, sty 6 corral
female: 3 cow, ewe, hen, sow 4 duck 5 goose, nanny
grub: 3 hay 4 corn, feed, oats, slop 5 swill
grunter: 3 hog, pig, sow 4 boar 5 shoat
swinger: 4 vane
Barolo: 3 red 4 wine 7 red wine
origin: 5 Italy
barometer: 4 norm 5 gauge, scale 8 standard
__ barometer: 3 cup 6 Fortin, marine 7 aneroid, cistern, mercury
barometric
line: 6 isobar
unit of ~ pressure: 4 torr
barometric __: 5 error 6 switch 8 pressure
baron: 4 lord, peer, rank 5 mogul, nawab, noble, title 6 tycoon 7 big boss, magnate 8 nobleman 9 blue-blood, financier, patrician 10 aristocrat
certain oil ~: 5 sheik 6 shaikh, sheikh
ender: 3 age, ess
superior: 8 viscount
__ baron: 5 press 6 cattle, robber
baroness: 4 dame, lady, peer 5 noble, title 10 noblewoman
baronet: 5 noble 8 nobleman
title: 3 Sir
wife: 4 dame, Lady
baronial: 5 noble 6 august, lordly
baron of __: 4 beef
__ Baron, The: 3 Red
Baron, The Red: 3 ace 5 pilot
baroque: 5 style 6 florid, ornate, quaint 10 decorative, ornamented
composer: 4 Bach
instrument: 4 lute, viol
Baroque: 3 Era
composer: 4 Bach 6 Handel
painter: 6 Rubens 9 Velázquez
barque: 4 boat
barquette: 7 dessert
Barr: 7 Douglas 8 Roseanne
Barrack-Room Ballads
author: Rudyard Kipling
part: 5 Tommy
barracks: 3 bed 4 camp, tent 6 billet, casern 7 bivouac, caserne 8 garrison, quarters 10 encampment, Quonset hut

assignment: 6 billet
officer: 3 NCO, sgt. 8 sergeant
picture: 5 pin-up
barracks ___: 3 bag 6 lawyer
barracuda: 4 fish, spet 6 sennet
habitat: 3 sea 5 ocean
Barracuda: 3 car 4 auto 8 Plymouth
barrage: 4 boom, fire, hail 5 blast, blitz, burst, salvo, shoot, storm, surge 6 attack, battle, deluge, launch, shower, volley 7 assault, battery, bombard, gunfire 8 enfilade, fire upon, plethora, shelling 9 avalanche, broadside, cannonade, crossfire, discharge, fusillade, onslaught, profusion 10 cannonfire
media ~: 4 hype 5 blitz
naval ~: 5 salvo 6 volley 7 barrage 9 broadside, cannonade, fusillade
Barranquilla: 4 city, port, town
locale: 8 Colombia
barre: 4 tail 8 handrail
bend at the ~: 4 plie
Barre: 4 city, town
locale: 7 Vermont
barred: 8 excluded 9 unwelcome
barred ___: 3 owl
barrel: 3 fly, hie, keg, rip, run, tub, vat, zip 4 cask, dart, dash, drum, flit, race, rush, tear, zoom 5 hurry, scoot, speed 6 ashcan, firkin, gallop, hasten, hustle, move it, rocket, scurry 7 floor it, hop to it, oil unit, quicken, scamper 8 hogshead, OPEC unit, step on it 9 hotfoot it, shake a leg, skedaddle 10 burn rubber, get a move on, hightail it
beer ~: 3 keg
bottom contents: 4 lees 5 dregs 8 sediment
bottom of the ~: 5 worst
component: 4 hoop 5 stave
diameter: 4 bore
ender: 4 head 5 house
filler: 4 beer, pork, wine
fraction: 6 gallon
groove: 5 croze
herring ~: 4 cade
hoop wood: 3 elm
into: 3 ram 7 collide, rear-end
lock, stock and ~: 6 in toto, wholly
maker: 6 cooper
of laughs: 4 card, riot
oil ~: 4 drum
open a ~: 3 tap
over a ~: 5 broke 7 trapped 8 helpless 9 penniless
pork ~: 9 patronage
stopper: 4 bung
barrel ___: 4 bolt, cuff, knot, race, roll, roof 5 chair, chest, organ 6 cactus, engine, racing
barrel-___: 5 racer 7 chested, vaulted
___ barrel: 4 pork 5 over a
___-barrel: 6 single 7 cracker
___ Barrel: 7 Cracker
barrel-back ___: 5 chair
___-barreled: 6 double
barreleye: 4 fish
___ barrelhead: 5 on the
barrelhouse: 3 bar
barrelmaker, name meaning: 6 Cooper
barrel of ___: 6 laughs 7 monkeys
Barrel-Organ, The author: Alfred Noyes
___ Barrel Polka: 4 Beer
barrels: 4 a lot, lots, tons 5 heaps, scads
barrel-shaped obj.: 3 cyl. 8 cylinder
barren: 3 dry 4 arid, bald, bare, dull, poor, vain, void 5 blank, bleak, empty, stark, vapid, waste 6 desert, devoid, effete, fallow, severe, used up, vacant 7 austere, drained, parched, Spartan, sterile, useless, vacated 8 depleted, deserted, desolate, infecund, lifeless 9 bare-bones, evacuated, exhausted, fruitless, infertile, unadorned 10 lackluster, profitless, unprolific
area: 6 desert, Sahara
barrenness: 9 austerity 10 desolation
barrens: 5 wilds 10 wilderness
___ barrens: 4 pine
Barrès, Maurice: 6 French, writer
Barrett: 3 Syd 4 Rona 5 Majel
___ Barrett Browning: 9 Elizabeth
barrette: 4 clip
Barretts of Wimpole Street, The (1934 film)
cast: Charles Laughton, Fredric March, Norma Shearer
barricade: 3 bar, dam 4 dike, jump, stop, wall, weir 5 block, fence 6 hurdle, shut in 7 bulwark, defense, rampart 8 obstruct, palisade 9 roadblock 10 difficulty, impediment
barbed-wire ~: 6 abatis
Barrie: 4 city, Mona, town 5 Chase, Wendy 7 Barbara 10 Pan creator
character: 4 Smee 5 Wendy 8 Peter Pan
locale: 6 Canada 7 Ontario
Barrie, Barbara: 7 actress
film: Breaking Away (1979)
Judy Berlin (2000)
One Potato, Two Potato (1964)
Barrie, James M.: 6 author 8 Scottish 10 playwright
dog: 4 Nana
work: The Admirable Crichton
Dear Brutus
Peter Pan
Quality Street
What Every Woman Knows
The Will
barrier: 3 bar, dam 4 dike, gate, moat, rail, reef, snag, wall, weir 5 block, fence, hedge, limit, minus 6 hurdle 7 embargo, railing, rampart 8 blockade, boundary, drawback, handicap, obstacle, weakness 9 detriment, hindrance, liability, partition, restraint 10 bottleneck, impediment, protection
build a better ~: 5 redam
court ~: 3 net
farm ~: 4 rail 5 fence
island: 3 cay, key
mosquito ~: 3 net
movable ~: 4 gate
openwork ~: 5 grill 6 grille
race-winner's ~: 4 tape
river ~: 4 dike 5 levee 10 embankment
room ~: 4 wall
water ~: 3 dam 4 dike, mole, weir 5 jetty, levee, wharf 7 sea wall 10 breakwater, embankment
zoo ~: 4 moat
barrier ___: 4 reef 5 beach 6 island
___ barrier: 4 heat 5 sonic, sound, trade, vapor 7 thermal
___ Barrier Reef: 5 Great
barring: 3 but 6 except, unless 7 besides 9 exception 10 leaving out
this: 4 else 9 otherwise
barrio: 4 slum 6 ghetto 7 quarter
city: 6 East L.A.
kid: 4 niña, niño 8 muchacha, muchacho
store: 6 bodega
Barrios, Eduardo: 6 writer 7 Chilean
Barris, Chuck: 2 MC 4 host 5 emcee
barrister: 3 att. 4 atty. 6 jurist, lawyer, legist 7 counsel 8 advocate, attorney 9 counselor, solicitor
org.: 3 ABA
wear: 3 wig
Barron: 5 Steve
Barron's
reader: 4 exec, lion, suit 6 broker, tycoon 7 magnate 8 investor
rival: 6 Forbes 7 Fortune
subject.: 2 co. 4 corp., firm 5 stock 7 company 8 business
barroom: 3 pub 4 dive 5 local 6 lounge, saloon, tavern 7 gin mill, taproom 8 alehouse, groggery, grog shop, taphouse 9 speakeasy
see also bar
barroom ___: 5 brawl, plant
barrow: 3 hog 4 cart, hill 5 dolly, mound, swine 7 tumulus 8 handcart, pushcart 9 hand truck
in America: 8 pushcart
starter: 4 hand 5 wheel
Barrow: 4 city, town 5 Clyde
locale: 6 Alaska
resident: 6 Eskimo
___ Barrow: 5 Point
Barry: 3 Len 4 Dave, Gene, Gibb, Jeff, Mann, Rick 5 Bonds, Morse, White, Young 6 Diller, Gordon, Kelley, Marion, Nelson, Newman, Philip, Sadler 7 Manilow, McGuire 8 Bostwick, DeVorzon, Levinson, Sullivan, Williams 9 Goldwater, Sharpless 10 Fitzgerald, Livingston, Sonnenfeld
Barry, Gene: 5 actor
film: China Gate (1957)
Thunder Road (1958)
The War of the Worlds (1953)
TV: Bat Masterson, Burke's Law, The Name of the Game
Barry Lyndon (1975 film)
cast: Marisa Berenson, Patrick Magee, Ryan O'Neal
director: Stanley Kubrick
Barrymore: 4 Drew, John 5 Ethel 6 Lionel
Barrymore, Diana to Ethel: 5 niece
Barrymore, Drew: 7 actress
film: Boys on the Side (1995)
Charlie's Angels (2000)
E.T. The Extra-Terrestrial (1982)
Ever After (1998)
Firestarter (1984)
Guncrazy (1992)
Irreconcilable Differences (1984)
Never Been Kissed (1999)
Scream (1996)
The Wedding Singer (1998)
Barrymore, Ethel: 7 actress
film: Deadline U.S.A. (1952)
The Farmer's Daughter (1947)
Just for You (1952)
Kind Lady (1951)
None But the Lonely Heart (1944, AA)
Pinky (1949)
Portrait of Jennie (1948)
Rasputin and the Empress (1932)
The Spiral Staircase (1946)
Barrymore, John: 5 actor
film: Arsene Lupin (1932)
The Beloved Rogue (1927)
A Bill of Divorcement (1932)
Counsellor-at-Law (1933)
Dinner at Eight (1933)
Don Juan (1926)
Dr. Jekyll and Mr. Hyde (1920)
Grand Hotel (1932)
The Great Man Votes (1939)
Hold That Co-ed (1938)
The Invisible Woman (1941)
The Mad Genius (1931)
Maytime (1937)
Midnight (1939)
Rasputin and the Empress (1932)
Reunion in Vienna (1933)
Romeo and Juliet (1936)
State's Attorney (1932)
Svengali (1931)
Tempest (1928)
Topaze (1933)
Twentieth Century (1934)
Barrymore, Lionel: 5 actor
film: Ah, Wilderness! (1935)
Arsene Lupin (1932)
Broken Lullaby (1932)
Camille (1937)
Captains Courageous (1937)
David Copperfield (1935)
The Devil-Doll (1936)
Dinner at Eight (1933)
Down to the Sea in Ships (1949)
A Family Affair (1937)
A Free Soul (1931, AA)
The Girl From Missouri (1934)
Guilty Hands (1931)
It's a Wonderful Life (1946)
The Little Colonel (1935)
Mark of the Vampire (1935)
Mata Hari (1932)
On Borrowed Time (1939)
Rasputin and the Empress (1932)
The Road to Glory (1936)
Sadie Thompson (1928)
The Stranger's Return (1933)
Sweepings (1933)
West of Zanzibar (1928)
A Yank at Oxford (1938)
The Yellow Ticket (1931)
You Can't Take It With You (1938)
Barry, Philip: 6 author, writer
work: The Philadelphia Story
Barry, Rick: 5 cager
milieu: 5 court
org.: 3 NBA
sport: 10 basketball
bars: 4 jail 6 prison
final ~: 4 coda
frequent ~: 4 tope 8 pub-crawl
game square with ~: 4 jail
mdse. ~: 3 UPC
one behind ~: 6 inmate 7 convict 8 prisoner
___ bars: 6 behind, killer, monkey
Barstow: 4 city, Stan, town
locale: 10 California
Barstow, Stan: 7 British 10 playwright
Bart: 5 Starr 6 Lionel 7 Simpson 8 Maverick 9 Braverman
sister: 4 Lisa
to Homer: 3 son
to Lisa: 3 bro 7 brother
bartender: 10 mixologist
band: 6 garter
request: 2 ID
see also bar
barter: 4 deal, sell, swap, swop 5 bandy, trade 6 change, dicker, haggle 7 traffic 8 exchange 10 quid pro quo
Bartered Bride, The: 5 opera
composer: 7 Smetana
barterer, birthright: 4 Esau
Barth: 4 John, Karl
Barthelme, Donald: 6 writer
Barthelmess, Richard: 5 actor
film: Broken Blossoms (1919)
Four Hours to Kill (1935)
Heroes for Sale (1933)
The Last Flight (1931)
Only Angels Have Wings (1939)
Tol'able David (1921)
Way Down East (1920)
Barth, John: 6 author, writer
work: Chimera
Coming Soon!!!
Giles Goat-Boy
Lost in the Funhouse
Sabbatical
The Sot-Weed Factor
The Tidewater Tales
Bartholdi: 8 Frédéric
contemporary: 5 Rodin

Bartholomew: **5** saint **7** Freddie
Bartholomew, Freddie: **5** actor
film: Anna Karenina (1935)
Captains Courageous (1937)
David Copperfield (1935)
Little Lord Fauntleroy (1936)
Lloyd's of London (1936)
Swiss Family Robinson (1940)
Bartles partner: **6** Jaymes
Bartlesville: **4** city, town
locale: **4** Okla. **8** Oklahoma
Bartlett: **4** city, Hall, John, pear, town **6** Bonnie **8** Jennifer
locale: **8** Illinois **9** Tennessee
relative: **4** Bosc **5** Anjou **6** Comice, Seckel
Bartlett, John: **6** writer **8** compiler
work: Familiar Quotations
Bartlett's entry: **4** anon., quot. **5** quote **9** anonymous
Bartok: **3** Eva
Bartók, Béla
work: Bluebeard's Castle
Concerto for Orchestra
Mikrokosmos
The Miraculous Mandarin
Petite Suite
Bartolomeo: **10** Cristofori
see also Italian
Bartolomeu: **4** Dias
Barton: **4** Enos, Fink **5** Clara, Derek **7** Charles, MacLane
Barton, Charles: **8** director
film: Abbott and Costello Meet Frankenstein (1948)
Africa Screams (1949)
Buck Privates Come Home (1947)
Dance With Me Henry (1956)
The Last Outpost (1935)
Mexican Hayride (1948)
The Noose Hangs High (1948)
The Shaggy Dog (1959)
The Time of Their Lives (1946)
The Wistful Widow of Wagon Gap (1947)
Barton, Clara: **5** nurse
Barton, Derek: **7** chemist **8** Nobelist
Barton Fink (1991 film)
cast: Judy Davis, John Goodman, John Turturro
director: Joel Coen
Barty: **5** Billy
Baruch: **7** Bernard, Spinoza **8** Blumberg
Baruntse: **4** peak **5** mount **8** mountain
locale: **4** Asia **5** Nepal **9** Himalayas
baryon: **8** particle
container: **4** atom
Baryshnikov, Mikhail: **6** dancer **7** danseur, Latvian, Russian
birthplace: **4** Riga **6** Latvia
specialty: **6** ballet
baryton: **6** string **8** bass viol
Barzona: **3** cow **4** bull **6** bovine, cattle
Barzun, Jacques: **6** author, writer
bas ___: **4** bleu **6** mizvah **7** mitsvah, mitzvah
bas-___: **6** relief
Bas-___: **4** Rhin
basal: **5** basic, least **6** bottom, lowest **7** minimum, organic, primary, radical **10** elementary, underlying
basal ___: **4** body, cell, disk **5** ridge **7** granule
basalt: **4** lava, rock **7** mineral
base: **3** bad, bag, bed, KOH, low **4** butt, camp, evil, foot, foul, home, lewd, mean, NaOH, post, root, sack, seat, site, ugly, vile **5** abode, cheap, crude, depot, first, found, hinge, lousy, lowly, model, seamy, small, snide, sorry, stand, third, wrong **6** abject, alkali, bottom, center, coarse, common, depend, derive, dismal, ground, humble, little, locate, menial, odious, origin, second, shoddy, sleazy, sneaky, sordid, trashy, unholy, vulgar, wicked **7** abysmal, accurst, beastly, bedrock, bestial, caddish, corrupt, footing, heinous, ignoble, immoral, knavish, lowdown, roguish, servile, squalid, station, support **8** accursed, backbone, beggarly, cowardly, degraded, depraved, dreadful, foothold, garrison, home port, indecent, plebeian, shameful, sinister, stinking, terminal, terrible, unworthy, wretched **9** abhorrent, construct, dastardly, establish, home plate, hydroxide, invidious, loathsome, nefarious, offensive, predicate, repugnant, revolting, underside **10** abominable, despicable, foundation, groundwork, indecorous, indelicate, iniquitous, lower-class, maleficent, settlement, substratum, traitorous, villainous
baseball ~: **3** bag **4** home **5** first, third **6** second
be off ~: **3** err
clearer: **5** homer
computer ~: **6** binary
ender: **3** man **4** ball, born, less, line **5** board **6** burner
formula: **3** KOH **4** NaOH
kind of ~ hit: **5** bloop **6** looper **9** line drive
neutralizer: **4** acid
numerical ~: **5** radix
off ~: **4** AWOL **5** amiss, wrong **6** afield **8** mistaken **10** inaccurate, inapposite
of operations: **7** station
reach ~ headfirst: **5** slide
set up ~: **4** camp **6** encamp **7** bivouac
starter: **4** data, fire **5** wheel
touch ~: **4** talk **5** phone, tag up **7** contact **9** telephone
see also army, military
base ___: **3** box, hit, map, pay **4** camp, line, load, pair, path, rate, unit, wage **5** house, level, metal, price **6** burner, estate, period, runner, salary, tenant **7** bullion, running, station
___ base: **3** air **4** data, home, rate **5** Attic, cloud, first, Lewis, power, third, touch **6** kettle, second
___-base: **3** off **4** zero
___ Base: **5** Ace of
baseball: **4** game **5** sport **6** sphere **8** card game
area: **5** mound **6** dugout **7** bullpen, infield **8** backstop, outfield **10** scoreboard
assistant: **6** bat boy
award: **3** MVP
base: **3** bag **4** home **5** first, third **6** second
bat first in ~: **7** lead off
bat wood: **3** ash
boss: **2** GM **3** mgr. **5** owner **7** manager
broadcaster: **4** Buck **5** Allen, Canel, Caray, Gowdy, Wolff **6** Barber, Hodges, Murphy, Nelson, Prince, Scully, Uecker **7** Harwell **8** Bob Wolff, Hamilton, Jack Buck, McCarver, Mel Allen **9** Bob Murphy, Bob Prince, Bob Uecker, Buck Canel, Curt Gowdy, Garagiola, Red Barber, Vin Scully **10** Brickhouse, Harry Caray, Russ Hodges
cap feature: **5** visor, vizor
card company: **5** Topps
class AAA ~: **6** minors
climax, usually: **5** ninth
club: **3** bat
contents of a ~ bag: **5** rosin
division: **6** inning
event: **3** fly, hit, out **4** foul, walk **5** bloop, drive, homer, pop-up, steal **6** looper, series **9** line drive
family name: **4** Alou
fare: **6** hot dog
feature: **4** seam
fourth hitter: **7** clean-up
fumble: **5** error **6** bobble
gear: **4** mitt **5** glove **6** helmet
Hall of Fame executive: **5** Frick, Giles, Veeck **6** Barrow, Landis, Rickey, Yawkey **7** Johnson **8** Chandler, Ed Barrow, Griffith, MacPhail, Spalding **9** Bill Veeck, Ford Frick, Tom Yawkey **10** Ban Johnson
Hall of Fame manager: **4** Mack **5** Lopez, Selee **6** Alston, Hanlon, Harris, McGraw, Weaver **7** Al Lopez, Huggins, Lasorda, Stengel **8** Anderson, Durocher, McCarthy **9** McKechnie, Ned Hanlon **10** Connie Mack, Earl Weaver, Frank Selee, John McGraw
Hall of Fame player: **3** Day, Fox, Ott **4** Babe, Bell, Cobb, Dean, Doby, Fisk, Ford, Foxx, Hoyt, Mays, Mize, Rice, Ruth, Ryan, Wynn, Yogi **5** Aaron, Anson, Banks, Bench, Brett, Brock, Carew, Combs, Doerr, Evers, Flick, Gomez, Grove, Irvin, Kiner, Klein, Lemon, Paige, Perez, Reese, Rixey, Roush, Rusie, Smith, Spahn, Terry, Vance, Waner, Wheat, Young, Yount **6** Bender, Carter, Cepeda, Cronin, Cuyler, Dihigo, Feller, Foster, Frisch, Gehrig, Gibson, Goslin, Hunter, Kaline, Koufax, Lajoie, Mantle, Mel Ott, Morgan, Murray, Musial, Niekro, Palmer, Seaver, Sisler, Snider, Sutton, Ty Cobb, Wagner, Wilson **7** Appling, Ashburn, Averill, Bunning, Carlton, Collins, Cy Young, Fingers, Hornsby, Hubbell, Jackson, Jenkins, Johnson, Lazzeri, Leon Day, Mathews, McCovey, Medwick, Puckett, Rizzuto, Roberts, Ruffing, Sam Rice, Schmidt, Speaker, Stearns, Traynor, Vaughan, Waddell, Wilhelm **8** Al Kaline, Aparicio, Babe Ruth, Bob Lemon, Boudreau, Cap Anson, Clemente, Cochrane, DiMaggio, Drysdale, Edd Roush, Lou Brock, Marichal, Marquard, Robinson, Rod Carew, Stargell, Williams, Winfield **9** Alexander, Amos Rusie, Bill Terry, Bob Feller, Bob Gibson, Dandridge, Dizzy Dean, Don Sutton, Early Wynn, Eppa Rixey, Greenberg, Hank Aaron, Jim Palmer, Joe Cronin, Joe Morgan, Killebrew, Larry Doby, Lou Gehrig, Mathewson, Mazeroski, Nap Lajoie, Nellie Fox, Newhouser, Nolan Ryan, Paul Waner, Radbourne, Slaughter, Tom Seaver, Tony Perez, Waite Hoyt, Yogi Berra, Zack Wheat **10** Bobby Doerr, Campanella, Charleston, Chuck Klein, Dazzy Vance, Duke Snider, Earle Combs, Elmer Flick, Ernie Banks, Gary Carter, Hack Wilson, Jim Bunning, Jimmie Foxx, Joe Medwick, Josh Gibson, Kiki Cuyler, Lefty Gomez, Lefty Grove, Lloyd Waner, Monte Irvin, Ozzie Smith, Phil Niekro, Pie Traynor, Ralph Kiner, Red Ruffing, Robin Yount, Rube Foster, Stan Musial, Whitey Ford, Willie Mays **11** Yastrzemski
Hall of Fame umpire: **4** Klem **6** Chylak, Conlan **7** Barlick, Hubbard **8** Bill Klem **9** Al Barlick
hit: **4** bunt **5** drive, homer **6** double, single, triple **7** home run **9** line drive
home run in ~: **6** dinger
hot corner: **5** third
infraction: **4** balk
inning: **5** frame
kind of ~ game: **5** no-run **8** no-hitter
league: **4** Amer., Natl. **8** American, National
list: **6** lineup, roster
miscue: **5** error
next in ~: **6** on deck
nickname: **3** Yaz
not fair in ~: **4** foul
not foul in ~: **4** fair
not out in ~: **4** safe
objective: **3** win **7** pennant
official in ~: **3** ump **6** umpire
pass: **4** walk
pitch: **6** sinker, slider **8** change-up, forkball, splitter
pitcher and catcher in ~: **7** battery
ploy: **4** bunt **5** slide, steal **7** squeeze **8** pitchout **9** sacrifice
pop fly: **5** bloop **6** looper
position: **2** CF, LF, RF, SS **7** baseman, catcher, pitcher **9** shortstop
rare ~ game: **5** no-hit **8** no-hitter
score: **3** run
scoreboard heading: **3** RHE
shoe piece: **5** cleat
situation: **5** one on, two on
solid hit, in ~: **5** liner **9** line drive
star: **3** Cey, Nen **4** Agee, Alou, Blue, Gant, Kaat, Mota, Nomo, Otis, Rose, Sosa, Valo, Yost **5** Bando, Belle, Boggs, Bonds, Brown, Burks, Davis, Evans, Grace, Gwynn, Jeter, Lopes, Maris, Oliva, Reese, Staub, Tatis, Tiant, Torre **6** Alomar, Baines, Baylor, Dawson, Franco, Garvey, Harrah, Hodges, Maddux, Maglie, Newsom, Olerud, Orosco, Pappas, Piazza, Pinson, Pujols, Raines, Ripken, Ron Cey, Suzuki, Tanana, Thomas, Walker **7** Bagwell, Canseco, Clemens, Glavine, Gossage, Griffey, Jim Kaat, Johnson, McGriff, McGwire, Molitor, Nettles, Ramirez, Robb Nen, Ron Gant, Ventura **8** Amos Otis, Blyleven, Joe Torre, Martinez, Palmeiro, Pete Rose, Sal Bando, Sandberg, Trammell, Vida Blue, Williams **9** Cal Ripken, Eddie Yost, Elmer Valo, Galarraga, Gil Hodges, Henderson, Hershiser, Hideo Nomo, Luis Tiant, Manny Mota, Mark Grace, Sal Maglie, Sammy Sosa, Schilling, Tim Raines, Tony Gwynn, Tony Oliva, Wade Boggs **10** Barry Bonds, Bobby Bonds, Bobo Newsom, Davey Lopes, Derek Jeter, Greg Maddux, John Franco, Ken Griffey, Mike Piazza, Milt Pappas, Moises Alou, Roger Maris, Rusty Staub, Toby Harrah, Tommie Agee, Vada Pinson
stat in ~: **2** AB, HR, SB **3** ERA, RBI **4** save **5** at bat, ribby **6** assist, putout **7** shutout
strikeout: **5** whiff
tag: **3** out
team: **4** Cubs, Mets, Reds **5** Expos, Twins **6** Angels, Astros, Braves, Giants, Padres, Red Sox, Royals, Tigers **7** Brewers, Dodgers, Indians, Marlins, Orioles, Pirates, Rangers, Rockies, Yankees **8** Blue Jays, Mariners, Phillies, White Sox **9** Athletics, Cardinals, Devil Rays
term: **3** bag, bat, fly, hit, out, RBI, run,

tag, ump **4** balk, bunt, fair, foul, home, safe, save, walk **5** at bat, bloop, error, fungo, homer, mound, no-hit, pitch, plate, slump, steal, swing, tag up, whiff **6** assist, batboy, bobble, clutch, dinger, double, inning, lineup, on base, on deck, pop fly, put-out, rubber, single, sinker, slider, strike, triple, umpire, windup **7** battery, bullpen, catcher, clean-up, fielder, home run, infield, lead off, pennant, pick off, pitcher, rundown, sandlot, shutout, slugger, squeeze **8** backstop, box score, change-up, farm team, forkball, grounder, no-hitter, outfield, pitchout, southpaw, splitter
throw: **3** peg
up, in ~: **5** at bat
VIP: **3** mgr, ump **5** coach **6** umpire **7** manager
woe: **4** loss **5** slump
baseball ___: **3** bat, cap **5** glove
___ baseball: **6** indoor **7** sandlot
baseball-card flaw: **6** crease
___ Baseball Confederacy, The: **4** Iowa
baseballer: **4** ALer, NLer
California ~: **5** Angel
Chicago ~: **3** Cub
Cincinnati ~: **3** Red
Detroit ~: **5** Tiger
Kansas City ~: **5** Royal
Minnesota ~: **4** Twin
New York ~: **3** Met **4** Yank **6** Yankee
San Diego ~: **5** Padre
San Francisco ~: **5** Giant
Texas ~: **5** Astro
Baseball is ___ of inches: **5** a game
Baseball Tonight network: **4** ESPN
baseborn: **3** low **5** lowly **6** common, vulgar **7** ignoble **8** plebeian, ungentle, untitled **10** lower-class
___-base budgeting: **4** zero
based: **7** located
be ~ on: **4** rest **6** depend
___-based: **5** broad **7** reality
based on ___ story: **5** a true
Basehart, Richard: **5** actor
film: Decision Before Dawn (1952)
Fourteen Hours (1951)
He Walked by Night (1948)
La Strada (1954)
Moby Dick (1956)
The Satan Bug (1965)
Time Limit (1957)
TV: Voyage to the Bottom of the Sea
___-base hit: **3** one, two **5** extra, three
Basel: **4** city, font, town **8** typeface
locale: Switzerland
river: **5** Rhine
Basel-___: **4** Land **5** Stadt
baseless: **4** idle **6** flimsy, untrue **7** invalid **8** fanciful, spurious **9** erroneous, unfounded, untenable **10** bottomless, fallacious, gratuitous, groundless, ill-founded
baseline
beyond the ~: **4** foul
in geometry: **5** x-axis
material: **4** lime
___ baseman: **5** first, third **6** second
Basemath husband: **4** Esau
basement: **5** floor **6** cellar
bargain ~ caveat: **3** irr. **4** as is **5** irreg.
fixture: **5** drier, dryer **6** boiler, washer **7** furnace
in the ~: **4** last **5** below
like a wet ~: **4** dank **5** moldy, musty **6** smelly **8** mildewed
opposite: **4** loft **5** attic
reading: **5** meter
seating: **5** stool
___ basement: **7** bargain
baseness: **4** evil **8** iniquity, venality **9** depravity **10** corruption
Basenji: **3** dog **5** canid, hound **6** canine
baby ~: **3** pup **5** puppy
base on ___: **5** balls
___-base paint: **3** oil **5** water **6** rubber
baserunner ploy: **4** lead **5** steal
bases
all ~ covered: **5** ready **8** prepared
column ~: **4** tori
___ base with: **5** touch
bash: **2** do **3** bit, hit **4** beat, belt, blow, club, fest, fete, gala, mall, maul, orgy, slam, slap, slug **5** abuse, blast, flail, knock, party, paste, pound, punch, smash, smite, spree, swipe, thump, whack, whang, wreck **6** assail, attack, batter, fiesta, strike, thwack, wallop **7** assault, blowout, clobber, rough up, shindig, trounce **8** jamboree, mistreat, uppercut, wingding **9** criticize, festivity
celebrity ~: **5** roast
old-style: **5** smite
throw a ~: **4** host
see also party
basher: **6** critic
___ Bashevis Singer: **5** Isaac
bashful: **3** coy, shy **5** aloof, chary, mousy, timid **6** demure, humble, modest, mousey, silent **7** ashamed, distant **8** blushing, reserved, reticent, retiring, sheepish, timorous **9** diffident, flinching, reclusive, shrinking, withdrawn **10** unassuming, uneffusive
Bashful: **5** dwarf
colleague: **3** Doc **5** Dopey, Happy **6** Grumpy, Sleepy, Sneezy
bashfulness: **7** modesty
Bashkir: **8** republic
capital: **3** Ufa
Basho, Matsuo: **4** poet **8** Japanese
verse: **5** haiku
basic: **3** key, raw **4** bare, easy, elem., main, real **5** basal, plain, stock, vital **6** bottom, earthy, innate, simple, staple **7** central, initial, minimal, organic, primary, radical, unfussy **8** alkaline, cardinal, inherent, integral, standard, ultimate **9** elemental, essential, innermost, intrinsic, necessary, primitive, principal, right-hand, uncomplex, vestigial **10** elementary, primordial, underlying
assumption: **5** axiom, given **9** principle
beliefs: **5** ethos
idea: **4** core, gist, pith **5** drift, heart **7** essence, keynote
not ~: **6** acidic
skills: **3** RRR **4** ABCs
solution: **6** alkali
unit: **4** atom **8** molecule
basic ___: **3** dye **4** rate, salt, slag, wage **5** dress, steel **6** salary, weight **7** fuchsin, magenta, plumage, process
BASIC: **8** language
alternative: **3** ADA, APL, SQL **4** Alef, html, Icon, Java, LISP, Logo, Orca, Perl **5** Algol, Cecil, COBOL, Dylan, SISAL **6** Delphi, Eiffel, Erlang, Oberon, Pascal, Prolog, Sather, Scheme, Snobol **7** Fortran
term: **3** rem **4** go to
basically: **7** at heart **8** in effect **9** in essence, primarily, radically, virtually **10** implicitly, inherently, originally, ultimately
Basic 4: **6** cereal
competitor: **3** Kix **4** Life, Trix **5** Kashi, Quisp, Total **6** Kaboom, Muesli, Oreo O's, Pablum, Smacks **7** All-Bran, Crispix, Harmony, Hunny B's, Mueslix, Oat Bran, Pokemon **8** Boo Berry, Cheerios, Corn Chex, Corn Pops, Fiber One, Rice Chex, Special K, Uncle Sam, Wheaties **9** Alpha Bits, Apple Zaps, Grape Nuts, Honey Comb, Just Right, Wheat Chex **10** Apple Jacks, Bran Flakes, Cap'n Crunch, Cocoa Puffs, Froot Loops, Mini-Wheats, Nutri-Grain, Puffed Rice, Quaker Oats, Smart Start **11** Cocoa Blasts, Cookie Crisp, Golden Crisp, Lucky Charms, Puffed Wheat, Sweet Crunch, Waffle Crisp
Basic Instinct (1992 film)
cast: Michael Douglas, George Dzundza, Sharon Stone
director: Paul Verhoeven
basics: **4** ABCs **5** needs **8** training **9** resources, rudiments
get down to ~: **6** lay out **7** explain **8** simplify, spell out
Basic Training of Pavlo Hummel, The
author: David Rabe
basidium: **6** fungus
Basie, Count: **7** pianist, William **10** bandleader
genre: **4** jazz
basil: **4** herb
sauce: **5** pesto
___ basil: **4** bush **5** sweet
Basil: **4** Toni **5** saint **7** Dearden, Radford **8** Rathbone
costar: **5** Nigel
in Russian: **6** Vasily
successor: **4** Ivan
Basilan ___: **7** Islands
Basile, Giambattista: **6** writer **7** Italian
basilica: **6** church, temple **9** cathedral **10** tabernacle
feature: **3** pew **4** apse, nave
treasure: **4** icon, ikon **5** eikon
Basilio, Carmen: **5** boxer
milieu: **4** ring
Basil, Toni song: Mickey (1982)
basin: **3** bay, pot, tub **4** bowl, ewer, font, lake, pond, pool, sink **5** fiord, fjord, inlet, lough **6** harbor, hollow, valley, vessel **7** harbour **8** boatyard, washbowl **9** container, reservoir, watershed **10** depression
catch ~: **4** sump
cirque ~: **4** tarn
companion: **4** ewer **7** pitcher
geological ~: **4** tala
holy-water ~: **4** font **5** stoup
mountain ~: **3** cwm **6** cirque
parker: **5** yacht
starter: **4** wash
stone ~: **6** lavabo
___ basin: **4** slop **5** catch, river, sugar, tidal **6** geyser, plunge **7** pouring
Basin ___: **6** Street
___ Basin: **4** Saar **5** Great, Minas, Tarim **6** Donets
Basinger, Kim: **7** actress
film: Batman (1989)
Cool World (1992)
Final Analysis (1992)
L.A. Confidential (1997, AA)
The Marrying Man (1991)
My Stepmother Is an Alien (1988)
Nadine (1987)
The Natural (1984)
Never Say Never Again (1983)
spouse: Alec Baldwin
basis: **3** bed, eat **4** core, crux, root **5** cause, gauge **6** ground, motive, origin, reason, source, theory **7** essence, footing, grounds, keynote, nucleus, premise, pretext, warrant **8** backbone, evidence, keystone, occasion, rudiment **9** authority, criterion, principle **10** antecedent, assumption, derivation, foundation, groundwork
movie ~ often: **4** book, play **5** novel
of comparison: **6** analog
of life: **6** carbon
tax ~: **5** ratal **10** assessment
without ~: **9** unfounded
basis ___: **5** point **6** weight
___ basis: **4** cash, gold **7** accrual
bask: **3** sun, tan **4** laze, loll **5** relax **6** lounge, wallow **8** sunbathe **9** luxuriate
in: **5** revel, savor **7** delight
basker acquisition: **3** tan
Baskerville: **4** font **8** typeface
Baskervilles beast: **5** hound
basket: **4** hoop **5** score **6** dosser, hamper **10** two-pointer
capacity: **4** peck **6** bushel
easy ~: **5** lay up, tap in
ender: **4** ball
farm ~: **4** peck, skep **6** bushel
filler: **4** eggs **5** fruit **6** apples **7** produce
for dried fruit: **5** frail
jai alai ~: **5** cesta
like a ~: **5** woven
made a ~: **4** sank, wove
make a ~: **4** sink **5** plait, score, weave
making: **5** craft
Mexican ~ grass: **5** otate
picnic ~: **6** hamper
starter: **5** bread, waste
weaver's twig: **5** osier, withe **6** willow
wicker ~: **5** creel
basket ___: **4** fern, fish, hilt, star **5** chair, weave **6** dinner, flower
___ basket: **3** tea **5** salad **6** market, picnic, pollen **7** pouring, steamer
basketball: **3** orb **4** game **5** hoops, sport **6** sphere
announcer's cry: **5** swish
area in ~: **5** court **8** foul line
brand: **4** Voit
call: **4** foul
center's position: **5** pivot
coach: **3** Iba, Yow **4** Daly, Rupp **5** Brown, Olson **6** Knight, Wooden **7** Holzman **8** Auerbach **10** Carnesecca
defunct ~ org.: **3** ABA
filler: **3** air
Hall of Famer: **3** Iba, Yow **4** Bing, Bird, Daly, Gola, Reed, Rupp, West **5** Barry, Brown, Cousy, Greer, Hayes, Issel, Jones, Lucas, Mikan, Olson **6** Baylor, Cowens, Erving, Gervin, Holman, Kay Yow, Knight, Lanier, Malone, McAdoo, Meyers, Monroe, Pettit, Thomas, Twyman, Unseld, Walton, Wooden **7** Bellamy, Bradley, Frazier, Holzman, Johnson, K.C. Jones, Russell, Schayes, Tom Gola, Wilkens **8** Auerbach, Bob Cousy, Dan Issel, Dave Bing, Goodrich, Hal Greer, Havlicek, Heinsohn, Maravich, Petrovic, Sam Jones, Thurmond **9** Ann Meyers, Archibald, Bob Lanier, Bob McAdoo, Bob Pettit, Jerry West, Larry Bird, Nat Holman, Robertson, Wes Unseld **10** Bill Walton, Carnesecca, Dave Cowens, Earl Monroe, Elvin Hayes, Jerry Lucas, John Wooden **11** Abdul-Jabbar, Chamberlain, DeBusschere
hoop site: **5** court **6** garage
infraction: **4** foul **7** palming
like many ~ pros: **4** tall **5** rangy
maneuver: **4** dunk, pass, pick, shot **5** block, press, steal **7** dribble, rebound
1997 ~ film: **6** Air Bud
org.: **3** NBA
path: **3** arc **5** curve
player: **5** cager **8** hoopster

position: 3 ctr. 5 guard 6 center 7 forward
shot: 4 dunk 5 lay up, tip-in 8 slam dunk
star: 3 Bol 4 Kidd 5 O'Neal 6 Bryant, Jordan, Malone, Parish, Pippen, Rodman 7 Gilmore, Iverson 8 Mourning, Olajuwon 9 Manute Bol
starter in ~: 6 tip-off
stat: 5 point 6 assist
substitute in ~: 8 sixth man
target: 3 net, rim 4 hoop
team: 4 Cavs, five, Heat, Jazz, Mavs, Nets, Suns 5 Bucks, Bulls, Hawks, Kings, Magic, Spurs 6 Knicks, Lakers, Pacers, Sixers 7 Celtics, Hornets, Nuggets, Pistons, Raptors, Rockets, Wizards 8 Clippers, Warriors 9 Cavaliers, Grizzlies, Mavericks
term: 3 rim 4 dunk, foul, hoop, pass 5 block, court, guard, lay up, press, shoot, steal, swish 6 center, period, tip-off 7 dribble, forward, palming, rebound, set shot, time-out 8 foul line, foul shot, hook shot, jump ball, jump shot, overtime, sixth man, slam dunk
tiebreaker: 2 OT 8 overtime
tourney: 3 NIT 4 NCAA
venue: 3 gym 5 arena, court
where ~ was first played: 4 YMCA
basketballer
Boston ~: 4 Celt 6 Celtic
Indiana ~: 5 Pacer
Los Angeles ~: 5 Laker
Miami ~: 4 Heat
New Jersey ~: 3 Net
Phoenix ~: 3 Sun
Sacramento ~: 4 King
San Antonio ~: 4 Spur
Seattle ~: 5 Sonic 10 SuperSonic
basketry palm: 4 nipa
Baskett: 5 James
basketwork material: 5 osier 6 willow
bit of: 4 twig 5 withe
Baskin-Robbins: 8 ice cream
competitor: 4 Edy's 7 Breyer's 9 Friendly's, Good Humor 10 Dairy Queen, Haagen Dazs, Turkey Hill
order: 4 cone
basmati: 4 rice 5 grain
Basov, Nicolay: 7 Russian 8 Nobelist 9 physicist
basque: 6 bodice
pas de ~: 4 step
saut de ~: 4 leap
Basque: 8 language
bonnet: 5 beret
port: 6 Bilbao
Basque __: 5 shirt
Basra: 4 city, port, town
locale: 4 Irak, Iraq
bass: 3 low 4 clef, deep, fish, male 5 Pinza, Ramey, range, voice 6 singer 7 caroler 8 game fish, low-toned, vocalist 9 Chaliapin, chorister, deep-toned, sport fish 10 low-pitched
booster: 3 amp
ender: 3 oon 4 wood
higher than ~: 5 tenor
instrument: 3 sax 4 viol 6 fiddle 9 saxophone
Italian ~: 5 Pinza
notation: 5 F clef
Russian ~: 9 Chaliapin
bass __: 3 sax 4 clef, drum, horn, viol 5 staff 6 fiddle, reflex
__ bass: 3 sea 4 kelp, rock 5 black, green, stone, white 6 calico, double, ground, silver, string 7 Alberti, channel, figured, striped, through, walking
Bass: 3 Sam 8 Fontella
Bass __: 3 Ale 6 Strait
Bassani, Giorgio: 6 writer 7 Italian
bass drum: 4 drum 8 gran casa
Basse-__: 5 Terre
Basses-__: 5 Alpes
basset __: 4 horn 5 hound, table
Basset: 3 dog 5 canid, hound 6 canine
comic-strip ~: 4 Fred
features: 4 ears
like ~ hounds' ears: 5 loppy 6 floppy
__ Basset: 4 Fred
Basse-Terre: 4 city, town 7 capital
locale: 10 Guadeloupe
Bassett, Angela: 7 actress
film: How Stella Got Her Groove Back (1998)
Malcolm X (1992)
Music of the Heart (1999)
The Score (2001)
Waiting to Exhale (1995)
What's Love Got to Do With It (1993)
Bassey, Shirley: 6 singer
song: Goldfinger (1965)
Bass, Fontella song: Rescue Me (1965)
bassinet: 3 bed 4 crib 6 cradle
bassist, jazz: 6 Mingus 7 Blanton 9 Pettiford
basslike fish: 5 snook
basso: 6 singer 9 chorister
basso-__: 7 relievo
bassoon: 4 reed, wind
cousin: 4 oboe
essentially: 4 tube
bass viol: 6 string 7 baryton
basswood: 4 tree 6 linden
bast: 4 hemp, jute, rope 5 fiber
fiber shrub: 5 urena
baste: 3 sew 4 beat, club, drub, lash, tack 5 pound, scold, whomp 6 batter, pummel, revile, stitch, thrash, wallop 7 clobber, moisten, trounce 9 castigate
basted: 5 moist
baster, turkey: 5 pipet 7 pipette
Bastia: 4 city, town
locale: 6 France
bastille: 4 gaol, jail 6 prison
Bastille __: 3 Day
Bastille locale: 5 Paris 6 France
bastinado: 6 cudgel 9 truncheon
basting, rip out: 5 unsew
__-basting turkey: 4 self
bastion: 4 rock, wall 7 bulwark, citadel, defense, parapet, rampart 8 fastness, fortress, mainstay 10 breastwork, stronghold
Basuto home: 6 Africa 7 Lesotho 8 Botswana
bat: 4 cane, club, flap, slam, slug, wink 5 blink, stick, whack 6 animal, cudgel, mammal 7 clobber, flutter, missile 8 bludgeon, rapidity 9 truncheon 10 fledermaus
again: 5 rehit
an eye: 4 wink 5 blink
around: 4 roam 5 drift, prowl 6 confer, debate, ramble, wander 7 discuss, meander 8 talk over
at ~: 4 turn 7 hitting
back and forth: 6 debate 7 discuss, hash out
baseball ~ wood: 3 ash
ender: 3 boy, man, men 4 fish, fowl, girl
eyelashes: 5 flirt
go to ~ for: 3 aid 4 back, help 6 assist, defend 7 endorse, indorse, stick by, support 8 advocate, champion 10 rally round, speak up for
haven: 4 cave 5 antre, attic 6 belfry
like a ~: 6 aliped
maker: 5 lathe
move like a ~: 4 flit
navigational aid: 4 echo 5 sonar
not ~ an eye: 8 keep cool 9 stay loose
of an eye: 4 jiff 5 jiffy 6 minute, second
right off the ~: 6 at once, pronto 7 quickly, rapidly, swiftly 8 in a flash, in no time, on the fly 9 instantly, like a shot
starter: 4 bull, ding 5 brick
swinger: 6 hitter
turns at ~: 6 inning
wield a ~: 5 swing
bat __: 3 boy, ray 4 girl, turn 6 mizvah 7 mitsvah, mitzvah
bat-__ fox: 5 eared
__ bat: 5 brown, fruit, fungo 7 mastiff, vampire
Bat: 9 Masterson
Bat*21 (1988 film)
cast: Danny Glover, Gene Hackman, Jerry Reed
batá: 4 drum
origin: 4 Cuba
Bataan: 6 battle 9 peninsula
Bataan (1943 film)
cast: George Murphy, Robert Taylor
director: Tay Garnett
Bataille, Georges: 6 French, writer
batajón: 4 drum
origin: 4 Cuba
Batan __: 7 Islands
Batang: 4 font 8 typeface
Batavia: 4 city, town
locale: 8 Illinois
batch: 3 lot, set 4 hunk, lump, mass, pack, pile, sort 5 array, bunch, clump, group, sheaf 6 amount, bundle 7 cluster, mixture 8 quantity, shipment 10 assemblage, assortment, collection, cumulation
color ~: 6 dye lot
miller's ~: 5 grist
Batdance (1989 song) artist: Prince
bate: 3 ebb 6 lessen, reduce, subdue 7 flutter 8 diminish, moderate, restrain
bateau: 4 boat 6 vessel
bated: 3 low 5 faint, piano, quiet
Bateman: 5 Jason 7 Justine
Bates: 2 H.E. 4 Alan 5 Kathy 6 Norman
establishment: 5 motel
Bates, Alan: 5 actor
film: Butley (1974)
The Entertainer (1960)
Far From the Madding Crowd (1967)
Georgy Girl (1966)
Gosford Park (2001)
Hamlet (1990)
Nothing but the Best (1964)
The Rose (1979)
Royal Flash (1975)
The Running Man (1963)
Three Sisters (1970)
An Unmarried Woman (1978)
We Think the World of You (1988)
Whistle Down the Wind (1961)
Women in Love (1969)
Zorba the Greek (1964)
Bates, H.E.: 6 writer 7 British
Bates, Kathy: 7 actress
film: At Play in the Fields of the Lord (1991)
Dolores Claiborne (1995)
Dragonfly (2002)
Fried Green Tomatoes (1991)
Misery (1990, AA)
Prelude to a Kiss (1992)
Primary Colors (1998)
Shadows and Fog (1992)
Titanic (1997)
The Waterboy (1998)
Bate, W. Jackson: 6 writer
__ bat for: 4 go to
bath: 2 WC 3 dip, loo, spa 4 pool, wash 6 laving, sponge 7 dunking, reverse, soaking 8 ablution, infusion, lavation, lavatory, restroom, washroom 9 cleansing, scrubbing 10 powder room
aftermath: 4 ring
combining form: 5 balne- 6 balneo-
decor: 4 tile
ender: 3 mat, tub 4 robe, room 5 house
item: 4 soap 5 towel 9 facecloth, washcloth
kind of ~: 3 dye
like a Turkish ~: 6 steamy
long ~: 4 soak
need a ~: 4 reek 5 smell, stink
powder: 4 talc 6 talcum
sponge: 5 loofa, luffa 6 loofah
starter: 3 sun 4 bird, foot
steam ~: 5 sauna
take a ~: 4 lose, wash 6 shower
bath __: 3 mat 5 salts, sheet, towel, water 6 sponge 7 mitsvah, mitzvah
__ bath: 3 dye, eye, mud 4 half, sitz, stop 5 blood, draw a, steam, take a, water 6 bubble, master, sponge 7 Turkish
Bath: 3 spa 4 city, town
brew: 3 tea
county: 4 Avon
locale: 5 Maine 7 England
river: 4 Avon
Bath __: 3 bun 5 chair
__ Bath and Beyond: 3 Bed
__ Bath Book: 6 Ernie's
bathe: 3 dip, lap, wet 4 lave, soak, swim, wade, wash 5 clean, cover, imbue, rinse, scrub, steep 6 splash 7 deterge, immerse, launder, moisten 8 saturate, submerse, surround 9 disinfect
starter: 3 sun
bathed: 5 clean 6 washed
bathetic: 5 mushy, trite 7 maudlin, mawkish 10 threadbare
__ Bathgate: 5 Billy
Bathgate, Andy: 6 skater 8 puckster
milieu: 3 ice 4 rink 5 arena
org.: 3 NHL
bathhouse: 6 bagnio, cabana
bathing: 9 immersion
go ~: 4 swim
starter: 3 sun
suit: 5 thong 6 bikini 7 maillot 8 one-piece, two-piece
suit top: 3 bra
bathing __: 3 cap 4 suit 6 beauty
Bathing Beauty (1944 film)
cast: Basil Rathbone, Red Skelton, Esther Williams
director: George Sidney
bathos: 5 nadir 7 schmalz, shmaltz 8 schmaltz 10 anticlimax
bathrobe: 6 kimono 7 cover-up
material: 4 wool 5 terry 6 fleece 8 chenille
bathroom: 2 WC 3 lav 4 john 7 latrine 8 lavatory
accessory: 5 towel 6 tissue
bottle: 5 iodin 6 iodine 8 peroxide
cabinet item: 4 Q-Tip 5 floss 6 lotion 9 ChapStick, hand cream 10 toothbrush, toothpaste
cleaner: 5 Comet, Tilex 7 Mr. Clean
device: 5 scale
feature: 4 tile
fixture: 3 tub 6 shower
tissue: 5 Scott 6 Marcal 7 Charmin 8 Northern, Soft Weve 10 Cottonelle, White Cloud
worker: 5 tiler
baths: 4 spas 7 thermae 10 hot springs
Bathsheba

father: 5 Eliam
husband: 5 David, Uriah
son: 7 Solomon
bathtub
ancient Roman ~: 6 labrum
feature: 4 plug 5 drain
gin: 5 hooch 6 hootch
toy: 4 boat, duck
bathtub __: 3 gin
Bathurst __: 6 Island
bathwater
like ~: 5 soapy
tester: 6 big toe
bathyscaphe operator: 5 diver
batik: 6 fabric 8 material
need: 3 dye
Batista, Fulgencio: 5 Cuban 8 dictator
batiste: 6 fabric
Batley: 4 city, town
locale: 7 England 9 Yorkshire
Batman: 4 hero 9 superhero 10 Bruce Wayne, comic strip
creator: 4 Kane
dog: 3 Ace
foe: 5 Joker 7 Penguin, Riddler, Two-Face
headquarters: 4 cave
like TV's ~: 4 camp
partner: 5 Robin
portrayer: 4 West 6 Keaton, Kilmer 7 Clooney
wear: 4 cape, mask
Batman (1989 film)
cast: Kim Basinger, Michael Keaton, Jack Nicholson
director: Tim Burton
Batman (ABC adventure)
cast: Madge Blake (Aunt Harriet)
Victor Buono (King Tut)
Yvonne Craig (Barbara Gordon/Batgirl)
Frank Gorshin (The Riddler)
Neil Hamilton (Commissioner Gordon)
Eartha Kitt (Catwoman)
Burgess Meredith (The Penguin)
Alan Napier (Alfred)
Julie Newmar (Catwoman)
Stafford Repp (Chief O'Hara)
Cesar Romero (The Joker)
Burt Ward (Dick Grayson/Robin)
Adam West (Bruce Wayne/Batman)
Batman __: 7 Forever, Returns
Batman and Robin: 3 duo 4 pair, team
Batman Forever (1995 film)
cast: Jim Carrey, Tommy Lee Jones, Nicole Kidman, Val Kilmer, Chris O'Donnell
director: Joel Schumacher
Batman Returns (1992 film)
cast: Danny DeVito, Michael Keaton, Michelle Pfeiffer, Christopher Walken
director: Tim Burton
Batman & Robin (1997 film)
cast: George Clooney, Chris O'Donnell, Arnold Schwarzenegger, Alicia Silverstone, Uma Thurman
director: Joel Schumacher
Bat Masterson (NBC western) cast: Gene Barry (Bat Masterson)
Batna: 4 city, town
locale: 7 Algeria
baton: 3 rod 4 club, mace, wand 5 staff, stick 6 cudgel 9 billy club, truncheon 10 nightstick
magician's ~: 4 wand
passer's race: 5 relay
perform with a ~: 5 twirl 7 conduct
Baton Rouge: 4 city, port, town
locale: 9 Louisiana
river: 11 Mississippi
school: 3 LSU
__ Bator: 4 Ulan
batrachophobe fear: 5 frogs
bats in the __: 6 belfry
battalion: 4 army, unit 5 corps, force, squad 6 legion 7 legions, phalanx 9 multitude 10 contingent
group: 3 rgt. 4 regt. 8 regiment
batted
object: 6 eyelid 7 eyelash
run ~ in: 5 ribby
strike: 4 foul
__ batted in: 3 run
batten: 3 tie 4 slat 6 fasten, secure, thrive 7 board up, bolster, cover up, tighten 8 grow rich, nail down 9 clamp down
batten down the __: 7 hatches
battened down: 4 fast, shut 6 secure
batter: 3 hit, mix, ram 4 bash, beat, drub, hurt, lash, maim, mall, maul, mush, pelt, slam 5 baste, dough, flail, knock, paste, pound, punch, smash, smite, thump, wreck 6 beetle, bruise, buffet, damage, hammer, injure, pommel, pummel, strike, thrash, thwack, wallop 7 assault, bombard, cake mix, clobber, lambast, mixture, rough up 8 lambaste
bane: 3 out 4 foul 5 slump 6 strike
challenge: 5 curve 8 forkball, splitter
ender: 4 cake
face the first ~: 5 start
goal: 3 hit 4 bunt 5 homer
hit the ~: 4 bean
ingredient: 3 egg 4 yolk 5 yeast
mix ~: 4 beat, stir
place: 3 box 4 home 5 plate
stat: 3 avg., RBI 7 average
to the pitcher: 3 foe
batter __: 4 pile 5 board, brace, bread
batter-__: 3 fry
battercake: 7 pancake 8 flapjack
battering ram: 6 engine
battery: 3 set 4 guns 5 array, group, suite 6 attack, felony, mayhem, series, volley 7 barrage, beating, offense, weapons 8 cannonry, violence 9 artillery, cannonade, onslaught
brand: 5 Delco
charge: 5 boost
chemical: 4 acid
part: 4 cell 5 anode 7 cathode
size: 2 AA 3 AAA 5 C cell, D cell
start a dead ~: 4 jump
terminal: 3 neg., pos. 5 anode 7 cathode 8 negative, positive
type: 5 D cell, NiCad, solar 7 dry cell, storage, Voltaic
word on a ~: 4 volt
__ battery: 3 AAA, air, dry 4 NiCd 5 nicad, solar 7 storage, Voltaic
Battery __: 4 Park
batting: 7 filling
order: 6 line-up
practice area: 4 cage
batting __: 3 eye 5 order 7 average
__ batting: 6 cotton
battle: 3 war 4 bout, feud, fray, to-do 5 brawl, clash, fight, mix-up, run-in, set-to, siege 6 action, affray, attack, combat, dustup, engage, fracas, go at it, have at, oppose, racket, resist, ruckus, rumpus, sortie, strife, tangle, tussle 7 assault, barrage, bombing, compete, contend, contest, crusade, dispute, grapple, mix it up, quarrel, rhubarb, ruction, warfare, wrangle, wrestle 8 brouhaha, campaign, conflict, fighting, long haul, skirmish, struggle 9 encounter, hostility, imbroglio, onslaught, scrimmage 10 blitzkrieg, contention, donnybrook, engagement, free-for-all, resistance
begin a ~: 6 attack, engage, invade
boldness in ~: 4 guts 5 valor 7 courage
conditioned by ~: 10 hard-bitten
cry: 5 motto, whoop 6 byword, charge, slogan, war cry 8 Geronimo, war whoop 9 catchword
doing ~: 5 at war
ender: 4 ship 5 field, front, wagon 6 ground
equip for ~: 3 arm 5 rearm
lineup: 5 array
name meaning ~: 5 Boris
of honor: 4 duel
prepare for ~ old-style: 5 enarm
ready for ~: 5 armed 7 psyched
remove from a ~ zone: 7 retreat 8 evacuate, withdraw
site: 5 arena
WWI ~: 5 Aisne, Marne, Somme, Ypres
WWII ~: 6 Bataan
1798 ~: 4 Nile
1806 ~: 4 Jena
1813 ~: 4 Erie
1836 ~: 5 Alamo
1914 ~: 4 Yser 5 Marne, Ypres
1916 ~: 5 Somme
1918 ~: 5 Marne
1944 ~: 4 Truk 5 Bulge, Leyte
battle __: 3 cry 4 line, plan, star 5 clasp, dress, group, royal, wagon 6 jacket 7 cruiser, fatigue, lantern, station
battle-__: 3 axe 7 scarred
__ battle: 5 proxy 7 pitched
Battle: 8 Kathleen
Battle __: 3 Cry 4 Hymn
Battle __ Bulge: 5 of the
Battle __ of Freedom, The: 3 Cry
Battle __ of the Republic, The: 4 Hymn
__ Battle Book, The: 6 Butter
Battle Creek: 4 city, town
locale: 8 Michigan
Battle Cry: 4 film 5 novel
author: Leon Uris
cast: Van Heflin, Tab Hunter, Aldo Ray
director: Raoul Walsh
battlefield: 5 arena, front
healer: 5 medic
battleground: 5 arena 8 landmark
1950s ~: 5 Korea
1960s ~: 3 Nam
Santa Anna ~: 5 Alamo
vehicle: 4 tank
Battleground (1949 film)
cast: John Hodiak, Van Johnson, Ricardo Montalban
director: William Wellman
Battle Hymn (1957 film)
cast: Rock Hudson, Martha Hyer
director: Douglas Sirk
Battle Hymn of the Republic, The
author: 4 Howe
starter: 4 mine
word: 5 glory, sword, wrath
Battle, Kathleen: 4 diva 6 singer 7 soprano
specialty: 4 aria 5 opera
battlement: 4 wall 5 redan 7 parapet, rampart
opening: 6 crenel 8 crenelle
Battle of Alcazar, The author: 5 Peele
Battle of Angels author: Tennessee Williams
Battle of Blenheim, The author: Robert Southey
Battle of New Orleans, The (1959 song) artist: Johnny Horton
battle of the __: 5 bands, sexes
Battle of the __: 5 Bulge
Battle of the Sexes, The (1960 film)
cast: Constance Cummings, Robert Morley, Peter Sellers
battle protector, name meaning: 10 Hildegarde
battler: 8 crusader 9 combatant 10 contestant
battleship: 4 boat 7 carrier, cruiser, flattop, frigate, gunboat 8 corvette, man-of-war 9 destroyer
blast: 5 salvo
letters: 3 USS
of 1898: 5 Maine
battleship __: 4 gray, grey
Battleship Potemkin, The locale: 6 Odessa
__ Battle's Opinions of Whist: 3 Mrs.
battle station, take a: 3 man
battuta: 4 beat 7 measure
batty: 3 mad 4 zany 5 flaky, inane 6 absurd, cuckoo, flakey 7 bananas, bonkers, touched 8 crackers 9 eccentric, half-baked, senseless 10 off-the-wall
Batu: 4 peak 5 mount 8 mountain
locale: 6 Africa 8 Ethiopia
Batumi: 4 city, town
locale: 7 Georgia
Bat Yam: 4 city, town
locale: 6 Israel
bauble: 3 gem, toy 5 curio, dodad, jewel 6 doodad, geegaw, gewgaw, locket, tinsel, trifle 7 jewelry, spangle, trinket 8 gimcrack, nicknack, ornament 9 bagatelle 10 decoration, knickknack
baud __: 4 rate
Baudelaire, Charles: 4 poet 6 French
work: The Flowers of Evil
Baudolino author: Umberto Eco
Baudrons: 3 cat 5 felid 6 feline
Bauer: 4 Hank 5 Eddie 6 Steven
Bauer, Steven spouse: Melanie Griffith
Baugh: 5 Laura, Sammy
Baugh, Laura: 6 golfer
milieu: 5 links 6 course
org.: 4 LPGA
Baugh, Sammy: 2 QB
sport: 8 football
Bauhaus: 4 font 8 typeface
name: 4 Klee, Rohe
bauhinia: 4 tree 5 shrub
baum: 4 tree 6 German
Baum: 5 Vicki 6 L. Frank
Bauman: 3 Jon
Baum, L. Frank: 6 author, writer
beast: 4 lion
dog: 4 Toto
work: Father Goose
The Wonderful Wizard of Oz
Baum, Vicki: 6 author, writer
work: Grand Hotel
Bauru: 4 city, town
locale: 6 Brazil
Bausch and __: 4 Lomb
bauxite: 3 ore 7 mineral
giant: 5 Alcoa
__ b'Av: 5 Tisha 6 Tishah
Bavaria
mountain range: 4 Harz, Rhon
peak: 3 Alp
river: 4 Isar 8 Naab. Eger
Bavarian cream __: 3 pie
Bavier: 7 Frances
bawbee: 5 money 9 halfpenny
bawdy: 4 blue, lewd, racy, rude 5 dirty, salty 6 coarse, ribald, risqué, unmeet, vulgar 7 naughty, obscene 8 off-color 9 low-minded 10 indecorous, indelicate
bawl: 3 cry, sob 4 bark, howl, mewl, pule, roar, wail, weep, yaup, yawp, yell, yowl 5 shout 6 bellow, boohoo, clamor, holler, lament, scream, shriek, snivel 7 blubber, bluster, screech, ululate, whimper 9 caterwaul, shed a tear 10 take it hard, vociferate

out: 4 lash, whip 5 scold 6 berate, rebuke 7 upbraid 8 reproval 9 castigate, reprehend 10 upbraiding, vituperate
bawl __: 3 out
bawler: 7 crybaby
bawling: 5 noisy 7 in tears, tearful 9 sniveling
out: 6 earful, rebuke 8 scolding 9 reprimand
sound: 3 wah
Bax: 6 Arnold
Baxter: 3 Les, Ted 4 Anne 5 James 6 Warner 8 Meredith
Baxter (1973 film)
cast: Scott Jacoby, Patricia Neal
Baxter and his Orchestra, Les
song: The Poor People of Paris (1956)
Unchained Melody (1955)
Wake the Town and Tell the People (1955)
Baxter, Anne: 7 actress
film: All About Eve (1950)
Angel on My Shoulder (1946)
The Blue Gardenia (1953)
Chase a Crooked Shadow (1958)
The Eve of St. Mark (1944)
Five Graves to Cairo (1943)
Guest in the House (1944)
The (1946, AA) Razor's Edge
Smoky (1946)
The Sullivans (1944)
Sunday Dinner for a Soldier (1944)
The Ten Commandments (1956)
A Ticket to Tomahawk (1950)
Yellow Sky (1948)
Baxter, James: 4 poet
Baxter, Meredith: 7 actress
spouse: David Birney
Baxter, Warner: 5 actor
film: 42nd Street (1933)
Broadway Bill (1934)
In Old Arizona (1929, AA)
Penthouse (1933)
The Prisoner of Shark Island (1936)
The Road to Glory (1936)
Slave Ship (1937)
The Squaw Man (1931)
Wife, Husband and Friend (1939)
bay: 3 arm, cry 4 bark, Coos, cove, Faxa, gulf, howl, Huna, nook, roar, tree, Vigo, wail, yowl 5 basin, bayou, bight, brown, Casco, color, Dvina, fiord, firth, fjord, frith, Fundy, Green, horse, inlet, James, Manta, niche, Onega, shout, shrub, Tampa 6 Abukir, alcove, Baffin, bellow, Bengal, Biscay, Botany, Brunei, cranny, Dublin, equine, harbor, Hudson, lagoon, laguna, laurel, Manila, Mobile, Naples, Newark, recess, Sagami, Sarera, Suruga, Ungava, Valona, Walvis, Whales 7 Delagoa, estuary, Glacier, harbour, Prudhoe, reddish, Saginaw, Setúbal, Thunder, ululate, Walfish 8 Biscayne, Buzzards, Cardigan, chestnut, Delaware, Georgian, Hangchow, Hangzhou, Humboldt, Jiaozhou, Kiaochow, Monterey, San Pablo 9 anchorage, Apalachee, caterwaul, Frobisher, Galveston, Guanabara, Magdalena, Penobscot, Pensacola, ululation 10 Chesapeake, Guantánamo, Port Philip
Alabama ~: 6 Mobile
Alaska ~: 7 Prudhoe
Albania ~: 6 Valona
Antarctica ~: 6 Whales
Arctic ~: 6 Baffin
at ~: 5 treed 6 caught, frozen 7 held off, in check, trapped 8 cornered, helpless 9 paralysed, powerless 10 motionless
Atlantic ~: 4 Faxa, Vigo 5 Fundy 6 Biscay, Walvis 7 Setúbal, Walfish 8 Biscayne, Delaware 9 Frobisher, Penobscot 10 Chesapeake
Australia ~: 6 Botany 10 Port Philip
away from the ~: 6 inland
Bangladesh ~: 6 Bengal
Beaufort Sea ~: 7 Prudhoe
bring to ~: 3 nab 4 trap, tree 5 catch 6 collar, corner 7 capture
California ~: 8 Monterey, San Pablo
Canada ~: 5 Fundy, James 6 Baffin, Hudson, Ungava 8 Georgian 9 Frobisher
China ~: 8 Hangchow, Hangzhou, Jiaozhou, Kiaochow
color kin: 3 dun, tan 4 bole, ecru, fawn, foxy, nude, seal 5 amber, beige, camel, cocoa, hazel, khaki, mocha, sepia, tawny, umber 6 auburn, bister, bistre, bronze, coffee, copper, ginger, russet, sienna, sorrel, suntan, walnut 7 biscuit, caramel, dogwood 8 chestnut, cinnamon, mahogany 9 butternut, chocolate
Cuba ~: 10 Guantánamo
Ecuador ~: 5 Manta
Egypt ~: 6 Abukir
ender: 4 side 5 berry
Florida ~: 5 Tampa 8 Biscayne 9 Apalachee, Pensacola
France ~: 6 Biscay
Greenland ~: 6 Baffin
Gulf of Mexico ~: 5 Tampa 6 Mobile 9 Galveston, Pensacola
hold at ~: 5 parry, repel 6 rebuff 7 fend off, repulse, ward off 8 stave off
Iceland ~: 4 Faxa, Huna
Indian Ocean ~: 6 Bengal 7 Delagoa
Indonesia ~: 6 Sarera
Ireland ~: 6 Dublin
Irish ~: 5 Sligo
Italy ~: 6 Naples
Japan ~: 6 Sagami, Suruga
Lake Huron ~: 7 Saginaw
Maine ~: 5 Casco 9 Penobscot
Malaysia ~: 6 Brunei
Maryland ~: 10 Chesapeake
Massachusetts ~: 8 Buzzard's
Mexico ~: 9 Magdalena
Michigan ~: 7 Saginaw
Mideast ~: 6 Abukir
Mozambique ~: 7 Delagoa
Myanmar ~: 6 Bengal
Namibia ~: 6 Walvis 7 Walfish
New Guinea ~: 6 Sarera
New Jersey ~: 6 Newark 8 Delaware
Norwegian ~: 5 fiord, fjord
Nova Scotia ~: 5 Fundy
Pacific ~: 5 Manta 8 Monterey
Philippines ~: 5 Subic 6 Manila
Portland's ~: 5 Casco
Portugal ~: 7 Setúbal
Ross Sea ~: 6 Whales
rum: 10 aftershave
Russia ~: 5 Dvina, Onega
sick ~: 8 hospital 9 infirmary
South China Sea ~: 6 Brunei
Spain ~: 4 Vigo 6 Biscay
starter: 4 rose, sick
Texas ~: 9 Galveston
transport: 5 ferry 9 hydrofoil
tree: 6 laurel
Virginia ~: 10 Chesapeake
Wales ~: 8 Cardigan
White Sea ~: 5 Dvina, Onega
window: 5 belly, oriel 6 paunch
Wisconsin ~: 5 Green
bay __: 3 ice, oil, rum 4 leaf, lynx, salt, tree 6 antler, laurel, poplar, window 7 scallop
__ bay: 3 red 4 bomb, bull, case, lock, sick 5 cargo, drive, sweet 7 payload
__ Bay: 3 Emu, Ise 4 Back, Coos, Faxa, Hilo 5 Casco, Dvina, Goose, Green, James, Manta, Onega, Subic, Tampa, Tiger, Tokyo 6 Baffin, Botany, Hudson, Manila, Mobile, Newark, Oyster, Sarera, Ungava, Walvis 7 Chaleur, Delagoa, Glacier, Montego, Prudhoe, Saginaw, Thunder
__-Bay: 5 Put-in
bayadere: 6 fabric
__ Ba Yah: 3 Kum
Bayamo: 4 city, town
locale: 4 Cuba
Bayamón: 4 city, town
locale: 10 Puerto Rico
Bay Area county: 4 Napa 5 Marin
bayberry: 4 tree 5 fruit, shrub 6 candle
__ Bay Buccaneers: 5 Tampa
Bay City: 4 town
locale: 8 Michigan
Bay City Rollers
homeland: Scotland
song: Money Honey (1976)
Saturday Night (1975)
You Made Me Believe in Magic (1977)
__ Bay Company: 7 Hudson's
bayer: 3 dog 4 wolf 5 husky 6 coyote
Bayer competitor: 3 APF 4 Cope 5 Advil, Aleve 6 Anacin, Datril, Motrin 7 Ecotrin, Tylenol 8 Bufferin, Excedrin, St. Joseph, Vanquish 9 Ascriptin
__ Bayer Sager: 6 Carole
Bayes: 4 Nora
Bayeux neighbor: 4 St. Lô
Bayh: 4 Evan 5 Birch
bay leaf: 4 herb
Bayle, Pierre: 6 French 11 philosopher
Baylor: 3 Don 4 univ. 5 Elgin 6 school 10 university
athletes: 5 Bears
conference: 9 Big Twelve
locale: 4 Waco 5 Texas
Baylor, Don sport: 8 baseball
Baylor, Elgin: 5 cager
milieu: 5 court
org.: 3 NBA
sport: 10 basketball
bayman: 7 clammer
Bay of __: 3 Uri 4 Acre, Pigs 6 Biscay
Bay of Bengal
city: 6 Madras
island: 7 Nicobar 8 Andamans
river to the ~: 6 Ganges 7 Cauvery, Hooghly, Krishna, Salween 8 Godavari 9 Irrawaddy
Bay of Biscay
ocean: 3 Atl. 8 Atlantic
peninsula: 6 Iberia
port: 5 Gijón 6 Bilbao
Bay of Fundy
feature: 4 tide
river to the ~: 6 St. John
Bay of Naples island: 5 Capri
Bay of Pigs locale: 4 Cuba
bayonet: 4 stab 5 knife 6 weapon
Bayonet Point: 4 city, town
locale: 7 Florida
Bayonne: 4 city, port, town
locale: 6 France 9 New Jersey
bayou: 3 arm, bay 4 gulf 5 inlet, swamp 6 lagoon
boat: 6 bateau
dweller: 5 Cajan, Cajun 6 Creole
feature: 5 marsh
__ Bayou: 4 Blue
__ Bay Packers: 5 Green
Bay Point: 4 city, town
locale: 10 California
Bayreuth: 4 city, town
locale: 7 Germany
Bay Shore: 4 city, town
locale: 7 New York
baysmelt: 4 fish
Bay State
see Massachusetts
Baytown: 4 city
locale: 5 Texas
Baywatch (NBC adventure)
cast: Traci Bingham (Jordan Tate)
Yasmine Bleeth (Caroline Holden)
Donna D'Errico (Donna Marco)
Nicole Eggert (Summer Quinn)
Carmen Electra (Lani McKenzie)
Erika Eleniak (Shauni McLain)
David Hasselhoff (Mitch Bucannon)
Pamela Anderson Lee (C.J. Parker)
Gena Lee Nolin (Neely Kapshaw)
Alexandra Paul (Stephanie Holden)
Parker Stevenson (Craig Pomeroy)
setting: 5 beach 6 Malibu
bazaar: 4 fair, fete, mart 6 market 7 benefit 8 emporium 10 flea market, fund-raiser
ancient ~: 5 agora
Arab ~: 3 suk, suq 4 souk
indoor ~: 4 mall
__ Bazaar: 7 Harper's
Bazna: 3 pig 5 swine
bazoo: 4 puss, trap 5 mouth 6 kisser
bazooka: 9 artillery
essentially: 4 tube
target: 4 tank
Bazooka: 3 gum 9 bubble gum
bazookas: 8 weaponry
BB: 4 ammo, shot 6 pellet
gun: 8 air rifle
gun sound: 4 ping
propellant: 3 air
BB __: 3 gun 4 shot
B&B: 3 inn
alternative: 5 motel
part of ~: 3 bed 9 breakfast
B.B.: 4 King
b-ball: 5 hoops
BBC
competitor: 3 ITV
home: 6 London
meridian: 3 GMT
nickname: 4 Beeb
receiver: 4 tele 5 telly
series: 5 Dr. Who
bbl.: 4 meas.
bigger than a ~: 3 hhd.
see also barrel
B.C.: 4 prov. 5 comic 8 province
cartoonist: 4 Hart
character: 4 Grog, Thor
currency: 4 clam
home: 4 cave
insect: 3 ant
neighbor: 3 Alb., Ida. 4 Alta.
sound: 3 zot
see also British Columbia
BCE, part of: 3 Era 6 Before 7 Current
B-complex: 7 vitamin
acid: 5 folic
component: 4 PABA 6 biotin, niacin 7 choline 8 inositol, Vitamin H
B.D.: 4 Wong
__ B. Davis: 3 Ann
__ B. DeMille: 5 Cecil
bdl.: 3 pkg.
see also bundle
Bd. of Ed. concern: 3 sch.
__ B. Driftwood: 4 Otis
be: 4 live, verb 5 exist, occur 6 happen, remain 7 breathe, subsist, survive 9 come about, take place, transpire 10 come to pass
at: 6 attend, show up
in French: 4 être
in Italian: 3 ser
in Latin: 4 esse
in Spanish: 3 ser
be __: 5 along

be __ as it may: 4 that
be-__: 3 bop, ins
__ be!: 5 Glory
__-be: 5 would
Be: 4 elem. 7 element 9 beryllium
 4 for ~: 4 at. no.
Be __, It's My Heart: 7 Careful
Be __ to Your School: 4 True
__ Be: 3 I'll 5 Let It
be a __: 3 pal 5 sport
Bea: 6 Arthur, Lillie 9 Benaderet
beach: 4 land 5 coast, shore, wreck 6 maroon, strand 8 littoral, seacoast, seashore 10 oceanfront, waterfront
 acquisition: 3 tan
 bird: 3 ern 4 erne, gull 7 seagull
 building: 3 hut 6 cabana
 cause of ~ erosion: 4 tide
 creation: 6 castle
 ender: 4 head, side, wear 5 front, scape 6 comber
 enjoy the ~: 5 bathe
 find: 5 shell
 impostor: 5 ho-dad
 item: 5 radio, towel 6 cooler, lotion
 like a ~ day: 5 sunny
 like the ~: 5 sandy
 location: 5 coast
 on the ~: 6 ashore
 patron: 6 basker
 prohibition: 6 no pets
 relax at the ~: 3 sun 4 bask 5 float
 residue: 4 grit
 surface: 4 sand
 terrace: 4 berm 5 berme
 toy: 4 ball, pail
 water: 4 surf
 wear: 5 thong 6 bikini, caftan, kaftan, sandal, shorts, trunks 7 cover-up, maillot 8 one-piece, swimsuit, two-piece
 woe: 4 burn 7 sunburn
beach __: 3 bum, pea 4 ball, berm, crab, face, flea, plum 5 aster, buggy, drift, grass, ridge, scarp
__ beach: 4 free 6 muscle 7 barrier
Beach __: 3 Red 4 Baby, Boys 5 Party
__ Beach: 4 Long, Palm, Vero 5 China, Cocoa, Dover, Miami, Omaha, On the, Pismo 6 Bikini, Delray, Laguna, Myrtle, Pebble 7 Daytona, Newport
Beacham: 9 Stephanie
Beach Baby (1974 song) artist: First Class
beach ball filler: 3 air
Beach Blanket Bingo (1965 film)
 cast: Frankie Avalon, Annette Funicello, Paul Lynde
 director: William Asher
Beach Boys
 members: Wilson, Love, Jardine
 song: Barbara Ann (1966)
  Be True to Your School (1963)
  California Girls (1965)
  Dance, Dance, Dance (1964)
  Don't Worry Baby (1964)
  Fun, Fun, Fun (1964)
  Good Vibrations (1966)
  Help Me, Rhonda (1965)
  I Get Around (1964)
  In My Room (1963)
  Kokomo (1988)
  Rock and Roll Music (1976)
  Sloop John B (1966)
  Surfer Girl (1963)
  Surfin' Safari (1962)
  Surfin' U.S.A. (1963)
  When I Grow Up (1964)
  Wouldn't It Be Nice (1966)
beachcomber: 6 loafer 7 forager 8 gadabout, scrounge, wanderer 9 scavenger
 find: 5 conch, shell
 tool: 4 pail 5 sieve 6 bucket
Beachcomber, The (1938 film)
 cast: Tyrone Guthrie, Elsa Lanchester, Charles Laughton
Beachcomber, The (1955 film)
 cast: Glynis Johns, Robert Newton
 director: Muriel Box
beached: 6 ashore 7 aground 8 stranded
Beaches (1988 film)
 cast: John Heard, Barbara Hershey, Bette Midler
 director: Garry Marshall
beachhead: 8 foothold, lodgment
Beachhead (1954 film)
 cast: Tony Curtis, Frank Lovejoy
Beach Party (1963 film)
 cast: Frankie Avalon, Bob Cummings, Annette Funicello, Dorothy Malone
 director: William Asher
__ Beach Party: 6 Muscle
Beach Red (1967 film)
 cast: Rip Torn, Cornel Wilde
 director: Cornel Wilde
__ Beach Story, The: 4 Palm
Beach, The (2000 film)
 cast: Guillaume Canet, Leonardo DiCaprio, Virginie Ledoyen, Tilda Swinton
 director: Danny Boyle
Be a Clown composer: 6 Porter
__ be a cold day...: 4 It'll
beacon: 4 beam, lamp, sign 5 flare, guide, light 6 Pharos, signal 7 lantern, lookout, warning 8 lodestar 9 indicator 10 lighthouse, watchtower
 radar ~: 5 racon
__ beacon: 5 radar, radio
Beacon __: 4 Hill
bead: 4 blob, drop, glob 6 bubble 7 driblet, droplet, globule, granule, trinket 8 spherule
 draw another ~ on: 5 reaim
 draw a ~ on: 3 aim 5 aim at, train
 ender: 4 work
 material: 5 coral, nacre 9 turquoise
 rosary ~: 3 ave 4 gaud
 tube-shaped ~: 5 bugle
bead __: 4 fern, test, tree 5 plane, plant 7 molding
__ bead: 4 rail, stop 5 borax, bugle, weave 7 glazing
beadle: 6 sexton
Beadle, George: 8 Nobelist 10 geneticist
__ bead on: 4 get a 5 draw a
beads: 4 peag 5 sewan 6 choker, rosary, seawan, wampum 7 jewelry 8 necklace, ornament
 certain ~: 5 sweat
 Indian ~: 4 peag 5 sewan 6 wampum
 item with ~: 6 abacus
 mantra ~: 4 mala 6 rosary
__ beads: 4 love 5 worry 6 Baily's, prayer
beady: 10 glittering
beady-__: 4 eyed
beagle: 3 dog 4 boat, ship 5 canid, hound, pooch 6 canine, Snoopy
 feature: 3 ear
beak: 3 neb, nib 4 bill, nose 5 mouth, snoot, snout 6 schnoz 7 schnozz 9 proboscis, schnozzle 10 schnozzola
 base: 4 cere
 bird ~: 3 neb, nib
 combining form: 5 rostr- 6 rhamph-, rostri-, rostro- 7 rhampho-
beaked: 8 aquiline
 vessel: 5 cruet 6 beaker, carafe 7 alembic
beaker: 3 cup 5 flask, glass, stein 7 alembic 9 container, glassware, lab vessel
 cousin: 4 vial 5 flask, phial
 material: 5 glass, Pyrex
Beale __ Blues: 6 Street
be-all and __-all: 3 end
Beals: 8 Jennifer
beam: 3 ray 4 boom, emit, grin, jamb, lath, pole, post, prop, rump, shed, slow, spar, stud 5 brace, flash, gleam, jambe, joist, level, shaft, shine, slant, smile, spark, stare, strut, train 6 beacon, column, girder, lintel, member, piling, pillar, rafter, regard, streak, timber 7 give off, glitter, radiate, send off, sparkle, trestle 8 crossbar, throw off, transmit 9 broadcast, emanation, irradiate, stanchion, two-by-four 10 cantilever, crosspiece
 balance ~: 5 event
 boat's ~: 5 width
 bright ~: 3 ray 5 laser 9 spotlight
 combining form: 5 actin- 6 actino-
 emit an intense ~: 4 lase
 ender: 3 ish
 fastener: 5 rivet
 floor ~: 6 header
 generator: 5 laser, maser
 make ~: 4 send 5 cheer, elate, liven 6 buoy up, lift up, perk up, please, puff up, thrill, tickle, turn on 7 delight, elevate, gladden, happify, hearten, lighten, overjoy, satisfy 9 enrapture, inebriate, make happy 10 exhilarate, intoxicate
 nautical: 7 carling, cathead
 off the ~: 4 loco, lost 6 astray 9 wandering
 on the ~: 5 adept, aware, right 6 posted, wise to 7 correct 9 cognizant 10 acceptable, conversant, proficient, unmistaken
 penetrating ~: 4 X-ray 5 laser
 railroad ~: 3 tie
 roof ~: 6 header
 ship ~: 4 keel
 splitter: 5 prism
 starter: 3 sun 4 horn, moon 5 cross
 steel ~: 4 I-bar, L bar 5 I-beam 6 girder
 supporting ~: 5 truss
beam __: 3 sea 4 fill, mill, wind 5 brick, light, reach, trawl 6 weapon 7 antenna, compass
__ beam: 3 box, low, tie 4 arch, grub, high, warp 5 cloth, laser, on the, radio 6 breast, dragon, flitch, ground, ledger, pencil, sealed 7 balance, primary, Tyndall, walking
Beam __, Scotty!: 4 me up
Beame: 3 Abe
beaming: 3 lit 5 aglow, happy, lit up, lucid, shiny, sunny 6 ablaze, bright, elated, flashy, joyful, lucent 7 blazing, fulgent, glowing, lambent, radiant, shining 8 cheerful, dazzling, euphoric, gleaming, luminous, lustrous, splendid 9 beautiful, brilliant, effulgent, refulgent, sparkling 10 flying high
Beamon, Bob: 10 long jumper
beams
 high ~: 7 brights
 low ~: 6 dimmer
beamy: 4 wide 5 broad
bean: 3 nob, nut, pea 4 conk, fava, lima, mung, navy, pole, snap, soya 5 green, pinto, tonka 6 adzuki, castor, coffee, cowpea, frijol, kidney, legume, lentil, noggin, noodle, string 7 frijole, haricot, refried, vanilla 8 garbanzo 9 vegetable
 Asian ~: 3 soy, urd
 chili ~: 5 pinto 6 kidney
 chocolate ~: 5 cacao
 cluster ~: 4 guar
 curd: 4 tofu
 ender: 3 bag 4 pole 5 stalk
 horse ~: 4 fava
 hull: 3 pod
 Japanese ~: 6 adzuki
 locust ~: 5 carob
 Mexican ~: 6 frijol 7 frijole
 paste: 4 miso
 pole: 5 stalk
 soup ~: 4 lima
 starter: 3 soy 4 buck, snap 5 broad, jelly
 use one's ~: 5 think
 vine of the ~ family: 5 vetch
bean __: 3 pod, pot 4 ball, curd, shot, tree 5 aphid, caper 6 beetle, weevil 7 counter, sprouts
__ bean: 3 pea, wax 4 bayo, buck, bush, ceci, fava, jack, lima, Lyon, moth, mung, navy, pole, rice, snap, soya, wild 5 azuki, black, broad, cacao, chile, chili, cocoa, green, horse, pinto, screw, shell, sieva, sword, tonka 6 adsuki, adzuki, butter, castor, chilli, French, Indian, kidney, locust, mescal, ordeal, poison, potato, runner, string, tepary, velvet, winged 7 Calabar, cluster, jumping, vanilla
Bean: 2 L.L. 3 Roy 4 Alan, Andy 5 Orson
Bean __, The: 5 Trees 6 Eaters
beanbag: 3 toy 6 pillow 7 cushion
beanbag __: 5 chair
beanball: 5 pitch
bean counter: 3 CPA 4 acct. 10 accountant
 top ~: 3 CFO
Bean Eaters, The author: Gwendolyn Brooks
beanery: 5 diner 6 eatery 10 restaurant
__ Beanfield War, The: 7 Milagro
beanie: 3 cap 8 skullcap
Beanie Babies: 3 fad 5 craze
beanpole: 4 slim 5 lanky, scrag, stick 7 slender
beans: 5 dough 6 annual
 full of ~: 5 wrong 8 mistaken
 partner: 4 pork
 prepare coffee ~: 5 grind
 prepare Mexican ~: 5 refry
 spill the ~: 3 rat 4 blab, blat, leak, sing, talk, tell 5 blurt, let on 6 tattle 7 confess
__ beans: 5 baked, jelly 7 refried
beanstalk: 4 slim 5 lanky 7 slender
 owner: 5 giant
Bean Town: 6 Boston
Bean Trees, The author: Barbara Kingsolver
bear: 2 go 3 lug 4 cart, have, hold, lump, Pooh, take, tend, tote 5 abide, allow, beget, breed, bring, brook, carry, ferry, grump, sloth, stand, stick, teddy, ursid, yield 6 accept, afford, animal, Boo-Boo, convey, endure, Fozzie, harbor, Kodiak, mammal, permit, Smokey, suffer, uphold 7 deliver, exhibit, grizzly, harbour, include, possess, produce, receive, ride out, signify, stomach, support, survive, sustain, undergo 8 cinnamon, engender, fructify, grumbler, maintain, omnivore, shoulder, tolerate, transfer 9 entertain, Gentle Ben, propagate, put up with, reproduce, send forth, silvertip, transport, withstand 10 bring forth, Paddington
 advice: 4 sell
 baby ~: 3 cub
 bring to ~: 3 use 5 apply, exert 6 employ 8 exercise
 cartoon ~: 4 Yogi 6 Boo Boo
 CBer's ~: 3 cop
 combining form: 4 arct- 5 arcto-
 constellation: 4 Ursa
 counterpart: 4 bull
 cross to ~: 4 onus 5 trial

down: 3 try 5 labor, press 6 reduce, strain, strive 9 overpower
down on: 6 burden, coerce, compel, strain 7 focus on 8 draw near, get after
ender: 3 cat, ish 4 skin 5 berry
female: 3 sow
food: 5 honey 7 berries
foot: 3 paw
grin and ~ it: 4 take 5 stick 6 adjust, submit 7 stomach 8 overlook
hair: 3 fur
home: 3 den, zoo 4 lair 5 woods 6 forest
hug: 6 clench
in Latin: 4 Ursa
in mind: 4 heed 6 recall 7 bethink 8 remember 9 recognize, recollect 10 reckon with
in Spanish: 3 oso
male: 4 boar
name meaning ~: 5 Bjorn 6 Ursula
of very little brain: 4 Pooh
on: 3 sit 4 lean 6 affect 7 concern, pertain 9 pertain to
out: 5 prove 6 attest, ratify, verify 7 certify, confirm, justify, reflect, warrant, witness 8 validate 10 strengthen
starter: 3 bug
stuffed ~: 5 Teddy
trap: 5 snare
up: 5 shore 6 endure, manage, resist 7 bolster, weather
upon: 5 touch 6 regard, relate
(upon): 5 weigh
up under: 5 stick 7 sustain
utterance: 3 grr 5 growl, grunt
with: 4 take 5 abide, stand 6 excuse, suffer 7 forgive, stomach, sustain 8 overlook, tolerate
woolly ~: 3 bug 6 insect

bear __: 3 hug, out 4 claw, down 5 fruit, grass 6 garden, leader
__ bear: 3 ant, sun 4 cave 5 black, brown, honey, Malay, panda, polar, sloth, teddy, water, white 6 Kodiak, woolly 7 grizzly
Bear: 4 peak 5 mount, river 6 Bryant 8 mountain
author: 5 Engel
rival: 3 Jet, Ram 4 Bill, Colt, Lion 5 Brown, Chief, Eagle, Giant, Niner, Raven, Saint, Texan, Titan 6 Bengal, Bronco, Cowboy, Falcon, Jaguar, Packer, Raider, Viking 7 Charger, Dolphin, Panther, Patriot, Redskin, Seahawk, Steeler 8 Cardinal 9 Buccaneer
River locale: 4 Utah 5 Idaho 7 Wyoming
Bear __: 7 Stearns
__ Bear: 4 Br'er, Papa, Yogi 5 Great 6 Edward, Lesser, Little, Smokey 7 Running
bearable: 7 livable 8 liveable, moderate 9 tolerable
bearably: 8 somewhat
bearberry: 5 fruit
beard: 4 fuzz, hair, mask 6 goatee 7 stubble, Vandyke 8 disguise, imperial, whiskers
combining form: 5 pogon- 6 pogono-
cut the ~ off: 5 shave
ender: 6 tongue
grain ~: 3 awn 6 arista
locale: 4 chin
pluck by the ~: 4 twit
remover: 5 razor
site: 3 jaw
starter: 4 blue, gray, grey 5 Black, goats
the lion: 4 face 5 brave 8 confront

Beard: 5 Frank, James 7 Charles
Beard, Charles: 6 writer
bearded: 5 hairy 7 barbate, bristly, goateed, hirsute, unshorn 8 unshaven 9 incognito, whiskered
animal: 3 gnu 4 goat 6 aoudad
as grain: 5 awned
brothers' surname: 5 Smith
flower: 4 iris
bearded __: 3 tit 4 iris, seal 6 collie, darnel 7 vulture
Beard, James: 4 chef
beardless: 5 green 6 callow 8 immature 10 adolescent
Beardmore __: 7 Glacier
Beardsley: 6 Aubrey
beard the __: 4 lion
bearer: 5 envoy, payee, toter 6 herald, porter, runner 7 carrier, courier 8 conveyer, emissary 9 consignee, messenger
combining form: 4 -pher, -phor 5 -phore
starter: 3 cup, fur 4 live, mace, tale 5 torch, train
bearer __: 4 bond
__ Bearer: 5 Water 7 Serpent
bear in __: 4 mind
bearing: 3 air, way 4 look, mien, pose, west 5 front, poise, style 6 aspect, import, manner, regard, stance 7 conduct, heading, kinship, meaning, posture, purport 8 attitude, behavior, carriage, demeanor, presence, relation, tendency 9 direction, relevance, semblance 10 appearance, connection, deportment, generation, pertinence
combining form: 6 -gerous, -parous, -phoria 7 -phorous
have a ~ on: 6 regard 7 concern
in heraldry: 6 charge 8 ordinary
on: 8 relevant
starter: 3 fur 4 ever, tale 5 child
bearing __: 4 rail, rein, wall 5 plate, sword
__ bearing: 4 ball 5 plain 6 roller, thrust
bearings: 3 aim 5 track 8 location, position 9 direction, situation
get one's ~: 6 orient
bearish: 5 corss, crass, crude, gruff, onery, rough, surly, testy 6 coarse, cranky, crusty, grumpy, ireful, lumpen, oafish, ornery, touchy, vulgar 7 bilious, boorish, doltish, grouchy, illbred, loutish, peevish, uncivil, uncouth 8 choleric, churlish, cloddish, growling, grumpish, snappish, snarling 9 crotchety, difficult, dyspeptic, irascible, irritable, querulous, splenetic 10 ill-natured, out of sorts, ungracious
bearlike
mammal: 5 koala, panda
name meaning ~: 5 Orson
béarnaise: 5 sauce
__ Be Around: 3 I'll
bear paw: 6 pastry
Bears: 4 team 6 eleven
home: 7 Chicago
org.: 3 NFC, NFL
sport: 8 football
see also Baylor, Brown
__ Bears: 5 Gummi, Teddy 6 Silver
Bearsden: 4 city, town
locale: 8 Scotland
Bearse: 6 Amanda
bearskin: 3 fur, rug
Béart: 10 Emmanuelle
Bear, The author: William Faulkner
bear: 4 Bart
Beasley: 6 Allyce
beast: 5 brute, churl, demon, devil, fiend, swine 6 animal, daemon, daimon, lummox, savage 7 critter, crittur, Lucifer, monster, varment, varmint, wild man 8 creature 9 archfiend, barbarian, hellhound 10 blackguard
combining form: 4 ther- 5 -there, thero- 6 therio-
of burden: 2 ox 3 ass, yak 4 mule 5 burro, camel, horse, llama 6 donkey
Beast author: Peter Benchley
beastly: 3 bad, low 4 base, evil, foul, grim, mean, poor, ugly, vile 5 awful, brute, cruel, feral, harsh, lousy, nasty, rabid, woful 6 animal, brutal, coarse, crumby, crummy, dismal, ferine, fierce, horrid, odious, rotten, savage, unkind, vulgar, wanton, woeful 7 accurst, baleful, baneful, bestial, boorish, brutish, callous, doleful, ghastly, heinous, hideous, hurtful, inhuman, untamed, vicious 8 accursed, barbaric, depraved, dreadful, fiendish, God-awful, grievous, horrible, inferior, inhumane, pitiless, ruthless, sadistic, shameful, stinking, terrible, unbroken, vengeful, wretched 9 abhorrent, appalling, atrocious, barbarous, cutthroat, defective, execrable, ferocious, frightful, insidious, loathsome, malicious, merciless, miserable, monstrous, offensive, repellant, repellent, revolting, truculent, unbridled 10 abominable, despicable, detestable, disastrous, disgusting, horrendous, outrageous, petrifying, vindictive
place: 3 zoo 9 menagerie
Beastmaster, The role: 4 Maax
beast of __: 4 prey 6 burden
Beast of Burden (1978 song) artist: Rolling Stones
Beast of the City, The (1932 film) cast: Jean Harlow, Walter Huston
beasts: 5 fauna, stock 6 cattle
king of ~: 4 lion
Beasts and Super Beasts author: Saki
Beast's companion: 5 Belle 6 Beauty
beat: 3 cap, hit, mix, ram, rap, top, win, zap 4 area, bang, bash, belt, best, cane, club, cuff, drop, drub, drum, flap, flog, foil, harm, lash, lick, mall, mash, maul, pelt, post, rime, rout, slam, slap, slug, sock, stir, swat, take, tick, trim, whip, whup, worn 5 abuse, all in, baste, blend, break, crush, flail, kaput, knock, meter, outdo, parry, pound, pulse, punch, rhyme, route, scoop, smack, spank, stamp, swing, tempo, throb, thump, tired, trump, upset, weary, whack, worst 6 accent, batter, beetle, better, bruise, buffet, bushed, cudgel, defeat, dished, exceed, gammon, hammer, injure, larrup, lather, outrun, outwit, patrol, patter, pommel, pooped, pummel, punish, puzzle, quiver, rebuff, resist, rhythm, ripple, rounds, stress, strike, subdue, switch, thrash, thwack, wallop 7 agitate, at a loss, cadence, cadency, circuit, clobber, conquer, drained, flutter, get past, hold off, lambast, measure, mystify, nose out, outplay, overrun, pulsate, repulse, scourge, surpass, trounce, vibrate, wearied, worn out 8 bludgeon, defeated, dragging, fatigued, give it to, knock out, lambaste, maltreat, outclass, out of gas, outrival, outscore, outshine, outsmart, outstrip, overcome, overtake, push back, turn back, undulate, vanquish 9 castigate, checkmate, exhausted, force back, itinerary, oscillate, overpower, overwhelm, palpitate, played out, pulsation, throbbing, vibration, withstand 10 knocked out, put to shame, undulation
around the bush: 5 fence, hedge, skirt, stall, waver 6 ramble, waffle 9 pussyfoot
as wings: 4 flap
at bridge: 3 set
back: 4 rout 5 repel 6 rebuff
badly: 4 rout 5 cream, skunk, stomp, thump, whomp
barely ~: 3 nip 4 clip, edge, nose 7 nose out 8 slip past
down: 5 quell 6 reduce 7 flatten, oppress 8 suppress 9 overpower
fast: 9 palpitate
for a poet: 5 meter
get ~: 4 lose
it: 2 go 3 git, lam, rip, run 4 exit, flee, scat, shoo 5 hurry, leave, scram, split 6 begone, decamp, depart, get out, go away 7 abscond, dash off, get lost, go south, make off, pull out, push off, retreat, ride off, take off 8 hightail, shove off, withdraw 9 skedaddle 10 go fly a kite, hightail it, hit the road
musical ~: 6 rhythm, stress 7 battuta
one's gums: 3 yak, yap 7 chatter
starter: 3 off 4 back, brow, dead, down, drum, fare 5 heart
the bushes: 4 hunt, seek 7 rummage 9 track down
the drums: 6 talk up 7 advance, promote 9 publicize
the rap: 4 walk 6 go free
up: 3 mug 4 mall, maul 5 knock, seedy, thump 6 pommel, pummel, thrash 10 threadbare
walker: 3 cop 9 policeman
walk the ~: 5 guard 6 patrol
beat __: 3 man, out 4 poet 6 hollow
beat __ to one's door: 5 a path
__ beat: 3 big 5 world 6 Mersey
__ Beat: 4 Teen 7 Foolish
beatable: 8 vincible
beat around the __: 4 bush
beaten: 6 broken, frothy, undone 8 overcome
get ~ by: 4 lose 6 lose to
go off the ~ path: 4 veer 5 stray 7 deviate
it may be ~: 3 egg, rap, rug 4 path
off the ~ path: 6 afield, lonely, remote 8 isolated, secluded
path: 5 trace, track, trail
starter: 4 brow
beaten __: 4 path 7 biscuit
__-beaten: 7 weather
beater: 5 mixer, whisk
__-beater: 4 fare
Beat Goes On, The (1967 song) artist: Sonny and Cher
beatific: 6 divine 7 angelic, elysian, radiant, saintly 8 blissful, ecstatic, heavenly 9 angelical, celestial, rapturous
vision: 8 afflatus
beatify: 4 laud 5 bless 6 revere 7 enthral, inthral, rejoice 8 canonize, enravish, enthrall, inthrall, venerate 9 enrapture, transport 10 consecrate
beating: 4 rout 5 abuse 6 athrob, defeat, hiding 7 ahead of, battery, licking 8 conquest, flitting 9 trouncing 10 punishment
it takes a ~: 4 drum
take a ~: 4 lose
__-beating: 6 breast
beat it: 4 away, scat, shoo 5 scram
Beat It (1983 song) artist: Michael Jackson
Beatles
award: 3 MBE
film: 4 Help
hairstyle: 3 mop
manager: Brian Epstein
members: McCartney, Lennon, Harrison, Starr, Best, Sutcliffe

record label: Apple
song: All You Need Is Love (1967)
And I Love Her (1964)
Baby You're a Rich Man (1967)
The Ballad of John and Yoko (1969)
Can't Buy Me Love (1964)
Come Together (1969)
Day Tripper (1965)
Do You Want to Know a Secret (1964)
Eight Days a Week (1965)
Eleanor Rigby (1966)
Free as a Bird (1995)
Get Back (1969)
Got to Get You Into My Life (1976)
A Hard Day's Night (1964)
Hello Goodbye (1967)
Help! (1965)
Hey Jude (1968)
I Feel Fine (1964)
I Saw Her Standing There (1964)
I Want to Hold Your Hand (1964)
Lady Madonna (1968)
Let It Be (1970)
The Long and Winding Road (1970)
Love Me Do (1964)
Nowhere Man (1966)
Paperback Writer (1966)
Please Please Me (1964)
P.S. I Love You (1964)
Revolution (1968)
She Loves You (1964)
She's a Woman (1964)
Something (1969)
Strawberry Fields Forever (1967)
Ticket to Ride (1965)
Twist and Shout (1964)
We Can Work It Out (1965)
Yellow Submarine (1966)
Yesterday (1965)
beatnik: 8 bohemian, longhair **10** unorthodox
affirmative: 4 I dig
buddy: 6 daddy-o
cousin: 5 hippy **6** hippie
drum: 5 bongo
exclamation: 3 man
home: 3 pad
topper: 5 beret
__ Beat of My Heart: 5 Every
Beaton: 5 Cecil
beat one's __: 4 gums
Beatrice: 4 Webb **6** Lillie **8** Straight
beau: 5 Dante
mother: 5 Sarah
to Charles: 5 niece
to Leonato: 5 niece
Beatrix: 6 Potter
beats me: 6 I dunno, no idea **8** who knows
beat the __: 3 rap **4** drum **6** bushes
Beat the Clock: 8 game show
activity: 5 stunt
host: Bud Collyer
Beat the Devil (1954 film)
cast: Humphrey Bogart, Jennifer Jones, Gina Lollobrigida
director: John Huston
Beattie: 3 Ann **5** James
Beattie, Ann: 6 author, writer
work: Another You
Chilly Scenes of Winter
The Doctor's House
Falling in Place
Park City
Perfect Recall
Picturing Will
Beattie, James: 8 Scottish **11** philosopher
beat to the __: 4 draw **5** punch
Beatty: 3 Ned **6** Warren
Beatty, Ned: 5 actor
film: 1941 (1979)
The Big Easy (1987)
Deliverance (1972)
Hear My Song (1991)
Hopscotch (1980)
Life (1999)
Prelude to a Kiss (1992)
Rudy (1993)
Spring Forward (2000)
Superman (1978)
Superman II (1980)
Switching Channels (1988)
Superman role: 4 Otis
Beatty, Warren: 5 actor
film: All Fall Down (1962)
Bonnie and Clyde (1967)
Bugsy (1991)
Bulworth (1998)
Dick Tracy (1990)
$ (Dollars) (1971)
Heaven Can Wait (1978)
Ishtar (1987)
Love Affair (1994)
McCabe & Mrs. Miller (1971)
The Only Game in Town (1970)
The Parallax View (1974)
Reds (1981, AA)
The Roman Spring of Mrs. Stone (1961)
Shampoo (1975)
Splendor in the Grass (1961)
spouse: Annette Bening
TV: The Many Loves of Dobie Gillis
beat-up: 4 worn **6** ragged, shabby **7** run-down **9** rusted-out **10** threadbare
beau: 4 date, love **5** dandy, fella, flame, honey, lover, swain, wooer **6** fellow, fiancé, squire, steady, suitor **7** admirer, beloved, sweetie **9** boyfriend, inamorato **10** sweetheart
ideal: 5 model **7** paragon **8** paradigm
monde: 6 jet set **7** society
beau __: 5 geste, ideal, monde **6** dollar
Beau: 7 Bridges **8** Brummell
Beau __: 4 Père **5** Geste, James **7** Brummel
Beau Brummel (1954 film)
cast: Stewart Granger, Elizabeth Taylor, Peter Ustinov
Beau Brummell: 3 fop **4** dude **5** dandy, swell **8** popinjay
Beauchamp: 6 Pierre
Beauchampe author: William Simms
beaucoup: 4 a lot, much **9** in a big way
__ beaucoup: 5 merci
Beaufort: 3 sea **7** Francis
locale: 6 Alaska
Beaufort Scale measure: 4 wind
Beaufort Sea bay: 7 Prudhoe
Beau Geste (1939 film)
cast: Gary Cooper, Brian Donlevy, Ray Milland, Robert Preston
director: William Wellman
Beau Geste author: 4 Wren
Beau Ideal, The composer: 5 Sousa
Beau James (1957 film)
cast: Bob Hope, Vera Miles
director: Melville Shavelson
Beaujolais: 3 red, vin **4** wine
color: 3 red
grape: 5 gamay
origin: 6 France
Beaumont: 3 Ned **4** city, Hugh, town **5** Harry
locale: 5 Texas
Beauport: 4 city, town
locale: 6 Canada, Québec
Beauregard: 3 gen. **6** Pierre **7** general
boss: 3 Lee
org.: 3 CSA
beaut: 3 gem, pip **4** lulu, oner **5** dandy, dilly, doozy **6** doozie **9** humdinger
beauteous: 6 lovely, pretty **8** gorgeous, stunning
beautician, often: 4 dyer
beauties, group of: 4 bevy
beautiful: 4 cute, fair, sexy, trim **5** grand, ideal, sweet **6** comely, dainty, divine, lovely, pretty, scenic, superb **7** angelic, beaming, elegant, radiant, sublime, winsome **8** alluring, becoming, enticing, esthetic, glorious, gorgeous, handsome, heavenly, pleasing, scenical, splendid, striking, stunning, tasteful **9** admirable, angelical, appealing, covetable, desirable, excellent, exquisite, marvelous, ravishing, wonderful **10** attractive, bewitching, delightful, ornamental, statuesque, well-formed
combining form: 4 call-, calo- **5** calli-, callo-
make more ~: 5 adorn **7** dress up, enhance **8** decorate
name meaning ~: 5 Shana **7** Belinda
people: 5 elite **6** jet set
person: 6 vision **7** stunner **8** knockout
beautiful __: 6 people
Beautiful __: 5 Girls **7** Dreamer
Beautiful __, A: 4 Mind **7** Morning
__ Beautiful: 5 House
__ Beautiful Doll: 5 Oh You
Beautiful Dreamer composer: 6 Foster
Beautiful Girls (1996 film)
cast: Matt Dillon, Noah Emmerich, Annabeth Gish, Lauren Holly, Timothy Hutton
director: Ted Demme
__ Beautiful Girl, The: 4 Most
Beautiful Mind, A (2001 film)
cast: Jennifer Connelly, Russell Crowe, Ed Harris
director: Ron Howard
Beautiful Morning, A (1968 song)
artist: Rascals
__ beautiful pea-green boat: 3 in a
__ Beautiful Sea: 5 By the
Beautiful Stranger (1999 song) artist: Madonna
beautify: 4 deck, gild, trim **5** adorn, array, grace, primp **6** bedeck, make up **7** develop, dress up, enhance, flatter, garnish, improve **8** decorate, emblazon, ornament, prettify **9** embellish, embroider, glamorize, smarten up
beauty: 3 pip **4** doll **5** asset, charm, class, dandy, doozy, grace, merit, style, value, Venus, worth **6** Adonis, allure, Apollo, appeal, eyeful, glamor, looker, vision **7** benefit, charmer, glamour, Miss U.S.A., stunner **8** artistry, elegance, radiance, radiancy **9** advantage, dreamboat, good looks, humdinger **10** attraction, loveliness, refinement
add ~ to: 5 adorn **7** dress up, enhance **8** decorate
aid: 4 kohl **5** gloss, liner, rouge **6** powder **7** blusher, mascara **8** cosmetic, lipstick, war paint **9** cosmetics **10** face powder
ender: 4 bush **5** berry
goddess of ~: 5 Venus **6** Hathor **9** Aphrodite
magazine: 4 Elle **5** Vogue **6** Allure
name meaning ~: 5 Jamal **6** Jamaal
parlor: 5 salon
preceder: 3 age
realm of ~: 3 art
beauty __: 4 mark, shop, spot **5** quark, salon, sleep **6** parlor **7** contest
__ beauty: 4 rock **6** meadow, spring **7** bathing, painted
Beauty __ the eye...: 4 is in
__ Beauty: 4 Rome **5** Black, She's a **7** Bathing
Beauty and the Beast (1992 song)
artist: Celine Dion, Peabo Bryson
Beauty and the Beast (CBS drama)
cast: Linda Hamilton (Catherine Chandler)
Ron Perlman (Vincent)
Vincent's home, in ~: 5 sewer
Beauty and the Beast (1946 film)
director: Jean Cocteau
__ Beauty apple: 4 Rome
beauty cream additive: 4 aloe
...beauty is __ forever: 4 a joy
Beauty is only skin-deep: 3 saw **5** adage **6** saying
Beauty Is Only Skin Deep (1966 song)
artist: Temptations
beauty pageant
accessory: 4 sash
award: 5 tiara, title **7** bouquet
title: 4 Miss
VIP: 5 judge
beauty parlor: 5 salon
application: 3 dye **4** tint **5** henna, rinse **6** bleach, mousse **7** mud pack
item: 3 dye, net **4** comb, tint **5** drier, dryer, rinse **6** curler, mousse, roller **7** hairpin, shampoo **9** blow dryer, hair spray
treatment: 3 set **4** perm, trim **5** rinse **6** dye job, facial **7** shampoo, touch-up **8** manicure
Beauty's beloved: 5 Beast
Beauty's Punishment author: Anne Rice
Beauty's Release author: Anne Rice
Beauvoir, Simone de: 6 French, writer
friend: Sartre
work: All Said and Done
The Mandarins
The Prime of Life
The Second Sex
She Came to Stay
beaux __: 4 arts **5** ideal **6** gestes, mondes **7** esprits
beaver: 3 fur, hat **6** animal, mammal, rodent
construction: 3 dam **5** lodge
eager ~: 6 dynamo
emulate a ~: 4 gnaw
ender: 5 board
female: 3 sow
like a ~: 5 eager
male: 4 boar
pelt: 3 plu **4** plew
relative: 3 rat **4** cavy, degu, jird, paca, vole **5** coypu, gundi, mouse, xerus **6** agouti, gerbil, gopher, jerboa, marmot, murine **7** hamster, lemming, muskrat, visacha **8** chipmunk, cricetid, dormouse, squirrel, tuco-tuco **9** chickaree, groundhog, guinea pig, porcupine, woodchuck **10** chinchilla, prairie dog
young: 3 kit
__ beaver: 5 eager
Beaver: 7 Cleaver
show: Leave It to Beaver
State: 3 Ore. **6** Oregon
Beaver __: 3 Dam
Beavercreek: 4 city, town
locale: 4 Ohio
Beavers: 6 Louise
Beaverton: 4 city, town
locale: 6 Oregon
Beavis: 4 teen, toon
Bebe: 7 Daniels **8** Neuwirth
bebop: 4 jazz **5** dance, music
Be-Bop-A-Lula (1956 song) artist: Gene Vincent
Be-Bop Baby (1957 song) artist: Ricky Nelson
be-bopper: 3 cat
becalm: 4 halt, lull, stop **5** quell, quiet, stall **6** soothe **7** compose
becalmed: 5 still **8** windless **10** motionless

becard: 4 bird
Be Careful, It's My Heart composer: Irving Berlin
because: 3 for 5 due to, since 6 in that 7 owing to, whereas 8 as long as, by reason, by virtue, in view of 10 inasmuch as, seeing that
of: 5 due to 7 owing to, through 8 thanks to
of this: 6 hereat
Because __ so: 5 I said
Because (1964 song) artist: Dave Clark Five
Because I Love You (1990 song) artist: Stevie B
Because of Love (1994 song) artist: Janet Jackson
Because of You (1951 song) artist: Tony Bennett
Because They're Young (1960 song) artist: Duane Eddy
Because You Loved Me (1996 song) artist: Celine Dion
béchamel __: 5 sauce
__-bêche: 4 tête
bêche-de-__: 3 mer
Bechet, Sidney: 11 clarinetist, saxophonist
genre: 4 jazz
Bech is Back author: John Updike
Bechke: 5 Elena
beck: 3 nod 6 signal 7 gesture, summons
at one's ~ and call: 5 ready
Beck: 4 Jeff, John 6 Martin 8 Kimberly
beck and __: 4 call
Becker: 4 Gary 5 Boris, Sandy 6 Harold
Becker (CBS sitcom)
cast: Ted Danson (Dr. John Becker), Terry Farrell (Reggie Costa)
Becker, Boris: 7 netster 9 tennis pro
rival: 5 Lendl
Becker, Gary: 8 Nobelist 9 economist
Becker, Harold: 8 director
film: The Black Marble (1979)
City Hall (1996)
Domestic Disturbance (2001)
Malice (1993)
Mercury Rising (1998)
The Onion Field (1979)
The Ragman's Daughter (1972)
Sea of Love (1989)
Becket (1964 film)
cast: Richard Burton, Sir John Gielgud, Peter O'Toole
__ Becket: 7 Thomas à
Beckett: 6 Samuel, Scotty
Beckett, Samuel: 5 Irish 6 writer 8 Nobelist
friend: James Joyce
work: Echo's Bones
Endgame
Malone Dies
Molloy
Murphy
The Unnamable
Waiting for Godot
Watt
Beckinsale, Kate: 7 actress
film: Cold Comfort Farm (1995)
The Golden Bowl (2001)
The Last Days of Disco (1998)
Laurel Canyon (2002)
Pearl Harbor (2001)
Serendipity (2001)
Beckmann: 3 Max
beckon: 3 nod 4 call, coax, draw, lure, wave 5 tempt 6 allure, entice, invite, motion, signal, summon 7 attract, gesture
beckoned: 4 bade
beckoning: 10 attractive
Becks: 4 beer
competitor: 5 Coors, Pabst 6 Amstel, Corona, Miller, Molson 7 Schlitz 8 Dos Equis, Heineken, Michelob 9 Lowenbrau 10 Ballantine
becloud: 3 dim, fog 4 blur, fade, hide, roil, veil 5 bedim, befog, shade 6 darken, puzzle, shadow 7 confuse, eclipse, mystify, obscure 8 bewilder, confound 9 adumbrate, obfuscate 10 overshadow
become: 3 fit, get 4 suit, turn 6 beseem, modify 7 enhance, flatter 8 emerge as, turn into 9 morph into 10 change into, evolve into, look good on, look well on, mature into
__ Becomes Her: 5 Death
becoming: 4 cute, fine, good, nice 6 comely, decent, pretty, proper, seemly 7 fitting 8 apposite, decorous, handsome, suitable 9 agreeable, beautiful, enhancing
becomingly: 4 well
becomingness: 9 propriety
Becquerel, Antoine: 6 French 8 Nobelist 9 physicist
__ Be Cruel: 4 Don't
bed: 3 cot 4 base, bunk, crib, doss, king, plot, sack, twin 5 basis, berth, futon, layer, patch 6 bottom, cradle, garden, ground 7 stratum, trundle 8 barracks, bassinet, mattress 9 furniture, underside 10 foundation, groundwork, substratum
and breakfast: 3 inn 7 lodging
baby ~: 4 crib 6 cradle 8 bassinet
board: 4 slat
camp ~: 3 cot 4 bunk
care for a ~: 3 hoe 4 make, weed
coal ~: 4 seam 7 stratum
combining form: 4 clin- 5 clino-
covering: 5 duvet, eider, quilt 6 canopy, spread 9 comforter
day ~: 4 sofa 5 divan
ender: 3 bug, rid 4 fast, mate, post, rock, roll, room, side, time 5 plate, stead, straw 6 fellow, ridden, spread, spring 7 chamber, clothes
fabric: 5 linen, sheet 10 pillowcase
flower ~: 4 plot 6 garden
frame: 5 stead
go to ~: 3 lie 5 sleep 6 retire, turn in 7 sack out 10 hit the sack
hop out of ~: 4 rise, wake 5 arise, awake, get up, rouse, waken 6 awaken, wake up
in ~: 5 not up 6 asleep, laid up 7 resting, retired 8 sleeping 9 sacked out
in England ~: 3 kip 4 doss
it can hide a ~: 4 sofa
Japanese ~: 3 mat 5 futon
material: 5 brass
Murphy ~ place: 6 closet
occupant: 4 seed 5 plant 6 flower 7 sleeper
of roses: 4 ease 6 luxury 7 comfort 8 good life, opulence
out of ~: 5 astir 6 arisen
portable ~: 3 cot 5 futon
put to ~: 5 close, print 6 finish 7 let roll 8 complete 10 consummate
roll out of ~: 4 rise, wake 5 awake, get up, rouse, waken 6 awaken, bestir, wake up
ship's ~: 4 bunk 5 berth
size: 4 king, twin 5 queen 6 double
starter: 3 day, hot, sea 4 flat, lake, road, seed, sick, snub 5 child, river, water 6 stream 7 feather
bed __: 3 bug 4 bolt, load, rest, tray 5 board, chair, check, linen, place, stone, table 6 jacket 7 molding
bed-__: 3 sit 6 sitter
__ bed: 3 air, box, car, day, hot, pie, pig 4 boat, bunk, camp, loft, mast, sofa, tent, twin 5 angel, chair, field, press, put to, stump 6 anchor, double, filter, French, Murphy, oyster, parade, sleigh 7 feather, tanning, truckle, trundle
__-bed: 4 flat
__-Bed: 5 Hide-A
bed and __: 5 board
bed-and-breakfast: 3 inn
visitor: 5 guest
__ be darned!: 3 I'll
bedaub: 4 blot, soil 5 smear, stain, touch 6 bedeck, blotch, doll up, dude up, smirch, smudge 7 bedizen, begrime, deck out, plaster 8 ornament 9 bespatter, overdress
bedaze: 4 stun 7 confuse
bedazzle: 4 stun 5 shine 7 enchant 9 captivate, overwhelm
bedazzled: 5 in awe
Bedazzled (1967 film)
cast: Eleanor Bron, Peter Cook, Dudley Moore
director: Stanley Donen
Bedazzled (2000 film)
cast: Brendan Fraser, Elizabeth Hurley, Frances O'Connor, Miriam Shor
director: Harold Ramis
Bed Bath and __: 6 Beyond
bedbug: 5 cimex 6 chinch, insect
bedclothes: 3 PJs 4 gown 6 nighty 7 nightie, pajamas 9 nightgown 10 sleep shirt
bedcover: 5 duvet, eider, quilt 6 canopy, spread 9 comforter
bedding: 5 cover, eider, linen, quilt, sheet 6 linens, pillow 7 blanket 9 comforter, down quilt, eiderdown 10 pillowcase
bedding __: 5 plane, plant
Beddoe: 5 Philo
beddy-__: 3 bye
Bede: 4 Adam 5 saint
bedeck: 4 gild, trim 5 adorn, array, grace 6 bedaub 7 bedizen, dress up, enhance, festoon, garnish 8 accouter, accoutre, beautify, decorate, ornament 9 caparison, embellish, embroider, glamorize
bedecked: 4 clad
Bedelia, Bonnie: 7 actress
film: Bad Manners (1998)
The Big Fix (1978)
The Boy Who Could Fly (1986)
Die Hard (1988)
Die Hard 2 (1990)
Fat Man and Little Boy (1989)
Lovers and Other Strangers (1970)
Speechless (1994)
Bedelia home, in a folk song: 4 Erin
bedevil: 3 bug, vex 4 bait, gall, jinx, roil 5 annoy, chaff, harry, haunt, tease, worry 6 badger, bother, harass, muddle, needle, noodge, obsess, pester 7 agonize, confuse, provoke, torment 8 befuddle, confound, distress, irritate
bedeviled: 7 accurst 8 accursed, obsessed 9 possessed
bedew: 3 wet 6 dampen 7 moisten 8 sprinkle
bedewed: 3 wet 4 damp 5 moist 10 glistening
bedfellow: 4 ally
Bedford: 4 city, town
locale: 5 Texas
Bedford Incident, The (1965 film)
cast: Sidney Poitier, Richard Widmark
Bedfordshire: 6 county
city: 5 Luton
locale: 7 England
river: 4 Ouse
bedim: 4 blur 5 cloud, shade 6 darken, shadow 7 becloud, obscure 9 adumbrate 10 overshadow
bedizen: 5 adorn 6 bedaub, bedeck 8 decorate, ornament
Bedknobs and Broomsticks (1971 film)
cast: Angela Lansbury, David Tomlinson
director: Robert Stevenson
bedlam: 3 din 4 mess, riot 5 chaos, noise 6 hubbub, mayhem, tumult, unrest, uproar 7 anarchy, ferment, turmoil 8 disarray, madhouse, shambles, upheaval 9 commotion, confusion, mobocracy 10 hullabaloo, hurly-burly, turbulence
Bedlam (1946 film)
cast: Boris Karloff, Anna Lee, Ian Wolfe
Bedloe's __: 6 Island
bed-making: 9 housework
Bednarik: 5 Chuck
Bednorz, Georg: 8 Nobelist 9 physicist
Bedny, Demyan: 4 poet 7 Russian
bed of __: 5 nails, roses
Bed of Flowers, A author: Auburon Waugh
bed of nails
user: 5 faker, fakir, faqir 6 faquir
Bed of Roses (1933 film)
cast: Constance Bennett, Joel McCrea
director: Gregory La Cava
Bed of Roses (1993 song) artist: Bon Jovi
bedog: 5 hound 6 harass
Bedouin: 4 Arab 5 tribe
headcord: 4 agal
language: 6 Arabic
leader: 5 sheik 6 shaikh, sheikh
mount: 5 camel
robe: 3 aba 4 abba
bedraggle: 4 muss, soil 6 rumple
bedraggled: 5 dowdy, grimy, seedy, soggy, soppy 6 blowsy, blowzy, filthy, frowsy, frowzy, frumpy, shabby, sloppy, sodden, soiled, unneat, untidy 7 blowsed, blowzed, dirtied, muddied, scruffy, sullied, unclean, unkempt 8 decrepit, drenched, dripping, slipshod, slovenly 9 ungroomed 10 besmirched, disheveled, disordered, threadbare
bedrape: 3 rig 4 deck, garb 5 array, cover, dress 6 attire, clothe, fit out, outfit, tog out 7 costume 8 accouter, accoutre 9 caparison
Bedrich: 7 Smetana
Bed Riddance author: Ogden Nash
bedridden: 3 ill 4 sick 6 ailing, infirm, laid up, sickly, unwell 7 unsound 8 confined 9 afflicted 10 indisposed
bedrock: 4 base 5 dance 10 foundation
deposit: 3 oil, ore 9 gemstones, petroleum 10 natural gas
Bedrock
see Flintstones
bedroll alternative: 3 cot 4 bunk
bedroom: 5 berth, bower 7 boudoir, chamber
adjunct: 6 closet
community: 4 burb 5 exurb 6 suburb 9 outskirts
furniture: 4 lamp 5 suite 6 bureau, vanity 7 dresser 8 wardrobe
bedroom __: 7 slipper 9 community
__ bedroom: 6 master
Bedroom at __: 5 Arles
Bedroom Farce author: Alan Ayckbourn
Bedroom Window (1987 film)
cast: Steve Guttenberg, Isabelle Huppert, Elizabeth McGovern
director: Curtis Hanson
Bedrosian: 5 Steve
Beds: 6 county

locale: 7 England
bedsheets: 5 linen
bedside
book: 5 diary
companion: 5 nurse
furnishing: 4 lamp 5 table 8 end table
item: 5 clock
bedside __: 6 manner
__ Beds National Monument: 4 Lava
bedspread: 5 cover 7 blanket 8 coverlet, coverlid
fabric: 8 chenille 10 marseilles
bedstead
light ~: 3 cot 4 bunk
part: 3 leg 4 slat 5 frame
bedtime: 5 night, sleep 6 curfew
approach ~: 5 laten
beverage: 4 milk 5 cocoa, toddy
in ads: 4 nite
late ~: 2 a.m. 3 two 4 four 5 one a.m., three, two a.m. 6 four a.m. 7 three a.m. 8 midnight, wee hours
reading: 5 novel, story
sound: 5 snore
bedtime __: 5 story
Bedtime for Bonzo (1951 film)
cast: Diana Lynn, Ronald Reagan, Walter Slezak
director: Frederick de Cordova
Bedtime Story (1941 film)
cast: Fredric March, Loretta Young
bee: 3 bug 5 drone, grade, party 6 insect, social, worker 7 stinger 9 carpenter, gathering, spelldown 10 pollinator
busy ~: 7 hustler 8 live wire
compete in a ~: 5 spell
defense: 5 sting 7 stinger
ender: 4 hive, line 5 bread 6 keeper
follower: 3 cee
genus: 4 apis
home: 4 hive 6 apiary
male ~: 5 drone
name meaning ~: 5 Debra 7 Deborah
participant: 6 husker 7 quilter, speller
product: 3 wax 4 comb 5 honey, quilt
starter: 5 honey 6 bumble, humble
stingless ~: 5 drone
target: 6 flower
bee __: 3 fly, gum 4 balm, bird, glue, moth, tree 5 block, plant 6 beetle, martin
bee-__: 5 eater, stung
__ bee: 4 king 5 apple, honey, mason, queen, sweat 6 bumble, killer, social, worker 7 husking
Bee: 4 aunt 5 paper 9 newspaper
locale: 6 Fresno 10 Sacramento
to Andy: 4 aunt
Bee __: 4 Gees
beebee: 4 ammo, shot 10 ammunition
Beebe, William: 8 explorer
milieu: 3 sea 4 deep 5 ocean
beech: 3 nut 4 fern, tree 9 shade tree
tree: 8 chestnut
beech __: 4 fern, mast 6 marten
__ beech: 6 copper, purple
Beech-__: 3 Nut
competitor: 6 Gerber
Beecham, Thomas: 3 Sir 7 British 9 conductor
Beecher, Henry Ward: 6 writer
daughter: Harriet
Beecher, Lyman: 8 preacher
__ Beecher Stowe: 7 Harriet
Beechwood 4-5789 (1962 song) artist: Marvelettes
bee-eater: 4 bird
beef: 4 kick, meat, moan 5 brawn, cavil, chuck, gripe, might, power, sinew 6 cattle, charge, grouse, muscle, plaint, repine, squawk, yammer 7 dispute, grumble, protest, quarrel, red meat 8 argument, complain, strength 9 bellyache, complaint, criticism, grievance, make a fuss, objection
cut: 3 eye 4 chop, loin, rump 5 chuck, filet, patty, roast, round, shank, steak, T-bone 6 pattie 7 sirloin 9 club steak, cube steak 11 filet migñon, porterhouse
designation: 5 prime 6 grade A
dish: 4 stew 6 fajita
dried ~: 5 jerky
ender: 4 wood 5 eater, steak
eschewer: 5 vegan 10 vegetarian
full of ~ fat: 5 suety
half a ~: 4 side
in French: 5 boeuf
large joint of ~: 5 baron
like some ~: 4 lean
product: 5 jerky
rating org.: 4 USDA
so to speak: 4 turf
up: 4 gird, grow, tone 5 bloat, boost, build, shore, steel, swell, widen 6 anneal, dilate, expand, fatten, harden, temper 7 amplify, augment, bolster, broaden, burgeon, develop, empower, enhance, enlarge, fortify, inflate, stiffen, toughen 8 bourgeon, buttress, energize, heighten, indurate, lengthen, vitalize 9 intensify, reinforce 10 aggrandize, invigorate, strengthen, supplement
young ~: 4 veal
beef __: 3 tea 4 stew 6 cattle 7 extract
__ beef: 4 baby, corn, Kobe 5 bully 6 corned 7 chipped, corn-fed
beefalo: 5 bovid 6 bovine, hybrid
relative: 3 yak 4 anoa, arna, gaur, urus, zebu 5 bison, gayal, takin 6 mithan, muskox 7 aurochs, banteng, banting, buffalo, carabao, kouprey, tamarao, tamarau, timarau
beefcake: 4 hunk, stud
beefiness: 3 vim 4 dint, thew 5 brawn, force, might, power, thews, vigor 6 energy, muscle 7 fitness, muscles, potence, potency, stamina 8 vitality 9 endurance, fortitude, puissance, toughness 10 brute force
beefsteak: 4 meat 6 tomato
relative: 4 Roma 6 Big Boy 9 Better Boy, Early Girl, Quick Pick
beefsteak __: 3 rye 6 fungus, tomato 7 begonia
beefwood: 4 tree
beefy: 4 hale, iron, wiry 5 bulky, burly, fubsy, hardy, heavy, hefty, hulky, hunky, husky, lusty, meaty, obese, plump, pudgy, pursy, solid, stout, tough 6 brawny, chubby, chunky, fleshy, hearty, mighty, portly, potent, pyknic, robust, rotund, rugged, sinewy, steely, stocky, strong, sturdy, virile, zaftig, zoftig 7 adipose, doughty, filling, hulking, massive, paunchy 8 athletic, forceful, indurate, muscular, powerful, puissant, roly-poly, stalwart, thickset, vigorous 9 Atlantean, corpulent, filled-out, Herculean, strapping, well-built 10 able-bodied, overweight, red-blooded
Bee Gees: 4 trio
member: Barry, Maurice, Robin, Gibb
song: How Can You Mend a Broken Heart (1971)
How Deep Is Your Love (1977)
I Started a Joke (1969)
I've Got to Get a Message to You (1968)
Jive Talkin' (1975)
Lonely Days (1970)
Love So Right (1976)
Love You Inside Out (1979)
Night Fever (1978)
Nights on Broadway (1975)
One (1989)
Stayin' Alive (1977)
Too Much Heaven (1978)
Tragedy (1979)
You Should Be Dancing (1976)
beehive: 4 coif, nest 6 apiary, hairdo 7 upsweep 8 coiffure 9 hairstyle
boss: 5 queen
cousin: 4 Afro
like a ~: 4 ahum, busy
sound: 4 buzz
straw ~: 4 skep
Beehive State
see Utah
beekeeper: 8 apiarist
beeline: 5 route
in a ~: 8 directly, straight
make a ~: 5 hurry 6 hasten
Beelzebub: 5 demon, devil, Satan 6 daemon, daimon 7 Lucifer
forte: 4 evil
been: 5 lived 6 stayed 7 existed
had ~: 3 was 4 were
__-been: 3 has
__ Been a Long, Long Time: 3 It's
Been Around the World (1998 song)
artist: Mase, Notorious B.I.G., Puff Daddy
Beene: 8 Geoffrey
__ been had!: 3 I've
__ Been Kissed: 5 Never
__ Been Lonely Too Long: 3 I've
__ been robbed!: 3 I've
__ been sleeping in my bed?: 4 Who's
been there, __ that: 4 done
__ been thinking...: 3 I've
__ Been Working on the Railroad: 3 I've
beep: 4 call, honk, page, tone, toot 6 signal, summon
Beep Beep (1958 song) artist: Playmates
beeper: 4 horn 5 alarm, pager
beer: 3 Bud 4 brew, suds 5 Becks, Coors, drink, Kirin, lager, Pabst, quaff 6 Amstel, chaser, Corona, liquor, Miller, Molson, stingo 7 brewski, cold one, pilsner, Schlitz 8 beverage, Dos Equis, Heineken, Michelob 9 Budweiser, inebriant, Lowenbrau 10 Ballantine
agave ~: 6 pulque
barrel: 3 keg
category: 4 lite 5 draft
characteristic: 4 body, foam, head 5 froth
corn ~: 6 chicha
dark ~: 4 bock
Dutch ~: 6 Amstel 8 Heineken
holder: 3 keg, mug 5 glass, stein 6 barrel, bottle, cooler, fridge 8 schooner
ingredient: 4 malt, wort 5 grain, yeast 6 barley
Japanese ~: 5 Kirin
joint: 3 bar, pub 6 saloon, tavern 8 alehouse 9 bierstube, roadhouse
keg adjunct: 3 tap
light ~: 5 lager
like bock ~: 4 aged
like some ~: 5 on tap
low-calorie ~: 4 lite
make ~: 4 brew
Mexican ~: 6 Corona 8 Dos Equis
nickname: 3 Oly
nonalcoholic ~: 6 Odoul's
old ~ brand: 5 Piels
Polynesian ~: 4 kava
quantity: 3 keg 4 case 6 barrel 7 six-pack
relative: 3 ale 5 stout
reminiscent of ~: 5 malty
Russian ~: 5 kvass, quass
spring ~: 4 bock
beer __: 4 bust, hall, pump 5 on tap 6 engine, garden
__ beer: 3 ice 4 bock, near, root 5 birch, draft, lager, small, steam, weiss 6 ginger, spruce
Beer __: 4 Nuts
Beer Barrel __: 5 Polka
beer-bellied: 6 flabby 10 abdominous
Beerbohm, Max: 6 writer 7 British
Beeri daughter: 6 Judith
Beernaert, Auguste: 7 Belgian 8 Nobelist
beer on __: 3 tap
Beersheba: 4 city, town
locale: 6 Israel
region: 5 Negeb
Beery: 4 Noah 7 Wallace
Beery, Wallace: 5 actor
film: Ah, Wilderness! (1935)
The Big House (1930)
The Bowery (1933)
The Champ (1931, AA)
China Seas (1935)
Dinner at Eight (1933)
Flesh (1932)
Grand Hotel (1932)
The Last of the Mohicans (1920)
A Message to Garcia (1936)
The Mighty Barnum (1934)
Min and Bill (1930)
Old Ironsides (1926)
Slave Ship (1937)
This Man's Navy (1945)
Three Ages (1923)
Treasure Island (1934)
Viva Villa! (1934)
spouse: Gloria Swanson
bees
do it: 5 sting
ender: 3 wax
group of ~: 5 swarm
of ~: 5 apian
bee's __: 5 knees
bee-sting result: 4 itch, welt
beet: 4 root 5 chard 6 veggie 9 vegetable
ender: 4 root
product: 5 sugar 6 borsch 7 borscht
beet __: 5 sugar
__ beet: 4 leaf 5 sugar
beet-faced: 3 red 5 ruddy 6 florid
Beethoven, Ludwig van: 6 German 8 composer
birthplace: 4 Bonn
piece: 4 opus 5 opera, rondo 6 sonata 8 concerto, symphony
work: Appassionata Sonata
Choral Symphony
Coriolanus Overture
Emperor Concerto
Eroica Symphony
Fidelio
Für Elise
Kreutzer Sonata
Leonore Overture
Missa Solemnis
Moonlight Sonata
Pastoral Symphony
Pathétique Sonata
Spring Sonata
Waldstein Sonata
Wellington's Victory
beetle: 3 bug, dor, ram 4 beat, dorr, form, mold, pelt, uang 5 crush, forge, lay on, pound, shape 6 batter, chafer, hammer, insect, pummel, scarab 7 firefly, ladybug, project 8 overhang, protrude, stand out 10 projecting, protruding
click ~: 6 elater
eater: 6 mantid, mantis
ender: 4 weed

larva: 4 grub
rhinoceros ~: 4 uang
starter: 4 lady
beetle-___: 6 browed
___ beetle: 3 bee, May, oil 4 bark, bean, fire, flea, gold, leaf, rose, rove, seed, stag 5 click, flour, snout, tiger, water 6 carpet, diving, flower, ground, khapra, larder, potato, sawyer, sexton, spruce, timber 7 Asiatic, blister, fiddler
Beetle: 2 VW 3 car 4 auto 6 German 10 automobile, Volkswagen
Beetle Bailey: 5 comic 10 comic strip
artist: Mort Walker
dog: 4 Otto
organization: 4 army
soldier: 4 Zero 5 Plato, Sarge 7 Snorkel
Beetlejuice (1988 film)
cast: Alec Baldwin, Geena Davis, Michael Keaton
director: Tim Burton
beetleweed: 5 galax
beetling: 9 prominent
___ beets: 7 Harvard, pickled
beeves: 6 cattle
beezer: 5 snoot 6 schnoz 7 schnozz 9 schnozzle 10 schnozzola
bef.: 4 prev.
befall: 4 pass 5 occur, visit 6 happen 7 occur to 8 happen to, overtake 9 come about, take place, transpire 10 come to pass
cause to ~: 5 incur
befit: 4 suit 6 beseem
befitting: 3 apt, fit 4 just, nice 5 right 6 beseem, kasher, kosher, proper, seemly 7 fitting 8 apposite, decorous, rightful, suitable 9 agreeable, behooving, beseeming, on the nose 10 applicable, conforming, felicitous
befog: 3 dim 4 blur, mist 5 cloud 6 darken, muddle 7 becloud, confuse, mystify, obscure, steam up 8 confound 9 obfuscate
befool: 5 trick 8 hoodwink
be for: 4 back 5 favor 7 support
before: 2 by 3 ago, ere 4 once, till 5 ahead, prior, until 6 erenow, gone by, hereto 7 ahead of, earlier, prior to, up to now 8 formerly, hitherto 9 a while ago, in advance, in front of, in the past, preceding 10 previously, previous to
combining form: 4 fore- 6 proter- 7 protero-
ender: 4 hand, time
in German: 3 von
old-style: 4 erst
prefix: 3 pre-, pro- 4 ante-, fore-
the present: 3 ago 4 past
the rest: 5 first 9 preceding
to a poet: 3 ere
before ___: 4 long
Before and After (1996 film)
cast: Edward Furlong, Liam Neeson, Meryl Streep
director: Barbet Schroeder
___ before beauty: 3 age
___ Before Dying: 5 A Kiss
beforehand: 5 ahead, early, first 6 sooner 7 advance, already, betimes, earlier 9 a while ago, in advance 10 in good time, precocious, previously
Before I Say Good-Bye author: Mary Higgins Clark
Before Night Falls (2000 film)
cast: Javier Bardem, Andrea Di Stefano, Olivier Martinez, Sean Penn
director: Julian Schnabel
___ before swine: 6 pearls
Before the Next Teardrop Falls (1975 song) artist: Freddy Fender
___ before the storm: 4 calm
beforetime: 8 formerly 10 previously
___ Before Time, The: 4 Land
___ before you leap: 4 look
Before You Walk out of My Life (1995 song) artist: Monica
befoul: 3 mar 4 soil 5 dirty, smear, spoil, stain, sully, taint 6 defile, malign, smudge 7 begrime, blacken, pollute, profane, tarnish 8 besmirch 9 desecrate
befouled: 5 grimy, sooty 6 filthy, grubby, grungy 7 unclean 8 maculate, slovenly 10 unsanitary
befriend: 7 promote, sustain, welcome 8 cotton to 9 buddy up to 10 take up with
___ be friends!: 4 Let's
befuddle: 4 daze 5 addle, mix up, throw 6 baffle, muddle, puzzle 7 bedevil, confuse, fluster, perplex 8 bewilder, confound, unsettle 9 disorient, dumbfound, inebriate 10 intoxicate
befuddled: 4 asea, dopy, hazy 5 at sea, dizzy, loopy 6 addled, in a fog 7 reeling 9 slaphappy 10 bewildered
beg: 3 ask, sue, woo 4 pray, seek, urge 5 cadge, hit up, mooch, plead, press 6 adjure, appeal, grovel 7 beseech, entreat, implore, request, solicit 8 freeload, petition, scrounge, sponge on 9 impetrate, importune, mendicate, panhandle 10 pass the hat, supplicate
off: 5 demur 6 bow out, refuse 7 decline
pardon: 5 sorry 8 excuse me 9 apologize
beg ___: 3 off
beget: 4 bear, have, sire 5 breed, cause, spawn 6 create, father 7 produce 8 engender, result in 9 procreate, propagate, reproduce 10 bring about, give rise to
beggar: 4 hobo, ruin 5 faker, fakir, faqir, tramp 6 faquir, pauper, rascal 7 have-not, vagrant 8 deadbeat, indigent, vagabond 9 mendicant, scrounger 10 impoverish, panhandler, ragamuffin, supplicant
request: 4 alms
beggarly: 4 base, mean, poor 5 broke, needy, sorry 6 bad off, hard up, ill off, in need, in want, meager, measly, paltry, shabby 7 pinched, pitiful, servile 8 badly off, bankrupt, indigent, piddling, strapped, wretched 9 destitute, insolvent, miserable, moneyless, penniless, penurious 10 down and out, inadequate, pauperized, straitened
Beggar Maid, The: 4 poem
author: Tennyson
Beggar-My-Neighbor: 4 game 8 card game
Beggar on Horseback author: George S. Kaufman
beggars can't be choosers: 3 saw 5 adage 6 saying
Beggar's Opera, The (1953 film)
cast: Stanley Holloway, Laurence Olivier
director: Peter Brook
Beggar's Opera, The author: John Gay
beggary: 4 need 6 penury, rabble 7 poverty 8 riffraff 9 indigence, neediness, pauperism 10 insolvency
begin: 4 dawn, open, rise 5 arise, enter, found, set in, set to, set up, start 6 appear, assume, crop up, emerge, fall to, go to it, launch, let rip, set off, set out, spring, tackle, wade in 7 aggress, develop, go ahead, jump off, kick off, lead off, preface, take off, usher in 8 activate, commence, embark on, get going, initiate, set about, set forth, touch off 9 actualize, come forth, enter into, establish, eventuate, germinate, get to work, institute, introduce, originate, strike out, undertake 10 inaugurate, plunge into
again: 5 renew 6 resume
a journey: 2 go 4 pack, sail 5 board, leave, start 6 embark, set off, set out 7 emplane, entrain, jump off, set sail, ship out 8 go aboard, set forth 9 leave port, undertake
a paragraph: 6 indent
business: 4 open
hostilities: 5 set on, storm 6 attack, engage, invade, strike 7 set upon
to develop: 3 bud 6 sprout 9 germinate
to like: 6 grow on
to ~ with: 5 first
Begin, Menachem: 2 P.M. 7 Israeli 8 Nobelist
Nobelist Peace partner: 5 Sadat
predecessor: 5 Rabin
successor: 6 Shamir
beginner: 3 cub 4 tiro, tyro 5 newie, pupil 6 greeny, newbie, novice 7 amateur, dabbler, entrant, learner, new hand, recruit, trainee 8 freshman, initiate, neophyte, newcomer, putterer 9 fledgling, greenhorn, novitiate 10 apprentice, dilettante, first-timer, tenderfoot
beginner's ___: 4 luck
beginning: 3 top 4 as of, dawn, germ, rise, seed 5 birth, early, first, front, gitgo, intro, onset, start 6 advent, day one, origin, outset, source, spring 7 genesis, infancy, initial, kickoff, leadoff, nascent, opening, preface, prelude, premier, primary 8 creation, entrance, original, preamble, premiere 9 emanation, etymology, inception, inceptive, incipient, induction, principle, square one, threshold 10 antecedent, conception, derivation, elementary, envisaging, generation, incipience, initiation
Beginning or the End, The (1947 film)
cast: Brian Donlevy, Robert Walker
director: Norman Taurog
beginnings: 4 root 6 origin 7 infancy
Beginnings (1971 song) artist: Chicago
___ Beginning to Look a Lot...: 3 It's
___ Begins at Forty: 4 Life
___ Begins for Andy Hardy: 4 Life
Begin the Beguine
bandleader: 4 Shaw
composer: Cole Porter
begird: 3 tie 4 belt, bind 5 bound, box in, hem in, truss 6 buckle, circle, fasten, shut in 7 confine, contain, enclose, inclose 8 cincture, encircle, surround 9 encompass
be glad to: 4 sure 6 no prob 8 of course, you got it 9 certainly, no problem
Begley, Ed: 5 actor
film: 12 Angry Men (1957)
Hang 'em High (1968)
Patterns (1956)
Sweet Bird of Youth (1962, AA)
The Unsinkable Molly Brown (1964)
Warning Shot (1967)
Begley Jr., Ed: 5 actor
film: Blue Collar (1978)
She-Devil (1989)
TV: St. Elsewhere
begone: 4 away, scat, shoo 5 scram 6 avaunt, beat it, get out 7 amscray, buzz off, get lost, push off, vamoose 9 take a hike 10 go fly a kite
starter: 3 woe
begonia: 5 plant 6 flower
___ begonia: 3 rex
___, Be Good!: 4 Lady
Be Good to Yourself (1986 song) artist: Journey
Beg pardon!: 4 ahem 5 sorry 8 excuse me
begrime: 4 foul, soil 5 dirty, stain, sully, taint 6 bedaub, befoul, smirch, smudge 7 besmear, blacken, pollute, tarnish 8 besmirch
begrimed: 5 dirty, grimy, smoky, sooty 6 filthy, grubby, grungy 7 unswept 8 maculate, polluted, slovenly, unwashed 10 unsanitary
begrudge: 4 envy 5 covet, spite, stint
begrudging: 7 envious, jealous 9 unwilling
beg to ___: 6 differ
beguile: 3 con, lie, wow 4 bait, coax, dupe, fool, lure, rook, scam, sell, snow, trap, vamp, wile 5 amuse, charm, cheat, tempt, trick 6 allure, cajole, delude, divert, entice, entrap, lead on, rope in, take in, tickle 7 attract, bewitch, deceive, defraud, delight, enchant, enthral, finesse, inthral, mislead, pretend, two-time 8 enthrall, entrance, flimflam, hoodwink, inthrall, inveigle 9 captivate, disinform, enrapture, entertain, fascinate, infatuate
beguiled: 4 rapt 5 led on 7 far gone 8 held fast, ravished 10 infatuated
Beguiled, The (1970 film)
cast: Clint Eastwood, Elizabeth Hartman, Geraldine Page
director: Don Siegel
beguiler: 4 vamp 5 siren 6 gigolo 7 charmer 9 inveigler, temptress 10 gold digger
beguiling: 5 siren 8 alluring, delusive, inviting, specious 9 deceitful, deceptive 10 enchanting, fallacious, misleading
beguine: 5 dance
relative: 5 rumba 6 rhumba
begum spouse: 3 aga 4 agha
begun: 8 underway 9 happening 10 in progress
behalf: 4 part, sake, side 7 account, benefit 8 interest
on ~: 6 in lieu
on ~ of: 3 for 7 instead 9 acting for, in place of
Behan, Brendan: 5 Irish 6 author, writer
work: Borstal Boy
The Hostage
The Quare Fellow
behave: 2 do 3 act 4 mind, work 5 react 6 acquit, deport 7 act well, comport, conduct, conform, go along, operate, perform, respond 8 function 10 act one's age, stay in line, toe the line
toward: 5 treat 6 handle
___-behaved: 4 well
behaved, badly: 7 naughty
___ Behaving Badly: 3 Men
behavior: 3 way 4 form 6 habits, manner, morals, policy 7 actions, bearing, conduct, manners 8 carriage, demeanor, protocol 9 treatment 10 deportment
brave ~: 5 valor 7 courage
code of ~: 5 ethic 6 ethics 8 morality, protocol
past ~: 6 record
pattern: 5 habit, type A, Type B 8 syndrome
well-mannered ~: 4 tact 7 decorum 8 breeding, civility, courtesy, protocol, urbanity 9 etiquette, gallantry,

gentility **10** politeness, refinement
__ **behavior: 4** good **6** animal
behavioral science: 10 psychology
behemoth: 5 giant **7** mammoth, monster **8** colossus **9** leviathan
behest: 4 word **5** order **6** charge, urging **7** bidding, command, dictate, mandate, precept, request **9** direction, directive, prompting
behind: 3 aft, for, off, pro **4** last, late, next, slow **5** after, tardy **6** astern, in back, in debt, latish, losing **7** backing, belated, causing, delayed, ensuing, lagging, overdue, past due **8** backside, backward, in back of, trailing **9** following, in arrears, later than **10** delinquent, succeeding, supporting
combining form: 7 opistho-
prefix: 4 meta-, post- **5** retro-
behind __: 4 bars
__ **behind: 3** lag **4** drop, fall
Behind Closed Doors (1973 song)
artist: Charlie Rich
Behind Enemy Lines (2001 film)
cast: Gene Hackman, Gabriel Macht, Owen Wilson
behindhand: 3 lax **5** tardy **7** belated, overdue **9** negligent, unheedful
Behind That Curtain hero: 4 Chan
behind the __: 5 times, wheel **6** scenes
behind the __ ball: 5 eight
__ **behind the ears: 3** wet
behind-the-scenes: 6 covert, secret
behold: 3 see **4** ecce, espy, look, ta-da, view **5** sight, ta-dah, voilà **6** look at, notice, peek at, regard, remark **7** discern, observe, witness **8** gaze upon, perceive **10** get a load of
in Latin: 4 ecce
something to ~: 6 eyeful
the man, in Latin: 8 ecce homo
__ **behold: 5** lo and
behold a son, name meaning:
6 Reuben
Behold competitor: 6 Endust, Pledge **10** Liquid Gold, Old English
beholden: 4 into **5** owing **6** in hock **7** obliged **8** grateful, indebted, thankful **9** obligated **10** honor-bound
be ~: 3 owe
beholder: 6 viewer **7** watcher, witness **8** observer, onlooker **9** spectator **10** eyewitness
__ **Be Home For Christmas: 3** I'll
behoof: 3 use **7** benefit **9** advantage
behoove: 5 befit **6** beseem
Behrman, S.N.: 6 author, writer
Beid: 4 star
Beiderbecke: 3 Bix
first name: Leon
genre: 4 jazz
instrument: 5 piano **6** cornet
beige: 4 gray, grey **5** brown, color **6** almond, suntan **7** neutral **8** brownish **9** earth tone
relative: 3 ash, bay, dun, tan **4** bole, dove, drab, ecru, fawn, foxy, nude, seal **5** amber, camel, cocoa, dusty, hazel, khaki, merle, mocha, pearl, putty, sepia, slate, taupe, tawny, umber **6** alesan, auburn, bister, bistre, bronze, coffee, copper, ginger, russet, sienna, silver, sorrel, suntan, walnut **7** biscuit, caramel, dogwood, grizzly **8** charcoal, chestnut, cinnamon, gunmetal, mahogany, platinum **9** butternut, chocolate
beignet: 6 pastry
Beijing: 4 city, town **7** capital
locale: 3 PRC **5** China
Beijing __: 4 duck
Beilan __: 4 Pass
Bei Mir Bist du Schoen (1938 song)
artist: Andrews Sisters

__ **be in England...: 4** Oh to
being: 4 body, esse, life, self, soul **5** human **6** animal, entity, matter, mortal, nature, person **7** essence, reality **8** creature, life form, organism **9** actuality, existence, something **10** individual, living soul
artificial ~: 5 droid, robot **9** automaton
big ~: 5 giant, titan **7** Cyclops, mammoth **9** leviathan
bring into ~: 4 make **5** breed **6** create
combining form: 3 ont- **4** onto-
come into ~: 5 arise, start **6** grow up, spring **7** develop
divine ~: 3 god **4** daka **5** deity **6** dakini **7** goddess
enjoy ~ alive: 4 live **5** party **7** have fun **9** delight in, whoop it up
for the time ~: 3 now **9** meanwhile, temporary
have ~: 3 are **5** exist
human ~: 3 man **4** life, soul **6** person **10** individual, living soul
in Latin: 4 esse
mode of ~: 5 state
strike one as ~: 4 seem **6** appear
that ~ the case: 2 so **4** ergo, if so, then, thus **5** hence
time ~: 5 nonce **7** present
__ **being: 5** human
__**-being: 3** ill **4** well
__ **Being: 7** Supreme
Being and Having author: Gabriel Marcel
Being and Nothingness author: Jean-Paul Sartre
Being John Malkovich (1999 film)
cast: John Cusack, Cameron Diaz, Catherine Keener, John Malkovich
director: Spike Jonze
Being There: 4 film **5** novel
author: Jerzy Kosinski
cast: Melvyn Douglas, Shirley MacLaine, Peter Sellers, Jack Warden
director: Hal Ashby
Being With You (1981 song) artist: Smokey Robinson
Beira: 4 city, port, town
locale: 10 Mozambique
Beirut: 4 city, port, town **7** capital
locale: 7 Lebanon
Be it __ so humble...: 4 ever
__ **be it from me: 3** far
Beja home: 5 Sudan **6** Africa
Béjart, Maurice: 6 dancer **7** danseur
bejewel: 5 adorn
bejeweled: 6 ornate **10** glittering
Be kind to your web-__ friends:
6 footed
bel __: 5 canto
Bel: 7 Kaufman
Bel __: 3 Air **5** Paese
Bela: 3 Kun **6** Bartók, Lugosi, Schick **7** Karolyi
father: 8 Benjamin
son: 3 Iri
Béla: 6 Bartók
belabor: 4 lash **6** overdo, rehash, stress **7** dwell on **8** go too far, overwork **9** dwell upon, go on about **10** hammer home
Belafonte: 5 Harry, Shari
Belafonte, Harry: 5 actor **6** singer
daughter: Shari
film: The Angel Levine (1970)
Carmen Jones (1954)
Odds Against Tomorrow (1959)
song: Day-O (1957)
Bel Air: 3 car **4** auto, city, town **5** Chevy **9** Chevrolet **10** automobile
locale: 8 Maryland **10** California
Belarus: 6 nation **7** country

capital: 5 Minsk
city: 5 Brest, Gomel, Orsha, Pinsk
neighbor: 6 Latvia, Poland, Russia **7** Ukraine **9** Lithuania
Belasco: 5 David
belated: 4 slow **5** tardy **6** behind, remiss **7** delayed, overdue **8** detained **10** behindhand, last-minute, unpunctual
belay: 4 stop **6** fasten
belaying __: 3 pin **5** cleat
belch: 4 burp, spew, spue **5** eruct **9** discharge
Belch, Toby: 3 sot
beldam: 3 hag **5** crone, shrew, witch **6** virago **8** harridan **9** henpecker
Beldar Conehead's daughter:
6 Connie
beleaguer: 4 bait **5** annoy, harry, tease, worry **6** assail, harass, noodge, plague **7** shut off, shut out **8** surround **9** persecute
beleaguerment: 5 siege
Belém: 4 city, port, town
locale: 6 Brazil
once: 4 Pará
belemnite: 5 shell **6** fossil **8** seashell
Belfast: 4 city, port, town
locale: 7 Ireland
org.: 3 IRA
town near ~: 6 Antrim
Belford: 4 peak **5** mount **8** mountain
locale: 7 Rockies **8** Colorado
Belfort: 4 city, town
locale: 6 France
belfry: 5 spire, tower **6** cupola **7** steeple **8** pinnacle **9** bell tower
dweller: 3 bat
sound: 4 bong, peal, ring, toll
Belg.
see Belgium
belga: 5 money
Bel Geddes: 6 Norman **7** Barbara
Bel Geddes, Barbara: 7 actress
film: Blood on the Moon (1948)
Caught (1949)
Fourteen Hours (1951)
I Remember Mama (1948)
Panic in the Streets (1950)
Vertigo (1958)
TV: Dallas
Belgian __: 4 hare **5** Congo **6** endive **7** griffon
Belgian Blue: 3 cow **4** bull **6** bovine, cattle
Belgian Malinois: 3 dog **5** canid **6** canine
Belgian Tervuren: 3 dog **5** canid **6** canine
Belgium: 6 nation **7** country
ancient ~: 4 Gaul
capital: 8 Brussels
chemist: 6 Solvay
city: 4 Mons **5** Aalst, Alost, Ghent, Liege, Ypres **6** Bruges, Ostend **7** Antwerp **9** Zeebrugge
marble: 5 rance
money: 5 belga, franc **7** centime
neighbor: 6 France **7** Germany, Holland **10** Luxembourg **11** Netherlands
Nobelist in Chemistry: 9 Prigogine
Nobelist in Literature:
11 Maeterlinck
Nobelist in Medicine: 6 Bordet, de Duve **7** Heymans
Nobelist in Peace: 4 Pire **9** Beernaert **10** La Fontaine
org.: 4 Leie, NATO
painter: 5 Ensor **8** Magritte
port: 5 Ghent **6** Ostend **7** Antwerp **9** Zeebrugge
province: 5 Namur

resort: 3 Spa
river: 3 Lys **4** Oise, Yser **5** Meuse, Senne
stew: 10 carbonnade
violinist: 5 Ysaye
Belgrade: 4 city, town **7** capital
city near ~: 5 Vrsac
locale: 10 Yugoslavia
native: 4 Slav
river: 4 Sava **6** Danube
Belial: 5 devil, Satan
belie: 4 mock **5** rebut **6** negate, refute **7** explode, gainsay, slander **8** backbite, disprove **10** calumniate, contradict, controvert
belief: 3 ism **4** idea, side, view **5** cause, credo, creed, dogma, faith, guess, logic, maxim, stand, tenet, trust **6** ethics, notion, school, theory, thesis **7** feeling, mindset, opinion, precept, thought **8** attitude, credence, doctrine, ideology, judgment, position, reliance, religion, standard **9** principle, rationale, sentiment, suspicion, teachings, tradition **10** acceptance, assumption, conclusion, confidence, conjecture, contention, conviction, dependance, dependence, estimation, hypothesis, impression, persuasion
prefix: 4 ideo-
beliefs: 4 lore **5** ethos **8** ideology **10** philosophy
set of ~: 5 credo, creed, dogma **6** mythos
believable: 6 honest, likely **7** tenable **8** credible, possible, probable, rational **9** authentic, fiduciary, plausible, thinkable **10** aboveboard, acceptable, convincing, creditable, imaginable, impressive, persuasive, presumable, reasonable, satisfying, supposable
believe: 3 buy **4** deem, feel, hold, hope, view **5** fancy, judge, sense, think, trust **6** accept, affirm, assume, bank on, credit, expect, gather, hold to, look to, reckon, regard, rely on **7** count on, imagine, presume, suppose, suspect, swallow, swear by **8** conceive, consider, depend on, gamble on, hold with, maintain, theorize **9** count upon, postulate **10** conjecture, presuppose, understand
hard to ~: 4 tall **10** incredible
in: 4 rely **5** trust **6** accept **7** swear by **10** put faith in
lead to ~: 4 hint **5** imply, infer, let on **6** tip off **7** suggest **8** indicate, intimate, persuade **9** brainwash, catechize, insinuate
make ~: 3 lie **4** fool, play, pose **5** dream, enact, feign **7** act as if, act like, imagine, playact, pretend **8** simulate **9** fantasize
old-style: 4 trow
__**-believe: 4** make
...believe __ the whole thing!: 4 I ate
Believe (1999 song) artist: Cher
believed: 7 reputed **8** reported
__ **Believe in Magic: 5** Do You
__ **believe in yesterday: 3** Oh I
Believe It or Not!
creator: 6 Ripley
entry: 6 oddity
believer: 7 apostle **8** adherent, canonist, disciple, follower, upholder **9** dogmatist, layperson, supporter
suffix: 3 -ist, -ite **5** -arian
__ **believer: 4** true
__ **Believer: 3** I'm a, Old **4** True
Believer, The (2002 film)
cast: Summer Phoenix, Theresa Russell, Billy Zane
director: Henry Bean

__ Believes in Me: 3 She
Believe What You Say (1958 song) artist: Ricky Nelson
believing: 4 sure 5 loyal 7 certain 8 positive, sanguine 9 convinced, credulous, satisfied 10 falling for, optimistic
Belinda: 4 moon 8 Carlisle
planet: 6 Uranus
__ Belinda: 6 Johnny
Belinda author: Anne Rice
belittle: 3 dis, pan, rip 4 gibe, jeer, jibe, mock, slam, slur, snub 5 abase, abuse, cavil, decry, knock, libel, lower, roast, scoff, scorn, smear, sneer, spurn, taunt 6 defame, demean, deride, dump on, heckle, impugn, jibe at, malign, offend, rebuff, show up, slight, vilify 7 affront, asperse, blister, cry down, degrade, detract, disdain, laugh at, mortify, put down, rank out, run down, scoff at, slander, sneer at, traduce 8 backbite, badmouth, denounce, derogate, diminish, discount, downplay, minimize, play down, ridicule, take down, talk down, tear down, vilipend 9 blaspheme, criticize, denigrate, deprecate, discredit, disparage, frown upon, humiliate, shoot down, underrate 10 calumniate, disrespect, undervalue
belittlement: 5 abuse 7 slander
belittler: 6 critic 8 vilifier 9 detractor
belittling: 8 critical 10 derogatory, detractive, minimizing
Beliveau: 4 Jean
Belize: 4 city, port, town 6 nation 7 country
capital: 8 Belmopan
money: 4 cent 6 dollar
neighbor: 6 Mexico 9 Guatemala
org.: 3 OAS
bell: 4 gong, sign 5 alarm, chime 6 curfew, densho, dinger, kenong, ringer, signal, tocsin 8 angklung, carillon 10 percussion
alternative: 4 gong
church ~: 7 angelus
ender: 3 boy, hop 4 bird, wort 6 flower
literary ~ town: 4 Atri 5 Adano
ring a ~: 6 recall 8 remember 9 recognize
ringer: 3 cow, ewe 4 lama 6 caller, priest 7 visitor
sound: 4 bong, ding, dong, peal, ring, ting, toll 5 clang, knell 6 jingle, tinkle
starter: 3 bar, cow 4 blue, door, dumb, hare, snow
tongue of a ~: 7 clapper
tower: 6 belfry 7 steeple
what a ~ ends: 5 round
bell __: 3 cow, jar, lap 4 arch, bird, book, buoy, frog, pull, push, seat, toad 5 crank, curve, glass, metal 6 beaker, pepper 7 captain, heather, housing
bell-__: 3 hop 6 bottom 7 cranked
__ bell: 3 air, tap 5 ring a 6 anchor, dinner, diving, jingle, Lutine, silver, vesper 7 Angelus, Sanctus
Bell: 2 Ma 3 Tom 4 city, town 5 Acton, Ellis 6 Archie, Currer
locale: 10 California
partner: 6 Howell
Watson to ~: 4 asst. 9 assistant
Bell __: 4 Labs
__ Bell: 4 Baby, Taco 5 Ellis, Glass 7 Liberty, Mission, Packard
Bella: 5 Abzug
Bellabella: 6 Indian 7 Amerind
Bellacoola: 6 Indian 7 Amerind
belladonna: 5 toxin
belladonna __: 4 lily
Bellamy: 4 Walt 5 Madge, Ralph
Bellamy, Ralph: 5 actor
film: Airmail (1932)
The Awful Truth (1937)
Carefree (1938)
The Court-Martial of Billy Mitchell (1955)
Dive Bomber (1941)
The Good Mother (1988)
Guest in the House (1944)
Hands Across the Table (1935)
His Girl Friday (1940)
Lady on a Train (1945)
The Narrow Corner (1933)
Picture Snatcher (1933)
Pretty Woman (1990)
Sunrise at Campobello (1960)
Trade Winds (1938)
Trading Places (1983)
Bellamy, Walt: 5 cager
milieu: 5 court
org.: 3 NBA
sport: 10 basketball
Bell and __: 6 Howell
Bellatrix: 4 star
__ Bell Blues: 7 Wedding
Bell, Book and Candle (1958 film)
cast: Jack Lemmon, Kim Novak, Janice Rule, James Stewart
cat: 9 Pyewacket
director: Richard Quine
bell-bottoms: 5 jeans, pants 8 trousers
like ~: 3 mod 6 flared
Bellboy, The (1960 film)
cast: Alex Gerry, Jerry Lewis
director: Jerry Lewis
Bell, Cool Papa: 10 outfielder
belle: 6 looker 8 ballgoer 9 debutante
admirer: 4 beau
époque: 3 era
of the ball: 3 deb 9 debutante
belle __: 6 époque
Belle: 4 Lulu 5 Starr 6 Albert
Belle, Albert sport: 8 baseball
Belleau Wood: 6 battle
Belle de Jour (1967 film)
cast: Catherine Deneuve, Michel Piccoli, Jean Sorel
director: Luis Buñuel
Belleek __: 4 ware
Bellefleur author: Joyce Carol Oates
Belle of the Ball composer: 8 Anderson
Belle of the Nineties (1934 film)
cast: Roger Pryor, Mae West
director: Leo McCarey
Bellerophon horse: 7 Pegasus
belles-lettres: 7 writing 10 literature
Belles on Their Toes (1952 film)
cast: Jeanne Crain, Myrna Loy
director: Henry Levin
belletristic: 8 literary
Belleville: 4 city, town
locale: 6 Canada 7 Ontario 8 Illinois 9 New Jersey
Bellevue: 4 city, town
locale: 8 Nebraska 10 Washington
Bellflower: 4 city, town
locale: 10 California
Bell for Adano, A: 4 film 5 novel
author: John Hersey
cast: William Bendix, John Hodiak, Gene Tierney
director: Henry King
Bell Gardens: 4 city, town
locale: 10 California
bellhop: 4 page 5 toter 6 porter 7 carrier
call for a ~: 5 front
Belli: 6 Melvin 8 Giuseppe
bellicose: 4 cold, cool, mean, ugly 5 nasty, onery, surly, upset 6 chilly, ornery 7 glacial, hateful, hawkish, hostile, martial, warlike, warring 8 contrary, factious, fighting, inimical, militant, ructious, spiteful 9 combative, litigious, malicious, wrangling 10 aggressive, jingoistic, malevolent, pugnacious, rebellious
god: 4 Ares, Mars
__-bellied sapsucker: 6 yellow
belligerence: 5 fight 8 acrimony 9 hostility
belligerent: 4 cold, mean 5 nasty, onery, surly, upset 6 fierce, ornery 7 fighter, glacial, hateful, hostile, martial, warlike, warring 8 battling, contrary, fighting, inimical, militant, spiteful 9 bellicose, combative, litigious, malicious, offensive, truculent, wrangling 10 aggressive, jingoistic, malevolent, pugnacious
stance: 6 akimbo
Belli, Giuseppe: 4 poet 7 Italian
Belli, Melvin: 3 att. 4 atty. 6 lawyer 8 attorney
org.: 3 ABA
Bellingham: 4 city, town
locale: 10 Washington
Bellingshausen: 3 sea
locale: 10 Antarctica
Belling the Cat
source: 4 Esop 5 Aesop
Bellini: 8 Giovanni, Vincenzo
Bellini, Vincenzo work: Norma
Bell Jar, The author: Sylvia Plath
Bell Labs creation: 4 Unix
Bellman, Carl: 4 poet 7 Swedish
bell metal: 5 alloy
component: 3 tin 6 copper
__ Bello: 5 Porto
Bello, Andrés: 4 poet 10 Venezuelan
Belloc, Hilaire: 6 writer 7 British
work: Cautionary Tales
Mr. Burden
On Everything
On Nothing
The Path to Rome
Bell of __, The: 4 Atri
Bellona brother: 4 Mars
bellow: 3 bay, cry 4 bark, bawl, bray, call, howl, rant, roar, wail, yaup, yawp, yell, yelp 5 growl, noise, shout, whoop 6 clamor, holler, scream, shriek 7 bluster, exclaim, resound, sing out, thunder 8 let loose 10 vociferate
bellowing: 4 loud 5 aroar, noisy
Bellows: 3 Gil
Bellow, Saul: 6 writer 8 Nobelist
work: The Adventures of Augie March
Dangling Man
The Dean's December
Henderson the Rain King
Herzog
Him With His Foot in His Mouth
Humboldt's Gift
It All Adds Up
More Die of Heartbreak
Mr. Sammler's Planet
Ravelstein
Seize the Day
A Theft
To Jerusalem and Back
The Victim
bell pepper: 6 veggie 9 vegetable
__ Bell Rock: 6 Jingle
bells: 8 carillon, gankogui
Canterbury ~: 5 plant 6 flower
eight ~: 6 midday
sound of ~: 4 bong, ding, dong, peal, ring, ting, toll 5 chime, clang 6 jingle, tinkle
with all the ~ and whistles: 6 deluxe 8 complete
__ bells: 5 coral, hell's 6 sleigh
__-bells: 5 Chile, merry 6 oconee
__ Bells: 3 Bow 6 Jingle, Silver 7 Tubular
Bells Are Ringing (1960 film): 7 musical
cast: Fred Clark, Judy Holliday, Dean Martin
character: 3 Sue 4 Ella 6 Sandor
composer: 5 Green, Styne 6 Comden
director: Vincente Minnelli
bell-shaped __: 5 curve
bell-shaped flower: 5 tulip
Bells of St. Mary's, The (1945 film)
cast: Ingrid Bergman, Bing Crosby, Henry Travers
director: Leo McCarey
Bell Song, The opera: 5 Lakme
bells on her __: 4 toes
Bellson, Louis: 7 drummer
genre: 4 jazz
spouse: Pearl Bailey
Bells, The: 4 poem
author: Edgar Allan Poe
bell the __: 3 cat
__ Bell, The: 7 Liberty
Bell, The author: Iris Murdoch
bellum opposite: 3 pax
starter: 4 ante
Bellview: 4 city, town
locale: 7 Florida
bellwether mate: 3 ewe
Bellwood: 4 city, town
locale: 8 Illinois
belly: 3 gut, pot, tum 4 craw 5 swell, tummy 6 inside, paunch 7 abdomen, gizzard, stomach 9 bay window, intumesce, spare tire 10 midsection
button: 5 navel 9 umbilicus
dancer accessory: 4 veil 5 zills 6 armlet
ender: 4 ache, band 6 button
fire in the ~: 5 drive 7 longing 8 ambition
flop: 4 dive
go on one's ~: 5 crawl
go ~ up: 4 fail, fold 6 topple
laugh: 4 boff, roar 6 guffaw
muscles: 3 abs
starter: 3 pot, sow
up to: 4 near 8 approach
yellow ~: 4 wimp 5 sissy 6 coward, craven 7 chicken, dastard 8 weakling 9 fraidy cat, jellyfish
belly __: 3 pan 4 bust, flop, girt, slam 5 dance, girth, laugh 6 buster, button, dancer 7 landing
belly-__: 4 land, wash 5 helve
__ belly: 4 pork
bellyache: 4 beef, carp, crab, fuss, moan 5 gripe, groan, whine 6 grouch, grouse, kvetch, repine, squawk, yammer 7 grumble, protest 8 complain 9 grievance, make a fuss
bellyacher: 5 grump 6 grouch, moaner 7 crybaby 8 grumbler
bellyband: 4 belt
belly-button variety: 5 innie, outie
bellyful: 6 enough 7 surfeit 8 up to here
Belly of Pairs author: Emile Zola
Belmondo, Jean-Paul: 5 actor
film: Breathless (1959)
Cartouche (1964)
Les Misérables (1995)
The Thief of Paris (1967)
Two Women (1961)
Belmont: 4 city, town 5 track 9 racetrack
locale: 10 California
racer: 6 equine
transaction: 3 bet 5 wager
Belmont Stakes: 4 race 9 horse race
Belmopan: 4 city, town 7 capital
locale: 6 Belize
Belo, Carlos: 8 Nobelist, Timorese

Belo Horizonte: 4 city, town
locale: 6 Brazil
Beloit: 4 city, town
locale: 9 Wisconsin
belong: 2 go 3 fit 4 bide, jibe, live, mesh, rank, suit, vest 5 agree, apply, fit in, lodge, relax, tie in 6 go with, inhere, reside, settle 7 blend in, connect, pertain, qualify 9 appertain, chime with, correlate, harmonize 10 be relevant, feel at home, go together
to: 6 relate 7 pertain 8 adhere to, be part of 9 appertain
belonging: 6 native 7 kinship, loyalty, rapport 8 affinity 9 commodity, inclusion 10 acceptance, attachment
cost of ~: 4 dues
to: 5 under
to thee: 5 thine
belongings: 4 gear 5 goods, stuff 6 assets, estate, things, wealth 7 effects 8 chattels, holdings, property 9 equipment
Belonging to Someone (1958 song)
artist: Patti Page
__ Belong to Me: 3 You
belote: 4 game 8 card game
beloved: 2 jo 3 pet 4 baby, beau, dear, idol, jill 5 amour, angel, chéri, cooky, cutey, cutie, deary, ducky, flame, honey, leman, novia, novio, sugar, sweet 6 adored, bon ami, chérie, cookie, dautie, dearie, fiancé, prized, steady, sweets 7 admired, darling, dearest, dear one, doted on, passion, pigsney, revered, schatzi, squeeze, sweetie, tootsie 8 cared for, chouchou, cutie pie, dowsabel, dulcinea, endeared, esteemed, hallowed, idolized, macushla, paramour, precious, previous, snookums, sugar pie, sweetums, truelove 9 bonne amie, boyfriend, cherished, dreamboat, inamorata, inamorato, petit chou, treasured, valentine, venerated, worshiped 10 girlfriend, heartthrob, honeybunch, mavourneen, sweetheart, sweetie pie, turtledove
by: 6 dear to
make ~: 6 endear
name meaning ~: 3 Amy 4 Cara 5 Aimee, David 6 Amanda 7 Erasmus
__ beloved...: 6 Dearly
Beloved author: Toni Morrison
Beloved Enemy (1936 film)
cast: Brian Aherne, Merle Oberon
Beloved Rogue, The (1927 film)
cast: John Barrymore, Conrad Veidt
director: Alan Crosland
below: 4 down 5 infra, neath, under 7 beneath, south of 8 inferior, less than 9 downwards 10 inferior to, too good for, underneath, unworthy of
combining form: 6 infero-
ender: 6 ground
in French: 4 à bas
prefix: 3 sub- 5 infra-, under- 6 contra-
belowdecks, put: 4 lade, load, stow
below the __: 4 belt, line
below the belt: 4 foul 5 dirty, nasty 6 unfair, unjust 8 cowardly 9 dishonest
Bel Paese: 6 cheese
Belson: 5 Jerry
belt: 3 bop, hit, obi 4 area, band, bash, beat, biff, blow, cuff, flog, gird, hurt, ring, road, sash, slam, slug, sock, swat, swig, whip, zone 5 blast, cinch, paste, punch, smack, smash, snort, spank, speed, strap, strip, swath, tract, whack, whang 6 begird, cestus, circle, fascia, fasten, girdle, hamaki, imbibe, locale, pommel, pummel, region, ribbon, swathe, thrash, thwack, wallop 7 baldric, clobber, expanse, scourge, section, swallow 8 baldrick, ceinture, cincture, conveyer, conveyor, district, locality, uppercut 9 bandoleer, bandolier, bellyband, haul off on, surcingle, territory, waistband 10 cummerbund, expressway
barber ~: 5 strop
below the ~: 4 foul 6 unfair, unjust
black ~: 4 rank 6 expert
clip-on: 4 mike 5 pager 6 beeper 8 tie clasp 10 microphone
combining form: 3 zon- 4 zono-
decorative ~: 3 obi 4 sash 5 patte
don a ~: 4 gird
ender: 3 way 4 line
holder: 4 loop
Japanese ~: 3 obi 6 hamaki
makeshift ~: 4 rope
out: 4 sing, yell 5 shout 8 vocalize
part: 6 buckle
quick ~: 3 tot 5 snort 6 jigger
seat ~: 5 strap
tightening: 6 layoff 7 cutback 8 decrease 9 lessening, reduction 10 diminution
tighten one's ~: 3 eke 4 save 5 skimp, stint 6 reduce 7 cut back 9 economize
belt __: 3 bag 4 line 6 course, sander 7 highway
__ belt: 3 fan, lap 4 farm, life, rust, seat 5 black, brown, chain, cinch, money, sword, white 6 marine, Orion's, safety, timing, weight 7 borscht, tornado
__ Belt: 3 Sun 4 Corn, Rust, Snow 5 Bible, Frost 6 Cotton
belt, black
see karate
belted: 4 girt 7 cinched
constellation: 5 Orion
belted __: 4 tire
Belted Galloway: 3 cow 4 bull 6 bovine, cattle
__-belted tire: 4 bias
beltless dress: 4 sack, tent 6 muu-muu, sheath
beltline: 5 waist
beltmaker tool: 3 awl
Belton: 4 city, town
locale: 8 Missouri
Beltran, Robert: 5 actor
film: Eating Raoul (1982)
Latino (1985)
TV: Star Trek: Voyager
beluga: 4 fish 5 whale 6 caviar 7 caviare 8 cetacean, sturgeon 9 leviathan
product: 3 roe
relative: 3 orc, sei 6 narwal 7 cowfish, dolphin, finback, grampus, narwhal, rorqual 8 narwhale, porpoise
Belushi: 3 Jim 4 John 5 James
Belushi, James: 5 actor
film: About Last Night ... (1986)
Diary of a Hitman (1992)
K-9 (1989)
Once Upon a Crime (1992)
Only the Lonely (1991)
The Principal (1987)
Red Heat (1988)
Belushi, John: 5 actor 8 comedian
film: 1941 (1979)
The Blues Brothers (1980)
Continental Divide (1981)
National Lampoon's Animal House (1978)
Neighbors (1981)
Belva: 5 Plain
belvedere: 6 cupola, gazebo 7 lookout
Belvedere: 3 car 4 auto 8 Plymouth
Belvidere: 4 city, town
locale: 8 Illinois

__ Belvoir: 4 Fort
Bely, Andrei: 4 poet 7 Russian
Belzer: 7 Richard
Belzoni, Giovanni: 7 Italian 8 explorer
bema: 9 sanctuary
neighbor: 4 apse, nave
Beman, Deane: 6 golfer
milieu: 5 links 6 course
org.: 3 PGA
Bemba home: 5 Congo 6 Africa, Malawi, Zambia
Bembo: 4 font 8 typeface
__ Be Me: 5 Let It
bemean: 5 lower
Bemelmans, Ludwig: 6 writer
work: Madeleine
bemire: 4 soil 5 dirty, muddy
__ Be Missing You: 3 I'll
bemoan: 3 rue 4 wail, weep 5 mourn 6 bewail, grieve, lament, regret, sorrow 7 cry over, deplore, weep for 9 grieve for 10 take it hard
bemuse: 4 daze, stun 5 addle 6 puzzle 7 confuse, mystify, nonplus, perplex, stupefy 8 bewilder, confound, distract, paralyse, paralyze 9 give pause, preoccupy
bemused: 4 asea, lost, rapt 5 at sea 10 spellbound
Be My Baby (1963 song) artist: Ronettes
__ Be My Girl: 5 Use Ta
be my guest: 3 yes 8 of course 9 certainly
Be My Guest (1959 song) artist: Fats Domino
Ben: 4 Blue, Bova, Gunn, Lyon 5 Casey, Cross, Hecht, Hogan, Shahn, Stein, uncle 6 Bernie, Jonson, Maddow, Murphy, Piazza, Savage, Turpin, Vereen 7 Affleck, Bradlee, Gazzara, Johnson, Matlock, Stiller, Stoloff 8 Crenshaw, Franklin, Kingsley 9 Alexander, Mottelson 10 Cartwright, Sharpsteen
in films ~: 3 rat
Ben __ process: 3 Day
Ben-__: 3 Hur 4 Ammi
__ Ben: 3 Big
Ben (1972 song) artist: Michael Jackson
Benacerraf, Baruj: 8 Nobelist
Benaderet: 3 Bea
__ Ben Adhem: 4 Abou
Benadryl competitor: 5 Afrin 6 Contac, Nyquil, Tavist 7 Actifed, Comtrex, Dayquil, Dristan, Sinutab, Sudafed 8 Dimetapp, Drixoral, TheraFlu 9 Coricidin, Triaminic 10 Robitussin
Ben-Ammi father: 3 Lot
Benatar, Pat
song: Hit Me With Your Best Shot (1980)
Invincible (1985)
Love Is a Battlefield (1983)
We Belong (1984)
Benavente, Jacinto: 6 writer 7 Spanish 8 Nobelist 10 playwright
Benazir: 6 Bhutto
father: 3 Ali
Benben, Brian: 5 actor
spouse: Madeleine Stowe
Benbrook: 4 city, town
locale: 5 Texas
Ben Casey (ABC drama)
cast: Vince Edwards (Dr. Ben Casey)
Sam Jaffe (Dr. David Zorba)
bench: 3 pew 4 seat 5 chair, court, judge, ledge, table 6 exedra, settee 7 exhedra 9 courtroom, furniture, judiciary, worktable
ender: 4 mark 6 warmer
judge's ~: 4 banc
locale: 6 church, dugout 9 courtroom
rapper: 5 gavel
ride the ~: 3 sit
starter: 4 work
warmer: 3 sub 5 scrub 9 alternate 10 substitute
wear: 4 robe 7 uniform
bench __: 3 dog 4 hook, mark, show, stop, test, work 5 check, press, screw, table 6 jockey, warmer 7 warrant
__ bench: 4 back, milk 5 front, piano, water 6 bucket 7 anxious, optical, Windsor
__ Bench: 5 King's 6 Queen's
bench-clearer: 5 brawl, fight, melee 10 free-for-all
benching, reason for a: 5 slump
Bench, Johnny: 3 Red 7 catcher
Benchley: 5 Peter 6 Robert
Benchley, Peter: 6 author, writer
work: Beast
The Deep
The Island
Jaws
Rummies
Shark Trouble
Benchley, Robert: 3 wit 5 actor 6 author, writer
film: I Married a Witch (1942)
It's in the Bag! (1945)
The Sky's the Limit (1943)
work: From Bed to Worse
My Ten Years in a Quandary
benchmark: 3 par 4 norm 5 gauge, index 7 measure 8 landmark, standard 9 criterion, yardstick 10 touchstone
bench-press target: 3 pec 4 pecs
bend: 3 arc, bow, jog, mar, nod, sag, tip, yaw 4 arch, curl, flex, fold, hook, kink, lean, loop, mold, sway, tack, tilt, turn, veer, warp 5 angle, budge, crook, curve, droop, hunch, shape, sinus, slant, slope, slump, stoop, sweep, twine, twist, yield 6 buckle, camber, crease, crouch, dog-ear, dogleg, hunker, slouch, soften, submit, swerve 7 contort, deflect, diverge, flexure, incline 8 flection, flecture, landmark, lean over, persuade 9 curvature, deviation, genuflect, influence, sinuosity 10 compromise, divergence, lumber flaw, predispose
an elbow: 3 sip 4 swig, tope 5 drink, snort 6 imbibe, tipple
ballet ~: 4 plié 5 fondu
down: 5 hunch, kneel, stoop 6 crouch 8 lean over
fairway ~: 6 dogleg
fisherman's ~: 4 knot
hawser ~: 4 knot
one's ear: 3 gab, yak 4 talk 5 run on
out of shape: 4 warp
over backward: 4 arch 6 strive
plumbing ~: 3 ell, ess 5 elbow
river ~: 5 bight, elbow, oxbow
the head: 3 nap, nod 4 doze 6 drowse
the knee: 3 bow 7 bow down 9 genuflect
to: 4 heed, mind, obey 5 agree 6 accept, follow, fulfil 7 abide by, fulfill, observe, respect, truckle 8 carry out
to one's will: 4 boss 5 bully, force 8 arm-twist, dominate, domineer, override, overrule 10 boss around, intimidate
U-shaped ~: 5 oxbow
bend __: 5 an ear 6 dexter
bend __ backward: 4 over
__ bend: 4 knee 5 cable, sheet 6 anchor, becket, hawser, return 7 carrick, Grecian, quarter

Bend: 4 city, town
locale: 6 Oregon
__ Bend: 4 Gila
bendable: 4 soft 6 lissom 7 lissome, pliable 8 flexible
bended knee, go on: 3 ask, beg, sue 4 urge 5 crawl, plead 7 beseech, declare, entreat, implore, propose 8 petition 9 importune 10 supplicate
bender: 3 jag 4 tear, toot 5 binge, spree
elbow ~: 3 sot 4 lush
eyeball ~: 5 op art
fender ~: 4 dent 5 crash
metal ~: 5 swage
of a sort: 4 knee 5 elbow
wire ~: 6 pliers
__ bender: 3 on a 4 mind 6 fender, gender
Bender, Chief: 7 pitcher 8 Athletic
bendir: 4 drum
origin: 7 Morocco
Bendix competitor: 5 Amana, Norge 6 Maytag, Tappan 7 Admiral, Jenn-Air, Kenmore 8 Hotpoint 9 Magic Chef, Whirlpool 10 Frigidaire, Kelvinator, KitchenAid
Bendix, William: 5 actor
film: A Bell for Adano (1945)
Big Steal (1949)
The Blue Dahlia (1946)
The Dark Corner (1946)
Detective Story (1951)
Guadalcanal Diary (1943)
Johnny Holiday (1949)
Lifeboat (1944)
The Web (1947)
Where There's Life ... (1947)
TV: The Life of Riley
Bend Me, Shape Me (1967 song)
artist: American Breed
__ Bend Mizell: 7 Vinegar
__ Bend National Park: 3 Big
Bend of the River (1952 film)
cast: Rock Hudson, Arthur Kennedy, James Stewart
director: Anthony Mann
__ bene: 4 nota
Ben E. __: 4 King
Be Near Me (1985 song) artist: ABC
beneath: 3 low 5 below, infra, lower, under 8 less than 10 inferior to, unworthy of
prefix: 4 hypo- 5 under-
__ Beneath My Wings: 4 Wind
Beneath the 12 Mile Reef (1953 film)
cast: Terry Moore, Gilbert Roland, Robert Wagner
director: Robert Webb
Benedetti, Mario: 6 writer 8 Uruguyan
Benedetto: 5 Croce
benedict: 5 groom 7 husband 10 bridegroom
Benedict: 4 Dirk, Paul, pope 5 saint 6 Arnold 7 pontiff
__ Benedict: 4 eggs
Benedictine: 4 monk 5 drink 8 beverage 9 religious
address: 6 frater 7 brother
title: 3 Dom
benediction: 2 OK 4 okay 5 grace 6 orison, prayer, thanks 8 blessing
give a ~: 5 bless
windup: 4 amen
Benedictsson, Victoria: 6 writer 7 Swedish
benefaction: 4 boon, gift 5 favor, grant 7 largess, present, service 8 blessing, courtesy, donation, good deed, good turn, kindness, largesse, offering 9 patronage
benefactor: 5 angel, donor, giver 6 backer, friend, patron 7 founder, grantor, sponsor 8 altruist, financer 9 assistant, protector, supporter 10 grubstaker, Santa Claus, subscriber, subsidizer, well-wisher
Benefactor, The author: Susan Sontag
benefice: 6 office 7 prebend, revenue, stipend 8 sinecure 9 emolument 10 preferment
ecclesiastical ~: 5 glebe
beneficence: 4 alms, boon, gift 5 heart 6 relief, succor 7 benefit, charity, present 8 altruism, blessing, donation, goodness, kindness, largesse, offering 10 generosity
beneficent: 4 good, kind 5 noble 6 kindly 7 liberal 8 generous, gracious, merciful, princely 10 benevolent, charitable
one: 5 donor, giver
beneficial: 4 fine, good, nice, okay 5 great, handy, legit, lucky, moral, noble, of use, utile 6 proper, useful 7 ethical, gainful, healthy, helpful, hopeful 8 all right, friendly, fruitful, laudable, pleasant, pleasing, positive, remedial, salutary, splendid, superior, valuable 9 admirable, agreeable, covetable, desirable, excellent, expedient, favorable, healthful, reputable, rewarding, wholesome, wonderful 10 acceptable, convenient, creditable, profitable, propitious, salubrious, worthwhile
least ~: 5 worst
beneficiary: 4 heir 5 donee, payee 6 bearer, coheir 7 grantee, heiress, legatee 8 assignee, receiver
benefit: 3 aid, use 4 boon, gain, gala, gift, good, help, perc, perk, plus, sake 5 asset, avail, bazar, edify, event, favor, fruit, merit, serve, value, worth 6 assist, bazaar, beauty, behalf, behoof, pay off, profit, raffle, return, virtue 7 enhance, further, godsend, improve, promote, service, utility, welfare, work for 8 bake sale, blessing, interest 9 advantage, privilege, well-being 10 betterment, expediency, fund-raiser, percentage
added ~: 4 perc, perk 5 bonus
fringe ~: 4 boon, ESOP, perc, perk, plus 5 bonus 6 reward
from: 5 enjoy, learn 6 profit
have the ~ of: 3 use 5 enjoy 6 access
reap the ~: 6 profit
unexpected ~: 4 boon 5 gravy
__ benefit: 6 fringe, strike
__-benefit: 4 cost, risk
benefit of the __: 5 doubt
Beneke, Tex: 11 saxophonist
genre: 4 jazz
Benelux
locale: 6 Europe 7 Belgium, Holland 10 Luxembourg 11 Netherlands
Benes: 6 Eduard
Benet, Juan: 6 writer 7 Spanish
Benet, Stephen Vincent: 6 writer
work: The Devil and Daniel Webster
John Brown's Body
Benét, William Rose: 4 poet
benevolence: 4 help, pity 5 amity, mercy 6 comity, lenity 7 charity 8 altruism, goodness, goodwill, humanity, kindness, lenience, sympathy 9 tolerance
benevolent: 3 big 4 good, kind 5 close, lofty, noble 6 benign, caring, chummy, clubby, decent, genial, gentle, humane, kindly, loving, tender 7 affable, amiable, clement, cordial, helpful, largess, lenient, liberal, saintly, sparing 8 all heart, amicable, friendly, generous, gracious, intimate, largesse, merciful, outgoing, parental, princely, sociable, tolerant 9 bounteous, bountiful, brotherly, convivial, favorable, unselfish 10 altruistic, beneficent, bighearted, buddy-buddy, charitable, chivalrous, free-handed, humanistic, neighborly, solicitous
order: 4 Elks
__ Ben Ezra: 5 Rabbi
Bengal: 3 bay 6 fabric 10 footballer
Bay of ~ city: 6 Madras
country: 5 India
rival: 3 Jet, Ram 4 Bear, Bill, Colt, Lion 5 Brown, Chief, Eagle, Giant, Niner, Raven, Saint, Texan, Titan 6 Bronco, Cowboy, Falcon, Jaguar, Packer, Raider, Viking 7 Charger, Dolphin, Panther, Patriot, Redskin, Seahawk, Steeler 8 Cardinal 9 Buccaneer
Bengal __: 4 rose 5 light, tiger 6 cashoo, lancer, quince 7 catechu
Bengali: 5 Indic 8 language
wrap: 4 sari 5 saree
bengaline: 6 fabric 8 material
Bengals: 4 team 6 eleven
home: 10 Cincinnati
org.: 3 AFC, NFL
sport: 8 football
Ben-Gay rival: 4 Heet
Benghazi: 4 city, port, town
locale: 5 Libya
Bengkulu: 4 city, town
locale: 9 Indonesia
Benguela __: 7 Current
Ben-Gurion Airport
client: 4 El Al
locale: 3 Lod 6 Israel
Ben-Gurion, David: 9 Israeli. P.M.
contemporary: 4 Meir
predecessor: 7 Sharett
successor: 6 Eshkol 7 Sharett
Benha: 4 city, town
locale: 5 Egypt
Ben-Hur: 4 epic 5 Judah, novel, slave
author: Lew Wallace
character: 4 Iras 5 Jesus 6 Ben Hur, Esther, Pilate, Tirzah 7 Messala, Quintus 9 Balthasar, Simonides
Ben-Hur (1926 film)
cast: Francis X. Bushman, May McAvoy, Ramon Novarro
director: Fred Niblo
Ben-Hur (1959 film)
cast: Stephen Boyd, Hugh Griffith, Jack Hawkins, Charlton Heston, Sam Jaffe, Martha Scott
costume designer: 4 Erté
director: William Wyler
garb: 4 toga
studio: 3 MGM
Beni: 5 river
locale: 7 Bolivia
Benicia: 4 city, town
locale: 10 California
Benicio: 7 Del Toro
benighted: 8 ignorant 9 in the dark 10 illiterate, uneducated
benign: 4 easy, good, kind, mild, soft 5 lucky, noble 6 aidful, genial, gentle, humane, kindly, useful 7 affable, amiable, healthy, helpful, lenient 8 friendly, gracious, harmless, merciful, obliging, parental, positive, remedial, salutary 9 congenial, effectual, favorable, healthful, temperate 10 benevolent, productive, propitious, worthwhile
Benigni, Roberto: 5 actor
Oscar: Life Is Beautiful
benignity: 5 favor
Benin: 5 river 6 nation 7 country
capital: 9 Porto-Novo
city on the Bight of ~: 5 Lagos
language: 3 Fon, Gbe 6 French
money: 5 franc
neighbor: 4 Togo 5 Niger 7 Nigeria
people: 3 Fon 6 Yoruba
port: 7 Cotonou
River locale: 7 Nigeria
ruler: 3 oba
Benin City: 4 town
locale: 7 Nigeria
Bening, Annette: 7 actress
film: American Beauty (1999)
The American President (1995)
Bugsy (1991)
The Great Outdoors (1988)
The Grifters (1990)
Guilty by Suspicion (1991)
Love Affair (1994)
Mars Attacks! (1996)
Regarding Henry (1991)
Richard III (1995)
The Siege (1998)
What Planet Are You From? (2000)
spouse: Warren Beatty
benison: 8 blessing 10 good wishes
Benito: 6 Juárez 9 Mussolini
Benito Cereno author: Herman Melville
benjamin: 4 coat 6 jacket 8 overcoat
Benjamin: 3 Orr 4 West 5 Bratt, Spock 7 Britten, Cardozo, Latrobe, Richard 8 Banneker, Disraeli, Franklin, Harrison 9 Netanyahu
brother: 3 Dan, Gad 4 Levi 5 Asher, Judah 6 Joseph, Reuben, Simeon 7 Zebulun 8 Issachar, Naphtali
father: 5 Jacob
mother: 6 Rachel
sister: 5 Dinah
son: 3 Ard, Ehi 4 Bela, Gera, Rosh 5 Nohah, Rapha 6 Ashbel, Becher, Huppim, Muppim, Naaman 7 Jediael
__ Benjamin: 7 Private
__ Benjamin Harrison: 4 Fort
Benjamin Moore: 5 paint
Benjamin, Richard: 5 actor 8 director
film: Catch-22 (1970)
City Heat (1984)
Diary of a Mad Housewife (1970)
Goodbye, Columbus (1969)
House Calls (1978)
Love at First Bite (1979)
Mermaids (1990)
The Money Pit (1986)
Mrs. Winterbourne (1996)
My Favorite Year (1982)
My Stepmother Is an Alien (1988)
Racing With the Moon (1984)
The Sunshine Boys (1975)
Westworld (1973)
spouse: Paula Prentiss
Ben Jelloun, Tahar: 6 writer 8 Moroccan
Ben & Jerry's: 8 ice cream
competitor: 4 Edy's 7 Breyer's 9 Friendly's, Good Humor 10 Dairy Queen, Haagen Dazs, Turkey Hill
Benji: 3 dog, pet 4 mutt 5 stray 6 canine
Benji (1974 film)
cast: Peter Breck, Edgar Buchanan, Deborah Walley
director: Joe Camp
__ Ben Jonson!: 5 O rare
Bennett: 4 Boyd, Cerf, Joan, Tony 5 Bruce, Hywel 6 Arnold 9 Constance, Gwendolyn
Bennett, Arnold: 6 writer 7 British
Bennett, Constance: 7 actress
film: Affairs of Cellini (1934)
Bed of Roses (1933)
Escape to Glory (1940)
Merrily We Live (1938)
Smart Woman (1948)
Topper (1937)
Topper Takes a Trip (1939)
Two-Faced Woman (1941)
What Price Hollywood? (1932)
Bennett, Gwendolyn: 6 writer

Bennett, Joan: 7 actress
film: Artists and Models Abroad (1938)
Bulldog Drummond (1929)
Disraeli (1929)
Father of the Bride (1950)
Father's Little Dividend (1951)
Hollow Triumph (1948)
Little Women (1933)
The Macomber Affair (1947)
Man Hunt (1941)
The Man I Married (1940)
The Man in the Iron Mask (1939)
The Man Who Reclaimed His Head (1934)
Me and My Gal (1932)
Mississippi (1935)
The Reckless Moment (1949)
Scarlet Street (1945)
She Couldn't Take It (1935)
The Son of Monte Cristo (1940)
Trade Winds (1938)
The Woman in the Window (1944)
Bennett, Tony
song: Because of You (1951)
Cold, Cold Heart (1951)
The Good Life (1963)
If I Ruled the World (1965)
I Left My Heart in San Francisco (1962)
In the Middle of an Island (1957)
I Wanna Be Around (1963)
Rags to Riches (1953)
Who Can I Turn To (1964)
Ben Nevis: 4 peak 5 mount 8 mountain
locale: 6 Europe 8 Scotland
Benn, Gottfried: 6 German, writer
Bennie and the Jets (1974 song)
artist: Elton John
__ Benning: 4 Fort
Benny: 4 Hill, Jack 6 Carter 7 Goodman 8 Mardones
Benny, Jack: 8 comedian
film: Artists and Models Abroad (1938)
Broadway Melody of 1936 (1935)
Buck Benny Rides Again (1940)
The Horn Blows at Midnight (1945)
The Meanest Man in the World (1943)
To Be or Not to Be (1942)
spouse: Mary Livingstone
to Rochester: 4 boss
Benny & Joon (1993 film)
cast: Johnny Depp, Mary Stuart Masterson, Aidan Quinn
Benoit, Joan: 6 runner 10 marathoner
__ Be Not Proud: 5 Death
__ Ben's: 5 Uncle
Bensenville: 4 city, town
locale: 8 Illinois
Benson: 4 Ezra 5 Robby 6 George
Benson (ABC sitcom)
cast: Missy Gold (Katie Gatling)
Robert Guillaume (Benson DuBois)
James Noble (Governor James Gatling)
Inga Swenson (Gretchen Kraus)
Benson, George
song: Give Me The Night (1980)
On Broadway (1978)
This Masquerade (1976)
Turn Your Love Around (1981)
Benson, Robby: 5 actor
film: The Chosen (1981)
Ice Castles (1979)
Jeremy (1973)
One on One (1977)
__ Ben Stein's Money: 3 Win
bent: 3 set 4 bias, firm, gift, head, turn, vein 5 askew, bandy, bound, bowed, flair, habit, knack, leant, slant, trait, trend 6 akimbo, angled, curved, gnarly, intent, liking, skewed, talent, warped, zigzag 7 ability, angular, crooked, faculty, impulse, leaning, sinuous, slouchy, stooped, twisted, winding 8 angulose, angulous, aptitude, attitude, cockeyed, facility, inclined, penchant, resolute, spurious, tendency, tortuous, velleity 9 insistent 10 determined, out of shape, preference, proclivity, propensity
be ~ upon: 4 want 6 desire 7 hope for
combining form: 4 cyrt- 5 curvi-, cyrto- 6 campto-
easily ~: 5 lithe 6 supple 7 elastic, plastic 8 flexible 9 lithesome
from the waist (ballet): 8 renverse
it may be ~: 3 ear 5 elbow
out of shape: 3 mad 5 angry, irate, upset 6 raging 7 furious, steamed 8 frothing 10 boiling mad
over: 6 astoop 7 hunched
__-bent: 4 hell
Bentham, Jeremy: 7 British 11 philosopher
Bentley: 2 E.C. 3 car 4 auto 10 automobile
model: 5 Azure, Turbo 6 Arnage 8 Mulsanne
Bentley, E.C.: 6 writer 7 British
creation: clerihew
sleuth: 5 Trent
work: Trent's Last Case
Benton: 4 city, town 5 Barbi, Brook 6 Robert
locale: 8 Arkansas
Benton, Brook
song: Baby (1960)
The Boll Weevil Song (1961)
Hotel Happiness (1962)
It's Just a Matter of Time (1959)
Kiddio (1960)
Rainy Night in Georgia (1970)
A Rockin' Good Way (1960)
So Many Ways (1959)
Benton, Robert: 8 director
film: Bad Company (1972)
Billy Bathgate (1991)
Kramer vs. Kramer (1979, AA)
The Late Show (1977)
Nadine (1987)
Nobody's Fool (1994)
Places in the Heart (1984)
Twilight (1998)
Benton, Thomas Hart: 6 artist 7 painter
Bentonville: 4 city, town
locale: 8 Arkansas
Bentsen: 5 Lloyd
Benue: 5 river
locale: 7 Nigeria 8 Cameroon
benumb: 4 dull, stun 5 blunt 6 deaden, freeze 7 petrify, stupefy 8 paralyse, paralyze
benumbed: 6 frozen, torpid 9 unfeeling
Benvenuti, Nino: 5 boxer
milieu: 4 ring
Benvenuto Cellini composer: 7 Berlioz
Benz: 4 Karl
benzene base: 3 tar
benzoate: 4 salt
benzocaine: 5 ester
benzoic __: 4 acid
benzoyl peroxide target: 3 zit 4 acne
Beowulf: 4 epic, hero, saga
beverage: 4 mead
character: 4 Hygd 5 Breca, Eofor, Onela, Scyld 6 Wiglaf 7 Beowulf, Eadgils, Eanmund, Grendel, Hrethel, Hygelac, Ohthere, Unferth, Wulfgar 8 Aeschere, Freawaru, Heardred, Hrethric, Hrothgar, Hrothulf 9 Hrothmund 10 Ongentheow, Wealhtheow
BEP
department: 5 Treas. 8 Treasury
part: 6 Bureau 8 Printing 9 Engraving
Beppo author: Byron
Beppu: 4 city, town
locale: 5 Japan
Be prepared: 5 motto
org.: 3 BSA
bequeath: 4 give, will 5 endow, leave 6 bestow, donate, legate 8 hand down, transmit 10 contribute
bequeathed: 10 handed down, hereditary
be ~: 7 inherit
__ be Queen o' the May: 4 I'm to
bequest: 4 gift, will 5 grant, leave 6 legacy 7 subsidy 8 donation, heirloom 9 endowment, patrimony
document: 4 will
testator's ~: 6 estate
Be quiet!: 3 shh 4 hush 5 can it, shush 6 shut up 8 pipe down
berate: 3 hit, jaw, nag, rag 4 drub, flay, lash, rail, ride, twit, whip 5 abuse, chide, scold 6 assail, rail at, rebuke, vilify 7 bawl out, censure, chew out, henpeck, lambast, lecture, put down, reprove, tell off, upbraid 8 admonish, chastise, harangue, lambaste, reproach 9 castigate, criticize, dress down, excoriate, exprobate, fulminate, fustigate, lash out at, reprehend, reprimand 10 take to task, tongue-lash, vituperate
Berber: 4 Moor, Riff 6 Hamite 8 language
people: 5 Riffi
region: 3 Rif
Berberian: 3 Ara
Berbice: 5 river
locale: 6 Guyana
Berbick, Trevor: 5 boxer
milieu: 4 ring
Berceo, Gonzalo de: 4 poet 7 Spanish
berceuse: 7 lullaby
Bercy __: 5 sauce
Berdyaev, Nikolai: 7 Russian 11 philosopher
Berea: 4 city, town
locale: 4 Ohio 8 Kentucky
bereave: 3 rob 5 strip 7 deprive, despoil 10 dispossess
bereaved: 3 sad 4 lorn 6 devoid 7 forlorn, missing 8 grieving, mourning
bereavement: 4 loss 5 grief 6 sorrow 8 distress, mourning
bereft: 4 lorn 6 devoid, robbed 7 forlorn, lacking, missing 8 deprived, divested 9 destitute
of: 7 needing
Berenger, Tom: 5 actor
film: At Play in the Fields of the Lord (1991)
The Big Chill (1983)
The Dogs of War (1980)
Gettysburg (1993)
Major League (1989)
One Man's Hero (1999)
Platoon (1986)
Someone to Watch Over Me (1987)
Training Day (2001)
Berenice: 6 Abbott
author: 3 Poe
composer: 6 Handel
Berenice's __: 4 Hair
__ Berenices: 4 Coma
Berenson: 6 Marisa 7 Bernard
Berenson, Bernard: 6 writer
Berenstain: 3 Jan 4 Stan
Beresford, Bruce: 8 director
film: 'Breaker' Morant (1979)
The Club (1980)
Crimes of the Heart (1986)
Don's Party (1976)
Double Jeopardy (1999)
Driving Miss Daisy (1989)
Tender Mercies (1983)
beret: 3 cap, hat, tam
site: 4 tête
__ Beret: 5 Green
Beretta: 3 car 4 auto 5 Chevy 9 Chevrolet 10 automobile
Berezina: 5 river
locale: 7 Belarus
berg: 4 floe 7 growler
feature: 3 tip
source: 7 glacier, ice pack 8 ice sheet
Berg: 3 Moe 4 Paul 5 Alban, Molly, Patty 8 Gertrude
Berg, Alban: 8 Austrain, composer
like ~ 's music: 6 atonal
work: Lulu
Wozzeck
bergamasca: 5 dance
Bergamo: 4 font 8 typeface
bergamot: 4 pear, tree 5 fruit 6 citrus
relative: 4 lime, Ugli 5 lemon, navel 6 orange, pomelo, tangor 7 kumquat, satsuma, Seville, tangelo 8 mandarin, shaddock, Valencia 9 tangerine 10 calamondin, grapefruit
Bergen: 4 city, port, town 5 Edgar, Polly 7 Candice
dummy: 5 Snerd 7 Klinker 8 McCarthy
locale: 6 Norway
prop: 5 dummy
Bergen, Candice: 7 actress
film: 11 Harrowhouse (1974)
Bite the Bullet (1975)
Carnal Knowledge (1971)
Gandhi (1982)
The Group (1966)
Rich and Famous (1981)
The Sand Pebbles (1966)
Starting Over (1979)
Sweet Home Alabama (2002)
spouse: Louis Malle
TV: Murphy Brown
Bergenfield: 4 city, town
locale: 9 New Jersey
Berger: 4 Erna 5 Senta 6 Helmut, Thomas
Bergerac: 7 Jacques
__ Bergère: 6 Folies
Berger, Erna: 6 singer 7 soprano
specialty: 5 opera
Berger, Thomas: 6 author, writer
work: Arthur Rex
Crazy in Berlin
Killing Time
Little Big Man
Neighbors
Nowhere
Orrie's Story
Reinhart in Love
Vital Parts
Bergius, Friedrich: 7 chemist 8 Nobelist
Bergman: 4 Alan 6 Andrew, Ingmar, Ingrid 7 Hjalmar, Marilyn, Sandahl
Bergman, Andrew: 8 director
film: The Freshman (1990)
Honeymoon in Vegas (1992)
It Could Happen to You (1994)
So Fine (1981)
Bergman, Hjalmar: 6 writer 7 Swedish
Bergman, Ingmar: 7 Swedish 8 director
film: Autumn Sonata (1978)
Cries and Whispers (1972)
Fanny and Alexander (1983)
The Passion of Anna (1969)
Persona (1966)
Sawdust and Tinsel (1953)
Scenes From a Marriage (1973)
The Seventh Seal (1957)
Shame (1968)
The Silence (1963)

Smiles of a Summer Night (1955)
Through a Glass, Darkly (1962)
Wild Strawberries (1957)
Bergman, Ingrid: 7 actress, Swedish
film: Anastasia (1956, AA)
Arch of Triumph (1948)
Autumn Sonata (1978)
The Bells of St. Mary's (1945)
Cactus Flower (1969)
Casablanca (1942)
Dr. Jekyll and Mr. Hyde (1941)
For Whom the Bell Tolls (1943)
Gaslight (1944, AA)
Goodbye Again (1961)
Indiscreet (1958)
The Inn of the Sixth Happiness (1958)
Intermezzo (1939)
Murder on the Orient Express (1974, AA)
Notorious (1946)
Spellbound (1945)
The Yellow Rolls-Royce (1964)
role: 4 Ilsa, Meir 5 Golda
spouse: Roberto Rossellini
Berg, Moe: 3 spy 7 catcher
Berg, Patty: 6 golfer
milieu: 5 links 6 course
org.: 4 LPGA
Berg, Paul: 7 chemist 8 Nobelist
Bergson, Henri: 6 French, writer 8 Nobelist 11 philosopher
Bergström, Sune: 8 Nobelist
Beriah father: 5 Asher
beribbon: 4 trim 5 adorn 8 decorate, pretty up
Berigan: 5 Bunny
Be right with you!: 6 coming 7 in a jiff 8 just a sec 9 in a minute
Bering: 3 sea 5 Vitus 6 strait 8 explorer
locale: 6 Alaska
Bering __: 3 Sea 4 Time 6 Strait
Bering Sea
island: 4 Attu 8 Pribilof
river to the ~: 5 Yukon
sighting: 4 floe
swimmer: 4 seal
Bering, Vitus: 6 Danish 8 explorer
Berke: 8 Breathed
Berkeley: 4 city, town 5 Busby 6 George, Xander
county north of ~: 4 Napa
locale: 10 California
Berkeley, George: 5 Irish 11 philosopher
Berkeley Square (1933 film)
cast: Heather Angel, Leslie Howard
director: Frank Lloyd
berkelium: 7 element
Berkley: 9 Elizabeth
Berkner __: 6 Island
Berkow: 3 Ira
Berks: 6 county
locale: 7 England
Berkshire: 3 pig 5 swine 6 county
city: 5 Ascot 6 Slough 7 Reading
locale: 7 England
school: 4 Eton
Berkshire Music Festival site: 5 Lenox
Berle, Milton: 5 actor, comic 8 comedian
contemporary: 6 Caesar
Berlin: 4 city, town 6 Irving, Isaiah 7 capital, Jeannie
composition: 4 song, tune 5 score
E. ~ locale, once: 3 GDR
had one: 4 wall
locale: 7 Germany
river: 5 Havel, Spree
Berlin __: 4 Wall, wool 7 Express
__ Berlin: 4 East, Judy, West
Berlin Alexanderplatz (1980 film)
director: Rainer Werner Fassbinder
Berliner: 5 Emile 6 German
Berlin Express (1948 film)
cast: Paul Lukas, Merle Oberon, Robert Ryan
Berling: 4 font 8 typeface
Berlin, Irving: 8 composer
musical: Annie Get Your Gun
As Thousands Cheer
Call Me Madam
The Cocoanuts
Face the Music
Louisiana Purchase
Miss Liberty
Mr. President
Music Box Revue
This Is the Army
org.: 5 ASCAP
score: Blue Skies
Carefree
Easter Parade
Follow the Fleet
Holiday Inn
Top Hat
White Christmas
song: Alexander's Ragtime Band
All Alone
All by Myself
Always
Anything You Can Do
Be Careful, It's My Heart
Blue Skies
Change Partners
Cheek to Cheek
Count Your Blessings Instead of Sheep
A Couple of Swells
Doin' What Comes Natur'lly
Easter Parade
The Girl That I Marry
God Bless America
Heat Wave
How Deep Is the Ocean
I Got the Sun in the Morning
I Love a Piano
It's a Lovely Day Today
Lazy
Let Me Sing and I'm Happy
Let's Face the Music and Dance
Let's Have Another Cup of Coffee
Let's Take an Old-Fashioned Walk
Let Yourself Go
Mandy
Oh, How I Hate to Get Up in the Morning
Play a Simple Melody
A Pretty Girl Is Like a Melody
Puttin' on the Ritz
Say It With Music
The Song Is Ended
Steppin' Out With My Baby
There's No Business Like Show Business
They Say It's Wonderful
This Is the Army, Mr. Jones
This Year's Kisses
Top Hat, White Tie and Tails
What'll I Do
When I Lost You
White Christmas
You Can't Get a Man With a Gun
You'd Be Surprised
Berlin Stories, The author: Christopher Isherwood
Berlin-to-Cologne dir.: 3 WSW
Berlioz, Hector: 6 French 8 composer
work: Benvenuto Cellini
The Damnation of Faust
Harold in Italy
Symphonie Fantastique
The Trojans
Berlitz, Charles: 8 linguist
berm: 4 bank, path 5 ledge, shelf
Berman: 3 Len, Ted 7 Shelley
Bermejo: 5 river
locale: 9 Argentina
Bermuda: 3 car 4 auto, isle 5 Edsel, grass 6 island, Willys 10 automobile
capital: 8 Hamilton
city: 8 Hamilton, St. George
hrs.: 3 AST
ocean: 3 Atl. 8 Atlantic
petrel: 5 cahow
vehicle: 5 moped
wear: 6 shorts
Bermuda __: 3 rig 4 high, lily 5 grass, onion 6 cutter, petrel, shorts
Bermudas: 5 pants 6 shorts
Bern: 4 city, town 6 canton 7 capital
city near ~: 4 Sion 6 Gstaad
lake: 6 Brienz
locale: Switzerland
river: 3 Aar 4 Aare
Bernadette: 3 Ste. 5 saint 6 Peters
Bernadette (1967 song) artist: Four Tops
Bernadette of __: 7 Lourdes
Bernanos, Georges: 6 French, writer
Bernard: 3 Lee 4 Kalb, Katz, Rose, Shaw 5 saint 6 Baruch, De Voto, Kliban 7 Crystal, Malamud 8 Berenson, Cornfeld, Herrmann 10 Mandeville
Saint ~ burden: 3 keg 6 brandy
Saint ~ home: 4 Alps
Saint ~ sound: 3 arf, grr 4 bark, woof 5 growl
Bernardi: 8 Herschel
__ Bernardino: 3 San
Bernardo: 7 Houssay 8 O'Higgins 10 Bertolucci
__ Bernard Shaw: 6 George
Bernays: 6 Edward
Berne: 4 Eric
see also Bern
Bernese Alps: 5 range
locale: 6 Europe 11 Switzerland
peak: 5 Eiger
river: 3 Aar 4 Aare
Bernhard: 6 Langer, Sandra, Thomas
Bernhardt: 5 Sarah 6 Curtis
Bernhard, Thomas: 6 writer 8 Austrian
Bernhardt, Sarah: 6 French 7 actress
birthplace: 5 Paris
contemporary: 4 Duse
Bernie: 3 Ben, Mac 5 Casey, Kosar 6 Kopell, Parent, Taupin 7 Federko 8 Williams
Berni, Francesco: 4 poet 7 Italian
Bernina: 4 peak 5 mount 8 mountain
locale: 4 Alps 5 Italy 6 Europe 11 Switzerland
Bernina __: 4 Alps, Pass
Bernsen, Corbin: 5 actor
film: Hello Again (1987)
Major League (1989)
Tales From the Hood (1995)
role: 5 Arnie
spouse: Amanda Pays
TV: L.A. Law
Bernstein: 4 Carl 5 Elmer 6 Eduard 7 Leonard
Bernstein, Carl spouse: Nora Ephron
Bernstein, Leonard: 8 composer 9 conductor
work: The Age of Anxiety
Chichester Psalms
Fancy Free
Jeremiah Symphony
Kaddish Symphony
Mass
Beroea today: 6 Aleppo
Berra, Yogi: 4 Yank 6 Yankee 7 catcher
gear for ~: 4 mitt 5 glove
Berriozabal: 4 city, town
locale: 6 Mexico 7 Chiapas
berry: 5 drupe, fruit, maqui, salal, toyon 6 acinus 7 currant 8 sea grape
Christmas ~: 5 toyon
combining form: 4 cocc- 5 bacci-, cocci-, cocco-
patch hazard: 5 briar, brier, thorn 7 prickle
purple ~: 5 maqui, salal 8 sea grape
red ~: 8 barberry 9 bearberry, raspberry 10 strawberry
starter: 3 bar, bay, cow, dew, dog, ink, tea, wax 4 bane, bear, blue, crow, hack, ling, poke, rasp, shad, snow, soap, twin, wolf 5 black, bunch, china, choke, cloud, coral, elder, goose, honey, nanny, sheep, spice, straw, sugar, young 6 beauty, candle, dangle, nannie, salmon, silver, winter 7 bramble, checker, service, sparkle, thimble, whortle 9 partridge
tree: 5 elder
__ berry: 5 wheat 7 buffalo, juniper, miracle
Berry: 3 Jan, Ken 5 Chuck, Gordy, Halle 7 Wendell
Berry, Chuck
song: Johnny B. Goode (1958)
Maybellene (1955)
My Ding-a-Ling (1972)
No Particular Place to Go (1964)
Rock & Roll Music (1957)
Roll Over Beethoven (1956)
School Day (1957)
Sweet Little Sixteen (1958)
__ Berry Farm: 6 Knott's
Berry, Halle: 7 actress
film: Bulworth (1998)
Die Another Day (2002)
Executive Decision (1996)
Losing Isaiah (1995)
Monster's Ball (2001, AA)
Swordfish (2001)
Berryman, John: 4 poet
work: The Dream Songs
Homage to Mistress Bradstreet
Love & Fame
Berry, Wendell: 6 author, writer
berseem: 5 plant 6 flower
berserk: 3 mad 4 amok, wild 5 amuck, manic, rabid 7 flipped, haywire, hog-wild, violent 8 in a furor, maniacal 9 possessed 10 hysterical
go ~: 4 rage, riot, snap 5 freak 6 lose it 7 rampage, run wild 8 have a fit
Bert: 4 Lahr 5 Convy, Jones, Parks 6 Kalmar 7 Bobbsey, Sakmann, Wheeler 8 Blyleven 9 Kaempfert
friend: 5 Ernie 6 Kermit
sister: 3 Nan
berth: 3 bed, cot, job 4 bunk, dock, land, moor, pier, quay, slip, spot 5 cabin, jetty, lower, place, upper, wharf 6 billet, harbor 7 bedroom, bunk bed, harbour 8 position 9 anchorage
come to ~: 4 dock, land
give a wide ~ to: 4 shun 5 avoid, elude, evade, scorn, skirt 6 eschew 8 flee from, sidestep 10 circumvent, recoil from, shrink from
place: 4 dock, pier, port, quay 5 wharf
wide ~: 6 leeway 7 license
__ berth: 3 mud 5 lower, upper
bertha: 6 collar
cousin: 5 fichu
like a ~: 4 lacy
Bertha: 3 gun 6 cannon 8 asteroid
__ Bertha: 3 Big
Berthe: 6 Sister 7 Morisot
Berthelot, Pierre: 6 French 7 chemist
Berthold: 8 Schwartz
Bertie: 7 Higgins
Bertil: 5 Ohlin
Bertinelli, Valerie: 7 actress
spouse: Eddie Van Halen
Bertolt: 6 Brecht
Bertolucci, Bernardo: 8 director
film: The Conformist (1971)

The Last Emperor (1987, AA)
Last Tango in Paris (1973)
Luna (1979)
Stealing Beauty (1996)
Bertram: 10 Brockhouse
Bertrand: 7 Russell 9 Tavernier
Bertrille: 3 nun 6 sister 9 Flying Nun
Berwick: 4 city, town
locale: 7 England
Berwick-upon-__: 5 Tweed
Berwyn: 4 city, town
locale: 8 Illinois
beryl: 4 blue 5 green 6 bluish 7 blueish, emerald, mineral 8 gemstone 9 morganite 10 aquamarine
color kin: 4 cyan, jade, sage 5 breen, olive, virid 6 myrtle, reseda 7 avocado, celadon, emerald 8 pea green 9 pistachio, turquoise 10 aquamarine, chartreuse
Beryl: 7 Markham 10 Bainbridge
beryllium: 5 metal 7 element
Berzelius, Jöns: 7 chemist, Swedish
bes: 6 Hebrew, letter
predecessor: 5 aleph
successor: 5 gimel
__ Be Sad Songs: 7 There'll
Bésame __: 5 Mucho
Besant, Annie Wood: 11 philosopher
beseech: 3 ask, beg, bid, sue 4 pray, urge 5 plead, press 6 adjure, appeal, exhort 7 entreat, implore, request, solicit 8 petition 9 impetrate, importune 10 supplicate
beseechment: 4 plea 6 prayer
__ Be Seeing You: 3 I'll
beseem: 4 suit 5 befit, match 6 become 7 behoove 9 befitting 10 accord with
beset: 3 dun, ply, rag 4 bait 5 annoy, haunt, hem in, hound, press, spite, storm, swamp, worry 6 assail, attack, harass, in a box, noodge 7 afflict, bombard, overrun, plagued, studded, trouble 8 embattle, fire upon, obsessed, surround, troubled 9 importune
besetting: 8 habitual 10 compulsive
beshow: 4 fish
beside: 4 near, next 5 along 6 next to 7 abreast, close to, lateral 8 abutting, adjacent 9 abreast of, adjoining 10 adjacent to, juxtaposed
combining form: 3 par- 4 para-
besides: 3 and, bar, too, yet 4 also, else, more, plus 5 again, along 6 as well, at that, beyond, except, to boot 7 barring, further, on top of 8 likewise, moreover, more than 9 apart from, aside from, excepting, excluding, other than, otherwise, outside of, what's more 10 in addition, in excess of, leaving out
prefix: 3 epi-
beside the __: 4 mark 5 point
besiege: 3 ply 4 rush 5 haunt, press, storm, swamp 6 assail, attack, harass 7 aggress, bombard, envelop, rip into 8 encircle, fire upon, surround 9 close in on, importune
besieged: 6 in a fix, in a jam 7 up a tree 10 in hot water, up the creek
one's remark: 5 why me 8 not again
besmear: 3 dab 4 blur, foul, soil 5 stain, sully 6 blotch, smirch, smudge 7 begrime, draggle 8 discolor
besmirch: 4 foul, slur, soil, spot 5 dirty, muddy, smear, stain, sully, taint 6 befoul, blotch, crud up, defame, defile, malign, smudge 7 begrime, blacken, draggle, pollute, slander, tarnish 8 backbite, discolor, disgrace, throw mud 9 denigrate 10 villainize
besmirched: 5 grimy, sooty 6 filthy, fouled, grubby, grungy 7 unclean 8 maculate, slovenly 10 bedraggled, unsanitary
__ Beso: 3 Eso
besom: 5 broom
material: 4 twig
use a ~: 5 sweep
__ Be So Nice...: 4 You'd
__ be sorry!: 5 You'll
besot: 7 stupefy 9 inebriate, infatuate 10 intoxicate
besotted: 5 tipsy 6 blotto 7 far gone 9 irrigated 10 infatuated
bespangle: 5 adorn
bespatter: 4 blot, spot 6 bedaub, malign
bespattered: 5 muddy
bespeak: 4 bode, show 6 ask for, bid for, reveal, secure, tell of 7 address, betoken, display, exhibit, portend, promise, reflect, request, reserve, signify, testify 8 indicate, register 9 predicate
bespeckle: 3 dot
besprinkle: 3 wet 6 dampen 7 asperse, scatter
__ Be Square: 5 Hip to
Bess: 6 Truman 7 Myerson 9 Armstrong
to Harry: 4 wife
Bessell: 3 Ted
Bessemer: 4 city, town 5 Henry
locale: 7 Alabama
Bessemer __: 5 steel 7 process
Bessemer, Henry: 3 Sir 7 British 8 inventor
product: 5 steel
Bessie: 4 Head, Love 5 Smith
Besson, Luc: 8 director
Bess Truman, __ Wallace: 3 née
Bess, You Is My Woman Now: 4 duet
composer: 8 Gershwin
best: 3 ace, cap, top 4 A-one, beat, lick, most, peak, pick, rout, tops, whip 5 cream, crown, elite, ideal, one up, outdo, prime, primo, trump, worst 6 defeat, exceed, finest, finish, grade A, select, superb, tiptop, unique, wallop 7 capital, conquer, highest, in front, leading, optimal, optimum, outplay, perfect, special, supreme, surpass, triumph, vintage 8 champion, choicest, foremost, four-star, greatest, outscore, overcome, peerless, surmount, top-grade, topnotch, top-rated, ultimate, vanquish 9 first-rate, high-class, matchless, nonpareil, number one, paramount, sovereign, strongest, top drawer, topflight, unequaled, unrivaled, virtuosic, worthiest 10 consummate, first-class, inimitable, preeminent, put to shame, unrivalled, world-class
at ~: 6 partly 7 ideally 9 maximally, optimally
barely ~: 4 clip, edge 7 nose out
combining form: 6 aristo-
come out second ~: 4 lose, show
condition: 4 pink
days: 5 prime
do one's ~: 3 try
ender: 6 seller
get the ~ of: 3 win 5 unarm 6 defeat, master, subdue 7 conquer 9 overpower
had ~: 5 ought 6 should 7 ought to
in one's ~ interests: 7 politic
in the ring: 2 KO
make the ~ of: 5 get by 6 make do, manage 8 tolerate 9 put up with, reconcile
man's ~ friend: 3 dog
of seven: 6 series
part: 4 lead, most 5 cream 6 flower 8 majority 9 highlight
roster of the ~: 5 A-list
select the ~: 4 cull, sift 6 screen 9 high-grade
Sunday ~: 4 duds, garb, gear, rags, togs, wear 5 array, dress, frock, getup, mufti 6 attire, civies, finery, livery, outfit, things 7 apparel, civvies, clothes, costume, raiment, regalia, threads 8 ensemble, frippery, garments, wardrobe 9 trappings 10 habiliment
wishes: 7 regards 8 respects
wish the ~ for: 5 bless
best __: 3 boy, man 5 of all
best __ and tucker: 3 bib
best __ possible worlds: 5 of all
best __ to be, the: 5 is yet
best- __ plans: 4 laid
best-__ scenario: 4 case
__ best: 6 second, Sunday
Best: 4 Edna, Pete 5 James 7 Charles
Best and the Brightest, The author: David Halberstam
Best Boy (1979 film) director: Ira Wohl
Best, Edna: 7 actress
film: Intermezzo (1939)
The Man Who Knew Too Much (1934)
South Riding (1938)
Swiss Family Robinson (1940)
Bester, Alfred: 6 author, writer
Best Foot Forward (1943 film)
cast: Lucille Ball, William Gaxton
director: Edward Buzzell
__ best friend: 4 man's
bestial: 3 low 4 base, mean, vile 5 cruel, feral 6 brutal, coarse, oafish, savage, sordid 7 brutish, debased, inhuman, loutish 8 barbaric, inhumane 9 barbarian, barbarous, primitive, unpitying 10 unmerciful
Be still!: 3 shh 4 hush 5 quiet
best in __: 4 show
Best in Show (2000 film)
cast: Christopher Guest, Eugene Levy, Michael McKean, Catherine O'Hara
director: Christopher Guest
bestir: 4 move, wake 5 rally, rouse, waken 6 arouse, awaken, kindle, vivify, wake up 7 actuate, inspire 8 motivate 9 get moving, impassion, stimulate
best is __ be, the: 5 yet to
Best Is __ Come, The: 5 Yet to
Best Laid Plans (1999 film)
cast: Josh Brolin, Rocky Carroll, Alessandro Nivola, Reese Witherspoon
Best Laid Plans, The author: Sidney Sheldon
best-loved: 3 pet 8 favorite 9 preferred
one: 4 fave
best man's offering: 5 toast
Best Man, The (1964 film)
cast: Edie Adams, Henry Fonda, Cliff Robertson
director: Franklin Schaffner
Best Man, The (1999 film)
cast: Morris Chestnut, Taye Diggs, Nia Long, Harold Perrineau
director: Malcolm D. Lee
Best of Enemies, The (1961 film)
cast: David Niven, Michael Wilding
director: Guy Hamilton
Best of Everything, The (1959 film)
cast: Stephen Boyd, Hope Lange, Suzy Parker
director: Jean Negulesco
Best of My Love (song) artist: Eagles, Emotions
Best of Times, The (1986 film)
cast: Holly Palance, Pamela Reed, Kurt Russell, Robin Williams
director: Roger Spottiswoode
Best of Times, The (1981 song) artist: Styx
bestow: 4 deal, give, vest 5 allot, award, endow, endue, grant, indue, lodge, share, spare, spend 6 afford, confer, devote, donate, extend, heap on, impart, lavish, return 7 furnish, hand out, present, provide 8 bequeath 9 apportion, vouchsafe 10 contribute, distribute
bestowal: 4 gift, will 5 award, grant 8 largesse 9 endowment
bestower: 5 donor 7 grantor
best-quality: 5 prime 6 choice, select
bestrew: 3 sow 6 spread 7 diffuse, radiate, scatter 8 disperse, sprinkle 9 broadcast, cast about
bestride: 4 span 7 overtop 8 dominate, step over, straddle 9 cross over, stand over, tower over
bestseller: 3 hit 4 book 5 novel
Best That You Can Do (1981 song)
artist: Christopher Cross
Best Things in Life Are Free, The (1992 song)
artist: Janet Jackson, Luther Vandross, Ralph Tresvant
Best Thing That Ever Happened to Me (1974 song) artist: Gladys Knight and the Pips
__ Best Thing, The: 4 Next
Best Western: 5 motel
competitor: 7 Days Inn 9 Ramada Inn 10 Comfort Inn, Econo Lodge, Hampton Inn, Holiday Inn, Quality Inn, Red Roof Inn, Travelodge
Best Years of Our Lives, The (1946 film)
cast: Dana Andrews, Hoagy Carmichael, Myrna Loy, Fredric March, Virginia Mayo, Harold Russell, Teresa Wright
director: William Wyler
studio: 3 RKO
__ be surprised!: 4 You'd
bet: 3 lay 4 ante, noir, play, risk 5 put up, rouge, stake, wager 6 chance, exacta, gamble, Hebrew, letter, parlay 7 lay odds, venture 8 chance it, long shot, make book, perfecta, trifecta 9 speculate
accepter: 5 taker
amount: 5 stake
collect a ~: 3 win
first: 4 open
meet a poker ~: 3 see
offset a ~: 5 hedge
on: 4 back 5 trust 6 chance 8 put money
one's bottom dollar: 4 rely 5 trust 6 depend 7 believe
predecessor: 5 aleph
roulette ~: 3 odd, red 4 even, noir 5 black, rouge
successor: 5 gimel
taker: 6 bookie
track ~: 4 show 5 place 6 exacta, parlay 8 perfecta, quinella, trifecta
you ~: 2 ay, da, ja, sí 3 aye, oui, yea, yep, yup 4 amen, fine, okay, sure, true, yeah 5 good-o, natch, quite, right, roger, uh-huh 6 agreed, and how, gladly, good-oh, indeed, just so, rather, righto, surely, yowzah 7 exactly, for sure, go ahead, granted, indeedy, mais oui, quite so, right on, ten-four 8 all right, for a fact, of course, thumbs up, very well 9 be my guest, certainly, darn right, naturally, precisely, sure thing 10 absolutely, by all means, definitely, positively, sure enough, that's right
__ bet: 3 you 4 side 6 if-come 7 pyramid

BET: 7 channel
alternative: 3 CMT, MTV, PAX, TBS, TLC, TNN, TNT, USA 4 ESPN, HGTV 5 A and E, C-SPAN, Style 6 Noggin, Tech TV, TV Land 7 Court TV, Ovation, SoapNet 8 Lifetime
beta: 5 Greek 6 letter 10 prerelease
preceder: 5 alpha
successor: 5 gamma
beta __: 3 ray 4 cell, iron, line, test, wave 5 brass, decay 6 rhythm 7 blocker
__ Beta Kappa: 3 Phi
betake: 4 move 6 repair 9 cause to go
Betamax: 3 VCR
creator: 4 Sony
Betcha By Golly, Wow (1972 song)
artist: Stylistics
betel: 3 nut 4 palm 5 areca
Betelgeuse: 4 star 5 M star
constellation: 5 Orion
bête noire: 4 bane, fear 7 bugbear 8 pet peeve
beth: 6 Hebrew, letter
preceder: 4 alef 5 aleph
successor: 5 gimel
Beth: 6 Daniel, Henley 7 Howland 9 Broderick
sister: 2 Jo 3 Amy, Meg
Beth __: 3 Din 6 Hillel 7 Midrash, Shammai
Beth (1976 song) artist: Kiss
Bethany: 4 city, town
locale: 8 Oklahoma
be that __ may: 4 as it
__ Be the Day: 6 That'll
Bethe, Hans: 8 Nobelist 9 physicist
bethel: 6 chapel, hostel 9 sanctuary
Bethel: 4 city, town 6 Leslie
locale: 6 Alaska
__ Be the One: 5 Let Me
__ Be There: 3 I'll 5 Got to, Let Me
Bethesda: 4 city, town
locale: 8 Maryland
__ be the tie that binds: 5 blest
__ Beth Hurt: 4 Mary
bethink: 6 recall, remind 8 remember 9 recognize, recollect 10 bear in mind, keep in mind
Bethlehem: 4 city, town
athletes: 9 Engineers
city near ~: 6 Easton
gift: 4 gold 5 myrrh 12 frankincense
locale: 4 Penn. 6 Jordan
school: 6 Lehigh
trio: 4 Magi
Bethlehem __: 4 sage 5 Steel
__ Bethlehem: 6 Star of
Bethlehem Steel for short: 6 Bessie
Bethune (1977 film)
cast: Kate Nelligan, Donald Sutherland
director: Eric Till
Bethune, Zina: 7 actress
betide: 5 occur 6 happen 7 turn out 8 happen to 9 take place, transpire 10 come to pass
__ be tied: 5 fit to
betimes: 4 anon, soon 5 early 9 in advance 10 beforehand
Beti, Mongo: 6 writer 11 Cameroonian
bêtise: 6 trifle 7 faux pas 9 absurdity
Betjeman, John: 4 poet 7 British
betoken: 4 bode, mark, mean, show 5 augur, imply 6 denote 7 bespeak, connote, portend, predict, presage, promise, signify 8 forebode, forecast, foreshow, foretell, indicate, prophesy, stand for 9 represent, symbolize 10 foreshadow
betony: 5 plant 6 flower
betray: 4 sell, sing 5 cross, rat on, spill 6 delude, desert, expose, fink on, reveal, squeal, take in, turn in 7 abandon, deceive, divulge, forsake, let slip, mislead, sell out 8 blurt out, disclose, give away, go back on, inform on, register 9 break with, disinform
a confidence: 4 blab, tell 6 gossip
betrayal: 6 dupery 7 perfidy, treason 8 exposure, giveaway 9 deception, treachery
betrayer: 5 enemy, Judas, knave, snake, viper 6 ratter 7 ratfink, traitor 8 apostate, forsaker, informer, recreant, renegade, turncoat 9 ill-wisher, informant
betroth: 6 engage 7 promise
betrothal: 6 plight 7 promise 8 espousal 10 affiancing, engagement
announcement: 4 bans 5 banns
betrothed: 4 love 6 fiancé 7 fiancée 8 intended, wife-to-be
Be True to Your School (1963 song)
artist: Beach Boys
bets
hedging one's ~: 4 sage, wary, wise 5 chary, leery 7 careful, guarded, politic, prudent 8 cautious 9 judicious, provident, sagacious, tentative
take ~: 8 give odds, make book
Betsey: 7 Johnson
Betsy: 4 Ross 5 Blair, Drake, Rawls 6 Palmer
__ Betsy From Pike: 5 Sweet
Betsy's Wedding (1990 film)
cast: Alan Alda, Joey Bishop, Anthony LaPaglia, Catherine O'Hara, Joe Pesci, Molly Ringwald, Ally Sheedy
director: Alan Alda
Betsy, The: 4 film 5 novel
author: Harold Robbins
cast: Robert Duvall, Tommy Lee Jones, Laurence Olivier, Katharine Ross
director: Daniel Petrie
betta: 4 fish
Bette: 5 Davis 6 Midler
nickname: 5 Miss M
__ Bette: 6 Cousin
Bette Davis Eyes (1981 song) artist: Kim Carnes
Bettelheim, Bruno: psychologist
Bettendorf: 4 city, town
locale: 4 Iowa
better: 3 cap, top, win 4 beat, help, more 5 amend, cured, finer, fix up, outdo, raise, trump 6 enrich, exceed, fitter, polish, refine, reform 7 advance, correct, enhance, forward, further, greater, improve, promote, recover, recruit, shape up, sharpen, surpass, touch up, upgrade 8 improved, not so bad, outshine, outstrip, souped up, spruce up, stronger, superior, surmount, worthier 9 cultivate, healthier, improving, meliorate, on the mend, sharpened, transcend 10 ameliorate, preferable, preferably, recovering
get ~: 4 heal, mend 5 rally 6 look up, pick up 7 rebound, recover 10 recuperate
get ~ in the bottle: 3 age 6 mellow
get into ~ condition: 7 restore, work out 8 exercise
get the ~ of: 5 one up, trump, upset, worst 6 defeat, outwit 7 conquer 8 outsmart, overcome
go one ~: 3 top 5 outdo 7 surpass
had ~: 5 ought 6 should 7 ought to
half: 4 mate, wife 6 spouse 7 husband
like ~: 6 prefer
make ~: 7 improve 10 ameliorate
none ~: 4 best, tops
old enough to know ~: 5 adult, grown, of age 6 mature 7 grown-up
part: 4 bulk, most 8 majority 10 lion's share
than: 5 above
than nothing: 4 fair, so-so 6 decent 8 adequate, bearable, mediocre, passable 9 something, tolerable 10 acceptable
think ~ of: 3 rue 6 regret
turn for the ~: 5 rally
better __: 3 off 4 half
better __ than never: 4 late
better __ than sorry: 4 safe
__ better: 5 go one
Better __ and Gardens: 5 Homes
Better Be Good to Me (1984 song)
artist: Tina Turner
__ better believe it!: 4 You'd
Better Boy: 6 tomato
relative: 4 Roma 6 Big Boy 9 beefsteak, Early Girl, Quick Pick
Better Business __: 6 Bureau
Better Days (1992 song) artist: Bruce Springsteen
Better Man (1994 song) artist: Pearl Jam
betterment: 7 advance, benefit 8 progress 9 amendment, promotion, upgrading 10 prosperity
__ better or for worse: 3 for
__ Betters: 3 Our
__ better to have loved...: 3 'Tis
__ Better Watch Out: 3 You
Bettger: 4 Lyle
betting
game: 4 faro 5 craps, poker 8 baccarat, roulette 9 blackjack, twenty-one
parameters: 4 odds
quit ~: 6 cash in
setting: 3 OTB 4 Reno 5 track, Vegas 6 casino 8 Las Vegas 9 racetrack
Betti, Ugo: 7 Italian 10 playwright
bettong: 9 marsupial
relative: 4 euro 5 bilbi, bilby, koala 6 numbat, wombat 7 dasyure, opossum, wallaby 8 kangaroo, wallaroo 9 bandicoot, phalanger
bettor: 5 taker 6 player, punter 7 gambler, plunger, wagerer 8 gamester 9 risk taker
concern: 3 nag 4 ante, pony 6 action
declaration: 5 banco
mecca: 3 OTB 4 Reno 5 track, Vegas 6 casino 8 Las Vegas 9 racetrack
note: 3 IOU
__ betty: 5 brown
Betty: 4 Ford 5 Field, Smith, White 6 Comden, Grable, Hutton, Rollin, Rubble, Thomas, Wright 7 Buckley, Everett, Friedan, Furness, Garrett, Johnson 8 Williams
Betty __: 4 Boop, Coed, lamp 7 Crocker
__ Betty: 5 Nurse
Betty Crocker product: 3 mix 7 cake mix
Bettye: 8 Ackerman
Betty Ford Center purpose: 5 rehab
between: 4 amid 5 among, 'twixt 6 amidst, middle, midway, mongst, within 7 amongst, through 9 bounded by 10 enclosed by, separating
in French: 5 entre
in Spanish: 5 entre
prefix: 5 inter-
us: 9 entre nous
between __ and a hard place: 5 a rock
between __ and me: 3 you
between-meal food: 4 nosh 5 snack
between-rounds area: 6 corner
Between Tears and Laughter author: Alden Nowlan
Between the Acts author: Virginia Woolf
__ between the cracks: 4 slip
Between the Devil and the Deep Blue Sea composer: 5 Arlen 7 Koehler
__ between the lines: 4 read
Between the Lines (1977 film)
cast: Lindsay Crouse, Jeff Goldblum, John Heard
director: Joan Micklin Silver
__ Between the States: 3 War
__ Between the Tates, The: 3 War
Between Walls author: William Carlos Williams
between you __: 5 and me
betwixt: 4 amid 5 among 6 amidst, mongst 7 amongst
betwixt and __: 7 between
__ Bet Your Life: 3 You
Betz: 4 Carl
Beulah: 5 Bondi
Beulah, peel __ grape: 3 me a
beurre __: 4 noir 5 blanc, fondu, manié
__ beurre: 5 petit
Bevans: 4 Clem
bevel: 4 cant, tilt 5 miter, slant, slope 6 angled, canted, tilted 7 chamfer, mitered, oblique, slanted, sloping 8 diagonal, inclined 9 at an angle
bevel __: 4 gear, neck 5 joint 6 siding, square
beveled: 6 skewed 8 diagonal
beverage: 3 ade, ale, gin, Joe, nog, pop, rum, rye, tea 4 beer, bock, brew, cola, fizz, flip, grog, kava, marc, maté, mead, milk, ouzo, port, raki, sake, saki, wine 5 anise, Bronx, cider, cocoa, decaf, drink, float, juice, julep, kvass, lager, mocha, negus, pekoe, perry, punch, shrub, sling, stout, toddy, vodka, water 6 bishop, brandy, cassis, coffee, Cognac, eggnog, gimlet, kirsch, kumiss, kummel, mai tai, malted, mescal, Mickey, mimosa, nectar, oolong, Pernod, porter, posset, pulque, rickey, rob roy, Scotch, shandy, tisane, whisky, zombie 7 aquavit, Bacardi, bourbon, Campari, collins, cordial, curaçao, herb tea, iced tea, limeade, liqueur, martini, mint tea, negroni, oenomel, pale ale, potable, ratafia, sangría, seltzer, sidecar, sloe gin, soda pop, stinger, tequila, whiskey 8 absinthe, anisette, apéritif, black tea, bouillon, calvados, club soda, coco loco, daiquiri, Drambuie, eau de vie, espresso, green tea, Guinness, highball, Jack Rose, lemonade, libation, pilsener, pink lady, potation, salty dog, schnapps, skim milk, souchong, spritzer, Tia Maria, vermouth 9 alexander, applejack, aqua vitae, Cointreau, cream soda, drinkable, ginger ale, hard cider, Manhattan, margarita, milk shake, mint julep, moonshine, moosemilk, orangeade, slivovitz, soda water, soft drink, ward eight, yerba maté 10 apple juice, Bloody Mary, buttermilk, café au lait, caffé latte, cappuccino, chartreuse, fruit juice, ginger beer, golden fizz, grape juice, horse's neck, Jamaica rum, malted milk, Mickey Finn, Moscow mule, piña colada, rock and rye, shandygaff, silver fizz, tonic water, Vichy water
alcoholic ~: 3 ale, gin, rum, rye 4 beer, bock, grog, mead, ouzo, port, sake, saki, wine 5 booze, hooch, julep, kvass, lager, sling, stout, toddy, vodka 6 bishop, brandy, bubbly, cassis, chicha, Cognac, gimlet, liquor, mai tai, mescal, mimosa, porter, pulque, redeye, rob roy, scotch, whisky,

zombie **7** aquavit, Bacardi, bourbon, Campari, Collins, cordial, curaçao, liqueur, martini, negroni, pale ale, ratafia, sangria, sidecar, sloe gin, spirits, stinger, tequila, whiskey **8** absinthe, anisette, aperitif, calvados, cocktail, coco loco, daiquiri, Drambuie, eau de vie, Galliano, Guinness, highball, Jack Rose, libation, nightcap, pilsener, pink lady, potation, salty dog, schnapps, Tia Maria, vermouth **9** alexander, applejack, aqua vitae, Champagne, Cointreau, firewater, hard cider, Manhattan, margarita, mint julep, moonshine, moosemilk, slivovitz **10** Bloody Mary, Jamaica rum, Moscow mule, piña colada, rock and rye
après-ski ~: **5** cocoa, toddy
autumn ~: **5** cider
bedtime ~: **4** milk **5** cocoa
Beowulf ~: **4** mead
brewed ~: **3** ale, tea **4** beer **5** lager, stout
British ~: **3** ale, tea
carbonated ~: **3** pop **4** cola, soda **8** root beer **9** ginger ale
chest: **6** cooler
diner ~: **3** joe **4** java **6** coffee
dinner ~: **4** wine
eggy ~: **3** nog
fermented ~: **3** ale **4** beer, mead, wine **5** cider, lager, stout **6** chicha, pulque
fruit ~: **3** ade **5** cider
green ~: **3** tea
herbal ~: **3** tea
holder: **3** cup, pot, urn **5** flute, glass **6** carafe
hot ~: **3** tea **5** cocoa, toddy **6** coffee
iced ~: **3** tea
in French: **3** thé, vin
Japanese ~: **4** sake, saki
malt ~: **3** ale **4** beer
Middle East ~: **4** arak **6** arrack
morning ~: **3** tea **4** milk **6** coffee
suffix: **3** -ade
Yuletide ~: **3** nog **6** eggnog
see also drink
Beverly: **4** city, town **5** Sills **6** Cleary **7** D'Angelo, Garland, Johnson
locale: **4** Mass.
Beverly Hillbillies, The (1993 film)
cast: Diedrich Bader, Dabney Coleman, Erika Eleniak, Cloris Leachman, Lily Tomlin, Jim Varney
director: Penelope Spheeris
Beverly Hillbillies, The (CBS sitcom)
cast: Max Baer Jr. (Jethro Bodine)
Raymond Bailey (Milburn Drysdale)
Donna Douglas (Elly May Clampett)
Buddy Ebsen (Jed Clampett)
Nancy Kulp (Jane Hathaway)
Irene Ryan (Granny)
dog: Duke
Beverly Hills: **4** city, town
Drive in ~: **5** Rodeo
home: **6** estate
locale: **10** California
__ Beverly Hills: **5** Troop
Beverly Hills Cop (1984 film)
cast: John Ashton, Eddie Murphy, Judge Reinhold
director: Martin Brest
role: **4** Axel **5** Foley
Beverly Hills 90210 (Fox drama)
cast: Shannen Doherty (Brenda Walsh)
Jennie Garth (Kelly Taylor)
Luke Perry (Dylan McKay)
Jason Priestley (Brendon Walsh)
Tori Spelling (Donna Martin)
Ian Ziering (Steve Sanders)
bevy: **4** band, herd, pack **5** bunch, covey, crowd, flock, group, horde, swarm **6** muster, throng, troupe **7** cluster **8** assembly **9** gathering **10** collection, whole bunch
member: **5** quail **6** beauty
bewail: **3** rue **4** moan, weep **5** mourn **6** bemoan, grieve, lament, regret, repent, sorrow **7** cry over, deplore **8** bawl over, weep over **9** grieve for, moan about **10** groan about, show sorrow, take it hard
beware: **4** look, mind, shun **5** avoid **6** caveat, danger **7** look out, pay heed, warning **8** mistrust, take care, take heed, watch out **9** keep alert **10** look out for
beware of the dog in Latin: **9** cave canem
beware the __ of March: **4** ides
bewhiskered: **5** hairy **7** bearded
animal: **3** cat **4** seal **5** otter **6** walrus
bewilder: **4** daze, snow, stun **5** addle, amaze, floor, mixup, stump, throw **6** baffle, bemuse, boggle, flurry, fuddle, muddle, outwit, puzzle, rattle **7** astound, becloud, confuse, fluster, mystify, nonplus, perplex, perturb, shake up, stupefy, unnerve **8** astonish, befuddle, confound, entangle, outsmart **9** give pause, overwhelm **10** disconcert
bewildered: **4** agog, asea, hazy, lost **5** agape, at sea, blank, dizzy **6** addled, in a fog, punchy **7** abashed, at a loss, fuddled, puzzled, reeling **9** astounded, awestruck, befuddled, delirious, flummoxed, flustered, in a dither, mystified, perplexed, staggered, stupefied, surprised, uncertain **10** astonished, bowled over, dumbstruck, flipped out, speechless, taken aback
response: **3** huh
bewildering: **7** complex **8** puzzling
system: **4** maze
bewilderment: **3** fog **4** haze **6** enigma, stupor
bewitch: **3** hex **4** draw, jinx, lure, take **5** charm, tempt **6** allure, dazzle, disarm, enamor, ravish **7** attract, beguile, conjure, enchant, engross, enthral, inthral **8** enthrall, entrance, inthrall, transfix **9** captivate, enrapture, fascinate, hypnotize, inebriate, infatuate, spellbind, transport **10** intoxicate
bewitched: **4** gaga **5** magic **7** far gone **8** obsessed **9** enchanted, entranced, fallen for, possessed **10** captivated, enraptured, fascinated, infatuated, mesmerized, spellbound
Bewitched (ABC sitcom)
cast: Marion Lorne (Aunt Clara)
Elizabeth Montgomery (Samantha Stevens)
Agnes Moorehead (Endora)
Dick Sargent (Darrin Stephens)
David White (Larry Tate)
Dick York (Darrin Stephens)
producer: **5** Asher
twitcher: **4** nose
Bewitched, Bothered and Bewildered
composer: **4** Hart **7** Rodgers
bewitching: **5** magic, siren, spell **6** lovely **7** lovable, magical, winning, winsome **8** alluring, inviting, loveable, magnetic **9** beautiful, disarming, glamorous **10** attractive, enchanting, magnetical
Bexhill: **4** city, town
locale: **6** Sussex **7** England
bey: **5** ruler, title **8** governor
locale: **5** Tunis **6** Turkey
robe: **3** aba **4** abba
Bey: **6** Turhan
Beymer: **7** Richard
beyond: **3** too **4** more, over, past **5** above, outer **6** across, free of, onward, yonder **7** ahead of, besides, clear of, further, onwards, outside, without **8** as well as **9** apart from **10** superior to, surpassing
combining form: **3** par- **4** para- **6** preter- **7** praeter-
in German: **4** über
prefix: **3** out- **4** meta-, para- **5** extra-, hyper-, trans-, ultra- **6** preter-
the horizon: **4** afar
beyond __: **5** price **6** number **7** compare, measure
beyond a __: **5** doubt
Beyond Good and Evil author: Friedrich Nietzsche
Beyond Peace author: **5** Nixon
Beyond Rangoon setting: **5** Burma
beyond the __: **4** pale
Beyond the Sea (1960 song) artist: Bobby Darin
Beyond the Valley of the Dolls (1970 film)
cast: Marcia McBroom, Cynthia Myers, Dolly Read
director: Russ Meyer
bezant: **4** coin **5** money
bezel: **3** rim **6** flange
contents: **5** jewel
Béziers: **4** city, town
locale: **6** France
bezillions: **4** lots, many, tons **5** heaps, scads
bezique: **4** game **8** card game
variety: **7** binocle
Bezons: **4** city, town
locale: **6** France
B.F.: **7** Skinner **8** Goodrich
BFA
part of ~: **4** arts, fine **8** bachelor
BFG, The author: Roald Dahl
__ B. Goode: **6** Johnny
__ B'Gosh: **7** OshKosh
Bhagalpur: **4** city, town
locale: **5** India
river: **6** Ganges
Bhagavad-Gita: **4** epic, poem
characters: **6** Arjuna **7** Krishna
original language: **8** Sanskrit
setting: **3** war **5** India
vehicle: **7** chariot
bharal: **5** sheep
relative: **4** geep **5** argal, shapu, urial **6** aoudad, argali, merino **7** bighorn, mouflon **8** cimarron, moufflon
Bharati, Subramania: **4** poet **6** Indian
bhaya: **4** drum
origin: **5** India
__ B. Hayes: **10** Rutherford
bhikshu: **4** monk **8** Buddhist
bhikshuni: **3** nun **8** Buddhist
Bhopal: **4** city, town
locale: **5** India
Bhutan: **6** nation **7** country
bovine: **4** Siri
capital: **6** Thimbu **7** Thimphu
locale: **4** Asia
mountain: **10** Chomo Lhari, Kula Kangri
neighbor: **5** Assam, China, India
people: **6** Lepcha
Bhutto, Benazir: **2** P.M. **9** Pakistani
bi-
predecessor: **3** uni-
successor: **3** tri-
bi-__: **5** level, swing
Bi: **4** elem. **7** bismuth, element
83 for ~: **4** at. no.
Bialik: **5** Chaim, Mayim
Bialik, Chaim: **4** poet **6** Hebrew
bialy: **4** roll **5** bread
flavoring: **5** onion
Bialystock: **3** Max
Bianca: **4** moon **6** Jagger
planet: **6** Uranus
Bianchi: **7** Daniela
bianci, opposite of: **4** neri
__ Bianco: **6** Tony Lo
Biarritz: **3** car **4** auto, city, town **8** Cadillac **10** automobile
locale: **6** France
bias: **4** bent, skew, sway, tilt, warp **5** angle, slant, slope, trend, twist **6** liking, racism **7** bigotry, distort, incline, leaning **8** attitude, diagonal, jaundice, penchant, tendency **9** appetence, influence, injustice, prejudice, sentiment **10** chauvinism, favoritism, narrowness, partiality, predispose, preference, proclivity, propensity, unfairness
on the ~: **6** aslant **7** athwart **8** diagonal **9** at an angle, crossways, crosswise, slantways, slantwise **10** diagonally
without ~: **4** fair, just **9** objective
bias-__ tire: **3** ply **6** belted
biased: **6** myopic, narrow, skewed, unfair, unjust **7** bigoted, leaning, not fair, oblique, partial **8** diagonal, disposed, on a slant, one-sided, partisan **9** arbitrary, parochial **10** intolerant, prejudiced, subjective, unbalanced
be ~: **4** tend **6** prefer
one: **5** bigot
bias-ply: **4** tire
biathlon: **5** event
equipment: **5** rifle
take part in a ~: **3** ski **5** shoot
bib: **6** napkin
and tucker: **6** attire, finery
ender: **4** cock
require a ~: **5** drool
wearer: **3** tot **7** toddler
bib and __: **6** tucker
bibb: **6** faucet, timber **7** bracket
Bibb: **6** county **7** lettuce
county seat: **5** Macon
locale: **7** Georgia
bibber: **3** sot **4** lush **5** toper **7** tippler
starter: **4** wine
Bibbidi __ Boo: **7** Bobbidi
bibble: **4** tope
bibcock: **3** tap
bibelot: **5** curio **6** trifle **7** trinket **8** nicknack **10** knickknack
Bibi: **9** Andersson, Osterwald
bible: **4** book **5** guide **6** manual **8** handbook **9** authority, guidebook, vade mecum
Bible: **7** the Word **8** holy book **9** scripture **10** scriptures
book: **3** Eph., Isa., Job, Lev., Mic., Neh., Num., Psa., Rev., Rom. **4** Acts, Amos, Exod., Ezra, Joel, John, Jude, Luke, Macc., Mark, Obad., Prov., Ruth, Thes. **5** Chron., Hosea, James, Jonah, Kings, Levit., Micah, Nahum, Peter, Thess., Titus, Tobit **6** Baruch, Daniel, Esdras, Esther, Exodus, Haggai, Isaiah, Joshua, Judges, Judith, Psalms, Romans, Samuel, Sirach **7** Azariah, Ezekiel, Genesis, Hebrews, Malachi, Matthew, Numbers, Obadiah, Susanna, Timothy **8** Habakkuk, Jeremiah, Manasseh, Nehemiah, Philemon, Proverbs **9** Ephesians, Galatians, Leviticus, Maccabees, Zechariah, Zephaniah **10** Chronicles, Colossians, Revelation
distributor: **7** Gideons
edition: **3** RSV **5** Douay **7** Vulgate
last word of the ~: **4** amen
line: **3** ver. **5** verse

Bible __: 4 Belt 6 school 7 Society
Bible Tells Me So, The (1955 song)
  artist: Don Cornell
Biblical
  beast: 3 ass
  boat: 3 ark
  brother: 4 Abel, Cain, Esau, Seth, Shem 5 Aaron
  city: 4 Zoar 5 Sodom 6 Bethel
  comforter: 5 staff
  food: 5 manna
  garden: 4 Eden
  gift: 4 gold 5 myrrh 12 frankincense
  hunter: 4 Cain, Esau
  idol: 4 Baal
  juniper: 5 retem
  king: 3 Asa 4 Saul 5 David, Herod 7 Solomon
  kingdom: 4 Elam, Moab 5 Ophir, Sheba
  land: 6 Goshen
  language: 5 Greek 6 Hebrew 7 Aramaic
  matriarch: 4 Leah 5 Sarah
  measure: 4 omer
  mountain: 4 Nebo 5 Horeb, Sinai 6 Ararat, Carmel, Pisgah
  name for Israel: 6 Beulah
  nation: 5 Magog
  ointment: 4 nard
  Palestine: 6 Canaan
  patriarch: 4 Enos 5 Isaac 7 Abraham
  pause: 5 selah
  preposition: 4 unto
  priest: 3 Eli
  prison escapee: 5 Peter
  pronoun: 3 thy 4 thee, thou 5 thine
  prophet: 4 Amos 5 Hosea, Micah, Moses
  scribe: 4 Ezra
  shepherd: 4 Abel
  stargazers: 4 Magi
  subject of a ~ miracle: 4 wine 6 loaves
  tax: 5 tithe
  topic: 3 sin
  tree: 5 algum, almug
  twin: 4 Esau 5 Jacob
  underworld: 5 Sheol
  verb: 4 hast, hath, wast, wert 5 didst, seest, shalt
  verb ender: 3 est, eth
  wall word: 4 mene 5 tekel
  wedding site: 4 Cana
  weed: 4 tare
bibliographic
  suffix: 3 ana 4 iana
bibliography: 4 list 6 record 7 catalog 9 catalogue
  abbr.: 4 auth., et al., ibid. 5 et seq., op. cit.
  phrase: 6 et alii
  word: 4 idem
bibliophile: 8 bookworm 9 booklover
  purchase: 4 book, tome 6 volume
bibliophobe fear: 5 books
bibliotheque item: 5 livre
bibulous: 6 spongy 7 soaking 9 absorbent, permeable
  one: 3 sot 4 wino 7 tippler
Bic: 3 pen 5 razor
  alternative: 5 Pilot 6 Parker, Schick 7 Uni-Ball 8 Gillette 9 PaperMate
  filler: 3 ink
bicarb: 7 antacid
__ bicarbonate: 6 sodium
bicarbonate of __: 4 soda
bice: 4 blue 5 color, green
Bicentennial Man (1999 film)
  cast: Wendy Crewson, Sam Neill, Robin Williams
  character: 5 robot
  director: Chris Columbus
  dog: 5 Woofy
biceps: 6 flexor, muscle
  band: 6 armlet
  exercise: 4 curl 6 chin-up
  show off the ~: 4 flex
biceps __: 7 brachii, femoris
Bichette: 5 Dante
bichir: 4 fish
Bichon Frise: 3 dog 5 canid 6 canine
bicker: 4 deal, feud, spar, tiff 5 argue, brawl, cavil, fight, scrap 6 haggle, hassle, niggle, rattle 7 dispute, quarrel, quibble, wrangle 8 disagree, pettifog, squabble 9 altercate, have words
bickering: 4 feud, fuss, spat, tiff 6 fracas, strife 7 dispute, quarrel 8 argument, friction, polemics, squabble 9 imbroglio 10 difficulty, dissension
Bickford, Charles: 5 actor
  film: Anna Christie (1930)
    The Court-Martial of Billy Mitchell (1955)
    Days of Wine and Roses (1962)
    Dynamite (1929)
    Jim Thorpe - All-American (1951)
    Johnny Belinda (1948)
    Mr. Lucky (1943)
    The Song of Bernadette (1943)
    A Star Is Born (1954)
    This Day and Age (1933)
Bickle, Travis drove one: 4 taxi
bicorne: 3 hat
bicuspid neighbor: 5 molar
bicycle: 4 ride 5 wheel 7 vehicle
  area: 4 lane, path
  kind of ~ seat: 6 banana
  part: 4 bell, gear, seat, tire 5 brake, pedal, spoke, wheel 9 handlebar
  power ~: 5 moped
  ride a ~: 5 pedal
  ten-speed ~: 5 racer
bicycle __: 4 kick, path, race, seat
__ bicycle: 4 push 6 tandem 8 ten-speed
Bicycle __ for Two: 5 Built
Bicycle Rider in Beverly Hills, The
  author: William Saroyan
Bicycle Thief, The (1947 film) director: Vittorio De Sica
bicycling: 5 sport
bicyclist: 5 rider
bid: 3 ask, say, try 4 tell, wish 5 crack, essay, offer, order, quote 6 ask for, demand, direct, effort, enjoin, exhort, invite, render, submit, summon, tender 7 attempt, beseech, command, invited, proffer, propose, request, require, venture 8 endeavor, offering, overture, proposal 9 make a play, quotation 10 invitation, make a pitch, submission
  bridge ~: 5 one no
  farewell: 4 wave 5 leave 6 depart
  first: 4 open
  make a ~: 3 try 5 offer
  proposal: 5 offer, quote
  silent ~: 3 nod
  to take no tricks: 5 nullo
bid __: 5 price
__ bid: 3 cue 4 dumb, free, jump 5 shift 6 asking, demand, sealed 7 psychic, reverse
bid and __: 5 asked
Bidart, Frank: 4 poet
biddable: 4 tame 8 resigned, yielding 9 tractable
Biddeford: 4 city, town
  locale: 5 Maine
bidder: 8 opponent
  after East: 5 South
  amount: 5 offer
bidding: 4 word 5 order 6 behest 7 command, dictate, mandate, precept 9 direction
  do one's ~: 4 obey
  old-style: 4 hest
Biddle: 8 Nicholas
biddy: 3 hen 4 fowl 6 pullet 7 cackler, chicken 10 fussbudget
  young ~: 5 chick
bide: 4 live, stay, wait 5 await, dwell, tarry 6 belong, endure, hold on, linger, remain, reside 7 sojourn 8 tolerate 10 hang around
  one's time: 4 wait 5 await, delay, tarry 6 lie low 7 stand by
Bide-__: 4 a-Wee
Biden: 6 Joseph
bide one's __: 4 time
Bidin' My Time composer: 8 Gershwin
Biehn, Michael: 5 actor
  film: The Abyss (1989)
    Aliens (1986)
    The Rock (1996)
    The Terminator (1984)
    Tombstone (1993)
Biel: 4 city, lake, town 7 Jessica
  locale: Switzerland
bien-__: 4 être
__ bien: 3 est, muy 4 está, tres
Bien Hoa: 4 city, town
  locale: 7 Vietnam
Bienne: 4 lake
  locale: 11 Switzerland
biennial: 5 event, plant
__ Bien Phu: 4 Dien
Bierce, Ambrose: 6 author, writer
  employer: Hearst
  friend: Harte, Twain
  work: The Devil's Dictionary
bierkäse: 6 cheese
Bierstadt: 4 peak 5 mount 8 mountain
  locale: 7 Rockies 8 Colorado
biff: 4 belt, blow, swat 5 punch, whack 8 uppercut
bifid: 5 cleft, in two
bifocals: 5 specs 7 glasses 10 eyeglasses
bifold: 6 double
biform: 4 dual 6 Sphinx 7 mermaid
bifurcate: 4 fork, part 5 forky, split 6 branch, forked, spread 7 deviate, diverge, radiate 8 separate
bifurcation: 4 fork 5 split
big: 4 free, full, high, huge, kind, tall, vast, wide 5 adult, ample, awash, broad, bulky, burly, giant, great, gross, grown, heavy, hefty, hippy, husky, jumbo, large, lofty, mondo, noble, proud, roomy, stout, super 6 goodly, kindly, mature, mickle, mighty, rugged, strong 7 bloated, copious, eminent, endless, haughty, hulking, immense, leading, liberal, mammoth, man-size, massive, monster, pompous, popular, selfish, serious, sizable, titanic, weighty 8 arrogant, boastful, bragging, brimming, colossal, enormous, far-flung, generous, gigantic, gracious, heavyset, imposing, infinite, inflated, king-size, outsized, oversize, powerful, selfless, sizeable, spacious, stalwart, sweeping, thumping, tolerant, whapping, whopping 9 boundless, capacious, conceited, cyclopean, excessive, expansive, extensive, front-page, full-grown, heavy-duty, herculean, humongous, imperious, important, leviathan, limitless, momentous, outspread, overblown, panoramic, paramount, ponderous, prominent, strapping, unbounded, universal, unlimited, walloping, well-built, well-known, whalelike, worldwide 10 altruistic, benevolent, commodious, embonpoint, exhaustive, family-size, flamboyant, gargantuan, meaningful, monumental, munificent, prodigious, staggering, stupendous, thundering, tremendous, voluminous, widespread
  and strong: 5 burly 9 strapping
  ape: 5 orang 6 galoot, lummox 7 galloot, gorilla
  as life: 5 plain 7 visible 8 apparent, manifest
  be ~: 3 let 4 give 5 allow
  break: 4 luck 7 opening
  deal: 3 ado 4 flap, stir, to-do 6 uproar
  do: 4 fete, gala 5 event
  ender: 3 eye, wig 4 head, horn, shot, time 5 mouth
  eyes: 6 hunger 8 ambition
  game: 4 lion 5 rhino, tiger 8 elephant
  go over ~: 3 wow 5 score 6 please, thrill, turn on 7 impress, succeed 8 blow away 9 electrify
  hand: 5 kudos 6 praise 7 ovation, plaudit 8 accolade, applause, cheering 9 standing O
  hit: 3 win 5 smash 6 winner 7 success, triumph, victory
  hit it ~: 6 arrive, do well, thrive 7 make out, prosper, succeed, triumph 8 fare well, flourish, get ahead, get lucky, go places, make good
  house: 3 jug, pen 4 gaol, jail 5 clink, manor, villa 6 castle, cooler, estate, lockup, palace, prison 7 palazzo 10 plantation
  house resident: 3 con 5 crook, felon, lifer 7 convict 8 criminal, jailbird, prisoner, yardbird 10 lawbreaker
  in a ~ way: 4 a lot, lots, much, tons 5 loads, no end 6 galore, highly, hugely, oodles, vastly 7 aplenty, grandly, greatly, largely 8 beaucoup, lavishly, terribly 9 copiously, extremely, immensely, liberally, profusely 10 abundantly, a great deal, enormously, prodigally
  make a ~ thing about: 4 carp, fuss 7 quibble
  name: 5 celeb 7 notable 8 luminary 9 celebrity
  picture: 4 plan 5 mural, whole 6 blowup, fresco 8 time line
  piece: 5 chunk
  shot: 3 VIP 4 head, king, lion, name 5 baron, chief, mogul, nabob, nawab, wheel 6 fat cat, kahuna, top dog, tycoon 7 magnate, notable 8 higher-up, kingfish, official 9 authority, celebrity, commander, dignitary, executive, key player, personage
  stink: 5 fetor 6 foetor 9 grievance
  talk ~: 4 brag, crow 5 boast, vaunt 6 overdo 7 bluster, lay it on 9 gasconade
big __: 3 end, gun, lie, one, toe, top 4 band, beat, deal, game, hair, hook, idea, mama, name, road, shot, talk, time, tree 5 bucks, daddy, house, labor, money, skate, stick, wheel 6 casino, cheese, kahuna, laurel, league, sister 7 brother, leaguer, picture, science
big __ elephant: 4 as an
big __ outdoors: 5 as all
big __ theory: 4 bang
big-__: 4 name 5 boned, timer 6 ticket 7 hearted
big-__ item: 6 ticket
__ big: 4 talk 5 hit it
Big (1988 film)
  cast: Tom Hanks, John Heard, Robert Loggia, Elizabeth Perkins
  director: Penny Marshall
Big __: 3 Ben, Mac, Man, Red, Sur, Ten 4 Bird, Blue, East, Five, Foot, Gulp, Love, Nate, Shot, Time 5 Apple,

Board, Daddy, Muddy, Poppa, Steal 6 Bertha, Bopper, Dipper 7 Brother, Trouble
Big __!: 4 deal
Big __ Conference: 3 Ten 4 East
Big __ Don't Cry: 5 Girls
Big __ Era: 4 Band
Big __ for the Little Lady, A: 4 Hand
Big __ Island: 7 Diomede
Big __ John: 3 Bad
Big __ Love, A: 5 Hunk O'
Big __ National Park: 4 Bend
Big __ One, The: 3 Red
Big __ Taxi: 6 Yellow
Big __, The: 3 Fix, Hit, Sea, Sky 4 Easy, Heat, Hurt, Town, Unit 5 Chill, Clock, Combo, House, Knife, Money, Sleep, Store, Tease, Trail 6 Kahuna, Parade, Valley 7 Country
Big __ Turner: 3 Joe
Bigamist, The (1953 film)
cast: Joan Fontaine, Edmond O'Brien
director: Ida Lupino
Big Apple: 3 NYC 6 Gotham 7 New York 9 Manhattan
airport: 3 JFK, LGA
ave.: 3 Lex.
commuter rte.: 4 LIRR
cultural center: 4 MOMA
force: 4 NYPD
hotel: 5 Plaza
initials: 3 NYC
neighborhood: 4 Soho 6 Bowery, Harlem 7 Tribeca
newspaper: 3 NYT 4 News, Post 5 Times
parade sponsor: 5 Macy's
player: 3 Met 4 Yank 7 Yankees
restaurant: 6 Lutèce, Sardi's 7 Elaine's
retailer: 4 Saks 5 Macy's
school: 3 NYU
stadium: 4 Shea
subway agency: 3 MTA
theater: 6 Apollo
transport: 6 A Train
big as __: 4 life
big as a __: 5 house
Big as Life author: E.L. Doctorow
Big Bad __: 4 John, Mama
Big Bad John
actor: 4 Dean, Elam
Big Bad John (1961 song) artist: Jimmy Dean
Big Bad Love (2002 film)
cast: Rosanna Arquette, Arliss Howard, Paul LeMat, Debra Winger
director: Arliss Howard
Big Bad Mama (1974 film)
cast: Angie Dickinson, William Shatner, Tom Skerritt
Big Bad Wolf, emulate the: 4 blow, huff, puff
Big Band music: 4 jazz, jive 5 swing
Big Ben
home: 6 London
numeral: 3 III, VII, XII 4 VIII
sound: 4 bong
Big Bend: 4 park
locale: 5 Texas
Big Bertha: 3 gun 6 cannon
birthplace: 5 Essen 7 Germany
milieu: 3 WWI
Big Bird
colleague: 4 Bert 5 Ernie, Piggy 6 Kermit 9 Miss Piggy
network: 3 PBS
street: 6 Sesame
Big Blue: 3 IBM
home: 6 Armonk 7 New York
product: 2 PC 8 computer
Big Board: 4 NYSE
alternative: 4 AMEX
initials: 3 IBM
street: 4 Wall
Big Boned Gal singer: 4 Lang
Big Bopper song: Chantilly Lace (1958)
Big Boss Man (1967 song) artist: Elvis Presley
Big Boy: 3 car 4 auto 6 Hudson, tomato
relative: 4 Roma 9 beefsteak, Better Boy, Early Girl, Quick Pick
__ Big Boy: 4 Bob's
Big Broadcast of 1938, The (1938 film)
cast: W.C. Fields, Bob Hope, Dorothy Lamour, Martha Raye
director: Mitchell Leisen
Big Broadcast, The (1932 film)
cast: Gracie Allen, George Burns, Bing Crosby, Kate Smith
Big Brother creator: 6 Orwell
Big Business (1988 film)
cast: Edward Herrmann, Bette Midler, Lily Tomlin, Fred Ward
director: Jim Abrahams
Big Carnival, The (1951 film)
cast: Kirk Douglas, Jan Sterling
director: Billy Wilder
big-cat hybrid: 5 liger 6 tiglon
Big Chill, The (1983 film)
cast: Tom Berenger, Glenn Close, Jeff Goldblum, William Hurt, Kevin Kline, Mary Kay Place, Meg Tilly, JoBeth Williams
director: Lawrence Kasdan
Big Clock, The (1948 film)
cast: Charles Laughton, Ray Milland, Maureen O'Sullivan
director: John Farrow
Big Combo, The director: 5 Lewis
Big Country, The (1958 film)
cast: Burl Ives, Gregory Peck
director: William Wyler
Big D: 6 Dallas
Big Daddy (1999 film)
cast: Joey Lauren Adams, Adam Sandler, Rob Schneider, Jon Stewart
Big Daddy portrayer: 4 Ives
Big Dance, The: 4 NCAA
Big deal!: 6 so what 8 who cares
Big Deal on Madonna Street (1958 film)
cast: Vittorio Gassman, Marcello Mastroianni
Big Diomede __: 6 Island
Big Dipper: 5 ladle 9 Ursa Major
constellation near the ~: 5 Draco
star: 5 Alcor
unit: 4 star
big-eared animal: 3 ass 5 bunny, burro, hound 6 basset, rabbit
Big East: 10 conference
school: 3 NDU 5 Miami, UConn 7 Rutgers, St. John's 8 Syracuse 9 Notre Dame, Seton Hall, Villanova 10 Georgetown, Pittsburgh, Providence 11 Connecticut
Big Easy: 10 New Orleans
Big Easy, The (1987 film)
cast: Ellen Barkin, Ned Beatty, Dennis Quaid
role: 4 Remy
Bigelow: 3 tea 7 Kathryn
competitor: 6 Lipton, Nestea, Salada, Tetley 7 Red Rose 8 Twinings
Bigelow, Kathryn spouse: James Cameron
bigeye: 4 fish
big-eyed: 4 owly
Big Fix, The (1978 film)
cast: Susan Anspach, Bonnie Bedelia, Richard Dreyfuss
Bigfoot cousin: 4 Yeti 9 Sasquatch
__ big for one's britches: 3 too
bigger
get ~: 3 wax 4 grow 6 expand, mature 7 enlarge, fill out
than life: 4 epic 6 heroic
__ bigger and better things!: 4 On to
Biggers, Earl Derr: 6 author, writer
creation: Charlie Chan
work: Seven Keys to Baldpate
__ bigger than a breadbox?: 4 Is it
Bigger Than Life (1956 film)
cast: James Mason, Barbara Rush
director: Nicholas Ray
biggest: 7 maximum
share: 4 bulk, most 8 majority
Biggest Little City, The: 4 Reno
Biggest Part of Me (1980 song) artist: Ambrosia
biggie: 3 VIP 5 mogul, mover 6 fat cat, shaker, tycoon 7 hotshot, magnate
biggin: 3 cap
Big Girls Don't Cry (1962 song) artist: Four Seasons
Big Green: 9 Dartmouth
Biggs: 5 Jason
Biggs-Dawson: 6 Roxann
Biggs, E. Power: 8 organist
Big Hand for the Little Lady, A (1966 film)
cast: Henry Fonda, Joanne Woodward
big-headed: 4 smug, vain 5 cocky 7 fustian, haughty, pompous, stuck-up 8 arrogant, boastful, snobbish 9 conceited
big-headedness: 5 pride 6 vanity 7 conceit 9 arrogance
big-hearted: 4 free, kind 5 noble 7 liberal 8 generous, gracious, princely, selfless 10 altruistic, benevolent, charitable, humanistic
one: 5 softy 6 softie
Big Heat, The (1953 film)
cast: Glenn Ford, Gloria Grahame
director: Fritz Lang
Big Hit, The (1998 film)
cast: Christina Applegate, China Chow, Lou Diamond Phillips, Mark Wahlberg
bighorn: 5 sheep 6 animal, mammal
covering: 4 wool
relative: 4 geep 5 argal, shapu, urial 6 aoudad, argali, bharal, merino 7 burrhel, mouflon 8 moufflon
Bighorn: 5 range, river
locale: 7 Montana, Wyoming
river to the ~: 8 Shoshone
__ Bighorn: 6 Little
Bighorns: 3 mts. 5 range 9 mountains
big house: 3 jug, pen 4 jail, stir 5 clink 6 cooler, prison
resident: 3 con 5 lifer 6 inmate 7 convict 8 prisoner
Big House, The (1930 film)
cast: Wallace Beery, Robert Montgomery, Chester Morris
bight: 3 bay 4 bend, gulf, loop 5 fiord, fjord, inlet
West African ~: 6 Biafra
Bight of Benin
city on the ~: 5 Lagos
Big Hunk O' Love, A (1959 song)
artist: Elvis Presley
Big Joe: 6 Turner
Big Kahuna, The (2000 film)
cast: Danny DeVito, Kevin Spacey
Big Knife, The (1955 film)
cast: Ida Lupino, Jack Palance, Shelley Winters
director: Robert Aldrich
Big Knife, The author: Clifford Odets
big-league: 3 pro 5 major 7 eminent, serious 9 high-level, important, prominent
Big Lebowski, The (1998 film)
cast: Jeff Bridges, Steve Buscemi, John Goodman, Julianne Moore
director: Joel Coen
Big Love (1987 song) artist: Fleetwood Mac
Biglow Papers, The author: James Russell Lowell
Big Mac: 6 burger 9 hamburger
ingredient: 4 beef, meat 5 patty 6 cheese, pattie, tomato 7 lettuce
__ Big Man: 6 Little
Big Money, The
author: John Dos Passos
trilogy: 3 USA
Big Mountain song: Baby, I Love Your Way (1994)
bigmouth: 4 fish 7 tattler 10 taleteller, tattletale
bigmouthed: 4 long 5 gabby, gassy, tumid, windy, wordy 6 prolix 7 diffuse, fustian, hyped up, lengthy, orotund, pompous, ranting, stilted, unterse, verbose, voluble 8 boastful, inflated, rambling 9 bombastic, garrulous, grandiose, high-flown, overblown, redundant, rhapsodic, talkative 10 big-talking, discursive, euphuistic, flamboyant, histrionic, long-winded, loquacious, palaverous, rhetorical
Big, Mr.: 3 VIP 4 boss, king 6 honcho, top dog 7 kingpin
Big Muddy: 5 river 11 Mississippi
locale: 4 Iowa 8 Illinois, Missouri 9 Louisiana, Tennessee
big-name: 5 noted 7 eminent 8 renowned 9 prominent 10 celebrated
bigness: 4 bulk, size 8 enormity, free hand 9 amplitude, immensity, largeness, magnitude 10 liberality
bignonia: 5 shrub
tree: 7 catalpa 8 calabash
bigos: 4 stew
bigot: 5 hater, jingo 6 zealot 7 diehard, fanatic 9 sectarian 10 chauvinist, monomaniac
bigoted: 5 rabid 6 biased, little, narrow, unfair 7 insular, partial 9 parochial, sectarian 10 intolerant, prejudiced
bigotry: 4 bias, hate 6 racism 9 prejudice 10 unfairness
Big Parade, The (1925 film)
cast: Renee Adoree, John Gilbert, Claire McDowell
director: King Vidor
Big Poison: 5 Waner
Big Poppa (1995 song) artist: Notorious B.I.G.
Big Red: 7 Cornell
home: 6 Ithaca
Big Red Dog, The dog: 8 Clifford
Big Red One, The (1980 film)
cast: Robert Carradine, Mark Hamill, Lee Marvin
Big Sea, The author: Langston Hughes
Big Shot (1979 song) artist: Billy Joel
Big Sky state: 4 Mont. 7 Montana
Big Sky, The (1952 film)
cast: Kirk Douglas, Arthur Hunnicutt, Dewey Martin, Elizabeth Threatt
director: Howard Hawks
Big Sleep, The: 4 film 5 novel
author: Raymond Chandler
cast: Lauren Bacall, Humphrey Bogart, Martha Vickers
composer: 7 Steiner
director: Howard Hawks
Big Spring: 4 city, town
locale: 5 Texas
Big Steal (1949 film)
cast: William Bendix, Jane Greer, Robert Mitchum
director: Don Siegel

Big Store, The (1941 film)
cast: Margaret Dumont, Tony Martin, Chico Marx, Groucho Marx, Harpo Marx
Big Sur: **4** city, town
attraction: **4** surf, view **5** ocean
locale: **10** California
Big 10
see Big Ten
Big 12
see Big Twelve
big-talking: **4** smug, vain **5** cocky, proud **6** la-de-da, la-di-da, stuffy **7** fustian, haughty, pompous, stuck-up **8** affected, arrogant, assuming, boastful, cocksure, immodest, lah-di-dah, puffed up, snobbish **9** bigheaded, bombastic, conceited, know-it-all, loudmouth **10** complacent, egocentric, hoity-toity
Big Ten school: **3** Ill., MSU, OSU, PSU **4** Iowa, Mich., Minn., Wisc. **6** Purdue **7** Indiana **8** Illinois, Michigan **9** Minnesota, Ohio State, Penn State, Wisconsin
Big Three site of 1945: **5** Yalta
big-ticket: **6** costly **9** expensive
big-ticket __: **4** item
big-time: **5** noted **7** eminent
operator: **4** doer **5** mover, wheel **6** shaker
Big Time (1987 song) artist: Peter Gabriel
big top: **6** circus
regular: **5** clown, tamer **7** acrobat **9** lion tamer **10** ringmaster
Big Top Pee-wee (1988 film)
cast: Valeria Golino, Pee-wee Herman, Kris Kristofferson, Penelope Ann Miller
director: Randal Kleiser
Big Town, The (1987 film)
cast: Matt Dillon, Tommy Lee Jones, Diane Lane, Tom Skerritt
director: Ben Bolt
Big Trail, The (1930 film)
cast: El Brendel, Marguerite Churchill, John Wayne
director: Raoul Walsh
Big Trouble (2002 film)
cast: Tim Allen, Rene Russo, Tom Sizemore, Stanley Tucci
director: Barry Sonnenfeld
Big Twelve school: **3** ISU, Kan., KSU, Neb., OSU, Tex., TTU **4** Colo., Nebr., Okla., TAMU **5** Texas **6** Baylor, Kansas **7** Texas A&M **8** Colorado, Missouri, Nebraska, Oklahoma **9** Iowa State, Texas Tech **11** Kansas State
Big Valley, The (ABC drama)
cast: Peter Breck (Nick Barkley) Linda Evans (Audra Barkley) Richard Long (Jarrod Barkley) Lee Majors (Heath Barkley) Barbara Stanwyck (Victoria Barkley)
big-voiced: **5** forte, noisy **7** blaring, booming, jarring, pealing, rackety, raucous, reboant, roaring **8** crashing, piercing, plangent, rumbling, sonorous, strident, turned up **9** clamorous, deafening **10** boisterous, resounding, stentorian, strepitous, thundering, uproarious, vociferous
Big West school: **4** UNLV
bigwig: **3** VIP **4** exec, head, lion, name, star **5** brass, chief, mogul, nabob **6** honcho, top dog **7** headman, hotshot, magnate, notable **9** authority, celebrity, dignitary, personage
Big Yellow Taxi (1975 song) artist: Joni Mitchell
Bihar capital: **5** Patna
Bijagos __: **7** Islands
bijou: **3** gem **5** jewel **6** locket **7** trinket
bike: **5** cycle, pedal, wheel **6** tandem **7** vehicle **8** ten-speed **10** go for a ride, two-wheeler
ender: **3** way
ride a ~: **5** cycle, pedal
starter: **4** mini **5** motor
see also bicycle
__ bike: **4** dirt **5** trail
Bikel, Theodore: **5** actor
film: The Defiant Ones (1958) The Enemy Below (1957) I Bury the Living (1958) The Little Ark (1972)
biker: **7** cyclist **10** Hell's Angel
aid: **4** clip
gear: **6** helmet
ride: **3** hog
roar: **5** vroom
selection: **5** speed
stop: **6** hostel
bikeway: **4** lane, path
Bikila, Abebe: **6** runner **10** marathoner
bikini: **8** swimsuit
part: **3** bra
Bikini: **4** isle **5** atoll **6** island
event: **4** test **5** A-test, N-test
Bikini Beach (1964 film)
cast: Frankie Avalon, Annette Funicello, Martha Hyer, Keenan Wynn
director: William Asher
Biko: **5** Steve
Bil: **5** Baird, Keane
bilateral: **6** mutual **8** two-sided **10** reciprocal, respective
Bilbao: **4** city, port, town
locale: **5** Spain
bilberry: **5** fruit
bilbi: **9** marsupial
relative: **4** euro **5** koala **6** numbat, wombat **7** bettong, dasyure, opossum, wallaby **8** kangaroo, wallaroo **9** bandicoot, phalanger
bilbo: **5** chain **7** trammel
bile: **4** gall **5** venom, wrath **6** choler, malice, rancor, temper **10** irritation
carrier: **4** duct
combining form: **4** chol- **5** chole-, cholo-
source: **5** liver
Biletnikoff, Fred: **10** footballer
bilge: **3** gas, rot **4** blah, bosh, bull, bunk, guff, jazz, jive, pooh, tosh **5** fudge, hokum, hooey, prate, stuff, trash, tripe **6** bunkum, bushwa, drivel, footle, gabble, gammon, gibber, havers, hot air, humbug, jabber, jargon, kibosh, piffle **7** baloney, blarney, blather, blether, boloney, bushwah, eyewash, flannel, flubdub, fustian, garbage, hogwash, inanity, malarky, rubbish, twaddle **8** buncombe, claptrap, falderal, falderol, flimflam, flummery, folderal, folderol, malarkey, nonsense, slipslop, tommyrot, trumpery **9** banana oil, gibberish, kidstakes, moonshine, poppycock, rigmarole **10** applesauce, balderdash, codswallop, double-talk, flapdoodle, galimatias, Jabberwock, mumbo jumbo, rigamarole, taradiddle
bilge __: **4** keel, pump, well **5** board, piece, water
bilimbi: **5** fruit
bilingual book: **6** diglot
bilious: **3** wan **5** onery, surly **6** ornery, peaked, queasy, queazy, sallow **7** bearish **8** liverish, snappish **9** splenetic **10** ill-humored, out of sorts
biliousness: **6** spleen
bilk: **2** do **3** con **4** burn, gull, nick, rook, shun, snow, take **5** cheat, cozen, gouge, pluck, screw, sting, trick **6** fleece, take in **7** deceive, defraud, mislead, swindle **8** flimflam, hoodwink **9** bamboozle, four-flush, shake down **10** overcharge, run a game on
Bilko: **3** NCO, Sgt. **5** Ernie **8** sergeant
bill: **2** ad **3** dun, fin, neb, nib, tab **4** beak, brim, chit, debt, list **5** bylaw, check, C-note, fiver, flyer, lobby, money, price, score, visor, vizor **6** dollar, poster, roster, tenner **7** account, invoice, lawsuit, leaflet, measure, placard, program, sawbuck, smacker, statute **8** banknote, circular, currency, frogskin, proposal, schedule, simoleon **9** broadside, greenback, liability, publicize, reckoning, statement **10** paper money
abbr.: **3** amt., inv. **4** stmt.
addition: **3** tax
and coo: **3** woo **4** neck **5** spoon **6** cuddle
attachment: **5** rider
bar ~: **3** tab
bird's ~: **3** neb, nib
blocker: **3** nay **4** veto
dollar ~: **3** one **6** single
enclosure: **3** SAE
ender: **3** bug **4** fish, fold, head, hook **5** board **6** poster
fill the ~: **4** suit **5** cater, serve **6** please **7** qualify, satisfy
five-dollar ~: **3** fin
foot the ~: **3** pay **5** spend, treat **6** defray
Franklin's ~: **5** C-note **7** hundred
Grant's: **5** fifty
Hamilton's ~: **3** ten **7** sawbuck
Jackson's: **6** twenty
Lincoln's ~: **3** fin **4** five
lowest ~: **3** one
monthly ~: **3** gas, tel. **4** util. **5** phone **8** electric, mortgage **9** utilities
of fare: **4** menu **5** carte, table
on a cap: **5** visor, vizor
pass a ~: **5** adopt, enact
restaurant ~: **5** check
sell a ~ of goods: **2** do **3** con, rob **4** bilk, burn, clip, dupe, fool, gull, have, hoax, nick, rook, scam, take, trim **5** cheat, cozen, fraud, gouge, mulct, pluck, set up, shaft, stiff, sting, trick **6** diddle, extort, fleece, hustle, outwit, rip off, sucker **7** deceive, defraud, finagle, sandbag, swindle **8** flimflam, hoodwink, outsmart **9** bamboozle, four-flush, shake down, victimize **10** run a game on
send a ~ collector: **3** dun
settler: **5** payer
starter: **3** wax, way **4** blue, boat, duck, hand, horn, play, shoe **5** cross, hawks, ivory, razor, spoon, sword **6** cranes, sheath, sickle, storks
thousand-dollar ~: **5** G-note
three-dollar ~: **4** fake, sham **5** phony **6** phoney
unpaid ~: **4** debt **6** arrear, red ink **7** arrears, deficit **9** liability, shortfall **10** obligation
utility ~ abbr.: **3** kwh
Washington's ~: **3** one
__ bill: **3** due **4** bank, show, time, true, twin **6** bottle, demand, dollar, double, inland, public, ripper **7** banker's, finance, foreign, private
Bill: **3** cat, Day, Nye **4** Dana, Klem, Macy, Tony **5** Bixby, Black, Blass, Conti, Cosby, Daily, Gates, Haley, Hayes, Krohn, Maher, Terry, Veeck, Walsh, Wyman **6** Cullen, Dickey, Gaines, Graham, Hunter, Justis, Medley, Monroe, Moyers, Murray, Paxton, Persky, Rigney, Tilden, Toomey, Walton, Willis, Wilson **7** Bradley, Buffalo, Clinton, Doggett, Forsyth, Hartack, Madlock, Mauldin, Pullman, Rodgers, Russell, Sharman, Travers, Withers **8** Anderson, Buchanan, Melendez, Parcells, Plympton, Robinson **9** Mazeroski, McKechnie, Shoemaker, Watterson **10** footballer, Smitrovich
rival: **3** Jet, Ram **4** Bear, Colt, Lion **5** Brown, Chief, Eagle, Giant, Niner, Raven, Saint, Texan, Titan **6** Bengal, Bronco, Cowboy, Falcon, Jaguar, Packer, Raider, Viking **7** Charger, Dolphin, Panther, Patriot, Redskin, Seahawk, Steeler **8** Cardinal **9** Buccaneer
Bill & __ Bogus Journey: **4** Ted's
Bill & __ Excellent Adventure: **4** Ted's
Bill __ and His Comets: **5** Haley
Bill __, the Science Guy: **3** Nye
__ Bill: **5** Pecos **6** Reform **7** Buffalo
bill and __: **3** coo
billboard: **2** ad **4** sign **5** lobby **6** poster **9** publicity, publicize
in Britain: **8** hoarding
Billboard: **3** mag **8** magazine
category: **3** rap **4** rock, soul **7** country
entry: **3** hit **4** song
list: **5** chart
billbug: **6** insect
__-billed auk: **5** razor
billed item: **3** cap
__-billed platypus: **4** duck
billet: **3** hut, job **4** bunk, live, post, slab, spot **5** berth, house, lodge, put up, rooms, stick **6** letter, living, reside, take in **7** housing, lodging, quarter, shelter **8** barracks, lodgings, lodgment, position, quarters **9** situation **10** employment
billet doux: **10** love letter
word in a: **4** cher **6** cherie
billfish: **3** gar
billfold: **6** wallet
filler: **3** fin, one, ten **4** cash **5** bucks, fiver, money **7** dollars
__ Bill Hickok: **4** Wild
billiard __: **4** ball, room **5** table **6** parlor
billiards: **4** game, pool **5** sport
black ball: **5** eight
cushion: **4** bank
glancing contact in ~: **4** kiss
need: **3** cue **4** rack **5** chalk **6** bridge
shot: **5** carom, massé **6** carrom
table cloth: **5** baize
__ billiards: **6** pocket
Billi Bi: **4** soup
Billie: **4** Dove **5** Burke **7** Holiday
hubby: **3** Flo
Billie, __, Lena, Sarah: **4** Ella
Billie Jean (1983 song) artist: Michael Jackson
Billie Jean King: **7** netster **9** tennis pro
opponent: **5** Riggs **6** Evonne
Billie Jean King, __ Moffitt: **3** née
billing: **9** publicity
cycle: **5** month
get top ~: **4** star
share ~: **6** costar
Billings: **4** city, Josh, town
locale: **7** Montana
school: **3** MSU
Billings, Josh: **6** author, writer
Billingsley: **4** John **5** Peter **7** Barbara
billion
about 6 ~ miles: **4** lt. yr. **9** light year
ender: **4** aire
prefix: **4** giga-
years, in geology: **3** eon **4** aeon
billionaire: **6** fat cat **9** moneybags, plutocrat
Billion Dollar Brain (1967 film)
cast: Michael Caine, Karl Malden

director: Ken Russell
billions: 4 mint, tons 5 loads, scads 6 hoards, scores 7 legions 11 lots and lots
Billions and billions... guy: 5 Sagan
billionth prefix: 4 nano-
Bill, Mr. cry: 4 oh no
bill of __: 4 fare, sale 5 entry, goods 6 health, lading
Bill of Divorcement, A (1932 film)
cast: John Barrymore, Billie Burke, Katharine Hepburn
director: George Cukor
__ bill of goods: 5 sell a
__ bill of health: 5 clean
bill-of-lading abbr.: 4 recd.
Bill of Rights advocacy grp.: 4 ACLU
billow: 4 flap, rise, roll, tide, wave 5 crest, heave, pitch, surge, swell 6 puff up, ripple, well up 7 balloon, breaker 8 undulate, whitecap 10 ebb and flow
out: 5 swell 7 balloon
billowing: 10 voluminous
garment: 4 cape 5 cloak
billowy: 5 puffy
bills: 3 oof 4 cash, gelt, jack, kail, kale, loot, peag, pelf 5 bread, bucks, dough, funds, lucre, money, moola, mopus, pesos, rhino, sewan 6 dinero, do-re-mi, mammon, mazuma, moolah, seawan, silver, specie, wampum, wealth 7 cabbage, capital, lettuce, ooftish, scratch, shekels 8 bankroll, cold cash, currency, hard cash 9 long green 10 green stuff
behind on ~: 5 owing 6 in debt 9 in arrears
fat roll of ~: 3 wad
have ~: 3 owe
like new ~: 5 crisp
run up ~: 3 buy 5 spend 6 charge
Bills: 4 team 6 eleven
home: 7 Buffalo
org.: 3 AFC, NFL
sport: 8 football
Bills, Bills, Bills (1999 song) artist: Destiny's Child
bill-signing souvenir: 3 pen
Bill & Ted's Excellent Adventure (1989 film)
cast: George Carlin, Bernie Casey, Keanu Reeves, Alex Winter
director: Stephen Herek
Bill the Cat comment: 3 ack
billy: 4 club, cosh, goat 5 baton, stick 6 cudgel 8 bludgeon 9 truncheon
billy __: 4 club, goat
__ billy: 5 silly
Billy: 4 Conn, Gray, Idol, Joel, Mumy, Paul, Rose, Swan, Vera, Welu, Zane 5 Barty, Bland, Hayes, Mauch, Ocean 6 Carter, Casper, Crudup, Curtis, Graham, Herman, Martin, Squier, Sunday, Vaughn, Wilder 7 Baldwin, Collins, Crystal, DeWolfe, Grammer, Hartack, Preston, Vaughan 8 Eckstine, Williams 9 Strayhorn
Billy & __: 6 Lillie
Billy __: 4 Budd, Liar 6 Elliot, the Kid
Billy __ and the Checkmates: 3 Joe
Billy __ Cyrus: 3 Ray
Billy __ Williams: 3 Dee
__ Billy: 6 Bronco
__-Billy: 5 Rock-A
Billy Bathgate: 4 film 5 novel
author: E.L. Doctorow
cast: Dustin Hoffman, Nicole Kidman, Bruce Willis
director: Robert Benton
Billy Bob: 8 Thornton
Billy Budd: 4 film 5 novel, opera
author: Herman Melville
cast: Melvyn Douglas, Robert Ryan, Peter Ustinov
composer: 7 Britten
director: Peter Ustinov
Billy, Don't Be a Hero (1974 song)
artist: Bo Donaldson and the Heywoods
billy goat: 4 male
feature: 5 beard
mate: 5 nanny 6 nannie
offspring: 3 kid
Billy Goats Gruff adversary: 5 troll
Billy Liar (1963 film)
cast: Julie Christie, Tom Courtenay
director: John Schlesinger
Billy Rose's Jumbo (1962 film)
cast: Stephen Boyd, Doris Day, Jimmy Durante, Martha Raye
director: Charles Walters
Billy Straight author: Jonathan Kellerman
Billy the Kid: 6 ballet
composer: 7 Copland
Biloxi: 4 city, port, town
state: 4 Miss.
Biloxi Blues: 4 film, play
author: Neil Simon
cast: Matthew Broderick, Matt Mulhern, Christopher Walken
director: Mike Nichols
biltong: 4 meat
Bimini __: 7 Islands
bimonthly: 3 mag 8 magazine
bin: 3 box 4 case, crib 5 hutch 6 bunker, coffer, hamper, hopper, manger 8 corn crib, Dumpster 9 container 10 receptacle
__ bin: 5 trash
Binaca competitor: 5 Certs 6 Mentos, Tic Tac 7 Altoids, Clorets, Dentyne
binal: 6 double 7 twofold
binary: 4 dual 6 double 7 twofold, two-part
digit: 3 one 4 zero
star: 6 Sirius
binary __: 4 cell, code, form, star 5 color, digit 6 number, pulsar, system 7 fission
binate: 4 dual 6 double 7 in pairs, two-fold
binaural: 6 stereo
Binchy, Maeve: 5 Irish 6 author, writer
work: Circle of Friends
The Copper Beech
Echoes
Evening Class
Firefly Summer
The Glass Lake
Light a Penny Candle
The Lilac Bus
Quentins
Scarlet Feather
Silver Wedding
Tara Road
bind: 3 fix, jam, pin, sew, tie, wed 4 bale, bond, know, lace, lash, link, rope, tape, weld, wrap, yoke 5 affix, cinch, clamp, force, hitch, leash, stick, tie up, truss 6 attach, begird, bundle, cement, compel, crunch, enlace, fasten, fetter, hamper, hobble, hogtie, hook up, inlace, lace up, ligate, lock up, oblige, pickle, pinion, ratify, secure, strait, tether 7 confine, conjoin, connect, dilemma, enchain, manacle, pin down, promise, require, shackle, tighten 8 enfetter, handcuff, hot water, make fast, obligate, quandary, restrain, restrict 9 constrain, constrict, deep water, indenture, interlace, prescribe, tight spot 10 difficulty
ender: 4 weed
in a ~: 5 stuck 7 up a tree 10 up the creek
nautically: 4 frap
starter: 5 spell
__ bind: 3 in a 6 double
binder: 8 notebook 9 loose-leaf
package ~: 4 cord, tape 5 twine
starter: 4 book 5 spell
__ binder: 4 ring
Binder: 5 Steve
binding: 4 band 5 cover, strap, valid 8 dressing, ligature, limiting, required 9 incumbent, mandatory, necessary, requisite, stringent 10 compulsory, imperative, obligatory, peremptory
legally ~: 5 valid
make ~: 4 pass, sign 6 decree 8 validate
material: 4 cord, rope 5 twine
molecule: 6 ligand
name meaning ~: 7 Rebecca, Rebekah
not ~: 4 null 5 loose 7 invalid
part: 5 cover, npard, spine
starter: 4 book 5 spell
type of book ~: 4 yapp
binding __: 4 post 6 energy, rafter, strake
__ binding: 4 full, half, seam, yapp 6 spiral 7 circuit, edition, library, perfect, quarter
bindlestiff: 3 bum 4 hobo 5 tramp
binds, tie that: 7 wedlock 8 marriage
bine: 4 stem
starter: 4 wood
__ bin ein Berliner: 3 Ich
Binet: 6 Alfred
Binet-Simon __: 4 test 5 scale
Bing: 4 Dave 6 cherry, Crosby, Rudolf
cherry relative: 7 marasca, morello, oxheart
film buddy: 3 Bob
Bing, Dave: 5 cager
milieu: 5 court
org.: 3 NBA
sport: 10 basketball
binge: 3 jag 4 tear, toot 5 fling, gorge, revel, spree 6 bender, pig out 7 blowout, rampage, splurge 8 carousal 10 all-nighter, gormandize
__ binge: 3 on a
Bingham: 5 Traci
Binghamton: 4 city, town
city near ~: 6 Elmira
locale: 7 New York
__ Bingle: 3 Der
bingo: 3 aha 4 game 5 right 8 you got it
call: 4 B one, B six, B ten, B two 5 B five, B four, B nine 6 B eight, B seven, B three 7 B eleven, B twelve
official: 6 caller
relative: 4 keno 5 beano, lotto
bingo __: 4 card, hall
Bingo Eli Yale composer: 6 Porter
Bingo Long..., The (1976 film)
cast: James Earl Jones, Richard Pryor, Billy Dee Williams
director: John Badham
Binh Dinh: 4 city, town
locale: 7 Vietnam
today: 6 An Nhon
biniou: 4 wind 7 bagpipe
Binnie: 6 Barnes
Binnig, Gerd: 8 Nobelist 9 physicist
Binoche, Juliette: 7 actress
Oscar: The English Patient
binocle: 4 game 8 card game
binocular
component: 5 prism
lens: 5 optic
Binyon, Laurence: 4 poet 7 British
bio: 4 life 5 story 6 memoir, résumé 7 memoirs, profile 9 life story
datum: 3 age, née
ender: 4 tech 7 science
final ~: 4 obit
job-seeker's ~: 4 vita 6 résumé
Bio-Bio: 5 river
locale: 5 Chile
biochemical
catalyst: 6 enzyme
compound: 5 lipid 6 lipide
energy source: 3 ATP
biodegradable: 5 green
biodynamics: 7 science
bioflavonoid: 5 rutin 6 citrin
biographer: 6 author, writer
Biographer's Tale, The author: A.S. Byatt
biography: 4 life, vita 5 genre, story 6 memoir 7 memoirs, profile 9 life story 10 adventures, literature
biol.: 3 sci.
branch: 4 anat.
course: 3 bot.
biological: 7 organic
breakdown: 5 lysis
class: 5 taxon
classes: 4 taxa
duct: 3 vas
grouping: 7 kingdom
map: 5 genom 6 genome
partition: 6 septum
partitions: 5 septa
process: 6 ecesis 7 osmosis
subdivision: 5 class, genus, order 6 phylum 7 species
biological __: 5 child, clock 6 parent, rhythm 7 control
biology: 7 science
branch of ~: 5 space 6 botany, marine, osmics 7 anatomy, bionics, ecology, zoology 8 genetics, mycology 9 molecular 10 biophysics, exobiology, morphology 11 biodynamics
lab stain: 5 eosin
prefix with ~: 5 macro, micro, neuro
strand: 3 DNA
study: 4 life
__ biology: 4 cell 5 space 6 marine 9 molecular
biome: 6 desert 10 rain forest
biomedical research agcy.: 3 NIH
Biondi, Matt: 7 swimmer
bionic, human: 6 cyborg
Bionic Woman, The (ABC/NBC adventure)
cast: Lindsay Wagner (Jaime Sommers)
dog: 3 Max
org.: 3 OSI
role: 6 cyborg
bionomics: 7 ecology 8 oecology
biopic: 4 film
biosphere: 5 earth, world 7 habitat
biota component: 5 fauna, flora
biotic: 7 organic
biotin: 8 B vitamin
biotite: 4 mica 7 mineral
Bioy Casares, Adolfo: 6 writer 9 Argentine
biped: 3 ape, emu, man 4 bird, duck, emeu, T-rex, yeti 5 chimp, goose, human, orang 7 chicken, gorilla, ostrich, primate 8 allosaur, theropod 9 orangutan 10 orangutang
biplane
support: 5 strut
WWI ~: 4 Spad
birch: 3 rod 4 beer, tree, whip, wood 5 alder, shrub 6 cudgel, thrash 10 flagellate
family shrub: 5 alder, hazel 8 hornbeam
product: 5 canoe
spike: 5 ament 6 catkin
tree: 5 alder, hazel 8 hornbeam
birch __: 4 beer
__ birch: 3 red 4 gray, grey 5 black,

canoe, paper, river, sweet, white
6 cherry, yellow
Birch: 4 Bayh 5 Thora
__ Birch: 5 Simon
birchbark: 5 canoe
Birches: 4 poem
author: Robert Frost
Birch Interval (1977 film)
cast: Eddie Albert, Rip Torn, Ann Wedgeworth
director: Delbert Mann
Birch, Thora: 7 actress
film: American Beauty (1999)
Ghost World (2001)
Monkey Trouble (1994)
Paradise (1991)
bird: 3 auk, emu, ern, hen, jay, kea, mew, moa, owl, pie, roc, tit, tui 4 chat, coot, crow, dodo, dove, duck, emeu, erne, guan, gull, hawk, huia, ibis, kagu, kaka, kite, kiwi, knot, lark, loon, lory, merl, mina, myna, nene, rail, rhea, rook, ruff, shag, skua, smew, sora, swan, teal, tern, tody, wren 5 biped, booby, brant, buteo, colin, crake, crane, dance, eagle, egret, eider, finch, galah, goony, goose, grebe, heron, jager, junco, koloa, macaw, mavis, merle, minah, murre, mynah, noddy, ousel, ouzel, oxeye, pewee, pewit, pipit, pitta, plane, potoo, quail, raven, robin, saker, scaup, serin, shama, snipe, solan, stilt, stint, stork, swift, twite, vireo, yager 6 avocet, barbet, becard, bishop, bonxie, brolga, bulbul, canary, chebec, chough, chukar, condor, conure, cuckoo, curlew, darter, dipper, drongo, dunlin, falcon, fulmar, gander, gannet, godwit, gooney, grouse, hoopoe, jabiru, jacana, jaeger, kakapo, lanner, linnet, magpie, martin, merlin, motmot, mud hen, oriole, osprey, parrot, parula, peewit, petrel, phoebe, pigeon, plover, pouter, puffin, quezal, roller, scoter, sea mew, shrike, siskin, takahe, thrush, tityra, tomtit, toucan, towhee, trogon, turaco, turkey, verdin, whidah, whydah, wigeon, willet 7 anhinga, babbler, barn owl, bittern, bluejay, bunting, bustard, buzzard, cariama, chicken, cotinga, courser, creeper, dottrel, dovekey, dovekie, elaenia, elepaio, fantail, finfoot, gadwall, goshawk, grackle, gray jay, graylag, greylag, halcyon, harrier, hen hawk, hoatzin, jacamar, jackdaw, kestrel, kinglet, lapwing, limpkin, mallard, manakin, marabou, mudlark, ortolan, ostrich, peacock, peafowl, pelican, penguin, phoenix, pochard, quetzal, redpoll, redwing, scooter, seagull, seriema, skimmer, skylark, sparrow, swallow, tanager, tattler, tinamou, titlark, touraco, vulture, wagtail, waxbill, waxwing, widgeon, wryneck 8 amadavat, avadavat, bee-eater, bellbird, blackcap, bluebill, boatbill, bobolink, bobwhite, bullneck, caracara, cardinal, cockatoo, coturnix, curassow, dabchick, didapper, dotterel, eagle owl, fish hawk, flamingo, garganey, grayback, grosbeak, guacharo, hawfinch, hemipode, hoactzin, hornbill, killdeer, kiskadee, landrail, longspur, lorikeet, manacode, marabout, megapode, moorfowl, murrelet, nightjar, notornis, nuthatch, oxpecker, parakeet, paraquet, paroquet, parroket, peetweet, pheasant, redshank, redstart, ringdove, screamer, sea eagle, shelduck, shoebill, shoveler, starling, thrasher, titmouse, tragopan, trembler, tremblor, troupial, water hen, wheatear, whimbrel, whinchat, whistler, white-eye, woodchat, woodcock, woodlark 9 albatross, broadbill, bullfinch, cassowary, chaffinch, chickadee, cockateel, cockatiel, cormorant, crossbill, currawong, dowitcher, fieldfare, flinthead, francolin, frogmouth, gallinule, gerfalcon, goldeneye, goldfinch, grassquit, guillemot, gyrfalcon, hammerkop, kittiwake, mallemuck, merganser, mollymawk, mollymoke, nighthawk, ossifrage, pardalote, parrakeet, parroquet, partridge, peregrine, phalarope, ptarmigan, razorbill, redbreast, sandpiper, seedeater, sharpbill, sheldrake, spoonbill, sprigtail, stonechat, thickhead, trumpeter, turnstone
10 budgerigar, budgerygah, chiffchaff, clay pigeon, demoiselle, dickcissel, flycatcher, goatsucker, greenfinch, greenshank, hammerhead, honeyeater, kingfisher, kookaburra, nutcracker, pratincole, sanderling, shearwater, sheathbill, sicklebill, turtledove, woodpecker, yellowlegs
aerie ~: 4 hawk 5 eagle 6 falcon
African ~: 4 coly 6 bishop, drongo, lanner, turaco, whidah, whydah 7 courser, finfoot, marabou, ostrich 8 lovebird, oxpecker, whinchat, woodchat 9 francolin, hammerkop 10 hammerhead, weaverbird
almost any ~: 5 flier, flyer
anserine ~: 5 goose
Antarctic ~: 6 adelie 7 emperor, penguin
aquatic ~: 4 coot, gull, swan, tern 5 grebe 6 jaçana 7 finfoot, penguin 8 flamingo 9 gallinule, phalarope
Arabian Nights ~: 3 roc
Arctic ~: 4 skua 5 brant 6 fulmar 9 gerfalcon, gyrfalcon
Argentine ~: 7 cariama, seriema
artificial ~: 5 decoy
Asian ~: 4 lory, ruff, smew 5 shama 6 bulbul, chukar, drongo, lanner 7 courser, finfoot, marabou, ostrich 8 amadavat, avadavat, dotterel, eagle owl, leafbird, lorikeet, megapode 9 cormorant, francolin, friarbird, frogmouth, ossifrage 10 greenfinch, honeyeater, weaverbird
attractor: 4 suet 6 feeder
Australian ~: 3 emu, iao 4 emeu, lory 5 galah 6 brolga, drongo 7 mudlark 8 cockatoo, lorikeet, lyrebird, megapode 9 bowerbird, cassowary, cockateel, cockatiel, currawong, friarbird, frogmouth, pardalote, riflebird 10 budgerigar, budgerygah, honeyeater, kookaburra
baby ~: 5 chick, owlet 6 eaglet 7 gosling 8 duckling, nestling 9 fledgling, hatchling
bald ~: 5 eagle
beak: 3 neb, nib
big ~: 3 emu 4 emeu, rhea 7 ostrich
black ~: 3 daw 4 crow, merl 5 raven 7 jackdaw 8 starling
black-and-orange ~: 6 oriole
blue ~: 3 jay 5 heron 7 bunting 8 bluebird
Brazilian ~: 7 cariama, seriema
brilliantly colored ~: 3 kea 5 macaw 6 parrot 8 parakeet
call: 3 caw 4 peep, pipe, twee 5 cheep, chirp, tweet 6 cuckoo 7 chirrup, twitter
cattle ~: 5 egret
Central American ~: 4 guan 5 potoo 7 quetzal, tinamou 8 caracara, curassow
Christmas ~: 5 goose
claw: 5 talon
coastal ~: 3 ern 4 erne, gull, tern 7 pelican
colonel's ~: 5 eagle
combining form: 3 avi- 5 -ornis 6 ornith- 7 ornitho-
crested ~: 3 jay 6 hoopoe 10 woodpecker
crop: 4 craw
crowlike ~: 4 huia 6 chough
diving ~: 3 auk 4 coot, loon 5 booby, grebe, murre, ousel, ouzel, solan 6 auklet, dipper 8 murrelet 10 kingfisher
dog: 5 hound 7 pointer 9 retriever
domestic ~: 3 hen 4 duck, fowl 5 drake, goose 6 gander 7 chicken, rooster
early ~ prize: 4 worm
eat like a ~: 4 peck, pick
Egyptian sacred ~: 4 ibis
ender: 3 dog, man, men 4 bath, cage, call, feed, lime, seed, shot 5 brain, house 6 feeder 7 watcher
European ~: 4 chat, lark, rook, ruff, shag, smew 5 ousel, ouzel, saker, twite 6 chough, cuckoo, hoopoe, lanner, linnet, siskin 7 babbler, graylag, greylag, jackdaw, lapwing, pochard, redwing, skylark, sunbird, wagtail, waxbill 8 coturnix, dotterel, eagle owl, garganey, hawfinch, ringdove, starling, whinchat, woodchat, woodlark 9 bullfinch, cormorant, fieldfare, francolin, goldfinch, ossifrage, stonechat 10 greenfinch, turtledove
extinct ~: 3 moa 4 dodo, huia
feature: 4 beak, wing 6 air sac 7 feather 8 feathers
fish-eating ~: 3 ern 4 erne, gull, tern 5 heron 7 pelican
flight feather: 5 remex
flightless ~: 3 emu, moa 4 dodo, emeu, kiwi, rhea 6 takahe 7 ostrich, penguin 8 notornis 9 cassowary
food: 4 seed, suet
fork-tailed ~: 4 tern
game ~: 5 quail 6 grouse 8 pheasant 10 wild turkey
gull-like ~: 6 bonxie, fulmar 7 skimmer
hangar ~: 5 plane
harsh-voiced ~: 3 jay, kea, pie 4 crow 5 macaw 6 parrot
Hawaiian ~: 2 oo 4 nene, omao 5 koloa, shama 7 elepaio
hieroglyphics ~: 4 ibis
home: 4 cage, nest, tree 5 aerie 6 aviary, hangar, jungle
honey-eating ~: 3 iao
house: 6 aviary 9 enclosure
hunter: 6 fowler
imitate a ~: 4 sing
in Latin: 4 avis
keelbone: 6 carina
larklike ~: 5 pipit
long-legged ~: 4 ibis 5 crane, egret, heron
long-necked ~: 4 swan
long-plumed ~: 5 egret 7 ostrich, peacock
marsh ~: 4 rail, sora, teal 5 crake, egret, snipe 6 mud hen 7 bittern 9 gallinule
Mexican ~: 5 potoo 7 quetzal
move like a ~: 3 fly, hop 4 dart, flit
name meaning ~: 5 Vogel
New Guinean ~: 7 mudlark 8 manacode 9 bowerbird, cassowary
New Zealand ~: 3 kea, moa, oii, tui 4 huia, kaka, kiwi, weka 6 kakapo, takahe 8 notornis
nocturnal ~: 3 owl
of peace: 4 dove
of prey: 4 hawk, kite 5 eagle, glede 6 elanet, falcon, lanner 7 kestrel
ostrichlike ~: 3 moa 4 rhea
Pacific ~: 4 kagu 5 goony 6 gooney
palindromic ~: 3 tit
pampas ~: 4 rhea
parson ~: 3 tui
passerine ~: 5 vireo
ploverlike ~: 6 jacana 7 courser
pouched ~: 7 pelican 9 cormorant
preacher ~: 5 vireo
quail-like ~: 8 hemipode
rare ~: 4 oner 7 prodigy
ratite ~: 3 emu 4 emeu
razor-billed ~: 3 auk
red-breasted ~: 5 robin
roost: 5 perch
sanctuary: 6 aviary
sandpiper-like ~: 9 phalarope
shelter: 4 cote, nest
small ~: 3 tit 4 wren 5 dicky, pewit 6 dickey, dickie, peewit
snipelike ~: 9 dowitcher
snowy ~: 3 owl 5 egret
South American ~: 4 guan, rhea, yeni 5 potoo 7 finfoot, hoatzin, quetzal, tinamou 8 caracara, curassow, guacharo, hoactzin, ovenbird, screamer, troupial
starter: 3 cat, cow, jay, oil, red, sun 4 bell, blue, fire, jail, king, lady, love, lyre, oven, rail, reed, rice, snow, song, surf, tick 5 black, bower, cedar, friar, moose, mound, rifle, shore, snake, sugar 6 tailor, tropic, wattle, weaver, yellow 7 butcher, humming, mocking, thunder
stomach: 4 craw
storklike ~: 8 shoebill
strigiform ~: 3 owl
swallowlike ~: 5 swift
swimming ~: 4 duck, loon, swan 5 goose 7 anhinga 9 snakebird
talking ~: 4 mina, myna 5 macaw, minah, mynah 6 parrot
that has red meat: 3 emu 4 emeu
that lays green eggs: 3 emu 4 emeu
throat: 6 gorget
thrushlike ~: 8 thrasher
thumb: 5 alula
titmouse-like ~: 6 verdin
top of a ~ head: 6 pileus
tropical ~: 4 guan, mina, myna 5 macaw, minah, mynah, pitta 6 barbet, becard, bulbul, motmot, parrot, tityra, toucan, trogon, turaco 7 antbird, elaenia, jacamar, manakin, oilbird, touraco 8 bee-eater, boatbill, hornbill, parakeet, puffbird, white-eye 9 broadbill, grassquit, seedeater, sharpbill 10 tailorbird
turkeylike ~: 4 guan
wading ~: 4 ibis, rail 5 crane, egret, heron, snipe, stilt, stork 6 avocet, jaçana 7 bittern, limpkin 8 boatbill, flamingo, shoebill 9 hammerkop, spoonbill 10 demoiselle, hammerhead
watcher's aid: 6 feeder 8 spyglass 10 binoculars
web-footed ~: 3 auk 4 duck, loon, swan 5 goose, solan
West Indies ~: 4 tody
white ~: 4 swan 5 egret
whose male hatches the eggs: 4 kiwi
wise ~: 3 owl
yellow-breasted ~: 4 chat
bird __: 3 dog 4 band, call, farm, feed, ring, shot, walk 5 grass, louse 6 cherry, feeder, pepper, plague, ringer

7 banding, colonel, watcher
bird-___: 7 brained, watcher
___ bird: 3 bee 4 bell, cage, dodo, game, tick 5 bosun, dough, early, goony, rifle, shore, state, water, widow 6 bishop, gooney, indigo, meadow, mutton, parson, regent, tropic, wading 7 apostle, buffalo, diamond, frigate, man-o'-war, peabody, teacher
___ bird..: 4 It's a
Bird: 5 Lance, Larry 7 Antonia
milieu: 3 NBA
of Paradise constellation: 4 Apus
played it: 3 sax 4 alto
Bird (1988 film)
cast: Diane Venora, Forest Whitaker, Michael Zelniker
director: Clint Eastwood
subject: Charlie Parker
Bird ___ Gilded Cage, A: 3 in a
___ Bird: 3 Big 4 Free 5 Do the 6 Silver, Yellow
birdbath organism: 4 alga
birdbrain: 3 ass, nit, oaf, sap 4 boob, clod, dodo, dolt, fool, simp, twit 5 chump, clown, cluck, dummy, dunce, joker, looby, ninny, patsy 6 dimwit, lummox, nitwit, sucker, turkey 7 buffoon, dingbat, dullard, fathead, half-wit, jackass, pinhead, saphead 8 bonehead, dumbbell, meathead, numskull 9 blockhead, numbskull, simpleton 10 dunderhead, nincompoop
birdbrained: 3 mad 4 daft, luny 5 loony, silly 6 looney 7 fatuous, vacuous
birdcage: 6 aviary, volary
device: 6 feeder
swing: 5 perch
birdcage ___: 5 clock
birdcage, the (1995 film)
cast: Gene Hackman, Nathan Lane, Dianne Wiest, Robin Williams
director: Mike Nichols
Birdcage, The artist: 4 Erté
birdcall: 4 song 5 cheep, chirp, tweet 7 twitter
bird-dog: 4 seek 5 stalk 6 pursue 9 track down
Bird Dog (1958 song) artist: Everly Brothers
Bird Falls Down, The author: Rebecca West
bird feeder staple: 4 suet 5 seeds
birdhouse: 4 cote 6 aviary, volary
birdie
beater: 5 eagle
plus one: 3 par
bird in ___: 4 hand
___ Bird Johnson: 4 Lady 5 Lynda
birdland: 5 dance
Bird, Larry: 5 cager
milieu: 5 court
org.: 3 NBA
sport: 10 basketball
birdman: 5 pilot
Birdman of Alcatraz: 5 lifer 6 Stroud
Birdman of Alcatraz (1962 film)
cast: Burt Lancaster, Karl Malden, Thelma Ritter
director: John Frankenheimer
bird of ___: 4 prey 7 passage
bird-of-paradise: 5 plant 6 flower
___ Bird of Youth: 5 Sweet
Bird on a Wire (1990 film)
cast: David Carradine, Mel Gibson, Goldie Hawn
director: John Badham
birds: 4 aves, fowl
do it: 3 fly 4 peck, sing, soar 5 chirp, glide, perch, roost, tweet 7 twitter
for the ~: 5 inane, silly 6 absurd 9 worthless 10 ridiculous
like ~: 5 alate, avian 6 alated
of a feather: 7 cohorts, cronies 10 colleagues
of a region: 5 ornis
partner: 4 bees
science: 11 ornithology
thumbs: 6 alulae
tops of ~ ' heads: 5 pilea
where ~ fly in the fall: 5 south
Birds ___, bees...: 4 do it
birds and ___: 4 bees
Birds, Beasts, and Flowers author: D.H. Lawrence
Birds Do It star: 5 Sales
Birdseye: 8 Clarence
rival: 5 Libby 6 Libby's
bird's-eye view: 8 panorama
bird's-nest ___: 4 fern, soup 6 fungus
birds of a ___: 7 feather
Birdsong: 4 Otis 5 Cindy
___ bird special: 5 early
Birds, The (1963 film)
cast: Tippi Hedren, Suzanne Pleshette, Jessica Tandy, Rod Taylor
director: Alfred Hitchcock
___ Birds, The: 5 Thorn
Birds, The author: Aristophanes
character: 4 Iris 5 Epops
Bird thou never ___: 4 wert
Birdy (1984 film)
cast: Nicolas Cage, John Harkins, Matthew Modine
director: Alan Parker
bireme: 4 boat 6 galley
equipment: 3 oar
projection: 3 ram
biretta: 3 cap, hat
Birgit: 7 Nilsson
birler need: 3 log
birling: 5 sport
competitor: 10 lumberjack
match: 5 roleo
Birman: 3 cat 5 felid 6 feline
Birmingham: 4 city, town
athletes: 7 Blazers 11 Crimson Tide
locale: 7 Alabama, England
school: 3 UAB
Birnbach: 4 Lisa
Birney, David spouse: Meredith Baxter
birr: 5 money 7 impetus
birrus: 5 cloak
birth: 4 dawn, rank 5 class, onset, start 6 origin, outset, source, spring 7 descent, genesis, infancy, lineage 8 ancestry, creation, delivery, heritage, nascency, natality, nativity, pedigree 9 awakening, beginning, emergence, inception 10 extraction
bird: 5 stork
by ~: 3 née 9 naturally 10 originally
ender: 3 day 4 mark, root, wort 5 place, right, stone
from ~: 6 innate
give ~: 4 yean 5 calve
give ~ to: 4 bear, have 5 begin, breed, spawn 6 create 7 deliver 8 engender, generate, initiate 9 originate 10 bring forth
high ~: 8 nobility 9 blue blood, gentility 10 upper class, upper crust
name meaning ~: 4 Edna
of ~: 5 natal
birth ___: 4 name, rate 6 family, father, mother, parent
birthday: 5 event 7 jubilee
celebration: 5 party
count: 5 years
expression: 4 wish
figure: 3 age
in one's ~ suit: 4 bare, nude 5 naked 8 starkers
mail: 4 card
name meaning ~: 7 Natalie
party item: 4 cake, gift 5 favor 6 candle, piñata 7 present
birthday ___: 4 cake, suit 5 party
Birthday Party, The: 4 film, play
author: Harold Pinter
cast: Patrick Magee, Robert Shaw
director: William Friedkin
___ Birthday to You: 5 Happy
birthing ___: 4 room 6 center
training: 6 Lamaze
birthmark: 4 mole 5 nevus 7 blemish
Birth of a Nation, The (1915 film)
cast: Lillian Gish, Mae Marsh, Henry B. Walthall
director: D.W. Griffith
Birth of the Blues, The (1941 film)
cast: Bing Crosby, Brian Donlevy
birthplace: 4 home 6 cradle, source
birthright: 5 claim 6 legacy 7 liberty 8 heritage 9 privilege
barterer: 4 Esau
birthstone: 3 gem 5 jewel
April ~: 7 diamond
August ~: 7 peridot
December ~: 9 turquoise
February ~: 8 amethyst
January ~: 6 garnet
July ~: 4 ruby
June ~: 5 pearl
March ~: 10 aquamarine
May ~: 5 agate 7 emerald
November ~: 5 topaz
October ~: 4 opal
September ~: 8 sapphire
Birtle: 4 city, town
locale: 6 Canada 8 Manitoba
bis: 5 twice 6 encore
Bisbee: 4 city, town
locale: 7 Arizona
Biscay, Bay of
feeder: 5 Loire
peninsula: 6 Iberia
port: 5 Gijón 6 Bilbao
Biscayne: 3 bay, car 4 auto, park 5 Chevy 9 Chevrolet 10 automobile
Biscayne Bay
county on ~: 4 Dade
locale: 5 Miami 7 Florida
Bischoff: 3 Sam
biscotto: 6 cookie
flavoring: 5 anise
biscuit: 3 bun, tan 5 bread, brown, cooky, scone, wafer 6 cookie, suntan 7 cracker
color kin: 3 bay, dun, tan 4 bole, ecru, fawn, foxy, nude, seal 5 amber, beige, camel, cocoa, hazel, khaki, mocha, sepia, tawny, umber 6 auburn, bister, bistre, bronze, coffee, copper, ginger, russet, sienna, sorrel, suntan, walnut 7 caramel, dogwood 8 chestnut, cinnamon, mahogany 9 butternut, chocolate
crisp ~: 4 rusk
Londoner's ~: 5 scone
saltless ~: 4 tack
thin ~: 5 wafer
biscuit ___: 4 ware 5 bread 7 tortoni
___ biscuit: 3 dog, sea, tea 4 drop, ship, soda 5 pilot, water 6 beaten 7 ratafia
bise: 4 wind
bisect: 3 cut, saw 4 fork 5 halve, sever, split 6 cleave, divide 7 split up 8 separate 9 branch off, intersect
bisected: 5 split 6 in half
bisection: 4 half 8 division
'B' Is for Burglar author: Sue Grafton
Bishkek: 4 city, town 7 capital
locale: 10 Kyrgyzstan
bishop: 3 man 4 bird, pope, rank 5 drink, piece 6 cleric, eparch, exarch, priest 7 pontiff, prelate, primate 8 beverage, cocktail, diocesan, minister, overseer 9 patriarch 10 archpriest, chesspiece
crosier: 5 crook
decree: 5 canon
domain: 3 see 7 diocese, prelacy
Eastern ~: 4 abba 6 exarch
ingredient: 4 port 6 cloves, orange
neighbor: 6 knight
of a ~: 9 episcopal
of Rome: 4 pope 7 pontiff
onetime TV ~: 5 Sheen
protector, maybe: 4 pawn
seat: 9 cathedral
South African ~: 4 Tutu
starter: 4 arch
topper: 5 miter, mitre
Bishop: 3 Jim 4 Joey 5 Elvin, Julie 7 Michael, Stephen
Bishop at Sea, The author: Andrew Greeley
Bishop, Joey: 2 MC 4 host 5 emcee
Bishop, Michael: 8 Nobelist
Bishop Orders His Tomb, The: 4 poem
author: Robert Browning
bishopric: 3 see 7 diocese, prelacy
bishops: 6 clergy
body of ~: 10 episcopacy
council: 5 synod
Bishop, Stephen
song: It Might Be You (1983)
On and On (1977)
Bishop's University
locale: 6 Canada, Quebec
Bishop's Wife, The (1947 film)
cast: Cary Grant, David Niven, Loretta Young
director: Henry Koster
dog: 7 Queenie
bismanol: 5 alloy
component: 7 bismuth 9 manganese
Bismarck: 3 sea 4 boat, city, ship, town
city near ~: 5 Minot
county: 8 Burleigh
locale: 4 N. Dak. 9 New Guinea
river: 8 Missouri
Bismarck ___: 3 Sea 7 herring
___ Bismarck: 7 Otto von
___-Bismol: 5 Pepto
bismuth: 5 metal 7 element
alloy: 8 bismanol 10 Wood's metal
Bisoglio: 3 Val
bison: 5 bovid 6 animal, bovine, cattle, wisent
feature: 4 hump
relative: 3 yak 4 anoa, arna, gaur, urus, zebu 5 gayal, takin 6 mithan, muskox 7 aurochs, banteng, banting, beefalo, buffalo, carabao, cattalo, kouprey, tamarao, tamarau, timarau
Bison: 6 Howard 8 Bucknell
bisque: 4 soup 5 color, gumbo 6 yellow
___ bisque: 7 lobster
Bissau: 4 city, town 7 capital
Bissell: 3 vac 4 Whit 6 vacuum
competitor: 5 Kirby, Oreck 6 Hoover 10 Electrolux
Bisset, Jacqueline: 7 actress
film: Airport (1970)
Bullitt (1968)
Dangerous Beauty (1998)
Day for Night (1973)
The Deep (1977)
The Grasshopper (1970)
Let the Devil Wear Black (2000)
The Mephisto Waltz (1971)
Murder on the Orient Express (1974)
Rich and Famous (1981)
Under the Volcano (1984)
Who Is Killing the Great Chefs of Europe? (1978)
bistre: 5 brown 9 yellowish
kin: 3 bay, dun, tan 4 bole, ecru,

fawn, foxy, nude, seal **5** amber, beige, camel, cocoa, hazel, khaki, mocha, sepia, tawny, umber **6** auburn, bronze, coffee, copper, ginger, russet, sienna, sorrel, suntan, walnut **7** biscuit, caramel, dogwood **8** chestnut, cinnamon, mahogany **9** butternut, chocolate

bistro: **3** bar **4** cafe **5** diner **6** eatery, lounge, tavern **7** cabaret **8** taphouse **9** brasserie, nightclub, nightspot **10** restaurant
menu: **5** carte
name word: **4** chez
patron: **5** diner, eater
patronize a ~: **3** eat, sup **4** dine

bit: **3** dab, dot, job, jot, tad **4** atom, bash, dash, iota, jiff, lick, lump, mite, mote, part, role, slab, snip, time, tool, whit, wisp **5** auger, crumb, drill, flake, fleck, grain, jiffy, money, piece, pinch, scrap, shard, sherd, shred, skosh, space, speck, spell, stint, taste, tinge, touch, trace **6** dollop, gobbet, little, moment, morsel, ration, sample, sliver, snatch, tidbit, trifle **7** driblet, droplet, granule, instant, modicum, oddment, portion, remnant, segment, shaving, smidgen, smidgin, snippet, trickle, went for **8** fraction, fragment, molecule, particle, pittance, smidgeon, specimen, spoonful **9** cameo role, scintilla, short time **10** jackhammer, sprinkling
attachment: **4** rein
part: **5** cameo
partner: **5** brace
starter: **3** hen, tid **4** back, rare **5** frost

bit __: **3** key, map **4** part, stop **5** gauge **6** player

__ bit: **3** in a **4** wing **5** auger, bergy, check, drill, every **6** center, parity **7** chamfer, snaffle

__-bit: **3** two **5** frog's, wait-a **6** devil's

bit-by-bit: **7** gradual **9** gradually
get ~: **5** amass, glean **6** gather **7** collect

bite: **3** fee, nip, tax, zip **4** burn, gnaw, kick, nosh, snap, tang, zest **5** champ, chill, chomp, lunch, munch, piece, punch, scrap, share, slice, snack, spice, sting, taste **6** charge, crunch, gnaw at, gnaw on, incise, injury, morsel, nibble, outlay, sample, tidbit **7** section **8** fraction, fragment, mouthful, piquancy, pungency, spoonful **9** crispness, liability, light meal, masticate, volunteer **10** percentage
bug ~: **4** welt
government's ~: **3** tax
grab a ~: **3** eat, sup **4** dine, nosh **5** lunch, snack **6** gobble, nibble **7** munch on, put away **8** chow down, wolf down **9** have a meal, scarf down
just a ~: **3** bit **5** taste **6** morsel, nibble, sample, tidbit, trifle **7** forkful, soupçon **8** mouthful, spoonful
like a mosquito ~: **5** itchy
not apt to ~: **4** tame
off too much: **6** overdo
one's lip: **7** forbear, refrain, repress
one's nails: **5** worry **7** agonize
process a ~: **4** chew
react to a ~: **4** itch **5** sting, swell
sound ~: **4** clip **5** blurb, piece **6** slogan **7** excerpt, snippet **8** buzzword, one-liner, spot news **9** newsbreak
starter: **4** back, flea **5** frost, snake
take the ~ out of: **5** allay **6** lessen
the dust: **3** bow **4** bomb, bust, fail, flop, lose, slip, trip **5** flunk **6** blow it, falter **7** blunder, founder, go under, go wrong, misstep, stumble, wash out **8** fall flat, flounder, lay an egg **9** strike out

bite-__: **4** size **5** sized

__ bite: **5** grab a, sound

bite one's __: **3** lip **6** tongue

biter: **3** dog **4** flea, gnat **5** midge **6** insect **7** incisor **8** mosquito
dog ~: **4** flea
night ~: **6** bedbug
target: **3** lip **4** nail **10** fingernail
tiny ~: **4** flea, gnat **5** midge

__ Bites: **4** Love **7** Reality

bite the __: **4** dust **6** bullet

Bite the Bullet (1975 film)
cast: Candice Bergen, James Coburn, Gene Hackman
director: Richard Brooks

biting: **3** dry, icy, raw **4** acid, cold, cool, sour, tart **5** acerb, brisk, chill, harsh, nippy, polar, rough, sharp, tangy **6** arctic, bitter, chilly, frigid, frosty, frozen, severe, strong, wintry **7** acerbic, caustic, cutting, glacial, intense, mordant, numbing, piquant, pungent, satiric, shivery, wintery **8** abrasive, freezing, incisive, piercing, poignant, scathing, stinging **9** corrosive, insulting, offensive, sarcastic, satirical, trenchant, withering **10** astringent
nail ~: **4** vice
pest: **4** flea, gnat **8** mosquito

Bit-o-__: **5** Honey

bit of talcum..., A author: **4** Nash

bit-part performer: **5** extra

__ bits: **3** two **4** four

__ Bits: **5** Alpha

Bits and Pieces (1964 song) artist: Dave Clark Five

bits partner: **6** pieces

bitsy: **3** wee **4** tiny **5** teeny **6** teensy

__-bitsy: **4** itsy

bitt: **4** post

__ bitten...: **4** Once

__-bitten: **4** flea, hard

bitter: **3** ale, icy, raw **4** acid, cold, dire, hard, sore, sour, tart **5** acerb, acrid, cruel, gelid, harsh, nasty, rough, sharp, stern, taste, woful **6** biting, crabby, fierce, frigid, frosty, frozen, heated, savage, severe, sullen, woeful **7** acerbic, caustic, cutting, cynical, galling, glacial, hateful, hostile, hurtful, ice-cold, intense, painful, pungent, satiric **8** alkaline, brackish, freezing, grievous, liverish, piercing, rigorous, ruthless, sardonic, scathing, stinging, vinegary, virulent **9** acidulous, alienated, corrosive, estranged, inclement, malicious, rancorous, resentful, sarcastic, satirical, vitriolic **10** astringent, calamitous, disturbing, unpleasant, vindictive
alternative: **5** stout
combining form: **4** picr- **5** picro-
dispute: **4** feud **7** quarrel
feel ~: **6** resent
it may be ~: **3** end
pill: **6** misery **7** letdown
plant: **5** vetch
purgative: **5** aloin
vetch: **3** ers

bitter __: **3** ale, end, rot **4** dock, herb, lake, pill, root **5** aloes, apple, cress, gourd, vetch **6** almond, orange **7** cassava

bitterling: **4** fish

bitterly: **6** keenly **9** viciously

bittern: **4** bird
milieu: **5** marsh
relative: **5** heron

bitterness: **4** gall, pain, rage **5** agony, venom **6** enmity, flavor, grudge, hatred, malice, rancor, regret **7** acidity, anguish, sarcasm **8** acerbity, acridity, acrimony, distress, mordancy, piquancy, pungency, tartness **9** animosity, harshness, hostility, sharpness, virulence **10** heartbreak

bitterroot: **5** plant **6** flower

Bitterroot: **5** range **9** mountains
locale: **5** Idaho **7** Montana, Rockies

bitters: **7** quinine

bittersweet: **6** ironic, orange

Bitter Sweet (1940 film)
cast: Nelson Eddy, Jeanette MacDonald
director: W.S. Van Dyke

Bittersweet author: Danielle Steel

Bitter Sweet Symphony (1998 song)
artist: Verve

Bitter Tea of General Yen, The (1933 film)
cast: Nils Asther, Gavin Gordon, Barbara Stanwyck
director: Frank Capra

bitty: **3** wee **4** baby, puny, tiny **5** small, teeny **6** atomic, bantam, little, minute, peewee, petite, teensy **8** atomical, atomlike **9** miniature, pint-sized **10** diminutive, teeny-weeny, vest-pocket

__-bitty: **4** itty **6** little

__ Bitty Pretty One: **6** Little

__ Bitty Tear, A: **6** Little

bitumen: **3** tar

bituminous deposit: **4** coal, seam

bivalve: **4** clam **5** capiz, shell **6** quahog **7** quahaug **8** seashell

bivouac: **4** camp **5** étape **6** casern, encamp **7** caserne **8** barracks, lodgment **10** encampment
quarters: **4** tent

biwa: **4** lute **6** string
origin: **5** Japan

Biwa: **4** lake
locale: **5** Japan

biweekly: **8** magazine **9** newspaper

Bixby, Bill: **5** actor
film: Clambake (1967)
The Kentucky Fried Movie (1977)
Speedway (1968)
TV: The Courtship of Eddie's Father, The Incredible Hulk, My Favorite Martian

biz: **7** pursuit **10** profession
show ~: **2** TV **5** stage **6** movies **10** television

__ biz: **4** show

Biz: **9** detergent
rival: **3** All, Era, Fab, Yes **4** Bold, Dash, Gain, Surf, Tide, Wisk **5** Cheer, Dreft, Purex **6** Calgon, Clorox, Dynamo, Oxydol **7** Octagon **9** Ivory Snow

Biz __: **6** Markie

bizarre: **3** odd **4** camp, eery, wild **5** crazy, eerie, funny, gonzo, kooky, outré, queer, weird **6** atypic, far out, freaky, kookie, quaint, quirky, way out **7** curious, deviant, erratic, oddball, offbeat, strange, surreal, unusual **8** aberrant, abnormal, atypical, freakish, peculiar, striking, uncommon **9** anomalous, divergent, eccentric, fantastic, grotesque, irregular, laughable, ludicrous, unnatural **10** off-the-wall, outlandish, ridiculous, unfamiliar, unorthodox
in a ~ way: **5** oddly

Bizet, Georges: **6** French **8** composer
work: Carmen
The Fair Maid of Perth
Ivan IV
L'Arlésienne
Le Docteur miracle
Les pêcheurs de perles
Marche Funèbre
The Pearl Fishers
Roma

Biz Markie song: Just a Friend (1990)

B.J.: **6** Thomas

__ B. Johnson: **6** Lyndon

Bjorn: **4** Borg

Bjornson, Bjornstjerne: **6** writer **8** Nobelist

bk.: **3** vol.
addendum: **3** app.
after Amos: **4** Obad.
after Exodus: **3** Lev. **5** Levit.
after Ezra: **3** Neh.
after Proverbs: **4** Eccl
Apocrypha ~: **4** Macc.
before Daniel: **4** Ezek.
before Job: **4** Esth.
before Jonah: **4** Obad.
before Numbers: **3** Lev. **5** Levit.
category: **3** ref. **4** biog., fict., hist. **5** sci fi
drug-reference ~: **3** PDR
large-size ~: **3** fol.
New Testament ~: **3** Eph **4** Thes.
old ~ collector: **5** antiq.
place: **3** lib.
writer: **4** auth.
see also book

Bk: **4** elem. **7** element **9** berkelium
97 for ~: **4** at. no.

bks.-to-be: **3** mss.

blab: **3** gab, yak **4** chat, leak, sing, tell **5** bleat, blurt, prate, run on, speak, spill **6** gossip, jabber, let out, patter, reveal, snitch, squeal, tattle, yammer **7** chatter, divulge, lay bare, let slip, prattle, tell all **8** babbling, disclose, give away, let it out, ramble on, rattle on **9** name names **10** chew the rag, yackety-yak

blabber: **10** chew the rag

blabbermouth: **5** sieve **6** gabber, gasbag, gossip, magpie, tattle, yapper **7** tattler, windbag **8** blowhard, gossiper, informer, jabberer **10** tattletale

black: **3** jet, tea **4** bear, dark, ebon, inky, onyx, ugly **5** dirty, ebony, mirky, murky, raven, sable, smoky, sooty **6** darken, dismal, filthy, gloomy, somber, swarth **7** joyless, ominous, shadowy, swarthy, unclean, unlucky **8** charcoal, darkness, hopeless, lowering, starless **9** cheerless, lightless, pitch-dark, unlighted **10** inexpiable, lugubrious, tenebrific, villainous
art: **10** necromancy
bird: **3** daw **4** crow, merl **5** raven **7** jackdaw **8** starling
box: **9** mechanism
brown and ~ butterfly: **5** comma
card: **4** club **5** spade
cat: **4** omen
cloud: **4** pall
color: **3** jet **4** inky, onyx **5** ebony, raven, sable, sooty
combining form: **3** mel- **4** atro-, mela-, melo- **5** melan- **6** melano-
deep ~: **3** jet **4** ebon, inky, onyx **5** ebony, raven **9** pitch-dark
ender: **3** cap, leg, out, top **4** ball, bird, body, buck, cock, damp, face, fish, head, jack, legs, list, mail, ness, poll, wash **5** berry, board, guard, smith, snake, strap, thorn
eye: **4** blot, slur **5** mouse, odium, stain **6** bruise, insult, shiner **7** slander
fuel: **3** oil **4** coal
gem: **4** opal
give a ~ eye: **3** hit **4** slur, sock **5** libel, shame, smear **6** defame, vilify **8** mistreat
gold: **3** oil
goo: **3** tar
hat wearer: **6** bad guy **7** villain

hole, once: 4 star
in ~ and white: 5 clear, plain 8 explicit
in French: 4 noir 5 noire
in heraldry: 5 sable
in the ~: 7 solvent 9 lucrative
lacquer: 5 japan
look: 5 frown, glare, scowl
magic: 5 magic 6 voodoo 7 sorcery 9 diabolism 10 necromancy, witchcraft
make ~ and blue: 4 hurt 6 bruise, injure 7 contuse 8 discolor
mark: 4 slur, smut 6 stigma
name meaning ~: 7 Melanie 8 Schwartz
out: 5 faint, swoon 6 censor, delete, go limp, stifle
piano key: 5 A flat, B flat, D flat, E flat, G flat 6 A sharp, C sharp, D sharp, F sharp, G sharp
pitch ~: 4 dark 5 unlit 8 moonless
plus white: 4 gray, grey
sheep: 5 rogue 6 bad guy, rascal 9 miscreant, scoundrel 10 delinquent
starter: 4 bone, boot, lamp
tea: 5 bohea, congo, oopak 6 congou, oopack
tie: 6 tuxedo
to a poet: 4 ebon
use ~ magic: 3 hex 5 curse 7 bewitch
wear ~: 5 mourn
wood: 5 ebony

black __: 3 art, box, cod, cow, dog, eye, fly, fog, fox, gum, hat, haw, ice, oak, out, rat, rot, tea, tie 4 bass, bean, bear, belt, bile, book, buck, duck, flag, flux, gang, gnat, gold, gram, hole, kite, knot, land, lead, mark, mold, opal, ring, ruff, rust, sage, spot, stem 5 alder, birch, bread, chaff, cumin, dwarf, frost, humor, light, magic, maple, molly, money, olive, perch, racer, shank, sheep, snake, whale, witch 6 acacia, balsam, bottom, bryony, butter, cherry, cohosh, comedy, copper, cosmos, grouse, letter, liquor, locust, market, pepper, pewter, poplar, powder, scoter, spruce, sucker, velvet, walnut, wattle 7 buffalo, crappie, currant, diamond, margate, mustard, pudding, skimmer, studies, vulture

black __ spider: 5 widow

__ black: 3 gas 4 bone, drop 5 in the, ivory 6 animal, carbon 7 aniline, channel

__-black: 3 jet 4 blue 5 pitch

Black: 3 sea 4 Bill, Hawk, Hugo, Noel 5 Cilla, Clint, James, Karen, range 6 Jeanne, Joseph
Sea locale: 7 Eurasia

Black __: 3 Box, Cat, Rod, Sea 4 Flag, Fury, Girl, Hand, Hawk, Mesa, Monk, Oxen, Pope, Rain 5 Angel, Angus, Friar, Hills, Maria, Shirt, Stump, Volta, Watch, Water, Widow 6 Armour, Beauty, Canyon, Comedy, Forest, Legion, Muslim, Plague, Prince, Stream, Sunday, Velvet 7 Orpheus, Panther, Rainbow, Russian, Tuesday

Black __ cake: 6 Forest

Black __ of Calcutta: 4 Hole

Black __, The: 3 Cat 4 City, Room, Rose, Swan 5 Arrow, Sheep, Tulip 6 Knight, Marble, Pirate, Riders

Black __ War: 4 Hawk

__ Black: 5 Men in

Black and __ Fantasy: 3 Tan

black-and-blue: 5 livid 7 bruised
mark: 4 hurt 5 mouse 6 boo-boo, bruise

black and tan: 5 drink 8 beverage, cocktail
ingredient: 3 ale 5 stout 6 porter

black-and-white: 5 print
animal: 3 auk 5 panda, skunk, zebra
snack: 4 Oreo

Black and White (2000 film)
cast: Robert Downey Jr., Bijou Phillips, Brooke Shields
director: James Toback

Black Angel (1946 film)
cast: Dan Duryea, Peter Lorre
director: Roy William Neill

Black Angus: 3 cow

Black Armour author: Elinor Wylie

black as __: 4 coal 5 night, pitch

Black as He's Painted author: Ngaio Marsh

blackball: 3 ban 4 oust, shun, snub, tabu, veto 5 debar, expel, spurn 6 bounce, pass on, rebuff, reject 7 disdain, dismiss, exclude 8 disallow, turn down 9 cast aside, exclusion, ostracize, repudiate

blackballed: 9 unwelcome

Black Bears
home of the ~: 5 Maine, Orono

Black Beauty: 5 horse 6 equine

Black Beauty (1994 film)
cast: Sean Bean, David Thewlis

black belt: 4 rank, sash 6 expert
gym: 4 dojo
move: 4 chop
sport: 4 judo 6 karate

blackberry: 5 fruit 8 ice cream
alternative: 5 lemon, mocha, peach 6 banana, coffee, Jamoca, toffee 7 caramel, coconut, vanilla 8 cinnamon, hazelnut 9 bubblegum, chocolate, pineapple, pistachio, raspberry, rocky road, rum raisin 10 cheesecake, Neapolitan, peppermint, strawberry
hybrid ~: 10 loganberry
variety of ~: 8 dewberry

Blackberry Winter author: Margaret Mead

Black Bess: 5 horse 6 equine

blackbird: 3 ani 4 merl, rook 5 merle 7 grackle
comment: 3 caw
European ~: 5 ousel, ouzel

...blackbirds baked in __: 4 a pie

Blackbirds' school: 3 LIU

blackboard: 5 slate
accessory: 6 eraser
erase the ~: 4 wash, wipe 5 clean
like a ~ eraser: 5 dirty, dusty 7 powdery, unclean 8 unwashed
marker: 5 chalk

Blackboard Jungle: 4 film 5 novel
author: Evan Hunter
cast: Glenn Ford, Anne Francis, Vic Morrow
director: Richard Brooks

blackbuck: 5 sasin 8 antelope
relative: 3 gnu, kob 4 guib, kudu, oryx, puku, topi 5 addax, bongo, chiru, eland, goral, korin, nyala, oribi, saiga, serow 6 chammy, dikdik, duiker, impala, koodoo, lechwe, nilgai, rhebok, shammy, shamoy 7 blaubok, blesbok, chamois, defassa, gazelle, gemsbok, gerenuk, grysbok, nylghai, nylghau, sassaby 8 blesbuck, bontebok, bushbuck, gemsbuck, reedbuck, steenbok, steinbok 9 pronghorn, sitatunga, springbok, waterbuck 10 hartebeest, wildebeest

Blackburn: 4 peak 5 mount 8 mountain
locale: 6 Alaska

Black Camel, The hero: 4 Chan

blackcap: 4 bird

Black Cat (1990 song) artist: Janet Jackson

Black Cat, The
author: 3 Poe
cat: 5 Pluto

Black Cat, The (1934 film)
cast: Boris Karloff, Bela Lugosi
director: Edgar G. Ulmer

Black City, The author: George Sand

Black, Clint: 6 singer
spouse: Lisa Hartman

Black Comedy author: Peter Shaffer

black-currant cordial: 6 cassis

Black & Decker rival: 4 Skil

black duck: 4 fowl
relative: 4 smew, teal 5 eider, Pekin, Rouen, scaup 6 Cayuga, scoter 7 gadwall, mallard, pintail, pochard, redhead, widgeon 8 garganey, mandarin, oldsquaw, shoveler 9 broadbill, goldeneye, goosander, greenhead, merganser, sprigtail 10 bufflehead, canvasback, surf scoter

blacked out: 4 dark 5 unlit 6 aswoon 7 fainted, swooned

blacken: 3 rip 4 char, foul, sear, slur, soil, soul 5 dirty, libel, shade, singe, smear, stain, sully, taint 6 befoul, crud up, darken, defame, defile, malign, scorch, smudge, vilify 7 asperse, begrime, contuse, ebonize, grow dim, pollute, slander, tarnish, traduce 8 badmouth, besmirch, dishonor, grow dark, throw mud 9 denigrate 10 calumniate

blackened: 4 inky 5 grimy, sooty 6 filthy, fouled, grubby, grungy 7 injured 8 maculate, slovenly 10 unsanitary

__ blackest dye: 5 of the

Blackett, Patrick: 8 Nobelist 9 physicist, scientist

black-eyed __: 3 pea 5 Susan

black-eyed pea: 6 legume

black-eyed Susan: 5 plant 6 flower

Black Flag: 11 insecticide
rival: 4 Raid
target: 3 ant, bug 6 insect

Blackfoot: 5 tribe 6 Indian 7 Amerind 8 language

Black Forest
city: 5 Baden
locale: 7 Germany
tree: 5 larch

Black Forest __: 4 cake

Black Fury (1935 film)
cast: William Gargan, Karen Morley, Paul Muni
director: Michael Curtiz

Black Girl (1972 film)
cast: Brock Peters, Leslie Uggams
director: Ossie Davis

blackguard: 3 cad, cur 4 heel, toad, worm 5 beast, churl, knave, rogue, scamp, viper 6 bad guy, bad hat, defame, malign, rascal, revile, rotter, vilify, wretch 7 bounder, run down, villain 8 blighter, picaroon, rakehell, scalawag 9 miscreant, reprobate, scallawag, scallywag, scoundrel, vulgarian 10 delinquent, ne'er-do-well, scapegrace, vituperate

Black Hand (1950 film)
cast: Gene Kelly, J. Carrol Naish

Black Hawk: 3 Sac, war 4 Sauk
foe: 6 Keokuk

Black Hawk Down (2001 film)
cast: Josh Hartnett, Ewan McGregor, Tom Sizemore
director: Ridley Scott

Blackhawk rival: 4 Blue, King, Star, Wild 5 Bruin, Devil, Flame, Flyer, Oiler, Sabre, Shark 6 Canuck, Coyote, Ranger 7 Capital, Panther, Penguin, Red Wing, Senator 8 Canadien, Islander, Predator, Thrasher 9 Avalanche, Hurricane, Lightning, Maple Leaf 10 Blue Jacket, Mighty Duck

Blackhawks: 3 six 4 team
home: 7 Chicago
milieu: 3 ice 4 rink
org.: 3 NHL
sport: 6 hockey

black-hearted: 4 evil 5 cruel 8 ruthless, sinister 9 malicious, merciless

Black Hills
locale: 4 S. Dak.
mountain: 6 Harney

Black Horse Troop, The composer: 5 Sousa

black-ink item: 5 asset

Black is Black (1966 song) artist: Los Bravos

Black Is the __ of My True Love's Hair: 5 Color

blackjack: 4 club, cosh, game 6 cudgel 8 bludgeon, card game 9 truncheon
alias: 7 pontoon 9 twenty-one, vingt-et-un
card: 3 ace, six, ten, two 4 five, four, jack, king, nine 5 deuce, eight, queen, seven, three
dealer: 4 bank 5 house
dealer's device: 4 shoe
dealer's headwear: 5 visor, vizor
option: 3 hit 4 stay
place: 4 Reno 5 Vegas 6 casino
play ~: 3 bet
request: 5 hit me
work at the ~ table: 4 deal

Black Jack: 7 general 8 Pershing
command: 3 AEF

Black, James: 8 Nobelist

__ Black Joe: 3 Old

Black, Joseph: 7 British, chemist

Black, Karen: 7 actress
film: Cisco Pike (1972)
The Day of the Locust (1975)
Easy Rider (1969)
Family Plot (1976)
Five Easy Pieces (1970)
The Great Gatsby (1974)
Nashville (1975)
The Pyx (1973)

Black Knight, The composer: 5 Elgar

Black Legion (1936 film)
cast: Humphrey Bogart, Erin O'Brien-Moore
director: Archie Mayo

Black Like Me (1964 film)
cast: Roscoe Lee Browne, James Whitmore
director: Carl Lerner

blacklist: 6 punish 7 exclude 9 ostracize, proscribe, repudiate 10 thumbs down

Black Magic Woman (1970 song)
artist: Santana

blackmail: 5 bleed, force 6 coerce, compel, extort, prey on, threat 8 coercion, threaten 9 extortion, hush money, shakedown 10 protection

Blackmail (1929 film)
cast: Sara Allgood, Anny Ondra
director: Alfred Hitchcock

Blackman: 4 Joan 5 Honor

Black Marble, The (1979 film)
cast: Barbara Babcock, Paula Prentiss, Harry Dean Stanton

black-market: 7 illegal, illicit, traffic

Black Mesa author: Zane Grey

Black Mischief author: Evelyn Waugh

Black Monday event: 5 crash, panic

Blackmun: 5 Harry

Black Narcissus: 4 film 5 novel
author: 5 Rumer

cast: Deborah Kerr, Sabu
Black Orpheus: 4 film
setting: 3 Rio **6** barrio **8** Carnival
Black or White (1991 song) artist: Michael Jackson
blackout ___: 4 skit
Black Pearl, The: 4 Pelé
author: 5 O'Dell
black-pudding ingredient: 4 pork
Black Rain (1989 film)
cast: Kate Capshaw, Michael Douglas, Andy Garcia
director: Ridley Scott
Black Rainbow (1991 film)
cast: Rosanna Arquette, Tom Hulce, Jason Robards
Black Riders, The author: Stephen Crane
Black Rose, The author: Thomas Costain
Black Russian: 5 drink **8** cocktail
ingredient: 5 vodka **6** Kahlúa
Blacksburg: 4 city, town
athletes: 6 Hokies **8** Gobblers
locale: 8 Virginia
school: 3 VPI
Black Sea
arm of the ~: 4 Azov
feeder: 4 Rion **5** Rioni
locale: 6 Crimea
port: 5 Odesa, Varna **6** Odessa
resort: 5 Sochi, Yalta
river to the ~: 7 Dnieper **8** Dniester
villa: 5 dacha
Black Sheep, The author: Honoré de Balzac
blacksmith
at times: 5 shoer
furnace: 5 forge
need: 4 rasp **5** anvil
target: 4 hoof
___ Blacksmith, The: 7 Village
Black Stallion, The (1979 film)
boy: 4 Alec
cast: Teri Garr, Kelly Reno, Mickey Rooney
Black Star, Bright Dawn author: 5 O'Dell
Blackstone: 5 Harry **7** William
Black Sunday (1977 film)
cast: Bruce Dern, Marthe Keller, Robert Shaw
director: John Frankenheimer
Black Swan, The (1942 film)
cast: Laird Cregar, Maureen O'Hara, Tyrone Power
director: Henry King
blackthorn: 4 sloe, tree **5** shrub
family: 4 rose
relative: 4 pear, plum **5** apple, peach **6** almond, cherry, medlar, quince **7** apricot **8** hawthorn, oiticica
black-tie: 6 dressy
affair: 4 ball, gala **6** formal **7** banquet
not ~: 6 casual
blacktop: 4 pave
___ Blacktop: 7 Two-Lane
Black Tuesday (1954 film)
cast: Peter Graves, Edward G. Robinson
Black Tulip, The author: Alexandre Dumas
black velvet: 5 drink **8** beverage, cocktail
ingredient: 5 stout **9** champagne
Black Velvet (1980 song) artist: Alannah Myles
Black Watch: 5 plaid
wear: 4 kilt
Black Water (1975 song) artist: Doobie Brothers
black water, name meaning: 7 Douglas
Blackwell: 4 Earl **9** Elizabeth
Black & White (1972 song) artist: Three Dog Night
black widow ___: 6 spider
Black Widow (1987 film)
cast: Dennis Hopper, Theresa Russell, Nicol Williamson, Debra Winger
director: Bob Rafelson
Blackwood, Algernon: 6 writer **7** British
Blackwood Farm author: Anne Rice
Blacula (1972 film)
cast: William Marshall, Denise Nicholas
director: William Crain
blade: 3 fop **4** edge, epee, foil, leaf, shiv **5** frond, kilij, knife, saber, straw, sword **6** cutlas, dagger, lancet, rapier **7** coxcomb, cutlass, scapula, sidearm, simitar **8** scimitar, scimiter **9** dapper Dan, pretty boy, swordsman **10** jack-a-dandy
British ~: 5 sabre
copter ~: 5 rotor
fencing ~: 4 épée
gay ~: 3 fop **4** dude **5** dandy, swell **10** jack-a-dandy
harrow ~: 4 disc, disk
holder: 5 razor **6** knight **9** Musketeer, swordsman
hood's ~: 4 shiv
hussar's ~: 5 saber
Malay ~: 4 kris **6** crease, creese
medieval ~: 4 snee **5** sword
mixer ~: 6 beater
nautical: 6 rudder
of yore: 4 snee **5** estoc
plow ~: 6 colter **7** coulter
rub a ~ on stone: 4 whet
sharpener: 5 strop
starter: 5 razor **6** switch
three-sided ~: 4 épée
turbine ~: 4 vane
windmill ~: 4 vane
___ blade: 5 razor, rotor
Blade: 5 paper **9** newspaper
locale: 6 Toledo
Blade (1998 film)
cast: Stephen Dorff, Kris Kristofferson, Wesley Snipes
Blade Runner (1982 film)
cast: Harrison Ford, Rutger Hauer, Edward James Olmos, Sean Young
director: Ridley Scott
Blades, Ruben: 5 actor **10** Panamanian
blaff: 4 stew
blah: 3 gas, rot **4** bosh, bull, bunk, drab, dull, flat, guff, jazz, jive, mild, pooh, punk, so-so, tosh **5** banal, bilge, bland, fudge, ho-hum, hokum, hooey, prate, stuff, trash, tripe, unfun, vapid **6** boring, bunkum, bushwa, drivel, footle, gabble, gammon, gibber, havers, hot air, humbug, jabber, jargon, jejune, kibosh, piffle, stuffy **7** baloney, blarney, blather, blether, boloney, bushwah, eyewash, flannel, flubdub, fustian, garbage, hogwash, humdrum, inanity, insipid, languid, prosaic, rubbish, twaddle **8** buncombe, claptrap, falderal, falderol, flimflam, flummery, folderal, folderol, lifeless, listless, mediocre, nonsense, slipslop, sluggish, tommyrot, trumpery, unsalted **9** apathetic, banana oil, dry-as-dust, gibberish, kidstakes, lethargic, moonshine, poppycock, prosaical, rigmarole, tasteless, wearisome **10** applesauce, balderdash, bilge water, codswallop, double-talk, dullsville, flapdoodle, flavorless, galimatias, Jabberwock, lackluster, monotonous, mumbo jumbo, pedestrian, rigamarole, spiritless, taradiddle, unexciting
blahs: 5 blues **7** languor, sadness **8** doldrums **10** depression, melancholy, woefulness
having the ~: 3 sad **4** blue **6** morose **8** dejected
blain: 4 sore **6** blotch **7** blister
Blaine: 4 city, town **6** Vivian
locale: 9 Minnesota
Blaine, Rick love: 4 Ilsa
Blainville: 4 city, town
locale: 6 Canada, Québec
Blair: 4 Tony **5** Betsy, Brown, Janet, Linda **6** Bonnie **9** Underwood
Blair, Bonnie: 6 skater
Blair, Janet: 7 actress
film: The Black Arrow (1948)
Broadway (1942)
Burn, Witch, Burn (1962)
I Love Trouble (1948)
Something to Shout About (1943)
Tonight and Every Night (1945)
Blair, Tony: 2 P.M. **7** British
predecessor: 5 Major
Blair Witch Project (1999 film)
cast: Heather Donahue, Joshua Leonard, Michael Williams
director: Daniel Myrick, Eduardo Sanchez
Blaise: 5 saint **6** Pascal **7** Modesty **8** Cendrars
Blais, Marie-Claire: 4 poet **6** writer **8** Canadian
Blake: 5 Eubie, Madge **6** Amanda, Robert **7** Edwards, Whitney, William
Blake, Colonel aide: 5 Radar
Blake, Eubie: 7 pianist **8** composer
collaborator: Noble Sissle
genre: 4 jazz
Blakely: 5 Colin, Susan
Blake, Robert: 5 actor
film: Electra Glide in Blue (1973)
In Cold Blood (1967)
Tell Them Willie Boy Is Here (1969)
TV: Baretta
Blake, William: 4 poet **7** British
homeland: England
work: The Book of Los
The Book of Thel
The Clod and the Pebble
The Four Zoas
The Sick Rose
The Song of Los
The Tyger
Blakey, Art: 7 drummer
genre: 4 jazz
Blakley: 5 Ronee
Blalock: 6 Jolene
blamable: 5 wrong **6** guilty, liable **7** at fault **8** culpable **9** imputable **10** answerable, chargeable, delinquent, in the wrong
blame: 3 rag, rap, tax **4** onus **5** blast, chide, decry, fault, guilt, odium, scold, thank **6** accuse, burden, charge, finger, impute, indict, pick on, rebuke, saddle, stigma **7** censure, condemn, obloquy, reproof, reprove, upbraid **8** credit to, denounce, disfavor, reproach, sentence **9** attribute, criticism, criticize, discredit, implicate, liability, reprimand, stick it to **10** accusation, credit with, denunciate, imputation, indictment, reflection, take to task, vituperate
assign ~ to: 5 pin on **6** accuse, charge
deflector: 5 alibi
ender: 6 worthy
free from ~: 5 clear **9** vindicate
her: 4 Mame
taker: 4 goat **5** patsy **9** scapegoat
take the ~: 5 admit, own up
to ~: 5 wrong **6** guilty, liable **7** at fault **8** culpable **10** in the wrong
Blame ___ the Bossa Nova: 4 it on
Blame It on Rio (1984 film)
cast: Joseph Bologna, Michael Caine, Valerie Harper, Michelle Johnson, Demi Moore
director: Stanley Donen
Blame It on the Bossa Nova (1963 song) artist: Eydie Gorme
Blame It on the Rain (1989 song)
artist: Milli Vanilli
blameless: 4 good, pure **5** clean, clear, moral **6** worthy **7** upright **8** innocent, spotless, unsoiled, virtuous **9** crimeless, exemplary, faultless, guilt-free, guiltless, not guilty, righteous, stainless, unspotted, unsullied **10** immaculate, impeccable, inculpable, in the clear
___ Blame Me: 4 Don't
blamer: 5 shrew **6** critic
___ blanc: 3 vin **6** ballet, beurre, boudin
Blanc: 3 alp, Mel **4** Mont
___ Blanc: 4 Mont **5** Pinot **6** Chenin
Blanca ___: 4 Peak
blanch: 3 wan **4** fade, pale **5** chalk, quail, start, steam, wince **6** flinch, recoil, shrink, whiten **7** parboil **8** etiolate
___ blanche: 5 carte, pomme
Blanche: 5 Sweet
blanched: 4 pale **5** ashen, livid, white **6** chalky **7** whitish **9** albescent, colorless
Blanche Fury (1948 film)
cast: Stewart Granger, Valerie Hobson
Blanchett, Cate: 7 actress
film: Bandits (2001)
The Gift (2000)
Pushing Tin (1999)
The Shipping News (2001)
The Talented Mr. Ripley (1999)
blancmange: 6 junket **7** dessert **8** flummery
ingredient: 4 milk
blanco: 4 vino
___ blanco: 3 oso
___ Blanco: 3 Rio
Blanco-Fombona, Rufino: 6 writer **10** Venezuelan
bland: 3 dry **4** blah, dull, flat, mild, soft, tame **5** balmy, banal, ho-hum, suave, vapid **6** boring, polite, smooth, stuffy, urbane **7** affable, humdrum, insipid, tedious **8** pleasant, soothing, unsalted, unsavory **9** calmative, innocuous, tasteless, wearisome **10** flavorless, monotonous, unexciting
fare: 3 pap
not ~: 3 hot **5** spicy, tangy **6** spicey
Blanda, George: 2 QB
sport: 8 football
Bland, Billy song: Let the Little Girl Dance (1960)
blandish: 4 coax **5** press **6** cajole **7** flatter, wheedle **8** butter up, inveigle, persuade, play up to, soft-soap **9** sweet-talk
blandishment: 7 blarney, coaxing **8** cajolery, flattery **9** adulation
Blane: 5 Ralph **6** Marcie
Blane, Marcie song: Bobby's Girl (1962)
blank: 4 bare, form, null, void, zero **5** clean, clear, dazed, empty, space, stony **6** absent, barren, bullet, cipher, glassy, lacuna, stoney, unused, vacant **7** deadpan, shut out, vacuous **8** masklike, omission, spotless, unfilled, unmarked **9** awestruck, impassive, untouched **10** bewildered, confounded, nonplussed, poker-faced, speechless
book: 5 album, diary **7** journal
contest entry ~: 4 name

document: 4 form
draw a ~: 6 forget
look: 5 stare
blank ___: 4 book, tape, wall 5 check, shell, verse
___ blank: 5 draw a, entry
___-blank: 5 point
blanked out: 9 forgotten, repressed 10 suppressed
blanket: 4 veil, wrap 5 cover, layer, quilt, sheet, throw 6 afghan, spread 7 bedding, coating, conceal, envelop, general, generic, overall, overlay 8 covering, sweeping 9 bedspread, comforter, extensive, generical, inclusive 10 spread over
adjustment: 4 tuck
hobo ~: 6 bindle
horse ~: 5 manta
light ~: 5 throw 6 afghan
material: 4 wool 6 fleece
Mexican ~: 6 sarape, serape
wet ~: 4 bore, drag, drip 7 killjoy 9 pessimist, worrywart
blanket ___: 4 roll, toss 5 chest, sheet 6 stitch
blanket-___: 6 flower, stitch
___ blanket: 3 wet 6 saddle 7 quarter
___ Blanket Bingo: 5 Beach
blankness: 4 void 7 vacuity 9 emptiness
blanquette: 4 stew
blanquillo: 4 fish
Blanton, Jimmy: 7 bassist
genre: 4 jazz
blare: 4 bray, honk 5 noise, sound 6 clamor, cry out, racket, scream, shriek 7 clangor, fanfare, tantara 9 broadcast
blaring: 4 loud 5 forte, noisy 6 brassy, shrill 7 booming, clarion, jarring, pealing, rackety, raucous, reboant, roaring 8 crashing, piercing, plangent, rumbling, sonorous, strident, turned up 9 big-voiced, clamorous, deafening 10 boisterous, resounding, stentorian, strepitous, thundering, uproarious, vociferant, vociferous
blarney: 3 gas, rot 4 blah, bosh, bull, bunk, guff, jazz, jive, pooh, tosh 5 bilge, fudge, hokum, hooey, prate, stuff, trash, tripe 6 bunkum, bushwa, drivel, dupery, footle, gabble, gammon, gibber, havers, hot air, humbug, jabber, jargon, kibosh, piffle 7 baloney, blather, blether, boloney, bushwah, coaxing, eyewash, flannel, flubdub, fustian, garbage, hogwash, inanity, lay it on, rubbish, twaddle 8 buncombe, cajolery, claptrap, falderal, falderol, fast talk, flattery, flimflam, flummery, folderal, folderol, nonsense, slipslop, tommyrot, trumpery 9 banana oil, deception, gibberish, kidstakes, moonshine, poppycock, rigmarole, sweet talk, wheedling 10 applesauce, balderdash, bilge water, codswallop, double-talk, empty words, flapdoodle, galimatias, Jabberwock, mumbo jumbo, overpraise, rigamarole, taradiddle
Blarney Stone
city near the ~: 4 Cork
site: 4 Eire, Erin 7 Ireland
___ Blas: 3 Gil, San
Blasco Ibañez, Vincente: 6 writer 7 Spanish
blasé: 5 bored, jaded, sated, weary 6 casual, cloyed 7 glutted, unmoved, worldly 8 satiated 9 apathetic, surfeited, unexcited 10 nonchalant, world-weary
hardly ~: 3 hot 4 awed 5 eager 6 gung-ho 7 excited
___ Blas Overture: 3 Ruy
blaspheme: 4 cuss 5 abuse, curse, swear 6 deride, impugn, oppugn, revile, vilify 7 profane, put down, run down, slander, traduce 8 badmouth, belittle, execrate 9 desecrate 10 vituperate
blasphemous: 4 vile 7 impious, profane, ungodly
blasphemy: 3 sin 6 heresy 7 impiety 8 swearing 9 indignity, invective, profanity, sacrilege, violation 10 execration, scurrility
Blass, Bill: 8 designer
rival: 5 Klein 6 Armani, Lauren 7 Versace
blast: 3 din 4 ball, bang, bash, belt, blow, bomb, boom, bray, damn, drub, fest, flay, gala, gale, gust, honk, nuke, peal, puff, rail, riot, roar, ruin, shot, slam, toot, wham, wind 5 blame, burst, crack, crash, draft, noise, party, roast, salvo, shoot, smash, storm, wreck 6 assail, attack, blow-up, deafen, hit out, impugn, kaboom, oppugn, rail at, report, squall, thrill, volley, wallop 7 assault, barrage, blowout, bombard, clobber, condemn, destroy, explode, fun time, lambast, scourge, shatter, tempest, thunder, torpedo, whistle 8 big party, demolish, denounce, dynamite, eruption, fire upon, good time, great fun, lambaste, open fire, outbreak, outburst, shivaree 9 castigate, criticism, criticize, discharge, explosion, festivity, great time, lash out at 10 annihilate, detonation, saturnalia
cannon ~: 5 salvo
from the past: 4 oldy 5 oldie
full ~: 6 in toto, wholly 7 flat out, totally, utterly 8 entirely 9 to the hilt 10 completely, thoroughly, to the limit
have a ~: 5 enjoy, party, revel
material: 3 TNT 5 nitro
sound: 3 pow 4 roar 6 kaboom 7 thunder 9 explosion
starter: 4 ecto, endo, sand
wind ~: 4 gust
blast ___: 3 off 4 cell, lamp, wave 7 furnace
___ blast: 3 air 4 full, rice
blasted: 6 damned 7 hateful 8 infernal
___-blasted: 3 dad
Blast From the Past (1999 film)
cast: Brendan Fraser, Alicia Silverstone, Sissy Spacek, Christopher Walken
director: Hugh Wilson
blast-furnace fuel: 4 coke
blasting: 5 noisy
cap: 4 fuse, fuze 7 lighter
compound: 3 TNT 5 nitro 6 amatol
starter: 4 sand
blast it: 4 damn, darn, drat, durn
blastoff: 5 start 9 departure
org.: 4 NASA
blat: 3 baa, cry 4 bray 8 blurt out
blatant: 4 loud, open, rank 5 campy, gross, naked 6 arrant, brassy, brazen, flashy, garish, patent, shrill, tawdry 7 glaring, obvious, raucous 8 flagrant, impudent, overbold, palpable, piercing, strident, unsubtle 9 barefaced, deafening, downright, flaunting, obtrusive, screaming, shameless, unabashed 10 unblushing
mistake: 5 gaffe 6 bêtise 7 faux pas
blather: 3 gab, gas, rot, yak, yap 4 blah, bosh, bull, bunk, guff, gush, jazz, jive, pooh, talk, tosh 5 bilge, bleat, fudge, hokum, hooey, prate, stuff, trash, tripe 6 babble, bunkum, bushwa, drivel, footle, gabble, gammon, gibber, gossip, havers, hot air, humbug, jabber, jargon, kibosh, piffle, ramble 7 baloney, blarney, boloney, bushwah, chatter, eyewash, flannel, flubdub, fustian, garbage, hogwash, inanity, malarky, palaver, prattle, rubbish, twaddle 8 babbling, buncombe, claptrap, falderal, falderol, fast talk, flimflam, flummery, folderal, folderol, malarkey, nonsense, ramble on, rattle on, slipslop, talk idly, tommyrot, trumpery 9 banana oil, gibberish, kidstakes, loquacity, moonshine, poppycock, rigmarole 10 applesauce, balderdash, bilge water, chew the rag, codswallop, double-talk, flapdoodle, galimatias, Jabberwock, mumbo jumbo, rigamarole, taradiddle
blathering: 4 long 5 gabby, gassy, tumid, windy, wordy 6 prolix 7 diffuse, fustian, hyped up, lengthy, orotund, pompous, ranting, stilted, unterse, verbose, voluble 8 boastful, inflated, rambling 9 bombastic, garrulous, grandiose, high-flown, overblown, redundant, rhapsodic, talkative 10 big-talking, discursive, euphuistic, flamboyant, histrionic, long-winded, loquacious, palaverous, rhetorical
blaubok: 8 antelope
relative: 3 gnu, kob 4 guib, kudu, oryx, puku, topi 5 addax, bongo, chiru, eland, goral, korin, nyala, oribi, saiga, serow 6 chammy, dik-dik, duiker, impala, koodoo, lechwe, nilgai, rhebok, shammy, shamoy 7 blesbok, chamois, defassa, gazelle, gemsbok, gerenuk, grysbok, nylghai, nylghau, sassaby 8 blesbuck, bontebok, bushbuck, gemsbuck, reedbuck, steenbok, steinbok 9 blackbuck, pronghorn, sitatunga, springbok, waterbuck 10 hartebeest, wildebeest
Blaue ___: 6 Reiter
blay: 4 fish
blaze: 4 burn, fire, lick, mark 5 burst, flame, flare, flash, glare, light, shine 6 flames 7 bonfire, burning, flare up, torrent 8 landmark, outburst, radiance, radiancy, wildfire 10 brilliance, combustion, effulgence, incandesce
a trail: 4 lead 5 guide 7 pioneer
remnant: 3 ash 4 coal 5 ember 6 cinder
up: 5 flare 6 ignite
Blaze (1989 film)
cast: Lolita Davidovich, Paul Newman
director: Ron Shelton
blaze a ___: 5 trail
Blaze of Glory (1990 song) artist: Bon Jovi
blazer: 4 coat 6 jacket
detail: 4 vent
starter: 5 trail
Blazer: 3 SUV 5 cager, Chevy 9 Chevrolet
rival: 3 Cav, Mav, Net, Sun 4 Buck, Bull, Hawk, Heat, Jazz, King, Spur 5 Knick, Laker, Magic, Pacer, Sixer, Sonic 6 Celtic, Hornet, Nugget, Piston, Raptor, Rocket, Wizard 7 Clipper, Grizzly, Warrior 8 Cavalier, Maverick 10 SuperSonic, Timberwolf
Blazers: 4 five, team
locale: 8 Portland
org.: 3 NBA
blazing: 3 hot, lit 5 afire, aglow, fiery, shiny 6 ablaze, aflame, aglare, bright, flashy, red-hot, torrid 7 flaring, fulgent, glaring, lambent, radiant 8 luminous, lustrous 9 brilliant 10 passionate
star: 5 plant 6 flower
Blazing Saddles (1974 film)
cast: Madeline Kahn, Harvey Korman, Cleavon Little, Gene Wilder
director: Mel Brooks
singer: 5 Laine
blazon: 7 display 8 proclaim 9 embellish
blazonry: 8 heraldry
bldg. unit: 3 apt.
see also building
bldr.: 3 mfr.
see also builder
bleach: 4 fade 5 chalk, Purex, Snowy, Vivid 6 bluing, Clorox, whiten 7 absolve, blueing, decolor, lighten, wash out 8 Borateem, etiolate 10 decolorize
bottle: 3 jug
needing ~: 4 gray 5 dingy 7 stained
target: 5 stain
bleached: 3 wan 4 pale 5 light, white 6 chalky 9 albescent, colorless, washed-out
bleachers: 5 seats 6 stands 7 benches, seating 9 Ruthville 10 grandstand
activity: 6 booing, waving 8 cheering, clapping
bum: 3 fan
feature: 3 row 4 tier
sound from the ~: 3 boo, rah, yea 4 yell 5 chant 6 go team
bleaching
agent: 5 lemon, ozone 8 peroxide
vat: 4 keir, kier
bleak: 3 raw, sad 4 bare, dark, dour, fish, grim 5 drear, dusky, gaunt, no-win, sorry, stark 6 barren, broody, dismal, dreary, gloomy, leaden, lonely, severe, somber, wintry 7 austere, drizzly, joyless, sterile, unhappy, wintery 8 blighted, dejected, desolate, hopeless, lowering, mournful 9 bulldozed, cheerless, saddening, woebegone 10 deforested, depressing, lugubrious, melancholy, oppressive, tenebrific
Bleak House
author: Charles Dickens
cat: 8 Lady Jane
character: 3 Ada 4 Rosa 6 Esther
bleakness: 5 gloom 7 sadness 10 depression, desolation, loneliness, woefulness
blear: 3 dim 4 blur, mist 5 cloud, fuzzy 6 blurry, dimmed, smudge 7 blurred, clouded, dimness, obscure, unclear 9 teary-eyed 10 cloudiness
bleared: 10 indistinct
bleary: 3 dim 4 dark, hazy 5 dusky, faded, fuzzy, mirky, misty, murky, muted, spent, tired, vague 6 blurry 7 blurred, joyless, shadowy, unclear 9 unfocused 10 indistinct, out of focus
bleary-___: 4 eyed
bleat: 3 baa, cry, maa 4 blab, call 5 whine 7 blather
bleater: 3 ewe, ram 4 lamb 5 sheep
bleb: 3 wen 4 cyst 6 bubble 7 blister 9 air bubble
blecch: 3 ugh, yek 4 yuck
Bledsoe: 8 Tempestt
bleed: 3 run, sap 4 milk, mope, ooze 5 drain, exude, mourn, screw 6 extort, fleece, grieve, lament, prey on, suffer 7 deplete, exhaust, flow out, squeeze 9 blackmail, empathize, percolate, shake down, strong-arm 10 overcharge, sympathize
dry: 5 drain 7 exhaust
for: 4 pity 10 sympathize
starter: 4 nose
bleeder ___: 4 pipe, tile 5 valve
bleeding heart: 5 plant 6 flower

bleep: **5** erase **6** censor, delete, signal **7** edit out **9** expurgate
Bleeth: **7** Yasmine
blemish: **3** mar, zit **4** blot, flaw, mark, scar, slur, spot, wart **5** fault, speck, spoil, stain, sully, taint **6** blotch, damage, defect, smudge, stigma **7** eyesore, scratch, tarnish **8** weakness **9** birthmark **10** beauty spot, imputation
  fender ~: **4** dent, ding
  skin ~: **3** wen, zit **4** wart
  wood ~: **4** knar, knot
blemished: **9** defective
blench: **4** fade **5** cower, quail, start, wince **6** flinch, recoil, whiten **7** shy away **10** shrink from
blend: **2** go **3** mix, wed **4** beat, brew, fuse, join, meld, olio, stir, tone, whip **5** admix, alloy, cross, elide, fit in, immix, marry, merge, unify, union, unite, weave **6** commix, fusion, make up, mingle **7** amalgam, combine, harmony, mixture **8** coalesce, compound, intermix, solution **9** admixture, commingle, composite, harmonize, immixture, integrate, potpourri, synthesis **10** adulterate, amalgamate, concoction, homogenize, interbreed, interweave, synthesize
  in: **6** belong **8** go native
  into: **4** melt **8** dissolve
  not ~ well: **5** clash
  with: **10** complement
blende: **3** ore
  starter: **4** horn **5** pitch
blended: **5** mixed **6** melded **7** kneaded **9** composite
blender: **5** mixer **9** appliance
  alternative: **5** whisk **9** eggbeater
  brand: **5** Oster
  setting: **3** mix **4** chop **5** purée, speed
  sound: **4** whir **5** whirr
  use the ~: **3** mix **4** chop, whip **5** purée
blending: **6** in tune
Blenheim: **6** battle
Blenheim __: **7** spaniel
blenny: **4** fish **6** gunnel
blesbok: **8** antelope
  relative: **3** gnu, kob **4** guib, kudu, oryx, puku, topi **5** addax, bongo, chiru, eland, goral, korin, nyala, oribi, saiga, serow **6** chammy, dikdik, duiker, impala, koodoo, lechwe, nilgai, rhebok, shammy, shamoy **7** blaubok, chamois, defassa, gazelle, gemsbok, gerenuk, grysbok, nylghai, nylghau, sassaby **8** bontebok, bushbuck, gemsbuck, reedbuck, steenbok, steinbok **9** blackbuck, pronghorn, sitatunga, springbok, waterbuck **10** hartebeest, wildebeest
bless: **4** laud **5** endow, ensky, exalt, extol, honor, thank **6** anoint, devote, extoll, hallow, ordain, permit, praise, ratify **7** approve, baptize, beatify, commend, glorify, magnify, smile on **8** canonize, dedicate, enshrine, eulogize, inshrine, sanctify, sanction **9** smile upon, subscribe **10** consecrate, panegyrize
  old-style: **4** sain
  opposite of ~: **4** damn **5** curse
blessed: **4** holy **5** happy, lucky **6** divine, joyful, joyous, sacred **7** saintly **8** blissful **9** celestial, fortunate, inviolate **10** auspicious, felicitous, fortuitous, inviolable
  abode of the ~: **7** Elysium
  be ~ with: **4** have **5** enjoy
  declare ~: **7** beatify
  event: **5** birth
  name meaning ~: **5** Zelig **8** Benedict
blessed __: **5** event
Blessed __: **6** Virgin
Blessed Damozel, The author: Dante Gabriel Rossetti
Blessed Event (1932 film)
  cast: Mary Brian, Dick Powell, Lee Tracy
  director: Roy Del Ruth
Blessed, Land of the: **6** Avalon
blessing: **2** OK **4** boon, luck, okay **5** asset, grace, mercy **6** thanks **7** backing, benefit, benison, consent, godsend, support **8** approval, sanction, windfall **9** advantage, hallowing **10** dedication, good wishes, invocation, lucky break, permission
  give one's ~: **6** concur, permit **7** approve, consent **9** acquiesce **10** condescend
  preceder: **5** achoo **6** ahchoo, sneeze **7** kerchoo
__ blessing: **5** mixed **6** second
Blessing, The author: Nancy Mitford
Bless the Beasts and Children (1972 film)
  cast: Miles Chapin, Billy Mumy, Barry Robins
  director: Stanley Kramer
Bless You (1961 song) artist: Tony Orlando & Dawn
blest: **4** holy **5** happy **6** gifted **7** favored **8** hallowed **10** sanctified
Blest Gana, Alberto: **6** writer **7** Chilean
blether: **3** gas, rot **4** blah, bosh, bull, bunk, guff, jazz, jive, pooh, tosh, wind **5** bilge, fudge, hokum, hooey, prate, stuff, trash, tripe **6** bunkum, bushwa, drivel, footle, gabble, gammon, gibber, havers, hot air, humbug, jabber, jargon, kibosh, piffle **7** baloney, blarney, boloney, bushwah, eyewash, flannel, flubdub, fustian, garbage, hogwash, inanity, malarky, rubbish, twaddle **8** buncombe, claptrap, falderal, falderol, fast talk, flimflam, flummery, folderal, folderol, malarkey, nonsense, rhetoric, slipslop, tommyrot, trumpery **9** banana oil, bombastic, gibberish, goofiness, kidstakes, moonshine, poppycock, rigmarole **10** applesauce, balderdash, bilge water, codswallop, double-talk, flapdoodle, galimatias, Jabberwock, mumbo jumbo, rigamarole, taradiddle
bleu __: **6** cheese
bleu-__: **5** de-roi
__ bleu: **5** Sacré **6** cordon
bleu cheese: **8** dressing
blewit: **6** fungus **7** blue-leg **8** mushroom
Blida: **4** city, town
  locale: **7** Algeria
Blige, Mary J.
  song: I'll Be There for You (1995)
    Not Gon' Cry (1996)
    Real Love (1992)
Bligh: **7** captain, William
blight: **3** mar, rot, woe **4** bane, dash, ruin, rust **5** decay, taint, wreck **6** foul up, infect, mess up, mildew, plague, wither **7** corrupt, destroy, eyesore, scourge **8** calamity, disaster **9** detriment, frustrate, nightmare, pollution, ruination **10** affliction
  urban ~: **4** slum, smog **6** litter, sprawl
__ blight: **3** elm **4** fire, halo, late, leaf, spur, twig **5** early **6** stamen, thread
blighted: **5** bleak **8** ill-fated
  tree: **3** elm
blighter: **3** cad **5** knave, rogue, scamp, swine **6** bad guy **8** scalawag **9** scallawag, scallywag **10** blackguard, scapegrace
blimp: **5** craft **7** airship, balloon **8** aircraft, zeppelin **9** dirigible
  home: **6** hangar
  like a ~: **3** LTA **5** rigid
  part: **3** pod **4** hull
__ Blimp: **7** Colonel
blind: **4** mask, rash, ruse **5** front, hasty, shade, tight, trick **6** dazzle, hidden, screen **7** covered, dead end, deceive, knavery, unaware **8** covering, heedless, mindless, obscured, partisan, reckless **9** concealed, impetuous, oblivious, senseless, unknowing, unmindful **10** camouflage, obstructed, regardless, subterfuge
  alley: **7** dead end, impasse **8** cul-de-sac
  cheat at ~ man's buff: **4** peek
  ender: **4** fold, side, worm
  name meaning ~: **5** Cecil **6** Cicely **7** Cecilia
  spot: **7** failing **8** weakness
  turn a ~ eye to: **8** overlook
  unit: **4** slat **6** louvre
blind __: **3** pig **4** copy, date, door, hole, seed, side, spot **5** alley, faith, floor, snake, tiger, trust **6** casing, flange, roller
blind __ bat: **3** as a
__ blind: **3** rob **4** duck **6** window **8** Venetian
__-blind: **5** color **6** double, single
Blind Ambition author: **4** Dean
Blind Date author: Jerzy Kosinski
Blinded by the Light (1976 song)
  artist: Manfred Mann
__ blind eye: **5** turn a
Blind Faith (1998 film)
  cast: Charles S. Dutton, Kadeem Hardison, Lonette McKee, Courtney B. Vance
Blind Fireworks author: Louis MacNeice
blindfold: **7** obscure **9** obfuscate
  get past the ~: **4** peek
blinding: **6** aglare **7** glaring **8** dazzling
  light: **6** dazzle
blindingly bright: **4** neon **10** florescent
blindly: **8** at random, pell-mell
  search ~: **5** grope
blindman's buff: **4** game
__ Blind Mice: **5** Three
__ Blindness: **5** On His
blindside: **6** ambush
blini: **7** pancake
  kin: **5** crêpe
  partner: **3** lox **6** butter, caviar **9** sour cream
blink: **3** bat **4** wink **5** flash **6** recoil, twitch **7** flicker, flutter, glimmer, glitter, nictate, shimmer, sparkle, twinkle **8** back down, bat an eye **9** nictitate
  at: **6** ignore **7** absolve **8** overlook, tolerate **9** disregard
  on the ~: **5** kaput **6** broken **7** damaged **9** defective, disrepair **10** broken-down
  starter: **3** ice **4** snow
__ blink: **5** on the
blinker: **6** eyelid, signal
  screen ~: **6** cursor
blintz: **7** pancake
  partner: **9** sour cream
blip: **6** signal **10** aberration
  on a polygraph: **3** lie
  radar ~: **4** ping
  sonar ~: **4** echo
Blish, James: **6** writer
  genre: **5** sci-fi
bliss: **3** joy **6** heaven, utopia **7** delight, ecstasy, elation, nirvana, rapture **8** euphoria, felicity, gladness, paradise, pleasure **9** happiness **10** ebullience
bliss __: **3** out
Bliss: **4** Fort **6** Carman
Bliss author: Katherine Mansfield
blissed out: **4** rapt **8** ecstatic
blissful: **4** glad **5** blest, happy, merry **6** blithe, cheery, divine, edenic, elated, golden, jovial, joyful, joyous, upbeat **7** blessed, gleeful, pleased, radiant, tickled **8** beatific, cheerful, ecstatic, euphoric, exultant, heavenly, jubilant, mirthful, thrilled **9** delighted, gladdened, in ecstasy, overjoyed, rapturous, rejoicing, rhapsodic **10** enraptured, flying high
  place: **4** Eden **6** Avalon, heaven, utopia **7** Elysium, nirvana
Bliss of Mrs. Blossom, The (1968 film)
  cast: Richard Attenborough, Shirley MacLaine
blister: **3** sac, wen **4** bleb, cyst, lash, slur, sore **5** blain, smear **6** bubble, insult, scorch, vilify **7** lambast, vesicle **8** belittle, lambaste, swelling **9** castigate, denigrate
  cause a ~: **3** rub
blister __: **4** pack, rust **5** steel **6** beetle, copper **7** package
blistered: **3** raw **4** sore
blistering: **3** hot **6** red-hot, torrid **8** white-hot
B.Lit.: **3** deg.
blithe: **3** gay **4** glad **5** happy, jolly, light, merry, sunny **6** breezy, cheery, chirpy, genial, jaunty, jocund, jovial, joyful, joyous, lively, upbeat **7** buoyant, gleeful, jocular, pleased, tickled **8** blissful, carefree, cheerful, ecstatic, euphoric, exultant, gladsome, heedless, jubilant, mirthful, thrilled **9** delighted, lightsome, overjoyed, rejoicing, sprightly **10** flying high, unbothered, unthinking, untroubled
Blithedale Romance, The author: Nathaniel Hawthorne
Blithe Spirit (1945 film)
  cast: Constance Cummings, Kay Hammond, Rex Harrison
  director: David Lean
  scene: **6** seance
Blithe Spirit author: Noël Coward
blitz: **4** raid, rush **5** storm **6** attack, charge, invade, strike, thrust **7** assault, barrage, bombard, bombing, offense **8** fire upon, gang up on, shelling **9** offensive, onslaught
blitz __: **3** can **5** chess
__ blitz: **5** media
blitzed-__: **3** out
Blitzen: **8** reindeer
  colleague: **5** Comet, Cupid, Vixen **6** Dancer, Dasher, Donder **7** Prancer
Blitzer, Wolf: **10** newscaster
blitzkrieg: **6** battle **7** offense **10** aggression
Blitzstein: **4** Marc
Blixen: **5** Karen **7** Dinesen **11** Isak Dinesen
Blix, Hans: **7** Swedish **8** diplomat
blizzard: **4** snow **5** storm **9** snowstorm
  configuration: **5** swirl
  pileup: **4** bank **5** drift
bloat: **4** grow, puff **5** bulge, swell, widen **6** beef up, dilate, expand, fatten, puff up, pump up, spread **7** augment, balloon, broaden, burgeon, distend, enlarge, inflate, swell up **8** bourgeon, heighten, lengthen, swell out **9** intumesce
bloated: **3** big **5** gassy, puffy, tumid **7** swollen
bloater: **4** fish
blob: **3** dab **4** bead, daub, drop, glob, lump, mark, mass, spot **5** clump, patch, smear **6** bubble, dollop,

smudge, splash **7** droplet, globule, splotch **8** spherule
blobby: 9 amorphous
Blobel, Günter: 8 Nobelist
Blob, move like the: 4 ooze
bloc: 4 bund, ring, sect **5** group, junta, party, union **6** cartel, clique, league, muster **7** combine, council, entente, faction **8** alliance **9** anschluss, coalition, syndicate **10** federation
en ~: 6 in full **8** as a whole **10** altogether
political ~: 5 labor
Bloch: 3 Ray **5** Felix **6** Ernest, Konrad
Bloch, Felix: 8 Nobelist **9** physicist
Bloch, Konrad: 8 Nobelist
block: 3 bar, dam, jam, lot, toy **4** bolt, cake, clog, cork, cube, halt, hunk, loaf, lock, lump, mass, plug, seal, shut, slab, snag, stem, stop, unit **5** brick, check, chock, choke, chunk, close, cross, dam up, delay, deter, embar, estop, hitch, ingot, jam up, latch, parry, solid, stall, stimy, stymy, wedge **6** arrest, clog up, cut off, defeat, forbid, hamper, hang up, hinder, hold up, impede, lock up, plug up, region, retard, seal up, secure, square, stop up, stymie, tackle, thwart **7** barrier, congest, exclude, obviate, occlude, prevent, seal off, section, segment, shut off, shutter, stopper, ward off **8** button up, close off, encumber, handicap, obstacle, obstruct, prohibit, sabotage, stoppage **9** barricade, foreclose, frustrate, hamstring, hindrance, intercept, stonewall, territory **10** bottleneck, impediment, limitation
a broadcast: 3 jam
and tackle: 5 hoist **6** lifter
builder's ~: 3 lot
building ~: 4 atom, unit
chip off the old ~: 3 lad, son **5** image, scion **9** offspring
down the ~: 4 near **5** close
ender: 3 ade, age **4** head **5** house **6** buster
hardwood ~: 5 rabot
illegally: 4 clip
make ~ letters: 5 print
marble ~: 4 slab
material: 6 cement **8** concrete
new kid on the ~: 3 cub **4** tiro, tyro **5** pupil **6** greeny, novice **7** amateur, dabbler, entrant, learner, recruit, trainee **8** beginner, freshman, initiate, neophyte, newcomer, putterer **9** fledgling, greenhorn, novitiate **10** apprentice, dilettante, first-timer, tenderfoot
off: 7 enclose, isolate
of ice: 4 berg, cube, floe
out: 4 form, plan **5** frame, shape **6** design, screen, sketch **7** shut off
patio ~: 5 paver
paving ~: 4 sett
plastic building ~: 4 Lego
road ~: 7 barrier
seller of old: 6 iceman
starter: 4 cell, road, wood **6** breech, cinder
stumbling ~: 3 bar, rub **4** snag **5** catch, hitch **6** hurdle, kicker **7** barrier, pitfall, problem, setback **8** drawback, handicap, obstacle **9** hindrance **10** impediment
sun ~: 3 oil **5** cloud, shade **6** lotion
unit: 4 cell
up: 3 dam **4** plug
block __: 3 out, tin **4** coal, lava, line, mast **5** chord, front, grant, house, party, plane, print, trade **6** caving, heater, letter, signal, system **7** booking, capital, diagram
__ block: 3 bee, fly, gin, sun **4** bull, jack, lead, tint, yule **5** dummy, fault, glass, horse, jewel, nerve, plate, sound, swage, tower **6** breeze, cinder, dasher, double, engine, impost, leader, monkey, office, pillow, plinth, raggle, snatch **7** auction, butcher, leading, mortise, writer's
Block __: 6 Island
blockade: 3 bar, dam **4** bolt, clog, cork, lock, plug, seal, shut, snag, stop **5** dam up, latch, siege **6** clog up, hold up, lock up, picket, plug up, seal up, secure, stop up **7** barrier, closure, enclose, inclose, seal off, shut off, shut out, shutter **8** button up, obstacle, obstruct, stoppage, surround **9** foreclose **10** impediment
__blockade: 5 naval
blockade-__: 6 runner
Blockade (1938 film)
cast: Madeleine Carroll, Henry Fonda
director: William Dieterle
Blockade Runners, The author: Jules Verne
blockage: 3 bar **4** clog, stop **5** tie-up **6** arrest, hurdle, logjam **7** embargo **8** gridlock, stoppage **9** impedance **10** congestion, impediment, traffic jam
reliever: 5 stent
remove a ~: 5 unjam **6** unclog
block and __: 6 tackle
Blockbuster
rental: 5 movie, video
section: 3 DVD **5** sci-fi **6** action, horror
blocked: 5 tight **6** stuffy **10** impassable
it may be ~: 5 sinus
it's ~ by sunblock: 5 UV ray
blocker
bill ~: 3 nay **4** veto
channel ~: 5 V-chip
river ~: 3 dam
sun ~: 3 fog, oil **4** tree **5** cloud, shade, smaze **6** awning, lotion
UV ~: 5 ozone
x-ray ~: 4 lead
__ blocker: 4 beta **5** alpha **7** calcium
Blocker, Dan: 5 actor
role: 4 Hoss **10** Cartwright
blockhead: 3 ass, lug, nit, oaf, sap **4** boob, clod, dolt, dope, fool, gowk, lunk **5** chump, clown, cluck, dummy, dunce, joker, klutz, looby, ninny, patsy, schmo **6** dimwit, lubber, lummox, nitwit, schmoe, sucker, turkey **7** buffoon, bungler, dingbat, dullard, half-wit, jackass **8** dumbbell, numskull **9** birdbrain, harebrain, ignoramus, lamebrain, numbskull, simpleton **10** nincompoop
blockheaded: 5 dense, silly, thick, unapt **6** cloddy
Block-Heads (1938 film)
cast: Oliver Hardy, Stan Laurel
Block, Lawrence: 6 writer
block-shaped: 5 cubic **6** chunky
Bloembergen, Nicolaas: 8 Nobelist **9** physicist
Blois: 4 city, town
locale: 6 France
river: 5 Loire
Blok, Aleksandr: 4 poet **7** Russian
bloke: 2 he **3** guy, sir **4** chap, gent, male **5** fella **6** feller, fellow, mister
British ~: 3 guv **4** chap, mate
friendly ~: 5 matey
that ~: 3 him
blond: 4 fair **5** flaxy, light, sandy **6** blonde, flaxen, yellow **7** towhead **9** towheaded **10** auricomous, fair-haired
go ~: 6 bleach
kin: 4 buff, corn, gold, lime, rust, sand **5** brass, coral, cream, flaxy, lemon, maize, ocher, ochre, peach, rusty, straw **6** canary, chammy, citron, crocus, flaxen, shammy, shamoy **7** apricot, chamois, citrine, jasmine, mustard, nankeen, old gold, saffron, xanthic **8** daffodil, primrose **9** champagne, goldenrod, jessamine
Blond Baboon, The author: Janwillem van de Wetering
__ blonde: 3 ash **8** platinum
__ Blonde: 7 Legally, Suicide
Blondell, Joan: 7 actress
film: Bullets or Ballots (1936)
Cry 'Havoc' (1943)
Dames (1934)
Desk Set (1957)
Footlight Parade (1933)
Gold Diggers of 1933 (1933)
The Greeks Had a Word for Them (1932)
Lawyer Man (1932)
Nightmare Alley (1947)
Night Nurse (1931)
Stand-In (1937)
Stay Away, Joe (1968)
There's Always a Woman (1938)
Three Men on a Horse (1936)
Three on a Match (1932)
Topper Returns (1941)
A Tree Grows in Brooklyn (1945)
Union Depot (1932)
spouse: Dick Powell, Mike Todd
Blonde Venus (1932 film)
cast: Marlene Dietrich, Cary Grant
director: Josef von Sternberg
blondie: 4 cake **7** dessert
Blondie (1938 film)
cast: Arthur Lake, Penny Singleton
Blondie (comic strip)
character: 4 Cora, Elmo, Herb **6** Cookie **7** Dagwood, Dithers **9** Alexander
dog: 5 Daisy
surname: 8 Bumstead
work like ~: 5 cater
Blondie (rock group)
leader: Debbie Harry
song: Call Me (1980)
Heart of Glass (1979)
Rapture (1981)
The Tide Is High (1980)
blondish: 4 fair **5** light, sandy
blood: 3 kin **4** race **6** origin, strain **7** descent, kinfolk, kinship, lineage **8** ancestry, pedigree, relative
bad ~: 4 feud **5** spite, venom **6** animus, enmity, grudge, hatred, malice, rancor **7** ill will **8** conflict, friction **9** animosity, antipathy, hostility, nastiness
be out for ~: 6 avenge **7** pay back, revenge
blue ~: 5 count, noble **8** nobleman **9** gentility, patrician **10** aristocrat
British blue ~: 6 aristo
carrier of white ~ cells: 5 lymph
classification: 3 ABO **4** O neg **5** type A, type B, type O
combining form: 3 hem- **4** -emia, hema-, hemo- **5** -aemia, hemat-, -hemia **6** -haemia, hemato-, sangui- **8** sanguine-
component: 5 serum **6** plasma **10** hemoglobin
ender: 4 bath, line, root, shed, shot, worm **5** guilt, hound, stain, stone **6** mobile, stream, sucker **7** letting, thirsty **8** curdling
flesh and ~: 3 kin **4** aunt, soul **5** being, uncle **6** cousin, family, sister **7** brother, kinfolk, sibling **8** relation, relative
fluids: 4 sera
in cold ~: 9 knowingly, on purpose, willfully
in the ~: 6 innate **9** ingrained
like ~: 5 thick
make one's ~ boil: 3 irk, vex **4** rile **5** anger, peeve, upset **6** insult, offend **9** infuriate
obstruction: 4 clot
vessel: 4 vein **5** aorta **6** artery **9** capillary
visit a ~ bank: 6 donate
blood __: 3 red **4** bank, bath, cell, clot, feud, heat, knot, lily, meal, test, type **5** count, donor, fluke, group, level, money, royal, serum, sport, sugar **6** orange, plasma, vessel **7** brother, pudding, sausage
__ blood: 3 bad, new **4** blue, full, half **5** whole, young **6** pigeon **7** dragon's
Blood __: 4 Test **5** Money, Sport **6** Simple
__ Blood: 3 Bad **4** Wise **5** First, Young **7** Captain
blood-and-__: 4 guts
Blood and Gold author: Anne Rice
__ Blood and Guts: 3 Old
Blood and Sand (1941 film)
cast: Linda Darnell, Rita Hayworth, Tyrone Power
director: Rouben Mamoulian
blood bank
depositor: 5 donor
quantity: 4 pint, unit
__ blood cell: 3 red **5** white
blood-chilling: 4 gory **5** eerie, lurid, scary **6** creepy **8** horrible **10** terrifying
bloodcurdling: 4 gory **5** eerie, lurid, scary **6** creepy **8** horrible **10** terrifying
__-blooded: 3 hot, red **4** blue, cold, full, warm
bloodfin: 4 fish
bloodhound: 3 dog **6** canine, shamus **9** detective
emulate a ~: 5 sniff, trace, track **6** follow
feature: 4 jowl **6** dewlap
like a ~: 5 jowly
lips: 5 flews
trail: 4 odor **5** scent, smell, spoor
Blood Knot, The author: Athol Fugard
bloodless: 3 wan **4** cold, pale **5** ashen, livid, pasty, white **6** chalky, pallid, sallow, unkind **8** unlively **9** albescent, colorless, impassive, unfeeling **10** insensible, spiritless
bloodline: 5 roots **9** forebears, genealogy
Bloodline author: Sidney Sheldon
Blood of Abraham, The author: 6 Carter
Blood of a Poet, The (1930 film) director: Jean Cocteau
Blood on the __: 3 Sun **4** Moon
Blood on the Moon (1948 film)
cast: Barbara Bel Geddes, Robert Mitchum
director: Robert Wise
Blood on the Sun (1945 film)
cast: James Cagney, Sylvia Sidney
director: Frank Lloyd
blood-red: 7 crimson
Blood Red, Sister Rose author: Thomas Keneally
bloodroot: 5 plant **6** flower
bloodshot: 3 red
Blood Simple (1984 film)
cast: John Getz, Dan Hedaya, Frances McDormand
director: Joel Coen
dog: 4 Opal
Blood Sport author: Dick Francis
bloodstone: 3 gem **10** chalcedony

Bloodstone song: Natural High (1973)
bloodsucker: 4 tick 5 leech 6 bedbug 8 parasite
Blood, Sweat & Tears
leader: David Clayton-Thomas
song: And When I Die (1969)
Spinning Wheel (1969)
You've Made Me So Very Happy (1969)
Blood Test author: Jonathan Kellerman
bloodthirsty: 4 mean 5 cruel, harsh, nasty 6 animal, brutal, fierce, lupine, savage, unkind, wanton 7 beastly, callous, hurtful, inhuman, vicious, violent, warlike 8 barbaric, fiendish, inhumane, pitiless, ruthless, sadistic, vengeful 9 cutthroat, ferocious, merciless, monstrous, predatory, truculent 10 vindictive
blood-tingling: 9 thrilling
blood-typing system: 3 ABO
bloodwood: 4 tree
bloody: 3 raw, red 4 gory 5 lurid
Bloody __: 4 Mary 6 Caesar
Bloody Mary: 5 drink, Tudor 8 cocktail
daughter: 4 Liat
ingredient: 5 vodka 11 tomato juice
blooey: 10 on the fritz, out of order
bloom: 3 bud 4 boom, grow, pink, posy 5 prime, ripen, youth 6 floret, flower, mature, open up, sprout, thrive 7 blossom, burgeon, develop, prosper, succeed 8 bourgeon, flourish, fructify, vegetate 9 bear fruit, freshness, germinate, luxuriate 10 effloresce, nasturtium
full ~: 8 maturity
see also flower
Bloom: 5 Bobby, Verna 6 Claire, Harold
Bloom, Bobby song: Montego Bay (1970)
Bloom, Claire: 7 actress
film: Alexander the Great (1956)
The Brothers Karamazov (1958)
The Buccaneer (1958)
Charly (1968)
Crimes and Misdemeanors (1989)
The Haunting (1963)
Limelight (1952)
Look Back in Anger (1958)
Mighty Aphrodite (1995)
Shadowlands (1985)
The Spy Who Came in From the Cold (1965)
The Wonderful World of the Brothers Grimm (1962)
spouse: Philip Roth, Rod Steiger
Bloom County: 5 strip 10 comic strip
cat: 4 Bill
penguin: 4 Opus
__ bloomer: 4 late
Bloomfield: 4 city, town
locale: 8 Michigan 9 New Jersey
Bloom, Harold: 6 writer
blooming: 4 ripe, rosy, well 5 ruddy, young 6 waxing 7 glowing, growing, healthy, radiant, verdant 8 fruitful, thriving 9 flowering 10 blossoming, prospering, prosperous, successful
early: 4 rath 5 rathe
starter: 4 ever
Bloomingdale: 4 city, town
locale: 8 Illinois
Bloomingdale's rival: 4 Saks
Bloomington: 4 city, town
athletes: 8 Hoosiers
locale: 7 Indiana 8 Illinois 9 Minnesota 10 California
...bloom in the spring, __: 5 tra la
Bloom, Molly last word: 3 yes
Bloom of Life, The author: Anatole France
bloop: 3 fly 6 looper, pop fly
blooper: 4 slip 5 boner, error, fluff, gaffe, lapse 6 boo-boo, bungle 7 blunder, faux pas, mistake
Blore: 4 Eric
blossom: 3 bud 4 posy 5 bloom, ripen, yield 6 floret, flower, mature, thrive, unfold 7 burgeon, develop, produce, prosper, succeed 8 bourgeon, flourish, fructify, progress, vegetate 9 germinate 10 effloresce
see also flower
__ blossom: 5 apple, peach 6 double, orange
Blossom: 4 Rock 6 Dearie
Blossom Fell, A (1955 song) artist: Nat King Cole
blossoming: 5 happy, young 6 abloom 9 fulfilled
Blossom (NBC sitcom) cast: Mayim Bialik (Blossom Russo)
__ Blossoms: 3 Gin 6 Broken
Blossoms in the Dust (1941 film)
cast: Greer Garson, Walter Pidgeon
director: Mervyn LeRoy
blossoms, of: 6 floral
blot: 3 dry, mar, sop 4 blur, flaw, mark, slur, soil, spot 5 dirty, fault, odium, patch, shame, smear, speck, spoil, stain, sully, taint 6 absorb, bedaub, defect, pat dry, smudge, stigma 7 balloon, blemish, calumny, slander, tarnish 8 black eye, disgrace 9 bespatter 10 imputation
out: 4 hide 5 erase 6 delete, efface, excise, rub off 7 destroy, eclipse, expunge 9 eliminate, eradicate 10 annihilate, extinguish
blotch: 4 mark, spot 5 blain, stain 6 bedaub, measle, smudge, stigma 7 besmear, blemish, ink spot 8 besmirch, mottling 9 gravy spot
combining form: 5 macul- 6 maculi-, maculo-
blotchy: 6 spotty 7 mottled
blotted out: 9 forgotten, repressed 10 suppressed
blotter
name on a police ~: 3 Doe, Roe 4 Jane, John
place for a ~: 4 desk
police ~ entry: 2 MO 3 AKA 5 alias
spot: 3 ink
subject: 4 perp 7 suspect
blotting __: 5 paper
blotto: 5 drunk 6 stewed 8 squiffed 10 inebriated
blouse: 3 top 5 middy, shirt, V-neck, waist 6 bodice, halter, huipil, T-shirt 7 garment, puff out 8 pullover, separate 10 turtleneck
adornment: 3 pin 5 cameo 7 corsage
fabric: 4 poly, silk 5 linen, nylon 6 cotton, eyelet
long ~: 5 tunic
loose ~: 5 middy
make a ~: 3 sew
part: 4 neck, yoke 8 neckline
sleeveless ~: 5 shell
trim: 5 jabot 6 ruffle
__ blouse: 5 middy
blouson: 5 shirt
bloviate: 4 rail, rant, rave 5 decry, orate, spout 7 declaim, thunder 8 denounce, harangue, perorate 9 fulminate, hold forth
blow: 3 bop, hit, jab, rap 4 bang, bash, belt, biff, flee, gale, gust, honk, hurt, jolt, kick, muff, pant, puff, sigh, slam, slap, slug, sock, stab, swat, tick, toot, waft, wind 5 blast, botch, clout, draft, knock, punch, shock, smack, sound, spend, spill, split, storm, swipe, thump, treat, use up, waste, whack, whomp 6 breeze, buffet, bungle, exhale, flurry, impact, mishap, strike, stroke, thwack, trauma, wallop 7 bad luck, debacle, explode, reverse, screw up, setback, take off, tempest, tragedy, typhoon, undoing, whistle 8 accident, calamity, disaster, hightail, run for it, squander, uppercut 9 bombshell, buffeting, collision, dissipate, fisticuff, hurricane, mishandle, take a hike, throw away 10 concussion, gamble away, hit the road, misfortune, run through
a fuse: 4 flip, rage, rant, rave 5 erupt, freak, go ape, storm 6 lose it, see red, seethe 7 explode, flare up, flip out 10 hit the roof
as the wind: 4 gust, howl, waft 5 sough
away: 3 awe 4 stun 5 amaze, crush, floor 6 delete, thrill 7 astound, impress, stupefy, triumph 8 astonish, surprise 9 dumbfound, go over big, overpower
deal a ~: 6 strike
ender: 3 fly, gun, off, out 4 fish, hard, hole, pipe 5 torch
glancing ~: 5 swipe
glancing ~ in cricket: 5 snick
hard ~: 4 gale, gust 5 blast, storm 6 squall 7 cyclone, tempest 9 windstorm
hot and cold: 4 sway, vary 5 hedge, shift, waver 6 falter 9 fluctuate, vacillate
in: 4 come, show 5 enter, pop up 6 appear, arrive, show up, turn up 7 turn out 8 get there
it: 3 err 4 bomb, bust, fail, flop, flub, goof, lose, miss, slip, trip 5 flunk, misdo 6 falter, foul up, goof up, mess up 7 blunder, founder, go under, go wrong, lose out, misstep, screw up, stumble, wash out 8 fall flat, flounder, lay an egg 9 mishandle, mismanage, strike out
karate ~: 4 chop
loud ~: 4 thud, wham, whap 5 thump, whang
low ~: 4 foul 6 insult 9 cheap shot
mark from a ~: 4 weal, welt 6 bruise
off: 5 spurn 6 reject
off steam: 4 rant, rave, vent, yell 6 holler, scream
one's horn: 4 toot
one's own horn: 4 brag, crow 5 boast
open-handed ~: 4 slap
out: 5 douse, dowse, quash 6 exhale, quench 7 smother 9 extirpate 10 extinguish
out of proportion: 7 magnify 8 overplay 10 exaggerate
out of the water: 4 beat, best, rout, stun 5 cream, crush 6 dazzle, defeat, thrash 7 astound, conquer, overrun, stagger, stupefy, trounce 8 astonish, bowl over, vanquish 9 devastate, dumbfound, overpower, overwhelm
over: 3 end 4 pass, wane 5 abate 7 subside 8 decrease, diminish 10 settle down
powerful ~: 4 kayo, swat 5 whomp
sky high: 5 rebut 6 refute 8 disprove, puncture 9 discredit, shoot down 10 invalidate
the joint: 2 go 4 exit 5 leave 6 bow out, cut out, decamp, depart, get out 7 abscond, bail out, pull out, push off 8 check out, hang it up, knock off, light out, pack it in, run out on, shove off, skip town 9 take a hike, walk out on 10 call it a day
the lid off: 4 leak, tell 6 reveal
the whistle: 3 rat 4 blab, halt, sing, tell 5 blame 6 accuse, betray, charge, expose, inform, squeal, turn in
up: 4 boil, bomb, fume, rage, rant, ruin 5 crack, erupt, swell 6 expand, get mad 7 balloon, bristle, enlarge, explode, fill out, inflate, magnify, stretch 8 detonate, dynamite, have a fit, mushroom 9 embroider, intumesce, overstate 10 exaggerate, hit the roof
blow __: 3 fly, off, out 4 away, over 5 a fuse, drier, dryer
blow __ steam: 3 off
blow-__: 3 dry 4 comb, hard 5 drier, dryer
__ blow: 3 at a, low 4 body
Blow: 3 Joe
blow a __: 4 fuse 6 gasket
blow-by-blow: 4 full 8 detailed, thorough 10 disclosure
blower: 3 fan 5 phone 9 hair dryer, telephone 10 ventilator
use the ~: 3 dry
__ blower: 4 snow 5 glass
__-blower: 7 whistle
blowfish: 4 fugu 6 puffer
blowfly: 3 bug 6 insect
Blow, Gabriel, Blow composer: 6 Porter
blowgun ammo: 4 dart
blowhard: 5 raver 6 gasbag, gascon 8 fanfaron 9 loud-mouth, swaggerer
blowhole: 4 vent
emanation: 5 spout
blow hot and __: 4 cold
blow-in: 8 newcomer, stranger
blowing: 5 windy 6 breezy
hot and cold: 6 fickle 7 erratic, flighty, mutable 8 hesitant, variable, volatile, wavering 9 impulsive, mercurial, undecided 10 capricious, changeable, inconstant, on the fence
__-blowing: 4 mind
Blowing Kisses in the Wind (1991 song) artist: Paula Abdul
Blowin' in the Wind (song) artist: Peter, Paul and Mary, Stevie Wonder
composer: 8 Bob Dylan
blown: 5 spent 8 misspent 10 dissipated
away: 5 in awe 8 overcome
it may be ~: 5 glass
it may be ~ off: 5 steam
over: 9 forgotten
__-blown glass: 4 hand
blow off __: 5 steam
blow one's __: 3 top 4 cool, mind 5 stack
blow one's own __: 4 horn
blowout: 4 bash, fete, flat, gala, luau, orgy 5 binge, blast, feast, party, revel, spree 6 spread 7 jubilee, shindig 8 jamboree 9 explosion, festivity 10 detonation
Blow Out (1981 film)
cast: Nancy Allen, John Lithgow, John Travolta
director: Brian De Palma
blowpipe emission: 6 gas jet
blows: 8 fighting
exchange ~: 3 box, row 4 duel, spar, swat 5 argue, brawl, brush, fight, punch, run-in, scrap, whack 6 attack, battle, bicker, combat, go at it, oppose, rumble, take on, tussle 7 assault, contend, contest, grapple, mix it up, quarrel, scuffle, vie with, wage war, wrangle, wrestle 8 do battle 9 altercate, slug it out, square off 10 fisticuffs, tangle with
blowsy: 5 dowdy, ruddy 6 frumpy

blow the ___: 4 coop 7 whistle
blow the ___ off: 3 lid
blowtorch, use a: 4 fuse, melt, weld
blowup: 3 enl., row 5 blast, burst, photo 6 strife 7 rampage, tantrum 8 argument, eruption, outbreak, upheaval 9 explosion 10 detonation, photograph
cause of a ~: 3 TNT 5 nitro 8 dynamite 9 explosive
Blowup (1966 film)
cast: David Hemmings, Sarah Miles, Vanessa Redgrave
director: Michelangelo Antonioni
___ Blow Your Horn: 4 Come
blowzy: 3 red 5 messy, ruddy 6 florid, sloppy, unneat, untidy 7 tousled, unkempt 8 red-faced, rubicund, sanguine, slovenly, uncombed 10 bedraggled, disheveled
B.L.S.: 3 deg.
holder: 9 librarian
part: 5 Labor 6 Bureau 10 Statistics
BLT: 8 sandwich
locale: 5 diner 6 eatery 10 restaurant
part of ~: 5 bacon 6 tomato 7 lettuce
spread: 4 mayo
blubber: 3 cry, sob 4 bawl, howl, mewl, pule, wail, weep 6 boohoo, snivel 7 whimper 9 caterwaul, shed tears
remove ~: 6 flench, flense
Blubber author: Judy Blume
bludgeon: 3 bat, hit, sap 4 bang, beat, club, cosh, mall, maul, whip 5 bully, clout, smite, stick 6 beat on, coerce, cudgel, hector, strike 7 clobber, lambast 8 browbeat, lambaste 9 billy club, blackjack, terrorize, truncheon 10 intimidate, nightstick
___ Blu Dipinto Di Blu: 3 Nel
blue: 3 low, sad 4 dark, down, foul, glum, lewd, mopy, navy, racy, teal 5 azure, bawdy, beryl, color, dirty, moody, mopey, ocean, royal, salty, skyey, spicy, woful 6 broody, cheese, cobalt, cyanic, dismal, erotic, gloomy, morose, ribald, risqué, somber, spicey, vulgar, wicked, woeful 7 crushed, doleful, forlorn, hangdog, in a funk, joyless, naughty, obscene, unhappy 8 cerulean, dejected, desolate, downcast, indecent, off-color, sapphire, troubled 9 bummed out, cheerless, depressed, heartsick, miserable, saturnine, sorrowful, turquoise, woebegone 10 chapfallen, despondent, dispirited, indelicate, lascivious, melancholy, spiritless, suggestive
and yellow: 5 green
baby ~: 3 eye
baby in ~: 3 boy
big ~ marble: 5 Earth
bird: 3 jay 5 heron 7 bunting 8 bluebird
blood: 4 duke, earl, peer 5 count, noble 8 nobleman 9 patrician 10 aristocrat
bloods: 5 elite, lords 8 nobility
British ~ blood: 6 aristo
chips: 5 stock
collar: 5 labor 6 worker
color: 4 anil, cyan, navy, Nile, teal 5 Alice, azure, perse, slate 6 cobalt, indigo, raisin, violet 7 peacock 8 cerulean, sapphire 9 turquoise 10 aquamarine, periwinkle
combining form: 4 cyan- 5 cyano-
dark ~: 4 navy 5 perse
dye: 4 anil, woad 6 indigo
earn a ~ ribbon: 3 win 7 succeed, triumph
ender: 4 bell, bill, bird, book, coat, fish, gill, nose, stem, weed 5 beard, berry, blood, curls, grass, jeans, point, print, stone 6 bonnet, bottle, jacket, tongue 8 stocking
flag: 5 plant 6 flower
flower: 4 flag, flax, iris 5 bluet, camas 6 camass, indigo, lupine, violet 7 aconite, gentian, veronia 8 aconitum, ageratum, boltonia, harebell, larkspur 9 columbine, ground ivy, hydrangea 10 cornflower, delphinium, periwinkle
greenish ~: 4 aqua, cyan, Nile, teal 7 peacock 9 robin's-egg, turquoise 10 aquamarine
in a ~ funk: 6 morose 7 unhappy 8 dejected 9 depressed 10 melancholy
in heraldry: 5 azure
it turns litmus ~: 6 alkali
jeans: 5 pants 6 denims 9 dungarees
language: 9 profanity
make black and ~: 4 hurt 6 bruise, injure 7 contuse 8 discolor
men in ~: 6 police
mineral: 5 beryl 6 iolite 9 turquoise 10 peacock ore
once in a ~ moon: 6 rarely, seldom 9 sometimes
out of the ~: 6 sudden 8 abruptly, suddenly 10 unexpected
ox: 4 Babe
pigment: 4 bice
plate: 8 luncheon
plate special: 4 meal
plate special spot: 4 café 5 diner 6 eatery
point: 3 cat 7 Siamese
reddish ~: 6 violet
ribbon: 5 prize 6 trophy 7 laurels
slightly ~: 4 racy 6 risqué 10 suggestive
spot on a map: 3 bay, sea 4 lake 5 ocean
sun: 5 O star
talk a ~ streak: 3 yak 5 prate, run on 7 chatter, prattle
the ~: 3 sky
toon: 5 Smurf
true ~: 4 fast 5 loyal
wildflower: 4 flax 5 bluet
wild ~ yonder: 3 sky 5 ether 6 aether
blue ___: 3 cat, flu, fox, gas, gum, ice, jay, law, mud, tit 4 book, bull, chip, crab, flag, funk, jack, line, lips, mass, mold, moon, note, onyx, pike, stem 5 alert, blood, coral, crane, curls, daisy, dicks, flash, giant, goose, grama, heron, jeans, lotus, peter, phlox, point, racer, shark, sheep, shift, wavey, whale 6 cheese, cohosh, grouse, marlin, Monday, myrtle, ribbon, runner, spirea, spruce, streak 7 catfish, dogwood, jasmine, melilot, norther, pointer, succory, swimmer, thistle, vitriol, walleye
blue ___ face: 5 in the
blue ___ special: 5 plate
blue-___: 3 leg, red, sky 4 eyed 5 black, green, rinse, water 6 collar, pencil 7 blooded
blue-___ law: 3 sky
___ blue: 3 ice, sky 4 baby, bice, code, cyan, iron, navy, Nile, teal, true 5 Alice, beryl, cadet, china, copen, king's, pearl, royal, slate, steel 6 alkali, cobalt, indigo, powder 7 Antwerp, peacock
___-blue: 4 true
Blue: 3 Ben 4 Vida 5 range 6 iceman
rival: 4 King, Star, Wild 5 Bruin, Devil, Flame, Flyer, Oiler, Sabre, Shark 6 Canuck, Coyote, Ranger 7 Capital, Panther, Penguin, Red Wing, Senator 8 Canadien, Islander, Predator, Thrasher 9 Avalanche, Blackhawk, Hurricane, Lightning, Maple Leaf 10 Blue Jacket, Mighty Duck
river: 4 Nile
Blue ___: 3 Sky 4 Army, Jean, Moon, Nile, Nose 5 Angel, Bayou, Cross, Denim, Flame, Magic, Money, skies, Swede, Tango 6 Collar, Demons, Grotto, Hawaii, Monday, Shield, Velvet, Voyage 7 Prelude
Blue ___ Mountains: 5 Ridge
Blue ___, The: 4 Lamp, Veil 5 Angel 6 Dahlia, Hammer, Lagoon 7 Lantern
Blue ___ Waltz: 6 Danube
___ Blue: 3 Am I, Big 4 Deep, Navy, N.Y.P.D., True 5 Misty 6 Desert, Jackie
Blue Angel (1960 song) artist: Roy Orbison
Blue Angel, The (1930 film)
cast: Marlene Dietrich, Emil Jannings
director: Josef von Sternberg
Blue Angel, The role: 4 Lola
blueback ___: 6 salmon
Blue Bayou (song) artist: Linda Ronstadt, Roy Orbison
Bluebeard's Castle composer: 6 Bartók
Bluebeard wife: 6 Fatima
bluebell: 5 plant 6 flower
blueberry: 5 fruit, shrub 8 bilberry
family: 5 heath
relative: 5 salal 6 azalea, kalmia 7 arbutus, rhodora 8 cassiope, cowberry 9 deerberry
Blueberry Hill (1956 song) artist: Fats Domino
opener: 6 I found
bluebill: 4 bird
bluebird residence: 4 nest
blue blood: 4 dame, duke, earl, lady, lord, peer 5 baron, elite 7 marquis 10 aristocrat, noblewoman
org.: 3 DAR
blue-blooded: 5 noble 8 highborn, wellborn, well-bred 9 patrician 10 upper-class
blue bloods: 5 elite 8 nobility
bluebonnet: 3 cap, hat 5 plant 6 flower, lupine
bluebottle: 3 bug, fly 5 plant 6 flower, insect
Blue Carbuncle, Sherlock's: 3 gem
blue channel ___: 3 cat 7 catfish
Blue Chips actor: 5 Nolte
BlueChoice: 3 HMO
bluecoat: 3 cop 9 policeman 11 policewoman
Blue Collar (1978 film)
cast: Ed Begley Jr., Harvey Keitel, Yaphet Kotto, Richard Pryor
director: Paul Schrader
blue-collar worker: 7 laborer
Blue Cross
alternative: 5 Aetna
offering: 3 HMO
Blue Dahlia, The (1946 film)
cast: William Bendix, Alan Ladd, Veronica Lake
director: George Marshall
Blue Danube Waltz composer: 7 Strauss
Blue Demons: 6 DePaul
Blue Denim (1959 film)
cast: Brandon de Wilde, Carol Lynley
director: Philip Dunne
Blue Devils: 4 Duke
Blue Eagle org.: 3 NRA
Blue Estuaries poet: 5 Bogan
Blue Eyes Crying in the Rain (1975 song) artist: Willie Nelson
bluefin: 4 fish, tuna 5 tunny
blue-flowered ground cover: 5 ajuga
Blue Gardenia, The (1953 film)
cast: Anne Baxter, Richard Conte
director: Fritz Lang
bluegill: 4 fish 5 bream 7 sunfish
blue-glazed pottery: 4 delf 5 delft
___ Blue Gown: 5 Alice
bluegrass: 5 music
genus: 3 poa
instrument: 5 banjo 6 fiddle
Bluegrass State: 3 Ken. 8 Kentucky
blue-gray: 6 steely
blue-green: 4 aqua, cyan 9 turquoise
organism: 4 alga
Blue Grotto locale: 5 Capri
Blue Hammer, The author: Ross Macdonald
Blue Hawaii (1961 film)
cast: Joan Blackman, Angela Lansbury, Elvis Presley
director: Norman Taurog
bluehead: 4 fish
Blue Hen State: 3 Del. 8 Delaware
___ blue heron: 5 great 6 little
Blue II painter: 4 Miró
blue in the ___: 4 face
Blue Island: 4 city, town
locale: 8 Illinois
bluejacket: 3 gob, tar 4 salt 6 seaman 7 jack-tar, mariner
Blue Jacket rival: 4 Blue, King, Star, Wild 5 Bruin, Devil, Flame, Flyer, Oiler, Sabre, Shark 6 Canuck, Coyote, Ranger 7 Capital, Panther, Penguin, Red Wing, Senator 8 Canadien, Islander, Predator, Thrasher 9 Avalanche, Blackhawk, Hurricane, Lightning, Maple Leaf 10 Mighty Duck
Blue Jackets: 3 six 4 team
home: 8 Columbus
org.: 3 NHL
sport: 6 hockey
blue jay: 4 bird
topper: 5 crest
Blue Jay rival: 3 Cub, Met, Red 4 Expo, Twin 5 Angel, Astro, Brave, Giant, Padre, Rocky, Royal, Tiger 6 Brewer, Dodger, Indian, Marlin, Oriole, Philly, Pirate, Ranger, Red Sox, Yankee 7 Mariner 8 Athletic, Cardinal, Devil Ray, White Sox
Bluejays: 9 Creighton
Blue Jays: 3 ten 4 team
home: 7 Ontario, Toronto
org.: 3 ALE, MLB
sport: 8 baseball
Blue Jean (1984 song) artist: David Bowie
Blue Knight, The dog: 3 Leo
Blue Lagoon, The (1980 film)
cast: Christopher Atkins, William Daniels, Leo McKern, Brooke Shields
director: Randal Kleiser
Blue Lantern, The author: Colette
___ Blue Line, The: 4 Thin
Blue Meridian author: Peter Matthiessen
blue mold: 6 fungus
Blue Monday (1957 song) artist: Fats Domino
Blue Money (1971 song) artist: Van Morrison
Blue Monster, The: 5 Doral
Blue Moon: 4 Odom, song, tune
composer: 4 Hart 7 Rodgers
Blue Moon (1961 song) artist: Marcels
blue moon, like a: 4 rare
Blue Nile: 5 river
explorer: 5 Baker
locale: 5 Sudan 7 Ethopia
source: 4 Tana 5 Tsana
bluenose: 4 prig 5 priss, prude 6 censor 9 formalist, nice Nelly
blue-nose: 4 prim 6 prissy 7 prudish 8 priggish 10 censorious

Blue on Blue (1963 song) artist: Bobby Vinton
blue-pencil: 4 edit 5 alter 6 censor, delete, excise, redact, revise 7 expunge 9 expurgate
notation: 4 dele, stet 5 caret
wielder: 6 editor
__ Blue Persuasion: 7 Crystal
blue plate __: 7 special
Blue Plate Special author: Damon Runyon
blue point: 3 cat 5 felid 6 feline 7 Siamese
blueprint: 4 plan 5 chart, draft, model 6 design, layout, scheme, sketch 7 diagram, formula, outline, picture, specify 8 game plan, strategy, time line 9 floor plan, visual aid
detail: 4 door, spec 5 stair 6 closet, window
...blue ribbon __: 4 on it
__ Blue Ribbon: 5 Pabst
blue-ribbon awarder: 4 fair
blues: 3 woe 4 funk, jazz, mood 5 angst, dolor, dumps, genre, gloom, mopes, music 6 misery, sorrow 7 anguish, despair, sadness 8 doldrums, glumness 9 dejection, heartache, moodiness 10 depression, heavy heart, melancholy, woefulness
baby ~: 4 eyes, orbs
guitarist: 4 King 6 B.B. King 7 Diddley 9 Bo Diddley
have the ~: 4 mope 5 brood
rhythm and ~: 5 music
singing the ~: 3 low 4 down 6 morose 8 downcast 9 sorrowful
street: 5 Basin, Beale
blues-__: 4 rock
__ blues: 4 baby
Blues: 3 six 4 team
home: 7 St. Louis
milieu: 3 ice 4 rink
org.: 3 NHL
sport: 6 hockey
Blues __ Night: 5 in the
__ Blues: 3 Yer 4 Navy 5 Miami, Moody, Paris, Po' Boy, Sugar 6 Biloxi, Outlaw, Wabash
Blues Brothers 2000 (1998 film)
cast: Dan Aykroyd, John Goodman, Joe Morton, Nia Peeples
director: John Landis
Blues Brothers, The (1980 film)
cast: Dan Aykroyd, John Belushi, Cab Calloway
director: John Landis
__ Blue Sea: 4 Deep
Blues for Mister Charlie author: James Baldwin
blue shark: 4 fish
__ blue shark: 5 great
Blues Image song: Ride Captain Ride (1970)
Blue singer: 5 Rimes
Blues in the Night
composer: 5 Arlen 6 Mercer
second word of ~: 4 mama
Blue Skies (1946 film)
cast: Fred Astaire, Joan Caulfield, Bing Crosby
Blue Skies composer: Irving Berlin
blue-sky __: 3 law
Blue Sky (1994 film)
cast: Powers Boothe, Tommy Lee Jones, Jessica Lange
director: Tony Richardson
bluesman's lick: 4 riff
__ Blue Something: 4 Deep
Blue Springs: 4 city, town
locale: 8 Missouri
Blues Suite choreographer: 5 Ailey
Bluest Eye, The author: Toni Morrison
bluestocking: 7 egghead
__ blue streak: 5 talk a
Blue Suede Shoes (1956 song)
artist: Carl Perkins, Elvis Presley
bluet: 5 plant 6 flower
Blue Tail Fly singer: 4 Ives
Blue Tango composer: 8 Anderson
__ blue terrier: 5 Kerry
Blue Triangle org.: 4 YWCA
bluette: 6 fungus
Blue Veil, The (1951 film)
cast: Charles Laughton, Jane Wyman
Blue Velvet (1986 film)
cast: Laura Dern, Dennis Hopper, Kyle MacLachlan, Isabella Rossellini
director: David Lynch
Blue Velvet (1963 song) artist: Bobby Vinton
Blue, Vida sport: 8 baseball
Blue Voyage author: Conrad Aiken
bluewood: 4 tree 5 shrub
blue wood __: 5 aster
bluff: 3 lie 4 fake, fool, hill, jive, ruse, sham, snow 5 blunt, cliff, feign, feint, frank, put on, ridge, spoof, trick 6 abrupt, assume, candid, deceit, delude, direct, humbug, take in, threat 7 bluster, deceive, fake out, finesse, mislead, pretend, pretext 8 headland, mountain, pretense, psych out, simulate 9 deception, disinform, four-flush, outspoken, precipice 10 false front, forthright, from the hip, prominence, promontory, subterfuge, unreticent
__ Bluff: 4 Pine 7 Coogan's
bluffer: 4 fake 5 fraud 8 imposter, impostor 9 hypocrite
bluing: 6 bleach
Blumberg, Baruch: 8 Nobelist
Blume in Love (1973 film)
cast: Susan Anspach, Kris Kristofferson, George Segal
director: Paul Mazursky
Blume, Judy: 6 author, writer
work: Blubber
Deenie
Double Fudge
Forever
Freckle Juice
Fudge-a-mania
Iggie's House
The Pain and the Great One
Smart Women
Summer Sisters
Superfudge
Then Again, Maybe I Won't
Tiger Eyes
Wifey
Blumenau: 4 city, town
locale: 6 Brazil
Blunden, Edmund: 4 poet 7 British
blunder: 3 dud, err 4 bomb, bust, flop, flub, goof, lose, loss, miss, muff, slip, trip 5 boner, botch, error, fault, fluff, flunk, gaffe, lapse, lurch, wrong 6 barney, blow it, boo-boo, bungle, defeat, falter, fiasco, foozle, foul up, fumble, goof up, howler, mishap, muddle, slip-up, totter, turkey 7 blooper, debacle, faux pas, founder, go under, go wrong, misstep, mistake, screwup, stumble, washout 8 downfall, fall flat, flounder, lay an egg 9 gaucherie, indecorum, mishandle, mismanage, oversight, strike out 10 inaccuracy
social ~: 5 gaffe 6 bêtise 7 faux pas
blunderbore: 4 ogre
blunderbuss: 3 oaf 4 boor 5 rifle 6 musket
blunderer: 2 ox 3 oaf 4 lout 5 klutz, looby 6 lummox
blundering: 6 clumsy 7 awkward, unadept 8 bungling, cloddish, inexpert, lubberly, tactless, unsubtle 9 maladroit
blunt: 3 sag, sap 4 curt, dull, flag, rude, tire, wane 5 allay, bluff, brusk, frank, gruff, plain, short, stark, terse, vocal 6 abrupt, benumb, candid, dampen, deaden, direct, honest, impair, obtund, obtuse, reduce, shrink, soften, weaken 7 brusque, deplete, exhaust, fatigue, mollify, rounded, uncivil 8 edgeless, enervate, enfeeble, impolite, mitigate, out-front, straight, succinct, tactless, undercut, unsubtle 9 attenuate, downright, outspoken, pointless, trenchant, undermine, water down 10 debilitate, devitalize, forthright, free-spoken, from the hip, point-blank, to the point, ungracious, unmediated, unpolished, unreserved, unreticent
combining form: 5 ambly- 6 amblyo-
end: 4 stub
blunted: 4 dull
bluntly: 7 up front 10 point-blank
bluntness: 7 honesty
Blunt, Wilfrid: 6 writer 7 British
blur: 3 dim, fog 4 blot, daze, fade, mist, spot 5 bedim, befog, blear, cloud, fog up, muddy, smear, stain, sully, taint 6 darken, fuzz up, smudge 7 becloud, besmear, dimness, obscure 8 discolor, haziness 9 adumbrate
blurb: 2 ad 4 puff 5 promo 6 review 9 promotion, publicity, puff piece, sound bite
blurred: 3 dim 4 hazy 5 blear, foggy, fuzzy, misty, muzzy, vague 6 bleary, cloudy 9 unfocused 10 indistinct
blurry: 4 dark, hazy 5 blear, dusky, faded, fuzzy, mirky, murky, muted 6 bleary, fogged 7 shadowy 9 unfocused 10 indistinct, out of focus
blurt out: 4 blab, blat 5 utter 6 betray 7 exclaim, lay bare, let slip
blush: 4 pink, wine 5 color, flush, rouge 6 makeup, redden 8 cosmetic, rosiness 9 reddening, ruddiness
first ~: 7 morning
make ~: 5 abash, shame 6 praise 9 embarrass 10 compliment
blush __: 4 wine
blusher: 5 paint, rouge 8 cosmetic
blushing: 3 coy, red 4 pink, rosy 5 ruddy, timid 6 demure, modest 7 ashamed, bashful, flushed
bluster: 3 cow, gas 4 bawl, brag, crow, flap, rage, rant, rave, roar 5 bluff, storm, swash 6 bellow, hector, hot air 7 bombast, bravado, clatter, show off, swagger, talk big, tempest 8 browbeat 9 arrogance, gasconade 10 intimidate
blusterer: 6 gasbag 7 windbag
blustering: 4 loud, wild 5 windy 6 raging 7 huffish, rampant 9 turbulent
blustery: 3 raw 4 wild 5 windy 6 breezy, raging, stormy 7 furious 9 turbulent
Bluth: 3 Don
Bluto: 3 gob, tar 4 salt 6 sailor
to Popeye: 5 rival
blvd.: 2 st. 3 ave. 4 pkwy.
__ Blvd.: 6 Sunset
Bly: 6 Nellie, Robert
Blyden: 5 Larry
Blyleven, Bert sport: 8 baseball
Blynken shipmate: 3 Nod 6 Wynken
Bly, Robert: 6 writer
Blyth: 3 Ann 4 city, town
locale: 7 England
Blyth, Ann: 7 actress
film: The Great Caruso (1951)
Killer McCoy (1947)
The King's Thief (1955)
Thunder on the Hill (1951)
A Woman's Vengeance (1947)
The World in His Arms (1952)
Blythe: 6 Danner
daughter: 7 Gwyneth
Blytheville: 4 city, town
locale: 8 Arkansas
Blyton: 4 Enid
__ B. Mayer: 5 Louis
__ B. McClellan: 6 George
BME awarder: 3 MIT
BMI rival: 5 ASCAP
BMOC: 3 VIP 5 celeb
house: 4 frat
part: 3 Big, Man 6 Campus
BMT locale: 3 NYC
kin: 3 IRT
BMW: 3 car 4 auto 6 German, import 10 automobile
alternative: 2 MG 3 Jag 4 Audi 5 Lexus
part: 5 Motor, Works 8 Bavarian
B'nai B'rith org.: 3 ADL
bn.com rival: 6 Amazon
bo: 4 tree 5 pipal 6 peepul
bo-__: 4 peep
__-bo: 3 tae
Bo: 5 Derek, Gritz 7 Diddley, Hopkins, Jackson, Svenson
Bo __: 6 Weevil
B&O: 2 RR
employee: 4 engr.
part of ~: 4 Ohio 9 Baltimore
stop: 3 sta., stn.
B.O.: 9 box office
buy: 3 tkt. 6 ticket
sign: 3 SRO
boa: 4 wrap 5 scarf, snake, stole, throw 6 animal 7 reptile 9 neckpiece
relative: 3 asp 5 aboma, adder, cobra, krait, mamba, racer, viper 6 dhaman, python, taipan 7 markhor, rattler 8 anaconda, moccasin, ringhals 9 boomslang, coachwhip 10 bushmaster, copperhead, sidewinder
boar: 3 hog, pig 5 swine 6 animal, tusker 9 razorback
ender: 4 fish 5 hound
mate: 3 sow
tooth: 4 tusk
__ boar: 4 wild
board: 4 eats, food, jury, lath, meal, sign, slab, slat 5 catch, get on, hop on, lodge, meals, panel, plank, put up, strip, table 6 bureau, harbor, take in, ticket, timber 7 aliment, cabinet, care for, climb on, council, emplane, enplane, entrain, harbour, quarter 8 trustees, victuals 9 committee, directors, syndicate 10 commission, department, executives, management, provisions
African ~ game: 3 bao
amateur on a ~: 5 ho-dad
bed ~: 4 slat
bring on ~: 4 hire 6 employ, engage
bulletin ~ material: 4 cork, felt
by the ~: 4 gone
cleaner: 6 eraser
clean the ~: 4 wash, wipe 5 erase
clear the cribbage ~: 5 unpeg
covering: 5 emery, paint, stain 6 enamel 7 shellac, varnish
drawing ~ original: 5 plan A 9 blueprint
emery ~: 4 file
ender: 4 room, walk 7 sailing
fasten to a ~: 4 tack 6 staple
flight ~: 4 sked 5 sched. 8 schedule
flight ~ datum: 3 ETA, ETD
game: 4 Clue, Risk 5 chess, pente, shogi, Sorry 7 Careers, pachisi 8 checkers, Monopoly, Scrabble 10 backgammon
game need: 3 man 4 dice 5 piece
get on ~: 6 embark 7 enplane, entrain

holder: 4 nail, vise 5 screw 8 sawhorse
imperfection: 4 hole, knot 5 crack
informally: 5 hop on
insert: 3 peg
Japanese ~ game: 5 shogi
lodging on ~: 5 cabin 9 stateroom
material: 4 pine, wood 6 timber
member: 3 CEO, dir. 4 exec, pres., suit 7 trustee 9 executive
membership: 4 seat
narrow ~: 4 lath, slat
not on ~: 6 ashore
on ~: 4 here 6 with us 7 present
put on ~: 4 lade, load, ship, stow
review ~: 5 panel 7 inquest 9 committee
room and ~: 4 keep 7 lodging, pension
spiritualist's ~: 5 Ouija
starter: 3 box, cup, key, lap, lee, mop, out, peg, sea 4 back, base, bill, buck, call, card, clap, clip, cork, dart, dash, duck, fall, fire, foot, free, hard, head, knee, mill, mold, over, sail, ship, side, sign, snow, star, surf, tail, wall, wash 5 above, barge, black, bread, chalk, chess, fiber, flash, floor, liner, match, paper, paste, press, punch, scale, score, skate, sound, story, straw 6 beaver, bridge, center, cradle, finger, mother, paddle, splash, spring, string, switch, teeter 7 checker, plaster, scraper, scratch, shuffle, weather 8 particle 9 container
trim a ~: 5 resaw
up: 5 cover 6 batten
went off the ~: 4 dove
work: 6 agenda

board __: 4 feet, foot, game, room, rule, side 5 check 7 measure
__ board: 3 bed, low 4 arch, hack, half, high, hunt, jute, lear, lens, snow, tilt, tote 5 altar, angle, bilge, broom, draft, emery, facia, idiot, layer, otter, Ouija, slant, table 6 batter, comber, county, cradle, diving, fascia, gypsum, leader, ledger, louver, Malibu, preset, school, scrive, signal, window 7 Bristol, circuit, control, cutting, drawing, ironing, molding, running, tilting, warping
__-board: 3 off 4 call
__ Board: 3 Big 6 Boogie
__-Board: 3 Peg
boarder: 5 guest, liver 6 lessee, lodger, tenant
starter: 4 sail, snow, surf 5 skate
boarding
device: 4 ramp 9 gangplank
house: 5 B and B 7 lodging 8 lodgment
house rental: 4 room
place: 4 dock, pier, stop 5 wharf 7 airport, station 8 terminal
school: 4 acad., prep 7 academy
starter: 4 sail, snow, surf 5 skate
boarding __: 4 pass, ramp 5 house, party 6 school
boarding house __: 5 reach
boardlike: 5 rigid, stiff 6 wooden
Boardman: 4 city, town
locale: 4 Ohio
Board of Elections concern: 6 ballot
__ Board of Trade: 7 Chicago
boardroom display: 5 graph
boards: 5 stage 6 lumber 7 theater, theatre
gone by the ~: 3 out 5 dated, fusty, hoary, passé, stale 6 démodé, old hat 7 archaic, outworn 8 obsolete, outdated, outmoded 9 forgotten, moss-grown, out-of-date 10 antiquated, superseded
tread the ~: 3 act 4 play 7 perform
__ Boards: 7 College
boardwalk: 9 promenade
section: 5 plank
structure: 4 pier
Boardwalk buy: 5 hotel, house
boar friend
name meaning ~: 5 Erwin, Irwin
Boas: 5 Franz
boast: 3 own 4 brag, crow, tout 5 claim, enjoy, gloat, pride, spout, swash, vaunt 6 flaunt, parade 7 bravado, lay it on, possess, show off, swagger, talk big, trumpet 9 gasconade 10 aggrandize, exaggerate, grandstand
boastful: 3 big 4 smug, vain 5 cocky, gassy, proud, windy 6 snooty 7 crowing, fustian, haughty, pompous, stuck-up 8 arrogant, bragging, snobbish, vaunting 9 bigheaded, bombastic, conceited, egotistic, strutting 10 big-talking, swaggering, triumphant
one: 6 crower, gasbag, gascon 7 showoff 8 braggart, fanfaron 9 loudmouth
what the ~ blow: 5 smoke
boastfulness: 3 ego 4 wind 6 vanity 7 bravado, conceit, ego trip 9 arrogance, gasconade
boat: 3 ark, dau, dow, gig, hoy, tub, tug 4 Argo, bark, brig, dhow, dory, hulk, junk, prao, prau, proa, punt, raft, scow, ship, yawl 5 barge, canoe, craft, ferry, float, kayak, ketch, liner, oiler, scull, shell, skiff, sloop, smack, umiak, xebec, yacht, zebec 6 argosy, barque, bateau, bireme, caique, carack, carvel, cutter, dinghy, drakar, dugout, galley, launch, lugger, packet, sampan, tanker, tender, trader, vessel, whaler, wherry, zebeck 7 caravel, carrack, chebeck, clipper, coaster, collier, coracle, corsair, cruiser, dredger, felucca, frigate, galleon, gondola, lighter, monitor, pinnace, pontoon, steamer, trawler, trireme, vehicle 8 car ferry, corvette, dahabeah, fireship, flagship, ironclad, man-of-war, runabout, schooner, trimaran 9 catamaran, destroyer, freighter, hydrofoil, minelayer, oil tanker, outrigger, privateer, steamship, submarine, troopship 10 barkentine, battleship, brigantine, Hovercraft, hydroplane, icebreaker, ocean liner, quadrireme, supply ship, tea clipper, watercraft, windjammer
aluminum ~: 5 canoe
animal ~: 3 ark
any ~: 3 her, she
Arab ~: 4 dhow 7 felucca 8 dahabeah
backbone: 4 keel
bark ~: 5 canoe
bayou ~: 6 bateau
big ~: 4 ship 5 liner, yacht 7 steamer 9 freighter, steamship
canal ~: 5 barge 7 gondola
Chinese ~: 4 junk 6 sampan
clumsy ~: 3 ark, tub 4 hulk, scow
coal carrier ~: 7 collier
combining form: 5 scaph- 6 scapho-
cruise ~: 5 liner 7 steamer 9 steamship
dip out a ~: 4 bail
don't rock the ~: 3 bow 4 mind 5 agree, yield 6 accede, accept, assent, comply, give in, relent, submit 7 go along, respect 8 play ball 9 acquiesce, cooperate 10 come around
Dutch fishing ~: 6 dogger
East Indies freight ~: 5 oolak
ender: 3 man, men 4 bill, lift, load 5 house, swain
end of a ~: 3 aft 5 stern 6 astern
Eskimo ~: 5 kayak, umiak
fast ~: 6 cutter 9 hydrofoil, speedboat 10 Hovercraft, hydroplane
fishing ~: 4 dory 5 smack 6 lugger, whaler 7 coaster, trawler
flat-bottomed ~: 4 dory, junk, punt, raft, scow 5 barge, float 7 lighter, pontoon
follower: 4 wake
for cars: 5 ferry
front of a ~: 3 bow 4 prow 7 forward
Greek ~: 6 galley
harbor ~: 3 tug
hazard: 3 fog, ice 4 berg, floe, gale, reef, snag 5 shoal 7 typhoon 9 hurricane
hold a ~ steady: 4 dock 5 lie to 6 anchor
Indian ~: 5 canoe 9 birchbark
Indonesian ~: 4 prao, prau, proa
jolly ~: 4 yawl
kitchen: 6 galley
lateen-rigged ~: 4 dhow 6 carvel 7 caravel, felucca
merchant ~: 6 argosy, carack, trader 7 carrack, clipper, galleon 8 schooner 9 freighter 10 brigantine, tea clipper
miss the ~: 3 err 4 fail 7 mistake 8 go astray
motor ~: 6 launch
narrow ~: 5 canoe, kayak, skiff 9 outrigger
oared ~: 3 gig 4 dory 5 scull, shell, skiff 6 caique, dinghy, dugout, sampan, wherry 9 outrigger
on a slow ~ to China: 4 asea 5 at sea
paddled ~: 5 canoe, kayak, umiak
pantry: 5 cuddy
part: 4 deck, helm, hold, hull, prow 5 cabin, hatch, stern 6 gunnel, tiller 7 gunwale 10 figurehead
patrol ~: 5 aviso
pea-green ~ passenger: 3 owl 8 pussycat
person: 7 refugee
pirate ~: 7 corsair 9 privateer 10 Jolly Roger
pleasure ~: 5 yacht 7 cruiser 8 trimaran 9 catamaran
poled ~: 4 punt, raft 5 float 7 gondola
portable ~: 5 canoe, kayak, umiak
propeller: 3 oar 4 sail 5 motor 6 engine, paddle
PT ~: 7 warship
racing ~: 5 scull, shell, yacht
Red Sea ~: 4 dhow
ritzy ~: 5 yacht
river ~: 4 raft 5 barge, canoe, ferry 8 car ferry
rock the ~: 5 rebel, upset 6 revolt
Roman ~: 6 bireme, galley 7 trireme 10 quadrireme
round ~: 7 coracle
runway: 4 ramp
sailing ~: 5 yacht 7 clipper 10 barkentine, tea clipper, windjammer
Scottish fishing ~: 6 baldie
secure a ~: 4 dock, moor 6 anchor
silt clearer ~: 7 dredger
single-masted ~: 5 sloop 6 cutter 8 dahabeah
small ~: 4 dory, yawl 5 canoe, skiff 7 coracle, rowboat 8 sailboat 9 outrigger
South Seas ~: 4 prao, prau, proa 9 outrigger
square-ended ~: 4 pram
square-rigged ~: 4 bark, brig 6 barque
starter: 3 air, cat, fly, gun, ice, pig, row, tow, tug 4 bull, cock, fire, flat, fold, john, keel, life, long, sail, show, surf, work 5 ferry, house, jolly, motor, power, river, sauce, speed, steam, whale 6 cockle, paddle
that ~: 3 her, she
three-masted ~: 5 xebec, zebec 7 clipper 10 tea clipper
trip: 4 sail 6 cruise, voyage
two-masted ~: 4 yawl 5 ketch
underwater ~: 3 sub 9 submarine
wake: 4 wash
with square sails: 4 junk 8 dahabeah
see also ship
boat __: 3 bed, bug 4 deck, hook, lily, nail, neck, tail 5 patch, spike, train 6 people
__ boat: 3 buy, jet, tag 4 bolt, buoy, mail, surf, York 5 crash, drift, gravy, hatch, Irish, jolly, party, pedal, pilot, stake, storm, water 6 advice, Bowser, diving, flying, killer, market, packet, picket, rowing 7 assault, pulling, sailing, torpedo, vedette
__ Boat: 4 Show
boatbill: 4 bird
boater: 3 hat, lid 8 straw hat 9 yachtsman
boathouse gear: 3 oar 6 paddle
Boating painter: 5 Manet
boatman: 3 gob 6 sailor, sea dog 7 jack tar
river: 5 Volga
water ~: 3 bug 6 insect
__ Boat Song, The: 6 Banana
boatswain's __: 4 call, pipe 5 chair
__ Boat, The: 4 Love, Open 6 Golden
__ boat to China: 4 slow
boatyard: 5 basin
Boaz
father of ~: 6 Salmon
son of ~: 4 Obed
wife: 4 Ruth
bob: 3 jig, wag 4 clip, coif, duck, jump, skip, toss, trim 5 float, money 6 bounce, curtsy, hairdo, jiggle, joggle, jounce, lollop, wabble, wobble 7 curtsey, pendant, shorten 8 coiffure, cut short, shilling 9 hairstyle, oscillate
ender: 3 cat 4 sled, stay, tail 5 white
fishing bait: 3 dap, dib
no siree ~: 3 nay
plumb ~: 6 weight
starter: 3 ear, ski 4 skee
up: 4 rise 6 appear, emerge
__ bob: 5 Dutch, plumb
Bob: 3 Rae 4 Abel, arum, Dole, Goen, Hope, Kane, Lind, Vila, Weir, Wynn 5 Clark, Cousy, Crane, Dishy, Dylan, Estes, Fosse, Hayes, Lemon, Lilly, Luman, Saget, Seger, Smith, Welch, Wills 6 Barker, Beamon, Brenly, Costas, Crosby, Dahlin, Denver, Eberly, Feller, Geldof, Gibson, Goalby, Greene, Griese, Gunton, Kerrey, Knight, Lanier, Mackie, Marley, McAdoo, Newman, Pettit, Uecker, Watson 7 Balaban, Elliott, Eubanks, Hartley, Hoskins, Keeshan, Kelljan, Mathias, Montana, Newhart, Seagren 8 Carlisle, Cummings, Rafelson, Richards, Woodward
bob and __: 5 weave
Bob and __: 3 Ray
Bobbettes song: Mr. Lee (1957)
__ Bobbidi Boo: 7 Bibbidi
Bobbie: 6 Gentry
bobbin: 5 spool
in Britain: 4 pirn
lace: 5 Cluny
bobble: 3 err 4 muff 5 botch, fluff 6 fumble, jiggle, joggle, jounce, mess up 7 mistake, screw up

Bobbsey twin: 3 Nan 4 Bert 7 Flossie, Freddie
bobby: 3 cop 6 copper 9 policeman
follower: 5 soxer
stick: 4 cosh
bobby __: 3 pin, sox 4 calf 5 socks, soxer 7 dazzler
Bobby: 3 Day, Orr, Van, Vee 4 Bare, Hart, Hebb, Hull 5 Bloom, Breen, Brown, Darin, Doerr, Ewing, Helms, Jones, Layne, Lewis, Mauch, Rahal, Riggs, Short, Troup, Unser 6 Fuller, Knight, Rydell, Vinton, Womack 7 Allison, Bonilla, Fischer, Freeman, Hackett, Pickett, Russell, Sherman, Thomson 8 Caldwell, Driscoll, Farrelly, McFerrin, Mitchell 9 Goldsboro
__ Bobby McGee: 5 Me and
Bobby's Girl (1962 song) artist: Marcie Blane
Bobby Shaftoe's gone __: 5 to sea
bobby-sock relative: 6 anklet
bobby-soxer: 4 girl, miss, teen
dance: 3 hop
wow a ~: 5 croon
Bobby Sox to Stockings (1959 song)
artist: Frankie Avalon
Bob & Carol & Ted & Alice (1969 film)
cast: Dyan Cannon, Robert Culp, Elliott Gould, Natalie Wood
director: Paul Mazursky
bobcat: 3 cat 4 lynx 5 felid 6 animal, feline 8 toboggan
relative: 4 eyra, lion, lynx, puma 5 chita, liger, ounce, tiger, tigon 6 cheeta, chetah, cougar, jaguar, margay, ocelot, serval, tiglon 7 caracal, cheetah, leopard, panther 9 catamount 10 jaguarundi
Bobcat: 3 car 4 auto 7 Mercury 10 automobile, Goldthwait
Bob Mathias Story, The (1954 film)
cast: Ward Bond, Bob Mathias
Bob Newhart Show, The (CBS sitcom)
cast: Peter Bonerz (Jerry Robinson)
Bill Daily (Howard Borden)
Bob Newhart (Bob Hartley)
Suzanne Pleshette (Emily Hartley)
Marcia Wallace (Carol Kester)
producer: MTM
setting: Chicago, Illinois
trains: 3 els
Bobo: 6 Newsom
bobolink: 4 bird 7 ortolan
relative: 6 oriole
Bob Roberts (1992 film)
cast: Giancarlo Esposito, Tim Robbins
director: Tim Robbins
Bob's __ Boy: 3 Big
bobsledding: 5 sport
track: 5 chute
bobstay: 3 rod 4 rope 5 chain
bobtail: 5 horse 6 equine
__ Bob Thornton: 5 Billy
bobwhite: 4 bird 5 colin, quail
family: 5 covey
Boca del Mar: 4 city, town
locale: 7 Florida
bocane: 5 dance
Boca Raton: 4 city, town
locale: 7 Florida
Boccaccio, Giovanni: 4 poet 7 Italian
work: Decameron
boccie: 4 game
boce: 4 fish
Bochco: 6 Steven
Bochil: 4 city, town
locale: 6 Mexico 7 Chiapas
Bochner: 4 Hart 5 Lloyd
Bochsa: 6 Robert
bock: 4 beer 5 drink 8 beverage
alternative: 3 ale 5 lager, stout
Bock: 5 Jerry
Bock's __: 3 Car
bod: 4 form 5 build 6 figure 8 physique
bodacious: 3 def, rad 4 aces, A-one, boss, braw, cool, dece, fine, gear, keen, neat, nice, phat, tuff 5 dandy, ducky, grand, great, marvy, neato, nobby, prime, slick, super, swell 6 bang on, bang-up, bonzer, bosker, choice, divine, dreamy, far-out, gnarly, groovy, lovely, peachy, slap-up, spot on, superb, terrif, tiptop, unreal, whizzo, wicked 7 amazing, awesome, capital, corking, perfect, ripping, skookum, stellar, sublime 8 dazzling, especial, eximious, fabulous, five-star, four-star, frabjous, glorious, heavenly, jim-dandy, slam-bang, smashing, splendid, standout, sterling, stickout, superior, terrific, top-level, topnotch, very good, wondrous 9 Endsville, excellent, exemplary, exquisite, first-rate, high-grade, hunky-dory, marvelous, memorable, sollicker, top-flight, wonderful 10 first-class, hotsy-totsy, jack-a-dandy, out of sight, peachy-keen, phenomenal, remarkable, stupendous, super-duper
bode: 5 augur 6 waited 7 bespeak, betoken, point to, portend, presage, promise, signify 8 foreshow, foretell 9 foretoken 10 foreshadow
bodega: 7 grocery 8 wine shop 9 warehouse
locale: 6 barrio
owner: 6 grocer
patron: 5 señor 6 Latina, Latino, señora
Bodel, Jean: 4 poet 6 French
Bodenheim, Maxwell: 4 poet
bodhi: 3 fig 4 tree
bodhran: 4 drum
origin: 7 Ireland
bodice: 3 top 6 basque, blouse 9 dress part
ripper: 7 romance
short-sleeved ~: 6 angiya
__-bodied: 4 able, full
__-bodied seaman: 4 able
bodies: 6 people, somata
bodiless: 9 lightsome, spiritual 10 discarnate, immaterial, impalpable, intangible, unphysical
bodily: 4 real 5 fully 6 wholly 7 en masse, organic, sensual, somatic, totally 8 as a group, corporal, entirely, personal, physical 9 corporeal 10 altogether, completely, in the flesh
bodily __: 4 harm
Bodily Harm author: Margaret Atwood
__-boding: 3 ill
bodkin: 3 awl 4 pick 6 dagger, needle 7 hairpin 8 stiletto
__ bodkins: 3 ods
Bodoni: 4 font 8 typeface
body: 3 mob, set, sum 4 band, bulk, crux, form, gist, mass, soma, sort, soul, team, zest 5 being, build, corps, frame, group, human, party, shape, suite, torso, total, troop, trunk 6 corpus, entity, figure, legion, makeup, matter, mortal, person 7 anatomy, chassis, company, essence 8 assembly, fuselage, majority, organism, physique 9 gathering, substance 10 contingent, individual, membership, opera omnia
auto ~: 7 chassis
build: 5 frame 8 physique
celestial ~: 3 orb 4 moon, star 5 comet 6 planet, sphere
check: 5 frisk
combining form: 4 -soma, -some 5 somat- 6 somato-
ender: 4 sera, surf, work 5 guard 6 fluids 7 builder
fluid: 5 blood, lymph, serum 6 saliva
governing ~: 5 board, House, panel 6 Senate 7 council 8 Congress, trustees 9 directors 10 commission, executives, management, parliament
heat: 5 fever 7 pyrexia
language: 4 pose 5 shrug 7 gesture, posture
main ~: 4 text
of an organism: 4 soma
of knowledge: 4 lore 6 mythos 7 science 9 tradition
of laws: 4 code 5 canon
of principles: 5 ethic, ethos
of soldiers: 4 army, unit 5 troop 6 cohort, legion 9 battalion
of water: 3 bay, sea 4 cove, lake, loch, pond, pool, tarn 5 inlet, ocean, sound 6 harbor, lagoon
of work: 6 oeuvre
part: 3 arm, ear, eye, hip, jaw, leg, lip, rib, toe 4 back, bone, brow, calf, chin, face, foot, gums, hair, hand, head, heel, iris, knee, lens, limb, lung, nape, neck, nose, pate, shin, skin, ulna, vein 5 ankle, aorta, belly, blood, brain, cheek, chest, colon, digit, elbow, femur, flesh, gland, heart, ileum, ilium, liver, lymph, molar, mouth, nares, navel, organ, pupil, scalp, shank, skull, spine, thigh, thumb, tibia, tooth, torso, trunk, uvula, velum, wrist 6 armpit, artery, biceps, canine, carpus, coccyx, cornea, eyelid, fibula, finger, gullet, instep, kidney, larynx, marrow, muscle, neuron, palate, pelvis, pinkie, retina, sacrum, septum, spleen, tarsus, temple, tendon, thorax, throat, thymus, tongue 7 abdomen, adenoid, adrenal, cranium, cuticle, deltoid, eardrum, eyeball, eyebrow, forearm, hipbone, ischium, knuckle, medulla, midriff, nostril, pharynx, scapula, sternum, stomach, synapse, thyroid, trachea, triceps 8 appendix, backbone, cerebrum, clavicle, forehead, ganglion, inner ear, ligament, mandible, pancreas, shinbone, shoulder, skeleton, voice box, windpipe 9 capillary, cartilage, cheekbone, corpuscle, diaphragm, esophagus, extremity, funny bone, hamstring, intestine, lymph node, middle ear, pituitary, thighbone, umbilicus, vocal cord 10 Adam's apple, breastbone, cerebellum, collarbone, epiglottis, optic nerve, quadriceps, spinal cord
politic: 4 weal 5 state 6 nation, people 10 population
political ~: 4 pact 5 union 8 alliance
rhythm: 5 pulse
shop: 3 gym 6 garage
starter: 3 any 4 anti, busy, home, some 5 black, every
body __: 3 art, rub 4 blow, drop, mike, plan, post, shop, slam, suit, type, wave 5 check, clock, image, press, shirt, track 6 artist, double, rhythm 7 bolster, English, politic
body-__: 4 surf 7 builder
__ body: 4 Barr, cell, gray, grey, main 5 basal, Golgi, polar, stake 6 astral 7 acetone, carotid, ciliary, olivary, student
...body __ body...: 5 meet a
Body __: 4 Heat 6 Double
Body and Soul (1947 film)
cast: Hazel Brooks, John Garfield, Lilli Palmer
director: Robert Rossen
Body Artist, The author: Don DeLillo
bodybuilder: 5 he-man
bane: 4 flab
exercise: 4 curl 5 shrug, squat
goal: 5 brawn 8 strength
iteration: 3 rep
material: 4 iron
need: 7 trainer 8 barbells, Nautilus 9 dumbbells
pride: 3 abs 4 pecs, quad, tone 5 delts 6 biceps, muscle 7 triceps 8 physique
Body Count actor: 4 Ice-T
Body Double (1984 film)
cast: Melanie Griffith, Deborah Shelton, Craig Wasson
director: Brian De Palma
bodyguard: 6 escort 8 defender, henchman, watchdog, watchman 9 custodian, protector
Body Heat (1981 film)
cast: Richard Crenna, William Hurt, Kathleen Turner
character: 3 Ned
director: Lawrence Kasdan
Body Language (1982 song) artist: Queen
__ body meet...: 3 If a
__-body plane: 4 wide
body-shop
job: 4 dent 6 repair
offering: 6 loaner
body-slamming gp.: 3 WWF
Body Snatcher, The (1945 film)
cast: Henry Daniell, Boris Karloff, Bela Lugosi
director: Robert Wise
Body Snatcher, The author: Robert Louis Stevenson
Boeing: 7 William
product: 3 jet 5 plane
rival: 6 Airbus 8 Lockheed
Boeing Boeing (1965 film)
cast: Tony Curtis, Jerry Lewis
Boeotia neighbor: 6 Attica
seaport: 6 Delium
Boer: 9 Afrikaner
Boer __: 3 War
Boesky: 4 Ivan
Boesman and Lena author: Athol Fugard
Boethius: 5 Roman 11 philosopher
Boetticher: 4 Budd
boff: 6 strike, wallop 10 belly laugh
boffo: 5 socko 8 smashing 9 first-rate
review: 4 rave
show: 3 hit 5 smash
Bofors guns: 3 AAs
Bofors Gun, The (1968 film)
cast: Ian Holm, David Warner, Nicol Williamson
bog: 3 fen 4 mire, quag, sink 5 marsh, swamp 6 morass, slough 7 lowland, wetland 8 quagmire, wetlands 9 backwater
combining form: 4 helo-
down: 4 mire, slow 6 detain, hold up, slow up 7 set back 8 slow down
fruit: 9 cranberry
fuel: 4 peat
bog __: 3 oak, ore 4 hole, moss 6 myrtle, turtle
__ bog: 4 peat
boga: 4 fish
Bogan, Louise: 4 poet 6 writer
Bogarde, Dirk: 5 actor
film: Agent 8 3/4 (1965)
Appointment in London (1953)
Cast a Dark Shadow (1955)
Damn the Defiant! (1962)
Darling (1965)
Death in Venice (1971)
Doctor in the House (1954)

Doctor's Dilemma (1958)
Justine (1969)
King and Country (1964)
The Servant (1963)
Simba (1955)
The Sleeping Tiger (1954)
So Long at the Fair (1950)
The Spanish Gardener (1956)
Stranger in Between (1952)
A Tale of Two Cities (1958)
Victim (1961)
The Woman in Question (1950)

Bogart: 4 Paul 8 Humphrey
Bogart, Humphrey: 5 actor
film: Action in the North Atlantic (1943)
The African Queen (1951, AA)
All Through the Night (1942)
Angels With Dirty Faces (1938)
The Barefoot Contessa (1954)
Beat the Devil (1954)
The Big Sleep (1946)
Black Legion (1936)
Brother Orchid (1940)
Bullets or Ballots (1936)
The Caine Mutiny (1954)
Casablanca (1942)
Dark Passage (1947)
Dark Victory (1939)
Dead End (1937)
Deadline U.S.A. (1952)
Dead Reckoning (1947)
The Desperate Hours (1955)
The Enforcer (1951)
The Harder They Fall (1956)
High Sierra (1941)
In a Lonely Place (1950)
Key Largo (1948)
Kid Galahad (1937)
The Left Hand of God (1955)
The Maltese Falcon (1941)
Marked Woman (1937)
The Oklahoma Kid (1939)
The Roaring Twenties (1939)
Sabrina (1954)
Sahara (1943)
Stand-In (1937)
They Drive by Night (1940)
To Have and Have Not (1944)
The Treasure of the Sierra Madre (1948)
spouse: Lauren Bacall
Bogatá: 4 city, town 7 capital
locale: 8 Colombia
Bogdanovich, Peter: 8 director
film: The Last Picture Show (1971)
Mask (1985)
Nickelodeon (1976)
Noises Off (1992)
Paper Moon (1973)
Saint Jack (1979)
Targets (1968)
Texasville (1990)
They All Laughed (1981)
What's Up, Doc? (1972)
bogey: 3 UFO 4 ogre 5 ghoul 7 monster 9 hobgoblin 10 apparition
minus one: 3 par
__ bogey: 6 double, triple
bogeyman: 4 ogre 5 ghoul 7 monster 10 apparition
boggle: 4 flub, muff 5 amaze, botch, demur, pause, waver 6 bungle, falter, foul up, fumble, goof up, mess up, wonder 7 astound, confuse, louse up, mystify, nonplus, perplex, screw up, stagger, stupefy 8 astonish, bewilder, bowl over, hang back, hesitate 9 dumbfound, overwhelm
Boggle: 8 word game
boggler: 2 ox 3 oaf 4 lout 6 enigma
__-boggling: 4 mind
Bogg, Phineas time travel device: 4 Omni
Boggs, Wade sport: 8 baseball
bogie: 5 ghost, shade 9 hobgoblin
Bogie costar: 6 Bacall
Bogor: 4 city, town
locale: 9 Indonesia
Bogosian: 4 Eric
Bogotá: 4 city, town
city near ~: 4 Cali
locale: 8 Colombia
see also Spanish
bogus: 4 fake, mock, sham 5 false, phony, put-on 6 ersatz, forged, phoney, pseudo, unreal 7 assumed, feigned 8 spurious 9 imitation, pretended, simulated, synthetic 10 artificial, fabricated, factitious, fictitious, fraudulent
not ~: 4 real 5 legit 7 genuine
bogyman
see bogeyman
Bohai: 4 gulf
locale: 5 China
sea: 6 Yellow
Bohay: 5 Heidi
bohea: 3 tea 8 black tea
bohemian: 4 arty 5 artsy, gypsy, hippy 6 hippie 7 beatnik, offbeat, raffish 8 left-bank 10 free spirit, iconoclast, unorthodox
Bohemian: 5 Czech
city: 5 Plzen
dance: 5 polka
saint: 10 Wenceslaus
Bohemian Girl, The (1936 film)
cast: Oliver Hardy, Stan Laurel, Thelma Todd
Bohemian Rhapsody (1976 song)
artist: Queen
Böhm, Karl: 9 conductor
Bohr: 4 Aage 5 Niels
Bohr, Aage: 6 Danish 8 Nobelist 9 physicist
Bohrer: 7 Corinne
Bohr, Niels: 6 Danish 8 Nobelist 9 physicist
concern: 4 atom
Boiardo, Matteo: 4 poet 7 Italian
boil: 4 brew, burn, cook, fume, heat, rage, rave, stew 5 anger, flare, froth, poach, steam, steep, storm, swirl 6 blow up, bubble, coddle, decoct, fire up, see red, seethe, simmer 7 bristle, flare up, smolder, swelter 8 smoulder 9 evaporate, fulminate
almost ~: 5 scald 6 simmer
down: 4 trim 6 decoct, digest 7 abridge, distill, shorten 8 compress, condense, simplify 9 capsulize, summarize, synopsize, telescope 10 abbreviate
in oil: 3 fry 5 sauté 7 deep-fry
make one's blood ~: 3 irk, vex 4 rile 5 anger, peeve, upset 6 offend
over: 4 rage, rant, rave 5 erupt 8 have a fit
Boileau, Nicholas: 4 poet 6 French
boiled: 10 a l'anglaise
combining form: 5 cocto-
down: 5 brief, short, terse 6 gnomic 7 compact, concise, refined 8 succinct
boiled __: 3 oil 5 shirt, sweet 6 dinner
__-boiled: 4 hard, soft
boiler: 3 pan 6 kettle 7 caldron, furnace 8 cauldron, saucepan
ender: 5 maker, plate
starter: 3 pot
tend the ~: 5 stoke
boiler __: 4 room, suit 5 plate
__ boiler: 5 steam 6 double
boilermaker
component: 4 beer 6 chaser, whisky 7 whiskey
Boilermakers: 6 Purdue
boilerplate: 8 standard
Boiler Room, The (2000 film)
cast: Ben Affleck, Vin Diesel, Nia Long
boil-in-__: 3 bag
boiling: 3 hot, mad 4 ired 5 angry, fiery, livid, wroth 6 asteam, red-hot, steamy, sultry, toasty, torrid 7 enraged, furious, summery 8 ovenlike, tropical, white-hot 9 indignant
at the ~ point: 3 hot 5 angry 6 raging 7 furious, steamed 8 bubbling, scalding 9 simmering 10 infuriated
boiling __: 5 point
bois __: 4 d'arc 5 brûlé
Boisbriand: 4 city, town
locale: 6 Canada, Québec
Bois de Boulogne: 4 parc
Bois de Boulogne artist: 4 Dufy
Boise: 4 city, town
athletes: 7 Broncos
conference: 3 WAC
county: 3 Ada
locale: 5 Idaho
school: 3 BSU
Boise __: 7 Cascade
__ Boise: 4 Fort
boisterous: 4 loud, wild 5 aroar, forte, noisy, rowdy 6 bouncy, hectic, hoiden, hoyden, robust, unruly 7 blaring, booming, jarring, lowbred, pealing, rackety, rampant, raucous, reboant, riotous, roaring 8 brawling, crashing, piercing, plangent, rumbling, sonorous, strident, turned up 9 big-voiced, clamorous, deafening, impetuous, turbulent 10 disorderly, in an uproar, resounding, rollicking, stentorian, strepitous, thundering, tumultuous, uproarious, vociferant, vociferous
boisterousness: 5 noise 8 hilarity
Boitano, Brian: 6 skater
boîte: 4 café 7 cabaret 9 nightclub, night spot
boîte de __: 4 nuit
Boito opera: 4 Nero
Bojer, Johan: 6 writer 9 Norwegian
bok __: 4 choy
Bok: 5 Derek
bok choy: 6 veggie 7 cabbage 9 vegetable
Bokhara __: 3 rug 6 clover
Bol.
see Bolivia
__-Bol: 3 Ty-D
bola alternative: 5 lasso, reata, riata 6 lariat
Boland: 4 Mary 5 Eavan
Boland, Eavan: 4 poet 5 Irish
Bolcom, William: 7 pianist
bold: 4 game, pert, rude 5 brash, brave, fresh, gutsy, manly, nervy, pushy, risky, sassy, saucy, showy, smart, stout, vivid 6 active, awless, brassy, brazen, cheeky, daring, flashy, gritty, heroic, hoiden, hoyden, jaunty, plucky, spunky, strong, virile 7 assured, aweless, dashing, defiant, doughty, forward, gallant, impavid, staunch, uncivil, valiant, visible 8 assuming, fearless, forceful, heroical, immodest, impudent, insolent, intrepid, manifest, resolute, spirited, stalwart, unafraid, valorous 9 ambitious, audacious, barefaced, confident, daredevil, dauntless, desperate, dreadless, foolhardy, outspoken, presuming, shameless, undaunted, unfearful, unfearing 10 chivalrous, courageous, forthright, incautious, mettlesome, pronounced, undismayed, ungracious, unreserved
be ~: 4 dare 7 venture 8 confront 9 challenge
be so ~: 7 presume, venture
ender: 4 face 5 faced
look: 4 leer
not ~: 3 shy 5 timid 7 bashful
woman: 4 vamp 5 hussy, siren 9 temptress
bold-__: 5 faced
Bold: 9 detergent
competitor: 3 All, Biz, Era, Fab, Yes 4 Dash, Gain, Surf, Tide, Wisk 5 Cheer, Dreft, Purex 6 Calgon, Dynamo, Oxydol 7 Octagon 9 Ivory Snow
Bold and the Beautiful, The (CBS): 4 soap 9 soap opera
Bold and the Brave, The (1956 film)
cast: Wendell Corey, Mickey Rooney
bold counsel, name meaning: 6 Conrad
boldface alternative: 4 Ital. 6 Italic
bold-faced: 6 brazen 8 impudent
boldness: 4 face, gall, guts, sass 5 cheek, heart, nerve, pluck, sauce, valor 6 daring, mettle, spirit, starch 7 bravery, courage, heroism, license, prowess 8 audacity, defiance, temerity 9 assurance, fortitude, gallantry, hardiness, impudence, insolence 10 confidence, effrontery, enterprise, knighthood
boldo: 4 tree 9 evergreen
bold peace, name meaning: 9 Ferdinand
bold people, name meaning: 7 Leopold
bole: 3 log 4 clay 5 trunk 7 reddish 8 brownish 9 tree trunk
color kin: 3 bay, dun, tan 4 ecru, fawn, foxy, nude, seal 5 amber, beige, camel, cocoa, hazel, khaki, mocha, sepia, tawny, umber 6 auburn, bister, bistre, bronze, coffee, copper, ginger, russet, sienna, sorrel, suntan, walnut 7 biscuit, caramel, dogwood 8 chestnut, cinnamon, mahogany 9 butternut, chocolate
__ Bolena: 4 Anna
bolero: 4 coat 5 dance, music 6 jacket
Bolero
actress: 5 Derek
composer: 5 Ravel
instrument in ~: 4 oboe
Boles, John: 5 actor 6 singer
film: Back Street (1932)
Craig's Wife (1936)
The King of Jazz (1930)
The Littlest Rebel (1935)
The Loves of Sunya (1927)
A Message to Garcia (1936)
Music in the Air (1934)
Only Yesterday (1933)
Stella Dallas (1937)
boletus: 6 fungus
Boleyn, Anne: 5 queen 7 British
Bolger, Ray: 5 actor 6 dancer
costar: 4 Lahr 5 Haley 7 Garland
film: The Daydreamer (1966)
The Harvey Girls (1946)
Where's Charley? (1952)
The Wizard of Oz (1939)
bolide: 6 meteor 8 fireball
Bolingbrook: 4 city, town
locale: 8 Illinois
bolivar: 5 money
Bolívar, Simón: 9 liberator, statesman 10 Venezuelan
birthplace: 7 Caracas
Bolivia: 6 nation 7 country
beast: 5 llama 6 alpaca
capital: 5 La Paz, Sucre
city: 5 Oruro 6 El Alto, Potosí, Tarija 9 Santa Cruz 10 Cochabamba
export: 3 tin
Indian: 4 Moxo 6 Aymara 7 Quechua
lake: 8 Titicaca

language: 6 Aymara 7 Quechua, Spanish
mining town: 5 Oruro
money: 4 peso 7 bolivar 9 boliviano
mountain: 6 Sajama 7 Illampu 8 Ancohuma, Illimani 9 Condoriri 10 Parinacota
neighbor: 4 Peru 5 Chile 6 Brazil 8 Paraguay 9 Argentina
org.: 3 OAS
range: 5 Andes
river: 4 Beni
tanager: 4 yeni
see also Spanish

boll: 3 pod 7 seed pod
cleaner: 3 gin
boll ___: 6 weevil
bollard: 4 post 5 kevel
Böll, Heinrich: 6 German, writer 8 Nobelist
Bolling: 7 Tiffany
bollix: 4 foil 5 botch, snafu 6 bungle, foul up, fumble, mess up 7 disrupt
bollixed: 7 puzzled, stumped
Boll Weevil Song, The (1961 song)
artist: Brook Benton
Bol, Manute: 5 cager
milieu: 5 court
org.: 3 NBA
sport: 10 basketball
bolo: 3 tie 5 knife 8 neckwear 9 string tie
kin: 7 machete
bolo ___: 3 tie 5 knife
bologna: 4 meat 7 sausage
unit: 5 slice
Bologna: 4 city, town 6 Joseph
locale: 5 Italy 6 Italia
Bologna, Joseph: 5 actor
film: Blame It on Rio (1984)
Cops and Robbers (1973)
Made for Each Other (1971)
My Favorite Year (1982)
spouse: Renee Taylor
bolon: 4 harp 6 string
origin: 6 Africa
Bolshevik: 3 Red 9 Communist
leader: 5 Lenin
victim: 4 czar, tsar
Bolshevism: 9 Communism, socialism
Bolshevist: 7 leftist
Bolshoi ___: 6 Ballet
rival: 5 Kirov
bolster: 3 aid, pad 4 abut, buoy, feed, gird, help, hold, prop, tone 5 boost, brace, build, shore, steel 6 anneal, assist, batten, bear up, beef up, buck up, expand, harden, hold up, prop up, temper, tone up, uphold 7 brace up, build up, bulwark, burgeon, develop, empower, enhance, fortify, promote, shore up, stiffen, support, sustain, toughen 8 advocate, bourgeon, buttress, energize, indurate, reassure, vitalize 9 cultivate, encourage, intensify, reinforce 10 invigorate, rally round, strengthen
bolt: 3 bar, dam, eat, fly, rod, run 4 clog, cork, dart, dash, flee, gulp, lock, plug, race, rush, seal, shut, skip, stud, T-bar, tear, wolf 5 arrow, block, close, dam up, elope, flash, gorge, latch, rivet, scoot, shoot, split, start 6 clog up, cut out, decamp, desert, devour, escape, fasten, gallop, gobble, guzzle, hasten, hurtle, inhale, lock up, plug up, run off, seal up, secure, spring, stop up 7 abscond, bail out, closure, consume, dart off, dash off, engorge, go south, javelin, make off, missile, run away, scamper, seal off, shutter, startle, swallow, take off 8 blockade, button up, fastener, fugitate, gulp down, hightail, material, obstruct, run for it, step on it, turn tail, wolf down 9 go swiftly, hotfoot it, lightning, scarf down, skedaddle, stabilize 10 burn rubber, hightail it, make tracks, projectile, take flight
contents: 5 cloth 6 fabric 8 material
cover: 6 cap nut
down: 3 eat 4 wolf 5 rivet
ender: 4 hole, rope
holder: 3 lug, nut 4 T-nut
lightning ~: 5 flash
location: 6 breech
part: 4 yard 5 shank
starter: 3 eye 4 dead, king, ring 7 thunder
upright: 5 rigid 8 vertical
___ bolt: 3 bed, box, fox, lag, rag, rod, tap 4 barb, dead, deck, hook, lift, rock, stud, wing 5 lewis, night, panic, stove, tower 6 anchor, barrel, bottom, toggle 7 cremone, machine
Bolt: 5 Tommy 6 Robert
Bolt author: Dick Francis
bolted: 4 firm, shut 5 tight
bolt from the ___: 4 blue
bolti: 4 fish
Bolton: 4 city, town 7 Michael
locale: 7 England
boltonia: 5 plant 6 flower
Bolton, Michael
real last name: Bolotin
song: How Am I Supposed to Live Without You (1989)
How Can We Be Lovers (1990)
Love Is a Wonderful Thing (1991)
Said I Loved You...But I Lied (1994)
Time, Love and Tenderness (1991)
When a Man Loves a Woman (1991)
When I'm Back on My Feet Again (1990)
Bolt, Robert: 7 British 10 playwright
bolts
bucket of ~: 3 car 4 auto, heap 5 crate, lemon 6 jalopy
nuts and ~: 3 nub 4 knub, pith 6 detail 7 reality
bolus: 4 pill
___-bolus: 5 holus
Boma: 4 city, town
locale: 5 Congo
bomb: 3 dud 4 ammo, bust, fail, flop, lose, loss, mine, rase, raze, slip, trip 5 blast, flunk, shell, speed 6 attack, blow it, blow up, defeat, falter, fiasco, mishap, rocket, turkey 7 blunder, debacle, failure, fizzler, founder, go under, go wrong, grenade, lose out, missile, misstep, stumble, torpedo, wash out, wipe out 8 backfire, downfall, fall flat, flounder, lay an egg, munition 9 explosive, strike out 10 ammunition, nonsuccess
A ~: 6 Fat Man 9 Little Boy
defective ~: 3 dud
do ~ squad work: 6 defuse, defuze
ender: 5 proof, shell, sight
sound: 5 blast 6 kaboom 9 explosion
starter: 4 fire
trial: 10 N-test A-test
bomb ___: 3 bay, run 4 rack 5 ketch, lance, squad 7 shelter
___ bomb: 4 atom, buzz, tear, time 5 depth, dirty, robot, smart, smoke, stink, water 6 atomic, cherry, flying, fusion, rocket, stench 7 aerosol, cluster, fission
___-bomb: 4 dive
Bombal, Maria: 6 author, writer 7 Chilean
bombard: 3 zap 4 pelt 5 beset, blast, blitz, hound, shell, shoot, storm, throw 6 assail, attack, batter, harass, launch, pester, strike 7 assault, barrage, besiege, rip into 8 fire upon, open fire 9 cannonade, haul off on
in Britain: 5 prang
Bombardier (1943 film)
cast: Pat O'Brien, Randolph Scott
bombardment: 4 fire 5 blitz, burst 6 volley 7 barrage 9 broadside, cannonade
bombast: 3 gas 4 rant, talk 6 hot air, speech 7 bluster, bravado, padding 8 claptrap, nonsense, rhetoric 9 gasconade, pomposity 10 empty words, pretension, vocalizing
bombastic: 4 long 5 gabby, gassy, tumid, windy, wordy 6 prolix 7 diffuse, fustian, hyped up, lengthy, orotund, pompous, ranting, stilted, unterse, verbose, voluble 8 boastful, inflated, rambling 9 garrulous, grandiose, high-flown, overblown, redundant, rhapsodic, talkative 10 big-talking, discursive, euphuistic, flamboyant, histrionic, long-winded, loquacious, palaverous, rhetorical
bombax: 4 tree 6 baobab, durian
Bombay: 3 cat 4 city, port, town 5 felid 6 feline
city near ~: 4 Puna 5 Poona, Thana 6 Indore
locale: 5 India
Bombay ___: 4 duck, hemp
bombazine: 6 fabric 8 material
bombe: 7 dessert
alternative: 6 frappe, sundae 10 peach Melba
ingredient: 8 ice cream
Bombeck, Erma: 3 wit 6 author 8 humorist
bomber: 4 coat 5 plane 6 jacket 8 airplane, warplane
crew: 6 airmen
dive ~ descent: 5 swoop
org.: 3 SAC
WWII ~: 5 Stuka 8 Bock's Car, Enola Gay
bomber ___: 6 jacket
___ bomber: 4 dive 5 heavy, light 6 medium
___-bomber: 7 fighter
bombinate: 3 hum
...bombs bursting ___: 5 in air
bombshell: 4 blow, jolt 5 shock 8 surprise 9 sensation 10 revelation
___ bombshell: 6 blonde
Bombshell (1933 film)
cast: Jean Harlow, Frank Morgan, Lee Tracy
director: Victor Fleming
bomb squad
do ~ work: 6 defuse, disarm
worker: 5 robot
bombycid: 4 moth
___ b'Omer: 3 Lag
Bomu: 5 river
locale: 5 Congo
source: 4 Uele
bon ___: 3 ami, mot, ton 4 soir 6 marché, vivant, voyage 7 appétit
Bon ___: 3 Ami 4 Jovi
Bona: 4 peak 5 mount 8 mountain
locale: 6 Alaska
Bona ___: 3 Dea
bonaci: 4 fish
Bonaduce: 5 Danny
bona fide: 4 good, just, real, safe, true 5 legit, right, solid, valid 6 actual, honest, kasher, kosher, lawful 7 genuine, literal, regular, sincere 8 official, rightful, verified 9 authentic, heartfelt, veritable
Bon Ami: 8 cleanser
alternative: 4 Ajax, Bab-O 5 Comet 9 Soft Scrub
bonanza: 3 ore 4 lode, mine, vein 7 cash cow 8 gold mine, windfall
Bonanza (NBC western)
cast: Dan Blocker (Hoss Cartwright)
David Canary (Candy)
Lorne Greene (Ben Cartwright)
Michael Landon (Little Joe Cartwright)
Pernell Roberts (Adam Cartwright)
Victor Sen Yung (Hop Sing)
setting: 5 ranch 6 Nevada 9 Ponderosa
Bonaparte: 8 Napoleon
fate: 5 exile
island: 4 Elba 8 St. Helena
symphony first called ~: 6 Eroica
Bonar: 3 Law
Bonaventure: 5 saint
St. ~ locale: 5 Olean 7 New York
bonbon: 5 candy, sweet 6 nougat 7 dessert, fondant 9 chocolate, sweetmeat 10 confection
Bon-Bon author: Edgar Allan Poe
bond: 3 fix, gum, tie, wed 4 bail, bind, fuse, gage, glue, link, lock, pact, pawn, rope, tape, weld, yoke 5 asset, chain, marry, paper, paste, stick, union, unite 6 adhere, cement, fasten, fetter, hookup, pledge, treaty 7 combine, compact, connect, loyalty, manacle, network, promise, rapport, shackle, stickum 8 alliance, contract, covenant, fastener, fixative, handcuff, junction, juncture, ligature, marriage, relation, security, vinculum, warranty 9 agreement, debenture, guarantee, indenture 10 attachment, collateral, connection, friendship, obligation
alternative: 5 stock
attachment: 6 coupon
combining form: 4 desm- 5 desmo-
emotional ~: 3 tie 4 love 9 affection
ender: 3 age, man, men 4 maid 5 woman, women 6 holder 7 servant
kind of ~: 3 deb. 4 Euro, muni 5 no par 9 debenture, municipal
rating: 3 AAA, BAA, BBB, CCC
return: 5 yield
short-term ~: 3 deb. 9 debenture
___ bond: 4 baby, bail, clip, flat, gold, junk, muni, pair 5 Dutch, ionic, strip 6 bearer, common, coupon, dative, double, flying, header, income, raking, single, triple, Yankee 7 assumed, English, Flemish, Liberty, payment, peptide, revenue, running, savings
Bond: 4 Ward 5 James 6 Julian
bondage: 4 yoke 6 chains 7 fetters, slavery 8 trammels 9 captivity, restraint, servitude 10 internment
place into ~: 6 enserf 7 capture, enslave
bonded ___: 6 whisky 7 whiskey
Bondi, Beulah: 7 actress
film: Back to Bataan (1945)
It's a Wonderful Life (1946)
Make Way for Tomorrow (1937)
On Borrowed Time (1939)
One Foot in Heaven (1941)
Penny Serenade (1941)
Remember the Night (1940)
So Dear to My Heart (1949)
The Southerner (1945)
___ bonding: 4 male, pair
bonding agent: 4 glue 5 epoxy
bond-issuing org.: 4 GNMA
Bond, James: 3 spy 4 hero 5 agent 7 British
portrayer: 5 Moore 6 Dalton 7 Brosnan, Connery, Lazenby
school: 4 Eton
bondman: 5 helot
bonds: 5 irons 6 chains 7 fetters 8 shackles, trammels 9 servitude
buy ~: 6 invest

how some ~ sell: 5 at par
like some ~: 5 risky
seller: 6 broker
stocks and ~: 6 assets, wealth
Bonds: 5 Barry, Bobby
Bonds, Barry sport: 8 baseball
bondservant: 4 serf 5 slave 6 thrall 7 chattel
bond-service employee: 5 rater
Bonds, Gary U.S.
song: Dear Lady Twist (1962)
New Orleans (1960)
Quarter to Three (1961)
School Is Out (1961)
Twist, Twist Senora (1962)
bondsman, ancient: 4 esne, serf 5 helot
___ Bonds Today?: 3 Any
bonduc: 4 tree
Bond, Ward: 5 actor
film: The Bob Mathias Story (1954)
Fort Apache (1948)
Hondo (1953)
The Maltese Falcon (1941)
On Dangerous Ground (1952)
Operation Pacific (1951)
Tall in the Saddle (1944)
TV: Wagon Train
Bondy: 4 city, town
locale: 6 France
bone: 3 jaw, rib 4 coxa, ulna 5 china, femur, filet, hyoid, ilium, incus, inion, jugal, malar, skull, talus, tibia, vomer, white 6 carpal, carpus, coccyx, concha, cuboid, fibula, fillet, hammer, pelvis, radius, sacrum, stapes, tarsal, tarsus, zygoma 7 carpale, cranium, ethmoid, humerus, ischium, malleus, maxilla, patella, phalanx, scapula, sternum, stirrup 8 clavicle, cuboidal, glabella, mandible, off-white, palatine, parietal, skeleton, sphenoid, vertebra 9 braincase, occipital, olecranon, trapezium, trapezoid, yellowish, zygomatic 10 astragalus, metacarpus, metatarsus, premaxilla
ankle ~: 5 talus 6 tarsus 10 astragalus, metatarsus
arm ~: 4 ulna 6 radius 7 humerus 9 olecranon
breast ~: 7 sternum
cavity: 5 fossa 6 antrum
cheek ~: 5 jugal, malar
color kin: 4 milk, snow 5 cream, ivory, milky 6 argent, oyster, silver 8 eggshell
combining form: 3 -ost 4 ossi-, oste- 5 osteo-
cranial ~: 5 vomer 6 zygoma 7 ethmoid 8 parietal, sphenoid 9 zygomatic
depression: 5 fovea
dinosaur ~: 6 fossil
ear ~: 5 incus 6 hammer, stapes 7 malleus, stirrup
ender: 3 set 4 fish, head 5 black
facial ~: 8 glabella
fide: 5 legit 6 lawful 7 genuine
fish: 5 filet
foot ~: 5 talus 6 cuboid, tarsal, tarsus 8 cuboidal
forearm ~: 4 ulna 6 radius 9 olecranon
head ~: 3 jaw 7 maxilla 8 mandible
hip ~: 5 ilium 6 pelvis
horn-shaped ~: 5 cornu
innominate ~: 4 coxa
jaw ~: 7 maxilla 8 mandible 10 premaxilla
knee ~: 7 patella
leg ~: 4 shin 5 femur, tibia 6 fibula
longest ~: 5 femur
middle-ear ~: 5 anvil, incus
mouth ~: 8 palatine
nasal ~: 5 vomer 6 concha 7 ethmoid
of contention: 5 issue 8 argument
of the hip ~: 5 iliac
opening: 6 meatus
pelvic ~: 4 coxa 7 ischium
postaxial ~: 4 ulna
shoulder ~: 7 scapula 8 clavicle
skull ~: 5 vomer 6 zygoma 7 cranium, ethmoid 8 parietal, sphenoid 9 braincase, occipital, zygomatic
spinal ~: 6 coccyx
starter: 3 hip, jaw 4 back, ring, shin, tail, wish 5 aitch, ankle, cheek, thigh, whale 6 breast, collar, marrow 7 feather, herring, knuckle
structure: 8 skeleton
tongue ~: 5 hyoid
to pick: 4 feud, spat, tiff 5 gripe 7 dispute, quarrel 8 argument, conflict, squabble 9 exception 10 contention, difference
turn to ~: 6 ossify
up on: 4 cram, read 5 study 6 master
vertebral ~: 3 rib 6 sacrum
work one's fingers to the ~: 4 toil 5 slave 6 drudge
wrist ~: 6 carpal, carpus, hamate 7 carpale 9 trapezium 10 metacarpus
zygomatic ~: 5 malar
bone ___: 3 ash, oil 4 cell, meal, up on 5 black, china, felon 6 marrow, shaker
bone-___: 3 dry
___ bone: 4 heel, keel, long 5 crazy, funny, jugal, malar 6 cannon, coffin, fetter, haunch, pulley, splint 7 frontal, mastoid, stirrup
...bone, ___ of hair: 5 a hank
___-Bone: 4 Milk
Bone Collector, The (1999 film)
cast: Angelina Jolie, Queen Latifah, Michael Rooker, Denzel Washington
director: Phillip Noyce
Bonecrack author: Dick Francis
___-boned: 3 big, raw
bone-dry: 4 arid, sere 7 thirsty 9 juiceless
bonehead: 3 ass, nit, oaf, sap 4 boob, clod, dolt, fool 5 chump, clown, cluck, dummy, dunce, idiot, joker, klutz, ninny, patsy, silly 6 dimwit, lummox, nitwit, sucker, turkey 7 buffoon, bungler, dingbat, dullard, half-wit, jackass 8 dumbbell, numskull 9 birdbrain, harebrain, lamebrain, numbskull, simpleton 10 nincompoop
boneheaded: 5 silly, thick 7 fatuous 9 half-baked 10 weak-minded
boneless cut: 5 filet
boner: 4 flub, goof, muff 5 error, gaffe, snafu 6 boo-boo, bungle, foulup, miscue, muddle, slipup 7 blooper, blunder, faux pas, misstep, mistake 8 dumb move 9 false move, indecorum
Boner's Ark dog: 4 Spot
Bonerz, Peter: 5 actor
film: Funnyman (1967)
Medium Cool (1969)
TV: The Bob Newhart Show
bones: 4 dice 6 doctor 8 skeleton 9 physician
ankle ~: 4 tali 5 tarsi
arm ~: 5 radii
back ~: 5 sacra
bare ~: 9 framework
foot ~: 4 tali 5 tarsi
in Latin: 4 ossa
leg ~: 6 femora
pelvic ~: 4 ilia 5 sacra
remove ~: 5 filet 6 fillet
skin and ~: 4 lean, thin 5 rangy, spare 9 emaciated
starter: 3 saw 4 lazy 5 cross
___ bones: 4 bare 6 oracle 7 Napier's
___ Bones: 4 Brom, Lazy 5 Bag of, Echo's
Bones, Brom prey: 5 Crane
Bonesetter's Daughter, The author: Amy Tan
Bonete: 4 peak 5 mount 8 mountain
locale: 9 Argentina
bone-tired: 5 all in, weary, wiped 6 bushed 7 drained 9 exhausted 10 knocked out
Bonet, Lisa: 7 actress
film: Enemy of the State (1998)
spouse: Lenny Kravitz
TV: A Different World, The Cosby Show
bone to ___: 4 pick
bonfire: 5 blaze
fuel: 4 wood 6 sticks
residue: 3 ash 4 coal 5 ember 6 cinder
started a ~: 3 lit
Bonfire of the Vanities, The: 4 film 5 novel
author: Tom Wolfe
cast: Kim Cattrall, Morgan Freeman, Melanie Griffith, Tom Hanks, Bruce Willis
director: Brian De Palma
bong: 4 peal, ring, toll 5 chime
bongo: 4 drum 8 antelope
relative: 3 gnu, kob 4 guib, kudu, oryx, puku, topi 5 addax, chiru, conga, eland, goral, korin, nyala, oribi, saiga, serow 6 chammy, dikdik, duiker, impala, koodoo, lechwe, nilgai, rhebok, shammy, shamoy 7 blaubok, blesbok, chamois, defassa, gazelle, gemsbok, gerenuk, grysbok, nylghai, nylghau, sassaby 8 blesbuck, bontebok, bushbuck, gemsbuck, reedbuck, steenbok, steinbok 9 blackbuck, pronghorn, sitatunga, springbok, waterbuck 10 hartebeest, wildebeest
Bonham Carter, Helena: 7 actress
film: Getting It Right (1989)
Hamlet (1990)
Howards End (1992)
Lady Jane (1985)
Mighty Aphrodite (1995)
Novocaine (2001)
Planet of the Apes (2001)
A Room With a View (1986)
Bonheur, Rosa: 6 artist 7 painter
homeland: 6 France
Bonhoeffer, Dietrich: 6 German 11 philosopher
Bonhomme ___: 7 Richard
boniface: 9 innkeeper
place: 3 inn
Boniface: 4 pope 5 saint 7 pontiff
Bonilla: 5 Bobby
Bonin ___: 7 Islands
boning ___: 5 knife
Bonita: 9 Granville
Bonita Springs: 4 city, town
locale: 7 Florida
bonito: 4 fish, tuna
bon jour: 5 hello 7 welcome
Bonjour Tristesse: 4 film 5 novel
author: Françoise Sagan
cast: Deborah Kerr, David Niven, Jean Seberg
director: Otto Preminger
Bon Jovi: 3 Jon
members: Bon Jovi, Sambora
song: Always (1994)
Bad Medicine (1988)
Bed of Roses (1993)
Blaze of Glory (1990)
Born to Be My Baby (1988)
I'll Be There for You (1989)
Lay Your Hands on Me (1989)
Living in Sin (1989)
Livin' on a Prayer (1987)
Wanted Dead or Alive (1987)
You Give Love a Bad Name (1986)
bonk: 6 strike
bonkers: 4 bats, daft, gaga, loco 5 batty, dotty, kooky, nutty 6 kookie 7 bananas, flipped, haywire, touched 10 over the top
drive ~: 3 irk 5 annoy 6 bother, pester 8 irritate
go ~: 5 crack, freak 6 lose it
bon mot: 4 jest, joke, quip 6 remark 7 epigram 8 repartee, wordplay 9 witticism 10 pleasantry
Bonn: 4 city, town
city near ~: 5 Essen
locale: 7 Germany
river: 5 Rhine
bonnang: 6 chimes 10 percussion
origin: 4 Java
bonne: 4 maid
amie: 2 jo 3 pet 4 baby, dear, jill, love 5 amour, angel, cooky, cutey, cutie, deary, ducky, flame, honey, leman, lover, lovey, novia, sugar, sweet 6 chérie, cookie, dautie, dearie, steady, sweets 7 beloved, dearest, dear one, pigsney, schatzi, squeeze, sweetie, tootsie 8 chouchou, cutie pie, dowsabel, dulcinea, ladylove, lovebird, macushla, paramour, precious, snookums, sugar pie, sweetums, truelove 9 dreamboat, inamorata, petit chou, valentine 10 girlfriend, heartthrob, honeybunch, mavourneen, sweetheart, sweetie pie, turtledove
bonne ___: 3 foi 4 amie, idée, nuit 5 femme 6 bouche, chance
Bonne ___!: 4 nuit 6 chance
bonne chance: 8 good luck
___ bonne heure: 3 à la
Bonner: 5 Elena, Frank 6 Junior
bonnet: 3 hat, lid 4 poke 8 covering 9 headdress
Brit's ~: 4 hood
bug: 3 bee
Easter ~: 6 finery
holder: 6 hatbox
starter: 3 sun 4 blue
bonnet ___: 3 top 5 glass, rouge, shark 6 monkey 7 macaque
___ bonnet: 3 war 4 poke 6 Easter
Bonneville: 3 car, dam 4 auto 7 Pontiac
Bonneville Salt Flats site: 4 Utah
bonnie: 4 cute, fair 6 comely, dainty, pretty 7 winsome 9 appealing 10 attractive
girl: 4 lass
Bonnie: 4 Hunt 5 Blair, Raitt, Tyler 6 Guitar, Parker 7 Bedelia 8 Bartlett, Franklin
Bonnie and Clyde (1967 film)
cast: Warren Beatty, Faye Dunaway, Gene Hackman, Estelle Parsons, Michael J. Pollard
director: Arthur Penn
Bonnies
where the ~ play: 3 SBU
bonny: 4 cute, fair 6 comely, dainty, pretty 7 winsome 10 attractive
one: 4 lass
___ bono: 3 cui, pro
Bono: 5 Sonny 8 Chastity
Bono, Chastity mom: 4 Cher
Bonoff: 5 Karla
Bono, Sonny spouse: Cher
___ bono work: 3 pro
bonsai: 3 art 4 tree 5 dwarf, plant 9 miniature
locale: 5 Japan

Bonsmara: 3 cow 4 bull 6 bovine, cattle
__ Bont: 5 Jan De
bontebok: 8 antelope
relative: 3 gnu, kob 4 guib, kudu, oryx, puku, topi 5 addax, bongo, chiru, eland, goral, korin, nyala, oribi, saiga, serow 6 chammy, dik-dik, duiker, impala, koodoo, lechwe, nilgai, rhebok, shammy, shamoy 7 blaubok, blesbok, chamois, defassa, gazelle, gemsbok, gerenuk, grysbok, nylghai, nylghau, sassaby 8 blesbuck, bushbuck, gemsbuck, reedbuck, steenbok, steinbok 9 blackbuck, pronghorn, sitatunga, springbok, waterbuck 10 hartebeest, wildebeest
Bontemps, Arna: 6 writer
bonus: 3 tip 4 gift, perc, perk, plum, plus 5 award, extra, goody, gravy 6 bounty, goodie, rebate, reward 7 premium, subsidy 8 addition, dividend, gratuity, largesse 9 lagniappe 10 percentage
buyer's ~: 6 coupon, rebate
concert ~: 6 encore
Cracker Jack ~: 5 prize
Bonus __: 4 Army 7 Eventus
bon vivant: 7 epicure, gourmet 8 hedonist, sybarite 9 epicurean 10 voluptuary
quality: 6 esprit
Bon Voyage, Charlie Brown (1980 film) director: Bill Melendez
bon voyage site: 4 deck, dock, pier, ship 5 berth, liner, wharf 7 steamer 10 cruise ship, waterfront
bonxie: 4 bird, skua
bony: 4 lank, lean, thin 5 gaunt, lanky, spare 6 ill-fed, knobby, meager, osteal, skinny 7 osseous, scrawny 8 indurate 9 emaciated 10 unfilleted
structure: 3 jaw 8 skeleton
bonze: 4 monk
bonzer: 3 def, rad 4 aces, A-one, boss, braw, cool, dece, fine, gear, keen, neat, nice, phat, tuff 5 dandy, ducky, grand, great, marvy, neato, nobby, prime, slick, super, swell 6 bang on, bang-up, bosker, choice, divine, dreamy, far-out, gnarly, groovy, lovely, peachy, slap-up, spot on, superb, terrif, tiptop, unreal, whizzo, wicked 7 amazing, awesome, capital, corking, perfect, ripping, skookum, stellar, sublime 8 dazzling, especial, eximious, fabulous, five-star, four-star, frabjous, glorious, heavenly, jim-dandy, slam-bang, smashing, splendid, standout, sterling, stickout, superior, terrific, top-level, topnotch, very good, wondrous 9 bodacious, Endsville, excellent, exemplary, exquisite, first-rate, high-grade, hunky-dory, marvelous, sollicker, top-flight, wonderful 10 first-class, hotsy-totsy, jack-a-dandy, out of sight, peachy-keen, phenomenal, remarkable, stupendous, super-duper
Bonzo: 5 chimp 10 chimpanzee
nosh: 6 banana
boo: 4 jeer 5 scoff, scorn, whoop 6 heckle, hiss at 7 catcall 9 raspberry
not saying ~: 5 quiet 6 silent
say ~: 5 scare 8 frighten
Boo __: 3 Hoo
boo and __: 4 hiss
boob: 3 ass, nit, oaf, sap 4 boor, clod, dolt, fool 5 chump, clown, cluck, dummy, dunce, joker, ninny, patsy 6 dimwit, lubber, lummox, nitwit, sucker, turkey 7 buffoon, bumbler, dingbat, dullard, fathead, half-wit, jackass, pinhead, saphead 8 bonehead, dumbbell, meathead, numskull 9 birdbrain, blockhead, lamebrain, numbskull, simpleton 10 dunderhead
like a ~: 5 inept
tube: 2 TV 5 TV set 8 idiot box 10 television
tube, in Britain: 5 telly
boob __: 4 tube
Boo Berry: 6 cereal
competitor: 3 Kix 4 Life, Trix 5 Kashi, Quisp, Total 6 Kaboom, Muesli, Oreo O's, Pablum, Smacks 7 All-Bran, Crispix, Harmony, Hunny B's, Mueslix, Oat Bran, Pokemon 8 Cheerios, Corn Chex, Corn Pops, Fiber One, Rice Chex, Special K, Uncle Sam, Wheaties 9 Alpha Bits, Apple Zaps, Grape Nuts, Honey Comb, Just Right, Wheat Chex 10 Apple Jacks, Bran Flakes, Cap'n Crunch, Cocoa Puffs, Froot Loops, Mini-Wheats, Nutri-Grain, Puffed Rice, Quaker Oats, Smart Start 11 Cocoa Blasts, Cookie Crisp, Golden Crisp, Lucky Charms, Puffed Wheat, Sweet Crunch, Waffle Crisp
boo-boo: 3 cut, err 4 goof, hurt, slip 5 boner, error, gaffe, lapse, wound 6 bruise, injury, scrape, slipup 7 blooper, blunder, faux pas, misstep, mistake, scratch 9 oversight
make a ~: 3 err 4 flub, goof
publishing ~: 4 typo 7 erratum
remover: 6 eraser
Boo-Boo: 4 bear
buddy: 4 Yogi
booby: 3 oaf 4 bird, fool 5 dunce, prize 6 gannet 7 seabird
deserving the ~ prize: 5 worst
trap: 4 mine, ruse, trap 5 snare 7 pitfall 8 obstacle 9 explosive
booby __: 4 trap 5 hatch, prize
boodle: 3 lot, wad 4 mint, pile, swag 5 booty, bribe, bunch, graft, money 7 jobbery 8 kickback
Boog: 6 Powell
boogaloo: 5 dance
boogie: 4 jazz 5 dance 7 get down
Boogie __: 4 Down 5 Board, Fever 6 Nights
Boogie Nights (1997 film)
cast: Heather Graham, Julianne Moore, Burt Reynolds, Mark Wahlberg
director: Paul Thomas Anderson
Boogie On Reggae Woman (1974 song) artist: Stevie Wonder
Boogie Oogie Oogie (1978 song) artist: A Taste of Honey
Boogie Wonderland (1979 song) artist: Earth, Wind & Fire, Emotions
boogie-woogie: 4 jazz 5 music
Boogie Woogie Bugle Boy (song) artist: Andrews Sisters
artist: Bette Midler
boo-hoo: 3 cry, sob 4 bawl, mewl, pule, wail, weep 6 snivel 7 blubber, whimper 9 shed tears
boojum: 4 tree
Boojum: 5 Snark
book: 3 log 4 hire, take, text, tome, work 5 album, atlas, bible, codex, diary, enter, novel, order, print, prose, set up, story 6 accuse, arrest, charge, engage, line up, manual, pick up, primer, reader, record, script, volume 7 account, charter, edition, lexicon, omnibus, procure, program, reserve, romance, speller, writing 8 hardback, libretto, register, schedule, textbook, thriller, whodunit 9 directory, hardcover, narrative, paperback, preengage, softcover, thesaurus 10 arrange for, bestseller, compendium, cyclopedia, dictionary, regulation, roman à clef
absorb a ~: 4 cram, read 5 study 6 peruse
accountant's ~: 6 ledger
art ~ publisher: 6 Abrams
autograph hound's ~: 5 album
bedside ~: 5 diary
bestselling ~: 5 Bible
bilingual ~: 6 diglot
binding: 5 cover, paper 7 leather
blank ~: 5 album
Buddhist sacred ~: 5 sutra 6 tantra
buyer: 6 editor, reader, school 7 library
by the ~: 5 legit, licit, stern 6 kasher, kosher, lawful, proper 7 allowed 8 methodic, orthodox, rightful 9 permitted, stringent 10 authorized, methodical, sanctioned
captain's ~: 3 log
cartographer's ~: 5 atlas
Chinese ~ of divination: 6 I Ching
closed ~: 6 enigma, riddle 7 mystery
combining form: 6 biblio-
corrections: 6 errata
cover: 6 jacket
crack a ~: 4 cram, read 5 study 6 peruse
ender: 3 end, let 4 case, lore, mark, rack, shop, worm 5 louse, maker, plate, shelf, stall, stand, store 6 binder, keeper, making, mobile, seller 7 bindery, binding, keeping
extra: 6 insert
feature: 5 index 6 dog-ear
genre: 4 play 5 drama, how-to, novel, sci-fi 6 horror, poetry 7 fiction, romance 10 non-fiction, short-story
heavy ~: 4 tome
Hindu sacred ~: 4 Gita, Veda
holder: 5 shelf
ID: 4 ISBN
illustration: 5 plate
item in a ~: 5 match
jacket feature: 3 bio 4 ISBN 5 blurb, price, title 6 author, review 7 bar code
large ~ size: 5 folio
like a ~: 6 wholly 8 entirely, from A to Z 10 completely, thoroughly
make ~: 3 bet 4 punt 5 stake, wager 6 gamble 8 give odds, take bets 9 speculate
map ~: 5 atlas
of photos: 5 album
of public records: 5 liber
page: 5 recto, verso
part: 4 flap 5 cover, pages, spine 6 jacket 7 binding
pew ~: 6 hymnal
pocket ~: 9 paperback
reference ~: 3 gaz., OED 4 dict., ency., text, tome 5 atlas, encyc. 6 encycl., manual 9 gazetteer, thesaurus 10 dictionary
repository: 7 library
reviewer: 5 rater 6 critic
sacred ~: 5 Bible, Koran, Quran
scholarly ~: 4 text, tome
school ~: 4 text
section: 4 chap., leaf, page, part 5 part I 6 part II 7 chapter, part III
starter: 3 day, log 4 bank, blue, case, cash, chap, code, cook, copy, flip, hand, horn, hymn, note, over, pass, play, stud, text, word, work, year 5 check, guide, match, scrap, story, style 6 pocket, prompt, school, sketch
throw the ~ at: 6 punish 7 condemn, convict 8 sentence
type of ~ binding: 4 yapp
book __: 3 bag 4 club, gill, list, lore, lung, tile 5 louse, match, share, value 6 jacket, review 7 burning, society
book-__: 4 work 8 learning
__ book: 3 fly 4 baby, bell, blue, code, fake, gill, make, Mass, open, rare, roll 5 audio, black, blank, comic, dream, funny, how-to, like a, phone, stock, trade, white 6 church, closed, phrase, pocket, prayer, sealed, sketch, source 7 account, cookery, picture, service, statute, talking, tell-all
__ Book: 4 Good 6 Jungle
__, Book and Candle: 4 Bell
bookbinder
material: 4 glue, roan 5 cloth 7 buckram, leather
bookcase: 9 furniture
part: 5 shelf
place: 4 wall 5 study 6 alcove
__ Book Club: 6 Oprah's
__ Book Confidential: 5 Comic
Booke: 7 Sorrell
booked: 7 engaged 8 reserved
Book 'em, __!: 4 Dano 5 Danno
Booker T. __: 10 Washington
Booker T. and the MGs
song: Green Onions (1962)
Hang 'Em High (1968)
Time Is Tight (1969)
bookie
alternative: 3 OTB
concern: 3 bet
protection: 5 hedge
quote: 4 odds
booking: 3 gig, job 5 order 10 engagement
booking __: 5 agent, clerk 6 office
bookish: 3 dry 5 fussy, stiff 6 brainy, formal, stuffy 7 donnish, erudite, learned, precise, stilted 8 academic, cerebral, highbrow, literary, longhair, pedantic, studious 9 pedagogic, scholarly 10 fastidious, pedantical, scholastic
type: 4 nerd, nurd 7 egghead
bookkeeper: 3 CPA 4 acct. 5 clerk 7 auditor 8 recorder 9 registrar 10 accountant, controller
abbreviation: 3 ROA
book: 6 ledger 7 journal
term: 3 net 5 asset, debit 6 credit, income, profit 7 expense 9 liability
booklet: 5 tract 8 brochure, pamphlet
book-lined room: 3 den 5 study 7 library
Bookman: 4 font 8 typeface
bookmark: 3 tab 6 dog-ear
bookmarked item: 3 URL
Book of __: 4 Odes 5 Books, Hours, Kells 6 Mormon 7 Changes
Book of __ Prayer: 6 Common
Book of Burlesques, A author: H.L. Mencken
Book of Changes: 6 I Ching
Book of Daniel, The author: E.L. Doctorow
Book of Hours, The poet: 5 Rilke
Book of Lights, The author: Chaim Potok
Book of Los, The author: William Blake
Book of Love (1958 song) artist: Monotones
Book of Merlyn, The author: T.H. White
Book of Nonsense, A author: Edward Lear
Book of Snobs, The author: William Makepeace Thackeray
Book of Songs, The author: 5 Heine
Book of Stars, The (2000 film)
cast: Karl Geary, Jena Malone, Mary Stuart Masterson, D.B. Sweeney
director: Michael Miner
Book of Thel, The author: William Blake

bookplate
phrase: 5 ex lib. 8 ex libris
books: 6 ledger 7 account 10 literature
check the ~: 5 audit
concerning ~: 8 literary
five ~ of Moses: 4 Tora 5 Torah
hit the ~: 4 cram, read 5 study 6 master
it's on the ~: 3 law 7 statute
like some kids' ~: 5 pop-up
manipulate the ~: 4 cook 6 tamper
one for the ~: 3 gem 5 doozy 6 marvel
wipe off the ~: 5 erase 6 cancel 7 rescind, scratch 8 dissolve 10 invalidate
bookseller, on-line: 4 eBay 6 Amazon
bookstore
category: 4 diet 5 how-to, humor, sci-fi 6 horror 7 fiction, history 9 biography
enjoy a ~: 6 browse
___ Book, The: 4 Foot 6 Jungle
bookworm: 4 nerd, nurd, wonk 6 reader 7 learner, scholar
what a ~ does: 4 pore, read 5 study
boola boola: 5 huzza 6 hoorah, hooray, hurrah, hurray, huzzah
singer: 3 Eli 5 Yalie 7 Bulldog
Boole, George: 7 British 8 logician
boom: 3 bar 4 bang, beam, mast, pole, roar, roll, slam, spar, wham 5 blast, bloom, burst, crack, crane, crash, noise, smash, sound, spirt, spurt 6 expand, flower, growth, report, rumble, thrive, timber, upturn 7 barrage, develop, explode, prosper, resound, succeed, thunder, upsurge, upswing 8 drumfire, flourish, increase, mushroom 9 barricade, cannonade, explosion, intensify 10 appreciate, detonation, prosperity
alternative: 4 bust
cannon ~: 5 salvo
go ~: 5 erupt 7 explode, thunder 8 detonate 9 discharge
lower the ~: 5 scold 6 berate 9 reprimand
nautical ~: 4 gaff, spar 5 sprit
support: 4 mast
time: 2 up 6 uptick 7 upswing
boom ___: 3 box 4 shot, town
___ boom: 3 jib 4 baby 5 sonic 7 whisker
boom-and-___: 4 bust
___ boom bah!: 3 Sis
boombox: 5 radio 6 stereo 8 CD player 10 tape player
button: 4 stop 5 pause 6 record, rewind
letters ~: 4 AMFM
sound: 5 blare, noise
boomer: 8 kangeroo
baby ~ offsprings: 4 Gen-X
___ boomer: 4 baby
Boomer: 7 Esiason
boomerang: 5 react 7 rebound 8 backfire 10 bounce back
like a ~: 6 curved
Boomerang! (1947 film)
cast: Dana Andrews, Lee J. Cobb, Jane Wyatt
director: Elia Kazan
booming: 4 loud 5 forte, large, noisy, palmy 7 blaring, orotund, rackety, raucous, reboant, roaring, wealthy 8 piercing, plangent, resonant, sonorous, strident, thriving, turned up 9 big-voiced, clamorous, deafening, doing well 10 boisterous, prosperous, stentorian, strepitous, successful, uproarious, vociferant, vociferous
boom-or-___: 4 bust
boomslang: 5 snake 6 animal 7 reptile
relative: 3 asp, boa 5 aboma, adder, cobra, krait, mamba, racer, viper 6 dhaman, python, taipan 7 markhor, rattler 8 anaconda, moccasin, ringhals 9 coachwhip 10 bushmaster, copperhead, sidewinder
Boom Town (1940 film)
cast: Claudette Colbert, Clark Gable, Spencer Tracy
boon: 3 aid 4 gift, help, plus 5 asset, favor, jolly 6 virtue 7 benefit, gleeful, godsend 8 blessing, largesse, windfall 9 advantage, convivial, endowment, privilege 10 lucky break
companion: 3 pal 5 buddy 6 friend 8 alter ego
boondocks: 4 town 5 wilds 6 Podunk, sticks 7 country 8 frontier 9 backwater, backwoods 10 wilderness
in the ~: 6 remote
Boone: 3 Pat 5 Debby 6 Daniel 7 Richard
Boone, Daniel: 4 hero 7 pioneer 8 explorer
Boone, Debby song: You Light Up My Life (1977)
Boone, Pat
real first name: Charles
song: Ain't That a Shame (1955)
April Love (1957)
At My Front Door (1955)
Chains of Love (1956)
Don't Forbid Me (1956)
Friendly Persuasion (1956)
I Almost Lost My Mind (1956)
If Dreams Came True (1958)
I'll Be Home (1956)
It's Too Soon to Know (1958)
Long Tall Sally (1956)
Love Letters in the Sand (1957)
Moody River (1961)
Remember You're Mine (1957)
Speedy Gonzales (1962)
Sugar Moon (1958)
Why Baby Why (1957)
A Wonderful Time Up There (1958)
Boone, Richard: 5 actor
film: Dragnet (1954)
Hombre (1967)
I Bury the Living (1958)
The Raid (1954)
Rio Conchos (1964)
The Shootist (1976)
The Tall T (1957)
The War Lord (1965)
TV: Have Gun Will Travel, Hec Ramsey, Medic
Boone's Lick author: Larry McMurtry
boonies
see boondocks
Boop, Betty: 4 toon 7 flapper
dog: 5 Pudgy
voice: 4 Kane
boor: 3 ape, cad, oaf 4 boob, clod, goon, hick, jerk, lout 5 brute, churl, clown, looby, swine, yahoo, yokel 6 baboon, lummox, rustic 7 buffoon, hayseed, peasant 9 barbarian, vulgarian 10 philistine
boorish: 3 dim 4 loud, rude 5 brash, crass, crude, dense, gross, gruff, nervy 6 clumsy, coarse, rustic, vulgar 7 awkward, bearish, beastly, ill-bred, loutish, lowbred, raffish, selfish, unadept, uncouth 8 barbaric, churlish, heedless, impolite, inurbane, tactless, unpoised 9 backwater, barbarian, barbarous, difficult, graceless, ungallant, unrefined 10 indecorous, outlandish, uncultured, ungracious, unpolished, unthinking
Boorman, John: 8 director
film: Deliverance (1972)
The Emerald Forest (1985)
Excalibur (1981)
Hell in the Pacific (1968)
Hope and Glory (1987)
Point Blank (1967)
The Tailor of Panama (2001)
Boorstin: 6 Daniel
Boosler: 6 Elayne
boost: 3 aid 4 back, buoy, gain, hand, help, hike, jump, laud, lift, loot, plug, puff, push, rise, tout 5 add to, build, exalt, heave, hoist, impel, leg up, lobby, raise, shove, speed 6 assist, beef up, expand, extend, foster, growth, haul up, jack up, jerk up, mark up, pilfer, praise, rip off, step up, thieve, thrust, uphold, upturn 7 advance, amplify, augment, bolster, buildup, elevate, endorse, enhance, enlarge, further, improve, indorse, inflate, inspire, magnify, nurture, promote, scale up, support, upgrade, upraise, upswing 8 addition, advocate, embolden, heighten, imbolden, increase, multiply, pick-me-up, shoplift 9 advertise, elevation, encourage, expansion, increment, intensify, promotion, publicity, publicize, reinforce, subscribe 10 aggrandize, assistance, exaggerate, exhilarate, rally round
give a ~ to: 3 aid 4 back, help 6 assist 7 bail out, further, promote, support
morale: 7 enthuse, hearten, support 9 encourage
booster: 5 urger 6 jaycee, patron, rooter, votary 7 admirer, devotee 8 advocate, exponent, partisan 9 flatterer, proponent
amount: 4 dose
club member: 4 alum, grad 6 alumna
rocket: 5 Agena
seat user: 3 kid, tot 5 child 7 toddler
shot: 4 hypo
booster ___: 4 dose, seat, shot 5 cable
boot: 2 ax 3 axe, can, pac 4 drop, fire, kick, muff, oust, sack, shoe 5 botch, eject, evict, expel, let go, match, wader 6 bounce, buskin, depose, galosh, golosh, lay off, mucluc, mukluk, ouster, patten, slip-up 7 cashier, dismiss, drum out, galoshe, heave-ho, kick out, release 8 chase out, drive out, footgear, footwear, furlough, get rid of, muckluck, overshoe, pink-slip, snow shoe, throw out 9 discharge, eighty-six, terminate 10 Wellington
attachment: 4 spur
ender: 3 leg 4 jack, lace, lick 5 black, strap
Europe's ~: 5 Italy
fisherman's ~: 5 wader
fix a ~: 4 sole 6 resole
hip ~: 5 wader
in America: 5 trunk
out: 3 axe, can 4 fire, oust, sack 5 evict, exile, expel 6 bounce, depose 9 discharge
part: 3 lug, toe 4 lace, sole, vamp 6 insole
snow ~ brand: 5 Sorel
starter: 4 free, jack
the ball: 3 err
to ~: 3 too, yet 4 also 6 as well 7 besides, further 8 moreover
wearer: 4 puss
boot ___: 4 camp, hook, tree
___ boot: 3 hip, ski, top 4 half, jump 6 chukka, combat, cowboy, Denver, Desert, riding 7 Hessian, jodhpur
Boot ___: 4 Hill
___ Boot: 3 Das
boot camp
command: 6 at ease, fall in
figure: 3 sgt. 6 gyrene, Marine 8 sergeant
reply: 3 sir 5 no sir 6 yes sir
routine: 5 drill
booted: 4 shod
bootee: 4 shoe 8 baby shoe, footgear, footwear
booth: 4 cell, coop, mart, seat 5 kiosk, stall, stand 6 alcove, carrel, market 7 carrell, cubicle 8 boutique 9 cubbyhole, enclosure 10 repository
Brit's phone ~: 5 kiosk
mall ~: 5 kiosk
occupant: 5 voter 6 caller
offering: 4 info
___ booth: 4 toll 5 phone 7 polling
Booth: 5 Edwin 6 Hubert 7 Shirley 10 Tarkington
___ Boothe Luce: 5 Clare
Boothe, Powers: 5 actor
film: Blue Sky (1994)
The Emerald Forest (1985)
Nixon (1995)
Tombstone (1993)
U Turn (1997)
Boothia: 4 gulf 9 peninsula
locale: 6 Canada
Booth, Shirley: 7 actress
film: About Mrs. Leslie (1954)
Come Back, Little Sheba (1952, AA)
The Matchmaker (1958)
TV: Hazel
bootie: 4 shoe 8 baby shoe
booties, make: 4 knit 7 crochet
Bootle: 4 city, town
locale: 7 England
bootleg: 5 hooch 6 hootch 7 illegal, illicit, smuggle, traffic 8 unlawful 9 moonshine 10 contraband
bootlegger: 5 felon 8 criminal 9 miscreant
material: 4 mash 5 hooch 6 hootch 9 moonshine
nemesis: 3 Fed 4 Ness
bootless: 4 vain 6 unshod 7 inutile, useless 8 unusable 9 for naught, pointless, to no avail, worthless 10 profitless, unavailing
bootlick: 4 fawn 5 toady 6 grovel 7 adulate, flatter 8 kowtow to
bootlicker: 5 toady 6 fawner, flunky, lackey, yes man 7 flunkey 8 courtier, kowtower 9 sycophant
bootlicking: 7 servile 8 flattery
Bootnose: 3 Sid 4 Abel
boots
shake in one's ~: 5 cower 6 cringe
Boots: 8 Randolph
___ Boots: 5 Puss 'N
boots and ___: 7 saddles
___ Boots Are Made...: 5 These
boot-shaped country: 5 Italy
Boots Malone (1952 film)
cast: William Holden, Johnny Stewart
booty: 4 haul, loot, pelf, swag, take 5 goods, trove 6 boodle, spoils, trophy 7 jobbery, pillage, plunder, takings
Bootylicious (2001 song) artist: Destiny's Child
booze: 5 drink, hooch, sauce 6 hootch, liquor, rotgut, whisky 7 alcohol, spirits, whiskey 9 inebriant, moonshine 10 hard liquor, intoxicant
bop: 3 pow 4 belt, blow, conk, jazz, sock 5 dance, music, punch 6 wallop 7 clobber
Bop ___ You Drop: 3 'Til
___ Bop: 3 She
Bo-Peep
call to ~: 3 baa 5 bleat
charge: 5 sheep
Bopha! (1993 film)
cast: Danny Glover, Malcolm McDowell, Alfre Woodard
director: Morgan Freeman

__-Bopp comet: 4 Hale
__-bopper: 5 teeny
__ Bopper: 3 Big
bora: 4 wind
Bora Bora: 4 isle 6 island
  locale: 9 Polynesia, South Seas
borage: 4 herb
Borah: 4 peak 5 mount 8 mountain
  locale: 5 Idaho
Boran: 3 cow 4 bull 6 bovine, cattle
borate: 4 salt
Borateem: 6 bleach
  competitor: 5 Purex, Snowy, Vivid 6 Clorox
borax: 3 ore
Boraxo: 4 soap
  rival: 3 Lux 4 Dial, Dove, Lava, Tone, Zest 5 Camay, Coast, Ivory, Lever 6 Caress, Shield 8 Lifebuoy 9 Palmolive, Safeguard 11 Irish Spring
__ Borch: 3 Ter
Borchert, Wolfgang: 6 German, writer
Bordeaux: 3 vin 4 city, port, town, wine 6 claret
  locale: 6 France
  river: 7 Garonne
  wine: 5 Médoc
Bordelaise __: 5 sauce
Borden: 4 Gail 6 Lizzie
  competitor: 5 Kraft
  cow: 5 Elmer, Elsie
  product: 4 glue, milk
  weapon: 3 axe
border: 3 hem, lip, rim 4 abut, brim, edge, join, lace, line, meet, side, trim 5 brink, frame, front, limit, shore, skirt, touch, verge 6 adjoin, edging, fringe, limbus, margin, stripe 8 boundary, division, frontier, land's end, lie along, neighbor, surround 9 extremity, outskirts, perimeter, periphery, state line, threshold
  circular ~: 4 band, belt, ring 6 collar, girdle 8 cincture
  ender: 4 line
  fabric ~: 3 hem 4 seam 6 edging, fringe
  on: 4 abut, join 5 touch 6 adjoin 9 juxtapose
  ornamental ~: 4 dado
  road ~: 4 curb 5 verge 8 shoulder
  water ~: 4 bank 5 beach, coast, shore 7 seaside 8 littoral, seaboard, seashore 9 shoreline
border __: 3 tax 4 line
Border __: 6 collie, States 7 terrier
Border Incident (1949 film)
  cast: Ricardo Montalban, George Murphy
  director: Anthony Mann
bordering: 4 near, nigh 6 at hand, nearby 8 adjacent, imminent, next-door 9 impending, proximate 10 contiguous, convenient, juxtaposed
  on: 4 near 6 beside 8 touching
borderline: 3 end 6 fringe, limbic 8 marginal, unstable 9 ambiguous, debatable, dubitable, equivocal, on the edge, uncertain, undecided, unsettled 10 ambivalent, indecisive, indefinite
Borderline (1984 song) artist: Madonna
borders: 5 limbi 8 confines
Borders: 9 bookstore 10 bookseller
Border, The (1982 film)
  cast: Harvey Keitel, Jack Nicholson, Warren Oates, Valerie Perrine
  director: Tony Richardson
Bordertown (1935 film)
  cast: Bette Davis, Paul Muni
  director: Archie Mayo
Bordet, Jules: 7 Belgian 8 Nobelist
Bordoni, Irene: 6 singer
bore: 3 dig 4 cloy, drag, drip, jade, mine, pain, pall, pest, pill, ream, tire, well 5 creep, drill, gouge, prick, stare, weary 6 burrow, gasbag, pierce, tunnel, yawner 7 dullard, fatigue, turn off, wear out, windbag 8 gouge out, irritant, nuisance, puncture 9 penetrate, perforate, tidal wave 10 discomfort, jackhammer, put to sleep, wet blanket
  broaden a ~: 4 ream
  tidal ~: 5 eager, eagre
__ bore: 5 snail, tidal
__-bore: 4 full 5 small
boreal: 4 wind 5 north 8 northern
__ borealis: 6 aurora, corona
boreas: 4 wind
Boreas: 3 god
  parent of: 3 Eos 6 Aeolus
borecole: 4 kail, kale
bored: 5 blasé, jaded, tired, weary 6 in a rut 7 worn out 8 listless 9 incurious 10 world-weary
  feeling: 4 blah
  get ~: 4 tire
  like ~ kids: 5 antsy, itchy 7 fidgety 8 restless 9 unsettled
  (of): 4 sick
  reaction: 4 yawn
boredom: 5 ennui 6 apathy, tedium 7 fatigue 8 flatness, lethargy, monotony 9 jadedness, lassitude, weariness 10 melancholy
  express ~: 4 sigh, yawn 5 ho-hum
borer: 3 bug 4 pest, worm 5 auger, drill, larva, tirer 6 insect 7 termite 8 white ant
  combining form: 6 trypan- 7 trypano-
  product: 4 hole
  starter: 4 wood
__ borer: 4 corn, twig 7 currant
bore to __: 5 tears
__ Boreum: 4 Mare
Borg, Bjorn: 5 Swede 7 netster 9 tennis pro
  milieu: 5 court
Borges, Jorge Luis: 6 writer 9 Argentine
Borge, Victor: 6 Danish 7 pianist
Borgia: 6 Cesare 8 Lucrezia
  in-law: 4 Este
  see also Italian
Borglum, Gutzon: 6 artist 8 sculptor
Borgnine, Ernest: 5 actor
  film: The Badlanders (1958)
    The Catered Affair (1956)
    The Dirty Dozen (1967)
    Emperor of the North (1973)
    Escape From New York (1981)
    Ice Station Zebra (1968)
    Jubal (1956)
    Law and Disorder (1974)
    Man on a String (1960)
    Marty (1955, AA)
    The Poseidon Adventure (1972)
    The Wild Bunch (1969)
  spouse: Katy Jurado, Ethel Merman
  TV: McHale's Navy
Bori, Lucrezia: 6 singer 7 soprano
  specialty: 5 opera
boring: 3 dry 4 arid, blah, drab, dull, flat, tame 5 bland, heavy, ho-hum, unfun, vapid, yawny 6 draggy, dreary, jejune, stodgy, stuffy 7 humdrum, insipid, nowhere, operose, prosaic, routine, tedious 8 dragging, tiresome 9 ponderous, prosaical, tasteless, wearisome 10 dullsville, enervating, lackluster, monotonous, pedestrian, uneventful
  experience: 4 drag, yawn
  get ~: 4 pale, pall
  person: 4 drag, pill
  tool: 3 awl, bit 5 auger, drill 10 jackhammer
Boris: 4 czar, tsar 6 Becker 7 Badenov, Godunov, Karloff, Spassky, Yeltsin 9 Goldovsky, Pasternak
  wife: 5 Naina
Boris Godunov: 5 opera
  composer: 10 Mussorgsky
  role: 5 Pimen, Xenia 6 Dmitri, Feodor 7 Gregory, Shuisky, Varlaam
  setting: 6 Poland, Russia
Bork: 6 Robert
Borlaug, Norman: 8 Nobelist 10 agronomist
Borman, Frank: 9 astronaut
born: 3 née 6 innate, living 7 hatched 8 destined, inherent 9 delivered, intrinsic 10 congenital
  be ~: 9 originate
  first: 5 elder, older 6 eldest
  loser: 4 dupe 5 patsy
  loser's question: 5 why me
  not ~ yesterday: 5 sharp, smart 6 astute
  starter: 3 low, new 4 base, free, high, last, true, twin, well 5 earth
  to the manner ~: 5 noble 7 genteel 9 patrician
  yesterday: 3 raw 4 naif 5 naive
born __: 5 loser
born-__: 5 again
__-born: 3 sea 4 city, last 5 first, twice 6 heaven, middle, native 7 foreign, natural
Born __: 4 Free 5 to Run
__ Born, A: 6 Star Is
born-again: 5 pious 9 religious
born and __: 4 bred
borne: 6 wafted 7 carried, endured
  starter: 3 air, sea 4 ship 5 space, water
Borneo: 4 isle 6 island
  archipelago: 5 Malay
  country on ~: 6 Brunei
  island near ~: 4 Bali, Java, Laut 7 Celebes 8 Sulawesi
  language: 5 Dayak
  port: 10 Balikpapan
  primate: 5 orang 9 orangutan 10 orangutang
  region: 5 Sabah
  sea: 4 Sulu
__ Bornes: 5 Mille
Born Free: 4 film, song
  artist: Roger Williams
  cast: Virginia McKenna, Bill Travers
  director: James Hill
  lioness: 4 Elsa
Born in the U.S.A. (1984 song) artist: Bruce Springsteen
bornite: 3 ore
Born Loser, The: 7 cartoon
  dog: 6 Kewpie
Born, Max: 7 British 8 Nobelist 9 physicist
Born on the Fourth of July (1989 film)
  cast: Tom Cruise, Willem Dafoe
  director: Oliver Stone
  setting: 3 Nam 7 Vietnam
Born to Be My Baby (1988 song)
  artist: Bon Jovi
Born to Be Wild (1968 song) artist: Steppenwolf
Born to Be With You (1956 song)
  artist: Chordettes
Born to Dance (1936 film)
  cast: Eleanor Powell, James Stewart
  composer: 6 Porter
  director: Roy Del Ruth
Born to Kill (1947 film)
  cast: Walter Slezak, Lawrence Tierney, Claire Trevor
  director: Robert Wise
Born Too Late (1958 song) artist: Poni-Tails
Born to Run (1975 song) artist: Bruce Springsteen
born to the __: 6 purple
Born Yesterday: 4 film 5 novel
  author: 5 Kanin
  cast: Broderick Crawford, William Holden, Judy Holliday
  director: George Cukor
Borodin, Aleksandr: 7 Russian 8 composer
  work: Prince Igor
boron: 7 element
  ore: 7 kernite
boron __: 5 oxide 7 carbide, hydride, nitride
Boros, Julius: 6 golfer
  milieu: 5 links 6 course
  org.: 3 PGA
borough: 4 town
  boss: 5 mayor
  London ~: 6 Barnet, Ealing
  New York ~: 5 Bronx 6 Queens 8 Brooklyn 9 Manhattan
Borowski, Tadeusz: 6 Polish, writer
Borromini, Francesco: 7 Italian 8 sculptor 9 architect
borrow: 3 bum, owe 4 copy, rent, take 5 adopt, mooch, usurp 6 assume, pirate 7 imitate 8 simulate 10 plagiarize
  a phrase: 4 cite 5 quote
  from: 5 hit up, mooch 7 imitate
  on: 4 hock, pawn 8 mortgage
  opposite: 4 lend
  trouble: 5 worry
borrowed: 10 derivative
  amount ~: 4 loan
  car: 6 loaner
borrowed __: 4 time
borrower
  back a ~: 6 cosign
  figure: 3 APR 8 interest
  funds: 4 loan
borscht: 4 soup
  base: 4 beet
borscht __: 4 belt 7 circuit
Borstal Boy author: Brendan Behan
Boru, Brian land: 4 Erin
Borzage, Frank: 8 director
  film: Bad Girl (1932, AA)
    Desire (1936)
    A Farewell to Arms (1932)
    History Is Made at Night (1937)
    I've Always Loved You (1943)
    Lazybones (1925)
    Little Man, What Now? (1934)
    Man's Castle (1933)
    The Mortal Storm (1940)
    Seventh Heaven (1927, AA)
    Strange Cargo (1940)
    Street Angel (1928)
    Three Comrades (1938)
    The Vanishing Virginian (1942)
borzoi: 3 dog 5 canid 6 canine
BOS
  see Boston
Bosc: 4 pear
  relative: 5 Anjou 6 Comice, Seckel 8 Bartlett
boscage: 5 copse 7 coppice
Boscán, Juan: 4 poet 7 Spanish
Bosch: 4 Carl 10 Hieronymus
Bosch, Carl: 6 German 7 chemist 8 Nobelist
Bosch, Hieronymus: 6 artist 7 Flemish, painter
Bosco: 4 John 6 Philip
Bosco, John: 5 saint
Bose rival: 4 TEAC
bosh: 3 gas, rot 4 blah, bull, bunk, guff, jazz, jive, pooh, tosh 5 bilge, fudge, hokum, hooey, prate, stuff, trash, tripe 6 bunkum, bushwa, drivel, footle, gabble, gammon, gibber, havers, hot air, humbug, jabber, jargon, kibosh, piffle

7 baloney, blarney, blather, blether, boloney, bushwah, eyewash, flannel, flubdub, fustian, garbage, hogwash, inanity, malarky, rubbish, twaddle 8 buncombe, claptrap, falderal, falderol, flimflam, flummery, folderal, folderol, malarkey, nonsense, slipslop, tommyrot, trumpery 9 banana oil, gibberish, goofiness, kidstakes, moonshine, poppycock, rigmarole, silliness 10 applesauce, balderdash, bilge water, codswallop, double-talk, flapdoodle, galimatias, Jabberwock, mumbo jumbo, rigamarole, taradiddle

bosker: 3 def, rad 4 aces, A-one, boss, braw, cool, dece, fine, gear, keen, neat, nice, phat, tuff 5 dandy, ducky, grand, great, marvy, neato, nobby, prime, slick, super, swell 6 bang on, bang-up, bonzer, choice, divine, dreamy, far-out, gnarly, groovy, lovely, peachy, slap-up, spot on, superb, terrif, tiptop, unreal, whizzo, wicked 7 amazing, awesome, capital, corking, perfect, ripping, skookum, stellar, sublime 8 dazzling, especial, eximious, fabulous, five-star, four-star, frabjous, glorious, heavenly, jim-dandy, slambang, smashing, splendid, standout, sterling, stickout, superior, terrific, top-level, topnotch, very good, wondrous 9 bodacious, Endsville, excellent, exemplary, exquisite, first-rate, high-grade, hunky-dory, marvelous, sollicker, top-flight, wonderful 10 first-class, hotsy-totsy, jack-a-dandy, out of sight, peachy-keen, phenomenal, remarkable, stupendous, super-duper

bosket: 5 grove 7 thicket

bosky: 6 silvan, sylvan, woodsy

Bosley: 3 Tom 8 Crowther

Bosley, Tom: 5 actor
  film: The World of Henry Orient (1964)
  TV: Happy Days, Murder, She Wrote

bo's'n: 3 off. 5 bosun 6 sailor 7 jack tar, officer
  boss: 4 cap'n, capt. 7 captain

Bosnia and Herzegovina
  capital: 8 Sarajevo
  city: 5 Doboj, Tuzla 6 Mostar, Zenica 8 Prijedor, Sarajevo 9 Banja Luka
  neighbor: 7 Croatia 10 Yugoslavia
  peacekeeping org.: 4 NATO
  writer: 6 Andric

bosom: 4 soul 5 chest 8 intimate
  buddy: 3 pal 4 chum 5 buddy, crony 6 friend 7 adviser, advisor, comrade 8 alter ego, intimate 9 companion, confidant

Bosom Buddies (ABC sitcom)
  cast: Tom Hanks (Kip Wilson)
  Peter Scolari (Henry Desmond)

boson: 4 pion 5 meson 6 photon 7 pi meson 8 particle

Bosox
  see Red Sox

boss: 3 def, rad, run, top 4 aces, A-one, braw, cool, dece, exec, fine, gear, good, head, keen, king, lord, neat, nice, phat, stud, supt., tuff 5 chief, dandy, ducky, grand, great, hirer, marvy, Mr. Big, neato, nobby, prime, ruler, slick, super, swell 6 bang on, bang-up, bonzer, bosker, cheese, choice, direct, divine, dreamy, far-out, gerent, gnarly, groovy, honcho, leader, lovely, manage, peachy, pretty, slap-up, spot on, superb, terrif, tiptop, top dog, tycoon, unreal, whizzo, wicked 7 amazing, awesome, capital, captain, control, corking, foreman, headman, manager, oversee, perfect, ripping, skipper, skookum, stellar, sublime 8 brass hat, dazzling, director, dominate, employer, especial, eximious, fabulous, five-star, four-star, frabjous, glorious, governor, heavenly, higher-up, jim-dandy, kingfish, official, overseer, slam-bang, smashing, splendid, standout, sterling, stickout, superior, terrific, top-level, topnotch, very good, wondrous 9 authority, bodacious, commander, Endsville, excellent, executive, exemplary, exquisite, first-rate, high-grade, hunky-dory, marvelous, officiate, organizer, sollicker, supervise, thrilling, top-flight, unrivaled, wonderful 10 administer, first-class, head honcho, hotsy-totsy, jack-a-dandy, out of sight, peachy-keen, phenomenal, politician, remarkable, stupendous, super-duper, supervisor, unrivalled
  around: 5 order 6 demand 8 domineer 9 trample on, tyrannize
  baseball ~: 3 mgr. 7 manager
  be the ~: 4 rule 6 govern 7 control 8 hold sway
  company ~: 3 CEO 4 exec, suit 9 executive
  echo: 5 toady 6 flunky, yes man 7 flunkey
  in Spanish: 3 amo 4 jefe
  mob ~: 3 don 4 capo
  note from the ~: 5 see me
  often: 5 firer, hirer, owner
  shield ~: 4 umbo
  straw ~: 6 gerent 7 manager 8 overseer 10 figurehead, supervisor
  workers: 5 staff

__ boss: 3 pit 4 fire 5 straw, trail, wagon 7 section

Boss __: 5 Tweed

bossa nova: 5 dance, music
  cousin: 5 samba

Bossa Nova Baby (1963 song) artist: Elvis Presley

bosses: 10 management

Bossier City: 4 town
  locale: 9 Louisiana

Boss Lady star: 4 Bari

Bosson, Barbara: 7 actress

Boss's Son, The director: 4 Roth

bossy: 4 firm, hard 5 cruel, picky, pushy, rigid, stern, tough 6 severe 7 austere, Spartan 8 arrogant, despotic, exacting, hard-line, rigorous, superior 9 arbitrary, demanding, draconian, imperious, officious, stringent, unbending, unsparing 10 commanding, despotical, inflexible, iron-fisted, ironhanded, no-nonsense, oppressive, peremptory, tyrannical

Bossy: 3 cow 4 Mike

Bossy, Mike: 8 puckster
  milieu: 3 ice 4 rink 5 arena
  org.: 3 NHL

Bostic: 4 Earl

Boston: 4 city, fern, game, port, town 5 dance, novel 8 Beantown, card game
  airport: 5 Logan
  athletes: 7 Huskies
  author: Upton Sinclair
  campus: 5 Tufts, U Mass
  county: 7 Suffolk
  entrée: 3 cod 5 scrod 7 chowder
  locale: 4 Mass.
  newspaper: 5 Globe 6 Herald
  nickname: 3 Hub
  pro team: 3 Sox 5 Celts 6 Bruins, Red Sox 7 Celtics
  river: 6 Mystic 7 Charles
  skyscraper, for short: 3 Pru
  song: Amanda (1986)
  Don't Look Back (1978)
  More Than a Feeling (1976)
  We're Ready (1986)
  suburb: 4 Lynn 6 Lowell
  zone: 3 EDT, EST

Boston __: 3 bag, ivy 4 bull, fern, Pops 5 Globe 6 Common, Market, Public, rocker, states 7 Brahmin, lettuce, terrier

Boston baked __: 5 beans

Boston College
  athletes: 6 Eagles
  conference: 7 Big East

Boston Common: 4 park

Boston cream __: 3 pie

Boston Garden: 5 arena
  player: 4 Celt 6 Celtic

Boston Harbor
  feature: 4 quay
  jetsam: 3 tea

Bostonians, The author: Henry James

Boston monkey: 5 dance

Boston Public (Fox drama)
  cast: Kathy Baker (Meredith Peters)
  Loretta Devine (Marla Hendricks)
  Fyvush Finkel (Harvey Lipschultz)
  Jessalyn Gilsig (Lauren Davis)
  Anthony Heald (Scott Guber)
  Rashida Jones (Louisa Fenn)
  Nicky Katt (Harry Senate)
  Sharon Leal (Marilyn Sudor)
  Chi McBride (Steven Harper)
  Jeri Ryan (Ronnie Cooke)
  extra: 4 teen

Boston Tea __: 5 Party

Bostwick: 5 Barry

bosun: 6 sailor 7 jack tar 9 boatswain
  boss: 4 cap'n, capt. 7 captain

Boswell: 5 James 6 Connee

Boswell, James: 6 writer 8 Scottish

Boswell, James subject: Johnson

Bosworth: 5 Brian

Bosworth Field: 6 battle
  locale: 7 England
  loser: 10 Richard III
  winner: 8 Henry VII

bot.: 3 sci.

bota: 8 wineskin

botanical __: 6 garden

botanist: 4 Cohn, Gray 5 Banks, Vries 6 Carver, Mendel, Torrey 8 Linnaeus
  angle: 4 axil
  Austrian ~: 6 Mendel
  bract: 5 palea
  British ~: 5 Banks
  bud: 5 gemma
  capsule: 5 theca
  creation: 6 hybrid
  Dutch ~: 5 Vries
  filament: 6 elater
  German ~: 4 Cohn
  opening: 5 stoma
  openings: 7 stomata
  ridge: 6 carina
  sac: 5 ascus
  scion: 5 graft
  space: 6 areola, areole
  study: 5 flora 6 plants
  suffix: 3 -ody 5 -aceae
  Swedish ~: 8 Linnaeus

botany: 7 science
  branch of ~: 8 bryology, pomology 9 phytology 10 dendrology, floristics

Botany __: 3 Bay 4 wool

Botany Bay, like: 5 penal

botch: 3 err, mar 4 blow, boot, flub, goof, mess, miss, muff, ruin 5 gum up, misdo, mix up, snafu, spoil, wreck 6 blow it, bobble, boggle, bollix, bumble, bungle, foozle, foul up, fumble, goof up, mess up, muck up, muddle, slip-up 7 blunder, louse up, mistake, screw up 8 flounder, shambles 9 mishandle, mismanage

Botch-a-Me (1952 song) artist: Rosemary Clooney

botched: 6 faulty, sloppy 8 slipshod, slovenly 10 unthorough
  effort: 4 goof 5 error 6 slip-up 7 mistake

botcher: 2 ox 3 oaf 4 lout 5 klutz

botfly: 3 bug 6 insect

both: 3 duo 5 alike, twain 6 either, the two 7 equally, pronoun
  combining form: 3 bis- 4 ambi- 5 amphi-, ampho-
  for ~ sexes: 4 coed 6 unisex

Botha, P.W.: 9 statesman 12 South African

Bothell: 4 city, town
  locale: 10 Washington

__ both ends meet: 4 make

bother: 3 ado, ail, bug, dog, eat, get, irk, kid, nag, rag, vex 4 bait, care, carp, drag, faze, fret, fuss, gall, goad, miff, pain, pest, ride, rile, to-do 5 annoy, chafe, eat at, get to, harry, hound, nag at, nudge, peeve, shake, taunt, tease, upset, worry 6 accost, badger, dismay, gnaw at, harass, hassle, heckle, impede, madden, molest, needle, nettle, noodge, obsess, pester, pick on, plague, pother, put out, rankle, rattle, ruffle 7 afflict, agitate, bedevil, concern, disturb, fluster, grate on, henpeck, perturb, problem, provoke, torment, trouble 8 browbeat, disquiet, distress, exercise, headache, irritant, irritate, nuisance, unsettle, vexation 9 aggravate, annoyance, discomfit, displease, give a darn, incommode, interrupt, take pains 10 difficulty, discompose, disconcert, exasperate, irritation
  don't ~: 9 never mind
  ender: 4 some

botheration: 3 ado 4 pest 6 hassle 7 anxiety, problem

bothered: 5 upset 6 uneasy 7 put upon, worried
  be ~ by: 4 mind
  no longer ~ by: 5 rid of

bothersome: 5 messy, pesky, pesty 6 thorny, trying, vexing 8 annoying, worrying 9 demanding, difficult, troubling, vexatious 10 disturbing, in one's hair, irritating

Bothe, Walther: 6 German 8 Nobelist 9 physicist

Bothnia: 4 gulf
  locale: 6 Sweden 7 Finland
  sea: 6 Baltic

Both Sides Now (1968 song) artist: Judy Collins

__ both ways: 3 cut

Bothwell: 4 Scot

Botkin: 5 Perry

Boton: 4 font 8 typeface

botrytis: 6 fungus

Botswana: 6 nation 7 country
  bovine: 6 Tswana
  capital: 8 Gaborone
  coin: 5 Thebe
  desert: 8 Kalahari
  lake: 5 Ngami
  money: 4 pula 5 thebe
  neighbor: 7 Namibia 8 Zimbabwe
  people: 5 Sotho 6 Basuto, Herero, Tswana

Botticelli, Sandro: 6 artist 7 Italian, painter
  work: 4 nude 5 Venus

bottle: 3 jar, jug 4 tree, vial 5 cruet, flask, glass, phial 6 carafe, carboy, flacon, flagon 7 canteen, repress 8 decanter, preserve, suppress 9 container
  British ~ size: 5 litre
  capacity: 4 pint 5 liter, quart
  dweller: 5 genie

edge: 3 lip
ender: 4 neck 5 brush
get better in the ~: 3 age 6 mellow
hit the ~: 4 tope 5 booze, drink
lab ~: 5 flask 6 aludel
material: 5 glass
medicine-chest ~: 6 iodine 7 alcohol 8 peroxide
open a ~: 5 uncap 7 unscrew
perfume ~: 4 vial 5 phial 6 flacon
returnable ~: 5 empty
spin the ~: 4 game
starter: 4 blue
stopper: 3 cap, lid, top 4 cork
top: 3 cap, lid 4 neck
up: 4 hold 5 cramp, quash 6 corner, hold in 7 confine, contain, repress 8 suppress 9 constrain
use a ~ opener: 5 uncap
whiskey ~: 5 fifth
wine ~: 6 carafe, flagon
withdraw from a ~: 4 wean
bottle __: 3 cap, imp 4 baby, bill, club, fern, shop, tree 5 glass, gourd, green, party 7 gentian, turning
bottle-__: 3 fed 4 feed 6 washer
bottle-__ dolphin: 5 nosed
__ bottle: 5 gemel, Klein 6 Nansen, siphon, vacuum 7 pilgrim, squeeze, thermos
bottlebrush: 4 tree 5 grass
bottled __: 3 gas 5 water 6 in bond
__-bottled: 6 estate
bottled-up: 4 pent 9 inhibited, repressed
bottleneck: 3 jam 4 snag 5 block, jam-up, tie-up 6 hangup, hinder, holdup, logjam 7 barrier 8 cul-de-sac, gridlock, obstacle 10 congestion, impediment, traffic jam
cause a ~: 3 jam 5 block 6 impede
bottle-nosed __: 5 whale 7 dolphin
bottom: 3 bed, end 4 base, foot, root, side, soul 5 basal, basic, floor, least, nadir 6 depths, ground, lesser, lowest, valley 7 minimum, radical, support 8 low point 9 lowermost, underside 10 foundation, underlying
at ~: 6 au fond
at the ~ of: 6 behind
bet one's ~ dollar: 4 rely 6 depend
deal from the ~: 5 cheat
dress ~: 3 hem
ender: 4 land, most
feeder: 4 carp
floor: 6 cellar
food-chain ~: 4 alga 5 algae
from the ~ of one's heart: 9 sincerely
get to the ~ of: 5 plumb, solve 6 fathom
hit ~: 4 fell, sink 6 go down, plunge 7 founder, go under 8 flounder, submerge
lake ~: 3 bed 7 benthos
line: 3 sum 4 cost, crux 5 limit, point, tally, total 6 outlay, payoff, profit 7 essence, meaning, reality, revenue 8 key point, receipts 9 essential, main point 10 conclusion
of the barrel: 5 worst
on the ~: 7 aground 10 underneath
river ~: 3 bed
rock ~: 4 zero 5 nadir, worst
sea ~: 3 bed 7 benthos
send to the ~: 4 sink
ship ~: 4 hull, keel
top to ~: 6 wholly 7 totally
touch ~: 4 sink
bottom __: 3 dog, ice, out 4 bolt, fish, gear, heat, land, line, time 5 grass, quark, round, yeast 6 drawer, feeder
__ bottom: 4 rock 5 false, top to
__-bottom: 4 bell 6 sulfur
__ Bottom: 5 Foggy
__ Bottom Boat, The: 5 Glass
bottomless: 4 deep 7 abysmal, abyssal, yawning 8 baseless, profound 9 cavernous, limitless, unfailing, unfounded, unsounded 10 fathomless, groundless, unfathomed, unmeasured
pit: 5 abysm, abyss
bottomless __: 3 pit
bottom-line: 5 vital 8 critical 9 essential
figure: 3 net, sum 5 count, score, tally, total 6 amount 9 aggregate, reckoning
bottom-of-the-__: 4 line
bottom-out: 7 decline 9 downswing, recession
bottoms: 5 swamp 6 meadow
like some ~: 5 false
Bottoms: 3 Sam 6 Joseph 7 Timothy
Bottoms, Timothy: 5 actor
film: The Last Picture Show (1971)
Love and Pain (and the Whole Damn Thing) (1972)
The Paper Chase (1973)
Texasville (1990)
bottoms up: 5 salud, skoal, toast 6 cheers, kampai, prosit
Bottrop: 4 city, town
locale: 7 Germany
Botts __: 4 dots
botulin: 5 toxin
Botvinnik, Mikhail forte: 5 chess
Botwood: 4 city, town
locale: 6 Canada
Bouaké: 4 city, town
locale: 10 Ivory Coast
__ bouche: 4 fine 5 bonne
Boucher: 8 François
Boucherville: 4 city, town
locale: 6 Canada, Québec
boucle: 4 yarn 6 fabric
boudin __: 4 noir 5 blanc
boudoir: 4 room 5 bower 7 bedroom
Boudreau, Lou: 6 Indian 9 shortstop
bouffant: 4 coif 6 hairdo 8 coiffure 9 hairstyle
__ bouffe: 5 opera
Bougainville: 4 isle 6 island
locale: 7 Pacific 8 Solomons
bougainvillea: 5 plant 6 flower
Bougainville, Louis Antoine de: 6 French 8 explorer
bough: 3 arm 4 limb 6 branch
place: 4 tree 5 trunk
stunted ~: 4 spur
take a ~: 3 lop 5 prune
boughpot: 4 vase
__-bought: 5 store
bought, just: 3 new 6 cherry 8 brand-new 9 never used
bougie: 6 candle
bouillabaisse: 4 soup, stew
base: 4 fish
bouillon: 4 soup 5 broth, stock 8 beverage, julienne
bouillon __: 3 cup 4 cube 5 spoon
__ bouillon: 4 beef 7 chicken
Boulanger: 5 Nadia
boulder: 4 rock, slab 5 stone
breaker: 3 TNT 5 nitro 8 dynamite
Boulder: 4 city, town
athletes: 9 Buffaloes
locale: 8 Colorado
newspaper: 6 Camera
sports org.: 4 USOC
Boulder __: 3 Dam 6 Canyon
Boulder Dam: 6 Hoover
lake: 4 Mead
boulevard: 3 way 4 mall, road 5 paseo, route 6 artery, avenue, street 7 ingress 9 concourse
divider: 6 island
liner: 4 tree
Los Angeles ~: 4 Pico 6 Sunset
boulevardier: 3 fop 5 dandy
Boulevard of Broken Dreams composer: 5 Dubin 6 Warren
Boulez, Pierre: 6 French 9 conductor
Boulle, Pierre: 6 French, writer
work: The Bridge Over the River Kwai
Planet of the Apes
Boulogne: 4 city, port, town
Bois de ~: 4 parc, park
see also French
Boulogne-sur-__: 3 Mer
Boult, Adrian: 3 Sir 7 British 9 conductor
Boulting: 3 Roy 4 John
Boulting, Roy: 8 director
film: The Family Way (1966)
The Risk (1960)
Run for the Sun (1956)
Sailor of the King (1953)
There's a Girl in My Soup (1970)
Thunder Rock (1942)
bounce: 2 ax 3 axe, bob, can, hop, jar, jog, pep, vim, zip 4 boot, bump, drop, echo, flop, jerk, jump, leap, life, oust, sack, shun, skip, veto, zest 5 carom, eject, evict, frisk, let go, spurn, start, vault, verve, vigor 6 carrom, depose, energy, glance, jiggle, joggle, jounce, lay off, pass on, rattle, rebuff, recoil, reject, remove, spring 7 boot out, cashier, disdain, dismiss, dribble, drum out, exclude, kick out, rebound, release, say no to 8 buoyance, buoyancy, disallow, dynamism, furlough, get rid of, pink-slip, ricochet, snap back, turn down, vitality, vivacity 9 animation, blackball, cast aside, discharge, eighty-six, élan vital, rejection, repudiate, terminate 10 elasticity, exuberance, friskiness, get up and go, liveliness, resilience, spring back
back: 4 echo 5 carom, rally, react 6 carrom, return, revive 7 rebound, recover 8 backfire, ricochet 9 boomerang 10 recuperate
checks: 4 kite
infield ~: 3 hop
off: 6 glance 7 deflect
on water: 3 dap 4 skip
sound ~: 4 echo
Bounce (2000 film)
cast: Ben Affleck, Natasha Henstridge, Gwyneth Paltrow
director: Don Roos
__ Bounce: 6 Jersey
Bounce competitor: 5 Downy 7 Snuggle 9 Cling Free 10 Final Touch
bounced-check letters: 3 NSF
bouncer: 5 guard
baby ~: 4 knee
demand: 2 ID 3 out
like a ~: 5 burly 6 strong
bounciness: 6 spring 10 elasticity
bouncing: 8 vigorous
off the walls: 4 edgy 5 antsy, hyper
bouncy: 3 gay 5 fresh, jolly, perky 6 frisky, jovial, lively, yeasty 7 buoyant, rocking, romping, rubbery, springy 8 cheerful, spirited 9 ebullient, energetic, exuberant, resilient, sprightly, vivacious 10 boisterous
gait: 3 jog 4 lope, skip, trot
melody: 4 lilt
bound: 3 end, hop, run 4 bent, edge, jump, leap, line, skip, sure 5 bourn, fated, fence, hem in, limit, lunge, start, tight, vault 6 apogee, begird, doomed, driven, forced, hasten, hurdle, intent, liable, margin, pounce, prance, secure, spring 7 captive, confine, hop over, limited, obliged, pledged 8 confined, destined, hemmed in, impelled, indebted, required, restrict, stalwart, surround 9 compelled, obligated 10 contracted, purposeful, relentless
and determined: 7 decided 8 resolute, stubborn
by: 9 subject to
by oath: 5 sworn
for: 5 off to
not ~ by: 6 exempt
starter: 3 fog, ice, pot 4 east, hard, hide, home, hoof, iron, snow, soft, west 5 brass, cloth, house, north, paper, south 6 strike
to happen: 4 sure 7 certain, cinched 8 definite, in the bag, positive 10 guaranteed, inevitable
up: 8 absorbed, immersed, obsessed
__ bound: 5 lower, upper
__-bound: 3 air 4 rock, tide 5 earth, honor 6 muscle, spiral 7 outward, weather
__ Bound: 7 Alabamy, Outward
boundaries: 4 area, term 5 limit, orbit, range, scope, sweep 6 bounds, region 7 borders, compass, purview, terrain 8 confines, environs 9 perimeter, periphery, territory
locate ~: 6 demark, survey
push back the ~: 5 widen
set ~: 6 define
boundary: 3 end, rim 4 edge, line, mete, side 5 ambit, brink, hedge, limit, verge 6 border, limbus, limits, margin, radius 7 barrier, compass 8 division, frontier 9 extremity, outskirts, perimeter, periphery, territory 10 outer limit
marker: 4 rail 5 fence, stake
boundary __: 4 line 5 layer, rider
Boundary Peak: 5 mount 8 mountain
locale: 3 Nev. 6 Nevada
bounded: 7 limited 9 qualified 10 measurable, terminable
by: 6 amidst 7 between
bounder: 3 cad 4 roué 5 knave, rogue, scamp, swine, yahoo 6 bad guy 8 scalawag 9 scallawag, scallywag, scoundrel 10 blackguard, scapegrace
Bound for Glory (1976 film)
cast: David Carradine, Ronny Cox, Melinda Dillon
director: Hal Ashby
bounding main: 3 sea 5 ocean
on the ~: 4 asea 5 at sea
ride the ~: 4 sail 6 cruise, voyage
boundless: 3 big 4 vast, wide 6 eonian, untold 7 abysmal, endless, immense 8 infinite, spacious, unending 9 countless, excessive, extensive, limitless, no-strings, unbounded, unfailing, unlimited 10 indefinite, tremendous, unconfined, unnumbered, widespread
bounds: 4 pale 5 ambit, limit, orbit, range, verge 6 extent, limits, reason 7 measure 8 confines, premises 9 perimeter
keep within ~: 4 curb 5 check, limit 6 temper 7 confine, contain 8 moderate, regulate, restrain, restrict 9 constrict
out of ~: 4 tabu 5 shady, taboo, ultra 6 banned, errant 7 illegal, illicit, naughty 8 outlawed, straying, unlawful, verboten 9 forbidden, frowned on, off-limits 10 closed-down, not allowed, prohibited, proscribed, unorthodox
within ~: 6 in line 9 allowable
__ bounds: 5 out of
bounteous: 4 full, rich 5 ample, noble, palmy 6 enough, plenty 7 copious, liberal, profuse 8 abundant, generous, handsome, prodigal 9 bountiful, plentiful 10 benevolent, munificent
bountiful: 4 many, rich 5 ample

6 divers, enough, gobs of, lavish, lots of, myriad, plenty, umteen, untold 7 copious, fertile, heaps of, liberal, no end of, piles of, profuse, scads of, umpteen 8 abundant, affluent, generous, handsome, manifold, numerous, oodles of, princely, prodigal, prolific, scores of, umpsteen 9 bounteous, countless, exuberant, luxuriant, plenteous, plentiful, quite a few, unsparing 10 benevolent, charitable, dime a dozen, hospitable, munificent, zillions of
name meaning ~: 5 Doris
Bountiful: 4 city, town
locale: 4 Utah
__ Bountiful: 4 Lady
bounty: 4 gift, loot 5 bonus, flood, grant, price 6 reward, wealth 7 premium, subsidy, tribute 8 largesse 9 abundance, endowment, plenitude, profusion 10 lavishness, liberality, prosperity
bounty __: 6 hunter
__ bounty: 5 king's 6 queen's
Bounty: 4 boat, ship 10 paper towel
competitor: 4 Viva 5 Scott 6 Brawny
event: 6 mutiny
port of call: 6 Tahiti
Bounty, The (1984 film)
cast: Mel Gibson, Anthony Hopkins, Laurence Olivier
bouquet: 4 nose, odor, posy 5 aroma, odour, scent, smell, spray 7 incense, nosegay, perfume 9 fragrance, redolence
element: 4 posy 6 flower
holder: 4 frog, vase
maker: 7 florist
wine ~: 4 nose 5 aroma, scent 9 fragrance
bouquet __: 5 garni
bouquet-by-phone: 3 FTD
bourbon: 6 whisky 7 whiskey
drink: 5 julep 9 mint julep
bourbon __: 4 rose 6 whisky 7 whiskey
Bourbon: 5 royal 6 street
see also French
Bourg: 7 commune
department: 3 Ain
locale: 6 France
bourgeois: 4 non-U 6 common, people 8 plebeian 9 hidebound, illiberal, landowner, Victorian 10 capitalist, philistine
__ bourgeois: 5 petit
__ bourgeoise: 6 petite
__ bourgeoisie: 5 haute, petty
Bourgeois, Léon: 8 Nobelist
Bourget, Paul: 6 French, writer
__ bourguignon: 4 beef 5 boeuf
Bourke-White, Margaret: 12 photographer
spouse: Erskine Caldwell
bourn: 4 pale, rill 5 bound, brook, creek, limit, realm, rille 6 domain, sphere, stream 7 rivulet 9 streamlet
bourne: 4 pale, rill 5 bound, brook, creek, limit, realm, rille 6 domain, sphere, stream 7 rivulet 9 streamlet
Bourne Identity, The: 4 film 5 novel
author: Robert Ludlum
cast: Chris Cooper, Matt Damon, Clive Owen
character: 5 Jason
director: Doug Liman
Bourne Supremacy, The author: Robert Ludlum
Bourne Ultimatum, The author: Robert Ludlum
Bournmouth: 4 city, town
locale: 6 Dorset 7 England
bourrée: 5 dance
pas de ~: 4 step
bourse: 6 market
Wall Street ~: 3 ASE 4 NYSE
Bousoño, Carlos: 4 poet 7 Spanish
bout: 4 duel, tilt, time 5 event, fight, match, round, scrap, set-to, shift, spell 6 attack, battle, tussle 7 contest, scuffle 8 conflict, struggle 9 encounter, fistfight, main event 10 engagement, fisticuffs
division: 5 round
ender: 2 KO 3 TKO 4 kayo
have a ~ with: 3 box 4 spar
locale: 4 ring 5 arena
long ~: 5 siege
wild ~: 5 binge, spree
see also boxing
__ bout: 5 title
boutique: 4 mart, shop 5 booth, salon, store 8 emporium 9 gift store
employee: 6 fitter
Bouton, Jim: 6 author, hurler 7 pitcher
work: Ball Four
boutonniere site: 5 lapel
Boutros-__: 5 Ghali
bouvardia: 5 shrub
family: 6 madder
relative: 5 ixora 6 coffee 8 cinchona, gardenia
Bouvier des Flandres: 3 dog 5 canid 6 canine
Bouvier, Jacqueline in 1947: 3 deb 9 debutante
bouzouki: 4 lute 6 string
origin: 6 Greece
Bova, Ben: 6 writer
genre: 5 sci-fi
bovarism: 3 ego
Bovary: 4 Emma
title: 3 Mme. 6 Madame
Bovet, Daniel: 7 Italian 8 Nobelist
bovine: 2 ox 3 cow, yak 4 anoa, arna, dull, gaur, urus, zebu 5 bison, dense, gayal, steer, takin 6 heifer, mithan, muskox, obtuse, oxlike, stolid 7 aurochs, banteng, banting, beefalo, buffalo, carabao, cattalo, cowlike, kouprey, lumpish, tamarao, tamarau, timarau 8 sluggish 9 impassive 10 cattlelike, phlegmatic
Africa ~: 4 Glan, Kuri, Tuli 5 Barka, Boran, Horro, Maure, N'dama, Nguni 6 Angeln, Ankole, Ovambo, Tswana 7 Mashona 8 Bonsmara, Gelbvieh
Arctic ~: 6 muskox
Australia ~: 10 Murray Grey
Azerbaijan ~: 5 Kurdi 6 Sarabi
Bhutan ~: 4 Siri
Bosnia ~: 4 Busa
Brazil ~: 6 Nelore 7 Canchim
breed: 3 Gir 4 Busa, Glan, Kuri, Rath, Siri, Tuli 5 Angus, Barka, Boran, Dajal, Dangi, Deoni, Devon, Fjall, Horro, Kerry, Kurdi, Luing, Malvi, Maure, N'dama, Nguni, Oropa, Rathi, Sanhe, Wagyu 6 Angeln, Ankole, Aubrac, Baladi, Channi, Dexter, Dhanni, Dulong, Gaolao, Herens, Jaulan, Jersey, Lohani, Mewati, Nagori, Nelore, Nimari, Ongole, Ovambo, Ponwar, Rojhan, Salers, Sarabi, Sussex, Tswana, Vosges 7 Alberes, Bachaur, Barzona, Brahman, Brahmin, Cachena, Canchim, Istoben, Mashona, Red Poll, Retinta, Sahiwal, Yanbian 8 Ayrshire, Bonsmara, Charbray, Chianina, Galloway, Gelbvieh, Guernsey, Hereford, Holstein, Limousin 9 Charolais, Shorthorn, Simmental 10 Lincoln Red, Murray Grey, Welsh Black
Cambodia ~: 7 kouprey
chew: 3 cud
China ~: 5 takin 6 Dulong 7 Yanbian
Croatia ~: 4 Busa
England ~: 5 Devon 6 Jersey, Sussex 7 Red Poll 8 Guernsey, Hereford 10 Lincoln Red
Eritrea ~: 5 Barka
extinct ~: 4 urus 7 aurochs
foot: 4 hoof
France ~: 6 Aubrac, Herens, Salers, Vosges 7 Alberes 8 Limousin 9 Charolais
gland: 5 udder
group: 4 herd
Himalayas ~: 3 yak 5 takin
humped ~: 4 zebu 5 bison 7 buffalo
hybrid: 6 catalo 7 beefalo, cattalo
India ~: 3 Gir 4 arna, Rath, Siri, zebu 5 Dajal, Dangi, Deoni, Malvi, Rathi 6 Channi, Gaolao, Mewati, Nagori, Nimari, Ongole, Ponwar, Rojhan 7 Bachaur, Brahman, Brahmin, Sahiwal
Indonesia ~: 4 anoa
Iran ~: 5 Kurdi 6 Sarabi
Ireland ~: 5 Kerry 6 Dexter
Israel ~: 6 Baladi
Italy ~: 5 Oropa 8 Chianina
Japan ~: 5 Wagyu
Jordan ~: 6 Baladi
Laos ~: 7 kouprey
Lebanon ~: 6 Baladi
Macedonia ~: 4 Busa
Malay ~: 4 gaur 5 gayal 6 mithan 7 banteng, banting
Mideast ~: 6 Baladi, Jaulan
Mongolia ~: 5 Sanhe
Myanmar ~: 5 takin
name: 5 Bossy
Netherlands ~: 8 Holstein
of ads: 5 Elsie
Pakistan ~: 6 Channi, Dhanni, Lohani 7 Sahiwal
Philippines ~: 7 carabao, tamarao, tamarau, timarau
Pyrenees ~: 7 Alberes
Russia ~: 7 Istoben
Scotland ~: 5 Angus, Luing 8 Ayrshire, Galloway
Serbia ~: 4 Busa
shaggy ~: 3 yak 5 bison 7 buffalo
Sikkim ~: 4 Siri
sound: 3 low, moo
Spain ~: 7 Alberes, Cachena, Retinta
stomach: 6 omasum
stomachs: 5 omasa
Sweden ~: 5 Fjall
Switzerland ~: 6 Herens 9 Simmental
Syria ~: 6 Baladi, Jaulan
Tibet ~: 3 yak
Turkey ~: 5 Kurdi
young ~: 4 calf
Yugoslavia ~: 4 Busa
bovines: 4 kine
bow: 3 arc, nod, sag 4 arch, bend, cave, flex, fore, loop, prow, stem 5 angle, curve, debut, front, greet, kotow, yield 6 cave in, comply, crouch, curtsy, give in, kowtow, launch, relent, salaam, salute, slouch, submit, suffer, weapon 7 concede, flexure, gesture, rainbow, succumb 8 anterior, crescent, flection, forepart 9 acquiesce, curvature, reverence, sinuosity, surrender 10 capitulate, salutation, semicircle
and scrape: 4 fawn 5 court, kneel, toady 6 grovel, kowtow 8 bootlick, fawn upon, suck up to 10 curry favor, pay court to
application: 5 rosin
bearer: 4 Amor, Eros 5 Cupid 6 hunter 7 warrior
boat with a high ~: 4 dory
component: 4 loop
down to: 5 kneel, thank 6 praise 9 genuflect, prostrate
ender: 3 fin, leg, man, men, wow 4 head, knot, line, shot 5 front, sprit 6 string
in music: 4 arco
lady's ~: 6 curtsy
make a ~: 3 tie
missile: 5 arrow
notch: 4 nock
opposite: 5 stern
out: 4 quit 5 leave 6 beg off, resign 7 abandon 8 withdraw
part of the ~: 5 hawse 10 figurehead
sound: 5 twang
starter: 3 fog, sun 4 down, long, rain, wing 5 cross 6 saddle
structure: 6 fo'c's'le
to: 4 heed, mind, obey 5 defer 6 accept, follow, fulfil, listen 7 abide by, conform, consent, fulfill, observe, respect, succumb 8 carry out 9 acquiesce
toward the ~: 4 fore
violin ~ part: 4 frog
wood: 3 yew
bow __: 3 net, oar, out, saw, tie 5 front, shock 6 rudder, window 7 compass
bow-__: 3 wow 4 iron
__ bow: 4 face, wing 5 sound, spoon 6 Cupid's, fiddle 7 Brocken, clipper
Bow: 5 Clara
Bowa: 5 Larry
bow and __: 6 scrape
bowdlerize: 4 edit 6 censor 8 mutilate 9 expurgate, red-pencil
Bowdoin: 6 school 7 college
locale: 5 Maine
bowed: 4 bent 5 bandy, round 6 zigzag 7 angular, crooked, winding 8 angulose, angulous, cockeyed
combining form: 3 tox- 4 toxi-, toxo-
Bo Weevil (1956 song) artist: Teresa Brewer
Bowen, Elizabeth: 6 author, writer 7 British
bower: 3 cot, hut 4 nook 5 arbor, cabin, house, lodge, shack 6 alcove, anchor, chalet, grotto, recess 7 bedroom, boudoir, close in, cottage, enclose, inclose, pergola 8 bungalow, encircle, surround
ender: 4 bird
Bower: 10 Antoinette
Bowe, Riddick: 5 boxer
milieu: 4 ring
Bowery Boys film: 5 Mr. Hex
Bowery denizen: 4 wino
Bowery, The (1933 film)
cast: Wallace Beery, Jackie Cooper, George Raft
director: Raoul Walsh
__ Bowes: 6 Pitney
Bowes, Major medium: 5 radio
bowfin: 4 amia, fish 7 dogfish, grindle, mudfish
Bowfinger (1999 film)
cast: Christine Baranski, Heather Graham, Steve Martin, Eddie Murphy
director: Frank Oz
dog: 5 Betsy
bowie __: 5 knife
Bowie: 3 Jim 4 city, Kuhn, town 5 David
locale: 8 Maryland
Bowie, David
producer for ~: 3 Eno
real last name: Jones
song: Blue Jean (1984)
China Girl (1983)
Dancing in the Street (1985)
Fame (1975)
Golden Years (1976)

Let's Dance (1983)
spouse: Iman
Bowie, Jim last stand: 5 Alamo
bowl: 4 roll 5 arena, basin, crock 6 saucer, tureen, vessel 7 stadium 8 coliseum 9 colosseum, container 10 receptacle
drinking ~: 5 mazer
dust ~: 9 wasteland
filler: 4 soup, stew 5 chili 6 cereal
game prelude: 6 parade
large ~: 5 jorum
mixing ~: 6 krater
of cherries, maybe: 4 life
ornamental ~: 5 tazza
over: 3 awe, wow 4 jolt, stun 5 amaze, floor, shock, upset 6 boggle, dazzle 7 astound, stagger, stupefy, unnerve 8 astonish, overcome, surprise 9 dumbfound, overwhelm, take aback
pedestal ~: 5 tazza
starter: 4 fish, wash
bowl __: 4 game, over
__ bowl: 4 fish, slop 5 float, punch, salad, sugar 6 bubble, finger, mixing
__ Bowl: 3 Pro 4 Dust, Hula, Rose, Yale 5 Alamo, Aloha, Gator, Sugar, Super 6 Fiesta, Orange
bowlegged: 5 bandy
bowler: 3 hat 4 Roth, Welu 5 Aulby, derby, Weber 6 Burton, Carter, kegler 7 Anthony, athlete, kegeler 9 Don Carter 10 cricketeer
strikes, to a ~: 3 xes
Bowles: 4 Jane, Paul 5 Sally
Bowles, Jane: 6 author, writer
Bowles, Paul: 6 author, writer
bowline: 4 knot, rope
bowling: 5 sport
alley button: 5 reset
alley part: 4 lane 6 gutter 7 channel 8 foul line
division: 5 frame
goal: 6 pocket
group: 6 league
lawn ~: 5 bocce, bocci 6 boccia, boccie
milieu: 4 lane 5 alley
pin: 5 maple
score: 4 mark 5 spare 6 strike
term: 3 tap 4 foul, hook, mark 5 alley, frame, spare, split 6 bucket, double, gutter, kegler, pocket, strike, triple, turkey 7 channel, headpin, kingpin 8 foul line, pushaway
three straight strikes in ~: 6 triple, turkey
two straight strikes in ~: 6 double
woe in ~: 3 tap 5 split
bowling __: 3 bag 4 ball 5 alley, green 6 center, crease
Bowling for Columbine (2002 film)
director: Michael Moore
Bowling Green: 4 city, town
athletes: 7 Falcons
conference: 3 MAC
locale: 4 Ohio 8 Kentucky
__ Bowl of Tea: 4 Eat a
bowman: 6 archer 9 Robin Hood
Bowman: 3 Lee
bownet: 4 trap
bowpot: 4 vase
bowser __: 3 bag
Bowser's pal: 4 Fido, Spot 5 Rover
bow-shaped: 5 arced
bowsprit: 4 spar
place: 4 prow
support: 3 fid
bowstring
groove: 4 nock
like a ~: 4 taut
protection: 3 wax
pull a ~: 4 draw
bowtie: 5 pasta 8 neckwear
style: 6 clip-on
bowwow: 3 arf, dog 4 bark, woof 5 pooch 6 canine
box: 3 bin, jam, pen 4 cage, case, cuff, duke, pack, slap, spar, swat, till 5 chest, crate, fight, hutch, punch, shrub, smack, spank, trunk, TV set, whack 6 bunker, carton, coffer, encage, encase, incase, packet, strike 7 confine, humidor, package 9 container, slug it out 10 receptacle, television
black ~: 9 mechanism
boom ~: 5 radio 6 stereo
boom ~ letters: 4 AMFM
buyer: 3 fan
carpenter's ~: 5 miter
cash ~: 4 till
contents: 5 lunch
corrugated ~: 6 carton
cylindrical ~: 5 pyxis
end: 4 flap
ender: 3 car 4 fish, haul, wood 5 board, thorn
food in a ~: 6 cereal
geisha's ~: 4 inro
goggle ~: 2 TV 4 tube 5 TV set 8 boob tube 10 television
grocery ~ letters: 3 RDA 5 net wt.
idiot ~: 2 TV 4 tube 5 TV set 8 boob tube 10 television
in: 4 trap 5 siege 6 begird, encase, entrap, hinder, shut up 7 confine 8 surround
jewelry ~: 6 casket
music ~: 5 phono 10 phonograph
office: 4 gate 10 attendance
office disaster: 4 bomb, flop
on a string: 4 kite
one in a ~: 5 juror
opera ~: 4 loge
picnic ~: 6 cooler
safe-deposit ~: 5 vault
social: 5 event 10 fundraiser
starter: 3 hat, hot, ice, sky 4 band, fire, gear, hell, juke, mail, pill, post, salt, sand, shoe, soap, tool 5 bread, match, sauce, snuff, sweat 6 letter, pepper, rattle, shadow, strong, tinder 7 chatter, squeeze
still in the ~: 3 new 6 unused
storage ~: 5 trunk
top: 3 lid
up: 4 wrap 5 crate 6 incase 7 enclose, package
voice ~: 6 larynx
warehouse ~: 5 crate 6 carton
box __: 3 bed, set, top 4 beam, bolt, calf, coat, iron, keel, kite, loom, nail, plot, room, seat, sill 5 elder, frame, lunch, plait, pleat, score, stall, stoop, store 6 camera, canyon, column, girder, gutter, office, social, spring, staple, turtle, wrench 7 cornice
__ box: 3 toe 4 bank, base, boom, call, coin, damp, drop, fuse, gear, gill, hunt, jury, poor, pump, rose, tote, wall 5 black, coach, ditty, glove, grout, idiot, jewel, knife, light, miter, money, music, press, steam, swell, voice 6 ballot, connex, dialog, flower, jockey, letter, orgone, outlet, paddle, pencil, pillar, pounce, puzzle, sentry, signal, sluice, squawk, switch, vanity, window 7 batter's, dealing, hunting, journal, lockout, packing, penalty, pouncet, pouring, Skinner
__-box: 3 out 4 salt 6 goggle, tucker 7 witness
Box: 4 play 5 drama
author: Edward Albee
__ Box: 5 Black, Demon, Music 7 Squeeze
boxcar: 5 train
contents: 7 freight
rider: 4 hobo
boxcars: 6 twelve
__ Box Derby: 4 Soap
boxed in: 4 pent
box elder genus: 4 acer
boxer: 3 Ali, dog, Pep, pet, pug 4 Baer, Bowe, Conn, Zale 5 Lewis, Louis, Moore, Tyson 6 canine, Hagler, Holmes, Liston, Norton, Spinks, Tunney 7 athlete, Basilio, Berbick, Charles, Corbett, Dempsey, fighter, Foreman, Frazier, Johnson, LaMotta, Leonard, Max Baer, Walcott, Willard 8 Braddock, Graziano, Griffith, Joe Louis, Marciano, pugilist, Robinson, Tony Zale 9 Benvenuti, Billy Conn, gladiator, Holyfield, Ken Norton, Mike Tyson, Patterson, Schmeling, Willie Pep 10 Gene Tunney, Joe Frazier, Joe Walcott, Leon Spinks
attire: 4 robe 6 trunks
baby ~: 3 pup 5 puppy, whelp
countenance: 5 scowl
cue: 4 bell
gear: 5 glove
glove of ancient Rome: 6 cestus
handicap: 8 glass jaw
injury: 3 cut 4 welt
match: 4 bout 10 fisticuffs
move: 3 bob 4 chop, kayo 5 feint, lunge, punch, weave 6 clinch
nickname: 5 Champ
official: 3 ref 7 referee
org.: 3 WBA, WBC
punch: 3 jab 4 hook, left 5 cross, right 8 haymaker, uppercut
quest: 5 title
ritual: 7 weigh-in
starter: 4 kick
stat: 2 KO 3 TKO 4 kayo 5 reach
target: 3 jaw
three minutes: 5 round
training: 8 roadwork
venue: 4 ring 5 arena
warning: 3 grr
weapon: 4 fist
boxer __: 6 shorts
Boxer: 7 Barbara
boxers: 6 shorts 7 jockeys 9 underwear
Boxers: 4 cult
home: 5 China
Boxer, The (1969 song) artist: Simon and Garfunkel
Boxiana author: 4 Egan
boxing: 4 ring 5 sport 8 pugilism, slugfest 10 fisticuffs
area: 4 ring 5 apron, ropes 8 ringside
term: 2 KO 3 bob, jab, pug, TKO 4 bell, bout, gate, hook, kayo, ring, spar 5 apron, count, cross, feint, ropes, round, weave 6 canvas, clinch, prelim 7 handler, weigh-in 8 glass jaw, haymaker, knockout, ringside, roadwork, uppercut
see also boxer
boxing __: 4 ring 5 glove
__ boxing: 4 kick
Boxing Day mo.: 3 Dec.
Boxleitner, Bruce spouse: Melissa Gilbert
box office
adjective: 5 socko
buy: 3 tix, tkt. 5 ducat 6 ticket
disaster: 3 dud 4 bomb, flop 6 turkey
figure: 4 gate, take 10 attendance
hit: 4 boff 5 boffo, smash 7 boffola
letters: 3 SRO
box score entry: 2 HR 3 hit, RBI, run 5 at bat, error
Box Socials author: W.P. Kinsella
Boxster: 3 car 4 auto 7 Porsche
__ Box, The: 5 Magic, Wrong 6 Oblong
boxtop piece: 3 tab
boxwood: 4 tree 5 shrub
boxy: 5 squat 6 square 8 thickset
boy: 3 cub, kid, lad, son, tad 4 male 5 cadet, child, minor, sonny, sprig, youth 6 fellow, junior, laddie, shaver, sprout, squirt 7 brother, sapling 8 half-pint, juvenile, small fry, young man 9 stripling, youngster
ender: 3 ish 6 friend
starter: 3 bat, bus, cow, fly, low, pot, tom 4 atta, bell, call, copy, foot, high, home, news, page, play, plow, tall 5 bully, choir, dough, house, paper 6 school
__ boy: 3 bat, bus, day, old, pin 4 atta, ball, best, copy, it's a, poor 5 altar, cabin, cover, mama's, ship's, stock, Teddy, water 6 chorus, office, powder, wonder 7 glamour
Boy __ Dolphin: 3 on a
__ Boy: 3 Bad 4 Best, It's a 5 Bugle, Danny, Rover, Sonny 6 Golden, Lonely, Nature 7 Borstal, Georgia, Soldier
__-Boy: 3 La-Z
boyar: 5 noble 7 Russian
__ Boy-Ar-Dee: 4 Chef
Boyce: 5 Tommy
boycott: 3 ban, bar 4 snub 5 avoid, rebel, spurn 6 eschew, ice out, picket, strike 7 embargo, protest, shut out 8 sanction 9 exclusion, ostracize, proscribe
Boyd: 7 Bennett, Stephen, William
__ Boyd: 6 Oil Can
__ Boyd Orr: 4 John
Boyd, Stephen: 5 actor
film: Ben-Hur (1959)
The Best of Everything (1959)
Billy Rose's Jumbo (1962)
The Bravados (1958)
The Fall of the Roman Empire (1964)
Fantastic Voyage (1966)
Boyer: 3 Ken 4 Paul 5 Clete 7 Charles
Boyer, Charles: 5 actor
film: Algiers (1938)
All This and Heaven Too (1940)
Arch of Triumph (1948)
Back Street (1941)
Barefoot in the Park (1967)
Cluny Brown (1946)
Confidential Agent (1945)
Conquest (1937)
The Constant Nymph (1943)
The Earrings of Madame de ... (1953)
Fanny (1961)
The First Legion (1951)
Flesh and Fantasy (1943)
Gaslight (1944)
History Is Made at Night (1937)
Hold Back the Dawn (1941)
How to Steal a Million (1966)
Love Affair (1939)
The Man From Yesterday (1932)
Tales of Manhattan (1942)
Together Again (1944)
Tovarich (1937)
A Woman's Vengeance (1947)
Boyer, Paul: 7 chemist 8 Nobelist
__ Boy Floyd: 6 Pretty
boyfriend: 2 jo 3 pet 4 baby, beau, date, dear, love, male 5 amour, angel, chéri, cooky, cutey, cutie, deary, ducky, flame, honey, leman, lover, lovey, novio, sugar, swain, sweet, wooer 6 bon ami, cookie, dautie, dearie, escort, steady, suitor, sweets 7 admirer, beloved, darling, dearest, dear one, pigsney, schatzi, squeeze, sweetie, tootsie 8 chou-chou, cutie pie, dowsabel, intimate, lovebird,

macushla, paramour, precious, snookums, sugar pie, sweetums, truelove **9** companion, confidant, dreamboat, inamorato, petit chou, valentine **10** heartthrob, honeybunch, mavourneen, sweetheart, sweetie pie, turtledove
in French: **3** ami
in Spanish: **5** amigo
Boy Friend, The (1971 film)
cast: Moyra Fraser, Christopher Gable, Twiggy
director: Ken Russell
Boy From New York City (song), The artist: Ad Libs, Manhattan Transfer
boyhood: **5** youth
Boy in __ Vest: **4** a Red
Boyington: **5** Pappy
boyish: **5** green, young **6** callow **8** childish, immature, innocent, juvenile, youthful **10** adolescent
Boy Is Mine, The (1998 song)
artist: Brandy, Monica
Boy King, The: **3** Tut
Boyle: **3** Kay **5** Peter **6** Robert
Boyle, Kay: **4** poet **6** author, writer
Boyle, Lara Flynn: **7** actress
film: Men in Black II (2002)
Red Rock West (1993)
The Temp (1993)
Threesome (1994)
Wayne's World (1992)
TV: The Practice
Boyle, Peter: **5** actor
film: The Brink's Job (1978)
The Candidate (1972)
Doctor Dolittle (1998)
The Dream Team (1989)
F.I.S.T. (1978)
The Friends of Eddie Coyle (1973)
Hammett (1983)
Monster's Ball (2001)
Red Heat (1988)
The Shadow (1994)
Slither (1973)
Steelyard Blues (1973)
Surrender (1987)
Taxi Driver (1976)
While You Were Sleeping (1995)
Yellowbeard (1983)
Young Frankenstein (1974)
TV: Everybody Loves Raymond
Boyle, Robert: **7** British, chemist **9** physicist
Boyle's __: **3** law
__ Boy Lost: **6** Little
Boy Meets Girl (1938 film)
cast: James Cagney, Pat O'Brien, Marie Wilson
director: Lloyd Bacon
boy-meets-girl event: **5** mixer
Boy Named Charlie Brown, A (1970 film) director: Bill Melendez
Boy Named Sue, A (1969 song) artist: Johnny Cash
Boyne: **5** river
locale: **7** Ireland
__-boy network: **3** old
boy next __: **4** door
Boynton Beach: **4** city, town
locale: **7** Florida
boys: **3** he's
club: **4** YMCA, YMHA
rural ~ org.: **3** FFA
Boys __: **4** Club, Town
__ Boys: **3** Bad, Jo's, Pep **5** Beach **6** Wonder **7** Beastie
Boy Scout
act: **4** deed
founder: **5** Beard
group: **3** den **6** patrol
like a ~: **4** kind, true **5** brave, clean, loyal **7** helpful, thrifty **8** cheerful, friendly, obedient, reverent **9** courteous
rank: **3** Cub **4** Life, Star **5** Eagle
wear: **4** sash
__ Boy Scout, The: **4** Last
Boys Don't Cry (1999 film)
cast: Peter Sarsgaard, Chloë Sevigny, Brendan Sexton III, Hilary Swank
director: Kimberley Peirce
boysenberry: **5** fruit
Boys for Pele singer: **4** Amos
Boys From Brazil, The: **4** film **5** novel
author: Ira Levin
boys: **6** clones
cast: James Mason, Laurence Olivier, Gregory Peck
Boys From Syracuse, The: **7** musical
songwriter: **4** Hart **7** Rodgers
Boys in the Band, The (1970 film)
cast: Leonard Frey, Kenneth Nelson, Peter White
director: William Friedkin
Boys' Night Out (1962 film)
cast: James Garner, Kim Novak, Tony Randall
Boys of Summer, The
author: **4** Kahn
name: **3** Gil, Roy **4** Carl **6** Jackie, Pee Wee **8** Preacher
subject: **3** Cox, Roe **5** Black, Reese **6** Hodges, Labine, Snider **7** Erskine, Furillo **8** Billy Cox, Joe Black, Newcombe, Robinson **9** Gil Hodges **10** Campanella, Clem Labine, Duke Snider
Boys of Summer, The (1984 song)
artist: Don Henley
Boys on the Side (1995 film)
cast: Drew Barrymore, Whoopi Goldberg, Matthew McConaughey, Mary-Louise Parker
director: Herbert Ross
Boys Town (1938 film)
cast: Mickey Rooney, Spencer Tracy
director: Norman Taurog
locale: **4** Nebr. **5** Omaha **8** Nebraska
Boy's Will, A: **4** poem
author: Robert Frost
__ Boy, The: **5** Stone **6** Errand **7** Persion, Winslow
Boy Who Cried Wolf, The
source: **4** Esop **5** Aesop
Boy Without a Girl, A (1959 song)
artist: Frankie Avalon
Boy With the Green Hair, The (1948 film)
cast: Pat O'Brien, Robert Ryan, Dean Stockwell
Boyz II Men
members: Morris, McCary, Stockman
song: 4 Seasons of Loneliness (1997)
End of the Road (1992)
I'll Make Love to You (1994)
In the Still of the Nite (1992)
It's So Hard to Say Goodbye to Yesterday (1991)
Motownphilly (1991)
On Bended Knee (1994)
One Sweet Day (1995)
A Song for Mama (1997)
Water Runs Dry (1995)
Boyz N the Hood (1991 film)
cast: Laurence Fishburne, Cuba Gooding Jr., Ice Cube, Nia Long
director: John Singleton
Boz: **6** Scaggs **7** Dickens
boy: **3** Pip, Tim **7** Tiny Tim
Bozeman: **4** city, town
locale: **7** Montana
school: **3** MSU
bozo: **3** oaf **4** dolt, fool, jerk, lout **5** clown, creep, dufus, dummy, dunce **6** dimwit, doofus, galoot, lummox **7** buffoon, galloot, halfwit **8** dummkopf, goofball **9** numbskull, roughneck **10** dunderhead, nincompoop
BPOE: **4** Elks
cousin: **4** IOOF
meeting site: **5** lodge
__-B-Q: **3** Bar
__-b-que: **3** bar
Br: **4** elem. **7** bromine, element
35 for ~: **4** at. no.
bra: **7** bandeau **8** lingerie
__-brac: **5** bric-a
Bracco, Lorraine: **7** actress
film: GoodFellas (1990)
Medicine Man (1992)
Radio Flyer (1992)
Someone to Watch Over Me (1987)
spouse: Harvey Keitel, Edward James Olmos
TV: The Sopranos
brace: **3** duo, leg, tie, two **4** beam, gird, grip, hold, pair, prop, stay **5** clamp, ready, shore, steel **6** couple, fasten, girder, hold up, prop up, rafter, steady, timber, uphold **7** bolster, fortify, prepare, refresh, shore up, stiffen, support, sustain, twosome **8** buttress, mainstay, reassure **9** reinforce, stabilize, stanchion, undergird, withstand **10** invigorate, strengthen
angle ~: **4** L bar
architectural ~: **5** strut
oneself: **4** gird **5** steel **6** hang on
relative: **5** paren
up: **4** gird, tone **5** build, rally, shore, steel **6** anneal, harden, temper **7** bolster, burgeon, develop, empower, enhance, enliven, fortify, stiffen, toughen **8** bourgeon, buttress, energize, indurate, vitalize **9** intensify, reinforce **10** invigorate
brace __: **4** jack, root **5** table **7** molding
__ brace: **4** arch, knee, main **5** stage **6** batter
braced: **3** set **4** firm **5** ready
bracelet: **5** chain **6** armlet, bangle **7** arm band, jewelry, manacle, trinket **8** ornament
dangler: **5** charm
site: **3** arm **5** ankle, wrist
__ bracelet: **5** charm, slave **6** tennis
bracelets: **5** cuffs, irons **8** manacles, shackles **9** handcuffs
snap the ~ on: **5** pinch, run in **6** arrest
bracer: **5** drink, tonic **8** libation, pick-me-up, stimulus **9** stimulant **10** invigorant
__ Bracer: **4** Skin
braces: **10** suspenders
Brach's: **5** candy
bracing: **4** cool **5** brisk, crisp, fresh **7** healthy, rousing **8** vigorous **10** energizing, fortifying, refreshing
braciola: **4** meat
bracken: **4** fern
Bracken: **3** Peg **5** Eddie
Bracken, Eddie: **5** actor
film: The Fleet's In (1942)
Hail the Conquering Hero (1944)
The Miracle of Morgan's Creek (1944)
Summer Stock (1950)
Too Many Girls (1940)
Brackenridge, Hugh: **6** author, writer
bracket: **3** tie **4** clip, hasp, join, kind, link, prop, sort, yoke **5** clamp, clasp, class, joint, ledge, range, stand **6** corbel, couple, holder, staple **7** butress, concole, connect, section, support **8** category, classify, division, fastener, grouping **9** underline **10** cantilever
cornice ~: **5** ancon
fixer: **5** screw
mast ~: **4** bibb
relative: **5** paren
bracket __: **3** saw **4** foot **5** clock, creep **6** fungus
__ bracket: **3** tax **5** angle **6** square
__-bracket creep: **3** tax
bracketed: **4** akin **6** allied, joined **7** related **8** coherent, relative **9** connected, continual, pertinent, undivided **10** affiliated, applicable, associated, continuous
brackish: **5** briny, salty **6** bitter, saline **7** saltish **8** stagnant **10** unpleasant
bract: **4** leaf **5** frond, palea **6** spathe
brad: **4** tack **8** fastener
Brad: **4** Hall, Park, Pitt **5** Davis **6** Dexter, Dourif, Renfro **7** Garrett, Johnson **8** Anderson
Bradbury: **3** Ray **7** Malcolm
Bradbury, Malcolm: **6** author, writer
Bradbury, Ray: **6** author, writer
genre: sci-fi
work: Dandelion Wine
Fahrenheit 451
The Golden Apples of the Sun
The Illustrated Man
I Sing the Body Electric!
The Martian Chronicles
Something Wicked This Way Comes
Urban Horrors
Braddock, Jim: **5** boxer
dethroned him: **4** Baer
milieu: **4** ring
Bradenton: **4** city, town
locale: **7** Florida
Bradford: **4** city, town **5** Jesse **7** Dillman, William
locale: **6** Canada **7** England, Ontario **9** Yorkshire
Bradlee, Ben: **6** editor
Bradley: **2** Ed **3** Tom **4** Bill, Omar
athletes: **6** Braves
colleague: **5** Kroft, Safer, Stahl **7** Wallace
locale: **6** Peoria **8** Illinois
rank: **3** gen. **7** general
Bradley, Bill: **5** cager
milieu: **5** court
org.: **3** NBA
sport: **10** basketball
Bradley Center: **5** arena
Bradley, Francis Herbert: **7** British **11** philosopher
Bradshaw, Terry: **2** QB
sport: **8** football
Bradstreet, Anne: **4** poet **6** writer
Bradstreet partner: **3** Dun
Brady: **5** Alice, James, Scott **6** Mathew **8** Nicholas
Brady, Alice: **7** actress
film: Beauty for Sale (1933)
The Gay Divorcee (1934)
In Old Chicago (1938, AA)
Joy of Living (1938)
Three Smart Girls (1936)
Young Mr. Lincoln (1939)
Brady Bill opponent: **3** NRA
Brady Bunch Movie, The (1995 film)
cast: Gary Cole, Shelley Long, Michael McKean
director: Betty Thomas
Brady Bunch, The (ABC sitcom)
cast: Ann B. Davis (Alice Nelson)
Florence Henderson (Carol Brady)
Christopher Knight (Peter Brady)
Mike Lookinland (Bobby Brady)
Maureen McCormick (Marcia Brady)
Susan Olsen (Cindy Brady)
Eve Plumb (Jan Brady)
Robert Reed (Mike Brady)
Barry Williams (Greg Brady)
dog: **5** Tiger
threesome: **4** sons **9** daughters

Brady, Mathew: 12 photographer
Braeden: 4 Eric
brag: 4 crow, game, tout **5** boast, extol, exult, gloat, pride, spout, vaunt **6** extoll, flaunt, hotdog, parade **7** bluster, show off, swagger, talk big **8** card game, showboat **9** gasconade, loudmouth **10** grandstand
  nothing to ~ about: 4 so-so **7** average **8** mediocre
Braga: 4 city, town **5** Sonia
  locale: 8 Portugal
Braga, Sonia: 7 actress
  film: Angel Eyes (2001)
    Dona Flor and Her Two Husbands (1978)
    Kiss of the Spider Woman (1985)
    The Milagro Beanfield War (1988)
    Moon Over Parador (1988)
Bragg: 4 Fort **7** Braxton, William
braggadocio: 3 gas **4** wind **5** boast **7** bravado, showoff
braggart: 4 snob **6** crower, egoist, gascon **7** showoff **8** fanfaron **9** know-it-all, loud-mouth, swaggerer
Bragg, William: 3 Sir **7** British **8** Nobelist **9** physicist
__ bragh: 6 Erin go
Brahe, Tycho: 6 Danish **10** astronomer
Brahm: 4 John
Brahma: 3 cow **4** bull, fowl, poem **5** steer **6** bovine, cattle **7** chicken
  bovine feature: 4 hump **6** dewlap
  chicken relative: 6 Bantam, Houdan, Sussex **7** Cornish, Dorking, Leghorn **8** Araucana, Langshan, Shanghai **9** Dominique, Orpington, Wyandotte
Brahman: 3 god **5** Atman, caste, Hindu
  co-equal: 5 Shiva **6** Vishnu
Brahmin: 4 snob **5** caste, elite
__ Brahmin: 6 Boston
Brahms, Johannes: 6 German **8** composer
  work: Academic Festival Overture
    German Requiem
    Lullaby
    Tragic Overture
braid: 4 coil **5** plait, queue, tress, twist, weave **6** cordon, enlace, inlace, splice **7** cornrow, entwine, intwine, pigtail **8** ponytail **9** hairstyle, interlace **10** decoration, intertwine, interweave
  burning ~: 4 wick
  crochet ~: 5 lacet
  gold ~: 5 orris
  ornamental ~: 4 gimp
braided
  bread: 6 hallah
  cord: 4 rope
  locks: 6 dreads **8** pigtails
braids: 4 coif **6** hairdo **8** coiffure
Braille: 5 Louis
  mark: 3 dot
  use ~: 4 read
  writing need: 6 stylus
brain: 3 ace, hit **4** conk, head, mind, sage, whiz, wonk **5** organ **6** genius, reason **7** clobber, creator, egghead, prodigy, scholar, thinker, whiz kid **8** cerebrum, Einstein, highbrow, longhair, virtuoso **9** intellect, mentality, professor **10** cerebellum, gray matter, mastermind
  combining form: 6 cerebr- **7** cerebro- **8** encephal- **9** encephalo-
  computer's ~: 3 CPU
  convolution: 5 gyrus
  ender: 3 pan **4** case, stem, wash, work **5** child, power, storm **6** teaser
  medical prefix: 5 neuro-
  membrane: 4 dura
  messenger: 5 nerve **6** neuron
  opening: 4 pyla
  part: 4 lobe **6** cortex
  passage: 4 iter
  protector: 5 skull **7** cranium
  starter: 3 end **4** bird, fore, hind, lame **5** crack **6** rattle **7** between, feather, scatter
  tissue: 4 tela **5** telae
  trust: 7 cabinet, council
  use one's ~: 5 think **8** cogitate
brain __: 4 case, cell, gain, scan, stem, wash, wave **5** child, coral, drain, trust **7** hormone
__ brain: 4 left **5** on the, right
Brain: 5 novel
  author: Robin Cook
__ Brain: 6 Broca's
Brainard: 3 Ned
braincase: 6 sconce **7** cranium
brainchild: 4 idea **6** scheme **7** concept, thought **8** creation, proposal **9** invention
brained starter: 4 bird, hare, lame **5** crack **7** scatter
Braine, John: 6 author, writer **7** British
brainless: 4 daft, dull **5** giddy, goosy, silly **6** simple, stupid **7** fatuous, foolish **8** headless **9** half-baked **10** irrational
brainpower: 2 IQ **3** wit **4** mind, wits **9** mentality
  measure: 6 IQ test
brains: 3 wit **4** mind, wits **5** asset, sense **6** acumen, reason, wisdom **9** erudition, ingenuity, intellect, mentality, smartness **10** cleverness, horse sense, mastermind
  cudgel one's ~: 4 mull **5** think **6** figure, puzzle **7** work out **8** ruminate **10** deliberate
  opposite: 5 brawn
  pick the ~ of: 7 consult **8** question
  rack one's ~: 4 mull **5** think **6** figure, puzzle **7** work out **8** ruminate **10** deliberate
brainstorm: 4 idea **5** hatch **6** confer, ideate, ponder **7** analyze, consult, imagine, thought **8** cogitate, conceive **9** fabricate, improvise, speculate
  in French: 4 idée
Brainstorm (1983 film)
  cast: Louise Fletcher, Christopher Walken, Natalie Wood
brainteaser: 5 poser **6** enigma, riddle **7** problem, stumper
Braintree: 4 city, town
  locale: 4 Mass.
brain-twister: 5 poser **6** enigma, riddle **7** problem, stumper
brainwash: 4 sway **5** teach, train **8** persuade **9** catechize, condition, inculcate, influence, pound into
brain wave chart: 3 EEG
brainwork: 7 thought **10** cogitation, reflection
brainy: 5 sharp, smart **6** astute, bright, clever, gifted, mental, shrewd **7** bookish, erudite, knowing, learned, sapient **8** cerebral, highbrow, skillful **9** astucious, brilliant, ingenious, inventive **10** insightful, thoughtful
  bunch: 5 Mensa
  not ~: 4 slow **5** dense, thick
  one, maybe: 4 nerd, nurd
braise: 4 cook, sear, stew **5** brown, sauté **6** simmer
brake: 4 curb, fern, halt, slow, snag, stop **5** check, delay, pedal, stall **6** dampen, damper, hamper, hinder, impede, pull up, retard, slow up **7** control, fetch up, inhibit **8** slow down **9** deterrent, hindrance, restraint **10** constraint, decelerate
  device: 4 shoe
  jockey's ~: 4 rein
  neighbor: 3 gas
  problem: 4 skid
  wagon ~: 5 sprag
brake __: 3 pad **4** band, drum, fade, shoe **5** fluid, light, pedal, wheel **6** lining
__ brake: 3 air **4** band, disc, disk, dive, drum, foot, hand **5** cliff, power, press, prony, speed, track **7** coaster, parking
brakes: 3 ABS **4** disc, disk
  fix the ~: 5 repad
  hit the ~: 4 slow, stop **6** ease up, hold up, rein in, slow up **7** ease off **8** hold back, moderate, slow down **10** decelerate
__ brakes: 5 power
Bram: 6 Stoker
bramble: 4 burr, bush **5** briar, brier, furze, gorse, shrub, spine, thorn **6** nettle **7** thistle
  family: 4 rose
  fruit: 9 raspberry **10** blackberry
  relative: 4 sloe **6** kerria, spirea **7** jetbead, spiraea **8** hardhack, ninebark, photinia **9** firethorn, raspberry
brambly: 6 thorny **7** prickly
Bramley: 5 apple
  relative: 4 crab, Gala, Lodi, Rome **5** Mutsu **6** Empire, Ida Red, medlar, Pippin, russet **7** Baldwin, costard, Freedom, Liberty, Spartan, Wealthy, Winesap **8** Cortland, Jonathan, McIntosh **10** Rome Beauty
Brampton: 4 city, town
  locale: 6 Canada **7** Ontario
Bram Stoker's Dracula (1992 film)
  cast: Anthony Hopkins, Gary Oldman, Keanu Reeves, Winona Ryder
  director: Francis Ford Coppola
bran: 5 grain **6** cereal **8** roughage **10** health food
  content: 5 fiber
  source: 3 oat, rye **4** corn **5** wheat
bran __: 6 muffin
__ bran: 3 oat **6** raisin
__-Bran: 3 All
Branagh, Kenneth: 5 actor **8** director
  film: Celebrity (1998)
    Dead Again (1991)
    Henry V (1989)
    How to Kill Your Neighbor's Dog (2001)
    Much Ado About Nothing (1993)
    Othello (1995)
    Peter's Friends (1992)
    Wild Wild West (1999)
  spouse: Emma Thompson
Branca: 5 Ralph
branch: 3 arm **4** bank, cion, fork, limb, part, stem, wing **5** annex, bough, creek, perch, prong, ramus, scion, split, sprig, stick **6** bureau, member, office, ramify, spread, stream **7** chapter, deviate, diverge, outpost, radiate, section **8** category, division, offshoot, position, separate **9** affiliate, bifurcate, confluent, extension, outgrowth, tributary **10** department, subsection, subsidiary
  combining form: 4 clad- **5** clado-
  dove ~: 5 olive
  graft a tree ~: 6 inarch
  hanger: 5 sloth
  off: 4 fork **6** bisect, ramble, spread
  olive ~: 5 peace, truce **7** amnesty **9** armistice, ceasefire **10** moratorium
  out: 4 grow **5** add to, widen **6** expand, extend **7** broaden, develop, enlarge, radiate **8** increase **9** diversify
  railroad ~: 4 spur **6** feeder
  river ~: 4 trib. **9** tributary
  small ~: 4 twig **5** shoot
  structure: 4 nest
  tree ~: 4 limb, rame **5** bough
branch __: 3 cut, out **4** line, wilt **5** point, water
__ branch: 5 olive
Branch: 6 Rickey
__ Branch: 3 Red **4** Long
branched: 6 ramous **8** arboreal
branches: 4 rami
  decorative ~: 6 bocage
  remove ~: 3 lop **5** prune
  tree ~: 6 canopy
branchlike: 6 ramose
Brancusi: 10 Constantin
brand: 3 ilk **4** kind, logo, mark, name, scar, sear, slur, sort, stab, type **5** badge, class, genre, genus, label, odium, stain, stamp, taint, title **6** accuse, kidney, manner, stigma **7** product, variety **8** flambeau, hallmark **9** trademark **10** impression, imputation, stigmatize
  name: 4 make, mark **5** label **9** trademark
__ brand: 4 name **5** house, store **7** private
Brand: 3 Max **7** Neville
Brand author: Henrik Ibsen
branded beasts: 6 cattle
Brandeis, Louis: 5 judge **6** jurist **7** justice
Brandenburg Concertos composer: 4 Bach
Brandenburg Gate site: 6 Berlin
branding iron, use a: 4 mark, sear
brandish: 4 show, wave **5** shake, wield **6** dangle, flaunt, parade **7** display, show off, swagger, trot out **8** flourish **10** wave around
brand-new: 3 new **4** mint **5** fresh, novel **6** cherry, red-hot, virgin **7** updated **8** up-to-date, virginal
Brand New Key (1971 song) artist: Melanie
Brando, Marlon: 5 actor
  adopted home: 5 Samoa
  birthplace: 3 Neb. **4** Nebr. **5** Omaha **8** Nebraska
  film: Apocalypse Now (1979)
    A Countess From Hong Kong (1967)
    Don Juan DeMarco (1995)
    The Freshman (1990)
    The Godfather (1972, AA)
    Guys and Dolls (1955)
    Julius Caesar (1953)
    Last Tango in Paris (1973)
    The Men (1950)
    One-Eyed Jacks (1961)
    On the Waterfront (1954, AA)
    Sayonara (1957)
    The Score (2001)
    A Streetcar Named Desire (1951)
    Superman (1978)
    The Teahouse of the August Moon (1956)
    Viva Zapata! (1952)
    The Wild One (1954)
    The Young Lions (1958)
Brandon: 3 Lee **4** city, Cruz, town **7** de Wilde
  locale: 6 Canada **7** Florida **8** Manitoba
Brandon University
  location: 6 Canada **8** Manitoba
Brandt, Willy: 6 German **8** Nobelist
brandy: 4 marc, raki **5** drink **6** cognac, grappa, liquor **8** beverage, eau de vie
  apple ~: 8 calvados
  cherry ~: 6 kirsch
  flavoring: 4 plum **5** apple, peach **6** cherry **10** blackberry

French ~: **4** marc
glass: **7** snifter
Italian ~: **6** grappa
letters: **3** VSO **4** VSOP
Peruvian ~: **5** pisco
plum ~: **9** slivovitz
ready to sell, as ~: **4** aged **8** mellowed
South American ~: **5** pisco
store ~: **3** age
brandy __: **4** mint **7** snifter
Brandy
last name: Norwood
song: Baby (1995)
The Boy Is Mine (1998)
Brokenhearted (1995)
Have You Ever? (1998)
I Wanna Be Down (1994)
Sittin' Up in My Room (1996)
What About Us? (2002)
Brandy (1972 song) artist: Looking Glass
Bran Flakes: **6** cereal
competitor: **3** Kix **4** Life, Trix **5** Kashi, Quisp, Total **6** Kaboom, Muesli, Oreo O's, Pablum, Smacks **7** All-Bran, Crispix, Harmony, Hunny B's, Mueslix, Oat Bran, Pokemon **8** Boo Berry, Cheerios, Corn Chex, Corn Pops, Fiber One, Rice Chex, Special K, Uncle Sam, Wheaties **9** Alpha Bits, Apple Zaps, Grape Nuts, Honey Comb, Just Right, Wheat Chex **10** Apple Jacks, Cap'n Crunch, Cocoa Puffs, Froot Loops, Mini-Wheats, Nutri-Grain, Puffed Rice, Quaker Oats, Smart Start **11** Cocoa Blasts, Cookie Crisp, Golden Crisp, Lucky Charms, Puffed Wheat, Sweet Crunch, Waffle Crisp
Branford: **8** Marsalis
Branigan, Laura
song: Gloria (1982)
Self Control (1984)
Solitaire (1983)
brannigan: **4** riot **5** melee **6** barney **7** quarrel, wrangle **10** difference
Branson: **4** city, town **7** Richard
locale: **8** Missouri
brant: **4** bird, fowl **5** goose
relative: **4** nene **7** graylag
Brant: **9** Sebastian
Brantford: **4** city, town
locale: **6** Canada **7** Ontario
Branting, Karl: **7** Swedish **8** Nobelist
Brant, Sebastian: **4** poet **6** German
Branwell: **6** Brontë
Braque, Georges: **6** artist **7** painter
homeland: **6** France
style: **6** Cubism
__ bras: **7** chapeau
__ Brasco: **6** Donnie
Bras d'Or: **4** lake
locale: **6** Canada **10** Cape Breton
brash: **4** bold, loud, pert, rash, rude **5** cocky, hasty, nervy, pushy, rough, sassy, saucy, unshy **6** brassy, brazen, cheeky, jaunty, madcap, unwary **7** boorish, forward, selfish, uncivil **8** cocksure, headlong, heedless, impolite, impudent, insolent, reckless, tactless, unsubtle **9** audacious, barefaced, foolhardy, hotheaded, impetuous, impolitic, imprudent, impulsive, shameless, unadvised, uncareful, untactful, vivacious **10** headstrong, ill-advised, incautious, indiscreet, sophomoric, ungracious, unthinking, vociferant
brashness: **4** gall, sass **5** cheek, nerve, sauce **10** confidence, effrontery
Brasilia: **4** city, town **7** capital
locale: **6** Brazil
Brasov: **4** city, town
locale: **7** Romania, Rumania **8** Roumania
brass: **4** gall, mgmt., tuba **5** alloy, cheek, metal, moxie, nerve, sauce **6** cornet, hubris, hybris, yellow **7** reddish, trumpet **8** audacity, chutzpah, official, rudeness, superior, temerity, trombone **9** arrogance, executive, impudence, insolence, personage **10** effrontery, executives, management, sousaphone
color kin: **4** buff, corn, gold, lime, rust, sand **5** blond, coral, cream, flaxy, lemon, maize, ocher, ochre, peach, rusty, straw **6** blonde, canary, chammy, citron, crocus, flaxen, shammy, shamoy **7** apricot, chamois, citrine, jasmine, mustard, nankeen, old gold, saffron, xanthic **8** daffodil, primrose **9** champagne, goldenrod, jessamine
combining form: **5** chalc-, chalk- **6** chalco-, chalko-
component: **4** zinc **6** copper
ender: **4** ware **5** bound
fanfare: **5** tusch
get down to ~ tacks: **6** detail **7** account, itemize, specify **9** make clear, stipulate
hat: **4** boss **6** top dog **7** manager **8** employer, superior **9** executive
instrument: **4** horn, tuba **5** bugle **6** cornet **7** trumpet **8** trombone **10** sousaphone
source of future ~: **3** OCS, OTC, OTS
tacks: **5** facts **7** reality **9** actuality, essential **10** foundation
top ~: **4** mgmt. **5** chief **7** officer **8** kingfish **9** commander, key player **10** management
brass __: **3** hat **4** band, ring **5** tacks **8** knuckles
__ brass: **3** low, red, top **4** beta **5** alpha, horse
brassardo: **5** armor
brass-colored: **7** aeneous
Brasselle: **5** Keefe
brasserie: **6** bistro, eatery **10** restaurant
brassie: **4** club, wood **8** golf club
brasslike alloy: **6** latten
Brass Monkey: **5** drink
brassy: **4** bold, loud, rude **5** brash, nervy, saucy, unshy **6** brazen, cheeky, daring, not shy, shrill, vulgar **7** blaring, blatant, forward, lowbred **8** fearless, flippant, impudent, insolent, overbold, strident **9** audacious, barefaced, clamorous, outspoken, shameless, unabashed **10** unblushing, vociferant
brat: **3** imp **4** punk, snip **5** child, kiddy **6** bad boy, urchin **7** hellion **9** prankster, rotten kid, youngster **10** holy terror
be a ~: **4** sass **5** act up **7** disobey **9** misbehave
Christmas present for a ~: **4** coal
ender: **5** wurst
smile: **5** smirk
__ brat: **4** army
Brat __: **4** Pack
Brat Farrar author: **3** Tey
Bratislava: **4** city, town **7** capital
locale: **8** Slovakia
river: **6** Danube
Brattain, Walter: **8** Nobelist **9** physicist
Bratt, Benjamin: **5** actor
spouse: Talisa Soto
bratty: **5** nasty **6** impish, spoilt, unruly **7** spoiled **8** impudent **10** ill-behaved
bratwurst: **4** meat **7** sausage
unit: **4** link
bräuhaus order: **4** bier
Braulio: **5** Baeza
Braun: **5** razor **6** shaver
alternative: **7** Norelco **9** Remington
Braun, Carl: **6** German **8** Nobelist **9** physicist
Braunschweiger: **4** meat **7** sausage
brava: **5** cheer
__ Brava: **5** Costa
Bravada: **3** SUV **4** Olds **10** Oldsmobile
bravado: **5** boast, pluck, spunk, swash **7** bluster, bombast **8** bragging, defiance **9** gasconade, pomposity **10** feistiness, pretension, swaggering
Bravados, The (1958 film)
cast: Stephen Boyd, Joan Collins, Gregory Peck
director: Henry King
brave: **4** bold, dare, defy, face, game, risk **5** gutsy, manly, nervy, stout **6** daring, endure, gritty, heroic, plucky, strong, suffer **7** dashing, defiant, doughty, gallant, impavid, ride out, valiant, venture, warrior, weather **8** confront, fearless, heroical, intrepid, resolute, spirited, stalwart, unafraid, valorous **9** audacious, challenge, confident, daredevil, dauntless, go through, herculean, stand up to, undaunted, unfearful, unfearing, withstand **10** chivalrous, courageous, mettlesome, undismayed
abode: **4** tipi **5** lodge, tepee **6** teepee
be ~: **4** dare, defy **5** fight **6** oppose **7** venture **9** challenge
deed: **4** coup
it out: **4** last, stay **6** endure, hang in **8** stand pat
name meaning ~: **5** Casey
one: **4** hero **7** heroine **8** explorer **10** adventurer
Brave
Hall-of-Famer: **5** Aaron, Spahn **7** Mathews **9** Ed Mathews, Hank Aaron **10** Henry Aaron
rival: **3** Cub, Met, Red **4** Expo, Twin **5** Angel, Astro, Giant, Padre, Rocky, Royal, Tiger **6** Brewer, Dodger, Indian, Marlin, Oriole, Philly, Pirate, Ranger, Red Sox, Yankee **7** Blue Jay, Mariner **8** Athletic, Cardinal, Devil Ray, White Sox
Brave __, The: **3** One **5** Bulls
Brave Bulls, The (1951 film)
cast: Mel Ferrer, Anthony Quinn
director: Robert Rossen
Braveheart (1995 film)
cast: Mel Gibson, Sophie Marceau, Patrick McGoohan
director: Mel Gibson
garb: **4** kilt
group: **4** clan
brave heart, name meaning: **6** Howard
Brave Little Toaster, The (1987 film)
director: Jerry Rees
Brave Men author: **4** Pyle
Brave New World
author: Aldous Huxley
character: **4** Marx, Mond **5** Linda **6** Lenina **7** Bernard
drug: **4** soma
Braverman: **4** Bart
bravery: **4** dash, grit, guts **5** heart, nerve, pluck, spunk, valor **6** daring, mettle, spirit, starch **7** courage, heroism, prowess **8** audacity, backbone, boldness, gumption, strength **9** assurance, endurance, fortitude, gallantry, hardiness **10** confidence, knighthood, moral fiber
Braves: **4** nine, team **7** Bradley
home: **7** Atlanta
org.: **3** MLB, NLE
sport: **8** baseball
brave spear, name meaning: **6** Gerard
bravo: **3** rah **5** cheer, huzza **6** hoorah, hooray, hurrah, hurray, huzzah
in Spanish: **3** olé
Bravo: **7** channel
alternative: **3** AMC, HBO, IFC, SHO, TMC **4** Flix **5** Starz **6** Encore **7** Cinemax **8** Showtime, Sundance
offering: **4** film **5** movie
__ Bravo: **3** Rio
bravos: **7** ovation
braw: **3** def, rad **4** aces, A-one, boss, cool, dece, fine, gear, keen, neat, nice, phat, tuff **5** dandy, ducky, grand, great, marvy, neato, nobby, prime, slick, super, swell **6** bang on, bang-up, bonzer, bosker, choice, divine, dreamy, far-out, gnarly, groovy, lovely, peachy, slap-up, spot on, superb, terrif, tiptop, unreal, whizzo, wicked **7** amazing, awesome, capital, corking, perfect, ripping, skookum, stellar, sublime **8** dazzling, especial, eximious, fabulous, five-star, four-star, frabjous, glorious, heavenly, jim-dandy, slambang, smashing, splendid, standout, sterling, stickout, superior, terrific, top-level, topnotch, very good, wondrous **9** bodacious, Endsville, excellent, exemplary, exquisite, first-rate, high-grade, hunky-dory, marvelous, sollicker, top-flight, wonderful **10** first-class, hotsy-totsy, jack-a-dandy, out of sight, peachy-keen, phenomenal, remarkable, stupendous, super-duper
brawl: **3** row **4** feud, fray, riot **5** argue, clash, fight, melee, mix-up, scrap, set-to **6** affray, barney, battle, bicker, fracas, go at it, racket, ruckus, rumble, rumpus, strife, tumult, tussle, uproar **7** contest, dispute, quarrel, rhubarb, rioting, scuffle, wrangle **8** argument, brouhaha, disorder, outbreak, squabble, struggle **9** altercate, brannigan, duke it out, imbroglio, raise Cain **10** donnybrook, free-for-all, roughhouse
weapon: **4** fist
Brawley: **4** city, town
locale: **10** California
brawling: **4** wild **5** rowdy **10** boisterous, disorderly
brawn: **3** vim **4** beef, dint, meat, thew **5** force, might, power, sinew, thews, vigor **6** energy, muscle **7** fitness, muscles, potence, potency, stamina **8** strength, vitality **9** beefiness, endurance, fortitude, hardiness, huskiness, puissance, stoutness, toughness **10** brute force, mightiness, robustness, ruggedness, sturdiness
brawny: **3** fit **4** hale, iron, wiry **5** beefy, burly, hardy, hefty, hunky, husky, lusty, macho, nervy, stout, tough **6** hearty, mighty, potent, robust, rugged, sinewy, steely, stocky, strong, sturdy, virile **7** doughty **8** athletic, forceful, indurate, muscular, powerful, puissant, Stallone, stalwart, thickset, vigorous **9** Atlantean, herculean, strapping, well-built **10** able-bodied, red-blooded
guy: **5** he-man
Brawny: **10** paper towel
competitor: **4** Viva **5** Scott **6** Bounty
Braxton: **4** Toni **5** Bragg
Braxton, Toni
song: Another Sad Love Song (1993)
Breathe Again (1993)
Un-Break My Heart (1996)
You Mean the World to Me (1994)
You're Makin' Me High (1996)

bray: 3 baa, cry 4 blat, honk, hoot, rasp, wail 5 blare, blast, bleat, crush, neigh 6 bellow, heehaw, whinny
half a ~: 3 haw, hee
brayer: 3 ass 4 mule 5 burro 6 donkey
Braz.
neighbor: 3 Arg., Bol., Uru., Ven.
see also Brazil
braze: 4 weld 6 solder
brazen: 4 bold, dare, flip, loud, pert, rude 5 brash, cocky, fresh, gutsy, nervy, sassy, saucy, smart 6 arrant, awless, brassy, cheeky, daring, flashy, snippy, tawdry 7 assured, aweless, blatant, defiant, forward, glaring, lowbred, uncivil 8 flagrant, flippant, immodest, impolite, impudent, insolent, overbold, snippety 9 audacious, barefaced, out of line, shameless, unabashed, unashamed 10 outrageous, unblushing, ungracious
female: 4 minx 5 hussy 7 Jezebel
brazen-__: 5 faced
brazenness: 4 gall, sass 5 cheek, nerve, sauce 8 defiance 9 insolence 10 effrontery
brazier: 5 grill
residue: 4 coal 5 ember 6 cinder
Brazil: 6 nation 7 country
airline: 5 Varig
bandleader: 5 Cugat
bird: 7 cariama, seriema
capital: 8 Brasilia
Christmas in ~: 5 Natal
city: 4 Mauá, Pará 5 Bauru, Belém, Natal, Serra 6 Aruana, Canoas, Cuiabá, Franca, Goiâna, Ilhéus, Lorena, Maceió, Manaos, Manaus, Olinda, Osasco, Recife, Santos 7 Aracaju, Caruaru, Diadema, Guarujá, Jundiaí, Limeira, Maringá, Niterói, Pelotas, Taubaté, Uberaba, Vitoria 8 Anápolis, Blumenau, Campinas, Contagem, Curitiba, Londrina, Paulista, Salvador, Santarém, Sorocaba, Teresina 9 Fortaleza, Guarulhos, Joinville, Vila Velha 10 Imperatriz, Juiz de Fora, Nova Iguaçu, Pórto Velho, Santo André 11 Pórto Alegre
dance: 5 samba 7 lambada 9 bossa nova
diamond-mining region: 5 Goias
emperor: 5 Pedro
explorer: 6 Cabral
fish: 5 piaba 8 arapaima
language: 4 Tupi 10 Portuguese
macaw: 3 ara
money: 3 rei 5 conto 7 milreis, moidore 8 cruzeiro
mountain: 9 Sugar Loaf 10 Serra do Mar
neighbor: 4 Peru 6 Guyana 7 Bolivia, Uruguay 8 Colombia, Paraguay, Suriname 9 Argentina, Venezuela
org.: 3 OAS
palm: 5 assai
people: 3 Oti 4 Tupi 8 Caingang
poet: 7 Andrade 8 Bandeira
port: 3 Rio 4 Pará 5 Bahia, Belem, Ceara, natal 6 Cuiabá, Ilhéus, Recife, Santos 9 Fortaleza
river: 4 Acre 5 Negro, Purus, Xingu 6 Amazon, Javari
soccer star: 4 Pelé
state: 4 Acre, Pará 5 Amapa, Bahia, Ceara, Goias, Piaui 6 Parana 7 Alagoas, Paraiba, Roraima, Sergipe 8 Amazonas, Maranhao, Rondonia, Sao Paulo 9 Tocantins 10 Mato Grosso
tennis pro: 5 Bueno
title: 3 dom 6 senhor 7 senhora
tree: 7 araroba, seringa 8 carnauba, oiticica
waterfall: 6 Iguaçu 7 Iguassú
writer: 5 Amado, Ramos 7 Alencar, Queirôs
Brazil (1985 film)
cast: Robert De Niro, Kim Greist, Jonathan Pryce
director: Terry Gilliam
Brazil __: 3 nut 7 Current
Brazilian __: 4 ruby 5 guava, plume 7 emerald, peridot, rhatany
brazilianite: 3 gem 8 gemstone
Brazos: 5 river
city on the ~: 4 Waco
locale: 5 Texas
Brazzaville: 4 city, port, town 7 capital
locale: 5 Congo
Brazzi, Rossano: 5 actor
film: Light in the Piazza (1962)
Rome Adventure (1962)
South Pacific (1958)
Summertime (1955)
Woman Times Seven (1967)
Brea: 4 city, town
locale: 10 California
breach: 3 gap 4 foul, gulf, hole, rent, rift, tear 5 break, chasm, clash, cleft, crack, lapse, split 6 cranny, hiatus, invade, schism, sunder 7 discord, dispute, dissent, fissure, infract, interim, offense, opening, quarrel, rupture, violate 8 argument, conflict, disunity, fracture, interval, invasion, trespass, variance 9 deviation, violation 10 alienation, contravene, disharmony, dissension, encroach on, falling-out, infraction
of contract: 4 tort 9 improbity
of judgment: 5 error, lapse
of law: 5 crime, wrong 6 felony 7 misdeed, offense 9 violation 10 misconduct, wrongdoing
of secrecy: 4 leak
breach of __: 5 faith, trust 7 promise
Breach of Faith author: Theodore H. White
bread: 3 bun, nan, oof, pay, rye 4 carb, cash, coin, food, gelt, jack, kail, kale, loaf, loot, peag, pelf, pita, pone, roll, rusk, wage 5 bagel, bialy, bills, bucks, clams, dough, funds, lucre, matzo, money, moola, mopus, pesos, poori, rhino, sewan, toast, wages, white 6 dinero, do-re-mi, mammon, mazuma, moolah, muffin, seawan, silver, specie, wampum, wealth 7 aliment, anadama, bannock, biscuit, brioche, cabbage, capital, challah, chapati, crouton, crumpet, dollars, lettuce, oatcake, ooftish, popover, pretzel, saltine, scratch, shekels 8 baguette, bankroll, cold cash, cracknel, currency, hard cash, hardtack, smackers, zwieback 9 banknotes, croissant, frogskins, long green, simoleons, sourdough, sweet roll 10 greenbacks, green stuff, johnnycake, melba toast, sustenance, whole-grain, whole-wheat
and butter: 6 living 7 aliment 10 livelihood
base: 5 flour
braided ~: 6 hallah
break ~: 3 eat, sup 4 dine
brown ~: 5 toast
chamber: 4 oven
choice: 3 rye 5 white 10 whole-grain, whole-wheat
combining form: 4 arto-
daily ~: 4 diet, food 10 sustenance
dry ~: 4 rusk
emanation: 5 aroma
end: 4 heel 5 crust
ender: 3 box, nut 4 root 5 board, fruit 6 basket, winner
Eucharist ~: 5 wafer
in French: 4 pain
in Italian: 4 pane
in Japanese: 3 pan
in Spanish: 3 pan
like old ~: 5 moldy, stale
make ~: 4 bake, earn 5 knead
mold: 6 fungus
morsel: 5 crumb
need: 5 yeast 6 gluten
pocket ~: 4 pita
pudding: 7 dessert
Southern ~: 4 pone
spread: 3 jam 4 mayo, oleo 5 honey, jelly 9 margarine, marmalade
starter: 3 bee 4 corn, flat 5 short, sweet 6 ginger
store: 6 bakery 10 patisserie
unbaked ~: 5 dough
unit: 4 loaf 5 slice
unleavened ~: 5 matzo 6 matzah, matzoh
bread __: 4 line, mold 5 flour, knife 7 pudding
__ bread: 3 rye, sea 4 corn, holy, loaf, pita, pone, ship, soda 5 altar, black, break, brown, light, pilot, quick, spoon, wheat, white 6 batter, French, garlic, gluten, Indian, monkey 7 anadama, biscuit, Italian
Bread
song: Baby I'm-a Want You (1971)
Everything I Own (1972)
If (1971)
It Don't Matter to Me (1970)
Lost Without Your Love (1976)
Make It With You (1970)
bread-and-breakfast: 3 inn 7 lodging
bread-and-butter: 8 economic
Bread and Circuses author: 4 Agar
Bread and Wine author: Ignazio Silone
breadbasket: 3 gut, tum 5 belly, tummy 7 abdomen, stomach
province: 3 Alt., Man. 4 Alta. 7 Alberta 8 Manitoba
state: 3 Ill., Kan., Neb. 4 Iowa, N. Dak., Nebr., S. Dak. 6 Kansas 8 Illinois, Nebraska
breadfruit: 4 tree
family: 8 mulberry
relative: 3 fig 4 upas 5 ficus, ramon 6 antiar, fustic
breadth: 4 area, size, span 5 gamut, range, reach, scale, scope, space, sweep, width 6 extent, length, spread 7 compass, expanse 8 diameter, distance, fullness, latitude, vastness, wideness 9 amplitude, broadness, dimension, full range, immensity, largeness, magnitude, ranginess, roominess 10 liberality
add ~ to: 5 widen 6 expand 7 broaden, educate
of view: 6 vision
__-breadth: 5 hand's
Bread, Wine, and Salt author: Alden Nowlan
breadwinner: 5 labor 6 earner, worker 8 employee
break: 2 go 3 fly, gap, mar, top 4 beat, bust, chip, flee, halt, harm, hole, hurt, luck, lull, rend, rent, rest, rift, rive, ruin, shot, snap, stay, stop, tame, tear, tilt, time, verb 5 cleft, crack, crash, crush, letup, occur, outdo, pause, smash, snack, split, start, wreck, yield 6 appear, breach, breath, catnap, cesura, chance, change, convey, cut out, damage, decamp, decode, demote, emerge, escape, exceed, get out, happen, hiatus, impair, impart, inform, injure, injury, lacuna, lessen, let out, ravine, recess, reduce, refute, relief, reveal, schism, soften, subdue, sunder, unglue, weaken 7 abandon, abscond, caesura, crumble, cushion, destroy, disable, disjoin, disobey, divulge, fissure, getaway, holiday, implode, infract, interim, lighten, opening, respite, run away, rupture, shatter, split up, surpass, suspend, take ten, time out, violate 8 announce, bankrupt, breather, clear out, cleavage, decipher, demolish, diminish, disclose, dispirit, disprove, division, downtime, fracture, fragment, go beyond, infringe, intermit, interval, leverage, moderate, omission, outstrip, proclaim, puncture, separate, straiten, take five, vacation 9 advantage, cessation, come forth, cut and run, disregard, downgrade, hesitancy, humiliate, interlude, interrupt, pauperize, punctuate, transpire, violation 10 alienation, come to pass, come undone, contravene, controvert, demoralize, disconfirm, disruption, divergence, impoverish, make public, separation, suspension, transgress
a bronc: 4 tame
abruptly: 4 snap 5 crack 7 shatter
a fast: 3 eat
afternoon ~: 3 nap 6 siesta, snooze
a habit: 4 kick, wean
a law: 3 sin 6 breach, offend 7 disobey, do wrong, infract, violate 8 encroach, infringe 9 disregard 10 transgress
a promise: 3 lie 6 renege 7 violate
a record: 5 excel 6 exceed
away: 5 leave, rebel 6 escape, revolt, secede
bad ~: 6 mishap 8 hard luck 9 adversity 10 misfortune
big ~: 4 luck 7 opening
bread: 3 eat, sup 4 dine
camp: 5 leave 6 depart, pack up
coffee ~: 4 lull, rest 5 pause
down: 3 cry, rot, sob 4 fail, weep, wilt 5 decay, erode, spoil 6 die out, fall in, go awry 7 conk out, crumple, dissect, founder, go kaput, succumb 8 collapse, dissolve, simplify 9 come apart, decompose, dismantle, fall apart, inculcate 10 go to pieces
ender: 4 away, down, fast, neck 5 front, point, water 7 dancing, through
even: 3 tie 10 keep up with
faith: 6 betray, renege 7 sell out 8 go back on
forth: 4 spew, spue 5 erupt, spout
ground: 4 plow 5 begin 7 advance, kick off, pioneer
in: 3 rob, use 4 open, raid 5 barge, enter, enure, inure, steal, teach, train 6 burgle, irrupt, meddle, school 7 educate, obtrude, prepare 8 accustom, instruct, trespass 9 condition, get used to, habituate, interrupt, penetrate 10 burglarize, inaugurate
in hostilities: 5 truce 9 ceasefire
in relations: 4 rift 6 breach, schism 7 quarrel 10 falling-out
in the action: 4 lull 5 lapse 6 recess
into pieces: 5 smash 6 shiver 7 shatter 8 fragment, splinter
in two: 5 halve 6 bisect
loose: 4 bail, flee 6 escape, run off 7 get away
lucky ~: 4 boon 5 fluke, mercy 6 chance 7 godsend 8 blessing, fortuity, windfall
make a ~: 2 go 3 run 4 bolt 6 escape 7 abscond, so south 8 skip town 10 fly the coop, go on the lam

of day: 4 dawn, morn 5 sunup 7 morning, sunrise
off: 3 end 4 halt, part, quit, snap, stop, wean 5 cease, sever, spall, split 6 cancel, desist, detach, divide, recess, unlink 7 disjoin, split up 8 disunite, separate, set apart, surcease, uncouple 9 close down 10 call it a day, disconnect
one's heart: 4 dump, jilt 6 bum out, sadden 7 abandon, depress, let down 8 dispirit, distress 9 throw over 10 disappoint, dishearten
one's neck: 4 toil 5 slave, sweat 6 hustle, strain, strive 8 bear down, struggle
open: 5 burst, crack, force
point: 5 ad out
price ~: 4 sale 6 rebate 9 reduction
sentence ~: 4 dash 5 colon, comma 6 hyphen 9 semi-colon
silence: 3 say 5 speak
soldier's ~: 5 leave 8 furlough
starter: 3 day 4 fire, jail, news, wind 5 heart, house
stride: 6 falter
take a ~: 4 rest 5 pause, relax 6 lay off, recess, rest up, unwind 8 loosen up
the ice: 5 begin, start 6 embark, launch 8 commence
the news: 3 air 4 leak, tell 6 advise, clue in, inform, report, reveal, tip off 7 let slip 8 announce, disclose 9 make known 10 make public
the peace: 4 riot
the record of: 3 top 4 beat, best, pass 5 outdo 6 better 7 eclipse, surpass 8 outshine, outstrip, surmount
the rules: 4 defy 5 cheat, flout 7 disobey 9 disregard
through: 4 loom 6 appear, pierce
up: 3 end 4 ha-ha, halt, part, quit, rend, ruin 5 cease, close, end it, laugh, loose, smash, split 6 cackle, divide, finish, giggle, guffaw, harrow, loosen, ravage, recess, titter, weaken 7 adjourn, chortle, chuckle, disband, suspend 8 conclude, convulse, disperse, levigate, pack it in, separate 9 decompose, dismantle, knock down, pulverize, terminate 10 call it a day
up with: 4 dump 7 divorce 8 separate 9 throw over
with: 5 rebel 7 quarrel 9 repudiate
break __: 3 off, out 4 a leg, camp, down, even, into, rank 5 bread, cover, dance, loose, of day, point 6 ground 7 dancing, through
break __ ground: 3 new
__ break: 3 tea 4 fast 5 take a, tough 6 coffee, spring, winter 7 service, station
__ Break: 4 Fast 5 Point
breakable: 5 frail 6 flimsy 7 brittle, fragile, rickety, unsound 8 delicate 9 frangible, splintery
breakage: 4 harm, loss 5 abuse, crack 6 damage, injury 9 liability 10 impairment
breakaway group: 4 cult, sect
Breakdance (1984 song) artist: Irene Cara
breakdown: 6 fiasco 7 debacle, failure 8 analysis, collapse 9 diagnosis 10 disruption
beacon: 5 flare
combining form: 4 -lyze
diplomacy ~: 4 rift
of cells: 5 lysis
societal ~: 5 anomy 6 anomie
breaker: 4 surf, wave 5 surge 6 billow
circuit ~: 4 fuse
combining form: 5 -clast
ground ~: 3 hoe 5 spade 6 shovel 7 pioneer 8 inventor
ice ~: 4 pick
sound-barrier ~: 3 SST
starter: 3 ice, jaw, law, tie 4 back 5 trail 6 ground, strike
breaker __: 4 card 5 point, strip
__ breaker: 7 circuit, prairie
Breaker Morant (1979 film)
cast: Bryan Brown, Jack Thompson, John Waters, Edward Woodward
director: Bruce Beresford
break-even amount: 4 cost
breakfast: 3 eat 4 meal
bed and ~: 3 inn 7 lodging
beverage: 2 OJ 3 tea 4 milk 5 cocoa, juice 6 coffee
British ~ item: 6 kipper
Brooklyn ~: 5 bagel
choice: 3 ham 4 eggs 5 bacon, juice, links, toast 6 cereal, Danish, omelet, waffle 7 hotcake, pancake, sausage 9 sweet roll
continental ~ item: 3 tea 4 milk 5 donut, fruit 6 coffee, Danish, muffin 8 doughnut
device: 3 urn 6 brewer, juicer 7 toaster
fish: 3 lox
fruit: 5 melon 6 orange 9 cantaloup 10 grapefruit
grain: 3 oat, rye 5 wheat 6 cereal
holder: 4 bowl, tray 6 eggcup
late ~ hour: 3 ten 5 ten a.m.
nook: 6 alcove
pancake ~: 7 benefit 10 fundraiser
pastry: 5 donut 6 Danish 8 doughnut 9 sweet roll
roll: 5 bagel 9 croissant
spread: 3 jam 4 oleo 5 honey, jelly 6 butter 9 margarine, marmalade
time: 7 morning
__ breakfast: 4 dog's 7 English
Breakfast Antiphonies composer: 4 Bach
Breakfast at Tiffany's: 4 book, film
author: Truman Capote
cast: Buddy Ebsen, Audrey Hepburn, Patricia Neal, George Peppard
composer: 7 Mancini
director: Blake Edwards
Breakfast Club, The: 5 radio
Breakfast Club, The (1985 film)
cast: Emilio Estevez, Anthony Michael Hall, Judd Nelson, Molly Ringwald, Ally Sheedy
director: John Hughes
Breakheart Pass (1976 film)
cast: Charles Bronson, Richard Crenna, Ben Johnson
break-in: 3 job 5 heist, theft 6 bag job 7 robbery 8 burglary, thievery
Break In author: Dick Francis
breaking: 3 hot
and entering: 5 crime 6 felony
combining form: 6 -clasis 7 -clastic
new ground: 5 fresh, novel 6 clever 7 unusual 8 creative, inspired, original, singular 9 ingenious, inventive 10 innovative
point: 5 limit 8 showdown
starter: 5 heart 6 ground
__-breaking: 4 back
Breaking Away (1979 film)
cast: Barbara Barrie, Dennis Christopher, Paul Dooley, Dennis Quaid, Daniel Stern
cat: 7 Fellini
director: Peter Yates
vehicle: 4 bike 7 bicycle
Breaking In (1989 film)
cast: Sheila Kelley, Burt Reynolds, Casey Siemaszko
Breaking Point, The (1950 film)
cast: John Garfield, Patricia Neal, Phyllis Thaxter
director: Michael Curtiz
Breaking the Sound Barrier (1952 film)
cast: Ralph Richardson, Ann Todd
director: David Lean
Breaking Up Is Hard to Do (1962 song) artist: Neil Sedaka
Breakin' in a Brand New Broken Heart (1961 song) artist: Connie Francis
Break It to Me Gently (song) artist: Brenda Lee, Juice Newton
Break My Stride (1983 song) artist: Matthew Wilder
breakneck: 4 fast 5 brisk, fleet, hasty, quick, rapid, steep, swift 6 flying, racing, snappy, speedy 7 express, hurried, instant 8 headlong, reckless 9 dangerous, foolhardy, rapid-fire, uncareful, whirlwind 10 double-time, hypersonic, supersonic
break new __: 6 ground
break of __: 3 day
Break of Day author: John Donne
break one's __: 4 neck 5 heart
Breakout (1975 film)
cast: Charles Bronson, Robert Duvall, Jill Ireland
Breaks of the Game, The author: David Halberstam
break the __: 3 ice
breakthrough: 5 boost 7 advance 8 advanced, progress 9 milestone
break-up: 5 split 7 divorce, parting 10 separation
Break Up to Make Up (1973 song) artist: Stylistics
breakwater: 4 mole, pier 5 jetty, levee, wharf 7 sea wall 10 embankment
__ Breaky Heart: 4 Achy
bream: 4 fish 5 porgy 7 sunfish 8 bluegill
relative: 4 dace 6 minnow
Bream: 3 Sid
breast: 5 chest
beat one's ~: 6 lament
ender: 4 bone, work 5 plate 6 stroke
make a clean ~ of: 5 admit 7 own up to
starter: 3 red
breastbone combining form: 5 stern- 6 sterno-
__-breasted: 6 double, single
Breasted: 5 James
breastwork: 7 bastion, rampart
breath: 4 gasp, gulp, hint, jiff, life, odor, pant, puff, rest, wind 5 aroma, break, jiffy, pause, shade, smell, touch, trace, vapor, whiff 6 eupnea, minute, murmur, wheeze 7 respite, soupçon, whisper 10 exhalation, inhalation, suggestion
baby's ~: 5 plant 6 flower
brief ~: 4 gasp, huff, pant, puff
catch one's ~: 4 rest 5 pause
combining form: 4 -pnea 5 -pnoea 6 pneumo- 7 pneumat- 8 pneumato-
deep ~: 4 sigh
draw ~: 4 live
ender: 6 taking
freshener: 4 mint 6 cachou
holder: 4 lung
mint: 4 Cert
of air: 4 wind 6 breeze
of life: 5 anima 6 spirit
out of ~: 5 puffy 7 gasping, panting 8 wheezing
take one's ~ away: 3 awe, wow 4 stun 5 amaze 6 boggle, excite, thrill 7 astound, stagger, stupefy 8 astonish 9 take aback
breath __: 4 test
__ breath: 3 bad 5 baby's, bated, in one, out of
breathe: 3 are, say 4 gasp, gulp, live, pant, puff, tell 5 exist, imbue, utter 6 draw in, exhale, impart, infuse, inhale, inject, instil, wheeze 7 confide, express, instill, respire, subsist, whisper 10 articulate
a word: 4 tell
easy: 5 relax
fire: 4 boil, fume, rage, stew 5 storm 6 see red, seethe 7 smolder 10 hit the roof
hard: 4 gasp, huff, pant, puff 5 heave
in: 5 sniff 6 inhale
live and ~: 3 are 5 exist
new life into: 6 revive 7 refresh 10 regenerate
out: 4 sigh 6 exhale
roughly: 6 wheeze
breathe __ of relief: 5 a sigh
Breathe (1999 song) artist: Faith Hill
Breathe Again (1993 song) artist: Toni Braxton
Breathed, Berke: 10 cartoonist
breathe down one's __: 4 neck
breather: 4 lull, lung, rest 5 break, pause, truce 6 recess, relief 7 respite 8 reprieve 10 suspension
take a ~: 4 rest, stop 5 pause, relax 6 recess
breath freshener: 5 Certs 6 Binaca, Mentos, Tic Tac 7 Altoids, Clorets, Dentyne
breathing: 4 live 5 alive 6 eupnea, living 7 animate 10 inhalation
combining form: 4 spir- 5 spiri-, spiro-
disorder: 5 apnea 6 apnoea, asthma
fire: 3 hot, mad 5 angry, livid, riled, surly, vexed, wroth 6 fuming, ireful, piqued, raging, red-hot 7 angered, annoyed, berserk, boiling, enraged, furious, steamed 8 incensed, inflamed, provoked, up in arms, volcanic, worked up, wrathful 9 indignant, irritated, seeing red, ticked off 10 infuriated
organ: 4 gill, lung
passage: 5 naris 6 airway
passages: 5 nares
sound: 4 rale, sigh 6 wheeze
spell: 4 lull, rest 5 pause 6 recess 7 respite 8 reprieve
underwater ~ apparatus: 4 gill 5 scuba 7 snorkel
breathing __: 4 room 5 space, spell
Breathing Lessons author: Anne Tyler
breathless: 4 agog 5 agasp 6 winded 7 anxious, excited, gasping, gulping, panting 9 astounded, exhausted, expectant, impatient 10 incoherent, stertorous
Breathless (1959 film)
cast: Jean-Paul Belmondo, Jean Seberg
director: Jean-Luc Godard
Breathless (1958 song) artist: Jerry Lee Lewis
breathtaking: 3 def, rad 4 aces, A-one, boss, braw, cool, dece, fine, gear, keen, neat, nice, phat, tuff 5 dandy, ducky, grand, great, marvy, neato, nobby, prime, slick, super, swell 6 bang on, bang-up, bonzer, bosker, choice, divine, dreamy, far-out, gnarly, groovy, lovely, peachy, scenic, slap-up, spot on, superb, terrif, tiptop, unreal, whizzo, wicked 7 amazing, awesome, capital, corking, perfect, ripping, skookum, stellar, sublime 8 dazzling, dramatic, especial, excit-

ing, eximious, fabulous, five-star, four-star, frabjous, glorious, heavenly, jim-dandy, scenical, slam-bang, smashing, splendid, standout, sterling, stick-out, superior, terrific, top-level, top-notch, very good, wondrous 9 bodacious, Endsville, excellent, exemplary, exquisite, first-rate, high-grade, hunky-dory, marvelous, sollicker, thrilling, top-flight, wonderful 10 first-class, hotsy-totsy, jack-a-dandy, out of sight, peachy-keen, phenomenal, remarkable, stupendous, super-duper

__ Breath You Take: 5 Every

breccia: 4 rock 5 stone

Brecht, Bertolt: 4 poet 6 German 10 playwright

collaborator: 5 Weill

work: Baal
The Life of Galileo
Mother Courage and Her Children
The Threepenny Opera

Breck: 5 Peter 7 shampoo

competitor: 5 Prell

__ Breckinridge: 4 Myra

Breck, Peter: 5 actor

film: Benji (1974)
Shock Corridor (1963)

TV: The Big Valley

__-bred: 3 ill 4 city, well 7 country

Breda: 4 city, town

locale: 4 Neth. 7 Holland 11 Netherlands

bred-in-the-__: 4 bone

bred starter: 3 low 4 high, home, pure 5 color, cross 8 standard

breech ender: 5 block, cloth, clout 6 loader

breeches: 5 jeans, pants 6 Capris, shorts, slacks 8 Bermudas, jodhpurs, knickers, trousers 9 plus fours

__ breeches: 4 knee 6 riding

breechloader: 3 gun 5 rifle 6 musket

breed: 4 bear, kind, line, race, rear, sire, sort, type 5 beget, cause, class, raise, spawn, stock 6 create, foster, kidney, manner, strain 7 bring up, develop, lineage, nourish, nurture, produce, species, variety 8 engender, generate, multiply, pedigree 9 cultivate, procreate, propagate, reproduce 10 give rise to

mixed ~: 3 cur, mut 4 mule, mutt 7 mongrel 8 alley cat

breeder __: 7 reactor

Breeder's Cup event: 4 race

breeding: 5 grace 6 polish 7 culture, lineage, manners 8 civility, courtesy, elegance, noblesse, prolific, urbanity 9 gentility, propriety 10 generation, refinement

good ~: 6 polish 7 conduct, culture, decorum, p's and q's 8 behavior, courtesy, urbanity 9 etiquette, politesse 10 deportment, politeness, refinement

ground: 6 hotbed

place: 4 nest

Breedlove, Craig: 5 racer 9 auto racer

Breed's __: 4 Hill

breeks: 5 pants

breen: 5 green 8 brownish

kin: 3 pea 4 cyan, jade, sage 5 beryl, olive, virid 6 myrtle, reseda 7 avocado, celadon, emerald, verdant 9 pistachio, turquoise 10 aquamarine, chartreuse

Breen: 5 Bobby

breeze: 3 air 4 blow, gust, puff, snap, wind 5 cinch, cushy, draft, speed 6 flurry, picnic, simple, zephyr 7 airflow, current 8 duck soup, kid stuff, painless, pushover, workable 9 no problem 10 child's play, effortless

ender: 3 way

faint ~: 4 waft 6 breath

float on the ~: 4 waft

hang in the ~: 3 dry 6 air-dry

in: 4 come 5 enter, pop up 6 appear, arrive, show up, turn up 8 get there

like a tropical ~: 5 balmy

make a ~: 3 fan

shoot the ~: 3 gab, jaw, rap 4 blab, chat 5 prate, speak 6 gossip, jabber 7 blather, blether, chatter 8 chitchat, talk idly 10 chew the fat, chew the rag

sudden ~: 4 gust

through: 3 ace, zip

__ breeze: 3 sea 4 lake, land 5 fresh, light 6 gentle, strong

Breeze: 3 car 4 auto 8 Plymouth

Breeze __, The: 4 and I

__ Breeze: 5 Lydie 6 Summer

breezeway terminus: 5 house 6 garage

breezy: 3 raw 4 airy, mild, pert 5 fresh, gusty, light, windy 6 blithe, casual, drafty, jaunty, lively, rakish 7 affable, blowing, buoyant, dashing, offhand 8 blustery, carefree, cheerful, debonair, informal 9 debonaire, easy-going, lightsome, sprightly, vivacious 10 debonnaire, unbothered, ventilated

__ brei: 5 matzo 6 matzah, matzoh

Breidha __: 5 Fjord

breketé: 4 drum

origin: 6 Africa

Brel: 7 Jacques

Bremen: 4 city, port, town

locale: 7 Germany

port near ~: 5 Emden

river: 5 Weser

Bremer: 7 Lucille 8 Fredrika

Bremer, Fredrika: 6 writer 7 Swedish

Bremerhaven: 4 city, port, town

locale: 7 Germany

Bremerton: 4 city, town

locale: 10 Washington

Bren: 3 gun 7 British 10 machine gun

Brenda: 3 Lee 5 Starr 7 Fricker, Russell, Vaccaro 8 Marshall

Brendan: 4 Gill 5 Behan 6 Fraser, Sexton

Brenda Starr (1989 film)

cast: Timothy Dalton, Diana Scarwid, Brooke Shields

Brendel, Alfred: 7 pianist 8 Austrian

Brendon: 8 Nicholas

Brenly: 3 Bob

Brennan: 6 Eileen, Walter 7 William

Brennan, Christopher: 4 poet 10 Australian

Brennan, Eileen: 7 actress

film: The Cheap Detective (1978)
Murder by Death (1976)
Private Benjamin (1980)

Brennan, Walter: 5 actor

film: Bad Day at Black Rock (1955)
Come and Get It (1936, AA)
The Gnome-Mobile (1967)
Home in Indiana (1944)
Kentucky (1938, AA)
My Darling Clementine (1946)
Nice Girl? (1941)
Nobody Lives Forever (1946)
Northwest Passage (1940)
The Pride of the Yankees (1942)
Red River (1948)
Sergeant York (1941)
Support Your Local Sheriff (1969)
Tammy and the Bachelor (1957)
Three Godfathers (1936)
To Have and Have Not (1944)
The Westerner (1940, AA)

song: Old Rivers (1962)

TV: The Real McCoys

Brenneman: 3 Amy

Brenner: 5 David 6 Sydney

Brenner Pass region: 5 Tirol, Tyrol

Brenner, Sydney: 7 British 8 Nobelist

Brent: 4 city, town 6 George, Spiner 9 Geiberger, Musberger

locale: 7 Florida

Brentano, Clemens: 4 poet 6 German

Brent, George: 5 actor

film: 42nd Street (1933)
Dark Victory (1939)
Female (1933)
The Great Lie (1941)
In This Our Life (1942)
Jezebel (1938)
My Reputation (1946)
The Old Maid (1939)
The Spiral Staircase (1946)
Tomorrow Is Forever (1946)

spouse: Ann Sheridan

Brenton: 4 Wood

Brentwood: 4 city, town

locale: 7 New York 9 Tennessee 10 California

Br'er: 3 Fox 4 Bear 6 Rabbit

Brescia: 4 city, town

locale: 5 Italy

Breslau: 4 city, town

river: 4 Oder, Odra

Breslin: 5 Jimmy

Breslow: 3 Lou

Bresnahan: 5 Roger

Brest: 4 city, port, town 6 Martin

locale: 6 France 7 Belarus

native: 6 Breton

Brest __: 7 Litovsk

Brest, Martin: 8 director

film: Beverly Hills Cop (1984)
Going in Style (1979)
Meet Joe Black (1998)
Midnight Run (1988)
Scent of a Woman (1992)

bret: 4 fish

Bret: 5 Harte 8 Maverick, Michaels 10 Saberhagen

brethren: 3 kin 6 parish 7 kinfolk 8 kinfolks, kinsfolk

Breton: 3 hat 4 cape, Celt 5 André

Breton __: 4 lace

Breton, André: 4 poet 6 French

__ Breton Island: 4 Cape

Brett: 5 Favre 6 Butler, George, Jeremy, Ratner, Somers

Brett, George: 5 Royal 10 baseballer

Bretton __ Conference: 5 Woods

Breuer __: 5 chair

breve: 4 mark, note 9 whole note

__ breve: 4 alla

brevet: 9 promotion

breviloquent: 4 curt 5 brief 7 concise, laconic

brevi manu: 7 offhand

brevity: 8 laconism 9 briefness, shortness

brew: 3 ale, tea 4 beer, boil, cook, form, make, perc, perk, plan, plot, stew, suds 5 blend, drink, hatch, lager, mocha, steep, stout 6 coffee, devise, foment, infuse, medley, porter, potion, scheme, stir up, whip up 7 concoct, develop, distill, ferment, Pilsner 8 beverage, contrive, infusion, Pilsener 10 concoction

breakfast ~: 3 joe, tea 4 java 6 coffee

ender: 3 pub 5 house 6 master

ingredient: 6 barley

milieu: 3 bar, pub 6 saloon, tavern 8 alehouse

sour ~: 6 alegar

witches' ~ need: 4 newt

see also beer

__ brew: 4 home 7 witches

brewed beverage: 3 ale, tea 4 beer 5 lager, stout 6 coffee

brewer: 3 urn 7 samovar

café ~: 4 urne

concern: 4 wort

need: 3 tun, vat 4 barm, malt, oast, wort 5 yeast 6 barley

product: 3 ale 4 beer 5 lager, stout

Brewer: 3 Gay 4 Mike 6 Teresa

Hall of Famer: 5 Yount 10 Robin Yount

rival: 3 Cub, Met, Red 4 Expo, Twin 5 Angel, Astro, Brave, Giant, Padre, Rocky, Royal, Tiger 6 Dodger, Indian, Marlin, Oriole, Philly, Pirate, Ranger, Red Sox, Yankee 7 Blue Jay, Mariner 8 Athletic, Cardinal, Devil Ray, White Sox

Brewer, Gay: 6 golfer

Brewers: 4 nine, team

home: 9 Milwaukee

org.: 3 MLB, NLC

sport: 8 baseball

Brewer, Teresa

song: Bo Weevil (1956)
Let Me Go, Lover (1954)
A Sweet Old Fashioned Girl (1956)
A Tear Fell (1956)
You Send Me (1957)

brewery starter: 5 micro

brewing: 8 imminent 9 in the wind

be ~: 4 loom 6 impend 8 threaten

leaf for ~: 3 tea 5 pekoe

brewski: 4 beer, suds 7 cold one

Brewster: 7 Jordana, William

Brewster __: 5 chair 7 McCloud

__ Brewster: 5 Punky

Brewster McCloud (1970 film)

cast: Bud Cort, Shelley Duvall, Sally Kellerman

director: Robert Altman

Brewster's Millions star: 5 Havoc

Breyer: 7 Stephen

Breyer's: 8 ice cream

competitor: 4 Edy's 9 Friendly's, Good Humor 10 Dairy Queen, Haagen Dazs, Turkey Hill

Brezhnev, Leonid: 7 Russian 9 statesman

domain: 4 USSR 7 Kremlin

Brian: 3 Eno, May 4 Boru, Mary 5 Friel, Jones, Keith, Kelly, Moore 6 Aherne, Aldiss, Benben, Hyland, Kerwin, Setzer, Wilson, Wimmer 7 Boitano, Dennehy, De Palma, Donlevy, Epstein, Holland, Piccolo 8 Bosworth, McKnight, Mitchell, Mulroney, Williams 9 Gottfried, Josephson

Briand, Aristide: 6 French 8 Nobelist 9 statesman

__-Briand Pact: 7 Kellogg

Brian's Song actor: 4 Caan

briar: 4 bush 5 shrub, spine, thorn 7 bramble, prickle

ender: 4 root, wood

starter: 5 sweet

briard: 3 dog 5 canid 6 canine

bribable: 5 venal 7 corrupt 9 mercenary

bribe: 3 buy, fix, sop 4 lure 5 get at, get to, graft, smear 6 boodle, buy off, grease, payoff, payola, ransom, square, suborn, tamper 7 corrupt, rake-off 8 kickback 9 hush money, influence, lubricate 10 inducement

bribery: 5 graft 8 venality 10 corruption

bric-a-brac: 5 curio 6 trifle 7 memento, whatnot 8 nicknack, souvenir 10 knickknack

place: 5 shelf

Brice: 5 Fanny 6 Marden

Brice, Fanny spouse: Billy Rose

brick: 3 red 4 cake 5 adobe, block, brown, color 6 cheese, fellow 9 vermilion

carrier: 3 hod

ender: 3 bat 4 work, yard 5 layer

food in a ~: 6 cheese

kin: 4 rose, ruby, rust, wine 5 coral,

grape, poppy, rusty, sandy **6** cerise, cherry, claret, garnet, maroon **7** carmine, crimson, fuchsia, magenta, pimento, scarlet, sultana, vermeil **8** amaranth, cardinal, dubonnet, geranium, rubicund **9** carnation, cranberry, vermilion **10** strawberry
material: **4** clay **5** straw
Southwestern ~: **5** adobe
starter: **4** fire, gold
worker: **5** layer, mason
brick __: **3** red **6** cheese
__ brick: **3** air **4** beam, iron **5** glass, Roman **6** salmon **7** pressed
Brick: **4** city, town
locale: **9** New Jersey
brickbat: **4** gibe, jibe, twit **7** affront **8** derision **9** criticism **10** imputation
Brickell, Edie
spouse: Paul Simon
Brick House (1977 song) artist: Commodores
bricklayer: **5** mason
implement: **3** hod
bricklaying: **5** craft, skill
__ brickle: **6** butter
Brickman: **4** Paul
__ Brick Road: **6** Yellow
bricks
hit like a ton of ~: **3** jar **4** daze, jolt, kayo, stun **5** shock **6** bedaze **7** astound, flummox, horrify, nonplus, outrage, stagger, stupefy, terrify **8** astonish, bewilder, blow away, bowl over, knock out, unsettle **9** dumbfound, overpower, overwhelm, take aback **10** discompose
hit the ~: **2** go **4** exit, move **5** leave **6** beat it, depart, go away, move on **7** make off, pull out, push off, take off, vamoose **8** shove off, slip away **10** shuffle off
partner: **6** mortar
Brickyard event: **4** race
bridal: **7** marital, nuptial, spousal, wedding **8** conjugal **9** connubial
accessory: **4** veil **6** garter, wreath **7** bouquet
gown feature: **5** train
month: **4** June
notice word: **3** née
wear: **4** lace **5** satin, tulle, white
bridal __: **4** gown, veil **5** party, suite **6** shower, wreath
Bridal Ballad author: Edgar Allan Poe
Bridal Veil __: **5** Falls
bride: **4** mate, wife **5** woman **6** missis, missus, spouse **8** helpmate, newlywed
acquisition: **4** band, ring **5** in-law
attendant: **10** flowergirl
bestowal: **5** dowry **6** dowery
companion: **5** groom
destination: **5** altar
ender: **5** groom
future: **7** fiancée
new title: **3** Mrs.
response: **3** I do
ride: **4** limo
walkway: **5** aisle
__ bride: **3** war **5** child
__ Bride: **4** June **7** Runaway
Bride Came __, The: **3** C.O.D.
Bride Elect, The composer: **5** Sousa
bridegroom: **4** mate **6** spouse **7** husband **8** benedict, newlywed
acquisition: **4** band, ring **5** in-law
attendant: **5** usher **7** best man **10** ring bearer
future ~: **6** fiancé
Bride of Frankenstein (1935 film)
cast: Colin Clive, Valerie Hobson, Boris Karloff, Elsa Lanchester, Una O'Connor
director: James Whale
Bride of Lammermoor, The
author: Walter Scott
character: **4** Lucy **5** Edgar
Brideshead: **6** estate
Brideshead Revisited
author: Evelyn Waugh
character: **3** Rex **4** Cara **5** Beryl, Celia, Ryder
__ Bride, The: **5** Tsar's **6** Devil's, Robber
Bride Wore Black, The (1968 film)
cast: Jean-Claude Brialy, Jeanne Moreau, Claude Rich
director: François Truffaut
bridge: **4** arch, game, join, link, span **5** cross **7** catwalk, connect, stretch, subtend, trestle, viaduct **8** arch over, card game, crossing, go across, overpass, traverse, vinculum **9** cross over, overpasse **10** connection, dental work
beat, at ~: **3** set
builder: **4** engr. **8** engineer
builder's concern: **6** stress
builder's deg.: **3** BCE
call: **3** bid **5** I pass, one no, rebid
coup: **4** slam
declaration: **5** trump
electric ~: **3** arc
end: **8** abutment
ender: **4** head, work
expert: **5** Goren **6** Sharif
fare: **4** toll
forerunner: **5** whist
group: **4** club
guard of folklore: **5** troll
holding: **4** hand
honor: **3** ace
in French: **4** pont
in Italian: **5** ponte
land ~: **7** isthmus
move: **5** raise
musical ~: **5** segue
need: **4** deck **5** cards
opening: **3** bid
pontoon: **6** bateau
position: **4** East, West **5** North, South
quorum: **4** four
response: **4** pass
ruff, in ~: **5** trump
site: **4** nose
starter: **4** draw, foot
support: **4** I-bar, pier **5** cable, pylon **6** girder
team: **3** duo **4** pair
term: **5** trick
the gap: **3** aid **6** assist **8** tide over **9** help along **10** see through
toll ~ unit: **4** axle
bridge __: **4** club, deck, lamp, loan **5** chair, cloth, house, table **7** circuit, fluting, passage
__ bridge: **3** ore **4** land, lift, rope, toll **5** ferry, float, Irish, light, paint, truss **6** Bailey, bateau, flying, monkey, rubber **7** auction, covered, docking, kissing, pontoon
Bridge __ Far, A: **3** Too
__ Bridge: **3** Mrs. **4** Eads **5** Adam's **6** London **7** Natural, Rainbow
Bridge at __: **5** Arles
Bridge at Remagen, The (1969 film)
cast: Bradford Dillman, Ben Gazzara, George Segal, Robert Vaughn
Bridge for Passing, A author: Pearl S. Buck
bridgehead: **8** foothold
Bridge of __: **5** Asses, Sighs
Bridge of Narni artist: **5** Corot
Bridge of San Luis Rey, The
author: Thornton Wilder
character: **3** Pio **5** Clara, Jaime **6** Pepita
Bridge on the Drina, The author: **3** Ivo
Bridge on the River Kwai, The (1957 film)
cast: Sir Alec Guinness, Jack Hawkins, Sessue Hayakawa, William Holden
director: David Lean
setting: **4** Siam
Bridge Over the River Kwai, The
author: Pierre Boulle
Bridge Over Troubled Water (song)
artist: Simon and Garfunkel
artist: Aretha Franklin
Bridgeport: **4** city, port, town
locale: **4** Conn.
town near ~: **6** Easton
Bridges: **4** Alan, Beau, Jeff, Todd **5** James, Lloyd **6** Alicia, Robert
__ Bridges: **4** Nash **7** Burning, Natural
Bridges, Alicia song: I Love the Nightlife (1978)
Bridges at Toko-Ri, The (1955 film)
cast: William Holden, Grace Kelly, Fredric March
director: Mark Robson
Bridges, Beau: **5** actor
film: The Fabulous Baker Boys (1989)
The Hotel New Hampshire (1984)
The Incident (1967)
The Landlord (1970)
Norma Rae (1979)
Your Three Minutes Are Up (1973)
Bridges, James: **8** director
film: Bright Lights, Big City (1988)
The China Syndrome (1979)
The Paper Chase (1973)
Perfect (1985)
Urban Cowboy (1980)
Bridges, Jeff: **5** actor
film: American Heart (1993)
Bad Company (1972)
The Big Lebowski (1998)
The Fabulous Baker Boys (1989)
Fat City (1972)
Fearless (1993)
The Fisher King (1991)
Hearts of the West (1975)
Jagged Edge (1985)
King Kong (1976)
The Last American Hero (1973)
The Last Picture Show (1971)
The Mirror Has Two Faces (1996)
The Muse (1999)
Nadine (1987)
Rancho Deluxe (1975)
Stay Hungry (1976)
Texasville (1990)
Thunderbolt and Lightfoot (1974)
Tucker: The Man and His Dream (1988)
White Squall (1996)
Bridges, Lloyd: **5** actor
film: Airplane! (1980)
The Goddess (1958)
High Noon (1952)
Jane Austen's Mafia! (1998)
Joe Versus the Volcano (1990)
Running Wild (1973)
son: **4** Beau, Jeff
TV: Sea Hunt
Bridges of Madison County, The (1995 film)
cast: Clint Eastwood, Meryl Streep
director: Clint Eastwood
setting: **4** Iowa
Bridges, Robert: **4** poet **7** British
Bridget: **5** Fonda
Bridge, The: **4** poem
author: Hart Crane
Bridget Jones's Diary (2001 film)
cast: Colin Firth, Hugh Grant, Gemma Jones, Renée Zellweger
Bridgeton: **4** city, town
locale: **9** New Jersey
Bridge Too Far, A
actor: **5** Caine
author: **4** Ryan
river: **5** Rhine
Bridgetown: **4** city **7** capital
locale: **8** Barbados
Bridgman, Percy: **8** Nobelist **9** physicist
bridle: **4** curb, rein, tame **5** check, leash **6** halter, muzzle, pull in, rear up, rein in, subdue **7** control, inhibit, repress **8** hold back, restrain, suppress, withhold **9** deterrent, restraint **10** keep in line
part: **3** bit **4** curb, rein
path: **5** trail
Brie: **6** cheese, French
alternative: **4** Edam **5** Gouda
covering: **4** rind
brief: **4** curt, memo, post **5** brusk, crisp, edify, hasty, pithy, prime, quick, ready, short, swift, teach, terse **6** abrupt, advise, digest, fill in, gnomic, inform, little, précis, report, sketch, skimpy, update **7** apprise, apprize, brusque, compact, concise, cursory, explain, hurried, laconic, limited, outline, pandect, passing, summary **8** abstract, fleeting, flitting, instruct, meteoric, succinct, synopsis **9** curtailed, enlighten, ephemeral, momentary, short-term, summarize, temporary, thumbnail, transient **10** abridgment, boiled down, compendium, compressed, evanescent, pro tempore, short-lived, to the point, transitory, unenduring
appearance: **5** cameo
attempt: **4** stab **5** whirl
but meaningful: **5** pithy
contact: **5** brush, graze
ender: **4** case
hold a ~ for: **6** defend, second **7** approve, endorse, indorse, support **8** champion, sanction, side with
look: **4** peek **5** recon **6** glance
statement: **5** flash, squib **9** news flash, sound bite
stay: **8** stopover
stop: **4** lull **5** pause
summary: **5** recap
time: **3** sec **4** jiff **5** jiffy, spell, trice **6** minute, moment, second
trip: **4** tour **5** drive **6** errand, outing **7** sojourn **9** excursion
__ brief: **4** news
briefcase: **3** bag **6** valise **7** attaché **9** portfolio
closer: **4** hasp
Brief Encounter (1945 film)
cast: Stanley Holloway, Trevor Howard, Celia Johnson
director: David Lean
doctor: **4** Alec
Brief History of Time, A author: Stephen Hawking
briefing: **6** fill-in **7** rundown
briefly: **7** briskly, hastily, in short, quickly, shortly, swiftly **8** suddenly **9** cursorily, hurriedly
briefs: **4** BVDs **5** pants **6** shorts, undies **7** jockeys **8** skivvies **9** underwear
__ Brief, The: **7** Pelican
Brienz: **4** lake
locale: **4** Bern **5** Berne **11** Switzerland
brier: **5** shrub, spine, thorn **7** bramble, prickle
starter: **3** cat **5** green, sweet
brig: **3** jug **4** boat, jail, ship **5** craft **6** argosy, cooler, lockup, prison **10** guardhouse
ender: **3** ade
brigade: **4** army, band, crew, unit **5** corps, fleet, force, group, squad,

troop **6** legion, outfit **7** company, phalanx **10** contingent, detachment
__ brigade: **4** fire **5** light **6** bucket
brigadier: **4** rank **7** general
Brigadoon (1954 film): **7** musical
cast: Cyd Charisse, Van Johnson, Gene Kelly
character: **3** Meg **5** Angus, Fiona, Tommy
director: Vincente Minnelli
songwriter: **5** Loewe **6** Lerner
brigand: **4** hood, thug **5** rogue, thief **6** bad guy, bandit, looter, mugger, outlaw, pirate, raider, robber, sacker, sea dog, vandal, viking **7** corsair, footpad, hoodlum, ruffian, sea wolf **8** criminal, gangster, marauder, picaroon, pillager, predator, rapparee, tough guy **9** buccaneer, desperado, plunderer, privateer **10** freebooter, highwayman
brigantine: **4** boat, ship **6** argosy
Brigati: **5** Eddie
Briggs: **5** Clare
Brigham City: **4** town
locale: **4** Utah
Brigham Young: **6** school **10** university
athletes: **7** Cougars
letters: **3** BYU
locale: **4** Utah **5** Provo
bright: **3** apt, gay, lit **4** fair, keen, pert, rich, rosy **5** aglow, alert, clean, clear, fresh, happy, jolly, light, lucid, merry, nitid, peppy, perky, quick, ready, sharp, shiny, smart, sunny, vivid, witty **6** ablaze, agleam, astute, brainy, clever, flashy, glossy, golden, joyful, joyous, limpid, lively, silver, strong, sunlit **7** beaming, blazing, burning, clement, fulgent, glowing, hopeful, knowing, lambent, moonlit, obvious, radiant, shining, well-lit **8** cheerful, colorful, dazzling, flashing, gleaming, incisive, keen-eyed, luminous, lustrous, polished, sanguine, spirited, splendid **9** astucious, brilliant, cloudless, effulgent, eggheaded, favorable, ingenious, inventive, lightsome, observant, promising, receptive, refulgent, sparkling, sprightly, unclouded, vivacious **10** auspicious, discerning, glittering, keen-witted, optimistic, precocious, shimmering
beam: **3** ray **5** laser **9** spotlight
blindingly ~: **4** loud, neon **5** gaudy **7** glaring **8** dazzling
group: **5** Mensa
looking on the ~ side: **7** hopeful **8** optimism **10** optimistic
make less ~: **3** dim **5** bedim, shade **6** soften
name meaning ~: **5** Clara, Clare **6** Bertha, Claire, Xavier
not ~: **4** dark, drab, dumb, gray, grey, slow **5** dense, dingy, thick
bright-__: **4** eyed
bright and __: **5** early
bright army, name meaning: **7** Herbert
brighten: **4** gild **5** cheer, light, liven, scrub, shine **6** buff up, buoy up, illume, kindle, perk up, polish, revive **7** burnish, cheer up, enliven, furbish, gladden, hearten, lighten, light up, relieve, spiff up **8** emblazon, illumine, ornament **9** embellish, intensify, irradiate, take heart **10** illuminate
bright-eyed: **4** pert **5** alert, eager, fresh, sunny **7** healthy **8** youthful
bright glory, name meaning: **6** Robert **7** Roberta
bright god, name meaning: **6** Osbert
bright land, name meaning: **7** Lambert
Bright Lights, Big City (1988 film)
cast: Phoebe Cates, Michael J. Fox, Swoosie Kurtz, Kiefer Sutherland
director: James Bridges
bright mind, name meaning: **6** Hubert
brightness: **4** glow **5** gleam, gloss, light, sheen, shine **6** gaiety, gayety, luster **7** glitter **8** optimism, radiance, radiancy, splendor **9** freshness, smartness **10** cleverness, effulgence
lose ~: **3** dim **4** fade
unit: **5** lumen **7** lambert
Brighton: **4** city, town
locale: **6** Sussex **7** England, New York **8** Colorado
town opposite ~: **6** Dieppe
Brighton Beach Memoirs: **4** film, play
author: Neil Simon
cast: Blythe Danner, Bob Dishy, Jonathan Silverman
character: **4** Kate, Nora **6** Eugene
director: Gene Saks
Brighton Rock: **4** film **5** novel
author: Graham Greene
cast: Richard Attenborough, Hermione Baddeley, Carol Marsh
director: John Boulting
bright pledge, name meaning: **7** Gilbert
bright raven, name meaning: **7** Bertram
brights: **9** high beams
bright sword, name meaning: **6** Egbert
Bright Victory (1951 film)
cast: Peggy Dow, Arthur Kennedy
director: Mark Robson
Brigid: **5** saint **6** Brophy
Brigitte: **6** Bardot **7** Nielsen
see also French
brill: **4** fish **6** turbot **8** flatfish
brilliance: **3** wit **4** glow **5** blaze, éclat, glare, gleam, gloss, light, shine **6** acumen, genius, luster, polish **7** glitter, sparkle **8** artistry, grandeur, radiance, radiancy, splendor **10** effulgence, virtuosity
brilliant: **3** ace, lit **4** star **5** aglow, light, lucid, noble, ready, sharp, shiny, slick, smart, sunny, vivid, witty **6** ablaze, astute, brainy, bright, clever, flashy, gifted, glossy, golden, lucent, ornate, strong, superb **7** beaming, blazing, flaming, fulgent, glowing, knowing, lambent, radiant, shining, vibrant **8** dazzling, gleaming, glorious, luminous, lustrous, masterly, readable, splendid, stunning **9** astucious, effulgent, eggheaded, excellent, ingenious, inventive, prominent, refulgent, sparkling, wonderful **10** celebrated, discerning, expressive, flamboyant, glittering, precocious
be ~: **4** glow, star **5** shine
not exactly ~: **4** slow **5** dense, thick
Brilliant Disguise (1987 song) artist: Bruce Springsteen
__ brillig...: **4** 'Twas
Brillo: **3** pad **7** soap pad
rival: **3** SOS
use ~: **5** scour, scrub
brim: **3** lip, rim **4** bill, edge, teem **5** brink, chime, limit, shore, skirt, verge, visor, vizor **6** border, flange, fringe, margin **7** run over **8** flow over, overflow, well over **9** periphery, spill over
ender: **5** stone
over: **4** fill **5** flood
Brim: **6** coffee
competitor: **5** Sanka
brimful: **4** full **5** awash **6** packed **7** teeming
__-brim hat: **4** snap
brimless hat: **5** toque **7** pillbox
Brimley: **7** Wilford
brimming: **3** big **4** full, rife **5** awash, laden **6** filled, imbued, jammed, loaded, packed **7** crammed, crowded, flooded, fraught, replete, stuffed **8** overfull
over: **4** full **5** awash **6** packed
Brindisi: **4** city, port, town
locale: **5** Italy
town near ~: **4** Oria
brindle: **3** cat **5** felid, tabby **6** feline
brindled: **4** pied **5** tawny **7** dappled, mottled, spotted, striped **8** speckled, streaked
brine: **8** sea water **9** salt water
steep in ~: **5** souse **6** pickle **8** preserve
brine-cured delicacy: **3** lox
Brinegar: **4** Paul
bring: **3** lug **4** bear, cart, draw, earn, haul, lead, take, tote **5** carry, cause, fetch, go get, guide, offer, truck, usher, yield **6** convey, escort, gather, induce, reduce, return, supply **7** conduct, deliver, drop off, provide, sell for **8** chaperon, engender, motivate, result in, transfer **9** accompany, chaperone, take along, transport
about: **4** form, make **5** beget, cause, spark, wreak **6** ask for, create, effect, induce, lead to **7** achieve, compass, produce, realize, trigger **8** conclude, engender, engineer, generate, occasion **9** hammer out, implement, instigate, originate **10** accomplish, effectuate, give rise to, make happen, put through
action: **3** sue **9** prosecute
along: **3** lug **4** tote **5** carry
around: **6** reason, revive **7** refresh, restore, win over **8** persuade **9** prevail on
a smile to: **5** amuse, cheer, elate
back: **5** rehab **6** revive **7** recover, restore **9** reinstate
bad luck: **3** hex **4** jinx **5** curse
before a judge: **3** try **5** retry
charges: **4** book **6** accuse, allege
down: **4** fell, land, ruin, sink, undo **5** abase, level, lower, shoot **6** bum out, deject, demean, dismay, humble, sadden, tackle, topple **8** dispirit, overturn, undercut **9** humiliate, overthrow, prostrate, undermine **10** dishearten
down the curtain on: **3** end **8** conclude
down the house: **3** wow **4** rase, raze **5** level **6** topple **7** delight, flatten **8** bulldoze, demolish, entrance
force to bear: **5** impel **6** compel **8** arm-twist, pressure **9** strong-arm
forth: **4** bear, make **5** evoke, hatch, spawn, yield **6** derive, elicit **7** produce **10** come up with
forward: **3** lay **6** adduce **7** advance, produce
home: **3** net **4** earn **7** clarify, clear up **8** manifest **9** elucidate, explicate, get across, make clear, make plain **10** illuminate, illustrate
home the bacon: **4** earn, work
in: **3** get, net, pay **4** earn, gain, land, make, pipe, reap **5** co-opt, fetch, gross, usher, yield **6** garner, return **7** acquire, realize, receive
into court: **4** haul
into existence: **4** cast, form, make, rear **5** beget, breed, hatch, order, set up, shape, spawn, train **6** cook up, create, effect, father, invent, mature **7** arrange, compose, concoct, develop, outline, pioneer, produce, think up, turn out **8** assemble, conceive, engineer, generate, initiate **9** actualize, construct, establish, fabricate, hammer out, originate, take shape **10** give life to, mastermind
into play: **3** use **5** apply, exert **6** entail, resort
into the open: **3** air **4** leak, tell, vent **6** reveal, unveil **7** display, exhibit, freshen, publish **8** disclose **9** broadcast, make known, talk about
into the world: **4** bear **5** beget
low: **4** bust, ruin **5** abase, crush, lower **6** defeat, demean, demote, humble, reduce, weaken **7** conquer, deflate, degrade **8** bankrupt, pull down, vanquish **9** humiliate, knock down, overpower, pauperize, subjugate **10** impoverish
off: **6** attain, effect, manage, wangle **7** achieve, execute, perform, realize, work out **10** accomplish, put through
on: **5** cause, incur **6** ask for, induce
on board: **4** hire **6** employ, engage
out: **3** say **4** show **5** educe, evoke, issue, stage, state, utter **6** elicit, expose **7** comment, extract **9** circulate, introduce
pressure to bear: **5** lobby **7** squeeze **8** arm-twist **9** strong-arm
to a close: **3** end **4** halt **6** finish, wrap up **9** terminate
to a screeching halt: **6** arrest, forbid, stifle **8** suppress
to a standstill: **4** stem **5** tie up **6** arrest, becalm, hinder **7** prevent **8** obstruct
to bay: **3** nab **4** trap, tree **5** catch **6** collar, corner **7** capture
to bear: **3** use **5** apply, exert **6** employ **8** exercise
to fruition: **7** realize **8** complete
together: **3** wed **4** join, weld **5** amass, group, rally, shape, unify, unite **6** adduct, center, gather, muster **7** compile, convene, convoke **8** assemble
to heel: **4** tame **6** subdue
to justice: **3** try **4** hear **9** prosecute **10** adjudicate
to light: **3** air **4** bare, find, show **5** admit, dig up **6** elicit, evince, expose, reveal, turn up, unmask, unveil **7** lay bare, uncover, unearth **8** disclose, discover **9** track down
to mind: **5** evoke **6** recall **7** suggest **9** visualize
to naught: **4** do in, raze, ruin, undo **5** annul **6** cancel, negate **7** abolish, destroy, nullify, reverse, wipe out **8** abrogate, bulldoze, demolish, sabotage **9** devastate **10** annihilate, invalidate, neutralize, obliterate
to pass: **5** cause **6** ask for **7** achieve **10** effectuate
to terms: **7** mediate **9** negotiate, reconcile
to the surface: **4** mine **5** dig up **6** dredge, exhume, uproot **7** uncover, unearth **8** excavate
to trial: **6** charge, indict **9** prosecute
up: **3** say **4** form, lift, rear, spew, spue, tell **5** breed, nurse, raise **6** broach, prompt **7** mention, nourish, nurture, refer to **8** throw out **9** introduce
upon oneself: **5** cause, incur **6** invite
up the rear: **3** lag **5** trail **6** follow
up to date: **5** refit **6** revise, update **7** remodel **9** modernize
bring __: **3** off, out **4** down, home **5** forth, round **6** around **7** forward
bring __ end: **4** to an
bring __ rear: **5** up the
bring down the __: **5** house

bringer
combining form: 4 -agog 6 -agogue
bringer of victory, name meaning: 7 Bernice 8 Berenice
...bring forth __: 4 a son
bring home the __: 5 bacon
Bringing Out the Dead (1999 film)
cast: Patricia Arquette, Nicolas Cage, John Goodman, Ving Rhames
director: Martin Scorsese
Bringing Up Baby (1938 film)
cast: Cary Grant, Katharine Hepburn, May Robson, Charlie Ruggles
director: Howard Hawks
leopard: 4 Baby
studio: 3 RKO
Bringing Up Buddy aunt: 4 Iris
Bringing Up Father: 5 strip 10 comic strip
character: 4 Nora 5 Jiggs 6 Maggie
dog: 4 Fifi 7 Pretzel
bring into __: 4 line, play
Bring It On (2000 film)
cast: Jesse Bradford, Kirsten Dunst, Eliza Dushku, Gabrielle Union
director: Peyton Reed
Bring Larks and Heroes author: Thomas Keneally
__ Bring Me Down: 4 Don't
Bring On the Night (1985 film)
cast: Omar Hakim, Sting
director: Michael Apted
Bring the Boys Home (1971 song)
artist: Freda Payne
bring to __: 4 bear, life, mind, pass, task 5 a boil, a halt, an end, light, terms
bring to a __: 4 halt
bring to one's __: 5 knees
bring up the __: 4 rear
brink: 3 eve, lip, rim 4 brim, edge 5 limit, shore, skirt, verge 6 border, fringe, margin 7 extreme 8 boundary, frontier 9 extremity, precipice, threshold
be on the ~: 6 teeter
on the ~: 5 ready
Brinker, Hans: 6 skater
Brinkley; 5 David 8 Christie
Brinkley, Christie
emulate ~: 4 pose 5 model
spouse: Billy Joel
Brinkley, David: 10 newscaster
partner: Chet Huntley
Brink's Job, The (1978 film)
cast: Peter Boyle, Peter Falk, Warren Oates
director: William Friedkin
Brinks truck protection: 5 armor
briny: 3 sea 4 deep, main 5 ocean, salty 8 brackish
drop: 4 tear
on the ~: 4 asea 5 at sea 8 cruising, off-shore
septet: 4 seas
brio: 3 vim, zip 4 dash, élan, fire, life, zing 5 gusto, punch, verve, vigor 6 energy, esprit, pizazz, spirit 7 panache 8 fervency, lyricism, vivacity 9 animation, élan vital 10 liveliness
__ brio: 3 con
brioche: 4 roll 5 bread
briolette: 3 gem
briquets: 8 charcoal
use ~: 5 grill
Brisbane: 4 city, port, town
locale: 9 Australia
brise-__: 4 bise 6 soleil
brisé: 4 leap
Brisebois: 8 Danielle
brisk: 4 busy, cool, fast, keen, pert, spry 5 agile, alive, crisp, fleet, fresh, hasty, nippy, peart, peppy, perky, quick, rapid, sharp, smart, stiff, swift, windy, zippy 6 active, biting, chilly, dapper, flying, lively, living, nimble, prompt, racing, snappy, speedy 7 bracing, express, hurried, instant, roaring, rocking, rousing 8 animated, bustling, vigorous 9 breakneck, efficient, energetic, sprightly, vivacious 10 double-time, fortifying, hypersonic, refreshing, supersonic
in music: 5 mosso
brisket: 4 meat, ribs 5 chest
briskly: 7 briefly, rapidly
briskness: 3 nip 4 snap 5 haste, speed, vigor 8 alacrity, celerity, rapidity 9 animation, diligence, quickness
brisling: 4 fish
bristle: 3 awn 4 boil, fume, hair, rage, seta, teem 5 thorn 6 arista, blow up, rear up, see red, seethe 7 flare up, prickle, stubble, whisker
combining form: 4 seti- 5 chaet- 6 chaeto-
ender: 4 tail
grain ~: 3 awn
bristlecone: 4 pine
bristles
having ~: 5 awned
tool with ~: 5 brush
bristling: 5 thick 7 fraught, teeming 8 swarming, thronged
bristly: 4 wiry 5 hairy, rough, setal, spiny 6 crabby, cranky, hispid, spined, thorny, touchy 7 bearded, prickly, stubbly, unshorn 8 prickled 9 irascible, irritable, whiskered
Bristol: 4 city, port, town 6 Johnny 7 channel
city near ~: 4 Bath
dance: 5 Stomp
fashion: 4 neat
locale: 7 England 9 Tennessee
partner: 5 Myers
river at ~: 4 Avon
see also British, English
Bristol __: 5 board, Stomp 7 Channel, fashion
Bristol-__: 5 Myers
Bristol Channel island: 5 Lundy
Bristol Stomp (1961 song) artist: Dovells
brit: 4 fish 5 sprat 7 herring 8 plankton
Brit.
corp: 3 ltd.
legislators: 3 MPs
lexicon: 3 OED
military branch: 3 RAF
money: 3 LSD
pilots: 3 RAF
pound: 4 ster.
__ Britain: 5 Great
Brit ally: 4 Yank
__ Britannia: 4 Rule
Britannia metal: 5 alloy
component: 3 tin 6 copper 8 antimony
Britannica: 3 enc. 4 ency. 5 encyc.
__ Britannica: 3 Pax
Britannicus author: Jean Racine
britches: 5 pants 8 trousers
Brite: 7 cleaner
competitor: 5 Lysol 6 Top Job 7 Lestoil, Mr. Clean, Pine Sol 9 Fantastik, Step Saver
__ B'rith: 4 B'nai
British
Airways former plane: 3 SST
ancient monument: 5 henge 10 Stonehenge
anthropologist: 6 Frazer, Leakey 10 Malinowski
archeologist: 7 Woolley
architect: 4 Nash, Wren
astronomer: 4 Ryle 6 Halley 7 Huggins
auto: 2 MG 3 MGB 5 Rolls, Rover 6 Austin, Jaguar 9 Land Rover 10 Rolls- Royce
ballet dancer: 5 Dolin 7 Fonteyn, Markova
beverage: 3 tea 6 hot tea
breakfast item: 6 kipper
brew: 3 ale 5 stout 6 porter
carbine: 4 sten
card game: 5 gleek 7 primero
cathedral town: 3 Ely 6 Exeter
cellist: 5 du Pré
charity: 5 Oxfam
cheese: 9 Leicester, Wiltshire
china: 5 Spode
cleric: 5 vicar
coat: 5 jemmy, tunic
composer: 4 Arne 5 Holst
conductor: 5 Boult 7 Beecham, Sargent 8 Goossens, Marriner 10 Barbirolli
conservative: 4 Tory
court of old: 4 leet
explorer: 3 Rae 5 Baker, Parry, Scott, Speke 6 Burton, Mawson 7 Markham, Stanley 8 Flinders, Franklin 9 Frobisher, Vancouver 10 Shackleton
FBI: 3 CID
figure skater: 7 Cousins
golfer: 5 Faldo
historian: 6 Gibbon
Honduras today: 6 Belize
honorary initials: 3 MBE
island: 3 Man 5 Lundy 6 Jersey
jacket: 5 jemmy, tunic 9 greatcoat
journalist: 6 Morris
legal society: 3 inn
medal: 3 DCM, DSO
medical journal: 6 Lancet
medical org.: 3 NHS
mil. branch: 3 RNR
money: 5 groat, pence, pound 6 guinea 7 coppers 8 shilling
Museum's marbles: 5 Elgin
Nobelist in Chemistry: 4 Todd 5 Aston, Kroto, Pople, Smith, Soddy, Synge 6 Barton, Harden, Martin, Porter, Ramsay, Sanger 7 Haworth, Hodgkin, Norrish 8 Mitchell, Robinson 9 Wilkinson 10 Rutherford 11 Hinshelwood
Nobelist in Economics: 5 Coase, Hicks, Lewis, Meade, Stone 8 Mirrlees
Nobelist in Literature: 5 Eliot 7 Golding, Kipling, Naipaul, Russell 9 Churchill 10 Galsworthy
Nobelist in Medicine: 4 Dale, Hill, Katz, Ross, Vane 5 Black, Chain, Jerne, Krebs, Nurse 6 Adrian, Florey, Huxley, Porter 7 Brenner, Fleming, Hodgkin, Hopkins, Medawar, Roberts, Sulston, Wilkins 8 Milstein 9 Tinbergen 10 Hounsfield 11 Sherrington
Nobelist in Peace: 3 Orr 5 Cecil 6 Angell, Cremer 9 Henderson, Noel-Baker 11 Chamberlain
Nobelist in Physics: 4 Born, Mott, Ryle 5 Bragg, Dirac, Gabor 6 Barkla, Hewish, Powell, Strutt, Wilson 7 Thomson 8 Appleton, Blackett, Chadwick 9 Cockcroft, Josephson 10 Richardson
noble: 4 dame, duke, earl, lady, lord, peer 6 knight 7 marquis
North America: 6 Canada
Order: 6 Garter
painter: 7 Hogarth 8 Reynolds 9 Constable 12 Gainsborough
Petroleum acquisition: 5 Amoco
philosopher: 6 Popper
physicist: 5 Dirac 6 Stokes
pianist: 4 Hess 8 Helfgott
playwright: 3 Fry, Gay, Kyd 4 Bolt, Gray, Shaw 5 Arden, Brome, Frayn 6 Cibber, Coward, Dekker, Dryden, Henley, Jonson 7 Barstow, Delaney, Heywood 8 Congreve, Farquhar, Fielding 9 Ayckbourn 10 Galsworthy
poet: 3 Gay, Pye 4 Gray, Gunn, Hood, Hunt, Rowe, Tate 5 Blake, Byron, Carew, Clare, Davie, Gower, Hardy, Keats 6 Arnold, Austin, Brontë, Brooke, Bryher, Cibber, Cotton, Cowley, Cowper, Crabbe, Daniel, Dryden, Empson, Eusden, Fuller, Henley, Hughes, Jonson, Motion, Warton 7 Bridges, Campion, Chaucer, Collins, Crashaw, Drayton, Herrick, Heywood, Hopkins, Housman, Johnson, Southey 8 Betjeman, Browning, Day Lewis, de la Mare, Shadwell, Tennyson 9 Cleveland, Coleridge, Masefield, Whitehead 10 Chatterton, FitzGerald, Wordsworth 12 Bulwer-Lytton
political party: 6 Labour
porcelain: 5 Spode
prep school: 4 Eton
racecourse: 5 Ascot, Epsom
record label: 3 EMI
resort: 4 Bath
rock group: 3 Who, XTC 6 Stones 7 Beatles 10 Spice Girls
royal house: 4 York 5 Tudor 6 Stuart 7 Windsor
rule in India: 3 raj
runner: 3 Coe 5 Ovett
scientist: 4 Ryle 5 Dirac 6 Leakey, Stokes 7 Huggins, Woolley 10 Malinowski 11 Sherrington
sculptor: 5 Moore
sheep breed: 5 Devon 6 Oxford, Romney 7 Cheviot, Lincoln, Ryeland, Suffolk 8 Cotswold, Dartmoor 9 Hampshire, Leicester, Southdown, Wiltshire 10 Dorset Horn, Shropshire
soprano: 6 Garden
sport: 4 polo 5 rugby 7 cricket
tenor: 5 Pears
title: 3 sir 4 dame, lady, lord
West Point: 3 RMA
writer: 4 Amis, Cary, Dahl, Ford, Glyn, Hall 5 Arlen, Auden, Bates, Blunt, Bowen, Byatt, Defoe, Doyle, Eliot, Frayn, Green, Hardy, James, Milne, Noyes, Powys, Wells 6 Aldiss, Ambler, Austen, Barnes, Binyon, Braine, Brontë, Brophy, Bryher, Bunyan, Butler, Evelyn, Fowles, Fraser, Gibbon, Graves, Greene, Hallam, Hilton, Hudson, Huxley, Morris, Popper 7 Bennett, Bentley, Blunden, Burgess, Carroll, Chatwin, Collins, Corelli, Douglas, Drabble, Durrell, Firbank, Fleming, Forster, Francis, Gissing, Golding, Grahame, Haggard, Hartley, Hazlitt, Johnson, Kipling, Ustinov 8 Beerbohm, Brookner, Connelly, Fielding, Forester, Jhabvala 9 Blackwood, Churchill, Goldsmith, Isherwood 10 Bainbridge, Chesterton, Galsworthy
see also England, Great Britain
British __: 3 gum 4 Open, warm 5 India, Isles 6 dollar, Empire, gallon, Guiana, Legion, Malaya, Museum 7 America, English, Library
British __ Indies: 4 West
British __ unit: 7 thermal
British Columbia: 8 province
city: 5 Delta, Kaslo, Lumby, Sooke

6 Fernie, Surrey, Vernon
7 Burnaby, Kelowna, Langley, Mission, Nanaimo, Osoyoos, Saanich 8 Kamloops, Richmond, Victoria 9 Coquitlam, Penticton, Port Moody, Vancouver
10 Abbotsford, Chilliwack, Maple Ridge
Indian: 5 Haida, Kaska 6 Nootka 7 Kutenai, Tlingit 8 Kwakiutl, Squamish 9 Tsimshian 10 Bellabella, Bellacoola
locale: 6 Canada
mountain: 6 Robson
river: 5 Liard 6 Fraser
school: 3 SFU, TWU 11 Simon Fraser
tribe: 5 Haida
waterfall: 5 Della
British Commonwealth
member: 4 Fiji 5 Ghana, India, Kenya, Malta, Nauru, Samoa, Tonga 6 Belize, Brunei, Canada, Cyprus, Gambia, Guyana, Malawi, Tuvalu, Uganda, Zambia
7 Bahamas, England, Grenada, Jamaica, Lesotho, Namibia, Nigeria, St. Lucia, Vanuatu
8 Barbados, Botswana, Cameroon, Dominica, Kiribati, Malaysia, Maldives, Sri Lanka, Tanzania
9 Australia, Mauritius, Singapore, Swaziland 10 Bangladesh, Mozambique, New Zealand, Saint Lucia, Seychelles 11 Sierra Leone, South Africa
British English words
aide-de-camp: 6 batman
apartment: 4 flat
auto accessory: 4 tyre
bed: 3 kip
bigwig: 3 nob
bloke: 3 guv 4 chap
blue blood: 6 aristo
bobbin: 4 pirn
boob tube: 5 telly
bottle size: 5 litre
bouquet: 5 odour
broke: 5 skint
buddy: 4 mate 5 matey
butter substitute: 5 marge
candy: 5 lolly
car hood: 6 bonnet
car trunk: 4 boot
cat: 3 mog 5 moggy
cavalry weapon: 5 sabre
chap: 4 mate 5 bloke, matey
chunk: 5 wodge
collide with: 5 prang
counsel: 4 rede
cow: 5 stirk
crankcase: 4 sump
crowded area: 3 wen
daft: 5 potty
dairy merchant: 6 eggler
ditch: 4 sike, syke
dog it: 5 skulk
drop feathers: 5 moult
eccentric: 5 potty
elevator: 4 lift
exam: 6 A level
exasperation: 5 aggro
exclamation: 4 I say 5 blimy 6 blimey, good-oh, rather, righto, whizzo 7 cheerio
expletive: 3 gor 5 blimy 6 blimey, bloody
farewell: 4 ta ta
fashion plate: 4 toff
fertilizer: 5 nitre
filament: 5 fibre
fishing reel: 4 pirn
flashlight: 5 torch
floor covering: 4 lino
fungus: 5 mould
glamorous: 5 dishy
goof off: 5 skulk
greeting: 5 hullo
gully: 4 sike, syke
hooligan: 3 yob
ice-cream cone: 6 cornet
inc.: 3 ltd.
inferior wine: 5 plonk
informer: 4 nark
irritable: 5 tilty
lavatory: 3 loo
length measure: 5 metre
letter: 3 zed
lockup: 4 gaol, quod
loose: 5 lowse
lout: 3 yob
maid: 4 char
male sheep: 3 tup
meddlesome: 5 nebby
metal: 9 aluminium
mime show: 5 panto
mother: 3 mum
neat: 4 trig
nightshirt: 4 sark
oath: 3 gor
pants: 6 breeks
parent: 3 mum 5 mater, pater
petty criminal: 4 spiv
phone booth: 5 kiosk
plan: 4 rede
potato chip: 5 crisp
pound: 4 quid
prison: 4 gaol
quaint: 4 twee
quart: 5 litre
raincoat: 3 mac
recall: 5 rub up
recon: 5 recce, recco
road edge: 4 kerb
room: 6 bed-sit
rooming house: 3 kip
sausage: 6 banger
scent: 5 odour
school test: 6 A level
shed feathers: 5 moult
sift: 3 lue
spool: 4 pirn
stench: 5 odour
stew: 6 hot pot
stoolie: 4 nark
street: 4 mews
streetcar: 4 tram
stroller: 4 pram
subway: 4 tube
sulk: 4 mump
sword: 5 sabre
tale: 4 rede
term of endearment: 3 luv
thanks: 2 ta
thread: 5 fibre
tout: 4 spiv
tree trunk: 4 stam
truck: 5 lorry
undergraduate: 5 sizar, sizer
verb ender: 3 ise
weight unit: 3 tod 5 stone
British Virgin Islands capital: 8 Road Town
Britney: 6 Spears
Briton: 7 Cockney, Oxonion 8 Londoner 9 mac wearer, Tony Blair 10 Englishman
ancient ~: 4 Celt, Gael, Jute, Pict 5 Angle, Iceni, Saxon
Britt: 3 May 4 Reid 6 Ekland
Brittain: 4 Vera
Brittany: 3 dog 5 canid, duchy 6 canine, Morgan, Murphy, region 8 province
city: 6 Rennes
locale: 6 France
native: 6 Breton
neighbor: 5 Anjou
Brittany __: 7 spaniel
Britten, Benjamin: 8 composer
collaborator: 5 Auden
work: Albert Herring
Billy Budd
Paul Bunyan
Peter Grimes
Simple Symphony
Spring Symphony
War Requiem
Welcome Ode
brittle: 5 crisp, frail, stiff 6 crispy, crusty 7 crumbly, crunchy, fragile, friable 9 breakable, frangible, unpliable 10 nondurable
ender: 4 bush
peanut ~: 5 candy 10 confection
resin: 5 copal
brittleness: 9 fragility
Britton: 6 Connie, Pamela 7 Barbara
Britz: 7 Jerilyn
Brno: 4 city, town
from ~: 5 Czech
bro: 3 pal, rel., sib 4 chum, mate 5 buddy, crony, kiddo 6 frater, friend 7 compeer, comrade, partner, sibling 8 intimate, relative 9 associate, colleague, good buddy
parent's ~: 3 unc, unk
unc's ~: 3 pop
broach: 3 tap 4 open, talk 5 raise 6 hint at, open up, pierce, uncork 7 bring up, mention, propose, suggest 8 puncture 9 introduce
broad: 3 big, lax 4 deep, full, vast, wide 5 ample, large, money, roomy, squat, thick 6 gaping, portly 7 copious, general, immense, liberal 8 extended, far-flung, spacious, sweeping, tolerant, unstrict 9 capacious, cavernous, expansive, extensive, inclusive, open-ended, outspread, universal, wholesale 10 indefinite, large-scale, ubiquitous, unspecific, voluminous, widespread
combining form: 4 eury-, plat- 5 platy-
ender: 3 axe 4 band, bean, cast, leaf, loom, side, tail 5 cloth, sheet, sword 6 caster 7 casting
foot: 3 EEE
in ~ daylight: 6 openly
not ~: 6 subtle
street: 3 ave. 4 blvd. 6 avenue 9 boulevard
valley: 4 dale, glen, lawn, park 5 field, green, plaza 6 common, meadow
broad __: 4 bean, gage, jump, seal 5 arrow, gauge, glass, reach 6 jumper 7 hatchet
broad-__: 5 based, brush 6 leafed, leaved, minded
Broadbent, Jim: 5 actor
film: The Avengers (1998)
Iris (2001, AA)
Moulin Rouge (2001)
Princess Caraboo (1994)
Richard III (1995)
Topsy-Turvy (2000)
The Wedding Gift (1993)
broadbill: 4 bird, duck, fowl
relative: 4 smew, teal 5 eider, Pekin, Rouen, scaup 6 Cayuga, scoter 7 gadwall, mallard, pintail, pochard, redhead, sea duck, widgeon 8 garganey, gray duck, mandarin, musk duck, oldsquaw, shoveler, surf duck, wood duck 9 black duck, goldeneye, goosander, greenhead, merganser, ruddy duck, sprigtail 10 bufflehead, canvasback, surf scoter, tufted duck
broadcast: 3 air, sow 4 beam, emit, news, on TV, seed, send, sown 5 blare, carry, cover, relay, strew 6 airing, flaunt, get out, herald, report, splash, spread 7 bestrew, divulge, lay bare, network, program, radiate, scatter, spatter 8 announce, disperse, proclaim, televise, transmit 9 advertise, circulate, propagate, publicize, telephone, ventilate 10 annunciate, disclosure, distribute, make public, promulgate, radiograph
again: 5 reair
agency: 3 FCC
bands: 4 AMFM
block a ~: 3 jam
component: 5 audio, video
initials: 3 ABC, CBS, NBC, PBS, UPN
instructional ~: 3 ETV, PBS
medium: 2 CB 5 radio 10 television
need: 4 mike 10 microphone
broadcaster: 4 DJ. VJ 6 anchor, deejay, veejay 7 station 9 announcer
baseball ~: 4 Buck 5 Allen, Canel, Caray, Gowdy, Wolff 6 Barber, Hodges, Murphy, Nelson, Prince, Scully 7 Harwell 8 Bob Wolff, Hamilton, Jack Buck, McCarver, Mel Allen 9 Bob Murphy, Bob Prince, Buck Canel, Curt Gowdy, Garagiola, Vin Scully
10 Brickhouse, Harry Caray, Russ Hodges
on wheels: 4 CBer
Broadcast News (1987 film)
cast: Albert Brooks, Holly Hunter, William Hurt
director: James L. Brooks
__ Broadcast, The: 3 Big
broadcloth: 6 fabric 8 material
broaden: 3 wax 4 grow 5 add to, bloat, flare, swell, widen 6 beef up, dilate, expand, extend, fatten, open up, spread 7 augment, burgeon, develop, enlarge, inflate, stretch 8 bourgeon, escalate, heighten, increase, lengthen 9 branch out, spread out 10 liberalize, supplement
broadening: 8 cultural, increase 9 expansion, extension, uplifting
broad-jump: 5 event, sport
broadloom: 3 rug 6 carpet 9 carpeting
broad-minded: 4 open 7 liberal 8 catholic, flexible, tolerant, unbiased
broad-mindedness: 9 tolerance
Broadmoor: 3 car 4 auto 10 Studebaker
broadness: 5 width 7 breadth 9 amplitude
broadside: 3 ram 4 bill 5 flyer, salvo, storm 6 attack, poster, volley 7 assault, barrage, censure, handout, placard 8 brochure, circular, fire upon, handbill, pamphlet 9 cannonade, criticism, onslaught
broadside __: 6 ballad
broad side of __: 5 a barn
broad-topped hill: 4 loma
Broadway: 4 font 5 stage 8 typeface
angel's delight: 3 hit, SRO 4 boff 5 boffo, smash
award: 4 Tony
backer: 5 angel
brightener: 4 neon
eatery: 6 Sardi's
figure: 5 actor, angel 7 actress 8 director, producer
musical: 3 Big 4 Cats, Coco, Hair, Mame, Nine, Rent 5 Annie, Dolly!, Evita, Gypsy, Hello, Zorba
6 Barnum, Can-Can, Grease, I Do! I Do!, Kismet, Les Miz, Oliver!, Pippin, Purlie, The Wiz 7 Allegro, Cabaret, Camelot, Chicago, Company, Follies, Pal Joey, Passion, Ragtime, Titanic,

Whoopee **8** Applause, Big River, Carousel, Fiorello!, Godspell, Oklahoma!, Peter Pan, Show Boat, Two by Two **9** Brigadoon, Funny Girl, Girl Crazy, No Strings, On the Town, Pipe Dream **10** Dreamgirls, Kiss Me Kate, Lady Be Good!, Miss Saigon, My Fair Lady, Shenandoah **11** A Chorus Line, Crazy For You, Damn Yankees, Leave It to Me, Me and Juliet, No No Nanette, Of Thee I Sing, Sweeney Todd, The King and I, The Lion King, The Music Man
offering: **4** show **5** drama, revue **6** review **7** musical
opener: **6** act one
see also theater
Broadway (1942 film)
cast: Janet Blair, Pat O'Brien, George Raft
director: William A. Seiter
Broadway ___: **3** Joe **4** Bill **5** Bound **6** Melody
___ Broadway: **5** Funky
Broadway Bill (1934 film)
cast: Warner Baxter, Walter Connolly, Myrna Loy
director: Frank Capra
Broadway Bound author: Neil Simon
Broadway Danny Rose (1984 film)
cast: Woody Allen, Mia Farrow, Nick Apollo Forte
director: Woody Allen
Broadway Limited: **5** train
Broadway Melody of 1936 (1935 film)
cast: Jack Benny, Eleanor Powell, Robert Taylor
director: Roy Del Ruth
Broadway Melody of 1940 (1940 film)
cast: Fred Astaire, George Murphy, Eleanor Powell
composer: **6** Porter
director: Norman Taurog
___-Broadway show: **3** off
Broadway's in Fashion artist: **4** Erté
broast: **4** cook
Brobdingnagian: **3** big **4** huge **5** giant **7** immense, titanic **8** gigantic
brocade: **6** fabric **8** material
Broca's Brain author: **5** Sagan
broccoli: **6** veggie **9** vegetable
bit: **6** floret
variety: **4** rabe
broccoli ___: **3** rab **4** raab, rabe
___ broche: **3** à la
brochette: **4** spit **5** kabab, kabob, kebab, kebob
Broch, Hermann: **6** writer **8** Austrian
brochure: **5** flyer, tract **7** booklet, handout, leaflet **8** circular, handbill, pamphlet **9** broadside **10** literature, prospectus
Brock: **3** Lou **6** Peters
brocket: **4** deer
relative: **3** elk, roe **4** axis, pudu, shou, sika **5** moose **6** chital, guemal, hangul, huemul, sambar, sambur, thamin, wapiti **7** caribou, muntjac, muntjak, sambhar, sambhur **8** reindeer **9** barasingh
Brockhouse, Bertram: **8** Nobelist **9** physicist
Brock, Lou: **10** outfielder
theft: **4** base
Brockovich: **4** Erin
Brockton: **4** city, town
city near ~: **6** Boston
locale: **4** Mass.
Brock University
location: **6** Canada **7** Ontario
Brockville: **4** city, town
locale: **6** Canada **7** Ontario
Brodber, Erna: **6** writer **8** Jamaican
Broderick: **4** Beth **5** Helen, James **7** Matthew **8** Crawford
Broderick, Matthew: **5** actor
film: Biloxi Blues (1988)
The Cable Guy (1996)
Election (1999)
Family Business (1989)
Ferris Bueller's Day Off (1986)
The Freshman (1990)
Glory (1989)
Godzilla (1998)
Ladyhawke (1985)
The Road to Wellville (1994)
WarGames (1983)
You Can Count on Me (2000)
spouse: Sarah Jessica Parker
Brodie: **5** Steve
Brodkey, Harold: **6** author, writer
Brodsky, Joseph: **4** poet **8** Nobelist
Brody: **4** Jane **6** Adrien
Brody, Adrien: **5** actor
film: Bread and Roses (2001)
Liberty Heights (1999)
The Pianist (2002, AA)
The Thin Red Line (1998)
brogan: **4** shoe **8** footgear, footwear
brogue: **4** shoe **6** accent, oxford **7** dialect **8** footwear
broil: **4** burn, cook, heat **5** grill, melee, roast **6** scorch, sizzle **7** quarrel, swelter **8** barbecue, brouhaha
starter: **4** char
___ broil: **6** London
___-broil: **3** pan
broiler: **4** oven **7** chicken
broiling: **3** hot **6** red-hot, sultry, toasty, torrid **7** boiling, summery **8** ovenlike, tropical **10** sweltering
Brokaw, Tom: **6** anchor **9** anchorman **10** newscaster
beat: **4** news
employer: **3** NBC **5** NBC-TV
broke: **4** poor **5** kaput, needy **6** bad off, busted, hard up, ill off, in need, in want, ruined **7** cracked, pinched **8** badly off, bankrupt, beggarly, deprived, indigent, strapped **9** destitute, insolvent, moneyless, penniless, penurious, tapped out **10** cleaned out, down and out, pauperized, straitened
go ~: **4** bust, fail, fold, sink
go for ~: **4** dare, risk **6** gamble, hazard, strain, strive **9** persevere
in Britain: **5** skint
starter: **5** house
___-broke: **5** stone
broken: **4** dead, tame, torn **5** cleft, kaput, rough, split, tamed **6** beaten, busted, docile, faulty, flawed, jagged, marred, pliant, ragged, undone, uneven **7** cracked, crushed, damaged, haywire, injured, smashed, subdued, trained, unsound **8** crumbled, fallible, impaired, in pieces, lamblike, obedient, sporadic, sundered **9** collapsed, compliant, defective, destroyed, fractured, imperfect, in the shop, irregular, shattered, tractable **10** disjointed, fragmented, incomplete, inoperable, manageable, on the blink, on the fritz, out of order, out of whack, spiritless, sporadical, submissive, vanquished
combining form: **6** fracto-
easily ~: **6** flimsy **7** rickety
ender: **7** hearted
glass: **6** cullet
isn't ~: **4** runs **5** works
it may be ~ at parties: **3** ice
not ~: **5** whole **6** entire, intact
starter: **5** heart, house
up: **3** sad **5** apart **7** in tears
broken ___: **3** lot **5** chord, heart
broken-___: **4** down
Broken ___: **5** Arrow, Lance, Wings **7** Lullaby, Rainbow
broken-arm holder: **5** sling
Broken Arrow: **4** city, town
locale: **8** Oklahoma
tribe: **6** Apache
Broken Arrow (1950 film)
cast: Jeff Chandler, James Stewart
director: Delmer Daves
Broken Arrow (1996 film)
cast: Delroy Lindo, Samantha Mathis, Christian Slater, John Travolta
director: John Woo
Broken Arrow (ABC western)
cast: Michael Ansara (Cochise) John Lupton (Tom Jeffords)
Broken Blossoms (1919 film)
cast: Richard Barthelmess, Donald Crisp, Lillian Gish
director: D.W. Griffith
broken-down: **5** tired **6** shoddy, sleazy **7** rickety, squalid **8** decrepit, timeworn **10** ramshackle
horse: **3** nag **4** jade
brokenhearted: **3** low, sad **4** blue, glum **5** upset, woful **6** gloomy, morose, somber, woeful **7** crushed, doleful, joyless, unhappy **8** dejected, downcast, troubled **9** bummed out, cheerless, heartsick, miserable, sorrowful, woebegone **10** chapfallen, dispirited, melancholy
Brokenhearted (1995 song) artist: Brandy
Broken Hearted Me (1979 song) artist: Anne Murray
Broken-Hearted Melody (1959 song) artist: Sarah Vaughan
Broken Lance (1954 film)
cast: Jean Peters, Spencer Tracy, Robert Wagner
director: Edward Dmytryk
Broken Lullaby (1932 film)
cast: Lionel Barrymore, Nancy Carroll
director: Ernst Lubitsch
Broken Wings (1985 song) artist: Mr. Mister
broker: **5** agent, fixer **6** dealer, jobber **7** Realtor **8** mediator, merchant **9** financier, go-between, middleman, negotiant **10** negotiator
concern: **3** Dow, mkt. **4** bond, DJIA **5** stock **6** assets, market, return **7** economy **8** dividend **9** portfolio
money ~: **4** bank **5** S and L **6** banker, lender, usurer
second mortgage, to a ~: **4** refi
starter: **4** pawn **5** power, stock
stat: **5** quote
suggestion: **3** buy **4** fund, muni, sell **6** invest
work with a ~: **4** hock, pawn, sell
___ broker: **4** bill, note **5** floor, power, stock **7** customs
brokerage: **7** percent **10** commission
Internet ~: **6** E-Trade
starter: **5** stock
term: **3** buy, put **4** bear, bull, call, muni, sell **5** share **6** invest, return **8** dividend **9** portfolio
brolga: **4** bird
Brolin: **4** Josh **5** James
Brolin, James: **5** actor
film: Capricorn One (1978)
Westworld (1973)
spouse: Barbra Streisand
TV: Hotel, Marcus Welby M.D.
brolly: **4** gamp **8** umbrella
Brome, Richard: **7** British **10** playwright
Bromfield, Louis: **6** author, writer
bromide: **3** saw **5** adage **6** cliché, saying **9** platitude
___ bromide: **6** methyl, silver, sodium
bromidic: **4** dull **5** corny, hokey, passé, stale, trite, vapid **6** common, jejune, old hat **7** clichéd, fatuous, humdrum, prosaic **8** outdated, outmoded **9** hackneyed, prosaical **10** uninspired, unoriginal
bromine: **7** element, halogen
combining form: **4** brom- **5** bromo-
compound: **6** halide
Bromo Seltzer: **7** antacid
competitor: **4** Tums **6** Maalox, Pepcid, Riopan, Zantac **7** Gelusil, Lactaid, Mylanta, Rolaids **8** Gaviscon **11** Alka-Seltzer, Pepto-Bismol
Bron: **4** city, town **7** Eleanor
locale: **6** France
bronc: **4** pony **5** horse, mount, steed **6** animal, equine
see also bronco
bronchial ___: **4** tube
bronchiole locale: **4** lung
bronco: **4** pony **5** horse, mount, steed **6** animal, equine
break a ~: **4** ride, tame
buster: **5** tamer **6** cowboy
catcher: **5** lasso, noose
emulate a ~: **4** buck, rear **5** throw
Bronco: **3** car, SUV **4** auto, Ford **5** oater **10** footballer
rival: **3** Jet, Ram **4** Bear, Bill, Colt, Lion **5** Brown, Chief, Eagle, Giant, Niner, Raven, Saint, Texan, Titan **6** Bengal, Cowboy, Falcon, Jaguar, Packer, Raider, Viking **7** Charger, Dolphin, Panther, Patriot, Redskin, Seahawk, Steeler **8** Cardinal **9** Buccaneer
Bronco Billy (1980 film)
cast: Clint Eastwood, Geoffrey Lewis, Sondra Locke
director: Clint Eastwood
broncobuster: **6** cowboy
meet: **5** rodeo
Broncos: **4** team **6** eleven **10** Boise State
home: **6** Denver
org.: **3** AFC, NFL
sport: **8** football
Bronfman: **5** Edgar **7** Charles
Bronko: **8** Nagurski
Bronowski: **5** Jacob
Bronson: **6** Alcott **7** Charles, Pinchot
___ Bronson Alcott: **4** Amos
Bronson, Charles: **5** actor
film: Breakheart Pass (1976)
Breakout (1975)
Death Wish (1974)
The Dirty Dozen (1967)
The Great Escape (1963)
Hard Times (1975)
The Magnificent Seven (1960)
Master of the World (1961)
Once Upon a Time in the West (1968)
The Sandpiper (1965)
Telefon (1977)
spouse: Jill Ireland
Bronstein: **3** Ena
Brontë: **4** Anne **5** Emily **8** Branwell **9** Charlotte
Brontë (1983 film)
cast: Julie Harris
director: Delbert Mann
Brontë, Anne: **4** poet **7** British
pseudonym: Acton Bell
work: Agnes Grey
The Tenant of Wildfell Hall
Brontë, Charlotte: **6** author, writer **7** British
pseudonym: Currer Bell
work: Jane Eyre
The Professor
Shirley
Villette

Brontë, Emily: 6 author, writer 7 British
hero: 10 Heathcliff
pseudonym: Ellis Bell
work: Wuthering Heights
Bronx: 5 drink 7 borough 8 cocktail
athletes: 4 Rams
attraction: 3 zoo
Bomber: 4 Yank 6 Yankee
cheer: 4 jeer, razz 8 derision 9 raspberry
give a ~ cheer: 4 jeer, mock 5 taunt
ingredient: 3 gin 8 vermouth
locale: 3 NYC 7 New York
school: 7 Fordham
Bronx __: 5 cheer
Bronx ___, The: 4 is up
Bronx? No, thonx!, The author: 4 Nash
Bronx Tale, A (1993 film)
cast: Robert De Niro, Chazz Palminteri
director: Robert De Niro
Bronx Zoo, The
actor: 5 Asner
author: 4 Lyle
bronze: 3 tan 5 alloy, brown, color, medal, metal 6 statue, suntan 8 brownish, preserve
coin: 4 cent
color kin: 3 bay, dun, tan 4 bole, ecru, fawn, foxy, nude, seal 5 amber, beige, camel, cocoa, hazel, khaki, mocha, sepia, tawny, umber 6 auburn, bister, bistre, coffee, copper, ginger, russet, sienna, sorrel, suntan, walnut 7 biscuit, caramel, dogwood 8 chestnut, cinnamon, mahogany 9 butternut, chocolate
combining form: 5 chalc-, chalk- 6 chalco-, chalko-
component: 3 tin 6 copper
disk: 4 gong
medal: 3 DSC 5 third
Roman ~ coin: 3 aes 5 uncia
__ bronze: 4 gilt, gold 7 cadmium, coinage, journal
Bronze __: 3 Age 4 Star 5 Medal
bronzed: 3 tan 9 suntanned
Bronze Horseman, The author: Aleksandr Pushkin
Bronze Star: 5 medal
reason: 5 valor 7 bravery
brooch: 3 pin 5 cameo, clasp 7 jewelry
remove a ~: 5 unpin
brood: 3 sit 4 fret, mope, pine, pout, stew, sulk 5 covey, flock, hatch, spawn, think, worry, young 6 chicks, clutch, family, grieve, lament, litter, ponder 7 agonize 8 children, incubate, languish, look back, ruminate 9 nestlings, offspring, posterity 10 hatchlings, introspect, take it hard
over: 4 mull, muse, stew 5 study, worry 6 ponder 8 remember
brooder: 3 hen 9 introvert
brooding: 4 blue, down, glum 5 moody 6 morbid, solemn, sullen 8 downcast, lowering, taciturn 10 unsociable
broodmare: 3 dam 5 horse
broody: 3 low, sad 4 blue, dark, down, glum, mopy 5 bleak, heavy, mopey 6 abject, dismal, gloomy, mopish, morose 7 doleful, hangdog, joyless, sagging, subdued, unhappy 8 cast down, dejected, desolate, downbeat, downcast, drooping, shot down, wretched 9 bummed-out, cheerless, depressed, heartsick, in the pits, miserable, prostrate, saturnine, sorrowful, woebegone 10 despondent, dispirited, meditative, melancholy, out of sorts
brook: 2 go 3 let 4 bear, lump, race, rill, take 5 abide, allow, bourn, creek, rille, stand 6 accept, endure, permit, runlet, stream 7 rivulet, stomach, sustain 8 accede to, assent to, live with, sanction, stand for, tolerate 9 approve of, authorize, put up with, streamlet, withstand
sound: 4 purl 6 babble, burble, gurgle, murmur
brook __: 5 trout
Brook: 5 Clive, Peter 6 Benton
Brooke: 5 Adams, Astor, Smith 6 Rupert 7 Hillary, Shields
groom: 5 André
Brooke, Hillary: 7 actress
film: Africa Screams (1949)
Sherlock Holmes Faces Death (1943)
Strange Impersonation (1946)
The Woman in Green (1945)
Brooke, Rupert: 4 poet 7 British
Brookfield: 4 city, town
locale: 9 Wisconsin
Brookhaven Laboratory site: 5 Upton
Brookline: 4 city, town
locale: 4 Mass.
Brooklyn: 7 borough
athletes: 10 Blackbirds
breakfast: 5 bagel
ender: 3 ese, ite
locale: 3 NYC 7 New York
pronoun: 5 youse
school: 3 LIU
what grows in ~: 5 a tree
Brooklyn Bridge artist: 5 Marin
Brooklyn Center: 4 city, town
locale: 9 Minnesota
Brooklyn Park: 4 city, town
locale: 9 Minnesota
Brookner, Anita: 6 writer 7 British
Brook Park: 4 city, town
locale: 4 Ohio
Brooks: 3 Kix, Mel 5 Avery, Garth, range 6 Albert, Donnie, Foster, Louise 7 Cleanth, Richard, Van Wyck 8 Atkinson, Robinson 9 Geraldine, Gwendolyn
peak: 4 Isto 6 Mt. Isto
range locale: 5 Yukon 6 Alaska, Canada 7 Rockies
Brooks, Albert: 5 actor
film: Broadcast News (1987)
Defending Your Life (1991)
Lost in America (1985)
The Muse (1999)
My First Mister (2001)
Brooks, Avery: 5 actor
film: 15 Minutes (2001)
TV: Spenser: For Hire, Star Trek: Deep Space Nine
Brooks Brothers buy: 3 tie 4 suit 5 shirt
Brooks, Cleanth: 6 writer
Brooks, Garth: 6 singer
birthplace: 5 Tulsa
song: Lost in You (1999)
Brooks, Gwendolyn: 4 poet
work: Aloneness
Annie Allen
The Bean Eaters
In the Mecca
Maud Martha
Brooks, James L.: 8 director
film: As Good as It Gets (1997)
Broadcast News (1987)
Terms of Endearment (1983, AA)
Brooks, Mel: 5 actor 8 comedian, director
film: Blazing Saddles (1974)
High Anxiety (1977)
The Producers (1968)
Robin Hood: Men in Tights (1993)
Silent Movie (1976)
Spaceballs (1987)
The Twelve Chairs (1970)
Young Frankenstein (1974)
spouse: Anne Bancroft
Brooks, Richard: 8 director
film: Bite the Bullet (1975)
Blackboard Jungle (1955)
The Brothers Karamazov (1958)
The Catered Affair (1956)
Cat on a Hot Tin Roof (1958)
Deadline U.S.A. (1952)
$ (Dollars) (1971)
Elmer Gantry (1960)
In Cold Blood (1967)
The Last Time I Saw Paris (1954)
Looking for Mr. Goodbar (1977)
Lord Jim (1965)
The Professionals (1966)
Something of Value (1957)
Sweet Bird of Youth (1962)
Take the High Ground (1953)
Brooks, Van Wyck: 6 author, writer
Brookville campus: 6 C.W. Post
Brookwood: 3 car 4 auto 5 Chevy 9 Chevrolet 10 automobile
broom: 5 besom, plant, sweep, whisk 6 flower 7 sweeper
ender: 4 ball, corn 5 stick
material: 5 straw
partner: 3 mop 7 dustpan
rider: 5 witch
starter: 5 whisk
use a ~: 5 sweep
__ broom: 4 bush, corn, push 5 brush, dyer's, whisk 6 Scotch 7 Spanish
broomball: 4 game
Broomfield: 4 city, town
locale: 8 Colorado
Broom-Hilda: 5 comic, witch 10 comic strip
creator: 5 Myers
Brophy, Brigid: 6 writer 7 British
Brosnan, Pierce: 5 actor
film: Die Another Day (2002)
GoldenEye (1995)
The Lawnmower Man (1992)
Mars Attacks! (1996)
Mrs. Doubtfire (1993)
The Tailor of Panama (2001)
The Thomas Crown Affair (1999)
Tomorrow Never Dies (1997)
The World Is Not Enough (1999)
role: 4 Bond 6 Steele 9 James Bond
TV: Remington Steele
Bross: 4 peak 5 mount 8 mountain
locale: 7 Rockies 8 Colorado
Brossard: 4 city, town
locale: 6 Canada, Québec
broth: 4 soup 5 stock 6 liquid, liquor 8 bouillon, consommé, julienne
clarify ~: 5 defat
brother: 3 boy, guy, kin, pal, sib 4 male, monk, twin 5 friar, padre, prior 6 feller 7 kinsman 8 relative
address: 3 fra
combining form: 7 adelpho-
starter: 4 step
__ brother: 3 big, lay 4 half, soul 5 blood, whole 6 foster
Brother __: 3 Rat 4 John 5 Louis 6 Orchid
__ Brother: 3 Big
Brother, Can You Spare __?: 5 a Dime
Brother From Another Planet, The (1984 film) director: John Sayles
brotherhood: 4 gild 5 guild, order, union, unity 6 league 7 coterie, society 8 alliance
Brotherhood, The (1968 film)
cast: Alex Cord, Kirk Douglas, Irene Papas
director: Martin Ritt
Brother John (1970 film)
cast: Bradford Dillman, Will Geer, Sidney Poitier
brotherly: 4 kind 9 comradely, forgiving, fraternal 10 altruistic, benevolent, charitable, solicitous
Brotherly Love (1969 film)
cast: Peter O'Toole, Susannah York
director: J. Lee Thompson
Brother Orchid (1940 film)
cast: Humphrey Bogart, Edward G. Robinson, Ann Sothern
director: Lloyd Bacon
__ Brothers: 3 Ice 4 Ames, Marx, Ritz 5 Isley, Joyce, Lever, Mills 6 Doobie, Everly 7 Statler
__ Brothers Band: 6 Allman
Brothers Four song: Greenfields (1960)
Brothers Karamazov, The: 4 film 5 novel
author: Fyodor Dostoyevsky
cast: Claire Bloom, Yul Brynner, Maria Schell
character: 4 Ivan 5 Mitya 6 Dmitri
director: Richard Brooks
Brothers McMullen, The (1995 film)
cast: Edward Burns, Mike McGlone, Jack Mulcahy
director: Edward Burns
__ Brothers, The: 5 Blues
brouhaha: 3 ado, din, row 4 flap, fray, spat, stir, to-do 5 brawl, broil, furor, melee, scene, set-to, stink 6 clamor, flurry, fracas, hoopla, hubbub, pother, ruckus, rumpus, uproar 7 dispute, ferment, scuffle, wrangle 9 commotion, imbroglio 10 free-for-all, hullabaloo, hurly-burly
Broun: 7 Heywood
Brouthers: 3 Dan
brow: 3 rim 4 edge, peak 8 forehead
ender: 4 beat 6 beaten
starter: 3 eye, low 4 high
browbeat: 3 cow, nag 4 carp 5 bully 6 badger, bother, coerce, harass, hector, lean on, menace 7 bluster, oppress 8 bludgeon, bulldoze, domineer, keep down, threaten 9 castigate, terrorize, trample on, tyrannize 10 intimidate
browbeaten: 5 timid 7 fearful
browbeater: 3 nag 5 bully 6 tyrant
browbeating: 6 duress 8 coercion
__-browed: 6 beetle
brown: 3 bay, fry, tan 4 cook, ecru, puce, rust, sear 5 amber, beige, brick, cocoa, hazel, khaki, mocha, ocher, ochre, sauté, sepia, tawny, toast, umber 6 auburn, braise, bronze, coffee, copper, ginger, russet, sorrel, tanned 8 chestnut, cinnamon, mahogany 9 chocolate, earth tone
be in a ~ study: 4 mull, muse 6 ponder 7 reflect
color: 3 bay, dun, tan 4 bole, ecru, fawn, foxy, nude, seal 5 amber, beige, camel, cocoa, hazel, khaki, mocha, sepia, tawny, umber 6 auburn, bister, bistre, bronze, coffee, copper, ginger, russet, sienna, sorrel, suntan, walnut 7 biscuit, caramel, dogwood 8 chestnut, cinnamon, mahogany 9 butternut, chocolate
do up ~: 3 ace
ender: 3 out 5 shirt, stone
flower: 7 bulrush, cattail 8 reed mace 10 aspidistra
get ~: 3 tan 6 bronze 8 sunbathe
light ~: 3 tan 4 ecru 5 beige 6 suntan
name meaning ~: 5 Bruno
pigment: 5 umber 6 bister, bistre
purplish ~: 4 puce
reddish ~: 3 bay 4 bole, foxy, rust 5 cocoa, henna, rusty, umber 6 auburn, copper, ginger, russet, sorrel, walnut 8 chestnut, cinna-

mon, mahogany
study: 6 revery, trance 7 reverie
brown ___: 3 bag, bat, off, rat, rot 4 alga, bear, belt, bent, coat, rice, spot 5 betty, bread, dwarf, goods, heart, hyena, sauce, soils, study, sugar, trout 6 butter, hackle, thrush 7 creeper, mustard
brown-___: 3 bag 6 bagger
___ brown: 4 Mars, seal 6 Cassel 7 Cologne, Vandyke
Brown: 3 Dee, Jim, Les, Ron, Tom 4 Foxy, H. Rap, John, Paul, Tina 5 Blair, Bobby, Bruce, Bryan, James, Jerry, Kevin, Larry, Peter 6 Arthur, Claude, Louise, Murphy 7 Charlie, Herbert, Michael, Rita Mae 8 Clarence, Sterling 10 footballer, university
athletes: 5 Bears
league: 3 Ivy
locale: 10 Providence
rival: 3 Jet, Ram 4 Bear, Bill, Colt, Lion, Yale 5 Chief, Eagle, Giant, Niner, Raven, Saint, Texan, Titan 6 Bengal, Bronco, Cowboy, Falcon, Jaguar, Packer, Raider, Viking 7 Charger, Dolphin, Panther, Patriot, Redskin, Seahawk, Steeler 8 Cardinal 9 Buccaneer
___ Brown: 5 Cluny 6 Father, Jackie, Murphy 7 Charlie
Brown Adam: 5 horse
brown-and-___: 5 serve
brown-bag contents: 4 meal 5 apple, candy, fruit, lunch 6 banana, cookie 8 sandwich
brown betty: 7 dessert
Brown, Bobby
song: Don't Be Cruel (1988)
Every Little Step (1989)
Good Enough (1992)
My Prerogative (1988)
On Our Own (1989)
Rock Wit'cha (1989)
Roni (1988)
She Ain't Worth It (1990)
spouse: Whitney Houston
___ brown bread: 6 Boston
Brown, Bryan: 5 actor
film: 'Breaker' Morant (1979)
Cocktail (1988)
F/X (1986)
Gorillas in the Mist (1988)
Brown, Charlie
exclamation: 4 rats
friend: 4 Lucy 5 Linus
strip: 7 Peanuts
toy: 4 kite
Brown, Clarence: 8 director
film: Ah, Wilderness! (1935)
Angels in the Outfield (1951)
Anna Christie (1930)
Anna Karenina (1935)
Come Live With Me (1941)
Conquest (1937)
The Eagle (1925)
Edison, the Man (1940)
Emma (1932)
Flesh and the Devil (1927)
A Free Soul (1931)
The Human Comedy (1943)
Idiot's Delight (1939)
Intruder in the Dust (1949)
The Last of the Mohicans (1920)
National Velvet (1944)
Possessed (1931)
Sadie McKee (1934)
The White Cliffs of Dover (1944)
A Woman of Affairs (1928)
The Yearling (1946)
film of 1932: 4 Emma
Brown, Claude: 6 author, writer
work: Manchild in the Promised Land
___ Brown collar: 6 Buster
Browne: 3 Dik 6 Thomas 7 Jackson
___ Browne belt: 3 Sam
Browne, Jackson
song: Doctor My Eyes (1972)
Somebody's Baby (1982)
Browne, Thomas: 6 writer 7 English
Brown Eyed Girl (1967 song) artist: Van Morrison
brown-eyed Susan: 5 plant 6 flower
Brown, Father house: 5 manse
Brown, Foxy song: I'll Be (1997)
Brown, Georg Sanford spouse: Tyne Daly
brown-haired: 6 brunet 8 brunette
Brown, Herbert: 7 chemist 8 Nobelist
Brownian ___: 6 motion
brownie: 3 elf 4 cake 5 dwarf, fairy, nisse 6 cookie, sprite 7 dessert 10 confection, leprechaun
like a fresh ~: 5 moist
Brownie: 5 scout 6 camera 9 Girl Scout
cap: 6 beanie
creator: 5 Kodak
points: 6 credit
Browning: 3 Tod 6 Robert
Browning, Elizabeth Barrett: 4 poet 7 British
husband: Robert
work: Aurora Leigh
Grief
The Lady's Yes
My Heart and I
Only a Curl
Sonnets From the Portuguese
Browning, Robert: 4 poet 7 British
work: Abt Vogler
Andrea del Sarto
Cleon
Fra Lippo Lippi
Give a Rouse
In a Gondola
The Inn Album
Love in a Life
My Last Duchess
Paracelsus
Pauline
The Pied Piper of Hamelin
Pippa Passes
Rabbi Ben Ezra
The Ring and the Book
Saul
Sordello
Browning, Tod: 8 director
film: The Devil-Doll (1936)
Dracula (1931)
Freaks (1932)
Mark of the Vampire (1935)
West of Zanzibar (1928)
Browning Version, The (1951 film)
cast: Jean Kent, Nigel Patrick, Michael Redgrave
director: Anthony Asquith
brownish
color: 3 tan 4 buff, drab, nude, puce, sand 5 beige, olive, putty, taupe 6 bronze 7 nankeen 10 terra cotta
purple: 4 puce
yellow: 4 buff
Brown, James
nickname: Godfather of Soul
song: Cold Sweat (1967)
I Got the Feelin' (1968)
I Got You (1965)
It's a Man's Man's Man's World (1966)
Living in America (1986)
Papa's Got a Brand New Bag (1965)
Say It Loud - I'm Black and I'm Proud (1968)
Brown, Jim: 4 back 5 actor
film: Dark of the Sun (1968)
The Dirty Dozen (1967)
Fingers (1978)
The Grasshopper (1970)
Ice Station Zebra (1968)
sport: 8 football
Brown, Joe E.: 5 actor
film: Alibi Ike (1935)
Elmer the Great (1933)
A Midsummer Night's Dream (1935)
Some Like It Hot (1959)
Son of a Sailor (1933)
You Said a Mouthful (1932)
___ Brown Jug: 6 Little
Brown, Kevin sport: 8 baseball
Brown, Larry: 5 coach
milieu: 5 court
org.: 3 NBA
sport: 10 basketball
Brown, Michael: 8 Nobelist
Brown, Paul: 5 coach
sport: 8 football
Brown, Peter song: Dance With Me (1978)
Brown, Rita Mae: 6 author, writer
___ browns: 4 hash
Browns: 4 team 6 eleven
home: 9 Cleveland
org.: 3 AFC, NFL
sport: 8 football
___ Brown's Schooldays: 3 Tom
Brown, Sterling: 4 poet
Brownstone Eclogues author: Conrad Aiken
brownstone feature: 5 stoop
Brown Sugar (1971 song) artist: Rolling Stones
Brownsville: 4 city, port, town
locale: 5 Texas
Brown, Tina: 6 editor
brown warrior, name meaning: 6 Duncan
brown-winged butterfly: 5 satyr
browse: 4 leaf, look, read, scan, skim 5 graze 6 forage, peruse 7 examine, meander 8 glance at 9 check over 10 look around, window-shop
on-line without posting: 4 lurk
the Internet: 4 surf
through: 4 leaf, page, scan 5 thumb
browser: 6 reader 8 Explorer, Netscape
address for a: 3 URL
spot: 3 Web 6 stacks 7 library 8 Internet
Broz, Josip: 4 Slav, Tito
Brubaker (1980 film)
cast: Jane Alexander, Yaphet Kotto, Robert Redford
Brubeck, Dave: 7 pianist
genre: 4 jazz
song: Take Five (1961)
Bruce: 3 Lee 4 Dern 5 Brown, Cabot, Lenny, Nigel, Wayne 6 Catton, Geller, Jenner, Willis 7 Babbitt, Bennett, Channel, Chatwin, Davison, Hornsby 8 Virginia 9 Beresford 10 Boxleitner
Robert the ~: 4 Scot
Bruce ___ Friedman: 3 Jay
Bruce, Nigel: 5 actor
film: The Adventures of Sherlock Holmes (1939)
The Corn Is Green (1945)
The Hound of the Baskervilles (1939)
The House of Fear (1945)
Limelight (1952)
The Pearl of Death (1944)
The Scarlet Claw (1944)
The Scarlet Pimpernel (1935)
Sherlock Holmes and the Secret Weapon (1942)
Sherlock Holmes Faces Death (1943)
The Spider Woman (1944)
The Woman in Green (1945)
Bruce, Virginia: 7 actress
film: Downstairs (1932)
Hired Wife (1940)
The Invisible Woman (1941)
The Mighty Barnum (1934)
The Murder Man (1935)
Pardon My Sarong (1942)
There Goes My Heart (1938)
Bruch: 3 Max
Bruckheimer: 5 Jerry
Bruckner, Anton: 8 Austrian, composer
Bruegel, Pieter: 6 artist 7 Flemish, painter
Bruhn, Erik: 6 dancer 7 danseur
specialty: 6 ballet
Bruin: 5 UCLAn 6 iceman
rival: 4 Blue, King, Star, Wild 5 Devil, Flame, Flyer, Oiler, Sabre, Shark 6 Canuck, Coyote, Ranger 7 Capital, Panther, Penguin, Red Wing, Senator 8 Canadien, Islander, Predator, Thrasher 9 Avalanche, Blackhawk, Hurricane, Lightning, Maple Leaf 10 Blue Jacket, Mighty Duck
Bruins: 3 six 4 team, UCLA
hockey great: 3 Orr
home: 6 Boston
milieu: 3 ice 4 rink
org.: 3 NHL
sport: 6 hockey
bruise: 3 mar 4 beat, harm, hurt, mall, mark, mash, maul, welt 5 knock, wound 6 bang up, batter, boo-boo, damage, injure, injury, lesion, scrape, shiner, squash 7 contuse 8 aggrieve, black eye, discolor, swelling 9 contusion
one's shins: 4 bark
treatment: 3 ice 6 arnica
bruised: 3 raw 4 achy, hurt, lame, sore 5 livid 6 rotten, tender 8 reddened
easily ~ item: 3 ego
bruiser: 3 ape 4 goon 5 boxer, he-man 6 lummox 7 fighter 8 tough guy
bruit: 5 rumor
___ brûlé: 4 bois
Brulé: 6 Indian 7 Amerind
___ brûlée: 5 crème
___ brûlot: 4 café
brumal: 4 cold 6 wintry 7 ice-cold, wintery 8 freezing
brumby: 5 horse
brume: 3 fog 4 haze, mist
Brumel, Valery: 10 high jumper
brummagem: 6 geegaw, gewgaw 9 bagatelle
Brummell, Beau: 4 dude 5 dandy
brumous: 5 foggy
brunch: 3 eat 4 meal
choice: 3 lox 4 eggs 5 bagel, crape, crêpe 6 Danish, omelet, waffle 8 hotcakes, omelette, pancakes 9 sweet roll
Brundage: 5 Avery
Brunei: 3 bay 6 nation 7 country
locale: 4 Asia 6 Borneo
money: 3 sen 4 cent 6 dollar
neighbor: 8 Malaysia
brunette: 4 dark 5 brown
Bruni: 5 Carla
Brünnhilde
husband: 7 Gunther
mother: 4 Erda
Bruno: 5 Kirby, saint 6 Walter 8 Giordano 10 Bettelheim
Bruno (2000 film)
cast: Joey Lauren, Shirley MacLaine, Gary Sinise
director: Shirley MacLaine
___ Bruno: 3 San
Bruno, Giordano: 7 Italian 11 philosopher
Brunswick: 4 city, stew, town
locale: 4 Ohio 5 Maine

brunt: 5 force 6 impact, strain
brush: 3 rub 4 lick, wipe 5 clash, clean, copse, fight, gorse, graze, groom, melee, nudge, run-in, scour, scrap, scrub, sedge, set-to, shave, shine, sweep, touch, whisk 6 bushes, fracas, stroke, tickle, tussle 7 coppice, fox tail, thicket 8 conflict, kindling, skirmish, spruce up, struggle 9 chaparral, close call, encounter, shrubbery 10 engagement
aside: 6 ignore 7 neglect 8 overlook 9 disregard
broom: 5 besom
carelessly: 4 daub 5 smear
combining form: 5 scopi-
cut: 9 hairstyle
ender: 3 off 4 fire, wood, work
off: 4 snub 5 spurn, whisk 6 ignore, pass up, rebuff, refuse, reject, slight 7 dismiss, neglect 8 discount, sneeze at 9 disregard
past: 4 skim 5 graze
starter: 3 air 4 hair, nail, sage, snow 5 paint, tooth, under 6 bottle
up: 7 retouch
up on: 5 learn 6 polish, review 7 refresh
wield a ~: 5 paint
with liquid: 5 baste 7 moisten
with the law: 4 bust 5 pinch 6 arrest, collar
brush __: 3 cut, off 4 fire, up on 5 broom
__ brush: 3 end, fox 4 wire 5 dandy, scrub 6 pastry, pollen 7 shaving
__ Brush: 6 Fuller
brushed hide: 5 suede
brushing sound: 5 swish
brush-off: 4 snub 6 rebuff, slight 9 dismissal, rejection
Brush Up Your Shakespeare composer: 6 Porter
brusque: 4 curt, rude 5 blunt, brief, frank, gruff, rough, short, surly, terse 6 abrupt, candid, crusty, ireful, morose, snippy 7 laconic, offhand, raucous 8 impolite, snippety, succinct, tactless 9 impatient, outspoken 10 indelicate, ungracious, unmannerly
Brussels: 4 city, town 7 capital
city near ~: 5 Ghent
locale: 7 Belgium
org.: 3 EEC 4 NATO
river: 5 Senne
Brussels __: 4 lace 6 carpet 7 griffon, sprouts
Brussels Griffon: 3 dog 5 canid 6 canine
brussels sprouts: 6 veggie 9 vegetable
brut: 3 dry
relative: 3 sec
brutal: 4 hard, mean, ugly 5 cruel, feral, harsh, nasty, rough 6 animal, fierce, savage, severe, unkind, wanton 7 beastly, bestial, callous, hurtful, inhuman, vicious, violent 8 barbaric, fiendish, grueling, inhumane, pitiless, ruthless, sadistic, vengeful 9 barbarian, barbarous, cutthroat, draconian, ferocious, heartless, merciless, monstrous, murderous, truculent, unfeeling, unpitying 10 oppressive, unmerciful, vindictive
brutality: 7 cruelty 8 ferocity, iron hand, violence 9 barbarism, barbarity, grossness 10 fierceness, inhumanity, oppression, savageness
brutalize: 4 warp 6 ill-use, misuse 8 mistreat 10 demoralize
brute: 3 ape, lug 4 boor, jerk, lout, ogre 5 beast, bully, demon, devil, fiend, knave, rowdy, swine, yahoo 6 animal, bad guy, daemon, daimon, lummox, savage, strong 7 beastly, monster, ruffian, villain 8 lifeless 9 archfiend, barbarian, hellhound, vulgarian
force: 3 vim 4 dint, thew 5 brawn, might, power, thews, vigor 6 energy, muscle 7 fitness, muscles, potence, potency, stamina 8 strength, violence, vitality 9 beefiness, endurance, fortitude, hardiness, huskiness, puissance, stoutness, toughness 10 brawniness, mightiness, robustness, sturdiness
__, Brute: 4 et tu
Brute Force (1947 film)
cast: Hume Cronyn, Burt Lancaster
director: Jules Dassin
brutish: 3 bad 4 wild 5 cruel, nasty, rough, rowdy 6 animal, fierce 7 beastly, bestial 8 devilish, fiendish 9 ferocious
one: 4 ogre 5 bully, fiend, yahoo 6 tyrant
Brutus: 5 Roman
foe: 6 Antony
like ~: 5 noble
question to ~: 4 et tu
see also Latin
Brutus, Dennis: 4 poet 12 South African
Bryan: 4 city, town 5 Adams, Brown 6 Forbes, Singer 8 Trottier
locale: 5 Texas
Bryant: 4 Bear, Kobe 5 Anita 6 Gumbel
Bryant, Anita
song: In My Little Corner of the World (1960)
Paper Roses (1960)
__ Bryant Ford: 5 Edsel
Bryant, Kobe: 5 cager
milieu: 5 court
org.: 3 NBA
sport: 10 basketball
Bryant, Paul nickname: 4 Bear
Bryant, William Cullen: 4 poet
newspaper: Post
work: The Embargo
Thanatopsis
To a Waterfowl
Bryan, William Jennings: 6 orator
Bryce Canyon: 4 park
locale: 4 Utah
Bryher: 4 poet 7 British
Brynhild
brother: 4 Atli
husband: 6 Gunnar
Bryn Mawr: 4 coll. 7 college
grad: 5 woman 6 alumna
locale: 4 Penn.
Brynner, Yul: 5 actor
film: Anastasia (1956)
The Brothers Karamazov (1958)
The Buccaneer (1958)
Futureworld (1976)
The Journey (1959)
The King and I (1956, AA)
The Magnificent Seven (1960)
Solomon and Sheba (1959)
The Ten Commandments (1956)
Westworld (1973)
kingdom: 4 Siam
brynza: 6 cheese
bryology: 7 science
study: 4 moss 9 liverwort
bryony: 4 vine
bryophyte: 4 moss
Bryson, Peabo
song: Beauty and the Beast (1992)
If Ever You're in My Arms Again (1984)
Tonight, I Celebrate My Love (1983)
A Whole New World (1993)
Bryusov, Valery: 6 writer 7 Russian
Brzezinski: 8 Zbigniew
B.S.: 3 deg
B6: 7 vitamin
BSA: 3 org.
part: 3 Boy 5 Scout 7 America
unit: 3 den 5 troop
B-sharp equivalent: 5 C flat
BSN holder: 5 nurse
B's, one of the musical: 4 Bach 6 Brahms 9 Beethoven
BSU
see Ball State, Boise State
B12: 7 vitamin
__ B. Taney: 5 Roger
BTU
100,000 ~ s: 5 therm 6 therme
part: 4 unit 7 British, thermal
relative: 3 cal. 7 calorie
user: 2 AC
bub: 3 bud, mac 6 buster
Bubba: 5 Smith
__ Bubba: 5 Hubba
bubble: 4 bead, bleb, blob, boil, drop, fizz, foam, rave 5 froth 6 aerate, gurgle, seethe, simmer 7 blister, droplet, froth up, smolder, sparkle 8 smoulder 9 percolate 10 effervesce
air ~: 4 bleb
ender: 3 gum, top 4 head
enjoy ~ gum: 4 blow, chew
maker: 3 gum 4 pipe, soap 7 aerator 8 fountain 9 detergent
over: 4 boil, gush 7 enthuse 8 overflow
tool with a ~: 5 level
wrap: 7 padding
bubble __: 3 gum, top 4 bath, pack, wrap 6 memory 7 chamber
__ bubble: 4 soap
__-bubble: 6 hubble
Bubble __: 3 Yum
bubble and __: 6 squeak
bubble-bath feature: 4 foam, suds 5 froth
bubblegum: 8 ice cream
alternative: 5 lemon, mocha, peach 6 banana, coffee, Jamoca, toffee 7 caramel, coconut, vanilla 8 cinnamon, hazelnut 9 chocolate, pineapple, pistachio, raspberry, rocky road, rum raisin 10 blackberry, cheesecake, Neapolitan, peppermint, strawberry
bubblehead: 3 ass, lug, nit, oaf, sap 4 boob, clod, dolt, dope, fool, gowk, lunk, simp 5 chump, clown, cluck, dummy, dunce, joker, klutz, looby, ninny, patsy, schmo 6 dimwit, lubber, lummox, nitwit, schmoe, sucker, turkey 7 buffoon, bungler, dingbat, dullard, half-wit, jackass 8 dumbbell, numskull 9 birdbrain, harebrain, ignoramus, lamebrain, numbskull, simpleton 10 nincompoop
bubble-headed: 5 ditsy, ditzy, giddy 9 mercurial
bubbles: 4 fizz, foam, soap, suds 5 froth 6 lather
fill with ~: 6 aerate
make ~: 4 blow
minus ~: 4 flat
__ Bubbles: 4 Tiny
Bubbles author: Beverly Sills
Bubbles in the Wine bandleader: 4 Welk
Bubbles, John: 6 dancer
bubble wrap, play with: 3 pop
bubbling: 5 fizzy
over: 4 avid, keen 5 aboil, eager, perky 6 elated 8 enthused 9 vivacious
quality: 3 zip 4 zest 5 oomph 9 happiness
bubbly: 4 fizz, soda 5 fizzy, jolly, peppy, perky 6 feisty, frothy 7 foaming, lathery 9 champagne
name: 4 Moet
Buber, Martin: 8 Austrian 11 philosopher
Bubka, Sergey: 11 pole vaulter
bubkes: 3 nil 4 nada 6 naught, nought 7 nothing
Buc
see Buccaneer, Pirate
Bucaramanga: 4 city, town
locale: 8 Colombia
bucatini: 5 pasta
alternative: 4 orzo, ziti 5 penne 6 noodle 7 lasagna, lasagne, pastina, ravioli 8 couscous, farfalle, linguine, linguini, macaroni, rigatoni 9 agnolotti, angelhair, cavatelli, manicotti, spaghetti 10 cannelloni, fettuccini, tortellini, vermicelli
buccal: 4 oral
buccaneer: 6 bandit, outlaw, pirate, robber, sea dog, viking 7 brigand, corsair, sea wolf 8 marauder, picaroon, rapparee, sea rover 9 privateer 10 freebooter
Buccaneer rival: 3 Jet, Ram 4 Bear, Bill, Colt, Lion 5 Brown, Chief, Eagle, Giant, Niner, Raven, Saint, Texan, Titan 6 Bengal, Bronco, Cowboy, Falcon, Jaguar, Packer, Raider, Viking 7 Charger, Dolphin, Panther, Patriot, Redskin, Seahawk, Steeler 8 Cardinal
Buccaneers: 4 team 6 eleven
home: 5 Tampa 8 Tampa Bay
org.: 3 NFC, NFL
sport: 8 football
Buccaneer, The (1938 film)
cast: Franciska Gaal, Fredric March
director: Cecil B. DeMille
Buccaneer, The (1958 film)
cast: Claire Bloom, Yul Brynner, Charlton Heston
director: Anthony Quinn
Buccaneer, The author: Maxwell Anderson
Bucephalus: 5 horse, steed 6 equine
Buchanan: 3 Pat 4 Bill, Edna, Jack 5 Edgar, James
Buchanan, Edgar: 5 actor
film: Abilene Town (1946)
Benji (1974)
The Walls Came Tumbling Down (1946)
TV: Petticoat Junction
Buchanan, James: 8 Nobelist 9 economist, president
alma mater: 9 Dickinson
former occupation: 6 lawyer
home: 9 Lancaster, Wheatland
opponent: 7 Frémont 8 Fillmore
veep: 12 Breckinridge
Buchanan Rides Alone (1958 film)
cast: Randolph Scott, Craig Stevens
Buchan, John: 6 author, writer 8 Scottish
Bucharest: 4 city, town 7 capital
locale: 7 Romania, Rumania 8 Roumania
river: 9 Dambovita, Dimbovita
Buch der Lieder poet: 5 Heine
Buchholz, Horst: 5 actor
film: The Magnificent Seven (1960)
One, Two, Three (1961)
Tiger Bay (1959)
Buchner, Eduard: 6 German 7 chemist 8 Nobelist
Büchner, Georg: 6 German 10 playwright
buchu: 5 shrub
Buchwald, Art: 3 wit 6 writer 8 humorist
buck: 3 dol., one, roe 4 bill, deer, defy, jerk, jump, kick, male, stag 5 fight, money, pitch, reach, repel, start,

throw 6 animal, dollar, oppose, resist, spring, unseat 7 contest, coxcomb, dispute, protest, smacker 8 banknote, dislodge, frogskin, simoleon, struggle 9 greenback, withstand 10 jack-a-dandy
baby ~: 4 fawn
cry: 5 troat
ender: 3 eye, saw 4 aroo, bean, eroo, horn, jump, shot, skin 5 board, hound, teeth, thorn, tooth, wheat
feature: 6 antler
fraction: 2 ct. 4 cent, dime 6 nickel 7 quarter
make a ~: 4 earn, work
mate: 3 doe 4 hind
pass the ~: 5 blame, refer
starter: 3 roe, saw 4 bush, reed 5 black, water 6 spring
the system: 4 defy 5 rebel 6 oppose, resist 7 protest
up: 3 aid 4 help, stir 5 cheer, liven, rouse, steel 6 arouse 7 bolster, console, enliven, hearten, inspire 8 embolden, enspirit, imbolden, inspirit, motivate 9 encourage, enhearten 10 invigorate
buck __: 4 bean, moth, slip 5 fever, sheet 6 passer
buck __ here, the: 5 stops
buck-__: 5 naked
__ buck: 4 door, fast, half 5 black, cross 6 golden
Buck: 5 cager, Henry, NBAer, Owens, Pearl 6 Rogers 7 Leonard 8 hoopster
partner: 3 Roy
rival: 3 Net, Sun 4 Bull, Hawk, Heat, Jazz, King, Spur 5 Knick, Laker, Magic, Pacer, Sixer 6 Celtic, Hornet, Nugget, Piston, Raptor, Rocket, Wizard 7 Clipper, Grizzly, Warrior 8 Cavalier, Maverick 10 SuperSonic, Timberwolf
buck and __: 4 wing
buckaroo: 6 cowboy 7 cowpoke 8 horseman, wrangler
Buck Benny Rides Again (1940 film)
cast: Jack Benny, Ellen Drew
director: Mark Sandrich
buckboard: 3 rig
bucket: 4 pail 5 scoop 6 vessel 9 container
brigade member: 7 fireman
champagne ~: 4 icer 6 cooler
defect: 4 hole
drop in the ~: 8 pittance
easy ~: 4 dunk
handle: 4 bail
like a certain ~: 5 oaken
locale: 4 barn, well
of bolts: 3 car 4 auto, heap 5 crate, lemon 6 jalopy 7 flivver
Sandburg's ~ of ashes: 4 past
starter: 3 gut
use a ~: 4 bail, fill 6 convey
wood: 3 oak
bucket __: 4 seat 5 bench 7 brigade
__ bucket: 3 ice 4 slop
bucket of ashes, a: 4 past
Bucket of Blood, A (1959 film) director: Roger Corman
buckets: 4 a lot, much
come down in ~: 4 pour, rain 6 deluge
buckeye: 3 nut 4 tree 5 shrub
Buckeyes: 3 OSU 9 Ohio State
Buckeye State: 4 Ohio
Buckingham: 7 Lindsey
Buckingham Palace
dweller: 4 king 5 queen, royal 6 prince 8 princess
inits.: 3 HRH
locale: 6 London 7 England
Buckinghamshire: 6 county
locale: 7 England
bucking the tiger: 4 faro
Buck in the Snow, The author: Edna St. Vincent Millay
buckle: 4 bend, clip, warp 5 catch, clasp, yield 6 begird, cave in, fasten, submit 7 contort, crumple, distort, give way, succumb 8 collapse, fastener
down: 4 work 5 fight 6 wade in 7 get busy, get to it, pitch in 10 launch into
holder: 4 belt, shoe 5 strap
starter: 4 turn 5 swash
Buckley: 5 Betty 7 William
Bucknell: 6 school 10 university
athletes: 5 Bison
locale: 4 Penn. 9 Lewisburg
Buckner: 4 Noel 5 Jerry
bucko: 3 bub, mac 4 chap
Buck, Pearl S.: 6 writer 8 Nobelist
heroine: 4 O-Lan
milieu: China
pseudonym: Sedges
work: A Bridge for Passing
Dragon Seed
The Exile
Far and Near
Fighting Angel
The Good Deed
The Good Earth
A House Divided
Imperial Woman
The Living Reed
Mandala
My Several Worlds
Sons
The Spirit and the Flesh
Buck Privates (1941 film)
cast: Bud Abbott, Lou Costello
director: Arthur Lubin
Buck Privates Come Home (1947 film)
cast: Bud Abbott, Lou Costello
director: Charles Barton
buckram: 6 fabric 8 material
Buck Rogers... (NBC sci-fi)
cast: Gil Gerard (Buck Rogers)
Erin Gray (Wilma Deering)
Felix Silla (Twiki)
bucks: 3 he's, oof 4 cash, gelt, jack, kail, kale, loot, peag, pelf 5 bread, dough, funds, lucre, money, moola, mopus, pesos, rhino, sewan 6 dinero, do-re-mi, mammon, mazuma, moolah, seawan, silver, specie, wampum, wealth 7 cabbage, capital, lettuce, ooftish, scratch, shekels 8 bankroll, cold cash, currency, hard cash 9 long green 10 green stuff
starter: 4 mega
__ bucks: 3 big 5 white
Bucks: 4 five, team 6 county
home: 9 Milwaukee
locale: 7 England
org.: 3 NBA
sport: 10 basketball
buckskin: 5 cloth 7 leather
buck stops here, The monogram: 3 HST
buckthorn: 4 tree 6 jujube
buckwheat: 5 grain 6 cereal
byproduct: 5 honey
dish: 5 kasha 8 hotcakes, pancakes 9 flapjacks
nutrient in ~: 5 rutin
buckwheat __: 4 coal, note 5 flour 8 pancakes
Buckwheat
dog: 4 Pete 5 Petey
friend: 5 Darla, Porky 6 Spanky 7 Alfalfa
Bucky: 4 Dent 6 Harris 7 Walters
__ buco: 4 osso
bucolic: 4 calm, idyl 5 idyll, rural 6 rustic 7 country 8 agrarian, Arcadian, farmlike, pastoral 10 provincial
plot: 4 acre
poem: 4 idyl 5 idyll
surroundings: 7 country 8 outdoors
Bucs
see Buccaneers, Pirates
bud: 3 guy 4 germ, node 5 bloom, graft, shoot 6 feller, floret, nodule, sprout 7 blossom, burgeon, compeer 8 bourgeon, vegetate 9 germinate, pullulate 10 burst forth, effloresce
combining form: 5 -blast 6 blasto-
eventually: 4 leaf 5 bloom 6 flower 7 blossom
holder: 4 limb, stem, twig, vase 5 bough, stalk
in botany: 5 gemma
in the ~: 5 early
nip in the ~: 4 foil, halt, stem, stop 5 avert, quash 6 arrest, put out, scotch 7 obviate, prevent, put down, squelch 8 preclude, stamp out 9 forestall 10 extinguish, put an end to
pickled flower ~: 5 caper
spicy flower ~: 5 clove
starter: 3 red 4 rose
bud __: 5 scale, sport, stick
__ bud: 4 leaf 5 brood, mixed, taste 6 flower 7 lateral
Bud: 4 beer, Cort 5 Grant 6 Abbott, Fisher, Yorkin 7 Collyer
partner: 3 Lou
see also Budweiser
Budapest: 4 city, port, town 7 capital
airline to ~: 5 MALEV
locale: 7 Hungary
river: 6 Danube
Budd: 5 Billy 9 Schulberg 10 Boetticher
Budd, Billy: 3 gob, tar 6 sailor
creator: 8 Melville
Buddenbrooks author: Thomas Mann
Buddha: 6 Gotama 7 Gautama 10 Siddhartha
attribute: 4 calm 10 compassion
contemporary: 6 Lao-tse, Lao-tze, Lao-tzu
cousin: 6 Ananda
discourse: 5 sutra
enemy of ~: 4 Mara
meditation spot: 6 bo tree
mother: 4 Maya
of the future: 8 Maitreya
title: 6 prince
Buddhism: 3 Zen 4 ch'an 6 tantra 8 Mahayana, religion 9 Theravada, Vajrayana
awakening to reality in ~: 5 bliss 7 nirvana
canon: 5 agama
chant: 2 om 6 mantra
community: 6 sangha
delusion about reality: 7 samsara
doctrine: 6 anatta, anicca, dharma, dukkha
drum: 6 damaru 7 mokugyo
energy: 5 prana
energy center: 6 chakra
energy channels: 4 nadi
eon: 5 kalpa
flower: 5 lotus
furnishing: 3 mat 5 tanka 6 candle 7 cushion, incense, thangka 10 butter lamp
gesture: 5 mudra
homage word: 4 namu
language of ~ scriptures: 4 Pali 8 Sanskrit
meditation cushion: 4 zafu
meditative state: 5 zhiné 6 satori 7 samadhi 8 dzogchen 10 shikantaza
monk: 4 lama 5 bonze 7 bhikshu 9 bhikshuni
monument: 4 tope 5 stupa
musical instrument: 4 bell, drum, gong 7 trumpet
ritual: 4 puja
ritual object: 4 bell 5 dorje, torma, vajra 6 bhumpo, phurba 7 mandala
sacred city: 4 Lasa 5 Lassa, Lhasa 8 Bodh-gaya
sacred mountain: 4 Meru, Omei
sacred syllable: 2 ah, om 3 aum, dza, hri, hum 4 hung
shrine: 5 stupa 6 Ajanta
sitting mat: 7 zabuton
symbol of the indestructible: 5 lotus, vajra
symbol of the universe: 7 mandala
symbol of Ultimate Reality: 5 lotus, vajra
teachings: 5 sutra 6 dharma, tantra
temple: 3 wat 5 zendo 8 lamasery
Tibetan ~ icon: 5 tanka 7 thangka
Tibetan school of ~: 4 Rimé 5 Kagyu, Sakya 7 Gelugpa, Nyingma
title: 4 guru, lama 5 geshe, Roshi 6 khenpo, sensei 7 Karmapa 8 Rinpoche 9 Dalai Lama
Ultimate Reality: 7 sunyata
virtue: 3 joy 4 love 8 paramita 10 bodhicitta, compassion, equanimity
vow: 6 samaya
wisdom: 5 jñana 6 prajna
__ Buddies: 5 Bosom
budding: 5 early, young 6 spring 8 juvenile, youthful 9 fledgling, incipient, potential, promising 10 developing, unrealized
buddleia: 5 shrub
buddy: 3 bro, guy, lad, mac, pal 4 ally, chum, dude, mate 5 amigo, crony, kiddo, pally 6 cohort, feller, frater, friend 7 compeer, comrade, partner 8 alter ego, intimate, roommate, sidekick 9 associate, colleague, companion, confidant 10 compatriot
beatnik ~: 6 daddy-o
cowboy's ~: 4 pard 7 pardner
good ~: 3 bro, pal 4 CBer
in Australian English: 4 mate
in British English: 4 mate
in French: 3 ami 4 amie
in Spanish: 5 amiga, amigo
buddy __: 4 seat 6 system
__ buddy: 4 good 5 bosom
Buddy: 3 Guy 4 Baer, Rich 5 Ebsen, Greco, Holly, Miles 6 Rogers 7 DeSylva, Hackett
to Bill: 3 dog, pet
buddy-buddy: 4 kind 5 close, thick 6 chummy, clubby, genial, kindly 7 affable, amiable, cordial 8 amicable, familiar, friendly, intimate, outgoing, sociable 9 convivial 10 benevolent, neighborly, solicitous
Buddy Buddy (1981 film)
cast: Jack Lemmon, Walter Matthau, Paula Prentiss
director: Billy Wilder
Buddy Holly Story, The (1978 film)
cast: Gary Busey, Charles Martin Smith, Don Stroud
budge: 4 bend, move, stir, sway 5 shift, yield 6 change 7 give way 8 convince, dislodge, persuade 9 influence 10 knock loose
don't ~: 4 stay 6 insist, refuse
Budge, Don: 7 netster 9 tennis pro
milieu: 5 court
budgerigar: 3 pet 4 bird 8 parakeet
budget: 5 funds, means, total 6 ration, upkeep 7 plan for, program 8 allocate 9 apportion, resources, statement 10 allocation

concern: 5 outgo
DC ~ watchdog: 3 GAO
item: 3 gas 4 elec., rent, util. 8 electric 9 utilities 10 car payment
limit: 3 cap 7 ceiling
starter: 4 fuss
stretch the ~: 3 eke 5 skimp, stint 6 eke out 9 economize
___ budget: 5 water 7 capital
___-budget: 3 low, off
Budget: 9 car rental 10 auto rental
competitor: 4 Avis 5 Alamo, Hertz 6 Dollar 7 Thrifty 8 National 10 Enterprise
budgetary: 6 fiscal 8 economic, monetary
budgeting: 7 finance 9 financial
abbr.: 3 YTD
budgie: 8 parakeet, paraquet, paroquet, parroket 9 parrakeet, parroquet
___ Bud Melman: 5 Larry
buds combining form: 7 -blastic
Budweiser: 4 beer
competitor: 5 Becks, Coors, Pabst 6 Amstel, Corona, Miller, Molson, Stroh's 7 Schlitz 8 Heineken, Michelob 9 Lowenbrau 10 Ballantine
dog: 5 Spuds
___ Bueller's Day Off: 6 Ferris
___ Buena: 5 Yerba
Buena Park: 4 city, town
locale: 10 California
buenas ___: 6 noches, tardes
Buenaventura: 4 city, port, town
locale: 8 Colombia
___ Buenaventura: 3 San
Buena Vista: 4 city, town 6 battle
locale: 6 Mexico
Bueno, Maria: 7 netster 9 tennis pro
milieu: 5 court
buenos ___: 4 días
Buenos Aires: 4 city, port, town 7 capital
city near ~: 5 Salto, Tigre
locale: 3 Arg. 9 Argentina
musical set in ~: 5 Evita
river: 5 Plata
see also Spanish
Buero Vallejo, Antonio: 7 Spanish 10 playwright
buff: 3 fan, nut, rub, tan 4 wipe 5 color, flaxy, freak, gloss, lover, maven, mavin, scour, scrub, shine 6 addict, flaxen, polish, rooter, suntan, yellow 7 admirer, burnish, devotee, furbish, groupie 8 brownish, follower, muscular 9 sandpaper 10 aficionado, enthusiast
cheat at blind man's ~: 4 peek
color kin: 4 corn, gold, lime, rust, sand 5 blond, brass, camel, coral, cream, flaxy, lemon, maize, ocher, ochre, peach, rusty, straw 6 almond, blonde, canary, chammy, citron, crocus, flaxen, shammy, shamoy 7 apricot, caramel, chamois, citrine, jasmine, mustard, nankeen, old gold, saffron, xanthic 8 daffodil, primrose 9 champagne, goldenrod, jessamine
in the ~: 4 nude 5 naked 9 unattired
up: 3 wax 5 shine 6 polish 8 brighten
buffa: 5 comic 8 humorous
opposite of ~: 5 seria
___ buffa: 5 opera
buffalo: 4 dupe, foil 5 bovid, bully, stump 6 animal, baffle, bovine, puzzle 7 deceive, mystify, nonplus, perplex, unnerve 8 hoodwink 10 intimidate
Cape ~ home: 6 Africa
feature: 4 hump
female: 3 cow
group: 4 herd
male: 4 bull
relative: 3 yak 4 anoa, arna, gaur, urus, zebu 5 bison, gayal, takin 6 mithan, muskox 7 aurochs, banteng, banting, beefalo, carabao, cattalo, kouprey, tamarao, tamarau, timarau 12 water buffalo
young: 4 calf 8 buffalo's
buffalo ___: 3 bug 4 bird, fish, gnat, robe 5 berry, cloth, grass, plaid, wings 7 currant, soldier
___ buffalo: 4 Cape 5 black, dwarf, water
Buffalo: 4 city, port, town
canal to ~: 4 Erie
conference: 3 MAC
county: 4 Erie
lake: 4 Erie
like ~ winters: 5 snowy
locale: 7 New York
newspaper: 4 News
pro team: 5 Bills 6 Sabres
suburb: 5 Depew
Buffalo ___: 4 Bill, Gals 5 Girls 6 Indian, Stance
buffalo berry: 5 fruit
Buffalo Bill: 4 Cody
buffaloed: 4 asea 5 stuck 7 stumped
buffaloes, water: 4 oxen
Buffalo Girls author: Larry McMurtry
Buffalo Grove: 4 city, town
locale: 8 Illinois
Buffalo Springfield song: For What It's Worth (1967)
Buffalo Stance (1989 song) artist: Neneh Cherry
buffer: 5 guard 6 shield 7 bulwark, cushion, defense, padding 9 safeguard 10 protection
buffer ___: 4 zone 5 state
Bufferin alternative: 3 APF 4 Cope 5 Advil, Aleve, Bayer 6 Anacin, Datril, Motrin 7 Ecotrin, Tylenol 8 Excedrin, St. Joseph, Vanquish 9 Ascriptin
buffet: 3 hit, jar 4 beat, blow, cuff, lash, meal, sock, swat, toss 5 crack, knock, pound, punch, smack, smite, spank, table, thump, whack, whang 6 batter, dinner, pommel, pummel, strike, supper, thrash, thwack, wallop 7 clobber 9 furniture, reception
choice: 3 ham 4 fish, food, soup 5 fruit, salad 6 entrée, shrimp, turkey 7 chicken, dessert 9 roast beef
enjoy the ~: 3 eat 5 gorge, stuff
patron: 5 diner, eater 8 gourmand
buffeting: 3 jar 4 blow 5 shock 6 impact 9 collision, explosion 10 concussion
Buffett: 5 Jimmy 6 Warren
Buffett, Jimmy: 6 singer
song: Margaritaville (1977)
Buffett, Warren
HQ: 3 Neb. 4 Nebr. 5 Omaha 8 Nebraska
bufflehead: 4 duck, fowl
relative: 4 smew, teal 5 eider, Pekin, Rouen, scaup 6 Cayuga, scoter 7 gadwall, mallard, pintail, pochard, redhead, sea duck, widgeon 8 garganey, gray duck, mandarin, musk duck, oldsquaw, shoveler, surf duck, wood duck 9 black duck, broadbill, goldeneye, goosander, greenhead, merganser, ruddy duck, sprigtail 10 canvasback, surf scoter, tufted duck
buffo: 5 comic 8 humorous
buffoon: 3 ass, nit, oaf, sap, wag 4 boob, boor, bozo, clod, dolt, fool, geek, joke, zany 5 chump, clown, cluck, comic, dummy, dunce, joker, ninny, patsy, sport 6 dimwit, jester, lummox, nitwit, sucker, turkey 7 dingbat, dullard, fathead, half-wit, jackass, pierrot, pinhead, saphead 8 bonehead, comedian, dumbbell, funnyman, meathead, numskull 9 birdbrain, blockhead, harlequin, lamebrain, legpuller, numbskull, simpleton 10 dunderhead
buffoonery: 3 fun 5 antic, farce, humor 7 fooling 8 zaniness 9 funniness, merriment 10 jocoseness
bit of ~: 4 joke 5 antic, prank
Buffy ___-Marie: 6 Sainte
Buffy the Vampire Slayer (1992 film)
cast: Paul Reubens, Donald Sutherland, Kristy Swanson
director: Fran Rubel Kuzui
Buffy the Vampire Slayer (WB sci-fi)
cast: Nicholas Brendon (Xander Harris)
Sarah Michelle Gellar (Buffy Summers)
bug: 3 ant, bee, bot, dor, dun, fad, flu, fly, get, irk, nag, nit, tap, tip, vex 4 flaw, flea, gall, germ, gnat, grub, lice, mite, moth, pest, pupa, rage, ride, rile, snag, tick, tine, wasp 5 annoy, aphid, aphis, borer, chafe, cimex, cooty, craze, drone, eat at, emmet, error, freak, get on, hound, imago, larva, louse, mania, midge, peeve, spy on, upset, virus, worry 6 abrade, acarid, badger, beetle, botfly, bother, chafer, chigoe, chinch, cicada, cocoon, cootie, defect, earwig, gadfly, glitch, grippe, harass, hassle, hornet, insect, larvae, locust, looper, maggot, malady, mantis, mayfly, needle, nettle, noodge, pester, plague, pother, punkie, pursue, put out, scarab, thrips, tipoff, tussah, vermin, weevil, work on 7 agitate, ailment, ant lion, bedevil, blowfly, chigger, cricket, disease, disturb, fanatic, firefly, hexapod, illness, katydid, microbe, no-see-um, perturb, pismire, provoke, termite, trouble, viceroy, wiretap 8 armyworm, bacillus, conenose, distress, firebrat, glowworm, honeybee, housefly, irritate, lacewing, listen to, mosquito, muckworm, reduviid, sickness, silkworm, woodworm 9 aggravate, bacterium, bumblebee, butterfly, chrysalis, cockroach, corn borer, damselfly, dobsonfly, dorbeetle, dragonfly, earthworm, eavesdrop, infection, influenza, obsession, saturniid, sheep tick, tarantula, woodborer 10 bluebottle, calicoback, deathwatch, deficiency, digger wasp, disconcert, froghopper, pear thrips, rose chafer, woolly bear
baby ~: 5 larva
back: 5 notum
bite: 4 welt 5 sting
bonnet ~: 3 bee
busy ~: 3 ant, bee
catch a ~: 3 ail
chest: 6 thorax
ender: 4 bane, bear 5 house
June ~: 3 dor 4 dorr 6 beetle
like a cold ~: 5 viral
like a ~ in a rug: 4 snug
mouth parts: 5 labra
off: 5 scram 7 get lost
out: 2 go 5 leave, scram 6 decamp 7 vamoose 8 fugitate, run for it 10 make tracks
pesky ~: 3 fly 4 gnat 5 midge 6 punkie 7 no-see-um 8 mosquito
phone ~: 3 tap 4 mike
pill ~: 6 isopod
science: 5 entom. 10 entomology
starter: 3 bed, hum, mud, red 4 bill, fire, lady 5 mealy, stink 6 doodle, jitter, litter, tumble 7 shutter
stinging ~: 3 bee 4 wasp 6 hornet
tiny ~: 4 gnat, mite 5 midge 6 punkie 7 no-see-um
user: 3 spy
see also insect
bug ___: 3 off, out 6 zapper
bug-___: 4 eyed
___ bug: 3 bed, mud, sow, tow 4 boat, flat, June, lace, leaf, love, pill, toad, true 5 cinch, grass, lygus, plant, shore, stilt, stink, water, wheel 6 ambush, calico, carpet, chinch, coreid, Croton, damsel, flower, fungus, potato, spider, squash 7 buffalo, cabbage, lygaeid
Bug: 2 VW 3 car 4 auto 5 river 10 automobile, Volkswagen
River locale: 6 Poland 7 Ukraine
river to the ~: 5 Narew
Buga: 4 city, town
locale: 8 Colombia
bugaboo: 4 bane, fear, jinx 7 problem
bugaku: 5 dance
Bugatti: 3 car 4 auto 6 Ettore 7 Italian 10 automobile
bugbear: 4 bane, bogy, ogre 6 fantom, goblin 7 bogyman, phantom, spectre 8 anathema, pet peeve 9 bête noire, hobgoblin, nightmare
bug-eyed: 4 agog, gaga
monster: 2 ET
Buggles song: Video Killed the Radio Star (1979)
buggy: 4 auto, loco, pram 5 wagon 7 vehicle 8 carriage
drivers: 5 Amish
dune ~: 3 ATV
venue: 4 dune
___ buggy: 4 baby, dune 5 beach, marsh, swamp 6 bundle
...bug in ___: 4 a rug
___ bug in one's ear: 4 put a
bugle: 4 horn, wind 7 trumpet
ender: 4 weed
play a ~: 4 blow
signal: 4 taps 6 charge 8 reveille
Bugle ___: 3 Boy
Bugler's Holiday composer: 8 Anderson
bugles, animal that: 3 elk
bugleweed: 5 ajuga
Bugliosi: 7 Vincent
Bugs: 4 Baer 5 Moran
Bugs Bunny: 4 hare 7 cartoon 9 comic book
adversary: 3 Taz 4 Fudd 9 Elmer Fudd
like ~: 5 eared
voice: Mel Blanc
bug's life, a (1998 film)
voice cast: Phyllis Diller, Julia Louis-Dreyfus, Kevin Spacey
Bug's Life, A
bug: 3 ant
role: 4 Atta
Bug Sur author: Jack Kerouac
Bugsy: 6 Siegel
wife: 4 Esta
Bugsy (1991 film)
cast: Warren Beatty, Annette Bening, Elliott Gould, Harvey Keitel, Ben Kingsley
director: Barry Levinson
___ Bug, The: 4 Gold, Love 5 Satan
buhr: 9 millstone
Buick: 3 car 4 auto 10 automobile
endorser: 5 Woods
model: 5 Regal 6 Apollo, Reatta 7 Century, Electra, Invicta, LeSabre, Limited, Riviera, Skyhawk, Skylark, Special, Wildcat 8 Somerset 9 Centurion, Gran Sport 10 Park Avenue,

Roadmaster, Sportwagon
build: 3 wax 4 body, form, gird, grow, make, mold, rear, rise, tone 5 add to, boost, erect, forge, found, frame, mount, put up, raise, set up, shape, shore, steel 6 accrue, anneal, beef up, create, enrich, expand, extend, figure, gather, harden, prop up, step up, temper, tone up 7 anatomy, augment, bolster, brace up, burgeon, compile, compose, develop, empower, enhance, enlarge, fashion, fortify, improve, produce, shore up, stiffen, throw up, toughen 8 assemble, bourgeon, buttress, energize, engineer, escalate, heighten, increase, indurate, initiate, multiply, physique, vitalize 9 construct, establish, fabricate, formulate, increment, institute, intensify, originate, reinforce, structure 10 accelerate, aggrandize, inaugurate, invigorate, strengthen, supplement
a wing: 3 add 5 add on, annex 6 adjoin, append, tack on
body ~: 5 frame 8 physique
castles in the air: 5 dream 7 imagine 9 fantasize
on: 3 add 4 rely 5 trust 6 depend
something to ~ on: 3 lot 4 spec 10 foundation
up: 3 get, wax 4 gird, grow, laud, lift, rise, tone 5 add to, amass, boost, build, exalt, lay by, lay up, lobby, shore, steel 6 accrue, anneal, enrich, expand, fatten, harden, praise, temper 7 amplify, augment, bolster, burgeon, develop, empower, enhance, fortify, improve, inflate, magnify, prepare, promote, recruit, stiffen, toughen 8 bourgeon, buttress, energize, escalate, heighten, increase, indurate, multiply, overrate, progress, vitalize 9 condition, increment, intensify, publicize, reinforce 10 exaggerate, invigorate, strengthen, supplement
build __ egg: 5 a nest
__-build: 5 jerry 6 custom
build a __ under: 4 fire
builder: 5 mason 6 framer 7 erector 8 engineer, inventer, inventor 9 architect, artificer, carpenter, developer 10 contractor, fabricator, mastermind
choice: 4 site
detail: 4 spec
empire ~: 5 baron, mogul, mover 6 bigwig, shaker, tycoon 7 magnate 9 financier, plutocrat 10 capitalist
starter: 4 home, ship
__ builder: 6 empire, master
__-builder: 4 body
__ Builders: 5 Mound
__ Builder, The: 6 Master
building: 4 barn, home 5 cabin, condo, house, shack 6 duplex, garage, lean-to, museum, palace 7 cottage, edifice, mansion, stadium 8 assembly, dwelling, high-rise 9 structure 10 skyscraper
block: 4 unit 5 brick
brace: 5 strut
circular ~: 4 dome 6 tholos
component: 4 beam, stud 5 I-beam, joist, truss 6 girder, rafter
crude ~: 4 shed 5 cabin, shack 6 lean-to
designers' org.: 3 AIA
detail: 4 spec
extension: 3 ell 4 wing 5 add-on, annex
feature: 4 deck 5 porch, spire, tower 6 column, cupola 7 balcony, steeple, veranda 9 bay window, bow window
govt. ~ agency: 3 HUD
level: 5 attic, story 6 cellar 8 basement
manager: 4 supe 5 super
material: 4 wood 5 adobe, brick, steel, stone 6 cement, thatch 8 concrete
nature's ~ block: 3 DNA, RNA 4 atom, cell, gene 10 chromosome
occupy an abandoned ~: 5 squat
office ~ area: 5 court, lobby 6 atrium 9 courtyard
plastic ~ block: 4 Lego
regulations: 4 code
religious ~: 5 zendo 6 chapel, church, pagoda, shrine, temple 8 lamasery 9 cathedral
site: 3 lot
site sight: 5 crane
starter: 4 body, ship
support: 4 beam 5 I-beam 6 girder
tall ~: 5 tower 10 skyscraper
tumbledown ~: 4 ruin
utility ~: 4 shed 6 garage, lean-to
building __: 4 code, line 5 block, paper 6 permit, trades 7 society
__ building: 4 body, loft 6 sliver
Building a Mystery (1997 song) artist: Sarah McLachlan
building-block material: 6 cement, cinder 8 concrete
buildings: 8 property
grounds and ~: 8 premises
Build Me Up Buttercup (1969 song) artist: Foundations
build on __: 4 spec
build-up: 4 gain, heap, hype 5 boost 6 growth, hoopla 7 accrual 8 increase, training 9 accretion, expansion, inflation, publicity, stockpile 10 escalation
household ~: 4 junk 5 trash 7 garbage
built: 5 put up
for speed: 5 sleek 8 souped-up
powerfully ~: 5 stout 8 muscular
to last: 5 solid, sound 6 rugged, strong, sturdy 8 well-made
built __: 6 to last
__-built: 3 cat 4 well 5 jerry, stick 6 carvel, custom 7 clinker, clipper
__ built a railroad...: 5 Once I
built-in: 6 innate, native 9 ingrained, intrinsic 10 deep-seated
built-up: 5 urban
area: 4 city, town 5 exurb 6 suburb 7 village 10 metropolis, settlement
buisine: 7 trumpet
Buisson, Ferdinand: 6 French 8 Nobelist
Bujold, Genevieve: 7 actress
film: The Act of the Heart (1970)
Anne of the Thousand Days (1969)
Choose Me (1984)
Coma (1978)
Dead Ringers (1988)
La Guerre Est Finie (1966)
The Thief of Paris (1967)
Bujones, Fernando: 6 dancer 7 danseur
milieu: 6 ballet
Bujumbura: 4 city, town 7 capital
locale: 7 Burundi
Bukavu: 4 city, town
lake: 4 Kivu
locale: 5 Zaire
Bukhara: 4 city, town
city near ~: 9 Samarkand
locale: 15 Asiam Uzbekistan
Bukowski, Charles: 6 author, writer
bulb
crocus ~: 4 corm
edible ~: 4 leek 5 camas, onion 6 camass, garlic
garden ~: 4 glad, iris 5 tulip 6 allium, scilla 8 daffodil, gladiola, hyacinth, snowdrop 9 Dutch iris, gladiolus, narcissus
hypo ~: 5 ampul 6 ampule 7 ampoule
light ~ filler: 4 neon 5 argon
light ~, in the comics: 4 idea
like a low-watt ~: 3 dim
place: 4 lamp 7 fixture 10 chandelier
planter: 5 spade 6 dibble
pungent ~: 5 onion 6 garlic
starter: 5 flash
within a bulb: 5 clove
__ bulb: 3 dim 5 flash, light
__ Bulba: 5 Taras
bulb-like stem: 4 corm
bulbous: 5 round, thick 7 rounded 8 globular
__-bulb thermometer: 3 dry, wet
bulbul: 4 bird 8 songbird
Bulfinch: 6 Thomas 7 Charles
Bulfinch, Charles: 9 architect
Bulgakov, Mikhail: 6 author, writer 7 Russian
Bulgaria: 6 nation 7 country
capital: 5 Sofia 6 Sofiya
city: 4 Ruse 5 Varna 6 Burgas, Dobric, Pleven, Sliven 7 Plovdiv
king: 5 Boris
money: 3 lev 4 leva 8 stotinka
mountain: 6 Musala 7 Rhodope
neighbor: 6 Greece, Turkey 7 Romania 9 Macedonia 10 Yugoslavia
Nobelist in Literature: 7 Canetti
port: 5 Varna
weight: 3 oke
Bulgarian: 4 Slav 6 Balkan 8 language
neighbor: 4 Turk 5 Greek
bulge: 3 jut, sag 4 bump, hump, knob, lump, node 5 bloat, heave, start, swell 6 dilate, expand, nodule, paunch 7 balloon, distend, enlarge, project, puff out, swell up 8 dilation, overhang, protrude, stand out, stick out, swelling, swell out 9 intumesce, outgrowth 10 distension, projection, prominence, protrusion
battle the ~: 4 diet, lose 6 reduce 7 work out 8 exercise
bulging: 5 puffy 6 convex 9 distended, obtrusive, prominent 10 lenticular
bulgur: 5 grain, wheat
bulk: 3 sum 4 body, girt, heft, lump, mass, most, size 5 girth, total, whole 6 extent, volume, weight 7 bigness 8 enormity, majority, quantity 9 aggregate, dimension, immensity, largeness, magnitude, plurality 10 dimensions, lion's share
buy in ~: 4 save
ender: 4 head
in ~: 9 wholesale
up: 3 pad 6 expand
bulk __: 4 mail 7 carrier, modulus
bulkhead: 4 wall 5 panel 9 partition
locale: 3 jet 4 ship 5 plane 8 airplane
bulkiness: 4 heft, mass 9 immensity 10 fleshiness
bulky: 3 big 4 huge 5 beefy, burly, great, gross, hefty, large, plump, stout, thick 6 portly 7 awkward, hulking, immense, mammoth, massive, unhandy, weighty 8 colossal, enormous, unwieldy 9 corpulent, ponderous 10 cumbersome, overweight, voluminous, well-padded
bull: 3 gas, lie, rot 4 blah, bosh, bunk, guff, jazz, jive, male, pooh, toro, tosh 5 bilge, fudge, hokum, hooey, prate, stuff, trash, tripe 6 animal, Brahma, bunkum, bushwa, drivel, footle, gabble, gammon, gibber, havers, hot air, humbug, jabber, jargon, kibosh, piffle 7 baloney, blarney, blather, blether, boloney, bushwah, eyewash, flannel, flubdub, fustian, garbage, hogwash, inanity, malarky, rubbish, twaddle 8 buncombe, claptrap, falderal, falderol, fast talk, flimflam, flummery, folderal, folderol, investor, malarkey, nonsense, optimist, slipslop, tommyrot, trumpery 9 banana oil, gibberish, goofiness, kidstakes, moonshine, poppycock, rigmarole 10 applesauce, balderdash, bilge water, codswallop, double-talk, flapdoodle, galimatias, Jabberwock, mumbo jumbo, rigamarole, taradiddle
advice: 3 buy
at times: 5 gorer
combining form: 4 taur- 5 tauri-, tauro-
constellation: 6 Taurus
delight: 5 rally 6 uptick 7 upswing
disarm a ~: 6 dehorn
ender: 3 bat, dog, ish, ock, pen 4 boat, doze, frog, head, horn, ring, whip 5 dozer, fight, finch 6 necked, roarer 7 fighter, mastiff
holder: 4 gate 6 corral 7 pasture
in a china shop: 3 oaf 5 klutz
in Britain: 5 stirk
in Spanish: 4 toro
market: 4 rise 5 rally 6 uptick 7 upswing
mate: 3 cow 6 heifer
meal: 5 grass
papal ~: 5 edict 6 decree
riding event: 5 rodeo
session: 3 gab, jaw, rap, yak 4 chat, talk 7 palaver 10 conference, discussion
session site: 4 dorm
shoot the ~: 3 gab, jaw, rap, yak 4 talk
sound: 5 snort 6 bellow
weapon: 4 horn
young ~: 4 calf
bull __: 3 ant, bay, gun, pen 4 gear, horn, rope 5 block, chain, float, shark, snake, trout, wheel 6 fiddle, header, riding, tongue 7 mastiff, session, terrier, thistle
bull-__: 3 bar 4 whip 6 necked, roarer
__ bull: 3 pit 4 blue 5 Irish, papal 6 Boston, Cretan
Bull: 3 May, Ole 4 Olaf, sign 5 April 6 Halsey, Taurus
follower ~: 5 Twins
preceder ~: 3 Ram
rival: 3 Net, Sun 4 Buck, Hawk, Heat, Jazz, King, Spur 5 Knick, Laker, Magic, Pacer, Sixer 6 Celtic, Hornet, Nugget, Piston, Raptor, Rocket, Wizard 7 Clipper, Grizzly, Warrior 8 Cavalier, Maverick 10 SuperSonic, Timberwolf
Bull __: 3 Run 5 Moose 6 Durham
__ Bull: 4 John 6 Golden, Raging 7 Sitting
bulla: 4 seal
bulldog
its logo is a ~: 4 Mack
like a ~: 6 jowled 9 tenacious 10 pugnacious
relative: 3 pug
bulldog __: 3 ant, jaw 4 clip 7 edition
__ bulldog: 6 French 7 English
Bulldog: 3 Eli 5 Yalie
school: 4 Yale 5 Drake 7 Citadel, Gonzaga
Bulldog Drummond (1929 film)
cast: Joan Bennett, Ronald Colman
bulldoze: 3 cow, dig 4 dupe, rase, raze, ruin 5 bully, level, outdo, press, shove, wreck 6 coerce, compel, hector, topple 7 destroy, dragoon, flatten,

unbuild **8** browbeat, demolish, domineer, pull down, take down, tear down **9** devastate, dismantle, knock down, overpower, take apart, terrorize **10** intimidate
bulldozing: **8** leveling **10** demolition
Bull Durham (1988 film)
cast: Kevin Costner, Tim Robbins, Susan Sarandon
director: Ron Shelton
bullet: **3** ace **4** ammo, shot, slug **6** dumdum **7** missile **9** cartridge **10** ammunition, projectile
ender: **5** proof
fake ~: **5** blank
poker ~: **3** ace
sound: **4** ping, zing **5** whine
bullet __: **4** tree, wood **5** train
__ bullet: **5** magic **6** silver, tracer
Bullet for Joey, A star: **4** Raft
bulletin: **4** news, word **6** notice **7** handout, message, program, tidings **8** dispatch, pamphlet **9** news flash **10** communiqué
all points ~: **7** dragnet
board material: **4** cork
like a news ~: **6** just in
police ~: **3** APB **5** alert
bulletin __: **5** board
__ bulletin: **4** news
bulletin-board
computer ~ manager: **5** sysop
fastener: **4** tack **7** pushpin **9** thumbtack
Bullet in the Head, A (1990 film) director: John Woo
Bullet Park author: John Cheever
bulletproof vest material: **6** Kevlar
__ bullets: **5** sweat
Bullets or Ballots (1936 film)
cast: Joan Blondell, Humphrey Bogart, Edward G. Robinson
director: William Keighley
Bullets Over Broadway (1994 film)
cast: John Cusack, Jennifer Tilly, Dianne Wiest
director: Woody Allen
bullfighter: **7** matador **8** toreador
cloak: **4** capa
maneuver: **4** pase
bullfighting: **5** sport
site: **5** arena
bullfinch: **4** bird
bullfrog genus: **4** rana
bullhead: **4** fish
Bullhead City: **4** town
locale: **7** Arizona
bullheaded: **5** rigid, stern **6** wilful **7** hard-set, willful **8** dogmatic, stubborn **9** tenacious **10** hard-bitten, iron-willed, refractory
Bullins, Ed: **6** author, writer
bullion: **4** gold
shape: **3** bar
site: **6** Ft. Knox
__ bullion: **4** base, gold
bullish: **10** optimistic
advice: **3** buy **6** invest
Bullitt (1968 film)
cast: Jacqueline Bisset, Steve McQueen, Robert Vaughn
director: Peter Yates
bullmastiff: **3** dog **5** canid **6** canine
Bull Moose: **5** party
name: **5** Teddy
bullneck: **4** bird
Bullock, Sandra: **7** actress
film: 28 Days (2000)
Demolition Man (1993)
Divine Secrets of the Ya-Ya Sisterhood (2002)
Gun Shy (2000)
Hope Floats (1998)
Miss Congeniality (2000)
Murder by Numbers (2002)
The Net (1995)
Practical Magic (1998)
Speed (1994)
A Time to Kill (1996)
While You Were Sleeping (1995)
film (voice): The Prince of Egypt (1998)
bullock's heart: **5** fruit
Bull, Olaf: **4** poet **9** Norwegian
Bull, Ole: **9** Norwegian, violinist
bullpen fixture: **3** ace **5** phone **6** closer, hurler **7** pitcher **8** reliever
bullring: **5** arena
figure: **4** toro **7** matador **8** toreador
Bull Run: **6** battle, stream **8** Manassas
boomer: **6** cannon
soldier: **3** Reb
victor: **3** Lee
bulls: **3** he's **6** cattle
Bulls: **4** five, team
home: **7** Chicago
org.: **3** NBA
sport: **10** basketball
bull's-eye: **5** candy **6** center, target **10** ground zero
eye the ~: **3** aim **5** point **6** target
hitter: **4** dart **5** arrow **6** bullet
__ Bulls, The: **5** Brave
__ Bull, The: **6** Lonely
Bullwinkle: **5** moose
foe: **5** Boris **7** Natasha
to Rocky: **3** pal
bully: **3** cow **4** goad, good, haze **5** brute, daunt, rowdy, snarl, tough **6** abaser, abuser, badger, coerce, extort, harass, hector, lean on, menace, pick on, prey on, rascal, tyrant **7** buffalo, coercer, control, dragoon, harrier, henpeck, oppress, ruffian, swagger, torment **8** bludgeon, browbeat, bulldoze, domineer, keep down, overbear, prey upon, threaten **9** despotize, miscreant, oppressor, persecute, shake down, strong-arm, swaggerer, terrorize, tormentor, trample on, tyrannize **10** browbeater, intimidate, persecutor, push around
ender: **3** boy
offering: **5** mouse **6** fat lip, shiner **8** black eye
bully __: **4** beef, tree **6** pulpit
__ Bully: **5** Wooly
bullyboy: **4** goon, thug **5** tough
bullyrag: **3** cow **5** tease **7** torment **8** aggrieve **10** intimidate
Bulmer: **4** font **8** typeface
Bulova: **5** watch **10** wristwatch
competitor: **4** Ebel, Rado **5** Casio, Elgin, Lorus, Omega, Rolex, Seiko, Timex **6** Fossil, Movado, Pulsar, Swatch **7** Citizen **8** Longines, Tag Heuer, Tourneau
Bülow, Hans von: **6** German **7** pianist
Bülow, Sunny von portrayer: **5** Close
bulrush: **4** reed, tule **5** sedge
Bulusan: **7** volcano
locale: **4** Asia **5** Luzon
bulwark: **4** wall **5** guard, shore **6** buffer, secure, shield **7** bastion, bolster, defense, fortify, protect, railing, rampart **8** buttress, fastness, mainstay **9** barricade, safeguard **10** protection, stronghold
Bulwark, The author: Theodore Dreiser
Bulwer-Lytton, Edward: **4** poet **6** author, writer **7** British
heroine: **4** Ione
work: Eugene Aram
Harold
The Last Days of Pompeii
Leila
Pelham
Rienzi
Zanoni
Bulworth (1998 film)
cast: Warren Beatty, Halle Berry, Don Cheadle, Oliver Platt, Paul Sorvino, Jack Warden
director: Warren Beatty
bum: **3** veg **4** hobo **5** cadge, idler, leech, louse, mooch, scamp, tramp **6** borrow, loafer, lounge, rascal, rotten **7** drifter, failure, outcast, solicit, sponger, vagrant **8** deadbeat, derelict, freeload, scrounge, spurious, vagabond, wanderer **9** do-nothing, nogoodnik **10** ne'er-do-well, panhandler, ragamuffin
around: **4** laze, loaf, roam, rove **7** goof off **10** knock about
bleacher ~: **3** fan
give a ~ steer: **8** misguide **9** misinform
out: **5** peeve **6** deject, dismay, sadden **7** depress, incense **8** dispirit **9** bring down **10** dishearten
rap: **5** frame **7** raw deal
starter: **7** stumble
bum __: **3** rap **5** steer
__ bum: **3** ski **5** beach
bumbershoot: **4** gamp **6** brolly **8** umbrella
bumble: **4** muff **5** botch, lurch **6** falter, fumble, muddle **7** stumble
ender: **3** bee
bumblebee: **3** bug **6** insect
Bumble Bee: **4** tuna
rival: **8** Star Kist
bumbler: **2** ox **3** ass, oaf **4** boob, clod, jerk, lout **5** klutz, looby **6** lubber
cry: **4** oops
bumbling: **5** gawky, inept **6** clumsy, gauche, klutzy, oafish, wooden **7** awkward, gawkish, halting, unadept **8** bungling, fumbling, inexpert, ungainly **9** all thumbs, graceless, lumbering, maladroit, stumbling, unskilled **10** unskillful
Bumbry: **5** Grace
bummed out: **3** sad **4** blue, down, glum **5** upset, woful **6** broody, gloomy, morose, somber, woeful **7** doleful, furious, hangdog, joyless, unhappy **8** dejected, downcast, troubled **9** cheerless, depressed, exanimate, heartsick, miserable, sorrowful, woebegone **10** chapfallen, despondent, dispirited, distressed, melancholy
bummer: **4** drag **6** downer **7** raw deal
Bummer!: **4** alas **6** too bad
bump: **3** hit, jar, jog **4** dent, jerk, jolt, lump, node, push **5** bulge, carom, dance, eject, elbow, gnarl, nudge, raise, shake, shock, wound **6** bounce, carrom, jostle, jounce, justle, move up, nodule, pimple, reduce, step up **7** advance, elevate, jostles, preempt, promote, upgrade **8** dislodge, displace, increase, obstacle, swelling **9** contusion, increment, smash into **10** knock loose, projection, prominence
down: **6** demote
heads: **5** argue **6** debate **7** wrangle **8** disagree
into: **4** find, jolt, meet **6** strike **8** chance on, happen on **9** encounter, run across **10** chance upon **11** collide with
into, in Britain: **5** prang
result: **6** bruise
skin ~: **3** wen, zit
sound: **4** thud **5** thump
up against: **4** abut **5** touch **6** adjoin
__ bump: **5** speed
bumpa: **4** wind **8** clarinet **10** instrument
bumper: **6** fender, shield **8** auto part **9** plentiful
adjunct: **6** air dam
coating: **6** chrome
flaw: **4** dent, ding
sticker words: **4** honk **5** I love **9** honk if you
bumper __: **3** car **4** crop, jack, pool **5** guard **7** sticker
bumper-car ride: **6** Dodgem
Bumpers: **4** Dale
bumper-to-bumper: **6** jammed **10** gridlocked
bumpkin: **3** oaf **4** clod, hick, lout, rube **5** looby, yokel **6** galoot, lummox, rustic **7** galloot, hayseed, peasant, plowboy, redneck **9** hillbilly **10** clodhopper, provincial
Bump 'n Grind (1994 song) artist: R. Kelly
bump on a log, like a: **5** inert
Bumppo, Natty
quarry: **4** deer
__ bumps: **5** chill, goose
bumps, have goose: **6** shiver, tingle
bumptious: **5** cocky, nervy, pushy **6** cheeky **7** forward **8** impudent **9** obtrusive **10** aggressive
bumpy: **5** jerky, lumpy, nubby, rough, warty **6** choppy, jouncy, knobby, rugged, rutted, uneven **7** jarring, knurled, nodular **8** potholed **9** irregular, turbulent **10** nonuniform
__ Bums: **3** Dem.
bum's rush, give the: **4** boot, oust **6** bounce **7** boot out, cast out, kick out, turn out **8** throw out **9** chase away
Bumstead: **6** Cookie **7** Blondie, Dagwood **9** Alexander
boss: **7** Dithers
boss's wife: **4** Cora
dog: **5** Daisy
neighbor: **4** Elmo, Herb
nickname: **3** Dag
__ Bums, The: **6** Dharma
bun: **4** coif, hair, loaf, roll **5** bread **6** Danish, hairdo **7** chignon, upsweep **8** coiffure **9** hairstyle, sweet roll
locale: **4** head, nape **5** diner **6** bakery
__ bun: **4** Bath **5** honey **6** sticky **7** Banbury **8** cinnamon
bunch: **3** gob, lot, set, ton, wad **4** bale, band, bevy, clan, gang, heap, herd, host, lump, mass, pack, pile, raft, ring, slew, team, unit **5** array, batch, clock, covey, crowd, flock, group, press, sheaf, stack, swarm, troop **6** boodle, bundle, gather, huddle, league, muster, passel, pileup, throng **7** cluster, numbers **8** assemble, assembly, quantity **9** gathering, multitude **10** assemblage, assortment, collection, congregate
ender: **5** berry, grass **6** flower
of: **6** divers, myriad, umteen, untold **7** copious, profuse, umpteen **8** abundant, manifold, numerous, umpsteen **9** bountiful, countless, quite a few
up: **4** heap, herd **5** crowd, group **6** gather, huddle **7** combine **9** squeeze in **10** congregate
wild ~: **3** mob **4** gang, pack **5** tribe
bunch __: **4** pink **5** grass, light
Bunche, Ralph: **8** diplomat, Nobelist
bunches: **5** reams
__ Bunch, The: **4** Wild **5** Brady
bunco: **3** con **4** scam **5** cheat **7** con game, swindle **8** flimflam
artist: **6** con man
buncombe: **3** gas, rot **4** blah, bosh, bull, guff, jazz, jive, pooh, tosh **5** bilge, fudge, hokum, hooey, prate, stuff, trash, tripe **6** bushwa, drivel, footle,

gabble, gammon, gibber, havers, hot air, humbug, jabber, jargon, kibosh, piffle **7** baloney, blarney, blather, blether, boloney, bushwah, eyewash, flannel, flubdub, fustian, garbage, hogwash, inanity, rubbish, twaddle **8** claptrap, falderal, falderol, flimflam, flummery, folderal, folderol, nonsense, slipslop, tommyrot, trumpery **9** banana oil, gibberish, kidstakes, moonshine, poppycock, rigmarole **10** applesauce, balderdash, bilge water, codswallop, double-talk, flapdoodle, galimatias, Jabberwock, mumbo jumbo, rigamarole, taradiddle

bund: **4** bloc

Bundesrat locale: **7** Austria, Germany

Bundestag locale: **7** Germany

bundle: **3** lot, pkg., set, tie, wad **4** bale, bind, heap, load, loot, mint, pack, pile, stow, wisp, wrap **5** array, batch, bunch, clump, group, means, money, sheaf, stack **6** fardel, packet, parcel **7** cluster, package, snuggle **10** accumulate, assortment, collection, cumulation

binder: **4** cord, rope **5** twine **6** string

drop a ~: **4** lose

hay ~: **4** bale **5** stack

of energy: **6** dynamo

off: **4** oust, rush, send, ship **5** split **6** decamp, depart, hustle, kidnap **7** vamoose

of joy: **3** tot **4** baby **6** infant **7** bambino, newborn, toddler **9** little one

of nerves: **5** antsy, itchy, jumpy, tense **6** uneasy **7** anxious, jittery, keyed up, nervous, restive, uptight **8** agitated, restless, skittish, troubled **9** concerned, excitable, ill at ease **10** high-strung

up: **4** wrap **6** enwrap, muffle **7** swarthe **9** dress warm

wheat ~: **5** sheaf

bundled software: **5** suite

bundle-of-joy bringer: **5** stork

bundler, hay: **5** baler

Bundt __: **3** pan **4** cake

Bundy: **2** Al **3** Peg

bung: **4** cork, dent, plug

up: **3** mar **4** dent, hurt **6** damage, injure

bungalow: **3** hut **4** home **5** bower, house **6** cabana, casita **7** cottage

language: **5** Hindi

__-Bungay: **4** Tono

bungee __: **4** cord **7** jumping

bungle: **3** err **4** blow, flub, goof, muff, slip, trip **5** boner, botch, gumup, lapse, misdo, shank **6** boggle, bollix, foozle, foul up, fumble, goof up, mess up, muddle, slip-up **7** blooper, blunder, failure, louse up, misstep, mistake, screw up **9** mishandle, mismanage

bungler: **2** ox **3** oaf **4** clod, dolt, fool, lout **5** dunce, idiot, klutz, looby **7** jackass **8** bonehead, cloddish, goofball **9** blockhead, harebrain **10** addlebrain

bungling: **5** gawky, inept **6** clumsy, klutzy, oafish **7** awkward, gawkish, loutish, unadept **8** botching, bumbling, fumbling, inexpert, lubberly, tactless, ungainly **9** all thumbs, graceless, lumbering, maladroit, stumbling, unskilled **10** blundering, ungraceful, unskillful

Bunin, Ivan: **4** poet **7** Russian **8** Nobelist

bunk: **3** bed, cot, gas, rot **4** blah, bosh, bull, guff, jazz, jive, live, pooh, stay, talk, tosh **5** berth, bilge, fudge, hokum, hooey, lodge, prate, put up, stuff, trash, tripe **6** billet, bushwa, drivel, footle, gabble, gammon, gibber, havers, hot air, humbug, jabber, jargon, kibosh, piffle **7** baloney, blarney, blather, blether, boloney, bushwah, eyewash, flannel, flubdub, fustian, garbage, hogwash, inanity, malarky, quarter, rubbish, twaddle **8** claptrap, falderal, falderol, fast talk, flimflam, flummery, folderal, folderol, malarkey, nonsense, rhetoric, slipslop, tommyrot, trumpery **9** banana oil, gibberish, kidstakes, moonshine, poppycock, rigmarole **10** applesauce, balderdash, bilge water, codswallop, double-talk, empty words, flapdoodle, galimatias, Jabberwock, mumbo jumbo, rigamarole, taradiddle

bed: **5** berth

ender: **4** mate, room **5** house

position: **3** top **5** on top **6** bottom

bunk __: **3** bed

bunker: **3** bin, box **4** trap **5** chest **6** coffer, hazard **8** sand trap **10** receptacle

club: **5** wedge

filler: **4** sand

machine-gun ~: **4** nest

Bunker, Archie: **5** bigot

wife: **5** Edith

Bunker Hill: **6** battle

locale: **4** Mass.

bunkhouse item: **3** bed, cot

bunko squad concern: **5** fraud

bunkum: **3** gas, rot **4** blah, bosh, bull, guff, jazz, jive, lies, pooh, tosh **5** bilge, fudge, hokum, hooey, prate, stuff, trash, tripe **6** bushwa, drivel, footle, gabble, gammon, gibber, havers, hot air, humbug, jabber, jargon, kibosh, piffle **7** baloney, blarney, blather, blether, boloney, bushwah, eyewash, flannel, flubdub, fustian, garbage, hogwash, inanity, malarky, rubbish, twaddle **8** claptrap, falderal, falderol, flimflam, flummery, folderal, folderol, malarkey, nonsense, rhetoric, slipslop, tommyrot, trumpery **9** banana oil, gibberish, goofiness, kidstakes, moonshine, poppycock, rigmarole **10** applesauce, balderdash, bilge water, codswallop, double-talk, empty words, flapdoodle, galimatias, Jabberwock, mumbo jumbo, rigamarole, taradiddle

Bunning, Jim: **3** sen. **6** hurler **7** pitcher, senator

bunny: **3** pet **6** rabbit **10** cottontail

dumb ~: **3** ass, nit, oaf, sap, wag **4** boob, boor, bozo, clod, dolt, fool, geek **5** chump, clown, cluck, dunce, joker, ninny, patsy **6** dimwit, lummox, nitwit, sucker, turkey **7** buffoon, dingbat, dullard, fathead, halfwit, jackass, pierrot, pinhead, saphead **8** bonehead, meathead, numskull **9** birdbrain, blockhead, lamebrain, numbskull, simpleton **10** dunderhead

emulate a ~: **3** hop

feature: **3** ear **4** ears

hop: **5** dance

hug: **5** dance

like a ~: **5** furry

tail: **4** scut

bunny __: **3** hop, hug

__ bunny: **4** dust **6** Easter

Bunny: **7** Berigan

Bunny __: **5** O'Hare

__ Bunny: **4** Bugs

bunny hop: **5** dance

bunny hug: **5** dance

bunnylike: **5** eared

Bunsen __: **6** burner

nozzle: **6** gas jet

Bunsen, Robert: **6** German **7** chemist

bunt: **3** hit

ender: **4** line

situation, perhaps: **5** one on

bunt __: **5** order **6** single

__ bunt: **4** drag

bunting: **4** bird, pape **5** cloth, finch, flags **6** fabric **7** ortolan, pennant **10** dickcissel

__ bunting: **4** lark, reed, snow **6** indigo **7** painted

buntline: **4** rope

Buntline, Ned: **5** alias **6** writer

real name: Judson

subject: Cody, Buffalo Bill

Bunton: **4** Emma

Bunts author: **4** Will

Buñuel, Luis: **8** director

film: Belle de Jour (1967)

Diary of a Chambermaid (1964)

The Discreet Charm of the Bourgeoisie (1972)

L'Age d'Or (1930)

Simon of the Desert (1965)

bunya-bunya: **4** tree

Bunyan, John: **6** author, writer **7** British

work: Grace Abounding

The Holy War

Pilgrim's Progress

Bunyan, Paul: **4** hero **5** giant, opera **10** lumberjack

blue ox: **4** Babe

composer: **7** Britten

cook: **3** Ole

dog: **4** Fido **5** Elmer

tool: **3** axe

buon __: **6** fresco, giorno

buona __: **4** sera **5** notte

Buona Sera, Mrs. Campbell (1969 film)

cast: Peter Lawford, Gina Lollobrigida

Buoniconti, Nick sport: **8** football

Buono, Victor: **5** actor

film: Hush ... Hush, Sweet Charlotte (1965)

Robin and the Seven Hoods (1964)

The Silencers (1966)

The Strangler (1964)

What Ever Happened to Baby Jane? (1962)

TV: Batman

buoy: **5** float **6** marker

place: **3** sea **5** ocean

sitter: **4** gull

unlit ~: **3** nun

up: **4** lift, prop **5** boost, cheer, elate, raise **6** uphold, uplift **7** bolster, cheer up, elevate, enliven, hearten, lighten, support, sustain **8** brighten, embolden, imbolden, reassure **9** encourage **10** exhilarate

__ buoy: **3** can, dan, nun **4** bell, gong, life, ring **5** cable **6** anchor **7** mooring

buoyancy: **3** pep **4** élan **6** bounce, gaiety, gayety, levity, spring **7** jollity, rapture **8** optimism **9** animation, jocundity, lightness **10** ebullience, exuberance, friskiness, liveliness

buoyant: **4** airy **5** happy, jolly, light, perky, sunny **6** afloat, blithe, bouncy, breezy, cheery, floaty, jaunty, jovial, lively, upbeat, yeasty **7** springy **8** animated, carefree, cheerful, floating, mirthful, sanguine, youthful **9** exuberant, lightsome, resilient **10** flying high, optimistic, unbothered

be ~: **5** float

Buoyant Billions author: George Bernard Shaw

bupkes: **3** nil **4** nada **6** naught, nought **7** nothing

bur: **7** sticker **8** irritant **9** annoyance

starter: **4** sand **6** butter, cockle

bur __: **3** oak **4** reed **6** clover

Burbank: **3** cat **4** city, town **6** Luther

locale: **8** Illinois **10** California

burberry: **6** fabric **8** material

burble: **3** lap **4** foam, purl **5** froth **6** murmur

burbling: **5** foamy

burbot: **3** cod **4** fish, ling

'burbs, The (1989 film)

cast: Bruce Dern, Carrie Fisher, Tom Hanks

director: Joe Dante

burden: **3** lay, tax **4** care, drag, duty, lade, levy, load, onus, task, yoke **5** blame, chore, point, tenor, trial, weary, weigh **6** charge, fardel, hassle, hinder, lading, lumber, misery, saddle, strain, stress, upshot, weight **7** afflict, concern, oppress, purport, refrain, trouble **8** encumber, entangle, handicap, hardship, irritant, overhead, overload, pressure **9** albatross, annoyance, hindrance, incommode, liability, millstone, substance, weigh down **10** affliction, bear down on, difficulty, impediment, imposition, infliction

beast of ~: **3** ass, yak **4** mule **5** burro, camel, horse, llama **6** donkey

beasts of ~: **4** oxen

name meaning ~: **4** Amos

burdened: **5** laden **10** encumbered

combining form: **6** -ridden

burden of __: **5** proof

Burden of Dreams (1982 film)

cast: Claudia Cardinale, Werner Herzog, Klaus Kinski

Burden of Proof, The author: Scott Turow

burdensome: **4** hard **5** heavy, hefty **6** leaden, taxing **7** arduous, onerous, weighty **8** exacting, tiresome, unwieldy **9** demanding, difficult, laborious, ponderous, unwieldly **10** cumbersome, disturbing, enervating, oppressive

Burdette, Lew: **6** hurler **7** pitcher

Burdick: **6** Eugene

burdock: **4** weed

Burdon, Eric group: **7** Animals

bureau: **5** board, chest **6** agency, branch, lowboy, office **7** dresser **8** division **9** committee, furniture, suite part **10** chiffonier, commission, department, news center

part: **4** knob **6** drawer

__ bureau: **5** press **6** credit, travel

__ Bureau: **4** Farm **7** Weather

bureaucracy: **4** maze **7** red tape **8** city hall

bureaucrat: **7** officer **8** official

paper: **4** form **10** triplicate

Bureau of __: **5** Mines **7** Customs

Bureau of __ Affairs: **6** Indian

Bureau of __ Management: **4** Land

Bureau of __ Statistics: **5** Labor

Bureau of the __: **6** Budget, Census

burg: **4** city, town **6** hamlet **7** village **10** metropolis

Burgas: **4** city, town

locale: **8** Bulgaria

burgee: **4** flag **6** banner **7** pennant

burgeon: **3** bud **4** gird, grow, rise, tone **5** bloat, bloom, build, shore, steel, swell, widen **6** anneal, beef up, dilate, expand, flower, harden, prop up, spread, spring, sprout, temper, thrive, tone up **7** augment, blossom, bolster, brace up, broaden, build up, develop, empower, enhance, enlarge, fortify, inflate, leaf out, shoot up, shore up, stiffen, toughen **8** buttress, energize, flourish, heighten, increase, indurate, lengthen, multiply, mushroom, put forth, shoot out, snowball, vegetate, vitalize **9** germinate, intensify, luxuriate, pullulate, reinforce **10** effloresce, invigorate, strengthen

burger: **4** meat **6** Big Mac **7** Whopper **8** fast food

partner: 3 pop 4 Coke 5 fries, Pepsi, shake 7 soda pop 9 milkshake
starter: 3 ham 5 chili 6 cheese
topper: 5 bacon, onion, Swiss 6 catsup, cheese, pickle, tomato 7 ketchup, lettuce, mustard 8 mushroom
Burger: 6 Warren 8 Hamilton
Burger, Hamilton: 2 DA
nemesis: 5 Mason
Burger King rival: 3 KFC 6 Subway, Wendy's 8 Pizza Hut 9 McDonald's
burgers, prepare: 5 grill
Burger, Warren: 5 judge 6 jurist 7 justice
Burgess: 6 Gelett 7 Anthony 8 Meredith
Burgess, Anthony: 6 writer 7 British
pseudonym: Kell
work: Any Old Iron
A Clockwork Orange
The Long Day Wanes
Burgess, Gelett: 6 writer
subject: Goops, Purple Cow
work: Are You a Bromide?
Burghoff, Gary: 5 actor
costar: 4 Alda, Farr
role: 5 Radar
show: 4 MASH
burglar: 4 yegg 5 crook, felon, thief 6 outlaw, robber 7 filcher, prowler, stealer 8 intruder, pilferer 9 purloiner
deterrent: 3 dog, grr 4 lock, safe 5 alarm, guard, vault 8 deadbolt, watchman
diamonds, to a ~: 3 ice
ender: 5 proof
need: 5 fence 7 lookout
potential ~: 5 caser
target: 4 loot, safe 7 jewelry 9 valuables
burglar ___: 5 alarm
___ burglar: 3 cat
burglarize: 3 rob 4 loot 5 rifle, steal 6 invade, thieve 7 break in
burglary: 3 job 5 caper, crime, heist, theft 6 felony, holdup 7 break-in, larceny, robbery 8 filching, stealing, thievery 9 pilferage
burgle: 3 rob 5 rifle, steal 6 thieve 7 break in 9 knock over
burgoo: 4 stew
Burgoyne, John: 7 British, general
burgundy: 3 red 4 wine 5 color
color kin: 4 plum 6 purple 8 eggplant, mulberry 9 raspberry
Burgundy: 3 vin 4 wine 5 pinot 6 region 8 province
kingdom: 5 Arles
locale: 6 France
region: 6 Bresse
river: 5 Saône
type of ~: 5 Mâcon 7 chablis
vessel: 3 vat 4 cask 5 cruet 6 carafe 7 pitcher 8 decanter
Burgundy ___: 5 sauce 7 trefoil
buried: 4 deep 6 hidden 8 immersed, overcome, ulterior 9 forgotten, unexposed 10 undivulged
Burien: 4 city, town
locale: 10 Washington
burin: 4 tool 5 flint
Burke: 4 city, Jack, Paul, town 5 Delta 6 Billie, Edmund, Johnny
locale: 8 Virginia
___ Burke: 6 Stoney
Burke, Billie: 7 actress
film: A Bill of Divorcement (1932)
The Cheaters (1945)
Craig's Wife (1936)
Doubting Thomas (1935)
Only Yesterday (1933)
She Couldn't Take It (1935)
Topper Takes a Trip (1939)
The Wizard of Oz (1939)
spouse: Flo Ziegfeld
Burke, Delta spouse: Gerald McRaney
Burke, Jack: 6 golfer
Burke's Law (ABC drama) cast: Gene Barry (Amos Burke)
Burkina Faso: 6 nation 7 country
money: 5 franc
neighbor: 4 Mali, Togo 5 Benin, Ghana, Niger 10 Ivory Coast
people: 5 Mossi 6 Senufo, Tuareg 7 Songhai
Burks, Ellis sport: 8 baseball
burl: 4 knar, knot, node, slub 6 nodule
Burl: 4 Ives
burlap: 6 fabric 8 material
carrier: 4 sack
fiber: 4 hemp, jute
Burleigh: 6 Grimes
Burleson: 4 city, town
locale: 5 Texas
burlesque: 4 show, twit 5 farce, mimic, sneer, spoof 6 comedy, parody, satire 7 imitate, lampoon, mockery, satiric, takeoff 8 ridicule, satirize, travesty 9 dramatize, ludicrous, satirical 10 caricature, lampoonery, vaudeville
bit: 3 act 4 skit, turn
show: 5 revue 6 review
burley: 7 tobacco
Burlingame: 4 city, town
locale: 10 California
Burlington: 4 city, town
athletes: 10 Catamounts
locale: 4 Iowa 6 Canada 7 Ontario, Vermont
Burlington Zephyr: 5 train
burly: 3 big, fit 4 hale, iron, wiry 5 beefy, bulky, hardy, hefty, hunky, husky, lusty, plump, stout, thick, tough 6 brawny, hearty, mighty, portly, potent, robust, rugged, sinewy, steely, stocky, strong, sturdy, virile 7 doughty, hulking, sizable 8 athletic, bruising, forceful, indurate, muscular, powerful, puissant, sizeable, stalwart, thickset, vigorous 9 Atlantean, corpulent, filled-out, Herculean, strapping, well-built 10 able-bodied, red-blooded, well-padded
___-burly: 5 hurly
Burma: 6 nation 7 country, Myanmar
bandit: 6 dacoit, dakoit
capital: 6 Yangon 7 Rangoon
export: 4 teak
former capital: 3 Ava
leader: 3 U Nu
measure: 3 lan
money: 3 pya 4 kyat
neighbor: 4 Laos 5 Assam, China, India 8 Thailand 10 Bangladesh
neighbor, once: 4 Siam
org.: 5 ASEAN
ox: 5 gayal
people: 4 Nosu
port: 6 Sittwe, Yangon 7 Rangoon
Burma ___: 4 Road 5 Shave
Burma Road terminus: 6 Lashio
Burma Shave creation: 5 verse
Burmese: 3 cat 5 Asian, felid 6 feline
Burmese ___: 3 cat 4 jade 5 glass
burn: 3 get 4 bake, bilk, bite, boil, char, cook, fume, gall, hurt, lick, pain, sear 5 anger, blaze, broil, cheat, flame, flare, light, parch, peeve, roast, scald, singe, smart, sting, toast, torch, use up, wound 6 chisel, fleece, ignite, injury, kindle, refute, reject, scorch, seethe, simmer 7 combust, deceive, defraud, smolder, swindle, two-time 8 enkindle, flimflam, hoodwink, irritate, overcook, smoulder, squander 9 carbonize, catch fire, cauterize, victimize 10 incandesce, incinerate, run a game on
cause: 3 lye, sun 4 fire 5 stove 9 hot coffee
do a slow ~: 4 fume 6 seethe 7 smolder
for: 4 want 6 desire
(for): 4 long, pant 5 yearn
out: 4 jade, tire
partner: 5 crash, slash
rubber: 3 hie, rev, zip 4 bolt, dash, race, rush, zoom 5 hurry, speed 6 barrel, career, hasten, hustle, scurry 8 step on it 9 hotfoot it, make haste, shake a leg 10 accelerate
slightly: 4 char, sear 5 singe
slow ~: 5 anger, pique 6 temper 9 surliness 10 irritation
soother: 3 ice 4 aloe, balm 5 salve 8 vitamin E
starter: 3 sun 4 wind 5 heart
the midnight oil: 4 cram, pore 5 learn, study
treatment: 3 ice 4 aloe, balm 5 salve, sulfa 8 vitamin E
up: 3 ire, sap 5 anger, annoy, drain, trash, waste 6 nettle 7 deplete, incense, outrage 8 fool away, squander 9 dissipate
up the road: 4 race, rush, zoom 5 speed
with liquid: 5 scald
burn ___: 3 bag, out 6 rubber
burn ___ in one's pocket: 5 a hole
___ burn: 4 slow 5 flash 7 freezer
burnable: 9 flammable
Burnaby: 4 city, town
locale: 6 Canada
school: 3 SFU
burned: 4 hurt 5 stung, taken 6 flambé, rooked 7 cheated, fleeced, injured, taken in, wounded 8 swindled 9 disabused
out: 4 worn 5 jaded, tired, weary 7 drained 9 exhausted
starter: 3 sun 4 wind
up: 4 sore 5 angry, irate, upset 7 furious, steamed 9 indignant 10 infuriated
burned ___ crisp: 3 to a
___-burned: 3 dad
burned-out shell: 4 hulk
burner: 6 gas log 7 furnace
Bunsen ~ nozzle: 6 gas jet
lab ~: 4 etna 6 Bunsen
on the back ~: 7 pending
place: 5 range, stove
put on the back ~: 5 table 6 shelve 7 suspend 8 postpone
starter: 4 barn, base 5 after
___ burner: 3 gas, oat, oil 4 back, base, lime, weed 5 front, Meker, pilot 6 Argand, Bunsen
Burnet, Frank: 3 Sir 8 Nobelist 10 Australian
Burnett: 5 Carol 7 Charles
Burnett, Carol: 10 comedienne
alma mater: 4 UCLA
film: The Four Seasons (1981)
The Front Page (1974)
Noises Off (1992)
TV: The Carol Burnett Show
Burnette: 5 Rocky 6 Johnny
Burnette, Johnny song: You're Sixteen (1960)
Burnette, Rocky song: Tired of Toein' the Line (1980)
Burney, Fanny: 6 author, writer 7 English
work: Evelina
___ Burnie: 4 Glen
burning: 3 hot, lit 4 dire, fire, live, sore 5 afire, aglow, blaze, eager, fiery, irate, itchy, smoky 6 ablaze, aflame, ardent, bright, fervid, heated, on fire, red-hot, torrid, urgent 7 caustic, crucial, excited, exigent, fervent, flaring, frantic, hurry-up, instant, intense, painful, zealous 8 critical, exigeant, feverish, frenzied, hopped up, in flames, kindling, pressing, sizzling, spirited, vehement, white-hot 9 fanatical, important, insistent, irritated, scorching 10 compelling, imperative, irritating, passionate, sweltering
braid: 4 wick
bush: 5 wahoo
combining form: 4 igni-
desire: 5 ardor
evidence of ~: 3 ash 5 coals, smoke 6 embers 7 cinders
malicious ~: 5 arson
start ~: 6 ignite
burning ___: 4 bush, ghat 5 glass
Burning ___: 4 Bush, Love 5 Heart 7 Bridges
Burning Bush author: Louis Untermeyer
Burning Down the House (1983 song) artist: Talking Heads
Burning Giraffe, The artist: 4 Dali
Burning Heart (1985 song) artist: Survivor
Burning Love (1972 song) artist: Elvis Presley
burnish: 3 rub 4 buff 5 gloss, scour, sheen, shine 6 luster, polish, smooth 7 furbish 8 brighten
burnished: 5 light, shiny 6 glassy, glossy 8 lustrous
Burnley: 4 city, town
locale: 7 England 10 Lancashire
burn one's ___: 7 bridges
burnoose: 5 cloak
wearer: 4 Arab 7 Bedouin
burnout: 7 fatigue 10 exhaustion
cause of ~: 6 stress 8 overwork
Burns: 3 Ken 6 George, Robert
see also Scottish
Burns and Allen: 3 duo 4 pair, team
Burns, Frank: 5 major
series: 4 MASH
Burns, George: 5 actor 8 comedian
cigar: 4 prop
film: 18 Again! (1988)
The Big Broadcast (1932)
College Swing (1938)
A Damsel in Distress (1937)
Going in Style (1979)
Oh, God! (1977)
Six of a Kind (1934)
The Sunshine Boys (1975, AA)
We're Not Dressing (1934)
role: 3 God
spouse: Gracie Allen
Burnside: 6 Andrew
Burns, Robert: 4 poet 8 Scottish
work: Afton Water
Anna
Auld Lang Syne
The Banks o'Doon
Comin' Thro' the Rye
Duncan Gray
For A' That
The Holy Fair
John Anderson My Jo
A Red, Red Rose
Sweet Afton
Tam Glen
Tam o'Shanter
To a Louse
To a Mountain Daisy
To a Mouse
Burnsville: 4 city, town
locale: 9 Minnesota
burnt
color: 5 umber 6 sienna
in cookery: 5 brulé 6 brulée
starter: 3 sun

up: 5 angry **7** furious, steamed **9** disgusted **10** infuriated
burnt ___: 4 lime **5** umber **6** almond, sienna
burnt ___ crisp: 3 to a
burnt almond: 8 ice cream
  alternative flavor: 5 lemon, mocha, peach **6** banana, coffee, Jamoca, toffee **7** caramel, coconut, vanilla **8** cinnamon, hazelnut **9** bubblegum, chocolate, pineapple, pistachio, raspberry, rocky road, rum raisin **10** blackberry, cheesecake, Neapolitan, peppermint, strawberry
Burn That Candle (1955 song) artist: Bill Haley and His Comets
burn the ___ at both ends: 6 candle
burn the midnight ___: 3 oil
Burnt Norton poet: 5 Eliot
burnt-offering spot: 5 altar
burnt-out: 5 jaded, spent, tired, weary **9** exhausted
Burnt Ship, A author: John Donne
burn up the ___: 4 road
burp: 5 belch, eruct **10** eructation
burp ___: 3 gun
Burpee offering: 4 bulb, flat, root, seed, tree **5** plant **6** hybrid
burr: 4 husk **6** accent **7** seed pod, sticker
burr ___: 3 cut **7** haircut
Burr: 5 Aaron **7** Raymond **9** Tillstrom
  to Hamilton: 3 foe
Burr author: Gore Vidal
burrhel: 5 sheep
  relative: 4 geep **5** argal, shapu, urial **6** aoudad, argali, merino **7** bighorn, mouflon **8** cimarron, moufflon
burrito: 8 tortilla
  cousin: 4 taco
  filler: 4 beef **5** beans **6** cheese
burro: 3 ass **6** animal, brayer, donkey, equine **7** jackass
  comment: 4 bray
  go by ~: 4 ride
  relative: 5 horse, kiang, zebra **6** onager, quagga **8** chigetai **9** dziggetai
burro's tail: 5 plant
Burroughs: 4 John **5** Edgar
  successor: 6 Unisys
Burroughs, Edgar Rice: 6 author, writer
  character: 3 ape **4** Jane **6** Tarzan
  creation: Tarzan
Burroughs, John: 6 author, writer
  friend: Whitman, Edison
  work: Riverby
Burroughs, William S.: 6 author, writer
  pseudonym: Lee
  work: Naked Lunch
    Nova Express
burrow: 3 den, dig **4** bore, grub, hole, lair, mine, root **5** delve, gouge, lodge, scoop **6** kennel, nestle, tunnel **7** snuggle **8** excavate, hideaway, scoop out **9** hollow out **10** excavation
burrowing rodent: 4 degu, jird **6** gerbil, gopher, rabbit **7** hamster, mole rat, visacha **8** tuco-tuco **9** groundhog, woodchuck **10** prairie dog
Burrows, Abe: 6 author, writer
Burr, Raymond: 5 actor
  film: Godzilla... (1954)
    Pitfall (1948)
    Rear Window (1954)
  TV: Ironside, Perry Mason
bursa: 3 sac **7** vesicle
Bursa: 4 city, town
  locale: 6 Turkey
bursar: 6 purser **7** cashier **9** treasurer **10** controller
  boss: 4 prex, prez **5** prexy
burst: 3 pop, rip **4** bang, boom, gush, gust, open, shot, slam, torn **5** blast, blaze, crack, erupt, flash, go off, laugh, lunge, sally, salvo, smash, sound, spasm, spate, spirt, split, spurt, storm **6** blow up, shiver, splash, volley **7** barrage, explode, fly open, give way, implode, rupture, shatter, torrent **8** break out, detonate, eruption, fracture, fragment, mushroom, outbreak, outburst, puncture, splinter **9** break open, cannonade, come apart, discharge, explosion, fusillade, gush forth
  artillery ~: 5 round, salvo
  at the seams: 4 teem
  forth: 3 bud **4** gush **5** erupt, issue **6** appear, emerge, sprout **7** leaf out **9** germinate
  in: 5 barge, enter **9** interrupt
  in on: 7 startle **8** surprise
  of laughter: 4 gale, roar
  of speed: 4 dash **5** spurt
  of wind: 4 gust
  out: 3 cry **7** exclaim
  starter: 3 air, sun **4** down, star **5** cloud
  with pride: 5 gloat, kvell, preen
bursting: 4 full, rife **7** teeming **8** thronged **9** chock-full
Burstyn, Ellen: 7 actress
  film: Alice Doesn't Live Here Anymore (1974, AA)
    The Ambassador (1984)
    Divine Secrets of the Ya-Ya Sisterhood (2002)
    The Exorcist (1973)
    Harry and Tonto (1974)
    How to Make an American Quilt (1995)
    The King of Marvin Gardens (1972)
    The Last Picture Show (1971)
    Resurrection (1980)
    Same Time, Next Year (1978)
    Tropic of Cancer (1970)
    Twice in a Lifetime (1985)
    When a Man Loves a Woman (1994)
Burt: 4 Ward **5** Young **7** Kennedy **8** Reynolds **9** Bacharach, Lancaster
Burton: 3 Tim **4** city, Lane, town **5** Edith, LeVar **6** Nelson **7** Richard, Richter **8** Cummings
  locale: 8 Michigan
Burton, LeVar: 5 actor
  film: Star Trek: Insurrection (1998)
  TV: Roots, Star Trek: The Next Generation
Burton, Nelson: 6 bowler
  milieu: 5 alley
  org: 3 PBA
Burton, Richard: 3 Sir **7** British **8** explorer
Burton, Richard (actor): 5 Welsh
  film: Alexander the Great (1956)
    Anne of the Thousand Days (1969)
    Becket (1964)
    Cleopatra (1963)
    The Desert Rats (1953)
    The Longest Day (1962)
    Look Back in Anger (1958)
    My Cousin Rachel (1952)
    The Night of the Iguana (1964)
    Nineteen Eighty-Four (1984)
    The Sandpiper (1965)
    The Spy Who Came in From the Cold (1965)
    The Taming of the Shrew (1967)
    The V.I.P.s (1963)
    Where Eagles Dare (1969)
    Who's Afraid of Virginia Woolf? (1966)
  spouse: Elizabeth Taylor
Burton, Tim: 8 director
  film: Batman (1989)
    Batman Returns (1992)
    Beetlejuice (1988)
    Edward Scissorhands (1990)
    Ed Wood (1994)
    Mars Attacks! (1996)
    Planet of the Apes (2001)
    Sleepy Hollow (1999)
Burton-upon-___: 5 Trent
Burundi: 6 nation **7** country
  capital: 9 Bujumbura
  it begins in ~: 4 Nile
  language: 7 Kirundi
  money: 5 franc
  neighbor: 5 Congo **6** Rwanda **8** Tanzania
  people: 4 Tusi **5** Rundi, Tussi, Tutsi **6** Watusi **7** Watutsi
bury: 4 hide, rout **5** cache, cover, embed, imbed, inter, outdo, plant, stash **6** engulf, ingulf, inhume, thrash **7** conceal, cover up, implant, repress, secrete, trounce **8** ensconce, enshroud, stow away, suppress **9** overpower, overwhelm
  the hatchet: 6 make up, pardon **7** forgive **9** negotiate, reconcile
Bury my heart at Wounded Knee originator: 5 Benét
Bury the Dead author: Irwin Shaw
bus: 5 coach **6** jitney **7** vehicle **9** Greyhound, transport
  alternative: 3 cab, car, jet **4** auto **5** plane, train **8** airplane
  depot: 3 sta. **7** station **8** terminal
  ender: 3 boy **4** load
  garage: 4 barn
  route: 4 line
  shuttle ~: 6 jitney
  sign: 5 local **7** express
  starter: 4 auto, mini, omni **5** motor
  station info: 3 arr., ETA **5** sched. **8** schedule
  take the ~: 4 ride **7** commute
  ticket price: 4 fare
  unit: 4 seat
bus ___: 3 bar, boy **4** girl, line **6** driver **7** station
___ bus: 6 school
Bus ___: 4 Stop
___ Bus: 5 Magic
Busa: 3 cow **4** bull **6** bovine, cattle
busboy burden: 4 tray
Busby: 8 Berkeley
Buscaglia, Leo: 5 Dr. Hug **6** writer
Buscemi, Steve: 5 actor
  film: Animal Factory (2000)
    The Big Lebowski (1998)
    Con Air (1997)
    Fargo (1996)
    Ghost World (2001)
    Living in Oblivion (1995)
Busch: 3 Mae **5** Fritz, Niven **7** Charles
Busch, Charles: 6 author, writer
Busch, Fritz: 9 conductor
Busch Gardens city: 5 Tampa
Busch Stadium team: 3 St. L. **4** Rams **7** St. Louis
Busey, Gary: 5 actor
  film: Barbarosa (1982)
    The Buddy Holly Story (1978)
    Carny (1980)
    Insignificance (1985)
    Lethal Weapon (1987)
    Point Break (1991)
    Rookie of the Year (1993)
    A Star Is Born (1976)
    Under Siege (1992)
Busfield: 7 Timothy
bush: 4 tire **5** briar, hedge, plant, shrub, wilds **6** jungle **7** bramble, fatigue, guayule, logania, outback, thicket **8** justicia, woodland **9** backwater, backwoods **10** hinterland, wilderness
  beat around the ~: 5 fence, hedge, skirt, stall, waver **6** ramble, waffle **9** hem and haw, pussyfoot
  burning ~: 5 wahoo
  combining form: 5 thamn- **6** thamno-
  decorative ~: 4 rose **6** azalea **7** jasmine **8** camellia, gardenia
  dweller: 6 Aussie **9** aborigine
  ender: 4 buck **5** whack **6** master, ranger
  protector: 3 bur **4** burr **5** briar, brier, spine, thorn **7** prickle
  starter: 4 rose, salt, shad, snow **6** beauty, button, fetter, hobble, pepper **7** brittle, stagger, steeple
  thorny ~: 7 bramble
bush ___: 3 hog, lot, pig, tit **4** baby, bean, coat **5** broom, pilot, poppy **6** clover, hammer, jacket, league, parole
___ bush: 5 sugar **6** calico **7** burning, flannel **8** creosote **9** butterfly, cranberry
Bush: 4 Kate **5** Laura **6** George **7** Barbara
bush baby: 7 primate
  relative: 3 ape **4** saki, titi **5** chimp, drill, jocko, lemur, loris, magot, orang, potto, shrew **6** aye-aye, baboon, Bandar, galago, gelada, gibbon, grivet, guenon, howler, langur, macaco, monkey, rhesus, uakari, vervet **7** colobus, gorilla, guereza, hoolock, macaque, sapajou, siamang, tamarin, tarsier **8** capuchin, mandrill, mangabey, marmoset, talapoin **9** orangutan **10** Barbary ape, chimpanzee, orangutang
bushbuck: 8 antelope
  relative: 3 gnu, kob **4** guib, kudu, oryx, puku, topi **5** addax, bongo, chiru, eland, goral, korin, nyala, oribi, saiga, serow **6** chammy, dik-dik, duiker, impala, koodoo, lechwe, nilgai, rhebok, shammy, shamoy **7** blaubok, blesbok, chamois, defassa, gazelle, gemsbok, gerenuk, grysbok, nylghai, nylghau, sassaby **8** blesbuck, bontebok, gemsbuck, reedbuck, steenbok, steinbok **9** blackbuck, pronghorn, sitatunga, springbok, waterbuck **10** hartebeest, wildebeest
Bush Christmas director: 5 Smart
bushed: 4 beat, worn **5** all in, spent, tired, weary **6** dished, pooped **7** worn-out **8** dog-tired, tired out **9** bone-tired, exhausted **10** knocked out
bushel
  Egyptian ~: 5 ardeb
  fraction: 4 peck
  Hebrew ~: 4 epha, omer **5** ephah
Bushel ___ Peck, A: 4 and a
bushels: 4 lots, many, tons **5** scads **6** hoards
bushes: 5 brush **9** shrubbery
  beat the ~: 4 hunt, seek **6** search **7** rummage **9** track down
  row of ~: 5 hedge
Bush, George: 3 Eli **9** president
  adviser: 6 Sununu
  alma mater: 4 Yale **7** Andover
  birthplace: 4 Mass. **6** Milton
  cabinet member: 4 Barr, Card, Dole, Kemp **5** Baker, Brady, Lujan **6** Cheney, Martin **7** Cavazos, Madigan, Skinner, Watkins, Yeutter **8** Sullivan
  child: 3 Jeb **4** Doro, Neil **6** Marvin
  former org.: 3 CIA
  home: 5 Texas
  middle name: 6 Walker **7** Herbert
  opponent: 7 Clinton, Dukakis
  parent: 7 Dorothy **8** Prescott

previous occupation: 6 oilman
veep: 6 Quayle
wife: 7 Barbara
word in a ~ quote: 4 lips, read
Bush, George W.: 3 Eli 9 president
advisor: 4 Rice
alma mater: 4 Yale 7 Andover, Harvard
birthplace: 8 New Haven
cabinet member: 4 Chao 5 Evans, Paige, Ridge 6 Mineta, Norton, O'Neill, Powell 7 Abraham, Veneman 8 Ashcroft, Martinez, Principi, Rumsfeld, Thompson
child: 5 Jenna 7 Barbara
degree: 3 MBA
home: 5 Texas 8 Crawford
middle name: 6 Walker
mother: 7 Barbara
opponent: 4 Gore 5 Nader
veep: 6 Cheney
wife: 5 Laura
bushido: 4 code 8 Japanese
follower: 7 samurai
virtue: 5 honor 7 bravery 10 simplicity
bush-league: 5 dinky, lower, minor, small 6 lesser 10 inadequate, low-ranking
bushman: 9 aborigine
bushmaster: 5 snake 6 animal 7 reptile
relative: 3 asp, boa 5 aboma, adder, cobra, krait, mamba, racer, viper 6 dhaman, python, taipan 7 markhor, rattler 8 anaconda, moccasin, ringhals 9 boomslang, coachwhip 10 copperhead, sidewinder
Bushmiller, Ernie: 10 cartoonist
creation: 5 Nancy
Bushnell: 5 David, Nolan
bushranger: 7 rustler
bushwa: 3 gas, rot 4 blah, bosh, bull, bunk, guff, jazz, jive, pooh, tosh 5 bilge, fudge, hokum, hooey, prate, stuff, trash, tripe 6 bunkum, drivel, footle, gabble, gammon, gibber, havers, hot air, humbug, jabber, jargon, kibosh, piffle 7 baloney, blarney, blather, blether, boloney, eyewash, flannel, flubdub, fustian, garbage, hogwash, inanity, malarky, rubbish, twaddle 8 buncombe, claptrap, falderal, falderol, flimflam, flummery, folderal, folderol, malarkey, nonsense, slipslop, tommyrot, trumpery 9 banana oil, gibberish, goofiness, kidstakes, moonshine, poppycock, rigmarole 10 applesauce, balderdash, bilge water, codswallop, double-talk, flapdoodle, galimatias, Jabberwock, mumbo jumbo, rigamarole, taradiddle
bushwhack: 4 trap 6 ambush, waylay 7 assault 8 surprise
bushy: 5 hairy, thick 6 shaggy 7 unshorn
hair: 3 mop 4 mane
mass: 3 tod
bushy-tailed: 5 furry
animal: 3 fox
bright-eyed and ~: 5 alert, fresh, perky, sunny 7 healthy
business: 3 job 4 duty, firm, line, mart, role, shop, task, work 5 field, house, store, thing, topic, trade 6 affair, career, cartel, market, matter, métier, office, outfit 7 calling, company, concern, factory, mission, project, pursuit, service, traffic 8 commerce, dealings, function, goings-on, industry, lifework, monopoly, practice, province, vocation 9 patronage 10 employment, enterprise, happenings, livelihood, occupation, profession, walk of life
aka: 3 DBA
arrangement: 4 deal 8 contract
attire: 3 tie 4 suit
bloc: 6 cartel
card symbol: 4 logo
channel: 4 CNBC
collapse: 5 crash
concern: 4 cost, loss 6 profit, red ink 7 economy 8 expenses, overhead 9 operation
confab: 3 mtg. 4 conf., conv. 7 meeting 10 conference, convention
consideration: 4 cost 7 expense 8 overhead
degree: 3 BBA, MBA
division: 4 dept. 10 department
do ~: 3 buy 4 deal, fire, hire, sell, ship 5 trade, truck 6 employ, export, import 7 bargain, deliver, traffic 8 transact
document: 4 memo 6 report
do ~ for: 9 represent
doing ~: 4 open
do ~ with: 9 patronize
drum up ~: 4 hype 6 hustle 7 promote 9 advertise
execs: 3 mgt. 4 mgmt. 10 management
expansion: 4 boom
for short: 3 inc., ltd., org. 4 assn. 5 estab.
funny ~: 5 antic, caper, humor, trick 6 deceit, levity 7 hijinks 8 mischief, trickery
get down to ~: 5 begin, start 7 shape up
give the ~ to: 3 bug, nag, rag 4 haze, ride 5 harry, hound, scold 6 berate, harass, hassle, heckle, needle, plague 7 chew out, upbraid 8 browbeat 14 put on the carpet
go out of ~: 4 fail, fold 6 fold up
letter notation: 3 enc. 4 attn., SASE
loss: 4 bath 7 reverse 8 reversal
magazine: 3 Inc. 6 Forbes 7 Barron's, Fortune
meaning ~: 7 serious 8 resolute 10 determined
minding other's ~: 4 nosy 5 nosey 6 prying, snoopy 7 curious, gossipy
misbehavior: 5 fraud
officer: 6 bursar 7 trustee 9 president
order of ~: 6 agenda 7 program 8 schedule
out of ~: 5 kaput 6 closed 8 bankrupt
partner, often: 3 son
phone: 3 ext. 9 extension
place of ~: 4 mall, mill, shop 5 kiosk, stall, store 6 office 7 factory 8 boutique
record: 5 check 7 receipt
records check: 5 audit
reduction of ~ activity: 9 downswing, recession 10 depression
risky ~: 4 dare, spec 5 wager 6 hazard
school: 4 GMAT
subject: 4 econ. 7 finance 9 economics
subordinate: 3 sec. 4 asst., sec'y 9 assistant, secretary
suit shade: 4 blue, gray, grey, navy
takeover: 3 LBO 6 buyout
VIP: 3 CEO, CFO, mgr. 4 exec 5 owner
business __: 3 end 4 card, case, park, suit 5 agent, class, cycle, reply 7 affairs, college, English, machine
__ business: 3 big, rag 4 mean, show 5 funny, stage 6 monkey
__ business!: 5 I mean
__ Business: 3 Big 5 Risky 6 Family, Monkey
business as __: 5 usual
__ Business Bureau: 6 Better
business letter
abbr.: 3 att., enc. 4 attn.
encl.: 4 SASE
word: 3 sir 4 sirs 6 madame 9 gentlemen
businesslike: 4 tidy 5 sober, staid 6 solemn, somber 7 deadpan, orderly, serious 8 methodic 9 humorless, practical, pragmatic, realistic, unamusing 10 no-nonsense, unhumorous
Business Man, The author: 3 Poe
Business of Strangers, The (2001 film)
cast: Stockard Channing, Julia Stiles, Frederick Weller
director: Patrick Stettner
business-related: 8 economic
Business Week: 3 mag 8 magazine
rival: 6 Forbes 7 Barron's, Fortune
buskin: 4 boot, shoe 5 drama 6 acting 7 tragedy 8 footwear
busman's __: 7 holiday
Busman's Honeymoon author: Dorothy Sayers
Buson: 4 poet 8 Japanese
genre: 5 haiku
Busoni: 9 Ferruccio
buss: 4 kiss 5 smack 6 smooch 8 osculate 10 osculation
Bus Stop: 4 film, play
author: William Inge
cast: Marilyn Monroe, Don Murray, Arthur O'Connell
director: Joshua Logan
Bus Stop (1966 song) artist: Hollies
bust: 3 dud, nab 4 bomb, fail, flop, fold, lose, loss, raid, ruin, slap, slip, tame, tear, trip 5 break, catch, flunk, pinch, run in, seize, spree 6 arrest, blow it, collar, defeat, demote, detain, falter, fiasco, fold up, mishap, pick up, pull in, reduce, statue, turkey 7 blunder, capture, debacle, failure, fizzler, founder, go under, go wrong, jailing, misstep, seizure, stumble, washout 8 bring low, disaster, downfall, fall flat, flounder, fracture, lay an egg 9 apprehend, downgrade, recession, sculpture, strike out 10 depression, impoverish, nonsuccess
go ~: 4 fail, fold
in: 5 barge, enter 9 interrupt
locale: 5 niche 6 alcove 8 pedestal
open: 3 pry 5 force, jimmy 7 break in
opposite: 4 boom
out: 6 escape
participant: 4 narc, nark 5 narco
Roman ~: 4 herm
__ bust: 4 baby, beer
Bust a Move (1989 song) artist: Young MC
bustard: 4 bird
Busta Rhymes
song: Dangerous (1998)
Turn It Up (1998)
What's It Gonna Be?! (1999)
Woo-Hah!! Got You All in Check (1996)
busted: 4 tame 5 broke, kaput, ran in, skint 6 broken 8 bankrupt, deprived, finished, indigent 9 destitute, insolvent, penniless 10 out of order
party: 4 perp
up: 4 hurt 7 damaged, injured
Busted (1963 song) artist: Ray Charles
buster: 3 bud, mac 5 kiddo
bronco ~: 6 cowboy 7 cowpoke 8 wrangler
clod ~: 3 hoe
starter: 3 sod 4 gang 5 block, crime, trust 6 bronco
__ buster: 5 union
Buster: 6 Crabbe, Keaton
Buster Brown: 3 boy 4 toon 6 collar
dog: 4 Tige
__ Bus, The: 4 Last 5 Lilac 7 Wayward
bustier: 3 top 5 shirt
Bustin' Loose (1981 film)
cast: Robert Christian, Richard Pryor, Cicely Tyson
director: Oz Scott
bustle: 3 ado, hum, run, zip 4 dash, fuss, move, rush, stir, teem, to-do, whir 5 furor, haste, hoo-ha, hurry, press, swirl, whirr 6 action, clamor, flurry, hasten, hoopla, hubbub, hustle, lather, scurry, tumult, uproar 7 clutter, ferment, mad rush, scamper, turmoil 8 activity, brouhaha, disorder, foofaraw, scramble 9 commotion, confusion 10 excitement, get hopping, hullabaloo
bustling: 4 busy, spry 5 alive, astir, brisk, perky 6 active, at work, lively 7 dynamic, working 8 animated 9 assiduous, energetic, sprightly
busts: 3 art 9 sculpture
busy: 4 at it, nosy, spry 5 astir, brisk, in use, nosey, perky 6 active, at work, engage, hectic, lively, on duty, ornate, prying, snoopy, snowed, tied up 7 crowded, dynamic, engaged, humming, immerse, on the go, popping, swamped, working 8 animated, bustling, employed, immersed, laboring, occupied, studious 9 assiduous, energetic, engrossed, officious, on the move, sprightly 10 in a meeting, in an uproar, meddlesome, overloaded
act ~: 4 toil, work 5 hurry, slave 6 bustle, hustle, scurry
as a phone: 5 in use
bee: 7 hustler 8 live wire
ender: 4 body, work
extremely ~: 4 ahum, at it 7 humming 8 occupied 10 overworked
get ~: 4 move 5 begin, start 6 fall to, jump in, tackle 7 hop to it, pitch in 8 get going 9 take steps 10 buckle down
insect: 3 ant, bee
keep ~: 5 tie up 6 employ, engage, occupy
not ~: 4 free, idle, slow 5 slack
period: 4 rush
place: 3 zoo 4 hive 6 hotbed
very ~ schedule: 5 whirl
busy __: 3 bee 6 signal
busy as a __: 3 bee 6 beaver
busybody: 3 hen 5 snoop 6 gossip 7 meddler, tattler 8 fat mouth, quidnunc 9 buttinsky 10 meddlesome, Nosy Parker, rubberneck, taleteller, tattletale, yenta. prier
be a ~: 3 pry 6 meddle
like a ~: 4 nosy 5 nosey 6 snoopy 7 curious 8 meddling
busy old fool, Donne's: 3 sun
but: 3 bar, yet 4 just, only, save 5 if not 6 and yet, except, merely, singly, solely, though, unless 7 barring, however, save for 9 other than 10 except that, leaving out, regardless
in Spanish: 3 más
but __: 3 yet
__ but: 3 all
...but __ has her way: 5 woman
...but __ itself: 4 fear
But __ art?: 4 is it
But __ for Me: 3 Not
But __ me, give me liberty...: 5 as for
But __ on forever: 3 I go
butane: 3 gas 4 fuel
form of ~: 3 LPG 5 LP gas
butch: 4 coif 6 hairdo 7 haircut
Butch: 7 Cassidy, Patrick
Butch Cassidy and the Sundance Kid (1969 film)
cast: Paul Newman, Robert Redford,

Katharine Ross
director: George Roy Hill
butcher: 4 ruin 5 wreck 7 louse up 8 bollix up
ender: 4 bird
implement: 3 saw
offering: 4 beef, chop, lamb, meat, pork, veal 5 joint, links, roast, shank, steak, T-bone, tripe 6 cutlet, mutton, rib eye 7 sausage, sirloin
scraps: 5 offal
shop fixture: 5 scale 6 cooler
unit: 2 lb. 5 pound
butcher __: 4 shop 5 block, knife, linen, paper, rayon
Butcher Boy, The star: 3 Rea
butcher, the __..., the: 5 baker
Butch Van __ Kolff: 5 Breda
Butenandt, Adolf: 7 chemist 8 Nobelist
buteo: 4 bird
But Gentlemen Marry Brunettes
author: Anita Loos
__ but goodies: 6 oldies
But I Do (1961 song) artist: Clarence Henry
...but I know what __: 5 I like
__ but known!: 4 Had I
Butkus, Dick: 7 analyst 10 linebacker
sport: 8 football
butler: 3 man 4 male 5 Lurch, valet 6 Alfred, flunky, Jeeves 7 flunkey 9 major-domo 10 manservant
sitcom ~: 5 Lurch
teammate: 4 chef, cook, maid 7 footman
butler __, The: 5 did it
__ butler: 6 silent
Butler: 4 Daws 5 Brett, David, Jerry 6 Murray, Samuel 7 Octavia 9 Gable role
Butler, David: 8 director
film: Calamity Jane (1953)
Caught in the Draft (1941)
A Connecticut Yankee (1931)
Doubting Thomas (1935)
Kentucky (1938)
The Little Colonel (1935)
The Littlest Rebel (1935)
Pigskin Parade (1936)
The Princess and the Pirate (1944)
Road to Morocco (1942)
San Antonio (1945)
Sunny Side Up (1929)
Thank Your Lucky Stars (1943)
Where's Charley? (1952)
Butler, Jerry
song: He Will Break Your Heart (1960)
Let It Be Me (1964)
Only the Strong Survive (1969)
Butler, Murray: 8 Nobelist
Butler, Octavia: 6 author, writer
Butler, Rhett love: 5 O'Hara 8 Scarlett
butler's __: 4 tray 5 table 6 pantry
Butler, Samuel: 4 poet 6 writer 7 British
work: Erewhon
Hudibras
The Way of All Flesh
__ Butler Yeats: 7 William
Butley (1974 film)
cast: Alan Bates, Richard O'Callaghan, Jessica Tandy
director: Harold Pinter
__, but no cigar: 5 Close
But Not for Me composer: 8 Gershwin
__ but not heard: 4 seen
__ but not least: 4 last
but only God can __ tree: 5 make a
Butor, Michel: 6 French, writer
buts: 10 objections
no ifs, ands or ~: 6 really 7 exactly 9 precisely 10 absolutely, definitely, positively
butt: 3 end, hit, ram, sap, tip 4 base, cask, dupe, poke, rear, stub 5 chump, patsy, sport, stump 6 pigeon, sucker, target, thrust, victim 7 fall guy, project, remnant, run into 8 easy mark 9 extremity, posterior, scapegoat
against: 5 touch 6 adjoin 8 neighbor
in: 3 pry 4 nose 6 jump in, kibitz, meddle, tamper 7 intrude, obtrude 8 trespass 9 intercede, interfere, interpose, interrupt, intervene
out: 7 project 8 protrude
butt __: 3 end 4 weld 5 hinge, joint, plate, shaft 6 chisel, stroke
butte
form a ~: 5 erode
kin: 4 mesa 7 plateau
Butte: 4 city, town
city near ~: 6 Helena
locale: 7 Montana
butter: 3 jam, ram 4 goat 6 spread 9 preserves
bread and ~: 6 living 7 aliment 10 livelihood
container: 3 tub 5 crock
ender: 3 bur, cup, fat, fly, nut 4 ball, fish, milk, weed, wort 6 scotch 7 fingers
holder: 3 tub 6 firkin
Indian ~: 4 ghee
like ~: 6 creamy, smooth
maker: 5 churn, dairy
rating: 6 grade A
spreader: 5 knife
substitute: 4 oleo 9 margarine
substitute, in Britain: 5 marge
unit: 3 pat 5 pound
up: 3 woo 4 coax 6 cajole 7 flatter, lay it on, wheedle 8 blandish, fawn over, kowtow to 9 get next to, shine up to 10 compliment
butter __: 4 bean, clam, tree 5 knife, sauce 6 cookie, muslin 7 brickle
__ butter: 4 shea 5 apple, black, brown, cacao, cocoa, drawn, peach 6 mowrah, peanut 7 coconut, kneaded
__ Butter: 3 Hot
butter-and-__ man: 3 egg
Butter and Egg Man, The author: George S. Kaufman
Butter Battle Book, The author: Dr. Seuss
butter bean: 4 lima
buttercup: 5 akene, plant 6 achene, flower
buttercup __: 6 squash
__ buttercup: 4 tall 7 Bermuda, bulbous
__ buttered rum: 3 hot
Butterfield 8: 4 film 5 novel
author: John O'Hara
cast: Eddie Fisher, Laurence Harvey, Elizabeth Taylor
director: Daniel Mann
Butterfinger: 5 candy 9 chocolate
alternative: 4 Mars, Twix 5 Clark, Heath 6 Kit Kat, Mounds, PayDay, Reese's, Zagnut 7 Krackel, Oh Henry 8 Baby Ruth, Hershey's, Milky Way, Snickers 9 Almond Joy, Mr. Goodbar 10 NutRageous
butterfingered: 5 inept, unapt 6 clumsy 8 lubberly 10 unskillful
butterfingers: 2 ox 3 oaf 4 clod, dolt, lout 5 klutz 6 lubber, lummox 7 bungler
cry: 4 oops
Butterflies Are Free (1972 film)
cast: Edward Albert, Goldie Hawn, Eileen Heckart
butterflies in the stomach: 6 nerves
butterfly: 3 bug 5 satyr 6 insect, stroke 7 monarch
catcher: 3 net
cousin: 4 moth
do the ~: 4 swim
emulate a ~: 4 flit
kin: 5 crawl 10 backstroke
social ~: 5 mixer
stage: 4 pupa 5 larva, pupae 6 cocoon
valve: 6 damper
butterfly __: 3 net, nut, pea 4 bomb, bush, roof, weed 5 chair, table, valve, wedge 6 damper, effect, flower, orchid 7 closure
__ butterfly: 3 owl, sea 4 leaf 5 satyr, zebra 6 sulfur 7 alfalfa, cabbage, emperor, monarch, thistle, troilus
Butterfly: 7 McQueen
Butterfly (1957 song)
artist: Andy Williams, Charlie Gracie
Butterfly (1981 film)
cast: Stacy Keach, Orson Welles, Pia Zadora
__ Butterfly: 4 Iron 6 Madama, Madame 7 Elusive
butterfly-bee analogist: 3 Ali
buttermilk: 8 beverage
make ~: 5 churn
Buttermilk: 5 horse 6 equine
rider: Dale Evans
__ Buttermilk Sky: 3 Ole
butternut: 4 tree 5 brown 6 squash
color kin: 3 bay, dun, tan 4 ecru, fawn, foxy, nude, seal 5 amber, beige, camel, cocoa, hazel, khaki, mocha, sepia, tawny, umber 6 auburn, bister, bistre, bronze, coffee, copper, ginger, russet, sienna, sorrel, suntan, walnut 7 biscuit, caramel, dogwood, hickory 8 chestnut, cinnamon, mahogany 9 chocolate
butter pecan: 8 ice cream
alternative: 5 lemon, mocha, peach 6 banana, coffee, Jamoca, toffee 7 caramel, coconut, vanilla 8 cinnamon, hazelnut 9 bubblegum, chocolate, pineapple, pistachio, raspberry, rocky road, rum raisin 10 blackberry, cheesecake, Neapolitan, peppermint, strawberry
butterscotch: 5 candy 8 ice cream 9 sweetmeat
alternative: 5 lemon, mocha, peach 6 banana, coffee, Jamoca, toffee 7 caramel, coconut, vanilla 8 cinnamon, hazelnut 9 bubblegum, chocolate, pineapple, pistachio, raspberry, rocky road, rum raisin 10 blackberry, cheesecake, Neapolitan, peppermint, strawberry
Butterworth: 3 Mrs. 7 Charles
Butterworth's, Mrs.: 5 syrup
buttery: 4 oily 6 creamy, smooth 9 adulatory 10 lubricious
__ but the Best: 7 Nothing
__ but the brave...: 4 None
__ But the Lonely Heart: 4 None
But there is __ in Mudville: 5 no joy
But thy __ summer shall not fade: 7 eternal
buttinsky: 4 pest 5 snoop 7 meddler 8 busybody 10 Nosy Parker
__ but to do...: 6 theirs
button: 4 stud 5 close 6 fasten, switch 8 fastener, mushroom
alternative: 4 snap 6 Velcro, zipper
belly ~: 5 navel 9 umbilicus
down: 6 secure 7 specify 8 identify 9 designate 10 categorize, consummate
ender: 4 ball, bush, hole, hook, mold, wood
material: 4 bone 5 nacre 7 plastic
neat as a ~: 4 tidy 7 orderly
one's lip: 5 quiet 6 clam up, shut up
panic ~: 5 alarm
replace a ~: 3 sew 5 sew on
ridge: 4 nurl 5 knurl
right on the ~: 5 exact, right, sharp 7 correct 8 accurate
starter: 4 push 5 belly
up: 4 bolt, lock, seal, shut 5 close, latch 6 fasten, secure 7 seal off
word: 4 push 5 press
button __: 3 ear, man 5 quail
button-__ shirt: 4 down
__ button: 3 hot 4 cuff, hold, hunt, push, turn 5 belly, egads, on the, panic 6 collar 7 Spanish
Button: 4 Dick 8 Gwinnett
buttonbush: 5 plant 6 flower
Button, Dick: 6 skater 7 analyst
button-down: 5 shirt, yuppy 6 square, yuppie
buttoned up: 4 done 5 quiet 6 silent 9 secretive 10 unspeaking
buttonhole: 4 slit 5 delay, press 6 accost, detain, hold up
button one's __: 3 lip
buttons
popping one's ~: 5 proud
push the ~: 7 control
__ Button Shoes: 4 High
Buttons, Red: 5 actor 8 comedian
film: Hatari! (1962)
The Longest Day (1962)
The Poseidon Adventure (1972)
Sayonara (1957, AA)
Your Cheatin' Heart (1964)
buttonwood: 4 tree
Buttram: 3 Pat
buttress: 4 gird, hold, pier, prop, stay, tone 5 brace, build, shore, steel 6 anneal, beef up, column, harden, prop up, temper, tone up, uphold 7 bolster, bulwark, burgeon, defense, develop, empower, enhance, fortify, shore up, stiffen, support, sustain, thicken, toughen 8 bourgeon, energize, indurate, mainstay, vitalize 9 intensify, reinforce, stabilize, stanchion, undergird 10 invigorate, strengthen, supplement
__ buttress: 6 flying
butut: 5 money
__ but wiser: 5 older
__ but world enough...: 5 Had we
butyl __: 6 rubber 7 acetate, alcohol, nitrite
__ but You: 6 Nobody
But You Know I Love You (1969 song) artist: Kenny Rogers
Butz: 4 Earl
buxom: 5 plump, pudgy 6 zaftig, zoftig 9 filled-out 10 Rubenesque
buy: 3 get, own 4 deal, shop, take 5 bribe, order, spend, steal, value, yield 6 accept, deal in, obtain, pay for, pick up, secure 7 acquire, bargain, believe, corrupt, fall for, procure, shop for, swallow 8 closeout, invest in, purchase, transact 9 subscribe 10 investment
alternative: 4 rent 5 lease 6 borrow 7 charter
opposite: 4 sell
time: 5 delay, stall, table 6 put off 8 postpone
buy __: 3 off, out 4 boat, into, time
buy __ in a poke: 4 a pig
__ Buy: 4 Best
buyback: 6 assent, patent 8 discount, giveback, rollback, yielding 9 admission, agreement, allowance, privilege, surrender 10 acceptance, adjustment, compliance, compromise, concession, confession, indulgence, permission
buyer: 5 owner, payer, taker 6 client, emptor, patron, vendee 7 end user 8 consumer, customer

bonanza: **4** sale **7** auction **9** clearance
bonus: **5** no tax **6** coupon, rebate
caution: **4** as is **6** beware
concern: **5** price **8** warranty **9** guarantee
find a ~: **4** push, sell **5** foist **7** promote **9** advertise
proposal: **3** bid **5** offer
request: **8** charge it
round ~ phrase: **4** on me
buyers: **6** public **9** clientele, consumers
buyer's __: **6** market
buying: **9** ownership, patronage
and selling: **5** trade **7** traffic **8** business, commerce, dealings, exchange, industry **9** patronage
shop without ~: **6** browse
buying __: **5** power
buy low, sell __: **4** high
__ Buy Me Love: **4** Can't
buy on __: **4** spec
buyout: **4** deal **8** takeover
Buz: **6** Sawyer
buzz: **3** hum, tip, yak **4** coif, kick, ring, talk, whir, whiz, zoom **5** drone, noise, phone, rumor, sound, whirr **6** clamor, gossip, hoopla, murmur, report, tipoff **7** chatter, hearsay, whisper **8** pleasure **9** grapevine, telephone **10** excitement
ender: **4** word
off: **4** scat, shoo **5** scram **6** begone, get out **10** go fly a kite
buzz __: **3** off, saw, wig **4** bomb
Buzz: **5** Kulik **6** Aldrin **8** Clifford
capsule-mate: **4** Neil
buzzard: **4** bird **5** buteo
honey ~: **4** pern
__ buzzard: **5** honey **6** turkey
Buzzard's __: **3** Bay
buzz-cut opposite: **4** Afro
buzzed: **4** high **5** tight, tipsy
Buzzell, Edward: **8** director
film: At the Circus (1939)
Best Foot Forward (1943)
Easy to Wed (1946)
Go West (1940)
Neptune's Daughter (1949)
A Woman of Distinction (1950)
buzzer: **3** bee, fly **5** alarm **6** cicada **8** doorbell
__ buzzer: **3** joy
Buzzi: **4** Ruth
buzzing: **4** ahum, go-go, talk **5** astir, noise **6** aswarm, lively, murmur
about: **4** stir, to-do
sound: **3** hum **4** zoom **5** drone
__ B. Vance: **8** Courtney
BVDs: **6** briefs, shorts **7** jockeys **9** underwear
rival: **5** Hanes **6** Jockey
B-vitamin source: **4** meat **5** yeast
__ B. Wallis: **3** Hal
bwana: **3** sir **4** boss **6** hunter, master
expedition: **6** safari
helper: **6** bearer
B'way
see Broadway
B.W.I. part: **4** West **6** Indies **7** British
by: **3** per, via **4** as of, away, near, over, past **5** along, aside **6** at hand, before, beside, beyond, nearby, next to **7** close to, through **9** abreast of, alongside, to one side
any chance: **4** ever
itself: **4** lone, solo **5** alone, per se **6** singly **8** solitary
prefix: **4** para-

by __: **3** far, gum **4** half, hand, Jove, rote **5** a hair, a mile, and by, golly, heart, the by, turns, way of **6** chance, cracky, rights **7** degrees, request
by __ and bounds: **5** leaps
by __ and starts: **4** fits
by __ means: **3** all, any
by __ of: **3** way **4** dint **5** means **6** reason, virtue
by __ or by crook: **4** hook
by __ shot: **5** a long
by-__: **4** blow, line, name, pass, path, play, plot, road, talk, work **6** bidder, street **7** product
by-__-leave: **4** your
__ by: **3** get, lay, lie, put, set **4** come, drop, stop **5** abide, by and, by the, stand, swear, swing **6** squeak **7** squeeze
__-by: **4** blow **5** close
By __: **4** Jove **7** Jupiter
by a __ shot: **4** long
by all means: **3** yep, yes **4** sure **8** of course **9** certainly, naturally, no problem
__ by an Angel: **7** Touched
by and __: **5** large
by any __: **5** means
__ by any other name...: **5** a rose
Byatt, A.S.: **6** author, writer **7** British
sister: Drabble
work: Babel Tower
The Biographer's Tale
The Game
Possession
The Shadow of a Sun
Still Life
bye: **4** pass, ta-ta **5** aloha, later, see ya **6** see you, so long **7** goodbye **8** au revoir, farewell, sayonara
__-bye: **4** good **5** beddy, rock-a
__ by ear: **4** play
__ by east: **5** north, south
bye-bye: **3** bye **4** ta-ta **5** adieu, aloha, later, see ya **6** so long **7** good-bye **8** farewell
in French: **5** adieu **8** au revoir
in Hawaiian: **5** aloha
in Italian: **4** ciao
in Japanese: **8** sayonara
in Latin: **3** ave **4** vale
in Portuguese: **5** adeus
in Spanish: **5** adios
make ~: **4** wave
Bye, Bye Baby (1965 song) artist: Four Seasons
Bye Bye Birdie (1963 film): **7** musical
cast: Ann-Margret, Janet Leigh, Paul Lynde, Maureen Stapleton, Dick Van Dyke
composer: **5** Adams **7** Strouse
director: George Sidney
role: **3** Kim **5** Rosie
song: **4** Kids
Bye Bye Bye artist: **5** 'Nsync
Bye Bye, Love (1995 film)
cast: Janeane Garofalo, Matthew Modine, Randy Quaid, Paul Reiser
Bye Bye Love (1957 song) artist: Everly Brothers
Byelorussia once: **3** SSR
__-Bye to All That: **4** Good
__ by fire: **5** trial
byform: **7** variant
__-by-four: **3** two
__ By Golly, Wow: **6** Betcha
bygone: **3** old **4** late, lost, once, over, past **5** dated, of old, olden, passé **6** former, of yore **7** ancient, archaic, defunct, extinct, old-time, one-time, quondam **8** obsolete, outmoded, out of use, previous, vanished **9** erstwhile, forgotten, grievance, out-of-date **10** back-number
bygones
let ~ be bygones: **5** let go **6** excuse, forget, pardon **7** forgive **8** overlook, play past
By gosh!: **3** wow **4** egad **5** egads
Byington, Spring: **7** actress
film: A Family Affair (1937)
The Vanishing Virginian (1942)
Walk Softly, Stranger (1950)
TV: December Bride
By Jove!: **4** egad, I say **5** egads
__ by jowl: **5** cheek
By Jupiter: **7** musical
songwriter: **4** Hart **7** Rodgers
__ by jury: **5** trial
by land __: **5** or sea
__ by land...: **5** One if
bylaw: **3** act **4** bill, code, fiat, rule **5** canon, edict, tenet **7** mandate, measure, precept, statute **9** enactment, guideline, ordinance **10** observance, regulation
by leaps and __: **6** bounds
byline: **6** credit
name: **6** author, editor
By Love Possessed author: James Gould Cozzens
__ by Me: **5** Stand
__ by Myself: **3** All
byname: **6** handle **8** cognomen
Byner: **4** John
__-by-night: **3** fly
by no __: **5** means
__ by north: **4** east, west
__ by Northwest: **5** North
BYOB part: **3** own **4** beer, your **5** booze, bring **6** bottle
__ by one's guns: **5** stand, stick
__ by one's wits: **4** live
bypass: **4** duck, jump, omit, shun, skip **5** avoid, dodge, evade, shirk, shunt, skirt **6** detour, eschew, ignore **7** abstain, neglect, rule out, shy from **8** flee from, go around, sidestep **9** get around, runaround **10** circumvent, work around
bypath: **4** lane, road, walk **6** detour
byproduct: **6** result **7** product, spinoff **8** offshoot **9** outgrowth **10** derivative
Byrd: **6** Donald, Robert **7** Charlie, Richard
Byrd, Charlie: **9** guitarist
genre: **4** jazz
__ Byrd Land: **5** Marie
Byrd, Richard: **8** explorer
book: **5** Alone
fox terrier: **5** Igloo
Byrds
song: Mr. Tambourine Man (1965)
Turn! Turn! Turn! (1965)
byre: **4** shed **7** cowshed
Byrne, Gabriel: **5** actor
film: Cool World (1992)
Defence of the Realm (1985)
Hello Again (1987)
Lionheart (1987)
Little Women (1994)
Polish Wedding (1998)
A Simple Twist of Faith (1994)
The Usual Suspects (1995)
spouse: Ellen Barkin
Byrnes, Edd: **5** actor **6** singer
song: Kookie, Kookie (1959)
byroad: **4** lane **8** short cut

Byron: **5** Allen, White **6** Haskin, Nelson **7** British **9** MacGregor
Byron, Lord: **4** poet **7** British
contemporary: **5** Keats **7** Shelley
daughter: **3** Ada
homeland: England
work: Beppo
Cain
Childe Harold's Pilgrimage
Don Juan
Hours of Idleness
Lara
Manfred
Parisina
The Prisoner of Chillon
She Walks in Beauty
__ by south: **4** east, west
__ Bysshe Shelley: **5** Percy
bystander: **7** witness **8** onlooker **9** spectator **10** eyewitness
__ by Starlight: **6** Stella
__ by storm: **4** take
bytalk: **8** chitchat
byte
part: **3** bit
starter: **4** giga, mega, tera
transmitter: **5** modem
__ by Temptation: **3** Def
bytes
1024 ~: **4** one K
what ~ measure: **6** memory
by that fact in Latin: **6** eo ipso
by the __: **3** way **7** numbers
by the __ of one's pants: **4** seat
by the __ of one's teeth: **4** skin
by the __ token: **4** same
__ by the bell: **5** saved
by-the-book: **5** rigid, stern **8** exacting
__ by the Dozen: **7** Cheaper
by the grace of God in Latin: **9** Dei gratia
By the Light of the Silvery __: **4** Moon
__ by the nose: **4** lead
By the Rivers of Babylon author: Nelson Demille
by the same __: **5** token
__-by-the-Sea: **6** Carmel
By the Time I Get to Phoenix (1967 song)
artist: Glen Campbell
composer: **4** Webb
By the Waters of Babylon author: Emma Lazarus
by the way in French: **9** en passant
__ by the wayside: **4** fall
BYU
church: **3** LDS
conference: **3** WAC
locale: **4** Utah **5** Provo
rival: **4** UTEP
byway: **4** lane, path, road, walk **5** route, trail **6** avenue, street **8** side road
__ by west: **5** north, south
__-by-wire: **3** fly
byword: **3** saw **5** adage, axiom, gnome, maxim, motto **6** dictum, phrase, saying, slogan **7** precept, proverb **8** aphorism **9** battle cry
by-your-__: **5** leave
__ By Your Man: **5** Stand
Byzantine: **7** complex **8** involved **9** entangled, intricate
coin: **6** besant, bezant **7** bezzant
division: **5** thema
empress: **5** Irene
image: **4** icon, ikon **5** eikon
ruler: **6** exarch **7** emperor, empress
Byzantine __: **4** rite **5** chant **6** Church, Empire
Byzantium author: William Butler Yeats

C: 3 key, pos., vit. 4 clef, elem., mark, note 5 grade, width 6 carbon, letter 7 vitamin
alias: 6 B sharp
almost ~: 5 D plus
and W: 5 music
get a ~: 4 pass
in phonetic alphabet: 7 Charlie
major relative: 6 A minor
measure: 3 deg. 6 degree
6 for ~: 4 at. no.
sharp: 5 D flat
vitamin ~: 4 acid
vitamin ~ source: 6 citrus
C ___: 3 in C 4 and W, clef, star 6 ration, supply 7 battery, horizon
C ___ cat: 4 as in
C'___ la vie!: 3 est
C-___: 4 axes, axis, bias, note, SPAN 5 clamp 6 scroll
C. ___ Koop: 7 Everett
___ C: 3 C in, Mel 6 middle 7 vitamin
___ C.: 3 K. of
'C' ___ Corpse: 5 Is for
Ca: 4 elem. 7 calcium, element
20 for ~: 4 at. no.
CA
clock setting: 3 PDT, PST
see also California
C.A.
country: 4 Guat., Hond.
see also Central America
Caan, James: 5 actor
film: Cinderella Liberty (1973)
Countdown (1968)
El Dorado (1967)
Eraser (1996)
For the Boys (1991)
Gardens of Stone (1987)
The Godfather (1972)
Hide in Plain Sight (1980)
Honeymoon in Vegas (1992)
Misery (1990)
The Rain People (1969)
Rollerball (1975)
Slither (1973)
Thief (1981)
cab: 4 hack, taxi 6 hansom, jitney 7 taxicab, vehicle 9 transport 10 conveyance
alternative: 2 el 3 bus 5 train
clock: 5 meter
cost: 4 fare
ender: 3 man, men 5 stand 6 driver
go by ~: 4 ride
horse-drawn ~: 6 hansom
illicit ~: 5 gypsy
of Asia: 6 gharri, gharry
signal a ~: 4 hail
starter: 4 pedi, taxi
cab ___: 6 driver
___ cab: 5 gypsy 6 hansom, livery
Cab: 8 Calloway
___ Cab: 6 Yellow
Cabada: 4 city, town
locale: 6 Mexico 8 Veracruz
cabal: 3 mob 4 ring 5 junta, junto, party 6 clique, scheme 7 collude, coterie, faction, in-group 8 intrigue, plotters, schemers 10 conspiracy
cabala: 6 secret 7 arcanum 9 esoterics, mysticism, occultism
Jewish ~ work: 5 zohar
cabalistic: 6 arcane, occult 8 oracular
caballero: 6 Latino 9 gentleman
cabana: 3 hut 5 house 7 cottage 8 bungalow 9 bathhouse
boy offering: 5 towel
cabaret: 5 boîte 6 bistro, eatery 9 nightclub, nightspot 10 supper club
group: 4 band 5 combo
number: 4 song, tune
cabaret ___: 3 tax
Cabaret (1972 film)
cast: Joel Grey, Liza Minnelli, Michael York
composer: 3 Ebb 6 Kander
director: Bob Fosse
role: 5 emcee
setting: 6 Berlin, Kit-Kat 7 Germany
cabasa: 6 shaker 10 percussion
origin: 6 Brazil
cabbage: 3 oof 4 cash, gelt, jack, kail, kale, loot, peag, pelf 5 bills, bread, bucks, dough, funds, lucre, money, moola, mopus, pesos, rhino, sewan 6 dinero, do-re-mi, mammon, mazuma, moolah, seawan, silver, specie, veggie, wampum, wealth 7 capital, dollars, lettuce, ooftish, scratch, shekels 8 bankroll, cold cash, currency, hard cash, smackers 9 banknotes, frogskins, long green, simoleons, vegetable 10 greenbacks, green stuff
color: 5 green
cousin: 4 kail, kale 5 cress
dish: 4 slaw
field: 5 patch
in French: 4 chou
skunk ~ family: 4 arum
unit: 4 head
cabbage ___: 3 bug 4 moth, palm, rose, tree 5 aphid 6 looper
___ cabbage: 3 red, sea 4 palm, stem 5 Savoy, skunk, swamp 6 celery, turnip 7 Chinese, stuffed
cabbagehead: 3 ass, oaf, sap 4 boob, bozo, clod, dodo, dolt, dope, fool 5 chump, clown, cluck, dummy, dunce, joker, ninny, patsy, stupe 6 dimwit, lummox, nitwit, sucker, turkey 7 buffoon, dingbat, dullard, half-wit, jackass, saphead 8 dumbbell, numskull 9 birdbrain, lamebrain, numbskull, simpleton
cabbage patch: 5 dance
Cabbage Patch Kids: 5 craze, dolls
company: 6 Coleco
cabbie: 4 hack 6 driver 9 chauffeur 10 taxi driver
credential: 3 lic. 7 license
income: 3 tip 4 fare
invite: 5 hop in
Cabell: 4 Enos
Cabernet: 3 red 4 wine 5 grape
origin: 6 France
relative: 5 Gamay, pinot, Tokay 6 Merlot 7 Catawba, Concord, Niagara 8 malvasia, muscatel 9 muscadine, Sauvignon, zinfandel 10 Chardonnay
caber tosser: 4 Scot
cabezon: 4 fish
cabin: 3 hut 4 home, room 5 abode, berth, bower, house, hutch, lodge, shack 6 chalet, shanty 7 cottage, lodging, retreat 8 dwelling, lodgment, log house, quarters 9 stateroom
cruiser: 4 boat 5 yacht
material: 3 log
wood: 4 pine
cabin ___: 3 boy 4 deck, hook 5 class, court, fever 7 cruiser
___ cabin: 3 log 4 poop 5 trunk
Cabin ___ Sky: 5 in the
cabinet: 4 wine 5 board, chest, hutch, white 6 closet, locker 7 council, dresser 8 advisors, cupboard 9 committee, furniture 10 brain trust, counselors, executives
department: 3 Agr., DoD, HUD, Int. 4 Educ. 5 Labor, State, Treas. 6 Energy 7 Defense, Justice 8 Interior, Treasury 9 Education
division: 4 dept. 10 department
ender: 4 work 5 maker 6 making
finish: 5 stain
former dept.: 3 HEW
former post: 3 PMG
medicine ~ item: 5 floss 6 iodine 7 aspirin 10 toothpaste
member: 4 secy. 8 minister 9 secretary
part: 4 door 5 hinge
wood: 5 alder, ebony
cabinet ___: 4 wine 7 picture, pudding, scraper
___ cabinet: 4 file 5 china 6 corner, liquor, shadow 7 Hoosier, kitchen
cabinetmaker: 6 joiner 10 woodworker
Cabin in the Sky (1943 film)
cast: Eddie Anderson, Lena Horne, Ethel Waters
director: Vincente Minnelli
cable: 4 line, news, rope, wire 5 media, pay TV, telex 6 report, stitch, strand 8 telegram 9 radiogram
anchor ~ hole: 5 hawse
award: 3 Ace
car: 4 tram
channel: 3 AMC, BET, CMT, CNN, HBO, HSN, IFC, MTV, PAX, QVC, SHO, TBS, TLC, TMC, TNN, TNT, USA 4 CNBC, ESPN, Flix, HGTV 5 A and E, Bravo, C-SPAN, MSNBC, Spike, Starz, Style 6 Encore, Noggin, Tech TV, TV Land 7 Cinemax, Court TV, Ovation, ShopNBC, SoapNet 8 Lifetime, Showtime, Sundance
ender: 3 way 4 cast, gram 6 vision
former cable ~: 3 TNT
hub: 5 spool
install ~: 3 lay
like some ~: 4 co-ax
nautical: 6 hawser
outlet: 2 TV 5 TV set
overseer: 3 FCC
post for a ship's ~: 4 bitt 7 bollard
power ~: 4 line
predecessor: 6 aerial
runway: 4 duct
service: 4 CATV
support: 5 pylon
TV worker: 5 wirer
cable ___: 3 car 4 bend, buoy 5 crane 6 length, stitch 7 molding, railway, release, tramway
cable-___: 5 ready
___ cable: 3 pay 5 power 6 ground, jumper, leader 7 armored, booster, coaxial
Cable, George Washington: 6 writer
cablegram: 4 wire 5 telex
Cable Guy, The (1996 film)
cast: Matthew Broderick, Jim Carrey, George Segal
director: Ben Stiller
cable stitch, make a: 4 knit
cabman: 4 hack 6 driver
Cabo ___ Lucas: 3 San
cabochon: 3 gem
lack: 5 facet
caboodle
kit and ~: 3 all 6 entire
caboose: 3 car
neighbor: 6 boxcar
position: 4 rear
Caborca: 4 city, town
locale: 6 Mexico, Sonora
Cabo San Lucas: 4 city, town
locale: 6 Mexico
Cabot: 3 str. 4 John 5 Bruce 6 strait 9 Sebastian
Cabot ___: 4 Cove 6 Strait
Cabot, Bruce: 5 actor
film: Fancy Pants (1950)
The Flame of New Orleans (1941)
King Kong (1933)
Murder on the Blackboard (1934)
Mystery of the White Room (1939)
Show Them No Mercy! (1935)
Cabot Cove doc: 4 Seth
Cabot, John: 7 Italian 8 explorer
___ Cabot Lodge: 5 Henry
Cabot, Sebastian: 5 actor 8 explorer
Cabral, Pedro Alvarez: 8 explorer
cabrilla: 4 fish
Cabrillo: 4 Juan
Cabrini, Mother: 3 nun 7 Frances
Cabrio: 2 VW 3 car 4 auto 10 automobile, Volkswagen
cabriole: 4 leap
Cabriolet: 3 car 4 Audi, auto 10 automobile
cacao: 4 tree 5 fruit 9 evergreen
exporter: 5 Ghana
cacao ___: 4 bean 6 butter
___ cacciatore: 4 alla
cache: 4 bury, hide, hold, keep, mask, mine, save, stow, veil 5 amass, cloak, couch, cover, hoard, kitty, put by, stash, stock, store, trove 6 garner, load up, retain, save up, supply 7 conceal, harvest, lay away, nest egg, obscure, put away, reserve, savings, secrete 8 disguise, ensconce, gold mine, hang onto, hold onto, magazine, maintain, put aside, salt away, stow away, treasure 9 hidey-hole, stockpile 10 accumulate, camouflage, depository, storehouse
like a ~: 6 hidden
cache ___: 6 memory 7 storage
Cachena: 3 cow 4 bull 6 bovine, cattle
cachet: 5 state 6 status 7 stature 8 position, prestige, standing
Cachi: 4 peak 5 mount 8 mountain
locale: 5 Andes 9 Argentina
cachinnate: 5 laugh
cachinnation: 8 laughter
cachou: 7 lozenge
cachucha: 5 dance
cack: 4 shoe 8 footwear
cackle: 3 cry 4 crow, ha-ha 5 clack, cluck, laugh, sound 6 babble, gabble, giggle, guffaw, rattle, squawk, titter 7 break up, chortle, chuckle, crack up 8 laughter
cackleberry: 3 egg
cackler: 3 hen 5 biddy
cackling: 8 giggling
ça, comme çi comme: 4 so-so
cacophonic: 8 jangling 9 unmusical
cacophonous: 4 loud 5 harsh, noisy 6 ablare, shrill 7 raucous 9 dissonant
cacophony: 3 din 5 Babel, noise 6 clamor, jangle 7 discord, grating 9 stridency 10 dissonance
cactus: 4 tuna 5 agave, nopal, plant 6 cereus, cholla, flower, maguey, mescal, peyote 7 opuntia, saguaro 9 succulent
bud: 6 areola, areole
defense: 5 spine
fruit: 5 nopal 7 saguaro 8 pitahaya
kin: 5 yucca
like ~: 5 spiny, xeric
milieu: 6 desert 7 Arizona
suitable for: 3 dry 4 arid
cactus ___: 4 moth, pear, wren 6 dahlia
___ cactus: 4 chin, crab, star, vine 6 barrel, Easter, old-man, orchid 7 rainbow, rat-tail
Cactus Flower (1969 film)
cast: Ingrid Bergman, Goldie Hawn, Walter Matthau, Jack Weston
director: Gene Saks
cad: 3 cur 4 boor, heel, jerk, lout, rake,

roué, toad 5 crumb, knave, louse, rogue, scamp, swine 6 bad guy, bad hat, rascal, rotter, varlet 7 bounder, dirtbag, lowlife, villain 8 blighter, rakehell, two-timer 9 miscreant, no-goodnik, scoundrel, vulgarian 10 blackguard, ne'er-do-well
rebuke: 4 slap
Cadbury: 5 candy 9 chocolate
caddie: 5 gofer, toter 7 carrier
burden: 3 bag 5 irons, woods
hire a ~: 4 golf
offering: 3 tee 4 club, iron, wood 6 driver, mashie, putter 7 niblick
caddie ___: 4 cart
caddish: 4 base 5 crude 7 ignoble, ill-bred, uncivil, uncouth 9 ungallant 10 unmannerly
Caddo: 3 Ree 6 Indian, Pawnee 7 Amerind 8 language
___ caddy: 3 tea
Caddy: 3 car 4 auto 10 automobile
competitor: 4 Linc
Caddyshack (1980 film)
cast: Chevy Chase, Rodney Dangerfield, Ted Knight, Bill Murray, Michael O'Keefe
director: Harold Ramis
cade: 3 tar
source: 7 juniper
cadence: 4 beat, lilt, rime, tone 5 meter, pulse, rhyme, swing, tempo 6 accent, rhythm 7 measure 10 intonation, modulation
word: 3 hup
___ cadence: 4 half 6 plagal 7 Landini, perfect
cadent: 8 rhythmic
Cadereyta: 4 city, town
locale: 6 Mexico 9 Nuevo León
cadet: 3 boy 4 pleb 5 plebe 7 soldier 9 legionary
Colorado: 6 airman
freshman ~: 4 pleb 5 plebe
meal: 4 mess
naval ~: 3 mid 5 middy
response: 5 no sir 6 yes sir
school: 3 VMI 9 West Point
cadet ___: 4 blue, gray, grey 5 cloth
___ cadet: 5 space
Cadets: 4 Army, USMA
Cadette: 5 scout 9 Girl Scout
cadge: 3 beg, bum 5 mooch 6 sponge 8 freeload, scrounge 9 impetrate, panhandle
cadger: 6 sponge 7 sponger 8 parasite 10 freeloader
cadi: 5 judge 6 Moslem, Muslim
Cadillac: 3 car 4 auto 10 automobile
model: 3 CTS, ESV 6 Calais, Catera 7 Allante, DeVille, Seville 8 Biarritz, Cimarron, Eldorado, Escalade 9 Fleetwood
Cadillac ___: 3 Man 4 Jack
like a ~ interior: 5 roomy
___ Cadillac: 4 Pink
Cadillac Jack author: Larry McMurtry
Cadillac Man (1990 film)
cast: Fran Drescher, Pamela Reed, Tim Robbins, Robin Williams
Cádiz: 4 city, gulf, port, town
city on the Gulf of ~: 6 Huelva
locale: 5 Spain
Cadmean ___: 7 victory
cadmium: 5 metal 7 element
cadmium ___: 3 red 4 cell 5 green 6 bronze, orange, yellow 7 sulfate, sulfide
___-cadmium battery: 6 nickel
Cadmus
brother of ~: 5 Cilix 6 Thasus 7 Phineus, Phoenix
daughter of ~: 3 Ino 5 Agave 6 Semele 7 Autonoe
parent of ~: 6 Agenor 10 Telephassa
sister of ~: 6 Europa
wife of ~: 8 Harmonia
cadre: 4 cell, core 5 force, staff 6 scheme 7 nucleus 9 framework, personnel
caduceus: 4 wand 5 staff
org. with a ~: 3 AMA
caducity: 7 frailty 8 weakness
Cady: 5 Frank
___ Cady Stanton: 9 Elizabeth
Caecilia: 4 font 8 typeface
Caedmon: 4 poet 7 British
___ caelo: 4 toto
Caen: 4 city, Herb, town
locale: 6 France
neighbor: 4 St. Lô
river: 4 Orne
Caerphilly: 6 cheese
caesar: 5 ruler, salad, title
Caesar: 3 Sid 4 Nero 5 Galba, Roman, ruler, salad, title, Titus 6 Adolph, Julius, Trajan 7 Hadrian 8 Augustus, Aurelian, Caligula, Tiberius 9 Vespasian 10 Diocletian
contemporary: 5 Berle
in Italian: 6 Cesare
month named for a ~: 3 Aug., Jul. 4 July 6 August
partner: 4 Coca
Caesar ___: 5 salad
___ Caesar: 6 Bloody, Julius, Little
___, Caesar!: 4 Hail
Caesar and Cleopatra author: George Bernard Shaw
___ Caesar, aut nihil: 3 aut
Caesar Cascabel author: Jules Verne
Caesarea: 4 city, port, town
Caesar, Julius: 5 Roman
city: 4 Rome
duds: 4 toga
early post of ~: 5 edile
foe: 4 Cato, Gaul 5 Casca 6 Brutus 7 Cassius
part of a ~ boast: 4 I saw, veni, vici, vidi 5 I came
question: 4 et tu
tongue: 3 Lat. 5 Latin
unlucky day for ~: 4 ides
___ Caesar's ghost!: 5 Great
Caesar, Sid: 8 comedian
film: The Cheap Detective (1978)
The Guilt of Janet Ames (1947)
It's a Mad Mad Mad Mad World (1963)
TV: Your Show of Shows
Caesar's Palace site: Las Vegas
caesura: 3 gap 4 halt, rest 5 break, pause 6 lacuna
café: 5 boîte, diner 6 bistro, coffee, eatery, French 7 cabaret 9 lunchroom, nightclub, nightspot 10 restaurant
addition: 4 lait
alternative: 3 thé
attraction: 5 aroma
container: 4 urne 5 tasse
customer: 5 diner, eater
feature: 4 menu 6 awning
royale ingredient: 6 cognac
waiter: 6 garçon
café ___: 3 car 4 noir 5 crème 6 au lait, brûlot, filtre, royale 7 curtain, society
café ___ leche: 3 con
___-café: 6 pousse
___ Cafe: 6 Bagdad
café au ___: 4 lait
cafeteria: 6 eatery 9 lunchroom 10 dining room, restaurant
item: 4 tray
patron: 5 eater
selection: 4 food
worker: 4 cook
cafeteria ___: 4 plan 7 benefit
cafeteria-___: 5 style
___ Cafe, The: 6 Atomic
caffè ___: 5 latte
caffeine source: 4 cola, kola 5 cacao
Cafferty: 4 John
caftan: 4 mumu, robe 5 dress 7 cover-up, garment 9 beachwear 10 loungewear
cage: 3 box, pen 4 cell, coop, jail, shut 5 frame, hutch 6 aviary, intern, lock up, shut up 7 capture, confine, enclose, impound, inclose, interne 8 backstop, imprison 9 enclosure, structure
dweller: 4 bird, myna 5 mynah 6 canary, parrot 8 parakeet
protector: 6 goalie
starter: 4 bird
___ cage: 3 rib 4 roll 7 Faraday
Cage: 4 John 7 Nicolas
caged: 4 pent 7 captive
Caged (1950 film)
cast: Agnes Moorehead, Eleanor Parker
director: John Cromwell
Cage, Nicolas: 5 actor
aunt: Talia Shire
film: Adaptation (2002)
Birdy (1984)
Bringing Out the Dead (1999)
Captain Corelli's Mandolin (2001)
City of Angels (1998)
Con Air (1997)
Face/Off (1997)
The Family Man (2000)
Guarding Tess (1994)
Honeymoon in Vegas (1992)
It Could Happen to You (1994)
Leaving Las Vegas (1995, AA)
Moonstruck (1987)
Peggy Sue Got Married (1986)
Racing With the Moon (1984)
Raising Arizona (1987)
Red Rock West (1993)
The Rock (1996)
Valley Girl (1983)
spouse: Patricia Arquette, Lisa Marie Presley
uncle: Francis Ford Coppola
cager: 5 NBAer 8 hoopster
former ~ org.: 3 ABA
like many ~ s: 4 tall 5 rangy
pro ~: 3 Cav, Mav, Net, Sun 4 Buck, Bull, Hawk, Heat, Jazz, King, Spur 5 Knick, Laker, Magic, Pacer, Sixer, Sonic 6 Celtic, Hornet, Nugget, Piston, Raptor, Rocket, Wizard 7 Clipper, Grizzly, Warrior 8 Cavalier, Maverick 10 SuperSonic, Timberwolf
see also basketball
cagey: 3 sly 4 arch, wary, wily 5 canny, chary, leery, slick 6 clever, crafty, shifty, shrewd, tricky 7 careful, cunning, elusive, elusory, evasive, guarded, mindful 8 cautious, guileful, slippery 9 sagacious, secretive 10 suspicious
cageyness: 5 craft
Cagliari: 4 city, town
locale: 5 Italy
Cagney: 3 cop 5 Chris, James
Cagney, James: 5 actor
film: Angels With Dirty Faces (1938)
Blood on the Sun (1945)
Boy Meets Girl (1938)
Captains of the Clouds (1942)
Ceiling Zero (1935)
City for Conquest (1940)
Each Dawn I Die (1939)
Footlight Parade (1933)
The Gallant Hours (1960)
'G' Men (1935)
Lady Killer (1933)
Love Me or Leave Me (1955)
Man of a Thousand Faces (1957)
The Mayor of Hell (1933)
A Midsummer Night's Dream (1935)
Mister Roberts (1955)
The Oklahoma Kid (1939)
One, Two, Three (1961)
Picture Snatcher (1933)
The Public Enemy (1931)
Ragtime (1981)
The Roaring Twenties (1939)
Shake Hands With the Devil (1959)
The Strawberry Blonde (1941)
Torrid Zone (1940)
Tribute to a Bad Man (1956)
White Heat (1949)
Yankee Doodle Dandy (1942, AA)
imitator word: 3 rat 5 dirty
role: 5 Cohan
Cagney & Lacey (CBS drama)
cast: Tyne Daly (Det. Mary Beth Lacey)
Sharon Gless (Det. Chris Cagney)
cagoule: 4 coat 6 jacket 8 raincoat
Caguas: 4 city, town
locale: 10 Puerto Rico
Cahn: 5 Sammy
collaborator: 5 Styne 9 Van Heusen
cahoots: 10 conspiracy
be in ~: 4 plan, plot 6 scheme, wangle 7 collude, connive 8 conspire, intrigue, maneuver 9 machinate
in ~: 6 allied, united 8 hooked up, in league
Cahuilla: 5 tribe 6 Indian 7 Amerind
Caicos: 4 isls. 5 isles 7 islands
locale: 7 Bahamas 10 West Indies
caiman: 4 croc 6 animal 7 reptile 9 crocodile
Cain: 4 Dean 6 eldest
brother: 4 Abel, Seth
dwelling place: 3 Nod
grandson of ~: 4 Irad
nephew: 4 Enos
parent: 3 Eve 4 Adam
query start: 3 am I
raise ~: 4 rave, riot 5 brawl, clash 6 clamor, squawk 7 carouse
raising ~: 5 noisy
son of ~: 5 Enoch
victim: 4 Abel
___ Cain: 5 raise
Cain author: Byron
Caine, Michael: 3 Sir 5 actor
film: Alfie (1966)
Billion Dollar Brain (1967)
Blame It on Rio (1984)
California Suite (1978)
The Cider House Rules (1999, AA)
Deathtrap (1982)
The Destructors (1974)
Dirty Rotten Scoundrels (1988)
Dressed to Kill (1980)
The Eagle Has Landed (1977)
Educating Rita (1983)
Gambit (1966)
Hannah and Her Sisters (1986, AA)
The Man Who Would Be King (1975)
Miss Congeniality (2000)
The Muppet Christmas Carol (1992)
Noises Off (1992)
Pulp (1972)
Quills (2000)
The Romantic Englishwoman (1975)
Silver Bears (1978)
Sleuth (1972)
Surrender (1987)
Sweet Liberty (1986)
Too Late the Hero (1970)
The Whistle Blower (1986)
The Wilby Conspiracy (1975)
The Wrong Box (1966)
Zulu (1964)
Caine Mutiny Court-Martial, The
author: Herman Wouk

Caine Mutiny, The (1954 film)
cast: Humphrey Bogart, José Ferrer, Van Johnson, Fred MacMurray
composer: **7** Steiner
director: Edward Dmytryk
Caingang: **6** Indian **7** Amerind
Cain, James M.: **6** author, writer
work: Double Indemnity
Mildred Pierce
The Moth
The Postman Always Rings Twice
Rainbow's End
Serenade
Three of a Kind
caique: **4** boat, ship
cairn: **4** heap **8** memorial, monument
South Sea ~: **3** ahu
Cairn ___: **7** terrier
Cairns: **4** city, town
locale: **9** Australia
Cairo: **4** city, port, town **7** capital
city near ~: **5** Tanta
it ends at ~: **4** Ohio
language: **6** Arabic
locale: **5** Egypt **7** Mideast
opera that premiered in ~: **4** Aïda
river: **4** Nile
caisson: **5** float **9** container
load: **4** ammo
caitiff: **6** bad guy **7** villain **9** miscreant
Caitlin
in English: **9** Catherine, Katherine
Caius: **4** pope **7** pontiff
caixa: **4** drum
origin: **6** Brazil
cajeput: **4** tree
relative: **5** guava **6** myrtle **10** eucalyptus
cajole: **4** coax, lure, urge, wile **5** tempt **6** entice, induce, pander, praise, work on **7** beguile, flatter, lay it on, wheedle **8** blandish, butter up, inveigle, persuade, play up to, soft-soap, suck up to **9** sweet-talk **10** compliment
cajolery: **7** blarney, coaxing, palaver **8** flattery, hard sell, humoring, jollying, soft soap, stroking **9** sweet talk, wheedling **10** compliment, enticement, persuasion
cajón: **4** drum
origin: **4** Peru
Cajun: **7** Acadian
cousin: **6** Creole
craft: **6** bateau
dish: **4** okra **5** gumbo
home: **5** bayou
like ~ cooking: **5** spicy **6** spicey
seasoning: **4** file
stew: **8** étouffée
___ Cajuns: **5** Ragin'
cake: **3** bar **4** baba, loaf, lump, mass, slab, soap, tart **5** babka, blini, block, brick, Bundt, crêpe, latke, pound, torte **6** blintz, danish, gâteau, harden, kuchen, marble, sponge, trifle, waffle **7** brownie, congeal, dessert, encrust, genoise, savarin, stollen, tartlet, thicken **8** flapjack, solidify **9** angel food, chocolate, dacquoise, jelly roll, madeleine, sally lunn **10** confection, devil's food, ladyfinger, upside-down
cousin: **3** pie **4** tart
decorate a ~: **3** ice **5** frost
decoration: **5** icing **6** dragée
decorator: **4** icer
ender: **4** walk
first name in ~: **4** Sara
fried ~: **5** donut **8** doughnut
frosting on the ~: **5** bonus
in French: **6** gateau
ingredient: **5** flour, mocha, sugar, yeast **6** batter **9** chocolate
like some ~: **4** iced, oaty, rich **5** moist, oaten
make a ~: **4** bake
makings: **3** mix
no piece of ~: **4** hard **5** tough
part: **5** layer
piece of ~: **4** easy, snap **5** cinch, crumb, cushy, slice, wedge **6** breeze, picnic, simple **8** duck soup, painless, pushover **10** child's play, effortless, unexacting
pro: **5** baker **10** pastry chef
rum ~: **4** baba
sale: **10** fundraiser
serving: **5** piece, slice
starter: **3** ash, cup, hoe, hot, oat, pan, tea **4** corn **5** fruit, short **6** batter, cheese, coffee, johnny, yellow **7** griddle
take the ~: **3** win **7** triumph
topper: **5** icing **6** candle
wedding ~ doll: **4** wife **5** bride, groom
cake ___: **3** mix, pan **5** eater, flour **6** makeup
___ cake: **3** hot, oil **4** corn, fish, rice, salt, soul **5** angel, Bundt, layer, pound, wheat, yeast **6** almond, cheese, coffee, cotton, funnel, groom's, icebox, marble, simnel, sponge **7** Banbury, flannel, linseed, wedding
___-cake: **4** pat-a **5** patty
caked: **5** muddy, thick
___-Cake makeup: **3** Pan
Cakes and Ale
author: W. Somerset Maugham
character: **3** Amy **4** Kear, Kemp **5** Alroy, Rosie
cakewalk: **4** romp, snap **5** cinch **6** breeze, picnic **8** pushover
in a ~: **6** easily
cal.
column: **3** Fri., Mon., Sat., Sun., Thu., Tue., Wed. **4** Thur., Tues. **5** Thurs.
notation: **4** appt.
page: **2** mo. **3** Apr., Aug., Dec., Feb., Jan., Jul., Jun., Mar., May, Nov., Oct., Sep.
unit: **2** mo., wk.
see also calendar
___-cal: **3** low
Cal: **5** Trask **6** Ripken, Thomas **7** Hubbard
rival: **3** USC
twin: **4** Aron
Cal ___: **4** Poly, Tech
Cal.
see California
calaba: **4** tree
Calabar: **5** river
locale: **7** Nigeria
Calabar ___: **4** bean
Calabasas: **4** city, town
locale: **10** California
calabash: **4** tree **5** gourd
relative: **7** catalpa **8** bignonia
___ Calabash: **3** Mrs.
calaboose: **4** jail, poky, stir **5** joint, pokey **6** lockup, prison
Calais: **3** car **4** auto, city, Olds, port, town **8** Cadillac **10** Oldsmobile
city near ~: **5** Lille
locale: **6** France
___ Calais: **5** Pas de
Calama: **4** city, town
locale: **5** Chile
calamanco: **6** fabric **8** material
calamari: **5** squid
calamine: **5** alloy
component: **3** tin **4** lead, zinc
lotion: **4** balm
target: **4** bite, itch
calamine ___: **5** brass **6** lotion
calamite: **6** fossil
calamitous: **4** dire **5** toxic, woful **6** bitter, malign, tragic, woeful **7** adverse, baleful, baneful, fateful, harmful, ruinous, unlucky **8** damaging, grievous, negative, tragical **9** blighting, dangerous, ill-omened, injurious **10** afflictive, deplorable, disastrous, lamentable, pernicious
calamity: **3** ill, woe **4** bane, blow, doom, loss, ruin **5** curse, event, havoc, shame **6** blight, misery, mishap, ordeal, plague **7** scourge, tragedy, undoing **8** accident, casualty, disaster, distress, hard luck, hardship **9** adversity, cataclysm, detriment, nightmare, ruination **10** affliction, misfortune
Calamity Jane (1953 film)
cast: Doris Day, Howard Keel
calamondin: **5** fruit **6** citrus
relative: **4** lime, Ugli **5** lemon, navel **6** orange, pomelo, tangor **7** kumquat, satsuma, Seville, tangelo **8** bergamot, mandarin, shaddock, Valencia **9** tangerine **10** grapefruit
calamus: **5** quill
calando: **6** slower, softer
Calaveras County jumper: **4** frog
calaverite: **3** ore
calc-___: **4** spar, tufa, tuff **6** sinter
Calchas: **4** seer
daughter of ~: **8** Cressida
calcify: **6** harden **8** indurate
calcite to Mohs: **5** three
calcium: **7** element
hydroxide: **6** alkali
like ~ oxide: **4** limy
oxide: **4** lime
source: **4** milk
calcium ___: **5** light, oxide **7** blocker, carbide, hydrate, nitrate, oxalate, sulfide
calculable: **9** countable, estimable **10** computable, imaginable, measurable, reckonable
calculate: **3** add, sum **4** find, make, plan, plot, tell **5** count, gauge, sum up, tally, total **6** assume, bank on, cipher, divide, figure, number, plan on, reckon, rely on **7** compute, count on, measure, project, work out **8** depend on, estimate, keep tabs, multiply, subtract **9** count upon, determine, enumerate, keep score **10** anticipate
roughly: **8** estimate
calculated: **7** studied **9** conscious, strategic **10** deliberate
calculated ___: **4** risk
calculating: **3** sly **4** keen, wary, wily **5** canny, chary **6** artful, crafty, shrewd **7** careful, cunning, devious, furtive, politic **8** cautious, discreet, guileful, scheming **9** observant
calculation: **3** age **4** area **5** count, ratio, yield **6** adding **7** caution, thought **8** dividing, estimate, figuring, forecast, planning, prudence **9** reckoning
calculator: **6** abacus **10** accountant
feature: **3** key, LCD, LED **6** keypad, memory **7** display
figure: **3** sum **5** total **6** addend **7** divisor **8** dividend
key: **3** CLR, cos, dot, sin, tan **4** plus, sine **5** clear, minus, times **6** cosine, equals **7** percent
use a ~: **3** add **6** divide **8** multiply, subtract
work: **4** math **10** arithmetic
___ calculator: **5** solar **6** pocket
calculus: **4** math
calculation: **3** lim., vol. **4** area **5** limit **6** volume **8** integral
pioneer: **5** Euler
Calcutta: **4** city, port, town
city near ~: **6** Howrah
clothing: **4** sari **5** saree
locale: **5** India **6** Bengal
Mother of ~: **6** Teresa
river: **5** Hugli
see also India
Calcutta (1960 song) artist: Welk
caldarium: **5** sauna
Caldecott ___: **5** medal
Calder: **9** Alexander **10** Willingham
Calder, Alexander: **6** artist **8** sculptor
work: **6** mobile
Calderón, Pedro: **6** author **7** Spanish **10** playwright
Caldwell: **3** Zoe **4** city, town **5** Bobby, Sarah **6** Taylor **7** Erskine
locale: **5** Idaho
Caldwell, Erskine: **6** author, writer
spouse: Margaret Bourke-White
work: Annette
Close to Home
Georgia Boy
God's Little Acre
Tobacco Road
Trouble in July
Caldwell, Sarah: **9** conductor
Cale: **10** Yarborough
Caleb: **4** Carr
son of ~: **4** Elah
Caledon: **4** city, town
locale: **6** Canada **7** Ontario
Caledonia: **4** city, town **8** Scotland
locale: **9** Wisconsin
Caledonian ___: **5** Canal
calefaction: **4** heat
calendar: **4** card, list **6** agenda, docket **7** daybook, Filofax, program **8** schedule **10** chronology
Chinese ~ year: **2** ox **3** dog, rat **4** boar **5** horse, sheep, snake, tiger **6** dragon, monkey, rabbit **7** rooster
church ~: **4** ordo
column: **3** Fri., Mon., Sat., Sun., Thu., Tue., Wed. **4** Thur., Tues. **5** Thurs. **6** Friday, Monday, Sunday **7** Tuesday **8** Saturday, Thursday **9** Wednesday
court ~: **6** docket
division: **2** mo., wk., yr. **3** day **4** date, week, year **5** month
for short: **4** sked
French Revolution ~ month: **6** Nivôse **7** Floréal, Ventôse **8** Brumaire, Frimaire, Germinal, Messidor, Pluviôse, Prairial **9** Fructidor, Thermidor **11** Vendémiaire
Hebrew ~ month: **2** Av **4** Adar, Elul, Iyar **5** Nisan, Sivan, Tevet **6** Kislev, Shevat, Tammuz, Tishri **7** Heshvan
Islamic ~ month: **4** Rabi **5** Rajab, Safar **6** Jumada, Shaban **7** Ramadan, Shawwal **8** Muharram **9** Dhu al-Qa'da **10** Dhu al-Hijja
model: **5** pin-up
page: **3** Apr., Aug., Dec., Feb., Jan., Jul., Jun., Mar., May, Nov., Oct., Sep. **4** July, June **5** April, March, month **6** August **7** January, October **8** December, February, November **9** September
Roman ~ day: **4** ides **5** nones **7** calends, kalends
run: **5** MTWTF
stone ~ user: **5** Aztec
calendar ___: **3** art, day **4** year **5** clock, month, watch
___ calendar: **4** desk **5** Hindu, Roman **6** church, Hebrew, Jewish, Julian, Moslem, Muslim **7** Chinese, Islamic
Calendar Girl (1960 song) artist: Neil Sedaka
calendario page: **3** mes
calends follower: **4** ides
calendula: **5** plant **6** flower
calescent: **3** hot
Calexico: **4** city, town
locale: **10** California

calf: **4** dogy, shin, veal **5** dogey, dogie **6** animal, heifer **7** foreleg **8** maverick
catcher: **5** reata, riata, roper **6** cowboy, lariat
cry: **5** bleat
ender: **4** skin
food source: **5** udder
front of the ~: **4** shin
golden ~: **4** idol
locale: **3** leg
lone ~: **4** dogy, waif **5** dogey, dogie, leppy, stray **6** doggie **8** maverick
look at with ~ eyes: **4** ogle
meat: **4** veal
muscle: **6** soleus
muscles: **5** solei
on the range: **4** dogy **5** dogey, dogie
starter: **4** moon
calf __: **4** love **6** roping
__ calf: **3** box, sea **5** bobby **6** fatted, golden
calf-length: **4** midi
calf-roping event: **5** rodeo
Calgary: **4** city, town
hockey player: **5** Flame
locale: **3** Alb. **4** Alta. **6** Canada **7** Alberta
newspaper: **3** Sun **6** Herald
Stampede: **5** rodeo
Stampeders' org.: **3** CFL
Calgon: **9** detergent
alternative: **3** All, Biz, Era, Fab, Yes **4** Bold, Dash, Gain, Surf, Tide, Wisk **5** Cheer, Dreft, Purex **6** Dynamo, Oxydol **7** Octagon **9** Ivory Snow
Calhern, Louis: **5** actor
film: The Asphalt Jungle (1950)
The Count of Monte Cristo (1934)
The Devil's Doorway (1950)
Duck Soup (1933)
Julius Caesar (1953)
The Magnificent Yankee (1950)
The Man With a Cloak (1951)
Men of the Fighting Lady (1954)
spouse: Ilka Chase
Calhoun, Rory: **5** actor
film: I'd Climb the Highest Mountain (1951)
A Ticket to Tomahawk (1950)
With a Song in My Heart (1952)
Cali: **4** city, town
locale: **8** Colombia
Caliban: **4** moon
planet: **6** Uranus
tormentor: **5** Ariel
caliber: **4** size **5** value, worth **6** degree, status **7** quality, stature **8** diameter **9** character, largeness
Calibra: **3** car **4** auto, Opel **10** automobile
calibrate: **5** align, aline, gauge, reset, scale **6** adjust **7** measure **8** fine-tune, graduate
anew: **5** reset
calico: **3** cat **5** cloth, felid **6** feline **7** spotted **9** patchwork
calico __: **3** bug, cat **4** bass, bush, clam, crab **6** flower
calicoback: **3** bug **6** insect
Calico Pie author: Edward Lear
calidity: **4** heat
__ caliente: **3** ojo
__ Caliente: **4** Agua
Calif.
campus: **3** USC
clock setting: **3** PDT, PST
neighbor: **3** Nev., Ore. **4** Ariz., Oreg.
school: **3** USC **4** UCLA
see also California
Califano: **6** Joseph
California: **4** gulf **5** state
airport: **3** LAX, SFO
animal on ~ flag: **4** bear
bay: **8** Monterey, San Pablo
city: **4** Bell, Brea, Galt, Lodi, Napa, Ojai **5** Arden, Azusa, Ceres, Chico, Chino, Davis, Hemet, Indio, Norco, Poway, Selma, Tracy, Vista, Wasco, Yreka **6** Arcade, Big Sur, Carmel, Carson, Clovis, Colton, Corona, Covina, Cudahy, Delano, Downey, Duarte, Dublin, East L.A., El Toro, Eureka, Florin, Folsom, Fresno, Frisco, Gilroy, Goleta, Graham, Irvine, Laguna, La Mesa, Lennox, Lomita, Lompoc, Madera, Marina, Merced, Newark, Novato, Oakley, Orange, Orcutt, Orinda, Oxnard, Perris, Pomona, Rialto, Santee, Sonoma, Sonora, Tulare, Tustin, Upland, Walnut **7** Alameda, Anaheim, Antioch, Arcadia, Ashland, Atwater, Banning, Barstow, Belmont, Benicia, Brawley, Burbank, Compton, Concord, Cypress, El Cajon, El Monte, Fontana, Fremont, Gardena, Hanford, Hayward, La Habra, La Presa, La Verne, Lemoore, Lynwood, Manteca, Maywood, Modesto, Norwalk, Oakland, Oildale, Ontario, Parkway, Redding, Reedley, Rocklin, Salinas, San Jose, Seaside, Stanton, Tarzana, Turlock, Valinda, Vallejo, Visalia, Windsor, Yucaipa **8** Alhambra, Altadena, Bay Point, Berkeley, Calexico, Campbell, Carlsbad, Cerritos, Coronado, Daly City, Danville, El Centro, Elk Grove, Fair Oaks, Florence, Glendale, Glendora, Hercules, Hesperia, Highland, Lakeside, Lakewood, La Mirada, La Puente, La Quinta, Lawndale, Los Altos, Los Banos, Los Gatos, Martinez, Millbrae, Milpitas, Monrovia, Monterey, Moorpark, Morro Bay, Murrieta, Pacifica, Palmdale, Palo Alto, Paradise, Pasadena, Petaluma, Redlands, Richmond, Rosemead, Rosemont, Rubidoux, San Bruno, San Diego, San Dimas, San Mateo, San Pablo, San Ramon, Santa Ana, Saratoga, Stockton, Temecula, Torrance, Westmont, Whittier, Woodland, Yuba City **9** Brentwood, Buena Park, Calabasas, Camarillo, Casa de Oro, Claremont, Coachella, Costa Mesa, Cupertino, Dana Point, El Cerrito, Encinitas, Escondido, Fairfield, Fallbrook, Fullerton, Hawthorne, Hollister, Inglewood, Isla Vista, Lafayette, Lancaster, Livermore, Long Beach, Los Nietos, Menlo Park, Montclair, Oceanside, Paramount, Pittsburg, Placentia, Riverside, Roseville, San Carlos, San Marcos, San Rafael, Santa Cruz, Santa Rosa, Seal Beach, South Gate, Sunnyvale, Union City, Vacaville **10** Aliso Viejo, Atascadero, Bellflower, Burlingame, Carmichael, Chino Hills, Chula Vista, Culver City, Diamond Bar, Foster City, Lake Forest, Lemon Grove, Los Angeles, Montebello, Morgan Hill, Mount Helix, Orangevale, Palm Desert, Pico Rivera, Pismo Beach, Pleasanton, Ridgecrest, Sacramento, San Gabriel, San Jacinto, San Leandro, San Lorenzo, Santa Clara, Santa Maria, Santa Paula, Simi Valley, Suisun City, Temple City, West Carson, West Covina, Yorba Linda
clock setting: **3** PDT, PST
cop grp.: **4** LAPD
county: **4** Inyo, lake, Napa **5** Marin **6** Orange
desert: **6** Mohave **7** Sonoran **11** Death Valley
fish: **7** alfiona, finspot, grunion, sculpin **8** halfmoon **10** yellowtail
former ~ congressman: **4** Bono
fort: **3** Ord
garlic center: **6** Gilroy
Indian: **4** Pomo, Yahi, Yana **5** Maidu, Miwok, Modoc, Piute, Washo, Wintu, Yurok **6** Mohave, Mojave, Paiute, Patwin, Wintun, Yokuts **7** Chumash **8** Cahuilla
industry: **4** film **6** cinema, movies
lake: **4** Mono **5** Tahoe **8** Lahontan **9** Salton Sea
motto: **6** Eureka
mountain: **4** Muir, Sill **5** Lyell **6** Lassen, Shasta, Wilson **7** Granite, Langley, Palomar, Russell, Tyndall, Whitney **8** Panamint **9** El Capitan **10** Williamson
national park: **7** Redwood, Sequoia **8** Yosemite **10** Joshua Tree
neighbor: **6** Mexico, Nevada, Oregon **7** Arizona
newspaper: **7** L.A. Times
peninsula: **4** Baja **8** Monterey
port: **7** Oakland **8** San Diego **10** Los Angeles
pro team: **5** Kings, the A's **6** Angels, Giants, Lakers, Niners, Padres, Sharks **7** Dodgers, Raiders **8** Chargers, Clippers, Warriors **9** Athletics **11** Mighty Ducks
racetrack: **6** Del Mar **10** Santa Anita
river: **3** Eel
school: **3** USC **4** UCLA **5** Menlo **6** Eureka **8** Stanford, Whittier **10** Pepperdine
seaside rte.: **3** PCH
state flower: **5** poppy
state gem: **9** benitoite
state marine fish: **9** garibaldi
state marine mammal: **9** gray whale
state mineral: **4** gold
state motto: **6** Eureka
state rock: **10** serpentine
state tree: **7** redwood
student: **5** UCLAn
tree: **5** toyon **7** redwood, sequoia
tribe: **4** Hupa **5** Wintu **6** Wintun
University of ~ campus: **5** Davis
volcano: **6** Lassen
waterfall: **7** Feather
wind: **8** Santa Ana
winery: **5** Gallo
wine valley: **4** Napa
California __: **3** Sun **4** gull, Love, mink, rose **5** Girls, poppy, quail, Suite **6** condor, laurel, nutmeg, privet **7** Current, oakworm, rosebay
__ California: **4** Alta, Baja **5** Hotel, Lower, Upper
California Dreamin' (1966 song) artist: Mamas & the Papas
California Girls (song) artist: Beach Boys, David Lee Roth
California, Here I Come! (1924 song)
artist: Al Jolson
composer: **5** Meyer
California Love (1996 song)
artist: Dr. Dre, Roger, Tupac
California Suite (1978 film)
cast: Alan Alda, Michael Caine, Bill Cosby, Jane Fonda, Walter Matthau, Elaine May, Richard Pryor, Maggie Smith
director: Herbert Ross
writer: Neil Simon
californium: **7** element
Calif.-to-Fla. route: **4** I-Ten
caliginous: **5** mirky, murky
Caligula: **5** Roman **6** Caesar
horse: **9** Incitatus
nephew: **4** Nero
Caligula author: Albert Camus
__ caliper: **6** inside **7** outside, vernier
caliph: **3** Ali **4** imam, male **5** imaum, ruler **6** gerent
Calisher, Hortense: **6** author, writer
Calista: **9** Flockhart
calisthenics: **7** workout **8** aerobics, exercise **9** athletics **10** daily dozen, gymnastics, isometrics
Calisto: **4** font **8** typeface
calix: **3** cup **7** chalice
Calixtus: **4** pope **7** pontiff
calk: **5** cleat
Calkiní: **4** city, town
locale: **6** Mexico **8** Campeche
Calkins, Mary: **11** philosopher
call: **3** cry, dub, tag **4** beep, dial, levy, name, need, page, peep, plea, ring, roar, term, wake, yell **5** alarm, bleat, cheep, chirp, guess, hallo, hillo, hullo, judge, label, phone, pop by, pop in, rally, rouse, run in, shout, style, title, tweet, visit, voice, waken **6** appeal, beckon, bellow, come by, cry out, demand, dial up, drop by, drop in, excuse, gather, halloa, halloo, hallow, hilloa, holler, hulloo, notice, notify, option, outcry, pursue, reason, reckon, ring up, signal, stop by, stop in, summon, warble **7** address, baptize, command, contact, convene, convoke, entitle, exclaim, grounds, intitle, predict, request, sing out, solicit, summons, swing by **8** announce, assemble, christen, come over, consider, estimate, nominate, occasion, proclaim, proposal, subpoena **9** designate, necessity, rehearsal, telephone, touch base **10** denominate, get a hold of, incitement, invitation, obligation, vociferate
a bet: **3** see
again, in poker: **5** resee
a halt to: **3** end **6** finish
a meeting: **6** gather, muster, summon **7** convene, convoke, marshal **8** assemble
at one's beck and ~: **5** ready
attention-getting ~: **2** yo **3** hey
attention to: **4** note **6** accent, advert, play up, stress **7** feature, mention, point up **8** point out **9** highlight, punctuate, spotlight, underline **10** underscore
back: **6** recant
bird ~: **3** caw **4** peep, pipe, twee **5** cheep, chirp, tweet **6** cuckoo **7** chirrup, twitter
bugle ~: **4** taps **8** reveille
cat ~: **3** mew **4** meow, yowl **5** miaou, miaow, miaul
cattle ~: **3** moo **7** meeting **9** interview
close ~: **5** brush **8** near miss
coin-toss ~: **5** heads, tails
director's ~: **3** cut **5** print **6** action
end a ~: **6** hang up
ender: **3** boy **4** back **5** board
for: **4** hail, need, page, take, want **5** claim, exact **6** demand, entail, invoke, pick up **7** request, warrant
(for): **3** ask
forth: **5** evoke **6** elicit, invoke **7** provoke **8** summon up
in: **6** recall, redeem **7** consult, convene
into question: **5** doubt **6** impugn, oppose **7** dispute **9** challenge
it a day: **3** end **4** halt, quit, stop **5** cease, close **6** finish, retire, turn in, wind up, wrap up **7** adjourn, break up **8** break off, conclude, finish up, knock off, pack it in **9** terminate

it quits: 4 stop 5 cease
make the ~: 6 decide
off: 3 end 4 drop 5 abort, scrub 6 cancel 7 abolish, retract
on: 3 ask 5 visit 6 drop by, invite, invoke 7 go to see 10 pay court to
on ~: 5 ready
one's own: 4 have 5 adopt
on the carpet: 5 chide 6 rebuke 8 admonish 9 reprimand
opposite: 3 put
out: 3 cry 5 shout 7 exclaim
partner: 4 beck
perhaps: 4 wake 5 waken 6 awaken
starter: 3 cat 4 bird
the shots: 4 boss, lead, rule 5 order 6 direct, govern, manage, settle 7 control, dictate, oversee 8 dominate 9 supervise
time: 5 pause 6 recess
to: 4 hail 6 summon 7 shout at 8 holler at, wave down
to account: 3 rag 5 blame, scold 6 rebuke 7 reprove 9 reprehend, reprimand 10 take to task
to arms: 5 alert, rally 6 alarum 7 recruit 8 mobilize
together: 6 muster 7 convoke 8 assemble
to mind: 5 think 6 recall, review 8 remember 9 recollect, visualize
trumpet ~: 7 fanfare, tantara 8 flourish
umpire: 3 out 4 balk, ball, foul, safe 6 strike
up: 4 dial, levy, ring 5 draft, evoke, phone, raise 6 enlist, muster, recall 7 convoke, recruit 8 activate, mobilize, remember 9 visualize
upon: 3 ask, use 4 pray, tell 5 visit 6 enjoin, exhort, invoke 7 require 10 fall back on
call __: 3 box, for, off, out 4 back, down, loan, rate, sign, slip, upon 5 forth, money, names 6 market, number, option 7 letters, waiting
call __ day: 3 it a
call __ question: 4 into
call __ to: 5 a halt
call-__: 5 board
__ call: 3 act 4 bird, cold, junk, mail, mess, open, roll, sick, toll, wolf 5 altar, close, crank, house, phone, trunk 6 cattle, margin, wake-up 7 collect, curtain
__-call: 4 will
Call __: 4 on Me
Call __ cab!: 3 me a
Call __ Wild, The: 5 of the
Callaghan, James: 2 P.M. 7 British
predecessor: 6 Wilson
successor: 8 Thatcher
Callaghan, Morley: 6 writer 8 Canadian
calla lily: 5 aroid, plant 6 flower
family: 4 arum
like a ~: 5 showy
milieu: 5 marsh
callaloo: 4 soup
ingredient: 4 crab 6 greens
Callan, Michael: 5 actor
film: Cat Ballou (1965)
The Interns (1962)
Lepke (1975)
You Must Be Joking! (1965)
Callao: 4 city, port, town
site: 4 Peru
Callas: 5 Maria 7 Charlie
Callas, Maria: 4 diva 6 singer 7 soprano
specialty: 4 aria 5 opera
called
also ~: 5 alias
for: 8 required 9 necessary
once ~: 3 née 4 born 8 formerly
called __: 6 strike
...called for his fiddlers __: 5 three
__ Called Horse: 4 A Man
__ Called To Say I Love You: 5 I Just
__ Called Wanda: 5 A Fish
__ Callender's: 5 Marie
caller: 5 guest 7 visitor 10 bell ringer
gentleman ~: 4 beau
identify a ~: 5 trace
play ~: 2 QB 11 quarterback
sports ~: 3 ref, ump 6 umpire 7 referee
__-caller: 4 name
callers: 7 company
accepting ~: 6 at home
calligrapher: 6 scribe
need: 3 ink, nib, pen 6 inkpot
calligraphy: 5 print 6 script 7 writing
line: 5 serif
calling: 3 gig, job 4 line, walk, work 5 craft, niche, trade 6 career, day job, métier, racket 7 mission, pursuit 8 business, lifework, vocation 9 life's work 10 occupation, profession, walk of life
a spade a spade: 6 candid
calling __: 4 card
__ calling: 4 Avon, cold
__-calling: 4 name
Calling all cars...: 3 APB
Calling America artist: 3 ELO
calliope: 8 keyboard 10 instrument
power: 5 steam
relative: 5 organ, piano
Calliope: 4 Muse
colleague: 4 Clio 5 Erato 6 Thalia, Urania 7 Euterpe 9 Melpomene 10 Polyhymnia 11 Terpsichore
lover of ~: 6 Apollo
parent of ~: 4 Zeus 9 Mnemosyne
son of ~: 5 Linus 7 Orpheus
Callisthenes: 5 Greek 11 philosopher
Callisto: 4 bear, moon
planet: 7 Jupiter
Callistus: 4 pope 7 pontiff
call it __: 4 a day 5 quits
Call It Love (1989 song) artist: Poco
Call It Sleep author: 4 Roth
Call Me __: 4 Anna 5 Bwana, Madam
Call Me Irresponsible composer: 4 Cahn 9 Van Heusen
Call Me Ishmael author: 5 Olson
Call Me Madam (1953 film): 7 musical
cast: Ethel Merman, Donald O'Connor
director: Walter Lang
inspiration: 5 Mesta
songwriter: 6 Berlin
__ Call Me MISTER Tibbs: 4 They
Call Me (song) artist: Al Green, Blondie, Johnny Mathis
Call Northside 777 (1948 film)
cast: Lee J. Cobb, Richard Conte, James Stewart
director: Henry Hathaway
Call of the Canyon author: Zane Grey
Call of the Toad, The author: Günter Grass
Call of the Wild, The: 4 film 5 novel
author: Jack London
cast: Clark Gable, Loretta Young
director: William Wellman
dog: 4 Buck, Dave 5 Spitz 7 Sol-leks
setting: 5 Yukon 6 Alaska
__ call on: 4 pay a
call one's __: 5 bluff
Call on Me (1974 song) artist: Chicago
callous: 4 hard, mean 5 cruel, harsh, nasty, stony, tough 6 animal, brutal, fierce, savage, stoney, unkind, wanton 7 beastly, coarsen, hurtful, roughen, vicious 8 barbaric, fiendish, hardened, indurate, inhumane, pitiless, ruthless, sadistic, uncaring, vengeful 9 cut-throat, ferocious, heartless, impassive, inclement, insensate, merciless, monstrous, truculent, unfeeling, unpitying, unstirred 10 hard-boiled, unaffected, vindictive
calloused, become: 6 harden
callow: 3 raw 4 naif 5 fresh, green, naive, young 6 boyish, jejune, tender 7 puerile 8 immature, juvenile, underage, untested, youthful 9 beardless, guileless, half-grown, untrained 10 sophomoric
one: 3 boy, cub, lad, pup 4 tiro, tyro 5 puppy, youth 6 novice 8 beginner 9 youngster 10 apprentice
Calloway: 3 Cab
callowness: 9 freshness, greenness, ignorance
call the __: 4 tune 5 shots
__ Call the Whole Thing Off: 4 Let's
__ Call the Wind Maria: 4 They
call to __: 4 arms, task 5 order 7 account
call-up: 5 draft, order 6 muster
org.: 3 SSS
status: 4 one A
__ call us...: 4 Don't
__ Call You Sweetheart: 5 Let Me
calm: 4 balm, cool, ease, easy, even, hush, lick, lull, mild, rest 5 allay, level, order, peace, poise, quell, quiet, relax, rural, sober, staid, still, stoic 6 defuse, defuze, gentle, hushed, low-key, mellow, pacify, placid, poised, repose, sedate, serene, settle, smooth, soften, soothe, stable, steady, temper 7 amiable, appease, assuage, at peace, bucolic, clement, compose, console, cool out, easeful, equable, halcyon, harmony, mollify, orderly, pacific, patient, placate, relaxed, relieve, restful, silence, stoical, unfazed 8 amicable, carefree, composed, coolness, inactive, in repose, laid-back, mitigate, moderate, pastoral, peaceful, quietude, rational, reassure, resigned, serenity, soothing, together, tranquil, waveless, windless 9 alleviate, bucolical, collected, composure, easygoing, impassive, nerveless, peaceable, placidity, quiescent, quiet down, quietness, reposeful, soft-pedal, soundless, stillness, stormless, temperate, unexcited, unextreme, unruffled, unstirred, unworried 10 coolheaded, dispassion, equanimity, harmonious, motionless, nonchalant, phlegmatic, placidness, propitiate, restrained, rippleless, sedateness, simmer down, stress-free, unaffected, unagitated, unbothered, untroubled
be ~: 5 relax
down: 4 lull, rest 5 quiet, relax 6 cool it, soothe, unwind 7 cool off 8 loosen up
in music: 7 placido
...calm, __ bright: 5 all is
__ Calm: 3 Sea 4 Dead
calmative: 5 bland 6 easing 7 anodyne 8 sedative
Calm down!: 4 easy 5 chill, relax 6 cool it 8 chill out
calming: 6 dreamy 8 narcotic 9 soporific
calmness: 4 ease, lull, rest 5 peace, poise, quiet, still 6 aplomb, repose, temper 7 concord, reserve 8 coolness, optimism, patience, presence, serenity 9 balminess, composure, placidity, quietness, sang-froid, stillness 10 dispassion, equanimity, moderation, steadiness
Cal. neighbor: 3 Nev., Ore., Pac. 4 Ariz.
caloric in ads, less: 4 lite
caloricity: 4 heat 8 warmness
calorie: 4 unit
counters' retreat: 3 spa
cousin: 3 BTU
__ calorie: 4 gram 5 empty, large, small
calories
count ~: 4 diet
loaded with ~: 4 rich
needing ~: 6 hungry
calorify: 4 heat 6 heat up
Calpulalpan: 4 city, town
locale: 6 Mexico 8 Tlaxcala
Calpurnia husband: 6 Caesar
Cal Tech
grad: 2 EE 3 Eng. 4 engr.
rival: 3 MIT
caltrop: 3 nut
Calumet City: 4 town
locale: 8 Illinois
calumniate: 3 hit 4 gibe, jeer, jibe, mock, slam, slur, snub 5 abuse, belie, decry, libel, scorn, smear, spurn, sully, taunt 6 defame, deride, dump on, heckle, impugn, malign, offend, rebuff, revile, slight, smirch, vilify 7 affront, asperse, blacken, degrade, disdain, put down, rank out, rip into, run down, slander, spatter, traduce 8 backbite, badmouth, belittle, denounce, ridicule, tear down, throw mud, vilipend 9 denigrate, discredit, disparage, humiliate 10 depreciate, disrespect, stigmatize
calumnious: 8 critical, libelous 9 invidious 10 defamatory, derogatory
calumny: 3 dig, lie 4 barb, blot, gibe, jibe, slam, slap, slur, snub 5 abuse, libel, scorn, taunt 6 attack, rebuff, slight, smrich 7 affront, catcall, disdain, mockery, obloquy, offense, put-down, slander, untruth 8 contempt, derision, reproach, ridicule 9 aspersion, cheap shot, contumely 10 backbiting, defamation, derogation, devalution, disrespect, impugnment, imputation, opprobrium, revilement
calvados: 5 drink 8 beverage
Calvados' capital: 4 Caen
Calvary __: 5 cross
Calvé, Emma: 6 singer 7 soprano
specialty: 5 opera
Calvert: 8 DeForest
calves: 5 young 6 cattle
bearer of ~: 3 cow 5 whale
calves' __: 5 liver
Calvet, Corinne: 7 actress
film: The Far Country (1955)
On the Riviera (1951)
Rope of Sand (1949)
Sailor Beware (1951)
Calvillo: 4 city, town
locale: 6 Mexico
Calvin: 4 John 5 Klein, Peete 6 Melvin, Murphy 7 Trillin 8 Coolidge
Calvin and Hobbes: 5 comic, strip 7 cartoon 10 comic strip
character: 3 Moe 5 Susie
tiger: 6 Hobbes
Calvin Klein competitor: 4 DKNY, Polo 5 Guess, Karan 6 Armani, Lauren
Calvin, Melvin: 7 chemist 8 Nobelist
Calvino, Italo: 6 author, writer 7 Italian
work: Cosmicomics
Invisible Cities
Mr. Palomar
calx: 5 oxide 9 quicklime
Calydon, king of: 6 Oeneus
calypso: 5 music, plant 6 flower
kin: 3 ska 4 soca
standard: 4 Dayo
Calypso: 4 moon 5 nymph
father of ~: 5 Atlas
planet: 6 Saturn
Calypso (1975 song) artist: Denver
calyx leaf: 5 sepal
cam: 3 cog 7 trippet 8 auto part
ender: 5 shaft 6 corder
__ cam: 5 heart 6 rocker
__-cam: 3 sky

Cam: 5 Neely, river
River locale: 7 England
camaca: 6 fabric 8 material
Camacho: 5 Avila 6 Hector
Camagüey: 4 city, town
locale: 4 Cuba
camaka: 6 fabric 8 material
camaraderie: 5 amity, cheer 7 jollity, society 8 intimacy
Camargo: 4 city, town
locale: 6 Mexico 9 Chihuahua
Camargue: 3 car 4 auto 10 Rolls-Royce
Camarillo: 4 city, town
locale: 10 California
Camaro: 3 car 4 auto, IROC 5 Chevy 9 Chevrolet 10 automobile
camass: 4 bulb 5 plant 6 flower
Camay: 4 soap
alternative: 3 Lux 4 Dial, Dove, Lava, Tone, Zest 5 Coast, Ivory, Lever 6 Boraxo, Caress, Shield 8 Lifebuoy 9 Palmolive, Safeguard 11 Irish Spring
camber: 4 bend, flex 5 curve, slant, toe-in 9 sinuosity
Cambodia: 6 nation 7 country
bovine: 7 kouprey
capital: 9 Phnom Penh
continent: 4 Asia
lake: 8 Tonle Sap
language: 5 Khmer
money: 3 sen 4 riel
neighbor: 4 Laos 7 Vietnam 8 Thailand
temple: 3 wat
Cambodian: 5 Asian, Khmer
neighbor: 3 Lao, Tai 4 Thai
Cambrian: 3 Era
Cambrian Mountains site: 5 Wales
cambric: 3 tea 5 linen 6 fabric
Cambridge: 3 car 4 auto, city, town 7 Godfrey 8 Plymouth 10 automobile
academic: 3 don 5 tutor
athletes: 7 Crimson
exam: 6 tripos
grad: 2 EE 3 eng. 4 engr.
locale: 4 Mass. 6 Canada 7 England, Ontario
school: 3 MIT 7 Harvard
student: 6 Cantab
Cambridgeshire: 6 county
locale: 7 England
Cambs: 6 county
locale: 7 England
camcorder
attachment: 3 VCR
button: 3 rec 5 focus 6 record
format: 3 VHS 4 Beta
maker: 4 Sony
use a ~: 4 tape
Camden: 4 city, town
locale: 9 New Jersey
Camden Yards: 5 arena 7 stadium 8 ballpark
player: 6 Oriole
see also baseball
came
I ~: 4 veni
to rest: 3 lit 4 alit
___ came a spider...: 5 Along
___ Came Bronson: 4 Then
___ Came C.O.D., The: 5 Bride
___ Came Home: 5 Sunny, Three
camel: 3 tan 5 brown, mount 6 animal, mammal 8 Bactrian 9 dromedary, yellowish
backbreaker: 5 straw
cousin: 5 llama 6 alpaca, vicuna 7 guanaco
driver's command: 5 kneel
ender: 4 back
execute a ~: 5 skate
feature: 4 hoof, hump
female: 3 cow
fermented ~ milk: 6 kumiss
go by ~: 4 ride
in India: 4 oont
male: 4 bull
metaphorically: 4 ship
milieu: 3 ice 4 rink 5 oasis 6 desert, Sahara 7 caravan
relative: 3 bay, dun, tan 4 bole, buff, ecru, fawn, foxy, nude, seal 5 amber, beige, cocoa, hazel, khaki, mocha, sepia, tawny, umber 6 almond, auburn, bister, bistre, bronze, coffee, copper, ginger, russet, sienna, sorrel, suntan, walnut 7 biscuit, caramel, dogwood 8 chestnut, cinnamon, mahogany 9 butternut, chocolate
young: 4 calf
camel ___: 3 hay 4 spin 5 grass 7 cricket
___ Camel: 7 Sopwith
camelhair fabric: 3 aba 4 abba
camellia: 5 plant, shrub 6 flower
Camellia State: 3 Ala. 7 Alabama
Camelot: 7 musical
actor: 4 Nero 6 Harris 8 Redgrave
songwriter: 5 Loewe 6 Lerner
camel's ___ coat: 4 hair
camel walk: 5 dance
Camembert: 6 cheese, French
cousin: 4 Brie
cameo: 3 bit 4 part, role 6 walk-on 7 bit part, jewelry 8 anaglyph
do a ~: 3 act 7 perform
make a ~: 6 emboss 7 engrave
shape: 4 oval
stone: 4 onyx
cameo ___: 4 role, ware 5 glass
camera: 3 SLR 4 Fuji 5 Canon, Kodak, Leica, Nikon, Ricoh 6 Konica, Pentax, Rollei 7 Brownie, Minolta, Olympus, Vivitar, Yashica 8 Polaroid
activate a ~: 6 expose
adjust a ~: 5 focus
ender: 3 man, men 5 woman, women 6 person 7 persons
filler: 4 film
follower: 6 action
lens scope: 5 field
lens shield: 4 gobo
part: 4 iris, lens, zoom 5 flash
prepare for the ~: 3 mug 4 pose
setting: 5 f-stop, speed, t-stop
shot: 6 fade-in 7 closeup
wheels: 5 dolly
camera ___: 4 tube 6 lucida 7 obscura
camera-___: 3 shy 5 ready
___ camera: 3 box, gun 4 disc, disk, view 5 gamma, Kodak, sound, video 6 candid, reflex 7 instant, pinhole
___-camera: 3 off
___ Camera: 4 I Am a 6 Candid
Cameron: 4 Diaz, Kirk, peak 5 Crowe, James, mount 8 Mitchell, mountain
locale: 7 Rockies 8 Colorado
Cameron, James: 8 director
film: The Abyss (1989)
Aliens (1986)
The Terminator (1984)
Titanic (1997, AA)
True Lies (1994)
spouse: Suzy Amis, Kathryn Bigelow, Linda Hamilton
___ Cameron Swayze: 4 John
Cameroon: 6 nation 7 country
bovine: 4 Kuri
capital: 7 Yaoundé
city: 5 Duala, Kaélé, Kumba 6 Douala, Garoua, Maroua 7 Bamenda, Yaoundé 9 Bafoussam
lake: 4 Chad, Nios, Nyos
locale: 3 Afr. 6 Africa
money: 5 franc
neighbor: 4 Chad 5 Congo, Gabon, Gabun 7 Nigeria
people: 3 Fan 4 Fang, Fula 6 Fulani, Kanuri, Pangwe 7 Pahouin
port: 5 Duala 6 Douala
river: 5 Benue
volcano: 3 Oku
writer: 4 Beti
___ Cameroons: 6 French 7 British
___ Came Running: 4 Some
___ Came, The: 5 Rains
___ Came You: 4 Then
Camiletti: 3 Rob
Camilla: 5 Sparv 8 asteroid
Camilla Parker-___: 6 Bowles
Camille: 4 film 5 novel 7 Pisarro 8 Pissarro 10 Saint-Saëns
author: Alexandre Dumas
cast: Lionel Barrymore, Greta Garbo, Robert Taylor
director: George Cukor
love: 6 Armand
see also French
Camillo: 5 Golgi
Camino Real author: Tennessee Williams
camion: 4 dray
camise: 5 shirt, smock
camisole: 5 shift 8 lingerie
camlet: 6 marble
camoca: 6 fabric 8 material
Camoes, Luis de: 4 poet 10 Portuguese
camomile: 3 tea
camouflage: 4 hide, lure, mask, veil 5 blind, cache, cloak, couch, cover, guise, shade 6 screen, shroud 7 conceal, obscure, secrete 8 disguise 9 dissemble, obfuscate 10 keep secret, masquerade, red herring
color: 5 green
one in ~: 5 hider
wearer: 6 hunter 7 soldier 8 commando
camouflaged: 6 covert, hidden, secret, unseen 7 furtive, private 8 hush-hush 10 undercover, under wraps
camp: 3 set 4 arch, base, sect, side, tent, wild 5 droll, étape, farce, lodge, weird 6 far-out, resort 7 bivouac, bizarre, comical, faction, jocular, Lejeune, lodging, rough it 8 affected, barracks, garrison, humorous 9 laughable, Pendleton 10 artificial, pitch a tent, theatrical
berth: 3 cot
boss: 2 CO
break ~: 5 leave 6 depart
cousin: 6 kitsch
craft: 5 canoe
employee: 4 cook
ender: 4 fire, oree, site 5 stool 6 ground
fixture: 4 tent
meal: 4 mess
name meaning ~: 7 Chester
opposite ~: 3 foe 5 enemy
order: 4 halt 5 march 6 at ease
prison ~: 5 gulag
routine: 5 drill
set up ~: 4 tent 5 pitch, roost
camp ___: 3 bed, car, out 4 it up 5 chair, shirt, stove 6 robber 7 meeting
___ camp: 3 day 4 base, boot, work 5 break, honor, sugar 6 strike, summer 7 trailer
___-camp: 5 aid-de 6 aide-de
Camp: 3 Joe 6 Walter 7 Colleen
Camp ___: 5 David 6 Swampy 7 Lejeune
Camp ___ Accords: 5 David
Camp ___ Girl: 4 Fire
___ Camp: 5 Space
Campagna di ___: 4 Roma
campaign: 3 bid 4 push, race 5 drive, fight, lobby, quest, stump 6 attack, battle 7 canvass, crusade, promote, tactics, warfare 8 movement, politick 9 barnstorm, offensive, operation 10 enterprise, expedition
button word: 4 vote 5 elect 7 reelect
campaign ___: 3 hat 4 fund 5 chest, medal 6 button, ribbon
donor: 3 PAC 6 fat cat
for: 7 support 8 advocate
(for): 3 run 5 lobby, stump 7 contend
political ~: 3 bid 4 race
pro: 3 pol 10 politician
promises: 8 platform
staffer: 4 aide
tactic: 3 mud 5 smear 6 attack, debate 7 slander
topic: 5 crime, issue 7 defense, economy
___ campaign: 5 smear
campaigner: 7 warrior 8 advocate, crusader, reformer 10 politician
corporate ~: 5 adman
campaign name
of 1936: 3 Alf
of 1952/1956: 3 Ike 5 Adlai
of 1992: 4 Bill, Ross
of 1996: 3 Bob 4 Bill, Dole, Ross
Campanella: 3 Joe, Roy
Campanella, Roy: 6 Dodger 7 catcher, slugger
teammate: 5 Reese 6 Hodges, Snider 8 Newcombe, Robinson
Campania
city: 4 Nola 6 Amalfi, Naples, Napoli 7 Salerno
locale: 5 Italy 6 Italia
stream: 4 Sele
campanile: 5 tower 7 steeple 8 pinnacle
feature: 4 bell
Campari: 5 drink 8 beverage
Campbell: 3 Kim 4 Earl, Glen, Neve, town 5 Naomi, Scott, Tevin, Tisha 6 Luther, Thomas
Campbell, Earl sport: 8 football
Campbell, Glen
song: By the Time I Get to Phoenix (1967)
Galveston (1969)
Gentle on My Mind (1968)
It's Only Make Believe (1970)
Rhinestone Cowboy (1975)
Southern Nights (1977)
Wichita Lineman (1968)
Campbell, Kim: 2 P.M. 8 Canadian
predecessor: 8 Mulroney
successor: 8 Chrétien
___ Campbell, KY: 4 Fort
Campbell, Neve: 7 actress
film: Drowning Mona (2000)
Panic (2000)
Scream (1996)
Wild Things (1998)
TV: Party of Five
Campbell River: 4 city, town
locale: 6 Canada
___ Campbell Scott: 6 Duncan
Campbell Soup: 7 company
competitor: 5 Knorr 9 Progresso
headquarters: 6 Camden
Campbell, Thomas: 4 poet 8 Scottish
Camp David Accords: 4 pact 6 treaty
conferee: 5 Begin, Sadat 6 Carter
nation: 5 Egypt 6 Israel
Campeche: 4 city, gulf, town 5 state
city: 6 Carmen 7 Calkiní 9 Champotón, Escárcega
locale: 6 Mexico
camper: 2 RV 9 Winnebago 10 mobile home
driver: 4 RVer
fuel: 3 LPG
relative: 3 van
___ camper: 5 happy, truck 6 pickup
campfire
remains: 5 ashes
starter: 5 spark

treat: 5 frank, Smore 6 hot dog, weiner
Camp Fire __: 4 Girl
campground: 4 site
convenience: 6 hookup
initials: 3 KOA
camphor: 4 tree
relative: 6 laurel 7 avocado 8 cinnamon 9 sassafras
camphor __: 3 ice, oil 4 ball, tree
__ camphor: 5 anise 6 Borneo 7 Malayan, Sumatra
Campinas: 4 city, town
locale: 6 Brazil
camping: 5 sport
__ campion: 4 moss, rose 5 white 7 bladder, evening
Campion: 4 Jane 6 Thomas
film: 8 The Piano
Campion, Thomas: 4 poet 7 British
Camp Meeting, The composer: 4 Ives
campo: 3 lea, ley 5 veldt 7 lowland, prairie 9 grassland
Campobello: 3 isl. 4 isle 6 island
locale: 6 Canada
monogram: 3 FDR
Campo Grande: 4 city, town
locale: 6 Brazil
camporee
attendee: 5 Scout 8 Boy Scout
unit: 4 tent
Camptown Races composer: 6 Foster
campus: 4 quad 7 grounds 10 university
cheer: 3 rah
disruption: 5 sit-in
facility: 3 gym, lab 4 dorm, hall, quad
like ~ walls: 5 ivied
misfit: 4 nerd, nurd
organization: 3 sor. 4 frat 6 Hillel 8 sorority 10 fraternity
outcast: 4 nerd, nurd
person: 4 dean, prof 6 bursar
sports org.: 4 NCAA
starter: 5 hippo
student: 4 BMOC, coed 5 frosh 6 junior, senior 8 freshman 9 sophomore
see also college
__-campus: 3 off
campy: 4 zany 5 banal, droll, funky, witty 6 absurd 7 blatant 8 affected, humorous, mannered, overdone 9 laughable 10 artificial, outlandish, theatrical
exclamation: 3 oof, pow 5 zowie
perhaps: 5 retro
Camry: 3 car 4 auto 6 Toyota
Camryn: 7 Manheim
Camus, Albert: 6 French, writer 8 Nobelist 10 playwright
birthplace: Algeria
work: Caligula
Cross Purpose
The Fall
L'Etranger
The Myth of Sisyphus
No Exit
The Plague
The Rebel
State of Siege
The Stranger
can: 2 ax 3 axe, tin 4 boot, drop, fire, jail, john, oust, poky, sack 5 expel, let go, pokey, put up, store 6 bounce, lay off, lockup, pickle, prison, record, vessel 7 cashier, deep-six, dismiss, drum out, hoosgow, kick out, latrine, package, process, release, slammer, turn out 8 furlough, get rid of, hoosegow, pink-slip, preserve 9 container, discharge, terminate
combining form: 5 scyph- 6 scyphi-, scypho-
covering: 5 label
do what one ~: 3 try 6 strive 7 attempt, have a go, venture 9 have a go at, have a shot, have a stab 10 have a whack
it: 5 quiet 6 shut up
of worms: 7 problem 9 adversity
opener: 3 tab 6 gadget
opener target: 3 lid
producer: 5 Alcoa
can __: 4 buoy 6 opener
__ can: 3 ash, oil, tin 5 blitz, jerry, spray, trash 6 squirt 7 aerosol, garbage
Can __ Top This?: 3 You
Can __ you?: 5 I help
Can.
currency: 3 dol.
neighbor: 3 Ida., USA 4 Alas., Mich., Minn., Mont., N. Dak., Wash.
police force: 4 RCMP
province: 3 Alb., Man., Nfd., Ont., PEI 4 Alba., Alta., Newf., Nfld., Sask.
region: 3 NWT
see also Canada
__ Can: 4 Yes I
Canaan
deity: 4 Baal
father of ~: 3 Ham
grandfather of ~: 4 Noah
land of ~: 6 Israel
canada: 5 cañon 6 canyon 8 riverbed
Canada: 3 Lee 6 nation 7 country
agreement with ~: 5 NAFTA
alphabet ender: 3 zed
Arctic explorer: 3 Rae
baseballer: 4 Expo 7 Blue Jay
bay: 5 Fundy, James 6 Baffin, Hudson, Ungava 8 Georgian 9 Frobisher
bird: 4 loon 5 goose
bird on a ~ $1 coin: 4 loon
capital: 6 Ottawa
city: 4 Ajax, Alma, Amos, Baie, Faro, Hull, Mayo, Olds 5 Anjou, Craik, Delta, Elgin, Hanna, Kaslo, Laval, Leduc, Lévis, Lumby, Rouyn, Sooke, Sorel, St. Luc, Taber, Truro, Unity 6 Argyle, Aurora, Aylmer, Barrie, Birtle, Brigus, Comeau, Dundas, Fernie, Granby, Guelph, Inuvik, Kanata, La Baie, London, Milton, Nepean, Onoway, Oshawa, Ottawa, Pictou, Québec, Regina, Sarnia, Scugog, Souris, Ste.-Foy, St. John, Surrey, The Pas, Val-d'Or, Verdun, Vernon, Whitby 7 Avonlea, Baddeck, Botwood, Brandon, Burnaby, Caledon, Calgary, Cap-Pele, Chambly, Chatham, Eastend, Grimsby, Halifax, Iqaluit, Kelowna, Lachine, Langley, La Salle, Lincoln, Markham, Melfort, Mirabel, Mission, Moncton, Nanaimo, Nipawin, Noranda, Old Crow, Orillia, Osoyoos, Red Deer, Saanich, St. John's, Sudbury, Timmins, Tisdale, Toronto, Vaughan, Welland, Weyburn, Windsor, Wynyard, Yorkton 8 Alberton, Ancaster, Beauport, Bradford, Brampton, Brossard, Carcross, Cornwall, Edmonton, Flin Flon, Fort Erie, Gatineau, Georgina, Hamilton, Hay River, Kamloops, Keno City, Kingston, Montréal, Moose Jaw, New Minas, North Bay, Oakville, Richmond, Rimouski, Sept-Iles, St. Albert, Ste.-Julie, St.-Hubert, St.-Jérôme, St. Thomas, Victoria, Waterloo, Winnipeg 9 Brantford, Cambridge, Coquitlam, Côte-St.-Luc, Dartmouth, Haldimand, Innisfail, Jonquière, Kitchener, Longueuil, Mascouche, Miramichi, Nanticoke, Newmarket, Outremont, Owen Sound, Penticton, Pickering, Port Elgin, Port Moody, Sackville, Saskatoon, St.-Georges, St.-Lambert, St.-Laurent, St.-Léonard, Stratford, Val-Belair, Vancouver, Westmount, Woodstock 10 Abbotsford, Belleville, Blainville, Boisbriand, Brockville, Burlington, Cape Breton, Chicoutimi, Chilliwack, Clarington, Cumberland, Dawson City, Gloucester, Lethbridge, Maple Ridge, Mount Lorne, Mount Pearl, New Glasgow, Repentigny, Sherbrooke, St.-Constant, Ste.-Thérèse, St.-Eustache, Strathcona, Terrebonne, Thunder Bay, Whitchurch, Whitehorse
coat: 7 kuletuk
conductor: 9 Pelletier
critic: 7 McLuhan
explorer: 9 Champlain
flag feature: 4 leaf 9 maple leaf
fliers: 4 RCAF
footballer: 6 Eskimo
gulf: 7 Boothia 10 St. Lawrence
Indian: 3 Han 4 Cree 5 Haida, Kaska 6 Abnaki, Micmac, Nootka, Ottawa 7 Abenaki, Kutchin, Kutenai, Naskapi, Tlingit 8 Kwakiutl, Malecite, Wabanaki 9 Saulteaux, Tsimshian 10 Assiniboin, Bellabella, Bellacoola
island: 6 Baffin 8 Victoria 9 Ellesmere, Vancouver
lake: 4 Erie 5 Huron, Rainy 6 Louise, Simcoe 7 Nipigon, Ontario 8 Manitoba, Michigan, Superior, Winnipeg 9 Athabasca, Great Bear 10 Great Slave
language: 6 French 7 English
leader: 2 p.m.
legislature: 6 Senate
money: 4 cent, dime 5 penny 6 dollar, loonie, toonie 7 quarter, twoonie
mountain: 4 King 5 Logan, Walsh 6 Robson, Steele 7 Lucania, Rockies, St. Elias 8 Caubvick, Columbia
native: 5 Inuit 6 Innuit, Inupik
neighbor: 3 Ida., USA 4 Alas., Mich., Minn., Mont., N. Dak., Wash. 5 Idaho, Maine 6 Alaska 7 Montana, New York, Vermont 8 Michigan 10 Washington 11 North Dakota, South Dakota 12 New Hampshire
Nobelist in Chemistry: 5 Taube 6 Marcus 7 Polanyi 8 Herzberg
Nobelist in Economics: 7 Mundell, Scholes, Vickrey
Nobelist in Medicine: 7 Banting
Nobelist in Peace: 7 Pearson
Nobelist in Physics: 6 Taylor 10 Brockhouse
org.: 3 OAS 4 NATO
pianist: 5 Gould 8 Peterson
pie: 5 rappe 6 rappie
poet: 4 Page 5 Blais, Dudek, Klein, Pratt, Purdy, Scott, Smith 6 Avison, Carman, Hébert 7 Garneau, Newlove, Service, Souster 8 Sangster 9 Choquette, Fréchette, Grandbois, Gustafson
police force: 4 RCMP
political party: 3 Lib. 7 Liberal
port: 7 Halifax, Toronto 8 Montreal 9 Churchill, Vancouver 10 Thunder Bay
province: 3 Alb., Man., Nfd., Ont., PEI, Que. 4 Alba., Alta., Newf., Nfld., Sask. 6 Quebec 7 Alberta, Nunavut, Ontario 8 Manitoba 10 Nova Scotia 12 New Brunswick, Newfoundland, Saskatchewan 15 British Columbia
region: 5 Gaspé, Yukon 6 Acadia
river: 4 Nass 5 Liard, Peace, Slave, Yukon 6 Fraser, Nelson, Ottawa, St. John, Thelon 7 Niagara, St. Clair 8 Columbia, Hamilton, Klondike, Kootenay, Saguenay 9 Churchill, Mackenzie, Richelieu 10 Coppermine, St. Lawrence
Rockies park: 5 Banff
school: 3 TWU 4 York 5 Brock, Laval, Trent 6 Acadia, McGill, Queen's 7 Bishop's, Brandon, Ryerson 8 Carleton, Lakehead, McMaster, Memorial 9 Concordia, Dalhousie
sea: 8 Labrador 9 Hudson Bay
town official: 5 reeve
tree: 5 maple
valley: 5 droke
waterfall: 5 Della 7 Niagara, Panther
wildcat: 4 lynx
writer: 3 Roy 5 Blais, Engel, Moore, Mowat, Munro, Wiebe 6 Atwood, Davies, Moodie, Nowlan, Parker, Wilson 7 Findley, Gallant, McLuhan, Richter 9 Callaghan 10 Haliburton, Montgomery
Canada __: 3 Act, Day, Dry, jay 4 lily, lynx 5 goose 6 balsam 7 hemlock, thistle
__ Canada: 3 Air 5 Lower, Upper
Canada Day month: 4 July
Canada Dry: 4 soda 9 soft drink
alternative: 3 TAB 4 Nehi 5 Fanta 6 Fresca, Sprite 8 Diet Rite, Dr Pepper 10 Mello Yello, Royal Crown
Canada goose: 4 fowl
relative: 4 nene 5 brant 7 graylag
Canada prime ministers:
2003– Paul Martin
1993–2003 Jean Chrétien
1993 Kim Campbell
1984–1993 Brian Mulroney
1984 John Turner
1980–1984 Pierre Trudeau
1979–1980 Joe Clark
1968–1979 Pierre Trudeau
1963–1968 Lester Pearson
1957–1963 John Diefenbaker
1948–1957 Louis St. Laurent
1935–1948 W.L. Mackenzie King
1930–1935 Richard Bennett
1926–1930 W.L. Mackenzie King
1926 Arthur Meighen
1921–1926 W.L. Mackenzie King
1920–1921 Arthur Meighen
1911–1920 Sir Robert Laird Borden
1896–1911 Sir Wilfrid Laurier
1896 Sir Charles Tupper
1894–1896 Sir Mackenzie Bowell
1892–1894 Sir John Thompson
1891–1892 Sir John Abbott
1878–1891 Sir John MacDonald
1873–1878 Alexander Mackenzie
1867–1873 Sir John MacDonald
Canadian: 5 river
locale: 8 Oklahoma 9 New Mexico
Canadian __: 5 bacon, Falls, goose 6 French, Legion, Shield, Sunset, whisky 7 English, hemlock, soldier
__ Canadian: 5 Royal 6 French, native 7 English
Canadian Bacon (1995 film)
cast: Alan Alda, John Candy, Rhea Perlman, Kevin Pollak
director: Michael Moore
Canadian Sunset (1956 song)
artist: Andy Williams, Eddie Heywood, Hugo Winterhalter
Canadien: 6 iceman
rival: 4 Blue, King, Star, Wild 5 Bruin, Devil, Flame, Flyer, Oiler, Sabre, Shark 6 Canuck, Coyote, Ranger 7 Capital, Panther, Penguin, Red Wing, Senator 8 Islander, Predator, Thrasher 9 Avalanche, Blackhawk, Hurricane, Lightning, Maple Leaf 10 Blue Jacket, Mighty Duck

Canadiens: 3 six 4 team
home: 8 Montreal
milieu: 3 ice 4 rink
org.: 3 NHL
sport: 6 hockey
canaille: 3 mob 6 rabble
canal: 4 duct, Erie, Göta, Kiel, Suez 5 Grand 6 artery, course, groove, Panama, Rideau, trench, trough 7 channel, conduit, passage, Welland 8 aqueduct, waterway 10 passageway
anatomical ~: 4 iter 5 lumen
bank: 4 berm 5 berme
feature: 4 lock
sight: 5 barge 7 gondola
site: 3 ear 4 root 5 tooth 7 isthmus
__ canal: 3 ear 4 root, ship 5 resin 6 spinal 7 lateral
Canal __: 4 Zone
__ Canal: 4 Erie, Kiel, Suez 5 Grand 6 Panama
__ Canals: 3 Soo
Canandaigua: 4 lake
locale: 7 New York
Cananea: 4 city, town
locale: 6 Mexico, Sonora
canapé: 4 nosh, sofa 5 snack, taste 7 munchie 9 appetizer 10 finger food
topping: 3 lox, roe 4 pâté 6 caviar, cheese, salmon 7 caviare
canard: 4 hoax, tale 5 rumor, story 6 report 7 falsity, untruth, whapper, whopper 9 falsehood
__ Canaria Island: 4 Gran
canary: 3 pet 4 bird, fink, nark, wine 5 color, dance, finch 6 singer, yellow 7 stoolie, tattler 8 informer, songbird 9 informant 10 taleteller, tattletale
bill: 3 nib
home: 4 cage 6 aviary
imitate a ~: 4 sing 6 warble
relative: 4 buff, corn, gold, lime, rust, sand 5 blond, brass, coral, cream, flaxy, lemon, maize, ocher, ochre, peach, rusty, serin, straw 6 blonde, chammy, citron, crocus, flaxen, shammy, shamoy 7 apricot, chamois, citrine, jasmine, mustard, nankeen, old gold, saffron, xanthic 8 daffodil, primrose 9 champagne, goldenrod, jessamine
seat: 5 perch
sound: 5 tweet
canary __: 4 seed 5 grass 6 yellow
Canary: 4 isls. 5 David, isles 7 islands
Canary Islands
island: 5 Palma 6 Hierro 7 La Palma 8 Tenerife 9 Teneriffe
owner: 5 Spain
port: 9 Las Palmas
canasta: 4 game 8 card game
cousin: 3 gin
holding: 4 meld, trey
Canatlán: 4 city, town
locale: 6 Mexico 7 Durango
Canaveral: 4 cape
org.: 4 NASA
__ Can Be Beautiful: 4 Life
Canberra: 4 city, town 7 capital
locale: 9 Australia
river: 8 Molonglo
__ can be told!: 5 Now it
__ Can Boyd: 3 Oil
Canby: 7 Vincent
cancan: 5 dance
do the ~: 4 kick
like ~ dancers: 5 leggy
Can-Can (1960 film): 7 musical
cast: Maurice Chevalier, Louis Jourdan, Shirley MacLaine, Frank Sinatra
composer: Cole Porter
director: Walter Lang
setting: 5 Paris 6 France
__ Can Can: 5 Yes We
cancel: 2 ax 3 axe, nix, zap 4 drop, kill, lift, undo, void, X out 5 abort, annul, erase, quash, remit, scrap, scrub 6 delete, efface, negate, offset, recall, recant, refute, repeal, revoke 7 abolish, call off, expunge, nullify, redress, rescind, retract, reverse, scratch, torpedo, wipe out 8 abrogate, break off, close out, cross out, disallow, dissolve, override, overrule, set aside, write off 9 discharge, eliminate, liquidate, repudiate, strike out, terminate 10 balance out, counteract, invalidate, neutralize, scratch out
a launch: 5 scrub
out: 6 negate, offset, refute 8 outweigh 10 compensate, counteract
(out): 5 equal
canceled: 3 off 4 no-go, void
canceled check notation: 3 NSF 4 paid
cancellation: 6 recall 7 receipt
avoid ~: 5 renew
Cancer: 4 crab, sign
month: 3 Jul., Jun. 4 July, June
predecessor: 6 Gemini
successor: 3 Leo
Cancer Ward author: Solzhenitsyn
Canchim: 3 cow 4 bull 6 bovine, cattle
__ Can Cook: 3 Yan
Cancún: 4 city, town
locale: 6 Mexico
see also Spanish
candescence: 6 luster
Candice: 6 Bergen
father: 5 Edgar
candid: 4 naif, open 5 bluff, blunt, brusk, frank, naive, photo, plain 6 abrupt, direct, honest 7 brusque, genuine, natural, sincere, up-front, upright 8 impolite, out-front, snapshot, straight, tactless, truthful, unartful 9 downright, guileless, impartial, ingenuous, outspoken, unfeigned, unguarded, unslanted 10 aboveboard, flat-footed, forthright, foursquare, free-spoken, from the hip, indelicate, point-blank, unaffected, unmediated, unreserved, unreticent
be ~: 5 level
don't be ~: 3 haw, hem 10 equivocate
Candid __: 6 Camera
Candida: 4 font 8 typeface
Candida (1970 song) artist: Tony Orlando & Dawn
Candida author: Shaw
candidate: 6 runner, seeker 7 entrant, hopeful, nominee 8 aspirant, opponent, prospect 9 applicant, appointee, contender, dark horse, job-hunter, pothunter, successor 10 competitor, contestant, handshaker, petitioner, solicitant
be a ~: 3 run
concern: 5 issue, slate, voter 6 ballot, debate
successful ~: 2 in
candidates: 5 field
Candidate, The (1972 film)
cast: Peter Boyle, Don Porter, Robert Redford
director: Michael Ritchie
Candid Camera (ABC/NBC/CBS comedy)
host: Allen Funt, Peter Funt
plant: 4 mike
request: 5 smile
Candide author: Voltaire
candidly: 4 true 5 truly 6 as it is, openly, simply 8 directly, straight 9 naturally, sincerely 10 point-blank
candied: 5 glacé, sweet 6 honied, sugary 7 honeyed, sugared 8 cajoling 9 adulatory 10 flattering, saccharine
candied __: 3 yam
candle: 5 light, taper 6 bougie, shames 7 shammes 8 bayberry 9 luminaria
circler: 4 moth
count: 3 age
ender: 3 nut, pin 4 fish, wick, wood 5 berry, light, power, stick 6 holder 7 snuffer
holder: 4 cake 6 sconce
ingredient: 3 wax 4 suet, wick
make a ~: 3 dip
poetically: 4 glim
use a ~: 5 light 6 censed
candle __: 5 power
__ candle: 4 rush 5 Roman 6 Easter, Hefner 7 paschal
__-candle: 4 foot 5 meter
candleberry: 3 nut 5 fruit
Candle in the Wind (1987 song) artist: Elton John
Candle in the Wind author: Maxwell Anderson
Candle in the Wind, The author: T.H. White
candlelight: 5 flame
candlelit: 3 dim
candlemaker, name meaning: 8 Chandler
candlemaking fruit: 8 bayberry
Candlemas __: 3 Day
candlenut: 4 tree 5 Asian
family: 6 spurge
tree: 5 kukui
candlepins: 4 game
candlepower: 5 light
unit: 5 lumen
Candler: 3 Asa 4 city, town
locale: 7 Georgia
__ Candles: 7 Sixteen
candlestick: 7 pricket 8 flambeau 9 girandole
maker's partner: 5 baker 7 butcher
Candlestick __: 4 Park
__ candle to: 5 hold a
can-do: 4 able 9 efficient
Can do!: 4 easy
candor: 5 truth 7 honesty, naiveté 8 openness, veracity 9 frankness, good faith, sincerity 10 simplicity
__ Can Dream: 3 If I
candy: 3 bar 4 bark, kiss, mint 5 crème, fudge, goody, snack, sweet, taffy 6 bonbon, comfit, dragée, goodie, halvah, jujube, nougat, red-hot, sucker, toffee 7 caramel, fondant, gumdrop, penuche, praline, process 8 bull's-eye, divinity, licorice, lollipop, marzipan, sourball 9 chocolate, jellybean, lemon drop, marchpane, nonpareil, sugarplum, sweetmeat 10 almond bark, confection, jawbreaker, peppermint
after-dinner ~: 4 mint
brand: 3 PEZ 4 Mars, Rolo, Twix 5 Clark, Heath, Lindt, Necco, Reese 6 Brach's, Charms, Godiva, Kit Kat, M and M's, Mounds, Nestle, PayDay, Reese's, Zagnut 7 Cadbury, Goobers, Hershey, Krackel, Oh Henry, Sno-Caps 8 Baby Ruth, Chuckles, Hershey's, Milk Duds, Milky Way, Perugina, Skittles, Snickers 9 Almond Joy, Mr. Goodbar, Raisinets, Starburst, Toblerone, Twizzlers 10 Jelly Belly, Lifesavers, NutRageous, Sweet-Tarts
British ~: 5 lolly
chewy ~: 5 taffy, toffy 6 toffee
chocolate ~: 3 bar 4 kiss
cost, once: 5 penny
ender: 4 tuft
hard ~: 4 drop 5 charm, lolly
ingredient: 5 anise, cocoa, sugar
like ~: 5 sweet
nut: 6 almond
peppermint ~: 5 patty 6 pattie
pillow ~: 4 mint
shape: 3 bar 4 drop
Turkish ~: 5 halva 6 halvah 7 halavah
candy __: 3 bar 4 cane, corn, dish, pull 5 apple, floss 6 stripe 7 striper
__ candy: 3 ear 4 hard, rock 5 sugar 6 barley, cotton
Candy: 4 Etta, John 5 Clark 8 Cummings
Candy __: 4 Girl, Land, Rain
Candy __, The: 3 Man
Candy (1991 song) artist: Iggy Pop
candy-apple color: 3 red 6 cerise
candy-coated: 5 sweet
Candy Girl (1963 song) artist: Four Seasons
Candy is dandy... poet: 4 Nash
Candy, John: 5 actor
film: Canadian Bacon (1995)
Cool Runnings (1993)
The Great Outdoors (1988)
Once Upon a Crime (1992)
Only the Lonely (1991)
Planes, Trains & Automobiles (1987)
Spaceballs (1987)
Splash (1984)
Stripes (1981)
Uncle Buck (1989)
Volunteers (1985)
Candyman (1992 film)
cast: Xander Berkeley, Virginia Madsen, Tony Todd
director: Bernard Rose
Candy Man, The (1972 song) artist: Sammy Davis Jr.
Candy-O band: 4 Cars
candy striper: 4 aide
candytuft: 5 plant 6 flower
cane: 3 bat, hit, rap, rod 4 beat, drub, flog, pole, prop, whip 5 grass, plant, ratan, spank, staff, stave, stick 6 bamboo, cudgel, Melaka, rattan, strike, thrash, thwack 7 Malacca, scourge 9 truncheon
for Chaplin: 4 prop
material: 6 bamboo
product: 3 rum 5 berry, chair, sugar
cane __: 4 reed 5 chair, sugar 6 cutter
__ cane: 4 dumb 5 candy, giant, large, small, sugar, sword 6 switch 7 Malacca
ça ne __ rien: 4 fait
__ Cane: 5 Mondo
Canea: 4 port
locale: 5 Crete 6 Candia
native: 6 Cretan
ça ne fait rien: 8 no matter
canella: 4 tree 9 condiment
__ canem: 4 cave
Canetti, Elias: 6 author, writer 8 Nobelist 9 Bulgarian 10 playwright
canfield: 4 game 8 card game
canful: 3 tin
Can I __ Witness?: 4 Get a
__ Can I Be Sure: 3 How
Caniff: 4 Milt 6 Milton
canine: 3 dog, fox, pet, pom, pug 4 Asta, fang, Odie, wolf 5 boxer, dhole, dingo, hound, husky, pooch, tooth 6 Bullet, corsac, coydog, coyote, cuspid, fennec, jackal, Lassie 8 Alsatian, Checkers, eyetooth, shepherd 9 Rin Tin Tin 10 snarleyyow
Africa: 6 fennec, jackal
Asia: 5 dhole 6 corsac, jackal
Australia: 5 dingo
bane: 4 flea 5 mange
cartilage: 5 lytta
category: 3 toy
cinema ~: 4 Asta, Toto 5 Balto 6 Lassie 9 Rin Tin Tin

comics ~: 4 Fuzz, Odie, Otto, Ruff 5 Barfy, Bitsy, Daisy, Snert 6 Grimmy 7 Dogbert 9 Marmaduke
command: 3 beg, sit 4 come, heel, stay 5 fetch, shake, sit up, speak 6 drop it 8 roll over
core of a ~: 4 pulp
cousin: 5 molar
covering: 3 cap, fur 6 enamel
cross: 3 mut 4 mutt
drink like a ~: 5 lap up
holder: 3 gum
hotel: 5 pound 6 kennel 7 shelter 8 doghouse
offspring: 3 pup 5 puppy, whelp
registry org.: 3 AKC
related: 6 dental
restraint: 5 leash
retrieval: 5 stick
small ~: 3 pom, pug 4 peke 5 corgi 6 lap dog
snatch a ~: 6 dognap
sound: 3 arf, grr 4 bark, howl, woof 5 gnarl, growl, snarl, whine 6 bowwow
tooth: 4 fang
wild ~: 3 fox 4 wolf 5 dingo 6 coyote, jackal
see also dog
Canine Cantata composer: PDQ Bach
Canio: 5 tenor
opera: 9 Pagliacci
wife: 5 Nedda
canis: 3 dog
Canis __: 5 Major, Minor 7 Majoris, Minoris
Canis Major
neighbor: 4 Argo
owner: 5 Orion
star in ~: 6 Sirius
Canis Major author: Robert Frost
Can I Steal a Little Love (1957 song) artist: Frank Sinatra
canistel: 5 fruit
canister: 4 case 9 container
Can it!: 3 shh 5 quiet 6 shut up
__ Can I Turn To: 3 Who
Canlaon: 7 volcano
locale: 4 Asia 11 Philippines
canned: 5 let go, put up
food: 4 corn, peas, Spam, tuna 5 beans
not ~: 5 fresh
Canned __: 4 Heat
cannel: 4 coal
cannelloni: 5 pasta 7 noodles
alternative: 4 orzo, ziti 5 penne 6 noodle 7 lasagna, lasagne, pastina, ravioli 8 bucatini, couscous, farfalle, linguine, linguini, macaroni, rigatoni 9 agnolotti, angelhair, cavatelli, manicotti, spaghetti 10 fettuccini, tortellini, vermicelli
Cannery Row: 4 film 5 novel
author: John Steinbeck
cast: Audra Lindley, Nick Nolte, Debra Winger
director: David S. Ward
Cannes: 4 city, port, town
group: 6 jet set
locale: 6 France
neighbor: 4 Nice
topic: 6 cinema
Cannibals and Missionaries author: Mary McCarthy
canniness: 3 art 5 craft 7 caution 8 keenness 9 foresight, smartness 10 cleverness, discretion, precaution
canning item: 3 jar 5 sieve
Cannock: 4 city, town
locale: 7 England
cannoli: 6 pastry 7 dessert, Italian
make ~: 5 stuff
cannoli, make: 5 stuff
cannon: 3 arm, gun 4 arty. 6 big gun, mortar 8 howitzer, ordnance 9 artillery
command: 4 fire
ender: 3 ade, eer 4 ball
fodder: 8 infantry
loose ~: 5 rogue
nickname: 6 Bertha 9 Big Bertha
part: 6 breech
roar: 4 boom 5 salvo
water ~ target, perhaps: 5 crowd
cannon __: 4 ball, bone 6 fodder
__ cannon: 5 loose, water
Cannon: 2 J.D. 4 Dyan 5 towel 6 Freddy
cannonade: 4 boom, fire, roll 5 burst, salvo, shell, storm 6 volley 7 assault, barrage, battery, bombard, thunder 8 fire upon, shelling 9 broadside
cannonball: 4 ammo 10 ammunition
human ~ terminus: 3 net
Cannonball: 5 train 8 Adderley
__ Cannonball: 6 Wabash
Cannonball Run, The (1981 film)
cast: Dom DeLuise, Jack Elam, Farrah Fawcett, Roger Moore, Burt Reynolds
director: Hal Needham
Cannon (CBS drama) cast: William Conrad (Frank Cannon)
Cannon, Dyan: 7 actress
film: The Anderson Tapes (1972)
Author! Author! (1982)
Bob & Carol & Ted & Alice (1969)
Deathtrap (1982)
Heaven Can Wait (1978)
Honeysuckle Rose (1980)
The Last of Sheila (1973)
Out to Sea (1997)
Shamus (1973)
Such Good Friends (1971)
spouse: Cary Grant
cannoneer often: 5 firer
cannonfire: 4 boom, fire, roll 5 burst, salvo, shell, storm 6 volley 7 assault, barrage, battery, bombard, thunder 8 fire upon, shelling 9 broadside
Cannon, Freddy
song: Palisades Park (1962)
Tallahassee Lassie (1959)
Way Down Yonder in New Orleans (1959)
cannonry: 7 battery
cannons: 4 arty. 8 materiel, weaponry 9 artillery, munitions
__ cannot wither her: 3 Age
canny: 3 sly 4 arch, cagy, foxy, wary, wily, wise 5 acute, cagey, quick, slick, smart 6 adroit, artful, astute, clever, crafty, shrewd 7 careful, cunning, guarded, heedful, knowing, politic, prudent, sunning, thrifty 8 cautious, dextrous, discreet, guileful, skillful, watchful 9 astucious, dexterous, ingenious, judicious, provident, sagacious 10 thoughtful
Canoa: 4 city, town
locale: 6 Mexico, Puebla
Canoas: 4 city, town
locale: 6 Brazil
canoe: 4 boat 5 craft, kayak, skiff 6 dugout, paddle, vessel 7 pirogue, vehicle 9 birchbark, outrigger 10 watercraft
anagram: 5 ocean
Eskimo ~: 5 kayak, umiak
paddle: 3 oar
spot: 4 lake 5 river 6 rapids
wood: 5 birch
canoe __: 5 birch 6 slalom
canoeing: 5 sport
can of __: 5 worms
__ can of worms: 5 open a
canola: 3 oil
canon: 3 law 4 code, rule 5 bylaw, creed, dogma, edict, tenet 6 cleric, decree, oeuvre 7 dictate, precept, statute 8 doctrine, standard 9 criterion, ordinance, principle 10 convention, regulation
Buddhist: 5 agama
composer: 4 Bach
marking: 5 presa
markings: 5 prese
canon __: 3 law 6 lawyer
__ canon: 4 crab 5 minor
Canon: 3 SLR 6 camera, copier
alternative: 4 Fuji, Mita 5 Kodak, Leica, Nikon, Ricoh, Xerox 6 Konica, Pentax, Rollei 7 Minolta, Olympus, Vivitar, Yashica 8 Polaroid
Canon City: 4 city, town
locale: 8 Colorado
cañon feature: 5 tilde
canonical: 5 jural, legal, sound 6 lawful 8 accepted, approved, clerical, dogmatic, official, orthodox, rightful, standard 9 classical, episcopal, religious, statutory 10 authorized, dogmatical, legitimate, recognized, sanctioned
hour: 4 sext 5 matin, nones, terce 7 worship
canonical __: 3 age 4 hour
canonicals: 3 alb 4 cope, garb 5 habit, stole 6 attire 7 cassock, maniple, vesture 8 surplice
canonist: 8 believer
canonize: 5 bless 7 beatify, glorify, idolize, worship 8 dedicate, sanctify 10 consecrate
canonized one: 2 st. 3 ste. 5 saint 6 sainte
canonry: 6 clergy
canoodle: 6 caress, fondle
Canopus: 4 star
canopy: 3 sky 5 cover, shade 6 awning, screen 7 marquee 8 covering, overhang, pavilion, sunshade 9 baldachin
it has a ~: 6 forest
canotier: 6 fabric 8 material
Canova: 4 Judy 5 Diana
__ Can Say Goodbye: 5 Never
__ can say that again!: 3 You
Canseco, José sport: 8 baseball
...can Spring be __ behind?: 3 far
canst relative: 6 mayest
cant: 3 sag, tip 4 keel, lean, sham, talk, tilt 5 argot, bevel, idiom, lingo, lurch, pitch, slang, slant, slope 6 deceit, humbug, jargon, patois, patter 7 dialect, incline, recline, tip over 8 language, parlance, pretense, shoptalk 9 hypocrisy 10 dishonesty, lip service, vernacular, vocabulary
can't
help but: 4 must 6 have to, should 7 ought to
live without: 5 crave 7 hurt for, require
stand: 4 hate 5 abhor 6 detest, loathe
Can't __: 4 Stop 5 Let Go, We Try
Can't __ Friends?: 4 We Be
Can't __ Love: 5 Buy Me
Can't __ Lovin' Dat Man: 4 Help
__ cantabile: 4 aria
Cantabrian: 5 range 9 mountains
locale: 6 Iberia
river: 4 Ebro
Cantabrigian: 4 Brit 6 Briton
river: 3 Cam
Cantab rival: 3 Eli 5 Yalie 7 Bulldog
cantaloupe: 4 pepo 5 melon 6 orange
kin: 6 casaba 7 cassaba
cantankerous: 4 dour, mean, sour, ugly 5 cross, huffy, moody, onery, surly, testy 6 crabby, cranky, crusty, grumpy, morose, ornery, stuffy, touchy 7 bearish, bristly, grouchy, loutish, peevish, prickly, waspish 8 captious, choleric, churlish, contrary, grumpish, petulant, snappish, stubborn 9 crotchety, difficult, irascible, irritable, obstinate, querulous, splenetic 10 ill-humored, out of sorts
one: 4 crab 5 grump 6 grouch
cantankerousness: 6 spleen, temper
__ cantante: 5 basso
Cantar de __ Cid: 3 Mio
Cantar de Rodrigo hero: 5 El Cid
cantata: 5 music
like a ~: 6 choral
maestro: 4 Bach
singers: 5 choir
tune: 4 aria
__ cantata: 5 missa
__ can't be!: 4 This
__ Can't Be Love: 4 This
Can't Buy Me Love (1964 song) artist: Beatles
__ Can't Cheat an Honest Man: 3 You
canted: 4 awry 5 askew, atilt, bevel, leant 6 askant 7 askance, crooked 8 cockeyed, lopsided
canteen: 5 flask 6 bottle 7 kitchen, thermos 9 container, lunchroom 10 chuck wagon, restaurant
initials: 3 USO
canter: 3 jog, run 4 gait, lope, pace, skip, step, trip, trot, walk 5 amble 6 gallop 7 dogtrot, saunter 9 gallopade
Canterbury: 4 city, town
bells: 5 plant 6 flower
locale: 4 Kent 7 England
Canterbury __: 5 bells, Tales
Canterbury Tales, The: 4 poem
author: Geoffrey Chaucer
character: 4 Cook, Dyer, Monk 5 Canon, Clerk, Friar, Harry, Reeve 6 Bailey, Doctor, Knight, Miller, Parson, Squire, Weaver, Yeoman 7 Chaucer, Plowman, Shipman 8 Franklin, Geoffrey, Manciple, Merchant, Pardoner, Prioress, Sergeant, Summoner 9 Carpenter, Second Nun 10 Nun's Priest, Wife of Bath 11 Haberdasher
drink: 4 mead
inn: 6 Tabard
Canterbury topper, Archbishop of: 5 mitre
Canterville Ghost, The (1944 film)
cast: Charles Laughton, Margaret O'Brien, Robert Young
director: Jules Dassin
Can't Fight This Feeling (1985 song) artist: REO Speedwagon
__ Can't Get a Man With a Gun: 3 You
Can't Get Enough of Your Love, Babe (1974 song) artist: Barry White
Can't Get It Out of My Head (1975 song) artist: ELO
Can't Get Used to Losing You (1963 song) artist: Andy Williams
__ Can't Go Home Again: 3 You
__ Can't Have Everything: 3 You
__ Can't Have You: 3 If I
Can't Help Falling in Love (1961 song) artist: Elvis Presley
__ Can't Help It, The: 4 Girl
Can't Help Lovin' Dat Man composer: 4 Kern 11 Hammerstein
Canth, Minna: 6 author, writer 7 Finnish
Can Tho: 4 city, town
locale: 7 Vietnam
__ Can't Hurry Love: 3 You
canticle: 3 ode 4 hymn, song 5 music, psalm 6 anthem
cantilever: 4 beam 5 truss 7 bracket
cantilever __: 6 bridge
cantillate: 4 sing
cantina: 3 bar 6 saloon
shout: 5 salud
snack: 4 taco, tapa

Cantique de Noël composer: 4 Adam
Can't Let Go (1991 song) artist: Mariah Carey
Can't Nobody Hold Me Down (1997 song)
artist: Mase, Puff Daddy
canto: 3 air 4 song 5 verse 6 melody
__ canto: 3 bel
canton: 4 ward 5 lodge, state 7 quarter 8 province
Swiss ~: 3 Uri, Zug 4 Bern, Vaud 5 Berne 6 Aargau, Valais
Canton: 4 city, town
attraction: 3 HOF 10 Hall of Fame
ender: 3 ese
locale: 4 Ohio 5 China 8 Michigan
river: 3 Hsi
cantor: 5 hazan 6 hazzan 7 chazzan
place: 4 shul 5 schul 9 synagogue
Cantor: 3 Ida 5 Eddie
Cantor, Eddie: 5 actor 8 comedian
film: The Kid From Spain (1932)
Kid Millions (1934)
Roman Scandals (1933)
Thank Your Lucky Stars (1943)
Whoopee! (1930)
Cantoria: 4 font 8 typeface
Cantos author: Ezra Pound
Cantrell: 4 Lana
cantrip: 3 hex 5 spell
Can't Smile Without You (1978 song)
artist: Barry Manilow
Can't Stay Away From You (1988 song) artist: Gloria Estefan
Can't Stop This Thing We Started (1991 song) artist: Bryan Adams
__ Can't Take It With You: 3 You
Can't Take My Eyes Off You (1967 song) artist: Frankie Valli
__ can't take that away...: 4 They
__ Can't We Be Friends?: 3 Why
Can't We Try (1987 song)
artist: Dan Hill, Vonda Shepard
Can't You Hear My Heartbeat (1965 song) artist: Herman's Hermits
Can't You See (1995 song)
artist: Notorious B.I.G., Total
Can't You See That She's Mine (1964 song) artist: Dave Clark Five
Can't you take __?: 5 a hint, a joke
Canuck rival: 4 Blue, King, Star, Wild 5 Bruin, Devil, Flame, Flyer, Oiler, Sabre, Shark 6 Coyote, Ranger 7 Capital, Panther, Penguin, Red Wing, Senator 8 Canadien, Islander, Predator, Thrasher 9 Avalanche, Blackhawk, Hurricane, Lightning, Maple Leaf 10 Blue Jacket, Mighty Duck
Canucks: 3 six 4 team
home: 9 Vancouver
milieu: 3 ice 4 rink
org.: 3 NHL
sport: 6 hockey
Canute: 4 king 6 Danish
foe: 4 Olaf, Olav
canvas: 3 art, oil 4 sail, tarp 6 fabric 7 picture, tenting 8 painting, portrait 9 sailcloth, still life, tarpaulin 10 watercolor
ender: 4 back
product: 4 tarp, tent 6 awning 9 sailcloth
support: 4 mast 5 easel
user: 6 artist, painer
canvasback: 4 duck, fowl
relative: 4 smew, teal 5 eider, Pekin, Rouen, scaup 6 Cayuga, scoter 7 gadwall, mallard, pintail, pochard, redhead, sea duck, widgeon 8 garganey, gray duck, mandarin, musk duck, oldsquaw, shoveler, surf duck, wood duck 9 black duck, broadbill, goldeneye, goosander, greenhead, merganser, ruddy duck, sprigtail 10 bufflehead, surf scoter, tufted duck
canvaslike fabric: 5 wigan
canvass: 3 ask 4 case, poll, talk 5 study 6 review, survey, voting 7 examine, inspect, solicit 8 campaign
__ Can Wait: 6 Heaven
Can we talk? lady: 6 Rivers
__ Can Whistle: 4 Some 6 Anyone
canyon: 4 gulf 5 Bryce, chasm, gorge, gulch, gully 6 arroyo, canada, coulee, gulley, ravine, valley
edge: 3 lip, rim
form a ~: 5 erode
mouth: 4 abra
phenomenon: 4 echo
canyon __: 4 wind
__ canyon: 3 box
__ Canyon: 5 Black, Bryce, Grand, Steve 6 Laurel 7 Boulder
__ Canyon Dam: 4 Glen
Canyonlands: 4 park
city near: 4 Moab
locale: 4 Utah
Canyon Passage (1946 film)
cast: Dana Andrews, Brian Donlevy
__ Canyon Suite: 5 Grand
Can you __?: 5 dig it
Can You Feel the Love Tonight (1994 song) artist: Elton John
__, Can You Hear Me?: 4 Papa
__ can you see: 4 O say 5 Oh say
Can You Top This?: 9 radio show
canzone: 3 ode
canzonet: 4 song 5 music
CaO, containing: 4 limy
Ca(OH)2: 6 alkali
cap: 3 fez, hat, lid, taj, tam, tip, top 4 beat, best, cork, kepi, seal, slur 5 beret, crest, crown, excel, limit, outdo 6 beanie, better, biggin, exceed, finial, letter, outwit, pileus, tipoff, top off, topper, vertex, wrap up, zenith 7 biretta, ceiling, eclipse, maximum, surpass 8 balmoral, berretta, birretta, coonskin, covering, outshine, outsmart, outstrip, round off, round out, surmount, yarmelke, yarmulka, yarmulke 9 balaclava, bottle top, cockscomb, culminate, Glengarry, headdress, transcend, zucchetto 10 bluebonnet, complement, consummate, crownpiece, upper limit
AL ~ letters: 3 SOX
and gown wearer: 4 grad
combining form: 8 calyptri-, calyptro-
conical ~ wearer: 5 dunce
doff the ~ to: 5 greet
ender: 5 stone
feather in one's ~: 4 fame 5 award, badge, glory, honor, kudos, medal, prize 6 credit, honors, praise, renown, reward, trophy 7 acclaim, laurels, triumph, victory 8 accolade, citation, gold star, prestige 10 decoration
French ~: 5 beret, shako
part: 4 bill 5 visor, vizor 6 earlap
plumed ~: 5 shako
polar ~: 3 ice
put on one's thinking ~: 8 meditate
set one's ~ for: 3 woo 4 date 5 court 6 pursue 7 take out 9 cultivate
sheepskin ~: 6 calpac 7 calpack
starter: 3 hub, ice, mad, mob, red, sky, toe 4 knee, snow 5 black, fools, night, skull, white
stocking ~: 5 toque, tuque
tasseled ~: 3 fez, tam
visored ~: 4 kepi
visorless ~: 3 tam 5 beret
cap __: 3 gun, jib 4 rock 5 cloud, screw 6 pistol, sleeve
cap-__: 4 à-pie
__ cap: 3 hot, ice 4 ball, drip, inky 5 cloud, dunce, fool's, gimme, legal, polar, screw, small, watch 6 bottle, cradle, dunce's, flight, forage, Gandhi, jockey, Juliet, oyster, salary, shaggy 7 bathing, bishop's, chimney, liberty, service
__-cap: 3 mid 7 bishop's
Cap: 5 Anson
capa: 5 cloak
Capa: 6 Robert
capabilities: 5 gifts 6 powers, skills 7 talents 9 aptitudes, faculties, potential
capability: 5 means, might, power, skill 6 talent 7 faculty, know-how, potence, potency, promise 8 adequacy, aptitude, efficacy, facility, resource 9 endowment, potential 10 competence, efficiency, right stuff
lessen the ~ of: 6 derate
Capablanca, José forte: 5 chess
capable: 3 apt, fit 4 deft, good 5 adept, handy, hardy, quick, slick 6 adroit, au fait, expert, nimble, strong, suited, up to it 7 skilled, trained 8 adequate, dextrous, graceful, masterly, powerful, seasoned, skillful, talented 9 competent, dexterous, effective, efficient, masterful, on the ball, practiced, qualified, up to snuff, up to speed 10 proficient
humorously: 3 ept
isn't ~ of: 4 can't
make ~: 10 capacitate
more ~: 5 abler
not ~: 5 unfit
of: 4 up to 6 open to 8 liable to, likely to
suffix: 3 -ile 4 -able, -ible
Capable of Honor author: Allen Drury
capably: 4 ably, well 5 aptly, great 6 deftly, nimbly 7 handily, rightly 8 laudably, worthily
capacious: 3 big 4 vast, wide 5 ample, broad, large, roomy 7 liberal, sizable 8 abundant, extended, far-flung, generous, sizeable, spacious, sweeping 9 dilatable, expansive, extensive, plentiful 10 commodious, expandable, voluminous, widespread
capaciousness: 4 room, size 5 space, sweep 9 amplitude
capacitance unit: 5 farad
capacitate: 6 enable 7 empower, qualify
__ capacitor: 4 flux, grid 6 bypass
capacity: 4 fill, gift, head, role, room, size 5 knack, limit, might, power, reach, scope, sense, skill, space, state 6 office, sphere, status, talent, volume 7 ability, faculty, makings, potence, potency, stature 8 adequacy, aptitude, facility, function, judgment, province, quantity, standing 9 amplitude, dimension, endowment, endurance, largeness, magnitude, potential, readiness 10 competence, leadership, propensity, right stuff
at ~: 4 full 9 chock-full
have a ~ for: 4 hold
in the ~ of: 3 qua
of large ~: 5 ample, roomy
suffix: 7 -ability, -ibility
unit of ~: 5 liter, litre, quart 6 gallon
__ capacity: 4 heat 5 field, vital 7 reserve
__ Capades: 3 Ice
cap and __: 4 gown 5 bells
cap-a-pie: 6 wholly
caparison: 3 rig 4 deck, gear 5 adorn, rig up 6 bedeck, clothe, dude up, finery, fit out, outfit, rig out 7 bedrape, clothes, deck out, dress up, full fig, rigging, turn out 8 accouter, accoutre, glad rags, housings 9 trappings
Capa, Robert: 12 photographer
Cap-de-la-Madeleine: 4 city, town
locale: 6 Canada, Québec
cape: 3 Ann, Bon, Cod, May, ras 4 Horn, Race, Roca, Skaw, wrap, York 5 Alava, amice, capot, cloak, Coral, fichu, Hafun, point, Sable, Wrath 6 almuce, Breton, capote, dolman, Helles, mantle, muleta, tabard, tippet 7 Agulhas, Comorin, Dezhnev, Froward, garment, Gris-Nez, La Hague, Lookout, manteau, mantlet, Matapan, mozetta, Nordkyn, Ortegal, paletot, pelisse 8 Columbia, Farewell, Flattery, foreland, Gallinas, Good Hope, Hatteras, headland, Land's End, mantilla, mozzetta, palatine, pelerine, San Lucas 9 Canaveral, Mendocino, Trafalgar 10 Chelyuskin, Finisterre, Lizard Head, promontory
Africa: 5 Verde
Alaska: 4 Nome
Antarctica: 5 Adare
Carolina: 4 Fear
church: 5 amice, fanon, orale 6 almuce 7 mozetta 8 mozzetta
Dakar: 5 Verde
ender: 4 skin
Gallipoli: 6 Helles
Hebrides: 5 Sleat
Japan: 3 Oma 4 mino
Massachusetts: 3 Ann, Cod
matador's ~ color: 4 rojo
New Jersey: 3 May
Nova Scotia: 5 Canso
Portugal: 4 Roca
South America: 4 Horn
Spanish: 8 mantilla
Washington: 5 Alava
cape __: 4 work 6 collar
Cape __: 3 Ann, Cod, fox, May 4 Fear, Horn, Roca, Town 5 Alava, Dutch, Verde 6 Colony 7 Agulhas, buffalo, Gris-Nez, jasmine, Kennedy
Cape __, AK: 4 Nome
Cape __ cottage: 3 Cod
Cape __ Island: 6 Breton
Cape __, Liberia: 6 Palmas
Cape __, MA: 3 Ann, Cod
Cape __, NC: 4 Fear
Cape __-Nez: 4 Gris
Cape __, NJ: 3 May
Cape __, Portugal: 4 Roca
Cape __, Senegal: 5 Verde
Cape Breton: 4 city, isle, town 6 island
locale: 6 Canada 10 Nova Scotia
Cape Canaveral
beach near ~: 5 Cocoa
locale: 3 Fla. 7 Florida
org.: 4 NASA
Cape Cod
cottage feature: 5 gable
island off ~: 9 Nantucket
sight: 4 dune
town: 5 Truro 7 Hyannis
Cape Cod __: 7 cottage, lighter
__ Cape Cod: 3 Old
Cape Codder ingredient: 5 vodka
Cape Cod Lighter, The author: 5 O'Hara
Cape Coral: 4 city, town
locale: 7 Florida
Cape Farewell author: Harry Matinson
Cape Fear (1962 film)
cast: Polly Bergen, Robert Mitchum, Gregory Peck
director: J. Lee Thompson
Cape Fear (1991 film)
cast: Robert De Niro, Jessica Lange, Juliette Lewis, Nick Nolte
De Niro in ~: 5 ex-con
director: Martin Scorsese

Cape Fear's loc.: 4 N. Car.
Cape Girardeau: 4 city, town
locale: 8 Missouri
Cape Gris-__: 3 Nez
Capek, Karel: 5 Czech 6 writer 10 playwright
work: The Insect Play
The Life of the Insects
Meteor
An Ordinary Life
Power and Glory
R.U.R.
The War With the Newts
capelin: 4 fish
Capella: 4 star
Capeman, The composer: 5 Simon
Cape May: 4 city, town
locale: 9 New Jersey
Cape of Good Hope country: 3 RSA
caper: 3 gag 4 jape, jest, joke, lark, leap, play, romp, skip 5 antic, frisk, heist, plant, prank, shrub, spree, stunt, theft, trick 6 cavort, frolic, gambol, prance 7 foolery, garnish, hijinks, robbery, rollick 8 burglary, escapade, mischief, thievery 9 condiment, have a ball, high jinks, horseplay, whoop it up 10 shenanigan, tomfoolery
__ caper: 4 bean, cut a
Caper author: Lawrence Sanders
capercaillie: 4 bird
Cape Roca locale: 6 Iberia 8 Portugal
Capet: 4 Hugh
Cape Town: 4 city, port
locale: 3 RSA
mountain: 5 Table
Cape Verde: 6 nation 7 country
capital: 5 Praia
city: 5 Dakar, Praia
Cape Verde Islands volcano: 4 Fogo
Cape Wrangell locale: 4 Attu 6 Alaska
capgun: 3 toy
Caph: 4 star
capibara: 6 animal, mammal, rodent
capillary: 4 vein
capillary __: 4 tube 6 action
cap in __: 4 hand
capital: 3 def, oof, rad 4 aces, A-one, best, boss, braw, cash, city, cool, dece, fine, gear, gelt, good, jack, kail, kale, keen, loot, main, neat, nice, peag, pelf, phat, seat, star, tops, tuff 5 asset, bills, bread, bucks, dandy, dough, ducky, funds, grand, great, lucre, marvy, means, money, moola, mopus, neato, nobby, pesos, prime, rhino, sewan, slick, stock, super, swell 6 assets, bang on, bang-up, bonzer, bosker, choice, deluxe, dinero, divine, do-re-mi, dreamy, far-out, gnarly, groovy, letter, lovely, mammon, mazuma, moolah, peachy, seawan, silver, slap-up, specie, spot on, superb, terrif, tiptop, unreal, utmost, wampum, wealth, whizzo, wicked 7 amazing, awesome, cabbage, corking, dollars, funding, lettuce, ooftish, optimum, perfect, reserve, ripping, savings, scratch, shekels, skookum, stellar, sublime 8 bankroll, cold cash, currency, dazzling, especial, eximious, fabulous, five-star, four-star, frabjous, glorious, hard cash, heavenly, jim-dandy, monetary, property, slam-bang, smackers, smashing, splendid, standout, sterling, stickout, superior, terrific, top-level, top-notch, very good, wondrous 9 banknotes, bodacious, Endsville, essential, excellent, exemplary, exquisite, financing, first-rate, frogskins, high-grade, hunky-dory, long green, majuscule, marvelous, paramount, principal, resources, simoleons, sollicker, top-flight, upper case, uttermost, wonderful 10 first-class, greenbacks, green stuff, hotsy-totsy, inexpiable, investment, jack-a-dandy, metropolis, out of sight, peachy-keen, phenomenal, remarkable, stupendous, super-duper, world-class
African: 4 Lomé 5 Abuja, Accra, Akkra, Cairo, Dakar, Rabat, Tunis 6 Asmara, Bamako, Bangui, Bissau, Dodoma, Harare, Kigali, Luanda, Lusaka, Malabo, Maputo, Maseru, Niamey 7 Abidjan, Algiers, Conakry, Kampala, Mbabane, Nairobi, Tripoli, Yaoundé 8 Cape Town, Djibouti, Freetown, Gaborone, Khartoum, Kinshasa, Lilongwe, Monrovia, Pretoria, Windhoek 9 Bujumbura, Mogadishu, Porto-Novo 10 Addis Ababa, Libreville, Nouakchott 11 Brazzaville, Ouagadougou
Alpine: 4 Bern 5 Berne 6 Vienna
Andean: 4 Lima 6 Bogotá 8 Santiago
Asia Minor: 6 Angora, Ankara
Asian: 4 Baku, Dili, Doha, Malé, Sana 5 Amman, Dacca, Dhaka, Hanoi, Kabul, Sanaa, Seoul, Tokyo 6 Ankara, Bagdad, Beirut, Manama, Muscat, Riyadh, Taipei, Tehran, Yangon 7 Baghdad, Bangkok, Beijing, Bishkek, Colombo, Jakarta, Rangoon, Teheran, Thimphu 8 Abu Dhabi, Beyrouth, Damascus, Djakarta, Dushanbe, Katmandu, New Delhi, Tashkent 9 Islamabad, Jerusalem, Phnom Penh, Pyongyang, Ulan Bator, Vientiane 10 Kuwait City 11 Kuala Lumpur, Ulaanbaatar
Baltic: 4 Riga 5 Vilna 7 Tallinn, Vilnius
Caribbean: 6 Havana, Nassau 7 St. John's 8 Castries, Kingston, Road Town 9 Kingstown, St. George's 10 Basseterre, Bridgetown, George Town, Oranjestad 11 Port of Spain 12 Fort-de-France, Port-au-Prince
Central American: 7 Managua, San José 8 Belmopan 10 Panama City 11 San Salvador, Tegucigalpa
European: 4 Bern, Kiev, Oslo, Riga, Roma, Rome, Wien 5 Berne, Minsk, Paris, Praha, Sofia, Vaduz, Vilna 6 Athens, Berlin, Dublin, Lisboa, Lisbon, London, Madrid, Moscow, Prague, Skopje, Sofiya, Vienna, Warsaw, Zagreb 7 Belfast, Cardiff, Den Haag, Nicosia, Tallinn 8 Belgrade, Brussels, Chisinau, Helsinki, Sarajevo, The Hague, Valletta 9 Amsterdam, Bucharest, Edinburgh, Ljubljana, Stockholm 10 Bratislava, Copenhagen
like venture ~ investments: 5 dicey 6 chancy, daring, unsafe 9 uncertain 10 precarious
make ~ out of: 3 use 7 exploit
Mideast: 4 Doha, Sana 5 Amman, Sanaa 6 Bagdad, Beirut, Manama, Muscat, Riyadh, Tehran 7 Baghdad, Teheran 8 Abu Dhabi, Beyrouth, Damascus 9 Jerusalem 10 Kuwait City
near the equator: 5 Quito
provide ~: 4 back, fund
South American: 4 Lima 5 La Paz, Quito, Sucre 6 Bogotá 7 Caracas, Cayenne 8 Asunción, Santiago, Brasilila 10 Montevideo, Paramaribo 11 Buenos Aires
South Pacific: 4 Apia, Suva 5 Agana 6 Majuro, Manila, Nouméa, Tarawa 7 Honiara, Papeete 8 Funafuti, Pago Pago, Port-Vila 9 Nuku'alofa
world's highest ~: 5 La Paz
capital __: 3 sum 4 gain, levy, loss, ship, sins 5 asset, crime, goods, stock 6 budget, flight, letter, outlay 7 account, surplus
__ capital: 4 risk 5 block, fixed, small 6 equity 7 venture, working
Capital __, The: 4 Gang
Capital Crimes author: Sanders
capital gains __: 3 tax
Capital Gang, The network: CNN
capitalism: 9 democracy 10 free market
capitalist: 6 tycoon 7 magnate 8 investor 9 bourgeois, financier, landowner, moneybags, plutocrat
capitalize: 3 use 4 fund 5 stake 7 finance 9 subsidize
on: 6 profit 7 exploit
Capital rival: 4 Blue, King, Star, Wild 5 Bruin, Devil, Flame, Flyer, Oiler, Sabre, Shark 6 Canuck, Coyote, Ranger 7 Panther, Penguin, Red Wing, Senator 8 Canadien, Islander, Predator, Thrasher 9 Avalanche, Blackhawk, Hurricane, Lightning, Maple Leaf 10 Blue Jacket, Mighty Duck
Capitals: 3 six 4 team
home: 10 Washington
milieu: 3 ice 4 rink
org.: 3 NHL
sport: 6 hockey
capitals (state) by city:
Albany - New York
Annapolis - Maryland
Atlanta - Georgia
Augusta - Maine
Austin - Texas
Baton Rouge - Louisiana
Bismarck - North Dakota
Boise - Idaho
Boston - Massachusetts
Carson City - Nevada
Charleston - West Virginia
Cheyenne - Wyoming
Columbia - South Carolina
Columbus - Ohio
Concord - New Hampshire
Denver - Colorado
Des Moines - Iowa
Dover - Delaware
Frankfort - Kentucky
Harrisburg - Pennsylvania
Hartford - Connecticut
Helena - Montana
Honolulu - Hawaii
Indianapolis - Indiana
Jackson - Mississippi
Jefferson City - Missouri
Juneau - Alaska
Lansing - Michigan
Lincoln - Nebraska
Little Rock - Arkansas
Madison - Wisconsin
Montgomery - Alabama
Montpelier - Vermont
Nashville - Tennessee
Oklahoma City - Oklahoma
Olympia - Washington
Phoenix - Arizona
Pierre - South Dakota
Providence - Rhode Island
Raleigh - North Carolina
Richmond - Virginia
Sacramento - California
Saint Paul - Minnesota
Salem - Oregon
Salt Lake City - Utah
Santa Fe - New Mexico
Springfield - Illinois
Tallahassee - Florida
Topeka - Kansas
Trenton - New Jersey
capitals (state) by state:
Alabama - Montgomery
Alaska - Juneau
Arizona - Phoenix
Arkansas - Little Rock
California - Sacramento
Colorado - Denver
Connecticut - Hartford
Delaware - Dover
Florida - Tallahassee
Georgia - Atlanta
Hawaii - Honolulu
Idaho - Boise
Illinois - Springfield
Indiana - Indianapolis
Iowa - Des Moines
Kansas - Topeka
Kentucky - Frankfort
Louisiana - Baton Rouge
Maine - Augusta
Maryland - Annapolis
Massachusetts - Boston
Michigan - Lansing
Minnesota - St. Paul
Mississippi - Jackson
Missouri - Jefferson City
Montana - Helena
Nebraska - Lincoln
Nevada - Carson City
New Hampshire - Concord
New Jersey - Trenton
New Mexico - Santa Fe
New York - Albany
North Carolina - Raleigh
North Dakota - Bismarck
Ohio - Columbus
Oklahoma - Oklahoma City
Oregon - Salem
Pennsylvania - Harrisburg
Rhode Island - Providence
South Carolina - Columbia
South Dakota - Pierre
Tennessee - Nashville
Texas - Austin
Utah - Salt Lake City
Vermont - Montpelier
Virginia - Richmond
Washington - Olympia
West Virginia - Charleston
Wisconsin - Madison
Wyoming - Cheyenne
capitals (world) by city:
Abidjan - Ivory Coast
Abu Dhabi - United Arab Emirates
Abuja - Nigeria
Accra - Ghana
Addis Ababa - Ethiopia
Agana - Guam
Algiers - Algeria
Amman - Jordan
Amsterdam - Netherlands
Andorra La Vella - Andorra
Ankara - Turkey
Antananarivo - Madagascar
Apia - Samoa
Ashkhabad - Turkmenistan
Asmara - Eritrea
Astana - Kazakhstan
Asunción - Paraguay
Athens - Greece
Bagdad - Iraq
Baku - Azerbaijan
Bamako - Mali
Bandar Seri Begawan - Brunei
Bangkok - Thailand
Bangui - Central African Republic
Banjul - Gambia
Basse-Terre - Guadeloupe
Basseterre - St. Kitts and Nevis
Beijing - China
Beirut - Lebanon
Belfast - Northern Ireland
Belgrade - Yugoslavia
Belmopan - Belize
Berlin - Germany
Bern - Switzerland

Bishkek - Kyrgyzstan
Bissau - Guinea-Bissau
Bogotá - Colombia
Brasilia - Brazil
Bratislava - Slovakia
Brazzaville - Congo (Republic)
Bridgetown - Barbados
Brussels - Belgium
Bucharest - Romania
Budapest - Hungary
Buenos Aires - Argentina
Bujumbura - Burundi
Cairo - Egypt
Canberra - Australia
Cape Town - South Africa
Caracas - Venezuela
Cardiff - Wales
Castries - St. Lucia
Cayenne - French Guiana
Chisinau - Moldova
Colombo - Sri Lanka
Conakry - Guinea
Copenhagen - Denmark
Dakar - Senegal
Damascus - Syria
Den Haag - Netherlands
Dhaka - Bangladesh
Dili - East Timor
Djakarta - Indonesia
Djibouti - Djibouti
Dodoma - Tanzania
Doha - Qatar
Dublin - Ireland
Dushanbe - Tajikistan
Edinburgh - Scotland
Fort-de-France - Martinique
Freetown - Sierra Leone
Funafuti - Tuvalu
Gaborone - Botswana
George Town - Cayman Islands
Georgetown - Guyana
Godthab - Greenland
Guatemala City - Guatemala
Hague, The - Netherlands
Hamilton - Bermuda
Hanoi - Vietnam
Harare - Zimbabwe
Havana - Cuba
Helsinki - Finland
Honiara - Solomon Islands
Islamabad - Pakistan
Jakarta - Indonesia
Jamestown - St. Helena
Jerusalem - Israel
Kabul - Afghanistan
Kampala - Uganda
Katmandu - Nepal
Khartoum - Sudan
Kiev - Ukraine
Kigali - Rwanda
Kingston - Jamaica
Kingstown - St. Vincent and the Grenadines
Kinshasa - Congo (Democratic Republic)
Koror - Palau
Kuala Lumpur - Malaysia
Kuwait City - Kuwait
La Paz - Bolivia
Libreville - Gabon
Lilongwe - Malawi
Lima - Peru
Lisbon - Portugal
Ljubljana - Slovenia
Lomé - Togo
London - United Kingdom
Luanda - Angola
Lusaka - Zambia
Luxembourg - Luxembourg
Madrid - Spain
Majuro - Marshall Islands
Malabo - Equatorial Guinea
Malé - Maldives
Managua - Nicaragua
Manama - Bahrain
Manila - Philippines
Maputo - Mozambique
Maseru - Lesotho
Mbabane - Swaziland
Minsk - Belarus
Mogadishu - Somalia
Monaco-Ville - Monaco
Monrovia - Liberia
Montevideo - Uruguay
Moroni - Comoros
Moscow - Russia
Muscat - Oman
Nairobi - Kenya
Nassau - Bahamas
N'Djamena - Chad
New Delhi - India
Niamey - Niger
Nicosia - Cyprus
Nouakchott - Mauritania
Nouméa - New Caledonia
Nuku'alofa - Tonga
Oranjestad - Aruba
Oslo - Norway
Ouagadougou - Burkina Faso
Pago Pago - American Samoa
Palikir - Micronesia
Panama City - Panama
Papeete - French Polynesia
Paramaribo - Suriname
Paris - France
Phnom Penh - Cambodia
Port-au-Prince - Haiti
Port Louis - Mauritius
Port Moresby - Papua New Guinea
Port of Spain - Trinidad and Tobago
Porto-Novo - Benin
Port Stanley - Falkland Islands
Port-Vila - Vanuatu
Prague, Praha - Czech Republic
Praia - Cape Verde
Pretoria - South Africa
Pyongyang - North Korea
Quito - Ecuador
Rabat - Morocco
Rangoon - Myanmar
Reykjavík - Iceland
Riga - Latvia
Riyadh - Saudi Arabia
Road Town - British Virgin Islands
Rome - Italy
Roseau - Dominica
Sanaa - Yemen
San José - Costa Rica
San Salvador - El Salvador
Santiago - Chile
Santo Domingo - Dominican Republic
Sarajevo - Bosnia and Herzegovina
Seoul - South Korea
Singapore - Singapore
Skopje - Macedonia
Sofia - Bulgaria
St. George's - Grenada
St. John's - Antigua and Barbuda
Stockholm - Sweden
Sucre - Bolivia
Suva - Fiji
Taipei - Taiwan
Tallinn - Estonia
Tarawa - Kiribati
Tashkent - Uzbekistan
Tbilisi - Georgia
Tegucigalpa - Honduras
Teheran - Iran
Tehran - Iran
Thimphu - Bhutan
Tirana - Albania
Tokyo - Japan
Tórshavn - Faeroe Islands
Tripoli - Libya
Tunis - Tunisia
Ulaanbaatar - Mongolia
Vaduz - Liechtenstein
Valletta - Malta
Victoria - Seychelles
Vienna - Austria
Vientiane - Laos
Vilnius - Lithuania
Warsaw - Poland
Wellington - New Zealand
Wien - Austria
Windhoek - Namibia
Yangon - Myanmar
Yaoundé - Cameroon
Yerevan - Armenia
Zagreb - Croatia

capitals (world) by country:

Afghanistan - Kabul
Albania - Tirana
Algeria - Algiers
American Samoa - Pago Pago
Andorra - Andorra La Vella
Angola - Luanda
Antigua and Barbuda - St. John's
Argentina - Buenos Aires
Armenia - Yerevan
Aruba - Oranjestad
Australia - Canberra
Austria - Vienna (Wien)
Azerbaijan - Baku
Bahamas - Nassau
Bahrain - Manama
Bangladesh - Dhaka
Barbados - Bridgetown
Belarus - Minsk
Belgium - Brussels
Belize - Belmopan
Benin - Porto-Novo
Bermuda - Hamilton
Bhutan - Thimphu
Bolivia - La Paz, Sucre
Bosnia and Herzegovina - Sarajevo
Botswana - Gaborone
Brazil - Brasilia
British Virgin Islands - Road Town
Brunei - Bandar Seri Begawan
Bulgaria - Sofia
Burkina Faso - Ouagadougou
Burundi - Bujumbura
Cambodia - Phnom Penh
Cameroon - Yaoundé
Cape Verde - Praia
Cayman Islands - George Town
Central African Republic - Bangui
Chad - N'Djamena
Chile - Santiago
China - Beijing
Colombia - Bogotá
Comoros - Moroni
Congo (Democratic Republic) - Kinshasa
Congo (Republic) - Brazzaville
Costa Rica - San José
Croatia - Zagreb
Cuba - Havana
Cyprus - Nicosia
Czech Republic - Prague (Praha)
Denmark - Copenhagen
Djibouti - Djibouti
Dominican Republic - Santo Domingo
Dominica - Roseau
East Timor - Dili
Ecuador - Quito
Egypt - Cairo
El Salvador - San Salvador
Equatorial Guinea - Malabo
Eritrea - Asmara
Estonia - Tallinn
Ethiopia - Addis Ababa
Faeroe Islands - Tórshavn
Falkland Islands - Port Stanley
Fiji - Suva
Finland - Helsinki
France - Paris
French Guiana - Cayenne
French Polynesia - Papeete
Gabon - Libreville
Gambia - Banjul
Georgia - Tbilisi
Germany - Berlin
Ghana - Accra
Greece - Athens
Greenland - Godthab
Grenada - St. George's
Guadeloupe - Basse-Terre
Guam - Agana
Guatemala - Guatemala City
Guinea-Bissau - Bissau
Guinea - Conakry
Guyana - Georgetown
Haiti - Port-au-Prince
Honduras - Tegucigalpa
Hungary - Budapest
Iceland - Reykjavík
India - New Delhi
Indonesia - Jakarta (Djakarta)
Iran - Teheran (Tehran)
Iraq - Bagdad (Baghdad)
Ireland - Dublin
Israel - Jerusalem
Italy - Rome (Roma)
Ivory Coast - Abidjan
Jamaica - Kingston
Japan - Tokyo
Jordan - Amman
Kazakhstan - Astana
Kenya - Nairobi
Kiribati - Tarawa
Kuwait - Kuwait City
Kyrgyzstan - Bishkek
Laos - Vientiane
Latvia - Riga
Lebanon - Beirut
Lesotho - Maseru
Liberia - Monrovia
Libya - Tripoli
Liechtenstein - Vaduz
Lithuania - Vilnius
Luxembourg - Luxembourg
Macedonia - Skopje
Madagascar - Antananarivo
Malawi - Lilongwe
Malaysia - Kuala Lumpur
Maldives - Malé
Mali - Bamako
Malta - Valletta
Marshall Islands - Majuro
Martinique - Fort-de-France
Mauritania - Nouakchott
Mauritius - Port Louis
Micronesia - Palikir
Moldova - Chisinau
Monaco - Monaco-Ville
Mongolia - Ulaanbaatar (Ulan Bator)
Morocco - Rabat
Mozambique - Maputo
Myanmar - Yangon (Rangoon)
Namibia - Windhoek
Nepal - Katmandu
Netherlands - Amsterdam, The Hague (Den Haag)
New Caledonia - Nouméa
New Zealand - Wellington
Nicaragua - Managua
Nigeria - Abuja
Niger - Niamey
Northern Ireland - Belfast
North Korea - Pyongyang
Norway - Oslo
Oman - Muscat
Pakistan - Islamabad
Palau - Koror
Panama - Panama City
Papua New Guinea - Port Moresby
Paraguay - Asunción
Peru - Lima
Philippines - Manila
Poland - Warsaw
Portugal - Lisbon (Lisboa)
Qatar - Doha
Romania - Bucharest
Russia - Moscow

Rwanda - Kigali
Samoa - Apia
Saudi Arabia - Riyadh
Scotland - Edinburgh
Senegal - Dakar
Seychelles - Victoria
Sierra Leone - Freetown
Singapore - Singapore
Slovakia - Bratislava
Slovenia - Ljubljana
Solomon Islands - Honiara
Somalia - Mogadishu
South Africa - Cape Town, Pretoria
South Korea - Seoul
Spain - Madrid
Sri Lanka - Colombo
St. Helena - Jamestown
St. Kitts and Nevis - Basseterre
St. Lucia - Castries
St. Vincent and the Grenadines - Kingstown
Sudan - Khartoum
Suriname - Paramaribo
Swaziland - Mbabane
Sweden - Stockholm
Switzerland - Bern (Berne)
Syria - Damascus
Taiwan - Taipei
Tajikistan - Dushanbe
Tanzania - Dodoma
Thailand - Bangkok
Togo - Lomé
Tonga - Nuku'alofa
Trinidad and Tobago - Port of Spain
Tunisia - Tunis
Turkey - Ankara
Turkmenistan - Ashkhabad
Tuvalu - Funafuti
Uganda - Kampala
Ukraine - Kiev
United Arab Emirates - Abu Dhabi
United Kingdom - London
United States - Washington
Uruguay - Montevideo
Uzbekistan - Tashkent
Vanuatu - Port-Vila
Venezuela - Caracas
Vietnam - Hanoi
Wales - Cardiff
Yemen - Sanaa
Yugoslavia - Belgrade
Zambia - Lusaka
Zimbabwe - Harare

capita, per: 4 each 6 apiece
Capitol
gofer: 4 page
group: 5 House, lobby 6 Senate
sight: 4 Mall
topper: 4 dome
VIP: 3 rep., sen. 7 senator
vote: 3 nay 7 abstain, present
Capitol ___: 4 Hill
Capitol ___, The: 5 Steps
Capitol-___: 3 EMI
Capitoline site: 4 Rome
Capitol Reef: 4 park
locale: 4 Utah
capitulate: 3 bow 4 fold, lose 5 yield 6 accept, cave in, fess up, give in, give up, relent, submit 7 concede, succumb 9 surrender 10 come across
caplet: 4 pill
caplin: 4 fish
Cap'n ___: 3 Eri 6 Crunch
Cap'n Crunch: 6 cereal
competitor: 3 Kix 4 Life, Trix 5 Kashi, Quisp, Total 6 Kaboom, Muesli, Oreo O's, Pablum, Smacks 7 All-Bran, Crispix, Harmony, Hunny B's, Mueslix, Oat Bran, Pokemon 8 Boo Berry, Cheerios, Corn Chex, Corn Pops, Fiber One, Rice Chex, Special K, Uncle Sam, Wheaties 9 Alpha Bits, Apple Zaps, Grape Nuts, Honey Comb, Just Right, Wheat Chex 10 Apple Jacks, Bran Flakes, Cocoa Puffs, Froot Loops, Mini-Wheats, Nutri-Grain, Puffed Rice, Quaker Oats, Smart Start 11 Cocoa Blasts, Cookie Crisp, Golden Crisp, Lucky Charms, Puffed Wheat, Sweet Crunch, Waffle Crisp
dog: 6 Seadog
capo: 3 don 9 beginning
group: 3 mob
capon: 4 bird, fowl, male, meat 7 chicken, poultry
caponata: 9 appetizer
Capone: 2 Al 8 gangster
nemesis: 3 IRS 4 Ness
rival: 5 Moran
Caponi, Donna: 6 golfer
milieu: 5 links 6 course
org.: 4 LPGA
capote: 4 cape, coat, wrap 5 cloak, cover 6 jacket, mantle 8 overcoat
Capote: 3 Tru 6 Truman
Capote, Truman: 6 author, writer
work: Breakfast at Tiffany's
The Grass Harp
In Cold Blood
Local Color
The Muses are Heard
Music for Chameleons
Other Voices, Other Rooms
Capp: 2 Al 4 Andy
Capp, Al
adjective: 3 Li'l
character: 5 Abner, Mammy, Pappy, Shmoo, Yokum 8 Daisy Mae
hyena: 4 Lena
cappa magna: 5 cloak
Capp, Andy wife: 3 Flo
___-capped: 4 snow 5 cloud
Cap-Pele: 4 city, town
locale: 6 Canada
cappella
a ~: 5 music 6 choral
a ~ style: 6 doo-wop
cappelletti: 5 pasta
alternative: 4 orzo, ziti 5 penne 6 noodle 7 lasagna, lasagne, pastina, ravioli 8 bucatini, couscous, farfalle, linguine, linguini, macaroni, rigatoni 9 agnolotti, angelhair, cavatelli, manicotti, spaghetti 10 cannelloni, fettuccini, tortellini, vermicelli
cappuccino: 5 drink 6 coffee 8 beverage
cousin: 5 latte
flavor: 5 mocha
place: 4 café
Capra, Frank: 8 director
film: American Madness (1932)
Arsenic and Old Lace (1944)
The Bitter Tea of General Yen (1933)
Broadway Bill (1934)
Here Comes the Groom (1951)
It Happened One Night (1934, AA)
It's a Wonderful Life (1946)
Lady for a Day (1933)
Lost Horizon (1937)
Meet John Doe (1941)
The Miracle Woman (1931)
Mr. Deeds Goes to Town (1936, AA)
Mr. Smith Goes to Washington (1939)
Platinum Blonde (1931)
Pocketful of Miracles (1961)
State of the Union (1948)
The Strong Man (1926)
You Can't Take It With You (1938, AA)
Capri: 3 car, isl. 4 Ahna, auto, isle 6 island 7 Lincoln, Mercury
attraction: 6 grotto
city near ~: 6 Naples
island near ~: 4 Elba
locale: 5 Italy
suffix: 3 ote
Capri ___: 5 pants
Capriati, Jennifer: 7 netster 9 tennis pro
foe: 4 Graf 5 Seles
milieu: 5 court
capriccio: 5 music, prank
caprice: 4 joke, whim 5 fancy, music, quirk 6 notion, vagary 7 impulse
Caprice: 3 car 4 auto 5 Chevy 9 Chevrolet 10 automobile
Caprichos artist: 4 Goya
capricious: 5 giddy, moody, timid 6 chancy, fickle, fitful, quirky, uneven 7 aimless, erratic, flighty, mutable, playful, unloyal, wayward 8 careless, fanciful, notional, skittish, ticklish, unstable, unsteady, variable, volatile 9 arbitrary, crotchety, eccentric, faithless, fantastic, humorsome, impulsive, irregular, mercurial, up-and-down, vagarious, whimsical 10 changeable, inconstant, lubricious, unreliable
Capricorn: 4 goat, sign
follower: Aquarius
months: 3 Dec., Jan. 7 January 8 December
preceder: Sagittarius
Capricorn Concerto composer: 6 Barber
Capricorn One (1978 film)
cast: James Brolin, Elliott Gould, Hal Holbrook
director: Peter Hyams
caprine: 7 goatish 8 goatlike
capriole: 4 jump
Capris: 5 pants
feature: 4 slit
Capris song: There's a Moon Out Tonight (1961)
Caps: 3 six 4 team
milieu: 3 ice 4 rink
org.: 3 NHL
Capshaw, Kate spouse: Steven Spielberg
capsicum: 9 condiment
capsize: 3 tip 4 sink, turn 5 upend, upset, wreck 6 invert, topple 7 tip over 8 keel over, overturn, turn over
Caps Lock neighbor: 3 Tab 5 Shift
capstan ___: 3 bar 5 table
capstone: 4 acme 6 climax, summit, zenith 8 high spot
capsule: 3 pod, sac 4 dose, pill 8 abridged, medicine, synopsis 9 condensed, container, shortened, synopsize 10 medication
botanical ~: 4 boll 5 theca
___ capsule: 4 time 5 space 7 aneroid, Bowman's
capsulize: 5 recap 9 summarize
capt.: 4 rank
employer: 3 USN 4 USAF, USCG
heading: 3 ENE, ESE, NNE, NNW, SSE, SSW, WNW, WSW
subordinate: 2 lt. 3 cdr. 4 cmdr. 5 lieut.
superior: 3 adm., col., maj.
captain: 4 boss, exec, head, rank 5 chief, pilot, steer 6 leader, manage, master, sailor, top dog 7 jack tar, mariner, officer, oversee, skipper 8 director, helmsman, kingfish, navigate 9 authority, commander, executive
book: 3 log
destination: 4 port
fictional ~: 4 Ahab, Hook, Kirk, Nemo
insignia: 3 bar
milieu: 3 sea 4 asea, helm, main 5 at sea, ocean 6 bridge
of industry: 4 czar 5 baron, mogul 6 tycoon 7 magnate
reply to a ~: 5 no sir 6 aye aye
superior: 5 major
see also nautical
___ captain: 3 sea 4 bell, port 5 field, staff
Captain ___: 3 Ron 4 Fury, Kidd 5 Blood, Video
Captain Blood (1935 film)
cast: Lionel Atwill, Olivia de Havilland, Errol Flynn
director: Michael Curtiz
Captain Brassbound's Conversion
author: George Bernard Shaw
Captain Carey, U.S.A. (1950 film)
cast: Wanda Hendrix, Alan Ladd
director: Mitchell Leisen
Captain Corelli's Mandolin (2001 film)
cast: Christian Bale, Nicolas Cage, Penélope Cruz, John Hurt
director: John Madden
Captain From Castile (1947 film)
cast: Jean Peters, Tyrone Power
director: Henry King
Captain Fury (1939 film)
cast: Brian Aherne, Victor McLaglen
director: Hal Roach
Captain Horatio Hornblower (1951 film)
cast: Robert Beatty, Virginia Mayo, Gregory Peck
director: Raoul Walsh
Captain Kidd: 6 pirate
Captain Lightfoot (1955 film)
cast: Rock Hudson, Barbara Rush
director: Douglas Sirk
Captain Newman, M.D. (1963 film)
cast: Eddie Albert, Tony Curtis, Angie Dickinson, Gregory Peck
director: David Miller
captain's ___: 3 bed 4 mast 5 chair, table
Captains Courageous: 4 film 5 novel
author: Rudyard Kipling
cast: Lionel Barrymore, Freddie Bartholomew, Melvyn Douglas, Spencer Tracy
character: 5 Disko, Troop 6 Harvey
director: Victor Fleming
Captain's Daughter, The author: Aleksandr Pushkin
Captains of the Clouds (1942 film)
cast: James Cagney, Dennis Morgan
director: Michael Curtiz
Captain's Paradise (1953 film)
cast: Yvonne De Carlo, Sir Alec Guinness, Celia Johnson
Captain's Tiger author: Athol Fugard
Captain's wife: 4 Toni 8 Tennille
Captain & Tennille
song: Do That to Me One More Time (1979)
Lonely Night (1976)
Love Will Keep Us Together (1975)
Muskrat Love (1976)
Shop Around (1976)
The Way I Want to Touch You (1975)
The Captain: Daryl Dragon
Captain Video (Dumont sci-fi) cast: Al Hodge (Captain Video)
foe: 5 Tobor
caption: 4 term 5 title 6 legend 7 heading, writing 8 headline, subtitle 9 underline
___-captioned: 6 closed
captious: 5 cross, testy 6 crabby, crusty 7 carping, finicky, fretful, nagging, peevish 8 caviling, contrary, critical, exacting, finiking, finnicky, fretsome, petulant, specious 9 demanding, fractious, irritable, querulous, sarcastic 10 censorious, nitpicking
Captiva: 3 isl. 4 isle 6 island
locale: 7 Florida

captivate: **4** draw, lure, take, vamp **5** charm, tempt **6** absorb, allure, appeal, dazzle, disarm, enamor, engage, ravish, rope in, turn on **7** attract, beguile, bewitch, enchain, enchant, engross, enthral, immerse, inthral **8** bedazzle, enthrall, entrance, inthrall, intrigue, transfix **9** enrapture, entertain, fascinate, hypnotize, infatuate, magnetize, mesmerize, spellbind, transport
captivated: **4** rapt **6** enrapt **7** far gone **8** held fast, obsessed, ravished **9** bewitched, delighted, engrossed, gladdened **10** fascinated, infatuated
be ~ by: **4** love **5** adore
captivating: **5** siren **6** lovely, pretty, quaint **7** darling, lovable, winning, winsome **8** adorable, alluring, loveable, magnetic, pleasing **10** magnetical
captive: **4** held **5** bound, caged, slave **6** in jail, jailed **7** convict, hostage, subject **8** confined, detainee, ensnared, internee, locked up, prisoner **9** in custody **10** imprisoned
hold ~: **3** net **4** take **5** seize **6** immure
captivity: **4** jail **6** prison **7** bondage, fetters, slavery **8** thraldom **9** committal, detention, restraint, servitude, thralldom, vassalage **10** constraint, entombment, internment, subjection
free from ~: **5** unpen **6** let out
captor: **6** jailer **7** officer **9** conqueror, kidnapper, policeman
capture: **3** bag, get, nab, net, win **4** bust, cage, gain, grab, hook, land, lure, nail, rope, take, trap **5** catch, pinch, run in, seize, snare **6** abduct, arrest, collar, corner, entrap, kidnap, obtain, occupy, pick up, ravage, rope in, secure, snatch **7** acquire, ensnare, insnare, round up, seizure **8** grab away, surprise **9** apprehend, extradite, lay hold of, track down **10** bring to bay, commandeer, confiscate, kidnapping, occupation, photograph
again: **5** rewin
elude ~: **4** hide **6** escape
Capture, The (1950 film)
cast: Lew Ayres, Victor Jory, Teresa Wright
director: John Sturges
Capuana, Luigi: **6** writer **7** Italian
capuche: **4** hood
capuchin: **3** sai **5** cloak, jocko **6** animal, coffee, mammal, monkey **7** primate
monkey: **3** sai
relative: **3** ape **4** saki, titi **5** chimp, drill, jocko, lemur, loris, magot, orang, potto, shrew **6** aye-aye, baboon, Bandar, galago, gelada, gibbon, grivet, guenon, howler, langur, macaco, rhesus, uakari, vervet **7** colobus, gorilla, guereza, hoolock, macaque, sapajou, siamang, tamarin, tarsier **8** bush baby, mandrill, mangabey, marmoset, talapoin **9** orangutan **10** Barbary ape, chimpanzee, orangutang
Capulet to Montague: **3** foe
capybara: **6** animal, mammal, rodent
relative: **3** rat **4** cavy, degu, jird, paca, vole **5** coypu, gundi, mouse, xerus **6** agouti, beaver, gerbil, gopher, jerboa, marmot, murine **7** hamster, lemming, muskrat, visacha **8** chipmunk, cricetid, dormouse, squirrel, tuco-tuco **9** chickaree, groundhog, guinea pig, porcupine, woodchuck **10** chinchilla, prairie dog
car: **2** MV **3** AMC, Geo, GMC, Jag, Kia, neo, Reo **4** Audi, auto, Colt, Fiat, Ford, heap, Jeep, Lada, limo, Nash, Olds, Opel, tram **5** Acura, Aries, Buick, Caddy, Chevy, Civic, coupe, diner, Dodge, Eagle, Edsel, Essex, Honda, Isuzu, Mazda, Pinto, Rolls, sedan, wagon **6** Bronco, Cougar, Daewoo, De Soto, Escort, Falcon, Fiesta, Hudson, Impala, Jaguar, jalopy, Kaiser, Kissel, Nissan, Pierce, Rabbit, Saturn, Subaru, Suburu, Suzuki, Taurus, Tercel, Toyota, wheels, Willys **7** Bentley, caboose, Checker, Citroen, clunker, compact, concern, Ferrari, flivver, hardtop, Hyundai, La Salle, Lincoln, Maxwell, Mercury, Mustang, Packard, phaeton, Pontiac, Porsche, Rambler, Renault, Skylark, sleeper, vehicle **8** Cadillac, Chrysler, Daihatsu, Plymouth, roadster, wagon-lit **9** Alfa Romeo, cabriolet, Chevrolet, hatchback, Hupmobile, limousine, transport, two-seater **10** automobile, conveyance, Duesenberg, gas guzzler, Mitsubishi, Oldsmobile, rattletrap, Rolls Royce, Studebaker, Volkswagen **11** Lamborghini
1920s: **3** Reo **5** Essex
1960s: **3** GTO
ad abbr.: **3** APR, EPA, MPG
AMC: **5** Pacer **7** Gremlin
assemblers' org.: **3** UAW
bar: **4** axle **5** strut
borrowed ~: **6** loaner
British: **2** MG **3** Jag, MGB **5** Rolls, Rover **6** Jaguar **10** Rolls-Royce
British ~ part: **4** boot, tyre **6** bonnet
buyer need: **4** loan
Chrysler: **4** Neon **5** Dodge **6** De Soto
classic: **3** GTO, Reo **4** Cord, Ghia, Nash **5** Aston, Essex, Stutz, T-bird
combining form: **4** auto-
dealer sign: **4** sold, used
defective ~: **4** heap **5** crate, lemon
document: **5** lease, title
drive the getaway ~: **4** abet
ender: **3** hop, top **4** fare, king, load, port, sick **5** maker, uncle
engine: **4** V-six **5** V-four **6** diesel, V-eight, Wankel
fast ~: **5** Lotus, racer **6** hot rod
feed the ~: **5** gas up
for hire: **3** cab **4** limo, taxi **9** limousine
fuel: **3** gas
General Motors: **4** Olds, Opel **5** Buick, Caddy **6** Saturn **7** Pontiac **8** Cadillac **10** Oldsmobile
German: **3** BMW **4** Audi, Opel **6** Beetle **10** Volkswagen
go by ~: **5** drive, motor
heater setting: **5** deice **7** defrost
interior material: **5** vinyl **7** leather
Italian: **4** Fiat, Ghia **7** Ferrari **8** Maserati **9** Alfa Romeo
Japanese: **5** Miata **6** Nissan, Toyota
job: **3** LOF **4** lube **6** repair, tuneup
Korean: **3** Kia
leave the ~: **4** park
lifter: **4** jack
like an old ~: **5** rusty
luxury ~: **3** BMW **4** limo, Linc **5** Lexus **7** Lincoln **8** Cadillac, Infiniti
metal: **5** steel **6** chrome **8** aluminum
necessity: **5** spare **6** engine
new ~ odometer reading: **5** OOOOO
owner's dread: **4** dent **7** scratch
parker: **5** valet
part: **4** axle, belt, carb, hood, hose, tire **5** brake, grill, motor, radio, strut, wheel, wiper **6** bumper, clutch, engine, fender, grille, heater, mirror **7** chassis, fan belt, starter **8** CD player **9** defroster **10** alternator, carburetor
part brand: **4** Fram **5** Delco
path: **4** road
problem: **4** rust **5** no oil
racing org.: **4** NHRA
radio feature: **4** scan **6** preset
registration info: **3** VIN **4** make **5** color, model, owner
repairer: **4** mech **6** garage **8** mechanic
ride: **4** lift, spin
roof: **4** T-top
Russian: **3** Zil **4** Lada
safety device: **6** airbag **8** seat belt
security device: **5** alarm
showroom ~: **4** demo
sporty ~: **3** Gto, Jag **5** coupe, T-bird, 'Vette **6** Camaro **8** Corvette
starter: **3** box **4** flat, hand, race, rail, side, tram **5** motor **6** street
Swedish: **4** Saab **5** Volvo
wax: **7** Simoniz
went by ~: **6** autoed
window: **4** vent
see also automobile
car __: **3** bed **4** card, coat, line, park, pool, seat, wash **6** pooler
__ car: **3** bar, tow, way **4** café, camp, club, coal, dome, life, mail, pace, rack, skip, slot, tank, town, trap **5** cable, chair, funny, kiddy, larry, panda, prowl, radio, scout, sport, squad, stock, world **6** buffet, bumper, cattle, cruise, dining, estate, hopper, kiddie, lounge, luxury, muscle, outfit, parlor, patrol, police, racing, safety, saloon, sports **7** armored, baggage, command, compact, foreign, freight, gondola, mid-size, Pullman, sleeper, touring, tourist, trailer, trolley
__-car: **5** rent-a
__-Car: **5** Econo
__ cara: **4** A te o
Cara: **5** Irene **8** Williams
Cara __: **3** Mia
carabao: **5** bovid **6** animal, bovine, mammal
relative: **3** yak **4** anoa, arna, gaur, urus, zebu **5** bison, gayal, takin **6** mithan, muskox **7** aurochs, banteng, banting, beefalo, buffalo, cattalo, kouprey, tamarao, tamarau, timarau
caracal: **3** cat **5** felid **6** animal, feline, mammal
relative: **4** eyra, lion, lynx, puma **5** chita, liger, ounce, tiger, tigon **6** bobcat, cheeta, chetah, cougar, jaguar, margay, ocelot, serval, tiglon **7** bay lynx, cheetah, leopard, panther **9** catamount **10** jaguarundi
caracara: **4** bird
Caracas: **4** city, town **7** capital
locale: **9** Venezuela
see also Spanish
Caractacus composer: **4** Arne
carafe: **3** jug **5** cruet, flask **6** bottle, flagon **7** alembic, pitcher **8** decanter **9** container **10** wine bottle
kin: **4** ewer
caragana: **4** tree **5** shrub
family: **3** pea
Cara, Irene
song: Breakdance (1984)
Fame (1980)
Flashdance...What a Feeling (1983)
carambola: **5** fruit
caramel: **3** tan **5** brown, candy, sweet **8** ice cream **9** sweetmeat, yellowish
alternative: **5** lemon, mocha, peach **6** banana, coffee, Jamoca, toffee **7** coconut, vanilla **8** cinnamon, hazelnut **9** bubblegum, chocolate, pineapple, pistachio, raspberry, rocky road, rum raisin **10** blackberry, cheesecake, Neapolitan, peppermint, strawberry
candy brand: **4** Rolo
custard: **4** flan
like ~: **5** chewy, gooey
relative: **3** bay, dun, tan **4** bole, buff, ecru, fawn, foxy, nude, seal **5** amber, beige, camel, cocoa, hazel, khaki, mocha, sepia, tawny, umber **6** almond, auburn, bister, bistre, bronze, coffee, copper, ginger, russet, sienna, sorrel, suntan, walnut **7** biscuit, dogwood **8** chestnut, cinnamon, mahogany **9** butternut, chocolate
Cara Mia (song) artist: Jay and the Americans, Mantovani
Car and __: **6** Driver
carapa: **4** tree
relative: **4** neem **6** acajou, sapele **7** avodire **8** mahogany
carapace: **4** skin **5** shell
carat: **6** weight **7** measure
fraction: **2** pt. **5** point
24 ~: **4** pure **7** sincere
caravan: **4** band **5** train **6** convoy, safari **7** cortege, journey **9** cavalcade **10** expedition, procession
animal: **5** camel
stop: **5** oasis, serai
Caravan: **3** van **5** Dodge
caravansary: **3** inn **5** hotel, serai **6** hostel
caravel: **4** boat, Niña, ship **5** Pinta **10** Santa Maria
caraway: **4** herb, seed
holder: **3** rye **5** bread
Caray: **5** Harry
carb: **4** rice, spud **5** bread, pasta, tater **6** potato
carbamide: **4** urea
__ carbide: **5** boron **7** calcium, silicon
__ Carbide: **5** Union
carbine, British: **4** sten
Carbine Williams (1952 film)
cast: Jean Hagen, James Stewart
carbo-__: **4** load **7** loading
carbohydrate: **3** poi, yam **4** rice, taro **5** pasta, sugar **6** manioc, potato, starch **7** cassava, dextrin, glucose, lactose, maltose, risotto, sucrose **8** couscous, dextrine, dextrose, fructose, kedgeree, semolina, wild rice **9** brown rice, home fries
plant-cell ~: **5** xylan
suffix: **3** -ose
__ carbohydrate: **6** simple **7** complex
carbolic: **4** acid
carbon: **4** copy **6** ectype **7** diamond, element, replica **8** graphite, likeness **9** lampblack, reproduce
add ~ dioxide to: **6** aerate
alloy: **5** steel **8** cast iron
carbonate form: **5** trona
coated with ~: **5** sooty
combining form: **7** anthrac- **8** anthraco-
compound: **4** enol **5** ester
compound suffix: **3** -ane, -ene
copy: **7** replica **8** likeness **9** duplicate, facsimile, identical, imitation, lookalike **10** equivalent
crystalline form of ~ gem: **7** diamond
deposit: **4** soot
form of ~: **4** coal **7** diamond **8** graphite
frozen ~ dioxide: **6** Dry Ice
hard crystallized ~: **7** diamond
carbon __: **3** arc, tet **4** copy, star **5** black, cycle, fiber, paper, steel **6** dating, tissue **7** dioxide, process
carbon-__: **4** date **6** dating
carbonate: **4** salt **6** alkali
__ carbonate: **4** lead **6** barium, sodium **7** calcium, lithium
carbonated: **5** fizzy, foamy
drink: **4** cola, soda
not ~: **5** still

carbonated __: 5 water
carbonation: 3 gas 4 fizz
Carbondale: 4 city, town
locale: 8 Illinois
carbon-14 expert: 5 dater
carbonic: 4 acid
__ Carboniferous: 5 Upper
carbonium: 3 ion
carbonize: 4 burn, char, heat, sear 5 singe 6 scorch
carbonized plants: 4 peat
carbonless paper: 3 NCR
carbonnade: 4 stew
carbon-nitrogen __: 5 cycle
carboy: 6 bottle
carcajou: 6 animal, mammal, weasel
relative: 4 mink 5 fitch, otter, ratel, sable, skunk, stoat, tayra 6 badger, ermine, ferret, marten 7 foumart, polecat 8 foulmart, kolinsky, muishond 9 wolverine
Carcassonne's department: 4 Aude
Carcross: 4 city, town
locale: 6 Canada
card: 3 ace, tag, wag, wit 4 jack, king, riot, trey, zany 5 comic, cutup, deuce, joker, knave, queen 6 agenda, docket, lineup, scream, ticket 7 program, punster 8 calendar, comedian, funnyman, humorist, jokester, kibitzer, quipster, schedule 9 character, leg-puller, timetable
baseball ~ company: 5 Fleer, Topps 6 Bowman 7 Donruss 9 Upper Deck
black ~: 4 club 5 spade
catalog abbr.: 5 illus.
catalogue datum: 5 title 6 author
collection: 4 deck, hand, pack
combo: 4 meld, pair
dealer's device: 4 shoe
dealer's offering: 3 cut
drawing ~: 4 lure, star 6 magnet 7 feature
ender: 5 board, sharp 6 holder 7 sharper
face ~: 4 jack, king 5 honor, queen
game stake: 4 ante
green ~ holder: 7 refugee 8 emigrant, newcomer 9 foreigner, immigrant 10 noncitizen
greeting ~ feature: 4 poem 5 rhyme 8 doggerel
greeting ~ word: 4 yule
high ~: 3 ace 4 jack, king 5 queen
honor ~: 3 ace, ten 4 king
low ~: 3 two 4 four, trey 5 deuce, three
(out): 3 log 5 punch
player's headwear: 5 visor, vizor
player's yell: 3 gin, uno
playing ~: 3 six, ten 4 five, four, jack, king, nine, trey 5 deuce, eight, heart, joker, queen, seven, spade, three
red: 5 heart 7 diamond
seer's ~: 5 tarot
select a ~: 4 draw
spot: 3 pip
starter: 4 time 5 score
top ~: 3 ace
use a credit ~: 3 owe 6 charge
used to jimmy spring locks: 4 loid
wild ~: 5 deuce, joker
card __: 4 game 5 index, punch, shark, table, trick 7 catalog, counter 9 catalogue
card-__: 3 cut, key
__ card: 3 car, cue, key, mag, red 4 bank, case, coat, cost, down, face, file, gray, grey, hole, long, Mass, post, rate, show, side, spot, unit, wild 5 altar, balop, bingo, chase, dance, debit, donor, entry, false, flash, green, honor, idiot, index, phone, place, punch, reply, smart, store, tally, trump, union 6 bubble, charge, credit, postal, report 7 breaker, calling, compass, drawing, get-well, landing, library, picture, playing, reentry, trading
Card: 4 NLer 6 Frisch, Musial, Sisler 10 baseballer
__ Card: 5 Green 7 Maximum
cardamom: 4 herb 5 spice
Cardamom: 5 range
locale: 4 Asia 5 India
__ card, any...: 5 Pick a
card-carrying: 5 legal 6 lawful 8 rightful
Cárdenas: 4 city, town
locale: 6 Mexico 7 Tabasco
carder's request: 2 ID
card game: 3 gin, loo, nap, uno, war 4 brag, faro, fish, jass, skat, snap, stud 5 beano, cinch, gleek, monte, omber, Pedro, pitch, poker, rummy, tarok, whist 6 belote, Boston, bridge, casino, ecarte, euchre, fan-tan, go fish, hearts, hold 'em, hombre, memory, piquet, red dog 7 authors, belotte, bezique, binocle, canasta, cooncan, high-low, lowball, old maid, pontoon, primero, seven-up 8 all fours, anaconda, baccarat, baseball, canfield, conquian, cribbage, forfeits, gin rummy, I doubt it, Michigan, napoleon, patience, pinochle, sixty-six, slapjack 9 blackjack, draw poker, freezeout, old sledge, penny ante, quadrille, solitaire, spoilfive, twenty-one, vingt-et-un 10 backgammon, klaberjass, knock rummy, panguingue 11 chemin de fer, crazy eights, high-low-jack, rouge et noir, speculation
British ~: 5 gleek 7 primero
European ~: 5 tarok
French ~: 6 belote
3-handed ~: 5 omber 6 hombre
cardiac __: 5 cycle 6 muscle, output
cardiac readout: 3 ECG, EKG
Cardiff: 4 city, Jack, port, town
Giant: 4 hoax
locale: 5 Wales
river: 4 Taff
cardigan: 6 jacket 7 sweater
craft a ~: 4 knit
Cardigan: 3 bay
locale: 5 Wales
Cardin: 6 Pierre
rival: 5 Klein 6 Armani, Lauren
cardinal: 2 no. 3 key, red 4 bird, main, male, rank 5 basic, chief, color, prime, vital 6 cleric, datary, number, ruling, utmost 7 central, leading, pivotal, prelate, primary, radical, supreme 8 headmost 9 essential, important, paramount, principal, strategic, uttermost, vermilion 10 overriding, preeminent, underlying
beak: 3 nib
color: 3 red
home: 4 nest
point: 4 east, west 5 north, south
point suffix: 3 ern
relative: 4 rose, ruby, rust, wine 5 brick, coral, grape, poppy, rusty, sandy 6 cerise, cherry, claret, garnet, maroon 7 carmine, crimson, fuchsia, magenta, pimento, scarlet, sultana, vermeil 8 amaranth, dubonnet, geranium, rubicund 9 carnation, cranberry, vermilion 10 strawberry
cardinal __: 3 sin 4 sign 5 point, tetra, trait, vowel 6 flower, number, system, virtue 7 numeral
Cardinal: 4 NLer 7 Cushing, Ernesto 9 Richelieu 10 baseballer, footballer
Hall of Famer: 4 Dean 5 Smith 6 Frisch, Gibson, Musial, Sisler 7 Medwick 12 Schoendienst
rival: 3 Cub, Jet, Met, Ram, Red 4 Bear, Bill, Colt, Expo, Lion, Twin 5 Angel, Astro, Brave, Brown, Chief, Eagle, Giant, Niner, Padre, Raven, Rocky, Royal, Saint, Texan, Tiger, Titan 6 Bengal, Brewer, Bronco, Cowboy, Dodger, Falcon, Indian, Jaguar, Marlin, Oriole, Packer, Philly, Pirate, Raider, Ranger, Red Sox, Viking, Yankee 7 Blue Jay, Charger, Dolphin, Mariner, Panther, Patriot, Redskin, Seahawk, Steeler 8 Athletic, Devil Ray, White Sox 9 Buccaneer
Cardinale, Claudia: 7 actress
film: 8 1/2 (1963)
Burden of Dreams (1982)
Cartouche (1964)
Don't Make Waves (1967)
Fitzcarraldo (1982)
The Leopard (1963)
Once Upon a Time in the West (1968)
__ Cardinal Egan: 6 Edward
Cardinal, Ernesto: 4 poet 10 Nicaraguan
Cardinals: 4 nine, team 6 eleven 9 Ball State
home: 7 Arizona, St. Louis
logo: 3 St. L.
org.: 3 MLB, NFC, NFL, NLC
sport: 8 baseball, football
Cardinal Sins, The author: Greeley
Cardinal Virtues author: Greeley
cardiogram starter: 4 echo
cardiologist concern: 5 aorta, heart
cardiology adjective: 6 aortal, aortic
cardio medication: 5 nitro
__-card monte: 5 three
cardoon: 6 veggie 9 vegetable
Cardozo: 5 judge 7 justice 8 Benjamin
cards
be in the ~: 4 loom 7 portend
hand out ~: 4 deal
in the ~: 4 luck, near 5 fated 6 at hand, likely 7 in store 8 destined, imminent, probable 9 impending
peek at the ~: 5 cheat
put one's ~ on the table: 6 reveal
__ cards: 5 in the, Zener
Cards: 4 nine, team 6 eleven
org.: 3 MLB, NFL
cardsharp: 6 rascal, robber
__-card stud: 4 five 5 seven
card-table project: 6 jigsaw
Carducci, Giosuè: 4 poet 7 Italian 8 Nobelist
care: 3 woe 4 duty, egis, heed, load, mind 5 aegis, alarm, pains, sweat, trial, trust, worry 6 bother, burden, charge, dismay, effort, escrow, object, regard, regret, strain, stress 7 anguish, anxiety, caution, concern, conduct, control, custody, keeping, thought, trouble 8 auspices, disquiet, distress, give a rap, hardship, industry, interest, prudence, tutelage, vexation, wardship 9 affection, alertness, assiduity, attention, diligence, exactness, give a damn, give a darn, give a hoot, hindrance, misgiving, precision, vigilance 10 affliction, discretion, foreboding, management, precaution, protection, solicitude, uneasiness, weather eye
don't ~ for: 4 hate 7 dislike
don't ~ to: 6 refuse 7 decline
ender: 4 free, worn 5 giver, taker
examine with ~: 4 sift
for: 4 keep, like, love, mind, rear, tend 5 adore, board, fancy, nurse, prize, raise, see to, serve, value, watch 6 admire, attend, dote on, esteem, manage, revere, take to, wait on 7 baby-sit, cherish, idolize, nourish, nurture, protect, support, worship 8 dote upon, enshrine, hold dear, inshrine, maintain, preserve, treasure, wait upon 9 look after, reverence 10 appreciate
freedom from ~: 4 ease 5 peace 8 calmness, serenity 9 composure
handle with ~: 6 caress
have a ~: 6 beware 7 look out
not taken ~ of: 5 unmet
prefix for ~: 4 Medi
starter: 3 day 5 after, child, elder 6 health
take ~: 6 beware
take ~ of: 3 pay 4 feed, mall, maul, tend 5 act on, nurse, see to, watch 6 advert, attend, foster, handle, reward 7 address, baby-sit, execute, nurture, protect, provide, shelter, sit with 8 attend to, cope with, deal with, keep safe, maintain, minister, see about, transact 9 cultivate, do justice, look after, overpower, watch over 10 accomplish, compensate, consummate
(to): 4 like 6 prefer
care __: 4 a rap 5 a hang, a hoot, label 7 package
__ care: 3 day 4 skin, take 6 foster, health 7 managed, primary
__-care: 4 easy, home 5 acute, child
__ Care: 5 I Don't
care a __: 4 hang, hoot
__ care!, A: 4 lot I
__-care center: 3 day
cared for: 7 beloved
careen: 3 tip 4 keel, lean, list, race, reel, rock, sway, tear, tilt, veer 5 lurch, pitch, weave 6 glance, hurtle, swerve, totter, wabble, wobble 7 stagger 8 heel over, ricochet
careening: 5 alist
career: 3 job, run 4 line, race, rush, tear, walk, work 5 craft, field, speed, sweep 6 living, métier, plunge, racket, record 7 banking, calling, pursuit 8 baseball, business, lifetime, lifework, position, practice, vocation 9 specialty 10 burn rubber, livelihood, occupation, profession, walk of life
criminal: 5 felon
soldier: 5 lifer
start: 5 debut
starter: 4 grad
summary: 4 vita 6 résumé
career __: 4 goal, move 5 woman 8 diplomat, planning
__ career: 9 checkered
Career (1959 film)
cast: Tony Franciosa, Shirley MacLaine, Dean Martin
Careers: 4 game 9 board game
carefree: 3 gay 4 airy, calm, cool, easy 5 happy, jolly, light, merry, staid, stoic, sunny 6 at ease, blithe, breezy, cheery, jaunty, jovial, low-key, mellow, placid, secure, sedate, serene 7 at peace, buoyant, halcyon, relaxed, romping, stoical 8 cheerful, composed, feckless, grooving, laid-back, reckless, tranquil, untaxing 9 collected, easygoing, footloose, impassive, lightsome, temperate, unanxious, unexcited, unruffled, unworried 10 flying high, insouciant, nonchalant, rollicking, unagitated, unbothered, untroubled
episode: 4 idyl, lark
in French: 9 sans souci
Carefree: 3 gum 4 city, town
alternative: 5 Extra, Orbit 7 Dentyne, Trident 8 Chiclets, Freedent 10 Doublemint, Juicy Fruit
locale: 7 Arizona
Carefree (1938 film)
cast: Fred Astaire, Ralph Bellamy, Ginger Rogers

composer: Irving Berlin
director: Mark Sandrich
Carefree Highway (1974 song) artist: Gordon Lightfoot
careful: 4 cagy, nice, safe, wary, wise 5 alert, cagey, canny, chary, exact, fussy, leery, sober 6 choosy, frugal, minute 7 choosey, finicky, guarded, heedful, mindful, precise, prudent, sparing, thrifty, wakeful 8 accurate, cautious, delicate, diligent, discreet, exacting, finiking, finnicky, keen-eyed, methodic, reliable, rigorous, studious, thorough, vigilant, watchful 9 assiduous, attentive, defensive, judicious, observant, provident, regardful, selective 10 deliberate, fastidious, methodical, meticulous, particular, protective, scrupulous, solicitous, suspicious, thoughtful
be ~: 4 mind 6 go slow 7 heads up, look out, watch it
be ~, old-style: 4 reck
not ~: 3 lax 4 rash 10 incautious
reasoning: 5 logic
__ careful!: 4 Do be
Careful!: 4 easy
carefully: 4 well 7 charily 8 gingerly 9 advisedly, anxiously, correctly, guardedly, heedfully, honorably, inside out, precisely, prudently, tactfully, uprightly 10 cautiously, delicately, dependably, discreetly, faithfully, rigorously, thoroughly, vigilantly, watchfully
carefulness: 4 heed 6 regard, thrift 7 caution, concern 9 chariness, precision, vigilance
__ care in the world: 4 not a
careless: 3 lax 4 lazy, rash 5 hasty, loose, messy, slack 6 remiss, shoddy, sloppy, unwary, wanton 7 cursory, offhand, raffish, unaware 8 derelict, fallible, heedless, indolent, listless, mindless, off-guard, pell-mell, reckless, slapdash, slipshod, slovenly, wasteful 9 desperate, forgetful, haphazard, imprecise, imprudent, impulsive, negligent, oblivious, unadvised, uncareful, unguarded, unheedful, unmindful, vagarious 10 capricious, delinquent, incautious, indiscreet, last-minute, neglectful, nonchalant, regardless, uncritical, unthinking, unthorough
be ~: 4 lose 7 neglect
__ care less: 7 couldn't
Careless Hands singer: Mel Torme
Careless Husband, The playwright: 6 Cibber
Careless Love author: 5 Adams
carelessly: 6 anyhow 7 lightly 8 absently, pell-mell 10 flippantly
carelessness: 5 haste 6 laxity 7 neglect 9 oversight
Careless Whisper (1984 song) artist: George Michael
__ care of: 4 take
__ Care Of Business: 5 Takin'
Care of Time, The author: Eric Ambler
CARE package: 3 aid 10 assistance
__ cares?: 3 Who
caress: 3 hug, pat, rub, woo 4 love 5 touch 6 clinch, clutch, cuddle, stroke, tickle 7 embrace, snuggle 8 make nice
Caress: 4 soap
alternative: 3 Lux 4 Dial, Dove, Lava, Tone, Zest 5 Camay, Coast, Ivory, Lever 6 Boraxo, Shield 8 Lifebuoy 9 Palmolive, Safeguard 11 Irish Spring
caretaker: 4 nana 5 super 6 keeper, sitter, warden 7 curator, janitor 8 gardener, watchdog 9 concierge, custodian, governess, nursemaid, protector 10 baby sitter, supervisor
Caretakers, The (1963 film)
cast: Polly Bergen, Joan Crawford, Robert Stack
Caretaker, The author: Harold Pinter
caret, use a: 6 insert
Carew: 3 Rod 6 Thomas
careworn: 5 tired 7 haggard 8 footsore 9 exhausted
Carew, Rod: 4 Twin 10 baseballer
Carew, Thomas: 4 poet 7 British
Carey: 4 Drew 5 Diane, Harry 6 Lowell, Mariah 9 Macdonald
Carey, Mariah
song: Always Be My Baby (1996)
Can't Let Go (1991)
Dreamlover (1993)
Emotions (1991)
Endless Love (1994)
Fantasy (1995)
Forever (1996)
Heartbreaker (1999)
Hero (1993)
Honey (1997)
I Don't Wanna Cry (1991)
I'll Be There (1992)
I Still Believe (1999)
Love Takes Time (1990)
Make It Happen (1992)
My All (1998)
One Sweet Day (1995)
Someday (1991)
Thank God I Found You (2000)
Vision of Love (1990)
Without You (1994)
Carey Treatment, The (1972 film)
cast: James Coburn, Pat Hingle, Jennifer O'Neill
director: Blake Edwards
Car 54, Where Are You? (NBC sitcom)
cast: Fred Gwynne (Francis Muldoon) Joe E. Ross (Gunther Toody)
creator: 5 Hiken
setting: Bronx, New York
cargo: 4 haul, load 5 goods 6 lading 7 baggage, exports, freight, imports, payload, tonnage, tunnage 8 contents, shipload, shipment 9 wagonload
area: 4 hold
deliver ~: 6 unload
handler: 3 van 5 lader 6 lumper 9 stevedore
ship: 5 oiler 6 argosy, tanker
take on ~: 4 lade, stow
tanker ~: 3 oil 5 crude
temporarily jettisoned ~: 5 lagan
unit: 3 ton
cargo __: 3 bay 4 cult, ship 5 liner 6 pocket
__ cargo: 3 air
carhop: 6 server, waiter 8 waitress
cariama: 4 bird
Carib: 6 Indian 7 Amerind 8 language
Caribbean: 3 sea
city: 5 Ponce 6 Havana, Nassau 7 San Juan, St. John's 8 Castries, Kingston, Road Town 9 Kingstown, St. George's 10 Basseterre, Bridgetown, George Town, Oranjestad 11 Port of Spain 12 Fort-de-France, Port-au-Prince
country: 4 Cuba 5 Haiti 6 Dom. Rep. 7 Bahamas, Grenada, Jamaica, St. Lucia 8 Barbados, Dominica 10 Saint Lucia
dance: 4 soca 5 limbo, mambo 7 beguine
explorer: 8 Columbus
fish: 10 yellow jack
gear: 5 scuba
gulf: 6 Darien, Gonâve 7 San Blas 8 Gonaïves, Honduras
island: 4 Saba 5 Aruba 6 Tobago 7 Grenada, Jamaica, St. Lucia 8 Barbados, Dominica, Trinidad 10 Guadeloupe, Martinique, Puerto Rico, Saint Lucia
islands: 3 BWI 6 Indies 7 Bahamas, Caymans 10 West Indies
liquor: 3 rum
music: 3 ska 4 zouk
native: 6 Arawak
river to the ~: 4 Coco, Ulúa 5 Hondo 6 Patuca 7 Chagres, Motagua 9 Magdalena
trip: 6 cruise
volcano: 5 Pelee
Caribbean __: 3 Sea 5 Plate, Queen 7 Current
__ Caribbean Cruises: 5 Royal
Caribbean Queen (1984 song) artist: Billy Ocean
caribe: 4 fish 7 piranha 8 predator
Cariboo: 5 range 9 mountains
locale: 6 Canada
caribou: 4 deer 6 animal, mammal
feature: 6 antler
hunter: 6 Eskimo
relative: 3 elk, roe 4 axis, deer, pudu, shou, sika 5 moose 6 chital, guemal, hangul, huemul, sambar, sambur, thamin, wapiti 7 brocket, muntjac, muntjak, sambhar, sambhur 8 reindeer 9 barasingh
Caribou: 4 city, town
locale: 5 Maine
caricature: 3 ape, art 4 draw, mock, sham 5 farce, mimic, put-on, sneer, spoof 6 parody, satire, send-up 7 burlesk, cartoon, drawing, imitate, lampoon, mockery, takeoff 8 ridicule, satirize, travesty 9 burlesque, imitation 10 distortion, exaggerate, pasquinade
feature: 4 nose
caricaturist: 4 mime 5 mimic
caries: 6 cavity 10 tooth decay
carillon: 4 bell 5 bells 6 chimes 10 percussion
__ Carinae: 3 Eta
caring: 4 fond 6 humane, loving, tender 7 helpful, thought, valuing 8 maternal, parental 9 concerned, fraternal 10 benevolent, empathetic, solicitous, thoughtful
carioca: 5 dance
home: 3 Rio
relative: 5 samba
Cariou: 3 Len
carious: 6 rancid
Carl: 4 Betz, Cori, Jung, Orff 5 Bosch, Braun, Icahn, Lewis, Rowan, Sagan 6 Albert, Czerny, Dreyer, Lerner, Milles, Rakosi, Reiner, Wieman, Wilson 7 Bellman, Carlton, Douglas, Furillo, Hubbell, Laemmle, Perkins, Schultz 8 Almqvist, Anderson, Franklin, Sandburg, Weathers 9 Bernstein, Spitteler, Zuckmayer 10 Ballantine
son: 3 Rob
Carl __ Gustav: 3 XVI
Carla: 5 Bruni, Hills 6 Gugino
in Cheers: 4 Rhea
Carle: 7 Frankie
Carleton: 7 William 8 Gajdusek
Carleton University
location: 6 Canada, Ottawa 7 Ontario
Carleton, William: 5 Irish 6 writer
__ Carl Fabergé: 5 Peter
Carlin: 4 Lynn 6 George
carling: 4 beam
Carlisle: 3 Bob 5 Kitty 7 Belinda
Carlisle, Belinda
song: Circle in the Sand (1988)
Heaven Is a Place on Earth (1987)
I Get Weak (1988)
Mad About You (1986)
Carlisle, Kitty spouse: Moss Hart
Carlito's Way (1993 film)
cast: Penelope Ann Miller, Al Pacino, Sean Penn
director: Brian De Palma
Carlo: 5 Gadda, Gozzi, Ponti 6 Rubbia 7 Cassola, Collodi, Goldoni 8 Imperato
in English: 7 Charles
Sophia, to ~: 4 wife
__ Carlo: 5 Monte
__ Carlo Menotti: 4 Gian
Carlos: 4 Belo, Juan 5 Lamas, Wendy 6 Chávez, Reyles, Walter 7 Bousoño, Fuentes, Montoya, Santana 9 Castaneda
in English: 7 Charles
see also Spanish
__ Carlos: 3 Don
__ Carlos Jobim: 7 Antonio
Carlotta in English: 9 Charlotte
Carlsbad: 4 city, town
locale: 9 New Mexico 10 California
Carlsbad Caverns: 4 park
locale: 9 New Mexico
Carlson: 4 Arne 7 Chester, Richard
Carlsson, Arvid: 8 Nobelist
Carlton: 4 Carl, Fisk 5 Steve
__ Carlton: 4 Ritz
Carlton House __: 4 desk 5 table
Carlton, Steve: 6 hurler 7 Phillie, pitcher
Carl von __: 5 Weber 9 Ossietzky 10 Clausewitz
Carly: 5 Simon
Carlyle: 6 Thomas
Carlyle, Thomas: 6 author, writer 8 Scottish 9 historian
carman: 9 conductor
Carman, Bliss: 4 poet 8 Canadian
Carme: 4 moon
planet: 7 Jupiter
Carmel: 4 city, town
locale: 7 Indiana 10 California
Carmel-__-Sea: 5 by-the
Carmela: 7 Soprano
Carmelite: 3 nun 5 friar 9 religious
Carmen: 4 city, Eric, town 5 McRae, opera 6 Dragon 7 Basilio, Electra, Miranda 9 Cavallaro
composer: 5 Bizet
Don José in ~: 5 tenor
locale: 6 Mexico 8 Campeche
role: 6 Zuniga 7 Don José, Micaëla, Moralès 8 Mercédès 9 Escamillo, Frasquita
setting: 5 Spain 7 Seville
solo: 4 aria
see also Spanish
Carmen author: Prosper Mérimée
Carmen, Eric
song: All by Myself (1976)
Hungry Eyes (1987)
Make Me Lose Control (1988)
Carmen Jones (1954 film)
cast: Pearl Bailey, Harry Belafonte, Dorothy Dandridge
director: Otto Preminger
lyricist: Hammerstein
Carmen Sandiego: 9 detective
need: 3 map
Carmichael: 3 Ian 4 city, town 5 Hoagy 7 Stokely
locale: 10 California
Carmina Burana composer: 4 Orff
carmine: 3 red 5 color 6 purply 7 crimson 8 purplish
relative: 4 rose, ruby, rust, wine 5 brick, coral, grape, poppy, rusty, sandy 6 cerise, cherry, claret, garnet, maroon 7 crimson, fuchsia, magenta, pimento, scarlet, sultana, vermeil 8 amaranth, cardinal, dubonnet, geranium, rubicund 9 carnation, cranberry, vermilion 10 strawberry
Carmine: 7 Coppola
Carnaby Street locale: 4 Soho

carnage: 4 gore 5 havoc 6 murder 8 massacre 9 bloodshed, mortality, slaughter
Carnal Knowledge (1971 film)
cast: Ann-Margret, Candice Bergen, Art Garfunkel, Rita Moreno, Jack Nicholson
director: Mike Nichols
carnallite: 3 ore
carnation: 3 red 5 plant 6 flower
relative: 4 nude, rose, ruby, rust, wine 5 brick, coral, grape, melon, poppy, rusty, sandy 6 cerise, cherry, claret, damask, garnet, maroon, salmon 7 apricot, carmine, crimson, fuchsia, magenta, pimento, scarlet, sultana, vermeil 8 amaranth, cardinal, dubonnet, flamingo, geranium, rubicund 9 cranberry, vermilion 10 strawberry
shade: 3 red 4 pink 5 white
spot: 5 lapel
carnauba: 3 wax 4 palm, tree 6 car wax
Carnegie: 4 Dale 6 Andrew
Carnegie __: 4 Hall, Tech, unit 6 Mellon
carnegiea: 6 cactus
Carne, Judy spouse: Burt Reynolds
carnelian: 3 gem 4 sard 7 sardine, sardius
Carnera: 5 boxer, Primo
he KO'd ~: 4 Baer
Carner, JoAnne: 6 golfer
milieu: 5 links 6 course
org.: 4 LPGA
Carnesecca, Lou: 5 coach
milieu: 5 court
sport: 10 basketball
Carnes, Kim
song: Bette Davis Eyes (1981)
Don't Fall in Love With a Dreamer (1978)
More Love (1980)
carney: 6 barker
Carney: 3 Art 4 city, town 8 Lansford
locale: 8 Maryland
Carney, Art: 5 actor
film: Going in Style (1979)
Harry and Tonto (1974, AA)
House Calls (1978)
Last Action Hero (1993)
The Late Show (1977)
TV: The Honeymooners
Carnic Alps: 5 range 9 mountains
locale: 5 Italy 6 Europe 7 Austria
Carniola: 4 font 8 typeface
carnitas: 5 snack
carnival: 4 fair, show 5 raree 6 circus 7 jubilee 8 festival 9 Mardi Gras 10 masquerade, street fair
attraction: 4 ride 6 go-cart, go-kart
give a ~ spiel: 4 bark
prize: 4 doll 6 kewpie 8 goldfish
prop: 5 stilt
ride cry: 4 whee
setup: 4 tent 5 booth 6 midway
worker: 4 geek 6 barker
carnival __: 5 glass
Carnival
day: 5 Mardi
locale: 3 Rio 6 Brazil
offering: 6 cruise
Carnival (1995 song) artist: Merchant
carnivore: 8 predator
quest: 4 meat, prey
carnotite: 3 ore
Carnovsky: 6 Morris
carny: 6 barker
Carny (1980 film)
cast: Gary Busey, Jodie Foster
carnyx: 4 wind 7 trumpet 10 instrument
carob: 3 pod 4 bean, tree 6 legume
relative: 3 koa 6 cassia, cercis, locust, padauk, padouk, redbud 7 araroba, mesquit 8 mesquite, tamarind 9 poinciana
carol: 3 air 4 hymn, noel, sing, song, tune 5 music, troll 6 ballad, intone
start: 4 hark 5 o come 6 adeste
syllables: 4 fa la, la la 6 fa la la
word: 3 'tis
Carol: 3 Alt 4 Kane, Mann, Reed 5 Haney, Heiss 6 Leifer, Lynley, Potter 7 Burnett 8 Channing, Lawrence
Carol Burnett Show, The (CBS variety)
cast: Carol Burnett
Tim Conway
Harvey Korman
Vicki Lawrence
Lyle Waggoner
Carol City: 4 town
locale: 7 Florida
Carole: 4 King 6 Landis 7 Lombard
Carole Bayer __: 5 Sager
caroler: 4 alto, bass 5 tenor 7 soprano 8 baritone, vocalist 9 chorister
carolers: 5 choir 6 chorus
Carolina: 4 city, rice, town
alternative: 6 Minute 7 Success 9 Uncle Ben's
cape: 4 Fear
locale: 10 Puerto Rico
team: 8 Panthers 10 Hurricanes
Carolina __: 3 ash, bay 4 lily, Moon, rail, wren 7 jasmine
Caroline: 4 Lamb, Rhea 5 Aaron 7 Kennedy
aunt of ~: 3 Pat 5 Ethel 6 Eunice
uncle of ~: 3 Ted
__ Caroline: 5 Sweet
Caroline in the City (NBC sitcom)
cast: Malcolm Gets (Richard Karinsky)
Eric Lutes (Del Cassidy)
Lea Thompson (Caroline Duffy)
cat: 5 Salty
Caroline Islands
part of the ~: 3 Yap 4 Truk 5 Palau
__ Carol Oates: 5 Joyce
Carol Stream: 4 city, town
locale: 8 Illinois
__ & Carol & Ted & Alice: 3 Bob
carolus: 5 money
Carolus: 8 Linnaeus
Carolyn: 5 Chute, Jones, Keene 6 Forché
carom: 4 bank, bump 6 bounce, glance, recoil 7 rebound 8 ricochet 10 bounce back
light ~: 4 kiss
carom __: 4 ball
caroms: 4 game
Caron, Leslie: 7 actress
film: An American in Paris (1951)
Daddy Long Legs (1955)
Doctor's Dilemma (1958)
Fanny (1961)
Father Goose (1964)
Gigi (1958)
Lili (1953)
The L-Shaped Room (1963)
Caro nome: 4 aria
__ carotene: 4 beta
Carothers: 7 Wallace
carotid __: 4 body 5 gland, sinus 6 artery
carousal: 3 jag 4 riot, tear 5 binge, spree 7 revelry
carouse: 4 play, romp 5 revel 6 frolic 7 have fun, roister 9 have a ball, make merry, raise Cain, whoop it up
carousel: 4 ride
Carousel (1956 film): 7 musical
cast: Shirley Jones, Gordon MacRae, Cameron Mitchell
composer: 7 Rodgers 11 Hammerstein
director: Henry King
carp: 3 koi, nag 4 dace, fish, harp, kick, moan, orfe, rail 5 cavil, gripe, groan, knock, prate, whine 6 bother, grouch, grouse, kvetch, niggle 7 censure, grumble, henpeck, nitpick, quarrel, quibble 8 browbeat, complain, goldfish 9 bellyache, criticize, find fault, make a fuss 10 tongue-lash
at: 3 nag 6 rebuke 7 censure
kin: 3 ide 4 chub, rudd
starter: 4 endo
carpaccio base: 4 beef
carpal: 4 bone
locale: 5 wrist
starter: 4 meta
carpal __: 6 tunnel
Carpathians: 5 range 9 mountains
locale: 6 Europe 7 Romania, Rumania 8 Slovakia
mountain range: 5 Tatra
river: 4 Oder, Odra
carpe: 5 Latin, seize
carpe __: 4 diem
carpenter: 3 ant, bee 6 joiner 7 artisan, builder 10 journeyman, woodworker
angle: 5 bevel
at times: 5 sawer
companion: 6 walrus
cut: 5 miter
fastener: 4 bolt, nail, T-nut 5 screw, U-bolt
groove: 4 dado
in an 1859 novel: 4 Bede
name meaning ~: 9 Zimmerman
need: 5 apron, dowel, stain 6 ladder 7 goggles 8 miter box
strap: 3 gib
strip: 4 lath
tool: 3 adz, saw 4 adze, vise 5 clamp, drill, lathe, level, plane, plumb 6 C-clamp, chisel, hammer, pliers
wedge: 4 shim
woe: 4 knot 8 splinter
carpenter __: 3 ant, bee 4 moth 6 gothic
Carpenter: 4 John 5 Karen, Scott 7 Richard
Carpenter, John: 8 director
film: Assault on Precinct 13 (1976)
Escape From New York (1981)
The Fog (1980)
Halloween (1978)
Carpenters: 3 duo
members: Richard, Karen
song: Close to You (1970)
For All We Know (1971)
Goodbye to Love (1972)
Hurting Each Other (1972)
Only Yesterday (1975)
Please Mr. Postman (1974)
Rainy Days and Mondays (1971)
Sing (1973)
Superstar (1971)
Top of the World (1973)
We've Only Just Begun (1970)
Yesterday Once More (1973)
Carpentersville: 4 city, town
locale: 8 Illinois
Carpentier, Alejo: 5 Cuban 6 writer
carpentry: 5 skill, trade
joint: 5 bevel
carper: 3 nag 4 prig 6 critic, kvetch
carpet: 3 rug, rya 4 Agra, shag 5 plush 6 Berber, runner, Saxony, toupee 7 Persian 8 Aubusson, tapestry 9 broadloom, cover over
alternative: 4 lino 7 parquet 8 linoleum
calculation: 4 area 5 sq. yds.
call on the ~: 5 chide 6 rebuke 8 admonish 9 reprimand
cleaner: 3 vac 6 vacuum 7 sweeper
ender: 3 bag 4 weed 5 grass 6 bagger
fabric: 4 wool 5 frisé, nylon
fastener: 4 tack
feature: 3 nap 4 pile
fiber: 4 kemp 5 istle, ixtle
install: 3 lay
maker: 4 loom
old-style: 5 tapis
roll out the red ~: 5 greet, honor 7 lionize, receive, welcome
spoiler: 5 stain
carpet __: 3 bug 4 moth, tack, tile 5 grass, shark, snake 6 beetle 7 slipper, sweeper
__ carpet: 3 red 5 magic, on the 6 flying, velvet, Wilton 7 Persian, Turkish
Carpetbaggers, The
author: Harold Robbins
character: 4 Rina
__-carpet treatment: 3 red
carping: 5 picky 7 fretful, nagging, peevish 8 captious, caviling, critical, fretsome 9 criticism, grumbling, querulous
critic: 5 momus
critics: 4 momi
carpoolers, lane for: 3 HOV
carport kin: 6 garage
carpus: 4 bone 5 wrist
neighbor: 4 ulna
starter: 4 meta
Carr: 5 Caleb, Cathy, Vikki 7 Darleen 8 Charmian
car-racing org.: 4 IROC, NHRA
carrack: 4 boat, ship 6 argosy, vessel 7 galleon
Carradine: 4 John 5 David, Keith 6 Robert
Carradine, David: 5 actor
film: Bird on a Wire (1990)
Bound for Glory (1976)
The Long Riders (1980)
Q (1982)
Roadside Prophets (1992)
TV: Kung Fu
Carradine, John: 5 actor
film: Bluebeard (1944)
The Grapes of Wrath (1940)
Stagecoach (1939)
The Ten Commandments (1956)
Carradine, Keith: 5 actor
film: Andre (1994)
The Bachelor (1993)
Choose Me (1984)
The Duellists (1977)
Emperor of the North (1973)
The Long Riders (1980)
Nashville (1975)
Pretty Baby (1978)
Thieves Like Us (1974)
song: I'm Easy (1976)
Carrara: 6 marble
Carrasquilla, Tomás: 6 author, writer 9 Colombian
Carré: 4 Otis
__ Carré: 6 John Le
Carrefour: 4 city, town
locale: 5 Haiti
carrel: 4 desk 5 booth 6 alcove, recess
Carrel, Alexis: 8 Nobelist 9 biologist
car rental: 4 Avis 5 Alamo, Hertz 6 Budget, Dollar 7 Thrifty 8 National 10 Enterprise
Carrera: 3 car 4 auto 7 Barbara, Porsche
Carreras, José: 5 tenor 6 singer
specialty: 5 opera
Carrere: 3 Tia
Carrey, Jim: 5 actor
film: Ace Ventura: Pet Detective (1994)
Batman Forever (1995)
The Cable Guy (1996)
Dumb & Dumber (1994)
Earth Girls Are Easy (1989)
How the Grinch Stole Christmas (2000)
Liar Liar (1997)
Man on the Moon (1999)
The Mask (1994)

Me, Myself & Irene (2000)
The Truman Show (1998)
spouse: Lauren Holly
carriage: 3 air, gig, rig 4 gait, mien, pose, shay, walk 5 buggy, coach, stand, sulky, wagon 6 chaise, landau, stance 7 bearing, conduct, freight, phaeton, posture, transit 8 attitude, behavior, delivery, demeanor, equipage, presence 9 transport 10 appearance, conveyance, deportment
baby ~: 4 pram 5 buggy 6 go-cart
Holmes ~: 4 shay
horse: 7 hackney
horse-drawn ~: 3 rig 6 calash, fiacre 7 caleche
horseless ~: 3 car 4 auto 7 vehicle 10 automobile
Javanese ~: 4 sado 5 sadoo
occupant: 4 baby, doll
of India: 6 gharri, gharry
part: 4 axle 5 while
Roman: 5 rheda
trade: 5 elite
carriage __: 3 dog 4 bolt 5 horse, house, piece, trade 6 return
__ carriage: 3 gun 4 baby, slip 6 saloon
carrick bend: 4 knot
Carrie: 3 Nye 4 film, Henn 5 novel 6 Fisher, Nation 9 Snodgress
author: Stephen King
cast: Amy Irving, William Katt, Piper Laurie, Sissy Spacek, John Travolta
director: Brian De Palma
Carrie-__ Moss: 4 Anne
__ Carrie: 6 Sister
Carrie-Anne (1967 song) artist: Hollies
carried: 5 borne
away: 4 gaga, rapt
be ~: 4 ride, waft
easily ~: 8 portable
get ~ away: 8 overplay
carrier: 5 dolly, envoy, toter 6 bearer, porter, runner 7 airline, frigate, vehicle 8 conveyer, conveyor, emissary 9 messenger, transport 10 battleship, conveyance
aircraft ~: 4 ship 7 warship 8 man-of-war
bag ~: 5 caddy, toter 6 caddie, porter, skycap 7 bellhop, bellman
coal ~: 3 car 4 scow, tram 5 barge
combining form: 3 -fer 4 -pher, -phor 5 -phore
commuter ~: 3 bus, car 4 auto 5 ferry, train 7 shuttle
fare ~: 4 hack, taxi 7 taxicab
freight ~: 3 van 5 barge, truck 6 boxcar
fuel ~: 5 oiler 6 coaler, tanker
letter ~: 5 stamp 7 mailman, postman 8 envelope
ore ~: 5 barge
quiver ~: 6 archer, bowman 9 Robin Hood 10 longbowman
water ~: 3 rut 4 duct, hose, line, pail, pipe, race 5 canal, ditch, drain, flume, gulch, gully 6 arroyo, furrow, gulley, gutter, outlet, siphon, strait, syphon, trench, trough 7 channel, conduit, culvert, passage 8 aqueduct
carrier __: 4 wave 6 pigeon
__ carrier: 3 air, hod 4 ball, bulk, data, jeep, mail 5 space, spear, troop, water 6 charge, common, escort, exempt, letter, postal 7 weapons
__-carrier: 4 puck 5 spear
Carrier rival: 5 Rheem, Trane 6 Lennox 7 Fedders 9 Friedrich
Carrillo: 3 Leo 4 city, town
locale: 6 Mexico 8 Veracruz
Carrington (1995 film)
cast: Jonathan Pryce, Emma Thompson
carrion: 5 offal 10 rottenness
Carroll: 3 Leo, Pat 5 Baker, David, Lewis 7 Diahann, O'Connor 9 Madeleine
Carroll, Diahann: 7 actress
film: Paris Blues (1961)
spouse: Vic Damone
TV: Dynasty, Julia
Carroll, Leo G.: 5 actor
film: North by Northwest (1959)
Spellbound (1945)
Tarantula (1955)
TV: The Man From U.N.C.L.E., Topper
Carroll, Lewis: 6 author, writer 7 British
contemporary: 4 Lear
heroine: 5 Alice
real last name: Dodgson
work: Alice's Adventures in Wonderland
The Hunting of the Snark
Sylvie and Bruno
Through the Looking-Glass
Carroll, Madeleine: 7 actress
film: The 39 Steps (1935)
Blockade (1938)
The General Died at Dawn (1936)
Honeymoon in Bali (1939)
Lloyd's of London (1936)
My Favorite Blonde (1942)
On the Avenue (1937)
The Prisoner of Zenda (1937)
Carrollton: 4 city, town
locale: 5 Texas
Carrollwood: 4 city, town
locale: 7 Florida
carrot: 4 lure, plum, root 6 orange, reward, veggie 7 premium 9 incentive, vegetable 10 enticement, inducement, rabbit food, temptation
dangle a ~: 5 tempt 6 entice
relative: 5 anise
source: 4 farm 6 garden
stick: 5 snack
carrot-__: 3 top
carrot-and-__: 5 stick
Carruth, Hayden: 4 poet
Carr, Vikki song: It Must Be Him (1967)
carry: 3 air, lug, run, win 4 bear, cart, draw, haul, have, hold, keep, lift, move, pack, sell, sway, take, tote, waft 5 bring, ferry, fetch, relay, shlep, stock, truck 6 convey, convoy, deal in, handle, schlep, shlepp, uphold 7 comport, conduct, deliver, include, prevail, signify, support, sustain, win over 8 relocate, shoulder, transfer, transmit 9 broadcast, reinforce, transport 10 accomplish
a torch: 4 long, pine
a torch for: 4 love 5 adore
a tune: 4 sing
away: 4 cart 6 abduct, remove 7 ablates, enchant 8 entrance 9 discharge, transport
back: 6 return
easy to ~: 5 light
ender: 3 all, out 4 over
hard to ~: 5 heavy 10 cumbersome
off: 4 take 5 seize, steal 6 abduct, kidnap 7 succeed
on: 2 go 3 ply 4 have, hold, keep, rage, rant, rave, wage, wail, work 5 act up, emote, fight, mourn, party, serve 6 cavort, endure, extend, gambol, manage, pursue, resume, sorrow 7 conduct, persist, proceed, prolong, survive 8 continue, maintain, practice, transact 9 misbehave, persevere
out: 2 do 4 heed, meet, mind, obey 5 bow to, enact, wreak 6 accept, bend to, commit, effect, follow, fulfil, manage, redeem 7 abide by, achieve, agree to, defer to, execute, fulfill, observe, perform, realize, respect 8 adhere to, complete, conclude, dispense, listen to, transact 9 conform to, consent to, discharge, implement 10 accomplish, administer, consummate, effectuate, make good on, perpetrate
out, old-style: 5 doest
over: 4 keep 6 retain
the day: 3 win 7 succeed, triumph
through: 4 make 6 effect, finish 7 achieve, perform, persist, play out, realize
to: 5 reach
to and fro: 5 ferry
too far: 6 overdo
weight: 4 tell 5 count, weigh 6 matter
carry __: 3 off, out 4 away, over 5 a tune, light 6 permit 7 forward, through
carry __ conversation: 3 on a
carry __ of weight: 4 a lot
__-carry: 4 hand
...carry __ stick: 4 a big
Carry: 6 Nation
carry a __: 5 torch
carryall: 3 bag 4 tote 5 pouch, purse 7 handbag
carry-in __: 6 dinner, supper
carrying: 4 with
a grudge: 4 sore 6 bitter
a weapon: 5 armed
capacity: 6 armful
carrying __: 5 place 6 charge
__-carrying: 4 card
Carry moonbeams home __: 6 in a jar
carry-on: 3 bag 7 luggage
carryout: 4 meal
carry-over: 9 remainder
carry the __: 3 day 4 ball
Cars
leader: Ric Ocasek
song: Drive (1984)
Shake It Up (1981)
Tonight She Comes (1985)
You Might Think (1984)
Cars (1980 song) artist: Gary Numan
Carsey: 5 Marcy
Carson: 3 Kit 4 city, Jack, John, town 6 Johnny, Rachel 9 McCullers
locale: 3 Cal. 5 Calif. 10 California
__ Carson: 3 Kit 4 Fort
Carson City: 4 town 7 capital
lake near ~: 5 Tahoe
locale: 3 Nev. 6 Nevada
__ Carson, CO: 4 Fort
Carson, Johnny: 4 host 5 emcee
predecessor: 4 Paar
successor: 4 Leno
theme composer: 4 Anka
Carson, Kit: 5 scout
homesite: 4 Taos
Carson, Rachel: 6 author, writer
work: The Edge of the Sea
The Sea Around Us
The Sense of Wonder
Silent Spring
Under the Sea-Wind
Cars That Ate Paris, The (1974 film)
director: Peter Weir
cart: 3 lug 4 bear, dray, haul, move, take, tote, wain 5 bring, carry, dolly, ferry, shlep, sulky, wagon 6 barrow, convey, gurney, schlep, shlepp 7 deliver, ricksha, rikisha, rikshaw, tumbrel, tumbril, vehicle 8 rickshaw, tea table, transfer 9 carry away, transport
away: 4 haul, move
brake: 5 sprag
ender: 3 age 4 load 5 loads, wheel
farm ~: 4 wain
hospital ~: 6 gurney
in Britain: 6 trolly 7 trolley
lawn ~: 6 barrow
leader: 2 ox 5 horse
part: 4 axle 5 wheel
starter: 3 dog, tea, tip 4 hand, push
cart __: 5 horse
__ cart: 3 bar 4 dust, golf 5 crash 6 caddie, tumble 7 grocery
__ Carta: 5 Magna
cartage: 7 traffic
Cartagena: 4 city, port, town
locale: 8 Colombia
Cartago: 4 city, town
locale: 8 Colombia
Car Talk network: 3 NPR
carte: 4 menu 8 wine list 10 bill of fare
blanche: 3 run 7 freedom, liberty, license, mandate 8 free hand
du jour: 4 list, menu 10 bill of fare
listing: 3 vin
carte __: 6 du jour 7 blanche, d'entrée
__ carte: 3 a la
cartel: 4 bloc, OPEC, ring, synd. 5 group, trust 6 treaty 7 combine 8 business, monopoly 9 syndicate 10 consortium
Carter: 3 Amy, Don, Mel 4 Chip, Gary, Jack, June, Nell, Nick 5 Benny, Billy, Dixie, Glass, Janis, Jimmy, Lynda, Terry 6 Howard 7 Hodding 8 Clarence, Maybelle, Rosalynn
__ Carter: 3 Get
Carter, Benny: 11 saxophonist
genre: 4 jazz
sax: 4 alto
__ Carter Cash: 4 June
Carter, Dixie spouse: Hal Holbrook
Carter, Don: 3 PBA 6 bowler
milieu: 5 alley
Carteret: 4 city, town
locale: 9 New Jersey
Carter, Gary: 7 catcher
Carter, Howard: 12 archeologist
discovery: 3 Tut 7 King Tut
Carteris: 8 Gabriela
Carter, Jimmy: 8 Nobelist 9 president
advisor: 5 Lance 6 Jordan
alma mater: 4 USNA 9 Annapolis
cabinet member: 4 Bell 5 Adams, Brown, Kreps, Vance 6 Andrus, Harris, Muskie 8 Califano, Landrieu
child: 3 Amy 4 Chip, Jack 7 Jeffrey
home: 6 Plains 7 Georgia
middle name: 4 Earl
mother: 7 Lillian
opponent: 4 Ford 6 Reagan
previous occupation: 6 farmer
sibling: 4 Ruth 5 Billy 6 Gloria
V.P.: 7 Mondale
wife: 8 Rosalynn
Carter, Jimmy, books by:
Always a Reckoning
The Blood of Abraham
Everything to Gain
The Hour Before Daylight
Keeping Faith
Living Faith
Sources of Strength
Talking Peace
Turning Point
The Virtues of Aging
Why Not the Best?
Carter, Nick: 3 spy 5 agent
Cartesian
conclusion: 3 I am, sum
connection: 4 ergo
line: 4 axis
Cartesian __: 5 devil, diver, doubt, plane, space 7 product
Carthage
ancient city near ~: 4 Zama 5 Utica
city near ~: 5 Tunis
language: 5 Punic
loc.: 3 Afr. 6 Africa
queen of ~: 4 Dido
Carthaginian: 5 Punic

Cartier-Bresson: 5 Henri
Cartier, Jacques: 6 French 8 explorer
cartilage: 6 tissue 7 gristle
canine ~: 5 lytta
combining form: 6 chondr- 7 chondro- 8 chondrio-
carting: 8 delivery
Cartland: 4 Dame 7 Barbara
cartographer: 6 mapper 8 Mercator
abbr.: 3 alt., Atl., isl., lat., mts., Pac., str., ter. 4 terr.
product: 3 map 5 atlas, inset
speck: 3 cay, key 4 isle 6 island
unit: 6 degree, minute, second
carton: 3 box 4 case 5 crate 6 packet, parcel 7 package, six-pack, ten-pack 9 container
cartoon: 4 film 5 short 6 sketch 7 drawing, picture 9 animation 10 caricature, comic strip
credit: 5 voice 8 animator
exclamation: 3 oof 4 yeow 7 omigosh
frame: 3 cel 4 cell
Japanese ~ genre: 5 Anime
sound effect: 4 bonk, wham 5 boing
TV ~: 6 kidcom
cartoonist: 4 Capp, Hart, Nast 5 Adams, Davis, Gould, Keane, Kelly, Young 6 Al Capp, artist, Browne, Caniff, drawer, Eisner, Foster, Larson, Mullin, Schulz, Searle, Soglow, Walker 7 Ketcham, Lazarus, Trudeau 8 Aragones, Bil Keane, Goldberg, Herblock, Jim Davis, Lasswell, Mac-Nelly, Oliphant 9 Chic Young, Dik Browne, Guisewite, Hal Foster, Walt Kelly, Watterson 10 Gary Larson, Johnny Hart, Mort Walker, Scott Adams, Thomas Nast
helper: 5 inker
need: 3 ink 6 eraser
org.: 3 NCS
tool: 6 Benday
cartouche: 4 oval
Cartouche (1964 film)
cast: Jean-Paul Belmondo, Claudia Cardinale, Odile Versois
director: Philippe de Broca
cartridge: 4 ammo, case 6 bullet 7 missile 10 ammunition
cartridge ___: 4 belt, clip 5 brass
Car Trouble (1985 film)
cast: Ian Charleson, Julie Walters
cartwheel: 6 tumble
Cartwright: 3 Ben, Joe 4 Adam, Hoss 5 Nancy 6 Angela 8 Veronica 9 Alexander, Little Joe
Cartwright, Ben: 7 rancher
child: 3 Joe 4 Adam, Hoss 9 Little Joe
portrayer: Lorne Greene
Caruaru: 4 city, town
locale: 6 Brazil
Caruso: 5 David 6 Enrico
Caruso, Enrico: 5 tenor 6 singer
portrayer: Mario Lanza
specialty: 4 aria 5 opera
___ Caruso, The: 5 Great
carve: 3 cut 4 etch, pare, stab 5 cut up, knife, model, sever, shape, slash, slice 6 chisel, cleave, emboss, incise, sculpt 7 engrave, whittle 9 sculpture
out: 4 take
up: 5 allot, split 6 parcel
wood: 5 thurm
carved: 6 graven 7 incised
combining form: 5 glypt- 6 glypto-
Greek ~ image: 6 xoanon
Greek ~ images: 5 xoana
carver: 7 artisan 9 craftsman
medium: 4 jade, lava 8 soap. Wood
Carver: 4 John 5 Steve 7 Raymond
Carver, George Washington: 8 botanist
Carver, Raymond: 6 writer
Carvey: 4 aper, Dana
Carville, James spouse: Mary Matalin
carving: 3 art 5 glyph, totem 8 division 9 totem pole
mineral: 9 alabaster
carving ___: 4 fork 5 knife
car-wash
machine: 5 waxer
need: 3 wax 5 spray, water 6 chammy, shammy, shamoy 7 chamois
step: 5 rinse
Car Wash (1976 song) artist: Rose Royce
Car Wash actor: 3 Mr. T
Cary: 4 city, town 5 Elwes, Grant, Joyce 10 Middlecoff
ex: 4 Dyan
locale: 4 N. Car.
Cary, Joyce: 6 author, writer 7 British
casa: 8 hacienda
grande: 5 villa
material: 5 adobe
Casa ___ Orchestra: 4 Loma
casaba: 5 fruit, melon 9 muskmelon
Casablanca: 4 city, port, town
city near ~: 4 Safi 5 Rabat, Saffi
locale: 3 Mor. 7 Morocco
Casablanca (1942 film)
cast: Ingrid Bergman, Humphrey Bogart, Sydney Greenstreet, Paul Henreid, Peter Lorre, Claude Rains, Conrad Veidt, Dooley Wilson
composer: 7 Steiner
director: Michael Curtiz
role: 3 Sam 4 Ilsa, Rick 6 Blaine, Laszlo, Victor 7 Renault
screenwriter: 4 Koch
setting: 4 café 5 Rick's 7 Morocco
Casa de Oro: 4 city, town
locale: 10 California
Casa Grande: 4 city, town
locale: 7 Arizona
Casa Loma Orchestra leader: Glen Gray
Casals: 5 Pablo, Rosie 8 Rosemary
Casals, Pablo: 7 cellist, Spanish
Casals, Rosemary: 7 netster 9 tennis pro
milieu: 5 court
Casanova: 4 roué 5 Romeo 7 Don Juan, Giacomo 8 lothario 9 libertine
Casanova's Big Night (1954 film)
cast: Joan Fontaine, Bob Hope
cat: 8 Leonardo
director: Norman Z. McLeod
Casas Adobes: 4 city, town
locale: 7 Arizona
Casbah
locale: 4 Oran 6 Africa 7 Algeria, Algiers
mall: 5 bazar 6 bazaar
wear: 3 fez
Casbah (1948 film)
cast: Yvonne De Carlo, Peter Lorre, Tony Martin
cascade: 4 fall, flow, gush, pour, spew, spue 5 flood, spout 6 deluge, onrush, stream 7 descend, torrent 8 cataract, downrush, overflow 9 avalanche, waterfall 10 inundation, outpouring
Cascade: 9 detergent
alternative: 3 Joy 4 Ajax, Dawn 8 Sunlight 9 Palmolive 10 Electrasol
___ Cascade: 5 Boise
Cascades: 5 range 9 mountains
locale: 6 Canada 10 Washington
mountain: 4 Hood 5 Adams 6 Lassen, Shasta 7 Rainier 8 St. Helens
Cascades, The: 3 rag
composer: Scott Joplin
Casco: 3 bay
locale: 5 Maine
case: 3 bag, bin, box, pod 4 bark, grip, husk, look, suit 5 chest, claim, crate, event, frame, scout, shape, shell, sneak, spy on, state, study, topic, trial, trunk, watch 6 action, carton, coffer, dative, jacket, pack up, plight, reason, sample, survey, valise 7 baggage, canvass, check up, context, dilemma, dispute, enclose, examine, example, inclose, inspect, lawsuit, lookout, luggage, patient 8 canister, check out, incident, instance, look over, magazine, occasion, petition, position, sampling, scope out, specimen 9 cartridge, condition, container, happening, objective, obsession, portfolio, sheathing, situation 10 integument, litigation, occurrence, receptacle, scrutinize
attaché ~: 3 bag 9 portfolio
breaker: 4 clew, clue
court ~: 3 res 5 trial 7 lawsuit
do the ~ over: 5 retry
ender: 4 book, load, mate, work 6 harden 8 hardened
get on one's ~: 3 bug, nag 4 harp 6 badger 9 find fault, persecute
grammatical ~: 3 abl., acc., nom., obj. 4 poss. 6 dative 8 ablative 9 objective 10 nominative, possessive
hard ~: 4 hull, husk, thug 8 carapace 10 integument
hear a ~: 3 try 5 judge
history: 4 file 6 record, report 7 dossier 8 document, specimen 10 background
hopeless ~: 5 goner
in ~: 4 lest 6 should 9 perchance
in any ~: 5 still 10 regardless
in that ~: 4 then
in the ~ of: 5 as for
legal ~ statement: 5 facta
list: 6 docket
lower ~: 5 small 9 minuscule
make a federal ~ of: 6 overdo
make one's ~: 5 prove
needle ~: 4 etui 5 etwee
nut ~: 3 bur 4 kook 5 crank, shell
one bringing a ~: 4 suer
on the ~: 4 at it 7 working
seed ~: 3 pod
solve a ~: 5 crack
starter: 4 book, show, slip, suit 5 brain, brief, crank, lower, smear, stair, upper, watch
state one's ~: 5 argue, plead
that being the ~: 2 so 4 ergo, if so 5 hence
upper ~: 7 capital 9 majuscule
wind up a ~: 4 rest 6 settle
case ___: 3 bay, law 4 card, shot 5 glass, goods, knife, study 6 ending, method, system, worker 7 grammar, history
___ case: 3 egg, job, key 4 hard, news, test, wing 5 brain, dairy, in any, index, jewel, spore, upper 6 pencil, vanity 7 attaché, federal, hunting, packing, Pullman, timbale, Wardian
___ case for: 5 make a
caseharden: 8 indurate
casein: 4 curd
case in ___: 5 point
Casella: 7 Alfredo
casement ___: 4 door 5 cloth 6 window
Case of Identity, A author: Doyle
Case of Libel, A star: 5 Asner
Case of Lucy Bending, The author: Lawrence Sanders
Case of Need, A author: Crichton
Case of Samples, A author: 4 Amis
Case of Sergeant Grischa, The author: Arnold Zweig
caserne: 7 bivouac 8 barracks, garrison
___-case scenario: 4 best 5 worst
Casey: 3 Ben 5 Jones, Kasem 6 Bernie 7 Stengel, William
club: 3 bat
org.: 3 CIA
Casey at the Bat ender: 3 out 9 strike-out
cash: 3 oof 4 coin, gelt, jack, kail, kale, loot, peag, pelf 5 asset, bills, bread, bucks, coins, dough, funds, lucre, money, moola, mopus, pesos, rhino, sewan 6 assets, change, dinero, dollar, do-re-mi, income, mammon, mazuma, monies, moolah, nickel, redeem, riches, seawan, silver, specie, wampum, wealth 7 cabbage, capital, dollars, lettuce, ooftish, savings, scratch, shekels 8 bankroll, currency, hard cash, monetary, smackers 9 banknotes, frogskins, liquidate, long green, simoleons 10 greenbacks, green stuff
advance: 4 loan
alternative: 5 check 6 charge
blow ~: 5 spend 8 squander
bundle: 3 wad 4 pile
cow: 7 bonanza 8 gold mine
ender: 3 ier 4 book, less
flow: 6 income 7 revenue 8 receipts
get ~ for: 4 hock, pawn, sell
holder: 3 ATM 4 safe, till 8 register
in: 6 redeem 7 collect 8 exchange 9 liquidate
in on: 3 use 7 exploit
on hand: 5 asset
partner: 5 carry
recipient: 5 payee
register calculation: 3 tax
register co.: 3 IBM, NCR
short of ~: 5 broke, needy
stash: 3 IRA 5 Keogh 7 account, nest egg 9 piggy bank
substitute: 3 IOU 5 scrip
see also coin, money
cash ___: 3 bar, cow, out 4 crop, flow 5 audit, basis, money, value 6 letter 7 account, journal, machine
cash ___ barrelhead: 5 on the
___ cash: 4 cold, hard 5 petty
Cash: 3 Pat 4 Norm 6 Johnny 7 Rosanne
cash and ___: 5 carry
cash-back offer: 6 rebate
cashew: 3 nut 4 nosh, tree 5 snack
relative: 5 mango, sumac 6 acajou, fustet, mastic, sumach 9 pistachio, sugarbush
cashier: 2 ax 3 axe, can 4 boot, drop, fire, oust, sack 5 clerk, expel, let go 6 bounce, bursar, depose, lay off, purser, reject, remove, teller 7 cast off, dismiss, drum out, release, turn out 8 displace, furlough, get rid of, pink-slip 9 discharge, paymaster, terminate
cry: 4 next
cashier's ___: 5 check
Cash, Johnny
song: A Boy Named Sue (1969) Folsom Prison Blues (1968) I Walk the Line (1956) Ring of Fire (1963)
wife: June Carter
cashless ___: 7 society
cashless deal: 4 swap, swop 5 trade 6 barter
cashmere: 4 goat, wool 6 fabric 7 sweater
Cashmere Bouquet: 4 soap
alternative: 3 Lux 4 Dial, Dove, Lava, Tone, Zest 5 Camay, Coast, Ivory, Lever 6 Boraxo, Caress, Shield 8 Lifebuoy 9 Palmolive, Safeguard 11 Irish Spring
Casimir of Poland: 5 saint
casing: 4 bark, hull, rind, skin 5 frame 6 jacket, sheath 7 wrapper 8 covering 9 framework 10 integument
casing ___: 4 nail 5 knife
___ casing: 3 air 5 blind 6 spiral

casino: 4 game 5 Sands 6 Sahara 7 Aladdin, Caesar's, Harrah's 8 card game, Foxwoods, MGM Grand, slot spot 9 nightclub
action: 3 bet
city: 4 Reno 5 Vegas 8 Las Vegas
cry: 5 banco, hit me
data: 4 odds
employee: 6 dealer 7 pit boss 8 croupier
furnishing: 4 deck 5 cards, table, wheel
game: 4 faro, keno 5 craps, poker, slots 6 écarté 8 baccarat, roulette 9 blackjack, twenty-one
implement: 4 rake, shoe
industry: 6 gaming
invocation: 4 luck
locale: 3 Nev. 6 Nevada
maximum: 5 limit
natural: 5 seven 6 eleven
patron: 6 better, bettor
show: 5 revue 6 review
sign: 4 neon
the ~ so to speak: 5 house
tip: 4 toke
Casino (1995 film)
cast: Robert De Niro, Joe Pesci, Sharon Stone, James Woods
director: Martin Scorsese
Casino ___: 6 Royale
Casino Royale: 4 film, song 5 novel
artist: Herb Alpert and the Tijuana Brass
author: Ian Fleming
cast: Woody Allen, Ursula Andress, David Niven, Joanna Pettet, Peter Sellers, Orson Welles
director: John Huston
Casio: 5 watch 10 wristwatch
alternative: 4 Ebel, Rado 5 Elgin, Lorus, Omega, Rolex, Seiko, Timex 6 Bulova, Fossil, Movado, Pulsar, Swatch 7 Citizen 8 Longines, Tag Heuer, Tourneau
casita: 8 bungalow
cask: 3 bbl., keg, tub, tun, vat 4 butt 6 barrel, firkin, foudre 8 hogshead 9 container
part: 5 stave
put a hole in a ~: 3 tap
stopper: 4 bung
Cask of Amontillado, The author: Edgar Allan Poe
Caslon: 4 font 8 typeface
casmerodius albus: 5 egret
Caspar: 5 magus 7 Van Dien 10 Weinberger 11 Milquetoast
et al.: 4 Magi
like ~: 4 wise
Caspary: 4 Vera
Casper: 4 city, Dave, town 5 Billy
locale: 3 Wyo. 7 Wyoming
the Ghost's uncle: 5 Fatso 6 Stinky 7 Stretch
Casper, Billy: 6 golfer
milieu: 5 links 6 course
org.: 3 PGA
Casper, Dave sport: 8 football
Caspian locale: 7 Eurasia
Caspian Sea: 4 lake
catch: 4 carp
city near the ~: 5 Rasht, Resht
feeder: 4 Kura, Ural 5 Atrak, Atrek, Volga
land: 4 Iran
neighbor: 4 Aral
port: 4 Baku
Cass: 4 Mama 5 Peggy 6 Elliot 7 Elliott, Gilbert
Cassandra: 4 seer 5 sibyl 7 prophet 10 prophetess
brother of ~: 5 Chaon, Paris 6 Hector, Pammon 7 Polites, Troilus 8 Antiphus 9 Deiphobus, Hipponous, Polydorus
parent of ~: 5 Priam 6 Hecuba
sister of ~: 6 Creusa, Iliona 7 Laodice 8 Polyxena
son of ~: 6 Pelops 9 Teledamus
twin of ~: 7 Helenus
Cassandra Compact, The author: Robert Ludlum
Cassandra Crossing, The (1977 film)
cast: Richard Harris, Burt Lancaster, Sophia Loren
producer: Carlo Ponti
Cassatt, Mary: 6 artist 7 painter
contemporary: 5 Degas
cassava: 6 legume
Cassavetes: 4 John, Nick
Cassavetes, John: 8 director
film: A Child Is Waiting (1963)
The Dirty Dozen (1967)
Edge of the City (1957)
Faces (1968)
The Fury (1978)
Minnie and Moskowitz (1971)
Opening Night (1977)
Rosemary's Baby (1968)
Saddle the Wind (1958)
Shadows (1960)
Whose Life Is It Anyway? (1981)
spouse: Gena Rowlands
Cass County seat: 5 Fargo
Casselberry: 4 city, town
locale: 7 Florida
casserole: 4 dish, stew 6 potpie 7 goulash 10 stroganoff
cook a ~: 4 bake
cover: 3 lid
ingredient: 4 tuna
cassette: 4 tape
alternative: 2 CD 4 disc, disk
contents: 5 movie, video
copy a ~: 3 dub
deck button: 3 rec, rew 4 stop 5 eject, pause 6 record, rewind
format: 3 DAT
half: 5 side A, side B
recorder letters: 3 mic
starter: 5 audio, video
cassette ___: 4 deck, tape 6 player 8 recorder
cassia: 4 tree 5 senna, shrub, spice 6 legume 8 cinnamon
relative: 3 koa 5 carob 6 cercis, locust, padauk, padouk, redbud 7 araroba, mesquit 8 mesquite, tamarind 9 poinciana
cassia ___: 3 pod 4 bark, pulp
Cassidy: 3 Ted 4 Jack 5 Butch, David, Shaun 6 Joanna 7 Patrick 8 Hopalong
Cassidy, Butch: 5 alias 6 outlaw
Cassidy, David
song: Cherish (1971)
spouse: Kay Lenz
TV: The Partridge Family
Cassidy, Jack spouse: Shirley Jones
Cassidy, Joanna: 7 actress
film: Bank Shot (1974)
Under Fire (1983)
Who Framed Roger Rabbit (1988)
Cassidy, Shaun
song: Da Doo Ron Ron (1977)
Hey Deanie (1977)
That's Rock 'N' Roll (1977)
cassimere: 6 fabric 8 material
Cassini: 4 Igor, Oleg
creation: 4 gown 5 dress
Cassini, Oleg spouse: Gene Tierney
___ Cassino: 5 Monte
Cassin, René: 6 French 8 Nobelist
Cassio adversary: 4 Iago
cassiope: 5 shrub
relative: 5 heath, salal 6 azalea, kalmia 7 arbutus, rhodora 8 cowberry 9 blueberry, deerberry
Cassiopeia
component: 4 star
daughter of ~: 9 Andromeda
Cassirer, Ernst: 11 philosopher
cassis: 5 drink 8 beverage
apéritif: 3 kir
cassiterite: 3 ore
Cassius: 4 Clay 5 Roman
and company: 5 cabal
opponent: 5 Sonny
___ Cassius has a lean...: 4 Yond
Cass, Mama
group: Mamas & The Papas
last name: Elliot
real name: Ellen Naomi Cohen
song: Dream a Little Dream of Me (1968)
cassock: 4 coat 6 jacket 10 canonicals
Cassola, Carlo: 6 writer 7 Italian
cassoulet: 4 stew
cassowary: 4 bird 6 ratite
kin: 3 emu 4 emeu
Cass Timberlane author: Sinclair Lewis
cast: 3 air, hue, log, peg, set 4 flip, form, hurl, lick, look, mien, mold, send, shed, tint, tone, toss, type 5 chuck, color, fling, heave, impel, level, light, model, pitch, shade, shape, sling, staff, stamp, strew, throw, tinge, trait 6 actors, kidney, launch, manner, matrix, nature, plunge, reckon, spread, troupe, visage 7 company, diffuse, plaster, players, project, radiate, reflect, scatter 8 bespread, demeanor, disperse, ejection, ensemble, throw out 9 actresses, expulsion, sculpture, semblance 10 appearance, complexion, distribute, impression
a ballot: 4 vote 6 choose
about: 4 seek 5 flail, grope, strew 6 forage, scheme, search 7 bestrew, look for 8 contrive, flounder
a fly: 4 fish 5 angle
a pall over: 6 dampen
around for: 4 hunt, seek
aside: 4 cede, drop, dump, jilt, sell, shed, shun, veto 5 chuck, ditch, forgo, spurn, yield 6 bounce, forego, give up, pass on, rebuff, reject 7 abandon, discard, disdain, dismiss, exclude, forfeit, forsake, say no to 8 disallow, forswear, get rid of, hand over, jettison, leave out, part with, throw out, turn down 9 abandoned, blackball, dispose of, foreswear, repudiate, surrender, throw away 10 relinquish
a slur on: 6 defame 7 slander
a spell: 3 hex 4 jinx
away: 4 lost 5 spend 6 maroon, strand 7 abandon 8 stranded 9 abandoned 10 high and dry
be in a ~: 3 act 7 perform
doubt on: 6 impugn 8 question
down: 4 sink 5 abase, lower, lowly 6 broody, humble 7 degrade 8 dejected, dispirit 9 humiliate 10 dishearten, spiritless
ender: 3 off 4 away
gently: 3 dap
head the ~: 4 star
join the ~ of: 5 act in
light on: 8 illumine
loose: 5 let go 7 release
member: 5 actor 7 actress
off: 4 molt, sail, shed 5 egest, eject, sluff 6 reject 7 cashier, dismiss, forsake 8 derelict, forsaken, forswear, jettison, renounce 9 foreswear, ownerless, repudiate, throw away 10 repudiated
out: 4 emit, oust, spew, spue, vent 5 egest, eject, exile, expel, exude, issue 6 banish, deport, reject 7 diffuse, dismiss, emanate, give off, radiate 8 exorcise, exorcize, supplant, throw off 9 eliminate, ostracize, send forth
slot: 4 role
something to ~: 4 line, role, vote 5 spell 6 ballot
starter: 3 mis 4 down, fore, news, over, tele, type 5 broad, cable, color, rough 6 narrow, sports 7 weather
supporter: 5 sling
cast ___: 3 off, out 4 iron 5 about, aside, steel, stone 6 adrift
cast ___ over: 5 a pall
cast-___ stomach: 4 iron
___ cast: 5 false 7 plaster
___-cast: 3 die, fly 4 open, sand, type
Cast ___: 4 Away
Cast a Dark Shadow (1955 film)
cast: Dirk Bogarde, Margaret Lockwood
director: Lewis Gilbert
Casta diva: 4 aria
cast against ___: 4 type
Castaneda: 6 Carlos
castanets: 8 clackers 10 percussion
dance: 4 jota 6 bolero 8 fandango
Castaños: 4 city, town
locale: 6 Mexico 8 Coahuila
castaway: 6 adrift, reject 7 discard, outcast 8 derelict, marooned, stranded, throw-out, unmoored
call: 3 SOS
home: 3 hut 4 isle 5 atoll 6 island
transport: 4 raft
Cast Away (2000 film)
cast: Tom Hanks, Helen Hunt
director: Robert Zemeckis
Castaways of the Flag, The author: Jules Verne
caste: 4 rank 5 class, order 6 estate, status 7 station, stratum 8 position, standing 10 immaculate
Hindu ~: 4 Ahir, Jati 5 Sudra 7 Brahman, Brahmin
member: 5 Hindu 6 Hindoo
Castel Gandolfo
lake: 6 Albano
locale: 5 Italy
resident: 4 pope 7 pontiff
Castellammare di Stabia: 3 spa 4 city, town 6 resort 7 seaport
locale: 5 Italy
Castellaneta: 3 Dan
Castellano: 7 Richard
castellated ___: 3 nut 4 beam
caster: 5 cruet, wheel 6 roller
need: 3 rod 4 line, reel
starter: 4 news, surf 5 broad, rough 6 sports 7 weather
castigate: 3 hit, rag, rip 4 beat, damn, flay, flog, lash, rail, slam, whip 5 abuse, baste, blast, chide, scold 6 berate, indict, punish, rebuke, scathe, thrash 7 bawl out, blister, censure, chasten, chew out, condemn, lambast, scourge, upbraid 8 browbeat, chastise, denounce, lambaste, penalize 9 criticize, dress down, excoriate, fulminate, reprehend, reprimand 10 come down on, discipline, tongue-lash, vituperate
castigation: 5 abuse, blame 6 rebuke 7 censure, lecture 8 diatribe
castigator: 5 scold, shrew 9 henpecker
castigatory: 5 penal
Castile: 4 soap
city: 5 Avila
locale: 5 Spain
partner: 6 Aragón
Castile ___: 4 soap
Castilian: 8 language
casting: 5 metal
starter: 4 surf, type 5 broad, rough 6 narrow

casting ___: 3 rod 4 vote 5 voice, wheel
___ casting: 3 die, fly 4 bait, plug, slip, surf 7 central
casting out ___: 5 nines
cast iron: 5 alloy
  component: 6 carbon
cast-iron ___: 7 stomach
castle: 4 fort, home, rook 5 house, manor, tower 6 palace 7 chateau, citadel, domicil, housing, lodging, mansion 8 domicile, dwelling, fastness, fortress 10 chess piece, donjon site, stronghold
  Cuban ~: 5 Morro
  feature: 4 keep, moat 5 tower 6 donjon 7 dungeon
  Havana ~: 5 Morro
  in chess: 4 rook
  in the air: 5 dream 7 fantasy 8 daydream 9 pipe dream
  protector, maybe: 4 pawn
  queenside ~ in chess notation: 3 OOO
  wall: 6 bailey 7 ballium
  worker: 4 serf
castle ___ air: 5 in the
___ castle: 3 air 4 sand
Castle: 5 Irene 6 Vernon 7 William
Castle ___: 4 walk
___ Castle: 4 Man's 5 Axel's, Morro, White 6 Maiden 7 Windsor
Castlebar's county: 4 Mayo
___ Castle, Cuba: 5 Morro
castle in ___: 5 Spain
castle in the ___: 3 air
Castle in the Sea, The author: 5 O'Dell
Castle, Nick film of 1989: 3 Tap
Castle of Otranto, The author: Horace Walpole
Castle of Saint ___: 4 Elmo
Castle of the Carpathians, The author: Jules Verne
Castle on the Hudson (1940 film)
  cast: John Garfield, Pat O'Brien
  director: Anatole Litvak
Castle Rock: 4 city, town
  locale: 8 Colorado
castles
  build ~ in the air: 9 speculate
  in the air: 6 revery 7 reverie
Castles in the Air (1972 song) artist: Don McLean
Castle, The author: Franz Kafka
  character: 4 Gisa, Olga 5 Klamm, Momus 6 Amalia, Frieda 7 Sortini
Castlewood: 4 city, town
  locale: 8 Colorado
castoffs: 4 junk, rags 7 rejects
cast one's ___ with: 3 lot
castor: 3 oil 4 bean
  bean protein: 5 ricin
castor ___: 3 oil 4 bean 5 sugar
Castor: 4 peak, star 5 Jimmy, mount 8 Argonaut, mountain
  constellation: 6 Gemini
  locale: 4 Alps 6 Europe 11 Switzerland
  parent of ~: 4 Leda, Zeus
  sister of ~: 5 Helen
  twin of ~: 6 Pollux
Castorini, Loretta portrayer: 4 Cher
Castres: 4 city, town
  locale: 6 France
Castries: 4 city, town 7 capital
  locale: 7 St. Lucia
Castro: 4 sofa 5 Fidel, Raoul
  capital: 6 Havana
  country: 4 Cuba
  see also Spanish
Castrogiovanni today: 4 Enna
Castro Valley: 4 city, town
  locale: 10 California
cast the ___ stone: 5 first
___ cast, the: 5 die is
casual: 3 lax 4 cool, easy, homy 5 blasé, homey, light, loose 6 breezy, chance, degage, folksy, little, mellow, random 7 aimless, cursory, liberal, offhand, raffish, relaxed, tieless 8 fireside, informal, laid-back, unstrict, untaxing 9 dress code, easygoing, haphazard, hit-or-miss, impromptu, irregular, leisurely, uncertain, unplanned 10 accidental, incidental, infrequent, nonchalant, occasional, off-the-cuff, unaffected, unagitated, uncritical, unexpected, unforeseen
  dress phrase: 5 no tie
  not ~: 6 dressy, formal
  participant: 7 amateur
  wear: 3 cap, tee 5 jeans, skort 6 chinos, denims, slacks, T-shirt 10 dishabille
casually: 4 idly 7 lightly 8 by chance 9 leisurely, naturally 10 flippantly
Casualties of War locale: 3 Nam
casualty: 4 loss 6 mishap, victim 7 debacle 8 accident, calamity, disaster, sufferer 10 misfortune
casuist: 8 logician, reasoner
casuistic: 7 evasive 9 illogical
casuistry: 6 dupery 7 fallacy 9 chicanery, deception, hypocrisy, sophistry
casus ___: 5 belli
cat: 3 guy, pet, tom 4 eyra, lion, lynx, Manx, puma, puss 5 chita, civet, fossa, genet, jiver, kitty, korat, liger, ounce, tabby, tiger, tigon, zibet 6 Angora, animal, calico, cheeta, chetah, cougar, feline, feller, jaguar, kitten, malkin, mammal, margay, mouser, ocelot, purrer, serval, tiglon 7 bay lynx, brindle, caracal, cheetah, hipster, leopard, Maltese, panther 8 bebopper, house pet, longhair 9 blue point, catamount, grimalkin, Himalayan, seal point, shorthair 10 colorpoint, jaguarundi, sabertooth
  Africa: 4 lion 5 chita, civet 6 cheeta, chetah, serval 7 caracal, cheetah, leopard
  alley ~: 5 stray
  Asia: 4 lion 5 chita, civet, ounce, tiger 6 cheeta, chetah 7 cheetah, leopard
  at times: 5 mewer, pawer 6 lapper, meower, purrer
  big ~: 4 lion, puma 5 tiger 6 ocelot 7 leopard
  black ~: 4 omen
  breed: 4 Manx 5 Korat 6 Birman, Bombay, Exotic, LaPerm, Ocicat, Somali, Sphynx 7 Burmese, Persian, Ragdoll, Siamese 8 Balinese, Devon Rex, Javanese, Oriental, Siberian 9 Chartreux, Maine Coon, Singapura, Tonkinese 10 Abyssinian, Cornish Rex, Selkirk Rex, Turkish Van
  British: 3 mog 5 moggy
  Canada: 4 lynx
  Central America: 6 margay
  coat: 3 fur
  combining form: 5 aelur-, ailur- 6 aeluro-, ailuro-
  comment: 3 mew 4 meow, purr, yowl 5 I'm hip, miaou, miaow, miaul
  cool ~: 6 daddy-o
  doc: 3 DVM, vet
  drink: 4 milk
  drink like a ~: 5 lap up
  ender: 3 gut, kin, nap, nip 4 bird, boat, call, cher, fish, head, mint, tail, walk 5 brier, fight
  fat ~: 5 mogul, nabob 6 tycoon 7 big shot, Pooh-bah 9 moneybags, plutocrat 10 man of means
  female: 5 queen
  foot: 3 paw
  fraidy ~: 4 wimp 5 sissy 7 chicken, dastard 9 jellyfish
  hangout: 5 alley
  hybrid: 5 liger, tigon 6 tiglon
  India: 7 caracal
  in French: 4 chat
  in Latin: 5 felis
  in Spanish: 4 gato
  let the ~ out of the bag: 3 air 4 bare, leak, tell 5 admit, blurt, spill 6 betray, expose, gossip, reveal, squeal, tattle 7 divulge, let slip 8 disclose, give away 9 make known
  like most ~ s: 4 neat
  like some ~: 3 hep 4 cool 5 feral
  lives: 4 nine 6 ennead
  male: 3 gib, tom
  maneuver: 4 arch
  Mexico: 6 ocelot
  mother ~ grip: 4 nape
  murmur: 3 pur 4 purr
  North America: 4 lynx, puma 6 cougar 7 panther 9 catamount
  of Egyptian mythology: 4 Bast
  palm: 3 pad
  play ~ and mouse: 7 torment
  quarry: 3 rat 5 mouse
  Siamese ~ marking: 5 point
  South America: 4 puma 6 cougar, margay, ocelot 7 panther
  spotted ~: 5 ounce 6 jaguar, ocelot, serval 7 leopard
  starter: 3 bob, hep, tom 4 bear, copy, hell, pole, wild 5 stone
  striped ~: 5 tiger
  tailless ~: 4 Manx
  Thailand: 5 korat
  to a flea: 4 host
  top ~: 4 boss 5 chief 7 headman
  tormentor: 4 flea
  toy: 4 yarn
  tropical ~: 4 eyra 5 civet 10 jaguarundi
  wild ~: 4 lion, puma 5 civet, tiger 6 cougar, jaguar 7 panther
  young: 6 kitten
cat ___: 3 rig 4 flea, suit, yawl 6 litter, tackle 7 burglar, whisker
cat-___: 4 eyed, foot 5 built, train 6 harpin
cat-___-tails: 5 o'-nine
___ cat: 3 fat, hep, mud 4 blue, coon, copy, manx, one o', palm, two o' 5 alley, civet, fossa, tiger 6 Angora, calico, fraidy, native 7 Burmese, channel, Maltese, Persian, Siamese
___-cat: 4 one-a, two-a 5 four-a 6 fraidy 7 scaredy
Cat: 7 Stevens
Cat ___: 6 Ballou, People
Cat ___ Hat, The: 5 in the
Cat ___ Hot Tin Roof: 3 on a
___ Cat: 3 Top 5 Alley, Black, Honky
___-Cat: 3 Sno
CAT ___: 4 scan 7 scanner
cataclysm: 4 doom, loss, ruin 5 flood, havoc 6 mishap 7 debacle, torrent, tragedy 8 calamity, collapse, disaster, upheaval 9 tidal wave 10 convulsion, earthquake, inundation, misfortune
cataclysmic: 4 dire 6 tragic 7 fateful, harmful, ruinous 8 tragical
catacomb: 4 tomb 5 vault 6 tunnel
  recess: 7 loculus
catacombs: 4 maze 9 labyrinth
catafalque: 4 bier
Catalan Landscape artist: 4 Miró
Catalán's country: 6 España
Catalina: 3 car, isl. 4 auto, isle 6 island 7 Pontiac
Catalina Foothills: 4 city, town
  locale: 7 Florida
___ Catalina Island: 5 Santa
catalog: 4 file, list, roll, sort 5 index, order, tally 6 assort, detail, litany, record, roster 7 archive, itemize, program 8 classify, identify, organize, register, tabulate 9 directory, inventory 10 pigeonhole, prospectus, stereotype
  items: 3 ads
  subject: 5 model
___ catalog: 4 card 5 title, union 6 author, on-line 7 Messier, subject
cataloguer: 5 Sears 6 L.L. Bean
Catalonian
  city: 6 Lérida
  river: 4 Ebro
catalpa: 4 tree 5 plant 6 flower
  relative: 8 bignonia, calabash
  tree: 9 jacaranda
catalyst: 4 goad, spur 5 agent 6 enzyme 7 impetus 8 reactant, stimulus 9 incentive, spark plug 10 motivation
catamaran: 4 boat 5 skiff 8 sailboat
catamount: 3 cat 4 puma 5 felid 6 animal, feline, mammal 7 panther
  relative: 4 eyra, lion, lynx 5 chita, liger, ounce, tiger, tigon 6 bobcat, cheeta, chetah, cougar, jaguar, margay, ocelot, serval, tiglon 7 bay lynx, caracal, cheetah, leopard 10 jaguarundi
cat and ___: 3 dog, rat 5 mouse
Cat and Mouse author: Günter Grass
Cat and the Canary, The (1927 film)
  cast: Laura LaPlante, Tully Marshall
  director: Paul Leni
Cat and the Canary, The (1939 film)
  cast: Paulette Goddard, Bob Hope
Cat and the Curmudgeon, The author: 5 Amory
Cat and the Fiddle, The (1934 film): 7 musical
  cast: Jeanette MacDonald, Frank Morgan, Ramon Novarro
  composer: 4 Kern 11 Hammerstein
Catania: 4 city, town
  locale: 5 Italy
  view from ~: 4 Etna 5 Aetna
catapult: 4 hurl 5 fling, heave, shoot, sling, throw 6 engine, hurler, hurtle, launch, propel, weapon
  in America: 9 slingshot
  missile: 5 stone
cataract: 7 cascade, torrent 8 overflow
  site: 4 lens
catarrh: 5 rheum
catastrophe: 4 blow, doom, loss 5 event, havoc 6 crisis, fiasco, misery, mishap, sorrow 7 debacle, reverse, scourge, tragedy, undoing 8 calamity, casualty, disaster, hardship, upheaval
catastrophic: 4 dire 5 woful 6 costly, tragic, woeful 7 fateful, ruinous, unlucky 8 ill-fated, luckless, tragical
Catawba: 4 wine 5 grape, river, white
  relative: 5 Gamay, pinot, Tokay 6 Merlot 7 Concord, Niagara 8 Cabernet, malvasia, muscatel 9 muscadine, Sauvignon, zinfandel 10 Chardonnay
Cat Ballou (1965 film)
  cast: Nat King Cole, Jane Fonda, Stubby Kaye, Lee Marvin
catbird seat: 7 lookout
catboat: 5 skiff
catcall: 3 boo, dig 4 barb, gibe, hiss, hoot, jeer, jibe, slam, slap, slur, snub, twit 5 abuse, libel, scorn, taunt 6 heckle, rebuff, slight 7 affront, calumny, disdain, mockery, obloquy, offense, put-down 8 contempt, derision, ridicule 9 aspersion, contumely 10 defamation, disrespect, opprobrium
catch: 3 bag, get, nab, net, nip, rub 4 bust, clip, game, grab, grip, hasp, hear, hook, lock, mesh, nail, pain, pawl, snag, snap, spot, take, trap

5 board, clasp, field, grasp, hitch, hop on, lasso, latch, lodge, marry, prize, seize, snare, stick, trick 6 arrest, buckle, collar, corner, corral, detect, enmesh, entrap, expose, follow, immesh, inmesh, jump at, kicker, listen, secure, snatch, take in 7 acquire, capture, climb on, discern, ensnare, find out, head off, hit upon, insnare, involve, observe, pitfall, proviso, realize, receive, reflect 8 contract, discover, drawback, entangle, fastener, glom on to, interest, lock part, obstacle, overtake, perceive, pounce on, smell out, surprise 9 apprehend, condition, get hold of, hindrance, intercept, lay hold of, provision, recognize, track down 10 bring to bay, comprehend, understand
a bug: 3 ail
advance after a ~: 5 tag up
again: 5 renab
a glimpse of: 3 see 4 espy, spot 6 descry, detect, notice 7 discern, make out
basin: 4 sump
easy ~: 5 pop up
ender: 3 all, fly 4 pole, poll, word 5 penny
fail to ~: 4 muff
fire: 4 burn 6 ignite, kindle, set off 8 enkindle 10 incinerate
flies: 4 shag, yawn
hard to ~: 4 eely 7 elusive
holder: 5 creel 6 basket
hold of: 3 nab 4 hook, land, nail, snag 5 seize 6 arrest, collar, corral, snap up, snatch 7 capture, ensnare 9 apprehend, latch onto
in a net: 6 enmesh, immesh
mechanical ~: 6 detent
off-guard: 5 shock 8 surprise
on: 3 dig, get, see 5 get it, grasp, learn, sense 6 follow 7 realize 10 understand
one's breath: 5 pause
on to: 3 get 4 know 5 learn, sense
red-handed: 3 bag, get, nab, net 4 bust, grab, nail, trap 5 catch, pinch, run in, seize 6 arrest, collar, snatch 7 capture, startle 8 surprise 9 apprehend, burst in on
sight of: 3 eye, see, spy 4 espy, find, spot 6 descry 7 discern, glimpse
some rays: 3 sun, tan 4 bask
some z's: 3 nap 4 doze, rest 5 sleep 6 turn in
the eye: 8 stand out
unprepared: 3 jar 4 numb, rock, stun 5 abash, floor 6 appall, dismay 7 astound, horrify, shake up, stagger, stupefy 8 astonish, bowl over, paralyze, surprise, unsettle 9 electrify, galvanize, overwhelm
up: 6 gain on 7 recover
up to: 5 reach 8 approach, overtake
catch __: 3 dog 4 colt, crop, fire, on to 5 a crab, basin 6 phrase, stitch
catch __ of: 4 wind 5 sight
catch-__: 3 can 4 colt, cord
__ catch: 4 fair 5 elbow 6 safety, spring
Catch __ You Can: 4 Me If, Us If
Catch!: 4 here
catch a __: 4 crab 6 Tartar
Catch a Falling Star (1958 song) artist: Perry Como
Catch a falling star author: 5 Donne
catchall: 9 inclusive
abbr.: 3 etc. 4 et al., misc.
term: 4 et al. 6 et alia, et alii, others
catch-as-catch-__: 3 can
catcher: 6 Piazza 7 athlete 10 baseballer
cow ~: 5 lasso, reata, riata 6 lariat
fly ~: 3 web 5 honey 6 cobweb
gear: 3 pad 4 mask, mitt 5 glove
Hall of Fame ~: 4 Fisk 5 Bench, Berra 6 Carter, Dickey, Gibson 8 Cochrane 9 Yogi Berra 10 Bill Dickey, Campanella, Gary Carter
man behind the ~: 3 ump 6 umpire
mouse ~: 3 cat 4 trap 6 feline
place: 3 rye
quotable ~: 4 Yogi 5 Berra
stance: 6 crouch
starter: 3 cow, dog, fly 4 gnat 6 oyster
__ catcher: 4 dust
Catcher in the Rye, The author: J.D. Salinger
catcher's __: 3 box 4 mitt 5 glove
catch in __: 4 a lie
catching: 5 viral 7 endemic 8 epidemic, pandemic 9 endemical, epizootic 10 contagious, epidemical, infectious, inoculable
some z's: 4 abed 6 asleep
start ~ up: 4 gain 7 close in
__-catching: 3 eye
catch one's __: 3 eye 6 breath
__ Cat Chow: 6 Purina
catchpenny: 4 mean 5 cheap 6 stingy
catchphrase: 3 saw 5 maxim, motto 6 slogan 7 proverb 8 laconism 9 battle cry, watchword 10 shibboleth
catch some __: 4 rays
Catch-22: 4 snag 7 dilemma, paradox, proviso 8 obstacle, quandary
Catch-22 (film, novel)
author: Joseph Heller
cast: Alan Arkin, Martin Balsam, Richard Benjamin, Art Garfunkel, Jack Gilford, Buck Henry, Bob Newhart, Anthony Perkins, Paula Prentiss, Martin Sheen, Jon Voight, Orson Welles
character: 3 Orr 4 Milo 5 Major 9 Yossarian
director: Mike Nichols
catchup
see ketchup
catch-up, play: 6 pursue
Catch Us If You Can (1965 song)
artist: Dave Clark Five
catchword
see catchphrase
catchy: 6 fitful, tricky 8 hummable, pleasing 9 deceptive
Catch you later!: 3 bye 4 ciao, ta ta 6 bye-bye 7 goodbye 8 au revoir, farewell
__-Cat Club: 3 Kit
Cate: 9 Blanchett
catechism: 4 book, test 9 education
catechize: 3 ask 4 quiz 5 drill, grill, probe, query, teach, train 7 educate, enquire, examine, inquire 8 instruct, question 9 enlighten 10 evangelize
catechumen: 4 tiro, tyro 5 pupil 6 novice 7 convert, learner 8 initiate, neophyte 9 fledgling, novitiate, proselyte
categorical: 4 firm, sure 5 plain 6 actual, all-out, direct 7 certain, express, flat-out 8 absolute, clear-cut, complete, definite, distinct, dogmatic, emphatic, explicit, forceful, positive, resolute, specific, straight, ultimate 10 conclusive, dogmatical, unswerving, unwavering
categorically: 5 truly 6 really, wholly
categorize: 3 peg 4 file, rank, sort 5 group, order, place, range 6 assort, divide 8 classify, identify, tabulate, typecast 9 put down as 10 button down, distribute, pigeonhole
category: 3 ilk 4 kind, rank, sort, tier, type 5 class, genre, genus, grade, group, level, state 6 branch, league, manner, rating, sector, series 7 bracket, heading, section, species, variety 8 division, grouping 10 department, pigeonhole
catchall ~: 4 misc. 5 other
category __: 6 killer
Catemaco: 4 city, town
locale: 6 Mexico 8 Veracruz
catenate: 5 tie in
catenation: 5 chain 6 series 8 sequence
cater: 4 host 6 outfit, purvey, supply 7 furnish, provide
to: 4 baby, feed, tend 5 do for, favor, humor, spoil 6 attend, coddle, cosset, dandle, oblige, pamper, pander, please, wait on 7 gratify, indulge, work for 8 give in to, wait upon 9 spoon-feed
(to): 8 minister
cater-__: 6 corner, cousin
Catera: 3 car 4 auto 8 Cadillac
Catered Affair, The (1956 film)
cast: Ernest Borgnine, Bette Davis, Debbie Reynolds
catered event: 6 affair 7 banquet
caterpillar: 3 bug 4 pest 5 egger, larva 6 insect
case: 6 cocoon
combining form: 5 -campa, eruci-
construction: 4 tent
like a ~: 5 hairy
__ caterpillar: 4 tent 7 tussock
caterwaul: 3 bay, cry 4 bawl, howl, meow, wail, yell, yowl 5 miaou, miaow, miaul 6 scream, shriek 7 blubber, screech
caterwauling: 3 din 5 noise
Cates: 6 George, Phoebe 7 Gilbert
Cates, Phoebe: 7 actress
film: Bright Lights, Big City (1988)
Gremlins (1984)
Gremlins 2 The New Batch (1990)
Princess Caraboo (1994)
spouse: Kevin Kline
catfight: 3 row 4 spat 5 set-to 7 quarrel
catfish: 4 raad 6 hassar, tandan 8 bullhead
catcher: 3 net
whisker: 6 barbel
__ catfish: 4 blue 7 channel, Chinese, walking
Catfish: 6 Hunter
Catfish Row: 4 slum 8 tenement
locale: 10 Charleston
resident: 4 Bess 5 Porgy
cat food: 5 Amore 6 Figaro, Purina 7 Whiskas 8 Friskies 10 Chef's Blend, Fancy Feast
Cath.: 5 relig.
leader: 4 msgr.
not ~: 4 Prot.
__ Cath.: 3 Rom.
catharsis: 5 purge 9 cleansing, purgation 10 abreaction, evacuation, lustration
cathartic plant: 5 senna
Cathay: 5 China
visitor: Marco Polo
cathead: 4 beam 6 timber
cathedra, ex: 8 official
cathedral: 6 church, temple 8 basilica 9 sanctuary 10 tabernacle
British ~ town: 3 Ely 6 Exeter
clergy: 5 canon
court: 6 parvis
feature: 3 pew 4 apse, arch, icon, ikon, nave 5 eikon, spire 6 chevet
French ~ town: 5 Reims 6 Amiens, Rheims
head: 4 dean 6 bishop
seat: 7 diocese
Spanish ~ town: 5 Avila
style: 6 Gothic
cathedral __: 4 hull 5 glass 7 ceiling
Cathedral author: Nelson Demille
Cathedral City: 4 town
locale: 10 California
Catherine: 3 Ste. 4 Bach, Parr 5 Hicks, O'Hara 6 Howard, Keener 7 Deneuve 8 de' Medici, Oxenberg 9 Zeta-Jones
in Irish: 7 Caitlin
Catherine __-Jones: 4 Zeta
Catherine of __: 5 Siena 6 Aragon 10 Alexandria
Catherine of Alexandria: 5 saint
Catherine of Siena: 5 saint
Catherines, husband of three: 5 Henry
Catherine the Great successor: 4 Paul 5 Paul I
Catherine Wheel, The author: Jean Stafford
Cather, Willa: 6 author, writer
work: Alexander's Bridge
Death Comes for the Archbishop
A Lost Lady
Lucy Gayheart
My Antonia
My Mortal Enemy
Obscure Destinies
One of Ours
O Pioneers!
Paul's Case
Shadows on the Rock
The Song of the Lark
The Troll Garden
Cathleen: 7 Nesbitt
cathode __: 3 ray 4 glow
cathode ray tube: 8 terminal
cathodes, like some: 3 neg., pos. 8 negative, positive
catholic: 4 wide 6 cosmic, global 7 general, generic, liberal 8 cosmical, tolerant 9 generical, inclusive, receptive, unbigoted, universal, worldwide 10 ecumenical, large-scale, open-minded
Catholic __: 6 Church
__ Catholic: 3 Old 5 Greek, Roman
catholicon: 7 panacea
Catholic service: 4 Mass
Cathryn: 5 Damon
Cathy: 4 Carr 5 comic, Rigby, strip 6 Dennis 8 Moriarty, O'Donnell 9 Guisewite
dog: 7 Electra
Cathy __ Crosby: 3 Lee
Cathy's Clown (1960 song) artist: Everly Brothers
Catiline author: Henrik Ibsen
Cat in the Hat, The author: Dr. Seuss
catkin: 5 ament, plant
tree: 5 alder
Catlett: 3 Sid 6 Walter
catlike: 5 agile, felid 6 feline 8 stealthy
carnivore: 5 civet
catman: 5 tamer 9 lion tamer
catnap: 4 doze 5 break, sleep 6 drowse, siesta, snooze 7 drop off, shuteye 8 downtime 10 fall asleep, forty winks
catnip: 4 herb
cat-o'-__-tails: 4 nine
Cato: 5 Roman 6 orator
garment for ~: 4 toga
see also Latin
Catoctin: 3 mts. 5 range 9 mountains
locale: 8 Maryland, Virginia
Cat on a Hot Tin Roof: 4 film, play
author: Tennessee Williams
cast: Burl Ives, Paul Newman, Elizabeth Taylor
character: 3 Mae 5 Brick, Dixie 7 Big Mama 8 Big Daddy
director: Richard Brooks
dog: 8 Bucky Boy
cat-o'-nine-tails: 4 whip
Caton-Jones, Michael: 8 director
film: Doc Hollywood (1991)
The Jackal (1997)
Rob Roy (1995)

Scandal (1989)
This Boy's Life (1993)
Catonsville: 4 city, town
locale: 8 Maryland
catoptrophobe fear: 7 mirrors
catorce, half of: 5 siete
Cato the __: 5 Elder 7 Younger
cats: 6 people
ender: 3 paw
fat ~: 4 rich
mice, to ~: 4 prey
rain ~ and dogs: 4 pour, teem
cats (advertising):
Leo (MGM)
Morris (Nine Lives cat food)
Tony (Frosted Flakes, tiger)
cats (comic strips/comics):
Arlene (Garfield)
Atilla (Mother Goose and Grimm)
Azrael (Smurfs)
Bill (Bloom County)
Bobo (The Piranha Club)
Catbert (Dilbert)
Garfield
Heathcliff
Hobbes (Calvin and Hobbes, tiger)
Hope (The Gumps)
Hot Dog (Dennis the Menace)
Kittycat (The Family Circus)
Mooch (Mutts)
Muffin (Pickles)
Sid (Ziggy)
Streaky (Supergirl)
World War II (Peanuts)
cats (films):
Am (Lady and the Tramp)
Baby (Bringing Up Baby, leopard)
Bambi (Earth Girls Are Easy)
Beeswax (Her Alibi)
Burbank (Lethal Weapon)
Cat (Breakfast at Tiffany's)
Catzilla (Mouse Hunt)
Clementine (Visit to a Small Planet)
Cosmic Creepers (Bedknobs and Broomsticks)
Elke (The Towering Inferno)
Fellini (Breaking Away)
Figaro (Pinocchio)
General Sterling Price (True Grit)
Italics (Runaway Bride)
Jacob (Dr. Dolittle, tiger)
Jake (The Cat From Outer Space)
Jarvis (The Man With Two Brains)
Jonesy (Alien)
Julius (Twins)
Leonardo (Casanova's Big Night)
Lucifer (Cinderella)
Milo (The Adventures of Milo and Otis)
Miss Kitty (Batman Returns)
Mr. Bigglesworth (Austin Powers)
Mr. Jinx (Meet the Parents)
Mufasa (The Lion King, lion)
Neutron (This Island Earth)
Oliver (Oliver & Company)
Orion (Men in Black)
Pyewacket (Bell, Book and Candle)
Rajah (Aladdin, lion)
Romeo (Romancing the Stone)
Ruby (Girl, Interrupted)
Rufus (Re-Animator)
Sassy (Homeward Bound)
Scar (The Lion King, lion)
Si (Lady and the Tramp)
Simba (The Lion King, lion)
Sweetie (The Fifth Element)
Sylvester (Warner Bros.)
Thomasina (The Three Lives of Thomasina)
Timer (The Specialist)
Tiny (Unlawful Entry)
Tom (Tom and Jerry)
Tonto (Harry and Tonto)
Whiskers (Last Action Hero)
cats (literature):
Bagheera (The Jungle Book, panther)
Bloomberg (Franny and Zooey)
Church (Pet Sematary)
Crookshanks (Harry Potter)
Dinah (Alice in Wonderland)
Grimalkin (Wuthering Heights)
Lady Jane (Bleak House)
Mehitabel (Archy and Mehitabel)
Mr. Paws (Harry Potter)
Mrs. Murphy (Rita Mae Brown)
Mrs. Norris (Harry Potter)
Pixel (The Cat Who Walks Through Walls)
Pluto (The Black Cat)
Puff (Dick and Jane)
Shere Khan (The Jungle Book, tiger)
Snowdrop (Alice in Wonderland)
Snowy (Harry Potter)
Tao (The Incredible Journey)
Tibbles (Harry Potter)
Tufty (Harry Potter)
White Nose (Happy Hollisters)
cats (TV):
Benny the Ball (Top Cat)
Bruce (Honey West, ocelot)
Choo Choo (Top Cat)
Clarence (Daktari, lion)
Elizabeth Barrett Browning (Cheers)
Felix
Henrietta (Mr. Rogers' Neighborhood)
Katnip (Herman and Katnip)
King Leonardo (lion)
Kitty Kat (The Addams Family, lion)
Kitty (South Park)
Lucky (ALF)
Minerva (Our Miss Brooks)
Nero (Remington Steele)
Rags (Crusader Rabbit, tiger)
Ruff (Ruff and Reddy)
Salem (Sabrina, the Teenage Witch)
Salty (Caroline in the City)
Scratchy (The Simpsons)
Snowball (The Simpsons)
Spartacus (Just Shoot Me)
Spot (Star Trek: The Next Generation)
Stimpy (Ren and Stimpy)
Toonces (Saturday Night Live)
Top Cat
cat's __: 4 meow 6 cradle 7 pajamas, whisker
cat's-__: 3 ear, paw 4 claw
cat's-__ marble: 3 eye
Cats: 7 musical
composer: 4 Rice 11 Lloyd Webber
inspiration: 5 Eliot
monogram: 3 ALW, TSE
role: 3 Gus 5 Plato, Quaxo 6 Alonzo, George, Jemima, Victor 7 Admetus, Demeter, Electra, Exotica, Genghis, Gilbert 8 Etcetera, Macavity, Sillabub, Victoria 9 Asparagus, Cassandra, Coricopat, Pouncival, Tantomile 10 Grizabella, Growltiger, Jellylorum, Munkustrap 11 Bombalurina, Carbucketty, Griddlebone, Mungojerrie 12 Jennyanydots, Rumpleteazer, Rum Tum Tugger
__ cats and dogs: 4 rain
CAT scan relative: 3 MRI
cat's cradle: 4 game
Cat's Cradle author: Kurt Vonnegut Jr.
cat's-eye: 3 gem 6 marble 8 gemstone
relative: 5 agate, aggie
Cat's Eye author: Margaret Atwood
Cat's in the Cradle (song) artist: Harry Chapin, Ugly Kid Joe
Catskills: 4 mtns. 5 range 9 mountains
locale: 7 New York
cat's-paw: 4 dupe, knot, pawn, prey, tool 5 patsy 6 jackal, puppet
catsup
see ketchup
cattail: 4 reed, rush 5 plant 6 flower
site: 5 marsh
cattalo: 5 bovid 6 animal, bovine, hybrid, mammal
relative: 3 yak 4 anoa, arna, gaur, urus, zebu 5 bison, gayal, takin 6 mithan, muskox 7 aurochs, banteng, banting, buffalo, carabao, kouprey, tamarao, tamarau, timarau
Cattaraugus County city: 5 Olean
__ Cat, The: 5 Black
cattiness: 5 spite
cattle: 3 mob 4 beef, cows, herd, kine, oxen, yaks 5 bison, bulls, steer, stock 6 beasts, beeves, calves, dogies, masses, steers 7 bovines, Brahmas, heifers 9 livestock, longhorns 10 shorthorns
African ~ enclosure: 5 craal, kraal
ancestor: 7 aurochs
at times: 5 lower, mooer
bird: 5 egret
black ~: 5 Angus
breed: 3 Gir 4 Busa, Glan, Kuri, Rath, Siri, Tuli 5 Angus, Barka, Boran, Dajal, Dangi, Deoni, Devon, Fjall, Horro, Kerry, Kurdi, Luing, Malvi, Maure, N'dama, Nguni, Oropa, Rathi, Sanhe, Wagyu 6 Angeln, Ankole, Aubrac, Baladi, Channi, Dexter, Dhanni, Dulong, Gaolao, Herens, Jaulan, Jersey, Lohani, Mewati, Nagori, Nelore, Nimari, Ongole, Ovambo, Ponwar, Rojhan, Salers, Sarabi, Sussex, Tswana, Vosges 7 Alberes, Bachaur, Barzona, Brahman, Brahmin, Cachena, Canchim, Istoben, Mashona, Red Poll, Retinta, Sahiwal, Yanbian 8 Ayrshire, Bonsmara, Charbray, Chianina, Galloway, Gelbvieh, Guernsey, Hereford, Holstein, Limousin 9 Charolais, Shorthorn, Simmental 10 Lincoln Red, Murray Grey, Welsh Black
call: 3 low, moo 7 meeting 9 interview
catcher: 5 lasso, reata, riata
chew: 3 cud
country: 5 ranch, range
enclosure: 3 pen 4 crib, yard 6 corral
food: 6 fodder, forage
genus: 3 bos
group: 4 herd 5 drove
handler: 6 cowboy, drover 7 cowpoke
herders: 5 Masai 6 Maasai
hip joint: 5 thurl
hornless ~: 5 Angus, muley 6 mulley
mover: 4 prod
of India: 4 zebu
prod: 4 goad
raise ~: 5 ranch
South America: 4 nata
steal ~: 6 rustle
work with ~: 4 herd, rope 5 drive 6 corral, dehorn
cattle __: 3 car, run 4 call, grub, prod, show, tick 5 egret, guard
__ cattle: 4 beef 5 dairy 6 humped
Cattle Annie and Little Britches (1980 film)
cast: Burt Lancaster, Amanda Plummer, Rod Steiger
cattlelike: 6 bovine
Catton, Bruce: 6 author 9 historian
work: The Coming Fury
Glory Road
Grant Moves South
Grant Takes Command
Mr. Lincoln's Army
Never Call Retreat
A Stillness at Appomattox
Terrible Swift Sword
Cattrall: 3 Kim
catty: 4 mean 5 nasty, snide 6 feline, unkind 7 hateful, hostile, vicious 8 spiteful, stealthy, venomous 9 malicious, rancorous 10 backbiting, evil-minded, ill-natured, malevolent
comment: 3 mew 4 meow 5 miaou, miaow, miaul, swipe
catty-__: 6 corner
Catull: 4 font 8 typeface
Catullus: 4 poet 5 Roman
catwalk: 6 bridge
Cat Who Came for Christmas, The
author: 5 Amory
Cat Who Walks Through Walls, The
cat: 5 Pixel
Catwoman foe: 5 Robin 6 Batman
C. Aubrey __: 5 Smith
Caubvick: 4 peak 5 mount 8 mountain
locale: 6 Canada 8 Labrador
Cauca: 5 river
locale: 8 Columbia
Caucasian: 5 Arian, Aryan, white
Caucasus: 3 mts. 5 range 9 mountains
extinct ~ volcano: 6 Kazbek
locale: 6 Europe, Russia 7 Georgia 10 Azerbaijan
mountain: 6 Elbrus, Elbruz
native: 5 Osset 6 Ossete
river: 4 Kurd, Rion 5 Rioni
caucho: 3 ule 6 rubber
caucus: 4 bloc, meet 6 parley, powwow 7 council, faction, meeting, session 8 assembly, conclave, congress 9 gathering 10 convention
state: 4 Iowa
caudal appendage: 4 tail
caudata member: 4 newt
caught: 5 at bay, stuck 10 interested
napping: 6 spacey 7 in a daze, out of it, unaware 8 heedless 9 negligent, unmindful, unwitting 10 out to lunch
up: 6 enrapt 9 engrossed
caught __: 5 short
Caught (1949 film)
cast: Barbara Bel Geddes, James Mason, Robert Ryan
director: Max Ophuls
caught in __: 4 a lie
Caught in the Draft (1941 film)
cast: Bob Hope, Dorothy Lamour
Caught you!: 3 aha 6 gotcha
cauldron: 3 pot, vat 5 crock 6 boiler, kettle 9 container
contents: 4 brew
ingredient: 4 newt
Caulfield: 4 Joan 7 Maxwell
cauliflower: 6 veggie 9 vegetable
bit: 6 floret
cauliflower __: 3 ear 6 fungus
caulk: 4 seal 5 close
caulking
in need of ~: 5 leaky 6 drafty
material: 5 oakum, putty
Caulkins: 5 Tracy
__ causa: 7 exempli, honoris
__ causa pro causa: 3 non
causation: 4 root 6 origin, reason 8 creation 9 invention
cause: 2 do 3 let 4 goal, lead, make, move, root, sake, seat, seed, side, soul, suit 5 agent, basis, beget, breed, bring, hatch, ideal, maker, raise 6 belief, compel, create, effect, elicit, entail, factor, incite, induce, kindle, lead to, motive, origin, parent, prompt, reason, source, spring 7 actuate, creator, crusade, dream up, genesis, grounds, lawsuit, produce, provoke, purpose, trigger 8 engender, generate, initiate, motivate, movement, occasion, producer, result in 9 instigate, necessity, objective, originate 10 antecedent, bring about, conviction, effectuate, enterprise, foundation, give rise to, inducement, litigation, motivation, originator, prime mover

a riot: **5** rouse **6** arouse, foment, set off, whip up, work up **7** agitate, inflame **9** instigate
combining form: **4** etio- **5** aetio-, ailio-
ender: **3** way
for alarm: **5** peril **6** danger
harm to: **3** mar **4** maim, ruin **5** abuse, spoil, stain, wound, wrong **6** batter, bruise, deface, defile, impair, injure, mangle, ravage **7** corrupt, pollute, scratch, tarnish **9** undermine
havoc: **5** wreck
help the ~: **6** chip in, donate **9** volunteer **10** contribute
horror: **5** scare **7** horrify, terrify **8** frighten **9** terrorize
irritation: **3** irk, vex **4** gall, rile **5** annoy, chafe, clash, peeve, pique **6** abrade, nettle, rankle **7** inflame, provoke **9** aggravate **10** exasperate
lost ~: **5** goner
of ruin: **6** plague **7** scourge **8** anathema, calamity, downfall
resentment: **3** vex **4** roil **5** anger, annoy, peeve, pique, upset **6** nettle, offend, put out **7** provoke **8** irritate **9** displease
to happen: **4** spur **5** incur, spark **6** incite, prompt, set off **7** produce, trigger **8** generate, motivate, touch off **9** stimulate **10** bring about
cause ___: **7** célèbre
___ cause: **4** lost **5** final **6** formal
cause and ___: **6** effect
Cause for Alarm (1951 film)
cast: Barry Sullivan, Loretta Young
director: Tay Garnett
causeless: **8** needless **10** gratuitous, groundless, unasked-for
___ cause order: **4** show
causerie: **4** chat **9** tête-à-tête
...cause the Bible tells ___: **4** me so
causeway: **4** path, road
causing: **6** behind
combining form: **3** -fic **5** -genic **7** -facient
joy: **8** cheering, pleasant, pleasing
Causing a Commotion (1987 song)
artist: Madonna
caustic: **3** dry, lye **4** acid, sour, tart **5** acerb, acrid, harsh, sharp, snide **6** biting, bitter, ireful, severe **7** acerbic, burning, cutting, erosive, mordant, pungent, satiric **8** abrasive, alkaline, incisive, sardonic, scathing, stinging **9** corrosive, sarcastic, satirical, trenchant
solution: **3** KOH, lye **4** NaOH **6** alkali
caustic ___: **4** lime, soda **5** curve **6** baryta, potash **7** alcohol, surface
cauterize: **4** burn, sear **5** scald **7** cleanse
Cauthen, Steve: **6** jockey
milieu: **5** track
caution: **3** tip **4** care, heed, sign, warn **5** alert **6** advice, advise, caveat, exhort, inform, notice, notify, remind, tip off **7** counsel, portent, red flag, reserve, warning **8** admonish, dissuade, forewarn, prudence, red light **9** alertness, attention, canniness, restraint, vigilance **10** admonition, discretion, precaution, providence
color of ~: **5** amber
throw ~ to the winds: **4** dare
with ~: **5** shyly **6** askant, warily **7** askance, charily, leerily, timidly **8** frugally **9** carefully, guardedly, heedfully, mindfully, sparingly, thriftily
word of ~: **4** don't **6** beware
Cautionary Tales author: Hilaire Belloc
cautious: **3** shy **4** cagy, safe, slow, wary **5** alert, cagey, canny, chary, fussy, leery **6** unsure **7** all ears, careful, dubious, finicky, guarded, heedful, mindful, politic, prudent **8** delicate, discreet, doubtful, doubting, exacting, finiking, finnicky, hesitant, keen-eyed, moderate, reserved, rigorous, thorough, vigilant, watchful **9** assiduous, attentive, farseeing, judicious, observant, provident, skeptical, tentative, uncertain **10** deliberate, fastidious, longheaded, meticulous, on one's toes, particular, scrupulous, suspicious, uneffusive
be ~: **4** care, mind **9** have a care
one: **6** heeder
cautiously: **7** charily **8** gingerly **9** advisedly, carefully, tactfully **10** delicately
cautious seldom ___, The: **3** err
Cauvery: **5** river
locale: **5** India
Cav
see Cavalier
___ cava: **4** vena
Cava: **4** wine
origin: **5** Spain
Cavafy, Constantine: **4** poet **5** Greek
cavalcade: **5** array **6** parade **7** caravan **9** march-past, promenade, spectacle **10** expedition, procession
Cavalcanti, Guido: **4** poet **7** Italian
cavalier: **4** curt **5** lofty, proud **6** lordly, rakish, snooty, suitor **7** haughty, offhand **8** arrogant, horseman, insolent, scornful, superior, wasteful **10** disdainful
Cavalier: **3** car **4** auto **5** Chevy **9** Chevrolet **10** automobile
Cavalier poet: **5** Carew **6** Waller **7** Herrick **8** Lovelace, Suckling
Cavalier rival: **3** Mav, Net, Sun **4** Buck, Bull, Hawk, Heat, Jazz, King, Spur **5** Knick, Laker, Magic, Pacer, Sixer, Sonic **6** Celtic, Hornet, Nugget, Piston, Raptor, Rocket, Wizard **7** Clipper, Grizzly, Warrior **8** Maverick **10** SuperSonic, Timberwolf
Cavaliers: **3** U. Va. **4** five, team
home: **9** Cleveland
org.: **3** NBA **4** NCAA
sport: **10** basketball
cavalla: **4** fish
Cavallaro: **6** Carmen
Cavalleria Rusticana: **5** opera
composer: **8** Mascagni
cavalry: **2** tp. **4** army **5** troop **8** dragoons
command: **6** charge
headquarters: **4** fort
horse: **7** charger, trooper
sitcom: **6** F Troop
weapon: **5** lance, saber, sabre, sword
___ cavalry: **3** air, sky
cavalryman: **6** hussar, lancer **7** soldier **10** equestrian
Algerian ~: **5** spahi **6** spahee
Prussian ~: **4** ulan **5** uhlan
cavatelli: **5** pasta
alternative: **4** orzo, ziti **5** penne **6** noodle **7** lasagna, lasagne, pastina, ravioli **8** bucatini, couscous, farfalle, linguine, linguini, macaroni, rigatoni **9** agnolotti, angelhair, manicotti, spaghetti **10** cannelloni, fettuccini, tortellini, vermicelli
cavatina: **3** air **4** song **5** music **6** melody
cave: **3** bow, den **4** hole, lair, room **5** antre **6** grotto, submit **7** shelter, succumb **8** hideaway **9** surrender **10** subterrane
art: **5** mural
dweller: **3** bat **5** troll **6** apeman
-dwelling combining form: **6** troglo-
ender: **3** man **4** fish
explorer: **9** spelunker
in: **3** bow, sag **4** give, sink, wilt **5** slump, yield **6** accede, buckle, fess up, relent **7** concede, crumple, give way **8** collapse **9** acquiesce **10** capitulate
(in): **5** stave
in verse: **4** grot
pigment used in ~ art: **5** ocher, ochre
sound: **4** echo
cave ___: **3** art, man **4** bear **5** canem **7** cricket, dweller
___ Cave: **4** Niah **6** Danger, Spirit **7** Fingal's, Lascaux, Mammoth, Ventana
caveat: **5** alarm **6** notice **7** caution, red flag, warning **10** admonition
buyer ~: **4** as is
issue a ~: **4** warn
caveat ___: **6** emptor
Cavell: **5** Edith
caveman
cartoon ~: **3** Oop
discovery: **4** fire
Caveman (1981 film)
cast: Barbara Bach, Shelley Long, John Matuszak, Ringo Starr
___ Cave National Park: **4** Wind **7** Mammoth
Cavendish: **5** Henry **6** banana
Cavendish, Henry: **7** chemist **9** physicist
birthplace: **4** Nice
cavern: **3** den **4** hole **5** antre, vault **6** grotto
see also cave
cavernous: **4** deep, huge, vast, wide **5** broad, large, roomy **6** gaping **7** abysmal, yawning **8** spacious **9** chambered **10** bottomless, commodious, fathomless, sepulchral, voluminous
opening: **3** maw
___ Caverns: **4** Howe **5** Luray
Caves of Steel, The author: Asimov
Cave Spring: **4** city, town
locale: **8** Virginia
Cavett, Dick
alma mater: **4** Yale
spouse: Carrie Nye
wife: **3** Nye
caviar: **3** ova, roe **4** eggs **6** canapé
companion: **5** blini, bliny
exporter: **4** Iran **6** Russia
source: **4** shad **6** beluga
cavil: **3** nag **4** beef, carp **5** whine **6** bicker, grouse, jibe at, pick at **7** censure, nitpick, quarrel, quibble **8** belittle, complain, pettifog **9** complaint, criticism, criticize, deprecate, disparage, find fault, make a fuss, objection **10** split hairs
caviler: **5** shrew **6** critic **9** henpecker
caviling: **5** cross **7** carping, fretful **8** captious, critical, fretsome **9** criticism, querulous
cavities, anatomical: **5** antra
cavity: **3** gap, pit **4** dent, hole, mold, nook, void **5** abysm, abyss, mouth, sinus **6** areola, areole, caries, crater, hollow, lacuna, pocket, recess, socket **7** opening, vacuity **10** depression, excavation, interspace
anatomical ~: **5** lumen, sinus **6** antrum
bone ~: **5** fossa **6** antrum
combining form: **4** -cele, coel- **5** -coele
detector: **4** X-ray
filler: **3** DDS, DMD **5** inlay **7** dentist
of a ~: **6** antral
of the nasal ~: **5** naric
oral ~: **5** mouth
plant ~: **6** locule
rock ~: **3** vug **4** vugg, vugh
volcano ~: **3** pit **6** cavity
___ cavity: **5** sinus **7** pleural
cavort: **4** lark, leap, play, romp, skip **5** caper, dance, frisk, revel **6** frolic, gambol, prance **7** carry on, rollick **9** have a ball, make merry **10** fool around
Cavs: **4** five, team
org.: **3** NBA
cavy: **4** paca **6** animal, mammal, rodent
relative: **3** rat **4** degu, jird, mara, paca, vole **5** coypu, gundi, mouse, xerus **6** agouti, beaver, gerbil, gopher, jerboa, marmot, murine **7** hamster, lemming, muskrat, visacha **8** chipmunk, cricetid, dormouse, squirrel, tuco-tuco **9** chickaree, groundhog, guinea pig, porcupine, woodchuck **10** chinchilla, prairie dog
caw: **5** croak **6** squawk **8** birdcall
Cawdor bigshot: **5** thane, thegn
Caxias do Sul: **4** city, town
locale: **6** Brazil
caxixi: **6** rattle **10** percussion
origin: **6** Africa, Brazil
Caxton: **4** font **8** typeface
cay: **4** eyot, isle, reef **5** islet **6** island **9** coral reef
Cayce: **5** Edgar
cayenne: **5** spice **6** pepper **9** condiment
Cayenne: **3** SUV **4** city, port, town **7** Porsche
___ Cayes, Haiti: **3** Les
cayman: **4** croc **6** animal **7** reptile **9** crocodile
___ Cayman: **5** Grand
Cayman Islands
capital: **10** George Town
money: **4** cent **6** dollar
Cayuga: **4** duck, fowl, lake **5** tribe **6** Indian **7** Amerind **8** Iroquois **10** Finger Lake
ally: **6** Mohawk, Oneida, Seneca **8** Onondaga **9** Tuscarora
locale: **7** New York
relative: **4** smew, teal **5** eider, Pekin, Rouen, scaup **6** scoter **7** gadwall, mallard, pintail, pochard, redhead, sea duck, widgeon **8** garganey, gray duck, mandarin, musk duck, oldsquaw, shoveler, surf duck, wood duck **9** black duck, broadbill, goldeneye, goosander, greenhead, merganser, ruddy duck, sprigtail **10** bufflehead, canvasback, surf scoter, tufted duck
cayuse: **4** hoss, pony **5** horse, mount **6** animal, equine
catcher: **6** lariat
Cayuse: **6** Indian **7** Amerind
Cazale, John: **5** actor
film: The Conversation (1974)
The Deer Hunter (1978)
Dog Day Afternoon (1975)
The Godfather (1972)
The Godfather Part II (1974)
CB: **5** radio
emergency ~ channel: **4** nine
knob: **3** vol. **6** volume **7** squelch
moniker: **6** handle
word: **4** over **7** ten-four
CBC: **7** network
CBer: **9** good buddy
cousin: **3** ham
CBS
HQ: **3** NYC
logo: **3** eye
part of ~: **3** Sys. **4** Syst. **8** Columbia
regulator: **3** FCC
rival: **3** ABC, Fox, NBC, UPN **5** ABC-TV, NBC-TV
cc.: **4** meas. **7** measure
C.C. ___: **5** Rider
___ C. Calhoun: **4** John
CCH: **7** Pounder
C-clamp: **4** vise **7** gripper
___ C. Clarke: **6** Arthur

cc, not a: 4 orig. 8 original
ccs.: 3 amt. 4 meas 6 amount, dosage 7 measure
CCU locale: 4 hosp. 8 hospital
Cd: 4 elem. 7 cadmium, element
  48 for ~: 4 at. no.
CD: 4 disc, disk 5 asset
  alternative: 2 LP 3 DAT 4 tape 5 album, T-bill, T-note 8 cassette
  earnings: 3 int. 8 interest
  enjoy a ~: 6 listen
  holder: 4 case 5 saver 9 jewel case
  part of ~: 3 dep., ROM 4 Cert., disc, disk 7 compact, deposit
  player: 2 DJ 6 deejay 7 boombox
  player ancestor: 4 hi-fi
  player maker: 3 RCA 4 Sony
  player part: 5 diode, laser
  put on ~: 6 encode
  selection: 5 track
  source: 4 bank 5 S and L
  type: 2 EP 3 IRA
CD __: 6 player, single
CD-__: 3 ROM
CDC: 4 agcy. 6 agency
  department: 3 HHS
  part of ~: 7 Centers, Control, Disease
cdr.: 4 rank
  employer: 3 USN
CD-ROM: 4 disc, disk
Ce: 4 elem. 6 cerium 7 element
  58 for ~: 4 at. no.
cease: 3 end 4 drop, halt, lull, quit, stop 5 abort, avast, can it, close, lapse, let up, pause 6 cool it, cut out, desist, expire, finish, give up, hold it, lay off, run out, stop it, wind up, wrap up 7 abstain, adjourn, back off, break up, die down, refrain, suspend 8 break off, close out, conclude, intermit, knock off, leave off, pack it in, shut down 9 close down, disappear, terminate 10 call it a day, knock it off, put an end to
  starter: 3 sur
  to a sailor: 5 avast
  work: 4 quit 5 leave 6 bow out, retire 8 hang it up, step down 10 give notice
cease and __: 6 desist
cease-fire: 5 truce 9 armistice, white flag
  region: 3 DMZ
ceaseless: 6 eterne, steady 7 abiding, chronic, endless, eternal, nonstop, undying 8 constant, enduring, timeless, unbroken, unending, untiring, unwaning 9 chronical, continual, incessant, perennial, perpetual, unabating, unceasing, unfailing 10 continuous
ceaselessly: 5 on end 7 forever
Cebalrai: 4 star
Cebu: 4 city, port, town
  city: 4 Naga
  island near ~: 5 Leyte
Ce Ce: 8 Peniston
Cech, Thomas: 7 chemist 8 Nobelist
Cecil: 4 Earl 5 Adams, Edgar 6 Beaton, Parker, Powell, Rhodes 7 DeMille 8 Hoffmann, Kellaway, language
  Agnes, to: 5 niece
  alternative: 3 ADA, APL, SQL 4 Alef, html, Icon, Java, LISP, Logo, Orca, Perl 5 Algol, Basic, COBOL, Dylan, SISAL 6 Delphi, Eiffel, Erlang, Oberon, Pascal, Prolog, Sather, Scheme, Snobol 7 Fortran
Cecil __ Lewis: 3 Day
Cecil, Edgar: 8 Nobelist
Cecilia: 3 ste. 5 saint 6 sainte
  in Irish: 6 Sheila
Cecilia (1970 song) artist: Simon and Garfunkel
cedant __ togae: 4 arma
cedar: 4 tree, wood 5 savin 6 deodar, savine 7 conifer, deodara 8 hardwood
  product: 4 cone
cedar __: 4 robe 5 apple, chest 7 waxwing
__ cedar: 3 red 4 salt 5 Atlas, Japan, white 6 Alaska, ground, Oregon, pencil 7 incense, Spanish
Cedar __, IA: 5 Falls 6 Rapids
Cedar City: 4 town
  locale: 4 Utah
Cedar Falls: 4 city, town
  locale: 4 Iowa
Cedar Hill: 4 city, town
  locale: 5 Texas
Cedar Park: 4 city, town
  locale: 5 Texas
Cedar Rapids: 4 city, town
  college: 3 Coe
  locale: 4 Iowa
  village near ~: 5 Amana
cedars of __: 7 Lebanon
cede: 4 drop, dump, give, sell, shed 5 chuck, ditch, forgo, grant, waive, yield 6 assign, convey, forego, fork up, give up, render 7 abandon, forfeit, forsake 8 abdicate, forswear, get rid of, hand over, jettison, part with, sign away, sign over, throw out, transfer 9 cast aside, dispose of, foreswear, sacrifice, surrender, throw away 10 relinquish
  starter: 4 ante 5 inter
cedi: 5 money
cedilla indication: 5 soft c
ceding: 10 abdication
Cedric: 5 Errol 7 Gibbons 9 Hardwicke
cee: 5 grade
  as a grade: 4 so-so
  follower: 3 dee
  preceder: 3 bee
  starter: 3 Jay
ceiba: 4 tree 5 kapok 6 cotton
ceiling: 3 cap, lim., top 4 dome, roof 5 limit, price, quota 6 height, record 7 maximum 8 covering
  arched ~: 5 vault
  device: 3 fan
  domed ~: 6 cupola
  hit the ~: 4 rage, rant, rave 5 freak 6 seethe
  make hit the ~: 5 anger 6 madden, offend, tee off 7 incense 9 infuriate
  opposite: 5 floor
  price ~: 3 cap
  support: 4 beam 5 joist
ceiling __: 3 fan 4 tile, zero 5 piece
__ ceiling: 5 glass
Ceiling Zero (1935 film)
  cast: James Cagney, Pat O'Brien
  director: Howard Hawks
ceinture: 4 belt
cel: 5 frame
  artist: 5 inker
  subject: 4 toon
Cel.
  not ~: 4 Fahr.
Cela, Camilo: 6 author, writer 7 Spanish 8 Nobelist
celadon: 5 color, green 7 grayish
  relative: 3 pea 4 cyan, jade, sage 5 beryl, breen, olive, virid 6 myrtle, reseda 7 avocado, emerald, verdant 9 pistachio, turquoise 10 aquamarine, chartreuse
Celaeno: 5 Harpy 6 Amazon, Pleiad
celandine: 5 plant, poppy 6 flower
Celanese: 6 fabric 8 material
Celan, Paul: 4 poet 6 German
Celaya: 4 city, town
  locale: 6 Mexico 10 Guanajuato
celeb: 3 VIP 4 name, star 6 phenom 7 notable 8 luminary 9 personage
Celebes: 3 sea 4 isle 6 island
  locale: 6 Borneo
  ox: 4 anoa
  sea: 5 Banda
  today: 8 Sulawesi
celebrant cry: 6 hoorah, hurray
celebrate: 4 fete, keep, laud, sing 5 exalt, extol, exult, feast, honor, party, revel 6 extoll, praise 7 acclaim, drink to, glorify, lionize, observe, rejoice, splurge, triumph, worship 8 eulogize, live it up 9 have a ball, make merry, publicize, raise heck, raise hell, recommend, ritualize, signalize, solemnize 10 compliment, consecrate, jump for joy
Celebrate (1970 song) artist: Three Dog Night
celebrated: 4 star 5 famed, great, known, noted 6 famous 7 big-name, eminent, notable, popular, revered, storied 8 glorious, historic, immortal, renowned, splendid 9 acclaimed, brilliant, important, legendary, memorable, prominent, topflight, well-known 10 preeminent
Celebrated Jumping Frog..., The
  author: Mark Twain
celebrating: 6 joyful, joyous 8 exultant, jubilant
celebration: 4 bash, fest, fete, gala, rite 5 blast, event, feast, party, rally, revel, spree, treat 6 fiesta, hoopla 7 acclaim, blowout, holiday, jubilee, liturgy, pageant, revelry, triumph 8 birthday, carousal, ceremony, festival, function, goings-on, jamboree, occasion, wingding 9 reception
  suffix: 3 -mas
Celebration (1980 song) artist: Kool and the Gang
celebratory: 4 gala 6 festal 8 honorary
__ célèbre: 5 cause
celebrities: 5 elite
celebrity: 3 VIP 4 fame, icon, idol, lion, name, star 5 éclat, glory, honor 6 bigwig, figure, renown, repute 7 big name, bigshot, hotshot, notable, stardom 8 eminence, grandeur, luminary, prestige, somebody 9 big cheese, dignitary, greatness, notoriety, personage, superstar 10 notability, popularity, prominence, reputation
  bash: 5 roast
  bit part: 5 cameo
Celebrity: 3 car 4 auto, Olds 5 Chevy 9 Chevrolet 10 Oldsmobile
Celebrity (1998 film)
  cast: Kenneth Branagh, Judy Davis, Leonardo DiCaprio, Famke Janssen, Joe Mantegna
  director: Woody Allen
celeriac: 6 veggie 9 vegetable
celeritous: 5 hasty, quick, rapid
celerity: 4 rush 5 haste, hurry, speed 6 hustle 8 alacrity, dispatch, legerity, rapidity, velocity 9 briskness, fleetness, quickness, swiftness 10 expedition, promptness, speediness
Celeron maker: 5 Intel
celery: 6 veggie 9 appetizer, vegetable
  Japanese ~: 3 udo
  portion: 5 stalk
celery __: 4 root, salt, soda 5 stalk 7 cabbage
__ celery: 4 knob, wild 7 Chinese
celesta: 8 keyboard 10 instrument
__ céleste: 4 voix
Celeste: 4 Holm 5 pizza
  alternative: 5 Jeno's, Tony's 6 Ellio's 7 Totino's 8 DiGiorno 9 Tombstone 10 Freschetta
Celeste Aïda: 4 aria
celestial: 4 holy 5 blest 6 astral, divine 7 angelic, blessed, elysian, godlike, sublime 8 beatific, empyreal, empyrean, ethereal, heavenly, seraphic, supernal 9 ambrosial, angelical, ineffable, spiritual, unworldly 10 immaterial, seraphical
  being: 5 angel 6 cherub, seraph
  body: 4 moon, star 5 comet 6 sphere
  science: 6 astron. 9 astronomy
  sphere: 3 sky
celestial __: 4 pole 5 globe 6 sphere 7 equator, horizon
Celestial __: 4 City 6 Empire
celestial mechanics: 7 science
  study: 6 motion 7 gravity
Celestial Navigation author: Anne Tyler
Celestine: 4 pope 5 Peter 7 pontiff
Celestine, Peter: 5 saint
celestite: 3 ore 7 mineral
Celia: 4 Cruz 6 Weston 7 Johnson
celibate: 4 abbé, pure 6 chaste 8 virtuous 9 continent
Celica: 3 car 4 auto 6 Toyota
Celine: 4 Dion
Céline, Louis-Ferdinand: 6 French, writer
cell: 3 egg 4 cage, coop, germ, jail 5 booth, cadre, spore 6 alcove, amoeba, recess 7 chamber, cubicle, dungeon, faction 8 cloister 9 corpuscle, cubbyhole, enclosure
  builder: 3 bee 5 drone
  combining form: 3 cyt- 4 -cyte, cyto- 5 -plast
  component: 4 gene 5 lipid 6 lipide
  dissolution: 5 lysis
  ender: 4 mate, ular 5 block
  feature: 3 bar
  germ ~: 4 seed 5 spore 6 gamete
  letters: 3 DNA, RNA
  nerve ~: 5 fiber
  nerve ~ part: 4 axon 5 axone
  occupant: 3 con, nun 4 monk 6 inmate 7 convict
  phone co.: 3 GTE, MCI 7 T-Mobile 8 Cingular
  phone kin: 5 pager
  phone maker: 5 Nokia 6 Nextel 8 Ericsson, Motorola
  place: 4 hive, jail 6 prison 7 beehive
  retina ~: 3 rod 4 cone
cell __: 3 sap 4 body, line, pack, wall 5 cycle, phone, plate 6 fusion, theory 7 biology
__ cell: 3 air, dew, dry, egg, fat, red, wet 4 acid, beta, bone, fuel, germ, glue, hair, Kerr, mast, stem, unit 5 basal, blast, blood, brain, flame, guard, nerve, pilot, sieve, solar, swarm, white 6 binary, collar, goblet, killer, memory, nettle, plasma, Weston 7 cadmium, gravity, pigment, primary, Schwann, somatic, storage, voltaic
cella: 4 naos 7 chamber
cellar: 4 bsmt. 5 floor 8 basement 9 last place
  contents: 4 salt, wine
  ender: 3 age
  in the ~: 4 last
  selection: 4 port, rosé
  starter: 4 salt
cellar __: 4 sash 6 fungus
__ cellar: 4 cold, root, wine 5 storm 7 cyclone
Cellini, Benvenuto: 6 artist 8 sculptor
  homeland: 5 Italy
  patron: 4 Este
cellist: 2 Ma 5 du Pré 6 Casals, Yo-Yo Ma 7 Starker 12 Rostropovich
  direction: 4 arco
  purchase: 5 rosin
cello: 6 string 10 instrument
  ending: 5 phane
  feature: 5 f hole
  kin: 5 viola 6 violin
  part: 4 neck 6 end pin

cellophane __: 4 tape 6 noodle
cells
add more ~: 4 grow
breakdown of ~: 5 lysis
carrier of white blood ~: 5 lymph
combining form: 7 -blastic
destroy, as ~: 4 lyse
like some nerve ~: 6 apolar
nervous system ~: 4 glia
Cell, The (2000 film)
cast: Vincent D'Onofrio, Jennifer Lopez, Vince Vaughn, Jake Weber
Cell, The author: Athol Fugard
cellular: 7 organic
cellular __: 5 phone
celluloid: 4 film 6 cinema
developer: 5 Hyatt
cellulose: 4 pulp
fabric: 5 rayon
cellulose __: 3 gum 7 acetate, nitrate
__ cellulose: 5 ethyl 6 methyl
Celsius, Anders: 7 Swedish 10 astronomer
Celt: 4 Gael, Scot 5 druid 6 Breton, Briton 8 Irishman, Welshman 9 Hibernian 10 Cornishman, Highlander
Celtic: 4 Bird, Erse 5 Cousy, Irish 8 Bob Cousy, Havlicek, language 9 Larry Bird
chariot: 5 essed
god: 3 Tiu
group: 4 clan
harvest festival: 6 lammas
instrument: 4 harp 5 rotta, rotte
language: 4 Erse, Gael, Manx 5 Welsh 6 Gaelic
Neptune: 3 Ler, Lir
paradise: 6 Avalon
poet: 4 bard
priest: 5 druid
rival: 3 Cav, Mav, Net, Sun 4 Buck, Bull, Hawk, Heat, Jazz, King, Spur 5 Knick, Laker, Magic, Pacer, Sixer, Sonic 6 Hornet, Nugget, Piston, Raptor, Rocket, Wizard 7 Clipper, Grizzly, Warrior 8 Cavalier, Maverick 10 SuperSonic, Timberwolf
tribe: 5 Iceni
Celtic __: 5 cross
Celtics: 4 five, team
home: 6 Boston
org.: 3 NBA
sport: 10 basketball
cembalo: 8 keyboard 10 instrument
cement: 3 fix, gum 4 bind, bond, fuse, glue, join, seal, weld 5 epoxy, grout, merge, paste, putty, stick, unite 6 adhere, attach, cohere, fasten, harden, mortar, secure, solder 7 combine, connect, encrust, incrust, plaster, sealant, stickum, stiffen 8 adhesive, concrete, fixative, mucilage
brand: 4 Duco
container: 4 form
fix, as in ~: 5 embed, imbed
lay ~: 4 pave, pour
packing ~: 4 lute
sealed with ~: 5 luted
section: 4 slab 5 block
cement __: 5 mixer, steel
__ cement: 4 slag 6 Keene's, rubber 7 alumina, contact, masonry
cemented: 3 set 4 firm 5 stiff 8 embedded
Cenci, The author: Shelley
Cendrars, Blaise: 6 French, writer
cen. fraction: 2 yr. 4 year
ceng ceng: 7 cymbals 10 percussion
origin: 4 Bali
cenobite: 4 monk 7 recluse 9 religious
Cenon: 4 city, town
locale: 6 France
cenotaph: 8 monument
Cenozoic: 3 Era
epoch: 6 Eocene
cense: 7 perfume
censer: 8 thurible
censor: 3 ban, cut 4 Cato, edit 5 bleep 6 critic, delete, excise, forbid, muzzle, purify, remove 7 abridge, monitor, repress, scissor, squelch 8 black out, bluenose, disallow, examiner, naysayer, prohibit, sanitize, suppress, vilifier 9 expurgate, interdict, red-pencil, strike out 10 blue-pencil, bowdlerize, scissor out
Roman ~: 4 Cato
censored, not: 5 uncut 8 complete
censoring device, TV: 5 V-chip
censorious: 8 captious, critical 9 cavillous, culpatory, querulous 10 accusatory, condemning, denouncing, derogatory
censorship: 3 ban 7 silence 10 blue-pencil, forbidding
anti-~ org.: 4 ACLU
censurable: 5 wrong 10 delinquent
censure: 3 hit, jaw, rag, rap, tax 4 carp, damn, lash, rail, snub, twit 5 blame, cavil, chide, decry, knock, odium, scold 6 accuse, assail, berate, carp at, impugn, indict, lesson, rebuff, rebuke, tirade, vilify 7 asperse, condemn, contemn, frown on, inveigh, lambast, lecture, obloquy, reproof, reprove, squelch, tell off, upbraid 8 admonish, chastise, denounce, lambaste, reproach, reproval, scolding, sentence 9 broadside, castigate, criticism, criticize, denigrate, deprecate, discredit, disparage, excoriate, exprobate, frown upon, fulminate, invective, lash out at, ostracize, proscribe, reprehend, reprimand 10 admonition, discipline, imputation, reflection, take to task, vituperate
census: 4 list, poll, roll 5 tally 6 survey 9 head count 10 demography
Bible ~ book: 3 Num. 7 Numbers
datum: 3 age, sex
period: 6 decade
census __: 5 taker, tract
cent: 4 coin 5 money, penny 6 copper
down to one's last ~: 5 needy
mill, to a ~: 5 tenth
starter: 3 per
cent __: 4 sign
__ cent: 3 per, red 4 half
centaur: 4 Abas 5 Areos, Hyles, Lycus, Medon, Mimas, Orius, Ureus 6 Agrius, Amycus, Arctus, Argius, Bienor, Bromus, Chiron, Clanis, Dictys, Doupon, Elatus, Elymus, Helops, Nessus, Ophion, Orneus, Pholus 7 Amphion, Anchius, Aphidas, Asbolus, Cheiron, Chromis, Daphnis, Dorylas, Dryalus, Eurytus, Gryneus, Hodites, Homadus, Hylaeus, Imbreus, Isoples, Latreus, Lycabas, Lycidas, Lycopes, Peuceus, Phrixus, Pisenor, Pylenor, Rhoecus, Rhoetus, Ripheus, Thaumas, Thereus 8 Aphareus, Crenaeus, Cyllarus, Demoleon, Echeclus, Eurytion, Hippasus, Hylonome, Iphinous, Melaneus, Mermerus, Monychus, Nedymnus, Petraeus, Pyracmus, Teleboas 9 Chthonius, Eurynomus, Hippotion, Perimedes, Phaecomes, Pyraethus, Styphelus 10 Antimachus, Phlegraeus
Centaur: 4 font 8 typeface
__ Centauri: 5 Alpha 7 Proxima
centavo: 4 coin 5 money
centavos, 100: 4 peso 6 escudo
Centennial author: James A. Michener
Centennial State: 3 Col. 4 Colo. 8 Colorado
center: 3 hub, mid, nub 4 base, core, gist, knub, pith, root, seat, Shaq 5 focus, heart, hiker, inner, midst, nexus, unify 6 inmost, inside, kernel, medial, mesial, middle, office 7 attract, collect, essence, fulcrum, keynote, lineman, nucleus, village 8 bull's-eye, converge, cynosure, focalize, interior, midpoint 9 innermost 10 crossroads, focal point, mainstream, midsection
basketball ~ position: 5 pivot
combining form: 3 mid- 4 medi- 5 medio-
ender: 4 fold, line 5 board, folds, lines, piece 6 pieces
in heraldry: 9 fess point 10 fesse point
in the ~: 4 amid 5 among 6 amidst, mongst 7 amongst
of operations: 2 HQ 4 base
point: 4 node
starter: 3 epi, sub 4 hypo, meta 5 ortho
center __: 3 bit, pin 4 back, jump, line 5 field, plate, punch, wheel 6 spread 7 fielder, forward
__ center: 3 rec 4 cost, data, dead, home, live 5 civic, guide, media, nerve, optic, storm 6 crisis, garden, profit 7 bowling, control, culture, day-care, message, optical, service
__-center: 3 off
__ Center: 5 Epcot 7 Garment, Medical
Centereach: 4 city, town
locale: 7 New York
__-centered: 4 body, face, self
Centerfold (1981 song) artist: J. Geils Band
centerless in heraldry: 6 voided
center of __: 4 mass 7 gravity
Center of the World, The (2001 film)
cast: Balthazar Getty, Carla Gugino, Molly Parker, Peter Sarsgaard
director: Wayne Wang
Center Point: 4 city, town
locale: 7 Alabama
center point of lower half in heraldry: 7 nombril
centers: 4 loca, loci
Centerville: 4 city, town
locale: 4 Ohio
centesimo: 4 coin 5 money
centi ender: 4 pede
centime: 4 coin 5 money
centimes, 100: 5 franc
__ centimeter: 5 cubic 6 square
centimeter-gram-second unit: 3 erg
centimo: 4 coin 5 money
centipede unit: 3 leg
central: 3 key, mid 4 main 5 basic, chief, focal, inner, polar, prime, urban, vital 6 inside, median, middle, ruling 7 crucial, nuclear, pivotal, primary, salient 8 cardinal, dominant, foremost, immanent, interior 9 essential, innermost, intrinsic, paramount, principal 10 overriding
idea: 5 motif, theme
idea, in music: 4 tema
of a ~ point: 5 nodal
part: 4 axis, body, yolk 5 spine 6 endall
point: 5 midst, navel, nodus, pivot 6 thesis
points: 4 loca, loci, nodi
position: 5 midst, pivot
central __: 4 bank, city 5 angle 6 moment, sulcus 7 casting, heating
central __ system: 7 nervous
central __ theorem: 5 limit
Central __: 4 Park, time 6 Powers, Valley 7 African, America, Sudanic
Central African Republic: 6 nation 7 country
capital: 6 Bangui
money: 5 franc
neighbor: 4 Chad 5 Congo, Sudan 8 Cameroon
Central Amer. country: 3 Nic. 4 Guat.
Central America
bird: 4 guan 5 potoo 7 quetzal, tinamou 8 caracara, curassow
capital: 7 Managua, San José 8 Belmopan 10 Panama City 11 San Salvador, Tegucigalpa
country: 6 Belize, Panama 8 Honduras 9 Costa Rica, Guatemala, Nicaragua 10 El Salvador
feline: 6 margay
fish: 7 helleri 9 swordtail
flower: 6 dahlia
fruit: 9 sapodilla
gulf: 6 Panama 7 Fonseca 8 Honduras
Indian: 4 Cuna, Maya 5 Carib, Lenca, Mayan 7 Miskito, San Blas
palm tree: 6 cohune
primate: 7 sapajou 8 capuchin, marmoset
river: 4 Coco, Ulúa 5 Hondo, Lempa 6 Patuca 7 Chagres, Motagua
rodent: 4 paca 6 agouti 8 spiny rat
sea: 9 Caribbean
shrub: 8 cat's-claw
volcano: 4 Póas 5 Fuego, Irazú, Tacan 6 Arenal, Masaya, Pacaya 9 Momotombo
weasel: 6 grison
see also Spanish
Central Daylight __: 4 Time
Central Islip: 4 city, town
locale: 7 New York
centralize: 5 focus, merge 9 integrate 10 accumulate, amalgamate, streamline
Central Michigan conference: 3 MAC
Central Michigan University athletes: 9 Chippewas
Central Okanagan: 4 city, town
locale: 6 Canada
Central Park
architect: 7 Olmsted
it's north of ~: 6 Harlem
locale: 3 NYC 9 Manhattan
sight: 6 hansom 9 reservoir
central processing __: 4 unit
Central Standard __: 4 Time
__ Centre, Toronto: 5 Eaton
Centreville: 4 city, town
locale: 8 Virginia
centrifugal __: 3 box, pot 5 force 7 casting
centrifuge stress: 6 G force
centripetal __: 5 force
cents: 5 money
British ~: 5 pence
put one's two ~ in: 3 add 5 opine 6 meddle
cents-__ coupon: 3 off
__ Cents a Dance: 3 Ten
__-cent store: 3 ten
__ cents worth: 3 two
cents' worth, two: 3 tip 4 view 6 advice, tipoff 7 comment 9 viewpoint
centum: 7 hundred
__ centum: 3 per
centuries, untold: 3 eon 4 aeon, eons 5 aeons
Centurion: 3 car 4 auto 5 Buick
__ Centurions, The: 3 New
century: 3 eon 4 aeon 7 hundred 8 eternity, long time
fraction: 4 year 6 decade
plant: 4 aloe 5 agave
twenty-first ~: 6 modern
Century: 3 car 4 auto, font 5 Buick 8 typeface 10 automobile
Century Schoolbook: 4 font 8 typeface

Century's Ebb author: John Dos Passos
CEO: 3 ldr., VIP 4 boss, exec 6 bigwig, cheese, leader 8 official, superior 9 executive
deg.: 3 MBA
métier: 4 corp. 5 board
often: 4 pres.
part of ~: 3 Off. 4 Exec. 5 Chief 7 Officer 9 Executive
cep: 6 fungus 8 mushroom
C.E., part of: 3 Era 9 Christian
___-ce pas?: 4 n'est
Cepeda, Orlando: 5 Giant
cephalalgia: 8 headache
cephalopod defense: 3 ink
Cepheus: 8 Argonaut
constellation near ~: 5 Draco
daughter of ~: 9 Andromeda
son of: 9 Narcissus
ceraceous: 4 waxy
ceramic
ancient Greek ~ piece: 6 kernos
coating: 5 glaze 6 enamel
square: 4 tile
worker: 5 tiler
ceramic ___: 4 tile
ceramics: 4 ware 5 china, craft, tiles 6 crocks, jasper 7 pottery 8 clayware, crockery 9 delft ware, ironstone, porcelain, stoneware 10 dinnerware
compound: 5 ceria
tool: 6 coggle
cerastes: 5 snake, viper
cerate: 8 ointment
Cerberus: 3 dog 8 guardian
cercis: 4 tree 5 shrub
family: 6 legume
relative: 3 koa 5 carob 6 cassia, locust, padauk, padouk, redbud 7 araroba, mesquit 8 mesquite, tamarind 9 poinciana
cereal: 3 Kix, oat, rye 4 bran, corn, Life, oats, rice, Trix 5 grain, Kashi, Maypo, Quisp, Total, wheat 6 farina, flakes, groats, Kaboom, millet, muesli, Oreo O's, Pablum, quinoa, Smacks 7 All-Bran, Crispix, granola, Harmony, Hunny B's, Mueslix, Oat Bran, oatmeal, Pokemon 8 Boo Berry, Cheerios, Corn Chex, Corn Pops, Fiber One, porridge, Rice Chex, Special K, Uncle Sam, Wheaties 9 Alpha Bits, Apple Zaps, buckwheat, Grape Nuts, Honey Comb, Just Right, Wheat Chex 10 Apple Jacks, bowl filler, bran flakes, Cap'n Crunch, Cocoa Puffs, corn flakes, Froot Loops, Mini-Wheats, Nutri-Grain, Puffed Rice, Quaker Oats, raisin bran, rolled oats, Smart Start 11 Cocoa Blasts, Cookie Crisp, Golden Crisp, Lucky Charms, Puffed Wheat, Sweet Crunch, Waffle Crisp
Asian ~ grass: 4 ragi 5 raggy 6 raggee
box abbr.: 3 RDA 4 nt. wt. 5 net wt.
breakfast ~: 4 bran
cooked ~: 5 gruel, kasha 6 farina
fungus: 5 ergot
grain: 3 oat, rye 4 corn, rice 5 wheat 6 barley
ingredient: 4 bran 5 fiber
kids' ~: 3 Kix 4 Trix
like some ~: 4 oaty 5 mushy, oaten 6 crispy
maker: 4 Post 7 Kellogg
serving: 4 bowl
sound: 3 pop 4 snap 7 crackle
spike: 3 awn, ear
tiger: 4 Tony
tool: 5 spoon
topper: 6 banana
cerebellum: 4 mind 5 brain
cerebral: 5 smart 6 brainy, mental 7 bookish, erudite 8 highbrow, long-hair, rational, thinking 9 scholarly 10 analytical, reasonable
set: 5 Mensa
cerebral ___: 6 cortex
cerebrate: 4 muse 5 think 6 reason 7 reflect 8 cogitate 10 deliberate
cerebrum: 4 mind 5 brain
ceremonial: 4 rite 5 state 6 august, formal, ritual, solemn 7 liturgy, stately 8 decorous 10 liturgical
ceremonious: 6 formal, ritual, solemn 7 courtly, pompous, stately 8 decorous 9 dignified
ceremony: 4 form, pomp, rite 5 state, toast 6 custom, nicety, ritual, starch 7 decorum, liturgy, service 8 courtesy, heraldry, protocol, splendor 9 etiquette, formality, propriety 10 graduation, observance, politeness
religious ~: 6 ritual 7 baptism, liturgy, service 9 communion, Eucharist, sacrament 10 observance
___ ceremony: 3 tea
Ceres: 4 city, town 8 asteroid
brother of ~: 5 Pluto 7 Jupiter, Neptune
daughter of ~: 10 Proserpina
equivalent: 7 Demeter
locale: 10 California
parent of ~: 3 Ops 6 Saturn
sister of ~: 4 Juno 5 Vesta
cereuses bloom, when: 5 night
Cerf, Bennett: 3 wit 9 publisher
specialty: 3 pun
spouse: Sylvia Sidney
Cergy: 4 city, town
locale: 6 France
Cerigo: 4 font 8 typeface
cerise: 3 red 5 color 9 vermilion
relative: 4 rose, ruby, rust, wine 5 brick, coral, grape, poppy, rusty, sandy 6 cherry, claret, garnet, maroon 7 carmine, crimson, fuchsia, magenta, pimento, scarlet, sultana, vermeil 8 amaranth, cardinal, dubonnet, geranium, rubicund 9 carnation, cranberry, vermilion 10 strawberry
cerium: 5 metal 7 element 9 rare earth 10 lanthanide
Cermak: 5 Anton
cero: 4 fish 8 mackerel
Cerritos: 4 city, town
locale: 6 Mexico 10 California
Cerro Azul: 4 city, town
locale: 6 Mexico 8 Veracruz
cert.: 4 guar.
certain: 3 set 4 firm, real, safe, sure, true 5 clear, fixed, on ice, valid 6 actual, secure, steady 7 assured, decided, ensured, express, for sure, settled, special, various 8 absolute, accurate, cocksure, decisive, definite, destined, fail-safe, implicit, inerrant, in the bag, ironclad, positive, reliable, singular, specific, unerring, verified 9 assertive, authentic, automatic, axiomatic, believing, confident, convinced, downright, foolproof, rock solid, satisfied, unfailing 10 conclusive, dependable, determined, guaranteed, inarguable, inevitable, infallible, legitimate, particular, unarguable, undeniable, undisputed, undoubtful, unimagined, verifiable
___ certain: 3 for 7 annuity
Certainement!: 3 oui
___ Certain Feeling: 4 That
certainly: 2 ay, da, ja, si, so 3 aye, oui, yea, yep, yes, yup 4 fine, okay, sure, very, yeah 5 good-o, natch, quite, right, roger, truly, uh-huh 6 agreed, and how, gladly, good-oh, indeed, just so, rather, really, righto, surely, you bet, yowzah 7 exactly, for sure, go ahead, indeedy, mais oui, quite so, right on, ten-four 8 all right, as you say, for a fact, of course, thumbs up, very well 9 assuredly, be my guest, darn right, decidedly, doubtless, naturally, no mistake, precisely, sure thing, you betcha, you said it 10 absolutely, by all means, definitely, far and away, inevitably, positively, sure as hell, sure enough, that's right
Certain Smile, A (1958 song) artist: Johnny Mathis
Certain Smile, A author: Sagan
certainty: 4 fact, lock 5 cinch, truth 6 surety 7 clarity, reality, sure bet 8 accuracy, firmness, optimism, security 9 assurance, certitude, constancy, dogmatism, fixedness, guarantee, sure thing 10 confidence, conviction, positivism, steadiness
say with ~: 4 aver, avow
certificate: 3 doc. 4 deed 5 paper, scrip 6 coupon, permit, ticket 7 diploma, license, receipt, voucher 8 document, warranty
___ certificate: 3 tax 4 gift, gold 5 birth, share, stock 6 silver, street 7 savings
certificate of ___: 5 stock 6 origin 7 deposit
certification: 5 proof 8 hallmark
certified: 4 sure 5 known, tried, valid 7 genuine 8 official 9 excellent, qualified 10 guaranteed
certified ___: 4 mail, milk 5 check
certified ___ accountant: 6 public
___-certified: 5 board
certify: 2 OK 3 let 4 aver, avow, okay 5 prove, swear, vouch 6 affirm, assure, attest, avouch, depone, ensure, ratify, verify 7 approve, bear out, confirm, endorse, indorse, license, qualify, testify, warrant, witness 8 accredit, sanction, validate, vouch for 9 ascertain, authorize, establish, guarantee, indemnify 10 asseverate, legitimize
certitude: 4 fact 5 trust 9 assurance, certainty 10 conviction
Certs: 4 mint 10 breath mint
alternative: 6 Binaca, Mentos, Tic Tac 7 Altoids, Clorets, Dentyne
cerulean: 4 blue 5 color 8 greenish
relative: 4 anil, cyan, navy, Nile, teal 5 Alice, azure, slate 6 cobalt, indigo, raisin, violet 7 peacock 8 sapphire 9 turquoise 10 aquamarine, periwinkle
cerulean ___: 4 blue 7 warbler
cerumen: 3 wax 6 earwax
cerussite: 3 ore
Cervantes, Miguel de: 6 writer 7 Spanish
work: Don Quixote
cerveza: 4 beer 7 Spanish
seller: 6 bodega
snack with ~: 4 tapa
cervid: 3 elk 4 deer 5 moose 7 caribou
___ Cervin: 4 Mont
cervine animal: 3 elk 4 deer 5 moose 7 caribou
Césaire, Aimé: 4 poet 10 Martinican
Cesar: 4 Moro, Ritz 5 Pelli, Pugni 6 Chavez, Franck, Romero 8 Milstein
Cesare: 5 Pugni, Siepi 6 Borgia, Danova, Pavese 8 Beccaria
in English: 6 Caesar
cesium: 5 metal 7 element 9 rare earth
cess: 4 luck
ender: 3 pit 4 pool
cessation: 3 end 4 halt, rest, stay, stop 5 break, close, letup, pause, quiet, truce 6 arrest, cutoff, ending, finish, freeze, hiatus, layoff, period, recess 7 closure, respite, time-out 8 curtains, stoppage 9 remission 10 conclusion, desistance, expiration, standstill, suspension
Cessna: 5 plane 8 airplane
drive a ~: 6 aviate
cesspool: 3 sty 4 sump
c'est ___ chose: 5 autre
c'est-___: 5 à-dire
C'est ___: 3 Moi 5 Si Bon
c'est autre ___: 5 chose
C'est la ___!: 3 vie 6 guerre
C'est La Vie (song) artist: B*Witched, Robbie Nevil, Sarah Vaughan
C'est magnifique!: 6 oo-la-la 7 ooh-la-la
C'est Magnifique composer: 6 Porter
___ c'est moi: 5 L'état
cestus: 4 belt
cetacean: 3 orc, sei 4 susu 5 whale 6 beluga, narwal 7 cowfish, dolphin, finback, grampus, narwhal, rorqual 8 narwhale, porpoise
Cetera, Peter
song: After All (1989)
Glory of Love (1986)
Hard to Say I'm Sorry (1997)
The Next Time I Fall (1986)
One Good Woman (1988)
ceteris ___: 7 paribus
Cetus, star in: 4 Mira
Cévennes: 5 range 9 mountains
locale: 6 Europe, France
C. Everett ___: 4 Koop
ceviche: 8 fish dish 9 appetizer
Cewa home: 6 Africa, Malawi, Zambia 10 Mozambique
Ceylon: 8 Sri Lanka
royal capital of ~: 5 Kandy
Cey, Ron sport: 8 baseball
Cézanne, Paul: 6 artist 7 painter
homeland: 6 France
Cf: 4 elem. 7 element 11 californium
98 for ~: 4 at. no.
CF: 3 pos. 8 position
C4H8: 6 alkene
CFC
destroyer: 5 ozone
part of ~: 6 chloro, fluoro
CFL award: 7 Grey Cup
___ C. Flippen: 3 Jay
___ C. Frémont: 4 John
cg.: 4 meas. 7 measure
Chablis: 3 vin 4 wine 5 white 9 white wine
like ~: 3 sec
origin: 6 France
Chacel, Rosa: 6 writer 7 Spanish
cha-cha: 4 step 5 dance 9 three-step
cousin: 5 mambo
Cha-Cha-Cha, The (1962 song) artist: Bobby Rydell
Chachi's cousin: 6 Fonzie
Chacksfield: 5 Frank
___ Chaco: 4 Gran
chaconne: 5 dance
chacun ___ goût: 4 à son
Chad: 4 lake, Lowe 6 nation, Stuart 7 country, Everett
bovine: 4 Kuri
capital: 8 N'Djamena
city: 7 Moundou 8 N'Djamena
lake: 4 Chad
lake locale: 5 Niger 6 Africa 7 Nigeria 8 Cameroon
money: 5 franc
neighbor: 5 Libya, Niger, Sudan 7 Nigeria 8 Cameroon
people: 4 Fula 6 Fulani, Kanuri
chador kin: 4 sari 5 saree
Chadwick: 5 James 8 Florence
Chadwick, James: 3 Sir 8 Nobelist 9 physicist
chafe: 3 bug, irk, rub, vex 4 fume, gall, mope, rage, roil, stew, warm, wear

5 annoy, erode, grate, graze, sweat, worry, yearn 6 abrade, bother, fester, harass, nettle, offend, pother, rankle, ruffle, scrape 7 enflame, incense, inflame, provoke 8 abrasion, exercise, irritate 9 excoriate 10 exasperate
chafed: 3 raw 4 sore 9 irritated
chafer: 3 bug 6 beetle, insect, scarab 10 scarabaeid
rose ~: 3 bug 6 insect
chaff: 3 kid, rib 4 husk, jeer, jest, joke, josh, junk, mock, pods, razz 5 dregs, dross, husks, straw, taunt, tease, trash, waste 6 banter, debris, deride, refuse, shards, shells 7 bedevil, remains, rubbish 8 raillery, ridicule
eliminate ~: 4 sift
grain ~: 5 husks, palea
Chaffee: 4 Suzy
Chaffey: 3 Don
chaffinch: 3 pet 4 bird
chafing: 8 friction 9 impatient
chafing __: 4 dish
Chagall, Marc: 6 artist 7 painter
homeland: 6 Russia
Museum locale: 4 Nice
Chagga home: 6 Africa 8 Tanzania
Chagres: 5 river
locale: 6 Panama
chagrin: 5 abash, shame, upset 6 dismay 7 letdown, mortify, perturb, umbrage 8 disquiet 9 abashment, annoyance, discomfit, displease, embarrass 10 disappoint, disconcert, dissatisfy, infelicity
exclamation: 4 oh-oh, oops, uh-oh 6 whoops
chagrined: 7 abashed 8 sheepish
Chagrin Falls: 4 city, town
locale: 4 Ohio
Chaim: 5 Potok, Topol 6 Bialik
chain: 3 row 4 band, bond, iron, moor, yoke 5 group, leash, queue, range, ridge, trite 6 catena, fasten, fetter, secure, sequel, series, stores, string, tether 7 confine, jewelry, manacle, pendant, shackle 8 bracelet, handcuff, restrain, sequence 9 lightning, syndicate 10 continuity, succession
ball and ~: 6 burden
gang member: 7 convict 8 prisoner
heavy ~: 4 rope
mountain ~: 5 range, ridge
nautical ~: 3 tye 7 bobstay
part: 3 mtn. 4 link 5 store 6 island 8 mountain
short ~: 3 fob
site: 4 neck 5 ankle
sound: 5 clank
chain __: 3 saw 4 belt, fern, gang, gear, mail, pump, rule, shot, wale 5 coral, drive, plate, store 6 letter, locker, stitch 7 measure, reactor
chain-__ fence: 4 link
__ chain: 3 key 4 bull, door, drag, food, jack, open, sash, side, skid, tire 5 choke, heavy, light, pitch, power, watch 6 closed, forked, golden, Markov, roller, timing 7 Gunter's, lateral, Markoff
Chained __: 4 Lady
Chain, Ernst: 8 Nobelist
Chain Gang (1960 song) artist: Sam Cooke
chain-link __: 5 fence
chain of __: 7 command
Chain of Fools (1967 song) artist: Aretha Franklin
chains: 5 bonds, gyves 7 bilboes, bondage, fetters, jewelry, slavery 8 manacles, shackles, trammels 9 handcuffs, restraint, servitude
Chains of Love (1956 song) artist: Pat Boone
chair: 4 lead, seat 5 bench, sedan, stool 6 chaise, head up, leader, rocker 7 instate, preside 8 director, moderate, recliner 9 furniture, judiciary, officiate, organizer, supervise
ender: 3 man, men 5 woman, women 6 person 7 persons
find another ~: 5 resit
fixer: 5 caner
grab a ~: 3 sit 4 park 5 perch
guide to a ~: 5 usher
leave the ~: 5 arise, get up, stand
like a good ~: 5 comfy
make a ~: 4 cane
mate: 5 table
offer a ~ to: 4 seat
part: 3 arm, leg 4 seat, slat, wing 5 splat 6 caster 7 cushion
starter: 3 arm 4 high, wing 5 wheel
take the ~: 7 preside 8 moderate
chair __: 3 bed, car 4 lift, rail 5 table 6 warmer
__ chair: 3 bed, LCM, tub 4 Bath, Brno, camp, cane, club, deck, easy, horn, lawn, page, sand, side, wing 5 acorn, Cesca, Dante, draft, Dutch, Eames, mammy, sedan, sling, tulip, yacht 6 barber, barrel, basket, Breuer, bridge, Carver, corner, curule, friar's, lounge, Morris, Paimio, porter, swivel, tablet 7 barber's, beanbag, Coxwell, Elijah's, folding, Harvard, Hogarth, hunting, peacock, periwig, reading, rocking, slipper, steamer, Wassily, Windsor
chairman __ board: 5 of the
__ chairman: 4 shop 5 board
__-chairman: 4 vice
Chairman __: 3 Mao
chairperson: 4 head 6 leader 7 captain 8 director
concern: 6 agenda
need: 5 gavel
__ chairs: 7 musical
Chairs, The author: Eugène Ionesco
chaise: 4 shay 5 coach 6 daybed 8 carriage
chaise __: 3 d'or 6 longue, lounge
Chaka: 4 Khan
chakay: 6 string, zither 10 instrument
Chakiris, George Oscar: West Side Story
chalcedony: 4 onyx, sard 5 agate, prase 7 mineral, sardine, sardius
Chalco: 4 city, town
locale: 6 Mexico
chalcocite: 3 ore
chalcopyrite: 3 ore
Chaldean: 4 seer 7 diviner 10 astrologer, soothsayer
chalet: 3 hut 5 bower, cabin, house, lodge 6 A-frame 7 cottage 8 dwelling, ski lodge
feature: 4 eave
Chaliapin: 4 bass 5 basso, Fëdor 6 Feodor, Fyodor, singer
specialty: 5 opera
chalice: 3 ama, cup 5 calix, grail 6 goblet
partner: 5 paten
__ Chalice, The: 6 Silver
chalk: 5 score, tally 6 blanch, bleach, crayon, marker, whiten 7 mineral 9 whitewash
and clay mixture: 4 malm
ender: 5 board, stone
out: 5 trace
relative: 6 crayon
remover: 6 eraser
talk: 4 talk 6 lesson, speech 7 address, lecture, oration 8 training
target: 3 cue
up: 3 get 5 notch, score, tally 6 obtain, record, secure
up to: 3 lay 6 charge, credit, impute 7 ascribe 8 accredit 9 attribute
chalk __: 4 line, talk 6 stripe
chalk __ to experience: 4 it up
__ chalk: 6 French 7 tailor's
chalkboard: 5 slate
erase a ~: 4 wipe
Chalk Garden, The (1964 film)
cast: Deborah Kerr, Hayley Mills, John Mills
director: Ronald Neame
chalky: 3 wan 4 pale 5 ashen, milky, white 6 pallid, sallow 7 powdery, whitish 8 blanched, bleached 9 albescent, bloodless 10 cretaceous
challah: 5 bread
make ~: 5 braid
challenge: 3 try, vie 4 dare, defy, gage, mock, test 5 brave, claim, fight, query, rally, rival, wager 6 accost, impugn, take on, threat 7 accosts, contest, dispute, protest, provoke, vie with 8 confront, defiance, denounce, face down, gauntlet, mistrust, question 9 demanding, discredit, objection, search out, stand up to, stimulate, ultimatum 10 contradict, controvert, invitation
authority: 5 rebel
medieval ~: 4 gage
meet the ~: 4 cope 7 succeed
respondent: 5 taker
__-challenge: 3 eco
__ Challenge: 6 Sports
challenger: 3 foe 5 darer, rival 8 opponent 10 competitor, contestant
quest: 5 title
Challenger: 3 car 4 auto 5 Dodge 10 automobile, Studebaker
org.: 4 NASA
Challengers, The: 8 game show
host: Dick Clark
challenging: 4 bold, hard 5 brave 6 brazen, daring 7 defiant 8 insolent, mutinous, rigorous 9 obstinate, resistant, truculent 10 aggressive, pugnacious, rebellious, refractory
challis: 6 fabric 8 material
__ Chalmers: 5 Allis
Chalmette: 4 city, town
locale: 9 Louisiana
Chalons: 6 battle
Châlons-sur-__: 5 Marne, Saône
chamber: 4 cell, hole, room 5 music 6 alcove, pocket 7 bedroom, council, cubicle, shelter 8 assembly, congress 9 container, enclosure
combining form: 4 -cele, coel- 5 -coele
ender: 4 maid
in Spanish: 4 sala
monastic ~: 4 cell
music instrument: 5 cello, viola 6 violin
piece: 4 trio 5 music, nonet, octet 7 octette, quartet
starter: 3 bed 4 ante
temple ~: 4 naos 5 cella
underground ~: 4 cave, kiva 5 crypt, vault 6 bunker, cavern, grotto
upper ~: 5 attic 6 dormer, garret
vaulted ~: 5 vault 6 recess
see also room
chamber __: 3 mug 5 music, opera 7 concert
__ chamber: 3 air, ion 4 echo, star 5 cloud, float, lower, privy, smoke, spark, state, surge, upper 6 bubble
__ Chamber: 3 Red 4 Star 5 First 6 Second
Chambered Nautilus, The author: Oliver Wendell Holmes
Chamberlain: 4 Owen, Wilt 6 Austen 7 Neville, Richard
Chamberlain, Austen: 8 Nobelist
Chamberlain, Neville: 2 P.M. 7 British
foreign secretary: 4 Eden
predecessor: 7 Baldwin
successor: 9 Churchill
Chamberlain, Owen: 8 Nobelist 9 physicist
Chamberlain, Richard: 5 actor
film: The Four Musketeers (1975)
Petulia (1968)
The Slipper and the Rose (1976)
The Three Musketeers (1974)
The Towering Inferno (1974)
song: Three Stars Will Shine Tonight (1962)
TV: Dr. Kildare
The Thorn Birds
Chamberlain, Wilt
milieu: 5 court
org.: 3 NBA
sport: 10 basketball
chamber of __: 7 horrors
Chamber of Deputies locale: 5 Italy
chambers: 5 suite 7 lodging 8 lodgment, quarters
in ~: 9 secretive
judge's ~: 6 camera
Chambers: 9 Whittaker
Chambertin: 3 red 4 wine
origin: 6 France
Chambly: 4 city, town
locale: 6 Canada, Québec
chambray: 6 fabric 8 material
chambre: 4 room 5 salle 6 French
chameleon: 5 anole 6 animal, lizard 7 reptile
kin: 5 agama 6 iguana
__ Chameleon: 5 Karma
chameleonlike: 5 fluid 7 erratic, mutable, protean 8 shifting, unstable, wavering 9 mercurial, uncertain 10 changeable
chamfer: 5 bevel
chamfron: 5 armor
Chamisso, Adelbert von: 4 poet 6 German
Chamlang: 4 peak 5 mount 8 mountain
locale: 4 Asia 5 Nepal 9 Himalayas
chamois: 5 cloth, color, izard 6 animal, mammal, yellow 7 grayish, leather 8 antelope
relative: 3 gnu, kob 4 buff, corn, gold, guib, kudu, lime, oryx, puku, rust, sand, topi 5 addax, blond, bongo, brass, chiru, coral, cream, eland, flaxy, goral, korin, lemon, maize, nyala, ocher, ochre, oribi, peach, rusty, saiga, serow, straw 6 blonde, canary, citron, crocus, dik-dik, duiker, flaxen, impala, koodoo, lechwe, nilgai, rhebok 7 apricot, blaubok, blesbok, citrine, defassa, gazelle, gemsbok, gerenuk, grysbok, jasmine, mustard, nankeen, nylghai, nylghau, old gold, saffron, sassaby, xanthic 8 blesbuck, bontebok, bushbuck, daffodil, gemsbuck, primrose, reedbuck, steenbok, steinbok 9 blackbuck, champagne, goldenrod, jessamine, pronghorn, sitatunga, springbok, waterbuck 10 hartebeest, wildebeest
use a ~: 4 wipe
chamomile: 3 tea 5 plant 6 flower
Chamonix, sight from: 3 alp
champ: 4 bite, gnaw 5 munch 6 top dog, victor, winner 9 number one
at the bit: 5 chafe
champ __ bit: 5 at the
champac: 4 tree
family: 8 magnolia
champagne: 3 vin 4 fizz, wine 5 color 6 bubbly, yellow 8 greenish
blended ~: 5 cuvee
bottle: 5 split 6 magnum

bucket: 4 icer 6 cooler
category: 3 sec 4 brut, doux
glass: 5 flute
grape: 5 pinot
name: 3 Dom 4 Moet, Mumm 8 Perignon
partner: 6 caviar 7 caviare
prepare ~: 3 ice 5 chill
relative: 4 buff, corn, gold, lime, rust, sand 5 blond, brass, coral, cream, flaxy, lemon, maize, ocher, ochre, peach, rusty, straw 6 blonde, canary, chammy, citron, crocus, flaxen, shammy, shamoy 7 apricot, chamois, citrine, jasmine, mustard, nankeen, old gold, saffron, xanthic 8 daffodil, primrose 9 goldenrod, jessamine
ritual: 5 toast
stopper: 4 cork

__ champagne: 4 pink

Champagne for Caesar (1950 film)
cast: Barbara Britton, Ronald Colman, Celeste Holm, Art Linkletter, Vincent Price

Champagne music man: 4 Welk

Champagne Supernova (1996 song)
artist: Oasis

Champagne Tony: 4 Lema

Champagne wishes guy: 5 Leach

champaign: 5 plain 7 lowland

Champaign: 4 city, town
athletes: 6 Illini
locale: 8 Illinois

champ at the __: 3 bit

champêtre, fête: 5 feast 6 repast, spread 7 banquet

champignon: 8 mushroom

champing at the bit: 4 avid 5 antsy, eager, ready 6 gung-ho, on edge

champion: 4 back, best, head, hero 5 chief, first, prime 6 backer, defend, foster, knight, master, patron, tip-top, top dog, uphold, victor, winner 7 apostle, endorse, espouse, forward, further, indorse, leading, paladin, premier, promote, protect, support 8 advocate, crusader, defender, endorser, exponent, fight for, foremost, greatest, medalist, plead for, reformer, side with, stand for, superior, thump for, top-notch 9 apologist, conqueror, nonpareil, number one, numero uno, paraclete, principal, proponent, protector, supporter, top-drawer, vindicate 10 go to bat for, rally round, speak up for, subjugator, triumphant, world-class
name meaning ~: 4 Neal, Neil
prize: 5 title

Champion: 3 car 4 auto 5 Gower, horse, Marge 10 automobile, Studebaker
rider: Gene Autry

Champion (1949 film)
cast: Kirk Douglas, Arthur Kennedy, Marilyn Maxwell
director: Mark Robson

__ Champion: 5 King's 6 Queen's

Champion, Gower spouse: Marge

championship: 4 egis 5 aegis, crown, prize, title 7 support, victory 8 espousal 9 patronage 10 protection

__ Championship Season: 4 That

Champlain: 4 lake
locale: 7 New York, Vermont

Champlain, Samuel de: 8 explorer

champlevé: 6 enamel, inlaid

Champlin: 4 city, town
locale: 9 Minnesota

Champotón: 4 city, town
locale: 6 Mexico 8 Campeche

Champs __: 7 Élysées

champs' cry: 5 we win, we won

Champs song: Tequila (1958)

Champ, The (1931 film)
cast: Wallace Beery, Jackie Cooper, Irene Rich
director: King Vidor

Chan: 6 Jackie 7 Charlie

chance: 3 bet, hap, lot, odd 4 fate, luck, odds, risk, room, shot, stab, time 5 bet on, break, fluky, lucky, occur, stake, wager 6 casual, danger, flukey, gamble, hazard, random, resort 7 aimless, attempt, fortune, leisure, lottery, oddball, offhand, venture 8 accident, endanger, fortuity, long shot, occasion, prospect 9 arbitrary, fair shake, fortunate, haphazard, hit-or-miss, liability, privilege, unplanned, unwitting 10 accidental, contingent, fortuitous, incidental, jeopardize, likelihood, lucky break, unexpected, unintended
blow the ~: 4 miss
by ~: 4 idly 5 haply 7 luckily 8 at random, casually, randomly
discover by ~: 5 hit on
even ~: 6 tossup
fat ~: 4 uh-uh
found by ~: 5 lit on
game of ~: 4 keno 5 craps, lotto, poker 6 raffle 7 lottery 8 baccarat, roulette
good ~: 10 likelihood
happening: 5 fluke, quirk 8 accident, fortuity
it: 3 bet 6 gamble
not a ~: 3 nah, naw, nay, nix, non 4 nein, nope, nyet, uh-uh 5 I won't, ixnay, never, no how, no way 6 no deal, noways, nowise 7 I refuse 8 forget it, I will not, negative, negatory 9 by no means, fat chance, I think not 10 count me out, thumbs down
on: 4 find, meet 8 bump into 9 encounter, run across 10 come across
run the ~ of: 4 risk
starter: 3 per 6 happen
take a ~: 4 bite, dare, risk 5 wager 6 gamble, hazard 7 venture 9 speculate
taking, for short: 4 spec
to play: 4 turn

chance __ lifetime: 3 of a

__ chance: 6 second

__ chance!: 3 Fat 4 Not a 5 Bonne

Chance: 5 Frank
teammate: 5 Evers 6 Tinker

Chance author: Joseph Conrad

chancel: 6 church 9 sanctuary
hanging: 6 dossal, dossel
neighbor: 4 apse, nave

chancellor: 8 official

__-chancellor: 4 vice

Chancellor: 4 John

Chancellor __ Exchequer: 5 of the

__ Chancellor: 4 Lord

Chancellorsville: 6 battle
winner at ~: 3 Lee

__ Chance on Me: 5 Take a

chances: 4 lots, odds 5 state 7 outlook 8 prospect

Chances Are (1989 film)
cast: Robert Downey Jr., Mary Stuart Masterson, Ryan O'Neal, Cybill Shepherd
director: Emile Ardolino

Chances Are (1957 song) artist: Mathis

chancy: 4 iffy 5 dicey, hairy, risky, rocky 6 touchy, tricky, unsafe, unsure 7 dubious, erratic, parlous 8 perilous, ticklish 9 ambiguous, dangerous, debatable, hazardous, uncertain, unsettled, vagarious 10 capricious, indefinite, precarious, unresolved, up for grabs, up in the air

chandelier: 5 light 7 fixture
hanging: 5 prism

Chandler: 4 city, Gene, Jeff, Otis, town 5 Estee, Happy 7 Dorothy, Raymond
locale: 7 Arizona

Chandler, Gene song: Duke of Earl (1962)

__ Chandler Harris: 4 Joel

Chandler, Raymond: 6 author, writer
sleuth: Marlowe
work: The Big Sleep
Farewell, My Lovely
The High Window
The Lady in the Lake
The Little Sister
The Long Goodbye
Playback

Chandrasekhar, Subramanyan: 8 Nobelist 9 physicist

Chanel: 4 Coco
product: 5 scent 7 perfume

Chaney Jr., Lon: 5 actor
film: Abbott and Costello Meet Frankenstein (1948)
Frankenstein Meets the Wolf Man (1943)
Of Mice and Men (1939)
Son of Dracula (1943)
The Wolf Man (1941)

Chaney, Lon: 5 actor
film: He Who Gets Slapped (1924)
The Hunchback of Notre Dame (1923)
Oliver Twist (1922)
The Phantom of the Opera (1925)
West of Zanzibar (1928)

chang: 6 string 8 dulcimer

Chang: 4 twin 7 Siamese
brother: 3 Eng

Changchun: 4 city, town
locale: 5 China

Changduk Palace site: 5 Seoul

change: 3 fit 4 cash, coin, flux, move, redo, swap, swop, vary, veer, warp 5 act on, adapt, alter, amend, break, budge, coins, dimes, money, morph, shift, swing, trade, waver 6 adjust, affect, barter, evolve, juggle, modify, motion, mutate, nickel, redeem, reform, remake, revise, silver, switch, tamper 7 act upon, assault, coinage, commute, convert, diverge, inflect, lighten, meander, nickels, novelty, pennies, permute, qualify, redress, remodel, replace, reshape, restyle, reverse, revisal, shuffle, variety 8 diminish, flip-flop, innovate, make over, modulate, movement, mutation, quarters, renovate, reversal, revision, supplant, transfer, upheaval, variance 9 about-face, alternate, amendment, departure, deviation, diversify, diversion, evolution, fluctuate, oscillate, redaction, reshaping, transform, translate, transmute, transpose, vacillate, variation 10 adjustment, alteration, conversion, correction, difference, emendation, innovation, modulation, new wrinkle, refinement, regenerate, remodeling, reorganize, reposition, revolution, substitute, tamper with, transition, turnaround
apt to ~: 6 fickle 7 flighty
back: 6 revert
combining form: 4 trop- 5 tropo-
complete ~ of mind: 5 U-turn
course: 3 cut, yaw, zig 4 tack, turn, veer
ender: 4 over
get used to ~: 4 cope 5 adapt
have a ~ of heart: 6 recant 7 reverse 8 pull back, withdraw 9 back-pedal
holder: 5 purse 6 pocket 9 piggy bank
into: 6 become
likely to ~: 6 labile
make a minor ~: 6 adjust
maker: 6 editor
of direction: 5 U-turn
off: 6 rotate 9 take turns
one's address: 4 move 8 relocate
one's mind: 4 bend 6 relent 7 retract 9 vacillate
one's ways: 4 mend 6 reform 7 shape up 10 make amends
positions: 5 reset, shift
radical ~: 7 shake-up 8 upheaval 10 revolution
residence: 6 uproot 7 migrate 8 relocate
sides: 4 turn 6 defect
slowly: 6 evolve
small ~: 3 cts. 4 cent, coin, dime 5 cents, coins, dimes, penny 6 nickel 7 nickels, pennies, quarter 8 quarters
starter: 5 inter, short 7 counter
subject to ~: 9 tentative
text: 4 edit 5 emend
the order: 5 mix up 6 jumble, muddle 8 disarray, scramble 9 rearrange 10 disarrange
to suit: 5 adapt, slant
unexpected ~: 5 twist

change __: 3 off 5 hands 7 ringing

__ change: 3 sea 5 chump, exact, small

__ Change: 4 Cool 5 Quick 7 Seasons

changeable: 5 fluid, moody 6 fickle, labile, mobile, uneven 7 erratic, mutable, protean, unloyal, wayward 8 shifting, slippery, ticklish, unstable, unsteady, variable, volatile, wavering 9 adaptable, faithless, impulsive, irregular, mercurial, revocable, spasmodic, temporary, transient, uncertain, unsettled, versatile, whimsical 10 capricious, inconstant, indecisive, irresolute, permutable, reciprocal, reversible, unreliable
one: 9 chameleon

__-change artist: 5 quick

changed: 7 unalike 9 different

changeless: 6 static, steady 7 abiding 8 constant, enduring, ironclad 9 immutable, permanent, steadfast 10 invariable, undecaying

Changeling, The
author: Thomas Middleton, William Rowley

Changeling, The (1979 film)
cast: George C. Scott, Trish Van Devere

changement de pied: 4 leap

change of __: 4 pace 5 habit, heart, venue

Change of Habit (1969 film)
cast: Barbara McNair, Mary Tyler Moore, Elvis Presley

Change of Heart (1983 song) artist: Tom Petty and the Heartbreakers

Change of Heart (1986 song) artist: Cyndi Lauper

change one's __: 4 mind, tune

changeover: 5 shift 8 apostasy 10 conversion

Change Partners composer: 6 Berlin

__ changer: 4 coin 6 record

Changes, Book of: 6 I Ching

changes to, make: 4 redo 5 adapt, alter, amend

Change the World (1996 song) artist: Eric Clapton

change-up: 5 pitch

changing: 7 migrant, mutable 8 variable 9 unsettled
place: 6 cabana
readily: 5 fluid

changing __: 3 bag 4 note, room, tone 5 table

Changing ___: **5** Faces, Lanes
Changing Lanes (2002 film)
cast: Ben Affleck, Toni Collette, Samuel L. Jackson, Sydney Pollack
director: Roger Michell
Chang Jiang, port on the: **4** Wuhu
changko: **4** drum
origin: **5** Korea
Chang, Michael: **7** netster **9** tennis pro
milieu: **5** court
rival: **6** Agassi
___ chango: **6** presto
Changsha: **4** city, town
locale: **5** China, Hunan
Changtzu: **4** peak **5** mount **8** mountain
locale: **4** Asia
Chanhassen: **4** city, town
locale: **9** Minnesota
Chani: **4** peak **5** mount **8** mountain
Chan, Jackie: **5** actor
film: Police Story (1985)
Project A (1983)
Rush Hour (1998)
Rush Hour 2 (2001)
Shanghai Noon (2000)
channel: **3** rut, str., way **4** dike, duct, flue, line, link, neck, race, slot **5** agent, canal, ditch, drain, flume, gouge, guide, gulch, gully, means, organ, route, sound, stria, track **6** agency, arroyo, artery, avenue, convey, course, direct, funnel, furrow, groove, gullet, gulley, gutter, medium, outlet, siphon, strait, syphon, trench, trough, tunnel, valley **7** conduct, conduit, culvert, fluting, narrows, passage, pathway, vehicle **8** aqueduct, transmit **9** influence **10** instrument, passageway
anatomical ~: **4** vein **5** aorta, lumen **6** artery
blocker: **5** V-chip
British ~: **3** BBC
cable: **3** AMC, BET, CMT, CNN, HBO, HSN, IFC, MTV, PAX, QVC, SHO, TBS, TLC, TMC, TNN, TNT, USA **4** CNBC, ESPN, Flix, HGTV **5** A and E, Bravo, C-SPAN, MSNBC, Spike, Starz, Style **6** Encore, Noggin, Tech TV, TV Land **7** Cinemax, Court TV, Ovation, ShopNBC, SoapNet **8** Lifetime, Showtime, Sundance
clear a ~: **6** dredge
combining form: **5** solen- **6** soleno-
control: **4** dial
designation: **3** UHF, VHF
marker: **4** buoy
port: **5** Brest **6** Calais
surfer's need: **2** TV **5** TV set
surfers zap past them: **3** ads
TV: **3** ABC, CBS, Fox, NBC, PBS, UPN
water ~: **5** ditch, flume
channel ___: **3** cat **4** back, bass, iron **5** black **6** surfer **7** catfish
channel-___: **4** surf **7** surfing
___ channel: **4** back **5** clear
___ Channel: **5** North **7** Ambrose, Bristol, English
Channel Islands
island: **4** Sark **6** Jersey **8** Guernsey
locale: **7** Britain, England
port: **8** St. Helier
channel-surf: **3** zap
Channelview: **4** city, town
locale: **5** Texas
Channi: **3** cow **4** bull **6** bovine, cattle
Channing: **5** Carol, Margo **8** Stockard
Channing, Stockard: **7** actress
film: The Business of Strangers (2001)
The Cheap Detective (1978)
Grease (1978)
Practical Magic (1998)
Six Degrees of Separation (1993)
Smoke (1995)
Up Close & Personal (1996)
chanson: **4** song **5** music
chanson ___: **6** d'amour **7** de geste
Chanson de ___: **6** Roland
chant: **2** om **4** sing, song, tune **5** drone, music, psalm, utter **6** incant, intone, litany, mantra, melody, recite **7** mantram, worship **8** vocalize **9** plainsong **10** repetition
starter: **5** plain
___ chantant: **4** café
chanter: **6** singer **8** vocalist
chanterelle: **6** fungus **8** mushroom
chanteuse: **6** singer **8** vocalist
chantey: **3** air **4** song, tune
singer: **3** gob, tar **6** sailor, sea dog
chanticleer: **4** cock, fowl **7** chicken, rooster
sound: **4** crow
Chantilly: **4** city, town **7** dessert
locale: **8** Virginia
Chantilly ___: **4** lace **5** sauce
Chantilly Lace (1958 song) artist: Big Bopper
chantry: **6** chapel, temple
Chanukah Song, The (1995 song)
artist: Adam Sandler
Chanukkah top: **7** dreidel
Chao Phraya: **5** river
locale: **8** Thailand
chaos: **4** mess, riot **5** havoc, mix-up, snafu, snarl **6** bedlam, huddle, jumble, jungle, mayhem, muddle, tumult, unrest, uproar **7** anarchy, clutter, discord, entropy, ferment, rioting, turmoil **8** disarray, disorder, madhouse, shambles, upheaval **9** confusion, mobocracy **10** hurly-burly, turbulence, unruliness
Chaos
daughter of ~: **3** Nyx **4** Gaea
son of ~: **4** Eros **6** Erebus
wife of ~: **3** Nyx
chaotic: **4** wild **5** messy, mussy, wooly **6** hectic, unneat, untidy, woolly **7** haywire, jumbled, lawless, riotous, tangled **8** anarchic, confused, pell-mell **9** turbulent **10** anarchical, disjointed, disordered, disorderly, in an uproar, incohesive, topsy-turvy, tumultuous, unpeaceful, upside-down
place: **3** zoo
chap: **2** he **3** egg, guy, man, sir **4** dude, gent, male, mate **5** bloke, bucko, crack, fella, sport **6** feller, fellow, mister, redden **7** roughen
ender: **4** book **6** fallen
young ~: **3** lad
___ chap: **3** old
Chap ___: **5** Stick
Chapala: **4** city, lake, town
locale: **6** Mexico **7** Jalisco
chaparajos: **8** leggings
chaparral: **5** brush
chaparral ___: **3** pea **4** bird, cock, lily
chapati: **5** bread
chapeau
see hat
chapel: **6** bethel, church, shrine, temple **7** chantry, oratory, worship **8** sacellum **9** sanctuary **10** tabernacle
___ Chapel: **5** Arena **7** Sistine
chapel de ___: **3** fer
Chapel Hill: **4** city, town
athletes: **8** Tar Heels
locale: **4** N. Car.
school: **3** UNC
___-Chapelle: **5** Aix-la
chapel of ___: **4** ease
Chapel of Love (1964 song) artist: Dixie Cups
chaperon: **4** lead **5** bring, guard, guide, watch **6** attend, convoy, duenna, escort, squire **7** conduct, oversee, protect, support **8** guardian, shepherd **9** accompany, attendant, companion, safeguard, supervise, watch over
one with a ~: **3** deb
chapfallen: **3** sad **4** blue, down, glum **5** woful **6** gloomy, morose, somber, woeful **7** doleful, hangdog, joyless, unhappy **8** dejected, downcast, lowering, troubled **9** bummed out, cheerless, heartsick, miserable, sorrowful, woebegone **10** dispirited, melancholy
Chapin: **5** Harry **6** Lauren
___ Chapin Carpenter: **4** Mary
Chapin, Harry
song: Cat's in the Cradle (1974)
Taxi (1972)
chaplain: **5** padre, rabbi, rebbe **6** cleric, parson, pastor, priest **8** minister, preacher
chaplet: **6** diadem, wreath **7** coronet, garland
Chaplin: **3** Syd **4** Oona, Saul **6** Sydney **7** Charles **9** Geraldine
Chaplin (1992 film)
cast: Dan Aykroyd, Geraldine Chaplin, Robert Downey Jr.
director: Richard Attenborough
Chaplin, Charles: **3** Sir **5** actor **8** director
contemporary: **5** Lloyd **6** Keaton
film: The Circus (1928)
City Lights (1931)
A Countess From Hong Kong (1967)
The Gold Rush (1925)
The Great Dictator (1940)
The Kid (1921)
A King in New York (1957)
Limelight (1952)
Modern Times (1936)
Monsieur Verdoux (1947)
A Woman of Paris (1923)
prop: **4** cane
spouse: Paulette Goddard, Oona O'Neill
Chaplin, Geraldine: **7** actress
film: Chaplin (1992)
Doctor Zhivago (1965)
The Hawaiians (1970)
Nashville (1975)
Remember My Name (1978)
Roseland (1977)
mother: **4** Oona
Chapman: **4** John **5** Tracy **6** George, Graham
Chapman, George: **4** poet **7** British **10** playwright
Chapman, Tracy
song: Fast Car (1988)
Give Me One Reason (1996)
chapped: **5** rough
chaps: **5** pants **8** leggings
chapter: **4** unit, wing **5** local, phase **6** branch, member **7** episode, section **8** division **9** affiliate
and verse: **6** detail
of history: **3** era
partner: **5** verse
poem ~: **5** canto
quote ~ and verse: **4** list, tell **6** relate, report **7** account, analyze, itemize, narrate, recount, specify **8** describe **9** elaborate, enumerate, expound on, make clear
start, usually: **5** recto
chapter ___: **4** head, ring **5** house
Chapter ___: **3** Two **6** Eleven
chapter and ___: **5** verse
Chapter 11: **10** bankruptcy
go into ~: **4** bust, fail
in ~: **5** broke **8** bankrupt
Chapter on Ears, A writer: **4** Elia, Lamb
Chapter Two: **4** film, play
author: Neil Simon
cast: James Caan, Valerie Harper, Marsha Mason
Chapultepec: **6** battle
locale: **6** Mexico
chaqueta: **4** coat **6** jacket
char: **4** burn, fish, heat, sear **5** singe **6** scorch **7** blacken **8** overcook **9** carbonize
ender: **4** coal **5** broil, woman
Chara: **4** star
char-à-banc: **3** bus **5** coach
characin: **4** fish
character: **3** air, ilk **4** aura, card, form, kind, kook, mold, mood, part, role, self, sort, soul, tone, type, vein **5** class, clown, crank, ethos, flake, genre, honor, human, state, style **6** aspect, cipher, credit, figure, flavor, kidney, letter, makeup, mettle, morale, nature, number, person, repute, scream, spirit, status, symbol, temper, virtue, weirdo **7** caliber, courage, essence, numeral, oddball, probity, quality, station, texture **8** attitude, good name, identity, ideogram, mystique, original, standing **9** attribute, eccentric, extrovert, integrity, mentality, personage, rectitude, reference **10** appearance, atmosphere, complexion, estimation, expression, hieroglyph, honestness, individual, principles, reputation
character ___: **3** set **5** actor, piece, study **6** sketch **7** builder, defense, witness
___ character: **4** flat, unit **5** out of, round, stock **7** control
character-building org.: **3** BSA
characteristic: **3** way **4** look, mark, sign **5** point, quirk, trait, typic **6** aspect, custom, innate, signal, unique **7** classic, earmark, feature, natural, quality, special, symptom, typical **8** hallmark, property, specific **9** mannerism
not ~ of: **6** unlike
of (suffix): **3** -ile, -ine, -ish
characteristic ___: **4** root, x-ray **5** curve, value **6** vector
characterization: **4** role **6** acting **7** profile **8** portrait
characterize: **3** peg **5** brand, label **6** define, depict, sketch, typify **7** feature, outline, portray, qualify **8** describe, identify, set apart **9** personify
characterized by: **4** with
characterless: **4** drab **8** ordinary
charade: **3** act **4** fake, pose **5** farce **6** dupery, riddle **8** disguise, pretense **9** deception, pantomime
Charade: **3** car **4** auto **8** Daihatsu
Charade (1963 film)
cast: Cary Grant, Audrey Hepburn, Walter Matthau
director: Stanley Donen
music: Henry Mancini
charades: **4** game
play ~: **4** mime **6** act out
Charbray: **3** cow **4** bull **6** bovine, cattle
Charcas: **4** city, town
locale: **6** Mexico
charcoal: **4** gray, grey **5** black, color **8** brownish
relative: **3** ash **4** dove, drab **5** beige, dusty, merle, pearl, putty, slate, taupe **6** silver **7** grizzly **8** gunmetal, platinum
trap, as ~: **6** adsorb
use ~: **4** cook **5** grill
charcoal ___: **3** rot **5** grill **6** burner
chard: **4** beet **6** veggie **9** vegetable
kin: **4** kail, kale
___ chard: **5** Swiss
Chardonnay: **3** vin **4** wine **5** grape, white
relative: **5** Gamay, pinot, Tokay

6 Merlot 7 Catawba, Concord, Niagara 8 Cabernet, malvasia, muscatel 9 muscadine, Sauvignon, zinfandel
___ Chardonnay: 5 Pinot
charge: 3 ask, fee, job, lay, owe, rap, tab, tax, zap 4 beef, bite, book, care, cost, dash, dues, duty, fare, levy, onus, push, rate, rush, task, tilt, toll, urge, ward 5 blame, blitz, claim, debit, forge, gripe, imbue, lunge, onset, order, price, quote, rally, runat, score, shoot, storm, trust 6 accuse, allege, amount, assess, attack, behest, burden, damage, direct, escrow, exhort, have at, hurtle, impose, impugn, impute, indict, invest, ionize, lading, lumber, office, outlay, plunge, sortie, tariff, thrill, towage 7 arraign, assault, command, conduct, contend, control, custody, damages, entrust, expense, impeach, intrust, keeping, mandate, mission, payment, pervade, release, tuition 8 accredit, auspices, delegate, instruct, permeate, province, purchase, relegate, reproach, stampede 9 complaint, direction, directive, electrify, explosive, implicate, inculpate, onslaught, oversight, quotation, reckoning, reprehend, statement 10 accusation, allegation, assessment, assignment, commitment, go pell-mell, imputation, indictment, management, obligation
  account: 6 credit
  alternative: 4 cash 5 check
  answer a ~: 5 plead, rebut
  be in ~: 3 run 4 head, lead, rule 5 steer 6 head up, manage 7 command, control, operate 9 supervise
  cabaret ~: 5 cover
  criminal ~: 3 rap
  false ~: 5 frame, smear 6 bad rap, bum rap 7 frame-up
  get a ~ out of: 4 like 5 enjoy
  group in ~: 3 mgt. 4 mgmt. 10 management
  in ~: 7 regnant 8 dominant, superior 10 commanding
  it: 3 buy, owe
  kind of ~: 3 neg., pos. 8 negative, positive
  one in ~: 3 ldr. 4 head 5 chief, Mr. Big 6 leader, master
  response: 6 denial, guilty 9 not guilty
  service ~: 3 fee
  starter: 3 sur 5 turbo 7 counter
  up: 5 liven 7 enliven
  with: 5 blame, lay on 6 impute 8 credit to
  without ~: 4 free 6 gratis, public 9 on the cuff 10 for nothing, on the house
charge ___: 4 card 5 plate 7 account, carrier
___ charge: 4 door, free, late, take 5 bound, cover, depth, fixed, point, space 6 access, powder, public, shaped 7 finance, service, trickle 8 carrying
chargeable: 6 liable 8 blamable 9 blameable 10 answerable, indictable
charge-card user: 4 ower
charged: 5 laden, ran at 6 loaded 7 replete 8 electric 10 electrical, encumbered, portentous
  electrically ~: 4 live 5 ionic
  particle: 3 ion 5 anion 6 cation, kation
  swimmer: 3 eel
chargé d'affaires: 5 agent, envoy 6 consul, legate 7 attaché 8 diplomat, emissary, minister 10 ambassador, negotiator, peacemaker
Charge of the Light Brigade author: Alfred Tennyson
Charge of the Light Brigade, The (1936 film)
  cast: Olivia de Havilland, Errol Flynn
  director: Michael Curtiz
charger: 5 horse, mount, steed 6 equine 7 palfrey, platter, trooper 8 destrier, war-horse
Charger: 3 car 4 auto 5 Dodge
Charger rival: 3 Jet, Ram 4 Bear, Bill, Colt, Lion 5 Brown, Chief, Eagle, Giant, Niner, Raven, Saint, Texan, Titan 6 Bengal, Bronco, Cowboy, Falcon, Jaguar, Packer, Raider, Viking 7 Dolphin, Panther, Patriot, Redskin, Seahawk, Steeler 8 Cardinal 9 Buccaneer
Chargers: 4 team 6 eleven
  home: 8 San Diego
  org.: 3 AFC, NFL
  sport: 8 football
charges
  answer ~: 5 plead
  bring ~: 3 sue 4 book 6 accuse, allege 8 litigate 9 prosecute
  one who ~: 4 ower 5 payer
  suspend ~: 6 pardon
Chari: 5 river
  locale: 6 Africa
charily: 5 shyly 6 askant, warily 7 askance, leerily, timidly 8 frugally 9 carefully, guardedly, heedfully, mindfully, sparingly, thriftily 10 cautiously
chariness: 8 mistrust, wariness 9 leeriness, nonbelief, suspicion 10 discretion
Charing ___: 5 Cross
chariot: 5 essed 7 vehicle
  builders: 6 Hyksos, Romans
Charioteer: 6 Auriga
Charioteer, The author: Mary Renault
Chariots of Fire (1981 film)
  cast: Ian Charleson, Ben Cross, Nigel Havers
  director: Hugh Hudson
  highlight: 4 race
  music: Vangelis
charisma: 4 aura, pull 5 charm, magic 6 allure, appeal, dazzle, glamor 7 glamour 8 mystique, presence 9 magnetism
charismatic: 7 dynamic, likable 8 magnetic 10 magnetical
Charisse, Cyd: 6 dancer 7 actress
  film: The Band Wagon (1953)
    Brigadoon (1954)
    Party Girl (1958)
    Silk Stockings (1957)
    Singin' in the Rain (1952)
    Two Weeks in Another Town (1962)
  spouse: Tony Martin
charitable: 4 good, kind, nice 5 noble 6 giving, humane, kindly 7 clement, largess, lenient, liberal 8 all heart, generous, gracious, largesse, merciful, obliging, tolerant 9 bountiful, brotherly, favorable, forgiving, indulgent, righteous, unselfish, unsparing 10 altruistic, beneficent, benevolent, bighearted, forbearing, free-handed, hospitable, humanistic, thoughtful, unstinting
  activity: 5 cause 6 bazaar 7 benefit 10 fundraiser
  be ~: 6 donate
  donation: 4 alms
  one: 5 donor, giver
  org.: 4 CARE 6 UNESCO, UNICEF
charity: 3 aid 4 alms, dole, gift, pity 5 grant, mercy 6 relief, virtue 7 handout, largess 8 altruism, clemency, donation, goodwill, humanity, kindness, largesse, lenience, leniency, offering 9 tolerance 10 compassion, foundation, generosity, liberality
  British ~: 5 Oxfam
  partner: 4 hope 5 faith
  seek ~: 3 beg
___ Charity: 5 Sweet
Charity begins ___: 6 at home
charlatan: 3 con 4 fake, liar, sham 5 cheat, faker, fraud, knave, phony, quack, rogue 6 phoney, rascal 8 imposter, impostor, swindler 9 hypocrite 10 adventurer, mountebank
Charlemagne: 3 roi 4 king 7 emperor
  capital: 6 Aachen
  father: 5 Pepin
  Pope who crowned ~: 3 Leo
Charlemont author: William Simms
Charlene: 6 Tilton
Charles: 3 Ray 4 Best, Dana, Drew, Haid, Ives, lake, Lamb, Lane, Mayo, Nash, Nick, Nora 5 Atlas, Beard, Boyer, Busch, Coody, Dawes, Drake, Eames, Frend, Gobat, Goren, Jimmy, Lyell, McKim, Münch, Olson, Peale, Péguy, Reade, river, saint, Shyer, Simic, Vidor 6 Addams, Barkla, Barton, Cioffi, Coburn, Conrad, Cotton, Curtis, Darwin, Ezzard, Finley, Fuller, Gounod, Grodin, Kuralt, Martel, McGraw, Mingus, Morgan, Napier, Norton, Osgood, prince, Richet, Schulz, Schwab, Townes, Wesley, Wilson, Wright 7 Babbage, Barkley, Berlitz, Bronson, Burnett, Chaplin, Coulomb, Dickens, Durning, Farrell, Guiteau, Huggins, Jarrott, Laveran, Nicolle, Nordoff, Richter, Ruggles, Siebert, Strouse, Walters, Windsor, Woolley 8 Aznavour, Bickford, Bukowski, Bulfinch, Crichton, de Gaulle, Goodyear, Laughton, Nordhoff, Pedersen, Perrault, Ringling, Sangster, Scribner, Van Doren, Williams 9 Fairbanks, Guillaume, Kimbrough, Lindbergh, MacArthur, Steinmetz, Winninger 10 Baudelaire
  city on the ~: 6 Boston
  dog: 4 Asta
  in German: 4 Karl
  in Italian: 5 Carlo
  in Spanish: 6 Carlos
Charles ___ Gibson: 4 Dana
Charles ___ Hughes: 5 Evans
Charles ___ Reilly: 6 Nelson
Charlesbourg: 4 city, town
  locale: 6 Canada, Québec
Charles, Ezzard: 5 boxer
  milieu: 4 ring
Charles I foe: 3 Pym
Charles in Charge (CBS sitcom) cast: Scott Baio (Charles)
___ Charles, LA: 4 Lake
Charleson: 3 Ian
Charles, Prince
  Beatrice, to ~: 5 niece
  parent: 6 Philip 9 Elizabeth
  princedom: 5 Wales
  sib: 4 Anne 6 Andrew, Edward
  son: 5 Harry, Henry, Wills 7 William
  sport: 4 polo
Charles, Ray
  song: Busted (1963)
    Crying Time (1966)
    Georgia on My Mind (1960)
    Hit the Road Jack (1961)
    I Can't Stop Loving You (1962)
    One Mint Julep (1961)
    Take These Chains From My Heart (1963)
    Unchain My Heart (1961)
    What'd I Say (1959)
    You Are My Sunshine (1962)
    You Don't Know Me (1962)
___ Charles spaniel: 4 King
Charles the ___: 5 Great
Charleston: 4 city, port, town 5 dance, Oscar
  athletes: 8 Bulldogs
  county: 7 Kanawha
  dance: 8 bunny hug
  locale: 3 W. Va. 4 S. Car. 8 Illinois
  river: 3 Elk 7 Kanawha
  school: 7 Citadel
Charles Van ___: 5 Doren
charley ___: 5 horse
Charley: 5 Pride 6 Weaver 7 Varrick
___ Charley?: 6 Where's
charley horse: 4 ache, kink 5 cramp, crick, spasm
Charley's Aunt: 4 play 5 farce
Charley Varrick (1973 film)
  cast: Joe Don Baker, Felicia Farr, Walter Matthau
  director: Don Siegel
Charlie: 4 Byrd, Chan, Rich, Rose, tuna 5 Brown, McCoy, Pride, Sheen, Watts 6 Barnet, Callas, Finley, Gracie, Keller, Louvin, Parker 7 Chaplin, Daniels, Ruggles 8 Comiskey 9 Gehringer, Leibrandt, Schlatter
  brother: 3 Syd 6 Emilio
  good-time ~: 5 sport
  preceder: 5 Baker
Charlie and the Chocolate Factory author: Roald Dahl
Charlie Brown (1959 song) artist: Coasters
  opener: 3 fee
Charlie Chan at the Opera (1936 film)
  cast: Boris Karloff, Warner Oland
Charlie Chan at Treasure Island (1939 film)
  cast: Cesar Romero, Sidney Toler
Charlie Chan in Egypt (1935 film)
  cast: Warner Oland, Pat Paterson
Charlie Chan in London (1934 film)
  cast: Drue Layton, Warner Oland
Charlie Chan on Broadway (1937 film)
  cast: Keye Luke, Warner Oland
Charlie Hustle: Pete Rose
Charlie's Angels: 4 trio
Charlie's Angels (2000 film)
  cast: Drew Barrymore, Cameron Diaz, Lucy Liu, Bill Murray
  director: McG
Charlie's Angels (ABC adventure)
  cast: David Doyle (John Bosley)
    Farrah Fawcett (Jill Munroe)
    John Forsythe (Charlie Townsend)
    Shelley Hack (Tiffany Welles)
    Kate Jackson (Sabrina Duncan)
    Cheryl Ladd (Kris Munroe)
    Tanya Roberts (Julie Rogers)
    Jaclyn Smith (Kelly Garrett)
Charlize: 6 Theron
charlotte: 7 dessert
Charlotte: 3 Rae 4 city, town 5 Lewis 6 Brontë, Gilman 8 Rampling
  in Italian: 8 Carlotta
  locale: 4 N. Car.
  newspaper: 8 Observer
  sister of ~: 4 Anne 5 Emily
  team: 7 Hornets
Charlotte ___, VI: 6 Amalie
___ Charlotte Islands: 5 Queen
charlotte russe: 4 cake 7 dessert
Charlottesville: 4 city, town
  athletes: 9 Cavaliers
  locale: 8 Virginia
  school: 3 U Va
Charlotte's Web
  author: E.B. White
  character: 3 rat 5 Avery
Charlottetown: 4 city
  locale: 6 Canada
Charlton: 6 Heston
Charly: 7 McClain
Charly (1968 film)
  cast: Claire Bloom, Cliff Robertson, Lilia Skala

charm: **3** hex, obi, woo **4** draw, juju, lure, mojo, send, take, vamp, zest **5** asset, grace, magic, obeah, spell, tempt **6** allure, amulet, appeal, bangle, beauty, disarm, enamor, endear, engage, glamor, grigri, lead on, please, ravish, scarab **7** amenity, attract, beguile, bewitch, charism, coaxing, delight, enchant, enthral, glamour, inthral, jewelry, periapt, trinket, wheedle, win over **8** charisma, elegance, enthrall, entrance, greegree, grisgris, inthrall, intrigue, inveigle, talisman, urbanity **9** captivate, enrapture, entertain, fascinate, hypnotize, inebriate, infatuate, magnetism, mesmerize, spellbind, tantalize, transport, wheedling **10** allurement, attraction, intoxicate, loveliness, tickle pink
magic ~: **4** mojo **6** amulet, fetich, fetish
charm __: **6** school **8** bracelet
Charm: **5** candy
Charmaine composer: **5** Rapee
__ charmant!: **4** Très
charmed: **4** rapt **5** blest, lucky **7** blessed, far gone, favored, on a roll **8** held fast **9** delighted, fortunate, gladdened, on a streak, overjoyed **10** auspicious, felicitous, fortuitous, infatuated, spellbound
charmed __: **4** life **5** quark **6** circle
Charmed (WB fantasy)
cast: Holly Marie Combs (Piper Halliwell)
Shannen Doherty (Pru Halliwell)
Alyssa Milano (Phoebe Halliwell)
character: **5** witch
__ charmed life: **5** lead a
Charmed Life, A author: Mary McCarthy
Charmed Lives author: **5** Korda
charmer: **5** cutey, cutie **6** beauty, wizard **8** beguiler, conjurer, conjuror, magician, sorcerer **9** bewitcher, enchanter
little ~: **4** pixy **5** cutey, cutie, pixie
partner: **5** cobra, snake
__ charmer: **5** snake
charmeuse: **6** fabric **8** material
Charmian: **4** Carr
Charmin alternative: **5** Scott **6** Marcal **8** Northern, Soft Weve **10** Cottonelle, White Cloud
charming: **4** cute, nice **5** suave, sweet **6** dainty, lovely, pretty, quaint, rakish **7** amiable, darling, likable, lovable, winning, winsome **8** adorable, alluring, debonair, engaging, esthetic, fetching, inviting, likeable, loveable, magnetic, mannerly, pleasant, pleasing, romantic, striking, tasteful, tempting **9** appealing, debonaire, desirable, exquisite, glamorous **10** debonnaire, delectable, delightful, magnetical, personable
__ Charming: **6** Prince
charms: **7** jewelry
Charms: **5** candy
Charm School author: Nelson Demille
Charnel Rose, The author: Aiken
Charo: **7** Spanish **8** flamenco **9** guitarist
spouse: Xavier Cugat
Charolais: **3** cow **4** bull **6** bovine, cattle
Charon: **4** moon
circles it: **5** Pluto
father of ~: **6** Erebus
planet: **5** Pluto
river: **4** Styx
Charpak, Georges: **8** Nobelist **9** physicist
charpoy: **3** cot **8** bedstead
charqui: **4** meat
Char, René: **4** poet **6** French
charro: **6** cowboy **8** horseman
need: **5** reata, riata
Charro! (1969 film)
cast: Ina Balin, Victor French, Lynn Kellogg, Elvis Presley
chart: **3** log, map **4** plan, plot **5** graph **6** design, layout, sketch, zodiac **7** diagram, outline **8** schedule, tabulate **9** adumbrate, blueprint, delineate, floor plan, horoscope, visual aid
anew: **5** remap
indication: **5** trend
shape: **3** bar, pie
starter: **4** flow
topper: **3** hit
chart __: **4** room **5** house
__ chart: **3** bar, eye, pie **4** flip, flow, star, time **5** chord, natal, pilot **7** control, Snellen
__ Charta: **5** Magna
charter: **3** let **4** book, code, deed, hire, pact, rent, take **5** lease **6** employ, engage, treaty **7** license, reserve **8** contract, document **9** agreement, concordat, franchise, privilege **10** commission
charter __: **5** party **6** colony, member
Charter __: **3** Oak
chartered: **5** legal
chartered __: **4** bank
Charterhouse of Parma, The author: Stendhal
Charteris: **6** Leslie
detective: **5** Saint, Simon **7** Templar
Chartier, Alain: **4** poet **6** French
Chartres: **4** city, town
locale: **6** France
river: **4** Eure
chartreuse: **5** color, drink, green **8** beverage **9** yellowish
relative: **3** pea **4** cyan, jade, sage **5** beryl, breen, olive, virid **6** myrtle, reseda **7** avocado, celadon, emerald, verdant **9** pistachio, turquoise **10** aquamarine
Chartreux: **3** cat **5** felid **6** feline
Chartwell, to Churchill: **6** estate
charvet: **6** fabric **8** material
charwoman: **4** maid **7** cleaner
chary: **3** shy **4** cagy, wary **5** cagey, leery **6** frugal, gun-shy, stingy, uneasy, unsure **7** bashful, careful, dubious, guarded, heedful, mindful, prudent, sparing, thrifty **8** cautious, discreet, doubtful, doubting, hesitant, keen-eyed, watchful **9** diffident, flinching, provident, reluctant, skeptical, uncertain **10** economical, fastidious, scrupulous, suspicious, uneffusive
Charybdis: **5** peril **9** whirlpool
parent of ~: **4** Gaea **8** Poseidon
chase: **3** dog, tag, woo **4** hunt, race, seek, shag **5** expel, hound, quest, shoot, stalk, track, trail **6** chivvy, follow, gun for, pursue, search **7** engrave, fox hunt, go after, pursuit, run down **8** quest for, run after, stampede **9** drive away, track down
anagram for ~: **5** aches
out: **4** boot, oust, rout, shoo **5** repel **6** dispel, run off **8** drive off, send away **9** drive away
scenes: **6** action
starter: **7** steeple
chase __: **4** card **7** mortise
__ chase: **4** give **5** paper
Chase: **3** Hal **4** Edna, Ilka **5** Chevy, David **6** Barrie
Chase a Crooked Shadow (1958 film)
cast: Anne Baxter, Herbert Lom, Richard Todd
chase-away word: **4** scat, shoo **5** scram **6** begone **8** scramola
Chase, Chevy: **5** actor **8** comedian
film: Caddyshack (1980)
Fletch (1985)
Foul Play (1978)
Modern Problems (1981)
National Lampoon's Christmas Vacation (1989)
National Lampoon's Vacation (1983)
Seems Like Old Times (1980)
Spies Like Us (1985)
Three Amigos! (1986)
TV: Saturday Night Live
Chase, Ilka spouse: Louis Calhern
Chase, Mary Ellen: **6** writer
__ Chase, MD: **5** Chevy
Chase of the Golden Meteor, The
author: Jules Verne
chaser: **4** beer, soda **5** drink, posse **6** whisky **7** whiskey
robber ~: **6** lawman **7** officer
without a ~: **4** neat **8** straight **10** straight up
Chase & Sanborn: **6** coffee
alternative: **5** Sanka, Yuban **7** Folgers, Melitta, Nescafe, Savarin **9** Hills Bros.
__ Chase Smith: **8** Margaret
__ Chase, The: **5** Paper
chasing: **5** after
chasm: **3** gap, maw, pit **4** gulf, hole, rift **5** abyss, cañon, gorge, gully, split **6** breach, canyon, crater, gulley, ravine, schism **7** crevice, fissure **8** cleavage, crevasse
like a ~: **6** gaping **7** yawning
chassé: **4** step **5** glide **8** movement
chassis: **4** body **5** frame, shape, shell **6** figure **8** fuselage **9** framework
Chast: **3** Roz
chaste: **4** good, pure **5** clean, moral, stark **6** decent, demure, modest, vestal **8** celibate, innocent, maidenly, spotless, unsoiled, virtuous **9** continent, incorrupt, lily-white, stainless, undefiled, unsullied, untainted, wholesome
name meaning ~: **5** Agnes
chasten: **5** scold **6** humble, punish, thrash **7** mortify **9** castigate, humiliate
chastened: **5** sorry **7** subdued **8** contrite **10** remorseful
chastise: **3** rag **4** flay, lash, whip **5** scold, spank **6** berate, lean on, punish, strike, thrash **7** censure, chew out, lay into, upbraid **8** penalize **9** castigate, criticize, excoriate, fustigate, reprehend **10** discipline
chastity: **6** virtue **7** modesty **8** morality **9** austerity **10** abstinence, simplicity
Chastity: **4** Bono
parent: **4** Cher **5** Sonny
chasuble, garment under a: **3** alb
chat: **3** gab, jaw, rap, yak, yap **4** bird, blab, chin, talk, word **5** prate, speak, visit **6** babble, confab, dialog, gossip, jabber, natter, parley, powwow, rattle, tattle, yammer **7** discuss, palaver, prattle, schmoos **8** causerie, converse, dialogue, schmoose, schmooze, songbird **9** discourse, tête-à-tête, touch base **10** chew the fat, chew the rag, conference, yackety-yak
online ~: **2** IM
pas de ~: **4** leap
prepare to ~ perhaps: **5** log on
room chuckle: **3** LOL
starter: **4** chit, wood
striped ~: **5** tigre
chat __: **4** room, show
__ chat: **4** palm **5** pas de
château: **4** keep **5** abode, house **6** castle, estate, palace, winery **7** mansion **8** fortress **10** manor house
château __: **4** d'eau, wine
Château __: **3** D'if
Château-__: **7** Thierry
Chateaubriand: **5** steak **8** François
novel: **4** René
Châteauguay: **4** city, town
locale: **6** Canada, Québec
Château Lafite product: **4** wine **6** claret
Château-Thierry: **6** battle
locale: **6** France
river: **5** Marne
Chatham: **4** city, earl, town
locale: **6** Canada **7** Ontario
chatroom offerer: **3** AOL
Chattanooga: **4** city, town **6** battle
locale: **4** Tenn. **9** Tennessee
Chattanooga Choo Choo composer: **6** Gordon, Warren
Chattanoogie __ Shine Boy: **4** Shoe
chattel: **4** serf **5** goods, slave **6** assets, things, thrall **7** effects, villein **8** property **9** commodity
chatter: **3** gab, gas, jaw, rap, yak, yap **4** blab, buzz, gush, talk **5** bilge, clack, noise, prate, run on, shake, sound, speak, spout **6** babble, drivel, gabble, gibber, gossip, jabber, natter, patter, pop off, ramble, rattle, tattle **7** blather, blether, maunder, palaver, prattle, twaddle, yakking **8** babbling, chitchat, rattle on **9** gibberish, loquacity, table talk **10** chew the rag
ender: **3** box
prone to ~: **9** talkative
__ chatter: **4** idle
chatterbox: **6** gabber, gasbag, gossip, magpie, yakker **8** prattler
chattering: **5** noisy, prate **8** babbling **9** garrulity, garrulous, talkative **10** loquacious
quit ~: **6** shut up
__ Chatterley's Lover: **4** Lady
Chatterton: **4** Ruth **6** Thomas
Chatterton, Thomas: **4** poet **7** British
chatty: **5** gabby, gassy, talky, wordy **7** gossipy, unterse **8** familiar, friendly, informal **9** garrulous, talkative **10** bigmouthed, colloquial, long-winded, loquacious
not ~: **4** curt
Chatwin, Bruce: **6** writer **7** British
Chaucer, Geoffrey: **4** poet **7** British
character: **4** Cook, Dyer, Monk **5** Canon, Clerk, Friar, Harry, Reeve **6** Bailey, Doctor, Knight, Miller, Parson, Squire, Weaver, Yeoman **7** Chaucer, Plowman, Shipman **8** Franklin, Geoffrey, Manciple, Merchant, Pardoner, Prioress, Sergeant, Summoner **9** Carpenter, Second Nun **10** Nun's Priest, Wife of Bath **11** Haberdasher
work: The Canterbury Tales
chauffeur: **5** drive, ferry **6** cabbie, driver
outfit: **6** livery **7** uniform
chauffeured car: **4** limo
Chausson: **6** Ernest
Chautauqua: **4** lake
locale: **7** New York
chauvinism: **4** bias **8** jingoism **9** prejudice **10** fanaticism, narrowness
chauvinist: **5** bigot, jingo
__ chauvinist: **4** male
Chavez: **5** Cesar **6** Carlos
Chavez __: **6** Ravine
chaw: **3** wad **4** quid
over: **4** mull
Chayefsky, Paddy: **6** author, writer
work: Altered States
Gideon
Marty
Middle of the Night
The Tenth Man
chayote: **5** fruit **8** mirliton
Chazz: **10** Palminteri
Che: **7** Guevara
Cheadle, Don: **5** actor
film: Bulworth (1998)

The Family Man (2000)
Swordfish (2001)
Traffic (2000)
Volcano (1997)
cheap: 3 low 4 base, mean 5 junky, lousy, petty, ratty, tacky, tatty, tight, tinny 6 cheesy, common, crumby, crummy, frugal, garish, little, low-end, modest, on sale, shabby, shoddy, sleazy, sordid, stingy, tawdry, trashy, two-bit, vulgar 7 bargain, chintzy, cut-rate, good buy, low-cost, miserly, nominal, raffish, reduced, slashed, thrifty 8 for a song, inferior, mediocre, moderate, schlocky, ungiving 9 half-price, low-priced, penurious, rinky-dink, tasteless, third-rate, worthless 10 despicable, economical, jerry-built, low-quality, marked down, reasonable, second-rate, skinflinty
be ~: 5 skimp
ender: 5 skate
not ~: 4 dear 6 costly 8 generous
sell ~: 4 dump
shot: 3 dig 4 barb, gibe, jibe, slam, slap, slur, snub 5 abuse, libel, scorn, taunt 6 insult, rebuff, slight 7 affront, calumny, catcall, disdain, low blow, mockery, obloquy, offense, put-down, slander 8 contempt, derision, ridicule 9 aspersion, contumely 10 defamation, disrespect, opprobrium
cheap __: 4 shot
cheap-__: 4 jack, john
__ cheap: 5 on the
__-cheap: 3 dog 4 dirt
cheap at __ the price: 5 twice
Cheap Detective, The (1978 film)
cast: Ann-Margret, Eileen Brennan, Sid Caesar, Stockard Channing, James Coco, Dom DeLuise, Peter Falk, Louise Fletcher, John Houseman, Madeleine Kahn, Fernando Lamas, Marsha Mason, Phil Silvers, David Ogden Stiers, Vic Tayback, Abe Vigoda, Nicol Williamson, Paul Williams
director: Robert Moore
cheapen: 6 debase, reduce 7 degrade, depress, detract, devalue 8 diminish, minimize 9 devaluate 10 adulterate
Cheaper by the Dozen (1950 film)
cast: Jeanne Crain, Myrna Loy, Clifton Webb
director: Walter Lang
cheaper than: 5 under
cheapskate: 5 miser, piker 7 miserly 8 tightwad 9 skinflint
Cheap Trick
song: Don't Be Cruel (1988)
The Flame (1988)
I Want You to Want Me (1979)
cheat: 2 do 3 con, gyp, rob, sin 4 bilk, burn, clip, crib, dupe, fake, foil, fool, gull, have, hoax, hose, liar, nick, rook, scam, sham, snow, take 5 bunco, cozen, crook, dodge, fraud, fudge, gouge, knave, mulct, pluck, quack, rogue, screw, shaft, shark, shirk, spoof, steal, thief, trick, wrong 6 chisel, con man, deceit, delude, diddle, dodger, euchre, fleece, hustle, outwit, racket, rascal, ripoff, robber, rope in, sucker, take in, thwart 7 beguile, deceive, defraud, fast one, finagle, grifter, hustler, mislead, pretend, sandbag, scammer, sharper, sharpie, snow job, swindle, two-time 8 chiseler, conniver, deceiver, flimflam, hoodwink, imposter, impostor, outsmart, simulate, swindler 9 bamboozle, charlatan, con artist, deception, defrauder, disinform, four-flush, frustrate, hypocrite, imposture, scoundrel, shell game, trickster, victimize 10 dirty trick, double-deal, hanky-panky, overcharge, run a game on
at Hide and Seek: 4 look
on an exam: 4 copy, peek
sheet: 4 crib, trot
cheaters: 5 specs 7 glasses 8 horn-rims 10 eyeglasses, spectacles
Cheaters, The (1945 film)
cast: Billie Burke, Joseph Schildkraut
director: Joseph Kane
Cheatham, Doc: 9 trumpeter
genre: 4 jazz
cheating: 6 deceit, racket, unfair 7 unloyal 8 disloyal, trickery 9 dishonest, faithless, two-timing, unethical 10 illegality, unfaithful
__ Cheatin' Heart: 4 Your
chebec: 4 bird
Chechen city: 6 Grozny
check: 3 nip, tab 4 balk, bill, curb, dike, foil, halt, page, quiz, rein, scan, slow, stay, stem, stop, tame, test, tick 5 abort, audit, baulk, block, brake, count, deter, draft, frisk, gauge, judge, leash, limit, money, proof, prove, quell, stall, trial 6 arrest, assess, bridle, dampen, damper, defeat, detain, halter, hamper, handle, hinder, impede, muzzle, oppose, pull in, rebuff, rein in, retard, review, search, slow up, stifle, thwart, ticket, verify 7 analyze, compare, confirm, control, enquiry, examine, eyeball, harness, inhibit, inquiry, inspect, measure, monitor, prevent, refrain, repress, reverse, suspend, ward off 8 analysis, evaluate, hold back, keep back, look into, look over, make sure, mitigate, moderate, obstacle, obstruct, overhaul, preclude, restrain, restrict, scrutiny, slow down, stoppage, suppress, withhold 9 abatement, ascertain, constrain, deterrent, hamstring, hindrance, intercept, interrupt, proofread, reckoning, restraint 10 comparison, constraint, counteract, discourage, effrontery, impediment, inhibition, inspection, limitation, scrutinize, standstill
add-on: 3 tax
blank ~: 7 mandate
casher: 5 payee 6 drawee
cashing need: 3 sig. 9 signature
electronically: 4 scan 5 sweep
ender: 3 off, out 4 book, list, mate, rein, room 5 point
European ~: 4 giro
for errors: 4 edit 5 proof 6 redact 9 proofread
for fit: 5 try on
for fraud: 6 go over 7 examine, inspect 9 go through 10 scrutinize
give a rain ~: 5 defer, delay 6 put off 7 suspend
hold in ~: 4 keep, rein 6 govern
in: 4 come 5 pop up, reach 6 appear, arrive, attend, report 8 get there, register
in ~: 5 at bay
item to ~: 2 ID 3 hat 4 coat 6 ID card
line: 4 date 6 amount 9 signature
manipulator: 5 kiter
mark: 4 tick
of business records: 5 audit
off: 4 mark
one's mail, perhaps: 5 log in
out: 3 eye, vet 4 case, ogle, quit, read, test, view 5 assay, gauge, leave, probe, prove, scout, split, spy on, study, tally, try on 6 assess, browse, peruse, size up, square, survey, verify 7 confirm, examine, glimpse, inspect, qualify 8 appraise, evaluate, follow up, look into, look over, withdraw 10 correspond
(out): 5 scope
pick up the ~: 3 pay 4 fund 5 spend, treat 6 defray 7 finance
prepare to ~ out: 4 pack
rain ~: 4 stub 10 invitation
redeem a ~: 4 cash
remainder: 4 stub
send a ~: 3 pay 5 remit
some ~ payees: 7 bearers
stamp: 3 NSF 4 paid
starter: 3 hat, pay 5 cross 7 counter
the fine print: 4 pore 5 study
up on: 4 case, quiz 6 verify 7 monitor, oversee 8 overlook 9 supervise
word on a sample ~: 4 void
words on a ~: 5 pay to
write a ~: 4 draw
write a bad ~: 4 kite 6 bounce
writer: 5 maker, payer
check __: 3 bit, out 4 line, list, mark, over, rail, stub, up on 5 it out, valve
check __ the mail!, The: 4 is in
__ check: 3 bed, hat 4 bank, body, door, Glen, hook, poke, rain, spot 5 bench, blank, board, sales, sweep 6 parity, rubber 7 banker's, counter, reality
__-check: 4 back, fore, spot 5 cross, spell 6 broken, double
checked: 4 safe 6 pent-up, silent 7 limited 8 reined in
checker: 3 man 5 inlay, piece 9 inspector
ender: 5 berry, bloom, board 6 blooms
__ checker: 5 spell
Checker: 3 cab, car 4 auto, taxi 10 automobile
model: 7 Superba 8 Marathon
operator: 6 cabbie
checkerberry: 5 fruit
Checker, Chubby
song: The Fly (1961)
Let's Twist Again (1961)
Limbo Rock (1962)
Pony Time (1961)
Popeye (1962)
Slow Twistin' (1962)
The Twist (1960)
checkered: 5 plaid 6 inlaid 9 patchwork, patterned 10 variegated
checkered __: 4 flag, lily, past 6 career
checkers: 4 game
capture, in ~: 4 jump
in Britain: 8 draughts
promote, in ~: 4 king 5 crown
side: 3 red 5 black
__ checkers: 7 Chinese
checking account
detail: 4 stmt. 9 statement
kind of: 5 no-fee
offerer: 4 bank 5 S and L
...checking it __: 5 twice
check-in place: 5 hotel, lobby, motel 7 airport
Check it out!: 4 look 6 lookee, oh look
Check It Out (1988 song) artist: John Cougar Mellencamp
checkless __: 7 society
checklist: 6 agenda
checkmark: 4 tick
checkmate: 3 win 4 beat, drub 6 defeat 7 conquer, triumph, trounce, victory 8 conquest, vanquish 9 discomfit
checkout
scanner ID: 3 UPC
worker: 6 bagger 7 cashier
checkout __: 7 counter
Checkpoint Charlie site: 6 Berlin
check's in the __!, The: 4 mail
checks off: 3 xes
check the __: 3 oil
checkup: 4 exam 6 review 10 inspection
command: 5 say ah
sound: 2 ah 3 aah
checkups, like some: 6 annual, dental
cheddar: 6 cheese 8 longhorn
like some ~: 4 aged 5 sharp, tangy
relative: 5 colby 7 Chester 8 American, Cheshire 9 Leicester
Cheech: 5 Marin
partner: 5 Chong
cheek: 3 lip 4 gall, jowl, sass 5 brass, mouth, nerve, sauce 6 hubris, hybris 8 audacity, back talk, boldness, chutzpah, rudeness, temerity 9 arrogance, brashness, flippancy, impudence, insolence 10 brazenness, effrontery, impishness
by jowl: 4 near 5 close, dense, thick 6 beside, packed 7 crowded 8 abutting, adjacent, touching 9 congested, jam-packed 10 near-at-hand
combining form: 3 mel- 4 melo- 5 bucco-
ender: 4 bone
feature: 6 dimple
insect ~: 5 bucca
makeup: 5 blush
of the ~: 5 jugal, malar 6 buccal
place: 4 face
tongue in ~: 5 in fun 6 in jest 7 as a joke 8 jokingly 9 jestingly, kiddingly
turn the other ~: 7 forgive
with tongue in ~: 5 campy, drily
cheek __: 5 pouch, strap, tooth
cheekbone: 5 malar
cheek by __: 4 jowl
__-cheeked: 4 mail, rosy
cheekiness: 5 sauce 9 flippancy 10 effrontery, impishness
Cheek to Cheek: 4 song, tune
composer: Irving Berlin
first word: 6 heaven
musical: 6 Top Hat
Cheektowaga: 4 city, town
locale: 7 New York
cheeky: 4 bold, flip, pert, rude 5 brash, fresh, nervy, sassy, saucy 6 awless, brassy, brazen, daring, snippy 7 aweless, forward, uncivil 8 arrogant, flippant, impolite, impudent, insolent, snippety 9 audacious, bumptious, out of line, shameless 10 irreverent
cheep: 4 call, peep, pipe 5 chirp, tweet 6 squeak, squeal 7 twitter 8 bird call
cheer: 3 joy, rah, yay 4 buoy, glee, hail, lift, yell, zest 5 amuse, elate, exult, huzza, liven, mirth, pep up, shout, whoop 6 buck up, gaiety, gayety, holler, hoorah, hooray, hurrah, hurray, huzzah, perk up, pick up, please, praise, revive, scream, solace, soothe, thrill, uplift 7 acclaim, applaud, comfort, console, delight, elevate, enliven, gladden, gratify, happify, hearten, hurrahs, lighten, rapture, refresh, root for, support, upraise 8 embolden, enspirit, gladness, hilarity, imbolden, inspirit, optimism, reassure 9 amusement, encourage, entertain, happiness, jocundity, merriment, untrouble 10 brighten up, exhilarate, joyousness, jump for joy, regalement, risibility, strengthen
Bronx ~: 4 razz 9 raspberry
ender: 6 leader 7 leading
French ~ word: 4 vive
gave a ~: 5 rahed
give a Bronx ~: 4 jeer, mock 5 sneer, taunt
good ~: 4 glee 7 jollity 8 optimism 9 geniality, happiness
holiday ~: 3 nog 6 eggnog
on: 4 root, urge 7 root for
opera ~: 5 brava, bravo
opposite: 3 boo
rousing ~: 3 yea

Spanish ~ word: **3** olé **4** viva
start: **3** hip, sis **4** viva
up: **4** buoy, perk **5** liven **6** solace **7** comfort, console, enliven, gladden, hearten, inspire, lighten, satisfy **8** brighten, reassure **9** encourage, take heart **10** exhilarate
Yale ~: **5** boola
__ cheer: **4** good **5** Bronx
Cheer: **9** detergent
alternative: **3** All, Biz, Era, Fab, Yes **4** Bold, Dash, Gain, Surf, Tide, Wisk **5** Dreft, Purex **6** Calgon, Dynamo, Oxydol **7** Octagon **9** Ivory Snow
cheerful: **3** gay **4** glad, high, nice, rosy, warm **5** happy, jolly, light, merry, peart, perky, riant, sunny **6** blithe, bouncy, breezy, bright, festal, genial, hearty, jaunty, jocund, jovial, joyful, joyous, lively, upbeat **7** beaming, buoyant, chipper, cordial, gleeful, jocular, pleased, radiant, romping, tickled, willing **8** blissful, carefree, ecstatic, euphoric, exultant, giggling, grooving, jubilant, laughing, likeable, mirthful, pleasant, sanguine, thrilled **9** contented, convivial, delighted, exuberant, lightsome, overjoyed, promising, rejoicing, sprightly, vivacious **10** heartening, optimistic, rollicking, unbothered
earful: **4** song, tune **5** music **6** ballad, jingle, number **7** lullaby
name meaning ~: **6** Hilary **7** Hillary
not ~: **3** low, sad **4** blue, dark, down, drab, dull, glum, grim, mopy **5** black, bleak, drear, mirky, mopey, murky, stark, surly, woful **6** broody, dismal, dreary, gloomy, morose, somber, sullen, woeful **7** austere, doleful, forlorn, in a funk, joyless, unhappy **8** dejected, desolate, dolorous, downbeat, downcast, lonesome, troubled, wretched **9** bummed out, dejecting, depressed, heartsick, miserable, saddening, sorrowful, woebegone **10** chapfallen, depressing, despondent, dispirited, drearisome, in the dumps, lugubrious, melancholy, oppressive, out of sorts, tenebrific
Cheerful Little Earful composer: **4** Rose **6** Warren **8** Gershwin
cheerfully: **6** gladly **7** readily **9** agreeably
cheerfulness: **4** glee **5** mirth **6** gaiety, gayety **8** buoyance, buoyancy, felicity, hilarity, optimism **9** merriment
cheering: **7** acclaim, big hand, ovation **8** exultant, gladsome **9** promising **10** optimistic
loudly: **5** aroar
Cheerio!: **3** bye **4** ta-ta **5** see ya, toast **6** so long **7** goodbye **8** farewell
Cheerios: **6** cereal
competitor: **3** Kix **4** Life, Trix **5** Kashi, Quisp, Total **6** Kaboom, Muesli, Oreo O's, Pablum, Smacks **7** All-Bran, Crispix, Harmony, Hunny B's, Mueslix, Oat Bran, Pokemon **8** Boo Berry, Corn Chex, Corn Pops, Fiber One, Rice Chex, Special K, Uncle Sam, Wheaties **9** Alpha Bits, Apple Zaps, Grape Nuts, Honey Comb, Just Right, Wheat Chex **10** Apple Jacks, Bran Flakes, Cap'n Crunch, Cocoa Puffs, Froot Loops, Mini-Wheats, Nutri-Grain, Puffed Rice, Quaker Oats, Smart Start **11** Cocoa Blasts, Cookie Crisp, Golden Crisp, Lucky Charms, Puffed Wheat, Sweet Crunch, Waffle Crisp
like ~: **4** oaty **5** oaten
cheerleader: **6** rooter
feat: **4** yell **5** split
group: **3** sqd. **5** squad
like a ~: **5** peppy, perky
prop: **3** pom **5** baton **6** pompom, pompon
quality: **3** pep
shout: **3** rah **6** go team
wear: **5** skirt
cheerless: **3** sad **4** blue, dark, down, drab, dull, glum, grim, mopy **5** black, bleak, drear, mirky, mopey, murky, stark, surly, woful **6** broody, dismal, dreary, gloomy, morose, somber, sullen, woeful **7** austere, doleful, forlorn, hangdog, in a funk, joyless, unhappy **8** dejected, desolate, dolorous, downbeat, downcast, lonesome, troubled, wretched **9** bummed out, dejecting, depressed, heartsick, miserable, saddening, sorrowful, unhopeful, woebegone **10** chapfallen, depressing, despondent, dispirited, drearisome, in the dumps, lugubrious, melancholy, oppressive, out of sorts, tenebrific
cheerlessness: **4** pall **5** gloom **7** sadness
cheers
round of ~: **5** salvo
three ~: **5** huzza **6** hoorah, hooray, hurrah, hurray, huzzah
__ cheers!: **5** Three
Cheers (NBC sitcom)
cast: Kirstie Alley (Rebecca Howe)
Nicholas Colasanto (Ernie Pantusso)
Ted Danson (Sam Malone)
Kelsey Grammer (Frasier Crane)
Woody Harrelson (Woody Boyd)
Shelley Long (Diane Chambers)
Bebe Neuwirth (Lilith Sternin)
Rhea Perlman (Carla Tortelli)
John Ratzenberger (Cliff Clavin)
Roger Rees (Robin Colcord)
George Wendt (Norm Peterson)
Norm's occupation: **3** CPA
Norm's wife: **4** Vera
order: **3** ale **4** beer, brew
prop: **5** stein, stool
setting: bar, Boston
Cheers!: **5** salud, skoal, toast **6** prosit
Cheers for Miss Bishop (1941 film)
cast: William Gargan, Martha Scott
director: Tay Garnett
cheery: **3** gay **4** glad **5** happy, jolly, light, merry, perky, sunny **6** blithe, elated, genial, hearty, jocund, jovial, joyful, joyous, upbeat **7** buoyant, chipper, festive, gleeful, pleased, radiant, tickled **8** blissful, carefree, ecstatic, euphoric, exultant, jubilant, laughing, mirthful, positive, thrilled **9** delighted, lightsome, overjoyed, rejoicing, sprightly **10** delightful, heartening, unbothered
cheese: **4** bleu, blue, Brie, Edam, feta, Roka **5** banon, brick, colby, dairy, Gouda, Kraft, nacho, Swiss **6** brynza, chevre, farmer, Leyden, mysost, Romano, Tilsit **7** cheddar, Chester, chevret, crottin, crowdie, fontina, gervais, Gjetost, Gruyère, Limburg, ricotta, sapsago, Stilton **8** American, Beaufort, Beaumont, Bel Paese, bierkäse, Cheshire, Emmental, Liptauer, longhorn, muenster, parmesan, pecorino **9** Camembert, Emmenthal, Jarlsberg, Leicester, Limburger, Port Salut, provolone, Roquefort, Wiltshire **10** caerphilly, Emmentaler, Gorgonzola, mascarpone, mozzarella, Neufchâtel
big ~: **3** CEO, VIP **4** boss, exec, lion, name **5** celeb, chief, mogul, nabob **6** top dog **7** headman, notable **8** kingfish **9** authority, celebrity, commander
coat: **4** rind
combining form: **3** tyr- **4** tyro-
dish: **5** fondu **6** fondue
Dutch: **4** Edam **5** Gouda **6** Leyden
ender: **4** cake **5** cloth **6** burger
factory: **5** dairy
French: **4** Brie **9** Camembert
goat ~: **6** chevre **7** chevret
improve ~: **3** age
in a mousetrap: **4** bait
it: **3** run **4** flee **5** scram
like ~: **7** caseous
like some ~: **4** aged, mild **5** moldy, sharp
like Swiss ~: **5** holey
lover: **5** mouse
prepare ~: **5** grate
product: **4** whey
Quebec Trappist ~: **3** oka
say ~: **4** grin, pose **5** smile
source: **4** milk
starter: **4** head
state: **3** Wis. **9** Wisconsin
unit: **4** cube, slab **5** brick, slice, wedge, wheel
cheese __: **3** pie **4** cake, tray **5** eater, steak **6** spread **7** product
__ cheese: **3** big, pot, rat **4** bleu, blue, coon, curd, Edam, goat, hard, jack **5** brick, colby, cream, Dutch, store, Swiss **6** farmer, Romano **7** cheddar, clabber, cottage, Gruyère, pimento, Stilton
__ cheese!: **3** Say
cheeseburger topping: **5** bacon, onion **6** catsup, tomato **7** ketchup, lettuce
cheesecake: **8** ice cream
alternative: **5** lemon, mocha, peach **6** banana, coffee, Jamoca, toffee **7** caramel, coconut, vanilla **8** cinnamon, hazelnut **9** bubblegum, chocolate, pineapple, pistachio, raspberry, rocky road, rum raisin **10** blackberry, Neapolitan, peppermint, strawberry
cheesecloth: **5** gauze **6** fabric
like ~: **4** wove **5** woven
Cheese Nips: **7** cracker
alternative: **4** Ritz **5** Zesta **6** Krispy **7** Cheez-It **8** Triscuit **10** Wheat Thins
cheeseparer: **5** miser **9** skinflint
cheesy: **3** bad **5** cheap **6** flimsy, shlock, shoddy **7** schlock **8** inferior **9** fifth-rate, third-rate **10** fourth-rate, second-rate
snack: **5** nacho
cheetah: **3** cat **5** felid **6** animal, feline, mammal
relative: **4** eyra, lion, lynx, puma **5** liger, ounce, tiger, tigon **6** bobcat, cougar, jaguar, margay, ocelot, serval, tiglon **7** bay lynx, caracal, leopard, panther **9** catamount **10** jaguarundi
Cheetah: **3** ape **5** chimp **10** chimpanzee
Cheetos: **4** nosh **5** snack
Cheever, John: **6** author, writer
work: Bullet Park
The Enormous Radio
Falconer
Oh What a Paradise It Seems
The Wapshot Chronicle
Cheevy, Miniver, like: **4** lean, slim
Cheez __: **4** Whiz
Cheez-It: **7** cracker
alternative: **4** Ritz **5** Zesta **6** Krispy **8** Triscuit **10** Wheat Thins
chef: **4** cook, Kerr **5** baker, Beard, Child **9** cuisinier, Escoffier
attraction: **5** aroma
cry: **4** done
fat strip: **6** lardon **7** lardoon
gadget: **5** corer, dicer, ricer **6** baster, beater, slicer
gravy: **3** jus
herb: **4** sage **5** thyme **7** parsley **8** rosemary
measure: **3** cup, tbs., tsp. **4** tbsp. **8** teaspoon **10** tablespoon
need: **3** pan, pot **4** mitt, oven **5** apron, knife **6** kettle
offerings: **4** menu
pastry ~, at times: **4** icer
phrase: **3** a la **5** au jus
serving: **4** dish **6** entrée
chef-__: **7** d'oeuvre
__ chef: **6** pastry
Chef __-Ar-Dee: **3** Boy
__ Chef: **5** Magic
chef de __: **7** cuisine
chef's __: **5** salad
Chef's Blend: **7** cat food
alternative: **5** Amore **6** Figaro, Purina **7** Whiskas **8** Friskies **10** Fancy Feast
Che gelida manina: **4** aria
Cheju: **4** city, town
locale: **10** South Korea
CHEKA successor: **4** OGPU
Chekhov, Anton: **6** author **7** Russian **10** playwright
character: **4** Olga **5** Irina, Masha
work: The Cherry Orchard
Ivanov
The Seagull
Three Sisters
Uncle Vanya
chela: **4** claw **5** organ **6** pincer
Chelmsford: **4** city, town
locale: **5** Essex **7** England
Chelsea: **4** city, town **5** Field **7** Clinton
locale: **4** Mass.
Chelyuskin: **4** cape
locale: **6** Russia
chem.: **3** sci. **4** subj.
compound: **3** alc.
reaction product: **3** ppt.
weak, in ~: **3** dil.
see also chemical, chemistry
__ chem.: **4** phys.
Chemax: **4** city, town
locale: **6** Mexico **7** Yucatán
chemical
abbreviation: **3** alc., mol., ppt.
banned ~: **3** DDT, PCB **4** Alar
compound: **4** enol **5** amide, amine, diene, ester, imide, imine, niter, oxide **8** diolefin
concentration: **5** titer
container: **3** vat
corrosive ~: **3** lye **4** acid
dye: **3** azo **6** litmus
extract: **5** educt
prefix: **3** iso-, oxa-, oxo-, oxy- **4** nitr- **5** pheno-
radical: **4** acyl **5** allyl
reaction: **5** redox **9** oxidation, reduction
starter: **3** bio **5** petro
suffix: **3** -ane, -ase, -ate, -ene, -ide, -ine, -ite, -nol, -ose, -yne **4** -olic **5** -phane
undergo ~ change: **5** react
chemical __: **4** bond, pulp **5** toner
__ Chemical: **3** Dow
chemin de fer: **4** game **8** card game
exclamation ~: **5** banco
chemise: **4** slip **5** dress, shift, shirt
British ~: **4** sark
chemist: **4** Berg, Davy, Hahn, Kuhn, Todd, Urey **5** Black, Boyle, Curie, Dewar, Libby, Nobel, Soddy **6** Bunsen, Dalton, Müller, Nernst, Perkin, Perrin, Ramsay, Remsen, Solvay **7** Crookes, Hodgkin, Pasteur, Pauling, Scheele **8** Avogadro, pharmacy, Sorensen **9** Arrhenius, Berthelot, Berzelius,

Cavendish, Gay-Lussac, Lavoisier, Mendeleev, Priestley **10** pharmacist
Belgian: **6** Solvay
British: **4** Davy **5** Black, Boyle, Soddy **6** Dalton, Perkin, Ramsay **7** Crookes, Hodgkin **9** Cavendish, Priestley
Danish: **8** Sorensen
deg.: **3** BCS, Sc.B.
French: **5** Curie **6** Perrin **7** Pasteur **9** Berthelot, Gay-Lussac, Lavoisier
German: **4** Hahn, Kuhn **6** Bunsen, Müller, Nernst
in America: **10** pharmacist
Italian: **8** Avogadro
Polish: **5** Curie
Russian: **9** Mendeleev
Scottish: **4** Todd **5** Dewar
Swedish: **5** Nobel **7** Scheele **9** Arrhenius, Berzelius
vessel: **4** etna **5** flask, pipet **6** beaker, carboy **7** pipette
chemistry: **7** science **10** attraction
abbreviation: **3** mol., ppm **5** mol. wt.
class cost: **6** lab fee
room: **3** lab
starter: **3** bio **5** petro
__ chemistry: **5** laser, legal **7** colloid, organic, quantum
Chemnitz: **4** city, town
locale: **7** Germany
Chen: **4** Joan
Chenab: **5** river
feeder: **6** Jhelum
locale: **5** India **8** Pakistan
Cheney: **4** Dick, veep
predecessor: **4** Gore
Chengchow's province: **5** Honan
Chengdu: **4** city, town
locale: **5** China
Chénier, André de: **4** poet **6** French
chenille: **6** fabric **8** material
Chenin Blanc: **3** vin **4** wine **5** grape
relative: **5** Gamay, pinot, Tokay **6** Merlot **7** Catawba, Concord, Niagara **8** Cabernet, malvasia, muscatel **9** muscadine, Sauvignon, zinfandel **10** Chardonnay
Chennai: **4** city, town
locale: **5** India
Chennault: **6** Claire
Chen Ning __: **4** Yang
cheongsam: **5** dress
Cheops, son of: **6** Khafre
__ che penso: **3** Piu
__ cher: **3** mon
Cher: **5** river **6** singer **7** actress
film: Mask (1985)
Mermaids (1990)
Moonstruck (1987, AA)
Silkwood (1983)
Suspect (1987)
The Witches of Eastwick (1987)
locale: **6** France
song: After All (1989)
Bang Bang (1966)
Believe (1999)
Dark Lady (1974)
Gypsys, Tramps & Thieves (1971)
If I Could Turn Back Time (1989)
I Found Someone (1988)
Just Like Jesse James (1989)
Take Me Home (1979)
The Way of Love (1972)
You Better Sit Down Kids (1967)
spouse: Gregg Allman, Sonny Bono
Cherán: **4** city, town
locale: **6** Mexico **9** Michoacán
Cherbourg: **4** city, port, town
locale: **6** France
cherchez la __: **5** femme
Cherenkov, Pavel: **8** Nobelist **9** physicist
chéri: **2** jo **3** pet **4** baby, dear, love **5** amour, angel, cooky, cutey, cutie, deary, ducky, flame, honey, leman, lover, lovey, novio, sugar, sweet **6** bon ami, cookie, dautie, dearie, steady, sweets **7** beloved, dearest, dear one, pigsney, schatzi, squeeze, sweetie, tootsie **8** chou-chou, cutie pie, dowsabel, lovebird, macushla, paramour, precious, snookums, sugar pie, sweetums, truelove **9** boyfriend, dreamboat, inamorato, petit chou, valentine **10** heartthrob, honeybunch, mavourneen, sweetheart, sweetie pie, turtledove
Chéri author: Colette
chérie: **2** jo **3** pet **4** baby, dear, jill, love **5** amour, angel, cooky, cutey, cutie, deary, ducky, flame, honey, leman, lover, lovey, novia, sugar, sweet **6** cookie, dautie, dearie, steady, sweets **7** beloved, dearest, dear one, pigsney, schatzi, squeeze, sweetie, tootsie **8** chou-chou, cutie pie, dowsabel, dulcinea, ladylove, lovebird, macushla, paramour, precious, snookums, sugar pie, sweetums, truelove **9** bonne amie, dreamboat, inamorata, petit chou, valentine **10** girlfriend, heartthrob, honeybunch, mavourneen, sweetheart, sweetie pie, turtledove
Cherie: **7** Johnson
cherimoya: **5** fruit
hybrid: **7** atemoya
cherish: **4** like, love **5** adore, go for, prize, savor, value **6** admire, dote on, ensoul, esteem, insoul, revere **7** care for, idolize, worship **8** dote upon, enshrine, hold dear, inshrine, treasure, venerate **9** care about, reverence **10** appreciate
cherished: **3** pet **4** dear **5** sweet **6** sacred **7** beloved, darling, welcome **8** precious, valuable **9** priceless
make ~: **6** endear
one: **7** darling **10** sweetheart
Cherish (song) artist: Association, David Cassidy, Kool and the Gang, Madonna
Chernenko: **10** Konstantin
Chernobyl: **4** city
city near: **4** Kiev
locale: **3** Ukr. **7** Ukraine
Cherokee: **3** SUV **4** Jeep **5** tribe **6** Indian **7** Amerind **8** language
kin: **4** Erie **5** Huron
Cherokee __: **4** rose **5** Strip
cheroot: **5** cigar, smoke
cherries
like ~ Jubilee: **6** flambé
prepare ~: **4** stem
cherries jubilee: **7** dessert
ingredient: **8** ice cream
cherry: **3** red **4** Bing, tree, wood **5** color, drupe, fruit **7** marasca, morello, oxheart **10** maraschino
brandy: **6** kirsch
ender: **5** stone
ground ~: **9** tomatillo
leftover: **3** pit **4** stem **5** stone
picker part: **4** boom
relative: **4** pear, plum, rose, ruby, rust, sloe, wine **5** apple, brick, coral, grape, peach, poppy, rusty, sandy **6** almond, cerise, claret, damson, garnet, maroon, medlar, quince **7** apricot, carmine, crimson, fuchsia, magenta, pimento, scarlet, sultana, vermeil **8** amaranth, cardinal, dubonnet, geranium, hawthorn, oiticica, rubicund **9** carnation, cranberry, greengage, myrobalan, vermilion **10** blackthorn, strawberry
starter: **5** choke
where a ~ may go: **5** on top
cherry __: **3** pie, red **4** bomb, coal, cola, plum, soda **5** birch **6** laurel, pepper, picker, tomato
cherry-__: **3** bob **4** pick
__ cherry: **3** pin **4** Bing, bird, fire, sand, sour, wild **5** black, dwarf, heart, sweet **6** ground, laurel, winter **7** mahaleb, Surinam
Cherry: **3** Don **5** Neneh **8** Eagle-Eye
Cherry __: **3** Pie **4** Bomb, Coke
Cherry Bomb (1987 song) artist: John Cougar Mellencamp
Cherry, Cherry (1966 song) artist: Neil Diamond
Cherry, Don song: Band of Gold (1955)
Cherry Hill: **4** city, town
locale: **9** New Jersey
Cherry, Neneh
song: Buffalo Stance (1989)
Kisses on the Wind (1989)
Cherry Orchard, The: **4** play
author: Anton Chekhov
character: **4** Anya, Gaev **5** Boris, Fiers, Varya, Yasha **6** Leonid, Simeon **7** Ivanova
Cherry Pink and Apple Blossom White (1955 song) artist: Perez Prado
cherrystone: **4** clam
cherry vanilla: **8** ice cream
alternative: **5** lemon, mocha, peach **6** banana, coffee, Jamoca, toffee **7** caramel, coconut **8** cinnamon, hazelnut **9** bubblegum, chocolate, pineapple, pistachio, raspberry, rocky road, rum raisin **10** blackberry, cheesecake, Neapolitan, peppermint, strawberry
cherub: **4** Amor, baby, Eros **5** angel, child, Cupid, putto **6** moppet **8** amoretto, innocent
Valentine's Day ~: **4** Amor, Eros **5** Cupid
cherubic: **7** angelic **9** angelical
chervil: **4** herb
Cheryl: **4** Ladd, Lynn **5** Tiegs **6** Miller **9** Holdridge
Chesapeake: **3** bay **4** city, town
locale: **8** Virginia
Chesapeake and __: **4** Ohio
Chesapeake author: James A. Michener
Chesapeake Bay
bird: **4** tern
ketch: **6** bugeye
river to ~: **7** Potomac
Chesebrough-Pond's product: **4** Q-Tip
Cheshire: **6** cheese, county
city: **5** Crewe **6** Widnes
locale: **7** Britain, England
Cheshire __: **3** cat **6** cheese
Cheshire Cat expression: **4** grin
chess: **4** game **9** board game
action: **4** move **6** castle, gambit
call: **5** check
choice: **5** black, white
coup: **4** fork, mate
device: **5** timer
ender: **3** man, men **5** board
Estonian ~ master: **3** Nei
Japanese ~: **5** shogi
piece: **2** kt., QP **3** man **4** king, pawn, rook **5** queen **6** bishop, castle
queenside castle, in ~ notation: **3** OOO
chess __: **3** pie, set **5** clock
__ chess: **5** blitz, speed **7** Chinese
chess champions (world):
2000– Vladimir Kramnik (Russia)
1985–2000 Garry Kasparov (Russia)
1975–1985 Anatoly Karpov (Russia)
1972–1975 Bobby Fischer (USA)
1969–1972 Boris Spassky (Russia)
1963–1969 Tigran Petrosian (Russia)
1961–1963 Mikhail Botvinnik (Russia)
1960–1961 Mikhail Tal (Russia)
1958–1960 Mikhail Botvinnik (Russia)
1957–1958 Vasily Smyslov (Russia)
1948–1957 Mikhail Botvinnik (Russia)
1937–1946 Alexander Alekhine (Russia)
1935–1937 Max Euwe (Netherlands)
1927–1935 Alexander Alekhine (Russia)
1921–1927 José Capablanca (Cuba)
1894–1921 Emanuel Lasker (Germany)
1886–1894 William Steinitz (Bohemia)
chessman: **4** king, pawn, rook **5** piece, queen **6** bishop, castle
Chessman portrayer: **4** Alda
Chess Players, The artist: **6** Eakins
chest: **3** box **4** case **5** bosom, hutch, trunk **6** breast, bunker, bureau, coffer, cooler, locker, lowboy, thorax **7** cabinet, commode, dresser **8** moneybox **9** container, furniture, strongbox **10** chiffonier
combining form: **6** stetho-, thorac- **7** thoraci-, thoraco-
covering: **3** bib **4** vest **5** shirt
ender: **3** nut
get off one's ~: **3** say **4** tell **5** spill **6** relate, unload **7** confess, confide, recount, tell all, unbosom **8** unburden
material: **5** cedar
muscle: **3** pec
part: **4** knob **6** drawer
pounder: **3** ape **7** gorilla
rattle: **4** rale
sacred ~: **3** ark **4** cist
Spanish Main ~: **4** arca
war ~: **4** fund **6** coffer **8** treasury **9** exchequer
__ chest: **3** ice, pyx, sea, war **4** high, hope, mule, slop **5** cedar, dower, oxbow, steam **6** Armada, arming, barrel, Hadley, powder **7** blanket, tilting, wedding
__-chested: **4** deep **6** barrel
Chester: **4** town **5** Gould, Himes **6** Arthur, cheese, Morris, Nimitz **7** Carlson, Conklin
locale: **4** Penn.
chesterfield: **4** coat, sofa **5** couch
Chesterfield: **4** city, earl, lord, town
locale: **8** Missouri
__ Chester French: **6** Daniel
Chesterton, G.K.: **6** writer **7** British
friend: Belloc
Chester White: **3** hog, pig **5** swine
home: **3** pen, sty
chestnut: **3** bay, nut, red **4** roan, tale, tree **5** brown, color, horse **6** cliché, equine **7** reddish **9** platitude
horse ~: **6** conker
hull: **3** bur
old ~: **3** saw **5** adage
Polynesian ~: **4** rata
prepare ~ s: **5** roast
relative: **3** bay, dun, tan **4** bole, ecru, fawn, foxy, nude, seal **5** amber, beech, beige, camel, cocoa, hazel, khaki, mocha, sepia, tawny, umber **6** auburn, bister, bistre, bronze, coffee, copper, ginger, russet, sienna, sorrel, suntan, walnut **7** biscuit, caramel, dogwood **8** cinnamon, mahogany **9** butternut, chocolate
water ~: **5** tuber
chestnut __: **3** oak **4** clam, coal **6** bottle
__ chestnut: **5** horse, liver, water **7** Chinese, Spanish
Chestnut Hill athletes: **6** Eagles
Chestnuts roasting __ ...: **4** on an
chest of __: **5** viols **7** drawers

chest protector wearer: 3 ump 6 umpire 7 catcher
chest-thumping: 5 macho
do some ~: 4 brag 5 boast, vaunt
chesty: 5 proud 9 conceited
Chet: 5 Baker 6 Atkins 7 Huntley
cheth: 6 Hebrew, letter
predecessor: 5 zayin
successor: 3 tet 4 teth
Chetumal: 4 city, town
locale: 6 Mexico
cheval __: 5 glass 6 screen
__ cheval: 5 pas de
cheval glass: 6 mirror
Chevalier, Maurice: 5 actor
film: Can-Can (1960)
Fanny (1961)
Folies Bergère (1935)
Gigi (1958)
Love in the Afternoon (1957)
Love Me Tonight (1932)
The Love Parade (1929)
The Merry Widow (1934)
One Hour With You (1932)
The Way to Love (1933)
Chevelle: 3 car 4 auto 5 Chevy 9 Chevrolet 10 automobile
chevet: 4 apse
Cheviot: 3 ewe, ram 4 lamb 5 sheep 6 fabric 8 material
home: 3 pen 4 cote
chèvre: 6 cheese
chevret: 6 cheese
Chevrolet: 3 car 4 auto 5 Louis 10 automobile
model: 3 Geo 4 Nova, Vega 5 Astro, Cobra, Monza, Nomad, Tahoe, 'Vette 6 Belair, Blazer, Camaro, Delray, Impala, Laguna, Lumina, Malibu, Yeoman 7 Beretta, Caprice, Corsica, Corvair, Tracker, Venture 8 Biscayne, Cavalier, Chevelle, Citation, Concours, Corvette, Parkwood, Sting Ray, Suburban, Townsman 9 Avalanche, Brookwood, Celebrity, Kingswood 10 Greenbrier, Monte Carlo 11 Trailblazer
rival: 4 Ford, Olds 7 Mercury
chevron: 5 badge 8 insignia
shape: 3 vee
three ~ wearer: 3 NCO
Chevron: 3 gas 8 gasoline
rival: 4 Arco 5 Amoco, Exxon
chevrotain: 4 deer
Chevy
see Chevrolet
Chevy Blazer: 3 SUV
Chevy Chase: 4 city, town
locale: 8 Maryland
chew: 3 eat 4 gnaw 5 chomp, graze, grind, munch, taste 6 crunch, nibble 9 masticate
cattle ~: 3 cud
hard to ~: 5 tough
on: 3 eat 7 reflect 9 masticate
out: 3 rag 4 flay, lash, rail, whip 5 abuse, scold 6 berate, rebuke 7 tell off, upbraid 8 chastise, harangue 9 castigate, reprehend, reprimand 10 vituperate
over: 4 mull, muse 8 consider, ruminate 9 speculate 10 deliberate
(over): 5 think
something to ~ on: 3 gum
the fat: 3 gab, jaw, rap, yak, yap 4 chat, talk 5 prate, speak 6 gossip, jabber, parley, patter 7 blabber, blather, chatter, prattle 8 chitchat, converse, schmooze 10 yakkety-yak
the scenery: 5 emote
chew __: 3 out
__ chew: 3 dog
Chewa home: 6 Africa, Malawi, Zambia 10 Mozambique
Chewbacca: 7 Wookiee
chewer, scenery: 3 ham 6 emoter
chewing gum: 5 Extra, Orbit 7 Dentyne, Trident 8 Carefree, Chiclets, Freedent 10 Doublemint, Juicy Fruit
base: 6 chicle
like some ~ gums: 5 minty
chewing-out: 6 rebuke 8 reproval 10 upbraiding
chew the __: 3 cud, fat, rag
chewy: 5 tough 7 crunchy
candy: 4 Rolo 5 taffy, toffy 6 toffee 7 caramel
__ Chex: 3 Oat 4 Corn, Rice 5 Wheat
Cheyenne: 4 city, town 5 oater, river, tribe 6 Indian 7 Amerind 8 language
county: 7 Laramie
home: 4 tipi 5 tepee 6 teepee
locale: 3 Wyo. 7 Wyoming
show: 5 rodeo
Cheyenne (ABC western) cast: Clint Walker (Cheyenne Bodie)
Cheyenne Autumn (1964 film)
cast: Carroll Baker, Dolores Del Rio, Karl Malden, Sal Mineo, Richard Widmark
director: John Ford
Cheyenne Social Club, The (1970 film)
cast: Henry Fonda, Shirley Jones, Sue Ane Langdon, James Stewart
director: Gene Kelly
chi: 5 Greek 6 letter
follower: 3 psi
preceder: 3 phi
chi-__ test: 6 square 7 squared
__ chi: 3 tai
Chi: 7 McBride 8 Coltrane
Chi-__: 3 Rho 5 Lites
__ Chi: 5 Sigma
chia: 5 plant
Chiang: 7 Kai-shek
adversary: 3 Mao
Chianina: 3 cow 4 bull 6 bovine, cattle
Chianti: 3 red 4 vino, wine
container: 6 carafe
origin: 5 Italy
Chiapa: 4 city, town
locale: 6 Mexico
Chiapas: 5 state 7 Mexican
city: 5 Acala 6 Bochil, Tonalá 7 Arriaga, Comitan, Huixtla, Reforma, Yajalón 8 Ocosingo, Palenque 9 Cintalapa, Tapachula
Chiautempan: 4 city, town
locale: 6 Mexico 8 Tlaxcala
Chiautla: 4 city, town
locale: 6 Mexico, Puebla
Chiba: 4 city, town
locale: 5 Hondo, Japan 6 Honshu
Chibcha: 6 Indian 7 Amerind
Chibchan language: 4 Cuna
chic: 3 hip, mod, now 4 mode, posh 5 class, faddy, fancy, flair, haute, natty, nifty, ritzy, sharp, smart, swank, swell, vogue 6 bon ton, classy, dapper, dressy, flossy, modish, rakish, snappy, trendy, urbane, with it 7 à la mode, current, dashing, elegant, fashion, in vogue, popular, stylish, voguish 8 up-to-date 9 fanciness, gussied up, high-class, high-toned, in fashion, nattiness 10 dapperness, dressiness, modishness, refinement, swankiness
not ~: 3 out 5 dowdy, passé 6 frumpy
__ chic: 4 trés 7 radical
Chic: 5 Young 7 Johnson
Chicago: 4 city, port, town
airport: 5 O'Hare 6 Midway
area: 4 Loop
athletes: 8 Ramblers 10 Blue Demons
city near ~: 4 Gary 5 Elgin, Niles 6 Cicero, Joliet
county: 4 Cook
Cub: 4 NLer
exchange, for short: 4 Merc
Fire starter: 3 cow
hrs.: 3 CDT, CST
like ~: 5 windy
Lincoln Park: 3 zoo
lines: 3 Els
locale: 3 Ill. 8 Illinois
newspaper: 4 Trib 7 Tribune 8 Sun-Times
opera company: 5 Lyric
planetarium: 5 Adler
pro team: 3 Sox 4 Cubs 5 Bears, Bulls 8 White Sox 10 Blackhawks
school: 6 DePaul, Loyola
superstation: 3 WGN
TV show: 5 Oprah
Chicago (2002 film)
cast: Richard Gere, Queen Latifah, Renée Zellweger, Catherine Zeta-Jones
character: 4 Hart 5 Roxie, Velma
composer: 3 Ebb 6 Kander
director: Rob Marshall
Chicago (rock group)
member: Cetera, Kath, Lamm, Loughnane, Pankow, Parazaider, Seraphine
song: 25 or 6 to 4 (1970)
Baby, What a Big Surprise (1977)
Beginnings (1971)
Call on Me (1974)
Does Anybody Really Know What Time It Is? (1970)
Feelin' Stronger Every Day (1973)
Hard Habit to Break (1984)
Hard to Say I'm Sorry (1982)
I Don't Wanna Live Without Your Love (1988)
If You Leave Me Now (1976)
Just You 'N' Me (1973)
Look Away (1988)
Make Me Smile (1970)
Old Days (1975)
Saturday in the Park (1972)
Searchin' So Long (1974)
What Kind of Man Would I Be? (1989)
Will You Still Love Me? (1986)
Wishing You Were Here (1974)
You're Not Alone (1989)
You're the Inspiration (1984)
Chicago __: 4 Fire, Hope 5 Poems, steak, style 6 School, window
Chicago __ of Trade: 5 Board
Chicago __ Sox: 5 White
__ Chicago: 5 In Old
Chicago Hope (CBS drama)
cast: Adam Arkin (Dr. Aaron Shutt)
Peter Berg (Dr. Billy Kronk)
Hector Elizondo (Dr. Phillip Watters)
Mark Harmon (Dr. Jack McNeil)
Roxanne Hart (Camille Shutt)
Christine Lahti (Dr. Kathryn Austin)
Mandy Patinkin (Dr. Jeffery Geiger)
extra: 2 RN 3 EMT
__ Chicago, IN: 4 East
Chicago Poems author: Carl Sandburg
Chicana: 6 Latina
chicane: 3 con 4 dupe, fool, hoax, ruse, wile 5 fraud 9 deception
chicanery: 3 con 4 ploy, ruse, wile 5 dodge, feint, fraud, guile, wiles 6 deceit, dupery 7 knavery, quibble 8 artifice, intrigue, jugglery, trickery 9 casuistry, deception, dirty work, duplicity, fourberie, sophistry, stratagem 10 dishonesty, hanky-panky, hocus-pocus, subterfuge
Chicano neighborhood: 6 barrio
chicha: 4 beer
Chichén Itzá native: 4 Maya 5 Mayan
Chichester Psalms composer: 9 Bernstein
chichi: 2 in 3 hip, mod 4 arty, tony 5 artsy, fancy, haute, ritzy, showy, swank, toney 6 dapper, frilly, modish, ornate, swanky, trendy 7 à la mode, current, elegant, in style, popular, stylish, voguish 8 affected, mannered 9 gussied up, in fashion 10 all the rage
__ chi ch'uan: 3 tai
chick: 4 bird 9 fledgling, hatchling
ender: 3 pea 4 weed
future ~: 3 egg
group: 5 brood
home: 4 coop, farm, nest 8 henhouse
like a ~: 5 downy, fuzzy
mother: 3 hen
starter: 3 dab
talk: 4 peep
Chick: 4 Webb 5 Corea, Hafey, Hearn
Chick-__: 5 a-Boom
chickadee: 4 bird
Chickadee, W.C. Fields': 3 Mae
Chickamauga: 6 battle
locale: 7 Georgia
chickaree: 6 animal, mammal, rodent 8 squirrel
morsel: 5 acorn
relative: 3 rat 4 cavy, degu, jird, paca, vole 5 coypu, gundi, mouse, xerus 6 agouti, beaver, gerbil, gopher, jerboa, marmot, murine 7 hamster, lemming, muskrat, visacha 8 chipmunk, cricetid, dormouse, squirrel, tuco-tuco 9 groundhog, guinea pig, porcupine, woodchuck 10 chinchilla, prairie dog
Chickasaw: 5 tribe 6 Indian 7 Amerind
chicken: 4 bird, cock, fowl, meat, wimp 5 biddy, biped, capon, sissy, timid 6 afraid, Ancona, bantam, Brahma, coward, craven, gun-shy, Houdan, pullet, scared, Sussex, trepid, yellow 7 alarmed, anxious, Cornish, dastard, daunted, Dorking, fearful, Leghorn, nervous, panicky, poultry, quitter, rooster, spooked, wimpish 8 Araucana, cowardly, fearsome, hesitant, Langshan, poltroon, recreant, Shanghai, timorous, weakling 9 Dominique, fraidy cat, jellyfish, Orpington, petrified, terrified, Wyandotte 10 frightened, scaredy-cat
and rice: 4 soup
appetizer: 8 drumette
Asian ~: 6 cochin
clean a ~: 5 dress
cooking ~: 5 capon, frier, fryer 7 roaster
eat like a ~: 4 peck
ender: 3 pox
feed: 4 mash 6 change 8 pittance
female: 3 hen
follower: 3 pox
group: 6 clutch
home: 4 coop, farm 8 henhouse
lack: 5 nerve 7 courage
little ~: 6 bantam
male: 7 rooster
noodle: 4 soup
out: 4 quit 5 panic, quail 7 abandon 9 run scared
(out): 4 wimp
part: 3 leg 4 neck, wing 5 thigh 6 breast
salad ingredient: 4 mayo
seat: 5 roost
spring ~: 5 youth
to a chicken hawk: 4 prey
wire: 4 mesh
young: 6 pullet
chicken __: 3 out, pox, run 4 coop, feed, hawk, Kiev, roll, soup, wire 5 adder, liver, snake 6 breast, ladder, switch, turtle 7 cholera, colonel, lobster
chicken __ king: 3 à la
chicken __ soup: 6 noodle

chicken-__: 3 fry 5 or-egg 7 hearted, livered
chicken-__ steak: 5 fried
__ chicken: 4 city, mock 5 Digby 6 spring 7 prairie
Chicken __: 6 Little
Chicken __ Sea: 5 of the
chicken-and-__: 3 egg
__-chicken circuit: 6 rubber
chicken-hearted: 4 weak 5 timid 6 craven 8 cowardly
chicken in __ pot: 5 every
Chicken of the Sea: 4 tuna
alternative: 8 Star Kist 9 Bumble Bee
chickenpox: 9 varicella
cause: 5 virus
symptom: 4 itch 5 fever
chickpea: 4 gram 6 legume, veggie 9 vegetable
dip: 6 hommos, hummus
__ Chicks: 5 Dixie
chicle
product: 3 gum
source: 5 latex
Chiclets: 3 gum 10 chewing gum
alternative: 5 Extra, Orbit 7 Dentyne, Trident 8 Carefree, Freedent 10 Doublemint, Juicy Fruit
Chico: 4 city, Marx, town
brother: 5 Gummo, Harpo, Zeppo 7 Groucho
locale: 10 California
Chico and the Man (NBC sitcom)
cast: Jack Albertson (Ed Brown)
Scatman Crothers (Louie)
Freddie Prinze (Chico Rodriguez)
setting: 6 East L.A.
Chicoloapan: 4 city, town
locale: 6 Mexico
Chicopee: 4 city, town
locale: 4 Mass.
chicory: 4 herb
relative: 6 endive
chicory relative: 6 endive
Chicoutimi: 4 city, town
locale: 6 Canada, Québec
chide: 3 nag, rag 4 rate 5 blame, scold 6 berate, rebuff, rebuke 7 censure, condemn, lecture, reprove, tell off, upbraid 8 admonish, reproach 9 castigate, criticize, lash out at, reprehend, reprimand
chider: 5 scold, shrew 6 parent 9 henpecker, termagant
chief: 3 key, ldr., top 4 arch, boss, head, jefe, king, main, star 5 first, grand, major, nawab, prime, ruler 6 bigwig, gerent, honcho, leader, master, ruling, sachem, staple, top cat, utmost 7 captain, central, crucial, headman, highest, leading, manager, officer, premier, primary, special, supreme, viceroy 8 big wheel, cardinal, champion, deciding, director, dominant, foremost, governor, headmost, higher-up, kingfish, overseer, superior, top brass 9 big cheese, commander, essential, executive, number one, organizer, paramount, president, principal, prominent, sovereign, uppermost 10 overriding, preeminent, supervisor
crew: 5 staff 9 personnel
executive: 4 pres., prez 5 prexy 8 director 9 president
prefix: 4 arch-
suffix: 4 -arch
chief __: 4 mate 7 justice
chief __ officer: 5 petty 7 warrant
__ chief: 3 den 4 crew, fire 7 talking
Chief: 6 Bender 7 gridder 10 footballer
rival: 3 Jet, Ram 4 Bear, Bill, Colt, Lion 5 Brown, Eagle, Giant, Niner, Raven, Saint, Texan, Titan 6 Bengal, Bronco, Cowboy, Falcon, Jaguar, Packer, Raider, Viking 7 Charger, Dolphin, Panther, Patriot, Redskin, Seahawk, Steeler 8 Cardinal 9 Buccaneer
Chief __ George: 3 Dan
chief executive __: 7 officer
chiefly: 6 mainly, mostly 7 at large, largely 8 above all 9 generally, primarily 10 especially
chief of __: 5 staff, state
Chief of __ Operations: 5 Naval
Chiefs: 4 team 6 eleven
home: 10 Kansas City
org.: 3 AFC, NFL
sport: 8 football
__ Chiefs of Staff: 5 Joint
chieftain: 4 amir, emir, head 5 ameer, emeer, ruler 6 gerent, leader, master 8 superior
Chieftain: 3 car 4 auto 7 Pontiac
chiffchaff: 4 bird
chiffon: 3 pie 5 filmy, gauze, ninon, sheer, voile 6 fabric, flimsy 10 diaphanous
like ~: 5 gauzy, sheer 6 clingy
chiffonier: 5 chest 6 bureau 7 dresser 8 wardrobe
Chiffons
song: He's So Fine (1963)
One Fine Day (1963)
Sweet Talkin' Guy (1966)
chigetai: 6 animal, equine, mammal
relative: 3 ass 5 burro, horse, kiang, zebra 6 donkey, onager, quagga 7 jackass
chigger: 3 bug 6 insect
chignon: 3 bun 4 coif, knot 6 hairdo 7 upsweep 8 coiffure
chigoe: 3 bug 4 flea 6 insect
genus: 5 tunga
Chihuahua: 3 dog 4 city, town 5 canid, pooch, state 6 canine 7 Mexican
city: 6 Juárez, Madera, Meoqui 7 Anáhuac, Camargo, Hidalgo, Jiménez, Ojinaga 8 Delicias, Saucillo 10 Cuauhtémoc, Juan Aldama
like ~: 4 tiny 5 small
toon: 3 Ren
see also Spanish
Chihuahuan: 6 desert
locale: 6 Mexico
Chilac: 4 city, town
locale: 6 Mexico, Puebla
Chilapa: 4 city, town
locale: 6 Mexico 8 Guerrero
Chilcat: 6 Indian 7 Amerind
child: 3 boy, imp, kid, lad, son, tad, tot 4 babe, baby, brat, cion, girl, mite, teen, tike, tyke, ward 5 bairn, human, kiddy, minor, scion, youth 6 cherub, infant, kiddie, laddie, moppet, nipper, person, squirt 7 bambino, kinsman, neonate, newborn, preteen, sapling, toddler 8 daughter, half-pint, juvenile, nonvoter, small fry, teenager 9 offspring, stripling, youngster 10 adolescent, descendant, individual
adopted ~: 4 ward
annoying ~: 3 imp 4 brat
bearer: 6 mother
chant: 5 me too
combining form: 3 ped- 4 paed-, paid-, pedo- 5 paedo-, paido-, tecno-
cry: 3 mom 4 mama 5 mamma, mommy
ender: 3 bed, ish 4 care, like 5 birth, proof 7 bearing
female ~: 4 girl 8 daughter
flower ~: 5 hippy 6 hippie 8 bohemian, longhair
forsaken ~: 4 waif 6 orphan 9 foundling
foster ~: 7 adoptee
game: 3 tag, war 5 jacks, potsy 6 go fish 7 old maid 9 hopscotch
getaway: 4 camp
inner ~: 6 psyche
in Spanish: 4 niña, niño
male ~: 3 boy, son
marker: 6 crayon
not a ~: 5 adult, grown, of age
play a ~ game: 4 hide
protest: 5 not me
question: 3 why
reading program: 3 RIF
ride: 4 pony 5 trike 7 scooter 8 tricycle
sibling's ~: 5 niece 6 nephew
song finish: 3 XYZ
song starter: 3 ABC
sponsored ~: 6 godson 11 goddaughter
starter: 3 god 4 moon, step 5 brain, grand 6 school
taboo: 4 no-no
toy: 3 top 4 ball 5 Legos 6 blocks
treat like a ~: 9 patronize
warning: 6 behave, be nice
watch a ~: 7 baby-sit
with ~: 6 gravid 8 enceinte, pregnant 9 expecting
child __: 4 wife 5 bride, labor 7 support, welfare
child-__: 4 care 5 proof
__ child: 3 lap 4 with 5 brain, inner 6 flower, foster, poster, wonder
__-child: 3 man
Child: 4 Jane 5 Julia, Lydia
__ Child: 3 O-o-h 4 Love
childbirth: 8 delivery
combining form: 4 toco-, toko-
method: 6 Lamaze 7 natural
Childe: 6 Hassam
Childe Harold's Pilgrimage author: Byron
childhood: 4 teen 5 youth 6 cradle 7 infancy, puberty 8 minority 9 juniority 10 immaturity, juvenility, schooldays
malady: 5 colic, croup, mumps 6 otitis 7 measles 10 chickenpox
second ~: 6 dotage
__ childhood: 6 second
Childhood's End author: Clarke
__ Child in the City: 3 Hot
Child Is Born, A (1940 film)
cast: Geraldine Fitzgerald, Jeffrey Lynn
director: Lloyd Bacon
childish: 5 silly, young 6 boyish, infant, jejune, simple, unwise 7 kiddish, peevish, puerile 8 immature, juvenile, youthful 9 frivolous, infantile
demand: 5 gimme, I want
retort: 4 am so, is so 5 am too, are so
Child Is Waiting, A (1963 film)
cast: Judy Garland, Burt Lancaster, Gena Rowlands
director: John Cassavetes
Child, Julia: 4 chef
cuisine: 6 French
childlike: 4 naif 5 naive, young 6 simple, tender 7 artless, kiddish, natural, puerile 8 immature, innocent, juvenile, lamblike, trustful, trusting, unartful, youthful 9 credulous, guileless, ingenuous, primitive, unfeigned 10 unaffected
Child, Lydia: 6 author, writer
Child of Fire author: 5 O'Dell
Child of the Morning author: Luce
children: 4 kids 5 brood, heirs, issue 7 kinfolk, progeny 8 kinfolks, kinsfolk 9 offspring, posterity
combining form: 5 proli-
of ~: 6 filial
starter: 3 god 4 moon, step 6 school
what ~ should be: 4 seen
__ Children: 4 Only 5 All My, Dream 6 Little, Today's
Children of a Lesser God (1986 film)
cast: William Hurt, Piper Laurie, Marlee Matlin
character: 4 Edna, Orin 5 Lydia, Sarah
director: Randa Haines
Children of Paradise director: 5 Carné
Children of Sanchez author: Oscar Lewis
Children of the Albatross author: 3 Nin
Children of the Night (1990 song)
artist: Richard Marx
Children of the Poor, The author: 4 Riis
children's __: 4 menu
Children's __: 3 Day 7 Crusade
Children's Hour, The
author: Henry Wadsworth Longfellow, Lillian Hellman
character: 4 Lois 6 Amelia 7 Rosalie
Children's Marching Song, The (1959 song) artist: Mitch Miller
Childress, Alice: 6 author, writer
Childress, Alvin role: 4 Amos
Childs: 7 Lucinda, Marquis
Child's Christmas in Wales, A poet: 6 Thomas
Child's Garden of Verses, A author: Robert Louis Stevenson
child's play: 4 easy, snap 5 cinch, cushy 6 facile, picnic, simple 7 no sweat 8 duck soup, painless, pushover 10 effortless, elementary, unexacting
Child's play!: 5 a snap
Child's Play (1988 film)
cast: Catherine Hicks, Chris Sarandon, Alex Vincent
__ Child, The: 4 Late
chile __: 7 relleno
chile __ carne: 3 con
Chile: 6 nation 7 country
airline: 3 LAN
capital: 8 Santiago
city: 5 Arica, Talca 6 Calama, Curicó, Osorno, Temuco 7 Chillán, Iquique, Quilpué 8 Coquimbo, La Serena, Rancagua, Santiago, Valdivia 10 Concepción, Puente Alto, Talcahuano, Valparaíso, Viña del Mar
desert: 7 Atacama
export: 5 niter
from ~: 6 Andean
fruit: 5 maqui
gulf: 5 Penas
Indian: 10 Araucanian
island: 6 Easter
lake: 4 Laja
language: 7 Spanish
money: 4 peso 6 condor, escudo
mountain: 4 Toro 5 Pular 6 Bonete, Juncal 7 San Juan 8 El Muerto, Tortolas 9 Incahuasi, Marmolejo, Tupungato 10 Mercedario, Parinacota, Tres Cruces
neighbor: 4 Peru 7 Bolivia 9 Argentina
Nobelist in Literature: 6 Neruda 7 Mistral
org.: 3 OAS
pianist: 5 Arrau
poet: 5 Parra 6 Neruda 7 Mistral
port: 5 Arica 10 Valparaiso
range: 5 Andes
river: 6 Biobío
shrub: 5 maqui
tree: 5 boldo, maqui 6 alerce, mayten
volcano: 6 Láscar
writer: 5 Rojas 6 Bombal, Donoso 7 Allende, Barrios, Dorfman, Edwards 9 Blest Gana
Chilean: 5 Latin
chile con __: 5 carne

Chiles: 4 Lois 6 Lawton
chili: 6 pepper 9 condiment
bean: 5 pinto 6 kidney
dip: 5 salsa
ender: 6 burger
ingredient: 4 bean, meat 5 carne 6 onions
pepper: 3 aji 5 spice
powder herb: 5 cumin
sauce: 5 salsa 6 relish 9 condiment
server: 5 ladle
chili ___: 3 dog, oil 4 bean 5 sauce, verde 6 pepper, powder
chili ___ carne: 3 con
___ chili: 7 five-way
Chili: 5 Davis
Chi-Lites
song: Have You Seen Her (1971) Oh Girl (1972)
Chilkat: 6 Indian 7 Amerind
Chilkoot Pass locale: 6 Alaska
chill: 3 ice, icy, nip, raw 4 ague, bite, cold, cool 5 alarm, deter, gelid, nippy, polar, stony 6 arctic, biting, dampen, dismay, freeze, frigid, frosty, frozen, murder, slight, stoney, wintry 7 glacial, horrify, hostile, ice-cold, iciness, numbing, petrify, rawness, shivery, stiffen, terrify, unnerve, wintery 8 coldness, cool down, coolness, freezing, frighten, gelidity 9 aloofness, crispness, frigidity 10 discourage, intimidate, unfriendly
again: 5 reice
out: 5 relax 6 cool it
put the ~ on: 4 snub
chill ___: 5 bumps 6 factor
Chill: 5 Wills
Chillán: 4 city, town
locale: 5 Chile
chilled: 4 cold, cool 5 on ice, stiff 6 frappé, frigid, frosty, frozen 8 freezing
chiller-___: 6 diller
___ chill factor: 4 wind
Chillicothe: 4 city, town
locale: 4 Ohio
chilling: 3 icy 4 eery 5 eerie, scary 9 frightful, harrowing
out: 6 at rest
Chilliwack: 4 city, town
locale: 6 Canada
chills and fever: 4 ague
___ Chill, The: 3 Big
Chillum: 4 city, town
locale: 8 Maryland
chilly: 3 icy, raw 4 cold, cool, dank, mean 5 algid, aloof, brisk, crisp, fresh, gelid, nasty, nippy, onery, polar, stony, surly 6 arctic, biting, drafty, frigid, frosty, frozen, ornery, remote, stoney, wintry 7 glacial, hateful, hostile, numbing, shivery, wintery 8 contrary, freezing, hibernal, inimical, lukewarm, spiteful 9 bellicose, malicious, withdrawn 10 malevolent, pugnacious, unfriendly
comment: 3 brr
in a ~ fashion: 5 icily
Chilly Scenes of Winter author: Ann Beattie
Chilpancingo: 4 city, town
locale: 6 Mexico 8 Guerrero
chimaera: 4 fish
Chimalhuacán: 4 city, town
locale: 6 Mexico
Chimborazo: 4 peak 5 mount 8 mountain
locale: 5 Andes 7 Ecuador
chime: 4 bell, bong, brim, gong, peal, ring, toll, tone 5 agree, clang 6 tinkle 8 ding-dong, doorbell 9 harmonize
in: 4 talk 5 agree, state, utter 6 jump in, meddle 8 throw out 9 interrupt
(in): 4 join
with: 6 belong
chimera: 5 dream, fancy 6 fantom 7 fantasy, figment, monster, phantom 8 delusion, illusion 9 pipe dream
Chimera author: John Barth
chimere: 4 robe
chimerical: 5 ideal 6 dreamy, irreal, unreal 7 fatuous 8 delusive, fanciful, illusive, illusory, quixotic 9 fantastic, imaginary 10 fictitious, groundless, quixotical
chimes: 7 bonnang 8 carillon 10 instrument, percussion
like some ~: 6 hourly
___ chimes: 4 wind
Chimes at Midnight (1967 film)
cast: Jeanne Moreau, Margaret Rutherford, Orson Welles
director: Orson Welles
chimney: 3 lum 4 flue, vent 5 stack
clean a ~: 5 sweep
coating: 4 soot
emission: 5 plume
like a ~: 5 sooty
nester: 3 daw 5 stork
part: 4 flue 6 ashpit
shelf: 3 hob
chimney ___: 3 cap, pot 4 rock 5 piece, place, sweep, swift, wheel 6 breast, corner 7 swallow, sweeper
chimp: 3 ape 5 biped, Bonzo, jocko 6 animal, mammal 7 Cheetah, primate
food: 6 banana
home: 3 zoo 6 Africa
like a ~: 5 apish
little ~: 6 apelet
NASA ~: 4 Enos
relative: 4 saki, titi 5 drill, jocko, lemur, loris, magot, orang, potto, shrew 6 aye-aye, baboon, Bandar, galago, gelada, gibbon, grivet, guenon, howler, langur, macaco, monkey, rhesus, uakari, vervet 7 colobus, gorilla, guereza, hoolock, macaque, sapajou, siamang, tamarin, tarsier 8 bush baby, capuchin, mandrill, mangabey, marmoset, talapoin 9 orangutan 10 Barbary ape, orangutang
chimta: 10 percussion, tambourine
origin: 5 India
chin: 3 gab, jaw, rap, yak 4 chat 5 utter 6 gossip, yammer 10 yackety-yak
combining form: 5 genio-, mento-
feature: 5 cleft 6 dimple, goatee
it's tucked under the ~: 5 viola 6 violin
smoother: 5 razor
chin ___: 4 rest 5 music, strap 6 cactus
ch'in: 6 string, zither
origin: 5 China
Chin: 7 Tiffany
china: 4 bone, dish 5 Lenox, Spode 6 dishes, Mikasa, Sèvres 7 Dresden, Limoges 8 ceramics, clayware, crockery, Wedgwood 9 porcelain, Rosenthal, tableware 10 dinnerware
bull in a ~ shop: 3 oaf 5 klutz
buy: 3 set
ender: 4 ware 5 berry
flaw: 5 crack
material: 4 clay
piece: 3 cup 4 dish 5 plate
china ___: 4 bark, blue, clay 6 closet 7 cabinet
___ china: 4 bone 5 set of, Spode, stone 7 Dresden, Nanking
China: 3 sea 6 Cathay, nation 7 country
ancient capital: 4 Sian, Xian 6 Singan
ancient ruler: 4 Wang
art material: 4 jade
association: 4 tong
attraction: 4 wall 9 Great Wall
bay: 8 Hangchow, Hangzhou, Jiaozhou, Kiaochow
benevolent spirit: 5 hsien
boat: 4 junk 6 sampan
book of divination: 6 I Ching
border river: 3 Ili 4 Amur, Yalu
bovine: 5 takin 6 Dulong 7 Yanbian
Buddhism of ~: 8 Mahayana
capital: 6 Peking 7 Beijing
cellist: 2 Ma 6 Yo-Yo Ma
cinnamon: 6 cassia
city: 4 Sian, Wuhu, Wuxi, Xian, Zibo 5 Jilin, Jinan, Tsuni, Tzepo, Tzupo, Wuhan, Wuhsi, Wusih, Yanan, Yenan 6 Anshan, Bengbu, Dairen, Dalian, Datong, Fushun, Harbin, Peking, Singan 7 Beijing, Chengdu, Lanzhou, Nanjing, Qingdao, Tianjin 8 Changsha, Hangzhou, Peiching, Shanghai, Shenyang, Tientsin 9 Changchun, Chongqing, Guangzhou, Zhengzhou
combining form: 4 Sino- 6 Sinico-
council: 4 yuan
date: 6 jujube
desert: 4 Gobi
Disney film set in ~: 5 Mulan
dog: 4 chow, peke 8 chow chow 9 Pekingese
dynasty: 3 chi, Han, Jin, Qin, Wei, Xia, Yin 4 Chan, Chen, Chin, Chou, Hsia, Ming, Tang, Tsin, Yuan 5 Liang, Shang
emperor: 4 P'u Yi, Wuti 6 Kang Xi
explorer: 4 Polo
fabric: 4 silk
farming area: 5 paddy
feminine principle: 3 yin
from ~: 5 Asian
fruit: 6 loquat
game: 5 salta 6 fan-tan 8 mah-jongg
gelatin: 4 agar 8 agar-agar
goddess: 5 Nukua
gooseberry: 4 kiwi
gulf: 5 Bohai, Pohai 8 Liaodong, Liaotung
idol: 4 joss
island off: 4 Amoy 5 Matsu 6 Quemoy, Taiwan 7 Formosa
lake: 5 Tai Hu 7 Koko Nor 9 Qinghai Hu
language: 4 Miao, Shan 5 Hmong, Kuoyu, Uigur 6 Hsiang, Kamtai, Manchu, Uighur 7 Chinese 8 Mandarin 9 Cantonese
leader: 3 Mao 4 Chou, Deng
locale: 4 Asia 6 Orient
Mahayana school in ~: 4 Chan
mammal: 5 panda
martial art: 5 wushu
masculine principle: 4 yang
measure: 4 tsun
money: 3 fen 4 tael, yuan 5 sycee
mountain: 6 Kungur, Kunlun 7 Nan Ling 8 Tian Shan, Tien Shan 9 Broad Peak 10 Amne Machin, Gasherbrum, Minya Konka, Muztagh Ata
mountain people of ~: 5 Hmong
mountain range: 5 Altai 6 Kunlun 7 Kuenlun
nanny: 3 ama 4 amah
neighbor: 4 Laos 5 Burma, India, Macao, Macau, Nepal, Tibet 6 Bhutan, Russia, Thibet, Xizang 7 Sitsang, Vietnam 8 Hong Kong, Mongolia, Pakistan 10 Kazakhstan, Kyrgyzstan, North Korea, Tajikistan
nut: 6 lichee, litchi 7 leechee
pagoda: 3 taa
parade feature: 6 dragon
path: 3 Tao
people: 2 Yi 4 Lolo, Miao 5 Hmong
philosopher: 4 Mo Ti 6 Lao-tzu
poet: 4 Li Po, Tufu 7 Wang Wei
porcelain: 4 Ming
port: 4 Amoy, Dagu, Wuhu 5 Macao, Macau 6 Fuzhou, Tianji, Weihai 7 Foochow, Yingkou 8 Shanghai, Tientsin
province: 5 Gansu, Henan, Honan, Hunan, Kansu 6 Fujian
rebel: 5 Boxer
river: 3 Han, Hsi 4 Liao, Yalu, Yuan, Yuen 5 Siang, Tarim
sea: 6 Yellow
shrub: 6 nardin, tobira 7 cumquat, kumquat, mahuang, nandina
sleeping platform: 4 kang
tea: 3 cha 5 bohea, congo 6 congou
tree: 5 yulan 6 gingko, ginkgo, lichee, litchi, longan, loquat, lungan 7 leechee 8 mandarin
vegetable: 3 udo
warehouse: 4 hong 6 godown
weight: 5 catty, Liang, picul
writer: 6 Lao She, Lao-tzu, Pa Chin
zodiac animal: 2 ox 3 dog, rat 4 boar 5 horse, sheep, snake, tiger 6 dragon, monkey, rabbit 7 rooster
China ___: 3 oil, Sea 4 Gate, Girl, rose, Seas, silk, tree 5 aster, Beach
___ China: 3 Red 6 Poland
___-China: 4 Indo 6 Cochin
China Beach (ABC drama)
cast: Dana Delany (Colleen McMurphy) K.C. Koloski (Marg Helgenberger)
extra: 2 RN 5 nurse
China Clipper airline: 5 Pan-Am
China Gate (1957 film)
cast: Gene Barry, Nat King Cole, Angie Dickinson
China Girl (1983 song) artist: Bowie
___ China Sea: 4 East 5 South
China Seas (1935 film)
cast: Wallace Beery, Clark Gable, Jean Harlow
director: Tay Garnett
China Sky actor: 3 Ahn
China Syndrome, The (1979 film)
cast: Michael Douglas, Jane Fonda, Jack Lemmon
director: James Bridges
Chinatown (1974 film)
cast: Faye Dunaway, John Huston, Jack Nicholson
director: Roman Polanski
chinch: 3 bug 6 bedbug, insect
chinchilla: 3 fur 6 animal, mammal, rodent
habitat: 5 Andes
relative: 3 rat 4 cavy, degu, jird, paca, vole 5 coypu, gundi, mouse, xerus 6 agouti, beaver, gerbil, gopher, jerboa, marmot, murine 7 hamster, lemming, muskrat, visacha 8 chipmunk, cricetid, dormouse, squirrel, tuco-tuco 9 chickaree, groundhog, guinea pig, porcupine, woodchuck 10 prairie dog
Chincoteague ___: 3 Bay 4 pony
Chindwin: 5 river
locale: 7 Myanmar
chine: 5 ridge, spine 8 backbone
Chinese: 5 Asian 8 language
food: 4 pu pu 6 lo mein, mei fun, wonton 7 chow fun, egg roll, pea pods 8 bean curd, chop suey, chow mein, dumpling, snow peas, spare rib 9 fried rice, roast pork 10 egg foo yung, moo shu pork, Peking duck, spring roll
see also China
Chinese ___: 3 ink, lug, red, tag, wax 4 date, Wall 5 anise, boxes, chess, white 6 banana, celery, Empire, houses, jujube, puzzle, radish

7 cabbage, catfish, gelatin, juniper, lacquer, lantern, mustard, parsley, Shar-Pei
Chinese checkers: **4** game
Chinese Connection, The (1972 film)
  cast: Bruce Lee
Chinese Crested: **3** dog **5** canid **6** canine
Chinese Nightingale, The author: Vachel Lindsay
Chinese Parrot, The hero: **4** Chan
Chinese restaurant
  additive: **3** MSG
  condiment: **7** mustard **8** soy sauce **9** duck sauce
  course: **4** pupu **6** dim sum, lo mein, mei fun, wonton **7** chow fun, egg roll, pea pods **8** bean curd, chop suey, chow mein, dumpling, snow peas, spare rib **9** fried rice, roast pork, spare ribs **10** egg foo yung, moo shu pork, Peking duck, spring roll, wonton soup
  drink: **3** tea **6** hot tea
  freebie: **3** tea **4** rice
  menu general: **3** Tso
  menu word: **3** hot **4** sour **5** spicy, sweet
  menu words: **5** no MSG
  pan: **3** wok
  soup ingredient: **4** nest **6** wonton
  style: **5** Hunan **8** Szechuan **9** Cantonese
chinfest: **6** confab, powwow
___ Ching: **5** Tao Te
chink: **4** leak, rift **5** cleft, crack, split **6** cranny, tinkle **7** fissure, opening
  in one's armor: **8** weakness
chino: **5** khaki, twill **6** fabric **8** material
Chino: **4** city, town
  locale: **10** California
Chino Hills: **4** town
chinook: **4** tyee, wind **6** salmon
Chinook: **5** tribe **6** Indian **7** Amerind **8** language
chinos: **5** jeans, pants **8** trousers
chinquapin: **3** nut **4** tree
chintz: **6** fabric **8** material
___ chintz: **5** India
chintzy: **4** loud **5** cheap, tacky **6** low-end, shabby, skimpy, stingy, tawdry **8** schlocky, ungiving
  one: **5** miser
chin-up: **8** exercise
  beneficiary: **3** arm **6** biceps
chionophobe fear: **4** snow
chip: **3** cut **4** clip, lump, nick, part **5** break, crack, flake, notch, piece, scrap, shard, sherd, slice **6** chisel, damage, sliver **7** crumble, shaving, whittle **8** fragment, splinter
  accompaniment: **3** dip
  away at: **5** erode
  bargaining ~: **8** leverage
  Brit's potato ~: **5** crisp
  dipping ~: **5** nacho
  erasable memory ~: **5** EPROM
  feature: **5** ridge
  in: **3** add, pay **4** ante **6** ante up, assist, donate, pay out, pony up **9** subscribe, volunteer **10** contribute
  ingredient: **4** corn, salt **6** chives, potato
  off the old block: **3** lad, son **4** cion **5** image, scion **7** replica **9** offspring
  PC ~ maker: **5** Intel
  prefix: **5** micro
  starter ~: **4** ante
  stone ~: **5** galet, spall **6** gallet, garret
  topping: **3** dip **5** salsa **9** sour cream
  toss in a ~: **3** bet **5** wager
  with a ~ on one's shoulder: **5** angry, upset **6** bitter, peeved
chip ___: **3** log **4** 'n dip, shot **7** carving
chip ___ the old block: **3** off
___ chip: **3** log **4** blue, corn **5** white **6** hybrid, potato
Chip ___: **5** 'n' Dale
chip and ___: **3** dip
chipmunk: **6** animal, mammal, rodent
  cartoon ~: **4** Chip, Dale **5** Alvin, Simon **8** Theodore
  cheek: **5** pouch
  like a ~: **5** furry
  relative: **3** rat **4** cavy, degu, jird, paca, vole **5** coypu, gundi, mouse, xerus **6** agouti, beaver, gerbil, gopher, jerboa, marmot, murine **7** hamster, lemming, muskrat, visacha **8** cricetid, dormouse, squirrel, tuco-tuco **9** chickaree, groundhog, guinea pig, porcupine, woodchuck **10** chinchilla, prairie dog
  snack: **5** acorn
Chipmunk Song, The (1958 song)
  artist: David Seville
chip 'n ___: **3** dip
Chip partner: **4** Dale
chipped ___: **4** beef
Chippendale: **6** Thomas
chipper: **3** gay **4** pert, spry, tidy, well **5** fresh, happy, jolly, light, merry, perky **6** cheery, genial, jovial, lively **7** dashing, healthy **8** cheerful, mirthful **9** ebullient, exuberant, lightsome, sprightly
Chippewa: **5** tribe **6** Indian **7** Amerind
chips: **4** nosh **5** dough, money, snack
  exchange ~: **6** cash in, redeem
  have ~: **3** eat **4** nosh **5** munch, snack
  in the ~: **4** rich **7** wealthy
  like ~: **5** salty **6** crispy
  make ~: **3** fry
  one in the ~: **6** fat cat
  partner: **4** fish
___ chips: **4** corn, soap **5** poker **6** potato
ChiPs (NBC drama)
  cast: Erik Estrada (Frank 'Ponch' Poncherello)
    Randi Oakes (Bonnie Clark)
    Larry Wilcox (Jon Baker)
  setting: **10** California, Los Angeles
Chips Ahoy!: **6** cookie
  alternative: **4** Oreo **7** Droxies **10** Fig Newtons, Lorna Doone
chip-shot destination: **5** green
Chips, Mr.
  portrayer: **5** Donat **6** O'Toole
  what ~ taught: **5** Latin
Chiquita product: **6** banana
Chiquitita (1979 song) artist: ABBA
Chirac: **7** Jacques
  see also French
Chiricahua: **5** tribe **6** Indian **7** Amerind
chiro: **4** fish
chirography: **7** writing
chiromancer: **4** seer
Chiron: **7** centaur **8** asteroid
  daughter of ~: **4** Thea **8** Ocyrrhoe
  father of ~: **6** Cronos, Cronus
chiropractor concern: **4** back **5** spine
chirp: **4** call, peep, pipe, sing, twee **5** cheep, tweet **7** twitter **8** vocalize
chirping insect: **6** cicada **7** cricket
chirpy: **3** gay **5** happy, jolly, light, sunny **6** blithe, genial, jovial, lively **9** sprightly
chirr: **5** trill
chirrup: **4** peep **5** trill
chiru: **8** antelope
  relative: **3** gnu, kob **4** guib, kudu, oryx, puku, topi **5** addax, bongo, eland, goral, korin, nyala, oribi, saiga, serow **6** chammy, dik-dik, duiker, impala, koodoo, lechwe, nilgai, rhebok, shammy, shamoy **7** blaubok, blesbok, chamois, defassa, gazelle, gemsbok, gerenuk, grysbok, nylghai, nylghau, sassaby **8** blesbuck, bontebok, bushbuck, gemsbuck, reedbuck, steenbok, steinbok **9** blackbuck, pronghorn, sitatunga, springbok, waterbuck **10** hartebeest, wildebeest
chisel: **3** cut, hew **4** burn, chip, rook, tool **5** carve, cheat, edger, gouge, pluck, shape **6** incise, sculpt **7** engrave, swindle **8** flimflam **9** victimize
  ancient ~: **4** celt **5** burin
  feature: **4** edge **5** bezel
  relative: **3** adz **4** adze
chisel ___: **4** plow **5** point
___ chisel: **3** set **4** butt, cold, mill, skew **5** drove, pitch, tooth **6** firmer, paring, pocket **7** drawing, framing, mortise, turning
chiseler: **5** cheat, knave, shark, thief **6** bad guy, robber **7** sharper, sharpie **8** swindler
Chisholm: **5** trail **7** Shirley
Chisholm Trail
  town: **4** Enid **7** Abilene **9** Fort Worth
  users: **6** cattle
Chisinau: **4** city, town **7** capital
  locale: **7** Moldova
Chisox: **3** ten **4** team
  see also White Sox
chi-square ___: **4** test
Chisum (1970 film): **5** oater
  cast: Geoffrey Deuel, Forrest Tucker, John Wayne
  setting: **9** New Mexico
chit: **3** IOU, tab **4** bill **6** marker, ticket **7** receipt, voucher **9** liability
  ender: **4** chat
  write a ~: **3** owe
  writer: **4** ower **5** maker
Chita: **6** Rivera
Chita author: Lafcadio Hearn
chital: **4** deer **6** mammal **8** antelope
  relative: **3** elk, roe **4** axis, pudu, shou, sika **5** moose **6** guemal, hangul, huemul, sambar, sambur, thamin, wapiti **7** brocket, caribou, muntjac, muntjak, sambhar, sambhur **8** reindeer **9** barasingh
chitchat: **3** gab, jaw, rap, yak **4** talk, word **5** prate **6** banter, bytalk, confab, gabble, gibber, gossip, parley **7** chatter, palaver **8** babbling, converse, idle talk, repartee **9** small talk, table talk **10** chew the rag
chiton: **5** shell, tunic **8** seashell
  cousin: **5** stola
Chitra author: Rabindranath Tagore
Chittagong: **4** city, port, town
  locale: **10** Bangladesh
chitter: **5** tweet
Chitty Chitty Bang Bang: **4** book, film
  author: Ian Fleming
  cast: Sally Ann Howes, Dick Van Dyke
  character: **5** Potts, Truly **11** Scrumptious
  dog: **6** Edison
  screenwriter: **4** Dahl
chivalrous: **4** bold, kind **5** brave, lofty **6** heroic, polite **7** courtly, gallant, genteel, valiant **8** gracious, heroical, highbred, knightly, romantic, valorous **9** courteous, honorable, unselfish **10** benevolent, courageous, high-minded, undismayed
  deed: **4** gest **5** geste
chivalry: **8** courtesy **10** knighthood
  participant: **6** damsel, knight
Chivas ___: **5** Regal
chive: **4** herb **6** veggie **9** vegetable
  kin: **4** leek **5** onion
chivvy: **3** nag, vex **4** bait, hunt **5** chase **6** pursue
Chloe: **4** Webb
  love: **7** Daphnis
Chloë: **7** Sevigny
___ chloride: **3** tin **4** gold, zinc **5** allyl, ethyl, vinyl **6** acetyl, barium, benzal, benzyl, ferric, methyl, silver, sodium **7** calcium, chromic, lithium, stannic, thionyl
chloride, sodium: **4** salt **9** table salt
chlorine: **3** gas **7** element, halogen
  compound: **6** halide
Chloris, son of: **6** Nestor
chloroform cousin: **5** ether
chlorophyll
  maker: **5** plant
  plant lacking ~: **6** albino, fungus
  respository: **4** leaf
chlorophyta: **5** algae
Chlumsky: **4** Anna
Cho: **8** Margaret
choate: **4** full **8** integral
chocalho: **6** shaker **10** percussion
  origin: **6** Brazil
chock: **5** block, wedge
chockablock: **4** full, rife **5** laden, solid **6** filled, jammed, loaded, packed **7** crammed, crowded, replete, stuffed, teeming **8** brimming
chock-full: **3** SRO **4** full, rife **6** filled, jammed, loaded, packed **7** crammed, crowded, replete, stuffed, teeming **8** bursting, thronged **9** congested, jam-packed, plentiful, to the roof
chocoholic: **6** addict
  favorite: **5** fudge
Chocolat (2000 film)
  cast: Juliette Binoche, Dame Judi Dench, Johnny Depp, Lena Olin
  director: Lasse Hallström
chocolate: **4** cake **5** brown, candy, color, sweet **6** bonbon, flavor **8** ice cream **9** sweetmeat
  alternative: **5** lemon, mocha, peach **6** banana, coffee, Jamoca, toffee **7** caramel, coconut, vanilla **8** cinnamon, hazelnut **9** bubblegum, pineapple, pistachio, raspberry, rocky road, rum raisin **10** blackberry, cheesecake, Neapolitan, peppermint, strawberry
  bar brand: **4** Mars, Twix **5** Clark, Heath, Lindt **6** Kit Kat, Mounds, Nestle, PayDay, Reese's, Zagnut **7** Cadbury, Krackel, Oh Henry **8** Baby Ruth, Hershey's, Milky Way, Snickers **9** Almond Joy, Mr. Goodbar, Toblerone **10** NutRageous
  bar ingredient: **5** sugar **6** almond
  bean: **5** cacao
  brand: **4** Mars **5** Lindt **6** Godiva **7** Cadbury, Hershey **8** Hershey's, Whitman's **9** Toblerone
  candy: **3** bar **4** kiss **5** fudge
  center: **5** cream, creme
  dish: **5** fondu **6** fondue
  hot ~: **5** cocoa
  hot ~ container: **3** mug
  make ~ curls: **5** shave
  mark: **5** stain
  marshmallow snack: **5** Smore
  relative: **3** bay, dun, tan **4** bole, ecru, fawn, foxy, nude, seal **5** amber, beige, camel, cocoa, hazel, khaki, mocha, sepia, tawny, umber **6** auburn, bister, bistre, bronze, coffee, copper, ginger, russet, sienna, sorrel, suntan, walnut **7** biscuit, caramel, dogwood **8** chestnut, cinnamon, mahogany **9** butternut
  substitute: **5** carob
  syrup brand: **4** U Bet **5** Bosco
  tree: **5** cacao
chocolate ___: **3** bar **4** cake, malt, milk, tree **5** syrup **6** malted **7** soldier

__ chocolate: 3 hot 4 dark, milk 5 white
chocolate chip __: 5 cooky 6 cookie
chocolate point: 3 cat 5 felid 6 feline
__ chocolates: 5 box of
Chocolate Soldier, The composer: 6 Straus
Choctaw: 5 tribe 6 Indian 7 Amerind
__ Chodesh: 4 Rosh
Chofu: 4 city, town
locale: 5 Japan
__-choi: 3 pak
choice: 3 def, rad, sel., top 4 aces, A-one, boss, braw, cool, dece, fine, gear, good, keen, neat, nice, phat, pick, plum, rare, tops, tuff, vote 5 crack, cream, dandy, ducky, elect, elite, fancy, first, grand, great, marvy, neato, nobby, prime, prize, slick, super, swell, voice 6 bang on, bang-up, bonzer, bosker, deluxe, divine, dreamy, far-out, gnarly, goodly, groovy, lovely, option, peachy, select, slap-up, spot on, superb, terrif, tiptop, unreal, whizzo, wicked, worthy 7 amazing, awesome, capital, corking, liberty, optimum, perfect, refusal, ripping, skookum, special, stellar, sublime, vintage 8 dazzling, decision, election, especial, eximious, fabulous, favorite, five-star, four-star, frabjous, free will, glorious, heavenly, jim-dandy, judgment, luscious, pleasure, slam-bang, smashing, splendid, standout, sterling, stickout, superior, terrific, top-level, topnotch, very good, volition, wondrous 9 bodacious, Endsville, excellent, exemplary, exquisite, first-rate, high-class, high-grade, hunky-dory, marvelous, preferred, selection, sollicker, top-drawer, top-flight, unrivaled, wonderful 10 assortment, discretion, first-class, hand-picked, hotsy-totsy, jack-a-dandy, nomination, out of sight, peachy-keen, phenomenal, preference, remarkable, stupendous, super-duper, unrivalled
list: 4 menu
__ choice: 7 dealer's, Hobson's
__ Choice: 6 O'Hara's 7 Critic's, Healthy, Sophie's, Taster's
choicest: 4 best 7 optimum 9 topflight
choices, top: 5 A-list
choir: 6 chorus 7 singers 8 ensemble 9 vocalists
area behind the ~: 4 apse
ender: 3 boy 4 girl 6 master
member: 4 alto, bass 5 basso, tenor, voice 7 soprano 8 baritone
members: 4 alti
place: 4 loft 5 riser
selection: 4 hymn 5 canto, motet 7 cantata
small ~: 5 nonet, octet 7 octette
tunic: 5 cotta
choir __: 4 loft
Chokai: 7 volcano
locale: 4 Asia 5 Japan 6 Honshu
choke: 4 clog, gulp, slow 5 block, quiet, wring 6 impede, shut up, stifle 7 congest, occlude, overrun, smother, squeeze 8 obstruct, throttle
back: 6 stifle
ender: 4 bore, damp, hold 5 berry, point 6 cherry
off: 3 dam 4 stop 7 silence
choke __: 3 off 4 back, coil 5 chain 6 collar
chokecherry: 5 fruit
choked up: 5 teary 10 tongue-tied
choker: 5 beads 7 jewelry 8 necklace 9 adornment
fastener: 5 clasp
cholent: 4 soup
choler: 3 ire 4 bile, rage 5 anger, wrath 6 temper 10 irritation, resentment
choleric: 3 hot, mad 4 ired, sore 5 angry, cross, fiery, huffy, irate, livid, onery, riled, surly, testy, wroth 6 crusty, fuming, ireful, morose, ornery, peeved, raging, raving, red-hot, touchy 7 bearish, enraged, furious, grouchy, peevish, peppery, ranting, uptight 8 critical, incensed, inflamed, liverish, maddened, outraged, snappish, wrathful 9 indignant, irascible, irritable, irritated, querulous, resentful, splenetic 10 freaked out, ill-humored, infuriated, out of sorts
cholesterol
bad ~: 3 LDL
good ~: 3 HDL
part: 5 lipid 6 lipide
__ cholesterol: 5 serum
Cholet: 4 city, town
locale: 6 France
choline starter: 6 acetyl
cholla: 6 cactus
Cholula: 4 city, town
locale: 6 Mexico, Puebla
Chomo Lhari: 4 peak 8 mountain
locale: 4 Asia 5 China, Tibet 6 Bhutan 9 Himalayas
chomp: 4 bite, chew, gnaw 5 gnash, munch 6 crunch
on: 3 eat
Chomsky: 4 Noam
chon: 5 money
Chong: 5 Tommy 6 Thomas 7 Rae Dawn
partner: 5 Marin 6 Cheech
Chongjin: 4 city, town
locale: 10 North Korea
Chongqing: 4 city, town
locale: 5 China
Chong, Rae Dawn: 7 actress
film: American Flyers (1985)
Commando (1985)
The Principal (1987)
Quest for Fire (1981)
The Visit (2000)
choose: 3 opt, sel., tab, tap 4 cull, like, name, pick, sort, take, vote, want, will 5 adopt, draft, elect, favor, go for, key on 6 anoint, assign, decide, desire, go into, opt for, prefer, select, settle, take up, winnow 7 appoint, embrace, excerpt, fix upon, pick out, vote for 8 bookmark, decide on, delegate, draw lots, handpick, nominate 9 designate, determine, flip a coin, preordain, single out, take sides 10 draw straws, settle upon
don't ~: 6 pass by 8 pass over
Choose Me (1984 film)
cast: Genevieve Bujold, Keith Carradine, Lesley Ann Warren
director: Alan Rudolph
chooser choice: 4 odds 5 evens
choose up __: 5 sides
choosy: 4 prim 5 fussy, picky 6 dainty 7 careful, finicky 8 finiking, finnicky 9 selective 10 fastidious, particular
Cho Oyu: 4 peak 5 mount 8 mountain
locale: 4 Asia 5 Nepal, Tibet 6 Thibet, Xizang 7 Sitsang 9 Himalayas
chop: 2 ax 3 axe, cut, hew, lop 4 crop, cube, dice, fell, hack, jowl, meat, slap, slur, sock, stab 5 cut up, mince, shear, slash, slice, smack 6 cleave, divide, reduce 7 abridge, curtail, scissor, shorten 8 truncate 9 roughness
down: 2 ax 3 axe, hew 4 fell 6 hack up 7 hack off 8 hack down
ender: 5 house, logic, stick 6 fallen
finely: 4 dice 5 mince
off: 3 lop 5 sever
chop __: 4 mark, shop, sooy, suey 6 stroke
__ chop: 4 pork, veal 5 grand 6 French, karate
chopa: 4 fish
chop-chop: 4 ASAP, stat
__ Chop Hill: 4 Pork
chophouse: 6 eatery 10 restaurant
order: 4 rare 8 well-done
Chopin: 4 Kate 8 Frédéric
chopine: 4 shoe 8 footwear
Chopin, Frédéric: 4 Pole 8 composer
friend: George Sand
genre: 5 étude, waltz 6 sonata 7 ballade, prelude, scherzo 8 nocturne 9 impromptu, polonaise
work: Minute Waltz
Revolutionary Etude
Chopin, Kate: 6 author, writer
Chopin's Étude __ Major: 3 in E
chopped: 4 hewn
liver: 4 pâté
chopped __: 5 chuck, liver, steak 7 sirloin
chopper: 2 ax 3 axe 4 helo 5 tooth 6 copter 8 aircraft 10 helicopter
emulate a ~: 3 fly 4 soar 5 hover, whirr
military ~: 6 Apache
starter: 4 wood
topper: 5 rotor 6 enamel
choppers: 5 plate, teeth 8 dentures
chopping __: 5 block
chopping firewood: 5 chore
choppy: 4 wild 5 bumpy, rough 6 jouncy 9 spasmodic, turbulent
Chopra: 6 Deepak
chops: 3 jaw, maw 4 jaws, meat 5 mouth 6 entrée
lick one's ~: 5 savor 6 relish
starter: 6 mutton
chop-shop supplier: 5 thief
Choquette, Robert: 4 poet 8 Canadian
choral: 4 sung 5 lyric, vocal 7 lyrical, musical 9 a cappella
ensemble: 5 octet 7 octette
member: 4 alto, bass 5 basso, tenor 7 soprano 8 baritone
members: 4 alti
work: 4 hymn 5 canto, motet 7 cantata
chorale: 4 hymn, song 5 music, psalm 9 vocalists
Choral Symphony: 5 ninth
composer: 9 Beethoven
chord: 5 notes, triad 6 tendon 7 harmony
strike a ~: 5 touch 6 affect
chord __: 5 chart, organ
__ chord: 5 block, major, minor, ninth, sixth 6 broken 7 altered, seventh
chorda: 5 algae
Chordettes
song: Born to Be With You (1956)
Just Between You and Me (1957)
Lollipop (1958)
Mr. Sandman (1954)
chore: 3 job 4 duty, task, work 5 grind, labor, stint 6 burden, errand, odd job, raking, sewing 7 dusting, ironing, laundry, mopping, project, washing 8 cleaning, sweeping 9 housework, vacuuming 10 assignment
choreography: 6 ballet 7 dancing
choreophobe fear: 7 dancing
chorister: 4 alto, bass 5 basso, tenor 6 singer 7 soprano 8 baritone, vocalist
chortle: 3 heh 4 ha-ha 5 laugh 6 cackle, giggle, guffaw, titter 7 break up, chuckle, crack up, snicker, snigger 8 laughter
chorus: 4 song, tune 5 choir, music 6 melody 7 refrain 8 carolers, ensemble, glee club 9 vocalists
for full ~: 4 SATB
full ~ in music: 5 tutti
girl: 6 dancer
Greek ~ part: 5 epode
join the ~: 4 sing
member: 4 alto, bass 5 basso, tenor, voice 7 soprano 8 baritone
members: 4 alti
preceder: 5 verse
show: 5 revue 6 review
syllable: 3 tra
syllables: 4 la la 6 la la la 7 tra la la
chorus __: 3 boy 4 frog, girl
__ Chorus: 5 Anvil
Chorus Line, A (1985 film): 7 musical
cast: Michael Douglas, Terrence Mann, Alyson Reed
character: 2 Al 3 Don, Roy, Tom, Val 4 Bebe, Greg, Judy, Lois, Mark, Mike, Paul, Zach 5 Bobby, Butch, Diana, Frank, Larry, Vikki 6 Cassie, Connie, Maggie, Sheila, Tricia 8 Kristine
director: Richard Attenborough
original producer: 4 Papp
song: 3 One
__ chose: 5 peu de
__-chose: 7 quelque
chosen: 5 elect, elite 6 select 7 favored 8 accepted 9 preferred, spoken for, voluntary 10 fair-haired
__-chosen: 4 well
Chosen, The: 4 film 5 novel
author: Chaim Potok
cast: Robby Benson, Maximilian Schell, Rod Steiger
director: Jeremy Paul Kagan
__ chou: 5 pâte à
Chou: 5 En-lai
chou-chou: 2 jo 3 pet 4 baby, dear, jill, love 5 amour, angel, chéri, cooky, cutey, cutie, deary, ducky, flame, honey, leman, lover, lovey, novia, novio, sugar, sweet 6 bon ami, chérie, cookie, dautie, dearie, steady, sweets 7 beloved, dearest, dear one, pigsney, schatzi, squeeze, sweetie, tootsie 8 cutie pie, dowsabel, dulcinea, ladylove, lovebird, macushla, paramour, precious, snookums, sugar pie, sweetums, truelove 9 bonne amie, boyfriend, dreamboat, inamorata, inamorato, petit chou, valentine 10 girlfriend, heartthrob, honeybunch, mavourneen, sweetheart, sweetie pie, turtledove
chough: 4 bird
chouse: 5 cheat 7 swindle
chow: 3 dog 4 eats, food, grub, meal, meat 5 spitz 7 aliment, victual, vittles 8 K rations, victuals 9 provender
Army ~: 3 MRE 4 mess, Spam
down: 3 eat, sup 4 feed 5 dig in 6 devour, ingest 7 consume 9 grab a bite
ender: 5 hound
like a ~: 7 Chinese
chow __: 4 down, line, mein
chowder: 4 soup
like Manhattan clam ~: 5 thymy
server: 5 ladle
__ chowder: 4 clam, corn
chowderhead: 3 ass, oaf, sap 4 boob, boor, bozo, clod, dodo, dolt, dope, fool, jerk, simp 5 chump, clown, cluck, dummy, dunce, joker, ninny, patsy, stupe 6 dimwit, lummox, nitwit, sucker, turkey 7 buffoon, dingbat, dullard, half-wit, jackass, saphead 8 dumbbell, numskull 9 birdbrain, lamebrain, numbskull, simpleton
chowhound: 7 glutton
__ choy: 3 bok
Chrétien, Jean preceder: 8 Campbell
Chris: 3 Rea 4 Lowe, Rock 5 Evert, Isaak 6 Barber, Cooper, Farley, Kenner, LeDoux, Lemmon, Montez, Tucker 7 DeBurgh, Elliott 8 Columbus, O'Donnell, Robinson, Sarandon

rival: 6 Evonne
Chris-__: 5 Craft
chrism: 3 oil 7 holy oil
apply ~: 5 anele 6 anoint
chrisom: 4 robe
Chrissie: 5 Evert, Hynde
rival: 6 Evonne
Christ: 5 Jesus 6 Savior 7 Messiah
Christa: 6 Miller 9 McAuliffe
Christabel: 4 poem
author: Samuel Taylor Coleridge
Christchurch: 4 city, town
locale: 10 New Zealand
christen: 3 dub, tag 4 call, name, term 5 title 7 baptize, entitle, intitle 8 sprinkle
christened: 3 née
christening initials: 3 USS
Christiaan: 7 Barnard, Eijkman, Huygens
Christian: 3 Era 4 Bale, Dior, Nyby 5 Lange, Linda, Roger 6 de Duve, Grabbe, Slater 7 Claudia, Doppler, Lacroix 8 Anfinsen, Fletcher
inscription: 4 INRI
symbol: 4 fish
temple: 6 church
Christian __: 3 Era 4 name, year 7 Brother, Science
__-Christian: 5 Judeo 6 Judaeo
__ Christian Andersen: 4 Hans
Christiania today: 4 Oslo
Christianity: 3 rel.
early ~ center: 6 Edessa
Christian Mysticism author: Inge
Christian Science founder: 4 Eddy
__, Christian Soldiers: 6 Onward
__ christie: 4 stem
Christie: 3 Lou 4 Anna 5 Julie 6 Agatha, Hefner 8 Brinkley
concoction: 4 plot
perform a ~: 3 ski 4 skee
__ Christie: 4 Anna
Christie, Agatha: 4 Dame 6 author, writer 7 British
sleuth: Poirot, Marple, Hercule, Jane
work: And Then There Were None
Curtain
Death on the Nile
The Mousetrap
The Murder of Roger Ackroyd
Murder on the Orient Express
The Mysterious Affair at Styles
The Pale Horse
Witness for the Prosecution
Christie, Julie: 7 actress
film: Billy Liar (1963)
Darling (1965, AA)
Demon Seed (1977)
Doctor Zhivago (1965)
Don't Look Now (1973)
Fahrenheit 451 (1967)
Far From the Madding Crowd (1967)
Heaven Can Wait (1978)
McCabe & Mrs. Miller (1971)
Petulia (1968)
Shampoo (1975)
Young Cassidy (1965)
role: 4 Lara
Christie's
action: 3 bid, nod 7 auction
patron: 6 bidder
Christina: 5 Ricci, saint, Stead 7 Onassis 8 Aguilera, Rossetti 9 Applegate
father: 3 Ari
Christina's World artist: 5 Wyeth
Christine: 5 Elise, Lahti, McVie 7 McGuire 8 Baranski
Christine author: Stephen King
title character: 3 car 4 auto
__ Christi, TX: 6 Corpus
Christmas: 4 isle, Noel, yule 6 island
berry: 5 toyon
bird: 5 goose
carol start: 4 hark 5 o come 6 adeste
Christmas-tree decoration: 6 icicle
ender: 4 tide, time
Eve flier: 5 Comet, Cupid, Vixen 6 Dancer, Dasher, Donder 7 Blitzen, Prancer, Rudolph 8 reindeer
goodies: 4 loot 5 gifts 8 presents
greenery: 5 holly 6 wreath
in French: 4 Noël
in Portuguese: 5 Natal
in Spanish: 7 Navidad
like a ~ tree: 5 lit up 9 decorated
naughty child's ~ gift: 4 coal
pageant figures: 4 Magi
pageant prop: 4 halo
poem opener: 4 'Twas
predecessor: 3 eve
quaff: 3 nog 6 eggnog
smelling of ~: 5 piney
song: 4 Noel 5 carol
sound: 6 hohoho
tableau: 6 crèche
tree: 3 fir 4 pine 6 balsam
tree base: 5 stand
tree ornament: 4 ball, cane, star 6 icicle, tinsel 9 candy cane
tree topper: 4 star 5 angel
trio: 4 Magi
white ~ need: 4 snow
Christmas __: 3 Day, Eve 4 card, club, fern, rose, seal, tree 5 berry 6 cactus, factor, Island 7 Holiday, pudding
Christmas __, A: 5 Carol, Story
__ Christmas: 4 Bush 5 Merry, White 6 Father
Christmas card word: 4 Noel 5 Peace
Christmas Carol, A
author: Charles Dickens
character: 3 Bob, Tim 5 ghost, Jacob 6 Marley 7 Scrooge, Tiny Tim 8 Cratchit, Ebenezer
cry: 3 bah 6 humbug
last word of ~: 3 one
setting: 6 London 7 England
Christmas Carol, A (1938 film)
cast: Terry Kilburn, Gene Lockhart, Reginald Owen
Christmas Carol, A (1951 film)
cast: Kathleen Harrison, Alastair Sim, Jack Warner
Christmas Club member: 5 saver
Christmas comes but __ year: 5 once a
Christmas Holiday (1944 film)
cast: Deanna Durbin, Gene Kelly
Christmas in __: 4 July 5 Aspen
Christmas in Connecticut (1945 film)
cast: Sydney Greenstreet, Dennis Morgan, Barbara Stanwyck
Christmas in July (1940 film)
cast: Ellen Drew, Dick Powell
director: Preston Sturges
Christmas Oratorio composer: 4 Bach
Christmas Song, The composer: 5 Torme
Christmas Story, A (1983 film)
cast: Peter Billingsley, Melinda Dillon, Darren McGavin
Christ of St. John of the Cross artist: 4 Dali
Christ of the __: 5 Andes
Christoph: 5 Gluck
Christopher: 3 Fry, Lee 4 Noth, Penn, pope, Wren 5 Burke, Cross, Guest, Lloyd, Reeve, saint, Smart 6 Atkins, Dennis, George, Hewitt, Knight, Morley, Norris, Walken, Warren 7 Brennan, Lambert, Marlowe, Plummer, pontiff 8 Columbus 9 Isherwood
friend: 4 Pooh 5 Robin
Christopher Columbus (1949 film)
cast: Florence Eldridge, Fredric March
Christ Stopped at Eboli author: 4 Levi
__ Christ Superstar: 5 Jesus
Christy: 4 Lane 9 Mathewson
__ Christy Minstrels: 3 New
chroma: 3 hue 4 tint 5 color
chroma __: 3 key
__ chromate: 4 lead 6 barium 7 bismuth
chromatic: 4 hued 8 colorful
chromatic __: 4 sign 5 scale
chrome: 4 trim 5 metal
chrome __: 3 red 4 alum, dome 5 green, steel 6 yellow 7 leather
chromic __: 4 acid 5 oxide 7 acetate
chromium: 5 metal 7 element
alloy: 7 Elinvar, Inconel 9 Vitallium
chromium __: 5 oxide, steel 7 acetate
chromosome
choice: 4 X or Y
component: 3 DNA, RNA
enzyme: 6 DNAase
factor: 3 sex
gene sites on a ~: 4 loca, loci
having an X ~: 6 female 8 feminine
having a Y ~: 4 male 9 masculine
locate a gene on a ~: 3 map
part: 4 gene
type of ~: 2 XX, XY
Chromosome 6 author: Robin Cook
chronic: 5 usual 6 inborn 7 abiding, lasting 8 constant, enduring, habitual, long-term, unwaning 9 ceaseless, continual, incessant, ingrained, perennial, sustained, unabating 10 deep-seated, inveterate, persistent, unyielding
become ~: 5 recur
malady (suffix): 4 -itis
not ~: 5 acute
chronicle: 4 saga, tale, tell 5 diary, enrol, story 6 annals, enroll, memoir, record, relate, report 7 account, history, journal, narrate, recount, set down, version 8 describe, register 9 expound on, narration, narrative, recountal
entry: 5 event
Chronicle: 5 paper 9 newspaper
locale: 7 Houston
chronicler: 6 scribe 8 annalist, recorder 9 historian
chronicles: 5 files 7 archive
Chronicles
follower: 4 Ezra
preceder: 5 Kings
Chronicles of Clovis, The
author: Saki
character: 4 Esme
Chronicles of Narnia, The author: C.S. Lewis
__ Chronicles, The: 5 Heidi 6 Marlow 7 Martian, Vampire
__ Chronium: 4 Mare
chronograph: 5 clock, watch 9 timepiece
chronological: 8 temporal
adjective: 5 horal
division: 3 era
chronological __: 3 age
chronology: 4 time 7 journal 8 calendar
element: 5 event
chronometer: 5 clock, watch 9 timepiece
chrysalis: 3 bug 4 pupa 6 insect
chrysanthemum: 4 kiku 5 plant 6 flower
Chrysler: 3 car 4 auto 6 Walter 10 automobile
acquisition: 3 AMC
car: 6 De Soto
model: 5 Royal 6 Cirrus 7 Cordoba, LeBaron, Newport, Sebring, Windsor 8 Concorde, Conquest, Imperial, Pacifica, Saratoga 9 New Yorker, PT Cruiser 11 Fifth Avenue
trademark: 4 Jeep
chrysoberyl: 3 gem 8 gemstone
chrysolite: 7 mineral
chrysoprase: 3 gem 8 gemstone
Chrysostom, John: 5 saint
chub: 4 bait, fish 9 whitefish
kin: 4 carp 6 minnow
chubby: 5 beefy, fubsy, hefty, husky, large, obese, plump, pudgy, pursy, round, stout, tubby 6 chunky, fleshy, portly, pyknic, rotund, stocky, zaftig, zoftig 7 adipose, paunchy 8 roly-poly 9 corpulent, filled-out 10 abdominous, overweight, well-padded
Chubby: 7 Checker
chuck: 3 lob 4 bail, beef, cast, cede, drop, dump, flip, hurl, sell, shed, toss 5 ditch, fling, forgo, heave, pitch, scrap, sling, steak, throw, yield 6 forego, give up, let fly, reject 7 abandon, discard, dismiss, forfeit, forsake 8 forswear, get rid of, hand over, jettison, part with, throw out, toss away 9 cast aside, dispose of, eighty-six, foreswear, surrender, throw away 10 relinquish
insert: 3 bit
starter: 4 wood
wagon: 7 canteen
wagon dinner: 4 chow, grub
wagon honcho: 4 cook
chuck __: 5 steak, wagon
chuck-__: 4 full, luck 5 a-luck
__ chuck: 4 salt 5 drill 7 balloon
Chuck: 4 Daly, Noll 5 Berry, Jones, Klein 6 Barris, Colson, Norris, Willis, Yeager 7 Connors, Woolery 8 Bednarik, Mangione 9 Fairbanks
Chuck __ Love: 4 E.'s in
chuck-a-luck: 4 game
need: 4 dice
Chuck E.'s in Love (1979 song) artist: Rickie Lee Jones
chuckle: 3 heh, yak, yok, yuk 4 ha-ha, yock, yuck 5 laugh 6 cackle, giggle, heehee, titter 7 snicker, snigger 8 laughter
chat room ~: 3 LOL
elicit a ~: 5 amuse
ender: 4 head
chucklehead: 3 ass, oaf, sap 4 boob, bozo, clod, dodo, dolt, dope, fool 5 chump, clown, cluck, dummy, dunce, joker, ninny, patsy, stupe 6 dimwit, lummox, nitwit, sucker, turkey 7 buffoon, dingbat, dullard, half-wit, jackass, saphead 8 dumbbell, numskull 9 birdbrain, lamebrain, numbskull, simpleton
Chuckles: 5 candy
__-chucks: 3 nun
chuff: 4 pant
chug
see chug-a-lug
chug-a-lug: 4 gulp, swig 5 swill 6 guzzle 7 swallow 8 gulp down
Chug-A-Lug (1964 song) artist: Roger Miller
chukar: 4 bird, fowl
relative: 5 poult, quail, snipe 6 grouse, peahen, turkey 7 peacock, peafowl 8 curassow, moorfowl, pheasant, woodcock 9 partridge 10 guinea fowl, jungle fowl, wild turkey
Chukchi __: 3 Sea
chukka: 4 boot, shoe 8 footwear
material: 5 suede
chukkers game: 4 polo
Chulalongkorn locale: 4 Siam
Chula Vista: 4 city, town
locale: 10 California
chum: 3 bro, pal 4 ally, bait, fish, mate 5 amigo, buddy, crony, pally 6 cohort, frater, friend 7 compeer, comrade, partner 8 alter ego, intimate, playmate, sidekick 9 associate, colleague, confi-

dant **10** bosom buddy, compatriot, well-wisher
Australian: 4 mate
British: 4 mate **5** matey
cowboy's ~: 4 pard
in French: 3 ami **4** amie
in Spanish: 5 amiga, amigo
(with): 6 hobnob, mingle **9** socialize
see also friend
Chumash: 6 Indian **7** Amerind
chummy: 4 cosy, cozy, kind **5** close, cozey, cozie, thick **6** clubby, genial, kindly **7** affable, amiable, cordial **8** amicable, familiar, friendly, intimate, outgoing, sociable **9** convivial **10** benevolent, buddy-buddy, neighborly, palsy-walsy, solicitous
get ~ with: 8 befriend
chump: 3 ass, oaf, sap **4** boob, butt, clod, dolt, dupe, fool, gull, lamb, lout, tool **5** clown, cluck, dummy, dunce, joker, looby, ninny, patsy **6** dimwit, lummox, nitwit, pigeon, sucker, turkey **7** buffoon, dingbat, dullard, fall guy, fathead, half-wit, jackass, pinhead, saphead **8** bonehead, dumbbell, easy mark, meathead, numskull, pushover **9** birdbrain, blockhead, harebrain, lamebrain, numbskull, simpleton **10** dunderhead
chump __: 6 change
chums, meet one's old: 5 reune
__ Chung: 4 Wang
Chung, Connie spouse: Maury Povich
chunk: 3 gob, wad **4** glob, hunk, lump, mass, part, pile, slab **5** block, clump, piece, quota, scrap, share, wedge **6** morsel, nugget, parcel **7** portion, section **8** fraction, fragment **10** percentage
in Britain: 5 wodge
take a ~ out of: 3 nip **4** bite
chunk-light __: 4 tuna
chunky: 5 beefy, heavy, husky, lumpy, plump, pudgy, squat, stout, thick **6** chubby, rotund, stocky **8** heavyset, thickset **9** filled-out
alternative: 5 plain **6** smooth
church: 4 fane, sect **5** abbey **6** chapel, parish, shrine, temple **7** chancel, mission **8** basilica, ecclesia, religion **9** cathedral, sanctuary **10** house of God, persuasion, tabernacle
assistant: 6 lector
banner: 7 labarum
bell: 7 angelus
calendar: 4 ordo
cape: 5 amice **6** almuce **7** mozetta **8** mozzetta **10** cappa magna
coat: 7 cassock
combining form: 7 ecclesi- **8** ecclesio-
container: 4 font **6** censer
council: 5 curia, synod
cover-up: 4 veil
desk: 4 ambo **5** ambon
donation: 5 tithe
Eastern ~ member: 5 Uniat **6** Uniate
ender: 3 man, men **4** yard **5** going, manly, woman **6** warden
exclamation ~: 4 amen **7** hosanna
fair: 5 bazar **6** bazaar
feature: 3 pew **4** apse, jube, loft, nave **5** aisle, altar, ambry, choir, organ, spire **6** atrium, belfry, chapel, pulpit, vestry **7** chancel, gallery, narthex, reredos, steeple **8** antenave, parclose, sacristy, transept, westwork
figure: 4 icon, ikon **5** cross, eikon, saint
group: 6 clergy
headdress: 5 miter, mitre
land: 5 glebe
Latin ~ service: 5 missa
law: 5 canon, dogma **7** precept **8** doctrine
medieval ~ music sign: 4 neum **5** neume
members: 5 laics, laity **6** parish
music: 4 hymn **5** motet
not of the ~: 3 lay **4** laic **6** laical
official: 3 rev. **4** msgr. **5** abbot, elder, prior, Rt. Rev., vicar **6** cleric, deacon, parson, warden **8** minister, reverend **9** monsignor
offshoot: 4 sect
of the ~: 8 clerical
plate: 5 paten
portico: 6 parvis
rite: 4 Mass **7** service, worship
robe: 6 chimar, chimer **7** chimere, chrisom
Scottish ~: 4 kirk
song: 5 psalm
songbook: 6 hymnal
teachings: 5 dogma **6** Gospel
vestment: 3 alb **5** amice
wall recess: 5 ambry **6** aumbry **8** armarium
church __: 3 key **4** book, mode, rate, text, year **6** father, school **7** council, visible
__ church: 4 free **5** state, union **6** mother **7** servant
Church: 5 Frank **9** Frederick
__ Church: 3 Low **4** High **5** Broad, Greek, Latin **6** Coptic, Mormon **7** Eastern, Russian, Western
churchgoing: 5 pious **9** religious
Churchill: 4 peak, port **5** mount, river, Sarah **7** Winston **8** mountain
River locale: 8 Manitoba
Churchill __: 5 Downs, Falls
Churchill Downs: 5 track
event: 4 race **5** Derby
locale: 8 Kentucky **10** Louisville
Churchill, Winston: 2 P.M. **3** Sir **7** British **8** Nobelist **9** statesman
gesture: 3 vee
one of a ~ quartet: 4 toil **5** blood, sweat, tears
predecessor: 6 Attlee **11** Chamberlain
prop: 4 cane
so few, to ~: 3 RAF
successor: 4 Eden **6** Attlee
work: Closing the Ring
The Gathering Storm
The Grand Alliance
The Hinge of Fate
Their Finest Hour
Triumph and Tragedy
Church of __: 3 God **4** Rome **7** England
Church of the Poison Mind (1983 song) artist: Culture Club
Churchy La __: 5 Femme
churl: 3 cur, oaf **4** boor, heel, lout, worm **5** beast, clown, knave, looby, miser, rogue, scamp, yahoo **6** bad guy, grouch, rascal **7** peasant **9** miscreant, reprobate, scoundrel, vulgarian **10** blackguard, clodhopper, curmudgeon
churlish: 4 mean, rude, sour **5** crass, cross, crude, gruff, onery, rough, surly **6** coarse, crusty, grumpy, morose, oafish, ornery, rustic, snippy, stingy, sullen, touchy **7** bearish, boorish, grouchy, loutish, lowbred, miserly, peevish, uncivil, vicious **8** cloddish, grumpish, impolite, snippety, ungiving **9** unfeeling **10** ill-natured, indecorous, uncultured, ungracious, unmannerly, unpleasant
churn: 4 mill, moil, roil **5** mix up, shake, swirl **6** seethe, simmer, stir up **7** agitate, shake up **9** container
creation: 6 butter
plunger: 6 dasher
churn __: 3 out **5** drill **7** molding
churr: 5 trill
Chu, Steven: 8 Nobelist **9** physicist
chute: 4 ramp **5** flume, slide, slope **6** gutter **7** incline **9** waterfall **10** water slide
alternative: 6 ladder
like a ~: 5 steep
material: 4 silk
starter: 4 para
Chutes and __: 7 Ladders
chutney: 5 sauce **6** relish **8** dressing **9** condiment
flavoring: 5 mango
chutzpah: 4 gall **5** brass, cheek, moxie, nerve, spunk **6** hubris, hybris **8** audacity, temerity, tenacity **9** arrogance, assurance, impudence, insolence **10** effrontery, feistiness
full of ~: 5 brash, nervy **6** daring
Chuvash poet: 4 Aigi
Chuzzlewit: 6 Martin
Chynna: 8 Phillips
CIA
agent: 3 spy
counterpart: 3 KGB
forerunner: 3 OSS
nautical cousin: 3 ONI
operative: 3 agt., spy **5** agent, spook
part of ~: 4 Agcy. **6** Agency **7** Central
relative: 3 NSA
ciao: 3 bye **4** ta-ta **5** later, see ya **6** so long **7** goodbye **8** au revoir, farewell
in French: 5 adieu
in Hawaiian: 5 aloha
in Latin: 3 ave **4** vale
in Spanish: 5 adios
Ciardi, John: 4 poet **6** critic
Cibber, Colley: 4 poet **6** author **7** British **10** playwright
cicada: 3 bug **6** buzzer, insect, locust **7** cricket
sound: 5 chirr, churr **6** chirre
cicatrix: 4 scar
Cicely: 5 Tyson
Cicero: 4 city, town **5** Roman **6** orator
emulate ~: 5 orate
locale: 8 Illinois
see also Latin
cicerone: 5 guide **6** docent
Cid, El: 4 hero **7** Spanish
cider: 5 drink **8** beverage
season: 4 fall
source: 5 apple
unit: 6 gallon
cider __: 5 press **7** vinegar
__ cider: 4 hard **5** sweet
Cider House Rules, The: 4 film **5** novel
author: John Irving
cast: Michael Caine, Delroy Lindo, Tobey Maguire, Charlize Theron
director: Lasse Hallström
Cielito __: 5 Lindo
Cielo __: 4 e mar
Cienfuegos: 4 city, town
locale: 4 Cuba
Ciera: 3 car **4** auto, Olds **10** Oldsmobile
cigar: 4 puro, rope **5** claro, smoke, stogy **6** corona, Havana, stogie **7** cheroot **8** panatela, perfecto
box wood: 5 cedar
brand: 5 Te Amo
end: 3 ash **4** butt, stub
have a ~: 5 smoke
producer: 4 Cuba **5** Tampa
cigar-__ Indian: 5 store
cigare filler: 5 tabac
__ cigar is a smoke: 5 a good
cilantro: 4 herb **9** coriander
Cilento, Diane spouse: Sean Connery, Anthony Shaffer
cilia: 5 hairs, setae **6** lashes **8** filament **9** eyelashes
of ~: 5 setal
ciliary __: 4 body **6** muscle **7** process
cilium: 4 hair, lash, seta **7** eyelash
Cilla: 5 Black
cimarron: 5 sheep
relative: 4 geep **5** argal, shapu, urial **6** aoudad, argali, bharal, merino **7** burrhel, mouflon **8** moufflon
Cimarron: 3 car **4** auto, film **5** novel, river **8** Cadillac **10** automobile
author: Edna Ferber
cast: Richard Dix, Irene Dunne
director: Wesley Ruggles
locale: 8 Oklahoma **9** New Mexico
studio: 3 RKO
cimex: 3 bug **6** bedbug, insect
Cimino, Michael Oscar: The Deer Hunter
__ Cimmerium: 4 Mare
cinch: 3 ice, tie **4** belt, bind, easy, game, girt, grip, lock, snap **5** cushy, girth, latch **6** assure, breeze, enfold, ensure, infold, picnic, secure, simple **7** no sweat, triumph **8** cakewalk, card game, duck soup, painless, pushover, workable **9** certainty, determine, guarantee, sure thing **10** child's play, effortless, unexacting
cinch __: 3 bug **4** belt
cinched: 4 sure **6** belted
cinchona: 4 tree **5** shrub
relative: 5 ixora **6** coffee, madder **8** gardenia **9** bouvardia
Cincinnati: 4 city, town **5** horse
athletes: 8 Bearcats **10** Musketeers
county: 8 Hamilton
fictional ~ station: 4 WKRP
locale: 4 Ohio
newspaper: 4 Post **8** Enquirer
pro team: 4 Reds **7** Bengals
rider: 5 Grant
river: 4 Ohio
school: 6 Xavier
Cincinnati Kid, The (1965 film)
cast: Ann-Margret, Karl Malden, Steve McQueen, Edward G. Robinson
director: Norman Jewison
Cincinnatus: 5 Roman **7** general
Cinco de Mayo: 3 día **7** holiday
cinco minus tres: 3 dos
cincture: 4 band, belt, gird, ring **6** begird, circle, collar, girdle **8** encircle, surround **9** encompass
cinder: 3 ash **4** slag **5** ember, fleck **7** residue
collector: 6 ashman
ender: 5 block
cinder __: 4 cone **5** block, patch, track
Cinder
ender: 4 ella
Cinderella (1950 film)
cat: 7 Lucifer
dog: 5 Bruno
event: 4 ball
headpiece: 5 tiara
like ~'s stepsisters: 4 ugly
mouse: 3 Gus, Jaq
setting: 4 ball
Cinderella __: 5 story **7** Liberty
Cinderella Liberty (1973 film)
cast: James Caan, Marsha Mason, Eli Wallach
director: Mark Rydell
cinderlike: 4 ashy **5** ashen **7** grayish
cinders
turn to ~: 4 char
Cinders: 4 Ella
Cindy: 5 Adams **6** Wilson **8** Crawford, Williams
Cindy, Oh Cindy (1956 song)
artist: Eddie Fisher, Tarriers
cine: 4 film **5** movie
cinema: 3 pic **4** film, show **5** films, movie, odeon, odeum **6** flicks, movies **7** drive-in, theater, theatre **9** big screen, celluloid, multiplex

admonition: 3 shh
chain: 5 Loews
list: 4 cast
local ~: 4 nabe
showing: 4 film 5 short 7 cartoon
sight: 5 queue
sign: 4 Exit
snack: 5 candy 6 nachos 7 Goobers, popcorn 8 Milk Duds 9 Raisinets
suffix: 4 -plex
technique: 3 pan 4 fade, iris
unit: 5 frame
see also film, movie
cinéma ___: 6 vérité
Cinemax: 7 channel
alternative: 3 AMC, HBO, IFC, SHO, TMC 4 Flix 5 Bravo, Starz 6 Encore 8 Showtime, Sundance
offering: 4 film 5 movie
Cineplex ___: 5 Odeon
cineplex offering: 4 film 5 movie
cineraria: 5 plant 6 flower
cinereous: 4 gray, grey 5 ashen
Cinna author: Pierre Corneille
cinnabar: 3 ore 7 mineral
cinnamon: 4 bear, fern, tree 5 brown, spice 7 reddish 8 ice cream 9 yellowish
alternative: 5 lemon, mocha, peach 6 banana, coffee, Jamoca, toffee 7 caramel, coconut, vanilla 8 hazelnut 9 bubblegum, chocolate, pineapple, pistachio, raspberry, rocky road, rum raisin 10 blackberry, cheesecake, Neapolitan, peppermint, strawberry
family: 6 laurel
relative: 3 bay, dun, tan 4 bole, ecru, fawn, foxy, nude, seal 5 amber, beige, camel, cocoa, hazel, khaki, mocha, sepia, tawny, umber 6 auburn, bister, bistre, bronze, coffee, copper, ginger, russet, sienna, sorrel, suntan, walnut 7 avocado, biscuit, camphor, caramel, dogwood 8 chestnut, mahogany 9 butternut, chocolate, sassafras
tree: 6 cassia
unit: 5 stick
cinnamon ___: 3 bun 4 bear, fern, roll, teal, vine 5 stone
___ cinnamon: 6 Saigon 7 Chinese
cinnamon bun: 6 pastry
Cinnamon Grahams: 6 cereal
competitor: 3 Kix 4 Life, Trix 5 Kashi, Quisp, Total 6 Kaboom, Muesli, Oreo O's, Pablum, Smacks 7 All-Bran, Crispix, Harmony, Hunny B's, Mueslix, Oat Bran, Pokemon 8 Boo Berry, Cheerios, Corn Chex, Corn Pops, Fiber One, Rice Chex, Special K, Uncle Sam, Wheaties 9 Alpha Bits, Apple Zaps, Grape Nuts, Honey Comb, Just Right, Wheat Chex 10 Apple Jacks, Bran Flakes, Cap'n Crunch, Cocoa Puffs, Froot Loops, Mini-Wheats, Nutri-Grain, Puffed Rice, Quaker Oats, Smart Start 11 Cocoa Blasts, Cookie Crisp, Golden Crisp, Lucky Charms, Puffed Wheat, Sweet Crunch, Waffle Crisp
cinnamon roll: 5 sweet 6 pastry
cinnamon teal: 4 duck, fowl
relative: 4 smew, teal 5 eider, Pekin, Rouen, scaup 6 Cayuga, scoter 7 gadwall, mallard, pintail, pochard, redhead, sea duck, widgeon 8 garganey, gray duck, mandarin, musk duck, oldsquaw, shoveler, surf duck, wood duck 9 black duck, broadbill, goldeneye, goosander, greenhead, merganser, ruddy duck, sprigtail 10 bufflehead, canvasback, surf scoter, tufted duck

Cinnamon Toast Crunch: 6 cereal
competitor: 3 Kix 4 Life, Trix 5 Kashi, Quisp, Total 6 Kaboom, Muesli, Oreo O's, Pablum, Smacks 7 All-Bran, Crispix, Harmony, Hunny B's, Mueslix, Oat Bran, Pokemon 8 Boo Berry, Cheerios, Corn Chex, Corn Pops, Fiber One, Rice Chex, Special K, Uncle Sam, Wheaties 9 Alpha Bits, Apple Zaps, Grape Nuts, Honey Comb, Just Right, Wheat Chex 10 Apple Jacks, Bran Flakes, Cap'n Crunch, Cocoa Puffs, Froot Loops, Mini-Wheats, Nutri-Grain, Puffed Rice, Quaker Oats, Smart Start 11 Cocoa Blasts, Cookie Crisp, Golden Crisp, Lucky Charms, Puffed Wheat, Sweet Crunch, Waffle Crisp
cinque: 4 five 7 Italian
ender: 4 foil
follower: 3 sei
preceder: 7 quattro
cinquefoil feature: 3 arc
Cintalapa: 4 city, town
locale: 6 Mexico 7 Chiapas
CIO: 5 union
chapter: 3 lcl. 5 local
members: 5 labor
partner: 3 AFL
Cio-Cio-San
accessory for ~: 3 obi
to Yakusidé: 5 niece
Cioffi: 7 Charles
cioppino: 4 stew
cipher: 3 nil, zip 4 code, sign, zero 5 aught, blank, count, ought, zilch 6 figure, legend, naught, nought, number, reckon 7 compute, nothing 8 goose egg 9 calculate, character, nonentity 10 encryption
code: 3 key
expert: 5 coder
put in ~: 6 encode
solve a ~: 6 decode
ciphering: 9 reckoning 10 arithmetic
circa: 5 about 6 approx., around, nearly 7 roughly
circadian: 5 daily 7 per diem
dysrhythmia: 6 jet lag
circadian ___: 6 rhythm
Circe: 8 conjurer 9 sorceress
brother of ~: 6 Aeetes 8 Apsyrtus
emulate ~: 5 tempt
lover of ~: 8 Odysseus
parent of ~: 5 Persa 6 Hecate, Helios
sister of ~: 5 Medea 8 Pasiphae
son of ~: 5 Romus 6 Agrius 7 Anteias, Ardeias, Latinus, Romanus 9 Telegonus
circle: 3 lap, mob, set 4 band, belt, club, disc, disk, gird, gyre, halo, hoop, loop, ring, turn 5 class, crowd, curve, group, hem in, junto, orbit, pivot, shape, wheel, whirl 6 begird, clique, engird, gyrate, league, rotate, sphere 7 academy, aureola, aureole, company, coterie, enclose, envelop, environ, faction, inclose, in-group, revolve, society 8 cincture, gloriole, go around, surround 9 encompass, enwreathe, following, hangers-on, perimeter 10 revolution
back: 6 return
combining form: 3 gyr- 4 gyro-
dance: 4 hora, kolo 9 farandole
diagram developer: 4 Venn
flattened ~: 4 oval 7 ellipse
formed into a ~: 5 orbed
in a vicious ~: 4 vain 5 inane 6 absurd, futile 7 insipid 9 for naught, frivolous, pointless, worthless 10 ridiculous
inner ~: 5 cabal, elite 6 clique, jet set 7 coterie, faction 10 upper crust

line across a ~: 3 dia. 4 diam. 5 chord 6 radius 8 diameter
measures: 5 radii
numbered ~: 4 dial
of flowers: 3 lei
of light: 4 halo 6 corona 7 aureola, aureole
portion: 3 arc
ratio: 2 pi
size: 4 area
tiny ~: 3 dot
to a poet: 3 orb
traffic ~: 6 rotary
unit: 6 degree
___ circle: 4 full, hour, unit 5 color, dress, great, inner, pitch, polar, small 6 family, sewing 7 azimuth, charmed, diurnal, parquet, quality, squared, traffic, transit, vicious, winner's
___ Circle: 5 Great, Inner 6 Arctic, Family
circled: 5 orbed
Circle Game, The author: Atwood
Circle in the Sand (1988 song) artist: Belinda Carlisle
Circle of Friends: 4 film 5 novel
author: Maeve Binchy
cast: Minnie Driver, Chris O'Donnell
circles
going in ~: 4 lost
run ~ around: 3 top 4 beat, best 5 outdo 6 outwit 8 outsmart 9 overwhelm
circlet: 6 bangle, diadem, wreath
circle the ___: 6 wagons
___ Circle, The: 5 First 6 Family
Circle, The author: Maugham
circling: 6 spiral
circuit: 3 lap 4 beat, loop, ring, tour, walk, zone 5 ambit, orbit, round, route, track, wheel 6 course, hookup, league 7 compass 9 itinerary, perimeter, round trip 10 revolution
component: 4 fuse
problem: 4 leak 5 short
rubber-chicken ~: 5 stump
tend to a ~ breaker: 5 reset
three-way ~: 3 wye
unit: 3 amp, ohm 4 watt 6 ampere
circuit ___: 4 edge 5 board, court, judge, rider 7 binding, breaker
___ circuit: 3 NOR, NOT 4 grid, NAND, open, side 5 AND-OR, logic, short 6 bridge, closed, safety 7 borscht, phantom, printed, sawdust, squelch
Circuit ___: 4 City
circuitous: 7 complex, devious, sinuous, winding 8 rambling, tortuous 10 collateral, meandering, roundabout
circuitry: 7 network
circular: 2 ad 3 rnd. 4 bill 5 flier, flyer, orbic, round 6 curved, insert, spiral 7 handout, leaflet 8 brochure, dislike, handbill, indirect, magazine, pamphlet, ringlike 9 broadside
border: 4 band, belt, ring 6 collar, girdle 8 cincture
follow a ~ path: 3 arc
motion: 4 gyre, spin 8 gyration
object: 4 disk
somewhat ~: 4 oval
word: 4 sale, save
circular ___: 3 mil, saw 4 file 5 error, light, pitch 7 measure, sailing
Circular Staircase, The author: Mary Roberts Rinehart
circulate: 3 air 4 flow, send, turn 5 issue, rumor, strew, swirl 6 mingle, report, spread, travel, wander 7 publish, radiate 8 bring out, disperse, proclaim 9 broadcast, get around, interview, make known, propagate, publicize, ventilate 10 distribute, mill around, move around, promulgate

circulating: 5 astir 7 current 8 in the air
circulating ___: 6 medium 7 capital, decimal, library
circulation: 4 flow 5 issue 6 spread
aid: 3 fan
circulatory system part: 4 vein 5 aorta, heart 6 artery
circumambulate: 4 ring, rove 5 skirt 6 wander
circumference: 3 rim 4 edge, girt, loop 5 ambit, girth 6 border, fringe 7 compass, outline 8 boundary 9 perimeter
ratio: 2 pi
segment: 3 arc
circumlocute: 5 dodge 6 wander
circumlocutory: 5 wordy 6 prolix 7 diffuse, verbose 9 redundant 10 discursive, long-winded, pleonastic
circumnavigate: 4 ring 5 round, skirt
circumnavigator: 4 Fogg, Gray 5 Drake 8 Magellan
circumscribe: 4 ring 5 bound, fence, hem in, limit 6 define, engird 7 compass, confine, delimit, enclose, environ, inclose, mark off, outline, qualify 8 encircle, restrain, restrict, surround
circumscribed: 6 narrow 7 insular, limited 8 definite, orthodox 9 qualified
circumspect: 3 shy 4 cagy, wary 5 alert, cagey, canny, chary, fussy, leery 7 careful, finicky, guarded, heedful, politic, prudent 8 cautious, discreet, exacting, finiking, finnicky, keen-eyed, rational, rigorous, thorough, vigilant, watchful 9 assiduous, attentive, judicious, observant, provident 10 fastidious, meticulous, particular, reasonable, scrupulous
circumspection: 4 care 7 caution, finesse 9 vigilance 10 precaution
circumspectly, act: 6 beware
circumstance: 4 case 5 event, state, thing 6 action, affair 7 destiny, episode 8 accident, exigence, exigency, fortuity, grandeur, incident, occasion
partner: 4 pomp
uncontrollable ~: 4 luck 6 chance
circumstances: 3 lot 4 life 5 state, terms 6 assets 7 capital 8 position 9 situation 10 livelihood
in different ~: 9 otherwise
in reduced ~: 4 poor 5 needy
under any ~: 5 at all
under what ~: 3 how
___ circumstances beyond...: 5 Due to
circumvent: 4 duck, foil, shun, trap 5 avert, avoid, dodge, elude, evade, parry, shirk, skirt 6 bypass, entrap, escape, eschew, outwit, thwart 7 abstain, defraud, shy from 8 flee from, outflank, outsmart, sidestep, surround 9 frustrate, get around, overreach 10 disappoint, work around
circumvention: 7 evasion
circus: 4 fair, show 6 big top 8 carnival 9 spectacle
animal: 3 dog 4 bear, flea, lion, seal 5 tiger
employee: 5 clown, tamer 6 barker 7 juggler 10 ringmaster
need: 3 net 4 hoop, ring, tent 5 knife, stilt, sword 6 cannon
routine: 3 act 5 stunt
sound: 4 roar
wear: 6 tights
circus ___: 3 act 4 tent
___ circus: 4 flea, tent 6 flying
Circus ___: 7 Maximus
___ Circus: 5 At the 6 Family
Circus Circus locale: 5 Vegas 8 Las Vegas

Circus Maximus: 5 arena
official: 5 edile
cirio: 4 tree
cirque: 3 cwm
basin: 4 tarn
Cirque du __: 6 Soleil
cirrocumulus: 4 wisp 5 cloud
cloud: 4 wisp
cirrostratus: 5 cloud
cirrus: 4 wisp 5 cloud
like a ~: 5 wispy 7 wispish
Cirrus: 3 car 4 auto 8 Chrysler
Cisalpine __: 4 Gaul
CIS ancestor: 4 USSR
cisco: 4 fish 9 whitefish
Cisco: 4 city
locale: 5 Texas
Cisco __: 3 Kid 4 Pike 7 Systems
Cisco Kid, The (TV western): 5 oater
cast: Leo Carrillo (Pancho) Duncan Renaldo (The Cisco Kid)
Cisco Kid, The (1973 song) artist: War
Cisco Pike (1972 film)
cast: Karen Black, Gene Hackman, Kris Kristofferson
ciseaux: 4 leap
'C' Is for Corpse author: Sue Grafton
Cissy: 7 Houston
Cistercian: 9 religious
cistern: 3 vat 4 sump, tank 9 container, reservoir
__ cit.: 3 loc. 5 in loc.
citadel: 4 fort, keep 5 tower 6 castle 7 bastion, defense, lookout, redoubt 8 fortress, garrison 10 stronghold
Citadel: 6 school
locale: 4 S. Car. 10 Charleston
student: 5 cadet 7 Bulldog
Citadel, The (1938 film)
cast: Robert Donat, Rex Harrison, Ralph Richardson, Rosalind Russell
director: King Vidor
citation: 5 award, prize, quote 6 praise, trophy 7 example, excerpt, extract, mention, passage, summons, tribute 8 encomium 9 extolment, quotation, reference 10 decoration, imputation
abbr.: 4 et al., ibid. 5 op. cit.
invite a ~: 5 speed
Citation: 3 car 4 auto 5 Chevy, Edsel, horse 9 Chevrolet 10 automobile
rider: 6 Arcaro
citations: 8 analecta, analects
__ citato: 4 loco 5 opere
cite: 3 lay 4 name, note 5 offer, order, quote, refer 6 accuse, adduce, assert, praise, recall, summon, ticket 7 commend, excerpt, extract, itemize, mention, recount, refer to, specify 8 allude to, decorate, point out, remember, spell out, subpoena 9 enumerate, exemplify, recognize, recollect, reference, single out
cithara cousin: 4 harp
cities: 5 urbia
change ~: 4 move, relo 8 relocate
of ~: 5 civic 9 municipal
__ Cities: 4 Quad, Twin
Cities of the Interior author: Anaïs Nin
citified: 5 urban
citify: 8 urbanize
citizen: 5 voter 6 native 7 dweller, resider 8 indigene, national, resident, taxpayer 9 indweller 10 inhabitant
U.S. ~ ID: 3 SSN
__ citizen: 4 dual 6 senior
Citizen: 5 watch 10 wristwatch
alternative: 4 Ebel, Rado 5 Casio, Elgin, Lorus, Omega, Rolex, Seiko, Timex 6 Bulova, Fossil, Movado, Pulsar, Swatch 8 Longines, Tag Heuer, Tourneau
Citizen Kane (1941 film)
cast: Joseph Cotten, Agnes Moorehead, Everett Sloane, Orson Welles
composer: 8 Herrmann
director: Orson Welles
prop: 4 sled 7 Rosebud 9 snow globe
studio: 3 RKO
citizen of (suffix): 3 ite
citizenry: 6 people, public 7 country 9 residents 10 population
citizens __ radio: 4 band
citizen's __: 6 arrest
citizenship __: 6 papers
Citizen Tom Paine author: Howard Fast
Citizen X star: 3 Rea
citrate: 4 salt 5 ester
citric: 4 acid 6 fruity, lemony
citrine: 3 gem 6 yellow 7 mineral
relative: 4 buff, corn, gold, lime, rust, sand 5 blond, brass, coral, cream, flaxy, lemon, maize, ocher, ochre, peach, rusty, straw 6 blonde, canary, chammy, citron, crocus, flaxen, shammy, shamoy 7 apricot, chamois, jasmine, mustard, nankeen, old gold, saffron, xanthic 8 daffodil, primrose 9 champagne, goldenrod, jessamine
Citroën: 3 car 4 auto 5 André 6 import 10 automobile
model: 4 Saxo 5 Xsara 6 Activa
citron: 4 tree 5 fruit 6 cedrat, yellow
ender: 4 ella
relative: 4 buff, corn, gold, lime, rust, sand 5 blond, brass, coral, cream, flaxy, lemon, maize, ocher, ochre, peach, rusty, straw 6 blonde, canary, chammy, crocus, flaxen, shammy, shamoy 7 apricot, chamois, citrine, jasmine, mustard, nankeen, old gold, saffron, xanthic 8 daffodil, primrose 9 champagne, goldenrod, jessamine
citron __: 4 wood 5 melon
citronella __: 3 oil 6 candle
citrus: 4 lime, ugli 5 fruit, lemon 6 orange, pomelo, tangor 7 cumquat, kumquat, satsuma, Seville, tangelo 8 bergamot, mandarin, shaddock, Valencia 9 tangerine 10 calamondin, grapefruit
city: 5 Ocala
colorant: 6 ethene
cover: 4 rind, skin 6 albedo
drink: 3 ade
grower bane: 5 frost 7 drought
Italian ~: 8 bergamot
peel: 4 zest
peel constituent: 5 rutin
tree: 3 bel 4 bael, lime 5 lemon 6 orange, pomelo, pumelo 7 pommelo, pummelo, tangelo 8 bergamot, mandarin, shaddock 9 tangerine 10 grapefruit
yield: 5 juice
Citrus Heights: 4 city, town
locale: 10 California
Citrus Park: 4 city, town
locale: 7 Florida
Città __ Vaticano: 3 del
cittern: 6 guitar, string
origin: 6 Europe
city: 4 burg, town 5 civic, civil, metro, place, urban 6 public 7 capital 8 downtown 9 municipal 10 metropolis
combining form: 5 metro-, -polis
ender: 4 wide 5 scape
like a ~ population: 5 dense
of a ~: 5 urban
city __: 4 desk, hall, plan, room 5 clerk 6 editor, father 7 chicken, council, edition, manager, planner, slicker
city-__: 4 born, bred 5 state
__ city: 3 fat 4 core, free 5 inner, strip 6 garden 7 central
City: 4 font 8 typeface
City __: 4 Girl, Hall, Heat 5 of God 6 Lights 7 Streets
__ City: 3 Bay, Del, Fat, Oil, Sim, Sin, Sun 4 Daly, Dark, Holy, Iowa, Neon, Open, Park, Spin, Surf 5 Dodge, Lanai, Mason, Naked, Ocean, Ponca, Queen, Quiet, Rapid, Sioux, Windy 6 Carson, Culver, Gotham, Jersey, Kansas, Mexico, Radium 7 Circuit, Emerald, Vatican 8 Atlantic, Salt Lake, Virginia 9 Forbidden
__ City, AZ: 3 Sun
__ City, CA: 4 Yuba
__ City Chiefs: 6 Kansas
__ City Confidential: 6 Kansas
__ City, FL: 4 Ybor 5 Plant 6 Haines, Panama
City for Conquest (1940 film)
cast: James Cagney, Ann Sheridan
director: Anatole Litvak
City Girl (1984 film)
cast: Laura Harrington, Joe Mastroianni, Carole McGill
director: Martha Coolidge
City Hall (1996 film)
cast: Danny Aiello, John Cusack, Bridget Fonda, Martin Landau, Al Pacino
City Hall boss: 5 mayor 8 hizzoner
City Heat (1984 film)
cast: Jane Alexander, Clint Eastwood, Madeline Kahn, Burt Reynolds
director: Richard Benjamin
__ City, HI: 5 Lanai
__ City, IA: 5 Sioux
City in the Sea, The author: Poe
City Lights (1931 film)
cast: Charles Chaplin
director: Charles Chaplin
__ City, NJ: 5 Ocean
__ City, NV: 6 Carson
City of __: 3 God, Joy 4 Elms, Hope 5 David, Light 6 Angels, Totems
City of Angels (1998 film)
cast: Andre Braugher, Nicolas Cage, Dennis Franz, Meg Ryan
dog: 4 Earl
City of Brotherly __: 4 Love
City of God author: E.L. Doctorow
City of Hope (1991 film)
cast: Tony Lo Bianco, Joe Morton, Vincent Spano
director: John Sayles
City of Industry (1997 film)
cast: Stephen Dorff, Timothy Hutton, Famke Janssen, Harvey Keitel
director: John Irvin
City of Joy setting: 5 India
City of Light, The: 5 Paree, Paris
City of New Orleans: 5 train
City of New Orleans, The (1972 song)
artist: Arlo Guthrie
City of Seven __: 5 Hills
City of the Beasts author: Allende
City of the Kings: 4 Lima
City of Trees, The: 5 Boise
__ City, OK: 3 Del
__ City, PA: 3 Oil
__ City Rollers: 3 Bay
__ City Royals: 6 Kansas
cityscape: 4 view 5 vista
__ City, SD: 5 Rapid
City Slickers (1991 film)
cast: Billy Crystal, Bruno Kirby, Jack Palance, Helen Slater, Daniel Stern, Patricia Wettig, Noble Willingham
city-state, ancient: 5 Argos, polis 6 Athens, Sparta
__ City steak: 6 Kansas
City Streets (1931 film)
cast: Gary Cooper, Sylvia Sidney
director: Rouben Mamoulian
__ City Sue: 5 Sioux
City That Never Sleeps (1953 film)
cast: Mala Powers, Gig Young
director: John H. Auer
__ City, The: 5 Black, Naked 7 Eternal
City Without Walls author: W.H. Auden
City Wit, The author: 5 Brome
__ City Woman: 5 Sweet
Ciudad del Este: 4 city, town
locale: 8 Paraguay
Ciudad Juárez neighbor: 6 El Paso
Ciudad Valles: 4 city, town
locale: 6 Mexico
civet: 3 cat 5 felid, rasse, zibet 6 animal, feline, mammal 7 wildcat
product: 4 musk
civic: 4 city 5 local, urban 6 public 8 internal 9 municipal
group: 4 Elks 7 Jaycees, Kiwanis
civic __: 6 center, leader
civic-__: 6 minded
Civic: 3 car 4 auto 5 Honda
civics: 8 politics
civil: 4 city, kind 5 suave 6 polite, public, social, urbane 7 cordial, genteel, refined, secular, tactful 8 domestic, gracious, ladylike, mannerly, obliging, outgoing, pleasant, temporal, well-bred 9 courteous, municipal 10 diplomatic, neighborly, respectful, thoughtful
disorder: 4 riot
liberty: 2 rt. 5 right
offense: 4 tort
servant: 5 mayor 7 officer 8 official 10 bureaucrat
war: 6 revolt 7 anarchy 8 sedition, uprising 9 rebellion 10 revolution
civil __: 3 day, law, war 4 year 6 rights 7 defense, servant, service
Civil __ Patrol: 3 Air
Civil Action, A (1998 film)
cast: Robert Duvall, William H. Macy, Tony Shalhoub, John Travolta
Civil Aeronautics __: 5 Board
Civil Disobedience: 5 essay
author: Henry David Thoreau
__ civile: 3 jus
civilian: 6 layman
attire: 5 mufti
civilian __: 7 clothes
civilian __ board: 6 review
Civilian Conservation __: 5 Corps
civility: 4 tact 5 mense 7 decorum, manners 8 breeding, courtesy, protocol, urbanity 9 etiquette, gallantry, gentility, propriety 10 politeness, refinement
act of ~: 6 devoir
civilization: 7 culture, society 8 progress
...civilization __ know it: 4 as we
Civilization director: 4 Ince, West
civilize: 6 refine 8 humanize
civilized: 4 nice, tame 5 suave 6 polite, urbane 7 genteel, refined 8 mannerly 9 courteous
__ Civilized Nations: 4 Five
civilizing: 8 cultural 9 uplifting
civil rights org.: 4 ACLU, CORE, EEOC, SCLC, SNCC 5 NAACP
Civil War
anthem: 5 Dixie
battle: 6 Shiloh 7 Bull Run 8 Antietam, Manassas 9 Vicksburg 10 Fort Sumter, Gettysburg, Wilderness
color: 4 blue, gray, grey
general: 3 Lee, Ord 5 Bragg, Buell, Early, Ewell, Grant, Meade 6 Custer, Hooker, Stuart 7 Forrest, Halleck, Hancock, Jackson, Pickett, Sherman, Sickles 8 Burnside, Johnston, Sheridan 9 Doubleday, McClellan 10 Beauregard, Longstreet
inits.: 3 CSA, REL, USG
nickname: 3 Abe

side: 5 North, South, union
soldier: 3 reb
veterans' org.: 3 GAR
weapon: 5 saber 6 cannon
___ Civil War: 7 English, Spanish
civvies: 5 dress, mufti 7 clothes
Cixous, Hélène: 6 French, writer
___ C. Kenton: 4 Erle
Cl: 4 elem. 7 element, halogen 8 chlorine
17 for ~: 4 at. no.
clabber: 4 clot, curd 5 dairy 6 cheese, curdle, gelate 7 thicken
clabbered: 4 sour 5 thick
clack: 3 yak, yap 4 snap, tick 5 click, cluck, noise, sound 6 cackle, rattle 7 chatter, clatter, palaver
clacker, dancer's: 4 zill
Clacton-on-___: 3 Sea
clad: 5 robed 6 decent, garbed 7 arrayed, attired, clothed, covered, dressed, enrobed 8 bedecked 9 decked out, outfitted
in: 7 wearing
starter: 4 iron
___-clad: 4 snow 5 armor
clafouti: 5 sweet 6 pastry
Claiborne: 3 Liz 4 Pell 5 Craig 7 Dolores
claim: 2 rt. 3 say 4 aver, avow, case, dibs, feud, hold, lien, plea 5 argue, boast, right, share, stake, title 6 action, allege, assert, avowal, charge, demand, insist, option, rights 7 call for, contend, declare, deserve, lawsuit, pretend, profess, purport, reserve 8 argument, arrogate, averment, interest, maintain, petition, pretense, property, stake out 9 assertion, challenge, ownership, postulate, privilege 10 allegation, birthright, contention, pretension
false ~: 4 hoax
file a ~: 3 sue 8 litigate
first ~: 4 dibs 6 option
have a ~: 5 merit
honor a ~: 5 repay 6 refund, settle 7 pay back 8 make good 9 reimburse
lay ~: 7 pretend
legal ~: 4 lien 5 droit 8 mortgage
reason for a ~: 4 loss 6 damage
relinquish a ~: 5 waive
starter: 4 quit 7 counter
to fame: 5 forte 9 specialty
claim-___: 6 jumper
claimant: 6 lienor 8 litigant 9 applicant
claiming ___: 4 race
Claiming of Sleeping Beauty, The
author: Anne Rice
___-claims court: 5 small
___ claim to: 3 lay
Clair: 4 René 5 saint 8 Huxtable
to Cliff: 4 wife 6 spouse
Clair de Lune composer: 7 Debussy
Claire: 3 Ina 5 Bloom, Danes 6 Trevor 7 Forlani 9 Chennault
___ Claire: 3 Eau 5 Marie
Claire, Ina: 7 actress
film: Claudia (1943)
The Greeks Had a Word for Them (1932)
Ninotchka (1939)
The Royal Family of Broadway (1930)
___ Claire, Que.: 6 Pointe
Clairol competitor: 6 L'Oreal
Clair, René: 8 director
film: And Then There Were None (1945)
The Flame of New Orleans (1941)
Forever and a Day (1943)
I Married a Witch (1942)
It Happened Tomorrow (1944)
A Nous la Liberté (1931)
clairvoyance: 3 ESP, psi 9 telepathy
clairvoyant: 3 fey 4 seer 5 augur, sibyl, vatic 6 medium, mental, oracle 7 aruspex, diviner, prophet, psychic, vatical 8 haruspex, oracular, telepath 9 prescient 10 predictive
need: 5 tarot 7 crystal
words: 4 I see
Clairvoyant, The (1934 film)
cast: Claude Rains, Fay Wray
clam: 4 buck 5 gaper, shell 6 dollar, gweduc, quahog 7 bivalve, coquina, geoduck, mollusc, mollusk, pompano, quahaug, relaxed, seafood, smacker, steamer, toheroa 8 seashell, simoleon 9 hard-shell, shellfish, soft-shell 10 littleneck
chowder: 4 soup
ender: 4 bake, worm 5 shell 7 diggers
giant ~: 5 shell 8 seashell
like Manhattan ~ chowder: 5 thymy
part: 5 valve
sauce alternative: 5 pesto 8 marinara
up: 5 quiet 6 stifle 7 be quiet, silence 8 withhold
clam ___: 5 sauce, shell 7 chowder, diggers
___ clam: 4 hard, king, long, soft, surf 5 giant, horse, pismo, razor, round 6 butter, calico 7 steamer
clamant: 5 noisy 6 urgent 8 pressing 10 compelling
clambake: 4 fete, gala, meal 5 feast, party, rally 6 picnic 9 festivity, gathering
Clambake (1967 film)
cast: Bill Bixby, Shelley Fabares, Will Hutchins, Elvis Presley
clamber: 4 shin 5 climb, crawl, mount, scale 6 ascend, ramble, shinny 7 shinney 8 scrabble, scramble
up: 5 mount
clam chowder: 4 soup
clamdiggers: 5 pants 8 knickers
clammed up: 3 mum 5 quiet 6 silent 9 secretive 10 speechless, unspeaking
clammy: 3 wet 4 cold, damp, dank 5 humid, moist, muggy, soggy, undry 6 steamy, sticky, stuffy, sultry, sweaty 7 viscose, viscous, wettish
clamor: 3 ado, cry, din, row 4 bawl, buzz, fuss, howl, peal, roar, to-do 5 blare, hoo-ha, noise, shout 6 bellow, bustle, hassle, holler, hubbub, lather, outcry, racket, ruckus, rumpus, tumult, uproar 7 clangor, cluster, ferment, protest, turmoil 8 brouhaha, disorder, hangover, proclaim 9 agitation, cacophony, commotion, hue and cry, make a fuss, raise Cain 10 clattering, hubba-hubba, hullabaloo, hurly-burly
for: 6 demand
(for): 3 ask
clamorous: 4 loud 5 aroar, forte, noisy, vocal 6 brassy 7 blaring, booming, exigent, hooting, jarring, pealing, rackety, rampant, raucous, reboant, roaring 8 crashing, exigeant, piercing, plangent, rumbling, sonorous, strident, turned up 9 big-voiced, deafening, demanding, insistent 10 boisterous, imperative, insatiable, resounding, stentorian, strepitous, thundering, tumultuous, uproarious, vociferant, vociferous
clamp: 4 bind, grip, join, lock, vise 5 brace, clasp, latch 6 clench, fasten, joiner, secure 7 bracket 8 fastener
down on: 5 quash 6 batten, stifle
clamp ___: 4 down
___ clamp: 3 bar 4 mast
Clampett: 3 Jed 7 Elly May
nephew: 6 Bodine, Jethro
portrayer: 5 Ebsen 7 Douglas
Clampitt, Amy: 4 poet
clams: 4 cash 5 bread, dough
prepare ~: 3 fry 5 steam
clams ___: 6 casino
clamshell ___: 4 door 6 bucket
clamshell material: 5 nacre
clan: 3 mob, set 4 band, club, gang, race, ring 5 bunch, folks, group, house, stock, tribe 6 clique, family, outfit, people 7 coterie, faction, ingroup, kindred, kinfolk, lineage, society 8 kinfolks, kinsfolk 10 fraternity
ancient Greek ~: 6 phyles
bigwig: 5 thane, thegn
clash: 4 feud
division: 4 sept
emblem: 5 totem
man: 4 Scot
member: 4 aunt 5 niece, uncle 6 cousin, nephew
wear: 4 kilt 5 plaid
see also family
Clancy Brothers member: 5 Makem
Clancy, Tom: 6 author 8 novelist
hero: Jack Ryan
subject: 3 CIA
work: Airborne
Armored Cav
The Cardinal of the Kremlin
Carrier
Clear and Present Danger
Debt of Honor
Executive Orders
Fighter Wing
The Hunt for Red October
Marine
Patriot Games
Rainbow Six
Red Rabbit
Red Storm Rising
SSN
Submarine
The Sum of All Fears
The Teeth of the Tiger
Without Remorse
clandestine: 3 sly 4 foxy 6 artful, closet, covert, hidden, masked, secret, sneaky, unseen, veiled 7 cloaked, furtive, illicit, on the QT, private 8 hush-hush, obscured, secluded, shrouded, sneaking, stealthy 9 concealed, disguised, underhand 10 undercover, under wraps
org.: 3 CIA, NSA, ONI
clandestinely: 7 sub rosa 8 on the sly, secretly 10 under cover
clang: 4 bong, gong, peal, ring, toll 5 chime, clink, knell, noise, sound 6 jangle, jingle 7 resound
clanger: 4 bell
clangor: 3 din 4 ring 5 blare, noise 6 clamor, hubbub, jangle, racket, tumult, uproar 7 clatter 8 clashing 10 clattering
clangorous: 4 loud 5 noisy 6 shrill 8 clashing
clank: 5 sound 6 jangle, rattle 7 clatter
clannish: 9 exclusive, sectarian
Clan of the Cave Bear, The
author: Jean Auel
character: 3 Aba, Iza, Oga, Uka 4 Ayla, Brun, Creb, Durc, Goov 5 Broud
clansperson: 4 aunt 5 uncle 6 cousin, father, mother, sister 7 brother 8 relative
Clanton: 3 Ike 5 Jimmy
foe: 4 Earp
Clanton, Jimmy
song: Go, Jimmy, Go (1959)
Just a Dream (1958)
Venus in Blue Jeans (1962)
clap: 4 peal, slam, slap 5 crack, smack, smash, sound 6 praise 7 acclaim, applaud, thunder
cuffs on: 5 run in 6 arrest
ender: 4 trap 5 board
one's hands on: 4 grab 6 snatch
starter: 4 hand 5 after 7 thunder
clapboard: 5 board 6 wooden
Clap for the Wolfman (1974 song)
artist: Guess Who
clapper: 6 tongue
place: 4 bell
clappers: 10 percussion
clapping: 7 ovation 8 applause
Clapping Song, The (1965 song) artist: Shirley Ellis
clap sticks: 8 hyoshigi
Clapton, Eric: 7 British 9 guitarist
band: 5 Cream 8 Roosters 9 Yardbirds 10 Blind Faith
song: Change the World (1996)
I Can't Stand It (1981)
I Shot the Sheriff (1974)
Lay Down Sally (1978)
Layla (1972)
Promises (1978)
Tears in Heaven (1992)
claptrap: 3 gas, rot 4 blah, bosh, bull, bunk, guff, jazz, jive, pooh, tosh, wind 5 bilge, fudge, hokum, hooey, prate, stuff, trash, tripe 6 bunkum, bushwa, drivel, footle, gabble, gammon, gibber, havers, hot air, humbug, jabber, jargon, kibosh, piffle 7 baloney, blarney, blather, blether, boloney, bombast, bushwah, eyewash, flannel, flubdub, fustian, garbage, hogwash, inanity, malarky, palaver, rubbish, twaddle 8 buncombe, falderal, falderol, flimflam, flummery, folderal, folderol, malarkey, nonsense, slipslop, tommyrot, trumpery 9 banana oil, gibberish, goofiness, kidstakes, moonshine, poppycock, rigmarole 10 applesauce, balderdash, bilge water, codswallop, double-talk, empty words, flapdoodle, galimatias, Jabberwock, mumbo jumbo, rigamarole, taradiddle
Clap Yo Hands composer: 8 Gershwin
claque: 7 fawners, rooters, toadies 9 applauder 10 applauders, flatterers, sycophants
Clara: 3 Bow 4 city, town 6 Barton, Spital 8 Schumann
locale: 6 Mexico 8 Veracruz
___ Clara, CA: 5 Santa
Clara of ___: 6 Assisi
Clare: 4 John, Luce 5 saint 6 Briggs
town in county ~: 5 Ennis
Clare ___ Luce: 6 Boothe
Clare, Angel wife: 4 Tess
Clare, John: 4 poet 7 British
Claremont: 4 city, town
locale: 10 California
Clarence: 3 cat, Day 4 lion, Nash 5 Brown, Henry 6 Carter, Darrow, Thomas 7 Gilyard, Mulford 8 Birdseye, Williams
Clarence, the Cross-Eyed Lion (1965 film)
cast: Betsy Drake, Marshall Thompson
Clare of ___: 6 Assisi
claret: 3 red, zin 4 wine 5 color, Médoc 6 purply 7 crimson 8 Bordeaux, purplish 9 table wine, zinfandel
origin: 6 France
relative: 4 rose, ruby, rust, wine 5 brick, coral, grape, poppy, rusty, sandy 6 cerise, cherry, garnet, maroon 7 carmine, crimson, fuchsia, magenta, pimento, scarlet, sultana, vermeil 8 amaranth, cardinal, dubonnet, geranium, rubicund 9 carnation, cranberry, vermilion 10 strawberry
claret ___: 3 cup, red

Clarice: 8 Starling
adversary: 8 Hannibal
clarification: 8 exegesis
words of ~: 5 I mean
clarify: 4 show, sort 5 clean, solve 6 answer, purify, refine, reword, unfold 7 explain, expound 8 illumine, simplify, spell out 9 bring home, elaborate, elucidate, interpret, make plain, translate 10 illuminate, illustrate
clarinet: 4 urua, wind 5 bumpa
cousin: 4 oboe
kind of ~: 4 alto
part: 4 reed
sound: 4 tone
clarinetist: 4 Shaw 6 Bechet, Herman 7 Goodman 8 Fountain
name: 4 Pete 5 Artie, Benny, Woody 6 Sidney
Clarington: 4 city, town
locale: 6 Canada 7 Ontario
clarion: 4 wind 6 shrill 7 blaring, trumpet 8 strident
Clarissa Explains It All (Nickelodeon sitcom)
cast: Melissa Joan Hart (Clarissa Darling)
Elizabeth Hess (Janet Darling)
Joe O'Connor (Marshall Darling)
Jason Zimbler (Ferguson Darling)
Clarissa Harlowe author: Samuel Richardson
clarity: 8 accuracy, lucidity 9 certainty, plainness, precision 10 directness, exactitude, legibility, simplicity
lacking ~: 4 hazy 5 fuzzy, muzzy
Clark: 3 Bob, Dee, Joe, Roy 4 Dane, Dave, Dick, Fred, Kent 5 Candy, Gable, Susan, Terri 6 Petula, Ramsey 7 Anthony, Gillies, Sanford, William 8 Claudine, Griffith 9 chocolate
colleague: 4 Lois 5 Jimmy, Lewis, Perry
__ & Clark: 4 Lois
Clark Bar: 5 candy, snack 9 chocolate
alternative: 4 Mars, Twix 5 Heath 6 Kit Kat, Mounds, PayDay, Reese's, Zagnut 7 Krackel, Oh Henry 8 Baby Ruth, Hershey's, Milky Way, Snickers 9 Almond Joy, Mr. Goodbar 10 NutRageous
Clark, Dee song: Raindrops (1961)
Clark, Dick: 2 MC 4 host 5 emcee
Clarke: 3 Mae 4 Alan, city, town
locale: 7 Georgia
Clarke, Arthur C.: 6 writer 7 British
home: Sri Lanka, Ceylon
work: Childhood's End
The Coast of Coral
Earthlight
A Fall of Moondust
The Fountains of Paradise
Rendezvous With Rama
__ Clarke Duncan: 7 Michael
Clarke, Mae: 7 actress
film: Frankenstein (1931)
Lady Killer (1933)
Night World (1932)
The Penguin Pool Murder (1932)
The Public Enemy (1931)
Turn Back the Clock (1933)
__ Clark Five: 4 Dave
Clark Five, Dave
song: Because (1964)
Bits and Pieces (1964)
Can't You See That She's Mine (1964)
Catch Us If You Can (1965)
Glad All Over (1964)
I Like It Like That (1965)
Over and Over (1965)
You Got What It Takes (1967)
Clark, Fred: 5 actor
film: Auntie Mame (1958)
Bells Are Ringing (1960)
The Solid Gold Cadillac (1956)
Clark, Joe: 2 P.M. 8 Canadian
predecessor: 7 Trudeau
successor: 7 Trudeau
Clark, Kenneth: 3 Sir
Clark, Mary Higgins: 6 author, writer
work: All Around the Town
Before I Say Good-Bye
The Cradle Will Fall
A Cry in the Night
Daddy's Little Girl
Double Vision
He Sees You When You're Sleeping
I'll Be Seeing You
Let Me Call You Sweetheart
The Lost Angel
The Lottery Winner
Loves Music, Loves to Dance
Lucky Day
Moonlight Becomes You
My Gal Sunday
The Night Awakens
On the Street Where You Live
Pretend You Don't See Her
Remember Me
Silent Night
Stillwatch
A Stranger Is Watching
Weep No More, My Lady
We'll Meet Again
Where Are the Children?
While My Pretty One Sleeps
You Belong to Me
Clark, Petula
song: Don't Sleep in the Subway (1967)
Downtown (1965)
I Couldn't Live Without Your Love (1966)
I Know a Place (1965)
My Love (1966)
This Is My Song (1967)
Clarksdale: 4 town
locale: 4 Miss.
Clarkson: 8 Patricia
Clark, Susan: 7 actress
film: Colossus: The Forbin Project (1970)
Coogan's Bluff (1968)
Night Moves (1975)
Skin Game (1971)
spouse: Alex Karras
TV: Webster
Clarksville: 4 city, town
locale: 7 Indiana 9 Tennessee
Clark, Walter van Tilburg: 6 author
work: The Ox-Bow Incident
Clark, William: 8 explorer
partner: 5 Lewis
claro: 5 cigar
clarsach: 4 harp 6 string
origin: 7 Ireland 8 Scotland
Clary: 6 Robert
clash: 3 jar, row 4 feud, fray, jolt, spat, tiff, tilt 5 argue, brawl, brush, fight, grate, melee, run-in, scrap, set-to, shock 6 affray, battle, breach, combat, differ, fracas, impact, jangle, racket, rumpus, strife, strike, tussle 7 collide, contend, discord, dispute, dissent, grapple, mix it up, quarrel, quibble, rupture, scuffle, wrangle 8 argument, conflict, disagree, disunity, do battle, friction, showdown, skirmish, squabble, struggle, variance 9 encounter, lock horns, raise Cain, scrimmage 10 difference, disharmony, donnybrook, engagement, falling-out
don't ~: 2 go 5 match
of arms: 3 war 7 warfare
they may ~: 4 egos 5 wills
with: 9 encounter
(with): 7 compete
Clash by Night: 4 film, play
author: Clifford Odets
cast: Paul Douglas, Marilyn Monroe, Robert Ryan, Barbara Stanwyck
director: Fritz Lang
clashing: 5 harsh 6 at odds, unlike 7 clangor, hostile, opposed 8 contrary, jangling, opposing, rattling, strident 9 differing 10 clangorous, discordant
clasp: 3 hug, pin 4 clip, fist, grab, grip, hold, join, lock, take 5 catch, clamp, grasp, press, seize, stick 6 broach, brooch, buckle, clench, clinch, clutch, enfold, fasten, infold, snatch 7 bracket, embrace, squeeze 8 fastener 9 fastening, handshake, hold tight, keep close
old-style: 4 ouch 5 tache
place for a jewelry ~: 4 nape, neck
starter: 4 hand
__ clasp: 3 tie 6 battle 7 service
class: 3 ilk, set 4 chic, form, kind, luxe, mold, rank, sort, tier, type 5 birth, brand, breed, caste, genre, genus, grade, group, label, order, range, sharp, style, taxon 6 assort, beauty, bon ton, circle, clique, course, estate, family, league, lesson, manner, nobles, pizazz, polish, rating, school, sphere, status, stripe 7 bracket, coterie, culture, dashing, echelon, lineage, quality, seminar, species, station, stratum, stylish, subject, variety 8 ancestry, category, division, elective, elegance, grouping, pedigree, position, standing, urbanity 9 character, first-rate, genealogy 10 refinement
conduct a ~: 5 teach 7 lecture
disrupt the ~: 5 cut up
division: 5 order
economy ~: 5 coach
ender: 4 bell, mate, room
get the ~ back together: 5 reune
head of the ~: 3 ace 4 best, tops 5 first 9 first-rate
keep after ~: 6 detain
leader: 4 prof 7 teacher 8 lecturer 9 professor 10 instructor
lower ~: 4 herd, scum 5 dregs 6 masses, rabble 8 riffraff 9 commoners, hoi polloi, peasantry
not in ~: 3 out 4 away 6 absent
one in a ~: 5 pupil, tutee 7 student
rank factor: 3 GPA
ruling ~: 5 elite 7 royalty 8 nobility
school ~: 3 art, bio., Eng., gym, soc. 4 chem.., hist., lect., math, shop, trig 6 home ec, phys ed 7 biology, English, history, lecture, physics, poli sci 8 calculus, geometry 9 chemistry, sociology 10 psychology
social ~: 5 caste
unlikely ~ president: 4 nerd, nurd
upper ~: 4 rich 5 haves, lords 6 gentry, jet set 7 society 8 nobility 9 gentility 10 haute monde
work: 6 lesson
class __: 3 act, day, war 4 mark 5 clown 6 action 7 meaning, warfare
class-__ suit: 6 action
__ class: 4 form, word 5 Bible, cabin, first, lower, third, upper 6 best in, master, middle, second, social 7 economy, tourist, working
__-class: 4 high 5 first, third, world 6 fourth
Class Action (1991 film)
cast: Colin Friels, Gene Hackman, Mary Elizabeth Mastrantonio
director: Michael Apted
classes
biological ~: 4 taxa
classic: 4 oldy, tome 5 model, oldie, typic 6 simple 7 regular, typical, vintage 8 standard 9 exemplary 10 consummate, definitive, magnum opus
starter: 3 neo
Classic: 3 car 4 auto 7 Rambler
classical: 5 Attic, Doric, Greek, Ionic, model, music, Roman, style 7 elegant, Grecian, Homeric 8 Hellenic, literary 9 canonical, exemplary, Virgilian 10 harmonious, historical, humanistic, restrained, scholastic
composer: 4 Arne, Bach, Ives, Lalo, Orff 5 d'Indy, Dukas, Elgar, Fauré, Gluck, Grieg, Haydn, Holst, Liszt, Ravel, Satie, Verdi, Weber 6 Bartók, Brahms, Chopin, Delius, Dvorák, Glinka, Gounod, Handel, Mahler, Mozart, Wagner, Webern 7 Bellini, Berlioz, Borodin, Britten, Debussy, Delibes, Milhaud, Poulenc, Puccini, Purcell, Rossini, Smetana, Strauss, Vivaldi 8 Bruckner, Clementi, Paganini, Respighi, Schubert, Schumann, Sibelius, Telemann 9 Beethoven, Buxtehude, Donizetti, Hindemith, Meyerbeer, Prokofiev, Scarlatti 10 Monteverdi, Saint-Saëns
language: 5 Greek, Latin
music: 4 trio 5 fugue, motet, opera, rondo, waltz 6 sonata 7 cantata, partita, quartet, toccata 8 concerto, nocturne, oratorio, serenade, symphony
scholar: 8 humanist
starter: 3 neo
Classical __: 3 Gas 5 Greek, Latin
Classical Gas (1968 song) artist: Mason Williams
classicism: 8 grandeur 9 formality, Hellenism, propriety, restraint, sublimity 10 excellence, proportion, refinement, regularity, simplicity
Classico: 5 sauce 10 pasta sauce
alternative: 4 Ragu 5 Prego 6 Prince 10 Newman's Own 11 Aunt Millie's
classics: 7 letters 10 literature
classification: 3 ilk 4 kind 5 genre, genus, grade, group, label, niche, order 6 branch, rating, series, system 7 bracket, echelon, section, sorting 8 category, grouping, ordering, sequence
blood ~: 5 type A, type B, type O 6 type AB
science of ~: 8 taxonomy
classified: 2 ad 6 inside, secret, want ad 7 private, regular 8 hush-hush
abbr.: 2 rm. 3 EEO, EIK, EOE 4 bsmt 6 apt. gar.
cost: 6 ad rate
listing: 3 job 8 personal, yard sale
classify: 4 file, list, name, rank, rate, size, sort, type 5 grade, group, index, label, order, place, range 6 assort, divide, number 7 arrange, bracket, catalog 8 evaluate, graduate, identify, organize, regulate, separate, tabulate 9 catalogue 10 categorize, distribute, pigeonhole
__-class mail: 5 first, third 6 second
classmate: 4 peer 6 friend
classmates, see the old: 5 reune
Class Reunion author: 5 Jaffe
classroom: 4 hall
clanger: 4 bell
item: 3 map 4 desk 5 chalk, globe 6 eraser
jotting: 5 notes
no-no: 3 gum
sound: 3 pst, shh 4 psst
classy: 4 chic, fine, luxe, posh, rich, tony 5 haute, ritzy, sharp, swank, swell, swish, toney 6 dapper, dressy,

modish, snappy, snazzy, spiffy, spruce, swanky **7** dashing, elegant, in vogue, refined, stylish, voguish **8** esthetic, tasteful **9** exclusive, first-rate, glamorous, high-toned
clatter: 3 din **4** bang, roar **5** clack, clank, noise, noisy, sound **6** clamor, hubbub, jangle, racket, rattle, rumpus, uproar **7** bluster, clangor **8** ballyhoo **9** commotion **10** hullabaloo
Claude: 4 King **5** Akins, Brown, McKay, Monet, Rains, saint, Simon **6** Albert, Harmon **7** Debussy, Lelouch, Lorrain
in Spanish: 7 Claudio
Claude, Albert: 8 Nobelist
__-Claude Duvalier: 4 Jean
__-Claude Killy: 4 Jean
Claudel, Paul: 4 poet **6** French
Claudette: 7 Colbert
__-Claude Van Damme: 4 Jean
Claudia: 8 Schiffer **9** Cardinale, Christian
colleague of ~: 4 Elle, Tyra **5** Cindy, Naomi
Claudia (1943 film)
cast: Ina Claire, Dorothy McGuire, Robert Young
Claudia and David (1946 film)
cast: Mary Astor, Dorothy McGuire, Robert Young
director: Walter Lang
Claudine: 5 Auger, Clark **6** Longet
Claudio: 5 Arrau **6** Abbado **10** Monteverde, Monteverdi
in English: 6 Claude
Claudius: 5 Roman **6** Caesar
home: 4 Rome
successor: 4 Nero
see also Latin
Claus __ Bülow: 3 von
clause: 7 article, codicil, passage, proviso, section **9** amendment, paragraph, provision **10** subsection
connector: 3 and, but, nor **4** conj. **7** however **11** conjunction
escape ~: 3 out
modifier: 6 adverb
separator: 5 comma **6** em dash
__ clause: 4 main, noun, stop **6** adverb, escape, finite **7** Delaney, elastic, no-trade, omnibus, reserve
__ Clause, The: 5 Santa
Clausewitz: 4 Carl
__ clausum: 4 mare
Claus von __: 5 Bulow
Clavell, James: 6 author, writer
work: Gai-Jin
King Rat
Noble House
Shogun
Tai-Pan
Whirlwind
Claverings, The author: Trollope
claves: 6 sticks **10** percussion
clavichord: 10 instrument
clavicle: 4 bone
locale: 8 shoulder
clavier: 8 keyboard
composer for the ~: 4 Bach
claw: 3 rip **4** mall, maul, tear **5** talon **6** mangle, pincer, scrape, ungual, unguis **7** scratch **8** lacerate **10** fingernail
at: 3 paw **6** attack
combining form: 4 chel- **5** cheli-, ungui-
crustacean ~: 5 chela
starter: 3 dew
claw __: 3 bar **4** foot **6** hammer
__ Claw, The: 7 Scarlet
claxon: 4 horn
clay: 4 loam, marl, soil **5** adobe, earth, loess **6** kaolin **7** earthen, kaoline, pottery **10** terra cotta
combining form: 3 pel- **4** pelo- **5** argil- **7** argilli-, argillo-
cooker: 4 kiln
plant that grows on ~ animals: 4 chia
product: 4 tile **5** adobe **7** ceramic, pottery **10** terra cotta
rock: 5 shale
type of ~: 4 gley, malm **5** argil **6** kaolin **7** biscuit, kaoline
work with ~: 5 knead, model, throw
clay __: 5 court, flour, stone **6** pigeon **7** mineral
__ clay: 3 red **4** ball, fire, pipe **5** china **7** boulder, potter's
Clay: 5 Henry **7** Cassius
today: 3 Ali
claybank: 5 horse
Clayburgh, Jill: 7 actress
film: It's My Turn (1980)
Luna (1979)
Semi-Tough (1977)
Silver Streak (1976)
Starting Over (1979)
An Unmarried Woman (1978)
spouse: David Rabe
Clayderman: 7 Richard
clayey: 5 gluey, gummy, pasty **6** earthy, sticky **7** plastic **8** flexible **9** malleable
material: 4 loam, marl **5** loess
Clay, Henry: 6 orator
claymore: 5 sword
clay pigeon
launcher: 4 trap
shooting: 5 skeet
Clay Pigeons (1998 film)
cast: Georgina Cates, Janeane Garofalo, Joaquin Phoenix, Vince Vaughn
clay-rich soil, like: 5 loamy, marly
Clayson: 4 Jane
Clayton: 3 Jan **4** Jack **5** Moore
__ Clayton Powell: 4 Adam
clayware: 5 china **7** pottery **8** ceramics, crockery **9** porcelain **10** terra cotta
Clea author: Lawrence Durrell
clean: 3 mop **4** dust, fair, lave, neat, pure, soak, soap, swab, swob, tidy, trim, wash, wipe **5** bathe, blank, brush, clear, erase, flush, fresh, groom, legal, mop up, moral, plain, rinse, scour, scrub, sharp, snowy, sop up, sweep, sweet, total, white **6** bathed, bright, chaste, decent, fairly, filter, neaten, neatly, polish, purify, refine, scrape, simple, sponge, spruce, tidy up, vacuum, washed **7** aseptic, clarify, clear up, correct, deterge, elegant, ethical, expunge, furbish, launder, legible, orderly, perfect, precise, refined, shampoo, shining, sinless, sterile, sweep up, unarmed, unfussy, upright **8** absolute, complete, decisive, definite, dirtless, distinct, drug-free, flawless, germfree, graceful, honestly, hygienic, innocent, pristine, purified, readable, sanitary, spotless, spruce up, thorough, unbribed, unfouled, unsoiled, vacuumed, virtuous, well-kept **9** blameless, deodorize, disinfect, exemplary, faultless, guilt-free, guiltless, honorable, judicious, laundered, sanitized, sparkling, stainless, sterilize, taintless, undefiled, unobscene, unsmudged, unspotted, unstained, unsullied, untainted, wholesome **10** antiseptic, conclusive, immaculate, impeccable, inculpable, in the clear, sterilized, unimpaired, uninfected, unpolluted, upstanding, weaponless
again: 5 remop
air org.: 3 EPA
come ~: 3 own **4** bare **5** admit, level, own up **6** fess up **7** confess
good ~ fun: 6 frolic
hands: 7 probity **9** innocence
house: 5 purge, sweep
keep one's nose ~: 6 behave **10** toe the line
not ~: 5 dirty, germy, grimy **6** filthy, impure, sloppy, soiled
out: 3 gut **4** ruin **5** empty, purge **7** shake up **8** evacuate
squeaky ~: 6 chaste **8** spotless **10** immaculate
sweep: 7 triumph, victory **9** landslide
thoroughly: 5 scour, scrub
up: 4 edit, lave, rake **5** sweep **6** neaten, profit, redact, reform, revise, settle **7** correct, rectify **8** legalize **9** expurgate, keep house, refurbish
up one's act: 5 atone **6** reform
wipe the slate ~: 6 pardon **7** absolve, forgive, release **8** overlook
clean __: 3 out **4** room **5** hands, house, sweep **6** energy
clean __ of health: 4 bill
clean __ whistle: 3 as a
clean-__: 3 cut **6** handed, limbed, living, shaven
__ clean: 4 come
__-clean: 3 dry **7** squeaky
clean and __: 4 jerk
Clean and Sober (1988 film)
cast: Kathy Baker, Morgan Freeman, Michael Keaton, M. Emmet Walsh
director: Glenn Gordon Caron
clean as a __: 7 whistle
__ clean breast of: 5 make a
clean-cut: 4 neat, nice, trim **5** clear, crisp **6** proper **7** regular **8** distinct, handsome **9** wholesome
cleaned out: 5 broke **9** penniless
cleaner: 3 lye, vac **4** char, maid, soap, wipe **5** Brite, broom, Lysol, Tilex **6** Top Job, vacuum **7** Lestoil, Pine Sol **9** detergent, Fantastik, Step Saver
like some ~ s: 4 piny **5** piney
partner: 4 dyer
pipe ~: 3 lye **5** Drano, snake
scent: 4 pine
target: 4 dust, spot **5** grime, stain
__ cleaner: 3 air, dry **4** pipe **6** street, vacuum
cleaning: 5 chore **7** laundry **9** housework **10** refinement
cloth: 3 rag **6** chammy, shammy, shamoy **7** chamois
device: 3 mop, vac **4** swab **5** broom, brush **6** dry mop, vacuum
needing ~: 5 dirty, dusty, messy
starter: 5 house
substance: 3 lye **4** soap
cleaning __: 4 lady **5** woman
__ cleaning: 3 dry **6** spring
__-cleaning oven: 4 self
cleanliness: 7 hygiene
clean-living: 4 pure **8** virtuous
Clean, Mr. rival: 5 Lysol **7** Lestoil, Pine Sol
clean one's __: 5 clock
cleanse: 4 swab, swob, wash **5** flush, purge, rinse, scour, scrub **6** purify, refine **7** freshen, launder **8** sanctify, sanitize **9** cauterize, disinfect, expurgate, sterilize
cleanser: 3 lye **4** Ajax, Bab-O, soap, suds **5** borax, Comet **6** Bon Ami, lather, polish **7** solvent, Woolite **8** abrasive, fumigant **9** detergent, germicide, Soft Scrub **10** antiseptic
clean-shaven: 9 beardless
cleansing: 4 bath **8** ablution, lavation **9** catharsis
Cleanthes: 5 Greek, Stoic **11** philosopher
cleanup: 5 purge
clean up one's __: 3 act
clear: 3 net, pay, rid **4** bare, earn, easy, fair, free, leap, make, mild, open, pure, rake, reap, safe, sure, void, wipe **5** blank, clean, empty, erase, exact, fresh, let go, light, lucid, overt, plain, sharp, shiny, stark, sunny, sweep, vault, vivid, white **6** acquit, bright, direct, excuse, exempt, glassy, hurdle, hyalin, in tune, in view, let off, limpid, lucent, marked, pardon, patent, profit, public, purify, remove, serene, settle, simple, smooth, square, unclog, unload, vacant, vacate **7** absolve, audible, certain, crystal, decided, evident, explain, exposed, express, graphic, hyaline, in focus, legible, logical, obvious, precise, realize, receive, release, relieve, set free, shining, through, unblock, unravel, vacuous, visible **8** apparent, clean-cut, coherent, definite, distinct, explicit, innocent, jump over, knowable, luculent, luminous, manifest, palpable, pass over, pellucid, pleasant, readable, resolved, shake off, simplify, surmount, take home, unburden, unhidden, unveiled, vitreous **9** blameless, cloudless, convinced, disengage, downright, eliminate, exculpate, exonerate, extricate, graphical, graspable, guilt-free, guiltless, melodious, navigable, negotiate, satisfied, trenchant, unblurred, unclouded, unimpeded, unlimited, unobscure, vindicate **10** articulate, conclusive, disculpate, easily read, observable, pronounced, see-through, spelled out, unarguable, undeniable, undoubtful, unhampered, unhindered, unshrouded, untroubled
a loan: 5 repay **7** pay back, satisfy **8** make good, settle up, square up **9** liquidate, reimburse **10** compensate
as mud: 5 mirky, murky, vague **9** equivocal **10** unexplicit
away: 5 scoop **6** remove
be ~: 5 add up **9** make sense
become ~: 3 gel **5** click **9** penetrate
crystal ~: 5 lucid **6** patent **7** obvious **8** apparent, knowable, manifest
cut: 8 apparent, knowable
fail to ~: 6 bounce
get ~ of: 4 duck, flee, lose **5** avoid, dodge, elude, evade, skirt **6** escape **7** fend off **8** sidestep **10** circumvent
in the ~: 4 safe **5** clean **8** innocent **9** blameless, guilt-free, guiltless **10** inculpable
it might be ~: 5 coast
it's not ~: 3 mud **4** blur
make ~: 4 look, show **5** state **6** decode, define, detail, evince, refine **7** exhibit, explain **8** decipher, describe, simplify **9** bring home, emphasize, explicate, expound on, get across, put across, translate **10** illuminate, illustrate
of: 4 past **6** beyond
of the bottom: 6 aweigh
out: 2 go **3** fly, run **4** flee, scat **5** break, leave, purge, scram, sweep **6** decamp, run off **7** abscond, make off, ride off, shake up, take off **8** hightail, run for it, shove off
sky: 5 ether **6** aether
steer ~ of: 4 duck, omit, shun **5** avoid, dodge, elude, evade, shirk, skirt, spurn **6** beware, bypass, eschew, lay off **7** shy from **8** flee from, sidestep **10** circumvent
the decks: 4 tidy **5** ready
the way: 3 aid **6** assist
thinking: 5 logic **6** wisdom

up: **5** clean, solve, sweep **6** settle, square, unfold **7** explain, resolve, satisfy, unravel **8** simplify, untangle **9** bring home, elucidate **10** illuminate, illustrate
clear ___: **3** ice, off, out **4** away, text **5** as mud **7** channel
clear ___ bell: **3** as a
clear-___: **3** cut, eye **4** eyed **6** headed **7** coating, sighted
___ clear: **3** all **5** in the
___-clear: **7** crystal
clearance: **2** OK **4** okay, room, sale **5** leave, say-so **7** consent, go-ahead **8** approval, headroom, sanction **9** acquittal, allowance, discharge, open space, unloading **10** evacuation, green light
phrase: **4** as is
clearance ___: **4** sale **6** papers
Clear and Present Danger (1994 film)
cast: Anne Archer, Willem Dafoe, Harrison Ford
director: Phillip Noyce
hero: Jack Ryan
clear as ___: **3** mud **5** a bell
Clearasil target: **3** zit **4** acne
clear-cut: **4** open **5** exact, lucid, plain, sharp, terse, tight **6** in view, patent, public, strong **7** assured, evident, exposed, express, obvious, precise, visible **8** definite, explicit, manifest, specific, unhidden, unveiled **9** definable, trenchant **10** definitive, observable, pronounced, reasonable, unshrouded
___ Clear Day...: **3** On a
cleared: **4** open **6** exempt **8** official **10** off the hook, vindicated
out: **4** gone
clear-eyed: **5** sober
Clearfield: **4** city, town
locale: **4** Utah
clearheaded: **4** calm, keen **5** acute, alert, lucid, sharp, smart, sober **6** astute, bright, steady, with it **7** heads-up, prudent, sapient **8** composed, rational, sensible **9** astucious, collected, judicious, on the ball, unruffled, wide-awake **10** discerning, on one's toes, on the stick, perceptive
clearheadedness: **5** sense
clearing: **4** yard **5** glade, space **6** region **7** expanse
clearing ___: **4** bath, loan, mark **5** house
clearly: **4** well **5** by far, plain, smack **6** easily, simply, surely **8** markedly
say ~: **10** articulate
seen: **5** plain **7** obvious
show ~: **5** prove **7** specify
clearness: **9** freshness **10** simplicity
___ clear of: **5** steer
clear one, name meaning: **8** Clarence
clear-sighted: **8** keen-eyed, lynx-eyed **9** observant, sagacious
clear the ___: **3** air **4** deck
Clearwater: **4** city, town **5** range
city near ~: **5** Largo
locale: **7** Florida
Cleary: **7** Beverly
cleat: **4** calk **5** wedge
cleavage: **3** cut, gap **4** rift, slit **5** break, chasm, cleft, split **6** divide, schism **8** division, fracture **10** separation
combining form: **5** -clase
cleave: **3** axe, cut, hew, rip **4** chop, join, link, part, plow, rend, rive, stab, tear **5** carve, cling, crack, sever, slash, slice, split, stick, unite **6** adhere, attach, be true, bisect, cohere, cut off, divide, fasten, sunder **7** cling to, disjoin, scissor, stand by, stick to **8** dissever, disunite, separate
cleaver: **3** axe **4** froe, frow **5** knife
use a ~: **3** hew **4** chop
Cleaver: **4** June, Ward **5** Wally **6** Beaver **8** Eldridge
Cleaver, Beaver: **8** Theodore
word: **3** gee **5** golly
Cleaver, Wally buddy: **5** Eddie
Cleavon: **6** Little
Cleburne: **4** city, town
locale: **5** Texas
___ Cleef: **6** Lee Van
cleek: **4** club **8** golf club
Cleese, John: **5** actor **7** British **8** comedian
film: And Now for Something Completely Different (1972)
Die Another Day (2002)
Fierce Creatures (1997)
A Fish Called Wanda (1988)
Monty Python's The Meaning of Life (1983)
The Out-of-Towners (1999)
The Secret Policeman's Other Ball (1982)
Time Bandits (1981)
clef: **4** bass **5** tenor **6** treble
letters: **4** FACE **5** EGBDF
locale: **5** staff
notation: **4** rest
roman à ~: **4** book **7** fiction
___ clef: **4** alto, bass **5** tenor, viola **6** roman à, treble, violin **7** soprano
cleft: **3** cut, gap **4** gulf, rent, rift, slit, torn **5** bifid, break, chink, crack, gorge, in two, riven, split **6** breach, broken, cranny, dimple, hollow, parted **7** cracked, crevice, fissure, incised, opening **8** cleavage, fracture, sundered **9** separated
combining form: **5** fissi-
Cleghorne: **5** Ellen
Clélie author: Madeleine de Scudéry
Clem: **6** Bevans, Labine
clematis: **4** vine **5** plant **6** flower
___ clematis: **5** curly **7** scarlet
Clemenceau: **7** Georges
clemency: **4** pity **5** grace, mercy **6** lenity, pardon **7** charity, quarter, release **8** kindness, lenience, leniency **9** tolerance **10** compassion, gentleness
Clemens: **3** Sam **5** Roger, Twain **6** Krauss **8** Brentano
Clemens, Roger sport: **8** baseball
clement: **3** lax **4** calm, easy, fair, kind, mild, soft, warm **5** balmy, loose, sunny **6** bright, decent, gentle, humane, kindly, tender **7** lenient, ruthful, sparing **8** flexible, gracious, laid-back, merciful, placable, tolerant **9** assuasive, compliant, easygoing, forgiving, indulgent, temperate, unextreme **10** altruistic, benevolent, charitable, forbearing, permissive, unexacting
Clement: **4** pope **5** Moore, saint **6** Attlee **7** pontiff
___ Clemente, CA: **3** San
Clemente, Roberto: **6** Pirate **10** outfielder
Clementine
father: **5** miner
shoe size: **4** nine
Clementi piece: **5** étude
Clements, Ron: **8** director
film: Aladdin (1992)
The Great Mouse Detective (1986)
The Little Mermaid (1989)
Clemson: **6** school **7** college
athlete: **5** Tiger
conference: **3** ACC
locale: **4** S. Car.
clench: **4** fist, grip, hold, lock **5** clamp, clasp, grasp, seize **6** clutch **7** bear hug, tighten **9** handshake, hold tight
clenched ___: **4** fist
Cleo: **5** Laine
Cleon author: Robert Browning
Cleopatra: **5** queen **8** Egyptian
attendant: **4** Iras
love: **4** Marc **6** Antony, Caesar
milieu: **4** Nile **5** Egypt
serpent: **3** asp
sister: **8** Berenice
star in 1917: **4** Bara
Cleopatra (1934 film)
cast: Claudette Colbert, Henry Wilcoxon, Warren William
director: Cecil B. DeMille
Cleopatra (1963 film)
cast: Richard Burton, Rex Harrison, Elizabeth Taylor
director: Joseph L. Mankiewicz
Cleopatra's ___: **6** Needle
Cleopatre artist: **4** Erté
cleped: **5** named
clergy: **4** nuns **6** curate, estate **7** bishops, canonry, prelacy, priests **8** deaconry, minister, ministry **9** ministers, pastorate, rabbinate **10** missionary, priesthood
deg.: **3** STB, STM
not ~: **5** laity
not of the ~: **3** lay **4** laic **6** laical
cleric: **3** rev. **4** abbé, dean, guru, imam, lama, Père, pope **5** abbot, canon, clerk, elder, imaum, padre, rabbi, rebbe, roshi, Rt. Rev., vicar **6** Becket, bishop, curate, deacon, divine, father, parson, pastor, priest, reader, rector, sensei, shaman **7** Brahman, Brother, dominie, karmapa, mahatma, pontiff, prelate, primate **8** cardinal, chaplain, minister, ordinary, preacher, reverend, rinpoche, sky pilot **9** ayatollah, churchman, Dalai Lama, deaconess, maharishi, monsignor, patriarch, precentor, religious, subdeacon, Tashi Lama **10** archbishop, archdeacon, prebendary
home: **5** manse
clerical: **5** papal, pious **7** monkish **8** churchly, hieratic, monastic, pastoral, prelatic, priestly **9** apostolic, canonical, episcopal, religious **10** monastical, parsonical, pontifical, rabbinical
court: **4** rota
garment: **3** alb **5** fanon, orale, rabat
headdress: **5** miter, mitre
subject: **3** rel. **8** religion
worker: **5** clerk **6** typist
clerical ___: **5** error **6** collar
clerihew: **4** poem **5** verse
clerk: **4** hand **5** filer, typer **6** scribe, typist **7** cashier, employe **8** employee **10** amanuensis, bookkeeper
concern: **4** file
Navy ~: **6** yeoman
spot: **4** desk
starter: **5** sales
___ clerk: **3** law, lay **4** bank, city, file, room, town **5** stock **6** county **7** booking
Clermont: **4** boat, ship
power source: **5** steam
Clete: **5** Boyer
Cletus: **4** pope **7** pontiff
Cleveland: **4** Abbe, city, John, town **5** Amory, James **6** Grover
county: **8** Cuyahoga
lake: **4** Erie
locale: **4** Ohio **9** Tennessee
org. founded in ~: **4** WCTU
pro team: **4** Cavs **6** Browns **7** Indians **9** Cavaliers
river: **8** Cuyahoga
time zone: **3** EDT, EST
town near ~: **4** Avon **5** Berea, Parma
___ Cleveland Alexander: **6** Grover
Cleveland, Grover: **9** president
biographer: **6** Nevins
former occupation: **6** lawyer
home: **7** Buffalo, New York **9** New Jersey
opponent: **6** Blaine **8** Harrison
real first name: **7** Stephen
V.P.: **9** Hendricks, Stevenson
wife: **7** Frances
Cleveland, John: **4** poet **7** British
Cleveland Plain ___: **6** Dealer
clever: **3** apt, sly **4** able, cagy, cute, deft, foxy, good, neat, wily, wise **5** acute, adept, cagey, canny, fresh, nifty, novel, quick, ready, savvy, sharp, slick, smart, swift, witty **6** adroit, artful, astute, brainy, bright, crafty, daedal, gifted, habile, nimble, shrewd, subtle **7** cunning, knowing, unusual **8** creative, dextrous, incisive, inspired, original, readable, skillful, talented **9** astucious, brilliant, dexterous, ingenious, inventive, masterful, sprightly, strategic **10** discerning, innovative, keen-witted, proficient
comments: **6** banter
move: **4** ploy, ruse **6** device **8** artifice
person: **3** wag, wit
remark: **4** quip **5** sally **6** bon mot
___ clever by half: **3** too
cleverness: **3** art, wit **4** wits **5** craft, guile, sense, skill **6** acumen, brains, esprit **7** finesse **8** aptitude, keenness **9** canniness, dexterity, handiness, ingenuity, quickness, sharpness, smartness **10** adroitness, astuteness, brightness, shrewdness
___ Cleves: **6** Anne of
Cliburn, Van: **7** pianist
cliché: **5** stale **6** homily, phrase, saying **7** bromide **8** chestnut **9** platitude **10** stereotype
clichéd: **4** dull, worn **5** corny, hokey, musty, passé, stale, trite, vapid **6** boring, common, jejune, old hat **7** fatuous, humdrum, prosaic, worn-out **8** bromidic, outdated, outmoded **9** hackneyed, prosaical **10** threadbare, uninspired, unoriginal
Clichy: **4** city, town
locale: **6** France
click: **4** snap, tick **5** clack, snick **6** pan out **8** hit it off
click ___: **4** stop **6** beetle
___-click: **6** double
clicker, mouse: **6** button
clickety-___: **5** clack
clicking: **4** tick
client: **3** acc. **4** acct., user **5** buyer, guest **6** patron **7** account, patient, regular, subject **8** customer
be a ~: **9** patronize
potential ~: **8** prospect
clientele: **5** trade **6** public **7** patrons **8** practice, regulars **9** clientage, following, patronage **10** dependents
Client, The (1994 film)
cast: Tommy Lee Jones, Brad Renfro, Susan Sarandon
director: Joel Schumacher
cliff: **4** crag, scar **5** bluff, scarp **6** escarp **8** overhang, overlook **9** precipice **10** escarpment, prominence, rocky ledge
debris: **5** scree
dweller: **3** ern **4** erne **5** eagle **6** eaglet
dwelling: **4** aery, eyry **5** aerie, eyrie
feature: **3** lip **4** crag **5** shelf
Hawaiian ~: **4** pali
inlet: **5** fiord, fjord
like a ~: **5** steep
cliff ___: **5** brake **7** dweller, swallow
cliff-___: **4** hang **6** hanger
Cliff: **5** Potts **6** Barnes, Gorman **7** Edwards, Richard **8** Arquette, Huxtable **9** Robertson

to Clair: **6** spouse **7** husband
to J.R.: **5** enemy
cliff brake: **4** fern
cliff-hanger: **5** story **6** serial **7** mystery **8** thriller **9** adventure
Cliffhanger (1993 film)
cast: John Lithgow, Sylvester Stallone
director: Renny Harlin
Clifford: **4** Buzz **5** Clark, Odets, Shull, Simak
Clifford __: **5** trust
Cliffs __: **5** Notes
Cliffside Park: **4** city, town
locale: **9** New Jersey
__ Cliffs of Dover, The: **5** White
Clift, Montgomery: **5** actor
film: Freud (1962)
From Here to Eternity (1953)
The Heiress (1949)
Judgment at Nuremberg (1961)
The Misfits (1961)
A Place in the Sun (1951)
Raintree County (1957)
Red River (1948)
The Search (1948)
Suddenly, Last Summer (1959)
Wild River (1960)
The Young Lions (1958)
Clifton: **4** city, town, Webb **5** Davis, James **7** Fadiman
locale: **9** New Jersey
climactic: **4** last **8** crowning, dramatic
climate: **4** mood **6** milieu **7** weather **8** elements **10** atmosphere
affecter: **6** El Niño **7** current
combining form: **6** meteor-
climate __: **7** control
Climate for Killing, A (1990 film)
cast: Steven Bauer, John Beck, Mia Sara
climatize: **7** toughen
climax: **4** acme, apex, head, peak **5** crest, crown **6** apogee, finale, height, payoff, summit, zenith **8** capstone, high spot, pinnacle, showdown **9** culminate, high point, punch line **10** denouement
starter: **4** anti
Climax, The (1944 film)
cast: Boris Karloff, Gale Sondergaard
climb: **3** top **4** go up, lift, move, rise, shin, soar **5** arise, crawl, mount, reach, scale, surge **6** ascend, ascent, move up, ramble, rocket, shinny **7** clamber, takeoff **8** escalate, scramble **9** crescendo
aboard: **4** join
all over: **5** chide **6** berate, rebuke
on: **5** board **7** entrain
to: **5** reach
climber: **5** plant
challenge: **3** alp **5** scarp
goal: **4** acme
mountain ~: **4** lift **6** iceman
need: **4** gaff, spur **5** ice ax, piton **6** ladder
porch ~: **5** thief
rest: **5** ledge
social ~: **4** snob **7** elitist, upstart
social ~ concern: **6** status
vacation spot: **5** Nepal
__ climber: **4** root **6** social
Climb Ev'ry Mountain composer: **7** Rodgers **11** Hammerstein
climbing: **6** uphill
device: **5** stair
plant: **3** ivy **4** nito, vine **5** cubeb, guaco, liana, liane, vetch **7** goldcup **8** bignonia, wistaria, wisteria
climbing __: **4** fern, iron, lily, rose **5** perch
climb the __: **5** walls
clime: **5** realm **7** weather **10** atmosphere
clinch: **3** hug, ice, tie **4** grab, grip, hold, lock, nail, seal, tell **5** clasp, grasp, seize, sew up **6** assure, caress, clutch, decide, enfold, fasten, finish, infold, secure, settle **7** embrace, squeeze **8** finalize, nail down, transact **9** determine, lay hold of **10** consummate
clinched: **4** sure **8** in the bag
clincher: **5** proof **6** payoff
Cline: **5** Patsy **6** Edward
Cline, Edward: **8** director
film: The Bank Dick (1940)
Crazy House (1943)
Ghost Catchers (1944)
Million Dollar Legs (1932)
My Little Chickadee (1940)
Never Give a Sucker an Even Break (1941)
Three Ages (1923)
Cline, Patsy
song: Crazy (1961)
I Fall to Pieces (1961)
Walkin' After Midnight (1957)
cling: **5** peach, stick **6** adhere, attach, cleave, cohere, hang on, hold on, linger, remain **7** embrace
ender: **4** fish **5** stone
to: **3** hug **4** love **6** cleave, clutch, retain **9** hold tight
cling __: **5** peach
__ cling: **6** static
clingfish: **6** testar, tetard
Cling Free alternative: **5** Downy **6** Bounce **7** Snuggle **10** Final Touch
clinging: **6** sticky **8** adhesive **9** tenacious
Clingmans Dome locale: **9** Tennessee
clingstone: **5** fruit, peach
clingy: **5** twiny **8** adhesive **9** tenacious
clothing: **4** knit
clinic: **8** hospital **9** infirmary
staffer: **2** GP, MD, RN **5** nurse **6** doctor
__ Clinic: **4** Mayo
clinical __: **5** trial
__-clinician: **5** nurse
Clinic, The author: Jonathan Kellerman
Clinique alternative: **4** Avon **5** Almay **6** Revlon **7** Lancome, Mary Kay **9** Cover Girl, Max Factor **10** Maybelline **11** Estée Lauder, Merle Norman
clink: **4** jail, poky, stir **5** clang, pokey, sound **6** cooler, jangle, jingle, lockup, prison, tinkle **7** hoosgow **8** hoosegow
one in the ~: **3** con **5** lifer **7** convict
clinker: **3** dud **4** goof
clinkety-__: **5** clank
Clint: **5** Black **6** Holmes, Howard, Walker **8** Eastwood
Clinton: **4** Bill, city, town **6** De Witt, George **7** Chelsea, Hillary **8** Davisson
locale: **4** Iowa **8** Maryland, Michigan
Clinton, Bill: **3** Eli **9** president
astrologically: **3** Leo
brother: **5** Roger
cabinet member: **4** Espy, Pena, Reno, West **5** Aspin, Brown, Cohen, Cuomo, Daley, Perry, Reich, Riley, Rubin **6** Herman, Kantor, O'Leary, Slater **7** Babbitt, Bentsen, Shalala, Summers **8** Albright, Cisneros
cat: **5** Socks
child: **7** Chelsea
home: **3** Ark. **7** New York **8** Arkansas
hometown: **4** Hope
idol: **5** Elvis
instrument: **3** sax
middle name: **9** Jefferson
mother: **8** Virginia
opponent: **4** Bush, Dole **5** Perot
original last name: **6** Blythe
party: **3** Dem. **8** Democrat
school: **4** Yale **6** Oxford **10** Georgetown
V.P.: **4** Gore
wife: **7** Hillary
Clinton, Hillary alma mater: **4** Yale
Clinton's Big Ditch: **4** Erie
Clio: **3** car **4** auto, Muse **5** award **7** Renault **10** automobile
candidate: **2** ad **5** adman **10** commercial
colleague: **5** Erato **6** Thalia, Urania **7** Euterpe **8** Calliope **9** Melpomene **10** Polyhymnia **11** Terpsichore
parent of ~: **4** Zeus **9** Mnemosyne
clip: **3** bob, cut, hit, mow, nip **4** chip, crop, dock, gait, join, pare, rate, snip, sock, stab, trim **5** catch, cheat, clasp, clout, groom, knock, lower, piece, prune, punch, shave, shear, slash, smack, speed, swipe, whack, wound **6** buckle, cut out, fasten, fleece, lessen, reduce, sample, wallop **7** abridge, bracket, curtail, cut back, defraud, excerpt, extract, scissor, shorten, squeeze, swindle **8** amputate, barrette, decrease, fast pace, fragment, truncate, uppercut **9** sound bite, victimize **10** abbreviate, run a game on
at a good ~: **4** fast **5** apace, quick
ender: **5** board, sheet
news ~: **5** video
on: **6** attach
clip __: **3** art, out **4** bond **5** joint
clip-__: **3** fed **4** clop
__ clip: **3** at a, gem, tie, toe **4** film, news, nose, wool **5** paper **7** bulldog
clip-on: **3** tie **8** neckwear
belt ~: **5** pager, phone **6** beeper
clipped: **5** shorn, terse **6** gnomic
clipper: **4** boat, ship **6** shears
coupon ~: **5** saver
on a ~: **4** asea **5** at sea
target: **4** nail
clipper __: **3** bow **4** ship
Clipper rival: **3** Cav, Mav, Net, Sun **4** Buck, Bull, Hawk, Heat, Jazz, King, Spur **5** Knick, Laker, Magic, Pacer, Sixer, Sonic **6** Celtic, Hornet, Nugget, Piston, Raptor, Rocket, Wizard **7** Grizzly, Warrior **8** Cavalier, Maverick **10** SuperSonic, Timberwolf
clippers: **4** tool **6** shears **8** scissors
use ~: **5** prune, shear
Clippers: **4** five, team
home: **10** Los Angeles
org.: **3** NBA
sport: **10** basketball
clippety-__: **4** clop
clipping: **3** cut **4** foul, snip **5** piece **7** cutting, snippet **8** fragment
shopper's ~: **6** coupon
__ clipping: **4** back, fore, hind **5** press
clique: **3** mob, set **4** band, bloc, clan, club, cult, gang, pack, ring **5** cabal, class, crowd, group, junto, troop **6** circle, outfit **7** company, coterie, faction, in-group, society
power-seeking ~: **5** cabal
cliquish: **9** exclusive, sectarian
Clive: **5** Brook, Colin **6** Barker, Barnes, Donner, Revill, Robert **7** Cussler
Clive, Colin: **5** actor
film: Bride of Frankenstein (1935)
Frankenstein (1931)
The Girl From 10th Avenue (1935)
Mad Love (1935)
One More River (1934)
cloak: **4** capa, cape, cowl, hide, mask, robe, veil, wrap **5** cache, capot, couch, cover, guise, manta, shawl **6** abolla, birrus, byrrus, capote, domino, enveil, facade, kaross, mantle, poncho, screen, shroud, veneer **7** burnous, conceal, cover up, envelop, garment, mandyas, manteau, mantlet, obscure, paenula, pelisse, pretext, secrete **8** burnoose, capuchin, covering, disguise, enshroud, pretense **9** dissemble, mandilion **10** camouflage, cappa magna, masquerade, roquelaure
African ~: **6** kaross
Arab ~: **7** burnous **8** burnoose
church ~: **10** cappa magna
ender: **4** room
hooded ~: **5** capot **6** capote
matador's ~: **4** capa
monk ~: **4** cowl **7** mandyas
mourning ~: **3** bug **6** insect
partner: **6** dagger
Roman ~: **6** abolla, birrus, byrrus **7** paenula
sleeveless ~: **3** aba **4** abba
Spanish ~: **5** manta
cloak-and-__: **5** sword **6** dagger, suiter
cloak-and-dagger org.: **3** CIA, KGB
Cloak & Dagger (1984 film)
cast: Dabney Coleman, Michael Murphy, Henry Thomas
cloaked: **6** covert, hidden, secret, unseen **7** furtive, private, sub rosa **8** hush-hush **9** out of view, unexposed **10** undercover, under wraps
Cloak, The: **5** opera
composer: **7** Puccini
clobber: **3** bat, bop, hit **4** bash, beat, belt, club, cuff, deck, drub, lick, slam, slug, swat, trim, whip **5** baste, blast, brain, clout, cream, paste, pound, smack, smash, smite, spank, stomp, tromp, whack, whang, worst **6** batter, buffet, hammer, strike, thrash, wallop **7** lambast, overrun, shellac, trounce **8** bludgeon, lambaste, shellack **9** criticize, haul off on, overpower
clobbered old-style: **4** smit
cloche: **3** hat
clock: **4** time **5** alarm, meter, timer, watch **6** ticker **9** timepiece **10** timekeeper
around the ~: **7** nonstop **10** all the time, constantly
at times: **6** chimer
change the ~: **5** reset
climber of rhyme: **5** mouse
digital ~ display: **3** LCD, LED
ender: **4** wise, work
feature: **4** dial, face, gear, hand **5** alarm, chime, radio, works **6** gimmal **8** movement
in: **4** come **5** pop up, reach **6** appear, arrive, attend, report
like ~ chimes: **5** horal
nos.: **3** hrs.
numeral: **3** III, VII, XII **4** IIII, VIII
obey the ~: **5** get up
punch a ~: **4** work
setting: **2** AM, PM **3** CDT, CST, EDT, EST, MDT, MST, PDT, PST
ship-shaped ~: **3** nef
sound: **4** tick, tock
standard setting: **3** GMT
summer ~ setting: **3** DST
watcher: **4** eyer
clock __: **4** jack **5** radio, watch **7** puncher, watcher
clock-__: **4** hour **5** timer
__ clock: **4** body, one o', shot, six o', ten o', time, two o' **5** acorn, alarm, Atmos, banjo, chess, five o', four o', nine o', quail, water **6** analog, atomic, cuckoo, eight o', lancet, pigeon, quartz, seven o', three o' **7** annular, balloon, bracket, digital, eleven o', gravity, twelve o'
Clockers (1995 film)
cast: Harvey Keitel, Delroy Lindo, John Turturro
director: Spike Lee
__ Clock Jump: **4** One o'
clock-radio switch: **4** AMFM
.... __ clock scholar: **5** a ten o'
Clock Symphony composer: **5** Haydn

Clock, The (1945 film)
cast: Judy Garland, James Gleason, Robert Walker
director: Vincente Minnelli
__ Clock, The: 3 Big
Clock Winder, The author: Anne Tyler
clockwise: 5 right 6 deasil
combining form: 5 dextr- 6 dextro-
starter: 7 counter
Clock without Hands author: Carson McCullers
clockwork: 9 precision 10 regularity, smoothness
like ~: 5 paced 6 steady 7 regular, uniform 8 reliable, reliably, steadily 9 every time, regularly, uniformly 10 invariably, on schedule
__ clockwork: 4 like
Clockwork Orange, A: 4 film 5 novel
author: Anthony Burgess
cast: Adrienne Corri, Patrick Magee, Malcolm McDowell
character: 4 Alex
director: Stanley Kubrick
clod: 2 ox 3 ass, oaf, sap 4 boob, boor, dolt, fool, gowk, hunk, lout, lump, rube 5 brute, chump, clown, cluck, dummy, dunce, joker, looby, ninny, patsy, yokel 6 dimwit, lubber, lummox, nitwit, sucker, turkey 7 buffoon, bumbler, bumpkin, bungler, dingbat, dullard, fathead, fumbler, half-wit, jackass, pinhead, saphead 8 bonehead, deadhead, dumbbell, dummkopf, lunkhead, meathead, numskull 9 birdbrain, blockhead, harebrain, lamebrain, numbskull, schlemiel, simpleton, thickhead 10 dunderhead
ender: 6 hopper
social ~: 4 nerd, nurd
Clod and the Pebble, The author: William Blake
cloddish: 4 dolt, dull 5 inept, unapt 6 clumsy, klutzy, oafish 7 awkward, bearish, bungler, doltish, loutish, unadept 8 churlish, fumbling, ungainly 9 all thumbs, maladroit 10 blundering, unskillful
clodhopper: 2 ox 3 oaf 4 hick, lout, shoe 5 churl, yokel 6 lubber, lummox, rustic 7 bumpkin, hayseed, peasant, plowboy 8 footwear 10 provincial
clodhopping: 6 rustic 7 loutish
Cloete, Stuart: 6 writer 12 South African
clog: 3 dam, jam, tie 4 bolt, cork, lock, plug, seal, shoe, shut, snag, stop 5 block, choke, close, cramp, dam up, dance, delay, gum up, latch, sabot, stick, tie up 6 hamper, hang up, hinder, impede, lock up, plug up, retard, seal up, secure, stop up 7 close up, congest, occlude, seal off, shutter 8 blockade, blockage, button up, close off, encumber, footgear, footwear, obstacle, obstruct, overfill 9 hindrance, impedance, occlusion 10 congestion
Japanese ~: 4 geta
kin: 5 sabot
locale: 4 sink 5 drain
clogged: 5 stuck 6 stuffy
like a ~ dryer vent: 5 fuzzy
cloisonné: 6 enamel
cloister: 3 den 4 cell, lair, nest, walk 5 abbey 6 arcade, friary, priory, temple 7 convent, nunnery, retreat, seclude 8 lamasery 9 courtyard, hermitage, monastery, peristyle, sanctuary, sequester
courtyard: 5 garth
Cloister and the Hearth, The
author: Charles Reade
character: 4 Kate 5 Denys, Elias, Giles 6 Gerard, Pietro
cloistered: 4 pent 6 hidden 7 recluse 8 secluded, shielded, solitary 9 insulated, out of view, reclusive, seclusive, sheltered, withdrawn 10 restricted
one: 3 nun 4 monk
clomp: 5 stamp, stump, tread 6 trudge
clone: 2 PC 4 copy, dupe, same, twin 5 ditto, model, Xerox, yuppy 6 double, ectype, repeat, yuppie 7 replica 8 computer, knockoff, likeness 9 duplicate, facsimile, imitation, look-alike, photocopy, replicate, reproduce
Dolly the ~: 3 ewe 5 sheep
unit: 4 cell 5 ramet
cloned: 9 identical
clonk: 4 thud 5 thump
Clooney: 4 Nick 6 George 8 Rosemary
Clooney, George: 5 actor
film: Batman & Robin (1997)
O Brother, Where Art Thou? (2000)
Ocean's Eleven (2001)
Out of Sight (1998)
The Perfect Storm (2000)
Three Kings (1999)
TV: ER
Clooney, Rosemary
song: Botch-a-Me (1952)
Come on-a My House (1951)
Hey There (1954)
Mambo Italiano (1954)
Mangos (1957)
This Ole House (1954)
spouse: José Ferrer
clop: 8 hoofbeat
__-clop: 4 clip
Clorets alternative: 5 Certs 6 Binaca, Mentos, Tic Tac 7 Altoids, Dentyne
Cloris: 8 Leachman
Clorox alternative: 5 Purex, Snowy, Vivid 8 Borateem
close: 3 bar, dam, end, zip 4 bolt, calk, clog, coda, cork, dear, fail, fast, fold, halt, kind, lace, lock, mean, near, next, nigh, plug, quit, seal, sell, shut, slam, snug, stop, warm, yard 5 anear, block, caulk, cease, dam up, dense, handy, humid, latch, muggy, quiet, sew up, sum up, terse, thick, tight, zip up 6 almost, at hand, at heel, button, chummy, clog up, clubby, desist, ending, expire, fasten, finale, finish, fold up, genial, hard by, kindly, lessen, lock up, loving, minute, narrow, nearby, packed, period, plug up, recede, run out, seal up, secret, secure, sticky, stingy, stop up, strict, stuffy, sultry, windup, wrap up 7 achieve, adjourn, affable, amiable, break up, compact, cordial, cramped, crowded, devoted, go under, literal, miserly, occlude, on the QT, play out, seal off, shut off, shut out, shutter, sparing, sweltry, thrifty, tighten, turn off 8 adjacent, amicable, button up, complete, conclude, confined, draw near, familiar, friendly, hush-hush, imminent, intimate, next-door, not quite, obstruct, outgoing, pack it in, put to bed, reserved, reticent, round off, round out, shut down, sociable, stifling, surcease, taciturn, taper off, terminus, transact, ungiving, wind down 9 cessation, confining, congested, convivial, culminate, illiberal, immediate, impending, jam-packed, make final, penurious, proximate, secretive, skintight, terminate 10 benevolent, buddy-buddy, call it a day, completion, conclusion, consummate, contiguous, convenient, denouement, desistance, expiration, juxtaposed, neighborly, nip and tuck, oppressive, palsy-walsy, resolution, solicitous, sweltering, ungenerous, unspeaking
behind: 6 at heel
be ~ to: 4 know
bring ~: 4 love 6 endear
by: 4 near, nigh 5 handy, unfar 6 around, at hand 7 locally 8 adjacent 9 alongside, proximate 10 convenient
call: 5 brush, scare
call comment: 4 phew, whew
combining form: 4 pycn-, sten- 5 plesi-, pycno-, steno- 6 plesio-
come ~ to: 8 approach, resemble
complimentary ~: 4 best, love 5 yours 6 warmly 9 sincerely 10 yours truly
down: 3 end 4 halt, shut, stop 5 cease 6 wind up 8 break off, dispatch, stamp out 9 eliminate 10 put an end to
ender: 3 out 4 down
forcefully: 4 slam
form ~ ties: 4 bond
getting ~: 4 warm
get ~ to: 6 gain on 8 approach
in: 3 pen 5 bower 6 encase, gain on, immure
in on: 4 near 7 besiege, envelop 8 approach, encircle, surround
in Scotland: 3 nar
keep ~: 3 hug 5 clasp, press, touch 6 clutch, cradle, cuddle, enfold, nestle, nuzzle 7 embrace, snuggle
not ~: 3 far
not even ~: 5 wrong 7 distant 8 mistaken 9 erroneous 10 inaccurate
of day: 6 curfew 7 bedtime 9 nightfall
off: 4 clog, seal, shut 5 block 6 impede 7 isolate, occlude 8 separate 9 segregate, sequester
out: 3 cut, end 5 cease, lower, slash 6 cancel, reduce 8 decrease, discount, mark down 9 dispose of, finish off, liquidate
ranks: 4 ally 5 merge, rally, unite 8 assemble, coalesce, converge 9 integrate
relative: 3 sib 4 twin 6 father, mother, sister 7 brother
securely: 4 seal, shut 6 batten
shave: 5 scare
starter: 4 fore
to: 2 by, on 4 like, near 5 about 6 almost, beside, hard by 7 nearing
to a poet: 4 nigh 5 anear
to (prefix): 3 epi
to the ground: 3 low 4 flat 5 short 8 knee-high, sea-level 10 unelevated
up: 3 zip 4 cork, lock, seal, shut 5 latch 6 immure 7 silence
up shop: 4 quit 10 call it a day
close __: 3 out 4 call, down, in on, shot 5 quote, ranks, reach, shave 6 helmet, quotes, stitch 7 harmony
close-__: 3 ups 4 knit 6 fisted, hauled, lipped, minded, reefed 7 cropped, fitting, grained, mouthed
close-__ drill: 5 order
Close __: 5 to You
closed: 4 dark, over, shut 6 locked, sealed 7 insular 8 airtight, shut down 9 exclusive 10 restricted
almost ~: 4 ajar
behind ~ doors: 6 inside 8 secretly 9 privately
book: 6 riddle 7 mystery 9 conundrum
combining form: 7 cleisto-
in: 4 pent 5 misty 6 pent-up
not ~: 4 open
remove the ~ sign: 6 reopen
closed __: 3 set 4 book, loop, plan, rule, shop 5 chain, shelf, shell, union 6 season, stance, system 7 circuit, cornice, couplet, gentian, primary
closed-__: 3 end 4 door 5 stack 6 minded
Closed: 4 sign
__ closed doors: 6 behind
Close Encounters... (1977 film)
cast: Melinda Dillon, Richard Dreyfuss, Teri Garr, François Truffaut
composer: 8 Williams
craft: 3 UFO
director: Steven Spielberg
Close Encounters of the Third Kind Theme (1978 song) artist: John Williams
closefisted: 4 mean, near 5 small, tight 6 greedy, skimpy, stingy 7 miserly, selfish, thrifty 8 grasping 9 illiberal, penurious 10 avaricious, pinch-penny, skinflinty, ungenerous
one: 5 piker 9 skinflint
closefistedness: 5 greed 7 avarice
close-fitting: 4 snug 5 tight
__ close for comfort: 3 too
Close, Glenn: 7 actress
film: 101 Dalmatians (1996)
Air Force One (1997)
The Big Chill (1983)
Cookie's Fortune (1999)
Dangerous Liaisons (1988)
Fatal Attraction (1987)
Hamlet (1990)
Immediate Family (1989)
Jagged Edge (1985)
Mars Attacks! (1996)
Maxie (1985)
The Natural (1984)
The Paper (1994)
Reversal of Fortune (1990)
The Stone Boy (1984)
Things You Can Tell Just by Looking at Her (2001)
The World According to Garp (1982)
film (voice): Tarzan (1999)
closely: 4 well 8 intently, narrowly
closemouthed: 3 mum 4 mute 5 quiet, terse 6 silent 8 hush-hush, reserved, reticent, taciturn 9 secretive, voiceless
one: 4 clam
Close My Eyes (1991 film)
cast: Clive Owen, Alan Rickman
Close My Eyes Forever (1989 song)
artist: Lita Ford, Ozzy Osbourne
closeness: 8 accuracy, affinity, intimacy, presence 9 affection, communion, immediacy, proximity 10 friendship, similarity
close-order __: 5 drill
closeout: 3 buy 7 bargain, special
close-packed: 5 dense, thick, tight
closer: 6 hurler 7 pitcher 8 reliever, salesman 9 dealmaker
gate ~: 3 bar 4 bolt, hasp, hook, lock 5 catch 7 padlock
inning: 5 ninth
stat: 3 ERA 4 save
Closer I Get to You, The (1978 song)
artist: Donny Hathaway, Roberta Flack
closest: 4 next 9 proximate
closet: 4 hide 6 locker, lock up, recess, secret 7 cabinet 8 cupboard, imprison, stow away, wardrobe 10 depository, repository
item: 3 tie 4 belt, shoe 5 dress, shelf, shirt 6 blouse, hanger 7 sweater
items: 4 junk 5 linen 6 attire
like some ~ doors: 6 bifold
like some ~ s: 5 mothy 9 cluttered
lining: 5 cedar
pest: 4 moth
put in the ~: 4 hang 6 hang up
skeleton in the ~: 5 shame 7 scandal
utility ~ item: 3 mop 4 pail 5 broom
water ~: 2 WC 3 lav., loo 7 latrine 8 bathroom, lavatory
__ closet: 5 china, linen, water 6 walk-in 7 clothes

closeted again: 5 rehid
close the __ on: 4 door
Close the Door (1978 song) artist: Teddy Pendergrass
Close to Home author: Erskine Caldwell
Close to My Heart (1951 film) cast: Ray Milland, Gene Tierney
close to one's __: 5 heart
__ close to schedule: 4 on or
Close to You (song) artist: Carpenters, Maxi Priest
closeup: 4 view 5 photo 10 photograph
prepare for a ~: 4 zoom 5 pan in
Close-Up: 10 toothpaste
alternative: 3 Aim 5 Crest, Gleem, Topol 7 Colgate, Viadent 9 Aquafresh, Mentadent, Pepsodent, Rembrandt, Sensodyne 10 Pearl Drops, Ultra Brite 11 Tom's of Maine
closing: 3 end 4 last 5 final 6 ending, finale, finish, latter 8 ultimate
in: 4 near
time: 6 curfew
closing __: 4 time 5 costs, error, price
Closing the Ring author: Churchill
Closing Time author: Joseph Heller
closure: 3 end, lid 4 bolt, cork, lock, plug, seal, seam, stop 5 latch 6 ending, finish, recess 7 padlock, stopper 8 blockade, curtains, stoppage 9 cessation 10 conclusion
combining form: 6 -clisis 7 -cleisis
clot: 3 gel, set 4 curd, jell, lump, mass 5 group 6 curdle, gelate, harden 7 acidify, clabber, clobber, congeal, stiffen, thicken 8 coalesce, solidify, thrombus 9 coagulate
combining form: 6 thromb- 7 thrombo-
cloth: 3 net, rag 4 felt, silk, wool 5 baize, denim, lisse, loden, plaid, ramee, ramie, satin, serge, stuff, terry, towel 6 calico, chintz, fabric, kersey 7 bunting, flannel, gingham, worsted 8 dry goods, jacquard, material, textiles 9 grosgrain, yard goods
absorbent ~: 6 diaper
altar ~: 6 dossal, dossel
billiard table ~: 5 baize
border: 3 hem
cleaning ~: 3 rag 6 chammy, shammy, shamoy 7 chamois
cotton ~: 6 calico, chintz
dealer: 6 draper, ragman
ender: 3 ier 5 bound
fold: 5 plait, pleat
hole: 6 eyelet
India: 6 Madras
in jai alai: 5 cinta
kitchen ~: 5 towel
made ~: 4 wove
made of whole ~: 4 fake 5 bogus
make ~: 4 spin 5 weave
man of the ~: 4 abbé 5 padre 6 cleric, priest
measure: 3 ell 4 bolt, yard
metallic ~: 4 lamé
not of the ~: 3 lay 4 laic 6 laical
Polynesian ~: 4 tapa
scrap: 3 rag
starter: 3 oil 4 back, dish, face, foot, hair, loin, sack, sail, wash 5 broad, table, waist 6 breech, cheese, saddle
surface: 3 nap
those not of the ~: 5 laics, laity
use a ~: 4 dust, wipe
woolen ~: 5 loden
worker: 4 dyer
see also fabric, material
__ cloth: 4 bark, drop, face, mast, piña, tapa, wire 5 altar, cadet, emery, grass, Janus, monk's, shade, suede, terry 6 beaver, bridge, covert, double, ground, melton, oxford, sponge, vision, waffle, zephyr 7 bolting, buffalo, hickory
cloth cleaner, name meaning: 6 Tucker
clothe: 3 rig, tog 4 deck, do up, garb 5 array, cover, drape, dress, endue, indue 6 attire, enrobe, fit out, outfit, tog out 7 bedrape, costume, cover up, deck out, furnish 8 accouter, accoutre
clothed: 4 clad 6 decent, enclad
be ~ in: 4 wear 6 have on
old-style: 5 yclad
clothes: 4 duds, garb, gear, rags, togs, wear 5 array, dress, frock, getup, mufti, robes 6 attire, civies, finery, livery, outfit, things 7 apparel, civvies, costume, raiment, regalia, threads, toggery 8 covering, ensemble, frippery, garments, wardrobe 9 caparison, trappings 10 habiliment, sportswear, Sunday best
abbr.: 3 irr. 5 irreg.
dirty ~: 4 wash 7 laundry
ender: 3 pin 4 line 5 horse, press
evening ~: 4 gown 5 dress 6 tuxedo
fine ~: 5 array
fresh ~: 6 change
gym ~: 6 shorts, sweats, T-shirt
holder: 6 closet, hamper, locker
iron ~: 4 mail 5 armor, press
line: 3 hem 4 seam
nostalgic ~ style: 5 retro
old ~: 4 rags
pole: 4 tree
presser: 4 iron
riding ~: 5 habit
shop for ~: 5 try on
sister's ~: 5 habit
starter: 3 bed 5 night, small
wearing ~: 4 clad
wearing no ~: 4 bare, nude 5 naked
work ~: 5 jeans 6 denims
see also clothing
clothes __: 4 moth, pole, rack, tree 6 closet
__ clothes: 5 plain 6 dinner, Sunday 7 evening, fatigue
Clothes for a Summer Hotel author: Tennessee Williams
clotheshorse: 3 fop 5 dandy, model, swell
clothesline: 4 rope
alternative: 5 drier, dryer
use a ~: 6 air-dry
clothespin: 3 peg
clothier: 6 fitter, tailor 9 outfitter
clothing: 3 RTW 4 garb, gear, need, suit, togs, wear 5 array, dress, getup, robes 6 attire, finery, livery, outfit, things, undies 7 apparel, costume, raiment 8 covering, ensemble, garments, wardrobe 9 trappings, underwear
category: 4 men's 6 women's
clingy ~: 4 knit
GI ~: 3 ODs 6 khakis
make ~: 3 sew 4 knit 5 weave
ordinary ~: 5 mufti
problem: 3 rip 4 fray, snag, tear 5 stain
protector: 3 bib 5 apron
specification: 2 lg., sm., XL 3 lge., med., XXL 4 long, size 5 cadet, large, short, small 6 medium, portly 10 extra large
store employee: 6 fitter
test ~: 5 try on
see also clothes
clothmaking apparatus: 4 loom
Clotho: 4 Fate
colleague: 7 Atropos 8 Lachesis
mother of ~: 6 Themis
clotted: 5 thick
clotted __: 5 cream
cloture ends, what: 6 debate
cloud: 3 dim, fog 4 blur, mist, roil, veil 5 addle, bedim, befog, blear 6 cirrus, dampen, darken, legion, muddle, nimbus, shadow 7 confuse, cover up, cumulus, obscure, perplex, stratus 8 confound, jaundice 9 adumbrate, disorient, mare's tail, obfuscate 10 overshadow
bit of a ~: 4 wisp
black ~: 4 pall
combining form: 4 neph- 5 nepho- 6 nephel- 7 nephelo-
contents: 4 rain 5 smoke, water
ender: 4 land 5 berry, burst, scape
fair-weather ~: 6 cirrus
formation: 4 bank
like a storm ~: 5 black
name starter: 4 alto
nine: 5 bliss 7 rapture 8 paradise
on ~ nine: 4 glad, high 5 happy, merry 6 blithe, cheery, elated, jovial, joyful, joyous, upbeat 7 gleeful, pleased, tickled 8 blissful, cheerful, ecstatic, euphoric, exultant, jubilant, mirthful, thrilled 9 delighted, overjoyed, rapturous, rejoicing, rhapsodic
over: 9 adumbrate
put on ~ nine: 5 elate, exult 6 buck up, perk up, uplift 7 delight, gladden, hearten 8 inspirit 10 exhilarate
region: 3 sky
roll ~: 5 arcus
seeding compound: 6 iodide
starter: 7 thunder
the issue: 7 confuse 8 confound 9 obfuscate
under a ~: 5 shady 7 suspect
up: 4 roil 6 darken
cloud __: 3 cap, ear 4 base, nine, rack 5 cover, grass, layer 6 banner 7 chamber, physics, seeding
cloud-__: 6 capped
cloud-__-land: 6 cuckoo
__ cloud: 3 cap, war 4 Oort, rain, roll, star 5 anvil, crest, rotor, scarf, white 6 banner, billow, funnel 7 pendant, tornado
__ Cloud: 3 Red
cloudberry: 5 fruit
cloudburst: 4 rain 5 storm 6 deluge 7 torrent 8 downpour 9 rainstorm
cloud chamber contents: 3 gas
clouded: 4 gray, grey, hazy 5 blear, foggy, milky, misty 6 hidden, turbid 8 overcast 9 equivocal, hard to see
Cloud Forest, The author: Peter Matthiessen
cloudiness: 5 blear
__ cloud in the sky: 4 not a
cloudless: 4 fair 5 clear, light, sunny 6 bright 8 sunshiny
clouds: 4 rack 5 nimbi 6 scores 7 legions
in the ~: 5 aloft 7 bemused, faraway 10 abstracted, starry-eyed
like some ~: 5 puffy, wispy 6 fleecy
low-lying ~: 3 fog 4 mist
move swiftly, as ~: 4 scud
treat ~: 4 seed
Clouds, The author: Aristophanes
Cloud, The: 4 poem
author: Percy Bysshe Shelley
cloudy: 3 dim 4 dark, gray, grey, hazy 5 mirky, misty, muddy, murky, shady, vague 6 dismal, dreary, gloomy, opaque, somber, sullen, turbid 7 blurred, obscure, sunless, unclear 8 confused, darkened, lowering, nebulous, overcast 9 imprecise, unsettled 10 indistinct
make ~: 4 roil
Clouseau: 7 Jacques, Sellers 9 Inspector
caper: 4 case
clout: 3 hit, rap 4 blow, clip, club, cuff, pull, slug, sock, swat, sway 5 crack, force, juice, knock, might, pound, power, punch, skill, smack, spank, swipe, thump, whack 6 credit, effect, muscle, strike, wallop, weight 7 clobber, control 8 bludgeon, leverage, pressure, prestige, standing, strength, uppercut 9 authority, fisticuff, influence
those with ~: 3 ins
clove: 4 bulb, tree 5 spice
clove __: 3 oil 4 pink 5 hitch
clove hitch: 4 knot
cloven: 5 forky, split 6 forked 7 incised
cloven __: 4 foot, hoof
clover: 5 alyce, plant 6 fodder, riches, wealth 7 alfalfa
be in ~: 9 luxuriate
ender: 4 leaf
in ~: 4 rich 5 flush 6 loaded, monied 7 moneyed, wealthy, well-off 8 affluent, well-to-do 9 well-fixed 10 privileged, propertied, prosperous, well-heeled
like a four-leaf ~: 5 lucky
__ clover: 3 bur, elk, hop, pin, red 4 bush, holy, owl's 5 alyce, dusty, Dutch, Japan, sweet, water, white 6 alsike, Ladino 7 Bokhara, crimson, Italian, prairie
cloverleaf: 8 crossing 9 underpass
part of a ~: 4 exit, loop, ramp
Cloverleaf: 4 city, town
locale: 5 Texas
cloves: 5 spice 6 garlic
__ cloves: 5 oil of
clove-scented flower: 4 pink
Clovis: 4 city, town
locale: 9 New Mexico 10 California
clown: 3 ass, kid, oaf, sap, wag 4 boob, boor, Bozo, clod, dolt, fool, jest, joke, mime, zany 5 chump, churl, cluck, comic, cutup, dummy, dunce, joker, ninny, patsy, Punch, yahoo 6 dimwit, jester, lubber, lummox, madcap, mummer, nitwit, sucker, turkey, victim 7 buffoon, dingbat, dullard, farceur, fathead, gagster, half-wit, jackass, pierrot, pinhead, saphead 8 bonehead, comedian, dumbbell, funnyman, humorist, kibitzer, meathead, numskull, quipster 9 birdbrain, blockhead, character, harlequin, kid around, lamebrain, leg-puller, numbskull, prankster, simpleton 10 dunderhead
around: 3 kid 4 jest, joke
be a ~: 5 amuse
bit: 5 stunt
like a ~: 5 funny
like ~ outfits: 5 baggy
locale: 6 big top, circus
often: 4 mime 5 mimer, mimic
prop: 3 wig 5 stilt 7 red nose
clown __: 4 fish 5 white 6 prince
__ clown: 5 class
__ Clown: 3 Be a 6 Cathy's
clowning: 3 fun 5 antic, humor 8 jocosity, zaniness 9 funniness, horseplay 10 jocoseness
clownish: 4 zany 5 daffy, droll 6 clumsy 7 loutish, unadept, uncouth
clownishness: 7 fooling 8 jocosity
Clown Prince of Basketball, The: 5 Lemon
Clown Prince of Denmark: 5 Borge
Clowns, The (1971 film) director: Federico Fellini
cloy: 4 bore, glut, jade, pall, sate 5 gorge, weary 7 satiate, satisfy, surfeit 8 overfill 10 gormandize
cloyed: 3 fed 4 full 5 blasé 10 world-weary

cloying: 5 sweet 6 sickly 7 maudlin, mawkish 10 saccharine
become ~: 4 pall
sweetness: 5 syrup 8 schmaltz
Clu: 7 Gulager
club: 3 bat, hit, org. 4 assn., band, bash, beat, clan, cosh, gang, gild, iron, mace, team, wood 5 assoc., baste, baton, billy, cleek, clout, disco, flail, group, guild, lodge, mashy, order, pound, spoon, staff, stick, wedge, whack 6 brassy, circle, clique, cudgel, driver, hammer, hurley, league, lounge, mallet, mashie, outfit, pommel, pummel, putter, strike, timber 7 brassey, brassie, clobber, coterie, faction, in-group, midiron, niblick, society 8 alliance, bludgeon 9 blackjack, truncheon 10 fellowship, fraternity, knobkerrie, membership, nightstick, shillelagh
aborigine war ~: 5 waddy 6 waddie
agricultural ~: 5 four H
ball ~: 4 team
billy ~: 4 cosh 5 baton, stick 6 cudgel 8 bludgeon
boys' ~: 4 YMCA, YMHA
carrier: 5 caddy 6 caddie
ceremonial ~: 4 mace
college ~: 3 sor. 4 frat 8 sorority 10 fraternity
combining form: 5 clavi- 6 rhopal- 7 rhopalo-
ender: 3 man, men 4 face, room 5 house, woman, women
girls' ~: 4 YWCA, YWHA
glee ~: 6 chorus 8 ensemble 9 vocalists
golf ~: 4 iron, wood 5 cleek, spoon, wedge 6 driver, mashie, putter 7 brassie, niblick 9 sand wedge
health ~: 3 gym, spa 9 gymnasium
high-IQ ~: 5 Mensa
one in a ~: 3 mem. 6 member
one ~ perhaps: 3 bid
payment: 4 dues
police ~ in India: 5 lathi 6 lathee
service ~: 4 Elks, YMCA 5 Amvet, Four H, lodge 7 Kiwanis
soda: 4 fizz 5 mixer
starter: 5 night
supper ~: 5 boîte 6 bistro, eatery 7 cabaret 9 nightspot
swing a ~: 4 putt 5 drive, pitch
up: 5 unite 7 go along 9 cooperate 10 join forces
war ~: 4 mace 6 cudgel 9 truncheon
without ~ soda: 4 neat
club ___: 3 bag, car 4 dues, foot, moss, soda, sofa 5 chair, grass, steak, wheat 6 fungus 7 fighter
___ club: 3 fan, key 4 ball, book, farm, glee, golf, men's 5 billy, yacht 6 bottle, bridge, devil's, golden, health, Indian, jockey, kennel, supper, women's 7 country, service
Club ___: 3 Med 7 Nouveau
___ Club: 4 Boys, Sam's 5 Four-H, Lions, Stork, Zonta 6 Escape, Kit-Cat, Kit-Kat, Rotary, Sierra 7 Culture, Horizon
clubby: 4 kind 5 close, thick 6 chummy, genial, kindly 7 affable, amiable, cordial 8 amicable, friendly, intimate, outgoing, sociable 9 congenial, convivial 10 benevolent, buddy-buddy, gregarious, neighborly, solicitous
clubhouse: 5 haunt
Club Nouveau song: Lean on Me (1987)
clubs: 4 suit
at times: 5 trump
five ~: 5 flush
club soda: 7 seltzer 8 beverage
___ Club, The: 6 Cotton
cluck: 3 ass, nit, oaf, sap, tut 4 boob, clod, dolt, fool, gowk 5 chump, clack, clown, dummy, dunce, joker, klutz, ninny, patsy 6 cackle, dimwit, lubber, lummox, nitwit, sucker, turkey, tut-tut 7 buffoon, dingbat, dullard, fathead, half-wit, jackass, pinhead, saphead 8 bonehead, dumbbell, meathead, numskull 9 birdbrain, blockhead, lamebrain, numbskull, simpleton 10 dunderhead
clucker: 3 hen 7 chicken
clue: 3 key, tip 4 hint, lead, mark, sign 5 index, trace 6 tipoff 7 hot lead, inkling, pointer 8 acquaint, evidence 9 footprint, indicator, suspicion 10 indication, intimation, suggestion
crime lab ~: 3 DNA 5 print 9 tire track
drop a ~: 4 hint 8 intimate
hound's ~: 5 scent, smell
in: 4 tell, warn 6 advise, inform, relate, tip off 8 instruct
Clue: 4 game 9 board game
character: 4 Plum 5 Boddy, Green, White 7 Mustard, Peacock, Scarlet
locale: 4 hall 5 study 6 lounge 7 kitchen, library 8 ballroom 10 dining room 12 billiard room, conservatory
weapon: 4 rope 5 knife 6 wrench 8 lead pipe, revolver 11 candlestick
clueless: 4 asea, lost 5 at sea 7 puzzled 8 confused
socially ~ one: 4 nerd, nurd
Clueless (1995 film)
cast: Stacey Dash, Brittany Murphy, Alicia Silverstone
catchphrase: 4 as if
character: 4 Cher
director: Amy Heckerling
clues
like some ~: 4 down 6 across
clump: 3 gob, set, wad 4 blob, glob, hunk, lump, mass, plod, thud, tuft 5 batch, chunk, divot, group, patch, stomp, stump, thump 6 bundle, lumber, nugget, trudge 7 cluster, thicket
clumsy: 3 oxy 5 gawky, inapt, inept, unapt 6 gauche, klutzy, oafish, sloppy, unable, wooden 7 awkward, boorish, gawkish, halting, hulking, labored, loutish, lumpish, unadept, uncouth, unhandy 8 bumbling, bungling, cloddish, clownish, fumbling, helpless, inexpert, lubberly, tactless, ungainly, unpoised, unsubtle, unwieldy 9 all thumbs, graceless, ham-handed, inelegant, lumbering, maladroit, ponderous, stumbling, unskilled, untactful, unwieldly 10 blundering, cumbersome, galumphing, leadfooted, left-handed, outlandish, unbecoming, unskillful
fix: 5 kluge 6 kludge
one: 3 ape, oaf 4 clod, hulk 5 klutz 6 lubber 7 bungler
one's comment: 4 oops 6 whoops
clunk: 4 thud 5 thump 6 lumber
clunker: 3 car 4 auto, bomb, heap 5 lemon 6 jalopy 10 automobile, hunk of junk, rattletrap
feature: 4 rust
clunky: 8 unwieldy 9 graceless, unwieldly 10 cumbersome
Cluny: 4 lace
Cluny Brown (1946 film)
cast: Charles Boyer, Jennifer Jones
director: Ernst Lubitsch
cluster: 3 set 4 band, bevy, gang, herd, lump, mass, nest, pack, tuft 5 array, batch, bunch, clump, covey, crowd, drift, group, swarm 6 bundle, clamor, gather, huddle 7 collect, round up 8 assembly 9 gathering 10 assemblage, collection, cumulation
flower ~: 5 ament, umbel 6 catkin
cluster ___: 3 cup, fly, leg 4 bean, bomb, pine 5 point 7 college
___ cluster: 4 open, star, tone 5 Virgo 7 Beehive, oak-leaf, Perseus
clustered: 5 dense
clutch: 3 hug, set 4 fist, grab, grip, hold, lock, snap, sort, take 5 brood, clasp, grasp, group, pedal, pluck, purse, seize 6 caress, clench, clinch, enfold, infold, retain, snatch 7 cling to, embrace, handbag, squeeze 8 quandary 9 keep close 10 pocketbook
neighbor: 5 brake
clutch ___: 3 bag 5 purse
___-clutch: 6 double
clutches: 4 grip 5 grasp 7 control, custody 10 possession
Clutha: 5 river
locale: 10 New Zealand
clutter: 4 mess, muss 5 snarl 6 bustle, jumble, jungle, litter, mess up, muddle, tangle 8 disarray, disorder, scramble, shambles 9 confusion 10 hodgepodge, untidiness
cluttered: 5 messy, mussy 6 unneat, untidy 10 disorderly, topsy-turvy
clutter-free: 4 neat, tidy 6 spruce
cluttering: 3 ado 4 daze, flap, fuss, mess, riot, stew 5 chaos, doubt, mix-up, panic, press, snarl, swirl 6 bedlam, bustle, dither, flurry, fracas, hubbub, huddle, jumble, jungle, lather, litter, mayhem, muddle, tangle, trauma, tumult, unrest, uproar 7 anarchy, clutter, mistake, turmoil 8 disarray, disorder, question, scramble, shambles 9 abashment, agitation, amazement, commotion, confusion, imbroglio, intricacy, labyrinth, patchwork 10 befuddling, bemusement, complexity, difficulty, excitement, hodgepodge, hurly-burly, perplexity, puzzlement, turbulence, untidiness, wilderness
Clyde: 4 Andy 5 river 6 Barrow, Jeremy 7 Drexler 8 Geronimi, Tombaugh 9 McPhatter
city on the ~: 7 Glasgow
Firth of ~ island: 5 Arran
Firth of ~ port: 3 Ayr
Firth of ~ tributary: 4 Doon
partner: 6 Bonnie
River locale: 7 Ireland
Clydesdale: 5 horse 6 equine
Clym's wife: 3 Vye 9 Eustachia
Clytemnestra
brother of ~: 6 Castor
daughter of ~: 7 Electra, Erigone 9 Iphigenia
husband of ~: 8 Tantalus 9 Agamemnon
mother of ~: 4 Leda
sister of ~: 5 Helen
son of ~: 6 Aletes 7 Orestes
cm.: 4 meas.
Cm: 4 elem. 6 curium 7 element
96 for ~: 4 at. no.
cmdr.: 3 ldr., off.
c'mon: 6 let's go
C'mon Marianne (1967 song) artist: Four Seasons
CMT alternative: 3 BET, MTV, PAX, TBS, TLC, TNN, TNT, USA 4 ESPN, HGTV 5 A and E, C-SPAN, Style 6 Noggin, Tech TV, TV Land 7 Court TV, Ovation, SoapNet 8 Lifetime
CN ___: 5 Tower
CNBC: 7 channel
alternative: 3 CNN 5 MSNBC
CNN: 4 news
alternative: 4 CNBC 5 MSNBC
anchorman: 4 Shaw
home: 7 Atlanta, Georgia
host: 4 King 9 Larry King
part of ~: 4 News 5 Cable 7 Network
piece: 4 rept. 6 report
receiver: 2 TV 5 TV set
word: 4 live
CNO: 3 VIP
grp.: 3 JCS, USN
C-note: 4 bill 7 hundred
change for a ~: 4 tens 8 twenties
ten ~ s: 3 gee 5 grand
co-___: 3 eds, ops, opt, own 4 host, star 5 occur, teach 6 anchor, author, manage, parent, winner, worker 7 edition, founder, manager, ordinal, produce, publish, venture
co.: 3 mfr., org. 4 corp., firm
component: 3 div. 5 R and D
VIP: 3 CEO, mgr. 4 pres.
Co: 4 elem. 6 cobalt 7 element
27 for ~: 4 at. no.
CO
see Colorado
C&O: 2 RR 8 railroad
Coacalco: 4 city, town
locale: 6 Mexico
coach: 3 bus 5 drill, edify, prime, stage, teach, train, tutor 6 advise, chaise, ground, leader, mentor, school 7 adviser, advisor, educate, manager, phaeton, prepare, teacher, trainer, vehicle 8 carriage, educator, initiate, instruct 9 abecedary, charabanc 10 instructor
concern: 4 team
ender: 3 man, men
leave the ~: 5 debus 9 disembark
puller: 4 team 5 horse 6 engine
starter: 5 stage
coach ___: 3 box, dog 5 horse, house
___ coach: 3 air, day 4 baby 5 motor, night 7 Concord, hackney, trolley
Coach (ABC sitcom)
cast: Shelley Fabares (Christine Fox) Craig T. Nelson (Hayden Fox) Jerry Van Dyke (Luther Van Dam)
dog: 6 Quincy
coach-and-___: 4 four
coached, one being: 5 tutee
Coachella: 4 city, town
locale: 10 California
coaching: 6 lesson 8 training 9 education
coachwhip: 5 snake 6 animal 7 reptile
relative: 3 asp, boa 5 aboma, adder, cobra, krait, mamba, racer, viper 6 dhaman, python, taipan 7 markhor, rattler 8 anaconda, moccasin, ringhals 9 boomslang 10 bushmaster, copperhead, sidewinder
coactively: 8 together
coadjutant: 4 aide 6 helper 8 henchman 9 assistant
coadjute: 9 cooperate
coagulate: 3 gel, set 4 clot, jell 6 curdle, gelate, harden 7 congeal, stiffen, thicken 8 coalesce, solidify 10 gelatinize, inspissate
coagulated: 5 thick 7 jellied 10 gelatinous
coagulation: 4 clot, mass
Coahuila: 4 city, town 5 state
city: 4 Nava 5 Acuña, Palau 7 Allende, Múzquiz, Sabinas, Torreón 8 Castaños, Frontera, Monclova, Saltillo, San Pedro, Zaragoza 9 Matamoros
locale: 6 Mexico
coal: 3 oil 4 coke, fuel 5 ember 6 cannel 7 lignite, mineral 8 resource 10 anthracite, bituminous, fossil fuel
add ~: 5 stoke
combining form: 7 anthrac-, carboni- 8 anthraco-

dust: 4 culm
ender: 4 fish 5 field
gem-grade ~: 3 jet
German ~ region: 4 Saar
holder: 3 bin, car, hod 4 scow, tram 5 barge 6 hopper
hot ~: 5 ember
product: 3 oil, tar 4 coke 7 diamond
residue: 6 cinder
size: 3 pea
slide: 5 chute
starter: 4 char
stratum: 4 seam, vein
tar derivative: 5 xylol 6 indene 7 creosol, cresote
unit: 3 ton 4 lump
user: 5 grill 7 furnace 8 barbecue
worker: 5 miner 6 stoker 7 collier

coal __: 3 car, gas, hod, oil, pit, tar 4 ball, mine, seam 5 field, miner 6 cutter, heaver, mining 7 measure, scuttle

__ coal: 3 cob, egg, gas, nut, pea 4 hard, rice, soft, wood 5 block, steam, stove, white 6 barley, bright, broken, cannel, cherry 7 boghead

Coal __ Daughter: 6 Miner's

coal-black: 4 ebon, inky 5 ebony

coaler: 4 ship

coalesce: 3 gel, mix, wed 4 clot, fuse, join 5 blend, merge, unify, unite 6 commix 7 combine, conjoin 9 coagulate, commingle, integrate 10 amalgamate

coalition: 4 bloc, ring 5 front, group, junta, junto, party, union 6 league, muster 7 amalgam, combine, faction 8 alliance 9 anschluss 10 conspiracy, federation, friendship, trade union

Coal Miner's Daughter (1980 film)
cast: Beverly D'Angelo, Tommy Lee Jones, Sissy Spacek
character: 4 Lynn 5 Cline, Patsy 7 Loretta 10 Patsy Cline
director: Michael Apted

coals
rake over the ~: 4 flay 5 chide, roast, scold 6 berate, rebuke 7 lambast, tell off 8 lambaste

coarse: 3 low, raw 4 base, foul, lewd, loud, rude, vile 5 bawdy, crass, crude, gross, gruff, harsh, nasty, nubby, raspy, rough, salty, seamy, tacky 6 common, earthy, gauche, grainy, hubbly, impure, ribald, rustic, smutty, unmeet, vulgar 7 bearish, beastly, bestial, boorish, ignoble, loutish, lowbred, obscene, profane, raffish, raucous, sketchy, uncivil, uncouth, unkempt 8 barbaric, churlish, degraded, immodest, impolite, impudent, indecent, off-color, plebeian, scratchy, unseemly 9 barbarian, barbarous, graceless, inelegant, low-minded, lubricous, makeshift, primitive, tasteless, unrefined 10 amateurish, indecorous, indelicate, lascivious, lower-class, regardless, scurrilous, uncultured, ungracious, unpolished
fabric: 5 chino, denim 6 burlap, linsey
fiber: 4 jute 5 istle, ixtle
file: 4 rasp
language: 9 invective, profanity
make ~: 9 granulate
one: 3 oaf 4 boor

coarse-grained: 6 gritty

coarsen: 5 enure, inure 6 harden 7 callous, roughen, toughen

coarseness: 4 woof 7 texture 8 lewdness 9 barbarism, bawdiness, crassness, harshness, indecency, roughness, vulgarity 10 disrespect, earthiness, indelicacy, smuttiness, unevenness

Coase, Ronald: 8 Nobelist 9 economist

coast: 4 bank, skim 5 beach, glide, relax, shore, short, slide, slink 6 cruise, strand 7 goof off, seaside, slither 8 littoral, seaboard, seashore, volplane 9 freewheel, shoreline 10 take it easy
away from the ~: 6 inland
ender: 4 land, line, ward, wise 5 wards
starter: 3 sea

coast-__ cutter: 5 guard

Coast: 4 soap
alternative: 3 Lux 4 Dial, Dove, Lava, Tone, Zest 5 Camay, Ivory, Lever 6 Boraxo, Caress, Shield 8 Lifebuoy 9 Palmolive, Safeguard 11 Irish Spring

Coast __: 5 Guard, Range

__ Coast: 4 East, Gold, Gulf, West 5 Caird, Ivory 6 Adélie, Murman, Pirate 7 Barbary, Malabar, Trucial

coastal: 6 marine 7 seaside 8 littoral, maritime
not ~: 6 inland 8 interior
phenomenon: 4 tide
recess: 4 cove 5 firth, frith

coastal __: 5 plain

coaster: 4 boat, ride, ship, sled
see also roller coaster

coaster __: 5 brake

__ coaster: 6 roller

Coasters
song: Along Came Jones (1959)
Charlie Brown (1959)
Poison Ivy (1959)
Searchin' (1957)
Yakety Yak (1958)
Young Blood (1957)

coast-guard __: 6 cutter

Coast Guard
alert: 3 SOS
like ~ rescues: 6 air-sea
officer: 3 CPO, ens. 6 ensign
woman of the ~: 4 Spar

coasting __: 4 lead 5 trade, wagon

coastline: 5 shore
calamity: 5 spill

Coast of Coral, The author: Clarke

coat: 3 fur, tog, tux 4 bark, pelt, rind, skin, tuck, wash, wrap 5 A-line, capot, cover, crust, frock, glaze, gloss, grego, jemmy, jibba, layer, loden, paint, parka, plate, rub on, sheet, shell, simar, smear, smock, tails, tunic, wamus 6 achkan, anorak, banian, banyan, blazer, bolero, bomber, capote, dolman, duffle, duster, ermine, finish, fleece, jacket, jerkin, lamina, raglan, reefer, spread, tabard, tuxedo, ulster, veneer, wammus, wampus 7 cagoule, cassock, cutaway, encrust, garment, incrust, kuletuk, lacquer, oilskin, overlay, paletot, plaster, slicker, spencer, surtout, varnish, zamarra 8 benjamin, chaqueta, covering, laminate, mackinaw 9 balmacaan, gloss over, Inverness, outerwear, pea jacket, petersham, redingote, sou'wester, whitewash 10 bush jacket, fearnought, flak jacket, lamination, macfarlane, mackintosh, protection
animal ~: 3 fur 4 pelt
arctic ~: 5 parka 6 anorak
British: 5 jemmy, tunic
Canada: 7 kuletuk
church ~: 7 cassock
close a ~: 5 zip up
cowboy ~: 8 chaqueta
ender: 4 room, tail 5 dress
expensive ~: 3 fur 4 mink 5 sable 6 ermine 10 chinchilla
fabric: 5 loden, serge 6 saxony 8 Burberry
fastener: 4 frog, snap 6 Velcro, zipper
for a house: 5 paint
formal ~: 6 tuxedo 7 cutaway
fox hunter's ~: 5 pinks
fruit ~: 4 rind
heavy ~: 5 loden, wamus 6 ulster, wammus, wampus 8 mackinaw
hooded ~: 5 grego 6 duffle
India: 6 achkan, banian, banyan
Japan: 5 haori, happi
length: 4 maxi
lose one's ~: 4 shed
makeshife ~ hanger: 4 nail
military ~: 5 tunic 9 Ike jacket 10 flak jacket
Moslem: 5 jibba
of arms: 4 seal 6 emblem 7 insigne 8 insignia
of paint: 5 layer
outer ~: 4 skin
part: 3 arm 4 vent 5 lapel 6 lining, sleeve
pedicurist's ~: 6 enamel
rack: 4 tree
remove the ~: 4 pare
seed ~: 4 aril 5 testa
shaggy ~: 4 hair
shed one's ~: 4 molt
shiny ~: 6 enamel
short ~: 5 grego 6 jerkin, reefer
Spain: 7 zamarra
starter: 3 red, top 4 blue, over, rain, tail, turn 5 great, house, petti, sugar, under, waist
thin ~: 6 lamina
words on a ~ of arms: 5 motto

coat __: 4 card, tree 6 flower, hanger 7 protein

__ coat: 3 box, car, fur, pea 4 bush, pink, polo, sack, seed, tail 5 brown, buffy, dress, frock, happi, jelly, privy, storm 6 brunch, double, duffel, duffle, finish, ground, trench 7 choroid, cutaway, hacking, morning, Norfolk, protein, scratch, stadium, swagger

__-Coat: 3 Glo

coated with ice: 5 gelid

Coatepec: 4 city, town
locale: 6 Mexico 8 Veracruz

Coates: 7 Phyllis

coati: 6 animal, mammal

coati-__: 5 mondi, mundi

coating: 4 film, peel, rind, rust, skin, wash 5 crust, glaze, layer, scale, sheet, shell 6 enamel, facing, finish, patina, patine, veneer 7 blanket, dusting, lacquer, varnish 8 covering 9 lubricant 10 integument, lamination

coat of __: 4 arms, mail

coat of arms: 5 crest 6 blazon
band: 4 orle
expert: 6 herald
figure: 5 beast

coat of arms panel in heraldry: 9 hatchment

coatroom accessory: 4 stub 6 hanger

Coat, The author: Athol Fugard

Coatzacoalcos: 4 city, town
locale: 6 Mexico 8 Veracruz

Coatzintla: 4 city, town
locale: 6 Mexico 8 Veracruz

coax: 3 get, nag 4 lure, urge, wile 5 egg on, tempt 6 allure, beckon, cajole, entice, incite, induce, rope in, wangle, work on 7 beguile, flatter, jawbone, wheedle 8 blandish, butter up, inveigle, persuade, soft-sell, soft-soap 9 encourage, importune, influence, sweet-talk
(into): 4 talk

coaxial __: 5 cable

coaxing: 5 charm 6 urging 7 blarney, palaver 8 cajolery, entreaty, flattery, humoring, jollying, soft soap, stroking 9 sweet talk, wheedling 10 persuasion

cob: 4 bird, male, swan 5 horse, money 6 animal, equine
attachment: 6 kernel
ender: 3 nut, web
mate: 3 pen
starter: 4 corn
young: 6 cygnet

cob __: 3 pie 4 coal

Cobain, Kurt spouse: Courtney Love

cobalt: 4 blue 5 azure, metal 7 element 8 greenish
alloy: 6 alnico 9 Vitallium
ore: 8 smaltite
relative: 4 anil, cyan, navy, Nile, teal 5 Alice, slate 6 indigo, raisin, violet 7 peacock 8 cerulean, sapphire 9 turquoise 10 aquamarine

cobalt __: 4 blue 5 bloom, green 6 yellow

Cobb: 2 Ty 5 Tiger, Tyrus 10 outfielder
surpasser: 4 Rose

Cobb (1994 film)
cast: Lolita Davidovich, Tommy Lee Jones, Robert Wuhl
director: Ron Shelton

Cobb, Irvin S.: 6 author, writer
work: Exit Laughing

cobble: 4 mend, sole 5 patch 7 patch up
ender: 5 stone

Cobb, Lee J.: 5 actor
film: 12 Angry Men (1957)
Anna and the King of Siam (1946)
Boomerang! (1947)
Call Northside 777 (1948)
Come Blow Your Horn (1963)
Coogan's Bluff (1968)
The Dark Past (1948)
Exodus (1960)
The Exorcist (1973)
Gorilla at Large (1954)
Green Mansions (1959)
Lawman (1971)
The Left Hand of God (1955)
Man of the West (1958)
The Moon Is Down (1943)
On the Waterfront (1954)
Party Girl (1958)
Thieves' Highway (1949)
The Three Faces of Eve (1957)
TV: The Virginian

cobbler: 3 pie 5 soler 7 dessert 9 shoemaker
concern: 4 heel, last, sole
ingredient: 4 pear 5 apple, berry, peach 6 cherry 7 rhubarb 9 cranberry, raspberry 10 blackberry, strawberry
tool: 3 awl

cobblestone: 4 road, rock

__ Cob, CT: 3 Cos

Cobh: 4 city, port, town
locale: 7 Ireland

cobia: 4 fish

Coblenz: 4 city, town
locale: 7 Germany
river: 5 Mosel 7 Moselle

cobnut: 3 nut 4 tree 5 hazel

COBOL: 8 language
alternative: 3 ADA, APL, SQL 4 Alef, html, Icon, Java, LISP, Logo, Orca, Perl 5 Algol, Basic, Cecil, Dylan, SISAL 6 Delphi, Eiffel, Erlang, Oberon, Pascal, Prolog, Sather, Scheme, Snobol 7 Fortran

cobra: 3 asp 5 snake, viper 6 animal, elapid 7 reptile
Asian ~: 5 krait
comment: 3 sss
cousin: 5 krait, mamba
genus: 5 elaps
like a ~: 6 hooded
relative: 3 boa 5 aboma, adder, racer, viper 6 dhaman, python, taipan 7 markhor, rattler 8 anaconda, moccasin, ringhals 9 boomslang, coach-

whip 10 bushmaster, copperhead, sidewinder
weapon: 4 fang 5 venom
___ cobra: 4 king 6 Indian
Cobra: 3 car, van 4 auto, Ford 5 Chevy 9 Chevrolet 10 automobile
Cobra Woman (1944 film)
cast: Jon Hall, Maria Montez, Sabu
coburg: 6 fabric 8 material
___-Coburg: 4 Saxe
Coburn: 5 James 7 Charles
Coburn, Charles: 5 actor
film: Bachelor Mother (1939)
The Devil and Miss Jones (1941)
Gentlemen Prefer Blondes (1953)
Heaven Can Wait (1943)
The Lady Eve (1941)
Louisa (1950)
Made for Each Other (1939)
Monkey Business (1952)
The More the Merrier (1943, AA)
Over 21 (1945)
Road to Singapore (1940)
Together Again (1944)
Wilson (1944)
Coburn, James: 5 actor
film: Affliction (1998, AA)
The Americanization of Emily (1964)
Bite the Bullet (1975)
The Carey Treatment (1972)
Cross of Iron (1977)
Dead Heat on a Merry-Go-Round (1966)
Eraser (1996)
The Great Escape (1963)
Hard Times (1975)
Harry in Your Pocket (1973)
The Last of Sheila (1973)
The Magnificent Seven (1960)
The Nutty Professor (1996)
The President's Analyst (1967)
Sky Riders (1976)
What Did You Do in the War, Daddy? (1966)
cobweb: 3 web 4 mesh 5 snare 8 filament
site: 5 attic 8 basement
cobweblike: 4 fine 5 filmy, gauzy 6 flimsy 8 delicate, finespun, gossamer 10 diaphanous
cobza: 4 lute 6 string
origin: 7 Romania, Rumania
Coca: 7 Imogene
cohort: 6 Caesar
Coca-Cola: 3 pop 4 soda 9 soft drink
alternative: 3 TAB 4 Nehi 5 Fanta, Pepsi 6 Fresca, Sprite 8 Diet Rite, Dr Pepper 9 Canada Dry 10 Mello Yello, Royal Crown 11 Mountain Dew
brand: 6 Fresca
flavor: 6 cherry 7 vanilla
sometimes: 5 mixer
Coca-Cola Kid, The (1984 film)
cast: Bill Kerr, Eric Roberts, Greta Scacchi
coccyx: 4 bone 8 tailbone
locale: 5 spine
Cochabamba: 4 city, town
locale: 7 Bolivia
___-cochere: 5 porte
Cochin: 4 city, port, town
locale: 5 India
Cochin China: 4 fowl 7 chicken
relative: 6 Bantam, Brahma, Houdan, Sussex 7 Cornish, Dorking, Leghorn 8 Araucana, Langshan, Shanghai 9 Dominique, Orpington, Wyandotte
cochlear: 6 spiral
cochlea site: 3 ear
Cochran: 5 Eddie, Steve 7 Johnnie 10 Jacqueline
Cochrane: 3 Tom 6 Mickey
Cochrane, Mickey: 7 catcher
cock: 4 bird 5 valve 7 chicken, rooster
crown: 4 comb
ender: 3 ade, pit 4 boat, crow, eyed, loft, sure 5 fight, horse, roach
starter: 3 bib, hay, pea, pet, sea 4 cold, game, stop, wood 5 billy, black, pinch, poppy 7 shuttle, weather
cock ___ walk: 5 of the
___ cock: 3 air 4 ball, moor, sage 5 heath 6 jungle, turkey
___-cock: 4 cold
cock-a-___: 3 poo 4 hoop 6 leekie
cock-a-doodle-doo: 4 crow 6 cackle, squawk
Cockaigne composer: 5 Elgar
cock-a-leekie: 4 soup
cockamamie: 5 inane, silly 7 foolish 10 irrational, weak-minded
cock-and-bull story: 4 tale
cockapoo: 3 dog 5 canid 6 canine
cockatiel: 4 bird
cockatoo: 4 bird 5 galah
feature: 5 crest
kin: 5 macaw
Cockcroft, John: 8 Nobelist 9 physicist
cockcrow: 4 dawn 5 sunup 7 morning, sunrise 8 daybreak, daylight
cocked ___: 3 hat
___-cocked: 4 half 6 return
Cocker, Joe
song: The Letter (1970)
Up Where We Belong (1982)
You Are So Beautiful (1975)
cocker spaniel: 3 dog 5 canid 6 canine
cockeyed: 4 agee, ajee, awry, bent, loco 5 amiss, askew, atilt, bowed, inane, silly, wacky 6 absurd, all wet, askant, aslant, canted, screwy, skewed, whacky, zigzag 7 angular, askance, crooked, fatuous, unsound, winding 8 angulose, angulous, lopsided, specious 9 illogical, irregular, ludicrous, senseless, untenable 10 groundless, ridiculous
Cockeyed Optimist, A composer: 7 Rodgers 11 Hammerstein
Cockfighter (1974 film)
cast: Warren Oates, Richard B. Shull, Harry Dean Stanton
___ cockhorse...: 5 Ride a
cockiness: 5 pride 6 hubris, hybris 8 audacity 9 flippancy 10 assumption
cockle: 5 shell 6 mussel, pucker 8 seashell
ender: 3 bur 4 boat 5 shell
cockles of one's ___: 5 heart
Cockney: 4 Brit 6 Briton
abode: 3 'ome
assistance: 3 'elp
assistant: 5 'elper
dropper: 5 aitch
endearment: 3 luv
greeting: 4 'ello
idol: 3 'ero
residence: 3 'ome
steed: 4 'orse
toast starter: 4 'eres
see also British
cock of the ___: 4 walk 5 woods
cockpit
abbr.: 3 alt., IAS
VIP: 5 pilot 7 copilot
work in the ~: 3 fly 6 aviate
Cockpit author: Jerzy Kosinski
cockroach: 3 bug 4 pest 6 insect
Cock Robin, like: 5 slain
cockscomb: 3 cap, hat 5 plant 6 flower
cockspur: 4 tree 8 hawthorn
cocksure: 4 smug, vain 5 brash, nervy 7 certain, hotshot 8 arrogant, impudent 9 conceited, confident, know-it-all, presuming 10 big-talking, swaggering
cocktail: 3 nog 4 flip, sour 5 Bronx, drink, sling 6 bishop, eggnog, Gibson, gimlet, mai tai, mimosa, posset, rickey, rob roy, zombie 7 Collins, martini, negroni, sidecar, stinger 8 coco loco, daiquiri, highball, Jack Rose, libation, pink lady, salty dog, vermouth 9 alexander, appetizer, Manhattan, margarita, moosemilk, ward eight 10 Bloody Mary, golden fizz, horse's neck, intoxicant, Moscow mule, piña colada, rock and rye, silver fizz
cooler: 3 ice 5 rocks
counter: 3 bar
garnish: 5 olive, twist
gin ~: 6 Gibson 7 martini
ingredient: 5 mixer 6 liquor 7 bitters
lounge: 3 bar 6 lounge, saloon
Molotov ~: 4 bomb
prepare a ~: 3 mix
cocktail ___: 4 hour 5 glass, party, sauce, table 6 lounge
___ cocktail: 5 fruit 6 shrimp 7 Molotov
Cocktail (1988 film)
cast: Bryan Brown, Tom Cruise, Elisabeth Shue
locale: 3 bar
Cocktail Party, The author: T.S. Eliot
Cocktails ___ Two: 3 for
cocky: 4 smug, vain 5 brash, nervy, proud 6 brazen, daring, jaunty 7 fustian, haughty, pompous, stuck-up 8 arrogant, boastful, fearless, impudent, snobbish, superior 9 big-headed, bumptious, conceited 10 big-talking
walk: 5 strut
Coco: 5 James, river 6 Chanel
competitor: 5 Estée
concern: 5 style
River locale: 8 Honduras 9 Nicaragua
cocoa: 5 brown, drink 7 reddish 8 beverage 9 yellowish
container: 3 mug
ender: 3 nut
relative: 3 bay, dun, tan 4 bole, ecru, fawn, foxy, nude, seal 5 amber, beige, camel, hazel, khaki, mocha, sepia, tawny, umber 6 auburn, bister, bistre, bronze, coffee, copper, ginger, russet, sienna, sorrel, suntan, walnut 7 biscuit, caramel, dogwood 8 chestnut, cinnamon, mahogany 9 butternut, chocolate
cocoa ___: 4 bean 6 butter
Cocoa ___: 5 Beach, Puffs
Cocoa Beach: 4 city, town
locale: 7 Florida
Cocoa Blasts: 6 cereal
competitor: 3 Kix 4 Life, Trix 5 Kashi, Quisp, Total 6 Kaboom, Muesli, Oreo O's, Pablum, Smacks 7 All-Bran, Crispix, Harmony, Hunny B's, Mueslix, Oat Bran, Pokemon 8 Boo Berry, Cheerios, Corn Chex, Corn Pops, Fiber One, Rice Chex, Special K, Uncle Sam, Wheaties 9 Alpha Bits, Apple Zaps, Grape Nuts, Honey Comb, Just Right, Wheat Chex 10 Apple Jacks, Bran Flakes, Cap'n Crunch, Cocoa Puffs, Froot Loops, Mini-Wheats, Nutri-Grain, Puffed Rice, Quaker Oats, Smart Start 11 Cookie Crisp, Golden Crisp, Lucky Charms, Puffed Wheat, Sweet Crunch, Waffle Crisp
Cocoa Frosted Flakes: 6 cereal
competitor: 3 Kix 4 Life, Trix 5 Kashi, Quisp, Total 6 Kaboom, Muesli, Oreo O's, Pablum, Smacks 7 All-Bran, Crispix, Harmony, Hunny B's, Mueslix, Oat Bran, Pokemon 8 Boo Berry, Cheerios, Corn Chex, Corn Pops, Fiber One, Rice Chex, Special K, Uncle Sam, Wheaties 9 Alpha Bits, Apple Zaps, Grape Nuts, Honey Comb, Just Right, Wheat Chex 10 Apple Jacks, Bran Flakes, Cap'n Crunch, Cocoa Puffs, Froot Loops, Mini-Wheats, Nutri-Grain, Puffed Rice, Quaker Oats, Smart Start 11 Cocoa Blasts, Cookie Crisp, Golden Crisp, Lucky Charms, Puffed Wheat, Sweet Crunch, Waffle Crisp
Cocoa Krispies: 6 cereal
competitor: 3 Kix 4 Life, Trix 5 Kashi, Quisp, Total 6 Kaboom, Muesli, Oreo O's, Pablum, Smacks 7 All-Bran, Crispix, Harmony, Hunny B's, Mueslix, Oat Bran, Pokemon 8 Boo Berry, Cheerios, Corn Chex, Corn Pops, Fiber One, Rice Chex, Special K, Uncle Sam, Wheaties 9 Alpha Bits, Apple Zaps, Grape Nuts, Honey Comb, Just Right, Wheat Chex 10 Apple Jacks, Bran Flakes, Cap'n Crunch, Cocoa Puffs, Froot Loops, Mini-Wheats, Nutri-Grain, Puffed Rice, Quaker Oats, Smart Start 11 Cocoa Blasts, Cookie Crisp, Golden Crisp, Lucky Charms, Puffed Wheat, Sweet Crunch, Waffle Crisp
Cocoanuts, The: 4 film, play 7 musical
author: George S. Kaufman
cast: Margaret Dumont, Chico Marx, Groucho Marx, Harpo Marx, Zeppo Marx
director: 6 Florey 7 Santley
songwriter: Irving Berlin
Cocoa Pebbles: 6 cereal
competitor: 3 Kix 4 Life, Trix 5 Kashi, Quisp, Total 6 Kaboom, Muesli, Oreo O's, Pablum, Smacks 7 All-Bran, Crispix, Harmony, Hunny B's, Mueslix, Oat Bran, Pokemon 8 Boo Berry, Cheerios, Corn Chex, Corn Pops, Fiber One, Rice Chex, Special K, Uncle Sam, Wheaties 9 Alpha Bits, Apple Zaps, Grape Nuts, Honey Comb, Just Right, Wheat Chex 10 Apple Jacks, Bran Flakes, Cap'n Crunch, Cocoa Puffs, Froot Loops, Mini-Wheats, Nutri-Grain, Puffed Rice, Quaker Oats, Smart Start 11 Cocoa Blasts, Cookie Crisp, Golden Crisp, Lucky Charms, Puffed Wheat, Sweet Crunch, Waffle Crisp
Cocoa Puffs: 6 cereal
competitor: 3 Kix 4 Life, Trix 5 Kashi, Quisp, Total 6 Kaboom, Muesli, Oreo O's, Pablum, Smacks 7 All-Bran, Crispix, Harmony, Hunny B's, Mueslix, Oat Bran, Pokemon 8 Boo Berry, Cheerios, Corn Chex, Corn Pops, Fiber One, Rice Chex, Special K, Uncle Sam, Wheaties 9 Alpha Bits, Apple Zaps, Grape Nuts, Honey Comb, Just Right, Wheat Chex 10 Apple Jacks, Bran Flakes, Cap'n Crunch, Froot Loops, Mini-Wheats, Nutri-Grain, Puffed Rice, Quaker Oats, Smart Start 11 Cocoa Blasts, Cookie Crisp, Golden Crisp, Lucky Charms, Puffed Wheat, Sweet Crunch, Waffle Crisp
cocobolo: 4 tree
coco-de-mer: 4 palm, tree 8 palm tree
Coco, James: 5 actor
film: The Cheap Detective (1978)
Murder by Death (1976)
Only When I Laugh (1981)
Such Good Friends (1971)
coco loco: 5 drink 8 beverage, cocktail
ingredient: 3 gin

coconut: 3 oil 4 bean, head, palm 5 fruit 6 noggin 8 ice cream
alternative: 5 lemon, mocha, peach 6 banana, coffee, Jamoca, toffee 7 caramel, vanilla 8 cinnamon, hazelnut 9 bubblegum, chocolate, pineapple, pistachio, raspberry, rocky road, rum raisin 10 blackberry, cheesecake, Neapolitan, peppermint, strawberry
dried ~: 5 copra 8 copperah
exporter: 4 Fiji
fiber: 4 coir
juice: 4 milk
layer: 4 husk
prepare ~: 5 grate
coconut __: 3 oil 4 milk, palm 6 butter
coconut __ pie: 5 cream
Coconut (1972 song) artist: Nilsson
Coconut Creek: 4 city, town
locale: 7 Florida
cocoon
creator: 5 larva
leave the ~: 6 emerge
made a ~: 4 wove
occupant: 4 pupa 5 pupae
product: 4 silk
Cocoon (1985 film)
cast: Don Ameche, Wilford Brimley, Hume Cronyn, Brian Dennehy, Jack Gilford, Steve Guttenberg, Maureen Stapleton, Jessica Tandy, Gwen Verdon, Tahnee Welch
craft: 3 UFO
director: Ron Howard
Cocos: 4 isls. 5 isles 7 islands
owner: 9 Australia
Cocteau, Jean: 6 artist, French, writer
friend: Picasso
Cocula: 4 city, town
locale: 6 Mexico 7 Jalisco
cod: 4 fish 6 burbot 7 seafood 8 lutefisk
alternative: 4 sole
boiled ~: 8 lutefisk
cousin: 4 hake, ling
ender: 4 fish
starter: 3 tom 4 ling 5 pease
young: 4 parr 5 sprag
cod __ oil: 5 liver
__ cod: 4 rock 5 black 6 Alaska 7 Pacific
__ Cod: 4 Cape
COD
not: 3 FOB, ppd. 7 prepaid
part: 4 cash 8 delivery
coda: 3 end 5 close 6 ending, epilog, finale 8 epilogue
__ Cod cottage: 4 Cape
coddle: 4 baby, boil, cook 5 humor, nurse, poach, spoil 6 cosset, dandle, dote on, pamper 7 cater to, gratify, indulge 8 dote upon 9 spoon-feed
starter: 5 molly
coddled __: 3 egg
code: 3 key, law 4 rule 5 bylaw, canon 6 cipher, cypher, ethics, legend, policy 7 charter, encrypt 8 standard 9 etiquette, ordinance, principle, semaphore 10 cryptogram, principles, regulation
breaker: 3 key
breaking org: 3 NSA
carrier: 4 gene
ender: 4 book
in ~: 9 encrypted 10 unreadable
inventor: 5 Morse
not up to ~: 5 unfit
of conduct: 5 ethic 8 protocol
part of a ~: 3 law
word: 4 Able, Zulu 5 Baker 7 Charlie
WWII ~ machine: 6 Enigma
code __: 4 blue, book, flag, name, word 6 dating, phrase
code-__: 7 sharing
__ code: 3 bar, tax, ten, zip 4 area, fire 5 color, dress, Morse, order, penal 6 access, binary, health, object, postal, source 7 airport, catalog, genetic, initial, machine
__-code: 5 color
Code __ West: 5 of the
__-coded: 5 color
codeine: 6 opiate
source: 5 opium
code of __: 6 ethics
Code of Scotland Yard, The (1946 film)
cast: Derek Farr, Oscar Homolka
Code of the West author: Zane Grey
Code of the Woosters, The author: P.G. Wodehouse
__-code reader: 3 bar
codex: 4 book 5 quire 6 volume 10 manuscript
codfish: 5 gadid, scrod, torsk 6 gadoid, schrod 7 bacalao
codger: 4 coot, fogy 5 fogey 6 galoot, geezer 7 galloot 9 eccentric, graybeard
query: 2 eh
codicil: 5 rider 6 clause 8 addendum, addition, appendix 9 amendment 10 postscript, supplement
codify: 5 order 6 embody, imbody 7 arrange 8 legalize, organize, tabulate 9 formulate, legislate
cod liver __: 3 oil
__ Cod, MA: 4 Cape
codswallop: 3 gas, rot 4 blah, bosh, bull, bunk, guff, jazz, jive, pooh, tosh 5 bilge, fudge, hokum, hooey, prate, stuff, trash, tripe 6 bunkum, bushwa, drivel, footle, gabble, gammon, gibber, havers, hot air, humbug, jabber, jargon, kibosh, piffle 7 baloney, blarney, blather, blether, boloney, bushwah, eyewash, flannel, flubdub, fustian, garbage, hogwash, inanity, rubbish, twaddle 8 buncombe, claptrap, falderal, falderol, flimflam, flummery, folderal, folderol, nonsense, slipslop, tommyrot, trumpery 9 banana oil, gibberish, kidstakes, moonshine, poppycock, rigmarole 10 applesauce, balderdash, bilge water, double-talk, flapdoodle, galimatias, Jabberwock, mumbo jumbo, rigamarole, taradiddle
Cody: 4 city, town
locale: 3 Wyo. 7 Wyoming
coed: 5 woman 7 scholar, student
quarters: 4 dorm
__ coefficient: 4 beta, drag 5 block 6 phenol 7 leading
coefficient of __: 4 drag
coelacanth: 4 fish
Coen: 4 Joel 5 Ethan
Coen, Joel: 8 director
film: Barton Fink (1991)
The Big Lebowski (1998)
Blood Simple (1984)
Fargo (1996)
The Hudsucker Proxy (1994)
The Man Who Wasn't There (2001)
O Brother, Where Art Thou? (2000)
Raising Arizona (1987)
spouse: Frances McDormand
__ coeptis: 6 annuit
coequal: 4 mate, peer 7 compeer, matched, partner
coerce: 3 cow 4 goad, make, push 5 bully, exact, force, press, wring 6 compel, extort, lean on 7 dragoon, shotgun 8 arm-twist, bludgeon, browbeat, bulldoze, pressure, threaten 9 blackmail, constrain, shake down, strong-arm, terrorize 10 bear down on, intimidate, pressurize
coercer: 5 bully, tough 7 hoodlum
coercion: 5 force 6 duress 7 tyranny 8 bullying, iron hand, menacing, pressure, violence 9 blackmail, extortion, restraint 10 compulsion, oppression
coercive: 5 stern 6 forced 7 violent
measure: 7 embargo 8 sanction
Coe, Sebastian: 5 miler 6 runner
emulate ~: 3 run 4 race
rival: 5 Ovett
Coetzee, J.M.: 6 writer 12 South African
__ coeur: 5 cri de, sacre
Coeur d'Alene: 4 city, town
locale: 3 Ida. 5 Idaho
Coeur de __: 4 Lion
__ Coeur, MO: 5 Creve
coeval: 4 same 9 attendant 10 coexistent, coincident, concurrent, concurring
coexist: 9 accompany
coexistent: 6 coeval 10 concurrent, synchronal
coextensive: 4 even 8 parallel
coffee: 3 joe, mud 4 bean, brew, java, Kona, tree 5 brown, decaf, drink, fluid, latte, mocha, Sanka, shrub, Yuban 6 jamoke 7 Folgers, Melitta, mugfuls, Nescafe, Savarin 8 awakener, beverage, capuchin, espresso, ice cream 9 demitasse, eye-opener, Hills Bros., Starbuck's, stimulant 10 brown shade, café au lait, cappuccino
additive: 4 lump 5 cream, sugar
alternative: 3 tea 5 lemon, mocha, peach 6 banana, Jamoca, toffee 7 caramel, coconut, vanilla 8 cinnamon, hazelnut 9 bubblegum, chocolate, pineapple, pistachio, raspberry, rocky road, rum raisin 10 blackberry, cheesecake, Neapolitan, peppermint, strawberry
brand: 5 Sanka, Yuban 7 Folgers, Melitta, Nescafe, Savarin 9 Hills Bros.
break: 4 lull, rest 5 pause 6 recess
break time: 5 ten a.m.
city: 6 Santos
companion: 3 bun 4 roll 5 bagel, donut 6 danish, éclair 7 cruller
emanation: 5 aroma
ender: 3 pot 4 cake 5 house, maker
family: 6 madder
get-together: 6 klatch
grind: 4 drip
grinder: 4 mill
grounds: 5 dregs
holder: 3 cup, mug, pot, urn 6 carafe
inferior ~: 3 mud
in French: 4 café
klatch: 5 party
liqueur: 6 Kahlúa
make ~: 4 brew, perc, perk
makeshift ~ table: 5 spool
Mideast ~ cup: 6 finjan
order: 5 black 6 au lait
prepare ~ beans: 5 grind, roast
relative: 3 bay, dun, tan 4 bole, ecru, fawn, foxy, nude, seal 5 amber, beige, camel, cocoa, hazel, ixora, khaki, mocha, sepia, tawny, umber 6 auburn, bister, bistre, bronze, copper, ginger, russet, sienna, sorrel, suntan, walnut 7 biscuit, caramel, dogwood 8 chestnut, cinchona, cinnamon, gardenia, mahogany 9 bouvardia, butternut, chocolate
source: 4 bean
spill ~ on, perhaps: 5 scald
unit: 5 pound
coffee __: 3 urn 4 cake, hour, mill, ring, shop, tree 5 break, cream, house, maker, royal, spoon, table 6 klatch 7 klatsch
coffee-__ book: 5 table
__ coffee: 4 drip, iced, Kona, perc, perk 5 Irish 7 Arabian, arabica, instant, robusta, Turkish
Coffee, __ Me?: 5 Tea or
Coffee, __ milk?: 5 tea or
Coffee-__: 4 Mate
coffeecake: 6 kuchen, pastry
Coffee Cantata composer: 4 Bach
coffeehouse: 4 café
music: 4 folk
order: 5 latte
__ coffee maker: 6 vacuum
coffeemaker need: 6 filter
Coffee or __?: 3 tea
coffeepot material: 5 Pyrex
coffee-table __: 4 book
Coffee, Tea, __?: 4 or Me
coffer: 3 bin, box 4 case, fisc 5 chest, trunk 6 bunker 7 lockbox 8 treasury, war chest 9 exchequer, strongbox 10 repository
Coffin: 4 Tris 8 Tristram
cog: 3 cam 4 gear 5 tooth 8 gridlock 9 component
ender: 5 wheel
cog __: 7 railway
__ cog: 5 slip a
Cogburn: 6 Reuben 7 Rooster
cogency: 5 logic, punch 6 weight 8 keenness, strength, validity
cogent: 3 apt 4 just 5 pithy, plain, solid, sound, valid, vivid 6 potent, strong 7 evident, express, fitting, logical, obvious, telling, tenable, weighty, well-put 8 analytic, apparent, apposite, coherent, distinct, explicit, forceful, luculent, manifest, methodic, palpable, powerful, rational, relevant, sensible, striking 9 effective, graspable, pertinent, pragmatic 10 analytical, compelling, conclusive, consistent, convincing, legitimate, meaningful, persuasive, satisfying, spelled out, unarguable
Coghlan, Eamonn: 5 miler 6 runner
cogitate: 4 mull, muse 5 think 6 ponder, reason 7 reflect 8 conceive, consider, meditate, mull over, ruminate 9 cerebrate, speculate, sweat over 10 brainstorm, deliberate, kick around
on: 8 mull over 9 entertain
cogitation: 7 thought 9 brainwork, deduction 10 conception, meditation, reflection, rumination
cogito: 5 Latin 6 I think
Cogito __ sum: 4 ergo
cognac: 5 drink 6 brandy, liquor 7 liqueur 8 beverage
kin: 6 kirsch
cognate: 4 akin, like 5 alike 6 allied, on a par 7 kindred, kinsman, related, similar 8 parallel, relative, relevant 9 analogous, kinswoman 10 affiliated, associated, comparable, equivalent
cognition: 9 knowledge 10 conception
cognitive: 8 rational 10 reasonable
ability: 5 logic
cognizance: 3 ken 4 heed 5 sense 6 memory, regard 8 keenness 9 awareness 10 perception
cognizant: 3 hep, hip 4 in on, up on, wise 5 alive, awake, aware, privy, savvy 6 posted, versed, with it 7 knowing, mindful, tuned in 8 apprised, familiar, informed, sensible 9 au courant, conscious, in the know, judicious, observant, on the beam, plugged in, sensitive 10 acquainted, conversant, perceptive
be ~ of: 3 see 4 know 7 realize
of: 4 onto 5 hip to 6 wise to 7 privy to
cognize: 3 see 4 know 5 grasp 6 fathom 7 discern 8 perceive 9 apprehend 10 comprehend, understand
cognomen: 4 name 5 title 6 byname, handle 7 epithet, pen name, surname

8 last name, nickname 9 pseudonym, sobriquet 10 family name, nom de plume, patronymic
cogon: 5 grass
cogwheel: 4 gear
Cohan, George M.: 5 Irish 8 composer
signature part: 3 Geo.
song: Give My Regards to Broadway
Harrigan
Mary's a Grand Old Name
Over There
The Yankee Doodle Boy
You're a Grand Old Flag
coheir: 7 legatee 9 inheritor
Cohen: 3 Rob 5 Myron 6 Morris 7 Leonard, Stanley 8 Frederic
Cohen, Morris: 11 philosopher
Cohen, Stanley: 8 Nobelist
Cohen-Tannoudji, Claude: 8 Nobelist 9 physicist
cohere: 4 fuse, glue, jell, join, link, yoke 5 agree, cling, fit in, merge, stick, unite 6 attach, cement, cleave, couple, fasten, hook up, relate, square 7 combine, conform, conjoin, connect, hitch on 8 be united, dovetail, hold fast 9 harmonize, hold water, make sense 10 correspond
coherence: 5 logic, unity 9 adherence, agreement, congruity, integrity, relations 10 attachment, conformity, connection, consonance, continuity, solidarity
coherent: 5 clear, lucid, sober, sound 6 cogent 7 legible, logical, orderly, tenable 8 analytic, methodic, rational, readable, reasoned, sensible 9 connected, organized, pragmatic 10 analytical, articulate, consistent, systematic
emit ~ light: 4 lase
cohesion: 8 sticking 9 adherence, integrity, stability 10 continuity
cohesive: 5 gluey, tough 10 integrated
become ~: 3 gel 4 jell
Cohn: 3 Roy 5 Harry, Mindy 9 Ferdinand
Cohn, Ferdinand: 8 botanist
coho: 4 fish 6 salmon
Cohoes: 4 city, town
locale: 7 New York
cohort: 3 pal 4 aide, ally, army, chum, mate 5 amigo, buddy, crony 6 fellow, friend, helper 7 comrade, partner 8 alter ego, confrere, follower, henchman, roommate, sidekick 9 assistant, associate, colleague, companion, confidant, supporter 10 accomplice, compatriot, well-wisher
cohost: 4 Ripa 5 Kelly, Regis, Rowan, Sajak, Vanna 6 Martin 7 McMahon 8 Dan Rowan, Pat Sajak 9 Ed McMahon, Kathie Lee, Kelly Ripa 10 Dick Martin, Vanna White
cohune: 4 palm
coif: 2 do 3 bob, bun, 'fro 4 Afro, buzz, conk, fade, flip, hair, pouf, punk, updo 5 bangs, butch, queue, style, twist 6 braids, hairdo, marcel, mohawk, plaits 7 beehive, chignon, crew cut, flattop, page boy, topknot, upsweep 8 bouffant, cornrows, ducktail, Dutch bob, pigtails, pin curls, ponytail, ringlets 9 hairstyle, headdress, permanent, pompadour, poodle cut, scalp lock, spit curls 10 cornbraids, dreadlocks, finger wave, Psyche knot
coign of ___: 7 vantage
coil: 4 curl, hank, kink, loop, roll, wind 5 braid, crimp, curve, helix, skein, snake, swirl, twine, twirl, twist, whorl 6 enwind, inwind, scroll, Slinky, spiral, spring, tangle, volute 7 entwine, intwine, meander, sinuate, wreathe 8 curlicue, curlycue, encircle 9 convolute, corkscrew, enwreathe, labyrinth, sinuosity 10 intertwine
combining form: 4 spir- 5 spiri-, spiro-
___ coil: 5 choke, field, spark, Tesla, voice 7 loading, tickler
coiled: 5 curly, kinky, round, snaky, spiry, wound 6 looped, spiral 7 helical, looping, sinuous
coin: 4 cash, cent, dime, duro, half, mint 5 bread, dough, franc, money, penny, piece, token 6 change, copper, create, invent, make up, nickel, silver 7 quarter 8 innovate 9 neologize, originate 10 half-dollar
bird on a ~: 5 eagle
catalogue rating: 3 unc. 4 fine
collectible ~: 5 proof
collector: 4 slot
counterfeit ~: 4 slug
ender: 3 age
factory: 4 mint
finish: 3 mat 5 matte
flipper's phrase: 6 call it
former 10-cent ~: 5 disme
holder: 5 purse 6 pocket
inscription: 5 motto
Kennedy ~: 4 half
like a new ~: 5 shiny
old gold ~: 5 dobla, ducat
other side of the ~: 8 opposite
ridge: 4 nurl 5 knurl
side: 3 obv. 7 obverse, reverse
sound: 5 plunk
stamp: 3 die
toss a ~: 4 flip 6 choose
toss call: 5 heads, tails
U.S. ~ word: 3 God 4 unum 5 trust 7 liberty 8 pluribus
worthless ~: 3 sou
see also money
coin ___: 3 box 4 lock, toss 5 purse 6 silver 7 changer, machine
coin ___ realm: 5 of the
coin-___: 3 ops
___ coin: 5 error, flip a, minor, token
coinage: 5 money 6 change 7 neology 8 creation, original 9 invention, neologism 10 concoction, innovation
coincide: 4 gybe, jibe, meet, mesh 5 agree, match, tally 6 concur, square 8 dovetail 10 correspond
coincidence: 6 chance, hazard
coincident: 4 same 6 coeval 7 similar 8 together 9 ancillary, attendant, attending, consonant 10 collateral, concurrent, concurring, coordinate, synchronal
coincidental: 5 fluky 6 chance, flukey 7 similar
coinciding: 6 in sync 7 similar 9 congruent 10 concurrent, synchronal
coiner: 8 inventer, inventor 9 neologist
coin of the ___: 5 realm
coin-op: 7 machine
feature: 4 slot
insert: 4 cash 5 money 6 change
place: 6 arcade
word: 6 insert
___ Coins in the Fountain: 5 Three
Cointreau: 5 drink 6 liquor 8 beverage
coir: 4 rope 5 fiber
coke: 4 coal, fuel
Coke: 4 cola, soda 6 Edward 9 soft drink
see also Coca-Cola
___ Coke: 4 Diet
Cokie: 7 Roberts
col ___: 5 legno
col.: 3 off. 4 rank
subordinate: 3 maj., sgt.
superior: 2 BG 3 gen.
Col.
neighbor: 3 Kan., Neb., Pan., Ven., Wyo. 4 Ariz., Ecua., Nebr.
see also Colombia, Colorado
___ Col.: 5 Lieut.
cola: 3 nut 4 Coke, Jolt, soda 5 drink, Pepsi 7 soda pop 8 beverage, Diet-Rite 9 soft drink 10 Royal Crown
buy: 3 can 5 liter
___-Cola: 4 Coca 5 Pepsi
___ colada: 4 piña
colander: 4 sift 5 sieve 8 strainer
Colasanto: 8 Nicholas
Colbert, Claudette: 7 actress
film: Boom Town (1940)
Cleopatra (1934)
Drums Along the Mohawk (1939)
The Egg and I (1947)
The Gilded Lily (1935)
It Happened One Night (1934, AA)
It's a Wonderful World (1939)
Maid of Salem (1937)
The Man From Yesterday (1932)
Midnight (1939)
The Palm Beach Story (1942)
Remember the Day (1941)
The Secret Fury (1950)
Since You Went Away (1944)
Skylark (1941)
Sleep My Love (1948)
So Proudly We Hail! (1943)
Three Came Home (1950)
Three-Cornered Moon (1933)
Thunder on the Hill (1951)
Tomorrow Is Forever (1946)
Tovarich (1937)
Under Two Flags (1936)
Without Reservations (1946)
colby: 6 cheese
Colchester: 4 city, port, town
locale: 5 Essex 7 England
Colchis-bound ship: 4 Argo
cold: 3 icy, nip, out, raw 4 arid, cool, iced, mean 5 algid, aloof, chill, crisp, frost, gelid, nasty, nippy, onery, polar, rheum, sharp, snowy, stark, stiff, stony, surly 6 arctic, biting, bitter, chilly, clammy, drafty, frigid, frosty, frozen, glassy, hiemal, ornery, remote, stoney, stormy, winter, wintry 7 chilled, cutting, distant, glacial, hateful, hostile, iciness, joyless, numbing, rawness, shivery, wintery 8 contrary, freezing, gelidity, hardened, indurate, inimical, lifeless, loveless, lukewarm, piercing, pitiless, positive, reserved, ruthless, Siberian, sniffles, spiteful, stinging, taciturn, unbiased 9 bellicose, below zero, bloodless, frigidity, heartless, impassive, inclement, insensate, malicious, unfeeling, withdrawn 10 chilliness, frostiness, impersonal, inclemency, insociable, malevolent, mechanical, pugnacious, unagitated, unamicable, unfriendly, unsociable
be ~: 6 shiver
blow hot and ~: 4 sway, vary, yo-yo 5 hedge, shift, waver 6 dither, falter, seesaw, waffle, wobble 8 straddle 9 fluctuate, hem and haw, pussyfoot, vacillate
blowing hot and ~: 4 torn 6 fickle 7 erratic, flighty, mutable, not sure 8 hesitant, variable, volatile, waffling, wavering 9 equivocal, impulsive, mercurial, uncertain, undecided, unsettled 10 ambivalent, capricious, changeable, inconstant, indecisive, irresolute, of two minds, on the fence
catch ~: 3 ail
combining form: 4 crym-, cryo- 5 crymo-, frigo- 7 psychro-
common ~: 6 coryza
cubes: 3 ice
cut: 3 ham 4 meat 6 salami, tongue 7 bologna 8 pastrami 9 roast beef 10 corned beef
cuts store: 4 deli
drink: 3 pop 4 cola, soda 5 juice, shake
duck: 4 wine
feet: 4 fear 5 alarm, panic 8 timidity 9 cowardice
get down ~: 5 learn 6 master
go ~ turkey: 4 quit
have a ~ one: 5 drink
have ~ feet: 5 cower, quail, quake, waver 6 cringe, falter, flinch, recoil, shrink, wobble 7 tremble 8 hang back, hesitate 9 hem and haw, vacillate 10 chicken out
having ~ feet: 5 jumpy, timid 6 afraid, craven, scared, yellow 7 chicken, daunted, fearful, panicky, spooked, wimpish 8 cowardly, fearsome, recreant, sheepish, timorous 9 nerveless, spineless, terrified, tremulous 10 frightened
kin: 3 flu
leave out in the ~: 4 shun, snub 5 spurn 6 ignore, rebuff, reject, slight 7 high-hat, neglect 8 overlook 9 ostracize
like a ~ fish: 6 chilly 7 distant 8 detached 9 apathetic, impassive 10 unfriendly, unsociable
like some ~ medicines: 3 OTC
one: 4 beer, brew 7 brewski
out ~: 5 inert 7 unaware 8 lifeless
out in the ~: 5 alone 9 unwelcome
out of the ~: 6 inside
period: 6 ice age
place for a ~ one: 3 bar, pub 6 saloon
precipitation: 4 snow 5 sleet 8 blizzard
protection from ~: 4 wrap 5 parka, scarf 6 anorak, gloves 7 mittens 8 earmuffs
remedy: 5 Afrin 6 Contac, Nyquil, Tavist 7 Actifed, Comtrex, Dayquil, Dristan, Sinutab, Sudafed 8 Benadryl, Dimetapp, Drixoral, TheraFlu 9 Coricidin, Triaminic 10 Robitussin
remedy name: 5 Vicks
resistant perhaps: 5 hardy
season: 6 winter
shoulder: 4 snub 6 rebuff, slight 7 refusal, repulse 9 rejection
snap: 5 frost
sound: 3 brr 5 achoo 6 ahchoo, hachoo 7 kerchoo
spell: 4 ague, snap
spot: 6 Arctic, fridge 7 Siberia 9 Antarctic, North Pole, South Pole
suffer from ~: 6 freeze
throw ~ water on: 5 deter 6 dampen, sadden 8 dispirit
weather drink: 3 tea 5 cocoa, toddy 6 eggnog, hot tea
weather need: 6 deicer 8 rock salt
cold ___: 3 cut, one, war 4 call, cash, cuts, deck, duck, feet, fish, pack, pole, snap, spot, tone, type, wave 5 as ice, color, cream, drink, frame, front, light, patch, spell, steel, store, sweat, water 6 cellar, chisel, fusion, rubber, turkey 7 calling, cathode, comfort, storage, warrior
cold ___ icicle: 4 as an
cold-___: 4 cock, draw, eyed, roll, weld, work 7 blooded, hearted
cold-___ flat: 5 water
___ cold: 4 down, head 5 knock 6 common
___-cold: 3 ice
Cold ___: 3 War 4 Fire 5 As Ice, Sweat 6 Turkey 7 Hearted
cold as ___: 3 ice
cold-blooded: 4 hard, mean 5 cruel, feral, harsh, nasty 6 animal, brutal,

fierce, savage, steely, unkind, wanton 7 beastly, callous, hurtful, inhuman, vicious 8 barbaric, fiendish, hardened, inhumane, pitiless, ruthless, sadistic, vengeful 9 cutthroat, ferocious, merciless, monstrous, truculent, unfeeling 10 hard-bitten, vindictive
Cold, Cold Heart (1951 song) artist: Tony Bennett
Cold Comfort Farm (1995 film)
cast: Eileen Atkins, Kate Beckinsale, Sheila Burrell
director: John Schlesinger
cold duck: 4 pink, wine
origin: 7 Germany
Colden, Cadwallader: 11 philosopher
Cold Fire author: Dean Koontz
cold-hearted: 5 stony 6 frigid, stoney 8 loveless, pitiless
Cold Hearted (1989 song) artist: Abdul
coldness: 5 chill, frost 7 cruelty, reserve 8 distance 9 frigidity 10 detachment
cold-shoulder: 4 shun, snub 5 scorn, spurn 6 ignore 9 ostracize
__ cold, starve...: 5 Feed a
Cold Sweat (1967 song) artist: James Brown
Cold Turkey (1971 film)
cast: Vincent Gardenia, Bob Newhart, Tom Poston, Pippa Scott, Dick Van Dyke
director: Norman Lear
Cold War
broadcaster: 3 VOA
capital: 4 Bonn 6 Moscow
initials: 3 KGB 4 NATO, USSR
news agcy.: 4 Tass
plane: 3 MIG 4 U-two
pres.: 3 DDE, HST, JFK, LBJ
soldier: 3 spy
threat: 5 H bomb
weapon: 2 MX 4 ICBM, MIRV
cold-water __: 4 flat
Coldwell __: 6 Banker
cole: 6 veggie 9 vegetable
cole __: 4 slaw
Cole: 3 Nat 4 Cozy, Gary, Tina 5 Paula 6 Porter, Thomas 7 Michael, Natalie, Younger
__ Cole: 7 Nat King, Old King
Coleco: rival: 5 Atari
Cole, Cozy: 7 drummer
song: Topsy II (1958)
Coleen: 4 Gray
Coleman: 2 Cy 4 Gary 6 Dabney 7 Hawkins, lantern, Ornette
Coleman, Dabney: 5 actor
film: The Beverly Hillbillies (1993)
Cloak & Dagger (1984)
The Man With One Red Shoe (1985)
Nine to Five (1980)
On Golden Pond (1981)
Tootsie (1982)
WarGames (1983)
You've Got Mail (1998)
Coleman, Ornette: 11 saxophonist
genre: 4 jazz
Cole, Natalie
song: I've Got Love on My Mind (1977)
Miss You Like Crazy (1989)
Our Love (1978)
Pink Cadillac (1988)
This Will Be (1975)
Unforgettable (1991)
Cole, Nat King
instrument: piano
song: A Blossom Fell (1955)
Darling Je Vous Aime Beaucoup (1955)
If I May (1955)
Looking Back (1958)
Ramblin' Rose (1962)
Send for Me (1957)
Those Lazy-Hazy-Crazy Days of Summer (1963)
Unforgettable (1961)
coleopteran: 6 beetle, insect
Cole Porter Song Book singer: 4 Ella 10 Fitzgerald
Coleridge, Samuel Taylor: 4 poet 7 British
colleague: Southey
friend: 4 Elia, Lamb
work: Christabel
Dejection: An Ode
France: An Ode
Frost at Midnight
Kubla Khan
Love
Osario
The Rime of the Ancient Mariner
To Asra
coleslaw: 4 side 5 salad
make ~: 5 shred
Colesville: 4 city, town
locale: 8 Maryland
Colette: 4 Toni 6 French, writer
work: The Blue Lantern
Chéri
Duo
Gigi
Mitsou
Sido
colewort: 4 kail, kale
Colfax: 8 Schuyler
Colgate: 10 toothpaste
alternative: 3 Aim 5 Crest, Gleem, Ipana, Topol 7 Close-Up, Viadent 9 Aquafresh, Mentadent, Pepsodent, Rembrandt, Sensodyne 10 Pearl Drops, Ultra Brite 11 Tom's of Maine
athletes: 7 Raiders
locale: 7 New York 8 Hamilton
unit: 4 tube
colic: 5 ileus
colicroot: 5 plant 6 flower
Colima: 4 city, town 7 volcano
city: 7 Armería, Tecomán 8 El Colomo 10 Manzanillo
locale: 6 Mexico
colin: 4 bird
Colin: 5 Clive, Firth 6 Friels, Powell, Wilson 7 Blakely, Farrell, Mochrie 8 MacInnes, Margaret
coliseum: 4 bowl 5 arena 7 stadium, theater, theatre 10 hippodrome
Coliseum, The author: Edgar Allan Poe
coll.: 3 sch. 4 acad., univ.
class: 4 lect.
club: 3 sor.
course: 3 bio., Eng., sem., soc. 4 geol., hist., stat. 10 chem.. phys. ed.
deg.: 3 BCE, BCS
senior's exam: 4 LSAT
student: 2 jr., sr. 3 jnr., snr. 4 soph.
see also college
collaborate (with): 4 join, work 6 assist, hook up, team up 8 interact
collaboration: 4 team 8 alliance
collaborative: 5 joint
group: 4 team
collaboratively: 8 mutually 9 in concert
collaborator: 4 ally 7 partner 8 co-worker, henchman, teammate
collage: 3 art 4 olio 7 mixture 8 pastiche
need: 4 glue
Collages author: Anaïs Nin
collapse: 2 go 3 sag 4 drop, fail, fall, flop, fold, give, sink, tire, wilt 5 crash, decay, faint, plotz, shock, slump, smash, yield 6 buckle, cave in, defeat, fall in, fizzle, perish, topple, trauma 7 conk out, crumble, crumple, debacle, deflate, descend, failure, founder, give way, plummet, subside, succumb, undoing 8 downfall, fall down, fall flat, pull down 9 breakdown, cataclysm, fall apart, recession, ruination 10 bankruptcy
about to ~: 5 shaky
collapsed: 4 fell, went 6 broken, fallen
collapsing: 4 beat 5 all in, tired
collar: 3 bag, cop, get, nab, net 4 bust, find, grab, hook, nail, take, trap, yoke 5 catch, dicky, grasp, pinch, run in, seize 6 abduct, arrest, corner, detain, dickey, dickie, flange, pick up, pull in, secure, snatch 7 capture, jailing, seizure 8 cincture 9 apprehend
blue ~: 5 labor 6 worker
ender: 4 bone
extension: 5 lapel
fastener: 4 stud
hot under the ~: 3 mad 4 ired, sore 5 angry, cross, fiery, huffy, irate, livid, onery, riled, surly, testy, wroth 6 crusty, fuming, ireful, morose, ornery, peeved, raging, raving, touchy 7 bearish, enraged, furious, grouchy, peevish, peppery, ranting, uptight 8 choleric, critical, incensed, inflamed, liverish, maddened, outraged, snappish, wrathful 9 indignant, irascible, irritable, irritated, querulous, resentful, splenetic 10 freaked out, ill-humored, infuriated, out of sorts
insert: 4 stay
lace: 5 ruche
lace ~: 4 ruff 6 bertha
site: 4 nape, neck
straightener: 4 iron
victim: 3 bug 4 flea, pest 6 insect
white ~: 6 worker
collar __: 3 rot 4 cell 5 point 6 button
__ collar: 3 dog 4 cape, Eton, flea, wing 5 angle, choke, horse, Roman, shawl 6 Johnny, rolled 7 notched, Vandyke
__-collar: 4 blue, pink 5 brass, horse, white 7 rainbow
collarbone combining form: 6 cleido-
collard __: 6 greens
collards: 7 veggies 10 vegetables
collared: 5 ran in 6 in jail
garment: 4 coat 5 shirt 6 jacket
one, for short: 4 perp
collate: 4 sort 5 group 6 assort, gather, verify 7 compare, compile, examine 8 assemble
collateral: 4 bail, bond, lien, pawn, side 5 funds 6 litter, pledge, surety 7 deposit, related 8 indirect, security 9 accessory, ancillary, assurance, attendant, auxiliary, dependant, dependent, guarantee, resources, satellite, secondary, tributary 10 adjunctive, circuitous, coincident, concurrent, coordinate, roundabout, subsidiary, supporting, synchronal
holder: 6 lienor
collation: 4 meal, nosh 5 snack 6 dinner, repast, spread, tidbit 10 comparison, validation
serving: 3 tea
colleague: 3 bro, pal 4 ally, chum, mate 5 amigo, buddy, crony 6 cohort, friend 7 compeer, comrade, partner 8 confrere, co-worker, henchman, sidekick, teammate, workmate 9 accessory, assistant, associate, auxiliary, coadjutor, companion, confidant 10 accomplice, compatriot, well-wisher
collect: 3 tap 4 cull, earn, herd, levy, mass, pile, rake, reap, save, take 5 amass, claim, dig up, flock, glean, group, hoard, raise, rally 6 accrue, cash in, center, corral, garner, gather, muster, obtain, pick up, rake in, secure 7 acquire, cluster, compile, convene, convoke, deposit, harvest, marshal, receive, round up, scare up 8 assemble, hold on to, muster up, scrape up 9 aggregate, stockpile 10 accumulate, congregate, pass the hat
a bet: 3 win
ender: 3 ive
on a surface: 6 adsorb
oneself: 5 relax
collect __: 4 call
collectanea: 8 analecta, analects 9 anthology 10 miscellany
collected: 4 calm, cool 5 quiet, sober, staid, stoic 6 at ease, low-key, mellow, placid, poised, sedate, serene 7 amiable, at peace, equable, pacific, relaxed, stoical, unmoved 8 amicable, carefree, composed, laid-back, peaceful, rational, reserved, together, tranquil 9 aggregate, confident, different, easygoing, impassive, nerveless, possessed, quiescent, temperate, unexcited, unruffled 10 nonchalant, phlegmatic, unagitated, untroubled
sayings: 3 ana
works: 5 canon
collectedness: 5 poise 6 aplomb
collectible: 3 due 5 curio 8 valuable
collection: 3 lot, set 4 band, bevy, heap, herd, levy, mass, pile 5 album, array, batch, bunch, flock, group, hoard, sheaf, stack, stock, store, troop, trove 6 bundle, corpus, medley 7 cluster, company, species, variety 8 assembly, ensemble, pastiche, quantity, treasury 9 aggregate, amassment, anthology, concourse, congeries, gathering, potpourri, repertory, selection, stockpile 10 assemblage, assortment, cumulation, depository, embodiment, hodgepodge, miscellany, opera omnia
suffix: 3 -age, -ana, -ery 4 -iana
collection __: 3 box 5 plate 6 agency
Collection, The author: Harold Pinter
collective: 5 joint, whole 6 mutual, shared, social, united 7 commune, general, generic, grouped, kibbutz, unified 8 combined, communal, compiled, conjoint 9 aggregate, assembled, composite, concerted, corporate, generical, undivided 10 cumulative
Russian ~: 5 artel
collective __: 4 farm, mark, noun
collectively: 5 as one 6 bodily, wholly 7 en masse 8 together
collector: 6 editor 7 pack rat. 8 gatherer
__ collector: 4 toll 5 solar 7 cyclone
collector's item: 5 curio, vertu, virtu
Collector, The: 4 film 5 novel
author: John Fowles
cast: Samantha Eggar, Terence Stamp
director: William Wyler
__ Collector, The: 4 Bone
colleen: 4 lass, maid, miss 5 woman 6 damsel, lassie, maiden 8 fraülein
home: 4 Eire, Erin 7 Ireland
Colleen: 4 Camp 5 Moore 8 Dewhurst 10 McCullough
Colleen (1936 film)
cast: Ruby Keeler, Jack Oakie, Dick Powell
college: 3 sch. 6 school 7 academy 8 univ. acad. 9 alma mater
army prog.: 4 ROTC
bill line: 4 room 5 board, meals 6 lab fee 7 tuition
book: 4 text
building: 4 dorm, hall
choice: 5 major, minor
club: 3 sor. 4 frat 8 sorority 10 fraternity
conferral: 6 degree

course: 3 art, bio., Eng., Ger., mus. 4 chem.., econ., geol., math 5 drama, music, psych 6 anthro, French, German, phys. ed. 7 biology, English, geology, physics, Spanish 9 chemistry, economics, sociology 10 psychology
courtyard: 4 quad
cred. units: 3 hrs.
deg.: 2 AA, AB, AS, BA, BE, MA. 3 BBA, BFA, BSC, DFA, MFA, MPA, Ph.D.
dining room: 7 commons
diploma word: 3 cum 5 laude, magna, summa 6 honors
do: 5 mixer
entrance exam: 3 SAT 4 PSAT
exam for ~ srs.: 3 GRE 4 GMAT, LSAT
freshman, usually: 4 teen
grad: 4 alum 6 alumna 7 alumnus
grounds: 6 campus
head: 4 prex, prez 5 prexy
keepsake: 2 yb. 4 ring 8 yearbook
like most ~ s: 4 coed
military ~: 3 VMI 4 USMA, USNA 5 USAFA 7 Citadel 9 West Point
offering: 6 course
official: 4 dean 6 bursar 9 registrar
paper: 6 thesis
party: 5 mixer
party site: 4 frat
party staple: 3 keg
protest: 5 sit-in
sport: 4 golf 5 track 6 hockey, soccer 7 bowling 8 baseball, football, lacrosse, swimming 9 wrestling 10 basketball, volleyball
sports org.: 3 AAU 4 NCAA
stat: 3 GPA
student: 4 soph 5 frosh 6 junior, seniod 8 freshman 9 sophomore
teacher: 4 prof 6 docent, lector 8 lecturer 9 professor 10 instructor
unit: 6 credit
website suffix: 3 edu
woman: 4 coed
women's ~: 5 Smith 7 Barnard 8 Bryn Mawr 9 Wellesley
word in some ~ nicknames: 4 Tech
college __: 3 try 5 radio
__ college: 3 cow 6 barber, junior 7 cluster
College __: 5 Humor, Swing 6 Boards
College __, The: 5 Widow
__ College: 3 Joe
College director: 5 Horne
College Humor (1933 film)
cast: Bing Crosby, Jack Oakie
director: Wesley Ruggles
__ College, NC: 4 Elon
College Park: 4 city, town
athletes: 5 Terps 9 Terrapins
locale: 8 Maryland
College Station: 4 city, town
athletes: 6 Aggies
locale: 5 Texas
school: 4 TAMU
College Swing (1938 film)
cast: Gracie Allen, George Burns, Martha Raye
director: Raoul Walsh
__ college try, the: 3 old
College Widow, The author: Ade
collegian: 4 coed, soph 5 frosh 6 junior, senior 8 freshman 9 sophomore
collegiate: 8 academic
starter: 5 inter
Colleyville: 4 city, town
locale: 5 Texas
collide: 4 meet 5 clash, crash, smash 6 hurtle, pile up, strike 7 quarrel 8 conflict, disagree
with: 3 hit, ram 4 bump, butt, jolt 6 impact, strike
with, in Britain: 5 prang
collie: 3 dog 5 pooch 6 canine, herder 8 sheepdog, shepherd
charge: 5 flock, sheep
fictional ~: 3 Lad 6 Lassie
name for a ~: 4 Shep
__ collie: 6 Border, smooth 7 bearded
collier: 4 boat 5 miner
Collier: 9 Constance
Collier's rival: 4 Life, Look
Collierville: 4 city, town
locale: 9 Tennessee
colliery exit: 4 adit
collimate: 5 align, aline 8 parallel
Collins: 4 Gary, Joan, Judy, Phil 5 Billy, drink, Eddie, Tyler 6 Jackie, Wilkie 7 Michael, Pauline, Stephen, William 8 beverage, cocktail
ingredient: 3 gin 4 lime, soda 9 lime juice 10 lemon juice
__ Collins: 3 Tom
Collins, Billy: 4 poet
__ Collins, CO: 4 Fort
Collins, Gary spouse: Mary Ann Mobley
collins ingredient: 4 lime
Collins, Joan: 7 actress
film: The Bravados (1958)
The Opposite Sex (1956)
The Road to Hong Kong (1962)
Seven Thieves (1960)
Up in the Cellar (1970)
The Virgin Queen (1955)
spouse: Anthony Newley
TV: Dynasty
Collins, Phil
lead singer of: Genesis
song: Against All Odds (1984)
Another Day in Paradise (1989)
Don't Lose My Number (1985)
Do You Remember? (1990)
Easy Lover (1984)
Groovy Kind of Love (1988)
I Wish It Would Rain Down (1990)
One More Night (1985)
Separate Lives (1985)
Sussudio (1985)
Take Me Home (1986)
Two Hearts (1988)
Collinsville: 4 city, town
locale: 8 Illinois
Collins, Wilkie: 6 writer 7 British
work: The Moonstone
The Woman in White
Collins, William: 4 poet 7 British
collision: 3 hit, jar 4 blow, jolt, tilt 5 crash, shock, smash, wreck 6 impact, pileup 7 contact 8 accident, conflict 9 encounter, rear-ender, sideswipe 10 concussion, percussion
avoid ~: 6 swerve
minor ~: 4 bump
result: 4 dent
sound: 3 bam 4 wham
collision __: 6 course 7 density
__ collision: 6 head-on 7 elastic
collocate: 8 parallel 10 accumulate
Collodi, Carlo: 6 author, writer 7 Italian
work: Pinocchio
colloid: 3 gel 5 algin
collop: 4 meat
colloquial: 5 slang 6 chatty, common, vulgar 8 informal 9 dialectal, idiomatic 10 vernacular
colloquialism: 5 idiom, slang 8 localism
colloquy: 4 talk, word 5 forum 6 dialog, parley 8 dialogue 9 discourse 10 conference, discussion
Colloquy of Monos and Una, The author: Edgar Allan Poe
collude: 4 abet, plot 5 cabal 6 scheme 7 connive 8 conspire, intrigue 9 machinate
collusion: 4 plot 8 intrigue 9 shell game, whitewash 10 complicity, connivance, conspiracy, guiltiness
Collyer: 3 Bud 4 June
Colm: 6 Meaney
Colman, Ronald: 5 actor
film: Bulldog Drummond (1929)
Champagne for Caesar (1950)
A Double Life (1947, AA)
If I Were King (1938)
The Late George Apley (1947)
The Light That Failed (1939)
Lost Horizon (1937)
The Prisoner of Zenda (1937)
Raffles (1930)
Random Harvest (1942)
A Tale of Two Cities (1935)
The Talk of the Town (1942)
Under Two Flags (1936)
Colmar: 4 city, town
locale: 6 France
Colo.
clock setting: 3 MDT, MST
neighbor: 3 Kan., Neb., Wyo. 4 Kans., Nebr., N. Mex.
sch.: 5 USAFA
see also Colorado
colobus: 6 mammal, monkey 7 primate
relative: 3 ape 4 saki, titi 5 chimp, drill, jocko, lemur, loris, magot, orang, potto, shrew 6 aye-aye, baboon, Bandar, galago, gelada, gibbon, grivet, guenon, howler, langur, macaco, rhesus, uakari, vervet 7 gorilla, guereza, hoolock, macaque, sapajou, siamang, tamarin, tarsier 8 bush baby, capuchin, mandrill, mangabey, marmoset, talapoin 9 orangutan 10 Barbary ape, chimpanzee, orangutang
cologne: 5 scent 7 perfume 9 fragrance
characteristic: 4 odor
container: 4 vial 5 phial
ingredient: 4 musk
Cologne: 4 city, town
city near ~: 5 Essen
locale: 3 Ger. 7 Germany
river: 5 Rhine
__ Cologne: 5 eau de
__ Colognie: 4 Odie
colombard: 4 wine 5 white
Colombia: 6 nation 7 country
capital: 6 Bogotá
city: 4 Buga, Cali 5 Neiva, Pasto, Tuluá, Tunja 6 Bogotá, Cúcuta, Ibagué, Itaguí, Soacha 7 Armenia, Cartago, Palmira, Pereira, Popayán, Soledad 8 Envigado, Medellín, Montería 9 Cartagena, Sincelejo 10 Santa Marta, Valledupar
clothing: 5 ruana
Indian: 4 Tama 7 Chibcha
money: 4 peso
neighbor: 4 Peru 6 Brazil, Panama 7 Ecuador 9 Venezuela
Nobelist in Literature: 7 Márquez
org.: 3 OAS
peak: 4 Ruiz
poet: 5 Silva 6 Rivera
port: 9 Cartagena
river: 4 Meta
volcano: 4 Ruiz 5 Huila, Pasto 6 Puracé 7 Galeras
writer: 6 Rivera 7 Márquez
see also Spanish
Colombo: 4 city, port, town 7 capital
locale: 8 Sri Lanka
colon: 5 money
half a ~: 3 dot
in analogies: 4 is to
Colón: 4 city, port, town
colonel: 4 rank 5 Klink 6 Potter
command: 3 rgt. 8 regiment
insignia: 5 eagle
see also Army
__ colonel: 4 bird 5 light 7 chicken
Colonel __: 5 Blimp
Colonel __ Parker: 3 Tom
__ Colonel, The: 6 Little
colonial: 3 era 6 quaint
dance: 4 reel 6 minuet 8 saraband 9 sarabande
descendants' org.: 3 DAR, SAR
flute: 4 fife
loyalist: 4 Tory
newscaster: 5 crier
rest stop: 4 inne
starter: 3 neo
word in ~ place names: 3 New
colonist: 7 pioneer, settler 8 emigrant 9 immigrant 10 inhabitant
colonize: 6 settle
colonizer: 7 settler
small ~: 3 ant, bee 5 emmet
Colonna: 5 Jerry 8 Vittoria
colonnade: 4 stoa 6 arcade 7 pergola
Colonna, Vittoria: 4 poet 7 Italian
colonus: 4 serf
colony: 4 hive, nest 5 swarm 7 outpost 8 ant group, offshoot, province 9 community, territory 10 dependency, possession, settlement
group: 5 swarm
member: 3 ant
__ colony: 5 crown, penal, royal
__ Colony: 4 Cape, Lost
Colony Park: 3 car 4 auto 7 Mercury
colophon: 6 device, emblem, symbol
colophony: 5 rosin
color: 3 ash, bay, dun, dye, hue, jet, pea, tan 4 anil, aqua, blue, bole, bone, buff, cast, corn, cyan, dove, drab, ecru, fake, fawn, foxy, gold, inky, jade, lime, milk, navy, Nile, nude, onyx, plum, puce, race, rose, ruby, rust, sage, sand, seal, snow, teal, tint, tone, warp, wine 5 adorn, Alice, amber, azure, beige, beryl, blond, brass, breen, brick, camel, cocoa, coral, cream, dusty, ebony, flame, flaxy, fudge, glaze, gloss, grape, hazel, henna, imbue, ivory, khaki, lemon, lilac, maize, mauve, melon, merle, milky, mocha, ocher, ochre, olive, paint, peach, pearl, poppy, putty, raven, rusty, sable, sandy, sepia, shade, slant, slate, smoke, sooty, spice, stain, straw, taupe, tawny, tinct, tinge, twist, umber, virid 6 almond, argent, auburn, bister, bistre, blonde, bronze, canary, cerise, chammy, cherry, chroma, citron, claret, cobalt, coffee, copper, crocus, dahlia, damask, damson, doctor, enamel, flaxen, garble, garnet, ginger, indigo, infuse, maroon, myrtle, nature, orange, orchid, oyster, purple, raisin, redden, reseda, russet, salmon, shammy, shamoy, sienna, silver, sorrel, suntan, violet, walnut 7 apricot, avocado, biscuit, caramel, carmine, celadon, chamois, citrine, crimson, distort, dogwood, emerald, enliven, falsify, fuchsia, grizzly, heather, jasmine, magenta, magnify, mustard, nankeen, old gold, peacock, petunia, pigment, pimento, pumpkin, saffron, scarlet, sultana, verdant, vermeil, xanthic 8 amaranth, amethyst, burgundy, cardinal, cerulean, charcoal, chestnut, cinnamon, daffodil, disguise, dubonnet, eggplant, eggshell, emblazon, flamingo, flesh out, geranium, gunmetal, hyacinth, jaundice, lavender, mahogany, mulberry, platinum, primrose, rubicund, sapphire, tincture 9 alabaster, butternut, carnation, champagne, chocolate, cranberry,

embellish, embroider, goldenrod, jessamine, misrender, overstate, pistachio, raspberry, robin's-egg, tangerine, turquoise, vermilion **10** aquamarine, chartreuse, complexion, exaggerate, heliotrope, illuminate, periwinkle, strawberry, terra cotta
black ~: **3** jet **4** inky, onyx **5** ebony, raven, sable, sooty
blackish ~: **8** burgundy
blue ~: **4** anil, cyan, navy, Nile, teal **5** Alice, azure, slate **6** cobalt, indigo, raisin, violet **7** peacock **8** cerulean, sapphire **9** turquoise **10** aquamarine, periwinkle
bluish ~: **4** jade, plum **5** beryl, mauve, merle, pearl, slate **6** myrtle, orchid **8** lavender, platinum **9** cranberry, turquoise
brown ~: **3** bay, dun, tan **4** bole, ecru, fawn, foxy, nude, seal **5** amber, beige, camel, cocoa, hazel, khaki, mocha, sepia, tawny, umber **6** auburn, bister, bistre, bronze, coffee, copper, ginger, russet, sienna, sorrel, suntan, walnut **7** biscuit, caramel, dogwood **8** chestnut, cinnamon, mahogany **9** butternut, chocolate
brownish ~: **4** buff, drab, nude, puce, sand **5** beige, breen, olive, putty, taupe **7** nankeen **8** charcoal **10** terra cotta
combining form: **5** chrom- **6** -chrome, chromo- **7** chromat- **8** chromato-
ender: **4** bred, cast, fast **5** blind, breed
gray ~: **3** ash **4** dove, drab **5** beige, dusty, merle, pearl, putty, slate, taupe **6** silver **7** grizzly **8** charcoal, gunmetal, platinum
grayish ~: **3** dun **4** nude, sage **5** Alice, sepia, slate **6** chammy, indigo, oyster, reseda, shammy, shamoy **7** celadon, chamois **8** mulberry
green ~: **3** pea **4** cyan, jade, sage **5** beryl, breen, olive, virid **6** myrtle, reseda **7** avocado, celadon, emerald, verdant **9** pistachio, turquoise **10** aquamarine, chartreuse
greenish ~: **4** aqua, cyan, lime, Nile, teal **6** cobalt **7** peacock **8** cerulean **9** champagne, robin's-egg, turquoise **10** aquamarine
in heraldry: **8** tincture
orange ~: **5** flame, henna **7** pumpkin, saffron **8** hyacinth **9** tangerine **10** terra cotta
orangish ~: **5** ocher, ochre, poppy **6** crocus **7** saffron
pink ~: **4** nude **5** melon **6** damask, salmon **7** apricot **8** flamingo **9** carnation
pinkish ~: **4** dove **5** coral, peach **7** apricot, heather
purple ~: **4** plum, puce **5** lilac, mauve **6** dahlia, damson, orchid **7** heather, petunia **8** amethyst, burgundy, eggplant, lavender, mulberry **9** raspberry **10** heliotrope
purplish ~: **4** dove **5** azure, grape **6** claret, raisin **7** carmine, crimson, fuchsia, magenta, sultana **8** amaranth, dubonnet
red ~: **4** rose, ruby, rust, wine **5** brick, coral, grape, poppy, rusty, sandy **6** cerise, cherry, claret, garnet, maroon **7** carmine, crimson, fuchsia, magenta, pimento, scarlet, sultana, vermeil **8** amaranth, cardinal, dubonnet, geranium, rubicund **9** carnation, cranberry, vermilion **10** strawberry
reddish ~: **3** bay **4** bole, foxy, plum, rust, sand **5** brass, cocoa, coral, flame, henna, lilac, ocher, ochre, rusty, umber **6** auburn, copper, ginger, orchid, russet, sorrel, walnut **7** petunia **8** chestnut, cinnamon, hyacinth, mahogany, rubicund **9** raspberry, tangerine **10** heliotrope
starter: **3** tri **5** water
tan ~: **4** buff **5** camel **6** almond **7** caramel
white ~: **4** bone, milk, snow **5** cream, ivory, milky **6** argent, oyster, silver **8** eggshell
whitish ~: **6** silver
yellow ~: **4** buff, corn, gold, lime, rust, sand **5** blond, brass, coral, cream, flaxy, lemon, maize, ocher, ochre, peach, rusty, straw **6** blonde, canary, chammy, citron, crocus, flaxen, shammy, shamoy **7** apricot, chamois, citrine, jasmine, mustard, nankeen, old gold, saffron, xanthic **8** daffodil, primrose **9** champagne, goldenrod, jessamine
yellowish ~: **3** tan **4** bone, drab, fawn, foxy, jade, nude, rust **5** amber, camel, cocoa, coral, cream, ivory, khaki, olive, putty, rusty, sandy, tawny **6** auburn, bister, bistre, ginger, russet, salmon, sienna, suntan **7** apricot, caramel, dogwood **8** cinnamon **9** alabaster **10** chartreuse
color __: **4** code **5** force, guard, index, phase, point, wheel **6** circle, filter, scheme **7** printer
color-__: **3** key **4** code **5** blind, coded, field
__ color: **3** ash, oil **4** cold, corn, dove, tone **5** Congo, earth, false, flame, flesh, king's, local, straw **6** binary, ground, muffle, poster, temper **7** albumen, albumin, primary
__-color: **3** two **4** four
Color __, The: **6** Purple
Colorado: **5** river, state **6** desert
city: **4** Vail **5** Aspen, Ouray **6** Arvada, Aurora, Denver, Golden, Parker, Pueblo **7** Boulder, Durango, Greeley **8** Brighton, Ken Caryl, Lakewood, Longmont, Loveland, Security, Thornton **9** Canon City, Columbine, Englewood, Estes Park, Lafayette, Littleton, Telluride, Widefield **10** Broomfield, Castle Rock, Castlewood, Northglenn, Southglenn, Wheat Ridge
city on the ~: **4** Yuma **6** Austin
college: **5** Regis
conference: **9** Big Twelve
county: **4** Yuma **5** Otero
Indian: **3** Ute **4** Yuma
mountain: **4** Yale **5** Bross, Eolus, Estes, Evans **6** Antero, Elbert, Oxford, Wilson **7** Belford, Cameron, Harvard, Laramie, Lincoln, San Juan, Sawatch, Shavano, Sherman **8** Columbia, Democrat, Sneffels **9** Bierstadt, Pikes Peak, Princeton
national park: **9** Mesa Verde
neighbor: **4** Utah **6** Kansas **7** Arizona, Wyoming **8** Nebraska, Oklahoma **9** New Mexico
resort: **4** Vail **5** Aspen
river: **5** Yampa
River locale: **4** Utah **7** Arizona
river to the ~: **4** Gila **10** Pedernales
state flower: **9** columbine
state gemstone: **10** aquamarine
state grass: **9** blue grama
state tree: **10** blue spruce
team: **7** Rockies **9** Avalanche
tributary: **4** Gila **7** Dolores
Colorado __: **6** Desert, spruce **7** Plateau
Colorado Springs: **4** city, town
athletes: **7** Falcons
county: **6** El Paso
school: **5** USAFA
student: **5** cadet **6** airman
Colorado State athletes: **4** Rams
Colorado Territory (1949 film)
cast: Virginia Mayo, Joel McCrea
director: Raoul Walsh
colorant: **3** dye **4** woad **5** paint, tinge **6** litmus **7** pigment
coloration: **4** tint **5** tinge **10** complexion
combining form: **6** -chroia
coloratura: **4** diva **5** lyric, voice **6** singer **7** soprano **8** vocalist
specialty: **4** aria **5** trill
colored: **5** tinct **7** partial **8** partisan
brightly ~: **4** neon **5** vivid
combining form: **6** -chroic **7** -chroous
prefix for ~: **5** multi
__-colored: **4** high, rust, wine **5** parti, party **6** coffee
__-colored glasses: **4** rose
colorfast, wasn't: **3** ran **4** bled
colorful: **4** hued **5** gaudy, juicy, vivid **6** bright, flashy, florid **7** dashing, graphic, vibrant **8** romantic **9** chromatic, graphical **10** expressive
coloring: **3** dye **4** tint, tone **5** paint, stain, tinct, tinge **8** infusion **10** complexion
agent: **4** dyer
combining form: **6** -chromy
device: **6** crayon
organic ~: **3** azo **6** azo dye
coloring __: **4** book
colorist: **4** dyer
colorless: **3** wan **4** arid, ashy, drab, dull, flat, pale, tame **5** ashen, faded, livid, mousy, vapid, waxen, white **6** common, doughy, dreary, mousey **7** grayish, hueless, insipid, prosaic **8** achromic, blanched, bleached, lifeless, mediocre, unlively **9** bloodless, prosaical, washed-out **10** achromatic, dullsville, impersonal, lackluster, monotonous
Color of Darkness author: James Purdy
Color of Money, The (1986 film)
cast: Tom Cruise, Mary Elizabeth Mastrantonio, Paul Newman
director: Martin Scorsese
prop: **3** cue **4** rack **5** chalk
colorpoint: **3** cat **5** felid **6** feline
Color Purple, The: **4** film **5** novel
author: Alice Walker
cast: Margaret Avery, Danny Glover, Whoopi Goldberg, Oprah Winfrey
director: Steven Spielberg
role: **5** Celie, Sofia
colors: **4** flag **6** ensign **7** pennant
flying ~: **7** success, triumph, victory
profusion of ~: **4** riot
with flying ~: **4** fine, well **5** great **6** easily **7** handily **8** adroitly, expertly, smoothly, very well **9** hands down **10** skillfully, swimmingly
__ colors: **5** false **6** flying, livery
Colors (1988 film)
cast: Maria Conchita Alonso, Robert Duvall, Sean Penn
director: Dennis Hopper
__ Colors: **4** True **7** Primary
Colors of the Wind (1995 song) artist: Vanessa Williams
colossal: **3** big **4** huge, vast **5** bulky, giant, great, hefty, jumbo, large **6** mighty **7** hulking, immense, mammoth, massive, sizable, titanic **8** enormous, gigantic, king-size, oversize, sizeable, towering, whapping, whopping **9** cyclopean, herculean, humongous, monstrous, overlarge **10** formidable, gargantuan, monumental, prodigious, stupendous, tremendous
Colosseum: **5** arena
denizen: **4** lion **9** gladiator
honoree: **6** Caesar
locale: **4** Rome
colossus: **5** giant, titan, whale **7** mammoth, monster **8** behemoth **9** leviathan
Colossus... (1970 film)
cast: Eric Braeden, Susan Clark
Colossus of __: **6** Memnon, Rhodes
Colossus of Maroussi, The author: Henry Miller
__ Colossus, The: **3** New
Colossus, The author: Sylvia Plath
Colotlán: **4** city, town
locale: **6** Mexico **7** Jalisco
Colour of Love, The (1988 song) artist: Billy Ocean
Colson: **5** Chuck **7** Charles
colt: **4** foal, male **5** horse **6** animal, equine **8** newcomer
mother: **3** dam **4** mare
sibling: **5** filly
Colt: **3** car, gun, Sam **4** auto **5** Dodge **6** pistol, Samuel **10** Mitsubishi
rival: **3** Jet, Ram **4** Bear, Bill, Lion **5** Brown, Chief, Eagle, Giant, Niner, Raven, Saint, Texan, Titan **6** Bengal, Bronco, Cowboy, Falcon, Jaguar, Packer, Raider, Viking **7** Charger, Dolphin, Panther, Patriot, Redskin, Seahawk, Steeler **8** Cardinal **9** Buccaneer
colter: **5** blade
Colter, Jessi song: I'm Not Lisa (1975)
coltish: **4** wild **6** frisky, lively, unruly **7** playful, romping, untamed **8** playsome, spirited, sportive **9** gamboling **10** frolicsome
Colton: **4** city, town
locale: **10** California
Coltrane: **3** Chi **4** John
Coltrane, John: **11** saxophonist
genre: **4** jazz
Coltrane, Roscoe deputy: **4** Enos
Colts: **4** team **6** eleven
org.: **3** AFC, NFL
sport: **8** football
coltsfoot: **5** galax, plant
Colum: **7** Padraic
Columba __: **4** Noae
Columba, Saint
site of ~ monastery: **4** Iona
Columbia: **3** riv. **4** cape, city, peak, town **5** mount, river **6** studio **8** mountain
athletes: **5** Lions **6** Tigers **9** Gamecocks
competitor: **3** Fox, MGM **6** Disney **7** Miramax, New Line **9** Paramount, Universal **10** Dreamworks, Warner Bros.
creation: **4** film **5** movie
league: **3** Ivy
locale: **6** Canada **7** Alberta, New York, Rockies **8** Colorado, Maryland, Missouri **9** Tennessee
offering: **5** movie
org.: **4** NASA
river: **8** Congaree
River explorer: **4** Gray
River locale: **6** Oregon **10** Washington
river to the ~: **5** Snake **8** Kootenay **9** Deschutes **10** Willamette
school: **3** USC
__ Columbia: **7** British
__, Columbia: **4** Hail
__-Columbian: **3** pre
Columbia Pictures: **6** studio
owner: **4** Cohn, Sony
Columbia, the __ of the Ocean: **3** Gem

Columbine: 4 city, town
locale: 8 Colorado
columbite: 3 ore 7 mineral
Columbo: 3 cop, tec 4 Russ 10 lieutenant
caper: 4 case
Columbo (TV drama)
cast: Peter Falk (Lt. Columbo)
employer: LAPD
Columbus: 4 city, town 5 Chris
athletes: 8 Buckeyes
county: 8 Franklin
locale: 4 Ohio 7 Georgia, Indiana 8 Nebraska
newspaper: 8 Dispatch
river: 6 Scioto
school: 3 OSU 9 Ohio State
Columbus ___: 3 Day
___, Columbus: 7 Goodbye
Columbus author: Joaquin Miller
Columbus, Chris: 8 director
film: Bicentennial Man (1999)
Harry Potter and the Chamber of Secrets (2002)
Harry Potter and the Sorcerer's Stone (2001)
Home Alone (1990)
Home Alone 2... (1992)
Mrs. Doubtfire (1993)
Nine Months (1995)
Only the Lonely (1991)
Columbus, Christopher: 8 explorer
contemporary: 5 Cabot
discovery: 7 Bahamas
home: 5 Genoa, Italy
ship: 4 Niña 5 Pinta 10 Santa Maria
sponsor: 5 Spain 8 Isabella 9 Ferdinand
Columbus Day
event: 4 sale
month: 3 Oct. 7 October
column: 3 leg, row 4 beam, line, pier, post, rank, stay 5 piece, pylon, queue, shaft, stela, stele, totem, tower, train 6 parade, pillar, review, series 7 article, feature, obelisk, support, upright, writing 8 buttress, monolith, monument, pedestal, pilaster 9 editorial 10 procession
addition ~: 4 ones, tens 5 units 8 hundreds 9 thousands
bases: 4 tori
calendar ~: 3 Fri., Mon., Sat., Sun., Thu., Tue., Wed. 4 Thur., Tues. 5 Thurs. 6 Friday, Monday, Sunday 7 Tuesday 8 Saturday, Thursday 9 Wednesday
combining form: 4 styl- 5 -style, stylo-
credit: 6 byline
ender: 3 ist
feature: 7 entasis
formatted in a single ~: 5 one up
gossip ~ subject: 5 actor, celeb 7 actress 9 celebrity, headliner
inscribed ~: 5 stela
part: 4 dado, orlo
ridge: 5 arris
row of ~ s: 6 arcade 7 pergola 9 colonnade
shaft: 5 scape
steel structural ~: 5 lally
support: 5 socle
type: 5 Doric, Ionic 6 Gothic 10 Corinthian
wall ~: 4 anta
column ___: 4 inch 6 krater, vector
___ column: 3 box 5 agony, fifth, Lally, sixth 6 flying, spinal 7 midwall, rostral
Column B, one from: 6 lo mein 7 chow fun 8 chow mein 9 fried rice, spare ribs 10 Peking duck
columnea: 5 shrub
columnist: 5 press 6 author, scribe, writer 7 analyst 8 reporter 9 wordsmith 10 ink slinger, journalist
fifth ~: 5 snake 7 traitor 8 quisling, turncoat
___ columnist: 5 fifth
Colum, Padraic: 4 poet 5 Irish 10 playwright
Colvin: 5 Shawn
___ com: 3 dot
coma: 6 torpor, trance 7 slumber 8 lethargy
Coma: 4 film 5 novel
author: Robin Cook
cast: Elizabeth Ashley, Genevieve Bujold, Michael Douglas
director: Michael Crichton
Comalcalco: 4 city, town
locale: 6 Mexico 7 Tabasco
.com alternative: 3 edu, net
Coman: 4 peak 5 mount 8 mountain
locale: 10 Antarctica
Comanche: 5 horse, tribe 6 equine, Indian 7 Amerind 8 language
language family: 5 Numic
Comancheros, The (1961 film): 5 oater
cast: Ina Balin, Jack Elam, Lee Marvin, John Wayne, Stuart Whitman
director: Michael Curtiz
Comaneci, Nadia: 7 gymnast 8 Romanian
comate: 5 hairy 6 tufted 7 partner 9 companion
comb: 4 rake, seek, sift, sort 5 groom, probe, scour, sweep, tease 6 dredge, forage, search 7 examine, inspect, ransack, rummage 8 untangle 10 scrutinize
combining form: 4 cten-, loph- 5 cteno-, lophi-, lopho- 6 lophio-
contents: 5 honey
impediment: 4 snag
manufacturer: 3 bee 4 hive
out: 7 unravel
part: 4 cell 5 tooth
partner: 5 brush
starter: 3 cox 5 curry, honey
with a fine tooth ~: 10 thoroughly
___ comb: 3 hot 4 blow, fine, rose 7 rattail
combat: 3 war 4 buck, defy, duel, fray, tilt 5 clash, fight, jihad, joust 6 action, affray, attack, battle, oppose, resist, strife 7 contest, service, warfare 8 battling, conflict, fighting, skirmish, struggle 9 encounter, withstand 10 contention, engagement, opposition, resistance
prepare for ~: 3 arm 8 embattle
unit: 4 army 5 corps 8 division, regiment 9 battalion
vehicle: 4 tank
zone: 5 arena, front
combat ___: 4 boot, team, zone 6 jacket
combat-___: 5 ready
Combat (ABC drama)
cast: Rick Jason (Lt. Gil Hanley) Vic Morrow (Sgt. Chip Saunders)
combatant: 3 foe 4 side, vier 5 enemy 6 dueler 7 battler, fighter, soldier, warrior 8 attacker 9 gladiator, ill-wisher, legionary 10 contestant
combative: 5 saucy 7 hawkish, martial, warlike 8 fighting, militant, military, ructious 9 bellicose, energetic, litigious, strenuous, truculent 10 aggressive, fire-eating, jingoistic, pugnacious, unfriendly
one: 6 bantam
combe: 4 glen
comber: 4 wave
starter: 5 beach
combination: 3 mix 4 bloc, gild, stew 5 alloy, blend, group, guild, union 6 cartel, fusion, hybrid, league, medley, merger 7 amalgam, faction, mixture 8 alliance, blending, compound 9 aggregate, potpourri, synthesis 10 miscellany
combination ___: 4 door, last, lock, shot 6 square 7 platter
combine: 3 mix, wed 4 band, bloc, bond, fuse, join, link, mesh, pool, ring, yoke 5 admix, alloy, blend, group, immix, marry, merge, party, trust, unify, unite 6 attach, cartel, cement, cohere, commix, couple, embody, hook up, imbody, league, make up, mingle, team up 7 bunch up, conjoin, connect, hitch on, mixture 8 coalesce, interact 9 affiliate, aggregate, coalition, commingle, integrate, interface, interlace, syndicate 10 amalgamate, interweave, synthesize
numbers: 3 sum, tot 5 add up, count, sum up, tally, total, tot up 6 figure 7 compute, count up 9 calculate
with: 5 add to
combined: 4 mixt 5 in all, joint, mixed 6 allied, joined, united 7 grouped 8 in league, in unison, together 9 undivided 10 collective
___ combined: 6 Alpine, Nordic
combining ___: 4 form 6 weight
combining forms
abdomen: 4 celi- 5 celio-, coeli-, ventr- 6 coelio-, ventri-, ventro-
abduct: 3 -nap
abnormal: 4 anom- 5 anomo-
acid: 3 oxy-
action: 3 cin-, kin- 4 cino-, kine-, kino-
activated by: 5 -ergic
active: 7 -kinetic
activity: 7 -kinesis
acute: 3 oxy-
addict: 5 -holic 6 -aholic
advocate: 4 -crat 5 -arian, -ocrat
air: 3 atm- 4 atmo- 6 pneumo- 7 pneumat- 8 pneumato-
algae: 4 phyc- 5 phyco-
alien: 3 xen- 4 xeno-
alive: 4 vivi-
all: 3 omn-, pan- 4 omni-, pano-, pant- 5 panta-, panto-
almond: 7 amygdal- 8 amygdalo-
almost: 3 pen- 4 pene-
aloft: 4 hyps- 5 hypsi-, hypso-
alone: 3 mon- 4 mono-, soli-
alternative: 6 allelo-
altitude: 4 hyps- 5 hypsi-, hypso-
amber: 6 succin- 7 succino-
ancient: 4 pale- 5 palae-, paleo- 6 archeo-, palaeo-, palaio- 7 archaeo-
ancillary: 3 par- 4 para-
angle: 4 goni- 5 gonio-
angular: 3 -gon
animal: 2 zo- 3 zoo- 4 -zoon
animals: 3 -zoa
ankle: 4 tali-
anklebone: 5 tarso-
ant: 6 myrmec- 7 myrmeco-
antibiotic: 5 -mycin
antimony: 4 stib- 5 stibi-, stibo- 6 stibio-
apart: 4 dich- 5 dicho-
ape: 6 pithec- 7 pitheco-
appearance: 5 -phany
appearing: 4 phen- 5 pheno-
appetite: 6 -orexia
apple: 4 pomi-
arched: 3 tox- 4 toxi-, toxo-
arid: 3 xer- 4 xero-
arm: 6 brachi- 7 brachio-
armless: 5 anopi- 6 anoplo-
around: 6 circum-
arrangement: 3 tax- 4 -nomy, taxi-, taxo-, -taxy 5 -taxis
arrow: 3 tox- 4 toxi-, toxo-
arsenic: 6 arseno-
art: 4 -urgy 6 techno-
artery: 6 arteri- 7 arterio-
assembly: 4 -fest
atmosphere: 3 aer- 4 aeri-, aero-
auger: 6 trypan- 7 trypano-
axis: 3 axi-, axo-
back: 3 not- 4 dors-, noto- 5 dorsi-, dorso- 7 opistho-
bad: 3 cac-, dys-, mal- 4 caco-
balance: 5 stato-
ball: 5 spher- 6 sphaer-, sphero- 7 sphaero-
band: 3 zon- 4 zono-
barb: 3 onc- 4 onch-, onci-, onco- 5 oncho-
bare: 4 gymn-, nudi-, psil- 5 gymno-, psilo-
bark: 6 phello-
bath: 5 balne- 6 balneo-
beak: 5 rostr- 6 rhamph-, rostri-, rostro- 7 rhampho-
beam: 5 actin- 6 actino-
bear: 4 arct- 5 arcto-
beard: 5 pogon- 6 pogono-
bearer: 4 -pher, -phor 5 -phore
bearing: 6 -gerous, -parous, -phoria 7 -phorous
beast: 4 ther- 5 -there, thero- 6 therio-
beautiful: 4 call-, calo- 5 calli-, callo-
bed: 4 clin- 5 clino-
before: 4 fore- 6 proter- 7 protero-
behind: 7 opistho-
being: 3 ont- 4 onto-
believer: 5 -arian
below: 6 infero-
belt: 3 zon- 4 zono-
bending: 7 sphingo-
bent: 4 cyrt- 5 curvi-, cyrto- 6 campto-
benzene: 4 benz- 5 benzo-
berry: 4 cocc- 5 bacci-, cocci-, cocco-
beside: 3 par- 4 para-
best: 6 aristo-
beyond: 3 par- 4 para- 6 preter- 7 praeter-
bile: 4 chol- 5 chole-, cholo-
billion: 4 giga-
billionth: 3 nan- 4 nano- 5 nanno-
bird: 3 avi- 5 -ornis 6 ornith- 7 ornitho-
bitter: 4 picr- 5 picro-
black: 3 mel- 4 atro-, mela-, melo- 5 melan- 6 melano-
blood: 3 hem- 4 -emia, hema-, hemo- 5 -aemia, hemat-, -hemia 6 -haemia, hemato-, sangui- 8 sanguine-
blotch: 5 macul- 6 maculi-, maculo-
blue: 4 cyan- 5 cyano-
blunt: 5 ambly- 6 amblyo-
boat: 5 scaph- 6 scapho-
body: 4 -soma, -some 5 somat- 6 somato-
bog: 4 helo-
boiled: 5 cocto-
bond: 4 desm- 5 desmo-
bone: 3 -ost 4 ossi-, oste- 5 osteo-
book: 6 biblio-
borer: 6 trypan- 7 trypano-
boron: 3 bor- 4 boro-
both: 3 bis- 5 amphi-, ampho-
bowed: 3 tox- 4 toxi-, toxo-
brain: 6 cerebr- 7 cerebro- 8 encephal- 9 encephalo-
branch: 4 clad- 5 clado-
brass: 5 chalc-, chalk- 6 chalco-, chalko-
bread: 4 arto-
break down: 4 -lyze
breaker: 5 -clast
breaking: 6 -clasis 7 -clastic
breaking down: 5 -lysis, -lytic
breastbone: 5 stern- 6 sterno-
breath: 4 -pnea 5 -pnoea 6 pneumo- 7 pneumat- 8 pneumato-
breathing: 4 spir- 5 spiri-, spiro-
bringer: 4 -agog 6 -agogue

bristle: 4 seti- 5 chaet- 6 chaeto-
broad: 4 eury-, plat- 5 platy-
broken: 6 fracto-
bromine: 4 brom- 5 bromo-
bronze: 5 chalc-, chalk- 6 chalco-, chalko-
brother: 7 adelpho-
brush: 5 scopi-
bud: 5 -blast 6 blasto-
buds: 7 -blastic
bull: 4 taur- 5 tauri-, tauro-
burdened: 6 -ridden
burning: 4 igni-
bush: 5 thamn- 6 thamno-
can: 5 scyph- 6 scyphi-, scypho-
cap: 8 calyptri-, calyptro-
car: 4 auto-
carbon: 7 anthrac- 8 anthraco-
carrier: 3 -fer 4 -pher, -phor 5 -phore
cartilage: 6 chondr- 7 chondro- 8 chondrio-
carved: 5 glypt- 6 glypto-
cat: 5 aelur-, ailur- 6 aeluro-, ailuro-
caterpillar: 5 -campa, eruci-
cause: 4 etio- 5 aetio-, ailio-
causing: 3 -fic 5 -genic 7 -facient
cave-dwelling: 6 troglo-
cavity: 4 -cele, coel- 5 -coele
cell: 3 cyt- 4 -cyte, cyto- 5 -plast
cells: 7 -blastic
center: 3 mid- 4 medi- 5 medio-
centered: 7 -centric
chamber: 4 -cele, coel- 5 -coele
change: 4 trop- 5 tropo-
channel: 5 solen- 6 soleno-
cheek: 3 mel- 4 melo- 5 bucco-
cheese: 3 tyr- 4 tyro-
chest: 6 stetho-, thorac- 7 thoraci-, thoraco-
child: 3 ped- 4 paed-, paid-, pedo- 5 paedo-, paido-, tecno-
childbirth: 4 toco-, toko-
children: 5 proli-
chin: 5 genio-, mento-
Chinese: 4 Sino- 6 Sinico-
church: 7 ecclesi- 8 ecclesio-
circle: 3 gyr- 4 gyro-
city: 5 metro-, -polis
claw: 4 chel- 5 cheli-, onych-, ungui- 6 onycho-
clay: 3 pel- 4 pelo- 5 argil- 7 argilli-, argillo-
cleavage: 5 -clase
cleft: 5 fissi-
climate: 6 meteor-
clockwise: 5 dextr- 6 dextro-
close: 4 pycn-, sten- 5 plesi-, pycno-, steno- 6 plesio-
closed: 7 cleisto-
closure: 6 -clisis 7 -cleisis
clot: 6 thromb- 7 thrombo-
cloud: 4 neph- 5 nepho- 6 nephel- 7 nephelo-
club: 5 clavi- 6 rhopal- 7 rhopalo-
coal: 7 anthrac-, carboni- 8 anthraco-
coil: 4 spir- 5 spiri-, spiro-
cold: 4 crym-, cryo- 5 crymo-, frigo- 7 psychro-
collarbone: 6 cleido-
color: 5 chrom- 6 -chrome, chromo- 7 chromat- 8 chromato-
coloration: 6 -chroia
colored: 6 -chroic 7 -chroous
coloring: 6 -chromy
column: 4 styl- 5 -style, stylo-
comb: 4 cten-, loph- 5 cteno-, lophi-, lopho- 6 lophio-
common: 3 cen- 4 caen-, ceno-, coen- 5 caeno-, coeno-
communication: 3 -log 5 -logue
complete: 3 tel- 4 tele-, telo-
completely: 3 pan- 4 pano-, pant- 5 panta-, panto-
completion: 6 teleut- 7 teleuto-
computer: 5 cyber-
concealed: 4 adel- 5 adelo-
conically: 9 turbinato-
constellation: 5 sider- 6 sidero-
containing: 6 -ferous
conversation: 3 -log 5 -logue
copper: 4 cupr- 5 chalc-, chalk-, cupri-, cupro 6 chalco-, chalko-
cork: 6 phello-
cornea: 5 cerat-, kerat- 6 cerato-, kerato-
correct: 4 orth- 5 ortho-
counterclockwise: 3 lev- 4 levo- 5 laevo-
countless: 4 myri- 5 myrio-
course: 4 drom- 5 -drome, dromo-
cover: 4 steg- 5 stego-
covering: 4 cole- 5 coleo- 7 cortico-
creeping: 6 herpet- 7 herpeto-
crest: 4 loph- 5 lophi-, lopho- 6 lophio-
crop: 4 agro-
cross: 6 stauro-
crow: 5 -corax
crown: 7 stephan- 8 stephano-
culture: 5 ethno-
cup: 5 cotyl-, cyath-, scyph- 6 cotyli-, cotylo-, cyatho-, scyphi-, scypho-
current: 4 rheo- 7 galvano-
curved: 4 cyrt- 5 cyrto- 6 campto- 7 -tropous
custom: 4 nomo-
cut: 4 -sect, tomo- 6 -tomous
cutter: 4 -tome
cutting: 4 -tomy
dance: 5 chore- 6 choreo-, chorio-
darkness: 5 scoto-
decline: 4 clin- 5 clino-
decompose: 4 -lyze
decomposing: 5 -lytic
decomposition: 3 lys- 4 lysi-, lyso- 5 -lysis
deer: 5 cervi-
defective: 4 atel- 5 atelo-
deficiency: 5 -penia
deficient: 6 -privic
deflection: 7 sphingo-
dense: 4 dasy-, pycn- 5 pycno-
depth: 5 batho-, bathy-
deputy: 4 vice-
deserving of: 6 -worthy
desire: 6 -orexia
destroyer: 5 -clast
destroying: 7 -clastic
devil: 6 diabol- 7 diabolo-
dice: 8 astragal- 9 astragalo-
different: 5 heter- 6 hetero-
dimmed: 5 ambly- 6 amblyo-
discoloration: 6 -chroia
disease: 3 nos- 4 noso- 5 patho-, -pathy
display: 5 -orama
distant: 3 tel- 4 tele-, telo-
distinct: 5 chori-
distribution: 4 -nomy
diver: 4 -dyta 5 -dytes
diverse: 4 vari- 5 vario-
divide: 4 -sect
divided: 3 -fid 5 fissi- 6 -tomous
divination: 5 -mancy
divining: 6 -mantic
doctrine: 4 -logy
dog: 3 cyn- 4 cyno-
double: 4 dipl- 5 diplo-
doubled: 3 bis-
down: 4 ptil- 5 ptilo-
drawing: 4 -gram 6 -graphy
drawn: 5 -graph
dream: 4 onir- 5 oneir-, oniro- 6 oneiro-
drug: 8 pharmaco-
dry: 3 xer- 4 xero-
dull: 5 brady-
dulled: 5 ambly- 6 amblyo-
dust: 4 coni- 5 conio-
ear: 2 ot- 3 aur-, oto- 4 auri-
earlier: 4 fore- 6 proter- 7 protero-
earliest: 4 prot- 5 proto-
early: 2 eo-
earth: 3 geo-
earthquake: 5 -seism 6 seismo-
eater: 4 -phag, -vore 5 -phage
eaters: 4 -vora
eating: 4 phag- 5 phago-, -phagy 6 -phagia, -vorous 7 -phagous
eddy: 4 dino-
effect: 4 -ergy
egg: 2 oo-, ov- 3 ovi-, ovo-
eight: 3 oct- 4 octa-, octo-
elderly: 6 presby- 7 presbyo-
eleven: 5 undec- 6 hendec- 7 hendeca-
embryo: 5 -blast 6 blasto-
emotion: 4 thym- 5 thymo-
empty: 3 ken- 4 keno-
end: 3 tel- 4 tele-, telo-
English: 5 Anglo-
engraving: 5 glypt- 6 glypto-
enthusiasm: 5 -mania
enthusiast: 4 -phil 5 -phile
entire: 3 hol- 4 holo-, toti- 7 integri-
environment: 3 eco-
equal: 3 iso- 4 pari-
even number: 5 artio-
evil: 4 male-
examination: 4 -opsy
excessive: 4 macr- 5 macro-
excision: 4 -tomy 6 -ectomy
exemplary: 4 arch-
existence: 3 ont- 4 onto-
experience: 7 empirio- 8 empirico-
experiment: 7 empirio- 8 empirico-
expert: 7 -meister
exposed: 4 gymn- 5 gymno-
external: 2 ex- 3 ect-, exo- 4 ecto-
extreme: 4 arch-
eye: 4 ocul-, opto- 5 oculo- 8 ophthalm- 9 ophthalmo-
eyelid: 7 blephar- 8 blepharo-
face: 6 -hedron, prosop- 7 prosopo-
faced: 6 -hedral
false: 5 pseud 6 pseudo-
fan: 5 rhipi- 6 rhipid- 7 rhipido- 8 flabelli-
far: 3 tel- 4 tele-, telo-
farming: 4 agri-
fast: 5 tachy-
fat: 3 lip- 4 adip-, lipo-, sebi-, sebo- 5 adipo-, lipar-, stear-, steat- 6 liparo-, stearo-, steato-
father: 4 patr- 5 patri-, patro-
fear: 4 phob- 5 phobo- 6 -phobia
fearer: 5 -phobe
fearing: 6 -phobic
feather: 3 pen- 4 pinn-, pter-, ptil- 5 penni-, penno-, pinni-, ptero-, ptilo- 7 pinnati-
feeding: 6 -trophy
feeling: 5 patho-, -pathy 8 esthesio- 9 aesthesio-
felt: 3 pil- 4 pilo-
female: 3 gyn- 4 gyne-, gyno-, -gyny 5 gynec-, thely- 6 gyneco-, -gynous
ferment: 3 zym- 4 zymo-
fern: 6 pterid- 7 pterido-
fever: 5 febri-, pyret- 6 pyreto-
few: 4 olig- 5 oligo-, pauci-
fibula: 6 perono-
field: 4 agro-
fifteen: 8 pentadec- 9 pentadeca-
fifth: 5 quint- 6 quinti-
fighting: 5 -machy
figure: 3 eid- 4 eido-
fillet: 4 taen- 5 taeni- 6 taenio-
film: 4 cine-
fin: 6 pteryg- 7 pterygo-
fine: 4 lept- 5 lepto-
finger: 6 dactyl-, digiti- 7 dactylo-
fingered: 9 -dactylous
Finnish: 5 Fenno-
fire: 3 pyr- 4 igni-, pyro-
first: 4 arch-, prot- 5 arche-, archi-, proto-
fish: 5 pisci- 6 ichthy- 7 ichthyo-
fit for: 6 -worthy
five: 4 pent- 5 penta- 6 quinqu- 7 quinque-
flake: 5 lepid-, -lepis 6 lepido-
flank: 5 lapar- 6 laparo-
flat: 4 plan-, plat- 5 plani-, plano-, platy-
flesh: 3 cre- 4 creo-, kreo-, sarc- 5 creat-, sarco- 6 creato-
flour: 6 aleuro-
flow: 4 -rhea, rheo- 5 -rrhea
flower: 4 anth-, flor- 5 antho-, flori-
flowered: 7 -anthous, -florous
flute: 3 aul- 4 aulo-
fly: 3 myi- 4 myio- 5 musci-
fold: 5 ptych- 6 ptycho-
food: 4 sito-
foot: 3 ped-, pod- 4 -pede, pedi-, pedo-, podo-
footed: 6 -podous
footlike part: 4 -pode 6 -podium
footstep: 4 ichn- 5 ichno-
fore: 6 antero-
foremost: 4 prot- 5 proto-
forest: 3 hyl- 4 hylo-
form: 5 -morph 6 morpho-
formation: 6 -plasty 7 -poiesis
former: 6 proter- 7 protero-
fossil: 4 -lite, -lyte 5 oryct- 6 orycto-
four: 4 tetr- 5 quadr-, tetra- 6 quadri-, quadru-, tessar- 7 quateer-, tessara-, tessera-
fourth: 5 quart- 6 tetart- 7 tetarto-
freedom: 8 eleuther- 9 eleuthero-
freeze: 4 cryo-
French: 5 Gallo- 6 Franco-
friction: 5 tribo-
frightful: 4 dino-
fringe: 6 thysan- 7 thysano-
frog: 4 rani- 7 batrach- 8 batracho-
front: 4 fore- 6 antero-
frost: 4 crym- 5 crymo-
fruit: 4 -carp 5 carpo-, fruct- 6 fructi-
fruited: 7 -carpous
full of: 3 -ous
fungus: 3 myc- 4 myco- 6 -mycete
funnel: 5 choan- 6 choano-
gall: 4 chol- 5 chole-, cholo-
garden: 4 -etum
gas: 4 mano-
gathering: 4 -fest
general: 3 cen- 4 caen-, ceno-, coen- 5 caeno-, coeno-
genetically engineered: 7 Franken-
germ: 6 bacter- 7 bacteri- 8 bacterio
gills: 7 branchi- 8 branchio-
gland: 4 aden- 5 adeno-
glass: 4 hyal-, vitr- 5 hyalo-, vitri-, vitro-
glue: 4 coll- 5 collo-
gnat: 5 culic- 6 culici-
goat: 5 capri-
god: 3 the- 4 theo-
gold: 3 aur- 4 auri- 5 chrys- 6 chryso-
good: 2 eu- 4 bene- 5 agath- 6 agatho-
government: 5 -archy, -cracy
graceful: 5 habro-
grain: 4 cocc-, sito- 5 cocci-, cocco-, grani- 6 chondr- 7 chondro- 8 chondrio-
grand: 3 meg- 4 mega- 5 megal- 6 megalo-
grapevine: 5 ampel- 6 ampelo-
gray: 4 poli- 5 glauc-, polio- 6 glauco-
grease: 4 sebi-, sebo-
great: 3 meg- 4 macr-, magn-, mega- 5 macro-, magni-, megal- 6 megalo-
Greek: 5 Greco- 6 Graeco- 7 Helleno-

green: 4 verd- 5 chlor-, verdo- 6 chloro-
ground: 5 chame- 6 chamae-
growth: 3 aux- 4 auxo- 5 -plasy 6 auxamo-, -plasia, -trophy
guard against: 3 par- 4 para-
guest: 3 xen- 4 xeno-
gums: 3 ulo- 6 gingiv- 7 gingivo-
hair: 3 pil- 4 pili-, pilo- 5 chaet-, crini-, trich- 6 chaeto-, -tricha, tricho-
hairy: 4 dasy-
half: 4 demi-, hemi-, semi-
halo: 7 stephan- 8 stephano-
hand: 5 chiro- 6 cheiro
hard: 5 scler- 6 sclera-, sclero-
hare: 3 lag- 4 lago-
hate: 3 mis- 4 miso-
head: 6 cephal- 7 cephalo-, -cephaly 8 -cephalic 9 -cephalous
healing: 5 iatro-, -iatry 7 -iatrics
heap: 5 cumul- 6 cumuli-, cumulo-
hearing: 4 acou- 5 acouo-, audio-
heart: 5 cardi- 6 -cardia, cardio- 7 -cardium
heat: 3 pyr- 4 pyro- 5 therm- 6 calori-, thermo-, -thermy
heavens: 4 uran- 5 urano-
heavy: 4 bary- 5 gravi-
height: 3 acr- 4 acro-, hyps- 5 hypsi-, hypso-
hidden: 4 adel- 5 adelo-, crypt-, krypt- 6 crypto-, krypto-
high: 3 alt- 4 alti-
hip: 4 coxa- 5 ischi-, ischo-
hole: 5 -trema
holy: 4 hagi-, hier- 5 hagio-, hiero-
hood: 8 calyptri-, calyptro-
hook: 3 onc- 4 onch-, onci-, onco- 5 oncho- 6 ancylo-, ankylo- 7 anchylo-
hormone: 5 kinin-
horn: 4 -corn 5 cerat-, kerat- 6 cerato-, kerato-
horse: 4 hipp- 5 hippo- 6 -hippus
human: 5 homin- 6 homini- 7 anthrop- 8 anthropo-
hundred: 4 cent-, hect-, hekt- 5 centi-, hecto-, hekto-
hundredth: 4 cent- 5 centi-
hybrid: 4 noth- 5 notho-
ill: 3 dys-, mal-
image: 3 eid-, typ- 4 eido-, icon-, ikon-, typo- 5 eicon-, icono-, idolo-, ikono- 6 eicono-, eidolo-
imperfect imitation: 5 -aster
implement: 4 -labe
incision: 4 -tomy
increase: 3 aux- 4 auxo- 6 auxamo-
indefinite: 4 myri- 5 myrio-
India: 4 Indo-
indigo: 3 ind- 4 indo-
in front: 5 proso-
inhabiting: 6 -colous
inhalation: 4 anem- 5 anemo-
inner: 3 eso-
insect: 6 entomo-
instrument: 4 -labe
internal: 3 end-, ent- 4 endo-, ento-
intestine: 5 enter- 6 entero-
invisible: 5 aphan- 6 aphano-
iodine: 3 iod- 4 iodo-
iris: 4 irid- 5 irido-
Irish: 7 Hiberno-
iron: 5 ferri-, ferro-, sider- 6 sidero-
irregular: 4 anom- 5 anomo-
island: 4 neso-
itch: 4 psor- 5 psoro-
jaw: 4 geny- 5 genyo-, gnath- 6 gnatho-
jawed: 8 -gnathous
joining: 3 gam- 4 gamo-
joint: 5 arthr- 6 ancylo-, ankylo-, arthro- 7 anchylo-
juice: 3 opo- 4 chyl- 5 chili-, chylo-
kernel: 5 caryo-, karyo-
key: 5 clavi-, clavo-
kidney: 4 reni-, reno- 5 nephr- 6 nephro- 7 -nephron, -nephros
kind: 4 phyl- 5 phylo-
knee: 4 genu-
knob: 3 tyl- 4 tylo-
knowing: 7 -gnostic 9 -gnostical
knowledge: 5 -gnomy, -sophy 6 -gnosis
lack: 5 -penia
lacking: 3 lyo- 4 lipo-
lake: 4 limn- 5 limni-, limno-
lance: 5 lonch- 6 loncho-
language: 4 -glot 5 glott- 6 glotto-
large: 3 meg- 4 macr-, magn-, maxi-, mega- 5 macro-, magni-, megal- 6 megalo-
lateral: 5 pleur- 6 pleuro-
law: 4 nomo-
layer: 5 ptych- 6 ptycho-, strati-
lead: 5 plumb- 6 plumbo-
leader: 4 -agog 6 -agogue
leaf: 5 phyll- 6 phyllo
leaved: 7 -folious
leaven: 3 zym- 4 zymo-
leaving: 4 lipo-
left: 3 lev- 4 levo- 5 laevo- 8 sinistro-
leg: 4 scel- 5 scelo-
lens: 4 phac-, phak- 5 phaco-, phako
lentil: 4 phac-, phak- 5 phaco-, phako
life: 3 bio-
lifeless: 4 abio-
ligament: 4 desm- 5 desmo- 7 syndesm- 8 syndesmo-
light: 4 luci-, phos-, phot- 5 lumin-, photo- 6 lumini-, lumino-
likeness: 4 icon-, ikon- 5 eicon-, icono-, ikono-, -opsis 6 eicono-
liking: 7 -philous
limb: 3 mel-
lined: 8 -stichous
lines: 5 -stich
lip: 5 cheil-, chilo-, labio- 6 cheilo-
listening: 4 acou- 5 acouo-
liver: 5 hepat- 6 hepato-
living: 4 vivi-
lizard: 4 saur- 5 -saura, sauro-
lobed: 3 -fid
local: 3 top- 4 topo-
loin: 4 lumb- 5 lumbo-
lonely: 4 erem- 5 eremo-
long: 3 mec- 4 macr-, meco- 5 macro- 7 dolicho-
long-running: 5 -athon
looking: 6 -scopic
looseness: 3 lyo-
lover: 4 -phil 5 -phile
loving: 4 phil- 5 philo- 6 -philic
low: 5 chame- 6 chamae-
lung: 5 pneum-, pulmo- 6 pneumo-, pulmon- 7 pneumon-, pulmoni-, pulmono- 8 pneumono-
maker: 3 -fex
making: 7 -facient, -poiesis
male: 4 andr- 5 andro-, -andry 7 -androus
man: 5 homin- 6 homini-
management: 4 -nomy
many: 4 mult-, poly- 5 multi-, pluri-
marriage: 4 -gamy 6 -gamous
marrow: 4 myel- 5 myelo-
Mars: 4 areo-
marsh: 4 helo- 6 paludi-
mass: 5 cumul- 6 cumuli-, cumulo-
matter: 3 hyl- 4 hylo-
measure: 5 -meter, metro-
measured: 6 -metric
measurement: 5 -metry
measuring science: 7 metrics
medicine: 5 iatro-, -iatry 7 -iatrics
member: 3 -mer
membrane: 5 chori- 6 chorio-, hymeno-
memory: 4 mnem- 5 mnemo-
mere: 4 psil- 5 psilo-
message: 4 -gram
middle: 3 mes- 4 meso- 5 centr- 6 centri-, centro-
mighty: 3 din- 4 dein-, dino- 5 deino-
milk: 4 lact- 5 lacti-, lacto- 6 galact- 7 galacto-
million: 3 meg- 4 mega-
mind: 3 noo- 5 menti-, phren-, psych- 6 phreni-, phreno-, psycho-
mineral: 4 -lite, -lyte 5 oryct- 6 orycto-
miracle: 8 thaumato-
misplaced: 7 chorist- 8 choristo-
mite: 4 acar- 5 acari-, acaro-
model: 3 typ- 4 typo-
mode of life: 6 -biosis
modified: 2 ne- 3 neo-
moist: 5 hygro-
molding: 6 -plasty
mole: 5 talpi-
monkey: 6 pithec- 7 pitheco-
monster: 5 terat- 6 terato-
month: 3 men- 4 meno-
moon: 4 luni- 5 selen- 6 seleni-, seleno-
more: 4 pleo-, plio 5 pleio-
mosquito: 5 culic- 6 culici-
moss: 3 bry- 4 bryo-, musc- 5 musci-, -musco
mother: 4 matr- 5 matri-, matro-
motion: 3 cin-, kin- 4 cino-, kine-, kino- 6 kinesi- 7 -cinesia, -kinesia, kinesio-
mountain: 3 ore-, oro- 4 oreo-
mouse: 3 -mys
mouth: 3 ori-, oro- 5 bucco-, -stoma, -stome 6 stomat- 7 stomato-
mouthed: 7 -stomous
movement: 6 kinesi- 7 -cinesia, -kinesia, kinesio-, -kinesis
movie: 4 cine-
moving: 4 plan- 5 -grade, plano- 6 kineto- 7 -kinetic
much: 4 poly-
mud: 3 pel- 4 pelo-
muscle: 2 my- 3 myo-
mushroom: 3 myc- 4 myco- 6 -mycete
nail: 4 helo- 5 onych-, ungui- 6 onycho-
naked: 4 gymn-, nudi- 5 gymno-
name: 4 -onym 7 onomato-
narrow: 4 sten- 5 steno- 7 augusti-, dolicho-
natural: 7 physico-
nature: 3 eco- 5 physi- 6 physio-
navel: 6 omphal- 7 omphalo-
near: 5 juxta-, plesi- 6 plesio-
neck: 3 der- 4 dero- 7 trachei 8 tra-cheio-
needle: 3 acu-
nerve: 4 neur- 5 neuro-
net: 5 dicty- 6 dictyo-
new: 2 ne- 3 neo-, nov- 4 ceno-, novo-
night: 4 noct-, nyct- 5 nocti-, nycti-, nycto-
nine: 3 non- 4 nona- 5 ennea-
nitrogen: 3 azo-
none: 5 nulli-
north: 4 arct- 5 arcto-
nose: 3 nas- 4 nasi-, naso-, rhin- 5 rhino-
notion: 4 ideo-
nourishment: 5 troph- 6 tropho-
nucleus: 5 caryo-, karyo-
number: 7 arithmo-
numerous: 4 myri- 5 myrio-
nut: 4 nuci- 5 caryo-, karyo-
nutrient: 5 troph- 6 tropho-
oar: 4 remi-
oblique: 3 lox- 4 loxo- 5 plagi- 6 plagio-
obsessed: 6 -ridden
occlusion: 6 -clisis 7 -cleisis
odor: 3 osm- 4 osmo-
offspring: 4 toco-, toko- 5 proli-
oil: 3 ole- 4 eleo-, olei-, oleo- 5 elaeo-, elaio-
old: 4 pale- 5 palae-, paleo- 6 archeo-, palaeo-, palaio- 7 archaeo-
old age: 6 geront- 7 geronto-
one: 3 mon-, uni- 4 heno-, mono-
one and a half: 6 sesqui-
one's own: 7 proprio-
onward: 5 proso-
opaque: 5 glauc- 6 glauco-
open: 6 phaner- 7 phanero-
opening: 5 -trema
opposite: 7 enantio-
order: 3 tax- 4 taxi-, taxo-, -taxy 5 -taxis
organism: 4 -zoon
organisms: 3 -zoa
origin: 4 -geny
original: 4 arch- 5 arche-, archi-
origination: 4 -gony
other: 3 all- 4 allo- 5 heter- 6 hetero-
outer: 2 ex- 3 ect-, exo- 4 ecto-
oyster: 5 ostre- 6 ostrei-, ostreo-
pad: 3 tyl- 4 tylo-
pain: 3 alg- 4 algo-, -algy, noci- 5 -algia 6 -odynia
painting: 6 -chromy
paired: 4 dipl- 5 diplo-
palate: 8 staphylo-
pale: 7 palladi-
pansy: 4 viol-
part: 4 -mere, -plex
partial: 3 mer- 4 mero-
parts: 6 -merous
past: 6 preter- 7 praeter-
peculiar: 4 idio-
pelvis: 4 pyel- 5 pyelo-
people: 3 dem- 4 demo- 5 ethno-
persisting: 4 meno-
person: 6 prosop- 7 prosopo-
personal: 4 idio-
perspiration: 4 hidr- 5 hidro-
pig: 3 hyo- 7 -choerus
pigment: 5 chrom- 6 -chrome, chromo-
pillar: 4 clon-, styl- 5 clono-, stylo-
pin: 6 perono-
pinnacle: 5 apico-
pipe: 3 aul- 4 aulo- 5 solen- 6 soleno-
pit: 5 bothr- 6 bothro-
place: 3 top- 4 loco-, topo- 5 -orium
plain: 4 pedi- 5 pedio-
plant: 4 phyt- 5 -phyte, phyto-
plate: 4 plac- 5 elasm-, placo- 6 elasmo-
pleasant: 4 hedy-
poisonous: 5 toxic- 6 toxico-
pond: 4 limn- 5 limni-, limno-
position: 5 stasi-
possessing: 3 -ous
power: 4 dyna- 5 dynam- 6 dynamo-
practicing: 6 -pathic
practitioner: 4 -path
prawn: 5 -caris
pressure: 3 bar- 4 baro-, tono- 5 piezo-
prickly: 5 echin- 6 echino-
priestly: 4 hier- 5 hiero-
primeval: 2 eo-
principal: 4 arch-
prior: 4 arch- 5 arche-, archi- 6 yester-
procession: 4 -cade
producer: 3 -gen 5 -arian
producing: 3 -fic 5 -genic 6 -ferous, -gerous, -parous
production: 4 -gony
prophesy: 5 -mancy
puberty: 4 hebe-
pulse: 7 sphygmo-
puncture: 5 -nyxis
purple: 7 purpuri-
quadrillion: 4 peta-

quadrillionth: 5 femto-
quintillion: 3 exa-
quintillionth: 4 atto-
race: 4 phyl- 5 ethno-, phylo-
racecourse: 5 -drome
rain: 4 hyet- 5 hyeto-, ombro-, pluvi- 6 pluvia-, pluvio-
raven: 5 -corax
ray: 5 actin- 6 actino-
reaction: 4 trop- 5 tropo-
rear: 7 opistho-
recent: 2 ne- 3 neo- 4 ceno-
receptacle: 7 -clinium
reciprocal: 6 allelo-
recording: 4 disc- 5 disci-, disco-
red: 5 pyrrh-, pyrro- 6 erythr-, pyrhho- 7 erythro-
reed: 5 calam- 6 calami-, calamo-
reesting: 5 stato-
regulator: 4 -stat
remaining: 4 meno-
removal: 6 -ectomy
repeller: 4 -fuge
reptile: 6 herpet- 7 herpeto-
resembling: 5 quasi-
resistant: 5 -proof
respiration: 4 -pnea 5 -pnoea
rib: 4 cost- 5 costo-, pleur- 6 pleuro-
ribbon: 4 taen-, -tene 5 taeni- 6 taenio-
rice: 4 oryz- 5 oryzi-, oryzo-
right: 4 orth-, rect- 5 dextr-, ortho-, recti- 6 dextro-
ring: 3 gyr- 4 cycl-, gyro- 5 cyclo-
river: 5 fluvi-, potam- 6 fluvio-, potamo-
road: 3 -ode
rock: 4 petr-, saxi- 5 petri-, petro-
rod: 6 -bacter, rhabdo-
root: 4 rhiz- 5 -rhiza, rhizo- 6 -rrhiza
rose: 4 rhod- 5 rhodo-
rotten: 4 sapr- 5 sapro-
rough: 6 trachy-
rowed: 8 -stichous
rows: 5 -stich
rule: 5 -archy, -cracy
ruler: 4 -crat 5 -ocrat
running: 4 drom- 5 -drome, dromo- 7 -dromous
sac: 3 asc- 4 asco-
sacred: 4 hier- 5 hiero-
sail: 5 histi- 6 histio-
saint: 4 hagi- 5 hagio-
saliva: 4 sial- 5 ptyal-, sialo- 6 ptyalo-
salt: 3 hal- 4 hali-, halo-, sali-
same: 3 aut-, hom- 4 auto-, equi-, homo-, taut- 5 tauto-
sand: 3 amm- 4 ammo- 5 psamm- 6 psammo-
sap: 3 opo-
sausage: 6 allant- 7 allanto-
saw: 3 pri- 5 prion-, serri- 6 priono-
scale: 5 lepid-, -lepis, squam- 6 lepido-, pholid-, squamo- 7 pholido-
scandal: 4 -gate
scenery: 5 -scape
science: 4 -logy 5 -sophy
scientific: 5 -logic
scrutiny: 5 -scopy
sea: 3 mer- 4 hali-, mari- 5 pelag- 6 pelago- 7 thalass- 8 thalasso-
seaweed: 4 phyc- 5 phyco-
second: 4 deut- 5 deuto- 6 deuter- 7 deutero-
secret: 5 crypt-, krypt- 6 crypto-, krypto-
section: 4 tomo-
seed: 4 cocc- 5 cocci-, cocco-
seeking: 5 -petal
segment: 4 -mere
self: 3 aut- 4 auto-
self-service: 5 -teria
sensation: 8 esthesio- 9 aesthesio-
sensitive to: 5 -ergic
separate: 4 idio-
separated: 4 dich- 5 chori-, dialy-, dicho- 7 chorist- 8 choristo-
septillion: 5 yotta-
septillionth: 5 yocto-
serpent: 4 ophi- 5 ophio-
seven: 4 hept-, sept- 5 hepta-, septi-
sextillion: 5 zetta-
sextillionth: 5 zepto-
shadow: 3 sci- 4 scia-, scio-, skia-
shaft: 5 scapi-
shaggy: 4 dasy-
shaped: 4 -form 7 -morphic 8 -morphous
sharp: 3 oxy-
sheath: 4 cole- 5 coleo-, -theca
shell: 5 conch- 6 concho-, ostrac- 7 ostraco-
shield: 4 scut- 5 aspid-, scuti- 6 aspido-
shining: 4 phen- 5 pheno-
short: 5 brevi- 6 brachy-
shoulder: 2 om- 3 omo-
shrimp: 5 -caris
Sicily: 6 Siculo-
side: 5 later-, pleur- 6 lateri-, latero-, pleuro-
sight: 4 -opia, opto- 5 -opsia
sign: 7 symbolo-
silk: 5 seric-
silver: 5 argyr- 6 argent-, argyro- 7 argenti-, argento-
similar: 5 homeo- 6 homeoe-, homoio-
simple: 4 hapl- 5 haplo-
single: 3 mon- 4 hapl-, mono- 5 haplo-
six: 3 hex-, sex- 4 hexa-, sexi- 5 sexti-
skill: 6 techno-
skin: 4 derm-, scyt- 5 -derma, dermo-, scyto- 6 dermat-, -dermis 7 dermato-
skinned: 9 -dermatous
skull: 5 crani- 6 cranio-
sleep: 4 hypn- 5 hypno-, somni-
slight: 4 lept- 5 lepto-
slime: 3 myx- 4 myxo-
slope: 4 clin- 5 -cline, clino- 6 -clinal
slow: 5 brady-
small: 4 micr-, mini-, parv- 5 micro-, parvi-, parvo-
smell: 3 osm-, ozo- 4 osmo-
smooth: 3 lio- 4 leio-
snake: 4 ophi- 5 ophio-
snout: 6 rhynch- 7 rhyncho-
snow: 4 chio- 5 chion- 6 chiono-
sodium: 4 natr- 5 natro-
soft: 5 malac- 6 malaco-
soil: 3 ped-, -sol 4 agro-, pedo-
sole: 4 pedi- 5 pedio-
solid: 5 stere- 6 stereo-
solitary: 4 erem-, soli- 5 eremo-
song: 4 melo-
soul: 4 thym- 5 psych-, thymo- 6 psycho-
sound: 3 son- 4 phon-, soni-, sono- 5 audio-, -phone, phono-, -phony
south: 5 austr- 6 austro-
space: 6 spatio-
spaceflight: 4 astr- 5 astro-
Spain: 7 Hispano-
spear: 4 dory-
spectacle: 4 -cade 5 -orama
speech: 3 log- 4 lalo-, -laly, logo- 5 gloss-, -lalia 6 glosso-, glotto-
speed: 4 drom- 5 dromo-, tacho-
spider: 6 arachn- 7 arachno-
spinal cord: 4 myel- 5 myelo-
spindle: 4 fusi-
spine: 5 rachi- 6 acanth-, rachio-, rhachi- 7 acantho-, rhachio-, vertebr-
spiral: 3 gyr- 4 gyro- 5 helic- 6 helico-
spirit: 4 thym- 5 psych-, thymo- 6 pneumo-, psycho- 7 pneumat- 8 pneumato-
spleen: 5 splen- 6 spleno-
split: 5 schiz- 6 schizo- 7 schisto-
spores: 4 coni- 5 conio-
spot: 5 macul- 6 maculi-, maculo-
spring: 4 cren- 5 creno-
sprout: 4 clad- 5 -blast, clado- 6 blasto-
spurious: 4 noth- 5 notho-
stabilizer: 4 -stat
stalk: 4 caul- 5 cauli-, caulo-
star: 4 astr- 5 -aster, astro-, sider- 6 -astero, sidero-
starch: 4 amyl- 5 amylo-
state: 6 -phoria
stealing: 5 klept- 6 klepto-
steam: 5 atmid- 6 atmido-
stem: 4 caul-, corm- 5 cauli-, caulo-, cormo-, scapi-
sticky: 5 gloeo-, gloio-
stomach: 4 celi- 5 celio-, coeli-, gastr-, ventr- 6 coelio-, gaster-, gastro-, ventri-, ventro- 7 gastero-
stone: 4 -lith, petr- 5 litho-, petri-, petro-
stoppage: 5 stasi-
straight: 4 orth-, rect- 5 ortho-, recti-
strange: 3 xen- 4 xeno-
stream: 4 rheo- 5 fluvi- 6 fluvio-
stretched: 4 tany-
stretching: 4 tono-
strong: 6 trachy-
structure: 5 -morph 6 morpho-
sufferer: 4 -path
suffering: 5 patho-, -pathy 6 -pathic
sugar: 4 gluc-, glyc-, sucr- 5 gluco-, glyco-, sucro- 7 sacchar- 8 sacchari-, saccharo-
sulfur: 3 thi- 4 thia-, thio- 5 thion- 6 thiono-
summit: 5 apico-
sun: 4 heli-, soli- 5 helio-
supporter: 4 -crat 5 -ocrat
surrounding: 6 circum-
suture: 6 -rhaphy 7 -rrhaphy
sweat: 4 hidr- 5 hidro-
swift: 5 tachy-
swimming: 4 nect- 5 necto-
swine: 3 hyo-
swollen: 4 phys- 5 physo-
swordlike: 4 xiph- 5 xiphi-, xipho-
tablet: 4 plac- 5 pinac-, pinak-, placo- 6 pinaco-
tail: 2 ur- 3 uro- 4 caud-, cerc- 5 caudi-, caudo-, cerco-
tallow: 5 steat- 6 steato-
tassel: 6 thysan- 7 thysano-
tawny: 5 fusco-, pyrrh-, pyrro- 6 pyrhho-
tear: 5 dacry- 6 dacryo-
tears: 7 lacrimo-
technique: 4 -urgy
temple: 7 temporo-
ten: 3 dec-, dek- 4 deca-, deka- 5 decem-
tendency: 6 -phoria
tendon: 4 teno-
tension: 4 tono-
tenth: 4 deci-
ten thousand: 5 myria-
terrible: 3 din- 4 dein-, dino- 5 deino-
terrifying: 4 dino-
Teutonic: 7 Germano-
theft: 5 klept- 6 klepto-
theory: 4 -logy
thick: 4 pycn- 5 pachy-, pycno-
thigh: 3 mer- 4 mero-
thin: 4 lept- 5 lepto-
third: 4 trit- 5 trito-
thought: 4 -noia
thousand: 4 kilo- 5 chilo-, milli-
thousandth: 5 milli-
thread: 3 mit-, nem- 4 fili-, mito-, nema-, nemo- 5 nemat- 6 nemato-
three: 3 tri-
thrice: 3 ter-
throat: 3 der- 4 dero- 6 bronch- 7 broncho-, pharyng- 8 pharyngo-
throughout: 4 -wide
time: 5 chron- 6 chrono-
tin: 5 stann- 6 stanno- 7 stannic-
tissue: 4 hist- 5 histi-, histo-, -plasm 6 histio-
toad: 7 batrach- 8 batracho-
toe: 6 dactyl- 7 dactylo-
toed: 9 -dactylous
tongue: 4 -glot 5 gloss- 6 glosso-, glotto-
tonsil: 7 amygdal- 8 amygdalo-
tooth: 4 dent- 5 denti-, dento-, odont- 6 odonto-
track: 4 ichn- 5 ichno-
transparent: 7 diaphan- 8 diaphano-
tree: 3 dry- 4 dryo- 5 dendr- 6 dendri-, dendro- 7 -dendron
tribe: 4 phyl- 5 phylo-
trillion: 4 tera-, treg- 5 trega-
trillionth: 4 pico-
tripled: 4 tris-
trough: 5 bothr- 6 bothro-
trunk: 4 corm- 5 cormo-
tube: 4 styl- 5 solen-, stylo- 6 siphon-, soleno-, syring- 7 siphoni-, siphono-, syringo-
tuft: 4 loph- 5 lophi-, lopho- 6 lophio-
Turkish: 5 Turco-
turn: 4 trop- 5 tropo-
turned: 7 -tropous
turned toward: 6 -tropic
turning: 6 stroph- 7 stropho-
turn toward: 5 -trope
twelve: 5 dodec- 6 dodeca-
twenty: 4 icos- 5 eicos-, icosa-, icosi- 6 eicosa-
twice: 2 bi-
twisted: 5 plect- 6 plecto-, strept- 7 strepsi-, strepto-
twisting: 6 stroph- 7 stropho-
two: 2 bi- 3 bin-, bis-, duo-, dyo-, twi-
two-part: 5 dicho-
unarmed: 5 anopi- 6 anoplo-
under: 6 infero-
unequal: 5 aniso-
uneven: 5 aniso-
union: 3 gam- 4 gamo-, -gamy 6 -gamous
unit: 4 -plex
universe: 4 cosm- 5 cosmo-
unpleasant: 3 cac- 4 caco-
unreal: 5 pseud 6 pseudo-
unusual: 4 anom- 5 anomo-
upward: 3 ano- 6 sursum-
urban: 5 metro-
usual: 5 normo-
uvula: 4 clon- 5 clono- 8 staphylo-
vapor: 4 mano- 5 atmid- 6 atmido-
various: 5 parti-, party- 6 poecil-, poikil- 7 poecilo-, poikilo-
vehicle: 6 -mobile
vein: 3 ven- 4 veni-, veno- 5 phleb- 6 phlebo-
vertebra: 7 spondyl- 8 spondylo-
vessel: 3 vas- 4 vaso- 5 angio-
view: 5 -scape
viewer: 5 -scope
viewing: 5 -scopy 6 -scopic
vine: 4 viti-
vinegar: 4 acet- 5 aceto-
viscera: 9 splanchno-
visible: 6 phaner- 7 phanero-
vision: 4 -opia, opto- 5 -opsia
voice: 4 phon- 5 phono-
voice box: 6 laryng- 7 laryngo-
walking: 5 -grade
wand: 6 rhabdo-
warfare: 5 -machy
water: 4 aqua-, aqui-, hydr- 5 hydat-,

hydro- **6** hydato-
waterless: 6 anhydr- **7** anhydro-
wave: 3 cym-, kym- **4** cymo-, kymo-
wax: 3 cer- **4** cero-
way: 3 -ode
weak: 4 lept- **5** lepto- **6** asthen- **7** astheno-
wealth: 4 plut- **5** Pluto-
weather: 6 meteor-
wedge: 5 embol-, sphen- **6** emboli-, embolo-, spheno-
weight: 3 bar- **4** baro-
well: 2 eu- **4** bene-
wet: 5 hygro-
whale: 3 cet- **4** ceto-
wheel: 5 troch- **6** trocho-
whirlpool: 4 dino-
white: 3 alb- **4** albo-, leuc-, leuk- **5** leuco-, leuko-
whole: 3 hol-, pan- **4** holo-, pano-, pant-, toti- **5** panta-, panto- **7** integri-
whorl: 7 spondyl- **8** spondylo- **9** verticill-
wide: 4 eury-
wild: 5 agrio-
will: 5 -bulia
wind: 4 anem- **5** anemo-, venti-, vento-
windpipe: 7 tracheo-
wine: 2 en- **3** eno-, oen-, vin- **4** oeno-, vini-, vino-
wing: 4 pter- **5** ptero- **6** pteryg- **7** pterygo-
winged: 7 -pterous
wisdom: 5 -sophy
within: 3 end-, ent- **4** endo-, ento-
woman: 3 gyn- **4** gyne-, gyno-, -gyny **5** gynec- **6** gyneco-, -gynous
wonder: 8 thaumato-
wood: 3 hyl-, xyl- **4** hylo-, lign-, xylo- **5** ligni-, ligno-
wool: 3 lan- **4** erio-, lani-, lano-
word: 3 log- **4** logo-, -onym **5** gloss- **6** glosso-, glotto- **7** onomato-
work: 3 erg- **4** ergo-, -ergy, -urgy
world: 4 cosm- **5** cosmo-
worm: 5 vermi- **6** scolec-, -scolex **7** scoleco-
worship: 5 -latry
worshiper: 5 -later
wound: 7 traumat- **8** traumato-
wrist: 5 carpo-
writing: 4 -gram **6** grapho-, -graphy
written: 5 -graph
wrongful: 3 mal-
yellow: 4 flav- **5** chrys-, flavo-, luteo-, xanth- **6** chryso-, xantho-
yoke: 3 zyg- **4** zygo-
yolk: 6 lecith- **7** lecitho-
zone: 3 zon- **4** zono-
combo: 3 duo, mix **4** band, trio **5** nonet, octet **6** medley **7** mélange, mixture, octette, quartet, variety **9** potpourri **10** miscellany
Combs, Earle: 4 Yank **6** Yankee **10** outfielder
combust: 4 burn **10** incinerate
combusted: 5 afire **7** blazing
combustible: 4 fuel **5** fiery **8** burnable, skittish, volatile
heap: 4 pyre
substance: 3 gas, oil **4** coal
combustion: 4 fire **5** blaze **7** flaming **8** ignition, kindling **9** agitation, commotion, explosion
criminal ~: 5 arson
evidence: 5 flame, smoke
product: 3 ash **6** fly ash
combustion __: 4 tube **6** engine
Comden: 5 Betty
collaborator: 5 Green
__ Comdr.: 5 Lieut.
come: 4 show **5** enter, get in, occur, pop in, pop up, reach, visit **6** appear, arrive, blow in, evolve, fall in, happen, make it, report, ring in, roll in, show up, sign in, spring, turn up **7** advance, check in, clock in, hit town, punch in, turn out **8** approach, breeze in, draw near, tag along **9** originate
aboard: 4 go in, go on **5** get in, get on **7** climb in, climb on, emplane, entrain **9** affiliate
about: 2 be **4** fall **5** arise, occur, pivot, rally **6** befall, evolve, happen, result **7** develop **9** eventuate, take place, transpire
a cropper: 4 bomb, bust, flop, lose, slip, trip **5** flunk **6** blow it, falter **7** blunder, founder, go under, go wrong, misstep, stumble, wash out **8** fall flat, flounder, lay an egg **9** strike out
across: 4 find, meet **5** dig up, spend **6** locate, strike **7** stumble **8** chance on **9** acquiesce, encounter, light upon **10** capitulate, chance upon, happen upon
across as: 4 seem
across with: 3 pay
after: 4 hunt **5** ensue, trail **6** follow, go next **7** go after, succeed
again: 5 recur **6** repeat, return **7** revisit **9** reiterate
along: 5 rally **6** look up **7** shape up **9** accompany **10** recuperate
and go: 5 recur **9** alternate, oscillate
apart: 4 open, snap, tear **5** burst, panic, ravel, split **7** unweave **8** fragment, separate **9** break down
around: 4 turn **5** adapt, awake, rally, visit, yield **6** accede, comply, mellow, relent, revive, soften, submit **7** recover **9** acquiesce, lighten up
ashore: 4 land **9** disembark
at: 5 reach **6** attack, charge **8** approach
away: 5 leave **8** separate
back: 5 reply **6** return **7** revisit
back to mind: 5 recur
back to school: 5 reune
before: 4 lead **7** precede, presage **8** antecede **9** go ahead of, introduce
between: 6 divide **7** rupture **8** alienate, separate **9** disaffect
by: 3 get, win **4** call, earn **5** visit **6** attain, obtain, secure **7** acquire, procure, receive **8** purchase
clean: 3 own **4** bare **5** admit, level, own up **6** fess up **7** confess
close: 4 near **8** approach
close to: 8 resemble
down: 4 land **5** light **6** alight, fall in
down hard: 4 pour, rain, teem **5** storm
down on: 5 chide, scold **6** berate, impugn, rebuke **7** censure, condemn, reprove, tell off, upbraid **8** admonish, restrict, surprise **9** castigate, criticize, dish it out, dress down, reprimand
down quickly: 5 swoop
down with: 3 get **4** have **5** catch **7** fall ill **8** contract
down with something: 3 ail
ender: 4 back, down
first: 4 lead **7** precede **8** antecede
forth: 5 begin, break **6** emerge **7** emanate
forward: 5 offer **7** advance **9** volunteer
(from): 4 hail, stem **6** derive, emerge, follow, spring **7** proceed **9** originate
from behind: 5 rally
hard to ~ by: 4 rare
home: 5 score **6** return
in: 4 land **5** enter
in a time to ~: 7 someday
in contact with: 4 meet
in first: 3 win **7** prevail, triumph
in handy for: 3 aid **4** help
in last: 3 lag **4** lose
in second: 4 lose **5** place
into: 3 win **5** enter **6** obtain **7** acquire, inherit, receive, succeed **9** get hold of, lay hold of
into being: 5 arise, begin, start **6** grow up, spring **9** originate
into view: 4 loom, rise **5** heave **6** appear, emerge
near: 5 verge
next: 5 ensue **6** follow **7** succeed
of age: 6 grow up, mature
off: 4 work **5** occur **6** happen **7** succeed
open: 4 undo
out: 4 leak **6** emerge, spring **9** transpire
out even: 7 balance
out of hiding: 4 show **6** appear, emerge **7** surface **10** break cover
out the same: 5 agree
out with it: 3 say **5** state, utter, voice **6** reveal **7** speak up
over: 4 call **5** visit **6** affect **8** happen to
through: 5 spend **7** produce, survive, weather **8** make good, stick out
to: 4 cost, make, stir, wake **5** awake, equal, reach, total, visit, waken **6** attain, attend, awaken, return, revive **8** reawaken
(to): 6 amount
to a decision: 6 settle
to a halt: 4 stop
to a head: 5 crest **6** climax **9** culminate
to an end: 2 do **3** fix **4** draw, halt, make, quit, rule, stop **5** cease, close, glean, infer, judge, sum up, think **6** assume, decide, deduce, effect, expire, finish, fulfil, gather, reason, reckon, run out, settle, wind up, wrap up **7** achieve, fulfill, imagine, play out, presume, pull off, resolve, suppose, surmise, suspect, work out **8** carry out, complete, conclude, dispatch, finalize, round off, round out, surcease **9** culminate, determine, terminate **10** accomplish, bring about, call it a day, consummate, put through
to a point: 5 taper
to be: 3 get **6** happen
to blows: 3 row **5** brawl, fight, scrap **7** grapple, mix it up, scuffle
to fruition: 5 ripen
together: 3 gel, mix, sit **4** jell, meet, mesh **5** merge, rally, reune, touch, unite **6** concur, gather, muster **7** collect, convene **8** assemble, coalesce, converge
to grips with: 4 face **6** handle, tackle **8** cope with, deal with **9** encounter **10** meet head on
to life: 6 revive
to light: 5 arise **6** emerge **7** surface
to mind: 4 dawn **5** arise, occur **6** recall, strike
to naught: 4 bomb, bust, fail, flop, sink, wane **6** fizzle, lessen, run dry, run out **7** dwindle, founder, misfire, run down, subside, tail off, thin out **8** backfire, collapse, fall flat, flounder, peter out, taper off **9** evaporate **10** run aground
to pass: 2 be **4** fall **5** break, ensue, occur **6** befall, betide, happen, pan out, turn up **9** eventuate, intervene, take place, transpire
to rest: 4 land **5** lodge **6** settle
to see: 5 visit **6** call on
to terms: 4 jibe **5** agree, level, yield **6** accord, make up, settle **7** bargain, concede, consent, go along, resolve, work out **8** cut a deal, play ball **9** acquiesce, harmonize, negotiate **10** capitulate
to the plate: 3 bat, hit
to the rescue: 3 aid **4** help, save
(toward): 4 move
undone: 3 rip **4** fray, open, tear, wear **5** break, burst, crack, shred, split **7** frazzle, give way, rupture **8** fragment, separate **9** disengage, pull apart **10** disconnect
unglued: 4 flip, rage, rail, rant, rave, snap, yell **5** break, go ape, go mad, shout, storm **6** bellow **7** carry on, explode, flare up, give way, go crazy, lash out, thunder **8** freak out, get angry, harangue **9** come apart, go bananas, raise Cain **10** hit the roof
up: 4 lift **5** arise, occur **6** appear, happen **7** surface **9** eventuate
up against: 4 abut, cope, defy, face, meet **5** brave **6** accost, oppose, resist, tackle **8** confront, face up to **9** challenge, encounter, pitch into, stand up to, withstand
up for air: 4 vent **6** emerge
up in the world: 4 rise **7** succeed
upon: 3 hit, spy **4** find **6** locate, look up **7** run into **8** discover, meet with, overtake **9** encounter, run across
up short: 3 owe **4** fail, lose
up to: 4 meet **5** reach, touch **7** satisfy
up with: 5 hatch, hit on **6** create, devise, supply **7** propose, think up **9** institute, originate, recommend **10** bring forth
what may: 6 surely **7** somehow **10** in any event
come __: 3 off, out **4** back, down, into, over, true, upon **5** about, again, along, and go, clean, in for, off it, round **6** across, around **7** between, forward, through, unglued **8** a cropper
come __ afar: 4 from
come __ are: 5 as you
come __ good: 4 to no
come __ head: 3 to a
come __ in the wash: 3 out
come __ it: 3 off
come __ line: 4 into
come __ may: 4 what
come __ of the rain: 5 in out
come __ on: 4 down
come __ one's own: 4 into
come __ or high water: 4 hell
come __ point: 3 to a
come __ the hammer: 5 under
come __ the pike: 4 down
come __ the wash: 5 out in
come __ to roost: 4 home
come __ with: 3 out **4** down
come-__: 3 ons **5** all-ye, outer **6** hither
__ come: 3 how **7** kingdom
__-come: 5 first
Come __: 4 to Me **6** Undone **7** Dancing, Running
Come __!: 4 on in **5** off it
Come __?: 5 again
Come __ About Me: 3 See
Come __, Come Tyre: 7 Nineveh
Come __ get it!: 3 and
Come __, Little Sheba: 4 Back
Come __ My House: 3 on-a
Come __ my parlor...: 4 into
Come __ or Come Shine: 4 Rain
Come __ to Me: 4 Back **6** Softly
Come __ With Me: 3 Fly **4** Live
Come __ Your Horn: 4 Blow
come a __: 7 cropper
Come again?: 3 huh **4** what
Come a Little Bit Closer (1964 song)
artist: Jay and the Americans
Come and __!: 5 get it

Come and Get It: 4 film 5 novel
 author: Edna Ferber
 cast: Edward Arnold, Frances Farmer, Joel McCrea
 director: Howard Hawks, William Wyler
Come and Get It (1970 song) artist: Badfinger
Come and Get With Me (1998 song) artist: Keith Sweat, Snoop Doggy Dogg
Come and Get Your Love (song) artist: Real McCoy, Redbone
come as you __: 3 are
Comeau: 4 city, town
 locale: 6 Canada, Québec
comeback: 4 echo 5 rally, reply 6 answer, remark, retort, return, ripost 7 rebound, revival, riposte 8 reaction, rebuttal, recovery, repartee, response 9 rejoinder 10 resurgence
 like some ~ s: 5 witty 6 clever, snappy
 make a ~: 5 rally 6 answer 7 rebound, recover, survive
 playground ~: 4 am so 5 am not, am too, are so
Come back, __: 5 Shane
__ Come Back: 4 Baby 5 Lover
Comeback author: Dick Francis
Come Back, Little Sheba: 4 film, play
 author: William Inge
 cast: Shirley Booth, Burt Lancaster, Terry Moore
 character: 3 Doc 4 Lola, Turk 5 Marie
 director: Daniel Mann
__ come back now!: 4 Y'all
Come Back to __: 4 Erin
__, Come Back to Me: 5 Lover
Come Back to Me (1990 song) artist: Janet Jackson
Come Back When You Grow Up (1967 song) artist: Bobby Vee
Come Blow Your Horn: 4 film, play
 author: Neil Simon
 cast: Lee J. Cobb, Molly Picon, Frank Sinatra
 director: Bud Yorkin
Come, come!: 3 tsk 4 pooh 6 tsk tsk
Come Dancing (1983 song) artist: Kinks
comedian: 3 wag, wit 4 card, zany 5 clown, comic, cutup, joker, mimic 6 amuser, jester, scream 7 buffoon, farceur 8 funnyman, humorist, jokester, quipster 9 leg-puller, performer, top banana
 see also comic
comedienne: 3 wag, wit 4 card, zany 5 clown, comic, cutup, joker, mimic 6 amuser, jester, scream 7 buffoon, farceur 8 humorist, jokester, quipster 9 performer, top banana
comedown: 7 decline 10 anticlimax
come down __: 4 with
come down the __: 4 pike
comedy: 4 play, show 5 farce, genre, humor, shtik, story 6 joking, satire, send-up, shtick 7 burlesk, jesting, takeoff 8 drollery, hilarity 9 burlesque, funniness, slapstick, spectacle
 bit of ~: 3 gag 4 joke, quip, skit 8 one-liner
 '80s ~ troupe: 4 SCTV
 starter: 5 tragi
 straight man: 4 foil 6 stooge
__ comedy: 3 low 4 high 5 black 7 musical
__ Comedy: 3 New, Old 5 Black, Love's 6 Middle
Comedy Central: 7 channel
 alternative: 3 BET, CMT, MTV, PAX, TBS, TLC, TNN, TNT, USA 4 ESPN, HGTV 5 A and E, C-SPAN, Style 6 Noggin, Tech TV, TV Land 7 Court TV, Ovation, SoapNet 8 Lifetime
comedy of __: 6 errors 7 manners
Comedy of Errors, The
 author: William Shakespeare
 character: 5 Pinch 6 Aegeon, Angelo, Dromio 7 Adriana, Aemilia, Luciana, Solinus 10 Antipholus
Comedy of Terrors, The (1964 film)
 cast: Boris Karloff, Peter Lorre, Vincent Price
__ Comedy, The: 5 Human 6 Divine
come from __: 4 afar
Come Go With Me (song) artist: Dell-Vikings, Exposé
come hell or __ water: 4 high
__ Come Home: 6 Lassie
__, Come Home: 6 Snoopy
come home to __: 5 roost
come in __: 3 for
come into __: 4 line
come into one's __: 3 own
__-come-lately: 6 Johnny
Come, let us __ Him: 5 adore
Come Live With Me (1941 film)
 cast: Hedy Lamarr, James Stewart
Come live with me and be my love...
 author: Christopher Marlowe
comely: 4 cute, fair, trim 5 bonny 6 bonnie, dainty, lovely, pretty, proper 7 shapely, winsome 8 adorable, alluring, becoming, fetching, gorgeous, handsome, pleasing, striking, stunning 9 beautiful, ravishing 10 attractive
Come Next Spring (1956 film)
 cast: Steve Cochran, Ann Sheridan
Come Nineveh, Come Tyre author: Allen Drury
come on __: 4 over 6 strong
come-on: 2 ad 4 bait, line, lure, trap 5 decoy, shill, snare 9 incentive 10 allurement, attraction, enticement, inducement, loss leader, temptation
 gesture: 4 wink
Come on!: 6 let's go
Come on-a My House (1951 song) artist: Rosemary Clooney
come one's __: 3 way
Come on in!: 5 enter
Come on Over (2000 song) artist: Christina Aguilera
come out in the __: 4 wash
comer: 7 hotshot 9 Young Turk 10 rising star, wunderkind
 former ~: 4 goer
 starter: 3 new 4 late
Comer: 9 Anjanette
Come Rain or Come Shine composer: 5 Arlen 6 Mercer
Come See About Me (1964 song) artist: Supremes
Come September (1961 film)
 cast: Sandra Dee, Rock Hudson, Gina Lollobrigida
 director: Robert Mulligan
__ Comes for the Archbishop: 5 Death
__ Come She Will: 5 April
__ Comes Mary: 5 Along
__ Comes Mr. Jordan: 4 Here
__ comes on little..., The: 3 fog
__ Comes Santa Claus: 4 Here
comestible: 4 good, meat 6 edible 7 victual 9 nutritive 10 alimentary
comestibles: 4 eats, food, grub 6 viands 7 aliment 8 victuals 9 provender 10 provisions
__ Comes to Harlem: 6 Cotton
__ Comes to the Forest: 6 Tigger
comet: 6 Encke's 7 Halley's 8 Hale-Bopp, Kohoutek 9 Hyakutake
 first to spot a ~ usually: 5 namer
 part: 4 coma, tail
 path: 3 arc
Comet: 3 car 4 auto 7 Mercury 8 cleanser, reindeer 10 automobile
 alternative: 4 Ajax, Bab-O 6 Bon Ami 9 Soft Scrub
 colleague: 5 Cupid, Vixen 6 Dancer, Dasher, Donder 7 Blitzen, Prancer
__ Cometh, The: 6 Iceman
come to __: 4 life, pass, play 5 a fork, a head, an end, blows, grief, light, terms
come to __ with: 5 grips
come to a __: 4 head
Come Together (1969 song) artist: Beatles
Come to Grief author: Dick Francis
Come to Me (1958 song) artist: Mathis
come to no __: 4 good
Come to the Stable (1949 film)
 cast: Celeste Holm, Hugh Marlowe, Loretta Young
 director: Henry Koster
come to think __: 4 of it
Comets' grp.: 4 WNBA
come under the __: 6 hammer
__ Come Undone: 4 She's
come up __: 4 with 5 roses, short 7 against
Come up and __: 5 see me
comeuppance: 3 due 6 rebuke, reward 7 deserts
 gain ~: 6 avenge
come what __: 3 may
COMEX rival: 4 Merc
comfit: 5 candy 10 confection
comfort: 3 aid 4 balm, ease, help, lift, pity 5 cheer, salve, style 6 assure, luxury, relief, smooth, solace, stroke, succor 7 amenity, anodyne, cheer up, console, hearten, lighten, relieve, satisfy, support, sustain 8 coziness, opulence, opulency, reassure, snugness, sympathy 9 encourage, entertain, happiness, well-being 10 assistance, bed of roses, prosperity, relaxation, sympathize
 companion: 3 aid
 sound of ~: 2 ah 3 aah
 station: 2 WC 3 lav, loo 7 latrine 8 bathroom, washroom
 words of ~: 5 it's OK
comfort __: 4 food, zone 6 letter 7 station
__ comfort: 4 cold
Comfort: 4 Alex
Comfort __: 3 Inn
comfortable: 4 cosy, cozy, easy, homy, nice, rich, snug, soft 5 cozey, cozie, cushy, flush, homey, roomy 6 at ease, at home, at rest, decent, loaded, monied, serene 7 easeful, livable, moneyed, relaxed, restful, wealthy, well-off 8 adequate, affluent, cared for, in clover, liveable, pleasant, relaxing, spacious, well-to-do 9 leisurely, luxurious, well-fixed 10 complacent, in the dough, in the money, privileged, propertied, prosperous, well-heeled
 be ~: 6 nestle 7 snuggle
 make ~: 5 greet 7 welcome
comforter: 4 puff 5 duvet, quilt, scarf 6 spread 7 bedding, blanket 8 coverlet, coverlid 9 eiderdown, supporter
 Biblical ~: 3 rod 5 staff
Comforter (1993 song) artist: Shai
comforting: 8 parental 9 analeptic, assuaging, consoling, relieving, remedying, restoring, softening, succoring, upholding 10 lightening, mitigating, reassuring, refreshing, sustaining
 word: 5 there
 words: 5 I care, I know
Comfort Inn: 5 motel
 alternative: 7 Days Inn 9 Ramada Inn 10 Econo Lodge, Hampton Inn, Holiday Inn, Quality Inn, Red Roof Inn, Travelodge 11 Best Western
comfortless: 5 bleak, harsh 6 lonely 7 forlorn
comfrey: 5 plant 6 flower
comfy: 4 cosy, cozy, easy, homy, snug, soft 5 cozey, cozie, cushy, homey 6 at ease 8 homelike, tucked in
 get ~: 6 curl up
 spot: 4 nest
comic: 3 wag, wit 4 card, zany 5 clown, cutup, droll, funny, joker 6 amuser, har-har, jester, scream 7 amusing, buffoon, farceur, jesting, jocular, risible 8 comedian, funnyman, humorist, humorous, jokester, quipster 9 facetious, jokesmith, laughable, leg-puller, ludicrous, performer, top banana
 beginning: 5 serio, tragi
 exaggeration: 4 camp 5 farce
 in music: 5 buffa, buffo
 job: 3 gig
 like a ~: 5 droll, funny, witty
 need: 4 mike 5 stool, water 8 material
 offering: 3 gag 4 joke, quip, skit 8 one-liner
 reward: 4 ha-ha 5 laugh
 silent ~: 4 mime 5 mimer
 writer: 6 gagman 7 gagster
comic __: 4 book 5 opera, strip 6 relief
comical: 4 camp, rich, zany 5 droll, funny, goofy, silly, wacky, witty 6 absurd, har-har, whacky 7 amusing, jesting, jocular, risible, waggish 8 farcical, humorous 9 facetious, hilarious, laughable, ludicrous, quizzical, whimsical 10 gut-busting, off-the-wall, ridiculous
 introduction: 5 serio, tragi
comicality: 5 humor
comic book
 character: 4 toon
 cry: 3 eek, ulp, wah 4 yeow
 genre: 5 sci-fi
 heroes: 4 X-Men
 sound effect: 3 arf, bam, oof, pow 5 splat
Comic Book Confidential (1989 film)
 cast: R. Crumb, Will Eisner, Jack Kirby
 director: Ron Mann
Comice: 4 pear, pome 5 fruit
 kin: 4 Bosc 5 Anjou 6 Seckel 8 Bartlett
comics: 7 funnies
comic strip: 7 cartoon
 artists' org.: 3 NCS
 finisher: 5 inker
Comin' __!: 4 at ya
Comin' __ the Mountain: 5 Round
Comin' __ the Rye: 4 Thro'
coming: 3 due 6 advent, earned, future 7 arrival, en route, ensuing, in store 8 eventual, expected, imminent, oncoming, on the way 9 following, impending, in the wind 10 appearance, receivable, subsequent
 after: 4 next 5 later
 down: 5 rainy 6 stormy 9 happening
 have ~: 4 earn, rate 5 merit 7 deserve
 next: 3 fol. 5 after 9 following
 on strong: 4 bold 7 zealous 9 undaunted
 out: 4 rise 5 debut
 say you're ~: 4 RSVP
 see ~: 7 portend, predict 8 prophesy 10 anticipate
 soon: 4 near, nigh 8 imminent
 starter: 4 home 5 forth, short
 up: 4 next
 up short: 7 lacking
coming __: 5 of age
__-coming: 5 up-and
Coming __: 4 Home
Coming __...: 4 soon
Coming __ in Samoa: 5 of Age
__ Coming: 4 Eli's 6 Second

Coming Fury, The author: Bruce Catton
Coming Home (1978 film)
cast: Bruce Dern, Jane Fonda, Jon Voight
director: Hal Ashby
subject: 3 Nam 7 Vietnam
Coming in __ wing...: 3 on a
Coming of Age in Samoa author: Mead
coming-of-age period: 5 teens
coming-out: 5 debut, party
Coming Out of the Dark (1991 song)
artist: Gloria Estefan
Coming Soon!!! author: John Barth
Coming to America (1988 film)
cast: John Amos, Arsenio Hall, James Earl Jones, Eddie Murphy
director: John Landis
role: 5 Akeem
Coming Up (1980 song) artist: Paul McCartney
Comin' Round the Mountain (1951 film)
cast: Bud Abbott, Lou Costello
Comin' Thro' the Rye author: Burns
__ comique: 5 opéra
Comique actor: 4 Tati
Comiskey: 7 Charles, Charlie
Comiskey Park locale: 7 Chicago
Comissiona, Sergiu: 9 conductor
Comitan: 4 city, town
locale: 6 Mexico 7 Chiapas
__ comitatus: 5 posse
comity: 4 tact 5 amity 7 harmony 8 courtesy, goodwill 10 friendship
comity of __: 7 nations
comma: 4 lull, mark 5 pause
what a ~ signals: 5 pause
__ comma: 6 serial, series, turned
Commack: 4 city, town
locale: 7 New York
command: 3 bid, law, run 4 call, fiat, grip, head, lead, rule, tell, wish, word, writ 5 edict, exact, force, grasp, might, order, power, reach, reign, skill 6 adjure, behest, biding, charge, compel, decree, dictum, direct, enjoin, firman, govern, handle, impose, insist, manage, ordain, summon 7 ability, bidding, control, dictate, enforce, know-how, mandate, mastery, oversee, potence, potency, precept, primacy, regency, require 8 dominate, dominion, hegemony, instruct, kingship, pleasure, sanction 9 authority, directive, influence, officiate, ordinance, prescribe, supervise, supremacy 10 ascendance, ascendancy, ascendence, ascendency, domination, government, injunction, leadership, management, take charge
a view: 4 face, look, view 6 survey 7 look out 8 prospect 9 look out on
be in ~: 6 direct, manage
computer ~: 3 cut 4 edit, find, go to, save, sort 5 enter, erase, macro, paste, print 6 delete
ender: 3 ant, eer
high ~: 5 brass 10 management
in ~: 5 on top
oater ~: 4 whoa 7 giddyap
officer ~: 4 halt, stop 6 freeze
old-style: 4 hest
second in ~: 2 VP 4 veep 6 veepee
soldier ~: 4 fire, halt 5 march 6 at ease, fall in 8 left face 9 right face
to a dog: 3 beg, sic, sit 4 come, down, heel, mush, stay 5 fetch, sic 'em, sit up, speak 6 drop it
command __: 3 car 4 post 6 module
command-__: 6 driven
__ command: 3 air 4 high
__ Command: 4 Dark, Lost 6 Secret
Command Decision (1948 film)
cast: Clark Gable, Walter Pidgeon
director: Sam Wood
commandeer: 4 take 5 annex, co-opt, seize, usurp 6 assume, hijack, snatch 7 capture, preempt, procure 8 arrogate, highjack, shanghai, take over 9 conscript, sequester 10 confiscate
commander: 4 amir, boss, czar, emir, exec, head, jefe, rank, tsar, tzar 5 ameer, chief, emeer, ruler 6 gerent, honcho, leader, master, top dog 7 captain, headman, kingpin, skipper 8 director, kingfish, top brass 9 big cheese, executive, key player, organizer, top banana 10 head honcho, mastermind
__ commander: 4 wing 7 supreme
Commander: 3 car 4 auto 10 Studebaker
commander in __: 5 chief
commander, in Arabic: 4 amir, emir 5 ameer, emeer
commanding: 5 bossy, lofty 6 lordly, potent 8 decisive, dominant, forceful, imposing, in charge, kinglike, powerful, striking, superior 9 arresting, assertive, imperious, sovereign 10 autocratic, compelling, dominating, impressive, peremptory
commanding __: 7 officer
commandment: 3 law 4 rule, word 5 canon 7 precept
break a ~: 3 sin 5 covet
number: 3 ten
starter: 4 thou
__ Commandment: 5 Fifth, First, Ninth, Sixth, Tenth, Third 6 Eighth, Fourth, Second 7 Seventh
__ Commandments: 3 Ten
commando: 7 soldier 9 legionary
action: 4 raid
weapon: 3 Uzi
Commando (1985 film)
cast: Rae Dawn Chong, Dan Hedaya, Arnold Schwarzenegger
director: Mark L. Lester
comme ci, comme ça: 4 so-so
Commedia dell'__: 4 Arte
comme il faut: 5 right 6 decent, proper, seemly 7 correct, fitting 8 decorous
commemorate: 4 keep 5 honor 6 salute 7 observe 8 remember
commemoration: 5 event, medal 7 tribute 8 ceremony, monument
Commemoration __: 3 Ode
commemorative: 5 stamp 8 memorial
stone: 5 stela, stele
verse: 3 ode
commence: 4 open, rise 5 arise, begin, dig in, enter, found, set in, start 6 launch, let rip, set off, set out, spring, take up 7 aggress, develop, get to it, kick off, lead off, preface 8 approach, embark on, get going, initiate, jump into, set forth 9 enter into, enter upon, get to work, introduce, originate, undertake 10 get started, inaugurate
commencement: 4 dawn, rise 5 birth, onset, start 6 advent, origin, outset, source 7 dawning, genesis, kickoff, leadoff, opening, prelude 8 exordium 9 inception
wear: 3 cap 4 gown
commend: 4 cite, hail, laud 5 bless, exalt, extol, honor 6 advise, extoll, praise, salute, tender 7 acclaim, applaud, approve, consign, endorse, entrust, flatter, glorify, indorse, intrust, proffer, suggest 8 hand it to, hand over, relegate, turn over 9 recommend 10 compliment, panegyrize
commendable: 4 fine, good, nice, okay 5 great, legit, model, moral, noble 6 proper, worthy 7 ethical 8 all right, laudable, pleasant, pleasing, splendid, superior 9 admirable, agreeable, excellent, reputable, wonderful 10 acceptable, beneficial, creditable
commendably: 4 well
commendation: 4 puff 5 honor, kudos 6 credit, eulogy, homage, praise, salute 7 acclaim, laurels, plaudit, tribute 8 accolade, approval, citation, encomium, flattery, good word 9 laudation, panegyric 10 exaltation
commensurate: 3 due, fit 4 even, like 5 equal, level 7 fitting 8 adequate
be ~: 6 equate
comment: 4 note, word 5 gloss, input, opine 6 assert, remark 7 expound, mention, observe, opinion 8 back talk, bring out, critique, feedback, footnote, point out, throw out 9 criticism, editorial, interject, statement, wisecrack 10 annotation, discussion
biting ~: 4 barb
unprepared ~: 5 ad-lib
Comment allez-__?: 4 vous
commentary: 6 review, speech 7 article, reading, remarks 8 analysis, critique, exegesis, treatise 9 criticism, discourse, editorial, narration, voice-over 10 annotation, definition, exposition, expression
commentator: 6 critic, pundit 7 analyst 8 lecturer, reporter, reviewer
page: 4 Op-Ed
__ commentator: 5 color
comments, clever: 6 banter
commerce: 5 trade 7 traffic 8 business, dealings, exchange, industry
acronym: 4 GATT 5 NAFTA
Commerce City: 4 town
locale: 8 Colorado
Commerce Dept. agency: 3 SBA 4 NOAA
commercial: 2 ad 4 advt., spot 5 pitch, promo 6 advert 7 request 8 economic, monetary 9 exploited, financial, for-profit, mercenary, pecuniary, publicity, retailing, wholesale 10 investment, marketable, mercantile, profitable
alliance: 5 trust 6 cartel
award: 4 Clio
endorsement: 4 plug
phrase: 6 act now
pro-bono: 3 PSA
promotion: 5 tie-in
skip past ~ s: 3 zap
song: 6 jingle
writer: 5 adman
commercial __: 3 art, law 4 bank, code, zone 5 break, paper, pilot 6 agency, artist, credit 7 attaché, college
Commercial Appeal: 9 newspaper
locale: 7 Memphis
commingle: 3 mix, wed 4 fuse, meld 5 admix, blend, immix, merge, unify, unite 6 commix 7 combine 8 coalesce, intermix 9 integrate 10 amalgamate
commingling: 9 confluent
comminute: 5 grind 9 granulate
commiserate: 4 pity 7 condole, console
commiseration: 4 pity 5 mercy 6 lenity, pathos 7 empathy 8 sympathy 10 condolence
commissary: 9 cafeteria 10 dining room
commission: 3 cut, fee, job, let, pay 4 hire, load, name, trim, work 5 board, place, share, slice, title, trust 6 agency, assign, bureau, employ, enable, engage, enlist, errand, office, ordain, ratify 7 appoint, charter, empower, entrust, intrust, license, mandate, mission, percent, qualify, station 8 accredit, delegate, deputize, kickback, nominate, sanction 9 allowance, authority, authorize, brokerage, committee, designate, factorage, indemnity 10 assignment, constitute, delegation, department, deputation, employment, engagement, inaugurate, obligation, percentage
in ~: 7 running, working 9 operating
out of ~: 3 ill 4 idle 5 kaput 6 broken, unable 7 injured 8 disabled, inactive 9 sidelined 10 broken-down, on the bench
put out of ~: 5 smash, wreck 7 disable 8 sabotage
__ commission: 4 into 5 out of
__ Commission: 6 Warren
commissioned __: 7 officer
commissioner: 6 deputy 8 official 9 appointee
__ commissioner: 4 high 6 county
commit: 3 put 4 give, send 5 trust 6 assign, decide, devote, employ, engage, pledge 7 achieve, consign, deliver, empower, entrust, intrust, perform, pull off, put away 8 carry out, dedicate, delegate, deputize, dispatch, relegate, turn over 9 authorize 10 accomplish, contribute, effectuate, perpetrate
oneself: 3 opt 6 decide
refuse to ~: 3 haw, hem 5 hedge 6 waffle 10 equivocate
commitment: 3 job, tie, vow 4 duty, must, word, work 6 charge, lock-in, pledge 7 promise, resolve 8 contract, covenant, devotion 9 assurance, guarantee, liability 10 dedication, engagement, obligation
like some ~ s: 5 prior
committal: 9 captivity 10 delegation
committed: 6 intent 7 engaged 9 dedicated 10 purposeful
committee: 5 board, group, panel 6 bureau, caucus 7 cabinet, council 8 congress, legation 9 task force 10 commission, executives
ender: 3 man, men 5 woman, women
head: 5 chair
committee __: 5 of one
__ committee: 5 ad-hoc, joint, rules 6 select 7 special
committee of the __: 5 whole
commix: 5 blend, merge 7 combine 8 coalesce 9 commingle 10 amalgamate
commode: 5 chest 9 furniture
commodious: 3 big 4 wide 5 ample, large, roomy 8 spacious 9 capacious, cavernous, expansive, extensive, uncrowded 10 convenient
commodities: 5 goods, stock, wares
commodity: 4 line, ware 5 asset, thing 6 future, object 7 article, chattel, product 8 material, valuable, vendible 9 belonging, specialty 10 possession
at hand: 6 actual
exchange area: 3 pit
commodore: 4 rank
service: 4 navy
__ commodore: 3 air
Commodore: 3 car 4 auto 6 Hudson
Commodores: 10 Vanderbilt
leader: Lionel Richie
song: Brick House (1977)
Easy (1977)
Just to Be Close to You (1976)
Lady (1981)
Nightshift (1985)
Oh No (1981)
Sail on (1979)
Still (1979)
Sweet Love (1976)
Three Times a Lady (1978)
common: 3 low 4 base, dull, hack, park, rife 5 banal, cheap, corny, crass, daily, green, hokey, joint, known, level,

lowly, passé, plaza, prosy, stale, stock, trite, typic, usual, vapid **6** coarse, humble, jejune, mutual, normal, old hat, public, shared, shoddy, simple, sleazy, social, square, tawdry, unmeet, vulgar, wonted **7** average, clichéd, current, fatuous, general, generic, humdrum, ignoble, lowbred, popular, prosaic, regular, routine, typical **8** accepted, baseborn, bromidic, déclassé, everyday, familiar, frequent, habitual, inferior, low-grade, ordinary, orthodox, outdated, outmoded, plebeian, standard, workaday **9** bourgeois, colorless, customary, generical, hackneyed, idiomatic, pervasive, prevalent, prosaical, quotidian, unanimous, universal, well-known, worldwide **10** accustomed, colloquial, dime-a-dozen, dullsville, indecorous, lower-class, pedestrian, prevailing, provincial, reciprocal, second-rate, uninspired, unoriginal, widespread
combining form: **3** cen- **4** caen-, ceno-, coen- **5** caeno-, coeno-
ender: **3** age **4** weal **5** place **6** wealth
common __: **3** era, law **4** bond, cold, cost, nail, name, noun, room, salt, teal, tern, time, weal, year **5** meter, pleas, ratio, sense, snipe, stock, topaz, touch **6** canary, factor, ground, mallow, prayer, rafter, rhythm, school, sennit, sulfur, tannin **7** carrier, council, divisor, grackle, measure
Common __: **3** Era **5** Sense **6** Market
Common Cause: **5** lobby
founder: **5** Nader
__ common denominator: **5** least **6** lowest
commoner: **4** pleb **7** peasant **8** plebeian
commoners: **4** raff **6** rabble **8** populace, riffraff **9** hoi polloi **10** lower class
commonly: **3** oft **6** simply **7** as a rule, usually **8** together **9** naturally, routinely **10** ordinarily
Common Market: **3** EEC
locale: **3** Eur. **6** Europe
money: **3** ecu **4** euro
prefix: **3** Eur-. **4** Euro-
__ common multiple: **5** least **6** lowest
commonplace: **3** dry, ord. **4** dull **5** corny, hokey, lowly, passé, prosy, stale, stock, trite, typic, usual, vapid **6** common, jejune, old hat **7** average, clichéd, fatuous, general, humdrum, mundane, prosaic, regular, trivial, typical, vanilla **8** bromidic, everyday, familiar, mediocre, ordinary, outdated, outmoded, workaday **9** hackneyed, platitude, prevalent, prosaical, quotidian **10** dullsville, uninspired, unoriginal
commons: **4** park **6** square **10** town square
common-sense: **4** sane **7** logical **9** realistic **10** reasonable
Common Sense and Nuclear Warfare author: Bertrand Russell
Common Sense author: Thomas Paine
commonwealth: **4** good **5** state **6** nation **7** country, kingdom, society **9** territory
__ Commonwealth: **7** British
Commonwealth Day month: **5** March
Commonwealth member: **4** Fiji **5** Ghana, India, Kenya, Malta, Nauru, Samoa, Tonga **6** Belize, Brunei, Canada, Cyprus, Gambia, Guyana, Malawi, Tuvalu, Uganda, Zambia **7** Bahamas, England, Grenada, Jamaica, Lesotho, Namibia, Nigeria, St. Lucia, Vanuatu **8** Barbados, Botswana, Cameroon, Dominica, Kiribati, Malaysia, Maldives, Sri Lanka, Tanzania **9** Australia, Mauritius, Singapore, Swaziland **10** Bangladesh, Mozambique, New Zealand, Saint Lucia, Seychelles **11** Sierra Leone, South Africa
Commonwealth of __: **7** England, Nations **8** Kentucky, Virginia
commotion: **3** ado, din, row **4** flap, fuss, riot, stew, stir, to-do **5** furor, hoo-ha, mania, mix-up, noise, scene, spirt, spurt, stink, storm **6** action, bedlam, bustle, clamor, dither, flurry, hassle, hoopla, hoorah, hooray, hubbub, hurrah, hurray, kickup, lather, mayhem, outcry, pother, racket, ruckus, rumpus, squall, tumult, uproar **7** clatter, clutter, dispute, ferment, quarrel, scuffle, trouble **8** ballyhoo, brouhaha, disquiet, outbreak, scramble **9** agitation, annoyance, confusion, hue and cry, rebellion, sensation **10** combustion, convulsion, excitement, hurly-burly, insurgence, turbulence
communal: **5** joint **6** mutual, public, shared, social **7** grouped **8** conjoint **9** corporate, unanimous **10** collective
word: **3** our **4** ours
commune: **4** talk **6** confer, parley **7** kibbutz **8** converse **9** discourse, touch base **10** collective
dweller: **5** hippy **6** hippie **10** kibbutznik
communicable: **8** catching **10** contagious, infectious
communicate: **3** air, say **4** call, give, send, talk, tell, wire **5** break, phone, relay, speak, utter, write **6** confer, convey, detail, impart, inform, pass on, recite, relate, report, reveal, signal **7** declare, divulge, mention, reflect, signify **8** advise of, converse, describe, disclose, hand down, interact, transmit, vocalize **9** make known, put across
silently: **3** nod **4** sign
with: **5** get to, reach **7** contact
communication: **4** info, mail, news, note, word **6** dialog, lesson, report, speech **7** contact, liaison, message, missive, tidings **8** briefing, bulletin, dialogue, dispatch, language **9** statement
combining form: **3** -log **5** -logue
device: **5** pager
facilitate ~: **6** liaise
oral ~: **4** talk **6** debate, homily, sermon **7** address, lecture, oration, oratory, pep talk **8** dialogue, rhetoric **9** chalk talk, discourse **10** discussion
system of ~: **8** language
wordless ~: **3** ESP
written ~: **4** line, memo, note **5** e-mail **6** letter **7** missive
communications: **5** media
company: **3** GTE, ITT
device: **3** TTY **5** phone
former ~ system: **5** telex
starter: **4** tele
communicative: **6** chatty, social **7** cordial **8** friendly, outgoing **9** convivial, talkative **10** gregarious
communion: **4** rite **5** unity **6** accord, prayer **7** harmony, rapport, rapture **8** affinity **9** agreement, closeness, Eucharist, good vibes, sacrament **10** fellowship
host: **5** wafer
plate: **5** paten
table: **5** altar
communion __: **3** cup **4** rail **5** cloth, plate, table
__ Communion: **4** Holy
communiqué: **4** memo, news, word **5** aviso **6** notice, report **7** message **8** bulletin, dispatch **9** statement
communism: **7** Marxism **8** Leninism **9** socialism **10** Bolshevism
Communist: **3** red **7** leftist
hero: **5** Lenin
old ~ state: **3** SSR
Communist __: **5** China, party
community: **4** town, turf **5** place, state **6** colony, hamlet, parish, public **7** kinship, society **8** affinity, locality **9** agreement, humankind, residents, territory **10** settlement, similarity
bedroom ~: **4** burb **5** exurb **6** suburb
Buddhist ~: **6** sangha
center: **4** the Y, YMCA, YMHA, YWCA, YWHA
ecological ~: **5** biome
of a ~: **5** local
community __: **5** chest **6** center, church **7** college, service
__ community: **4** base **5** gated **6** speech **7** village
Community Chest kin: **6** Chance
commutation: **6** switch, travel **8** exchange **9** shuffling
commutation __: **4** test **6** ticket
commutative __: **3** law **5** group
commute: **4** ride **5** drive **6** change, pardon, soften, travel **7** curtail, release, shorten **8** decrease, mitigate **9** transform, translate
starter: **4** tele
commuter: **5** rider **8** traveler **9** passenger
bane: **5** delay, tie up **6** detour
carrier: **3** bus, car **4** auto, rail **5** train **8** railroad
destination: **4** home, work **6** office
handhold: **5** strap
home: **5** burbs, exurb **6** suburb
starter: **4** tele
watering hole: **6** bar car
commuter __: **3** tax **4** belt **7** airline
__ commuter: **7** reverse
Como: **4** Lago, lake **5** Perry
locale: **5** Italy
¿Cómo __?: **4** está
Comonfort: **4** city, town
locale: **6** Mexico **10** Guanajuato
Como, Perry
record label: **3** RCA
song: And I Love You So (1973)
Catch a Falling Star (1958)
Don't Let the Stars Get in Your Eyes (1952)
Glendora (1956)
Home for the Holidays (1954)
Hot Diggity (1956)
It's Impossible (1970)
Juke Box Baby (1956)
Kewpie Doll (1958)
Ko Ko Mo (1955)
Magic Moments (1958)
More (1956)
Papa Loves Mambo (1954)
Round and Round (1957)
Till the End of Time (1945)
Tina Marie (1955)
Comorin: **4** cape
Comoros: **6** nation **7** country
capital: **6** Moroni
group: **10** Arab League
money: **5** franc
volcano: **8** Karthala
__ Como Va: **3** Oye
comp: **4** pass, test **7** freebee, freebie **8** free pass, free ride **10** recompense
comp __: **4** time
compact: **3** car **4** auto, bond, cram, deal, firm, snug, trim **5** brief, close, dense, pithy, short, solid, stuff, terse, thick, tight **6** league, narrow, packed, pocket, recede, reduce, shrink, treaty **7** abridge, concise, concord, crammed, crowded, curtail, entente, folding, laconic, pressed, promise, shorten, stuffed **8** alliance, compress, condense, contract, covenant, portable, protocol, succinct **9** agreement, concordat, condensed, indenture, jam-packed **10** abbreviate, automobile, boiled down, compressed, hard-packed, settlement, to the point
material: **5** rouge
reading: **5** brief **7** summary **8** abstract, synopsis
compact __: **3** car **4** disc, disk
compact __ player: **4** disc, disk
__ compact: **6** social
Compacta: **4** font **8** typeface
compacted: **4** hard **5** solid, tight **8** squeezed **9** condensed **10** compressed, synopsized
__ compactor: **5** trash
compadre: **5** amigo
compañera: **5** amiga
compañero: **5** amigo
companion: **3** pal **4** aide, ally, date, mate, wife **5** buddy, crony, guide, match **6** cohort, convoy, escort, fellow, friend, spouse, squire **7** compeer, consort, partner **8** alter ego, chaperon, handbook, henchman, intimate, playmate, roommate, sidekick **9** assistant, associate, attendant, auxiliary, boyfriend, chaperone, colleague, confidant, duplicate, protector, safeguard **10** accomplice, bosom buddy, complement, girlfriend, reciprocal, sweetheart
ender: **3** way
companion __: **4** cell, star **5** piece
__ companion: **4** boon, free **6** native
companionable: **4** kind, nice **5** close, sweet **6** chummy, clubby, genial, kindly, social **7** affable, amiable, cordial **8** amicable, friendly, intimate, outgoing, pleasant, sociable **9** convivial **10** benevolent, buddy-buddy, gregarious, neighborly, solicitous
companionless: **4** sole, solo, stag **5** alone **6** lonely, single **8** desolate, lonesome, solitary
companions: **7** retinue **9** entourage
company: **3** mob **4** band, body, cast, crew, firm, gang, pack, team **5** corps, covey, crowd, flock, group, guest, hands, house, label, party, squad, troop **6** agency, circle, clique, guests, league, legion, outfit, throng, troupe **7** brigade, callers, concern, coterie, platoon, retinue, society, visitor **8** assembly, business, employer, ensemble, presence, visitors **9** entourage, gathering, retainers, syndicate **10** assemblage, collection, enterprise, fellowship, membership
abbr.: **3** inc.
honcho: **3** CEO **4** pres. **9** president
company __: **3** man **4** town **5** grade, store, union **7** officer
__ company: **4** fire, free, road, twos **5** ship's, stock, trust **6** engine, growth, ladder, livery, parent, public **7** finance, holding, limited, private
__ company...: **4** Two's
Company: **7** musical
songwriter: **8** Sondheim
Company __ Keeps, The: **3** She
__ Company: **3** Bad **5** Mixed **6** London, Three's
Company She Keeps, The author: Mary McCarthy
Company, The: **3** CIA
Compaq: **2** PC **8** computer
rival: **3** IBM, Mac **4** Dell **5** Apple **7** Gateway
comparable: **4** akin, like, same, such **5** alike, equal, level **6** allied, on a par **7** cognate, kindred, similar **8** matching, parallel **9** analogous, consonant **10** equivalent, tantamount

be ~ to: 8 approach
make ~: 6 equate
to: 4 like, near
comparably: 5 alike
comparative: 7 similar 8 relative
extent: 5 ratio
comparatively: 6 rather
compare: 5 check, liken, weigh 6 equate, oppose, size up 7 analyze, balance, collate, examine, inspect, stack up 8 contrast, parallel 9 correlate 10 correspond, scrutinize
beyond ~: 4 best 5 ideal 7 perfect 8 peerless 9 unequaled
notes: 3 gab 4 chat, meet, talk 6 confer, huddle, parley, powwow 7 consult, discuss 8 converse 9 interface, touch base 10 brainstorm, chew the fat, deliberate
to: 5 rival, touch 8 rank with
compare __: 5 notes
__ compare: 6 beyond
compared to: 7 against, vis-à-vis
comparison: 5 check, ratio 6 simile 7 analogy 8 contrast, likeness, likening, metaphor 9 analyzing, balancing, collating, collation, measuring, semblance 10 connection, estimation, opposition, separation, similarity
basis of ~: 6 analog
make a ~: 5 liken
numeric ~: 5 ratio
test item: 6 Brand X
word of ~: 4 best, less, than 5 worse
words: 3 as a
comparison __: 4 test 7 shopper
comparison-__: 4 shop
compartment: 3 bay 4 cell, nook, slot 5 berth, booth, cubby, niche, stall 6 alcove, carrel, corner, locker, pocket 7 carrell, chamber, cubicle, portion, section, segment 8 division 9 cubbyhole 10 pigeonhole
cover: 5 hatch
secure ~: 4 safe 5 vault
__ compartment: 5 glove
compartmentalize: 8 separate
compás point: 3 sur 4 este 5 norte, oeste
compass: 4 area, loop, ring, room 5 ambit, field, gamut, grasp, hem in, limit, orbit, range, reach, realm, scope, sweep, width 6 attain, domain, effect, extend, extent, length, obtain, radius, sphere, spread 7 achieve, breadth, circuit, enclose, fulfill, horizon, inclose, procure, purview, realize 8 boundary, confines, distance, encircle, environs, latitude, surround 9 dimension, incidence, magnitude, perimeter, ranginess 10 accomplish, boundaries, bring about, comprehend
creation: 3 arc 6 circle
direction: 3 ENE, ESE, NNE, NNW, SSE, SSW, WNW, WSW 4 east, west 5 north, point, rhumb, south 7 heading 9 northeast, northwest, southeast, southwest
holder: 6 gimbal 8 binnacle
pointer: 6 needle
Spanish ~ point: 3 sur 4 este 5 norte, oeste
use a ~: 6 orient
user: 5 hiker 9 orienteer
compass __: 3 saw 4 card, rose 5 north, plane, plant 6 course, rafter
__ compass: 3 bow, dry, sky, wet 4 beam, dumb, pole 5 radio 6 liquid, spirit 7 vernier
compassion: 4 pity, ruth 5 heart, mercy 6 lenity, pathos 7 charity, empathy, quarter 8 clemency, kindness, lenience, sympathy 9 tolerance 10 condolence, humaneness, tenderness
feel ~: 4 ache, pity
lacking ~: 4 cold 8 ruthless
words of ~: 5 I care, I know
compassionate: 3 big, lax 4 easy, kind, mild, nice, soft, warm 5 loose 6 caring, decent, gentle, humane, kindly, tender 7 clement, lenient, piteous, ruthful, sparing 8 all heart, flexible, gracious, laid-back, merciful, placable, tolerant 9 assuasive, compliant, easygoing, forgiving, indulgent 10 altruistic, benevolent, bighearted, forbearing, permissive, responsive, unexacting
one: 5 carer
compatibility: 7 fitness, harmony, rapport 8 affinity
compatible: 3 fit 4 like, same 7 fitting 8 suitable 9 accordant, according, adaptable, agreeable, congenial, congruent, congruous, consonant, in harmony, in keeping, simpatico 10 concurrent, consistent, harmonious, in sync with, like-minded, synchronal
be ~: 5 agree, click
__-compatible: 3 IBM 4 plug
compatriot: 3 pal 4 ally, chum 5 amigo, buddy, crony 6 cohort, friend 7 comrade 8 indigene, sidekick 9 associate, colleague, confidant 10 well-wisher
compeer: 3 bro, bud, pal 4 chum, peer 5 buddy, equal, match 6 fellow, friend 7 coequal, comrade 8 intimate, roommate, sidekick 9 colleague, companion
compel: 4 bind, make 5 cause, drive, exact, force, impel, press 6 coerce, demand, impose, oblige 7 command, dragoon, require 8 bulldoze, persuade, pressure 9 blackmail, constrain, force upon, influence, strong-arm 10 bear down on, pressurize
compelled: 5 bound 9 unwilling
be ~: 4 have, must 6 have to
compelling: 5 valid 6 cogent, potent, strong, urgent 7 burning, driving, dynamic, logical 8 luculent, powerful, pressing, striking 9 effective, mandatory, necessary, stringent 10 commanding, compulsive, conclusive, engrossing, unarguable
compendiary: 5 short 7 laconic
compendious: 5 short, terse 7 concise, laconic 9 condensed
compendium: 3 ana, set 4 book 5 brief, table 6 digest, manual, précis, sketch, survey 7 epitome, pandect, summary 8 abstract, handbook, overview, synopsis, treasury 9 anthology 10 abridgment, conspectus, tabulation
compensate: 3 pay 5 atone, cover, repay 6 make up, offset, recoup, redeem, refund, reward 7 balance, recover, redress, replace, requite, satisfy 8 outweigh 9 cancel out, indemnify, make up for, reimburse 10 counteract, invalidate, make amends, neutralize, remunerate, take care of
for: 7 expiate 10 make good on
compensation: 3 fee, pay, tip 4 wage 5 bonus, price, wages 6 amends, profit, ransom, refund, return, reward, salary, tipoff 7 benefit, comfort, damages, deserts, payment, redress, stipend 8 earnings, reaction 9 emolument, expiation
__ compensation: 7 workers'
compensatory __: 7 damages
compete: 3 run, try, vie 4 play, race 5 clash, joust, rival 6 battle, strive, take on 7 contend, face off 8 scramble, struggle 9 lock horns
competely: 6 in toto
competence: 5 craft, might, power, savvy, skill 7 ability, finesse, fitness, know-how, stature 8 adequacy, aptitude, capacity 9 expertise 10 capability, efficiency, right stuff
competency: 5 skill 10 efficiency
competent: 3 fit 4 able, deft, good, sane 5 quick, savvy, slick, sound 6 adroit, au fait, expert, nimble, up to it, versed 7 capable, knowing, skilled, trained 8 adequate, dextrous, graceful, masterly, seasoned, skillful, suitable 9 all-around, dexterous, effective, efficient, masterful, on the ball, pertinent, qualified, up to snuff, up to speed 10 proficient, sufficient
humorously: 3 ept
more ~: 5 abler
not ~: 5 inept, unfit
competently: 4 ably, well 7 handily
more ~: 6 better
competition: 4 bout, duel, game, meet, race, side 5 clash, event, fight, match, sport 6 Brand X, strife 7 contest, rivalry 8 struggle, tug-of-war
component: 3 lap, leg
-free: 5 no-bid
Competition, The (1980 film)
cast: Richard Dreyfuss, Amy Irving, Lee Remick
competitive: 5 rival, type A 8 athletic
not ~: 5 type B
competitor: 3 foe 4 vier 5 enemy, match, rival 6 player 7 athlete, entrant, fighter 8 opponent 9 adversary, candidate, contender, dark horse, ill-wisher, job-hunter 10 antagonist, challenger, contestant, opposition
prize: 5 medal, purse
ranked ~: 4 seed
competitors: 5 field
compilation: 3 ana 6 corpus 7 omnibus 8 analecta, analects, pastiche
compile: 4 cull 5 amass, build 6 digest, garner, gather, muster 7 arrange, collate, collect, marshal 8 assemble, hold on to, organize 9 summarize 10 accumulate, congregate
compiled: 7 grouped 10 collective
compiler: 6 editor
complacency: 7 comfort, license 8 smugness 10 confidence
complacent: 4 smug 6 placid 7 pleased 8 gloating 9 conceited, confident, contented, easygoing, egotistic, gratified, presuming, satisfied 10 obsequious
complain: 4 beef, carp, crab, fuss, harp, kick, mind, moan, rage, rail, rant, sigh, wail, weep, yell 5 cavil, demur, gripe, groan, growl, grump, mourn, whine 6 grouch, grouse, holler, kvetch, mutter, repine, squawk, squeal, yammer 7 grumble, protest, quarrel, whimper 8 sound off 9 bellyache, find fault, make a fuss
about: 6 bemoan, lament, report
constantly: 3 nag 4 carp
to: 5 nag at
complainant: 4 suer
complainer: 3 nag 4 crab 5 grump, scold, shrew 6 critic, grouch, moaner, noodge 7 crybaby, killjoy 9 henpecker, pessimist, termagant
complaining: 5 whiny 6 crabby, lament, whiney 7 fretful, peevish 8 fretsome 9 grumbling, querulous
complaint: 4 ache, beef, fuss, kick, moan 5 cavil, gripe, stink, whine 6 charge, grouse, lament, malady, outcry, squawk 7 ailment, disease, grumble, illness, protest, quarrel, quibble, trouble 8 disorder, jeremiad, sickness, syndrome 9 annoyance, condition, criticism, grievance, infirmity, objection 10 accusation, affliction, discontent
lodge a ~: 3 sue 4 cite 5 blame 6 accuse, allege, charge, impute, indict 7 arraign 8 denounce
__ complaint: 5 file a
complaints: 4 flak 5 flack
list of ~: 6 litany
complaisance: 7 amenity 8 courtesy, kindness 9 deference, gentility 10 cordiality, indulgence
complaisant: 4 easy, kind, mild 5 civil 6 benign, polite 7 amiable, lenient 8 gracious, obliging, tolerant 9 tractable
Compleat Angler, The author: Walton
complement: 3 add, cap 4 crew, foil, mate, unit 5 add to, match, quota 6 amount, fulfil, top off 7 enhance, flatter, fulfill, perfect 8 quantity, round off, round out 9 aggregate, companion, correlate, integrate, remainder 10 accomplish, constitute, consummate, correspond, enrichment
full ~: 4 load
complementary: 7 related, similar 10 reciprocal
complementary __: 4 base, cell 5 angle, color 6 strand
complete: 2 do 3 all, end 4 done, fini, flat, form, full, rank 5 clean, close, crown, ended, gross, mop up, plumb, sew up, sheer, solid, sound, thoro, total, uncut, utter, whole 6 all-out, effect, entire, fill in, finish, fulfil, intact, make up, mature, settle, strict, wind up, wrap up 7 achieve, all over, execute, fill out, fulfill, overall, perfect, perform, play out, plenary, radical, realize, satisfy, through 8 absolute, achieved, carry out, conclude, definite, detailed, finalize, finished, implicit, integral, outright, put to bed, round off, round out, surcease, thorough, wholehog 9 concluded, determine, full-dress, intensive, inviolate, out-and-out, plentiful, searching, terminate, undivided, unlimited, unreduced, wholesale 10 accomplish, consummate, definitive, effectuate, exhaustive, get through, integrated, put through, soup to nuts, supplement, unabridged
combining form: 3 tel- 4 tele-, telo-
easily: 3 ace
name meaning ~: 5 Gomer
sorks: 6 corpus, oeuvre 10 collection, opera omnia
Complete Book of Running, The
author: 4 Fixx
completed: 4 done, over 5 ended, ready 9 fulfilled
in French: 4 fini
to a poet: 3 o'er
completely: 3 all 4 A to Z, just, well 5 fully, in all, plumb, quite, right, sheer, stark 6 bodily, in full, in toto, purely, simply, solely, wholly 7 en masse, in depth, totally, utterly 8 entirely, whole hog 9 all the way, every inch, full blast, inside out, like a book, literally, perfectly, to the hilt 10 absolutely, altogether, thoroughly, to the limit, to the teeth, ultimately
combining form: 3 pan- 4 pano-, pant- 5 panta-, panto-
in Latin: 6 in toto
completeness: 8 entirety
completion: 3 end 4 last 5 close 6 ending, finish, result, windup 8 fruition, maturity 9 execution, finishing 10 attainment, complement, conclusion, expiration, perfection
combining form: 6 teleut- 7 teleuto-
complex: 3 web 4 deep, maze 5 heavy

6 hang-up, knotty, lively, system, thorny, tricky 7 network, tangled 8 abstract, abstruse, fixation, involved, manifold, syndrome, tortuous 9 Byzantine, composite, Daedalean, difficult, elaborate, enigmatic, intricate, obsession, structure 10 circuitous, convoluted, perplexing
not ~: 4 easy 5 clear 6 simple
complex ___: 3 ion 5 plane 6 number 7 machine
___ complex: 6 immune 7 culture, Electra, Oedipus
complexion: 4 cast, glow, look, tint, vein 5 color, guise, style, tinge 6 aspect, makeup, nature 8 coloring, skin tone 9 character, semblance 10 appearance, coloration
dark ~: 5 olive
kind of ~: 4 fair 5 ruddy
woe: 4 acne
complexity: 4 knot 5 snarl 6 muddle 9 confusion, imbroglio, intricacy, labyrinth
points of ~: 4 nodi
compliance: 6 assent 7 consent 9 agreement, deference, obedience, orthodoxy, passivity 10 acceptance, adaptation, concession, conformity, observance, submission
compliant: 3 lax 4 easy, kind, meek, mild, soft, tame 5 loose, mousy 6 broken, docile, gentle, kindly, mousey, pliant 7 clement, dutiful, lenient, obeying, passive, ruthful, sparing, subdued, trained, willing 8 amenable, flexible, gracious, laid-back, lamblike, merciful, obedient, obliging, placable, resigned, tolerant, yielding 9 adaptable, agreeable, assenting, assuasive, easygoing, forgiving, indulgent, malleable, tractable 10 forbearing, governable, law-abiding, manageable, permissive, submissive, unexacting
complicate: 5 mix up, snarl 6 foul up, impede, jumble, mess up, muck up, muddle 7 confuse, snarl up 8 compound, confound, entangle 9 aggravate, convolute, elaborate, interfuse, make waves 10 disarrange, interweave
complicated: 4 deep, hard, ugly 5 fancy, heavy 6 knotty, tricky 7 complex, prickly 8 abstruse, involved, tortuous 10 convoluted, perplexing
make less ~: 4 ease 8 simplify
not ~: 4 easy 6 simple
complication: 3 rub 4 kink, knot, snag 5 mix-up, nodus, snarl 6 hurdle, muddle 7 dilemma, problem 8 drawback, intrigue, obstacle 9 labyrinth
complications: 4 nodi
complicity: 4 plot 9 agreement, collusion 10 connivance, conspiracy, guiltiness
compliment: 4 hail, kudo, laud 5 exalt, extol, honor, toast 6 cajole, extoll, praise 7 acclaim, applaud, commend, flatter, glorify, tribute 8 butter up, cajolery, encomium, flattery, good word, hand it to 9 adulation, celebrate, laudation, panegyric, recommend, sentiment, warm fuzzy 10 admiration, attentions, felicitate, panegyrize
in a way: 3 ape 7 imitate
left-handed ~: 3 cut, dig 4 slam, snub 6 insult, slight, zinger 7 affront, offense, put-down
react to a ~: 4 beam 5 smile
complimentary: 4 free 6 gratis 7 as a gift, glowing 8 costless 9 laudatory, on the cuff 10 for nothing, on the house
close: 4 best, love 5 yours 6 warmly 9 sincerely 10 yours truly
word: 4 cool, fine
complimentary ___: 5 close 7 closing
compliments: 7 regards 8 flattery, respects
comply: 3 bow 4 heed, meet, mind, obey, okay 5 admit, adopt, agree, allow, defer, go for, yield 6 accede, accept, assent, concur, follow, fulfil, give in, give up, listen, relent, submit 7 abide by, approve, conform, consent, fulfill, go along, include, observe, perform, respect 8 adhere to, play ball 9 acquiesce, cooperate 10 come around, give the nod, keep in step, toe the line
with: 4 meet, obey 5 act on, bow to 6 bend to, follow, fulfil 7 abide by, act upon, fulfill, observe, satisfy 8 adhere to, carry out 9 cooperate, recognize, sign off on
component: 3 cog 4 item, link, part, unit 5 piece 6 detail, factor, member 7 element, feature, fitting, fixture, section, segment 9 accessory, elemental, intrinsic 10 ingredient, peripheral
components: 8 workings 9 mechanism
comport: 4 gybe, jibe 5 agree, carry 6 acquit, behave, concur, square 7 conduct 9 harmonize 10 correspond
oneself: 3 act 6 behave
comportment: 3 air 4 mien 7 bearing, conduct, manners 8 behavior, carriage, demeanor
compose: 3 pen 4 calm, draw, form, lull, make 5 allay, build, draft, frame, quell, relax, set up, write 6 author, becalm, create, indite, make up, pacify, solace, soothe 7 appease, assuage, mollify, placate, produce 8 organize 9 construct, fabricate, formulate, harmonize, originate, reconcile, untrouble 10 simmer down, straighten
for printing: 3 set 7 typeset
composed: 4 calm, cool, even, sure 5 quiet, sober, staid, stoic 6 at ease, low-key, mellow, placid, poised, sedate, serene 7 amiable, assured, at peace, equable, pacific, relaxed, stoical, unmoved 8 amicable, carefree, laid-back, peaceful, reserved, together, tranquil 9 collected, easygoing, impassive, possessed, quiescent, temperate, unexcited, unruffled, unworried 10 nonchalant, unagitated, untroubled
be ~ of: 7 contain, include
___-composed: 4 self 7 through
composer: 3 Bax, Cui 4 Arne, Bach, Berg, Cage, Foss, Ives, Kern, Lalo, Orff, Wolf 5 Arlen, Auric, Bizet, Bliss, Bloch, Bruch, Cohan, Crumb, d'Indy, Dukas, Elgar, Fauré, Glass, Gluck, Gould, Grieg, Grofé, Haydn, Holst, Ibert, Lawes, Lehár, Liszt, Loewe, Lully, Ravel, Satie, Sousa, Styne, Verdi, Weber, Weill 6 Arnold, artist, author, Barber, Bartók, Berlin, Boulez, Brahms, Busoni, Carter, Chávez, Chopin, Coates, Cowell, Delius, Dvorák, Enesco, Foster, framer, Franck, Glière, Glinka, Gounod, Handel, Hanson, Harris, Kodály, Krenek, Ligeti, lyrist, Mahler, Mennin, Mozart, Piston, Porter, Previn, Schütz, Taylor, Varèse, Wagner, Walton, Warren, Webern 7 Antheil, Babbitt, Bellini, Berlioz, Borodin, Britten, Copland, Debussy, Delibes, Diamond, Gilbert, Janácek, Menotti, Milhaud, Nielsen, Poulenc, Puccini, Purcell, Rodgers, Rossini, Schuman, Smetana, Strauss, Thomson, Tiomkin, Vivaldi 8 Anderson, Bruckner, Chabrier, Chausson, Clementi, Couperin, Gershwin, Grainger, Korngold, Mascagni, Massenet, musician, Paganini, Respighi, Schubert, Schumann, Scriabin, Sessions, Sibelius, Sondheim, Sullivan, Telemann 9 Beethoven, Bernstein, Buxtehude, Cherubini, Donizetti, Hindemith, MacDowell, Meyerbeer, Offenbach, Prokofiev, Scarlatti, Schönberg, Van Heusen 10 Blitzstein, Gottschalk, Monteverdi, Mussorgsky, Paderewski, Palestrina, Ponchielli, Rubinstein, Saint-Saëns, Stravinsky, Villa-Lobos 11 Leoncavallo, Mendelssohn, Siegmeister, Tchaikovsky 12 Khachaturian, Rachmaninoff, Shostakovich
American: 4 Cage, Ives, Kern 5 Arlen, Bloch, Crumb, Glass, Gould, Grofé, Sousa, Styne 6 Barber, Berlin, Carter, Cowell, Foster, Hanson, Harris, Mennin, Piston, Previn, Taylor, Varèse, Warren 7 Antheil, Babbitt, Copland, Diamond, Menotti, Rodgers, Schuman, Thomson 8 Gershwin, Grainger, Korngold, Sessions, Sondheim 9 Bernstein, Hindemith, MacDowell 10 Blitzstein, Gottschalk 11 Siegmeister
Austrian: 4 Berg, Wolf 5 Haydn, Lehár 6 Krenek, Mahler, Mozart, Webern 7 Strauss 8 Bruckner, Schubert 9 Schönberg
Brazilian: 10 Villa-Lobos
British: 3 Bax 4 Arne 5 Bliss, Elgar, Holst, Lawes 6 Arnold, Coates, Handel, Walton 7 Britten, Gilbert, Purcell 8 Sullivan 15 Vaughan Williams
Czech: 6 Dvorák 7 Janácek, Smetana
Danish: 7 Nielsen 9 Buxtehude
Finnish: 8 Sibelius
French: 4 Lalo 5 Auric, Bizet, d'Indy, Dukas, Fauré, Ibert, Lully, Ravel, Satie 6 Boulez, Delius, Franck, Gounod 7 Berlioz, Debussy, Delibes, Milhaud, Poulenc 8 Chabrier, Chausson, Couperin, Massenet 9 Offenbach 10 Saint-Saëns
German: 4 Bach, Foss, Orff 5 Bruch, Gluck, Weill 6 Brahms, Schütz, Wagner 7 Strauss 8 Schumann, Telemann 9 Beethoven, Meyerbeer 11 Mendelssohn
Hungarian: 5 Liszt 6 Bartók, Kodály
Italian: 5 Verdi 6 Busoni 7 Bellini, Puccini, Rossini, Vivaldi 8 Mascagni, Paganini, Respighi 9 Cherubini, Donizetti 10 Monteverdi, Palestrina, Ponchielli 11 Leoncavallo
Mexican: 6 Chávez
Norwegian: 5 Grieg
org.: 3 BMI 5 ASCAP
output: 4 opus, trio 5 fugue, motet, nonet, opera, rondo, waltz 6 sonata 7 cantata, partite, quartet, toccata 8 concerto, nocturne, oratorio, serenade, symphony
Polish: 6 Chopin 10 Paderewski
Romanian: 6 Enesco, Ligeti
Russian: 3 Cui 6 Glière, Glinka 7 Borodin 8 Scriabin 9 Prokofiev 10 Mussorgsky, Rubinstein, Stravinsky 11 Tchaikovsky 12 Khachaturian, Rachmaninoff, Shostakovich
Scottish: 8 Hamilton
Spanish: 5 Falla 7 Albéniz
Swiss: 8 Honegger
composing: 3 art
composing ___: 4 room 5 stick
composite: 3 mix 5 alloy, blend, mixed, union 6 fusion, hybrid, medley, melded 7 amalgam, blended, complex, grouped, mixture 9 aggregate, immixture, synthesis 10 collective, commixture
composite ___: 4 shot 5 print 6 family, number, school
composition: 4 opus, poem, song, tune, work 5 essay, music, paper, piece, prose, score, setup, theme 6 format, layout, makeup, melody, thesis 7 anatomy, article, content, texture 8 concerto, rhapsody, symphony, treatise 10 literature
literary ~: 4 opus 6 column, sketch 7 article, passage, writing 9 editorial
musical ~: 4 opus, song, trio 5 fugue, motet, nonet, octet, opera, rondo, waltz 6 sonata 7 cantata, octette, partite, quartet, toccata 8 concerto, nocturne, oratorio, serenade, symphony
compositor concern: 6 layout
compos mentis: 4 sane 5 lucid, right, sound
___ compos mentis: 3 non
compost: 3 rot 5 decay, humus, mulch 9 fertilize 10 fertilizer
item: 4 peel, rind
composure: 4 calm, cool, ease 5 poise 6 aplomb, temper 7 balance, dignity 8 calmness, evenness, presence, serenity 9 assurance, fortitude, placidity, sang-froid, stability 10 dispassion, equanimity, moderation, sedateness
compote: 7 dessert 9 preserves
cousin: 3 jam 5 jelly
ingredient: 4 pear 5 apple, fruit
compound: 3 mix 4 make 5 add to, admix, blend, union 6 make up, recipe, worsen 7 amalgam, mixture 8 multiply, solution 9 aggravate, aggregate, intensify, synthesis 10 exacerbate
compound ___: 3 eye 4 leaf, lens, time 5 sugar 6 flower, magnet, number 7 winding 8 fracture
Compound W target: 4 wart
Compoz: 8 sleep aid
alternative: 5 Nytol 6 Unisom 7 Sominex
comprehend: 3 dig, get, see 4 grok, know, tell 5 catch, get it, grasp, savvy, seize, think 6 absorb, fathom, follow, intuit, master, take in 7 cognize, compass, make out, realize 8 conceive, perceive, relate to 9 apprehend, encompass, penetrate, recognize 10 appreciate, assimilate, understand
comprehensibility: 7 clarity
comprehensible: 4 easy 5 clear, lucid, plain, vivid 6 cogent, limpid 7 evident, express, obvious 8 apparent, coherent, distinct, explicit, luculent, luminous, manifest, palpable, readable 9 graspable 10 spelled out
comprehension: 3 ken, wit 4 wits 5 grasp, light 6 acumen, reason, sanity, uptake, wisdom 7 empathy, mastery, purview 8 judgment 10 perception
words of ~: 3 ohs 4 I see
comprehensive: 3 big 4 full, incl., vast, wide 5 broad, large, roomy, total, uncut, whole 6 entire, global 7 blanket, general, generic, overall, plenary, sizable 8 catholic, complete, detailed, far-flung, finished, sizeable, spacious, sweeping, synoptic, thorough 9 capacious, expansive, extensive, generical, universal, unreduced, wholesale, worldwide 10 exhaustive, synoptical, unabridged, widespread
work: 5 summa
comprehensive ___: 4 exam 6 school

comprehensively: **6** wholly **7** in depth, largely, totally
comprehensiveness: **5** scope **7** breadth
Comprende?: **3** see **5** get it
compress: **3** jam, nip, wad **4** cram **5** crush, pinch, press, smush, stuff, wring **6** crunch, digest, narrow, pucker, recede, reduce, shrink, squash **7** abridge, compact, curtail, flatten, shorten, squeeze, tighten, wrinkle **8** abstract, boil down, condense, contract **9** capsulize, constrict, summarize, telescope **10** abbreviate
as a data file: **3** zip
wet ~: **5** stupe
compressed: **3** cut **4** firm, hard **5** brief, dense, scant, short, solid, thick, tight **6** cut off, narrow, packed **7** compact, concise, crammed, crowded, cutback, cut down, reduced, stuffed **8** abridged, cut short, squeezed **9** compacted, condensed, confining, curtailed, shortened **10** abstracted, hard-packed, summarized, synopsized
compressed __: **3** air **6** speech
compression __: **4** wave **5** ratio
comprise: **4** form, have, make, span **5** cover, total **6** embody, imbody, make up, take in **7** add up to, contain, embrace, include, involve **9** consist of, encompass **10** constitute
comprising: **4** incl. **9** including
compromise: **4** bend, deal, pact, risk **6** accord, settle **7** bargain, imperil, work out **8** endanger, trade off **9** agreement, arbitrate, discredit, embarrass, implicate, make a deal, negotiate, prejudice **10** adjustment, concession, conciliate, jeopardize, settlement
don't ~: **6** insist
compromise __: **4** rail **5** joint **6** choice
compromising: **8** moderate
not ~: **5** rigid
Compromising Positions (1985 film)
cast: Edward Herrmann, Judith Ivey, Raul Julia, Susan Sarandon
Compton: **3** Ann **4** city, town **6** Arthur **9** MacKenzie
locale: **10** California
Compton, Arthur: **8** Nobelist **9** physicist
Compton-Burnett, Ivy: **6** author **7** British
comptroller: **3** CPA **6** bursar **8** official **9** treasurer **10** accountant, bookkeeper
task: **5** audit
Comptroller __: **7** General
compulsion: **3** yen **4** need, urge **5** drive, force, mania **6** duress **8** coercion, neurosis, pressure, violence **9** emergency, extortion, liability, necessity, obsession, restraint **10** constraint, obligation
Compulsion (1959 film)
cast: Dean Stockwell, Diane Varsi, Orson Welles
compulsive: **6** forced **7** driving **9** besetting, obsessive **10** compelling, passionate
behavior: **5** habit
compulsively, do: **6** devour
compulsory: **6** forced **7** binding **8** required **9** de rigueur, mandatory, necessary, requisite **10** imperative, inevitable, inexorable, obligatory
compunction: **5** qualm **6** regret **7** remorse, scruple **9** penitence **10** repentance
compunctions, have: **3** rue
compunctious: **5** sorry **6** humble, rueful **8** contrite, penitent **9** chastened, regretful, repentant **10** apologetic, remorseful
CompuServe
acquirer: **3** AOL
correspondence: **5** E-mail
patron: **4** user
computation: **5** count **9** reckoning
compute: **3** add, sum **4** plot, tell **5** add up, count, gauge, tally, total **6** assess, cipher, divide, figure, number, reckon **7** measure **8** keep tabs, multiply, subtract **9** calculate, keep score
computer: **2** PC **3** CPU, Mac **4** iMac, mini **5** clone, micro **6** laptop **7** machine **8** notebook **9** mainframe
abbr.: **3** RAM, ROM
access a ~ network: **5** log in
accessory: **5** mouse
acronym: **3** GUI, ram, ROM **4** gigo, RISC **5** MSDOS
aid: **5** macro
alter, as a ~ image: **5** morph
Apple ~: **3** Mac **4** iMac
attacker: **5** virus
base: **5** octal **6** binary
brain: **3** CPU
bulletin-board manager: **5** sysop
button: **5** reset
capacity: **3** meg
central ~: **4** host
chip element: **5** wafer
chip technology: **3** LSI
classification: **4** mini **5** micro
combining form: **5** cyber-
command: **4** edit, save, sort **5** enter, erase, macro, print **6** delete
communication device: **5** modem
component: **4** chip
correspondence: **5** E-mail
czar: **5** Gates
data: **4** file
data format: **5** ASCII
datum: **3** bit **4** byte
dept.: **3** EDP
device: **5** mouse
display: **6** bit map
dot: **5** pixel
early ~: **5** Eniac **6** abacus
early home ~: **5** Atari
early IBM ~ model: **2** AT, XT
end a ~ session: **6** log off
ender: **3** dom, ese
enthusiast: **4** geek **6** hacker
felon: **6** hacker
fictional ~: **3** Hal
fix a ~ program: **5** debug
fodder: **4** data
gain ~ access: **5** log in
game: **4** Myst **6** Tetris
game award: **5** Arkie
game brand: **3** NES **4** Sega **7** Genesis
geek: **4** guru, nerd, nurd
handheld ~ (abbr.): **3** PDA
hardware company: **5** Intel **6** Iomega
hazard: **5** surge
image file: **3** gif, tif
industry, briefly: **3** ADP
instruction: **5** macro
key: **3** alt, del, end, esc, tab **4** crtl, home, pg dn, pg up **5** arrow, enter, shift **6** delete, escape **7** control **9** backslash, backspace
kids' ~ language: **4** Logo
kind of ~ monitor: **3** LCD
kind of ~ port: **4** SCSI
knockoff: **5** clone
language: **3** ADA, APL, SQL **4** Alef, html, Icon, Java, LISP, Logo, Orca, Perl **5** Algol, Basic, Cecil, COBOL, Dylan, SISAL **6** Delphi, Eiffel, Erlang, Oberon, Pascal, Prolog, Sather, Scheme, Snobol **7** Fortran
lib.: **5** CD/ROM
like some ~ monitors: **5** hi-res **6** low-res
mag: **4** Byte
maker: **3** IBM, NEC **4** Acer, Cray, Dell, Sony **5** Apple **6** Compaq **7** Gateway, Toshiba
marker: **6** cursor
memory: **3** ram, ROM **4** core
message: **5** e-mail, error
monitor: **3** VDT, VGA
need: **3** ptr. **5** input **7** printer
network: **3** LAN
old ~ memory: **4** core
operating system: **3** DOS **4** Unix **5** MSDOS **7** Windows
options: **4** menu
owner: **4** user
perch: **3** lap
pictograph: **4** icon
prefix: **5** cyber-
printer brand: **5** Epson
printer device: **5** laser
printer speed: **3** lpm
problem: **3** bug **6** glitch
program: **6** applet
program function: **6** export
programmer: **5** coder
programmer, perhaps: **4** nerd, nurd
question: **4** fail **5** abort, retry
RAM ~ program: **3** TSR
reseller: **3** OEM
save ~ files: **6** back up
screen: **3** CRT **7** monitor **8** terminal
select, on a ~: **5** click
shortcut: **5** macro
shutdown: **5** crash
sound: **4** beep
speed unit: **3** MHz **4** mips
spreadsheet company: **5** Lotus
start a ~: **4** boot **6** boot up
storage: **4** bits, disc, disk **5** bytes, cache, CD/ROM **6** buffer
terminal (abbr.): **3** VDT
text scanner (abbr.): **3** OCR
timesaver: **5** macro
typeface: **5** Arial
type of home ~: **5** tower
user's annoyance: **4** spam
view a ~ file: **6** access
virus: **4** worm
write a ~ program: **4** code **6** encode
computer __: **3** law **4** nerd **5** crime, error, virus **6** memory, vision **7** science
__ computer: **4** home, host **6** analog, hybrid **7** digital, network, optical
__ Computer: **4** Dell **5** Apple **6** Compaq
computer-assisted __: **6** design, makeup
computerese: **5** lingo **6** jargon
comrade: **3** bro, pal **4** ally, chum, mate **5** amigo, buddy, crony **6** cohort, fellow, frater, friend **7** compeer, partner **8** alter ego, co-worker, intimate, sidekick **9** associate, colleague, confidant **10** bosom buddy, compatriot, well-wisher
comrade in __: **4** arms
comradeship: **5** unity **7** society
Comsat: **9** Early Bird
Comstock: **3** Ada **4** mine
deposit: **3** ore **4** lode
locale: **3** Nev. **6** Nevada
Comstock __: **4** Lode
Comte __: **3** Ory
Comte, Auguste: **6** French **11** philosopher
Comte de la Fere: **5** Athos
Comte Ory composer: **7** Rossini
Comtrex alternative: **5** Afrin **6** Contac, Nyquil, Tavist **7** Actifed, Dayquil, Dristan, Sinutab, Sudafed **8** Benadryl, Dimetapp, Drixoral, TheraFlu **9** Coricidin, Triaminic **10** Robitussin
Comus author: John Milton
Comus composer: **4** Arne
con: **2** do **3** lie, rob **4** anti, bilk, dupe, fool, gull, have, hoax, nick, rook, scam, take, with **5** bunco, cheat, cozen, felon, fraud, grift, learn, lifer, study, trick **6** delude, dupery, fleece, humbug, inmate, manage, outlaw, outwit, rip off, take in **7** against, beguile, chicane, deceive, defraud, loath to, mislead, snooker, swindle, wheedle **8** artifice, averse to, flimflam, hoodwink, internee, inveigle, jailbird, opponent, opposing, outsmart, persuade, pettifog, prisoner, talk into **9** bamboozle, charlatan, chicanery, counter to, deception, disinform, four-flush, hostile to, imposture, sweet-talk, victimize **10** at odds with, imposition, run a game on
cubicle: **4** cell
game: **4** hoax, lure, scam **5** bunco, dodge, fraud, sting **6** dupery, hosing, humbug, racket **7** knavery, swindle **8** trickery **9** deception **10** illegality
like a ~ artist: **5** shady
man: **4** liar **5** cheat, crook, knave, quack, rogue, shark, sneak, taker **6** bad guy, robber **7** grifter, hustler, sharper, sharpie **8** imposter, impostor, swindler **9** hypocrite **10** bamboozler, Harold Hill, scam artist
man's accomplice: **5** shill
opposite: **3** pro
pro and ~: **6** debate
votes: **4** noes **7** nays nos
con __: **3** job, man, men **4** brio, game, moto **5** amore, anima, fuoco **6** artist, dolore, maestà **7** sordino, spirito
Con: **6** Conrad
Con __: **3** Air **6** Edison
Con Air (1997 film)
cast: Steve Buscemi, Nicolas Cage, John Cusack, John Malkovich, Ving Rhames
director: Simon West
Conakry: **4** city, town **7** capital
locale: **6** Guinea
Conan: **6** O'Brien
__ Conan Doyle: **6** Arthur
Conan the Barbarian (1982 film)
cast: Sandahl Bergman, James Earl Jones, Arnold Schwarzenegger
director: John Milius
Conan the Destroyer character: **4** Zula
Conaway: **4** Jeff
conc.
not ~: **3** dil.
__ con carne: **5** chile, chili **6** chilli
concatenate: **4** bind, hook, join, link **5** bound, chain, unite **6** couple, joined, linked, united **7** chained, conjoin, connect **8** seriatim **9** connected, interlink, interlock
concatenation: **5** chain, nexus, queue, train **6** series **8** junction, juncture, sequence
concave: **5** round **6** curved, dented, dished, hollow, sunken **7** sagging **8** indented **9** depressed, excavated **10** scooped out
become ~: **4** sink
concavity: **4** dent, hole **5** curve **10** depression
conceal: **4** bury, hide, mask, palm, stow, veil **5** cache, cloak, couch, cover, shade, stash **6** enveil, harbor, inhume, pocket, screen, shield, shroud **7** blanket, cover up, envelop, harbour, obscure, seclude, secrete, shelter, shut off, shut out **8** disguise, ensconce, enshroud, stow away, suppress, withhold **9** adumbrate, dissemble, whitewash **10** camouflage
a message: **6** encode **7** encrypt
oneself: **4** lurk **6** hole up, lie low
concealed: **4** dark **5** blind, perdu, privy **6** covert, hidden, latent, occult, perdue, secret, unseen **7** furtive, private,

unknown **8** hush-hush, ulterior **9** covered up, incognito, invisible, non-public, out of view, potential, recondite, underhand, unexposed **10** enshrouded, tucked away, undercover, underlying, under wraps, undetected, unviewable
again: 5 rehid
by: 5 neath, under **10** underneath
combining form: 4 adel- **5** adelo-
concealment: 4 mask, veil **5** cover, front **6** hiding **7** eclipse, privacy, secrecy **8** covering, darkness, disguise **9** seclusion **10** camouflage
in ~: 5 doggo
concede: 3 bow, let, own **4** avow, fold, give, quit **5** admit, agree, allow, grant, let on, own up, yield **6** accede, accept, accord, cave in, fess up, give up, reveal **7** confess **8** say uncle **9** recognize, surrender **10** capitulate, understand
conceit: 3 ego **4** idea **5** pride, quirk **6** egoism, vanity **7** egotism, hauteur, swagger **8** self-love, smugness **9** arrogance, immodesty, vainglory **10** narcissism, pretension, stuffiness
conceited: 3 big **4** smug, vain **5** cocky, proud **6** chesty, la-de-da, la-di-da, stuffy **7** fustian, haughty, pompous, stuck-up **8** affected, arrogant, assuming, boastful, cocksure, immodest, lah-di-dah, puffed up, snobbish **9** bigheaded, hubristic, know-it-all, loudmouth **10** big-talking, complacent, egocentric, egoistical, hoity-toity
one: 6 egoist **7** coxcomb, egotist
smile: 5 smirk
conceitedness: 6 hubris, hybris, vanity
conceivable: 6 doable, likely, viable **7** earthly **8** credible, feasible, knowable, possible, workable **9** plausible, potential, practical, thinkable **10** achievable, attainable, imaginable
conceivably: 5 maybe **7** perhaps **8** possibly
conceive: 4 deem, form, plan **5** frame, hatch, think **6** cook up, create, design, device, devise, ideate, make up **7** believe, dream up, imagine, realize, suppose, think up, trump up **8** cogitate, engineer, envisage, envision **9** formulate, originate **10** appreciate, brainstorm, comprehend, mastermind, understand
of: 5 fancy **6** ideate, invent **7** picture **9** visualize
__-conceived: 3 ill
concentrate: 3 fix, put **4** join, mass, meet **5** amass, focus, merge, slant, spend, think, unite **6** center, fixate, gather, huddle, listen, muster, shrink, zero in **7** abridge, cluster, collect, compact **8** assemble, boil down, coalesce, compress, condense, converge
on: 7 address **8** mull over
concentrated: 4 firm **5** solid, thick **6** potent, robust, strong **7** compact, crammed, crowded, intense **8** straight **9** condensed, undivided **10** compressed
concentrating: 6 intent
concentration: 4 army, care, game, heap, mass **5** array, group, horde, swarm **7** cluster **8** card game, strength **9** specialty
alias: 6 memory
field of ~: 5 forte **9** specialty
Concentration: 8 game show
conjunction: 3 oar
genre: game show
host: Hugh Downs
objective: 5 match
puzzle: 5 rebus
Concepción: 4 city, Dave, town
locale: 5 Chile
river: 6 Bíobío
concept: 4 idea, seed, view, word **5** image, thing **6** notion, theory, vision **7** thought **10** brainchild, hypothesis, impression, perception
combining form: 4 ideo-
form a ~: 5 think **6** ideate
concept __: 3 art
__ concept: 4 high
conception: 4 idea, view **5** image, start **6** design, notion, origin, outset, theory, vision **7** genesis, infancy, inkling, opinion, reading, thought **8** creation, ideality **9** beginning, cognition, formation, imagining, invention, launching **10** cogitating, envisaging, exposition, impression, initiation
conceptual __: 3 art **6** artist **7** realism
conceptualize: 6 ideate **7** imagine **10** brainstorm
concern: 3 car, job, TLC **4** care, fear, firm, heed, part, sake **5** alarm, house, query, refer, stake, touch, worry **6** absorb, affair, bear on, bother, burden, domain, moment, outfit, regard, regret, relate, unease **7** anxiety, apply to, company, disturb, emotion, gravity, involve, pertain, project, thought, trouble, valuing **8** bear upon, business, deal with, disquiet, distress, function, interest, province, relate to **9** attention, curiosity, pertain to, relevance **10** enterprise, importance, solicitude
exclamation: 4 alas, oh-oh, uh-oh, yipe **5** alack, yikes, yipes
__ concern: 5 going
concerned: 5 antsy, itchy, jumpy, tense, upset **6** caring, loving, pacing, polite, uneasy **7** anxious, at stake, fearful, in a stew, jittery, keyed up, nervous, restive, uptight, worried **8** restless, skittish **9** attentive, disturbed, excitable, exercised, ill at ease, perturbed **10** distraught, distressed, high-strung, implicated, interested, solicitous, thoughtful
be ~: 4 care **9** give a darn
be ~ about: 4 fear
one: 5 carer
one ~ with (suffix): 3 -eer
response: 5 I care
with: 4 into **5** about
concerning: 4 as to, in re **5** about, anent, as for **6** toward **7** towards **8** relative, relevant **9** as regards
this: 6 hereof
concert: 3 gig **4** show **6** accord, unison **7** harmony, recital **8** musicale **9** agreement **10** jam session
act in ~: 4 join **5** unite **6** club up
bonus: 6 encore
ender: 5 going **6** finale, master **8** mistress
hall: 5 odeon, odeum, venue **7** theater, theatre
hall equipment: 3 amp
halls: 4 odea
in ~: 5 as one, at one **7** jointly **8** in unison, mutually, together **10** coactively, harmonious
income: 4 gate, take
instrument: 5 grand, piano
work: 5 piece
concert __: 5 grand, party, pitch
__ concert: 3 pop **4** pops **7** chamber
concerted: 5 as one, joint **6** mutual, united **7** grouped **9** unanimous, undivided **10** agreed upon, collective, concurrent, synchronal
concertedly: 8 together
concertina: 8 keyboard **10** instrument
concerto: 5 music, piece
conclusion: 4 coda
instrument: 4 harp, horn, oboe **5** piano, viola
movement: 5 rondo
concerto __: 6 grosso
Concerto __: 3 in F
__ Concerto: 7 Emperor
__ Concerto, A: 6 Lover's
Concerto for Orchestra composer: 6 Bartók
Concerto for the Left Hand composer: 5 Ravel
Concerto in F composer: 8 Gershwin
concession: 3 sop **4** bone **6** assent, patent **7** buyback **8** discount, giveback, rollback, yielding **9** admission, agreement, allowance, privilege, surrender **10** acceptance, adjustment, compliance, compromise, confession, indulgence, permission
ender: 4 aire
concessions for, make: 5 allow
Concetta: 5 Tomei
conch: 5 shell **8** seashell
kin: 6 limpet
liner: 5 nacre
concha: 4 apse, bone
locale: 3 ear **4** nose
Conchata: 7 Ferrell
conchiglie: 5 pasta
__ Conchita Alonso: 5 Maria
Conchos: 5 river
locale: 6 Mexico
concierge place: 5 hotel, lobby
conciliate: 6 pacify, soothe **7** appease, assuage, mediate, mollify, patch up, placate, reunite, satisfy, sweeten, win over **9** arbitrate, intervene, reconcile, untrouble **10** compromise
conciliation: 5 peace **6** pardon **7** redress **9** mediation
conciliator: 3 ref, ump **6** umpire **7** referee
conciliatory: 6 dovish, irenic, polite **8** irenical, yielding **9** peaceable
move: 8 overture
concise: 4 curt **5** brief, crisp, pithy, short, terse, tight **6** gnomic **7** compact, laconic **8** abridged, succinct **9** condensed **10** boiled down, compressed, synopsized, to the point
concisely: 7 in short
describe ~: 5 sum up
conciseness: 7 brevity
conclave: 5 synod **6** caucus, powwow **7** council, meeting, reunion **8** assembly, congress **9** gathering
conclude: 2 do **3** end, fix **4** draw, halt, make, quit, rule, stop **5** cease, close, end up, glean, infer, judge, sew up, sum up, think **6** assume, decide, deduce, effect, expire, finish, fulfil, gather, reason, reckon, run out, settle, wind up, wrap up **7** achieve, adjourn, break up, fulfill, imagine, play out, presume, pull off, resolve, suppose, surmise, suspect, work out **8** carry out, complete, dispatch, finalize, pack it in, round off, round out, surcease, theorize **9** culminate, determine, terminate **10** accomplish, bring about, call it a day, consummate, put through, understand
concluded: 3 o'er, set **4** done, fini, over **7** through **8** complete **9** fulfilled
concluding: 4 last **5** final **6** latter **8** eventual, terminal, ultimate **10** definitive
part: 4 coda **5** envoi **6** finale
conclusion: 3 end **4** stop, tail **5** close, finis **6** belief, ending, epilog, finale, finish, payoff, period, result, sequel, upshot, windup, wrap-up **7** closure, finding, opinion, outcome, surmise, thought, verdict **8** curtains, decision, judgment, last word, surcease, terminus **9** agreement, cessation, corollary, deduction, diagnosis, discovery, induction, inference **10** bottom line, completion, conjecture, conviction, denouement, desistance, expiration, hypothesis, resolution, settlement
come to a ~: 6 decide, settle
come to a hasty ~: 4 leap **8** misjudge
draw a ~: 6 deduce, reason
in ~: 4 last, thus **6** lastly **7** finally **9** at the last **10** ultimately
preceder: 4 ergo **5** hence
ultimate ~: 6 end-all
__ conclusion...: 4 So in
conclusions, jumping to: 4 rash **5** hasty **8** careless, heedless, reckless **9** foolhardy, hotheaded, impetuous, imprudent, impulsive, overhasty **10** headstrong, incautious
conclusive: 3 net, ult. **4** firm, last, sure **5** clean, clear, final, valid **6** all-out, cogent **7** assured, certain, decided, flat-out, for sure, obvious, settled, telling **8** absolute, accurate, critical, deciding, decisive, definite, emphatic, forceful, in the bag, official, positive, resolute, resolved, ultimate, verified **9** clinching, effectual, revealing **10** compelling, convincing, definitive, determined, guaranteed, inarguable, unarguable, undeniable, undoubtful, unswerving, unwavering
conclusively: 6 surely
concoct: 3 lay, lie **4** brew, form, plan, plot **5** frame, hatch, weave **6** cook up, create, design, devise, invent, make up **7** dream up, prepare, think up, trump up **8** contrive, engineer, simulate **9** fabricate, formulate, improvise, originate
concocted: 4 fake, made **5** bogus, false **10** fictitious
concoction: 3 mix **4** brew, tale, work **5** blend **7** coinage, mixture **8** creation **9** invention
concomitant: 7 related
concord: 4 pact **5** amity, peace, union, unity **6** accord, treaty, unison **7** compact, entente, harmony, rapport **8** calmness, goodwill, protocol, serenity **9** agreement, congruity, consensus, propriety, unanimity **10** friendship, solidarity
Concord: 3 AMC, car, red **4** auto, city, town, wine **5** grape **8** Plymouth
county: 9 Merrimack
locale: 10 California
relative: 5 Gamay, pinot, Tokay **6** Merlot **7** Catawba, Niagara **8** Cabernet, malvasia, muscatel **9** muscadine, Sauvignon, zinfandel **10** Chardonnay
river: 9 Merrimack
Concord __: 5 coach, grape
concordance: 6 unison **9** congruity
concordant: 6 united **9** according, congruous, consonant, unanimous **10** harmonious
concordat: 4 pact **6** accord, treaty **7** charter, compact, concord **8** contract, protocol **10** convention
Concorde: 3 car, jet, SST **4** auto, font **5** plane **8** airplane, Chrysler, typeface
home: 6 hangar
take the ~: 3 fly
Concord Hymn: 4 poem
author: 7 Emerson
Concordia University
location: 6 Canada **8** Montreal
Concord Sonata composer: 4 Ives
__ concours: 4 hors
Concours: 3 car **4** auto **5** Chevy **9** Chevrolet **10** automobile

concourse: 4 hall, path, road 5 crowd, foyer, group 6 avenue, street, throng 7 meeting, passage, session 8 assembly, junction, juncture 9 boulevard, gathering, multitude 10 assemblage, collection, concursion, confluence, passageway

concrete: 3 set 4 firm, hard, real 5 rigid, rocky, solid, stony 6 actual, cement, steely, stoney 7 factual, precise 8 accurate, definite, detailed, explicit, indurate, material, palpable, physical, positive, specific, tangible 9 touchable 10 inarguable, unimagined
foundation: 4 slab
kin: 6 cement
lay ~: 4 pave
like fresh ~: 5 unset
make ~: 8 solidify
mixer: 5 paver
set in ~: 9 permanent
smoothed ~: 5 luted
strengthener: 5 rebar

concrete ___: 4 noun, poet 5 mixer, music 6 number, poetry

concreteness: 7 reality

concretion: 4 mass

concur: 3 fit, nod 4 gybe, heed, jibe 5 agree, unite, yield 6 accede, accord, assent, comply, league 7 approve, comport, consent, go along 8 coincide 9 acquiesce, cooperate 10 give the nod
with: 4 okay 5 admit, adopt, allow, go for 6 accept, assent 7 approve, include, welcome 8 stand for 9 recognize, sign off on

concurrence: 5 unity 6 accord, assent 8 approval 9 agreement, congruity, proximity 10 solidarity
word of ~: 3 yea 4 amen 5 ditto
words of ~: 5 as am I, me too

concurrent: 6 coeval 9 concerted, confluent 10 coexistent, coexisting, coincident, coinciding, collateral, compatible, consistent, convergent, converging, harmonious, incidental, like-minded, synchronal

concurrently: 8 meantime, together 9 at one time, meanwhile 10 hand in hand
with: 6 during

concurring: 5 at one 6 coeval 9 agreeable, congruent 10 coincident

concursion: 4 hall, path, road 5 crowd, foyer, group, union 6 avenue, street, throng 7 meeting, passage, session 8 assembly, junction, juncture 9 boulevard, concourse, gathering, multitude 10 assemblage, collection, confluence, passageway

concuss: 7 agitate, shake up

concussion: 3 jar 4 blow 5 shock 6 impact 9 buffeting, collision, explosion

Condé: 4 Nast 6 Maryse

condemn: 3 hit, rap 4 damn, defy, doom, hiss 5 blame, blast, chide, curse, decry, knock, sneer 6 outlaw, rail at 7 censure, convict, deplore, dislike, reprove, upbraid 8 denounce, penalize, reproach, sentence 9 castigate, criticize, deprecate, excoriate, fulminate, fustigate, imprecate, proscribe, reprehend 10 come down on, vituperate

condemnation: 3 hit 4 slam 5 blame, knock, odium 6 rebuke, tirade 7 censure 8 sentence

condemned: 6 doomed 7 accurst 8 accursed

condensation: 3 dew 4 mist, rain 5 brief, frost, vapor 6 digest, précis 7 epitome, summary 8 abstract, synopsis

condensation ___: 5 point, trail 7 nucleus

condense: 3 cut 4 edit, trim 5 press, prune, recap, sum up 6 decoct, digest, narrow, recede, reduce, shrink 7 abridge, compact, curtail, distill, shorten, stiffen, thicken, tighten 8 abstract, boil down, compress, contract, solidify 9 capsulize, summarize, synopsize, telescope 10 abbreviate
on a surface: 6 adsorb

condensed: 3 abr., cut 4 firm 5 dense, short, solid, terse, thick 6 cut off, gnomic, packed 7 capsule, compact, concise, crammed, crowded, cut back, cut down, partial, reduced, sketchy, stuffed 8 abridged, cut short, digested, squeezed, succinct 9 compacted, curtailed, shortened 10 abstracted, compressed, hard-packed, summarized, synopsized, unfinished

condensed ___: 4 milk

condescend: 5 agree, deign, lower, stoop, yield 6 see fit 9 acquiesce, patronize, vouchsafe 10 talk down to

condescending: 5 lofty 6 lordly, snobby, snooty 8 arrogant, cavalier, snobbish, superior
type: 4 snob 5 snoot

condescendingly, behave: 5 deign

condescension: 5 pride 7 hauteur 9 patronage

condign: 4 fair, just, meet 5 right 6 lawful, proper 7 fitting 8 deserved, rightful, suitable

condiment: 4 NaCl, salt 5 caper, chili, gravy, onion, salsa, sauce, spice 6 catsup, garlic, pepper, relish, sambal, wasabi 7 canella, catchup, cayenne, chutney, ketchup, mustard, paprika, saffron, zedoary 8 capsicum, dressing, turmeric 9 flavoring, rocambole, seasoning
holder: 5 cruet 6 caster

___ con dios: 4 Vaya

condition: 2 if 4 case, must, term, tone, trim 5 adapt, catch, enure, equip, inure, light, phase, shape, state, train 6 fettle, health, malady, modify, plight, season, status, tone up 7 ailment, break in, build up, disease, fitness, illness, posture, prepare, proviso, qualify, quality, shape up, sharpen, specify 8 accustom, indurate, position, sickness, standing, syndrome 9 brainwash, complaint, determine, essential, exception, exemption, fine print, habituate, infirmity, necessity, provision, requisite, situation, status quo, stipulate, toughen up 10 appearance, limitation, occurrence, reputation, sine qua non, small print
best ~: 4 pink
general ~: 6 repair
get into better ~: 7 restore
good ~: 5 order 6 health, kilter 7 fitness
in good ~: 3 fit 4 hale, neat 5 hardy, right, sound 7 healthy 9 untouched
in poor ~: 5 ratty, unfit 6 beat-up 10 ramshackle
on ~: 2 if 9 providing
out of ~: 4 soft 6 flabby 7 run-down
perfect ~: 4 mint
physical ~: 6 health
suffix: 3 -dom, -ism, -ure 4 -ence, -ness, -ship

___ condition: 4 mint

conditional: 4 iffy 7 subject 8 relative 9 qualified, tentative
word: 3 may
words: 4 if so

conditioned ___: 6 reflex

___-conditioned: 3 ill

conditioner: 5 rinse
ingredient: 4 aloe

___ conditioner: 3 air 4 soil

conditioning: 7 workout 8 exercise

conditions: 3 ifs 5 terms 7 strings
under different ~: 9 otherwise

condo: 3 apt. 4 flat, home, unit 5 abode, house 6 duplex 7 domicil, habitat, housing, shelter 8 domicile, lodgment, quarters 9 apartment, residence
asset: 4 view
kin: 4 co-op

condole: 6 solace 7 hearten

condolence: 6 solace 10 compassion

condominium
see condo

Condominium author: MacDonald

Condon: 5 Eddie 7 Richard

condonable: 7 tenable 9 excusable 10 defensible, remittable, vindicable

condone: 6 excuse, wink at 7 forgive, let ride 8 overlook, stand for, tolerate 9 put up with

condor: 4 bird, coin 5 money 7 vulture
country: 4 Peru
emulate a ~: 3 fly 4 soar
home: 4 aery, eyry, nest 5 aerie, eyrie

___ condor: 6 Andean

conduce: 4 lead, tend 7 redound 9 gravitate

conducive: 9 accessory, efficient, promotive 10 convenient
be ~ (to): 4 tend
to: 3 for

conduct: 3 act, run, way 4 care, form, head, hold, keep, lead, mien, rule, take, wage 5 bring, carry, guide, pilot, steer, usher 6 acquit, behave, charge, convey, convoy, deport, direct, escort, govern, handle, manage, manner, pursue, record, stance 7 bearing, carry on, channel, comport, control, manners, operate, oversee, posture, preside 8 attitude, behavior, carriage, chaperon, demeanor, engineer, guidance, handling, morality, organize, regulate, shepherd, transact, transmit 9 accompany, chaperone, direction, officiate, oversight, prosecute, supervise, transport, treatment 10 administer, deportment, discipline, leadership, management, principles, ride herd on
disorderly ~: 4 riot
oneself: 6 behave
path of virtuous ~: 3 Tao

conductance unit: 3 mho 5 abmho

___ Conduct Medal: 4 Good

conductor: 3 Oue 4 Böhm, Foss, Graf, Muti 5 Adler, Boult, Busch, Engel, Faith, guide, Krips, Masur, Mehta, metal, Morel, Münch, Ozawa, Rudel, Solti, Szell 6 Abbado, Boulez, carman, Dorati, Hillis, Iturbi, Krauss, Kunzel, leader, Levine, Maazel, Mahler, Perlea, Previn, Reiner, Rudolf, Thomas, Walter 7 Beecham, De Waart, Fiedler, Karajan, Kleiber, Kubelik, maestro, Monteux, Ormandy, Salonen, Sargent 8 Ansermet, Caldwell, Damrosch, director, Goossens, Lockhart, Marriner, musician, Smallens, Whiteman, Williams 9 Barenboim, Bernstein, Goldovsky, Klemperer, Leibowitz, Leinsdorf, Markevich, Pelletier, Rodzinski, Rosenthal, Schippers, Steinberg, Stokowski, Toscanini 10 Barbirolli, Comissiona, Mantonvani, supervisor 11 Furtwängler, Kostelanetz, Mitropoulos 12 Koussevitzky
American: 5 Engel, Faith 6 Hillis, Kunzel, Levine, Maazel, Previn, Thomas 7 Fiedler 8 Caldwell, Lockhart, Whiteman, Williams 9 Barenboim, Bernstein, Rodzinski, Schippers, Steinberg, Stokowski
Austrian: 4 Böhm, Graf 5 Adler, Krips, Rudel 6 Krauss, Mahler 7 Karajan, Kleiber 9 Leinsdorf
British: 5 Boult 7 Beecham, Sargent 8 Goossens, Marriner 10 Barbirolli
Canadian: 9 Pelletier
cheer: 5 bravo
concern: 5 tempo
cry: 6 aboard 9 all aborad
Czech: 5 Adler 7 Kubelik
Dutch: 7 De Waart
electrical ~: 4 wire 5 shunt 6 dynode
Finnish: 7 Salonen
French: 5 Morel, Münch 6 Boulez 7 Monteux 9 Leibowitz, Rosenthal
German: 4 Foss 5 Busch, Masur 6 Rudolf, Walter 8 Damrosch 9 Klemperer 11 Furtwängler
good ~: 5 metal
Greek: 11 Mitropoulos
heat ~: 4 coil
Hungarian: 5 Solti, Szell 6 Dorati, Reiner 7 Ormandy
Indian: 5 Mehta
information ~: 5 nerve
Italian: 4 Muti 6 Abbado 9 Toscanini 10 Mantonvani
Japanese: 3 Oue 5 Ozawa
places: 5 podia
Romanian: 6 Perlea 10 Comissiona
Russian: 8 Smallens 9 Goldovsky, Markevich 11 Kostelanetz 12 Koussevitzky
Spanish: 6 Iturbi
stick: 5 baton
Swiss: 8 Ansermet

___-conduct pass: 4 safe

conduit: 4 duct, main, pipe, tube 5 canal, drain, flume, sewer, spout 6 artery, course, gutter 7 channel, culvert, passage 8 aqueduct, pipeline

cone: 5 shape 7 volcano 8 strobile
bearer: 3 fir 4 pine, tree 5 alder, cedar, larch
British ice-cream ~: 6 cornet
half a ~ in geometry: 5 nappe
partner: 3 rod
shape: 6 funnel
traffic ~: 5 pylon
unit: 5 scoop

cone ___: 5 plant, shell, snail 6 pepper

___ cone: 4 nose, pine, snow, tail, wind 5 pitch, Seger, sugar 6 cinder, growth 7 shatter, spatter

Cone: 5 David 6 hurler 7 pitcher

___ Cone: 5 Honey

___-Cone: 3 Sno

Coneheads (1993 film)
cast: Dan Aykroyd, Michelle Burke, Jane Curtin

conenose: 3 bug 6 insect

cone of ___: 7 silence

___-cone pine: 3 big

cone-shaped heater: 4 etna

Conestoga ___: 5 wagon

coney: 3 fur 4 fish, pika 5 hyrax 6 dassie, rabbit

Coney Island (1943 film)
cast: Betty Grable, George Montgomery, Cesar Romero
director: Walter Lang

conf.: 3 mtg. 4 sess.

confab: 3 mtg. 4 chat, meet, talk, word 6 dialog, huddle, powwow 7 council, meeting 8 assembly, chinfest, chitchat, dialogue 9 tête-à-tête 10 convention, discussion

confabulate: 3 rap, yak, yap 4 chat, talk 6 huddle, parley 7 palaver 8 chitchat, converse 10 chew the fat

confection: 3 jam, mix 4 cake, kiss 5 candy, fudge, halva, lolly, sweet, torte 6 bonbon, halvah, kuchen, pastry 7 halavah, mixture 8 gumdrops 9 jelly roll, preserves, sweetmeat

confectioner: **4** chef
confectioners' ___: **5** sugar
confederacy: **4** ring **5** union **6** league **8** alliance
Confederacy: **5** Dixie
opponent: **5** North, Union
Confederacy of Dunces, A author: **5** Toole
confederate: **4** ally, band **5** party, unify, unite **6** allied, league, united **7** abetter, abettor, comrade, conjoin, partner **8** combined
Confederate
general: **3** Lee **5** Early **6** Stuart **7** Forrest, Jackson **10** Beauregard, Longstreet
soldier: **3** reb **4** gray, grey
state: **3** Ala., Fla., Tex. **4** Miss., N. Car., S. Car. **5** Texas **7** Alabama, Ark. Tenn., Florida, Georgia **8** Arkansas, Virginia **9** Louisiana, Tennessee **11** Mississippi **13** North Carolina, South Carolina
confederated: **6** united
confederation: **4** bloc **5** union, unity **6** league **7** society **8** alliance **9** coalition **10** fraternity
confer: **3** gab **4** give, show, talk, vest **5** award, endow, grant, speak, spend, trust **6** accord, bestow, donate, heap on, huddle, impart, parley, powwow **7** commune, consult, discuss, palaver, present **8** converse **9** bat around, discourse, negotiate, touch base **10** brainstorm, contribute, deliberate
ender: **4** ence
upon: **4** give **5** award
with: **3** see **4** meet
conference: **4** chat **5** forum **6** Big Ten, dialog, huddle, league, Pac Ten, parley, powwow **7** Big East, council, hearing, meeting, seminar, session **8** assembly, colloquy, congress, dialogue **9** gathering, interview, symposium **10** colloquium, convention, discussion, groupthink, round robin, round table
in ~: **4** busy
questioners: **5** media, press
record: **4** proc.
site: **5** hotel
starter: **5** video
conference ___: **4** call, room
___ conference: **4** news **5** press **6** summit
conferral: **5** award
confess: **3** own **4** aver, avow, bare, sing, talk, tell **5** admit, allow, grant, let on, own up **6** affirm, assert, attest, avouch, fess up, reveal **7** concede, confirm, declare, divulge, lay bare, own up to, profess **8** disclose, unburden **9** come clean, recognize
confession: **5** story **6** avowal, exposé **9** admission, allowance, assenting, assertion, narration, statement, utterance **10** concession, disclosure, divulgence, profession, recitation, revelation, unbosoming
starter: **3** mea
words of ~: **4** I did **6** I did it **7** it was me
Confession (1937 film)
cast: Kay Francis, Basil Rathbone
director: Joe May
confessional
subject: **3** sin
visitor: **4** ruer **6** atoner
___ Confessions: **4** True
Confessions author: Rousseau
Confessions of Boston Blackie (1941 film)
cast: Harriet Hilliard, Chester Morris
director: Edward Dmytryk
Confessions of Felix Krull author: Thomas Mann
Confessions of Nat Turner, The
author: William Styron
confessor: **6** father **8** minister
father ~: **6** priest
___ confessor: **6** father
confetti, make: **5** rip up, shred
confidant: **3** pal **4** ally, chum **5** amigo, buddy, crony **6** cohort, friend **7** adviser, advisor, comrade **8** alter ego, intimate, roommate, sidekick **9** associate, boyfriend, colleague, companion **10** bosom buddy, compatriot
confidante: **3** pal **4** ally, chum **5** amigo, buddy, crony **6** cohort, friend **7** adviser, advisor, comrade **8** intimate, roommate, sidekick **9** associate, colleague, companion **10** bosom buddy, compatriot, girlfriend, well-wisher
confide: **4** talk **5** admit **6** impart, reveal **7** breathe, entrust, intrust, whisper **8** disclose, relegate, unburden
in: **5** trust
confidence: **4** cool, dash, ease, grit **5** faith, heart, nerve, pluck, poise, spunk, stock, trust **6** aplomb, belief, credit, daring, mettle, morale **7** bravery, courage, secrecy **8** backbone, boldness, credence, optimism, reliance, security, sureness, tenacity **9** assurance, brashness, certainty, fortitude, hardihood, impudence **10** conviction, dependance, dependence, equanimity, expectancy, resolution
betray a ~: **4** blab, talk, tell
game: **4** hoax, lure, scam **5** bunco, dodge, fraud, sting **6** dupery, hosing, humbug, racket **7** knavery, swindle **8** trickery **9** deception
give ~ to: **6** affirm, assure **7** hearten **8** reassure
have ~ in: **4** rely **5** trust **6** bank on **7** swear by **8** depend on
have ~ (in): **7** believe
in ~: **8** secretly
confidence ___: **3** man **4** game **5** limit
___-confidence: **4** self
confident: **4** bold, sure **5** brave **6** secure, upbeat **7** assured, certain, hopeful, valiant **8** cocksure, fearless, intrepid, positive, sanguine, unafraid **9** assertive, collected, convinced, dauntless, expectant, expecting, presuming, satisfied, undaunted, unfearing **10** complacent, counting on, courageous, optimistic, undismayed
be ~: **6** assert
not ~: **3** shy **5** timid
overly ~: **5** cocky
___-confident: **4** self
confidential: **5** inner, privy **6** closet, inside, inward, secret **7** inwards, private **8** backdoor, esoteric, hush-hush, intimate, personal **10** privileged
Confidential Agent (1945 film)
cast: Lauren Bacall, Charles Boyer
confidentiality: **7** privacy, secrecy
confidentially: **7** sub rosa **9** between us, entre nous **10** off the cuff
confiding: **5** naive
configuration: **3** cut **4** form **5** setup, shape **6** design, format, sketch **7** contour, outline **9** structure
___ Configuration, The: **5** Ninth
confine: **3** box, pen, tie **4** bind, cage, hold, jail, shut **5** bound, box in, chain, cramp, fence, hedge, hem in, hutch, lay up, limit, tie up **6** begird, cage in, coop up, detain, encage, encase, fetter, ground, hamper, hinder, hogtie, immure, incase, intern, lock up, remand, shut in, shut up **7** delimit, enclose, impound, inclose, isolate, put away, repress, seclude **8** bottle up, hold back, imprison, restrain, restrict, sentence, straiten, surround **9** constrain
to home: **6** ground
confined: **4** pent, sick **5** bound, close, local, on ice, stied **6** in jail, jailed, laid up, pent-up, shut in **7** captive, limited **8** fenced in, hemmed in **9** bedridden
confinement: **4** jail **5** bonds **6** arrest, bounds, chains, prison **7** control, custody **8** solitude **9** restraint, servitude
confines: **4** area, term **5** limit, orbit, range, scope, sweep **6** bounds, region **7** borders, compass, purview, terrain **8** environs **9** perimeter, periphery, territory **10** boundaries
confining: **5** close, scant **6** narrow **7** cramped, limited **8** limiting **10** compressed, contracted, oppressive, restricted
confirm: **2** OK **4** aver, avow, back, okay, seal, sign, test **5** admit, check, prove, vouch **6** affirm, assure, attest, ensure, look up, ratify, settle, uphold, verify **7** approve, bear out, certify, confess, endorse, indorse, justify, sustain, witness **8** check out, evidence, make sure, sanction, validate, vouch for **9** ascertain, establish, guarantee, recommend, respond to, sign off on **10** strengthen
confirmation: **2** OK **3** nod **4** okay, rite, seal, test **5** check, proof **6** assent, avowal **7** consent, go-ahead **8** approval, evidence, sanction **9** collation, sacrament, testimony
exclamation: **5** uh-huh
confirmed: **3** set **4** true **5** tough, valid **6** actual **8** habitual, verified **9** customary, hard-shell, ingrained **10** accustomed, deep-rooted, deep-seated, entrenched, guaranteed, habituated, inveterate, unimagined
confiscate: **4** grab, take **5** seize **6** assume **7** capture, impound, preempt **8** arrogate **9** sequester **10** commandeer
confiscation: **7** seizure **8** takeover
confiture: **9** preserves
conflagrant: **5** fiery **6** ablaze, aflame **7** flaming
conflagrate: **4** burn
conflagration: **4** fire, pyre **5** blaze **7** bonfire, burning, flaming, inferno **8** wildfire
conflate: **4** meld **7** combine
conflict: **3** row, war **4** bout, duel, feud, flap, fray, tilt **5** argue, brush, clash, fight, jihad, run-in, scrap, set-to **6** action, battle, breach, combat, differ, fracas, hot war, ruckus, strife, tussle **7** collide, contend, contest, discord, dispute, dissent, diverge, quarrel, quibble, rivalry, warfare **8** argument, bad blood, disagree, disunity, fighting, friction, skirmish, struggle, tug-of-war, variance **9** animosity, collision, encounter, hostility, interfere, lock horns, take issue **10** antagonism, contention, difference, disharmony, dissension, dissonance, engagement, opposition
in armed ~: **5** at war
site: **5** arena
1910s: **3** WWI
1940s ~: **4** WWII
___ conflict: **4** role **5** armed, class
conflicting: **5** rival **6** at odds, unlike **7** adverse, counter, opposed **8** clashing, contrary, opposing, opposite **10** face-to-face
confluence: **5** union **7** meeting **8** junction, juncture **9** concourse, gathering, multitude **10** assemblage, concursion
confluent: **6** branch, feeder **7** joining, meeting **8** blending, mingling **9** tributary **10** concurrent, synchronal
conform: **2** go **3** fit **4** gybe, heed, jibe, meet, suit, tune **5** adapt, agree, defer, fit in, match, tally **6** adhere, adjust, behave, cohere, comply, listen, orient, square **7** abide by, consent, observe **8** dovetail **9** acclimate, acquiesce, harmonize, play along, reconcile **10** assimilate, correspond, toe the line
don't: **6** differ **7** dissent **8** disagree
to: **4** mind, obey **5** act on **6** accept, follow, fulfil **7** abide by, act upon, fulfill, respect, satisfy **9** agree with
(with): **2** go **6** square
conformable: **5** alike **6** docile, proper **7** similar **8** amenable, obedient
conformation: **5** shape **6** nature **7** outline **9** structure
conforming: **4** like **6** in step **7** correct **9** accordant, befitting, congruent
conformist: **5** sheep, toady **6** yes man **7** Babbitt **8** emulator, orthodox
starter: **3** non
Conformist, The (1971 film)
cast: Dominique Sanda, Stefania Sandrelli, Jean-Louis Trintignant
director: Bernardo Bertolucci
conformity: **4** tune **7** harmony, keeping **8** likeness, symmetry **9** agreement, coherence, congruity, obedience, orthodoxy **10** allegiance, compliance, congruence, consonance, exactitude, observance, similarity, submission
confound: **3** vex **4** dash, daze, faze, lose, stun **5** abash, addle, amaze, befog, elude, floor, mix up, put on, rebut, stimy, stump, stymy, throw, upset **6** baffle, bemuse, defeat, foul up, jumble, muddle, puzzle, rattle, stymie **7** becloud, bedevil, confuse, flummox, fluster, mislead, mistake, mortify, mystify, nonplus, perplex, perturb, stagger, stupefy, unhinge, unnerve **8** astonish, befuddle, bewilder, disorder, surprise, throw off, unsettle **9** discomfit, disorient, overwhelm **10** complicate, disconcert
confounded: **4** damn **5** blank, fazed, sheer **6** darned **7** abashed, at a loss, fuddled, hateful **8** mistaken, unstrung **9** execrable
Confound it!: **4** dang, darn, drat
confrere: **3** pal **4** mate **5** amigo, equal **6** cohort **9** colleague
Confrey: **3** Zez
confront: **4** cope, defy, face, meet **5** brave **6** accost, accuse, breast, oppose, resist, tackle **8** face up to **9** challenge, encounter, pitch into, stand up to, withstand **10** meet head on
confrontation: **5** brush, clash, fight, mix-up, run-in, scene, set-to **6** affray, battle, crisis **7** dispute **8** conflict, defiance, showdown, skirmish **9** encounter
confronter: **5** facer
confronting: **6** across **7** opposed **8** opposing **10** face-to-face
Confucian principle: **3** shu, Tao
Confucius: **4** sage **11** philosopher
confuse: **3** fog **4** daze, faze, lose, stun, trip **5** addle, befog, cloud, floor, mix up, muddy, put on, snarl, stump, throw **6** baffle, bedaze, bemuse, boggle, flurry, foul up, fuddle, garble, jumble, litter, muddle, outwit, puzzle, rattle **7** becloud, bedevil, disturb, flummox, fluster, mislead, mistake, mystify, nonplus, perplex, perturb, screw up,

shuffle, snarl up, stupefy, unhinge 8 befuddle, bewilder, confound, disorder, entangle, outsmart, surprise, throw off, unsettle 9 adumbrate, discomfit, disorient, dumbfound, overwhelm 10 complicate, discompose, disconcert

confused: 4 asea, hazy, lost 5 aback, at sea, dizzy, foggy, messy, muddy, muzzy, spacy, stuck, upset, wooly 6 cloudy, hectic, in a fog, punchy, spacey, woolly 7 abashed, at a loss, chaotic, fuddled, haywire, out of it, puzzled, reeling, shook up 8 anarchic, darkened, mistaken, nebulous, pell-mell, rambling 9 flummoxed, misguided, quizzical, slaphappy, spaced out, unsettled 10 anarchical, disjointed, disorderly, in an uproar, incohesive, indefinite, in disarray, indistinct, out to lunch, topsy-turvy, upside-down
 easily ~: 5 ditzy

confusing: 5 vague 6 arcane 7 cryptic, obscure, unclear 8 abstruse, involved, nebulous, puzzling 9 cryptical, difficult, enigmatic, obscuring, upsetting 10 disruptive, disturbing, embroiling, indistinct, misleading, perplexing, unsettling

confusion: 3 ado 4 daze, flap, fuss, maze, mess, riot, stew 5 Babel, chaos, doubt, havoc, mix up, panic, press, snarl, swirl 6 bedlam, bustle, dither, flurry, fracas, hubbub, huddle, jumble, jungle, lather, litter, mayhem, muddle, tangle, trauma, tumult, unrest, uproar 7 anarchy, clutter, ferment, mistake, turmoil 8 disarray, disorder, question, scramble, shambles, upheaval 9 abashment, agitation, amazement, commotion, imbroglio, intricacy, labyrinth, mobocracy, patchwork 10 bemusement, complexity, difficulty, excitement, hodgepodge, hurly-burly, perplexity, puzzlement, turbulence, untidiness, wilderness
 exclamation: 3 hey, huh 4 what
 state of ~: 3 fog, zoo 4 haze, mess 5 snafu 6 muddle

confute: 5 parry, rebut 6 naysay, negate, oppugn, refute 7 dispute, explode 8 disagree, disprove, overturn 9 disaffirm, discredit 10 contradict, contravene, controvert, disconfirm, invalidate

___ Cong: 4 Viet

conga: 4 drum 5 dance
 like a ~ line: 5 snaky
 origin: 4 Cuba

conga ___: 4 drum, line

Conga (1985 song) artist: Estefan

Congaree: 5 river
 city on the ~: 8 Columbia
 locale: 4 S. Car.

congé: 8 farewell 9 discharge, dismissal

congeal: 3 gel, set 4 cake, clot, jell 6 curdle, freeze, gelate, harden 7 stiffen, thicken, tighten 8 solidify 9 coagulate 10 gelatinize

congealed: 5 stiff, thick 7 jellied

congenial: 4 kind, warm 6 benign, clubby, jovial, kindly, mellow, social 7 addable, affable, cordial 8 amicable, friendly, gracious, likeable, pleasant, pleasing, sociable 9 agreeable, congruous, consonant, convivial, favorable 10 compatible, consistent, delightful, harmonious, like-minded
 not ~: 4 cool 5 aloof

___ Congeniality: 4 Miss

congenital: 4 born 6 inborn, innate 9 ancestral, essential, ingrained, inherited, intrinsic 10 connatural, indigenous, indwelling, inveterate, unacquired

conger: 3 eel 4 fish
 hunter: 5 eeler
 Old English ~: 3 ele
 relative: 5 moray 7 lamprey
 young ~: 5 elver

congeries: 4 heap, mass, pile 10 assemblage, collection, cumulation

congest: 3 jam 4 clog, fill, glut, pack, plug, stop 5 block, choke, crowd, flood, stuff 6 impede 7 occlude 8 obstruct, overfill, overload 9 overcrowd 10 overburden

congested: 5 close 6 packed 9 chockfull, jam-packed, stoppered, stuffed-up 10 gridlocked, obstructed, overfilled

congestion: 3 jam 4 clog 5 snarl, tie-up 6 logjam 7 squeeze 8 blockage, clogging, crowding, gridlock, overflow 9 impedance, profusion 10 bottleneck, traffic jam
 spot: 5 sinus

___ congestion: 5 nasal

conglomerate: 3 mix 4 firm, pool 5 chain, merge, trust 6 cartel, empire, motley, varied 7 combine 9 syndicate

conglomeration: 3 mix 4 heap, mass, pile 5 hoard 6 medley 7 cluster, mixture, variety 8 scramble 9 congeries

Congo: 5 river
 beast: 3 ape
 city on the ~: 8 Kinshasa
 language: 3 Ebo, Ibo 4 Eboe, Igbo 5 Bantu
 mountain: 7 Mitumba
 people: 3 Fan 4 Fang, Luba 5 Bemba, Lunda, Mongo, Rundi, Zande 6 Azande, Pangwe 7 Pahouin
 region: 5 Shaba
 river: 4 Uele 5 Ebola
 river to the ~: 6 Ubangi
 tributary: 5 Kasai
 volcano: 10 Nyiragongo

Congo (Democratic Republic)
 capital: 8 Kinshasa
 city: 4 Boma 5 Uvira 6 Bukavu, Kikwit, Likasi, Matadi 7 Kananga, Kolwezi 8 Kinshasa 9 Kisangani 10 Lumumbashi
 formerly: 5 Zaire
 locale: 3 Afr. 6 Africa
 money: 5 franc
 neighbor: 5 Sudan 6 Angola, Rwanda, Uganda, Zambia 7 Burundi 8 Tanzania

Congo (Republic)
 capital: 11 Brazzaville
 city: 6 Gemena, Kamina, Likasi
 locale: 3 Afr. 6 Africa
 money: 5 franc
 neighbor: 5 Gabon 6 Angola 8 Cameroon

Congo ___: 3 dye, eel, red 5 color

___ Congo: 6 French, Middle 7 Belgian

Congo author: Michael Crichton

Congo, The author: Vachel Lindsay

congou: 3 tea 8 black tea

congratulate: 4 hail, laud 5 toast 6 praise, salute 7 applaud 8 hand it to

congratulations: 5 kudos 6 praise

congregate: 4 herd, meet 5 bunch, crowd, flock, group, rally, swarm 6 gather, muster 7 bunch up, collect, compile, convene, hang out, round up 8 assemble 9 forgather 10 gang around, rendezvous

congregation: 3 set 4 crew, mass 5 array, crowd, flock, group, laity, swarm 6 confab, muster, parish, throng 7 company, meeting, turnout 8 assembly, audience, ecclesia 9 multitude
 home: 4 shul 5 schul 6 church 9 synagogue
 leader: 5 rabbi, rebbe
 member: 6 layman
 response: 4 amen

congress: 4 gild 5 guild, union 6 caucus, league 7 chamber, council, meeting 8 assembly, conclave 9 committee, delegates, gathering 10 conference, convention, delegation

Congress: 5 taxer
 body: 5 House 6 Senate
 caucus: 4 bloc
 employee: 4 aide, page
 meeting: 4 sess. 7 session
 member: 3 rep., sen. 4 whip 7 senator 8 lawmaker
 output: 3 act, law
 send back to ~: 4 veto
 some ~ spending: 4 pork
 vote: 3 aye, nay

Congressional ___: 6 Record

Congressional ___ of Honor: 5 Medal

Congress of ___: 6 Vienna

Congress shall make ___...: 5 no law

Congreve, William: 7 British 10 playwright
 friend: Pope, Swift, Steele

congruence: 5 unity 6 accord 7 fitness 9 agreement, coherence, congruity 10 conformity, consonance, friendship

congruent: 7 logical, similar 9 agreeable, identical 10 coinciding, compatible, concurring, conforming, consistent, harmonious
 be ~: 5 match

congruity: 6 accord, parity 7 concord, fitness, harmony 9 agreement, coherence 10 accordance, conformity, consonance, proportion, similarity

congruous: 4 same 7 regular, similar 8 relevant 9 accordant, according, agreeable, congenial, consonant 10 compatible, concordant, consistent, harmonious

conic ___: 7 section

conical: 10 strobilate
 dwelling: 4 tipi 5 tepee 6 teepee

conifer: 3 fir 4 pine 5 cedar, cycad, larch 8 longleaf
 covering: 4 bark
 part: 4 cone 6 needle
 stand: 5 taiga

coniferous: 4 piny 5 piney

conjectural: 4 iffy, moot 6 chancy, unsure 8 academic 9 ambiguous, uncertain, unsettled 10 indefinite, unresolved, up for grabs, up in the air

conjecture: 3 say 4 feel, shot, view 5 guess, hunch, infer, think 6 assume, belief, reckon, theory, wonder 7 believe, imagine, opinion, predict, presume, suggest, suppose, surmise, suspect, thought 8 estimate, theorize 9 guesswork, induction, inference, postulate, speculate, suspicion, take a shot, take a stab 10 anticipate, assumption, conclusion, expectancy, hypothesis, impression

conjoin: 3 mix, tie, wed 4 ally, bind, join, link, mesh, yoke 5 hitch, unite 6 append, attach, cohere, couple, hook up, league, team up 7 combine, connect, hitch on 8 coalesce, federate 9 associate, integrate

conjoint: 6 mutual 7 grouped 8 communal 10 collective

conjointly: 4 also 5 as one 8 in unison, mutually, together 10 altogether

conjugal: 6 bridal, wedded 7 marital

conjugality: 8 marriage 9 matrimony

conjugate: 4 link 7 inflect

conjunct: 5 joint 8 combined

conjunction: 3 and, but, for, nor, tho, yet 4 lest, word 5 and/or, union 6 either, hookup, unless 7 meeting, neither 8 alliance, although
 French: 3 que
 German: 3 und
 Latin: 3 sed
 Spanish: 4 pero

conjuncture: 4 crux 6 crisis, crunch 9 emergency 10 crossroads

conjuration: 3 hex 5 spell

conjurer: 5 Circe, Kirke, witch 6 Hecate, Hekate, Merlin, wizard 7 charmer 8 magician, sorcerer 9 enchanter
 prop: 4 wand
 word: 5 hocus, pocus 6 presto

conjure up: 5 evoke, raise 6 devise, invoke 7 imagine 8 remember 9 recollect, visualize

conjuring: 5 magic 10 hocus-pocus, necromancy, witchcraft

conk: 3 bop, rap 4 bean, coif, cosh 5 brain, knock, smite 6 hairdo, strike, thwack 8 coiffure
 out: 3 die 4 fail, quit 5 sleep 7 fatigue, go kaput 8 collapse, languish 9 break down
 (out): 5 peter

Conklin: 6 Osgood 7 Chester

Conkling: 6 Roscoe

Conlan: 5 Jocko

___ con leche: 4 café

Conn: 4 Didi 5 Billy
 foe: 5 Louis
 U. ~ home: 6 Storrs

Conn.
 neighbor: 4 Mass.
 school: 5 USCGA, Yale U
 zone: 3 EDT, EST
 see also Connecticut

Connacht county: 5 Sligo

connate: 7 related 10 indigenous

connatural: 4 born 6 inborn 7 related 9 ancestral, essential, ingrained, inherited, intrinsic 10 congenital, indigenous, indwelling, inveterate, unacquired

Conn, Billy: 5 boxer
 milieu: 4 ring

connect: 3 tie, wed 4 ally, bind, bond, join, link, meet, mesh, span, weld, yoke 5 annex, hitch, refer, tie in, tie on, unite 6 adjoin, attach, belong, bridge, cement, cohere, couple, dial in, enlink, fasten, hook on, hook up, plug in, relate 7 bracket, combine, conjoin, hitch on, pertain 8 go across, interact, neighbor 9 affiliate, attribute, correlate, implicate, interface, interlink
 with: 5 tie to 7 contact

connect ___: 4 time

connected: 3 kin, one 4 akin 6 allied, joined, looped 7 related 8 coherent, in league, relative 9 bracketed, continual, pertinent, undivided 10 affiliated, applicable, associated, continuous
 not ~: 5 apart

___-connected: 4 well 6 simply

Connecticut: 5 river, state
 city: 6 Darien, Haddam, Hamden, Mystic, Storrs, Wilton 7 Ansonia, Bristol, Danbury, Meriden, Milford, Norwalk, Norwich, Old Lyme, Shelton 8 East Lyme, Hartford, New Haven, Stamford, Trumbull, Westport 9 East Haven, Fairfield, Greenwich, Naugatuck, Newington, New London, Stratford, Waterbury, West Haven 10 Bridgeport, Manchester, Middletown, New Britain, North Haven, Torrington
 city on the ~: 8 Hartford
 collegian: 3 Eli 7 Bulldog
 conference: 7 Big East
 Indian: 6 Pequot
 neighbor: 4 Mass. 7 New York
 prep school: 6 Choate

school: 4 Yale 5 Yale U
state animal: 10 sperm whale
state bird: 5 robin
state hero: 10 Nathan Hale
state mineral: 6 garnet
state shellfish: 6 oyster
state tree: 8 white oak
Connecticut Yankee, A: 7 musical
songwriter: 4 Hart 7 Rodgers
Connecticut Yankee, A (1931 film)
cast: Myrna Loy, Maureen O'Sullivan, Will Rogers
Connecticut Yankee..., A author: Mark Twain
connecting: 6 hookup 9 adjoining, reference 10 juxtaposed
word: 4 conj. 11 conjunction
connection: 3 tie 4 bond, link, lock, node, seam, spot 5 agent, joint, logic, nexus, segue, tie-in, union 6 access, bridge, friend, hookup, linkup, mentor, regard, source 7 bearing, contact, kinship, liaison, sponsor 8 affinity, coupling, junction, ligature, relation, relative, sympathy, vinculum 9 associate, coherence, fastening, go-between, messenger, relevance 10 attachment, comparison, continuity
in ~ with: 4 as to
make a ~: 6 attach, liaise
make a new ~: 5 retap
__ connection: 3 sea 5 delta 6 ground
__ Connection, The: 6 French 7 Chinese
connective: 3 and, nor 4 link 8 vinculum
tissue: 6 fascia
connector: 2 or 3 and, nor 6 either 7 neither 10 attachment
connect-the-__: 4 dots
conned, easily: 5 naive
Connee: 7 Boswell
Connelly: 4 Marc 5 Cyril 8 Jennifer
Connelly, Cyril: 6 writer 7 British
Connelly, Jennifer: 7 actress
film: A Beautiful Mind (2001, AA)
Dark City (1998)
Labyrinth (1986)
Pollock (2000)
The Rocketeer (1991)
Waking the Dead (2000)
Connelly, Marc: 6 author, writer
collaborator: Kaufman
work: Dulcy
The Farmer Takes a Wife
The Green Pastures
Connery: 4 Scot, Sean 5 Jason
Connery, Jason spouse: Mia Sara
Connery, Sean: 3 Sir 5 actor
film: The Anderson Tapes (1972)
The Avengers (1998)
Cuba (1979)
Darby O'Gill & the Little People (1959)
Diamonds Are Forever (1971)
Dr. No (1962)
Entrapment (1999)
Family Business (1989)
Finding Forrester (2000)
A Fine Madness (1966)
First Knight (1995)
From Russia With Love (1963)
Goldfinger (1964)
The Great Train Robbery (1979)
Highlander (1986)
The Hill (1965)
The Hunt for Red October (1990)
Indiana Jones and the Last Crusade (1989)
The Longest Day (1962)
The Man Who Would Be King (1975)
Marnie (1964)
Medicine Man (1992)
Murder on the Orient Express (1974)
The Name of the Rose (1986)
Never Say Never Again (1983)
The Next Man (1976)
Rising Sun (1993)
Robin and Marian (1976)
The Rock (1996)
The Russia House (1990)
Thunderball (1965)
Time Bandits (1981)
The Untouchables (1987, AA)
You Only Live Twice (1967)
film (voice): Dragonheart (1996)
spouse: Diane Cilento
Connick Jr., Harry: 7 pianist
spouse: Jill Goodacre
Connie: 4 Mack 5 Chung, Hines 7 Britton, Francis, Stevens 8 Corleone, Sellecca
Conniff: 3 Ray
conning __: 5 tower
Conning Tower monogram: 3 FPA
conniption: 3 fit 5 anger, pique 6 cat fit 7 tantrum 8 outburst 9 hysterics
connivance: 9 collusion 10 complicity, conspiracy
connive: 4 plot 6 scheme, wangle 7 collude, finagle, wrangle 8 conspire, intrigue 9 machinate
conniver: 5 cheat 8 swindler
quest: 5 angle
conniving: 3 sly 4 foxy 6 shifty 7 knavish 8 scheming 9 designing
connoisseur: 3 ace, fan 4 buff 5 adept, maven, mavin 6 critic, expert, master 7 devotee, epicure, esthete, gourmet 8 aesthete
Connolly: 6 Walter 7 Maureen
Connolly, Maureen: 7 netster 9 tennis pro
milieu: 5 court
Connors: 4 Mike 5 Chuck, Jimmy
Connors, Jimmy: 7 netster 9 tennis pro
colleague: 4 Ashe 5 Evert
milieu: 5 court
connotation: 4 hint 5 usage 6 nuance 7 meaning 8 overtone
connote: 4 hint, mean 5 imply, spell 6 hint at 7 betoken, purport, signify, suggest 8 indicate, intimate 9 insinuate, predicate, symbolize
Conn Smythe Trophy winner: 3 MVP
connubial: 6 bridal, wedded 7 marital, nuptial
connubiality: 8 marriage 9 matrimony
Conoco rival: 5 Amoco, Exxon, Mobil, Shell 7 Chevron
Conon: 4 pope 7 pontiff
__ con pollo: 5 arroz
conquer: 3 win, zap 4 beat, best, drub, lick, rout, tame, whip 5 cream, crush, floor, quell, upset, worst 6 defeat, humble, master, obtain, occupy, outwit, reduce, subdue 7 prevail, subvert, succeed, triumph 8 overcome, shut down, suppress, surmount, vanquish 9 checkmate, overpower, overthrow, overwhelm, subjugate
conquerable: 4 weak
conquering __: 4 hero
conqueror: 4 hero 6 captor, master, victor, winner 8 champion 10 subjugator, vanquisher
of 1066: 6 Norman
pride: 6 empire
Conqueror Worm, The author: 3 Poe
__ conquers all: 4 love
conquest: 3 win 4 coup, feat, rout, tour 5 score 6 defeat 7 beating, triumph, victory 9 checkmate, landslide, overthrow 10 occupation
Conquest: 3 car 4 auto 8 Chrysler
Conquest (1937 film)
cast: Charles Boyer, Greta Garbo, Reginald Owen
__ Conquest: 6 Norman
conquian: 4 game 8 card game
conquistador
homeland: 6 España
quest: 3 oro
trait: 5 greed
Conquistador author: MacLeish
Conrack (1974 film)
cast: Hume Cronyn, Madge Sinclair, Jon Voight, Paul Winfield
director: Martin Ritt
Conrad: 3 Con 4 Bain 5 Aiken, Janis, Nagel, Veidt 6 Hilton, Joseph, Robert 7 Charles, Michael, Richter, William
Conrad, Joseph: 6 writer 7 British
birthplace: Ukraine
setting: 3 sea
work: Chance
Heart of Darkness
Lord Jim
Nostromo
The Secret Sharer
Typhoon
Under Western Eyes
Victory
Conrad, William: 5 actor
film: The Ride Back (1957)
TV: Cannon, Jake and the Fatman
Conrail colleague: 6 Amtrak
Conried: 4 Hans
Conroe: 4 city, town
locale: 5 Texas
Conroy, Pat: 6 author, writer
work: Beach Music
The Boo
The Great Santini
The Lords of Discipline
My Losing Season
The Prince of Tides
The Water Is Wide
consanguine: 7 related
consanguineous: 3 kin 4 akin
consanguinity: 8 relation
consarn it: 4 dang
conscience: 4 soul 5 qualm 6 ethics, regret 7 scruple 8 scruples, superego 10 inner voice, principles
bad ~: 5 guilt, shame 7 remorse
be stung by ~: 3 rue
in all ~: 9 seriously, sincerely
without ~: 6 amoral
conscience __: 5 money 6 clause
Conscience, Hendrik: 6 writer 7 Belgian
conscience-stricken: 5 sorry 7 ashamed 8 contrite, penitent
conscientious: 5 fussy, moral 7 careful, dutiful, ethical, finicky, mindful, prudent, upright 8 cautious, diligent, exacting, faithful, finiking, finnicky, hustling, punctual, reliable, rigorous, sedulous, studious, thorough 9 assiduous, attentive, judicious, motivated, observant, reputable 10 fastidious, meticulous, particular, scrupulous
conscientiously: 4 hard, well
conscientiousness: 4 care 9 attention
conscious: 4 live 5 alert, alive, awake, aware 6 posted, wilful, with it 7 mindful, studied, willful 8 rational, sensible, sentient, vigilant, watchful 9 attentive, au courant, cognizant, observing, reasoning, sensitive 10 acquainted, calculated, conversant, deliberate, discerning, perceiving, perceptive, percipient, purposeful, reasonable, reflective, responsive
become ~: 4 wake 5 waken
be ~ of: 3 see 4 know 7 realize
of: 4 on to 6 wise to
__-conscious: 4 half, self 5 class
consciousness: 3 ken 4 life, mind 5 sense 6 memory, regard 7 concern, feeling 9 sensation 10 perception
component: 3 ego 8 superego
lose ~: 5 faint, swoon 7 crumple, pass out 8 black out, keel over
regain ~: 4 stir, wake 5 awake, waken 6 awaken, come to, return, revive 7 recover 10 come around
suspend ~: 5 sleep
conscribe: 5 draft 6 enlist
conscript: 4 levy 5 draft, force 6 enlist, induct 7 impress, recruit, soldier, warrior 8 inductee, shanghai 10 commandeer
conscription: 5 draft
agcy.: 3 SSS
consecrate: 4 keep 5 bless, deify, honor 6 anoint, devote, hallow, ordain 7 beatify, hallows 8 canonize, dedicate, enshrine, inshrine, sanctify 9 celebrate
consecrated: 4 holy 5 blest 6 divine, sacred 7 blessed
consecration: 8 blessing, devotion 10 commitment, dedication
consecution: 6 sequel, series, string 8 sequence
consecutive: 5 solid 6 serial 8 straight
consecutively: 6 in a row 7 running
consensus: 5 pulse, unity 6 accord 7 concord, harmony, rapport 9 agreement, unanimity
consent: 2 OK 3 bow, nod 4 bend, okay 5 abide, agree, defer, leave, say OK, yield 6 accede, assent, comply, concur, give in, permit, ratify 7 approve, conform, go-ahead, go along, license, promise 8 approval, blessing, sanction 9 acquiesce, clearance 10 compliance, give the nod, permission
age of ~: 8 majority
give ~: 2 OK 3 let 4 okay 5 agree, allow, grant, yield 6 accord, assent, cave in, comply, concur, permit 7 concede, consent 9 acquiesce, cooperate 10 come around
refuse ~: 4 deny, veto 6 forbid, reject 7 decline 8 disallow, prohibit, turn down 9 interdict, proscribe 10 disapprove
to: 2 go, OK 4 heed, mind, obey, okay 5 grant 6 accept, follow, fulfil, listen 7 abide by, fulfill, observe, respect 8 carry out, tolerate
word of ~: 2 ay 3 aye, yes
consent __: 6 decree
__ consent: 5 age of 7 implied
consenting: 7 willing 9 agreeable
words: 3 I do
consequence: 4 note, rank 5 state, value, worth 6 cachet, effect, impact, import, moment, payoff, renown, repute, result, sequel, status, upshot, weight 7 fallout, gravity, outcome, product, stature 8 eminence, interest, position, prestige, reaction, standing 9 magnitude, outgrowth
as a ~: 4 then, thus 9 therefore
be of ~: 4 rate 6 matter
of ~: 7 serious 9 important
__ consequence: 4 of no
consequences: 5 price 6 impact
alternative: 5 truth
like some ~: 4 dire
suffer ~: 3 pay
consequent: 4 next 5 sound 7 ensuing, logical 8 eventual 9 attendant, deducible, following, inferable, resultant, resulting, secondary 10 reasonable, subsequent, successive
consequential: 3 big 4 high 6 cogent 8 historic, pregnant 9 momentous 10 portentous
consequently: 4 ergo, then, thus 5 hence 9 therefore

conservation: 4 care 6 saving 7 economy 9 salvation
area: 9 sanctuary
practice ~: 5 reuse 7 recycle
__ conservation: 4 land, soil 8 wildlife
conservation of __: 4 mass 6 charge, energy, matter
conservative: 4 fogy, safe, Tory 5 chary, fogey, fusty, quiet, right, staid 6 narrow, square 7 diehard, prudent, thrifty 8 cautious, loyalist, moderate, old-guard, orthodox, straight, undaring 9 parochial, provident, temperate 10 economical, reasonable
British ~: 4 Tory
starter: 3 neo 5 ultra
Conservative __: 3 Jew 5 party 7 Baptist, Judaism
Conservatives: 5 party
wing: 5 right
conservator: 6 keeper, savior 7 curator, saviour 8 guardian
conservatory: 7 nursery 8 hothouse 10 greenhouse
deg.: 4 B.Mus.
graduate: 6 artist 8 musician
conserve: 4 keep, save 5 hoard, lay by, lay up, skimp, stash 6 ration, scrimp 7 cut back, protect, store up 8 maintain, preserve, retrench, sock away 9 economize, safeguard 10 underspend
conserves: 3 jam 5 jelly 9 marmalade, preserves
consider: 4 call, deem, feel, heed, mull, muse, view 5 count, judge, study, think, weigh 6 credit, debate, digest, esteem, look at, look on, ponder, reckon, regard, take up 7 balance, believe, examine, inspect, presume, reflect, sleep on, suppose, surmise, suspect 8 allow for, chew over, cogitate, deal with, envisage, factor in, look upon, meditate, mull over, pore over, ruminate, see about, turn over 9 enter into, reflect on, speculate, think over 10 reckon with, toss around, understand
don't ~: 6 ignore 7 rule out
considerable: 3 big 4 good, huge, lots, much, tidy 5 ample, great, heavy, hefty, large, lotsa, major, mondo 6 divers, gobs of, goodly, lavish, lots of, marked, mighty, myriad, pretty, umteen, untold 7 copious, heaps of, no end of, piles of, profuse, scads of, sizable, umpteen, weighty 8 abundant, handsome, manifold, material, numerous, oodles of, scores of, sizeable, umpsteen 9 bountiful, countless, momentous, quite a few 10 zillions of
considerably: 3 far 4 a lot, much, well 5 extra, no end, quite 6 rather 7 greatly, largely 8 markedly, somewhat, very much 9 like crazy
considerate: 3 big 4 good, kind, nice 5 lofty, sweet 6 gentle, humane, kindly, loving, polite 7 gallant, helpful, mindful, tactful 8 discreet, generous, gracious, mannerly, moderate, obliging, sportive, well-bred 9 regardful 10 bighearted
one: 5 carer
consideration: 3 fee, pay 4 care, heed, sake, tact, wage 5 price, study 6 debate, esteem, factor, reason, regard, review, reward, salary, spring 7 concern, payment, respect, stipend, thought 8 analysis, courtesy, kindness, scrutiny, thinking 9 emolument
in ~ of: 3 for
open for ~: 4 iffy 8 doubtful 9 dependent, provisory, uncertain, undecided, unsettled 10 contingent, indefinite
considered: 6 wilful 7 advised, express, reputed, willful 8 moderate 9 designful, judicious, voluntary 10 deliberate, thought-out, well-chosen
everything ~: 5 in all
__-considered: 3 ill 4 well
considering: 5 since 7 whereas
Consider it done: 6 I'm on it
Consider the Lilies author: Waugh
Consider Yourself musical: 6 Oliver!
Considine: 3 Bob, Tim
consign: 3 put 4 give, send, ship 5 leave, route, trust 6 commit, convey, devote 7 address, commend, deliver, entrust, forward, intrust 8 dedicate, delegate, hand over, relegate, transfer, transmit, turn over 9 surrender
consignee: 6 bearer
consignment: 3 lot 4 load 6 ration
consignment __: 4 note, shop 5 store
consignor: 6 jobber 8 merchant
consist
ender: 3 ent 4 ency
of: 7 contain, include 8 comprise
consistency: 6 parity 7 harmony, texture 9 congruity
consistent: 4 even, firm, like, same 5 level, sound 6 cogent, steady 7 equable, logical, regular, tenable, uniform 8 analytic, coherent, constant, methodic, of a piece, rational, sensible 9 accordant, according, agreeable, congenial, congruent, congruous, consonant, pragmatic, rock solid, unanimous, unfailing, unvarying 10 analytical, compatible, concurrent, dependable, harmonious, homogenous, invariable, legitimate, persistent, reasonable, synchronal, true-to-type, unchanging
be ~: 5 agree 6 cohere
be ~ with: 6 follow
not ~: 6 patchy 7 erratic
consistently: 4 ever 6 always, firmly 8 steadily 9 naturally, regularly, staunchly 10 dependably, faithfully, resolutely
consolation: 4 balm, ease 5 cheer 6 refund, relief, solace, succor 7 comfort 8 sympathy
word: 5 there
words: 5 I know, it's OK
consolation __: 5 prize
Consolato __ Mare: 3 del
console: 4 calm, lift, pity 5 cheer, quiet, shelf, table 6 buck up, solace, soothe, uphold 7 assuage, cheer up, comfort, gladden, hearten, relieve, upraise 8 enspirit, inspirit, reassure 9 encourage, untrouble
console __: 5 piano, table 10 television
consoler's offering: 3 hug
consolidate: 4 band, meld, pool 5 amass, blend, merge, unify, unite 6 cement, center, embody, firm up, harden, imbody, league 7 build up, bunch up, combine, compact, compile, connect, fortify 8 coalesce, solidify 10 synthesize
consolidated: 5 joint, solid, thick 6 united
consolidation: 5 union 6 merger 8 junction, juncture
consolidation __: 4 loan
consommé: 4 soup 5 broth 8 julienne
consonance: 5 unity 7 fitness 9 agreement, coherence, congruity, orthodoxy 10 conformity, congruence, friendship
consonant: 4 akin 6 in step, in sync, in tune, on a par 7 regular, similar, uniform 8 relevant 9 accordant, according, agreeable, analogous, congenial, congruous, unanimous 10 coincident, comparable, compatible, concordant, consistent, harmonious, true to type
be ~: 3 fit
smooth ~: 4 lene
sound: 5 soft c, soft g
voiceless ~: 4 surd
with: 4 like
consonants, like some: 5 velar
consort: 3 mix 4 mate, wife 5 group 6 friend, hobnob, mingle, spouse 7 hang out, husband, partner 8 roommate 9 accompany, associate, companion, pal around, socialize 10 fraternize
with: 3 see 4 date
(with): 3 run 6 take up
__ consort: 5 queen 6 prince
consortium: 4 pool 5 union 6 cartel, league 8 monopoly
conspectus: 7 epitome 8 abstract 10 compendium
conspicuous: 4 bold, open 5 clear, famed, great, noted, plain, showy, vivid 6 famous, flashy, garish, in view, marked, patent, public, signal 7 blatant, eminent, evident, exposed, glaring, notable, obvious, pointed, salient, splashy, unusual, visible 8 apparent, clear-cut, distinct, explicit, flagrant, manifest, palpable, renowned, singular, striking, unhidden, unveiled 9 arresting, prominent, well-known 10 noticeable, observable, remarkable, unshrouded
be ~: 5 shine 8 stand out
conspiracy: 4 plot, trap 5 cabal 6 racket, scheme 7 cahoots, frame-up 8 intrigue 9 coalition, collusion, treachery 10 complicity, connivance, disloyalty
conspiracy __: 6 theory
conspiracy of __: 7 silence
__ Conspiracy, The: 4 Open 5 Wilby
Conspiracy Theory (1997 film)
cast: Mel Gibson, Julia Roberts, Patrick Stewart
director: Richard Donner
conspiratorial: 6 secret 7 furtive
conspirators: 4 ring 5 cabal
conspire: 4 plan, plot 6 scheme, wangle 7 collude, connive 8 intrigue, maneuver 9 machinate
constable: 3 cop 6 lawman 7 officer 9 policeman
Constable, John: 6 artist 7 painter
homeland: 7 England
constabulary: 6 police
Constance: 4 lake 5 Moore 6 Towers 7 Bennett, Collier 8 Cummings
locale: 7 Austria, Germany 11 Switzerland
constancy: 6 fixity 7 loyalty 8 devotion, fidelity, firmness 9 adherence, certainty, diligence, eagerness, endurance, fixedness, fortitude, frequency, integrity, stability 10 allegiance, attachment, continuity, doggedness, permanence, perpetuity, regularity, resolution, steadiness, trustiness, uniformity
constant: 3 set 4 even, fast, firm, same, sure, true 5 fixed, level, loyal, paced, solid, usual 6 ardent, rooted, stable, static, steady, trusty 7 abiding, chronic, devoted, dutiful, endless, equable, lasting, nonstop, regular, settled, staunch, undying, uniform 8 definite, enduring, faithful, habitual, ironclad, lifelong, reliable, resolute, true-blue, unbroken, unending, untiring, unwaning 9 allegiant, ceaseless, chronical, continual, deathless, dedicated, immutable, incessant, parameter, perennial, permanent, perpetual, steadfast, sustained, unabating, unfailing, unvarying 10 changeless, consistent, continuous, dependable, invariable, inveterate, inviolable, monotonous, persistent, relentless, unchanging, unflagging, unwavering
__ constant: 3 gas 4 time 5 decay, solar 7 Hubble's, lattice, Planck's
Constant __, The: 4 Wife 5 Nymph 7 Husband
constantan: 5 alloy
component: 6 copper, nickel
Constant Craving singer: 4 Lang
Constant Husband, The (1955 film)
cast: Rex Harrison, Kay Kendall, Margaret Leighton
Constantin: 8 Brancusi
Constantine: 4 city, pope, town 5 saint 6 Cavafy 7 Michael, pontiff
locale: 7 Algeria
mother of ~: 6 Helena
wife of ~: 6 Fausta
Constantinople: 4 port 8 Istanbul
locale: 6 Turkey
Constantinopolitan __: 4 rite 5 Creed
constantly: 3 e'er 4 ever 6 always 9 gradually 10 unendingly
Constant Nymph, The (1943 film)
cast: Charles Boyer, Joan Fontaine, Alexis Smith
Constant Wife, The author: Maugham
constellation: 7 pattern
Altair's ~: 6 Aquila
altar: 3 Ara
Arcturus' ~: 6 Boötes
belted ~: 5 Orion
Betelgeuse's ~: 5 Orion
brightest star in a ~: 5 alpha 6 lucida
combining form: 5 sider- 6 sidero-
Deneb's ~: 6 Cygnus
near Cepheus: 5 Draco
near Hercules: 4 Lyra
near Hydra: 3 Leo
near Indus: 4 Grus
near Serpens: 5 Libra
near the Big Dipper: 5 Draco
near Virgo: 5 Libra 6 Corvus
Regulus' ~: 3 Leo
Rigel's ~: 5 Orion
Ring Nebula ~: 4 Lyra
second brightest star in a ~: 4 beta
Southern ~: 3 Ara 4 Argo, Grus, Vela 5 Mensa 6 Octans
Spica's ~: 5 Virgo
unit: 4 star
Vega's ~: 4 Lyra
constellations:
Andromeda (Chained Lady)
Antlia (Air Pump)
Apus (Bird of Paradise)
Aquarius (Water Bearer)
Aquila (Eagle)
Ara (Altar)
Aries (Ram)
Auriga (Charioteer)
Boötes (Herdsman)
Caelum (Chisel)
Camelopardalis (Giraffe)
Cancer (Crab)
Canes Venatici (Hunting Dogs)
Canis Major (Large Dog)
Canis Minor (Small Dog)
Capricorn (Goat)
Carina (Keel)
Cassiopeia (Seated Lady)
Centaurus (Centaur)
Cepheus (the King)
Cetus (Whale)
Chamaeleon (Chameleon)
Circinus (Pair of Compasses)
Columba (Dove)
Coma Berenices (Berenice's Hair)
Corona Australis (Southern Crown)
Corona Borealis (Northern Crown)
Corvus (Crow)

Crater (Cup)
Crux (Southern Cross)
Cygnus (Swan)
Delphinus (Dolphin)
Dorado (Swordfish)
Draco (Dragon)
Equuleus (Colt)
Eridanus (a river)
Fornax (Furnace)
Gemini (Twins)
Grus (Crane)
Hercules
Horologium (Clock)
Hydra (Water Monster)
Hydrus (Water Snake)
Indus (Indian)
Lacerta (Lizard)
Leo (Lion)
Lepus (Hare)
Libra (Balance)
Lupus (Wolf)
Lynx
Lyra (Lyre)
Mensa (Table)
Microscopium (Microscope)
Monoceros (Unicorn)
Musca (Fly)
Norma (T-square)
Octans (Octant)
Ophiuchus (Serpent Holder)
Orion (the Hunter)
Pavo (Peacock)
Pegasus (Winged Horse)
Perseus
Phoenix
Pictor (Painter's Easel)
Pisces (Fish)
Piscis Austinus (Southern Fish)
Puppis (Stern)
Pyxis (Mariner's Compass)
Reticulum (Net)
Sagitta (Arrow)
Sagittarius (Archer)
Scorpio (Scorpion)
Sculptor
Scutum (Shield)
Sextans (Sextant)
Taurus (Bull)
Telescopium (Telescope)
Triangulum Australe (Southern Triangle)
Triangulum (Triangle)
Tucana (Toucan)
Ursa Major (Large Bear)
Ursa Minor (Small Bear)
Vela (Sails)
Virgo (Virgin)
Volans (Flying Fish)
Vulpecula (Little Fox)

consternate: **5** alarm, appal, daunt **6** appall **7** stagger, startle
consternation: **4** care, fear **5** panic, shock **6** dismay, terror **8** surprise **9** abashment
  cause ~: **6** appall, dismay
Constitución: **4** city, town
  locale: **6** Mexico
constituency: **4** ward **6** people, public, voters **7** faction **8** district, electors, precinct
constituent: **4** link, part, unit **5** voter **6** factor, member **7** citizen, element, feature, portion **8** fraction, material
constituents: **6** voters **8** contents **10** electorate
constitute: **4** form, make **5** draft, found, frame, set up **6** create, depute, embody, imbody, make up, ordain **7** appoint, empower, include **8** comprise, deputize, legalize, validate **9** aggregate, authorize, construct, designate, establish, integrate, legislate **10** commission, complement
constitution: **3** law **4** code, form **5** build, frame, shape **6** design, fabric, health, nature, temper **7** charter, content **8** physique, vitality
  add-on: **5** bylaw **9** amendment
Constitution: **4** boat, ship **6** avenue
  articles in the ~: **3** VII **5** seven
  guarantee: **5** right
Constitution ___: **5** clock **6** mirror
___ Constitution: **3** USS **7** Federal
constitutional: **4** hike, turn, walk **5** jaunt, legal, licit **6** innate, lawful, ramble, stroll **7** organic, radical, saunter, workout **8** exercise, inherent
constitutional ___: **8** monarchy
Constitution Hall org.: **3** DAR
Constitution State: **11** Connecticut
Constitution State coll.: **5** U Conn
constitutive: **5** vital
constrain: **3** bar **4** bind, curb, make **5** check, cramp, force, hem in, impel, limit, stint **6** coerce, compel, hogtie, keep in, oblige, rein in, stifle **7** abstain, confine, control, harness, inhibit, require, trammel **8** bottle up, hold back, moderate, pressure, prohibit, restrain **9** constrict **10** intimidate, keep a lid on, keep in line, pressurize
constrained: **5** bound, sober, stiff **6** pent-up, uneasy **7** limited, stilted
constraint: **3** bar **4** curb, rein **5** brake, check, cramp, leash, stint **6** arrest, damper **7** reserve, shyness, slavery, trammel **8** timidity **9** captivity, detention, deterrent, hindrance, impulsion, necessity, restraint, timidness **10** compulsion, diffidence, imposition, inhibition, limitation, repression
constrict: **4** bind, curb **5** cramp, limit **6** corset, shrink, tauten **7** inhibit, squeeze, tighten **8** compress, restrict **9** attenuate, constrain
constricted: **5** tight **6** narrow
constriction: **7** tension
constrictor: **3** boa **5** noose, snake
construct: **4** base, form, make, mold, rear **5** build, erect, forge, frame, put up, raise, set up, shape **6** create, devise **7** compose, fashion, prepare, produce, work out **8** assemble, engineer **9** establish, fabricate, formulate, hammer out **10** constitute
  in haste: **5** rig up
construction: **3** cut **4** form **5** frame, shape **7** edifice, reading **8** assembly, building
  area: **3** lot **4** site
  detail: **4** spec
  junction: **4** weld
  machine: **5** crane, dozer, hoist **6** loader **9** bulldozer
  material: **4** iron, wood **5** steel **6** cement
  piece: **4** H-bar, I-bar, L-bar, stud, T-bar, Z bar **5** I-beam, joist, rebar, strut, T-beam
  site tray: **3** hod
  toy: **4** Lego
construction ___: **4** loan, site **5** paper
constructive: **6** aidful, benign, useful **7** helpful **8** positive, remedial, salutary, valuable **9** effectual, favorable, practical **10** productive, worthwhile
constructor: **5** maker **6** framer **9** artificer
construe: **4** read **5** infer, solve **6** deduce, define **7** analyze, explain **8** decipher, spell out **9** interpret, translate
Consuelo author: George Sand
consuetude: **4** wont
consul: **5** envoy **6** legate **7** attaché **8** delegate, diplomat, emissary, minister **10** ambassador
consul ___: **7** general
___-consul: **4** vice
consular ___: **5** agent
consulate: **7** embassy
consult: **3** ask, see **4** talk **5** refer **6** call in, confer, huddle, look to, parlay, powwow, turn to **9** negotiate **10** brainstorm
  with: **6** advise **8** approach
consultant: **7** adviser, advisor
  offering: **6** advice
consultation: **4** talk, word **6** indaba, powwow **7** hearing
consume: **3** eat, use **4** bolt, down, gulp, ruin, wolf **5** drain, drink, eat up, empty, erode, gorge, put in, scarf, spend, use up **6** absorb, devour, digest, engulf, expend, feed on, finish, guzzle, imbibe, ingest, ingulf, inhale, nosh on, obsess, prey on, ravage **7** corrode, deplete, destroy, engross, exhaust, feast on, partake, play out, put away, scarf up, smolder, snack on, swallow, utilize, wear out **8** chow down, gobble up, nibble on, smoulder, squander, toss down **9** devastate, dissipate, go through, polish off, preoccupy, scarf down **10** lay waste to, monopolize, run through
  don't ~: **4** fast **6** starve
  safe to ~: **6** edible
consumed: **4** lost **5** spent, tired **8** immersed, obsessed **9** possessed
  was ~: **4** went
consumer: **4** user **5** buyer, eater **6** emptor, vendee **7** shopper **8** customer **9** purchaser
  affairs topic: **5** fraud
  concern: **5** price, value
  conspicuous ~: **5** yuppy **6** yuppie
  crusader: **5** Nader
  goods: **4** mdse.
  lure: **2** ad **4** sale **6** rebate
  protection org.: **3** BBB, FDA, FTA
consumer ___: **5** goods **6** credit, strike
consumer ___ index: **5** price
Consumer Reports: **3** mag **8** magazine
  employee: **5** rater **6** tester
  lack: **3** ads
consuming: **7** erosive **9** absorbing, corrosive **10** engrossing
___-consuming: **4** time
consummate: **3** cap, end **4** arch, best, rank **5** close, crown, first, great, ideal, sew up, stark, total, utter **6** clinch, effect, finish, fulfil, superb, wind up, wrap up **7** achieve, classic, execute, fulfill, perfect, realize, supreme **8** absolute, carry out, complete, conclude, crowning, finalize, flawless, outright, peerless, profound, put to bed, thorough, ultimate **9** downright, exquisite, faultless, just right, masterful, matchless, out-and-out, perfected, polish off, practiced, terminate, unrivaled, virtuosic **10** accomplish, button down, complement, effectuate, impeccable, inimitable, preeminent, take care of, unrivalled
consummated: **4** done **8** complete
consummately: **4** to a T **9** perfectly
consummation: **3** end **4** goal **5** crest **6** ending, result, wrap-up **8** fruition
consumption: **3** use **6** eating, intake **7** burning **8** drinking
  unfit for ~: **4** rank **5** moldy **6** rancid, rotten **8** inedible
consumption ___: **3** tax **4** weed **5** goods
cont.: **3** Afr., Eur. **4** Aust. **5** N. Amer., S. Amer.
Contac alternative: **5** Afrin **6** Nyquil, Tavist **7** Actifed, Comtrex, Dayquil, Dristan, Sinutab, Sudafed **8** Benadryl, Dimetapp, Drixoral, TheraFlu **9** Coricidin, Triaminic **10** Robitussin
contact: **3** get **4** call, lens, link, meet, talk **5** get to, phone, reach, touch **6** impact, liaise, talk to **7** liaison, meeting, speak to, write to **8** approach, touching **9** check with, collision, telephone, touch base **10** connection, contiguity, get a hold of
  be in ~ with: **4** abut **6** adjoin
  brief ~: **5** brush
  via pager: **4** beep
contact ___: **4** lens, mine **5** paper, patch, print, sheet, sport **6** binary, cement, flight, flying **7** printer, process
Contact: **4** film **5** novel
  author: Carl Sagan
  cast: Jodie Foster, John Hurt, Matthew McConaughey, Tom Skerritt, James Woods
  director: Robert Zemeckis
contacts
  alternative: **5** specs **7** glasses
  big name in ~: **4** Lomb **6** Bausch
  candidate: **5** myope
  contact: **6** cornea
  like some ~: **4** soft
Contagem: **4** city, town
  locale: **6** Brazil
contagion: **6** plague **7** disease **9** infection, pollution **10** corruption, pestilence
Contagion author: Robin Cook
contagious: **5** viral **8** catching **9** epizootic, pestilent, poisonous, spreading **10** impartible, infectious, inoculable
contain: **4** curb, have, hold, take **5** cover, house **6** begird, embody, govern, hogtie, hold in, imbody, record, rein in, stifle, take in **7** add up to, control, embrace, enclose, harness, inclose, include, involve, repress, subsume **8** bottle up, comprise, hold back, restrain, restrict, suppress **9** consist of, encompass **10** keep a lid on
___-contained: **4** self
container: **3** bag, bin, box, can, cup, hod, jar, jug, keg, kit, mug, pan, pod, pot, sac, tin, tub, tun, urn, vat **4** bowl, case, cask, dish, ewer, flat, mold, pail, sack, skin, tank, tray, tube, vase, vial **5** ampul, basin, chest, churn, crate, crock, flash, flask, hutch, phial, pouch, purse, shell, stein, trunk **6** ampule, barrel, basket, beaker, bottle, bucket, carafe, carton, cradle, firkin, flacon, flagon, hamper, holder, hopper, kettle, magnum, packet, vessel **7** amphora, ampoule, caisson, caldron, canteen, capsule, chamber, cistern, humidor, package, scuttle **8** canister, cauldron, crucible, envelope **9** portfolio, reliquary, reservoir **10** receptacle, repository
  flat ~: **4** tray **5** plate **7** platter
container ___: **3** car **4** ship **5** board
containing: **4** with **9** including
  combining form: **6** -ferous
  nothing: **4** bare, void **5** empty **6** barren, hollow, vacant **7** vacated **9** evacuated
containment: **7** control
contaminant: **3** PCB **8** impurity
contaminate: **3** mar **4** foul, soil **5** dirty, spoil, stain, sully, taint **6** befoul, damage, debase, defile, infect, poison, rancid, smudge **7** begrime, blacken, corrupt, pollute, tarnish, vitiate **8** besmirch
contaminated: **4** foul **5** dirty, grimy, sooty **6** filthy, grubby, grungy, impure **7** corrupt, unclean **8** maculate, slovenly **10** unsanitary
contamination: **5** filth **6** damage **8** impurity **9** pollution **10** defilement
conte: **5** fable
Conte: **7** Richard
contemn: **4** hate, snub, twit **5** scorn, sneer, spurn **6** demean, deride, slight

7 censure, despise, disdain, dislike, sniff at 9 disregard 10 look down on, take to task
contemplate: 3 eye, see 4 mull, muse, plan, view 5 study, think, weigh 6 behold, digest, expect, gaze at, intend, look at, ponder, reason, regard, survey 7 foresee, inspect, observe, propose, reflect, stare at 8 aspire to, chew over, cogitate, consider, envisage, envision, meditate, mull over, muse over, ruminate, turn over 9 speculate 10 reckon with
contemplation: 4 look 5 study 6 musing, revery 7 reverie, thought 8 planning
object of ~: 5 navel
contemplative: 4 wise 6 intent 7 pensive, wistful 8 studious, thinking 9 religious
contempo: 6 modern, recent
contemporaneous: 6 coeval 7 present 10 coexistent
contemporary: 3 new, now 4 peer 5 in use 6 coeval, extant, living, modern, modish, recent, trendy 7 abreast, à la mode, current, in vogue, present, topical 8 up-to-date 10 coexistent
contempt: 3 dig 4 barb, gibe, jibe, sass, slam, slap, slur, snub 5 abuse, libel, odium, scorn, shame, spite, taunt 6 hatred, infamy, malice, nausea, rebuff, slight 7 affront, calumny, catcall, disdain, hauteur, mockery, obloquy, offense, put-down, sarcasm, slander 8 aversion, defiance, derision, disfavor, dishonor, distaste, ignominy, loathing, ridicule 9 antipathy, aspersion, contumely, disregard, disrepute, insolence 10 defamation, disrespect, opprobrium
exclamation: 3 aha, bah, boo, boy, huh, pah, tsk, tut, yah 4 as if, pfui, phoo, pish, pooh, posh, tush 5 faugh, ho-hum, humph, pshaw, shame 6 phooey, tsk tsk, tut-tut 8 for shame
express ~: 4 hiss, pooh 5 sniff, snort
feel ~ for: 4 hate, shun 5 abhor, scorn, spurn 6 detest, loathe, reject, revile, slight 7 despise, disdain, dislike, sneer at 8 execrate 9 abominate 10 look down on
treat with ~: 3 dis 4 jeer, mock 5 flout, scoff, spurn 6 deride, slight
Contempt (1963 film)
cast: Brigitte Bardot, Jack Palance
director: Jean-Luc Godard
contemptible: 3 bad, low 4 base, mean, vile 5 cheap, crass, dirty, lousy, mangy, nasty, seamy, slimy, sorry 6 abject, little, mangey, odious, paltry, ragged, rotten, shabby, sneaky, sordid, wicked 7 hateful, ignoble, knavish, lowdown, pitiful 8 baseborn, shameful, stinking, unworthy, wretched 9 miserable, repellant, repellent
one: 3 cad, cur 4 heel, toad, worm 5 skunk, swine, twerp, twirp 6 insect
contemptuous: 5 proud 6 cheeky 7 cynical, haughty 8 arrogant, cavalier, derisive, insolent, sardonic, scornful 9 sarcastic, vitriolic
contend: 3 run, vie, war 4 aver, avow, cope, feud, play, tilt 5 argue, claim, clash, fight, rival 6 affirm, allege, assert, battle, charge, insist, reason, refute, resist, strive, submit 7 compete, face off, grapple, purport, quarrel, vie with, wrestle 8 conflict, maintain, struggle 9 have words, lock horns, square off
(for): 2 go 5 quest 8 campaign
with: 4 face 5 rival 6 take on
contender: 4 vier 5 rival 6 player 7 fighter, nominee 9 candidate, disputant, job-hunter 10 antagonist, competitor, contestant
__ contendere: 4 nolo
contender with God, Hebrew for: 6 Israel
content: 4 glad, size, smug, text 5 happy, value 6 at ease, matter, please, serene 7 appease, at peace, gratify, meaning, pleased, satisfy, suffice, willing 8 relieved, thankful 9 fulfilled, gratified, satisfied, substance
full of ~: 5 meaty, pithy
not ~: 5 itchy 8 restless
rich in ~: 5 meaty
starter: 3 dis, mal
substantial ~: 4 meat
contented: 4 easy, smug 5 happy, quiet 8 cheerful 9 gratified, satisfied 10 complacent
sound: 2 ah 3 aah, pur 4 purr
contention: 3 war 4 feud, view 5 claim, fight, issue, posit, set-to, stand 6 battle, belief, combat, debate, static, strife, thesis 7 discord, dispute, dissent, feuding, opinion, quarrel, rivalry, wrangle 8 argument, conflict, disunity, friction, question, squabble, struggle 9 assertion, dialectic, discord, encounter, hostility, wrangling 10 allegation, antagonism, deposition, difference, discussion, disharmony, dissension, dissidence, dissonance, hypothesis, litigation, opposition, profession
bone of ~: 5 issue 8 argument
still in ~: 5 alive
contentious: 4 cold, cool, mean 5 aloof, nasty, onery, surly, testy 6 chilly, ornery, remote 7 glacial, hateful, hostile, warlike 8 contrary, factious, fighting, inimical, militant, spiteful 9 bellicose, litigious, malicious, truculent, withdrawn 10 malevolent, pugnacious
be ~: 5 argue 6 bicker
one: 6 arguer
contentment: 4 ease 5 bliss, peace 7 comfort, rapture, welfare 8 felicity, gladness, pleasure, serenity
contents: 4 list, load, text 5 cargo 6 topics, volume 7 details, filling, freight, innards, insides 8 chapters, subjects 9 substance
Conte, Richard: 5 actor
film: The Blue Gardenia (1953)
Call Northside 777 (1948)
Full of Life (1956)
Guadalcanal Diary (1943)
House of Strangers (1949)
I'll Cry Tomorrow (1955)
Ocean's Eleven (1960)
Thieves' Highway (1949)
Tony Rome (1967)
A Walk in the Sun (1945)
Whirlpool (1949)
contest: 3 row, sue, vie 4 bout, buck, duel, fray, game, meet, race, tilt 5 argue, brawl, event, fight, match, run-in, scrap, set-to, sport, trial 6 affray, attack, battle, combat, debate, defend, oppose, rumble, strife 7 dispute, lawsuit, quarrel, rivalry, wrangle 8 conflict, litigate, long jump, object to, question, skirmish, struggle, tug-of-war 9 athletics, challenge, encounter, fight over, prosecute 10 engagement, make a stand, tournament
ancient ~: 4 agon
faked ~: 5 setup
no ~: 9 hands down
orator ~: 8 polemics
qualifying ~: 4 heat
submission: 5 entry
venue: 5 arena, track
__ contest: 6 beauty
contestable: 4 moot
contestant: 4 side, vier 6 player 7 battler, entrant, fighter, hopeful, nominee, warrior 8 opponent 9 adversary, candidate, combatant, contender, contester, dark horse, disputant 10 antagonist, challenger, competitor
become a ~: 5 enter
rank a ~: 4 seed
__ contested: 5 hotly
contest, no: 4 plea
context: 4 case 5 light 7 meaning, setting
take out of ~: 8 misquote
Conti: 3 Tom 4 Bill
Conti, Bill song: Gonna Fly Now (1977)
contiguity: 7 abuttal, contact, joining, meeting 8 abutment, abutting, touching 9 adjacence, adjacency, proximity
contiguous: 4 near 5 close 6 nearby 8 abutting, adjacent, next door, touching 9 adjoining, bordering, immediate, in contact 10 approximal, contactual, convenient, juxtaposed, near-at-hand
be ~: 4 abut 8 neighbor
to: 4 near 6 beside
continence: 9 austerity 10 abstinence
continent: 3 Afr., Eur. 4 Asia, land, pure 5 N. Amer., S. Amer., sober 6 Africa, chaste, Europe 8 celibate 9 abstinent, Antartica, Australia, inhibited, temperate, unextreme 10 abstemious, Antarctica, restrained
continental
alliance: 3 OAS, OAU
breakfast item: 3 tea 4 milk 5 bagel, donut 6 banana, coffee, danish 8 doughnut
connector: 7 isthmus
divider: 3 sea 5 ocean, Urals
drifter: 5 plate
prefix: 3 Eur- 4 Afro-, Euro- 5 trans
continental __: 4 code, rise 5 drift, quilt, shelf, slope 6 divide, margin, system 7 cuisine, seating
Continental: 3 car 4 auto, Linc 7 airline, Lincoln 10 automobile
Airlines Arena team: 4 Nets
allies: 6 France, French
alternative: 5 Delta 6 United 7 Jet Blue 8 American 9 Southwest, US Airways 11 America West
former competitor: 5 USAir
to a Redcoat: 3 foe 5 enemy
Continental __: 4 Army 6 Celtic, Divide
Continental Congress meeting site: 4 York
Continental Divide (1981 film)
cast: John Belushi, Blair Brown
director: Michael Apted
Continental Op, The author: Hammett
continental walk: 5 dance
Continent, The: 6 Europe
contingencies: 3 ifs
contingency: 4 case 5 event 6 chance 9 liability
detail: 5 plan B
contingency __: 3 fee, tax 4 fund, plan 5 table 7 reserve
contingent: 4 body, team 5 corps, fluky, group, quota, troop 6 chance, flukey, likely, random 7 brigade, subject 8 not final, possible, probable, relative 9 battalion, dependant, dependent, disciples, haphazard, qualified, secondary, tentative, uncertain 10 accidental, delegation, deputation, detachment, fortuitous, incidental, unexpected, unforeseen
be ~: 4 hang, rest 5 hinge, pivot 6 depend
on: 9 providing, subject to
contingent __: 3 fee 4 fund 7 reserve
continual: 6 serial, steady 7 chronic, endless, eternal, lasting, regular, running 8 constant, enduring, frequent, habitual, unbroken, unending, untiring, unwaning 9 ceaseless, chronical, connected, incessant, perennial, permanent, perpetual, recurrent, unabating, unceasing, unfailing, unvarying 10 persistent, persisting, relentless, repetitive, unchanging, unflagging
continually: 4 ever 6 always 8 evermore
continuance: 4 life, time 6 length 8 lifetime, sequence
continuation: 6 sequel
continue: 2 go 3 run 4 go on, hold, last, live, stay 5 abide, exist, recur, renew, run on, segue, stand 6 endure, extend, hang in, hold on, keep at, keep on, keep up, linger, live on, pick up, pursue, push on, remain, reopen, resume, stream, take up 7 advance, carry on, draw out, persist, press on, proceed, prolong, restart, stick to, subsist, survive, sustain 8 go on with, lengthen, maintain, preserve, progress, protract, return to 9 go forward, persevere 10 forge ahead, perpetuate, recommence, stay a while
to: 5 reach
unable to ~: 8 overcome
uninterrupted: 3 run, yak, yap 4 talk 5 run on 6 rattle 7 maunder
continued: 5 ran on, solid 6 serial 8 untiring 9 recurrent
continuing: 6 living, serial 7 abiding, lasting, ongoing, pending, undying 8 lifelong, long-term, residual, standing, untiring 9 lingering, perennial 10 inveterate
continuity: 4 flow 5 chain, train 6 course, series 7 linking, stamina 8 cohesion, duration, monotony, sequence, survival 9 coherence, constancy, endurance, extension, fixedness, stability 10 connection, durability, perpetuity, succession
__ continuo: 5 basso
continuous: 5 level, solid 6 direct, entire, looped, smooth, steady 7 endless, nonstop, ongoing, running 8 constant, straight, unbroken, unending 9 ceaseless, connected, incessant, insistent, perpetual, prolonged, unceasing, undivided, unfailing
change: 4 flux
flow: 6 stream
continuous __: 4 wave 5 hinge, miner 6 cutter 7 casting
continuous-__ paper: 4 form
continuously: 5 on end 7 non-stop
continuum: 5 scale 10 perpetuity
Contla: 4 city, town
locale: 6 Mexico 8 Tlaxcala
conto: 5 money
contort: 4 bend, curl, warp 5 gnarl, screw, twist, wring 6 buckle, deform, mangle, wrench, writhe 8 misshape 9 convolute
contorted: 3 wry 6 atwist, skewed 7 crooked 9 malformed
expression: 5 scowl, sneer
contortion: 7 grimace 9 asymmetry, deformity 10 distortion
contortionist, like a: 5 lithe 6 limber
contour: 4 edge, form, line 5 curve, shape 6 figure 7 outline, profile, terrain 8 side view 9 lineament, sculpture 10 silhouette, topography
contour __: 3 map 4 line 5 sheet

7 curtain, feather
Contour: **3** car **4** auto, Ford
Contours song: Do You Love Me (1962)
contra: **4** anti **6** versus **7** against, reverse **8** opposite
per ~: **7** however
Contra ___, CA: **5** Costa
___-Contra: **4** Iran
contraband: **7** illegal, illicit **9** forbidden, moonshine, smuggling **10** bootlegged, prohibited, proscribed, rum-running
run ~: **7** smuggle
contrabass: **4** wind **6** string **10** instrument
contrabassoon: **4** wind **10** instrument
cousin: **4** oboe
contract: **3** ebb, get, job **4** bond, deal, pact, sell, tuck, wane, work **5** catch, incur, paper **6** engage, lessen, narrow, pledge, policy, pucker, recede, reduce, shrink, take in, treaty **7** abridge, bargain, charter, compact, curtail, decline, deflate, develop, dwindle, fall off, promise, reserve, shorten, shrivel, squeeze, subside, tighten **8** compress, condense, covenant, decrease, diminish, marriage, warranty **9** agreement, attenuate, concordat, epitomize, guarantee, indenture, liability, negotiate, stipulate, undertake **10** abbreviate, commitment, engagement, obligation, settlement
add-on: **5** rider
athlete's ~ clause: **5** no cut
detail: **4** spec, term **6** clause
for: **3** buy **4** hire **5** order **6** employ **7** charter
issue: **5** hours, raise **6** rights **8** benefits
negotiator: **3** rep **5** agent
signer: **5** inker, party
term: **6** hereby, herein
try for a ~: **3** bid **5** bid on
contract ___: **4** bond **5** labor **6** bridge
___ contract: **4** land **5** no-bid, no-cut, quasi **6** social **7** no-trade
___ contracta: **4** vena
contract bridge: **4** game **8** card game
contracted: **5** bound, scant, stiff, tight **6** narrow **9** confining
contraction: **3** tic **5** spasm **7** elision, falloff **8** decrease
common ~: **3** he'd, I'll, it'd, it's, I've **4** can't, don't, he'll, isn't, she'd, we'll, won't **5** aren't, didn't, hasn't, she'll, they'd, wasn't **6** doesn't, mustn't, they'll **7** couldn't, wouldn't **8** shouldn't
Dixie ~: **4** y'all
nonstandard ~: **4** ain't
old-style ~: **5** mayn't, shan't
poetic: **3** e'en, e'er, o'er, 'tis **4** ne'er, 'twas **5** neath, 'twere
contractor: **5** party **7** builder
at times: **5** paver, tiler
contractual: **5** legal
contradict: **4** defy, deny **5** belie, cross, rebut **6** impugn, naysay, negate, oppose, recant, refute **7** confute, dispute, gainsay **8** disagree, disprove **9** challenge, disaffirm, discredit, repudiate **10** contravene, counteract, prove wrong
contradiction: **6** denial **7** paradox **8** defiance, negation, variance
contradictory: **6** unlike **8** converse, opposite
contraire, au: **2** no **3** nah, naw, nay, nix, non **4** nein, nope, nyet, uh-uh **5** I won't, ixnay, never, no how, no way **6** no deal, noways, nowise **7** I refuse **8** forget it, I will not, negative, negatory **9** by no means, fat chance, I think not **10** count me out, not a chance, thumbs down
contralto: **5** voice **6** singer **8** Anderson, vocalist
colleague: **4** bass **5** basso, mezzo, tenor **7** soprano **8** baritone
contraption: **3** rig **4** tool **5** gismo, gizmo **6** device, gadget, widget **7** machine **9** machinery
contrapuntal song: **5** motet
contrariety: **7** inverse, obverse, reverse **8** converse, flip side, opposite, polarity **10** antithesis, opposition
contrariwise: **9** otherwise, vice versa
contrary: **4** cold, cool, mean **5** alien, aloof, balky, nasty, onery, polar, rigid, surly **6** averse, chilly, feisty, gainst, mulish, ornery, remote, unlike, unruly **7** adverse, counter, defiant, glacial, hateful, hostile, naughty, opposed, piggish, restive, reverse, unalike, wayward **8** captious, clashing, factious, indocile, inimical, negative, obdurate, opposing, opposite, perverse, spiteful, stubborn, untoward **9** bellicose, crotchety, different, dissident, malicious, obstinate, pigheaded, resistive, withdrawn **10** antithetic, dissimilar, hard-bitten, headstrong, inflexible, malevolent, pugnacious, rebellious, refractory, unfriendly
one: **4** anti
on the ~: **2** no **3** but, nah, naw, nay, nix, non **4** nein, nope, nyet, uh-uh **5** I won't, ixnay, never, no how, noway **6** no deal, noways, nowise **7** I refuse **8** forget it, I will not, negative, negatory **9** by no means, fat chance, I think not **10** count me out, not a chance, thumbs down
prefix: **5** retro- **7** counter-
to: **6** versus **7** athwart
to fact: **5** false **6** untrue **9** incorrect **10** fabricated, fallacious, fictitious, inaccurate
vote: **3** nay
___ contrary: **5** on the
contrast: **4** foil, vary **6** accent, differ, oppose, set off **7** compare, deviate, diverge **8** mismatch, separate **9** disparity, diversity, variation **10** comparison, difference, divergence, separation
in ~ to: **7** against, vis-à-vis
like some ~ s: **5** stark
contrasted: **6** unlike **10** antithetic
contrasting: **5** other **7** diverse **8** opposite
contravene: **4** deft **5** abort, annul, break, cross, spurn **6** abjure, breach, impugn, naysay, negate, oppose, refute, reject, resist, thwart **7** confute, disobey, dispute, gainsay, infract, intrude, violate **8** disagree, disclaim, disprove **9** disaffirm, discredit, go against, interfere, interpose, repudiate **10** contradict, counteract, transgress
contre-___: **4** jour **6** partie
contretemps: **4** goof **5** gaffe, run-in **6** boo-boo, mishap, slip-up **7** blooper, blunder, faux pas
contribute: **3** add **4** give, lead, lend **5** endow, grant, pay in, put in, put up, spend **6** ante up, bestow, chip in, commit, confer, devote, donate, impart, join in, kick in, pony up, render, supply, tender **7** dole out, hand out, pitch in, present, produce, proffer, promote, provide **8** bequeath, dispense **9** cooperate, reinforce, sacrifice, subscribe, subsidize **10** administer, strengthen, supplement
to: **4** help **6** assist **7** benefit
contribution: **4** alms, gift, help **5** grant, share, tithe **7** charity, handout, present, subsidy **8** bestowal, donation, offering
contributor: **5** donor, giver **6** backer, factor, patron, writer **8** reporter **9** columnist, supporter **10** benefactor, journalist, subscriber
campaign ~: **3** PAC **6** fat cat
contrite: **5** sorry **6** humble **8** penitent **9** chastened, regretful, repentant **10** apologetic, remorseful
be ~: **3** rue **6** repent
one: **4** ruer **6** atoner
contrition: **3** rue **5** shame **6** regret **7** penance, remorse **9** attrition, hair shirt, penitence **10** repentance
contrivance: **4** plan, plot, ploy, ruse, tool **5** angle, craft, dodge, gismo, gizmo, shift, thing, trick **6** design, device, engine, gadget, scheme, widget **7** gimmick, machine **8** artifice, intrigue **9** machinery, mechanism
contrive: **3** lay, rig **4** brew, form, plan, plot **5** frame, hatch, weave **6** affect, cook up, create, design, device, devise, invent, make up, manage, whip up **7** arrange, concoct, devises, dream up, fashion, finagle, prepare, project, think up, trump up, work out **8** assemble, engineer, intrigue, maneuver **9** formulate, improvise, machinate **10** manipulate
contrived: **3** pat **4** fake, made, sham, wove **5** false, hokey, phony, woven **6** forced, phoney **7** labored, stopgap **8** affected, overdone, spurious, strained **9** unnatural **10** artificial, factitious, jury-rigged
contriving: **4** wily **6** shifty
control: **3** own, run, say, use **4** boss, care, curb, head, helm, hold, keep, lead, rule, stem, sway, tact, work **5** brake, bully, check, clout, guide, leash, limit, might, pilot, quell, steer, wield **6** arrest, bridle, charge, direct, govern, halter, handle, head up, manage, police, ration, rein in, rudder, subdue **7** command, conduct, contain, dictate, harness, mastery, monitor, oversee, potence, potency, preside, repress, smother **8** clutches, deal with, dominate, domineer, dominion, guidance, hegemony, hold back, moderate, prestige, regulate, restrain **9** abatement, authority, constrain, direction, influence, mesmerize, occupancy, oversight, ownership, reign over, restraint, supervise, supremacy, upper hand **10** administer, ascendance, ascendancy, ascendence, ascendency, discipline, domination, government, keep in line, leadership, management, manipulate, monopolize, occupation, oppression, possession, regulation
be in ~: **4** rule **6** govern
device: **4** rein **5** lever, valve **6** button
easy to ~: **4** tame **6** docile
firm ~: **4** grip **5** grasp **6** clench, clinch **7** command, mastery
lose ~: **4** skid, snap **5** freak, go ape, panic **6** go wild
one out of ~: **5** rager
out of ~: **4** amok, wild **5** amuck, loose **6** adrift, unruly **7** haywire, rampant, runaway
under ~: **4** cool **6** in hand, in line
control ___: **3** rod **4** room, unit **5** board, chart, freak, group, panel, point, stick, tower **6** center, rocket, survey **7** account, surface
___ control: **3** gun **4** arms, ball, fire, rent, spin, tone **5** flood, price **6** cruise, damage, flight, ground, remote, social **7** balance, climate, mission, portion, quality
___-control: **4** dual, self
Control (1986 song) artist: Janet Jackson
CONTROL foe: **4** KAOS
___ control language: **3** job
controlled: **5** sober **7** limited, orderly, subject **8** discreet, governed, moderate, obsessed **9** nerveless **10** reasonable
controller: **6** bursar, leader, master **8** director **10** bookkeeper
controlling: **5** bossy **6** ruling **8** dominant, powerful **9** principal
control tower
device: **5** radar
dot: **3** pip **4** blip
controversial: **4** moot, open **7** at issue, dubious, suspect **8** arguable, disputed
controversy: **3** row **4** feud, flak, fuss, spat, tiff **5** fight, flack, issue, scrap **6** battle, debate, rumpus, strife, unrest **7** dispute, polemic, quarrel, wrangle **8** argument, question, squabble
controvert: **4** deny **5** argue, belie, break, rebut **6** debate, negate, oppose, oppugn, refute **7** confute, dispute, gainsay **8** disprove, question **9** challenge **10** disconfirm, prove wrong
contumacious: **6** wilful **7** defiant, lawless, wayward, willful **8** contrary, perverse **9** obstinate
contumacy: **8** defiance **10** fanaticism
contumely: **3** dig **4** barb, gibe, jibe, slam, slap, slur, snub **5** abuse, libel, scorn, taunt **6** insult, rebuff, slight **7** affront, calumny, catcall, disdain, mockery, obloquy, offense, put-down, slander **8** contempt, derision, ridicule **9** aspersion, cheap shot, indignity, insolence, invective **10** defamation, disrespect, opprobrium
contuse: **4** hurt **5** wound **6** bruise, injure **7** blacken **8** discolor
contused: **4** hurt **5** livid
contusion: **4** bump, hurt, welt **5** wound **6** bruise, injury **8** swelling
conundrum: **4** koan **5** poser, vexer **6** enigma, puzzle, riddle, teaser **7** arcanum, mystery, problem **10** closed book, puzzlement
conurbation: **4** city
conure: **4** bird **6** parrot
home: **4** cage, nest
conv.: **3** mtg. **4** sess.
convalesce: **4** heal, mend **6** look up, perk up **7** rebound, recover **10** recuperate
convalescent: **6** better **7** patient
convalescing: **9** on the mend
convection ___: **4** cell, oven
convene: **3** sit **4** call, hold, meet, open **5** rally **6** call in, corral, gather, muster, summon **7** collect, convoke, round up, scare up **8** assemble **9** forgather **10** congregate
again: **5** resit **6** remeet
convenience: **3** aid, use **4** ease, help **5** avail **6** luxury **7** amenity, benefit, comfort, leisure, liberty, service, utility **8** facility **9** handiness
at one's ~: **7** anytime
convenience ___: **4** food **5** store
convenience store
item: **3** gum, pop **4** cola, soda **5** candy, frank **6** hot dog **8** ice cream, magazine, sandwich **9** newspaper **10** chewing gum
convenient: **3** fit **4** good, near, nigh, snug **5** close, handy, happy, of use, on tap, ready **6** at hand, nearby, timely, useful, wieldy **7** close by, helpful, hopeful, in reach **8** adjacent, apposite, imminent, next-door, portable, suitable

9 adaptable, adjoining, agreeable, all-around, available, bordering, conducive, easy to use, expedient, favorable, fortunate, immediate, impending, opportune, proximate 10 acceptable, accessible, beneficial, commodious, contiguous, seasonable, time-saving
convent: 5 abbey 7 nunnery, retreat 8 cloister 9 monastery, sanctuary
attire: 5 habit
dweller: 3 nun 6 abbess
room: 4 cell
convention: 4 form, meet, mode, wont 5 canon, habit, rally, usage 6 caucus, confab, custom, powwow, praxis, treaty 7 council, fashion, meeting, precept, reunion 8 assembly, congress, jamboree, niceties, practice 9 concordat, covenance, delegates, etiquette, formality, gathering, propriety, tradition 10 assemblage, conference, delegation
site: 4 hall 5 arena, hotel
wear: 3 fez 5 badge, ID tag 7 name tag
convention __: 6 center
__ convention: 4 open
__ Convention: 6 Geneva, Warsaw
conventional: 3 std. 4 dull, tame 5 corny, hokey, moral, passé, plain, rigid, sober, stale, stock, trite, typic, usual, vapid 6 common, formal, jejune, narrow, normal, old hat, proper, ritual, square, stuffy, wonted 7 clichéd, correct, current, fatuous, general, humdrum, insular, popular, prosaic, prudish, regular, routine, typical, uptight 8 accepted, bromidic, decorous, dogmatic, everyday, expected, habitual, mediocre, ordinary, orthodox, outdated, outmoded, plebeian, standard, straight 9 customary, hackneyed, prosaical, unwritten 10 dogmatical, prevailing, uninspired, unoriginal
conventional __: 6 weapon, wisdom
conventions: 5 mores 6 praxes 8 protocol 9 propriety
conventual: 3 nun
Conventual __: 4 Mass
converge: 4 meet 5 flock, focus, merge, touch, unite 6 center, gather, huddle 8 assemble, focalize 9 intersect
on: 3 mob 4 near 8 approach
convergence: 8 junction, juncture
convergent: 7 joining, meeting, merging 8 blending 10 concurrent, synchronal
conversable: 8 obliging 9 agreeable 10 accessible
conversant: 3 hep, hip 5 aware 6 at home, au fait, versed, wise to 7 knowing, learned, skilled 8 familiar, informed 9 au courant, cognizant, conscious, observant, on the beam, plugged in, practiced 10 acquainted, perceptive, percipient, proficient
be ~ in: 4 know
with: 4 up on
conversation: 3 gab 4 chat, talk, word 6 confab, dialog, gossip, parley, powwow, speech 7 palaver 8 chitchat, colloquy, dialogue, exchange, language, repartee 9 tête-à-tête
center of ~: 5 topic
combining form: 3 -log 5 -logue
filler: 2 er, um 4 I see 5 I mean
make idle ~: 3 gab, rap, yak 4 chat
piece: 5 curio 6 oddity
starter: 5 hello
conversation __: 3 pit 5 chair, piece
conversational: 5 gabby, talky 6 chatty 7 gossipy 8 friendly 9 garrulous, talkative 10 big-mouthed, long-winded, loquacious
Conversation of Eiros and Chamion, The author: Edgar Allan Poe
Conversation, The (1974 film)
cast: John Cazale, Frederic Forrest, Gene Hackman
director: Francis Ford Coppola
converse: 3 gab, rap, yak 4 chat, chin, talk 5 speak, visit 6 confer, parley 7 commune, palaver, reverse, schmoos 8 antipode, antipole, chitchat, opposite, schmoose, schmooze 9 antipodal, discourse 10 antithesis, antithetic, chew the fat
Converse competitor: 4 Avia, Keds 6 Adidas, Reebok
conversely: 9 vice versa
conversion: 5 shift 6 change, reform 8 exchange, flip-flop 9 about-face, refitting 10 adaptation, alteration, changeover
lane ~: 5 spare, split
conversion __: 3 van 5 ratio, table
__ conversion: 3 van 6 equity
__ Convers Wyeth: 6 Newell
convert: 3 win 4 lead, sway, turn 5 adapt, alter, co-opt 6 change, decode, modify, novice, reform, switch 7 baptize, recruit, win over 8 disciple, follower, neophyte, persuade, transfer 9 liquidate, novitiate, transform, translate 10 catechumen
converted __: 4 rice 5 steel
__ converter: 6 rotary, torque
convertible: 3 car 4 auto, sofa 6 daybed, landau, liquid, mutual 7 mutable, related 9 alterable 10 automobile, changeable, modifiable, reciprocal
convertible __: 4 bond, lens
__ convertible: 7 hardtop
convertible preferred __: 5 stock
convertiplane acronym: 4 STOL
convex: 5 lobed 6 arched 7 bulging, rounded 9 outcurved
molding: 5 ovolo, torus
moldings: 4 tori 5 ovoli
tile: 6 imbrex
convexity, architectural: 7 entasis
convey: 3 lug, say, tow 4 bear, cart, cede, draw, give, haul, mean, move, pipe, send, take, tell, tote, waft 5 break, bring, carry, ferry, fetch, grant, shlep, speak, truck 6 funnel, impart, pass on, recite, relate, schlep, shlepp 7 channel, conduct, consign, deliver, express, forward, purport, recount, signify, sustain 8 describe, disclose, dispatch, transfer, transmit, vocalize 9 get across, make known, put across, transport 10 distribute
lightly: 4 waft
conveyance: 3 cab, car 4 deed 7 carrier, transit, vehicle 8 carriage, delivery 9 transport 10 delegation
see also vehicle
conveyor: 4 belt 6 bearer 7 carrier
convict: 5 felon, lifer 6 inmate, refute 7 captive, condemn 8 criminal, internee, jailbird, prisoner, sentence 9 miscreant
convicted: 6 guilty
conviction: 4 idea, view 5 cause, dogma, faith, slant, tenet, trust 6 belief, fervor, surety 7 feeling, opinion, thought, verdict 8 credence, doctrine, firmness, reliance, sureness 9 assurance, certainty, certitude, principle, sentiment 10 conclusion, condemning, confidence, enthusiasm, impression, persuasion
erroneous ~: 5 frame 6 bad rap, bum rap 7 frame-up
lack of ~: 5 doubt
lose ~: 5 waver
state with ~: 4 aver, avow 6 assert
Convicts (1991 film)
cast: Robert Duvall, Lukas Haas, James Earl Jones
Convicts 4 (1962 film)
cast: Ben Gazzara, Ray Walston, Stuart Whitman
convince: 3 get, win 4 hook, sell 5 budge 6 assure, induce 7 satisfy, win over 8 overcome, persuade, reassure, talk into 9 prevail on, put across
convinced: 4 sold, sure 5 clear 7 certain 8 positive, sanguine 9 believing, confident, obstinate, presuming, satisfied 10 optimistic
be ~: 4 feel 5 think, trust 6 accept, assume, bank on, rely on 7 believe, count on 8 depend on 9 believe in, count upon
easily ~: 5 naive
convincing: 5 solid, sound, valid 6 cogent, moving, potent, strong 7 logical, telling 8 credible, faithful, luculent, powerful, rational 9 authentic, disarming, effective, plausible 10 acceptable, believable, conclusive, dependable, felicitous, imaginable, impressive, persuasive, presumable, reasonable, satisfying, unarguable
be ~: 4 sell, wash
convivial: 3 fun, gay 4 boon, gala, kind 5 close, happy, jolly, merry 6 chummy, clubby, festal, genial, hearty, jocund, jovial, kindly, lively, social 7 affable, amiable, cordial, festive 8 amicable, cheerful, friendly, intimate, mirthful, outgoing, pleasant, sociable 9 congenial, fun-loving, hilarious, vivacious 10 benevolent, buddy-buddy, gregarious, hospitable, neighborly, solicitous
conviviality: 6 gaiety, gayety 9 happiness, merriment
convocation: 4 diet, meet 5 rally, synod 6 confab, powwow 7 council, meeting 8 assembly, conclave, congress 9 symposium
convoke: 4 call 6 call up, gather, muster, summon 7 collect, convene, marshal, round up 8 assemble
convolute: 4 coil, curl 7 contort, sinuate 10 complicate
convoluted: 5 snaky 6 ornate 7 complex, sinuous, winding 8 flexuous, involved, tortuous 9 entangled, intricate 10 meandering
convolution: 4 coil, loop, maze 5 helix, swirl, twirl, twist 6 spiral 7 coiling, snaking 8 curlicue, curlycue 9 labyrinth
convoy: 5 carry, fleet, guard, guide, train, usher 6 escort 7 caravan, conduct, protect 8 chaperon 9 accompany, chaperone, companion, safeguard
component: 4 semi 5 truck
Convoy (1975 song) artist: C.W. McCall
convulse: 5 shake, upset 6 quiver, tickle 7 agitate, break up, crack up, disturb, shake up, shudder 8 unsettle 10 discompose
convulsed, be: 4 roar 5 laugh 6 guffaw
convulsion: 5 quake, spasm, start, storm 6 tumult 7 seizure, tempest 8 paroxysm 9 agitation, cataclysm, commotion 10 earthquake
convulsive: 5 jerky 9 explosive, spasmodic 10 hysterical
Convy: 4 Bert
Conway: 3 Tim, Tom 4 city, Jack, town 5 Kevin 6 Twitty
locale: 8 Arkansas
Conway, Tim: 5 actor 8 comedian
film: The Shaggy D. A. (1976) The World's Greatest Athlete (1973)
TV: The Carol Burnett Show, McHale's Navy
cony: 3 fur 4 hare, pika 5 hyrax 6 animal, dassie, mammal, rabbit
coo: 4 peep 6 gurgle, murmur
bill and ~: 4 neck 5 spoon 6 cuddle
Cooder: 2 Ry
Coody, Charles: 6 golfer
cooer: 4 dove 6 pigeon 8 lovebird
Coogan: 5 Keith 6 Jackie
Coogan, Jackie: 5 actor
film: The Kid (1921)
Oliver Twist (1922)
Peck's Bad Boy (1921)
spouse: Betty Grable
TV: The Addams Family
Coogan's Bluff (1968 film): 5 oater
cast: Susan Clark, Lee J. Cobb, Clint Eastwood, Tisha Sterling
director: Don Siegel
cook: 3 fix, fry 4 bake, boil, brew, burn, chef, make, nuke, sear, stew, warm 5 baker, broil, brown, curry, devil, grill, outdo, poach, roast, sauté, scald, shirr, steam, steep, toast 6 braise, broast, coddle, decoct, doctor, heat up, panfry, scorch, simmer, sizzle, tamper 7 escalop, griddle, parboil, prepare, servant, swelter 8 barbecue, escallop, rational 9 fricassee, microwave
accessory: 4 mitt, peel 5 apron, timer 7 spatula
don't ~: 6 eat out
ender: 3 out 4 book, ware
exhortation: 5 dig in
for a crowd: 5 cater
in a microwave: 4 nuke
measure: 3 cup, tbs., tsp. 4 dash, tbsp. 5 pinch 6 cupful 8 teaspoon 10 tablespoon
need: 3 pan, pot, wok 4 oven 5 grill, stove 6 frypan, kettle, teapot, tureen, vessel 7 dishpan, roaster, skillet 8 barbecue, saucepan
one way to ~: 3 fry 4 bake, boil, sear, stew 5 broil, grill, poach, roast, sauté, scald, shirr, steam 6 braise, broast, coddle, panfry 7 parboil 8 barbecue 9 fricassee, microwave
quickly: 5 fry up
up: 4 form, make, plan, plot 5 frame, hatch 6 devise, ideate, invent 7 concoct, fashion, imagine 8 conceive, contrive, intrigue 9 fabricate, formulate
Zen ~: 5 tenzo
cook-__: 3 off, out
__ cook: 3 fry
Cook: 2 mt. 3 mtn., str. 4 isle, peak 5 James, mount, Peter, Robin 6 Elisha, island, strait 7 Fielder 8 mountain
locale: 10 New Zealand
offering: 4 tour
rival: 5 Peary
Cook __: 5 Inlet 6 Strait 7 Islands
cookbook: 6 manual
amt.: 3 tbs., tsp. 4 tbsp.
direction: 3 add, fry 4 beat, boil, chop, dice, heat, stew, stir 5 baste, purée, roast, sauté, scald, steam, toast
phrase: 3 a la 5 add in
Cooke: 3 Sam 8 Alistair
cooked: 4 done 5 ready
lightly ~: 4 pink, rare
not ~: 3 raw
cooked-up: 5 bogus, false 10 fictitious
cooker: 3 pan, pot, wok 4 oven 5 crock, grill, stove 6 frypan 8 barbecue
__ cooker: 4 slow
cookery: 4 food 7 kitchen 10 gastronomy
burnt, in ~: 5 brulé 6 brulée
stuffed, in ~: 5 farci

term: 5 au jus, garni 7 à la mode 8 au gratin
Cooke, Sam
song: Another Saturday Night (1963)
Chain Gang (1960)
Shake (1965)
Twistin' the Night Away (1962)
You Send Me (1957)
Cookeville: 4 city, town
locale: 9 Tennessee
cookhouse: 7 kitchen
cookie: 2 jo 3 bar, pet 4 baby, dear, jill, kiss, love, Oreo, snap 5 amour, angel, chéri, cutey, cutie, deary, ducky, flame, goody, honey, leman, lover, lovey, novia, novio, sugar, sweet, wafer 6 bon ami, butter, chérie, dautie, dearie, Droxie, fig bar, goodie, hermit, jumble, steady, sweets 7 beloved, biscuit, brownie, dearest, dear one, fortune, hibachi, oatmeal, pigsney, ratafia, schatzi, squeeze, sweetie, tootsie 8 biscotto, chou-chou, cutie pie, dowsabel, dulcinea, ladylove, lovebird, macaroon, macushla, paramour, precious, seed cake, snookums, sugar pie, sweetums, truelove 9 bonne amie, boyfriend, Chips Ahoy, dreamboat, Fig Newton, inamorata, inamorato, krummkake, lebkuchen, petit chou, tollhouse, valentine 10 gingersnap, girlfriend, heartthrob, honeybunch, lady finger, Lorna Doone, mavourneen, shortbread, sugar wafer, sweetheart, sweetie pie, turtledove
box stat.: 5 net wt.
cooker: 4 oven
crisp ~: 4 snap
dough container: 4 tube
holder: 3 box, jar 5 crock
ingredient: 3 fig, nut, oat 5 anise, crème, dough 6 ginger
maker: 5 baker 6 bakery
manufacturer: 7 Archway, Keebler, Nabisco 8 Sunshine 9 Mrs. Fields 10 Famous Amos, Peak Freans
mix: 6 batter
molasses ~: 6 hermit
nugget: 4 chip
partner: 4 milk
quantity: 5 batch 6 jarful
sheet: 3 tin
the way the ~ crumbles: 3 lot 4 fate
thin ~: 5 wafer
tidbit: 5 crumb
topping: 5 icing 9 chocolate
cookie ___: 3 jar 5 press, sheet 6 cutter
___ cookie: 4 drop 6 butter 7 fortune
Cookie: 8 Bumstead 9 Lavagetto
Cookie (1989 film)
cast: Peter Falk, Emily Lloyd, Dianne Wiest
director: Susan Seidelman
Cookie Crisp: 6 cereal
competitor: 3 Kix 4 Life, Trix 5 Kashi, Quisp, Total 6 Kaboom, Muesli, Oreo O's, Pablum, Smacks 7 All-Bran, Crispix, Harmony, Hunny B's, Mueslix, Oat Bran, Pokemon 8 Boo Berry, Cheerios, Corn Chex, Corn Pops, Fiber One, Rice Chex, Special K, Uncle Sam, Wheaties 9 Alpha Bits, Apple Zaps, Grape Nuts, Honey Comb, Just Right, Wheat Chex 10 Apple Jacks, Bran Flakes, Cap'n Crunch, Cocoa Puffs, Froot Loops, Mini-Wheats, Nutri-Grain, Puffed Rice, Quaker Oats, Smart Start 11 Cocoa Blasts, Golden Crisp, Lucky Charms, Puffed Wheat, Sweet Crunch, Waffle Crisp
cookie dough: 8 ice cream
alternative: 5 lemon, mocha, peach 6 banana, coffee, Jamoca, toffee 7 caramel, coconut, vanilla 8 cinnamon, hazelnut 9 bubblegum, chocolate, pineapple, pistachio, raspberry, rocky road, rum raisin 10 blackberry, cheesecake, Neapolitan, peppermint, strawberry
Cookie Monster cohort: 4 Bert 5 Ernie, Piggy 6 Kermit 7 Big Bird 9 Miss Piggy
cookies and cream alternative: 5 lemon, mocha, peach 6 banana, coffee, Jamoca, toffee 7 caramel, coconut, vanilla 8 cinnamon, hazelnut 9 bubblegum, chocolate, pineapple, pistachio, raspberry, rocky road, rum raisin 10 blackberry, cheesecake, Neapolitan, peppermint, strawberry
Cookie's Fortune (1999 film)
cast: Glenn Close, Julianne Moore, Chris O'Donnell, Liv Tyler
director: Robert Altman
cooking: 4 food 5 aboil 7 cuisine 8 thriving 9 housework 10 gastronomy
class: 6 home ec
direction: 3 fry 4 bake, beat, boil, heat, stew, stir 5 baste, roast, sauté, scald, steam
implement: 5 dicer, parer, ricer, sieve 6 beater 8 colander
ingredient: 3 egg, oil 4 lard, mace, sage 5 flour, spice, sugar, thyme 6 nutmeg 7 parsley, vanilla 8 cinnamon, rosemary
pot: 4 olla 6 copper
style: 5 Cajun 6 Creole
utensil: 3 pan, pot, wok 6 frypan, tureen 7 skillet
utensil coating: 6 enamel
cooking ___ gas: 4 with
Cooking Egg, A: 4 poem
author: T.S. Eliot
cooking oil: 6 canola, Crisco, Mazola, Wesson 7 Puritan
source: 4 corn 5 olive 9 sunflower
Cook Islands island: 9 Rarotonga
Cook, James: 7 British 8 explorer
cook one's ___: 5 goose
cookout: 3 bbq, fry 4 meal 5 bar-b-q 6 picnic 8 barbecue
fare: 4 fish 5 cabob, frank, kabab, kabob, kebab, kebob, steak, wurst 6 burger, hot dog, weiner 7 chicken 9 hamburger
Hawaiian ~: 4 luau
intruder: 3 ant
need: 3 gas 4 fire 5 grill 7 propane 8 barbecue, charcoal
remnant: 3 ash 6 cinder
site: 4 deck, park, yard 5 patio
Cook, Peter: 5 actor 8 comedian
film: Bedazzled (1967)
Getting It Right (1989)
The Secret Policeman's Other Ball (1982)
Cook, Rachael Leigh: 7 actress
film: All I Wanna Do (1998)
Antitrust (2001)
Get Carter (2000)
She's All That (1999)
Cook, Robin: 6 author, writer
work: Acceptable Risk
Brain
Chromosome 6
Coma
Contagion
Fatal Cure
Fever
Godplayer
Harmful Intent
Mindbend
Mortal Fear
Mutation
Outbreak
Seizure
Shock
Sphinx
Terminal
Toxin
Vector
Vital Signs
The Year of the Intern
Cook's ___: 4 tour
cook the ___: 5 books
cookware: 8 utensils
coating: 4 lard
name: 4 Ekco 5 Pyrex
cool: 3 def, hep, hip, icy, rad 4 aces, A-one, boss, braw, calm, cold, dece, even, fine, gear, keen, lull, mean, mild, neat, nice, phat, tuff 5 abate, algid, allay, aloof, brisk, chill, crisp, dandy, ducky, fresh, frost, gelid, grand, great, lucid, marvy, nasty, neato, nifty, nippy, nobby, onery, poise, prime, quiet, slake, slick, sober, sound, staid, stoic, suave, super, surly, swell, tepid, zingy 6 aplomb, arctic, at ease, bang on, bang-up, biting, bonzer, bosker, casual, chilly, choice, dampen, divine, dreamy, far out, freeze, frigid, frosty, gentle, gnarly, groovy, lovely, low-key, mellow, offish, ornery, peachy, placid, poised, quench, remote, sedate, serene, slap-up, spot on, steady, stolid, superb, temper, terrif, tiptop, unreal, whizzo, wicked, wintry 7 amazing, amiable, assuage, assured, at peace, awesome, bracing, capital, chilled, corking, distant, equable, glacial, hateful, hostile, mollify, neutral, offhand, pacific, perfect, politic, rapture, refresh, relaxed, ripping, shivery, skookum, stellar, stoical, sublime, unfazed, unmoved, warmish, wintery, zinging 8 amicable, carefree, composed, contrary, dazzling, detached, especial, eximious, fabulous, five-star, four-star, frabjous, glorious, heavenly, informal, inimical, jim-dandy, laid-back, loveless, lukewarm, mitigate, moderate, not so hot, peaceful, pleasant, rational, reserved, skillful, slam-bang, smashing, spiteful, splendid, standout, sterling, stickout, superior, terrific, together, top-level, topnotch, tranquil, very good, wondrous 9 apathetic, bellicose, bodacious, collected, composure, easygoing, Endsville, excellent, exemplary, exquisite, first-rate, high-grade, hunky-dory, impassive, incurious, malicious, marvelous, nerveless, quiescent, reconcile, sollicker, temperate, top-flight, unexcited, unextreme, unruffled, unstirred, unworried, withdrawn, wonderful 10 confidence, cool-headed, detachment, first-class, fortifying, hotsy-totsy, impersonal, impressive, insociable, jack-a-dandy, malevolent, nonchalant, out of sight, peachy-keen, phenomenal, phlegmatic, pugnacious, reasonable, refreshing, remarkable, restrained, sedateness, speechless, stupendous, super-duper, unaffected, unagitated, unfriendly, unsociable, untroubled
down: 3 ice 5 chill
drink: 3 ade, pop 4 cola, soda 5 beeer
dude: 3 cat 6 daddy-o, hepcat
flavor: 4 mint
in a ~ way: 5 icily
it: 3 nix 4 halt, stop, wait 5 cease, quiet, relax 6 desist, lay off, relent 7 silence 8 calm down, chill out, loosen up 9 lighten up, seriously
lose one's ~: 4 boil, rant, rave 5 go ape 6 blow up, get mad
not ~: 5 nerdy, unhip
off: 3 fan 4 calm, lull 5 quiet, relax 6 die out, soothe, unwind 8 calm down 10 settle down, simmer down
one's heels: 4 wait 5 tarry 8 sit tight
playing it ~: 7 careful 8 cautious
spot: 5 shade
time: 4 fall
cool ___: 3 out 4 jazz
cool ___ cucumber: 3 as a
cool-___: 6 headed
___ cool!: 3 Way
___-cool: 3 air 5 water
Cool ___: 4 Jerk, Love, Whip 5 It Now, World 6 Change
Cool ___ Bell: 4 Papa
Cool ___ Luke: 4 Hand
___ Cool: 3 Joe 6 Johnny, Medium
coolabah: 4 tree
coolant: 5 Freon, sweat
Cool, Dry Place, A (1999 film)
cast: Joey Lauren Adams, Monica Potter, Devon Sawa, Vince Vaughn
cooler: 3 ade, fan, ice, pen 4 coop, icer, jail, poky, stir 5 clink, pokey, rocks 6 fridge, icebox, lockup, prison 7 freezer, hoosgow, slammer 8 hoosegow
contents: 3 ice 4 beer, cola, soda
in the ~: 5 on ice
room ~: 2 AC 3 fan
summer ~: 3 ade, ice, pop 4 cola, soda 5 slush 6 breeze 7 iced tea
___ cooler: 4 wine 5 water
Cooley High (1975 film)
cast: Lawrence Hilton-Jacobs, Garrett Morris, Glynn Turman
Cool Hand Luke (1967 film)
cast: Lou Antonio, J.D. Cannon, George Kennedy, Strother Martin, Paul Newman
dog: 4 Blue
cool-headed: 4 calm 5 quiet, sober 10 farsighted, unagitated
Coolidge: 3 Cal 4 Rita 5 Grace 6 Calvin, Martha
Coolidge, Calvin: 9 president
alma mater: 7 Amherst
birthplace: 7 Vermont
former occupation: 6 lawyer
home: 4 Mass. 7 Vermont
like ~: 5 terse
opponent: 5 Davis 10 LaFollette
real first name: 4 John
V.P.: 5 Dawes
wife: 5 Grace
Coolidge, Martha: 8 director
film: Angie (1994)
City Girl (1984)
Lost in Yonkers (1993)
Out to Sea (1997)
Rambling Rose (1991)
Valley Girl (1983)
Coolidge, Rita
song: Higher and Higher (1977)
We're All Alone (1977)
spouse: Kris Kristofferson
cooling
agent: 6 Dry Ice
capacity unit: 3 BTU
device: 2 AC 3 fan 6 ice bag 7 ice pack
off: 5 truce 7 détente
cooling-off period: 5 delay, truce 6 autumn
Coolio: 9 Artis Ivey, rap artist
Cool it!: 4 stop 5 chill
Cool Love (1981 song) artist: Cruise
Cool Mission, A author: Nathanael West
Cool, Mr., no: 4 nerd, nurd 5 dweeb
coolness: 4 calm 5 chill, nerve, shade 6 apathy 7 neglect, reserve 8 calmness, distance 9 assurance, restraint, sang-froid 10 detachment, equanimity, moderation, neutrality

cool one's __: 5 heels
Cool Papa: 4 Bell
Cool Runnings (1993 film)
cast: John Candy, Doug E. Doug
director: Jon Turteltaub
Cool World (1992 film)
cast: Kim Basinger, Gabriel Byrne, Brad Pitt, Frank Sinatra Jr.
director: Ralph Bakshi
coon __: 3 cat, dog 6 cheese
cooncan: 4 game 8 card game
__ coon cat: 5 Maine
coon dog: 5 hound 10 bloodhound
Cooney: 5 Gerry
Coon Rapids: 4 city, town
locale: 9 Minnesota
coon's __: 3 age
__ coon's age: 3 in a
coonskin: 3 cap, hat
coop: 3 pen 4 cage, cell, cote, jail, nest 5 booth, fence, house, hutch 6 cooler, lockup, prison 7 hoosgow, housing, slammer 8 henhouse, hoosegow 9 enclosure
dweller: 3 hen 5 layer
fly the ~: 2 go 4 flee, skip 6 decamp, escape 7 abandon, abscond, go south 8 fugitate, jump bail, run for it 9 break away
group: 4 eggs, hens
sound: 3 coo 4 peep 6 cackle
starter: 3 hen
up: 3 pen 4 hold 5 cramp 6 encage 7 confine, enclose, impound, inclose
co-op: 4 flat, home, mart 5 abode, house 6 market 7 domicil, habitat, housing, shelter 8 domicile 9 residence
kin: 5 condo
__ coop: 7 chicken
cooped up: 4 pent 5 stied 8 fenced in
cooper: 7 artisan 9 craftsman
product: 4 cask 6 barrel
tool: 3 adz 4 adze
Cooper: 3 Pat 4 font, Gary, Leon 5 Alice, Chris 6 Gladys, Jackie 8 Melville, typeface
Cooper, Alice
song: Poison (1989)
School's Out (1972)
You and Me (1977)
cooperate: 3 aid 4 help 5 agree, align, aline, unite 6 accede, assist, club up, comply, concur, join in, league 7 go along, pitch in, promote 8 interact, play ball, take part 9 harmonize, lend a hand, play along 10 assist with, comply with, contribute, coordinate, join forces
with: 4 abet, join
(with): 4 side
cooperating: 6 united
cooperation: 3 aid 4 help 5 unity 6 assist 7 cahoots, harmony, synergy 8 teamwork
cooperative: 5 joint 6 shared, united 7 commune, helpful, unified 8 amenable, communal, obliging, synergic 9 concerted
cooperative __: 4 bank 5 store
cooperatively: 8 mutually 9 in concert
cooperator: 9 assistant, associate
Cooper, Chris: 5 actor
film: Adaptation (2002, AA)
The Bourne Identity (2002)
Great Expectations (1998)
Matewan (1987)
October Sky (1999)
The Patriot (2000)
Cooper City: 4 city, town
locale: 7 Florida
Cooper, Gary: 5 actor
deadline: 4 noon
film: Along Came Jones (1945)
Ball of Fire (1941)
Beau Geste (1939)
City Streets (1931)
The Court-Martial of Billy Mitchell (1955)
Design for Living (1933)
Desire (1936)
A Farewell to Arms (1932)
For Whom the Bell Tolls (1943)
Friendly Persuasion (1956)
The General Died at Dawn (1936)
The Hanging Tree (1959)
High Noon (1952, AA)
If I Had a Million (1932)
The Lives of a Bengal Lancer (1935)
Love in the Afternoon (1957)
Man of the West (1958)
Meet John Doe (1941)
Morocco (1930)
Mr. Deeds Goes to Town (1936)
One Sunday Afternoon (1933)
Peter Ibbetson (1935)
The Plainsman (1936)
The Pride of the Yankees (1942)
The Real Glory (1939)
Sergeant York (1941, AA)
Souls at Sea (1937)
Ten North Frederick (1958)
Vera Cruz (1954)
The Westerner (1940)
role: 4 York 5 Deeds, Geste 6 Gehrig
Cooper, Jackie: 5 actor
film: The Bowery (1933)
The Champ (1931)
The Return of Frank James (1940)
Skippy (1931)
Superman (1978)
Treasure Island (1934)
Cooper, James Fenimore: 6 author
work: The Deer Slayer
The Last of the Mohicans
Leather-Stocking Tales
The Pathfinder
The Pioneers
The Prairie
The Spy
Cooper, Leon: 8 Nobelist 9 physicist
Cooper Mountain, resort near: 4 Vail
Cooperstown
locale: 7 New York
member: 3 Day, Fox, Ott 4 Babe, Bell, Cobb, Dean, Doby, Fisk, Ford, Foxx, Hoyt, Klem, Mack, Mays, Mize, Rice, Ruth, Ryan, Wynn, Yogi 5 Aaron, Anson, Banks, Bench, Brett, Brock, Carew, Combs, Doerr, Evers, Flick, Frick, Giles, Gomez, Grove, Irvin, Kiner, Klein, Lemon, Lopez, Paige, Perez, Reese, Rixey, Roush, Rusie, Selee, Smith, Spahn, Terry, Vance, Veeck, Waner, Wheat, Young, Yount 6 Alston, Barrow, Bender, Carter, Cepeda, Chylak, Conlan, Cronin, Cuyler, Dihigo, Feller, Foster, Frisch, Gehrig, Gibson, Goslin, Hanlon, Harris, Hunter, Kaline, Koufax, Lajoie, Landis, Mantle, McGraw, Mel Ott, Morgan, Murray, Musial, Niekro, Palmer, Rickey, Seaver, Sisler, Snider, Sutton, Ty Cobb, Wagner, Weaver, Wilson, Yawkey 7 Al Lopez, Appling, Ashburn, Averill, Barlick, Bunning, Carlton, Collins, Cy Young, Fingers, Hornsby, Hubbard, Hubbell, Huggins, Jackson, Jenkins, Johnson, Lasorda, Lazzeri, Leon Day, Mathews, McCovey, Medwick, Puckett, Rizzuto, Roberts, Ruffing, Sam Rice, Schmidt, Speaker, Stearns, Stengel, Traynor, Vaughan, Waddell, Wilhelm 8 Al Kaline, Anderson, Aparicio, Babe Ruth, Bill Klem, Bob Lemon, Boudreau, Cap Anson, Chandler, Clemente, Cochrane, DiMaggio, Drysdale, Durocher, Ed Barrow, Edd Roush, Griffith, Lou Brock, MacPhail, Marichal, Marquard, McCarthy, Robinson, Rod Carew, Spalding, Stargell, Williams, Winfield 9 Al Barlick, Alexander, Amos Rusie, Bill Terry, Bill Veeck, Bob Feller, Bob Gibson, Dandridge, Dizzy Dean, Don Sutton, Early Wynn, Eppa Rixey, Ford Frick, Greenberg, Hank Aaron, Jim Palmer, Joe Cronin, Joe Morgan, Killebrew, Larry Doby, Lou Gehrig, Mathewson, Mazeroski, McKechnie, Nap Lajoie, Nellie Fox, Newhouser, Nolan Ryan, Paul Waner, Radbourne, Slaughter, Tom Seaver, Tom Yawkey, Tony Perez, Waite Hoyt, Yogi Berra, Zack Wheat 10 Ban Johnson, Bobby Doerr, Cal Hubbard, Campanella, Charleston, Chuck Klein, Connie Mack, Dazzy Vance, Duke Snider, Earle Combs, Earl Weaver, Elmer Flick, Ernie Banks, Frank Selee, Gary Carter, Hack Wilson, Jim Bunning, Jimmie Foxx, Joe Medwick, John McGraw, Josh Gibson, Kiki Cuyler, Lefty Gomez, Lefty Grove, Lloyd Waner, Monte Irvin, Ozzie Smith, Phil Niekro, Pie Traynor, Ralph Kiner, Red Ruffing, Robin Yount, Rube Foster, Stan Musial, Whitey Ford, Willie Mays 11 Carl Hubbell, Yastrzemski
site: 10 Hall of Fame
co-opt: 5 adopt, usurp 6 absorb, draw in 7 bring in, convert, include, preempt 8 take over 10 assimilate, commandeer
coordinate: 3 run 4 mate, mesh, pool 5 agree, align, aline, equal, match, synch, tie in 6 adjust, attune 7 coequal 8 mobilize, organize, parallel, regulate 9 cooperate, correlate, equalized, harmonize, integrate, reconcile 10 coincident, collateral, equivalent, proportion, reciprocal, tantamount
coordinate __: 4 bond 5 paper 6 clause, system
coordinated: 6 in sync
__-coordinated: 5 color
coordinates: 8 ensemble
use ~: 5 graph
__ coordinates: 5 polar 7 oblique
__ coordination: 7 eye-hand, hand-eye
coordinaton loss: 5 ataxy 6 ataxia
Coors: 4 beer
alternative: 5 Becks, Pabst 6 Amstel, Corona, Miller, Molson, Stroh's 7 Schlitz 8 Heineken, Michelob 9 Lowenbrau 10 Ballantine
brand: 4 Zima
Coos: 3 bay 5 tribe
locale: 6 Oregon
coot: 4 bird 6 codger, geezer, mud hen 8 water hen
cooter: 6 animal, turtle 7 reptile
cootie: 3 bug 5 louse 6 insect
Cootie: 4 game
cooties: 4 lice
Coover, Robert: 6 writer
co-owned: 5 joint
cop: 3 get, nab, rob 4 lift, narc, nark 5 bobby, filch, narco, pinch, swipe 6 collar, Friday, lawman, obtain, pilfer, rip off, shamus 7 acquire, Columbo, officer, procure, receive 8 bluecoat, Drummond, flatfoot 9 detective, patrolman 10 Dirty Harry
California ~ grp.: 4 LAPD, SFPD
catch: 4 perp 5 felon 8 criminal
drug ~: 4 narc, nark 5 narco
group: 2 PD 3 FOP, PBA 5 squad 8 precinct
London ~: 5 bobby
order: 6 freeze
out: 4 quit 5 evade, shirk 6 desert, renege 7 abandon 8 go back on, slack off 9 back-pedal
Paris ~: 4 flic
route: 4 beat
TV ~: 5 Lacey 6 Cagney, Friday 7 Columbo
undercover ~: 4 narc, nark 5 agent, narco
cop __: 3 out 5 a plea
__ cop: 7 traffic
__-Cop: 5 Rent-a
Copacabana: 5 beach 6 resort
locale: 3 Rio 6 Brazil
sculptor: 4 Erté
Copacabana (1978 song) artist: Barry Manilow
copacetic: 3 A-OK 4 jake 9 admirable 10 acceptable
copal: 5 resin 6 fossil
cope: 5 get by, stand 6 make do, manage, suffer 7 contend, grapple, make out, wrestle 8 confront, stand for, struggle 9 withstand 10 canonicals
with: 4 face, meet 6 endure, handle 8 face up to 10 meet head on, take care of
(with): 4 deal, live 6 reckon
Cope alternative: 3 APF 5 Advil, Aleve, Bayer 6 Anacin, Datril, Motrin 7 Ecotrin, Tylenol 8 Bufferin, Excedrin, St. Joseph, Vanquish 9 Ascriptin
Cope Book name: 4 Erma
Copeland: 7 Stewart
copenhagen __: 4 blue
Copenhagen: 4 city, port, town 5 horse 6 equine 7 capital
locale: 7 Denmark
rider: 10 Wellington
Swedish port near ~: 5 Malmö
Copenhagen author: Michael Frayn
Copernicus: 6 crater 8 Nicolaus 10 astronomer
Copiague: 4 city, town
locale: 7 New York
copier: 4 aper 6 scribe 7 epigone, machine 8 imitator 10 amanuensis
button: 5 reset
chemical: 5 toner 6 imager
company: 5 Canon, Ricoh, Xerox
for short: 5 mimeo
part: 4 drum
starter: 5 photo
coping __: 3 saw
copious: 3 big 4 full, many, much, rich, rife 5 ample, broad, large 6 divers, gobs of, lavish, lots of, myriad, plenty, umteen, untold 7 heaps of, liberal, no end of, opulent, piles of, profuse, scads of, umpteen 8 abundant, affluent, detailed, fruitful, generous, manifold, numerous, oodles of, princely, prodigal, prolific, scores of, umpsteen 9 abounding, bounteous, bountiful, countless, extensive, exuberant, luxuriant, plenteous, plentiful, quite a few, unsparing 10 inordinate, voluminous, zillions of
copiously: 4 much 6 vastly 7 largely 10 adequately
Cop Land (1997 film)
cast: Robert De Niro, Janeane Garofalo, Harvey Keitel, Ray Liotta, Sylvester Stallone
director: James Mangold
Copland, Aaron: 8 composer
work: Appalachian Spring
Billy the Kid
El Salon Mexico

Fanfare for the Common Man
A Lincoln Portrait
Quiet City
Rodeo
Short Symphony
Symphonic Ode
Copley: 4 Teri
Copley, John Singleton: 6 artist 7 painter
cop-out: 5 alibi 6 excuse 7 evasion, pretext
Coppell: 4 city, town
locale: 5 Texas
copper: 4 cent, coin, fuzz 5 bobby, brown, color, metal, pence, penny 7 element, reddish 8 flatfoot
alloy: 5 brass, Monel 6 bronze, latten, oreide, ormolu, oroide, tambac, tombac 7 Everdur, Mumetal 8 gunmetal, Manganin, pot metal 9 barberite, bell metal, duralumin, Dutch foil, Dutch gold, Dutch leaf, pinchbeck, platinoid 10 constantan, Dutch metal, gold bronze, mosaic gold
coin: 4 cent
combining form: 4 cupr- 5 chalc-, chalk-, cupri-, cupro 6 chalco-, chalko-
containing ~: 6 cupric 7 cuprous
ender: 4 head, leaf, ware 5 plate, smith
exporter: 5 Chile
ore: 7 azurite 9 malachite
relative: 3 bay, dun, tan 4 bole, ecru, fawn, foxy, nude, seal 5 amber, beige, camel, cocoa, hazel, khaki, mocha, sepia, tawny, umber 6 auburn, bister, bistre, bronze, coffee, ginger, russet, sienna, sorrel, suntan, walnut 7 biscuit, caramel, dogwood 8 chestnut, cinnamon, mahogany 9 butternut, chocolate
source: 3 ore
tone: 3 red 6 bronze
copper ___: 4 iris, spot 5 beech 7 cyanide, pyrites, sulfate
copper-___: 4 leaf 5 toned
Copper: 5 river
locale: 6 Alaska
Copperas Cove: 4 city, town
locale: 5 Texas
Copper Beech, The author: Binchy
Copperfield, David: 8 magician
first wife: 4 Dora
mother: 5 Clara
prop for ~: 4 wand
copperhead: 5 snake 6 animal 7 reptile
relative: 3 asp, boa 5 aboma, adder, cobra, krait, mamba, racer, viper 6 dhaman, python, taipan 7 markhor, rattler 8 anaconda, moccasin, ringhals 9 boomslang, coachwhip 10 bushmaster, sidewinder
weapon: 5 venom
Copperhead Road singer: 5 Earle
coppers, British: 5 pence
Copper Sun author: Countee Cullen
Coppertone: 6 lotion
ingredient: 4 PABA
no.: 3 SPF
coppice: 4 wood 5 brush, copse, grove, woods 7 boscage, coppice, thicket
Coppola: 5 Sofia 7 Carmine
Coppola, Francis Ford: 8 director
film: Apocalypse Now (1979)
Bram Stoker's Dracula (1992)
The Conversation (1974)
The Cotton Club (1984)
Finian's Rainbow (1968)
Gardens of Stone (1987)
The Godfather (1972)
The Godfather Part II (1974, AA)
The Godfather Part III (1990)
Jack (1996)
Peggy Sue Got Married (1986)
The Rainmaker (1997)
The Rain People (1969)
Rumble Fish (1983)
Tucker: The Man and His Dream (1988)
You're a Big Boy Now (1966)
nephew: Nicolas Cage
sister: Talia Shire
Coppola, Sofia spouse: Spike Jonze
coprolite: 6 fossil
cops and ___: 7 robbers
Cops and Robbers (1973 film)
cast: Joseph Bologna, Cliff Gorman
director: Aram Avakian
copse: 4 mott, wood 5 brush, grove, motte, woods 7 boscage, coppice, thicket
copter: 4 helo 7 chopper 8 aircraft 9 eggbeater 10 whirlybird
blade: 5 rotor
forerunner: 4 giro
noise: 4 whir 5 whirr
Coptic: 6 church 8 language
copula: 4 link
copy: 2 do 3 ape, dup., fac., fax 4 draw, dupe, echo, fake, lift, mock, news, sham, stat, text, type 5 clone, ditto, image, issue, mimeo, mimic, print, repro, steal, trace, write, Xerox 6 backup, borrow, carbon, depict, double, ectype, follow, mirror, parody, parrot, pirate, record, repeat, script, sketch 7 emulate, extract, forgery, imitate, portray, reflect, replica, reprint, rewrite, set down, tracing 8 knockoff, likeness, make like, simulate, specimen 9 duplicate, facsimile, imitation, look-alike, photocopy, Photostat, replicate, reproduce 10 mimeograph, photograph, plagiarize, repetition, simulacrum, transcribe, transcript
carbon ~: 7 replica 8 likeness 9 duplicate, facsimile, identical, imitation, look-alike 10 equivalent
ender: 3 boy, cat 4 book, edit, girl 5 right 6 holder, reader, writer
not a ~: 4 orig. 8 original
starter: 5 photo
copy ___: 3 boy, cat 4 desk, girl 5 paper 6 editor 7 machine
copy-___: 4 edit
___ copy: 4 fair, hard, line, soft, time 5 blind 6 carbon, ribbon 7 release
copycat: 3 ape 4 aper, mime 5 mimer, mimic 6 echoer, parrot 8 follower, imitator 9 imitative
comment: 5 ditto, me too
Copycat (1995 film)
cast: Holly Hunter, Dermot Mulroney, Sigourney Weaver
director: Jon Amiel
copyist: 6 scribe, sopher 9 scrivener, secretary 10 amanuensis
copyread: 4 edit
copyright: 6 patent 8 monopoly 10 monopolize
letter: 3 cee
relative: 2 TM 9 trademark
coq ___: 5 au vin
coquette: 3 toy 4 minx, vamp 5 flirt, tease 6 trifle 10 make eyes at
act the ~: 5 flirt, tease
Coquette sculptor: 4 Erté
coquettish: 3 coy 6 fickle 9 frivolous, kittenish
coquilles St. ___: 7 Jacques
Coquimbo: 4 city, town
locale: 5 Chile
coquina: 4 clam
Coquitlam: 4 city, town
locale: 6 Canada
coquito: 4 palm
cor: 4 oboe
cor ___: 7 anglais
Cora: 5 Baird 6 Sandel 7 Dithers
coracle: 4 boat
coral: 3 gem, red, sea 4 pink, rosy 5 color, polyp 6 orange, yellow 7 pinkish, reddish 9 yellowish
ender: 4 root 5 berry
formation: 3 cay, key 4 reef 5 atoll
reef denizen: 5 moray
reef pool: 6 lagoon
relative: 4 buff, corn, gold, lime, rose, ruby, rust, sand, wine 5 blond, brass, brick, cream, flaxy, grape, lemon, maize, ocher, ochre, peach, poppy, rusty, sandy, straw 6 blonde, canary, cerise, chammy, cherry, citron, claret, crocus, flaxen, garnet, maroon, shammy, shamoy 7 apricot, carmine, chamois, citrine, crimson, fuchsia, jasmine, magenta, mustard, nankeen, old gold, pimento, saffron, scarlet, sultana, vermeil, xanthic 8 amaranth, cardinal, daffodil, dubonnet, geranium, primrose, rubicund 9 carnation, champagne, cranberry, goldenrod, jessamine, vermilion 10 strawberry
coral ___: 4 lily, pink, reef, tree, vine 5 bells, plant, snake 6 fungus
___ coral: 3 cup, red 4 blue, leaf, seed 5 brain, chain, stony
Coral ___: 3 Sea 6 Gables 7 Springs
___ Coral, FL: 4 Cape
Coral Gables: 4 city, town
athletes: 10 Hurricanes
locale: 7 Florida
Coral Sea: 6 battle
inlet: 5 Papua
strait off the ~: 6 Torres
Coral Springs: 4 city, town
locale: 7 Florida
Coral Terrace: 4 city, town
locale: 7 Florida
Coram: 4 city, town
locale: 7 New York
cor anglais: 4 wind 10 instrument
Corazon: 6 Aquino
corbel: 7 bracket
corbel ___: 4 arch 5 table, vault
Corbett: 5 Glenn
Corbett, James J.: 5 boxer
milieu: 4 ring
Corbin: 7 Bernsen
corbina: 4 fish
Corby: 5 Ellen
Corcoran: 5 Kevin 6 Noreen
cord: 3 tie 4 lace, line, rope, wick 5 twine 6 bungee, cordon, girdle, lacing, riband, string, tether 8 ligature 10 drawstring
Arab ~: 4 agal
contents: 4 wood
ender: 3 age 4 wood
fishing ~: 4 line
loom ~: 6 heddle
starter: 3 rip 4 whip
cord ___: 4 foot 5 grass
___ cord: 3 rip 4 neck, sash 5 nerve, patch, shock 6 bungee, spinal
Cord: 3 car 4 Alex, auto 10 automobile
corda: 6 string
___ corda: 3 una 6 sursum
cordage: 4 rope 5 twine 7 lanyard
fiber: 5 istle, ixtle, sisal
source: 4 bast 5 ramee, ramie
Corday: 4 Mara
victim: 5 Marat
see also French
corde: 7 strings
___ corde: 3 tre
corded fabric: 3 rep 4 repp
fabric: 3 rep 4 repp
Cordelia: 4 moon
father: 4 Lear
planet: 6 Uranus
sister: 5 Regan 7 Goneril
Cordell: 4 Hull
Cordero, Angel: 6 jockey
milieu: 5 track
corder starter: 3 cam
Cordia: 3 car 4 auto 10 Mitsubishi
cordial: 4 kind, nice, warm 5 civil, close, drink, suave, tonic 6 cassis, chummy, clubby, genial, hearty, jovial, kindly, loving, mellow, polite, social, tender 7 affable, amiable, liqueur, sincere 8 amicable, beverage, cheerful, familiar, fireside, friendly, gracious, intimate, inviting, likeable, outgoing, pleasant, sociable 9 agreeable, congenial, convivial, courteous, welcoming 10 benevolent, buddy-buddy, gregarious, harmonious, hospitable, invigorant, neighborly, personable, solicitous
drink: 6 cassis, kummel 7 liqueur
flavoring: 5 anise
not ~: 4 cold 5 aloof
___ cordiale: 7 entente
cordiality: 5 amity 6 warmth 7 amenity 8 courtesy, goodwill, kindness 9 geniality, mutuality, sincerity 10 affability, amiability, good nature, heartiness
cordially: 8 heartily 9 favorably
cordite, co-inventor of: 4 Abel
cordlike: 4 ropy 5 ropey
cordoba: 5 money
Cordoba: 3 car 4 auto 8 Chrysler
Córdoba: 4 city, town
locale: 5 Spain 6 Mexico 8 Veracruz 9 Argentina
cordon: 4 cord, sash 5 badge, braid 6 riband, ribbon 7 enclose, inclose 8 surround 10 police line
off: 5 siege
Cordon Bleu
graduate: 4 chef
phrase: 3 à la
cordovan: 7 leather 8 goatskin
cords: 5 jeans, pants 8 trousers
make ~: 3 saw 5 saw up
___ cords: 5 vocal
corduroy: 6 fabric
alternative: 5 denim
feature: 3 rib 4 wale 5 ridge
like ~: 5 ridgy
corduroys: 5 jeans, pants 8 trousers
cordwood
like ~: 4 sawn
measure: 5 stere
stack: 4 rick
core: 3 hub, nub 4 crux, gist, knub, meat, pith, root, seed 5 basis, cadre, focus, heart, midst, sense 6 bowels, center, inside, kernel, marrow, middle, thrust, upshot 7 essence, keynote, nucleus, summary 8 interior, main idea 9 framework, innermost, lifeblood, main point, substance 10 foundation, midsection
to the ~: 7 utterly
core ___: 4 city, dump 6 barrel, memory 7 drawing
___ core: 4 hard
Corea, Chick: 7 pianist
genre: 4 jazz
Corel, home of: 4 Orem
Corelli: 5 Marie 6 Franco
Corelli, Franco: 5 tenor 6 singer
specialty: 5 opera
Corelli, Marie: 6 writer 7 British
corer: 4 tool
Coretta ___ King: 5 Scott
Corey: 4 Haim, Hart, Jeff 5 Elias, Irwin, Pavin 7 Feldman, Wendell
___ Corey: 7 Richard
Corey, Elias: 7 chemist 8 Nobelist

Corfu: 3 isl. 4 isle 6 island
island group: 6 Ionian
locale: 6 Greece
corgi: 3 dog, pet 5 pooch 6 canine
__ corgi: 5 Welsh
coriaceous: 8 leathery
coriander: 4 herb, seed 5 spice
Cori, Carl: 8 Nobelist
Coricidin alternative: 5 Afrin 6 Contac, Nyquil, Tavist 7 Actifed, Comtrex, Dayquil, Dristan, Sinutab, Sudafed 8 Benadryl, Dimetapp, Drixoral, Ther-aFlu 9 Triaminic 10 Robitussin
Cori, Gerty: 8 Nobelist
Corin: 5 Nemec
Corinne: 6 Bohrer, Calvet
Corinne author: Madame de Staël
Corinth: 4 gulf 7 isthmus
ancient Gulf of ~ region: 6 Achaea
locale: 6 Greece
rival of ~: 5 Argos
Corinthian: 5 order
alternative: 5 Doric, Ionic
Corinthians
follower: 9 Galatians
preceder: 6 Romans
Coriolanus
author: William Shakespeare
costume: 4 toga
setting: 4 Rome
Coriolanus Overture composer: 9 Beethoven
Coriolis __: 5 force 6 effect
cork: 3 cap, dam, gag, top 4 bolt, bung, clog, lock, plug, seal, shut, stop, tree 5 block, close, cover, dam up, latch, limit 6 clog up, lock up, plug up, seal up, secure, stifle, stop up 7 close up, closure, prevent, repress, seal off, shutter, stopper, stopple 8 blockade, button up, obstruct, prohibit
combining form: 6 phello-
ender: 3 age 4 wood 5 board, screw
fisherman's ~: 5 float
sound: 3 pop
source: 4 bark
up: 4 hold, seal
cork __: 3 oak 4 tree 7 cambium
Cork: 4 city, port, town 6 county
locale: 3 Ire. 4 Eire, Erin 7 Ireland
port for ~: 4 Cobh
river: 3 Lee
corkboard item: 4 tack 7 pushpin
corker: 3 pip 4 joke, lulu, oner 5 beaut, dilly, doozy 6 doozie
corking: 3 def, rad 4 aces, A-one, boss, braw, cool, dece, fine, gear, keen, neat, nice, phat, tuff 5 dandy, ducky, grand, great, marvy, neato, nifty, nobby, prime, slick, super, swell 6 bang on, bang-up, bonzer, bosker, choice, divine, dreamy, far-out, gnarly, groovy, lovely, peachy, slap-up, spot on, superb, terrif, tiptop, unreal, whizzo, wicked 7 amazing, awesome, capital, perfect, ripping, skookum, stellar, sublime 8 dazzling, especial, eximious, fabulous, five-star, four-star, frabjous, glorious, heavenly, jim-dandy, slam-bang, smashing, splendid, standout, sterling, stickout, superior, terrific, top-level, topnotch, very good, wondrous 9 bodacious, Endsville, excellent, exemplary, exquisite, first-rate, high-grade, hunky-dory, marvelous, sol-licker, top-flight, unrivaled, wonderful 10 first-class, hotsy-totsy, jack-a-dandy, out of sight, peachy-keen, phe-nomenal, remarkable, stupendous, super-duper, unrivalled
corkscrew: 4 coil, wind 5 curly, helix, twine, twist, whorl 6 spiral, volute 7 entwine, intwine, sinuate
corkwood: 5 balsa, shrub
Corky: 5 Nemec
Corleone: 3 Kay 4 Vito 5 Fredo, Sonny 6 Connie 7 Michael
Corleone, Sonny portrayer: 4 Caan
__ Corliss Archer: 4 Meet
corm: 4 bulb, taro 5 tuber
Cormack, Allan: 8 Nobelist
Corman, Roger: 8 director
film: A Bucket of Blood (1959)
Gas-s-s-s (1970)
House of Usher (1960)
The Intruder (1961)
The Little Shop of Horrors (1960)
The Masque of the Red Death (1964)
Pit and the Pendulum (1961)
The Raven (1963)
The Secret Invasion (1964)
Tales of Terror (1962)
The Undead (1957)
cormorant: 4 bird, shag
corn: 3 oil 4 ears, feed 5 grain, maize 6 annual, cereal, fodder, veggie, yellow 7 schmalz, shmaltz 8 preserve, schmaltz, swelling 9 vegetable
amount: 4 peck, rick 6 bushel
bearing ~: 5 eared
bit of ~: 3 ear 6 kernel
borer: 3 bug 6 insect
chip flavor: 5 nacho
color: 5 maize
ender: 3 cob, fed, row 4 ball, cake, crib, husk, meal, pone 5 braid, bread, crake, stalk 6 dodger, flower, husker, starch
ground ~: 4 samp
holder: 3 bin, can, cob, ear 4 crib 5 shuck, stalk
Indian ~: 5 maize
Indian ~ genus: 3 zea
kin: 6 bunion
lily genus: 4 ixia
lover: 4 crow
Mexican ~ flour: 4 masa
pest: 5 borer
prepare ~: 4 husk 5 shuck
product: 3 oil 4 oleo, pone
protein: 4 zein
relative: 4 buff, gold, lime, rust, sand 5 blond, brass, coral, cream, flaxy, lemon, maize, ocher, ochre, peach, rusty, straw 6 blonde, canary, chammy, citron, crocus, flaxen, shammy, shamoy 7 apricot, chamois, citrine, jasmine, mustard, nankeen, old gold, saffron, xanthic 8 daffodil, primrose 9 champagne, goldenrod, jessamine
rows: 8 coiffure
salad: 5 mache
starter: 3 pop, tri, uni 5 broom 6 barley, pepper
state: 3 Kan., Neb. 4 Iowa, Nebr. 6 Kansas 8 Nebraska
tassel: 4 silk 5 floss
corn __: 3 dog, oil, row 4 beef, cake, chip, lily, meal, pone, silk, smut, snow 5 borer, bread, broom, color, crake, flour, grits, plant, poppy, salad, snake, stack, stalk, sugar, syrup 6 cockle, dodger, flakes, gluten, liquor, muffin, picker, whisky 7 earworm, whiskey
corn __ cob: 5 on the
corn-__ beef: 3 fed
__ corn: 4 dent, seed 5 candy, ear of, field, flint, green, horse, sugar, sweet, table 6 barley, Guinea, hybrid, Indian, mutton
Corn __: 3 Law 4 Belt, Chex
cornball: 5 hokey, trite 7 maudlin
cornbraids: 4 coif 6 hairdo 8 coiffure
cornbread: 5 bread
Corn Chex: 6 cereal
competitor: 3 Kix 4 Life, Trix 5 Kashi, Quisp, Total 6 Kaboom, Muesli, Oreo O's, Pablum, Smacks 7 All-Bran, Crispix, Harmony, Hunny B's, Mueslix, Oat Bran, Pokemon 8 Boo Berry, Cheerios, Fiber One, Special K, Uncle Sam, Wheaties 9 Alpha Bits, Apple Zaps, Grape Nuts, Honey Comb, Just Right 10 Apple Jacks, Bran Flakes, Cap'n Crunch, Cocoa Puffs, Froot Loops, Mini-Wheats, Nutri-Grain, Puffed Rice, Quaker Oats, Smart Start 11 Cocoa Blasts, Cookie Crisp, Golden Crisp, Lucky Charms, Puffed Wheat, Sweet Crunch, Waffle Crisp
manufacturer: 12 General Mills
corn chip: 4 nosh 5 snack
name: 6 Fritos
corncob __: 4 pipe
corncob kin: 5 briar
cornea
combining form: 5 cerat-, kerat- 6 cerato-, kerato-
cover: 3 lid 6 eyelid
corned beef: 7 cold cut
dish: 4 hash
Corneille: 6 Pierre 7 Heymans
Corneille, Pierre: 4 poet 6 author, French 10 playwright
work: Cinna
Horace
Le Cid
Médée
cornel: 4 tree 5 shrub 7 dogwood
Cornel: 5 Wilde
Cornelia: 5 Guest, Roman
Cornelia __ Skinner: 4 Otis
cornelian __: 6 cherry
Cornelius: 4 pope, Ryan 7 pontiff, Tacitus 10 Vanderbilt
Cornell: 3 Don 4 Eric, Ezra 5 Lydia 9 Katherine
athletes: 6 Big Red
lake: 6 Cayuga
league: 3 Ivy
locale: 6 Ithaca 7 New York
Cornell, Eric: 8 Nobelist 9 physicist
corner: 3 fix, jam, nab 4 nook, trap, tree 5 angle, catch, crook, hem in, joint, niche, place, stimy, stymy 6 alcove, collar, cranny, pickle, plight, recess, scrape, stymie, vertex 7 capture, dilemma, hideout, impasse, retreat 8 bottle up, hideaway, junction, monopoly, quagmire, quandary 9 tight spot 10 monopolize, standstill
around the ~: 4 near 5 close
diamond ~: 4 home 5 first, third 6 second
ender: 4 back, ways, wise 5 stone
hard to ~: 4 eely 5 cagey
just around the ~: 4 near 7 close by 8 adjacent 10 accessible, conven-ient
off in a ~: 5 apart
sign: 4 Stop
sitter: 5 dunce
starter: 5 cater
the market: 5 buy up, sew up 7 possess 10 monopolize
turn the ~: 5 shift
corner __: 4 back, kick 5 chair, table 7 cabinet
__ corner: 3 hot 4 amen 5 turn a 6 coffin 7 chimney, neutral, witness
__-corner: 5 cater, catty
__ Corner: 4 Pooh 5 Poets
Corner Brook: 4 city, town
locale: 6 Canada
cornered: 5 at bay 6 in a fix, in a jam
__-cornered: 5 cater, catty, kitty
Cornered (1945 film)
cast: Dick Powell, Walter Slezak
director: Edward Dmytryk
__-cornered hat: 5 three
corners
cut ~: 4 save 5 skimp, stint 6 scrimp 8 retrench 9 economize 10 under-spend
lacking ~: 4 oval 5 round
__ corners: 3 cut 6 Oxford
__ Corners: 4 Five, Four
cornerstone: 4 base, rock 5 basis, coign, quoin 6 coigne 7 support 8 linchpin, lynchpin, mainstay
abbr.: 3 est. 4 estd. 5 estab.
feature: 4 date
Corner That Held Them, The author: Sylvia Warner
__ Corner, VA: 6 Tysons
cornet: 4 horn, wind 6 pastry 7 brasses
play ~: 4 blow
corn-fed __: 4 beef
cornfield
array: 4 ears, rows 6 stalks
cry: 3 caw
Mayan ~: 5 milpa
preyer: 4 crow
Cornflake Girl singer: 4 Amos
corn flakes: 6 cereal
Cornforth, John: 7 chemist 8 Nobelist
cornhusker: 6 farmer
Cornhuskers author: Carl Sandburg
Cornhusker State: 3 Neb. 4 Nebr. 8 Nebraska
cornice
bracket: 5 ancon
molding: 4 cyma
ornament: 6 dentil
support: 6 corbel, frieze
__ cornice: 3 box 5 boxed 6 closed
Corniche: 3 car 4 auto 10 Rolls-Royce
__ Corning: 5 Owens
Corning competitor: 5 Pyrex
Corn Is Green, The: 4 film, play
author: Emlyn Williams
cast: Nigel Bruce, John Dall, Bette Davis
director: Irving Rapper
Cornish: 4 fowl 7 chicken
relative: 6 Bantam, Brahma, Houdan, Sussex 7 Dorking, Leghorn 8 Arau-cana, Langshan, Shanghai 9 Dominique, Orpington, Wyandotte
__ Cornish game hen: 4 Rock
Cornishman: 4 Celt
Cornish Rex: 3 cat 5 felid 6 feline
cornmeal: 5 grain
product: 4 mush
cornmeal product: 4 mush, pone
corn on the __: 3 cob
Corn Pops: 6 cereal
competitor: 3 Kix 4 Life, Trix 5 Kashi, Quisp, Total 6 Kaboom, Muesli, Oreo O's, Pablum, Smacks 7 All-Bran, Crispix, Harmony, Hunny B's, Mueslix, Oat Bran, Pokemon 8 Boo Berry, Cheerios, Fiber One, Rice Chex, Special K, Uncle Sam, Wheaties 9 Alpha Bits, Apple Zaps, Grape Nuts, Honey Comb, Just Right, Wheat Chex 10 Apple Jacks, Bran Flakes, Cap'n Crunch, Cocoa Puffs, Froot Loops, Mini-Wheats, Nutri-Grain, Puffed Rice, Quaker Oats, Smart Start 11 Cocoa Blasts, Cookie Crisp, Golden Crisp, Lucky Charms, Puffed Wheat, Sweet Crunch, Waffle Crisp
cornrow: 5 braid, plait
cornrows: 4 coif 6 hairdo 8 coiffure
alternative: 4 Afro
cornstalks: 6 fodder
cornstarch name: 4 Argo
cornu: 4 horn
cornucopia: 4 horn 6 wealth 9 plenitude, profusion
item: 5 fruit

Cornwall: **4** city, town **6** county
locale: **6** Canada **7** England, Ontario
town: **5** Truro
Cornwallis alma mater: **4** Eton
Cornwell: **8** Patricia
corny: **4** dull **5** banal, hokey, mushy, passé, sappy, stale, tired, trite, vapid **6** common, jejune, old hat **7** clichéd, fatuous, humdrum, mawkish, prosaic **8** bromidic, outdated, outmoded, romantic, schmalzy, shmaltzy, shopworn **9** hackneyed, prosaical, schmaltzy **10** uninspired, unoriginal
__ corny as...: **4** I'm as
Corolla: **3** car **4** auto **6** Toyota
corolla part: **5** petal
corollary: **9** deduction, induction, inference **10** conclusion, end product
corona: **3** gas **4** halo, ring **5** cigar, crown **7** aureola, aureole **8** gloriole **9** flower top
part: **5** petal
Corona: **4** beer, city, font, town **8** typeface
alternative: **5** Becks, Coors, Pabst **6** Amstel, Miller, Molson, Stroh's **7** Schlitz **8** Heineken, Michelob **9** Lowenbrau **10** Ballantine
locale: **10** California
Coronado: **4** city, town
locale: **10** California
Coronado, Francisco de: **8** explorer
coronary __: **4** vein **5** sinus **6** artery, bypass **7** cushion
coronary-__ unit: **4** care
coronate: **5** crown **6** anoint
Coronation Ode composer: **5** Elgar
coronet: **5** crown, tiara **6** anadem, diadem, wreath **7** chaplet, garland **8** headband
Coronet: **3** car **4** auto **5** Dodge
Coropuna: **4** peak **5** mount **8** mountain
locale: **4** Peru **5** Andes
Corot, Jean: **6** artist **7** painter
homeland: **6** France
corp.: **3** org.
see also corporate
__ corp.: **3** hab.
corporal: **3** NCO **4** rank **6** bodily **7** somatic **8** anatomic, physical **10** anatomical
denial: **5** no sir
__ corporal: **5** lance
__ Corporal: **6** Little
corporate: **5** joint **6** allied, shared, united **8** communal **9** aggregate **10** collective
abbr.: **3** inc., ltd.
alias: **3** DBA
concern: **4** debt **5** image
coverage ~: **3** HMO
cutback: **3** RIF
czar: **5** mogul
deal: **3** LBO **8** takeover
department: **5** legal, R and D, sales
employee: **2** GM **3** CEO, CFO, COO, mgr. **4** exec, pres., secy. **5** treas
entity: **4** firm
ID: **2** TM **4** logo
illustration: **5** chart
jet: **4** Lear
section: **3** div. **4** dept.
structure: **5** rungs **6** ladder
corporate __: **3** jet **4** park **5** image **6** ladder, raider **7** culture, welfare
corporation: **4** firm **5** house, trust **6** outfit **7** company, concern, society **8** business, employer **9** syndicate
dummy ~: **5** front
__ corporation: **5** close, Crown **6** public
corporeal: **4** real **5** somal **6** bodily **8** anatomic, material, physical, tangible **9** earthborn, objective, touchable **10** anatomical, phenomenal
corps: **4** army, band, body, crew, team, unit **5** force, group, hands, squad, troop **6** outfit **7** brigade, company, workers **8** division, regiment, squadron **9** battalion, combatant, personnel **10** contingent, detachment
esprit de ~: **6** morale
__ corps: **4** army, drum **5** drill, press **6** signal
__ Corps: **3** Air, Job **5** Peace **6** Marine
corps de __: **6** ballet
corpsman: **5** medic
corpulent: **5** beefy, bulky, burly, fubsy, heavy, hefty, husky, large, obese, plump, pudgy, pursy, stout **6** chubby, fleshy, portly, pyknic, rotund, stocky, zaftig, zoftig **7** adipose, paunchy **8** roly-poly **9** filled-out, ponderous **10** abdominous, embonpoint, overweight, well-padded
corpus: **4** body **5** whole **6** oeuvre **8** entirety **10** collection, cumulation, opera omnia
habeas ~: **4** writ
corpus __: **5** juris **7** delicti
__ corpus: **6** habeas
Corpus Christi: **4** city, town
county: **6** Nueces
locale: **5** Texas
corpuscle: **4** cell
__ corpuscle: **3** red **5** blood, white **7** Krause's, tactile
corral: **3** pen **4** find, grab, herd, trap, yard **5** amass, catch, fence, grasp, group, hedge, penin, snare **6** garner, gather, obtain **7** acquire, collect, convene, enclose, inclose, paddock, receive, round up **8** assemble **9** enclosure
part: **5** fence
put back in the ~: **5** repen
sound: **5** neigh, snort **6** whinny
corralled: **4** pent **8** fenced in
correct: **2** OK, so **3** fit, fix **4** cure, edit, good, just, mend, nice, okay, prim, true **5** alter, amend, clean, debug, emend, exact, fix up, moral, reset, right, scrub, sound, valid **6** actual, adjust, better, dead-on, decent, direct, doctor, formal, modify, polish, proper, punish, rebuke, redact, reform, repair, revise, seemly **7** clean up, factual, fitting, improve, launder, on track, perfect, precise, rectify, redress, regular, shape up, touch up, veridic **8** accurate, decorous, faithful, flawless, ladylike, make over, official, on target, orthodox, penalize, regulate, rigorous, set right, standard, straight, suitable, truthful, unerring **9** do justice, equitable, errorless, faultless, make right, on the beam, on the nose, reconcile, veracious, veridical **10** acceptable, ameliorate, conforming, diplomatic, fiddle with, impeccable, legitimate, make good on, meticulous, on the money, put in order, scrupulous, straighten, turn around, unimagined, unmistaken
a correction: **4** stet
a mistake: **5** erase
combining form: **4** orth- **5** ortho-
Correct!: **3** yes **5** bingo, right **7** exactly **8** you got it **10** that's right
correction: **6** change, rebuke **7** editing, mending, redress, revisal **8** revising, revision **9** amendment **10** adjustment, admonition, alteration, discipline, emendation, punishment, reparation
house of ~: **3** pen **4** jail, stir **6** prison **7** slammer
mid-course ~: **8** variance
correction __: **5** fluid **7** officer
correctional: **5** penal
corrections: **6** errata
officer: **6** jailer, warden **7** turnkey
corrective: **5** penal **6** curing, remedy **8** cosmetic, curative, punitive, remedial, sanative **9** antidotal **10** palliative
it may be ~: **4** lens
correctly: **4** to a T, well **5** right **6** aright, dead-on, just so, nicely **7** rightly **8** very well **9** carefully, fittingly, just right, perfectly, precisely **10** accurately, decorously, virtuously
position ~: **5** align, aline
correctness: **5** order, right, truth **6** bon ton **7** decency, decorum, fitness **8** accuracy, civility, fidelity, veracity **9** precision, propriety
Correggio: **6** artist **7** Antonio
Corregidor: **6** battle
correlate: **4** link **5** match, tie in **6** belong, equate **7** compare, connect **8** organize, parallel **9** associate, duplicate, harmonize **10** complement, coordinate
correlation: **4** link **5** match **6** analog **8** analogue, parallel
correlative: **3** and, nor **7** similar
Correo __: **5** Aereo
correspond: **2** go **3** fit **4** gybe, jibe **5** agree, equal, match, tally, write **6** cohere, equate, square **7** compare, comport, conform **8** check out, coincide, dovetail, resemble **9** correlate, drop a line, drop a note, harmonize, make sense, partake of **10** assimilate, complement, epistolize
ender: **3** ent **4** ence
(to): **6** equate
correspondence: **4** mail, note **5** match, media **6** accord **7** harmony, letters, message, reports **8** likeness, symmetry, sympathy, writings **9** congruity
afterthought: **2** PS
computer ~: **5** e-mail
numerical ~: **5** ratio
correspondence __: **6** course, school
correspondent: **5** press **6** pen pal, writer **7** related **8** epistler, reporter, stringer
correspondent __: **4** bank **7** banking
__ correspondent: **3** war **7** foreign
corresponding: **4** akin, same, such **5** alike, equal **6** agnate, allied **7** cognate, kindred, similar **8** matching, opposite, parallel, relative **9** analogous **10** comparable, equivalent, reciprocal
to: **4** like
correspondingly: **5** alike **6** in kind **8** likewise
corrida
beast: **4** toro **6** el toro
floor: **5** arena
shout: **3** olé
corridor: **4** hall **5** aisle, alley, foyer, lobby **6** airway, artery **7** hallway, ingress, passage **10** passageway
Corridors of Power author: C.P. Snow
Corriedale: **5** sheep
Corrientes: **4** city, town
locale: **9** Argentina
Corrigan: **7** Douglas, Mairead **8** Wrong Way
Corrigan, Mairead: **8** Nobelist
corrigenda: **6** errata, errors
corrigendum: **5** error **7** erratum, mistake **8** misprint
Corrina, Corrina (1994 film)
cast: Don Ameche, Joan Cusack, Whoopi Goldberg, Ray Liotta
corroborate: **5** prove, vouch **6** attest, back up, ratify, verify **7** bear out, certify, confirm, endorse, indorse, justify, support, testify, witness **8** document, evidence, validate **9** vindicate
corroboration: **4** test **5** proof **8** evidence **9** testimony
corroborator: **7** witness **10** eyewitness
corroboree: **5** dance
corrode: **3** eat, rot **4** rust, wear **5** decay, eat at, erode **6** damage, gnaw at **7** consume, destroy, eat away, oxidize, tarnish **8** wear away **10** degenerate
corroded: **5** rusty
corrosion: **3** rot **4** rust, wear **5** decay **6** damage **7** erosion **9** iron oxide
corrosive: **5** acerb, acrid **6** biting, bitter **7** acerbic, caustic, cutting, erosive **8** virulent **9** consuming, sarcastic, trenchant
solution: **3** HCl **5** oleum
corrugate: **4** fold **5** crimp **6** crease, ruffle **7** wrinkle
corrugated: **5** rough **6** fluted, ridged **7** creased, grooved **8** crinkled, furrowed, wrinkled **9** roughened **10** channelled
container: **6** carton
corrugated __: **4** iron **5** paper
corrugation: **4** fold **5** ridge **6** crease, groove **7** wrinkle
corrupt: **3** bad, buy, fix, rot **4** base, evil, foul, gamy, harm, hurt, ruin, soil, vile, warp **5** abase, abuse, bribe, dirty, false, gamey, loose, shady, spoil, stain, taint, venal **6** blight, crud up, damage, debase, defile, demean, filthy, impair, impure, infect, louche, misuse, poison, ravage, rotten, sordid, square, suborn, tamper, unholy, wicked **7** crooked, debased, defiled, degrade, deprave, despoil, ignoble, immoral, knavish, pollute, subvert, tainted, unclean, ungodly, vitiate **8** bribable, criminal, degraded, depraved, disgrace, dishonor, doctored, infamous, infected, maltreat, mistreat, perverse, polluted, shameful, sinister, suborned, two-faced, vitiated **9** dishonest, dissolute, distorted, faithless, falsified, graceless, mercenary, miscreant, nefarious, on the take, poisonous, shameless, undermine, unethical **10** adulterate, degenerate, demoralize, fraudulent, iniquitous, licentious, outrageous, perfidious, profligate, unfaithful, virtueless
corrupted: **3** bad **5** loose **6** sordid **7** immoral **8** maculate **9** abandoned, debauched, dissolute, reprobate **10** dissipated, licentious, profligate
corruptible: **5** venal
corrupting: **7** harmful **9** injurious
corruption: **4** evil, ruin, vice **5** crime, decay, filth, fraud, graft **6** damage, infamy, payoff, payola, racket **7** bribery, jobbery **8** atrocity, baseness, foulness, impurity, iniquity, nepotism, venality **9** barbarism, contagion, decadence, depravity, doctoring, extortion, fourberie, looseness, lubricity, pollution, shadiness, turpitude, vitiation, vulgarity **10** debasement, defilement, degeneracy, dishonesty, distortion, illegality, immorality, profligacy, rottenness, wickedness
Corsa: **3** car **4** auto, Opel **10** automobile
corsac: **5** canid **6** canine, mammal
relative: **3** dog, fox **4** wolf **5** dhole, dingo **6** coydog, coyote, fennec, jackal
corsage: **5** spray **8** ornament
flower: **3** mum
corsair: **4** boat **6** pirate, raider, robber, viking **7** brigand **8** marauder, rapparee, sea rover **9** buccaneer, privateer **10** freebooter
quest: **5** booty **7** plunder
ship: **6** zebeck **7** chebeck **10** xebec zebec
Corsair: **3** car **4** auto **5** Edsel
corset: **5** stays **6** enlace, girdle, inlace **8** lingerie **9** constrict, girdle kin, underwear **10** foundation

material: 6 baleen
stiffener: 4 bone, stay
tightener: 5 lacer
Corsica: 3 car, isl. 4 auto, isle 5 Chevy 6 island 9 Chevrolet 10 automobile
hero: 5 Paoli
locale: 5 Medit.
neighbor: 3 Sar. 4 Elba, Sard. 8 Sardinia
port: 6 Bastia 7 Ajaccio
sheep: 7 mouflon 8 moufflon
see also French
Corsicana: 4 city, town
locale: 5 Texas
Corsican Brothers, The (1941 film)
cast: Douglas Fairbanks Jr., Akim Tamiroff, Ruth Warrick
Corso, Gregory: 6 author, writer
genre: Beat
Corso, Gregory genre: Beat
Cortazar: 4 city, town
locale: 6 Mexico 10 Guanajuato
Cortázar, Julio: 6 writer 9 Argentine
Cort, Bud: 5 actor
film: Brewster McCloud (1970)
Gas-s-s-s (1970)
Harold and Maude (1972)
Why Shoot the Teacher? (1977)
cortege: 5 suite, train 6 parade 7 caravan, retinue 9 entourage, following 10 procession
Cortés: 6 Hernán 8 Hernando
Cortés, Hernando: 7 Spanish 8 explorer
foe: 5 Aztec
see also Spanish
cortex: 4 bark, peel, rind 9 brain part 10 memory site, outer layer
__ cortex: 5 motor 6 visual 7 adrenal, sensory
Cortez: 4 Dave 7 Ricardo
Cortland: 5 apple
relative: 4 crab, Gala, Lodi, Rome 5 Mutsu 6 Empire, Ida Red, medlar, Pippin, russet 7 Baldwin, Bramley, costard, Freedom, Liberty, Spartan, Wealthy, Winesap 8 Jonathan, McIntosh 10 Rome Beauty
Cortot, Alfred: 5 Swiss 7 pianist
corundum: 4 ruby 5 emery, oxide, topaz 7 mineral 8 sapphire
to Mohs: 4 nine
coruscate: 5 flame, flash, gleam, shine 7 glimmer, glisten, glitter, sparkle, twinkle 10 incandesce
coruscating: 3 lit 5 aglow, shiny 6 ablaze, bright, flashy 7 fulgent, lambent, radiant 8 luminous, lustrous 9 brilliant, sparkling
coruscation: 5 flash, gleam, light 7 glimmer, glitter, sparkle 10 brilliance
Corvair: 3 car 4 auto 5 Chevy 9 Chevrolet 10 automobile
critic: 5 Nader
Corvallis: 4 city, town
athletes: 7 Beavers
locale: 6 Oregon
school: 3 OSU
corvette: 4 boat 7 frigate, warship 10 battleship
Corvette: 3 car 4 auto 5 Chevy 9 Chevrolet 10 automobile
producer: 3 GMC
Corvette K-225 (1943 film)
cast: James Brown, Ella Raines, Randolph Scott
director: Richard Rossen
corvina: 4 fish
corvo: 4 wine 7 Italian 8 Sicilian
corybantic: 7 frantic 8 frenetic, frenzied 9 delirious
corydalis: 5 plant 6 flower
coryphaeus: 6 leader, singer
coryphée: 6 dancer 9 ballerina
coryza: 4 cold 10 common cold
cos: 6 veggie 7 lettuce, romaine 9 vegetable
__ cos: 3 arc
Cos __, CT: 3 Cob
Cosa __: 6 Nostra
__ Cosa: 4 Cosi
Cosby, Bill: 5 actor 8 comedian
film: California Suite (1978)
Let's Do It Again (1975)
Mother, Jugs & Speed (1976)
A Piece of the Action (1977)
song: Little Ole Man (1967)
TV: The Cosby Show, I Spy
Cosby Show, The (NBC sitcom)
cast: Tempestt Bledsoe (Vanessa Huxtable)
Lisa Bonet (Denise Huxtable)
Bill Cosby (Dr. Cliff Huxtable)
Keshia Knight Pulliam (Rudy Huxtable)
Phylicia Rashad (Clair Huxtable)
Malcolm-Jamal Warner (Theo Huxtable)
cosecant reciprocal: 4 sine
cosec. subj.: 4 trig.
Cosell: 6 Howard
cosh: 3 sap 4 club, conk 6 cudgel 8 bludgeon 9 billy club, blackjack, truncheon
cosher: 6 pamper
Cosi __: 4 Cosa
Così fan tutte: 5 opera
composer: 6 Mozart
role: 7 Alfonso, Despina 8 Ferrando 9 Dorabella, Guglielmo 10 Don Alfonso, Fiordiligi
setting: 5 Italy 6 Naples
cosign: 9 guarantee 10 underwrite
Cosimo: 8 de'Medici
cosine: 5 ratio
Cosmas: 5 saint
cosmetic: 4 kohl 5 blush, cream, liner, paint, rouge 6 lotion, makeup, powder 7 surface 9 enhancing, improving 10 corrective, decorative
ancient ~: 4 kohl
applicator: 4 wand
brand: 4 Avon 5 Almay, Arden 6 Revlon 7 Lancome, Mary Kay 8 Clinique 9 Cover Girl, Max Factor 10 Maybelline 11 Estée Lauder, Merle Norman
ingredient: 4 aloe 6 acetal, jokoba
purchase: 3 dye 4 soap, talc, tint 5 blush, gelee, gloss, liner, rinse, toner
safety org.: 3 FDA
cosmic: 4 huge, vast 5 grand 7 immense 8 enormous, infinite 9 grandiose, limitless, universal 10 ecumenical, large-scale, stupendous
principle: 5 karma
ray particle: 4 muon 5 meson
cosmic __: 3 ray 4 dust 5 noise
Cosmicomics author: Italo Calvino
Cosmo: 3 mag 6 Topper 7 Spacely 8 magazine
reader: 5 woman
cosmochemistry: 7 science
Cosmological Eye, The author: Henry Miller
cosmology: 7 science
study: 8 universe
cosmonaut: 9 rocketeer
home: 3 Mir
cosmopolitan: 5 ritzy, urban 6 global, urbane 7 worldly 8 catholic, cultured
area: 3 urb 4 city
not ~: 5 rural
Cosmopolitan rival: 4 Elle 5 Vogue
cosmos: 5 plant, world 6 flower, galaxy, nature 8 universe
diagram: 7 mandala
Cosmos: 4 font 8 typeface
Cosmos author/host: 5 Sagan
Cossack: 8 horseman 10 equestrian
chief: 6 ataman
headquarters: 4 Omsk
Cossacks, The author: Leo Tolstoy
cosset: 3 pet 4 baby, love 6 coddle, cuddle, dandle, dote on, fondle, pamper 7 cater to, indulge 8 dote upon
cost: 3 fee, tab 4 bite, loss, rate, toll 5 price, quote, run to, value, worth 6 amount, charge, come to, damage, outlay, tariff 7 damages, expense, penalty, require, sell for, tuition 8 amount to, overhead 9 detriment, quotation, reckoning, sacrifice 10 bottom line, forfeiture
at ~: 9 wholesale
at any ~: 10 regardless
bear the ~: 3 pay 6 defray
effective: 10 worthwhile
of operation: 8 overhead
per unit: 4 rate
set a ~: 3 ask
cost __: 4 card, unit 5 sheet 6 center, keeper, ledger 7 overrun
cost __ and a leg: 5 an arm
cost-__: 4 plus 5 share 7 benefit, cutting, justify 9 effective
__ cost: 4 at no, unit 5 at any, fixed, prime 6 actual, common, direct 7 current
__-cost: 3 low
costa: 3 rib
Costa __: 4 Mesa, Rica 5 Brava, Rican 6 del Sol
Costa __, CA: 4 Mesa
Costa __ Sol: 3 del
Costa __, Spain: 5 Brava
Costa-__: 6 Gavras
__ Costa: 6 Contra
Costa del Sol attraction: 5 beach, playa
Costa-Gavras: 8 director
film: Missing (1982)
Music Box (1989)
Z (1969)
Costain, Thomas: 6 author, writer
work: The Black Rose
The Silver Chalice
Costa Mesa: 4 city, town
locale: 10 California
Costa, Michael oratorio: 3 Eli
cost an arm __ leg: 4 and a
costard: 5 apple
relative: 4 crab, Gala, Lodi, Rome 5 Mutsu 6 Empire, Ida Red, medlar, Pippin, russet 7 Baldwin, Bramley, Freedom, Liberty, Spartan, Wealthy, Winesap 8 Cortland, Jonathan, McIntosh 10 Rome Beauty
Costa Rica: 6 nation 7 country
capital: 7 San José
city: 5 Limon 7 San José
export: 7 bananas
gulf: 8 Papagayo
leader: 5 Arias
money: 5 colon 7 centimo
neighbor: 6 Panama 9 Nicaragua
Nobelist in Peace: 7 Sanchez
org.: 3 OAS
volcano: 4 Póas 5 Irazu 6 Arenal
see also Spanish
Costa Rican: 4 Tico
Costas: 3 Bob 8 Mandylor
__ cost averaging: 6 dollar
cost-conscious: 6 frugal 7 sparing
cost-control agcy., '40s: 3 OPA
Costco rival: 3 BJ's 8 Sam's Club
Costello: 3 Lou 5 Elvis
part of an Abbott and ~ routine: 4 Who's
costing little: 3 low 5 cheap 6 modest, on sale 7 cut-rate, reduced, slashed 8 for a song 9 half-price 10 economical, marked down, reasonable
costless: 4 free 6 gratis 10 on the house
costly: 4 dear, high, rich 5 plush, pricy, steep 6 deluxe, lavish, pricey 7 harmful, premium, ruinous 8 damaging, precious, splendid, valuable 9 big-ticket, excessive, expensive, luxurious, priceless, sumptuous 10 disastrous, exorbitant, high-priced
Costner, Kevin: 5 actor
film: 3000 Miles to Graceland (2001)
American Flyers (1985)
Bull Durham (1988)
Dances With Wolves (1990, AA)
Dragonfly (2002)
Field of Dreams (1989)
For Love of the Game (1999)
JFK (1991)
Message in a Bottle (1999)
No Way Out (1987)
A Perfect World (1993)
Revenge (1990)
Robin Hood: Prince of Thieves (1991)
Silverado (1985)
Thirteen Days (2000)
Tin Cup (1996)
The Untouchables (1987)
Waterworld (1995)
Wyatt Earp (1994)
role: 4 Earp, Hood, Ness
cost-of-living stat: 3 CPI
costs: 6 upkeep
absorb, as ~: 3 eat
gross less ~: 3 net
including mailing ~: 3 ppd. 8 postpaid
__ costs: 5 at all 7 closing
costume: 3 rig 4 duds, garb, gear, gown, suit 5 dress, getup, guise, habit, robes, style 6 attire, clothe, livery, outfit 7 apparel, bedrape, clothes, fashion, garment, uniform 8 clothing, disguise, ensemble 9 trappings 10 masquerade, Sunday best
attend in ~: 4 go as
kind of ~: 5 clown, ghost, witch
party: 6 masque 10 masquerade
costume __: 5 party 7 jewelry
costumes: 6 guises 8 wardrobe
costume-shop item: 3 wig
cosy: 4 homy, nice, safe, snug, soft, warm 5 comfy, cushy, homey 6 chummy, folksy, secure 7 livable, nestled, restful 8 familiar, intimate, liveable, tucked in 9 cuddled up, sheltered
cot: 3 bed 4 bunk 5 bower, hutch 6 gurney 7 charpai, charpoy, trundle
on wheels: 6 gurney
__ cot: 3 arc
cote: 9 sheepfold
dweller: 3 ewe, ram 4 dove, lamb
sound: 3 baa, coo, maa 5 bleat 6 baa baa, baaing
starter: 4 dove 5 sheep
__ côté: 5 pas de
Côte __: 3 d'Or 5 d'Azur 7 d'Ivoire
Côte d'Azur resort: 4 Nice
Côte d'Ivoire: 6 nation 7 country
see also Ivory Coast
coterie: 3 mob, set 4 band, clan, club, gang, pack, ring, team 5 cabal, class, crowd, group, junto, lodge, party 6 circle, clique, outfit 7 company, faction, in-group 8 sorority 9 following, hangers-on 10 fellowship, fraternity
coterminous: 4 even
Côte-St.-Luc: 4 city, town
locale: 6 Canada, Québec
cothamore: 6 fabric 8 material
Cotija: 4 city, town
locale: 6 Mexico 9 Michoacán
cotillion: 5 dance 9 festivity
attendee: 3 deb

cotinga: 4 bird
Cotler: 4 Kami
Cotonou: 4 city, port, town
locale: 5 Benin
Cotopaxi: 7 volcano
locale: 7 Ecuador
Cotswold: 5 sheep
cotta
terra ~: 4 clay 6 orange 7 pottery 8 brownish, clayware, crockery
cottage: 3 hut 4 home 5 bower, cabin, hovel, hutch, lodge, shack 6 cabana, chalet, lean-to, shanty 8 bungalow, lodgment, quarters
cottage ___: 5 fries, tulip 6 cheese, window 7 pudding 8 industry
cottage cheese bit: 4 curd 5 chive
cottage cheese relative: 7 ricotta
Cottage Grove: 4 city, town
locale: 9 Minnesota
Cottage Lake: 4 city, town
locale: 10 Washington
Cottage, The author: Danielle Steel
Cotten, Joseph: 5 actor
film: The Abominable Dr. Phibes (1971)
Citizen Kane (1941)
Duel in the Sun (1946)
The Farmer's Daughter (1947)
Gaslight (1944)
The Grasshopper (1970)
Hush ... Hush, Sweet Charlotte (1965)
Journey Into Fear (1942)
The Magnificent Ambersons (1942)
The Man With a Cloak (1951)
Niagara (1953)
Portrait of Jennie (1948)
Shadow of a Doubt (1943)
Since You Went Away (1944)
The Third Man (1949)
Walk Softly, Stranger (1950)
cotter: 5 wedge
cotter ___: 3 pin 4 slot
Cottian Alps: 5 range
locale: 5 Italy 6 Europe, France
cotton: 4 crop, duck, lawn 6 dimity, fabric 7 padding, rapport
alternative: 5 Orlon, rayon
ball of ~: 3 wad
Egyptian ~: 3 sak
ender: 4 seed, tail, weed, wood 5 mouth
fabric: 3 rep 4 duck, lawn, leno, pima, repp 5 baize, chino, crape, crepe, denim, dhoti, dhuti, khaki, piqué, plush, scrim, terry, toile, voile 6 calico, canvas, chally, chintz, damask, dhooti, dimity, gloria, madras, moreen, muslin, oxford, pongee, poplin, sateen, wadmal 7 buckram, bunting, cambric, challie, challis, dhootie, duvetyn, etamine, flannel, foulard, fustian, galatea, gingham, jaconet, khaddar, nankeen, oilskin, organdy, percale, satinet, silesia, ticking, tiffany, Viyella 8 Burberry, chambray, corduroy, Indienne, marcella, moleskin, nainsook, oilcloth, organdie, shantung, tarlatan 9 crinoline, flannelet, gabardine, paramatta, percaline, sailcloth, satinette, silkaline, velveteen 10 balbriggan, marseilles, seersucker
fiber: 4 noil
gin name: 3 Eli 7 Whitney
knot: 3 nep
like unginned ~: 5 seedy
machine: 3 gin 5 baler
matted ~: 4 batt
mesh: 4 leno
on a stick: 4 Q-Tip
pod: 4 boll
thread: 5 lisle
to: 5 enjoy 8 befriend
unit: 4 bale
cotton ___: 3 gin, gum, tie, top 4 cake, mill, wool 5 candy, grass, press 6 picker 7 batting, flannel, stainer, thistle
cotton-___: 7 picking
___ cotton: 4 Java, Pima, silk 5 pearl, perle 6 sewing, upland
Cotton: 6 Mather 7 Charles
Land of ~: 5 Dixie
Cotton ___: 4 Belt
Cotton ___, The: 4 Club
Cotton ___ to Harlem: 5 Comes
___ Cotton: 4 King
Cotton Bowl site: 5 Texas 6 Dallas
Cotton-Broker's Office artist: 5 Degas
Cotton Candy artist: 4 Hirt
Cotton, Charles: 4 poet 7 British
Cotton Club, The (1984 film)
cast: Richard Gere, Gregory Hines, Diane Lane
director: Francis Ford Coppola
setting: 6 Harlem
Cotton Comes to Harlem: 4 film 5 novel
author: Chester Himes
cast: Godfrey Cambridge, Calvin Lockhart, Raymond St. Jacques
director: Ossie Davis
Cottonelle alternative: 5 Scott 6 Marcal 7 Charmin 8 Northern, Soft Weve 10 White Cloud
cottonlike fiber: 5 ramee, ramie
cottonmouth: 5 snake
cottonmouthed: 7 parched, thirsty
cotton-pickin': 6 dad-gum, darned
cottonseed ___: 3 oil 4 cake, meal
cottontail: 6 mammal, rabbit, rodent
tail: 4 scut
Cottontail: 5 Peter
sibling of ~: 5 Mopsy 6 Flopsy
cottonwood: 4 tree 5 alamo 6 poplar
cousin: 5 aspen
Cottonwood Heights: 4 city, town
locale: 4 Utah
cottony fiber: 5 floss
coturnix: 4 bird
Coty: 4 René
couch: 3 lie, put 4 hide, mask, seat, sofa, veil, word 5 cache, cloak, cover, divan, frame, lodge, lower, utter 6 daybed, indite, lounge, phrase, settee 7 conceal, express, obscure, seating, secrete 8 disguise, love seat 9 davenport, formulate, furniture, tête-à-tête 10 camouflage
emulate a ~ potato: 4 laze, loll
leave the ~: 4 rise 5 arise, get up
couch ___: 4 roll 5 grass 6 potato
___ couch: 6 studio, tuxedo
couch potato: 5 idler, sloth 6 loller
choice: 5 cable
like a ~: 4 lazy 5 inert
need: 2 TV 3 VCR 4 dish, tube 5 TV set 7 cable TV
spot: 3 den 4 sofa
unlike a ~: 6 active
what a ~ does: 3 veg 4 .loll
cougar: 3 cat 4 puma 5 felid 6 animal, feline, mammal 7 panther, wildcat
color: 5 tawny
genus: 5 felis
relative: 4 eyra, lion, lynx 5 chita, liger, ounce, tiger, tigon 6 bobcat, cheeta, chetah, jaguar, margay, ocelot, serval, tiglon 7 bay lynx, caracal, cheetah, leopard, panther 9 catamount 10 jaguarundi
Cougar: 3 car 4 auto, Merc 7 Mercury 10 automobile
___ Cougar Mellencamp: 4 John
Cougars: 3 WSU
cough: 4 hack 6 wheeze
syrup ingredient: 4 tolu 6 ipecac
syrup measure: 4 tbsp. 10 tablespoon
up: 3 pay 4 ante 5 spend 6 pay out 8 fork over, hand over 10 recompense
cough ___: 4 drop 5 syrup
cough drop: 6 troche 7 lozenge
flavoring: 4 mint 5 anise, lemon
like ~ s: 3 OTC
name: 5 Smith 6 Luden's
could: 3 may 5 might
...could ___ fat: 5 eat no
it ~ be: 5 maybe
...could ___ horse!: 4 eat a
...could ___ lean: 5 eat no
Could ___ Magic: 4 It Be
Could ___ Use Me?: 3 You
...could eat ___: 5 no fat
Could I Have This Kiss Forever (2000 song) artist: Whitney Houston
Could It Be I'm Falling in Love (1973 song) artist: Spinners
Could It Be Magic (1975 song) artist: Barry Manilow
couldn't ___ less: 4 care
Couldn't agree more!: 6 I'll say
___ Could Read My Mind: 5 If You
___ Could Turn Back Time: 3 If I
Could You Use Me? composer: 8 Gershwin
coulee: 5 cañon, gulch 6 arroyo, canyon, ravine, valley
___ Coulee Dam: 5 Grand
Coulomb, Charles de: 9 physicist
coulomb per second: 3 amp
council: 4 bloc, diet 5 board, divan, house, junta, panel, synod 6 caucus, confab, jurors, powwow 7 academy, cabinet, chamber 8 assembly, conclave, congress, ecclesia 9 committee, gathering, syndicate 10 brain trust, conference, convention, executives
African ~: 6 indaba
Anglo-Saxon ~: 5 witan
chamber: 5 divan
Chinese ~: 4 yuan
church ~: 5 curia, synod
ender: 3 man, men 5 woman, women
honcho: 5 chair
member: 3 ald. 8 alderman, lawmaker
military ~: 5 junta
Moslem ~: 5 ulema
post-Reformation ~: 5 Trent
Roman ~: 6 Senate
Russian ~: 4 Duma
council ___: 4 fire 5 of war
___ council: 4 city 5 great, privy, trade, works 6 church, common 7 student
___ Council: 6 Nicene 7 Lateran, Supreme, Vatican
Council Bluffs: 4 city, town
locale: 4 Iowa
neighbor: 5 Omaha
council, literally,: 6 Soviet
council of ___: 3 war 5 state
Council of ___: 3 Ten 4 Pisa 5 Trent
counsel: 3 att. 4 atty., urge, warn 5 guide, steer 6 advice, advise, direct, enjoin, exhort, inform, jurist, lawyer, legist, prompt 7 adviser, advisor, caution, propose, suggest 8 admonish, advocate, attorney, guidance, instruct, persuade 9 barrister, recommend, solicitor 10 mouthpiece
in Britain: 4 rede
seek ~ from: 6 look to
___ counsel: 5 house 6 junior
___ Counsel: 5 King's 6 Queen's
counsel and rule, name meaning: 6 Ronald 8 Reginald
Counsellor-at-Law (1933 film)
cast: John Barrymore, Bebe Daniels, Doris Kenyon
director: William Wyler
counselor: 3 att. 4 atty. 5 guide 6 jurist, lawyer, leader, legist, mentor 7 adviser, advisor, teacher 8 advocate, attorney 9 abecedary, barrister, solicitor 10 instructor, legal eagle, mouthpiece
deg.: 2 JD 3 LL.B., MSW
female ~: 6 egeria
counselor-___: 5 at-law
counselors: 7 cabinet 10 brain trust
Counselors-at-Law author: Weidman
counsel protection, name meaning: 7 Raymond
count: 3 add, sum 4 deem, poll, rank, rate 5 add up, check, gauge, judge, noble, score, stock, sum up, tally, title, total, tot up 6 cipher, figure, matter, number, reckon, regard, voting 7 compute, figures, include, itemize, tick off 8 consider, look upon, nobleman, numerate 9 blueblood, calculate, enumerate, keep score, numbering, reckoning
ender: 3 ess 4 down
in England: 4 earl
count ___: 3 out 4 coup, down, noun, upon 5 heads, noses
___ count: 3 red 4 head 5 blood, point 6 pollen
___-count: 3 low 4 fast, high
Count: 5 Basie, title
Count ___!: 4 me in, on me 5 me out
Count ___ Blessings: 4 Your
countable: 10 calculable, explicable
Countach: 3 car 4 auto 11 Lamborghini
Count Chocula: 6 cereal
competitor: 3 Kix 4 Life, Trix 5 Kashi, Quisp, Total 6 Kaboom, Muesli, Oreo O's, Pablum, Smacks 7 All-Bran, Crispix, Harmony, Hunny B's, Mueslix, Oat Bran, Pokemon 8 Boo Berry, Cheerios, Corn Chex, Corn Pops, Fiber One, Rice Chex, Special K, Uncle Sam, Wheaties 9 Alpha Bits, Apple Zaps, Grape Nuts, Honey Comb, Just Right, Wheat Chex 10 Apple Jacks, Bran Flakes, Cap'n Crunch, Cocoa Puffs, Froot Loops, Mini-Wheats, Nutri-Grain, Puffed Rice, Quaker Oats, Smart Start 11 Cocoa Blasts, Cookie Crisp, Golden Crisp, Lucky Charms, Puffed Wheat, Sweet Crunch, Waffle Crisp
countdown
delay: 4 hold
discontinue the ~: 5 abort
number: 3 one, six, ten, two 4 five, four, nine, zero 5 eight, seven, three
word: 5 minus
Countdown (1968 film)
cast: James Caan, Robert Duvall, Joanna Moore
director: Robert Altman
___ Countdown, The: 5 Final
counted, first to be: 4 eeny
Countee: 6 Cullen
countenance: 3 mug 4 back, bear, cast, face, look, mien, puss, spur 5 brook, nod at, stand 6 accept, aspect, endure, handle, kisser, suffer, uphold, visage 7 applaud, approve, condone, endorse, indorse, smile on, support 8 calmness, features, hold with, live with, sanction, stand for, tolerate
don't ~: 5 scorn 6 deride
put out of ~: 6 rattle
counter: 4 desk, foil, loth 5 loath, parry, polar, react, rebut, reply, shelf, stand 6 answer, gainst, offset, oppose, refute, resist, retort, thwart 7 adverse, against, hit back, obviate, opposed, prevent, respond, reverse 8 contrary, opposing, opposite 9 antipodal, dia-

metric, frustrate, retaliate **10** antithetic
ender: **3** act, man, men, spy, sue, top **4** blow, coup, foil, glow, mine, move, pane, part, plan, play, plea, plot, pose, sign, sink, suit **5** check, claim, force, march, offer, point, poise, punch, shaft, stain, tenor, trade, weigh, woman, women **6** attack, change, charge, person, terror **7** balance, culture, current, example, factual, measure, persons, shading **8** argument, cyclical, irritant, proposal **9** clockwise, espionage, insurgent, offensive **10** productive, revolution
go ~ to: **4** defy, vary **5** cross, flout, rebel **6** differ, ignore, oppose **7** deviate, disobey, diverge, violate **8** conflict, contrast, disagree **9** disregard **10** contravene
seat: **5** stool
to: **3** con **4** anti **6** versus **7** against, athwart **8** opposing **10** at odds with
counter __: **5** check, image, table
counter-__: **3** ion **6** boulle, worker
__ counter: **4** bean, card, dust **5** lunch **6** Geiger **7** bargain, nucleus
counteract: **4** foil, undo **5** annul, check **6** cancel, hinder, negate, offset, oppose, thwart **7** balance, obviate, prevent, rectify, redress **9** cancel out, frustrate, go against **10** antagonize, compensate, contradict, contravene, invalidate, neutralize
counteractant: **4** cure **8** antidote
counterargue: **5** rebut
Counter-Attack and Other Poems author: Siegfried Sassoon
counterbalance: **5** weigh **6** cancel, offset, redeem **8** outweigh, reaction **9** stabilize **10** neutralize
countercharge: **5** reply **6** answer
counterclockwise: **4** levo
combining form: **3** lev- **4** levo- **5** laevo-
counterculturist: **5** rebel
countercurrent: **4** eddy
counterevidence, offer: **5** rebut
counterfactual: **5** wrong **7** in error
counterfeit: **3** bad **4** copy, fake, imit., mock, sham **5** bogus, faked, false, forge, fraud, phony, put-on, quack, queer **6** copied, ersatz, forged, phoney, pseudo, unreal **7** assumed, feigned, forgery, pretend **8** knockoff, simulate, spurious **9** imitation, pretended, simulated, synthetic **10** artificial, fabricated, fictitious, fraudulent
counterfeiter: **5** faker **6** forger **8** swindler
nemesis: **4** T-man
Counterfeiters, The author: André Gide
Counterfeit Traitor, The (1962 film)
cast: Hugh Griffith, William Holden, Lilli Palmer
director: George Seaton
counterfoil: **4** stub **7** receipt
counterirritant: **5** salve **8** ointment
countermand: **3** nix **4** kill, lift **5** annul, quash **6** cancel, negate, recall, recant, repeal, revoke **7** rescind, retract, reverse **8** override, overrule, overturn
counterpane: **5** quilt, throw **8** coverlet, coverlid **9** bedspread, comforter, eiderdown
counterpart: **4** copy, mate, twin **5** equal, match **6** analog **7** coequal **8** analogue, likeness, opposite
counterperson: **5** clerk
counterpoint: **5** music **7** descant, discant
master: **4** Bach
counterpoise: **6** redeem, weight **8** reaction **9** stabilize
countersign: **4** word **7** endorse, indorse, witness **8** password
countersink: **4** ream **5** drill
countertenor: **4** alto **5** voice **8** vocalist
countervail: **6** redeem
countess: **4** lady, peer, rank **5** noble, title, woman
husband: **4** earl
Countess Cathleen, The author: William Butler Yeats
Countess From Hong Kong, A (1967 film)
cast: Marlon Brando, Sydney Chaplin, Tippi Hedren, Sophia Loren
director: Charles Chaplin
counting: **4** with **8** addition **9** including
aid: **6** abacus **7** fingers **9** slide rule **10** calculator
ender: **5** house
everything: **6** in toto, wholly **7** totally **10** altogether, completely
game: **3** nim
Inca ~ device: **5** quipu
not ~: **7** besides **9** apart from, aside from, other than
on: **9** confident, dependant, dependent, presuming
unit: **5** dozen, gross
counting __: **4** room **5** house **6** number
counting-out word: **3** moe **4** eeny **5** meeny, miney
Counting the Ways author: Albee
countless: **4** many **6** divers, gobs of, legion, lots of, myriad, umteen, untold **7** copious, endless, heaping, heaps of, no end of, piles of, profuse, scads of, umpteen **8** abundant, infinite, manifold, numerous, oodles of, prodigal, scores of, umpsteen, unending **9** boundless, bountiful, limitless, quite a few, unlimited **10** innumerous, numberless, unnumbered, zillions of
combining form: **4** myri- **5** myrio-
Count me in!: **4** sure **6** I'm game
Count Me In (1965 song) artist: Gary Lewis and the Playboys
Count of Monte Cristo, The: **4** film **5** novel
author: Alexandre Dumas
cast: Louis Calhern, Robert Donat, Elissa Landi
character: **4** Abbé **5** Julie, Louis, Luigi, Renée, Vampa **6** Dantès, Debray, Edmond, Haidée, Lucien, Morrel **7** Assunta, Eugénie, Gaspard, Herbaut, Morcerf, Peppino **8** Danglars, Mercédès **9** Villefort
director: Rowland Lee
Count on Me (song) artist: Jefferson Starship, Whitney Houston
countrified: **4** farm, naif **5** naive, rural **6** rustic **7** bucolic **8** agrarian, downhome **9** backwoods, bucolical, parochial **10** provincial
country: **4** land, soil **5** genre, music, place, realm, rural, state **6** nation, public, region, rustic, voters **7** bucolic, grounds, kingdom, terrain **8** agrarian, Arcadian, citizens, dominion, homeland, outdoors, pastoral, populace **9** backwoods, boondocks, bucolical, citizenry, territory **10** provincial
addr.: **2** RR **3** RFD, rte. **5** rte. RR
Africa: **4** Chad, Mali, Togo **5** Benin, Congo, Egypt, Gabon, Ghana, Kenya, Libya, Niger, Sudan **6** Angola, Gambia, Malawi, Uganda, Zambia **7** Algeria, Eritrea, Lesotho, Morocco, Namibia, Nigeria, Senegal, Somalia, Tunisia **8** Botswana, Cameroon, Ethiopia, Tanzania, Zimbabwe **9** Swaziland **10** Ivory Coast, Madagascar, Mauritania, Mozambique **11** Burkina Faso, Côte d'Ivoire, Sierra Leone, South Africa **12** Guinea-Bissau
Asia: **3** Isr., Leb., Nam, Pak., Syr. **4** Irak, Iran, Iraq, Laos, Oman **5** China, India, Japan, Korea, Nepal, Qatar, Syria, Tibet, Yemen **6** Brunei, Israel, Taiwan, Thibet, Turkey, Xizang **7** Lebanon, Myanmar, Sitsang, Vietnam **8** Cambodia, Malaysia, Maldives, Mongolia, Pakistan, Sri Lanka, Thailand **9** Indonesia, Kirghizia, New Guinea **10** Kazakhstan, North Korea, South Korea, Uzbekistan **11** Philippines
ender: **3** man, men **4** side, wide **5** woman, women
Europe: **3** Aus., Lux., Rus., Swe. **4** Aust., Belg., Bulg., Eire, Erin, Gr. Br., Gt.Br., Holl., Icel., Lith., Neth., Norw., Swed. **5** Italy, Spain **6** Bosnia, España, France, Greece, Latvia, Monaco, Norway, Poland, Russia, Serbia, Sweden, Turkey **7** Albania, Andorra, Belarus, Belgium, Croatia, Denmark, England, Estonia, Finland, Germany, Holland, Hungary, Iceland, Ireland, Moldova, Romania, Ukraine **8** Bulgaria, Portugal, Slovakia, Slovenia **9** Lithuania **11** Netherlands, Switzerland, Vatican City **13** Liechtenstein
home: **5** villa **6** estate
South America: **4** Peru **5** Chile **6** Brazil, Guyana **7** Bolivia, Ecuador, Uruguay **8** Colombia, Paraguay, Suriname **9** Argentina, Venezuela
starter: **4** back
country __: **3** ham **4** club, mile, rock **5** fries, house, music, store **6** cousin, singer **7** kitchen
country-__: **4** bred **5** dance **7** western
__ country: **3** cow, old **4** back, God's **6** mother
__-country: **3** out **5** cross
Country (1984 film)
cast: Wilford Brimley, Jessica Lange, Sam Shepard
Country __ McDonald: **3** Joe
Country __, The: **4** Girl, Wife **6** Doctor
__ Country: **4** A Far, God's **5** North **7** Another, Mustang
country club
cry: **4** fore
fee: **4** dues
instructor: **3** pro **7** golf pro
Country Club: **4** city, town
locale: **7** Florida
Country Doctor, The author: Balzac
Country Girl, The: **4** film, play
author: Clifford Odets
cast: Bing Crosby, William Holden, Grace Kelly, Anthony Ross
character: **4** Dodd **5** Elgin **6** Bennie **7** Georgie
director: George Seaton
Country Joe: **8** McDonald
Country Life (1995 film)
cast: Sam Neill, Greta Scacchi
countryman: **8** indigene
country music
guitar: **5** Dobro
superstar: **4** Cash, Ford, Gill, Hall, Hill, Lynn, Reba, Snow, Tubb **5** Acuff, Autry, Black, Cline, Fargo, Foley, Gayle, Husky, Owens, Price, Pride, Tritt, Twain, Wells, Wills, Young **6** Arnold, Brooks, McGraw, Milsap, Nelson, Parton, Ritter, Strait, Tillis, Twitty **7** Haggard, Robbins, Wagoner, Willams, Wynette, Wynonna **8** Bob Wills, Campbell, Hank Snow, Jennings, Loveless, McEntire, Ray Price, Red Foley, Roy Acuff, Tom T. Hall, Yearwood **9** Buck Owens, Ernie Ford, Faith Hill, Gene Autry, Mel Tillis, Pam Tillis, Tex Ritter, Tim McGraw, Vince Gill **10** Clint Black, Donna Fargo, Eddy Arnold, Ernest Tubb, Faron Young, Kitty Wells, Patsy Cline **11** Shania Twain
countryside: **4** land **6** nature **8** outdoors **9** landscape
of the ~: **5** rural **8** pastoral
Country Squire: **3** car **4** auto, Ford
__ Country, The: **3** Big, Far **4** Back, Hi-Lo
Country Waif author: George Sand
countrywide: **4** natl. **8** national
Country Wife, The author: William Wycherley
__ count the ways: **5** let me
county: **5** shire **8** district, province
ender: **4** wide
England: **4** Beds, Kent, Oxon **5** Berks, Bucks, Cambs, Devon, Essex, Hants, Herts, Hunts, Lancs, Leics, Lincs, Middx, Notts, Salop, Warks, Wilts, Worcs, Yorks **6** Derbys, Dorset, Durham, Gloucs, Staffs, Surrey, Sussex **7** Norfolk, Rutland, Suffolk **8** Cheshire, Cornwall, Hereford, Somerset **9** Berkshire, Hampshire, Middlesex, Northants, Wiltshire, Yorkshire **10** Cumberland, Derbyshire, Lancashire, Shropshire
fair feature: **5** booth
Ireland: **4** Cork, Mayo **5** Cavan, Clare, Kerry, Louth, Meath, Sligo **6** Carlow, Dublin, Galway, Offaly **7** Donegal, Kildare, Leitrim, Wexford, Wicklow **8** Kilkenny, Laoighis, Limerick, Longford, Monaghan **9** Roscommon, Tipperary, Waterford, Westmeath
county __: **3** pin **4** fair, farm, line, seat **5** agent, board, clerk, court
__ County: **5** Bloom
County Cavan, river through: **4** Erne
County Chairman, The author: Ade
County Donegal islands: **4** Aran
Count Your Blessings (1954 song) artist: Eddie Fisher
Count Your Blessings... composer: Irving Berlin
coup: **4** deed, feat **5** purge **6** revolt, stroke **7** exploit, triumph **8** conquest **10** revolution, usurpation
coup __: **5** d'état, d'oeil, stick **6** d'essai
__ coup: **5** après, count, grand **6** palace
coup de __: **3** feu **4** main **5** grâce, poing **6** foudre, maître, soleil **7** théâtre
Coup de Grâce author: Yourcenar
coup d'état: **10** revolution
pull off a ~: **5** usurp
coupe: **3** car **4** auto **7** dessert, two-door **10** automobile
cousin: **5** sedan
coupé: **4** step
Coupe de Ville: **3** car **4** auto **8** Cadillac
Couperus, Louis: **5** Dutch **6** writer
couple: **2** pr. **3** duo, tie, two, wed **4** duad, dyad, item, join, link, pair, yoke **5** brace, deuce, hitch, match, twain, unite **6** adjoin, attach, cohere, fasten, hook on, hook up **7** bracket, combine, conjoin, connect, doublet, harness, hitch on, twosome **9** associate, newlyweds
a ~ of times: **5** twice
half of a ~: **3** one **4** wife **5** bride, groom **7** husband
new ~: **4** item
two-career ~: **4** dink
two ~ s: **4** four
coupled: **4** dual **6** double
with: **3** and
(with): **5** along

Couple Days Off (1991 song) artist: Huey Lewis and the News
Couple of Swells, A composer: 6 Berlin
coupler: 4 link, yoke 8 vinculum
Couples, Fred: 6 golfer
milieu: 5 links 6 course
org.: 3 PGA
couplet: 3 duo, two 4 rime 5 rhyme, verse
__ couplet: 4 open 6 closed, heroic
__ Couple, The: 3 Odd
coupling: 4 link, yoke 5 joint 6 hookup 8 junction, juncture 10 attachment, connection
coupon: 6 ticket 7 voucher 10 order blank
clipper: 5 saver
save, as a ~: 4 clip 6 cut out
site: 2 ad 5 paper 9 newspaper
use a ~: 4 save 6 redeem
coupon __: 4 bond, rate 7 clipper
__ coupon: 4 food 8 cents-off
__-coupon bond: 4 zero
courage: 4 dash, grit, guts, soul 5 heart, moxie, nerve, pluck, spine, spunk, valor 6 daring, mettle, spirit, starch 7 bravery, bravura, heroism, prowess, resolve 8 audacity, backbone, boldness, firmness, gumption, rashness, strength, temerity, tenacity 9 assurance, character, endurance, fortitude, gallantry, hardiness 10 confidence, enterprise, knighthood
deprive of ~: 5 unman
ending: 3 ous
lose ~: 6 falter
restore ~: 5 reman
Courage __ Fire: 5 Under
__ Courage and Her Children: 6 Mother
courageous: 4 bold, game 5 brave, gutsy, hardy, manly, nervy, stout, tough 6 awless, daring, gritty, heroic, plucky, spunky, strong 7 assured, aweless, defiant, doughty, gallant, impavid, leonine, staunch, valiant 8 fearless, heroical, intrepid, resolute, spirited, stalwart, unafraid, valorous 9 audacious, confident, daredevil, dauntless, dreadless, herculean, tenacious, undaunted, unfearful, unfearing, venturous 10 chivalrous, fire-eating, mettlesome, red-blooded, undismayed
be ~: 4 dare
not ~: 3 shy 4 weak 5 faint, timid 6 afraid, craven, scared, yellow 7 fearful, gutless, panicky 8 cowardly, recreant, timorous 9 dastardly, nerveless, spineless, tremulous 10 frightened
one: 4 hero, lion 5 darer
Courage Under Fire (1996 film)
cast: Matt Damon, Meg Ryan, Denzel Washington
director: Edward Zwick
Courant: 5 paper 9 newspaper
locale: 8 Hartford
courant, au: 3 new 5 aware, newsy 6 posted, versed, wise to 7 abreast, updated 8 familiar, informed, up-to-date 9 cognizant, conscious, in fashion, observant 10 conversant
courante: 5 dance
coureur de __: 4 bois
Couric: 5 Katie
courier: 5 envoy 6 bearer, herald, legate, runner 8 emissary 9 messenger
Courier: 4 font 8 typeface
Courier, Jim: 7 netster 9 tennis pro
milieu: 5 court
Courier Journal: 5 paper 9 newspaper
locale: 10 Louisville
Cournand, André: 8 Nobelist
course: 3 lap, run, way 4 dish, duct, flow, mode, path, pour, race, road, rush, soup, tack, term, tide, tier, west 5 canal, class, layer, march, orbit, round, route, salad, speed, spell, steps, sweep, track, trail, train, trend 6 access, artery, avenue, entrée, length, method, period, policy, resort, scheme, series, stream 7 advance, channel, circuit, conduit, current, dessert, heading, ingress, measure, passage, process, program, regimen, seminar, subject, tactics 8 approach, aqueduct, duration, elective, lifetime, movement, progress, sequence, tendency 9 direction, golf links, itinerary, procedure, racetrack, unfolding 10 continuity, discipline, procession, succession, trajectory
audit a ~: 5 sit in
change ~: 3 yaw, zag, zig 4 tack, turn, veer 5 sheer
change of ~: 5 U-turn
college ~: 3 art, bio., bot., eco., Eng., geo., mus., sci., sem., soc. 4 chem.., econ., geol., hist., math., phys, stat. 5 drama, music, psych 6 botany, Eng. Lit., French, German, phys. ed. 7 biology, English, geology, history, physics, science, seminar, Spanish 8 calculus 9 chemistry, economics, sociology 10 English Lit, literature, psychology, statistics
combining form: 4 drom- 5 -drome, dromo-
dinner ~: 4 soup 5 salad 6 entrée 7 dessert 9 appetizer
down a ~: 3 eat
finale: 4 exam, test
first ~: 4 soup 5 salad
first ~ of action: 5 plan A
golf ~: 5 links
go off ~: 3 err, yaw, zag 4 roam, rove, skid, slue, tack, turn, veer 5 drift, lurch, range, slide, stray, swing 6 divert, ramble, swerve, wander 7 deflect, deviate, digress, diverge, maunder, meander 8 sideslip
high school ~: 3 alg., bio., Eng., geo., gym, lit, mus. 4 biol., chem., econ., hist., math., trig 5 music 7 algebra, biology, English, physics 8 . Geometry 9 chemistry 10 literature
in due ~: 3 yet 4 anon, soon 10 eventually, ultimately
in the ~ of: 4 amid 5 along, among 6 amidst, during, mongst 7 amongst
length: 4 term 8 semester
listing: 4 menu
main ~: 4 meat 6 entrée
main ~ of study: 5 major
marker: 5 pylon
math ~: 3 alg. 4 calc., geom., stat., trig 7 algebra 8 calculus, geometry 10 statistics
of ~: 2 ay, da, ja, sí 3 aye, oui, yea, yep, yes, yup 4 fine, okay, sure, yeah 5 good-o, natch, quite, right, roger, truly, uh-huh 6 agreed, and how, gladly, good-oh, indeed, just so, rather, really, righto, surely, you bet, yowzah 7 exactly, for sure, go ahead, indeedy, mais oui, no doubt, quite so, ten-four 8 all right, as you say, thumbs up, very well 9 assuredly, be my guest, certainly, darn right, naturally, obviously, precisely, sure thing, you betcha, you said it 10 absolutely, as expected, by all means, definitely, far and away, positively, sure enough, that's right
of action: 3 way 4 line, plan 6 policy 7 process 10 proceeding
of events: 4 tide
off ~: 4 awry 6 afield, astray
of thought: 5 logic, tenor
par for the ~: 4 norm 5 typic, usual 7 typical 8 expected
plot a ~: 5 chart 8 navigate
pursue one's ~: 4 wend
reading: 4 text 8 textbook
run its ~: 3 ebb 4 ease, fade, flag, stop, wane 5 abate, let up, relax 6 ease up, lessen, recede 7 die down, dwindle, ease off, slacken, subside, tail off 8 blow over, diminish, fade away, moderate, peter out, taper off 10 slacken off
science ~: 3 bio. 4 biol., chem., geol., phys. 7 biology, geology, physics, science 9 chemistry
seafood ~: 4 bisk, sole, tuna 6 bisque, salmon, scampi, shrimp 7 lobster 8 flounder
secondary ~: 6 bypath
secondary ~ of action: 5 plan B
short ~: 6 clinic
starter: 4 race 5 water 6 string
stay the ~: 5 stand 7 persist 8 stand for, tolerate 9 persevere
take a ~: 5 enrol, learn, study 6 enroll
take a refresher ~: 6 bone up
through the ~ of: 4 amid 6 amidst
throw off ~: 6 derail
unit: 6 credit, lesson
__ course: 4 belt, cram, golf, lay a, main, snap, true 5 barge, crash, in due 6 honors, lacing, plinth, raking, survey 7 compass, heading
courser: 3 dog 4 bird 5 canid, horse, steed 6 canine, equine
court: 3 bar, woo 4 date, love, quad, walk, yard 5 bench, forum, judge, motel, patio, plaza, spark, spoon, staff 6 atrium, call on, garden, piazza, pursue, square, street 7 retinue, take out, wheedle 8 fawn over, kowtow to, tribunal 9 cultivate, enclosure, entourage, go out with, importune, Old Bailey, shine up to 10 attendants, quadrangle
appointee: 6 elisor 7 eslisor
award: 7 damages
barrier: 3 net
bring back to ~: 5 retry
bring into ~: 4 haul
British ~ of old: 4 leet
calendar: 6 docket
call: 3 let, out 4 ad in, foul
case: 3 res 5 trial 7 lawsuit
central ~ s: 5 atria
clerical ~: 4 rota 6 parvis
come before the ~: 6 appear
concern: 3 law 4 case, suit 5 trial
contest: 5 match
cry: 4 oyes, oyez 6 hear ye
decision: 3 let 5 award, guilt
ender: 3 ier 4 room, ship, side, yard 5 house
entertain the ~: 4 jest
evidence: 3 DNA
expel from ~: 6 disbar
figure: 3 att. 4 atty., suer 5 juror 6 arguer, lawyer 7 jurists 8 attorney
furnishing: 5 Bible
game: 6 tennis 10 basketball
go to ~: 3 sue 6 appeal 7 contest, dispute 8 file suit, litigate 9 prosecute
group: 3 ABA, NBA 4 jury, USTA 5 USLTA 9 grand jury, petit jury
hearing: 4 oyer
Indian ~ officials: 5 omlah
in jai alai: 6 cancha 7 fronton
injustice: 5 frame 6 bad rap, bum rap
introduce in ~: 5 enter
judgment: 4 fiat, writ 5 edict, order 6 decree, dictum, ruling 7 mandate, verdict 8 sanction 9 directive 10 injunction
kid at ~: 4 page
like a kangaroo ~: 4 fake, sham 5 bogus, false, hokey, phony 6 ersatz, parody, pseudo 8 so-called, spurious, travesty 9 pretended
motor ~: 8 rest stop
old Indian ~: 6 adalat
order: 4 writ 5 paper
Ottoman ~: 5 porte
personage: 2 DA 3 ref 5 clerk, judge, steno 6 umpire 7 bailiff, referee
phrase: 3 I do
Scottish ~ official: 5 macer
seat: 4 banc
session: 5 trial 6 assize
silencer: 5 gavel
starter: 4 back, down
statement: 4 oath, plea 5 alibi 9 testimony
system: 3 bar
take back to ~: 5 resue
take to a higher ~: 6 appeal
unbiased ~ advisor: 6 amicus
see also basketball, tennis
court __: 4 hand, shoe 5 dance, dress, of law, order 6 jester, tennis 7 packing, plaster
court-__: 7 martial
__ court: 3 law 4 auto, clay, food, hard, moot 5 cabin, day in, deuce, front, grass, motor, night, trial 6 county, family, mayor's, police 7 appeals, circuit, federal, people's, probate, provost, service, tourist, traffic, trailer
__-court: 5 out-of
Court: 8 Margaret
Court __ James's: 4 of St.
__ Court: 4 High 5 Night, World 7 General, Supreme
Courtenay, Tom: 5 actor
film: Billy Liar (1963)
King and Country (1964)
King Rat (1965)
The Loneliness of the Long Distance Runner (1962)
Courteney: 3 Cox 8 Arquette
courteous: 4 kind, nice, soft 5 civil, moral, suave, sweet 6 decent, gentle, kindly, polite, proper, subtle, urbane 7 affable, cordial, gallant, genteel, politic, refined, tactful 8 amicable, debonair, discreet, gracious, ladylike, likeable, mannerly, well-bred 9 attentive, civilized, debonaire, judicious, sensitive 10 chivalrous, cultivated, debonnaire, diplomatic, hospitable, respectful, soft-spoken, thoughtful, well-spoken
be ~: 5 thank
name meaning ~: 6 Curtis
not ~: 4 rude 7 brusque
courtesy: 4 gift, tact 5 favor 6 comity 7 amenity, manners, respect, service, suavity 8 breeding, ceremony, chivalry, civility, kindness, niceties, protocol, urbanity 9 deference, etiquette, gallantry, gentility, propriety, suaveness 10 cordiality, indulgence, knighthood, politeness, refinement
env.: 3 SAE 4 SASE
courtesy __: 3 car 4 call, card 5 light, title
courtier: 5 toady 6 fawner, squire, suitor 7 flunkey 8 adulator, follower, kowtower, servitor 9 attendant, flatterer, sycophant 10 bootlicker
courtiers: 9 entourage
courting __: 5 chair 6 mirror
Courting at Burnt Ranch, The, ballet: 5 Rodeo

courting one: 5 wooer
Court Jester (1956 film)
cast: Glynis Johns, Danny Kaye, Angela Lansbury, Basil Rathbone
courtliness: 8 elegance
courtly: 5 noble, regal, royal, suave 6 august, formal, polite, ritual, urbane 7 elegant, gallant, genteel, pompous, refined, stately 8 cultured, decorous, gracious, high-bred, polished, well-bred 9 dignified 10 chivalrous, respectful
courtly __: 4 love
Court, Margaret: 7 netster 9 tennis pro
milieu: 5 court
court-martial: 3 try
__ court-martial: 7 general, special, summary
Court Martial (1955 film)
cast: Margaret Leighton, David Niven
director: Anthony Asquith
Court-Martial of Billy Mitchell, The (1955 film)
cast: Ralph Bellamy, Charles Bickford, Gary Cooper
director: Otto Preminger
Courtney: 4 Love 5 Vance
Courtney __-Smith: 6 Thorne
court of __: 3 law 5 honor 6 claims, equity, record 7 appeals, inquiry
court of common __: 5 pleas
__-court press: 4 full
courtroom: 9 judiciary
see also court
courtship: 4 suit 6 dating, wooing 7 pursuit, romance 10 engagement
animal ~ site: 3 lek
Courtship of Eddie's Father, The (1963 film)
cast: Glenn Ford, Ron Howard, Shirley Jones, Stella Stevens
director: Vincente Minnelli
Courtship of Eddie's Father, The (ABC sitcom)
cast: Bill Bixby (Tom Corbett) Brandon Cruz (Eddie Corbett) Miyoshi Umeki (Mrs. Livingston)
Courtship of Miles Standish, The
author: Longfellow
character: 5 Alden 7 Mullins 9 Priscilla
__ Court, The: 7 People's
__ court to: 3 pay
Court TV: 7 channel
alternative: 3 BET, CMT, MTV, PAX, TBS, TLC, TNN, TNT, USA 4 ESPN, HGTV 5 A and E, C-SPAN, Style 6 Noggin, Tech TV, TV Land 7 Ovation, SoapNet 8 Lifetime
courtyard: 4 quad, yard 5 patio 6 atrium 8 cloister 9 enclosure, peristyle 10 quadrangle
cloister ~: 5 garth
of a ~: 6 atrial
courtyards: 5 atria
Courvoisier: 5 drink 8 beverage
couscous: 4 stew 5 grain
alternative: 4 orzo, ziti 5 penne 6 noodle 7 lasagna, lasagne, pastina, ravioli 8 bucatini, farfalle, linguine, linguini, macaroni, rigatoni 9 agnolotti, angelhair, cavatelli, manicotti, spaghetti 10 cannelloni, fettuccini, tortellini, vermicelli
cousin: 3 kin 7 kinsman 8 relative 9 kinswoman
__ cousin: 4 full 5 first 6 second 7 country, kissing
Cousin __: 3 Itt 4 Pons 5 Bette, Bobby
Cousin Bette: 4 film 5 novel
author: Honoré de Balzac
cast: Bob Hoskins, Jessica Lange, Hugh Laurie, Elisabeth Shue
director: Des McAnuff
Cousin Bobby (1991 film) director: Jonathan Demme
Cousin Itt: 6 Addams
Cousin Pons author: Honoré de Balzac
Cousins: 5 Robin 6 Norman
Cousins (1989 film)
cast: Ted Danson, Isabella Rossellini, Sean Young
director: Joel Schumacher
Cousins, Robin: 6 skater
Cousteau, Jacques-Yves: 8 explorer
milieu: 3 mer, sea 5 ocean
Cousy, Bob: 4 Celt 6 Celtic
milieu: 5 court
org.: 3 NBA
sport: 10 basketball
couter: 5 armor
couth: 7 refined 8 urbanity 9 suaveness
coutil: 6 fabric 8 material
__ couture: 5 haute
couturier: 6 fitter, tailor 8 designer 9 outfitter 10 dressmaker
French ~: 3 YSL 4 Dior
cove: 3 arm, bay 4 gulf 5 fiord, fjord, inlet 6 armlet, ensure, grotto, harbor, insure, recess 7 harbour, shelter
shelter, as in a ~: 5 embay
__ Cove: 5 Cabot
Coveleski: 4 Stan
covellite: 3 ore
covenant: 3 law, vow 4 bond, deal, deed, pact 5 trust 6 pledge, treaty 7 compact, promise 8 contract, protocol, warranty 9 agreement, testament 10 commitment, settlement
Covenant, The author: Michener
coven member: 5 witch
Covent Garden
locale: 6 London 7 Britain, England
offering: 4 aria 5 opera
performer: 4 diva
Coventry: 4 city, town
locale: 7 England
send to ~: 4 shun 5 exile
__ Cove, NY: 4 Glen
cover: 2 do 3 lap, lee, lid, sit, top 4 bury, coat, cork, garb, hide, mask, peel, rind, skin, span, veil, wrap 5 alibi, bathe, cache, capot, cloak, couch, dress, front, glaze, guard, guise, haven, layer, liner, paint, patch, quilt, rub on, shade, smear, touch 6 asylum, awning, canopy, capote, clothe, defend, embody, encase, ensure, enveil, harbor, imbody, incase, inhume, insure, invest, mantle, offset, pepper, reason, redeem, refuge, relate, safety, screen, secure, shadow, shield, shroud, spread, survey, take in, tell of, veneer 7 bedding, bedrape, binding, blanket, board up, conceal, contain, defense, eclipse, embrace, enclose, encrust, envelop, harbour, hideout, inclose, include, incrust, involve, lodging, obscure, overlay, plaster, pretext, protect, recount, retreat, secrete, shelter, shut off, shut out, smother, stretch, suffuse, surface, touch on, varnish, write up 8 comprise, deal with, disguise, ensconce, enshroud, envelope, overflow, pinch-hit, pretense, report on, security, traverse 9 adumbrate, bedspread, broadcast, encompass, make up for, reinforce, safeguard, sanctuary, touch upon, watch over 10 camouflage, compensate, keep a lid on, keep secret, protection, provide for, spread over
bed ~: 5 duvet, quilt 6 canopy 7 blanket 9 comforter
combining form: 4 steg- 5 stego-
ender: 3 age, lid
face ~: 4 mask
for: 8 pinch-hit 10 substitute
(for): 6 double, fill in 7 stand in
give ~: 6 shield
ground: 3 fly, hie, run 4 rush, trot 5 speed 6 travel 8 progress
ground ~: 3 sod 4 lawn 5 grass, mulch, plant, sedum
nautically: 6 batten
neck ~: 5 dicky, scarf 6 collar, dickey, dickie 7 muffler
one under ~: 5 hider
snugly: 4 tuck 6 tuck in
starter: 4 hard, slip, soft 6 ground
story: 5 alibi 7 pretext
take ~: 4 hide 6 lie low 7 hide out
the eyes: 7 obscure 9 obfuscate
thickly: 4 slab 7 slather
under ~: 8 on the sly, secretly, ulterior 9 concealed
up: 4 bury, hide, hush, mask, veil 5 cloak, cloud, shade 6 batten, clothe, enrobe, hush up, inhume, shield, stifle 7 conceal, protect, secrete, shelter 8 suppress 9 dissemble, keep quiet, misinform, stonewall, whitewash
with veneer: 4 coat 5 layer 7 overlay
words on the ~: 5 title 6 author 9 publisher
cover __: 3 boy 4 crop, girl, slip, text 5 glass, point, story 6 charge, ground, letter 7 version
cover-__: 3 ups
__ cover: 3 air, sky 4 dust, mast, open, snow, take 5 break, cloud, extra, under 6 ground, tongue
__-cover: 4 soft
Cover: 8 Franklin
coverage: 9 insurance
get ~ for: 6 ensure, insure 7 protect, warrant 9 indemnify
covered: 4 clad 5 blind, ready, shady 6 hidden 9 concealed, out of view, unexposed 10 enshrouded, tucked away
by: 5 neath, under 10 underneath
by, to a poet: 5 neath
not ~: 4 open 7 exposed
passage: 4 slip, stoa 5 slype 6 arcade
way: 4 stoa 7 gallery, portico 9 colonnade
with water: 5 soggy, soppy 6 soaked, sodden 7 sopping 8 drenched, dripping 9 saturated
covered __: 5 wagon 6 bridge
cover girl: 5 model, poser
Cover Girl: 6 makeup
alternative: 4 Avon 5 Almay 6 Revlon 7 Lancome, Mary Kay 8 Clinique 9 Max Factor 10 Maybelline 11 Estée Lauder, Merle Norman
Cover Girl (1944 film)
cast: Lee Bowman, Rita Hayworth, Gene Kelly
director: Charles Vidor
covering: 2 on 3 cap, hat, lid, top 4 coat, cowl, garb, gear, hide, hull, husk, over, peel, rind, robe, roof, tarp, tent, wrap 5 blind, cloak, crust, dress, glaze, layer, scarf, shade, shawl, sheet, shell 6 awning, bonnet, canopy, casing, facing, hiding, jacket, mantle, spread, veneer 7 blanket, ceiling, clothes, coating, drapery, garment, housing, lacquer, outside, surface, wrapper 8 clothing, disguise, envelope, frosting, kerchief, mantilla, rambling 9 tarpaulin 10 integument, protection
combining form: 4 cole- 5 coleo- 7 cortico-
cut the ~ off: 5 shave
floor ~: 3 mat, rug 4 lino, tile 6 carpet 8 linoleum 9 broadloom
flower-bed ~: 5 humus 7 compost
foot ~: 3 pac 4 boot, hose, shoe, sock 5 socks 9 stockings
head ~: 3 cap, hat, tam 4 cowl, hair, hood 5 beret, scarf, shawl
hot-dog ~: 4 skin 6 casing
leg ~: 4 spat 6 puttee 7 gambado
outer ~: 4 husk, rind, skin
protective ~: 4 tarp 5 armor
remove the ~: 4 peel, skin
thin ~: 4 film 5 scale
window ~: 5 drape, glass, grill, shade 6 grille, screen 7 curtain, drapery
see also cover
covering __: 5 power 6 letter
__ covering: 4 wall 5 floor, short
coverlet: 5 quilt, throw 6 afghan 9 bedspread, comforter, eiderdown
Cover Me (1984 song) artist: Bruce Springsteen
Cover of Rolling Stone, The (1973 song) artist: Dr. Hook
cover one's __: 6 tracks
covers, under the: 4 abed 5 not up
covert: 3 sly 5 privy 6 hidden, latent, masked, refuge, secret, veiled 7 cloaked, furtive, on the QT, private, shelter 8 hideaway, hush-hush, obscured, secluded, shrouded, sneaking, stealthy, ulterior 9 concealed, disguised, invisible, nonpublic, potential, sanctuary, secretive, sheltered 10 enshrouded, undercover, under wraps, undivulged, unviewable
operative: 5 ninja
org.: 3 CIA
covert __: 5 cloth 6 action
covertly: 7 on the QT, sub rosa 8 on the sly, secretly
covertness: 7 secrecy
cover-up: 4 sham 5 front, shirt, smock 6 anorak, caftan, kaftan 7 pretext 8 disguise 10 masquerade
see also cover, covering
covet: 4 envy, long, lust, need, seek, want, wish 5 crave, fancy, yearn 6 desire 7 ache for, itch for, long for, wish for 8 aspire to, begrudge, yearn for 9 hanker for, thirst for
ending: 3 ous
covetable: 4 good 6 sultry, useful 7 helpful, lovable 8 adorable, enticing, enviable, fetching, loveable 9 beautiful, desirable, excellent 10 attractive, beneficial, gratifying, profitable, worthwhile
covetous: 5 itchy 6 greedy, hungry, sordid 7 envious, jealous, lustful, miserly, wishful 8 desirous, grasping, ravenous 9 mercenary 10 avaricious, gluttonous
covetousness: 3 sin 4 envy, lust 5 greed 6 desire 7 avarice 8 cupidity
covey: 3 set 4 band, bevy, crew, gang, herd, nest 5 brood, bunch, flock, group, swarm 7 cluster, company 10 hatchlings
member: 5 quail
Covina: 4 city, town
locale: 10 California
Covington: 3 Wes 4 city, town
locale: 3 Ken. 8 Kentucky
cow: 3 awe, she 5 bully, daunt, deter, scare 6 animal, bovine, coerce, dampen, female, hector, heifer, mammal, rattle, subdue 7 bluster, critter, crittur, overawe, unnerve 8 browbeat, bulldoze, dispirit, dissuade, frighten, threaten 9 give pause, strong-arm, terrorize 10 dishearten, intimidate
ankle: 4 hock
ant ~: 5 aphid
Asian ~: 4 zebu
bellow: 3 low, moo
breed: 3 Gir 4 Busa, Glan, Kuri, Rath, Siri, Tuli 5 Angus, Barka, Boran,

Dajal, Dangi, Deoni, Devon, Fjall, Horro, Kerry, Kurdi, Luing, Malvi, Maure, N'dama, Nguni, Oropa, Rathi, Sanhe, Wagyu 6 Angeln, Ankole, Aubrac, Baladi, Channi, Dexter, Dhanni, Dulong, Gaolao, Herens, Jaulan, Jersey, Lohani, Mewati, Nagori, Nelore, Nimari, Ongole, Ovambo, Ponwar, Rojhan, Salers, Sarabi, Sussex, Tswana, Vosges 7 Alberes, Bachaur, Barzona, Brahman, Brahmin, Cachena, Canchim, Istoben, Mashona, Red Poll, Retinta, Sahiwal, Yanbian 8 Ayrshire, Bonsmara, Charbray, Chianina, Galloway, Gelbvieh, Guernsey, Hereford, Holstein, Limousin 9 Charolais, Shorthorn, Simmental 10 Lincoln Red, Murray Grey, Welsh Black
bunch: 4 herd
cash ~: 7 bonanza 8 gold mine
catcher: 5 lasso, reata, riata 6 lariat
chew: 3 cud
emulate a ~: 5 graze
ender: 3 boy, man, men, pea, pox 4 bane, bell, bird, fish, girl, hand, herb, herd, hide, lick, poke, rite, shed, slip 5 berry 7 catcher, puncher
follower: 4 town
genus: 3 bos
hip joint: 5 thurl
holy ~: 4 yipe 5 yikes, yipes
home: 4 barn 5 dairy
hornless ~: 5 muley 6 mulley
in Britain: 5 stirk
lunch: 5 grass
male: 4 bull
milking the ~: 5 chore
name: 5 Bossy 6 Bossie
offering: 4 milk
pampas ~ catcher: 4 bola
part: 4 hoof, tail 5 udder
sacred ~: 4 idol
sea ~: 6 dugong 7 manatee
shed: 4 byre
stomach: 5 rumen 6 omasum
stomachs: 5 omasa
trademark ~: 5 Elmer, Elsie
unbranded ~: 4 calf 5 stray 8 maverick
young: 4 calf 6 heifer
see also cattle
cow ___: 4 lily, pony, town 5 horse, pilot, shark, vetch 7 college, country, parsnip
___ cow: 3 ant, sea 4 bell, cash, holy, milk 5 black, have a, milch 6 sacred
___ cow!: 4 Holy
Cow ___: 6 Palace
coward: 4 baby, wimp 5 mouse, sissy 6 craven 7 chicken, dastard, milksop, quitter 8 deserter, poltroon, recreant, weakling 9 fraidy-cat, jellyfish 10 scaredy-cat
lack: 4 guts 5 nerve, spine
Coward ___ County: 5 of the
cowardice: 4 fear 8 cold feet, timidity
cowardly: 3 shy 4 base, weak 5 faint, timid 6 afraid, craven, scared, trepid, yellow 7 alarmed, anxious, chicken, daunted, fearful, gutless, jittery, nervous, panicky, spooked, wimpish 8 fearsome, hesitant, recreant, timorous 9 dastardly, nerveless, petrified, spineless, terrified, tremulous 10 frightened
Cowardly Lion portrayer: 4 Lahr
Coward, Noël: 3 Sir 6 author 7 British 8 composer 10 playwright
work: Blithe Spirit
Design for Living
Future Indefinite
Not Yet the Dodo
Present Indicative
Private Lives
Coward of the County (1979 song) artist: Kenny Rogers
cowberry: 5 fruit, shrub
relative: 5 heath, salal 6 azalea, kalmia 7 arbutus, rhodora 8 cassiope 9 blueberry, deerberry
cowboy: 5 rider 6 drover, gaucho, herder 7 rancher, vaquero 8 buckaroo, herdsman, horseman, stockman, wrangler 9 ranch hand 10 equestrian
at times: 5 roper 6 herder 7 brander
be a drugstore ~: 6 loiter
bed: 4 bunk
buddy: 4 pard 7 pardner
coat: 8 chaqueta
companion: 5 horse
competition: 5 rodeo
concern: 4 dogy, herd 5 dogey, stray 6 cattle, doggie
drugstore ~: 5 ogler
exclamation ~: 4 heck 5 howdy, wahoo 6 giddap 7 giddyap, giddyup
flick: 5 oater 7 western 10 horse opera
food: 4 chow, grub
gear: 4 rope 5 reata, riata 6 lariat
home: 5 ranch, range
instrument: 6 guitar
Mexican ~: 6 charro
nickname: 3 Tex 5 Dusty
response: 3 yep, yup 4 nope
South American ~: 6 gaucho
strap: 4 rein
sweetie: 3 gal
walk like a ~: 5 mosey
wear: 3 hat 4 boot, spur
cowboy ___: 3 hat 4 boot
___, cowboy!: 6 Ride 'em
Cowboy (1958 film)
cast: Glenn Ford, Jack Lemmon
director: Delmer Daves
___ Cowboy: 4 Neon 5 Urban 10 Rhinestone
Cowboy Philosopher on Prohibition, The author: Will Rogers
Cowboy rival: 3 Jet, Ram 4 Bear, Bill, Colt, Lion 5 Brown, Chief, Eagle, Giant, Niner, Raven, Saint, Texan, Titan 6 Bengal, Bronco, Falcon, Jaguar, Packer, Raider, Viking 7 Charger, Dolphin, Panther, Patriot, Redskin, Seahawk, Steeler 8 Cardinal 9 Buccaneer
Cowboys: 4 team 6 eleven
home: 6 Dallas
org.: 3 NFC, NFL
sport: 8 football
___ Cowboys: 5 Space
cowboys and ___: 7 Indians
Cowboys Work Is Never Done, A (1972 song) artist: Sonny and Cher
cowcatcher: 5 grill 6 grille
cowed: 5 timid 6 afraid 9 awestruck
easily ~ one: 5 softy 6 softie
Cowens, Dave
milieu: 5 court
org.: 3 NBA
sport: 10 basketball
cower: 4 fawn, hide 5 hunch, kotow, quail, quake, slink, sneak, toady, wince 6 blench, cringe, flinch, grovel, kowtow, recoil, shrink 7 slither, tremble, truckle
at: 5 dread
cowfish: 8 cetacean
relative: 3 orc, sei 5 whale 6 beluga, narwal 7 dolphin, finback, grampus, narwhal, rorqual 8 narwhale, porpoise
___ Cowgirls Get the Blues: 4 Even
cowhide: 7 leather
puncher: 3 awl
cowl: 4 hood 5 cloak 8 covering
wearer: 4 monk
Cowley, Abraham: 4 poet 7 British
cowlick: 4 hair, tuft 6 strand
cowlike: 6 bovine
cowlneck: 7 sweater
cowman: 7 rancher
coworker: 4 ally, mate 6 fellow 7 comrade, partner 9 associate, colleague
Cow Palace: 5 arena
cowpea: 4 bean 6 legume
Cowper, William: 4 poet 7 British
cowpoke: 6 drover, gaucho 7 rancher, vaquero 8 buckaroo, herdsman, wrangler
see also cowboy
cowrie: 5 shell 8 seashell
ridge: 5 varix
cows: 4 kine 5 stock 6 cattle 9 livestock
old-style: 4 kine
till the ~ come home: 7 forever
Cowsills
song: Hair (1969)
Indian Lake (1968)
The Rain, the Park & Other Things (1967)
cowslip: 5 plant 6 flower
cox: 9 steersman
ender: 4 comb 5 swain
Cox: 4 Alex 5 Nikki, Ronny, Wally 7 Deborah 9 Archibald, Courteney
coxa: 4 bone
site: 3 hip 6 pelvis
coxcomb: 3 fop 4 buck, dude 5 blade, dandy, spark, swell 8 popinjay 9 pretty boy 10 jack-a-dandy
Cox, Courteney: 7 actress
film: 3000 Miles to Graceland (2001)
Ace Ventura: Pet Detective (1994)
Scream (1996)
spouse: David Arquette
TV: Friends
Cox's Orange Pippin: 5 apple
relative: 4 crab, Gala, Lodi, Rome 5 Mutsu 6 Empire, Ida Red, medlar, Pippin, russet 7 Baldwin, Bramley, costard, Freedom, Liberty, Spartan, Wealthy, Winesap 8 Cortland, Jonathan, McIntosh 10 Rome Beauty
coxswain: 5 pilot 6 sailor 7 jack tar
concern: 4 crew 5 rower
obey a ~: 3 oar
coy: 3 shy, sly 4 arch, prim 5 timid 6 artful, cutesy, demure, modest 7 bashful, cutesie, evasive 8 affected, blushing, reserved, retiring, skittish 9 diffident, flinching, reluctant, secretive, shrinking, unwilling 10 coquettish, overmodest
act: 4 wink
coydog: 5 canid 6 canine
relative: 3 fox 4 wolf 5 dhole, dingo 6 corsac, coyote, fennec, jackal
___ Coy Mistress: 5 To His
coyness: 7 modesty
coyote: 3 fur 5 bayer, canid 6 animal, canine, howler, mammal
kin: 6 jackal
relative: 3 dog, fox 4 wolf 5 dhole, dingo 6 corsac, coydog, fennec, jackal
Coyote: 5 Peter, Wile E.
city on the ~: 7 San Jose
plaint: 4 howl
rival: 4 Blue, King, Star, Wild 5 Bruin, Devil, Flame, Flyer, Oiler, Sabre, Shark 6 Canuck, Ranger 7 Capital, Panther, Penguin, Red Wing, Senator 8 Canadien, Islander, Predator, Thrasher 9 Avalanche, Blackhawk, Hurricane, Lightning, Maple Leaf 10 Blue Jacket, Mighty Duck
State: 4 S. Dak.
Coyotes: 3 six 4 team
home: 7 Phoenix
milieu: 3 ice 4 rink
org.: 3 NHL
sport: 6 hockey
Coyote State sch.: 3 USD
Coyote Ugly (2000 film)
cast: Maria Bello, Adam Garcia, John Goodman, Piper Perabo
director: David McNally
Coyote, Wile E. mail-order company: 4 Acme
coypu: 6 animal, mammal, nutria, rodent
relative: 3 rat 4 cavy, degu, jird, paca, vole 5 gundi, mouse, xerus 6 agouti, beaver, gerbil, gopher, jerboa, marmot, murine 7 hamster, lemming, muskrat, visacha 8 chipmunk, cricetid, dormouse, squirrel, tuco-tuco 9 chickaree, groundhog, guinea pig, porcupine, woodchuck 10 chinchilla, prairie dog
Coyuca: 4 city, town
locale: 6 Mexico 8 Guerrero
cozen: 3 con 4 bilk, dupe, fool, gull, rook 5 cheat, trick 6 delude, fleece 7 deceive, defraud, mislead, pretend, swindle, two-time 8 hoodwink 9 bamboozle, disinform, victimize
coziness: 7 comfort 8 snugness
coz's father: 3 unc, unk 5 uncle
Cozumel: 4 city, town
locale: 6 Mexico
see also Spanish
cozy: 4 homy, nice, safe, snug, soft, warm 5 comfy, cushy, homey 6 chummy, folksy, secure 7 livable, nestled, restful 8 familiar, homelike, intimate, liveable, tucked in 9 cuddled up, sheltered
get ~: 6 curl up, nestle 7 snuggle
make ~: 4 tuck 6 tuck in
spot: 3 den 4 nest, nook 5 niche 6 hearth 9 fireplace
___ cozy: 3 tea
Cozy: 4 Cole
Cozzens, James Gould: 6 writer
work: By Love Possessed
Guard of Honor
C.P.: 4 Snow
CPA: 4 acct. 7 auditor 10 accountant, bookkeeper
abbr.: 3 ROA, YTD
concern: 2 bk. 3 acc., aud., irc, net 4 acct. 5 audit, books 6 ledger
employer: 3 IRS
forte: 3 nos. 7 numbers
part of ~: 4 Acct., Cert. 6 Public 9 Certified
record: 3 rct. 4 rcpt. 7 receipt
CPI
agency: 3 BLS
part of ~: 5 Index, Price 8 Consumer
cpl.: 3 NCO
like a ~: 3 enl.
subordinate: 3 PFC, pvt.
superior: 3 sgt.
see also corporal
CPO: 3 NCO
employer: 3 USN 4 Navy 6 US Navy
part of ~: 5 Chief, Petty 7 Officer
C.P.O. Sharkey (NBC sitcom) cast: Don Rickles (Otto Sharkey)
CPR
expert: 3 EMT 9 paramedic
teacher: 4 the Y, YMCA, YMHA
CPSC part: 6 Safety 7 Product 8 Consumer 10 Commission
CPU: 2 PC 8 computer 9 mainframe
part: 4 Unit 7 Central 10 Processing
Cr: 4 elem. 7 element 8 chromium
24 for ~: 4 at. no.

crab: 5 apple, crank, gripe, groan, grump, spite 6 Cancer, chider, grouch, grouse, hermit, kvetch, sidler 7 fiddler, grumble, seafood 8 complain, grumbler, sourball, sourpuss, windlass 9 bellyache, hard-shell, horseshoe, Sebastian, shellfish, soft-shell, termagant 10 complainer, curmudgeon, malcontent
claw: 5 chela
constellation: 6 Cancer
ender: 4 meat, wise 5 apple, stick
feature: 4 claw
fiddler ~: 3 uca
grass: 4 weed
larva: 4 zoea
month: 4 July
move like a ~: 5 sidle
relative: 4 Gala, Lodi, Rome 5 Mutsu 6 Empire, Ida Red, medlar, Pippin, russet 7 Baldwin, Bramley, costard, Freedom, Liberty, Spartan, Wealthy, Winesap 8 Cortland, Jonathan, McIntosh 10 Rome Beauty
crab ___: 4 legs, tree 5 apple, canon, grass, louse 6 cactus, spider
___ crab: 3 pea 4 blue, kelp, king, lady, land, mole, palm, rock, sand, snow, tree 5 beach, ghost, giant, green, Jonah, purse, shore, stone, white 6 Alaska, calico, hermit, mantis, market, mussel, oyster, spider, sprite 7 coconut, cracked, fiddler 8 cocoanut
Crab: 4 sign 6 Cancer
month: 3 Jul., Jun. 4 July, June
predecessor: 5 Twins
successor: 4 Lion
the ~: 4 sign
Crab ___: 6 Nebula
crab apple: 4 tree
___ crab apple: 5 showy, sweet 6 Oregon 7 garland, prairie
Crabbe: 6 Buster, George
Crabbe, Buster: 7 swimmer
crabbed: 4 dour, glum, mean, rude, sour, tart, ugly 5 cross, gruff, huffy, moody, nasty, onery, sulky, surly, testy 6 bitter, crusty, gloomy, grumpy, ireful, morose, ornery, snappy, sullen, touchy 7 bristly, cynical, fretful, grouchy, huffish, peevish, prickly, waspish 8 captious, fretsome, grumpish, liverish, petulant, snappish 9 crotchety, difficult, fractious, irascible, irritable, querulous, saturnine, splenetic 10 ill-natured, out of sorts, unsociable
Crabbe, George: 4 poet 7 British
crabbiness: 6 spleen 8 asperity, ill humor
crabby: 4 dour, glum, mean, rude, sour, tart, ugly 5 cross, gruff, huffy, moody, nasty, onery, sulky, surly, testy 6 bitter, crusty, fretty, gloomy, grumpy, ireful, morose, ornery, snappy, sullen, touchy 7 bristly, cynical, fretful, grouchy, huffish, peevish, prickly, waspish 8 captious, fretsome, grumpish, liverish, petulant, snappish 9 crotchety, difficult, fractious, irascible, irritable, querulous, saturnine, splenetic 10 ill-natured, out of sorts, unsociable
___-crab soup: 3 she
Crab, the: 4 sign
Crab, The: 5 Evers
crabwise: 8 sideways 9 laterally
crack: 2 go 3 ace, bid, cut, dig, gag, gap, hit, pop, pro, rap, try 4 bang, boom, chap, chip, clap, deft, flaw, flip, good, gybe, harm, hole, hurt, jest, jibe, joke, leak, open, peal, quip, rent, rift, shot, slam, slap, slit, snap, stab, tear, tops 5 adept, blast, break, burst, chasm, chink, cleft, clout, crash, fling, go ape, noise, smack, smash, sneer, solve, split, super, taunt, whack, whirl, wreck 6 adroit, blow up, breach, buffet, choice, cleave, damage, decode, expert, go wild, impair, injure, insult, lose it, outlet, remark, report, shiver, sunder 7 attempt, crevice, decrypt, fissure, opening, roughen, rupture, shatter, skilled, thunder, work out 8 aperture, breakage, crevasse, decipher, dextrous, discover, division, fracture, masterly, skillful, splinter, superior, talented 9 break open, dexterous, excellent, explosion, figure out, first-rate, go bonkers, penetrate, practiced, puzzle out, witticism 10 first-class, infiltrate, interspace, interstice, proficient
a book: 4 read 5 learn, study
down on: 4 halt, stop 5 quash 6 stifle 8 restrain, suppress
ender: 3 pot 4 down 5 brain
filler: 5 grout
have a ~ at: 3 try 7 attempt
jokes: 4 jest
of dawn: 5 sunup 7 morning
open: 5 force, jimmy
open a ~: 4 ajar
something to ~: 4 whip 5 smile
starter: 4 wise
take another ~ at: 5 retry
tough nut to ~: 5 poser 6 enigma 7 mystery, stumper
up: 4 ha-ha 5 amuse, laugh, wreck 6 cackle, giggle, guffaw, titter 7 chortle, chuckle 8 convulse
wise: 4 jest, joke
crack ___: 4 down, wise 5 a book
crack a ___: 4 book, joke 5 smile
___ crack at it: 5 take a
___ Crack'd, The: 6 Mirror
cracked: 4 torn 5 broke, cleft, split 6 broken, faulty, hoarse, rimose, rimous, solved 7 chipped, damaged, injured 8 fissured, sundered 9 fractured 10 deciphered
in a way: 4 ajar
it may be ~: 4 book, safe 5 smile
cracked ___: 3 ice 4 crab 5 wheat
cracked ___ be: 4 up to
cracked grain cereal: 6 groats
Cracked rival: 3 MAD
cracker: 4 Hi-Ho, Ritz, whip 5 Zesta 6 Krispy 7 biscuit, Cheez-It, saltine 8 Triscuit 10 Cheese Nips, Wheat Thins
box: 4 safe
ender: 4 jack
relative: 5 matzo 6 matzah, matzoh
shape: 6 animal
snack: 6 canapé
starter: 3 nut 4 fire, safe, wise
topper: 3 dip 4 Brie, pâté 6 caviar, cheese 7 caviare
vault ~: 4 yegg 5 thief 7 burglar
wanter: 5 Polly
cracker-___: 6 barrel
___ cracker: 4 soda 6 animal, graham, oyster
Cracker ___: 4 Jack 6 Barrel
crackerjack: 3 ace, def, rad 4 aces, A-one, boss, braw, cool, dece, deft, fine, gear, keen, neat, nice, phat, tuff, whiz 5 adept, dandy, ducky, grand, great, marvy, neato, nobby, prime, slick, solid, super, swell 6 adroit, bang on, bang-up, bonzer, bosker, choice, clever, divine, dreamy, expert, far-out, gnarly, groovy, lovely, master, peachy, slap-up, spot on, superb, terrif, tiptop, unreal, whizzo, wicked, wizard 7 amazing, awesome, capital, corking, perfect, ripping, skookum, stellar, sublime 8 dazzling, especial, eximious, fabulous, five-star, four-star, frabjous, glorious, heavenly, jim-dandy, masterly, skillful, slam-bang, smashing, splendid, standout, sterling, stickout, superior, terrific, top-level, topnotch, very good, wondrous 9 bodacious, Endsville, excellent, exemplary, exquisite, first-rate, high-grade, humdinger, hunky-dory, marvelous, practiced, sollicker, top-flight, wonderful 10 first-class, hotsy-totsy, jack-a-dandy, out of sight, peachy-keen, phenomenal, remarkable, stupendous, super-duper
Cracker Jack: 4 nosh 5 candy, snack
dog: 5 Bingo
ingredient: 5 prize 7 peanuts, popcorn
crackers: 3 mad 4 loco 5 batty, wiggy
___ Crackers: 6 Animal
cracking: 5 smart, swift
get ~: 3 hie 4 rush 5 begin, speed, start 6 go to it 7 pitch in 8 commence
needing ~: 5 coded 6 in code
starter: 4 safe, wise
___ cracking!: 3 Get
Crack in the Mirror (1960 film)
cast: Juliette Greco, Orson Welles
crackle: 4 snap 6 rustle, sizzle
ender: 4 ware
___! Crackle! Pop!: 4 Snap
crackling: 6 crispy 7 crunchy
Cracklin' Oat Bran: 6 cereal
competitor: 3 Kix 4 Life, Trix 5 Kashi, Quisp, Total 6 Kaboom, Muesli, Oreo O's, Pablum, Smacks 7 All-Bran, Crispix, Harmony, Hunny B's, Mueslix, Pokemon 8 Boo Berry, Cheerios, Corn Chex, Corn Pops, Fiber One, Rice Chex, Special K, Uncle Sam, Wheaties 9 Alpha Bits, Apple Zaps, Grape Nuts, Honey Comb, Just Right, Wheat Chex 10 Apple Jacks, Bran Flakes, Cap'n Crunch, Cocoa Puffs, Froot Loops, Mini-Wheats, Nutri-Grain, Puffed Rice, Smart Start 11 Cocoa Blasts, Cookie Crisp, Golden Crisp, Lucky Charms, Puffed Wheat, Sweet Crunch, Waffle Crisp
Cracklin' Rosie (1970 song) artist: Neil Diamond
crack of ___: 4 dawn, doom
crackpot: 4 kook, loon, wack 5 crank 6 maniac 7 lunatic
cracks
creep through the ~: 4 ooze, seep
let fall between the ~: 4 omit 5 let go 6 forget, ignore 7 let pass, neglect 8 let slide, overlook 9 disregard
crack the ___: 4 whip
crackup: 5 smash, split, wreck 8 accident, collapse, laughter 9 collision
Crack-Up (1946 film)
cast: Pat O'Brien, Claire Trevor
director: Irving Reis
Cracow river: 7 Vistula
cradle: 3 bed, hug 4 crib, hold 6 hotbed, nestle, origin, rocker 7 infancy, nurture, protect, support 8 babyhood, bassinet 9 childhood, container 10 birthplace
ender: 4 song 5 board
holder of song: 5 bough
propel a ~: 4 rock
cradle ___: 3 cap 4 roof 5 board, vault 6 scythe
___ cradle: 3 sea 4 cat's
Cradle of Love (song) artist: Billy Idol, Johnny Preston
Cradle of Texas Liberty, The: 5 Alamo
cradlesong: 7 lullaby
Cradle Song author: Sierra
Cradle Will Fall, The author: Mary Higgins Clark
Cradle Will Rock (1999 film)
cast: Hank Azaria, Ruben Blades, Joan Cusack, John Cusack
director: Tim Robbins
craft: 3 art, dau, dow, hoy, job 4 bark, boat, brig, dhow, dory, line, make, raft, ruse, ship, work 5 barge, blimp, canoe, forge, guile, knack, liner, oiler, plane, razee, skill, sloop, trade, wiles, yacht 6 career, coaler, deceit, device, devise, dinghy, scheme, talent, vessel, wherry 7 ability, airship, calling, cunning, fashion, felucca, finesse, knavery, know-how, macramé, orbiter, slyness, vehicle, weaving 8 airplane, aptitude, artifice, artistry, ceramics, foxiness, runabout, strategy, subtlety, trickery, vocation, wiliness, zeppelin 9 adeptness, cageyness, canniness, dexterity, diplomacy, duplicity, expertise, hydrofoil, ingenuity, smartness, stratagem, technique 10 adroitness, cleverness, competence, embroidery, expertness, hydroplane, icebreaker, livelihood, occupation, profession, shrewdness, subterfuge, virtuosity
Alaskan ~: 5 kayak, umiak
Cajun ~: 6 bateau
Indian ~: 5 canoe
lateen-rigged ~: 3 dau, dow 4 dhow
lunar ~: 6 lander
motorless ~: 4 punt, raft 5 canoe, sloop 6 glider
partner: 3 art
racing ~: 5 scull, shell, yacht
rower's ~: 5 canoe, kayak, scull, skiff
starter: 3 air 4 hand, king, wood 5 hover, rotor, space, stage, state, trade, water, witch 6 needle 7 shuttle
suffix: 4 -ship
to pole: 4 punt
ungainly ~: 3 tub
water ~: 3 dau, dow 4 boat, dhow, punt, raft, ship 5 canoe, kayak, liner, scull, sloop, umiak
see also boat, ship
craft ___: 5 union
___ craft: 6 gentle 7 landing
___-Craft: 5 Chris
___ craft advisory: 5 small
craftiness: 3 art 5 craft, guile 6 deceit, dupery 7 finesse 8 artifice 9 deception 10 imposition
craftsmanship: 3 art
craftsperson: 4 hand 5 maker, smith 6 artist, worker, wright 7 artisan, builder 9 artificer
___-craftsy: 5 artsy
crafty: 3 sly 4 arch, cagy, foxy, wily 5 cagey, canny, sharp, slick, smart, snaky 6 artful, astute, clever, shifty, shrewd, smooth, tricky 7 cunning, devious, furtive, vulpine 8 guileful, scheming, slippery, stealthy 9 astucious, deceitful, deceptive, designing, ingenious, insidious, underhand 10 serpentine, streetwise
in a ~ way: 5 slyly
one: 3 fox
___-crafty: 4 arty
crag: 3 tor 4 peak, rock 5 arête, cliff, stone 8 mountain, pinnacle 9 precipice 10 escarpment, prominence
craggy: 5 harsh, ridgy, rocky, rough 6 jagged, ridged, rugged, uneven 7 unlevel
abode: 4 aery, eyry 5 aerie, eyrie
Craig: 4 Mack, Wood 5 James, Jenny 6 Nelson, Wasson, Yvonne 7 Kilborn, Sheffer, Stadler, Stevens 9 Breedlove, Claiborne
Craig, James: 5 actor

film: The Devil and Daniel Webster (1941)
Kitty Foyle (1940)
Marriage Is a Private Affair (1944)
Our Vines Have Tender Grapes (1945)
Side Street (1949)
Craig's Wife (1936 film)
cast: John Boles, Billie Burke, Rosalind Russell
Craig T. __: 6 Nelson
Craik: 4 city, town
locale: 6 Canada
Crain, Jeanne: 7 actress
film: Apartment for Peggy (1948)
Belles on Their Toes (1952)
Cheaper by the Dozen (1950)
The Fastest Gun Alive (1956)
Home in Indiana (1944)
The Joker Is Wild (1957)
Leave Her to Heaven (1945)
A Letter to Three Wives (1949)
The Man Without a Star (1955)
Margie (1946)
The Model and the Marriage Broker (1951)
People Will Talk (1951)
Pinky (1949)
State Fair (1945)
You Were Meant for Me (1948)
crake: 4 bird **8** landrail
milieu: 5 marsh
__ crake: 4 corn
cram: 3 jam, ram **4** fill, glut, load, pack, tamp, tuck, wolf **5** crowd, crush, force, jam in, learn, press, ram in, shove, study, stuff, wedge **6** bone up, gobble, master, pack in, squash **7** bunch up, compact, crowd in, engorge, force in, jam-pack, shove in, squeeze, stuff in, surfeit **8** compress, overfill, overpack **9** lucubrate, overcrowd, overstuff, squeeze in
cram __: 6 course
cram-__: 4 full
Cram, Donald: 7 chemist **8** Nobelist
Cramer, Floyd: 7 pianist
song: Last Date (1960)
On the Rebound (1961)
San Antonio Rose (1961)
cram-full: 5 sated **6** loaded
crammed: 4 full, rife **5** dense, laden, thick **7** compact, replete, teeming **8** brimming, squeezed, thronged **9** chock-full, condensed **10** compressed, hard-packed
cramp: 4 ache, clog, hurt, kink, knot, pain, pang **5** box up, crick, limit, pinch, press, stimy, stymy **6** coop up, hamper, hinder, hobble, impede, injury, stymie, thwart, twinge **7** confine, inhibit, shackle, tighten **8** bottle up, encumber, obstruct, restrain, restrict **9** constrain, constrict, hamstring, stiffness **10** constraint, impediment, keep in line
one's style: 8 obstruct
__ cramp: 7 writer's
cramped: 4 tiny **5** close, scant, small, teeny, tight **6** little, narrow, teensy **7** crowded, limited **8** hemmed in **9** confining
quarters: 4 coop **5** booth **6** alcove, recess **7** chamber, cubicle, dungeon **8** cloister
cramp one's __: 5 style
cranberries
like ~: 4 tart
where ~ grow: 3 bog
cranberry: 3 red **5** fruit **6** bluish **7** blueish, crimson
family: 5 heath
relative: 4 rose, ruby, rust, wine **5** brick, coral, grape, poppy, rusty, sandy **6** cerise, cherry, claret, garnet, maroon **7** carmine, crimson, fuchsia, magenta, pimento, scarlet, sultana, vermeil **8** amaranth, cardinal, dubonnet, geranium, rubicund **9** carnation, vermilion **10** strawberry
cranberry __: 3 bog **4** bush, tree **5** glass
Cranbrook: 3 car **4** auto **8** Plymouth
Cranbury: 4 city, town
locale: 9 New Jersey
crane: 4 bird, boom **5** davit, hoist, wader **6** brolga, lifter **7** derrick, stretch **8** sandhill **10** demoiselle
arm: 3 jib
cousin: 4 ibis, rail **5** egret, heron **7** bustard
operator's perch: 3 cab
ship's ~: 5 davit
sound: 5 whoop
__ crane: 3 jib **4** blue **5** cable **7** Goliath
Crane: 3 Bob, Les **4** Hart **5** Niles **7** Frasier, Ichabod, Stephen
Crane, Hart: 4 poet **6** writer
work: The Bridge
Crane, Les song: Desiderata (1971)
Crane, Roy captain: 4 Easy
Crane, Stephen: 6 author, writer
work: The Black Riders
Maggie
The Open Boat
The Red Badge of Courage
War Is Kind
Cranford: 4 city, town
locale: 9 New Jersey
cranial __: 5 index, nerve
cranium: 4 bone, head **5** skull **6** noggin, noodle, sconce **9** braincase
bulge: 5 inion
cavity: 5 sinus
nerve: 5 vagus
nerves: 4 vagi
crank: 3 arm, bar, gin, nut, rev **4** crab, kook, spin, turn **5** grump, lever, start, winch **6** grouch, handle, maniac, wind up, zealot **7** capstan, fanatic, lunatic **8** crackpot, sourball, sourpuss, turn over, windlass **9** character, eccentric, intensify **10** curmudgeon
ender: 3 pin **4** case **5** shaft
up: 5 begin **8** get going **10** get started
(up): 3 rev **4** wind
crank __: 3 out, pin **4** call, down **6** letter
crankcase
contents: 3 oil
in Britain: 4 sump
problem: 5 no oil
crankiness: 6 spleen
cranky: 3 odd **5** cross, moody, onery, surly, testy, whiny **6** crusty, grumpy, morose, ornery, touchy, whiney **7** bearish, bristly, fretful, grouchy, huffish, peevish, peppery, waspish **8** fretsome, grumpish, liverish, petulant, snappish **9** crotchety, dyspeptic, irascible, querulous, splenetic **10** out of sorts
be ~: 5 gripe, grump, whine
Cranmer: 6 Thomas
cranny: 3 bay, gap **4** hole, nook, rift **5** chink, cleft, niche **6** alcove, breach, corner, hollow, recess **7** crevice, fissure, opening **10** interspace
partner: 4 nook
Cranston: 3 sen. **4** Alan, city, town **7** senator
crapaud: 4 frog **9** amphibian
craps: 4 game
action: 3 bet
locale: 4 Reno **5** Vegas **8** Las Vegas
natural: 5 seven **6** eleven
need: 4 dice
player: 7 gambler, shooter
crash: 3 jar, ram **4** bang, boom, drop, fall, jolt, live, peal, roar, slam, wham **5** blast, break, crack, lodge, noise, panic, shock, sleep, slump, smash, sound, total, wreck **6** fabric, hurtle, impact, invade, pileup, racket, strike, topple, tumble **7** collide, crackup, descend, descent, pancake, plummet, shatter, smashup, thunder, wrack up **8** accident, collapse, fall flat, fracture, fragment, horn in on, stampede **9** collision, hit the hay, interrupt, rear-ender, sideswipe **10** depression, percussion
into: 3 hit, ram **6** impact
(into): 4 plow **6** plunge
pad: 4 home **5** house **7** housing
place to ~: 3 bed, pad
sound: 3 bam, pow **4** thud **5** thump
the gates: 8 trespass
crash __: 3 pad **4** boat, cart, diet, dive **5** truck **6** course, helmet **7** landing
crash-__: 4 land
Crash __ Dummies: 4 Test
crash and __: 4 burn
Crashaw, Richard: 4 poet **7** British
__-crasher: 4 gate
crashing: 4 loud **5** forte, noisy **7** blaring, booming, jarring, rackety, raucous, reboant **8** piercing, plangent, sonorous, strident, turned up **9** big-voiced, clamorous, deafening **10** boisterous, resounding, stentorian, strepitous, uproarious, vociferous
crashing __: 4 bore
Crash Into Me (1997 song) artist: Dave Matthews Band
crash-investigation org.: 4 NTSB
crass: 3 low, raw **4** loud, rude **5** crude, dense, gross, nervy, rough, tacky **6** coarse, common, obtuse, unmeet, vulgar **7** bearish, boorish, lowbred, lowbrow, uncouth **8** churlish, inurbane **9** inelegant, low-minded, tasteless, unfeeling, ungallant, unrefined **10** indecorous, indelicate, unmannered
one: 3 oaf **4** boor
crassness: 10 coarseness, smuttiness
Crassus: 5 Roman
Cratchit: 3 Bob, Tim
dinner: 5 goose
like young ~: 4 tiny
crate: 3 box **4** auto, case, heap **5** boxup, truck, wreck **6** carton, encase, incase, jalopy, wheels **7** flivver, package, vehicle **9** container **10** automobile, rattletrap
amount: 3 doz. **5** dozen
put in a ~: 6 encase
remove from a ~: 5 unbox
still in the ~: 3 new
up again: 5 rebox
crater: 3 pit **4** hole, scar, vent **5** chasm, mouth, Tycho **6** cavity, hollow **7** lake bed **9** Haleakala **10** Copernicus, depression
contents: 4 lava
volcanic ~: 4 maar
Crater __: 4 Lake **5** Mound
__ Crater: 6 Meteor
Crater Lake: 4 park
locale: 3 Ore. **6** Oregon
cravat: 3 rep, tie **4** repp **5** ascot, scarf, stock **6** bow tie **7** foulard, necktie **8** neckwear **10** four-in-hand
fix a ~: 5 retie
crave: 4 long, lust, miss, need, pant, seek, sigh, want, will, wish **5** covet, fancy, go for, yearn **6** desire, die for, hanker **7** ache for, hope for, itch for, long for, pine for, require, sigh for, solicit **8** yearn for **9** cry out for, drool over, hunger for, thirst for
craven: 4 weak, wimp **5** sissy, timid, wimpy **6** coward, scared, yellow **7** chicken, dastard, fearful, gutless, ignoble, servile, wimpish **8** cowardly, poltroon, recreant, timorous **9** dastardly, fraidy-cat, jellyfish, tremulous, weak-kneed **10** scaredy-cat
Craven, Wes: 8 director
film: Music of the Heart (1999)
A Nightmare on Elm Street (1984)
Scream (1996)
Wes Craven's New Nightmare (1994)
craving: 3 yen **4** ache, itch, lust, need, urge, want, will **5** itchy, mania **6** desire, greedy, hunger, thirst **7** athirst, longing, passion, starved, thirsty **8** ambition, appetite, cupidity, munchies, starving **9** appetence, esurience, hankering
craw: 3 maw **4** crop **5** belly **6** gullet **7** gizzard, stomach
stick in one's ~: 4 rile
__ crawfish: 3 sea **4** Cape
Crawford: 3 Sam **4** Joan, John **5** Cindy **6** Johnny **7** Michael **9** Broderick
Crawford, Broderick: 5 actor
film: All the King's Men (1949, AA)
Born Yesterday (1950)
The Fastest Gun Alive (1956)
Larceny, Inc. (1942)
Night People (1954)
Scandal Sheet (1952)
Crawford, Cindy
emulate ~: 4 pose **5** model
spouse: Richard Gere
Crawford, Joan: 7 actress
film: Above Suspicion (1943)
The Caretakers (1963)
Dancing Lady (1933)
Flamingo Road (1949)
Goodbye, My Fancy (1951)
Grand Hotel (1932)
Harriet Craig (1950)
Humoresque (1946)
Johnny Guitar (1954)
The Last of Mrs. Cheyney (1937)
Mildred Pierce (1945, AA)
Our Dancing Daughters (1928)
Our Modern Maidens (1929)
Possessed (1931)
Possessed (1947)
Queen Bee (1955)
Rain (1932)
Sadie McKee (1934)
Strange Cargo (1940)
Sudden Fear (1952)
What Ever Happened to Baby Jane? (1962)
A Woman's Face (1941)
The Women (1939)
spouse: Douglas Fairbanks Jr., Franchot Tone
crawl: 4 drag, fawn, inch, move, plod, swim, tire, worm **5** climb, creep, plead, slink, sneak, swarm, toady **6** grovel, linger, writhe **7** clamber, truckle, wriggle
do the ~: 4 swim
ender: 5 space
make one's flesh ~: 5 chill, panic, scare, spook **6** appall, revolt **7** horrify, petrify, terrify **8** frighten **9** terrorize
(with): 4 teem **6** abound
crawl __: 5 space
__ crawl: 3 pub
crawler: 3 ant, tot **4** baby, worm **5** snake **6** infant, insect
bar ~: 5 toper
__ crawler: 5 night
Crawley: 4 city, town
locale: 6 Sussex **7** England
__-crawlies: 6 creepy
crawling: 4 poky, slow **5** itchy **6** draggy **7** gradual, impeded, languid **8** dilatory, drawn-out, hesitant, plodding, popu-

lous, slothful, sluggish, toddling 9 leisurely, lethargic, prolonged, snail-like, unhurried 10 deliberate, protracted
  (with): 5 thick 7 profuse, teeming 8 abundant
crawlingly: 8 bit by bit
crawlway: 6 tunnel
crawly: 4 eery 5 eerie 6 creepy
__-crawly: 6 creepy
Cray: 7 Seymour
__ crayfish: 3 sea 4 Cape
Crayola
  choice: 3 hue 5 color, shade
  color: 3 red, tan 4 blue, fern, gold, gray, plum 5 black, brown, denim, green, lemon, maize, melon, peach, sepia, umber, white 6 almond, beaver, canary, carrot, cerise, copper, maroon, orange, orchid, purple, salmon, shadow, sienna, silver, violet, yellow 7 apricot, fuchsia, magenta, manatee, pig pink, sky blue, sunglow, thistle 8 blue bell, blue gray, brick red, cerulean, chestnut, eggplant, lavender, mahogany, mulberry, navy blue, raw umber, sea green, shamrock, teal blue, torch red, wisteria 9 asparagus, blue green, brink pink, cadet blue, cranberry, dandelion, goldenrod, green blue, magic mint, mauvelous, orange red, pine green, raw sienna, red orange, red violet, violet red 10 aquamarine, blue violet, cornflower, desert sand, hot magenta, laser lemon, neon carrot, olive green, outer space, periwinkle, radical red, razzmatazz, timber wolf, tumbleweed, violet blue
  former ~ color: 5 flesh
crayon: 5 chalk 9 wax pencil
craze: 3 bug, fad 4 mode, rage 5 fever, mania, style, thing, trend, vogue 6 madden 7 derange, in thing, passion, Pokémon 8 fixation, Pet Rocks 9 Hula-Hoops, mood rings, obsession
crazed: 3 mad 4 amok, loco, wild 5 amuck, manic, rabid, wacky, wiggy 6 looney, savage, whacky 7 demonic, unsound 8 daemonic, in a furor, maniacal, wild-eyed 9 demonical, fanatical, possessed, wrought-up 10 hysterical, infuriated
craziness: 5 folly, mania 6 lunacy 8 nonsense 9 absurdity
crazy: 3 mad 4 gaga, loco, wild, zany 5 dotty, gonzo, goony, inane, manic, sappy, silly, wacky, weird 6 absurd, gooney, hectic, in love, madcap, whacky 7 bananas, bizarre, fatuous, foolish, oddball, smitten, strange, touched 8 maniacal 9 fanatical, fantastic, foolhardy, half-baked, imprudent, ludicrous, senseless 10 infatuated, outrageous, ridiculous
  about: 4 into 6 fond of 9 far gone on 10 infatuated
  be ~ about: 4 dote, love 5 adore 6 admire
  drive ~: 3 irk 5 annoy 6 pester
  go ~: 4 flip, rave 5 freak 7 rampage
  in a ~ way: 5 madly
  like ~: 4 a lot 5 madly 6 vastly, wildly 7 greatly, rabidly 8 ardently 9 fervently, furiously, intensely 10 recklessly
  like a fox: 3 sly 4 wily
  plumb ~: 4 loco
  quilt: 4 olio 6 jumble, medley 7 mélange 8 mishmash, mixed bag, pastiche 9 pasticcio, patchwork, potpourri 10 assortment, hodgepodge, miscellany, salmagundi
  wild and ~ guy: 5 yahoo
crazy __: 3 top 4 bone 5 quilt 6 eights
crazy __ loon: 3 as a
__ crazy: 4 like
__-crazy: 4 stir
Crazy __: 4 Love, Mama, Moon 5 Horse, House 6 Horses
Crazy __, The: 4 Otto
Crazy __ You: 3 for
__ Crazy: 3 Get, Gun, I Go, Man 4 Girl, Stir 5 Movie
Crazy About Her (1989 song) artist: Rod Stewart
crazy as __: 5 a loon
crazy eights: 4 game 8 card game
Crazy for You: 7 musical
  songwriter: 8 Gershwin
Crazy for You (1985 song) artist: Madonna
CrazyGlue competitor: 4 Duco
Crazy Horse foe: 6 Custer
Crazy Horses (1972 song) artist: Osmonds
Crazy House (1943 film)
  cast: Chic Johnson, Ole Olsen
  director: Edward Cline
Crazy in Alabama (1999 film)
  cast: Lucas Black, Melanie Griffith, Cathy Moriarty, David Morse
  director: Antonio Banderas
Crazy in Berlin author: Thomas Berger
Crazylegs: 6 Hirsch
Crazy Love (song) artist: Paul Anka, Poco
Crazy Mama (1975 film)
  cast: Cloris Leachman, Ann Sothern, Stuart Whitman
  director: Jonathan Demme
Crazy Moon (1986 film)
  cast: Peter Spence, Kiefer Sutherland
Crazy Otto, The (1955 song) artist: Johnny Maddox and the Rhythmasters
Crazy (song) artist: Patsy Cline, Seal
__ Crazy Summer: 3 One
creak: 5 grate, groan, sound 6 squeak, squeal
creaky: 5 stiff 7 ancient 8 decrepit
cream: 3 tan, top 4 balm, best, mash, milk, pick, plum, rout, skim, soda 5 color, dairy, elite, outdo, pride, salve, white 6 choice, defeat, finest, flower, lather, lotion, marrow, ravage, yellow 7 clobber, conquer, destroy, lambast, neutral, shellac, unguent 8 cosmetic, emulsion, lambaste, liniment, ointment, shellack 9 emollient, lubricate, overpower, yellowish
  add ~ to: 6 enrich
  get the ~: 4 skim 5 defat
  of the crop: 4 A-one, best, tops 5 A-list, elect, elite
  puff: 4 wimp 8 weakling
  relative: 4 bone, buff, corn, gold, lime, milk, rust, sand, snow 5 blond, brass, coral, flaxy, ivory, lemon, maize, milky, ocher, ochre, peach, rusty, straw 6 argent, blonde, canary, chammy, citron, crocus, flaxen, oyster, shammy, shamoy, silver 7 apricot, chamois, citrine, jasmine, mustard, nankeen, old gold, saffron, xanthic 8 daffodil, eggshell, primrose 9 champagne, goldenrod, jessamine
  serving: 4 glob 6 dollop
  soothing ~: 4 balm
  whipping tool: 5 whisk
  without ~: 5 black
cream __: 3 ice 4 pail, puff, soda 5 sauce 6 cheese
cream __ crop: 5 of the
__ cream: 3 egg, ice 4 cold, sour 5 Devon, heavy, light 6 coffee, double, triple 7 clotted, shaving
Cream
  leader: Eric Clapton
  song: Sunshine of Your Love (1968) White Room (1968)
Cream (1991 song) artist: Prince
cream cheese partner: 3 lox 5 bagel
cream-colored: 5 flaxy 6 flaxen
creamer relative: 4 ewer
creamery: 5 dairy
cream of __: 6 tartar 7 coconut 8 cocoanut, mushroom
Cream of __: 5 Wheat
cream of mushroom: 4 soup
cream of the __: 4 crop
__ cream pie: 6 Boston 7 coconut 8 cocoanut
cream puff: 3 car 4 auto, nerd, wimp 5 sissy 6 pastry 7 chicken, dessert 8 mama's boy, weakling 9 fraidy cat, jellyfish 10 automobile
  kin: 6 éclair
  sometimes: 3 car
cream soda: 8 beverage
__-cream soda: 3 ice
creamy: 4 lush, oily, rich, soft 5 gooey, white 6 fluffy, smooth 7 buttery, velvety 8 feathery, luscious
  cheese: 4 Brie 7 gervais 9 Camembert 10 mascarpone, Neufchâtel
creamy garlic: 8 dressing
creamy Italian: 8 dressing
crease: 4 bend, fold, line, ruck 5 crimp, plait, pleat, purse, ridge 6 dog-ear, furrow, groove, pucker, ruffle, rumple 7 crinkle, crumple, fluting, wrinkle 9 corrugate
__ crease: 4 goal 7 bowling, popping
create: 2 do 4 coin, form, make, work 5 beget, breed, build, cause, erect, forge, found, hatch, model, put up, set up, shape, spawn, start 6 author, design, devise, effect, father, invent, make up, whip up 7 compose, concoct, develop, dream up, fashion, imagine, pioneer, produce, think up, trump up 8 assemble, conceive, contrive, engender, engineer, generate, initiate, occasion, organize 9 actualize, construct, establish, fabricate, formulate, institute, originate 10 bring about, come up with, constitute, mastermind
creation: 4 opus, work 5 birth, world 6 making, nature, origin 7 coinage, figment, genesis, product 8 original, universe 9 beginning, causation, formation, handiwork, inception, invention 10 brainchild, conception, concoction, foundation, generation, production
Creation of the World, The composer: 7 Milhaud
Creation, The: 8 oratorio
  basis for ~: 7 Genesis
  composer: 5 Haydn
  role: 3 Eve 4 Adam
  setting: 4 Eden
creative: 3 new 5 fresh, novel 6 clever, gifted 7 fertile, unusual 8 artistic, esthetic, inspired, original, prolific 9 aesthetic, ingenious, inventive, visionary 10 artistical, innovative, productive
  impulse: 3 ego 4 idea 8 afflatus
  start: 3 neo
  type: 6 artist, author, genius, writer 8 composer, designer 9 innovator, visionary
  work: 3 art 4 opus 5 music, novel 6 design 7 fiction 9 blueprint, invention
creativity: 3 art 8 artistry 9 invention
creator: 4 sire 5 brain, cause, maker 6 artist, author, framer, mother, origin 7 founder 8 begetter, designer, inventer, inventor, producer 9 architect, artificer, fashioner, initiator, innovator 10 fabricator, mastermind, originator
Creator: 3 God 5 deity, Maker 8 Almighty
  Hindu ~: 6 Brahma
  Moslem ~: 5 Allah
Creator (1985 film)
  cast: Mariel Hemingway, Virginia Madsen, Peter O'Toole
creature: 4 pawn, soul 5 beast, being, thing 6 animal, entity, jackal, mortal, puppet 8 organism 10 individual
creature __: 7 comfort
Creature From the Black Lagoon (1954 film)
  cast: Julie Adams, Richard Carlson, Richard Denning
__ Creatures: 6 Fierce
__ creature was stirring...: 4 not a
crèche trio: 4 Magi
Crécy: 6 battle
credence: 5 faith, trust 6 belief, credit 8 reliance 10 confidence, conviction
  give ~ to: 7 believe
credential: 6 ID card, ticket
credentials: 5 proof 6 papers 7 diploma 8 passport 9 reference
credenza: 6 buffet 7 cabinet 9 furniture, sideboard
credibility: 5 trust 8 solidity, validity
credibility __: 3 gap
credible: 4 sane 5 frank, legit, sound, valid 6 doable, honest, likely, square, viable 7 factual, sincere, tenable, upright 8 feasible, possible, probable, rational, reliable, straight, workable 9 authentic, plausible, potential, practical, veracious 10 achievable, attainable, believable, convincing, dependable, forthright, imaginable, on the level, persuasive, reasonable, scrupulous
credit: 4 deem, fame, give, loan, name 5 asset, clout, faith, glory, honor, kudos, merit, thank, trust, worth 6 accept, bank on, bar tab, byline, esteem, impute, notice, praise, regard, rely on, renown, repute, status, thanks 7 acclaim, advance, ascribe, believe, laurels, plastic, voucher 8 approval, assign to, consider, credence, depend on, gamble on, good name, mortgage, prestige, relegate, reliance, standing 9 ascribe to, attribute, authority, chalk up to, character, deduction, influence 10 confidence, reputation
  author ~: 6 byline
  card action: 5 swipe 6 charge
  ender: 6 worthy
  extend ~: 4 bill, lend, loan 7 advance
  give ~ for: 5 allow
  letters: 3 IOU
  maintain good ~: 3 pay 5 repay
  opposite: 5 debit
  recipient: 4 ower
  source: 4 bank 6 lender
  use ~: 3 owe 6 charge
  with: 5 blame, lay on 6 impute 7 ascribe 9 attribute
credit __: 4 card, hour, line, memo, risk, slip 5 limit, union 6 agency, bureau, rating 7 manager, squeeze
creditable: 4 fine, good, nice, okay 5 great, legit, moral, noble 6 proper, worthy 7 ethical 8 all right, laudable, pleasant, pleasing, splendid, superior 9 admirable, agreeable, authentic, deserving, estimable, excellent, exemplary, honorable, praisable, reputable, wonderful 10 acceptable, believable, beneficial
credit card color: 4 gold 8 platinum

creditor: 5 payee 6 debtee, lender, loaner, usurer 7 Shylock
right: 4 lien
writ: 6 elegit
credo: 5 tenet 6 belief 8 doctrine, ideology 9 principle 10 philosophy
credulity: 7 naiveté 9 greenness
credulous: 4 naif 5 green, naive 6 simple, unwary 8 gullable, gullible, trusting 9 accepting, believing, childlike, fanatical 10 uncritical
Cree: 5 tribe 6 Indian 7 Amerind 8 language 10 Algonquian
creed: 3 ism 5 canon, dogma, faith, tenet 6 belief, canons 8 doctrine, ideology, religion 9 principle, teachings 10 persuasion, philosophy, principles
ender: 4 amen
Creed: 6 Apollo
___ Creed: 6 Nicene
Creedence Clearwater Revival
leader: John Fogerty
song: Bad Moon Rising (1969)
Down on the Corner (1969)
Green River (1969)
Have You Ever Seen the Rain (1971)
Lookin' Out My Back Door (1970)
Proud Mary (1969)
Sweet Hitch-Hiker (1971)
Travelin' Band (1970)
Up Around the Bend (1970)
creek: 3 ria, run 4 race, rill 5 bourn, brook, rille 6 branch, runlet, runnel, stream 7 rivulet 9 streamlet, tributary
cross a ~: 4 wade
up the ~: 6 in a fix, in a jam 8 helpless, hopeless 9 desperate
___ creek: 5 up the
Creek: 5 tribe 6 Indian 7 Amerind
___ Creek: 5 Cross 7 Coroner, Dawson's
___ Creek Pass: 4 Wolf
Creeley, Robert: 4 poet
creel, one for the: 6 keeper
creep: 3 pad 4 bore, bozo, edge, inch, jerk, lurk, pest, pill 5 crawl, loser, prowl, sculk, skulk, slink, snake, sneak, steal, twerp, twirp 6 bad guy, tingle, writhe 7 lowlife, slither, villain, wriggle 9 pussyfoot, scoundrel
through: 4 ooze, seep 10 infiltrate
up on: 5 stalk 8 approach
___ creep: 4 soil 7 bracket
Creep (1994 song) artist: TLC
creeper: 3 ivy, tot 4 bird, vine 5 plant
starter: 5 honey
trumpet ~: 5 plant 6 flower
___ creeper: 4 tree, wall 5 brown 7 trumpet
___ Creepers: 7 Jeepers
creepers, abounding in: 4 viny
creeping: 4 poky, slow 6 draggy 7 gradual, halting, impeded, lagging, languid 8 dilatory, drawn-out, hesitant, slothful, sluggish, toddling 9 leisurely, lethargic, prolonged, snaillike, unhurried 10 deliberate, protracted
combining form: 6 herpet- 7 herpeto-
creeping ___: 5 Jenny 6 fescue, Jennie 7 Charlie, juniper
Creeping Flesh, The (1973 film)
cast: Peter Cushing, Christopher Lee
creepingly: 8 bit by bit
creeps: 7 jimjams
give one the ~: 5 alarm, scare
Creepshow: 4 book, film
author: Stephen King
cast: Adrienne Barbeau, Ted Danson, Ed Harris, Hal Holbrook, Viveca Lindfors, E.G. Marshall, Leslie Nielsen, Carrie Nye, Fritz Weaver
director: George Romero
creepy: 4 eery 5 dread, eerie, scary, weird 6 crawly, spooky 7 dreaded, macaber, macabre, ominous, uncanny 8 dreadful, ghoulish, gruesome, peculiar, sinister 9 loathsome, repellant, repellent 10 terrifying, unsettling
creepy-crawly: 3 bug 6 insect
Creeque Alley (1967 song) artist: Mamas & the Papas
Cregar: 5 Laird
Creighton: 10 university
athletes: 8 Bluejays
locale: 5 Omaha 8 Nebraska
Creil: 4 city, town
locale: 6 France
creme: 5 candy, sweet
crème ___: 6 brûlée 7 d'ananas, fraîche
___ crème: 4 café 6 double, triple
crème brûlée: 7 dessert
crème de ___: 5 cacao 6 banane, cassis, fraise, menthe 7 bananes
crème de cacao: 5 drink 8 beverage
crème de la crème: 4 pick 5 elite, prize 6 choice
crème de menthe: 5 drink 8 beverage
Cremer, William: 8 Nobelist
Cremona: 4 city, font, town 8 typeface
collectible: 5 Strad
locale: 5 Italy
violinmaker: 5 Amati 10 Stradivari
crenel: 4 slit
Crenna, Richard: 5 actor
film: Body Heat (1981)
Breakheart Pass (1976)
First Blood (1982)
The Flamingo Kid (1984)
Rambo: First Blood Part II (1985)
Rambo III (1988)
Red Sky at Morning (1970)
The Sand Pebbles (1966)
Star! (1968)
Table for Five (1983)
Wait Until Dark (1967)
TV: Our Miss Brooks, The Real McCoys
Crenshaw: 3 Ben 5 melon
kin: 6 casaba 7 cassaba
Crenshaw, Ben: 6 golfer
org.: 3 PGA
creole ___: 6 tomato
___ creole: 3 à la 6 shrimp
Creole: 7 cuisine 8 language
vegetable: 4 ocra, okra, okro
___ Creole: 4 King 7 Haitian
Creon
daughter of ~: 6 Creusa
father of ~: 8 Heracles
sister of ~: 7 Jocasta
creosote source: 3 tar 7 coal tar
crepe: 6 fabric 7 pancake
relative: 5 blini, bliny 6 blintz 7 blintze
crepe ___: 4 hair 5 paper 6 myrtle, rubber 7 suzette
like ~ s suzette: 6 flambé
crepe de ___: 5 Chine
crêpe suzette: 7 dessert
crepitate: 7 crackle
crepon: 6 fabric 8 material
crepuscular: 5 dusky
crepuscule: 4 dusk 9 nightfall
crescendo: 4 apex, peak 5 climb, crest, surge, swell 6 summit, zenith 7 upsurge 8 building, increase, pinnacle
Crescendos song: Oh Julie (1958)
crescent: 3 arc, bow 4 lune, moon 5 lunet 6 pastry 7 falcate, rainbow 8 falcated, meniscus
fingernail ~: 6 lunula, lunule
moon end: 4 cusp, horn
-shaped: 6 bicorn, lunate
crescent ___: 4 moon, roll 5 truss
___ crescent: 7 Chinese, Turkish
___ Crescent: 3 Red 7 Fertile
Crescent Moon, The author: Rabindranath Tagore
Crespin, Règine: 6 singer 7 soprano
specialty: 5 opera
cress: 5 green, salad 6 veggie 7 garnish 9 vegetable
starter: 5 penny, water 6 pepper
___ cress: 4 rock 5 marsh 6 bitter, garden, Indian, winter
Cressida: 3 car 4 auto, moon 6 Toyota
father of ~: 7 Calchas
planet: 6 Uranus
to Pandarus: 5 niece
crest: 3 cap, top 4 acme, apex, head, peak, rise, sign, wave 5 crown, plume, ridge, spire, title 6 apogee, billow, climax, device, emblem, height, summit, symbol, vertex, zenith 7 hilltop, insigne, maximum, topknot 8 heraldry, high spot, insignia, meridian, pinnacle 9 crescendo, high point 10 coat of arms, prominence
combining form: 4 loph- 5 lophi-, lopho- 6 lophio-
ender: 6 fallen
inscription: 4 name 5 motto
mountain ~: 5 arete, ridge
on the ~: 4 atop
crest ___: 4 rail 5 cloud 7 coronet
Crest: 10 toothpaste
alternative: 3 Aim 5 Gleem, Topol 7 Close-Up, Colgate, Viadent 9 Aquafresh, Mentadent, Pepsodent, Rembrandt, Sensodyne 10 Pearl Drops, Ultra Brite 11 Tom's of Maine
unit: 4 tube
___ Crest: 6 Falcon
crested ___: 4 fern, iris 5 swift 6 lizard
Crested Butte: 4 city, town 6 resort
locale: 8 Colorado
crestfallen: 3 low, sad 4 blue, down, glum 5 heavy, moody, sorry, woful 6 gloomy, morose, somber, woeful 7 doleful, in a funk, joyless, subdued, unhappy 8 dejected, downcast, lowering, troubled, wretched 9 bummed out, cheerless, heartsick, miserable, sorrowful, woebegone 10 dispirited, melancholy
Creston, Paul: 8 composer
cretaceous: 6 chalky
Cretan: 5 Minos 7 Ariadne, El Greco
Cretan ___: 4 bull
Crete: 4 isle 6 island
ancient city: 7 Cnossus, Gnossus, Knossos
peak: 3 Ida 5 Mt. Ida
port: 5 Canea 6 Candia
where ~ is: 5 Medit.
cretonne: 6 fabric
Creüsa
brother of ~: 5 Paris 6 Hector
father of ~: 5 Creon, Priam 7 Priamus
husband of ~: 5 Eneas 6 Aeneas
mother of ~: 4 Gaea 6 Hecuba
sister of ~: 9 Cassandra
son of ~: 3 Ion
crevalle: 4 fish
crevasse: 4 gulf, rift 5 chasm, crack, gorge, gully 6 gulley, ravine 7 fissure
crevice: 3 gap 4 hole, leak, nook, rent, rift, slit 5 abyss, chasm, cleft, crack, split 6 cranny, ravine 7 fissure, opening 10 interstice
crew: 3 mob, set 4 band, gang, pack, team 5 corps, covey, crowd, force, group, hands, party, posse, sport, squad, staff, troop 6 league, muster, outfit, troupe 7 brigade, company, faction, oarsmen, retinue, sailors, sea dogs, workers 9 deckhands, personnel, shipmates 10 complement, stagehands
cut: 6 hairdo 8 coiffure 9 hairstyle
ender: 3 cut 4 mate
hire a ~: 3 man
hire a new ~: 5 reman
implement: 3 oar
member: 3 cox 4 hand 5 rower
work ~: 4 unit 5 corps
crew ___: 3 cut 4 neck, sock 5 chief
___ crew: 3 air, gun 6 ground
crew cut: 4 coif 6 hairdo 8 coiffure
give a ~: 4 crop 5 shear
opposite: 4 Afro
Crew-Cuts
song: Earth Angel (1955)
Gum Drop (1955)
Ko Ko Mo (1955)
Crewe: 4 city, town
locale: 7 England 8 Cheshire
crewel: 4 yarn 5 craft 10 embroidery, needlework
create with ~: 4 knit, purl
ender: 4 work
tool: 6 needle
Crewe Train author: Rose Macaulay
crewman: 3 gob, tar 4 hand, salt 6 sailor 7 jack tar
affirmative: 3 aye 6 aye aye
Crew, The (2000 film)
cast: Richard Dreyfuss, Dan Hedaya, Burt Reynolds
crib: 3 bed, bin 4 lift, pony, trot 5 cheat, filch, pinch 6 cradle, manger, pilfer 8 bassinet 9 furniture 10 cheat sheet, plagiarize
cry: 3 wah 4 mama 5 mamma
datum: 6 answer
occupant: 3 tot 4 baby, corn 6 infant 7 neonate, newborn
starter: 4 corn
use a ~: 5 cheat
crib ___: 5 sheet
cribbage: 4 game 8 card game
clear the ~ board: 5 unpeg
jack, in ~: 3 nob 7 his nobs
marker: 3 peg
cribbage ___: 5 board
cribwear: 3 PJs 7 pajamas
cricetid: 6 animal, mammal, rodent
relative: 3 rat 4 cavy, degu, jird, paca, vole 5 coypu, gundi, mouse, xerus 6 agouti, beaver, gerbil, gopher, jerboa, marmot, murine 7 hamster, lemming, muskrat, visacha 8 chipmunk, dormouse, squirrel, tuco-tuco 9 chickaree, groundhog, guinea pig, porcupine, woodchuck 10 chinchilla, prairie dog
Crichton: 5 James 7 Charles, Michael
Crichton, Charles: 8 director
film: Against the Wind (1948)
The Battle of the Sexes (1960)
Dead of Night (1945)
The Divided Heart (1954)
A Fish Called Wanda (1988)
The Lavender Hill Mob (1951)
Stranger in Between (1952)
The Titfield Thunderbolt (1953)
Crichton, Michael: 6 author, writer 8 director
film: Coma (1978)
The Great Train Robbery (1979)
Westworld (1973)
work: Airframe
The Andromeda Strain
A Case of Need
Congo
Disclosure
The Great Train Robbery
Jurassic Park
The Lost World
Rising Sun
Sphere
The Terminal Man
Timeline
crick: 3 ria 4 ache, kink, pain, rill 5 cramp, rille, spasm 6 twinge
spot: 4 neck

cricket: 3 bug, toy 4 game 5 sport 6 cicada, insect 10 percussion
ball: 6 googly
division: 6 inning
glancing blow in ~: 5 snick
jiminy ~: 4 gosh 5 golly
need: 3 bat 4 ball 6 wicket
sides: 3 ons
sound: 5 chirp, chirr, churr 6 chirre
squad: 6 eleven
term: 3 bye
wicket: 3 end
cricket ___: 4 frog 5 table
___ cricket: 4 cave, mole, sand, tree 5 camel, field, house 6 Mormon
cricketeer: 6 bowler
Cricket on the Hearth author: Dickens
Crickets song: 5 Oh Boy 6 Rave On 8 Peggy Sue 9 Maybe Baby
Crick, Francis: 8 Nobelist 10 geneticist
concern: 3 DNA
partner: 6 Watson
cri de ___: 5 coeur
cri, dernier: 3 fad 4 mode, rage 5 vogue 6 latest 7 fashion 8 last word
crier: 4 baby 6 hawker, herald, pedlar, pedler, vender, vendor, weeper 7 peddler 8 huckster 9 announcer, messenger 10 proclaimer
cry: 6 hear ye
___ crier: 4 town
Cries and Whispers (1972 film)
cast: Harriet Andersson, Ingrid Thulin, Liv Ullmann
director: Ingmar Bergman
___ C. Riley: 7 Jeannie
crime: 3 DWI, sin 4 pity, tort, vice 5 arson, bribe, graft, heist, lapse, theft, usury, wrong 6 felony, holdup, murder, racket 7 bad deed, larceny, misdeed, offense, outrage, scandal, treason 8 atrocity, burglary, delictum, iniquity, thievery, trespass 9 inside job, sacrilege, violation 10 corruption, infraction
aid in ~: 4 abet
anti-organized ~ act: 4 RICO
help in ~: 7 collude
lab clue: 3 DNA
lure into ~: 6 entrap
partner in ~: 4 ally 6 cohort
pin a ~ on: 5 frame
prevention dog: 7 McGruff
scene evidence: 5 print
scene of the ~: 5 venue
statistic: 6 arrest
syndicate head: 4 capo
crime-___: 7 fighter
Crime ___ Punishment: 3 and
___ Crime: 4 True 5 It's No
___ Crime?: 5 Is It a
Crimean ___: 3 War 5 Tatar 6 Gothic
Crime and Punishment: 4 film 5 novel
author: Fyodor Dostoyevsky
cast: Edward Arnold, Peter Lorre, Marian Marsh
character: 5 Rodya, Sonia 6 Dmitri, Rodion
director: Josef von Sternberg
Crimean port: 5 Yalta
crimebuster: 3 cop 4 G-man, narc, nark, T-man
Crimes and Misdemeanors (1989 film)
cast: Caroline Aaron, Alan Alda, Woody Allen, Claire Bloom, Mia Farrow
director: Woody Allen
Crimes of the Heart: 4 film, play
author: Beth Henley
cast: Diane Keaton, Jessica Lange, Sam Shepard, Sissy Spacek
character: 3 Meg 4 Babe 5 Chick, Lenny
director: Bruce Beresford
Crime Without Passion (1934 film)
cast: Whitney Bourne, Margo, Claude Rains
director: Ben Hecht, Charles MacArthur
criminal: 3 bad 4 evil, perp, punk, tabu, thug, yegg 5 crook, felon, rogue, taboo, thief, wrong 6 bad guy, bandit, banned, guilty, gunsel, outlaw, sinner, unfair 7 brigand, convict, corrupt, crooked, culprit, hoodlum, illegal, illicit, lawless, mobster, villain 8 culpable, evildoer, fugitive, hooligan, improper, internee, offender, outlawed, prisoner, scofflaw, unlawful, verboten, wrongful 9 desperado, felonious, forbidden, miscreant, murderous, nefarious, purloiner, racketeer, wrongdoer 10 cat burglar, delinquent, fraudulent, indictable, lawbreaker, outrageous, pickpocket, prohibited, shoplifter, trespasser
activity: 6 racket
band: 3 mob 4 gang, ring 10 underworld
charge: 3 rap
Indian ~: 6 dacoit, dakoit
law concept: 6 intent
not ~: 5 legal, legit 6 lawful
pattern: 2 MO
petty ~ in Britain: 4 spiv
slang: 5 argot
subduer: 5 taser
criminal ___: 3 law 4 code 5 court 6 lawyer 7 justice
criminality: 4 evil 5 guilt
criminate: 6 indict
criminology: 7 science
crimp: 4 coil, curl, fold, friz, kink, snag, undo, wave 5 frizz, plait, pleat, stimy, stymy, swirl 6 crease, dog-ear, groove, hamper, hinder, rumple, stymie, thwart 7 crinkle, crumple, fluting, sinuate, wrinkle 8 obstacle 9 corrugate
put a ~ in: 6 hinder, hobble
crimped: 5 kinky
crimson: 3 red 5 color, ruddy
relative: 4 rose, ruby, rust, wine 5 brick, coral, grape, poppy, rusty, sandy 6 cerise, cherry, claret, garnet, maroon 7 carmine, fuchsia, magenta, pimento, scarlet, sultana, vermeil 8 amaranth, cardinal, dubonnet, geranium, rubicund 9 carnation, cranberry, vermilion 10 strawberry
crimson ___: 4 flag 6 clover
Crimson: 7 Harvard
rival: 4 Elis 6 Yalies 8 Bulldogs
Crimson ___: 4 Tide 6 Pirate 7 Romance
Crimson and Clover (song) artist: Joan Jett and the Blackhearts, Tommy James and the Shondells
Crimson Pirate (1952 film)
cast: Eva Bartok, Nick Cravat, Burt Lancaster
Crimson Tide: 4 'Bama 7 Alabama
rival: 4 Vols
Crimson Tide (1995 film)
cast: Matt Craven, Gene Hackman, Denzel Washington
director: Tony Scott
cringe: 4 fawn 5 cower, kotow, quail, wince 6 flinch, grovel, kowtow, quiver, recoil, shrink 7 tremble 8 draw back
at: 5 dread
crinite: 6 fossil
crinkle: 4 fold, tuck 5 crimp, ridge 6 crease, furrow, pucker, ruffle, rumple, rustle 7 wrinkle 9 corrugate
crinkled fabric: 5 crape, crepe, lisse
crinkly: 5 rough
crinoid: 5 shell 8 seashell
crinoline: 5 skirt 6 fabric 8 material
Cripple ___, CO: 5 Creek
Crisco: 3 oil 10 cooking oil
alternative: 6 Mazola, Wesson 7 Puritan 8 olive oil
crisis: 4 pass, stew 5 panic, pinch 6 crunch, danger, plight, strait, unrest 7 dilemma, trouble, urgency 8 disaster, exigence, exigency, juncture, landmark, showdown, zero hour 9 deep water, emergency, imbroglio 10 depression, difficulty
crisis ___: 6 center
___ Crisium: 4 Mare
crisp: 3 cry, net, raw 4 cold, cool, curt, tidy 5 brief, brisk, fresh, nippy, pithy, sharp, short, smart, terse, toast 6 chilly, crusty, gnomic, snappy, spruce, wintry 7 bracing, brittle, concise, crumbly, crunchy, dessert, friable, laconic, orderly, wintery 8 clean-cut, spirited, succinct, unwilted 9 trenchant 10 fortifying, refreshing, to the point
not ~: 5 soggy, stale
___ crisp: 6 potato
Crisp: 6 Donald 7 Quentin
Crisp, Donald: 5 actor
film: The Adventures of Mark Twain (1944)
The Hills of Home (1948)
How Green Was My Valley (1941, AA)
Knute Rockne, All American (1940)
Lassie Come Home (1943)
The Little Minister (1934)
The Man From Laramie (1955)
National Velvet (1944)
Saddle the Wind (1958)
Svengali (1931)
The Uninvited (1944)
The Valley of Decision (1945)
Crispin: 5 saint 6 Glover
product: 4 shoe
Crispix: 6 cereal
competitor: 3 Kix 4 Life, Trix 5 Kashi, Quisp, Total 6 Kaboom, Muesli, Oreo O's, Pablum, Smacks 7 All-Bran, Harmony, Hunny B's, Mueslix, Oat Bran, Pokemon 8 Boo Berry, Cheerios, Corn Chex, Corn Pops, Fiber One, Rice Chex, Special K, Uncle Sam, Wheaties 9 Alpha Bits, Apple Zaps, Grape Nuts, Honey Comb, Just Right, Wheat Chex 10 Apple Jacks, Bran Flakes, Cap'n Crunch, Cocoa Puffs, Froot Loops, Mini-Wheats, Nutri-Grain, Puffed Rice, Quaker Oats, Smart Start 11 Cocoa Blasts, Cookie Crisp, Golden Crisp, Lucky Charms, Puffed Wheat, Sweet Crunch, Waffle Crisp
crispness: 3 nip 4 bite 5 chill, frost
lose ~: 4 wilt
Crispus: 7 Attucks
crispy: 5 chewy 6 crusty 7 brittle, crumbly, crunchy, friable 9 crackling
crisscross: 5 weave 7 athwart 8 traverse 9 intersect
Criss Cross: 7 musical
songwriter: 4 Kern
Criss Cross (1949 film)
cast: Yvonne De Carlo, Dan Duryea, Burt Lancaster
Criss-Cross author: Hal Porter
Cristina: 7 Ferrare
Crist, Judith: 6 critic 8 reviewer
___ Cristo: 5 Monte
Cristobal: 4 city, port, town
___ Cristóbal: 3 San
Cristo, Sangre de: 5 range 9 mountains
___-crit: 3 lit
criterion: 3 law, std. 4 norm, rule, test 5 basis, canon, gauge, model 7 measure, paragon 8 paradigm, standard 9 archetype, benchmark, parameter, precedent, principle, prototype, yardstick 10 foundation, touchstone
scholarship ~: 4 need 5 merit
critic: 3 nag 4 Reed 5 Crist, Ebert, judge, momus, rater 6 basher, blamer, carper, censor, expert, gadfly, moaner, nagger, noodge, panner, pundit, Shalit, writer 7 analyst, arbiter, caviler, crybaby, defamer, doubter, Rex Reed, scholar, scolder 8 attacker, disputer, maligner, quibbler, reviewer, Spingarn, vilifier 9 authority, belittler, detractor, evaluator, muckraker, nitpicker 10 complainer, disparager, Gene Shalit, Roger Ebert
at times: 5 raver 6 panner
unit: 4 star
critical: 3 key 4 dire, main 5 acute, fatal, fussy, grave, hairy, major, nasty, picky, sharp, tight, vital 6 minute, severe, urgent 7 burning, carping, crucial, cutting, exigent, fateful, finicky, fretful, nagging, peevish, pivotal, serious, weighty 8 captious, caviling, choleric, deciding, decisive, exacting, exigeant, finiking, finnicky, fretsome, pregnant, pressing, scathing, scolding, ticklish 9 demanding, desperate, high-level, important, memorable, momentous, querulous, sarcastic, strategic, trenchant 10 belittling, censorious, conclusive, derogatory, detracting, detractive, discerning, imperative, minimizing, nitpicking, particular, portentous, underlying
not ~: 5 minor 7 trivial
point: 5 brink
reaction: 4 rave
regard: 8 analysis 10 inspection
remark: 4 barb 5 swipe
critical ___: 4 mass 5 angle, point, ratio, state, value 6 region, volume 7 density
criticism: 3 rap 4 beef, flak, slam 5 abuse, blame, blast, cavil, flack, input, knock, lumps, whine 6 attack, earful, rebuke, review 7 carping, censure, comment, lecture, obloquy, opinion, panning, quibble, reproof, sarcasm 8 analysis, berating, caviling, diatribe, feedback, reproach, reproval 9 appraisal, aspersion, brickbats, broadside, complaint, objection, reprimand, sideswipe, stricture, talking-to 10 assessment, bawling-out, Bronx cheer, commentary, dissection, evaluation, exposition, impugnment, nitpicking, opprobrium, reflection, upbraiding
unjust ~: 6 bad rap
criticize: 3 hit, jaw, pan, rap, rip 4 bash, carp, damn, flay, lash, rail, slam, zing 5 blame, blast, cavil, chide, cut up, decry, fault, judge, knock, probe, roast, scold, snipe, study, trash, whine 6 assail, assess, berate, impugn, jump on, lean on, oppugn, peck at, pick at, rail at, rebuke, review, scathe, vilify 7 affront, analyze, censure, clobber, condemn, examine, lambast, lay into, lecture, nitpick, quibble, reprove, run down, upbraid 8 admonish, backbite, badmouth, belittle, chastise, denounce, evaluate, lambaste, reproach, talk down 9 castigate, cut to bits, disparage, dress down, excoriate, find fault, frown upon, fustigate, interpret, lash out at, pick apart, reprehend, reprimand, reprobate 10 come down on, denunciate, disapprove, scrutinize
Critic's Choice author: Ira Levin
critique: 4 barb 5 essay, input 6 review, survey 7 comment 8 analysis, exegesis, judgment 9 editorial 10 commen-

tary, exposition, literature
Critique of Judgment author: 4 Kant
Critique of Pure Reason author: 4 Kant
critter: 3 cow 5 beast 6 animal
Crius: 4 seer 5 giant, Titan
Cro-__: 6 Magnon
croak: 3 caw 5 grunt 6 mutter, squawk
croaker: 4 fish, frog 5 raven
croaking: 6 froggy 10 laryngitic
croaky: 5 gruff, husky 6 froggy, hoarse 8 gravelly
Croat: 4 Slav
  neighbor: 4 Serb
Croatia: 6 nation 7 country
  bovine: 4 Busa
  capital: 6 Zagreb
  city: 5 Sisak, Sisek, Split 6 Osijek, Rijeka, Zagreb
  island: 3 Vis
  legislature: 5 Sabor
  mountain: 7 Triglov
  neighbor: 7 Hungary 8 Slovenia 10 Yugoslavia
  port: 4 Pulj 5 Zadar
  river: 4 Sava
__-Croatian: 5 Serbo
croc: 6 animal 7 reptile
  relative: 5 gator
Croce: 3 Jim 9 Benedetto
Croce, Jim
  song: Bad, Bad Leroy Brown (1973)
    I Got a Name (1973)
    I'll Have to Say I Love You in a Song (1974)
    Time in a Bottle (1973)
    You Don't Mess Around With Jim (1972)
crochet: 4 knit, lace, note 6 stitch
  item: 5 doily, scarf 6 afghan, bootee, bootie, doyley
  need: 4 hook, wool 6 needle
crock: 3 jar, pot 4 bowl 6 cooker, flagon, vessel 7 amphora, caldron 8 cauldron 9 container, inebriate 10 intoxicate
  product: 4 stew
Crock __: 3 Pot
Crocker: 5 Betty
crockery: 5 china 7 pottery 8 ceramics, clayware 9 porcelain 10 dinnerware, terra cotta
Crockett: 4 Davy 5 Sonny
  beat: 5 Miami
  partner: 5 Tubbs
Crockett, Davy: 4 hero
  last stand: 5 Alamo
crocodile: 6 animal, caiman, cayman, gavial, lizard 7 gharial, leather, reptile
  female: 3 cow
  habitat: 4 Nile
  like ~ tears: 4 fake 5 false
  male: 4 bull
  neighbor: 5 hippo
  young: 8 crocklet
crocodile __: 4 bird 5 tears
Crocodile Dundee (1986 film)
  cast: Paul Hogan, Linda Kozlowski
  role: 3 Sue 4 Mick
Crocodile Rock (1972 song) artist: Elton John
crocus: 5 plant 6 flower, yellow 8 orangish
  bulb: 4 corm
  relative: 4 buff, corn, gold, iris, lime, rust, sand 5 blond, brass, coral, cream, flaxy, lemon, maize, ocher, ochre, peach, rusty, straw 6 blonde, canary, chammy, citron, flaxen, shammy, shamoy 7 apricot, chamois, citrine, jasmine, mustard, nankeen, old gold, saffron, xanthic 8 daffodil, primrose 9 champagne, goldenrod, jessamine
Croesus: 9 plutocrat
  like ~: 4 rich 7 wealthy
croft: 4 farm
Crofton: 4 city, town
  locale: 8 Maryland
Crofts: 4 Dash 7 Freeman
  partner: 5 Seals
Crofts, Freeman: 5 Irish 6 writer
  sleuth: French
__ Croft: Tomb Raider: 4 Lara
croissant: 5 bread
  shape: 4 lune
croissant shape: 4 lune, moon 5 lunar
Croix de __: 6 Guerre
Croix native, St.: 6 Cruzan
__ Croix, Que.: 3 Ste.
Cro-Magnon: 5 human 7 caveman
Crome Yellow author: Aldous Huxley
Cromwell: 4 John 5 James 6 Oliver 7 Richard
  victory site: 6 Dunbar
Cromwell, John: 8 director
  film: Abe Lincoln in Illinois (1940)
    Algiers (1938)
    Anna and the King of Siam (1946)
    Banjo on My Knee (1936)
    Caged (1950)
    Dead Reckoning (1947)
    The Goddess (1958)
    In Name Only (1939)
    Little Lord Fauntleroy (1936)
    Made for Each Other (1939)
    Of Human Bondage (1934)
    The Prisoner of Zenda (1937)
    The Racket (1951)
    Since You Went Away (1944)
    So Ends Our Night (1941)
    Son of Fury (1942)
    Sweepings (1933)
    Victory (1940)
    Village Tale (1935)
crone: 3 hag 5 harpy, witch 6 beldam 7 beldame 8 harridan
  like a ~: 5 anile
Cronin: 2 A.J. 3 Joe 5 James
Cronin, A.J.: 6 writer 8 Scottish
Cronin, James: 8 Nobelist 9 physicist
Cronin, Joe: 6 Red Sox 9 shortstop
Cronkite: 6 Walter
  network: 3 CBS 5 CBS-TV
Cronus: 5 giant, Titan
  brother of ~: 5 Coeus, Crius 7 Iapetus, Oceanus 8 Hyperion
  daughter of ~: 4 Hera 6 Hestia 7 Demeter
  equivalent: 6 Saturn
  parent of ~: 4 Gaea 6 Uranus
  sister of ~: 4 Rhea, Thia 5 Dione 6 Phoebe, Tethys, Themis 9 Mnemosyne
  son of ~: 4 Zeus 5 Hades, Pluto 6 Chiron 7 Cheiron 8 Poseidon
  wife of ~: 4 Rhea
crony: 3 bro, pal 4 ally, chum, mate 5 amigo, buddy 6 cohort, frater, friend 7 comrade, partner 8 alter ego, intimate, roommate, sidekick 9 associate, colleague, companion, confidant 10 accomplice, bosom buddy, compatriot, confidante, well-wisher
cronyism: 9 patronage
Cronyn, Hume: 5 actor
  film: Brute Force (1947)
    Cocoon (1985)
    Conrack (1974)
    The Postman Always Rings Twice (1946)
    The Seventh Cross (1944)
    Sunrise at Campobello (1960)
    There Was a Crooked Man ... (1970)
  spouse: Jessica Tandy
crook: 4 bend, flex, loop, wind, yegg 5 angle, cheat, curve, felon, fraud, ganef, gonef, gonif, knave, rogue, shark, staff, thief 6 bad guy, bandit, con man, corner, dogleg, goniff, outlaw, robber 7 burglar, filcher, flexure, rustler 8 criminal, gangster, pilferer, swindler 9 purloiner, racketeer, scoundrel
  a finger: 6 entice, invite, signal
  alternative: 4 hook
  assist a ~: 4 abet
  by hook or ~: 7 somehow, someway 8 someways
  ender: 4 back, neck
  move like a ~: 5 sculk, skulk
  story: 5 alibi
crooked: 3 sly, wry 4 agee, ajee, alop, awry, bent, evil, foul, wily 5 askew, bandy, bowed, dirty, false, lying, shady, snaky, wrong 6 angled, aslant, canted, hooked, louche, rotten, shifty, skewed, tricky, unfair, warped, zigzag 7 angular, corrupt, devious, illegal, knavish, sinuous, slanted, twisted, winding 8 angulose, angulous, cockeyed, criminal, delusive, guileful, lopsided, thieving, thievish, tortuous, twisting, unlawful 9 contorted, deceitful, dishonest, distorted, falsified, insincere, irregular, larcenous, malformed, nefarious, unaligned, underhand, unethical 10 asymmetric, fraudulent, meandering, mendacious, nonuniform, serpentine, untruthful, virtueless
  follow a ~ path: 3 zag, zig
  not ~: 6 direct
  scheme: 3 con 4 scam
Crooked Hearts (1991 film)
  cast: Peter Berg, Vincent D'Onofrio, Jennifer Jason Leigh
crooked mouth, name meaning: 8 Campbell
crookedness: 9 improbity
Crookes, William: 7 chemist 9 physicist, scientist
Crooklyn (1994 film)
  cast: Zelda Harris, Delroy Lindo, Alfre Woodard
  director: Spike Lee
crookneck: 6 veggie 9 vegetable
croon: 3 hum 4 sing 6 intone, warble 8 vocalize
crooner: 4 Como 6 Crosby, singer 7 Bennett, Sinatra 8 vocalist
  song: 6 ballad
crop: 3 cut, hew, lop, maw, mow 4 chop, clip, corn, craw, oats, pare, rice, snip, trim, whip 5 fruit, grain, prune, shave, shear, slash, wheat, yield 6 barley, cotton, cut off, detach, forage, fruits, gullet, lessen, nibble, output, reduce 7 curtail, harvest, produce, scissor, shorten, sorghum, trim off, veggies, vintage 8 cut short, gleaning, soybeans, truncate 10 vegetables
  animal's ~: 3 maw 4 craw
  combining form: 4 agro-
  cover ~: 6 legume
  cream of the ~: 4 best 5 elite
  eater: 4 crow 6 beetle, thrips
  ender: 4 land
  forage ~: 3 urd 5 vetch 6 clover
  land: 5 field
  plane: 6 duster
  raising: 7 farming
  science: 3 agr. 8 agronomy
  second grass ~: 5 rowen
  starter: 5 share, stone
  unit: 3 row 4 acre
  up: 4 rise 5 arise, begin, occur 6 appear, emerge, happen 7 surface
  up again: 5 recur
crop-__: 4 dust 5 eared 6 duster
__ crop: 4 cash, root 5 catch, cover, field, nurse, truck 6 riding
__-cropped: 5 close
cropper
  come a ~: 4 bomb, bust, flop, lose, slip, trip 5 flunk 6 blow it, falter 7 blunder, founder, go under, go wrong, misstep, stumble, wash out 8 fall flat, flounder, lay an egg 9 strike out
crop production
  science of: 8 agrology
crops: 7 harvest, produce
  bring in the ~: 4 reap
  fit for ~: 6 arable
  like some ~: 4 oaty 5 oaten
  raise ~: 4 farm, till
  treat ~: 4 dust
croquet: 4 game 5 sport
  site: 4 lawn, yard
  variation: 5 roque
  wicket: 4 hoop
croquette: 4 meat 5 patty
  relative: 5 latke 7 pancake
croquis: 6 sketch
Crosby: 3 Bob 4 Bing, Mary, Norm 5 David 6 Denise
  colleague: 4 Nash 5 Young 6 Stills
Crosby, Bing: 5 actor 6 singer
  costar: 4 Hope 6 Lamour
  film: Anything Goes (1936)
    The Bells of St. Mary's (1945)
    The Big Broadcast (1932)
    The Birth of the Blues (1941)
    Blue Skies (1946)
    College Humor (1933)
    The Country Girl (1954)
    Dixie (1943)
    Going Hollywood (1933)
    Going My Way (1944, AA)
    Here Comes the Groom (1951)
    Here Come the Waves (1944)
    High Society (1956)
    Holiday Inn (1942)
    Just for You (1952)
    Little Boy Lost (1953)
    Mississippi (1935)
    Rhythm on the River (1940)
    Road to Bali (1952)
    The Road to Hong Kong (1962)
    Road to Morocco (1942)
    Road to Rio (1947)
    Road to Singapore (1940)
    Road to Utopia (1945)
    Road to Zanzibar (1941)
    Robin and the Seven Hoods (1964)
    She Loves Me Not (1934)
    Sing, You Sinners (1938)
    Star Spangled Rhythm (1942)
    Waikiki Wedding (1937)
    Welcome Stranger (1947)
    We're Not Dressing (1934)
    White Christmas (1954)
  song: Amor (1944)
    Dinah (1932)
    True Love (1956)
    White Christmas (1955)
  spouse: Kathryn Grant
Crosby, Stills & Nash
  song: Just a Song Before I Go (1977)
    Marrakesh Express (1969)
    Our House (1970)
    Suite: Judy Blue Eyes (1969)
    Teach Your Children (1970)
    Wasted on the Way (1982)
    Woodstock (1970)
Crosetti: 5 Frank
crosier: 5 crook, staff
  carrier: 5 abbot
Crosland: 4 Alan
cross: 3 hot, mad, mix 4 foil, ford, ired, rood, sell, sore, span, tick 5 angry, blend, block, huffy, irate, livid, moody, onery, punch, riled, surly, testy, upset, vexed, wroth 6 betray, bridge, crabby, cranky, crusty, divide, foul up, fretty, fuming, go over, grumpy, hinder, hybrid, impede, impugn, ireful, mingle,

morose, oppose, ordeal, ornery, peeved, put out, raging, raving, red-hot, snappy, sullen, thwart, touchy **7** annoyed, bearish, enraged, fretful, furious, grouchy, huffish, in a snit, jaywalk, jewelry, louse up, mixture, mongrel, peevish, peppery, ranting, sell out, waspish **8** captious, caviling, choleric, churlish, fretsome, grumpish, incensed, inflamed, maddened, navigate, obstruct, outraged, pass over, petulant, traverse, wrathful **9** crotchety, fractious, frustrate, hybridize, indignant, intersect, irascible, irritable, irritated, querulous, resentful, splenetic, truculent **10** contradict, contravene, freaked out, ill-humored, infuriated, interbreed, interweave, misfortune, out of sorts, transverse
a creek: **4** ford, wade
align the ~ hairs: **3** aim **5** sight
at ~ purposes with: **7** athwart
canine ~: **3** mut **4** mutt
combining form: **6** stauro-
Egyptian ~: **4** ankh
ender: **3** bar, bow, cut, tie, way **4** beam, bill, bred, cuts, fire, hair, head, ness, over, road, ruff, talk, town, tree, walk, wind, wise, word **5** bones, breed, check, court, hatch, patch, piece **6** bowman **7** current
one's heart: **3** vow **4** avow **5** swear **6** pledge **7** promise
one's mind: **5** occur **7** occur to
out: **4** dele, x out **6** cancel, delete, efface, excise, remove **7** mark off, redline **9** red-pencil
over: **4** span **6** bridge **8** bestride
paths with: **4** meet
section: **6** sample **8** specimen
starter: **3** out **4** auto, back, test
swords: **4** buck, defy, duel, spar, tilt **5** argue, clash, fight **6** attack, battle, bicker, combat, debate, engage, oppose, resist, tussle **7** contend, contest, dispute, quarrel, wrangle **8** conflict, disagree, do battle, struggle **9** duke it out, have it out, lock horns, slug it out, withstand
the ocean: **4** sail **5** pilot **6** cruise, voyage **7** captain, journey **8** navigate
the plate: **5** score
the threshold: **4** go in **5** enter
to bear: **4** onus **5** trial **6** burden
weapons with: **4** face **6** attack, take on
where axes ~: **5** graph **6** origin
with: **5** mad at
cross __: **3** fox, out, sea **4** buck, fire, over, talk, wind **5** hairs, ratio, wires **6** street, stroke, swords **7** product, section **8** purposes
cross __ bear: **3** as a
cross-__: **4** eyed, fade, file, link, vein, vine **5** check, match, staff, trade, train **6** action, bearer, bedded, border, cousin, garnet, legged, stitch, string **7** country, examine, grained, indexed, utilize
cross-__ tire: **3** ply
__ cross: **3** tau **4** Iona **5** Greek, Latin, Mills, papal **6** ansate, Celtic, Geneva, single **7** Calvary, Maltese, Passion
__-cross: **5** cyclo **6** double, single
Cross: **3** Ben **6** Amanda, Marcia
__ Cross: **3** Red **4** Blue, Holy, Iron, Navy **5** Criss **7** Charing
cross as __: **5** a bear
crossbar: **4** beam, yoke **6** lintel
try to clear the ~: **5** vault
crossbeam: **5** trave **6** rafter
crossbill: **4** bird
genus: **5** loxia
crossbones partner: **5** skull
crossbow
arrow: **4** bolt
ready a ~: **3** aim
user: **6** archer
cross-bred: **4** mixt **5** mixed **6** hybrid
crossbreed: **3** cur, mut **4** mule, mutt **7** mongrel
__ cross bun: **3** hot
Cross, Christopher
song: Best That You Can Do (1981)
Ride Like the Wind (1980)
Sailing (1980)
Think of Laura (1983)
cross-country, go: **4** hike, ride, tour **5** drive **6** travel
Cross Creek (1983 film)
cast: Peter Coyote, Malcolm McDowell, Mary Steenburgen, Rip Torn
director: Martin Ritt
crosscurrent: **4** eddy
crosscut: **3** saw **6** tunnel
crossed
keep one's fingers ~: **4** hope, wish **5** dream **6** aspire, expect **7** look for **10** anticipate
out: **3** x'ed
__-crossed: **4** star
cross-examine: **3** ask **4** pump, quiz **5** grill **8** question
cross-eyed, look: **6** squint
crossfire: **7** barrage
Crossfire (1947 film)
cast: Robert Mitchum, Robert Ryan, Robert Young
director: Edward Dmytryk
Crossfire network: **3** CNN
crossing: **4** walk **6** bridge, cruise, voyage **7** meeting, opposed, passage, pathway, transit, viaduct **8** junction, juncture, opposing, overpass **9** traversal, underpass **10** cloverleaf
the ocean: **4** asea **5** at sea
crossing __: **5** guard
__ crossing: **5** grade, level, zebra
Crossing Brooklyn Ferry author: Walt Whitman
Crossing Delancey (1988 film)
cast: Amy Irving, Peter Riegert
director: Joan Micklin Silver
Crossing Guard, The author: Rabe
Crossing, The author: Howard Fast
Crossing the Bar author: Tennyson
Crossing the Border author: Oates
Cross my __ with silver: **4** palm
crossness: **8** asperity
cross of __: **7** Calvary
Cross of __: **4** gold, Iron
Cross of Gold orator: **5** Bryan
Cross of Iron (1977 film)
cast: James Coburn, James Mason, Maximilian Schell
director: Sam Peckinpah
Cross of Lorraine, The (1943 film)
cast: Jean-Pierre Aumont, Sir Cedric Hardwicke, Gene Kelly
director: Tay Garnett
cross one's __: **4** mind, palm, path **5** heart **7** fingers
crossover __: **5** voter **7** network
crosspatch: **6** grouch
crosspiece: **3** bar **4** beam, rung **6** lintel
door ~: **6** lintel
cross-ply __: **4** tire
cross-pollinate: **3** mix
Cross Purpose author: Albert Camus
cross-purposes: **4** odds
at ~: **7** opposed **8** opposing
cross-reference: **5** index
crossroads: **3** jct. **4** junc. **6** center **7** parting, village **8** junction, juncture
Crossroads (1942 film)
cast: Hedy Lamarr, William Powell, Claire Trevor
Crossroads (2002 film)
cast: Taryn Manning, Anson Mount, Zoë Saldana, Britney Spears
director: Tamra Davis
cross-section: **7** variety
__ Cross the Mersey: **5** Ferry
crossthreads: **4** weft
crosswalk user: **3** ped. **6** walker **10** pedestrian
crossways: **6** aslant, skewed **7** athwart **8** diagonal, opposite **9** at an angle, on the bias **10** diagonally
crosswise: **6** aslant, skewed **7** athwart **8** diagonal, opposite **9** at an angle, on the bias **10** diagonally
at sea: **5** abeam
crossword: **6** puzzle
clue abbr.: **3** var.
complete a ~: **5** solve
like ~s in 1913: **3** new
tool: **6** eraser, pencil
where the first ~ appeared: **5** World **7** NY World
__-Crostic: **6** Double
crotale: **7** cymbals **10** percussion
origin: **6** Brazil
crotchet: **4** hook, kink, whim **5** quirk **6** vagary
Crotchet Castle author: Peacock
crotchety: **5** cross, huffy, moody, onery, surly, testy **6** crabby, cranky, crusty, fretty, grumpy, ornery **7** bearish, fretful, grouchy, peevish, waspish **8** contrary, fretsome, grumpish, snappish, vinegary **9** difficult, eccentric, fractious, irritable, obstinate, querulous, splenetic **10** capricious, ill-natured, out of sorts
one: **4** coot **5** crank, grump
Crothers: **7** Scatman
crottin: **6** cheese
crouch: **3** bow, dip **4** bend, duck, lurk **5** hunch, squat, stoop **6** huddle, shrink, slouch **8** huddle up **10** hunker down
crouching: **3** low **5** squat
Crouching Tiger, Hidden Dragon (2000 film)
cast: Michelle Yeoh, Chow Yun-Fat, Zhang Ziyi
director: Ang Lee
croupier: **6** banker
colleague: **6** dealer
customer: **6** better, bettor
milieu: **4** Reno **5** Vegas **6** casino **8** Las Vegas
often: **5** raker
tool: **4** rake
croupy: **6** hoarse
Crouse: **6** Russel **7** Lindsay
partner: **7** Lindsay
Crouse, Lindsay: **7** actress
film: The Arrival (1996)
Between the Lines (1977)
Daniel (1983)
House of Games (1987)
Iceman (1984)
The Indian in the Cupboard (1995)
Places in the Heart (1984)
Slap Shot (1977)
spouse: David Mamet
crouton: **4** cube **5** bread
crow: **3** daw **4** bird, brag, rook **5** boast, exult, gloat, laugh, pride, vaunt **6** cackle, squawk **7** bluster, rub it in, swagger, talk big, triumph **8** jubilate, laughter **9** black bird **10** jump for joy
abounding in ~s: **5** rooky
as the ~ flies: **6** direct, in a row, linear, unbent **7** unbowed **8** directly, straight **10** unswerving
combining form: **5** -corax
eat ~: **6** grovel
ender: **3** bar **4** feet, foot **5** berry
Hawaiian ~: **5** alala
home: **4** nest
relative: **3** jay **5** raven **6** magpie **7** bluejay, gray jay **10** nutcracker
sound: **3** caw
starter: **4** cock **5** scare
__ crow: **3** ate, eat **4** fish **5** house **6** hooded, hoodie
Crow: **5** tribe **6** Indian, Sheryl **7** Amerind **8** language
home: **4** tipi **5** tepee **6** teepee
crowbar: **3** pry **5** force, jimmy, lever, prier, pryer
crowd: **3** jam, mob, set **4** army, bevy, cram, crew, fill, gang, herd, host, mass, pack, pile, pour, prod, push, teem **5** array, bunch, crush, flock, flood, group, horde, press, ram in, shoal, shove, sqush, stuff, swamp, swarm, troop **6** abound, circle, clique, deluge, gather, huddle, legion, masses, muster, people, rabble, squash, squish, squush, throng **7** bunch up, cluster, company, congest, coterie, faction, hearers, in-group, jam-pack, numbers, squeeze, squoosh, turnout **8** assembly, audience **9** concourse, gathering, listeners, multitude **10** assemblage, attendance, concursion, congregate, spectators
acknowledge the ~: **3** bow **4** wave
be part of the ~: **5** fit in
disappear in the ~: **5** blend
ender: **7** pleaser **8** pleasing
in: **5** enter, troop **9** interrupt
in ~: **5** elite **6** jet set
in a ~: **4** amid **5** among **6** amidst, mongst **7** amongst
(into): **6** stream
like a stadium ~: **5** aroar
noise: **3** rah **4** roar
out: **8** displace
pleaser: **6** parade
pleasing: **7** popular
proverbially: **5** three
scene actor: **4** supe **5** extra
together: **3** mob **5** flock
together, old-style: **5** serry
work the ~: **5** stump **8** campaign **10** kiss babies
crowd __: **7** pleaser
__ Crowd: **5** The In
crowded: **3** SRO **4** busy, full, rife **5** awash, close, dense, laden, thick, tight **6** filled, loaded, packed **7** compact, cramped, replete, sold out, teeming **8** brimming, populous, squeezed, thronged **9** chock-full, jam-packed, to the roof **10** compressed, hard-packed, wall-to-wall
area, in Britain: **3** wen
place: **3** zoo
crowdie: **6** cheese
crowds: **4** lots **6** flocks, scores **7** legions
like some ~: **4** ugly
Crowe: **7** Cameron, Russell
Crowe, Cameron: **8** director
film: Almost Famous (2000)
Jerry Maguire (1996)
Say Anything ... (1989)
Vanilla Sky (2001)
crower: **8** braggart
Crowe, Russell: **5** actor
film: A Beautiful Mind (2001)
Gladiator (2000, AA)
The Insider (1999)
L.A. Confidential (1997)
Proof of Life (2000)
The Quick and the Dead (1995)
__ crow flies: **5** as the
Crowley: **3** Pat **8** Patricia
crowlike bird: **6** chough
crown: **3** cap, tip, top **4** acme, apex, best, coin, head, pate, peak **5** crest, endow, endue, ensky, exalt, honor, indue, money, prize, ruler, spire, tiara,

title 6 anadem, climax, corona, diadem, finish, fulfil, height, instal, invest, reward, summit, thwack, tipoff, top off, trophy, vertex, wreath, zenith 7 coronet, ennoble, festoon, fulfill, install, instate, jewelry, laurels, monarch, perfect, royalty 8 complete, coronate, pinnacle 9 culminate, sovereign 10 consummate
at the ~: 4 atop
combining form: 7 stephan- 8 stephano-
covering: 6 enamel
earn the ~: 3 win
material: 4 gold 6 laurel
name meaning ~: 6 Steven 7 Stephen
of light: 4 halo
wearer: 4 czar, king, tsar, tzar 5 queen, ruler 7 monarch 9 sovereign
wear the ~: 4 rule 5 reign 6 govern
crown __: 3 rot, saw 4 fire, gall, land, lens, post, rust, wart 5 daisy, glass, graft, jewel, roast, vetch, wheel 6 antler, canopy, colony, cutter, octavo, prince, quarto
__ crown: 4 half 5 king's, mural 6 double
Crown
foe: 5 Porgy
__ Crown: 6 Triple
Crown Colony, former: 6 Guyana
crowned, get: 4 rule 5 reign 6 accede
Crowned Heads author: Thomas Tryon
Crowne Plaza: 5 hotel
alternative: 4 Omni 5 Hyatt 6 Hilton, Westin 7 Wyndham 8 Marriott, Radisson, Sheraton 10 DoubleTree 11 Four Seasons
crowning: 4 last 5 final 7 supreme 8 ultimate 9 climactic, paramount, principal, virtuosic 10 consummate
point: 4 acme 6 climax
crown of __: 6 thorns
crownpiece: 3 cap
Crown Point: 4 city, town
locale: 7 Indiana
Crown Victoria: 3 car 4 auto 7 Mercury
crow's-__: 4 feet, foot, nest
crow's-foot: 7 wrinkle
Crow, Sheryl
song: All I Wanna Do (1994)
If It Makes You Happy (1996)
Strong Enough (1995)
crow's nest: 7 lookout, station
cry: 4 ahoy, land 6 land ho
site: 4 mast
Crow, The (1994 film)
cast: Ernie Hudson, Brandon Lee, Michael Wincott
Crowther: 6 Bosley
CRT: 3 VDT 8 terminal
cousin: 3 LCD
pointer: 6 cursor
__ Cru: 5 Grand 7 Premier
__ Cruces, NM: 3 Las
crucial: 3 key 4 dire, high, main 5 acute, chief, grave, major, vital 6 needed, urgent 7 burning, central, exigent, fateful, hurry-up, pivotal, primary, serious, weighty 8 critical, deciding, decisive, exigeant, pressing, required 9 desperate, essential, high-level, important, mandatory, memorable, momentous, necessary, operative, right-hand, strategic 10 imperative, portentous, underlying
not ~: 5 minor 7 trivial
point: 6 crunch
crucible: 4 test 5 trial 6 ordeal, retort, vessel 7 alembic 9 container, probation
crucible __: 5 steel
Crucible, The: 4 film, play
author: Arthur Miller
cast: Yves Montand, Simone Signoret
event: 5 trial
setting: 4 Mass. 5 Salem
crucifix: 4 rood 5 cross
letters: 3 IHS 4 INRI
Crucifixion artist: 4 Dali
Crucifixion of Saint Peter artist: 4 Reni
cruciverbalist direction: 4 down 6 across
crud: 4 dirt, gunk, muck 5 filth, grime, slime 9 sleazebag
up: 5 taint
cruddy: 6 filthy, grungy 10 disgusting
crude: 3 low, oil, raw 4 base, loud, poor, rude 5 crass, gross, harsh, nervy, rough, tacky, unref. 6 abrupt, coarse, earthy, garish, gauche, Gothic, ragged, ribald, risqué, rustic, simple, smutty, tawdry, unmeet, vulgar 7 bearish, boorish, caddish, ill-bred, loutish, lowbred, natural, profane, raffish, sketchy, uncouth, unkempt 8 barbaric, churlish, degraded, fumbling, homemade, immature, impolite, impudent, indecent, inexpert, tactless, unseemly, unsubtle, untaught 9 barbarian, barbarous, graceless, inelegant, low-minded, lubricous, makeshift, primitive, tasteless, unevolved, ungallant, unrefined, untrained, unwrought 10 amateurish, indecorous, indelicate, lascivious, regardless, uncultured, unfinished, ungracious, unpolished, unskillful
one: 3 oaf 4 boor, lout
crude __: 3 oil
crudely: 5 rawly, rough
crudeness: 8 lewdness 9 barbarity, grossness, ignorance
crude oil: 9 petroleum
component: 6 ethane 8 dimethyl
measure: 3 bbl. 6 barrel
crudités: 9 appetizer 10 vegetables
companion: 3 dip
ingredient: 6 carrot
like ~: 3 raw
crudity: 7 lowness 9 gaucherie, indecency, vulgarity 10 incivility, inelegance
with ~: 5 rawly
Crudup, Billy: 5 actor
film: Almost Famous (2000)
The Hi-Lo Country (1998)
Waking the Dead (2000)
Without Limits (1998)
__ Crüe: 6 Motley
cruel: 3 bad 4 evil, firm, grim, hard 5 bossy, catty, harsh, nasty, picky, rigid, rough, stern, stiff, stony, tough 6 bitter, brutal, fierce, flinty, savage, severe, sinful, stoney, unfair, unkind, wanton, wicked 7 austere, beastly, bestial, brutish, callous, hateful, hellish, hurtful, inhuman, Spartan, vicious, violent 8 barbaric, demoniac, despotic, diabolic, exacting, fiendish, hardened, hard-line, horrible, inhumane, pitiless, rigorous, ruthless, sadistic, scathing, spiteful, vengeful 9 barbarian, barbarous, cutthroat, demanding, draconian, ferocious, heartless, inclement, merciless, monstrous, murderous, stringent, unbending, unfeeling, unpitying, unsparing 10 despotical, diabolical, implacable, inexorable, inflexible, iron-fisted, malevolent, no-nonsense, oppressive, relentless, tyrannical, unmerciful, vindictive, virtueless
one: 4 ogre 5 beast, brute
treatment: 6 misuse
Cruel __: 5 Shoes 6 Summer
Cruel __ Kind: 4 to be
Cruel __, The: 3 Sea
Cruella: 5 De Vil
cruellest month: 3 Apr. 5 April
Cruel Sea, The (1953 film)
cast: Denholm Elliott, Jack Hawkins
Cruel Summer (song) artist: Ace of Base, Bananarama
cruelty: 5 spite, venom, wrong 6 malice 7 tyranny 8 coldness, ferocity, iron hand, savagery, severity, violence 9 barbarism, brutality, depravity, despotism, harshness, nastiness 10 inclemency, inhumanity, oppression
exemplar of ~: 4 Sade 6 de Sade
__ Cruel World: 7 Goodbye
Crüe, Mötley
members: Neil, Mars, Sixx, Lee
song: Don't Go Away Mad (1990)
Dr. Feelgood (1989)
Girls, Girls, Girls (1987)
Smokin' in the Boys Room (1985)
Without You (1990)
cruet: 6 bottle, carafe 7 alembic 8 decanter
contents: 3 oil 7 vinegar 8 dressing
cruise: 3 gad 4 ride, sail, tour, trip 5 coast, jaunt, prowl, range 6 junket, patrol, ramble, travel, voyage, wander 7 journey, meander, sailing 8 crossing, navigate, vacation 9 excursion, gallivant
accommodation: 5 cabin, suite
activity: 4 tour 6 eating
along: 5 motor
amenity: 3 gym 4 pool 5 sauna 6 buffet, casino 7 sun deck
company: 6 Cunard 8 Princess 9 Celebrity
ship: 4 QE II 5 liner 6 vessel 7 steamer
stop: 3 POC, Rio 4 isle, port 5 Aruba 6 Alaska, harbor, Mexico, Nassau 7 Bermuda, Cozumel, Curaçao, Grenada, harbour, Jamaica, San Juan, St. Croix 8 Barbados, St. Thomas 9 Caribbean 10 port of call
taking a ~: 4 asea 5 at sea
(through): 6 breeze
cruise __: 3 car 4 ship 7 control, missile
Cruise: 3 Tom 5 Pablo
__ Cruise: 3 Sea
cruiser: 4 boat, ship 5 yacht 6 vessel 7 frigate 10 battleship
ender: 6 weight
__ cruiser: 3 day 5 cabin, heavy, light 6 battle, timber
Cruise, Tom: 5 actor
film: All the Right Moves (1983)
Born on the Fourth of July (1989)
Cocktail (1988)
The Color of Money (1986)
Days of Thunder (1990)
Eyes Wide Shut (1999)
Far and Away (1992)
A Few Good Men (1992)
The Firm (1993)
Interview With the Vampire: The Vampire Chronicles (1994)
Jerry Maguire (1996)
Magnolia (1999)
Minority Report (2002)
Mission: Impossible (1996)
Mission: Impossible II (2000)
Rain Man (1988)
Risky Business (1983)
Top Gun (1986)
Vanilla Sky (2001)
spouse: Nicole Kidman, Mimi Rogers
cruising: 4 asea 5 at sea
cruising __: 6 radius
cruller: 4 cake 6 pastry
kin: 5 donut 6 churro, éclair 8 doughnut
__ cruller: 6 French
crumb: 3 bit, cad, ort 4 atom, iota, lump, mite, mote, snip, soil, whit 5 grain, pinch, scrap, shred, speck, trace 6 morsel, nibble, sliver, tidbit 7 granule, modicum, ratfink, smidgen, smidgin 8 fragment, leftover, particle, pittance
coat with ~ s: 5 bread
Crumb: 6 Robert
crumble: 2 go 3 eat, rot 4 chip, fall, rust, wear 5 break, crush, decay, erode, grind, mince, spoil 6 molder, perish, powder, weaken, wither 7 give way 8 collapse, dissolve, fragment 9 decompose, granulate, pulverize, triturate 10 go to pieces
crumbled: 6 broken 8 in pieces
crumbles
how the cookie ~: 3 lot 4 fate
Crumblin' Down (1983 song) artist: John Cougar Mellencamp
crumbling: 3 old 5 musty 6 rotten 7 powdery, run-down 8 timeworn, untended 9 weathered 10 ramshackle, tumbledown
crumbly: 5 crisp, light, mealy 6 crispy 7 brittle, crunchy, fragile, friable 9 frangible 10 nondurable
crumbum: 5 louse
crumby: 3 low 6 no-good 9 worthless
crummy: 3 bad, low 4 foul, grim, poor, punk 5 awful, cheap, lousy, seedy, woful 6 dismal, filthy, horrid, no-good, odious, rotten, shabby, woeful 7 accurst, baleful, baneful, beastly, doleful, ghastly, run-down 8 accursed, dreadful, God-awful, grievous, horrible, inferior, pathetic, shameful, stinking, terrible, unusable, wretched 9 abhorrent, appalling, atrocious, defective, depressed, execrable, fifth-rate, frightful, insidious, loathsome, miserable, offensive, revolting, third-rate, worthless 10 abominable, despicable, detestable, disastrous, fourth-rate, horrendous, pathetical, second-rate
crumpet: 5 bread 6 pastry
accompaniment: 3 tea
crumple: 3 wad 4 give, muss 5 crush, grind, swoon, wad up, yield 6 buckle, cave in, crease, pucker, ruck up, rumple 7 give way, wrinkle 8 collapse 9 break down
Crumpled Papers artist: 3 Arp
crunch: 4 bind, bite, chew, gnaw, snag 5 chomp, crush, grind, munch 6 crisis, impact, powder, stress 7 problem, shatter, squeeze, trouble 8 pressure 9 adversity, emergency, masticate, pulverize, tight spot 10 misfortune
benefactors: 3 abs
into: 3 hit, ram
on: 4 chew 9 masticate
crunch __: 4 time
__ Crunch: 4 Cap'n 7 Nestle's
cruncher, number: 3 CPA 4 acct. 7 analyst 10 accountant
crunchy: 5 chewy, crisp 6 crispy, crusty 7 brittle, crumbly 9 crackling
food: 4 chip 6 celery, cereal 8 corn chip 10 cornflakes, potato chip
crus: 5 shank
site: 3 leg
crusade: 3 war 4 push 5 cause, drive, quest 6 battle 8 campaign, movement 10 enterprise, expedition, pilgrimage
Crusade in Europe author: 10 Eisenhower
crusader: 6 zealot 7 battler, fighter 8 advocate, champion, reformer 9 expounder 10 campaigner
__ Crusader: 5 Caped
Crusader Rabbit partner: 4 Rags 5 Tiger

Crusaders: 9 Holy Cross
Crusades
  destination: 4 East 5 Syria
  important ~ fortress: 5 Haifa
Crusades, The (1935 film)
  cast: Ian Keith, Henry Wilcoxon, Loretta Young
  director: Cecil B. DeMille
cruse: 3 jar, pot 6 bottle
crush: 3 hug, jam, mob, zap 4 beat, bray, cram, maim, mash, mill, pile, pulp, rout, ruin 5 break, crowd, grind, horde, munch, pound, press, quash, quell, smash, sqush, stamp, stave, stomp, swarm, total, tramp, tread, wad up, worst, wreck 6 beetle, crunch, defeat, grieve, impact, mangle, powder, quench, ravage, reduce, refute, rumple, scotch, squash, squish, squush, subdue, thrash, throng, wallop 7 conquer, crumble, crumple, destroy, embrace, flatten, oppress, passion, put down, repress, shatter, squeeze, squelch, squoosh, tighten, trample, trounce, wrinkle 8 blow away, compress, demolish, keep down, levigate, overcome, stamp out, suppress, vanquish 9 affection, granulate, multitude, obsession, overpower, overwhelm, pulverize, puppy love, subjugate 10 annihilate, dishearten, obliterate
  have a ~ on: 4 love 5 adore, fancy, yearn 7 care for, idolize, worship 9 care about
  underfoot: 5 stamp 7 trample
crushed: 3 low, sad 4 blue, hurt 6 broken, undone 7 abashed 8 wretched
crushed ___: 6 velvet
___ crusher: 3 jaw
crushing: 3 sad 5 tight 6 tragic 7 onerous, weighty 8 grueling, tragical
  news: 4 blow
___-crushing: 4 bone
Crusoe: 8 castaway, Robinson
  carved one: 5 canoe
  creator: 5 Defoe
  like ~ before Friday: 5 alone
crust: 4 bark, coat, edge, gall, hull, rind, rock, scum, skin 5 layer, nerve, shell 7 coating 8 audacity, covering 9 arrogance, impudence 10 effrontery, integument
  between faults: 5 horst
  earth's ~ layer: 4 moho, sial, sima 5 plate
  upper ~: 4 rich 5 elite, lords 6 gentry, jet set 7 society 8 nobility 9 exclusive, gentility 10 haute monde
___ crust: 4 snow 5 upper
crustacean: 4 crab 5 krill, prawn 6 isopod, mussel, shrimp 7 decapod, gribble, lobster, mollusc, mollusk, sandbug 8 amphipod, barnacle, cirriped, crayfish, macruran, mole crab 9 beach flea, shellfish, wood louse
  abdomen: 5 pleon
  claw: 5 chela 6 nipper
  larva: 4 zoea
  sense organ: 4 palp 6 palpus
  sense organs: 5 palpi
crusty: 4 dour 5 brusk, crisp, cross, gruff, huffy, moody, onery, rough, stern, surly, testy 6 abrupt, crabby, cranky, crispy, ornery, touchy 7 bearish, brittle, brusque, crunchy, friable, grouchy, peevish, waspish 8 captious, choleric, churlish, snappish, snarling, vinegary 9 crotchety, irascible, irritable, querulous, saturnine, splenetic 10 ill-humored, ironwilled, out of sorts
crutch: 4 prop 6 recess 7 support
Crutzen, Paul: 7 chemist 8 Nobelist
crux: 3 nub 4 body, core, gist, knub, meat, pith 5 basis, heart, joint, point 6 enigma, kernel, thrust 7 essence, keynote 10 bottom line
Cruz: 5 Celia 7 Brandon 8 Penélope
___ Cruz: 4 Vera 5 Santa
cruzado: 4 coin 5 money
cruzeiro: 4 coin 5 money
Cruz, Penélope: 7 actress
  film: All About My Mother (1999)
    All the Pretty Horses (2000)
    Captain Corelli's Mandolin (2001)
    Vanilla Sky (2001)
Cruz, Sor Juana: 4 poet 7 Mexican
CRV: 3 SUV 5 Honda
crwth: 4 lyre 5 rotta, rotte 6 string
  kin: 5 rebec 6 rebeck
  origin: 7 Ireland
cry: 3 aha, bay, eek, hah, oho, ooh, rah, sob 4 ahoy, bark, bawl, boom, bray, call, hoot, howl, mewl, moan, roar, wail, weep, yell, yowl 5 avast, bleat, crisp, hallo, hillo, hullo, motto, mourn, shout, utter, voice, whine, whoop 6 bellow, boo-hoo, cackle, clamor, halloa, halloo, hallow, hilloa, holler, hulloo, lament, scream, shriek, snivel, squawk, squeak, uproar 7 blubber, call out, exclaim, screech, sing out, whimper 9 break down, caterwaul, shed tears 10 hullabaloo, take it hard, vociferate
  barnyard ~: 3 baa, moo 4 bray, crow, oink 5 bleat
  ender: 4 baby
  see also exclamation
cry ___: 3 off 4 down, wolf 5 havoc, uncle
cry ___ spilled milk: 4 over
___ cry: 3 far, war 4 a far 6 battle
Cry ___: 4 Baby 5 Havoc 6 Danger, Terror 7 Freedom
Cry ___ River: 3 Me a
___ Cry: 4 Don't 6 Battle
Cry (1951 song) artist: Johnnie Ray
crybaby: 4 wimp 5 sissy 6 bawler, critic, griper, moaner, whiner 8 grumbler, recreant, weakling 10 bellyacher, complainer, malcontent
  be a ~: 4 bawl, moan, pule 5 gripe
Cry-Baby (1990 film)
  cast: Johnny Depp, Amy Locane, Susan Tyrrell
  director: John Waters
___ Cry Daddy: 4 Don't
Cry Danger (1951 film)
  cast: Richard Erdman, Rhonda Fleming, Dick Powell
Cryer: 3 Jon
Cry for Help (1991 song) artist: Rick Astley
Cry Freedom (1987 film)
  cast: Kevin Kline, Denzel Washington
  director: Richard Attenborough
Cry 'Havoc' (1943 film)
  cast: Joan Blondell, Margaret Sullavan
crying: 5 tears, teary, weepy 6 urgent 7 glaring, heinous, tearful 8 pressing 9 insistent, querulous, sniveling 10 lachrymose, waterworks
  need: 6 hankie
  noise: 3 wah
  shame: 4 pity
Crying Game, The (1992 film)
  cast: Jaye Davidson, Stephen Rea, Miranda Richardson, Forest Whitaker
Crying in the Chapel (1965 song)
  artist: Elvis Presley
Crying in the Rain (1962 song) artist: Everly Brothers
Crying of Lot 49, The author: Pynchon
___ crying out loud!: 3 For
Crying (song) artist: Don McLean, Roy Orbison
Crying Time (1966 song) artist: Ray Charles
Cry in the Dark, A (1988 film)
  cast: Bruce Myles, Sam Neill, Meryl Streep
  director: Fred Schepisi
Cry in the Night, A author: Mary Higgins Clark
Cry Like a Baby (1968 song) artist: Box Tops
Cry Me a River (1955 song) artist: Julie London
___ Cry of Freedom, The: 6 Battle
Cry of the Halidon, The author: Ludlum
cryolite: 7 mineral
cry one's ___ out: 4 eyes 5 heart
cryonics, practice: 6 freeze
___ Cry Out Loud: 4 Don't
cry over ___ milk: 5 spilt 7 spilled
crypt: 4 code, tomb 5 vault 6 recess
cryptanalyze: 6 decode 8 decipher
cryptic: 4 dark 5 mirky, murky, terse, vague 6 arcane, gnomic, hidden, secret 7 obscure, unclear 8 abstruse, esoteric, nebulous, oracular, puzzling, ulterior 9 confusing, enigmatic, recondite, secretive 10 indistinct, mysterious, perplexing
cryptogram: 4 code 6 cipher
  make a ~: 6 encode
  maker: 5 coder
  solve a ~: 6 decode
cryptographic org.: 3 NSA
crystal: 3 gem 5 clear, glass, stone 6 glassy 8 luminous, vitreous 9 unblurred
  clear: 5 lucid, plain 6 hyalin, limpid, patent 7 hyaline 8 apparent, knowable, luminous, manifest
  gaze: 4 scry
  gazer: 4 seer 5 sibyl 7 prophet, psychic
  gazer phrase: 4 I see
  gazing: 10 divination, prediction
  laser ~: 4 ruby
  plane: 4 face
  set: 5 radio
  twin ~: 5 macle
  use a ~ ball: 4 gaze
crystal ___: 3 set, tea 4 ball 5 gazer, pleat, radio 6 defect, gazing, pickup, system, violet 7 lattice
crystal-___: 5 clear
___ crystal: 4 rock, snow 6 leaded, liquid, quartz
Crystal: 4 city, town 5 Billy, Gayle 6 Waters 7 Bernard
  locale: 9 Minnesota
Crystal ___: 6 Palace
Crystal, Billy: 5 actor 8 comedian
  film: America's Sweethearts (2001)
    Analyze This (1999)
    City Slickers (1991)
    Forget Paris (1995)
    Memories of Me (1988)
    Mr. Saturday Night (1992)
    My Giant (1998)
    Throw Momma From the Train (1987)
    When Harry Met Sally... (1989)
  TV: Soap
Crystal Blue Persuasion (1969 song)
  artist: Tommy James
Crystal Cave, The author: Mary Stewart
___-crystal display: 6 liquid
crystal-filled rock: 5 geode
Crystal Lake: 4 city, town
  locale: 8 Illinois
Crystal Light: 9 soft drink
crystalline: 5 lucid 6 glassy, hyalin, limpid 7 hyaline
  antiseptic: 5 iodol
  rock: 4 spar
crystallize: 3 gel, ppt., set 4 form, jell 5 shape 6 harden 7 stiffen 8 solidify
crystals
  ice ~: 6 frazil
  rock-cavity ~: 5 druse
  wet ~: 4 snow
Crystals
  song: Da Doo Ron Ron (1963)
    He's a Rebel (1962)
    Then He Kissed Me (1963)
___ Crystal, The: 4 Dark
Cry Terror (1958 film)
  cast: James Mason, Rod Steiger, Inger Stevens
  director: Andrew Stone
Cry, the Beloved Country (1951 film)
  cast: Charles Carson, Canada Lee, Sidney Poitier
  director: Zoltan Korda
Cry, the Beloved Country (1995 film)
  cast: Charles S. Dutton, Richard Harris, James Earl Jones
Cry, the Beloved Country author: Alan Paton
Cry to Heaven author: Anne Rice
___ Cry Tomorrow: 3 I'll
Cs: 4 elem. 6 cesium 7 caesium, element
  55 for ~: 4 at. no.
  like some ~: 4 soft
C.S.: 5 Lewis 8 Forester
CSA: 4 Gray, Grey 5 Dixie, Grays, Greys
  end of a ~ signature: 4 E. Lee
  fighter: 3 reb
  monogram: 3 REL
  song: 5 Dixie
  state: 3 Ala., Fla., Tex. 4 Miss., N. Car., S. Car. 5 Texas 7 Alabama, Ark. Tenn., Florida, Georgia 8 Arkansas, Virginia 9 Louisiana, Tennessee 11 Mississippi 13 North Carolina, South Carolina
___ csc: 3 arc
___ C. Scott: 6 George
C-sharp alias: 5 D flat
Csonka, Larry sport: 8 football
C-SPAN: 7 channel
  alternative: 3 BET, CMT, MTV, PAX, TBS, TLC, TNN, TNT, USA 4 ESPN, HGTV 5 A and E, Style 6 Noggin, Tech TV, TV Land 7 Court TV, Ovation, SoapNet 8 Lifetime
  part: 3 Net., Pub. 5 Cable 6 Public 7 Affairs, Network 9 Satellite
CST, part of: 3 Std. 4 Time 7 Central 8 Standard
Ct.
  neighbor: 4 Mass.
  region: 4 N. Eng.
  see also Connecticut
CT ___: 4 scan 7 scanner
C2H4: 6 ethene
C2H5OH: 3 alc. 7 alcohol
C2H6: 6 ethane 8 dimethyl
C3H5N3]O9: 5 nitro
C-3P0: 5 droid, robot
C. Thomas ___: 6 Howell
ctn.: 3 pkg.
  handler: 3 UPS
  place for: 4 whse.
C-to-C sequence: 5 scale
ctr.: 3 mid. 5 midpt.
  community ~: 4 the Y, YMCA, YMHA, YWCA, YWHA
CTRL-___-DEL: 3 ALT
CTS: 3 car 4 auto 8 Cadillac
cts, 100: 3 dol.
Cu: 4 elem. 6 copper 7 element
  29 for ~: 4 at. no.
___ Cuarto, Argentina: 3 Rio
cuatro: 4 four 6 guitar 7 Spanish
  follower: 5 cinco
  preceder: 4 tres
  twice ~: 4 ocho

Cuauhtémoc: 4 city, town
locale: 6 Mexico 9 Chihuahua
Cuautitlán: 4 city, town
locale: 6 Mexico
Cuautla: 4 city, town
locale: 6 Mexico 7 Morelos
cub: 3 boy, kid, lad, tot 4 tiro, tyro, wolf 5 youth 6 greeny, lionet, novice 7 learner 8 beginner, reporter 9 off-spring, youngster 10 apprentice
home: 3 den 4 lair
parent: 4 bear, lion
cub __: 5 shark 8 reporter
__ cub: 4 wolf
Cub: 5 scout 10 baseballer
Hall of Famer: 5 Banks, Evers 6 Wilson 8 Williams 10 Ernie Banks
rival: 3 Met, Red 4 Expo, Twin 5 Angel, Astro, Brave, Giant, Padre, Rocky, Royal, Tiger 6 Brewer, Dodger, Indian, Marlin, Oriole, Philly, Pirate, Ranger, Red Sox, Yankee 7 Blue Jay, Mariner 8 Athletic, Cardinal, Devil Ray, White Sox
__ Cub: 5 Piper
Cuba: 3 isl. 4 isle 6 island, nation 7 country, Gooding
ballet dancer: 6 Alonso
bay: 10 Guantánamo
capital: 6 Havana
castle: 5 Morro
city: 6 Bayamo, Havana 7 Holguín 8 Camaguey, Matanzas, Santiago 10 Cienfuegos, Guantánamo
dance: 5 conga, mambo, rumba 6 cha-cha, rhumba 8 habanera
island: 5 Pines
leader: 6 Castro
money: 4 peso
neighbor: 5 Haiti
org.: 3 OAS
poet: 5 Diego 7 Guillén
product: 5 cigar
writer: 5 Martí 6 Arenas, Barnet 10 Carpentier
see also Spanish
Cuba (1979 film)
cast: Brooke Adams, Sean Connery, Jack Weston
director: Richard Lester
Cuba __: 5 libre
cubage: 6 volume
Cuban: 5 Latin
Cuban __: 4 heel
Cuban Overture composer: 8 Gershwin
cubby: 4 nook 5 niche
ender: 4 hole
Cubby: 6 O' Brien
cubbyhole: 4 cell, nook, room 5 booth, niche 6 alcove 7 cubicle
place into ~ s: 6 assort
cube: 3 die 4 chop, dice, loaf, lump 5 block, mince, power, solid 8 multiply 10 hexahedron
starter: 5 flash
cube __: 4 root 5 steak
__ cube: 3 ice 5 sugar
__ Cube: 3 Ice 6 Rubik's
cubeb: 5 fruit, shrub 6 veggie 9 vegetable
relative: 4 kava 6 pepper
cubes: 3 ice 4 dice 5 rocks
cubic: 5 solid 6 three-D
measure: 5 liter, stere 6 volume
cubicle: 4 cell, nook, room 5 booth, cubby, stall 6 alcove, recess 7 chamber 8 work area 9 cubbyhole, workplace 10 pigeonhole
library ~: 6 carrel 7 carrell
Cubism: 3 art 5 style
Cubist: 4 Gris 5 Léger 6 Braque 7 Duchamp, Picasso
cubit relative: 4 span
cuboid: 4 bone
locale: 4 foot
cubs: 6 litter
Cubs: 4 nine, team
home: 3 Chi. 7 Chicago
org.: 3 BSA, MLB, NLC
rivals: 3 Sox 8 White Sox
sport: 8 baseball
Cub Scout
group: 3 den 4 pack
leader: 5 Akela
__ Cucamonga, CA: 6 Rancho
cucaracha: 5 roach 9 cockroach
cuchia: 4 fish
Cuchulainn's wife: 4 Emer
cucking __: 5 stool
cuckoo: 3 ani, mad 4 bats, bird, daft, loco 5 batty, silly 7 jackass, touched 8 bird call, rainbird 9 harebrain, simpleton
ender: 4 pint 6 flower
Malay ~: 4 koel
cuckoo __: 4 wasp 5 clock
__-cuckoo-land: 5 cloud
cuckoopint: 4 arum 5 aroid, plant
__ Cuckoo, The: 7 Sterile
cucullate: 6 hooded
cucumber: 4 pepo 5 gourd 6 pickle, veggie 9 vegetable
__ cucumber: 3 bur, sea 6 horned, Indian
cucumberlike: 4 cool 6 as cool
Cúcuta: 4 city, town
locale: 8 Colombia
Cudahy: 4 city, town
locale: 10 California
cud chewers: 4 cows 6 camels, cattle, llamas
cuddle: 3 hug 4 hold, love 5 spoon, touch 6 caress, cosset, dandle, nestle, nuzzle 7 embrace, snuggle, squeeze 8 huddle up 10 bill and coo
cuddled up: 4 cosy, cozy, snug 5 cozey, cozie 8 tucked in
cuddly: 4 soft 7 lovable, snuggly 8 huggable, loveable
cuddy: 3 ass, oaf, sap 4 boob, butt, clod, dolt, dupe, fool, gull, lamb, lout, tool 5 chump, clown, cluck, dummy, dunce, joker, looby, ninny, patsy 6 dimwit, donkey, lummox, nitwit, pigeon, sucker, turkey 7 buffoon, dingbat, dullard, fall guy, fathead, half-wit, jackass, pinhead, saphead 8 bonehead, dumbbell, easy mark, meathead, numskull, pushover 9 birdbrain, blockhead, harebrain, lamebrain, numbskull, simpleton 10 dunderhead
cudgel: 3 bat, hit, rod, sap 4 beat, cane, club, cosh, flog, mace, slam 5 baton, billy, birch, pound, smite, stick 6 ferule, paddle, switch, weapon 7 lambast, war club 8 bludgeon, lambaste 9 bastinado, billy club, blackjack, truncheon 10 nightstick, shillelagh
cue: 3 tip 4 hint, prod, sign 6 prompt, signal, tipoff 7 inkling 8 mnemonic, reminder 10 indication, intimation
accessory: 5 chalk
bandleader ~: 5 hit it
fix a pool ~: 5 retip
game: 4 pool 7 snooker 9 billiards, eight ball
give a ~ to: 6 remind
on ~: 10 as expected
shot: 5 break, carom, massé
starter: 5 curly
cue __: 3 bid 4 ball, card 5 sheet, stick
__ cue: 5 miss a
Cuéllar, Pérez de home: 4 Peru
Cuenca: 4 city, town
locale: 7 Ecuador
Cuernavaca: 4 city, town
locale: 3 Mex. 6 Mexico 7 Morelos
cuesta: 5 ridge, slope
cuff: 3 box, hit 4 beat, belt, iron, slap, sock, swat 5 clout, knock, punch, smack, spank, swipe, thump, whack 6 arrest, buffet, pummel, strike 7 clobber, manacle, scuffle 9 wristband
accessory: 4 link
off the ~: 7 offhand 9 impromptu 10 informally
on the ~: 4 free 6 gratis 10 for nothing
place: 5 shirt 6 sleeve
starter: 4 hand
cuff __: 4 link 6 button
__ cuff: 5 on the 6 barrel, French, off the 7 rotator
cuff link: 4 stud
material: 5 nacre
Cuff Links song: Tracy (1969)
cuffs: 5 irons 8 shackles 9 bracelets
slap the ~ on: 3 nab 5 run in 6 arrest
cu. ft.: 3 vol. 4 meas.
Cugat, Xavier: 10 bandleader
Music: 5 rumba 6 rhumba
spouse: Charo, Abbe Lane
cui __: 4 bono
Cuiab: 4 city, town
locale: 6 Brazil
Cuiaba: 5 river
locale: 6 Brazil
cuica: 4 drum
origin: 6 Brazil
cuirass: 5 armor, plate 6 lorica
cuisine: 4 fare, food, menu, Thai 5 Cajun, Hunan, table 6 creole, dishes, French 7 cooking 10 gastronomy
enlivener: 5 spice
__ cuisine: 3 new 5 haute
__ Cuisine: 4 Lean
cuisinier: 4 chef
cuisse: 5 armor, plate
Cujo: 4 film 5 novel
author: Stephen King
cast: Daniel Hugh-Kelly, Danny Pintauro, Dee Wallace
director: Lewis Teague
Cukor, George: 8 director
film: Adam's Rib (1949)
A Bill of Divorcement (1932)
Born Yesterday (1950)
Camille (1937)
David Copperfield (1935)
Dinner at Eight (1933)
A Double Life (1947)
Gaslight (1944)
Girls About Town (1931)
Holiday (1938)
It Should Happen to You (1954)
Justine (1969)
Keeper of the Flame (1943)
Les Girls (1957)
Let's Make Love (1960)
Little Women (1933)
The Marrying Kind (1952)
The Model and the Marriage Broker (1951)
My Fair Lady (1964, AA)
One Hour With You (1932)
Pat and Mike (1952)
The Philadelphia Story (1940)
Rich and Famous (1981)
Romeo and Juliet (1936)
The Royal Family of Broadway (1930)
A Star Is Born (1954)
Sylvia Scarlett (1935)
Two-Faced Woman (1941)
What Price Hollywood? (1932)
A Woman's Face (1941)
The Women (1939)
Culbertson: 3 Ely
contemporary: 5 Goren
forte: 6 bridge
cul-de-sac: 5 alley 7 dead end, impasse 10 blind alley, bottleneck
Cul-de-Sac (1966 film)
cast: Françoise Dorléac, Donald Pleasence, Lionel Stander
director: Roman Polanski
Culebra __: 3 Cut
culex kin: 5 aedes
Culiacán: 4 city, town
locale: 6 Mexico 7 Sinaloa
culinary
concoction: 4 dish, soup 5 sauce 6 entrée
directive: 3 fry 4 beat, boil, chop, cool, dice, heat, stew, stir, warm 5 baste, roast, sauté, scald, steam, toast
see also cook, cooking
Culkin: 6 Kieran 8 Macaulay
cull: 3 opt 4 pick, pull, sort, take 5 amass, glean, pluck, unmix 6 assort, choose, garner, gather, prefer, screen, select, winnow 7 collect, compile, discard, extract, harvest, pick out, round up 8 handpick, hold on to, pick over 10 accumulate, settle upon
Cullen: 4 Bill 7 Countee
__ Cullen Bryant: 7 William
Cullen, Countee: 4 poet
work: Copper Sun
The Lost Zoo
cullis: 6 gutter
neighbor: 4 eave
Cullman: 4 city, town
locale: 7 Alabama
Cullum: 4 John
culminate: 3 cap, end 4 peak 5 close, crown 6 climax, finish, mature, pan out, result, top off, wind up 8 conclude, round off, round out 9 terminate
culmination: 3 cap, end, top 4 acme, apex, peak 5 close, crest, crown 6 apogee, capper, climax, ending, finale, finish, height, payoff, summit, upshot, vertex, windup, wrap-up, zenith 8 pinnacle, showdown, terminus 10 denouement
__-culotte: 4 sans
culottes: 5 pants, skirt
kin: 5 skort
Culp: 6 Robert, Steven
culpability: 4 onus 5 blame, fault, guilt 9 liability
culpable: 5 wrong 6 guilty, liable, unholy 7 at fault, to blame 8 blamable, criminal 9 blameable, red-handed 10 delinquent, in the wrong
culpa, mea: 5 sorry 7 apology, I'm sorry
__ Culp Hobby: 5 Oveta
culprit: 8 criminal, evildoer 9 miscreant 10 delinquent
Culp, Robert: 5 actor
film: Bob & Carol & Ted & Alice (1969)
Sky Riders (1976)
TV: I Spy
cult: 4 sect 5 group 6 clique 7 faction 8 religion 10 persuasion
follower: 3 ism, ist, ure
cultivable: 6 arable
cultivar: 5 plant
cultivate: 3 hoe, woo 4 farm, plow, rear, tend, till, work 5 breed, court, labor, raise, teach, train 6 better, enrich, follow, foster, garden, harrow, pursue, refine, school 7 advance, bolster, develop, educate, further, improve, nourish, nurture, produce, promote 9 brown-nose, encourage, fertilize, get in with, get next to, patronize, propagate, shine up to 10 discipline, take care of
again: 5 rehoe 6 replow, retill
fit to ~: 6 arable
cultivated: 4 nice, tame 5 noble, suave 6 urbane 7 elegant, genteel, learned, refined 8 educated, ladylike, lettered,

literate, polished, tasteful, well-bred 9 courteous
earth: 5 tilth
cultivation: 5 taste 6 growth, polish 7 farming, manners, plowing, tillage, tilling 8 agronomy, breeding, civility, delicacy, elegance, literacy
in need of ~: 5 weedy
cultivator: 3 hoe 4 plow 6 farmer, grower, harrow 8 gardener
adjunct: 4 disk
cultural: 6 ethnic 7 refined 8 artistic, refining 9 elevating, enriching, nurturing, uplifting 10 artistical, broadening, civilizing
character: 5 ethic, ethos
group: 6 ethnos
pursuit: 4 arts 5 music, opera 7 theater
cultural __: 3 lag
__-cultural: 5 cross
cultural anthropology: 7 science
Cultural Revolution leader: 3 Mao
culture: 4 race 5 class, ethos, grace, mores, taste 6 polish, values 7 customs, manners, society 8 breeding, delicacy, elegance, folklore, folkways, learning, nobility, noblesse, training, urbanity 9 education, erudition, ethnology, gentility, good taste, tradition 10 perception, refinement
combining form: 5 ethno-
medium: 4 agar 8 agar-agar
sign of ~: 5 poise, taste
starter: 3 api, avi 4 aero, agri, aqua, mari, seri, urbi, vini, viti 5 citri, flori, horti, micro, perma, pisci, silvi 7 counter
culture __: 3 lag 4 area, hero 5 pearl, shock, trait 6 center, factor, medium 7 complex, pattern, vulture
__ culture: 4 fish, pure 6 Corded, tissue, Wessex
__ Culture: 6 Desert 7 Ethical
Culture Club
leader: Boy George
song: Church of the Poison Mind (1983)
Do You Really Want to Hurt Me (1983)
I'll Tumble 4 Ya (1983)
Karma Chameleon (1983)
Miss Me Blind (1984)
Time (1983)
cultured: 4 nice 5 suave 6 mature, polite, urbane 7 courtly, genteel, learned, refined 8 educated, esthetic, finished, highbred, highbrow, ladylike, lettered, literate, polished, tasteful, well-bred 9 scholarly
not ~: 4 non-U 6 coarse
superficially ~: 4 arty 5 artsy
cultured __: 5 pearl
cultureless environment: 5 wilds 6 desert 9 wasteland 10 wilderness
Culture of Cities, The author: Mumford
cultures, science of: 9 ethnology
culver: 4 dove 6 pigeon
__-Culver: 7 Alberto
Culver City: 4 town
locale: 10 California
culvert: 4 duct 5 ditch, drain, gully, sewer 6 gulley, gutter 7 channel, conduit
cum __: 5 laude
cumber: 3 tax 4 load 5 weigh 6 hinder, lumber 9 weigh down
Cumberland: 4 city, town 5 river 6 county
city on the ~: 9 Nashville
locale: 6 Canada 7 England, Ontario 8 Maryland
River locale: 8 Kentucky 9 Tennessee
river to the ~: 5 Stone
Cumberland __: 3 Gap 7 Plateau
cumbersome: 5 bulky, heavy, hefty 6 clumsy, clunky 7 awkward, hulking, massive, onerous, unhandy, weighty 8 unwieldy 9 ponderous, unwieldly, wearisome 10 burdensome, galumphing, oppressive
Cumbrian: 5 range 9 mountains
cumin: 4 herb 5 spice
__ cum laude: 5 magna, summa
cum-laude stat: 3 GPA
cummerbund: 4 belt, sash
site: 5 waist
Cumming, Alan: 5 actor
film: The Anniversary Party (2001)
Get Carter (2000)
Titus (1999)
Urbania (2000)
Cummings: 3 Bob 5 Candy, Quinn 6 Burton, Irving, Robert 9 Constance
cummings, e.e.: 4 poet
work: Eimi
The Enormous Room
him
ViVa
XLI Poems
Cummings, Robert: 5 actor
film: The Accused (1948)
The Devil and Miss Jones (1941)
Dial M for Murder (1954)
It Started With Eve (1941)
Kings Row (1942)
The Lost Moment (1947)
Moon Over Miami (1941)
Reign of Terror (1949)
Saboteur (1942)
Sleep My Love (1948)
Spring Parade (1940)
cumulate: 5 lay by, lay up, merge, store 6 garner
cumulation: 4 heap, mass, pile 5 array, batch, group, hoard, stack, store 6 bundle, corpus, medley 7 cluster, variety 8 increase, pastiche, quantity, treasury 9 aggregate, amassment, anthology, congeries, gathering, potpourri, stockpile 10 assemblage, assortment, collection, depository, hodgepodge, miscellany
cumulative: 7 grouped 9 advancing, aggregate 10 augmenting, collective, increasing, increscent
cumulative __: 6 voting 7 scoring
cumulonimbus: 5 cloud
cumulus: 5 cloud
starter: 4 alto
Cuna: 6 Indian 7 Amerind
fabric: 4 mola
Cunard ship: 4 QE II
cunctation: 5 delay 8 lateness
cunctatious: 4 late 5 tardy
cuneiform: 7 writing
stroke: 5 wedge
cunner: 4 fish
cunning: 3 art, sly 4 arch, cagy, deft, foxy, keen, wily 5 cagey, canny, craft, guile, sharp, skill, slick, smart, wiles 6 acumen, adroit, artful, astute, clever, crafty, deceit, dupery, feline, shifty, shrewd, tricky 7 devious, evasive, furtive, knavery, knavish, knowing 8 dextrous, guileful, keenness, scheming, skillful, slippery, stealthy, strategy, thievish 9 astucious, deceitful, deception, deceptive, designing, dexterous, duplicity, ingenious, insidious, masterful, strategic, underhand 10 serpentine
bit of: 4 wile
not ~: 4 naif 5 naive
one: 3 fox
with ~: 5 slyly
Cunningham: 4 Liam 5 Merce 6 Imogen
Cunning Peasant, The composer: 6 Dvorák
Cuomo: 5 Mario 6 Andrew
Cuore: 3 SUV 8 Daihatsu
cup: 3 mug 4 zarf, zurf 5 calix, drink, glass, grail, mazer, prize 6 beaker, goblet, trophy, trough 7 chalice, tumbler 9 container, demitasse 10 receptacle
ancient Greek: 5 cylix, kylix
assayer's ~: 5 cupel
chemist's ~: 6 beaker
coffee ~: 3 mug
combining form: 5 cotyl-, cyath-, scyph- 6 cotyli-, cotylo-, cyatho-, scyphi-, scypho-
edge: 3 lip, rim
ender: 4 cake 5 board 6 bearer, flower
fraction: 5 ounce
go for the ~: 4 putt
golf ~: 4 hole 5 Ryder
handle: 3 ear
Last Supper ~: 5 Grail
Mideast coffee ~: 4 zarf, zurf 6 finjan
miss the ~: 5 spill
of tea: 3 bag 5 field, thing 7 leaning 9 specialty 10 preference
something 'twixt ~ and lip: 4 slip
starter: 3 egg, eye, tea 4 king 6 butter
tennis ~: 5 Davis
cup __: 5 coral, of tea, plant, shake, towel 6 fungus
__ cup: 4 dice 5 Adam's, assay, Dixie, force, fruit, gourd, grace, spout 6 caudle, claret, double, grease, loving 7 cluster, custard, Elijah's, feeding, painted, scarlet, steeple, stirrup, suction
__ Cup: 3 Tin 5 Davis, Dixie, Ryder, World 6 Walker 7 Stanley
cup and __: 5 cover 6 saucer
cupboard: 5 hutch, shelf 6 closet, larder, pantry 7 cabinet 8 wardrobe 9 furniture
church ~: 5 ambry 6 aumbry 8 armarium
item: 3 can, tin
part: 4 door, knob 5 shelf
__ cupboard: 4 dole 5 court, Dutch, press 6 livery 7 tridarn
Cupertino: 4 city, town
locale: 10 California
Cupid: 4 Amor, Eros 7 love god 8 reindeer 10 matchmaker
colleague: 5 Comet, Vixen 6 Dancer, Dasher, Donder 7 Blitzen, Prancer
master: 5 Santa
mother of ~: 5 Venus
target: 5 heart
weapon: 3 bow 4 dart 5 arrow
__ Cupid: 6 Stupid
cupidinous: 4 avid
cupidity: 4 lust 5 greed 6 hunger 7 avarice, avidity, craving, longing 8 rapacity, voracity 10 grabbiness
Cupid's __: 3 bow 6 arrows
__ cup of tea: 5 not my
cupola: 4 dome 6 belfry 7 furnace, lantern, lookout 9 belvedere
topper: 4 vane
cuppa: 3 tea
Cuppy: 4 Will
cupric __: 7 sulfate
cuprite: 3 ore
cupronickel: 5 alloy
cups
four ~: 5 quart
in one's ~: 5 tipsy
two ~: 4 pint
cup-shaped: 6 dished, hollow
cur: 3 cad, dog, mut, rat 4 heel, mutt, toad, worm 5 canid, churl, feist, knave, rogue, scamp, skunk, snake, sneak, stray, swine 6 bad egg, canine, hybrid, rascal, wretch 7 dastard, lowlife, mongrel, stinker, villain 8 dirty dog 9 miscreant, reprobate, scoundrel, vulgarian 10 blackguard, crossbreed, ne'er-do-well, scapegrace
cur's comment: 3 grr 5 growl
curaçao: 5 drink 8 beverage
ingredient: 4 peel
Curaçao: 3 isl. 4 isle 6 island
neighbor: 5 Aruba 9 Venezuela
port: 10 Willemstad
Curad: 7 bandage
alternative: 3 Ace 7 Band-Aid
curare: 4 inee 5 toxin 8 alkaloid
curassow: 4 bird, fowl
relative: 5 poult, quail, snipe 6 chukar, grouse, peahen, turkey 7 peacock, peafowl 8 moorfowl, pheasant, woodcock 9 partridge 10 guinea fowl, jungle fowl, wild turkey
curate: 4 abbé 5 padre 6 clergy, cleric, father, parson 8 minister, preacher 9 clergyman
curative: 5 tonic 6 iatric 7 healing, medical 8 remedial, salutary, sanative 9 antidotal, healthful, medicinal
curator: 6 keeper 7 manager, steward 8 director, guardian, watchdog 9 caretaker, custodian, organizer
degree: 3 MFA
curb: 3 rim, tie 4 drop, edge, rein, slow, snag, stay, stem, tame 5 brake, check, delay, leash, limit, lower, stint, tie up 6 bridle, dampen, fetter, govern, halter, hamper, hinder, hobble, impede, lessen, modify, muzzle, pull in, reduce, rein in, shrink, stifle, subdue, temper, thwart 7 abstain, contain, control, curtail, cut down, dwindle, fall off, harness, inhibit, refrain, repress, trammel 8 decrease, diminish, hold back, keep from, moderate, obstruct, peter out, preclude, restrain, restrict, straiten, suppress 9 abatement, constrain, constrict, deterrent, hindrance, intercept, restraint 10 constraint, discourage, impediment, keep a lid on, keep in line, limitation
ender: 4 side 5 stone
it: 4 park
curb __: 3 cut 4 ball, roof 6 market, weight 7 service
curbed: 6 pent-up, silent 7 limited 8 reined in
curbside cry: 4 taxi
curch: 5 scarf 8 kerchief
curd: 4 clot 6 casein 7 clabber, clobber, thicken
bean ~: 4 tofu
__ curd: 4 bean
curdle: 4 clot, sour, turn 5 go bad, spoil 6 gelate, go sour, harden 7 acidify, clabber, clobber, congeal, stiffen, thicken 9 coagulate
curdled: 4 sour 5 thick 6 rancid
curds partner: 4 whey
cure: 3 fix 4 heal, mend, salt 5 right, smoke, treat 6 elixir, kipper, pickle, reform, remedy, repair 7 correct, nostrum, panacea, rectify, redress, relieve, restore, therapy 8 antidote, medicine, palliate, preserve 9 alleviate, treatment 10 medication
leather: 3 tan
past ~: 8 hopeless 10 irremedial
something to ~: 3 ham 5 bacon
starter: 3 epi 4 mani, pedi
take the ~: 4 quit 7 refrain
cure-__: 3 all
__ cure: 5 faith, water
curé: 6 father, priest
cure-all: 6 elixir, potion, remedy 7 nostrum, panacea
cured: 9 good as new
cheese: 6 brynza
meat: 5 jerky
Curel: 6 lotion

alternative: 4 Keri 5 Nivea 6 Aveeno 7 Eucerin, Jergens, Pacquin 9 Lubriderm
curer: 6 doctor, healer 9 physician
curfew: 4 bell 7 bedtime 8 deadline 9 nightfall, time limit
after ~: 4 late
maybe: 3 ten 5 ten p.m. 6 eleven 8 eleven p.m., midnight
__ curiae: 5 amici 6 amicus
Curicó: 4 city, town
locale: 5 Chile
Curie: 3 Eve 4 Pole 5 Marie 6 Madame, Pierre
Curie, Marie: 6 Polish 7 chemist 8 Nobelist 9 physicist
daughter: 5 Irene
title: 3 Mme. 6 Madame
Curie, Pierre: 6 French 7 chemist 8 Nobelist 9 physicist
curio: 5 relic 6 bauble, geegaw, trifle 7 antique, bibelot, novelty, trinket, whatnot 8 nicknack, souvenir 9 bric-a-brac, objet d'art 10 knickknack
curios: 5 vertu, virtu
curiosity: 6 marvel, oddity, prying, rarity, regard, wonder 7 anomaly, concern 8 interest, nicknack, nosiness, snooping 9 eagerness, objet d'art, spectacle 10 knickknack, phenomenon, snoopiness
indulge one's ~: 3 ask 8 question
victim: 3 cat
__ Curiosity Shop, The: 3 Old
curious: 3 odd 4 nosy 5 funny, nosey, queer, weird 6 exotic, prying, quaint, snoopy 7 bizarre, oddball, peeping, peering, strange, unusual 8 abnormal, meddling, peculiar, puzzling, singular, uncommon 9 inquiring, quizzical, whimsical 10 interested, meddlesome, mysterious, outlandish, remarkable, unfamiliar
be ~: 3 ask 6 wonder
in a ~ way: 5 oddly
one: 5 asker
Curious George author: 3 Rey
curiously: 9 unusually 10 especially
Curitiba: 4 city, town
locale: 6 Brazil
curium: 5 metal 7 element
curl: 3 set 4 bend, coil, flex, friz, kink, lock, loop, turn, wave, wind 5 crimp, curve, frizz, helix, snake, swirl, tress, twine, twirl, twist, whorl 6 spiral 7 contort, entwine, frizzle, intwine, ringlet, scallop, scollop, sinuate, wreathe 8 flourish, squiggle, undulate 9 convolute, sinuosity
a lip: 4 mock, slam 5 flout, scoff, scorn, smirk, sneer 6 slight 7 grimace, put down, sniff at, snigger 8 ridicule 9 disparage 10 look down on
around: 9 enwreathe
one's hair: 5 alarm, spook 7 horrify, terrify 8 frighten
shoot the ~: 4 surf
up: 4 furl, kink 6 nestle 7 snuggle
__ curl: 3 pin 4 side, spit 7 sausage
curled: 5 round 6 spiral 7 helical
curlew: 4 bird 8 whimbrel 9 shorebird 10 sicklebill
kin: 6 avocet
curlicue: 3 ess 4 coil 5 twist 6 spiral 8 flourish 10 decoration
curling: 4 game, wavy 5 sport 6 spiral
period: 3 end
target: 3 tee
use a ~ iron: 5 crimp
curling __: 4 iron 5 stone, tongs
curl one's __: 3 lip 4 hair
Curl, Robert: 7 chemist 8 Nobelist
curly: 4 wavy 5 kinky, nappy 6 coiled, frizzy, permed 7 frizzly, looping, twisted, winding 9 corkscrew
coiffure: 4 Afro
ender: 3 cue
curly __: 3 top 4 palm
Curly: 6 Howard 7 Lambeau
brother: 3 Moe 5 Shemp
colleague: 5 Larry
Curly __: 3 Sue, Top
curmudgeon: 4 crab 5 churl, crank, cynic, grump 6 grouch 8 grumbler, sourball, sourpuss
word: 3 bah
curmudgeonly: 4 sour 5 surly 6 crusty, stingy 9 crotchety
Curnow, Allen: 4 poet
currant: 5 berry, fruit, shrub 6 raisin
__ currant: 3 red 5 black 6 Alpine, golden, Indian 7 buffalo
currawong: 4 bird
currency: 3 oof 4 bill, cash, gelt, jack, kail, kale, loot, peag, pelf 5 bills, bread, bucks, dough, funds, lucre, money, moola, mopus, pesos, rhino, sewan, usage 6 dinero, do-re-mi, mammon, mazuma, moolah, seawan, silver, specie, wampum, wealth 7 cabbage, capital, dollars, lettuce, ooftish, scratch, shekels 8 banknote, bankroll, cold cash, hard cash, smackers 9 banknotes, frogskins, long green, simoleons 10 greenbacks, green stuff, popularity
convert to ~: 4 cash 6 redeem
premium: 4 agio
substitute: 5 scrip
__ currency: 4 hard 7 managed, reserve
current: 2 AC, DC 3 hep, hip, mod, new, now 4 chic, eddy, flow, live, race, tide, tony, wind 5 draft, drift, faddy, fresh, going, in use, tenor, toney, trend, usual 6 breeze, chi-chi, common, course, El Niño, extant, latest, living, modern, modish, recent, ruling, stream, trendy 7 a la mode, flowing, in style, in vogue, ongoing, popular, present, stylish, topical, updated, voguish 8 accepted, tendency, up-to-date 9 customary, effective, immediate, in fashion, in the news, prevalent 10 all the rage, ebb and flow, in progress, present-day, prevailing, widespread
amount: 3 bal. 7 balance
circular ~: 4 eddy
combining form: 4 rheo- 7 galvano-
discharge: 3 arc
events: 4 news
medium: 4 wire 5 cable
practice: 5 vogue
problem: 5 short, surge
producer: 6 dynamo 9 generator
South American ~: 6 El Niño
starter: 5 cross 7 counter
stay ~: 6 keep up
terminal: 5 anode 7 cathode
unit: 3 amp, ohm 4 volt 6 ampere
with: 4 up on
current __: 4 cost 5 ratio, yield 6 assets, events, return 7 account, affairs, balance, density, limiter
__ current: 3 rip 4 eddy, grid 5 field 6 direct, Guiana 7 account, density
__ Current: 4 Peru 5 Japan 6 Alaska, Arctic, Brazil, Guinea, Rossel, Somali 7 Agulhas, Florida, Okhotsk, Oyashio
currently: 3 now 5 today 8 recently
Currents of Space, The author: Asimov
curriculum: 7 courses, program
range: 4 elhi
section: 4 unit
vitae: 3 bio 4 vita 6 digest, précis, record, résumé 7 outline, summary 8 synopsis
curriculum __: 5 vitae
__ curriculum: 4 core
Currier: 3 Nat 9 Nathaniel
partner: 4 Ives
curry: 4 cook 5 groom 9 condiment
favor: 3 woo 4 fawn 5 court 8 fawn over 9 get next to, insinuate, shine up to
loaded with ~: 3 hot
powder ingredient: 5 cumin
curry __: 5 favor 6 powder
Curry: 3 Tim
currycomb target: 4 mane
Cursa: 4 star
curse: 3 hex, pox 4 bane, damn, jinx, oath 5 swear 6 hoodoo, malign, misery, ordeal, plague, vilify, whammy 7 condemn, epithet, evil eye, profane, scourge, slander, torment, trouble 8 calamity 9 blaspheme, expletive, imprecate, profanity 10 affliction, imputation, infliction, vituperate
cover-up: 5 bleep
one's folly: 3 rue 6 bemoan, bewail, lament, regret, repent
cursed: 6 doomed 7 hapless, hateful, heinous, unblest, unhappy, unlucky 8 devilish, ill-fated, infernal, luckless 9 execrable, ill-omened, possessed, unblessed, unfavored 10 abominable, ill-starred
Curse of the Cat People (1944 film)
cast: Jane Randolph, Simone Simon, Kent Smith
director: Robert Wise
Curse of the Jade Scorpion, The (2001 film)
cast: Woody Allen, Dan Aykroyd, Helen Hunt, Charlize Theron
director: Woody Allen
Curses!: 4 oh no
Curses! __ again!: 6 Foiled
__ Curse, The: 4 Dain
cursing: 8 swearing 9 profanity
cursive: 7 running
cursor: 5 arrow, I-beam 7 flasher, pointer
mover: 5 mouse
cursory: 4 fast 5 brief, hasty, quick, rapid, short, swift 6 casual 7 hurried, offhand, passing, shallow, sketchy 8 careless, fleeting, slapdash 9 desultory, haphazard, momentary, negligent, unheedful 10 last-minute, mechanical, uncritical
curt: 4 rude 5 blunt, brief, brusk, crisp, gruff, huffy, pithy, quick, rough, sharp, short, terse 6 abrupt, snippy, unkind 7 brusque, concise, huffish, laconic, offhand, summary, uncivil 8 cavalier, snappish, snippety, succinct, taciturn 9 impatient 10 peremptory, to the point, ungracious
Curt: 5 Flood, Gowdy 7 Jurgens 9 Schilling
curtail: 3 cut 4 chop, clip, crop, curb, drop, slow, stem, trim 5 elide, limit, lower, prune, slash 6 lessen, narrow, recede, reduce, shrink 7 abridge, commute, compact, cut down, dwindle, fall off, shorten, whittle 8 compress, condense, contract, cut short, decrease, diminish, downsize, minimize, pare down, peter out, restrain, truncate 10 abbreviate
curtailed: 3 cut 5 brief, lower, short 7 partial, sketchy 9 condensed 10 compressed, synopsized
curtailment: 3 cut 7 cutback 8 decrease, shortage, stoppage 9 reduction, restraint
curtain: 4 veil 5 drape, shade 6 screen 7 drapery, secrete 8 portiere
bring down the ~ on: 3 end 6 finish 8 conclude
close a ~: 4 draw
fabric: 4 iron, lace 5 ninon, voile 6 chintz, dimity, Madras, moreen
holder: 3 rod
part: 6 edging
put up a ~: 4 hang
raiser: 4 Act I, play 5 event, intro 6 act one 7 opening, prelude
stage ~: 5 scrim
curtain __: 3 rod 4 call, line, time, wall 6 raiser, speech 7 lecture, shutter
__ curtain: 3 act, air, dog 4 café, draw, drop, fire, iron 5 glass, house, water 6 safety 7 contour, tableau
__ Curtain: 4 Iron, Torn 6 Bamboo
Curtain author: Agatha Christie
curtain-call follower: 6 encore
curtained off: 6 unseen
curtainlike partitions: 4 vela
Curtain of Green, A author: Welty
curtains: 6 the end
like some ~: 4 lacy 5 sheer
Curtin, Jane: 7 actress
film: Coneheads (1993)
role: 5 Allie
TV: 3rd Rock from the Sun, Kate & Allie, Saturday Night Live
Curtis: 3 Dan, Ken, Lee 4 Tony 5 Billy, LeMay 6 Hanson 7 Charles, Strange 8 Jamie Lee, Mayfield 9 Bernhardt
Curtis, Jamie Lee: 7 actress
film: Dominick and Eugene (1988)
Drowning Mona (2000)
Fierce Creatures (1997)
A Fish Called Wanda (1988)
The Fog (1980)
Forever Young (1992)
Grandview, U.S.A. (1984)
Halloween (1978)
Halloween H20: 20 Years Later (1998)
Love Letters (1983)
My Girl (1991)
Perfect (1985)
Prom Night (1980)
The Tailor of Panama (2001)
Terror Train (1980)
Trading Places (1983)
True Lies (1994)
parent: Janet Leigh, Tony
spouse: Christopher Guest
Curtiss: 5 Glenn
Curtis, Tony: 5 actor
film: Beachhead (1954)
Boeing Boeing (1965)
Captain Newman, M.D. (1963)
The Defiant Ones (1958)
Don't Make Waves (1967)
The Great Impostor (1961)
The Great Race (1965)
Houdini (1953)
Insignificance (1985)
Kings Go Forth (1958)
The Last Tycoon (1976)
Lepke (1975)
The List of Adrian Messenger (1963)
Not With My Wife You Don't! (1966)
Operation Petticoat (1959)
The Outsider (1961)
The Rat Race (1960)
Sex and the Single Girl (1964)
Some Like It Hot (1959)
Spartacus (1960)
Sweet Smell of Success (1957)
Trapeze (1956)
Who Was That Lady? (1960)
spouse: Janet Leigh
TV: Vega$
Curtiz, Michael: 8 director
film: 20,000 Years in Sing Sing (1933)
The Adventures of Huckleberry Finn (1960)

The Adventures of Robin Hood (1938)
Angels With Dirty Faces (1938)
Black Fury (1935)
The Breaking Point (1950)
Captain Blood (1935)
Captains of the Clouds (1942)
Casablanca (1942, AA)
The Charge of the Light Brigade (1936)
The Comancheros (1961)
Daughters Courageous (1939)
Dive Bomber (1941)
Dodge City (1939)
Female (1933)
Flamingo Road (1949)
Four Daughters (1938)
Jim Thorpe - All-American (1951)
The Kennel Murder Case (1933)
Kid Galahad (1937)
King Creole (1958)
Life With Father (1947)
The Mad Genius (1931)
Mildred Pierce (1945)
Mission to Moscow (1943)
Night and Day (1946)
The Private Lives of Elizabeth and Essex (1939)
The Proud Rebel (1958)
Romance on the High Seas (1948)
Roughly Speaking (1945)
The Sea Hawk (1940)
The Sea Wolf (1941)
The Story of Will Rogers (1952)
This Is the Army (1943)
The Walking Dead (1936)
White Christmas (1954)
Yankee Doodle Dandy (1942)
Young Man With a Horn (1950)

curtsy: **3** bob, bow, dip, nod **7** gesture **8** girl's bow, greeting, lady's bow **9** reverence
curvature: **3** arc, bow **4** arch, bend **5** shape **7** flexure **10** deflection
curve: **3** arc, bow, ess, sag **4** arch, bend, coil, curl, flex, hook, loop, ogee, turn, veer, warp, wind **5** crook, orbit, pitch, snake, sweep, swing, twist, whorl **6** camber, circle, slider, spiral **7** contour, ellipse, rainbow, scallop, scollop, sinuate **8** parabola **9** concavity, hyperbola, sinuosity **10** trajectory
double ~: **3** ess **4** ogee
ender: **4** ball
hairpin ~: **3** zag, zig
overhead ~: **4** arch
throw a ~: **4** stun **6** delude **7** stupefy **8** misquote, surprise
curve __: **4** ball **7** fitting
__ curve: **4** bell, sine **5** level, light, Peano **6** French, Jordan, Laffer, normal **7** caustic, derived, reverse
curveball: **4** ruse **5** pitch **8** surprise
curved: **4** bent **5** bandy, round, snaky **6** swirly **7** concave, sigmoid, sinuous, S-shaped **8** aquiline, circular, flexuous **9** sigmoidal **10** elliptical, serpentine
combining form: **4** cyrt- **5** cyrto- **6** campto- **7** -tropous
letter: **3** ess
line: **3** arc
molding: **4** ogee
not ~: **8** straight
outward: **6** convex
roof: **6** cupola
travel a ~ path: **3** arc **4** ring **5** orbit
curvet: **4** jump, leap
curving: **4** wavy **7** flexure, winding **8** tortuous
inward, as a beak: **5** adunc
curvy: **4** wavy **5** arced, round **7** sinuous, winding
Cusack: **4** Joan, John **5** Cyril
Cusack, Joan: **5** actress
film: Addams Family Values (1993)
Corrina, Corrina (1994)
Cradle Will Rock (1999)
Grosse Pointe Blank (1997)
Hero (1992)
In & Out (1997)
Married to the Mob (1988)
Men Don't Leave (1990)
Mr. Wrong (1996)
My Blue Heaven (1990)
Nine Months (1995)
Runaway Bride (1999)
Working Girl (1988)
Cusack, John: **5** actor
film: America's Sweethearts (2001)
Being John Malkovich (1999)
Bullets Over Broadway (1994)
City Hall (1996)
Con Air (1997)
Cradle Will Rock (1999)
Eight Men Out (1988)
Fat Man and Little Boy (1989)
Floundering (1994)
The Grifters (1990)
Grosse Pointe Blank (1997)
High Fidelity (2000)
The Journey of Natty Gann (1985)
Midnight in the Garden of Good and Evil (1997)
Pushing Tin (1999)
The Road to Wellville (1994)
Say Anything ... (1989)
Serendipity (2001)
Shadows and Fog (1992)
Cush
father of ~: **3** Ham
grandfather of ~: **4** Noah
son of ~: **6** Nimrod
cushaw: **6** squash **9** vegetable
Cushing: **4** font **5** Peter **8** Cardinal, typeface
Cushing, Peter: **5** actor
film: The Beast Must Die (1974)
The Creeping Flesh (1973)
Revenge of Frankenstein (1958)
The Risk (1960)
Star Wars (1977)
cushion: **3** mat, pad **4** seat **5** break **6** buffer, deaden, muffle, pillow **7** beanbag, hassock, mollify, padding, protect **8** headrest
Buddhist meditation ~: **4** zafu
fix a ~: **5** repad
starter: **3** pin
cushion __: **3** cut **4** pink **6** rafter
__ cushion: **3** air **7** whoopee, whoopie
__-cushioned: **3** air
cushionlike seat: **4** pouf
cushiony: **4** soft **5** downy, furry, nappy, plush **6** fleecy, fluffy, spongy **7** squishy, velvety
cushy: **4** cosy, cozy, easy, lush, plum, snug, soft **5** comfy, cozey, cozie, downy **6** simple **8** duck soup, painless **10** child's play, effortless, unexacting
job: **4** plum
cusk: **4** fish
cusk __: **3** eel
cusp: **3** end, tip, top **4** apex **5** point, wedge **6** height, tipoff
cuspid: **5** tooth **6** canine
cuspidor, sound near a: **4** ptui
cuss: **5** swear **6** geezer, vilify **7** profane **9** blaspheme, expletive
cussing: **4** vice **8** swearing **9** profanity
Cussler, Clive: **6** author **8** novelist
hero: Dirk Pitt
work: Atlantis Found
Blue Gold
Cyclops
Deep Six
Dragon
Fire Ice
Flood Tide
Golden Buddha
Iceberg
Inca Gold
Mayday
The Mediterranean Caper
Night Probe
Pacific Vortex
Raise the Titanic
Sahara
The Sea Hunters
Serpent
Shockwave
Treasure
Trojan Odyssey
Valhalla Rising
White Death
cussword: **4** oath **9** profanity
custard: **4** flan **6** junket **7** dessert, pudding **8** flummery
apple: **5** papaw **6** pawpaw
ingredient: **3** egg **4** yolk
like ~: **4** eggy **5** yolky
custard __: **3** cup, pie **5** apple
__ custard: **6** frozen
Custer: **4** city, town **6** George **10** Yellowhair
colleague: **4** Reno
horse: **8** Comanche
locale: **4** S. Dak.
Custer's __ Stand: **4** Last
custodial: **10** protective
custodian: **5** super **6** keeper, warden **7** curator, janitor, manager, steward **8** executor, guardian, overseer, watchdog **9** attendant, bodyguard, caretaker, concierge, protector **10** baby sitter, doorkeeper, supervisor
of goods: **6** bailee
custody: **4** care, egis **5** aegis, trust **6** arrest, charge, escrow **7** jailing, keeping **8** auspices, clutches, wardship **9** detention, oversight **10** internment, possession, protection
give ~: **7** entrust, intrust
have ~ of: **4** keep
in ~: **6** jailed **7** captive
keep in ~: **4** hold, jail **6** arrest, detain, immure, intern, lock up, remand **7** confine, impound, put away **8** imprison, sentence
one in ~: **4** ward
release from ~: **4** bail
take into ~: **3** nab **4** book, nail **5** pinch, run in, seize **6** arrest **9** apprehend
custom: **3** rut, tax, use, way **4** form, levy, mode, rule, wont **5** habit, style, usage, vogue **6** impost, manner, method, policy, praxis, ritual, system, towage **7** fashion, pattern, routine **8** ceremony, exaction, folkways, habitude, localism, practice **9** etiquette, formality, patronage, precedent, procedure **10** convention, observance, stereotype
according to ~: **7** à la mode, usually
combining form: **4** nomo-
house: **6** douane
custom __: **5** house
custom-__: **4** made, make **5** build, built, order **6** tailor
Custom: **3** car **4** auto, Ford
customarily: **3** usu. **6** mostly **7** as a rule, as usual, usually **9** naturally
customary: **3** set **5** stock, typic, usual **6** common, normal, proper, wonted **7** average, current, general, natural, popular, regular, routine, typical **8** accepted, everyday, familiar, frequent, habitual, ordinary, orthodox, standard **9** confirmed, household, prevalent, universal, unwritten **10** accustomed, inveterate, legitimate, prevailing, recognized, regulation, stipulated, understood
in French: **7** de règle
practice: **4** rite **5** habit
customer: **5** buyer, guest, taker **6** client, emptor, patron, person, vendee **7** account, habitué, shopper **8** consumer, purchase **10** frequenter
be a ~: **8** frequent **9** patronize
with a ~: **4** busy
__ customer: **4** cash, ugly **5** tough **6** one to a
customers, admitting: **4** open
customize: **6** modify **7** reshape
Customline: **3** car **4** auto, Ford
custom-made: **5** fancy **8** tailored
customs: **4** lore, ways **5** mores **6** morals, praxes **7** culture **8** folkways, protocol **9** ethnology, tradition **10** ins and outs
charge: **3** tax **4** duty **6** impost
document: **6** carnet
duty: **3** tax **6** impost
customs __: **5** house, union **6** broker
custos morum: **6** censor
cut: **2** ax **3** axe, hew, jag, lop, lot, mow, rip, saw **4** barb, chip, chop, clip, crop, dice, edit, fall, gash, hack, hurt, kerf, nick, omit, pare, part, reap, rift, sawn, skip, slab, slit, slot, snip, snub, stab, take, tear, trim, verb, wage **5** carve, cleft, crack, erase, gouge, lower, lunge, mince, notch, piece, prune, quota, score, sever, share, shave, shear, shorn, shred, slash, slice, snick, spurn, stamp, style, taunt, wages, wound **6** bisect, boo-boo, censor, chisel, cleave, delete, digest, dilute, divide, excise, furrow, groove, gullet, hairdo, incise, injury, insult, kidney, lesion, lessen, mangle, parcel, pierce, ration, ravine, rebuff, record, reduce, revise, slight, spoils, tamper, trench, weaken **7** abridge, curtail, diluted, expunge, fashion, fissure, incised, injured, jobbery, offense, opening, partial, percent, portion, put-down, reduced, sarcasm, scissor, scratch, section, segment, sketchy **8** abridged, cleavage, clipping, close out, condense, decrease, deletion, detached, diminish, dividend, division, excision, fraction, incision, kickback, lacerate, leave out, lowering, mark down, puncture, sundered, truncate **9** allotment, allowance, broken off, capsulize, condensed, curtailed, decrement, expurgate, hairstyle, indignity, interrupt, intersect, lacerated, lessening, ostracize, perforate, reduction, sculpture, selection, shortened, telescope, water down **10** adulterate, commission, compressed, diminished, diminution, diminution, expurgated, interspace, laceration, percentage, proportion, synopsized, unfinished
a ~ above: **4** rare **8** superior **9** unrivaled **10** unrivalled
across: **8** go beyond, traverse **9** intersect, transcend
a deal: **5** agree **9** acquiesce, negotiate
again: **5** remow, resaw
along: **5** speed
and dried: **4** dull **5** fixed, trite **6** boring **7** settled **9** hackneyed, wearisome **10** unoriginal
and paste: **4** edit
and run: **3** fly **4** flee, part **5** break **6** depart, desert, escape **7** abscond, go south, make off **8** fugitate, turn tail
apart: **5** sever **8** separate
a rug: **5** dance
back: **4** clip, pare, slow, snip, thin, trim **5** limit, lower, prune, shave, shear, skimp, slash **6** lessen, reduce **7** curtail, shorten **8** conserve, downsize, lessened **9** condensed

10 abbreviate, compressed, synopsized
barely ~: 4 nick
beef ~: 4 chop, loin, rump 5 chuck, filet, flank, roast, round, shank, steak, T-bone 6 fillet 7 sirloin 10 tenderloin
clear ~: 7 obvious 8 apparent
closely: 4 crop
cold ~: 3 ham 4 meat 6 salami 7 bologna 8 pastrami 10 corned beef
combining form: 4 -sect, tomo- 6 -tomous
corners: 4 save 5 skimp, stint 6 scrimp 8 retrench 9 economize 10 underspend
deep ~: 4 gash
down: 2 ax 3 axe, hew 4 curb, drop, fell, slow, trim 5 abase, abate, limit, lower, shave, slash 6 hack up, lessen, reduce, shrink 7 curtail, distill, dwindle, fall off, hack off, lighten, shorten 8 decrease, diminish, hack down, peter out, simplify 9 condensed, economize, summarize 10 abbreviate, compressed
down to size: 5 shame 6 demean, humble 7 deflate 8 belittle, minimize 9 humiliate
drastically: 5 slash
ender: 3 off, out 4 away, back, over, work, worm 5 grass, purse, water 6 throat
ice: 5 count 6 matter
in: 5 share 7 intrude 9 interpose, interrupt
into: 4 etch, snip 5 notch 6 incise 7 incised
into logs: 5 saw up
into small pieces: 5 mince, shred
in two: 5 halve, sever 6 bisect 8 separate
in zigzags: 4 pink
it may be ~: 4 deck 5 price, slack
it out: 4 quit, stop 5 cease 6 desist
lesser ~ usually: 5 side B
loose: 4 free 5 let go, revel 6 escape, untied 7 abandon, run wild 9 disengage
make the ~: 6 hack it 7 qualify, survive
narrow ~: 4 slit
not ~ out for: 5 unfit 6 unable
oblique ~: 5 bevel, miter
off: 3 end, lop, top 4 crop, pare, part, skin, snip, stem, trim 5 apart, block, sever, shave, shear, split 6 cleave, detach, disown, divide, excise, hang up, impede, unlink 7 disjoin, insular, isolate, silence, split up 8 disunite, obstruct, secluded, separate, set apart, suppress, uncouple 9 condensed, intercept, interrupt, segregate, sequester, terminate 10 abbreviate, compressed, disconnect, disinherit
off (from): 4 wean
old-style: 4 snee
open: 4 slit, torn 5 lance
out: 3 run 4 bolt, clip, flee, omit, quit, stop, trim 5 break, cease, erase, leave, split, usurp 6 delete, depart, excide, excise, exsect, remove 7 exscind, make off 8 fugitate, run for it 9 eliminate, extirpate, skedaddle 10 abbreviate
partner: 3 run 5 paste
price ~: 6 saving 8 discount
razor ~: 2 do 4 coif 8 coiffure
roughly: 6 hackle, heckle 7 hatchel
saw ~: 4 kerf
short: 3 bob, end, nip 4 crop, ruin, stop 5 abort, elide, shave 7 curtail, silence, suspend 9 condensed, interrupt, telescope, terminate 10 compressed, synopsized, unfinished
short ~: 3 bob 5 route 6 byroad
slanting ~: 4 bias
small ~: 4 snip
some slack: 6 relent
staff ~: 3 RIF 6 layoff
starter: 4 crew, hair, wood 5 cross, short, upper
take a ~: 5 swing
the grass: 3 mow 4 trim
through: 6 pierce
timber: 3 hew, log, saw
to bits: 9 criticize, pick apart
to fit: 4 trim 5 adapt 6 tailor
too close: 5 scalp
to the quick: 4 slur 5 wound 6 insult
treatment: 6 iodine
trees: 3 hew, saw 4 chop, fell
up: 4 chop, dice, hurt, joke, romp, slur 5 carve, divvy 6 defame, divide 7 dissect, quarter 9 apportion, criticize, misbehave, partition
venison ~: 4 rump, side 5 flank, thigh
cut ___: 3 off, out 4 a rug, back, down, drop, nail, rate, time 5 a deal, glass, grass, loose, no ice, short, stone 6 across, flower, square, velvet 7 corners
cut ___ chase: 5 to the
cut ___ for: 3 out
cut ___ on: 4 back, down
cut ___ quick: 5 to the
cut ___ swath: 5 a wide
cut ___ to size: 4 down
cut ___ ways: 4 both
cut-___: 4 pile, rate
___ cut: 4 burr, cold, crew, curb, jump, line, star, step, trap 5 brush, Dutch, eight, final, price, rough, table 6 branch, lentil, modern, single 7 cushion, emerald
___-cut: 4 card, fast, fine, full, open 5 clean, clear, sharp, short 6 double, French
___ Cut: 5 Prime 7 Culebra
cut a ___: 3 rug 5 caper, swath 6 figure
cut a ___ swath: 4 wide
cut and ___: 4 fill 5 paste
cut-and-___: 3 dry, try 5 cover, dried, paste
cut-and-dried: 5 usual 8 methodic
cut and paste: 4 edit
cutaneous: 6 dermal, dermic
cutaway: 4 coat 6 jacket
cutaway ___: 4 coat, dive, shot
cut a wide ___: 5 swath
cutback: 3 RIF 6 layoff 7 decline 8 decrease, lowering 9 abatement, decrement, lessening, reduction 10 diminution
cut both ___: 4 ways
cut down to ___: 4 size
cute: 4 pert 5 bonny, ducky, perky 6 bonnie, clever, comely, dainty, lovely, pretty, quaint, shrewd 7 darling, winning, winsome 8 adorable, alluring, becoming, charming, gorgeous, handsome, precious, striking, stunning 9 appealing, baby-faced, beautiful, ravishing 10 attractive
cute ___ button: 3 as a
cutesy: 3 coy 8 affected, too sweet
cutesy ___: 3 pie
cutesy-___: 3 poo
Cuthbert: 5 saint
cutie: 2 jo 3 pet 4 baby, dear, dish, doll, jill, love 5 amour, angel, chéri, cooky, deary, ducky, flame, honey, leman, lover, lovey, novia, novio, sugar, sweet 6 bon ami, chérie, cookie, dautie, dearie, steady, sweets 7 beloved, charmer, dearest, dear one, pigsney, schatzi, squeeze, sweetie, tootsie 8 chou-chou, dowsabel, dulcinea, ladylove, lovebird, macushla, paramour, precious, snookums, sugar pie, sweetums, truelove 9 bonne amie, boyfriend, dreamboat, inamorata, inamorato, petit chou, valentine 10 girlfriend, heartthrob, honeybunch, mavourneen, sweetheart, sweetie pie, turtledove
cutie ___: 3 pie
cutis ___: 4 vera
cutlass: 5 blade, knife, sword 6 dagger 7 sidearm
cousin: 4 épée 5 saber
material: 5 steel
Cutlass: 3 car 4 auto, Olds 10 automobile, Oldsmobile
cutler product: 5 knife
Cutler Ridge: 4 city, town
locale: 7 Florida
cutlery: 6 knives
metal: 5 steel
cutlet: 4 meat, veal
Cut me some ___!: 5 slack
cut no ___: 3 ice
cutoff: 4 halt, stop 6 recess 7 due date 8 deadline, stoppage 9 cessation 10 suspension
point: 5 limit, valve
cutoffs: 6 denims, shorts
cut one's ___: 6 losses
cut one's ___ on: 5 teeth
cut out ___: 3 for
cutout dress originator: 4 Erté
cutpurse: 3 dip 5 thief 10 pickpocket
cut-rate: 3 low 5 cheap 6 on sale 7 bargain, good buy, low-cost 8 moderate, uncostly 9 half-price, low-priced 10 economical, reasonable
___ cuts: 4 cold
cutter: 3 axe, saw 4 boat 5 knife, mower, parer, razor 6 barber, shears, stylus
combining form: 4 -tome
control a ~: 5 steer
cousin: 5 sloop
starter: 4 hair, wood 5 stone
wave ~: 4 prow
cutter ___: 3 bar 4 deck
___ cutter: 4 cane, coal, pipe, weed, wire 5 cooky, crown, glass, paper 6 cookie 7 Bermuda, revenue
___-cutter: 3 rug 5 daisy, plant
Cut that out!: 4 stop 6 quit it, stop it
cut the ___: 7 mustard
cutthroat: 4 mean 5 cruel, harsh, nasty, trout 6 animal, brutal, fierce, killer, savage, unkind, wanton 7 beastly, callous, hurtful, vicious 8 barbaric, fiendish, inhumane, murderer, pitiless, ruthless, sadistic, vengeful 9 barbarous, desperado, dog-eat-dog, ferocious, merciless, monstrous, truculent, unpitying 10 relentless, vindictive
cutthroat ___: 5 trout 6 bridge
Cutthroat Island (1995 film)
cast: Geena Davis, Frank Langella, Matthew Modine
director: Renny Harlin
cutting: 3 dry, raw 4 acid, cold, keen, slab, snip, sour, tart 5 acute, nasty, plant, sharp, shoot, snide, sprig, tight 6 barbed, biting, bitter, severe, shrewd 7 acerbic, caustic, hateful, hurtful, ice-cold, intense, mordant, pointed, satiric 8 abrasive, clipping, critical, incisive, sardonic, scathing, stinging, virulent 9 corrosive, malicious, offensive, quotation, sarcastic, satirical, trenchant 10 astringent
affix a ~: 5 graft
combining form: 4 -tomy
edge: 3 new 4 lead 6 modern 7 current 8 advanced, up-to-date, vanguard
remark: 3 dig 4 barb 7 sarcasm
room figure: 6 editor
tool: 3 axe, die, saw 5 blade, knife 6 bowsaw, stylus
up: 8 division 10 dissection
utensil: 5 parer
cutting ___: 3 oil 4 edge, room 5 board, fluid, horse 6 garden, stylus
___ cutting: 5 price
___-cutting: 4 cost, free
cuttlefish
cousin: 5 squid 7 octopus
defense: 3 ink
organ: 6 ink sac
pigment: 5 sepia
cut to ___: 6 shreds 7 ribbons
cut to the ___: 4 bone 5 chase, quick
Cutty Sark: 4 boat, ship
cutup: 3 imp, wag 4 card, zany 5 clown, comic, joker 6 fooler, jester 8 comedian, funnyman, humorist, kibitzer 9 leg-puller, prankster
cutworm: 5 larva
Cuvier: 7 Georges
Cuxhaven: 4 port
locale: 7 Germany
river: 4 Elbe
Cuyahoga, city on the: 9 Cleveland
Cuyahoga Falls: 4 city, town
locale: 4 Ohio
Cuyler, Kiki: 10 outfielder
Cuzco: 4 city, peak, town 5 mount 8 mountain
dweller: 4 Inca 5 Incan
locale: 4 Peru 5 Andes
see also Spanish
C.W.: 6 McCall
Post is part of it: 3 LIU
cwm: 5 basin 6 cirque, valley
CWO employer: 3 USN
C&W showplace: 4 Opry
Cy: 5 Young 7 Coleman 8 Endfield
cyan: 4 blue 5 green 8 greenish 9 blue-green
relative: 3 pea 4 anil, jade, navy, Nile, sage, teal 5 Alice, azure, beryl, breen, olive, slate, virid 6 cobalt, indigo, myrtle, raisin, reseda, violet 7 avocado, celadon, emerald, peacock, verdant 8 cerulean, sapphire 9 pistachio, turquoise 10 aquamarine, chartreuse, periwinkle
___ cyanide: 6 copper, sodium 7 cuprous
Cybele: 8 asteroid
son of ~: 5 Midas
cyber-bidders site: 4 eBay
cyber-crook: 6 hacker
cyber-guffaw: 3 LOL
cyberhead place: 3 net, Web 8 Internet
cyberphobe fear: 9 computers
cyber-shopping, place for: 5 e-mall
cyberspace: 3 Web 8 Internet
address: 3 URL
conversation: 4 chat
enter ~: 5 log in, log on
frequenter: 4 user
inits.: 3 AOL
junk mail: 4 spam
messages: 5 e-mail
return from ~: 6 log off
cyber tycoon: 5 Gates
Cybill: 8 Shepherd
Cybill character: 3 Ira
cyborg: 7 RoboCop
science: 7 bionics
Cyclades: 4 isls. 5 isles 7 islands
island: 3 Kea, Zea 4 Keos, Milo 5 Delos, Melos, Milos, Naxos, Paros, Thera, Thira 8 Santorin 9 Santorini
largest of the ~: 5 Naxos
locale: 5 Egean 6 Aegean
neighbor: 5 Crete 6 Candia
cyclamen: 5 plant 6 flower

cyclas: **4** robe **5** tunic **7** surcoat
cycle: **3** age, era, hog, run **4** bike, life, ring, turn **5** pedal, phase, recur, round, trike, wheel **6** Harley, period, series **7** routine **8** sequence, ten-speed **10** procession, revolution, succession, two-wheeler
billing ~: **5** month
kin: **5** moped
laundry ~: **4** soak, spin, wash **5** rinse
part: **5** phase
solar ~: **4** year
starter: **3** epi, tri, uni **4** giga, hemi, kilo, mega, mini, mono **5** motor **6** quadri
cycle __: **4** shop **7** billing
__ cycle: **4** cell, life, Otto, push, song **5** Krebs, lunar, solar **6** carbon, Carnot, diesel, Fenian, oxygen, Sothic **7** billing, cardiac, Metonic, Rankine, sunspot
__ Cycle: **4** Ring
cyclical: **7** regular **8** periodic **9** recurrent, recurring
in a way: **5** tidal
cycling: **5** sport
cyclist: **5** biker
need: **4** bike **6** helmet
cycloid section: **3** arc
cyclone: **4** gale, gust, wind **5** storm **7** tempest, tornado, twister **9** hurricane, whirlwind, windstorm
center: **3** eye
refuge: **6** cellar
cyclone __: **6** cellar **7** furnace
__ cyclone: **4** kona, wave **7** frontal
Cyclone __: **5** fence
Cyclones home: **4** Ames, Iowa
Cyclopean: **3** big **4** huge **5** giant, jumbo **7** immense **8** colossal, gigantic
cyclopedia: **4** book, list **7** lexicon **9** reference **10** dictionary
Cyclops: **5** Arges, giant **7** Acamans, Brontes, monster **8** Elatreus, Euryalus, Pyracmon, Steropes, Trachius **9** Argilipus, Halimedes **10** Polyphemus
had one: **3** eye
parent: **4** Gaea **6** Uranus
Cyclops author: Euripides
cyclotron target: **4** atom
Cyd: **8** Charisse
hubby: **4** Tony
Cydnus: **5** river
locale: **9** Asia Minor
cygnet: **4** bird **8** nestling **9** fledgling
parent: **3** cob, pen **4** swan
Cygnus: **4** swan
neighbor: **4** Lyra **6** Aquila
star in ~: **5** Deneb
cylinder: **3** rod **4** pipe, roll, tube
metal ~: **6** gabion
cylinder __: **3** saw **4** desk, head, seal **5** block, front, glass, press
__ cylinder: **3** air **5** pitch **6** master **7** central
__ cylinders: **5** on all
cylinders, firing on all: **4** sane
cylindrical: **5** round, tubal
container: **4** cask **6** barrel
fastener: **5** dowel
instrument: **4** oboe
structure: **4** silo
cyma __: **5** recta **7** reversa
cymbal: **3** zil **10** instrument
finger ~: **4** zill
relative: **4** gong
sound: **5** clang, clash
cymbalom: **6** string **8** dulcimer
origin: **7** Hungary
cymbals: **5** hi-hat **6** piatti **7** crotale, high-hat **8** ceng ceng **10** percussion
of India: **3** tal
Cymbeline author: Shakespeare
character: **6** Cloten, Imogen **7** Pisanio
song: **5** dirge
Cymric: **5** Welsh
Cymry: **5** Welsh
Cynda: **8** Williams
Cyndi: **6** Lauper
Cynewulf: **4** poet
cynic: **7** doubter, killjoy, sceptic, scoffer, skeptic **8** naysayer **9** pessimist **10** curmudgeon, questioner
response: **4** I bet, sure
cynical: **3** dry, wry **4** sour **6** bitter, crabby **7** mocking, satiric **8** doubtful, negative, sardonic, scornful, sneering **9** resistive, sarcastic, satirical, skeptical **10** suspicious
look: **5** sneer
cynicism: **7** dim view, sarcasm **8** glumness **9** nonbelief, pessimism, suspicion
cynophobe fear: **4** dogs
cynosure: **4** hero **5** focus **6** center, leader **7** paragon **8** lodestar, polestar **10** apotheosis, focal point
Cynthia: **4** Gibb, moon, poem **5** Geary, Ozick, Scott, Sikes **7** Gregory
Cynthia author: Walter Raleigh
cypress: **4** tree **7** juniper **8** sandarac **9** evergreen **10** arborvitae
growth: **4** knee
Japanese ~: **6** hinoki
Cypress: **4** city, town
locale: **10** California
Cypress Gardens locale: **3** Fla. **7** Florida
cyprinoid fish: **3** ide
Cyprus: **3** isl. **4** isle **6** island, nation **7** country
capital: **7** Nicosia
city: **6** Paphos **7** Nicosia
locale: **5** Medit.
money: **4** cent
wine: **7** retsina
Cyrano
friend of ~: **6** LeBret
prominent feature: **4** nose
Cyrano de Bergerac: **4** film, play
author: Edmond Rostand
cast: José Ferrer, Mala Powers, William Prince
director: Michael Gordon
Cyril: **5** saint **6** Cusack **8** Connelly, Ritchard **9** Kornbluth
Cyrus: **5** Vance **9** McCormick
cyst: **3** sac, wen **4** bleb **7** blister, vesicle
Cy Young __: **5** Award
C.Z.: **5** Guest
czar: **4** king, male **5** baron, mogul, ruler **6** despot, dynast, gerent, leader, tyrant **7** emperor, magnate, monarch **8** autocrat, kingfish, overlord **9** authority, commander, potentate, sovereign
decree: **5** ukase
ender: **3** dom, ina, ist
parliament: **4** Duma
Russian ~: **4** Ivan, Paul **5** Ivan V, Paul I, Peter **6** Feodor, Ivan IV, Ivan VI, Peter I **7** Feodor I, Ivan III, Peter II, Romanov **8** Nicholas, Peter III **9** Alexander **10** Alexander I
czardas: **5** dance **9** Hungarian
czarina: **5** noble, queen, ruler **6** gerent
Czech: **4** Slav **8** Bohemian, language, Moravian, Silesian
Czech Republic: **6** nation **7** country
capital: **5** Praha **6** Prague
city: **4** Brno **5** Plzen, Praha, Tábor **6** Prague **7** Ostrava
composer: **6** Dvorák **7** Smetana
conductor: **5** Adler **7** Kubelik
export: **5** glass **7** crystal
leader: **5** Benes, Havel **6** Dubcek **7** Masaryk
money: **6** korona, koruna
mountain: **3** Erz **6** Snezka **7** Sudeten
neighbor: **6** Poland **7** Austria, Germany **8** Slovakia
Nobelist in Chemistry: **9** Heyrovsky
Nobelist in Literature: **7** Seifert
org.: **4** NATO
playwright: **5** Capek, Havel **7** Jirásek
play written in ~: **3** R.U.R.
poet: **5** Havel, Holub **6** Neruda **7** Seifert
publisher: **8** Koudelka
river: **4** Eger, Elbe, Hron, Iser, Oder, odra, Ohre
runner: **7** Zatopek
tennis pro: **5** Kodes, Lendl **10** Mandlikova **11** Navratilova
violinist: **7** Kubelik
writer: **5** Capek, Hasek, Klíma **6** Hrabal **7** Jirásek, Kundera **9** Skvorecky
Czech Suite composer: **6** Dvorák
Czerny: **4** Carl, Karl **5** Henry

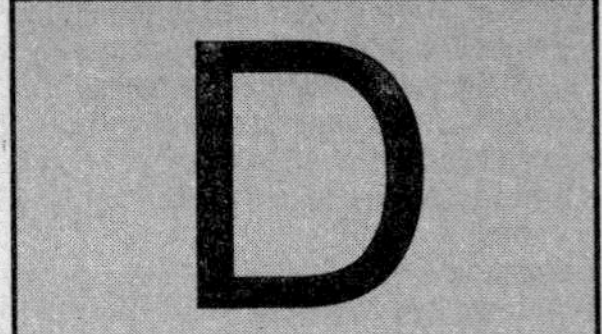

d __: 5 quark
__ d': 6 maître
D: 3 ltr., vit. 4 cell, mark 5 grade, width 6 letter 7 vitamin
flat alias: 6 C sharp
get a ~: 4 pass
get below ~: 5 flunk
in code: 5 delta
D __: 4 ring 5 layer, meson 7 battery
D __ day: 4 as in
D-__: 3 Day 4 Mark 6 notice
D. __: 3 Lit., Mus. 4 Litt., Surg.
__ D: 3 Big 4 Mike, R and 7 vitamin
'D' __ Deadbeat: 5 Is for
__-D: 5 three
da: 2 ay, ja, sí 3 aye, oui, yea, yep, yup 4 fine, okay, sure, yeah 5 good-o, natch, quite, right, roger, uh-huh 6 agreed, gladly, good-oh, indeed, just so, rather, righto, surely, you bet, yowzah 7 exactly, go ahead, indeedy, mais oui, quite so, ten-four 8 all right, as you say, of course, thumbs up, very well 9 be my guest, certainly, darn right, naturally, precisely, sure thing, you betcha, you said it 10 absolutely, by all means, definitely, positively, sure enough, that's right
opposite: 4 nyet
da __: 4 capo
__-da: 4 la-de, la-di
Da __ Ron Ron: 3 Doo
Da __, Vietnam: 4 Nang
DA: 6 hairdo
degree: 2 JD
org.: 3 ABA
part of ~: 3 att. 4 atty., dist. 8 attorney, district
quest: 5 proof
__ D.A.: 4 asst.
Daalder: 5 Renee
dab: 3 bit, pat 4 blob, drop, fish, lick, lump, spot, wipe 5 fleck, flick, rub on, smear, speck, touch, trace 6 dollop, expert, little, smudge 7 besmear, driblet, minimum, smidgen, smidgin, soupçon 8 flatfish, flounder, smidgeon
a ~ hand: 8 skillful
ender: 5 chick
preceder: 5 smack
smack ~: 8 directly
dab __: 4 hand
__ Daba Honeymoon, The: 3 Aba
__-dabba: 4 abba
__ dabba doo!: 5 Yabba
dabble: 5 dally 6 fiddle, loiter, paddle, play at, putter, splash, tinker, trifle 10 fool around, mess around, play around
dabbler: 4 tiro, tyro 5 toyer 6 novice 7 amateur 8 beginner, putterer, tinkerer 9 greenhorn 10 dilettante, uninitiate
dabbling duck: 4 fowl
relative: 4 smew, teal 5 eider, Pekin, Rouen, scaup 6 Cayuga, scoter 7 gadwall, mallard, pintail, pochard, redhead, widgeon 8 garganey, mandarin, oldsquaw, shoveler 9 broadbill, goldeneye, goosander, greenhead, merganser, sprigtail 10 bufflehead, canvasback, surf scoter
dabchick: 4 bird 8 didapper
Dabih: 4 star
__ dab'll do ya, A: 6 little
Dabney: 7 Coleman
d'Abo: 6 Maryam, Olivia
__ da braccio: 4 lira 5 viola
d'Abruzzo, Alphonso: 4 Alda
__ da capo: 4 aria
Dacca: 4 city, town 7 capital
locale: 10 Bangladesh
dace: 4 bait, fish 6 minnow
dacha: 6 estate 9 residence
dachshund: 3 dog, pet 5 pooch 6 canine
like a ~: 3 low
__ Dachshund, The: 4 Ugly
Dacia, people of ancient: 4 Avar
DaCosta: 6 Morton
dacquoise: 4 cake 7 dessert
Dacron: 5 fiber 6 fabric 9 polyester
dactyl: 3 toe 4 foot 5 digit 6 finger
relative: 4 iamb 7 anapest, pyrrhic, spondee, trochee
starter: 5 ptero
__ da Cunha: 7 Tristan 8 Euclides
dad: 2 pa 3 pop 4 male, papa, pops, sire 5 pappy, pater, poppa 6 father, old man, parent 8 relative
brother of ~: 3 unc, unk 5 uncle
dad of ~: 5 gramp 6 gramps 7 grandpa
in French: 4 père
mate: 3 mom
mom of ~: 4 nana 7 grandma
related on ~ 's side: 6 agnate
starter: 5 grand
dad-__: 3 gum 6 blamed, burned, gummed 7 blasted
__ Dad: 5 Major
dada: 4 papa 8 baby talk
Dada
artist: 3 Arp, Ray 4 Erté 5 Ernst 6 Man Ray 7 Duchamp, Hans Arp, Jean Arp
ender: 3 ism
__ Dada: 7 Idi Amin
da-DAH: 4 iamb
dadaiko: 4 drum
origin: 5 Japan
daddy: 2 pa 3 pop 4 male, papa, pops 5 poppa 6 father
longlegs: 3 bug 6 insect
mate: 5 mommy 6 mommie
sis: 5 aunty 6 auntie
starter: 5 grand
Daddy __ Legs: 4 Long
__ Daddy: 3 Big 4 Puff 5 Sugar
Daddy author: Danielle Steel
Daddy Don't You Walk So Fast (1972 song) artist: Wayne Newton
Daddy Long Legs (1955 film)
cast: Fred Astaire, Leslie Caron, Thelma Ritter
director: Jean Negulesco
daddy-o: 6 hepcat 7 cool cat
Daddy's __-hunting: 5 gone a
Daddy's Girls actor: 5 Moore
Daddy's Home (song) artist: Jermaine Jackson, Shep and the Limelites
Daddy's Little Girl author: Mary Higgins Clark
Dade: 6 county
city: 5 Miami
state: 3 Fla. 7 Florida
dad-gum: 7 doggone
dado: 3 die 6 groove
Da Doo Ron Ron (song) artist: Crystals, Shaun Cassidy
__ Dads: 5 My Two
daedal: 6 clever 7 complex 9 ingenious, intricate
Daedalus: 6 artist 8 Athenian, engineer, inventor
son of ~: 5 Iapyx 6 Icarus
__ Dae Jung: 3 Kim
daemon: 3 god 5 ghoul 10 evil spirit
Daewoo: 3 car 4 auto 10 automobile
model: 5 Lanos 6 Nubira 7 Leganza
__-da-fé: 4 auto
__ d'affaires: 5 homme 6 chargé
daffodil: 4 bulb 5 color, plant 6 flower, yellow
relative: 4 buff, corn, gold, lime, rust, sand 5 blond, brass, coral, cream, flaxy, lemon, maize, ocher, ochre, peach, rusty, straw 6 blonde, canary, chammy, citron, crocus, flaxen, shammy, shamoy 7 apricot, chamois, citrine, jasmine, mustard, nankeen, old gold, saffron, xanthic 8 primrose 9 champagne, goldenrod, jessamine
daffy: 4 bats, loco, zany 5 dotty, goofy, goosy, inane, loony, nutty, silly, wacky 6 absurd, looney, whacky 7 foolish 8 clownish 10 off the wall, ridiculous, weak-minded
Daffy: 4 Dean, Duck
Daffy Duck, talk like: 4 lisp
Dafoe, Willem: 5 actor
film: Affliction (1998)
Animal Factory (2000)
Born on the Fourth of July (1989)
Clear and Present Danger (1994)
The English Patient (1996)
The Last Temptation of Christ (1988)
Light Sleeper (1992)
Mississippi Burning (1988)
Platoon (1986)
Shadow of the Vampire (2000)
Spider-Man (2002)
Tom & Viv (1994)
Triumph of the Spirit (1989)
White Sands (1992)
daft: 3 mad 4 gaga, loco, luny, soft 5 balmy, dingy, dotty, flaky, goosy, inane, kooky, loony, loopy, nutty, potty, silly, wacky 6 absurd, cuckoo, flakey, kookie, looney, whacky 7 asinine, bonkers, doltish, foolish, idiotic, touched, unsound, witless 9 brainless, half-baked, idiotical, senseless 10 off-the-wall, ridiculous, squirrelly, weak-minded
daftness: 5 folly
da Gama, Vasco: 8 explorer 10 Portuguese
stop for ~: 5 India
__ da gamba: 5 viola
dagger: 4 dirk, snee 5 blade, knife, knive, point 6 cutlas 7 cutlass, obelisk, poniard, sidearm 8 stiletto
Celtic ~: 5 skean, skene
handle: 4 haft, hilt
Malay ~: 4 kris 6 crease, creese
partner: 5 cloak
printer's ~: 6 obelus
Sikh ~: 6 kirpan
thrust: 4 stab
__ dagger: 6 double 7 Spanish
daggers at, look: 4 rage 5 glare, scowl 6 glower 8 threaten
__ Dagh: 3 Ala
Dagnabbit!: 4 darn
Daguerre: 5 Louis
daguerreotype: 5 photo 7 picture
Dagwood: 8 Bumstead
boss: 7 Dithers
boss's wife: 4 Cora
dog: 5 Daisy
frequent request: 5 raise
kid: 6 Cookie 9 Alexander
neighbor: 4 Elmo, Herb
sweetheart before Blondie: 4 Irma
wife: 7 Blondie
__-dah: 5 lah-di
dahl: 4 stew
Dahl: 4 John 5 Roald 6 Arlene
Dahl, Arlene: 7 actress
film: Journey to the Center of the Earth (1959)
Reign of Terror (1949)
A Southern Yankee (1948)
spouse: Lex Barker, Fernando Lamas
dahlia: 5 plant 6 flower, purple, violet 8 amethyst
relative: 4 plum, puce 5 lilac, mauve 6 damson, orchid 7 heather, petunia 8 amethyst, burgundy, eggplant, lavender, mulberry 9 raspberry 10 heliotrope
Dahlia: 4 Lavi
__ Dahlia, The: 4 Blue
Dahl, Roald: 6 writer 7 British
birthplace: Wales
spouse: Patricia Neal
work: The BFG
Charlie and the Chocolate Factory
Going Solo
James and the Giant Peach
The Twits
Dahomey today: 5 Benin
dahoon: 4 tree 5 fruit, shrub
dah partner: 3 dit
dahs, dits and: 4 code 9 Morse code
__ Dai: 3 Bao
Daihatsu: 3 car 4 auto 10 automobile
model: 5 Cuore, Rocky 7 Charade
Dail Eireann locale: 7 Ireland
Dailey: 3 Dan 5 Janet
Dailey, Dan: 5 actor
film: I Can Get It for You Wholesale (1951)
It's Always Fair Weather (1955)
Mother Wore Tights (1947)
A Ticket to Tomahawk (1950)
You Were Meant for Me (1948)
daily: 5 paper 6 common 7 diurnal, journal, per diem, regular, routine 8 magazine, ordinary, periodic 9 circadian, newspaper, quotidian 10 periodical
delivery: 4 mail 5 paper 9 newspaper
dozen: 5 drill 8 exercise
drama: 4 soap
record: 5 diary
report: 4 news
routine: 3 job, rut 4 work 5 grind, habit, labor 6 groove 7 routine
daily __: 5 dozen 6 double
Daily: 4 Bill
Daily __: 4 News 5 Bruin 6 Planet
...__ daily bread: 3 our
Daily Bruin: 5 paper 9 newspaper
publisher: 4 UCLA
daily double: 3 bet 5 wager
Daily Planet: 5 paper 9 newspaper
reporter: 4 Kent, Lane, Lois 5 Clark, Olsen 8 Lois Lane 9 Clark Kent 10 Jimmy Olsen
Daimler: 8 Gottlieb
partner: 4 Benz
Dain Curse, The author: Hammett
daintiness: 8 delicacy
dainty: 4 cute, fine, lacy, lank, lean, neat, nice, slim, thin, twee, wiry 5 bonny, frail, fussy, lanky, light, spare, sweet, tasty, treat, wispy 6 bonnie, choosy, comely, gangly, lovely, petite, pretty, skinny, slight, slinky, svelte, twiggy 7 choosey, darling, finicky, fragile, gracile, mincing, refined, scraggy, scrawny, slender, spidery, willowy, wispish 8 charming, delicacy, delicate, ethereal, feathery, finiking, finnicky, gangling, graceful, precious 9 beautiful, delicious, exquisite, sweetmeat, sylphlike 10 attractive, delectable, fastidious, particular, weightless
overly ~: 6 cutesy 7 cutesie
daiquiri: 5 drink 8 beverage, cocktail
ingredient: 3 rum 4 lime 9 lime juice 10 lemon juice
__ daiquiri: 6 banana, frozen
dairy: 4 farm 5 ranch 8 creamery
animal: 3 cow
British ~ merchant: 6 eggler
ender: 3 man, men 4 maid 5 woman, women

implement: 5 churn
prefix: 4 lact- 5 lacto-
product: 4 curd, eggs, milk, whey 5 cream, curds, kefir, leben 6 butter, cheese, junket, yogurt 7 clabber 8 ice cream, skim milk 9 goat's milk, sour cream 10 buttermilk, heavy cream, light cream, lowfat milk, nonfat milk
rating: 6 grade A
sound: 3 moo
starter: 3 non
unit: 3 cup 4 pint 5 quart 6 gallon
dairy __: 4 farm 5 breed 6 cattle
Dairy __: 5 Queen
dairy case buy: 4 milk, oleo, skim
dairymaid's seat: 5 stool
Dairy Queen: 8 ice cream 9 soft serve
alternative: 4 Edy's 7 Breyer's 9 Friendly's, Good Humor 10 Haagen Dazs, Turkey Hill
order: 4 cone 5 float, shake, split
dais: 6 podium 7 rostrum 8 platform
covering: 5 drape
do ~ duty: 5 orate
VIP: 4 host 5 emcee, guest 7 speaker
daisy: 5 gowan, oxeye, plant 6 flower 7 blossom 10 marguerite, wildflower
center: 4 disk
daisy __: 3 ham 5 wheel
look-alike: 5 aster
daisy-__: 6 cutter
__ daisy: 4 blue 5 aster, crown, oxeye, Paris, white 6 Arctic, Easter, Shasta, yellow 7 African, English, seaside 10 Michaelmas
__-daisy: 4 upsa, upsy
Daisy: 6 Miller 7 Fuentes 9 Girl Scout
__ Daisy Clover: 6 Inside
Daisy Mae
boyfriend: 5 Abner
creator: 4 Capp 6 Al Capp
father-in-law: 5 Pappy
son: 3 Abe
Daisy Miller author: Henry James
Daito: 4 city, town
locale: 5 Japan
Dajal: 3 cow 4 bull 6 bovine, cattle
Dakar: 4 city, port, town 7 capital
cape: 5 Verde
locale: 7 Senegal
Dakota: 5 Sioux, tribe 6 Indian 7 Amerind 8 language
abode: 4 tent, tipi 5 tepee 6 teepee
dialect: 5 Teton
Indian: 3 Ree 5 Sioux 7 Arikara
__ Dakota: 5 North, South
Daktari lion: 8 Clarence
dal __: 5 segno
Dal: 5 river
locale: 6 Sweden
DAL: 5 Delta
former rival: 3 TWA 7 Braniff, Eastern
Dalai Lama: 4 rank 6 cleric 8 Nobelist
city: 4 Lasa 5 Lassa, Lhasa
country: 5 Tibet 6 Thibet, Xizang
dalasi: 5 money
dale: 4 glen 6 dingle, valley
companion: 4 hill
__-dale: 5 Alan-a
Dale: 3 Jim 4 Alan 5 Evans, Henry 6 Murphy 7 Bumpers, Jarrett, Messick, Midkiff 8 Carnegie 9 Earnhardt, Robertson
partner: 3 Roy 4 Chip
Dale City: 4 city, town
locale: 8 Virginia
Dale, Henry: 7 British 8 Nobelist
__ d'Alene: 5 Coeur
Dalén, Nils: 7 Swedish 8 Nobelist 9 physicist
daleth: 6 Hebrew, letter
predecessor: 5 gimel
successor: 2 he 3 heh
Daley: 5 Rosie 7 Richard
city: 3 Chi 7 Chicago
Dalgliesh: 4 Adam
Dalhousie University
location: 6 Canada 7 Halifax
Dalian: 4 city, town
locale: 5 China
dal ingredient: 6 lentil
Dali, Salvador: 6 artist 7 painter, Spanish
colleague: 4 Miró 5 Lorca
like ~ watches: 4 limp
Dall: 4 John
Dallas: 4 city, soap, town 6 George
athletes: 8 Mustangs
city near ~: 5 Ennis, Plano 6 Denton, De Soto
commodity: 3 oil
locale: 3 Tex. 5 Texas
pro team: 4 Mavs 5 Stars 7 Cowboys 9 Mavericks
river: 7 Trinity
school: 3 SMU
Dallas (CBS drama)
cast: Barbara Bel Geddes (Ellie Ewing)
Jim Davis (Jock Ewing)
Patrick Duffy (Bobby Ewing)
Linda Gray (Sue Ellen Ewing)
Larry Hagman (J.R. Ewing)
Ken Kercheval (Cliff Barnes)
Victoria Principal (Pam Ewing)
Charlene Tilton (Lucy Ewing)
setting: 5 ranch 9 Southfork
__ Dallas: 6 Stella
Dallas County city: 5 Selma
__ Dallas Forty: 5 North
Dallas-to-Reno dir.: 3 WNW
Dalla sua pace: 4 aria
dalliance: 9 loitering, puttering 10 carrying on, flirtation, frittering, frolicking, hanky-panky
dallier: 9 latecomer
__ Dalloway: 3 Mrs.
dally: 3 haw, lag, toy 4 drag, idle, laze, loaf, poke, stay, wait 5 amble, delay, flirt, mosey, stall, tarry, trail 6 dabble, dawdle, linger, loiter, put off, trifle 7 saunter 8 footdrag, gain time, hesitate, lollygag, lose time, slack off, straggle 9 poke along, waste time 10 boondoggle, fool around, mess around, play around
__-dally: 5 dilly
dallying: 4 lazy 6 otiose 7 unready 8 dilatory, indolent, slothful 9 apathetic, frivolity, negligent, shiftless 10 neglectful
Dalmatian: 3 dog, pet 5 canid, pooch 6 canine 7 fire dog
feature: 4 spot
seaport: 5 Zadar
Daloa: 4 city, town
locale: 10 Ivory Coast
Dalrymple: 3 Ian 4 Scot
Dalton: 4 Abby, city, John, town 7 Timothy
gang victim: 5 train
locale: 7 Georgia
Dalton, John: 7 British, chemist
Dalton, Timothy: 5 actor
film: Agatha (1979)
Brenda Starr (1989)
Licence to Kill (1989)
The Living Daylights (1987)
The Rocketeer (1991)
Wuthering Heights (1970)
Daltrey: 5 Roger
Daly: 4 John, Tyne 5 Chuck, James 7 Timothy
Daly, Chuck: 5 coach
sport: 10 basketball
Daly City: 4 city, town
locale: 10 California
Daly, James: 5 actor
film: The Resurrection of Zachary Wheeler (1971)
The Young Stranger (1957)
TV: Medical Center
Daly, John: 6 golfer
milieu: 5 links 6 course
org: 3 PGA
Daly, Tyne: 7 actress
film: The Enforcer (1976)
Telefon (1977)
spouse: Georg Sanford Brown
TV: Cagney & Lacey
dam: 3 bar, mom 4 bank, bolt, clog, cork, dike, lock, mama, mare, plug, seal, shut, stem, wall, weir 5 block, close, jam up, latch, levee, mamma 6 clog up, female, hinder, impede, lock up, plug up, seal up, secure, stop up 7 barrier, block up, choke up, prevent, seal off, shutter 8 blockade, button up, hold back, keep back, obstruct, restrain 9 barricade, broodmare 10 embankment
agcy.: 3 TVA
build a ~: 6 embank
builder: 6 beaver
Egyptian ~: 5 Aswan
Lake Mead ~: 6 Hoover
mate: 4 sire
Panama Canal ~: 5 Gatún
__ dam: 3 air 4 arch, wing 6 splash 7 gravity, tinker's
__ Dam: 5 Aswan, Gatún 6 Beaver, Hoover, Wilson 7 Boulder
dama: 6 señora
damage: 3 mar 4 chip, cost, harm, hurt, loss, maim, nick, ruin, scar, tear, toll 5 abuse, break, crack, erode, price, split, spoil, stain, wound, wreck, wrong 6 bang up, batter, bruise, charge, deface, defile, deform, impair, injure, injury, mangle, mess up, outlay, ravage, riddle, trauma, weaken 7 blemish, corrode, corrupt, disable, expense, pollute, scratch, slander, tarnish, vitiate 8 aggrieve, breakage, mischief, mutilate, sabotage 9 corrosion, detriment, liability, pollution, prejudice, undermine, vandalism, vandalize 10 corruption, impairment, knock about, tamper with
irrevocable ~: 7 debacle 8 calamity, disaster 9 cataclysm, perdition 10 extinction
minor ~: 4 dent, ding
widespread ~: 5 havoc
damage __: 7 control
damaged: 4 hurt, shot, torn, worn 5 kaput 6 broken, faulty, flawed 7 cracked, injured, unsound 8 fallible 9 defective, imperfect 10 on the blink, on the fritz, out of whack
easily ~: 5 frail 7 fragile
damages: 4 cost, fine 5 award, price 6 charge 7 expense, penalty 9 indemnity 10 punishment, reparation
__ damages: 7 nominal
damaging: 3 bad, ill 5 toxic 6 costly, malign, nocent 7 adverse, baleful, baneful, harmful, hurtful, ruinous 8 grievous, negative 9 dangerous, injurious 10 calamitous, derogatory, disastrous, pernicious
__, Daman, and Diu: 3 Goa
__ d'amandes: 4 lait
damaru: 4 drum
origin: 5 India
Damascene: 4 Arab
Damascus: 4 city, town 7 capital
locale: 3 Syr. 5 Syria
river: 6 Barada
VIP: 5 Assad
damask: 4 pink, rose, silk 5 linen 6 fabric
relative: 4 nude 5 melon 6 salmon 7 apricot 8 flamingo 9 carnation
damask __: 4 rose 5 steel
damask rose: 5 plant 6 flower
product: 4 atar, otto 5 athar, attar, ottar
Damasus: 4 pope 7 pontiff
D'Amato: 2 Al 7 Alfonse
d'Amboise, Jacques
specialty: 5 dance 6 ballet
Dambovita, city on the: 9 Bucharest
dame: 3 gal 4 lady 5 noble, title, woman 6 matron 7 dowager, peeress 8 baroness 9 blueblood 10 aristocrat, noblewoman
__ dame: 6 grande
__ Dame: 5 Notre
Dames (1934 film)
cast: Joan Blondell, Ruby Keeler, ZaSu Pitts, Dick Powell
director: Ray Enright
Dames __: 5 at Sea
Dam, Henrik: 6 Danish 8 Nobelist 10 biochemist
Damian: 5 saint 7 Michael
daminozide: 4 Alar
Damita: 2 Jo 4 Lili
Damita, Lili spouse: Errol Flynn
damn: 4 slam 5 blast, curse 6 outlaw, punish, vilify 7 censure, condemn 8 denounce 9 castigate, criticize, excoriate, imprecate, proscribe 10 confounded, denunciate
give a ~: 4 care, mind
not worth a ~: 5 lousy
__ damn: 7 tinker's
damnable: 4 evil 8 infernal
Damn: A Book of Calumny author: H.L. Mencken
damnation: 4 doom 9 perdition 10 execration
Damnation of Faust, The composer: 7 Berlioz
Damn the Defiant! (1962 film)
cast: Dirk Bogarde, Sir Alec Guinness
damn with faint __: 6 praise
Damn Yankees (1958 film)
cast: Tab Hunter, Gwen Verdon, Ray Walston
character: 3 Joe, Meg 4 Lola 5 Doris, Satan 6 Gloria 9 Applegate
composer: 4 Ross 5 Adler
director: George Abbott, Stanley Donen
song: 5 Heart
team: 4 Nats 8 Senators
Damon: 4 Mark, Matt 6 Runyon, Wayans 7 Cathryn
to Pythias: 3 pal 6 friend
Damone, Vic
song: On the Street Where You Live (1956)
spouse: Pier Angeli, Diahann Carroll
Damon, Matt: 5 actor
film: All the Pretty Horses (2000)
The Bourne Identity (2002)
Courage Under Fire (1996)
Dogma (1999)
Good Will Hunting (1997)
The Legend of Bagger Vance (2000)
Ocean's Eleven (2001)
The Rainmaker (1997)
Rounders (1998)
Saving Private Ryan (1998)
School Ties (1992)
The Talented Mr. Ripley (1999)
__ d'amore: 4 oboe 5 viola
D'amor sull'ali rosee: 4 aria
__ d'amour: 4 oboe 7 affaire, chanson
damp: 3 wet 4 dank, dewy, oozy 5 boggy, deter; humid, misty, moist, muddy, muggy, musty, soggy, steep, undry 6 clammy, deaden, drippy,

hydric, liquid, sodden, steamy, sticky, stuffy, sultry, swampy, sweaty, watery **7** depress, drizzly, mildewy, moisten, sopping, wettish **8** moisture **9** saturated **10** demoralize
habitat: **3** bog, fen **5** bayou, marsh, swamp
damp-___: **3** dry, mop
dampen: **3** cow, wet **4** cool, curb, dash, dull, mute, slow, soak **5** abate, allay, bedew, blunt, brake, check, chill, cloud, daunt, delay, deter, rinse, spoil, spray, water **6** deaden, deject, hamper, hinder, impede, lessen, muffle, quench, rain on, retard, sadden, slow up, stifle, temper **7** deflate, depress, humdify, inhibit, moisten, silence, slacken, wet down **8** diminish, dispirit, dissuade, humidify, irrigate, moderate, restrain, saturate, slow down, sprinkle, tone down **10** besprinkle, demoralize, discourage, dishearten, intimidate
dampened: **3** low **5** faint, moist, piano, quiet
damper: **5** brake, check, pedal **10** constraint
put a ~ on: **5** quash, slake **6** sadden
Dampier, William: **7** British **8** explorer
dampness: **3** dew, wet **5** vapor **7** wetness **8** humidity, moisture **9** sogginess
Damrosch, Walter: **6** German **9** conductor
damsel: **4** girl, lass, maid, miss **5** houri, woman **6** female, lassie, maiden **7** colleen **8** fraülein **9** young lady **10** demoiselle, young woman
cry: **4** help **5** never **6** my hero, save me
ender: **3** fly **4** fish
saver: **4** hero **6** knight
damselfly: **3** bug **6** insect
Damsel in Distress, A (1937 film)
cast: Gracie Allen, Fred Astaire, George Burns, Joan Fontaine
director: George Stevens
damson: **4** plum **5** color **6** purple
relative: **4** puce, sloe **5** lilac, mauve **6** cherry, dahlia, orchid **7** heather, petunia **8** amethyst, burgundy, eggplant, lavender, mulberry **9** greengage, myrobalan, raspberry **10** heliotrope
Dan: **4** Hill **5** Fouts, Issel, Patch, Rowan, Seals **6** Curtis, Dailey, Duryea, Frazer, Hedaya, Lauria, Marino, McGrew, O'Brien, Quayle, Rather **7** Aykroyd, Blocker, Hampton, Hartman, Majerle **8** Haggerty, Jacobson, O'Herlihy **9** Brouthers, Fogelberg
fancy ~: **4** dude **5** blade, swell **10** jack-a-dandy
parent: **5** Jacob **6** Bilhah
sibling: **3** Gad **4** Levi **5** Asher, Dinah, Judah **6** Joseph, Reuben, Simeon **7** Zebulun **8** Benjamin, Issachar, Naphtali
___ Dan: **5** fancy **6** Granny, Steely **7** England
Dana: **3** Vic **4** Bill **5** Elcar, Plato **6** Carvey, Delany, Scully, Wynter **7** Andrews, Charles
Danae
lover of ~: **4** Zeus
son of ~: **7** Perseus
___ Dana Gibson: **7** Charles
Danakil: **6** desert
locale: **6** Africa, Jibuti **7** Eritrea **8** Djibouti, Ethiopia
___ d'ananas: **5** crème
Da Nang: **4** city, town
locale: **7** Vietnam
Dana Point: **4** city, town
locale: **10** California
Dana, Richard Henry: **6** writer
work: Two Years Before the Mast
Danbury: **4** city, town
locale: **4** Conn.
dance: **2** ET **3** art, bop, dog, fly, hop, jig **4** ball, bird, bump, clog, dive, frug, gala, haka, hora, hula, jerk, jive, jota, juba, jump, khon, kolo, pogo, pony, prom, reel, rock, shag, skip, slop, step, sway, swim, walk **5** ballo, bebop, conga, disco, fling, frisk, galop, gavot, gigue, gopak, guess, hopak, horah, limbo, lindy, mambo, mixer, mouse, nasty, party, pavan, pavin, polka, rumba, salsa, samba, shake, skate, smurf, snake, stomp, strut, swing, tango, twine, twist, valse, vogue, waltz **6** ballet, bocane, bolero, boogie, Boston, bugaku, canary, cancan, cavort, cha-cha, formal, frolic, gambol, german, gyrate, hoof it, hustle, joropo, kathak, medium, minuet, monkey, morris, pavane, prance, rhumba, shimmy, stroll, trepak, Watusi **7** alegras, bedrock, beguine, bourrée, carioca, courant, csardas, cut a rug, czardas, djanger, foxtrot, freddie, gavotte, hoedown, lambada, lancers, ländler, le freak, mazurka, moshing, NY slide, one-step, peabody, perform, popcorn, shuffle, slauson, sock hop, sparkle, two-step **8** birdland, boogaloo, bunny hop, bunny hug, cachucha, cakewalk, chaconne, courante, Egyptian, fandango, flamenco, galliard, habanera, handjive, hornpipe, hula-hula, kazatsky, L.A. hustle, lindy hop, macarena, mazourka, merengue, moonwalk, rigadoon, saraband, soft-shoe, special K, tush push **9** acid house, allemande, alligator, bossa nova, breakdown, camel walk, cotillion, écossaise, farandole, festivity, hitchhike, jitterbug, malaguena, pas de deux, paso doble, passepied, Philly dog, polonaise, promenade, quadrille, sarabande, siciliano, tambourin, zapateado **10** achy-breaky, bergamasca, Charleston, corroboree, hucklebuck, hully gully, loco-motion, running man, saltarello, seguidilla, strathspey, tarantella, turkey trot, villanella
acrobatic ~: **5** limbo **9** jitterbug
African ~: **4** juba
all night: **5** revel **9** celebrate, make merry
Andalusian ~: **8** flamenco
Argentine ~: **5** tango
art form ~: **6** ballet
Austrian ~: **5** waltz **7** ländler
award: **6** Bessie
back-bending ~: **5** limbo
Balinese ~: **7** djanger
ballet: **7** pas seul **9** pas de deux **10** pas d'action
ballroom ~: **5** conga, mambo, rumba, samba, tango, waltz **6** cha-cha, rhumba **7** beguine, fox trot, lambada, one-step, peabody, two-step **8** habanera **9** bossa nova, polonaise **10** Charleston
band: **5** combo
bar-mitzvah ~: **4** hora
barn ~: **4** reel
bobbysoxer's ~: **3** hop
Bohemian ~: **5** polka
bolerolike ~: **8** cachucha
Brazilian ~: **5** samba **7** lambada **9** bossa nova
Bristol ~: **5** stomp
British ~: **6** morris
Bucharest ~: **4** hora
Caribbean ~: **4** soca **5** limbo, mambo **7** beguine
castanet ~: **4** jota **6** bolero **8** fandango
chain ~: **5** conga
circle ~: **4** hora, kolo
colonial ~: **4** reel **6** minuet **8** saraband **9** sarabande
combining form: **5** chore- **6** choreo-, chorio-
costume ~: **6** morris
Cuban ~: **5** conga, mambo, rumba **6** rhumba **8** habanera
Dixieland ~: **5** stomp
Dominican ~: **8** merengue
ender: **4** hall, wear
flamenco ~: **7** alegras
formal ~: **4** ball, prom
French ~: **5** gavot, valse **6** branle, cancan **7** bourrée, gavotte **9** cotillion, farandole, passepied, quadrille, tambourin
genre: **3** tap
German ~: **7** ländler
grass-skirt ~: **4** hula
half a ~: **3** can, cha
hand-clapping ~: **4** juba
hand gesture, in Indian ~: **5** mudra
handkerchief ~: **9** siciliano
Hawaiian ~: **4** hula **8** hula-hula
heavily: **5** stomp
heel-stomping ~: **5** gopak, hopak
high-kicking ~: **6** cancan
highland ~: **4** reel **5** fling
hippy ~: **4** hula
Hungarian ~: **7** csardas, czardas
Indian ~: **6** kathak
in French: **3** bal
in wooden shoes: **4** clog
Irish ~: **3** jig
Israeli ~: **4** hora **5** horah
Italian ~: **5** ballo, gigue **9** siciliano **10** bergamasca, saltarello, tarantella, villanella
Japanese ~: **6** bugaku, Bukavu
jazz ~: **4** jive **5** bebop, stomp, swing **9** jitterbug
Latin ~: **5** conga, mambo, raspa, salsa, samba, tango **6** cha-cha **9** zapateado
line ~: **5** conga
lively ~: **3** jig **4** reel **5** fling, galop, polka **6** bolero, joropo **7** mazurka, peabody **8** fandango, galliard, mazourka, rigadoon **9** breakdown, cotillion, paso doble **10** bergamasca, seguidilla, tarantella
Maori war ~: **4** haka
men-only ~: **4** khon **6** bugaku, trepak **8** kazatsky
movement: **4** step **5** glide
noisy ~: **9** breakdown
no-taps tap ~: **8** soft-shoe
NYC ~ co.: **3** ABT
partner: **4** song
Peppermint Lounge ~: **5** twist
Polish ~: **7** mazurka **8** mazourka **9** polonaise
ragtime ~: **6** shimmy **10** turkey trot
recklessly: **4** mosh
Romanian ~: **4** hora **5** horah
round ~: **4** hora **5** galop
running step ~: **7** courant **8** courante
salsa club ~: **5** rumba **6** rhumba
Savoy ~: **5** stomp
school ~: **3** hop **4** prom **5** mixer
Scottish ~: **4** reel **5** fling **9** écossaise **10** strathspey
Serbian ~: **4** kolo
sing and ~: **5** party
site: **4** barn **5** disco
slangily: **4** hoof **7** cut a rug
Slavic ~: **4** kolo **8** kazatsky
slow ~: **5** pavan, pavin **6** bocane, minuet, pavane **8** chaconne, habanera **9** allemande, polonaise **10** strathspey
song and ~: **4** line, yarn **5** pitch, spiel **6** reason **9** rationale
Spanish ~: **4** jota **6** bolero **7** alegras, bourrée **8** chaconne **9** malaguena, paso doble, zapateado **10** seguidilla
starter: **4** folk
stately ~: **5** pavan, pavin **6** minuet, pavane **8** chaconne, saraband **9** sarabande
step: **6** chassé, do-si-do **7** dos-à-dos
studio rail: **3** bar **5** barre
syllable: **3** cha
Thai ~: **4** khon
Ukraine ~: **5** gopak, hopak **6** trepak
under a bar: **5** limbo
Venezuelan ~: **6** joropo
version of a song: **5** remix
Viennese ~: **5** waltz
West Indies ~: **5** limbo
with a kick: **5** conga
16th-century ~: **5** ballo, pavan, pavin **6** canary, pavane **8** galliard
17th-century ~: **7** courant **8** courante, galliard **9** allemande, passepied
18th-century ~: **4** juba **9** cotillion, passepied
19th-century ~: **4** juba **5** galop
1920s ~: **6** shimmy **10** Charleston
1930s ~: **4** shag **5** lindy
1950s ~: **4** slop **5** shake **6** stroll **8** birdland, handjive **10** hucklebuck, hully gully
1960s ~: **3** dog, fly **4** bird, frug, jerk, pony, swim **5** skate, twine, twist **6** monkey, Watusi **7** freddie, slauson **8** boogaloo **9** alligator, camel walk, hitchhike, Philly dog **10** loco-motion
1970s ~: **4** bump, sway **5** disco **6** hustle **7** popcorn, shuffle **8** L.A. hustle, special K
1980s ~: **2** ET **4** pogo, walk **5** guess, nasty, salsa, snake, vogue **7** bedrock, le freak, neutron **8** Egyptian, moonwalk **9** acid house
1990s ~: **3** hop **4** dive **5** smurf **7** moshing, NY slide **8** macarena, tush push **10** achy-breaky, running man
dance ___: **4** band, card, form, hall, step **5** drama
___ dance: **3** hat, sun, tap, tea, toe, war **4** barn, clog, file, folk, line, rain, ring, slam **5** belly, break, cooch, court, ghost, round, snake, sword **6** apache, dinner, modern, morris, nautch, shadow, square, waggle **7** neutron
Dance ___ Hours: **5** of the
___ Dance: **4** Last, Let's **5** I Can't, I Won't, Sabre **7** Neutron
dance-club employee: **6** deejay
Dance, Dance, Dance (song) artist: Beach Boys, Chic
___ dance notation: **5** Laban
Dance of Death: **4** film, play
author: August Strindberg
cast: Geraldine McEwan, Laurence Olivier
Dance of Life, The author: **5** Ellis
Dance of the Hours composer: **10** Ponchielli
Dance of the Nymphs artist: **5** Corot
Dance on Little Girl (1961 song) artist: Paul Anka
dancer: **5** Bruhn, Dolin, Jooss, Kelly, Lifar, Tharp **6** Alonso, Béjart, Duncan, hoofer **7** Astaire, Bujones, Farrell, Fonteyn, Markova, Martins, Massine, Nureyev, Pavlova, Shearer, Ulanova **8** coryphée, d'Amboise, Danilova, De Valois, Eglevsky, figurant, Mitchell, Nijinsky, Rockette, Villella **9** ballerina, Gene Kelly, Tallchief **10** Balanchine, chorus girl **11** Baryshnikov, Youskevitch

ballet ~: **7** danseur **8** coryphée, danseuse, figurant
displace a ~: **5** cut in
garment: **4** tutu **6** tights
poor ~: **5** stiff
__ dancer: **3** tap **4** go-go, taxi **5** belly, gandy **6** ballet
Dancer: **8** reindeer
colleague: **5** Comet, Cupid, Vixen **6** Dasher, Donder **7** Blitzen, Prancer
handler: **5** Santa
__ Dancer: **4** I Am a **7** Private
Dancer at the Bar painter: **5** Degas
Dancer, The artist: **4** Erté
Dances With Wolves (1990 film)
animal: **5** bison
cast: Kevin Costner, Graham Greene, Mary McDonnell
director: Kevin Costner
foe: **6** Pawnee
home: **4** tipi **5** tepee **6** teepee
language: **6** Lakota **7** Lakhota
Dance the Night Away (1979 song) artist: Van Halen
Dance to Death author: Emma Lazarus
Dance to the Music (1968 song) artist: Sly and the Family Stone
Dance to the Music of Time, A author: Anthony Powell
Dance With a Stranger (1985 film)
cast: Rupert Everett, Ian Holm, Miranda Richardson
director: Mike Newell
Dance With Me (1998 film)
cast: Kris Kristofferson, Joan Plowright, Vanessa Williams
director: Randa Haines
Dance With Me (song)
artist: Betty Wright, Orleans, Peter Brown
Dance With Me Henry (1956 film)
cast: Bud Abbott, Lou Costello, Gigi Perreau
Dance With Me Henry (1955 song)
artist: Georgia Gibbs
__ dancing: **3** ice **4** slam **5** break **6** social, square **7** aerobic
Dancing __: **4** Lady **5** Queen **7** Machine
__ Dancing: **4** Come, Slow **5** Dirty **6** Shadow
__ Dancing!: **5** That's
Dancing Class, The artist: **5** Degas
Dancing Couple, The artist: **5** Steen
Dancing in the Dark (1984 song) artist: Bruce Springsteen
Dancing in the Street (song)
artist: David Bowie, Martha & the Vandellas, Mick Jagger
Dancing Lady (1933 film)
cast: Joan Crawford, Clark Gable, May Robson, Franchot Tone
Dancing Machine (1974 song) artist: Jackson 5
Dancing on the Ceiling (1986 song)
artist: Lionel Richie
Dancing Queen (1977 song) artist: ABBA
dandelion: **4** weed, wine **5** plant **6** flower
down: **5** pappi **6** pappus
stalk: **5** scape
Dandelion (1967 song) artist: Rolling Stones
Dandelion Wine author: Ray Bradbury
dander: **3** ire **4** rage **5** anger, Irish, pique, wrath **6** temper **9** huffiness, surliness
get one's ~ up: **4** rile **5** anger, peeve **7** bristle
Dandie Dinmont: **3** dog, pet **5** pooch **6** canine **7** terrier
dandle: **3** pet **5** spoil **6** coddle, cosset, cuddle, pamper **7** cater to, indulge
Dandridge: **3** Ray **7** Dorothy
dandruff: **5** scall, scurf **6** flakes
dandy: **3** A-OK, def, fop, gem, pip, rad **4** aces, A-one, beau, boss, braw, cool, dece, dude, fine, gear, keen, neat, nice, phat, prig, toff, tuff **5** beaut, boffo, ducky, grand, great, marvy, natty, neato, nifty, nobby, prime, prize, slick, super, swank, swell **6** bang on, bang-up, beauty, bonzer, bosker, choice, dapper, divine, dreamy, far-out, gnarly, groovy, lovely, peachy, rakish, slap-up, snazzy, spiffy, spot on, spruce, superb, swanky, terrif, tiptop, unreal, whizzo, wicked **7** amazing, awesome, boffola, capital, corking, coxcomb, foppish, perfect, ripping, skookum, stellar, sublime **8** dazzling, especial, eximious, fabulous, five-star, four-star, frabjous, glorious, heavenly, jim-dandy, just fine, popinjay, slam-bang, smashing, splendid, standout, sterling, stickout, superior, terrific, top-level, topnotch, very good, wondrous **9** agreeable, bodacious, Endsville, excellent, exemplary, exquisite, first-rate, high-grade, humdinger, hunky-dory, marvelous, prettyboy, sollicker, topflight, wonderful, wunderbar **10** first-class, hotsy-totsy, jack-a-dandy, out of sight, peachy-keen, phenomenal, remarkable, stupendous, super-duper
British ~: **4** toff
partner: **4** fine
__-dandy: **3** jim **5** handy, jack-a
Dandy (1966 song) artist: Herman's Hermits
__ d'âne: **3** pas
Dane: **5** Clark **9** Zealander
ender: **3** law
__ Dane: **5** Great
Danes, Claire: **7** actress
film: Les Misérables (1998)
Little Women (1994)
The Mod Squad (1999)
Polish Wedding (1998)
The Rainmaker (1997)
Romeo & Juliet (1996)
To Gillian on Her 37th Birthday (1996)
dang: **4** darn, drat, heck, oath **5** nerts, nertz **6** darn it, durn it **9** consarn it
__ d'angelo: **7** capelli
D'Angelo, Beverly: **7** actress
film: American History X (1998)
Coal Miner's Daughter (1980)
Every Which Way But Loose (1978)
Maid to Order (1987)
National Lampoon's Christmas Vacation (1989)
National Lampoon's Vacation (1983)
__ Dan George: **5** Chief
danger: **4** disk, risk **5** peril **6** beware, chance, crisis, hazard, menace, threat **7** pitfall, thin ice, trouble **8** exposure, jeopardy, unsafety **10** insecurity
ending: **3** ous
free from ~: **4** safe
in ~: **6** at risk, liable **7** exposed **8** vincible
in ~ of: **9** subject to
lure into ~: **6** entrap
out of ~: **4** safe **8** unharmed **9** untouched
response to ~: **4** fear
signal: **3** red **5** alert
Danger __: **4** Cave, Zone
Dangerfield, Rodney: **8** comedian
persona: **5** loser
dangerous: **3** bad **4** mean, ugly **5** hairy, nasty, risky, shaky, tight, toxic **6** chancy, lethal, malign, nocent, no joke, severe, thorny, unsafe, wicked **7** adverse, baleful, baneful, hurtful, noisome, ominous, parlous, rickety, ruinous, serious, unsound, vicious **8** alarming, damaging, headlong, menacing, negative, perilous, terrible, ticklish, unstable **9** breakneck, desperate, explosive, harrowing, hazardous, impending, injurious, insidious, malignant, murderous, pestilent, troubling, unhealthy **10** calamitous, disastrous, formidable, incendiary, jeopardous, pernicious, petrifying, portentous, precarious, serpentine, touch-and-go, vulnerable
group: **3** mob
make less ~: **6** defuse, defuze
not ~: **4** safe **8** harmless
partner: **5** armed
Dangerous (1935 film)
cast: Bette Davis, Franchot Tone
Dangerous Beauty (1998 film)
cast: Jacqueline Bisset, Catherine McCormack, Oliver Platt
__ Dangerous Game, The: **4** Most
Dangerous Liaisons (1988 film)
cast: Glenn Close, Swoosie Kurtz, John Malkovich, Mildred Natwick, Michelle Pfeiffer, Keanu Reeves, Uma Thurman
director: Stephen Frears
Dangerous (song) artist: Busta Rhymes, Roxette
Dangerous When Wet (1953 film)
cast: Fernando Lamas, Esther Williams
director: Charles Walters
Danger, The author: Dick Francis
Danger Zone (1986 song) artist: Kenny Loggins
Dangi: **3** cow **4** bull **6** bovine, cattle
Dang it!: **4** nuts **5** nerts, nertz
dangle: **3** sag **4** flop, hang, loll, pend, sway, wave **5** droop, sling, swing, trail **6** flaunt, follow **7** draggle, suspend **8** brandish, flourish, hang down **9** hang about, hang loose, oscillate
a carrot: **4** lure **5** tempt **6** entice
dangling: **4** limp **5** baggy, slack **6** droopy, floppy **7** flaccid, pendant, pendent **9** pendulous
Dangling Conversation, The (1966 song) artist: Simon and Garfunkel
Dangling Man author: Saul Bellow
Dang Me (1964 song) artist: Roger Miller
Dania Beach: **4** city, town
locale: **7** Florida
Daniel: **4** Beth, Mann, Tsui, Yuly **5** Boone, Bovet, Defoe, Mason, Shays, Stern **6** Inouye, Petrie, Samuel **7** Baldwin, Benzali, Deronda, Nathans, Webster **8** Boorstin, Ellsberg, Kahneman, McFadden, Travanti **9** Barenboim **10** Fahrenheit
follower: **5** Hosea
locale: **3** den
preceder: **7** Ezekiel
Daniel (1983 film)
cast: Edward Asner, Ellen Barkin, Lindsay Crouse, Timothy Hutton, Mandy Patinkin
director: Sidney Lumet
Daniel __ French: **7** Chester
Daniel __ Lewis: **3** Day
Daniel (1973 song) artist: Elton John
Daniela: **7** Bianchi
Daniel arap __: **3** Moi
Daniel, Beth: **6** golfer
Daniel Boone (NBC western)
cast: Ed Ames (Mingo)
Fess Parker (Daniel Boone)
Daniel Boone poet: **5** Benét
Daniel Deronda author: George Eliot
Daniel J. __: **8** Travanti
Danielle: **5** Steel **8** Darrieux **9** Brisebois
Daniels: **4** Bebe, Jeff **5** Faith **7** Charlie, William
Daniel, Samuel: **4** poet **7** British
Daniels, Bebe: **7** actress
film: 42nd Street (1933)
Counsellor-at-Law (1933)
The Maltese Falcon (1931)
Daniels, Jeff: **5** actor
film: 101 Dalmatians (1996)
Arachnophobia (1990)
Dumb & Dumber (1994)
Gettysburg (1993)
Heartburn (1986)
Marie (1985)
Pleasantville (1998)
The Purple Rose of Cairo (1985)
Radio Days (1987)
Rain Without Thunder (1992)
Speed (1994)
Sweet Hearts Dance (1988)
Terms of Endearment (1983)
Trial and Error (1997)
Daniels, William: **5** actor
film: 1776 (1972)
The Blue Lagoon (1980)
The Graduate (1967)
Ladybug Ladybug (1963)
The Parallax View (1974)
TV: St. Elsewhere
Daniel, Yuly: **6** writer **7** Russian
Danilova, Alexandra: **6** dancer **8** danseuse **9** ballerina
danio: **4** fish
danish: **4** cake **6** pastry **9** sweet roll
flavor: **5** prune
Danish: **5** bread **6** pastry **8** language
see also Denmark
Danish __: **3** oil **6** Modern, pastry
Danish __ Indies: **4** West
Danish __ Islands: **6** Virgin
__-Danish War: **6** Prusso
dank: **3** raw, wet **4** damp, dewy **5** humid, moist, muggy, musty, soggy, undry **6** chilly, clammy, steamy, sticky, stuffy, sultry **7** mildewy, odorous, wettish
danke: **6** thanks **7** spasibo **8** thank you
danke __: **5** schön **6** schoen
Danke Schoen (1963 song) artist: Wayne Newton
Dannay: **8** Frederic
Danner, Blythe: **7** actress
daughter: Gwyneth Paltrow
film: Alice (1990)
Brighton Beach Memoirs (1986)
Futureworld (1976)
Husbands and Wives (1992)
Man, Woman and Child (1983)
Meet the Parents (2000)
Mr. & Mrs. Bridge (1990)
The Prince of Tides (1991)
Danning: **5** Sybil
D'Annunzio, Gabriele: **4** poet **7** Italian
Danny: **4** Kaye **6** Aiello, DeVito, Elfman, Glover, O'Keefe, Thomas **8** Bonaduce, Pintauro, Williams
daughter: **5** Marlo
Danny __: **3** Boy **6** Deever
Danny and the Juniors song: At the Hop (1957)
Danny Boy (1959 song) artist: Conway Twitty
caller: **5** pipes
locale: **4** glen **6** meadow
Danny Deever author: Rudyard Kipling
Danny's Song (1973 song) artist: Anne Murray
Danny Thomas Show (ABC/CBS sitcom)
cast: Angela Cartwright (Linda Williams)
Hans Conried (Uncle Tonoose)
Jean Hagen (Margaret Williams)
Rusty Hamer (Rusty Williams)
Sherry Jackson (Terry Williams)
Marjorie Lord (Kathy Williams)

Sid Melton (Charley Halper)
Danny Thomas (Danny Williams)
Dano: 5 Linda, Royal
Danova: 6 Cesare
Dan Patch: 5 horse 9 racehorse
emulate: 4 race, trot
__ dansant: 3 thé
Danse __: 7 Macabre
danse du __: 6 ventre
__ danseur: 7 premier
danseuse: 9 ballerina
support: 3 bar 5 barre
Danson, Ted: 5 actor
film: 3 Men and a Baby (1987)
Cousins (1989)
spouse: Mary Steenburgen
TV: Becker, Cheers
Dante: 3 Joe 4 font, poet 7 Italian, Lavelli 8 Bichette, Rossetti, typeface 9 Alighieri
love: Beatrice
work: The Divine Comedy
The New Life
Dante __ Rossetti: 7 Gabriel
Dante, Joe: 8 director
film: The 'burbs (1989)
Gremlins (1984)
Gremlins 2 The New Batch (1990)
The Howling (1981)
Innerspace (1987)
Matinee (1993)
Piranha (1978)
Small Soldiers (1998)
Dantes: 6 Edmond
Dante Symphony composer: 5 Liszt
Dantley: 6 Adrian
Danton: 3 Ray 7 Georges
Danton (1982 film)
cast: Patrice Chereau, Gérard Depardieu, Wojciech Pszoniak
director: Andrzej Wajda
Danube: 5 river
city on the ~: 3 Ulm 4 Linz 6 Braila, Galati, Vienna 8 Belgrade, Budapest 10 Bratislava
feeder: 3 Inn, Olt 4 Enns, Hron, Isar, Prut, Raab, Raba, Sava 5 Drava, Iller, Pruth, Siret, Tisza 6 Morava
in Hungary: 4 Duna
locale: 3 Aus. 7 Austria, Germany, Hungary, Romania, Rumania 8 Roumania, Slovakia
Roman province near the ~: 5 Dacia
to Czechs: 5 Dunaj
__ Danube Waltz: 4 Blue
Danvers: 4 city, town
locale: 4 Mass.
Danville: 4 city, town
locale: 8 Illinois, Virginia 10 California
Danza, Tony: 5 actor
film: Angels in the Outfield (1994)
TV: Taxi, Who's the Boss?
Danzig: 4 city, gulf, port 6 Gdansk
locale: 6 Poland
river: 7 Vistula
__ d'Aosta: 5 Valle
dap: 4 skip 7 fly-fish
daphne: 5 plant, shrub
Daphne: 4 seer 5 oread 6 Zuniga 8 asteroid 9 du Maurier
lover of ~: 6 Apollo
Daphnis: 5 nymph 7 centaur
god offended by ~: 4 Eros
lover: 5 Chloe
parent: 6 Hermes
Daphnis and Chloë: 6 ballet
composer: 5 Ravel
dapper: 4 chic, neat, pert, spry, trim 5 agile, brisk, dandy, natty, nifty, sharp, sleek, smart, swank 6 chichi, classy, jaunty, lively, nimble, rakish, snappy, snazzy, spiffy, sporty, spruce, swanky 7 dashing, groomed, stylish, voguish 8 handsome 9 decked out, gussied up, in fashion, sprightly
fellow: 3 Dan, fop 4 dude 5 blade, swell
dapple: 3 dot 4 spot 5 fleck, horse 6 equine, mottle 10 variegated
dapple-__: 4 gray, grey
dappled: 4 pied 6 motley 7 brindle, flecked, mottled, piebald 8 brindled, freckled, speckled 9 multihued 10 multicolor, variegated
darabuka: 4 drum
Darby: 3 Kim
Darby O'Gill & the Little People (1959 film) cast: Sean Connery, Janet Munro, Albert Sharpe
D'Arby, Terence Trent
song: Sign Your Name (1988)
Wishing Well (1988)
__ d'arc: 4 bois
Darcel: 6 Denise
d'Arc, Jeanne: 3 Ste. 5 woman 6 leader, martyr, sainte
Dardan: 5 Priam 6 Hector, Trojan
Dardanelles end: 5 Egean 6 Aegean
Darden: 6 Severn
__-dardy: 5 lardy
dare: 4 defy, risk 5 brave, tempt 6 brazen, gamble, hazard 7 go for it, presume, venture 8 defiance 9 adventure, challenge, speculate, take a risk 10 go for broke, make a stand, take a flier
alternative: 5 truth
ender: 3 say 5 devil
__ dare: 3 on a
Dare: 8 Virginia
__ Dare: 6 Double
daredevil: 4 bold, rash 5 brave, risky 6 hotdog, madcap, risker 7 hotspur, show-off 8 headlong, heedless, overbold, reckless, stuntman 9 audacious, foolhardy, impulsive, uncareful 10 adventurer, courageous
feat: 5 stunt
lack: 3 net 5 sense
need: 5 nerve 7 courage
no ~: 5 sissy
dared old-style: 5 durst
daresay: 5 guess, think 7 suppose
Dar es Salaam: 4 city, port, town
locale: 8 Tanzania
__ dare to eat a peach?: 3 Do I
d'Arezzo: 5 Guido
daric: 4 coin 5 money
Darien: 4 city, gulf, town
locale: 4 Conn. 6 Panama 8 Colombia, Illinois
Darin, Bobby
song: 18 Yellow Roses (1963)
Beyond the Sea (1960)
Dream Lover (1959)
If I Were a Carpenter (1966)
Mack the Knife (1959)
Queen of the Hop (1958)
Splish Splash (1958)
Things (1962)
You Must Have Been a Beautiful Baby (1961)
You're the Reason I'm Living (1963)
spouse: Sandra Dee
daring: 4 bold, game, grit, guts, rash 5 brave, cocky, fresh, gutsy, moxie, nerve, nervy, pluck, risky, spunk, valor 6 active, awless, brassy, brazen, cheeky, gritty, heroic, plucky, risqué, spunky 7 aweless, bravery, courage, dashing, defiant, doughty, forward, gallant, heroism, impavid, prowess, staunch, valiant 8 audacity, boldness, fearless, headlong, heroical, impudent, intrepid, reckless, resolute, stalwart, temerity, unafraid, valorous 9 audacious, dauntless, desperate, dreadless, foolhardy, gallantry, unabashed, uncareful, undaunted, unfearful, unfearing 10 confidence, courageous, enterprise, feistiness, undismayed
act: 5 stunt
Daring Young Man on the Flying Trapeze, The author: William Saroyan
Darío, Rubén: 4 poet 10 Nicaraguan
Darius: 4 king 7 Milhaud, Persian
son of ~: 6 Xerxes 10 Achaemenes
Darius the __: 5 Great
Darjeeling: 3 tea 4 city
locale: 5 India
dark: 3 dim, dun, sad 4 blue, dour, drab, dusk, ebon, evil, glum, grim, inky, mirk, murk, ugly, vile 5 black, bleak, dingy, dusky, ebony, faded, fuzzy, gloom, loury, mirky, misty, murky, muted, night, sable, shady, sober, sooty, surly, swart, unlit, vague 6 arcane, bleary, blurry, broody, closed, cloudy, dismal, dreary, gloomy, hidden, ill-lit, lowery, morbid, morose, occult, opaque, secret, shadow, sinful, somber, sullen, swarth, unseen, veiled, wicked 7 cryptic, doleful, evening, joyless, obscure, ominous, satanic, shadowy, stygian, sunless, swarthy, unknown 8 abstruse, baffling, dejected, dolorous, hopeless, horrible, ignorant, infamous, infernal, jetblack, lowering, moonless, nebulous, overcast, puzzling, sinister, ulterior 9 cheerless, concealed, cryptical, depressed, enigmatic, lightless, murkiness, nightfall, nighttime, obscurity, recondite, satanical, sorrowful, tenebrous, unlighted 10 forbidding, indistinct, lugubrious, lusterless, melancholy, mysterious, mystifying, pitch-black, tenebrific, unknowable
after ~: 5 night 7 nightly 9 nighttime, nocturnal
area: 5 umbra 8 penumbra
companion: 4 tall 8 handsome
ender: 4 ling, room
get ~: 5 bedim, laten 7 becloud, blacken
horse: 8 long shot, opponent, underdog 9 candidate 10 competitor, contestant
hunt in the ~: 6 fumble 9 feel about
in the ~: 5 unlit 6 hidden, secret 7 out of it 8 ignorant 9 benighted, secretive, unadvised, unknowing, unmindful 10 uninformed
look: 5 scowl
make ~: 6 shadow
not ~: 5 light
not in the ~: 5 aware, hep to
shadow: 4 pall
shot in the ~: 3 bet 4 risk, stab 5 guess 6 gamble 9 guesswork
side: 4 evil
to a poet: 4 ebon
dark __: 4 meat, star 5 horse, slide 6 matter, nebula 7 lantern, mineral
__ dark: 5 first, in the
__-dark: 5 pitch
Dark __: 4 Ages, City, Eyes, Lady, Moon 5 Horse 7 Command, Journey, Passage, Shadows, Victory
Dark __ of the Moon: 4 Side
Dark __, The: 4 Half, Past 5 Angel, Arena, Tower 6 Corner, Mirror 7 Crystal
__, dark, and handsome: 4 tall
Dark Angel star: 4 Alba
Dark Arena, The author: Mario Puzo
Dark at the Top of the Stairs, The: 4 film 5 novel
author: William Inge
cast: Eve Arden, Dorothy McGuire, Robert Preston
character: 4 Cora 5 Rubin 6 Lottie, Reenie
director: Delbert Mann
Dark Canoe, The author: 5 O'Dell
Dark City (1998 film)
cast: Jennifer Connelly, Kiefer Sutherland
Dark Command (1940 film)
cast: Walter Pidgeon, Claire Trevor, John Wayne
director: Raoul Walsh
Dark Continent: 3 Afr. 6 Africa
Dark Corner, The (1946 film)
cast: Lucille Ball, William Bendix, Clifton Webb
director: Henry Hathaway
Dark Crystal, The (1982 film)
director: Jim Henson, Frank Oz
darken: 3 dim, mat, tan 4 blur, dull 5 bedim, befog, black, cloud, shade 6 deaden, deject, dim out, sadden, shadow 7 becloud, blacken, cloud up, depress, obscure, tarnish 8 dispirit, tone down 9 adumbrate, obfuscate 10 overshadow
darkened: 3 dim 4 gray, grey 5 mirky, muddy, murky, shady 6 cloudy, dismal, gloomy, opaque, somber, sullen, turbid 7 obscure, sunless, unclear 8 confused, lowering, overcast 9 unsettled 10 indistinct
Dark Eye in Africa, The author: Laurens Van der Post
Dark Eyes (1987 film)
cast: Marthe Keller, Silvana Mangano, Marcello Mastroianni
Darkfall author: Dean Koontz
Dark Half, The author: Stephen King
Dark Horse author: Fletcher Knebel
__ Dark House, The: 3 Old
Dark Intruder director: 4 Hart
darkish: 3 dim
Dark Journey (1937 film)
cast: Vivien Leigh, Conrad Veidt
Dark Lady (1974 song) artist: Cher
Darkman (1990 film)
cast: Colin Friels, Frances McDormand, Liam Neeson
director: Sam Raimi
Dark Mirror, The (1946 film)
cast: Lew Ayres, Olivia de Havilland, Thomas Mitchell
Dark Moon (1957 song)
artist: Bonnie Guitar, Gale Storm
darkness: 4 mirk, murk 5 black, gloom, night, shade 6 shadow 7 secrecy 8 blackout 9 ignorance, murkiness, nightfall, obscurity
combining form: 5 scoto-
Darkness at Noon
author: Arthur Koestler
character: 6 Arlova, Ivanov
Darkness, Prince of: 5 devil, Satan 7 Lucifer
Dark of the Moon author: Sara Teasdale
Dark of the Sun (1968 film)
cast: Jim Brown, Yvette Mimieux, Rod Taylor
Dark Passage (1947 film)
cast: Lauren Bacall, Bruce Bennett, Humphrey Bogart
director: Delmer Daves
Dark Past, The (1948 film)
cast: Lee J. Cobb, Nina Foch, William Holden
director: 4 Maté
Dark Rivers of the Heart author: Dean Koontz
darkroom
chemical: 6 amidol
equipment: 3 enl. 8 enlarger
image: 3 neg. 8 negative
product: 5 proof
solution: 5 fixer, toner

__ Dark Shadow: 5 Cast a
Dark Shadows (ABC): 4 soap 9 soap opera
dark-skinned: 6 swarth 7 swarthy
name meaning ~: 6 Morris 7 Maurice
Dark Tower, The author: Stephen King
Dark Victory (1939 film)
cast: Humphrey Bogart, George Brent, Bette Davis, Geraldine Fitzgerald
composer: 7 Steiner
director: Edmund Goulding
Darla: 4 Hood
Darleen: 4 Carr
Darlene: 4 Love
__ Darlin': 3 Li'l 5 Susie 6 Little
darling: 3 hon, luv, pet 4 baby, cute, dear, doll, idol, lamb, love 5 angel, child, deary, flame, honey, jewel, loved, lover, sugar, sweet 6 dainty, dearie, lovely, pretty, prized, valued 7 beloved, dearest, dear one, favored, lovable, sweetie, winsome 8 adorable, alluring, charming, engaging, favorite, heavenly, ladylove, loveable, precious, truelove 9 boyfriend, cherished, inamorata, treasured 10 delectable, delightful, enchanting, fair-haired, girlfriend, honeybunch, sweetheart
little ~: 3 tot 4 baby 5 angel 6 cherub, infant, moppet 7 neonate, newborn, toddler 8 cutie pie, dumpling, snookums 10 sweetie pie
Darling: 4 Erik 5 range, river, Wendy
dog: 4 Nana
friend: 3 Pan 5 Peter 8 Peter Pan
locale: 9 Australia
Darling (1965 film)
cast: Dirk Bogarde, Julie Christie, Laurence Harvey
director: John Schlesinger
Darling Be Home Soon (1967 song)
artist: Lovin' Spoonful
Darling Je Vous Aime Beaucoup (1955 song) artist: Nat King Cole
Darling Lili (1970 film)
cast: Julie Andrews, Rock Hudson
director: Blake Edwards
darn: 3 sew 4 dang, drat, heck, mend 5 patch, resew 6 repair 9 doggone it 10 confound it
give a ~: 4 care, heed, mind 5 sweat, worry 6 bother, object, regret 9 make a fuss
right: 2 ay, da, ja, sí 3 aye, oui, yea, yep, yup 4 fine, okay, sure, yeah 5 good-o, natch, quite, roger, uh-huh 6 agreed, gladly, good-oh, indeed, just so, rather, surely, you bet, yowzah 7 exactly, for sure, go ahead, indeedy, mais oui, quite so, ten-four 8 all right, as you say, of course, thumbs up, very well 9 be my guest, certainly, naturally, precisely, sure thing, you betcha, you said it 10 absolutely, by all means, definitely, positively, sure enough
something to ~: 4 sock
__ darn: 5 give a
Darn __!: 5 it all
Darn!: 4 dang, drat, heck, nuts, rats 5 nerts, nertz, shoot 6 cripes
in German: 3 ach
__ Darn Cat!: 4 That
darned: 4 very 10 confounded
__ darned!: 5 I'll be
darnel: 5 grass
Darnell: 5 Linda 6 Martin
Darnell, Linda: 7 actress
film: Anna and the King of Siam (1946)
Blood and Sand (1941)
Everybody Does It (1949)
Forever Amber (1947)
Hangover Square (1945)
It Happened Tomorrow (1944)
A Letter to Three Wives (1949)
The Mark of Zorro (1940)
My Darling Clementine (1946)
No Way Out (1950)
Summer Storm (1944)
Unfaithfully Yours (1948)
darner: 6 needle 9 dragonfly
__ Darn Hot: 3 Too
darning __: 3 egg 6 needle
darning, in need of: 5 holey
Darnley, Lord: 4 Scot
__ darn tootin'!: 3 Yer
Darn tootin'!: 6 I'll say
DAR part: 3 Rev. 4 Amer. 8 American 9 Daughters 10 Revolution
Darrell: 5 Evans
Darren: 5 James 7 McGavin
Darren, James: 5 actor 6 singer
film: All the Young Men (1960)
Let No Man Write My Epitaph (1960)
song: Goodbye Cruel World (1961)
Her Royal Majesty (1962)
TV: The Time Tunnel, T.J. Hooker
Darrieux: 8 Danielle
Darrow: 3 Ann 8 Clarence
Darryl: 6 Zanuck 7 Hickman 10 Strawberry
dart: 3 fly, hie, rip, run, zig, zip 4 bolt, dash, flap, flit, lick, race, rush, shot, skim, tear, whiz, zoom 5 hurry, lunge, scoot, shoot, spank, speed, start, swoop, whisk 6 barrel, gallop, hasten, hurtle, hustle, move it, rocket, scurry, sprint, whoosh 7 floor it, hop to it, missile, quicken, scamper 8 hightail, step on it 9 fulgurate, hotfoot it, shake a leg, skedaddle 10 get a move on, hightail it
part: 5 shaft
player's drink: 3 ale 5 lager, stout
shooter: 4 Amor, Eros 5 Cupid
__ d'art: 5 objet
Dart: 3 car 4 auto 5 Dodge 10 automobile
d'Artagnan: 9 Musketeer
friend: 5 Athos 6 Aramis 7 Porthos
prop: 4 épée 5 sword
dartboard wood: 3 elm
darter: 4 bird, fish
__ darter: 5 snail 7 fantail, rainbow
Dartmoor: 5 sheep
city near ~: 6 Exeter
locale: 7 England
Dartmouth: 4 city, town 7 college
athletes: 8 Big Green
league: 3 Ivy
locale: 4 Mass. 6 Canada 7 Hanover 10 Nova Scotia 12 New Hampshire
darts: 4 game 5 sport
locale: 3 pub
Darwell, Jane: 7 actress
film: Captain Tugboat Annie (1945)
The Grapes of Wrath (1940, AA)
Mary Poppins (1964)
Darwin: 4 city, town 7 Charles
locale: 9 Australia
Darwin, Charles: 7 British 10 naturalist
Darwinian __: 7 fitness
__ Darya: 3 Amu, Syr
Daryl: 4 Duke, Hall 6 Dragon, Hannah 7 Dawkins 8 Anderson
Das __: 4 Boot 7 Kapital
Das __ von der Erde: 4 Lied
Das Boot (1981 film)
cast: Herbert Gronemeyer, Jürgen Prochnow
craft: 3 sub 5 U-boat
director: Wolfgang Petersen
dash: 3 bit, fly, hie, nip, ram, rip, run, vim, zip 4 bolt, brio, dart, drop, élan, fire, flit, foil, lick, life, line, race, ruin, rush, slam, snap, tear, tick, tint, whit, zing, zoom 5 éclat, flair, haste, hurry, lunge, oomph, pinch, scoot, shade, shoot, spank, speed, style, taste, throw, tinge, touch, trace, verve, vigor, whiff, whisk, wreck 6 barrel, blight, bon ton, bustle, charge, dampen, dollop, energy, esprit, gallop, hasten, hustle, hyphen, little, move it, pizazz, plunge, rocket, scurry, spirit, splash, sprint, streak, thwart, trifle 7 bravery, bravura, courage, deflate, floor it, hop to it, modicum, panache, pizzazz, quicken, scamper, shatter, smidgen, smidgin, soupçon, sparkle, take off 8 confound, dispirit, flourish, smidgeon, spoonful, sprinkle, stampede, step on it, vivacity 9 animation, élan vital, frustrate, hotfoot it, shake a leg, skedaddle 10 burn rubber, confidence, disappoint, discourage, enterprise, enthusiasm, get a move on, get hopping, hightail it, liveliness, sprinkling
ender: 3 pot 5 board
hopes: 6 dismay, thwart 7 let down 10 dishearten
length: 2 em, en
Morse ~: 3 dah
off: 4 type 5 write 9 improvise
partner: 3 dot
starter: 4 slap
dash __: 3 off 4 down 5 light
__ dash: 3 jim, mut, nut 5 swung 6 pebble 7 spatter
Dash: 6 Crofts, Stacey 9 detergent
alternative: 3 All, Biz, Era, Fab, Yes 4 Bold, Gain, Surf, Tide, Wisk 5 Cheer, Dreft, Purex 6 Calgon, Dynamo, Oxydol 7 Octagon 9 Ivory Snow
Dash __!: 5 it all
__ Dashan, Ethiopia: 3 Ras
dashboard
device: 3 odo 4 dial, tach 5 gauge, radio 6 airbag, dimmer 8 CD player, odometer 10 tape player
reading: 3 mph, rpm
dashed off: 9 impromptu
Dasher: 8 reindeer
colleague: 5 Comet, Cupid, Vixen 6 Dancer, Donder 7 Blitzen, Prancer
handler: 5 Santa
dashi: 4 soup
Dashiell: 7 Hammett
contemporary: 4 Erle 6 Agatha
dog: 4 Asta
dashiki: 7 African, garment
dashing: 4 bold, chic, fast 5 brave, class, faddy, peppy, sharp, showy, smart, swank 6 breezy, classy, dapper, daring, jaunty, lively, modish, plucky, rakish, snappy, sporty 7 chipper, elegant, gallant, raffish, rousing, stylish, voguish 8 animated, colorful, dazzling, debonair, fearless, spirited 9 debonaire, impetuous, in fashion, sprightly, vivacious 10 debonnaire, flamboyant
fellow: 4 dude 5 blade, dandy, swell
Dasht-e-Kavire: 6 desert
locale: 4 Asia, Iran
Dasht-e-Lut: 6 desert
locale: 4 Asia, Iran
da Silva, Howard: 5 actor
film: 1776 (1972)
David and Lisa (1962)
Mommie Dearest (1981)
They Live by Night (1949)
Das Kapital author: Karl Marx
Das Lied von der Erde composer: 6 Mahler
Das Rheingold: 5 opera
character: 4 Erda, Froh, Loge, Mime, Norn 5 Freia, Wotan 6 Donner, Fafner, Fasolt, Fricka 8 Alberich, Woglinde 9 Wellgunde 10 Flosshilde
composer: 6 Wagner
setting: 5 Rhine 7 Germany
dassie: 5 hyrax
Dassin, Jules: 8 director
film: Brute Force (1947)
The Canterville Ghost (1944)
The Naked City (1948)
Never on Sunday (1960)
Rififi (1954)
Thieves' Highway (1949)
Topkapi (1964)
Up Tight (1968)
dastard: 3 cur 4 heel, wimp 5 devil, fiend, knave, rogue, scamp, sissy 6 bad guy, coward, craven 7 chicken 8 poltroon, recreant 9 fraidy cat, hellhound, jellyfish
dastardly: 3 low 4 base, mean, vile 5 timid 6 craven, rotten 7 ignoble, knavish, wimpish 8 recreant, shameful
dasyure: 9 marsupial
relative: 4 euro 5 bilbi, bilby, koala 6 numbat, wombat 7 bettong, opossum, wallaby 8 kangaroo, wallaroo 9 bandicoot, phalanger
dat
not ~: 3 dis
data: 4 info, news 5 facts, proof 6 notice 7 details, figures, numbers 8 evidence, material 10 statistics
computer ~ format: 5 ASCII
copy: 6 backup
disk: 5 CD/ROM 6 floppy
ender: 4 bank, base
enter ~: 4 type 5 input, key in
locate, as ~: 6 access
processing equipment: 2 PC
seek ~: 3 ask
sender: 4 ISDN 5 cable, modem
storage medium: 4 disk 5 CD/ROM 6 floppy 7 Zip disk 10 floppy disk
transfer rate: 4 baud
transmission science: 9 telemetry
unit: 3 bit 4 byte
data __: 3 set 4 bank, base 6 center 7 carrier, highway
database
function: 4 sort 6 select
Internet ~: 5 Lexis, Nexis
data-entry
area: 6 keypad
goof: 4 typo
person: 5 typer
data-sharing acronym: 3 LAN
data transmission, science of: 9 telemetry
date: 3 see, woo 4 appt., palm, time 5 court, fruit, go out, tryst 6 ask out, escort, go with, jujube, pursue, squire, suitor 7 meeting, partner, step out, take out 9 boyfriend, companion, go out with 10 engagement, girlfriend, invitation, rendezvous
at an early ~: 4 anon
bring up to ~: 6 revamp, revise, update 9 modernize
Chinese ~: 6 jujube
disappointing ~: 4 nerd, nurd
due ~: 3 end 5 limit 6 cutoff 8 deadline, zero hour
effective ~ in law: 4 nisi
ender: 4 line
entertainer's ~: 3 gig 7 booking
gal's ~: 5 fella 6 fellow
guy's ~: 3 gal 4 doll
have a ~: 5 go out
invite on a ~: 6 ask out
on a ~: 3 out
on that ~: 4 as of, then
out of ~: 5 passé 7 archaic
producer: 5 Yemen

provide a ~: 5 fix up, set up
regularly: 3 see
Roman ~: 4 ides 5 nones
starter: 3 air, pre 4 ante
to ~: 3 yet 5 as yet, so far 7 as of now 8 until now
tree: 4 palm
way to go on a ~: 5 Dutch
date ___: 4 line, palm 5 stamp 6 mussel
___ date: 3 due, pub 4 pack, play, pull, rain, sell, set a, up to, wild 5 blind, out of, value 6 cut-off, double, target 7 Chinese, release
___ date!: 4 It's a
___-date: 4 up-to 5 out-of 6 carbon, double
datebook
abbr.: 3 Mon., Sat., Sun., Thu., Tue., Wed. 4 Tues. 5 Thurs.
duration: 4 year
dated: 3 obs., old, out 5 dowdy, passé, stale 6 bygone, old hat, square 7 archaic, outworn 8 obsolete, outdated, outmoded, out of use, timeworn 10 antiquated, out of style
dateless: 4 stag 5 alone
date palm, name meaning: 6 Tamara
dater: 5 stamp 9 time stamp
date-setting phrase: 4 as of
___ D.A., The: 6 Shaggy
dating: 4 with 9 courtship
___ dating: 4 code, open 6 carbon 7 uranium
Dating Game, The host: Jim Lange
dating-service objective: 5 match
dative: 4 case
Datong: 4 city
locale: 5 China 6 Shanxi
Datril alternative: 3 APF 4 Cope 5 Advil, Aleve, Bayer 6 Anacin, Motrin 7 Ecotrin, Tylenol 8 Bufferin, Excedrin, St. Joseph, Vanquish 9 Ascriptin
datum: 4 fact, stat 9 statistic
datura: 10 jimsonweed, nightshade
daub: 3 pat 4 blob, spot 5 paint, smear, stain 6 smudge, spread, streak 7 plaster, spatter
daube: 4 stew
Dauber author: John Masefield
Daudet: 4 Léon 8 Alphonse
Daudet, Alphonse: 6 French, writer
Daudet, Léon: 6 French, writer
daughter: 3 kid, she 4 cion, girl 5 child, scion, woman 6 female 7 kinsman 9 offspring 10 descendant
starter: 3 god 4 step 5 grand
daughter-___: 5 in-law
___ Daughter: 5 Ryan's
daughterly: 6 filial
Daughter of Fortune author: Allende
Daughter of the Dragon star: 5 Oland
daughter of the oath, name meaning: 9 Bathsheba
Daughter of Time, The author: Josephine Tey
daughters: 5 issue 7 kinfolk 8 kinfolks, kinsfolk 9 offspring
Daughters and Rebels author: Mitford
Daughters Courageous (1939 film)
cast: Fay Bainter, John Garfield, Priscilla Lane, Claude Rains
director: Michael Curtiz
Daughters of the Dust director: 4 Dash
___ Daughter, The: 7 Farmer's, Ragman's
dauli: 4 drum
origin: 6 Greece
Daumier: 6 Honoré
daunt: 3 cow 4 faze 5 alarm, appal, bully, deter, scare, shake 6 appall, dampen, dismay, menace 7 depress, overawe, terrify, unnerve 8 dispirit, dissuade, frighten, paralyse, paralyze, unstring 10 demoralize, discourage, dishearten, intimidate, scare stiff
daunted: 4 down 5 timid 6 afraid, trepid 7 anxious, chicken, fearful, nervous, panicky 8 cowardly, downcast, fearsome, hesitant, timorous 9 awestruck
daunting: 5 scary 7 awesome 9 frightful 10 forbidding, formidable
dauntless: 4 bold, game 5 brave, gutsy, nervy, stout 6 awless, daring, gritty, heroic, plucky, spunky 7 aweless, defiant, doughty, gallant, impavid, staunch, valiant 8 fearless, heroical, intrepid, resolute, spirited, stalwart, unafraid, valorous 9 audacious, confident, dreadless, undaunted, unfearful, unfearing 10 courageous, invincible, mettlesome, undismayed
dauntlessness: 4 grit, guts 5 heart, nerve, valor 6 mettle, spirit 7 bravery, prowess 8 audacity
dauphin: 3 son 5 title 6 prince
Dauphine: 3 car 4 auto 7 Renault
Dausset, Jean: 6 French 8 Nobelist
dautie: 3 hon, luv, pet 4 baby, dear, doll, lamb, love 5 angel, deary, flame, honey, jewel, lover, sugar, sweet 6 dearie 7 beloved, darling, dearest, dear one, sweetie 8 ladylove, precious, truelove 9 boyfriend, inamorata 10 girlfriend, honeybunch, sweetheart
Davao: 4 city, gulf, port, town
locale: 11 Philippines
Dave: 4 Bing 5 Barry, Clark, Mason 6 Casper, Cortez, Cowens, Grusin, Parker, Thomas 7 Brubeck, Edmunds, Loggins, McNally, Navarro, Stewart 8 Garroway, Matthews, Winfield 9 Letterman
singing partner: 3 Sam
TV rival: 3 Jay
Dave (1993 film)
cast: Ben Kingsley, Kevin Kline, Frank Langella, Sigourney Weaver
director: Ivan Reitman
Dave ___ Five: 5 Clark
davenport: 4 desk, seat, sofa 5 couch, divan, table 6 daybed, settee 7 seating 9 furniture
Davenport: 4 city, town 5 Nigel 7 Lindsay
locale: 4 Iowa
Davenport, Lindsay: 7 netster 9 tennis pro
Daves, Delmer: 8 director
film: 3:10 to Yuma (1957)
The Badlanders (1958)
Broken Arrow (1950)
Cowboy (1958)
Dark Passage (1947)
The Hanging Tree (1959)
Jubal (1956)
Kings Go Forth (1958)
The Last Wagon (1956)
Pride of the Marines (1945)
The Red House (1947)
Rome Adventure (1962)
A Summer Place (1959)
Dave's World
network: 3 CBS 5 CBS-TV
secretary: 3 Mia
Davey: 5 Lopes
Davi: 6 Robert
David: 3 Hal, Lee 4 camp, Cone, Frye, Groh, Hume, king, Lean, Levy, Rabe, Rose, Soul, Toms 5 Bowie, Chase, Doyle, Dukes, Duval, Essex, Frost, Hubel, Keith, Kersh, Louis, Lynch, Mamet, Morse, Niven, saint, Selby, Spade, Swift, Wayne, White 6 Birney, Butler, Canary, Caruso, Crosby, Geddes, Geffen, Kelley, Lander, Miller, Nelson, Paymer, Rasche, Rudkin, Ruffin, Souter, Storey, Warner, Zucker 7 Belasco, Brenner, Carroll, Cassidy, Charvet, Coulier, Diamond, Dinkins, Garrick, Hartman, Hedison, Hockney, Houston, Ignatow, Janssen, Leisure, Manners, Merrick, Packard, Ricardo, Sarnoff, Seville, Thewlis, Trimble 8 Anspaugh, Arquette, Brinkley, Bushnell, Duchovny, Farragut, Faustino, Frizzell, Helfgott, Hemmings, Johansen, McCallum, Naughton, Oistrakh, Opatoshu, Robinson, Selznick, Susskind, Thompson 9 Baltimore, Ben-Gurion, Carradine, Letterman, Rappaport, Schwimmer, Tomlinson 10 Eisenhower, Halberstam, Hasselhoff, McCullough, Strathairn
army commander: 5 Abner
co-anchor: 4 Chet
daughter: 5 Tamar
father: 5 Jesse
grandfather: 4 Obed
great-grandmother: 5 Naomi
instrument: 4 harp
king before ~: 4 Saul
nephew: 5 Amasa
sibling: 4 Ozem 5 Eliab, Ricky 6 Raddai, Shimei 7 Abigail, Shammah, Zeruiah 8 Nethanel
son: 5 Amnon, Ibhar, Nogah 6 Eliada, Nepheg 7 Absalom, Chileab, Elishua, Ithream, Shammua, Solomon 8 Adonijah, Elishama 9 Eliphilet 10 Shephatiah
song of ~: 5 psalm
to Goliath: 3 foe 5 enemy 9 adversary
warrior: 3 Ira
wife: 5 Eglah 6 Abital, Maacah, Michal 7 Abigail, Haggith 9 Bathsheba
David ___ George: 5 Lloyd
David ___-Gurion: 3 Ben
David ___ Pierce: 4 Hyde
David ___ Roth: 3 Lee
David ___ Stiers: 5 Ogden
___ David: 4 Camp 5 Magen, Mogen 6 Star of 7 Tol'able
Davida: 8 asteroid
David and Lisa (1962 film)
cast: Howard da Silva, Keir Dullea, Janet Margolin
David Copperfield
author: Charles Dickens
character: 3 Ham 4 Dora, Em'ly, Emma, Heep, Jane, Mell, Rosa, Tipp 5 Agnes, Clara, Crupp, Sophy, Uriah 6 Barkis, Betsey, Daniel, Dartle, Demple, Edward, Mr. Dick, Tiffey 7 Creakle, Crewler, Francis, Jorkins, Lavinia, Markham, Quinion, Spenlow, Wilkins 8 Clarissa, Grainger, Gummidge, Littimer, Micawber, Peggotty, Traddles, Trotwood 9 Murdstone, Uriah Heep, Wickfield 10 Little Em'ly, Rosa Dartle, Steerforth
dog: 3 Jip
David Copperfield (1935 film)
cast: Lionel Barrymore, Freddie Bartholomew, Madge Evans, W.C. Fields, Edna May Oliver, Maureen O'Sullivan, Basil Rathbone, Roland Young
director: George Cukor
David E. ___: 6 Kelley
David H. ___: 6 Souter
David L. ___: 6 Lander
David-Neel, Alexandra: 6 French 8 explorer
David O. ___: 8 Selznick
Davidovich, Lolita: 7 actress
film: Blaze (1989)
Cobb (1994)
Gods and Monsters (1998)
Leap of Faith (1992)
The Object of Beauty (1991)
Play It to the Bone (1999)
Davidson: 2 Jo 4 Jaye, John
partner: 6 Harley
___ David Thoreau: 5 Henry
Davie: 4 city, town 6 Donald
locale: 7 Florida
Davie, Donald: 4 poet 7 British
Davies: 6 Marion 9 Robertson
Davies, Marion: 7 actress
film: The Florodora Girl (1930)
Going Hollywood (1933)
Marianne (1929)
Peg o' My Heart (1933)
Show People (1928)
Davies, Robertson: 6 writer 8 Canadian
work: The Deptford Trilogy
da Vinci Airport locale: 4 Rome
da Vinci, Leonardo: 6 artist 7 Italian, painter
Davis: 3 Jim, Mac 4 Brad, Eric, Erin, Gail, Hope, Joan, Judy, Love, Owen, Paul, town 5 Bette, Chili, Geena, Miles, Nancy, Ossie, Patti, Peter, Sammi 6 Adelle, Andrew, Angela, Tyrone 7 Clifton, Kristin, Raymond, Skeeter 9 Jefferson
Davis ___: 6 Strait
___-Davis: 4 Ziff
Davis, Andrew: 8 director
film: Above the Law (1988)
The Fugitive (1993)
A Perfect Murder (1998)
Stony Island (1978)
Under Siege (1992)
Davis, Bette: 7 actress
film: 20,000 Years in Sing Sing (1933)
All About Eve (1950)
All This and Heaven Too (1940)
Bordertown (1935)
The Catered Affair (1956)
The Corn Is Green (1945)
Dangerous (1935, AA)
Dark Victory (1939)
Deception (1946)
Fashions (1934)
The Girl From 10th Avenue (1935)
The Great Lie (1941)
Hush ... Hush, Sweet Charlotte (1965)
In This Our Life (1942)
It's Love I'm After (1937)
Jezebel (1938, AA)
Juarez (1939)
June Bride (1948)
Kid Galahad (1937)
The Letter (1940)
The Little Foxes (1941)
The Man Who Came to Dinner (1941)
Marked Woman (1937)
Mr. Skeffington (1944)
Now, Voyager (1942)
Of Human Bondage (1934)
Old Acquaintance (1943)
The Old Maid (1939)
Payment on Demand (1951)
The Petrified Forest (1936)
Phone Call From a Stranger (1952)
Pocketful of Miracles (1961)
The Private Lives of Elizabeth and Essex (1939)
Return From Witch Mountain (1978)
The Sisters (1938)
The Star (1952)
Three on a Match (1932)
The Virgin Queen (1955)
Watch on the Rhine (1943)
The Whales of August (1987)
What Ever Happened to Baby Jane? (1962)
The Working Man (1933)
Davis, Chili sport: 8 baseball
Davis Cup
former ~ captain: 4 Ashe
sport: 6 tennis

__ Davis Eyes: 5 Bette
Davis, Geena: 7 actress
 film: The Accidental Tourist (1988, AA)
  Angie (1994)
  Beetlejuice (1988)
  Cutthroat Island (1995)
  Earth Girls Are Easy (1989)
  The Fly (1986)
  Hero (1992)
  A League of Their Own (1992)
  Quick Change (1990)
  Speechless (1994)
  Stuart Little (1999)
  Thelma & Louise (1991)
  Tootsie (1982)
 spouse: Jeff Goldblum, Renny Harlin
__ Davis Group: 7 Spencer
Davis, Jefferson org.: 3 CSA
Davis, Jim dog: 4 Odie
__ Davis Jr.: 5 Billy, Sammy
Davis Jr., Billy spouse: Marilyn McCoo
Davis Jr., Sammy: 5 actor 6 singer
 film: Johnny Cool (1963)
  Ocean's Eleven (1960)
  Porgy and Bess (1959)
  Robin and the Seven Hoods (1964)
  Tap (1989)
 song: The Candy Man (1972)
  I've Gotta Be Me (1969)
  Something's Gotta Give (1955)
  What Kind of Fool Am I (1962)
Davis, Judy: 7 actress
 film: Alice (1990)
  Barton Fink (1991)
  Celebrity (1998)
  Husbands and Wives (1992)
  Impromptu (1991)
  My Brilliant Career (1979)
  A Passage to India (1984)
Davis, Mac
 song: Baby Don't Get Hooked on Me (1972)
  Stop and Smell the Roses (1974)
Davis, Miles: 9 trumpeter
 accessory: 4 mute
 genre: 4 jazz
 spouse: Cicely Tyson
Davis, Nancy: 7 actress
 film: Donovan's Brain (1953)
  Night Into Morning (1951)
  Shadow on the Wall (1950)
 spouse: Ronald Reagan
Davison: 5 Bruce
Davis, Ossie: 5 actor
 film: Black Girl (1972)
  Cotton Comes to Harlem (1970)
  Doctor Dolittle (1998)
  Do the Right Thing (1989)
  Get on the Bus (1996)
  Gone Are the Days (1963)
  Gordon's War (1973)
 film (voice): Dinosaur (2000)
 spouse: Ruby Dee
 TV: Evening Shade
Davis partner: 5 Parke
Davis, Raymond: 8 Nobelist 9 physicist
Davis, Skeeter
 song: The End of the World (1963)
  I Can't Stay Mad at You (1963)
Davisson, Clinton: 8 Nobelist 9 physicist
davit: 5 crane, hoist 7 derrick
Davos: 7 commune
 enjoy ~: 3 ski
 locale: 11 Switzerland
davul: 4 drum
 origin: 6 Greece, Turkey
Davy: 5 Jones 7 Humphry 8 Crockett
Davy __: 4 lamp 5 Jones
Davy Crockett... (1955 film)
 cast: Buddy Ebsen, Fess Parker
Davy, Humphry: 3 Sir 7 British, chemist
Davy Jones' locker: 3 sea 5 ocean
Davys, John: 7 British 8 explorer
daw: 6 magpie 7 grackle
 kin: 3 ani 5 raven
 starter: 4 jack
Dawa: 5 river
 locale: 5 Kenya 8 Ethiopia
Dawber, Pam spouse: Mark Harmon
dawdle: 3 lag 4 drag, idle, laze, loaf, loll, poke 5 amble, dally, delay, mosey, stall, tarry, trail 6 linger, loiter, lounge, put off, trifle 7 goof off, saunter 8 foot-drag, lallygag, lose time, slack off, straggle 9 poke along, waste time 10 dillydally, fool around, hang around, mess around, wait around
dawdler: 4 poke 5 idler, sloth, snail 7 laggard, lie-abed, lounger, trifler 8 layabout, lingerer, loiterer, slowpoke, slugabed, sluggard 9 latecomer, lazy-bones
dawdling: 4 poky, slow 5 delay, tardy 6 draggy 7 gradual, impeded, languid 8 dilatory, drawn-out, hesitant, slothful, sluggish 9 leisurely, lethargic, lingering, prolonged, snaillike, unhurried 10 deliberate, protracted
Dawes __: 4 plan
Dawes, Charles: 4 veep 8 Nobelist
Dawkins, Daryl sport: 10 basketball
dawn: 4 morn, rise 5 begin, birth, light, onset, prime, start, sunup 6 advent, aurora, emerge, origin, outset, unfold 7 genesis, infancy, morning, opening, sunrise 8 cockcrow, daybreak, daylight 9 beginning, emergence, inception, originate, threshold 10 break of day, first light, incipience
 dusk to ~: 5 night
 goddess: 3 Eos 4 Usha 5 Ushas 6 Aurora
 meet the ~: 4 rise, wake 5 arise, awake, waken 6 awaken, wake up
 music: 4 alba 6 aubade
 name meaning ~: 7 Roxanne
 of the ~: 4 eoan
 on: 7 occur to
dawn __: 5 horse 6 patrol 7 redwood
Dawn: 3 Lyn 5 O'Hara, Steel, Wells 6 Fraser, Upshaw
 alternative: 3 Joy 4 Ajax 7 Cascade 8 Sunlight 9 Palmolive 10 Electrasol
__ Dawn: 3 Red 4 Zulu 5 Delta
__ Dawn Chong: 3 Rae
__ Dawn I Die: 4 Each
dawning: 5 onset, start 6 origin, source 7 genesis
Dawn of the Dead (1978 film) director: George A. Romero
Dawn O'Hara author: Edna Ferber
Dawn Patrol, The (1938 film)
 cast: Errol Flynn, David Niven, Basil Rathbone
 director: Edmund Goulding
dawnward: 4 east
Daws: 6 Butler
Dawson: 3 Len 5 Andre 7 Richard
Dawson, Andre: 10 baseballer
Dawson City: 4 city, town
 locale: 6 Canada
Dawson Creek: 4 city, town
 locale: 6 Canada
 road: 5 Alcan
Dawson, Len: 2 QB 11 quarterback
 sport: 8 football
Dawson, Richard spouse: Diana Dors
Dawson's Creek (WB drama)
 cast: Katie Holmes (Joey Potter)
  Joshua Jackson (Pacey Witter)
  James Van Der Beek (Dawson Leery)
  Michelle Williams (Jen Lindley)
Dax: 4 city, town
 locale: 6 France
day: 3 era 4 time 6 period 10 generation
 a ~: 7 per diem 9 diurnally
 after day: 3 oft 5 often 10 all the time
 any ~: 4 anon, soon 8 sometime 10 imminently
 before: 3 eve
 break of ~: 4 dawn, morn 5 sunup 7 morning, sunrise
 call it a ~: 3 end 4 halt, quit, stop 5 cease, close 6 finish, retire, turn in, wind up, wrap up 7 adjourn, break up 8 break off, conclude, finish up, knock off, pack it in 9 terminate
 carry the ~: 3 win 7 prevail, succeed, triumph
 close of ~: 5 night 6 curfew 7 bedtime 9 nightfall
 ender: 3 bed, fly, hop 4 book, care, lily, long, pack, side, star, time, wear 5 break, dream, light, shift 6 flower 7 dreamer
 every eighth ~: 5 octan
 feast ~: 7 jubilee
 field ~: 4 bash 5 binge, fling, revel, spree 6 junket
 first part of the ~: 7 morning
 forever and a ~: 3 eon 4 aeon, ages 8 long time
 holy ~: 5 feast 6 Easter 9 Christmas
 in Latin: 4 diem
 in this ~ and age: 3 now 4 here 5 today
 light: 3 sun
 lily: 5 plant 6 flower
 make one's ~: 5 elate 6 please
 middle of the ~: 4 noon
 midmonth ~: 4 ides
 night and ~: 7 nonstop 9 endlessly 10 unendingly
 not give the time of ~: 3 cut 4 shun, snub 5 spurn 6 ignore, rebuff, slight 8 brush off
 of rest: 3 Sab., Sun. 6 Sunday 7 Sabbath 8 vacation
 of the week: 3 Fri., Mon., Sat., Sun., Thu., Tue., Wed. 4 Thur., Tues. 5 Thurs.
 one: 5 git-go, onset, start 6 origin 9 beginning
 one ~: 4 soon 10 eventually
 opposite: 5 night 7 evening
 rainy ~ fund: 7 nest egg, reserve, savings
 Roman calendar ~: 4 ides 5 nones 7 calends
 save for rainy ~: 8 salt away
 saver: 4 hero
 seize the ~: 4 live
 starter: 3 hey, may, mid, pay, Sun 4 holy, noon, sick, some, wash, week, work 5 birth, dooms, every
 start the ~: 4 rise, wake 5 arise, awake, get up, waken
 the other ~: 8 recently
 time of ~: 4 dawn, dusk, hour, morn, noon 5 sunup 6 sunset 7 evening, morning, sunrise
 to this ~: 5 still 8 hitherto, until now
 trip: 5 jaunt 9 excursion
 units: 3 hrs. 5 hours
day __: 3 bed, boy, job, man, one 4 camp, care, lily, loan, name, room 5 coach, labor, shift 6 letter, sailer, school 7 cruiser, jasmine, laborer, nursery, student
day __ day: 5 after
day-__: 4 care, trip 5 by-day, liner, to-day 6 trader 7 neutral, tripper
__ day: 3 lay, tag 4 fast, fete, good, high, holy, leap, name, sick, snow, term 5 civil, class, Ember, feast, field, First, Lord's, lunar, rainy, solar 6 banner, dollar, saint's, school 7 quarter, wedding, working
__-day: 3 all, dog, man 4 long 5 day-by, day-to, short, woman 6 degree, latter, person 7 present, working
Day: 3 Pat 4 Bill 5 Bobby, Doris 6 Dennis 7 Dorothy, Laraine 8 Clarence
Day __ Day: 5 After
Day-__: 3 Glo
__ Day: 3 Dre, May 4 Flag, Lady 5 Anzac, Arbor, Day by, Earth, Great, Green, Labor, Lucky, Rizal, Union 6 Boxing, Canada, Empire, Julian, Labour, Ladies', Lammas, Muster, School, Woman's 7 Another, Father's, Jackson, Mother's, Pioneer, Twelfth
__-Day: 3 May 4 One-A
__ Day, A: 5 Foggy
__-Day Adventist: 7 Seventh
__ Day Afternoon: 3 Dog
Dayak: 8 language
Dayan: 5 Moshe
__ day and age: 4 this 6 in this
__ day at a time: 3 one
__ Day at Black Rock: 3 Bad
Da Ya Think I'm Sexy? (1978 song)
 artist: Rod Stewart
Day at the Races, A (1937 film)
 cast: Margaret Dumont, Allan Jones, Chico Marx, Groucho Marx, Harpo Marx, Maureen O'Sullivan
 director: Sam Wood
daybed: 4 sofa 5 couch, futon 6 chaise 7 seating 9 davenport
Day, Bobby song: Rock-in Robin (1958)
daybook: 3 log 5 diary 6 ledger 7 Filofax, journal 8 calendar
daybreak: 4 dawn, morn 5 light, prime, sunup 6 aurora 7 morning, sunrise 8 cockcrow 10 first light
Day by Day author: Robert Lowell
day-care candidate: 3 kid, tot 4 tike, tyke 5 child
Day, Clarence: 6 author, writer
 work: Life With Father
  Life With Mother
__-day cover: 5 first
Day, Dennis employer: Jack Benny
Day, Doris: 6 singer 7 actress
 film: Billy Rose's Jumbo (1962)
  Calamity Jane (1953)
  The Glass Bottom Boat (1966)
  Love Me or Leave Me (1955)
  Lover Come Back (1961)
  The Man Who Knew Too Much (1956)
  Midnight Lace (1960)
  The Pajama Game (1957)
  Pillow Talk (1959)
  Please Don't Eat the Daisies (1960)
  Send Me No Flowers (1964)
  Teacher's Pet (1958)
  The Thrill of It All (1963)
  The Tunnel of Love (1958)
  Young at Heart (1954)
  Young Man With a Horn (1950)
 song: Again (1949)
  Everybody Loves a Lover (1958)
  If I Give My Heart to You (1954)
  Que Sera, Sera (1956)
daydream: 4 hope, moon, wish 5 fancy 6 ideate, revery, trance, vision 7 fantasy, figment, imagine, picture, reverie 8 delusion, illusion, space out 9 fantasize, imagining 10 woolgather
Daydream (1966 song) artist: Lovin' Spoonful
Daydream Believer (song) artist: Anne Murray, Monkees
daydreamer: 5 Mitty 8 escapist
Daydreamer, The (1966 film)
 cast: Ray Bolger, Jack Gilford
Daydreamin' (1998 song) artist: Tatyana Ali
Day Dreaming (1972 song) artist: Aretha Franklin

daydreamy: 6 vacant 7 unaware, wistful 8 mindless 9 unmindful
dayfly: 3 bug 6 insect
Day for Night (1973 film)
cast: Jean-Pierre Aumont, Jacqueline Bisset, Valentina Cortese
director: François Truffaut
__ Day George: 5 Lynda
day in __: 5 court
Day in the __, A: 4 Life 7 Country
Day in the Country, A (1946 film)
director: Jean Renoir
Day, Laraine: 7 actress
film: Foreign Correspondent (1940)
The High and the Mighty (1954)
Journey for Margaret (1942)
Mr. Lucky (1943)
The Third Voice (1960)
Unholy Partners (1941)
spouse: Leo Durocher
Day Lewis: 5 Cecil 6 Daniel
Day Lewis, Cecil: 4 poet 5 Irish 7 British 8 laureate
colleague: Auden, Spender
son: Daniel
Day Lewis, Daniel: 5 actor
film: The Age of Innocence (1993)
In the Name of the Father (1993)
The Last of the Mohicans (1992)
My Beautiful Laundrette (1985)
My Left Foot (1989, AA)
The Unbearable Lightness of Being (1988)
daylight: 4 dawn 5 light, sunup 6 aurora 7 morning, sunrise 8 cockcrow, sunshine
in broad ~: 6 openly
let ~ in: 6 expose, reveal 8 simplify
see ~: 7 realize
daylight-__ time: 6 saving
daylights, living: 4 wits
__ Daylights, The: 6 Living
__ Daylight Time: 7 Central, Eastern, Pacific 8 Mountain
Dayne, Taylor
song: Don't Rush Me (1988)
I'll Always Love You (1988)
I'll Be Your Shelter (1990)
Love Will Lead You Back (1990)
Prove Your Love (1988)
Tell It to My Heart (1987)
With Every Beat of My Heart (1989)
__ day now: 3 any
Day-O (1957 song) artist: Harry Belafonte
__ Day O'Connor: 6 Sandra
day of __: 4 rest
Day of __: 6 Infamy 9 Atonement
Day of Atonement author: Kellerman
Day of Doom, The author: Wigglesworth
Day of Fury, A (1956 film)
cast: Mara Corday, Dale Robertson
Day of the Jackal, The (1973 film)
cast: Alan Badel, Tony Britton, Edward Fox
director: Fred Zinnemann
Day of the Locust: 4 film 5 novel
author: Nathanael West
cast: Karen Black, Burgess Meredith, Donald Sutherland
director: John Schlesinger
Day of the Triffids, The author: John Wyndham
Day, Pat: 6 jockey
__ Day People: 5 Rainy
Dayquil alternative: 5 Afrin 6 Contac, Tavist 7 Actifed, Comtrex, Dristan, Sinutab, Sudafed 8 Benadryl, Dimetapp, Drixoral, TheraFlu 9 Coricidin, Triaminic 10 Robitussin
maker: 5 Vicks
days: 4 life 8 lifetime
from ~ of yore: 5 olden
in olden ~: 3 ago 4 once, past, then 6 before 7 earlier, long ago, time was, way back 8 back when, formerly, years ago 9 at one time, in the past 10 heretofore, previously
off: 7 holiday 8 vacation
old ~: 3 eld 4 past, yore 7 earlier, history, long ago 8 back when 9 antiquity, yesterday 10 yesteryear
one of these ~: 4 anon, soon 9 presently
seven ~: 4 week
starter: 4 nowa
these ~: 3 now 6 lately
days __: 5 of old, on end
__ days: 3 dog 5 olden, salad
__ Days: 3 Old 4 Last 5 Ember, End of, Glory, Happy, Radio 6 Better, Lonely, School 7 Hundred
__ Day's A Holiday: 5 Every
__-day Saint: 6 Latter
__ Days and Mondays: 5 Rainy
Days and Nights of Molly __, The: 4 Dodd
__ Days Are Here Again: 5 Happy
__ Days a Week: 5 Eight
day's end: 5 night 7 evening 9 nightfall
__ Days in May: 5 Seven
Days Inn: 5 motel
alternative: 9 Ramada Inn 10 Comfort Inn, Econo Lodge, Hampton Inn, Holiday Inn, Quality Inn, Red Roof Inn, Travelodge 11 Best Western
__ Day's Journey into Night: 4 Long
__ Day's Night: 5 A Hard
days of __: 4 yore 5 grace
Days of Grace author: 4 Ashe 10 Arthur Ashe
Days of Heaven (1978 film)
cast: Brooke Adams, Richard Gere, Sam Shepard
Days of Our Lives (NBC): 4 soap 9 soap opera
Emmy winner: 5 Carey
town: 5 Salem
__ Days of Pompeii, The: 4 Last
__ Days of the Condor: 5 Three
Days of Thunder (1990 film)
cast: Tom Cruise, Robert Duvall, Nicole Kidman, Randy Quaid
director: Tony Scott
Days of Wine and Roses: 4 film, song
artist: Andy Williams, Henry Mancini
cast: Charles Bickford, Jack Lemmon, Lee Remick
director: Blake Edwards
dayspring: 7 morning
__ Days Seven Nights: 3 Six
daystar: 3 sun
Days Without End author: O'Neill
__ days' wonder: 4 nine
__ Day, The: 6 Eighth, Wicked 7 Longest
Day the Earth Stood Still, The (1951 film)
cast: Sam Jaffe, Hugh Marlowe, Patricia Neal, Michael Rennie
composer: 8 Herrmann
director: Robert Wise
robot: 4 Gort
Day the World Went Away, The (1999 song) artist: Nine Inch Nails
__ day this has been...: 5 What a
day-to-day: 5 usual 6 normal 7 diurnal, mundane 9 quotidian
Dayton: 4 city, town
city near ~: 4 Lima 5 Xenia
locale: 4 Ohio
Daytona: 3 car 4 auto, race 10 Studebaker
Daytona Beach: 4 city, town
locale: 7 Florida
day-tripper: 7 tourist 10 vacationer
Day Tripper (1965 song) artist: Beatles
__-Day vitamins: 4 One-a
__-Day War: 3 Six
__ Day Will Come: 3 Our
Day Without Rain, A singer: 4 Enya
__ Day Women: 5 Rainy
__-day wonder: 4 nine
Dazai Osamu: 6 writer 8 Japanese
daze: 3 fog 4 blur, jolt, stun 5 shock, whirl 6 baffle, bemuse, muddle, stupor, trance 7 astound, confuse, nonplus, stupefy 8 astonish, befuddle, bewilder, confound, surprise 9 confusion
in a ~: 4 asea 5 at sea 7 unaware 9 perplexed
__ daze: 3 in a
__ Daze: 6 School
dazed: 4 numb 5 blank, dizzy, silly, spacy, tipsy 6 glassy, groggy, in a fog, spacey, stupid 7 fuddled, reeling 10 speechless
__-Dazs: 6 Häagen
__ d'Azur: 4 Cote
dazzle: 3 awe 4 daze 5 amaze, blind, éclat, flash, glare, shine 6 luster 7 bewitch, charism, impress, sparkle, stupefy 8 astonish, bowl over, charisma, entrance, radiance, radiancy, splendor, surprise 9 captivate, electrify, fascinate, hypnotize, overwhelm
__-dazzle: 6 razzle
Dazzle author: Judith Krantz
dazzler: 6 eyeful, vision
dazzling: 3 def, lit, rad 4 aces, A-one, boss, braw, cool, dece, fine, gear, keen, neat, nice, phat, tuff 5 aglow, dandy, ducky, grand, great, marvy, neato, nobby, prime, shiny, slick, super, swell 6 ablaze, bang on, bang-up, bonzer, bosker, bright, choice, divine, dreamy, far-out, flashy, gnarly, groovy, lovely, ornate, peachy, slap-up, spot on, strong, superb, terrif, tiptop, unreal, whizzo, wicked 7 amazing, awesome, beaming, capital, corking, dashing, fulgent, lambent, perfect, radiant, ripping, shining, skookum, stellar, sublime 8 especial, eximious, fabulous, five-star, four-star, frabjous, glorious, gorgeous, heavenly, jim-dandy, luminous, lustrous, meteoric, slam-bang, smashing, spending, splendid, standout, sterling, stickout, striking, stunning, superior, terrific, top-level, topnotch, very good, wondrous 9 arresting, bodacious, brilliant, Endsville, excellent, exemplary, exquisite, first-rate, glamorous, high-grade, hunky-dory, marvelous, ravishing, refulgent, sollicker, sparkling, top-flight, unrivaled, wonderful 10 first-class, glittering, hotsy-totsy, jack-a-dandy, out of sight, peachy-keen, phenomenal, remarkable, stupendous, super-duper, unrivalled
light: 5 glare
Dazzy: 5 Vance
D.B.: 7 Sweeney
DBA name: 5 alias
DC
agent: 4 G-man, T-man
airport: 6 Dulles, Reagan 8 National
bank name: 5 Riggs
body: 3 Sen., USS 4 Cong. 6 Senate 8 Congress
budget watchdog: 3 GAO
campus: 3 GWU
clock setting: 3 EDT, EST
dept.: 3 Agr.
figure: 3 rep., sen. 4 pres.
group: 3 NSC
gun lobby: 3 NRA
hostess: 5 Mesta
hundred: 6 Senate
hush-hush ~ grp.: 3 NSA
initials: 3 GOP
lobby: 3 PAC
mortgage insurers: 3 FHA
network: 3 NPR
part of ~: 4 Dist. 8 Columbia, District
party: 3 Dem., Rep.
publisher: 3 GPO
record-keeping org.: 3 GSA
school: 6 Howard 10 Georgetown
stadium: 3 RFK
suburb: 5 Olney
subway: 5 Metro
tax org.: 3 IRS
type: 3 pol
see also Washington D.C.
D.C. Cab (1983 film)
cast: Adam Baldwin, Irene Cara, Mr. T
director: Joel Schumacher
DCM: 5 medal
DD: 6 degree
institution: 3 sem. 8 seminary
D-Day
beach: 4 Gold, Juno, Utah 5 Omaha, Sword
commander: 3 DDE, Ike 10 Eisenhower
craft: 3 LCT, LST
time: 4 June 5 H Hour
town: 4 Caen, St. Lô
D-Day the Sixth of June (1956 film)
cast: Robert Taylor, Richard Todd, Dana Wynter
director: Henry Koster
DDE: 3 gen., Ike 4 pres. 7 general 9 president 10 Eisenhower
alma mater: 4 USMA
command: 4 NATO 5 SHAEF
milieu: 3 ETO
opponent: 3 AES
predecessor: 3 HST
successor: 3 JFK
veep: 3 RMN
see also Eisenhower
DDS: 6 degree 7 dentist
org.: 3 ADA
relative: 3 DMD
DDT: 9 herbicide
DDT-banning org.: 3 EPA
de __: 4 fide, jure, luxe, novo, Sade, trop 5 facto, plano, règle 6 gratia 7 rigueur
De __, IL: 4 Kalb
De __ Poetica: 4 Arte
DE
see Delaware
dea: 4 Juno 5 Venus 7 Minerva
DEA
agent: 3 Fed 4 narc, nark 5 narco
department: 7 Justice
part of ~: 4 Drug 6 Agency
deacon: 4 rank 5 title 6 clergy, cleric, doctor, warden 7 falsify 8 minister 9 clergyman
Deacon: 5 Jones 7 Richard
deaconess: 6 cleric
Deacon, Richard: 5 actor
film: The Gnome-Mobile (1967)
TV: The Dick Van Dyke Show, Leave It to Beaver
deactivate: 6 defuse, defuze
__ de Açúcar: 3 Pao
dead: 3 out 5 kaput, spent, tired 7 sterile 8 lifeless, obsolete, outmoded 9 exanimate, insensate 10 broken-down, insentient, lackluster, motionless
air: 5 quiet 7 silence
end: 7 impasse 8 cul-de-sac 10 blind alley, standstill
ender: 3 eye, pan 4 beat, bolt, fall, head, line, lock, wood 5 light
heat: 3 tie 4 draw
knock ~: 5 amuse 6 divert, regale 8 enthrall 9 entertain
letter: 5 nixie

ringer: 4 twin 5 image, match 6 double 7 picture 8 likeness 9 duplicate, facsimile, identical, look-alike 10 equivalent
set: 5 rigid 8 resolute, stalwart 9 immovable, obstinate 10 inexorable, purposeful, relentless, unwavering, unyielding
stop: 10 standstill
weight: 4 load, onus 10 impediment
dead __: 3 air, end, pan, run, set 4 bolt, drop, duck, heat, lift, load, mail, slow, spot, time 5 metal, water 6 center, firing, letter, matter, ringer, weight 7 freight, spindle, storage
dead __ doornail: 3 as a
Dead: 3 sea
locale: 6 Israel, Jordan
Dead __: 3 End, Man, Sea 4 Calm, Cert 5 Again, Alive, Skunk, Souls 7 Ringers
Dead __ Kids: 3 End
Dead __ Scrolls: 3 Sea
Dead Again (1991 film)
cast: Kenneth Branagh, Andy Garcia, Derek Jacobi
director: Kenneth Branagh
deadbeat: 3 bum 4 ower 5 leech, loser 6 beggar, debtor, loafer, sponge 7 moocher 8 parasite 10 freeloader
deadbolt: 4 lock
release a ~: 5 unbar
Dead Calm (1989 film)
cast: Nicole Kidman, Sam Neill, Billy Zane
dead-center: 6 middle
hit ~: 4 nail
Dead Cert author: Dick Francis
deaden: 4 damp, dull, mute, numb, stun 5 abate, blunt, quiet 6 benumb, dampen, darken, muffle, obtund, reduce, soften, stifle, subdue 7 cushion, repress, silence 8 diminish, suppress, tone down 9 alleviate 10 soundproof
dead-end: 5 blind, stimy, stymy 6 stymie
Dead End (1937 film)
cast: Humphrey Bogart, Joel McCrea, Sylvia Sidney
director: William Wyler
deadened: 3 low 4 numb 5 bated, faint, muted, piano, quiet 7 muffled 9 unfeeling 10 anesthetic, insentient
deadening: 8 narcotic 9 soporific 10 anesthetic
deadeye: 7 shooter 8 marksman
prowess: 3 aim
Deadeye __: 4 Dick
Deadeye Dick author: Kurt Vonnegut Jr.
__ Dead Gorgeous: 4 Drop
deadhead: 3 oaf 4 clod 6 lummox
Dead Heat on a Merry-Go-Round (1966 film)
cast: James Coburn, Aldo Ray, Camilla Sparv
dead-level: 6 candid, honest 7 sincere
Deadlier Than the __: 4 Male
deadline: 3 end 5 limit 6 curfew, cutoff 7 due date 8 pressure, zero hour
after the ~: 4 late 5 tardy
before the ~: 5 early 6 in time, on time
Deadline U.S.A. (1952 film)
cast: Ethel Barrymore, Humphrey Bogart
deadlock: 3 jam, tie 4 halt 5 tie up 6 logjam 7 impasse 8 standoff 9 stalemate 10 difficulty, standstill
deadlocked: 4 even 6 static
Deadly Affair, The (1967 film)
cast: James Mason, Maximilian Schell, Simone Signoret
director: Sidney Lumet
__ deadly sins: 5 seven
__ Deadly Sin, The: 5 First, Third 6 Fourth, Second
Deadly Strangers (1974 film)
cast: Hayley Mills, Simon Ward
Dead Man (1996 film)
cast: Johnny Depp, Gary Farmer
director: Jim Jarmusch
Dead Man's Curve (1964 song) artist: Jan & Dean
dead man's hand pair: 4 aces 6 eights
Dead Man's Walk author: Larry McMurtry
Dead Man Walking (1995 film)
cast: Sean Penn, Robert Prosky, Susan Sarandon
director: Tim Robbins
role: 3 nun
Dead Men Don't Wear Plaid (1982 film)
cast: Steve Martin, Carl Reiner, Reni Santoni, Rachel Ward
director: Carl Reiner
Dead of Winter (1987 film)
cast: Roddy McDowall, Mary Steenburgen
director: Arthur Penn
dead-on: 4 nice 5 exact, right 7 correct, exactly, perfect 8 specific 9 correctly, perfectly, precisely 10 unmistaken
__ Dead or Alive: 6 Wanted
deadpan: 5 blank, sober, staid, stony 6 solemn, somber, stoney, vacant, wooden 7 serious 9 humorless, unamusing 10 no-nonsense, unhumorous
Dead Poets Society (1989 film)
cast: Ethan Hawke, Robert Sean Leonard, Robin Williams
director: Peter Weir
Dead Pool, The (1988 film)
cast: Patricia Clarkson, Clint Eastwood, Evan C. Kim, Liam Neeson
director: Buddy Van Horn
Dead Reckoning (1947 film)
cast: Humphrey Bogart, Lizabeth Scott
Dead Ringers (1988 film)
cast: Genevieve Bujold, Jeremy Irons
Dead Sea: 4 lake
feeder: 6 Jordan
kingdom: 4 Edom, Moab
locale: 6 Israel, Jordan
region: 6 Canaan
Scrolls writer: 6 Essene
Dead Skunk (1973 song) artist: Loudon Wainwright III
Dead Souls author: Nikolai Gogol
Dead, The (1987 film)
cast: Rachael Dowling, Anjelica Huston, Donal McCann
director: John Huston
dead-tired: 10 knocked out
dead to __: 6 rights
Dead Toreador, The painter: 5 Manet
Deadwood: 4 city, town
locale: 4 S. Dak.
Dead Zone, The: 4 film 5 novel
author: Stephen King
cast: Brooke Adams, Tom Skerritt, Christopher Walken
topic: 3 ESP
deaf: 7 unaware 8 heedless 9 insensate, oblivious, unhearing, unheeding 10 regardless, unyielding
turn a ~ ear to: 4 deny 5 scorn 6 refuse, slight
__-deaf: 4 tone
deafen: 5 blast 7 thunder 9 overwhelm
deafening: 4 loud 5 forte, noisy 6 shrill 7 blaring, blatant, booming, jarring, rackety, raucous, reboant, roaring 8 crashing, piercing, plangent, rumbling, sonorous, strident, terrific, turned up 9 big-voiced, clamorous, screaming 10 boisterous, resounding, stentorian, strepitous, thundering, thunderous, tremendous, uproarious, vociferant, vociferous
deafness, tone: 6 asonia
deal: 3 buy 4 mete, pact, sale, swap, swop 5 allot, share, trade 6 accord, amount, assign, barter, bestow, bicker, buyout, dicker, extent, merger, ration, render 7 bargain, compact, deliver, dish out, divvy up, dole out, give out, good buy, hand out, inflict, mete out, pass out, portion, project, smuggle, traffic 8 contract, covenant, disburse, dispense, disperse, exchange, fork over, quantity 9 agreement, apportion, indenture, negotiate 10 administer, buy and sell, compromise, distribute, do business, horse trade, settlement
a blow: 5 lay to 6 damage, strike
big ~: 3 ado 4 fuss, to-do 5 hoo-ha
cashless ~: 4 swap, swop 5 trade
close the ~: 3 ice 4 sell 5 shake
cut a ~: 5 agree 9 acquiesce, negotiate
ender: 4 fish 5 maker
from the bottom: 5 cheat 7 swindle
good ~: 3 lot 4 a lot, heap, lots, mass, pile 5 no end, sight, stack, steal 6 plenty 7 bargain
in: 3 buy 4 sell 5 carry, stock 6 handle 7 traffic 8 exchange, purchase 10 distribute
make a ~: 4 sell 7 mediate 8 transact 9 arbitrate, negotiate 10 compromise
maker: 3 rep 5 agent
no ~: 3 nah, naw, nay, nix, non 4 nein, nope, nyet, uh-uh 5 I won't, ixnay, never 7 I refuse 8 forget it, I will not, negative, negatory 9 fat chance, I think not 10 count me out, not a chance, thumbs down
no big ~: 6 trifle 10 immaterial
out: 4 give, mete 5 issue 6 divide, parcel, ration 7 divvy up, inflict 8 disburse, dispense 10 distribute
partner: 5 wheel
preceder: 4 ante
refuse to ~ with: 4 shun, snub 5 spurn 6 ignore, rebuff, reject 7 disavow, disdain, neglect, scoff at 8 turn down
shady ~: 4 scam 5 cheat 6 con job, ripoff 7 swindle 9 injustice 10 corruption
with: 4 cope, meet 5 cover, field, solve, treat 6 accept, attack, handle, join in, manage, reckon, tackle, take on 7 concern, control, embrace, grapple, process, touch on 8 consider, face up to, take part 9 get to know, partake of, patronize, touch upon 10 meet head on, speak about, take care of
deal __: 4 me in, with
__ deal: 3 big, raw 4 done 6 square 7 one-shot, package
__ deal!: 3 Big 4 It's a 5 No big
Deal!: 4 fine, okay 6 agreed
__ Deal: 3 New, Raw 4 Fair
de Alarcón: 5 Pedro
dealer: 4 bank 5 owner 6 banker, broker, grocer, jobber, seller, trader, vender, vendor 8 marketer, merchant, retailer 10 franchisee, wholesaler
concern: 4 ante, deck 5 stock
device: 4 shoe
directive: 6 ante up
employer: 6 casino
headwear: 5 visor, vizor
illegal ~: 5 fence
nemesis: 4 narc, nark
offering: 3 cut 5 lease 6 rebate
price: 3 net
take-back: 4 repo
__-dealer: 7 wheeler
__ Dealer: 3 New 5 Plain
dealer's __: 6 choice
dealing: 8 business, exchange
dirty ~: 5 guile 6 deceit
__ dealing: 5 plain
__-dealing: 6 double
dealings: 5 trade 6 doings 7 affairs, matters, traffic 8 business, commerce 9 relations
have ~: 4 know 5 truck
dealmaker: 6 closer 10 negotiator
dealt
hand one is ~: 3 lot 4 life
not ~ with: 5 unmet
dean: 4 head, king 5 doyen 6 cleric, leader 8 educator, minister 9 authority, principal 10 headmaster
Dean: 4 Cain, John, Rusk 5 Daffy, Dizzy, Estus, James, Jimmy, Jones, Loren 6 Jagger, Koontz, Martin 7 Acheson, Riesner 8 Torrence 9 Stockwell
singing partner: 3 Jan
Dean __: 6 Witter
__ Dean Anderson: 7 Richard
Dean, Dizzy: 6 hurler 7 pitcher 8 Cardinal
Deane: 5 Beman, Silas
__ Dean Foster: 4 Alan
__ Dean Howells: 7 William
Dean, James: 4 idol 5 actor
film: East of Eden (1955)
Giant (1956)
Rebel Without a Cause (1955)
persona: 5 rebel
role: 3 Cal 4 Jett, Rink
Dean, Jimmy
song: Big Bad John (1961)
P.T. 109 (1962)
Deanna: 4 Troi 6 Durbin
Dean's December, The author: Saul Bellow
dean's list fig.: 3 GPA
__ Dean Stanton: 5 Harry
dear: 2 jo 3 hon, luv, pet 4 baby, high, jill, love, near 5 amour, angel, chéri, close, cooky, cutey, cutie, ducky, flame, honey, leman, loved, lover, lovey, novia, novio, pricy, steep, stiff, sugar, sweet 6 bon ami, chérie, cookie, costly, dautie, loving, pricey, prized, steady, sweets 7 beloved, darling, pet name, pigsney, schatzi, sincere, squeeze, sweetie, tootsie 8 adorable, chou-chou, cutie pie, dowsabel, dulcinea, esteemed, intimate, ladylove, lovebird, loved one, macushla, paramour, precious, snookums, sugar pie, sweetums, truelove, valuable 9 bonne amie, boyfriend, cherished, dreamboat, expensive, heartfelt, important, inamorata, inamorato, petit chou, priceless, sumptuous, treasured, valentine 10 at a premium, exorbitant, girlfriend, heartthrob, high-priced, honeybunch, mavourneen, overpriced, sweetheart, sweetie pie, turtledove
hold ~: 4 like, love 5 adore, go for, prize, value 6 esteem, revere 7 care for, cherish, idolize, worship 8 remember, treasure 9 care about
in French: 4 cher
in Italian: 4 cara
me: 4 alas, egad, gosh, my my 5 alack, egads, golly 7 heavens, my stars 10 I do declare, my goodness
partner: 4 near
Dear __: 3 Sir 4 Abby, Mama, Sirs 5 Heart 6 Brutus, Madame
Dear __ and Gentle People: 6 Hearts
Dear __ or Madam...: 3 Sir
__, Dear: 3 Yes
Dearborn: 4 city, town
locale: 8 Michigan
__ Dearborn: 4 Fort
Dearborn Heights: 4 city, town

locale: 8 Michigan
Dear Brutus author: James M. Barrie
Dearden: 5 Basil, James
__ Dearest: 6 Mommie
Dearest Enemy: 7 musical
songwriter: 4 Hart 7 Rodgers
Dear Heart (1964 film)
cast: Glenn Ford, Geraldine Page
director: Delbert Mann
Dear Heart (1964 song) artist: Andy Williams
Dearie: 7 Blossom
Dear Lady Twist (1962 song) artist: Gary U.S. Bonds
Dear Mama (1995 song) artist: Tupac
dear old __: 3 dad
dearth: 4 lack, need, want 6 famine 7 absence, paucity, poverty 8 exiguity, scarcity, shortage, sparsity 9 scantness 10 deficiency, inadequacy, meagerness
Death __: 4 Wish 6 Valley
__ Death: 4 Ase's
Death and the Maiden (1994 film)
cast: Ben Kingsley, Sigourney Weaver, Stuart Wilson
director: Roman Polanski
Death Becomes Her (1992 film)
cast: Goldie Hawn, Isabella Rossellini, Meryl Streep, Bruce Willis
director: Robert Zemeckis
Death Be Not Proud author: Gunther
Death be not proud poet: 5 Donne
Death Comes for the Archbishop
author: Willa Cather
Death in the Afternoon author: Ernest Hemingway
Death in the Family, A author: Agee
Death in Venice (1971 film)
cast: Dirk Bogarde, Mark Burns
director: Luchino Visconti
Death in Venice author: Thomas Mann
Death Kit author: Susan Sontag
Death of a Salesman: 4 film, play
author: Arthur Miller
cast: Mildred Dunnock, Fredric March, Kevin McCarthy, Cameron Mitchell
character: 3 Ben 4 Biff 5 Happy, Linda, Loman, Willy 6 Howard, Wagner 7 Bernard, Charley 8 Uncle Ben
Death of Bessie Smith, The author: Edward Albee
Death of Ivan Ilyich, The author: Leo Tolstoy
Death of the Hired Man, The author: Robert Frost
Death on the Nile author: Christie
__-death overtime: 6 sudden
Death Takes a Holiday (1934 film)
cast: Fredric March, Guy Standing, Evelyn Venable
director: Mitchell Leisen
Death to Smoochy (2002 film)
cast: Danny DeVito, Catherine Keener, Edward Norton, Robin Williams
director: Danny DeVito
Deathtrap: 4 film, play
author: Ira Levin
cast: Michael Caine, Dyan Cannon, Christopher Reeve, Irene Worth
character: 4 Myra 5 Bruhl, Helga 6 Sidney
director: Sidney Lumet
Death Valley: 4 park 6 desert
locale: 6 Nevada 10 California
Death Valley Days (TV western)
host: Stanley Andrews, Ronald Reagan, Robert Taylor, Dale Robertson
deathwatch: 3 bug 6 insect
Death Watch (1980 film)
cast: Harvey Keitel, Romy Schneider, Harry Dean Stanton
Death Wish (1974 film)
cast: Charles Bronson, Vincent Gardenia, Hope Lange
__ d'eau: 4 Jeux 7 château
debacle: 3 dud 4 blow, bomb, bust, flop, loss, rout, ruin 5 havoc, smash, wreck 6 defeat, fiasco, mishap, turkey 7 blunder, failure, misstep, stumble, washout 8 casualty, collapse, disaster, downfall 9 breakdown, cataclysm, ruination, trouncing 10 misfortune
Debacle author: Emile Zola
De Bakey: 7 Michael
__ de bal: 4 robe
__ de ballet: 5 corps 6 maître
__ de banane: 5 crème
debar: 3 ban, nix 4 veto 5 eject 6 abjure, enjoin, except, forbid, hinder, punish, reject 7 exclude, keep out, prevent, shut off, shut out, suspend 8 disallow, leave out, preclude, prohibit 9 blackball, foreclose, interdict, proscribe
debark: 4 land 6 alight, get off 8 go ashore
debarment: 9 exception, exclusion, expulsion
debase: 4 ruin, sink, soil, warp 5 dirty, lower, shame, spoil, stain, taint 6 crud up, defile, demean, humble, impair, insult, reduce, vilify, weaken 7 cheapen, corrupt, degrade, deprave, depress, devalue, pollute, profane, put down, subvert, vitiate 8 disgrace, dishonor, take down 9 devaluate, humiliate, shoot down, undermine 10 adulterate
oneself: 6 grovel
debased: 4 vile 6 impure, wicked 7 ashamed, bestial, corrupt 8 degraded, maculate
debasement: 5 abuse 8 disgrace 9 decadence, depravity, vitiation 10 corruption, defilement, degeneracy
__ de basque: 3 pas 4 saut
debatable: 4 iffy, moot, open 6 chancy 7 dubious 8 arguable, doubtful, forensic 9 in dispute, uncertain, undecided, unsettled 10 ambivalent, borderline, disputable, touch and go
__ de bataille: 6 cheval
debate: 4 feud 5 argue, fight, forum, study 6 oppose, ponder, reason, refute, speech 7 contest, discuss, dispute, hash out, polemic 8 argument, consider, hash over, polemics, question 9 bat around, bump heads, lock horns, negotiate, pro and con, sweat over, thrash out 10 contention, controvert, deliberate, discussion, kick around, toss around, war of words
answer in a ~: 5 rebut
open to ~: 4 moot
side: 3 con, for, pro 4 anti
debater: 6 arguer 8 rebutter 9 disputant
Debbe: 7 Dunning
Debbi: 6 Fields, Morgan
Debbie: 5 Allen, Harry, Meyer 6 Gibson 8 Reynolds
daughter: 6 Carrie
Debby: 5 Boone
de Beauvoir: 6 Simone
de bene __: 4 esse
debenture: 3 IOU 4 bond, debt
de Bergerac: 6 Cyrano
Debi: 5 Mazar 6 Thomas
__-de-biche: 4 pied
debilitate: 3 sag, sap 4 flag, jade, tire, wane 5 blunt, drain, weary 6 impair, reduce, shrink, soften, weaken 7 deplete, exhaust, fatigue, tire out, vitiate, wear out 8 enervate, enfeeble 9 attenuate, extenuate, prostrate, undermine 10 demoralize, devitalize
debilitated: 3 low 4 puny, sick, weak 5 frail, spent, unfit, wimpy 6 anemic, atonic, effete, feeble, flabby, flimsy, infirm 7 anaemic, fragile, run-down, wimpish 8 delicate, helpless, pithless 9 faltering, lethargic, nerveless, powerless, unhealthy 10 vulnerable
debility: 6 anemia 7 anaemia, fatigue, frailty, malaise 8 puniness, weakness 9 fragility, infirmity 10 feebleness, infirmness, unwellness
debit: 4 loss 7 expense 9 liability
partner: 6 credit
debit __: 4 card
debits-and-credits book: 6 ledger
__-de-boeuf: 4 oeil
debonair: 3 gay 5 suave 6 breezy, jaunty, rakish, urbane 7 dashing, elegant, refined 8 charming, gracious, polished 9 courteous, lightsome
debone: 5 filet 6 fillet
De Bont, Jan film of 1994: 5 Speed
Deborah: 3 Cox 4 Kerr 5 Harry 6 Raffin, Walley 8 Norville
dancing partner: 3 Yul
déboulé: 8 half turn
__ de Boulogne: 4 Bois
__ de bourrée: 3 pas
Debra: 5 Paget 6 Winger 7 Messing
Debrah: 9 Farentino
Debralee: 5 Scott
__ de bras: 4 port
Debrecen: 4 city, town
locale: 7 Hungary
Debreu, Gerard: 6 French 8 Nobelist 9 economist
debris: 4 chad, junk 5 chaff, dregs, dross, offal, ruins, scree, trash, waste, wreck 6 jetsam, jetsom, litter, refuse, rubble, shards, sherds 7 flotsam, garbage, rejects, rubbish 8 detritus, leftover, sediment, wreckage 9 driftwood
nautical ~: 6 jetsam, jetsom 7 flotsam
rocky ~: 5 scree, talus
de Broglie, Louis: 6 French 8 Nobelist 9 physicist
de Brunhoff: 4 Jean
Debs: 6 Eugene
debt: 3 IOU, tab 4 bill, hock, loan, loss, mtge. 5 score 6 arrear, bar tab, marker, red ink 7 arrears, poverty 8 mortgage 9 arrearage, debenture, liability, reckoning 10 obligation
be in ~: 3 owe
holder: 6 lienor
home buyer's ~: 4 mtge. 8 mortgage
in ~: 5 owing 6 behind 9 insolvent, mortgaged 10 straitened
marker: 3 IOU 4 chit
one in ~: 4 ower 6 lienee
recipient: 5 payee 8 creditor
satisfy a ~: 3 pay 5 pay up, repay 6 settle 9 discharge
security: 4 lien
debt __: 5 issue, limit 7 service
__ debt: 6 funded, oxygen, public, senior
debtee: 6 lienor 8 creditor
debt of __: 5 honor
debug: 3 fix 6 repair, revise 7 correct, rectify 8 overhaul
debunk: 6 expose 7 deflate, explode, flatten, lampoon 8 puncture, ridicule 9 disparage, shoot down
DeBurgh: 5 Chris
DeBusschere, Dave: 8 hoopster
Debussy, Claude: 6 French 8 composer
contemporary: 5 Faure, Satie
piece: 5 étude
work: Clair de lune
Jeux
Pelléas et Mélisande
Prelude to l'après-midi d'un faune
Vingt
debut: 3 bow 4 rise 5 intro 6 arrive 7 baptism, kickoff 8 premiere 9 coming out 10 appearance, incipience, initiation
debutante: 4 girl, lass 5 belle
Debutante Ball, The author: Henley
Debye, Peter: 5 Dutch 7 chemist 8 Nobelist
dec-
halved: 4 pent-
Dec.: 2 mo.
day: 4 Xmas
predecessor: 3 Nov.
successor: 3 Jan.
see also December
deca-: 3 ten
__ de cacao: 5 crème
__ de cachet: 6 lettre
decade: 3 ten 8 ten years
fraction: 3 one 4 year
__ decade: 5 mauve
decadence: 5 lapse 6 excess 7 decline 9 downgrade 10 corruption, debasement, degeneracy, devolution, regression, sensuality, sybaritism
decadent: 6 effete 11 fin de siècle
decaf: 8 beverage
brand: 5 Sanka
__ de café: 5 tasse
decal: 5 label 6 iron-on
__ de Calais: 3 Pas
Decalogue verb: 5 shalt
Decameron author: Giovanni Boccaccio
decamp: 2 go 3 fly, run 4 bolt, exit, flee, quit 5 break, elope, leave, scram, split 6 beat it, bug out, depart, desert, escape, get out, go away, pack up, retire 7 abscond, go hurry, go south, head out, make off, pull out, retreat, ride off, run away, take off, vamoose 8 clear out, evacuate, fugitate, hightail, march off, run for it, shove off 9 bundle off, disappear, skedaddle 10 fly the coop, hightail it, hit the road
__-de-camp: 3 aid 4 aide
De Camp: 8 Rosemary
decampment: 7 getaway 9 departure, egression
De Camptown Races
composer: 6 Foster
word: 6 doo-dah
decant: 4 pour 5 empty 7 draw off, pour out 8 rebottle
decanter: 5 crùet 6 bottle, carafe, flagon, vessel 7 pitcher
De Carlo, Yvonne: 7 actress
film: Captain's Paradise (1953)
Casbah (1948)
Criss Cross (1949)
The Ten Commandments (1956)
Tonight's the Night (1954)
TV: The Munsters
__ de cassis: 5 crème
decathlete: 6 Jenner, Thorpe, Toomey 7 Johnson, Mathias
decathlon: 5 sport
event: 3 run 6 discus, hurdle, sprint 7 javelin, shot-put 8 high jump, long jump 9 pole vault
Decatur: 4 city, town
city near ~: 4 Pana
locale: 7 Alabama 8 Illinois
decay: 3 eat, ebb, rot 4 fade, fail, ruin, rust, sink, slip, turn, wane, wear 5 erode, go bad, slide, slump, spoil, taint, waste 6 blight, fading, molder, perish, weaken, wither 7 atrophy, compost, corrode, crumble, decline, dwindle, entropy, failing, go stale, putrefy, shrivel 8 collapse, decrease, downfall, go to seed, spoilage, stagnate, wear away 9 aggravate, break down, corrosion, crumbling, decompose, withering 10 corruption, degen-

erate, depreciate, exacerbate, impairment, retrogress, spoliation
sign of ~: **4** rust
__ decay: **4** beta **5** alpha, gamma, tooth
decayed: **3** bad, old **4** worn **5** musty, rusty, seedy, stale **6** rotten, shabby **7** squalid, unclean **8** overripe **10** malodorous
Deccan Plateau region: **6** Kanara
dece: **3** def, rad **4** aces, A-one, boss, braw, cool, fine, gear, keen, neat, nice, phat, tuff **5** dandy, ducky, grand, great, marvy, neato, nobby, prime, slick, super, swell **6** bang on, bang-up, bonzer, bosker, choice, divine, dreamy, far-out, gnarly, groovy, lovely, peachy, slap-up, spot on, superb, terrif, tiptop, unreal, whizzo, wicked **7** amazing, awesome, capital, corking, perfect, ripping, skookum, stellar, sublime **8** dazzling, especial, eximious, fabulous, five-star, four-star, frabjous, glorious, heavenly, jim-dandy, slam-bang, smashing, splendid, standout, sterling, stickout, superior, terrific, top-level, topnotch, very good, wondrous **9** bodacious, Endsville, excellent, exemplary, exquisite, first-rate, high-grade, hunky-dory, marvelous, sollicker, top-flight, wonderful **10** first-class, hotsy-totsy, jack-a-dandy, out of sight, peachy-keen, phenomenal, remarkable, stupendous, super-duper
deceit: **3** art, lie **4** cant, hoax, ruse, sham, tale, wile **5** bluff, cheat, craft, feint, fraud, guile, lying, spoof, trick **6** fakery, humbug **7** cunning, fallacy, falsity, gimmick, slyness, snow job, swindle **8** artifice, bad faith, cheating, flimflam, foxiness, pretense, trickery, wiliness **9** chicanery, dirty pool, dirty work, duplicity, falsehood, falseness, fourberie, hypocrisy, imposture, invention, treachery, two-timing, whitewash **10** craftiness, defrauding, dishonesty, inveracity, subterfuge
deceitful: **3** sly **4** foxy, wily **5** dirty, false, lying, slick, snaky **6** artful, crafty, hollow, rotten, shifty, sneaky, tricky **7** crooked, cunning, devious, elusive, elusory, evasive, furtive, knavish, roguish, unloyal **8** delusive, delusory, forsworn, guileful, illusive, illusory, scheming, spurious, stealthy, two-faced **9** beguiling, designing, dishonest, faithless, insidious, insincere, underhand **10** fallacious, fraudulent, mendacious, misleading, unfaithful, unreliable, untruthful
deceivable: **4** easy, naif **5** naive
deceive: **2** do **3** con, fox, lie **4** bilk, burn, dupe, fool, gull, have, hoax, hoke, hook, jive, scam, sell, snow, take, trap **5** blind, bluff, cheat, cozen, hocus, lie to, put on, sneak, spoof, trick **6** betray, delude, entrap, fleece, lead on, outwit, suck in, take in **7** beguile, buffalo, defraud, ensnare, insnare, mislead, pretend, sell out, swindle, two-time **8** flimflam, hoodwink, outsmart, pettifog, simulate, throw off **9** bamboozle, disinform, four-flush, misinform, victimize **10** run a game on
deceived: **5** led on **9** misguided
deceiver: **4** liar **5** cheat, fraud, knave, rogue **7** traitor **9** hypocrite
decelerate: **4** slow **5** brake **6** retard, slow up **8** slow down **9** lose speed
December: **5** month
birthstone: **9** turquoise
current: **6** El Niño
day: **4** Xmas **9** Christmas
flyer: **8** reindeer
follower: **3** Jan. **7** January
January to ~: **4** year
like a ~ day: **4** cold **5** nippy **6** frosty
preceder: **3** Nov. **8** November
sign: **4** Goat **6** Archer **9** Capricorn
song: **4** Noel **5** carol
sound: **6** hohoho
temp: **5** Santa
December 1963 (1976 song) artist: Four Seasons
December Bride (CBS sitcom) cast: Spring Byington (Lily Ruskin)
December 5: **5** nones
décembre: **4** mois **6** French
janvier to ~: **5** année
decency: **5** honor **6** ethics **7** dignity, modesty, probity **8** fairness, goodness, kindness, morality, niceties **9** etiquette, good faith, propriety, rectitude
decennial event: **6** census
decent: **3** apt, fit **4** clad, fair, good, just, kind, nice, okay, tidy **5** ample, clean, moral, right, solid **6** chaste, garbed, gentle, honest, kindly, polite, proper, seemly, square, tender, worthy **7** clement, clothed, correct, dressed, ethical, fitting, helpful, lenient, sizable, sparing, upright **8** adequate, all right, becoming, decorous, friendly, generous, gracious, likeable, mannerly, mediocre, merciful, middling, obliging, passable, sizeable, spotless, straight, suitable, virtuous **9** courteous, honorable, tolerable, wholesome **10** acceptable, altruistic, benevolent, immaculate, reasonable, sufficient, thoughtful, upstanding
deception: **3** con, fib, lie **4** fake, flam, hoax, jive, ruse, scam, sham, tale, trap, wile **5** bluff, cheat, decoy, dodge, feint, fraud, guile, hokum, lying, setup, shill, snare, spoof, sting, trick **6** device, dupery, hustle **7** blarney, charade, chicane, con game, cunning, fallacy, falsity, fast one, gimmick, hogwash, malarky, pretext, snow job, sophism, swindle, untruth **8** artifice, bad faith, betrayal, delusion, flimflam, illusion, jugglery, malarkey, pretense, trickery **9** casuistry, chicanery, duplicity, falsehood, fourberie, hypocrisy, imposture, mare's nest, mendacity, stratagem, treachery, whitewash **10** boondoggle, craftiness, hanky-panky, hocus-pocus, imposition, inaccuracy, masquerade, misleading, subterfuge, trickiness
free from ~: **8** disabuse
Deception (1946 film)
cast: Bette Davis, Paul Henreid, Claude Rains
director: Irving Rapper
deceptive: **3** sly **4** fake, foxy, wily **5** false, lying, phony, slick **6** crafty, phoney, shifty, sneaky, tricky, untrue **7** cunning, elusive, elusory, evasive, roguish **8** deluding, delusive, delusory, guileful, illusive, illusory, scheming, slippery, specious, spurious, two-faced **9** ambiguous, beguiling, designing, dishonest, imaginary, imitative, insidious, insincere, invisible, plausible, underhand **10** fallacious, fictitious, fraudulent, inexplicit, mendacious, misleading, serpentine, unreliable
__ de chambre: **5** valet
__-de-chambre: **4** robe
de Champlain: **6** Samuel
__ de change: **6** bureau, lettre
__ de chat: **3** pas
__ de cheval: **3** pas
__ de chine: **5** crêpe
__ de chose: **3** peu
decibels, low in: **5** quiet
decide: **3** fix, opt, say, set **4** deem, pick, rule, take, vote **5** agree, elect, judge, solve **6** choose, clinch, commit, decree, define, figure, opt for, prefer, reason, settle **7** adjudge, agree on, chooses, pick out, resolve **8** conclude, draw lots, finalize, nominate **9** arbitrate, determine, preordain, single out **10** adjudicate, settle upon, take a stand
against: **3** nix **6** pass on
unable to ~: **4** torn **8** wavering **10** of two minds, on the fence
decided: **3** set **4** firm, sure **5** clear, fixed **6** intent, marked, mulish **7** assured, certain, earnest **8** absolute, definite, emphatic, finished, in the bag, positive, resolute **9** assertive, iron-jawed, unbending **10** conclusive, deliberate, inevitable, inflexible, pronounced, purposeful, unwavering, unyielding
not ~: **4** open, tied
yet to be ~: **9** ambiguous, debatable **10** in question, unresolved, up in the air
decidedly: **3** far **4** real, very **5** quite, truly **6** easily, highly, surely, vastly **7** but good, flat out **8** for a fact, in spades, markedly, terribly **9** certainly, downright, expressly **10** absolutely, by all means, decisively, definitely, distinctly, far and away, inevitably, positively
Decider author: Dick Francis
deciding: **3** key **5** chief, prime **7** crucial **8** critical, decisive **9** principal **10** conclusive
decile: **5** tenth
decimal
base: **3** ten
marking: **3** dot **5** point
point, in Europe: **5** comma
starter: **3** duo
decimal __: **5** place, point **6** system
__ decimal system: **5** Dewey
decimate: **3** gut **4** ruin **5** smash **6** defeat, quench **7** wipe out **8** demolish, massacre **9** slaughter **10** annihilate
decime: **4** coin **5** money
decipher: **2** do **4** read **5** break, crack, solve **6** decode, deduce, reveal **7** analyze, decrypt, dope out, explain, make out, unravel **8** construe, untangle **9** figure out, interpret, make clear, penetrate, puzzle out, translate **10** understand, unscramble
decipherable: **7** legible **8** readable
decision: **4** will **5** spine, voice **6** accord, choice, result, ruling **7** finding, liberty, outcome, resolve, verdict **8** backbone, election, firmness, judgment, sentence **9** agreement, fortitude, selection, will power **10** conclusion, preference, resolution, settlement
come to a ~: **6** settle
formal ~: **3** act
make a ~: **3** act **4** deem, rule **6** choose, direct, settle
make a judicial ~: **4** find **5** order **6** decide, decree, ordain **7** preside, resolve **8** sentence **9** prescribe, pronounce
makers: **4** jury
reverse a ~: **8** override, overrule
decision __: **4** tree **6** theory
decision-__: **5** maker **6** making
__ decision: **5** split **7** command
Decision Before Dawn (1952 film)
cast: Richard Basehart, Gary Merrill, Oskar Werner
director: Anatole Litvak
decision-making power: **5** say-so
__ decisis: **5** stare
decisive: **3** key, set **4** firm **5** acute, clean, fatal, final, vital **6** all-out, intent **7** assured, certain, crucial, fateful, flat-out, pivotal, precise, settled, telling **8** absolute, critical, definite, forceful, positive, pregnant, resolute, settling, ultimate **9** assertive, important, memorable, momentous, necessary, strategic **10** commanding, conclusive, definitive, determined, inarguable, peremptory, portentous, unarguable, undeniable
be ~: **3** act, opt **6** commit
period: **2** OT **8** overtime
De Civitate __: **3** Dei
deck: **2** KO **4** drop, gild, kayo, pack, slug, tier, trim **5** adorn, array, dress, equip, floor, grace, primp **6** attire, clothe, defeat, wallop **7** bedrape, clobber, festoon, flatten, garnish, gussy up **8** accouter, accoutre, beautify, emblazon, ornament, prettify **9** caparison, embellish, embroider, glamorize, knock down, prostrate
backyard ~: **5** patio
break the ~: **3** cut **7** shuffle
clean the ~: **3** mop **4** swab, swob
clear the ~: **4** tidy **5** ready
foreman: **4** bo's'n **5** bosun
fortuneteller's ~: **5** tarot
hands: **4** crew
hit the ~: **4** wake **5** arise, awake, get up, waken
member: **3** ace, six, ten, two **4** five, four, jack, king, nine, trey **5** deuce, eight, joker, queen, seven, three
not on ~: **5** below
on ~: **4** next, open **6** aboard **7** present **10** obtainable
opening: **5** hatch
out: **3** tog **4** garb, vest **5** adorn, array, equip, primp, prink **6** attire, bedaub, clothe, outfit **7** furnish **8** accouter, accoutre, spruce up **9** caparison
part: **4** card
protector: **5** stain
ship ~: **4** poop **5** orlop **6** fo'c's'le
stack the ~: **5** cheat **9** victimize
starter: **5** after **7** quarter
worker: **4** hand **6** sailor **7** jack tar
deck __: **3** lid, log **4** bolt, gang, hand, hook, load **5** chair, light, plate, watch **6** tennis **7** officer, passage
__ deck: **3** gun, sun **4** boat, cold, half, laid, main, poop, rear, spar, tape **5** cabin, lower, mower, orlop, shade, texas, upper **6** anchor, awning, bridge, cutter, flight **7** shelter, tonnage, weather
decked out: **4** clad **5** natty **6** dapper
__-decker: **5** three **6** double, triple
Decker: **4** Mary
partner: **5** Black
decker, hall: **5** holly
deckhand: **3** ABS, gob, tar **4** mate, salt **6** barger, sailor, seaman **7** mariner
Deck of Cards (1959 song) artist: Wink Martindale
Deck the Halls: **4** noel **5** carol
syllables: **3** fas, las **4** fa la, la la **6** fa la la, la la la
word: **3** 'tis
declaim: **4** rail, rant, rave, talk **5** decry, orate, speak, spout, utter **6** recite **7** lecture, thunder **8** bloviate, denounce, harangue, perorate **9** fulminate, hold forth
rhythmically: **5** chant
declamation: **6** speech **7** oration **8** harangue **10** recitation
declamatory: **5** stagy **6** stagey **7** pompous, stilted **9** bombastic **10** oratorical, rhetorical, theatrical
declaration: **3** bid **4** oath, plea **5** claim, edict, say-so **6** avowal, dictum, notice, remark **7** receipt **8** averment, bulletin, doctrine **9** manifesto, statement, testimony, utterance

__ Declaration: 7 Balfour
Declaration of Independence starter: 4 When
declarative: 8 positive 9 assertive 10 expository
declare: 3 air, own, say, vow 4 aver, avow, name, tell 5 admit, claim, plead, speak, state, swear, utter, voice, vouch 6 affirm, allege, assert, attest, avouch, depone, herald, remark, reveal 7 confess, deliver, divulge, express, observe, present, profess, promise, speak up, testify, warrant 8 announce, disclose, maintain, manifest, proclaim, propound, set forth, speak out 9 enunciate, make known, predicate, pronounce 10 asseverate, promulgate, put forward
false: 5 rebut 6 impugn, negate, recant, reject 7 disavow, dispute, gainsay 8 disclaim, renounce 9 repudiate 10 contradict, controvert
I do ~: 4 my my 6 dear me 8 goodness
déclassé: 6 common 8 inferior 10 second-rate
declension: 4 tilt 5 slope 7 descent
declination: 2 no 5 slant, slope 6 denial 7 descent, refusal
decline: 3 dip, ebb, nix, rot, sag 4 balk, dive, drop, fade, fail, fall, flag, lose, pass, sink, slip, veto, wane, wilt 5 abate, baulk, decay, demur, drain, droop, lapse, lower, say no, slant, slide, slump, spurn, waive 6 beg off, ebbing, lessen, loathe, pass up, perish, rebuff, recede, refuse, reject, shrink, waning, weaken, worsen 7 abstain, cutback, descend, descent, drop off, dwindle, entropy, failing, falloff, forbear, inflect, plummet, refrain, subside, tail off 8 comedown, contract, decrease, diminish, downturn, languish, level off, lowering, moderate, nosedive, peter out, slowdown, stagnate, turn down, twilight 9 abatement, backslide, decadence, downgrade, downslide, downswing, dwindling, lessening, recession, reduction, remission, retrocede, weakening, withering, worsening 10 anticlimax, depreciate, diminution, falling off, retrograde
combining form: 4 clin- 5 clino-
economic ~: 4 bust 9 recession 10 depression
in ~: 6 sickly 9 unhealthy
period of ~: 3 ebb
Decline and Fall author: Evelyn Waugh
Decline and Fall of the Roman Empire, The author: Edward Gibbon
declining: 4 sick 8 downhill
declivity: 4 drop 5 scarp, slope 7 descent, incline 8 gradient 9 downgrade
DEC 1970s computer: 3 VAX
__ Deco: 3 Art
decoct: 4 boil, cook 7 extract 8 boil down, condense
decoction: 6 liquor 7 extract
decode: 4 read 5 break, crack, parse, solve 6 deduce, reveal, unlock 7 analyze, convert, decrypt, dope out, explain, unravel 8 decipher, untangle 9 figure out, interpret, puzzle out, translate 10 understand, unscramble
decoders, U.S. military: 3 NSA
__ de coeur: 3 cri 7 affaire
__ de Cologne: 3 eau
decolorize: 4 fade 6 bleach, whiten
__ de combat: 4 hors
decompose: 3 eat, rot 4 turn 5 decay, spoil 6 molder 7 break up, crumble 8 dissolve 9 break down, fall apart
combining form: 4 -lyze
decomposing: 6 rancid, rotten
combining form: 5 -lytic
decomposition: 3 rot
combining form: 3 lys- 4 lysi-, lyso- 5 -lysis
decompression __: 5 table 7 chamber
DeConcini: 6 Dennis
decongestant form: 5 spray
decontainerize: 5 unbox 7 uncrate
decontaminate: 4 wash 5 bathe, clean, scrub 6 purify 7 cleanse, deterge, launder 8 fumigate, sanitize 9 disinfect, sterilize
decontaminated: 4 safe 5 clean 7 sterile
decor: 4 mode 5 style
change the ~: 4 redo
decorate: 4 cite, do up, edge, gild, trim 5 adorn, array, dress, grace, honor, paint 6 bedeck, emboss, enrich, jazz up 7 bedizen, dress up, encrust, enhance, festoon, flatter, furbish, furnish, garnish, gussy up, incrust, varnish 8 accouter, accoutre, beautify, emblazon, ornament, spruce up 9 embellish, embroider
decorated: 5 fancy, showy 6 flashy, frilly, glitzy, lavish 7 opulent 9 elaborate, garnished, luxurious, sumptuous
__ **Decorated My Life:** 3 You
decoration: 4 gilt, lace, palm, trim 5 award, badge, braid, dodad, frill, honor, inlay, medal, prize, title 6 accent, bauble, doodad, emblem, facing, geegaw, gewgaw, ribbon, sequin, stripe, tinsel, trophy 7 dingbat, festoon, garnish, gilding, insigne, laurels, pattern, pennant, spangle, tooling, trinket 8 accolade, appliqué, citation, curlicue, curlycue, filagree, filigree, flourish, fretwork, frippery, froufrou, furbelow, insignia, ornament, trapping, trimming 9 accessory, adornment, arabesque, bedecking, designing, fandangle, fillagree, garniture, gimcracks, parquetry 10 embroidery, enrichment, festooning, garnishing
object of ~: 3 fir 4 hero, tree
see also medal
Decoration __: 3 Day
decorative: 5 fancy 6 florid, frilly, ornate 7 baroque, for show 8 adorning, cosmetic 9 enhancing 10 ornamental
decorator
asset: 5 flair, style, taste
concern: 5 color, motif
de Cordova: 4 Fred 6 Arturo
decorous: 3 fit 4 nice, prim 5 moral, staid 6 au fait, august, decent, formal, proper, ritual, sedate, seemly 7 correct, courtly, elegant, fitting, orderly, pompous, refined, stately, stilted 8 becoming, highbred, highbrow, ladylike, mannerly, suitable 9 befitting, dignified 10 ceremonial
__ de corps: 6 esprit
decorticate: 4 peel, skin 5 strip
decorum: 4 form 5 taste 7 dignity, manners 8 ceremony, civility, niceties, protocol 9 etiquette, formality, gentility, propriety
__ de côté: 3 pas
de Coubertin: 6 Pierre
decoy: 4 bait, fake, lure, trap 5 shill, snare, tempt, trick 6 allure, come-on, entice, entrap, facade, lead on, rope in, suck in 8 inveigle, pretense 9 deception 10 allurement, enticement, red herring, temptation
decrease: 3 cut, dip, ebb, lag 4 clip, curb, drop, ease, fade, fall, lack, leak, loss, lull, pale, pare, sink, slow, thin, wane 5 abate, allay, decay, drain, droop, let up, lower, remit, slack, slash, slump 6 deduct, dilute, lessen, modify, muffle, narrow, rebate, recede, reduce, retard, shrink, slow up, waning, weaken, wither 7 abridge, commute, curtail, cutback, cut down, decline, deflate, deplete, die down, drop off, dwindle, erosion, falloff, lighten, mollify, plummet, shorten, shrivel, slacken, subside, tail off, take off, take out, thin out, whittle 8 blow over, close out, contract, diminish, discount, downsize, downturn, level off, mark down, minimize, moderate, peter out, roll back, slow down, subtract, take away, taper off, withhold 9 abatement, deduction, devaluate, downtrend, dwindling, evaporate, extenuate, lessening, reduction, remission, retrocede, shrinkage, withering 10 depreciate, diminution, falling off
the volume: 3 gag 4 calm, hush, lull, mute 5 quiet, shush 6 deaden, muffle, muzzle, shut up, stifle, subdue 7 be quiet 8 pipe down, suppress 9 quiet down 10 extinguish
velocity: 4 slow 5 brake 6 retard, slow up 8 slow down 10 decelerate
volume: 4 mute 7 silence 8 turn down
de-crease: 4 iron
decreased: 5 lower, short 8 lessened
by: 4 less 5 minus
decreasing: 9 on the wane
decree: 3 law, set 4 bull, fiat, rule, will, word, writ 5 canon, edict, irade, judge, order, ukase 6 decide, dictum, diktat, enjoin, firman, impose, ordain, ruling 7 adjudge, command, dictate, enforce, finding, mandate, precept, statute, verdict 8 judgment, legalize, sanction 9 directive, legislate, ordinance, papal bull, prescribe, pronounce 10 injunction, promulgate, regulation
church ~: 4 bull 5 canon
divine ~: 7 destiny
Muslim ~: 5 irade
decree __: 4 nisi
__ **decree:** 7 consent
decreed: 5 legal 6 lawful, vested 10 inevitable
decrement: 3 cut 7 cutback 9 deduction, reduction
decrepit: 4 weak, worn 5 mangy, musty, seedy, tatty, unfit 6 creaky, feeble, flimsy, mangey, shabby 7 fragile, rickety, run-down, unsound 8 timeworn, untended, well-used 10 antiquated, bedraggled, broken-down, ramshackle, threadbare, tumbledown
decrepitude: 7 malaise 8 weakness
decriminalize: 8 legalize
__ de Cristo: 6 Sangre
decry: 3 pan, rap 4 gibe, hiss, jeer, jibe, mock, slam, slur, snub 5 abuse, blame, knock, libel, lower, scorn, sneer, spurn, taunt 6 defame, deride, dump on, heckle, impugn, malign, offend, rail at, rebuff, slight, vilify 7 affront, asperse, censure, condemn, declaim, degrade, disdain, put down, rank out, run down, slander, traduce 8 backbite, badmouth, belittle, bloviate, denounce, derogate, pooh-pooh, ridicule, vilipend 9 criticize, denigrate, discredit, disparage, humiliate, reprehend 10 calumniate, disrespect, take to task, villainize
decrypt: 5 crack 6 decode 8 decipher
__ de cuisine: 4 chef
decussate: 9 intersect
DeDe Dinah (1958 song) artist: Avalon
__-de-dee: 6 fiddle
__ de dents: 3 mal
__ de deux: 3 pas
Dedham: 4 city, town
locale: 4 Mass.
river: 7 Charles
dedicate: 5 allot, apply, bless, put in 6 anoint, assign, commit, devote, donate, hallow, pledge 7 consign 8 canonize, give over, sanctify, set apart 9 apportion 10 consecrate, inaugurate
dedicated: 3 wed 4 avid, true 5 loyal 6 sacred, strong 7 devoted, dutiful, staunch, zealous 8 constant, faithful, true-blue, untiring, yeomanly 9 allegiant, committed, steadfast 10 purposeful, undeterred, unwavering
to: 3 for
Dedicated to the One I Love (1967 song) artist: Mamas & the Papas
Dedicated to the One I Love (song) artist: Shirelles
dedication: 7 loyalty, passion 8 blessing, devotion 9 adherence, hallowing 10 allegiance, commitment, fanaticism
stanza: 5 envoi
dedicatory: 8 memorial
work: 3 ode
__ de Dios: 4 Casa
__-de-do: 4 hoop 5 whoop
__-de-Dôme: 3 Puy
deduce: 4 draw, make, tell 5 glean, guess, infer, judge, think 6 assume, decode, derive, gather, reason, take it 7 imagine, make out, surmise 8 conclude, construe, decipher, estimate, perceive 9 figure out, reason out 10 understand
deducer's need: 5 logic 6 reason
deducible: 7 logical 9 derivable, following, inferable, traceable 10 consequent, reasonable
deduct: 4 dock, take 5 allow 6 lessen, reason, rebate, reduce 7 take off, take out 8 discount, roll back, subtract, take away, withhold, write off
__-deductible: 3 tax
deduction: 5 logic 6 answer, credit, reason, rebate, saving 7 finding, surmise, theorem, thought 8 decrease, discount, judgment, write-off 9 abatement, allowance, corollary, decrement, dialectic, inference, pondering, reasoning, reduction 10 assumption, cogitation, conclusion, derivation, diminution, hypothesis, meditation, reflection, rumination, withdrawal
game of ~: 4 Clue 5 Jotto
make a ~: 5 add up, infer
payroll ~: 3 tax 4 FICA 9 insurance
weight ~: 4 tare
__ **deduction:** 3 tax
deductions
after ~: 3 net
before ~: 5 gross
deductive: 7 a priori 8 rational 10 scientific
de Duve, Christian: 7 Belgian 8 Nobelist
dee: 5 grade
ender: 3 jay
Dee: 4 Joey, Kiki, Ruby 5 Brown, Clark, river 6 Sandra, Snider 7 Frances, Wallace
River locale: 8 Scotland
Dee and the Starliters, Joey song: Peppermint Twist (1961) Shout (1962)
deed: 3 act, job 4 coup, feat, move, turn, work 5 doing, geste, paper, stunt, title 6 action, effort 7 charter, exploit, reality 8 covenant, document, transfer 9 adventure, indenture, occupancy, ownership, quitclaim 10 conveyance
bad ~: 3 sin 5 crime, wrong
brave ~: 4 coup
chivalrous ~: 4 gest 5 geste
do a good ~: 4 help
good ~: 3 aid 4 help 5 favor 7 service

8 courtesy, kindness 10 kindliness
__ deed: 3 tax 5 title, trust
Dee Dee: 5 Myers, Sharp
Deed I Do singer: 5 Horne
__-Dee-Doo-Dah: 4 Zip-a
deeds: 4 acta 7 heroics 9 res gestae
Deeds: 10 Longfellow
Dee, Frances: 7 actress
film: Blood Money (1933)
If I Were King (1938)
I Walked With a Zombie (1943)
Of Human Bondage (1934)
So Ends Our Night (1941)
Souls at Sea (1937)
Wells Fargo (1937)
deejay: 5 Kasem 9 announcer
alternative: 4 band
material: 2 CD, LP 4 demo
Dee, Kiki song: Don't Go Breaking My Heart (1976)
deem: 4 feel, hold, rate, take, view 5 count, judge, think, value 6 assume, credit, decide, look on, reckon, regard, repute 7 believe, imagine, presume, suppose, surmise 8 conceive, consider, estimate, look upon
de-emphasize: 8 play down
Deenie author: Judy Blume
deep: 3 low, sea 4 bass, full, loud, rapt, rich 5 briny, broad, heavy, husky, ocean, sound, thick 6 arcane, buried, hidden, occult, secret, shrewd, strong, subtle, tricky 7 abysmal, abyssal, complex, Delphic, intense, learned, low down, obscure, orotund, serious, weighty 8 absorbed, abstract, abstruse, baritone, barytone, esoteric, guttural, immersed, intimate, profound, resonant, sonorous, unbroken 9 cavernous, engrossed, heartfelt, innermost, intensely, intensive, recondite 10 bottomless, fathomless, impressive, low-pitched, meaningful, mysterious, passionate, thoughtful, unknowable
be knee ~ in: 4 teem 5 swarm 6 infest
down: 6 inside
go ~ into: 5 probe 11 investigate
in ~: 5 stuck 7 trapped 8 strapped
off the ~ end: 9 foolhardy
water: 3 fix, jam 4 bind, mess 5 pinch 6 crisis, pickle, plight, scrape, strait 7 dilemma, problem, trouble 8 quandary 9 adversity 10 difficulty
deep __: 3 fat 4 down 5 floor, focus, fryer, space 6 breath, freeze 7 pockets
deep __ bend: 4 knee
deep-__: 3 fry, sea, set, six 4 dish, draw, dyed, laid 5 fried, water 6 frozen, rooted, seated, voiced 7 chested
__-deep: 4 knee, skin 5 ankle, waist
Deep __: 4 Blue 5 South 6 Impact, Purple, Valley
Deepak: 6 Chopra
Deep Blue Good-by, The author: John D. MacDonald
Deep Blue Sea (1999 film)
cast: Saffron Burrows, Samuel L. Jackson, Thomas Jane, Jacqueline McKenzie
director: Renny Harlin
Deep Cover rapper: 5 Dr. Dre
deep-dish __: 3 pie 5 pizza
deepen: 4 grow 5 mount, shade 6 dig out, dredge, expand, extend 7 develop, magnify, thicken 8 excavate, increase, scoop out 9 aggravate, intensify 10 strengthen
Deep End of the Ocean (1999 film)
cast: Whoopi Goldberg, Jonathan Jackson, Michelle Pfeiffer, Treat Williams
director: Ulu Grosbard
Deeper and Deeper (1992 song) artist: Madonna
__ deepest dye: 5 of the
deep-felt: 4 keen 5 acute
Deep Impact (1998 film)
cast: Robert Duvall, Morgan Freeman, Téa Leoni, Vanessa Redgrave, Maximilian Schell, Elijah Wood
director: Mimi Leder
__ Deep Is the Ocean: 3 How
__ Deep Is Your Love: 3 How
deeply: 4 very 6 highly, vastly 9 sincerely 10 to the quick
Deep Purple
song: Hush (1968)
Smoke on the Water (1973)
deep-rooted: 4 firm 5 inner 6 stable 7 lasting 8 embedded, lifelong 9 confirmed, ingrained 10 habituated, inveterate
deep-sea: 5 naval 6 marine 8 maritime, nautical
explorer: 5 diver
deep-sea diving: 5 sport
deep-seated: 3 gut 5 fixed, inner 6 inborn, inbred, rooted 7 built-in, chronic, radical 8 habitual, inherent, longtime, profound 9 chronical, confirmed, essential, ingrained, intrinsic, unabating 10 habituated, inveterate
deep-six: 3 can 4 dump 5 ditch, scrap 7 discard 8 jettison, throw out
Deep South: 5 Dixie
Deep, The: 4 film 5 novel
author: Peter Benchley
cast: Jacqueline Bisset, Louis Gossett Jr., Nick Nolte, Robert Shaw
director: Peter Yates
deep-toned: 4 alto, bass, rich 8 sonorous
Deep Valley (1947 film)
cast: Dane Clark, Ida Lupino
director: Jean Negulesco
deer: 3 doe, elk, roe 4 axis, buck, fawn, hart, hind, pudu, shou, sika, stag 5 Bambi, moose 6 animal, cervid, chital, guemal, hangul, huemul, mammal, sambar, sambur, thamin, wapiti 7 brocket, caribou, muntjac, muntjak, roebuck, sambhar, sambhur 8 reindeer, ruminant 9 barasingh, whitetail 10 chevrotain
Asia: 4 axis, shou, sika 6 chital, hangul, sambar, sambur, thamin 7 muntjac, muntjak, sambhar, sambhur 9 barasingh
combining form: 5 cervi-
Disney ~: 3 Ena 5 Bambi
ender: 3 fly 4 skin, yard 5 hound 7 stalker
feature: 6 antler
female: 3 doe 4 hind
foot: 4 hoof
genus: 4 rusa
male: 4 buck, hart, stag
North America: 3 elk 6 wapiti 7 caribou
South America: 4 pudu 6 guemal, huemul 7 brocket
tail: 4 scut
where ~ and antelope play: 5 range
young: 4 fawn
deer __: 3 fly 4 fern, lick, weed 5 grass, mouse
__ deer: 3 Key, red, roe 4 axis, mule, musk 5 marsh, mouse 6 Andean, fallow 7 barking, spotted
Deer __: 4 Xing
Deer __, The: 4 Park 6 Hunter, Slayer
__ deer, a female...: 4 Doe a
deerberry: 5 shrub
relative: 5 heath, salal 6 azalea, kalmia 7 arbutus, rhodora 8 cassiope, cowberry 9 blueberry
Deere: 4 John
product: 5 mower 7 tractor
rival: 4 Toro
Deerfield Beach: 4 city, town
locale: 7 Florida
Deer Hunter, The (1978 film)
cast: John Cazale, Robert De Niro, John Savage, Meryl Streep, Christopher Walken
director: Michael Cimino
__ Dee River: 3 Pee
Deer Park: 4 city, town
locale: 5 Texas 7 New York
Deer Park, The author: Norman Mailer
deerskin: 7 leather
Deer Slayer, The author: James Fenimore Cooper
character: 5 Hetty, Natty 6 Bumppo
deerstalker: 3 cap, hat
Dee, Ruby: 7 actress
film: Do the Right Thing (1989)
Gone Are the Days (1963)
The Jackie Robinson Story (1950)
A Raisin in the Sun (1961)
Up Tight (1968)
spouse: Ossie Davis
Dees: 4 Rick
Dee, Sandra: 7 actress
film: Come September (1961)
Imitation of Life (1959)
Romanoff and Juliet (1961)
Rosie! (1967)
A Summer Place (1959)
spouse: Bobby Darin
de-escalate: 5 lower 6 lessen 7 subside 8 level off
de-escalation: 5 truce
Dees, Rick song: Disco Duck (1976)
Deever: 5 Danny
__ Dee Williams: 5 Billy
def: 3 rad 4 aces, A-one, boss, braw, cool, dece, drum, fine, gear, keen, neat, nice, phat, tuff 5 dandy, ducky, grand, great, marvy, neato, nobby, prime, slick, super, swell 6 bang on, bang-up, bonzer, bosker, choice, divine, dreamy, far-out, gnarly, groovy, lovely, peachy, slap-up, spot on, superb, terrif, tiptop, unreal, whizzo, wicked 7 amazing, awesome, capital, corking, perfect, ripping, skookum, stellar, sublime 8 dazzling, especial, eximious, fabulous, five-star, four-star, frabjous, glorious, heavenly, jim-dandy, slam-bang, smashing, splendid, standout, sterling, stickout, superior, terrific, top-level, topnotch, very good, wondrous 9 bodacious, Endsville, excellent, exemplary, exquisite, first-rate, high-grade, hunky-dory, marvelous, sollicker, top-flight, wonderful 10 first-class, hotsy-totsy, jack-a-dandy, out of sight, peachy-keen, phenomenal, remarkable, stupendous, super-duper
Def __: 7 Leppard
DEF
predecessor: 3 ABC
successor: 3 GHI
telephone's ~: 5 three
__ de fábrica: 5 marca
deface: 3 mar 4 harm, maim, ruin, scar 5 score, spoil, sully, trash 6 damage, impair, injure, mangle 7 scratch, tarnish 8 mutilate 9 vandalize
defacement: 8 graffiti
defacer: 6 vandal
de facto: 4 real 5 truly 6 actual, in fact, really 8 actually 9 actuality, in reality 10 unimagined
defalcate: 5 steal 8 embezzle
de Falla: 6 Manuel
defamation: 3 dig, lie, mud 4 barb, dirt, gibe, jibe, slam, slap, slur, snub 5 abuse, libel, scorn, smear, taunt 6 rebuff, slight 7 affront, calumny, catcall, disdain, mockery, obloquy, offense, put-down, slander 8 contempt, derision, ridicule 9 aspersion, cheap shot, contumely 10 backbiting, detraction, disrespect, impugnment, muckraking, opprobrium
defamatory: 7 abusive, vicious 8 libelous 9 injurious, insulting, invidious, maligning, traducing, vilifying 10 calumnious, derogatory, detracting, detractive, scandalous, slanderous
defame: 3 hit, pan 4 gibe, jeer, jibe, mock, slam, slur, snub 5 abuse, cut up, decry, knock, libel, roast, scorn, smear, spurn, sully, taint, taunt, wrong 6 deride, dump on, heckle, impugn, malign, offend, rebuff, slight, vilify 7 affront, asperse, blacken, degrade, disdain, put down, rank out, run down, slander, tarnish, traduce 8 backbite, badmouth, belittle, besmirch, denounce, disgrace, dishonor, ridicule, vilipend 9 denigrate, discredit, disparage, humiliate, knock down 10 blackguard, calumniate, disrespect, scandalize, stigmatize, throw mud at, villainize, vituperate
defamer: 5 enemy 6 critic 8 vilifier 9 detractor, ill-wisher
Defarge: 3 Mme. 6 Madame
emulate ~: 4 knit
defassa: 6 mammal 8 antelope
relative: 3 gnu, kob 4 guib, kudu, oryx, puku, topi 5 addax, bongo, chiru, eland, goral, korin, nyala, oribi, saiga, serow 6 chammy, dik-dik, duiker, impala, koodoo, lechwe, nilgai, rhebok, shammy, shamoy 7 blaubok, blesbok, chamois, gazelle, gemsbok, gerenuk, grysbok, nylghai, nylghau, sassaby 8 blesbuck, bontebok, bushbuck, gemsbuck, reedbuck, steenbok, steinbok 9 blackbuck, pronghorn, sitatunga, springbok, waterbuck 10 hartebeest, wildebeest
defat: 4 skim, trim
default: 4 fail, lack, lose, miss 5 lapse, shirk, stiff 7 failure, lose out, neglect 8 inaction, omission 9 oversight 10 bankruptcy, insolvency, nonpayment
on: 6 run out
security against ~: 4 lien
defaulter: 7 failure 10 delinquent
defaulting: 10 delinquent
Def by Temptation (1990 film)
cast: Cynthia Bond, James Bond III, Kadeem Hardison
director: James Bond III
defeat: 2 KO 3 ace, dud, get, tan, top, zap 4 beat, best, bomb, bust, deck, drub, edge, fall, flop, foil, kayo, kill, lick, loss, mate, rout, ruin, sink, skin, trim, undo, veto, whip, whup 5 block, check, cream, crush, floor, outdo, pound, quash, quell, repel, skunk, smash, stimy, stymy, swamp, trash, trump, unarm, upend, upset, whack, whomp, worst 6 fiasco, finish, hammer, lacing, master, mishap, outhit, outwit, pommel, pummel, rebuff, reduce, show up, stymie, subdue, thrash, thwart, turkey, wallop 7 beating, beat out, blunder, conquer, debacle, failure, lambast, licking, misstep, mow down, nose out, nullify, outplay, overrun, put down, repulse, scuttle, setback, shellac, stumble, trample, trounce, undoing, victory, washout, win over, wipe out 8 collapse, confound, conquest, decimate, demolish, downfall, drubbing, fight off, knock out, lam-

baste, outclass, outflank, outscore, outsmart, overcome, shellack, suppress, surmount, trashing, vanquish, Waterloo **9** breakdown, checkmate, discomfit, eliminate, force back, frustrate, landslide, overpower, overthrow, overwhelm, plow under, pulverize, slaughter, steamroll, subjugate, thrashing, trouncing **10** annihilate, neutralize, nonsuccess, obliterate
admit ~: **4** quit **5** yield
barely ~: **3** nip **4** edge **7** nose out
decisively: **3** wap **4** bury, drub, rout, skin, whap, whip, whop, whup **5** cream, roust, skunk, stomp, thump, tromp, whomp **7** trounce **8** vanquish
defeated: **4** beat **6** broken **8** overcome
be ~: **4** fail, fall, lose **5** yield **6** go down **7** get beat, lose out
not yet ~: **4** in it **5** alive
one's cry: **5** uncle
__-defeating: **4** self
defeatist: **7** killjoy **8** downbeat **9** pessimist, unhopeful
word: **4** can't **6** cannot
defect: **3** bug **4** blot, flaw, kink, lack, scar, turn, vice, wart **5** error, fault, leave, speck, stain, taint **6** desert, foible, glitch, run out **7** abscond, blemish, failing, forsake, go south, pull out, scratch **8** drawback, renounce, weakness **10** disability, faultiness, inaccuracy, inadequacy, inefficacy
__ defect: **4** mass **7** crystal, lattice
defection: **8** apostasy **9** desertion, forsaking, rebellion, recreancy, rejection, secession, severance, sundering **10** alienation, deficiency, disloyalty, disownment, separation, withdrawal
defective: **3** bad, irr. **4** foul, grim, poor, sick **5** amiss, awful, lousy, woful **6** broken, crumby, crummy, dismal, faulty, flawed, horrid, marred, odious, rotten, woeful **7** baleful, baneful, beastly, damaged, doleful, ghastly, haywire, lacking, sketchy, unsound, wanting **8** dreadful, fallible, God-awful, grievous, horrible, impaired, inferior, shameful, stinking, terrible, wretched **9** appalling, atrocious, blemished, deficient, erroneous, execrable, frightful, imperfect, insidious, irregular, loathsome, miserable, offensive, revolting, subnormal **10** despicable, detestable, disastrous, horrendous, inaccurate, inadequate, incomplete, on the blink, on the fritz, out of order
combining form: **4** atel- **5** atelo-
vehicle: **3** dud **6** jalopy **7** clunker **10** hunk of junk
defector: **7** escapee, refugee, traitor **8** apostate, deserter, forsaker, recreant, renegade
__ defects: **4** zero
defects and all: **4** as is
Defence of the Realm (1985 film)
cast: Gabriel Byrne, Denholm Elliott, Greta Scacchi
defend: **4** hold, save **5** cover, fight, guard **6** assert, back up, embank, ensure, foster, insure, patrol, screen, secure, shield, uphold **7** contest, endorse, espouse, explain, indorse, justify, protect, shelter, support, sustain, ward off **8** advocate, champion, fight for, keep safe, maintain, preserve, stave off **9** fight over, keep guard, look after, safeguard, vindicate, watch over **10** go to bat for, rally round, speak up for, stand up for, stick up for
against: **7** prevent
defendable: **5** valid **8** verified
defendant: **4** resp., reus **5** party **8** litigant **10** respondent
answer: **4** plea **5** alibi
of 1925: **6** Scopes
option: **6** appeal
plea: **4** nolo **6** guilty **9** not guilty
defender: **5** guard **6** backer, jurist, keeper, knight, lawyer, legist, savior, votary **7** paladin, saviour **8** advocate, champion, exponent, guardian, watchman **9** apologist, bodyguard, paraclete, proponent, protector, supporter
__ defender: **6** public
Defender __ Faith: **5** of the
defender of men, name meaning: **9** Alexander
Defenders, The (CBS drama)
cast: E.G. Marshall (Lawrence Preston)
Robert Reed (Kenneth Preston)
Defending Your Life (1991 film)
cast: Albert Brooks, Meryl Streep, Rip Torn
director: Albert Brooks
defense: **4** fort, plea, wall **5** alibi, cover, fence, guard, reply **6** answer, buffer, excuse, reason, retort, shield **7** apology, bastion, bulwark, citadel, parapet, rampart, redoubt, shelter, tactics **8** advocacy, buttress, fortress, garrison, palisade, response, security **9** barricade, rejoinder, safeguard, sanctuary **10** embankment, opposition, precaution, protection, resistance, stronghold
acronym: **4** NATO **5** SEATO
advisory grp.: **3** NSC
close the ~: **4** rest
major ~ contractor: **5** Loral
mechanism: **6** denial
__ defense: **4** zone **5** civil
__-defense: **4** self
Defense Dept. org.: **3** ONI, SAC, USA, USN **4** USAF **5** NORAD
defenseless: **4** weak **5** naked **7** exposed, unarmed **8** helpless, wide open **9** powerless, unguarded
render ~: **5** unarm **6** disarm
defensible: **5** sound, valid **6** proper **7** logical, tenable **9** excusable, plausible **10** condonable, pardonable, remittable, vindicable
defensive: **4** wary **7** careful, opposed **8** opposing, watchful **9** resistive, thwarting **10** preventive, protecting, protective
on the ~: **5** at bay **7** uptight
defensive __: **3** end **4** back
defer: **4** stay **5** agree, delay, remit, table, waive, yield **6** comply, listen, put off, submit **7** conform, consent, neglect, respect, suspend **8** file away, hesitate, hold over, lay aside, postpone, put aside **10** pigeonhole, reschedule
to: **3** bow **4** heed, mind, obey **5** kotow **6** accept, follow, fulfil, kowtow, revere **7** abide by, fulfill, give way **8** carry out
__ de fer: **6** chapel, chemin
__-de-fer: **4** main **6** martel
deference: **5** honor **6** homage, regard **7** regards, respect, valuing **8** courtesy **9** attention, gallantry, obedience, obeisance, reverence **10** admiration, allegiance, attentions, compliance, politeness, submission, veneration
deferential: **4** meek, mild **5** civil **6** humble, polite **7** fawning **8** gracious **9** courteous, regardful **10** respectful
deferment: **4** stay **5** delay **7** respite **8** reprieve **10** suspension
deferments, having no: **4** one A
deferral: **8** abeyance, lateness
deferred __: **5** share **6** charge **7** annuity
__-deferred annuity: **3** tax
defiance: **3** lip **4** dare, sass **5** spite **6** mutiny, revolt **7** affront, bravado, refusal **8** audacity, back talk, boldness, contempt, temerity **9** challenge, contumacy, disregard, impudence, insolence, rebellion **10** brazenness, effrontery, insurgence, opposition, resistance
exclamation of ~: **3** yah **4** nuts **5** I won't, nerts, nertz, never
in ~ of: **7** despite
defiant: **4** bold, game **5** brave, gutsy, nervy, onery, sassy **6** awless, brazen, daring, feisty, gritty, heroic, ornery, plucky, spunky, unruly **7** aweless, doughty, gallant, naughty, staunch, valiant, wayward **8** contrary, factious, fearless, heroical, insolent, intrepid, mutinous, resolute, stalwart, stubborn, unafraid, valorous **9** audacious, dauntless, dreadless, obstinate, resistant, truculent, undaunted, unfearful **10** aggressive, courageous, pugnacious, rebellious, refractory
one: **5** darer
Defiant: **4** boat, ship
Defiant Ones, The (1958 film)
cast: Theodore Bikel, Tony Curtis, Sidney Poitier
director: Stanley Kramer
deficiency: **3** bug **4** flaw, lack, loss, need, want **5** fault, minus **6** dearth, glitch **7** absence, failing, paucity, poverty **8** drawback, exiguity, scarcity, shortage, sparsity, weakness **9** privation **10** inadequacy, meagerness, scantiness
combining form: **5** -penia
deficient: **3** bad, low, shy **4** poor, slim, sort, weak **5** amiss, rusty, scant, short **6** faulty, flawed, meager, scanty, scarce, skimpy **7** failing, ill-done, lacking, slender, wanting **8** deprived, impaired, inferior **9** defective, destitute, imperfect, subnormal **10** inadequate, incomplete, unfinished
be ~: **4** lack, need
combining form: **6** -privic
prove ~: **4** fail
deficit: **4** lack, loss **5** minus **6** red ink **7** arrears **8** shortage, underage **9** shortfall **10** inadequacy
__ deficit: **5** trade
defier: **5** rebel
defile: **4** foul, harm, pass, soil **5** abuse, dirty, shame, smear, spoil, stain, sully, taint, trash **6** befoul, crud up, damage, debase, embrue, imbrue, infect, malign, ravine, smudge **7** blacken, corrupt, degrade, pollute, profane, slander, tarnish, violate, vitiate **8** besmirch, disgrace, dishonor, maculate **9** desecrate **10** adulterate
defiled: **5** dirty **6** impure **7** corrupt, unclean **8** maculate
defilement: **4** harm **5** abuse, filth, taint **8** impurity, sullying **9** pollution, profaning, violation **10** corruption, debasement
definable: **5** exact, fixed **6** finite **7** fixable, precise **8** clear-cut, definite, specific
define: **3** fix **4** name **5** label, limit, shape **6** decide, demark, detail, lay out, set out, settle **7** delimit, enclose, explain, fence in, inclose, mark out, outline, specify **8** construe, describe, encircle, nail down, pinpoint, restrict, spell out **9** ascertain, delineate, demarcate, designate, determine, encompass, establish, formalize, formulate, interpret, make clear **10** stereotype
__-defined: **3** ill **4** well
defining __: **6** moment
definite: **3** set **4** firm, real, sure, true **5** clean, clear, exact, final, fixed, overt, plain, sharp, vivid **6** actual, limpid, marked, rooted, secure, stable, static **7** assured, audible, certain, decided, express, for sure, graphic, limited, obvious, precise, settled, special, visible **8** absolute, accurate, clear-cut, complete, concrete, constant, decisive, distinct, emphatic, explicit, implicit, incisive, in the bag, ironclad, palpable, positive, resolved, singular, specific, tangible, verified **9** definable, downright, graphical, permanent **10** conclusive, determined, forthright, guaranteed, inarguable, particular, pronounced, unarguable, unchanging, undeniable, undoubtful, unimagined, well-marked
not ~: **4** iffy **10** up in the air
definite __: **7** article
definitely: **2** ay, da, ja, sí, so **3** aye, oui, yea, yep, yes, yup **4** fine, just, okay, sure, yeah **5** good-o, natch, quite, right, roger, truly, uh-huh **6** agreed, easily, gladly, good-oh, indeed, just so, rather, righto, surely, you bet, yowzah **7** exactly, for sure, go ahead, indeedy, mais oui, quite so, ten-four **8** all right, as you say, for a fact, of course, thumbs up, very well **9** be my guest, certainly, darn right, decidedly, doubtless, expressly, naturally, no mistake, obviously, precisely, sure thing, you betcha, you said it **10** absolutely, by all means, explicitly, far and away, inevitably, positively, sure as hell, sure enough, that's right, undeniably
in Spanish: **4** sí sí
definition: **5** sense **7** meaning **9** diagnosis, outlining, rationale, rendering, rendition **10** annotation, commentary, denotation, expounding, expression
by ~: **5** per se
__-definition television: **4** high
definitive: **4** last **5** final, fixed **6** actual **7** classic, express, flat-out, precise **8** absolute, accurate, clear-cut, complete, decisive, emphatic, explicit, reliable, specific, standard, ultimate, verified **9** downright, finishing, full-dress **10** completing, concluding, conclusive, exhaustive, nailed down, unarguable, unimagined
definitude: **8** accuracy **9** exactness, precision
Def Jam genre: **3** rap
deflate: **4** dash, void **5** abase, empty, lower **6** dampen, debunk, humble, reduce, shrink, squash **7** depress, devalue, exhaust, flatten, mortify, put down **8** collapse, contract, decrease, diminish, dispirit, puncture, ridicule, take down **9** devaluate, humiliate, shoot down **10** depreciate
deflated: **5** empty
deflating sound: **3** sss
deflationary __: **6** spiral
deflator maybe: **3** pin
deflect: **4** bend, skew, veer, warp **5** avert, parry, shine **6** divert, glance, swerve **7** fend off, ward off **8** ricochet **9** bounce off, glance off, intercept, sidetrack, turn aside
deflection: **4** skew **5** shift, slant, slope **7** veering **9** curvature, departure, deviation, diversion **10** digression, divergence
combining form: **7** sphingo-
Defoe, Daniel: **6** writer **7** British
work: Journal of the Plague Year
Moll Flanders
Robinson Crusoe

__ de foie gras: **4** paté
__ de force: **4** tour
DeFore, Don: **5** actor
  film: Romance on the High Seas (1948)
    Without Reservations (1946)
  TV: The Adventures of Ozzie and Harriet, Hazel
deforest: **5** strip **8** clearcut
DeForest: **3** Lee **4** John **6** Kelley **7** Calvert
deform: **3** mar **4** warp **5** gnarl, twist **6** damage, mangle **7** contort, distort **8** misshape
__ de foudre: **4** coup
__ de fraise: **5** crème
__ de framboise: **5** crème
__ de France: **3** île **4** Tour **5** Marie
defraud: **2** do **3** con, gyp, rob **4** bilk, burn, clip, dupe, flay, gull, hoax, jive, milk, nick, ream, rook, scam, take **5** cheat, cozen, gouge, mulct, pluck, shaft, steal, trick **6** delude, fleece, hustle, outwit, rip off, suck in, take in **7** beguile, deceive, mislead, swindle **8** flimflam, hoodwink, outsmart **9** bamboozle, disinform, victimize **10** circumvent, run a game on
defrauder: **3** con **5** cheat, rogue **6** con man **9** charlatan, trickster
defray: **3** pay **4** fund **5** spend **6** pay for, redeem **7** finance
defrayal: **7** funding, payment
__-de-frise: **6** cheval
defrost: **4** thaw **7** get soft, thaw out **8** dissolve, fluidize, unfreeze
deft: **3** ace, apt **4** able, neat **5** adept, agile, crack, handy, quick, ready, slick **6** adroit, au fait, clever, expert, facile, habile, limber, nimble **7** capable, cunning, skilled, trained **8** delicate, dextrous, graceful, masterly, seasoned, skillful, talented **9** competent, dexterous, efficient, ingenious, masterful, practiced **10** proficient
deftness: **5** asset, skill, touch **7** ability, agility, mastery, sleight **8** facility, legerity **9** dexterity, expertise, lightness, readiness **10** nimbleness
__ de Fuca Strait: **4** Juan
defunct: **4** gone, late, past **5** kaput **6** bygone **7** expired, extinct
defuse: **4** calm **6** disarm, lessen, pacify, soften, soothe, weaken **7** disable, mollify **8** moderate **9** alleviate **10** deactivate, smooth over
defy: **4** buck, dare, face, foil, mock **5** brave, elude, fight, flout, rebel, repel, scorn, spurn **6** combat, deride, ignore, oppose, resist, revolt, slight, thwart **7** condemn, disobey, provoke, repulse, violate **8** confront, face down, ridicule **9** challenge, disregard, frustrate, stand up to, withstand **10** contradict
degage: **6** casual
Degas, Edgar: **6** artist, French **7** painter
  contemporary: **5** Manet
de Gaulle: **6** French **7** airport, Charles **9** statesman
  alternative: **4** Orly
degauss a tape: **5** erase
degenerate: **3** rot **4** rust, sink, slip **5** decay, lapse, slide, slump **6** worsen **7** corrode, fall off, regress **8** degraded **9** aggravate, backslide **10** disimprove, exacerbate, go to pieces, retrogress
degeneration: **4** drop, fall **5** decay, lapse **7** atrophy, decline, descent **9** vitiation, worsening
DeGeneres: **5** Ellen
de Gennes, Pierre-Gilles: **6** French **8** Nobelist **9** physicist
degerm: **5** clean **6** purify **8** sanitize **9** disinfect, sterilize
__ de geste: **7** chanson
de Givenchy: **6** Hubert
__ de grâce: **4** coup
degradable starter: **3** bio
degradation: **3** rot **5** shame **8** disgrace, dishonor, ignominy
degrade: **3** pan, rot **4** gibe, jeer, jibe, mock, ruin, sink, slam, slur, snub, soil **5** abase, abuse, decry, libel, lower, scorn, shame, spurn, taunt **6** debase, defame, defile, demean, demote, deride, dump on, heckle, humble, impugn, insult, lessen, malign, offend, rebuff, reduce, slight, vilify, weaken **7** affront, asperse, cheapen, corrupt, deprave, disdain, put down, rank out, run down, slander, traduce, vitiate **8** belittle, cast down, denounce, derogate, ridicule, take down, tear down, vilipend **9** denigrate, discredit, disparage, humiliate, shoot down **10** adulterate, calumniate, disrespect
degraded: **3** low **4** base, mean, vile **5** crude, gross, seamy **6** abject, coarse, sordid, vulgar **7** corrupt, debased, ignoble, low-down **8** depraved, shameful **9** worthless
degrading: **6** menial **8** shameful, unworthy **9** unhealthy **10** derogatory, despicable, pejorative
__ de grandeur: **5** folie
degree: **2** BA, BE, BS, MA, MD, MS **3** BBA, BCE, BCS, BFA, BPE, BSC, BSN, DDS, D.Ed., DFA, DMD, DVM, Ed.B, Ed.M., LL.D., MBA, MFA, MLS, MNA, MPA, MSE, MSN, MSW, Ph.D., Sc.D. **4** D.Lit., Lit.B, Lit.D., M.Agr., MSEd., rate, rung, step, unit **5** grade, level, limit, notch, order, phase, pitch, plane, range, scale, scope, shade, stage, title **6** amount, extent, length, rating, status, volume **7** caliber, diploma, doctor's, master's, measure **8** severity, strength **9** associate, doctorate, gradation, intensity, sheepskin **10** proportion
  architectural ~: **3** MFA
  art ~: **3** MFA
  bridge builder ~: **3** BCE
  business ~: **3** BBA, MBA
  chemist ~: **3** BCS, Sc.B.
  conservatory ~: **3** B.Mu.
  dentist ~: **3** DDS, DMD
  draftsman ~: **3** BME
  English ~: **4** Lit.B., Lit.D.
  entrepreneur ~: **3** MBA
  extreme ~: **3** nth
  farming ~: **3** MSA **4** M.Agr.
  give the third ~: **4** pump, quiz **5** grill, probe **7** torture **8** question
  greatest ~: **4** most
  gym teacher ~: **3** BPE
  holder: **4** alum, grad **6** alumna **7** alumnus **8** graduate
  journalism ~: **2** MJ
  law ~: **2** BL, JD **3** DCL, LL.B., LL.M., MCL, SJD
  librarian ~: **3** BLS, MLS
  medical ~: **3** DDS **4** M.Sc.D.
  MIT ~: **2** EE **3** BME
  nth ~: **3** max **7** extreme **8** ultimate
  nurse ~: **3** BSN, MNA, MSN
  physics ~: **3** Sc.B., Sc.D.
  piano instructor ~: **3** BME
  religious ~: **3** SSD, STB, STM, Th.D.
  requirement: **6** thesis
  slight ~: **5** tinge
  suffix: **4** -ness
  teacher ~: **3** Ed.B., Ed.M., MSE **4** MSEd.
  therapist ~: **3** MSW
  to a ~: **4** a bit **5** quite **6** kind of, partly, rather, sort of **8** slightly, somewhat **10** moderately
  to a high ~: **4** very **5** quite **6** deeply, rather, vastly **7** acutely, greatly **8** terribly **9** decidedly, extremely, seriously, supremely, unusually **10** enormously, especially, profoundly, remarkably, thoroughly, uncommonly
  to any ~: **5** at all
  to the nth ~: **6** in full, in toto, wholly **7** utterly **9** all the way, extremely **10** altogether, thoroughly
  to the same ~: **5** alike
  writer ~: **3** MFA **4** Lit.B., Lit.D.
  zoo staffer ~: **3** VMD
degree __: **4** mill
degree-__: **3** day
__ degree: **3** nth, to a **4** pass **5** third **7** doctor's, master's **9** bachelor's
__-degree: **5** first, third **6** second
Degree: **9** deodorant
  alternative: **3** Ban **4** Sure **5** Arrid, Tussy **6** Secret **7** Dry Idea, Mitchum **10** Right Guard, Soft and Dri, Speed Stick
__ degree-day: **7** growing, heating
degree of __: **5** curve **7** freedom
degrees
  above the equator: **4** N. Lat.
  below the equator: **4** S. Lat.
  by ~: **7** gradual **8** bit by bit **9** gradually, partially, piecemeal
  move by ~: **4** inch
__ Degrees of Separation: **3** Six
degu: **6** animal, mammal, rodent
  relative: **3** rat **4** cavy, jird, paca, vole **5** coypu, gundi, mouse, xerus **6** agouti, beaver, gerbil, gopher, jerboa, marmot, murine **7** hamster, lemming, muskrat, visacha **8** chipmunk, cricetid, dormouse, squirrel, tuco-tuco **9** chickaree, groundhog, guinea pig, porcupine, woodchuck **10** chinchilla, prairie dog
__ de guerre: **3** nom
__ de Guerre: **5** Croix
degust: **5** savor
dehair: **5** shear
__-de-Haute Provence: **5** Alpes
De Haven, Gloria spouse: John Payne
de Havilland, Olivia: **7** actress
  film: The Adventures of Robin Hood (1938)
    Alibi Ike (1935)
    Anthony Adverse (1936)
    Captain Blood (1935)
    The Charge of the Light Brigade (1936)
    The Dark Mirror (1946)
    Dodge City (1939)
    Gone With the Wind (1939)
    The Great Garrick (1937)
    Hard to Get (1938)
    The Heiress (1949, AA)
    Hold Back the Dawn (1941)
    Hush ... Hush, Sweet Charlotte (1965)
    In This Our Life (1942)
    It's Love I'm After (1937)
    Lady in a Cage (1964)
    Light in the Piazza (1962)
    The Male Animal (1942)
    My Cousin Rachel (1952)
    Not as a Stranger (1955)
    The Private Lives of Elizabeth and Essex (1939)
    The Proud Rebel (1958)
    The Snake Pit (1948)
    The Strawberry Blonde (1941)
    They Died With Their Boots On (1941)
    To Each His Own (1946, AA)
  sister: Joan Fontaine
de Hevesy, George: **7** chemist **8** Nobelist **9** Hungarian
dehire: **2** ax **3** axe **4** fire **5** let go **6** lay off **9** discharge
Dehmel, Richard: **4** poet **6** German
Dehmelt, Hans: **6** German **8** Nobelist **9** physicist
dehumidify: **3** dry **9** evaporate
dehydrate: **3** dry **4** sear **5** parch **7** process, shrivel **8** preserve **9** anhydrate, desiccate, evaporate, exsiccate
dehydrated: **3** dry **4** arid, sere **5** unwet **7** parched, thirsty **8** droughty **9** juiceless, waterless
Dei __: **6** gratia
__ Dei: **5** Agnus
deice: **4** salt **7** thaw out **8** unfreeze
Deidre: **4** Hall
deific: **5** godly **6** divine **7** godlike **8** almighty
deify: **4** love **5** adore, ensky, exalt, extol **6** extoll **7** elevate, ennoble, glorify, idolize, worship **8** sanctify, venerate **10** consecrate
Deighton, Len: **6** author, writer
  character: **3** spy
deign: **5** lower, stoop **6** see fit **8** be so kind **9** patronize, vouchsafe **10** condescend
Deimos: **4** moon
  neighbor: **6** Phobos
  parent: **4** Ares **9** Aphrodite
  planet: **4** Mars
  sibling: **6** Phobus **8** Harmonia
Deion: **7** Sanders
Deisenhofer, Johann: **6** German **7** chemist **8** Nobelist
__ D. Eisenhower: **6** Dwight
deistic: **6** divine **9** religious
deity: **3** god **7** creator, goddess **8** divinity
  see also god
__ de Janeiro: **3** Rio
__ de Javelle: **3** eau
déjà vu: **10** paramnesia
  clothing style: **5** retro
Déjà Vu (1998 film)
  cast: Glynis Barber, Stephen Dillane, Victoria Foyt, Vanessa Redgrave
  director: Henry Jaglom
deject: **4** tire **6** bum out, dampen, darken, dismay, sadden **7** depress **8** dispirit **9** bring down **10** demoralize, discourage, dishearten
dejected: **3** low, sad **4** blue, dark, down, glum, mopy **5** bleak, heavy, mopey, sorry, woful **6** abject, broody, dismal, gloomy, mopish, morose, somber, woeful **7** doleful, hangdog, in a funk, joyless, sagging, subdued, unhappy **8** cast down, desolate, downbeat, downcast, drooping, shot down, wretched **9** bummed-out, cheerless, depressed, exanimate, heartsick, in the pits, miserable, prostrate, saturnine, sorrowful, unhopeful, woebegone **10** chapfallen, despondent, dispirited, melancholy, out of sorts, spiritless
  be ~: **4** mope
dejection: **3** woe **5** blues, dolor, gloom, grief **6** misery, sorrow **7** anguish, despair, sadness **8** distress, doldrums, glumness, the blues **9** heartache, pessimism **10** depression, desolation, heartbreak, heavy heart, loneliness, melancholy, woefulness
Dejection: An Ode author: Coleridge
__ déjeuner: **5** petit
déjeuner dish: **6** salade
Déjeuner sur l'herbe painter: **5** Manet
de jure: **7** by right
__ de justice: **3** lit
De Kalb: **4** city, town
  athletes: **7** Huskies
  locale: **8** Illinois
  school: **3** NIU
deke: **4** fake **5** feint

victim: 6 goalie
Deke: 7 Slayton
Dekker: 6 Albert, Thomas 7 Desmond
Dekker, Thomas: 7 British 10 playwright
de Klerk: 2 F.W. 4 Boer 9 president
homeland: 3 RSA 11 South Africa
de Kooning, Willem: 5 Dutch 6 artist 7 painter
Del: 5 Ennis 6 Amitri, Reeves 7 Shannon
Del __: 3 Rio 4 City 5 Monte, Norte
Del.
see Delaware
__ de la Cité: 3 île
Delacroix, Eugène: 6 artist, French 7 painter
__ de Lafayette: 7 Marquis
Delagoa: 3 bay
locale: 10 Mozambique
Delahanty: 2 Ed
__ de Lahore: 5 Le roi
de la Hoya: 5 Oscar
__ de la Madeleine: 4 îles
de la Mare, Walter: 4 poet 7 British
delaminate: 4 peel
__-de-lance: 3 fer
de Lancie: 4 John
DeLand: 4 city, town
athletes: 7 Hatters
locale: 7 Florida
school: 7 Stetson
Delaney: 3 Kim 7 Shelagh
Delaney, Shelagh: 7 British 10 playwright
Delano: 4 city, town
locale: 10 California
__ Delano Roosevelt: 8 Franklin
Delany, Dana: 7 actress
film: Light Sleeper (1992)
Wide Awake (1998)
TV: China Beach
__ de la Paix: 3 Rue
de Laplace: 6 Pierre
__ de la Plata: 3 Rio
de la Renta, Oscar: 8 designer
rival: 5 Blass, Klein 6 Armani, Lauren 7 Versace
__ de la Réunion: 3 île
de Larrocha: 6 Alicia
__ de la Société: 4 îles
delate: 6 accuse
De Laurentiis: 4 Dino
Delaware: 3 bay 4 city, town 5 river, state 6 Indian 7 Amerind
capital: 5 Dover
city: 5 Dover, Lewes 6 Newark 10 Wilmington
city on the ~: 6 Camden, Easton 7 Trenton
dynast: 6 DuPont
feeder: 6 Lehigh 10 Schuylkill
Indian: 5 Unami 6 Lenape 9 Nanticoke
locale: 4 Ohio
neighbor: 8 Maryland 9 New Jersey
nickname: 10 First State
River locale: 4 Penn. 7 New York 9 New Jersey
state beverage: 4 milk
state fish: 8 weakfish
state insect: 7 ladybug
state tree: 5 holly
Delaware __ Gap: 5 Water
delay: 3 gap, jam, lag, tie 4 clog, curb, drag, mire, poke, slow, stay, stop, wait 5 block, brake, dally, defer, deter, hedge, hitch, pause, remit, sit on, stall, table, tarry, tie up, trail, waive 6 dampen, dawdle, detain, hamper, hang-up, hinder, holdup, impede, linger, loiter, put off, remain, retard, shelve, slow up 7 adjourn, hold off, inhibit, lay over, neglect, problem, prolong, red tape, respite, setback, slacken, suspend 8 dawdling, demurral, downtime, encumber, file away, footdrag, hesitate, hold over, interval, keep back, lateness, lay aside, obstruct, postpone, prohibit, protract, reprieve, slowdown, stoppage, surcease, tarrying 9 deferment, detention, extension, hindrance, interlude, interrupt, lingering, runaround, stalemate 10 dillydally, filibuster, hesitation, impediment, standstill, suspension
after a ~: 5 later 6 at last
cause ~: 4 slow 6 hang up
don't ~: 6 act now
legal ~: 4 hold, stop 5 waive 8 reprieve 9 deferment, remission 10 suspension
without ~: 3 now 4 ASAP, stat 5 apace, right, short, today 6 at once 7 readily 8 directly, promptly, right now, right off 9 at present, forthwith, presently, right away, summarily 10 at this time, here and now, this minute
delayed: 4 late, slow 5 tardy 6 behind 7 belated, overdue 8 detained 9 leisurely
delayed-__: 6 action
delaying: 4 slow 8 dilatory, hesitant 10 hesitation
Delbert: 4 Mann 9 McClinton
Delbrück, Max: 8 Nobelist
__ del Carmen: 5 Playa
Del City: 4 city, town
locale: 8 Oklahoma
__ del Corso: 3 Via
dele: 4 drop, edit, x off, x out 5 erase 6 excise, remove 7 edit out, expunge, take out 8 cross off, cross out 9 eliminate, expurgate, red-pencil, strike out
undo a ~: 4 stet
delectable: 5 sapid, sweet, tasty, yummy 6 dainty, divine, goodie, lovely, savory, toothy 7 darling 8 adorable, charming, enticing, fragrant, heavenly, inviting, luscious 9 agreeable, ambrosial, delicious, enjoyable, exquisite, flavorful, good to eat, nectarous, palatable, toothsome 10 appetizing, delightful, enchanting, gratifying, satisfying
delectate: 7 delight, enchant, gratify
delectation: 3 joy 4 zest 5 charm, gusto 7 delight, rapture 8 pleasure 9 enjoyment
Deledda, Grazia: 6 writer 7 Italian 8 Nobelist
delegate: 4 make, name, send 5 agent, envoy, proxy, trust, vicar 6 assign, charge, choose, commit, consul, depute, deputy, invest, nuncio, ordain, regent 7 appoint, consign, empower, entrust, intrust, license, stand-in 8 accredit, deputize, emissary, hand over, minister, nominate, relegate, settle on, transfer, turn over 9 appointee, authorize, designate, messenger, parcel out, surrogate 10 ambassador, commission, negotiator, settle upon
delegation: 8 congress 9 committal, gathering, reference, referring, submittal 10 assignment, commission, consigning, contingent, convention, conveyance, deputation, nomination, ordination, relegation
__ de León: 5 Ponce
de Lesseps: 9 Ferdinand
__ de l'est: 4 Gare
__ del Este: 5 Punta
delete: 3 cut 4 drop, omit, snip, trim, x out 5 annul, bleep, elide, erase, purge, scrub 6 cancel, censor, cut out, efface, excise, remove, rub off, rub out, strike 7 blot out, edit out, exclude, expunge, redline, scissor, scratch, take out, wipe out 8 black out, blow away, cross off, cross out, white out 9 eliminate, eradicate, expurgate, red-pencil, strike out 10 blue-pencil, obliterate
deleted: 3 x'ed
deleterious: 3 bad, ill 5 toxic 6 costly, malign, nocent 7 adverse, baleful, baneful, corrupt, harmful, hurtful, nocuous, noxious, ruinous 8 damaging, negative, sinister 9 dangerous, injurious, poisonous, unhealthy 10 calamitous, disastrous
deleteriousness: 4 harm
Delfonics
song: Didn't I (1970)
La-La - Means I Love You (1968)
Delft: 4 city, port, town
locale: 7 Holland 11 Netherlands
ware: 8 ceramics
__ del Fuego: 6 Tierra
Delhi: 4 city, town
city SSE of ~: 4 Agra
locale: 5 India
river: 5 Jumna 6 Yamuna
__ Delhi: 3 New, Old
deli: 4 mart, shop 5 store 6 eatery, market 10 restaurant
item: 3 BLT, ham, lox, rye, sub 4 chub, hero, mayo, slaw, to go 5 bagel, bialy, derma, Genoa, hoagy, knish, latke, wurst 6 hoagie, kishka, salami, tongue 7 bologna 8 pastrami 9 roast beef 10 corned beef
patron: 5 eater
scale word: 4 tare
shout: 4 next
unit: 2 lb., oz. 5 dozen, ounce, pound
Delia: 6 Ephron
Delian: 7 Artemis
League member: 5 Samos
deliberate: 3 sit 4 mull, muse, poky, slow 5 argue, meant, pause, study, sweat, think, waver, weigh 6 confer, debate, draggy, parley, ponder, reason, sedate, wanton, wilful 7 careful, decided, discuss, express, gradual, halting, impeded, lagging, languid, planned, reflect, revolve, serious, studied, willful, witting 8 cautious, chew over, cogitate, crawling, creeping, dawdling, dilatory, dragging, drawn-out, hesitant, intended, meditate, methodic, moderate, mull over, plodding, rational, resolute, ruminate, slothful, sluggish, talk over, toddling, turn over 9 cerebrate, conscious, designful, entertain, leisurely, lethargic, projected, prolonged, provident, purposive, snaillike, speculate, strategic, unhurried, voluntary 10 calculated, considered, excogitate, kick around, meticulous, protracted, purposeful, scrupulous, thoughtful, thought out, well-chosen
deliberately: 8 bit by bit, by design 9 leisurely, purposely
deliberation: 4 heed 6 debate, parley 7 caution, thought
without ~: 5 ad-lib 9 extempore 10 off-the-cuff
Delibes, Léo: 6 French 8 composer
delicacy: 4 tact 5 style, taste, treat, viand 6 dainty, luxury, morsel, nuance, tidbit 7 culture, finesse, frailty, modesty 8 airiness, ambrosia, elegance, fineness, subtlety, weakness 9 diplomacy, euphemism, fragility, frailness, lightness, propriety 10 daintiness, refinement
lacking ~: 4 rude 5 brash, crass
delicate: 4 deft, fine, lacy, nice, puny, sick, soft, thin, weak 5 adept, filmy, frail, gauzy, light, sheer, silky, wimpy, wispy 6 anemic, atonic, dainty, effete, feeble, flabby, flimsy, lovely, pastel, petite, pretty, sickly, slight, sticky, subtle, tender, tricky 7 anaemic, awkward, careful, elegant, fragile, mincing, netlike, politic, precise, refined, rickety, skilled, subdued, tactful, unsound, wimpish, wispish 8 cautious, discreet, ethereal, finespun, gossamer, graceful, helpless, masterly, perilous, pithless, skillful, ticklish, volatile 9 breakable, difficult, exquisite, faltering, frangible, powerless, sensitive, squeamish, unhealthy 10 cobweblike, diaphanous, diplomatic, ornamental, precarious, proficient, vulnerable
name meaning ~: 7 Delilah
Delicate Balance, A author: Albee
__ Delicate Condition: 5 Papa's
Delicate Delinquent, The (1957 film)
cast: Martha Hyer, Jerry Lewis
delicatessen
see deli
Delicias: 4 city, town
locale: 6 Mexico 9 Chihuahua
delicious: 3 mmm, yum 4 good, nice, rich 5 apple, sapid, sweet, tasty, yummy 6 dainty, divine, lovely, savory, toothy, yum-yum 8 adorable, fragrant, heavenly, luscious, noshable 9 agreeable, ambrosial, enjoyable, exquisite, fantastic, flavorful, good to eat, nectarous, palatable, succulent, toothsome 10 appetizing, delectable, delightful, gratifying
__ Delicious apple: 3 Red 6 Golden
__ delicti: 6 corpus
delicto, find in flagrante: 5 catch
delictum: 5 crime
delight: 3 joy, wow 4 glee, send, zest 5 amuse, bliss, charm, cheer, elate, exult, gusto, peach, revel 6 divert, excite, fulfil, luxury, please, ravish, regale, thrill, tickle, turn on, wallow 7 beguile, disport, ecstasy, elation, enchant, fulfill, gladden, gratify, happify, hearten, rapture, rejoice, satisfy, triumph 8 entrance, euphoria, felicity, intrigue, jubilate, knock out, pleasure, radiance, radiancy 9 amusement, delectate, enrapture, entertain, fascinate, happiness, jocundity, luxuriate, transport 10 ebullience, effervesce, exhilarate, exultation, jump for joy, regalement
cry of ~: 2 ah 3 aah, ooh 4 good, whee 5 goody, oh boy, zowie 6 goodie, hotcha, hot dog
in: 4 bask, like, love 5 adore, eat up, enjoy, revel, savor 6 relish 9 feast upon, luxuriate
show ~: 4 glow, grin 5 smile
__ delight: 6 Idiot's 7 Turkish
delighted: 4 glad, rapt 5 happy, merry 6 blithe, cheery, enrapt, jovial, joyful, joyous, upbeat 7 charmed, gleeful, pleased, radiant 8 blissful, cheerful, ecstatic, euphoric, exultant, jubilant, mirthful, ravished 9 delirious, enchanted, entranced, fulfilled, gladdened, gratified, overjoyed, rejoicing, rhapsodic 10 captivated, fascinated, flying high
be ~: 4 rave 5 exult
__ delighted!: 4 I'd be
delightful: 4 nice 5 sweet 6 cheery, clever, dreamy, golden, jovial, lovely, pretty 7 amusing, darling, lovable, sensual, winsome 8 adorable, charming, engaging, glorious, heavenly, inviting, loveable, pleasant, pleasing 9 agreeable, ambrosial, beautiful, congenial, delicious, enjoyable, ineffable, nectarous, palatable, rapturous, rav-

ishing, thrilling **10** acceptable, attractive, delectable, enchanting, gratifying, refreshing, satisfying
place: 4 Eden
Delight in Disorder: 4 poem
author: 7 Herrick
Delilah: 5 Jones
lover: 6 Samson
Delilah (1968 song) artist: Tom Jones
Delilah Jones (1956 song) artist: McGuire Sisters
DeLillo, Don: 6 author, writer
work: Americana
The Body Artist
End Zone
Libra
Mao II
The Names
Running Dog
Underworld
White Noise
Delima: 4 font **8** typeface
delimit: 6 define **7** confine **9** determine
delineate: 3 map, set **4** draw, etch, limn, mark, plot **5** chart, paint, trace **6** define, depict, design, detail, lay out, map out, recite, sketch **7** outline, picture, portray, recount **8** block out, describe **9** adumbrate, interpret **10** illustrate
delineation: 3 map **4** tale **5** chart, draft, story **6** design, report, sketch **7** account, diagram, drawing, outline, profile **8** likeness **9** depiction, narration, rendition
delinquency: 5 abuse, fault, guilt **7** neglect, offense **9** oversight
delinquent: 3 bad, lax **4** AWOL, lack, late, punk **5** felon, slack, tardy **6** behind, guilty, outlaw, rascal, remiss, unpaid **7** culprit, hoodlum, overdue, runaway, wayward **8** blamable, careless, criminal, culpable, derelict, hooligan, offender, recreant **9** blameable, defaulter, desperado, miscreant, negligent, offending, red-handed, reprobate, wrongdoer **10** blackguard, black sheep, censurable, defaultant, defaulting, lawbreaker, malefactor, neglectful
be ~: 3 owe
__ de Lion: 5 Coeur
deliquesce: 4 melt, thaw **7** liquefy, liquify **8** dissolve, fluidize
delirious: 4 wild **5** rabid **7** excited, frantic **8** ecstatic, frenetic, frenzied, thrilled, wild-eyed **9** delighted, disturbed, gladdened, overjoyed, rapturous, unsettled, wandering **10** bewildered, corybantic, disordered, distracted, flipped out, hysterical, incoherent, irrational
be ~: 4 rave **7** carry on
Delirious (1983 song) artist: Prince
delirium: 4 zeal **5** mania **6** fervor, frenzy **7** ecstasy, passion, rapture **8** hysteria **10** enthusiasm
__-de-lis: 5 fleur
Delishious composer: 8 Gershwin
Deli, The rapper: 4 Ice-T
Delius: 9 Frederick
deliver: 3 fax **4** bear, cart, deal, free, give, have, hurl, read, save, send, ship, take **5** bring, carry, fetch, fling, loose, pitch, relay, remit, serve, speak, throw, truck, utter **6** acquit, commit, convey, fork up, hand in, launch, loosen, ransom, recite, redeem, rescue, supply, turn in, wait on **7** achieve, consign, declare, dish out, drop off, express, forward, inflict, lecture, present, produce, provide, recruit, release **8** announce, dispatch, dispense, fork over, hand down, hand over, liberate, make good, proclaim, transfer, transmit, turn over, wait upon **9** discharge, extricate, give forth, pronounce, transport, unshackle **10** administer, distribute, emancipate
a speech: 4 rant, talk **5** orate
prepare to ~: 5 lie in
something to ~: 4 mail **5** cargo **6** letter **7** freight, package
the goods: 7 perform
up: 4 sell **5** yield **6** turn in **7** sell out **8** hand over **9** surrender
deliverance: 6 ransom, relief **7** freedom, liberty, release **9** salvation
Deliverance: 4 film **5** novel
author: James Dickey
cast: Ned Beatty, Ronny Cox, Burt Reynolds, Jon Voight
director: John Boorman
instrument: 5 banjo
delivered: 4 born
be ~ of: 4 bear
deliverer: 6 savior **7** messiah, saviour
of old: 6 iceman **7** milkman
way: 5 route
...deliver us from __: 4 evil
delivery: 3 pkg. **4** drop, mail **5** birth, issue **6** rescue **7** arrival, carting, diction, freeing, liberty, mailing, package, receipt, recital, release **8** carriage, dispatch, shipment, transfer **9** elocution, rendition, salvation, utterance **10** childbirth, conveyance, inflection, intonation, liberation, modulation, recitation, transferal
accept ~: 7 receive
acknowledgment: 4 rcpt. **7** receipt
daily ~: 4 mail **5** paper **9** newspaper
extra: 5 setup
letters: 3 COD
person: 9 messenger
service: 3 UPS **4** USPS **5** FedEx
vehicle: 3 van **5** truck
delivery __: 3 boy, end **4** room
__ delivery: 4 free **7** drive-by, express, forward, general, special
dell: 4 glen **6** dingle, hollow, valley **8** clearing
dweller: 6 farmer
Dell: 2 PC **4** Gabe **7** Gabriel **8** computer
competitor: 3 IBM **7** Gateway
Della: 5 falls, Reese **6** Street **9** waterfall
creator of ~: 4 Erle
Della Robbia: 4 Luca
delle Puglie: 4 Bari
Dello Joio: 6 Norman
__ del Mar: 4 Viña
Delmas: 4 city, town
locale: 5 Haiti
Delmer: 5 Daves
Delmonico __: 5 steak
Delmont: 3 car **4** auto, Olds **10** automobile, Oldsmobile
Del Monte: 6 catsup **7** ketchup
alternative: 5 Heinz, Hunt's **6** Libby's
Delmore: 8 Schwartz
__ De L'Omelette, The: 3 Duc
Delon, Alain: 5 actor
film: The Leopard (1963)
Lost Command (1966)
Texas Across the River (1966)
__ de Londres: 4 gros
DeLorean: 4 John
Delos: 4 isle **6** island
locale: 6 Greece **8** Cyclades
de los Angeles: 8 Victoria
__-de-loup: 4 trou
__ De-Lovely: 3 It's
Delphi: 4 town **8** language
alternative: 3 ADA, APL, SQL **4** Alef, html, Icon, Java, LISP, Logo, Orca, Perl **5** Algol, Basic, Cecil, COBOL, Dylan, SISAL **6** Eiffel, Erlang, Oberon, Pascal, Prolog, Sather, Scheme, Snobol **7** Fortran
god: 6 Apollo
oracle site: 6 Phocis
priestess: 6 oracle
Delphian: 4 deep **5** vatic **7** fatidic **8** oracular **9** enigmatic, prophetic, vaticinal
Delphine author: Madame de Staël
delphinium: 5 plant **6** flower
__ del Plata: 3 Mar
Delpy: 5 Julie
Delray: 3 car **4** auto **5** Chevy **9** Chevrolet
Delray Beach: 4 city, town
locale: 7 Florida
del Rey: 6 Lester
__ del Rey, CA: 6 Marina
Del Rio: 3 car, Los **4** auto, city, Ford, town **7** Dolores
locale: 5 Texas
__ del Rio, Cuba: 5 Pinar
Del Rio, Dolores: 7 actress
film: Cheyenne Autumn (1964)
Flying Down to Rio (1933)
The Fugitive (1947)
Journey Into Fear (1942)
Lancer Spy (1937)
What Price Glory? (1926)
Delroy: 5 Lindo
Del Ruth: 3 Roy
del Sarto: 6 Andrea
__ del Sol: 5 Costa
Del Sol: 3 car **4** auto **5** Honda
delt: 6 muscle
kin: 2 ab **3** pec **4** quad
delta: 5 Greek, mouth **6** letter **7** deposit
deposit: 4 silt
follower: 7 epsilon
locale: 5 mouth, river
preceder: 5 gamma
delta __: 3 ray **4** iron, team, wave, wing **6** rhythm **8** function
Delta: 3 car **4** auto, font, Olds, town **5** Burke **7** airline **8** typeface **10** automobile, Oldsmobile
alternative: 6 United **7** Jet Blue **8** American **9** Southwest **11** America West, Continental
former competitor: 3 TWA **5** Pan-Am, USAir **7** Braniff, Eastern **8** National
hub: 7 Atlanta
overseer: 3 FAA
Delta __: 4 Dawn, team **6** Center **7** Wedding
Delta Dawn (1973 song) artist: Reddy
Delta Factor, The author: Spillane
Delta of Venus, The author: Anaïs Nin
Delta Wedding author: Eudora Welty
deltoid: 6 muscle **10** triangular
Deltona: 4 city, town
locale: 7 Florida
Del Toro, Benicio: 5 actor
film: The Pledge (2001)
Snatch (2000)
Traffic (2000, AA)
deludable: 4 easy, naif **5** naive
delude: 3 con, lie **4** dupe, fool, hoax, jive, nick, sell, snow **5** bluff, cheat, cozen, sneak, trick **6** betray, lead on, rope in, sucker, take in **7** beguile, deceive, defraud, mislead, pretend, two-time **8** hoodwink, misguide, pettifog, throw off **9** bamboozle, disinform, four-flush
deluge: 4 gush, pour, rain, rush, teem **5** crowd, drown, flood, souse, spate, surge, swamp **6** drench, engulf, ingulf, lavish, onrush **7** barrage, cascade, overrun, torrent **8** downpour, inundate, overflow, overload, plethora, submerge **9** avalanche, overwhelm, snow under **10** cloudburst, inundation, outpouring
refuge: 3 ark
Delugg: 6 Milton
DeLuise: 3 Dom **5** Peter
DeLuise, Dom: 5 actor **8** comedian
film: The Cannonball Run (1981)
The Cheap Detective (1978)
The End (1978)
Silent Movie (1976)
The Twelve Chairs (1970)
__ de Lune: 5 Clair
delusion: 4 myth **5** dream **6** dupery, fantom, mirage **7** chimera, eidolon, fallacy, fantasm, fantasy, figment, mistake, phantom **8** chimaera, daydream, phantasm **9** deception, fairy tale, mare's nest, misbelief, obsession, pipe dream **10** aberration, apparition
freedom from ~: 7 nirvana
in Buddhism: 7 samsara
delusive: 3 sly **5** false, lying **6** irreal, tricky, unreal, untrue **7** crooked, devious **8** fanciful, guileful, quixotic, specious, spurious **9** beguiling, deceitful, deceptive, dishonest, imaginary, insincere **10** chimerical, fallacious, mendacious, misleading, quixotical, unreliable, untruthful
delusory: 5 lying **9** deceitful, deceptive, visionary **10** fallacious, misleading
deluxe: 4 fine, lush, nice, posh, rich **5** fancy, grand, plush, ritzy, swank, swell **6** choice, costly, loaded, select, swanky **7** capital, elegant, opulent **8** palatial, splendid, superior, top-shelf **9** exclusive, expensive, high-class, luxuriant, luxurious, sumptuous, unrivaled **10** first-class, unrivalled
DeLuxe: 3 car **4** auto **5** Dodge **8** Plymouth **10** automobile
__ del Vaticano: 5 Città
delve: 3 dig **4** grub, mine, root, seek **5** plumb, probe **6** burrow, dredge **7** rummage, unearth **8** excavate, research
into: 4 look, pore, sift **5** plumb, probe **7** examine, explore **8** read up on
Delvecchio: 4 Alex
Del Verrocchio: 6 Andrea
__-de-lys: 5 fleur
demagogue: 7 fanatic, hothead, inciter **8** agitator, fomenter, inflamer **9** firebrand **10** incendiary, instigator, politician
__ de main: 4 coup
__ de maître: 4 coup
__ de Mallorca: 5 Palma
demand: 3 bid, tax **4** call, levy, need, plea, take, urge, want, will **5** claim, exact, force, order, press, price **6** appeal, compel, enjoin, impose, insist, sue for **7** call for, enquire, enquiry, implore, inquire, inquiry, proviso, request, require, solicit **8** entreaty, insist on, occasion, petition, press for, pressure **9** clamor for, cry out for, impetrate, importune, necessity, provision, requisite, ultimatum **10** imposition, injunction, insistence, popularity, supplicate, union issue, urgent need
as a price: 3 ask
companion: 6 supply
heavy ~: 3 run
in ~: 3 hot **6** staple **7** popular **8** valuable **10** at a premium, marketable
payment: 3 dun
demand __: 3 bid **4** bill, loan, note **5** draft **7** deposit
demand-__: 4 side
demanding: 4 firm, hard **5** bossy, cruel, exact, fussy, picky, rigid, rough, stern, tough **6** rugged, severe, strict, taxing, thorny, trying, uphill, urgent **7** arduous, austere, exigent, finicky, nagging, onerous, Spartan **8** captious, critical, despotic, exacting, exigeant, finiking, finnicky, grueling, hard-line, pressing, rigorous, tiresome, toilsome **9** ambi-

tious, assertive, challenge, clamorous, difficult, draconian, impatient, imperious, insistent, intensive, laborious, querulous, strenuous, stringent, unbending, unsparing **10** bothersome, burdensome, despotical, enervating, exhausting, fastidious, formidable, inflexible, insatiable, iron-fisted, nononsense, oppressive, particular, tyrannical, unamenable
not ~: **4** easy **5** cushy, light
one: **5** taker **8** martinet **9** nit-picker
demantoid: **3** gem **8** gemstone
demarcate: **5** limit **6** define **7** delimit **9** determine
demarcation: **4** line **5** limit **6** margin **8** boundary, division, terminus
line of ~: **4** edge **5** verge **6** border, margin **8** frontier **9** perimeter, periphery
Demarest, William: **5** actor
film: Along Came Jones (1945)
The First Legion (1951)
Jolson Sings Again (1949)
The Jolson Story (1946)
The Miracle of Morgan's Creek (1944)
Salty O'Rourke (1945)
TV: My Three Sons
Demaret, Jimmy: **6** golfer
__-de-Marne, France: **3** Val
dematerialize: **6** vanish
de Maupassant: **3** Guy
__ de Mayo: **5** Cinco
demean: **3** dis, pan **4** haze, sink **5** abase, lower, scorn **6** debase, dump on, humble, lessen **7** contemn, corrupt, cry down, degrade, put down **8** badmouth, belittle, bring low, derogate, diminish, play down, take down **9** bring down, disparage, humiliate, knock down
oneself: **5** stoop **6** grovel, kowtow
demeaning: **6** menial **10** derogatory, detractive, pejorative
demeanor: **3** air, set **4** cast, look, mien **5** front, guise, poise **6** aspect, manner **7** bearing, conduct, fashion **8** attitude, behavior, carriage, presence **10** appearance, deportment
de'Medici: **6** Cosimo **7** Lorenzo
in-law: **4** Este
de Médicis: **5** Marie **9** Catherine
__ de menthe: **5** crème
Demento: **2** Dr.
__ de mer: **3** mal
__-de-mer: **4** coco **5** bêche
Demerara: **5** river
locale: **6** Guyana
demesne: **6** estate, region **8** province
Demeter: **7** goddess
daughter: **4** Cora, Kore **8** Despoena **10** Persephone
epithet: **5** Chloe, Evius, Lusia, Mysia **6** Erinys, Stiria **7** Cabirea, Lernaea, Thesmia **8** Despoena, Pelasgus **9** Anesidora **10** Malophorus
equivalent: **5** Ceres
lover: **4** Zeus **6** Iasion **8** Poseidon
parent: **4** Rhea **6** Cronos, Cronus
sibling: **4** Hera, Zeus **5** Hades **6** Hestia **8** Poseidon
son: **5** Arion **6** Plutus **7** Eubulus **8** Dionysus **10** Philomenus
demi-: **4** half
demi-__: **3** sec **4** plié **6** cannon, hunter, pointe **7** pension
Demi: **5** Moore
Demian author: **5** Hesse
demi ender: **4** urge **5** monde, tasse
__ de mieux: **5** faute
demilitarized zone: **5** limbo
de Mille: **5** Agnes
DeMille, Cecil B.: **8** director
film: The Buccaneer (1938)
The Cheat (1915)
Cleopatra (1934)
The Crusades (1935)
Dynamite (1929)
The Greatest Show on Earth (1952)
The King of Kings (1927)
Madam Satan (1930)
The Plainsman (1936)
Reap the Wild Wind (1942)
The Road to Yesterday (1925)
Samson and Delilah (1949)
The Squaw Man (1931)
The Ten Commandments (1923)
The Ten Commandments (1956)
This Day and Age (1933)
Union Pacific (1939)
genre: **4** epic
Demille, Nelson: **6** writer
work: By the Rivers of Babylon
Cathedral
Charm School
The General's Daughter
The Gold Coast
The Lion's Game
Mayday
Plum Island
Spencerville
The Talbot Odyssey
Up Country
Word of Honor
__ de Milo: **5** Venus
Demi-Paradise, The (1943 film)
cast: Leslie Henson, Laurence Olivier, Penelope Dudley Ward
director: Anthony Asquith
demise: **3** end **5** lease **8** downfall
demisemiquaver: **4** note
demit: **4** quit **5** lower **6** resign **8** abdicate, renounce
demitasse: **3** cup **6** coffee
demiurgic: **8** original **9** inventive
Demme: **3** Ted **8** Jonathan
Demme, Jonathan: **8** director
film: Cousin Bobby (1991)
Crazy Mama (1975)
Handle With Care (1977)
Last Embrace (1979)
Married to the Mob (1988)
Melvin and Howard (1980)
Philadelphia (1993)
The Silence of the Lambs (1991, AA)
Stop Making Sense (1984)
demobilize: **7** disband
democracy: **6** nation **7** freedom **8** republic **10** capitalism
participant: **5** voter
world's largest ~: **5** India
Democracy author: Joan Didion
Democrat: **3** FDR, HST, JFK, LBJ, pol **4** peak **5** mount **8** mountain
certain ~: **7** liberal
locale: **7** Rockies **8** Colorado
opponent: **3** GOP, Ind., Rep.
__ Democrat: **6** Social
Democrat-Gazette: **5** paper **9** newspaper
locale: **8** Arkansas **10** Little Rock
democratic: **4** free **8** populist **9** socialist **10** autonomous, self-ruling
Democratic: **5** party
donkey creator: **4** Nast
early ~ opponent: **4** Whig
Democratic-Republican: **5** party
Democritus: **5** Greek **11** philosopher
démodé: **3** old, out **5** passé **8** outdated **9** out-of-date
demographic datum: **3** age, sex **4** race **6** gender
demography: **6** census **7** science
demoiselle: **4** bird, girl **5** crane, woman **6** damsel, maiden
demolish: **4** rase, raze, ruin, sack, sink, undo **5** blast, break, crush, level, scrap, smash, spoil, total, trash, wreck **6** defeat, quench, ravage, refute, topple, uproot **7** destroy, flatten, shatter, subvert, torpedo, unbuild **8** bulldoze, decimate, dissolve, pull down, spoliate, take down, tear down **9** devastate, dismantle, eradicate, extirpate, knock down, pulverize, take apart **10** annihilate, obliterate
demolished: **4** lost **5** kaput
demolition: **5** wreck **6** razing **8** leveling, sabotage **9** explosion **10** bulldozing
material: **3** TNT **5** nitro
demolition __: **5** derby
Demolition Man (1993 film)
cast: Sandra Bullock, Nigel Hawthorne, Wesley Snipes, Sylvester Stallone
demon: **3** imp **4** ogre **5** afrit, beast, brute, devil, fiend, ghoul, jinni, lamia, rogue **6** afreet, goblin, rascal **7** fanatic, hellion, incubus, monster, villain **8** succubus **9** archfiend, speedster
Arabian ~: **5** afrit **6** afreet
speed ~: **5** racer **6** hot rod
demon __: **3** rum
__ demon: **5** speed **7** Maxwell
Demon __: **3** Box **4** Seed, Star
Demon Box author: Ken Kesey
Demond: **6** Wilson
Demon Deacons: **10** Wake Forest
demonic: **3** bad **4** evil, vile **5** cruel, manic **6** crazed, savage, wicked **7** frantic, hellish, lunatic, satanic, violent **8** devilish, diabolic, fiendish, frenzied, infernal, maniacal **9** satanical **10** diabolical
__ Demons: **4** Blue
Demon Seed (1977 film)
cast: Julie Christie, Gerrit Graham, Fritz Weaver
Demon Seed author: Dean Koontz
demonstrate: **4** cite, give, show, test **5** argue, march, prove, rally, sit in, teach **6** evince, parade, picket, reason, unfold, verify **7** bespeak, confirm, declare, display, exhibit, explain, express, produce, protest, reflect, roll out, show off, trot out **8** describe, evidence, indicate, manifest, proclaim, set forth
demonstrated, which was to be: **3** QED
demonstration: **4** show **5** flash, lie-in, march, proof, rally, sit-in, token **6** love-in, parade **7** display, protest **8** evidence **9** spectacle, testimony
sight: **6** banner, poster **10** picket line
demonstrative: **6** loving, tender **7** certain, gushing **8** decisive, definite, outgoing, specific
pronoun: **4** that, this
demonstrator: **8** militant **9** protester
demoralize: **4** damp, rout **5** abash, break, daunt, shake, stain, upset **6** dampen, deject, rattle, unglue **7** corrupt, depress, nonplus, unnerve **8** dispirit, psych out, unsettle, unstring **9** brutalize, discomfit, disparage, embarrass, give pause, overwhelm, undermine **10** debilitate, disconcert, discourage, dishearten
demoralized: **6** broken **7** crushed, daunted **8** dejected, downcast **9** depressed, dispirited **10** spiritless
DeMornay: **7** Rebecca
Demosthenes: **5** Greek **6** orator
demote: **4** bust, drop **5** break, lower **6** humble, reduce **7** degrade **8** bring low, bump down, reassign, relegate **9** downgrade, humiliate, knock down
__ de mots: **3** jeu
Dempsey: **4** Jack **7** Patrick
Dempsey, Jack: **5** boxer
demulcent: **4** balm **6** lotion **7** anodyne, unction **8** ointment, soothing **9** emollient **10** mollifying, palliative
demur: **3** haw **4** balk **5** baulk, tarry **6** beg off, boggle, object, recoil, refuse, regret, resist, shrink **7** decline, protest, scruple **8** complain, disagree, hesitate, hold back, question **9** make a fuss **10** disapprove, put up a fuss
demure: **3** coy, shy **4** meek, prim **5** sober, staid, timid **6** chaste, humble, modest, prissy, proper, sedate **7** bashful, prudish **8** affected, blushing, reserved, retiring, skittish **9** diffident **10** unassuming, uneffusive
in England: **3** mim
demureness: **7** modesty **8** humility
demurral: **5** delay **10** hesitation
demurring: **9** reluctant, unwilling
demy: **5** paper
Demy, Jacques film of 1961: **4** Lola
den: **4** cave, hold, lair, nest, nook, room **5** haunt, lodge, study **6** burrow, cavern, hotbed, kennel, refuge, TV room **7** atelier, hideout, library, rec room, retreat, sanctum, shelter **8** cloister, dwelling, hideaway, playroom, snuggery **9** media room, sanctuary **10** family room, rumpus room, trophy room
denizen: **3** cub **4** bear
need: **2** TV **4** sofa **5** TV set **6** settee
den __: **5** chief **6** father, mother
Den __: **4** Haag
__ de nacre: **5** L'Etui
Denain: **4** city, town
locale: **6** France
Denali: **3** GMC, SUV **4** park, peak **5** mount **8** McKinley, mountain
locale: **6** Alaska
denarius: **4** coin **5** money
denary: **7** tenfold
denatured __: **7** alcohol
Dench, Judi: **4** Dame **7** actress
film: 84 Charing Cross Road (1987)
Chocolat (2000)
Die Another Day (2002)
GoldenEye (1995)
Iris (2001)
Shakespeare in Love (1998, AA)
The Shipping News (2001)
Tomorrow Never Dies (1997)
The World Is Not Enough (1999)
dendrite
counterpart: **4** axon **5** axone
locale: **5** nerve **6** neuron
dendritic: **8** arboreal
dendrology: **6** botany
dendrophobe fear: **5** trees
Deneb: **4** star
constellation: **6** Cygnus
Denebola: **4** star
Deneuve, Catherine: **6** French **7** actress
film: Belle de Jour (1967)
Repulsion (1965)
Time Regained (1999)
Deng: **7** Chinese **8** Xiaoping
predecessor: **3** Mao
Den Haag: **4** city, town **7** capital
locale: **7** Holland **11** Netherlands
Denholm: **7** Elliott
denial: **2** no **3** nah, nay **4** nope, not I, uh-uh, veto **5** not me **6** rebuff **7** refusal **8** negation, nihilism, refusing, turndown **9** disavowal, disbelief, dismissal, rejection **10** abnegation, disclaimer, gainsaying, refutation, retraction
French ~: **3** non
German ~: **4** nein
military ~: **5** no sir
phrase: **4** not I **5** not me
Russian: **4** nyet
Scottish ~: **3** nae
Security Council ~: **4** veto

slangy ~: **3** nah, naw **4** nope, uh-uh **6** ain't so
__-denial: **4** self
Deniece: **8** Williams
denier: **7** atheist **8** Alibi Ike, naysayer
denigrate: **3** dis, hit, rip **4** gibe, jeer, jibe, mock, slam, slur, snub **5** abuse, decry, knock, libel, roast, scorn, smear, spurn, sully, taunt **6** defame, deride, dump on, heckle, humble, impugn, malign, offend, rebuff, revile, slight, vilify **7** affront, asperse, blacken, blister, censure, cry down, degrade, detract, disdain, put down, rank out, run down, slander, traduce **8** backbite, belittle, besmirch, denounce, derogate, mudsling, ridicule, tear down, throw mud, vilipend **9** discredit, disparage, downgrade, humiliate **10** calumniate, depreciate, disrespect, scandalize, villainize
denigration: **3** dig **4** barb, gibe, jibe, slam, slap, slur, snub **5** abuse, libel, scorn, taunt **6** rebuff, slight **7** affront, calumny, catcall, disdain, mockery, obloquy, offense, put-down, slander **8** contempt, ridicule **9** cheap shot, contumely **10** disrespect, opprobrium
denim: **5** cloth **6** fabric **8** material
denims: **5** jeans, pants **7** cutoffs **8** trousers **9** blue jeans, dungarees
De Niro, Robert: **5** actor
film: 15 Minutes (2001)
The Adventures of Rocky and Bullwinkle (2000)
Analyze This (1999)
Awakenings (1990)
Backdraft (1991)
Bang the Drum Slowly (1973)
Brazil (1985)
A Bronx Tale (1993)
Cape Fear (1991)
Casino (1995)
Cop Land (1997)
The Deer Hunter (1978)
Falling in Love (1984)
The Fan (1996)
The Godfather Part II (1974, AA)
GoodFellas (1990)
Greetings (1968)
Guilty by Suspicion (1991)
Heat (1995)
Hi, Mom! (1970)
Jacknife (1989)
The King of Comedy (1983)
The Last Tycoon (1976)
Mad Dog and Glory (1993)
Mean Streets (1973)
Meet the Parents (2000)
Men of Honor (2000)
Midnight Run (1988)
New York, New York (1977)
Once Upon a Time in America (1984)
Raging Bull (1980, AA)
The Score (2001)
Showtime (2002)
Sleepers (1996)
Stanley & Iris (1990)
Taxi Driver (1976)
This Boy's Life (1993)
True Confessions (1981)
The Untouchables (1987)
Wag the Dog (1997)
Denis: **5** Leary, saint **6** Potvin **7** Diderot
Denise: **3** Loo **6** Crosby, Darcel **8** Huxtable, Levertov, Nicholas, Richards
Denison: **4** city, town
locale: **5** Texas
denizen: **5** liver, voter **6** native **7** citizen, dweller, resider **8** habitant, occupant, resident **9** indweller **10** inhabitant
__ den Linden: **5** Unter
Denmark: **6** nation, strait **7** country
astronomer: **5** Brahe
ballet dancer: **5** Bruhn **7** Martins
capital: **10** Copenhagen
chemist: **8** Sorensen
city: **5** Arhus **6** Ålborg, Odense **7** Aalborg **9** Helsingör **10** Copenhagen
explorer: **6** Bering **9** Rasmussen
island off ~: **3** Fyn **4** Fano
islands: **5** Faroe
king: **4** Eric
legislature: **9** Folketing
money: **3** ore **4** oras **5** krone **9** rixdollar
neighbor: **7** Germany
Nobelist in Chemistry: **4** Skou
Nobelist in Literature: **6** Jensen **9** Gjellerup **11** Pontoppidan
Nobelist in Medicine: **3** Dam **5** Krogh **6** Finsen **7** Fibiger
Nobelist in Peace: **5** Bajer
Nobelist in Physics: **4** Bohr **9** Mottelson
org.: **4** NATO
physician: **6** Finsen
physicist: **4** Bohr **7** Oersted
pianist: **5** Borge
scientist: **4** Bohr **5** Brahe **6** Finsen **7** Oersted **8** Sorensen
tenor: **8** Melchior
toast: **5** skoal
toy company: **4** Lego
weight: **4** eser
writer: **4** Bang, Nexö **6** Jensen **7** Dinesen, Holberg **8** Andersen, Jacobsen **9** Gjellerup
Dennehy, Brian: **5** actor
film: Cocoon (1985)
First Blood (1982)
F/X (1986)
Gorky Park (1983)
Legal Eagles (1986)
Never Cry Wolf (1983)
Presumed Innocent (1990)
Romeo & Juliet (1996)
Denning: **7** Richard
Dennis: **3** Day **5** Cathy, Dugan, Franz, Gabor, Quaid, Sandy **6** Brutus, Coffey, Farina, Hopper, Miller, Morgan, O'Keefe, Potter, Rodman, Weaver, Wilson **7** DeYoung, Patrick, Ralston **8** Haysbert, Mitchell **9** DeConcini
Dennis, Patrick aunt: **4** Mame
Dennis, Sandy: **7** actress
film: The Four Seasons (1981)
The Fox (1968)
The Out-of-Towners (1970)
Thank You All Very Much (1969)
Up the Down Staircase (1967)
Who's Afraid of Virginia Woolf? (1966, AA)
Dennis the Menace: **3** imp **4** brat, pest **5** comic **10** comic strip
artist: **7** Ketcham
cat: **6** Hot Dog
character: **4** Gina, Joey **5** Alice, Henry **6** Wilson **8** Margaret
dog: **4** Ruff
like ~: **5** pesky, pesty
Dennis the Menace (CBS sitcom)
cast: Herbert Anderson (Henry Mitchell)
Gloria Henry (Alice Mitchell)
Joseph Kearns (George Wilson)
Jay North (Dennis Mitchell)
dog: **7** Fremont
Denny: **6** Martin, McLain **8** Reginald
Denny's competitor: **4** IHOP
denominate: **4** call, name, term **5** style, title **9** designate
denomination: **3** ilk **4** cult, kind, name, sect, sort, term, type, unit **5** brand, class, creed, faith, grade, group, label, title, value **6** belief, church **7** variety **8** category, religion
__ denominator: **6** common
denotation: **4** sign **5** sense **6** symbol **7** meaning **10** definition, importance, indication
denotative: **8** symbolic **10** figurative, indicative
denote: **4** mark, mean, name, show **5** imply, spell **6** signal **7** betoken, express, purport, signify, suggest **8** evidence, indicate, pinpoint, point out, stand for **9** adumbrate, designate, represent, symbolize
denouement: **3** end **5** close **6** climax, ending, finale, finish, result, upshot, windup, wrap-up **7** last act **8** terminus **10** conclusion, resolution
denounce: **3** hit, rap **4** damn, gibe, jeer, jibe, mock, rail, slam, slur, snub **5** abuse, blame, blast, decry, knock, libel, roast, scold, scorn, smear, spurn, taunt **6** accuse, attack, defame, deride, dump on, heckle, impugn, indict, malign, offend, rail at, rebuff, rebuke, revile, slight, vilify **7** affront, asperse, censure, condemn, declaim, degrade, deplore, disdain, impeach, lambast, put down, rank out, reprove, slander, traduce, upbraid **8** belittle, bloviate, derogate, lambaste, reproach, ridicule, vilipend **9** castigate, challenge, criticize, denigrate, discredit, disparage, dress down, excoriate, fulminate, fustigate, humiliate, proscribe, reprehend, reprimand **10** calumniate, disrespect, make a stand, stigmatize, take to task, vituperate
de novo: **3** new **4** anew **5** again **6** afresh **10** from the top
dense: **3** dim **4** dopy, dull, dumb, firm, hard, lush, rank, slow **5** close, crass, dopey, heavy, solid, thick, tight **6** bovine, jammed, oafish, obtuse, packed, simple, stolid, stupid **7** boorish, compact, crammed, crowded, doltish, fatuous, foolish, loutish, lumpish, teeming, weighty, witless **8** mindless, populous, thickset **9** close-knit, condensed, dimwitted, jam-packed, luxuriant, pigheaded **10** compressed, hard-packed, slow-witted, synopsized
combining form: **4** dasy-, pycn- **5** pycno-
one: **2** ox **3** ass, nit, oaf, sap **4** boob, bozo, clod, dodo, dolt, dope, fool, geek, gowk, lunk, simp, twit, yo-yo **5** chump, clown, cluck, dummy, dunce, goose, joker, klutz, looby, moron, ninny, patsy, schmo **6** dimwit, galoot, lubber, lummox, nitwit, schmoe, sucker, turkey **7** airhead, buffoon, bungler, dingbat, dullard, fathead, galloot, half-wit, jackass, pinhead, saphead **8** bonehead, cloddish, dumbbell, lunkhead, meathead, numskull **9** birdbrain, blockhead, ding-a-ling, harebrain, ignoramus, lamebrain, numbskull, simpleton **10** dunderhead, dunderpate, loggerhead, nincompoop, noodlehead
densho: **4** bell **10** percussion
origin: **5** Japan
density: **6** weight **8** firmness, hardness
__ density: **4** flux **6** weight **7** current, surface
__-density: **3** low **4** high
dent: **3** mar, pit **4** bump, bung, ding, mark, nick **5** notch **6** bang up, cavity, dimple, hollow, push in, recess **7** headway, press in **8** disallow **9** concavity **10** depression, impression
location: **6** fender
make a ~: **5** begin, solve
Dent: **5** Bucky
dental __: **4** lisp, pulp **5** floss, plate **7** hygiene, implant **9** insurance
dental floss option: **3** wax
dental-rinse brand: **4** Plax
dented: **7** concave
dentist
advice: **5** brush, floss
concern: **3** gap **4** ache, chip **5** crown, decay, inlay, lower, teeth, tooth, upper **6** braces, bridge, caries, cavity, enamel **9** toothache
deg.: **3** DDS, DMD
need: **4** X-ray **5** drill **6** cement
office call: **4** next
office music: **5** Muzak
org.: **3** ADA
request: **4** bite, open **5** rinse
supply, once: **5** ether
dentistry: **7** science
Denton: **4** city, town
athletes: **9** Mean Green
locale: **5** Texas
school: **3** UNT **10** North Texas
__ d'entrée: **5** carte
__ dents: **5** mal de
Dentyne: **3** gum
alternative: **5** Certs, Extra, Orbit **6** Binaca, Mentos, Tic Tac **7** Altoids, Clorets, Trident **8** Carefree, Chiclets, Freedent **10** Doublemint, Juicy Fruit
denude: **4** bare, peel **5** strip **6** expose, fleece **7** disrobe, lay bare, uncover, undress
__ de nuit: **5** boîte
denunciate: **4** damn **5** blame, knock, scold **6** rail at **7** upbraid **9** criticize, fulminate **10** take to task
denunciation: **4** slam **5** abuse, blame **6** attack, tirade **7** reproof **8** diatribe
Denver: **3** Bob **4** city, John, Pyle, town
college: **5** Regis
height: **4** mile
locale: **7** Rockies **8** Colorado
newspaper: **4** Post
pro team: **7** Broncos, Nuggets, Rockies
river: **11** South Platte
suburb: **6** Arvada
zone: **3** MDT, MST
Denver __: **4** boot **6** omelet **8** omelette
Denver, John
album: **5** Aerie
song: Annie's Song (1974)
Back Home Again (1974)
Calypso (1975)
I'm Sorry (1975)
Rocky Mountain High (1973)
Sunshine on My Shoulders (1974)
Take Me Home, Country Roads (1971)
Thank God I'm a Country Boy (1975)
deny: **3** bar, nix **4** veto **5** rebut **6** disown, forbid, impugn, negate, oppose, rebuff, recant, refuse, refute, reject **7** disavow, dispute, gainsay, mortify **8** disclaim, go back on, prohibit, renounce, turn down, withhold **9** repudiate **10** contradict, controvert, cut off from
oneself: **7** abstain
use: **3** bar **5** debar, expel **6** censor, forbid, outlaw **7** boycott, exclude, rule out **8** disallow, prohibit **9** blackball, ostracize, proscribe
Denys: **5** saint
Denzel: **10** Washington
deo: **4** Mars **7** Jupiter, Mercury, Neptune
deo __: **7** gratias, volente
deodar: **4** tree **5** cedar
deodorant: **3** Ban **4** Sure **5** Arrid, Tussy **6** Degree, Secret **7** Dry Idea, Mitchum

9 fumigator 10 Right Guard, Soft and Dri, Speed Stick
form: 5 spray 6 roll-on
deodorize: 4 wash 5 clean 6 purify 7 cleanse, freshen, refresh, sweeten 8 sanitize 9 disinfect
Deoni: 3 cow 4 bull 6 bovine, cattle
__ de Oro: 3 Rio
deoxyribonucleic: 4 acid
De Palma, Brian: 8 director
film: Blow Out (1981)
Body Double (1984)
The Bonfire of the Vanities (1990)
Carlito's Way (1993)
Carrie (1976)
Dressed to Kill (1980)
The Fury (1978)
Greetings (1968)
Hi, Mom! (1970)
Mission: Impossible (1996)
Phantom of Paradise (1974)
Scarface (1983)
Sisters (1973)
The Untouchables (1987)
spouse: Nancy Allen
Depardieu, Gérard: 5 actor 6 French
film: Cyrano de Bergerac (1990)
Danton (1982)
Green Card (1990)
Man in the Iron Mask (1998)
My Father, The Hero (1994)
depart: 2 go 3 fly, run 4 exit, flee, move, quit, vary 5 go off, leave, scram, split, start, stray 6 beat it, cut out, decamp, desert, escape, get out, go away, move on, pop off, ramble, recede, retire, secede, set off, set out, vacate 7 abscond, entrain, get away, head out, make off, migrate, pull out, push off, retreat, ride off, take off 8 abdicate, bid adieu, blast off, emigrate, evacuate, hightail, light out, run along, separate, set forth, shove off, slip away, withdraw 9 break camp, bundle off, cut and run, disappear, take leave 10 hit the road, make tracks, shuffle off
ender: 3 ure
(from): 6 differ 7 deviate
departed: 4 away, gone, left, went 9 withdrawn
departing: 8 outgoing
department: 3 arm, job 4 area, duty, slot, unit, ward 5 board, field, realm 6 agency, branch, bureau, domain, office, sphere 7 section, station 8 category, division, function, precinct, province, vocation 9 bailiwick, expertise, specialty 10 assignment, commission, occupation
head: 4 prof 9 professor
heads: 5 board 7 cabinet, council 8 advisors 9 committee 10 brain trust, counselors
department __: 5 store
__ department: 4 fire 6 police
Department of __: 5 Labor, State 6 Energy 7 Defense, Justice 8 Commerce 9 Education
department store: 4 mart 5 K Mart, Kohl's, Macy's, Sears 6 market, Target 7 Wal-Mart 8 J.C. Penney, retailer
event: 4 sale 9 white sale
staffer: 5 buyer, clerk 7 cashier
store section: 4 boy's, men's 5 girl's 6 women's
departure: 4 exit 5 adieu, going, leave 6 change, egress, escape, exodus, flight 7 getaway, goodbye, liftoff, novelty, parting, removal, retreat, takeoff, veering, walkout 8 blastoff, farewell, straying, variance 9 avoidance, desertion, deviation, diversion, egression, exception, going away, migration, recession, secession, taking off, variation, wandering 10 aberration, decampment, deflection, difference, digression, discursion, divergence, emigration, evacuation, expiration, innovation, new wrinkle, retirement, separation, setting out, withdrawal
from the norm: 3 pip 4 blip 8 variance 9 deviation, disparity, variation 10 aberration, divergence
hasty ~: 3 lam 6 flight
listing: 4 sked 8 schedule
point of ~: 4 gate 9 threshold
verbal ~: 10 digression
__ de Pascua: 4 Isla
__ de pasto: 4 vino
de Paul: 4 Gene 7 Vincent
DePaul
athletes: 10 Blue Demons
locale: 7 Chicago 8 Illinois
__ de pays: 3 vin
depend: 4 bank, base, hang, rely, rest, ride 5 count, hinge, pivot
ender: 3 ent 4 ence
on: 5 trust 6 accept, assume, credit, look to, reckon 7 believe, require, swear by 9 calculate 10 set store by
(on): 3 bet 4 bank, hang, lean, rely, rest 5 count, hinge 6 gamble 8 fall back
dependability: 5 trust 7 loyalty 8 fidelity 9 stability
dependable: 4 even, good, just, sure, true 5 level, loyal, solid, sound, tried 6 honest, secure, stable, steady, trusty, worthy 7 careful, certain, durable, regular, staunch, uniform 8 constant, credible, faithful, inerrant, punctual, reliable, stalwart 9 authentic, goofproof, honorable, reputable, rock solid, steadfast, unfailing, veracious 10 consistent, convincing, infallible, true to type, unchanging
not ~: 5 shaky 7 erratic, flighty
dependence: 5 faith, stock, trust 6 belief 8 reliance 9 addiction 10 confidence
free from ~: 4 wean
dependency: 6 colony
__ Dependency: 4 Ross
dependent: 4 ward, weak 5 child, minor, needy 6 hooked, mutual 7 related, reliant, subject 8 helpless, immature, relative 9 ancillary, powerless, provisory, reckoning, secondary, tentative 10 collateral, contingent, counting on, reciprocal, vulnerable
be ~ (on): 4 hang
on: 7 relying 9 subject to
dependent __: 6 clause
__ Depends on You: 5 It All
De Pere: 4 city, town
locale: 9 Wisconsin
depict: 4 copy, draw, limn, show, tell 5 limns, paint 6 detail, map out, relate, render, sketch 7 narrate, outline, picture, portray, recount 8 describe, rehearse 9 delineate, exemplify, interpret, represent 10 illustrate
distinctly: 4 etch
unfairly: 4 skew
depiction: 5 image 6 acting, design, sketch 7 drawing, outline, tableau 8 likeness, portrait 9 enactment, portrayal, rendering, rendition
__-de-piété: 4 mont
depilatory
name: 4 Nair, Neet
target: 4 hair
deplane: 5 light 6 alight, arrive 7 descend 9 disembark
deplete: 3 dry, sag, sap, use 4 flag, milk, tire, void, wane 5 bleed, blunt, drain, dry up, eat up, empty, spend, trash, use up, waste 6 burn up, expend, finish, frivol, reduce, run out, shrink, soften, unload, weaken 7 consume, dig into, exhaust, fatigue, sell out, wear out 8 bankrupt, decrease, diminish, enervate, enfeeble, evacuate, fool away, squander 9 attenuate, dissipate, undermine 10 debilitate, devitalize, impoverish
depleted: 3 low 4 bare, gone, poor 5 all in, empty, spent 6 barren, devoid, effete, vacant 7 sold out, worn out 8 bankrupt 9 destitute
depletion: 4 lack, loss
deplorable: 3 sad 4 dire, grim, poor 5 awful, lousy, sorry, woful 6 abject, rotten, tragic, woefeul 7 piteous, pitiful 8 dolorous, dreadful, grievous, mournful, pathetic, pitiable, shameful, stinking, terrible, tragical, wretched 9 egregious, execrable, loathsome, miserable 10 afflictive, calamitous, disastrous, horrifying, lamentable, melancholy, pathetical, scandalous, unbearable
act: 3 sin
deplore: 3 rue 4 hate, moan, wail, weep 5 abhor, mourn 6 bemoan, bewail, lament, regret, repent, sorrow 7 condemn, dislike 8 denounce, object to 9 deprecate 10 recoil from
deploy: 7 arrange, marshal, station 8 maneuver
__ Deployment Force: 5 Rapid
__ de plume: 3 nom
__ de poing: 4 coup
Depok: 4 city, town
locale: 9 Indonesia
depone: 4 avow 7 testify, witness
__ de pont: 4 tête
deport: 3 out 5 exile, expel 6 acquit, banish, behave 7 cast out, conduct, kick out 8 relegate, send away 9 ostracize, transport 10 expatriate
deportee: 5 exile 7 outcast 10 expatriate
deportment: 3 air, set 4 mien 6 aspect, manner, stance 7 actions, bearing, conduct, manners, posture 8 behavior, carriage, demeanor 9 etiquette, expulsion 10 appearance
depose: 4 oust 5 eject, swear 6 attest, avouch, bounce, depone, remove, unseat 7 boot out, cashier, dismiss, drum out, kick out, subvert, testify, toss out, witness 8 attest to, dethrone, displace, throw out 9 interview, overthrow
deposit: 3 lay, put, set 4 drop, gage, keep, lees, mine, park, plop, save, seam, silt, stow 5 amass, delta, dregs, drift, embed, imbed, place, plant, put by, stash, store 6 garner, instal, locate 7 advance, collect, drop off, grounds, install, lay away, put away, savings 8 alluvium, gold mine, lodgment, put aside, retainer, salt away, sediment, sock away 9 formation, plunk down, settlings 10 collateral
deposit __: 4 slip 5 money
__ deposit: 4 bank, time 6 demand, direct
__-deposit box: 4 safe 6 safety
deposition: 5 proof 6 ouster 7 removal 8 ejection, evidence 9 admission, affidavit, discharge, dismissal, overthrow, testimony 10 allegation, contention, dethroning, unfrocking
give a ~: 4 aver, avow 6 allege, assert, attest 7 certify, declare
depositor: 5 saver
check ~: 5 payee
watchdog: 4 FDIC 5 FSLIC
depository: 4 bank, safe, slot 5 cache, depot, vault 6 closet 7 archive, arsenal 8 magazine, treasury 9 repertory, warehouse 10 collection, repository, storehouse
depot: 4 base, stop, yard 5 store 6 armory, garage 7 station 8 landfill, magazine, terminal 9 warehouse 10 bus station, depository, repository, storehouse
abbr.: 3 arr., ETA, ETD, sta.
posting: 4 sked 8 schedule
__ Depot: 4 Home 5 Union 6 Office
Depp, Johnny: 5 actor
film: Benny & Joon (1993)
Chocolat (2000)
Cry-Baby (1990)
Dead Man (1996)
Don Juan DeMarco (1995)
Donnie Brasco (1997)
Edward Scissorhands (1990)
Ed Wood (1994)
From Hell (2001)
Sleepy Hollow (1999)
deprave: 4 warp 5 stain 6 debase 7 corrupt, degrade, subvert, vitiate 10 lead astray
depraved: 3 bad, low 4 base, evil, ugly, vile 5 seamy 6 rakish, rotten, sinful, unholy, wanton, wicked 7 beastly, corrupt, immoral, twisted, ungodly, vicious 8 degraded, uncurbed 9 dissolute, low-minded, miscreant, nefarious, shameless 10 licentious, outrageous, profligate, villainous, virtueless
depravity: 3 ill 4 evil, vice 7 cruelty 8 baseness, enormity, iniquity 9 vitiation, ybaritism 10 corruption, debasement, degeneracy, immorality, profligacy, wickedness
deprecate: 3 rip 4 hate 5 abuse, cavil, knock, scorn 6 jibe at, malign, regret, vilify 7 asperse, censure, condemn, deplore, detract, put down, run down 8 backbite, badmouth, belittle, derogate, disfavor, minimize, play down, take down 9 disesteem, disparage, poor-mouth 10 depreciate, disapprove, discommend, discourage
deprecation: 5 abuse 7 dislike
depreciate: 4 sink 5 decay, lower 6 reduce 7 asperse, decline, deflate, depress, detract, devalue, slander 8 decrease, talk down 9 denigrate, deprecate, devaluate, discredit, disparage, dispraise, downgrade, underrate 10 adulterate, calumniate, devalorize, look down on, undervalue
depreciation: 4 wear 5 decay, libel, slump 7 decline, slander 8 overhead
depredate: 3 gut, rob 4 loot, raid, sack 5 spoil, strip 6 harrow, maraud, pirate, prey on, ravage 7 despoil, pillage, plunder, ransack 8 freeboot, prey upon 9 desecrate, devastate 10 lay waste to
depress: 4 damp, faze, push, sink, tire 5 abase, daunt, drain, lower, upset, weary, worry 6 bum out, dampen, darken, debase, deject, impair, lessen, reduce, sadden, squash, unglue 7 cheapen, deflate, devalue, flatten, let down, oppress, torment 8 desolate, diminish, dispirit, distress, enervate, keep down, push down 9 devaluate, downgrade, weigh down 10 demoralize, depreciate, devitalize, discourage, dishearten
depressed: 3 low, sad 4 blue, dark, down, glum, grim, mopy 5 heavy, moody, mopey, sorry 6 broody, crumby, crummy, gloomy, hollow, morbid, morose, sunken 7 concave, doleful, forlorn, hangdog, in a funk, joyless, let down, set back, unhappy, way down 8 dejected, desolate, downcast, indented, liverish, recessed, wretched 9 aggrieved, bummed-out,

cheerless, destitute, in the pits, miserable, on a downer, saturnine, sorrowful, taken down, woebegone **10** despairing, despondent, dispirited, distressed, down and out, in the dumps, lugubrious, melancholy, out of sorts, spiritless
act ~: **4** mope **5** brood
depressed __: **4** area
depressing: **3** sad **4** grim **5** bleak, mirky, murky, no fun, sorry, stark **6** dismal, dreary, gloomy, somber **7** joyless **8** hopeless, mournful **9** cheerless, dejecting, saddening, upsetting **10** lugubrious, melancholy, oppressive, tenebrific
event: **6** bummer, downer
depression: **3** dip, pit, sag, woe **4** bust, dent, funk, hole, mold, mood, pall, sink **5** basin, blahs, blues, crash, dolor, gloom, grief, panic, scoop, slump **6** cavity, crater, crisis, dimple, furrow, groove, hollow, misery, recess, sorrow, trench, trough, valley **7** anguish, despair, dim view, foxhole, malaise, sadness **8** bad times, distress, doldrums, glumness, sinkhole, the blues **9** abasement, abjection, bleakness, concavity, deflation, dejection, hard times, heartache, inflation, pessimism, recession **10** abjectness, affliction, bankruptcy, bear market, desolation, difficulty, discontent, dreariness, excavation, gloominess, heartbreak, heavy heart, impression, inactivity, loneliness, low spirits, melancholy, stagnation, woefulness
Depression __: **5** glass
__ Depression: **5** Great
__ depressor: **6** tongue
deprivation: **4** lack, loss, need, want **6** denial **8** hardship
deprive: **3** rob **4** oust **5** strip, wrest **6** divest **7** bereave **10** dispossess
of (prefix): **3** dis-
of wind: **5** stall
deprived: **4** poor **5** broke, needy **6** bereft, busted **7** forlorn, lacking, wanting **8** bankrupt, indigent, strapped, wiped out **9** dead broke, deficient, destitute, flat broke, insolvent, moneyless, penniless, penurious **10** down-and-out, on the rocks, straitened
be ~: **4** need
be ~ of: **4** lose **7** forfeit
of: **7** needing
old-style: **4** reft
De profundis: **5** psalm
De Profundis author: Oscar Wilde
dept.: **3** bur., div. **4** sect.
Deptford Trilogy, The author: Robertson Davies
depth: **4** drop, gulf **5** abyss, nadir, scope **6** acuity, acumen, wisdom **7** insight, lowness **8** keenness, sagacity, strength **9** dimension, intellect, intensity, sharpness, thickness **10** astuteness, profundity
charge: **6** ashcan
combining form: **5** batho-, bathy-
go out of one's ~: **4** risk
having no ~: **4** one-d, two-d
in ~: **5** fully **8** from A to Z, whole hog **9** inside out **10** completely, thoroughly, to the limit
measure ~: **5** plumb, sound
out of one's ~: **4** asea **5** at sea **6** afield
sailor's ~ unit: **3** fth. **4** fath. **6** fathom
depth __: **4** bomb **6** charge, finder **7** sounder
__ depth finder: **5** sonic
depthless: **4** idle **7** sketchy
depth of __: **5** field, focus
depths: **5** abyss, midst, nadir **6** bottom, bowels, recess **9** innermost
Depths of Glory author: Irving Stone
deputation: **8** legation **10** commission, contingent, delegation
depute: **8** delegate, transfer **9** designate **10** constitute
deputies: **4** help **5** staff
on horseback: **5** posse
deputize: **4** name **6** assign, commit **7** appoint, empower **8** delegate **9** authorize, designate **10** commission, constitute
deputy: **3** rep, sub **4** aide, help, vice **5** agent, envoy, proxy, vicar **6** acting, backup, helper, lawman, legate, regent **7** bailiff, officer, staffer **8** delegate, emissary, henchman, minister **9** appointee, assistant, go-between, man Friday, surrogate, underling **10** ambassador, legislator, lieutenant, substitute
combining form: **4** vice-
deputy __: **7** sheriff
Deputy __: **4** Dawg
__ de quatre: **3** pas
de Queiroz: **3** Eca
De Quincey: **6** Thomas
Der __: **4** Alte
deracinate: **9** eradicate, extirpate
derail: **5** wreck **6** foul up **8** go astray
Derain: **5** André
Deranged cowriter: **3** Eno
derate: **6** reduce
Der Blaue Reiter artist: **3** Arp
derby: **3** hat **4** race **6** bowler **9** horse race
material: **4** felt
__ derby: **6** roller
Derby: **4** city, race, town **6** county
also-ran: **3** nag
entrant: **5** horse
ground: **4** turf
like ~ enthusiasts: **5** horsy **6** horsey
locale: **7** England
prize: **5** purse
river: **7** Derwent
track: **4** oval
winner's flower: **4** rose
Derbyshire: **5** chair **6** county
locale: **7** England
de règle: **9** customary
deregulate: **7** leave be **8** let alone **9** decontrol
Derek: **2** Bo **3** Bok **4** John **5** Jeter **6** Barton, Jacobi **7** Walcott
Derek, Bo: **7** actress
film: 10 (1979)
Bolero (1984)
Orca (1977)
spouse: John Derek
Derek, John: **5** actor
film: Exodus (1960)
Scandal Sheet (1952)
The Ten Commandments (1956)
spouse: Ursula Andress, Bo Derek, Linda Evans
derelict: **3** bum, lax **4** hobo, lorn, wino **5** slack, tramp, wreck **6** remiss **7** cast off, drifter, outcast, run-down, vagrant **8** careless, castaway, deserted, desolate, forsaken, homeless, renegade, untended, vagabond **9** abandoned, discarded, neglected, negligent, ownerless, unmindful **10** delinquent, ne'er-do-well, neglectful, ragamuffin, ramshackle, regardless, unreliable
dereliction: **5** fault, guilt **6** breach, laxity **7** default, neglect **9** oversight
__ de résistance: **5** pièce
deride: **3** dis, kid, pan, rag, rib, rip **4** defy, gibe, hiss, hoot, jeer, jibe, mock, razz, slam, slur, snub, twit **5** abuse, chaff, decry, fleer, flout, knock, libel, roast, scoff, scorn, sneer, spurn, taunt **6** banter, defame, dump on, heckle, hoot at, impugn, insult, jibe at, malign, offend, parody, rebuff, slight, vilify **7** affront, asperse, contemn, degrade, disdain, laugh at, put down, rank out, scoff at, slander, traduce **8** belittle, denounce, pooh-pooh, ridicule, vilipend **9** blaspheme, denigrate, discredit, disparage, humiliate, make fun of, poke fun at **10** calumniate, disrespect
de rigueur: **10** obligatory
derision: **3** dig **4** barb, gibe, jibe, slam, slap, slur, snub **5** abuse, libel, scorn, shame, sport, taunt **6** insult, rebuff, slight **7** affront, calumny, catcall, disdain, mockery, obloquy, offense, put-down, razzing, sarcasm, slander **8** brickbat, contempt, ridicule, scoffing, sneering **9** cheap shot, contumely **10** Bronx cheer, disrespect, impugnment, opprobrium
exclamation: **3** aha, bah, fie, hah, yah **4** ha-ha, he he **5** hello, te-hee **6** haw-haw, la-de-da, la-di-da, tee-hee **7** big deal **8** lah-di-dah
express ~: **4** hiss, hoot, jeer **5** snort
object of ~: **4** goat
derisive: **5** sassy, snide **7** jeering, mocking, mordant **8** sardonic, scoffing, scornful, taunting **9** insulting, laughable, quizzical, sarcastic, vitriolic **10** disdainful, irreverent, pejorative, ridiculing
derivable: **9** available, deducible, inferable, resultant, traceable **10** obtainable
derivation: **4** root **5** basis **6** origin, source **7** descent **8** ancestry, pedigree **9** beginning, deduction, emanation, etymology, genealogy, inception **10** extraction, foundation, hypothesis, provenance, wellspring
word ~: **9** etymology
derivative: **6** copied **7** product, spinoff **8** acquired, borrowed, inferred, offshoot, rehashed **9** ancestral, by-product, emulative, imitative, outgrowth, secondary **10** descendant, hereditary, secondhand, unoriginal
__ derivative: **5** first **6** second **7** partial
derive: **3** get **4** base, draw, earn, make, reap, rise, stem, take **5** educe, glean, hatch, infer, reach **6** deduce, elicit, gather, obtain, result, spring **7** descend, develop, emanate, extract, proceed, procure, receive **8** arrive at, come from, flow from, stem from, take from **9** arise from, determine, formulate, grow out of, originate, reason out **10** bring forth
derived __: **4** form, unit **5** curve
(from): **4** come, stem **5** arise **9** originate
from reasoning: **5** infer **6** deduce, deduct, induce, induct
derived form: **7** variant **10** inflection
__ de Rivoli: **3** Rue
derma: **4** skin **5** layer **6** kishka, kishke, kiskha
casing: **3** gut
dermal: **9** cutaneous
vent: **4** pore **5** stoma **10** sweat gland
dermis: **4** skin
plus epidermis: **5** cutis
starter: **3** epi
Dermot: **8** Mulroney
Dern: **5** Bruce, Laura
Dern, Bruce: **5** actor
daughter: Laura
film: After Dark, My Sweet (1990)
Black Sunday (1977)
The 'burbs (1989)
Coming Home (1978)
The Driver (1978)
Family Plot (1976)
The Glass House (2001)
The Great Gatsby (1974)
Hush ... Hush, Sweet Charlotte (1965)
The King of Marvin Gardens (1972)
Posse (1975)
Silent Running (1971)
Smile (1975)
spouse: Diane Ladd
dernier cri: **3** fad **4** mode, rage **5** vogue **6** latest **7** fashion **8** last word
Dern, Laura: **7** actress
film: Blue Velvet (1986)
Focus (2001)
Jurassic Park (1993)
Novocaine (2001)
October Sky (1999)
A Perfect World (1993)
Rambling Rose (1991)
parent: Bruce, Diane Ladd
derogate: **5** abuse, decry, libel **6** demean, malign, vilify **7** asperse, degrade, detract, put down, run down, slander **8** belittle, denounce, diminish, disgrace, minimize, play down, talk down **9** denigrate, deprecate, disparage
derogation: **7** calumny **10** detraction, muckraking, reflection
derogatory: **5** snide **8** critical, damaging, decrying, libelous, scornful, spiteful **9** aspersing, degrading, demeaning, injurious, malicious, maligning, offensive, sarcastic, slighting, vilifying **10** belittling, calumnious, censorious, defamatory, detracting, detractive, disdainful, malevolent, minimizing, pejorative, slanderous
__-de-roi: **4** bleu
__ de Roland: **7** Chanson
Deronda: **6** Daniel
__ de rose oil: **4** bois
derrick: **5** crane, davit, hoist **6** lifter
arm: **3** jib
__ derrick: **3** oil
D'Errico: **5** Donna
Der Ring des Nibelungen: **5** cycle
composer: **6** Wagner
derring-do: **5** pluck, spunk, valor **7** heroics, prowess **9** gallantry
bit of ~: **4** feat
tale of ~: **4** gest, saga **5** geste
derringer: **6** pistol
Derringer: **5** Yancy
Der Rosenkavalier: **5** opera
Annina in ~: **4** alto
composer: **7** Strauss
role: **4** Ochs **6** Annina, Sophie **8** Marianne, Octavian
setting: **6** Vienna **7** Austria
Derry: **4** city, port, town
college: **5** Magee
locale: **7** Ireland
Dershowitz, Alan: **6** lawyer **8** attorney
Der Spiegel: **5** paper **6** German **9** newspaper
Dersu Uzala (1975 film) director: Akira Kurosawa
dervish: **5** faker, fakir, faqir **6** faquir **9** religious
movement: **4** spin **5** whirl
religion: **5** Islam
__ dervish: **7** howling **8** whirling
Derwent: **5** river
locale: **5** Derby **6** Hobart **7** England **8** Tasmania
Des: **7** Barlett, McAnuff, O'Connor
Des __: **6** Moines **7** Plaines
__-de-sac: **3** cul
__ de Sade: **7** Marquis

Desafinado (1962 song) artist: Getz
Desai, Anita: 6 Indian, writer
de Sales: 7 Francis
desalt: 6 purify 7 distill
DeSario: 4 Teri
___ des Beaux Arts: 5 École, Musée
___ de scandale: 6 succès
descant: 4 sing, talk 6 melody, ramble, strain 7 monolog 8 perorate 9 discourse, expatiate, monologue
Descartes, René: 6 French 8 geometer 11 philosopher
  conclusion: 3 I am, sum
descend: 3 dip, set 4 dive, drop, fall, land, sink, step 5 crash, lapse, light, lower, slant, slide, slope, slump, swoop 6 alight, derive, get off, go down, hop off, plunge, settle, spring, tumble 7 cascade, decline, deplane, detrain, plummet 8 collapse, dismount, nosedive, submerge 9 disembark, originate, swoop down
  ender: 3 ant, ent
  on: 4 land, raid, rush 5 visit 6 assail, invade
descendant: 3 son 4 cion, heir 5 child, issue, scion 8 daughter, grandson, offshoot 9 offspring, posterity 10 derivative
  suffix: 3 -ite
___ descendant: 6 lineal
descendants: 4 seed 5 issue 7 kinfolk, lineage, progeny 8 kinfolks, kinsfolk 9 posterity
  colonial ~ org.: 3 DAR, SAR
  line of ~: 5 stirp
descended: 4 alit
  be ~ (from): 5 arise 6 spring
descending: 4 down 8 downhill, downward
___ Descending: 7 Orpheus
___ Descending a Staircase: 4 Nude
descent: 3 dip 4 dive, drop, fall, line, raid 5 birth, blood, crash, foray, lapse, roots, slide, slope, slump, stock, swoop 6 attack, origin, plunge, strain, tumble 7 decline, falling, incline, lineage, sinking 8 ancestry, downfall, downturn, heredity, invasion, lowering, nosedive, pedigree, plunging, tailspin 9 declivity, downgrade, etymology, forebears, genealogy, incursion 10 declension, derivation, extraction, plummeting
  steep ~: 6 escarp
Descent from Xanadu author: Harold Robbins
Descent into Hell author: Charles Williams
Descent Into the Maelstrom, A author: Edgar Allan Poe
Deschamps, Eustache: 4 poet 6 French
Deschutes: 5 river
  locale: 6 Oregon
describe: 4 limn, tell, term 5 label, paint, state, sum up 6 convey, define, depict, detail, impart, recite, relate, report, set out, sketch, unfold 7 explain, express, narrate, outline, picture, portray, qualify, recount, specify, write up 8 rehearse, set forth, subtitle 9 adumbrate, chronicle, delineate, elucidate, explicate, expound on, make clear, represent 10 illustrate
  briefly: 4 limn 5 sum up 6 sketch 7 outline
  vividly: 5 paint 6 depict 10 illustrate
description: 3 ilk 4 kind, mold, sort, tale, type 5 class, genre, label, stamp, story, title 6 detail, nature, report, sketch, stripe 7 account, heading, profile, recital, species, variety 8 category, portrait 9 narration, narrative, rehearsal, statement
___ description: 3 job
descriptive: 5 vivid 7 graphic 9 graphical
  word: 9 adjective
descry: 4 espy, hear, spot 5 sight 6 detect, notice 7 discern, glimpse, make out 8 discover, perceive 9 recognize
Desdemona: 4 moon
  enemy: 4 Iago
  handkerchief: 4 prop
  husband: 7 Othello
  planet: 6 Uranus
desecrate: 4 ruin, sack 5 abuse, spoil 6 befoul, defile, misuse, ravage 7 despoil, pillage, pollute, profane, violate 8 dishonor, spoliate 9 blaspheme, depredate, devastate
desecration: 3 sin 6 misuse 7 outrage 9 sacrilege, violation 10 defilement
desensitize: 4 dull, numb 5 blunt 6 benumb, deaden 7 coarsen
Deseret
  News: 5 paper 9 newspaper
  today: 4 Utah
desert: 3 dry 4 arid, bare, bolt, fail, flee, Gobi, jilt, quit, skip, Tahr, Thar, Tuhr 5 biome, ditch, leave, Namib, Negeb, Negev, split, waste, wilds 6 barren, betray, cop out, decamp, defect, depart, escape, Gibson, go AWOL, Libyan, maroon, Mohave, Mojave, Nubian, reward, Sahara, strand, Syrian 7 abandon, abscond, Arabian, aridity, Atacama, bail out, forsake, hot spot, Kara Kum, Painted, Sechura, Simpson, Sonoran, sterile, take off 8 desolate, forswear, hightail, Kalahari, Kyzyl Kum, lifeless, rainless, renounce, run out on, sneak off 9 cut and run, Dasht-e Lut, foreswear, Great Salt, infertile, leave flat, skip out on, throw over, walk out on, wasteland 10 Chihuahuan, go away from, Great Sandy, Patagonian, punishment, Sturt Stony, Taklamakan, wilderness 11 Death Valley
  Africa: 5 Namib, Sahel 6 Libyan, Nubian, Sahara 7 Arabian 8 Kalahari
  ancient ~ kingdom: 5 Nubia
  animal: 5 camel
  Arizona: 7 Sonoran 10 Chihuahuan
  Asia: 4 Gobi, Tahr, Thar, Tuhr 6 Syrian 7 Arabian, Kara Kum 8 Kyzyl Kum 9 Dasht-e Lut, Great Salt
  Australia: 6 Gibson 7 Simpson 10 Great Sandy, Sturt Stony
  basin floor: 5 playa
  California: 6 Mohave 7 Sonoran 11 Death Valley
  Egypt: 6 Libyan, Sahara 7 Arabian
  feature: 4 dune, reif 5 oasis
  fruit: 4 date
  in Arabic: 6 Sahara
  India: 4 Tahr, Thar, Tuhr
  inn: 5 serai
  Iran: 9 Dasht-e Lut, Great Salt
  lake: 6 mirage 8 illusion
  largest ~: 6 Sahara
  like a ~: 3 dry 4 arid, sere 6 barren
  Mexico: 7 Sonoran 10 Chihuahuan
  Mideast: 5 Dahna, Nafud, Nefud, Negeb, Negev, Sinai 6 Syrian
  Mongolia: 4 Gobi
  North America: 6 Mohave 7 Sonoran 10 Chihuahuan 11 Death Valley
  Pakistan: 4 Tahr, Thar, Tuhr
  plant: 5 agave, athel, retem, sotol, yucca 6 cactus, jojoba 7 saguaro
  prince: 4 amir, emir 5 ameer, emeer
  rodent: 5 gundi
  South America: 7 Atacama, Sechura 10 Patagonian
  state: 6 Nevada 7 Arizona 9 New Mexico
  Sudan: 6 Libyan, Nubian 7 Arabian
  surface: 4 rock, sand
desert ___: 3 rat 6 father, iguana, locust 7 varnish
Desert ___: 3 Fox 4 Blue, boot, Gold, Moon 5 Bloom, Storm 6 Attack, Shield 7 Culture
Desert ___, The: 3 Fox 4 Rats 5 of Ice
___ Desert: 3 Lut, Red 4 Thar 5 Kavir, Namib, Nefud 6 Gibson, Indian, Libyan, Mohave, Mojave, Nubian, Syrian 7 Arabian, Atacama, Painted
Desert Attack (1960 film)
  cast: John Mills, Sylvia Syms
  director: J. Lee Thompson
Desert Bloom (1986 film)
  cast: Ellen Barkin, Annabeth Gish, Jon Voight, JoBeth Williams
  subject: 5 A-test
Desert Blue (1999 film)
  cast: Kate Hudson, Christina Ricci, Brendan Sexton III, Daniel von Bargen
  director: Morgan Freeman
deserted: 4 bare, lone, lorn, wild 5 empty 6 barren, lonely, vacant 7 forlorn 8 derelict, desolate, forsaken, isolated, lonesome, secluded, solitary, stranded 9 abandoned, neglected 10 high and dry, unoccupied
Deserted Village, The author: Oliver Goldsmith
deserter: 4 AWOL 6 coward, dodger 7 escapee, quitter, refugee, runaway, traitor 8 apostate, defector, forsaker, recreant, renegade 9 absconder
Desert Fox, The (1951 film)
  cast: Cedric Hardwicke, James Mason, Jessica Tandy
  director: Henry Hathaway
Desert Gold author: Zane Grey
deserting: 10 abdication
desertion: 8 apostasy 9 avoidance, defecting, defection, departure, disavowal, falseness, forsaking, marooning, recreancy, rejection, secession, treachery 10 abdication, abrogation, absconding, withdrawal
Desert of Ice, The author: Jules Verne
Desert of Love, The author: Mauriac
Desert of Wheat, The author: Zane Grey
Desert Rats, The (1953 film)
  cast: Richard Burton, James Mason, Robert Newton
  director: Robert Wise
deserts: 3 due 6 reward 10 punishment, recompense
  just ~: 3 due 5 merit 7 payback 10 recompense
___ deserts: 4 just
Desert Storm: 3 war
  cuisine: 3 MRE
  target: 4 Irak, Iraq 5 Basra, Busra 6 Busrah
deserve: 4 earn, rate 5 claim, merit 7 warrant 10 have coming
deserved: 3 due 4 fair, just, meet 5 right 6 earned 7 condign, fitting, merited 8 rightful, suitable 9 equitable, justified 10 reasonable
___ deserved: 6 richly
___-deserved: 4 well
deserving: 6 worthy 7 fitting 8 laudable 9 admirable, estimable, praisable, righteous 10 creditable
  suffix: 6 -worthy
___ des Flandres: 7 Bouvier
___ des gens: 5 droit
DeShannon, Jackie
  song: Put a Little Love in Your Heart (1969)
    What the World Needs Now Is Love (1965)
Desi: 5 Arnaz
  daughter: 5 Lucie
  Lucy, to ~: 6 costar
De Sica, Vittorio: 8 director
  film: The Bicycle Thief (1947)
    The Earrings of Madame de ... (1953)
    The Garden of the Finzi-Continis (1971)
    Shoeshine (1946)
    Two Women (1961)
    Umberto D (1952)
    Woman Times Seven (1967)
    Yesterday, Today and Tomorrow (1964)
desiccate: 3 dry 4 sear 5 parch, wizen 6 wither 7 shrivel 9 anhydrate, dehydrate, evaporate 10 devitalize
desiccated: 5 unwet 9 juiceless
Desiderata (1971 song) artist: Crane
desiderate: 4 want, wish
desideratum: 3 aim 4 need, want 9 necessity, requisite
Desiderius: 7 Erasmus
___ de siècle: 3 fin
design: 3 aim, map 4 draw, form, goal, mold, plan 5 chart, décor, draft, forge, frame, hatch, label, model, motif, setup, study, style 6 create, devise, intend, invent, layout, makeup, reason, recipe, scheme, sketch, symbol 7 arrange, concoct, diagram, dope out, drawing, fashion, outline, pattern, produce, program, project, propose, purpose, think up, thought 8 block out, conceive, contrive, game plan, heraldry, maneuver, ornament, scenario, skeleton, strategy 9 blueprint, delineate, depiction, floor plan, formation, give shape, intention, invention, make plans, objective, originate, structure, treatment 10 conception, mastermind
  add a ~ to: 6 emboss
  by ~: 9 on purpose, purposely
  criterion: 4 spec
  heraldic ~: 4 ente
___ design: 7 graphic
designate: 3 dub, peg, set, tag, tap 4 call, make, mark, name, pick, slot, term 5 elect, key on, label, place, point, style, title 6 anoint, assign, choose, define, denote, depute, direct, finger, record 7 appoint, earmark, entitle, intitle, qualify, specify 8 allocate, delegate, deputize, handpick, indicate, nominate, set aside 9 apportion, authorize, prescribe, single out, stipulate 10 button down, commission, constitute, denominate, put down for, settle upon
Designate a Driver sponsor: 4 MADD
designated ___: 6 driver, hitter
designation: 4 mark, name, term, word 5 class, label, title 7 epithet 8 nickname
designedly: 9 knowingly, on purpose, purposely, willfully, wittingly 10 purposedly, studiously
designer: 5 maker 7 creator, deviser, founder, planner 8 engineer, inventer, inventor 9 architect, artificer, contriver, fashioner 10 mastermind, originator
  collection: 4 line
  deg.: 3 MFA
  item: 3 tie 4 gown, suit 5 A-line, dress
  label: 3 YSL 4 Dior, DKNY 5 Klein 6 Armani, Lauren 7 Versace
designer ___: 4 gene 5 jeans
___ designer: 7 fashion
Design for Living: 4 film, play
  author: Noël Coward
  cast: Gary Cooper, Miriam Hopkins, Fredric March
  director: Ernst Lubitsch

designful: **10** considered, deliberate
designing: **3** sly **4** wily **6** artful, crafty, shrewd, subtle, tricky **7** cunning, devious, knavish **8** plotting, scheming **9** ambitious, conniving, deceitful, deceptive, dishonest, insidious, observant **10** conspiring, intriguing
Designing Woman (1957 film)
cast: Lauren Bacall, Dolores Gray, Gregory Peck
director: Vincente Minnelli
Designing Women (CBS sitcom)
cast: Delta Burke (Suzanne Sugarbaker)
Dixie Carter (Julia Sugarbaker)
Annie Potts (Mary Jo Shively)
concern: **5** decor
setting: **7** Atlanta, Georgia
designless: **6** random **9** haphazard
designs, dizzying: **5** op art
Desilu formerly: **3** RKO
__ des Invalides: **5** Hôtel
desirability: **5** value, worth
desirable: **4** good **5** swell **6** sultry, useful **7** helpful, lovable, welcome **8** adorable, charming, enticing, enviable, fetching, loveable **9** advisable, agreeable, beautiful, covetable, excellent, expedient **10** acceptable, attractive, beneficial, gratifying, preferable, profitable, worthwhile
least ~: **5** worst
less ~: **5** worse
make ~: **6** endear
more ~: **6** better
most ~: **4** best, tops
thing: **4** plum
desire: **3** aim, yen **4** ache, envy, hope, itch, like, long, lust, miss, mood, need, pant, pine, seek, urge, want, whim, will, wish **5** ardor, covet, crave, fancy, go for, letch, yearn **6** appeal, ask for, choose, fervor, hunger, intent, liking, prefer, pursue, relish, thirst **7** avidity, craving, dream of, emotion, hope for, impulse, long for, longing, passion, pine for, purpose, request, require, solicit, wish for **8** ambition, appetite, aspire to, entreaty, fondness, languish, pleasure, velleity, volition, voracity, yearn for, yearning **9** affection, appetence, eagerness, esurience, hankering, intention, obsession, thirst for, will to win **10** aspiration, incitement, preference, settle upon, sweet tooth
combining form: **6** -orexia
insatiable ~: **4** urge **5** greed **6** fervor, thirst **7** avidity, craving **8** cupidity **9** appetence
personified: **4** Eros
seat of ~ to the ancients: **5** liver
show excessive ~: **5** drool
Desire (1936 film)
cast: Gary Cooper, Marlene Dietrich, John Halliday
director: Frank Borzage
__ Desire: **4** All I
Desire (1980 song) artist: Andy Gibb
desired: **7** welcome **8** enviable
Desirée (1977 song) artist: Diamond
Desire Under the Elms: **4** film, play
author: Eugene O'Neill
cast: Burl Ives, Sophia Loren, Anthony Perkins
character: **4** Eben **5** Abbie, Cabot **6** Simeon
director: Delbert Mann
desirous: **4** avid, keen **5** eager, itchy **6** ardent, hungry **7** anxious, athirst, hopeful, jealous, longing, lustful, thirsty, wanting, willing, wishing, wistful **8** aspiring, covetous, grasping, ravenous, yearning **9** ambitious **10** passionate
desist: **3** end **4** halt, quit, stop **5** can it, cease, close, forgo, pause, yield **6** cool it, forego, lay off, refuse, stop it **7** abstain, forbear, refrain **8** break off, cut it out, knock off, leave off, surcease **10** knock it off
desistance: **5** close **6** ending, finish **9** cessation **10** conclusion
desk: **5** table **6** carrel **7** carrell, counter, lectern, rolltop **8** kneehole, vargueno **9** davenport, furniture, secretary, workplace **10** escritoire
church ~: **4** ambo **5** ambon
ender: **3** man, men, top
feature: **4** lamp **5** in-box **6** drawer
Italian ~: **5** stipo
item: **3** pen **4** lamp **6** eraser, pencil **8** calendar, computer
library ~: **6** carrel **7** carrell
material: **4** wood
reading ~: **7** lectern
reference: **9** thesaurus **10** dictionary
site: **3** den **5** study **6** office
desk __: **3** job, pad, set **4** work **6** copier, jockey
__ desk: **4** city, copy **5** front, Salem **7** reading, roll-top, writing
desk-bound: **9** sedentary
Desk Set (1957 film)
cast: Joan Blondell, Katharine Hepburn, Spencer Tracy, Gig Young
director: Walter Lang
Des Moines: **4** city, town **5** river
athletes: **8** Bulldogs
city near ~: **4** Ames
county: **8** Humboldt
locale: **4** Iowa **10** Washington
newspaper: **8** Register
river: **7** Raccoon
school: **5** Drake
Desmond: **4** Paul, Tutu **5** Norma **6** Dekker, Johnny, O'Grady
Desmond, Johnny
song: Play Me Hearts and Flowers (1955)
The Yellow Rose of Texas (1955)
Desmond, Paul: **11** saxophonist
genre: **4** jazz
instrument: **3** sax **7** alto sax
Desna: **5** river
locale: **6** Russia
Desnos, Robert: **4** poet **6** French
__ de société: **4** vers
__ de soie: **4** peau
__-de-soie: **5** poult
desolate: **4** bare, blue, down, lorn, ruin, sack, wild **5** alone, bleak, empty, gaunt, spoil, stark **6** barren, broody, desert, dismal, dreary, gloomy, lonely, ravage, shabby, somber, vacant **7** depress, destroy, forlorn, in a funk, joyless, pillage, private, run-down, sterile, unknown **8** dejected, derelict, deserted, dolorous, downcast, forsaken, lonesome, solitary, spoliate, wretched **9** abandoned, cheerless, depressed, devastate, miserable **10** despondent, lay waste to, melancholy, unoccupied
spot: **4** moor **6** desert
desolation: **3** woe **4** pall, ruin **5** gloom, grief, havoc **6** misery, pathos, sorrow **7** anguish, despair, sadness **8** bareness, distress, solitude **9** bleakness, dejection, emptiness, heartache, isolation **10** barrenness, depression, extinction, gloominess, heartbreak, loneliness, melancholy, woefulness
__ de Soleil: **4** Bain
DeSoto: **3** car **4** auto, city, town **10** automobile
contemporary: **4** Nash
locale: **5** Texas
model: **8** Firedome **9** Fireflite, Firesweep **10** Adventurer **11** Powermaster
de Soto, Hernando: **7** Spanish **8** explorer
despair: **3** woe **4** mope **5** dolor, gloom, grief **6** misery, sorrow **7** anguish, dim view, emotion, malaise, travail **8** glumness, the blues **9** dejection, heartache, lose faith, lose heart, pessimism **10** depression, desolation, give up hope, heartbreak, infelicity, loneliness, melancholy, woefulness
cry of ~: **4** alas, oh no
in ~: **3** low, sad **4** blue, glum, mopy **5** mopey **6** gloomy, morbid, morose **7** doleful, forlorn, unhappy **8** dejected, desolate, grieving, hopeless, wretched **9** all torn up, bummed-out, cheerless, depressed, desperate, miserable, sorrowful, woebegone **10** despondent, melancholy
despairing: **3** sad **7** forlorn **8** wretched **9** depressed, desperate, in the pits, miserable, oppressed **10** despondent, in the dumps, melancholy
desperado: **4** thug **6** bad guy, bad man, bandit, gunman, outlaw, robber **7** brigand **8** criminal, gangster **9** cutthroat **10** delinquent, gunslinger, lawbreaker
Desperadoes, The (1943 film)
cast: Glenn Ford, Randolph Scott
director: Charles Vidor
__ desperandum: **3** nil
desperate: **4** bold, dire, rash, vain **5** acute, grave, hasty, no-win, risky **6** daring, fierce, hard up, urgent **7** crucial, drastic, extreme, forlorn, frantic, intense, parlous, useless **8** careless, critical, downcast, frenzied, headlong, hopeless, reckless, shocking, terrible, vehement, wretched **9** atrocious, audacious, dangerous, foolhardy, hazardous, impetuous, in the soup, monstrous, uncareful **10** despairing, despondent, determined, headstrong, incautious, outrageous, petrifying, scandalous, up the creek
Desperate __, The: **5** Hours, Trail
Desperate Characters (1971 film)
cast: Shirley MacLaine, Kenneth Mars, Gerald O'Loughlin
director: Frank D. Gilroy
Desperate Hours, The (1955 film)
cast: Humphrey Bogart, Arthur Kennedy, Fredric March
director: William Wyler
Desperate Journey (1942 film)
cast: Errol Flynn, Raymond Massey
director: Raoul Walsh
desperately: **5** madly **8** terribly
Desperately Seeking Susan (1985 film)
cast: Rosanna Arquette, Madonna, Aidan Quinn
director: Susan Seidelman
Desperate People, The author: Mowat
Desperate Trail, The (1994 film)
cast: Sam Elliott, Linda Fiorentino, Craig Sheffer
Desperation author: Stephen King
despicable: **3** low **4** base, foul, grim, mean, poor, ugly, vile **5** awful, cheap, dirty, lousy, nasty, seamy, slimy, sorry, woful, wrong **6** abject, crumby, crummy, dismal, filthy, horrid, no-good, odious, rotten, shabby, sordid, woeful **7** accurst, baleful, baneful, beastly, doleful, ghastly, hateful, ignoble, pitiful, satanic, servile, squalid **8** accursed, dreadful, God-awful, grievous, horrible, inferior, shameful, stinking, terrible, wretched **9** abhorrent, appalling, atrocious, defective, degrading, execrable, frightful, insidious, loathsome, miserable, offensive, repellant, repellent, revolting, satanical, worthless **10** abominable, detestable, disastrous, horrendous
one: **3** cad **4** heel, toad, worm **5** slime, swine, twerp, twirp
Despina: **4** moon
planet: **7** Neptune
despisable: **5** sorry
despise: **4** hate, shun **5** abhor, scorn, spurn **6** detest, loathe, reject, revile, slight **7** contemn, disdain, dislike **8** execrate **9** abominate **10** look down on
despised: **7** unloved **8** loveless **9** unpopular
despite: **3** tho, yet **5** altho **6** even so, though **8** although, even with
Des Plaines: **4** city, town **5** river
locale: **8** Illinois
despoil: **3** mar, rob **4** loot, raid, ruin, sack **5** rifle, steal, strip, waste, wreck **6** harrow, maraud, ravage **7** bereave, corrupt, destroy, pillage, plunder, ransack **8** freeboot **9** depredate, desecrate, devastate, vandalize
old-style: **5** reave
despoiler: **6** vandal
despondency: **3** woe **5** blues, dolor, dumps, gloom, grief, mopes **6** misery, sorrow **7** anguish, despair, emotion, sadness **8** doldrums, glumness, the blues **9** dejection, heartache, pessimism **10** depression, heartbreak, melancholy
despondent: **3** low, sad **4** blue, down, glum, mopy **5** heavy, mopey, sorry **6** broody, gloomy, morbid, morose, rueful **7** doleful, forlorn, hangdog, in a funk, unhappy **8** dejected, desolate, downcast, grieving, wretched **9** all torn up, bummed-out, cheerless, depressed, desperate, in despair, in the pits, miserable, sorrowful, woebegone **10** despairing, dispirited, melancholy
Desportes, Philippe: **4** poet **6** French
despot: **4** czar, tsar, tzar **6** satrap, tyrant **7** autarch, monarch **8** autocrat, dictator **9** oppressor
word: **3** law
despotic: **4** firm, hard **5** bossy, cruel, harsh, picky, rigid, stern, tough **6** kingly, lordly, severe, strict **7** austere, lawless, Spartan **8** absolute, dogmatic, dominant, exacting, hard-line, imperial, rigorous **9** arbitrary, demanding, draconian, imperious, stringent, tyrannous, unbending, unsparing **10** autocratic, dogmatical, high-handed, inflexible, iron-fisted, ironhanded, iron-willed, no-nonsense, oppressive, peremptory, tyrannical
despotism: **7** cruelty, fascism, tyranny **8** iron hand **9** autocracy **10** domination, oppression
despotize: **5** bully **7** oppress
__ d'esprit: **3** jeu **5** point
desquamate: **4** molt, peel **5** flake
Des'ree song: You Gotta Be (1994)
__ d'essai: **4** coup **6** ballon
__ des Saintes: **4** îles
Dessau: **4** city, town
locale: **7** Germany
__ des Sauvages: **3** été
dessert: **3** ice, pie **4** cake, duff, flan, fool, meal, tart **5** bombe, coupe, crape, crepe, crisp, donut, glace, grunt, Jello, slump, sweet, torte **6** bonbon, course, éclair, frappe, gateau, gelati, gelato, junket, mousse, mud pie, pashka,

sorbet, sundae, trifle **7** blondie, cobbler, compote, custard, gelatin, parfait, pudding, sherbet, soufflé, supreme, tortoni **8** ambrosia, apple pie, doughnut, dumpling, flummery, fruit cup, fruit pie, ice cream, meringue, mince pie, peach pie, pecan pie, streusel, syllabub, tiramisu **9** barquette, Chantilly, cherry pie, dacquoise, mincemeat, raisin pie **10** blancmange, brown betty, peach Melba, pumpkin pie, rhubarb pie, zabaglione **11** crème brulée
ender: 5 spoon
frozen ~ chain: 4 TCBY
like some ~ s: 6 flambé
preceder: 6 entrée
to a Brit: 6 afters
to dieters: 4 no-no
topping: 5 sauce, sirup, syrup
trolley: 4 cart
dessert ___: 4 cart, fork, menu, tray, wine **5** knife
desserts
get one's just ~: 4 earn, rate **7** deserve **10** have coming
give just ~: 5 spite **6** avenge **7** get even, hit back, pay back, requite **9** get back at, stick it to
___ de Staël: 6 Madame
___ d'Este: 5 Villa
___ d'estime: 6 succès
destination: 3 aim, end **4** goal, port, stop **6** target **8** ambition, terminus **9** intention, objective
reach a ~: 6 arrive **8** get there
destine: 4 doom **6** likely, ordain **9** preordain **10** foreordain
destined: 4 born **5** bound, fated, meant **6** doomed, likely, sealed **7** certain, in store **8** impelled **10** inevitable, inexorable, in the cards, undoubtful
destiny: 3 lot **4** doom, fate, luck **5** karma **6** future, kismat, kismet **7** fortune
individual ~: 5 moira
Norse goddess of ~: 3 Urd
Roman goddess of ~: 5 Parca
Destiny's Child
song: Bills, Bills, Bills (1999)
Bootylicious (2001)
Emotions (2001)
Independent Woman (2000)
Jumpin', Jumpin' (2000)
No, No, No (1997)
Say My Name (2000)
Survivor (2001)
destitute: 4 poor **5** broke, needy, sorry **6** bad off, bereft, busted, hard up, ill off, in need, in want, lonely, pauper **7** pinched, wanting **8** badly off, bankrupt, beggarly, depleted, deprived, helpless, indigent, starving, strapped, wiped out **9** dead broke, deficient, depressed, exhausted, flat broke, insolvent, miserable, moneyless, penniless, penurious, played out **10** down-and-out, on the rocks, pauperized, straitened
destitution: 4 lack, need, ruin, want **6** dearth, misery, penury **7** beggary, paucity, poverty **8** hardship **9** indigence, mendicity, neediness, pauperdom, pauperism **10** starvation
d'Estournelles de Constant, Paul: 6 French **8** Nobelist
destrier: 5 horse **6** equine **7** charger **8** war-horse
destroy: 3 axe, end, gut, sap **4** do in, nuke, rase, raze, ruin, sack, sink, slay, undo **5** blast, break, cream, crush, erase, fordo, level, quash, rip up, smash, spoil, total, trash, waste, wrack, wreck **6** blight, devour, finish, mangle, quench, ravage, topple, uproot **7** abolish, blot out, consume, corrode, despoil, expunge, nullify, pillage, scuttle, shatter, subvert, torpedo, unbuild, wipe out **8** bulldoze, demolish, desolate, dissolve, dynamite, paralyse, paralyze, pull down, sabotage, spoliate, stamp out, take down, tear down **9** devastate, dismantle, eradicate, extirpate, knock down, liquidate, overwhelm, slaughter, take apart **10** annihilate, extinguish, lay waste to
documents: 5 shred
gradually: 5 erode
destroyed: 4 gone, lost **5** kaput **6** broken, undone **7** in ruins **9** miserable
not ~: 6 extant
old-style: 4 smit
destroyer: 4 ship **6** vandal **7** frigate, warship **8** man-of-war **10** battleship
combining form: 5 -clast
letters: 3 USS
name meaning ~: 6 Gideon
Destroyer, Hindu: 5 Shiva
destroying combining form: 7 -clastic
___-destruct: 4 auto, self
destruction: 3 end **4** doom, loss, ruin **5** havoc, smash **6** damage, defeat, mayhem **7** rampage, undoing **8** downfall, sabotage
___ Destruction: 5 Eve of
destructive: 4 dire, fell **5** toxic **6** lethal, malign, savage, tragic, wicked **7** adverse, baleful, baneful, caustic, erosive, harmful, hurtful, ruinous, vicious, violent **8** damaging, negative, tragical, virulent, wasteful **9** dangerous, injurious, malignant, murderous **10** calamitous, disastrous
force: 7 scourge
one: 3 Hun **4** Goth **6** Vandal **8** Visigoth
destructiveness: 8 violence
Destructors, The (1974 film)
cast: Michael Caine, James Mason, Anthony Quinn
Destry Rides Again (1939 film)
cast: Marlene Dietrich, Brian Donlevy, James Stewart, Charles Winninger
___ de suite: 4 tout
desultory: 6 fitful, ragged, random, spotty **7** aimless, cursory **8** rambling **9** excursive, haphazard, irregular **10** occasional, willy-nilly
DeSylva: 2 B.G. **5** Buddy
detach: 3 lop **4** crop, part **5** loose, sever, split, unfix, unpeg, unpin **6** cut off, divide, loosen, remove, rip off, unlink **7** disjoin, divorce, isolate, pull off, split up, tear off, unhitch **8** break off, disunite, liberate, separate, set apart, uncouple, unfasten **9** disengage, take apart **10** disconnect
gradually: 4 wean
detached: 3 cut, icy **4** cool, free **5** alone, aloof, apart, loose, split, stoic **6** remote, untied **7** distant, insular, neutral, stoical **8** discrete, reserved, separate, unbiased **9** apathetic, impartial, objective, unslanted, withdrawn **10** impersonal, insociable, nonchalant, unagitated
in music: 4 stac. **5** stacc. **8** staccato
detachment: 4 army, cool, unit **5** corps, force, party, squad, troop **6** detail, patrol **7** brigade, divorce, platoon, split-up **8** coldness, coolness, disunion, division, solitude **9** aloofness, partition, task force, unconcern **10** contingent, disjoining, dreaminess, equanimity, neutrality, remoteness, separation
detail: 4 army, item, list, part, send, show, spec, tell, unit **5** force, point, squad, thing, touch, trait, troop **6** aspect, define, depict, factor, lay out, nicety, patrol, recite, regard, relate, report, reveal, set out, sketch **7** account, analyze, catalog, element, exhibit, feature, itemize, minutia, narrate, portray, recount, respect, specify **8** describe, division, instance, loose end, set forth, specific, spell out **9** catalogue, component, delineate, elaborate, embellish, enumerate, epitomize, expound on, fine point, formulate, make clear, punctilio, stipulate, task force **10** detachment, particular
attention to ~: 4 care
go into ~: 4 list **5** brief, gloss **6** lay out **7** analyze, clarify, explain, itemize, specify **8** annotate, describe, spell out **9** blueprint, elaborate, elucidate, enumerate, expound on, make clear, put across
in ~: 8 whole hog **9** inside out **10** item by item, thoroughly
product ~: 4 spec
trivial ~: 3 nit
detail ___: 3 man **7** drawing
detailed: 4 full, vast **6** minute **7** copious, graphic, precise **8** accurate, complete, concrete, seriatim, specific, thorough **9** elaborate, full-dress, graphical, technical **10** blow-by-blow, exhaustive, meticulous
details: 4 data, dope **5** facts, terms **6** trivia **7** program **8** contents, minutiae, niceties **9** fine print **10** conditions, ins and outs
add ~: 6 fill in **7** augment **8** flesh out
handler: 4 aide
press for ~: 4 pump
tend to final ~: 5 mop up
___ Detail, The: 4 Last
detain: 3 nab **4** bust, hold, jail, keep, mire, nail, slow, stay **5** check, delay, pinch, run in, seize **6** arrest, collar, hang up, hinder, hold up, impede, intern, lock up, pick up, pull in, remand, retard **7** bog down, confine, inhibit, interne, set back **8** hold back, hold on to, hold over, imprison, keep back, make late, restrain, slow down **9** apprehend, extradite **10** buttonhole
detained: 4 slow **5** tardy
detainee: 7 captive **8** internee, prisoner
detainment: 10 internment
___ d'état: 4 coup **6** raison
detect: 3 see, spy **4** espy, find, note, spot **5** catch, dig up, hit on, learn, scent, sense, smell, sniff, trace **6** descry, expose, locate, notice, pick up, turn up, unmask **7** discern, make out, observe, uncover **8** discover, identify, pinpoint, smell out, sniff out **9** ascertain, recognize, stumble on, track down
detectable: 7 audible, visible **8** palpable, tangible
detection: 4 find **6** espial **8** exposure **9** discovery, unmasking **10** disclosure, revelation, uncovering, unearthing
device: 5 radar, sonar
detective: 2 PI **3** cop, fed, spy **4** dick, narc, nark **5** agent, narco, snoop **6** shamus, sleuth **7** gumshoe, officer **9** constable, operative **10** bloodhound, private eye, prosecutor
cry: 3 aha
discovery: 4 clew, clue
do ~ work: 5 trace
duo's dog: 4 Asta
Fed. medical ~: 3 CDC
fictional ~: 4 Chan, Fell, Rome **5** Dupin, Lupin, McGee, Queen, Small, Spade, Tibbs, Trent, Vance, Wolfe **6** Alleyn, Archer, Carter, Hammer, Holmes, Marple, Poirot, Shayne, Wimsey **7** Charles, Maigret, Marlowe, Templar **8** Drummond, Sam Spade, Sherlock, The Saint, Tony Rome **9** Honey West, Lew Archer, Nero Wolfe **10** David Small, Mike Hammer, Nick Carter, Philo Vance
first name in ~ fiction: 4 Erle
rabbi ~: 5 Small
skill: 5 logic
story pioneer: 3 Poe
work: 4 case
___ detective: 5 house **7** private
Detective Story (1951 film)
cast: William Bendix, Kirk Douglas, Eleanor Parker
director: William Wyler
Detective, The (1968 film)
cast: Ralph Meeker, Lee Remick, Frank Sinatra
___ Detective, The: 5 Cheap
___ detector: 3 lie **4** mine **5** metal, smoke **7** crystal
detent: 4 pawl **7** ratchet
détente: 4 thaw **5** truce **10** cooling off
detention: 5 delay **6** arrest **7** custody, jailing, keeping **9** captivity, hindrance, restraint, retention **10** constraint, detainment, immurement, impediment, indictment, internment, quarantine
place of ~: 4 jail **5** gulag **6** prison
deter: 3 cow **4** damp, turn **5** block, check, chill, daunt, delay, scare **6** dampen, hinder, impede, put off **7** fend off, inhibit, obviate, prevent, trammel, ward off **8** dispirit, dissuade, frighten, hold back, obstruct, preclude, redirect, restrain, scare off, slow down, stave off **9** foreclose, forestall, give pause, talk out of **10** discourage, dishearten, intimidate, keep in line
opposite: 4 abet
deterge: 4 lave, wash **5** bathe, clean, scrub **6** purify **7** launder **9** disinfect
detergent: 3 All, Biz, Era, Fab, Yes **4** Ajax, Bold, Dash, Gain, soap, Surf, Tide, Wisk **5** Cheer, Dreft, Ivory, Purex **6** Calgon, Dynamo, Oxydol **7** cleaner, Octagon, Woolite **8** cleanser **9** Ivory Snow
feature: 4 suds
ingredient: 5 borax **6** alkali
old ~ brand: 3 Duz **5** Rinso
target: 5 grime, stain **6** grease
deteriorate: 3 ebb, rot **4** fade, fail, flag, rust, sink, slip, wane, wear, wilt **5** decay, erode, lapse, slide, slump, spoil **6** suffer, weaken, worsen **7** corrode, crumble, decline, degrade, fall off, regress, relapse, rot away, vitiate **8** decrease, languish, stagnate, vegetate, wear away **9** aggravate, fall apart **10** degenerate, exacerbate, go downhill, go to pieces, retrogress
deteriorated: 4 worn **6** shabby **7** worn-out **8** decrepit
deterioration: 3 ebb **4** fall, ruin, slip, wear **5** decay, lapse **6** damage **7** decline, entropy **8** downturn
determinant: 5 cause **6** factor, motive, reason, source
determinate: 4 spot **7** limited, special **8** definite
determination: 4 grit, guts, push, will, zeal **5** drive, heart, nerve, pluck, spine, spunk, stand, valor **6** choice, energy, result **7** bravery, courage, purpose, resolve, verdict **8** backbone, boldness, decision, firmness, judgment, sentence, solution, tenacity, volition **9** hardiness, stability, willpower **10** resolution
___-determination: 4 self

determine: **3** fix, set **4** find, mean, rate, rule, show, tell, vote **5** cinch, elect, gauge, impel, judge, learn, place, prove, solve, think **6** affect, assess, choose, clinch, decide, define, derive, figure, govern, locate, orient, settle, size up, verify **7** delimit, dictate, find out, measure, pin down, propose, resolve, specify, unearth, work out **8** complete, conclude, discover, draw lots, identify, nail down, pinpoint, regulate **9** arbitrate, ascertain, calculate, condition, establish, ferret out, figure out, get a fix on, get to know, influence, preordain **10** adjudicate, boil down to, foreordain, have a hunch, predestine, predispose, settle upon
determined: **3** set **4** bent, firm, sure **5** rigid, stout **6** dogged, driven, gritty, intent, steely, strong, sturdy, wilful **7** adamant, certain, earnest, serious, willful **8** decisive, definite, hellbent, in the bag, positive, resolute, sedulous, stalwart, stubborn, tireless, untiring **9** ambitious, desperate, obstinate, steadfast, strenuous, tenacious **10** conclusive, hardboiled, headstrong, inevitable, inflexible, persistent, purposeful, undeterred, unflagging, unwavering
be ~: **7** persist **9** persevere
determinedly: **4** hard **8** for keeps
determining: **5** chief, final **7** crucial, pivotal, supreme **8** critical, deciding, decisive **9** important **10** conclusive, definitive
__ de terre: **5** pomme
Deterrence (2000 film)
cast: Sean Astin, Timothy Hutton, Kevin Pollak, Sheryl Lee Ralph
deterrent: **3** bar **4** curb, rein **5** brake, check **6** bridle, lesson **7** trammel **8** obstacle **9** hindrance, restraint **10** constraint, impediment, preventive
detest: **4** hate **5** abhor, leech **6** loathe **7** despise, dislike **8** can't take, execrate **9** abominate, can't stand **10** recoil from, shrink from
old-style: **5** spise
detestable: **3** bad **4** foul, grim, poor **5** awful, lousy, seamy, sorry, woful, wrong **6** crumby, crummy, dismal, horrid, odious, rotten, woeful **7** accurst, baleful, baneful, beastly, doleful, ghastly, hateful, heinous, hideous, satanic **8** accursed, dreadful, God-awful, grievous, horrible, inferior, shameful, shocking, stinking, terrible, wretched **9** abhorrent, appalling, atrocious, defective, execrable, frightful, insidious, invidious, loathsome, miserable, monstrous, nefarious, obnoxious, offensive, repellant, repellent, repugnant, repulsive, revolting, satanical **10** abominable, despicable, disastrous, disgusting, horrendous, outrageous
detestation: **4** hate **5** odium **6** enmity, hatred **7** disgust, dislike **8** aversion, distaste, loathing **9** repulsion, revulsion
detested: **7** unloved **9** unpopular
__ de tête: **3** mal
__ de théâtre: **4** coup
dethrone: **4** oust **6** depose, remove, unseat **8** displace **9** overthrow
de Tocqueville: **6** Alexis
__ de toilette: **3** eau
detonate: **4** fire **5** burst, erupt, go off, sound **6** blow up, go boom, set off **7** explode, thunder **8** shoot off, touch off **9** discharge, fulminate
detonation: **5** blast, noise **6** blow-up, report **7** blowout **9** discharge, explosion
sound: **4** bang, boom, roar **6** kaboom
detonative: **9** explosive
detonator: **3** cap **4** fuze **7** lighter
__ de toros: **5** plaza **6** fiesta
de Toth, Andre: **8** director
film: House of Wax (1953)
The Indian Fighter (1955)
Man on a String (1960)
None Shall Escape (1944)
Pitfall (1948)
detour: **3** err **4** turn **5** route, skirt **6** bypass, bypath **7** reroute **8** sidestep **9** deviation, diversion **10** digression, divergence
detract: **3** mar **4** slur **5** lower, sneer **6** divert, lessen, malign, reduce **7** cheapen, run down, slander **8** belittle, diminish, draw away, minimize, subtract **9** devaluate
detracting: **8** critical **9** invidious **10** defamatory, derogatory, minimizing
detraction: **7** slander **9** aspersion, disesteem, injustice, maligning, traducing **10** backbiting, defamation, derogation, muckraking, pejorative, revilement, scurrility
detractive: **8** critical, libelous **9** aspersive, demeaning, invidious **10** belittling, defamatory, derogatory
detractor: **4** hack **5** enemy **6** critic **7** defamer, reviler **8** asperser, impugner, maligner, vilifier **9** belittler, derogater, ill-wisher **10** denigrator, deprecator, disparager
detrain: **5** light **6** alight, get off **7** descend, jump off **9** disembark
where to ~: **5** depot **7** station **8** terminal
__ Detrick: **4** Fort
detriment: **4** bane, cost, harm, hurt, loss **5** minus **6** blight, damage, hurdle, injury, plague **7** barrier **8** calamity, disaster, drawback, handicap, obstacle, weakness **9** hindrance, liability, nightmare, prejudice, ruination **10** disservice, impairment, impediment
detrimental: **3** bad, ill **5** toxic **6** malign **7** adverse, baleful, baneful, harmful, hurtful, nocuous, ruinous **8** damaging, inimical, negative **9** dangerous, injurious, unhealthy **10** calamitous, disastrous
__ de Triomphe: **3** Arc **4** l'Arc
detritus: **5** scree **6** debris, gravel, litter **7** garbage **8** leavings
rock ~: **4** sand
__ de trois: **3** pas
Detroit: **4** city, port, town **5** river
arena: **4** Cobo
brew: **6** Stroh's
city near ~: **6** Ecorse
company: **3** GMC **4** Ford
county: **5** Wayne
labor group: **3** UAW
locale: **8** Michigan
newspaper: **4** News **9** Free Press
product: **3** car **4** auto **5** sedan
pro team: **5** Lions **6** Tigers **7** Pistons **8** Red Wings
River destination: **4** Erie
Detroit __ Wings: **3** Red
__ Detroit: **6** Doctor
Detroit-to-Denver dir.: **3** WSW
de trop: **7** surplus, too much **9** redundant
detrude: **5** lower
Deucalion author: John Ruskin
deuce: **3** tie, two **4** card **7** two-spot
beater: **4** trey
point after ~: **4** ad in **5** ad out
Deuce Coupe choreographer: **5** Tharp
deuces __: **4** wild
__ Deuces, The: **6** Flying
__-deucy: **4** acey
Deuel: **5** Peter
deus ex __: **7** machina
__ deus in nobis: **3** est
Deus Ramos, Joao de: **4** poet
deuterium discoverer: **4** Urey
deuteron: **8** particle
Deuteronomy
follower: **6** Joshua
peak: **4** Nebo
preceder: **7** Numbers
Deuteronomy, Old: **3** cat
Deutsch: **6** German **7** Babette
Deutsch, Babette: **4** poet
Deutsche __: **4** mark
Deutschland
see German
Deutschland __ Alles: **4** über
deutzia: **5** shrub
deux: **3** two **6** French
follower: **5** trois
preceder: **3** une
__ deux: **5** entre, pas de
Deux-Sèvres: **10** department
capital: **5** Niort
__ de vache: **4** bois
De Valera, Eamon: **5** Irish **9** statesman
De Valois, Ninette: **5** Irish **6** dancer **8** danseuse **9** ballerina
devalorize: **9** downgrade **10** depreciate
devaluate: **5** abase, lower **6** debase, impair **7** detract **8** decrease
devalue: **5** lower **6** debase, impair **7** cheapen, deflate, depress **8** mark down, take down, write off **9** downgrade, underrate, write down **10** adulterate, depreciate
Devane, William: **5** actor
film: Family Plot (1976)
Marathon Man (1976)
Testament (1983)
Yanks (1979)
TV: Knots Landing
devastate: **4** raid, rase, raze, ruin, sack, sink **5** harry, level, smash, spoil, total, trash, waste, wreck **6** ravage, topple **7** consume, despoil, destroy, pillage, plunder, shatter, stagger, unbuild **8** bulldoze, demolish, desolate, freeboot, spoliate, take down, tear down **9** depredate, desecrate, dismantle, knock down, overwhelm, take apart
devastated: **4** lost **7** in a funk, in ruins **8** finished
devastating: **6** lethal **7** ruinous, telling, violent **8** stunning
devastation: **4** ruin **5** havoc, waste **7** debacle
__ de veau: **3** ris **4** tête
de Vega: **4** Lope
develop: **2** go **3** age, wax **4** boom, brew, form, gird, grow, rise, stem, tone **5** arise, begin, bloom, breed, build, educe, forge, occur, ripen, shape, shore, start, steel, train, widen **6** anneal, beef up, create, deepen, derive, emerge, enrich, enroot, evolve, expand, extend, foster, grow up, happen, harden, mature, mellow, polish, prop up, refine, result, sketch, spread, spring, sprout, temper, thrive, tone up, unfold, work up **7** advance, amplify, augment, blossom, bolster, brace up, broaden, build up, burgeon, empower, enhance, enlarge, exploit, fortify, improve, magnify, nurture, perfect, pioneer, prepare, produce, promote, prosper, realize, shape up, shore up, stiffen, toughen, work out **8** beautify, bourgeon, buttress, commence, contract, energize, engender, flourish, generate, heighten, increase, incubate, indurate, maturate, progress, take root, vitalize **9** actualize, branch out, come about, cultivate, elaborate, establish, formulate, germinate, intensify, originate, reinforce, transpire **10** invigorate, liberalize, mastermind, strengthen
begin to ~: **3** bud
gradually: **6** evolve
into: **6** become
developed: **4** ripe **5** adult **6** mature
not ~: **6** latent
developer: **7** builder, pioneer, planner
offering: **3** lot **4** land
output: **3** pix **6** photos **8** pictures
developing: **5** young **7** budding, ongoing **8** thriving **9** half-grown, incipient
development: **4** rise **5** boost, event, phase **6** course, growth, result, spread **7** advance, buildup, outcome, process, stature **8** addition, breeding, incident, increase, maturity, offshoot, progress, ripening **9** gestation, outgrowth **10** perfection
housing ~: **5** tract
unexpected ~: **5** twist
unit: **5** house
development __: **6** rights
__ Devens: **4** Fort
de Vere, Aubrey Thomas: **4** poet **5** Irish
Devereux: **4** Earl
__ de verre: **4** pâte
Devers, Gail: **6** runner **8** sprinter
Devi: **4** Kali **6** mother, Shakti **7** goddess, Parvati **9** Annapurna
consort: **5** Shiva
like ~: **5** Vedic
__ Devi: **5** Nanda
deviant: **3** odd **4** eery **5** eerie, weird **6** atypic, errant, freaky, off-key, quirky **7** bizarre, oddball, offbeat, strange, unusual, variant, wayward **8** aberrant, abnormal, atypical, freakish, peculiar, uncommon **9** anomalous, different, divergent, eccentric, fantastic, heretical, irregular **10** unorthodox
deviate: **3** err, sin, yaw **4** part, sway, turn, vary, veer **5** shift, slant, split, stray **6** branch, differ, spread, swerve, wander **7** digress, diverge, radiate **8** aberrate, contrast, divagate, separate **9** bifurcate, misbehave
deviating: **6** errant **7** unalike **8** abnormal **9** different, divergent
by extremes: **7** radical
deviation: **3** yaw **4** bend, flaw **5** error, shift, slope **6** breach, change, detour **7** anomaly, veering **8** mutation, neurosis, variance **9** departure, disparity, diversion, exception, variation **10** aberration, alteration, deflection, difference, digression, divergence, innovation
standard ~ symbol: **5** sigma
__ deviation: **4** mean **7** average, compass **8** standard
device: **4** logo, plot, ploy, ruse, tool, trap, wile **5** badge, craft, crest, dodge, feint, gizmo, thing, trick **6** emblem, engine, gadget, gambit, legend, scheme, symbol, widget **7** gimmick, insigne, machine, utensil **8** artifice, colophon, conceive, contrive, heraldry, insignia, loophole, maneuver **9** accessory, apparatus, appliance, deception, expedient, flotation, implement, invention, mechanism, stratagem, strategem **10** expediency, instrument, subterfuge
__ device: **6** homing **8** mnemonic **9** flotation
deviceful: **6** clever, shrewd **9** ingenious, inventive **10** innovative
devices: **9** equipment, machinery
__ de vie: **3** eau
devil: **3** imp **4** cook, ogre **5** beast, brute, demon, fiend, rogue, Satan, tease

6 Belial, daemon, daimon, diablo, pester, rascal 7 dastard, evil one, Lucifer, monster, torment, villain 8 evildoer 9 archfiend, Beelzebub, scoundrel 10 jackanapes
between the ~ and the deep blue sea: 6 in a fix, in a jam
combining form: 6 diabol- 7 diabolo-
doll: 4 mojo
domain: 5 Hades 10 underworld
dust ~: 4 eddy
emulate the ~: 5 tempt
ender: 3 ish, try 4 fish, wood
little ~: 3 imp 4 brat 5 scamp
paintbrush: 5 plant 6 flower
poor ~: 6 wretch
ray: 5 manta
starter: 4 dare
Tasmanian ~: 6 animal 8 predator 9 marsupial
devil __: 3 dog, ray 4 tree
devil __, the: 5 to pay
devil-__-care: 3 may
__ devil: 3 sea 4 dust, heat, king
Devil: 5 Satan 8 puckster
rival: 4 Blue, King, Star, Wild 5 Bruin, Flame, Flyer, Oiler, Sabre, Shark 6 Canuck, Coyote, Ranger 7 Capital, Panther, Penguin, Red Wing, Senator 8 Canadien, Islander, Predator, Thrasher 9 Avalanche, Blackhawk, Hurricane, Lightning, Maple Leaf 10 Blue Jacket, Mighty Duck
__ Devil: 5 Bwana 6 Little
__-Devil: 3 She
Devil and Daniel Webster, The (1941 film)
cast: Edward Arnold, James Craig, Walter Huston
Devil and Daniel Webster, The author: Stephen Vincent Benet
Devil and Miss Jones, The (1941 film)
cast: Jean Arthur, Charles Coburn, Robert Cummings
director: Sam Wood
Devil-Doll, The (1936 film)
cast: Lionel Barrymore, Maureen O'Sullivan
director: Tod Browning
deviled egg: 9 appetizer
devilfish: 5 manta 8 manta ray
Devil in a Blue Dress (1995 film)
cast: Jennifer Beals, Tom Sizemore, Denzel Washington
director: Carl Franklin
Devil in Disguise (1963 song) artist: Elvis Presley
Devil Inside (1988 song) artist: INXS
Devil in the Belfry, The author: Poe
Devil Is a Woman, The (1935 film)
cast: Lionel Atwill, Marlene Dietrich
director: Josef von Sternberg
devilish: 4 evil 5 curst 6 cursed, impish, wicked 7 accurst, brutish, demonic, hellish, inhuman, satanic 8 accursed, daemonic, demoniac, diabolic, fiendish, infernal, inhumane 9 demonical, execrable, nefarious, satanical 10 diabolical, villainous
devilkin: 3 imp 4 brat
DeVille: 3 car 4 auto 8 Cadillac
devil-may-care: 3 gay, lax 4 rash 5 blasé 6 jaunty, rakish, sporty 7 raffish, reckess 8 carefree, careless, heedless, rakehell, reckless, sporting, sportive 9 foolhardy, impetuous 10 rollicking, swaggering
devilment: 8 mischief 9 nastiness
__ Devil Moon: 3 Old
Devil or Angel (1960 song) artist: Bobby Vee
Devil Ray: 10 baseballer
rival: 3 Cub, Met, Red 4 Expo, Twin 5 Angel, Astro, Brave, Giant, Padre, Rocky, Royal, Tiger 6 Brewer, Dodger, Indian, Marlin, Oriole, Philly, Pirate, Ranger, Red Sox, Yankee 7 Blue Jay, Mariner 8 Athletic, Cardinal, White Sox
Devil Rays: 3 ten 4 team
home: 5 Tampa 8 Tampa Bay
org.: 3 ALE, MLB
sport: 8 baseball
devil's __ cake: 4 food
devil's __ needle: 7 darning
devil's-__: 3 bit 6 tongue
Devils: 3 six 4 team
disk: 4 puck
home: 9 New Jersey
milieu: 3 ice 4 rink
org.: 3 NHL
sport: 6 hockey
Devil's __: 5 Waltz 6 Island
Devil's __, The: 3 Own 4 Pool 5 Bride 7 Brother, Doorway, General
Devil's Advocate, The (1997 film)
cast: Jeffrey Jones, Al Pacino, Keanu Reeves, Charlize Theron
director: Taylor Hackford
Devil's Advocate, The author: West
Devil's Brother, The (1933 film)
cast: Oliver Hardy, Stan Laurel, Thelma Todd
director: Hal Roach
Devil's Dictionary, The author: Ambrose Bierce
Devil's Disciple, The: 4 film, play
author: George Bernard Shaw
cast: Kirk Douglas, Burt Lancaster, Laurence Olivier
character: 5 Essie
director: Guy Hamilton
Devil's Doorway, The (1950 film)
cast: Louis Calhern, Paula Raymond, Robert Taylor
director: Anthony Mann
Devilseed author: Frank Yerby
devil's food __: 4 cake
Devil's General, The author: Carl Zuckmayer
Devil's Own, The (1997 film)
cast: Ruben Blades, Margaret Colin, Harrison Ford, Brad Pitt
director: Alan J. Pakula
Devil's Playground, The (1976 film)
cast: Arthur Dignam, Nick Tate
director: Fred Schepisi
Devil's Pool, The author: George Sand
Devil's Tail ingredient: 5 vodka
Devils, The (1971 film)
cast: Vanessa Redgrave, Oliver Reed
director: Ken Russell
Devil's Waltz author: Kellerman
deviltry: 4 evil, vice 7 knavery, roguery, sorcery 8 iniquity, mischief 9 nastiness, rascality 10 friskiness, wickedness
Devil With a Blue Dress On (1966 song) artist: Mitch Ryder
Devil Woman (1976 song) artist: Cliff Richard
Devin: 4 font 8 typeface
Devine: 4 Andy 7 Loretta
Devine, Andy: 5 actor
film: Never Say Die (1939) Stagecoach (1939)
TV: ...Wild Bill Hickok
__ de violette: 5 crème
devious: 3 sly 4 foxy, wily 5 false, shady, snaky 6 artful, crafty, louche, shifty, sneaky, subtle, tricky, zigzag 7 crooked, cunning, evasive, oblique, sinuous 8 delusive, guileful, indirect, scheming, slippery, tortuous 9 deceitful, designing, dishonest, insidious, insincere, underhand 10 circuitous, fraudulent, mendacious, misleading, roundabout, untruthful
act: 4 ploy 6 gambit
purpose: 5 angle
devise: 3 lay 4 brew, form, make, mold, plan, plot 5 ad-lib, craft, draft, forge, frame, hatch, shape 6 cook up, create, design, invent, legacy, make up, map out, whip up 7 arrange, concoct, dream up, fashion, imagine, prepare, produce, project, think up, trump up, work out 8 conceive, contrive, engineer, intrigue 9 conjure up, construct, fabricate, formulate, improvise 10 come up with, mastermind
devisee: 4 heir 7 heiress
deviser: 6 framer 8 designer 9 artificer, fashioner 10 fabricator
devitalize: 3 sag, sap 4 flag, jade, tire, wane 5 blunt, drain, weary 6 impair, reduce, shrink, soften, weaken 7 deplete, depress, exhaust, fatigue, tire out, vitiate, wear out 8 enervate, enfeeble 9 attenuate, desiccate, undermine 10 debilitate, emasculate
DeVito: 5 Danny, Karla
DeVito, Danny: 5 actor 8 director
film: Batman Returns (1992)
The Big Kahuna (2000)
Death to Smoochy (2002)
Drowning Mona (2000)
Get Shorty (1995)
Heist (2001)
Hoffa (1992)
Jack the Bear (1993)
The Jewel of the Nile (1985)
Junior (1994)
Living Out Loud (1998)
Man on the Moon (1999)
Other People's Money (1991)
The Rainmaker (1997)
Renaissance Man (1994)
Romancing the Stone (1984)
Ruthless People (1986)
Terms of Endearment (1983)
Throw Momma From the Train (1987)
Tin Men (1987)
Twins (1988)
The War of the Roses (1989)
What's the Worst That Could Happen? (2001)
spouse: Rhea Perlman
TV: Taxi
__ de vivre: 4 joie
devoid: 5 bleak, empty, stark 6 absent, barren, bereft 7 wanting 8 depleted, desolate, lifeless
of: 7 lacking, without
(of): 4 bare, free
of interest: 4 flat 5 vapid 6 boring, jejune 7 prosaic 9 tasteless, wearisome 10 dullsville, flavorless, lackluster
devoirs: 7 regards 8 respects 10 good wishes
DeVol: 5 Frank
devolution: 5 lapse 9 decadence
Devon: 3 cow 4 bull 5 sheep 6 bovine, cattle, county
city: 6 Exeter 8 Plymouth
locale: 7 England
river: 3 Exe
Devon __: 5 cream
Devonian subdivision: 5 Erian
Devon Rex: 3 cat 5 felid 6 feline
Devonshire __: 5 cream
DeVorzon: 5 Barry
devote: 4 give 5 allot, apply, bless, put in, spend 6 assign, bestow, commit, direct, donate, hallow, pledge 7 consign, earmark, reserve 8 allocate, dedicate, sanctify, set apart, set aside 9 apportion 10 consecrate, contribute
oneself to: 2 do 6 tackle 7 address 9 undertake
devoted: 4 true 5 close, liege, loyal, pious, thick 6 ardent, doting, fervid, filial, loving 7 adoring, dutiful, earnest, staunch, valuing, zealous 8 constant, faithful, intimate, maternal, parental, reliable, true-blue, untiring, yeomanly 9 allegiant, attentive, dedicated, fraternal, steadfast, unselfish 10 solicitous, undeterred
be ~: 6 adhere, cleave
be ~ to: 5 adore 6 follow
to God, name meaning: 6 Lemuel
devotedly: 5 madly 7 rabidly
devotedness: 4 love 7 loyalty
Devoted to You (1958 song) artist: Everly Brothers
devotee: 3 fan, nut 4 buff 5 fiend, freak, junky, lover 6 addict, rooter 7 admirer, booster, fanatic, fancier, groupie, habitué 8 adherent, disciple, follower, partisan 9 supporter, worshiper 10 aficionado, enthusiast, specialist
suffix: 3 -ist, -ite
devotion: 4 love, zeal 5 ardor, piety 6 fealty, fervor, homage, liking, prayer, regard 7 loyalty, passion, worship 8 fidelity, fondness 9 adherence, adoration, affection, constancy, fixedness, intensity, puppy love, reverence, sincerity 10 allegiance, attachment, commitment, dedication, enthusiasm, friendship
Hindu ~: 6 bhakti
letters of ~: 3 TLC
medieval ~: 7 angelus
object of ~: 4 icon, idol, ikon 5 eikon
__-devotion: 4 self
devotional: 6 solemn 9 spiritual
De Voto: 7 Bernard
devour: 3 eat 4 bolt, gulp, read, take, wolf 5 eat up, gorge, scarf 6 absorb, engulf, feed on, finish, gobble, guzzle, ingest, ingulf, inhale, prey on, relish, take in 7 consume, destroy, engorge, feast on, partake, pillage, put away, revel in, scarf up, swallow 8 chow down, gobble up, wolf down 9 polish off, scarf down, swallow up 10 annihilate, gormandize, monopolize
devout: 4 holy, pure 5 godly, pious 6 ardent, fervid, hearty 7 adoring, angelic, earnest, fervent, intense, saintly, serious, sincere, zealous 8 faithful, orthodox, reverent 9 angelical, heartfelt, religious, righteous 10 passionate, worshipful
devoutness: 5 piety 6 fervor 9 godliness, reverence
De Vries: 4 Hugo 5 Peter
De Vulgare Eloquentia author: 5 Dante
dew: 4 mist 5 vapor, water 8 dampness, moisture 9 sogginess
bit of ~: 4 bead, drop
ender: 3 lap 4 claw, drop, fall 5 berry, point
mountain ~: 6 whisky 7 whiskey
opposite: 5 frost
starter: 3 sun 5 honey
time: 4 morn 5 sunup 7 morning
dew __: 4 cell, line, worm 5 plant, point
dew __ the thorn, The: 4 is on
DEW __: 4 line
De Waart, Edo: 5 Dutch 9 conductor
Dewar: 3 Sir 4 Scot 5 James
Dewar __: 5 flask 6 vessel
Dewar, James: 7 chemist 8 Scottish 9 physicist, scientist
dewberry: 5 fruit
dewdrop: 4 bead 7 globule
__ Dewdrop: 5 Daddy
Dew Drop __: 3 Inn
Dewey: 3 Tom 4 John 6 George, Melvil
brother: 4 Huey 5 Louie

uncle: 6 Donald
Dewey __ system: 7 decimal
Dewey, John: 8 educator 11 philosopher
Dewhurst, Colleen: 7 actress
film: Anne of Green Gables (1985)
Ice Castles (1979)
Man on a String (1960)
McQ (1974)
spouse: George C. Scott
de Wilde, Brandon: 5 actor
film: Blue Denim (1959)
The Member of the Wedding (1952)
Shane (1953)
Those Calloways (1965)
Dewitt: 7 Wallace
DeWitt: 5 Joyce
dewlap: 4 jowl 6 wattle
Dew Line acronym: 3 SAC 5 NORAD
DeWolf: 6 Hopper
DeWolfe: 5 Billy
dewy: 3 new, wet 4 damp, dank 5 fresh, humid, misty, moist, undry 7 wettish 8 unwilted
dewy-__: 4 eyed
dexter: 5 right 9 right hand
Dexter: 3 cow 4 Brad, bull 6 bovine, cattle, Gordon, Manley
Dexter, Colin inspector: 5 Morse
dexterity: 3 art 4 ease 5 craft, knack, skill 7 ability, agility, aptness, faculty, finesse, know-how, mastery, sleight 8 artistry, deftness, facility, legerity 9 adeptness, expertise, handiness, ingenuity, quickness, readiness 10 adroitness, cleverness, expertness, nimbleness, smoothness
dexterous: 3 ace, apt 4 able, deft, good, neat 5 adept, agile, canny, crack, handy, quick, ready, slick 6 adroit, artful, au fait, clever, expert, facile, habile, nimble, smooth 7 capable, cunning, skilled, trained 8 graceful, masterly, seasoned, skillful 9 competent, efficient, ingenious, inventive, masterful 10 diplomatic, effortless, proficient
dexterously: 4 neat 7 handily
dextro- opposite: 4 levo-
dextrose: 5 sugar
Dey: 5 Susan
DeYoung: 6 Dennis
Dezhnev: 4 cape
locale: 6 Russia
DFC: 5 medal
DFM awarder: 3 RAF
DFW: 7 airport
locale: 3 Tex. 5 Texas
DH: 6 batter
stat: 3 RBI
D.H.: 8 Lawrence
DHA: 9 fatty acid
__ Dhabi: 3 Abu
Dhaka: 4 city, town 7 capital
locale: 10 Bangladesh
dhaman: 5 snake 6 animal 7 reptile
relative: 3 asp, boa 5 aboma, adder, cobra, krait, mamba, racer, viper 6 python, taipan 7 markhor, rattler 8 anaconda, moccasin, ringhals 9 boomslang, coachwhip 10 bushmaster, copperhead, sidewinder
Dhanni: 3 cow 4 bull 6 bovine, cattle
Dharma Bums, The author: Kerouac
Dharma & Greg (ABC sitcom)
cast: Jenna Elfman (Dharma Finkelstein)
Thomas Gibson (Greg Montgomery)
dog: 6 Nunzio, Stinky
Dhaulagiri: 4 peak 5 mount 8 mountain
locale: 4 Asia 5 Nepal
Dheigh, Khigh TV series: 4 Khan
dhola: 4 drum
origin: 5 India

dhole: 3 dog 5 canid 6 canine
relative: 3 dog, fox 4 wolf 5 dingo 6 corsac, coydog, coyote, fennec, jackal
d'honneur, affaire: 4 duel
dhooti: 6 fabric 8 material
__ d'horizon: 4 tour
__ d'hôte: 5 table
__ d'hôtel: 6 maitre
dhoti: 6 fabric 8 material
dhow: 4 boat, ship 5 craft 6 vessel 10 watercraft
dhuti: 6 fabric
__ diable: 3 à la
__ Diable: 5 île du
diablo: 5 demon, devil, fiend, Satan 6 daemon, daimon 7 evil one, Lucifer 9 archfiend
Diablo: 3 car 4 auto 11 Lamborghini
diabolical: 3 bad 4 evil, mean, vile 5 cruel, nasty 6 wicked 7 demonic, hellish, impious, satanic, vicious 8 daemonic, demoniac, devilish, fiendish, infernal, shameful 9 atrocious, demonical, monstrous, nefarious, satanical 10 maleficent, unhallowed, villainous
one: 5 demon, devil, fiend, Satan
Diabolique (1955 film)
cast: Vera Clouzot, Paul Meurisse, Simone Signoret
director: Henri-Georges Clouzot
diabolism: 4 evil 10 black magic
diacritical mark: 4 shwa 5 breve, hacek, schwa, tilde 6 obelus
diadem: 5 crown, tiara 6 wreath 7 chaplet, circlet, coronet, jewelry 8 headband, headgear
Diadem: 4 star
Diadema: 4 city, town
locale: 6 Brazil
diag.: 5 illus.
Diaghilev: 5 Serge 6 Sergey
diagnose: 4 spot 5 place 8 identify, pinpoint 9 recognize
diagnosis: 9 breakdown, discovery, prognosis 10 conclusion, definition
Diagnosis: 14 Murder (1976 film)
cast: Judy Geeson, Christopher Lee
Diagnosis Murder (CBS drama) cast: Dick Van Dyke (Dr. Mark Sloan)
diagnostic: 10 indicative
test: 3 EEG, MRI 4 scan, X-ray
diagonal: 4 bias 5 askew, bevel, slant, slope 6 angled, biased, skewed, zigzag 7 beveled, oblique, on a bias, slanted 8 slanting 9 crossways, crosswise, on the bias 10 transverse
mover: 6 bishop
diagonally: 5 askew, slant 6 aslant, aslope 9 at an angle, crossways, crosswise, obliquely, on the bias, slantways, slantwise 10 cornerways, cornerwise
move ~: 3 zag, zig 6 zigzag
diagram: 3 map 4 plan 5 chart, graph, parse, table 6 design, figure, layout, scheme, sketch 7 drawing, outline, picture, profile 9 adumbrate, blueprint, floor plan, visual aid 10 tabulation
__ diagram: 4 flow, Laue, tree, Venn 5 block, phase 6 Argand, Euler's 7 Feynman, Mollier, scatter
diagrammatic: 7 graphic 9 graphical
Diahann: 7 Carroll
dial: 4 call, knob, ring, tune 5 gauge, phone, tuner 6 call up, tune in 7 pointer 9 indicator, telephone, touch base
choices: 2 AM, FM
in: 5 log on 7 connect
letters: 3 ABC, DEF, GHI, JKL, MNO, PRS, TUV, WXY 4 oper.

starter: 3 sun
dial __: 4 tone 5 train
__ dial: 4 jump 6 miner's, rotary
__-dial: 4 auto 6 direct
Dial: 4 soap
alternative: 3 Lux 4 Dove, Lava, Tone, Zest 5 Camay, Coast, Ivory, Lever 6 Boraxo, Caress, Shield 8 Lifebuoy 9 Palmolive, Safeguard 11 Irish Spring
dialect: 4 cant, talk 5 argot, idiom, lingo, slang 6 brogue, jargon, patois, speech, tongue 8 language, localism, locution 10 vernacular
dialectal: 9 idiomatic 10 colloquial
dialectic: 5 logic 8 forensic 9 deduction, polemical, reasoning 10 contention, discussion, persuasion, persuasive
dialectics: 6 reason 9 reasoning
__ dialing: 4 tone 5 pulse
Dial M for Murder (1954 film)
cast: Robert Cummings, Grace Kelly, Ray Milland
character: 3 Max 4 Tony 6 Sheila
composer: 7 Tiomkin
director: Alfred Hitchcock
dialog: 4 chat, talk 6 confab, parley, powwow, script, speech 8 colloquy 9 discourse, tête-à-tête 10 conference, discussion
bit of ~: 4 line
dialog __: 3 box
Dialog: 4 font 8 typeface
dialogue: 10 vocalizing
Dialogues author: 5 Plato
dial-up device: 5 modem
diamante: 6 fabric 8 material
Diamante: 3 car 4 auto 10 Mitsubishi
diameter: 5 width 6 length 7 breadth, caliber
half: 6 radius
diametrical: 5 polar 7 counter 8 opposite
diamond: 3 gem 5 field, jewel, shape 6 carbon 7 jewelry, mineral, sandlot, stadium 8 ballpark, gemstone
defect: 4 flaw
dust: 4 bort 5 boart, bortz
in heraldry: 7 lozenge
jubilee number: 5 sixty
low-quality ~: 4 bort 5 boart, bortz
month: 5 April
once: 4 coal
pattern: 6 argyle
plane: 5 facet
shape: 5 rhomb
slangily: 4 rock
Smithsonian ~: 4 Hope
source: 4 mine
to Mohs: 3 ten
weight: 2 ct. 5 carat
see also baseball
diamond __: 4 bird, dust, lane, ring 5 drill, point 6 willow 7 jubilee
diamond __ rough: 5 in the
__ diamond: 4 Hope 5 black 6 Jonker, Matara, Matura
Diamond: 4 Legs, Neil 5 David, Selma
Diamond __: 3 Jim, Lil, Men 4 Girl, Head
Diamond __ Brady: 3 Jim
diamondback: 4 moth 5 snake 7 rattler
danger: 4 fang 5 venom
Diamondback: 10 baseballer
rival: 3 Cub, Met, Red 4 Expo, Twin 5 Angel, Astro, Brave, Giant, Padre, Rocky, Royal, Tiger 6 Brewer, Dodger, Indian, Marlin, Oriole, Philly, Pirate, Ranger, Red Sox, Yankee 7 Blue Jay, Mariner 8 Athletic, Cardinal, Devil Ray, White Sox
Diamondbacks: 4 nine, team
home: 7 Arizona, Phoenix
org.: 3 MLB, NLW
sport: 8 baseball
Diamond Bar: 4 city, town
locale: 10 California

Diamond Girl (1973 song) artist: Seals and Crofts
Diamond Head locale: 4 Oahu 6 Hawaii
diamond in the __: 5 rough
Diamond Jim (1935 film)
cast: Edward Arnold, Jean Arthur, Binnie Barnes
Diamond Men (2001 film)
cast: Bess Armstrong, Jasmine Guy, Donnie Wahlberg
Diamond, Neil
song: America (1981)
Cherry, Cherry (1966)
Cracklin' Rosie (1970)
Desirée (1977)
Girl, You'll Be a Woman Soon (1967)
Heartlight (1982)
Hello Again (1983)
Holly Holy (1969)
I Am...I Said (1971)
Kentucky Woman (1967)
Longfellow Serenade (1974)
Love on the Rocks (1980)
Play Me (1972)
September Morn (1980)
Solitary Man (1970)
Song Sung Blue (1972)
Sweet Caroline (1969)
Yesterday's Songs (1981)
You Don't Bring Me Flowers (1978)
__ Diamond Phillips: 3 Lou
Diamond Queen, The actress: 4 Dahl
__ Diamond Ring: 4 This
diamonds: 3 bid, ice 4 suit 7 jewelry
at times: 5 trump
fake ~: 5 paste
like raw ~: 5 uncut
Diamonds
song: Little Darlin' (1957)
Silhouettes (1957)
The Stroll (1958)
Diamonds (1999 film)
cast: Dan Aykroyd, Lauren Bacall, Kirk Douglas
director: John Asher
Diamonds (1987 song) artist: Alpert
Diamonds and Pearls (1991 song)
artist: Prince
Diamonds and Rust singer: 4 Baez
Diamonds Are a Girl's Best Friend
composer: 5 Styne
Diamonds Are Forever: 4 film 5 novel
author: Ian Fleming
cast: Sean Connery, Charles Gray, Jill St. John
director: Guy Hamilton
Dian: 6 Fossey 9 Parkinson
Diana: 4 Dors, Lynn, Nyad, Rigg, Ross 5 Roman, Sands 6 Canova, Hyland 7 goddess, Muldaur, Scarwid, Spencer, Wynyard
equivalent: 7 Artemis
parent: 7 Jupiter
twin: 6 Apollo
Diana (1957 song) artist: Paul Anka
Diane: 4 Ladd, Lane 5 Arbus, Baker, Carey, Duane, Kurys, Renay, Varsi 6 Keaton, McBain, Sawyer, Venora 7 Cilento
to Woody: 6 costar
Diane __ Fürstenberg: 3 von
__ Diane: 5 steak
Diane (1964 song) artist: Bachelors
Dianne: 5 Wiest 6 Lennon 9 Feinstein
dianthus: 5 plant 6 flower
diapason: 6 melody 7 harmony
diaper: 4 Luvs 5 nappy 7 Drypers, Huggies, Pampers
fix a ~: 5 repin
holder: 3 pin 9 safety pin
diaphanous: 4 airy, fine, lacy, thin 5 filmy, gauzy, lucid, sheer 6 flimsy 7 chiffon 8 delicate, finespun, gossamer, pellucid 10 cobweblike, see-through

diaphoresis: **5** sweat
diarist: **5** Frank, noter, Pepys **6** writer **7** Johnson **8** Anaïs Nin **9** Anne Frank
diarist, British: **5** Pepys
diary: **3** log **4** book **6** memoir, record **7** account, daybook, journal, writing **8** longhand, register **9** chronicle, recountal
capacity: **4** year
notation: **5** entry
put in one's ~: **3** log **5** enter
starter: **4** dear
__ Diary: **4** Dear, Eve's **6** Turtle
Diary of a Chambermaid (1964 film)
cast: Georges Geret, Jeanne Moreau, Michel Piccoli
director: Luis Buñuel
Diary of a Genius author: **4** Dali
Diary of a Hitman (1992 film)
cast: James Belushi, Forest Whitaker
Diary of a Mad Housewife (1970 film)
cast: Richard Benjamin, Frank Langella, Carrie Snodgress
Diary of a Madman author: Gogol
Diary of Anne Frank, The (1959 film)
cast: Millie Perkins, Joseph Schildkraut, Shelley Winters
director: George Stevens
Diary of a Yuppie author: Auchincloss
Diary, The (1958 song) artist: Sedaka
__ dias: **6** buenos
Dias: **10** Bartolomeu
diaskeuast: **6** editor
diaspora: **5** exile
Diaspora author: **4** Egan
diatom: **4** alga **5** algae
diatomaceous earth: **7** mineral
diatribe: **4** rant **5** abuse **6** screed, speech, tirade **8** harangue, jeremiad **9** criticism, invective, philippic **10** impugnment, vocalizing
__ diavolo: **3** fra
Diaz: **7** Cameron **8** Porfirio
Diaz, Cameron: **7** actress
film: Any Given Sunday (1999)
Being John Malkovich (1999)
Charlie's Angels (2000)
The Mask (1994)
My Best Friend's Wedding (1997)
The Sweetest Thing (2002)
There's Something About Mary (1998)
Things You Can Tell Just by Looking at Her (2001)
Vanilla Sky (2001)
film (voice): Shrek (2001)
dibble: **4** tool **10** garden tool
dibs: **5** claim, title **6** rights
DiCaprio, Leonardo: **5** actor
film: The Beach (2000)
Celebrity (1998)
Man in the Iron Mask (1998)
The Quick and the Dead (1995)
Romeo & Juliet (1996)
This Boy's Life (1993)
Titanic (1997)
nickname: **3** Leo
dice: **3** cut **4** chop, cube **5** bones, cubes, cut up, mince **6** cleave, gamble, reduce
action: **4** roll, toss **5** throw
combining form: **8** astragal- **9** astragalo-
five, in ~: **6** cinque
game: **5** craps
lucky ~ throw: **5** seven **6** eleven
no ~: **8** forget it
one, in ~: **3** ace
six, in ~: **4** sise
spot: **3** pip
tamper with ~: **3** fix, rig **4** load
throw: **3** six, ten, two **4** aces, five, four, nine **5** eight, seven, three **6** eleven, twelve **7** boxcars, doubles **9** snake eyes

__ dice: **5** liars, poker
__ Dice Clay: **6** Andrew
dicey: **5** risky **6** chancy, touchy, tricky **8** perilous **9** hazardous, uncertain **10** precarious
dichotomize: **4** part **5** sever, split
dichotomy: **5** split **8** disunion, division
Dichter, Misha: **7** pianist
DiCillo, Tom: **8** director
film: Johnny Suede (1991)
Living in Oblivion (1995)
The Real Blonde (1998)
Dick: **2** A.B. **4** Andy, Lane, York **5** Clark, Foran, Hyman, Motta, Shawn, Tracy, Weber **6** Butkus, Button, Cavett, Cheney, Haymes, Martin, Powell, Turpin, Vitale **7** Fosbury, Francis, Gautier, Grayson, Gregory, Sargent, Van Dyke **8** Gephardt, Smothers **9** Van Patten
Dick (1999 film)
cast: Kirsten Dunst, Dave Foley, Dan Hedaya, Michelle Williams
Dick __: **4** test
__ Dick: **6** Ragged **7** Deadeye
__-Dick: **4** Moby
__, Dick and Harry: **3** Tom
Dick and Jane
cat: **4** Puff
dog: **4** Spot
verb: **3** run, see
dickcissel: **4** bird
dickens: **4** heck
little ~: **3** imp **4** brat, pest **6** urchin
Dickens, Charles: **6** writer **7** British
character: **3** Pip, Tim **4** Nell **5** Uriah
exclamation: **3** bah
illustrator: Phiz
pseudonym: Boz
work: American Notes
Barnaby Rudge
Bleak House
A Christmas Carol
Cricket on the Hearth
David Copperfield
Dombey and Son
Great Expectations
Hard Times
Little Dorrit
Martin Chuzzlewit
The Mystery of Edwin Drood
Nicholas Nickleby
The Old Curiosity Shop
Oliver Twist
Our Mutual Friend
Pickwick Papers
A Tale of Two Cities
dicker: **4** deal **5** argue **6** barter, haggle, higgle **7** bargain **9** negotiate
Dickerson, Eric: **10** footballer
dickey: **4** vest **6** collar **9** neck scarf, small bird
fastener: **4** stud
Dickey: **3** Lee **4** Bill **5** James
Dickey, Bill: **6** Yankee **7** catcher
Dickey, James: **6** author, writer
work: Deliverance
Dickey, James work: Deliverance
Dickinson: **5** Angie, Emily **8** Richards
Dickinson, Angie: **7** actress
film: Big Bad Mama (1974)
Captain Newman, M.D. (1963)
China Gate (1957)
Dressed to Kill (1980)
Ocean's Eleven (1960)
The Outside Man (1973)
Point Blank (1967)
Pretty Maids All in a Row (1971)
The Resurrection of Zachary Wheeler (1971)
Rome Adventure (1962)
spouse: Burt Bacharach
TV: Police Woman
Dickinson, Emily: **4** poet
home: Amherst

Dick, Philip K.: **6** writer
__ Dickson Carr: **4** John
__ Dick, The: **4** Bank
Dick Tracy (1990 film)
cast: Warren Beatty, Glenne Headly, Madonna, Al Pacino
director: Warren Beatty
Dick Van __: **4** Dyke **6** Patten
Dick Van Dyke Show, The (CBS sitcom)
cast: Morey Amsterdam (Buddy Sorrell)
Richard Deacon (Mel Cooley)
Larry Mathews (Ritchie Petrie)
Mary Tyler Moore (Laura Petrie)
Rose Marie (Sally Rogers)
Dick Van Dyke (Rob Petrie)
__ di Como: **4** Lago
dictate: **3** law, say, set **4** fiat, read, rule, talk, word **5** canon, edict, order, speak, utter **6** behest, decree, dictum, direct, enjoin, govern, impose, ordain **7** bidding, command, control, mandate, precept **8** dominate **9** determine, direction, preordain, prescribe, principle, ultimatum, verbalize **10** incitement, injunction, regulation
to: **9** tyrannize
dictating __: **7** machine
dictation pro: **5** steno
dictator: **4** czar, duce, tsar, tzar **5** ruler **6** despot, gerent, tyrant **7** emperor **8** autocrat **9** oppressor
Dictator: **3** car **4** auto **10** Studebaker
dictatorial: **4** firm, hard **5** bossy, cruel, picky, rigid, stern, tough **6** severe **7** austere, haughty, pompous, Spartan **8** absolute, arrogant, despotic, dogmatic, exacting, hard-line, imperial, rigorous **9** demanding, draconian, officious, stringent, unbending, unsparing **10** despotical, dogmatical, inflexible, iron-fisted, no-nonsense, oppressive, peremptory, tyrannical
dictatorship: **7** tyranny **9** autocracy
__ Dictator, The: **5** Great
diction: **5** style, usage **6** phrase, speech **7** oratory, wording **8** delivery, language, locution, phrasing, verbiage **9** elocution, eloquence
obsolete ~: **8** archaism **10** archaicism
dictionary: **4** book, list **5** lexis **7** lexicon **8** language **9** reference **10** cyclopedia, vocabulary
abbr.: **3** adj., adv., obs., OED, syn., var. **4** conj., etym., pron. **5** deriv.
digital ~: **5** CD/ROM
material: **10** vocabulary
range: **4** A to Z
unit: **4** word **5** entry **10** definition
use a ~: **6** look up
__ dictionary: **7** reverse **9** crossword
__ Dictionary, The: **6** Devil's
dictum: **3** saw **4** fiat, rule, word **5** adage, axiom, dogma, gnome, irade, maxim, moral, motto, order, say-so **6** byword, decree, ruling, saying, truism **7** command, decrees, mandate, precept, proverb, theorem **8** aphorism, apothegm, sentence **9** ordinance, principle, statement **10** apophthegm, principium
obiter ~: **6** remark **7** comment **9** assertion, statement, utterance
__ dictum: **6** obiter
Did __!: **3** not, too
didact: **10** instructor
didactic: **8** pedantic **9** pedagogic **10** pedantical
__-di-dah: **3** lah
didapper: **4** bird **5** grebe
didaskaleinophobe fear: **6** school
diddle: **5** cheat **6** loiter, putter **7** swindle **9** waste time

Diddley, Bo: **9** guitarist
genre: **5** blues
Diddling author: Edgar Allan Poe
diddly: **3** nix **6** trifle
less than ~: **3** nil
diddly-__: **5** squat
__ Diddy: **5** Do Wah
Diderot, Denis: **6** French, writer **11** philosopher
__ Did For Love: **5** What I
Didi: **4** Conn
Didion, Joan: **6** author, writer
work: After Henry
Democracy
Miami
Play It as It Lays
Political Fictions
Run River
Salvador
Slouching Towards Bethlehem
The White Album
Did It in a Minute (1982 song) artist: Hall and Oates
__ Didn't Believe Me: **4** They
__ Didn't Care: **3** If I
Didn't I (1970 song) artist: Delfonics
Didn't I (Blow Your Mind) (1989 song) artist: New Kids on the Block
__ Didn't Say Yes: **3** She
Didn't We Almost Have It All (1987 song) artist: Whitney Houston
dido: **5** antic, prank
Dido: **5** queen
husband: **5** Eneas **6** Aeneas **8** Sychaeus
parent: **5** Belus
sibling: **4** Anna **9** Pygmalion
Dido and Aeneas composer: **4** Arne
Didot: **4** font **8** typeface
didrachma: **4** coin **5** money
Didrikson: **4** Babe **7** Mildred
Did you __!: **4** ever
__, Did You Evah!: **4** Well
Did you ever __ lassie...: **4** see a
Did You Ever __ Dream...: **4** See a
die: **3** ebb **4** cube, dado, fade, fail, mold, wane **5** abate, lapse, stall **6** fizzle, perish, recede, vanish **7** conk out, dwindle, ease off, fade out, slacken, subside, succumb **8** fade away, melt away, peter out
down: **3** ebb **4** lull, wane **5** abate, cease, let up **6** lessen, recede, relent **7** dwindle, subside, tail off, thin out **8** decrease, fade away, head away, level off, moderate, taper off **9** retrocede
ender: **4** back, hard **5** stock
for: **5** crave
high: **3** six
on the vine: **3** ebb, rot, sag **4** fade, wilt **5** decay, lapse **6** go soft, worsen **7** decline, dwindle **8** languish, vegetate **9** fizzle out, waste away **10** degenerate, retrogress
out: **3** ebb **4** fade **5** let up **6** vanish **7** cool off **8** decrease **9** break down
partner: **4** tool
surface: **4** face, side
die __: **4** down **7** casting
die-__: **4** cast, hard
__ die: **4** do or, open, sine, trim
Die __: **7** Walküre
Die Another Day (2002 film)
cast: Halle Berry, Pierce Brosnan, John Cleese, Dame Judi Dench
director: Lee Tamahori
Diedrich: **5** Baker
Diefenbaker, John: **2** P.M. **8** Canadian
successor: **7** Pearson
dieffenbachia: **5** aroid, plant
Die Fledermaus: **5** opera

composer: 7 Strauss
role: 3 Ida 5 Adele, Falke 6 Alfred 7 Gabriel 9 Rosalinde
setting: 4 jail 6 Vienna 7 Austria
Die Frau ohne Schatten: 5 opera
composer: 7 Strauss
Diego: 6 Eliseo, Rivera 9 Velázquez
in English: 5 James
__ Diego: 3 San
Diego, Eliseo: 4 poet 5 Cuban
diehard: 4 firm, fogy 5 bigot, fogey, loyal, rigid 6 zealot 7 fogyish, old-line 8 loyalist, mossback, orthodox, partisan 9 extremist, immovable 10 inflexible
cry: 5 never
Diehard: 7 battery
rival: 5 Delco
Die Hard (1988 film)
cast: Bonnie Bedelia, Alan Rickman, Reginald VelJohnson, Bruce Willis
director: John McTiernan
Die Hard 2 (1990 film)
cast: William Atherton, Bonnie Bedelia, Bruce Willis
director: Renny Harlin
Die Hard With a Vengeance (1995 film)
cast: Jeremy Irons, Samuel L. Jackson, Bruce Willis
director: John McTiernan
die is __, the: 4 cast
Diels, Otto: 6 German 7 chemist 8 Nobelist
__ diem: 3 per 5 carpe
Die Meistersinger: 5 opera
composer: 6 Wagner
role: 3 Eva 4 Hans 5 David, Sachs 6 Pogner 7 Walther 9 Magdalena
setting: 7 Germany 9 Nuremburg
__ Diemen's Land: 3 Van
__ dien: 3 Ich
Dien Bien Phu: 6 battle
Die Nibelungen (1924 film) director: Fritz Lang
Dieppe: 4 city, port, town
locale: 6 France
Dies __: 4 Irae
diesel: 3 gas 4 fuel 6 engine 8 gasoline 10 locomotive
diesel __: 3 oil 4 fuel 5 cycle 6 engine
Diesel: 3 Vin 6 Rudolf
Diesel, Vin: 5 actor
film: The Boiler Room (2000)
The Fast and the Furious (2001)
Saving Private Ryan (1998)
XXX (2002)
film (voice): The Iron Giant (1999)
Die Sonnette an Orpheus poet: 5 Rilke
diet: 4 fare, food, menu 5 lo-fat 6 intake, low-cal, reduce, viands 7 aliment, council, edibles, regimen 8 slim down, victuals 9 nutriment, nutrition, treatment 10 sustenance
Atkins ~ no-no: 5 sugar
component: 3 fat 5 fiber
crash ~: 4 fast
food: 4 lite 5 no-cal, no-fat
go on a ~: 4 lose 6 reduce 8 slim down 10 lose weight
successfully: 4 lose
target: 4 flab
diet __: 4 soda 7 kitchen
__ diet: 3 fad 5 crash
Diet
locale: 5 Japan
site: 5 Worms
Diet __: 4 Coke, Rite 5 Pepsi
dietary: 9 nutritive 10 alimentary
figure: 3 RDA
need: 4 iron, zinc 5 fiber
dietary __: 3 law 5 fiber
dieter
concern: 5 waist 6 figure
device: 5 scale
dread: 4 gain
fare: 5 salad 6 celery 8 skim milk
no-no: 3 fat 5 snack 7 dessert
of rhyme: 5 Sprat
resort: 3 spa
suitable for ~: 5 lo-cal, lo-fat, no-cal, no-fat
unit: 4 gram 7 calorie
Dieterle, William: 8 director
film: The Accused (1948)
Blockade (1938)
Boots Malone (1952)
The Devil and Daniel Webster (1941)
Dr. Ehrlich's Magic Bullet (1940)
Dr. Socrates (1935)
Fashions (1934)
The Hunchback of Notre Dame (1939)
Jewel Robbery (1932)
Juarez (1939)
The Last Flight (1931)
Lawyer Man (1932)
The Life of Emile Zola (1937)
A Midsummer Night's Dream (1935)
Portrait of Jennie (1948)
Rope of Sand (1949)
The Story of Louis Pasteur (1936)
diethyl __: 5 ether, oxide
Diet of __: 5 Worms
Dietrich: 7 Marlene 10 Bonhoeffer
Dietrich, Marlene: 7 actress
film: Blonde Venus (1932)
The Blue Angel (1930)
Desire (1936)
Destry Rides Again (1939)
The Devil Is a Woman (1935)
The Flame of New Orleans (1941)
Follow the Boys (1944)
A Foreign Affair (1948)
Judgment at Nuremberg (1961)
The Lady Is Willing (1942)
Manpower (1941)
Morocco (1930)
No Highway in the Sky (1951)
Rancho Notorious (1952)
The Scarlet Empress (1934)
Shanghai Express (1932)
Witness for the Prosecution (1957)
Diet Rite: 3 pop 4 cola, soda 9 soft drink
alternative: 3 TAB 4 Nehi 5 Fanta 6 Fresca, Sprite 8 Dr Pepper 9 Canada Dry 10 Mello Yello, Royal Crown 11 Mountain Dew
Dietz: 6 Howard
__-dieu: 4 prie
Dieu __ droit: 5 et mon
Dieu __ garde: 4 vous
__ Dieu!: 3 Mon
Die Walküre: 5 opera
composer: 6 Wagner
Die Winterreise divisions: 6 lieder
differ: 4 vary 5 argue, clash, range 6 depart 7 deviate, dissent, diverge, protest, quarrel, quibble 8 conflict, contrast, disagree 10 stand apart
ender: 3 ent 4 ence
__ differ: 5 beg to
difference: 3 gap, row 4 feud, spat, tiff 5 clash, scrap, split 6 acedia, change, strife 7 anomaly, dispute, quarrel, variety 8 argument, conflict, contrast, squabble, variance 9 asymmetry, departure, deviation, disaccord, disparity, diversity, exception, gradation, variation 10 aberration, alteration, antagonism, antithesis, contention, digression, disharmony, dissension, dissidence, dissonance, divergence, inequality, opposition, separation, unlikeness
make a ~: 5 count 6 affect, impact, matter
no ~: 4 same
of opinion: 4 rift, spat, tiff 5 break, clash 7 dispute, quarrel 8 argument, squabble, variance
slight ~: 5 shade
__ difference!: 4 Same
different: 3 new, odd 4 else 5 alien, apart, mixed, novel, other 6 atypic, sundry, unique, unlike, varied 7 altered, changed, deviant, diverse, oddball, offbeat, several, special, strange, unalike, unequal, unusual, variant, various 8 aberrant, assorted, atypical, contrary, discrete, distinct, manifold, multiple, opposite, peculiar, separate, specific, uncommon 9 alternate, collected, deviating, disparate, dissonant, divergent, fantastic, irregular, multiform, otherwise, startling, unheard-of, unrelated, unsimilar 10 antithetic, discordant, discrepant, dissimilar, individual, mismatched, poles apart, refreshing, unfamiliar, unorthodox, variegated
be ~: 4 vary
combining form: 5 heter- 6 hetero-
completely ~: 6 unlike 8 opposite
in Spanish: 4 otra, otro
make ~: 5 alter 6 change
meaning: 5 twist
one: 5 other 7 another, oddball
under ~ conditions: 9 otherwise
Different Corner, A (1986 song) artist: George Michael
Different Drum (1967 song) artist: Linda Ronstadt
differential __: 4 gear, rate
differential part: 4 axle, gear
differentiate: 4 tell 6 winnow 8 contrast, set apart 9 tell apart
differentiation: 8 contrast
differently: 4 else 9 otherwise
__ different tune: 5 sing a
Different World, A (NBC sitcom)
cast: Lisa Bonet (Denise Huxtable)
Jasmine Guy (Whitley Gilbert)
differing: 6 at odds, uneven 7 unequal, variant 8 clashing, opposite 9 dissident, dissonant, divergent, heretical 10 discrepant
difficult: 4 hard, rude 5 fussy, hairy, heavy, messy, picky, rigid, risky, rocky, rough, stiff, tight, tough 6 Augean, crabby, feisty, knotty, oafish, opaque, rugged, severe, sticky, thorny, tricky, trying, uphill, vexing 7 arduous, bearish, boorish, complex, finicky, hard-won, obscure, onerous, operose, painful, prickly, problem, serious, tangled, unclear, weighty 8 abstract, baffling, delicate, esoteric, exacting, finiking, finnicky, grueling, involved, puzzling, strained, ticklish, tiresome, toilsome 9 ambitious, confusing, crotchety, demanding, effortful, enigmatic, entangled, fractious, hazardous, herculean, insoluble, intricate, irritable, laborious, murderous, obstinate, recondite, strenuous, wearisome 10 bothersome, burdensome, exhausting, fastidious, formidable, gargantuan, irritating, meandering, mysterious, mystifying, perplexing, refractory, unamenable, unsettling, unyielding
make less ~: 4 ease 8 simplify
make more ~: 8 encumber
not ~: 4 easy 6 simple
position: 3 fix 4 bind, spot 5 nodus
to handle: 5 bulky 7 awkward 10 cumbersome
to understand: 6 arcane 7 labored
difficulty: 3 ado, fix, jam, rub, woe 4 bind, fuss, kink, mess, need, pain, snag, spot, to-do 5 hitch, pinch, snarl, trial 6 bother, burden, crisis, hang-up, hassle, hiccup, holdup, hurdle, kicker, matter, misery, ordeal, pickle, plight, scrape, strain, strait, strife, weight 7 anxiety, dilemma, impasse, problem, quarrel, setback, trouble 8 deadlock, distress, drawback, exigence, exigency, hardness, hardship, headache, hiccough, hot water, obstacle, quagmire, quandary, question, struggle 9 adversity, annoyance, barricade, bickering, confusion, deep water, emergency, grievance, hindrance, imbroglio, millstone, suffering 10 affliction, bafflement, depression, falling-out, harassment, impediment, irritation, misfortune, oppression, perplexity
involve in ~: 4 mire 7 bog down
without ~: 6 easily 7 handily
diffidence: 7 modesty, reserve, shyness 8 meekness, timidity 9 hesitancy, mousiness, timidness 10 constraint, hesitation, insecurity, reluctance
diffident: 3 coy, shy 4 meek 5 aloof, chary, timid 6 demure, humble, modest 7 abashed, bashful, distant, fearful 8 hesitant, reserved, reticent, retiring, sheepish 9 blenching, flinching, reclusive, reluctant, shrinking, unassured, withdrawn 10 suspicious, unassuming, uneffusive
__ diffraction: 4 x-ray
Diff'rent Strokes (NBC sitcom)
cast: Conrad Bain (Philip Drummond)
Todd Bridges (Willis Jackson)
Gary Coleman (Arnold Jackson)
Dana Plato (Kimberly Drummond)
diffuse: 4 cast, emit, long, melt, shed, soft, spew, spue, thin 5 eject, expel, exude, gabby, issue, loose, spray, strew, wordy 6 instil, prolix, spread, strewn 7 bestrew, cast out, emanate, general, give off, instill, lengthy, radiate, scatter, verbose, voluble 8 disperse, rambling, throw off, transmit 9 bombastic, dispersed, garrulous, propagate, scattered, send forth, spread out, talkative, universal 10 digressive, discursive, large-scale, long-winded, loquacious, palaverous, unspecific, widespread
diffuse __: 6 nebula
diffusion: 6 spread 9 dispersal, expansion 10 dispersion, propaganda, scattering
__ diffusion: 7 culture, gaseous, thermal
DiFranco: 3 Ani
dig: 3 get, hoe 4 barb, bore, gibe, grok, grub, jibe, like, mine, poke, root, seek, slam, slap, slur, snub, till, work 5 abuse, adore, crack, delve, enjoy, get it, gouge, grasp, libel, probe, scorn, stick, study, taunt 6 burrow, dredge, follow, garden, insult, rebuff, relish, search, slight, tunnel 7 affront, calumny, catcall, catch on, disdain, mockery, obloquy, offense, put-down, sarcasm, slander 8 bulldoze, contempt, derision, excavate, relate to, ridicule, scoop out 9 aspersion, cheap shot, contumely, hollow out, lucubrate, undermine, wisecrack 10 appreciate, comprehend, defamation, disrespect, excavation, opprobrium, understand
discovery: 5 shard, sherd
for: 4 hunt, mine, seek
for info: 3 ask 8 research
in: 3 eat 4 wolf 5 eat up 7 scarf up 8 chow down, entrench 9 scarf down
in one's heels: 4 balk 5 baulk 6 refuse, resist
into: 4 look, pore, sift 5 plumb 6 plunge 7 deplete, examine, explore

into the past: 6 recall 8 remember
out: 5 scoop 6 deepen, elicit, hollow, remove 7 rummage 8 dislodge, excavate
starter: 4 shin
up: 4 find, mine 5 learn, raise 6 detect, dredge, exhume, locate, uproot 7 collect, rout out, uncover, unearth 8 discover, disinter, excavate, research 9 ferret out, search out 10 come across
dig __: 3 out 4 into
__ dig: 5 infra
Digby, Kenelm: 7 British 11 philosopher
digest: 3 cut, eat 4 lump, trim 5 brief, study, sum up 6 absorb, aperçu, ingest, ponder, précis, reduce, report, résumé, survey, take in 7 abridge, analyze, compile, consume, epitome, pandect, scissor, shorten, summary, swallow 8 abstract, boil down, compress, condense, consider, magazine, synopsis 9 summarize, synopsize, think over 10 abbreviate, abridgment, assimilate, compendium, paraphrase
__ Digest: 7 Reader's
digestible: 5 light 6 edible 10 alimentary
digestion: 10 absorption
aid: 4 bile 6 bicarb, enzyme
digestive: 10 alimentary
organ: 5 liver 7 stomach
digestive __: 5 gland, tract 6 system
digestive-tract part: 5 ileum
digger: 4 mole 5 miner 6 badger, gopher 9 groundhog, woodchuck
org.: 3 UMW
tool: 4 pick, spud 5 spade 6 shovel
wasp: 3 bug 6 insect
__ digger: 4 gold
Digger: 5 O'Dell 6 Barnes, Phelps
digging __: 5 stick
Diggin' on You (1995 song) artist: TLC
__ Diggity: 3 Hot
Diggs: 4 Taye
DiGiorno: 5 pizza
alternative: 5 Jeno's, Tony's 6 Ellio's 7 Celeste, Totino's 9 Tombstone 10 Freschetta
digit: 3 one, six, toe, two 4 five, four, nine, unit 5 eight, pinky, seven, three, thumb 6 big toe, dactyl, figure, finger, member, number, pinkie 7 numeral 9 appendage
binary ~: 3 one 4 zero
double-looped ~: 5 eight
lower ~: 3 toe
opposable ~: 5 thumb
top ~: 4 nine
use a ~: 5 point
__ digit: 6 binary
__-digit: 6 double, single, triple
digital
adjunct: 4 nail
device: 2 PC
display: 4 time
not ~: 6 analog
watch display: 3 LCD, LED
digital __: 5 clock, watch 7 display, readout
digitize: 4 scan
dignified: 5 grand, great, lofty, noble, proud, regal, staid 6 august, formal, lordly, ritual, sedate, solemn 7 courtly, elegant, eminent, exalted, gallant, pompous, refined, stately 8 decorous, elevated, highbred, highbrow, imperial, imposing, ladylike 9 honorable, imperious, respected, venerable
dignify: 4 lift 5 exalt, grace, honor, raise 6 praise 7 elevate
dignitary: 3 VIP 4 lion, name, star 5 nabob 6 big gun, bigwig, figure, kahuna, leader 7 bigshot, notable, officer 8 luminary, official, somebody 9 celebrity, personage
dignity: 4 rank 5 glory, honor, merit, poise, state, worth 6 regard, status, virtue 7 decency, decorum, hauteur, majesty, respect, stature 8 elegance, eminence, grandeur, nobility, prestige, standing 9 composure, etiquette, greatness, propriety, solemnity 10 kingliness, refinement, sedateness, self-esteem, worthiness
digress: 4 roam, turn, vary 5 drift, stray 6 ramble, wander 7 deviate, diverge 8 divagate
..__ digress!: 4 But I
digression: 5 aside 6 detour 7 veering 8 drifting, straying 9 departure, deviation, diversion, excursion, variation, wandering 10 apostrophe, deflection, difference, discursion, divagation, divergence
digressive: 7 diffuse 8 episodic, rambling 9 excursive 10 discursive, episodical, tangential
digs: 3 pad 4 home 5 abode, house 7 habitat, housing 8 dwelling, lodgment, quarters 9 residence
crude ~: 3 hut 5 hovel, lodge, shack 6 lean-to
fancy ~: 5 manor, villa 6 estate 7 chateau, mansion 10 plantation
see also home
Dijon: 4 city, town
locale: 6 France
river: 5 Ouche
Dijon __: 7 mustard
Dik: 6 Browne
dik-dik: 6 animal 8 antelope
relative: 3 gnu, kob 4 guib, kudu, oryx, puku, topi 5 addax, bongo, chiru, eland, goral, korin, nyala, oribi, saiga, serow 6 chammy, duiker, impala, koodoo, lechwe, nilgai, rhebok, shammy, shamoy 7 blaubok, blesbok, chamois, defassa, gazelle, gemsbok, gerenuk, grysbok, nylghai, nylghau, sassaby 8 blesbuck, bontebok, bushbuck, gemsbuck, reedbuck, steenbok, steinbok 9 blackbuck, pronghorn, sitatunga, springbok, waterbuck 10 hartebeest, wildebeest
dike: 3 bar, dam 4 bank, foss, wall, weir 5 check, fosse, levee 6 embank, trench 7 barrier, channel, sea wall 8 causeway, obstacle, retainer 9 barricade 10 embankment, impediment
problem: 4 leak
diktat: 7 penalty 10 punishment, settlement
__ di Lammermoor: 5 Lucia
dilapidated: 4 shot, worn 5 dingy, ratty, seedy, tacky 6 beat-up, crumby, crummy, grungy, ragged, shabby, shoddy, sleazy 7 damaged, decayed, in ruins, rickety, run-down, unkempt 8 decaying, decrepit, derelict, timeworn 10 ramshackle, tumbledown
dilapidation: 4 wear 5 decay 6 blight 7 neglect
dilate: 3 wax 4 grow 5 bloat, bulge, swell, widen 6 expand, extend, spread 7 augment, balloon, broaden, burgeon, distend, enlarge, inflate, magnify, stretch 8 bourgeon, heighten, lengthen
dilated: 4 wide
dilation: 5 bulge 6 spread 8 swelling 9 expansion
dilator's place: 3 eye 5 pupil
dilatory: 3 lax 4 late, lazy, poky, slow 5 slack, tardy 6 draggy, remiss 7 gradual, halting, impeded, laggard, lagging, languid, unready 8 crawling, creeping, dallying, dawdling, delaying, dragging, drawn-out, hesitant, plodding, slothful, sluggish, tarrying, toddling 9 leisurely, lethargic, lingering, prolonged, snaillike, unhurried 10 deliberate, last-minute, protracted
maneuver: 5 stall
Dilbert: 5 strip 10 comic strip
cartoonist: Scott Adams
character: 4 Asok, Tina 5 Alice, Carol, Wally 7 Catbert, Dogbert, Ratbert, The Boss
place: 4 desk 6 office
dilemma: 3 fix, jam, rub 4 bind, case, knot, mess, spot 6 corner, crisis, muddle, pickle, plight, scrape, strait 7 problem, trouble 8 exigence, exigency, juncture, quagmire, quandary 9 deep water 10 difficulty
in a ~: 4 torn
dilettante: 4 tiro, tyro 6 novice 7 amateur, dabbler 8 beginner, putterer 9 greenhorn, layperson, unskilled 10 amateurish, tenderfoot, uninitiate
dilettantish: 4 arty 5 artsy
Dili: 4 city, town 7 capital
locale: 9 East Timor
diligence: 4 care, zeal 5 labor, rigor, vigor 6 effort 8 exertion, industry, keenness, patience, tenacity 9 alertness, assiduity, attention, briskness, constancy, fixedness, intensity, quickness 10 intentness
diligent: 6 active 7 careful, earnest, intense 8 resolute, sedulous, studious, tireless 9 assiduous, attentive, laborious, unfailing 10 persistent, unflagging, unwearying
diligently: 4 hard
dill: 4 anet, herb
dill __: 6 pickle
Dillard, Annie: 6 author, writer
__-diller: 6 killer 7 chiller
Diller: 5 Barry 7 Phyllis
Dillinger: 4 John
foe: 3 FBI 4 G-man 6 Hoover
Dillinger (1945 film)
cast: Anne Jeffreys, Edmund Lowe, Lawrence Tierney
Dillinger (1973 film)
cast: Richard Dreyfuss, Ben Johnson, Cloris Leachman, Warren Oates, Michelle Phillips
Dillman, Bradford: 5 actor
film: The Bridge at Remagen (1969) Brother John (1970) Escape From the Planet of the Apes (1971) Mastermind (1976) Piranha (1978) The Resurrection of Zachary Wheeler (1971) Sudden Impact (1983) The Way We Were (1973)
Dillon: 4 Matt 7 Melinda
Dillon, Matt: 5 actor
film: Beautiful Girls (1996) The Big Town (1987) Drugstore Cowboy (1989) The Flamingo Kid (1984) In & Out (1997) One Night at McCool's (2001) Over the Edge (1979) Rumble Fish (1983) Tex (1982) There's Something About Mary (1998) To Die For (1995) Wild Things (1998)
Dillon, Melinda: 7 actress
film: Bound for Glory (1976) A Christmas Story (1983) Close Encounters of the Third Kind (1977) F.I.S.T. (1978)
Dill Pickle, A author: Mansfield
dilly: 3 pip 4 lulu, oner 5 beaut, doozy, poser 6 corker, doozie 10 ripsnorter
dillydallier: 5 idler 9 lazybones
dillydally: 3 haw, lag 4 idle, laze, loaf, poke 5 amble, delay, mosey, stall, tarry, waver 6 dawdle, linger, loiter, put off, trifle 7 saunter, whiffle 8 hesitate, lollygag, straggle 9 waste time
dilute: 3 cut 4 thin, weak 5 water 6 impair, lessen, reduce, watery, weaken 7 lighten, vitiate 8 decrease, diminish 9 attenuate, water down 10 adulterate
diluted: 3 cut 4 tame, thin, weak 6 impure, watery
not ~: 4 neat, pure 5 uncut
dim: 3 fog 4 blur, dark, fade, hazy, mist, pale, slow, soft, veil, wane, weak 5 befog, blear, cloud, dense, dingy, dusky, faded, faint, fuzzy, lower, mirky, misty, muddy, murky, muted, shade, shady, thick, vague 6 bleary, cloudy, darken, gloomy, ill-lit, oafish, obtuse, opaque, shadow, somber, stupid 7 becloud, blacken, blurred, boorish, darkish, doltish, obscure, shadowy, Stygian, subdued, tarnish, unclear 8 darkened, lowering, nebulous, obscured, tone down, turn down 9 adumbrate, candlelit, lightless, obfuscate, tenebrous, toned down, uncertain, unlighted 10 ill-defined, indistinct, lackluster, lusterless, overshadow, pedestrian
ender: 3 wit
suddenly: 5 go out
take a ~ view of: 5 knock, scorn 7 censure, deplore, put down, run down 8 belittle, derogate, disfavor 9 deprecate, disesteem, disparage, poor-mouth 10 disapprove
view: 5 gloom 7 despair, sadness 8 cynicism, glumness 9 dejection, pessimism 10 depression, gloominess, melancholy, woefulness
dim __: 3 sum 4 bulb
DiMaggio: 3 Dom, Joe 5 Vince
DiMaggio, Joe: 6 Yankee 10 outfielder
spouse: Marilyn Monroe
uniform number: 4 five
Dim All the Lights (1979 song) artist: Donna Summer
dimanche: 6 French, Sunday
follower: 5 lundi
preceder: 6 samedi
__ Dimas: 3 San
Dimbovita: 5 river
city on the ~: 9 Bucharest
locale: 7 Romania
dime: 4 coin 5 money 6 change
18th-century ~: 5 disme
like a ~: 4 clad, thin
like a new ~: 5 shiny
store: 4 mart 6 market
symbol on a ~: 5 torch
without a ~: 5 broke 9 penniless
word on a ~: 3 God, one 4 unum 5 trust 6 States, United 7 America, liberty 8 pluribus
dime __: 5 novel, store
dime-a-dozen: 6 common 7 humdrum, liberal, profuse 9 bountiful
dimension: 4 bulk, size 5 ambit, depth, range, reach, realm, scale, scope, width 6 aspect, extent, format, height, length, volume 7 breadth, compass, measure 8 capacity 9 amplitude, magnitude
fourth ~: 4 time
give ~: 8 flesh out
rectangular ~: 5 width 6 length
to a builder: 4 spec

__ **dimension:** 5 fifth, first, third 6 fourth, second
__ **Dimension:** 5 Fifth
Dimetapp: 10 cough syrup
alternative: 5 Afrin 6 Contac, Nyquil, Tavist 7 Actifed, Comtrex, Dayquil, Dristan, Sinutab, Sudafed 8 Benadryl, Drixoral, TheraFlu 9 Coricidin, Triaminic 10 Robitussin
diminish: 3 cut, ebb, lag, sag 4 bate, curb, drop, fall, lull, pale, pare, sink, slow, wane 5 abate, break, drain, dwarf, let up, lower, prune, relax, slack, taper 6 change, dampen, deaden, deduct, demean, dilute, lessen, rebate, recede, reduce, shrink, soften, weaken, worsen 7 abridge, cheapen, curtail, cut down, decline, deflate, deplete, depress, detract, drop off, dwindle, fall off, mollify, put down, qualify, run down, shorten, slacken, subside, tail off, take off, take out, thin out, whittle 8 belittle, blow over, contract, decrease, derogate, discount, downsize, head away, minimize, mitigate, moderate, peter out, subtract, take away, taper off, tear down, withhold 9 extenuate, retrocede 10 abbreviate
diminished: 3 cut 4 less 5 let up, lower, short 7 limited, partial 8 lessened
by: 4 less 5 minus
diminishing: 8 decrease 9 on the wane
diminishing __: 7 returns
diminution: 3 cut, ebb 4 drop, fall, slip 7 cutback, decline 8 decrease, discount 9 abatement, deduction, lessening, reduction, remission, weakening
diminutive: 3 wee 4 baby, itsy, puny, tiny 5 bitty, dwarf, elfin, pigmy, pygmy, short, small, teeny, weeny 6 atomic, bantam, little, midget, minute, peewee, petite, pocket, slight, teensy 7 stunted, trivial 8 atomical, atomlike, nickname 9 itsy-bitsy, itty-bitty, miniature, pint-sized, undersize 10 teeny-weeny, undersized, vest-pocket
Spanish suffix: 3 -ita, -ito
suffix: 3 -cle, -ine, -kin, -let, -nik, -ock, -rel, -ula, -ule 4 -ella, -elle, -ette, -kins, -ling
Dimitri: 7 Tiomkin
__ **Dimittis:** 4 Nunc
dimity: 6 cotton, fabric 8 material
dimmed: 5 blear 6 bleary
combining form: 5 ambly- 6 amblyo-
dimmer __: 6 switch
dimness: 4 blur, haze, pall 5 blear, gloom, shade 6 shadow
dimple: 3 pit 4 dent 5 cleft 6 hollow 10 depression
site: 4 chin
dim sum: 9 appetizer
additive: 3 MSG
cooker: 3 wok
Dim Sum: a Little Bit of Heart (1984 film)
cast: Kim Chew, Laureen Chew, Victor Wong
director: Wayne Wang
dimunition: 3 cut
__ **dim view:** 5 take a
dimwit: 3 ass, nit, oaf, sap 4 boob, bozo, clod, dolt, dope, fool, gowk, simp, twit 5 chump, clown, cluck, dummy, dunce, goose, joker, ninny, patsy, stupe 6 baboon, lubber, lummox, stupid, sucker, turkey 7 buffoon, dingbat, dullard, fathead, jackass, pinhead, saphead 8 bonehead, dumbbell, meathead, numskull 9 birdbrain, blockhead, harebrain, lamebrain, numbskull, simpleton 10 dunderhead, nincompoop
dimwitted: 4 dopy, dull, slow 5 dense, dopey, silly, thick 6 obtuse, simple 7 doltish, foolish, witless 8 mindless
din: 4 roar, stir 5 babel, blast, hoo-ha, noise, sound 6 bedlam, clamor, hubbub, jangle, racket, ruckus, rumpus, tumult, uproar 7 clangor, clatter, discord, thunder 8 brouhaha, disquiet 9 cacophony, commotion, hue and cry 10 clattering, hullabaloo
Din: 4 Beth 5 Gunga
Dina: 5 Meyer 6 Spybey 7 Merrill
Dinah: 3 cat 5 Shore 6 Manoff 10 Washington
brother: 3 Dan, Gad 4 Levi 5 Asher, Judah 6 Joseph, Reuben, Simeon 7 Zebulun 8 Benjamin, Issachar, Naphtali
parent: 4 Leah 5 Jacob
uncle: 4 Esau
__ **Dinah:** 4 De De
Dinah Shore Classic org.: 4 LPGA
dinar: 4 coin 5 money
country: 4 Irak, Iran, Iraq 5 Libya
Dinaric: 4 Alps
din-din: 4 meal 6 supper
d'Indy: 7 Vincent
dine: 3 eat, sup 5 feast
at home: 5 eat in
partner: 4 wine
wine and ~: 3 woo 4 feed, fete 5 treat 9 entertain
diner: 3 car 4 café 5 eater 6 bistro, eatery 8 gourmand 9 hash house, lunchroom 10 restaurant
add-on: 3 tip
ad words: 5 eat at
beverage: 3 joe, tea 4 milk, soda 6 coffee 7 iced tea
choice: 6 entrée
employee: 4 cook 6 waiter 7 cashier 8 waitress
fare: 4 eats
freebie: 4 mint, salt 5 jelly, sugar, syrup, water 6 catsup, napkin, pepper 7 ketchup, mustard
go to a ~: 6 eat out
handout: 4 menu
offering: 3 BLT, pie 5 chile, chili, lunch 6 chilli, omelet 8 omelette
order, with the: 5 usual
patron: 7 trucker
sign: 4 eats, neon
sitcom ~: 4 Mel's
tab: 5 check
see also restaurant
Diner (1982 film)
cast: Kevin Bacon, Ellen Barkin, Steve Guttenberg, Paul Reiser, Mickey Rourke, Daniel Stern
director: Barry Levinson
__ **Diner:** 4 Mel's, Tom's
dinero: 3 oof 4 cash, gelt, jack, kail, kale, loot, peag, pelf 5 bills, bread, bucks, dough, funds, lucre, money, moola, mopus, pesos, rhino, sewan 6 do-re-mi, mammon, mazuma, moolah, seawan, silver, specie, wampum, wealth 7 cabbage, capital, dollars, lettuce, ooftish, scratch, shekels 8 bankroll, cold cash, currency, hard cash, smackers 9 banknotes, frogskins, long green, simoleons 10 greenbacks, green stuff
con mucho ~: 4 rico
unit: 4 peso
where el ~ is: 5 banco
Diner's Club: 10 credit card
use: 3 owe 6 charge
Dinesen, Isak: 6 Danish, writer
on film: Streep
real name: Karen Blixen
work: Out of Africa
Seven Gothic Tales
Winter's Tales
dinette: 4 nook
piece: 5 chair
place: 6 alcove
dinette __: 3 set
ding: 3 mar 4 dent, nick, slam, sock, swat 5 whack 6 jingle, tinkle
ender: 3 bat
starter: 4 wing
ding-__: 4 dong 5 a-ling
__**-ding:** 4 wing
ding-a-ling: 3 ass, oaf, sap 4 boob, clod, ditz, dolt, fool, kook, yo-yo 5 chump, clown, cluck, dummy, dunce, joker, ninny, patsy 6 dimwit, lubber, lummox, nitwit, sucker, turkey 7 buffoon, dullard, fathead, half-wit, jackass, pinhead, saphead 8 bonehead, dumbbell, meathead, numskull 9 birdbrain, blockhead, harebrain, lamebrain, numbskull, simpleton 10 decoration, dunderhead, nincompoop
dingbat: 3 ass, oaf, sap 4 boob, clod, ditz, dolt, fool, kook, yo-yo 5 chump, clown, cluck, dummy, dunce, joker, ninny, patsy 6 dimwit, lubber, lummox, nitwit, sucker, turkey 7 buffoon, dullard, fathead, half-wit, jackass, pinhead, saphead 8 bonehead, dumbbell, meathead, numskull 9 adornment, birdbrain, blockhead, harebrain, lamebrain, numbskull, simpleton 10 decoration, dunderhead, nincompoop
Dingbat: 5 Edith
daughter: 6 Gloria
ding-dong: 5 chime
Ding dong __...: 4 bell
dinger: 4 bell 5 homer 7 home run
dinghy: 4 boat 5 craft, skiff 7 rowboat
need: 3 oar
propel a ~: 3 row
dingle: 4 dale, dell, glen 6 hollow, valley
Dingle Bay locale: 7 Ireland
dingo: 3 dog 5 canid 6 animal, canine 10 Australian
relative: 3 fox 4 wolf 5 dhole 6 corsac, coydog, coyote, fennec, jackal
__ **Dings:** 4 Ring
dingus: 5 dodad, thing 6 doodad, widget
dingy: 3 dim 4 daft, dark, drab, gray, grey 5 dirty, grimy, mirky, murky, seedy, smoky, tacky 6 dismal, dreary, ill-lit, ragged, shabby, shoddy, somber 7 run-down, squalid 8 slovenly 10 broken-down, lusterless, threadbare
__ **Dinh Diem:** 3 Ngo
dining
amenity: 5 doily 6 doyley, napkin
area: 4 hall 6 alcove
car sandwich: 4 club
enticement: 5 aroma
room: 4 mess 7 commons 8 chow hall, mess hall 9 cafeteria, refectory 10 triclinium
utensil: 4 fork 5 knife, spoon
dining __: 3 car 4 hall, room 5 table
dining-room
piece: 5 hutch
staffer: 6 busboy, waiter 8 waitress
__**-dink:** 5 rinky
Dinka: 5 Nilot
home: 5 Sudan 6 Africa
__ **Dinka Doo:** 4 Inka
Dinkins: 5 David
dinkum: 4 real 9 authentic
__ **dinkum:** 4 fair, hard
dinky: 4 punk, tiny 5 minor, small, teeny 6 lesser, little, shabby, teensy 8 picayune, trifling 9 small-time 10 bush-league, second-rate
__ **Dinky Parlay Voo:** 5 Hinky
__ **Dinmont:** 6 Dandie
dinner: 4 meal 5 feast, party 6 buffet, entrée, repast, supper 7 banquet 9 collation, reception
and a movie: 4 date
beverage: 4 port, wine
bird: 4 duck 5 capon, frier, fryer 6 turkey 7 chicken, roaster
celebrity ~: 5 roast
ceremonial ~: 5 seder
chuck wagon ~: 4 grub
course: 4 soup 5 salad 6 entrée 7 dessert 9 appetizer
ender: 4 time, ware
faux pas: 4 burp
follower: 5 movie
formal ~: 4 fete, meal 5 feast, party 6 repast, spread 7 banquet
get ready for ~: 5 dress
GI ~: 4 mess
have ~: 3 eat, sup 5 feast 10 break bread
invite to ~: 4 feed 6 ask out
jacket: 3 tux 4 tuck 6 tuxedo
make ~: 4 bake, cook 7 prepare
order for ~: 3 get 4 have 5 enjoy 7 procure
part: 6 entrée
party: 5 salon 6 soiree
preceder: 5 grace
put out ~: 5 serve
scraps: 4 orts
setting: 5 place
signal: 4 bell
stay home for ~: 5 eat in
dinner __: 4 bell, fork, ring 5 dance, dress, knife, plate, table 6 jacket 7 clothes, theater, theatre
__ **dinner:** 5 shore 6 basket, boiled 7 carry-in, potluck
__**-dinner:** 5 after
Dinner at Antoine's author: 5 Keyes
Dinner at Eight: 4 film, play
author: 6 Ferber 7 Kaufman
cast: John Barrymore, Lionel Barrymore, Wallace Beery, Marie Dressler, Jean Harlow
character: 3 Dan 4 Dora, Tina 5 Kitty, Paula, Ricci, Vance 6 Hattie, Oliver 7 Gustave 8 Carlotta 9 Millicent
director: George Cukor
Dinner at the Homesick Restaurant
author: Anne Tyler
__**-dinner mint:** 5 after
Dinner Party, The author: Howard Fast
dinnerware: 5 china 6 dishes 8 ceramics, crockery 9 porcelain
item: 4 bowl 5 plate 6 saucer
Dinner With Drac (1958 song) artist: John Zacherle
Dinning, Mark song: Teen Angel (1960)
Dino: 3 pet
master: 4 Fred
Dino De __: 10 Laurentiis
dino follower: 4 saur
dinornis robustus: 3 moa
dinosaur: 4 T-rex 6 animal, lizard 7 reptile 8 allosaur, obsolete, sauropod, theropod 9 iguanodon, leviathan, pterosaur, stegosaur, supersaur 10 brontosaur, diplodocus, megalosaur, titanosaur 11 brachiosaur, ichthyosaur, triceratops, tyrannosaur
bone: 6 fossil
DNA preserver: 5 amber
preserver: 3 bog, tar 6 tar pit
Dinosaur (2000 film)
voice cast: Ossie Davis, D.B. Sweeney, Alfre Woodard
dinosaurian: 3 big
dinothere: 8 elephant
dinotherian: 3 big
Dinsmore: 5 Elsie
dint: 3 vim 4 thew 5 brawn, force, might, power, thews, vigor 6 effort, energy, muscle 7 fitness, muscles, potence,

potency, stamina **8** exertion, strength, vitality **9** beefiness, endurance, fortitude, hardiness, huskiness, puissance, stoutness, toughness **10** brawniness, brute force, mightiness, robustness, sturdiness
Dinty: **5** Moore
diocese: **3** see **7** prelacy **9** bishopric **10** episcopacy, episcopate
Diocletian: **5** Roman **6** Caesar
__ diode: **5** zener
Diogenes: **5** Greek **11** philosopher
specialty: **8** Cynicism
Diomede: **4** isls. **5** isles **7** islands
Dion
last name: Di Mucci
song: Abraham, Martin and John (1968)
Donna the Prima Donna (1963)
Drip Drop (1963)
Little Diane (1962)
Love Came to Me (1962)
Lovers Who Wander (1962)
Ruby Baby (1963)
Runaround Sue (1961)
The Wanderer (1961)
Dion and the Belmonts
song: A Teenager in Love (1959)
Where or When (1960)
Dion, Celine
homeland: Canada
song: All by Myself (1997)
Beauty and the Beast (1992)
Because You Loved Me (1996)
If You Asked Me to (1992)
I'm Your Angel (1998)
It's All Coming Back to Me Now (1996)
My Heart Will Go On (1998)
A New Day Has Come (2002)
The Power of Love (1993)
That's the Way It Is (1999)
Where Does My Heart Beat Now (1991)
Dione: **4** moon **5** giant, Titan
daughter: **9** Aphrodite
parent: **4** Gaea **6** Uranus
planet: **6** Saturn
son: **6** Pelops
Dionne: **5** Marie **6** Farris, Marcel **7** Warwick
Dionne, Marcel: **8** puckster
see also hockey
Dionysius: **4** pope **5** saint, Thrax **7** Exiguus, pontiff
mountain where ~ was hidden: **4** Nysa
Dionysus
animal sacred to ~: **4** goat, lion, lynx **5** tiger **7** dolphin, panther
attendant: **5** satyr
daughter: **8** Deianira, Pasithea
epithet: **6** Lyaeus **7** Lenaeus **9** Pyrigenes, Thriambus
equivalent: **7** Bacchus
lover: **4** Aura, Hera **5** Carya **6** Nicaea **7** Althaea, Ariadne, Physcoa **9** Aphrodite
parent: **4** Zeus **6** Semele **7** Demeter
plant sacred to ~: **3** ivy **4** rose, vine **6** laurel **8** asphodel
son: **5** Thoas **6** Phlias **7** Ceramus, Iacchus **8** Narcaeus, Oenopion **9** Eurymedon, Staphylus **10** Peparethus
Dior, Christian: **6** French **8** designer
design: **5** A-line
Dioscorus: **4** pope **7** pontiff
Diotima: **4** font **8** asteroid, typeface
__ dioxide: **4** lead **6** barium, carbon, sulfur **7** silicon, uranium
dip: **3** nod, sag, set, wet **4** bath, dive, drop, duck, dunk, fade, fall, sink, skim, soak, swim, tilt, wash **5** bathe, droop, fondu, lower, pitch, rinse, salsa, scoop, slide, slope, slump, souse, swoop **6** crouch, drench, fondue, go down, plunge, recede, swerve, tumble **7** curtsey, decline, descend, descent, dunking, falloff, immerse, incline, moisten, plummet, soaking **8** downturn, drop down, infusion, lowering, nose-dive, submerge, submerse **9** guacamole, immersion, sour cream, worsening **10** depression, pickpocket
ender: **5** stick
ingredient: **5** chive, onion **9** sour cream
into: **4** read, scan
landscape ~: **4** glen **6** dingle, valley
out a boat: **4** bail
place for a ~: **4** pool
take a ~: **4** swim
__ dip: **4** head **5** chip 'n **6** French
__-dip: **5** sheep **6** double
__ di pesce: **5** zuppa
...Dipinto __: **5** di Blu
diplodocus: **8** dinosaur
diploma: **5** paper **6** degree **9** sheepskin
holder: **4** grad **6** alumna **7** alumnus **8** graduate
word: **3** cum **4** arts **5** laude, magna, summa **7** science
diploma __: **4** mill
diplomacy: **4** tact **5** craft, poise, skill **7** finesse **8** delicacy, politics, subtlety **10** artfulness, discretion, expedience, statecraft
alternative: **3** war
breakdown: **4** rift
__ diplomacy: **6** dollar **7** gunboat, shuttle
Diplomacy for the Next Century
author: **4** Eban
diplomat: **3** amb. **5** envoy, fixer **6** consul, legate **7** attaché **8** emissary, minister **10** ambassador, negotiator, peacemaker
home: **3** emb. **7** embassy
Diplomat: **3** car **4** auto **5** Dodge
diplomate: **8** graduate
diplomatic: **4** wise **5** civil, suave **6** artful, irenic, polite, subtle **7** correct, politic, prudent, tactful **8** delicate, dextrous, discreet, gracious, irenical, pleasant **9** conniving, courteous, dexterous, judicious, sensitive, strategic **10** contriving, intriguing, thoughtful
code: **8** protocol
success: **4** pact **6** accord
diplomatic __: **4** body **5** corps, pouch
Diplomatic Courier (1952 film)
cast: Stephen McNally, Patricia Neal, Tyrone Power
director: Henry Hathaway
dipole: **6** two-rod **10** rabbit ears
dipole __: **6** moment **7** antenna
dipper: **4** bail, bird **5** ladle, ousel, ouzel, scoop **6** bailer, ladler
__ Dipper: **3** Big **6** Little
dipping: **8** downhill **9** immersion
dippy: **5** goofy, inane, silly **6** absurd **9** eccentric
dipsy-__: **6** doodle
Dipsy: **9** Teletubby
dir.: **2** NE, NW, SE, SW **3** EbN, EbS, ENE, ESE, hdg., NNE, NNW, SSE, SSW, WbN, WbS, WNW, WSW
Dirac, Paul: **7** British **8** Nobelist **9** physicist, scientist
dire: **4** grim **5** acute, awful, dread, grave, sorry, woful **6** bitter, horrid, mortal, somber, tragic, urgent, woeful **7** baleful, burning, crucial, drastic, dreaded, exigent, extreme, fearful, harmful, hurry-up, instant, ominous, painful, ruinous, serious **8** alarming, critical, dreadful, exigeant, fearsome, grievous, horrible, horrific, pressing, terrible, tragical **9** appalling, desperate, frightful, ill-boding, ill-omened, insistent **10** calamitous, deplorable, disastrous, formidable, lamentable, petrifying
in ~ straits: **5** needy **6** hard-up
straits: **6** crisis, penury **7** trouble
__ dire: **4** voir
__-dire: **3** oui **5** c'est-à
dirección: **4** este
direct: **3** aim, bid, run, set **4** boss, head, lead, mail, open, rule, send, ship, show, tell, true, turn **5** apply, bluff, blunt, clear, drive, edify, exact, focus, frank, guide, level, order, pilot, plain, point, prime, refer, right, route, short, slant, steer, swing, teach, train, tutor **6** abrupt, advise, candid, charge, devote, enjoin, govern, handle, head-on, head up, honest, inform, jockey, linear, manage, orient, simple **7** address, arrange, channel, command, conduct, control, correct, counsel, dictate, express, natural, nearest, nonstop, operate, oversee, precise, preside, produce, require, sincere **8** absolute, accurate, dominate, engineer, explicit, instruct, navigate, out-front, outright, personal, positive, regulate, shepherd, shortest, straight, unbroken **9** designate, downright, firsthand, immediate, influence, officiate, outspoken, prescribe, supervise **10** administer, continuous, face-to-face, flat-footed, forthright, foursquare, from the hip, give orders, manipulate, mastermind, point-blank, ride herd on, run the show, show the way, to the point, unaffected, unmediated, unreserved, unreticent, unswerving
elsewhere: **5** refer
ender: **3** ion, ive, ory **5** orate
in ~ opposition: **10** face-to-face, unmediated
direct __: **3** sum, tax **4** cost, mail **5** labor **6** action, cinema, method, object **7** address, current, deposit, primary, product
direct-__: **4** dial **6** access, acting **7** examine
directed __: **7** verdict
__ directed: **5** Use as
__-directed: **5** inner, other
direction: **3** way **4** east, left, path, side, tack, tide, west **5** drift, north, order, route, slant, south, tenor, track, trend **6** behest, charge, course, recipe **7** bearing, bidding, conduct, control, dictate, heading, outlook, precept, purpose, quarter, running **8** bearings, guidance, tendency **9** education, guideline, influence, objective, ordinance, viewpoint **10** advisement, aspiration, government, indication, leadership, likelihood, management, proclivity, regulation, standpoint, trajectory
change ~: **3** yaw, zag **4** tack, turn, veer, wind
change of ~: **3** uey **5** U-turn **9** one-eighty
compass ~: **2** NE, NW, SE, SW **3** ENE, ESE, NNE, NNW, SSE, SSW, WNW, WSW **4** east, west **5** north, point, south
cookbook ~: **3** add, fry **4** bake, boil, chop, dice, heat, stir, warm **5** baste, chill, roast, sauté, scald, slice
finding: **5** radar
French ~: **3** est, sud **4** nord **5** ouest
German ~: **3** ost **5** osten, süden **6** norden, westen
in another ~: **4** away
it can move in any ~: **5** queen
musical ~: **5** dolce, forte, largo, secco **6** arioso, da capo
nautical ~: **3** aft, EbN, EbS, SbE **4** alee, fore **5** abeam, aport **6** astern
provide ~: **5** steer
show the ~: **5** point
sign: **5** arrow
Spanish ~: **3** sur **4** este **5** norte, oeste
stage ~: **4** exit **5** enter **6** exeunt
suffix: **3** -ern
direction __: **5** angle **6** cosine, finder, number
__ direction: **5** stage
directional __: **6** signal **7** antenna
directionless: **5** blind **6** adrift **7** erratic
directions: **5** specs **6** advice, recipe **7** formula **10** indication
follow ~: **4** mind, obey
needing ~: **4** lost
directive: **4** memo, rule, word **5** edict, order, ukase **6** behest, charge, decree, firman, ruling **7** command, mandate, message **9** ordinance **10** injunction, memorandum, regulation
directly: **3** due, new **4** anon, ASAP, soon **5** ad rem, plumb, right, smack, spang **6** at once, openly, pronto, simply **7** exactly, frankly, quickly, shortly **8** candidly, honestly, in person, promptly, smack dab, straight, verbatim **9** forthwith, in a moment, in a second, instantly, literally, posthaste, precisely, presently, right away **10** face-to-face, forthright, personally, point-blank, unswerving
directness: **6** candor **7** clarity
director: **4** boss, exec, head **5** chair, chief, super **6** gerent, honcho, leader, master, regent, top dog, tycoon **7** captain, curator, foreman, headman, kingpin, manager, officer, skipper **8** governor, kingfish, official, overseer, superior **9** commander, conductor, executive, organizer, principal **10** controller, headmaster, mastermind, supervisor
award: **5** Oscar
shoot: **4** take **6** retake
viewing: **6** rushes **7** dailies
windup: **4** wrap
yell: **3** cut **5** print **6** action
director __: **7** general
__ director: **3** art **5** stage **6** cruise **7** casting, program **8** managing
directors: **5** board, panel **7** council **10** management
director's __: **5** chair
directory: **4** book, list, roll **5** guide, index **6** lineup, record, roster **7** catalog, who's who **8** handbook, register **9** catalogue **10** white pages
entry: **4** name
dirge: **4** hymn, tune **5** elegy, music **6** lament, melody, monody **7** requiem **8** threnody
tempo: **5** lento
dirham: **5** money
country: **4** Iraq, Irak **5** Libya, Qatar **6** Kuwait **7** Morocco, Tunisia
dirigible: **5** blimp **7** airship, balloon **8** aircraft, zeppelin
filler: **6** helium
like a ~: **3** LTA **5** rigid
Dirigo is its motto: **5** Maine
dirk: **4** shiv, snee **5** knife, skean, skene **6** dagger, weapon **7** sidearm
Dirk: **4** Pitt **7** Bogarde **8** Benedict
dirndl: **5** dress, skirt
dirt: **3** mud **4** crud, grit, guck, gunk, info, land, loam, mire, muck, scum, soil **5** earth, filth, grime, rumor **6** gossip, ground, grunge, skinny **7** earthen,

lowdown, scandal, slander, topsoil 8 impurity 10 defamation
cheap: 8 a good buy 10 economical
chunk of ~: 4 clod
devoid of ~: 5 clean
dish ~: 6 gossip
do ~ to: 5 wrong
fling ~: 4 slur 5 libel, smear, sully, taint 6 defame, impugn, malign, vilify 7 asperse, slander, traduce 8 backbite, besmirch, throw mud 9 disparage 10 calumniate
get rid of ~: 4 wash 5 scour, scrub
hit pay ~: 5 score 7 prevail
hit the ~: 4 fall 5 slide 6 topple
path: 5 trail
pay ~: 3 ore 4 lode 8 solution
poor: 5 needy 8 strapped 9 penniless
remover: 4 soap
smear: 6 smudge
wet ~: 3 mud
dirt __: 4 bike, farm, road 6 farmer
dirt-__: 4 poor 5 cheap
__ dirt: 3 pay
dirtbag: 3 cad 6 bad egg
dirtied: 5 sooty 8 maculate, vitiated 10 bedraggled, insanitary
dirtiness: 4 mess 9 pollution
dirtless: 5 clean 6 washed 8 unsoiled 9 laundered
dirty: 4 blot, blue, foul, lewd, mean, soil, spot, ugly, vile 5 bawdy, black, dingy, dusty, germy, grimy, grody, lousy, mangy, messy, muddy, nasty, slimy, smear, sooty, stain, sully, taint 6 befoul, bemire, crud up, debase, defile, embrue, filthy, fouled, frowsy, frowzy, grotty, grubby, grungy, imbrue, impure, litter, mangey, mess up, ribald, rotten, sleazy, sloppy, smudge, smutty, soiled, sordid, unfair, untidy, vulgar 7 begrime, blacken, corrupt, crooked, defiled, illicit, muddied, naughty, obscene, pollute, profane, smudged, spatter, spotted, squalid, stained, sullied, tarnish, unclean, unkempt, unswept 8 begrimed, besmirch, indecent, maculate, off-color, polluted, slovenly, spiteful, stagnant, undusted, unwashed 9 deceitful, dishonest, low-minded, lubricous, tarnished, uncleaned, unethical 10 despicable, germ-ridden, insanitary, lamentable, lusterless, scurrilous, suggestive, unhygienic, unsanitary
not ~: 5 clean 8 spotless
work: 5 fraud, guile 6 deceit, dupery, racket 7 falsity, knavery, misdeed, perfidy, swindle 8 artifice 9 chicanery, deception, duplicity, hypocrisy, treachery 10 dishonesty
dirty __: 3 war 4 bomb, look, pool, rice, word, work 5 linen 6 tricks 7 laundry
Dirty __: 5 Diana, Hands, Harry 7 Dancing, Laundry
Dirty Dancing (1987 film)
cast: Jennifer Grey, Jerry Orbach, Patrick Swayze
director: Emile Ardolino
nickname: 4 Baby
dirty-dealing: 9 underhand, unethical
Dirty Diana (1988 song) artist: Michael Jackson
Dirty Dingus Magee (1970 film)
cast: Anne Jackson, George Kennedy, Frank Sinatra
Dirty Dozen, The (1967 film)
cast: Ernest Borgnine, Charles Bronson, Jim Brown, John Cassavetes, Richard Jaeckel, George Kennedy, Trini Lopez, Lee Marvin, Robert Ryan, Telly Savalas, Donald Sutherland, Clint Walker
director: Robert Aldrich
Dirty Hands author: Jean-Paul Sartre
Dirty Harry: 3 cop 8 Callahan
employer: 4 SFPD
Dirty Harry (1972 film)
cast: Clint Eastwood, Harry Guardino, Reni Santoni
director: Don Siegel
__ dirty job but...: 4 It's a
Dirty Laundry (1982 song) artist: Don Henley
Dirty Mary Crazy Larry (1974 film)
cast: Peter Fonda, Susan George
__ dirty rat!: 3 You
Dirty Rotten Scoundrels (1988 film)
cast: Michael Caine, Glenne Headly, Steve Martin
director: Frank Oz
dis: 4 gibe, jibe 5 knock, scorn 6 demean, deride, heckle, insult 7 put down 8 badmouth, belittle, mouth off 9 denigrate
not ~: 3 dat
Dis: 5 Hades 10 underworld
disabuse: 3 rid 8 set right 9 enlighten, unbeguile, undeceive 10 disenchant
disaccord: 4 feud 6 refuse 8 variance 10 contention, difference, disharmony, dissension, dissidence, dissonance, heterodoxy
disaccustom: 4 wean
disadvantage: 4 flaw, harm, hurt, lack, loss, snag 5 fault, minus 6 burden, damage, defect, hamper, hurdle, injury, kicker 7 barrier, failing, problem 8 drawback, handicap, hardship, obstacle, weakness, weak spot 9 detriment, hindrance, liability 10 impediment
__ disadvantage: 3 at a
disadvantaged: 4 poor 5 broke, needy, sorry 6 bad off, hard up, ill off, in need, in want 7 pinched 8 badly off, bankrupt, beggarly, deprived, indigent, strapped 9 destitute, insolvent, moneyless, penniless, penurious 10 down and out, pauperized, straitened
disadvantageous: 7 adverse, harmful, hurtful, useless 8 contrary, damaging
disadvise: 5 deter 10 discourage
disaffect: 6 divide 8 alienate, disunite, embitter, estrange, imbitter 10 antagonize, discompose, drive apart
disaffection: 5 break 6 breach, unrest
disaffiliate: 6 detach, secede
disaffirm: 6 impugn, naysay, negate, refute 7 confute, gainsay 10 contradict, contravene
disagree: 4 spat, vary 5 argue, clash, demur 6 bicker, differ, naysay, negate, oppose, refute 7 collide, confute, dissent, diverge, protest, quarrel, quibble, wrangle 8 conflict, squabble 9 have words, square off, take issue 10 contradict, contravene
disagreeable: 3 bad 4 mean, rude, sour, ugly 5 awful, brusk, cross, nasty, onery, seamy, surly, whiny, woful 6 bitter, feisty, ornery, rancid, rotten, snappy, unruly, whiney, woeful 7 brusque, defiant, grating, grouchy, naughty, painful, peevish, waspish, wayward 8 annoying, brackish, churlish, contrary, horrible, liverish, petulant, snappish, stubborn, unsavory 9 crotchety, offensive, repulsive, splenetic, thankless, unsightly, unwelcome 10 out of sorts, rebellious, unfriendly
disagreeing: 6 at odds 7 opposed 8 clashing, opposing
disagreement: 3 gap 4 feud, rift, spat, tiff 5 break, clash, fight, scrap 6 battle, breach, debate, hassle, strife 7 discord, dispute, dissent, faction, ill will, problem, quarrel, tension 8 argument, conflict, disunion, disunity, division, friction, squabble, variance 10 opposition
exclamation of ~: 3 nay, rot 4 bosh, uh-uh 7 baloney, rubbish
disallow: 3 ban, bar, nix 4 dent, shun, tabu, veto 5 debar, spurn 6 abjure, bounce, cancel, censor, except, forbid, negate, outlaw, pass on, rebuff, refuse, reject, revoke 7 disavow, disdain, dismiss, embargo, exclude, shut out 8 disclaim, override, overrule, prohibit, turn down 9 blackball, cast aside, interdict, proscribe, repudiate
disallowance: 4 veto 6 denial 7 refusal
__-disant: 3 soi
disappear: 2 go 3 ebb, end, fly, set 4 exit, fade, flee, lift, melt, sink, wane 5 cease, leave, scram 6 begone, decamp, depart, escape, perish, recede, vacate, vanish 7 abscond, go south, retreat, take off, vamoose 8 dissolve, evanesce, hightail, vaporize, withdraw 9 dissipate, evaporate 10 take flight
in the crowd: 5 blend
slowly: 5 erode
Disappear (1990 song) artist: INXS
disappearance: 4 exit, loss 6 exodus, flight
exclamation: 4 poof
disappeared: 4 gone, lost 7 missing
disappearing
do a ~ act: 4 flee 5 elude
__ disappearing act: 3 do a
disappoint: 4 dash, fail, foil, mock, sell 6 dismay, sadden, thwart 7 chagrin, let down, sell out 8 embitter, fall down, imbitter 9 displease, dumbfound, frustrate 10 circumvent, disconcert, disenchant, disgruntle, dishearten, dissatisfy
disappointed: 4 down 5 burnt, upset 6 aghast, burned 7 let down, unhappy 8 downcast, shot down 9 regretful
disappointing: 3 off, sad 5 rocky
disappointment: 3 dud 4 blow, drag 6 bummer, defeat, downer, fiasco, regret 7 chagrin, failure, letdown, licking, setback, washout
exclamation of ~: 2 aw 4 darn, drat, jeez, oh no, rats, sigh 5 fudge, zooks 6 phooey, shucks, zounds 7 brother, horrors, Odzooks 8 Gadzooks
Disappointment: 4 cape
locale: 10 Washington
disapproval: 5 odium 6 denial, rebuke 7 censure, dislike, dissent, refusal, reproof 8 reproach
cry of ~: 3 boo, fie, och, tsk, tut 4 hiss, hoot, nuts, pooh, posh, uh-uh 5 hooey, nerts, nertz, pshaw 6 tsk tsk, tut-tut 7 big deal
show ~: 3 boo 4 hiss, hoot 5 frown
disapprove: 4 mind, veto 5 demur, spurn 6 object, oppose, refuse, regret, reject 7 frown on, quarrel 8 turn down 9 criticize, deprecate, disesteem, dispraise, reprehend, reprobate 10 discommend, look down on
of: 4 mind 5 decry 7 condemn, deplore, dislike
disapproved: 4 tabu 5 taboo
disapprover: 6 critic
disapproving: 4 cool 7 hostile, injured 8 critical
disapprovingly: 6 askant 7 askance
disarm: 3 win 4 melt 5 charm 6 defuse, defuze 7 bewitch, enchant, unnerve, win over 8 entrance 9 captivate, fascinate 10 smooth over
disarming: 7 winning, winsome 10 bewitching, convincing, inveigling, persuasive, saccharine
disarrange: 4 mess, muss 5 mix up, upset 6 jumble, litter, mess up, ruffle, tangle, tumble, untidy 7 disturb, shuffle 8 scramble, unsettle 10 complicate, disconcert
disarranged: 5 messy, mussy, upset 6 untidy 7 tousled, unkempt 8 pell-mell
disarrangement: 5 mix-up 6 jumble
disarray: 4 mess, muss 5 chaos, snarl 6 bedlam, huddle, jumble, jungle, litter, mayhem, muddle, muss up, tumult, unrest, uproar 7 anarchy, clutter, derange, ferment, shuffle, turmoil 8 disorder, shambles, unsettle, upheaval 9 confusion, mobocracy 10 dishabille, turbulence, untidiness
in ~: 5 upset 6 untidy 8 confused 10 disheveled
disassemble: 4 undo 5 unrig 8 take down
disassociated: 5 apart 8 separate
disaster: 3 woe 4 bane, blow, bust, doom, flop, loss, rout, ruin 5 smash 6 blight, crisis, fiasco, misery, mishap, plague 7 debacle, tragedy, washout 8 accident, calamity, casualty, hardship, upheaval 9 adversity, cataclysm, detriment, nightmare, ruination 10 infliction, misfortune, nonsuccess
box-office ~: 4 bomb, flop
natural ~: 5 flood 8 blizzard 9 hurricane
relief org.: 4 FEMA
disaster __: 4 area
disastrous: 3 bad 4 dire, foul, grim, poor 5 awful, fatal, lousy, toxic, woful 6 costly, crumby, crummy, dismal, horrid, malign, odious, rotten, tragic, woeful 7 accurst, adverse, baleful, baneful, beastly, doleful, fateful, ghastly, harmful, ruinous, unlucky 8 accursed, damaging, dreadful, God-awful, grievous, horrible, ill-fated, inferior, luckless, negative, shameful, sinister, stinking, terrible, tragical, untoward, wretched 9 abhorrent, appalling, atrocious, dangerous, defective, execrable, frightful, ill-omened, injurious, insidious, loathsome, miserable, offensive, revolting 10 abominable, calamitous, deplorable, despicable, detestable, horrendous, ill-starred, petrifying
disavow: 4 deny 5 annul, scorn 6 abjure, impugn, recant, reject 7 forsake, gainsay, retract 8 disallow, forswear, go back on, renounce, take back, withdraw 9 back-pedal, foreswear, repudiate
disavowal: 6 denial 7 refusal 8 negation 9 desertion
words of ~: 4 not I 5 not me
disband: 4 fold 5 demob, sever, split 7 break up, scatter 10 demobilize
disbar: 5 eject 7 exclude
disbelief: 3 awe 5 doubt 6 denial 7 atheism, dubiety 8 mistrust, nihilism 9 dubiosity, rejection 10 skepticism
exclamation of ~: 2 aw 3 huh, pah 4 nuts, oh no, pooh, posh, rats, umph, what 5 hooey, humph, pshaw, zooks 6 zounds 7 baloney, Odzooks 8 Gadzooks, honestly
disbelieve: 5 doubt, query, scorn 6 be wary, reject, wonder 7 be leery, scoff at, suspect 8 discount, mistrust, question 9 discredit, repudiate, smell a rat
disbeliever: 7 sceptic, skeptic
disbelieving: 9 quizzical, skeptical
disburden: 3 rid 4 ease, free, help, shed 6 solace 7 lighten 9 discharge, exonerate, extricate
disburse: 3 pay 4 deal, fork, give, mete

5 issue, spend 6 ante up, divide, expend, lay out, pay out, ration 7 deal out, dish out, divvy up, dole out, hand out, mete out, pass out 8 dispense, shell out 10 administer, distribute
disbursement: 5 outgo, price 6 outlay 7 expense, payment 8 spending
disc: 2 CD 3 DVD 5 album, plate 6 circle 7 Frisbee, platter
jockey: 6 deejay 9 announcer
starter: 5 video
see also disk
disc __: 4 film 5 brake 6 camera, jockey, player
__ disc: 4 Airy 5 laser 7 compact, optical
discard: 4 cull, doff, drop, dump, jilt, junk, omit, shed, toss 5 chuck, ditch, scrap 6 banish, give up, reject 7 abandon, deep-six, forsake, let go of 8 castaway, get rid of, give up on, jettison, lay aside, part with, shake off, write off 9 cast aside, dispose of, eliminate, supersede, sweep away, throw away 10 relinquish
discarded: 8 derelict 9 ownerless
discards: 4 junk 5 trash 6 jetsam, jetsom 7 flotsam, garbage, rejects
discarnate: 8 bodiless 10 immaterial
discern: 3 see 4 espy, feel, find, know, note, spot, tell, view 5 catch, judge, learn, sense, sight 6 behold, descry, detect, fathom, notice 7 cognize, make out, observe, pick out, realize 8 perceive, smell out 9 apprehend, ascertain, figure out, penetrate, recognize 10 understand
discernible: 5 clear, plain, vivid 6 cogent, visual 7 audible, evident, express, obvious, sensory, visible 8 apparent, distinct, explicit, manifest, palpable, tangible 9 graspable, sensorial 10 spelled out
discerning: 4 keen, sage, sane, wise 5 acute, quick, sharp, smart 6 astute, bright, clever, shrewd 7 logical, prudent, refined, thought 8 critical, keen-eyed, lynx-eyed, profound, rational, sensible 9 astucious, brilliant, conscious, ingenious, judicious, observant, provident, sagacious, selective, sensitive 10 farsighted, insightful, perceptive, percipient
discernment: 3 eye, wit 4 wits 5 depth, sense, taste 6 acumen, reason, vision, wisdom 7 insight 8 elegance, judgment, keenness 10 perception
discharge: 2 ax 3 axe, can, pay 4 bang, boot, drop, emit, fire, flow, free, gush, leak, meet, ooze, oust, pour, sack, shot, spew, spit, spue, vent, void 5 annul, belch, blast, burst, congé, drain, egest, eject, empty, erupt, expel, exude, let go, loose, round, salvo, serve, shoot, spill, spirt, spout, spurt, storm, yield 6 acquit, bounce, cancel, congee, dehire, efflux, finish, firing, fulfil, go boom, launch, layoff, let off, let out, loosen, pardon, parole, pay off, recall, redeem, refund, remove, report, set off, settle, unlade, unload, vacate, volley 7 abide by, achieve, barrage, cashier, deliver, dismiss, drum out, emanate, execute, explode, freeing, fulfill, give off, heave-ho, kick out, manumit, off-load, payment, perform, pouring, receipt, release, satisfy, secrete, seepage, set free, spatter, thunder 8 abrogate, carry out, detonate, disgorge, effluent, ejection, emission, emptying, eruption, furlough, get rid of, liberate, outburst, pink slip, shoot off, transact, unlading 9 acquittal, annulment, carry away, clearance, disburden, dismissal, effluence, eliminate, emanation, exclusion, exculpate, execution, exemption, exonerate, explosion, expulsion, exudation, fusillade, liquidate, muster out, pour forth, probation, secretion, send forth, supersede, terminate, unloading, unshackle 10 accomplish, deposition, detonation, disembogue, evacuation, liberation, observance, remittance, settlement
gradually: 4 leak, ooze, seep 5 exude 7 secrete
discharge __: 4 lamp, tube
__ discharge: 4 glow 5 brush 6 corona 7 general 9 honorable
discharged matter: 6 egesta
disciple: 3 fan 5 pupil 7 admirer, apostle, convert, devotee, learner, student 8 adherent, believer, follower 9 proselyte, supporter, worshiper
suffix: 3 -ist, -ite
__ Disciple, The: 6 Devil's
disciplinarian: 5 bully 6 tyrant 7 teacher 8 enforcer, martinet, stickler 10 taskmaster
legislative ~: 4 whip
disciplinary: 4 firm, hard 5 bossy, cruel, penal, picky, rigid, stern, tough 6 severe 7 austere, Spartan 8 despotic, exacting, hard-line, punitive, rigorous 9 demanding, draconian, stringent, unbending, unsparing 10 despotical, inflexible, iron-fisted, no-nonsense, oppressive, tyrannical
discipline: 3 job, rod 4 area, walk, whip, will 5 drill, field, order, rigor, teach, train 6 course, punish, school, sphere 7 censure, conduct, control, penalty, regimen, science, subject 8 activity, chastise, exercise, penalize, practice, punition, training 9 castigate, cultivate, education, habituate, restraint, specialty, willpower 10 correction, curriculum, limitation, punishment, regulation, strictness
__-discipline: 4 self
disciplined: 4 tame 5 sober 7 orderly 8 methodic, moderate
not ~: 3 lax 4 wild 6 unruly
disclaim: 4 deny 5 waive 6 abjure, recant, refute, reject, revoke 7 forsake, gainsay, retract 8 abdicate, abnegate, disallow, forswear, renounce, take back, withdraw 9 foreswear, repudiate 10 contravene
disclaimer: 6 denial, waiver 7 refusal 8 negation
disclose: 3 air, say 4 bare, blab, leak, open, show, tell 5 admit, break, let on, spill, unrip, utter 6 betray, convey, expose, impart, let out, relate, report, reveal, unfold, unmask, unveil 7 confess, confide, declare, divulge, exhibit, lay bare, let slip, mention, signify, uncover 8 announce, disinter, give away, proclaim, register, unburden 9 make known 10 make public
disclosed: 4 open 8 knowable, manifest
disclosure: 4 news 6 exposé 8 giveaway 9 admission, broadcast, detection, discovery, unveiling 10 blow-by-blow, confession, divulgence, revelation, unbosoming, uncovering, unveilment
Disclosure: 4 film 5 novel
author: Michael Crichton
cast: Michael Douglas, Demi Moore, Donald Sutherland
director: Barry Levinson
Discman maker: 4 Sony
disco: 3 fad 4 club 5 dance, music 9 dance hall, nightclub, nightspot
Caribbean ~: 4 zouk
dancing: 4 go-go
spinner: 2 DJ 6 deejay
Disco __: 4 Duck, Lady
Disco Duck (1976 song) artist: Dees
Disco Lady (1976 song) artist: Johnnie Taylor
discolor: 3 mar 4 blur, soil 5 smear, stain, sully, taint 6 bruise 7 besmear, contuse, tarnish 8 besmirch
discoloration: 4 blot, scar, spot 5 stain 6 blotch, bruise, defect 7 blemish 9 contusion
combining form: 6 -chroia
discombobulate: 3 jar 4 stun 5 abash, addle, upset 6 fuddle, muddle, puzzle, rattle 7 confuse, fluster, perplex, unnerve 8 confound
discombobulated: 4 asea 5 at sea 7 abashed, puzzled 8 unstrung
discomfit: 4 faze 5 abash, scare, shake, spite, upset 6 baffle, bother, defeat, dismay, heckle, rattle, ruffle, thwart, unglue 7 chagrin, confuse, disturb, fluster, mortify, nonplus, perplex, perturb 8 confound, unsettle, unstring 9 checkmate, embarrass, frustrate, humiliate, take aback 10 demoralize, discompose, disconcert, disgruntle
discomfiting: 5 scary
discomfiture: 7 chagrin 9 abashment
discomfort: 4 ache, bore, hurt, pain 5 alarm, upset 6 misery, regret 7 malaise, perturb, trouble 8 distress, frighten, hardship, irritate, soreness 9 annoyance, embarrass, suffering 10 discompose, inquietude, irritation, uneasiness
cause of ~: 5 thorn
exclamation: 2 ow 3 ack, ick, oof, ugh, yow 4 moan, ouch, phew, yelp, yeow, yuck 5 groan, yecch
show ~: 5 wince
discomforting: 5 hairy 6 sticky
discommend: 9 deprecate 10 disapprove
discommode: 6 put out 8 unsettle 9 disoblige, incommode, interfere
discompose: 3 irk, jar, vex 4 faze, jolt, stun 5 abash, addle, annoy, harry, shake, upset 6 bother, flurry, harass, nettle, plague, rattle, ruffle 7 agitate, confuse, disturb, fluster, perplex, perturb, shuffle, unhinge 8 convulse, irritate, psych out, unsettle, unstring 9 disaffect, discomfit, displease, embarrass 10 discomfort, disconcert
discomposed: 6 uneasy 8 unstrung
disconcert: 3 bug 4 faze, jolt, trip 5 abash, addle, annoy, appal, get to, mix up, shake, shame, throw, upset 6 appall, baffle, bother, dismay, flurry, foul up, heckle, hinder, mess up, puzzle, rattle, ruffle, unglue 7 agitate, chagrin, confuse, disturb, fluster, nonplus, perplex, perturb, shake up, trouble, unnerve 8 bewilder, confound, frighten, psych out, surprise, unsettle, unstring 9 discomfit, embarrass, frustrate, take aback, unbalance 10 demoralize, disappoint, disarrange, discompose, disgruntle
disconcerted: 5 upset 6 shaken, thrown 7 abashed, unglued 8 unstrung
disconfirm: 5 break, rebut 6 negate, refute 7 confute, gainsay 8 disprove 10 controvert
disconnect: 4 part, undo 5 loose, sever, split, unpeg, unrig, untie 6 cut off, detach, divide, hang up, loosen, unlink 7 divorce, isolate, split up, tear off 8 break off, separate, set apart, uncouple 9 break it up, disengage, dislocate, interrupt, segregate, take apart 10 break it off, come undone, dissociate
disconnected: 5 apart, loose 6 broken 7 asunder, garbled, jumbled, mixed up, muddled 8 confused, discrete, rambling, separate 9 excursive
disconnection: 5 split 8 division
disconsolate: 3 low, sad 4 blue, down, glum, mopy 5 heavy, mopey, sorry, woful 6 abject, dreary, gloomy, lonely, morose, somber, woeful 7 crushed, doleful, forlorn, hurting, joyless, unhappy, wistful 8 dejected, desolate, downcast, troubled, wretched 9 bummed out, cheerless, heartsick, miserable, plaintive, prostrate, sorrowful, woebegone 10 chapfallen, dispirited, melancholy
disconsolateness: 5 gloom 6 sorrow
discontent: 6 unrest 8 friction 9 annoyance, complaint, displease, grumbling 10 depression, uneasiness, woefulness
show ~: 4 moan 5 groan 6 kvetch 8 complain
discontented: 4 sour 5 weary 7 grouchy 9 miserable, querulous
discontinuance: 3 end 4 stop 6 disuse, ending, finish, period 7 closing 8 abeyance, stoppage
discontinue: 3 end 4 drop, halt, quit, stay, stop 5 break, cease, close, lapse, pause, scrub, sever 6 desist, finish, wind up, wrap up 7 abandon, adjourn, back off, break up, shut off, shut out, suspend 8 break off, conclude, intermit, knock off, leave off, pack it in, separate, shut down, surcease 9 close down, terminate 10 call it a day
discontinuity: 3 gap 5 break, crack 6 hiatus, lacuna 7 opening 8 cleavage, fracture 10 disruption
discontinuous: 6 broken
discord: 3 din 4 feud 5 chaos, clash, noise, split 6 breach, jangle, racket, rancor, strife, unrest 7 dissent, faction, quarrel, trouble, warfare 8 argument, conflict, disunity, friction, sour note, variance 9 animosity, antipathy, cacophony, harshness, hostility, mobocracy, wrangling 10 antagonism, contention, disharmony, dissension, dissonance, turbulence
apple of ~ contender: 4 Hera
Greek goddess of ~: 4 Eris
discordance: 9 cacophony
discordant: 4 ajar 5 harsh, noisy 6 atonal, off-key, shrill, unlike 7 grating, jarring, raucous, unalike 8 clashing, improper, jangling, strident 9 different, disparate, dissident, dissonant, divergent, unmusical 10 discrepant, incoherent, quarreling
be ~: 8 disagree
Discordia counterpart: 4 Eris
discount: 4 sale 5 lower, price, scoff, slash 6 deduct, forget, ignore, rebate, reduce, refund, reject, saving, slight 7 bargain, cut-rate, neglect, put down, scoff at 8 belittle, brush off, close out, decrease, diminish, markdown, minimize, mistrust, overlook, pass over, rollback, subtract, take away 9 abatement, deduction, discredit, disregard, reduction, underplay 10 concession, diminution, disbelieve, percentage
store: 6 outlet
ticket: 6 coupon
discount __: 4 rate 5 house, store 6 broker, market
__ discount: 4 bank, cash, deep, time 5 trade
discounted: 4 less 6 on sale
not ~: 4 list 6 retail
discountenance: 3 irk 4 faze 5 abash, shame, upset 6 oppose, rattle, reject 7 chagrin, condemn, frown on, nonplus 8 object to

discounting: 4 save 9 except for
discount-rack abbr.: 3 irr. 5 irreg.
discourage: 4 curb, dash 5 check, chill, daunt, deter, scare 6 dampen, deject, dismay, hinder, impede, rebuff, sadden, unglue 7 depress, inhibit, overawe, repress, unnerve 8 dispirit, dissuade, frighten, hold back, obstruct, restrain 9 deprecate, disadvise, disparage, frustrate, give pause, indispose, interfere, prostrate, talk out of, turn aside 10 demoralize, dishearten, disincline, intimidate, keep in line
discouraged: 3 sad 4 blue, down, glum 6 abject, broken 7 in a funk 8 dejected, downcast 9 saturnine
discouragement: 5 gloom 6 dismay, rebuff
discouraging: 3 bad, dim 5 bleak, mirky, murky, rocky 6 dismal, dreary, gloomy
discourse: 4 chat, lect., talk, word 5 orate, speak, theme 6 confer, dialog, homily, parley, reason, recite, sermon, speech, thesis 7 address, commune, lecture, monolog, oration, writing 8 colloquy, converse, dialogue, harangue, language, perorate, rhetoric, treatise 9 elaborate, expatiate, hold forth, monograph, monologue, sermonize, utterance 10 commentary, commentate, discussion, dissertate, exposition, literature, recitation, vocalizing
topic: 5 thema
Discourse on Method: 5 essay
author: 9 Descartes
discourteous: 4 curt, flip, pert, rude 5 brusk, fresh, gruff, harsh, nervy, rough, sassy, saucy, short, surly 6 abrupt, awless, brazen, cheeky, snippy 7 aweless, boorish, brusque, ill-bred, uncivil, uncouth 8 churlish, flippant, impolite, impudent, insolent, inurbane, snippety, tactless 9 offensive, out of line
discourtesy: 4 sass 6 insult, slight
discover: 3 see, spy 4 espy, find, hear, read, show, spot, tell 5 catch, crack, dig up, glean, hit on, learn, trace 6 descry, detect, intuit, locate, look up, notice, strike, turn up, unfold, unveil 7 find out, glimpse, hit upon, light on, nose out, observe, pioneer, realize, rout out, uncover, unearth 8 come upon, identify, perceive, smell out, surprise 9 ascertain, determine, ferret out, get to know, get wind of, light upon, originate, track down
Discover: 8 magazine 10 credit card
rival: 4 Omni, Visa
use ~: 3 owe 6 charge
discovered, just: 3 new
discovery: 4 find, news 5 trove 6 espial, strike 7 finding 9 detection, diagnosis, encounter, invention, principle 10 conclusion, disclosure, exposition, innovation, perception, revelation, uncovering, unearthing
cry of ~: 3 aha, oho 6 eureka
Discovery: 4 ship 10 spacecraft
captain: 6 Baffin, Hudson
org.: 4 NASA
passenger: 4 Garn
Discovery __: 3 Day 4 Club 5 Inlet
discredit: 4 gibe, jeer, jibe, mock, slam, slur, snub 5 abuse, blame, decry, doubt, libel, odium, rebut, scoff, scorn, shame, smear, spurn, taint, taunt, wrong 6 defame, deride, dump on, expose, heckle, humble, impugn, malign, naysay, negate, offend, rebuff, refute, reject, show up, slight, vilify 7 affront, asperse, censure, confute, degrade, explode, put down, rank out, run down, scandal, scoff at, slander, subvert, traduce 8 belittle, denounce, discount, dishonor, distrust, mistrust, reproach, ridicule, take down, tear down, throw mud, vilipend 9 challenge, denigrate, disesteem, disparage, disrepute, frown upon, humiliate, reflect on 10 calumniate, compromise, contradict, contravene, depreciate, disbelieve, invalidate, reflection, stigmatize
discreditable: 3 bad 4 poor 6 shoddy, unfair 8 unseemly
discreet: 4 safe, wary, wise 5 canny, chary, right 6 modest, polite, simple, subtle 7 careful, guarded, politic, private, prudent, tactful 8 cautious, delicate, keen-eyed, sensible 9 courteous, farseeing, judicious, provident, sensitive, temperate 10 controlled, diplomatic, longheaded, reasonable, restrained, thoughtful
Discreet Charm of the Bourgeoisie, The (1972 film)
cast: Stephane Audran, Fernando Rey, Delphine Seyrig
director: Luis Buñuel
Discreet Music composer: 3 Eno
discreetness: 7 caution, modesty
discrepancy: 3 gap 5 split 8 conflict, variance 9 variation
discrepant: 7 unalike 9 different, differing, disparate, dissonant, divergent 10 at variance, discordant, inaccurate
discrete: 5 apart 6 unlike, varied 7 diverse, unalike, variant, various 8 detached, distinct, separate 9 different, unrelated 10 individual
discretion: 4 care, tact 6 choice, option 7 caution, finesse 8 judgment, prudence, volition 9 attention, canniness, chariness, diplomacy, foresight, good sense, vigilance 10 precaution, providence, shrewdness, solicitude
at one's ~: 6 freely
discretionary: 8 optional 9 voluntary
discretionary __: 6 income 7 account
discriminate: 4 tell 8 separate 9 segregate, victimize
discriminating: 4 fine, keen 5 acute, fussy, picky, sharp 6 astute, choose, choosy, select, shrewd, subtle 7 careful, choosey, finical, finicky, logical, refined 8 critical, eclectic, finiking, finnicky, lynx-eyed, rational, sensible, tasteful 9 astucious, observant, sagacious, selective
discrimination: 3 ear, eye, wit 4 bias, care, wits 5 sense, taste 6 acumen, wisdom 7 bigotry, culture 8 inequity, judgment, keenness 9 prejudice
discriminatory: 6 biased, unfair, unjust 7 partial 8 one-sided, partisan 9 arbitrary, selective 10 prejudiced, unbalanced
disculpate: 5 clear 6 acquit 9 vindicate
discursion: 5 aside 8 drifting, straying 9 departure, wandering 10 apostrophe, digression
discursive: 4 long 5 gabby, wordy 6 prolix 7 diffuse, erratic, lengthy, unterse, verbose, voluble 8 rambling 9 bombastic, excursive, garrulous, talkative 10 digressive, loquacious, palaverous
discus: 5 event
competition: 4 meet
discuss: 4 chat, talk 5 touch, treat 6 confer, debate, go into, reason, rehash, review 7 address, mention, speak of 8 hash over, talk over, vocalize 9 bat around, negotiate, talk about, touch base 10 deliberate, kick around, speak about, toss around
discussing, no longer worth: 4 moot
discussion: 4 talk, word 5 input 6 airing, confab, debate, dialog, huddle, parley, powwow, review, speech 7 comment, hearing, meeting, session 8 colloquy, dialogue, question 9 dialectic, discourse, interview, symposium, tête-à-tête, wrangling 10 conference, contention, exposition, groupthink, literature, recitation
group: 5 forum, panel
matter for ~: 5 issue
up for ~: 4 open
__ discussion: 5 panel 6 heated
disdain: 3 dig 4 barb, gibe, hate, jeer, jibe, mock, shun, slam, slap, slur, snub, veto 5 abhor, abuse, decry, libel, scoff, scorn, sneer, snoot, spurn, taunt 6 bounce, defame, deride, dump on, hatred, heckle, impugn, malign, offend, pass on, rebuff, reject, slight, vilify 7 affront, asperse, calumny, catcall, contemn, degrade, despise, exclude, hauteur, mockery, neglect, obloquy, offense, put down, rank out, slander, sniff at, traduce 8 aversion, belittle, contempt, denounce, derision, pooh-pooh, ridicule, turn down, vilipend 9 antipathy, arrogance, aspersion, blackball, cast aside, contumely, denigrate, disparage, disregard, humiliate, repudiate 10 calumniate, defamation, disrespect, ill feeling, look down on, opprobrium, recoil from
cry of ~: 3 bah, pah, tsk, tut 4 egad, pish, pooh, posh, tush 5 egads, pshaw, shame 6 tsk tsk, tut-tut 8 for shame
show ~: 4 jeer 5 shrug, sniff, snoot
with ~: 5 icily 8 snootily
disdainful: 5 lofty, proud 6 snooty 7 haughty, jeering 8 arrogant, cavalier, derisive, insolent, sardonic, superior 9 despising, egotistic, rejecting, vitriolic 10 contemning, derogatory, hoity-toity, intolerant, minimizing
disdainfulness: 5 pride 7 hauteur 9 arrogance, insolence
disease: 3 bug, ill, pox 4 rust 6 blight, malady, plague 7 ailment, illness 8 disorder, sickness 9 complaint, condition, contagion, ill health, infection, infirmity 10 affliction, unwellness
combining form: 3 nos- 4 noso- 5 patho-, -pathy
plant ~: 4 rust, wilt 5 ergot 6 blight, mildew 10 damping-off
prevent ~: 8 immunize 9 vaccinate
science of ~: 8 medicine
disease-fighting org.: 3 NIH
disease-proof: 6 immune
disembark: 4 land 5 light 6 alight, arrive, get off 7 deplane, descend, detrain, step out 8 get there, go ashore 10 come ashore
disembarkation: 7 arrival
disembarrass: 3 rid 8 liberate
disembodied: 8 bodiless, separate 9 spiritual 10 discarnate, immaterial
disenchant: 4 sour 7 let down, turn off 8 disabuse 9 undeceive 10 disappoint
disenchanted: 5 blasé, burnt, fed up 6 burned, soured 7 cynical, let down
Disenchanted, The author: Schulberg
disencumber: 3 rid 5 clear 6 unload 7 lighten, relieve 8 unburden, untangle
disengage: 3 pry 4 free, undo, wean 5 clear, let go, loose, split, unpeg, untie, unzip 6 detach, loosen, opt out, unbind 7 isolate, release, retreat 8 cut loose, separate, uncouple, unfasten, withdraw 9 dislocate, extricate, weasel out 10 come undone, disconnect, dissociate
disengaged: 3 lax 4 free, idle, lazy 5 inert 6 asleep, draggy, torpid, untied 7 dormant, neutral, passive 8 inactive, indolent, slothful, sluggish 9 lethargic, sedentary
disentangle: 4 comb, free, undo 5 clear, let go, ravel, solve, untie 6 decode, unwind 7 clear up, resolve, sort out, unravel, unsnarl, untwist, work out 8 decipher, separate, simplify, untangle 10 unscramble
disenthrall: 4 free 5 loose 6 loosen, redeem 10 emancipate
__ d'Isère: 3 Val
disestablish: 4 void 5 annul 7 abolish
disesteem: 9 deprecate, discredit, disregard, disrepute, ill repute 10 detraction, disapprove, muckraking
disfavor: 5 blame, odium, shame 7 refusal 8 aversion, contempt, mistrust 9 deprecate, ill repute
disfavorable: 8 critical, libelous 9 aspersive, demeaning, invidious 10 belittling, defamatory, derogatory, detractive
'D' Is for Deadbeat author: Sue Grafton
disgorge: 4 spew, spue 5 egest, eject, empty, expel, spill 6 unload 9 discharge
disgrace: 4 blot, slur, soil 5 guilt, lower, odium, shame, spoil, stain, sully, taint 6 debase, defame, defile, infamy, rascal, stigma 7 attaint, corrupt, mortify, obloquy, scandal, tarnish, undoing 8 besmirch, derogate, ignominy, take down 9 humiliate, ill repute 10 debasement, opprobrium, stigmatize
sign of ~: 4 blot 5 stain 9 black mark
disgraced: 6 fallen
disgraceful: 3 low 4 base, foul, grim, mean, poor, vile 5 awful, lousy, nasty, shady, sorry, woful, wrong 6 crumby, crummy, dismal, horrid, odious, rotten, shabby, shoddy, woeful 7 accurst, baleful, baneful, beastly, doleful, ghastly, ignoble 8 accursed, dreadful, flagrant, God-awful, grievous, horrible, infamous, inferior, shameful, shocking, stinking, terrible, unworthy, wretched 9 abhorrent, appalling, atrocious, defective, execrable, frightful, insidious, loathsome, miserable, monstrous, offensive, revolting 10 abominable, despicable, detestable, disastrous, horrendous, scandalous
disgrade: 6 reduce
disgruntle: 5 abash, annoy, shame, upset 6 dismay, offend 7 mortify, perturb 9 discomfit, displease, embarrass 10 disappoint, disconcert
disgruntled: 5 huffy, sulky, testy, vexed 6 crabby, cranky, grumpy, peeved, put out, sullen 7 annoyed, grouchy, injured, peevish, unhappy 8 grumpish
disgruntlement: 7 chagrin
disguise: 4 fake, hide, mask, veil 5 alter, beard, cache, capot, cloak, color, couch, cover, feign, front, shade, trick 6 encode, facade, shroud 7 charade, conceal, costume, cover-up, falsify, obscure, secrete 8 covering, illusion, pretense, simulate 9 dissemble, obfuscate 10 camouflage, false front, keep secret, masquerade
item: 3 wig 5 beard 7 glasses 8 mustache
wear the ~ of: 4 go as 6 pass as
disguised: 5 false, incog 6 covert, hidden, masked, secret, unseen, veiled 7 furtive, private 8 hush-hush 9 incognito, invisible, out of view 10 undercover, under wraps
disgust: 4 hate, tire 5 appal, odium, repel, shock, weary 6 appall, hatred, insult, offend, revolt, sicken 7 fend off,

hold off, horrify, outrage, repulse, turn off 8 alienate, aversion, drive off, gross out, loathing 9 abominate, antipathy, repulsion, revulsion 10 abhorrence, repellence, repugnance
cry of ~: 3 ack, bah, fie, huh, ick, pah, rot, ugh, yah 4 bosh, darn, drat, heck, nuts, pfui, phew, phoo, pooh, posh, rats, yeck, yuck 5 faugh, fudge, nerts, nertz, pshaw, yecch, zooks 6 darn it, phooey, shucks, zounds 7 brother, goldarn, goldurn, Odzooks, rubbish 8 Gadzooks
disgusted: 4 sick 5 fed up, weary 7 teed off, unhappy 8 outraged 9 squeamish, turned off 10 displeased, fastidious, grossed out
be ~ by: 6 detest
with: 6 sick of
disgusting: 4 foul, icky, rank, ugly, vile 5 awful, gross, nasty, yucky 6 cruddy, grungy, horrid, odious, rancid, rotten, sleazy, vulgar 7 beastly, ghastly, hateful, hideous, noisome, squalid 8 gruesome, inedible, shocking, stinking 9 atrocious, execrable, frightful, loathsome, low-minded, monstrous, obnoxious, offensive, repellant, repellent, repugnant, repulsive, revolting, shameless 10 abominable, detestable, outrageous, scandalous
dish: 4 bowl, food, meal 5 china, plate, stein 6 course, entrée, gossip, recipe, saucer 7 platter 8 scoop out 9 casserole, container, tableware
alternative: 5 cable
ancestor: 6 aerial
delectable ~: 5 viand
dirt: 6 gossip
dryer: 5 towel
ender: 3 pan, rag 4 ware 5 cloth, towel, water 6 washer
fragment: 5 shard, sherd
holder: 4 rack, tray
it out: 7 lambast, lay it on 8 lambaste 10 come down on
main ~: 4 meat 6 entrée
name words: 3 à la
out: 3 pay 4 deal, give, mete 5 issue, ladle, serve 6 divide, ration 7 deliver, divvy up 8 disburse, dispense 10 distribute
partner: 5 spoon
serving ~: 4 boat 7 platter
side ~: 4 rice, slaw 5 pasta, salad 6 potato, veggie 8 coleslaw, macaroni 9 vegetable
up: 5 serve
dish ___: 3 out, top 5 gravy, it out, night 7 antenna
___ dish: 4 side, soap 5 candy, petri 7 chafing
___-dish: 4 deep
disharmony: 4 feud 5 clash 6 breach, strife 7 discord, faction 8 conflict, friction, sour note 9 disaccord 10 contention, difference, dissension, dissidence, dissonance, heterodoxy, turbulence
dishcloth: 3 rag
dishearten: 3 cow 4 tire 5 abash, appal, crush, daunt, deter, unman, weary 6 appall, bum out, dampen, deject, dismay, sadden, unglue 7 depress, oppress, unnerve 8 cast down, dispirit, dissuade 9 bring down, disparage, frustrate, give pause, humiliate, indispose 10 demoralize, disappoint, discourage, disincline, intimidate
disheartened: 3 low, sad 4 blue, down, glum 5 woful 6 abject, broken, gloomy, morose, somber, woeful 7 doleful, joyless, unhappy 8 dejected, downcast, troubled 9 bummed out, cheerless, exanimate, heartsick, miserable, sorrowful, woebegone 10 chapfallen, melancholy
disheartening: 3 sad 5 bleak, mirky, murky, sorry 6 dismal, gloomy
disheartenment: 7 despair
dished: 4 beat 5 all in, spent 6 bushed, cupped, done in, pooped 7 concave, drained, wearied, worn out 8 dog-tired, tired out 9 dead tired, exhausted, played out
dishes: 4 menu 5 china 7 cuisine 10 dinnerware, gastronomy
do the ~: 4 wash
help with the ~: 3 dry 4 wipe
remove ~ from the table: 3 bus
dishevel: 4 mess, muss 6 jumble, mess up, muss up, ruck up, ruffle, rumple, tangle 7 snarl up
disheveled: 4 wild 5 dowdy, messy, mussy, ratty, seedy, upset 6 blowsy, blowzy, frowsy, frowzy, grungy, sloppy, unneat, untidy 7 blowsed, blowzed, rumpled, squalid, tousled, unkempt 8 slipshod, slovenly, wrinkled 9 bagged out 10 bedraggled, disarrayed, disordered, disorderly, unbuttoned
dish it ___: 3 out
dishonest: 3 sly 4 foul 5 dirty, false, lying, shady 6 louche, rotten, shifty, sneaky, tricky, unfair, unholy, untrue 7 corrupt, crooked, devious, immoral, knavish 8 cheating, delusive, guileful, sinister, slippery, thieving, thievish, wrongful 9 deceitful, deceiving, deceptive, designing, faithless, insidious, insincere, strategic, swindling, two-timing, underhand, unethical 10 backbiting, fictitious, fraudulent, mendacious, misleading, perfidious, traitorous, untruthful, villainous
be ~: 3 con, lie 4 bilk, burn, dupe, fool, gull, have, hoax, hook, scam, sell, snow, take, trap 5 bluff, cheat, cozen, lie to, put on, sneak, trick 6 betray, delude, entrap, fleece, lead on, outwit, suck in, take in 7 beguile, buffalo, deceive, defraud, ensnare, insnare, mislead, pretend, sell out, swindle 8 flimflam, hoodwink, outsmart, pettifog, simulate, throw off 9 bamboozle, four-flush, misinform, victimize
one: 4 liar 5 crook, rogue, sneak
dishonesty: 3 lie 4 cant 5 guile, lying 6 deceit, racket 7 falsity, knavery 8 bad faith, venality 9 chicanery, dirty work, duplicity, falsehood, fourberie, hypocrisy, improbity, mendacity, rascality, treachery 10 corruption, hanky-panky, hocus-pocus, illegality, infidelity, trickiness
dishonor: 5 abase, guilt, odium, shame, stain, sully, taint, wrong 6 debase, defame, defile, infamy, insult, stigma 7 attaint, blacken, corrupt, obloquy, scandal, slander 8 contempt, ignominy 9 abasement, desecrate, discredit, humiliate, ill repute, notoriety, violation 10 opprobrium
dishonorable: 3 low, sly 4 base, foul, grim, poor 5 awful, dirty, false, lousy, seamy, shady, woful 6 abject, crumby, crummy, dismal, horrid, odious, rotten, shabby, shoddy, unfair, woeful 7 accurst, baleful, baneful, beastly, corrupt, crooked, doleful, ghastly, ignoble 8 accursed, degraded, dreadful, God-awful, grievous, horrible, inferior, shameful, stinking, terrible, unworthy, wretched, wrongful 9 abhorrent, appalling, atrocious, defective, execrable, frightful, insidious, loathsome, miserable, notorious, offensive, revolting, underhand, unethical 10 abominable, despicable, detestable, disastrous, horrendous
one: 3 cad 4 heel 5 rogue
dishonored: 6 fallen
dishpan: 4 bowl 5 basin
dishpan ___: 5 hands
___-dish pie: 4 deep
dishrag
like a ~: 4 limp
use a ~: 4 wipe
dish the ___: 4 dirt
dishwasher: 9 appliance
cycle: 3 dry 5 rinse
phase: 5 cycle
sinkful: 4 suds
dishwashing detergent: 3 Joy 4 Ajax, Dawn 7 Cascade 8 Sunlight 9 Palmolive 10 Electrasol
dishwater
like ~: 4 dull 5 soapy
source: 6 faucet
dishy: 6 pretty 7 gossipy
Dishy: 3 Bob
disillusion: 6 dismay 7 let down 8 disabuse, embitter, imbitter 9 unbeguile, undeceive 10 disenchant
disillusioned: 4 sour 5 blasé, burnt 6 burned 7 let down
disillusionment: 6 dismay 7 letdown
disimprison: 6 redeem
disinclination: 5 qualm 8 aversion
disincline: 10 discourage, dishearten
disinclined: 4 loth, slow 5 loath 6 afraid, averse 7 uneager 9 reluctant, unwilling
disinfect: 4 wash 5 bathe, clean, scrub 6 degerm, purify 7 cleanse, deterge, launder 8 fumigate, sanitize 9 deodorize, sterilize
disinfectant: 6 cresol 7 cleaner 8 cleanser, fumigant, purifier 9 germicide, sanitizer 10 antiseptic, sterilizer
brand: 5 Lysol
target: 4 germ 5 staph
disinfected: 4 pure 5 clean 7 sterile
disinform: 3 con, lie 4 dupe, fool, hoax, jive, sell, snow 5 bluff, cheat, cozen, trick 6 betray, delude, lead on, rope in, sucker, take in 7 beguile, deceive, defraud, mislead, pretend 8 hoodwink, misguide, pettifog, throw off 9 bamboozle, four-flush
disinformation: 3 lie 4 tale
disingenuity: 4 line, ruse, wile 5 craft, guile 6 deceit, device, scheme 7 cunning, knavery, slyness 8 artifice, foxiness, trickery, wiliness 9 cageyness, duplicity, stratagem 10 cleverness, craftiness, shrewdness, subterfuge
disingenuous: 3 sly 6 crafty, sneaky 7 unfrank 8 guileful, uncandid
exclamation: 5 who me
disinherit: 3 rob 4 lose, oust 6 cut off, disown 7 exclude 9 repudiate
disintegrate: 3 eat, rot 4 ruin, sink 5 burst, decay, erode, grind, smash, spoil 6 molder, soften 7 break up, crumble, decline, give way, rot away 8 collapse, evanesce, fragment, splinter 9 decompose
disintegrated: 4 gone
disintegration: 3 rot 4 ruin 5 decay 7 decline, erosion
disinter: 5 dig up 6 exhume 7 uncover, unearth 8 disclose
disinterest: 7 boredom 8 lethargy
show ~: 4 yawn
disinterested: 4 fair, just, open 5 aloof, tepid 6 square 7 neutral 8 balanced, detached, unbiased 9 equitable, impartial, objective, uncolored, unselfish 10 even-handed
disjoin: 3 pry, rip 4 part, rend 5 break, loose, sever, split, untie, unzip 6 cleave, cut off, detach, divide, loosen, sunder, unlink 7 divorce, split up, tear off 8 break off, disunite, separate, set apart, uncouple 9 interrupt 10 disconnect
disjoined: 7 asunder
disjoint: 5 sever 8 disunite, separate
disjointed: 5 apart, loose 6 broken 7 aimless, chaotic, jumbled, muddled 8 confused, rambling, separate 9 displaced, disunited, separated, spaced-out, spasmodic 10 disordered, incoherent, incohesive, irrational, unattached
disjointly: 5 apart
disjunction: 4 rent 5 break, cleft, split 6 breach 8 cleavage, disunion, disunity, division, fracture 9 severance 10 separation
disk: 2 LP 5 CD/ROM, shape, wafer, wheel 6 circle, danger, floppy, harrow, medium, record, saucer 7 Frisbee, platter
bronze ~: 4 gong
contents: 4 data
data ~: 5 CD/ROM 6 floppy
deejay's ~: 4 demo
1990s toy ~: 3 pog
obsolete: 2 LP
put on ~: 3 cut
rotary ~: 3 cam
slot: 6 A drive
solar ~: 4 Aten, Aton
spinner: 2 DJ 6 deejay
starter: 5 video
disk ___: 4 pack 5 brake, crank, drive, wheel 6 floret, flower, harrow, jockey, sander
___ disk: 3 sun 4 hard 5 audio, basal, laser, optic, pedal 6 floppy, Masson 7 compact, optical
diskette: 6 floppy
clean a ~: 6 delete
prepare a ~: 6 format 10 initialize
disk operating ___: 6 system
___ disk player: 7 compact
disk-shaped: 5 round 8 circular
dislike: 4 hate, shun 5 abhor, avoid, odium 6 animus, detest, enmity, eschew, grudge, hatred, loathe, resent 7 condemn, contemn, deplore, despise 8 aversion, execrate, loathing, object to 9 abominate, animosity, antipathy, hostility, revulsion 10 abhorrence, antagonism, execration, repellence, repugnance
disliked: 5 lousy 7 unloved 9 unpopular
dislocate: 4 pull 5 mix up, shift, upset 6 jumble, luxate, wrench 7 disrupt, shuffle, unhinge 8 dislodge, disorder 9 disengage 10 disconnect, knock loose
dislocation: 8 luxation 10 disruption
sense of ~: 5 anomy 6 anomie
dislodge: 4 buck, bump, oust 5 budge, eject, evict 6 dig out, remove, uproot 8 force out, shake off 9 dislocate, extricate 10 knock loose
disloyal: 3 bad 5 false 6 untrue 8 apostate, cheating, factious, forsworn, recreant, renegade, two-faced 9 faithless, seditious, two-timing 10 inconstant, perfidious, rebellious, subversive, traitorous, unfaithful
be ~ to: 6 betray 7 sell out
one: 3 rat 7 traitor 8 quisling
disloyalty: 7 perfidy, treason 8 bad faith 9 defection, falseness, recreancy, treachery, violation 10 conspiracy, infidelity, untrueness
dismal: 3 low, sad 4 base, blue, dark, dour, foul, glum, grim, poor 5 awful,

black, bleak, dingy, drear, dusky, gaunt, heavy, lousy, lurid, mirky, moody, murky, sorry, surly, woful **6** broody, cloudy, crumby, crummy, dreary, gloomy, horrid, leaden, odious, rotten, somber, sullen, woeful **7** accurst, baleful, baneful, beastly, doleful, forlorn, ghastly, joyless, ominous, pitiful, unhappy **8** accursed, darkened, dejected, desolate, dolorous, dreadful, God-awful, grievous, hopeless, horrible, inferior, liverish, lowering, overcast, shameful, stinking, terrible, wretched **9** abhorrent, appalling, atrocious, cheerless, defective, execrable, frightful, insidious, loathsome, miserable, offensive, revolting, saddening, saturnine, sorrowful, tenebrous, unlighted, woebegone **10** abominable, depressing, despicable, detestable, disastrous, horrendous, lugubrious, melancholy, oppressive, tenebrific

Dismal __: **5** Swamp

dismals: **7** sadness **10** melancholy

dismantle: **4** lift, part, ruin, undo **5** level, strip, unrig, wreck **6** ravage, recall, topple **7** break up, destroy, undress **8** bulldoze, demolish, pull down, take down, tear down **9** break down, devastate, knock down, take apart **10** annihilate

Dismas: **5** saint

dismay: **4** care, faze, fear **5** abash, alarm, appal, chill, daunt, dread, panic, scare, shake, shock, upset **6** appall, bother, bum out, deject, fright, put off, rattle, sadden, terror **7** agitate, anxiety, chagrin, disturb, letdown, nonplus, perturb, petrify, terrify, unnerve **8** affright, dispirit, disquiet, distress, frighten, surprise, unstring **9** abashment, agitation, bring down, discomfit, give pause, terrorize, trepidity **10** disappoint, disconcert, discourage, disgruntle, dishearten

cry of ~: **2** ow, oy **3** yow **4** alas, oh no, oh oh, oops, ouch, whew, yeow, yipe **5** alack, oyvey, yipes **6** crikey, whoops **7** caramba, horrors **8** gracious, honestly

dismayed: **5** upset **6** aghast, uneasy **9** awestruck

disme: **4** coin

dismiss: **3** axe, can, cut **4** boot, drop, fire, free, omit, oust, sack, send, shun, veto **5** chuck, eject, evict, expel, let go, purge, spurn **6** banish, bounce, depose, lay off, let off, pass on, pass up, punish, rebuff, recall, reject, remove, revoke, shelve, unseat **7** cashier, cast off, cast out, disdain, drum out, exclude, kick out, neglect, put down, release, relieve, rule out, say no to, send off, turn out **8** brush off, disallow, drive out, exorcise, exorcize, force out, furlough, get rid of, laugh off, pink-slip, pooh-pooh, relegate, send away, sneeze at, turn down **9** blackball, cast aside, discharge, eliminate, freeze out, repudiate, terminate

from one's mind: **6** forget

dismissal: **4** boot **5** congé, exile, the ax **6** congee, denial, layoff, waiver **7** deposal, release, removal **8** brush-off, eviction, pink slip **9** acquittal, discharge, exclusion, expulsion, ostracism, rejection **10** banishment, deposition, liberation, old heave-ho, relegation, suspension, unfrocking

dismount: **4** land **5** light **6** alight, arrive, get off, hopoff **7** descend, get down, jump off

Disney: **3** Roy **4** Walt **6** studio

car: **6** Herbie

character: **3** Doc **4** Chip, Cleo, Dale, Duey, Huey **5** Ariel, Bambi, Daisy, Dopey, Dumbo, Dwarf, Goofy, Happy, Louie, Pongo, Remus **6** Donald, Faline, Figaro, Flower, Grumpy, Ludwig, McDuck, Mickey, Minnie, Oswald, Sleepy, Sneezy **7** Bashful, Cruella, Monstro, Perdita, Scrooge, Thumper **8** Geppetto, Von Drake **9** Daisy Duck, Pinocchio, Snow White **10** Cinderella, Donald Duck, Uncle Remus

competitor: **3** Fox, MGM **7** Miramax, New Line **8** Columbia **9** Paramount, Universal **10** Dreamworks, Warner Bros.

contemporary: **5** Lantz

creation: **4** film **5** movie **7** cartoon

dog: **4** Lady **5** Pluto, Tramp

frame: **3** cel **4** cell

middle name: **5** Elias

network: **3** ABC **4** ESPN **5** ABC-TV

theme park: **5** Epcot

__ Disney: **4** Euro

__ Disney World: **4** Walt

disobedience: **3** sin **6** mutiny **8** defiance **9** rebellion

__ disobedience: **5** civil

disobedient: **3** bad **4** wild **6** unruly **7** defiant, lawless, naughty, wayward **8** contrary, indocile, perverse

disobey: **4** defy **5** break, evade, flout, rebel **6** ignore, mutiny, revolt **7** infract, violate **9** disregard **10** contravene

disoblige: **6** offend, put out **9** displease, incommode **10** discommode

disobliging: **5** loath **9** unwilling

disorder: **4** fuss, mess, muss, riot, stir, to-do **5** brawl, chaos, havoc, mania, mix up, snafu, snarl, swirl, upset **6** bustle, clamor, dither, fracas, hubbub, huddle, jumble, litter, malady, mayhem, mess up, muddle, muss up, ruckus, rumple, rumpus, tumble, tumult, unrest, uproar **7** ailment, anarchy, clutter, confuse, disease, illness, license, mob rule, rioting, scatter, shuffle, snarl up, trouble, turmoil **8** confound, disarray, nihilism, outbreak, shambles, sickness, syndrome, unsettle, violence **9** complaint, confusion, dislocate, imbroglio, infirmity, looseness, mobocracy, patchwork, rebellion **10** affliction, hullabaloo, turbulence, unruliness, untidiness, unwellness

civil ~: **4** riot

disordered: **4** wild **5** messy, mussy, rough, upset **6** hectic, untidy **7** chaotic, haywire, lawless, tousled, unglued **8** pell-mell, slovenly **9** delirious, stirred up, turbulent, unsettled **10** bedraggled, disheveled, disjointed, in an uproar, incoherent, incohesive, out-of-place

disorderly: **4** wild **5** dowdy, messy, mix up, mussy, noisy, rough, rowdy **6** random, unruly, untidy **7** chaotic, jumbled, lawless, muddled, on a tear, raucous, riotous, tangled, unkempt, wayward **8** anarchic, confused, factious, pell-mell, slovenly, unlawful **9** cluttered, fractious, haphazard, irregular, out-of-line, out-of-step, scattered, scrambled, termagant, turbulent, unsettled, untrained **10** anarchical, boisterous, disheveled, disruptive, licentious, out-of-order, out-of-whack, rebellious, refractory, topsy-turvy, tumultuous, unpeaceful, upside down, vociferant

disorderly __: **6** person **7** conduct

Disorderly Orderly, The (1964 film)

cast: Glenda Farrell, Jerry Lewis, Susan Oliver

director: Frank Tashlin

disorganization: **4** mess **5** chaos, mix-up **6** muddle **8** shambles **10** disruption, turbulence

disorganize: **5** mix up **6** jumble, ravage **7** derange, shuffle **8** unsettle

disorganized: **5** messy, upset, wooly **6** ragged, woolly **7** chaotic, haywire, jumbled, mixed up, muddled **8** anarchic, confused, messed up, pell-mell **10** anarchical, disorderly

situation: **3** zoo

disorient: **4** lose **5** addle, cloud **6** muddle **7** confuse **8** befuddle, confound

disorientation: **3** fog

disoriented: **4** asea, lost **5** at sea, spacy **6** adrift, astray, spacey **7** mixed up **8** confused, unhinged, unstable, unstrung

__ di sortita: **4** aria

disown: **4** deny **5** scorn **6** abjure, cut off, recant, reject **7** abandon, forsake **8** abdicate, abnegate, forswear, renounce **9** foreswear, repudiate **10** disinherit

disownment: **9** defection, sundering

disparage: **3** pan, rap **4** gibe, jeer, jibe, mock, slam, slur, snub **5** abase, abuse, cavil, decry, knock, libel, roast, scold, scorn, smear, sneer, spurn, taunt **6** debunk, defame, demean, deride, dump on, heckle, impugn, jibe at, malign, offend, rebuff, slight, vilify **7** affront, asperse, censure, cry down, degrade, detract, put down, rank out, run down, slander, traduce **8** backbite, badmouth, belittle, denounce, derogate, minimize, play down, ridicule, take down, talk down, throw mud, vilipend **9** criticize, denigrate, deprecate, discredit, dispraise, disregard, downgrade, frown upon, fustigate, humiliate, shoot down, underrate **10** calumniate, demoralize, depreciate, discourage, dishearten, undervalue, villainize

disparagement: **3** dig **4** barb, gibe, jibe, slam, slap, slur, snub **5** abuse, blame, libel, scorn, taunt **6** rebuff, slight **7** affront, calumny, catcall, disdain, mockery, obloquy, offense, put-down, sarcasm, scandal, slander **8** contempt, derision, ridicule **9** aspersion, cheap shot, contumely **10** defamation, disrespect, opprobrium

disparager: **6** critic

disparaging: **5** snide **7** abusive **8** captious, critical, libelous **9** sarcastic **10** detractive, pejorative

one: **6** abaser

disparate: **5** other **6** motley, uneven, unlike, varied **7** distant, diverse, unalike, unequal, various **9** different, divergent, unsimilar **10** at variance, discordant, discrepant, dissimilar, poles apart

disparity: **3** gap **7** variety **8** contrast, mismatch **9** deviation, imbalance, otherness, variation **10** difference, dissonance, divergence, divergency, inequality, unevenness, unlikeness

dispassion: **4** calm **8** calmness **9** composure **10** sedateness

dispassionate: **4** calm, cool, fair, just, numb **5** quiet, sober, staid, stoic, stony **6** at ease, low-key, mellow, placid, sedate, serene, square, stoney **7** amiable, at peace, equable, neutral, pacific, relaxed, stoical, unmoved **8** amicable, balanced, carefree, composed, detached, laid-back, moderate, peaceful, tranquil, unbiased **9** collected, easy-going, equitable, impartial, impassive, objective, quiescent, temperate, uncolored, unexcited, unruffled **10** even-handed, nonchalant, unagitated, untroubled

dispatch: **3** eat, zap **4** ease, mail, memo, news, send, ship, slay, word, zeal **5** haste, hurry, issue, remit, route, speed **6** commit, convey, finish, hasten, hustle, launch, letter, report, settle **7** deliver, forward, message, missive, quicken, swallow **8** alacrity, bulletin, celerity, conclude, delivery, rapidity, transfer, transmit, velocity **9** close down, fleetness, news flash, order to go, polish off, quickness, readiness, swiftness **10** communiqué, expedition, memorandum, promptness

boat: **5** aviso

with ~: **3** PDQ **5** apace **6** presto **7** fleetly, hastily, quickly, rapidly, swiftly **8** in a flash, in a jiffy, in no time, pell-mell, speedily **9** forthwith, hurriedly, instantly, like a shot, posthaste

dispatch __: **4** boat, case

Dispatch: **5** paper **9** newspaper

locale: **4** Ohio **8** Columbus

__ Dispatch: **3** Ems

dispel: **3** rid **4** rout **6** banish **7** scatter **9** chase away, drive away

dispensable: **5** spare **8** needless

dispensary: **6** clinic **8** pharmacy

stock: **5** serum **7** vaccine **8** medicine **10** antobiotic

dispensation: **4** dole, gift **5** award, favor, leave **7** amnesty, liberty, license, portion, release, service, serving **8** bestowal, courtesy, kindness

dispense: **3** ply **4** deal, dole, dose, give, mete **5** allot, apply, issue, share, spare, spend, spray **6** assign, divide, manage, ration, render, supply **7** deal out, deliver, dish out, divvy up, dole out, execute, furnish, give out, hand out, inflict, mete out, pass out, portion, provide, release **8** allocate, carry out, disburse, shell out **9** apportion, implement **10** administer, contribute, distribute, measure out

with: **4** shed **5** scrap, spare, waive **6** refuse **7** discard **8** sign away **9** throw away

dispensed amount: **4** dose **6** dosage

dispenser: **6** jobber **7** machine **9** container

like a ~: **6** coin-op

dispersal: **6** spread **9** diffusion

disperse: **4** cast, deal, lift, melt, thin **5** strew **6** divide, fan out, spread **7** bestrew, break up, diffuse, divvy up, dole out, scatter, send off, spatter **9** broadcast, circulate, propagate **10** distribute

dispersed: **4** sown, thin **6** sparse **7** diffuse **10** fractional

dispersion: **5** issue **6** spread **9** diffusion **10** scattering

dispirit: **3** cow **4** dash, tire **5** break, daunt, deter, unman **6** bum out, dampen, darken, deject, dismay, sadden, unglue **7** deflate, depress, oppress, unnerve **8** cast down, dissuade **9** bring down, give pause **10** demoralize, discourage, dishearten, intimidate

dispirited: **3** low, sad **4** blue, down, glum, mopy **5** mopey, woful **6** broody, gloomy, morose, somber, woeful **7** doleful, hangdog, joyless, unhappy **8** dejected, downbeat, downcast **9** bummed-out, cheerless, depressed, exanimate, heartsick, miserable, satur-

nine, sorrowful, unhopeful, woebegone 10 chapfallen, despondent, melancholy
be ~: 4 mope
dispiritedness: 4 funk 8 the blues
dispiriting: 3 sad 5 mirky, murky 6 dismal, dreary, somber
displace: 4 bump, fire, lose, move, oust, sack, vary 5 eject, evict, exile, expel, shift, strip, usurp 6 banish, depose, follow, remove, uproot 7 cashier, replace, succeed 8 crowd out, dethrone, force out, relegate, relocate, supplant, unsettle 9 ostracize, supersede, transport 10 expatriate, infringe on, reposition, substitute, transplant
displaced person: 5 exile 6 émigré 7 outcast, refugee 8 emigrant
group: 3 IRO
displacement: 5 exile, shift
displacement __: 3 ton 4 hull 6 engine 7 current, tonnage
__ displacement: 4 load 5 light 7 angular
display: 3 act, air 4 bare, face, give, look, pomp, show, wear 5 array, exude, flash, front, model, sight, sport, state 6 blazon, effect, evince, expose, flaunt, hold up, layout, parade, reveal, sample, set out, splash, spread, unfold, unfurl, unmask, unroll, unveil 7 arrange, bespeak, example, exhibit, feature, pageant, perform, present, produce, promote, reflect, showing, show off, trot out, uncover 8 brandish, emblazon, evidence, exposure, flourish, indicate, manifest, panorama, pretense, register, showcase, splendor, terminal 9 advertise, exemplify, make known, promenade, spectacle 10 exhibition, exposition, illustrate, pretension, promulgate, revelation
brilliant ~: 5 blaze
combining form: 5 -orama
grand ~: 4 show 5 state 7 fanfare, panoply 8 ceremony, heraldry 9 pageantry
model: 4 demo
put on ~: 4 show 5 array, shown 6 expose
wild ~: 3 mob 4 flap 5 brawl, chaos, scene 6 bedlam, fracas, mutiny, rabble, racket, ruckus, rumble, rumpus, tumult, uproar 7 rampage, turmoil 8 disorder, uprising, violence 9 commotion, imbroglio 10 donnybrook, free-for-all
display-case material: 5 glass
__ display terminal: 5 video 6 visual
displease: 3 irk, vex 4 fret, gall, hurt, miff, rile, roil, tire 5 anger, annoy, peeve, pique, repel, shock, upset 6 bother, enrage, nettle, offend, put out, revolt 7 chagrin, incense, provoke, turn off 8 irritate 9 aggravate, disoblige, frustrate 10 antagonize, disappoint, discompose, discontent, disgruntle, dissatisfy, exasperate
displeased: 3 mad 4 sick 5 angry, upset 8 wrathful 9 disgusted, indignant
look ~: 4 pout 5 frown, scowl
with: 5 mad at
displeasing: 3 off 4 sour 6 bitter 8 brackish 9 offensive, unwelcome
displeasure: 3 ire 5 anger, pique, wrath 6 hatred 7 chagrin, offense, umbrage 8 vexation 9 annoyance
cry of ~: 2 ow 3 boo, boy, yow 4 hiss, moan, ouch, yeow 5 groan
show ~: 4 jeer, pout, sulk 5 frown, scoff, scowl, whoop 6 deride 7 catcall 8 ridicule
disport: 4 play, romp 5 amuse, sport 6 divert 7 delight, refresh 9 amusement, diversion, entertain 10 recreation

disposable: 9 available, throwaway 10 expendable
disposable __: 6 income
disposal: 4 sale 8 riddance
area: 8 landfill
at one's ~: 6 usable 7 useable
put at one's ~: 5 offer 9 volunteer
dispose: 3 set 4 sell, tend 5 array, order, stand 6 locate, settle 7 arrange, incline, marshal, prepare, swallow 8 motivate, organize, regulate 10 predispose
of: 3 rid 4 cede, drop, dump, junk, sell, shed, toss, vend 5 chuck, ditch, forgo, yield 6 finish, forego, give up, peddle, refute, remove, settle, unload 7 abandon, discard, forfeit, forsake 8 close out, forswear, hand over, jettison, part with, throw out, unburden 9 cast aside, eighty-six, eliminate, foreswear, liquidate, polish off, surrender, throw away 10 auction off, do the trick, relinquish, take care of
disposed: 3 apt 4 game 5 prone, ready 6 biased, liable, likely 7 of a mind, partial, tending, willing 8 inclined, prepared
be ~: 4 lean, tend 6 likely
__-disposed: 3 ill 4 well
disposition: 4 mood, side, soul, vein 5 humor 6 esprit, makeup, mettle, morale, nature, spirit, temper 7 impulse, leaning, mindset, posture, tactics 8 aptitude, attitude, decision, ordering, tendency 9 mentality, reception, sentiment 10 propensity
suffix: 3 -ive
dispositions, like some: 5 sunny
dispossess: 3 rob 4 lose, oust 5 eject, evict, expel, usurp 6 divest, put out 7 bereave, deprive 10 disinherit, infringe on
dispossessed: 6 bereft
dispossession: 4 loss
disproportional: 8 lopsided
disproportionate: 5 undue, wrong 6 uneven 7 unequal 8 lopsided 9 overblown
disproportionately: 6 unduly
disprove: 5 belie, break, rebut 6 answer, expose, naysay, negate, refute 7 confute, explode 8 puncture, tear down 9 disaffirm, vindicate 10 contradict, contravene, controvert, disconfirm, invalidate
Dispur: 4 city, town
locale: 5 Assam, India
disputable: 4 moot 7 dubious 8 arguable, doubtful 9 debatable, litigious, uncertain
disputant: 5 rival 6 arguer 7 agonist, debater, fighter 8 litigant, opponent 9 contender 10 antagonist, contestant, polemicist
disputation: 7 quarrel 8 polemics
disputatious: 6 ornery 9 bellicose
dispute: 3 row 4 beef, buck, case, deny, feud, fuss, spar, spat, tiff 5 argue, brawl, clash, fight, query, rebut, run-in, scrap 6 answer, barney, battle, bicker, breach, debate, fracas, hassle, hubbub, impugn, jangle, naysay, negate, oppose, reason, refute, resist, rumpus, strife, tirade, uproar 7 confute, contest, discord, dissent, gainsay, lawsuit, polemic, problem, quarrel, quibble, wrangle 8 argument, brouhaha, conflict, disunity, friction, litigate, mistrust, question, skirmish, squabble, variance 9 bickering, challenge, commotion, disaffirm, encounter, fireworks, go to court, imbroglio 10 contention, contradict, contravene, controvert, difference, falling-out, litigation
in ~: 4 iffy, moot, open 7 dubious 8 arguable, doubtful 9 debatable, uncertain, undecided, unsettled 10 borderline
settler: 6 umpire 7 arbiter, referee
disqualification cause: 4 foul
disqualify: 3 bar 6 recall 7 disable 9 disenable, eighty-six, eliminate 10 disentitle, invalidate
disquiet: 3 din, jar, vex 4 care, fret, jolt, roil, stir, to-do 5 alarm, angst, annoy, noise, qualm, shake, shock, upset, worry 6 bother, dismay, harass, pester, unrest 7 agitate, anxiety, chagrin, concern, ferment, fidgets, fluster, malaise, perturb, shake up, tension, trouble, turmoil, unhinge 8 distress, frighten, unsettle, unstring 9 commotion 10 foreboding, inquietude, solicitude, uneasiness
more than ~: 5 dread 6 terror
disquieted: 5 jumpy, upset 6 uneasy 7 anxious, fearful 9 ill at ease
be ~ about: 4 fear 5 dread
disquieting: 5 queer 8 grievous, sinister
disquietude: 4 fear 5 noise
disquisition: 5 essay 6 thesis 7 lecture, monolog 8 treatise 9 discourse, monologue 10 exposition, literature
Disraeli: 2 P.M. 4 earl 7 British 8 Benjamin
to Gladstone: 5 rival
Disraeli (1929 film)
cast: Florence Arliss, George Arliss, Joan Bennett
Disraeli author: André Maurois
disrate: 6 reduce
disregard: 4 defy, miss, omit, skip, snub 5 break, flout, rebel, scorn, spurn, waive 6 apathy, forget, ignore, laxity, oppose, pass by, rebuff, resist, revolt, slight, wink at 7 abandon, blink at, contemn, disdain, disobey, let pass, neglect, rule out, tune out, violate 8 brush off, contempt, defiance, discount, ignoring, laugh off, lay aside, lethargy, live with, omission, overlook, override, overrule, pass over, pooh-pooh, shrug off, sneeze at, vilipend 9 brush away, disesteem, disparage, eliminate, ignorance, lassitude, oversight, pay no mind, slighting, unconcern 10 brush aside, disrespect, negligence
disregardful: 3 lax 5 slack 8 derelict, heedless 9 negligent
disregarding: 9 in spite of
disrelish: 4 hate 6 loathe
disremember: 6 forget
disrepair, in: 4 worn 6 broken 10 broken-down, on the blink, on the fritz, out of order, out of whack, tumbledown
disreputable: 3 bad, low 4 vile 5 loose, lowly, seamy, seedy, shady 6 abject, louche, no good, shabby, shoddy, sleazy, sordid 7 raffish 8 infamous, shameful, unseemly, unworthy 9 notorious, unethical 10 scandalous
disrepute: 5 odium, shame, taint 6 infamy, stigma 7 obloquy, scandal 8 contempt, ignominy 9 discredit, disesteem, notoriety 10 opprobrium
disrespect: 3 dig 4 barb, gibe, jeer, jibe, mock, sass, slam, slap, slur, snub 5 abuse, decry, libel, scorn, spurn, taunt 6 defame, deride, dump on, heckle, impugn, insult, malign, offend, rebuff, slight, vilify 7 affront, asperse, calumny, catcall, degrade, disdain, impiety, mockery, neglect, obloquy, offense, put down, rank out, slander, traduce 8 belittle, contempt, denounce, derision, ridicule, rudeness, vilipend 9 aspersion, cheap shot, contumely, denigrate, disparage, disregard, flippancy, humiliate, impudence, indignity, insolence, sacrilege 10 calumniate, coarseness, defamation, effrontery, incivility, opprobrium
disrespectful: 4 flip, pert, rude 5 fresh, nervy, rough, sassy, saucy 6 awless, cheeky, snippy 7 aweless, ill-bred, impious, uncivil 8 flippant, impolite, impudent, insolent, inurbane, snippety 9 offensive, sarcastic
be ~: 4 sass
disrobe: 4 peel 5 strip 6 denude 7 take off, undress 8 get out of, unclothe
disrobed: 4 bare, nude 5 naked 8 in the raw 9 in the buff, unattired
disrupt: 4 ruin, stop 5 cut up, mix up, smash, upset 6 bollix, heckle, impede, mess up, muck up, muddle, rattle, ravage 7 agitate, disturb, rupture, shuffle, violate 8 disunite, psych out, sabotage, unsettle 9 dislocate
disruption: 4 ruin, stop 5 break, split, upset 6 schism 7 breakup 8 division, outbreak, sabotage, upheaval 9 breakdown 10 earthquake, separation
business ~: 6 strike
disruptive: 9 confusing, out-of-line, upsetting 10 aggressive, disorderly, disturbing, unsettling
dissatisfaction: 6 regret, unrest 7 anxiety, chagrin 9 annoyance, grumbling
dissatisfied: 6 grumpy 7 unhappy 8 grumpish 9 querulous
dissatisfy: 7 chagrin, let down 9 displease 10 disappoint
dissect: 5 cut up, parse, sever, slice, study 7 analyze, examine, inspect 8 separate 9 anatomize, break down, take apart 10 scrutinize
dissection: 8 analysis 9 breakdown, criticism 10 experiment, inspection
dissemblance: 5 guile
dissemble: 3 lie 4 fake, hide, mask 5 cloak, feign 6 shroud 7 conceal, cover up, deceive, falsify, pretend, profess 8 disguise 9 four-flush, pussyfoot, stonewall, whitewash 10 camouflage, double-talk, masquerade, play possum
dissembler: 5 knave 9 hypocrite
dissembling: 5 lying 6 deceit
disseminate: 3 air, sow 4 deal 5 issue, print, spray, strew 6 effuse, spread 7 bestrew, diffuse, publish, radiate, scatter 8 disperse, proclaim, sprinkle, transmit 9 propagate
dissemination: 5 issue 6 spread
dissension: 4 feud 5 fight, split 6 breach, heresy, strife, unrest 7 discord, faction, quarrel 8 conflict, friction, variance 9 bickering, disaccord 10 antagonism, contention, difference, disharmony, dissidence, dissonance, heterodoxy
sow ~: 6 divide
dissent: 4 balk, flak, vary 5 argue, clash, flack, rebel 6 breach, differ, heresy, object, refuse, revolt, schism, strife 7 discord, dispute, diverge, protest, quarrel, refusal 8 argument, conflict, disagree, disunity, variance 9 objection, rebellion 10 contention, opposition, resistance
religious ~: 9 blasphemy, sacrilege
slangy ~: 3 nah, naw 4 nope
dissenter: 5 rebel 7 heretic, sceptic, skeptic 8 maverick, naysayer, renegade 9 dissident 10 iconoclast, malcontent

dissenting: **8** clashing, negative **9** dissident, heretical, skeptical
vote: **3** nay
dissenting __: **7** opinion
dissertate: **5** speak, write **9** discourse, expatiate
dissertation: **5** essay, paper, theme, tract **6** speech, thesis **7** address, writing **8** critique, treatise **9** discourse **10** exposition
topic: **5** thema
Dissertation on Roast Pig, A author: Charles Lamb
disserve: **4** harm
disservice: **9** detriment, injustice, prejudice **10** unkindness
dissever: **3** saw **5** split **6** cleave **8** disunite
dissidence: **6** strife **7** quarrel **8** variance **9** disaccord **10** contention, difference, disharmony, dissension, dissonance, heterodoxy
dissident: **5** rebel **7** heretic **8** agitator, contrary, factious, renegade **9** differing, dissenter, heretical, heterodox, protester, sectarian **10** discordant, dissenting, rebellious, schismatic, separatist, unorthodox
quest: **6** asylum
dissimilar: **3** new **5** other **6** motley, unlike **7** diverse, unalike, unequal, various **8** contrary, distinct, opposite **9** different, disparate, divergent, unrelated, unsimilar **10** antonymous, individual, mismatched, poles apart
be ~: **6** differ **8** disagree
dissimilarity: **8** contrast **9** variation
dissimulate: **3** lie **4** fake, hide, mask **5** beard, cloak, feign **7** conceal, pretend **8** disguise
dissimulation: **5** guile **8** disguise, pretense
dissimulator: **4** liar
dissipate: **3** eat, sap **4** blow, lift, lose **5** abuse, drain, spend, trash, use up, waste **6** burn up, expend, frivol, lavish, run out, vanish **7** ablates, consume, deplete, exhaust, play out, scatter **8** evanesce, fool away, melt away, misspend, squander **9** attenuate, disappear, drive away, evaporate, throw away **10** fail to keep, gamble away, run through, trifle away
dissipated: **4** gone, lost **5** blown, kaput, loose, spent **6** rakish **7** all gone, immoral **8** misspent **9** abandoned, corrupted, dissolute, excessive, exhausted, played out, scattered **10** gone to seed, profligate, squandered
dissipation: **4** tear, toot **5** binge, waste **6** bender, misuse **10** recreation
dissociate: **5** sever **8** distance **9** disengage, segregate **10** disconnect
dissoluble: **7** endable **9** divisible, separable, severable **10** terminable
dissolute: **3** lax **4** wild **5** loose **6** rakish, wanton, wicked **7** corrupt, immoral, lustful, raffish, wayward **8** depraved, uncurbed **9** abandoned, corrupted, indulgent, libertine, low-minded, on the take, reprobate, shameless, sybaritic **10** dissipated, lascivious, licentious, profligate
one: **4** rake, roué
dissolution: **3** end **5** decay, split **6** ending **7** divorce, parting, split-up **8** division
dissolve: **3** eat, end **4** fade, melt, ruin, thaw, void **5** annul, lysee, mix in, quash, sever **6** cancel, recess, repeal, soften, vanish **7** abolish, adjourn, crumble, defrost, destroy, liquefy, liquify, shatter **8** abrogate, demolish, evanesce, fluidify **9** break down, decompose, disappear, evaporate, liquidate, terminate **10** deliquesce, invalidate
__ dissolve: **3** lap
dissolved: **4** gone **6** liquid
dissolving, remove by: **5** elute
dissonance: **5** noise **6** jangle, strife **7** discord **8** conflict **9** cacophony, disaccord, disparity, harshness **10** antagonism, contention, difference, disharmony, dissension, dissidence
dissonant: **5** harsh, noisy **6** atonal, off-key, unlike **7** grating, jarring, raucous **8** jangling, strident **9** anomalous, different, differing, divergent, irregular, out of tune, unmusical **10** cacophonic, discordant, discrepant, inharmonic
not ~: **5** tonal **7** melodic
dissuade: **3** cow **4** warn **5** daunt, deter **6** advise, dampen, reason **7** caution, prevent **8** dispirit **9** talk out of **10** discourage, dishearten, intimidate
dist. __: **4** atty.
distaff: **5** woman **6** female **8** maternal
distance: **3** gap, lap, way **4** span **5** range, reach, scope, space, width **6** extent, length, spread **7** breadth, compass, reserve, setting, stretch **8** coldness, coolness, interval **9** stiffness **10** dissociate, remoteness, separation
across: **5** width **7** breadth
around: **4** girt **5** girth
at a ~: **3** far, off **4** afar, away **5** apart **6** remote **7** far away **8** outlying
at a ~ from: **6** beyond
at a short ~: **5** anear
British ~ measure: **5** metre
close ~: **4** near
down: **5** depth
elbow-to-fingertip ~: **5** cubit
from the equator: **3** lat. **8** latitude
galactic ~: **4** lt. yr. **9** light year
go the ~: **4** last
keep one's ~: **4** shun, snub **5** evade, scorn, shirk, spurn **6** bypass, ignore, put off, rebuff, slight **7** disdain, dismiss, tune out **8** brush off, shrug off **9** disregard, pay no mind **10** disrespect, leave alone
long ~ line: **4** WATS
measure: **2** km **3** rod **4** mile, pace **5** block, meter, metre **6** fathom, league **7** furlong **9** kilometer
nautical ~: **6** fathom, league
prefix: **3** tel- **4** tele-
short ~: **3** hop **4** inch, step
__ distance: **3** at a **4** long, mean, skip **5** focal, from a, go the, lunar, polar **6** finite, middle, object, social, zenith **7** braking, hailing, horizon, psychic
distant: **3** far, icy, shy **4** afar, away, cold, cool **5** aloof, apart, faint, other, stiff **6** far off, frigid, modest, remote, unlike, yonder **7** bashful, faraway, foreign, outside, removed, unequal, unknown **8** detached, far-flung, outlying, reserved, reticent, retiring, separate, solitary, taciturn **9** diffident, disparate, reclusive, unbending, withdrawn **10** insociable, out of range, out of reach, unagitated, unamicable, unfriendly, unsociable
combining form: **3** tel- **4** tele-, telo-
keep ~ from: **4** shun **5** avoid, skirt
least ~: **7** closest, nearest
less ~: **6** closer, nearer
more ~: **7** farther
most ~: **7** extreme **8** farthest, ultimate
distaste: **4** hate **6** hatred **8** aversion, contempt, loathing **9** antipathy, hostility, repulsion, revulsion **10** abhorrence, repellence, repugnance
cry of ~: **3** ack, ick, rot, ugh **4** bosh, yuck **5** yecch **7** rubbish
having ~ for: **8** averse to
distasteful: **4** icky, ugly, vile **5** nasty, seamy, yucky **6** bitter, odious **7** galling, hateful, insipid, painful **8** annoying, brackish, grievous, unsavory **9** offensive, repellant, repellent, repugnant, repulsive, revolting, thankless, unwelcome **10** unpleasant
Disteghil Sar: **4** peak **8** mountain
locale: **4** Asia **8** Pakistan **9** Himalayas
distend: **4** puff **5** bloat, bulge, swell, widen **6** dilate, expand, fatten, puff up, pump up **7** balloon, enlarge, inflate **8** lengthen **9** intumesce
distended: **5** puffy, tumid **6** turgid **7** bulging, swollen
distention: **5** bulge **8** swelling **9** expansion, extension, inflation
distill: **4** brew, drip **6** desalt, filter, purify, refine **7** cut down, draw out, dribble, extract, ferment, trickle **8** boil down, condense, vaporize **9** evaporate **10** desalinate, desalinize
distillate: **7** extract
distillation: **4** brew
product: **5** ester
distilled: **7** refined **9** alcoholic
distilled __: **5** water
distiller: **6** brewer **7** alembic
distinct: **4** fine **5** apart, clean, clear, exact, lucid, other, plain, sharp, vivid **6** cogent, limpid, marked, patent, single, strong, unique, unlike **7** audible, diverse, evident, express, graphic, legible, obvious, precise, several, unalike, variant, various **8** apparent, clean-cut, definite, discrete, explicit, manifest, palpable, readable, separate, specific **9** different, graphical, graspable, trenchant, unrelated **10** articulate, dissimilar, individual, noticeable, particular, pronounced, spelled out, well-marked
be ~: **8** stand out
combining form: **5** chori-
make less ~: **4** blur, fuzz
not ~: **3** dim **5** fuzzy **6** bleary
distinction: **4** fame, mark, name, note, rank **5** asset, flair, glory, honor, merit, shade, style, value, worth **6** credit, nicety, renown, repute, status **7** earmark, feature, laurels, quality **8** contrast, elegance, eminence, grandeur, prestige, subtlety **9** variation
distinctive: **4** rare **5** novel, sharp **6** proper, signal, unique **7** special **8** discrete, original, peculiar, separate, singular, uncommon
feature: **9** specialty
mark: **6** cachet
quality: **4** aura **5** aroma
distinctly: **8** markedly **9** decidedly, expressly
distinctness: **7** clarity **8** identity
distinguish: **3** see **4** know, spot, tell, view **5** judge, sight **6** define, descry, detect, notice, select, set off, winnow **7** discern, make out, mark off, observe, sort out, specify **8** classify, contrast, estimate, identify, perceive, pinpoint, separate, set apart **9** recognize
between: **7** compare
oneself: **4** star **5** excel, shine
distinguishable: **5** clear, plain **7** evident, visible **8** definite, manifest **10** noticeable, well-marked
distinguished: **3** ace **4** high, star **5** famed, great, lofty, noble, noted **6** famous, signal, single **7** big-name, classic, eminent, honored, notable, special, unusual **8** esteemed, glorious, laureate, renowned, splendid, striking **9** memorable, prominent **10** celebrated, preeminent
be ~ (from): **6** differ
one: **3** VIP **5** great
Distinguished Gentleman, The (1992 film)
cast: Eddie Murphy, Sheryl Lee Ralph, Lane Smith
distinguishing: **8** specific
feature: **5** trait **7** quality **9** specialty
distort: **3** lie **4** bias, skew, warp **5** alter, color, fudge, gnarl, screw, slant, twist, wrest **6** buckle, deform, doctor, garble, injure, mangle, squash, strain, wrench **7** falsify, phony up **8** misquote **9** prejudice
distorted: **3** wry **6** skewed, untrue **7** corrupt, crooked **9** grotesque, jaundiced, malformed
distortion: **3** lie **5** slant **8** travesty **9** asymmetry, falsehood, hyperbole **10** aberration, caricature, contortion, corruption
distract: **5** mix up, upset **6** bemuse, divert, madden, rattle **7** unnerve **8** lead away **9** entertain, preoccupy
distracted: **4** lost, wild **7** worried **9** delirious, forgetful **10** distraught, distressed, hysterical
not ~: **6** intent **7** focused
distractedly: **5** madly **8** absently
distraction: **3** fun **5** feint, hobby **6** escape **7** pastime **10** recreation
drive to ~: **6** enrage, madden
distrait: **4** lost
distraught: **3** mad **6** pacing **7** frantic, worried **8** frenetic, frenzied **9** concerned, flustered, in a lather, perturbed, tormented, unscrewed **10** distracted, distressed, hysterical, irrational, nonplussed
distress: **3** ail, bug, irk, try, vex, woe **4** ache, bane, care, fear, fret, hurt, lack, need, pain, pang, rack, rend, rive, tire **5** agony, alarm, dolor, get to, gloom, grief, harry, hound, peeve, shake, shock, spook, tears, tense, trial, upset, worry, wound **6** affect, bother, dismay, grieve, harass, harrow, injure, injury, misery, needle, offend, ordeal, pester, pick on, plague, prey on, put out, sadden, sorrow, strain, strait **7** afflict, agitate, agonize, anguish, anxiety, bad luck, bedevil, concern, depress, malaise, oppress, sadness, shake up, tick off, torment, torture, travail, trouble, turmoil, weigh on **8** aggrieve, calamity, disquiet, exercise, exigence, exigency, hangover, hardship, hard time, irritate, unstring **9** adversity, aggravate, dejection, grievance, heartache, indigence, privation, suffering **10** affliction, bitterness, depression, desolation, difficulty, discomfort, heartbreak, heavy heart, loneliness, misfortune, woefulness
be in ~: **3** ail **4** ache **5** sweat
cause ~: **4** hurt
cause of ~: **4** bane
cry of ~: **2** oy **4** dear, help, oh no, oh oh, yowl
express ~: **4** moan, wail
one in ~: **6** damsel
signal: **3** SOS **5** flare **7** warning
distress __: **3** gun **4** call, flag, sale **6** signal
distressed: **4** down, hurt **5** sorry, tense, tired, upset, wired, woful **6** afraid, pacing, woeful **7** anxious, doleful, frantic, in a stew, nervous, tearful, uptight, worried **8** downcast, fluttery, frenetic, frenzied, in a tizzy, wretched **9** afflicted, all torn up, bummed-out,

concerned, depressed, exercised, in a lather, miserable, perturbed, sniveling, strung out, tormented, up the wall **10** distracted, distraught

distressed __: 4 area **5** goods

distressing: 3 bad **4** hard, sore **5** sharp, sorry, tight **6** bitter, severe **7** fearful, hurtful, onerous, painful, piteous, pitiful **8** dreadful, grievous, pathetic, poignant, pressing, shocking **9** sorrowful, vexatious **10** lamentable, pathetical

distribute: 4 cast, deal, give, mete, sort **5** allot, divvy, group, issue, order, serve, share, split, strew **6** assign, assort, bestow, convey, deal in, deploy, divide, parcel, ration, spread **7** deal out, deliver, dish out, divvy up, dole out, hand out, mete out, pass out, portion, publish, radiate, scatter, slice up **8** allocate, classify, disburse, dispense, disperse, separate **9** apportion, broadcast, circulate, parcel out, partition, propagate **10** administer, categorize, measure out

distribution: 4 dole **5** issue, order **6** ration **7** dealing, mailing **8** delivery, disposal, dividend, division, grouping, handling, ordering **9** allotting, publicity

agency: 3 syn. **4** synd. **9** syndicate

center: 4 whse. **9** warehouse

combining form: 4 -nomy

__ distribution: 6 normal **7** Poisson

distributor: 6 dealer, jobber **8** auto part

part: 5 rotor

district: 4 area, belt, land, ward, zone **5** local, place, tract **6** county, locale, parish, region, sector **7** grounds, quarter, section **8** locality, location, precinct, province, vicinity **9** territory

ecclesiastical ~: 3 see **7** prelacy **9** bishopric **10** episcopacy

of a ~: 5 zonal **6** zonary

outlying ~: 4 burb

voting ~: 4 area, zone **6** canton, parish **8** district, precinct **9** territory

district __: 3 man **5** court, judge **7** council, manager

__ district: 5 urban **6** school **7** low-rent

__ District: 4 Lake **7** Federal, Garment

Distrito Federal city: 6 México

distrust: 5 doubt, qualm, query **7** suspect **8** bad vibes, mistrust, question, wariness **9** discredit, misgiving, nonbelief, pessimism, smell a rat, suspicion **10** skepticism

distrustful: 3 shy **4** wary **5** chary, leery **6** uneasy, unsure **7** cynical, dubious, fearful, guarded, jealous **8** cautious, doubting, hesitant **9** skeptical, uncertain **10** suspicious

disturb: 3 ail, bug, irk, jar, vex **4** fret, gall, jolt, move, muss, rend, rile, rock, roil **5** alarm, annoy, harry, mix up, peeve, rouse, roust, shake, shift, shock, tease, throw, touch, upset, worry **6** affect, arouse, badger, bother, dismay, excite, flurry, foul up, harass, heckle, jumble, mess up, molest, muddle, needle, nettle, noodge, offend, pester, plague, pother, put out, rattle, ruffle, whip up **7** afflict, agitate, concern, confuse, disrupt, fluster, perturb, provoke, shake up, shuffle, trouble, unnerve **8** convulse, exercise, irritate, mess with, psych out, unsettle, unstring **9** discomfit, incommode, interrupt, overwhelm **10** disarrange, discompose, disconcert

do not ~: 5 let be **10** leave alone

__ Disturb: 5 Do Not

disturbance: 3 row **4** flap, fray, fuss, riot, stir, to-do **5** brawl, furor, scene, shock, storm, upset, worry **6** bother, clamor, flurry, fracas, hoo-hah, hubbub, racket, ruckus, rumble, rumpus, squall, tumult, unrest, uproar **7** ferment, quarrel, rampage, scuffle, trouble, turmoil **8** brouhaha, disorder, upheaval, uprising

stop a ~: 5 quell

disturbing: 5 messy, scary, tight **6** bitter **8** grievous, terrible, untoward **9** agonizing, annoyance, confusing, harrowing, vexatious **10** aggressive, bothersome, burdensome, disruptive, petrifying, unsettling

disunion: 5 split **6** schism **7** divorce, rupture **8** division **9** dichotomy **10** detachment, separation

disunite: 4 part, rend **5** sever, split, untie **6** cleave, cut off, detach, divide, unlink **7** disjoin, disrupt, divorce, scatter, split up **8** alienate, break off, disjoint, dissever, estrange, fragment, separate, set apart, uncouple **9** disaffect, dismember, fall apart, interrupt, set at odds **10** disconnect

disunited: 5 split **10** disjointed

disunity: 4 feud **5** clash **6** breach, strife **7** discord, dispute, dissent, faction **8** argument, conflict, variance **10** contention

disuse: 7 neglect

fallen into ~: 5 passé

sign of ~: 6 cobweb

disused: 5 passé **8** obsolete, outmoded

dit: 3 dot **4** code

partner: 3 dah

ditali: 5 pasta **7** noodles

ditat __: 4 Deus

ditch: 3 pit, rut **4** cede, dike, drop, dump, hide, hole, jilt, junk, moat, sell, shed, shun **5** chuck, drain, forgo, gully, leave, scrap, yield **6** desert, forego, furrow, give up, groove, gullet, gulley, gutter, ravine, reject, trench, trough **7** abandon, channel, culvert, deep-six, discard, forfeit, forsake, foxhole, let go of, scuttle **8** forswear, get rid of, give up on, hand over, jettison, part with, throw out **9** cast aside, dispose of, eighty-six, foreswear, surrender, throw away **10** excavation, relinquish

defensive ~: 5 fosse

in Britain: 4 sike, syke

make a ~: 3 dig

side of a ~: 6 escarp

__-ditch: 4 last

Dith: 4 Pran

dither: 3 fit **4** flap, halt, stew **5** shake, tizzy, waver **6** lather, shiver, tumult **7** shudder, stagger, whiffle **8** disorder, fence-sit **9** commotion, confusion, vacillate **10** excitement, mill around

get into a ~: 4 fret, fuss, stew **5** sweat, worry **7** agonize

in a ~: 4 wild **10** bewildered

Dithers, Mr.: 4 boss **6** Julius

creator: Chic Young

employee: 7 Dagwood **8** Bumstead

wife: 4 Cora

dits and dahs: 4 code **9** Morse code

ditto: 4 also, copy, mock, same **5** again, clone, mimic, Xerox **6** double, ectype, repeat **7** imitate, replica, the same **8** knockoff, likeness, likewise **9** duplicate, facsimile, imitation, photocopy, reiterate

relative: 3 etc.

ditto __: 4 mark

Ditto!: 4 also **5** me too, so am I, so do I **6** agreed, I do too **8** likewise

ditty: 3 air **4** lilt, rime, song, tune **5** music, rhyme **6** ballad, jingle, number **7** lullaby

ditty __: 3 bag, box

ditz: 5 flake, ninny **7** airhead, dingbat

ditzy: 5 giddy, goofy

diurnal: 5 daily **7** per diem **8** day-to-day, everyday **9** quotidian

more than ~: 5 horal

diurnal __: 3 arc **6** circle, motion

div.: 3 seg. **4** dept.

diva: 4 Alda **5** Melba, Moffo, Sills **6** artist, Callas, Norman, Peters, singer **7** actress, Tebaldi **8** Mitchell, musician, vocalist **9** Anna Moffo **10** prima donna, Sutherland

accolade: 5 brava **6** encore

asset: 5 voice

performance: 4 aria, song **5** opera

see also opera, singer

__ Diva: 5 Casta

divagate: 5 stray **6** ramble **7** deviate, digress

divagation: 5 slant **10** digression, divergence

divan: 4 seat, sofa **5** couch **6** day bed, lounge, settee **7** council, ottoman, seating **9** davenport

dive: 3 bar, dip, pub **4** drop, dump, fall, jump, sink, slum, swim, zoom **5** dance, haunt, joint, lunge, pitch, slide, swoop, twist **6** gainer, go down, header, lounge, plunge, pounce, saloon, tavern, tumble **7** barroom, cutaway, decline, descend, descent, hangout, plummet, taproom **8** taphouse **9** belly flop, jackknife, nightclub, worsening **10** cannonball, restaurant, submersion

in: 5 begin, start

starter: 3 sky **4** nose

take a ~: 4 lose, tank

dive __: 5 brake **6** bomber, tables

dive-__: 4 bomb

__ dive: 4 back, nose, swan **5** crash, fancy, front, power, take a **7** cutaway, forward, swallow

__-dive: 4 skin **5** scuba

Dive Bomber (1941 film)

cast: Ralph Bellamy, Errol Flynn, Fred MacMurray

director: Michael Curtiz

diver: 3 auk **4** loon **5** grebe **7** frogman **8** Louganis

combining form: 4 -dyta **5** -dytes

danger: 5 moray, shark

destination: 4 reef **5** coral, wreck

gear: 3 air **4** tank **5** scuba **7** goggles

milieu: 3 sea **5** ocean

Navy ~: 4 Seal

pearl ~: 3 ama

perfect score for a ~: 3 ten

quest: 5 pearl

starter: 3 sky **4** hell

weapon: 5 spear

__ diver: 3 sky **4** skin **5** pearl, scuba

diverge: 4 bend, fork, skew, turn, vary **5** slant, split, stray **6** branch, change, differ, ramble, spread, swerve, wander **7** deviate, digress, dissent, radiate, scatter **8** conflict, contrast, disagree, separate **9** bifurcate

divergence: 3 gap **4** bend, fork, skew **5** break, slant, split **6** detour, schism **7** parting, turning, variety, veering **8** contrast, variance **9** departure, deviation, disparity, gradation, otherness, radiation, variation **10** aberration, alteration, deflection, difference, digression, divagation, separation, unlikeness

divergent: 3 odd, off **4** eery **5** eerie, other, weird **6** atypic, freaky, off-key, quirky, unlike **7** bizarre, deviant, offbeat, strange, unalike, unequal, unusual, variant, various **8** aberrant, abnormal, atypical, freakish, peculiar, separate, uncommon **9** anomalous, deviating, different, differing, disparate, dissonant, eccentric, factional, fantastic, irregular, unnatural, unsimilar, untypical **10** discordant, discrepant, dissimilar, nonuniform, poles apart, unorthodox

divers: 6 sundry, varied **7** several, various **8** assorted

diverse: 4 mixt **5** mixed, other **6** motley, sundry, unlike, varied **7** several, unalike, unequal, variant, various, varying **8** assorted, discrete, distinct, manifold, multiple, opposite, separate **9** different, disparate **10** dissimilar

combining form: 4 vari- **5** vario-

diversify: 3 mix **4** vary **5** alter **6** change, expand, modify **9** branch out, spread out, variegate

diversion: 3 fun **4** game, play **5** hobby, party, sport **6** change, detour, end run, laughs, relief **7** disport, pastime, turning, veering **8** interest, pleasure **9** amusement, avocation, departure, deviation, enjoyment, frivolity, variation **10** aberration, alteration, deflection, digression, recreation, red herring, regalement, relaxation

diversity: 5 range **6** medley **7** variety **8** contrast, mixed bag, variance **9** variation **10** assortment, difference, inequality, miscellany, unlikeness

divert: 4 turn, veer **5** alter, amuse, drain, shunt, steal **6** modify, occupy, please, regale, swerve, switch, tickle **7** beguile, deflect, delight, detract, disport, gladden, gratify, reroute, ward off **8** distract, draw away, interest, lead away, recreate, redirect **9** entertain, preoccupy, sidetrack, turn aside

diverting: 3 fun **4** rich **5** droll, funny, kicky, light, witty **9** laughable

divertissement: 10 recreation

divest: 3 rid, rob **4** bare, dump, lose, oust **5** strip **6** free of, remove, unload **7** deprive, sell off, strip of, take off **8** get rid of **9** liquidate **10** dispossess

divested: 4 bare **5** naked **6** bereft

divide: 3 cut, gap **4** chop, fork, mete, part, sort, tear **5** allot, cross, cut up, grade, group, halve, order, sever, share, slice, split **6** assort, bisect, cleave, cut off, detach, parcel, ration, sunder, unlink **7** arrange, break up, compute, deal out, dish out, disjoin, dole out, hand out, portion, prorate, quarrel, rope off, rupture, scatter, slice up, split up **8** alienate, allocate, break off, classify, cleavage, disburse, dispense, disperse, disunite, estrange, separate, set apart, shell out, uncouple **9** apportion, calculate, disaffect, interrupt, intersect, intervene, parcel out, partition, punctuate, segregate, set at odds **10** categorize, disconnect, distribute, measure out

combining form: 4 -sect

in four: 7 quarter

in three: 7 trisect

in two: 4 half **5** halve **6** bisect

divided: 4 torn **5** apart, in two, split **7** asunder **8** separate **9** sectional **10** fractional

combining form: 3 -fid **5** fissi- **6** -tomous

not ~: 5 whole **6** entire

divided __: 7 highway

__ Divided, A: 5 House

...divided against itself __ stand: 6 cannot

Divided Self, The author: 5 Laing

dividend: 3 cut **4** perc, perk, plum **5** bonus, extra, gravy, prize, share **6** income, return, reward **7** portion, premium, revenue **8** addition, interest **9** allotment

__ dividend: 3 cum **5** extra, peace, scrip, stock **7** accrued, special

divider: 3 net 4 wall 5 fence, panel 6 screen 9 partition
__ divider: 3 bow 4 room 7 voltage
divi-divi: 4 tree 5 shrub
divination: 4 sign 5 magic 6 augury, oracle 7 sorcery 8 prophecy 9 intuition 10 necromancy, prediction
  Chinese book of ~: 6 I Ching
  combining form: 5 -mancy
divinator: 6 oracle 7 prophet
divine: 3 def, rad 4 abbé, aces, A-one, boss, braw, cool, dece, fine, gear, holy, keen, look, neat, nice, phat, tell, tuff 5 blest, dandy, dowse, ducky, godly, grand, great, guess, marvy, neato, nobby, prime, sense, slick, super, swell, tasty 6 bang on, bang-up, bonzer, bosker, choice, cleric, deific, dreamy, far-out, fathom, gnarly, groovy, intuit, lovely, peachy, priest, sacred, scared, slap-up, solemn, spot on, superb, terrif, tiptop, toothy, unreal, whizzo, wicked 7 amazing, angelic, awesome, blessed, capital, corking, deistic, exalted, godlike, perfect, predict, ripping, saintly, skookum, stellar, sublime, supreme 8 almighty, anointed, beatific, blissful, dazzling, especial, ethereal, eximious, fabulous, five-star, foretell, four-star, frabjous, glorious, heavenly, jim-dandy, perceive, preacher, prophesy, slam-bang, smashing, splendid, standout, sterling, stickout, superior, supernal, terrific, theistic, top-level, topnotch, very good, wondrous 9 ambrosial, angelical, beautiful, bodacious, celestial, delicious, Endsville, excellent, exemplary, exquisite, first-rate, high-grade, hunky-dory, ineffable, marvelous, nectarous, palatable, religious, sollicker, spiritual, succulent, top-flight, unearthly, unrivaled, wonderful 10 appetizing, delectable, first-class, hotsy-totsy, jack-a-dandy, omnipotent, omniscient, out of sight, peachy-keen, phenomenal, remarkable, sanctified, stupendous, super-duper, superhuman, unrivalled
  name meaning ~: 5 Diana, Diane
  one: 3 god 5 deity 7 goddess
  spirit: 5 numen
  will: 4 fate 7 destiny
divine __: 5 right 6 office 7 healing, service
Divine __: 4 Mind 5 Poems 6 Mother 7 Liturgy
Divine __, The: 4 Lady 5 Miss M 6 Comedy, Milieu
Divine Comedies author: James Merrill
Divine Comedy, The: 4 epic, epos, poem
  author: Dante
  character: 4 Adam, Cato, Nino 5 Aruns, Capet, Dante, Guido, Jason, Manto, Minos, Paolo, Sapia, Sinon 6 Charon, Chiron, Nessus, Nimrod, St. Lucy, Virgil 7 Cheiron 8 Beatrice
Divine Elegies poet: 5 Rilke
divine helmet, name meaning: 6 Anselm
Divine Milieu, The author: Pierre Teilhard de Chardin
Divine Miss M, The: 5 Bette 6 Midler
divine peace, name meaning: 7 Jeffrey 8 Geoffrey
Divine Poems author: John Donne
diviner: 4 seer 5 augur, magus, sibyl 6 oracle, wizard 7 aruspex, prophet 8 Chaldean, haruspex, magician, sorcerer 9 predictor 10 astrologer, forecaster, soothsayer
Divine Secrets of the Ya-Ya Sisterhood (2002 film)
  cast: Sandra Bullock, Ellen Burstyn, Fionnula Flanagan, Ashley Judd
  director: Callie Khouri
divine strength, name meaning: 6 Astrid
diving: 5 sport 10 water sport
  area: 4 pool
  bird: 3 auk 4 coot, loon 5 grebe, murre, ousel, ouzel, solan 6 auklet, dipper
  duck: 5 scaup 6 scoter 7 pochard, scooter 9 goldeneye, merganser
  position: 4 tuck
  starter: 3 sky
diving __: 4 bell, boat, duck, suit 5 board 6 beetle, petrel, reflex
__ diving: 3 sky 4 free, skin 5 fancy, scuba
diving-bell inventor: 4 Eads
diving-suit material: 5 latex
divining: 5 vatic 8 oracular
  combining form: 6 -mantic
  rod: 4 twig 6 dowser
  rod shape: 3 wye
  use a ~ rod: 5 dowse
divinity: 3 God 5 candy, deity 7 goddess, godhood 8 holiness 9 godliness
divinity __: 5 fudge 6 school 7 circuit
__ divinum: 3 jus
divisible: 10 dissoluble
  by two: 4 even
  not ~ by two: 3 odd
division: 3 arm, cut, gap 4 army, link, part, rift, sect, side, unit, ward, wing 5 break, class, corps, crack, force, piece, round, share, slice, split, squad, stage 6 border, branch, bureau, detail, legion, member, parcel, ration, region, schism, sector 7 bracket, carving, chapter, divorce, fission, parting, phalanx, portion, rending, rupture, section, segment, species 8 boundary, breaking, category, cleavage, disunion, fraction, grouping, precinct, province, variance 9 affiliate, bisection, detaching, dichotomy, partition 10 department, detachment, disruption, disuniting, proportion, separation
  word: 4 into
division __: 4 ring, sign 7 algebra
__ division: 3 air 4 cell, long, root 5 first, short 6 Encke's, second 7 benthic, Cassini, pelagic
division of __: 5 labor
Divo: 4 city, town
  locale: 10 Ivory Coast
__ d'Ivoire: 4 Cote
divorce: 5 sever, split 6 detach, sunder 7 breakup, disjoin, rupture 8 disunion, disunite, division, separate 10 detachment, disconnect, separation
Divorce American Style (1967 film)
  cast: Debbie Reynolds, Jason Robards, Jean Simmons, Dick Van Dyke
  director: Bud Yorkin
divorced: 5 apart, split, unwed 6 single 9 unmarried
divorcée: 2 ex
__ Divorcee, The: 3 Gay
Divorce-Italian Style (1962 film)
  cast: Marcello Mastroianni, Daniela Rocca, Stefania Sandrelli
  director: Pietro Germi
divot: 3 sod 4 turf
divulge: 3 air, say 4 bare, blab, leak, show, talk, tell 5 admit, break, let on, spill, utter, voice 6 betray, expose, impart, let out, relate, reveal, unfold, unmask, unveil 7 confess, declare, exhibit, lay bare, let slip, mention, uncover 8 announce, disclose, give away, proclaim, unburden 9 broadcast, make known 10 make public
divulgence: 6 exposé 9 admission 10 confession, disclosure, revelation, unbosoming
divulse: 4 tear
divvy up: 4 deal, give 5 allot, halve, issue, share, split 6 ration 7 deal out, dish out, dole out, hand out, mete out, pass out, portion 8 allocate, disburse, dispense, disperse 9 apportion, parcel out, partition 10 distribute, measure out
Dix: 4 Fort 7 Dorothy, Richard 8 Dorothea
Dix Hills: 4 city, town
  locale: 7 New York
Dixie: 4 toon 5 mouse, South 6 Carter 9 Deep South
  ender: 4 land
  fighter: 3 reb
  once: 3 CSA
  pronoun: 4 y'all
Dixie (1943 film)
  cast: Bing Crosby, Billy DeWolfe, Dorothy Lamour
  director: A. Edward Sutherland
Dixie __: 3 Cup 4 Land 6 Chicks
__ Dixie: 7 whistle
__-Dixie: 4 Winn
Dixiebelles song: Papa Joe's (1963)
Dixiecrat: 5 party
Dixie Cups song: Chapel of Love (1964)
Dixieland: 4 jazz 5 music
  dance: 5 stomp
  instrument: 5 banjo 7 trumpet
__ dixit: 4 ipse
Dixon: 4 Ivan 5 Donna, Jeane
  colleague: 5 Cayce, Mason
Dixon, Donna spouse: Dan Aykroyd
__-Dixon line: 5 Mason
dizain: 4 poem
dizzy: 4 gaga, hazy, zany 5 aswim, dazed, faint, flaky, giddy, inane, light, mix up, queer, rocky, shaky, silly, tipsy, woozy 6 addled, flakey, giggly, groggy, punchy, wabbly, wobbly 7 flighty, foolish, fuddled, muddled, reeling 8 confused, skittish, unstable, unsteady, whirling 9 befuddled, slaphappy, squeamish 10 bewildered, staggering, weak-minded
  be ~: 4 reel, swim 5 swirl, whirl
Dizzy: 4 Dean 9 Gillespie
Dizzy (1969 song) artist: Tommy Roe
dizzying: 5 heady, steep 10 immoderate, inordinate
  designs: 5 op art
  itinerary: 6 flurry
DJ: 10 disc jockey
  need: 2 CD, LP 3 amp, mic 4 mike 5 album 10 microphone
D.J. __ Jeff: 5 Jazzy
Djakarta: 4 city, town 7 capital
  locale: 9 Indonesia
djanger: 5 dance
Djebar, Assia: 6 writer 8 Algerian
djellabah: 4 robe
  wearer: 4 Arab
djembé: 4 drum
  origin: 6 Africa
Djibouti: 4 city, town 6 nation 7 capital, country
  capital: 8 Djibouti
  group: 10 Arab League
  gulf east of ~: 4 Aden
  language: 6 Somali
  locale: 6 Africa
  money: 5 franc
  neighbor: 7 Eritrea, Somalia 8 Ethiopia
  people: 4 Afar, Issa 6 Somali 7 Danakil
D.J. Jazzy Jeff: 6 rapper, singer
djun djun: 4 drum
  origin: 6 Africa
DLO org.: 4 USPS
__ D. MacDonald: 4 John
__-D.M.C.: 3 Run
Dmitri: 7 Tiomkin 9 Karamazov, Mendeleev
DMV document: 3 lic. 7 license
Dmytryk, Edward: 8 director
  film: Back to Bataan (1945)
    Broken Lance (1954)
    The Caine Mutiny (1954)
    Confessions of Boston Blackie (1941)
    Cornered (1945)
    Crossfire (1947)
    Hitler's Children (1943)
    The Left Hand of God (1955)
    Mirage (1965)
    Murder, My Sweet (1944)
    Raintree County (1957)
    The Sniper (1952)
    Soldier of Fortune (1955)
    So Well Remembered (1947)
    Till the End of Time (1946)
    Warlock (1959)
    The Young Lions (1958)
DMZ, part of: 4 zone
DNA
  ender: 3 ase
  part of ~: 4 acid 5 deoxy
  segment: 3 ATP 4 exon, gene 5 helix
DNA __: 4 test 5 probe, virus
__ DNA: 4 junk 7 genomic
Dnieper: 5 river
  city on the ~: 4 Kiev 5 Orsha
  locale: 6 Russia 7 Belarus, Ukraine
  river to the ~: 5 Desna 6 Pripet 8 Berezina
Dniester: 5 river
  city on the ~: 5 Odesa 6 Odessa
  locale: 6 Russia
do: 3 act, ape, con 4 ball, bash, bilk, copy, dupe, fare, fest, fete, gala, hoax, note, play, suit, tour, verb, wage, work 5 adapt, avail, cause, cheat, cover, event, get by, party, see to, serve, solve, trick, visit 6 act for, affair, behave, create, effect, finish, fleece, fulfil, look to, render, take on, wrap up 7 achieve, arrange, deceive, defraud, execute, explore, fulfill, jubilee, operate, perform, portray, prepare, produce, pull off, realize, resolve, satisfy, suffice, swindle, two-time, work out 8 attend to, carry our, carry out, coiffure, complete, conclude, decipher, flimflam, function, get along, ponytail, practice, transact, travel in 9 festivity, figure out, hairstyle, reception 10 accomplish, effectuate, feather cut, perpetrate, rejuvenate
  again: 6 repeat 7 run over 8 practice 9 reiterate
  agree to ~: 6 take on 9 undertake
  all right: 3 win 6 hack it, make it, manage, thrive 7 make out, prevail, prosper, triumph 8 flourish, go places, make good
  a number: 4 sing 5 croon 6 warble 8 vocalize
  a number on: 4 bilk, dupe, gull, rook 5 cheat, shaft 6 defame, delude, take in 7 deceive, defraud, swindle 8 flimflam
  away with: 3 ban, end, rid 4 kill, slay, stop 5 purge, scrub 6 efface, murder, remove, uproot 7 abolish, obviate, root out 8 dissolve, get rid of 9 eliminate, eradicate, liquidate, slaughter 10 put an end to
  can't ~ without: 4 need
  fail to ~: 4 miss, omit, shun, skip, snub 5 avoid, evade, scorn, shirk, spurn

6 bypass, eschew, forget, ignore, pass by 7 let pass, neglect 8 brush off, let slide, overlook, pass over 9 disregard, gloss over
for: 4 tend 5 serve 7 cater to 8 minister
have to ~ with: 6 belong, regard, relate 7 concern 9 as regards
how do you ~: 2 hi 4 ciao, hail 5 aloha, hello, howdy 7 bon jour, welcome
like: 4 echo 5 mimic 6 follow 7 imitate 8 simulate
make ~: 3 eke 4 cope 5 adapt, get by 6 eke out, manage 7 survive 8 get along, scrape by 9 just get by
make ~ with: 3 use
nothing: 3 sit, veg 4 idle, laze, loll 5 sit by, slack 6 rest up 7 slacken 8 lally-gag
nothing about: 5 sit on 6 stifle 7 squelch 8 suppress, withhold
offhand: 5 ad-lib 6 wing it 7 dash off
old-style: 4 dost
one's utmost: 3 aim, try, vie 4 moil, push, toil 5 essay, fight, labor, sweat 6 strain, tackle, take on 7 attempt, compete, contend 8 bear down, endeavor, go all out, scramble, shoot for, struggle 10 go for broke, go the limit
on one's own: 5 offer 6 enlist, sign up 7 pitch in, proffer, recruit, stand up, venture 9 undertake 10 put forward
out of: 3 con, rob 5 steal
over: 6 repeat, replay 7 remodel 8 rehearse 9 replicate 10 redecorate
perfectly: 3 ace 4 nail
preceders: 4 la ti
repeatedly: 5 drill
say I ~: 5 marry 10 get hitched, tie the knot
something: 3 act
things to ~: 6 agenda
up: 3 tie 4 lace, wrap 6 clothe, fasten 8 decorate, emblazon 9 embellish, refurbish 10 rejuvenate
voraciously: 6 devour
well: 3 ace 5 excel 6 make it, thrive 7 make out, prosper 8 flourish, hit it big, make good
what one can: 3 try 6 strive 7 attempt, have a go, venture 9 have a go at, have a shot, have a stab 10 have a whack
without: 4 need 5 forgo, spare 6 forego 7 abstain, refrain 8 keep from
wrong: 3 err, sin 10 transgress
do ___: 3 for 4 over, to a T, with 5 or die 6 battle 7 without
do ___ burn: 5 a slow
do ___ on: 4 a job
do ___ T: 3 to a
do ___ to: 6 credit 7 justice
do ___ turn: 5 a good
do ___ with: 4 away
do-___: 3 all, rag 4 good, re-mi, si-do 5 or-die 6 gooder 7 nothing
___ do: 4 make
___-do: 3 can 4 do-si 7 derring
Do ___: 4 Re Mi
Do ___!: 4 tell
Do ___ a Waltz?: 5 I Hear
Do ___ Believe in Love: 3 You
Do ___ Believe in Magic: 3 You
Do ___ Diddy Diddy: 3 Wah
Do ___ gently...: 5 not go
Do ___ others...: 4 unto
Do ___ say...: 3 as I
Do ___ to eat a peach?: 5 I dare
___ Do: 4 But I 5 No Can
do a ___ deed: 4 good
D.O.A. (1950 film)
cast: Luther Adler, Pamela Britton, Edmond O'Brien
director: Rudolph Maté
doable: 4 easy 6 likely, viable 8 credible, feasible, possible, workable 9 plausible, potential, practical 10 achievable, attainable, imaginable
Doak: 6 Walker
Doakes: 3 Joe
do-all: 8 factotum, handyman 9 man Friday 10 girl Friday
___ do anything better...: 4 I can
___ Doats: 6 Mairzy
DOB: 4 stat.
dobbin: 5 horse, mount 6 equine 9 farm horse
Dobbs Ferry: 4 city, town
college: 5 Mercy
locale: 7 New York
Dobbs, Lou: 8 reporter 10 newscaster
network: 3 CNN
Doberman Pinscher: 3 dog 5 canid 6 canine
Dobie: 4 Gray 6 Gillis
Döblin, Alfred: 6 German, writer
doblon: 5 money
Doboj: 4 city, town
locale: 6 Bosnia
Dobric: 4 city, town
locale: 8 Bulgaria
Dobro: 6 guitar, string
dobson: 3 fly
Dobson: 5 Kevin
dobsonfly: 3 bug 6 insect
Doby, Larry: 6 Indian 10 outfielder
Dobyns, Stephen: 6 writer
doc
see doctor
doc.: 3 lic. 4 cert. 6 certif.
Doc: 5 Adams, dwarf 6 Savage 8 Cheatham, Holliday 10 Severinsen
colleague: 5 Dopey, Happy 6 Grumpy, Sleepy, Sneezy 7 Bashful
friend: 5 Wyatt
___ d'occasion: 5 pièce
___ Doc Duvalier: 4 Papa
docent: 5 guide 8 lecturer
Doc Hollywood (1991 film)
cast: Bridget Fonda, Michael J. Fox, Barnard Hughes, Julie Warner
director: Michael Caton-Jones
Doc Horne author: George Ade
docile: 4 easy, meek, mild, soft, tame 5 lowly, mousy, quiet 6 broken, gentle, mellow, mousey, pliant 7 dutiful, orderly, passive, pliable, subdued, trained 8 amenable, lamblike, obedient, resigned, sheepish, yielding 9 adaptable, compliant, easygoing, tractable 10 manageable, submissive
one: 5 sheep
docility: 8 humility 10 submission
dock: 3 top 4 clip, fine, land, moor, pare, pier, port, quay, slip, trim 5 berth, jetty, levee, lieup, prune, put in, tie up, wharf 6 anchor, deduct, harbor, hook up, link up, marina 7 harbour, landing, shorten 8 penalize 9 anchorage 10 waterfront
crane: 5 davit
do ~ work: 4 lade
ender: 3 age 4 hand, side, yard 6 worker
fitting: 5 cleat
leave the ~: 4 sail 8 shove off
submarine ~: 3 pen
support: 4 pile
___ dock: 3 dry, ice, wet 4 sour 5 scene 6 bitter 7 graving, loading, spinach
docked, not: 4 asea 5 at sea
docket: 4 card, file, list 5 index 6 agenda, ticket 7 program 8 calendar, schedule 9 timetable
detail: 4 item 5 trial
word: 6 People, versus
___ docket: 5 trial
docking ___: 4 keel 6 bridge 7 station
Dockstader: 3 Lew
dockworker: 5 lader
org.: 3 ILA
doctor: 2 GP, MD 3 fix, rig, vet 4 cook, cure, edit, heal, mend 5 alter, color, fix up, fudge, medic, taint, treat 6 adjust, deacon, garble, healer, intern, juggle, medico, modify, remedy, repair, revise, tamper 7 correct, distort, falsify, interne, patch up, rectify, retouch, surgeon, touch up 8 graduate, medicate, minister, overhaul, sawbones 9 internist, physician 10 specialist, tamper with
advice: 5 relax
animal ~: 3 DVM, vet
assistant: 2 RN 3 LPN 5 nurse
assn.: 3 HMO
baby ~ for short: 2 OB
bk.: 3 PDR
circuit: 6 rounds
device: 5 pager 6 beeper
display: 6 degree
disreputable ~: 5 quack
ender: 3 ate
eye ~: 7 oculist
fam. ~: 2 GP
future ~ exam: 4 MCAT
GI ~: 5 medic
income: 3 fee
Islamic ~: 5 ulema
London ~ street: 6 Harley
need a ~: 3 ail
new ~: 6 intern 7 interne
office: 6 clinic
office call: 4 next
order: 2 Rx 4 dose, stat 5 say ah
org.: 3 AMA
picture: 4 X-ray
prescription: 4 drug 6 dosage
spin ~: 5 pr man
vessel: 5 ampul 6 ampule 7 ampoule
word for the ~: 3 aah
doctor ___, The: 4 is in
___ doctor: 3 eye 4 fish, foot, herb, play, root, spin 5 house, juris, snake, witch 6 family, flying, script, silver 7 medical
Doctor ___: 3 Sax, Who 5 Spock 6 Pascal 7 Detroit, Zhivago 9 Doolittle
Doctor ___ House: 5 in the
doctoral
exam: 4 oral
presentation: 6 thesis
doctorate: 3 Ph.D. 6 degree
Doctor Detroit (1983 film)
cast: Dan Aykroyd, Donna Dixon, Howard Hesseman
Doctor! Doctor! (1984 song) artist: Thompson Twins
Doctor Dolittle (1967 film)
cast: Richard Attenborough, Samantha Eggar, Rex Harrison, Anthony Newley
director: Richard Fleischer
dog: 3 Jip
Doctor Dolittle (1998 film)
cast: Peter Boyle, Ossie Davis, Eddie Murphy, Oliver Platt
director: Betty Thomas
dog: 5 Lucky
tiger: 5 Jacob
doctored: 9 falsified
doctoring: 9 treatment 10 corruption
Doctor My Eyes (1972 song) artist: Jackson Browne
Doctorow, E.L.: 6 writer
alma mater: Kenyon
first name: Edgar
work: Big as Life
Billy Bathgate
The Book of Daniel
City of God
Loon Lake
Ragtime
The Waterworks
Welcome to Hard Times
World's Fair
Doctor Pascal author: Emile Zola
doctor's ___: 6 degree, orders
Doctor Sax author: Jack Kerouac
Doctor's Dilemma (1958 film)
cast: Dirk Bogarde, Leslie Caron, Alastair Sim
director: Anthony Asquith
Doctor's House, The author: Beattie
Doctor Takes a Wife, The (1940 film)
cast: Reginald Gardiner, Ray Milland, Loretta Young
Doctor, The (1991 film)
cast: William Hurt, Christine Lahti, Elizabeth Perkins
director: Randa Haines
___ Doctor, The: 4 Good 7 Country
Doctor Zhivago: 4 film 5 novel
author: Boris Pasternak
cast: Geraldine Chaplin, Julie Christie, Alec Guinness, Omar Sharif, Rod Steiger
character: 4 Lara, Nika, Yuri 5 Pasha, Tania, Tonia
director: David Lean
locale: 5 Urals 6 Russia
doctrinaire: 5 bigot 8 believer, pedantic 9 sectarian 10 pedantical
doctrinal: 8 dogmatic, orthodox 9 religious 10 dogmatical
doctrine: 3 ism 4 lore 5 axiom, canon, credo, creed, dogma, faith, tenet 6 belief, gospel, policy, theory 7 article, precept 8 position, religion, teaching 9 principle, teachings 10 conviction, philosophy, propaganda
combining form: 4 -logy
___ Doctrine: 5 Nixon 6 Monroe, Truman
document: 4 deed, form, page, show, text, writ 5 paper, prove, title 6 policy, record, report, script, ticket, verify 7 charter, itemize, license, writing 8 evidence 9 indenture 10 prospectus
addendum: 5 rider
auto ~: 5 lease, title
blank ~: 4 form
business ~: 3 rpt. 6 report
legal ~: 4 deed, will, writ 5 brief, lease 7 warrant
ownership ~: 4 deed 5 title
part: 6 clause
storage medium: 5 fiche 9 microfilm
travel ~: 4 visa 8 passport
___ Document: 4 The R
documentary: 4 film 5 drama, genre 6 report 10 production
documentation: 5 proof 6 record 8 evidence
documented: 4 sure 5 valid 8 verified 10 historical
DOD
division: 3 USN 4 USAF, USMC
part of ~: 4 dept. 7 defense
place: 7 Cabinet
program: 3 SDI
VIP: 3 CNO
weapon: 3 ABM 4 ICBM
dodder: 4 limp 5 shake, weave 6 hobble, totter 7 tremble
doddering: 5 anile 6 infirm 9 faltering, tottering, trembling
Dodecanese island: 5 Leros 6 Patmos, Rhodes, Rhodos
dodeca-, one-third of: 5 tetra-
dodge: 4 duck, hoax, juke, lose, plot, ploy, ruse, scam, shun, veer, wile 5 avoid, cheat, elude, evade, feint, fence, fudge, hedge, lurch, parry, shake, shift, shirk, skirt, slack, trick, wince 6 bypass, device, dupery,

escape, eschew, racket, recoil, refuse, scheme **7** abstain, con game, evasion, fend off, gimmick, quibble, slacken **8** artifice, flee from, get out of, intrigue, maneuver, shake off, sidestep, strategy, trickery **9** chicanery, deception, get around, hem and haw, pussyfoot, runaround, skip out on, stratagem **10** circumvent, equivocate, subterfuge
Dodge: **3** car **4** auto **10** automobile
model: **4** Colt, Dart, Neon, Omni **5** Aries, Aspen, Royal, Viper **6** DeLuxe, Lancer, Magnum, Mirada, Monaco, Polara, Seneca, Shadow, Sierra, Spirit **7** Avenger, Caravan, Charger, Coronet, Durango, Dynasty, Matador, Phoenix, Pioneer, Stealth, Stratus, St. Regis, Swinger **8** Diplomat, Intrepid, Suburban, Wayfarer **9** Medallion **10** Challenger
partner: **6** Phelps
dodgeball: **4** game
Dodge City: **4** city, town
locale: **6** Kansas
marshal: **4** Earp
Dodge City (1939 film)
cast: Olivia de Havilland, Errol Flynn, Ann Sheridan
director: Michael Curtiz
Dodge, Mary Mapes: **6** writer
work: Hans Brinker
dodger: **5** cheat **6** evader **7** escapee **8** deserter, swindler **9** throwaway
___ dodger: **4** corn **5** draft
Dodger: **4** NLer **10** baseballer
great: **5** Reese, Vance, Wheat **6** Hodges, Koufax, Snider, Sutton **8** Drysdale, Robinson **9** Don Sutton, Gil Hodges, Zach Wheat **10** Campanella, Dazzy Vance, Duke Snider
rival: **3** Cub, Met, Red **4** Expo, Twin **5** Angel, Astro, Brave, Giant, Padre, Rocky, Royal, Tiger **6** Brewer, Indian, Marlin, Oriole, Philly, Pirate, Ranger, Red Sox, Yankee **7** Blue Jay, Mariner **8** Athletic, Cardinal, Devil Ray, White Sox
Dodgers: **4** nine, team
home: **10** Los Angeles
old ~ field: **6** Ebbets
org.: **3** MLB, MLW
sport: **8** baseball
dodging: **6** escape, shifty **7** evasion
dodgy: **7** evasive
Dodie: **5** Smith
dodo: **3** ass, nit **4** bird, dolt **5** dummy, dunce **7** airhead, dullard, old fogy **8** dumbbell, numskull **9** birdbrain, lamebrain, numbskull, simpleton **10** dunderhead, fuddy-duddy, nincompoop
dodo ___: **4** bird **5** split
Do Do Do composer: **8** Gershwin
Dodoma: **4** city, town **7** capital
locale: **8** Tanzania
Do do that ___...: **6** voodoo
Dodsworth: **4** film **5** novel
author: Sinclair Lewis
cast: Mary Astor, Ruth Chatterton, Walter Huston, Paul Lukas, David Niven
character: **3** Sam, Tub **4** Fran, Hurd, Ross **5** Brent, Emily, Matey
director: William Wyler
Dody: **7** Goodman
doe: **3** she **4** deer, hind **6** animal, female
ender: **4** skin
mate: **4** buck, hart, stag
offspring: **4** fawn
doe-___: **4** eyed
Doe: **4** Jane, John
Doe, a ___...: **4** deer
___ d'oeil: **4** coup
Doe, Jane: **5** woman **6** female
Doe, John: **3** man **4** male
doer: **6** dynamo, worker **7** hustler **8** achiever, activist, effector, go-getter, live wire, operator
good: **4** hero
good-deed ~: **4** hero **7** heroine
starter: **4** evil **5** wrong
suffix: **3** -ist **4** -ator
doer of good, name meaning: **8** Boniface
Doerr, Bobby: **6** Red Sox **10** baseballer
Does ___, or doesn't...: **3** she
Does Anybody Really Know What Time It Is? (1970 song) artist: Chicago
___ does it: **4** easy, that
___ Does It Better: **6** Nobody
doeskin: **7** leather
Doesn't Anybody Love Me? (1955 song) artist: McGuire Sisters
___ Doesn't Live Here Anymore: **5** Alice
Doesn't Really Matter (2000 song) artist: Janet Jackson
Does the Spearmint ___...: **4** lose
Does Your Chewing Gum ... (1961 song) artist: Lonnie Donegan
___-d'oeuvre: **4** chef
do-fa filler: **4** re mi
doff: **3** tip **4** shed **5** unhat **6** remove **7** discard, take off, undress **8** get out of
opposite: **3** don
the cap to: **5** greet **6** salute
___ Do Fools Fall in Love: **3** Why
___ do for now!: **4** It'll
dog: **3** cur, Lab, mut, nag, pet, pug, pup, tag **4** chow, Fido, flop, foot, mutt, peke, puli, tail **5** boxer, canid, chase, corgi, dance, dhole, dingo, feist, haunt, hound, husky, knave, pooch, puppy, spitz, stalk, tease, track, trail, worry **6** animal, bad guy, barker, beagle, borzoi, bother, bowwow, briard, canine, collie, follow, harass, heeler, hunter, kelpie, kuvasz, mammal, Nipper, pester, plague, poodle, pursue, saluki, setter, shadow, vizsla **7** basenji, bulldog, courser, harrier, lowchen, Maltese, mastiff, mongrel, pit bull, pointer, samoyed, sheltie, shih tzu, spaniel, terrier, tootsie, whippet **8** alsatian, Brittany, chow chow, cockapoo, elkhound, foxhound, Havanese, house pet, keeshond, komondor, papillon, run after, shepherd, shiba inu, springer **9** Chihuahua, dachshund, Dalmatian, gazehound, great Dane, greyhound, Lhasa apso, Marmaduke, Pekingese, persecute, retriever, schnauzer, track down **10** bloodhound, fox terrier, otterhound, Pomeranian, rottweiler, schipperke, weimaraner, Welsh corgi **14** wolfhound akita
astronomical ~: **5** Canis
baby ~: **3** pup **5** puppy
bad ~: **5** biter
bane: **4** flea, lice **5** mange
bird ~: **5** hound, scout
black-tongued ~: **4** chow
breed: **3** Lab, pug **4** chow, peke, puli **5** akita, boxer, corgi, spitz **6** beagle, borzoi, briard, collie, kuvasz, poodle, saluki, vizsla **7** basenji, bulldog, harrier, lowchen, Maltese, mastiff, pit bull, pointer, samoyed, sheltie, shih tzu, terrier, whippet **8** Brittany, chow chow, elkhound, foxhound, Havanese, keeshond, komondor, papillon, shiba inu **9** Chihuahua, dachshund, Dalmatian, great Dane, greyhound, Lhasa apso, Pekingese, schnauzer **10** bloodhound, fox terrier, otterhound, Pomeranian, rottweiler, schipperke, weimaraner, Welsh corgi
breeder org.: **3** AKC
brush the ~: **5** groom
chain: **5** leash
combining form: **3** cyn- **4** cyno-
command: **3** beg, sic, sit **4** come, heel, mush **5** shake, sic 'em, sit up, speak **8** roll over
curly-tailed ~: **5** Akita
doc: **3** vet, VMD
document: **3** lic. **7** license
drink like a ~: **5** lap up
ender: **3** ear, leg, nap **4** bane, cart, face, fish, gone, sled, trot, wood **5** berry, fight, house, tooth, watch **7** catcher
feat: **5** trick
fennel: **4** weed
food: **6** kibble
genus: **5** canis
greet a ~: **3** pat
hot ~: **3** ham **5** frank, huzza, weeny **6** hoorah, hooray, hurrah, hurray, huzzah **10** grandstand
incite a ~: **3** sic
it: **3** lag, run **4** loaf **5** shirk **7** goof off **9** goldbrick
it, in Britain: **5** sculk, skulk
junkyard ~: **3** cur **4** mutt **5** biter **7** mongrel **10** crossbreed
lap ~: **3** pom **4** peke **6** Yorkie **7** Shih Tzu **9** Pekingese **10** Pomeranian
like a ~: **5** loyal
like a junkyard ~: **3** bad **4** ugly **5** dirty, mangy **7** lowdown, scruffy, vicious **8** churlish **9** dangerous **10** despicable, ill-natured
like a mad ~: **5** rabid
like a ~ tail: **4** awag
like some ~ ears: **5** loppy **6** droopy
name: **3** Rex **4** Fido, Shep, Spot **5** Rover
name meaning ~: **5** Caleb
one-third of a ~ name: **3** Rin
owner shout: **4** here
paddle: **4** swim
part of a ~ tongue: **5** lytta
place: **3** lap
prairie ~: **6** animal, mammal, rodent
presidential ~: **3** Her, Him **4** Fala
put on the ~: **6** flaunt **7** show off **9** put on airs
red ~ in football: **5** blitz
relative: **3** fox **4** wolf **5** dhole, dingo **6** corsac, coydog, coyote, fennec, jackal
retrieval: **5** stick
reward: **3** pat
river for which a ~ was named: **4** Aire
salty ~: **6** sailor **7** jack tar
sea ~: **3** gob, tar **4** salt **6** sailor **7** brigand, jack tar, mariner **9** buccaneer
sitter: **6** kennel
snack: **4** bone
sound: **3** arf, grr, yip **4** bark, gnar, woof **5** whine **6** bow-wow
starter: **3** fog, hot, sun **4** bird, bull, fire, hang **5** chili, sheep, under, watch
Stephen Foster ~: **4** Tray
stray ~: **3** mut **4** mutt
tag: **2** ID **7** license
tag wearer: **2** GI
top ~: **4** boss, exec, head, jefe, king, star **5** champ, first, Mr. Big, ruler **6** bigwig, gerent, honcho, leader, master, winner **7** captain, headman, manager, premier **8** big wheel, brass hat, cardinal, champion, director, foremost, governor, higher-up, kingfish, official, overseer, superior **9** authority, big cheese, commander, executive, key player, number one, personage, president, principal, sovereign **10** supervisor
walking the ~: **5** chore
walk like a ~: **3** pad
water ~: **6** sailor **7** jack tar
wild ~: **5** dhole, dingo **6** coyote, jackal
with a wavy white coat: **6** kuvasz
without papers: **3** mut **4** mutt
work like a ~: **4** toil **8** struggle
dog ___: **3** fox, tag **4** chew, days, flea, hook, iron, nail, rose, show, sled, tick, work **5** Latin, shift, tooth, watch, whelk **6** clutch, collar, fennel, paddle, salmon, sledge, warden **7** biscuit, curtain
dog ___ manger: **5** in the
dog-___: **3** day, ear **4** poor **5** cheap, eared, tired **6** paddle, walker
dog-___-dog: **3** eat
___ dog: **3** cur, gun, hot, lap, red, sea, top, toy **4** bird, cant, coon, corn, moon, seal, sled, wolf **5** bench, black, catch, chile, chili, coach, devil, guard, guide, hound, puppy, salty, stray, water **6** attack, bottom, chilli, Eskimo, monkey, police, yellow **7** driving, hearing, herding, Maltese, prairie, raccoon, tolling, working
___ dog!: **3** Bad **4** Good
___-dog: **3** coy, pye, red **5** plate, spoke
___ Dog: **4** Bird, Lad a **5** Great, Hound, Stray **6** Lesser, Little **7** Running
dog-and-___ show: **4** pony
___ Dog and Glory: **3** Mad
dog ate my homework, the: **5** alibi
dogbane: **5** plant
family shrub: **7** karanda **8** oleander **10** frangipani
tree: **7** karanda
Dog Barking at the Moon painter: **4** Miró
dogberry: **5** fruit
dogcatcher's catch: **5** stray
___ Dog Chow: **6** Purina
dog-collar attachment: **5** ID tag
___-dog contract: **6** yellow
Dog Day Afternoon (1975 film)
cast: John Cazale, Charles Durning, Al Pacino
character: **3** Sal **4** Leon
director: Sidney Lumet
dog days: **6** summer
forecast: **3** hot **5** humid
month: **3** Aug. **6** August
dog-ear: **4** bend, fold **5** crimp **6** crease **8** bookmark, fold over
dog-eared: **4** worn **5** ratty **10** threadbare
dog-eat-dog: **8** pitiless, ruthless **9** cutthroat, merciless, unpitying
dogface: **2** GI **3** pvt. **5** grunt **7** private
Dogfight (1991 film)
cast: Richard Panebianco, River Phoenix, Lili Taylor
director: Nancy Savoca
dogfight expert: **3** ace
dogfish: **4** huss **6** bowfin
___ dogfish: **5** piked, spiny **6** smooth
dog food: **4** Alpo, Iams **5** Nutro **6** Purina **8** Eukanuba **10** Ken-L Ration
Dogg: **4** Nate **5** Snoop
genre: **3** rap
dogged: **4** grim **6** gritty, wilful **7** patient, willful **8** obsessed, perverse, resolute, stubborn, untiring **9** impliable, insistent, obstinate, tenacious, unbending **10** determined, hard-bitten, inflexible, persistent, relentless, undeterred, unflagging
doggedly: **4** hard **6** keenly
doggedness: **4** grit **5** spunk **8** tenacity **9** constancy, fixedness
___-dogger: **3** hot
doggerel: **4** rime **5** rhyme, verse **6** poetry

doggone: **4** dang, darn, heck, rats **5** nerts, nertz **6** dad-gum
it: **4** darn, drat, rats **5** shoot
doggy: **3** pup **5** pooch, puppy **8** woof-woof
doggy bag bits: **4** orts
__ Doggy Dogg: **5** Snoop
__ dog has his day: **5** every
doghouse: **6** kennel
dogie: **3** cow **4** calf, waif **5** stray **6** estray
call: **3** maa
catcher: **4** rope **5** lasso, noose, reata, roper **6** lariat
dog in the __: **6** manger
dogleg: **4** bend **5** angle, crook
dog-license org.: **5** ASPCA
doglike scavenger: **5** hyena **6** hyaena
dog lover, name meaning: **6** Connor
dogma: **3** ism **5** canon, creed, faith, tenet **6** belief, dictum, gospel, tenets **7** precept **8** doctrine, ideology **9** principle, teachings **10** conviction
Dogma (1999 film)
cast: Ben Affleck, Matt Damon, Linda Fiorentino, Alan Rickman
dogmatic: **6** narrow **8** arrogant, despotic, orthodox, reasoned, unerring **9** arbitrary, canonical, doctrinal, fanatical, imperious, obstinate, pigheaded, sectarian **10** bullheaded, despotical, peremptory, tyrannical
dogmatist: **8** believer **9** sectarian
__ Dog Night: **5** Three
Dog of Flanders, A
actor: **4** Ladd
author: **5** Ouida
Dogon home: **4** Mali **6** Africa
Dogpatch: **4** town **6** hamlet
adjective: **3** Li'l
creator: **4** Capp
dad: **3** paw
expletive: **4** dang
possessive: **4** ourn
resident: **5** Abner **9** Daisy Maee
sufficient, in ~: **4** enuf, nuff
verb: **3** git
dog racing: **5** sport
dogs (advertising/products):
Beauty (Barbie)
Bingo (Cracker Jack)
Dinky (Taco Bell)
Ginger (Barbie)
McGruff (crime prevention)
Newton (Maytag)
Nipper (RCA)
Seadog (Cap'n Crunch)
Spuds MacKenzie (Budweiser)
Tige (Buster Brown)
Wags (Barbie)
dogs (comics):
Ace (Batman)
Andy (Mark Trail)
Barfy (The Family Circus)
Beauregard (Pogo)
Bitsy (Marvin)
Buck (The Gumps)
Daisy (Blondie)
Dawg (Hi and Lois)
Dogbert (Dilbert)
Dollar (Richie Rich)
Earl (Mutts)
Electra (Cathy)
Fifi (Bringing Up Father)
Fifi (Minnie Mouse)
Flip (Happy Hooligan)
Fuzz (Ziggy)
Grimmy (Mother Goose and Grimm)
Hot Dog (Jughead)
Kewpie (The Born Loser)
Killer (All Dogs Go to Heaven)
Krypto (Superman)
Marmaduke
Odie (Garfield)
Offisa Pupp (Krazy Kat)
Ol' Bullet (Snuffy Smith)
Otto (Beetle Bailey)
Poochie (Nancy)
Pretzel (Bringing Up Father)
Pudgy (Betty Boop)
Queenie (Dondi)
Roscoe (Pickles)
Rowdy (One Big Happy)
Ruff (Dennis the Menace)
Sam (The Family Circus)
Sandy (Little Orphan Annie)
Slivers (Little Nemo)
Smiley (Hazel)
Snert (Hagar the Horrible)
Spot (Boner's Ark)
Woofie (Mutts)
Zero (Little Annie Rooney)
dogs (films):
Alfie (Serpico)
Algonquin (Elvira, Mistress of the Dark)
Andromeda (The Parent Trap)
Attila (Phenomenon)
Barney (Gremlins)
Beau (WarGames)
Betsy (Bowfinger)
Bix (All of Me)
Blue (Cool Hand Luke)
Boomer (Independence Day)
Brinkley (You've Got Mail)
Bruiser (Legally Blonde)
Brutus (The Invisible Man's Revenge)
Bucky Boy (Cat on a Hot Tin Roof)
Buddy (Regarding Henry)
Buster (Nutty Professor II)
Butkus (Rocky)
Caesar (Our Man Flint)
Calico (With Six You Get Eggroll)
Carface (All Dogs Go To Heaven)
Chance (The Incredible Journey)
Charlie (All Dogs Go to Heaven)
Charlie (The Absent Minded Professor)
Charlie (The Final Countdown)
Chaucer (Foul Play)
Cheyenne (Jack the Bear)
Chiffon (The Shaggy Dog)
Chow Mein (Gypsy)
Cooper (What Lies Beneath)
Copernicus (Back to the Future)
Daphne (Look Who's Talking Now)
Dave (My Stepmother Is an Alien)
DeSoto (Oliver & Company)
Dodger (Oliver & Company)
Duke (Swiss Family Robinson)
Earl (City of Angels)
E. Buzz (Poltergeist)
Eddie (American Flyers)
Edison (Chitty Chitty Bang Bang)
Edward (The Accidental Tourist)
Einstein (Back to the Future)
Einstein (Oliver & Company)
Flo (All Dogs Go to Heaven)
Fly (Babe)
Francis (Oliver & Company)
Fred (Smokey and the Bandit)
Fritz (The Little Colonel)
Grunt (Flashdance)
Hansel (All Through the Night)
Harry (The Amityville Horror)
Harvey (E.T. the Extra Terrestrial)
Hearsay (The Firm)
Hobo (Please Don't Eat the Daisies)
Hosehead (Strange Brew)
Indiana (Indiana Jones)
Itchy (All Dogs Go to Heaven)
Jerry Lee (K-9)
Jerry (Tom and Jerry)
Kenny (Drop Dead Gorgeous)
Lafayette (The Aristocats)
Little Brother (Mulan)
Lucky (Dr. Dolittle)
Lucky (Married to the Mob)
Mandy (The Yellow Rolls Royce)
Matisse (Down and Out in Beverly Hills)
Max (Terminator 2: Judgment Day)
Max (The Little Mermaid)
Max (Volcano)
Meathead (Sudden Impact)
Merlin (Labyrinth)
Milo (The Mask)
Missy (Beethoven's 2nd)
Moose (Twister)
Muffy (Anatomy of a Murder)
Mutki (To Be or Not to Be)
Myron (Murder by Death)
Nanook (The Lost Boys)
Napoleon (The Aristocats)
Nemo (Avalon)
Opal (Blood Simple)
Pard (High Sierra)
Percy (Pocahontas)
Perdita (101 Dalmatians)
Pippet (Jaws)
Pluto (The Truman Show)
Pongo (101 Dalmatians)
Pongo (Robin Hood: Men in Tights)
Puffy (There's Something About Mary)
Queenie (The Bishop's Wife)
Rags (Sleeper)
Red (Visit to a Small Planet)
Rex (Babe)
Rhett (Steel Magnolias)
Rita (Oliver & Company)
Roach (The First Wives Club)
Rocks (Look Who's Talking Now)
Romulus (Reap the Wild Wind)
Rooney (Mr. Robinson Crusoe)
Roscoe (Oliver & Company)
Rusty (Mars Attacks)
Sam (Lethal Weapon)
Scraps (Airplane!)
Scud (Toy Story)
Shadow (The Incredible Journey)
Shane (Radio Flyer)
Skipper (Runaway Bride)
Sparky (Michael)
Speck (Pee Wee's Big Adventure)
Sport (The Egg and I)
Spot (Fun With Dick and Jane)
Taffy (With Six You Get Eggroll)
Talbot (The Sword in the Stone)
Tiger (The Sword in the Stone)
Tito (Oliver & Company)
Toby (Twister)
Tom Dooley (The Misfits)
Toto (The Wizard of Oz)
Turk (Swiss Family Robinson)
Uncas (Young Sherlock Holmes)
Verdell (As Good as It Gets)
Vladimir (The Glass Bottom Boat)
Waffles (Manhattan)
Walter (To Die For)
Willie (Patton)
Woofy (Bicentennial Man)
dogs (literature):
Alec (Tortilla Flat)
Argus (Odyssey)
Asta (The Thin Man)
Athos (Ulysses)
Balthasar (The Forsyte Saga)
Bluebell (Animal Farm)
Boatswain (Omoo)
Bob (Watership Down)
Bodger (The Incredible Journey)
Bonkers (The World According to Garp)
Bruno (Cinderella)
Buck (The Call of the Wild)
Bull's-eye (Oliver Twist)
Bunchie (Portrait of a Lady)
Cerberus (Hades)
Clematis (Seventeen)
Clifford (The Big Red Dog)
Crab (Two Gentlemen of Verona)
Cujo (Stephen King)
Dave (The Call of the Wild)
Diogenes (Dombey and Son)
Dougal (Little Lord Fauntleroy)
Elmer (Paul Bunyan)
Enrique (Tortilla Flat)
Fido (Paul Bunyan)
Flopit (Seventeen)
Fluff (Tortilla Flat)
Fluffy (Harry Potter and the Sorcerer's Stone)
Gnasher (Wuthering Heights)
Hector (Natty Bumppo)
Jessie (Animal Farm)
Jip (David Copperfield)
Jip (Doctor Dolittle)
Juno (Wuthering Heights)
Kazak (The Sirens of Titan)
Knave (Lad: A Dog)
Kojak (The Stand)
Luath (The Incredible Journey)
Max (How the Grinch Stole Christmas!)
Nana (Peter Pan)
Pajarito (Tortilla Flat)
Pilot (Jane Eyre)
Pincher (Animal Farm)
Rudolph (Tortilla Flat)
Skulker (Wuthering Heights)
Sol-leks (The Call of the Wild)
Spitz (The Call of the Wild)
Spot (Dick and Jane)
Toby (Sherlock Holmes)
Weenie (Eloise)
Wolf (Rip Van Winkle)
Wolf (Wuthering Heights)
Yap (The Mill on the Floss)
Zip (Happy Hollisters)
dogs (TV):
Antonio (The Drew Carey Show)
Apollo (Magnum, p.i.)
Arnold (Life Goes On)
Astro (The Jetsons)
Bandie (Life With Elizabeth)
Bandit (Jonny Quest)
Bandit (Little House on the Prairie)
Barney (Lou Grant)
Bijoux (Hooperman)
Black Tooth (Soupy Sales Show)
Boots (Emergency)
Bowser (Mr. Magoo)
Brain (Inspector Gadget)
Brandon (Punky Brewster)
Bridget (Lucas Tanner)
Buck (Married...With Children)
Buddy (Taxi)
Buddy (Veronica's Closet)
Butch (I Love Lucy)
Buttons (Animaniacs)
Chester (The Nanny)
Chipper (Land of the Giants)
Claude (The Beverly Hillbillies)
Cleo (The People's Choice)
Comet (Full House)
Cynthia (Green Acres)
Djinn Djinn (I Dream of Jeannie)
Dog (Columbo)
Dreyfuss (Empty Nest)
Duke (The Beverly Hillbillies)
Eddie (Frasier)
Flash (The Dukes of Hazzard)
Fred (I Love Lucy)
Freeway (Hart to Hart)
Fremont (Dennis the Menace)
Ginger (What Dreams May Come)
Grendel (thirtysomething)
Gulliver (The Andy Griffith Show)
Jasper (Bachelor Father)
King (Sergeant Preston of the Yukon)
Ladadog (Please Don't Eat the Daisies)
Leo (The Blue Knight)
Lord Nelson (The Doris Day Show)
Lucky (The Honeymooners)
Manfred (Tom Terrific)
Marlowe (Simon and Simon)

Max (Jake and the Fatman)
Max (The Bionic Woman)
Meatball (Baa Baa Black Sheep)
Mignon (Green Acres)
Mr. Peabody (Rocky and His Friends)
Murray (Mad About You)
Neil (Topper)
Nunzio (Dharma & Greg)
Old Blue (No Time for Sergeants)
Oliver (Family Affair)
Pax (Longstreet)
Pete/Petey (Little Rascals/Our Gang)
Porkchop (Doug)
Porthos (Enterprise)
Queequeg (The X-Files)
Quincy (Coach)
Rags (Spin City)
Reckless (The Waltons)
Reddy (Ruff and Reddy)
Ren (Ren and Stimpy)
Rex (The Life of Riley)
Rowlf (The Muppet Show)
Scruffy (The Ghost and Mrs. Muir)
Shamsky (Everybody Loves Raymond)
Simone (The Partridge Family)
Snow (The Monroes)
Snuffles (Quick Draw McGraw)
Sparky (South Park)
Speedy (The Drew Carey Show)
Sprocket (Fraggle Rock)
Spunky (Happy Days)
Stinky (Dharma & Greg)
Stormy (Life With Elizabeth)
Tet (Airwolf)
Tiger (The Brady Bunch)
Tiger (The Patty Duke Show)
Trader (Jungle Jim)
Tramp (My Three Sons)
Waldo (Nanny and the Professor)
White Fang (Soupy Sales Show)
Willie (Mama)
Wolf (Dr. Quinn, Medicine Woman)
Woofer (Winky Dink and You)
Zeus (Magnum, p.i.)

dog's __: 3 age 4 life 6 chance, letter
__ Dogs: 5 Straw
dog's age: 3 eon 4 aeon
__ Dogs and Englishmen: 3 Mad
dog-show org.: 3 AKC
dogsled pullers: 4 team
__ dog's life: 5 lead a
Dogs of War, The (1980 film)
cast: Tom Berenger, Christopher Walken
Dog star: 6 Sirius, Sothis
neighbor: 5 Orion
__-dog story: 6 shaggy
__ Dog, The: 6 Shaggy
dog-tired: 4 worn 5 spent, tired, weary, wiped 6 bushed, dished 8 fatigued 9 exhausted 10 knocked out
__ Dog Tray: 3 Old
dogtrot: 3 jog 6 canter
dogwood: 4 tree 5 brown, osier, plant, shrub 6 cornel, flower, kapuka 7 assagai, assegai 9 yellowish
relative: 3 bay, dun, tan 4 bole, ecru, fawn, foxy, nude, seal 5 amber, beige, camel, cocoa, hazel, khaki, mocha, sepia, tawny, umber 6 auburn, bister, bistre, bronze, coffee, copper, ginger, russet, sienna, sorrel, suntan, walnut 7 biscuit, caramel 8 chestnut, cinnamon, mahogany 9 butternut, chocolate
Dog Years author: Günter Grass
__-Doh: 4 Play
Doha: 4 city, town 7 capital
locale: 5 Katar, Qatar
Doherty: 5 Peter 7 Shannen
Doherty, Peter: 8 Nobelist 10 Australian
Doherty, Shannen: 7 actress
film: Heathers (1989)
TV: Beverly Hills 90210, Charmed
Do I dare to eat a peach? poet: 5 Eliot
Do I Do (1982 song) artist: Wonder
Do I Hear a Waltz?: 7 musical
songwriter: 7 Rodgers 8 Sondheim
__ Do I Love You?: 3 Why
doily: 3 mat 6 napkin 8 place mat
make a ~: 3 tat
material: 4 lace
doing: 3 act 4 deed 5 event 6 action 7 exploit 9 execution, handiwork, operation
keep from ~: 5 avoid 6 eschew, resist 7 back off, inhibit, refrain 8 restrain 9 interrupt
nothing: 4 idle, lazy 5 inert 6 otiose, torpid 7 dormant, jobless, loafing, resting 8 inactive, indolent, slothful, sluggish, stagnant 9 lethargic, loitering, out of work, sedentary, shiftless 10 motionless, on the shelf, stationary
nothing ~: 2 no 3 nah, naw, nay, nix, non 4 nein, nope, nyet, uh-uh 5 I won't, ixnay, never, no how, no way 6 no deal, noways, nowise, rebuff 7 I refuse 8 forget it, I will not, negative, negatory 9 by no means, fat chance, I think not, rejection 10 count me out, not a chance, thumbs down
starter: 4 evil 5 wrong
well: 4 rich 7 booming 8 affluent 10 prospering, prosperous, successful
__ doing: 7 nothing
__ Doing All Right: 4 I Was
Doing It All for My Baby (1987 song)
artist: Huey Lewis and the News
doings: 7 matters 8 dealings, goings-on 10 happenings
Doings of Raffles Haw, The author: Arthur Conan Doyle
Doin It (1996 song) artist: LL Cool J
Doin' What Comes Natur'lly composer: 6 Berlin
__ Do Is Dream of You: 4 All I
Doisy, Edward: 8 Nobelist
doit: 4 coin 5 money
__ do it: 4 Just
__ Do It: 4 Let's
__ Do It Again: 4 Let's
Do It Again (1972 song) artist: Steely Dan
Do It Again composer: 8 Gershwin
Do It Baby (1974 song) artist: Miracles
__ do it, bees...: 5 Birds
__ Do It Every Time: 6 They'll
do-it-yourself: 8 homemade
heading: 5 how to
purchase: 3 kit
trailer: 5 U-Haul
vehicle: 3 van 5 truck
dojo activity: 4 judo 6 karate
__-doke: 4 okey
Dolby: 6 Thomas
dolce: 7 sweetly
dolce __: 4 vita
dolce __ niente: 3 far
Dolcetto: 3 red 4 wine
origin: 5 Italy
doldrums: 4 funk, mood 5 blahs, blues, dumps, ennui, gloom 6 apathy, tedium, torpor 7 inertia, malaise 8 glumness 9 dejection, lassitude 10 depression, heavy heart, stagnation, woefulness
economic ~: 5 slump 8 slowdown 10 depression
in the ~: 3 low, sad 4 blue, mopy 5 moody, mopey
dole: 4 alms, gift, mete 5 allot, grant, grief 6 ration, regret, relief 7 charity, give out, handout, portion, welfare 8 donation, largesse 9 allotment, allowance 10 allocation
on the ~: 5 needy 8 leisured 9 unengaged 10 unemployed
out: 4 deal, give, mete 5 allot, divvy, issue, share 6 assign, divide, parcel, ration 7 divvy up, portion 8 disburse, dispense, disperse 9 apportion, partition 10 administer, contribute, distribute
__ dole: 5 on the
Dole: 3 Bob 6 Robert 9 Elizabeth
doleful: 3 sad 4 blue, dark, down, foul, glum, grim, poor 5 awful, lousy, moody, woful 6 broody, crumby, crummy, dismal, dreary, gloomy, horrid, morose, odious, rotten, rueful, somber, tragic, woeful 7 accurst, baleful, baneful, beastly, elegiac, forlorn, ghastly, hangdog, joyless, piteous, pitiful, unhappy 8 accursed, dejected, dolorous, downcast, dreadful, God-awful, grieving, grievous, horrible, inferior, mournful, shameful, stinking, terrible, tragical, troubled, wretched 9 abhorrent, appalling, atrocious, bummed out, cheerless, defective, depressed, execrable, frightful, heartsick, insidious, loathsome, miserable, offensive, plaintive, revolting, sorrowful, woebegone 10 abominable, chapfallen, despicable, despondent, detestable, disastrous, dispirited, distressed, horrendous, lamentable, lugubrious, melancholy
sound: 5 knell
Dolenz: 3 Ami 5 Micky 6 Mickey
colleague: 4 Tork 5 Jones 7 Nesmith
dolerite: 7 mineral
Dole, Robert: 3 pol 7 senator
state: 6 Kansas
Dolin, Anton: 6 dancer 7 British, danseur
__ Dolittle: 6 Doctor
doll: 3 Ken, toy 5 cutey, cutie, GI Joe, honey 6 Barbie, beauty, figure, kewpie, looker, prince, puppet 7 darling, gussy up, kachina, katcina, sweetie 8 cutie pie, figurine, katchina 9 dreamboat, plaything 10 honeybunch, marionette, sweetheart, sweetie pie
carnival ~: 5 prize 6 kewpie
counterpart: 3 guy
ender: 4 face 5 house
fad ~: 5 troll
male ~: 3 Ken 5 GI Joe
paper ~: 6 cutout
raggedy ~: 3 Ann 4 Andy
up: 5 adorn, dress, preen, primp, prink 6 attire, bedaub
wedding cake ~: 4 wife 5 bride
word: 4 mama
__ doll: 3 rag 4 baby 5 paper 6 Barbie, kewpie 7 kachina
__ Doll: 3 Rag 4 Baby 5 Devil, Paper, Party, Satin 6 Kewpie
dollar: 3 ace, one, tip 4 bill, buck, cash, clam 5 money 6 single 7 one-spot, smacker 8 banknote, frogskin, simoleon 9 greenback
fraction: 2 ct. 3 bit 4 cent, dime 5 penny 6 nickel 7 quarter
half ~: 4 coin
sign, basically: 3 ess
starter: 4 euro 5 petro
word on a ~: 3 God, one 4 Bank, Note, ordo, Seal, unum 5 debts, Great, legal, trust 6 annuit, public, Series, States, tender, United 7 America, coeptis, Federal, private, Reserve 8 pluribus, seclorum, Treasury 9 Secretary, Treasurer 10 Washington
dollar __: 3 day, gap 4 area, bill, sign
dollar __ averaging: 4 cost
dollar-__ man: 5 a-year
__ dollar: 3 top 4 beau, fast, half, sand, yuan 5 trade 6 Levant, silver 7 Anthony, British, quarter
__-dollar: 3 rix
Dollar: 9 car rental 10 auto rental
alternative: 4 Avis 5 Alamo, Hertz 6 Budget 7 Thrifty 8 National 10 Enterprise
Dollard-des-Ormeaux: 4 city, town
locale: 6 Canada, Québec
__ Dollar Legs: 7 Million
dollars: 4 cash, gelt, jack, kail, kale, loot, peag, pelf 5 bread, dough, funds, lucre, money, moola, mopus, pesos, rhino, sewan 6 dinero, do-re-mi, mammon, mazuma, monies, moolah, seawan, silver, specie, wampum, wealth 7 cabbage, capital, lettuce, ooftish, scratch, shekels 8 bankroll, cold cash, currency, hard cash 9 long green 10 green stuff
fistful of ~: 3 wad
to donuts: 8 probably 9 sure thing
$ (Dollars) (1971 film)
cast: Warren Beatty, Gert Frobe, Goldie Hawn
director: Richard Brooks
dollars-and-__: 5 cents
dollars to __: 6 donuts
Dolley: 7 Madison
dollface: 7 darling 10 sweetheart
dollop: 3 bit, dab, gob, pat 4 blob, dash, glob, glop, lump, spot 5 piece 7 portion 8 spoonful
Doll's House, A: 4 play
author: Henrik Ibsen
character: 4 Nils, Nora 5 Linde 6 Helmer
dolly: 4 cart 5 truck 6 barrow 7 carrier 9 hand truck
Dolly: 3 ewe 4 Levi 5 clone, sheep 6 Parton
Dolly __: 6 Varden
__, Dolly!: 5 Hello
Dolly Madison: 8 ice cream
alternative: 4 Edy's 7 Breyer's 9 Friendly's, Good Humor 10 Dairy Queen, Haagen Dazs, Turkey Hill
Dolly Sisters, The star: 5 Haver
Dollywood locale: 4 Tenn. 9 Tennessee
dolman: 4 cape, coat, robe, wrap 5 coats 6 mantle, sleeve
dolomite: 3 ore 6 marble 7 mineral
deposit: 4 marl
Dolomites: 3 mts. 4 Alps, mtns. 5 range
locale: 5 Italy 6 Europe
dolor: 3 woe 4 ache 5 agony, gloom, grief 6 misery, sorrow 7 anguish, despair, sadness 8 distress, the blues 9 dejection, heartache, suffering 10 depression, heartbreak, heavy heart, melancholy, woefulness
__ dolore: 3 con
Dolores: 4 Hart, Hope 6 Del Rio
Dolores Claiborne: 4 film 5 novel
author: Stephen King
cast: Kathy Bates, Jennifer Jason Leigh, Judy Parfitt
director: Taylor Hackford
Dolores Hidalgo: 4 city, town
locale: 6 Mexico 10 Guanajuato
__ dolorosa: 3 via 5 mater
dolorous: 3 sad 4 dark 5 woful 6 dismal, woeful 7 doleful, elegiac, painful, tearful 8 desolate, grievous, mournful, wretched 9 afflicted, anguished, cheerless, miserable, plaintive, sniveling, sorrowful, woebegone 10 deplorable, lamentable, lugubrious, melancholy
Dolph: 5 Sweet 7 Schayes 8 Lundgren
dolphin: 6 animal, dorado 8 cetacean
communication: 5 sonar

female: 3 cow
habitat: 3 sea 5 ocean
hazard: 3 net
largest ~: 4 orca
male: 4 bull
meal: 5 squid
relative: 3 orc, sei 5 whale 6 beluga, narwal 7 cowfish, finback, grampus, narwhal, rorqual 8 narwhale, porpoise
school: 3 pod
young: 3 pup 4 calf
dolphin ___: 4 kick
dolphinfish, half a Hawaiian: 4 mahi
dolphinlike cetacean: 4 susu
Dolphin rival: 3 Jet, Ram 4 Bear, Bill, Colt, Lion 5 Brown, Chief, Eagle, Giant, Raven, Saint, Texan, Titan 6 Bengal, Bronco, Cowboy, Falcon, Jaguar, Packer, Raider, Viking 7 Charger, Panther, Patriot, Redskin, Seahawk, Steeler 8 Cardinal 9 Buccaneer
Dolphins: 4 team 6 eleven
home: 5 Miami
org.: 3 AFC, NFL
sport: 8 football
dolphin-safe ___: 4 tuna
Dolphin, The author: Robert Lowell
dolt: 2 ox 3 ass, nit, oaf, sap 4 boob, bozo, clod, dodo, dope, fool, geek, gowk, lunk, simp, twit, yo-yo 5 chump, clown, cluck, dummy, dunce, goose, joker, klutz, looby, ninny, patsy, schmo 6 dimwit, galoot, lubber, lummox, nitwit, schmoe, sucker, turkey 7 airhead, buffoon, bungler, dingbat, dullard, fathead, galloot, half-wit, jackass, pinhead, saphead 8 bonehead, cloddish, dumbbell, lunkhead, meathead, numskull 9 birdbrain, blockhead, ding-a-ling, harebrain, ignoramus, lamebrain, numbskull, simpleton 10 dunderhead, dunderpate, loggerhead, nincompoop, noodlehead
old-style: 4 mome
doltish: 3 dim 4 daft, dopy, dull, dumb 5 dense, dopey, silly 6 obtuse 7 bearish, foolish, loutish, witless 8 cloddish, mindless 9 dim-witted 10 weak-minded
Dolton: 4 city, town
locale: 8 Illinois
dom: 9 religious
Dom: 5 abbot, title 6 Moraes 7 DeLuise 8 DiMaggio, Pérignon
Dom. ___: 3 Rep.
Domagk, Gerhard: 6 German 8 Nobelist
domain: 3 job 4 area, turf 5 arena, bourn, field, orbit, range, realm, world 6 dot-com, empire, estate, locale, nation, region, sphere 7 compass, concern, element, grounds, habitat, kingdom, quarter, terrain 8 locality, province 9 authority, bailiwick, specialty, territory 10 department
___ domain: 6 public 7 eminent
Domain of Arnheim, The author: Poe
___ do Mar: 5 Serra
Dombey and Son
author: Charles Dickens
dog: 8 Diogenes
dome: 4 head, roof 5 vault 6 cupola, noggin 7 ceiling 8 mountain
cover: 3 wig
home: 4 iglu 5 igloo
opening: 6 oculus
dome ___: 3 car, top 5 light
___ dome: 4 salt 5 onion, smoke 6 chrome, saucer
___ Dome: 6 Teapot
domed
projection: 4 apse
roof: 6 cupola
Domenico: 7 Modugno 9 Sçarlatti

Dome of Many-Coloured Glass, A
author: Amy Lowell
Domesday ___: 4 Book
domestic: 4 home, maid, tame 5 civil 6 au pair, native 7 servant 8 interior, internal, national 9 home-grown, household, launderer 10 indigenous
not ~: 7 foreign
domestic ___: 4 fowl 6 animal 7 partner, prelate, science
domesticate: 4 tame
domesticated: 4 tame 6 broken, docile, gentle, pliant 8 lamblike, obedient 9 compliant, tractable 10 manageable, submissive
not ~: 4 wild 5 feral
Domestic Disturbance (2001 film)
cast: Teri Polo, John Travolta, Vince Vaughn
___ domestic product: 5 gross
domicile: 3 pad 4 co-op, crib, home, nest 5 abode, condo, house, joint, lodge, place, put up, roost 6 castle, harbor 7 address, habitat, harbour, housing, lodging, mansion, quarter 8 dwelling, fireside, lodgment, quarters 9 apartment, residence
domicilio: 4 casa
dominance: 4 rule 7 mastery 9 advantage, authority, influence, supremacy, upper hand 10 ascendance, ascendancy, ascendence, ascendency, government, prepotency
dominant: 3 top 4 main, star 5 chief, first, major, on top, prime 6 ruling 7 central, leading, primary, rampant, regnant, supreme 8 despotic, forceful, in charge, powerful, reigning, superior, unbeaten 9 imperious, paramount, prevalent, principal, sovereign, unrivaled, uppermost 10 commanding, despotical, overriding, preeminent, prevailing, triumphant, unrivalled
feature: 5 motif
dominate: 3 hog 4 boss, head, lead, loom, rule, sway 5 reign, tower 6 direct, govern, handle, manage, obsess 7 command, control, dictate, prevail, triumph 8 bestride, loom over, outshine, override, overrule 9 reign over, subjugate, tyrannize 10 monopolize, overshadow, run the show, tower above
dominating: 5 macho
domination: 4 rule, sway 7 command, control, tyranny 8 hegemony 9 authority, despotism, influence, supremacy 10 ascendance, ascendancy, ascendence, ascendency, government, oppression, prepotency, repression, subjection
domineer: 4 rule 5 bully 6 hector, menace 7 control, henpeck, oppress, swagger 8 browbeat, bulldoze, keep down 9 trample on, tyrannize 10 boss around, intimidate
domineering: 4 firm, hard 5 bossy, cruel, macho, picky, proud, pushy, rigid, stern, tough 6 severe 7 austere, Spartan 8 arrogant, coercive, despotic, dogmatic, exacting, hard-line, imperial, rigorous 9 demanding, draconian, stringent, unbending, unsparing 10 despotical, dogmatical, inflexible, iron-fisted, no-nonsense, oppressive, peremptory, tyrannical
one: 5 bully
Domingo: 6 Sunday 7 Plácido, Spanish 9 Sarmiento
follower: 5 lunes
preceder: 6 sábado
___ Domingo: 5 Santo
Domingo, Plácido: 5 tenor 6 singer
milieu: 5 opera

piece: 4 aria
specialty: 5 opera
___ Domini: 4 Anno
Dominic: 5 saint 7 Keating
Dominica: 4 isle 6 island, nation 7 country
capital: 6 Roseau
money: 4 cent 6 dollar
org.: 3 OAS
Dominican: 4 monk 5 friar 7 brother
dance: 8 merengue
Dominican Republic: 6 nation 7 country
capital: Santo Domingo
city: 4 Moca 6 La Vega 8 Santiago
money: 4 peso
neighbor: 5 Haiti
org.: 3 OAS
Dominick: 5 Dunne
Dominick and Eugene (1988 film)
cast: Jamie Lee Curtis, Tom Hulce, Ray Liotta
dominie: 6 cleric
dominion: 4 area, hold, rule, sway 5 orbit, power, reach, realm, reign, state 6 empery, empire, nation, region, sphere 7 command, control, country, potence, potency, regency, terrain, victory 8 hegemony, kingship, province 9 authority, bailiwick, influence, ownership, supremacy, territory 10 ascendance, ascendancy, ascendence, ascendency, governance, government, possession
hold ~: 4 rule 5 reign 6 direct 7 command, control, oversee
in India: 3 raj
Dominion ___: 3 Day
Dominique: 4 fowl 7 chicken
relative: 6 Bantam, Brahma, Houdan, Sussex 7 Cornish, Dorking, Leghorn 8 Araucana, Langshan, Shanghai 9 Orpington, Wyandotte
Dominique (1963 song) artist: Singing Nun
domino: 4 cape, mask, tile 5 cloak 9 game piece 10 masquerade
certain ~: 3 ace 4 trey 5 deuce
spot: 3 pip
domino ___: 5 paper 6 effect, theory
Domino (1970 song) artist: Morrison
dominoes: 4 game
Domino, Fats
real first name: Antoine
song: Ain't That a Shame (1955)
Be My Guest (1959)
Blueberry Hill (1956)
Blue Monday (1957)
I'm in Love Again (1956)
I'm Walkin' (1957)
It's You I Love (1957)
I Want to Walk You Home (1959)
Valley of Tears (1957)
Walking to New Orleans (1960)
Whole Lotta Loving (1958)
Domino's specialty: 5 pizza
Domitian: 6 Caesar
___ dommage!: 4 C'est, Quel
___-domo: 5 major
Dom Pedro's wife: 4 Ines
don: 4 capo, wear 5 put on, sport 6 slip on 7 dress in, get into 8 slip into 9 godfather, professor
apparel: 5 dress 6 clothe
the feedbag: 3 eat
Don: 2 Ho 4 Imus, King, Owen, Weis 5 Adams, Bluth, Budge, Grady, Pardo, river, Rondo, Sharp, Shula, title 6 Ameche, Baylor, Carter, Cherry, DeFore, Everly, Gibson, Henley, Hewitt, Knotts, Larsen, Martin, McLean, Murray, Porter, Siegel, Sutton, Taylor, Zimmer 7 Chaffey, Cheadle, Cornell, DeLillo, Garlits, Johnson, Marquis, Maynard, McGuire, Medford, Messick, Novello, Quixote, Rickles 8 Drysdale, Galloway, Meredith, Mitchell, Williams 9 Kirschner, Mattingly, Robertson
River locale: 6 Russia
river to the ~: 6 Donets
sea fed by the ~: 4 Azov
Don ___: 4 Juan 6 Carlos 7 Quixote
Don ___ de la Vega: 5 Diego
Don ___ DeMarco: 4 Juan
dona: 7 senhora
dona ___ pacem: 5 nobis
Doña: 5 title
Dona Flor and Her Two Husbands: 4 film 5 novel
author: Jorge Amado
cast: Sonia Braga, Jose Wilker
director: Bruno Barreto
Donahue: 4 Phil, Troy 6 Elinor
Donahue, Phil spouse: Marlo Thomas
Donahue, Troy spouse: Suzanne Pleshette
Donald: 4 Byrd, Cram, Duck, Hall 5 Crisp, Davie, Trump 6 Glaser, Moffat, Petrie 7 O'Connor 8 Hamilton, McMillan 9 Barthelme, Pleasence 10 Sutherland
daughter: 6 Ivanka
in Irish: 5 Donal
in Italian: 4 Aldo
son: 6 Kiefer
Donald Duck
friend: 5 Daisy
nephew: 4 Huey 5 Dewey, Louie
to his nephews: 4 unca
voice of ~: 4 Nash
Donald E. ___: 8 Westlake
Donaldson: 3 Sam 5 Roger
network: 3 ABC 5 ABC-TV
Donaldson, Roger: 8 director
film: The Bounty (1984)
Cadillac Man (1990)
Cocktail (1988)
Marie (1985)
No Way Out (1987)
Species (1995)
Thirteen Days (2000)
White Sands (1992)
dona nobis ___: 5 pacem
donate: 4 give 5 award, endow, grant, offer, spend, tithe 6 bestow, chip in, confer, devote, kick in, pony up, render 7 hand out, present, provide, throw in 8 bequeath, dedicate 9 subscribe 10 contribute
Donatello: 6 artist 7 Italian 8 sculptor
Donath: 6 Ludwig
donation: 3 aid 4 alms, dole, gift, hand 5 grant 7 bequest, charity, largess, present, subsidy 8 gratuity, largesse, offering 9 endowment 10 assistance
make a ~: 4 give
religious ~: 5 tithe
Donat, Robert: 5 actor
film: The 39 Steps (1935)
The Citadel (1938)
The Count of Monte Cristo (1934)
Goodbye, Mr. Chips (1939, AA)
The Inn of the Sixth Happiness (1958)
The Magic Box (1951)
The Private Life of Henry VIII (1933)
Vacation From Marriage (1945)
___ Don Baker: 3 Joe
Don Carlos: 4 play 5 opera
author: Friedrich von Schiller
composer: 5 Verdi
role: 5 Eboli 7 Rodrigo 8 Theobald 9 Elizabeth
setting: 5 Spain 6 France
Doncha' Think It's Time (1958 song)
artist: Elvis Presley

Donder: 8 reindeer
colleague: 5 Comet, Cupid, Vixen 6 Dancer, Dasher 7 Blitzen, Prancer
Dondi: 6 orphan 7 cartoon 10 comic strip
dog: 7 Queenie
done: 3 old 4 fini, over, past, thru 5 ended, ready, spent, wrapt 6 cooked, finito 7 all over, through, wrapped, wrought 8 achieved, complete, executed, finished, over with, realized, rendered 9 completed, concluded, performed 10 buttoned up, terminated
by hand: 6 manual
easily ~: 6 facile, simple
for: 4 sunk 5 kaput, tired 6 doomed 7 accurst 8 accursed, obsolete, washed-up 9 vicarious
get ~: 3 end 4 cook 5 mop up 6 finish 7 achieve 10 put through
get the job ~: 4 work 6 hack it
in: 5 kaput, spent, tired, weary 6 dished 8 fatigued, finished 9 enervated, played out 10 knocked out
nicely ~: 4 neat 10 impressive
not ~: 4 no-no, rare 5 wrong
not well ~: 5 messy 6 shabby, shoddy, sloppy, untidy 7 unkempt 8 careless, fouled-up, slapdash, slipshod 9 haphazard, hit-or-miss, neglected
things to be ~: 6 agenda
to a poet: 3 o'er
with: 4 over 5 rid of 7 all over
done __ turn: 3 to a
__-done: 4 well
Done!: 5 there 6 agreed
__ Done: 5 Day Is
donee: 5 taker 8 receiver
Donegal: 4 port 5 tweed
locale: 7 Ireland
river: 4 Erne
Donegan, Lonnie
song: Does Your Chewing Gum ... (1961)
Rock Island Line (1956)
__ Done Him Wrong: 3 She
__ Donelson: 4 Fort
Donen, Stanley: 8 director
film: Arabesque (1966)
Bedazzled (1967)
Blame It on Rio (1984)
Charade (1963)
Damn Yankees (1958)
Funny Face (1957)
The Grass Is Greener (1960)
Indiscreet (1958)
It's Always Fair Weather (1955)
Movie Movie (1978)
On the Town (1949)
The Pajama Game (1957)
Royal Wedding (1951)
Seven Brides for Seven Brothers (1954)
Singin' in the Rain (1952)
Two for the Road (1967)
Donets: 5 river
locale: 6 Russia 7 Ukraine
Donetsk: 4 city, town
locale: 7 Ukraine
dong: 4 coin 5 money
__-dong: 4 ding
Don Giovanni: 5 opera
character: 4 Anna 5 Pedro 6 Elvira 7 Ottavio, Zerlina
composer: 6 Mozart
highlight: 4 duel
setting: 5 Spain 7 Seville
__ Dong School: 4 Ding
Donizetti, Gaetano
work: Anna Bolena
Don Pasquale
L'Elisir d'Amore
Lucia di Lammermoor
Lucrezia Borgia
donjon: 4 keep
site: 6 castle
Don Juan: 4 epic, poem, roué 5 opera, Romeo 6 ballet 8 lothario, tone poem 9 libertine
author: Byron, Strauss
composer: 5 Gluck
mother: 4 Ines, Inez
portrayer: 5 Errol
Don Juan (1926 film)
cast: Mary Astor, John Barrymore, Willard Louis
director: Alan Crosland
Don Juan DeMarco (1995 film)
cast: Marlon Brando, Johnny Depp, Faye Dunaway
director: Jeremy Leven
donkey: 3 ass 5 burro, genet, jenny, kiang, neddy 6 animal, brayer, equine, jennet, onager 7 jackass
cry: 4 bray 6 heehaw
Democratic ~ creator: 4 Nast
dinner: 4 feed
enticement: 6 carrot
feature: 3 ear
female ~: 5 genet, jenny 6 jennet
fix a ~ tail: 5 repin
foot: 4 hoof
in French: 3 ane
male: 7 jackass
relative: 5 horse, zebra 6 quagga 8 chigetai 9 dziggetai
young: 4 colt, foal
donkey __: 6 engine 7 topsail
Donkey __: 4 Kong
donkeys
when ~ fly: 5 no how, no way 8 forget it 9 fat chance 10 impossible, not a chance
donkey's __: 4 tail 5 years
Donkey Serenade composer: 5 Friml
donkeys fly, when: 5 never
Donkey's Years author: Michael Frayn
Donleavy, J.P.: 5 Irish 6 writer
Donlevy, Brian: 5 actor
film: Beau Geste (1939)
The Beginning or the End (1947)
The Birth of the Blues (1941)
Canyon Passage (1946)
The Creeping Unknown (1956)
Destry Rides Again (1939)
The Glass Key (1942)
The Great McGinty (1940)
Impact (1949)
Killer McCoy (1947)
Kiss of Death (1947)
A Southern Yankee (1948)
Wake Island (1942)
When the Daltons Rode (1940)
__ donna: 5 prima
Donna: 4 Reed 5 Dixon, Fargo, Karan, Lewis, Loren, Mills 6 Caponi, Pescow, Summer 7 D'Errico, Douglas, Shalala
Donna (1958 song) artist: Valens
Donna Reed Show, The (ABC sitcom)
cast: Carl Betz (Dr. Alex Stone)
Shelley Fabares (Mary Stone)
Paul Petersen (Jeff Stone)
Donna Reed (Donna Stone)
Donna the Prima Donna (1963 song)
artist: Dion
Donne, John: 4 poet 7 British
last lamenting thing for ~: 4 kiss
start of a ~ quote: 5 no man
work: Air and Angels
The Bait
Break of Day
A Burnt Ship
Divine Poems
The Extasy
A Fever
The Flea
The Good Morrow
The Legacy
Love's Alchemy
The Message
Songs and Sonnets
The Sunne Rising
The Triple Fool
The Undertaking
A Valediction
Donner: 3 Ral 5 Clive 7 Richard
Donner __: 4 Pass
Donner, Richard: 8 director
film: Assassins (1995)
Conspiracy Theory (1997)
Ladyhawke (1985)
Lethal Weapon (1987)
Lethal Weapon 2 (1989)
Lethal Weapon 3 (1992)
Lethal Weapon 4 (1998)
Maverick (1994)
Radio Flyer (1992)
Scrooged (1988)
Superman (1978)
Donnie Brasco (1997 film)
cast: Johnny Depp, Bruno Kirby, Michael Madsen, Al Pacino
director: Mike Newell
donnish: 7 bookish 8 pedantic 9 pedagogic 10 pedantical
Donny: 4 Most 6 Osmond 8 Hathaway
sister: 5 Marie
donnybrook: 3 row 4 fray, riot, to-do 5 brawl, clash, fight, melee, mix-up, set-to 6 affray, barney, battle, fracas, rumble, tussle, uproar 7 rhubarb, scuffle, turmoil 8 skirmish, slugfest, squabble 9 brannigan 10 free-for-all
D'Onofrio, Vincent: 5 actor
film: The Cell (2000)
Crooked Hearts (1991)
Full Metal Jacket (1987)
Household Saints (1993)
Mystic Pizza (1988)
Donohoe: 6 Amanda
donor: 5 angel, giver 6 backer, patron 7 grantor 8 altruist, bestower 10 benefactor
campaign ~: 3 PAC
no ~: 5 miser 9 skinflint
universal ~: 5 type O
donor __: 4 card
Donoso, José: 6 writer 7 Chilean
Do not __: 6 pass Go 7 disturb
Do not go gentle... author: Dylan Thomas
do-nothing: 3 bum 4 idle, lazy 5 drone, idler, slack 6 loafer, otiose, truant 7 goof-off, moocher, slacker 8 fainéant, indolent, loiterer, slothful, slugabed, sluggard 9 goldbrick, lazybones, shiftless 10 ne'er-do-well
bane: 4 work
Do not open __ Christmas!: 5 until
Donovan: 3 Art 6 Marion
daughter: Ione Skye
last name: Leitch
song: Atlantis (1969)
Hurdy Gurdy Man (1968)
Mellow Yellow (1966)
Sunshine Superman (1966)
Donovan's __: 4 Reef 5 Brain
Donovan's Brain (1953 film)
cast: Lew Ayres, Nancy Davis, Gene Evans
director: Felix Feist
Donovan's Reef (1963 film)
cast: Elizabeth Allen, Lee Marvin, John Wayne
director: John Ford
Donovan, Wild Bill agcy.: 3 OSS
Don Pasquale
composer: 9 Donizetti
setting: 4 Rome
Don Quixote: 5 novel 9 visionary
author: Miguel de Cervantes
don't: 4 no-no, tabu 5 taboo
Don't __: 3 Cry 4 Stop 5 Let Go, Speak, Worry
Don't __!: 3 ask
Don't __ boy to...: 5 send a
Don't __ cow, man!: 5 have a
Don't __ it!: 5 bet on
Don't __, It's Only Thunder: 3 Cry
Don't __ me!: 3 ask 6 look at
Don't __ Me: 4 Rush 5 Blame 6 Answer, Forbid, Forget
Don't __ Me in: 5 Fence
Don't __ Nothin' Bad: 3 Say
Don't __ on me: 5 tread
Don't __ on My Parade: 4 Rain
Don't __ the Small Stuff: 5 Sweat
Don't __, we'll...: 6 call us
Don't __ With Bill: 4 Mess
Don't (1958 song) artist: Elvis Presley
Don't Ask Me Why (1980 song) artist: Billy Joel
Don't be __!: 4 late 5 silly
Don't Be Cruel (song)
artist: Bobby Brown, Cheap Trick, Elvis Presley
Don't bet __!: 4 on it
Don't bother: 6 no need, skip it
Don't Bother __ Can't Cope: 3 Me I
Don't Bring Me Down (1979 song)
artist: ELO
Don't Come Around Here... (1985 song) artist: Tom Petty
Don't count __!: 4 on it
Don't Cry, __ Only Thunder: 3 It's
__ Don't Cry: 4 Boys
Don't Cry Daddy (1969 song) artist: Elvis Presley
Don't Cry for Me Argentina (1997 song): 5 tango
artist: Madonna
musical: 5 Evita
Don't Cry Out Loud (1979 song) artist: Melissa Manchester
composer: 5 Allen
Don't Cry (song) artist: Asia, Guns N' Roses
Don't Do Me Like That (1979 song)
artist: Tom Petty
Don't do that!: 4 stop 6 stop it
__ Don't Eat the Daisies: 6 Please
Don't Expect Me to Be Your Friend (1973 song) artist: Lobo
__, don't fail me now!: 4 Feet
Don't Fall in Love With a Dreamer (song) artist: Kim Carnes
artist: Kenny Rogers
Don't Fence Me In composer: 6 Porter
Don't Fight It (1982 song)
artist: Kenny Loggins, Steve Perry
Don't Get Me Wrong (1986 song)
artist: Pretenders
Don't Give Up On Us (1977 song)
artist: David Soul
Don't Give Up the Ship (1959 film)
cast: Jerry Lewis, Dina Merrill
director: Norman Taurog
Don't Go __ the Water: 4 Near
__ Don't Go: 4 Baby 6 Please
Don't Go Away Mad (1990 song) artist: Mötley Crüe
Don't Go Breaking My Heart (1976 song) artist: Elton John, Kiki Dee
Don't Hang Up (1962 song) artist: Orlons
Don't have __, man!: 4 a cow
dontic starter: 5 ortho
Don't It Make My Brown Eyes Blue (1977 song) artist: Crystal Gayle
Don't It Make Ya Wanna Dance singer: 5 Raitt
Don't Knock My Love (1971 song)
artist: Wilson Pickett
Don't Know Much (1989 song)
artist: Aaron Neville, Linda Ronstadt

Don't Leave Me This Way (1977 song) artist: Thelma Houston
Don't let go!: 6 hang on
Don't Let Go (1996 song) artist: En Vogue
Don't Let It End (1983 song) artist: Styx
Don't Let the Green Grass Fool You (1971 song) artist: Wilson Pickett
Don't Let the Stars Get in Your Eyes (1952 song) artist: Perry Como
Don't Let the Sun Catch You Crying (1964 song) artist: Gerry and the Pacemakers
Don't Let the Sun Go Down on Me (song) artist: Elton John, George Michael
Don't look ___!: 3 now **4** at me
Don't look ___ horse...: 5 a gift
Don't Look Back (1978 song) artist: Boston
Don't Look Now (1973 film)
cast: Julie Christie, Donald Sutherland
director: Nicolas Roeg
Don't Lose My Number (1985 song) artist: Phil Collins
Don't make ___ of me!: 5 a liar
Don't Make Me Over (1963 song) artist: Dionne Warwick
Don't Make Waves (1967 film)
cast: Claudia Cardinale, Tony Curtis, Sharon Tate
Don't Mess with Bill (1966 song) artist: Marvelettes
Don't mind if ___!: 3 I do
___ Don't Own Me: 3 You
___ Don't Preach: 4 Papa
Don't Pull Your Love (1971 song) artist: Hamilton, Joe Frank & Reynolds
Don't quit your ___!: 6 day job
Don't Rain on My Parade composer: 5 Styne **7** Merrill
Don't rub ___!: 4 it in
___-Don't Run: 4 Walk
Don't Rush Me (1988 song) artist: Taylor Dayne
___ Don't Say: 3 You
Don't Say a Word (2001 film)
cast: Michael Douglas, Famke Janssen, Brittany Murphy
Don't Sleep in the Subway (1967 song) artist: Petula Clark
Don't Stand So Close to Me (1981 song) artist: Police
Don't Stop (1977 song) artist: Fleetwood Mac
Don't Stop 'Til You Get Enough (1979 song) artist: Michael Jackson
Don't sweat it: 6 no loss **9** no big deal
Don't Take It to Heart director: 4 Dell
Don't Talk to Strangers (1982 song) artist: Rick Springfield
Don't tell ___!: 5 a soul
Don't Think Twice, It's All Right (1963 song) artist: Peter, Paul and Mary
Don't throw bouquets ___: 4 at me
Don't Throw It All Away (1978 song) artist: Andy Gibb
Don't touch ___ dial!: 4 that
Don't tread on me: 5 motto
Don't Turn Around (1994 song) artist: Ace of Base
Don't Walk Away (1993 song) artist: Jade
Don't Wanna Lose You (1989 song) artist: Gloria Estefan
Don't Want to Be a Fool (1991 song) artist: Luther Vandross
Don't Worry Baby (1964 song) artist: Beach Boys
Don't Worry Be Happy (1988 song) artist: Bobby McFerrin
Don't Worry Kyoko singer: 3 Ono
Don't you ___!: 4 dare
Don't You Care (1967 song) artist: Buckinghams
Don't You Know (1959 song) artist: Della Reese
Don't You Know What the Night Can Do? (1988 song) artist: Winwood
Don't You Want Me (song) artist: Human League, Jody Watley
Donus: 4 pope **7** pontiff
donut: 6 dunker, pastry, sinker
drown a ~: 4 dunk
feature: 4 hole **5** cream, glaze, jelly
kin: 5 bagel **7** cruller, kruller
order: 5 dozen
place: 6 bakery
shape: 5 torus
donuts
like some ~: 5 fried **6** glazed
___ Donuts: 6 Dunkin'
donut-shaped: 5 toric
doo-___: 3 wop
___-Doo: 6 Scooby
Doobie Brothers
song: Black Water (1975)
The Doctor (1980)
Listen to the Music (1972)
Long Train Runnin' (1973)
Real Love (1980)
What a Fool Believes (1970)
doodad: 5 frill, gismo, gizmo, thing **6** bauble, dingus, gadget, geegaw, gewgaw, whosis, widget **7** trinket, whatsis **8** nicknack, ornament **9** adornment, bagatelle, invention **10** decoration, instrument, knickknack
doodle: 3 jot **4** draw **6** putter, scrawl, sketch, tinker, trifle **7** drawing **8** graffiti, scribble **10** marginalia, mess around
ender: 3 bug
starter: 4 flap
___-doodle: 5 dipsy
___ Doodle: 6 Yankee
doodlebug: 6 insect
___-doodle-doo: 5 cock-a
doodly-squat: 3 nil **5** zilch **7** nothing
Doody: 6 Alison
___ Doody: 5 Howdy
doofus: 2 ox **3** ass, nit, oaf, sap **4** boob, bozo, clod, dodo, dolt, dope, fool, geek, gowk, lunk, nerd, nurd, simp, twit, yo-yo **5** chump, clown, cluck, dummy, dunce, goose, joker, klutz, looby, ninny, patsy, schmo, stupe **6** dimwit, galoot, lubber, lummox, nitwit, schmoe, sucker, turkey **7** airhead, buffoon, bungler, dingbat, dullard, fathead, galloot, half-wit, jackass, pinhead, saphead **8** bonehead, cloddish, dumbbell, goofball, lunkhead, meathead, numskull **9** birdbrain, blockhead, ding-a-ling, harebrain, ignoramus, lamebrain, numbskull, simpleton **10** dunderhead, dunderpate, loggerhead, nincompoop, noodlehead
Doogie Howser, M.D. (ABC sitcom)
cast: Neil Patrick Harris (Doogie Howser)
Doohan: 5 James
doohickey: 5 gismo, gizmo, thing **6** gadget, widget **7** whatsis **9** apparatus, mechanism
Dooley: 3 Tom **4** Paul **6** Wilson
Doolittle: 5 Eliza, Hilda
Doolittle, Eliza: 7 Cockney
Doolittle, Hilda: 4 poet
colleague: Pound, Eliot
subject: Freud
doom: 3 end, lot **4** ruin **7** condemn, destine, destiny, portion, tragedy, undoing **8** calamity, disaster, downfall **9** cataclysm, damnation, preordain, ruination **10** apocalypse, extinction, foreordain
ender: 5 sayer
partner: 5 gloom
prophet of ~: 9 Cassandra, pessimist
doomed: 4 lost, sunk **5** bound, curst, fated **6** cursed, ruined, undone **7** accurst, done for, ominous, unlucky **8** accursed, destined, ill-fated, luckless **9** condemned, ill-omened **10** inevitable
one: 5 goner
doomful: 7 fateful **8** sinister
Doomsday ___: 4 Book
Doomsday Conspiracy, The author: Sidney Sheldon
Doon: 5 river
locale: 8 Scotland
Doone: 5 Lorna
do one's ___: 3 bit
do one's ___ good: 5 heart
do one's ___ thing: 3 own
Doonesbury: 7 cartoon **10** comic strip
artist: 7 Trudeau
character: 2 B.D. **3** Kim, Sam **4** Alex, Duke, Mark, Mike **5** Honey **6** Hedley, Roland, Zonker **7** Boopsie **8** Samantha
locale: 6 Walden
do one's heart ___: 4 good
do one's own ___: 5 thing
door: 4 exit, gate, trap **5** entry, hatch, storm, way in **6** access, egress, portal **7** ingress, opening, postern **8** entrance, entryway, hatchway **9** revolving, threshold **10** passageway
aircraft ~: 5 hatch
back ~: 7 postern
ender: 3 man, mat, men, way **4** bell, jamb, knob, nail, post, sill, step, stop, yard **5** woman, women **6** keeper
feature: 3 mat **4** bolt, hook, jamb, knob, lock, sill **5** hinge, jambe, latch **6** lintel
hinge site: 4 jamb **5** jambe
install a ~: 4 hang
it may be checked at the ~: 6 ID card
keep the wolf from the ~: 4 work **7** peg away **9** grind away
lay at one's ~: 3 tax **5** blame **6** accuse, charge, finger **7** censure **8** sentence **9** attribute, implicate
like a French ~: 5 paned
next ~ to: 4 near **5** close **6** at hand, nearby **8** abutting, adjacent, touching **9** adjoining, bordering, immediate **10** contiguous, convenient, juxtaposed
open ~: 6 entrée
open a ~ illegally: 4 loid
opener: 3 key **7** key card
open the ~: 4 go in **5** let in, usher
position: 4 ajar
show the ~: 4 oust
sliding ~: 6 fusuma
sliding ~ groove: 5 regle
sound: 4 slam **5** creak
starter: 3 out **4** back
sub ~: 5 hatch
take through the ~: 6 lead in
word: 3 men **4** exit, pull, push **5** enter, women
door ___: 4 buck, jack **5** chain, check, money, prize **6** charge, closer, handle, opener
do-or-___: 3 die
___ door: 3 air **4** back, fire, flap, open, trap **5** blind, Dutch, dwarf, front, stage, storm, swing **6** French, joiner, pocket **7** falling, folding
___ Door: 5 Stage
doorbell: 5 chime **6** buzzer, ringer
eschew the ~: 5 knock
response: 6 come in
ringer: 6 caller
ring ~ s: 3 run **5** stump **8** campaign
sound: 4 dong, ring
Doorbell Rang, The author: Rex Stout
___ Door Canteen: 5 Stage
do-or-die: 7 crucial **9** last-ditch
doorframe: 4 jamb **5** jambe
Door Is Still Open to My Heart, The (1964 song) artist: Dean Martin
___-door Johnny: 5 stage
doorkeeper: 5 guard, tiler, usher **6** porter, sentry, warden **7** janitor, ostiary, turnkey **8** guardian, sentinel, watchdog **9** custodian
doorman's job, do a: 5 admit, let in
doormat: 5 patsy, toady **6** jackal, lackey **7** lacquey **8** kowtower **9** sycophant
use a ~: 4 wipe
___-door neighbor: 4 next
___-door opener: 6 garage
___-door policy: 4 open
doorpost: 4 jamb **5** jambe
doors
behind closed ~: 6 inside **8** secretly **9** privately
like some ~: 5 paned **6** bifold
open ~: 3 aid **4** ease, help **6** assist **10** facilitate
path to some ~: 5 stoop
Doors
leader: Jim Morrison
song: Hello, I Love You (1968)
Light My Fire (1967)
Touch Me (1969)
door's open!, The: 5 enter **6** come in
doorstep: 9 threshold
not leave on the ~: 5 ask in
welcomer: 3 mat
Doors, The (1991 film)
cast: Kevin Dillon, Val Kilmer, Meg Ryan, Frank Whaley
director: Oliver Stone
doorstop: 5 wedge
Door, The author: Rinehart
Door to December, The author: Dean Koontz
doorway: 4 exit, gate **5** entry, lobby **6** entrée, portal **7** ingress **8** entrance **9** threshold
accessory: 3 mat
part: 4 jamb, sill **5** jambe
do-over: 3 let **8** mulligan
doo-wop: 5 music, style
syllable: 3 dah, dum
Doo Wop (1998 song) artist: Lauryn Hill
doozie: 3 pip **4** lulu, oner **5** beaut, dilly **6** beauty, killer **8** standout **9** humdinger **10** ripsnorter
dope: 3 ass, tip **4** dolt, fool, gowk, info, jerk, news **5** dummy, dunce, facts, goods **6** dimwit, gossip, lubber, nitwit, notice, tipoff **7** details, half-wit, jackass, lackwit, lowdown **8** numskull **9** blockhead, harebrain, knowledge, lamebrain, numbskull, simpleton **10** dunderhead, nincompoop
out: 6 decode, design, figure, unfold **7** measure, unravel **8** decipher
dope ___: 3 out **5** sheet, story
___-dope: 5 rope-a
dopey: 5 dense, inane, silly, thick **6** obtuse, sleepy, stupid, torpid **7** doltish, foolish, languid, lumpish, out of it, witless **8** mindless, sluggish **9** befuddled, dim-witted, lethargic, senseless, soporific **10** weak-minded
Dopey: 5 dwarf
colleague: 3 Doc **5** Happy **6** Grumpy, Sleepy, Sneezy **7** Bashful
doppelgänger: 4 twin **5** ghost, image **7** specter
Doppler ___: 5 radar **6** effect
Doppler, Christian: 8 Austrian **9** physicist
dor: 3 bug **6** beetle, insect **7** June bug **8** elaterid

__ d'or: 5 louis 6 chaise, siècle
__ d'Or: 3 Val 4 Côte, L'Age 5 Le Coq, Palme
__ Dora: 4 dumb
dorado: 7 dolphin 8 mahimahi
do-rag: 5 scarf 8 kerchief
Doran: 3 Ann
Dorati, Antal: 9 conductor, Hungarian
dorbeetle: 3 bug 6 insect
Dorcas, emulate: 3 sew
Dordogne: 5 river
locale: 6 France
doré: 6 gilded, golden
Doré: 7 Gustave
do-re-mi: 3 oof 4 cash, gelt, jack, kail, kale, loot, peag, pelf 5 bills, bread, bucks, dough, funds, lucre, money, moola, mopus, pesos, rhino, sewan 6 dinero, mammon, mazuma, moolah, seawan, silver, specie, wampum, wealth 7 cabbage, capital, dollars, lettuce, ooftish, scratch, shekels 8 bankroll, cold cash, currency, hard cash, smackers 9 banknotes, frogskins, long green, simoleons 10 greenbacks, green stuff
Do Re Mi: 7 musical
songwriter: 5 Styne
Do-Re-Mi composer: 7 Rodgers 11 Hammerstein
Dorff: 7 Stephen
Dorfman, Ariel: 6 writer 7 Chilean
__ Doria: 6 Andrea
Dorian: 4 Gray, mode
Doric: 5 order 6 column 9 classical
alternative: 5 Ionic 10 Corinthian
column ridge: 5 arris
Do-Right, Dudley girl: 4 Nell
Doris: 3 Day 4 Duke, Hart 7 Lessing, Roberts 8 asteroid
daughter of ~: 7 Galatea
Doritos: 5 snack 9 taco chips
Dorking: 4 fowl 7 chicken
relative: 6 Bantam, Brahma, Houdan, Sussex 7 Cornish, Leghorn 8 Araucana, Langshan, Shanghai 9 Dominique, Orpington, Wyandotte
__ d'Orléans: 3 Ile
dorm: 4 hall, home 5 lodge 7 bedroom, lodging 8 quarters 9 residence
drudge: 4 wonk
inhabitant: 4 coed 7 student
item: 3 bed 5 pin-up
overseer: 2 RA
sound: 5 snore
view, perhaps: 4 quad
dormancy: 5 sleep 6 torpor 7 latency, slumber 8 abeyance 10 suspension
dormant: 3 lax 4 idle, lazy, logy 5 inert, still 6 asleep, dozing, draggy, fallow, latent, torpid 7 abeyant, napping, passive 8 dreaming, inactive, indolent, in repose, listless, sleeping, slothful, sluggish, snoozing 9 lethargic, potential, quiescent, sacked out, sedentary, sidelined, somnolent, suspended 10 disengaged, on the shelf, slumbering, unrealized
lie ~: 3 sit 6 hole up 8 go unused 9 hibernate
dormer: 4 loft 6 garret, window
build a ~: 5 add on
dormouse: 4 loir 5 lerot 6 animal, mammal, rodent
relative: 3 rat 4 cavy, degu, jird, paca, vole 5 coypu, gundi, xerus 6 agouti, beaver, gerbil, gopher, jerboa, marmot, murine 7 hamster, lemming, muskrat, visacha 8 chipmunk, cricetid, squirrel, tuco-tuco 9 chickaree, groundhog, guinea pig, porcupine, woodchuck 10 chinchilla, prairie dog
Dormouse's Tale, The, sister in: 5 Lacie
Dorn: 4 Erik 6 Philip 7 Michael
__ d'Oro: 6 Stella
Dorobo home: 5 Kenya 6 Africa 8 Tanzania
Dorothea: 3 Dix 5 Lange
Dorothy: 3 Day, Dix 4 Gish 5 Lyman, Moore, Tutin, Uhnak 6 Fields, Fisher, Gilman, Hamill, Lamour, Loudon, Malone, Parker, Sayers 7 Hodgkin, McGuire, Provine 8 Chandler 9 Bredehorn, Dandridge, Kilgallen 10 Richardson
co-panelist of ~: 6 Arlene 7 Bennett
dog: 4 Toto
slipper material: 4 ruby
to Em: 5 niece
dorp: 6 hamlet 7 village
dorper: 5 sheep
__ Dorrit: 6 Little
dorsal: 3 fin 4 back, rear 7 fin type 9 posterior
insect's ~ surface: 5 notum
dorsal __: 3 fin, lip 4 root
__ d'Orsay: 4 Quai
D'Orsay: 4 Fifi
Dors, Diana spouse: Richard Dawson
Dorset: 6 county
city: 5 Poole 10 Bournmouth
locale: 7 England
Dorset Horn: 5 sheep
Dorsetshire: 6 county
capital: 10 Dorchester
town: 5 Poole
Dorsett, Tony: 10 footballer
Dorsey: 5 Jimmy, Tommy
Dorsey, Jimmy: 11 saxophonist
instrument: alto sax, clarinet
song: So Rare (1957)
The Yam
Dorsey, Tommy: 10 trombonist
theme song: 5 Marie
tune: 3 You 4 Nola 5 Marie
dorsum: 4 back
Dortmund: 4 city, town
locale: 7 Germany
Dortmund-__ Canal: 3 Ems
dory: 4 boat, fish 5 barge, craft, skiff 6 vessel 7 rowboat 8 sailboat
move a ~: 3 oar, row
__-dory: 5 hunky
Dory: 6 Previn
dos: 3 two 6 numero 7 Spanish
follower: 4 tres
preceder: 3 uno
Dos __: 5 Equis 6 Passos
DOS
alternative: 4 Unix 5 Linux 7 Windows
command: 3 del, dir 4 copy, more, sort, type 5 erase 6 rename
part: 4 disk 6 system 9 operating
popularizer: 3 IBM
runner: 2 PC
dos-à-dos: 4 step
dosage: 6 amount
amount.: 2 cc. 3 tsp. 4 tbsp.
schedule: 3 q.i.d., t.i.d.
do's and don'ts: 4 code 5 rules 6 policy 7 customs 8 standard
dose: 4 pill 5 share, treat 6 tablet 7 capsule, measure, portion 8 dispense, medicine, quantity 10 medicament, medication
holder: 4 hypo 5 ampul 6 ampule, caplet, tablet 7 ampoule
starter: 4 mega
Doshisha University
locale: 5 Japan, Kioto, Kyoto
do-si-do: 4 step
__ Do Something to Me: 3 You
Dos Passos, John: 6 author, writer
work: The 42nd Parallel
The Big Money
Century's Ebb
Manhattan Transfer
Three Soldiers
U.S.A.
Dos Quebradas: 4 city, town
locale: 8 Colombia
doss: 3 bed
dossier: 4 file 6 folder, papers, record, report 7 archive, profile 9 portfolio
Dostoyevsky, Fyodor: 6 author, writer 7 Russian
work: The Brothers Karamazov
Crime and Punishment
The Double
The Gambler
The House of the Dead
The Idiot
Notes From the Underground
Poor Folk
The Possessed
dot: 3 bit, jot, pip 4 atom, iota, mark, mite, mote, spot 5 dowry, fleck, grain, pixel, point, speck 6 dapple, dowery, pepper, period, tittle 7 freckle, lentigo, spatter, stipple 8 flyspeck, particle, pinpoint, sprinkle 9 bespeckle
computer ~: 3 pel 5 pixel
follower: 3 com, edu, gov, net, org
map ~: 3 cay, key 4 isle, town 5 islet 6 island
on the ~: 5 exact, right, sharp 6 prompt 7 exactly, precise 8 accurate, promptly, punctual
dot __: 6 matrix 7 etching, product
dot-__: 3 com
__ dot: 5 flock, on the, polka
DOT
agency: 3 FAA
part of ~: 4 Dept. 10 Department
dot-com: 7 company
auction site: 4 eBay
dream: 3 IPO
stock: 6 Amazon
dote on: 4 baby, like, love 5 adore, enjoy, spoil 6 coddle, cosset, pamper 7 cherish, idolize, indulge, worship 8 fawn over, fuss over, give in to 9 care about
Dothan: 4 city, town
locale: 7 Alabama
__ Do That: 4 I Can
Do That to Me One More Time (1979 song) artist: Captain & Tennille
do the __: 4 math 5 trick
Do the Bird (1963 song) artist: Sharp
Do the Clam (1965 song) artist: Elvis Presley
Do the Right Thing (1989 film)
cast: Danny Aiello, Ossie Davis, Ruby Dee, Spike Lee
director: Spike Lee
pizzeria: 4 Sal's
__ doth protest..., The: 4 lady
doting: 4 fond 6 loving 7 amatory, amorous, devoted, fatuous, valuing 8 lovesick 9 amatorial, indulgent
dot-matrix __: 7 printer
Dotrice: 3 Roy 5 Karen
__ dots: 5 Botts
dotted __: 4 line 5 swiss
dotterel: 4 bird
Dottie: 4 West
dottle: 3 ash
dotty: 4 daft, gaga, loco 5 balmy, daffy, goofy, goosy, loopy 6 absurd 7 bonkers, foolish, touched 9 eccentric 10 off-the-wall
Douai: 4 city, town
locale: 6 France
Douala: 4 city, port, town
locale: 8 Cameroon
Douay Bible
book: 4 Osee 6 Tobias
Jacob's son in the ~: 4 Aser
Shem's father in the ~: 3 Noe
double: 3 duo, hit 4 copy, dual, fold, mate, rise, same, twin 5 binal, clone, ditto, image, match, Xerox 6 bifold, binary, binate, duplex, paired 7 coupled, replica, stand-in, twofold 8 knockoff, likeness, multiply 9 alternate, dualistic, duplicate, facsimile, imitation, look-alike, photocopy 10 dead ringer, reciprocal
agent: 3 spy 4 mole 8 turncoat
back: 4 turn 6 return 7 reverse
combining form: 4 dipl- 5 diplo-
curve: 3 ess 4 ogee
Dutch: 4 game 8 jump rope
ender: 3 ton 4 tree, wide, word 5 speak, think 6 header
entendre: 3 pun 8 wordplay
(for): 5 cover 6 fill in 10 substitute
on the ~: 4 anon, ASAP, fast, stat 5 apace, quick 6 pronto 7 hastily, quickly, rapidly, swiftly, tantivy 8 promptly 9 posthaste
over: 4 fold 5 stoop
prefix: 2 bi- 3 twi-
take: 8 reaction, response
trouble: 6 plight 8 quandary
whammy: 5 shock
Windsor: 4 knot
double __: 3 bar, bed, cup, run 4 axel, bass, bill, bind, bond, coat, date, demy, flat, ikat, jump, knit, play, reed, room, salt, star, stop, take, tape, tide, time, whip, wing 5 agent, altar, block, bogey, cloth, cream, crème, crown, drift, dummy, eagle, ender, entry, fault, first, fugue, helix, hitch, modal, piece, rhyme, sharp, steal, sugar, truck 6 batten, boiler, dagger, magnum, paddle, quotes, sculls, spread, tackle, wicket 7 bassoon, blossom, coconut, dresser, dribble, entente, feature, glazing, harness
double-__: 3 cut, dip 4 bank, book, crop, date, dome, duty, knit, lock, park, reed, ring, talk, team, time, wide 5 blind, check, click, cross, digit, edged, ended, faced, quick, sided, space 6 acting, action, bottom, clutch, decker, figure, glazed, minded, nickel, ripper, runner, tailed, tongue 7 dealing, jointed
double-__ bookkeeping: 5 entry
double-__ inflation: 5 digit
double-__ sword: 5 edged
double-__ window: 4 hung
__ double: 3 see 4 body 5 daily, on the 7 penalty, takeout
__-double: 6 triple
Double __: 4 Dare 5 Dutch, Fudge 6 Vision 7 Trouble, Wedding
Double-__: 7 Crostic
__ Double: 4 Body 5 On the
double-blind: 4 test
double-check: 2 OK 4 back, okay, seal, sign, test 5 admit, check, prove, vouch 6 affirm, attest, ensure, look up, ratify, settle, uphold, verify 7 approve, bear out, certify, confess, confirm, endorse, indorse, justify, sustain, witness 8 check out, evidence, make sure, sanction, validate, vouch for 9 ascertain, establish, guarantee, recommend, respond to, sign off on 10 strengthen
double-cross: 3 con 4 dupe 5 cheat, guile, trick 6 betray, delude, take in 7 deceive, defraud, mislead, sell out, swindle, two-time 8 hoodwink 9 treachery
double-crosser: 3 rat 5 cheat, knave, louse, snake, sneak 7 traitor 8 turncoat
double-crossing: 5 lying 7 knavish, perfidy 8 disloyal 9 underhand, unethical

doubled: 4 dual
combining form: 3 bis-
Double Dare: 8 game show
host: Mark Summers
double-daters: 4 four
Doubleday: 5 Abner 6 Nelson
double-deal: 5 cheat 7 two-time
double-dealer: 5 cheat, fraud, snake 7 traitor 8 swindler
double-dealing: 3 sly 5 dirty, false, fraud, lying 6 artful, deceit, dupery, rotten, sneaky, tricky 7 chicane, corrupt, crooked, devious, falsity, knavish, perfidy, swindle 8 bad faith, betrayal, cheating, delusive, guileful, intrigue, pretense, recreant, trickery, two-faced 9 deceitful, deception, dishonest, duplicity, insincere, treachery 10 mendacious, traitorous, untruthful
double-decker: 3 bus
double eagle: 4 coin
double-edged: 6 ironic
Double Fantasy artist: 3 Ono
Double Fudge author: Judy Blume
double-hook shape: 3 ess
double-hung: 6 window
Double Indemnity: 4 film 5 novel
author: James M. Cain
cast: Fred MacMurray, Edward G. Robinson, Barbara Stanwyck
director: Billy Wilder
Double Jeopardy (1999 film)
cast: Annabeth Gish, Bruce Greenwood, Tommy Lee Jones, Ashley Judd
director: Bruce Beresford
double-jointed: 5 agile
Double Life, A (1947 film)
cast: Ronald Colman, Signe Hasso, Edmond O'Brien
director: George Cukor
Double Lovin' (1971 song) artist: Osmonds
Double Man, The author: W.H. Auden
Doublemint: 10 chewing gum
alternative: 5 Extra, Orbit 7 Dentyne, Trident 8 Carefree, Chiclets, Freedent 10 Juicy Fruit
double or ___: 7 nothing
Double or Nothing: 9 radio show
double-quick: 5 apace, swift 7 hastily, swiftly 9 posthaste
double-reed: 4 oboe
___ doubles: 5 mixed
doublespeak: 6 jargon 8 language 9 misinform
doublet: 3 duo, set, two 4 duad, pair 6 couple, jacket, jerkin
___ double take: 3 do a
double-talk: 3 gas, rot 4 blah, bosh, bull, bunk, guff, jazz, jive, pooh, tosh 5 bilge, fudge, hokum, hooey, prate, stuff, trash, tripe 6 bunkum, bushwa, drivel, footle, gabble, gammon, gibber, havers, hot air, humbug, jabber, jargon, kibosh, piffle 7 baloney, blarney, blather, blether, boloney, bushwah, eyewash, flannel, flubdub, fustian, garbage, hogwash, inanity, rubbish, twaddle 8 buncombe, claptrap, falderal, falderol, flimflam, flummery, folderal, folderol, nonsense, slipslop, tommyrot, trumpery 9 banana oil, dissemble, gibberish, kidstakes, moonshine, poppycock, rigmarole 10 applesauce, balderdash, bilge water, codswallop, equivocate, flapdoodle, galimatias, Jabberwock, mumbo jumbo, rigamarole, taradiddle
Double, The author: Dostoyevsky
double-time: 3 hie 4 fast 5 brisk, fleet, hasty, quick, rapid, speed, swift 6 flying, racing, speedy 7 express, hurried, instant 9 breakneck, instantly
DoubleTree: 5 hotel
alternative: 4 Omni 5 Hyatt 6 Hilton, Westin 7 Wyndham 8 Marriott, Radisson, Sheraton 11 Crowne Plaza, Four Seasons
Double Trouble (1967 film)
cast: Annette Day, Elvis Presley
director: Norman Taurog
Double Vision (1978 song) artist: Foreigner
Double Vision author: Mary Higgins Clark
Double Wedding (1937 film)
cast: Myrna Loy, William Powell
doubloon: 4 coin, gold 5 money
doubly: 5 extra, twice 7 twofold
Doubs: 5 river
locale: 6 France
doubt: 5 qualm, query, worry 6 wonder 7 dubiety, problem, scruple, suspect 8 bad vibes, distrust, mistrust, quandary, question, suspense, wariness 9 ambiguity, confusion, disbelief, discredit, dubiosity, hesitancy, leeriness, misgiving, nonbelief, smell a rat, suspicion 10 disbelieve, hesitation, indecision, insecurity, skepticism
cry of ~: 2 uh, um 3 bah, hah 4 I bet 5 humph
express ~: 5 demur, query, waver 6 impugn 8 question
free from ~: 4 sure 5 prove 6 assure 7 certify, satisfy 8 convince 9 guarantee
have ~: 8 mistrust
have no ~: 4 know
no ~ should: 7 had best
without a ~: 3 yep, yes 4 amen, okay, sure, true 5 by far, quite, right, truly 6 and how, indeed, rather, really, righto, surely, verily, you bet 7 clearly, exactly, for real, for sure, quite so, readily 8 as you say, of course, to be sure 9 assuredly, certainly, darn right, decidedly, hands down, naturally, obviously, you betcha, you said it 10 absolutely, definitely, far and away, positively, sure enough, undeniably
___-doubt: 4 self
doubter: 5 cynic 6 critic 7 sceptic, scoffer, skeptic 8 agnostic 10 questioner
___ Doubtfire: 3 Mrs.
doubtful: 4 iffy, moot, open, wary 5 chary, leery, queer, rocky, shaky, vague 6 louche, unfirm, unsure 7 cynical, dubious, guarded, puzzled, suspect, tenuous 8 agnostic, cautious, hesitant, unlikely, unstable 9 ambiguous, debatable, equivocal, skeptical, tentative, uncertain, undecided, unsettled 10 disputable, hesitating, improbable, indecisive, indefinite, infeasible, precarious, suspicious, unresolved
doubting: 4 wary 5 leery 8 hesitant 9 skeptical
Thomas: 7 sceptic, skeptic
Doubting Thomas (1935 film)
cast: Billie Burke, Will Rogers, Alison Skipworth
doubtless: 4 sure 6 easily, likely, surely 8 for a fact, probably 9 assuredly, certainly, evidently, precisely, seemingly 10 absolutely, apparently, definitely, far and away, most likely, ostensibly, positively, presumably, supposedly
doubtlessly: 6 indeed
douceur: 5 bonus 9 lagniappe
Doug: 4 Ford 6 Flutie, McKeon, Savant 7 Henning, McClure, Sanders
dough: 3 mix, oof 4 cash, coin, gelt, jack, kail, kale, loaf, loot, peag, pelf 5 beans, bills, bread, bucks, chips, clams, funds, lucre, means, money, moola, mopus, pesos, rhino, sewan 6 batter, dinero, do-re-mi, mammon, mazuma, moolah, seawan, silver, specie, wampum, wealth 7 cabbage, capital, dollars, lettuce, mixture, ooftish, scratch, shekels 8 bankroll, cold cash, currency, hard cash, smackers 9 banknotes, frogskins, long green, simoleons 10 greenbacks, green stuff
component: 5 yeast
does it: 4 rise
ender: 3 boy, nut 4 face
lover: 5 miser 9 skinflint
Mideast ~: 4 filo
one with ~: 5 baker
prepare ~: 5 knead 6 leaven
rolling in ~: 4 rich 5 flush 6 loaded, monied 7 moneyed, wealthy, well-off 8 affluent, in clover, well-to-do 9 well-fixed 10 in the money, privileged, propertied, prosperous, well-heeled
doughboy: 2 GI 4 Yank
conflict: 3 WWI
doughtiness: 4 grit 5 nerve, pluck, valor 7 bravery, heroism
doughty: 4 bold, game, hale, iron, wiry 5 beefy, brave, burly, gutsy, hardy, hefty, hunky, husky, lusty, nervy, stout, tough 6 awless, brawny, daring, gritty, hearty, heroic, mighty, plucky, potent, robust, rugged, sinewy, spunky, steely, stocky, sturdy, virile 7 aweless, defiant, gallant, impavid, staunch, valiant 8 athletic, fearless, forceful, heroical, indurate, intrepid, muscular, powerful, puissant, resolute, stalwart, unafraid, valorous, vigorous 9 Atlantean, audacious, dauntless, dreadless, Herculean, strapping, undaunted, unfearful, unfearing, well-built 10 able-bodied, courageous, red-blooded, undismayed
doughy: 4 pale, soft 5 pasty 6 pallid
Douglas: 3 fir 4 Barr, Carl, city, Kirk, Mike, Paul, Sirk 5 Donna, Moore 6 Gordon, Hickox, Mawson, Melvyn, Norman 7 capital, Illeana, Michael, Stephen, Stewart 8 Corrigan, Osheroff, Trumbull 9 Fairbanks, MacArthur
locale: 9 Isle of Man
Douglas ___: 3 bag, fir 4 pine 6 spruce
Douglas, Gordon: 8 director
film: The Black Arrow (1948)
The Detective (1968)
Follow That Dream (1962)
The McConnell Story (1955)
Rio Conchos (1964)
Robin and the Seven Hoods (1964)
Saps at Sea (1940)
Them! (1954)
Tony Rome (1967)
Young at Heart (1954)
Douglas-Home, Alec: 2 P.M. 7 British
predecessor: 9 Macmillan
successor: 6 Wilson
Douglas, Kirk: 5 actor
film: 20,000 Leagues Under the Sea (1954)
The Bad and the Beautiful (1952)
The Big Carnival (1951)
The Big Sky (1952)
The Brotherhood (1968)
Champion (1949)
Detective Story (1951)
The Devil's Disciple (1959)
Diamonds (1999)
The Final Countdown (1980)
The Fury (1978)
Gunfight at the O.K. Corral (1957)
The Hook (1963)
The Indian Fighter (1955)
The Last Sunset (1961)
Last Train From Gun Hill (1959)
A Letter to Three Wives (1949)
Lonely Are the Brave (1962)
Lust for Life (1956)
The Man From Snowy River (1982)
The Man Without a Star (1955)
Out of the Past (1947)
Paths of Glory (1957)
Posse (1975)
Seven Days in May (1964)
Spartacus (1960)
The Strange Loves of Martha Ivers (1946)
There Was a Crooked Man ... (1970)
Tough Guys (1986)
Town Without Pity (1961)
Two Weeks in Another Town (1962)
The War Wagon (1967)
Young Man With a Horn (1950)
Douglas, Lloyd C. novel: The Robe
Douglas, Melvyn: 5 actor
film: The Americanization of Emily (1964)
Annie Oakley (1935)
Being There (1979, AA)
Billy Budd (1962)
Captains Courageous (1937)
The Guilt of Janet Ames (1947)
Hud (1963, AA)
I Never Sang for My Father (1970)
The Lone Wolf Returns (1935)
Mary Burns, Fugitive (1935)
Mr. Blandings Builds His Dream House (1948)
Ninotchka (1939)
The Old Dark House (1932)
That Uncertain Feeling (1941)
Theodora Goes Wild (1936)
There's Always a Woman (1938)
This Thing Called Love (1941)
Too Many Husbands (1940)
Two-Faced Woman (1941)
A Woman's Face (1941)
spouse: Helen Gahagan
Douglas, Michael: 5 actor
father: 4 Kirk
film: Adam at 6 A.M. (1970)
The American President (1995)
Basic Instinct (1992)
Black Rain (1989)
The China Syndrome (1979)
A Chorus Line (1985)
Coma (1978)
Disclosure (1994)
Don't Say a Word (2001)
Fatal Attraction (1987)
The Game (1997)
It's My Turn (1980)
The Jewel of the Nile (1985)
A Perfect Murder (1998)
Romancing the Stone (1984)
Shining Through (1992)
Traffic (2000)
Wall Street (1987, AA)
The War of the Roses (1989)
Wonder Boys (2000)
spouse: Catherine Zeta-Jones
TV: The Streets of San Francisco
Douglas, Norman: 6 writer 7 British
Douglas, Paul: 5 actor
film: Angels in the Outfield (1951)
Clash by Night (1952)
Everybody Does It (1949)
Forever Female (1953)
Fourteen Hours (1951)
It Happens Every Spring (1949)
The Mating Game (1959)
Panic in the Streets (1950)
The Solid Gold Cadillac (1956)
Douglass: 5 North 9 Dumbrille, Frederick 10 Montgomery
Douglas, Stephen A.: 6 orator

Douglasville: 4 city, town
locale: 7 Georgia
Do unto ___...: 6 others
dour: 3 sad 4 dark, glum, grim, sour, ugly 5 bleak, grave, moody, sulky, surly 6 crabby, crusty, dismal, dreary, gloomy, morose, severe, sullen 8 lowering, taciturn 9 saturnine, unsmiling 10 forbidding, ill-humored
Dourif: 4 Brad
dourness: 9 austerity
Douro: 5 river
locale: 5 Spain 8 Portugal
douroucouli: 7 primate
relative: 3 ape 4 saki, titi 5 chimp, drill, jocko, lemur, loris, magot, orang, potto, shrew 6 aye-aye, baboon, Bandar, galago, gelada, gibbon, grivet, guenon, howler, langur, macaco, monkey, rhesus, uakari, vervet 7 colobus, gorilla, guereza, hoolock, macaque, sapajou, siamang, tamarin, tarsier 8 bush baby, capuchin, mandrill, mangabey, marmoset, talapoin 9 orangutan 10 Barbary ape, chimpanzee, orangutang
douse: 3 wet 4 kill, soak, wash 5 plash, snuff, souse, water 6 drench, embrue, imbrue, put out, quench, splash 7 blow out, immerse, smother, spatter, turn off 8 saturate, snuff out, submerge 10 extinguish
doused: 3 out
douser need: 4 hose 7 hydrant
___-doux: 6 billet
douze: 6 French, twelve
dove: 4 bird, gray, grey 5 cooer 6 culver, purply 7 pinkish 8 pacifist, peacenik, purplish
branch: 5 olive
ender: 3 cot 4 cote, tail
home: 4 cote
intention: 5 peace
name meaning ~: 5 Jonah, Jonas 6 Jemima
opposite: 4 hawk
relative: 3 ash 4 drab 5 beige, dusty, merle, pearl, putty, slate, taupe 6 silver 7 grizzly 8 charcoal, gunmetal, platinum
sound: 3 coo
starter: 4 ring 6 turtle
___ dove: 4 rock 5 peace, quail, stock 6 ground
Dove: 4 Rita, soap 6 Billie
alternative: 3 Lux 4 Dial, Lava, Tone, Zest 5 Camay, Coast, Ivory, Lever 6 Boraxo, Caress, Shield 8 Lifebuoy 9 Palmolive, Safeguard 11 Irish Spring
Dove ___: 3 Bar 5 prism
dovecote: 6 aviary, volary
dovekie: 3 auk 4 bird
dovelike: 6 gentle 8 peaceful
Dovells
song: Bristol Stomp (1961)
You Can't Sit Down (1963)
Dover: 4 city, port, town 6 strait
county: 4 Kent
fish: 4 sole
locale: 3 Del. 4 Kent 7 England 8 Delaware
sight: 5 cliff
the white cliffs of ~: 5 chalk
town opposite ~: 6 Calais
Dover ___: 4 sole 5 Beach
Dover Beach author: Matthew Arnold
Dove, Rita: 4 poet
Doves in immemorial ___: 4 elms
Dove's Nest, The author: Mansfield
dovetail: 2 go 3 fit 4 gybe, jibe, link, mesh 5 match, tenon 6 cohere 7 conform 8 coincide, junction, juncture 9 harmonize, interlink, interlock, make sense 10 correspond
dovetail ___: 3 saw 5 hinge, plane
___-dovey: 5 lovey
dovish: 6 irenic 8 irenical, peaceful
Dow: 4 Tony 5 index, Peggy
partner: 5 Jones
Do-Wacka-Do (1965 song) artist: Roger Miller
dowager: 4 dame 5 woman 6 female 10 noblewoman
___ dowager: 5 queen
Do Wah Diddy Diddy (1964 song)
artist: Manfred Mann
Dowd's friend: 5 pooka 6 Harvey, rabbit
dowdy: 4 drab 5 dated, messy, passé, tacky 6 blowsy, frowsy, frowzy, frumpy, old hat, shabby, sordid, stodgy, unneat, untidy 7 unkempt 8 outdated, outmoded, slovenly 9 out-of-date, unstylish 10 antiquated, bedraggled, disheveled, disorderly
not ~: 4 neat
one: 5 frump
___ dowdy: 5 apple
dowel: 3 peg, rod
___-do-well: 4 ne'er
dowel-shaping tool: 4 nogg
dower ___: 5 chest, house
dowitcher: 4 bird
Dow Jones
figure: 3 low 4 high 5 close 7 average
firm: 3 IBM 5 Exxon, Kodak 7 Wal-Mart
index: 4 rail 7 utility 10 industrial
unit: 5 point
down: 3 eat, fur, low, nap, sad 4 blue, fell, fuzz, glum, lick, moor, mopy, pile, sick, take 5 below, drink, fluff, level, lower, moody, mopey, not up, outdo, quaff, under, woful 6 broody, gloomy, imbibe, ingest, lonely, morose, sickly, somber, woeful 7 consume, daunted, doleful, falling, forlorn, hangdog, in a funk, plumage, sinking, swallow, unhappy 8 brooding, dejected, desolate, dropping, inactive, listless, overcome, sluggish, troubled 9 bummed-out, cheerless, depressed, heartsick, miserable, polish off, woebegone 10 chapfallen, descending, despondent, dispirited, distressed, in the dumps, melancholy, out of order, out of sorts, spiritless, underneath
combining form: 4 ptil- 5 ptilo-
ender: 3 bow 4 beat, cast, fall, haul, hill, link, load, play, pour, side, size, spin, tick, time, town, turn, wind, zone 5 burst, court, draft, field, grade, range, right, river, scale, shift, slide, spout, stage, state, swing, trend 6 market, rigger, stairs, stater, stream 7 hearted, trodden
not ~: 6 across
prefix: 3 cat- 4 cata-, cath-, hypo-
starter: 3 hoe, let, low, put, rub, run, sun 4 come, draw, face, look, mark, melt, push, show, shut, slow, take, tear, turn 5 break, bring, build, clamp, climb, close, count, crack, eider, knock, paste, phase, shake, shoot, spell, stand, swans, touch 6 splash, tumble 7 thistle
the road: 4 soon 5 later
down ___: 4 card, cold, East 5 quark, under 7 payment
down ___ mouth: 5 at the, in the
down ___ wire: 5 to the
down-___: 3 bow 4 home, zone 6 easter, market
down-___-heel: 5 at-the
___ down: 3 cry, cut, die, get, lay, let, lie, mow, pat, pin, put, rub, run, set, sit, tie 4 back, bear, boil, call, chow, come, dash, deep, draw, dumb, face, fall, gear, hand, hold, keep, live, mark, nail, pare, pipe, play, pull, ride, salt, shut, slap, slim, step, take, talk, tear, tone, turn, wash, wear, wind, wolf 5 break, bring, clamp, climb, close, count, crack, crank, dress, eider, first, knock, phase, plunk, scarf, shake, shoot, shout, stand, stare, touch, track, water, weigh, write 6 buckle, powder, settle, simmer, splash, strike, thumbs, upside 7 drawing, knuckle, ratchet, talking
___ down!: 4 Pipe
___-down: 3 low, put, sit, top 4 fold 5 build, derry, hands, up-and 6 broken, tumble
Down ___: 3 Low 4 East 5 Under
Down ___ Riverside: 5 by the
___ Down: 3 Get, Lay, Way 4 Take 6 Boogie, Upside
down-and-___: 3 out 5 dirty, outer
down-and-dirty: 5 funky, nasty
down-and-out: 4 poor 5 needy 8 deprived, wretched 9 destitute, penniless
down-and-outer: 5 loser
Down and Out in Beverly Hills (1986 film)
cast: Richard Dreyfuss, Bette Midler, Nick Nolte
director: Paul Mazursky
dog: 7 Matisse
Down and Out in Paris and London
author: George Orwell
___ down a peg: 4 take
Down Argentine Way (1940 film)
cast: Don Ameche, Betty Grable, Carmen Miranda
Down at ___ Joe's: 4 Papa
down at the ___: 5 mouth
down-at-the-heel: 4 mean 5 seedy
downbeat: 4 glum 5 tempo 6 broody, gloomy, rhythm, solemn, thesis 7 unhappy 8 dejected, negative 9 cheerless, defeatist, unhopeful 10 dispirited
in music: 6 thesis
Down by the ___: 4 Erie
Down by the Lazy River (1972 song)
artist: Osmonds
Down by the Old Mill ___: 6 Stream
Down by the Salley Gardens author: William Butler Yeats
___-down cake: 6 upside
downcast: 3 low, sad 4 blue, glum, mopy 5 heavy, moody, mopey, sorry, woful 6 broody, dreary, gloomy, morose, somber, woeful 7 daunted, doleful, forlorn, hangdog, in a funk, joyless, subdued, unhappy 8 brooding, dejected, desolate, listless, troubled, wretched 9 bummed-out, cheerless, depressed, desperate, exanimate, heartsick, miserable, saturnine, sorrowful, woebegone 10 chapfallen, despondent, dispirited, distressed, melancholy, out of sorts, spiritless
one: 5 moper
___-down-drag-out: 5 knock
Down East: 5 Maine
Downeaster ___, The: 5 Alexa
downer: 4 drag 5 slump 6 bummer 7 bad luck, bad news, killjoy, sadness 8 bad scene, narcotic 9 pessimist, rough time
on a ~: 4 blue 9 depressed
starter: 3 sun
Downers Grove: 4 city, town
locale: 8 Illinois
Downey: 4 city, Roma, town 6 Morton, Robert
locale: 10 California
Downey Jr., Robert: 5 actor
film: Air America (1990)
Black and White (2000)
Chances Are (1989)
Chaplin (1992)
Heart and Souls (1993)
Only You (1994)
Restoration (1995)
Soapdish (1991)
True Believer (1989)
U.S. Marshals (1998)
Wonder Boys (2000)
Downey, Morton: 5 tenor 6 singer
downfall: 3 dud 4 bane, bomb, bust, doom, flop, loss, ruin 5 decay, smash, wrack 6 defeat, demise, fiasco, mishap, turkey 7 blunder, debacle, descent, failure, misstep, stumble, undoing, washout 8 collapse, Waterloo 9 perdition, ruination
downgrade: 4 bust 5 abase, break, lower, slope 6 demote, reduce 7 decline, degrade, depress, descent, devalue 8 relegate, write off 9 decadence, declivity, denigrate, devaluate, disparage, overwhelm 10 degeneracy, depreciate, devalorize, undervalue
downhearted: 3 low, sad 4 blue, glum, mopy 5 moody, mopey, woful 6 gloomy, morose, somber, woeful 7 daunted, doleful, forlorn, joyless, unhappy 8 brooding, dejected, listless, troubled 9 bummed out, cheerless, heartsick, miserable, saturnine, sorrowful, woebegone 10 chapfallen, dispirited, melancholy
downhill: 7 dipping, falling 8 dropping 9 declining 10 descending
go ~: 4 fail, sink 5 slide, slump 6 worsen 7 decline 10 degenerate
racer: 4 luge, sled 5 skier 7 bobsled 8 skeleton
see also ski
Downhill Racer (1969 film)
cast: Gene Hackman, Robert Redford, Camilla Sparv
director: Michael Ritchie
down-home: 6 folksy
___ Down in Darkness: 3 Lie
___ down in green pastures: 5 to lie
Downing Street
number: 3 ten
resident: 2 P.M.
Down in the Boondocks (1965 song)
artist: Billy Joe Royal
Down in the Delta (1998 film)
cast: Mary Alice, Al Freeman Jr., Wesley Snipes, Alfre Woodard
director: Maya Angelou
Down, Lesley-Anne spouse: William Friedkin
downlooker: 4 snob 5 snoot
Down Low (1996 song) artist: R. Kelly
___ down on: 3 cut 4 come, look, shut
___ down one's nose at: 4 look
___ down one's throat: 3 ram 5 shove
down on one's ___: 4 luck
Down on the Corner (1969 song)
artist: Creedence Clearwater Revival
___ down on the job: 3 lie
down partner: 5 dirty
downplay: 8 belittle, minimize 9 extenuate, whitewash 10 understate
downpour: 4 rain 5 flood, spate, storm 6 deluge 7 monsoon, torrent 8 drencher 9 rainstorm 10 cloudburst, inundation
downreaching: 4 deep
downright: 4 open, pure, rank, sure, very 5 blunt, clear, frank, gross, plain, plumb, sheer, stark, total, utter 6 arrant, candid, direct, honest, wholly 7 blatant, certain 8 absolute, definite, explicit, outright, specific, straight, thorough 9 arbitrary, decidedly, out-and-out 10 consummate, definitive, thoroughly, unmediated

downrush: **5** swoop **6** pounce **7** cascade
Downs: **4** Hugh
___ Downs: **5** Epsom, North, South
downscale: **6** low-end
___-down shirt: **6** button
downsize: **4** pare, trim **5** lower **6** lessen, reduce, shrink **7** abridge, curtail, cut back **8** decrease, diminish, roll back
downslide: **3** sag **4** drop **5** slump **7** decline **9** worsening
downs partner: **3** ups
downspout: **6** leader
___ Down Staircase: **5** Up the
Downstairs (1932 film)
  cast: Virginia Bruce, John Gilbert, Paul Lukas
downstairs worker: **4** maid
___-down strike: **3** sit
downswing: **5** slump **7** decline **9** worsening
down the ___: **4** line, road **5** drain, hatch, tubes
___ down the curtain: **4** ring
___ down the garden path: **4** lead, take
___ down the gauntlet: **5** throw
Down the hatch!: **5** toast
___ down the hatches: **6** batten
___ down the house: **5** bring
___ down the law: **3** lay
___-down theory: **7** trickle
___ down the pike: **4** come
___ down the river: **4** sell
downtime: **4** lull, rest, wait **5** break, delay, pause **6** catnap, recess **7** interim, respite **8** interval, stoppage **9** interlude **10** suspension
down-to-___: **5** earth
___ down to: **5** speak
___ down to cases: **3** get
down-to-earth: **4** real, sane **5** sober **6** common, folksy **7** mundane **8** rational, sensible **9** practical, pragmatic, realistic
___ Down to Rio: **6** Flying
___ down to size: **3** cut
down to the ___: **4** wire
Down to the Sea in Ships (1949 film)
  cast: Lionel Barrymore, Dean Stockwell, Richard Widmark
  director: Henry Hathaway
downtown: **3** urb **4** city **5** urban
Downtown (1965 song) artist: Petula Clark
Downtown Train (1989 song) artist: Rod Stewart
downtrend: **4** drop **5** slump
downtrodden: **6** abject
downturn: **3** dip, sag **4** drip, drop, fall **5** panic, slide, slump **6** plunge **7** decline, descent, plummet, retreat **8** decrease, slowdown **9** recession, worsening
Down Under
  see Australia
Down Under (1982 song) artist: Men at Work
___ down upon: **4** look
downward: **5** under **10** descending
  glide ~: **5** sweep
  slope: **3** dip **4** drop **7** descent, incline **8** gradient **9** declivity
downwards: **5** below
downwind: **4** alee
___ down with: **4** come
down with in French: **4** à bas
Down with the King (1993 song) artist: Run-D.M.C.
downy: **4** soft **5** cushy, furry, fuzzy, light, linty, nappy, plush, wooly **6** fleecy, flossy, fluffy, napped, woolly **7** squishy, velvety **8** cushiony
  duck: **5** eider
  fruit: **5** peach
  surface: **3** nap **4** pile
Downy: **8** softener
  alternative: **6** Bounce **7** Snuggle **9** Cling Free **10** Final Touch
downy-cheeked: **5** young
dowry: **3** dot
  of a ~: **5** dotal
dowsabel: **2** jo **3** pet **4** baby, dear, jill, love **5** amour, angel, chéri, cooky, cutey, cutie, deary, ducky, flame, honey, leman, lover, lovey, novia, novio, sugar, sweet **6** bon ami, chérie, cookie, dautie, dearie, steady, sweets **7** beloved, dearest, dear one, pigsney, schatzi, squeeze, sweetie, tootsie **8** chou-chou, cutie pie, dulcinea, ladylove, lovebird, macushla, paramour, precious, snookums, sugar pie, sweetums, truelove **9** bonne amie, boyfriend, dreamboat, inamorata, inamorato, petit chou, valentine **10** girlfriend, heartthrob, honeybunch, mavourneen, sweetheart, sweetie pie, turtledove
dowse: **6** divine, put out **10** waterwitch
dowser tool: **3** rod
doxology: **6** Gloria
___ doxology: **5** great **6** lesser **7** greater
Do Ya artist: **3** ELO **5** Oslin
doyen: **4** dean, king **5** elder **6** leader
Doyle: **5** David
Doyle, Arthur Conan: **3** Sir **6** author, writer **7** British
  work: A Case of Identity
    The Doings of Raffles Haw
    The Firm of Girdlestone
    The Five Orange Pips
    The Great Shadow
    The Hound of the Baskervilles
    The Land of Mist
    The Lost World
    The Maracot Deep
    Micah Clarke
    The Mystery of Cloomber
    The Parasite
    The Poison Belt
    The Red-Headed League
    The Refugees
    The Ring of Thoth
    A Scandal in Bohemia
    The Sign of Four
    Sir Nigel
    A Study in Scarlet
    The Tragedy of Korosko
    The Valley of Fear
    The White Company
Doyle, Popeye: **4** narc, nark
D'Oyly Carte: **7** Richard
Do you ___?: **4** mind
Do You Believe in Love (1982 song)
  artist: Huey Lewis and the News
Do You Believe in Magic (1965 song)
  artist: Lovin' Spoonful
Do You Believe in Us (1992 song)
  artist: Jon Secada
___ do you do: **3** how
Do You Feel Like We Do (1976 song)
  artist: Peter Frampton
___ do you good!: **4** It'll
Do you have two fives for ___?: **4** a ten
Do You Know the Way to San José (1968 song) artist: Dionne Warwick
Do You Love Me (1962 song) artist: Contours
Do you mean that?: **6** really
Do You Really Want to Hurt Me (1983 song) artist: Culture Club
Do You Remember? (1990 song)
  artist: Phil Collins
___ Do You Trust?: **3** Who
Do You Want Me (1991 song) artist: Salt-n-Pepa
Do You Want to Dance (song) artist: Bette Midler, Bobby Freeman
Do You Want to Know a Secret (1964 song) artist: Beatles
doze: **3** nap, nod **4** rest, yawn **5** sleep **6** catnap, drowse, nod off, siesta, snooze **7** drop off, shuteye, slumber **8** drift off **9** get sleepy **10** fall asleep, forty winks
  starter: **4** bull
doze ___: **3** off
dozen: **3** qty. **6** twelve **8** quantity
  courtroom ~: **4** jury
  daily ~: **5** drill **8** exercise
  dime a ~: **5** usual **6** common **7** humdrum, liberal, profuse **9** bountiful
  moons: **4** year
  one of a ~: **3** Apr., Aug., Dec., Feb., Jan., Jun., Mar., May, Nov., Oct., Sep. **4** July, Sept. **5** April, March, month **6** August **7** January, June. Jul., October **8** December, February, November **9** September
  twelve ~: **5** gross
___ dozen: **4** long **5** daily **6** baker's
dozens: **4** many
___ Dozen, The: **5** Dirty
dozer: **7** machine, vehicle **10** earth mover
  starter: **4** bull
Dozier: **6** Lamont
dozing: **6** asleep **7** dormant **9** sacked out, somnolent
  sound: **3** zzz
dozy: **6** drowsy, sleepy **9** heavy-eyed, lethargic, somnolent, soporific **10** half-asleep
DP: **7** refugee
Dr. ___: **3** Dre, Zee **4** Bull, Evil, Hook, John, Ruth **5** Quinn, Seuss **6** Jekyll, Pepper, Scholl **7** Demento, Kildare
drab: **3** tan **4** arid, blah, dark, dull, flat, gray, grey **5** dingy, dowdy, faded, ho-hum, mirky, mousy, murky, stale, vapid **6** boring, dreary, frumpy, mousey, shabby, somber **7** humdrum, insipid, neutral, prosaic, run-down, tedious **8** brownish, lifeless **9** cheerless, colorless, prosaical, washed-out, yellowish **10** lackluster, lusterless, tenebrific, uninspired
  color: **5** khaki, olive
  olive ~: **4** garb **5** dress, khaki **6** attire **7** uniform
  relative: **3** ash **4** dove **5** beige, dusty, merle, pearl, putty, slate, taupe **6** silver **7** grizzly **8** charcoal, gunmetal, platinum
Drabble, Margaret: **6** writer **7** British
  sister: Byatt
drabness: **6** tedium
drabs: **8** fatigues
drachma: **4** coin **5** money
  country: **6** Greece
  fraction: **4** obol **6** lepton
Draco: constellation
  neighbor: **7** Cepheus
  star in ~: **4** Adib
draconian: **4** firm, hard **5** bossy, cruel, harsh, picky, rigid, rough, sever, stern, tough **6** brutal, severe, strict **7** austere, drastic, extreme, Spartan **8** despotic, exacting, hard-line, rigorous **9** demanding, inclement, stringent, unbending, unsparing **10** despotical, inflexible, iron-fisted, no-nonsense, oppressive, tyrannical
Dracula: **7** vampire
  airborne ~: **3** bat
  author: Bram Stoker
  character: **4** Lucy, Mina **6** Harker
  outerwear: **4** cape
  portrayer: **3** Lee **6** Lugosi
  target for ~: **4** neck, vein
  weapon: **4** bite
Dracula (1931 film)
  cast: Helen Chandler, Bela Lugosi, David Manners
  director: Tod Browning
draft: **3** air, ale, map, pen, tap **4** blow, draw, eddy, gust, levy, make, plan, plot, puff, swig, wind **5** blast, check, drink, enrol, force, forge, frame, quaff, write **6** breeze, call up, cheque, choose, design, devise, draw up, enlist, enroll, indite, induct, inflow, layout, muster, sign on, sign up, sketch, summon **7** compose, current, fashion, impress, outline, prepare, project, recruit **8** nominate, potation, proposal, rough out, shanghai, skeleton **9** adumbrate, blueprint, conscribe, conscript, fabricate, formulate **10** air current, call of duty, constitute, money order, settle upon
  accept a ~: **5** go pro
  activity: **6** call-up
  allowing a ~: **4** ajar
  animal: **2** ox **5** horse
  avoid the ~: **5** dodge **6** enlist
  bar: **4** yoke
  board initials: **3** SSS
  classification: **4** one A, two A **5** four F
  first ~: **5** rough
  horse: **9** Percheron **10** Clydesdale
  improve a ~: **4** redo **5** repen
  info: **5** payee
  org.: **3** NBA, NFL
  starter: **2** up **4** down
draft ___: **3** ale **4** beer, mark, mill, tube **5** board, chair **6** animal, dodger
___ draft: **4** bank, time **5** light, share, sight **6** demand
draftable: **4** one A
Draft Dodger Rag singer: **4** Ochs
draftee: **2** GI **3** rct. **7** recruit, soldier **9** legionary
  like a rejected ~: **5** unfit
drafting ___: **4** yard **5** board
draftsman's deg.: **3** BME
drafty: **4** cold **5** windy **6** breezy, chilly
drag: **3** lag, lug, tow, tug **4** bore, haul, move, pain, pest, pill, plod, puff, pull, race, road, tide, toke **5** crawl, dally, delay, force, shlep, tarry, trail, trawl, trial **6** bother, bummer, burden, dawdle, downer, inhale, loiter, ration, schlep, shlepp, street **7** shuffle **8** haul away, leverage, mark time, nuisance, stagnate, straggle, tiresome, traction **9** annoyance, hindrance, influence, liability **10** impediment, imposition, inhalation, wet blanket
  a ~: **5** no fun
  down: **6** burden, impede, sadden
  ender: **3** net, oon **4** lift, line, ster
  in: **5** foist
  into court: **3** sue **8** litigate
  main ~: **4** road **7** highway
  off: **6** remove
  on: **8** protract
  oneself: **6** trudge
  one's feet: **3** lag **4** idle, laze, loaf **5** amble, dally, mosey, stall, tarry **6** dawdle, linger, loiter, put off **7** saunter **8** lollygag, obstruct, straggle **9** waste time **10** dillydally
  out: **5** roust **6** expand, extend **7** prolong, stretch **8** lengthen
  prepare to ~: **3** rev
  strip: **5** track
  through the mud: **5** libel, smear, sully, taint **7** tarnish **10** calumniate
  up: **5** raise
drag ___: **4** bunt, hunt, link, race, rake, sail **5** chain, strip **6** racing
___ drag: **3** ice **4** form, main, wave **7** induced
dragged, being: **5** in tow
dragging: **4** beat, dull, long, poky

5 unfun 6 boring, sickly 7 gradual, humdrum, impeded, languid, lengthy, tedious 8 dilatory, drawn-out, hesitant, overlong, slothful, sluggish, tiresome 9 leisurely, lethargic, prolonged, snail-like, unhurried, wearisome 10 deliberate, monotonous, protracted

__-dragging: 4 foot

draggle: 5 trail 6 dangle 7 besmear 8 besmirch

draggy: 3 lax 4 dull, flat, idle, lazy, poky, slow 5 inert 6 asleep, boring, jejune, sleepy, torpid 7 dormant, gradual, halting, impeded, lagging, languid, passive 8 crawling, creeping, dawdling, dilatory, dragging, drawn-out, hesitant, inactive, indolent, lifeless, plodding, slothful, sluggish, toddling 9 leisurely, lethargic, prolonged, sedentary, snaillike, unhurried 10 deliberate, disengaged, lackluster, protracted, spiritless

dragnet: 3 APB 4 hunt, seek, trap 5 trawl 6 search 7 manhunt
- **get in a ~:** 3 nab 4 bust, grab, nail, trap 5 catch, pinch, run in, seize 6 arrest, collar, corner, pick up, pull in, snatch 7 capture 9 apprehend

Dragnet (1954 film)
- **cast:** Ben Alexander, Richard Boone, Jack Webb
- **director:** Jack Webb

Dragnet (1987 film)
- **cast:** Dan Aykroyd, Tom Hanks, Harry Morgan, Christopher Plummer
- **director:** Tom Mankiewicz

Dragnet (NBC drama)
- **cast:** Ben Alexander (Frank Smith) Harry Morgan (Bill Gannon) Jack Webb (Sgt. Joe Friday)
- **employer:** LAPD

dragon: 4 Puff 5 Draco, Ladon, Ollie, Smaug 6 animal, Tiamat 7 monster, reptile
- **constellation:** 5 Draco
- **ender:** 3 fly 4 head, root
- **green ~:** 5 plant
- **100-headed ~:** 5 Ladon
- **in heraldry:** 6 wyvern
- **Komodo ~:** 6 animal 7 reptile
- **like a ~:** 5 scaly
- **of 1950s TV:** 5 Ollie
- **starter:** 4 snap

dragon __: 4 beam, lady, tree 5 piece 6 lizard

__ dragon: 5 green 6 flying, Komodo

Dragon: 5 Daryl 6 Carmen

Dragon __: 4 Lady, Seed 5 Tears

__ Dragon: 3 Red 5 Pete's

drag one's __: 4 feet 5 heels

dragonet: 4 fish

dragonfly: 3 bug 6 darner, insect
- **emulate a ~:** 4 dart 5 hover
- **young ~:** 5 naiad

Dragonfly (2002 film)
- **cast:** Kathy Bates, Kevin Costner, Joe Morton, Ron Rifkin
- **director:** Tom Shadyac

Dragonfly author: Dean Koontz

Dragonheart (1996 film)
- **cast:** Sean Connery, Dennis Quaid, David Thewlis
- **director:** Rob Cohen

Dragon in the Sea, The author: Frank Herbert

dragon's __: 4 head, tail 5 blood, mouth

Dragon Seed author: Pearl S. Buck

dragon's mouth: 5 plant 6 flower

Dragons of Eden, The author: Sagan

Dragon Tears author: Dean Koontz

Dragon: The Bruce Lee Story (1993 film)
- **cast:** Lauren Holly, Jason Scott Lee, Robert Wagner
- **director:** Rob Cohen

Dragonwyck author: Anya Seton

dragoon: 4 ulan 5 bully, force, uhlan 6 coerce, compel, hussar 7 oppress, trooper 8 bulldoze, horseman 9 terrorize 10 cavalryman, equestrian

dragoons: 7 cavalry

Dragoti: 4 Stan

dragster: 4 auto 5 racer 6 hot rod
- **org.:** 4 NHRA

__ Drag, The: 7 Varsity

drain: 3 dry, eat, sap, tap 4 duct, leak, lose, milk, ooze, pipe, pour, pump, seep, sift, tire, vent, void 5 abate, bleed, ditch, empty, exude, leach, sewer, spend, trash, use up, waste, weary 6 burn up, divert, expend, filter, finish, gutter, lessen, osmose, outlet, reduce, remove, run off, siphon, syphon, unload 7 channel, conduit, consume, culvert, decline, deplete, depress, draw off, drink up, dwindle, exhaust, fatigue, flow out, pump out, suck dry, tire out 8 bankrupt, decrease, diminish, evacuate, fool away, get rid of, squander, taper off, wear down 9 discharge, dissipate, filter off, percolate, prostrate 10 debilitate, devitalize, impoverish
- **cleaner:** 3 lye 5 Drano 11 Liquid-Plumr
- **down the ~:** 4 gone, lost, shot 5 kaput, spent 8 misspent
- **ender:** 3 age 4 pipe
- **off:** 4 bail 5 bleed
- **pour down the ~:** 5 waste 8 squander
- **problem:** 4 clog
- **rain ~:** 4 sump
- **rain ~ locale:** 4 curb
- **storm ~:** 5 sewer

__ drain: 5 brain, storm 6 French

drainage __: 4 area, wind 5 basin

drainage area: 4 sump 5 basin, bilge, ditch, gully 6 gulley

drained: 3 dry 4 bare, beat, void, worn 5 all in, spent, tired, trite, unwet, weary 6 barren, dished, pooped, vacant 7 fargone, refined, run-down, vacuous, worn out 8 wiped out 9 burned out, exhausted, prostrate 10 knocked out
- **of color:** 4 ashy, pale 5 ashen
- **poorly ~:** 5 boggy, seepy 6 marshy, swampy

drainer: 5 sieve 8 colander

draining: 9 unstopped

drainpipe section: 4 trap

drakar: 4 boat, ship

drake: 4 bird, duck, male

Drake: 3 Tom 4 Paul, Stan 5 Betsy, Edwin, Larry 6 Alfred 7 Charles, Francis
- **athletes:** 8 Bulldogs
- **locale:** 4 Iowa 9 Des Moines

Drake author: Alfred Noyes

Drake, Charles: 5 actor
- **film:** The Glenn Miller Story (1954) It Came From Outer Space (1953) No Name on the Bullet (1959) To Hell and Back (1955) You Never Can Tell (1951)

Drake, Francis: 3 Sir 7 British 8 explorer

Drakensburg: 5 range
- **locale:** 7 Lesotho

drakes: 3 he's

dram: 3 nip, tot 4 shot, unit 8 libation
- **fraction:** 5 minim

dram. __: 4 pers.

__ dram: 5 fluid

drama: 3 noh 4 play, show, work 5 genre, stage, story 6 hoopla, kabuki, medium, pathos 7 fiction, tension, theater, theatre, tragedy 9 soap opera, spectacle, stage play, stage show 10 grand opera, horse opera, production, tearjerker
- **award:** 4 Obie, Tony
- **daily ~:** 4 soap 9 soap opera
- **ender, maybe:** 4 Act V 5 Act II, Act IV 6 Act III
- **Japanese ~:** 3 noh 6 kabuki
- **musical ~:** 5 opera
- **start:** 4 Act I
- **starter:** 4 melo 5 photo
- **unit:** 3 act 5 scene

__ drama: 4 epic 5 dance, music, video 6 closet, heroic

dramatic: 5 vivid 6 moving, scenic 8 exciting, powerful, scenical, striking 9 affecting, climactic, emotional, startling, thrilling 10 expressive, histrionic, impressive, theatrical
- **activity:** 6 acting
- **be ~:** 5 emote 8 overplay
- **conflict:** 4 agon
- **device:** 5 aside, irony
- **intro:** 4 ta-da 5 ta-dah
- **overly ~:** 5 lurid, stagy 6 stagey

dramatic __: 5 irony, lyric 7 unities

Dramatics
- **song:** In the Rain (1972) Whatcha See Is Whatcha Get (1971)

dramatis personae: 4 cast

dramatist: 6 writer 10 librettist, playwright

dramatize: 3 act 5 emote, enact 6 act out, recite 7 burlesk, perform 8 overplay 9 burlesque, embroider, emphasize, overstate 10 exaggerate, illuminate

Drambuie: 5 drink 8 beverage

Dram Shop, The author: Emile Zola

Drancy: 4 city, town
- **locale:** 6 France

Drang partner: 5 Sturm

Drano alternative: 11 Liquid-Plumr

drape: 4 garb, hang, veil, wrap 5 array 6 attire, clothe, outfit, sprawl 7 arrange, curtain, festoon

Draper: 4 city, town 5 Henry, Polly, Rusty
- **locale:** 4 Utah

Draper, Henry: 10 astronomer

draper measure: 3 ell 4 yard

drapery: 5 arras, scrim 7 curtain, hanging 8 covering, portiere, tapestry
- **fabric:** 5 ninon 6 chintz 7 tabaret 8 cretonne
- **support:** 3 rod

Drapier's Letters author: Jonathan Swift

drastic: 4 dire 5 harsh, rough, stiff, ultra 6 severe, strong 7 extreme, radical 8 forceful 9 desperate, draconian, ill-omened 10 immoderate
- **change:** 8 upheaval

drastically: 4 very 8 terribly

drat: 4 dang, darn, heck, nuts, oath, rats 5 fudge 9 doggone it, expletive 10 confound it
- **in German:** 3 ach

draught: 3 ale 4 gulp, puff, wind 5 whiff 8 libation
- **deep ~:** 5 swill
- **place:** 3 pub

draughts: 4 game
- **in America:** 8 checkers

Drava: 5 river
- **locale:** 7 Austria, Croatia, Hungary 8 Slovenia 10 Yugoslavia

Draveil: 4 city, town
- **locale:** 6 France

Dravidian: 4 Gond 5 Asian
- **language:** 5 Gondi, Tamil

draw: 3 get, tap, tie, tow, tug 4 bait, copy, earn, etch, haul, hook, lead, limn, lure, plot, pull, shut, star, yank 5 bring, carry, charm, draft, evoke, fetch, graph, incur, infer, paint, pluck, poker, start, tempt, trace, trail 6 allure, beckon, convey, deduce, depict, derive, design, doodle, elicit, entice, father, gather, pull in, siphon, sketch, syphon 7 attract, bewitch, compose, enchant, extract, portray, receive, win over 8 appeal to, conclude, dead heat, intrigue, lengthen, motivate, persuade, standoff 9 captivate, delineate, fascinate, formulate, magnetize, stalemate 10 attendance, attraction, caricature, illustrate
- **a bead:** 3 aim 5 aim at, train
- **a blank:** 6 forget
- **a conclusion:** 5 infer 6 deduce, reason
- **a line through:** 4 x-out 8 cross off, cross out
- **a parallel:** 6 equate
- **apart:** 8 separate
- **a picture:** 7 specify 8 simplify
- **a salary:** 4 earn, work
- **attention to:** 6 accent 7 attract 9 spotlight, underline
- **away:** 4 wick 6 divert 7 detract
- **back:** 5 quail, start, wince 6 cringe, flinch, recede, recoil, retire, shrink 7 retreat 8 withdraw 9 sequester
- **close:** 4 love, near 8 approach
- **ender:** 3 bar 4 back, down, tube 5 knife, shave 6 bridge, string
- **forth:** 5 educe, evoke 7 provoke
- **in:** 5 co-opt, sop up 6 entice, entrap, gather, ingest, inhale, osmose, soak up, suck up 7 attract, breathe, involve, retract, swallow 9 implicate 10 assimilate
- **lots:** 4 pick 6 choose, decide, select 9 determine 10 settle upon
- **luck of the ~:** 6 chance 7 lottery
- **near:** 4 come 6 go up to 8 approach 9 close in on 10 bear down on
- **off:** 4 bail, milk, wick 5 drain 6 decant
- **on:** 3 tap, use 7 utilize
- **on glass:** 4 etch
- **out:** 4 milk, pump 5 educe 6 elicit, extend, retard 7 distill, extract, prolong, stretch 8 continue, elongate, lengthen, protract
- **starter:** 4 with
- **straws:** 6 choose
- **the latch:** 4 open
- **the line:** 3 bar, fix 4 halt, stop 5 check, limit 6 cut off, depart, step in 8 restrict
- **to a close:** 3 end 4 wane 6 finish
- **together:** 5 array, unite 6 adduct, center, huddle, pucker 7 compile
- **top ~:** 4 star
- **tournament ~:** 3 bye
- **toward evening:** 5 laten
- **up:** 4 lift, make, stop 5 draft, frame, raise, write 6 shrink 7 marshal, prepare 9 formulate
- **water:** 4 pump

draw __: 3 out, top 4 away, down, game, play, shot, slip 5 a bath, poker, slide, table 6 a blank, runner, straws, weight 7 curtain

draw __ in the sand: 5 a line

draw __ of: 5 ahead

draw __ on: 5 a bead

draw __ reins: 5 in the

__ draw: 5 quick

__-draw: 3 hot 4 cold, deep, fine

drawback: 3 rub 4 flaw, snag 5 catch, fault, hitch, minus 6 defect, hurdle 7 barrier, failing, pitfall 8 handicap, obstacle, weakness 9 detriment, hindrance, liability 10 deficiency, difficulty, impediment, inadequacy, inefficacy, limitation

drawbacks, with no: 5 ideal 7 optimum, perfect

drawer: 4 till 6 artist 10 cartoonist
attachment: 4 knob
holder: 4 desk 6 bureau
top ~: 4 A-one, best 5 A-list, elite 7 society
__-drawer: 3 top
drawing: 3 map 4 plan 6 design, doodle, raffle, scheme, sketch 7 cartoon, diagram, etching, graphic, lottery, outline, picture, profile, tracing 8 portrait 9 depiction, floor plan, graphical, work of art 10 caricature
architectural ~: 4 plan, spec 5 epure 6 detail
board output: 6 design
card: 4 lure, star 6 magnet 7 feature 9 headliner
combining form: 4 -gram 6 -graphy
copy a ~: 5 trace
device: 4 flue
near: 6 at hand
need: 6 crayon, pencil
place: 4 well
power: 4 pull 7 charism 8 charisma 9 magnetism
represent by ~: 4 limn
room: 5 salon 6 parlor
rough ~: 6 sketch 7 croquis
starter: 4 with
drawing __: 3 pin 4 card, down, room 5 board, frame, knife, table 6 chisel 7 account
drawing-__ comedy: 4 room
__ drawing: 4 core, line, wash 5 stick 6 detail 7 working
draw in one's __: 5 horns
draw in the __: 5 reins
drawl: 4 talk 5 twang 6 accent, intone, speech 8 localism
__ Draw McGraw: 5 Quick
drawn: 4 taut, worn 5 gaunt, tense, tight 6 in a tie, jangly, peaked, sapped 7 haggard, starved, worn-out 8 fatigued, fluttery, starving, stressed 10 interested
battle: 3 tie 9 stalemate
character: 4 toon
combining form: 5 -graph
fine: 8 specific
it may be ~: 4 bath
lightly ~ line: 5 trace
starter: 4 wire, with
tight: 4 taut 5 tense
drawn-out: 4 long, poky 6 draggy 7 gradual, halting, impeded, lagging, languid, lengthy 8 crawling, creeping, dawdling, dilatory, dragging, extended, hesitant, plodding, slothful, sluggish, toddling 9 elongated, leisurely, lethargic, prolonged, snaillike, unhurried 10 deliberate, protracted
__-drawn-out: 4 long
drawstring: 4 cord
draw the __: 4 line
dray: 4 cart 5 wagon 6 camion, sledge
ender: 3 age, man, men
place: 4 farm
Drayton, Michael: 4 poet 7 British
Drazen: 8 Petrovic
Dr. Brown's: 4 soda 9 soft drink
Dr. Bull (1933 film)
cast: Ralph Morgan, Marian Nixon, Will Rogers
director: John Ford
Dr. Dentons: 3 PJs 9 nightwear
Dr. Dre: 6 rapper
born: Andre Young
song: California Love (1996)
Dre Day (1993)
Keep Their Heads Ringin' (1995)
No Diggity (1996)
Nuthin' But a 'G' Thang (1993)
dread: 3 awe 4 dire, fear 5 alarm, angst, awful, panic 6 creepy, dismay, fright, horror, phobia, stress, terror 7 cower at 8 affright, alarming, aversion, cringe at, horrible, terrible 9 frightful, trepidity 10 foreboding, petrifying, recoil from, shrink from, terrifying, worry about
ender: 5 locks 6 nought
dreaded: 4 dire 6 creepy 7 fearful 8 alarming, horrible, terrible 9 frightful 10 terrifying
dreadful: 3 bad 4 base, dire, fell, foul, grim, poor 5 awful, gross, lousy, woful 6 creepy, crumby, crummy, dismal, grisly, horrid, odious, rotten, tragic, unholy, wicked, woeful 7 accurst, baleful, baneful, beastly, doleful, fearful, ghastly, hideous, ill-done, ungodly 8 accursed, alarming, flagrant, God-awful, grievous, horrible, horrific, inferior, shameful, shocking, stinking, terrible, terrific, tragical, wretched 9 abhorrent, appalling, atrocious, defective, execrable, frightful, insidious, loathsome, miserable, monstrous, nefarious, offensive, revolting 10 abominable, deplorable, despicable, detestable, disastrous, formidable, horrendous, petrifying
event: 4 blow 7 tragedy 8 calamity, disaster 10 misfortune
penny ~: 5 novel
Dreadful Lemon Sky, The author: John D. MacDonald
dreadless: 4 bold, game 5 brave, gutsy, nervy 6 daring, gritty, heroic, plucky, spunky 7 defiant, doughty, gallant, staunch, valiant 8 heroical, intrepid, resolute, stalwart, unafraid, valorous 9 audacious, undaunted, unfearful 10 courageous
dreadlocks: 2 do 4 coif 6 hairdo 8 coiffure 9 hairstyle
wearer: 5 rasta
dreadnought: 4 ship 10 battleship
dream: 4 goal, hope, loaf, muse, sigh, wish 5 angel, fancy, ideal, quest, yearn 6 aspire, revery, trance, vision 7 aim high, chimera, fantasy, figment, imagine, reverie, utopian 8 ambition, chimaera, delusion, illusion, stargaze 9 fantasize, nightmare 10 aspiration
acronym: 3 REM
bad ~: 9 nightmare
combining form: 4 onir- 5 oneir-, oniro- 6 oneiro-
ender: 4 land 5 scape
environment: 5 sleep
impossible ~: 7 fantasy
of: 5 fancy 6 desire 7 hope for, imagine, long for, pine for
starter: 3 day
up: 4 form, make 5 cause, fancy, frame, hatch, think 6 create, devise, ideate, invent 7 concoct, fashion, imagine 8 conceive, contrive 9 formulate, improvise, visualize 10 mastermind
dream __: 4 book, team 5 world 6 vision
__ dream: 4 pipe
Dream __: 4 Baby, Team 5 Lover 6 Weaver 7 Academy, Catcher, Weavers
Dream __, The: 4 Team 5 Lover, Songs
__ Dream: 4 Pipe 5 Elsa's, Just a 6 Gemini
Dream, A author: Edgar Allan Poe
Dream a Little Dream of Me (1968 song) artist: Mama Cass
Dream Along With Me singer: Como
Dream author: Emile Zola
Dream Baby (1962 song) artist: Roy Orbison
dreamboat: 2 jo 3 pet 4 baby, dear, doll, jill, love 5 amour, angel, chéri, cooky, cutey, cutie, deary, ducky, flame, honey, leman, lover, lovey, novia, novio, sugar, sweet 6 beauty, bon ami, chérie, cookie, dautie, dearie, steady, sweets 7 beloved, dearest, dear one, pigsney, schatzi, squeeze, sweetie, tootsie 8 chou-chou, cutie pie, dowsabel, dulcinea, ladylove, lovebird, macushla, paramour, precious, snookums, sugar pie, sweetums, truelove 9 bonne amie, boyfriend, inamorata, inamorato, petit chou, valentine 10 girlfriend, heartthrob, honeybunch, mavourneen, sweetheart, sweetie pie, turtledove
Dreamboat (1952 film)
cast: Jeffrey Hunter, Ginger Rogers, Clifton Webb
__ Dream, Can't I?: 4 I Can
Dreamcast company: 4 Sega
Dream Catcher author: Stephen King
Dream Children
author: Charles Lamb, Elia
Dream Deferred author: Hughes
__ Dreamed: 5 I Have
dreamed-up: 9 imaginary
dreamer: 8 escapist, idealist 9 visionary
Dream Girl sculptor: 4 Erté
Dreamin' (1989 song) artist: Vanessa Williams
dreaming: 4 lost 6 asleep, dozing, vacant 7 dormant, napping 8 snoozing 9 sacked out, somnolent 10 slumbering
__ dreaming?: 3 Am I
Dreaming (1980 song) artist: Cliff Richard
Dream Is __ Your Heart Makes, A: 5 a Wish
Dream Is Still Alive, The (1991 song) artist: Wilson Phillips
dreamland: 3 nod 5 sleep 7 fantasy 8 illusion 9 unreality
in ~: 4 abed 6 asleep
leave ~: 5 awake 6 awaken
Dream-Land author: Edgar Allan Poe
dreamlike: 5 vague 6 aerial, unreal 8 fanciful 9 imaginary 10 immaterial
Dream Lover (1959 song) artist: Darin
Dreamlover (1993 song) artist: Carey
Dream Lover, The author: Sanders
Dream Merchants, The author: Harold Robbins
Dream of Gerontius, The composer: 5 Elgar
Dream of Kings, A (1969 film)
cast: Irene Papas, Anthony Quinn, Inger Stevens
director: Daniel Mann
Dream On (1976 song) artist: Aerosmith
Dream Palace author: James Purdy
__ Dreams: 4 Hoop, In My 5 Sweet, These 6 Street
Dreams (1977 song) artist: Fleetwood Mac
Dreams and Projects author: 3 Arp
Dreams author: Edgar Allan Poe
Dreamscape (1984 film)
cast: Christopher Plummer, Dennis Quaid, Max von Sydow
director: Joseph Ruben
Dreams Die First author: Harold Robbins
__ Dreams May Come: 4 What
Dream Songs, The author: Berryman
Dream Team letters: 3 USA
Dream Team, The (1989 film)
cast: Peter Boyle, Stephen Furst, Michael Keaton, Christopher Lloyd
Dreamtime (1986 song) artist: Daryl Hall
...__ Dream Walking?: 5 Seen a
Dream Weaver (1976 song) artist: Gary Wright
Dream Within a Dream, A author: Poe
Dreamworks: 6 studio
competitor: 3 Fox, MGM 6 Disney 7 Miramax, New Line 8 Columbia 9 Paramount, Universal 10 Warner Bros.
creation: 4 film 5 movie
dreamy: 3 def, rad 4 aces, A-one, boss, braw, cool, dece, fine, gear, keen, lost, neat, nice, phat, rapt, slow, tuff 5 dandy, ducky, grand, great, marvy, moony, neato, nobby, prime, slick, super, swell, vague 6 bang on, bang-up, bonzer, bosker, choice, divine, far off, far-out, gnarly, groovy, irreal, lovely, peachy, pretty, slap-up, spot on, superb, terrif, tiptop, unreal, vacant, whizzo, wicked 7 amazing, awesome, calming, capital, corking, pensive, perfect, ripping, skookum, stellar, sublime, utopian, wistful 8 adorable, dazzling, especial, eximious, fabulous, fanciful, five-star, four-star, frabjous, glorious, heavenly, illusive, illusory, jim-dandy, listless, quixotic, relaxing, romantic, slam-bang, smashing, soothing, splendid, standout, sterling, stickout, superior, terrific, top-level, topnotch, very good, wondrous 9 bodacious, Endsville, excellent, exemplary, exquisite, first-rate, high-grade, hunky-dory, imaginary, marvelous, sollicker, top-flight, unworldly, visionary, whimsical, wonderful 10 chimerical, delightful, first-class, hotsy-totsy, idealistic, immaterial, intangible, jack-a-dandy, out of sight, peachy-keen, phenomenal, quixotical, remarkable, stupendous, super-duper
state: 3 kef
drear: 5 bleak 6 dismal, gloomy, leaden 7 forlorn 9 cheerless 10 lugubrious
dreariness: 5 gloom 6 tedium 8 drabness, monotony 10 depression
dreary: 3 sad 4 arid, dark, dour, drab, dull, flat, glum 5 bleak, dingy, gaunt, mirky, murky, sober, stark, unfun 6 boring, cloudy, dismal, gloomy, leaden, somber 7 doleful, forlorn, humdrum, joyless, tedious, unhappy 8 desolate, downcast, lonesome, lowering, mournful, overcast, tiresome, unlively, wretched 9 cheerless, colorless, ponderous, saddening, sorrowful, unlighted, wearisome, woebegone 10 depressing, enervating, lugubrious, melancholy, monotonous, pedestrian, tenebrific, uneventful
...dreary ev'rywhere __...: 5 I roam
Dred: 5 Scott
Dred author: Harriet Beecher Stowe
Dre Day (1993 song)
artist: Dr. Dre, Snoop Doggy Dogg
dredge: 3 dig 4 comb 5 delve, dig up, gouge, scoop 6 deepen 7 scooper, unearth 8 sprinkle 9 excavator 10 earth mover
up: 5 raise 7 unearth
dredger: 4 ship
Dreft: 9 detergent
alternative: 3 All, Biz, Era, Fab, Yes 4 Bold, Dash, Gain, Surf, Tide, Wisk 5 Cheer, Purex 6 Calgon, Dynamo, Oxydol 7 Octagon 9 Ivory Snow
dregs: 3 end 4 lees, scum, slag 5 chaff, swill, trash, waste 6 bottom, debris, rabble, refuse 7 deposit, garbage, grounds, remnant, residue, rubbish 8 deposits, residuum, riffraff, sediment 9 leftovers, remainder, settlings 10 lower class
full of ~: 5 silty
of society: 6 proles, rabble 8 riffraff, unwashed 9 hoi polloi

Dr. Ehrlich's Magic Bullet (1940 film)
cast: Ruth Gordon, Otto Kruger, Edward G. Robinson
drei: **4** four **6** German
dreidel: **3** top, toy
Dreiser, Theodore: **6** author, writer
work: An American Tragedy
The Bulwark
The Financier
The 'Genius'
Jennie Gerhardt
Sister Carrie
The Stoic
The Titan
drench: **3** dip, sog, sop, wet **4** dunk, hose, pour, soak, wash **5** douse, dowse, drown, flood, flush, imbue, souse, steep, swamp, water **6** deluge, embrue, imbrue, rain on, sodden, splash **7** immerse, moisten **8** inundate, irrigate, permeate, saturate, submerge
drenched: **3** wet **5** soggy, soppy **6** sweaty
drencher: **4** rain **5** flood **6** deluge **8** downpour **9** rainstorm **10** inundation
Drescher, Fran: **7** actress
film: American Hot Wax (1978)
Cadillac Man (1990)
like ~'s speech: **5** nasal
TV: The Nanny
Dresden: **4** city, town **5** china
city near ~: **5** Pirna
locale: **6** Saxony **7** Germany
river: **4** Elbe
Dresden __: **4** ware **5** china
Dresden-to-Leipzig dir.: **3** WNW
dress: **3** rig, tog **4** deck, duds, garb, gear, gown, izar, robe, sack, sari, tent, till, togs, trim **5** A-line, array, cover, frock, getup, habit, ihram, saree, shift, skirt, tog up, treat **6** attire, caftan, civies, clothe, dirndl, enrobe, fit out, kaftan, kimono, kirtle, livery, muumuu, outfit, sacque, sheath, suit up, swathe **7** apparel, bandage, bedrape, chemise, civvies, clothes, costume, garment, raiment, skimmer, threads, uniform **8** accouter, accoutre, bundle up, clothing, covering, decorate, ensemble, garments, ornament, pinafore, vestment, wardrobe **9** cheongsam, polonaise, redingote, strapless, trappings **10** appearance, habiliment, shirtwaist, Sunday best
accessory: **4** sash
African ~: **4** izar
ankle-length ~: **4** maxi
as: **7** emulate
a turkey: **5** stuff
beltless ~: **4** tent
bottom: **3** hem
calf-length ~: **4** midi
carefully: **5** primp, prink
casual ~: **6** slacks
ceremonial ~: **4** robe
change a ~ length: **5** rehem
code: **6** casual, formal
code concern: **6** attire
disorderly ~: **10** dishabille
down: **3** rag **4** whip **5** scold **6** berate, punish, rebuke, vilify **7** upbraid **8** denounce **9** castigate, criticize, reprehend, reprimand **10** come down on, tongue-lash
East Asian ~: **9** cheongsam
ender: **3** age **5** maker
evening ~: **4** gown
fabric: **5** crash, tulle, voile **6** coburg, dimity
fancy ~: **6** finery **9** caparison
fastener: **4** hook, snap **6** zipper
feature: **4** slit
Hawaiian ~: **6** muumuu
in: **3** don **4** wear
India ~: **4** sari **5** saree
informal ~: **3** tee **5** jeans
Japanese ~: **6** kimono
junior ~ size: **4** nine
long ~: **4** izar
loose-fitting ~: **4** tent
make a ~: **3** sew
Moslem ~: **5** ihram
old ~: **3** rag
ornament: **4** pouf
panel: **5** inset
paper-doll ~ part: **3** tab
part: **3** hem **4** yoke **5** skirt, waist **6** bodice
peasant ~: **6** dirndl
size: **2** lg. **3** lge. **6** petite
sleeveless ~: **6** jumper
starter: **3** sun **4** coat, head **5** house, night, shirt
style: **4** mini, sack, tent **5** A-line, shift **6** Empire
up: **4** doll, gild, trim **5** adorn, array, preen, primp, prink **6** attire, bedeck **8** beautify, decorate, ornament **9** caparison, embellish, glamorize, interlard
dress __: **4** coat, code, down, ship, suit **5** goods, shirt **6** circle **7** uniform
__ dress: **4** full, sack, tent **5** basic, court, fancy **6** battle, dinner, granny **7** evening, grannie, morning
__-dress: **4** full, side, suit **5** shirt
dressage: **5** sport
factor: **4** gait
horse: **10** Lippizaner
leap: **6** curvet
dressed: **4** clad **6** decent
be ~ in: **4** wear **5** sport **6** have on
elegantly ~: **5** natty, sharp, smart **6** dapper
poorly ~: **5** dowdy **6** ragged
dressed __ nines: **5** to the
__-dressed: **4** well
Dressed to Kill (1980 film)
cast: Nancy Allen, Michael Caine, Angie Dickinson
director: Brian De Palma
dresser: **5** chest, table **6** bureau **7** cabinet, highboy **9** furniture **10** chiffonier
fancy ~: **3** fop **4** dude **5** dandy, swell
feature: **4** knob
fussy ~: **5** dandy **7** coxcomb **8** popinjay **10** jack-a-dandy
shabby ~: **5** frump
starter: **4** hair
__ dresser: **5** Welsh **6** double, triple, window
Dresser: **4** Paul **6** Louise
dressiness: **4** chic **5** style
dressing: **3** pad **5** salve, sauce, spica **6** relish **7** bandage, binding, chutnee, chutney, plaster **8** liniment, ointment, stuffing **9** condiment, seasoning
down: **6** rebuke **7** censure, lecture **8** scolding **9** reprimand
gown: **4** robe **6** kimono
hair ~: **3** gel
leather ~: **6** dubbin **7** dubbing
place for ~: **5** salad
room: **5** bower **7** boudoir
use a ~ room: **5** try on
window ~: **4** mask **5** front **6** facade, veneer
wood ~ tool: **4** adze
dressing __: **4** case, gown, room, sack **5** glass, table **7** station
__ dressing: **3** ore **4** side **5** salad **6** boiled, French, window **7** Russian
Dressler, Marie: **7** actress
film: Anna Christie (1930)
Dinner at Eight (1933)
Emma (1932)
Min and Bill (1930)
Oscar: Min and Bill
role: **3** Min
dressmaker: **5** sewer **6** cutter, fitter, tailor **7** modiste **9** outfitter, tailoress **10** courturier, seamstress
cut: **4** bias
insert: **5** godet
need: **4** form **5** cloth, dummy
use ~ shears: **4** pink
dressy: **4** chic **5** fancy, natty, ritzy, sharp, smart, swank **6** classy, flossy, formal, frilly, ornate, swanky **7** elegant, for show, in style, stylish, voguish **8** black-tie **9** like gowns, not casual **10** ornamental
event: **4** gala **6** dinner **7** banquet **8** ceremony
material: **4** lamé **5** satin
not ~: **6** casual
Dress You Up (1985 song) artist: Madonna
Dreux: **4** city, town
locale: **6** France
Drew: **4** John **5** Carey, Ellen, Nancy **7** Charles, Pearson **9** Barrymore
Drew Carey Show, The (ABC sitcom)
cast: Diedrich Baker (Oswald Harvey)
Drew Carey (Drew Carey)
Kathy Kinney (Mimi Bobeck)
Christa Miller (Kate O'Brien)
Ryan Stiles (Lewis Kinski)
dog: **6** Speedy **7** Antonio
setting: **4** Ohio **9** Cleveland
Drew co-star: **5** Rehan
Drew, Nancy: **4** teen **9** detective
boyfriend: **3** Ned
help for ~: **4** clue
Drexel: **10** university
athletes: **7** Dragons
locale: **4** Penn. **5** Phila.
Drexel Heights: **4** city, town
locale: **7** Arizona
Drexel Hill: **4** city, town
locale: **4** Penn.
Drexler: **5** Clyde
Dreyfus: **6** Alfred
Dreyfuss, Richard: **5** actor
film: Always (1989)
American Graffiti (1973)
The Apprenticeship of Duddy Kravitz (1974)
The Big Fix (1978)
Close Encounters of the Third Kind (1977)
The Competition (1980)
The Crew (2000)
Dillinger (1973)
Down and Out in Beverly Hills (1986)
The Goodbye Girl (1977, AA)
Jaws (1975)
Lost in Yonkers (1993)
Moon Over Parador (1988)
Mr. Holland's Opus (1995)
Nuts (1987)
Postcards From the Edge (1990)
Stakeout (1987)
Tin Men (1987)
What About Bob? (1991)
Whose Life Is It Anyway? (1981)
Dr. Feelgood (1989 song) artist: Mötley Crüe
Dr. Hook
song: The Cover of Rolling Stone (1973)
Only Sixteen (1976)
Sexy Eyes (1980)
Sharing the Night Together (1978)
Sylvia's Mother (1972)
When You're in Love With a Beautiful Woman (1979)
__ Dri: **5** Wash 'n
dribble: **4** drip, drop, leak, ooze, seep, spit **5** drool, spill **6** bounce **7** distill, slobber, spatter, trickle **8** particle
__ dribble: **6** double
driblet: **3** bit, dab **4** bead, drop **7** globule **8** pittance
dribs and __: **5** drabs
dried
cut and ~: **4** dull **5** fixed, trite **6** boring **7** settled **9** hackneyed, wearisome **10** unoriginal
up: **4** arid, gone, sere **5** stale, wrung **7** parched, wizened **9** juiceless
__-dried: **3** air, sun **6** freeze
Driesch, Hans: **6** German **11** philosopher
drift: **3** aim, gad, run, yaw **4** bank, flit, flow, gist, heap, loaf, move, pile, ride, roam, rove, sail, skid, tend, tide, tone, turn, veer, waft **5** amble, float, glide, mosey, mound, point, range, sense, shift, slide, spend, stack, stray, tenor, trend **6** effect, import, intent, linger, motion, object, ramble, stream, wander **7** cluster, current, deposit, digress, essence, flutter, leaning, meander, meaning, migrate, purport, saunter, thought **8** alluvium, snowbank, straggle, tendency **9** bat around, direction, gallivant, intention, substance **10** knock about
along: **4** waft **5** float
by: **4** slip **6** elapse
ender: **4** wood
get the ~: **3** see **5** sense
material: **4** snow
off: **3** nap, nod **4** doze **6** drowse
starter: **4** snow, spin **5** spoon
to leeward: **3** sag
drift __: **3** ice, net **4** boat, lead, mine, tube **5** angle, meter **6** anchor, netter
__ drift: **5** beach **6** double **7** genetic, glacial
drifter: **3** bum **4** hobo **5** nomad, rover, tramp **6** outlaw **7** migrant, vagrant **8** derelict, runagate, stranger, traveler, vagabond, wanderer **9** itinerant, journeyer, transient **10** hitchhiker
Drifters
members: King, Thomas, Green, Hobbs, Lewis
song: On Broadway (1963)
Save the Last Dance for Me (1960)
There Goes My Baby (1959)
Under the Boardwalk (1964)
Up on the Roof (1962)
drifting: **4** asea **5** at sea **6** afloat **7** aimless, migrant, nomadic **8** rootless, vagabond **9** migratory, wayfaring **10** digression, discursion
Drift to a Dream singer: **5** Tritt
driftwood: **6** debris **8** kindling
destination: **5** beach, shore
drill: **3** bit **4** bore, sink, tool **5** auger, borer, coach, groom, march, punch, teach, train, tutor **6** lesson, pierce, review, school, season, warm-up **7** primate, riveter, routine, workout **8** aerobics, exercise, instruct, maneuver, marching, practice, puncture, rehearse, teaching, training, war games **9** catechize, implement, inculcate, maneuvers, penetrate, perforate, rehearsal, reptition **10** assignment, daily dozen, discipline, jackhammer, run-through
command: **4** halt **5** march **6** at ease, fall in **8** left face **9** right face
ender: **5** stock **6** master
grip: **5** brace
insert: **3** bit
relative: **3** ape **4** saki, titi **5** chimp, jocko, lemur, loris, magot, orang, potto, shrew **6** aye-aye, baboon, Bandar, galago, gelada, gibbon, grivet, guenon, howler, langur,

macaco, monkey, rhesus, uakari, vervet **7** colobus, gorilla, guereza, hoolock, macaque, sapajou, siamang, tamarin, tarsier **8** bush baby, capuchin, mangabey, marmoset, talapoin **9** orangutan **10** Barbary ape, chimpanzee, orangutang
starter: **3** man
drill ___: **3** bit, rig **4** pipe, team **5** chuck, corps, press, tower **6** string
___ drill: **3** air **4** fire, gang, hand, star **5** churn, power, twist **6** breast **7** diamond
driller
see dentist
drilling ___: **3** mud, rig **5** fluid
Drin: **5** river
locale: **7** Albania **9** Macedonia
Drina: **5** river
locale: **6** Bosnia, Serbia
drink: **3** ade, ale, cup, gin, lap, nog, pop, rum, rye, sip, Tab, tea **4** beer, bock, brew, cola, down, fizz, flip, grog, gulp, kava, marc, mead, ouzo, port, raki, sake, saki, shot, slug, soda, spot, swig, take, Tang, wine **5** anise, booze, Bronx, cider, cocoa, draft, glass, juice, julep, kvass, lager, mocha, negus, ocean, perry, quaff, sling, slurp, snort, stout, toast, toddy, tonic, touch, vodka, water **6** absorb, bishop, brandy, cassis, coffee, cognac, eggnog, gimlet, guzzle, imbibe, ingest, kirsch, kumiss, kummel, liquid, liquor, mai tai, mescal, Mickey, mimosa, nectar, Pernod, porter, posset, potion, pulque, rickey, rob roy, Scotch, shandy, soak up, tipple, whisky, zombie **7** alcohol, aquavit, Bacardi, bourbon, Campari, Collins, consume, cordial, curaçao, iced tea, limeade, liqueur, martini, negroni, oenomel, pale ale, potable, ratafia, sangría, sidecar, sloe gin, spirits, stinger, swallow, tequila, wassail, whiskey **8** absinthe, anisette, apéritif, beverage, calvados, cocktail, coco loco, daiquiri, Drambuie, eau de vie, Guinness, highball, Jack Rose, lemonade, libation, pilsener, pink lady, potation, salty dog, schnapps, spritzer, Tia Maria, vermouth **9** alexander, applejack, aqua vitae, Cointreau, hard cider, hoist a few, inebriant, jiggerful, Manhattan, margarita, mint julep, moonshine, moosemilk, slivovitz, ward eight **10** Bloody Mary, chartreuse, golden fizz, horse's neck, intoxicant, Jamaica rum, Mickey Finn, Moscow Mule, piña colada, rock and rye, shandygaff, silver fizz
after-dinner ~: **4** port **6** brandy, cognac
apple ~: **5** cider, juice **9** hard cider
Asian nomad's ~: **6** kumiss
astronaut's ~: **4** Tang
bar ~: **3** ale, rye **4** beer, shot, sour, wine **5** draft, julep, quaff, sling, snort, stout, vodka **6** brandy, cassis, chaser, cognac, gimlet, liquor, mai tai, mimosa, porter, rob roy, Scotch, whisky, zombie **7** alcohol, aquavit, Bacardi, bourbon, Collins, cordial, liqueur, martini, pale ale, sidecar, sloe gin, spirits, stinger, tequila, whiskey **8** apéritif, cocktail, daiquiri, Drambuie, Guinness, highball, pilsener, pink lady, potation, salty dog, schnapps, spritzer, Tia Maria, vermouth **9** Alexander, Cointreau, Manhattan, margarita, mint julep **10** Bloody Mary, Moscow Mule, piña colada, Tom Collins
big ~: **4** swig
breakfast ~: **2** OJ **5** cocoa, juice
British ~: **3** ale, tea
by the yard: **3** ale
carbonated ~: **3** pop **4** cola, soda **9** ginger ale
Chinese ~: **3** tea
citrus ~: **3** ade **7** limeade **8** lemonade **9** orangeade
cola ~: **4** Coke **5** Pepsi
cold ~: **3** ade **4** soda **5** juice, shake
cold-weather ~: **3** tea **4** grog **5** cocoa **6** eggnog, hot tea
container: **3** cup, mug **5** glass, stein
cooler: **3** ice
credit: **6** bar tab
curative ~: **5** tonic
extra: **5** lemon, straw, twist
fast: **4** chug, swig **5** swill **6** guzzle **8** chugalug
fermented ~: **3** ale **4** beer **5** kefir
French ~: **3** eau, thé, vin **4** lait
from a flask: **5** snort **6** guzzle, imbibe
fruit ~: **3** ade **5** juice, punch **6** frappé
fruit juice ~: **7** sangría
Greek ~: **4** ouzo
heartily: **5** quaff
honey ~: **4** mead
hot ~: **3** tea **5** cocoa, mocha, toddy **6** coffee
hot rum ~: **4** grog
in: **3** sip **5** learn, sop up **6** absorb, gather, ingest, osmose, soak up, suck up **7** swallow **10** assimilate
in a way: **3** lap
in baby-talk: **4** wawa
Japanese ~: **3** tea **4** sake, saki
knockout ~: **6** Mickey **10** Mickey Finn
like a pet: **3** lap **5** lap up
lo-cal ~: **3** Tab **4** diet, lite **6** Fresca
noisily: **5** slurp
noncarbonated ~: **3** tea **6** coffee **7** iced tea
of old: **4** mead
opener: **3** tab
order: **4** neat **5** round **10** on the rocks
Polynesian ~: **4** kava
prepare a ~: **3** mix
preprandial ~: **8** apéritif
quick ~: **3** tot **5** snort
Russian ~: **5** kvass, vodka
sailor's ~: **3** rum
sample a ~: **3** sip
slowly: **3** sip **5** nurse
small ~: **4** dram
soft ~: **3** ade, pop, Tab **4** Coke, cola, Nehi, soda **5** Moxie, Pepsi **8** Dr Pepper
stiff ~: **6** bracer
suffix: **3** ade
to: **5** toast **9** celebrate
to excess: **4** tope **6** tipple
wine ~: **6** bishop **7** sangria
Yuletide ~: **3** nog **6** eggnog
see also beverage
___ drink: **4** cold, soft, tall **5** mixed
Drink ___ only...: **4** to me
drinkable: **6** liquor **7** potable **8** beverage
make ~: **6** desalt, purify **10** desalinate, desalinize
drinker: **3** sot **4** lush **5** toper **7** tippler
drinkery: **6** lounge
drinking: **4** vice
age: **8** majority
aid: **5** straw
bowl: **5** mazer
cup of ancient Greece: **5** cylix, kylix
Greek ~ horn: **6** rhyton
vessel: **3** cup, mug **5** stein
drink-mix brand: **6** Wyler's **7** Kool-Aid
drinks, like some: **4** hard, soft
drip: **4** bore, jerk, leak, nerd, nurd, ooze, pest, plop, seep, slop, weep **5** exude, spill, sweat **7** distill, dribble, nebbish, slobber, trickle **8** downturn, perspire, sprinkle **9** percolate **10** wet blanket
locale: **4** eave, roof **6** faucet
drip ___: **3** cap, pan **5** grind **6** coffee
Drip Drop (1963 song) artist: Dion
drip-feed tube: **2** IV
dripping: **3** wet **5** juicy, leaky, moist, soggy, soppy, undry **6** sodden, sweaty **10** bedraggled
dripping ___: **3** pan
drippings: **6** grease
drippy: **4** damp, oozy **5** moist, sappy, undry **7** mawkish, wettish **8** sluggish **10** spiritless
Dr. I.Q.: **9** radio show
Driscoll, Bobby: **5** actor
film: So Dear to My Heart (1949)
Song of the South (1946)
Treasure Island (1950)
When I Grow Up (1951)
The Window (1949)
Dristan alternative: **5** Afrin **6** Contac, Nyquil, Tavist **7** Actifed, Comtrex, Dayquil, Sinutab, Sudafed **8** Benadryl, Dimetapp, Drixoral, TheraFlu **9** Coricidin, Triaminic **10** Robitussin
drive: **2** go **3** pep, ram, run, zip **4** fire, gear, goad, herd, lift, make, move, prod, push, ride, road, roll, send, sink, spin, spur, stab, take, tour, trip, urge, will, zeal **5** force, hurry, impel, jaunt, labor, lunge, motor, moxie, pitch, pound, punch, rouse, spunk, stamp, steer, stick, surge, vigor **6** appeal, arouse, avenue, compel, direct, effort, energy, incite, jockey, junket, launch, motive, outing, propel, reduce, strain, street, strike, tee off, thrust, travel, urge on, whip up **7** actuate, advance, animate, commute, crusade, impetus, impulse, journey, joyride, operate, passion, roundup **8** ambition, campaign, gumption, momentum, motivate, pressure, vitality **9** appetence, chauffeur, encourage, excursion, impulsion, incentive, inner fire, stimulate, willpower **10** accelerate, compulsion, enterprise, enthusiasm, fund-raiser, get up and go, horsepower, incitement, initiative, motivation, ride herd on
apart: **9** disaffect
a semi: **4** haul
at: **4** mean
away: **4** oust, rout, shoo **5** chase, eject, repel, roust **6** banish, dispel, offend **7** disgust, repulse **8** alienate, chase out **9** dissipate, force back
bungle a ~: **4** hook **5** shank, slice
crazy: **3** bug, irk, nag **4** rile **5** annoy, peeve **6** enrage, harass, madden, pester **7** derange, torment, trouble
creative ~: **3** ego
ender: **3** way **4** line **5** shaft
fast: **4** race **6** hot rod
forward: **5** impel **6** compel, urge on
home: **7** impress **9** reiterate
in: **5** embed, enter, imbed, infix
inner ~: **4** urge
kind of ~: **3** ZIP **4** hard **5** CD/ROM **6** floppy **8** diskette
out: **4** boot, oust, pump, rout **5** exile, expel, roust **7** dismiss, exclude **8** chase off, exorcise, exorcize **9** eliminate, order to go
prepare to ~: **5** tee up
recklessly: **5** weave **6** careen
short ~: **4** spin **5** jaunt
something to ~: **4** nail
drive ___: **3** bay, fit **4** time **5** shaft, train
drive ___ the ground: **4** into
drive-___: **4** thru **7** through
___ drive: **4** disk, hard, line, tape, worm **5** chain, fluid, motor, stern
___-drive: **4** test **5** front
___ Drive: **5** Rodeo
___ Drive by Night: **4** They
drive-in: **5** movie **6** cinema **7** theater, theatre **10** restaurant
load: **6** carful
waiter: **6** carhop
drive-in ___: **5** movie
drivel: **3** gab, gas, pap, rot **4** blah, bosh, bull, bunk, guff, jazz, jive, pooh, tosh **5** bilge, drool, fudge, hokum, hooey, prate, stuff, trash, tripe **6** babble, bunkum, bushwa, footle, gabble, gammon, gibber, havers, hot air, humbug, jabber, jargon, kibosh, piffle, ramble, slaver **7** baloney, blarney, blather, blether, boloney, bushwah, chatter, eyewash, flannel, flubdub, fustian, garbage, hogwash, inanity, prattle, rubbish, slobber, twaddle **8** babbling, buncombe, claptrap, falderal, falderol, flimflam, flummery, folderal, folderol, nonsense, slipslop, tommyrot, trumpery **9** banana oil, gibberish, goofiness, kidstakes, moonshine, poppycock, rigmarole, silly talk **10** applesauce, balderdash, bilge water, codswallop, double-talk, flapdoodle, galimatias, Jabberwock, mumbo jumbo, rigamarole, taradiddle
driven: **5** bound **8** hellbent, impelled, obsessed **10** determined
be ~: **4** ride
___-driven software: **4** menu
driver: **4** club, hack, wood **6** cabbie, cabman, hackie, jockey **8** golf club, motorist, operator **9** chauffeur
aid: **3** AAA, map
backseat ~: **3** nag **6** critic
bane: **4** flat, hook **5** slice
be in the ~'s seat: **3** run **4** lead **5** pilot, steer **6** direct **7** operate, oversee **9** supervise
camper ~: **4** RVer
goal: **5** green **7** fairway
ID: **3** lic. **7** license
license: **2** ID
license datum: **3** DOB, hgt. **4** name **5** photo **6** gender, height, weight
maneuver: **5** U-turn
org.: **3** AAA, PGA **4** USGA
peg: **3** tee
pro ~: **5** cabby, racer **6** cabbie
purchase: **3** gas **8** gasoline
shout: **4** fore
slave ~: **6** despot, master, tyrant **8** autocrat, dictator **10** taskmaster
train element: **4** axle
use a ~: **4** golf
with a handle: **4** CBer
see also golf
___ driver: **3** bus, cab **4** pile, taxi **5** quill, slave, stage **6** Sunday
Driver, Minnie: **7** actress
film: Circle of Friends (1995)
Good Will Hunting (1997)
Grosse Pointe Blank (1997)
Hard Rain (1998)
High Heels and Low Lifes (2001)
Return to Me (2000)
film (voice): Tarzan (1999)
driver's ___: **4** seat **7** license
driver's seat: **4** helm **7** command **9** supremacy
Driver, The (1978 film)
cast: Isabelle Adjani, Bruce Dern, Ryan O'Neal
director: Walter Hill
Drive (song) artist: Cars
artist: R.E.M.
drive-through order: **4** to go
driveway: **4** road **6** egress **7** ingress
do the ~: **3** tar **4** pave, seal **5** retar, retop **6** repave
ending: **6** garage

material: 3 tar 5 paver 6 gravel 8 blacktop, concrete
driving: 4 go-go 6 lively, urgent 7 dynamic, en route 8 forceful, vigorous 9 energetic, on the road, trenchant 10 compelling, compulsive, propulsive
area: 5 range
force: 4 birr 6 engine 7 impetus
hazard: 3 fog, ice 4 mist, rain, snow 5 glare, sleet 7 drizzle
driving ___: 3 dog 4 iron, rain, sail, time 5 range, wheel 6 barrel
driving-away word: 4 scat, shoo 5 scram 6 begone 8 scramola
Driving Force author: Dick Francis
Driving Miss Daisy (1989 film)
cast: Dan Aykroyd, Morgan Freeman, Jessica Tandy
director: Bruce Beresford
Drivin' My Life Away (1980 song)
artist: Eddie Rabbitt
Drixoral alternative: 5 Afrin 6 Contac, Nyquil, Tavist 7 Actifed, Comtrex, Dayquil, Dristan, Sinutab, Sudafed 8 Benadryl, Dimetapp, TheraFlu 9 Coricidin, Triaminic 10 Robitussin
drizzle: 3 wet 4 mist, rain 5 spray 8 fine rain, moisture, sprinkle
drizzly: 3 wet 4 damp 5 bleak, misty, moist, rainy, undry 7 wettish 8 sprinkly
Dr. J
see Erving
Dr. Jekyll and Mr. Hyde (1932 film)
cast: Rose Hobart, Miriam Hopkins, Fredric March
character: 5 Carew, Poole 7 Enfield
director: Rouben Mamoulian
Dr. Jekyll and Mr. Hyde (1941 film)
cast: Ingrid Bergman, Spencer Tracy, Lana Turner
director: Victor Fleming
Dr. K: 6 Gooden
Dr. Kildare (NBC drama)
cast: Richard Chamberlain (Dr. James Kildare)
Raymond Massey (Dr. Leonard Gillespie)
hospital: Blair
___ Dr. Malone: 5 Young
Dr. No: 4 film 5 novel
author: Ian Fleming
cast: Ursula Andress, Sean Connery, Joseph Wiseman
director: Terence Young
___ D. Rockefeller: 4 John
droid: 5 golem, robot 9 automaton
droit: 5 claim, right
droit ___ gens: 3 des
droll: 3 dry, wry 4 camp, rich 5 campy, comic, funny, queer, silly, witty 6 absurd, har-har, jocose, quaint 7 amusing, comical, jesting, jocular, risible, waggish 8 clownish, farcical, humorous 9 diverting, facetious, laughable, ludicrous, priceless, quizzical, whimsical 10 outlandish, ridiculous
drollery: 3 wit 4 jest, joke, quip 5 humor 6 comedy 7 waggery 8 jocosity, wordplay, zaniness 9 funniness, witticism 10 jocoseness, jocularity
dromedary: 5 camel 6 animal, mammal
feature: 4 hump
relative: 5 llama 6 alpaca, vicuna 7 guanaco 8 Bactrian
stop: 5 oasis
drome starter: 4 aero, velo 5 hippo
drone: 3 bee, bug, hum 4 buzz, male, slug, talk 5 chant, idler, noise, sound, thrum, whine, whirr 6 drudge, insect, jackal, loafer, murmur 7 lounger, sponger 8 parasite, sluggard 9 do-nothing, vibration 10 ne'er-do-well
home: 4 hive 6 apiary
drongo: 4 bird
droning: 10 monotonous
sound: 3 hum 4 buzz
Drood, Edwin betrothed: 4 Rosa
drool: 4 gush, leak, spit 5 water 6 drivel, saliva, slaver 7 dribble, enthuse, lay it on, slobber 8 salivate 10 salivation
over: 4 want 5 crave 6 desire
droop: 3 dip, lop, nod, sag 4 bend, flag, flop, lean, loll, mope, sink, tire, wilt 5 lower, quail, slump, stoop, trail 6 dangle, go limp, settle, slouch, suffer, weaken, wither 7 decline 8 decrease, get tired, hang down, languish, peter out 9 get sleepy, hang loose 10 fall asleep
drooping: 4 limp 5 baggy, tired, weary 6 broody, flabby 7 flaccid, languid 8 dejected 9 pendulous 10 knocked out
droopy: 4 alop, limp 5 baggy, loppy, saggy, slack, tired 6 flabby, floppy, wilted 7 flaccid, hanging, joyless, sagging, slouchy, stooped 8 dangling, fatigued 9 pendulous 10 melancholy, spiritless
drop: 3 axe, can, dab, dip, ebb, end, err, nip, sag, set 4 bead, beat, blob, boot, cede, curb, dash, deck, dele, dive, duck, dump, fall, fire, flop, iota, leak, loll, lose, omit, ooze, oust, quit, sack, sell, send, shed, sink, slip, spot, stop, tilt, tire, whit, wilt, x off, x out 5 cease, chuck, crash, depth, ditch, forgo, grain, lapse, leave, let go, level, light, lower, reach, scrub, slash, slide, slope, slump, speck, spend, spill, spurn, swoop, taste, tinge, touch, trace, yield 6 bounce, bubble, cancel, delete, demote, forego, fumble, give up, go down, lay off, lessen, let off, morsel, plunge, recede, recess, reduce, relent, remove, shelve, shrink, supply, trifle, tumble, unload 7 abandon, call off, cashier, curtail, cut down, decline, deposit, descend, descent, discard, dismiss, dribble, driblet, drum out, dwindle, falloff, forfeit, forsake, globule, kiss off, lay down, let fall, let go of, lozenge, mark off, modicum, plummet, redline, release, scratch, smidgen, smidgin, swallow, tail off, toss out, trickle 8 abdicate, collapse, cross off, cross out, decrease, delivery, diminish, downturn, file away, forswear, furlough, get rid of, give up on, hand over, jettison, lay aside, lowering, nosedive, particle, part with, peter out, pink-slip, renounce, shake off, smidgeon, throw out, trapdoor, write off 9 cast aside, declivity, discharge, dispose of, downslide, downtrend, eighty-six, eliminate, foreswear, lessening, ostracize, parachute, plump down, precipice, reduction, repudiate, surrender, terminate, throw away, throw over 10 diminution, go away from, relinquish
about a ~: 5 minim
abruptly: 3 axe 4 dump 5 plunk
a bundle: 4 lose
a letter: 4 send, slur
a line: 4 fish 5 write 10 correspond, epistolize
anchor: 4 land 6 arrive 8 get there
architectural ~: 5 gutta
away: 5 slope
back: 3 ebb 5 trail
by: 3 see 4 call 5 pop in, run in, visit 6 show up 7 go to see 8 pay a call
clues: 4 hint 5 let on
cough ~: 7 lozenge
down: 3 dip 4 duck, fall
down on: 6 pounce, snatch
ender: 3 let, out 4 wort 5 forge, light
eye ~: 4 tear
feathers: 4 molt, shed 5 moult
from a list: 4 x off, x out 8 cross off, cross out
from the team: 3 cut
have a ~: 5 drink
in: 3 see 4 call 5 enter, visit 6 appear, arrive, attend, show up, stop by 7 turn out 8 pay a call
in a letter box: 4 mail
in the bucket: 8 pittance
letter ~: 7 opening 8 aperture
mail ~: 3 box, GPO 4 slot, USPS
noisily: 4 plop
off: 3 ebb, nap, nod, sag 4 doze, fall, shed, sink, slip, wane 5 abate, bring, leave, slack, sleep, slide, slump 6 catnap, lessen, shrink, snooze, unload 7 decline, deliver, deposit, dwindle, present, saw logs, slacken 8 decrease, diminish, hand over 10 fall asleep, grab some z's
one's guard: 3 nap 5 relax
one's jaw: 4 gape, gawk 5 stare 6 goggle, marvel
out: 4 quit 5 leave, rebel 6 resign, secede 8 withdraw 10 apostatize
pounds: 4 slim 8 slim down
ready to ~: 4 worn 5 spent, tired, weary 9 exhausted
saline ~: 4 tear
sheer ~: 9 precipice
shot: 4 dink
starter: 3 air, dew, ear, gum 4 back, rain, snow, tear 5 eaves
target: 3 ear, eye 4 nose
the ball: 3 err 4 miss, slip 6 bumble, bungle, falter, fumble 7 blunder 8 misjudge
the curtain: 3 end 4 shut 6 finish 8 complete 9 terminate
drop ___: 3 box, ell, off, out, tee 4 arch, girt, keel, kick, leaf, pass, seat, shot, zone 5 a hint, a line, black, cloth, cooky, elbow, forge, front, panel, press, scene, table, valve 6 behind, cookie, hammer, letter, rudder, siding, window 7 biscuit, curtain, initial
drop ___ to: 5 a line, a note
drop-___: 4 ship
drop-___ table: 4 leaf
___ drop: 3 act, cut, leg 4 acid, body, dead, line, mail 5 cough, lemon 6 letter, pigeon
___-drop: 4 name
Drop Dead Fred star: 5 Cates
Drop Dead Gorgeous (1999 film)
cast: Kirstie Alley, Ellen Barkin, Kirsten Dunst, Denise Richards
dog: 5 Kenny
drop-in: 5 guest 7 visitor
___ Drop Kid, The: 5 Lemon
droplet: 3 bit 4 bead, blob, tear 6 bubble
droplets: 3 dew 4 mist 5 spray, vapor 8 dampness, moisture
drop like ___: 5 a rock
drop like ___ potato: 4 a hot
___ drop of a hat: 5 at the
drop-off: 8 slowdown 9 precipice
drop of golden sun, A: 3 ray
dropped ___: 3 egg 4 seat 5 waist
dropped jaw, with: 6 aghast, amazed 9 astounded, awestruck, stupefied, surprised 10 astonished, bewildered, dumbstruck, spellbound
dropper: 4 tube
cry: 4 oops
kin: 5 pipet 7 pipette
starter: 3 eye
___-dropper: 4 name
dropping: 4 down 8 downhill
drops: 5 spill
form ~: 4 bead 6 bead up
on the grass: 3 dew
___ drop soup: 3 egg
drop the ___ shoe: 5 other
dross: 4 scum, slag 5 chaff, trash, waste 6 debris, refuse 7 garbage, remnant, residue, rubbish 8 impurity, leavings, residuum
drossy: 9 worthless
drought: 6 thirst 7 absence 8 dry spell, shortage
causer: 6 El Niño
droughty: 4 arid, sere 7 parched, thirsty 9 waterless 10 dehydrated
drove: 3 mob 4 herd, pack 5 flock, horde, press, score, swarm, troop 6 legion, rabble, throng 7 legions, numbers 9 gathering, multitude
Drove my Chevy to the ___...: 5 levee
drover: 6 cowboy 7 cowpoke 8 herdsman, wrangler 9 ranch hand, trail boss
charge: 4 herd 6 cattle 9 livestock
droves: 6 flocks, hoards 7 legions
drown: 3 wet 4 dunk, sink 5 flood, souse, swamp 6 deluge, drench, embrue, engulf, imbrue, ingulf, muffle, splash 7 immerse 8 inundate, overcome, overflow, submerge 9 overpower, overwhelm
drowned ___: 6 valley
Drowned and the Saved, The author: 4 Levi
Drowning (2001 song) artist: Backstreet Boys
Drowning by Numbers (1987 film)
cast: Bernard Hill, Joan Plowright
director: Peter Greenaway
Drowning Mona (2000 film)
cast: Neve Campbell, Jamie Lee Curtis, Danny DeVito, Bette Midler
drowse: 3 nap, nod 4 doze, rest, yawn 5 sleep 6 catnap, nod off, snooze 7 slumber 8 drift off 9 get sleepy 10 fall asleep, grab some z's
drowsiness: 8 laziness, lethargy
sign of ~: 4 yawn
drowsy: 4 dozy, dull, lazy, logy, slow 5 tired, weary 6 sleepy, snoozy, torpid 7 languid 8 listless, sluggish 9 heavy-eyed, lethargic, somnolent, soporific 10 half-asleep, knocked out
make ~: 9 hypnotize
Droxies: 6 cookie
alternative: 4 Oreo 9 Chips Ahoy! 10 Fig Newtons, Lorna Doone
Dr Pepper: 4 soda 9 soft drink
alternative: 3 TAB 4 Coke, Nehi 5 Fanta, Pepsi 6 Fresca, Sprite 8 Diet Rite 9 Canada Dry 10 Mello Yello, Royal Crown 11 Mountain Dew
Dr. Pepper: 3 pop 4 cola, soda 9 soft drink
competitor: 4 Coke 5 Pepsi 8 Diet Rite
Dr. Quinn, Medicine Woman (CBS drama)
cast: Jane Seymour (Dr. Mike Quinn)
dog: 4 Wolf
Dr. Ruth: 10 Westheimer
___ Dr. Ruth: 3 Ask
Dr. Scholl product: 6 insole
Dr. Seuss character: 3 Cat, Gox, Ned, Pam, Vug, Who, Zax 4 Gack, Grox, Jake, Mack, Rolf 5 Glunk, Lorax, Yekko 6 Grinch, Horton, Huffle, Norval, Sam I Am, Yertle 8 Thidwick 9 Sneetches
locale: 8 Whoville
Dr. Socrates (1935 film)
cast: Ann Dvorak, Barton MacLane, Paul Muni
Dr. Strangelove (1964 film)
cast: Sterling Hayden, James Earl Jones, Slim Pickens, George C. Scott, Peter Sellers, Keenan Wynn

director: Stanley Kubrick
drub: 3 hit, tan, zap 4 beat, cane, flog, lick, mall, maul, rout, trim, whip 5 baste, blast, knock, paste, pound, worst 6 batter, defeat, hammer, pommel, pummel, thrash, wallop 7 clobber, conquer, overrun, shellac, trounce 8 shellack 9 checkmate, overpower, overwhelm
drubbing: 4 loss, rout 6 defeat 7 licking
Drucker: 4 Mort 5 Peter
drudge: 4 grub, hack, moil, peon, plod, toil, wade, work 5 drone, grind, labor, slave 6 jackal, menial, toiler 7 laborer, plodder, servant, slavery 8 factotum, work hard 9 grind away
ender: 4 work
Drudge: 4 Matt
drudgery: 3 job, rut 4 moil, toil, work 5 grind, labor, sweat 7 rat race, slavery, travail 8 hardship, hard work, scutwork 9 grunt work
drudging: 7 tedious 8 tiresome
drug: 5 sulfa, tonic 6 opiate, remedy, sedate 7 stupefy 8 laudanum, medicate, medicine, narcotic, sedative 9 stimulant 10 anesthetic, antibiotic, biological, depressant, medication, penicillin
amount: 4 dose
combining form: 8 pharmaco-
company: 5 Lilly, Merck 6 Pfizer
cop: 4 narc, nark 5 narco
ender: 5 store
label letters: 3 USP
science: 8 pharmacy
drug __: 4 czar
drug __ market: 5 in the, on the
__ drug: 5 sulfa 6 orphan, wonder 7 miracle
drug-bust org.: 3 ATF
drug-free: 5 clean
drugget: 6 fabric 8 material
druggist: 4 phar. 5 pharm. 10 apothecary, pharmacist, posologist
container: 4 vial 5 phial
drug-overseeing org.: 3 FDA
drug-reference bk.: 3 PDR
drugstore: 4 mart, phar. 5 pharm. 6 market 8 pharmacy 10 apothecary
be a ~ cowboy: 6 loiter 7 hang out
cowboy: 5 ogler
Drugstore Cowboy (1989 film)
cast: Matt Dillon, James LeGros, Kelly Lynch, James Remar
director: Gus Van Sant
druid: 4 Celt 7 prophet
Dru, Joanne: 7 actress
brother: Peter Marshall
film: All the King's Men (1949)
Red River (1948)
She Wore a Yellow Ribbon (1949)
Thunder Bay (1953)
Wagon Master (1950)
Red River role: 4 Tess
spouse: Dick Haymes
drum: 3 def, rap, tap, tar, udu 4 batá, beat, ekwe, fish, krin, roar 5 bhaya, bongo, caixa, cajón, conga, cuica, dauli, davul, dhola, kakko, kundu, lobby, ngoma, okedo, pound, pulse, sabar, snare, surdo, taber, tabla, tabor, taiko, tapan, thump, tupan, wheel 6 barrel, bendir, damaru, djembé, dun dun, nakers, naqara, ntenga, odaiko, patter, poëtti, quinto, rattle, tabour, tam-tam, tom-tom 7 atumpan, batajón, bodhran, breketé, changko, dadaiko, dugdugi, ingungu, isigubu, kalungu, murumbu, pulsate, talamba, tambour, terbang, thunder, timbale, tsuzumi 8 bass drum, darabuka, djun djun, gran casa, tympanum 10 kettledrum, tambourine
accompaniment: 4 fife
Afro-Cuban ~: 5 conga
attachment: 5 snare
beatnik's ~: 5 bongo
beat the ~ for: 4 sell 6 talk up 7 advance, espouse 9 publicize
emulate a ~ major: 5 strut, twirl
ender: 4 beat, fire, head 5 stick
flourish: 5 tusch
Indian: 5 tabla
into: 5 train, tutor 6 repeat 9 inculcate
major need: 5 baton, shako
material: 5 steel
Moorish ~: 6 atabal
out: 3 axe, can 4 boot, drop, fire, oust, sack 5 expel, let go 6 bounce, depose, expell, lay off 7 cashier, dismiss, release 8 furlough, get rid of, pink-slip 9 discharge, terminate
roll exclamation: 4 ta-da 5 ta-dah
small ~: 5 bongo, taber, tabor 6 tabour
sound: 4 roll
starter: 3 ear, hum 6 kettle
twin ~: 5 bongo
up: 6 hustle, invent, obtain 7 solicit
drum __: 3 out 5 brake, corps, major, table 6 memory 7 printer
__ drum: 3 red 4 bass, side 5 bongo, brake, conga, snare, steel
Drum __ Symphony: 4 Roll
__ Drum: 4 Fort
drum and __ corps: 5 bugle
drumbeat: 4 roll
two-note ~: 4 flam
drumfire: 4 boom
drummer: 4 Moon, Rich, Webb 5 Krupa, Roach, Starr, Watts 6 Blakey, Puente 7 Bellson
jazz ~: 4 Rich, Webb 5 Krupa, Roach 6 Blakey, Puente 7 Bellson
rock ~: 4 Moon 5 Starr, Watts
__ Drummer Boy, The: 6 Little
__ Drummer Girl, The: 6 Little
__ drummers drumming...: 4 nine
Drummond: 3 Ace, cop 7 Bulldog
Drummondville: 4 city, town
locale: 6 Canada, Québec
__ Drum, NY: 4 Fort
Drum Roll Symphony composer: 5 Haydn
Drums (1938 film)
cast: Raymond Massey, Sabu
director: Zoltan Korda
Drums Along the Mohawk (1939 film)
cast: Claudette Colbert, Henry Fonda, Edna May Oliver
character: 3 Gil 4 Lana, Yost 5 Brant
director: John Ford
__ Drum Song: 6 Flower
drumstick: 3 leg 4 meat 10 finger food
neighbor: 5 thigh
__ Drum, The: 3 Tin
drunk: 5 tipsy 6 loaded 10 inebriated
not ~: 5 sober
drupe: 4 kaki, plum 5 berry, fruit, mamey, peach 6 cherry 7 apricot 9 manzanita
drupelet: 6 acinus
Drury: 4 Lane 5 Allen, Janes
Drury, Allen: 6 writer
work: Advise and Consent
Capable of Honor
Come Nineveh, Come Tyre
Preserve and Protect
The Promise of Joy
Public Men
A Shade of Difference
The Throne of Saturn
Drury Lane composer: 4 Arne
druthers: 6 option 8 penchant 10 partiality, preference, proclivity
Dr. Who network: 3 BBC
dry: 3 sec, wry 4 arid, blot, brut, dull, sear, sere, wipe 5 baked, bland, drain, droll, dusty, empty, mealy, parch, plain, salty, stale, toast, towel, unwet, wizen 6 barren, biting, boring, desert, harden, jejune, kipper, season, sponge, torrid, wither 7 acerbic, athirst, bookish, caustic, cutting, cynical, deplete, drained, insipid, parched, powdery, process, prosaic, raucous, Saharan, shrivel, sterile, tedious, thirsty, unmoist, weather, wizened 8 ironical, lifeless, pedantic, preserve, rainless, sardonic, scorched, shrunken, withered 9 anhydrate, anhydrous, dehydrate, desiccate, evaporate, exhausted, infertile, juiceless, ponderous, prosaical, sarcastic, shriveled, unfertile, waterless 10 dehumidify, dehydrated, desertlike, desiccated, dullsville, enervating, evaporated, lackluster, monotonous, pedantical, teetotaler, unbuttered
bleed ~: 5 drain 7 exhaust
cleaner's challenge: 5 stain
combining form: 3 xer- 4 xero-
dock: 4 port
ender: 4 wall, well
fruit: 3 nut 5 prune, regma 6 raisin
goods: 5 cloth
have a ~ run: 6 try out
having a ~ environment: 5 xeric
high and ~: 7 aground 8 cast away, deserted, marooned, stranded 9 abandoned
ink: 5 toner
in the sun: 4 bake
leave high and ~: 4 jilt 6 desert, maroon, strand 8 abdicate
not ~: 3 wet 4 damp 5 teary
off: 4 blot, wipe 5 towel
org.: 4 WCTU
out: 4 wilt 5 parch 9 evaporate
place: 6 desert
run: 4 test 5 trial 8 practice, rehearse 9 rehearsal
spell: 5 slump 7 drought
squeeze ~: 5 wring
up: 4 sear, wilt 5 parch, wizen 6 run out, wither 7 deplete, shrivel, silence 8 emaciate, peter out 9 evaporate
dry __: 3 fly, fog, ice, law, lot, mop, rot, run 4 bulk, cell, dock, hole, kiln, lake, milk, rent, sink, suit, wall, wash, well 5 goods, plate, spell 6 freeze, fresco, offset 7 battery, cleaner, compass, measure
dry __ bone: 3 as a
dry-__: 4 eyed, farm, salt, shod 5 clean, gulch 7 footing, roasted
__-dry: 3 air 4 blow, bone, damp, drip, kiln, pale, spin 5 rough, smoke 6 freeze, tumble
Dry __: 3 Ice
__ Dry: 6 Canada
dryad: 5 nymph 9 tree nymph, wood nymph
dwelling: 4 tree
dry as __: 4 dust 5 a bone
dry-as-dust: 4 blah, dull, tame
Dryden: 3 Ken 4 John
Dryden, John: 4 poet 7 British 10 playwright
work: 3 ode 5 essay
dryer
dish ~: 5 towel
hair ~: 6 blower
like a clogged ~ vent: 5 fuzzy
loss, perhaps: 4 sock
residue: 4 lint 5 fluff
tear ~: 5 hanky 6 hankie
__-dryer: 4 blow 6 washer
Dryer: 4 Fred
__ dry eye: 4 not a
dry field, name meaning: 6 Dudley
dry-goods
measure: 4 yard
merchant: 6 draper
Dry Idea: 9 deodorant
alternative: 3 Ban 4 Sure 5 Arrid, Tussy 6 Degree, Secret 7 Mitchum 10 Right Guard, Soft and Dri, Speed Stick
drying
oven: 4 kiln, oast
spread for ~: 3 ted
dryness: 6 thirst 7 aridity 8 monotony 10 insipidity
Drypers alternative: 4 Luvs 7 Huggies, Pampers
__, Dry Place: 5 A Cool
dry rot: 4 mold 5 decay, fungi
Drysdale, Don: 6 Dodger, hurler 7 pitcher
Dry Tortugas: 4 isle, park 6 island
locale: 7 Florida
Dschubba: 4 star
D-sharp: 5 E flat
DSM: 5 award, medal
DSO: 5 medal
DST end: 3 Oct. 7 October
duad: 3 two 4 pair 6 couple 7 doublet, twosome
dual: 4 twin 6 biform, binary, binate, double, paired 7 coupled, doubled, twofold, two-part 8 biformed, two-sided 9 two-person
not ~: 4 unal
dual __: 5 space 7 citizen, highway
dual-__: 4 carb 7 purpose
Duane: 4 Eddy 5 Diane 6 Allman
Duane's Depressed author: Larry McMurtry
Duarte: 3 Eva 4 city, town
locale: 10 California
dub: 3 tag 4 call, name, term 5 label, style, title 6 knight, record 7 baptize, entitle, intitle 8 christen, nickname 9 designate 10 stereotype
in: 3 add
something to ~: 4 tape
__-dub: 4 rub-a
Dubai: 4 city, town
locale: 3 UAE
native: 4 Arab
DuBarry Was a Lady (1943 film): 7 musical
cast: Lucille Ball, Gene Kelly, Red Skelton
composer: 6 Porter
director: Roy Del Ruth
dubbed one: 3 Sir 4 Dame
dubbing need: 5 sword
Dubble Bubble: 3 gum
Dubhe: 4 star
dubiety: 5 doubt 9 disbelief 10 hesitation, indecision, skepticism
dubious: 4 iffy, moot, open, wary 5 chary, fishy, leery, queer, rocky, shady, shaky, vague 6 chancy, gun-shy, louche, unfirm, unsure 7 guarded, obscure, suspect, tenuous, unclear 8 arguable, cautious, doubtful, doubting, hesitant, unlikely, unstable 9 ambiguous, debatable, equivocal, skeptical, uncertain, undecided, unsettled 10 disputable, far-fetched, improbable, indefinite, infeasible, left-handed, precarious, suspicious, unreliable
be ~: 5 doubt 8 question
of ~ honesty: 5 shady 7 corrupt, crooked, devious 8 slippery, unsavory 9 notorious, unethical 10 fly-by-night
Dublin: 3 bay 4 city, port, town 7 capital
legislature: 4 Dail
locale: 4 Eire, Erin, Ohio 7 Ireland 10 California
river: 6 Liffey
theatre: 5 Abbey

Dubliners, The author: James Joyce
___ du bois: 6 fraise
Du Bois: 3 WEB 5 Marta
dubonnet: 3 red 4 wine 8 purplish
relative: 4 rose, ruby, rust, wine 5 brick, coral, grape, poppy, rusty, sandy 6 cerise, cherry, claret, garnet, maroon 7 carmine, crimson, fuchsia, magenta, pimento, scarlet, sultana, vermeil 8 amaranth, cardinal, geranium, rubicund 9 carnation, cranberry, vermilion 10 strawberry
Dubos: 4 René
DuBose: 7 Heyward
Dubrovnik: 4 city, port
locale: 7 Croatia
Dubuffet, Jean: 6 artist, French 7 painter 8 sculptor
Dubuque: 4 city, town
college: 5 Loras 6 Clarke
locale: 4 Iowa
ducat: 5 money 6 ticket
word: 3 row 4 seat 5 admit
ducats: 3 tix
Duc De L'Omelette, The author: Poe
Duchamp, Marcel: 6 artist, French 7 Dadaist, painter
subject: 4 nude
duchess: 4 lady, peer, rank 5 noble, title, woman
Duchess of ___: 4 Alba, York
Duchess of Alba, The painter: 4 Goya
Duchess of Malfi, The author: John Webster
duchess' spouse: 4 duke
Duchin: 4 Eddy 5 Peter
Duchin, Eddy: 7 pianist 10 bandleader
son: Peter
Duchin, Peter: 7 pianist
Duchovny, David: 5 actor
film: Kalifornia (1993)
The Rapture (1991)
Return to Me (2000)
spouse: Téa Leoni
TV: The X-Files
duchy: 5 Hesse, Pinsk, Savoy 6 Saxony, Valois 7 Bavaria, Brabant, Tuscany 8 Holstein 9 Aquitaine, Franconia 10 Luxembourg, Westphalia
duck: 3 bob, dip, nod 4 bird, drop, fowl, hide, lose, meat, shun, smew, snub, teal 5 avoid, biped, dodge, eider, elude, evade, hedge, koloa, lurch, parry, pekin, Rouen, ruddy, scaup, shirk, skirt, stoop, wince 6 bypass, Cayuga, cotton, crouch, escape, eschew, fabric, hunker, plunge, scoter, swerve 7 abandon, abstain, gadwall, immerse, mallard, Muscovy, pintail, pochard, redhead, shy from, widgeon 8 bluebill, bullneck, drop down, flee from, garganey, get out of, mandarin, oldsquaw, shoveler, sidestep, submerge 9 broadbill, goldeneye, goosander, greenhead, harlequin, leap aside, merganser, sprigtail, waterfowl 10 bufflehead, canvasback, circumvent, get clear of, surf scoter
blind user: 6 hunter
cold ~: 4 wine
cousin: 5 goose
dwelling: 4 nest
ender: 3 pin 4 bill, ling, tail, weed 5 board
European ~: 4 smew 9 sheldrake
fake ~: 5 decoy
foot feature: 3 web
genus: 5 anser
haunt: 4 pond
Hawaiian ~: 5 koloa
hunter's boot: 5 wader
lame ~: 5 goner
male ~: 5 drake
out: 6 escape 7 abscond
Peter and the Wolf ~: 4 oboe
responsibility: 5 evade 6 cop out, renege
sea ~: 4 coot 5 eider
sitting ~: 4 butt, dupe, goat, prey 6 pigeon, sucker, target, victim
sound: 5 quack
soup: 4 easy, snap 5 cinch, cushy 6 picnic, simple 7 no sweat 8 easy task, painless, pushover, workable 9 uncomplex 10 child's play, effortless, elementary, unexacting
walk like a ~: 6 waddle
duck ___: 4 foot, hawk, hook, soup 5 blind
duck ___ rock: 3 on a 5 on the
duck-___: 3 egg 4 walk 6 legged
duck-___ platypus: 6 billed
___ duck: 3 sea 4 cold, dead, fish, gray, grey, lame, musk, surf, wood 5 black, eider, ruddy, scaup 6 Bombay, canvas, Cayuga, diving, Peking, tufted 7 Beijing, Muscovy, pressed, sitting
Duck: 5 Daffy, Daisy 6 Donald
duck à ___: 7 l'orange
___ Duck Amendment: 4 Lame
Duck, Donald voice: 4 Nash
ducking ___: 5 stool
ducklike bird: 4 coot
___ duckling: 4 ugly
duckpins, play: 4 bowl
ducks: 5 pants 6 slacks 8 trousers
ducks-and-drakes: 4 game
___-duck session: 4 lame
ducks in ___: 4 a row
Duck Soup (1933 film)
cast: Louis Calhern, Margaret Dumont, Chico Marx, Groucho Marx, Harpo Marx, Zeppo Marx
director: Leo McCarey
___ Ducks, The: 6 Mighty
ducktail: 2 do 4 coif 6 hairdo 7 haircut 8 coiffure 9 hairstyle
___ Duck, The: 4 Wild
duckweed: 5 plant 6 flower
ducky: 2 jo 3 def, pet, rad 4 aces, A-one, baby, boss, braw, cool, cute, dear, dece, fine, gear, jill, keen, love, neat, nice, phat, tuff 5 amour, angel, chéri, cooky, cutey, cutie, dandy, deary, flame, grand, great, honey, leman, lover, lovey, marvy, neato, nobby, novia, novio, prime, slick, sugar, super, sweet, swell 6 bang on, bang-up, bon ami, bonzer, bosker, chérie, choice, cookie, dautie, dearie, divine, dreamy, far-out, gnarly, groovy, lovely, peachy, slap-up, spot on, steady, superb, sweets, terrif, tiptop, unreal, whizzo, wicked 7 amazing, awesome, beloved, capital, corking, dearest, dear one, perfect, pigsney, ripping, schatzi, skookum, squeeze, stellar, sublime, sweetie, tootsie 8 chou-chou, cutie pie, dazzling, dowsabel, dulcinea, especial, eximious, fabulous, five-star, four-star, frabjous, glorious, heavenly, jim-dandy, just fine, ladylove, lovebird, macushla, paramour, pleasing, precious, slam-bang, smashing, snookums, splendid, standout, sterling, stickout, sugar pie, superior, sweetums, terrific, top-level, topnotch, truelove, very good, wondrous 9 bodacious, bonne amie, boyfriend, dreamboat, Endsville, excellent, exemplary, exquisite, first-rate, high-grade, hunky-dory, inamorata, inamorato, marvelous, petit chou, sollicker, top-flight, valentine, wonderful 10 first-class, girlfriend, heartthrob, honeybunch, hotsy-totsy, jack-a-dandy, mavourneen, out of sight, peachy-keen, phenomenal, remarkable, stupendous, super-duper, sweetheart, sweetie pie, turtledove
Ducommun, Élie: 5 Swiss 8 Nobelist
duct: 4 flue, main, pipe, tube, vein, vent 5 canal, drain, shaft 6 artery, course, gutter, outlet, trough 7 air vent, channel, conduit, culvert, passage
air ~: 4 flue, vent
anatomical ~: 3 vas 5 lumen
ender: 4 work
starter: 3 ovi, via
duct ___: 4 keel, tape
___ duct: 3 air 4 bile 5 resin 7 hepatic
ductile: 4 soft 6 supple 7 plastic 8 formable 9 malleable
material: 4 gold, iron, lead 6 copper, nickel, silver 8 aluminum, platinum
ductless ___: 5 gland
ductlike: 5 tubal
dud: 4 bomb, bust, flop, loss 5 lemon, loser 6 defeat, fiasco, mishap, turkey 7 blunder, clinker, debacle, failure, fizzler, misstep, stumble, washout 8 downfall 10 nonsuccess
___-duddy: 5 fuddy
dude: 3 cat, fop, guy 4 chap, gent, toff 5 buddy, dandy, fella, kiddo 6 feller, fellow, hepcat 7 coxcomb 8 fancy Dan, gay blade, macaroni, popinjay 9 ladies' man, maccaroni, pretty boy 10 jack-a-dandy, tenderfoot
up: 5 array, groom, preen, primp, prink 6 attire, bedaub 9 caparison
dude ___: 5 ranch
___, dude!: 5 Later
duded up: 5 natty, smart 6 dapper
Dudek, Louis: 4 poet 8 Canadian
Dude Ranger, The author: Zane Grey
Dudevant pseudonym: 4 Sand
dudgeon: 3 ire 4 rage 5 anger, pique, wrath 6 rancor 7 umbrage 10 irritation, resentment
___ du Diable: 3 île
Dudley: 4 city, Earl, town 5 Moore 10 Herschbach
friend: 4 Nell
locale: 7 England
Dudley Do-Right (1999 film)
cast: Brendan Fraser, Eric Idle, Alfred Molina, Sarah Jessica Parker
duds: 4 garb, gear, togs 5 array, dress, robes 6 attire, things 7 apparel, clothes, costume, raiment 8 garments, wardrobe 10 Sunday best
see also clothing
___ Duds: 4 Milk
Dudweiler: 4 city
locale: 4 Saar 7 Germany
due: 3 two 4 fair, just, owed, ripe 5 jural, legal, owing, right, share, title 6 coming, earned, lawful, proper, reward, served, unpaid, vested 7 deserts, exactly, fitting, Italian, merited, overdue, payable 8 arriving, deserved, directly, expected, required, rightful, straight, suitable 9 equitable, in arrears, justified, liability, privilege, reckoning, repayment, requisite, scheduled, unsettled 10 receivable, recompense, sufficient
a ~: 8 together
balance ~: 7 arrears
date: 3 end 5 limit 6 cutoff 8 deadline, zero hour
follower: 3 tre
get one's ~: 4 earn 5 merit
in ~ time: 3 yet 4 soon 10 eventually, ultimately
past ~: 5 tardy 6 behind, unpaid
preceder: 3 uno
process: 3 law 7 justice
process championer: 4 ACLU
to: 5 since 7 because 9 because of 10 by reason of, by virtue of
to get: 5 in for
to the fact that: 7 whereas
due ___: 4 bill, date 7 process
due ___ of law: 6 course 7 process
___ due: 4 past 7 postage
due and ___: 6 proper
duel: 4 bout, tilt 5 fence, fight, joust 6 combat 7 contest 8 conflict, shootout, showdown 10 engagement, sword fight
maneuver: 5 lunge
weapon: 4 épée, foil 5 saber, sabre, sword 6 pistol
with words: 4 spar 6 banter
Duel at Diablo (1966 film)
cast: Bibi Andersson, James Garner, Sidney Poitier
dueler: 4 Burr 8 Hamilton 9 combatant
Duel in the Sun (1946 film)
cast: Joseph Cotten, Jennifer Jones, Gregory Peck
director: King Vidor
Duellists, The (1977 film)
cast: Keith Carradine, Edward Fox, Harvey Keitel
director: Ridley Scott
duenna: 6 escort 8 chaperon 9 chaperone, governess
Duenna, The author: Richard Sheridan
due process ___: 5 of law
dues: 3 fee, tax 4 rate 5 price 7 charges 10 assessment, reparation
payer: 6 member
pay one's ~: 5 atone 7 rectify, redress
Duesenberg: 3 car 4 auto 6 Samuel 10 automobile
dues-paying group: 4 club, frat
duet: 3 two 4 pair 7 twosome
___, due, tre: 3 uno
duff: 4 coal, fake 5 cheat, slack 7 dessert, pudding
Duff: 6 Howard 7 McKagan
duffel: 3 bag, kit 4 coat, gear 6 jacket, kitbag 7 holdall 8 knapsack 9 haversack
duffer: 2 ox 3 oaf 4 lout, tyro 5 looby 7 amateur 8 beginner
see also golf
Duff, Howard spouse: Ida Lupino
Duffy: 5 Julia, Karen 7 Patrick
Duffy's ___: 6 Tavern
Duffy's Tavern: 9 radio show
___ du Flambeau, WI: 3 Lac
Dufy, Raoul: 6 artist, French 7 painter
dug
ender: 3 out
in: 9 immovable, unbending 10 entrenched
Dugan: 6 Dennis
___ Dugan Returns: 3 Max
du Gard, Roger: 6 French, writer 8 Nobelist
dugdugi: 4 drum
origin: 5 India
dugong: 6 animal, mammal, sea cow
dugout: 3 pit 4 abri, boat 5 canoe, skiff 6 trench 7 foxhole 10 excavation
see also baseball
Duhamel, Georges: 6 French, writer
DUI fighter: 4 MADD
duiker: 8 antelope
relative: 3 gnu, kob 4 guib, kudu, oryx, puku, topi 5 addax, bongo, chiru, eland, goral, korin, nyala, oribi, saiga, serow 6 chammy, dik-dik, impala, koodoo, lechwe, nilgai, rhebok, shammy, shamoy 7 blaubok, blesbok, chamois, defassa, gazelle, gemsbok, gerenuk, grysbok, nylghai, nylghau, sassaby 8 blesbuck, bontebok, bushbuck, gemsbuck, reedbuck, steenbok, steinbok 9 blackbuck, pronghorn, sitatunga, springbok, waterbuck 10 hartebeest, wildebeest

Duino Elegies, The author: Rilke
Duisburg: 4 city, town
  locale: 7 Germany
  river: 4 Ruhr 5 Rhine
___ du jour: 4 plat, soup 5 carte
Dukakis: 5 Kitty 7 Michael, Olympia
Dukakis, Olympia: 7 actress
  film: Look Who's Talking (1989)
    Mighty Aphrodite (1995)
    Moonstruck (1987, AA)
    Mr. Holland's Opus (1995)
    Steel Magnolias (1989)
Dukas, Paul: 6 French 8 composer
  work: The Sorcerer's Apprentice
duke: 3 box 4 fist, hand, lord, male, peer, rank 5 noble, title 8 nobleman
  daughter: 4 lady
  domain: 5 duchy
  ender: 3 dom
  it out: 5 brawl, fight
  starter: 4 arch
Duke: 5 Daryl, Doris, Patty, title 6 Snider, Vernon 9 Ellington
  athletes: 10 Blue Devils
  conference: 3 ACC
  Indigo for ~: 4 mood
  locale: 4 N. Car. 6 Durham
  org.: 4 NCAA
Duke of ___: 4 Earl, York 10 Wellington
Duke of Earl (1962 song) artist: Gene Chandler
  genre: 6 doo-wop
Duke, Patty
  Oscar: The Miracle Worker
  real first name: Anna
  song: Don't Just Stand There (1965)
  spouse: John Astin
Dukes: 5 David 8 Duquesne
___ Dukes: 5 Amboy
Dukes of Hazzard, The (CBS adventure)
  cast: Catherine Bach (Daisy Duke)
    James Best (Sheriff Roscoe P. Coltrane)
    Sorrell Booke (Boss Hogg)
    Denver Pyle (Jesse Duke)
    John Schneider (Bo Duke)
    Tom Wopat (Luke Duke)
  deputy: 4 Enos
  dog: 5 Flash
  spinoff: Enos
Duke, The: 5 Wayne
___ Duke, The: 4 Iron 5 Grand
Dukono: 7 volcano
  locale: 4 Asia 9 Indonesia
___ du Lac, WI: 4 Fond
Dulbecco, Renato: 7 Italian 8 Nobelist
Dulce: 4 gulf
  locale: 9 Guatamala
Dulce et Decorum Est author: Wilfrid Owen
dulcet: 4 soft 5 sweet 6 in tune, liquid 7 lilting, lyrical, melodic, musical, tuneful 8 sonorous, soothing 9 melodious 10 euphonious
dulcimer: 5 chang 6 santir, string, zither 8 cymbalom
dulcinea: 2 jo 3 pet 4 baby, dear, jill, love 5 amour, angel, cooky, cutey, cutie, deary, ducky, flame, honey, leman, lover, lovey, novia, sugar, sweet 6 chérie, cookie, dautie, dearie, steady, sweets 7 beloved, dearest, dear one, pigsney, schatzi, squeeze, sweetie, tootsie 8 chou-chou, cutie pie, dowsabel, ladylove, lovebird, macushla, paramour, precious, snookums, sugar pie, sweetums, truelove 9 bonne amie, dreamboat, inamorata, petit chou, valentine 10 girlfriend, heartthrob, honeybunch, mavourneen, sweetheart, sweetie pie, turtledove
Dulcy author: George S. Kaufman, Marc Connelly
___ du Lieber!: 3 Ach
dull: 3 dry 4 arid, blah, drab, flat, gray, grey, lazy, logy, mild, slow, soft, tame 5 bland, blunt, corny, dense, empty, faded, faint, hoary, ho-hum, hokey, leady, matte, mirky, mousy, muddy, murky, musty, muzzy, passé, pasty, plain, prosy, quell, slack, sober, stale, thick, tired, trite, unapt, unfun, vapid 6 barren, benumb, boring, bovine, common, dampen, darken, deaden, draggy, dreary, drowsy, glassy, hollow, jejune, leaden, mousey, muffle, obtund, obtuse, old hat, opaque, sallow, simple, sleepy, somber, stodgy, stolid, stuffy, stupid, sullen, torpid, wooden 7 blunted, clichéd, doltish, fatuous, humdrum, insipid, languid, lumpish, muffled, nowhere, prosaic, relieve, routine, shallow, silence, tarnish, tedious, unwaxed, vacuous, witless, worn-out 8 bromidic, cloddish, dragging, familiar, lifeless, listless, lubberly, mediocre, mitigate, ordinary, outdated, outmoded, overcast, pedantic, sluggish, stagnant, tiresome, unlively, unsavory 9 brainless, cheerless, colorless, dimwitted, dry-as-dust, hackneyed, lethargic, pointless, ponderous, prosaical, soporific, tasteless, unpointed, washed-out, wearisome 10 dullsville, enervating, flavorless, glassy-eyed, lackluster, lusterless, monotonous, pedantical, pedestrian, slow-witted, spiritless, tenebrific, threadbare, uneventful, unexciting, uninspired, unoriginal
  as writing: 5 prosy
  become ~: 4 pale 8 languish
  color: 3 dun 4 drab, gray, grey
  combining form: 5 brady-
  grow ~: 4 fade
  not ~: 4 keen 5 sharp
  one: 4 bore, nerd, nurd 5 schmo
  routine: 3 rut 4 drag, rote
  sound: 4 thud 5 clonk, clunk, thump, thunk
  surface: 3 mat 5 matte
dull-___: 6 witted
dullard: 3 ass, nit, oaf, sap 4 boob, bore, clod, dodo, dolt, fool, gowk, jerk, simp 5 chump, clown, cluck, dummy, dunce, joker, klutz, looby, ninny, patsy 6 dimwit, lubber, lummox, nitwit, sucker, turkey 7 airhead, buffoon, dingbat, fathead, halfwit, jackass, pinhead, saphead 8 bonehead, dumbbell, lunkhead, meathead, numskull 9 birdbrain, blockhead, harebrain, lamebrain, numbskull, simpleton 10 dunderhead, nincompoop
Dullea, Keir: 5 actor
  film: 2001: A Space Odyssey (1968)
    David and Lisa (1962)
    The Fox (1968)
    The Hoodlum Priest (1961)
dulled combining form: 5 ambly- 6 amblyo-
Dulles, Allen onetime org.: 3 CIA
___ dull moment!: 6 Never a
dullness: 5 sleep 6 stupor, tedium 7 languor 8 drabness, flatness, laziness, lethargy, loginess, monotony 9 heaviness, indolence, inertness, lassitude 10 inactivity, insipidity
  cure: 5 strop 9 whetstone
dullsville: 3 dry 4 blah, dull, flat, tame 5 hoary, ho-hum, prosy, stale, tired, trite, unfun, vapid 6 boring, common 7 humdrum, insipid, nowhere, routine, tedious, worn-out 8 familiar, ordinary, tiresome, unlively 9 colorless, hackneyed, soporific
dull-witted: 4 slow 5 thick 6 obtuse
  one: 3 ass, nit, oaf, sap 4 boob, bore, clod, dodo, dolt, fool, gowk, jerk, simp 5 chump, clown, cluck, dummy, dunce, joker, klutz, looby, ninny, patsy 6 dimwit, lubber, lummox, nitwit, sucker, turkey 7 airhead, buffoon, dingbat, fathead, halfwit, jackass, pinhead, saphead 8 bonehead, dumbbell, lunkhead, meathead, numskull 9 birdbrain, blockhead, harebrain, lamebrain, numbskull, simpleton 10 dunderhead, nincompoop
Dulong: 3 cow 4 bull 6 bovine, cattle
dulse: 5 algae 7 seaweed
Duluth: 4 city, port, town
  locale: 7 Georgia 9 Minnesota
duly: 6 aright 10 as expected, punctually
  bound: 5 sworn
dum ___, spero: 5 spiro
Duma locale: 6 Russia
Dumas ___: 4 fils, père
Dumas, Alexandre: 6 French, writer
  character: 5 Athos 6 Aramis 7 Porthos 9 d'Artagnan
  one ~: 4 fils, père
  work: The Black Tulip
    Camille
    The Count of Monte Cristo
    La Tulipe Noire
    The Three Musketeers
    Twenty Years After
  see also French
du Maurier: 6 Daphne, George
du Maurier, Daphne: 4 Dame 6 writer 7 British
  work: Rebecca
du Maurier, George: 6 writer 7 British
  work: Trilby
dumb: 4 slow 5 dense, goosy, quiet, thick 6 obtuse, simple, stolid, stupid 7 asinine, doltish, foolish, vacuous 9 dimwitted, voiceless 10 speechless
  ender: 4 bell 5 found 6 struck, waiter
  move: 5 boner 6 booboo
  one: 4 bozo 6 lummox
  play ~: 3 act
  strike ~: 4 stun 7 silence, stagger, stupefy 8 surprise
dumb ___: 3 bid 4 cane, Dora, down, luck 6 barter, sheave 7 compass
dumb ___ ox: 4 as an
Dumbarton: 4 city
  locale: 8 Scotland
  river: 5 Clyde
Dumbarton ___: 4 Oaks
dumbbell: 3 ass, nit, oaf, sap 4 boob, clod, dodo, dolt, fool, gowk, jerk 5 chump, clown, cluck, dunce, joker, looby, ninny, patsy 6 dimwit, lubber, lummox, nitwit, sucker, turkey 7 airhead, buffoon, dingbat, dullard, fathead, halfwit, jackass, pinhead, saphead 8 bonehead, lunkhead, meathead, numskull 9 birdbrain, blockhead, harebrain, lamebrain, numbskull, simpleton 10 dunderhead, nincompoop
  unit: 5 pound 8 kilogram
  use a ~: 4 curl, lift 7 work out 8 exercise
Dumbbell: 6 nebula
dumbbells: 3 wts. 7 weights
Dumb & Dumber (1994 film): 5 farce
  cast: Jim Carrey, Jeff Daniels, Teri Garr, Lauren Holly
  director: Peter Farrelly
dumbfound: 3 awe, wow 4 faze, stun 5 amaze, floor, stump, throw 6 baffle, boggle, puzzle 7 astound, confuse, nonplus, perplex, petrify, shatter, stagger, stupefy 8 astonish, befuddle, blow away, bowl over, surprise 9 embarrass, overwhelm, take aback 10 disappoint
dumbfounded: 5 blank, dizzy 6 aghast
Dumbo: 8 elephant
  wing: 3 ear
Dumbrille: 8 Douglass
dumbstruck: 5 agape, in awe 6 amazed, jolted 7 shocked, stunned 8 startled 10 bewildered, tongue-tied
dumbwaiter: 6 lifter 8 elevator
Dumb Waiter, The author: Harold Pinter
dumdum: 6 bullet
Dum Dum (1961 song) artist: Brenda Lee
Dumfries: 4 city, town
  locale: 8 Scotland
  notable: 5 Burns
dummy: 3 ass, nit, oaf, sap 4 boob, bozo, clod, dodo, dolt, dope, fool, gowk, jerk, mock, sham 5 chump, clown, cluck, dunce, front, joker, looby, model, ninny, patsy 6 dimwit, effigy, lummox, nitwit, sucker, turkey 7 airhead, buffoon, dingbat, dullard, fathead, halfwit, jackass, pinhead, saphead 8 bonehead, dumbbell, lunkhead, meathead, numskull, spurious 9 birdbrain, blockhead, harebrain, ignoramus, lamebrain, mannequin, numbskull, simpleton 10 dunderhead, nincompoop
  corporation: 5 front
  dressmaker ~: 4 form
  in America: 8 pacifier
  perch: 4 knee
  protest ~: 6 effigy
  ventriloquist ~ home: 5 trunk
___ du monde: 4 gens 5 homme
Du Mont: 5 Allen
Dumont, Margaret: 7 actress
  film: Animal Crackers (1930)
    At the Circus (1939)
    The Big Store (1941)
    The Cocoanuts (1929)
    A Day at the Races (1937)
    Duck Soup (1933)
    A Night at the Opera (1935)
dump: 3 axe, hut, rid, sty, tip 4 cede, dive, drop, jilt, junk, sell, shed, slum, void 5 chuck, ditch, eject, empty, expel, forgo, hovel, joint, scrap, sneer, spurn, throw, yield 6 ashcan, divest, forego, give up, pigpen, pigsty, refuse, shanty, unlade, unload 7 abandon, ash heap, deep-six, discard, forfeit, forsake, let go of, piggery 8 empty out, forswear, get rid of, hand over, jettison, junkyard, landfill, part with, renounce, throw out, unburden 9 cast aside, dispose of, foreswear, repudiate, surrender, throw away, throw over 10 relinquish
  ender: 4 site 5 truck
  on: 4 gibe, jeer, jibe, mock, slam, slur, snub 5 abuse, decry, libel, scorn, spurn, taunt 6 attack, defame, demean, deride, heckle, impugn, insult, malign, offend, rebuff, slight, vilify 7 affront, asperse, degrade, disdain, put down, rank out, slander, traduce 8 badmouth, belittle, denounce, mistreat, ridicule, vilipend 9 denigrate, discredit, disparage, humiliate 10 calumniate, disrespect
  out: 5 spill, unbag
___ dump: 4 core 6 screen
dumping ground: 8 landfill
dumpling: 4 baby 6 dim sum 7 dessert
dumps: 4 mood 5 blues, slump 7 sadness 8 doldrums, glumness
  in the ~: 3 low, sad 4 blue, down, glum 5 moody, woful 6 gloomy, morose,

somber, woeful 7 doleful, forlorn, joyless, unhappy 8 dejected, troubled 9 bummed out, cheerless, depressed, exanimate, heartsick, miserable, sorrowful, woebegone 10 chapfallen, despairing, dispirited, melancholy
Dumpster: 3 bin
locale: 5 alley
material: 5 trash
relative: 6 ashcan
__ Dumpty: 6 Humpty
dumpy: 5 pudgy, squat 7 rundown
dum spiro, __: 5 spero
dun: 3 bug, nag 4 bill, dark 5 beset, brown, horse, hound, press 6 equine, gloomy, mayfly, pester, plague 7 grayish 9 importune, keep after 10 lusterless
relative: 3 bay, tan 4 bole, ecru, fawn, foxy, nude, seal 5 amber, beige, camel, cocoa, hazel, khaki, mocha, sepia, tawny, umber 6 auburn, bister, bistre, bronze, coffee, copper, ginger, russet, sienna, sorrel, suntan, walnut 7 biscuit, caramel, dogwood 8 chestnut, cinnamon, mahogany 9 butternut, chocolate
Dunagiri: 4 peak 5 mount 8 mountain
locale: 4 Asia 5 India 9 Himalayas
Dunant, Jean: 5 Swiss 8 Nobelist
Dunaway, Faye: 7 actress
film: Barfly (1987)
Bonnie and Clyde (1967)
Chinatown (1974)
Don Juan DeMarco (1995)
Eyes of Laura Mars (1978)
The First Deadly Sin (1980)
Little Big Man (1970)
Mommie Dearest (1981)
Network (1976, AA)
Oklahoma Crude (1973)
The Temp (1993)
The Thomas Crown Affair (1968)
Three Days of the Condor (1975)
The Towering Inferno (1974)
Voyage of the Damned (1976)
Dunbar: 4 Paul 7 William
Dunbar, Paul: 4 poet 6 author, writer
Dunbar, William: 4 poet 8 Scottish
Duncan: 4 city, Gray, Todd, town 5 Hines, Phyfe, Sandy 6 Robert 7 Isadora, Renaldo
locale: 8 Oklahoma
Duncan Gray author: Robert Burns
Duncan Hines product: 3 mix 7 cake mix
Duncan, Isadora: 6 dancer 8 danseuse 9 ballerina
Duncan, Robert: 4 poet
Duncan, Todd: 6 singer 8 baritone
specialty: 5 opera
Duncanville: 4 city, town
locale: 5 Texas
dunce: 3 ass, nit, oaf, sap 4 boob, bozo, clod, dodo, dolt, dope, fool, gowk, jerk, simp, slow, yo-yo 5 booby, chump, clown, cluck, dummy, dunce, joker, klutz, looby, ninny, patsy 6 dimwit, lubber, lummox, nitwit, sucker, turkey 7 airhead, buffoon, bungler, dingbat, dullard, fathead, halfwit, jackass, pinhead, saphead 8 bonehead, dumbbell, lunkhead, meathead, numskull, peabrain 9 birdbrain, blockhead, harebrain, ignoramus, lamebrain, numbskull, simpleton 10 dunderhead, nincompoop
cap shape: 4 cone
seat: 5 stool
Dunciad, The author: Alexander Pope
Dundalk: 4 city, town
locale: 8 Maryland
Dundas: 4 city, town
locale: 6 Canada 7 Ontario
Dundee: 4 city, port, town 9 Crocodile
locale: 8 Scotland
Dundee, Crocodile
girl: 3 Sue
see also Australia
dunderhead: 3 ass, nit, oaf, sap 4 boob, bozo, clod, dodo, dolt, dope, fool, gowk, simp 5 chump, clown, cluck, dummy, dunce, joker, looby, ninny, patsy, schmo 6 dimwit, lummox, nitwit, schmoe, sucker, turkey 7 buffoon, dingbat, dullard, fathead, half-wit, jackass, pinhead, saphead 8 bonehead, dumbbell, meathead, numskull 9 birdbrain, blockhead, lamebrain, numbskull, simpleton 10 nincompoop
dun dun: 4 drum
origin: 6 Africa
dune: 4 hill, sand, seif 5 mound, ridge
buggy: 3 ATV
dune __: 5 buggy, grass
__ dune: 4 sand
Dune author: Frank Herbert
Dune composer: 3 Eno
Dunedin: 4 city, town
locale: 7 Florida 10 New Zealand
Dungaree Doll (1955 song) artist: Eddie Fisher
dungarees: 5 jeans, Levi's, pants 6 denims 8 trousers
dungeon: 4 cell, hole, jail 5 vault 6 prison 9 oubliette
item: 4 rack 5 irons
like a ~: 4 dank 5 mirky, murky
place: 6 castle, cellar
Dungeons & Dragons
beast: 3 Orc 4 ogre
company: 3 TSR
fan: 5 gamer
locale: 6 castle
spellcaster: 4 mage
Dunham: 9 Katherine
Dunhill competitor: 5 Zippo
dunk: 3 dip 4 soak 5 souse 6 drench, plunge 7 immerse 8 saturate, submerge
alternative: 5 lay up
one: 5 score
dunk __: 4 shot
__ dunk: 4 slam
dunker: 5 donut 8 doughnut
target: 4 goal 6 basket
Dunkin' __: 6 Donuts
dunking: 3 dip 4 bath, wash 5 rinse, souse 6 plunge 7 soaking 9 immersion
Dunkirk: 4 city, port, town
locale: 6 France
Dun Laoghaire: 4 city, port
locale: 7 Ireland
dunlin: 4 bird 9 sandpiper, shorebird
Dunlop: 4 tire
Dunn: 4 Nora 5 James 7 Michael
Dunne: 5 Irene 6 Philip 7 Griffin 8 Dominick
dunned amount: 6 arrear 7 arrears
Dunne, Finley Peter: 6 author, writer
character: Dooley
Dunne, Irene: 7 actress
film: Anna and the King of Siam (1946)
The Awful Truth (1937)
Back Street (1932)
Cimarron (1931)
I Remember Mama (1948)
Joy of Living (1938)
Life With Father (1947)
Love Affair (1939)
Magnificent Obsession (1935)
The Mudlark (1950)
My Favorite Wife (1940)
Over 21 (1945)
Penny Serenade (1941)
Roberta (1935)
Show Boat (1936)
Theodora Goes Wild (1936)
Together Again (1944)
The White Cliffs of Dover (1944)
Dunning: 5 Debbe
Dunninger claim: 3 ESP
Dunn, James Oscar: A Tree Grows in Brooklyn
__-du-Nord: 5 Côtes
Duns __: 6 Scotus
Dunsinane: 4 fort, hill
locale: 8 Scotland
Dunstan: 5 saint
Dunst, Kirsten: 7 actress
film: All I Wanna Do (1998)
Bring It On (2000)
Dick (1999)
Drop Dead Gorgeous (1999)
Jumanji (1995)
Small Soldiers (1998)
Spider-Man (2002)
The Virgin Suicides (2000)
Dunwoody: 4 city, town
locale: 7 Georgia
duo: 3 two 4 both, dyad, pair, team 5 brace, combo, twain, twins 6 couple, double 7 couplet, doublet, twosome
Duo author: Colette
duomo: 6 temple 9 cathedral
__ du pays: 3 mal
dupe: 3 con, lie, sap 4 butt, copy, fish, fool, gull, have, hoax, jerk, lamb, mark, mock, naif, nick, pawn, prey, rook, same, scam, snow, take, tool, trap 5 cheat, chump, clone, cozen, hocus, mimeo, patsy, repro, shaft, trick 6 delude, ectype, jackal, lead on, outwit, pigeon, puppet, rip off, rope in, softie, stooge, sucker, suck in, take in, victim 7 beguile, buffalo, cat's-paw, chicane, deceive, defraud, fall guy, mislead, pretend, replica, swindle, two-time 8 bulldoze, easy mark, flim-flam, hoodwink, outsmart, pushover, sucker in 9 bamboozle, disinform, four-flush, imitation, photocopy, reproduce, scapegoat, victimize 10 run a game on
not a ~: 8 original
duped: 5 taken 7 taken in 8 mistaken
easily ~: 4 naif 5 naive
__-duper: 5 super
dupery: 3 con, fib, lie 4 hoax, jive, ruse, scam, sham, trap, wile 5 dodge, feint, fraud, guile, hokum, lying, snare, sting, trick 6 hustle 7 blarney, charade, con game, cunning, falsity, fast one, gimmick, hogwash, malarky, snow job, sophism, swindle, untruth 8 artifice, bad faith, betrayal, delusion, flimflam, foul play, jugglery, malarkey, pretense, trickery 9 casuistry, chicanery, deception, dirty work, duplicity, falsehood, hypocrisy, imposture, mare's-nest, mendacity, stratagem, treachery, whitewash 10 craftiness, hanky-panky, hocus-pocus, masquerade, subterfuge
Dupin, Auguste creator: 3 Poe
Dupin, Lucile pseudonym: 4 Sand
duple: 7 twofold
duple __: 4 time 6 rhythm 7 measure
duplex: 4 twin 5 condo 6 double, paired 7 twofold, two-unit 8 two-sided 9 apartment
duplicate: 3 fax 4 copy, echo, mate, same, stat, twin 5 clone, ditto, equal, match, mimeo, model, trace, Xerox 6 double, ectype, repeat 7 imitate, replica, twofold 8 knockoff, likeness, matching 9 companion, correlate, facsimile, identical, imitation, lookalike, photocopy, Photostat, replicate, reproduce 10 carbon copy, dead ringer, equivalent, reciprocal, recurrence, reflection, repetition, tantamount, transcribe, transcript
duplicate bridge: 4 game 8 card game
duplicating __: 7 machine
duplicative remark: 5 ditto, me too
duplicitous: 4 wily 5 false, shady 6 crafty, sneaky 7 devious 8 cheating, guileful, two-faced 9 underhand
be ~: 3 lie
duplicity: 3 art 4 wile 5 craft, fraud, guile 6 deceit, dupery 7 cunning, falsity, perfidy, treason 8 artifice, bad faith 9 chicanery, deception, dirty pool, dirty work, falsehood, falseness, hypocrisy, Judas kiss, treachery 10 craftiness, dirty trick, dishonesty, infidelity
dupondius: 4 coin 5 money
DuPont
HQ: 8 Delaware
product: 5 Lycra, Orlon 6 Kevlar, Lucite, Teflon
Dupree, Robbie song: Steal Away (1980)
Duprees song: You Belong to Me (1962)
du Pré, Jacqueline: 7 British, cellist
Duque de Caxias: 4 city, town
locale: 6 Brazil
Duquesne: 10 university
athletes: 5 Dukes
locale: 4 Penn. 10 Pittsburgh
__ Duquesne: 4 Fort
dur: 5 major
dura __: 5 mater
durability: 4 grit, guts 5 heart, moxie 7 stamina 8 firmness, strength 9 endurance, longevity, stability 10 continuity, permanence
durable: 5 solid, sound, tough 6 stable, steady, strong, sturdy 7 abiding, lasting 8 leathery, reliable 9 heavy-duty, long-lived, tenacious 10 dependable, reinforced
be ~: 4 last, wear
not ~: 5 tinny 6 flimsy
durable __: 5 goods, press
duralumin: 5 alloy
component: 6 copper 8 aluminum
Duran: 7 Roberto
Duran Duran
song: Come Undone (1993)
Hungry Like the Wolf (1983)
I Don't Want Your Love (1988)
Is There Something I Should Know (1983)
Notorious (1986)
Ordinary World (1993)
The Reflex (1984)
Union of the Snake (1983)
A View to a Kill (1985)
The Wild Boys (1984)
Durango: 3 SUV 4 city, town 5 Dodge, state 6 estado 7 Mexican
city: 5 Lerdo 6 Poanas 8 Canatlán
locale: 6 Mexico 8 Colorado
see also Spanish
Durant: 4 Will 5 Ariel
Durant, Ariel: 6 writer 9 historian
durante __: 4 vita
Durante, Jimmy: 5 actor 8 comedian
film: Billy Rose's Jumbo (1962)
It's a Mad Mad Mad Mad World (1963)
On an Island With You (1948)
Palooka (1934)
Speak Easily (1932)
Start Cheering (1938)
This Time for Keeps (1947)
trademark: 4 nose
Durant, Will: 6 writer 9 historian
work: The Age of Napoleon
Rousseau and Revolution
The Story of Civilization
The Story of Philosophy

Duras, Marguerite: **6** French, writer
duration: **3** run **4** life, span, term, time **5** space **6** course, extent, length, period, tenure **7** stretch **9** longevity **10** continuity, perpetuity
for the ~: **8** meantime **9** meanwhile
Durban: **4** city, port, town
locale: **3** RSA **5** Natal
Durbeyfield: **4** Tess
pursuer: **4** Alec
Durbin, Deanna: **7** actress
film: Christmas Holiday (1944)
First Love (1939)
It Started With Eve (1941)
Lady on a Train (1945)
Mad About Music (1938)
Nice Girl? (1941)
One Hundred Men and a Girl (1937)
Spring Parade (1940)
Three Smart Girls (1936)
Three Smart Girls Grow Up (1939)
Durc parent: **4** Ayla
__ dure: **4** pâte
Düren: **4** city, town
locale: **7** Germany
Dürer, Albrecht: **6** artist, etcher, German **7** painter **8** engraver
duress: **5** force **8** bullying, coercion, pressure, violence **10** compulsion
Durham: **4** city, town **6** county
athletes: **8** Wildcats **10** Blue Devils
city: **6** Seaham
locale: **4** Conn., N. Car. **7** England
school: **3** UNH **4** Duke
__ Durham: **4** Bull
durian: **4** tree **5** fruit
relative: **6** baobab, bombax
during: **4** amid, when **5** while **6** amidst, just as, whilst **7** through **8** all along **10** throughout
prefix: **3** dia- **5** intra-
durn: **4** dang, darn **6** shucks
Durning, Charles: **5** actor
film: Dog Day Afternoon (1975)
The Final Countdown (1980)
Lakeboat (2001)
The Man With One Red Shoe (1985)
Mass Appeal (1984)
North Dallas Forty (1979)
Sisters (1973)
Spy Hard (1996)
Tootsie (1982)
Tough Guys (1986)
True Confessions (1981)
duro: **4** coin
Duroc: **3** hog, pig **5** swine
young ~: **5** shoat, shote, shott
Durocher, Leo: **7** manager
nickname: **3** Lip **5** Lippy **6** The Lip
spouse: Laraine Day
durra: **5** grain **7** sorghum
Durrell, Lawrence: **6** author, writer **7** British
work: Acte
Alexandria Quartet
Balthazar
Clea
The Ikons
Justine
Livia
Mountolive
durum: **5** flour, grain, wheat
durum wheat: **5** grain
Durward: **5** Kirby **7** Quentin
Durwent: **5** river
locale: **8** Tasmania
Duryea, Dan: **5** actor
film: Another Part of the Forest (1948)
Black Angel (1946)
Criss Cross (1949)
Night Passage (1957)
Scarlet Street (1945)
Slaughter on Tenth Avenue (1957)
The Underworld Story (1950)
Winchester '73 (1950)
The Woman in the Window (1944)
__ du Salut: **4** îles, Port
Duse: **8** Eleonora
__ du seigneur: **5** droit
Dusenberry: **3** Ann
Dushanbe: **4** city, town **7** capital
locale: **9** Tajikstan **10** Tajikistan
dusk: **3** e'en **4** dark **6** shadow, sunset **7** evening, sundown **8** gloaming, twilight **9** nightfall **10** crepuscule
after ~: **4** dark **5** night
of yore: **5** gloam
dusky: **3** dim **4** dark, gray, grey, soft **5** bleak, faded, fuzzy, livid, mirky, murky, muted, shady **6** bleary, blurry, dismal, gloomy, somber, swarth, twilit **7** fuscous, joyless, shadowy, swarthy **8** lowering, overcast **9** lightless, poorly lit, tenebrous, unlighted **10** indistinct
Dussault: **5** Nancy
Düsseldorf: **4** city, town
city near ~: **4** Köln **5** Essen, Neuss
locale: **7** Germany
river: **5** Rhine
dust: **3** mop **4** lint, soil, wipe **5** clean, motes, spray **6** powder, refuse, tidy up **7** trounce **8** sprinkle **9** sweepings **10** sprinkling
bit: **5** speck
bite the ~: **3** bow **4** bomb, bust, fail, flop, lose, slip, trip **5** flunk **6** blow it, falter, fizzle **7** blunder, founder, go under, go wrong, misstep, stumble, wash out **8** fall flat, flounder, lay an egg **9** strike out
collector: **3** rag
combining form: **4** coni- **5** conio-
cover item: **3** bio **5** blurb **6** review
devil: **4** eddy, wind
diamond ~: **4** bort **5** boart, bortz
ender: **3** bin, off, pan
gathering ~: **4** idle **8** inactive, not in use
leave in the ~: **6** run off **9** leap ahead
starter: **3** saw **4** star
use a ~ rag: **4** wipe
valuable ~: **4** gold
dust __: **3** gun, mop, off **4** ball, cart, shot, well **5** bunny, cover, devil, kitty, mouse, storm, whirl **6** jacket, kitten, ruffle **7** catcher, counter
__ dust: **4** acid, gold, rock **5** dry as **6** cosmic **7** diamond
__-dust: **4** crop **5** dry-as
__ Dust: **3** Red **4** Star **6** Purple
Dust Bowl
like the ~: **3** dry **4** arid
migrant: **4** Okie
Dustbuster: **3** vac **6** vacuum
dustcloth: **3** rag
duster: **3** mop, rag **4** coat, maid **5** plane, smock **6** jacket **8** airplane, overcoat **9** housecoat
__ duster: **3** red **7** feather
__-duster: **4** crop **7** knuckle
Duster: **3** car **4** auto **8** Plymouth
Dustin: **6** Farnum **7** Hoffman
dusting: **5** chore **7** coating **9** housework **10** sprinkling
powder: **4** talc
dusting __: **6** powder
__-dusting: **4** crop
Dust in the Wind (1978 song) artist: Kansas
Dust of Snow: **4** poem
author: Robert Frost
__ dust shalt thou return: **4** unto
____, dust to...: **5** ashes
Dust Tracks on a Road author: Zora Neale Hurston
dustup: **3** ado, row **4** spat, tiff **5** run-in, set-to **6** barney, rumpus **7** quarrel **8** skirmish, squabble **9** brannigan
dusty: **3** dry **4** arid, gray, grey **5** dirty, grimy **6** unused **7** powdery, tedious, unclean, unswept **8** obsolete, outdated, timeworn, unwashed **9** out-of-date, uncleaned **10** lusterless
relative: **3** ash **4** dove, drab **5** beige, merle, pearl, putty, slate, taupe **6** silver **7** grizzly **8** charcoal, gunmetal, platinum
Dusty: **5** Baker **6** Rhodes
Dutch: **4** font **8** language, typeface
speaking island: **5** Aruba
uncle: **7** adviser, advisor
see also Netherlands
Dutch __: **3** bob, cut, lap **4** bond, door, gold, oven, rush, wife **5** chair, lunch, treat, uncle **6** Belted, Borneo, cheese, clover, Guiana, settle **7** auction
Dutch __ disease: **3** elm
Dutch __ Guinea: **3** New
Dutch __ Indies: **4** East, West
__ Dutch: **3** Old **4** Cape **6** Double, Middle
Dutch Belted: **3** cow **4** bull **6** bovine, cattle
Dutch bob: **4** coif **6** hairdo **8** coiffure
Dutch Courtezan, The author: John Marston
Dutch gold: **5** alloy
component: **4** zinc **6** copper
Dutchman's-pipe: **5** plant **6** flower
__ Dutchman, The: **6** Flying
Dutch metal: **5** alloy
component: **4** zinc **6** copper
Dutch New __: **6** Guinea
Dutch oven: **3** pot **6** cooker
Dutch West __: **6** Indies
dutiful: **4** good, true **5** lowly, loyal, moral **6** docile, filial **7** devoted, staunch, willing **8** amenable, constant, faithful, gracious, obedient, true-blue, yielding **9** agreeable, allegiant, compliant, dedicated, regardful, righteous, steadfast, tractable **10** law-abiding, respectful, scrupulous, submissive
be ~ to: **5** serve
__ du tout: **3** pas
Dutra: **4** Olin
Dutton, Charles S.: **5** actor
film: Blind Faith (1998)
Cry, the Beloved Country (1995)
Get on the Bus (1996)
TV: Roc
duty: **3** job, tax, tie **4** care, levy, must, need, onus, part, role, task, toll, work **5** chore, ought, place, stint, thing, watch **6** affair, burden, charge, excise, impost, office, tariff, towage **7** loyalty, mission, service, station **8** business, exaction, function, province **9** liability **10** assessment, assignment, commitment, department, engagement, obligation
call of ~: **5** draft
customs ~: **3** tax **6** impost
do ~: **5** serve
GI ~: **2** KP
ignore one's ~: **5** shirk **8** slack off
on ~: **4** busy **6** active, at work **8** employed
roster: **4** rota
sentry ~: **5** vigil, watch
tour of ~: **5** hitch, spell, stint
word of ~: **4** must **5** ought **6** should
duty-__: **4** free
__ duty: **3** sea **5** civic, guard **6** active
__-duty: **3** off **5** heavy, light **6** double
__ Duty: **5** Ode to
Duun, Olav: **6** writer **9** Norwegian
Duval, David: **6** golfer
Duvall: **6** Robert **7** Shelley
Duvall, Robert: **5** actor
film: The 6th Day (2000)
Angelo, My Love (1983)
Apocalypse Now (1979)
The Apostle (1997)
The Betsy (1978)
Breakout (1975)
A Civil Action (1998)
Colors (1988)
Convicts (1991)
Countdown (1968)
Days of Thunder (1990)
Deep Impact (1998)
The Eagle Has Landed (1977)
The Godfather (1972)
The Godfather Part II (1974)
John Q (2002)
Lawman (1971)
MASH (1970)
The Natural (1984)
Network (1976)
The Paper (1994)
Phenomenon (1996)
The Rain People (1969)
Rambling Rose (1991)
The Seven-Per-Cent Solution (1976)
The Stone Boy (1984)
Tender Mercies (1983, AA)
To Kill a Mockingbird (1962)
Tomorrow (1972)
True Confessions (1981)
Duvall, Shelley: **7** actress
film: 3 Women (1977)
Brewster McCloud (1970)
Popeye (1980)
Roxanne (1987)
The Shining (1980)
Thieves Like Us (1974)
Time Bandits (1981)
__ du Vent: **4** îles
__ du ventre: **5** danse
duvet: **5** quilt **9** comforter
duvetyn: **6** fabric **8** material
du Vigneaud, Vincent: **7** chemist **8** Nobelist
Duz rival: **5** Rinso
DVD
alternative: **3** VCR
attachment: **2** TV **5** TV set
Dvina: **3** bay **5** river
city on the ~: **4** Riga
locale: **6** Russia
DVM: **3** vet
Dvořák: **3** Ann **5** Anton **7** Antonín
Dvorak, Ann: **7** actress
film: Abilene Town (1946)
Dr. Socrates (1935)
'G' Men (1935)
The Private Affairs of Bel Ami (1947)
Scarface (1932)
Thanks a Million (1935)
The Way to Love (1933)
Dvořák, Antonín: **5** Czech **8** composer
work: The Cunning Peasant
Czech Suite
New World Symphony
Rhapsody for Orchestra
Slavonic Dances
D.W.: **8** Griffith
Dwan, Allan: **8** director
film: Chances (1931)
Frontier Marshal (1939)
The Iron Mask (1929)
The River's Edge (1957)
Sands of Iwo Jima (1949)
Suez (1938)
The Three Musketeers (1939)
Up in Mabel's Room (1944)
dwarf: **3** Doc **4** runt, star, tiny **5** Dopey, gnome, Happy, stunt, teeny **6** Grumpy, petite, Sleepy, Sneezy, teensy **7** Bashful **8** diminish, minimize **9** miniature, tower over, undersize **10** diminutive, homunculus, overshadow
tree: **6** bonsai

__ dwarf: 3 red 5 black, brown, white
dwarfs: 6 heptad
Dwarf, The author: Pär Lagerkvist
__ D. Watson: 5 James
Dwayne: 7 Hickman
dweeb: 4 geek, jerk, nerd, nurd, wimp, wonk 5 loser, twerp, twirp
like a ~: 6 uncool
dwell: 4 bide, harp, live, nest, stay 5 abide, exist, lodge, roost 6 inhere, linger, locate, occupy, remain, reside, settle 7 inhabit, sojourn 8 populate
on: 5 savor 6 ponder, ramble, stress 7 belabor, iterate 8 reassert, remember 9 emphasize
dweller: 5 liver 6 tenant 7 citizen, denizen, resider 8 indigene, occupant, resident 10 inhabitant
suffix: 3 -ian, -ite
__ dweller: 4 cave, lake 5 cliff
dwelling: 3 den, pad, res. 4 digs, home 5 abode, cabin, house, lodge, place 6 castle, chalet, palace 7 address, domicil, habitat, housing, lodging, mansion, shelter 8 building, domicile, dwelling, fireside, lodgment, quarters 9 residence
Amerind ~: 4 tipi 5 hogan, tepee 6 teepee
arctic ~: 4 iglu 5 igloo
bird ~: 4 nest
cliff ~: 4 aery, eyry 5 aerie, eyrie
cozy ~: 4 nest
crude ~: 3 hut 5 hovel, shack 6 lean-to
dryad ~: 4 tree
elevated ~: 4 aery, eyry 5 aerie, eyrie
frontier ~: 5 cabin
Herr ~: 4 haus
magnificent ~: 5 manor 6 castle
outdoor ~: 4 tent
prehistoric ~: 4 cave
rundown ~: 4 dive, dump, slum 5 hovel
ski ~: 5 lodge
Southwestern ~: 5 adobe
urban ~: 4 co-op, flat 5 condo 6 duplex 9 apartment
see also home, house
dwelling __: 5 place
__ dwelling: 3 pit 4 lake 5 cliff
__-dwelling: 4 cave
Dwight: 5 Evans, Moody 6 Gooden, Yoakam 7 Timothy, Twilley 10 Eisenhower
nickname: 3 Ike
opponent: 5 Adlai
wife: 5 Mamie
Dwight, Timothy: 6 writer
dwindle: 3 die, ebb 4 curb, drop, fade, fall, lull, sink, wane, wilt 5 abate, decay, drain, lower, peter, slack, taper 6 lessen, recede, reduce, shrink, weaken 7 curtail, cut down, decline, die down, drop off, fall off, shrivel, slacken, subside, tail off, thin out 8 contract, decrease, diminish, head away, languish, level off, peter out, slack off, taper off 9 retrocede
dwindling: 3 ebb 4 fall 7 decline 8 decrease 9 remission
__ D. Wood Jr.: 6 Edward
Dy: 4 elem. 7 element 10 dysprosium
66 for ~: 4 at. no.
dyad: 3 duo, two 4 pair 5 brace 6 couple 7 twosome
dyadic: 6 paired
Dyan: 6 Cannon
dye: 3 azo, hue 4 anil, tint, weld, woad 5 color, eosin, henna, paint, stain, tinct, tinge 6 anatto, eosine, indigo, kamala, litmus, madder, orchil, redden 7 alkanet, cudbear, fuchsin, gallein, genipap, logwood, pigment, recolor 8 amaranth, colorant, tincture, turmeric 9 cochineal 10 quercitron
acid ~: 5 eosin 6 eosine
azo ~: 8 amaranth
bin: 3 vat 4 keir
blue ~: 4 anil, woad 6 indigo
brown ~: 5 henna 7 gallein, genipap
chemical ~: 3 azo
chemist ~: 6 litmus
Egyptian ~: 5 henna
ender: 4 wood 5 stuff
green ~: 7 gallein
hair ~: 5 henna
ingredient: 4 alum
lab slide ~: 5 eosin 6 eosine
lot: 10 color batch
name: 3 Rit
nitrogen-based ~: 3 azo
organic ~: 3 azo 6 kermes
plant: 4 anil
purple: 7 alkanet, logwood 8 amaranth
red ~: 3 azo 5 eosin, henna 6 eosine, kermes, madder, orchil 7 alkanet, cudbear, genipap, logwood 8 amaranth 9 cochineal
yellow ~: 4 weld 6 kamala 8 turmeric 10 quercitron
yellow-red ~: 6 anatto
__ dye: 3 azo, vat 4 acid 5 azine, azoic, basic, Congo 6 sulfur, Tyrian 7 aniline, sulfide
__-dyed: 3 tie 4 deep, yarn 5 piece
dyed-in-the-wool: 4 avid 5 loyal, stern 6 enured, inured 7 diehard 8 absolute, complete, deep-down, faithful, hardcore, hardened 9 confirmed, stringent 10 inveterate
dyeing instruction: 5 rinse
dyer: 8 colorist
Dyer: 5 Wayne
dyer's __: 4 moss 5 broom 6 rocket
dye-with-wax technique: 5 batik 6 battik
Dying Animal, The novelist: 4 Roth
dying away in music: 7 calando
dying to know: 6 prying, snoopy 7 curious 8 meddling 9 butting in, intrusive, obtrusive 10 meddlesome
Dyken, Amy Van: 7 swimmer
Dykstra: 3 Len 5 Lenny
Dylan: 3 Bob 5 Baker, Jakob 6 Thomas 8 language 9 McDermott
alternative: 3 ADA, APL, SQL 4 Alef, html, Icon, Java, LISP, Logo, Orca, Perl 5 Algol, Basic, Cecil, COBOL, SISAL 6 Delphi, Eiffel, Erlang, Oberon, Pascal, Prolog, Sather, Scheme, Snobol 7 Fortran
contemporary: 4 Baez
Dylan, Bob
son: Jakob
song: Knockin' on Heaven's Door (1973)
Lay Lady Lay (1969)
Like a Rolling Stone (1965)
Positively 4th Street (1965)
Rainy Day Women (1966)
Dymphna: 5 saint
dynamic: 4 busy, go-go, live, spry 5 alive, astir, lusty, peppy, perky, ready, vital, zippy 6 active, at work, lively, living, moving, potent 7 animate, driving, hyped-up, intense, kinetic, vibrant, working 8 animated, bustling, electric, emphatic, forceful, powerful, vigorous 9 assiduous, energetic, masterful, sprightly, strenuous 10 aggressive, compelling, electrical, productive, unflagging
starter: 4 aero
dynamic __: 5 range 7 braking
Dynamic __: 3 Duo
dynamics: 6 motion
__ dynamics: 5 fluid, group 6 social
dynamism: 5 force, power, vigor 6 bounce 10 initiative
dynamite: 3 fab, TNT 4 rase, raze 5 blast 6 blow up 7 destroy, explode, shatter, sublime, unbuild 8 perilous, striking 9 explosive, wonderful 10 precarious, stupendous
ingredient: 5 nitro
sound: 3 pow 5 kapow 6 kaboom
Dynamite (1929 film)
cast: Charles Bickford, Kay Johnson, Conrad Nagel
director: Cecil B. DeMille
dynamize: 9 galvanize
dynamo: 4 doer, Turk 5 mover 6 shaker 7 hotshot, hustler, whiz kid 8 achiever, fireball, go-getter, live wire 9 generator, spark plug 10 ball of fire
part: 5 rotor 6 stator
Dynamo: 9 detergent
alternative: 3 All, Biz, Era, Fab, Yes 4 Bold, Dash, Gain, Surf, Tide, Wisk 5 Cheer, Dreft, Purex 6 Calgon, Oxydol 7 Octagon 9 Ivory Snow
dynast: 4 czar, king, tsar, tzar 5 queen, ruler 6 gerent, prince 7 czarina, emperor, empress, tsarina, tzarina 8 princess
dynastic: 5 royal
Dynasts, The author: Thomas Hardy
dynasty: 4 rule 5 house 6 empire, regime 7 kingdom
Chinese ~: 3 Chi, Jin, Qin, Wei, Xia, Yin 4 Chan, Chen, Hsia, Liao, Ming, T'ang, Tsin, Yuan 5 Liang, Shang
first Chinese ~: 4 Hsia
Dynasty: 3 car 4 auto 5 Dodge
Dynasty (ABC drama)
cast: Diahann Carroll (Dominique Deveraux)
Joan Collins (Alexis Colby)
Sammy Jo Dean (Heather Locklear)
Linda Evans (Krystle Carrington)
John Forsythe (Blake Carrington)
Pamela Sue Martin (Fallon Colby)
Emma Samms (Fallon Colby)
setting: 6 Denver 8 Colorado
dyne-centimeter: 3 erg
Dynel: 6 fabric 8 material
Dysart: 7 Richard
dysfunctional: 7 useless
dyspeptic: 6 cranky 7 bearish 9 irritable 10 ill-natured
dysprosium: 7 element
dysrhythmia, circadian: 6 jet lag
dziggetai: 6 equine
relative: 3 ass 5 burro, horse, kiang, zebra 6 donkey, onager, quagga 7 jackass
Dzundza, George: 5 actor
film: Basic Instinct (1992)
Impulse (1990)
White Hunter, Black Heart (1990)
TV: Law & Order

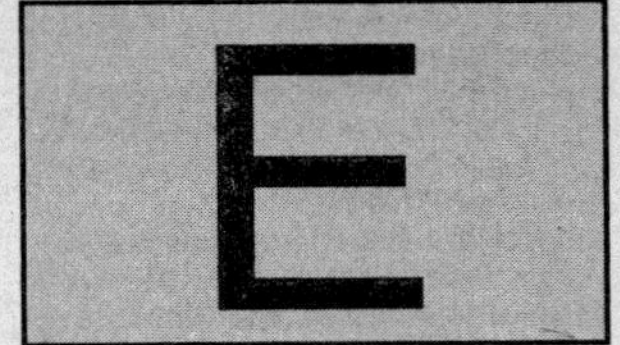

8
on a phone: 3 TUV
8 1/2 (1963 film)
cast: Anouk Aimée, Claudia Cardinale, Marcello Mastroianni
director: Federico Fellini
musical based on ~: 4 Nine
11%, about: 5 ninth
11:00 feature: 4 news
11 Harrowhouse (1974 film)
cast: Candice Bergen, Charles Grodin, James Mason
director: Aram Avakian
11th-grader: 6 junior
11-year-old: 5 'tween
18
holes: 5 round
play ~: 4 golf
__ 18: 4 Mila
18 Again! (1988 film)
cast: George Burns, Anita Morris, Tony Roberts, Charlie Schlatter
director: Paul Flaherty
18 and Life (1989 song) artist: Skid Row
18th-Amendment
subject: 6 liquor
supporter: 3 dry
18-wheeler: 4 semi 5 truck
18 Yellow Roses (1963 song) artist: Bobby Darin
80-day circumnavigator: 4 Fogg
84 Charing Cross Road (1987 film)
cast: Anne Bancroft, Dame Judi Dench, Anthony Hopkins
director: David Jones
84 Charing Cross Road author: 5 Hanff
86: 3 nix 5 agent
87th Precinct setting: 5 Isola
88: 5 piano
800 Leagues on the Amazon author: Jules Verne
800-no. relative: 4 WATS
808 (1999 song) artist: Blaque
867-5309/Jenny (1982 song) artist: Tommy Tutone
__-1138: 3 THX
1800: 5 six p.m.
1812 Overture composer: 11 Tchaikovsky
1857 mutineer: 5 Sepoy
1876 author: 5 Vidal
1898 rebel: 5 Boxer
e-__: 4 mail, mall, tail 7 tailing
E: 3 dir., vit. 5 vowel, width 6 letter 7 vitamin
flat: 3 key 6 D sharp 8 major key
in phonetic alphabet: 4 Echo
part of ~ = mc2: 4 mass 6 energy
to W line: 3 hor.
E __: 5 layer 6 galaxy, region
E __ dell' anima: 5 il sol
E __ eagle: 4 as in
E. __ Biggs: 5 Power
E. __ Hunt: 6 Howard
E. __ Proulx: 5 Annie
__ E: 4 T and 6 Sheila
'E' __ Evidence: 5 Is for
__-E: 4 Eazy
each: 3 per 4 a pop 5 a head, a shot, every 6 apiece, a throw, either, for one, singly 7 per head, per unit 9 per capita, per person 10 respective
one: 3 all 9 everybody
each __: 5 other
each and __: 5 every
Each Dawn I Die (1939 film)
cast: James Cagney, George Raft
__ each life...: 4 Into
__ Each Other: 7 Hurting
Each sack had __ cats...: 5 seven
Eadie __ a Lady: 3 Was
Eads __: 6 Bridge
Eagan: 4 city, town
locale: 9 Minnesota
eager: 3 hot 4 agog, avid, game, keen, wild 5 antsy, itchy, lanky, ready, wired 6 aflame, ardent, fervid, gung ho, hearty, hungry, intent, on edge, prompt, red-hot, strong 7 anxious, athirst, burning, earnest, excited, fervent, fired up, glowing, intense, longing, psyched, thirsty, willing, wishful, zealous, zestful 8 animated, aspiring, desirous, hopped up, juiced up, spirited, studious, tireless, vehement, yearning 9 ambitious, expectant, exuberant, hot to trot, impatient, impetuous, psyched up, strenuous, voracious 10 inspirited, passionate, raring to go, solicitous
about: 6 keen on
be ~: 4 jump
beaver: 4 doer 6 dynamo 7 busy bee, hustler 8 go-getter, live wire 10 ball of fire, hard worker
feel ~: 4 ache, long, lust, pang, pine, want 5 crave, throb, yearn 6 hanker
for company: 4 lone 5 alone 6 lonely 7 forlorn 8 desolate, forsaken, isolated, lonesome, rejected, solitary, unsocial 9 by oneself, destitute, reclusive, withdrawn 10 unattended
make ~: 4 whet
to do: 5 up for
to hear: 7 all ears 9 attentive
eager __: 6 beaver
__ Eager: 6 Johnny
eagerly: 4 hard 6 keenly 7 readily
eagerness: 4 fire, zeal, zest, zing 5 ardor, gusto, speed 6 desire, fervor, hunger, thirst 7 avidity, longing 8 alacrity, ambition, fervency, keenness, voracity, yearning 9 constancy, curiosity, fixedness, quickness, readiness, vehemence 10 aspiration, enterprise, enthusiasm, excitement, exuberance, greediness, heartiness, impatience, initiative, intentness, promptness, solicitude
showed ~, old-style: 5 rared
eagle: 3 ern 4 bird, coin, erne 5 money 6 raptor 10 bird of prey
a par-three hole: 3 ace
attack like an ~: 5 swoop
constellation: 6 Aquila
emulate an ~: 4 soar 5 glide, swoop
eye: 5 stare, vigil, watch 6 acuity 7 lookout 8 scrutiny
feature: 4 claw 5 talon
home: 4 aery, eyry, nest 5 aerie, eyrie
legal ~: 6 lawyer 8 attorney 9 counselor
like an ~: 8 aquiline
Muppet ~: 3 Sam
name meaning ~: 4 Erna 5 Adler
plus one: 6 birdie
plus two: 3 par
sea ~: 3 ern 4 bird, erne
wearer: 3 col. 7 colonel
eagle __: 3 eye, owl, ray
eagle-__: 4 eyed
__ eagle: 3 sea 4 bald, half 5 harpy, legal 6 double, golden, spread 7 quarter
Eagle: 3 AMC, car, LEM 4 auto 5 scout 7 Pennell 8 Boy Scout 10 automobile
rival: 3 Jet, Ram 4 Bear, Bill, Colt, Lion 5 Brown, Chief, Giant, Niner, Raven, Saint, Texan, Titan 6 Bengal, Bronco, Cowboy, Falcon, Jaguar, Packer, Raider, Viking 7 Charger, Dolphin, Panther, Patriot, Redskin, Seahawk, Steeler 8 Cardinal 9 Buccaneer
where the ~ landed: 4 moon
Eagle __: 5 Scout
__ Eagle: 4 Iron, Lone
Eagle and the Arrow, The
source: 4 Esop 5 Aesop
Eagle and the Hawk, The (1933 film)
cast: Cary Grant, Carole Lombard, Fredric March, Jack Oakie
eagle-eyed: 4 wary 8 keen-eyed 9 observant
Eagle Has Landed, The (1977 film)
cast: Michael Caine, Robert Duvall, Donald Sutherland
director: John Sturges
Eagle Pass: 4 city, town
locale: 5 Texas
Eagles: 4 band, team 6 eleven
member: Frey, Henley
org.: 3 BSA, NFC, NFL
song: Best of My Love (1974)
Heartache Tonight (1979)
Hotel California (1977)
I Can't Tell You Why (1980)
Life in the Fast Lane (1977)
The Long Run (1979)
Lyin' Eyes (1975)
New Kid in Town (1976)
One of These Nights (1975)
Take It to the Limit (1976)
Witchy Woman (1972)
sport: 8 football
__ Eagles Dare: 5 Where
eagle, star whose name means: 6 Altair
eaglet: 6 raptor 8 nestling 9 fledgling
Eagle, The (1925 film)
cast: Vilma Banky, Louise Dresser, Rudolph Valentino
__ Eagle, The: 4 Lone
Eakins, Thomas: 6 artist 7 painter
Eames: 4 Emma 5 chair 7 Charles
Eames, Emma: 6 singer 7 soprano
specialty: 4 aria 5 opera
Eamon: 8 De Valera
in English: 6 Edmond, Edmund
E. Annie: 6 Proulx
EAP
part of ~: 3 Poe 5 Allan, Edgar
ear: 4 corn, heed 5 organ, spike 6 handle 7 auricle 8 audience, listener 9 attention 10 perception
assault the ~: 6 deafen
bend an ~: 4 hark, talk 5 lobby, run on 7 hearken 9 eavesdrop
bone: 5 incus 6 stapes 7 stirrup
cleaner: 4 Q-Tip, swab, swob
collection: 3 wax 7 cerumen
combining form: 2 ot- 3 aur-, oto- 4 auri-
cover: 4 husk
ender: 3 bob, lap, wax, wig 4 ache, drop, drum, flap, lobe, mark, muff, plug, ring, shot, worm 5 phone, piece 9 splitting
feature: 5 canal
flea in one's ~: 3 tip 4 clue 6 tip-off 7 glimmer, inkling, whisper 10 glimmering, suggestion
give ~ to: 4 care, hear, heed, mind, obey 6 attend, follow, listen, notice 7 abide by, observe 8 adhere to, consider, listen to 10 bear in mind, take care of, toe the line
grain ~: 5 spica
hard on the ~: 4 loud 5 noisy 6 atonal 7 raucous
insert: 4 plug
lend an ~: 4 heed 6 listen 7 hearken, hear out
malady: 6 otitis
of an ~ part: 5 lobar
of the ~: 4 otic 5 aural 6 audial
opening: 6 meatus
outer ~: 6 concha
part: 3 cob 4 lobe 5 canal 6 hammer, kernel, tragus
play by ~: 5 ad-lib 6 invent, make up, whip up, wing it 9 improvise
pollution: 3 din 4 roar, stir 5 noise 6 bedlam, clamor, hubbub, jangle, racket, scream, shriek, tumult, uproar 7 clangor, clatter, discord 8 brouhaha, disquiet 9 commotion, hue and cry 10 hullabaloo
tin ~: 6 asonia
turn a deaf ~: 5 scorn 6 refuse, slight
winter ~ wear: 4 muff
ear __: 3 tag 4 band, lobe, plug, wrap 5 canal, candy, drops, sewer 6 fungus 7 trumpet
__ ear: 3 tin 4 deaf, tree, wood 5 bear's, cloud, inner, on its, outer, third 6 button, middle
__-ear: 3 dog 4 cat's, dog's
Earache My Eye (1974 song) artist: Cheech and Chong
__ ear and out...: 5 in one
__-ear dog: 7 hearing
eared __: 4 seal
__-eared: 3 dog, lop 4 crop, dog's, flop 5 sharp
__-eared bunny: 3 lop
earful: 4 info, talk 5 rumor 6 advice, gossip, rebuke, report 7 message 8 scolding 10 bawling out, revelation, telling-off, upbraiding
cheerful ~: 4 song, tune 5 ditty, music 6 ballad, jingle, number 7 lullaby
get an ~: 4 hear, heed 6 listen, take in 7 receive 8 discover, listen in, listen to 9 eavesdrop, get wind of 10 understand
Earhart, Amelia: 5 flier, flyer 7 aviator 8 aviatrix, explorer
earing: 4 rope
earl: 4 lord, male, peer, rank 5 noble, title 8 nobleman
ender: 3 dom
equivalent: 5 count
in German: 4 graf
Earl: 4 Butz, Grey, Wild 5 Cecil, Grant, Hines, Klugh, noble, Sande, title 6 Baring, Bostic, Dudley, Monroe, Scheib, Warren, Weaver, Wilson 7 Anthony, Averill, Scruggs 8 Campbell, Holliman 9 Blackwell 10 Sutherland
Earl __ Biggers: 4 Derr
Earl __ Hines: 5 Fatha
Earl __ tea: 4 Grey
earlap: 4 lobe 7 cap flap, hat part
Earle: 5 Combs, Hagen, Hyman, Steve
earless __: 4 seal 6 lizard
earlet: 6 tragus
Earl Grey: 3 tea
earlier: 3 ago, ere, yet 4 once, past 5 above, afore, ahead, older, prior 6 before, former 7 advance, one-time 8 foregone, formerly, previous, until now 9 a while ago, foregoing, preceding 10 beforehand, heretofore, previously
combining form: 4 fore- 6 proter- 7 protero-
prefix: 3 pre-, pro- 4 ante-
than: 3 ere 7 ahead of, prior to 10 previous to
earlier, the better, the: 4 ASAP, stat
earliest: 5 first, prime 6 maiden 7 initial, premier, primary 8 original, primeval 9 inceptive, primaeval, primitive, vestigial 10 primordial
combining form: 4 prot- 5 proto-
earlike projection: 5 pinna

__ Earl Jones: 5 James
Earl of __: 4 Avon 5 Essex
Earl of Avon: 4 Eden
Earl of Greystoke love: 4 Jane
early: 3 old, wee 5 ahead, young 6 prompt 7 advance, ancient, betimes, budding, forward, initial, morning, nascent, pioneer, too soon 8 germinal, immature, in the bud, original, primeval, punctual 9 beginning, embryonic, in advance, inceptive, premature, primaeval, primitive, unevolved 10 aboriginal, beforehand, in good time, precocious, primordial
early __: 4 bird, wood 5 riser 6 blight
early-__ system: 7 warning
Early: 4 Wynn 5 Jubal
Early __, early...: 5 to bed
Early Bird: 6 Comsat 9 satellite
early-blooming: 4 rath
Early Girl: 6 tomato
relative: 4 Roma 6 Big Boy 9 beefsteak, Better Boy, Quick Pick
Early in the Morning (1988 song)
artist: Robert Palmer
earmark: 3 tab, tag 4 mark, slot 5 stamp, trait 6 assign, devote 7 feature, insigne, quality, reserve 8 allocate, insignia, set apart, set aside 9 attribute, designate
have ~ of: 4 seem 8 resemble
earmarked: 7 special
earn: 3 get, net, win 4 draw, gain, make, rate, reap, take 5 bring, clear, fetch, gross, merit, score, yield 6 attain, come by, derive, effect, garner, gather, obtain, pick up, profit, return, secure, take in 7 achieve, acquire, bring in, collect, deserve, procure, realize, receive, support, warrant, work for, wrangle 8 pull down, take home 9 bring home, knock down, make money 10 have coming, qualify for
after taxes: 3 net 5 clear
a living: 4 live, work
homophone for ~: 3 ern, urn 4 erne
one's wings: 4 pass 5 cut it, train 6 make it 9 measure up 10 pass muster
earned: 3 due 4 owed 6 coming 7 fitting, merited 8 deserved, expected, rightful, suitable 9 justified 10 reasonable, sufficient
money ~: 8 receipts
earned __: 3 run 6 income 7 surplus
earned __ average: 3 run
__-earned: 4 well
earner: 6 worker 7 employe 8 employee, taxpayer
wage ~: 4 hand 5 prole 6 worker 7 employe 8 employee 9 jobholder
wage ~ cry: 4 TGIF
earnest: 4 avid, keen, pawn, warm 5 eager, staid, token 6 ardent, devout, fervid, hearty, infelt, intent, loving, pledge, urgent 7 decided, devoted, fervent, genuine, intense, promise, serious, sincere, weighty, zealous 8 diligent, resolute, security, sedulous, studious, vehement 9 heartfelt, important, strenuous, unfeigned 10 determined, meaningful, no-nonsense, passionate, purposeful, scrupulous, solicitous
begin in ~: 5 set to
in ~: 4 real 6 really
money of a sort: 4 bail
earnest __: 5 money
earnestly: 4 hard 6 keenly 8 for keeps, urgently 9 sincerely 10 thoroughly
earnestness: 4 will, zeal 5 ardor 6 fervor, spirit 7 loyalty, resolve 8 ambition, decision, devotion 9 sincerity
Earnhardt, Dale: 9 auto racer
milieu: 5 track
earnings: 3 pay 4 gain, gate, wage 5 lucre, wages, yield 6 income, payoff, profit, return, salary 7 revenue 8 proceeds, receipts 9 emolument, royalties
CD ~: 3 int. 8 interest
earnings __ share: 3 per
__-earnings ratio: 5 price
earn one's __: 5 spurs, wings
Earp: 5 Wyatt 6 Morgan, Virgil
ear-piercing: 4 loud 5 noisy 6 shrill 7 raucous
earring: 4 drop, hoop, stud 7 jewelry
kind of ~: 4 drop, loop, stud
like an ~: 6 clip-on, hooped
part: 4 wire
site: 4 lobe
Earrings of Madame de..., The (1953 film)
cast: Charles Boyer, Danielle Darrieux, Vittorio De Sica
ears: 4 corn 6 feeler 7 antenna
all ~: 4 rapt 5 alert 8 cautious, watchful 9 attentive, listening
animal with big ~: 4 hare 7 leveret
be all ~: 6 listen, perk up 9 eavesdrop
be up to one's: 4 teem 6 abound
easy on the ~: 4 soft 6 dulcet 7 lyrical, melodic, musical, tuneful 9 melodious
like ~: 5 lobed 6 lobate 7 lobated
like some dog ~: 4 alop 5 loppy 6 droopy
of the ~: 4 otic 5 aural 7 sensory 8 acoustic
prick up one's ~: 6 listen
rabbit ~: 6 aerial, dipole 7 antenna
spot between the ~: 4 nape
up to one's ~: 4 at it, busy 5 awash 6 hectic, tied up 7 swamped 8 bustling, immersed, occupied 9 engrossed 10 overloaded
use one's ~: 4 hear, heed, mind, obey 5 audit, catch, watch 6 attend, listen, tune in 7 hear out, monitor, observe, receive 8 hear tell, overhear, pick up on 9 eavesdrop 10 get a load of, give heed to, take advice, take notice
wet behind the ~: 4 naif 5 green, naive, young 6 callow, tender 8 immature
with eyes and ~ open: 4 wary
__ ears: 3 all 4 pig's 5 lamb's 6 rabbit
__ ears!: 5 I'm all
ears, CBer's: 5 radio
earshot: 5 range 7 hearing 9 listening
within ~: 4 near 7 audible 10 detectable
earsplitting: 4 loud 5 forte, harsh, noisy 6 shrill 7 blaring, blatant, booming, jarring, pealing, rackety, raucous, reboant, roaring 8 crashing, piercing, plangent, rumbling, sonorous, strident, turned up 9 big-voiced, clamorous, deafening 10 boisterous, resounding, stentorian, strepitous, thundering, uproarious, vociferous
earsplittingly: 4 loud 5 aloud, brash, noisy, vocal 6 brassy, strong 7 blaring, booming, intense, raucous, roaring 8 crashing, piercing 9 clamorous, deafening 10 blustering, boisterous, clangorous, loud-voiced, resounding, stentorian, thundering, uproarious, vociferous
earth: 3 sod 4 clay, dirt, lair, land, loam, marl, soil, turf 6 ground, nature 7 subsoil, topsoil 8 alluvium 9 undersoil 10 terra firma
cultivated ~: 5 tilth
depression: 6 graben
ender: 3 man, men, nut 4 born, ling, rise, star, work, worm 5 bound, light, mover, quake, shine 7 shaking
fine ~: 4 dust
in French: 5 terre
in Italian: 5 terra
in Latin: 5 terra
layer of ~: 4 turf
like rich ~: 5 loamy
like the ~ in a forest: 5 rooty
mound of ~: 4 berm 5 berme
mover: 3 hoe 5 dozer 6 dredge 9 bulldozer
rare ~: 5 metal 6 cerium, cesium, erbium 7 caesium, holmium, terbium, thulium, yttrium 8 europium, lutetium, samarium, scandium 9 neodymium, ytterbium 10 dysprosium, gadolinium, promethium 12 praseodymium
tone: 5 beige, brown, ocher, ochre, umber
wet ~: 3 mud
earth __: 3 art, god 4 sign, tone, wave 5 auger, color, lodge 6 almond, mother, pillar, tongue 7 goddess, science, station
__ earth: 4 rare 5 green, run to 6 Cassel, mother, rammed 7 fuller's
__-earth: 6 Middle
Earth: 3 orb 5 globe, world 6 planet, sphere 7 mankind 9 biosphere
atmosphere: 3 sky
bowels of the ~: 5 abyss
center: 4 core
combining form: 3 geo-
conscious org.: 3 EPA
crust part: 5 plate
end of the ~: 4 pole
envelope: 3 air 5 ether 6 aether
force: 4 one G
gap in ~ surface: 5 gulch, gully 6 canyon, ravine
goddess: 4 Gaea
heaven on ~: 4 Eden 6 utopia 7 Arcadia, Elysium 8 paradise 9 Shangri-la
inheritors: 4 meek
in the bowels of the ~: 4 deep
layer: 4 moho, sial, sima 5 crust 6 mantle
model: 3 map, orb 5 globe 6 sphere
most of the ~: 3 sea 5 ocean
nearest star to ~: 3 Sol, sun
neighbor: 4 Mars 5 Venus
not of this ~: 5 alien 6 cosmic 8 cosmical
of the ~: 5 gaean
on ~: 4 here 7 present
orbiter: 3 Mir 4 moon
returned to ~: 3 lit 4 alit
return to ~: 4 land 5 light 6 alight
science: 4 ecol. 7 ecology 9 geography 10 geophysics
-sky boundary: 3 hor. 7 horizon
surface: 4 land
Teutonic ~ goddess: 4 Erda
turning point: 4 axis
walk the ~: 4 last, live, stay 5 dwell, exist 6 occupy, reside, settle, thrive 7 breathe, subsist, survive
Earth __: 3 Day 5 Angel
Earth __ Are Easy: 5 Girls
Earth, __ & Fire: 4 Wind
Eartha: 4 Kitt
Earth Angel (song) artist: Crew-Cuts, Penguins
Earth author: Emile Zola
earthborn: 5 human 6 mortal 9 corporeal
earthen: 3 mud 4 clay, dirt
ender: 4 ware
earthenware: 5 crock 7 faience, pottery 8 ceramics, crockery 9 stoneware 10 terra cotta
Dutch: 4 delf 5 delft
Japanese ~: 4 raku
piece of ~: 3 jar, jug, pot 4 ewer, olla 5 crock, cruse, shard, sherd 6 bottle, carafe
__-earther: 4 flat
earthfall: 8 mudslide 9 avalanche, landslide, rockslide, snowslide
Earth Girls Are Easy (1989 film)
cast: Jim Carrey, Geena Davis, Jeff Goldblum, Damon Wayans
cat: 5 Bambi
Earth in the Balance author: 4 Gore
Earthlight author: Arthur C. Clarke
earthling: 3 man 5 human, woman 6 mortal, person
Earthlink: 3 ISP
earthly: 6 global, likely, mortal 7 mundane, secular, terrene, worldly 8 feasible, material, possible, probable, temporal 9 potential, practical 10 imaginable
Earthly Possessions author: Anne Tyler
earth measurement, science of: 7 geodesy
earthnut: 6 veggie 9 vegetable
earthquake: 4 jolt 5 quake, seism, shake, shock 6 tremor 7 temblor 8 upheaval 9 cataclysm 10 convulsion, disruption, macroseism, microseism, undulation
combining form: 5 -seism 6 seismo-
tremor: 5 L wave
earthquakes, science of: 10 seismology
earth-shaking: 9 momentous
not ~: 5 minor, petty 7 trivial
__ Earth, The: 4 Good
Earth, Wind & Fire
song: After the Love Has Gone (1979)
Boogie Wonderland (1979)
Got to Get You Into My Life (1978)
Let's Groove (1981)
September (1978)
Shining Star (1975)
Sing a Song (1975)
earthwork: 6 trench 7 foxhole, rampart
earthworm: 3 bug 6 insect
earthy: 3 raw 4 homy 5 basic, crude, funky, homey, lusty, salty 6 animal, clayey, coarse, folksy, ribald, robust, simple 7 clayish, natural 8 down home, indecent, off-color 9 elemental, practical, realistic, unrefined 10 indelicate, unromantic
color: 3 tan 4 ecru 5 brown 7 neutral
deposit: 4 marl, silt
pigment: 5 umber
'eart is, where the: 3 'ome
Earvin: 5 Magic 7 Johnson
earwax: 7 cerumen
earwig: 3 bug 4 pest 6 insect
ease: 3 ebb 4 calm, fall, help, rest, snap 5 abate, allay, let up, loose, peace, poise, quell, quiet, relax, salve, skill, slack, still, style, unzip 6 aplomb, lessen, loosen, luxury, pacify, plenty, relent, relief, remedy, repose, smooth, soften, soothe, temper 7 assuage, comfort, fluency, further, leisure, lighten, mollify, redress, relieve, slacken, subside, tail off 8 calmness, decrease, dispatch, expedite, facility, fluidity, free time, good life, go slowly, humanize, idleness, mitigate, moderate, palliate, pleasure, presence, security, serenity, simplify, unburden 9 affluence, alleviate, composure, dexterity, disburden, idle hours, passivity, quietness, readiness, sugar-coat, untighten, untrouble, well-being 10 adroitness, affability, ameliorate, bed of roses, confidence, efficiency, expertness, facileness, facilitate, inac-

tivity, legibility, liberalize, nimbleness, prosperity, quiescence, recreation, relaxation, simplicity, smoothness
at ~: **4** cool, rest **5** comfy, loose, relax, staid, stoic **6** low-key, mellow, placid, secure, sedate, serene **7** content, lolling, relaxed, resting, stoical **8** carefree, composed, laid-back, lounging, relaxing, tranquil **9** collected, impassive, temperate, unanxious, unexcited, unruffled **10** knock it off, nonchalant, unagitated, unbothered, unstressed, untroubled
away (from): **4** wean
epitome of ~: **3** ABC, pie
ill at ~: **4** edgy **5** antsy, itchy, jumpy, tense **6** on edge, uneasy **7** abashed, anxious, awkward, jittery, keyed up, nervous, restive, uptight **8** agitated, restless, skittish, troubled **9** concerned, disturbed, excitable, faltering, unrelaxed, unsettled **10** disquieted, high-strung, out of place, suspicious
off: **3** die, ebb **4** lull, rest, slow, wane **5** abate, let up, loose, relax, slack **6** loosen, relent, unwind, weaken **7** slacken **8** head away, moderate
out: **4** part **8** withdraw
put at ~: **5** allay **6** assure **7** satisfy
up: **8** head away
ease __: **3** off, out
__ ease: **5** ill at
__-ease: **6** heart's
easeful: **4** calm **5** quiet **6** placid **7** relaxed, restful **8** peaceful, pleasant, pleasing, relaxing, tranquil **9** agreeable, unruffled **10** untroubled
easel: **5** stand **6** tripod
display: **3** art **6** canvas, sketch **7** collage, picture **8** painting
part: **3** leg
easement: **4** balm, lull **6** relief, remedy, solace **7** anodyne, comfort **9** emollient **10** mitigation, palliative
Ease On Down the __: **4** Road
easier __ than done: **4** said
Easier Said Than Done (1963 song)
artist: Essex
easily: **4** well **5** by far **6** really, simply, surely **7** clearly, handily, lightly, plainly, readily **8** for a fact, very well **9** decidedly, doubtless, going away, hands down, leisurely, naturally **10** definitely, far and away, positively, swimmingly, undeniably
easiness: **8** lenience, optimism **10** simplicity
easing: **5** letup **7** anodyne, respite **8** soothing **9** abatement, assuasive, calmative, relieving, remission, softening **10** mitigation, palliation
east: **2** pt. **5** point **8** dawnward **9** direction
ender: **3** ern **4** ward **5** bound, wards
god of the ~ wind: **5** Eurus
in French: **3** est
in Spanish: **4** este
opposite: **4** west
starter: **3** Mid **5** North, south
East: **5** river **6** Orient
bidder after ~: **5** South
much of the ~: **4** Asia
River locale: **3** NYC **7** New York
East __: **3** End **4** Asia, Goth, Side **5** Coast, Lynne, River, Timor **6** Anglia, Bengal, Berlin, Indies, Punjab **7** Germany
East __ Company: **5** India
East-__ relations: **4** West
__ East: **3** Big, Far **4** down, Near **6** Middle
__ East Africa: **6** German **7** Belgian, British, Italian
East Asian
language: **3** Lao
river: **4** Amur
Eastbourne: **4** city, town
locale: **6** Sussex **7** England
East Brunswick: **4** city, town
locale: **9** New Jersey
east by __: **5** north, south
East Carolina
athletes: **7** Pirates
locale: **10** Greenville
East Chicago: **4** city, town
locale: **7** Indiana
East China: **3** sea
island: **4** Mazu **5** Matsu **6** Kiushu, Kyushu
locale: **5** China, Japan **6** Taiwan **10** South Korea
Eastend: **4** city, town
locale: **6** Canada
__-easter: **4** down
Easter: **4** isle **5** Pasch **6** island **7** holy day, Rapa Nui
dish: **3** ham **4** lamb
ender: **4** tide
event: **6** parade
need: **3** dye **4** eggs **6** basket
preceder: **4** Lent
wear: **6** bonnet, finery
Easter __: **3** egg **4** lily **5** bunny, daisy, Seals **6** bonnet, cactus, candle, Island, Monday, Parade, Sunday
Easter Island: **7** Rapa Nui
explorer: **9** Heyerdahl
head: **5** stela
owner: **5** Chile
easterly starter: **5** north
eastern: **8** Oriental **9** Levantine
ender: **4** most
starter: **5** north, south
Eastern __: **4** rite, time **5** Ghats, Hindi, shore, Slavs **6** Church, Empire, Europe, Thrace **7** Sudanic
__ Eastern: **3** Far **4** Near **6** Middle
Eastern Church
bishop: **6** exarch
member: **5** Uniat **6** Uniate
title: **4** abba
Eastern Daylight __: **4** Time
eastern lowland __: **7** gorilla
Eastern Michigan
athletes: **6** Eagles
conference: **3** MAC
locale: **9** Ypsilanti
Eastern Standard __: **4** Time
Eastern title: **3** aga **4** agha, amir, emir **5** ameer, emeer
Easter Oratorio composer: **4** Bach
Easter Parade (1948 film)
cast: Fred Astaire, Judy Garland, Peter Lawford
director: Charles Walters
Easter Parade composer: **6** Berlin
easter starter: **3** nor
East German secret police: **5** Stasi
East Greenland __: **7** current
East Haven: **4** city, town
locale: **4** Conn.
East Hill: **4** city, town
locale: **10** Washington
East India Company
headquarters: **6** Bombay
product: **5** spice
__ East India Company: **5** Dutch
East Indian: **5** Hindu **6** Hindoo
boat: **5** oolak
cedar: **6** deodar **7** deodara
chief: **4** raja
fruit: **5** cubeb **10** mangosteen
mast wood: **4** poon
sailor: **6** lascar **7** lashkar
shrub: **4** sunn
stew: **4** dahl
tree: **4** nipa **5** rohan
East Indian __: **5** lotus **6** walnut
East Indies: **7** islands
__ East Indies: **5** Dutch
Eastlake: **4** city, town
locale: **4** Ohio
East Lake: **4** city, town
locale: **7** Florida
East Lansing: **4** city, town
athletes: **8** Spartans
locale: **8** Michigan
school: **3** MSU
East Lyme: **4** city, town
Locale: **4** Conn.
Eastman: **3** Max **6** George
Eastman __: **5** Kodak
East Meadow: **4** city, town
locale: **7** New York
East Millcreek: **4** city, town
locale: **4** Utah
East of Eden: **4** film **5** novel
author: John Steinbeck
cast: James Dean, Julie Harris, Burl Ives, Raymond Massey, Jo Van Fleet
character: **3** Cal, Lee **4** Abra, Adam, Ames, Aron, Faye, Liza, Will **5** Bacon, Caleb, Cathy, Trask **6** Samuel **7** Charles **8** Hamilton
director: Elia Kazan
Easton: **4** city, town **6** Sheena
athletes: **8** Leopards
locale: **4** Penn.
school: **9** Lafayette
Easton, Sheena
homeland: Scotland
real last name: Orr
song: For Your Eyes Only (1981)
The Lover in Me (1988)
Morning Train (1981)
Strut (1984)
Sugar Walls (1985)
Telefone (1983)
We've Got Tonight (1983)
East Orange: **4** city, town
locale: **9** New Jersey
East Point: **4** city, town
locale: **7** Georgia
Eastpointe: **4** city, town
locale: **8** Michigan
East Ridge: **4** city, town
locale: **9** Tennessee
East River author: Sholem Asch
East Siberian: **3** sea
locale: **6** Russia
__ East Side: **5** Lower, Upper
East St. Louis: **4** city, town
locale: **8** Illinois
East Timor: **6** nation **7** country
capital: **4** Dili
eastward starter: **5** north, south
Eastwood, Clint: **5** actor **8** director
costar: **5** Locke
film: Absolute Power (1997)
Any Which Way You Can (1980)
The Beguiled (1970)
Bird (1988)
The Bridges of Madison County (1995)
Bronco Billy (1980)
City Heat (1984)
Coogan's Bluff (1968)
The Dead Pool (1988)
Dirty Harry (1972)
The Eiger Sanction (1975)
The Enforcer (1976)
Escape From Alcatraz (1979)
Every Which Way But Loose (1978)
Fistful of Dollars (1964)
For a Few Dollars More (1966)
The Gauntlet (1977)
The Good, the Bad, and the Ugly (1966)
Hang 'em High (1968)
Heartbreak Ridge (1986)
High Plains Drifter (1973)
Honkytonk Man (1982)
In the Line of Fire (1993)
Kelly's Heroes (1970)
Magnum Force (1973)
Midnight in the Garden of Good and Evil (1997)
The Outlaw Josey Wales (1976)
Paint Your Wagon (1969)
Pale Rider (1985)
A Perfect World (1993)
Pink Cadillac (1989)
Play Misty for Me (1971)
Space Cowboys (2000)
Sudden Impact (1983)
Thunderbolt and Lightfoot (1974)
True Crime (1999)
Two Mules for Sister Sara (1970)
Unforgiven (1992, AA)
Where Eagles Dare (1969)
White Hunter, Black Heart (1990)
TV: Rawhide
easy: **3** lax **4** calm, idly, kind, mild, naif, soft **5** a snap, basic, clear, comfy, cushy, handy, light, loose, naive, plain, quiet **6** a cinch, benign, casual, doable, docile, facile, fluent, gentle, kindly, serene, simple, smooth **7** affable, amiable, a picnic, clement, dupable, languid, lenient, natural, no sweat, obvious, relaxed, ruthful, sparing **8** amenable, apparent, carefree, duck soup, flexible, gullable, gullible, informal, laid-back, manifest, merciful, no bother, obedient, obliging, outgoing, painless, peaceful, placable, pleasant, readable, relaxing, sociable, tolerant, tranquil, trusting, unstrict, untaxing, workable, yielding **9** a pushover, assuasive, compliant, contented, deludable, forgiving, indulgent, leisurely, luxurious, no problem, no trouble, temperate, tractable, uncomplex, unextreme, unhurried, unworried **10** accessible, child's play, deceivable, effortless, elementary, forbearing, manageable, permissive, submissive, unexacting, unhardened, untroubled
breathe ~: **5** relax
ender: **5** going
free and ~: **3** lax **5** homey, loose **6** breezy, casual, folksy, mellow, simple **7** lenient, patient, relaxed **8** everyday, informal, laid back, outgoing, tolerant **9** indulgent **10** forbearing, off-the-cuff, open-minded, permissive
go ~: **5** let up, relax **10** take it slow
going ~: **3** lax **4** mild, soft **6** benign, gentle, humane **7** clement, lenient, liberal, sparing **8** allowing, excusing, merciful, obliging, tolerant, yielding **9** condoning, forgiving, indulgent, pampering, pardoning **10** charitable, permissive
go ~ on: **4** pity **5** spare **6** relent **7** absolve, release
in Portuguese: **5** facil
make ~: **8** simplify
mark: **3** sap **4** butt, dupe, goat, lamb, simp, tool **5** chump, patsy, softy **6** pigeon, softie, sucker, victim **8** pushover
on the ears: **4** soft **6** dulcet **7** lyrical, melodic, musical, tuneful **9** melodious
on the eyes: **4** fair **6** lavish, lovely **8** dazzling, gorgeous, handsome, imposing, stunning **9** beautiful, exquisite, ravishing, sumptuous **10** attractive
partner: **4** free, nice
shot: **4** dunk **5** gimme, lay up, tap in
something ~: **4** snap **5** cinch **6** picnic

starter: 5 speak
take it ~: 3 sit 4 idle, laze, loaf, lull, rest 5 coast, relax, slide, unlax 6 lounge, repose, rest up, unwind 9 luxuriate
taking it ~: 5 still 6 at rest 8 inactive, unmoving 10 motionless
task: 4 plum, snap 5 cinch 6 breeze, picnic 8 cakewalk, duck soup, sinecure 10 child's play
to steer: 3 yar 4 yare
to teach: 3 apt 5 quick, sharp
to understand: 5 clear, exact, lucid, overt, sharp, stark, vivid 6 direct, marked, simple, square 7 audible, crystal, evident, graphic, legible, logical, precise, visible 8 apparent, coherent, distinct, explicit, knowable, manifest, palpable, readable 9 graspable, unclouded, unimpeded 10 observable, pronounced, spelled out, unarguable, unhampered, unhindered
to use: 6 nearby, wieldy 7 close by 8 portable 10 accessible, convenient, time-saving
undertaking: 4 snap 5 cinch 6 breeze 8 duck soup, kid stuff 9 no trouble 10 child's play
win: 4 romp, rout 5 waltz
easy __: 5 as ABC, as pie, chair, money
easy __, easy go: 4 come
easy-__: 4 care 5 going
__ easy: 4 over 7 breathe
Easy: 6 Street 7 Rollins
Easy __: 4 Aces 5 Lover, Rider, to Wed 6 Living, Street
Easy __ Hard: 4 to Be
Easy __ it!: 4 does
Easy-__: 3 Off
__ Easy: 5 It's So, Nice 'N'
Easy (1977 song) artist: Commodores
Easy Aces: 9 radio show
easy as __: 3 ABC, pie
Easy Come, Easy Go (1967 film)
cast: Elsa Lanchester, Elvis Presley, Pat Priest
Easy Come, Easy Go (1970 song)
artist: Bobby Sherman
easygoing: 3 lax 4 calm, cool, kind, mild, soft 5 light, loose, slack, type B 6 breezy, casual, docile, genial, gentle, kindly, low-key, placid, serene 7 clement, equable, lenient, offhand, patient, relaxed, ruthful, sparing 8 carefree, composed, familiar, fireside, flexible, informal, laid-back, listless, merciful, placable, tolerant, unstrict 9 adaptable, assuasive, collected, compliant, forgiving, hang-loose, indulgent, unhurried 10 complacent, forbearing, insouciant, nonchalant, permissive, personable, unaffected, unagitated, unbothered, uncritical, unexacting, unhardened
not ~: 5 type A
easygoingness: 5 mercy 6 lenity 8 clemency, lenience, mildness, softness, sympathy 9 tolerance 10 compassion, gentleness, indulgence, moderation, tenderness, toleration
Easy Living (1937 film)
cast: Edward Arnold, Jean Arthur, Ray Milland
director: Mitchell Leisen
Easy Living (1949 film)
cast: Lucille Ball, Victor Mature, Lizabeth Scott
Easy Lover (1984 song)
artist: Phil Collins, Philip Bailey
easy on the __: 4 eyes
__ Easy Pieces: 4 Five
Easy Rider (1969 film)
cast: Karen Black, Peter Fonda, Dennis Hopper, Jack Nicholson
director: Dennis Hopper
Easy Street
actor: 4 Elam
on ~: 4 rich 5 flush 6 loaded, monied 7 moneyed, wealthy, well-off 8 affluent, in clover, well-to-do 9 well-fixed 10 in the dough, in the money, privileged, propertied, well-heeled
__ Easy, The: 3 Big
Easy to Be Hard (1969 song) artist: Three Dog Night
Easy to Be Hard musical: 4 Hair
Easy to Love (1953 film)
cast: Van Johnson, Tony Martin, Esther Williams
director: Charles Walters
Easy to Love composer: 6 Porter
Easy to Wed (1946 film)
cast: Lucille Ball, Van Johnson, Esther Williams, Keenan Wynn
director: Edward Buzzell
eat: 3 irk, rot, sup 4 bolt, chew, dine, down, gnaw, gulp, have, nosh, rust, take, wolf 5 annoy, basis, decay, dig in, drain, erode, feast, gorge, graze, lunch, munch, scarf, snack, taste, touch, use up, waste, worry 6 absorb, bother, brunch, chew on, devour, digest, dine on, feed on, gobble, guzzle, incept, ingest, inhale, live on, nibble, nosh on, picnic, pig out, prey on, sample, take in, tuck in 7 chomp on, consume, corrode, crumble, do lunch, exhaust, feast on, munch on, partake, put away, scarf up, snack on, swallow 8 bolt down, chow down, dispatch, dissolve, fill up on, gobble up, nibble on, pack away, pack it in, shovel in, squander, take food, tuck away, wear away, wolf down 9 breakfast, decompose, dissipate, feast upon, finish off, have a bite, have a meal, masticate, partake of, polish off, scarf down 10 break bread, gormandize, have dinner, take tiffin
at: 3 bug 4 gnaw, rust 5 annoy, erode, get to, worry 6 bother, gnaw on, nibble 7 corrode
away: 4 gnaw, rust 5 erode, waste 7 corrode 9 undermine
bite to ~: 4 nosh 5 snack
don't ~: 4 fast 7 abstain 8 go hungry
fit to ~: 4 good 5 tasty 6 edible
get ready to ~: 4 wash
good to ~: 4 rich 5 spicy, yummy 6 delish, savory, toothy 8 heavenly, luscious 9 delicious, flavorful, palatable, succulent, toothsome 10 appetizing, delectable
grass: 4 feed 5 graze
hungrily: 4 wolf
in German: 5 essen
like a bird: 4 peck, pick
like a horse: 5 chomp, gorge 10 gormandize
more sensibly: 4 diet
noisily: 4 gnaw 5 chomp, munch, slurp 6 crunch
not fit to ~: 3 bad 4 sour 5 fetid, yucky, yukky 6 putrid, rotten, turned 7 spoiled, tainted 8 inedible 10 disgusting
one's heart out: 4 fret, mope 5 mourn 6 grieve, lament, sorrow
one's words: 6 grovel, recant 7 retract 9 back-pedal
quickly: 4 bolt 5 scarf 6 devour, inhale 7 scarf up 8 wolf down 9 scarf down
ready to ~: 4 done 6 cooked
something to ~: 4 meal 5 lunch
through: 9 penetrate
too much: 5 stuff
up: 3 use 5 dig in, enjoy 6 devour, gobble, relish 7 consume, deplete, exhaust, feast on, revel in 9 delight in, finish off, luxuriate, polish off, scarf down
up the road: 4 zoom
well: 4 dine 5 feast
what you ~: 4 diet, fare, food 6 intake 7 aliment, edibles, regimen 8 victuals 9 nutriment 10 sustenance
eat __: 4 away, crow, into
eat __ a bird: 4 like
eat __ eaten: 4 or be
eat __ house and home: 5 out of
eat __ off the hog: 4 high
eat __ of one's hand: 3 out
eat __ pie: 6 humble
eatables: 4 fare 6 viands 7 aliment 8 victuals 9 provender 10 provisions, sustenance
eat-all: 8 omnivore
eat and __: 3 run
Eat at __: 4 Joe's
__ Eat Cake: 5 Let 'em
Eat, drink __ merry...: 5 and be
__-eaten: 4 moth, worm
eater: 5 diner 6 nosher 7 epicure, glutton, gobbler, luncher, nibbler, snacker 8 consumer, devourer, gourmand, predator
combining form: 4 -phag, -vore 5 -phage
selective ~: 3 cat 5 vegan 6 dieter
starter: 3 ant 4 beef, seed, toad 5 honey
__-eater: 3 bee 4 fire 5 lotus
__ Eaters: 4 Odor
__ Eaters, The: 4 Bean 6 Potato
__ Eater, The: 7 Biscuit, Pumpkin
eatery: 4 café 5 diner 6 bistro 7 cabaret 9 brasserie, cafeteria, hash house, lunchroom, trattoria 10 restaurant
chain ~: 3 KFC 4 HoJo, IHOP 5 Arby's 8 Pizza Hut 9 Applebee's, McDonald's, Roy Rogers 10 Burger King, TGI Friday's
listing: 4 menu
lure: 5 aroma
NYC ~: 4 deli 6 Lutèce, Sardi's 7 Elaine's
order: 3 BLT
eat high __ the hog: 3 off
eating: 10 at the table
away: 7 erosion, wearing 8 decrease 9 attrition, corrosion
combining form: 4 phag- 5 phago-, -phagy 6 -phagia, -vorous 7 -phagous
good ~: 7 cuisine 10 gastronomy
place: 5 table
utensil: 4 fork 5 spoon, spork
__ Eating Gilbert Grape?: 5 What's
Eating Raoul (1982 film)
cast: Paul Bartel, Robert Beltran, Mary Woronov
Eat It (1984 song) artist: Weird Al Yankovic
eat like __: 5 a bird
Eaton: 7 Shirley
eat one's __: 4 fill 5 words
eat one's __ out: 5 heart
eat out of __ and home: 5 house
eat out of one's __: 4 hand
eats: 4 chow, fare, food, grub, meal 5 board, snack 7 aliment, goodies 8 victuals 9 provender 10 provisions
Eat your broccoli __ dessert!: 4 or no
eau __: 5 de vie
Eau Claire: 4 city, town
locale: 9 Wisconsin
eau de __: 3 vie 7 Cologne, Javelle
eau de Cologne: 5 scent 7 perfume
eau de vie: 5 drink 8 beverage
eave: 8 overhang 10 projection
adornment: 6 icicle
locale: 4 roof
eave __: 5 spout 6 trough
eavesdrop: 3 bug, pry, spy, tap 4 hear 5 snoop 6 listen 7 monitor, wiretap 8 listen in, overhear 9 bend an ear
eavesdropper: 5 snoop, yenta 6 gossip 7 meddler 8 busybody, quidnunc 9 buttinsky 10 nosy Parker
what an ~ gets: 6 earful
eavesdropping: 4 nosy 5 nosey
eaves ender: 4 drop 7 dropper
eaves-trough: 4 duct 5 chute, drain 6 groove, gutter, sluice, trough
E.B.: 5 White
Eban: 4 Abba
Ébano: 4 city, town
locale: 6 Mexico
ebb: 3 die, lag 4 bate, drop, ease, fade, fall, flag, lull, sink, tide, wane, wilt 5 abate, decay, go out, let up, relax 6 die out, ease up, go down, lessen, recede, reflux, relent, shrink, waning 7 decline, die down, drop off, dwindle, ease off, fall off, low tide, outflow, outflux, regress, retreat, slacken, subside, tail off 8 backflow, contract, decrease, diminish, drop back, fade away, fall away, fall back, flagging, flow away, flow back, languish, low water, moderate, peter out, slack off, twilight, withdraw 9 abatement, disappear, dwindling, lessening, recession, refluence, remission, retrocede 10 diminution, fading away, regression, slackening, withdrawal
and flow: 4 flux, tide, wash 5 swing 6 billow 7 current 9 fluctuate, oscillate
lowest ~: 5 nadir
opposite: 4 flow
ebb __: 4 tide
__ ebb: 5 at low
Ebb: 4 Fred
Ebbets Field great: 5 Reese 6 Hodges 7 Furillo 8 Newcombe, Robinson 10 Campanella
ebbing: 7 decline 9 on the wane, remission
Ebb Tide (1965 song) artist: Righteous Brothers
Ebel: 5 watch
alternative: 4 Rado 5 Casio, Elgin, Lorus, Omega, Rolex, Seiko, Timex 6 Bulova, Fossil, Movado, Pulsar, Swatch 7 Citizen 8 Longines, Tag Heuer, Tourneau
Ebenezer: 7 Scrooge
exclamation: 3 bah
partner: 5 Jacob 6 Marley
Eberhard-Faber: 6 pencil
part: 5 point 6 eraser
Eberhart, Richard: 6 writer
Eberle: 3 Ray
Eberly: 3 Bob
Eber, son of: 5 Peleg
Ebert: 5 rater, Roger 9 Friedrich
emulate ~: 4 rate
Ebetsu: 4 city, town
locale: 5 Japan
Ebina: 4 city, town
locale: 5 Japan
Eboli: 4 city, town
locale: 5 Italy
Eboli (1979 film)
cast: Irene Papas, Gian Maria Volonté
ebon: 3 jet 4 dark 5 black, sable 9 coal-black, unlighted
ebonize: 5 shade 6 darken, smudge 7 blacken
ebony: 4 dark, tree 5 black, color 8 hardwood, jet-black 9 coal-black
relative: 3 jet 4 inky, onyx 5 raven, sable 14 sooty. persimmon
Ebony: 3 mag 8 magazine

rival: 3 Jet 7 Essence
Ebony and Ivory (1982 song)
artist: Paul McCartney, Stevie Wonder
Ebony Eyes (1961 song) artist: Everly Brothers
Ebony Tower, The author: John Fowles
Ebro: 3 río 5 river
locale: 5 Spain 6 Aragón
__ E. Brown: 3 Joe
Ebsen, Buddy: 5 actor
film: Breakfast at Tiffany's (1961) Davy Crockett... (1955)
TV: Barnaby Jones, The Beverly Hillbillies
ebullience: 3 joy, zip 4 zest 5 bliss 6 gaiety, gayety 7 delight, ecstasy, elation, rapture 8 buoyance, buoyancy, euphoria, felicity, vitality, vivacity 9 agitation, animation, happiness 10 enthusiasm, excitement, exuberance, exuberancy, friskiness, liveliness
ebullient: 4 agog 5 sunny, zippy 6 bouncy, elated, hearty, yeasty 7 chipper, excited, gushing, zestful 8 animated, effusive 9 explosive, exuberant, vivacious
be ~: 7 enthuse
Eb wife: 3 Flo
__ ec: 4 home
EC
member: 3 Den., Eng., Ger., Nor. 4 Ital.
part of ~: 3 Eur.
E.C.: 5 Segar 7 Bentley
écarté: 4 game 8 card game
E casta al par di neve! singer: 5 Tonio
Ecatepec: 4 city, town
locale: 6 Mexico
ecce: 6 behold
ecce __: 4 homo 6 signum
Ecce Homo painter: 5 Grosz
eccentric: 3 odd 4 card, coot, eery, geek, kook, luny, zany 5 balmy, batty, crank, dippy, dotty, eerie, flaky, gonzo, kooky, loony, loopy, nutty, outré, potty, queer, wacko, wacky, weird, wiggy 6 atypic, codger, far-out, flakey, freaky, fruity, galoot, geezer, kookie, looney, quaint, quirky, weirdo, whacky 7 bizarre, deviant, erratic, galloot, oddball, offbeat, strange, touched, unusual 8 aberrant, abnormal, atypical, freakish, original, peculiar, singular, uncommon 9 anomalous, character, crotchety, divergent, fantastic, irregular, laughable, off-center, queer duck, quizzical, unnatural, unscrewed, vagarious, whimsical 10 capricious, off-the-wall, outlandish, unbalanced, unorthodox
Eccentricities of a Nightingale, The author: Tennessee Williams
eccentricity: 3 tic 4 kink 5 quirk 6 foible, oddity 7 anomaly, oddness 8 crotchet 9 mannerism
Eccles: 4 city, town
locale: 7 England
ecclesia: 5 synod 6 church 7 council 8 assembly
Ecclesiastes preceder: 8 Proverbs
ecclesiastic: 4 abbé 5 abbot, padre, prior, vicar 6 bishop, cleric, father, parson, pastor, priest 8 clerical, minister, preacher
ecclesiastical: 4 holy 5 pious 8 churchly, clerical, hieratic, pastoral 9 religious
adjective: 5 papal
assembly: 5 synod
deg.: 3 Th.D.
district: 3 see 7 diocese, prelacy 9 bishopric 10 episcopacy
headdress: 5 miter
law: 5 canon
office: 6 curacy
title: 3 rev. 4 msgr. 5 Rt. Rev.
wear: 5 amice, orale, pilei
see also church
ecclesiastical __: 5 court 7 society
ecclesiastics: 6 clergy
Eccles, John: 8 Nobelist
ecdysis: 7 molting
ECG: 4 test 5 chart
concern: 5 heart
user: 2 MD 4 hosp.
échappé: 4 leap
Echegaray, José: 6 writer 8 Nobelist
echelon: 4 rank, tier 5 class, grade, level, order 7 ranking 8 position
__ echelon: 3 top 4 rear 7 forward
echelons: 9 hierarchy
echidna: 6 animal, mammal
feature: 5 spine
food: 3 ant
Echidna, daughter of: 6 Sphinx
echinoderm: 9 sea urchin
echo: 3 ape 4 copy, ring, roll 5 mimic, recur, sound 6 answer, bounce, do like, go like, mirror, parrot, repeat 7 imitate, iterate, rebound, recount, reflect, resound, run over, thunder, vibrate 8 imitator, make like, parallel, reaction, response 9 duplicate, imitation, parroting, reiterate, reproduce 10 bounce back, reflection, repetition
area: 5 cañon, gorge 6 canyon, valley
ender: 4 gram 5 virus 8 location 10 cardiogram
echo __: 7 chamber
Echo: 3 car 4 auto 5 nymph, oread 6 Toyota 10 automobile
daughter of ~: 4 lynx
lover of ~: 3 Pan
echoer: 5 mimic 6 parrot, yes-man 7 copycat
Echoes author: Maeve Binchy
echoic: 9 emulative, imitative 10 resounding
Echoi composer: 4 Foss
echoing: 8 resonant
echolocation device: 5 sonar
Echo's Bones author: Samuel Beckett
Eckerd competitor: 3 CVS 4 Osco 7 Rite-Aid 8 Walgreen
Eckhart: 8 Johannes
Eckstine: 5 Billy
éclair: 4 cake 6 pastry 7 dessert
emporium: 6 bakery
éclat: 4 dash, fame, pomp 5 flair, glory, kudos 6 dazzle, praise, renown, repute 7 acclaim, fanfare, success 8 applause, eminence, plaudits, prestige, splendor 9 celebrity 10 brilliance
eclectic: 8 rarefied
eclipse: 3 cap, top 4 hide, veil 5 cover, outdo 6 exceed, shadow, show up 7 becloud, blot out, obscure, surpass 8 outshine, outstrip, outweigh 9 adumbrate, darkening, shadowing, transcend 10 extinguish, overshadow, put to shame, tower above
feature: 5 umbra 6 corona
maybe: 4 omen
__ eclipse: 5 lunar, solar, total 7 annular
Eclipse: 3 car 4 auto 10 Mitsubishi
eclipsed: 5 inner 6 hidden, unseen, veiled 7 cloaked, clouded, covered 8 shielded, shrouded 9 concealed, disguised, incognito, out of view, unexposed 10 cloistered, tucked away, undercover
eclogue: 4 idyl 5 idyll, verse 8 pastoral
Eclogues
character: 4 Amor 5 Delia
ecodisaster: 5 spill
eco-friendly, be: 5 reuse
école: 6 French, school
attender: 5 élève
kin: 5 lycée
session: 5 lecon 6 classe
__ école: 5 haute
École __ Beaux-Arts: 3 des
ecol. no-no: 3 CFC
ecological: 5 green
adjective: 5 seral
grouping: 5 biome, biota
hazard: 5 radon
ecology: 7 science 9 bionomics
concern: 3 air 5 ozone, water
org.: 3 EPA
practice ~: 5 reuse
Econoline: 3 van 4 Ford
Econo Lodge: 5 motel
alternative: 7 Days Inn 9 Ramada Inn 10 Comfort Inn, Hampton Inn, Holiday Inn, Quality Inn, Red Roof Inn, Travelodge
economic: 6 fiscal 8 monetary 9 budgetary, financial, pecuniary 10 commercial, industrial, mercantile
decline: 4 bust 5 slump 9 recession 10 depression
global ~ grp.: 3 WTO
prefix: 5 socio
rise: 4 boom 5 spurt 6 growth, upturn 7 upsurge, upswing 10 prosperity
stat: 3 CPI, GDP, GNP 5 index
economic __: 4 good, rent 5 cycle, model 6 strike 7 geology
economical: 3 low 5 chary, cheap, spare 6 frugal, modest, on sale, stingy 7 bargain, cut-rate, low-cost, prudent, sparing, thrifty 8 a good buy, moderate, uncostly, ungiving 9 dirt cheap, efficient, half-price, low-priced, penny-wise, penurious, practical, provident, scrimping 10 avaricious, dime a dozen, marked down, methodical, prudential, reasonable, time-saving, unwasteful, work-saving
be ~: 5 reuse
not ~: 8 wasteful
economics: 7 banking, finance, science 10 Wall Street
prefix for ~: 5 macro, micro
__ economics: 3 new 4 home 6 social 7 welfare
economize: 4 save 5 skimp, stint 6 scrape, scrimp 7 cut down, lay away 8 conserve 9 save money 10 cut corners, underspend
economy: 4 size 6 saving, thrift 8 prudence 9 frugality, restraint, scrimping 10 efficiency
class: 5 coach
size: 3 big 5 jumbo, large
__ economy: 5 mixed, token 7 planned
ecophobe fear: 4 home
__ e Core: 5 Anema
eco-rich: 8 abundant
écossaise: 5 dance
ecosystem part: 5 fauna, flora
Ecotrin alternative: 3 APF 4 Cope 5 Advil, Aleve, Bayer 6 Anacin, Datril, Motrin 7 Tylenol 8 Bufferin, Excedrin, St. Joseph, Vanquish 9 Ascriptin
Eco, Umberto: 6 writer 7 Italian
work: Apocalypse Postponed
Baudolino
Foucault's Pendulum
Il nome della rosa
Il pendolo di Foucault
The Island of the Day Before
The Limits of Interpretation
Misreadings
The Name of the Rose
A Theory of Semiotics
__ E. Coyote: 4 Wile
Ecrins: 4 peak 5 mount 8 mountain
locale: 4 Alps 6 Europe, France
ecru: 3 tan 5 beige, brown, color 6 suntan 7 neutral 8 eggshell 10 light brown
relative: 3 bay, dun, tan 4 bole, fawn, foxy, nude, seal 5 amber, beige, camel, cocoa, hazel, khaki, mocha, sepia, tawny, umber 6 auburn, bister, bistre, bronze, coffee, copper, ginger, russet, sienna, sorrel, suntan, walnut 7 biscuit, caramel, dogwood 8 chestnut, cinnamon, mahogany 9 butternut, chocolate
ecstasy: 3 joy 5 bliss 6 heaven, raptus, trance 7 delight, elation, emotion, passion, rapture 8 delirium, euphoria, felicity, lyricism, paradise 9 happiness 10 ebullience, exaltation, joyfulness
opposite: 5 agony
ecstatic: 4 glad, high, rapt, wild 5 happy, merry 6 blithe, cheery, elated, jovial, joyful, joyous, upbeat 7 gleeful, glowing, pleased, radiant, tickled 8 beatific, blissful, cheerful, euphoric, exultant, floating, jubilant, mirthful, thrilled 9 delighted, delirious, emotional, gladdened, overjoyed, rapturous, rejoicing, rhapsodic, very happy 10 enraptured, flying high
exclamation: 5 whoop, zowie
make ~: 5 elate, liven 6 lift up, please, thrill 7 delight, elevate, gladden, hearten, satisfy 9 enrapture, transport 10 exhilarate
wax ~: 4 rave
ecto- ending: 5 -plasm
ectomorphic: 4 slim
ecto- opposite: 4 endo, ento
ectype: 3 fax 4 copy, dupe 5 clone, ditto, mimeo, repro, xerox 6 carbon 7 replica, reprint, tracing 8 likeness 9 duplicate, facsimile, look-alike, photocopy, Photostat 10 mimeograph, transcript 12 reproduction
ecu: 5 money
Ecuador: 6 nation 7 country
bay: 5 Manta
bird: 4 yeni
capital: 5 Quito
city: 5 Manta, Quito 6 Ambato, Cuenca 7 Machala, Milagro 9 Guayaquil 10 Portoviejo
gulf: 9 Guayaquil
Indian: 6 Jivaro
islands: 9 Galápagos
language: 6 Jivaro
money: 5 sucre 6 condor
mountain: 10 Chimborazo
neighbor: 4 Peru 8 Colombia
org.: 3 OAS
river: 4 Napo
tennis pro: 6 Segura
volcano: 6 Sangay 8 Cotopaxi
writer: 5 Adoum 8 Montalvo
see also Spanish
ECU issuer: 3 EEC
ecumenical: 6 cosmic 8 catholic, cosmical 9 inclusive, universal, worldwide
ecumenical __: 7 council
ed.
request: 3 SAE 4 SASE
__ ed: 4 phys 6 driver 7 driver's
Ed: 3 Ott 4 Ames, Koch, Wood, Wynn 5 Asner, horse, Lopat, Walsh 6 Begley, Harris, Lauter, McBain, Nelson, Norton, O'Neill 7 Bradley, Bullins, McMahon 8 Flanders, Marinaro, Sullivan 9 Delahanty, Kranepool
son: 6 Keenan
__ Ed: 6 Mister
Eda: 6 LeShan
edacious: 5 unfed 6 greedy, hungry 7 peckish, piggish, starved 8 esurient, famished, ravenous 9 insatiate, voracious 10 gluttonous

edacity: 5 greed 6 hunger 8 gluttony
Edam: 5 Dutch 6 cheese
alternative: 5 Gouda 6 Leyden
Edberg: 5 Swede 6 Stefan 9 tennis pro
rival: 5 Lendl 6 Agassi
Edd: 4 Hall 5 Roush 6 Byrnes
__ Edda: 5 Elder, Prose 6 Poetic 7 Younger
Eddie: 3 Foy 4 Egan, Yost 5 Bauer, Lopat, Mekka, Money, Plank, Shore 6 Albert, Arcaro, Cantor, Condon, Felson, Fisher, Hodges, Holman, Murphy, Stanky, Vedder 7 Bracken, Brigati, Cochran, Collins, Haskell, Heywood, Holland, Mathews, Munster, Rabbitt 8 Anderson, Van Halen 9 Kendricks
cop character: 4 Axel
__ Eddie Felson: 4 Fast
Eddington, Arthur: 9 physicist 10 astronomer
eddo: 4 taro
product: 3 poi
eddy: 4 tide, turn, wash 5 draft, surge, swirl, whirl, whorl 6 rotate, vortex 7 current 8 backflow 9 dust devil, maelstrom, whirlpool
combining form: 4 dino-
Eddy: 5 Duane, Grant 6 Arnold, Duchin, Merckx, Nelson
Eddy, Duane
song: Because They're Young (1960)
Forty Miles of Bad Road (1959)
Rebel-Rouser (1958)
eddying: 6 aswirl
Eddy, Nelson: 5 actor
film: Bitter Sweet (1940)
Maytime (1937)
Phantom of the Opera (1943)
Rosalie (1937)
Rose Marie (1936)
Ede: 4 town
locale: 7 Holland 11 Netherlands
Edel, Leon: 6 writer 10 biographer
subject: James, Cather, Thoreau
Edelman: 4 Herb 6 Gerald
Edelman, Gerald: 8 Nobelist
edelweiss: 5 plant 6 flower
Edelweiss composer: 7 Rodgers 11 Hammerstein
Eden: 6 utopia 7 Anthony, Arcadia, Barbara, Elysium, nirvana 8 paradise 9 Shangri-la 10 Phillpotts
event: 4 fall
exile: 3 Eve 4 Adam
he went east of ~: 4 Cain
place east of ~: 3 Nod
__ Eden: 6 Martin
Eden, Anthony: 3 sir 4 earl
earldom: 4 Avon
predecessor: 9 Churchill
successor: 9 Macmillan
Eden, Barbara: 7 actress
character: 5 genie
film: 7 Faces of Dr. Lao (1964)
Flaming Star (1960)
spouse: Michael Ansara
TV: I Dream of Jeannie
Harper Valley PTA
edenic: 5 ideal 7 Utopian 8 blissful, heavenly
Eden Prairie: 4 city, town
locale: 9 Minnesota
Eder: 5 river
locale: 7 Germany
Ederle: 5 Trudy 8 Gertrude
Edessa: 4 city, town, Urfa
locale: 6 Greece
__ ed Euridice: 5 Orfeo
__ E. Dewey: 6 Thomas
Edgar: 5 award, Cayce, Cecil, Degas, Guest, opera 6 Adrian, Bergen, Selwyn, Winter 7 Kennedy, Wallace 8 Bronfman, Buchanan, Martinez 9 Burroughs
composer: 7 Puccini
Edgar __ Burroughs: 4 Rice
Edgar Allan: 3 Poe
Edgard: 6 Varèse
__ Edgar Hoover: 4 John
Edgar Lee: 7 Masters
edge: 3 end, hem, lip, rim, tip 4 brim, curb, lead, line, odds, side, trim, whet 5 blade, bound, brink, creep, crust, frame, grind, ledge, leg up, limit, sidle, skirt, start, strop, verge 6 border, defeat, flange, fringe, limbus, margin, slip by, tipoff 7 contour, molding, nose out, outline 8 boundary, decorate, frontier, handicap, keenness, leverage, purchase, slip past, surround, trimming 9 advantage, extremity, head start, outskirts, perimeter, periphery, precipice, sharpness, squeeze by, threshold, upper hand
cutting ~: 4 lead 8 up-to-date, vanguard
ender: 4 ways, wise
gain an ~ on: 5 one up
improve an ~: 4 hone, whet 5 grind, strop 7 sharpen
in: 3 add, fit 5 enter 6 arrive 9 interpose, interrupt
ocean ~: 4 sand 5 beach, coast 8 littoral, seacoast 10 waterfront
on ~: 4 avid, keen, sour 5 antsy, eager, jumpy, nervy, tense, testy 6 jangly, uneasy 7 excited, fidgety, jittery, nervous, psyched, uptight, worried 8 fluttery, hopped up, restless 9 expectant, ill at ease, impatient, perturbed, tremulous, unsettled 10 raring to go
on the ~: 4 iffy 5 minor 7 minimal 8 marginal 10 borderline, negligible, peripheral
(out): 3 win 4 nose
(past): 5 sidle
pole along an ~: 4 rail 7 railing
projecting ~: 4 eave 6 flange
starter: 4 hard 7 feather 8 straight
take the ~ off: 4 ease, lull 5 blunt 6 lessen, pacify, smooth, soothe, temper 8 mitigate, tone down
to the ~: 7 outward, sideway 8 sideways, sidewise
edge __: 3 out 4 tool, wave 6 effect 7 molding
__ edge: 4 fore 5 knife, on the 6 deckle, ragged 7 circuit, cutting
__-edge: 4 gilt 7 leading
__ Edge: 6 Jagged, River's
edged: 4 keen 5 honed, sharp 7 fringed 9 sarcastic, trenchant
__-edged: 3 two 4 gilt, hard 5 sharp 6 double
edgeless: 4 curt 5 blunt, frank, gruff, plain, short, vocal 6 abrupt, direct 7 brusque 8 straight, succinct, unsubtle 9 outspoken 10 forthright, free-spoken, from the hip, point-blank, unpolished
Edge of Darkness (1943 film)
cast: Errol Flynn, Walter Huston, Ann Sheridan
director: Lewis Milestone
Edge of Heaven, The (1987 song)
artist: George Michael
Edge of Night, The (CBS/ABC): 4 soap 9 soap opera
Edge of Seventeen (1982 song) artist: Stevie Nicks
Edge of the City (1957 film)
cast: John Cassavetes, Sidney Poitier, Jack Warden
director: Martin Ritt
Edge of the Sea, The author: Rachel Carson
Edge of the Storm, The author: Augustín Yañez
edger: 4 tool 6 chisel 7 trimmer
__ Edge, The: 6 Razor's, River's
Edge, The author: Dick Francis
edgewise: 5 end on 7 sideway 8 sideways 9 laterally
Edgewood: 4 city, town
locale: 8 Maryland
Edgeworth, Maria: 5 Irish 6 writer
edginess: 7 fidgets, tension 9 tightness 10 impatience, inquietude
edging: 3 hem 4 lace, tape, trim 5 picot 6 border, fringe, ribbon
edgy: 5 antsy, itchy, jumpy, tense, testy, wired 6 fretty, ireful, jangly, snappy, touchy, uneasy 7 anxious, excited, fretful, jittery, keyed up, nervous, restive, uptight 8 fluttery, fretsome, restless, skittish, snappish 9 all nerves, excitable, ill at ease, impatient, irritable, querulous, tremulous, unsettled 10 highstrung
edible: 4 food, good 5 yummy 6 vittle 8 esculent, fit to eat, non-toxic 9 nutritive, palatable, toothsome, vegetable, wholesome 10 comestible, digestible, nourishing
become ~: 5 ripen
bulb: 4 leek 5 camas, onion 6 camass
no longer ~: 5 stale
root: 3 oca, oka, yam 4 beet, taro 6 carrot
seaweed: 4 agar 5 arame, dulse, laver 8 agar-agar
seed: 3 nut 4 chia 5 pinon 6 cashew, walnut
trendy ~: 4 tofu 8 bean curd
tuber: 3 oca, oka
edibles: 4 diet, fare, food, grub, meat 6 viands 7 aliment, produce, victual 8 victuals 9 provender 10 provisions, sustenance
edict: 3 act, law 4 fiat, rule, word 5 canon, irade, order, ukase 6 decree, firman, ruling 7 command, mandate, precept, statute 8 sentence 9 directive, manifesto, ordinance 10 injunction, regulation
Edict of __: 6 Nantes
Edie: 5 Adams, Falco 6 Magnus 7 McClurg 8 Brickell, Sedgwick
Edie author: 5 Stein
edifice: 5 tower 8 building 9 structure 10 skyscraper
edify: 5 brief, coach, guide, teach, tutor 6 direct, inform, school, uplift 7 benefit, educate, raise up 8 illumine, initiate, instruct 9 enlighten, inculcate 10 illuminate
edifying: 9 rewarding, wholesome
Edina: 4 city, town
locale: 9 Minnesota
Edinburg: 4 city, town
locale: 5 Texas
Edinburgh: 4 city, port, town
city near ~: 5 Perth 6 Dundee
locale: 8 Scotland
Edipo composer: 10 Mussorgsky
Edirne: 4 city, town
locale: 6 Turkey
Edison: 4 city, town 6 Thomas
locale: 9 New Jersey
Edison __: 6 effect
Edison Lighthouse song: Love Grows (1970)
Edison, the Man (1940 film)
cast: Rita Johnson, Lynne Overman, Spencer Tracy
Edison, Thomas: 8 inventor
birthplace: 4 Ohio 5 Milan
contemporary: 5 Tesla
middle name: 4 Alva
sneezer in ~'s first film: 3 Ott
Edisto: 3 isl. 4 isle 5 river 6 island
locale: 4 S. Car.
edit: 3 cut 4 dele, omit, redo, thin, trim 5 adapt, alter, amend, emend 6 censor, doctor, insert, mark up, polish, redact, refine, revise, rework 7 arrange, correct, improve, massage, rewrite, scissor, shorten, tighten, touch up 8 annotate, condense, copyread, fine-tune, rephrase 9 expurgate, proofread 10 blue-pencil, bowdlerize
a film: 3 cut, dub 5 recut, redub
out: 4 dele 5 bleep 6 censor, delete 8 cross out 9 expurgate
problems: 6 errata
starter: 4 copy
edited, not: 5 rough, uncut
Edith: 4 Head, Piaf 5 Evans, Meeks 6 Bunker, Wilson 7 Sitwell, Wharton 8 Hamilton
cousin: 5 Maude
husband: 6 Archie
editing: 8 revision 10 correction, emendation
edition: 3 ver. 4 book 5 issue 6 volume 7 reprint, version 8 printing 10 reprinting
Bible ~: 3 KJV, RSV 5 Douay 7 Vulgate
limited ~ perhaps: 5 print
magazine ~: 3 iss. 5 issue
newspaper ~: 5 extra, final
__ edition: 4 city, text 5 first, trade 6 pocket, school 7 bulldog, library, limited
__ Edition: 3 New 6 Inside
editor: 4 Pohl 6 Monroe, Strand, writer 7 Bradlee, emender, Greeley, newsman, Perkins, reviser, Shapiro 8 compiler, polisher, redactor, rewriter 9 annotator, collector, Podhoretz, Tina Brown, wordsmith 10 Ben Bradlee, diaskeuast, Perry White
compilation: 6 errata
concern: 3 mss. 4 text, typo 5 style 6 errata
notation: 4 dele, stet 5 caret
req.: 3 SAE 4 SASE
__ editor: 3 art 4 city, copy, text 5 night 7 linkage
editorial: 5 input, piece, prose 6 column 7 article, comment, opinion, writing 8 critique 10 commentary, exposition
editorialist: 5 press 6 author, scribe, writer 7 analyst 8 reporter 9 columnist 10 journalist
editor in __: 5 chief
Edmond: 4 city, town 5 Hoyle 6 Dantes, O'Brien 7 Fischer, Rostand 8 Goncourt
in Irish: 5 Eamon 6 Eamonn
locale: 8 Oklahoma
Edmonds: 4 city, town 5 Kevon
locale: 10 Washington
Edmonton: 4 city, town
locale: 6 Canada 7 Alb. Alta., Alberta
newspaper: 3 Sun 7 Journal
team: 6 Oilers
Ed, Mr.: 5 horse, steed
Edmund: 4 Kean, Lowe 5 Burke, Gwenn 6 Halley, Muskie, Waller, Wilson 7 Blunden, Hillary, Husserl, Spenser, Stedman 8 Goulding
in Irish: 5 Eamon 6 Eamonn
Edmund Fitzgerald cargo: 3 ore
Edmunds: 4 Dave
Edna: 4 Best 5 Chase 6 Ferber, Millay, O'Brien 7 Everage, Stengel 8 Buchanan 9 Purviance
Edna __ Oliver: 3 May
Edna St. __ Millay: 7 Vincent
Edo: 7 de Waart 8 Nigerian
home: 6 Africa 7 Nigeria
today: 5 Tokio, Tokyo

Edom
capital of ~: 5 Petra
kingdom near ~: 4 Moab
Edomites ancestor: 4 Esau
Édouard: 4 Lalo 5 Manet 8 Glissant, Vuillard
in English: 6 Edward
see also French
Edsel: 3 car 4 auto, Ford 5 lemon 10 automobile
model: 5 Pacer 6 Ranger 7 Bermuda, Corsair, Roundup 8 Citation, Villager
Edsel Ford Range locale: 10 Antarctica
Edsels song: Rama Lama Ding Dong (1961)
Ed Sullivan Show routine: 3 act
Ed TV (1999 film)
cast: Jenna Elfman, Woody Harrelson, Sally Kirkland, Matthew McConaughey
director: Ron Howard
Eduard: 5 Benes, Franz 6 Mörike 7 Buchner 9 Bernstein
Eduardo: 7 Barrios 8 Marquina
see also Spanish
educ.
institution: 2 HS 3 JHS, sch. 4 acad., coll., inst., univ.
union: 3 AFT, NEA, UFT
educate: 4 form, rear 5 coach, edify, groom, teach, train, tutor 6 inform, school 7 break in, nurture 8 instruct 9 catechize, cultivate, enlighten 10 evangelize
educated: 4 wise 6 taught, versed 7 erudite, learned 8 cultured, lettered, literate, prepared 9 scholarly 10 cultivated
guess: 3 est. 7 opinion, surmise 8 estimate, forecast, judgment 9 appraisal, reckoning, valuation 10 assessment, conjecture, evaluation, prediction, projection
___-educated: 4 self, well
Educating Rita (1983 film)
cast: Michael Caine, Julie Walters
education: 5 light, study 6 lesson 7 culture, reading, tuition 8 coaching, guidance, learning, literacy, pedagogy, teaching, training, tutoring 9 catechism, direction, erudition, grounding, knowledge, paedagogy, schooling 10 background, discipline, refinement, upbringing
basic ~ letters: 3 RRR
public ~ pioneer: 4 Mann
recipient: 5 pupil, tutee 7 learner, student, trainee
___ education: 5 adult 6 driver, higher 7 further, liberal, special
educational: 8 cultural, didactic 9 pedagogic 10 didactical
institution: 6 lyceum, school 7 academy, college
org.: 2 HS 3 JHS, PTA, sch. 4 acad., coll., inst., univ.
pursuit: 6 degree 7 diploma, master's 9 doctorate, sheepskin
Education of ___ K*A*P*L*A*N, The: 5 Hyman
educator: 4 dean 5 coach, tutor 6 mentor 7 teacher, trainer 8 lecturer 9 abecedary, professor 10 instructor
educe: 5 infer 6 derive, elicit, recall 7 develop, draw out, extract, work out 8 bring out 9 draw forth
Eduskunta locale: 7 Finland
Edvard: 5 Grieg, Munch
Edward: 3 Fox 4 Coke, Lear 5 Abbey, Albee, Asner, Cline, Doisy, Elgar, Gorey, Heath, Hicks, Lewis, Tatum, Young, Zwick 6 Albert, Arnold, Gibbon, Hopper, Jenner, Ludwig, Norton, Teller 7 Bernays, Buzzell, Dmytryk, Furlong, Kendall, Mulhare, Purcell 8 Appleton, Flanagan, Herrmann, Hoagland, Sedgwick, Steichen, Villella, Woodward 10 FitzGerald
in French: 7 Edouard
in German: 6 Eduard
in Spanish: 7 Eduardo
Edward ___: 3 VII 4 Bear
Edward ___ Horton: 7 Everett
Edward ___-Lytton: 6 Bulwer
Edward ___ Olmos: 5 James
Edward ___ Robinson: 9 Arlington
Edward Cardinal ___: 4 Egan
Edward D. ___ Jr.: 4 Wood
Edward G.: 8 Robinson
Edwardian ___: 3 Era
___ Edward Island: 6 Prince
Edward James: 5 Olmos
Edward M.: 7 Kennedy
Edward R.: 6 Murrow
Edwards: 3 AFB, Gus 5 Blake, Cliff, Jorge, Ralph, Tommy, Vince 7 Anthony 8 Jonathan
Edwards, Blake: 8 director
film: 10 (1979)
Breakfast at Tiffany's (1961)
The Carey Treatment (1972)
Darling Lili (1970)
Days of Wine and Roses (1962)
Experiment in Terror (1962)
The Great Race (1965)
Micki + Maude (1984)
Operation Petticoat (1959)
The Party (1968)
The Pink Panther (1964)
The Pink Panther Strikes Again (1976)
A Shot in the Dark (1964)
SOB (1981)
Sunset (1988)
The Tamarind Seed (1974)
That's Life! (1986)
This Happy Feeling (1958)
Victor/Victoria (1982)
What Did You Do in the War, Daddy? (1966)
Wild Rovers (1971)
spouse: Julie Andrews
Edward Scissorhands (1990 film)
cast: Johnny Depp, Vincent Price, Winona Ryder, Dianne Wiest
director: Tim Burton
hands: 6 shears
Edwards, Cliff nickname: Ukulele Ike
Edwards, Jorge: 6 writer 7 Chilean
Edwards, Tommy song: It's All in the Game (1958)
Edwardsville: 4 city, town
locale: 8 Illinois
Edwards, Vince: 5 actor
film: The Killing (1956)
The Victors (1963)
TV: Ben Casey
Edward the Confessor: 5 saint
Edwin: 4 Land, Muir 5 Abbey, Booth, Drake, Krebs, Meese, Moses, Starr 6 Hubble, McCain, Newman 7 Fischer, Hubbell, Markham, O'Connor 8 McMillan 9 Armstrong
Ed Wood (1994 film)
cast: Patricia Arquette, Johnny Depp, Martin Landau, Bill Murray, Sarah Jessica Parker
director: Tim Burton
role: 4 Bela 5 Orson 6 Lugosi, Welles
Edy's: 8 ice cream
alternative: 7 Breyer's 9 Friendly's, Good Humor 10 Dairy Queen, Haagen Dazs, Turkey Hill
e.e.: 8 cummings
EE: 4 shoe, wide 5 width
awarder: 3 MIT, RPI
EEC
member: 3 Den., Eng., Ger., Nor. 4 Ital.
money: 3 ecu 4 euro
part of ~: 3 Eur. 4 Comm., Econ.
prefix: 4 Euro-
EEE: 4 shoe, wide 5 width
eek: 4 yipe 6 a mouse
eel: 4 fish, grig, snig 5 moray 6 conger 7 lamprey, seafood 8 wriggler 9 ichthyoid 10 spitchcock
emulate an ~: 5 slide 7 slither
ender: 4 worm 5 grass
like an ~: 6 apodal 7 apodous
mud ~: 5 siren 9 amphibian 10 salamander
young ~: 4 grig 5 elver
___ eel: 3 mud 4 cusk, pike, sand 5 Congo, glass, moray 6 conger, lamper 7 lamprey, vinegar
___-eel: 4 rock, wolf
eelblenny: 4 fish
eelgrass: 6 enalid
eellike fish: 6 gunnel
eelpot: 4 trap
eelpout: 4 fish, quab
eelworm: 4 nema
eely: 7 elusive, elusory, wriggly 8 slippery, slithery
e'en: 4 dusk 7 evening, gloamin' 8 gloaming, twilight 9 nightfall
not ~ once: 4 ne'er
eensie-___: 7 weensie
eensy: 4 tiny 9 itty-bitty, miniature
eensy-___: 6 weensy
eeny follower: 5 meeny
EEOC
part of ~: 3 Emp. 4 Comm. 5 Equal
e'er: 2 ay 3 aye 5 alway
not quite ~: 3 oft
eerie: 3 odd 5 queer, scary, weird 6 atypic, crawly, creepy, freaky, occult, quirky, spooky, unreal 7 bizarre, deviant, eidolic, fearful, ghostly, haunted, macaber, macabre, offbeat, strange, uncanny, unusual 8 aberrant, atypical, chilling, eldritch, freakish, haunting, peculiar, spectral, uncommon 9 anomalous, divergent, eccentric, fantastic, ghostlike, grotesque, irregular, unearthly, unnerving 10 mysterious, outlandish, paranormal, unorthodox
feeling: 6 déjà vu
sound: 4 moan
Eero: 8 Saarinen
to Eliel: 3 son
...eether and ___ eyether: 4 I say
Eeyore: 6 donkey
creator: 5 Milne
friend: 3 owl, Roo 4 Pooh
Eeyore Has a Birthday author: A.A. Milne
Eeyore Loses a Tail author: A.A. Milne
E.F.: 6 Hutton
eff.: 3 apt.
efface: 4 rase, raze 5 erase 6 cancel, delete, rub out 7 blot out, expunge, wipe out 8 cross out, wear away 9 eliminate, eradicate, extirpate, sponge out 10 do away with, extinguish, obliterate, scratch out
___-effacing: 4 self
effect: 2 do 3 get 4 earn, look, show 5 cause, clout, drift 6 action, create, fulfil, impact, import, induce, obtain, render, result, secure, splash, thrust, upshot 7 achieve, actuate, compass, display, execute, fallout, fulfill, meaning, outcome, perform, procure, produce, product, pull off, purport, realize 8 bring off, carry out, complete, conclude, generate, occasion 9 actualize, aftermath, get across, implement, influence, outgrowth, put across 10 accomplish, bring about, consummate, give rise to, importance, impression, perpetrate, possession, put through
appreciable ~: 4 dent, mark 10 impression
be in ~: 4 hold, last, take 5 apply, carry, stand 6 endure, remain 7 carry on, contain, control, include, persist 8 stand for
carry into ~: 4 obey
combining form: 4 -ergy
go into ~: 6 kick in
have an ~: 4 take, tell, work
have an ~ on: 6 impact 8 register 9 influence 10 impression
have the opposite ~: 6 recoil 7 rebound 8 backfire 9 boomerang 10 bounce back
in ~: 5 truly, valid 6 active, almost, nearly, really, verily 8 actually 9 basically, so to speak, virtually 10 implicitly
not in ~: 4 null
put into ~: 4 vote 5 enact, order 8 legalize 9 establish, institute, legislate
starter: 5 after
take ~: 4 tell, work 5 enure, inure, set in 6 happen
to no ~: 4 vain 6 futile, hollow, in vain 7 inutile, sterile, useless 8 gainless 9 for naught, fruitless, pointless, thankless 10 profitless, unavailing
___ effect: 4 Bohr, edge, Gunn, Hall, halo, Kerr, lake, shot, side, skin, take 5 Auger, Hertz, Joule, moiré, pinch, Raman, sound, stage, Stark, Volta 6 domino, Edison, Magnus, Munroe, ripple, tunnel, Zeeman 7 Compton, Doppler, Faraday, Forbush, founder, knock-on, Pasteur, Peltier, placebo, ratchet, Seebeck, Thomson, Villari
___ Effect: 4 Zero
effective: 4 able, neat 5 quick, smart, sound, valid 6 active, cogent, potent, strong, up to it, useful 7 capable, current, in force, telling, working 8 adequate, forceful, powerful 9 competent, efficient, expedient, on the ball, operative, practical, sovereign, trenchant 10 compelling, convincing, impressive, infallible, persuasive, powerhouse, productive, proficient
be ~: 6 pan out 7 work out
cost-~: 6 doable 9 lucrative 10 worthwhile
date in law: 4 nisi
effective ___: 4 dose 7 current
effectively: 4 well
effectiveness: 5 avail, clout, force, power, punch, teeth, vigor 6 weight 7 potence, potency, success 8 strength, validity
lose ~: 4 pall
effector: 4 doer
effects: 4 gear 5 goods, stuff 6 assets, things 8 chattels, holdings, property 9 trappings 10 belongings
___ effects: 7 optical, special 8 personal
effectual: 5 quick, sound 6 aidful, benign, useful 7 helpful, telling 8 positive, powerful, remedial, salutary 9 achieving, efficient, favorable 10 conclusive, fulfilling, infallible, persuasive, productive, successful, worthwhile
effectually: 6 almost 9 just about, virtually
effectuate: 2 do 4 work 5 cause 6 commit, fulfil 7 execute, fulfill, perform, produce, realize 8 carry out, complete, transact 9 implement 10 accomplish, bring about, consummate, make happen

effendi: 3 sir 4 boss 5 title
in India: 5 saheb, sahib
effervesce: 4 fizz, foam, rave 5 exult, froth, spume 6 bubble, simmer 7 delight, enthuse, rejoice, sparkle
effervescence: 3 gas, joy, vim 4 fizz, foam, glee, zing 5 froth 6 gaiety, gayety 7 bubbles 8 bubbling, buoyance, buoyancy, frothing, vitality, vivacity
effervescent: 5 alive, fizzy, happy, jolly, light, merry, perky, zingy 6 bouncy, breezy, bubbly, frothy, joyful, joyous, lively, yeasty 7 buoyant, excited, gleeful, zinging 8 animated, jubilant, mirthful, spirited 9 sprightly, vivacious
make ~: 6 aerate 7 freshen 9 oxygenate, ventilate
effete: 4 puny, weak, worn 5 frail, spent, wimpy 6 anemic, atonic, barren, feeble, flabby, flimsy 7 anaemic, fragile, wimpish, worn-out 8 decadent, delicate, depleted, helpless, outmoded, pithless 9 exhausted, faltering, infertile, powerless, sissified 10 vulnerable
efficacious: 6 aidful, benign, potent, useful 7 capable, helpful 8 adequate, positive, powerful, puissant, remedial, salutary 9 effectual, favorable 10 productive, worthwhile
be ~: 4 take
efficacy: 5 avail, force, power 7 potence, potency, utility 8 strength, validity 10 capability
efficiency: 4 ease 5 skill 7 ability, economy, faculty, know-how, prowess 8 adequacy, facility 9 abundance, adeptness, expertise, readiness 10 capability, competence, competency
efficiency ___: 6 expert
___ efficiency: 4 hull 7 thermal
efficient: 3 apt 4 able, deft, good, lean, neat 5 adept, brisk, can-do, handy, slick 6 adroit, au fait, expert, nimble, prompt, up to it, useful 7 capable, regular, skilled, trained 8 adequate, dextrous, graceful, masterly, methodic, seasoned, skillful, thorough 9 competent, conducive, dexterous, effective, effectual, masterful, organized, practical, practiced, qualified 10 economical, methodical, productive, proficient, profitable, systematic
___-efficient: 4 cost, fuel
efficiently: 4 ably, well
effigy: 5 dummy, image, model 6 statue 7 picture 8 likeness, straw man
effloresce: 3 bud 4 grow 5 bloom 6 flower, sprout, thrive 7 blossom, burgeon, develop, prosper, succeed 8 flourish, fructify
effluence: 7 outflow 8 emission, emptying 9 discharge, emanation 10 outpouring
effluent: 4 flow, gush 6 oozing 7 outflow 9 discharge, emanation, exudation 10 exhalation
effluvial: 4 fumy 5 gassy 8 vaporous
effluvious: 7 odorous
effluvium: 3 gas 4 fume, odor, reek 5 miasm, vapor 6 miasma, stench 7 exhaust 10 exhalation
efflux: 7 outflow 8 emission 9 discharge, emanation 10 outpouring
ef follower: 3 gee
effort: 3 bid, job, try 4 care, deed, dint, feat, pain, push, shot, stab, toil, work 5 drive, essay, fling, force, labor, oomph, pains, sweat 6 action, strain 7 attempt, measure, trouble, venture 8 endeavor, exercise, exertion, industry, striving, struggle 9 diligence, operation 10 enterprise
best ~: 3 all
exert minimal ~: 5 glide, slide 6 cruise
futile ~: 5 waste
make an ~: 3 try 4 toil, work 5 exert, lay to, sweat 6 bother, strive, tackle 7 trouble 8 struggle
move without ~: 5 coast, glide, slide
reduce ~: 5 relax
with no ~: 6 easily, simply 7 lightly 9 leisurely, naturally
___ effort: 4 A for, E for
effortful: 6 uphill 7 hard-won, labored 9 difficult, laborious, strenuous 10 formidable
effortless: 4 easy, glib, soft 5 a snap, cushy, light 6 facile, fluent, simple, smooth 7 no sweat 8 dextrous, duck soup, painless, untaxing 9 dexterous, no problem 10 child's play, unexacting
effortlessly: 4 well 7 handily, lightly, readily 9 hands down 10 swimmingly
effortlessness: 4 ease
effrontery: 3 lip 4 face, gall, guff, sass 5 brass, check, cheek, crust, nerve 7 license 8 audacity, boldness, chutzpah, defiance, rudeness, temerity 9 arrogance, assurance, brashness, impudence, insolence, smart talk 10 brazenness, cheekiness, disrespect, incivility
effulgence: 4 glow 5 blaze, gleam, light, shine 6 luster 7 aureola, aureole, sparkle 8 radiance, radiancy, splendor 10 brightness, brilliance
effulgent: 5 lucid, nitid 6 bright 7 beaming, radiant 8 luminous, lustrous 9 brilliant
effuse: 4 emit, gush, pour 5 exude, spirt, spout, spurt 7 diffuse, emanate, flow out, pour out, profuse, secrete 9 ooze forth, pour forth, scattered, spread out
effusion: 5 spirt, spurt, surge 7 torrent
effusive: 4 avid, warm 5 gushy, mushy 6 hearty, lavish 7 fulsome, gushing, profuse 9 ebullient, expansive, exuberant, talkative 10 bigmouthed, unreserved
be ~: 7 enthuse
Efik
home: 6 Africa 7 Nigeria
kin: 6 Ibibio
EFL cousin: 3 ESL
Efrem: 9 Zimbalist
eft: 4 newt 9 amphibian 10 salamander
Efuru author: Flora Nwapa
___-E. Fyne: 4 Sylk
e.g.: 4 abbr. 10 for example
E.G.: 8 Marshall
egad: 3 fie, gee 4 darn, drat, oath, oh my, rats, yipe 5 yikes, yipes 6 zounds 9 expletive
in German: 3 ach
___, égalité, fraternité: 7 liberté
Egan: 5 Eddie 6 Pierce, Walter 7 Richard
Egan, Richard: 5 actor
film: Love Me Tender (1956)
Pollyanna (1960)
Slaughter on Tenth Avenue (1957)
A Summer Place (1959)
These Thousand Hills (1959)
Violent Saturday (1955)
Egan, Walter song: Magnet and Steel (1978)
Egbert: 4 king 5 Saxon
Eger: 4 city, Ohre, town 5 river
locale: 7 Germany, Hungary
Egeria: 5 nymph 8 asteroid
husband of ~: 4 Numa
egest: 4 spew, spue 5 expel, exude 7 cast off, cast out, spew out 8 disgorge, perspire 9 discharge
egesta: 5 sweat, tears
egg: 3 roe 4 cell, chap, ovum, prod, seed, urge 5 taunt 6 embryo, fellow, gamete, needle, origin, urge on 7 oospore, provoke
Australian ~: 4 goog
bad ~: 3 cad, cur 5 rogue 6 rotter 7 dirtbag, stinker, villain 9 nogoodnik, scoundrel
beater: 5 whisk
cell: 4 ovum 5 ootid
combining form: 2 oo-, ov- 3 ovi-, ovo-
concoction: 3 nog 6 omelet, quiche 8 omelette
contents: 5 fetus 6 embryo, foetus
deposit: 5 spawn
distibutor: 5 bunny, dairy 6 rabbit
ender: 3 cup, nog 4 head 5 fruit, plant, shell 6 beater
examiner: 5 sexer
golden ~ producer: 5 goose
good ~: 6 mensch
goose ~: 3 nil, zip 4 nada, none, null, zero 5 zilch, zippo 6 cipher, naught, nought 7 nothing
holder: 4 case, nest 5 crate 6 carton
immature ~: 5 ovule
insect ~: 3 nit
lay an ~: 4 bomb, bust, fail, flop, lose, slip, trip 5 flunk 6 blow it, falter 7 blunder, founder, go under, go wrong, misstep, stumble, wash out 8 fall flat, flounder 9 strike out
layer: 3 hen 4 bird
like ~ whites: 6 beaten
nest ~: 3 IRA 5 cache, funds, means, store 7 reserve, savings 9 resources
on: 4 abet, coax, goad, prod, push, spur, urge 5 annoy, impel, press 6 fillip, incite, kindle, prompt, stir up 7 actuate, agitate, incense, provoke 8 motivate 9 encourage, instigate
part: 4 yolk 5 glair, white 6 glaire
prepare an ~: 3 fry 4 boil 5 devil, poach, shirr 8 scramble
produce an ~: 3 lay
quantity: 3 doz. 5 dozen
rating: 6 grade A
size: 5 jumbo, large 10 extra large
egg ___: 3 nog 4 case, cell, coal, roll 5 cream, salad, stone, timer, tooth, white 7 rolling
egg ___ soup: 4 drop
egg ___ yung: 3 foo
___ egg: 3 ant, bad 4 good, nest 5 goose, lay an 6 Easter, Scotch 7 curate's, darning, dropped, thunder
egg and ___: 4 dart
egg and ___ race: 5 spoon
Egg and I, The (1947 film)
cast: Claudette Colbert, Percy Kilbride, Fred MacMurray, Marjorie Main
dog: 5 Sport
Eggar, Samantha: 7 actress
film: The Collector (1965)
Doctor Dolittle (1967)
Return From the Ashes (1965)
Walk, Don't Run (1966)
Why Shoot the Teacher? (1977)
eggbeater: 5 mixer 6 copter, gadget
___-egg blue: 6 robin's
egg-cream ingredient: 4 milk 5 sirup, syrup 7 seltzer
egg drop: 4 soup
egg-dyeing time: 6 Easter
egger: 4 moth
Eggert: 6 Nicole
egg foo ___: 4 yong, yung
egghead: 3 ace 4 dork, geek, nerd, nurd, whiz, wonk 5 brain 6 genius 7 prodigy, scholar, thinker 8 Einstein, hairless, highbrow, longhair, virtuoso 9 intellect, know-it-all, professor 10 mastermind
pride: 2 IQ 4 mind 5 brain, ideas 6 brains 9 intellect
eggheaded: 5 smart 6 bright 9 brilliant
eggnog: 5 drink 8 beverage, cocktail
ingredient: 3 egg, rum 4 milk 6 brandy 7 liqueur
egg on one's ___: 4 face
eggplant: 6 veggie 9 vegetable
appetizer: 8 caponata
color: 4 puce 6 purple
relative: 4 plum, puce 5 lilac, mauve 6 dahlia, damson, orchid 7 heather, petunia 8 amethyst, burgundy, lavender, mulberry 9 raspberry 10 heliotrope
___ eggplant: 6 tomato 7 scarlet
egg roll: 9 appetizer
time: 6 Easter
eggs: 3 ova, roe 5 dairy 6 caviar 7 caviare
color Easter ~: 3 dye
companion: 3 ham 4 hash 5 bacon, steak, toast 7 sausage 9 home fries
fish ~: 3 roe 6 caviar
goose ~: 3 OOO 4 OOOO 5 OOOOO
group of ~: 6 clutch
in Latin: 3 ova
like robins' ~: 4 blue 6 bluish 7 blueish
lobster ~: 3 roe
walking on ~: 4 wary 5 alert, chary, leery 7 careful, heedful, mindful, prudent 8 cautious, delicate, vigilant, watchful 9 tentative 10 deliberate
walk on ~: 6 tiptoe 9 pussyfoot
eggs ___ suisse: 3 à la
...eggs ___ basket: 5 in one
___ Eggs and Ham: 5 Green
Eggs Benedict, prepare: 5 poach
egg-shaped: 4 ooid, oval 5 ovate, ovoid, round 7 oviform 8 lopsided 9 ellipsoid 10 elliptical
eggshell: 4 ecru 5 color, white
relative: 4 bone, milk, snow 5 cream, ivory, milky 6 argent, oyster, silver
___ Egg, The: 6 Herne's, Square
egg-timer filler: 4 sand
eggy: 4 rich 9 yellowish
Egham: 4 city, town
locale: 6 Surrey 7 England
Egil: 5 Krogh
egis: 5 favor 6 shield, surety 7 support 8 auspices, guaranty, umbrella 9 patronage, safeguard 10 protection
eglantine: 5 plant 6 flower
Eglevsky, André: 6 dancer 7 danseur
specialty: 6 ballet
Egmont author: 6 Goethe
ego: 4 self, soul 5 pride 6 psyche, vanity 7 big head, conceit 8 bovarism, identity 9 arrogance, self-image 10 narcissism, self-esteem, self-regard
alter ~: 3 pal 4 ally, chum, mate 5 buddy, crony 6 backer, cohort, friend 7 comrade, consort, partner 8 intimate, playmate, sidekick, soul mate 9 associate, companion, confidant 10 bosom buddy, compatriot
companion: 2 id
trip: 5 pride 6 vanity
ego ___: 4 trip 5 ideal
ego-___: 5 alien 7 tripper
___ ego: 5 alter
Ego and the Id, The
author: Sigmund Freud
egocentric: 4 vain 6 stuffy 7 selfish 9 conceited 10 big-talking, egoistical, self-loving
egoism: 5 pride 6 vanity 7 conceit, hauteur 9 arrogance 10 narcissism, self-esteem
egoist: 4 snob 8 braggart 10 narcissist, self-seeker, self-server

egoistical: 4 smug, vain 5 proud 7 selfish 9 conceited, hubristic 10 egocentric, self-loving
Egoist, The author: George Meredith
Egon: 7 Schiele
egotism: 5 pride 6 vanity 7 conceit, hauteur 9 arrogance 10 narcissism
egotist: 7 showoff
obsession: 4 self
egotistic: 7 fustian, haughty, pompous, selfish 8 arrogant, assuming, boastful, snobbish 9 grandiose 10 complacent, disdainful
egotistical: 4 smug, vain 5 proud 7 haughty, pompous, selfish, stuck-up 8 affected, boastful, cocksure, inflated, prideful, puffed up, snobbish
egregious: 4 foul, rank 5 gross, utter 6 wicked 7 extreme, glaring 8 flagrant, grievous, uncommon 9 atrocious, monstrous, nefarious, notorious 10 deplorable, immoderate, outrageous, scandalous
egress: 4 door, exit, gate 5 go out, leave 6 escape, exodus, outlet, way out 7 exiting 9 departure 10 withdrawal
egression: 4 exit 6 escape 7 parting, walkout 9 departure 10 decampment, evacuation
egret: 4 bird 5 heron, wader 9 marsh bird 10 cattle bird
cousin: 4 ibis
emulate an ~: 4 wade
__ egret: 5 snowy 6 cattle, little
Eguren, José María: 4 poet 8 Peruvian
Egypt: 6 nation 7 country
ancient city: 4 Sais 5 Tanis 6 Abydos, Thebes
ancient ~ lighthouse: 6 Pharos
ancient ~ sacred flower: 5 lotus
and Syr., once: 3 UAR
Arabic name of ~: 4 Misr
archeological site: 5 Luxor 6 Amarna, Karnak
bay: 6 Abukir
bird: 4 ibis
bushel: 5 ardeb
capital: 5 Cairo
carriage: 6 gharri, gharry
cat of ~ mythology: 4 Bast
Christian: 4 Copt
city: 4 Giza, Qena, Suez 5 Aswan, Asyut, Benha, Cairo, Luxor, Tanta 6 Assiut, Assuan 7 Assouan 8 Port Said 10 Alexandria
cobra: 3 asp 6 uraeus
conquerors of ~: 6 Hyksos
cotton: 3 sak
dam: 5 Aswan
desert: 6 Libyan, Sahara 7 Arabian
dyestuff: 5 henna
father of ~: 3 Ham
god: 2 Ra 3 Bes, Set 4 Aten, Aton, Nunu, Ptah, Seth 5 Horus, Sebek, Thoth 6 Amon-Ra, Anubis, Osiris 7 Taueret
goddess: 3 Mut, Nut 4 Bast, Isis, Maat 6 Hathor 7 Sekhmet 8 Nephthys
god of wisdom: 5 Thoth
grandfather of ~: 4 Noah
group: 10 Arab League
gulf: 5 Akaba, Aqaba
home: 6 Africa
image in ~ art: 3 asp
it's n. of ~: 3 Eur. 5 Medit.
king: 3 Tut 4 Fuad 6 Ramses 7 Rameses
lake: 6 Nasser
language: 6 Arabic, Coptic
money: 5 asper 7 piaster, piastre 8 millieme
month: 4 Ahet
neighbor: 3 Isr., Leb. 5 Libya, Sudan 6 Israel
Nobelist in Literature: 7 Mahfouz
Nobelist in Peace: 5 Sadat
opera set in ~: 4 Aïda
peasant: 6 fellah
peninsula: 5 Sinai
port: 4 Suez 5 Cairo 8 Port Said 10 Alexandria
president: 5 Sadat 6 Nasser 7 Mubarak
province: 6 Faiyum
queen: 4 Cleo
river: 4 Nile
scientist: 7 Ptolemy
solar disk: 4 Aten, Aton
source of ocher: 6 dakhla
strip between Israel and ~: 4 Gaza
temple site: 6 Karnak
tree: 7 ambatch
waterwheel: 5 sakia
wind: 7 khamsin
writer: 9 el Saadawi
Egyptian: 4 Arab 5 dance 8 language
Egyptian __: 5 cobra, lotus 6 clover, cotton
Egyptian Mau: 3 cat 5 felid 6 feline
Egypt Lake: 4 city, town
locale: 7 Florida
Egyptologist: 5 Young 6 Petrie 7 Belzoni
symbol: 5 glyph
eh: 3 huh 4 what 5 query
E. Howard __: 4 Hunt
Ehrlichman: 4 John
Ehrlich, Paul: 8 Nobelist
Ehud: 5 Barak
Eichhorn: 4 Lisa
eider: 4 bird, duck, fowl 10 diving duck
ender: 4 down
relative: 4 smew, teal 5 Pekin, Rouen, scaup 6 Cayuga, scoter 7 gadwall, mallard, pintail, pochard, redhead, sea duck, widgeon 8 garganey, gray duck, mandarin, musk duck, oldsquaw, shoveler, surf duck, wood duck 9 black duck, broadbill, goldeneye, goosander, greenhead, merganser, ruddy duck, sprigtail 10 bufflehead, canvasback, surf scoter, tufted duck
eider __: 4 down, duck
eiderdown: 5 fluff, quilt 7 bedding 8 coverlet, coverlid 9 comforter
eidolic: 5 eerie 6 spooky 7 ghostly, haunted 10 phantasmal, wraithlike
eidolon: 5 ghost, ideal 6 fantom 7 phantom 8 delusion 10 apparition
Eiffel: 8 language 9 Alexandre
alternative: 3 ADA, APL, SQL 4 Alef, html, Icon, Java, LISP, Logo, Orca, Perl 5 Algol, Basic, Cecil, COBOL, Dylan, SISAL 6 Delphi, Erlang, Oberon, Pascal, Prolog, Sather, Scheme, Snobol 7 Fortran
Eiffel Tower locale: 5 Paris
Eigen, Manfred: 7 chemist 8 Nobelist
Eiger: 3 alp 4 peak 5 mount 8 mountain
locale: 4 Alps 6 Europe 11 Switzerland
Eiger Sanction, The (1975 film)
cast: Jack Cassidy, Clint Eastwood, George Kennedy, Vonetta McGee
director: Clint Eastwood
setting: 4 Alps
eight
base ~: 5 octal
behind the ~ ball: 6 in a fix, in a jam 7 trapped, unlucky
bells: 4 noon 6 midday
bits: 4 byte
combining form: 3 oct- 4 octa-, octo-
composition for ~: 5 octet 7 octette
cube root of ~: 3 two
figure of ~: 4 knot
furlongs: 2 mi. 4 mile
gills: 2 qt. 5 quart
group of ~: 5 octad, octet 7 octette
half a figure ~: 3 ess
homophone for ~: 3 ait, ate
in French: 4 huit
in German: 4 acht
in Italian: 4 otto
in Japanese: 5 hachi
in Latin: 4 octo
in Portuguese: 4 oito
in Spanish: 4 ocho
ounces: 3 cup
pints: 3 gal. 6 gallon
prefix: 4 octa-, octo-
quarter of ~: 3 two
quarts: 4 peck
to Mohs: 5 topaz
__ eight: 4 ward 6 figure
eightball: 4 game
maneuver: 5 massé
requirement: 3 cue
Eight Bells artist: 5 Homer
Eight Cousins author: Louisa May Alcott
Eight Days a Week (1965 song) artist: Beatles
eighteen-wheeler: 4 semi 5 truck
Eightfold __: 3 Way 4 Path
eighth: 5 grade 6 octave
every ~ day: 5 octan
letter: 5 aitch
mo.: 3 Aug. 6 August
eighth __: 4 note, rest
Eighth Commandment, The author: Lawrence Sanders
Eighth Day, The author: Thornton Wilder
Eighth Wonder of the World, The: 4 Kong
eight-legged creatures: 6 octopi
Eight Men Out (1988 film)
cast: John Cusack, Clifton James, Michael Lerner, Christopher Lloyd, John Mahoney, Charlie Sheen, David Strathairn, D.B. Sweeney
director: John Sayles
Eight Mortal Ladies Possessed author: Tennessee Williams
eightpenny __: 4 nail
__ eights: 5 crazy
eights, do figure: 5 skate
eight-track __: 4 tape
eighty: 9 fourscore
__-eighty: 3 one
Eighty-Eight: 3 car 4 auto, Olds 10 automobile, Oldsmobile
Eighty-Five Poems author: Louis MacNeice
eighty-six: 3 nix 4 boot, drop, kill, toss 5 chuck, ditch, eject, scrap 6 bounce 7 let go of 9 dispose of, throw over 10 disqualify
eighty-sixed: 4 beat, fini, over, shot, sunk 5 kaput 6 done in, no more, ruined, undone 7 all over, belly-up, defunct, done for, extinct, totaled, wrecked 8 finished, washed-up, wiped out 9 destroyed 10 demolished
Eijkman, Christiaan: 8 Nobelist
Eikenberry, Jill spouse: Michael Tucker
Eilat: 4 city, port, town
locale: 6 Israel
Eilbacher: 4 Lisa
Eileen: 4 Ford 6 Fulton 7 Brennan, Farrell, Heckart
Eilers: 5 Sally
ein: 3 one 6 German
in French: 3 une
in Italian: 3 uno
in Spanish: 3 uno
Eine __ in Venedig: 5 Nacht
Eine Kleine Nachtmusik composer: 6 Mozart
einkorn: 5 grain
Einsam in trüben Tagen singer: 4 Elsa
eins doubled: 4 zwei
Einstein: 3 ace 4 whiz 5 brain 6 Albert, genius 7 egghead, prodigy, thinker 8 highbrow, virtuoso 9 intellect 10 mastermind
Einstein __: 5 model, shift 6 theory
Einstein, Albert: 8 Nobelist 9 physicist
birthplace: 3 Ger., Ulm 7 Germany
colleague: 4 Bohr
forte: 4 math 7 physics
part of an ~ equation: 4 mass
see also German
einsteinium: 7 element
Einthoven, Willem: 8 Nobelist
Eire: 6 Old Sod 7 Ireland 9 Innisfail, Innisfree
__ Éireann: 4 Dáil 6 Seanad
Eisaku: 4 Sato
eisen: 4 iron 6 German
Eisenhower: 3 Ike 5 David, Mamie 6 Dwight, Milton
Eisenhower __: 6 jacket
Eisenhower, Dwight D.: president
alma mater: 4 USMA 9 West Point
birthplace: 5 Texas 7 Denison
book: 6 At Ease
cabinet member: 5 Gates, Hobby, McKay, Weeks 6 Benson, Dulles, Durkin, Folsom, Herter, Rogers, Wilson 7 McElroy 8 Anderson, Brownell, Flemming, Humphrey, Mitchell
former occupation: 7 general, soldier
home: 6 Kansas 7 Abilene 10 Gettysburg
HQ in '45: 5 Reims 6 Rheims
middle name: 5 David
nickname: 3 Ike
opponent: 9 Stevenson
real first name: 5 David
V.P.: 5 Nixon
wife: 5 Mamie
Eisenhut: 3 alp
Eisenstaedt: 6 Alfred, photog
Eisenstein, Sergei: 8 director
film: Alexander Nevsky (1938) Ivan the Terrible, Part One (1943) Potemkin (1925)
'E' Is for Evidence author: Sue Grafton
Eisley: 7 Anthony
Eisner: 7 Michael
either: 3 too 4 also, both, each 6 as well 8 likewise 9 whichever 10 this or that
or both: 5 and/or
eject: 3 rid 4 boot, bump, dump, emit, fire, oust, pump, rout, spew, spue, vent, void 5 debar, empty, evict, expel, exude, issue, purge, spout 6 banish, bounce, depose, disbar, launch, propel, remove, squirt 7 bail out, cast off, cast out, diffuse, dismiss, emanate, exclude, extrude, give off, kick out, radiate, spit out, toss out, turn out, unloose 8 disgorge, dislodge, displace, drive off, force out, get rid of, heave out, jettison, relegate, shoot out, throw off, throw out 9 discharge, eighty-six, eliminate, eradicate, send forth 10 dispossess
ejecta: 4 lava
ejection: 4 cast 8 emission, eruption, exorcism 9 discharge, exclusion, expulsion 10 deposition, evacuation, unfrocking
ejection __: 4 seat 7 capsule
ejector __: 4 seat
Ekberg: 5 Anita, Swede
eke: 5 skimp 6 make do, scrape 7 augment, scratch, squeeze, stretch 10 supplement, underspend
out: 6 make do, manage 7 squeeze 8 scrape by 10 supplement
eke __ a living: 3 out

__ E. Kelley: 5 David
Ekelöf, Gunnar: 4 poet 7 Swedish
EKG: 4 test 5 chart
  concern: 5 heart
  user: 2 MD 4 hosp.
__ E. King: 3 Ben
Ekland, Britt: 7 actress
  film: Endless Night (1971)
    The Man With the Golden Gun (1974)
    The Night They Raided Minsky's (1968)
    The Wicker Man (1973)
  spouse: Peter Sellers
ekwe: 4 drum
  origin: 7 Nigeria
Ekwensi, Cyprian: 6 writer 8 Nigerian
el: 2 RR 8 railroad
  cousin: 3 the
  follower: 2 em
  initials: 3 CTA
  locale: 3 Chi 4 Loop 7 Chicago
  preceder: 3 kay
  stop: 3 sta., stn. 7 station
el __: 4 toro 6 cheapo
El __: 3 Cid 4 Niño, Paso 5 Greco, Norte, Super 6 Diario, Dorado 7 Capitan 8 Cordobés
El __ Brujo: 4 Amor
El __, CA: 4 Toro
El __ Campeador: 3 Cid
El __ Grande: 6 Rancho
El __ Mexico: 5 Salón
El __ Pasa: 6 Condor
El __, TX: 4 Paso
E.L.: 8 Doctorow
elaborate: 4 rich 5 fancy, ritzy, showy 6 detail, expand, flashy, florid, frilly, glitzy, knotty, lavish, ornate, unfold 7 amplify, clarify, complex, develop, explain, flowery, for show, opulent, specify, work out 8 detailed, involved, thorough 9 ambitious, decorated, discourse, embellish, embroider, expatiate, extensive, garnished, interpret, intricate, luxuriant, luxurious, perfected, sumptuous 10 complicate, flamboyant, ornamental, ornamented, overworked, prodigious
  inlay: 4 buhl 5 boule 6 boulle
  on: 4 list, show, tell 6 detail, lay out, report, reveal, sketch 7 itemize, narrate, portray, recount, specify 8 describe, set forth, spell out 9 delineate, embellish, enumerate, make clear
elaboration, without: 6 simply
elaenia: 4 bird
Elaine: 3 May 5 Zayak 7 Stewart, Stritch
Elaine, the lily ___: 4 Maid
El Al: 7 airline
  destination: 3 Lod
El Alamein: 6 battle
El Alto: 4 city, town
  locale: 7 Bolivia
Elam: 4 Jack
  capital of ~: 4 Susa
  father of ~: 4 Shem
  grandfather of ~: 4 Noah
__ el Amarna: 3 Tel
élan: 3 vim, zip 4 brio, dash, fire, life, snap, soul, zest, zing 5 ardor, flair, flash, gusto, oomph, spunk, style, verve, vigor 6 bounce, energy, esprit, gaiety, gayety, pizazz, psyche, spirit 7 abandon, panache, pizzazz, sparkle 8 activity, buoyance, buoyancy, fervency, flourish, vitality, vivacity 9 animation 10 enthusiasm, excitement, exuberance, get-up-and-go, liveliness, vital spark
Elan: 4 font 8 typeface
eland: 6 animal, mammal 8 antelope
  land: 5 veldt
  relative: 3 gnu, kob 4 guib, kudu, oryx, puku, topi 5 addax, bongo, chiru, goral, korin, nyala, oribi, saiga, serow 6 chammy, dik-dik, duiker, impala, koodoo, lechwe, nilgai, rhebok, shammy, shamoy 7 blaubok, blesbok, chamois, defassa, gazelle, gemsbok, gerenuk, grysbok, nylghai, nylghau, sassaby 8 blesbuck, bontebok, bushbuck, gemsbuck, reedbuck, steenbok, steinbok 9 blackbuck, pronghorn, sitatunga, springbok, waterbuck 10 hartebeest, wildebeest
elanet: 4 hawk, kite 10 bird of prey
Elantra: 3 car 4 auto 7 Hyundai
elapid: 5 cobra, snake 6 animal 7 reptile
elapse: 2 go 3 fly 4 flow, go by, pass 5 fly by, lapse 6 expire, pass by, roll by, roll on, run out, slip by 7 glide by, slide by 8 slip away, tick away 9 glide away, intervene, transpire
elapsed: 4 gone, past 6 lapsed
elapsed __: 4 time
Elara: 4 moon
  planet: 7 Jupiter
elastic: 4 soft 6 limber, lissom, spongy, supple 7 lissome, plastic, pliable, springy 8 flexible, yielding 9 resilient
  device: 6 bungee
  fabric: 7 spandex
elastic __: 4 wave 5 limit 6 clause, tissue 7 modulus
__ elastic: 3 gum
elasticity: 4 give, tone 6 bounce, spring
Elat: 4 city, port, town
  locale: 6 Israel
elate: 4 send 5 cheer, liven 6 buoy up, lift up, perk up, please, puff up, thrill, tickle, turn on 7 delight, elevate, gladden, happify, hearten, lighten, overjoy, satisfy 9 enrapture, inebriate, make happy 10 exhilarate, intoxicate
elated: 4 glad, high, sent 5 happy 6 cheery, flying, joyful, joyous 7 beaming, gleeful, pleased 8 blissful, bubbling, ecstatic, enthused, euphoric, exultant, in heaven, jubilant, sanguine 9 ebullient, overjoyed, rapturous, rejoicing, rhapsodic 10 flying high, triumphant
  be ~: 4 glow 5 exult 9 walk on air
elaterid: 3 dor 4 dorr 6 beetle, insect
Elath: 4 city, town
  locale: 6 Israel
elation: 3 joy 4 glee, zest 5 bliss 6 gaiety, gayety 7 delight, ecstasy, emotion, jollity, rapture, triumph 8 euphoria, felicity, optimism 9 happiness, joviality, lightness 10 ebullience, exultation, jubilation
  show ~: 4 beam 5 exult 7 light up
Elayne: 7 Boosler
Elba: 3 isl. 4 isle 6 island
Elbe: 5 river
  city on the ~: 5 Pirna 7 Dresden, Hamburg
  locale: 7 Germany
  river to the ~: 4 Eger, Iser, Ohre 6 Moldau, Vltava
Elbert: 4 peak 5 mount 7 Hubbard 8 mountain
  locale: 7 Rockies 8 Colorado
elbow: 4 bump, poke, prod, push 5 hinge, joint, nudge, shove 6 jostle, justle, thrust 7 flexure 8 shoulder 9 push aside
  armor: 6 couter
  at one's ~: 4 near 5 close, handy, ready, utile 6 nearby, useful 7 close by 9 available 10 accessible, convenient
  bend an ~: 3 sip 4 swig, tope 5 drink, snort 6 imbibe, tipple
  bender: 3 sot 4 lush 5 toper
  counterpart: 4 knee
  ender: 4 room
  grease: 4 work 6 effort 8 exertion
  locale: 3 arm
  room: 5 space 6 leeway
  use ~ grease: 3 ply 4 buff 5 apply, scour, sweat, wield 6 employ, polish, strain 7 trouble, try hard, utilize 8 put forth
elbow __: 4 room 5 catch 6 grease
__ elbow: 4 drop 6 tennis
elbow grease: 4 toil
  use ~: 5 exert, scrub
elbowing, like: 4 rude 7 uncouth
elbowroom: 3 way 4 play 5 scope, space 6 leeway 7 freedom 8 latitude 9 free space, open space
elbows: 5 pasta 7 noodles 8 macaroni 9 maccaroni
  out at the ~: 5 broke, needy, seedy 6 bad off, hard up, ill off, in need, in want, shabby 7 pinched 8 badly off, bankrupt, beggarly, indigent, strapped 9 destitute, insolvent, moneyless, penniless, penurious 10 pauperized, straitened
  rub ~: 3 mix 6 hobnob 9 socialize 10 fraternize
  up to one's ~: 4 full 5 awash 7 crowded 8 brimming
__ elbows with: 3 rub
elbow-to-elbow: 3 SRO 5 dense, tight 6 packed 7 cramped, crowded, teeming 8 brimming, populous, squeezed 9 chock-full, jam-packed 10 wall-to-wall
elbow-to-fingertip distance: 5 cubit
Elbridge: 5 Gerry
Elbrus: 4 peak 5 mount 8 mountain
  locale: 6 Europe, Russia 8 Caucasus
Elburz: 5 range
  locale: 4 Asia, Iran
El Cajon: 4 city, town
  locale: 10 California
El Capitan: 4 peak 5 mount, train 8 mountain
  locale: 8 Yosemite 10 California
El Capitan composer: 5 Sousa
Elcar: 4 Dana
El Centro: 4 city, town
  locale: 10 California
El Cerrito: 4 city, town
  locale: 10 California
El Cid (1961 film): 4 epic
  cast: Charlton Heston, Sophia Loren, Raf Vallone
  director: Anthony Mann
El Cid foe: 4 Moor
El Colomo: 4 city, town
  locale: 6 Colima, Mexico
El Condor: 4 peak 5 mount 8 mountain
  locale: 5 Andes 9 Argentina
El Condor Pasa (1970 song) artist: Simon and Garfunkel
El Cordobés: 6 torero 7 matador 8 toreador
  see also Spanish
eld: 4 yore 9 antiquity 10 days of yore, yesteryear
elder: 4 tree 5 doyen, genro, older, shrub 6 cleric, senior 8 superior 9 firstborn, matriarch, patriarch, presbyter 10 golden ager
  ender: 4 care 5 berry
  marsh ~: 3 iva
  relative: 6 abelia 8 snowball
elder __: 4 hand 6 hostel
__ elder: 3 box 5 marsh 6 ruling
Elder: 3 Lee
Elder __: 4 Edda
elderberry: 4 wine 5 fruit
Elder, Katie brood: 4 sons
elderly: 3 old 4 aged 5 aging 6 ageing 7 ancient, wizened 8 grizzled 9 geriatric, getting on, senescent, up in years, venerable 10 gray-haired
  combining form: 6 presby- 7 presbyo-
Elders: 8 Joycelyn
Eldersburg: 4 city, town
  locale: 8 Maryland
eldest: 4 heir 9 born first, firstborn
  in law: 4 aine
eldest, Jr.'s maybe: 3 III
Eldorado: 3 car 4 auto 8 Cadillac
El Dorado: 4 city, town
  locale: 8 Arkansas
  treasure: 3 oro
  see also Spanish
El Dorado (1967 film): 5 oater 7 western
  cast: James Caan, Robert Mitchum, John Wayne
  director: Howard Hawks
Eldorado artist: 3 ELO
Eldorado author: Edgar Allan Poe
Eldoret: 4 city, town
  locale: 5 Kenya
Eldridge: 3 Roy 7 Cleaver 8 Florence
Eldridge, Roy: 9 trumpeter
  genre: 4 jazz
eldritch: 4 eery 5 eerie, weird
__ e Leandro: 3 Ero
Eleanor: 4 Bron 5 Rigby 6 Parker, Porter, Powell, Steber 7 Hibbert 9 Roosevelt
  mother-in-law: 4 Sara
  successor: 4 Bess
  to Franklin: 4 wife
  to Teddy: 5 niece
Eleanor and Franklin author: 4 Lash
Eleanor of __: 9 Aquitaine
Eleanor Rigby (1966 song) artist: Beatles
Eleanor Roosevelt, __ Roosevelt: 3 née
Eleazar, father of: 5 Aaron
elec.: 3 pwr.
  charge: 3 neg., pos.
  company: 4 util.
  cooler: 2 AC
  device: 4 rheo
  measure: 3 amp, kwh
elect: 3 opt 4 make, name, pick, take, vote 5 go for 6 accept, assign, choice, choose, chosen, decide, opt for, prefer, select, vote in 7 chooses, pick out, vote for 8 handpick, nominate, settle on 9 designate, determine, single out 10 decide upon, settle upon
  ender: 3 ion 5 orate
elected: 9 preferred, voluntary
  be ~: 3 win 5 get in
  ones: 3 ins
  try to get ~: 3 run
election: 4 race 5 event 6 choice, option, voting 7 primary 8 choosing, decision 9 balloting, franchise, selection 10 nomination, referendum
  campaign for ~: 5 stump
  committee: 6 caucus 8 congress
  district: 3 pct. 4 ward 8 precinct
  ender: 3 eer
  losers: 4 outs
  need: 4 poll 6 ballot
  participant: 5 voter
  result: 5 tally
  selection: 5 slate 9 candidate
  tactic: 5 smear
  time: 3 Nov. 4 fall 8 November
  winners: 3 ins
election __: 4 cake 5 board
__ election: 7 general, primary
Election (1999 film)
  cast: Matthew Broderick, Jessica Campbell, Chris Klein, Reese Witherspoon
Election Day: 3 Tue. 4 Tues.

Election Day (1985 song) artist: Arcadia
electioneer: **4** back, hype, plug, push **5** stump **6** talk up **7** advance, canvass, promote, support **8** campaign, plump for, politick
elective: **5** class **6** course **7** seminar **8** optional
electoral __: **4** vote **7** college
Electoral College member: **5** proxy
electorate: **5** party **6** public, voters
elector ender: **3** ate
Electra: **3** car, cat **4** auto, font **5** Buick **6** Carmen, Pleiad **8** typeface
brother of ~: **7** Orestes
daughter of ~: **4** Iris
father of ~: **5** Atlas **9** Agamemnon
husband of ~: **7** Pylades
lover of ~: **4** Zeus
sister of ~: **9** Iphigenia
son of ~: **5** Medon **9** Strophius
Electra __: **7** complex
Electra author: Euripides, Sophocles
Electra, Carmen spouse: Dennis Rodman
Electrasol: **9** detergent
alternative: **3** Joy **4** Ajax, Dawn **7** Cascade **8** Sunlight **9** Palmolive
electric: **5** kicky **7** charged, dynamic, voltaic **8** exciting, stirring **9** automatic, thrilling
company: **4** util. **7** utility
device: **5** relay **6** switch
discharge: **3** arc
meter: **5** gauge
power network: **4** grid
sign: **4** neon
starter: **6** dynamo
swimmer: **3** eel
electric __: **3** arc, eel, eye, ray **4** blue, cell, flux, glow, wave **5** field, light, meter, motor, organ, razor, storm, torch **6** charge, guitar, needle **7** catfish, circuit, current, furnace
__-electric: **5** turbo **6** diesel
__ Electric: **7** General
electrical: **9** automated, motorized **10** electronic, mechanized
conductor: **4** wire **5** shunt **6** dynode
connector: **4** plug
cord in Britain: **4** flex
junction: **3** wye
problem: **5** short, surge
switch: **5** on/off
unit: **3** amp, mho, ohm **4** volt, watt **5** farad, gauss **7** coulomb **8** ampere. mV
electrical __: **5** storm **6** degree
Electric Avenue (1983 song) artist: Eddy Grant
Electric Blue (1988 song) artist: Icehouse
electric-dart firer: **5** taser
electric eel: **4** fish
electric guitar hookup: **3** amp
Electric Horseman, The (1979 film)
cast: Jane Fonda, Willie Nelson, Valerie Perrine, Robert Redford
director: Sydney Pollack
electrician: **5** wirer
film ~: **6** gaffer
need: **6** pliers
electricity: **2** AC, DC **5** juice, power **7** current, utility, voltage
demand for ~: **4** load
generator: **3** eel, ray
install ~: **4** wire
__ electricity: **6** static **7** voltaic
Electric Kool-Aid Acid Test, The author: Tom Wolfe
electric-plug projection: **5** prong
electric slide: **5** dance
electrify: **4** fire, send, stir, wire **5** rouse, shock **6** arouse, charge, dazzle, excite, thrill **7** enthuse **8** energize, surprise **9** galvanize, go over big, magnetize, stimulate, transport **10** invigorate
electrifying: **7** vibrant **8** dramatic, striking **9** arresting, thrilling
fish: **3** eel, ray
electro-__: **6** optics **7** osmosis
electrochemistry: **7** science
electrode: **5** anode **7** cathode
bridge: **3** arc
of an ~: **6** anodal, anodic **8** cathodic
__ electrode: **7** calomel, control
electro ending: **4** lyte
Electrolux: **3** vac **6** vacuum
competitor: **5** Kirby, Oreck **6** Eureka, Hoover
electrolysis migrator: **5** anion
electromagnetic
amplifier: **5** maser
storm: **6** aurora
unit: **5** abohm
electromagnetic __: **4** pump, tape, unit, wave **5** field, pulse
electromotive force unit: **4** volt
electron: **6** lepton **8** particle
charge: **3** neg., pos. **8** negative, positive
free ~: **3** ion
gainer: **5** anion
high speed ~: **4** beta
site: **4** atom
tube: **5** diode
electron __: **3** gun **4** lens, tube **6** camera, optics
electron-__: **4** volt
__ electron: **4** free **7** valence
electronic: **6** hi-tech **9** automated, automatic
control system: **5** servo
info source: **5** CD/ROM
instrument: **4** Moog **5** synth
not ~: **5** print
reading: **4** scan
signal: **4** beep, blip, page **5** bleep
summoner: **5** pager **6** beeper
electronic __: **4** game, mail, tube **5** brain, crime, flash, music **7** banking, editing, imaging
electronic __ transfer: **5** funds
Electronic __ Systems: **4** Data
electronic music pioneer: **3** Eno
electronics: **7** science
company: **3** RCA **4** Aiwa, Koss, Sony **5** Casio, Sanyo, Sharp
device: **5** diode
electron tube part: **5** anode
electrostatic __: **4** lens, unit
electrum: **5** alloy, metal
component: **4** gold **6** nickel, silver
__ Elect, The: **5** Bride
__ E. Lee: **4** Robt. **6** Robert
eleemosynary: **7** liberal **10** almsgiving, altruistic, beneficent, benevolent, charitable, gratuitous
Elegaic Stanzas author: William Wordsworth
elegance: **4** luxe, ritz **5** charm, class, flair, grace, poise, style, taste **6** beauty, luxury, polish **7** culture, dignity, hauteur **8** breeding, delicacy, felicity, grandeur, lushness, nobility, noblesse, poshness, splendor **9** gentility, good looks **10** refinement
elegant: **4** chic, fine, haut, lacy, luxe, nice, posh **5** clean, fancy, grand, haute, plush, ritzy, slick, smart, swank, swell, swish **6** august, chichi, classy, deluxe, dressy, modish, ornate, proper, spruce, superb, urbane **7** courtly, dashing, genteel, opulent, refined, shapely, stately, stylish, voguish **8** artistic, debonair, decorous, esthetic, finished, gorgeous, graceful, handsome, highbred, highbrow, ladylike, majestic, polished, splendid, superior, tasteful **9** beautiful, classical, debonaire, dignified, exquisite, glamorous, high-toned, in fashion, luxurious, processed, sumptuous **10** artistical, cultivated, debonnaire, majestical
not ~: **5** crass, tacky
elegant fowl, Lear's: **3** owl
Elegants song: Little Star (1958)
elegiac: **3** sad **5** bleak **6** dismal, somber **7** doleful **8** dolorous, funereal, mournful **9** sorrowful, woebegone **10** lugubrious, melancholy
elegit: **4** writ
elegy: **4** poem **5** dirge **6** lament, plaint **7** requiem **8** threnody
Elegy Written in a Country Churchyard author: Thomas Gray
__ eleison: **5** kyrie
Elektra: **8** asteroid
element: **3** tin **4** gold, iron, item, lead, link, neon, part, unit, zinc **5** argon, boron, facet, field, iodin, piece, radon, state, xenon **6** aspect, barium, carbon, cerium, cesium, cobalt, copper, curium, detail, domain, erbium, factor, helium, indium, iodine, member, milieu, nickel, osmium, oxygen, radium, silver, sodium, sphere, streak, sulfur **7** arsenic, bismuth, bohrium, bromine, cadmium, caesium, calcium, dubnium, feature, fermium, gallium, habitat, hafnium, hahnium, hassium, holmium, iridium, krypton, lithium, mercury, niobium, portion, rhenium, rhodium, section, silicon, sulphur, terbium, thulium, uranium, wolfram, yttrium **8** actinium, aluminum, antimony, astatine, chlorine, chromium, europium, fluorine, francium, hydrogen, lutetium, material, nitrogen, nobelium, platinum, polonium, rubidium, samarium, scandium, selenium, tantalum, thallium, titanium, tungsten, vanadium **9** aluminium, americium, berkelium, beryllium, component, germanium, lanthanum, magnesium, manganese, neodymium, neptunium, palladium, plutonium, potassium, ruthenium, strontium, tellurium, ytterbium, zirconium **10** dysprosium, gadolinium, ingredient, lawrencium, molybdenum, particular, phosphorus, promethium, technetium **11** californium, einsteinium, mendelevium **12** protactinium **13** rutherfordium
class: **5** metal **8** nonmetal
component: **4** atom
distinguishing ~: **4** qual. **7** quality
having one ~: **5** unary
ID: **4** at. no.
inactive ~: **4** neon **5** argon, radon, xenon **6** helium **7** krypton
in alchemy: **3** air **4** fire **5** earth, water
magnetic ~: **6** cobalt
out of one's ~: **4** asea, lost **5** at sea
radioactive ~: **5** radon **6** curium, radium **7** bohrium, dubnium, fermium, hassium, thorium, uranium **8** actinium, astatine, francium, nobelium, polonium **9** americium, berkelium, neptunium, plutonium **10** lawrencium, meitnerium, promethium, seaborgium, technetium **11** californium, einsteinium, mendelevium **12** protactinium **13** rutherfordium
rare earth ~: **6** cerium, cesium, erbium **7** caesium, holmium, terbium, thulium, yttrium **8** europium, lutetium, samarium, scandium **9** neodymium, ytterbium **10** dysprosium, gadolinium, promethium **12** praseodymium
suffix: **3** -ium
unit: **4** atom **8** particle
__ element: **4** unit **5** major, minor, trace **6** typing
Element: **3** SUV **5** Honda
elemental: **5** basic **6** earthy **7** organic, primary **8** integral, ultimate **9** component, essential, intrinsic **10** primordial, underlying
state: **3** gas **5** solid **6** liquid **7** gaseous
elementary: **4** easy **5** basal, basic, plain **6** facile, simple **7** initial, primary **8** duck soup, original **9** beginning, essential, incipient, primitive, uncomplex **10** child's play, simplified, substratal, underlying
particle: **4** muon **5** meson, quark **6** baryon, lepton
elementary __: **6** charge, school **7** process
elements: **6** matter **7** climate, weather
basic ~: **4** ABCs
one of the four ~: **3** air **4** fire **5** earth, water
safe from the ~: **6** indoor, inside **7** indoors
elements by atomic number:
1 - hydrogen (H)
2 - helium (He)
3 - lithium (Li)
4 - beryllium (Be)
5 - boron (B)
6 - carbon (C)
7 - nitrogen (N)
8 - oxygen (O)
9 - fluorine (F)
10 - neon (Ne)
11 - sodium (Na)
12 - magnesium (Mg)
13 - aluminum (Al)
14 - silicon (Si)
15 - phosphorus (P)
16 - sulfur/sulphur (S)
17 - chlorine (Cl)
18 - argon (Ar)
19 - potassium (K)
20 - calcium (Ca)
21 - scandium (Sc)
22 - titanium (Ti)
23 - vanadium (V)
24 - chromium (Cr)
25 - manganese (Mn)
26 - iron (Fe)
27 - cobalt (Co)
28 - nickel (Ni)
29 - copper (Cu)
30 - zinc (Zn)
31 - gallium (Ga)
32 - germanium (Ge)
33 - arsenic (As)
34 - selenium (Se)
35 - bromine (Br)
36 - krypton (Kr)
37 - rubidium (Rb)
38 - strontium (Sr)
39 - yttrium (Y)
40 - zirconium (Zr)
41 - niobium (Nb)
42 - molybdenum (Mo)
43 - technetium (Tc)
44 - ruthenium (Ru)
45 - rhodium (Rh)
46 - palladium (Pd)
47 - silver (Ag)
48 - cadmium (Cd)
49 - indium (In)
50 - tin (Sn)
51 - antimony (Sb)
52 - tellurium (Te)
53 - iodine (I)
54 - xenon (Xe)
55 - cesium (Cs)
56 - barium (Ba)

57 - lanthanum (La)
58 - cerium (Ce)
59 - praseodymium (Pr)
60 - neodymium (Nd)
61 - promethium (Pm)
62 - samarium (Sm)
63 - europium (Eu)
64 - gadolinium (Gd)
65 - terbium (Tb)
66 - dysprosium (Dy)
67 - holmium (Ho)
68 - erbium (Er)
69 - thulium (Tm)
70 - ytterbium (Yb)
71 - lutetium (Lu)
72 - hafnium (Hf)
73 - tantalum (Ta)
74 - tungsten/wolfram (W)
75 - rhenium (Re)
76 - osmium (Os)
77 - iridium (Ir)
78 - platinum (Pt)
79 - gold (Au)
80 - mercury (Hg)
81 - thallium (Tl)
82 - lead (Pb)
83 - bismuth (Bi)
84 - polonium (Po)
85 - astatine (At)
86 - radon (Rn)
87 - francium (Fr)
88 - radium (Ra)
89 - actinium (Ac)
90 - thorium (Th)
91 - proactinium (Pa)
92 - uranium (U)
93 - neptunium (Np)
94 - plutonium (Pu)
95 - americium (Am)
96 - curium (Cm)
97 - berkelium (Bk)
98 - californium (Cf)
99 - einsteinium (Es)
100 - fermium (Fm)
101 - mendelevium (Md)
102 - nobelium (No)
103 - lawrencium (Lr)
104 - rutherfordium (Rf)
105 - hahnium/dubnium (Ha/Db)
106 - seaborgium (Sg)
107 - bohrium (Bh)
108 - hassium (Hs)
109 - meitnerium (Mt)

Elements of Style, The author: E.B. White
__ Element, The: 5 Fifth
__ elemi: 3 gum
Elena: 6 Bechke, Bonner, Valova 7 Verdugo 9 Nikolaidi
in English: 5 Ellen, Helen
__ Elena: 5 Maria
Eleni (1985 film)
cast: Linda Hunt, John Malkovich, Kate Nelligan
director: Peter Yates
Eleniak, Erika: 7 actress
film: The Beverly Hillbillies (1993)
Under Siege (1992)
TV: Baywatch
Eleni author: 4 Gage
Elenore (1968 song) artist: Turtles
Eleonora: 4 Duse
Eleonora author: Edgar Allan Poe
elepaio: 4 bird
elephant: 5 Dumbo, Jumbo, mount 6 animal, mammal 9 pachyderm
counterpart: 6 donkey
dinner: 6 baobab
ender: 3 ine, oid
feature: 3 ear 4 tusk 5 trunk
female: 3 cow
GOP ~ creator: 4 Nast
group: 4 herd
home: 3 zoo 6 big top, circus
lone ~: 5 rogue
male: 4 bull
owner: 4 raja
party: 3 GOP
prehistoric ~: 7 mammoth 8 stegodon 9 dinothere
seat: 6 houdah, howdah
sound: 6 bellow 7 trumpet
trap: 5 kheda 6 keddah, khedah
young: 4 calf
elephant __: 3 ear, gun 4 bird, fish, seal 5 folio, grass, shrew
__ elephant: 3 sea 4 pink 5 rogue, white 6 Indian 7 African, Asiatic
Elephant Boy (1937 film)
cast: Walter Hudd, Sabu
director: Robert Flaherty, Zoltan Korda
elephantine: 3 big 4 huge, vast 5 giant, great, jumbo, large 7 hulking, immense, lumpish, mammoth, massive, sizable, titanic 8 colossal, enormous, gigantic, king-size, oversize, sizeable, towering, whapping, whopping 9 Herculean, humongous, monstrous, overlarge, ponderous 10 gargantuan, monumental, prodigious, stupendous, tremendous
Elephant Man, The (1980 film)
cast: Anne Bancroft, Sir John Gielgud, Anthony Hopkins, John Hurt
director: David Lynch
Elephant of the Celebes artist: 5 Ernst
elephant's-ear: 4 taro
Eleuthera locale: 7 Bahamas
Eleutherius: 4 pope 7 pontiff
elev.: 2 mt. 3 alt., hgt., mtn.
elevate: 4 bump, hike, lift, rise 5 boost, cheer, deify, elate, ensky, exalt, grace, heave, hoist, raise, set up 6 bump up, buoy up, enrich, haul up, hike up, jack up, jerk up, lift up, move up, perk up, praise, prefer, refine, uphold, uplift 7 advance, dignify, enhance, ennoble, further, glorify, hearten, improve, inspire, magnify, promote, raise up, upgrade, upheave, upraise 8 heighten, levitate, nominate 9 intensify, transport
elevated: 4 high, tall 5 grand, great, lofty, moral, noble 6 aerial, alpine, high up, superb 7 eminent, ethical, exalted, soaring, stately, sublime, uprisen 8 empyreal, empyrean, rarefied, towering, upraised, virtuous 9 dignified, honorable, righteous 10 high-minded, upstanding
area: 4 mesa 5 ridge 7 plateau 8 highland
dwelling: 4 aery, eyry 5 aerie, eyrie 9 tree house
elevated __: 7 railway
elevation: 4 hill, hump, rise, side 5 boost, knoll, level, raise, ridge 6 ascent, glacis, height, zenith 7 hillock, plateau, rampart, stature 8 altitude, eminence, grandeur, mountain, nobility, platform 9 acclivity, loftiness, promotion, sublimity, upgrading 10 apotheosis, exaltation, high ground, levitation, preferment, prominence
elevator: 4 lift, shoe 5 hoist
alternative: 5 stair 9 escalator
button: 2 up 4 down, stop 8 door open 9 door close
compartment: 3 cab, car
contents: 5 grain, wheat
inventor: 4 Otis
music: 5 Muzak
passage: 5 shaft
sound: 5 whish
stop: 4 deck 5 floor, level, story 6 cellar 9 mezzanine
take the ~: 4 go up, rise 5 climb 6 ascend
elevator __: 3 car 4 shoe
__ elevator: 5 grain 7 service
élève locale: 5 école, lycée
__ Eleven: 6 Ocean's 7 Chapter
eleven combining form: 5 undec- 6 hendec- 7 hendeca-
elevenses: 3 tea
eleventh-day gift: 6 pipers
eleventh-hour: 4 late 5 tardy 7 belated, delayed, overdue 10 behind time, last-minute, unpunctual
elf: 3 fay, hob, imp 4 nixy, peri, pixy 5 faery, fairy, gnome, nisse, nixie, ouphe, pixie 6 faerie, goblin, kobold, sprite 7 brownie, gremlin 8 toymaker 9 hobgoblin 10 leprechaun
ender: 4 lock
product: 3 toy
elf counsel, name meaning: 6 Elvira
elf friend, name meaning: 5 Alvin
elfin: 3 fey 6 impish, little, petite 7 puckish 8 prankish 9 fairylike, sprightly, undersize 10 diminutive, leprechaun
elfish: 5 small 6 impish 8 spritely
Elfman: 5 Danny, Jenna
Elfman, Jenna: 7 actress
film: Ed TV (1999)
Keeping the Faith (2000)
TV: Dharma & Greg
elf ruler, name meaning: 6 Aubrey
Elgar, Edward: 7 British 8 composer
work: The Apostles
The Black Knight
Cockaigne
Coronation Ode
Enigma Variations
The Kingdom
Pomp and Circumstance
Elgart: 3 Les 5 Larry
Elgin: 4 city, town 5 watch 6 Baylor
alternative: 4 Ebel, Rado 5 Casio, Lorus, Omega, Rolex, Seiko, Timex 6 Bulova, Fossil, Movado, Pulsar, Swatch 7 Citizen 8 Longines, Tag Heuer, Tourneau
locale: 6 Canada 7 Ontario 8 Illinois
Elgin Marbles locale: 6 Athens
Elgon: 4 peak 5 mount 8 mountain
locale: 5 Kenya 6 Africa, Uganda
El Greco: 6 artist 7 painter
birthplace: 5 Crete 6 Candia
home: 5 Spain 6 Toledo
museum: 5 Prado
El Grullo: 4 city, town
locale: 6 Mexico 7 Jalisco
Eli: 4 Bush 5 Lilly, Terry, Yalie 7 Bulldog, Wallach, Whitney
cheer: 5 boola
rival: 6 Cantab
Elia: 4 Lamb 5 Kazan
product: 5 essay
Elias: 4 Howe 5 Corey 7 Canetti
elicit: 3 get, pry 4 draw, milk 5 cause, educe, evoke, fetch 6 arouse, derive, dig out, obtain, prompt, recall 7 draw out, extract, get from, provoke, trigger 8 bring out, occasion 9 call forth 10 bring forth
elide: 4 omit, slur 5 blend 6 delete, excise, ignore 7 abridge, curtail 8 cut short, leave out, pass over, slur over, suppress 9 gloss over, slide over, strike out, syncopate
Elie: 4 Abel 6 Wiesel 8 Ducommun, Nadelman
Eliel's son: 4 Eero
Eliezer, parent of: 5 Moses 8 Zipporah
eligible: 3 fit 5 unwed 6 in line, single, suited, vested, worthy 8 wifeless 9 qualified, unmarried 10 acceptable, employable, privileged
make ~: 6 enable, permit 7 empower, entitle, intitle, qualify 8 christen 9 authorize, designate, privilege 10 legitimize
Eligius: 5 saint
Elihu: 4 Root, Yale
friend of ~: 3 Job
Elijah: 4 Wood 5 McCoy 8 Muhammad
anathema for ~: 4 Baal
in Russian: 4 Ilya
in the Douay: 5 Elias
Elijah's __: 3 cup 5 chair
Elimelech, wife of: 5 Naomi
eliminate: 2 ax 3 axe, lop, rid 4 dele, drop, omit, oust, slay, x out 5 clear, eject, erase, evict, expel, purge 6 cancel, cut out, defeat, delete, efface, put out, reject, remove, screen, uproot 7 blot out, cast out, discard, dismiss, exclude, rule out, scratch, take out, wipe out 8 count out, drive out, get rid of, knock out, leave out, phase out, stamp out, throw out 9 close down, discharge, dispose of, disregard, eradicate, extirpate, liquidate, polish off, terminate 10 annihilate, disqualify, do away with, extinguish, invalidate
elimination: 3 ebb 4 test 5 letup 6 fading, relief, waning 7 anodyne, decline 8 decrease, quelling, stoppage 9 abatement, abolition, annulment, deduction, lessening, reduction, tempering, weakening 10 arrestment, diminution, prevention, subsidence
Eliminator artist: 5 ZZ Top
Elinor: 4 Glyn 5 Wylie 7 Donahue
Elinvar: 5 alloy
component: 4 iron 6 nickel 8 chromium
Elio: 5 Petri 6 Chacon 8 Fiorucci
__ Eli Olds: 6 Ransom
Elion, Gertrude: 8 Nobelist
Eliot: 2 T.S. 4 Ness 6 George 7 Janeway
Eliot, George: 5 alias 6 writer 7 British
homeland: England
real last name: Evans
work: Adam Bede
Daniel Deronda
Felix Holt
Middlemarch
The Mill on the Floss
The Radical
Romola
Silas Marner
__ Eliot Morison: 6 Samuel
Eliot, T.S.: 4 poet 6 writer 7 British 8 Nobelist 10 playwright
birthplace: St. Louis
colleague: Pound
first name: Thomas
middle name: Stearns
work: Ash Wednesday
Aunt Helen
The Cocktail Party
A Cooking Egg
The Family Reunion
The Hollow Men
The Love Song of J. Alfred Prufrock
Murder in the Cathedral
Portrait of a Lady
The Sacred Wood
The Waste Land
Eliphaz, parent of: 4 Adah, Esau
Elis
see Yale
Elisabeth: 4 Shue
Eli's Coming (1969 song) artist: Three Dog Night
Elise: 4 Neal 8 Kimberly 9 Christine
__ Elise: 3 Für
Eliseo: 5 Diego
Elisha: 4 Cook, Otis
Elisheba, husband of: 5 Aaron
Elissa: 4 Dido 5 Landi
elite: 3 top 4 best, font, pick, type 5 A-

list, cream, haves, noble, prime, upper **6** aristo, choice, chosen, flower, gentry, jet set, select, tip-top **7** favored, in crowd, society **8** literati, nobility, old money, selected, top-class, top-notch **9** blue blood, exclusive, gilt-edged, haut monde, highbrows, high-class, top drawer, topflight **10** blue bloods, first-class, glitterati, illuminati, main liners, privileged, upper-class, upper crust, world-class
alternative: **4** pica
___ elite: **5** power
Elite: **3** car, Reo **4** auto, font **8** typeface
Elite Syncopations: **3** rag
elitist: **4** snob **7** pompous **8** highbrow
elixir: **4** cure **5** tonic **6** liquid, liquor, nectar, potion, remedy **7** arcanum, cure-all, nostrum, panacea **8** medicine, pick-me-up, solution **10** invigorant, medication
___ Eli Yale: **5** Bingo
Eliza: **9** Doolittle
where ~ urged Dover: **5** Ascot
Elizabeth: **4** city, Dole, Peña, town **5** Allen, Arden, Bowen, Kenny, queen, ruler, Seton **6** Ashley, Hurley, Jolley, Taylor **7** Berkley, Hartman, Perkins, Shannon **8** Gilbreth, McGovern **9** Blackwell **10** Montgomery
in Germany: **4** Ilse
in Spanish: **6** Isabel
locale: **9** New Jersey
Elizabeth ___ Browning: **7** Barrett
Elizabeth ___ Seton: **3** Ann
Elizabeth ___ Stanton: **4** Cady
Elizabethan: **3** Age, Era **6** sonnet
epithet: **4** Bess
Elizabeth and ___: **5** Essex
Elizabeth Appleton author: John O'Hara
Elizabeth Arden: **6** makeup
alternative: **4** Avon **5** Almay **6** Lauder, Revlon **7** Lancome, Mary Kay **8** Clinique **9** Cover Girl, Max Factor **10** Maybelline
Elizabeth I: **5** queen, royal, ruler, Tudor
father: **5** Henry
mother: **6** Boleyn
Elizabeth II: **5** queen, royal, ruler **7** Windsor
award bestowed by ~: **3** OBE
child: **4** Anne **6** Andrew, Edward **7** Charles
father: **6** George
spouse: **6** Philip
to Edward VIII: **5** niece
Elizabeth II, Queen: **4** boat, ship **5** liner
milieu for ~: **3** sea **5** ocean
___ Elizabeth Mastrantonio: **4** Mary
Elizabeth the Queen author: Maxwell Anderson
Elizabethtown: **4** city
locale: **8** Kentucky
Eliza composer: **4** Arne
Elizondo, Hector: **5** actor
film: The Flamingo Kid (1984)
Frankie and Johnny (1991)
Nothing in Common (1986)
The Princess Diaries (2001)
Runaway Bride (1999)
TV: Chicago Hope
elk: **4** deer **6** animal, mammal, wapiti
ender: **5** hound
feature: **4** horn **6** antler
female: **3** cow
male: **4** bull
relative: **3** roe **4** axis, pudu, shou, sika **5** moose **6** chital, guemal, hangul, huemul, sambar, sambur, thamin **7** brocket, caribou, muntjac, muntjak, sambhar, sambhur **8** reindeer **9** barasingh
young: **4** calf
elk ___: **5** grass **6** clover
Elk: **5** range, river
city on the ~: **10** Charleston
Elke: **6** Sommer
Elk Grove: **4** city, town
locale: **8** Illinois **10** California
Elkhart: **4** city, town
locale: **7** Indiana
elkhound: **3** dog **5** canid **6** canine
Elkin, Stanley: **6** writer
Elko: **4** city, town
locale: **6** Nevada
Elkridge: **4** city, town
locale: **8** Maryland
Elks: **4** BPOE **5** lodge
Elkton: **4** city, town
locale: **8** Maryland
ell: **4** wing **5** annex, joint **8** addition
build an ~: **5** add on
Ella: **5** Joyce, Logan **6** Grasso, Raines **7** Cinders **10** Fitzgerald
contemporary: **4** Lena
specialty: **4** scat
Ellas: **6** Greece
elle: **3** she **6** French
Elle: **3** mag **5** model **10** Macpherson
rival: **5** Vogue
Elle et lui author: George Sand
Ellen: **4** Drew **5** Corby, Terry **6** Barkin, Greene **7** Burstyn, Glasgow, Goodman **9** Cleghorne, DeGeneres
in French: **6** Elaine
in Italian: **5** Elena
in Russian: **6** Yelena
in Spanish: **5** Elena
___-Ellen: **4** Vera
___ Ellen Ewing: **3** Sue
Eller: **4** aunt
Ellerbee: **5** Linda
Ellery colleague: **3** Rex **4** Erle **6** Agatha
Ellesmere: **4** isle **6** island
Ellie: **5** Ewing **9** Greenwich
to J.R.: **4** mama
Ellie ___: **4** Rhee
Elliman, Yvonne song: If I Can't Have You (1978)
Ellington: **4** Duke **6** Mercer
contemporary: **5** Basie **9** Armstrong
Ellington, Duke: **6** Edward **7** pianist
genre: **4** jazz
Ellio's: **5** pizza
alternative: **5** Jeno's, Tony's **7** Celeste, Totino's **8** DiGiorno **9** Tombstone **10** Freschetta
Elliot: **4** Cass **8** Mama Cass
Elliott: **3** Bob, Sam **4** Cass **5** Chris, Gould, Missy **6** Nugent **7** Denholm **8** Mama Cass
Elliott, Denholm: **5** actor
film: The Cruel Sea (1953)
Defence of the Realm (1985)
Indiana Jones and the Last Crusade (1989)
The Night My Number Came Up (1955)
Noises Off (1992)
Nothing but the Best (1964)
A Room With a View (1986)
Saint Jack (1979)
Trading Places (1983)
Elliott, Missy
song: Get Ur Freak On (2001)
Hot Boyz (1999)
Make It Hot (1998)
Not Tonight (1997)
One Minute Man (2001)
Trippin' (1998)
Elliott, Sam: **5** actor
film: The Desperate Trail (1994)
The Hi-Lo Country (1998)
Mask (1985)
Prancer (1989)
Shakedown (1988)
We Were Soldiers (2002)
spouse: Katharine Ross
ellipse: **5** curve, orbit **9** sinuosity
part: **3** arc
ellipsis component: **3** dot
elliptic: **4** oval **5** ovoid **9** egg-shaped
elliptical: **4** oval **5** ovate, ovoid, round, terse **6** curved, oblong **7** egglike **9** egg-shaped **10** oval-shaped
elliptical ___: **5** light **6** galaxy
Ellis: **3** isl. **4** Bell, isle **5** Burks, Jimmy, Perry **6** island **7** Shirley **8** Havelock, Marsalis, Patricia
Island locale: **3** NYC
Ellison: **5** James, Ralph **6** Harlan
Ellison, Harlan: **6** author, writer
genre: **5** sci-fi
Ellison, Ralph: **6** author, writer
work: Going to the Territory
Invisible Man
Shadow and Act
Ellis, Shirley
song: The Clapping Song (1965)
The Name Game (1965)
The Nitty Gritty (1963)
Ellmann, Richard: **6** writer
Ellsberg: **6** Daniel
Elly ___ Clampett: **3** May
elm: **4** tree, wych **8** hardwood **9** shade tree
tree: **7** zelkova **9** hackberry
___ elm: **4** rock, wych **5** water **6** winged **7** English
Elm: **2** st. **6** street
Elman: **5** Ziggy **6** Mischa
Elman, Mischa: **7** Russian **9** violinist
El Mante: **4** city, town
locale: **6** Mexico **10** Tamaulipas
Elm City collegian: **3** Eli **5** Yalie **7** Bulldog
___ elm disease: **5** Dutch
Elmer: **4** Fudd, Rice, Valo **5** Flick **6** Gantry, Sperry **9** Bernstein, Nordstrom
mate: **5** Elsie
to Bugs: **3** doc
Elmer Gantry: **4** film **5** novel
author: Sinclair Lewis
cast: Dean Jagger, Shirley Jones, Burt Lancaster, Jean Simmons
director: Richard Brooks
Elmer's ___: **4** Glue, Tune
Elmer the Great (1933 film)
cast: Joe E. Brown, Patricia Ellis, Frank McHugh
director: Mervyn LeRoy
Elmhurst: **4** city, town
locale: **8** Illinois
Elmira: **4** city, town
locale: **7** New York
El Misti: **7** volcano
fallout: **3** ash
locale: **4** Peru **5** Andes
Elmo: **5** Roper, saint **6** Muppet **7** Lincoln, Zumwalt
on Eek the Cat: **3** elk
street: **6** Sesame
Elmont: **4** city, town
locale: **7** New York
El Monte: **4** city, town
locale: **10** California
Elmore: **7** Leonard
___ Elmo's fire: **5** Saint
Elmwood Park: **4** city, town
locale: **8** Illinois
Elnath: **4** star
ELO
song: Can't Get It Out of My Head (1975)
Don't Bring Me Down (1979)
Evil Woman (1975)
Hold on Tight (1981)
Shine a Little Love (1979)
Telephone Line (1977)
Xanadu (1980)
elocution: **5** voice **6** speech **7** diction, oratory **8** delivery, rhetoric, verbiage **9** eloquence, utterance **10** expression, vocalizing
elocutionist: **6** orator
eloge: **6** eulogy **8** encomium **9** panegyric
elohim: **3** God **7** Creator, Jehovah
eloign: **4** flee **5** elope, leave **6** beat it, decamp, desert, escape, go AWOL, run off **7** abscond, duck out, run away, vamoose **9** cut and run, disappear, skedaddle, sneak away, steal away **10** fly the coop, make a break
Eloisa to Abelard author: Alexander Pope
Eloise's dog: **6** Weenie
elongate: **6** extend **7** enlarge, lengthy, stretch **8** lengthen **9** string out
elongated: **7** lengthy **8** drawn out, expanded, extended
shape: **4** oval **7** ellipse
elongation: **4** limb, wing **5** annex **6** branch, growth, length **7** adjunct **8** addition, appendix, increase, widening **9** appendage, expansion, extension, inflation **10** attachment, distension, perpetuity, projection, stretching, supplement
elongator: **5** stilt
Elon, son-in-law of: **4** Esau
elope: **3** run **4** bolt, flee **5** leave **6** decamp, escape, run off **7** abscond, run away, take off **8** skip town, slip away, sneak off **9** steal away
eloper: **5** lover, Romeo **6** Juliet **8** lothario **9** inamorato
need: **2** JP **6** ladder
of rhyme: **4** dish **5** spoon
eloquence: **4** rhet. **7** diction, fluency, oratory **8** facility, rhetoric **9** elocution, gift of gab, loquacity, readiness, wittiness **10** expression, volubility
eloquent: **4** glib **5** vivid, vocal **6** fluent, moving **7** graphic **8** poignant, readable, stirring, touching **9** graphical, talkative **10** articulate, expressive, impressive, meaningful, passionate, persuasive, rhetorical
wax ~: **3** act **4** gush **5** orate **7** carry on, overact, perform, playact **9** dramatize
El Paso: **4** city, town
athletes: **6** Miners **9** Longhorns
campus: **4** UTEP
fort: **5** Bliss
locale: **5** Texas
river: **9** Rio Grande
___ El Paso: **3** Old
El Paso (1959 song) artist: Marty Robbins
Elpis: **8** asteroid
El Prado: **5** museo **6** museum
El Pueblito: **4** city, town
locale: **6** Mexico **9** Querétaro
El Rosario: **4** city, town
locale: **6** Mexico **7** Sinaloa
Elroy: **6** Hirsch, Jetson
pet: **5** Astro
Els: **5** Ernie
Elsa: **7** Klensch, lioness, Maxwell, Morante, Peretti **10** Lanchester, Martinelli
dad: **4** lion
el Saadawi, Nawal: **6** writer **8** Egyptian
El Salón Mexico composer: **7** Copland
El Salto: **4** city, town
locale: **6** Mexico **7** Jalisco
El Salvador: **6** nation **7** country
city: **5** Apopa **8** Santa Ana **9** Mejicanos, San Miguel, Soyapango
currency: **5** colón
Indian: **5** Lenca
neighbor: **8** Honduras **9** Guatemala
org.: **3** OAS
see also Spanish

Elsa's Dream: **4** aria
else: **4** more **5** if not, other **7** besides, further, instead **9** different, otherwise **10** additional, in addition
before anything ~: **5** first **6** maiden, mainly **7** chiefly, initial, leading, lead-off, opening, pioneer, premier, to start **8** above all, earliest, foremost, original **9** in advance, inaugural, initially, primarily, primitive, prototype **10** originally
ender: **5** where
everything ~: **4** rest **9** remainder
nothing ~ but: **5** fully **6** really, wholly
or ~: **9** otherwise
or ~ in music: **5** ossia
something ~: **4** neat **5** doozy, grand, novel, other **6** marvel, unique **7** another, unusual **9** wonderful
somewhere ~: **4** away, gone **6** absent
__ else fails...: **5** If all
Els, Ernie: **6** golfer
milieu: **5** links **6** course
org.: **3** PGA
elsewhere: **3** off, out **4** away, gone **5** not in **6** abroad, absent **7** missing, not here **8** vanished **9** out of here **10** on vacation
direct ~: **5** refer
Elsie: **3** cow **5** Janis **8** Dinsmore
comment from ~: **3** low, moo
spouse: **5** Elmer
Elsie Venner author: Oliver Wendell Holmes
Eltanin: **4** star
El Tejar: **4** city, town
locale: **6** Mexico **8** Veracruz
Elton: **4** John
eluant: **7** solvent
Éluard, Paul: **4** poet **6** French
elucidate: **4** show **5** gloss, solve, state **6** set out, unfold **7** clarify, clear up, explain, resolve **8** describe, illumine, simplify, spell out **9** bring home, enlighten, exemplify, explicate, expound on, get across, interpret, make plain, translate **10** account for, illuminate, illustrate
elucidation: **5** gloss, light **7** comment **8** exegesis, solution
elude: **4** defy, duck, flee, foil, lose, shun **5** avoid, dodge, evade, parry, shake, shirk, skirt **6** baffle, escape, eschew, outrun, outwit, thwart **7** mystify, retreat **8** confound, get out of, shake off, sidestep, slip past, throw off **9** frustrate, get around **10** circumvent, get clear of
Elul: **5** month **6** Hebrew
predecessor: **2** Av
successor: **6** Tishri
elusive: **3** sly **4** cagy, eely **5** cagey **6** shifty, tricky **7** evasive, furtive **8** baffling, puzzling, slippery **9** deceitful, deceptive **10** intangible, mysterious
one: **3** eel **6** dodger
elute: **7** extract, wash out
elver: **3** eel **4** fish **5** moray **8** glass eel
Elvin: **5** Hayes, Jones **6** Bishop
Elvira (1981 song) artist: Oak Ridge Boys
Elvis: **4** idol **6** Stojko **7** Presley **8** Costello
daughter: **4** Lisa
like ~ ' shoes: **4** blue **5** suede
recording: **4** oldy **5** oldie
elvish: **5** short, small **6** impish
Elway, John: **2** QB **11** quarterback
sport: **8** football
Elwes, Cary: **5** actor
film: Glory (1989)
Hot Shots! (1991)
Kiss the Girls (1997)
Lady Jane (1985)
The Princess Bride (1987)
Robin Hood: Men in Tights (1993)
Shadow of the Vampire (2000)
Twister (1996)
film (voice): Quest for Camelot (1998)
Elwood: **4** Dowd
friend: **5** pooka **6** Harvey, rabbit
Ely: **3** Joe, Ron **4** city, isle, town **10** Culbertson
locale: **3** Nev. **6** Nevada
Elyria: **4** city, town
locale: **4** Ohio
__ Élysées: **6** Champs
elysian: **8** beatific, empyreal, empyrean **9** ambrosial, celestial
Elysian Fields: **6** utopia
Elysium: **4** Eden **6** heaven **7** Nirvana, rapture, Valhall, Walhall **8** paradise, Valhalla, Walhalla **9** Shangri-la
Elytis, Odysseus: **4** poet **5** Greek **6** writer **8** Nobelist
em: **3** ltr. **6** letter
follower: **2** en
preceder: **2** el
em __: **4** dash, pica, quad
__ 'em: **3** sic **4** hold
Em
to Dorothy: **4** aunt
E.M.: **7** Forster
emaciate: **5** dry up **6** wither **7** atrophy, shrivel **9** waste away **10** degenerate
emaciated: **4** bony, lank, lean, puny, thin **5** boney, gaunt **6** ill-fed, meager, peaked, skinny **7** haggard, starved **8** starving, underfed **9** atrophied **10** attenuated
e-mag: **7** webzine
e-mail: **3** msg. **4** memo **7** message
address part: **3** com, dot, edu, org
alternative: **3** fax **6** letter
ancestor: **5** telex
angry ~: **5** flame
command: **4** send **5** reply
guffaw: **3** LOL
header: **4** from
need: **5** modem
nuisance: **4** spam
prepare to check ~: **5** log in
server: **3** AOL
emanate: **4** emit, flow, gush, rise, spew, spue, stem **5** arise, eject, expel, exude, issue **6** derive, effuse, spring **7** cast out, diffuse, give off, proceed, radiate **8** flow from, throw off **9** arise from, come forth, discharge, originate, send forth
emanation: **4** aura, beam, flow, glow, gush, odor, vibe **5** aroma, light, smell, vibes **6** efflux, oozing **7** arising, flowing, gushing, issuing, outflow **8** effluent, emerging, issuance **9** beginning, discharge, effluence, emergence, exudation, radiation **10** derivation, exhalation
emancipate: **4** free, save **5** loose **6** loosen, redeem **7** deliver, manumit, release **8** liberate **9** unshackle **10** disenthral
emancipation: **7** freedom, liberty, release **8** delivery **9** salvation
emancipator: **6** savior **7** saviour
__ 'em and weep: **4** read
Emanuel: **2** Ax **6** Lasker, Leutze **10** Swedenborg
embank: **4** dike **5** guard **6** defend, secure, shield **7** protect
embankment: **3** dam **4** berm, dike, wall **5** berme, levee, mound, shore **6** escarp **7** defense, landing, rampart **10** breakwater
build an ~: **5** revet
embar: **5** block **6** hinder, lock up **8** imprison
embargo: **3** ban, bar **4** stop, veto **6** forbid, outlaw **7** barrier, boycott, exclude **8** blockage, disallow, sanction **9** exclusion, interdict, restraint **10** keeping out
Embargo, The author: William Cullen Bryant
embark: **2** go **4** sail, ship **5** leave, start **6** set off, set out **7** emplane, entrain, head out, jump off, set sail, ship out, take off **8** approach, go aboard, set forth, start off **9** get to work, leave port, undertake
on: **5** begin, enter **6** assume, launch, tackle **8** commence
embarkation: **5** start **6** origin
embarked: **6** aboard **7** en route, on board **9** in transit, traveling
embarrass: **3** vex **4** faze **5** abash, shame **6** humble, rattle, show up, unglue **7** chagrin, fluster, mortify, nonplus **9** discomfit, dumbfound, humiliate **10** compromise, demoralize, discomfort, discompose, disconcert, disgruntle
embarrassed: **3** red **6** ablush **7** abashed, bashful **8** blushing, sheepish
embarrassing: **6** sticky, touchy **7** awkward **8** delicate, ticklish **9** offensive
episode: **5** gaffe, scene **7** faux pas
embarrassment: **5** shame **6** fiasco, strait, unease **7** chagrin, faux pas, scandal **8** distress **9** abashment
exclamation of ~: **4** oops **6** whoops
show ~: **5** blush **6** redden
embarrassment of __: **6** riches
embassy: **7** mission **8** legation **9** consulate, residence
at times: **6** asylum
worker: **3** amb. **4** aide **6** consul, legate
embattle: **3** arm **5** beset, equip **7** besiege, fortify **8** mobilize **10** militarize
embay: **8** surround
Embden: **5** goose
embed: **3** fix, put, set **4** bury, nest, root, sink **5** imbue, infix, inlay, lodge, plant, stick **6** insert, instal, thrust **7** deposit, drive in, engrain, implant, ingrain, install, stuff in **8** hammer in, thrust in
embedded: **3** set **4** firm, hard **5** dense, fixed, inset **6** nailed, rooted, steely, welded **7** adamant, secured **8** anchored, cemented, concrete, fastened, hardened, hard-line, ironclad **9** condensed, screwed in, tightened **10** compressed, deep-rooted, stationary
embellish: **4** deck, do up, gild, trim **5** adorn, array, color, fudge, grace **6** bedeck, blazon, detail, enrich, expand, jazz up **7** dress up, encrust, enhance, festoon, flatter, garnish, gussy up, incrust, magnify, spiff up, varnish **8** beautify, brighten, decorate, misquote, ornament, spruce up **9** elaborate, embroider, glamorize, overstate **10** exaggerate, illustrate
embellished: **4** tall **5** fancy, showy **6** flashy, florid, frilly, glitzy, lavish, ornate **7** flowery, opulent **9** decorated, elaborate, garnished, luxurious, sumptuous
embellishment: **4** note, trim **5** frill **7** garnish, gilding **8** flourish, froufrou, ornament **9** adornment
ember: **3** ash **4** coal **6** cinder **7** hot coal
Ember __: **3** day **4** Days
embezzle: **3** rob **4** loot **5** filch, steal **6** pilfer, thieve **7** purloin **8** peculate **9** defalcate
embezzlement: **5** theft **6** misuse **7** larceny **8** filching, skimming, stealing
embezzler: **5** thief
dread: **3** aud. **5** audit
embitter: **4** sour **5** anger, upset **6** rankle **7** envenom **8** acerbate, alienate, irritate **9** acidulate, aggravate, disaffect, frustrate **10** disappoint
embittering: **7** onerous
emblazon: **4** deck, do up, trim **5** adorn, color **6** jazz up **7** display, gussy up **8** beautify, brighten, decorate, ornament, spruce up
emblem: **3** tag **4** flag, logo, mark, seal, sign **5** badge, crest, patch, stamp, token, totem **6** banner, device, ensign, figure, symbol **7** imprint, insigne, pennant **8** colophon, hallmark, heraldry, insignia, standard **9** adumbrate, trademark **10** coat of arms, decoration, fleur-de-lis
in heraldry: **6** device
emblematic: **5** typic **6** iconic **7** typical **8** iconical, symbolic **10** figurative, indicative, symbolical
...emblem of the __ love: **5** land I
embodied: **4** real **8** tangible **9** incarnate, touchable
embodiment: **4** form **5** image, model, shape **6** avatar, symbol **7** epitome, example, picture **8** exemplar, specimen **9** archetype, formation **10** apotheosis, collection, expression
embody: **4** have **5** cover, merge, shape, unite **6** codify, typify **7** combine, contain, express, include **8** comprise, manifest, organize, stand for **9** encompass, exemplify, integrate, personify, represent, symbolize **10** amalgamate, assimilate, constitute, illustrate
embog: **4** mire **6** bemire
emboîté: **4** step
embolden: **4** abet, buoy, goad, spur, stir **5** boost, cheer, rouse, steel **6** arouse, buck up, stir up **7** fortify, hearten, inspire, psych up **8** energize, enspirit, inspirit, motivate, psyche up **9** encourage, enhearten **10** invigorate, revitalize, strengthen
embonpoint: **3** big **5** large, obese **9** corpulent **10** well-padded
emboss: **5** carve, raise **7** encrust, impress, incrust **8** decorate, ornament
embossing tool: **4** seal
embouchure: **3** lip, rim **5** mouth
embow: **4** arch
embrace: **3** hug **4** grip, hold, lock, love **5** admit, adopt, clasp, cling, cover, crush, greet, let in, press, seize, touch **6** accept, caress, choose, clinch, clutch, cuddle, enfold, infold, nuzzle, take in, take on, take up **7** contain, enclose, espouse, inclose, include, involve, squeeze, welcome **8** comprise, deal with, encircle, surround **9** encompass, keep close
Embraceable You composer: **8** Gershwin
Embraced by the Light author: **5** Eadie
__-embracing: **3** all
embrasure: **6** recess
embrocate: **3** oil **5** apply **6** anoint **9** lubricate
embrocation: **6** lotion **8** lenitive, liniment, ointment
embroider: **3** sew **4** deck, gild, trim **5** color, fudge **6** bedeck, blow up, overdo, play up, puff up, stitch **7** falsify, gussy up, lay it on, magnify **8** beautify, decorate, misquote, ornament **9** dramatize, elaborate, embellish, overstate **10** aggrandize, exaggerate
maybe: **3** fib, lie **7** falsify, untruth **9** falsehood, mendacity **10** taradiddle
embroidered: **6** ornate
embroidery: **5** craft **6** crewel **9** adornment, arabesque **10** decoration, needlework

archaic ~: 5 brede
loop: 5 picot
purchase: 5 spool 6 needle, thread 10 pin cushion
thread: 5 floss
trim: 6 eyelet
embroil: 4 mire 5 snarl 6 enmesh, entrap, immesh, inmesh, tangle 7 ensnare, insnare, involve, quarrel 8 entangle
embryo: 3 egg 4 germ, seed 5 fetus, ovule 6 foetus 7 nucleus 8 rudiment
combining form: 5 -blast 6 blasto-
ender: 7 genesis
membrane: 6 amnion
nourishment for an ~: 4 yolk
embryology: 7 science
embryonic: 5 early, fetal 6 foetal, little 7 initial 8 evolving, germinal, immature, original 9 incipient, potential
area: 6 anlage
emcee: 4 host 9 officiate 10 auctioneer, ringmaster
jointly: 6 cohost
line: 5 intro
need: 3 mic 4 mike
place: 4 dais 6 podium 7 lectern, rostrum 8 platform
quiz show ~: 5 asker
__ 'em, cowboy: 4 Ride
Emden: 4 city, port, town
locale: 7 Germany
__ 'Em Eat Cake: 3 Let
emeer: 4 Arab 5 Osman, ruler 6 leader, Othman, prince 7 Kuwaiti 8 kingfish 9 chieftain, commander, potentate
emend: 3 fix 4 edit, mend 5 right 6 redact, reform, repair, revise 7 correct, improve, rectify, touch up
emendation: 6 change 7 editing, rewrite 8 revision 9 polishing, redaction 10 alteration, correction
emerald: 3 gem 5 beryl, color, green, jewel, virid 6 grassy 7 mineral 8 gemstone
ersatz ~: 5 paste
month: 3 May
name meaning ~: 9 Esmeralda
relative: 3 pea 4 cyan, jade, sage 5 beryl, breen, olive, virid 6 myrtle, reseda 7 avocado, celadon, verdant 9 pistachio, turquoise 10 aquamarine, chartreuse
surface: 5 facet
emerald __: 3 cut 5 green
Emerald __: 4 City, Isle
Emerald City
visitor: 4 lion, Toto 6 Tin Man 7 Dorothy 9 scarecrow
Emerald Forest, The (1985 film)
cast: Powers Boothe, Meg Foster
director: John Boorman
Emerald Isle: 4 Eire, Erin 7 Ireland
from the ~: 5 Irish
Emerald Point __: 3 NAS
emerge: 4 dawn, exit, loom, peep, peer, rise, show 5 arise, begin, bob up, break, pop up, spirt, spurt 6 appear, crop up, fade in, loom up, result, spring, sprout, stream 7 come out, develop, peep out, surface 8 break out, spring up, stand out 9 come forth, grow out of, originate, transpire 10 issue forth
as: 6 become
(from): 4 come
emergence: 4 dawn, rise 5 birth 6 origin 7 genesis, infancy 9 emanation 10 appearance, incipience
emergency: 4 need, pass 5 event, pinch, spare 6 crisis, crunch, plight, strait 7 stopgap, straits 8 exigence, exigency, juncture, meltdown, zero hour 9 crossroad, extremity, necessity 10 compulsion, difficulty, occurrence
fund: 7 nest egg, reserve
money: 5 scrip
signal: 3 SOS 5 alarm, flare, siren
worker: 3 EMT 5 medic 9 paramedic
emergency __: 4 boat, exit, room 5 brake
Emergency (NBC drama)
cast: Robert Fuller (Dr. Kelly Brackett)
Julie London (Dixie McCall)
Randolph Mantooth (John Gage)
Kevin Tighe (Roy DeSoto)
Bobby Troup (Dr. Joe Early)
dog: 5 Boots
producer: Jack Webb
emerging __: 6 market
Emeril exclamation: 3 bam
emeritus: 3 ret. 4 retd. 5 title 7 retired 9 professor
Emerson: 2 TV 3 Roy 4 Faye 5 TV set 10 Fittipaldi, television
alternative: 3 JVC, NEC, RCA 4 Sony 6 Quasar, Zenith 7 Hitachi, ProScan, Toshiba 8 Magnavox, Sylvania 9 Panasonic
Emerson, __ and Palmer: 4 Lake
Emerson, Ralph Waldo: 4 poet 6 writer 8 essayist
alma mater: Harvard
essay topic: 3 art
hometown: Boston
work: May-Day
Nature
Self-Reliance
Emerson, Roy: 7 netster 9 tennis pro
milieu: 5 court
emery: 7 mineral 8 abrasive, corundum
board: 4 file
emery __: 5 board, cloth, wheel
emeu: 4 bird
émeute: 4 riot 6 tumult 8 outbreak, uprising, violence
__ 'em Flying: 4 Keep
EMF unit: 4 volt
__ 'Em Hell, Harry!: 4 Give
__ 'em High: 4 Hang
EMI: 5 label
emigrant: 5 alien 7 refugee 8 colonist 10 expatriate
emigrate: 5 leave 6 depart 7 migrate 10 transplant
emigration: 6 exodus, moving 8 trekking 9 departure 10 relocation, resettling
émigré: 5 exile 7 refugee 9 foreigner 10 expatriate
hope: 6 asylum
Emil: 5 Sitka 6 Gilels, Kocher, Ludwig, Scaria 7 Zátopek 8 Jannings 10 von Behring
Emile: 4 Zola 8 Ardolino, Berliner, de Becque, Griffith
see also French
Emilia's husband: 4 Iago
Émilie: 6 Dionne
Emilio: 5 Pucci, Segrè 7 Estefan, Estevez 8 Pericoli
Emily: 4 Post 5 Balch, Lloyd 6 Brontë 7 Saliers 9 Dickinson
to Charlotte: 3 sis
Eminem: 6 rapper
eminence: 4 fame, hill, name, note, rise 5 éclat, glory, honor, title 6 esteem, height, leader, renown, repute, status, zenith 7 dignity, stature, success 8 altitude, grandeur, luminary, mountain, nobility, prestige, standing 9 authority, celebrity, elevation, greatness, loftiness, magnitude, personage 10 high ground, importance, kingliness, notability, prominence, reputation
__ eminence: 4 gray, grey
Éminence __: 5 grise
eminent: 3 big 4 high, loft 5 famed, grand, great, noble, noted, upper 6 august, famous 7 big-name, big-time, exalted, notable, storied 8 elevated, esteemed, glorious, immortal, renowned, singular, splendid, superior 9 big-league, dignified, honorable, important, prominent, topflight, well-known 10 celebrated
eminent __: 6 domain
eminently: 7 greatly 9 extremely 10 especially, remarkably, strikingly
emir: 4 Arab 5 Osman, ruler 6 gerent, leader, Othman, prince 7 Kuwaiti 8 kingfish 9 chieftain, commander, potentate
emirate: 5 Dibai, Dubai, Katar, Qatar 6 Kuwait
resident: 4 Arab 6 Qatari 7 Kuwaiti
emissary: 3 amb., spy 5 agent, envoy 6 bearer, consul, deputy, legate, nuncio 7 carrier, courier 8 delegate, diplomat 9 appointee, go-between, messenger, negotiant 10 ambassador, interceder
emission: 5 issue 6 efflux 7 venting 8 ejection, issuance 9 discharge, effluence, exudation, radiation 10 exhalation
emissions watchdog: 3 EPA
__-emission vehicle: 4 zero
emit: 4 beam, gush, ooze, pour, reek, send, shed, spew, spue, vent, void 5 eject, eruct, erupt, expel, exude, issue, loose, shine, shoot, sound, spill, spout 6 effuse, evolve, exhale, let off, put out, squirt, stream 7 cast out, diffuse, emanate, extrude, give off, give out, radiate, release, secrete, send out 8 shoot out, throw off, throw out 9 broadcast, cast forth, discharge, give forth, send forth
coherent light: 4 lase
__-emitting diode: 5 light
EMK: 3 sen., Ted 7 Kennedy
Emlyn: 8 Williams
Emma: 4 Peel 5 Calvé, Eames, Samms 6 Bovary, Bunton, Lathen 7 Goldman, Lazarus, Tennant, Willard 8 Hamilton, Thompson 9 Woodhouse
portrayer: 3 Uma 5 Diana
successor on The Avengers: 4 Tara
Emma (1932 film)
cast: Richard Cromwell, Marie Dressler, Jean Hersholt, Myrna Loy
Emma (1996 film)
cast: Toni Collette, Jeremy Northam, Gwyneth Paltrow, Greta Scacchi
Emma author: Jane Austen
Emmanuel: 5 Lewis 9 Rosenthal
Emmanuelle: 5 Béart
Emmeline: 9 Pankhurst
Emmenthaler: 5 Swiss 6 cheese
Emmerich: 4 Noah 6 Roland
Emmerich, Noah: 8 director
film: Beautiful Girls (1996)
Love & Sex (2000)
The Truman Show (1998)
Emmerich, Roland: 8 director
film: Godzilla (1998)
Independence Day (1996)
The Patriot (2000)
Stargate (1994)
emmet: 3 ant, bug 6 insect 7 pismire
Emmett: 5 Kelly
Emmitt: 5 Smith
Emmy: 5 award
Emmylou: 6 Harris
Emo: 7 Philips
emollient: 4 aloe, balm 5 cream, salve 6 lotion 7 lenient, unction, unguent 8 balsamic, lenitive, liniment, ointment, soothing 9 demulcent
emolument: 3 fee, pay 4 tips, wage 5 wages 6 income, profit, salary 7 payment, revenue, stipend 8 benefice, earnings, gratuity 10 honorarium, recompense
Emona: 4 font 8 typeface
Emory University site: 7 Atlanta, Georgia
__ E. Mosley: 5 Roger
emote: 3 act 4 gush 7 carry on, enthuse, ham it up, overact, perform, playact 9 dramatize, play a role
for a photo: 3 mug
emoter: 3 ham 5 actor 6 hot dog 7 actress, overact
emotion: 3 awe, ire, joy 4 fear, hate, love, mood, rage, soul, zeal 5 agony, anger, angst, ardor, grief, heart, odium, pique, pride, scorn, shame, spite, wrath 6 animus, bathos, desire, enmity, fervor, hoopla, malice, pathos, rancor, sorrow, spirit, thrill, warmth 7 concern, despair, disgust, ecstasy, elation, empathy, feeling, ill will, impulse, offense, outrage, passion, remorse, sadness, umbrage 8 acrimony, loathing, lyricism, sympathy, vexation 9 affection, agitation, animosity, antipathy, happiness, intensity, petulance, revulsion, sensation, sentiment, vehemence 10 abhorrence, enthusiasm, excitement, melancholy, repugnance
burst of ~: 5 spasm
combining form: 4 thym- 5 thymo-
feel ~: 5 throb
Hindu ~: 4 rasa
negative ~: 4 rage 5 odium, pique, scorn, spite, wrath 6 animus, enmity, malice, rancor 7 disgust, ill will, offense, outrage, umbrage 8 acrimony, loathing, vexation 9 animosity, antipathy, petulance, revulsion 10 abhorrence, repugnance
outburst of ~: 6 fantod
sans ~: 5 dryly, icily
show ~: 3 cry 4 rage, vent 5 react
touch the ~ of: 4 move 6 affect
emotional: 3 gut 4 warm 5 fiery, inner, mushy, teary 6 ardent, fervid, heated, moving, tender 7 fervent, lyrical, mawkish, nervous, soulful, zealous 8 dramatic, ecstatic, exciting, poignant, stirring, touching, visceral 9 affecting, affective, disturbed, excitable, fanatical, impetuous, impulsive, intuitive, sensitive, thrilling 10 histrionic, hot-blooded, hysterical, irrational, passionate, responsive, subjective
event: 5 drama
heat: 3 ire 4 fury, rage 5 pique, wrath 6 choler, enmity 7 offense, outrage 10 antagonism
onrush: 4 pang 5 throe
outburst: 3 cry, sob 4 bawl, wail, weep 5 scene 6 lament, scream
overly ~: 4 agog 5 gushy, lurid, mushy
tone: 4 mood
Emotional Rescue (1980 song) artist: Rolling Stones
Emotion in Motion (1986 song) artist: Rick Ocasek
emotionless: 3 icy 4 cold, cool 5 aloof 6 chilly, remote 7 glacial 9 withdrawn
one: 6 icicle
__ emotions: 5 mixed
Emotions (song) artist: Brenda Lee, Destiny's Child, Mariah Carey
emotive: 4 avid 8 touching 10 histrionic
empale: 6 pierce 8 transfix
Empalme: 4 city, town
locale: 6 Mexico, Sonora
empanada: 9 appetizer
empath
skill: 3 ESP 9 intuition, telepathy
empathetic: 4 warm 6 caring 9 vicarious 10 responsive

empathic: 8 merciful 10 responsive
empathize: 4 grok 5 bleed, mourn 6 grieve, lament, suffer
empathy: 4 pity 7 emotion, rapport 8 affinity, sympathy 9 good vibes 10 compassion, friendship
have ~: 4 care, heed, mind 5 worry 6 regard, regret, relate 7 anguish, concern 8 distress, interest 9 give a darn
lacking ~: 3 icy 4 hard, mean 5 cruel, rigid, rough, stern, tough 6 bitter, brutal, severe, strict, unkind 7 austere, callous, harshly, hostile 8 despotic, grueling, indurate, pitiless, rocklike, ruthless, savagely, severely, stubborn, wearying 9 difficult, insensate, merciless, obstinate, stringent, unbending, unfeeling, unsparing, viciously 10 adamantine, inflexible, pitilessly, relentless, unmerciful, unpleasant
Empedocles on Etna author: Matthew Arnold
emperor: 4 czar, male, tsar, tzar 5 noble, ruler 6 dynast, gerent, sultan 7 monarch, viceroy 8 dictator, imperial 9 potentate, sovereign
Roman ~: 4 Nero 6 Caesar
emperor __: 4 moth 7 penguin
Emperor and Galilean author: Henrik Ibsen
Emperor Concerto composer: 9 Beethoven
Emperor Jones, The
author: 6 O'Neill
character: 3 Lem 6 Brutus
Emperor of Ice Cream, The author: Wallace Stevens
Emperor of the North (1973 film)
cast: Ernest Borgnine, Keith Carradine, Lee Marvin
director: Robert Aldrich
Emperor's New Groove, The (2000 film)
voice cast: John Goodman, Eartha Kitt (voice), David Spade (voice)
__ Emperor, The: 4 Last
Emperor Waltz composer: 7 Strauss
empery: 5 realm 6 domain 8 dominion
emphasis: 4 tone 5 force, slant 6 accent, import, stress, weight 8 priority 9 attention, intensity 10 importance, insistence, prominence
exclamation of ~: 3 gee, wow 4 gosh 5 by gum, golly 6 far out 8 by cracky
give ~: 6 accent, play up, stress 7 bracket, feature, point up 9 highlight, italicize, punctuate, reinforce 10 accentuate, underscore
musical ~: 3 sfz. 9 sforzando
emphasize: 5 press, voice 6 accent, assert, harp on, play up, stress 7 dwell on, feature, impress, iterate 8 headline, insist on 9 dramatize, dwell upon, highlight, intensify, italicize, make clear, pronounce, punctuate, reinforce, reiterate, spotlight, underline 10 accentuate, articulate, exaggerate, illustrate, make a point, make much of, underscore
emphatic: 4 firm, loud 6 all-out, strong 7 decided, dynamic, express 8 absolute, accented, definite, explicit, forceful, powerful, resolute, stressed, striking, vehement, vigorous 9 assertive, energetic, insistent, trenchant 10 conclusive, definitive, expressive, pronounced, resounding, unswerving, unwavering, vociferant
be ~: 6 assert, demand, insist
turndown: 5 never, no how, no sir, no way
type: 6 italic
emphatically: 4 hard, very 7 greatly
empire: 4 rule, sway 5 realm 6 domain, nation 7 dynasty, kingdom 8 dominion 9 supremacy, territory
ancient ~ builder: 4 Inca, Maya 5 Incan, Mayan
builder: 5 baron, mogul 6 bigwig, tycoon 7 magnate 9 financier, plutocrat 10 capitalist
former ~: 4 USSR
Empire: 5 apple
relative: 4 crab, Gala, Lodi, Rome 5 Mutsu 6 Ida red, medlar, Pippin, russet 7 Baldwin, Bramley, costard, Freedom, Liberty, Spartan, Wealthy, Winesap 8 Cortland, Jonathan, McIntosh 10 Rome Beauty
__ Empire: 5 First, Roman 6 Fulani, Indian, Mongol, Second 7 British, Chinese, Eastern, Ottoman, Persian, Russian, Turkish, Western
Empire author: Gore Vidal
Empire of the Sun (1987 film)
cast: Christian Bale, John Malkovich, Miranda Richardson
director: Steven Spielberg
Empire State Bldg. site: 3 NYC 4 NY NY
Empire Strikes Back, The (1980 film)
cast: Carrie Fisher, Harrison Ford, Mark Hamill, Billy Dee Williams
composer: 8 Williams
director: Irvin Kershner
planet: 4 Hoth
empirical: 7 factual 9 practical, pragmatic
emplane: 5 board, get on 6 embark 8 go aboard
employ: 3 ply, put, use 4 hire, turn, work 5 apply, exert, spend, treat, wield 6 commit, engage, enlist, handle, hire on, occupy, resort, retain, sign on, sign up, take on 7 charter, exploit, harness, operate, utilize 8 exercise, keep busy, work with 9 make use of, put to work 10 commission, fall back on, manipulate
employable: 6 usable 7 useable 8 eligible 10 accessible
employed: 4 busy 5 in use 6 active, at work, on duty 7 working 8 laboring, occupied, on the job 9 on the move
be ~: 4 help, moil, plod, tend, toil, work 5 grind, labor, sweat 8 endeavor, exercise, plug away 9 grind away, moonlight 10 apprentice
be ~ by: 5 serve 7 work for
__-employed: 4 self
employee: 4 hand, hire 5 agent, clerk, labor 6 earner, worker 7 laborer 8 commuter, hireling, operator 9 assistant, hired hand, jobholder 10 apprentice, wage earner
badge: 6 ID card
entry-level ~: 5 clerk, gofer 6 gopher
health plan: 3 HMO, PPO
ID, often: 3 SSN
last words: 5 I quit
live-in ~: 4 maid 5 nanny 6 au pair, butler
reward: 4 perk 5 bonus, raise
transferred ~ benefit: 4 relo 10 relocation
underpaid ~: 5 slave 6 drudge
__ employee: 6 exempt
employees: 4 help 5 staff, union 9 personnel
Employees __: 4 Only
Employees' Entrance (1933 film)
cast: Wallace Ford, Warren William, Loretta Young
director: Roy Del Ruth
employer: 4 boss, firm 5 hirer 6 master 7 company, manager 8 brass hat 10 management, supervisor
like some ~ s: 5 bossy 8 arrogant, despotic 9 imperious 10 autocratic, commanding, oppressive, tyrannical
temp's ~: 4 firm 6 agency, office 7 company 10 department
employment: 3 job, use 4 line, post, work 5 labor, place, trade, usage 6 billet, sphere 7 pursuit, service, station 8 adoption, business, exercise, handling, position, vocation 9 appliance, avocation, enrolment, operation, signing on, situation 10 assignment, commission, enlistment, enrollment, livelihood, occupation, profession
change ~ frequently: 6 job-hop
gainful ~: 4 post, work 8 position
proof of ~: 5 badge 6 ID card
seek ~: 5 apply 8 petition
employment __: 6 agency
employment-data agcy.: 3 BLS
Emporia: 4 city, town
locale: 6 Kansas
emporium: 4 mart, shop 5 bazar, store 6 bazaar, market, outlet 8 boutique
event: 4 sale 8 closeout 9 clearance
empower: 4 gird, tone, vest 5 allow, build, shore, steel 6 anneal, assign, beef up, commit, enable, harden, invest, permit, prop up, temper, tone up 7 bolster, brace up, build up, burgeon, develop, enhance, entitle, entrust, fortify, intitle, intrust, license, qualify, shore up, stiffen, toughen, warrant 8 accredit, bourgeon, buttress, delegate, deputize, energize, indurate, nominate, sanction, vitalize 9 authorize, intensify, reinforce 10 capacitate, commission, constitute, invigorate, strengthen
empowered: 4 able 6 vested 10 privileged
empress: 4 Lady 5 noble, queen, ruler 6 gerent 7 monarch 8 imperial 9 potentate, sovereign
Empson, William: 4 poet 7 British
emptiness: 4 need, void 6 vacuum 7 vacancy, vacuity 8 solitude 9 blankness 10 desolation, exhaustion, hollowness, loneliness
emptor: 5 buyer 6 patron, vendee 7 end user 8 consumer, customer
__ emptor: 6 caveat
empty: 3 dry, gut, tip 4 bare, dull, dump, flat, idle, null, pump, vain, vent, void 5 blank, clear, drain, eject, expel, inane, leach, purge, scoop, silly, spend, spill, strip, tired, unfed, unlet, use up, vapid 6 absent, barren, decant, devoid, finish, glassy, hollow, hungry, jejune, lonely, unload, vacant, vacate 7 all gone, consume, deflate, deplete, exhaust, fatuous, insipid, lighten, pour out, sold out, starved, sterile, trivial, untaken, vacated, vacuous 8 clean out, deflated, depleted, deserted, desolate, disgorge, evacuate, famished, finished, ill-spent, lifeless, out of gas, ravenous, starving, unburden, unfilled 9 abandoned, discharge, evacuated, excavated, exhausted, frivolous, fruitless, senseless, valueless, worthless 10 groundless, unoccupied, unprofound
be on ~: 6 run out
combining form: 3 ken- 4 keno-
in one gulp: 4 chug 5 swill 6 guzzle
(into): 3 run 4 flow 6 stream
leave ~: 6 vacate
leave no part ~: 4 cram, fill, pack, sate 5 crowd 6 occupy, top off 7 jampack, pervade, satiate 8 brim over, permeate
literally, ~ hand: 6 karate
near ~: 3 low 4 down 5 below, lower, lowly, under 6 meager, paltry, sparse, sunken 7 nominal, reduced, shallow 8 depleted, subsided, uncostly 9 in the pits 10 down and out, marked down, rock-bottom
(of): 3 rid
of water: 4 bail 7 draw off 8 drain off
out: 4 dump 5 purge 6 hollow
space: 3 vac. 6 vacuum 8 headroom 9 clearance
words: 3 gas, pap, rot 4 bunk, wind 5 prate, stuff, tripe 6 bunkum, humbug 7 blarney, bombast, fustian, hogwash, malarky, palaver 8 buncombe, claptrap, malarkey, nonsense 9 gibberish, moonshine 10 mumbo jumbo
empty __: 4 word 5 morph 6 nester 7 calorie
empty __ syndrome: 4 nest
empty-__: 6 handed, headed
empty-handed: 4 poor
empty-headed: 4 daft 5 dizzy, giddy, goofy, inane, silly, thick 6 vacant 7 flighty, shallow, vacuous 8 ignorant
emptying: 4 flow, gush, ooze 5 burst, spill, spurt 7 seepage 8 ejection, emission, eruption, outburst, unlading 9 departure, discharge, effluence, excretion, explosion, expulsion, exudation, purgation, secretion, unloading 10 evacuation, withdrawal
Empty Nest (NBC sitcom)
cast: Dinah Manoff (Carol Weston) Kristy McNichol (Barbara Weston) Richard Mulligan (Dr. Harry Weston)
dog: 8 Dreyfuss
__ empty stomach: 4 on an
empyreal: 5 lofty, noble 7 elysian, exalted, sublime 8 elevated, ethereal, heavenly, majestic, ultimate 9 ambrosial, celestial, ineffable 10 majestical
empyrean: 3 sky 5 azure 6 heaven 8 ethereal, heavenly, paradise, ultimate 9 celestial, firmament 10 atmosphere
__ 'em, Rover!: 3 Sic
__ Ems, Germany: 3 Bad
EMT: 5 medic 9 paramedic
destination: 2 ER 4 hosp.
part of ~: 3 Med. 4 Emer., Tech.
procedure: 3 CPR
emu: 4 bird 5 biped 6 Aussie, ratite
relative: 4 kiwi, rhea
emulate: 3 ape 4 copy 5 equal, mimic, rival 6 follow, mirror 7 dress as, imitate, pattern, reflect 9 take after
emulating: 3 à la 4 like
emulative: 5 apish, rival 6 copied, echoic 9 imitative, mimicking, simulated 10 derivative, reflective, secondhand, unoriginal
emulator: 4 aper 5 rival, sheep, toady 6 yes man 7 Babbitt, epigone 8 assenter, imitator 10 conformist
remark: 5 ditto, me too
emulsifying agent: 5 algin 8 lecithin
emulsion: 5 cream, paint 8 solution
__-'em-up: 5 shoot
en __: 3 ami 4 bloc, dash, quad 5 carré, clair, garde, masse, prise, règle, route, suite 6 brosse, croûte, soleil 7 famille, passant, rapport
en __ air: 5 plein
En __: 5 Vogue
En __!: 5 garde
enable: 2 OK 3 let 4 fund, okay 5 allow, equip 6 permit, turn on 7 empower, entitle, intitle, license, qualify 8 accredit, activate, energize 9 authorize 10 capacitate, commission, facilitate

enact: **3** tax **4** make, pass, vote **5** order, stage **6** ordain, recite **7** achieve, perform, portray **8** carry out, legalize, recreate, transact **9** dramatize, establish, institute, interpret, legislate, prescribe **10** perpetrate
enacted: **5** legal **6** lawful, passed **7** decreed, ordered **8** enforced, enjoined, mandated, ordained **9** legalized, statutory **10** authorized, legislated
enactment: **3** law **7** measure, passage, playing, statute **9** depiction, execution, ordinance, portrayal **10** playacting, regulation
enamel: **5** color, glaze, gloss, inlay, japan, paint **6** finish, polish, veneer **7** coating, encrust, incrust, lacquer, varnish **9** champlevé, cloisonné **10** nail polish
crack, as ~: **5** craze
ender: **4** ware
neighbor: **6** dentin **7** dentine
target: **4** nail
__ enamel: **4** nail **6** Canton **7** mottled
enamelware: **4** tole
enamor: **5** charm **6** endear, entice **7** bewitch, enchant, enthral, inthral **8** enthrall, entrance, inthrall **9** captivate, enrapture, fascinate, infatuate, sweet-talk
enamored: **4** fond **6** loving **7** smitten
be ~ of: **4** love **5** fancy **6** dote on
of: **6** caring, doting, loving, tender **7** adoring, amatory, amorous **8** intimate, mad about, romantic
enantiosis: **5** irony **6** satire **7** sarcasm
E natural alias: **5** F flat
en bloc: **6** in full **8** as a whole, together **10** altogether
enc.: **3** env., SAE **4** SASE
part: **3** vol.
encage: **3** box **6** coop up, lock up **7** confine
encaged: **4** pent **6** pent up
encamp: **6** settle **7** bivouac **8** settle in **10** pitch a tent
encampment: **5** étape **7** bivouac **8** barracks, garrison
South African ~: **5** lager **6** laager
encapsulate: **5** sum up **6** digest **7** abridge, sheathe, shorten **8** condense **9** summarize
encarmine: **6** redden
Encarnación: **4** city, town
locale: **6** Mexico **7** Jalisco
encarnadine: **6** redden
encase: **3** box **4** pack, wrap **5** box in, box up, cover, crate, frame, house **6** pack up **7** close in, confine, enclose, envelop, inclose, package, protect, sheathe **8** preserve, surround
enceinte: **8** pregnant **9** expectant, expecting, with child
Enceladus: **4** moon
planet: **6** Saturn
encephalogram: **4** x-ray
enchain: **4** bind **5** rivet **6** fetter **7** engross, manacle, shackle, trammel **8** enfetter, handcuff, hold fast **9** captivate
enchant: **3** hex, wow **4** draw, grip, lure, send, take **5** charm **6** allure, appeal, disarm, enamor, engage, entice, please, ravish, thrill, tickle, turn on **7** attract, beguile, bewitch, delight, enthral, inthral **8** bedazzle, enthrall, entrance, inthrall, intrigue, transfix **9** captivate, carry away, delectate, enrapture, fascinate, hypnotize, inebriate, mesmerize, spellbind **10** intoxicate
enchanted: **3** fey **5** magic **6** enrapt **7** magical **9** bewitched, delighted, gladdened, possessed **10** fascinated, spellbound
be ~ by: **4** feel, like, love **5** adore, fancy, go for, prize **6** admire, dote on, regard, revere **7** care for, cherish, cling to, fall for, idolize, long for, romance, worship **8** be mad for, hold dear, treasure, venerate **9** delight in
state: **5** spell
Enchanted (1959 song) artist: Platters
Enchanted April (1991 film)
cast: Joan Plowright, Miranda Richardson
director: Mike Newell
setting: **5** Italy
__ Enchanted Evening: **4** Some
enchanter: **6** wizard **7** charmer **8** conjurer, conjuror, magician, sorcerer **9** bewitcher
enchanting: **4** fair, glam **5** magic, siren, spell **6** lovely, quaint **7** darling, lovable, magical, sirenic, winning, winsome **8** loveable, pleasant, pleasing, romantic **9** appealing, beguiling, endearing, glamorous, ravishing, sirenical, thrilling **10** attractive, bewitching, delectable, delightful, entrancing, intriguing
enchantment: **4** love **5** charm, magic, spell **6** allure **7** ecstasy, rapture, sorcery **9** magnetism
Enchantment (1948 film)
cast: Evelyn Keyes, David Niven, Teresa Wright
enchantress: **4** vamp **5** Aeaea, Circe, Kirke, Medea, siren, witch **7** charmer, Lorelei **9** sorceress
enchilada
filling: **5** chile, chili **6** chilli
sauce: **5** salsa
whole ~: **3** all **4** A to Z **8** entirety
__ enchilada: **3** big **5** whole
enchiridion: **5** bible, guide **8** handbook
Encina, Juan del: **4** poet **7** Spanish **10** playwright
Encinitas: **4** city, town
locale: **10** California
Encino: **4** city
locale: **10** California
Encino Man (1992 film)
cast: Sean Astin, Brendan Fraser, Pauly Shore
encircle: **3** orb **4** band, coil, gird, girt, hoop, lock, loop, ring, wind, wrap **5** bower, fence, girth, hem in, orbit, siege, twine **6** begird, define, emball, engird, gird in **7** besiege, compass, embrace, enclose, environ, inclose **8** cincture, surround **9** close in on, encompass, enwreathe
encirclement: **5** siege
encircling: **7** ambient
Encke's __: **5** comet
encl.: **3** env., SAE **4** SASE
enclad: **7** clothed
enclave: **4** area **7** country **8** district **9** territory
enclose: **3** hem, pen **4** cage, case, fold, gird, hold, lock, ring, shut, veil, wall, wrap **5** bower, box up, cover, fence, frame, hedge, hem in **6** begird, circle, coop up, cordon, corral, define, encase, engird, immure, incase, insert, intern, lock in, shut in, wall in **7** compass, confine, contain, embrace, envelop, environ, impound, include, rope off, seclude, shelter **8** blockade, block off, encircle, fence off, surround **9** encompass
enclosed: **5** inner **6** herein, indoor
enclosure: **3** pen, sty **4** area, cage, cell, coop, yard **5** booth, court, frame, hutch **6** aviary, corral, insert **7** chamber, fencing **8** stockade **9** birdhouse, courtyard **10** quadrangle
encode: **8** disguise, scramble
encoded: **6** secret
encoil: **4** wind
encomiastic: **7** glowing **9** adulatory, approving, favorable, laudatory, praiseful **10** eulogistic, flattering
encomium: **4** pean **5** eloge, honor, kudos, paean **6** eulogy, homage, praise, salute **7** acclaim, plaudit, tribute **8** accolade, citation, flattery, good word, plaudits **9** extolment, laudation, panegyric **10** compliment, exaltation
encompass: **4** gird, have, loop, ring, span **5** cover, hem in, range, reach **6** begird, circle, define, embody, engird, girdle, imbody, take in **7** contain, embrace, enclose, envelop, environ, inclose, include **8** cincture, comprise, encircle, surround **9** enwreathe **10** comprehend
encompassed by: **4** amid **5** among, 'twixt **6** amidst **7** between, betwixt
encompassing: **5** round **6** around **7** all over, ambient **9** embracing **10** encircling, enveloping
__-encompassing: **3** all
encore: **3** bis **4** more **5** again, rerun **6** repeat **7** reprise **8** once more **9** extra song **10** repetition
request an ~: **4** clap **5** cheer **7** applaud
Encore: **7** channel
alternative: **3** AMC, HBO, IFC, SHO, TMC **4** Flix **5** Bravo, Starz **7** Cinemax **8** Showtime, Sundance
encounter: **3** see **4** bout, face, find, flap, fray, meet, spot, tilt **5** brush, clash, fight, run-in, scrap, set-to, shock, stand, taste **6** action, attack, battle, combat, rumpus **7** contest, dispute, hit upon, liaison, meeting, quarrel, receive, run into, undergo **8** argument, bump into, chance on, come upon, conflict, confront, happen on, meet with, skirmish, squabble, struggle **9** clash with, collision, discovery, get to know, interview, reception, run across **10** alight upon, chance upon, come across, contention, engagement, experience, fall in with, happen upon, meet up with, rendezvous
encounter __: **5** group **7** session
__ Encounter: **5** Brief
__ Encounters...: **5** Close
encourage: **3** aid **4** abet, back, buoy, coax, feed, goad, help, prod, push, spur, stir, urge **5** boost, cheer, drive, egg on, rally, rouse, steel **6** advise, ask for, assist, buck up, buoy up, excite, exhort, foment, foster, incite, invite, praise, prop up, second, solace, succor, uphold **7** advance, animate, applaud, bolster, cheer up, comfort, console, endorse, enliven, forward, further, gladden, hearten, help out, indorse, inspire, lighten, nurture, promote, psych up, pull for, root for, support **8** advocate, embolden, energize, enspirit, imbolden, inspirit, reassure, revivify, sanction, side with **9** cultivate, galvanize, get behind, instigate, reinforce, smile upon, subsidize **10** exhilarate, predispose, revitalize, strengthen
falsely: **6** lead on
in evil: **6** incite **7** collude **9** instigate
encouragement: **3** aid **4** help, lift, spur **5** boost, cheer **6** succor, urging **7** backing, comfort, support **8** advocacy, optimism, sanction, stimulus
cry: **3** olé, rah, yay, yea, yes **4** c'mon, good **5** huzza **6** chin up, hoorah, hooray, hurrah, hurray, huzzah, let's go **7** attaboy **8** alley-oop, attagirl
encouraging: **4** rosy **6** bright, upbeat **7** hopeful **8** probable **9** promising **10** supportive
not ~: **4** dark **5** bleak, dusky **6** dismal, dreary, gloomy, somber **7** doleful, ominous **8** hopeless **9** miserable, saddening, saturnine, sorrowful, woebegone **10** depressing
encrinite: **6** fossil
encroach: **5** poach **6** invade, meddle **7** violate **8** trespass **9** intrude on, penetrate
on: **4** raid **5** storm, usurp **6** assail, breach, infest, invade, maraud, occupy, ravage **7** overrun, pillage, plunder, violate **8** permeate, trespass **9** penetrate
encroachment: **6** attack, inroad **8** invasion, trespass **9** incursion, violation
encrust: **4** cake **8** solidify
encrypted: **5** coded **6** in code
encrypting org.: **3** NSA
encryption: **4** code **6** cipher
encumber: **3** lay, tax **4** clog, fill, load **5** block, cramp, delay, tie up **6** burden, fetter, hamper, hand up, hinder, hogtie, hold up, impede, lumber, saddle **7** oppress, perplex **8** handicap, obstruct, overload, slow down **9** hamstring, weigh down
encumbered: **5** taxed **7** charged, fraught **8** burdened, hampered, weighted **9** laden. full, oppressed **10** loaded down
encumbrance: **3** bar **4** debt, drag, duty, lien, load, onus **6** burden, weight **7** barrier **8** handicap, obstacle **9** liability
encumbrances: **4** gear **5** goods
encyclopedia: **3** ref., set **7** Grolier **9** Americana, reference, World Book **10** Britannica
book: **3** vol. **5** index **6** volume
medium: **5** CD/ROM **6** online
encyclopedic: **4** a to z, vast, wide **5** broad **7** general **8** complete, far-flung, sweeping **9** expansive, extensive, universal **10** exhaustive, widespread
end: **3** aim, tip, top, use **4** butt, cusp, doom, drop, edge, goal, halt, heel, last, lees, lift, quit, rear, ruin, stop, stub, tail **5** abort, bound, cease, close, dregs, final, finis, lapse, limit, omega, point, quash, reach, sew up, stump **6** bottom, cut off, demise, desist, epilog, expire, expiry, finale, finish, intent, lay off, motive, object, payoff, period, quench, reason, result, run out, settle, target, tipoff, top off, upshot, windup, wrap up **7** abolish, adjourn, athlete, break up, call off, closing, closure, destroy, due date, extreme, get done, kiss off, last act, mission, outcome, passing, purpose, quietus, remnant, residue, resolve, selvage, sign off, undoing **8** abrogate, blow over, boundary, break off, close out, complete, conclude, curtains, cut short, deadline, dissolve, epilogue, get rid of, intermit, knock off, last gasp, last word, leave off, pack it in, rearmost, round off, round out, selvedge, shut down, stamp out, surcease, swan song, terminal, terminus, twilight, ultimate **9** cessation, close down, culminate, disappear, extremity, finish off, intention, interrupt, objective, punchline, remainder, ruination, terminate **10** aspiration, borderline, call it a day, completion, conclusion, consummate, denouement, do away with, expiration, extinguish, finish line, limitation, put through, relinquish, resolution

at: 4 abut
bad ~: 4 doom
combining form: 3 tel- 4 tele-, telo-
ender: 3 pin 4 game, long, most, note, play, ways, wise 5 brain, paper, point
in music: 4 fine
of a series: 5 omega 6 finale
starter: 4 book, week, year
to the ~ in Latin: 5 ad fin.
to the ~ in music: 6 al fine
end __: 3 man, men, run, use 4 bulb, game, leaf, line, mill, user, zone 5 brush, grain, organ, paper, plate, rhyme, sheet, table 6 around, matter, member 7 product
end __ high note: 3 on a
end __ line: 5 of the
end __ road: 5 of the
end __ world: 5 of the
end-__: 3 all 5 blown 7 stopped
__ end: 3 big, tag, the 4 at an, butt, dead, mill, poll, rear, tail 5 gable, in the, loose, split, tight 6 bitter, living, spread, sticky
__-end: 3 low 4 high, open, rear, year 5 front 6 closed
__ End: 4 Dead, East, West 5 Land's 6 Stoney, World's 7 Howards
end-all: 3 ult. 8 ultimate
endanger: 4 risk 5 peril 6 chance, hazard, menace 7 imperil, lay open 8 overhang, threaten 10 compromise, jeopardize
endangered: 4 rare 6 at risk 7 at stake 10 in jeopardy
endangered __: 7 species
endangerment: 4 risk 5 peril 8 jeopardy
endear: 5 charm 6 enamor 7 attract, win over 10 ingratiate
endeared: 5 amour 6 adored, prized 7 beloved, revered 8 cared for, esteemed, hallowed, idolized, precious 9 cherished, venerated, worshiped
endearing: 7 lovable, winning, winsome 8 loveable 10 enchanting
__ Endearing Young Charms: 5 Those
endearment: 3 hon 5 honey 7 pet name 8 fondness 9 affection, sweet talk 10 attachment, attraction
British term of ~: 3 luv
term of ~: 3 hon, pet 4 baby, dear, love 5 angel, honey, kiddo, sugar, sweet 7 darling 8 snookums 10 sweetheart
endeavor: 3 aim, bid, try 4 seek, shot, stab, toil 5 assay, essay, labor, offer, trial 6 effort, intend, strain, strive, take on 7 attempt, venture 8 activity, exertion, striving, struggle 9 undertake 10 enterprise
Endeavour org.: 4 NASA
ended: 3 o'er, out 4 done, fini, gone, over, past 7 all over, through 8 complete, over with 9 completed
__-ended: 4 open 6 double, single
endemic: 5 local 6 native 8 catching, regional 10 aboriginal, indigenous
__ ender: 4 nose 6 double
__-ender: 6 bitter
Ender, Kornelia: 7 swimmer
Enders, John: 8 Nobelist
Endgame author: Samuel Beckett
end in __: 4 a tie 5 a draw
ending: 4 coda, last, stop 5 close, final, finis, omega 6 epilog, finale, finish, sequel, upshot, windup, wrap-up 7 closing, closure, last act, outcome 8 epilogue, last page, surcease, swan song, terminus 9 cessation, summation 10 completion, conclusion, denouement, desistance, expiration, resolution
__ ending: 4 case, weak 5 happy, trick 8 surprise
__-ending: 5 never
Ending Up author: Kingsley Amis
end is __, The: 4 near
endive: 4 herb 6 veggie 9 vegetable
__ endive: 6 French 7 Belgian
__ End Kids: 4 Dead
endless: 3 big 4 much, vast 6 eonian, eterne, myriad, steady, untold 7 abiding, eternal, heaping, lasting, nonstop, tedious, undying 8 constant, enduring, infinite, timeless, unbroken, unending, unwaning 9 ceaseless, continual, countless, deathless, incessant, limitless, perennial, perpetual, unbounded, unceasing, unfailing, unlimited 10 continuous, enervating, innumerous, persistent, unnumbered
Endless __: 4 Love 5 Night, Sleep 6 Nights
Endless Love (song)
artist: Diana Ross, Lionel Richie, Luther Vandross, Mariah Carey
endlessly: 4 ever 7 forever, on and on 8 evermore 9 eternally
endlessness: 6 length 8 eternity 9 immensity
Endless Night (1971 film)
cast: Britt Ekland, Hayley Mills
Endless Nights (1987 song) artist: Eddie Money
Endless Sleep (1958 song) artist: Jody Reynolds
Endless Summers Nights (1988 song) artist: Richard Marx
Endless Summer, The (1966 film)
cast: Robert August, Mike Hynson
endman: 7 Mr. Bones
endnotes phrase: 6 et alia, et alii
endo-: 6 winner
ending: 5 plasm
opposite: 3 exo-
endocrine: 5 gland
endodontist deg.: 3 DDS, DMD
end of __: 5 an era
end of __, the: 5 an era
end-of-__: 4 file
__ end of one's rope: 5 at the
end-of-page abbreviation: 3 PTO
end-of-scene direction: 4 exit 6 exeunt
end-of-semester
event: 4 exam, test 5 final
end of the __: 4 line
End of the Battle, The author: Evelyn Waugh
End of the Innocence, The (1989 song) artist: Don Henley
End of the Road (1992 song) artist: Boyz II Men
End of the Road, The author: 5 Barth
End of the Romance, The artist: 4 Erté
__ end of the stick, the: 5 short
End of the World, The (1963 song) artist: Skeeter Davis
end-of-week cry: 4 TGIF
end on __ note: 5 a high
Endor
beast: 4 Ewok
dweller: 5 witch
endorse: 2 OK 3 ink, let 4 back, okay, sign 5 boost, favor 6 affirm, defend, permit, praise, ratify, second, uphold 7 approve, certify, commend, confirm, promote, support, sustain, warrant, witness 8 accredit, attest to, champion, notarize, sanction, stump for, validate, vouch for 9 authorize, autograph, encourage, get behind, guarantee, indemnify, recommend, subscribe 10 go to bat for, speak up for, stand up for, underwrite
endorsed: 3 Ok'd 4 OK'ed 8 official 9 preferred
item: 5 check 7 voucher
endorsement: 2 OK 4 amen, okay, plug 7 backing, go-ahead, support 8 adoption, advocacy, approval, sanction 9 reference
endorser: 6 backer, master, patron 7 apostle, paladin 8 advocate, champion, crusader, defender, exponent 9 paraclete, proponent, supporter
at times: 3 xer
endorsing: 3 for, pro 9 agreement
endow: 4 fund, give, vest, will 5 award, bless, crown, endue, equip, found, grant, indue 6 accord, bestow, confer, donate, enrich, invest, supply 7 finance, furnish, prepare, qualify, sponsor, support 8 bequeath, confer on 9 establish, subsidize 10 contribute, underwrite
endowed with, be: 4 have 5 boast 7 possess
endowment: 4 boon, fund, gift 5 award, flair, grant 6 bounty, legacy, talent 7 ability, bequest, faculty, funding, largess, present, quality, subsidy 8 aptitude, bestowal, capacity, donation, largesse 9 allowance, attribute, provision 10 capability, foundation, investment
recipient: 4 heir 5 donee
end-run: 6 outwit 8 outsmart
ends
at loose ~: 6 adrift 8 dallying, drifting, wavering 9 uncertain, unsettled
make ~ meet: 3 eke 4 live, save 5 skimp, stint 7 subsist
odds and ~: 4 bits, misc., olio, rest 5 melee, scrap, trash 6 debris, job lot, jumble, litter, medley, scraps, things 7 mélange, remnant, rubbish, rummage 8 et cetera, leavings, leftover, remnants, snatches, snippets 9 fragments, leftovers, potpourri, remainder 10 miscellany
partner: 4 odds
where ~ meet: 4 seam
__ ends: 5 loose, split
__ ends of the earth: 5 to the
Endsville: 3 def, rad 4 aces, A-one, boss, braw, cool, dece, fine, gear, keen, neat, nice, phat, tuff 5 dandy, ducky, grand, great, marvy, neato, nobby, prime, slick, super, swell 6 bang on, bang-up, bonzer, bosker, choice, divine, dreamy, far-out, gnarly, groovy, lovely, peachy, slap-up, spot on, superb, terrif, tiptop, unreal, whizzo, wicked 7 amazing, awesome, capital, corking, perfect, ripping, skookum, stellar, sublime 8 dazzling, especial, eximious, fabulous, five-star, four-star, frabjous, glorious, heavenly, jim-dandy, slam-bang, smashing, splendid, standout, sterling, stickout, superior, terrific, top-level, topnotch, very good, wondrous 9 bodacious, excellent, exemplary, exquisite, first-rate, high-grade, hunky-dory, marvelous, sollicker, top-flight, unrivaled, wonderful 10 first-class, hotsy-totsy, jack-a-dandy, out of sight, peachy-keen, phenomenal, remarkable, stupendous, super-duper, unrivalled
end-table item: 4 lamp 5 clock, radio
End, The (1978 film)
cast: Dom DeLuise, Sally Field, Burt Reynolds
director: Burt Reynolds
End, The (1958 song) artist: Earl Grant
__ end to: 5 put an
endue: 5 crown, endow, honor 6 assume, bestow, clothe, instal, invest 7 install, instate 9 transfuse
endurable: 7 livable 8 liveable 9 tolerable 10 sufferable
endurance: 3 vim 4 dint, grit, guts, thew, will 5 brawn, force, heart, might, moxie, pluck, power, spunk, thews, vigor 6 energy, mettle, muscle 7 bravery, courage, fitness, muscles, potence, potency, prowess, stamina 8 capacity, lifetime, patience, tenacity, vitality 9 allowance, beefiness, constancy, existence, fixedness, fortitude, gutsiness, hardiness, huskiness, longevity, puissance, restraint, stability, stoutness, suffering, tolerance, toughness 10 browniness, brute force, continuity, durability, indulgence, mightiness, permanence, resistance, resolution, robustness, sturdiness, submission, sufferance, toleration
endurance __: 4 race 5 ratio
endure: 2 go 4 bear, bide, go on, have, hold, last, live, lump, stay, take 5 abide, brave, brook, exist, stand, stick 6 accept, bear up, hang on, hold on, hold up, keep on, linger, live on, manage, permit, remain, resist, stay on, submit, suffer, wear on 7 carry on, hold out, make out, outlast, persist, prevail, receive, ride out, stomach, subsist, survive, sustain, swallow, undergo, wait out, weather 8 continue, cope with, meet with, stand for, sweat out, tolerate, wear well 9 go through, persevere, put up with, withstand 10 get through, sit through, stick it out, tough it out
enduring: 3 old 4 firm, sure 5 fixed, stoic, tight 6 stable, steady, strong 7 abiding, chronic, endless, eternal, lasting, nonstop, passive, patient, stoical, undying 8 constant, lifelong, residual, timeless, unending, unwaning 9 ceaseless, chronical, continual, incessant, indelible, long-lived, memorable, perennial, permanent, perpetual, steadfast, unabating, unceasing 10 changeless, habituated, inerasable, inveterate, monumental, persistent, unchanging, undecaying, unwavering
enduringly: 4 ever 6 always 7 finally, forever, for good, lasting 8 evermore 9 endlessly, eternally 10 unendingly
enduro: 4 test 8 auto race
Endust: 6 polish
alternative: 6 Behold, Pledge 10 Liquid Gold, Old English
endways: 7 upright 10 lengthways, lengthwise
Endymion: 4 poem
author: 5 Keats
lover of ~: 6 Selene
mother of ~: 6 Calyce
parent of ~: 4 Zeus 6 Calyce
son of ~: 5 Epeus, Paeon 7 Aetolus 9 Narcissus
End Zone author: Don DeLillo
ENE: 3 dir. 5 point 9 direction
opposite: 3 WSW
__ en el Rancho Grande: 4 Alla
enemies
like some ~: 5 sworn
make ~: 5 anger 6 enrage, fire up, madden 7 incense, inflame, provoke 8 irritate 9 displease, infuriate 10 exasperate
Enemies, A Love Story (1989 film)
cast: Anjelica Huston, Lena Olin, Ron Silver
director: Paul Mazursky
enemy: 3 foe 4 them 5 rival 6 bad guy, foeman 7 bad guys, defamer, hostile, invader, nemesis, opposer, traitor, villain 8 attacker, betrayer, opponent, saboteur 9 adversary, aggressor, assailant, combatant, detractor, ill-wisher, other side, terrorist 10 antagonist, competitor, opposition

join the ~: **4** turn **6** defect, desert, run out **7** forsake, pull out, sell out
meet one's ~: **4** face **6** attack, engage, line up, take on **7** assault **9** fight with
opposite: **4** ally
starter: **4** arch
survey: **5** recon
__ enemy: **6** public
__ Enemy: **7** Beloved, Dearest
...enemy, and they __: **4** is us **7** are ours
Enemy at the Gates (2001 film)
cast: Joseph Fiennes, Ed Harris, Jude Law, Rachel Weisz
director: Jean-Jacques Annaud
Enemy Below, The (1957 film)
cast: Theodore Bikel, Curt Jurgens, Robert Mitchum
director: Dick Powell
vessel: **3** sub **5** U-boat
Enemy Gods, The author: Oliver La Farge
__ enemy lines: **6** behind
Enemy Mine (1985 film)
cast: Louis Gossett Jr., Dennis Quaid
director: Wolfgang Petersen
Enemy of the People, An
author: Henrik Ibsen
character: **4** Kiil **5** Ejlif, Petra **6** Morten **7** Hovstad
Enemy of the State (1998 film)
cast: Lisa Bonet, Gene Hackman, Will Smith, Jon Voight
director: Tony Scott
__ Enemy, The: **6** Public **7** Violent
energetic: **4** busy, go-go, hale, live, racy, spry **5** alive, astir, brisk, fresh, hardy, lusty, peppy, perky, quick, smart, vital, zesty, zippy **6** active, at work, bouncy, hearty, lively, rugged, snappy, strong, virile, yeasty **7** animate, driving, dynamic, hyped-up, intense, kinetic, rousing, vibrant, willing, working, zestful **8** animated, bustling, emphatic, forceful, grooving, powerful, spirited, tireless, untiring, vigorous **9** ambitious, assiduous, combative, exuberant, sprightly, strenuous, vivacious **10** expressive, full of life, productive, red-blooded, undeterred, unflagging, unwearying
one: **4** doer **6** dynamo
energetically: **4** hard **5** madly **8** mightily
energize: **4** fuel, gird, pump, stir, tone **5** brace, build, hop up, liven, pep up, power, shore, steel **6** anneal, beef up, enable, excite, harden, jazz up, prop up, pump up, temper, tone up, turn on, vivify **7** actuate, animate, bolster, brace up, build up, burgeon, develop, empower, enhance, enliven, fortify, inspire, juice up, liven up, quicken, refresh, shore up, stiffen, toughen **8** activate, bourgeon, buttress, embolden, enspirit, imbolden, indurate, inspirit, motivate, vitalize **9** electrify, encourage, galvanize, intensify, reinforce, stimulate **10** invigorate
energizer: **5** tonic **8** pick-me-up **9** stimulant
energy: **3** pep, vim, zap, zip **4** brio, dash, dint, élan, fire, fuel, life, push, soul, thew, zeal, zest, zing **5** ardor, brawn, drive, force, juice, labor, might, moxie, oomph, power, punch, steam, thews, verve, vigor **6** action, bounce, bustle, muscle, pizazz, spirit, starch **7** fitness, muscles, pizzazz, potence, potency, stamina, voltage **8** activity, exertion, fervency, gumption, industry, momentum, strength, vitality, vivacity **9** animation, beefiness, élan vital, endurance, fortitude, hardiness, huskiness, intensity, puissance, stoutness, toughness **10** browniness, brute force, enterprise, enthusiasm, exuberance, get up and go, horsepower, initiative, liveliness, mightiness, resolution, robustness, sturdiness
biochemical ~ source: **3** ATP
Buddhist: **5** prana
bundle of ~: **6** dynamo
burst of ~: **5** spasm, spirt, spurt
center: **6** chakra
channel: **4** nadi
dynamo's ~: **3** EMF
field: **4** aura **8** ambience **9** emanation **10** atmosphere
full of ~: **4** go-go **5** alive, lusty, peppy, vital
lacking ~: **4** lazy, logy **6** effete **7** languid **8** listless
lack of ~: **6** anemia, anergy **7** anaemia
lose ~: **3** sag **4** tire, wilt
meas.: **3** BTU
nuclear ~ watchdog: **3** AEC
sap, as ~: **4** tire **5** drain, leach, use up **6** expend, lessen **7** deplete, exhaust, fatigue, suck dry, tire out **8** diminish, wear down **10** debilitate, devitalize, impoverish
science of ~: **7** physics
source: **3** sun **4** atom, carb, fuel **5** hydro
unit: **2** eV **3** cal. **4** ft. lb. **5** joule **7** calorie **9** degree-day, foot-pound
energy __: **4** band **5** audit, level
__ energy: **4** free, rest, soft, wind **5** clean, solar **6** atomic, orgone **7** binding, kinetic, nuclear, psychic, radiant
__-energy: **4** high
enero: **3** mes **5** month **7** January, Spanish
enervate: **3** sag, sap **4** flag, jade, tire, wane **5** blunt, weary **6** impair, reduce, shrink, soften, weaken **7** deplete, depress, exhaust, fatigue, tire out, unnerve, vitiate, wear out **8** enfeeble **9** attenuate, indispose, undermine **10** debilitate, devitalize, emasculate
enervated: **4** limp, logy, weak **5** faint, spent, tired, weary **6** done in, feeble **7** far-gone, languid, run-down, worn out **8** listless, out of gas **9** enfeebled, exhausted, lethargic, nerveless, paralyzed, prostrate, washed-out **10** gone to seed, knocked out, languorous, on the ropes, out of shape, spiritless
enervating: **6** taxing **7** tedious **8** tiresome
enervation: **6** anemia **7** anaemia, fatigue, frazzle, malaise **9** weariness **10** exhaustion, feebleness
Enesco, Georges: **8** Romanian, Rumanian **9** Roumanian, violinist
enfant terrible: **3** imp **4** brat **5** devil, scamp
enfeeble: **3** sag, sap **4** flag, tire, wane **5** blunt, waste, weary **6** impair, reduce, shrink, soften, weaken **7** deplete, exhaust, fatigue, tire out, unnerve, vitiate, wear out **8** enervate, paralyse, paralyze **9** attenuate, indispose, undermine **10** debilitate, devitalize
enfeebled: **6** infirm **7** injured
enfetter: **3** pin, tie **4** bind, bond, link, weld, wrap, yoke **5** affix, clamp, hitch, tie up **6** attach, bundle, cement, fasten, hook up, secure, tether **7** conjoin, connect, enchain, shackle, tighten
Enfield: **5** rifle
enfilade: **5** salvo **6** volley **7** barrage
enfin: **6** at last **7** finally **8** in the end
enflame: **3** bug, get, irk, vex **4** bait, gall, rage, rile, roil **5** anger, annoy, chafe, grate, peeve, pique, rouse, upset **6** abrade, bother, harass, offend, plague, rankle, ruffle **7** bedevil, disturb, provoke, torment, trouble **8** irritate **9** aggravate, displease, excoriate **10** exasperate
enfold: **3** hug, lap **4** hold, veil, wrap **5** cinch, clasp, press **6** clinch, clutch, swathe, wrap up **7** embrace, envelop, squeeze **8** surround **9** keep close
enforce: **3** use **5** apply, order, press **6** decree, demand, direct, enjoin, impose, invoke **7** command, entreat **9** implement, proscribe
enforceable: **4** just **5** legal, legit, licit, valid **6** kosher, lawful, proper **7** allowed, decreed **8** judicial **9** allowable, juridical, justified, statutory, warranted **10** authorized, legitimate, prescribed, sanctioned
enforcement: **6** duress **8** coercion, exaction
power: **5** teeth
Enforcer, The: **5** Nitti
Enforcer, The (1951 film)
cast: Humphrey Bogart, Zero Mostel
Enforcer, The (1976 film)
cast: Tyne Daly, Clint Eastwood, Harry Guardino
director: James Fargo
enfranchisement: **4** vote **6** choice **7** liberty **8** autonomy, decision, sanction, suffrage **10** liberation
eng.
part: **4** carb.
school: **4** tech.
see also engine, engineering
Eng.: **4** lang., subj.
course: **3** lit.
neighbor: **3** Ire. **4** Scot.
see also British, English
Eng. __: **3** Lit.
engage: **3** use **4** book, busy, face, grab, grip, hire, lock, meet, mesh, rent **5** apply, charm, enrol, lease, order, tie up **6** absorb, allure, appeal, arrest, assail, attack, commit, employ, enlist, enroll, line up, occupy, retain, secure, sign on, sign up, take on **7** appoint, assault, attract, betroth, charter, enchant, engross, enthral, immerse, inthral, involve, promise, recruit, reserve, takes on **8** activate, affiance, backbite, contract, enthrall, entrance, interest, inthrall, keep busy, switch on, take part **9** captivate, fascinate, fight with, interlace, interlock, intermesh, preoccupy, put to work **10** commission, monopolize
an entertainer: **4** hire **5** set up **6** line up, pick up **7** procure **8** register, schedule
in: **3** ply **4** have, wage **6** pursue, tackle, take up **7** address **8** practice **9** undertake
(in): **8** take part
engage __ test of wills: **3** in a
engaged: **4** busy **5** in use **6** active, at work, in gear, intent, signed, tied up **7** focused, working **8** involved, occupied, plighted, reserved **9** committed, on the move, operating, spoken for, wrapped up **10** performing
in: **4** up to
(in): **7** dealing
one: **6** fiancé **7** fiancée
one ~ in (suffix): **3** -eer
engagement: **3** gig, job, vow **4** bout, date, duel, duty, fray, meet, oath, pact, work **5** brush, clash, fight, match, stand, stint, troth, tryst **6** action, battle, combat, errand, pledge, wooing **7** booking, contest, meeting, promise **8** conflict, contract, skirmish **9** assurance, betrothal, blind date, courtship, encounter, enrolment, interview, situation **10** absorption, commission, commitment, enrollment, enterprise, invitation, obligation, rendezvous
engagement __: **4** ring
engaging: **4** nice **5** sweet **6** lovely, pretty **7** amiable, darling, likable, lovable, winning, winsome **8** charming, inviting, loveable, pleasant, pleasing, readable **9** appealing **10** attractive, delightful
En garde! follower: **4** duel
Engel: **6** Lehman, Marian **7** Georgia
Engel, Lehman: **9** conductor
Engel, Marian: **6** writer **8** Canadian
Engels: **9** Friedrich
colleague: **4** Marx
engender: **4** bear, give, make **5** beget, breed, bring, cause, hatch, plant, rouse, spark, spawn **6** arouse, create, foment, incite, induce, instil, lead to **7** develop, instill, produce, provoke **8** generate, occasion **9** instigate, propagate, stimulate **10** bring about, give rise to
engine: **4** tool, V-six **5** means, motor, turbo, V-four **6** barney, device, diesel, fanjet, V-eight, Wankel **7** machine, turbine **8** auto part, catapult, outboard, turbojet **9** apparatus, fire truck, generator, implement, machinery, mechanism **10** instrument, locomotive, powerhouse, power train
additive: **3** STP
cover: **4** hood
gun an ~: **3** rev **4** race
housing: **3** pod
meas.: **2** hp **3** rps
part: **3** cam, cyl., fan **4** pump **8** cylinder
problem: **5** no oil
small ~: **6** donkey
sound: **3** hum, pur **4** chug, ping, purr, putt, roar **5** cough, knock, vroom **6** varoom
engine __: **5** block, house **7** company, turning
__ engine: **3** gas, ion, jet **4** beer, fire, heat **5** goods, I-head, L-head, pilot, steam, trunk, V-type **6** arc-jet, barrel, Carnot, diesel, donkey, in-line, Jordan, piston, radial, ramjet, rocket, rotary, search, switch, Wankel **7** freight, hotbulb, jacking, propjet, resojet, uniflow, vernier
Engine Engine #9 (1965 song) artist: Roger Miller
engineer: **3** rig **4** plan, plot, tech. **5** build, set up, stage **6** create, devise, direct, manage **7** arrange, builder, concoct, conduct, finagle, operate, planner **8** conceive, contrive, designer, maneuver, organize **9** construct, fashioner, machinate, negotiate, originate **10** bring about, manipulate, mastermind, put through
furry ~: **6** beaver
__ engineer: **4** port **5** civil **6** flight, marine, mining **7** systems **8** domestic **10** mechanical
__-engineer: **7** reverse
engineering
branch: **4** mech. **5** civil **10** mechanical
datum: **4** spec **6** detail
feat: **3** dam **4** dike **6** bridge
subject: **4** math, phys. **7** physics
toy: **4** Lego
univ.: **3** MIT, RPI
__ engineering: **4** tool **5** human, ocean **6** social **7** ceramic, genetic, traffic
Engineers school: **6** Lehigh
Engine Number 9 (1970 song) artist: Wilson Pickett
__-engine plane: **4** twin
__-engine red: **4** fire

engird: **4** ring, wind **6** circle **7** enclose, environ, inclose **8** encircle, surround **9** encompass
England: **4** isle **6** Albion
ancient god: **3** Tiu
archaeologist: **5** Evans **6** Petrie
astronomer: **6** Halley **8** Herschel **9** Eddington
biochemist: **6** Sanger **7** Hopkins
biologist: **6** Huxley
biophysicist: **7** Hodgkin
botanist: **5** Banks
bovine: **5** Devon **6** Jersey, Sussex **7** Red Poll **8** Guernsey, Hereford **10** Lincoln Red
boys' school: **4** Eton
cathedral city: **3** Ely
cheese: **7** Chester, Stilton **8** Cheshire
chemist: **4** Davy **5** Black, Boyle, Soddy **6** Dalton, Perkin, Ramsay **7** Crookes, Hodgkin **9** Cavendish, Priestley
city: **4** Bath, Ryde, York **5** Blyth, Crewe, Derby, Dover, Egham, Leeds, Luton, Otley, Poole, Rugby **6** Batley, Bolton, Bootle, Dudley, Eccles, Exeter, Havant, Jarrow, Kendal, London, Oldham, Ossett, Oxford, Seaham, Slough, Stroud, Widnes, Yeovil **7** Banbury, Berwick, Bexhill, Bristol, Burnley, Cannock, Crawley, Ipswich, Margate, Norwich, Reading, Staines, Sunbury, Swindon, Telford, Walsall, Watford **8** Bradford, Brighton, Coventry, Hastings, Hereford, Plymouth **9** Cambridge, Leicester, Liverpool, Rotherham, Sheffield, Stockport, Worcester **10** Birmingham, Bournmouth, Chelmsford, Colchester, Eastbourne, Gloucester, Manchester, Nottingham, Sunderland
clergyman: **6** Wesley
combining form: **5** Anglo-
composer: **4** Arne **5** Elgar, Holst, Lawes **7** Britten
country festival: **3** ale
county: **4** Beds, Kent, Oxon **5** Berks, Bucks, Cambs, Devon, Essex, Hants, Herts, Hunts, Lancs, Leics, Lincs, Middx, Notts, Salop, Warks, Wilts, Worcs, Yorks **6** Derbys, Dorset, Durham, Gloucs, Staffs, Surrey, Sussex **7** Norfolk, Rutland, Suffolk **8** Cheshire, Cornwall, Hereford, Somerset **9** Berkshire, Hampshire, Middlesex, Northants, Wiltshire, Yorkshire **10** Cumberland, Derbyshire, Lancashire, Shropshire
courtier: **6** Sidney **7** Raleigh **8** Suckling
dance: **6** morris
designer: **6** Morris
diarist: **5** Pepys
dukedom: **4** York
Egyptologist: **5** Young **6** Petrie
essayist: **4** Lamb **5** Lewis, Pater, Powys **6** Pinero, Steele **9** Priestley, Stapledon
explorer: **4** Cook, Ross **5** Cabot, Davys, Drake **6** Baffin, Hudson **7** Dampier, Gilbert, Hawkins, Hillary, Raleigh
French port nearest ~: **6** Calais
garden feature: **4** maze
geneticist: **5** Crick **6** Galton
geologist: **5** Lyell
historian: **7** Toynbee, Walpole **8** Runciman, Strachey
humanist: **4** More
humorist: **9** Wodehouse
hymn writer: **5** Watts **6** Wesley
illustrator: **6** Potter
invader of ~: **5** Saxon **6** Norman
island: **3** Ely, Man **5** Wight **6** Jersey **8** Guernsey
journalist: **5** Smart
king: **4** Edwy, John **5** Edgar, Edred, Henry, James **6** Alfred, Canute, Edmund, Edward, Egbert, George, Harold, Henry I, Henry V, James I **7** Charles, Edward I, Edward V, George I, George V, Henry II, Henry IV, Henry VI, James II, Richard, Stephen, William **8** Charles I, Edward II, Edward IV, Edward VI, Ethelred, George II, George IV, George VI, Henry III, Henry VII, Richard I, William I **9** Athelstan, Charles II, Edward III, Edward VII, Ethelbald, Ethelbert, Ethelwulf, George III, Henry VIII, Richard II, William II, William IV **10** Edward VIII, Richard III, William III
lake: **8** Grasmere **10** Windermere
lexicographer: **7** Johnson **9** Partridge
mathematician: **7** Russell **9** Whitehead
money: **3** mil **5** broad, groat, noble, unite **6** guinea, tester, teston **7** carolus, jacobus, testoon **9** rose-noble
natural historian: **3** Ray **6** Darwin **7** Wallace
neighbor: **4** Eire **5** Wales **7** Ireland **8** Scotland
network: **3** BBC
of ancient ~: **6** Anglic
pamphleteer: **5** Paine
philosopher: **5** Locke **7** Russell, Spencer **9** Stapledon, Whitehead
philsopher: **4** Ryle
physicist: **5** Boyle, Bragg, Hooke, Joule **6** Kelvin, Newton **7** Crookes, Faraday, Thomson, Tyndall **8** Blackett, Chadwick, Rayleigh **9** Cavendish, Eddington **10** Rutherford
physiologist: **6** Adrian
pianist: **4** Hess
playwright: **5** Eliot, Nashe, Orton, Peele **6** Morgan, Pinero, Pinter, Rowley, Rudkin, Savage, Steele, Storey, Wesker **7** Chapman, Marlowe, Nichols, Osborne, Shaffer, Shirley, Webster, Whiting **8** Rattigan, Sheridan, Stoppard **9** Middleton, Priestley, Wycherley **11** Shakespeare
poet: **4** Owen, Pope, Read **5** Donne, Eliot, Monro, Peele, Powys, Raine, Rowse, Smart, Smith, Swift, Wyatt **6** Morris, Sidney, Symons, Waller **7** Chapman, Marlowe, Marvell, Peacock, Quarles, Raleigh, Sassoon, Shelley, Sitwell, Skelton, Southey, Spender, Spenser **8** Lovelace, Overbury, Richards, Rossetti, Suckling, Tennyson **9** Sackville, Southwell, Swinburne **10** Wordsworth **11** Shakespeare **13** Sackville-West
port: **4** Hull **5** Dover **6** London **8** Falmouth, Newhaven, Penzance, Plymouth, Sandwich, Weymouth **9** Liverpool, Newcastle **10** Colchester, Folkestone, Portsmouth
professor's deg.: **4** Lit.D.
publisher: **7** Newbery
queen: **4** Anne, Mary **5** Mary I **6** Mary II **8** Victoria **9** Elizabeth **10** Elizabeth I **11** Elizabeth II
racetrack: **5** Ascot, Epsom
ritual: **3** tea
river: **3** Cam, Usk, Wye **4** Aire, Avon, Leam, Ouse, Tyne **5** Leame, Tamar, Trent **6** Thames
royal house: **4** York **5** Blois, Tudor **6** Stuart **7** Hanover, Windsor **8** Normandy **9** Lancaster **11** Plantagenet
saint: **4** Bede **5** Alban, Baeda **6** Anselm **7** Dunstan **8** Boniface, Cuthbert **10** Thomas More **18** Edward the Confessor
satirist: **4** Pope **5** Nashe, Swift **9** Thackeray
scientist: **3** Ray **4** Davy, Snow **5** Banks, Black, Boyle, Bragg, Crick, Evans, Hooke, Joule, Lyell, Soddy, Young **6** Adrian, Dalton, Darwin, Galton, Halley, Huxley, Kelvin, Newton, Perkin, Ramsay, Sanger **7** Crookes, Faraday, Hodgkin, Hopkins, Thomson, Tyndall, Wallace **8** Blackett, Chadwick, Herschel, Rayleigh **9** Cavendish, Eddington, Priestley **10** Rutherford
sea: **5** Irish, North
spa: **4** Bath
to America: **4** ally
writer: **3** Pym **4** Amis, Lamb, Lear, More, Rhys, Ryle, Snow, Wain, West **5** Lewis, Locke, Mason, Menen, Moore, Murry, Orczy, Paine, Pater, Pepys, Powys, Reade, Rolfe, Shute, Watts, Waugh, White, Woolf, Young **6** Browne, Burney, Clarke, Conrad, Milton, Morgan, Morris, Orwell, Petrie, Potter, Powell, Ruskin, Sansom, Sayers, Sterne, Storey, Symons, Walton, Warner, Warton, Wilson **7** Dickens, le Carré, Marryat, Marston, Maugham, Meynell, Mitford, Montagu, Painter, Peacock, Renault, Russell, Shelley, Sitwell, Spencer, Stephen, Stewart, Surtees, Tolkien, Toynbee, Walpole **8** Christie, Lawrence, Macaulay, Matineau, Meredith, Mortimer, Quennell, Runciman, Sillitoe, Smollett, Strachey, Trollope, Williams **9** du Maurier, Masefield, Massinger, Mitchison, Partridge, Priestley, Pritchett, Radcliffe, Stapledon, Thackeray, Whitehead, Wodehouse **10** Muggeridge, Richardson **11** Shakespeare
see also British, Great Britain
England __: **6** Swings
__ England: **3** New
England Dan and John Ford Coley
song: I'd Really Love to See You Tonight (1976)
Love Is the Answer (1979)
Nights Are Forever Without You (1976)
We'll Never Have to Say Goodbye Again (1978)
England Swings (1965 song) artist: Roger Miller
Englewood: **4** city, town
locale: **7** Florida **8** Colorado **9** New Jersey
English: **4** Alex **8** language
body ~: **6** motion
deg.: **4** Lit.B.
homework: **5** essay, theme, vocab. **10** vocabulary
horn: **3** cor **4** reed
in plain ~: **6** namely **8** straight
English __: **3** elm, ivy, Lit, pea, red, yew **4** bond, horn, iris, Pale, sole **5** daisy, holly **6** finish, laurel, muffin, saddle, sennit, setter, sonnet, Suites, system, walnut **7** bulldog, Channel, sparrow
English __ spaniel: **3** toy **6** cocker
__ English: **3** Bad, New, Old **4** body, Sign **5** Basic, Early, Irish, king's **6** Middle, Modern, pidgin, queen's, signed **7** British, reverse, running
English at the North Pole, The author: Jules Verne
English Channel
feeder: **4** Orne **5** Seine, Somme
gulf: **6** St. Malo
isle: **5** Wight **6** Jersey **8** Guernsey
town: **5** Dover, Poole **6** Dieppe
English Derby locale: **5** Epsom
English horn kin: **4** oboe, reed
Englishman: **4** Brit **6** Briton
exclamation: **4** I say **8** good show
English muffin alternative: **4** roll **5** bagel, bialy, toast **9** croissant
English Patient, The (1996 film)
cast: Juliette Binoche, Willem Dafoe, Ralph Fiennes, Kristen Scott Thomas
director: Anthony Minghella
role: **4** Hana
setting: **6** Sahara
English setter: **3** dog **5** canid **6** canine
__ English sheepdog: **3** Old
English Suites composer: **4** Bach
Englund: **6** Robert
englut: **4** gulp **6** guzzle **8** wolf down
engorge: **4** bolt, glut, sate, wolf **5** raven, stuff **6** devour **8** gulp down **10** gobble down
oneself on: **3** eat **4** bolt **6** devour, feed on, finish, ingest, relish **7** consume, feast on, put away, scarf up **8** chow down, gobble up, wolf down **9** polish off, scarf down **10** gormandize
engr.
kind of ~: **4** mech.
sch.: **3** MIT, RPI
engrain: **8** entrench
engrave: **4** etch **5** carve, chase, infix, print, stamp **6** chisel, incise, instil **7** impress, imprint, instill, scratch **8** inscribe **9** mezzotint
engraved pillar: **5** stela, stele
engraver: **5** Dürer **6** etcher **7** jeweler **8** lapidary **10** lapidarist
need: **5** burin **6** dabber, stylus
engraver __: **6** beetle
engraving: **5** print **7** etching, picture, woodcut **8** intaglio **9** mezzotint **10** impression, lithograph
combining form: **5** glypt- **6** glypto-
__ engraving: **4** line, wood **5** steel
engross: **4** grip, hook **5** rivet, write **6** absorb, arrest, engage, engulf, ingulf, occupy **7** bewitch, consume, enchain, enthral, immerse, inthral **8** enthrall, interest, inthrall, transfix **9** captivate, enrapture, entertain, fascinate, preoccupy **10** monopolize
engrossed: **4** busy, deep, lost, rapt **6** intent **7** focused, wound up **8** caught up, held fast, obsessed, occupied **9** assiduous, impressed, intrigued, submerged, undivided, wrapped up **10** captivated, enthralled, fascinated, interested, really into, thoughtful, up to here in
engrossing: **8** readable **9** absorbing, consuming, obsessing **10** compelling, intriguing
engrossment: **4** grip, lure, stir **6** allure, regard, turn-on **7** concern, dousing, dunking, passion, pastime **8** interest, intrigue **9** attention, curiosity, diversion, immersion **10** absorption, attraction, enthusiasm, excitement, motivation, saturating, saturation, submerging
engulf: **4** bury, sink **5** drown, flood, swamp, whelm **6** absorb, deluge, devour **7** consume, engross, envelop, immerse, overrun, swallow **8** inundate, overflow, overtake, submerge, surround **9** overwhelm, snow under, swallow up
enhance: **4** gild, gird, lift, tone **5** add to,

adorn, amend, boost, build, exalt, fix up, grace, raise, shore, steel **6** anneal, become, bedeck, beef up, better, enrich, harden, polish, prop up, reform, temper, tone up **7** amplify, augment, benefit, bolster, brace up, build up, burgeon, develop, elevate, empower, flatter, fortify, garnish, improve, magnify, shape up, sharpen, shore up, spice up, stiffen, touch up, toughen, upgrade **8** beautify, bourgeon, buttress, decorate, energize, heighten, increase, indurate, spruce up, vitalize **9** embellish, glamorize, intensify, meliorate, reinforce **10** ameliorate, complement, invigorate, strengthen, supplement

enhancement: 4 gain, plus **5** bonus, extra **8** addition, increase **10** supplement

__ enhancement: 7 revenue

enhancer

flavor ~: 3 MSG **4** herb, salt **5** spice

enhancing: 8 cosmetic **10** decorative, ornamental

enhearten: 4 stir **5** rouse **6** arouse, buck up, stir up **7** inspire **8** embolden, enspirit, imbolden, inspirit, motivate, psyche up

Enid: 4 city, town **6** Blyton, Markey **7** Bagnold

husband of ~: 7 Geraint

locale: 8 Oklahoma

Enid Is Sleeping (1990 film)

cast: Jeffrey Jones, Elizabeth Perkins, Judge Reinhold

Enif: 4 star

enigma: 4 crux, knot, prob. **5** poser, vexer **6** puzzle, riddle, secret, sphinx, teaser **7** arcanum, baffler, boggler, mystery, paradox, problem, puzzler, stumper **8** question **9** conundrum **10** mind-bender, perplexity

Enigma

song: Return to Innocence (1994) Sadeness (1991)

Enigma (2001 film)

cast: Jeremy Northam, Dougray Scott, Kate Winslet

director: Michael Apted

Enigma, An author: Edgar Allan Poe

enigmatic: 4 dark **5** mirky, murky, vague **6** arcane, mystic **7** complex, cryptic, obscure, unclear **8** abstruse, Delphian, esoteric, nebulous, puzzling, stealthy, ulterior **9** ambiguous, confusing, cryptical, difficult, secretive **10** indistinct, inexplicit, mysterious, perplexing

Enigma Variations composer: 5 Elgar

enisle: 6 maroon, strand **7** isolate, seclude **8** set apart **10** place apart, quarantine

Eniwetok: 4 isle **5** atoll **6** island

event: 5 A test, N test

test subject: 5 H bomb

enjoin: 3 ban, bar, bid, put **4** tell, urge, warn **5** debar, force, order, plead, press **6** adjure, decree, demand, direct, forbid, impose, indite, ordain **7** command, counsel, dictate, enforce, inhibit, require **8** call upon, preclude, prohibit, restrain **9** prescribe, proscribe, recommend

enjoinment: 7 refusal

enjoy: 3 dig, own, use **4** grok, have, like, love **5** adore, boast, dig in, eat up, fancy, go for, revel, savor, taste **6** dote on, relish, wallow **7** have fun, possess, rejoice, revel in **8** cotton to, dote upon, flip over, thrill to **9** delight in, get high on, luxuriate **10** appreciate, experience, have a blast

enjoyable: 3 fun **5** jolly, kicky, merry, nifty, sweet **6** lively, lovely **7** likable, welcome **8** heavenly, pleasant, pleasing, readable **9** agreeable, delicious, flavorful, marvelous, palatable **10** delectable, delightful, gratifying, preferable, relishable, satisfying

enjoyment: 3 fun **4** kick, life, love, play, zest **5** gusto, sport **6** luxury, relish, thrill **7** rapture **8** felicity, pleasure **9** amusement, diversion, happiness, merriment, ownership **10** indulgence, possession, recreation, relaxation

exclamation of ~: 3 yum **6** yum-yum

Enjoy the Silence (1990 song) artist: Depeche Mode

Enjoy Yourself (1976 song) artist: Jackson 5

Enke, Karin: 6 skater

enkindle: 4 burn **5** light, rouse, spark **6** arouse, ignite **7** inspire **9** catch fire, impassion

enl.: 4 incr.

see also enlarge, enlist

enlace: 3 tie **4** bind **5** braid, twine, twist **6** bind up, corset, thread **8** surround, tangle up **9** interfold, interlock **10** intertwine, interweave

En-lai: 4 Zhou

enlarge: 3 add, pad, wax **4** grow, puff **5** add on, add to, bloat, boost, build, bulge, mount, raise, swell, widen **6** accrue, beef up, blow up, dilate, expand, extend, gather, jack up, puff up, pump up, ramble, recite, spread **7** add on to, advance, amplify, augment, balloon, broaden, burgeon, develop, distend, fill out, inflate, magnify, stretch, thicken, upsurge **8** bourgeon, elongate, escalate, heighten, increase, lengthen, multiply, snowball **9** branch out, expatiate, intumesce, reinforce, spread out **10** aggrandize, exaggerate, strengthen

a hole: 4 ream

enlarged: 5 puffy, tumid **7** swollen

enlargement: 4 incr. **6** blowup, growth, spread **7** buildup **8** addition, increase, swelling

maybe: 5 inset

enlighten: 5 brief, edify, guide, solve, teach, train **6** inform, school, wise up **7** apprise, apprize, educate **8** acquaint, advise of, disabuse, initiate, instruct **9** catechize, elucidate, exemplify, undeceive **10** illuminate

enlightened: 3 hep, hip **4** wise **5** aware, right, savvy **6** with it **7** knowing, learned, liberal, mindful, refined, tuned in **8** profound, rational **9** cognizant, in the know, plugged in

one: 5 arhat **6** Buddha

enlightening: 5 lucid, vivid **6** bright **7** evident, fulgent, refined **8** artistic, cultural, luminous, lustrous **9** brilliant, effulgent, elevating, enriching, graspable, inspiring, refulgent, uplifting

enlightenment: 4 info, life **5** light **6** wisdom **7** culture, liberty

enlink: 3 tie, wed **4** bind, bond, join, meet, mesh, yoke **5** annex, hitch, unite **6** adjoin, attach, bridge, cement, cohere, couple, fasten, hook up **7** combine, conjoin, connect **8** meld with **9** affiliate, interface

enlist: 3 get **4** hire, join, levy **5** draft, enrol, enter **6** assign, call up, employ, engage, enroll, induct, join up, muster, obtain, secure, sign on, sign up, take on **7** appoint, procure, recruit **8** initiate, mobilize, persuade, register, shanghai **9** conscribe, conscript, volunteer **10** commission

again: 4 reup

enlisted __: 3 man **5** woman **6** person

enlisted one: 2 GI **3** PFC **5** GI Joe **7** private, recruit, soldier, warrior

enlistment: 6 sign-up **9** enrolment, mustering **10** employment, enrollment

enliven: 4 buoy, fire, wake **5** awake, cheer, color, hop up, pep up, rally, renew, rouse, spark, spice, waken **6** arouse, awaken, buck up, buoy up, excite, fire up, jazz up, perk up, pick up, pump up, turn on, vivify, wake up **7** animate, brace up, cheer up, fortify, freshen, gladden, hearten, inspire, juice up, punch up, quicken, refresh, spice up **8** activate, brighten, energize, enspirit, inspirit, vitalize **9** encourage, entertain, galvanize, impassion, stimulate **10** exhilarate, intoxicate, invigorate, rejuvenate, strengthen

en masse: 6 bodily, wholly **8** in unison, mutually, together **10** altogether, completely

enmesh: 3 net **4** hook, mire, trap **5** catch, snare, snarl, twine **6** entrap, tangle **7** embroil, ensnare, entwine, insnare, intwine, involve, related **8** entangle, tangle up **9** interlace **10** intertwine

enmity: 3 ire, war **4** feud, hate **5** anger, odium, spite, venom **6** animus, grudge, hatred, malice, rancor, spleen **7** dislike, ill will **8** acrimony, aversion, bad blood, loathing **9** animosity, antipathy, hostility, nastiness, prejudice **10** abhorrence, alienation, antagonism, bitterness, unkindness

Enna: 4 city, town

locale: 5 Italy

ennea-: 4 nine

preceder: 4 octo-

successor: 3 dec-

ennead: 4 nine **5** Muses, nonet

less one: 5 octad

one of a mythical ~: 4 Clio **5** Erato **6** Thalia, Urania **7** Euterpe **8** Calliope **9** Melpomene **10** Polyhymnia **11** Terpsichore

Ennio: 9 Morricone

Ennis: 4 city, town **7** Skinnay

locale: 5 Texas **7** Ireland

ennoble: 5 crown, deify, exalt, honor **6** praise **7** elevate, magnify, promote **10** aggrandize

ennui: 4 tire **6** apathy, tedium **7** boredom, languor **8** doldrums, flatness, monotony **9** lassitude, weariness **10** melancholy

causing ~: 5 ho-hum

exhibit ~: 4 yawn

Ennui author: Langston Hughes

Eno: 5 Brian

Enoch: 5 Arden, Light

cousin: 4 Enos

father of ~: 4 Cain **5** Jared

grandmother of ~: 3 Eve

son of ~: 4 Irad **6** Lamech

Enoch Arden: 4 poem

author: Alfred Tennyson

Enola Gay: 5 plane **6** bomber **8** airplane

payload: 5 A bomb **6** Fat Man

enormity: 4 bulk, evil, size **6** horror **7** bigness, outrage **8** atrocity, evilness, hugeness, rankness, vastness, vileness **9** depravity, flagrancy, greatness, grossness, immensity, magnitude **10** infinitude

enormous: 3 big **4** huge, vast **5** bulky, giant, great, gross, jumbo, large **6** cosmic, mighty **7** hulking, immense, mammoth, massive, sizable, titanic **8** colossal, cosmical, gigantic, king-size, oversize, sizeable, spacious, terrific, towering, whapping, whopping **9** excessive, fantastic, Herculean, humongous, monstrous, overlarge, whalelike **10** astronomic, gargantuan, monumental, prodigious, stupendous, tremendous

enormously: 4 a lot, much, very **6** vastly **7** big time **9** in a big way, like crazy **10** incredibly

Enormous Radio, The author: John Cheever

Enormous Room, The author: e.e. cummings

Enos: 5 6 Barton, Cabell **9** Slaughter

father: 4 Seth

Enosh

father of ~: 4 Seth

grandfather of ~: 4 Adam

grandmother of ~: 3 Eve

enough: 5 ample, amply, uncle **6** fairly, plenty, rather **8** abundant, adequate **9** bounteous, bountiful, plenteous, plentiful **10** abundantly, acceptable, acceptably, moderately, reasonably, sufficient, unbearable

already: 4 OK OK

barely ~: 5 light, scant

be ~: 2 do **4** suit, work **5** get by, serve **6** render **7** fulfill, perform, realize, satisfy, suffice, work out

be good ~: 2 do **4** pass, suit, work **5** avail, get by, serve **6** answer **7** content, deliver, qualify, satisfy, suffice **10** hit the spot

good ~: 4 fine **7** up to par **8** adequate, very well **9** tolerable

more than ~: 5 ample, spare, undue **6** excess, galore, oodles

not good ~: 7 lacking, wanting **8** inferior **9** deficient, half-baked, imperfect **10** inadequate, incomplete

old ~: 5 of age

old ~ to know better: 5 adult, grown, of age **6** mature **7** grown-up

sure ~: 7 sincere **10** absolutely, guaranteed

well ~: 4 so-so **9** tolerably **10** acceptably, adequately, fairly well

__ enough: 4 good, sure **5** oddly

Enough (2002 film)

cast: Bill Campbell, Juliette Lewis, Jennifer Lopez

director: Michael Apted

Enough!: 5 can it, uncle **6** no more, quit it, stop it

__ Enough: 4 Good, High **5** Never, One Is **6** Strong

__ Enough and Time: 5 World

Enough Rope author: Dorothy Parker

enounce: 5 state

en passant: 7 by the by **8** by the way **9** in passing

capture: 4 pawn

enplane: 5 board, get on, hop on

__-en-Provence: 3 Aix

Enquirer: 5 paper **9** newspaper

locale: 10 Cincinnati

Enquiry author: Dick Francis

enrage: 3 ire **4** rile **5** anger, steam, upset **6** fire up, ireful, madden, rile up, tee off, work up **7** enflame, incense, inflame, make mad, provoke, steam up, tick off **8** irritate, make boil **9** displease, infuriate, make angry **10** exasperate

enraged: 3 hot, mad **4** ired, sore **5** angry, cross, huffy, irate, livid, riled, wroth **6** fierce, fuming, ireful, raging, raving, red-hot **7** angered, boiling, furious, ranting, violent **8** choleric, incensed, inflamed, volcanic, white-hot, wrathful **9** indignant, resentful, splenetic **10** aggravated, infuriated

enrapt: 6 joyful **7** all eyes **8** absorbed, caught up, turned on **9** attentive, delighted, enchanted, entranced

10 captivated, enthralled, fascinated, mesmerized, spell-bound, starry-eyed, transfixed
enrapture: 4 send 5 charm, elate 6 allure, enamor, ravish 7 attract, beatify, beguile, bewitch, delight, enchant, engross, enthral, inthral 8 enthrall, entrance, inthrall 9 captivate, fascinate, spellbind, transport
enraptured: 4 rapt 6 joyful, joyous 7 far gone 8 blissful, ecstatic, held fast, jubilant 9 bewitched 10 fascinated, infatuated
enravish: 7 beatify 8 enthrall 9 enrapture
enrich: 4 lard 5 add to, adorn, build, endow, fix up 6 better, fatten, fulfil, polish, reform, uplift 7 build up, develop, elevate, enhance, fortify, fulfill, improve, shape up, sharpen, sweeten, upgrade 8 decorate, ornament, spruce up 9 cultivate, embellish, fertilize, make finer, meliorate 10 aggrandize, ameliorate, supplement
enrichment: 7 enhance 8 flourish, ornament 9 accessory, adornment, bedecking 10 complement, completion, decoration, festooning, garnishing, supplement
Enrico: 5 Fermi 6 Caruso 9 Colantoni
in English: 5 Henry
Enright: 3 Dan, Ray
Enright, Ray: 8 director
film: Alibi Ike (1935)
Bad Men of Missouri (1941)
Coroner Creek (1948)
Dames (1934)
Flaming Feather (1951)
Hard to Get (1938)
Enrique in English: 5 Henry
enrobe: 4 garb 5 dress 6 attire, clothe 7 cover up
enrobed: 4 clad
enroll: 3 reg. 4 join, list 5 admit, draft, enter, learn, start 6 accept, engage, enlist, join up, line up, muster, record, sign on, sign up, wrap up 7 recruit 8 register 9 chronicle, subscribe
enrollment: 9 accession, admission, induction, reception 10 acceptance, employment, engagement, enlistment, initiation
__ enrollment: 4 open
enroot: 3 fix 5 plant 6 attach, foster 7 develop, implant 8 take hold 9 establish
__ en Rose: 5 La Vie
en route: 6 aboard, coming, midway 7 driving 8 embarked, motoring, on the way 9 advancing, in transit, on the road, traveling
on a ship: 4 asea 5 at sea
__ en scène: 4 mise 7 metteur
ensconce: 3 set, sit 4 bury, hide 5 cache, cover, plant, stash 6 instal, locate, nestle, occupy, settle 7 conceal, install, shelter, situate, snuggle 8 stow away, tuck away 9 establish, sequester
enseal: 5 stamp 8 notarize
ensemble: 4 band, cast, garb, suit, togs, trio 5 array, choir, dress, group, nonet, octet, suite 6 attire, chorus, livery, outfit, septet, sestet, sextet, troupe 7 clothes, company, costume, octette, quartet, quintet 8 entirety, glee club, sextette, totality 9 aggregate, gathering, orchestra, quintette, vocalists 10 assemblage, collection, Sunday best
furniture ~: 5 suite
leading part: 5 primo
musical ~: 4 band, orch., trio 5 choir, combo, nonet, octet 6 chorus, sestet, sextet 7 octette, quartet 8 sextette 9 orchestra, vocalists
ensemble __: 4 cast 6 acting
__ ensemble: 4 tout
Ensenada: 4 city, town
locale: 6 Mexico
enshrine: 5 adore, bless, ensky, exalt 6 hallow, revere 7 cherish 8 remember, sanctify, treasure 9 care about 10 consecrate, hold sacred
enshroud: 4 bury, hide, mask, veil, wrap 5 cloak, cover 7 conceal
enshrouded: 6 covert, hidden, mystic, secret, unseen 9 concealed, covered up, incognito, invisible 10 tucked away, undercover, under wraps
ensign: 4 flag, rank 5 badge 6 banner, colors, emblem, sailor 7 pennant 8 gonfalon, standard, streamer 9 banderole
asst.: 3 CPO
evil ~: 4 Iago
org.: 3 USN
Ensign Pulver actor: 4 Ives 5 Sands
ensilage: 5 straw
ensile: 5 store
ensky: 4 hail, laud, lift 5 bless, boost, crown, deify, exalt, extol, honor, raise 6 esteem, praise, revere 7 acclaim, commend, dignify, elevate, ennoble, glorify, idolize, lionize, magnify, promote, worship 8 enshrine, enthrone, eulogize 9 celebrate, recommend 10 aggrandize, compliment
enslave: 4 tame 9 indenture, subjugate
enslavement: 4 yoke 6 chains 9 servitude
ensnare: 3 bag, get, nab, net 4 grab, hook, lure, mesh, mire, snag, take, trap 5 catch, snarl, trick 6 enmesh, entrap, immesh, inmesh, rope in, suck in, tangle 7 capture, deceive, embroil, mislead 8 entangle, inveigle
ensorcelled: 5 magic 7 magical 8 wizardly, wizardry 9 bewitched 10 bewitching, enchanting, entrancing, miraculous
Ensor, James: 6 artist 7 painter
homeland: 7 Belgium
ensoul: 4 love 5 adore, prize, savor, value 6 admire, dote on, esteem, revere 7 care for, cherish, idolize, worship 8 enshrine, hold dear, treasure, venerate
ensue: 5 arise, occur, trail 6 follow, happen, result 7 go after, proceed, succeed 8 come next 9 arise from, come after, eventuate, intervene, supervene, transpire 10 come to pass
ensuing: 4 next 5 after, later 6 behind, coming, serial 8 eventual, in back of 9 following, resultant 10 consequent, subsequent, succeeding, successive
ensure: 3 ice 4 lock, mind, seal 5 cinch, guard 6 lock in, lock up, secure 7 certify, confirm, protect, warrant 8 attest to, make safe, nail down 9 guarantee, safeguard
ensured: 3 gtd. 7 certain 10 guaranteed
ENT
part of ~: 3 ear 4 nose 6 throat
entablature part: 6 frieze
entail: 4 mean 5 cause, imply 7 call for, include, involve, require
entangle: 3 net 4 hook, mesh, mire, snag, trap 5 catch, mix up, ravel, snare, snarl, twine 6 burden, enmesh, entrap, hamper, immesh, impede, inmesh, jumble, muddle, puzzle, tangle 7 confuse, embroil, ensnare, entwine, insnare, intwine, involve, perplex 8 bewilder 9 implicate, interlace 10 complicate, intertwine, interweave
entangled: 6 knotty, tricky 7 complex 8 abstruse, tortuous 9 Byzantine, difficult, elaborate, intricate 10 convoluted, perplexing
entanglement: 3 web 4 knot, mesh, mess, node, trap 5 mix-up, skein, snare, snarl, tieup 6 affair, cobweb, jumble, muddle, tangle 7 liaison, pitfall 8 disorder, intrigue, quagmire 9 labyrinth
Entebbe: 4 city, town
action: 4 raid
locale: 6 Uganda
entendre
double ~: 3 pun 8 wordplay
__ entendu: 4 bien
entente: 4 bloc, pact 6 accord, treaty 7 compact, concord 8 alliance 9 agreement
__ Entente: 6 Triple
enter: 3 key, log 4 book, come, go in, join, type 5 begin, enrol, get in, input, key in, pop in, probe, reach 6 access, appear, arrive, blow in, bust in, come in, drop in, ease in, edge in, enlist, enroll, fill in, go into, horn in, invade, join up, jump in, move in, muster, pierce, pile in, record, roll in, rush in, show up, sign on, sign up, slip in, step in, type in, walk in, worm in 7 barge in, break in, burst in, crowd in, drive in, ingress, intrude, punch in, put down, set down, sneak in, turn out 8 breeze in, come into, commence, embark on, enroll in, initiate, inscribe, mark down, pass into, register, set about, set out on 9 penetrate, set foot in 10 inaugurate, infiltrate, take part in
a harbor: 4 dock 5 put in
a highway: 5 merge
allow to ~: 5 admit, greet, let in 6 accept 7 embrace, receive, welcome
a plea: 3 sue
cyberspace: 5 log on
data: 4 type 5 input, key in 6 type in
how actors ~: 5 on cue
into: 4 join, open 5 begin, start, study 6 assume, launch 7 analyze, kick off, lead off, partake 8 commence, consider, get going, initiate 9 originate, undertake 10 inaugurate, scrutinize
one by one: 6 file in
enter __: 4 into, upon
__ Enter: 5 Do Not
Enter neighbor: 5 Shift
enterprise: 3 job, try 4 dash, firm, plan, push, task, zeal 5 cause, drive, pluck, quest, trade, vigor 6 action, affair, daring, effort, energy, hustle, outfit, spirit 7 attempt, company, concern, courage, crusade, project, pursuit, venture 8 activity, ambition, audacity, boldness, business, campaign, endeavor, gumption, industry 9 adventure, alertness, eagerness, foresight, happening, operation, readiness 10 engagement, enthusiasm, expedition, experiment, get-up-and-go, initiative
lack of ~: 5 sloth
enterprise __: 4 zone
__ enterprise: 4 free 7 private
Enterprise: 4 city, town 9 car rental 10 auto rental
alternative: 4 Avis 5 Alamo, Hertz 6 Budget, Dollar 7 Thrifty 8 National
journey: 4 trek
letters: 3 NCC, USS
locale: 7 Alabama
officer: 4 Data, Sulu, Troi 5 Bones, McCoy, Scott, Spock, Uhura 6 Chekov
speed: 4 warp
Enterprise (UPN sci-fi)
cast: Scott Bakula (Capt. Jonathan Archer)
John Billingsley (Dr. Phlox)
Jolene Blalock (T'Pol)
John Fleck (Silik)
Dominic Keating (Lt. Malcolm Reed)
Anthony Montgomery (Ens. Travis Mayweather)
Linda Park (Ens. Hoshi Sato)
Connor Trinneer (Cmdr. Trip Tucker)
dog: 7 Porthos
__ Enterprise: 3 USS 4 Free
enterprising: 4 bold, busy, go-go, spry 5 astir, eager, perky 6 active, at work, daring, lively 7 dashing, driving, dynamic, zealous 8 animated, aspiring, bustling, diligent, hustling, intrepid, vigorous 9 assiduous, energetic, sprightly
Enter Sandman (1991 song) artist: Metallica
entertain: 4 bear, fete, host 5 amuse, charm, cheer, lodge, put up, treat 6 absorb, divert, harbor, listen, occupy, please, regale, tickle 7 beguile, comfort, delight, disport, engross, enliven, enthral, gratify, harbour, inthral, receive, welcome 8 distract, enthrall, interest, inthrall 9 captivate, knock dead, make merry, recognize, socialize, spring for, stimulate, think over, titillate 10 anticipate, cogitate on, deliberate, keep in mind
an idea: 4 muse 5 study 6 ponder 7 reflect 8 cogitate, consider, mull over, ruminate 9 think over 10 deliberate, introspect
entertainer: 2 DJ 4 host, mime, name 5 actor, clown, comic, mimer 6 amuser, dancer, deejay, singer 7 acrobat, actress 8 comedian, humorist, musician, thespian 9 ballerina, chanteuse, performer 10 comedienne
engage an ~: 4 book, hire 5 set up 6 line up, pick up 7 procure 8 register, schedule
medieval ~: 4 bard, poet 8 minstrel
entertainers' union: 3 SAG 5 AFTRA
Entertainer, The: 3 rag
Entertainer, The (1960 film)
cast: Alan Bates, Roger Livesey, Laurence Olivier, Joan Plowright
director: Tony Richardson
Entertainer, The (1974 song) artist: Marvin Hamlisch
entertaining: 3 fun 5 funny, jolly, light, merry, witty 6 clever, lively, moving, social 7 piquant, rousing 8 humorous, pleasant, readable, stirring 9 laughable
entertainment: 3 fun 4 play, show 5 party, sport 6 affair, frolic 7 delight, pastime, revelry 8 pleasure 9 reception 10 recreation
center: 6 arcade
center component: 2 TV 3 VCR 5 TV set 9 DVD player
charge: 5 cover
choice: 4 show 5 movie, revue 6 comedy, review 7 theater
conglomerate: 3 MCA 4 Sony 6 Viacom
home ~ letters: 3 VHS
inflight ~: 5 movie
__ entertainment: 4 home, live
__ Entertainment: 5 That's
Entertainment Tonight
host: 4 Hart, Tesh
__ Entertain You: 5 Let Me
Enter the Dragon (1973 film)
cast: Bruce Lee, John Saxon
enthrall: 4 grab, grip, hook, send

5 charm, rivet 6 absorb, enamor, engage, ravish 7 attract, beatify, beguile, bewitch, enchant, engross, satisfy 8 entrance, interest 9 captivate, enrapture, entertain, fascinate, hypnotize, indenture, infatuate, knock dead, mesmerize, preoccupy, spellbind, subjugate, transport
enthralled: 4 agog, rapt 6 enrapt 8 held fast 9 attentive, engrossed, possessed 10 fascinated
enthralling: 7 lovable 8 loveable, readable
enthrallment: 7 slavery
enthrone: 4 king, seat 5 ensky, exalt 6 invest 7 glorify, instate, raise up
enthuse: 4 gush, rave, send 5 drool, emote, flush, psych 6 excite, fire up, thrill, work up 7 get into, impress, psych up 8 interest 9 electrify, go on about 10 bubble over, effervesce, get excited
enthused: 4 keen 6 elated, fervid, gung-ho 7 fervent 8 inspired
about: 5 big on
enthusiasm: 3 vim, zip 4 dash, élan, fire, life, zeal, zest, zing 5 ardor, drive, gusto, mania, oomph, spark, verve, vigor 6 energy, esprit, fervor, relish, spirit 7 ardency, avidity, emotion, passion, rapture 8 alacrity, ambition, delirium, devotion, fervency, interest, keenness, optimism, vivacity 9 animation, eagerness, élan vital, fieriness, intensity, obsession, transport, vehemence 10 conviction, ebullience, enterprise, excitement, exuberance, fanaticism, initiative, joyfulness
combining form: 5 -mania
lack of ~: 5 ennui 6 apathy, tedium 7 boredom, languor 8 doldrums, monotony 9 lassitude, weariness
show ~: 5 eat up, lap up 10 effervesce
enthusiast: 3 fan, nut 4 buff, jock 5 fiend, freak, lover 6 addict, maniac, rooter, votary, zealot 7 admirer, devotee, fanatic 8 adherent, partisan 9 proponent, supporter 10 aficionado, monomaniac
combining form: 4 -phil 5 -phile
enthusiastic: 3 hot, mad 4 agog, avid, busy, gaga, keen, spry, warm, wild 5 afire, astir, eager, fiery, het up, manic, peppy, perky, rabid, ready, wired 6 ablaze, active, aflame, ardent, at work, fervid, gung ho, hearty, intent, lively, yeasty 7 anxious, athirst, bananas, devoted, dynamic, earnest, excited, fervent, fired up, glowing, gushing, keyed up, willing, working, zealous 8 animated, bustling, effusive, juiced up, sanguine, spirited, thrilled, tireless, vigorous, youthful 9 assiduous, dedicated, energetic, rhapsodic, sprightly
about: 4 into 6 all for, keen on
affirmative: 6 yes yes
not ~: 4 loth 5 loath, tepid
sort: 5 tiger
entice: 4 bait, coax, draw, hook, lure, pull, wile 5 decoy, shill, snare, tempt 6 allure, appeal, arouse, beckon, cajole, draw in, enamor, entrap, lead on, pull in, rope in 7 attract, beguile, enchant, mislead, wheedle 8 appeal to, interest, inveigle, persuade 9 fascinate, sweet-talk, tantalize
enticement: 4 bait, lure, trap 5 decoy, savor, snare 6 allure, carrot, come-on 8 cajolery 9 incentive, mousetrap, sweetener 10 allurement, attraction, inducement, invitation, persuasion, temptation
enticer: 4 vamp 5 lurer
enticing: 4 sexy 6 lovely 8 alluring, inviting, tempting 9 beautiful, covetable, desirable 10 attractive, delectable, persuasive, voluptuous
entire: 3 all 4 full 5 gross, round, sound, total, uncut, utter, whole 6 intact 7 perfect, plenary, radical 8 absolute, all-in-one, complete, finished, integral, livelong, outright, the works, thorough, unbroken 9 aggregate, full-dress, inclusive, inviolate, undamaged, undivided, universal, unlimited, unreduced, untouched 10 continuous, exhaustive, in one piece, unabridged
combining form: 3 hol- 4 holo-, toti- 7 integri-
scale: 4 A to Z 5 field, gamut, range, reach, scope, sweep 6 extent 7 breadth 8 panorama, spectrum
entirely: 3 all 4 just, only, well 5 fully, plumb, quite, right, sheer 6 bodily, in full, in toto, purely, solely, wholly 7 totally, utterly 8 whole hog 9 every inch, like a book, perfectly, to the hilt 10 absolutely, altogether, completely, thoroughly, to the limit, to the teeth
not ~: 6 in part, mostly, partly
use ~: 5 eat up 7 exhaust 9 polish off
entirety: 3 all, sum 5 gross, total, whole 6 corpus 8 ensemble, totality 9 aggregate 10 opera omnia
entitle: 3 dub 4 call, name 5 allow, label, title 6 enable, permit 7 baptize, empower, qualify, warrant 8 christen, nickname 9 authorize, designate, privilege 10 legitimize
entitled: 6 vested
entitled to, be: 4 earn, rate 5 merit 7 deserve
entitlement: 3 due 4 dibs 5 right, title 7 license 9 privilege
org.: 3 SSA
entitlement __: 7 program
entity: 3 ens 4 body, item, unit 5 being, thing, whole 6 matter, nature, object 7 article, essence, reality, someone 8 creature, organism, presence, quiddity 9 actuality, existence, something 10 individual
single ~: 4 unit 5 monad
starter: 3 non
entom.: 3 sci.
entomb: 6 inhume
entomological stage: 4 pupa 5 imago, larva
entomologist accessory: 3 net
entomology: 7 science
branch of ~: 11 myrmecology
study: 7 insects
entomophobe fear: 7 insects
entourage: 5 court, staff, suite, train 6 escort 7 company, cortege, retinue 9 courtiers, followers, following, hangers-on, retainers 10 associates, attendants, companions, sycophants
entr'__: 4 acte
entrain: 5 board, get on, hop on 6 depart, embark 8 go aboard
entrammel: 3 tie 5 tie up
entrance: 3 way, wow 4 adit, door, gate, grip, hall, ramp 5 charm, inlet, lobby, mouth, start, way in 6 access, advent, allure, dazzle, disarm, enamor, engage, influx, portal, ravish, thrill 7 arrival, attract, beguile, bewitch, delight, doorway, enchant, enthral, gateway, ingress, inthral, passage, postern 8 anteroom, enthrall, hatchway, inthrall 9 admission, beginning, captivate, carry away, enrapture, fascinate, hypnotize, inception, inebriate, mesmerize, spellbind, threshold, transport, vestibule 10 admittance, appearance, initiation, intoxicate, passageway
allow ~: 5 let in 6 lead in 7 receive
curved ~: 4 arch
ender: 3 way
estate ~: 6 portal 7 doorway, ingress
fee: 4 ante
hall: 5 foyer, lobby 6 atrium 9 vestibule
hotel ~ feature: 6 awning, canopy 8 overhang
in France ~: 5 porte
mine ~: 4 adit
requirement: 4 exam, test
stairway: 5 stoop
__ entrance: 7 service
entranced: 4 lost, rapt 6 enrapt 8 held fast 9 bewitched, delighted, gladdened 10 fascinated
entrancement: 3 hex 5 spell
entrancing: 5 magic 7 lovable, magical 8 heavenly, loveable, magnetic 9 glamorous 10 enchanting, magnetical
entrant: 6 novice 8 aspirant, beginner, initiate, neophyte, newcomer 9 candidate 10 competitor, contestant, tenderfoot
entrants: 5 field 7 entries, runners 8 nominees 10 applicants, candidates
entrap: 3 bag, net 4 hook, lure, mire, take, trap 5 box in, catch, decoy, set up, snare, sting, tempt, trick 6 allure, ambush, draw in, enmesh, entice, immesh, inmesh, lay for, lead on, reel in, rope in, suck in, tangle 7 beguile, capture, deceive, embroil, ensnare, insnare 8 entangle, inveigle 10 circumvent
Entrapment (1999 film)
cast: Sean Connery, Will Patton, Ving Rhames, Catherine Zeta-Jones
director: Jon Amiel
entreat: 3 ask, beg, sue, woo 4 pray, seek, urge 5 plead, press 6 adjure, appeal, exhort, invoke 7 beseech, implore, request, solicit 8 appeal to, petition 9 impetrate, importune, plead with 10 supplicate
entreaty: 4 plea, suit 6 appeal, demand, desire, prayer 7 coaxing, request 8 petition 9 wheedling 10 invocation
make an ~: 3 ask, beg 4 seek, urge 5 plead, probe, query 6 appeal 7 beseech, implore, inquire, request 8 call upon, petition
entrechat: 4 leap
entrée: 2 in 3 cod, ham 4 bass, beef, chop, crab, dish, duck, fish, lamb, meal, meat, pork, pull, ribs, sole, stew, tuna, veal 5 chops, clams, filet, liver, roast, scrod, squab, steak, tacos, trout, way in 6 access, course, cutlet, dinner, pot pie, salmon, shrimp, ticket, turkey 7 chicken, codfish, doorway, halibut, ingress, lasagna, lasagne, lobster, mussels, oysters, ravioli, sea bass, serving, venison, welcome 8 beef stew, bluefish, fresh ham, lamb stew, main dish, meat loaf, open door, osso buco, passport, pheasant, pork loin, pot roast, scallops 9 admission, crab cakes, fried fish, influence, lamb chops, leg of lamb, meatballs, pork chops, roast duck, roast pork, smoked ham, spaghetti, spare ribs, swordfish, tortillas, veal chops 10 admittance, Cornish hen, enchiladas, fettuccine, main course, rack of lamb, red snapper, stroganoff, tenderloin, tortellini, veal cutlet
Boston ~: 5 scrod 6 schrod
brunch ~: 6 omelet 8 omelette
equine ~: 5 straw
French ~: 4 roti, veau
garnish: 5 cress 7 parsley
give ~ to: 6 take in
list: 4 menu
topping: 5 garni, gravy, sauce
entrench: 3 fix, peg, pin, set, tie 4 bind, bond, camp, glue, lock, nail, nest, root, stay, tack, weld 5 embed, imbed, infix, lodge, paste, perch, plant, roost, squat, stick 6 anchor, cement, enroot, fasten, harden, hole up, secure, settle 7 implant, ingrain, install, instill, station, stiffen, tighten 8 nail down, position, rigidify, solidify 9 establish, stabilize, thumbtack
entrenched: 3 set 9 confirmed 10 inveterate
become ~: 5 dig in
entrenching __: 4 tool
entre nous: 7 sub rosa 8 in secret, secretly 9 between us, privately
entrepreneur: 6 backer, tycoon 7 founder 8 promoter
letters: 3 DBA, SBA
entropy: 5 chaos, decay 7 decline 9 mobocracy
entrust: 4 lend, vest 5 leave, trust 6 assign, charge, commit, invest 7 commend, confide, consign, empower, present 8 accredit, delegate, hand over, relegate, turn over 9 surrender 10 commission
entry: 3 way 4 adit, door, gate, item 5 way in 6 access, portal, record 7 doorway, ingress 8 hatchway, notation, register 9 admission, threshold, vestibule 10 admittance
acct. ~: 2 cr.
ender: 3 way
fee: 4 ante 5 stake
forbid ~: 3 bar
gain ~: 4 come 5 get in 6 arrive, come in, show up
grant ~ to: 5 admit, greet 6 accept 7 include, receive, welcome
illegal ~: 6 bag job 8 trespass
ledger ~: 4 item, loss 5 asset, debit 6 credit
make an ~: 4 note 6 notate
permit ~: 5 let in 7 allow in
requirement: 5 badge 6 ID card
entry __: 4 card, form, word 5 blank
entry-__ job: 5 level
__ entry: 4 main, post 5 added, title 6 double
__-entry bookkeeping: 6 double, single
Entry of Christ Into Brussels artist: 5 Ensor
entryway: 4 door, gate 6 access, portal 7 ingress, postern 9 vestibule
Entwhistle: 4 John
entwine: 4 coil, curl, join, knit, lace, lock, wind 5 braid, plait, snake, snarl, twist, weave 6 enmesh, immesh, inmesh, spiral, splice 7 sinuate 8 entangle 9 corkscrew, interlace 10 interweave
__ Enuff: 4 Tuff
Enugu's country: 6 Biafra
enumerate: 3 add 4 cite, list, name, tell 5 add up, count, state, sum up, tally, total 6 detail, figure, number, recite, reckon, record, run off 7 itemize, mention, recount, run down, specify, tick off 8 spell out, tabulate 9 calculate, inventory, keep count, keep score 10 count noses
enumeration: 5 count, tally 6 census, litany 7 recital
enunciate: 3 say 5 speak, state, utter, voice 6 affirm, intone 7 declare, express 8 proclaim, set forth, vocalize 9 pronounce 10 articulate, promulgate
enunciation: 5 voice 6 speech 8 delivery
enure: 6 harden, season 7 break in, toughen 8 accustom 9 acclimate, con-

dition, get used to, habituate, withstand 10 take effect
(to): 6 harden
env.: 3 SAE 4 SASE
contents: 3 enc., ltr. 4 encl.
designation: 5 PO Box
see also envelope
enveil: 4 bury, wrap 5 cloak, cover, dress, guise, hider, layer 6 clothe, encase, screen, shield, shroud 7 conceal, enclose, envelop, obscure, protect 8 disguise, enshroud, traverse 9 adumbrate 10 spread over
envelop: 3 hug, lap 4 fold, hide, veil, wind, wrap 5 cloak, cover 6 circle, encase, enfold, engulf, enwrap, incase, infold, ingulf, inwrap, muffle, wrap up 7 besiege, blanket, conceal, enclose, inclose, smother 8 muffle up, surround 9 close in on, encompass
envelope: 5 cover 6 jacket, packet 7 wrapper 8 covering 9 container, portfolio 10 atmosphere, integument
abbr.: 3 att. 4 addr., attn.
earth's ~: 3 air 5 ether 6 aether
letters: 4 SWAK
need: 3 gum 4 glue 5 stamp
number: 3 Zip
open an ~: 4 slit
part: 4 flap 5 clasp
phrase: 6 care of
shape: 4 rect. 9 rectangle
wet an ~: 4 lick, seal
___ envelope: 3 pay 6 floral, window
envelopment: 5 siege
envenom: 4 sour 8 embitter, imbitter
enviable: 5 lucky 7 desired 8 superior 9 covetable, desirable, excellent, fortunate
assignment: 4 plum
Envigado: 4 city, town
locale: 8 Colombia
envious: 5 green 7 jealous 8 covetous 9 green-eyed, malicious, resentful 10 begrudging
be ~: 4 lust, seek 5 covet, crave 6 desire 7 ache for, itch for, long for, wish for 8 aspire to, yearn for 9 hanker for, thirst for
environ: 4 area, ring 6 circle, engird 7 enclose, inclose 8 encircle, surround 9 encompass
environment: 4 aura 5 state, world 6 milieu, nature, sphere 7 climate, context, element, habitat, setting, terrain 8 ambiance, ambience, backdrop, vicinity
combining form: 3 eco-
cultureless ~: 5 wilds 6 desert 9 wasteland 10 wilderness
organism modified by ~: 4 ecad
rapid growth ~: 3 den 4 nest 6 cradle, hotbed
science of ~: 7 ecology
environmental: 8 physical
agcy.: 3 DNR, EPA
problem: 4 smog 6 litter 9 pollution
science: 4 ecol. 7 ecology 8 oecology
environmental ___: 3 art 6 design 7 science
environment-minded: 5 green
environs: 4 area 6 region, suburb 7 compass, grounds, suburbs 8 confines, purlieus, vicinity 9 outskirts 10 boundaries
envisage: 4 plan 5 fancy, think 7 foresee, imagine, picture, predict, realize 8 conceive, consider, envision 9 visualize 10 anticipate
envisaging: 4 idea, view 5 image, start 6 design, notion, origin, outset, theory, vision 7 infancy, inkling, opinion, reading, thought 8 creation, ideality 9 beginning, cognition, formation, imagining, invention, launching 10 cogitating, conception, exposition, impression, initiation
envision: 3 see 5 fancy, think 7 foresee, imagine, picture, predict, project, realize 8 conceive, envisage 9 fantasize, visualize 10 anticipate
En Vogue
song: Don't Let Go (1996)
Free Your Mind (1992)
Giving Him Something He Can Feel (1992)
Hold on (1990)
My Lovin' (1992)
Whatta Man (1994)
envoy: 3 amb. 5 agent, vicar 6 bearer, consul, deputy, legate, nuncio 7 apostle, attaché, carrier, courier 8 delegate, diplomat, emissary, minister 9 appointee, go-between, messenger 10 ambassador, interceder
envy: 3 sin 4 wish 5 covet 8 begrudge, coveting, jealousy
enwind: 4 coil, curl, kink, loop 5 braid, crimp, curve, helix, snake, swirl, twirl, twist, whorl 6 spiral, tangle 7 wreathe 9 corkscrew 10 intertwine
enwrap: 6 shroud 7 envelop, swaddle 8 bundle up, surround
enwreathe: 3 arc 4 arch, coil, curl, gird, hoop, knot, loop, ring, roll 5 curve, twirl, twist, whorl 6 circle, girdle, spiral 7 circuit, scallop 8 encircle 9 encompass
Enya homeland: Ireland
Enzo: 3 car 4 auto 7 Ferrari, Stuarti
enzyme: 5 lyase, renin 6 lipase, pepsin 7 pepsine
genetic ~: 5 DNAse, RNAse
suffix: 3 ase
enzymes, science of: 8 zymology
eo ___: 4 ipso 6 nomine
eoan: 7 auroral
Eocene: 5 Epoch
eohippus: 5 horse 6 equine
eo ipso: 10 by that fact
Eola locale: 5 Texas
Eolus: 4 peak 5 mount 8 mountain
locale: 7 Rockies 8 Colorado
E.O.M. item: 4 bill 7 invoice 9 statement
eon: 3 age 4 ages 6 period 7 century, dog's age 8 eternity, long time 10 time period
Buddhist ~: 5 kalpa
Hindu ~: 4 yuga
eonian: 7 endless, eternal 8 infinite, unending 9 boundless, limitless, unbounded, unlimited 10 without end
Eos
brother of ~: 6 Helios
equivalent: 6 Aurora
lover of ~: 4 Ares 5 Orion 8 Astraeus, Cephalus, Tithonus
parent of ~: 4 Thea, Thia 8 Hyperion
sister of ~: 6 Selene
son of ~: 5 Eurus, Notus 6 Boreas, Memnon 7 Adymnus 8 Emathion, Phaethon, Zephyrus
eosin: 3 dye 6 red dye
EPA
concern: 3 mpg, PCB 4 ecol., smog
part of ~: 3 Env. 6 Agency 10 Protection
eparch: 6 bishop 7 prefect 8 praefect
EPCOT ___: 6 Center
EPCOT site: 3 Fla. 7 Florida, Orlando
épée: 5 blade, sport, sword 9 swordplay
alternative: 4 foil
move: 5 lunge
wield an ~: 5 fence, parry
Épernay's river: 5 Marne
ephah fraction: 4 omer
ephahs, ten: 3 kor
ephemeral: 5 brief, short 6 mortal 7 passing 8 episodic, fleeting, flitting, meteoric, temporal, volatile 9 fugacious, momentary, temporary, transient 10 episodical, evanescent, short-lived, transitory, unenduring
Ephesians preceder: 9 Galatians
ephod: 8 vestment
Ephron: 4 Nora 5 Delia, Henry
Ephron, Nora spouse: Carl Bernstein
epi: 6 finial
ender: 4 cure 6 center
epi-: 4 near, over, upon
epic: 4 poem, saga, tale 5 grand, story, verse 6 epopee, heroic 7 Homeric 8 fabulous, heroical, sweeping 9 grandiose, narrative 10 monumental
Greek ~: 5 Iliad 6 Aeneid 7 Odyssey
hero of a Hindu ~: 4 Rama
Norse ~: 4 edda, saga
of ~ proportions: 3 big 4 huge, vast 5 giant, great, gross, heavy, jumbo, large 6 cosmic 7 immense, mammoth, massive, monster, titanic 8 colossal, enormous, gigantic, oversize, spacious, terrific, towering, whopping 9 extensive, herculean, humongous, monstrous, walloping 10 gargantuan, monumental, overweight, prodigious, tremendous
poetry: 6 epopee 8 epopoeia
reciter: 4 bard
___ epic: 4 mock 5 beast
epical: 5 grand, great 6 heroic 8 heroical, majestic 9 grandiose 10 impressive, majestical
epicarp: 4 peel
Epicene author: Ben Jonson
epicure: 5 eater 6 foodie 7 gourmet 8 gourmand 10 gastronome
delicacy: 5 snail, viand 8 escargot
epicurean: 7 sensual 8 sensuous 9 bon vivant, libertine, luxurious, sybaritic 10 gastronome, gluttonous, hedonistic, sensualist, voluptuous
epidemic: 4 rife 6 plague 7 rampant 8 catching, outbreak 9 infection 10 infectious, widespread
epidemiology HQ: 3 CDC
epidermis: 4 pelt, skin
dermis plus ~: 5 cutis
opening: 5 stoma
epidote: 3 gem 7 zoisite
epigone: 3 ape 5 mimic, phony 6 copier, monkey, parrot, shadow 7 copycat 8 emulator, follower, imitator, impostor 10 plagiarist
epigram: 3 saw 4 quip 5 moral, motto, truth 6 bon mot, saying 7 proverb 8 aphorism, laconism 9 witticism
epigrammatic: 5 brief, meaty, pithy, short, terse, witty 7 concise, pointed 8 succinct 9 ingenious 10 to the point
tale: 4 myth, tale, yarn 5 fable, story 6 legend 7 parable 8 allegory
epigraph: 5 motto 6 legend, rubric
epilogue: 3 end 4 coda 6 ending, finale, sequel, wrap-up 9 afterword 10 conclusion, postscript
epimeliad: 5 nymph
Epimetheus: 4 moon 5 giant, Titan
brother of ~: 5 Atlas 10 Prometheus
planet: 6 Saturn
Épinal: 4 city, town
locale: 6 France, Vosges
épinglé: 6 fabric
epinicion: 3 ode 4 poem
epiphany: 7 insight 10 appearance, perception
Epiphany figures: 4 Magi
epiphyte: 5 plant
episcopal: 5 papal 8 churchly, clerical, pastoral, prelatic, priestly 9 canonical, religious 10 pontifical, rabbinical
Episcopal ___: 5 vicar 6 Church
episcopate: 3 see 7 diocese, prelacy
episode: 5 event, scene, story, thing 6 affair, matter 7 chapter 8 incident, occasion 9 adventure, happening, interlude 10 experience, occurrence
histrionic ~: 7 tantrum 8 outburst
violent ~: 5 quake 10 earthquake
episodic: 8 rambling 9 ephemeral 10 digressive
epistle: 6 letter 7 message, missive
apostle: 4 Paul
appendage: 2 PS 3 PPS
Epistle to Dr. Arbuthnot author: Alexander Pope
epistolary ___: 5 novel
epistolize: 5 write 9 drop a line, drop a note 10 correspond
epitaph: 5 elegy 6 legend
starter: 4 here
Epitaph: 5 paper 9 newspaper
locale: 9 Tombstone
Epitaph for a Spy author: Eric Ambler
epithalamic: 6 bridal 7 marital, nuptial 8 conjugal
epithet: 4 name 5 curse, label, title 6 insult 8 cognomen, nickname 9 expletive, sobriquet
mild ~: 4 dang, egad, rats 5 egads
epitome: 3 sum 4 type 5 ideal, model 6 digest 7 essence, paragon, summary 8 abstract, exemplar, synopsis 9 archetype 10 abridgment, apotheosis, compendium, conspectus, embodiment
epitomize: 5 sum up 6 detail, typify 8 contract, stand for 9 exemplify, represent, symbolize 10 illustrate
epizootic: 8 catching 9 pestilent, spreading 10 contagious, infectious
E Pluribus Unum: 5 Latin, motto
epoch: 3 age, era 4 time 6 period 7 vintage 10 generation
Cenozoic ~: 6 Eocene
N. Amer. geologic ~: 5 Erian
of an ~: 4 eral
Pleistocene ~: 6 ice age
Tertiary Period ~: 6 Eocene
epoch-___: 6 making
___ epoch: 7 glacial
Epoch: 6 Eocene 7 Miocene
epochal: 8 periodic 9 momentous
epode: 4 poem 5 verse
like an ~: 6 heroic 8 heroical
Epodes author: Horace
eponym: 4 name 8 namesake
noted: 7 Romulus 8 Quisling, Shrapnel
epopee: 4 epic 5 Iliad 7 Odyssey
___ époque: 5 belle
E. Power ___: 5 Biggs
epoxy: 5 resin 6 cement 8 adhesive
Eppa: 5 Rixey
Epperly: 4 peak 5 mount 8 mountain
locale: 10 Antarctica
Epping ___: 6 Forest
Epps, Omar: 5 actor
film: In Too Deep (1999)
Love and Basketball (2000)
The Mod Squad (1999)
The Wood (1999)
epsilon: 5 Greek 6 letter
follower: 4 zeta
preceder: 5 delta
Epsom: 3 spa
event: 5 Derby 9 horse race
locale: 7 England
Epsom ___: 4 salt 5 Downs, salts
Epsom and ___: 5 Ewell
Epstein: 3 Rob 5 Brian, Jacob
equable: 4 calm, cool, even, mild 5 level, quiet 6 low-key, mellow, placid, sedate, serene, stable, steady 7 amiable, at peace, pacific, relaxed, stoical, uniform, unmoved 8 amicable,

composed, constant, laid-back, moderate, peaceful, tranquil **9** collected, easygoing, impassive, quiescent, temperate, unexcited, unextreme, unruffled, unvarying **10** consistent, phlegmatic, true to type, unagitated, unchanging, untroubled
equal: **3** iso-, tie **4** even, fair, like, peer, same, tied **5** alike, level, match, reach, rival, total, touch **6** come to, fellow, on a par, square **7** abreast, add up to, compeer, emulate, identic, matched, sum up to, uniform **8** amount to, balanced, confrere, one to one, parallel, rank with, unbiased **9** duplicate, identical, impartial, objective **10** comparable, coordinate, correspond, evenhanded, fifty-fifty, homologous, synonymous, tantamount
be ~ to: **3** can **5** rival **7** emulate
combining form: **3** iso- **4** pari-
footing: **3** par
make ~: **5** level
not ~ to: **5** unfit **6** unable **9** incapable
on an ~ footing: **4** fair **5** level **6** square **7** uniform **8** balanced, matching **10** fifty-fifty
out: **6** cancel, offset **7** redress, rescind **10** balance out, counteract, neutralize
portion: **4** half **9** bisection
score: **3** tie
to: **4** like **5** ready **8** as good as
to the task: **3** fit **4** able, deft, keen **5** adept **6** adroit, expert, gifted **7** knowing, skilled **9** competent, masterful, qualified **10** proficient
without ~: **5** alone **6** single, unique **8** peerless
equal __: **4** sign, time
equal-__ projection: **4** area
Equal __ Amendment: **6** Rights
equality: **3** lib, par **6** parity **7** balance, isonomy **8** evenness, fairness, fair play, likeness, sameness, symmetry
org. promoting ~: **4** CORE **5** NAACP
equalize: **4** even **5** level, match **6** even up, offset, square **7** balance **8** square up **9** stabilize **10** commeasure, recompense
equalizer: **3** gun
equally: **4** both **5** alike, as one **9** uniformly
equals __: **4** sign
equal-sided: **6** square **7** rhombic
equanimity: **4** calm **5** peace, poise **6** aplomb, temper **7** ataraxy, balance **8** calmness, coolness, patience, serenity **9** assurance, composure, placidity, sangfroid **10** confidence, detachment, neutrality, sedateness, steadiness
equate: **5** level, liken, match **7** balance, compare **8** parallel **9** associate, correlate, make alike **10** correspond
equation: **5** ratio **7** formula **10** proportion
part: **3** var. **8** variable
__ equation: **4** heat, wave **5** polar **6** linear, simple, stable **7** Laplace, Riccati
equation of __: **4** time **5** state **6** motion
equator: **4** line
capital near the ~: **5** Quito
deg. above the ~: **4** N. Lat.
dist. from the ~: **3** lat. **8** latitude
equatorial: **3** hot **5** humid **6** sultry, torrid, tropic **8** steaming, stifling, tropical **10** sweltering
equatorial __: **4** tide **5** plane, plate **6** trough
Equatorial __: **6** Guinea **7** Current
__ Equatorial Africa: **6** French
__ Equatorial Current: **5** North, South
Equatorial Guinea: **6** nation **7** country
capital: **6** Malabo
city: **6** Malabo
neighbor: **5** Gabon **8** Cameroon
people: **3** Fan **4** Fang **6** Pangwe **7** Pahouin
equerry: **4** page **5** groom **8** horseman
equestrian: **5** rider **6** cowboy, gaucho, jockey, knight, lancer **7** Cossack, cowgirl, dragoon **8** buckaroo, horseman **10** cavalryman
mishap: **5** spill
need: **4** crop, tack **5** habit
sport: **4** polo
equiangular figure: **6** isogon, square
Equiano, Olaudah: **6** writer **8** Nigerian
equi- cousin: **3** iso-
equidistant: **6** median, middle **8** parallel
equilateral figure: **5** rhomb **6** square **7** rhombus
equilibrium: **3** par **4** calm **5** poise **6** aplomb, stasis **7** ataraxy, balance **8** calmness, coolness, serenity, symmetry **9** equipoise
equilibrium __: **5** price, valve
equine: **3** ass, bay, cob, dun, nag **4** Arab, barb, colt, foal, hack, jade, mare, moke, mule, plug, pony, roan **5** bronc, burro, filly, horse, horsy, kiang, mount, pacer, paint, pinto, steed, zebra **6** bronco, cayuse, dapple, dobbin, donkey, gee-gee, horsey, hunter, jumper, onager, quagga, sorrel, tarpan **7** Arabian, bobtail, charger, courser, cow pony, gelding, hackney, jackass, mustang, palfrey, piebald, trooper, trotter, unicorn **8** chestnut, chigetai, destrier, eohippus, palomino, polo pony, skewbald, stallion **9** appaloosa, dziggetai, packhorse, Percheron **10** Clydesdale, Lippizaner
African ~: **5** zebra **6** quagga
armor: **4** bard
Asian ~: **5** kiang **6** onager **8** chigetai **9** dziggetai
comment: **4** bray **5** neigh **6** heehaw, whinny
dad: **4** sire
entrée: **3** hay **4** oats **5** straw
extinct ~: **6** quagga
loquacious ~: **4** Mr. Ed
mom: **4** mare **5** filly
ornery ~: **3** ass **4** mule **5** burro
restraint: **4** rein
shade: **4** roan
small ~: **3** ass **4** pony **5** burro
stockade: **3** pen **6** corral **9** enclosure
TV ~: **4** Fury, Mr. Ed **8** Mister Ed
youngster: **4** colt, foal **5** filly
see also horse
equinoctial __: **4** line, year **5** point, rains, storm **6** circle
equinox
month: **3** Mar., Sep. **4** Sept. **5** March **9** September
sign: **5** Aries
__ equinox: **4** fall **6** spring, vernal
equip: **3** arm, fit, rig **4** deck, gear, gird **5** array, endow, ready, rig up, stock, train **6** enable, fit out, gear up, get set, outfit, purvey, rig out, supply **7** appoint, deck out, furnish, plenish, prepare, provide, qualify, satisfy, turn out **8** accouter, accoutre, embattle **9** condition, provision
ender: **3** age
with weapons: **7** fortify **8** embattle
equipage: **3** rig **4** gear **6** outfit **7** baggage **8** carriage **9** munitions
equipment: **3** kit, rig **4** gear **5** means, plant, stuff, thing, tools **6** tackle **7** baggage, devices **8** fittings, fixtures, supplies, utensils **9** apparatus, furniture, implement, machinery, trappings **10** appliances, belongings, facilities, instrument, provisions
change the ~: **5** refit
equipment design, science of: **10** ergonomics
equipoise: **5** level **6** aplomb, stasis **7** balance **8** evenness, symmetry **9** stability **10** equanimity, sedateness
equipped: **4** able **5** armed, ready **9** qualified
__-equipped: **3** ill **4** well
__ Equis: **3** Dos
equitable: **3** due **4** even, fair, just **5** right **6** proper, square **7** correct, ethical **8** balanced, deserved, straight, unbiased **9** impartial, objective, uncolored, unslanted **10** evenhanded, impersonal, reasonable
equitableness: **5** right **6** virtue **7** justice, redress **8** evenness, fairness, fair play, justness, morality **9** rectitude **10** due process, lawfulness
equity: **5** right **6** assets **7** justice **8** fairness, fair play, justness, property
equity __: **5** stake, stock **7** capital
__ equity: **5** sweat
__ Equity: **6** Actors'
__ equity loan: **4** home
Equity member: **5** actor **9** performer
equivalence: **3** tie **5** match **6** parity **7** balance **8** evenness, identity, likeness, sameness, synonymy
equivalent: **4** akin, even, like, same, such **5** alike, level, rival **6** agnate, allied, on a par **7** cognate, kindred, similar **8** matching, parallel **9** alternate, analogous, duplicate, identical **10** carbon copy, comparable, coordinate, dead ringer, homologous, reciprocal, substitute, synonymous, tantamount
be ~ to: **6** offset
is ~ (to): **6** amount
make ~: **5** level **6** equate **7** balance
to: **4** akin, like, same **5** equal **6** in kind, on a par, same as **7** close to, equal to, related, similar, uniform **8** as good as, matching, parallel **9** analogous, identical, virtually **10** comparable, compatible, resembling, synonymous, tantamount
word: **3** syn. **7** synonym
__ equivalent: **3** air **4** dose, gram
equivalently: **4** akin, same **5** alike, equal **6** on a par **7** cognate, equally, related, the same, uniform **8** in common **9** analogous, identical, similarly, uniformly **10** comparable, comparably, equivalent, the same way
equivocal: **4** hazy, open **5** fuzzy, muzzy, vague **7** clouded, dubious, evasive, muddled, oblique, unclear **8** doubtful, ulterior **9** ambiguous, tenebrous, uncertain, undecided **10** ambivalent, apocryphal, borderline, clear as mud, indefinite, indistinct, inexplicit, left-handed, misleading, suspicious, unexplicit, unverified
linker: **3** but **5** and/or
equivocate: **3** haw, lie **5** dodge, evade, fence, hedge, skirt, stall, swing, waver **6** waffle **7** quibble, whiffle **8** footdrag, hesitate, misquote, simulate **9** hem and haw, oscillate, pussyfoot, run around, stonewall **10** double-talk, mince words, tergiverse
equivocating: **5** lying **6** shifty **7** evasive
equivocation: **5** shift **7** evasion **9** runaround **10** hesitation
without ~: **6** flatly **9** sincerely **10** foursquare
equivocator: **4** liar **6** fibber **7** deluder **8** deceiver, perjurer **9** chameleon, con artist, falsifier, trickster **10** fabricator
response: **5** maybe
equivoque: **3** pun **8** wordplay
equus: **3** ass, nag **4** Arab, colt, foal, mare, mule, pony, roan **5** burro, filly, horse, pinto, steed, zebra **6** donkey, equine, Morgan **7** gelding, mustang, trotter **8** Shetland, stallion **10** Clydesdale
Equus: **4** play
author: Peter Shaffer
character: **4** Alan, Dora **6** Dysart, Strang
er
relative: **2** uh, um
Er: **7** element **10** elem.. erbium
68 for ~: **4** at. no.
ER
command: **4** stat
part: **4** emer., room **9** emergency
procedure: **3** CPR, EKG
setting: **3** ICU
staffer: **2** Dr., MD, RN **3** EMT **5** nurse **6** doctor
supply: **2** IV **4** sera **5** serum
unit: **2** cc.
ER (NBC drama)
cast: George Clooney (Dr. Douglas Ross)
Anthony Edwards (Dr. Mark Greene)
Laura Innes (Dr. Kerry Weaver)
Eriq LaSalle (Dr. Peter Benton)
Julianna Margulies (Carol Hathaway)
Noah Wyle (Dr. John Carter)
setting: Chicago
era: **3** age, day **4** time **5** cycle, epoch **6** period **7** vintage **10** generation, time period
bygone ~: **4** past, then **7** old days
in this ~: **3** now **5** today **9** currently
many ~ s: **3** age, eon **4** aeon, ages **6** period **8** long time
of the same ~: **6** coeval **10** coexistent, coincident
__ era: **6** common
Era: **5** Mogul **6** Moslem, Muslem, Muslim **7** Baroque **8** Cambrian, Cenozoic, Colonial, Gaslight, Mesozoic, Sassanid **9** Christian, detergent, Mycenaean, Paleozoic, Victorian
alternative: **3** All, Biz, Fab, Yes **4** Bold, Dash, Gain, Surf, Tide, Wisk **5** Cheer, Dreft, Purex **6** Calgon, Dynamo, Oxydol **7** Octagon **9** Ivory Snow
__ Era: **6** Common, Gaslit, Moslem, Muslim
ERA: **4** stat
part of ~: **3** Avg. **4** Runs **5** Equal **6** Earned, Rights **7** Average **9** Amendment
proponent: **3** NOW
__ Era and Out the Other: **5** In One
eradicate: **3** rid **4** lose, rase, raze **5** eject, erase, purge, trash **6** banish, delete, efface, excise, remove, rub off, rub out, uproot **7** abolish, blot out, destroy, expunge, lighten, mow down, pluck up, root out, weed out, wipe out **8** demolish, stamp out **9** eliminate, extirpate, liquidate, shoot down **10** annihilate, deracinate, do away with, extinguish, obliterate
eradication: **4** dele **7** erasure, removal **8** deletion **9** abatement, pulling up, uprooting **10** demolition, extinction, pulling out, rooting out, rubbing out, tearing out
Era of __ Feeling: **4** Good
erase: **3** cut, rub **4** dele, slay, trim, undo, wipe, X out **5** annul, clean, clear, purge, scrub **6** cancel, cut out, delete, efface, excise, forget, negate, remove,

revoke, rub off, rub out, strike **7** abolish, blot out, destroy, expunge, nullify, scissor, scratch, take out, wipe out **8** blank out, bleep out, get rid of, stamp out **9** eliminate, eradicate, expurgate, extirpate, sponge out, strike out **10** annihilate, extinguish, obliterate, scratch out

eraser: **6** art gum, rubber **9** eliminate
like a blackboard ~: **5** dirty, dusty **7** powdery, unclean **8** unwashed
material: **3** gum
use an ~: **4** X out **6** cancel, cut out, delete, excise, remove, rub out **7** expunge, scratch, wipe out **8** black out **9** eliminate, strike out

___ eraser: **3** gum

Eraser (1996 film)
cast: James Caan, James Coburn, Arnold Schwarzenegger, Vanessa Williams

Eraserhead (1978 film)
cast: Allen Joseph, Jack Nance, Charlotte Stewart
director: David Lynch

Erasmus, Desiderius: **5** Dutch **6** writer **8** humanist

Erastus: **6** Thomas

erasure: **8** deletion

___ erat demonstrandum: **4** quod

___ erat faciendum: **4** quod

Erato: **4** Muse
colleague: **4** Clio **6** Thalia, Urania **7** Euterpe **8** Calliope **9** Melpomene **10** Polyhymnia **11** Terpsichore
lover of ~: **8** Heracles
parent of ~: **4** Zeus **9** Mnemosyne

Eratosthenes: **10** astronomer

Erbil: **4** city, town **6** Arbela
locale: **4** Irak, Iraq

erbium: **7** element

Erdman: **4** Paul

Erdrich, Louise: **6** writer
subject: Chippewa

ere: **3** ago **4** once **5** afore, prior **6** before, gone by **7** earlier, prior to **9** in the past, preceding **10** previously, previous to
ender: **3** now **4** long **5** while

...ere ___ Elba: **4** I saw

ereb: **3** eve **6** Hebrew

Erebus: **4** peak **5** mount **7** volcano **8** mountain
daughter of ~: **6** Hemera **7** Hespera, Nemesis
locale: **10** Antarctica
parent of ~: **3** Nyx **5** Chaos
son of ~: **6** Charon, Hypnos

erect: **4** form, lift, make, rear **5** build, forge, found, frame, on end, pitch, plumb, put up, raise, set up, sheer, stand, steep **6** create, uprear **7** fashion, produce, upraise, upright **8** assemble, initiate, standing, straight, vertical **9** construct, establish, fabricate, institute **10** upstanding
be ~: **5** stand

Erector ___: **3** Set

___ erectus: **4** Homo

...ere I saw ___: **4** Elba

erelong: **4** anon, soon **10** in good time

eremite: **4** monk **5** loner **6** hermit **7** isolato, recluse **8** anchoret, solitary **9** anchoress, anchorite

eremitic: **4** line **5** alone **7** recluse **8** isolated, solitary **9** reclusive **10** antisocial

erenow: **4** once **5** afore, as yet **6** before **7** long ago **9** in the past **10** heretofore, previously

Eres Tu (1974 song) artist: Mocedades

Eretz ___: **6** Israel **7** Yisrael

erev: **3** eve **6** sunset **9** day before

Erewhon: **6** utopia

Erewhon author: Samuel Butler

character: **4** Yram **5** Senoj, Thims **6** Strong, Ydgrun, Zulora

Erfurt: **4** city, town
locale: **7** Germany

ergate: **3** ant

ergo: **4** then, thus **5** hence **9** as a result, therefore

ergo-: **4** work

ergonomics: **7** science

ergophobe fear: **4** work

___, ergo sum: **6** cogito

ergot: **4** mold **6** fungus, mildew

Erhard: **6** Werner
discipline: **3** Est

Eri
father: **3** Gad

Eric: **4** Idle, Thal, Till **5** Berne, Blore, Davis, Lutes, Scott **6** Ambler, Burdon, Carmen, Heiden, Hoffer, Kandel, Knight, Rochat, Rohmer, Stoltz **7** Braeden, Clapton, Cornell, Fleming, Lindros, Portman, Roberts **8** Bogosian, Mitchell, Sevareid **9** Dickerson, Lustbader, McCormack, Partridge, Weissburg, Wieschaus
son: **4** Leif

Eric ___: **6** the Red

Eric ___ Lustbader: **3** Van

erica: **4** tree **5** heath, shrub **7** heather **9** evergreen
relative: **6** azalea, sorrel **7** arbutus, madrone

Erica: **4** Jong, Kane

Erich: **5** Fromm, Segal **6** Kunzel **7** Kleiber **9** Leinsdorf

Erich ___ Korngold: **8** Wolfgang

Erich ___ Remarque: **5** Maria

Erich ___ Stroheim: **3** von

Ericson, Leif: **5** Norse **6** Viking **8** explorer

Ericsson: **5** phone **9** cell phone
alternative: **5** Nokia **6** Nextel **8** Motorola

Eric the Red: **5** Norse **6** Viking **8** explorer

Erie: **4** city, lake, port, town **5** canal, Mills, tribe **6** Indian **7** Amerind **9** Great Lake
locale: **4** Penn. **5** Penna. **6** Canada
neighbor: **5** Huron
vessel: **5** laker

Erie Canal
city: **6** Albany
craft: **5** barge

Erie Lackawanna: **2** RR **3** rwy. **8** railroad

___ Erie, Ont.: **4** Fort

erigeron: **5** plant **6** flower

Erik: **5** Bruhn, Satie **7** Darling, Erikson, Estrada **8** Lindberg **9** Karlfeldt

Erik ___ Karlfeldt: **4** Axel

Erika: **6** Morini, Slezak **7** Eleniak

Erik Dorn author: Ben Hecht

___-Erik Hexum: **3** Jon

Erikson: **4** Erik

Eriksson: **4** Leif

Erin: **4** Eire, Gray **5** Davis, Moran **6** Old Sod **7** auld sod, Ireland **8** Hibernia **9** Innisfail, Innisfree
tongue: **4** Erse **6** Gaelic

Erin Brockovich (2000 film)
cast: Albert Finney, Marg Helgenberger, Julia Roberts
director: Steven Soderbergh

Erin go ___!: **5** bragh

Erinyes: **6** Furies

Eriq: **7** LaSalle

Eris
daughter of ~: **3** Ate **5** Lethe
parent of ~: **3** Nyx **4** Hera, Zeus
twin of ~: **4** Ares

Eritrea: **6** nation **7** country
bovine: **5** Barka
capital: **6** Asmara
neighbor: **5** Sudan **8** Djibouti, Ethiopia
people: **4** Afar, Beja **7** Danakil

Erl-___, The: **4** King

Erlang: **8** language
alternative: **3** ADA, APL, SQL **4** Alef, html, Icon, Java, LISP, Logo, Orca, Perl **5** Algol, Basic, Cecil, COBOL, Dylan, SISAL **6** Delphi, Eiffel, Oberon, Pascal, Prolog, Sather, Scheme, Snobol **7** Fortran

Erlanger, Joseph: **8** Nobelist

Erle: **6** Kenton **7** Gardner
colleague of ~: **3** Rex **6** Agatha, Ellery

Erle ___ Gardner: **7** Stanley

Erle C. ___: **6** Kenton

Erlenmeyer ___: **5** flask

Erl-King, The author: Goethe

Erma: **7** Bombeck

ermine: **3** fur **4** coat, pelt, wrap **5** stoat **6** animal, weasel
relative: **4** mink **5** fitch, otter, ratel, sable, skunk, tayra **6** badger, ferret, marten **7** foumart, polecat **8** carcajou, foulmart, kolinsky, muishond **9** wolverine

Ermine, The author: Jean Anouilh

Ermont: **4** city, town
locale: **6** France

-er, more than: **3** -est

ern: **4** bird **5** eagle **7** seabird **8** sea eagle **9** shorebird **10** bird of prey
starter: **4** east, west **5** north, south

Ern: **8** Westmore

Erna: **6** Berger **7** Brodber

Ernani: **5** opera
composer: **5** Verdi

erne: **4** bird **5** eagle **7** seabird **8** sea eagle **9** shorebird **10** bird of prey

Ernest: **4** Ball, Gold, Papa, Tubb **5** Bloch, Gallo, Renan, Seton, Truex **6** Dowson, Lehman, Solvay, Walton **7** Worrell **8** Ansermet, Borgnine, Chausson, Hollings, Lawrence, Thompson, Torrence **9** Hemingway **10** Rutherford, Shackleton
nickname: **4** Papa

Ernest Goes to ___: **4** Camp

Ernest J. ___: **6** Gaines

Ernest K. ___: **4** Gann

Ernesto: **6** Moneta, Sábato **7** Guevara **8** Cardinal, Maserati
nickname: **3** Che
see also Spanish

Ernie: **3** Els **4** K-Doe, Pyle **5** Banks, Bilko, Shore **6** Fields, Hudson, Kovacs, Muppet, Nevers **7** Freeman, Maresca **8** Stautner **10** Bushmiller
colleague: **4** Bert **5** Piggy **6** Kermit **7** Big Bird

___ Ernie Ford: **9** Tennessee

Ernie K-___: **3** Doe

Erno: **5** Rubik

Ernst: **3** Max **4** Mach, Toch **5** Chain, Ruska **6** Jünger **7** Fischer, Haeckel, Richard **8** Cassirer, Lubitsch

Ernst, Max: **6** artist **7** painter
homeland: **7** Germany

Ernst, Richard: **7** chemist **8** Nobelist

Ernst & Young
staffer: **3** aud., CPA **4** acct. **7** auditor

erode: **3** eat, sap **4** rust, wear **5** chafe, decay, eat at **6** ablate, abrade, damage, lessen, ravage, weaken **7** consume, corrode, crumble, eat away, eat into, rub away, rub down, wash out **8** undercut, wear away, wear down **9** break down, grind down, undermine **10** chip away at

eroded: **3** ate **4** worn **8** timeworn

Eroica: **8** symphony
composer: **9** Beethoven
key: **5** E flat

Eros: **3** god **4** Amor **5** Cupid **6** libido **7** love god **8** amoretto, asteroid
brother of ~: **7** Anteros, Anterus
daughter of ~: **7** Volupta
equivalent: **4** Amor **5** Cupid
lover of ~: **6** Psyche
parent of ~: **3** Nyx **5** Chaos **9** Aphrodite

Eros and Civilization author: Herbert Marcuse

erose: **6** ragged, uneven **8** wind-worn

erosion: **4** wear **7** wearing **8** abrasion, decrease **9** attrition, corrosion
cause of ~: **4** tide, wind **5** river, water
result: **5** gully **6** canyon, gulley

___ erosion: **4** wind **5** sheet **6** splash

erosive: **7** caustic, wearing **8** abrading, abrasive **9** attritive, consuming, corrosive

___ E. Ross: **3** Joe

erotic: **3** hot **4** blue, lewd, racy, sexy **5** funky, spicy **6** loving, rated X, risqué, spicey, steamy, sultry, torrid, X-rated **7** amatory, naughty, sensual **8** alluring, magnetic, romantic **9** amatorial **10** magnetical, voluptuous

Erotica (1992 song) artist: Madonna

err: **3** sin **4** flub, goof, miss, muff, slip, trip **5** botch, fluff, lapse, misdo, snafu, stray **6** blow it, bobble, boo-boo, bungle, detour, foozle, foul up, fumble, go awry, mess up, misadd, miscue, slip up, wander **7** blunder, deviate, do wrong, go wrong, louse up, misdeal, misplay, misstep, mistake, snarl up, stumble **8** bollix up, go astray, misjudge, misspeak, misspell, slip a cog **9** misbehave, mishandle, mismanage, misreckon **10** transgress

errand: **3** job **4** task, trip **5** chore **7** mission **10** assignment, commission, engagement
assign to an ~: **4** send
do an ~: **3** run
helpful ~: **3** aid **5** favor **7** service **8** courtesy, goodwill, kindness
on an ~: **3** out **4** away
runner: **4** page **5** gofer **6** gopher, legman **9** messenger

___ errand: **4** on an **5** fool's

errant: **4** wild **5** stray, wrong **6** roving **7** aimless, deviant, naughty, off-base, roaming, wayward **8** fallible, questing, rambling, straying, vagabond **9** deviating, itinerant, off-course, off-target, traveling, wandering **10** journeying, meandering, off the mark, unorthodox, unreliable

___-errant: **6** knight

errantly: **3** off **5** amiss **6** astray

errare humanum ___: **3** est

errata: **5** goofs, slips, typos **6** boners, lapses **7** boo-boos **8** bloopers, mistakes **9** misprints **10** corrigenda
free of ~: **5** clean **7** correct, perfect **8** accurate

erratic: **3** odd **5** flaky, fluid, moody, queer, wacky, weird, wrong **6** chancy, fickle, flakey, patchy, quaint, random, roving, spotty, uneven, whacky, zigzag **7** aimless, bizarre, mutable, oddball, protean, strange, wayward **8** freakish, on-and-off, peculiar, periodic, rambling, shifting, sporadic, unstable, unsteady, variable, volatile, wavering **9** arbitrary, eccentric, fluctuant, haphazard, irregular, mercurial, spasmodic, uncertain, vagarious, wandering, whimsical **10** capricious, changeable, discursive, flickering, inconstant, meandering, nonuniform, outlandish, sporadical, unbalanced, undirected, unreliable, willy-nilly
move: **3** zag, zig **5** weave

erratum: **4** typo **7** mistake **8** misprint **10** inaccuracy

erring: **5** wrong **6** adrift, astray, faulty

7 peccant 8 fallible, mistaken 9 incorrect 10 inaccurate
Errol: 4 Leon 5 Flynn 6 Le Cain, Morris
Erroll: 6 Garner
erroneous: 3 bad 5 false, wrong 6 all wet, faulty, flawed, untrue 7 inexact, invalid, unsound 8 improper, mistaken, specious, spurious 9 defective, falsified, incorrect, misguided, unfounded 10 fallacious, ill-founded, inaccurate, mendacious, ungrounded, unreliable
conviction: 5 frame 6 bum rap
erroneously: 4 awry 5 afoul, amiss, badly, wrong 7 wrongly 8 erringly, faultily 9 foolishly 10 mistakenly, out of joint, unsuitably
error: 3 bad, bug, sin 4 flaw, foul, goof, miss, slip, trip, typo 5 boner, fault, fluff, gaffe, lapse, snafu, wrong 6 barney, boo-boo, defect, glitch, howler, lapsus, miscue, slipup 7 blooper, blunder, erratum, fallacy, falsity, faux pas, louse-up, misdeed, misplay, misstep, mistake, stumble 8 misprint, omission, solecism, trespass 9 deviation, misbelief, oversight, veniality 10 inaccuracy, infraction
check for ~ s: 5 proof
free from ~: 5 right 6 aright 7 correct 8 debugged, disabuse
in ~: 5 false, wrong 6 all wet, astray, faulty, untrue 7 inexact, unsound 8 specious 10 inaccurate, ungrounded
make an ~: 4 muff
margin for ~: 4 room 5 range, slack, space 6 leeway 8 latitude 9 elbowroom 10 room to move
partner: 5 trial
remover: 6 eraser
see the ~ of ways: 6 repent
service ~: 5 fault
show the ~ of one's ways: 6 reason
sports: 4 balk, foul 5 fault
___ error: 5 Type I 6 random, Type II 7 closing
errorless: 4 just 5 exact, right, valid 7 correct, factual, precise 8 accurate, flawless, unerring 9 faultless 10 immaculate, impeccable
error-prone: 5 human 6 clumsy 8 careless
ers: 5 vetch
ersatz: 4 fake, mock, sham 5 bogus, false, phony, put-on 6 forged, phoney, pseudo, unreal 7 assumed, feigned, plastic, stopgap 8 spurious 9 imitation, imitative, simulated, synthetic, unnatural 10 artificial, fabricated, fictitious, fraudulent, substitute
not ~: 4 real
Erse: 6 Celtic, Gaelic 8 language
Erskine: 4 John 8 Caldwell
erst: 4 once 6 whilom 7 quondam 8 formerly
ender: 5 while
erstwhile: 3 old 4 late, once, past 6 bygone, former 7 old-time, onetime, quondam 8 previous 9 preceding 10 previously
Erta-Ale: 7 volcano
locale: 6 Africa 8 Ethiopia
Erté: 6 artist 7 Russian
style: 4 deco
Ertegun: 5 Ahmet
eruct: 4 burp, emit 5 belch
erudite: 4 wise 5 savvy, smart 6 brainy 7 bookish, learned, sapient 8 academic, cerebral, educated, highbrow, lettered, literary, literate, longhair, pedantic, profound, well-read 9 scholarly 10 pedantical
erudition: 4 info, lore 5 savvy 6 brains, wisdom 7 culture, letters, reading 8 learning, literacy 9 education, knowledge 10 refinement
___ 'er up!: 4 Fill
erupt: 4 emit, gush, rage, spew, spue, vent 5 burst, go off, spirt, spout, spurt 6 blow up, go boom 7 explode, rupture, spew out 8 boil over, break out, detonate, have a fit, shoot off 9 discharge, pour forth 10 break forth, shoot forth
erupter: 7 volcano
erupting: 6 aburst
eruption: 4 gust, rash 5 blast, burst, noise, spasm, spirt, spurt 6 blow-up 8 ejection, outbreak, outburst, paroxysm, upheaval 9 discharge, explosion
fallout: 3 ash 4 lava 5 ember 6 cinder
ervil: 5 vetch
Ervin: 3 Sam
Erving, Julius: 3 Dr. J
milieu: 5 court
org.: 3 NBA
sport: 10 basketball
Erwin: 3 Stu 5 Neher 6 Rommel, Stuart
Erykah: 4 Badu
___ Erythraeum: 4 Mare
erythrocyte: 4 cell 9 blood cell, corpuscle
erythrophobe fear: 3 red 8 blushing
Erz: 5 range
locale: 6 Europe 7 Germany
Es: 4 elem. 7 element 11 einsteinium
99 for ~: 4 at. no.
E-6, Army: 4 SSgt.
E-7, Army: 3 SFC
Esa-___ Salonen: 5 Pekka
Esai: 7 Morales
Esaki, Leo: 8 Nobelist 9 physicist, scientist
Esa-Pekka: 7 Salonen
Esau
father-in-law of ~: 4 Elon
grandson of ~: 4 Omar 5 Gatam, Kenaz, Korah, Zepho, Zerah 6 Amalek, Mizzah, Nahath, Shamah
parent of ~: 5 Isaac 7 Rebekah
son of ~: 5 Jalam, Korah, Reuel 7 Eliphaz
twin of ~: 5 Jacob
wife of ~: 6 Judith 8 Basemath, Mahalath 10 Oholibamah
Esc: 3 key
Escalade: 3 SUV 8 Cadillac
Escalante: 5 Jaime
escalate: 4 go up, grow, leap, rise, soar 5 add to, arise, build, climb, mount, raise, swell, widen 6 ascend, expand, extend, jack up, move up, spread, step up 7 advance, amplify, augment, broaden, build up, enlarge, magnify, scale up 8 heighten, increase 9 go forward, increment, intensify 10 supplement
escalation: 4 leap, rise 6 spread 7 buildup 8 increase 9 inflation
escalator
alternative: 5 stair, steps 8 elevator
direction: 4 down 5 lower 10 descending
essentially: 5 stair
part: 4 axle, step 5 motor, tread
escalator ___: 6 clause
Escales composer: 5 Ibert
escallop: 4 bake, cook 5 brown, shell, steam 8 seashell
Escamillo: 6 torero 8 toreador 11 bullfighter
see also Spanish
escapade: 4 game, joke, lark 5 antic, caper, fling, prank, sport 6 frolic, gambol 7 exploit, rollick
Escapade (1990 song) artist: Janet Jackson
escape: 2 go 3 fly, lam, run 4 bolt, duck, evac., flee, leak, lose, ooze, seep, shun, skip 5 avert, avoid, break, dodge, elope, elude, evade, lam it, leave, skirt 6 decamp, depart, desert, egress, flight, get out, outlet, refuge, run off, run out, tunnel, vanish, way out 7 abscond, bailout, bust out, dodging, duck out, elusion, evasion, getaway, go south, leakage, make off, mystify, pastime, retreat, run away, slip off 8 breakout, cut loose, fugitate, get out of, light out, loophole, magic act, skip town, slip away, throw off, turn tail 9 avoidance, break away, break jail, cut and run, departure, disappear, salvation, steal away 10 break loose, circumvent, fly the coop, get clear of, ivory tower, take flight
artist: 7 Houdini 8 magician
button: 5 eject
cut off from ~: 4 trap 5 hem in 6 corner
from: 5 avoid, evade 8 shake off
means of ~: 3 out 4 exit 6 ladder
vehicle: 3 pod
escape ___: 3 pod 5 hatch, valve, wheel 6 artist, clause
___ escape: 4 fire 6 narrow
Escape: 3 SUV 4 Ford
Escape (1940 film)
cast: Alla Nazimova, Norma Shearer, Robert Taylor, Conrad Veidt
director: Mervyn LeRoy
Escape (1948 film)
cast: Peggy Cummins, Rex Harrison, William Hartnell
director: Joseph L. Mankiewicz
Escape (1979 song) artist: Rupert Holmes
escaped: 4 free, wild 5 loose 7 at large 10 on the loose
escapee: 5 fleer, hider 6 dodger, émigré 7 refugee, runaway 8 defector, deserter, fugitive, renegade
like an ~: 5 loose 7 at large 8 on the run
Escape From Alcatraz (1979 film)
cast: Clint Eastwood, Patrick McGoohan
director: Don Siegel
Escape From Fort Bravo (1953 film)
cast: John Forsythe, William Holden, Eleanor Parker
director: John Sturges
Escape from Freedom author: 5 Fromm
Escape From New York (1981 film)
cast: Ernest Borgnine, Donald Pleasence, Kurt Russell, Lee Van Cleef
director: John Carpenter
Escape From the Planet of the Apes (1971 film)
cast: Bradford Dillman, Kim Hunter, Roddy McDowall
director: Don Taylor
role: 4 Milo
___ escapement: 5 lever 6 anchor, Brocot, recoil 7 gravity
___ Escape, The: 5 Great
Escape to Glory (1940 film)
cast: Alan Baxter, Constance Bennett, Pat O'Brien
Escape to Witch Mountain (1975 film)
cast: Eddie Albert, Ray Milland, Kim Richards
escapist: 7 dreamer, ostrich 8 idealist 9 fantasist 10 daydreamer, non-realist
Escárcega: 4 city, town
locale: 6 Mexico 8 Campeche
escargot: 5 snail 9 appetizer
escarole alternative: 6 endive
escarp: 5 cliff 9 precipice 10 embankment
eschew: 4 duck, shun, skip 5 avoid, dodge, elude, evade, forgo, shirk 6 abjure, bypass, forgo, give up 7 abstain, boycott, dislike, forbear, refrain, shy from 8 flee from, forswear, keep from, renounce, swear off 9 foreswear 10 circumvent
humility: 4 crow 5 boast, exult, gloat, vaunt 6 hotdog 7 bluster, show off, swagger, talk big 8 showboat 9 gasconade 10 grandstand
Escobar
see Spanish
Escoffier: 4 chef 7 Auguste
see also French
escolar: 4 fish
Escondido: 4 city, town
locale: 10 California
escort: 3 see, ush 4 date, lead, seat, show, take, walk 5 bring, fetch, guard, guide, lover, scout, see in, steer, train, usher 6 attend, convoy, duenna, go with, lead in, squire 7 conduct, retinue, step out 8 chaperon, guardian 9 accompany, attendant, bodyguard, boyfriend, chaperone, companion, entourage, protector, safeguard
offering: 3 arm 4 limb 9 extremity
escort ___: 7 carrier, fighter
Escort: 3 car 4 auto, Ford 10 automobile
escorting: 4 with
escorts: 5 train 7 retinue
escritoire: 4 desk 5 table 7 rolltop 9 secretary
accessory: 3 pen
escrow: 4 care 5 aegis, owner 6 charge 7 custody 9 oversight 10 possession, protection
escudo: 4 coin 5 money
country: 8 Portugal 9 Cape Verde
escuela child: 4 niña, niño 10 estudiante
esculent: 4 good 5 tasty 6 edible
escutcheon: 4 seal 5 plate 6 shield
border: 4 orle
mark: 4 blot 5 stain
___ escutcheon: 6 thread
ESE: 3 dir. 5 point 9 direction
opposite: 3 WNW
___ e sempre: 3 ora
Esenin, Sergei: 4 poet 7 Russian
___, es, est: 3 sum
Esfahan: 4 city, town
locale: 4 Iran
ESG
part of ~: 4 Erle 7 Gardner, Stanley
___ E. Sherwood: 6 Robert
Eshkol, Levi: 7 Israeli
predecessor: 9 Ben-Gurion
successor: 4 Meir
Esiason, Boomer: 2 QB 11 quarterback
sport: 8 football
eskers: 4 osar 6 ridges
Eskimo: 5 Aleut, Inuit, Yupik 6 Innuit, Inupik 8 Aleutian
ancient ~ culture: 6 Dorset
coat: 6 anorak
home: 4 iglu 5 igloo 6 Alaska, Arctic
knife: 3 ulu
language: 5 Aleut, Inuit 6 Innuit, Inupik 8 Aleutian
pole: 5 totem
relative: 5 Aleut 8 Aleutian
vehicle: 4 sled 5 kayak, umiak
Eskimo ___: 3 dog, Pie 6 curlew
ESL: 6 course
cousin: 3 EFL
part of ~: 3 Eng. 4 Lang. 6 Second
Esme author: Saki
Esmeralda pet: 4 goat
___ Esme-with Love and Squalor: 3 For
___ Esmond: 5 Henry
esne: 4 serf 6 thrall
place: 4 fief 5 manor
Eso Beso (1962 song) artist: Paul Anka

esophagus: 3 maw 6 gullet, throat 7 pharynx
esoteric: 4 deep 6 arcane, hidden, inside, mystic, occult, Orphic, secret 7 cryptic, learned, obscure, private 8 abstruse, mystical, profound, rarefied 9 cryptical, difficult, enigmatic, innermost, recondite 10 mysterious, unknowable
esoterics: 6 cabala, kabala 7 cabbala, kabbala
ESP: 9 intuition, telepathy 10 sixth sense
espagnole ___: 5 sauce
espalier: 5 train
España: 5 Spain 6 nación
esparto: 5 grass
especial: 3 def, rad 4 aces, A-one, boss, braw, cool, dece, fine, gear, keen, neat, nice, phat, tuff 5 dandy, ducky, grand, great, marvy, neato, nobby, prime, slick, super, swell 6 bang on, bang-up, bonzer, bosker, choice, divine, dreamy, far-out, gnarly, groovy, lovely, peachy, single, slap-up, spot on, superb, terrif, tiptop, unreal, whizzo, wicked 7 amazing, awesome, capital, corking, perfect, ripping, skookum, stellar, sublime 8 dazzling, eximious, fabulous, favorite, five-star, four-star, frabjous, glorious, heavenly, jim-dandy, slam-bang, smashing, splendid, standout, sterling, stickout, superior, terrific, top-level, topnotch, very good, wondrous 9 bodacious, Endsville, excellent, exemplary, exquisite, first-rate, high-grade, hunky-dory, marvelous, sollicker, top-flight, wonderful 10 first-class, hotsy-totsy, individual, jack-a-dandy, occasional, out of sight, particular, peachy-keen, phenomenal, remarkable, stupendous, super-duper
especially: 4 such, very 5 extra 6 mainly, namely 7 chiefly, notably 8 above all, markedly, signally, uniquely 9 curiously, eminently, expressly, primarily, specially, strangely, supremely, unusually 10 abnormally, peculiarly, remarkably, singularly, strikingly, uncommonly
Esperanto: 6 tongue 8 language
Esperanza: 4 city, town
  locale: 6 Mexico, Sonora
espial: 6 notice 8 exposure, sighting 9 detection, discovery, unmasking 10 uncovering
___ E. Spingarn: 4 Joel
espionage: 6 spying
  name in ~: 4 Hari, Mata
  org.: 3 CIA, KGB
  starter: 7 counter
esplanade: 4 mall, path, walk 7 walkway
ESPN: 7 channel, network
  alternative: 3 BET, CMT, MTV, PAX, TBS, TLC, TNN, TNT, USA 4 HGTV 5 A and E, C-SPAN, Style 6 Noggin, Tech TV, TV Land 7 Court TV, Ovation, SoapNet 8 Lifetime
  fare: 6 sports
  feature: 3 NBA
Espoo: 4 city, town
  locale: 7 Finland
esposa de su padre: 5 madre
Esposito: 4 Phil 9 Giancarlo
Esposito, Phil
  milieu: 3 ice 4 rink 5 arena 6 hockey
  org.: 3 NHL
espousal: 5 match, troth 7 support, wedding 8 adoption, advocacy, marriage, nuptials 9 betrothal, fosterage, promotion
espouse: 3 wed 4 back 5 adopt, marry 6 defend, take on, take up 7 embrace, promote, support 8 advocate, champion 10 speak up for, stand up for
espouser: 5 urger 9 proponent, supporter
___ espressione: 3 con
espresso: 3 joe 4 java 5 drink, latte 6 coffee 8 beverage
  place: 4 café 6 bistro, eatery 10 restaurant
esprit: 3 vim, wit 4 brio, dash, élan, life, mood, zing 5 verve, vigor 6 morale, spirit, temper 7 sparkle 8 vivacity 9 animation, élan vital, intuition, mother wit 10 cleverness, enthusiasm, liveliness
  de corps: 6 morale
___ esprit: 4 jeu d'
Esprit: 4 font 8 typeface
espy: 3 see 4 find, spot, view 5 sight, watch 6 behold, descry, detect, notice, remark 7 discern, glimpse, make out, observe, witness 8 discover, smell out 9 lay eyes on, recognize
Espy: 4 Mike 7 Willard
-esque cousin: 3 -ine, -ish, -oid 4 -like
esquire: 4 male
Esquivel: 5 Laura
Esquivel, Adolfo Pérez: 8 Nobelist
ess: 5 curve, sigma 8 curlicue, curlycue, sibilant
  curve: 4 ogee
  follower: 3 tee
  preceder: 2 ar
___ es Salaam: 3 Dar
essay: 3 aim, bid, try 4 Op-Ed, seek, test 5 paper, prose, theme, tract, trial 6 effort, intend, strive, thesis, tryout 7 article, attempt, venture, writing 8 critique, endeavor, struggle, treatise 9 give it a go, undertake 10 experiment, exposition, literature, think piece
___ essay: 5 photo
Essay ___, An: 5 on Man
Essay Concerning Human Understanding, An author: John Locke
essayist: 5 Royce 6 author, scribe, writer 8 novelist 9 Podhoretz, wordsmith
  alias: 4 Elia
  Argentinian ~: 6 Sábato
  British ~: 4 Lamb 5 Lewis, Pater, Powys 6 Pinero, Steele 9 Priestley, Stapledon
  Czech ~: 9 Skvorecky
  Ecuadorian ~: 8 Montalvo
  French ~: 5 Péguy 7 Reverdy, Rolland, Romains
  German ~: 4 Mann
  Mexican ~: 5 Reyes
  Nigerian ~: 7 Soyinka
  West Indian ~: 7 Naipaul
Essay on Criticism, An author: Alexander Pope
Essay on Man, An author: Alexander Pope
Essays of Elia author: 4 Lamb
esse: 4 to be 5 being 6 entity 7 reality 9 actuality, existence
  form of ~: 3 est 4 erat
esse ___ percipi: 3 est
esse ___ videri: 4 quam
Essen: 4 city, town
  locale: 7 Germany
  river: 4 Ruhr
essence: 3 nub, sum 4 atar, aura, body, core, crux, germ, gist, knub, meat, odor, otto, pith, root, soul 5 athar, attar, basis, being, drift, fiber, heart, ottar, point, scent, smell, tenor 6 center, entity, flavor, kernel, marrow, nature, spirit 7 epitome, keynote, nucleus, perfume, summary, texture 8 backbone, key point, main idea, quiddity 9 character, flavoring, lifeblood, necessity, substance 10 bottom line, sine qua non
  in ~: 5 per se 6 nearly 8 innately 9 basically, primarily, virtually 10 implicitly
  of roses: 4 atar, otto 5 athar, attar, ottar
essence ___: 7 d'orient
___ essence: 5 of the, pearl
Essence: 3 mag 8 magazine
  rival: 3 Jet 5 Ebony
Essenes: 4 sect
essential: 3 key 4 high, main, must, need 5 basic, chief, inner, prime, typic, vital 6 inmost, needed, staple, urgent 7 capital, central, crucial, minimal, needful, organic, pivotal, primary, radical, typical 8 cardinal, foremost, inherent, integral, material, required 9 condition, elemental, groceries, important, intrinsic, mandatory, necessary, necessity, principal, principle, requisite, right-hand, substance, vital part 10 bottom line, brass tacks, congenital, deep-seated, elementary, imperative, sine qua non, substratal, underlying
  be ~: 6 inhere
  beginning: 5 quint
  mineral: 4 iron, zinc
  oil: 4 atar, otto 5 athar, attar, ottar
  part: 3 nub 4 core, knub, meat, pith 5 heart, vital
essential ___: 3 oil
essential ___ acid: 5 amino, fatty
essentially: 5 per se 6 mainly, mostly, purely 8 above all, in effect 9 primarily, virtually
essentials: 4 ABCs
esses, mispronounce: 4 lisp
Essex: 3 car 4 auto, city, earl, town 5 David, shire 6 county 10 automobile
  city: 10 Chelmsford, Colchester
  locale: 7 England 8 Maryland
  model: 9 Pacemaker 10 Terraplane
  rival: 3 Reo
Essex ___: 5 Junto, table
Essex, David song: Rock On (1974)
Essex song: Easier Said Than Done (1963)
Esso competitor: 4 Arco
est ___ in nobis: 4 deus
est.: 5 guess 6 approx. 9 valuation
establish: 3 fix, lay, set 4 base, form, make, rule, seat, show 5 argue, begin, build, enact, endow, erect, forge, found, learn, plant, prove, put up, set at, set up, start 6 create, define, enroot, impose, instal, invest, locate, occupy, ratify, reason, settle, verify 7 arrange, certify, confirm, develop, find out, install, instate, pioneer, produce, specify, station, support 8 assemble, ensconce, entrench, identify, organize, validate 9 ascertain, authorize, construct, determine, fabricate, formalize, formulate, hammer out, inculcate, institute, introduce, legislate, originate, predicate, preordain, prescribe, stabilize 10 constitute, generalize, inaugurate, strengthen
  as fact: 6 verify 7 certify, confirm, warrant 8 document, validate 9 ascertain, determine
established: 3 set 4 sure 5 known, set at, sound, tight, usual 6 formal, lawful, proper, rooted, secure, stable 7 certain, regular 8 definite, habitual, official, ordinary, orthodox, standard 9 prevalent, steadfast 10 prevailing
  be ~ in: 6 occupy
  fact: 5 axiom, given 7 premise 9 postulate
  get ~: 5 set in 6 locate, settle 8 make good, take root
  less ~: 5 newer
  not yet ~: 3 new 5 unset
  position: 4 base 6 anchor 7 support 8 foothold, lodgment 9 beachhead 10 bridgehead, foundation
establishment: 3 ins 4 firm 5 abode, house, joint, plant, setup, start 6 office, outfit, regime, system 7 company, concern, factory 8 business, creation, founding, old guard, quarters 9 stability
  frontier ~: 3 bar, inn 6 saloon 7 barroom 10 restaurant
  happy hour ~: 3 pub 6 saloon, tavern 7 taproom 8 alehouse, taphouse
  roadside ~: 3 inn 5 diner, motel, stand
  seedy ~: 4 dive 5 joint
Establishment, The author: Howard Fast
___ Estacado: 5 Llano
estado: 5 state 7 Spanish
estamin: 6 fabric 8 material
estancia: 5 ranch
estate: 4 land, park, rank, seat, Tara 5 acres, caste, class, dacha, manor, means, press, ranch, villa 6 assets, clergy, datcha, domain, legacy, nobles, spread, status, wealth, Xanadu 7 acreage, chateau, demesne, fortune, grounds, mansion, station 8 hacienda, holdings, net worth, property 9 Chartwell, farmstead, Graceland, homestead, patrimony, residence 10 belongings, Brideshead, journalism, Monticello, plantation
  document: 4 will
  English ~ feature: 4 maze
  entrance: 4 gate 6 portal 7 doorway, ingress
  first ~: 6 clergy, curate 7 prelacy 8 ministry 9 pastorate, rabbinate 10 priesthood
  fourth ~: 5 press
  measure: 4 acre
  medieval ~: 4 fief, odal 5 manor
  of India: 5 taluk 7 talooka
  plus: 5 asset
  real ~: 3 lot 4 land 6 assets, ground 7 acreage, grounds 8 property
  real ~ abbr.: 2 rm. 3 EIK, MLS 4 bdrm.
  sharer: 4 heir 6 coheir
  staffer: 4 cook, maid 5 valet 6 butler
estate ___: 3 car, tax 5 agent 8 planning
estate-___: 7 bottled
___ estate: 4 base, real 5 fifth, first, third 6 fourth, second 7 housing
Estates ___: 7 General
estates, like many: 5 gated
Estats: 4 peak 5 mount 8 mountain
  locale: 5 Spain 6 Europe 8 Pyrenees
___ est celare artem: 3 ars
est deus in ___: 5 nobis
Estéban
  in English: 6 Steven 7 Stephen
  see also Spanish
Estée Lauder: 6 makeup
  alternative: 4 Avon 5 Almay 6 Revlon 7 Lancome, Mary Kay 8 Clinique 9 Cover Girl, Max Factor 10 Maybelline
esteem: 4 fame, like, love, rank, rate 5 exalt, extol, favor, honor, kudos, prize, think, value 6 admire, credit, extoll, homage, honors, praise, reckon, regard, repute, revere 7 cherish, idolize, respect, tribute, valuing, worship 8 approval, consider, eminence, good name, hold dear, hold high, look up to, prestige, treasure, venerate 9 adoration, care about, recommend, reverence 10 admiration, appreciate, importance, popularity, reputation, set store by, veneration
  don't ~: 5 scorn
  gain ~: 4 rate 6 enamor, endear

lower in ~: 5 shame 6 debase, defile, demean, vilify 7 cheapen, degrade, deprave, devalue, profane, put down, vitiate 8 disgrace, dishonor, take down 9 humiliate, shoot down, undermine 10 adulterate
__-esteem: 4 self
Esteem: 3 car 4 auto 6 Suzuki
esteemed: 4 dear 5 noted 7 beloved, eminent 8 glorious, renowned, valuable 9 honorable, reputable, venerable
Estefan: 6 Emilio, Gloria
Estefan, Gloria
home: 5 Miami
song: 1-2-3 (1988)
Anything for You (1988)
Bad Boy (1986)
Can't Stay Away From You (1988)
Coming Out of the Dark (1991)
Conga (1985)
Don't Wanna Lose You (1989)
Here We Are (1990)
Music of My Heart (1999)
Rhythm Is Gonna Get You (1987)
Words Get in the Way (1986)
Estelí: 4 city, town
locale: 9 Nicaragua
Estella to Miss Havisham: 4 ward
Estelle: 5 Getty 6 Harris 7 Parsons
ester: 6 oleate 7 acetate, citrate, nitrate, nitrite, oxalate, stearin 8 glycerin, stearate, stearine, tartrate, urethane 9 banana oil, glyceride, glycerine 10 benzocaine, salicylate
ester __: 3 gum
__ ester: 7 acrylic
Esterhaus: 4 Phil
__ est errare: 7 humanum
Estes: 3 Bob, Rob 5 Shawn, Simon 8 Kefauver
running mate: 5 Adlai
Estes, Bob: 6 golfer
milieu: 5 links 6 course
org.: 3 PGA
Estes Park: 4 city, town
locale: 8 Colorado
Estes, Simon: 4 bass 6 singer 8 baritone
specialty: 5 opera
Estevez, Emilio: 5 actor
father: Martin Sheen
film: The Breakfast Club (1985)
The Mighty Ducks (1992)
Mission: Impossible (1996)
Repo Man (1984)
Stakeout (1987)
St. Elmo's Fire (1985)
Young Guns (1988)
spouse: Paula Abdul
Esther: 5 Rolle 6 Forbes 8 Phillips, Williams
cousin of ~: 8 Mordecai
festival: 5 Purim
foe: 5 Haman
follower: 3 Job
husband of ~: 6 Xerxes 9 Ahasuerus
preceder: 3 Neh. 8 Nehemiah
Esther composer: 6 Handel
esthetic: 8 tasteful
Esth neighbor: 4 Lett
est, id: 3 viz. 5 to wit 6 namely, that is
estimable: 4 good 5 solid 6 worthy 8 laudable 9 admirable, deserving, excellent, exemplary, honorable, meritable, praisable, reputable, respected, venerable 10 calculable, creditable
estimate: 3 set 4 call, deem, make, rank, rate 5 assay, gauge, guess, judge, price, sum up, think, weigh 6 assess, deduce, figure, reckon, regard, size up, survey 7 measure, opinion, predict, project, suppose, surmise 8 appraise, evaluate, forecast, judgment 9 appraisal, calculate, reckoning, valuation 10 assessment, conjecture, evaluation, prediction, projection
expenses: 6 ration 8 allocate 9 apportion
financial ~: 5 quote 6 budget 9 quotation
estimated: 5 rough 7 inexact
estimation: 5 favor, stock, worth 6 belief, regard 7 opinion, respect, thought, valuing 8 judgment, standing 9 adoration, appraisal, character, ciphering, measuring, reckoning, valuation, viewpoint 10 admiration, arithmetic, assessment, comparison, evaluation, impression, veneration
estimator phrase: 4 or so
estivation: 5 sleep
Estonia: 6 nation 7 country
capital: 7 Tallinn
chess master: 3 Nei
city: 5 Narva, Tartu 6 Tallin 7 Tallinn
from ~: 6 Baltic
lake: 6 Peipus
money: 5 kroon
neighbor: 6 Latvia, Russia
once: 3 SSR
Estonian: 4 Balt 8 language
estop: 3 ban, bar 5 block
EST, part of: 3 std. 4 time 7 Eastern
__ est percipi: 4 esse
Estrada: 4 Erik
estrange: 6 divide 8 disunite, separate 9 disaffect 10 antagonize
estranged: 6 bitter, lonely 10 friendless, unfriendly
estrangement: 4 feud, rift 5 break, split 6 breach, schism 7 rupture 8 disunity, division
estray: 4 dogy 5 dogey, dogie 8 wanderer
Estrela, Serra da: 5 range
estrin: 7 hormone
estuary: 3 arm, bay, ria 5 fiord, firth, fjord, frith, inlet, marsh, mouth
surge: 5 eager, eagre
Esultate!: 4 aria
esurience: 3 yen 4 itch, lust, need, want, wish 5 greed 6 desire, hunger, thirst 7 avarice, craving, longing 8 appetite, rapacity, venality, yearning 9 eagerness, hankering 10 famishment
esurient: 5 unfed 6 greedy, hungry 7 peckish, starved 8 edacious, famished, ravenous 9 insatiate, voracious
ESV: 3 van 8 Cadillac
Eszterhas: 3 Joe
et __: 3 seq., sqq., vir 4 alia, alii, seqq., uxor 6 cetera
et __ genus omne: 3 hoc
ET: 5 alien, dance, Orkan 6 Vulcan 7 Martian 8 Venusian
vehicle: 3 UFO
E-2, Army: 3 pvt.
eta: 5 Greek 6 letter
follower: 5 theta
preceder: 4 zeta
eta __: 5 meson
ETA: 5 guess
part of ~: 3 arr., est. 4 time 7 arrival 9 estimated
place: 3 sta., stn. 4 sked 5 depot, sched. 7 station
étagère piece: 5 china, curio, dodad, objet 6 doodad
e-tailer offering: 3 CDs 5 books, music
big ~ season: 4 Xmas
et al.: 9 and others
part of ~: 4 alia, alii
relative: 3 etc.
etamine: 6 fabric 8 material
etaoin __: 6 shrdlu
étape: 7 bivouac 9 warehouse
__ et armis: 7 virtute
__ États-Unis: 3 Les
etc.: 7 and so on 10 and so forth
category: 4 misc.
cousin: 4 et al. 6 et alia, et alii
etch: 4 draw 5 carve, stamp 6 incise 7 cut into, engrain, engrave, impress, imprint, ingrain, scratch 8 inscribe 9 delineate 10 illustrate
Etch a __: 6 Sketch
__ et Chandon: 4 Moet
etched in __: 5 stone
etcher: 4 Goya, Graf 5 Goyen 6 artist 8 engraver, Whistler
need: 4 acid 5 glass 6 stylus
__-et-Cher: 4 Loir
etching: 3 art 5 print 7 drawing, picture 9 engraving, mezzotint
__ etching: 3 dot 6 freeze
ETD: 5 guess
part of ~: 3 arr., dep., est. 4 time 9 departure, estimated
place: 3 sta., stn. 4 sked 5 depot, sched. 7 station
__ et Decorum Est: 5 Dulce
été: 6 French, saison, summer
__ E. Tee: 3 Lil
eternal: 4 ever, vast 6 eonian, steady 7 abiding, ageless, endless, lasting, undying 8 almighty, enduring, immortal, infinite, timeless, unending, unwaning 9 ceaseless, continual, deathless, incessant, perennial, perpetual, Sisyphean, unceasing, unfailing 10 unchanging
Eternal __: 4 City, Fire 5 Flame
Eternal City, The: 4 Roma, Rome
Eternal Fire author: Calder Willingham
eternally: 3 e'er 4 ever 5 no end 6 always 7 forever 8 evermore, for keeps 9 endlessly, regularly 10 unendingly
Eternal, the: 3 God 4 Lord
eterne: 7 ageless, endless, forever 8 timeless, unending 9 ceaseless, perpetual
eternity: 3 eon 4 aeon, ages, time 7 century, forever
Ethan: 4 Coen 5 Allen, Canin, Frome, Hawke 8 Phillips
ethane: 3 gas 4 fuel
Ethan Frome author: Edith Wharton
character: 3 Ned 5 Zeena 6 Mattie 7 Zenobia
ethanol to dimethyl ether: 6 isomer
Ethel: 5 Mertz 6 Merman, Waters, Wilson 7 Kennedy 9 Barrymore
brother of ~: 4 John 6 Lionel
Diana Barrymore, to ~: 5 niece
husband: 4 Fred
Ethelbert: 5 Nevin
Ethelred the __: 7 Unready
ether: 3 sky 7 heavens 10 anesthetic
__ ether: 5 ethyl, vinyl 6 acetic, ozonic 7 diethyl, divinyl, nitrous
ethereal: 4 airy 5 filmy, light 6 aerial, dainty, divine 7 angelic, sublime, tenuous 8 delicate, empyreal, empyrean, gossamer, heavenly, supernal 9 ambrosial, angelical, celestial, exquisite, ineffable, lightsome, spiritual, unearthly, unworldly 10 immaterial, intangible, unphysical
Etheridge: 6 Knight 7 Melissa
Etheridge, Melissa song: I'm the Only One (1994)
ethic: 6 morals 9 principle, tradition
__ ethic: 4 work 7 Puritan
ethical: 4 fair, fine, good, just, nice, okay 5 clean, great, legit, moral, noble, right, sound 6 decent, honest, humane, proper, square, trusty 7 upright 8 all right, elevated, laudable, pleasant, pleasing, splendid, straight, superior, virtuous 9 admirable, agreeable, equitable, excellent, high-toned, honorable, reputable, righteous, veracious, wholesome, wonderful 10 acceptable, beneficial, creditable, high-minded, principled, scrupulous, upstanding
Ethical Culture originator: 5 Adler
ethically: 9 honorably 10 virtuously
ethics: 4 code 5 mores 6 belief, values, virtue 7 decency, honesty 8 morality, precepts, standard 9 integrity 10 conscience, honestness, principles
lacking ~: 6 amoral
Ethiopia: 6 nation 7 country
ancient city: 4 Axum 5 Aksum, Meroe
bishop: 4 abba
bovine: 5 Barka, Boran, Horro
capital: 10 Addis Ababa
city: 5 Adowa, Harar 10 Addis Ababa
fossil site: 5 Hadar
lake: 4 Tana 5 Abaya, Tsana
language: 6 Somali
money: 4 birr, cent
mountain: 4 Batu, Guna 5 Gughe 9 Ras Dashan
neighbor: 5 Kenya, Sudan 7 Eritrea, Somalia 8 Djibouti
people: 4 Afar 5 Galla, Oromo, Tigré 6 Amhara, Sidamo, Somali 7 Danakil
primate: 6 gelada, grivet
province: 4 Shoa
royal name: 5 Haile
runner: 6 Bikila
title: 3 Ras
volcano: 7 Erta-Ale
waterfall: 6 Fincha
ethmoid: 4 bone
locale: 5 skull 7 cranium 9 braincase
ethnic: 6 native, racial, tribal 8 cultural, national 10 indigenous
group: 4 race 5 tribe
prefix: 4 poly- 5 Italo-
suffix: 3 -ese
ethnic __: 4 food 5 pride
ethnobotany: 4 lore 5 tales 6 fables 7 beliefs, customs, legends 8 doctrine, folklore, teaching 9 mythology 10 traditions
ethnology: 4 race 5 mores 6 custom, values 7 culture, customs, science, society 8 folklore, folkways
study: 8 cultures
et hoc __ omne: 5 genus
ethos: 5 mores 7 culture 8 folkways 9 character, standards
without ~: 3 bad 5 wrong 6 amoral, wicked
ethyl: 3 gas 4 fuel
acetate: 5 ester
ender: 3 -ene
hydride: 6 ethane 8 dimethyl
ethyl __: 5 ether, oxide 7 acetate, alcohol, hexoate, nitrate, nitrite, sulfide, urethan
ethylene __: 5 oxide 6 glycol 7 alcohol, bromide
et id __ omne: 5 genus
Étienne
in English: 6 Steven 7 Stephen
see also French
etiolate: 4 fade 6 blanch, bleach, whiten 7 wash out 8 enfeeble
etiquette: 4 code, form 6 custom 7 decency, decorum, dignity, fashion, manners, p's and q's 8 ceremony, civility, courtesy, niceties, protocol 9 amenities, formality, gentility, politesse, propriety, suavities 10 convention, deportment, politeness, seemliness
error: 4 no-no 5 gaffe 7 faux pas
name: 3 Amy 4 Post 5 Emily 7 Letitia 8 Baldrige 10 Vanderbilt
__ et labora: 3 ora

__-et-Loir: 4 Eure
__-et-Loire: 5 Indre, Maine, Saône
__ et lui: 4 Elle
__ et lumière: 3 son
__ et mon droit: 4 Dieu
Etna: 4 cone 7 volcano 10 Mongibello
emulate ~: 4 spew, spue 5 erupt
locale: 5 Italy 6 Europe
output: 3 ash 4 lava
view from ~: 6 Ionian
__ et noir: 5 rouge
ETO
commander: 3 DDE
nickname: 3 Ike
part: 3 Eur. 7 Theater 8 European 10 Operations
étoile: 4 star 6 dancer 9 ballerina
when ~ s come out: 4 nuit
Eton: 6 collar, jacket, school
like an ~ collar: 5 stiff
ref. for ~: 3 OED
rival: 6 Harrow
river: 6 Thames
Eton __: 6 collar, jacket 7 College
Etonian parent: 5 mater, pater
__ et orbi: 4 urbi
étouffée: 4 stew
__ et praeterea nihil: 3 vox
__ et quarante: 6 trente
__-être: 4 bien, peut
Etruscan: 8 Etrurian, language
city founded by ~ s: 5 Siena
god: 5 Tinia
town: 4 Veii, Veio 5 Adria
Etruscan __: 4 ware 6 Places
Etruscan Places author: D.H. Lawrence
ETs: 6 aliens 8 Martians
ETS exam: 3 GRE, SAT 4 GMAT, LSAT, PSAT
Etta: 4 Kett 5 James, Jones, Place
E.T. The Extra-Terrestrial (1982 film)
cast: Drew Barrymore, Peter Coyote, Henry Thomas, Dee Wallace
composer: 8 Williams
director: Steven Spielberg
dog: 6 Harvey
Etting: 4 Ruth
Ettore: 7 Bugatti
in English: 6 Hector
Et tu, __?: 5 brute
Et tu time: 4 Ides
__ et tuum: 4 meum
__ et ubique: 3 hic
etude: 5 music, study
__-et-un: 5 vingt
__ et Veritas: 3 Lux
__-et-Vilaine: 4 Ille
etymology: 4 root 6 origin, source 7 descent 8 ancestry 9 beginning 10 derivation, extraction, provenance
__ etymology: 4 folk 7 popular
etymon: 4 root 6 origin
Etzatlán: 4 city, town
locale: 6 Mexico 7 Jalisco
Eu: 4 elem. 7 element 8 europium
63 for ~: 4 at. no.
Eubanks: 3 Bob
Eubie: 5 Blake
eucalyptus: 4 tree, yate
eater: 5 koala
ether in ~ oil: 6 cineol
relative: 5 guava 6 myrtle 7 cajeput
yield: 3 gum 4 kino 5 resin
Eucerin: 6 lotion
alternative: 4 Keri 5 Curel, Nivea 6 Aveeno 7 Jergens, Pacquin 9 Lubriderm
Eucharist: 4 rite 9 communion, sacrament
box: 3 pix, pyx
bread: 5 wafer
plate: 5 paten
rite: 4 Mass
table: 5 altar
euchre: 4 game 5 cheat 7 swindle 8 card game, hoodwink
kin: 6 écarté
Eucken, Rudolf: 6 writer 8 Nobelist 11 philosopher
euclase: 3 gem 8 gemstone
Euclid: 4 city, town
locale: 4 Ohio
Euclidean __: 5 group, space 8 geometry
Eudora: 5 Welty
Eugene: 4 city, Debs, List, pope, town 5 Field, Fodor, Roche, Ysaye 6 O'Neill, Wigner 7 Burdick, Istomin, Ormandy, pontiff 8 Goossens, McCarthy
athletes: 5 Ducks
in Russian: 7 Yevgeni, Yevgeny
locale: 3 Ore. 6 Oregon
Eugene __: 4 Aram 6 Onegin
Eugène: 3 Sue 7 Ionesco 9 Delacroix
Eugene Aram author: Edward Bulwer-Lytton
Eugene Onegin: 5 novel, opera
author: Aleksandr Pushkin
character: 4 Olga 5 Tanya
composer: 11 Tchaikovsky
Eugenia: 8 asteroid
Eukanuba: 7 dog food
alternative: 4 Alpo, Iams 5 Nutro 6 Purina 10 Ken-L Ration
Eulabus: 4 pope 7 pontiff
Eulalie author: Edgar Allan Poe
__ Eulenspiegel: 4 Till
Euler, Leonhard: 13 mathematician
Euler's __: 7 diagram, formula
Euless: 4 city, town
locale: 5 Texas
eulogize: 4 laud 5 bless, ensky, exalt, extol, honor 6 extoll, praise 7 acclaim, applaud, glorify, lionize, magnify 9 celebrate, recommend 10 panegyrize
eulogy: 5 eloge, psalm 6 praise, speech 7 acclaim, oration, plaudit, tribute 8 accolade, encomium 9 extolment, laudation, panegyric 10 exaltation
Eumenides author: Aeschylus
Eunice: 7 Shriver
brother of ~: 3 JFK, Ted
daughter of ~: 5 Maria
son of ~: 7 Timothy
Eunomia: 8 asteroid
euonymus: 5 shrub
euphemism: 8 delicacy 9 inflation, pomposity 10 floridness
swearer's ~: 4 dang, darn, drat
euphemistic: 4 mild 5 vague 8 indirect, softened
euphonic: 5 sweet 6 dulcet
euphonious: 5 in key, sweet 6 dulcet, in tune 7 lyrical, melodic, musical, tuneful 8 sonorous 9 melodious, well-tuned 10 harmonious
euphonium: 4 horn, tuba, wind
euphony: 4 tune 5 music 6 melody 7 harmony
euphoria: 3 joy 4 glee 5 bliss 7 delight, ecstasy, elation, rapture 8 felicity 9 happiness 10 ebullience, exaltation, exultation, joyousness, jubilation
euphoric: 4 glad 5 giddy, happy, merry 6 blithe, cheery, elated, jovial, joyful, joyous, upbeat 7 beaming, gleeful, pleased, tickled 8 blissful, cheerful, ecstatic, exultant, jubilant, mirthful, thrilled 9 delighted, overjoyed, rapturous, rejoicing
state: 4 high 5 happy, tipsy 6 elated, joyful, pumped 7 psyched, soaring 9 exuberant 10 optimistic
Euphrates: 5 river
it joins the ~: 6 Tigris
locale: 4 Irak, Iraq 5 Syria 6 Turkey
river to the ~: 5 Murat 6 Khabur
Euphrosyne: 5 Grace 8 asteroid
colleague: 6 Aglaia, Thalia
euphuistic: 5 wordy 7 orotund, pompous, verbose 8 inflated 9 bombastic, grandiose, rhapsodic 10 big-talking, flamboyant, long-winded, rhetorical
eupnea: 4 puff 6 breath 9 breathing 10 exhalation, inhalation
Eur.: 4 cont.
alliance: 4 NATO
former ~ country: 3 GDR
historic ~ realm: 3 HRE
nation: 3 Aus., Lux., Rus., Swe. 4 Aust., Belg., Bulg., Gr. Br., Gt.Br., Holl., Icel., Lith., Neth., Norw., Swed.
south of ~: 3 Afr. 5 Medit.
speedometer reading in ~: 3 kph
Eurasia
bird: 4 smew, tern
language family: 6 Altaic
range: 4 Alai 5 Urals
sea: 5 Black 7 Caspian
shrub: 6 daphne 8 mezereon, mezereum, oleander, oleaster, tamarisk
Eure-et-__: 4 Loir
Eureka: 3 vac 4 city, town 5 motto 6 vacuum
locale: 10 California
rival: 5 Kirby, Oreck 6 Hoover 10 Electrolux
Eureka!: 3 aha, cry, hah, oho
Eureka author: Edgar Allan Poe
Euripides: 5 Greek 10 playwright
work: Alcestis
Andromache
Bacchae
Cyclops
Electra
Hecuba
Helen
Hippolytus
Ion
Iphigenia in Aulis
Medea
Orestes
The Trojan Women
euro: 4 coin 5 money 8 wallaroo 9 marsupial
competitor: 3 dol. 6 dollar
country: 5 Italy, Spain 6 France, Greece 7 Austria, Belgium, Finland, Germany, Holland, Iceland 8 Portugal 10 Luxembourg 11 Netherlands
replacer: 5 franc 6 peseta 7 drachma, guilder
Euro __: 6 Disney
Euromoney: 3 ecu
Europa: 4 moon 8 asteroid
brother of ~: 5 Cilix 6 Cadmus, Thasus 7 Phineus, Phoenix
father of ~: 6 Agenor 10 Telephassa
lover of ~: 4 Zeus
planet: 7 Jupiter
sister of ~: 4 Asia 6 Cadmus
son of ~: 5 Minos 8 Sarpedon
Europe: 8 Old World 9 continent
airline: 3 KLM, SAS 5 MALEV 6 Iberia
bird: 4 chat, lark, rook, ruff, shag, smew 5 ousel, ouzel, saker, serin, tarin, twite 6 chough, cuckoo, hoopoe, lanner, linnet, siskin 7 babbler, graylag, greylag, jackdaw, lapwing, pochard, redwing, skylark, sunbird, wagtail, waxbill 8 coturnix, dotterel, eagle owl, garganey, hawfinch, ringdove, starling, whinchat, woodchat, woodlark 9 bullfinch, cormorant, fieldfare, francolin, goldfinch, ossifrage, stonechat 10 greenfinch, turtledove
boot: 5 Italy
buy from ~: 6 import
capital: 4 Bern, Kiev, Oslo, Riga, Roma, Rome, Wien 5 Berne, Minsk, Paris, Praha, Sofia, Vaduz, Vilna 6 Athens, Berlin, Dublin, Lisboa, Lisbon, London, Madrid, Moscow, Prague, Skopje, Sofiya, Vienna, Warsaw, Zagreb 7 Belfast, Cardiff, Den Haag, Nicosia, Tallinn 8 Belgrade, Brussels, Chisinau, Helsinki, Sarajevo, The Hague, Valletta 9 Amsterdam, Bucharest, Edinburgh, Ljubljana, Stockholm 10 Bratislava, Copenhagen
car: 3 BMW 4 Fiat, Opel, Saab, Yugo
coal region: 4 Saar
ctry.: 3 Alb., Den., Eng., Ger., Ire., Nor., Rom. 4 Ital.
defense org.: 4 NATO
do ~: 4 tour
fish: 3 dab, ide 4 blay, boce, dory, ling, rudd 5 bleak, brill, guasa, loach, pargo, perch, tench 6 barbel, beluga, maigre, turbot, weever, zander 7 gudgeon, pigfoot 8 John Dory, pilchard 10 bitterling
former money: 4 lira, mark 5 ducat, franc 6 markka, peseta 7 drachma, pistole 9 schilling
grass: 7 esparto
gulf: 7 Bothnia
herb: 6 borage, lovage
in ~: 6 abroad 7 touring 8 overseas
it's s. of ~: 3 Afr. 5 Medit. 6 Africa
lake: 5 Onega
language: 3 Ger. 4 Erse, Ital. 5 Czech, Dutch, Greek, Irish 6 Danish, French, German, Polish 7 English, Finnish, Flemish, Italian, Latvian, Russian, Spanish, Swedish 8 Albanian, Estonian, Romanian 9 Hungarian, Icelandic, Norwegian 10 Lithuanian, Portuguese
language group: 6 Finnic
money: 4 euro 5 zloty 6 forint
mountain: 3 alp 4 Rysy, Zupo 5 Aneto, Eiger, Kekes, Korab, Teide 6 Castor, Ecrins, Elbrus, Elbruz, Estats, Musala, Posets, Snezka 7 Aragats, Bernina, Olympus, Triglov 8 Ben Nevis, Jungfrau 9 Mont Blanc, Monte Rosa 10 Matterhorn, Monte Corno
mountains: 4 Alps 5 Urals 8 Pyrenees 9 Apennines
nation: 3 Aus., Lux., Rus., Swe. 4 Aust., Belg., Bulg., Eire, Erin, Gr. Br., Gt.Br., Holl., Icel., Lith., Neth., Norw., Swed. 5 Italy, Spain 6 Bosnia, España, France, Greece, Latvia, Monaco, Norway, Poland, Russia, Serbia, Sweden, Turkey 7 Albania, Andorra, Belarus, Belgium, Croatia, Denmark, England, Estonia, Finland, Germany, Holland, Hungary, Iceland, Ireland, Moldova, Romania, Ukraine 8 Bulgaria, Portugal, Slovakia, Slovenia 9 Lithuania 11 Netherlands, Switzerland, Vatican City 13 Liechtenstein
neighbor: 4 Asia
old ~ country: 4 USSR 6 Latium
peninsula: 5 Italy 6 Iberia
region: 5 Scand. 6 Kosovo 7 Balkans
river: 3 Aar, Bug, Cam, Dal, Dee, Don, Inn, Lek, Lot, Lys, Oka, San, Tay, Ume, Usk, Wye 4 Aare, Adda, Aire, Aube, Avon, Cher, Doon, Drin, Ebro, Eder, Eger, Elbe, Ille, Isar, Kama, Maas, Main, Miño, Neva, Oder, Odra, Ohre, Oise, Oulu, Ouse, Prut, Ruhr, Saar, Sava, Styr, Taff, Tees, Tyne, Ural, Waal, Yser 5 Adige,

Aisne, Boyne, Clyde, Desna, Doubs, Douro, Drava, Drina, Dvina, Isère, Kuban, Loire, Marne, Memel, Meuse, Minho, Mures, Narew, Neman, Onega, Peene, Piave, Rhine, Rhone, Saône, Seine, Siret, Somme, Tagus, Tiber, Tisza, Trent, Tweed, Volga, Warta, Weser **6** Allier, Danube, Donets, Glomma, Humber, IJssel, Isonzo, Liffey, Mersey, Moldau, Morava, Neckar, Neisse, Niemen, Pripet, Sambre, Severn, Struma, Thames, Thjórs, Vardar, Vltava, Yarrow **7** Derwent, Dnieper, Garonne, Livenza, Maritsa, Moselle, Pechora, Rubicon, Schelde, Scheldt, Shannon, Trebbia, Vistula **8** Berezina, Dniester, Dordogne, Guadiana, Volturno
rodent: 6 suslik **7** hamster, mole rat, souslik
sea: 5 North **6** Baltic
starter: 3 Pan- **4** Indo-
tree: 4 sorb, wych **5** rowan
volcano: 4 Etna **8** Vesuvius **9** Santorini, Stromboli
weasel: 5 fitch, sable **6** ermine **7** foumart, polecat **8** foulmart
yard: 5 meter
European: 4 Balt, Brit, Dane, Esth, Finn, Gael, Lett, Pole, Serb, Slav, Turk **5** Greek, Swede, Swiss **6** German **7** Belgian, Bosnian, Italian, Latvian, Russian, Serbian **8** Albanian, Austrian, Croatian, Estonian, Moldovan, Romanian, Spaniard **9** Bulgarian, Frenchman, Hungarian, Norwegian, Slovakian, Slovenian, Ukrainian **10** Lithuanian, Monegasque
European __: 3 elk **4** plan **5** beech, elder, finch, larch, Union **6** chafer, linden
Europeans, The author: Henry James
europium: 7 element
Eurovan: 2 VW **10** Volkswagen
Eurus, mother of: 3 Eos
Euryale: 6 Amazon
father of ~: 4 Ares **5** Minos
lover of ~: 8 Poseidon
sister of ~: 6 Medusa
son of ~: 5 Orion
Euryclea, mother of: 3 Ops
Eurydice
husband of ~: 6 Nestor **7** Orpheus
lover of ~: 5 Eneas **6** Aeneas
son of ~: 5 Etias
Eurythemis, daughter of: 4 Leda
Eurythmics
song: Here Comes That Rain Again (1984)
Sweet Dreams (1983)
Would I Lie to You? (1985)
Eusden, Lawrence: 4 poet
Eusebius: 4 pope **7** pontiff
Eustace: 5 saint
Eustache: 9 Deschamps
Eustachian tube site: 3 ear
Eustachius: 5 saint
Eustatius, St. neighbor: 4 Saba
Eustis: 4 city, town
locale: 7 Florida
__ Eustis, VA: 4 Fort
Euterpe: 4 Muse
area: 3 mus. **5** music
parent of ~: 4 Zeus **9** Mnemosyne
sister: 4 Clio **5** Erato **6** Thalia, Urania **8** Calliope **9** Melpomene **10** Polyhymnia **11** Terpsichore
Eutychian: 4 pope **7** pontiff
Euwe, Max forte: 5 chess
Eva: 5 Gabor, Novak, Perón **6** Bartok, Duarte, Marton **7** Tanguay
sister of ~: 5 Magda **6** Zsa Zsa
Eva (1962 film)
cast: Stanley Baker, Virna Lisi, Jeanne Moreau
Eva __ Saint: 5 Marie
__ Eva: 6 Little
EVA: 9 spacewalk
org.: 4 NASA
evacuate: 2 go **4** void **5** drain, empty, leave, purge, use up **6** decamp, depart, get out, remove, unload **7** consume, deplete, exhaust, pull out
evacuated: 4 bare **5** empty **6** barren
evacuation: 4 exit **6** exodus **7** retreat **8** ejection, emptying **9** catharsis, clearance, departure, discharge, expulsion, purgation **10** withdrawal
evade: 4 duck, flee, jump, loaf, lose, shun **5** avoid, dodge, elude, fudge, hedge, parry, shirk, skirt, sneak **6** bypass, cop out, escape, eschew, ignore, put off, refuse **7** abstain, disobey, fend off, neglect, quibble, shy from **8** flee from, get out of, keep from, shake off, sidestep, throw off **9** get around, hem and haw, pussyfoot **10** circumvent, equivocate, escape from, get clear of, work around
a haymaker: 3 bob **4** duck **5** weave
the issue: 6 waffle **10** equivocate
the seeker: 4 hide
evader: 5 cheat **7** escapee **8** deserter **9** goldbrick
work ~: 5 idler **6** loafer, truant **7** goof-off, shirker, slacker **8** fainéant **9** do-nothing, lazybones **10** ne'er-do-well
evaluate: 3 try, vet **4** case, rank, rate, sift **5** assay, check, gauge, grade, judge, price, think, weigh **6** assess, ponder, reckon, review, screen, size up, survey, try out **7** analyze, balance, inspect, measure **8** appraise, check out, classify, estimate, factor in, keep tabs, look over **9** criticize, figure out, pick apart
evaluation: 4 test **5** stock **6** rating **7** opinion **8** analysis, estimate, feedback, judgment **9** appraisal, criticism, probation, valuation **10** assessment, estimation
evaluator: 5 judge **6** critic, expert, pundit **7** analyst, arbiter, scholar **8** reviewer **9** authority
Eva Luna author: Isabel Allende
Eva Marie __: 5 Saint
Evan: 4 Bayh **6** Hunter, Mecham
Evan-__: 6 Picone
Evander: 9 Holyfield
evanesce: 4 fade, melt **6** vanish **8** dissolve, fade away, vaporize **9** disappear, dissipate, evaporate
evanescent: 5 brief, short **6** mortal **7** passing, trivial **8** fleeting, flitting, temporal **9** ephemeral, momentary, temporary, transient **10** intangible, unenduring
Evangeline: 4 poem
author: Longfellow
character: 5 Basil, Mowis **7** Gabriel, Lilinau
setting: 6 Acadia
evangelist: 8 minister, preacher
Evangelista: 5 Linda **10** Torricelli
evangelize: 5 drill, teach, train **6** preach **7** educate **8** instruct **9** catechize
Evans: 3 Gil, Ray **4** Dale, Gene, Joan, Paul, peak **5** Edith, Faith, Janet, Linda, Madge, mount **6** Arthur, Dwight, Harold, Oliver, Robert, Walker **7** Connell, Darrell, Maurice, Rowland **8** mountain
locale: 7 Rockies **8** Colorado
partner: 5 Novak
Evans, Arthur: 12 archeologist
excavation site: 5 Crete **6** Candia
Evans, Dale
horse: 10 Buttermilk
spouse: Roy Rogers
Evans, Darrell sport: 8 baseball
Evans, Edith: 4 Dame
__ Evans Hughes: 7 Charles
Evans, Janet: 7 swimmer
Evans, Linda spouse: John Derek
Evans, Mary Ann pseudonym: 5 Eliot
Evans, Robert
spouse: Phyllis George, Ali MacGraw, Catherine Oxenberg
Evanston: 4 city, town
athletes: 8 Wildcats
locale: 8 Illinois
Evansville: 4 city, town
locale: 7 Indiana
sch.: 3 USI
Evans, Walker collaborator: 4 Agee
evaporate: 3 dry **4** boil, fade **5** dry up **6** dry out, vanish **7** distill **8** decrease, dissolve, evanesce, fade away, peter out **9** anhydrate, dehydrate, desiccate, disappear, dissipate **10** dehumidify
evaporated __: 4 milk
evaporation: 5 decay **6** fading **8** drying up **9** abatement
residue: 4 salt
Evaristus: 4 pope **7** pontiff
evasion: 3 lie **4** ruse, tale **5** dodge, shift, trick **6** cop-out, escape, excuse **7** dodging, elusion, pretext, quibble **8** pretense, shirking, shunning, trickery **9** avoidance, runaround **10** subterfuge
__ evasion: 3 tax
evasive: 3 coy, sly **4** cagy **5** cagey, dodgy, vague **6** shifty, tricky **7** cunning, devious, elusive, elusory, furtive, oblique, unclear **8** slippery **9** ambiguous, casuistic, deceitful, deceptive, equivocal, insincere, unwilling **10** inexplicit, misleading, roundabout, unexplicit, unobliging
phrase: 4 not I **5** not me
tactic: 3 zag, zig **6** end run
eve: 5 brink, verge **6** sunset **9** nighttime, threshold
Hebrew ~: 4 ereb, erev
opposite: 4 morn
Eve: 5 Arden, Curie, Plumb **6** Queler **7** Merriam **10** Harrington
domain: 4 Eden
grandson of ~: 4 Enos **5** Enoch
husband of ~: 4 Adam
son of ~: 4 Abel, Cain, Seth
source: 3 rib
tempter: 5 apple, snake **7** serpent
Eve __ Agnes, The: 4 of St.
Eve __ Mark, The: 4 of St.
Eve composer: 8 Massenet
Evel: 7 Knievel **9** daredevil
Evelina author: Fanny Burney
Evelina composer: 5 Arlen
Evelyn: 4 John, King, Lear, Wood **5** Keyes, Waugh **6** Ankers **7** Ashford, Venable
Evelyne: 5 Accad
Evelyn, John: 6 writer **7** British
even: 3 yet **4** calm, cool, fair, flat, just, tied **5** align, aline, equal, flush, level, match, plane, still **6** honest, in a tie, on a par, placid, serene, smooth, square, stable, steady **7** balance, equable, flatten, regular, uniform **8** balanced, composed, constant, equalize, matching, moderate, parallel, peaceful, smoothly, so much as, straight, tranquil, unbiased, unbroken **9** equitable, identical, impartial, smooth out, stabilize, temperate, unextreme, uniformly, unruffled, unvarying **10** all the more, consistent, deadlocked, dependable, equivalent, fifty-fifty, nose to nose, rhythmical, straighten, true to type, unagitated, unchanging, unwavering
a little: 3 any **5** at all
chance: 6 tossup
come out ~: 3 tie **7** balance
ender: 4 fall, song, tide **6** handed
get ~: 3 fix, tie **5** repay, spite **6** avenge **7** pay back, requite, revenge **9** pay in kind, retaliate
if: 3 tho, yet **5** altho, while **6** albeit, though, whilst **7** despite **8** although
nearly ~: 5 close, tight **8** not quite, round off, round out **9** proximate
not ~: 3 odd **4** nary
not ~ close: 4 cold **5** wrong **6** all wet **7** distant **8** mistaken **9** erroneous **10** inaccurate
not ~ once: 4 ne'er **5** never
not ~ one: 4 nada **5** zilch
now: 3 yet **5** still
on an ~ keel: 4 calm **5** alike, equal, level **6** in line, smooth, stable, steady **7** aligned, equable, lined up, matched, regular **8** balanced, constant, parallel, straight, unbroken **9** identical **10** comparable, consistent, equivalent
once: 4 ever **5** at all **9** at any time **10** at any point
one: 3 any **4** a bit **5** at all **7** a little
opposite: 4 morn
out: 5 level **6** spread **7** flatten, redress
(out): 7 average
so: 3 yes, yet **5** still **10** all the same
stay ~: 6 keep up **8** maintain, preserve
supposing: 6 though
temper: 8 patience **9** composure **10** sedateness
up: 3 tie **4** tied, trim **5** align, aline, level, plane **6** square **7** balance **8** equalize
even __: 5 money
even-__: 6 minded, steven
__ even: 3 get **5** break, odd or
...__ even a mouse: 3 not
evenhanded: 4 fair, just **5** equal **6** honest, square **7** neutral, upright **8** balanced, straight, unbiased **9** equitable, impartial, objective, uncolored, unslanted
evenhandedness: 6 equity **7** justice **8** fairness, fair play, justness **9** rightness **10** lawfulness
evening: 3 e'en **4** dark, dusk, nite **5** night **6** sunset **7** sundown **8** gloaming, twilight **9** nightfall, nighttime
draw toward ~: 5 laten
each ~: 7 nightly
ender: 4 wear
have an ~ meal: 3 sup **4** dine **5** feast
hour: 2 p.m. **3** six **4** nine **5** eight, seven
in French: 4 soir
in Italian: 4 sera
meal: 6 dinner, repast, supper
part of the ~: 5 shank
party: 6 soiree
star: 5 Venus **6** planet, Vesper
wear: 3 PJs, tux **4** gown **5** dress, stole **6** formal
evening __: 3 bag **4** gown, star **5** dress, watch **6** prayer, school **7** campion, clothes, emerald
__ evening: 4 good
Evening __: 4 Star **5** Class, Shade
Evening at Pops network: 3 PBS
Evening Class author: Maeve Binchy
Evening Shade (CBS sitcom)
cast: Ossie Davis (Ponder Blue)
Marilu Henner (Ava Newton)
Hal Holbrook (Evan Evans)
Burt Reynolds (Wood Newton)
setting: 3 Ark. **8** Arkansas
Evening Star author: Edgar Allan Poe

Evening Star, The: 4 film 5 novel
author: Larry McMurtry
cast: Juliette Lewis, Shirley MacLaine, Bill Paxton, Miranda Richardson
Evening with Richard Nixon, An
author: Gore Vidal
__ even keel: 4 on an
evenly: 5 alike, right 9 pari passu, uniformly
__ even more than anyone...: 3 E is
evenness: 7 balance, isonomy, justice 8 equality, monotony, symmetry 9 composure, equipoise 10 legibility
Even Now (song) artist: Barry Manilow, Bob Seger
even number combining form: 5 artio-
__-even point: 5 break
evensong: 4 hymn 6 vesper 7 vespers
even-steven, go: 3 tie 5 split
event: 2 do 4 bash, bout, case, expo, fair, fete, gala, game, meet, race 5 big do, match, mixer, party, pro-am, scene, state, thing 6 affair, discus, mishap, prelim, slalom 7 benefit, contest, episode, holiday, javelin, shot put 8 accident, birthday, calamity, election, fortuity, high jump, incident, landmark, long jump, marathon, occasion 9 box social, emergency, happening, milestone, pole vault, situation, spectacle, triathlon 10 barnburner, casus belli, centennial, experience, graduation, occurrence, phenomenon, tournament
blessed ~: 5 birth
host: 2 MC 5 emcee
important ~: 4 rite 8 landmark 9 milestone
in any ~: 5 still 6 anyhow, anyway 7 at least 9 at any rate 10 regardless
in that ~: 4 then 9 therefore
in the ~: 9 given that
main ~: 4 bout, duel 5 fight, match, round 7 contest, feature 8 showcase 9 headliner, highlight 10 engagement
sporting ~: 4 bout, bowl, dash, game, meet, race 5 fight, match, relay, rodeo 6 discus 10 prizefight
event __: 7 horizon, planner
__ event: 4 main 5 field, in any, media, track 7 blessed
even-tempered: 4 cool 6 placid 7 equable, patient 8 tranquil
not ~: 5 moody
eventful: 7 fateful 8 pregnant 9 memorable, momentous
even the __: 5 score
Even the Nights Are Better (1982 song) artist: Air Supply
eventide: 5 night 6 sunset 8 twilight 9 nightfall, nighttime
events: 4 proc. 6 doings 8 goings-on 10 happenings
course of ~: 4 tide
current ~: 4 news
order of ~: 7 program
past ~: 6 annals 7 account, history 9 chronicle, olden days, posterity, recountal
events list: 4 sked 5 sched., slate
__ event that: 5 in the
eventual: 4 last 5 final, later 6 coming, future, latter 7 ensuing 8 terminal, ultimate, upcoming 9 resulting 10 concluding, consequent, inevitable, subsequent
eventuality: 4 case 5 state 6 result, upshot
eventualize: 5 occur 6 result
eventually: 3 yet 4 anon, soon, then 5 after 6 at last, in a bit, in time, not now, one day 7 by and by, finally, for good, later on, someday 8 after all, in a while, in the end, sometime 9 afterward, hereafter 10 before long, ultimately
eventuate: 2 go 4 rise 5 begin, ensue, occur 6 follow, happen, pan out, result 7 turn out 9 come about, take place, terminate, transpire 10 come to pass
even-up: 10 fifty-fifty
Eve of Destruction (1965 song) artist: Barry McGuire
Eve of St. Agnes, The: 4 poem
author: John Keats
Eve of St. Mark, The author: Maxwell Anderson
eve. preceder: 3 aft
ever: 3 too 5 at all, no how 6 always 7 for good 8 even once, for keeps, in any way, sometime, unending 9 at any time, endlessly, eternally 10 at all times, at any point, constantly, enduringly, for all time, invariably, unendingly
and anon: 3 oft
as ~: 6 always, surely 10 invariably
ender: 4 more 5 glade, green, where, which 6 glades 7 bearing, lasting 8 blooming
hardly ~: 6 little, rarely, seldom 8 scarcely
not ~: 4 ne'er 5 never
partner: 4 anon
since: 4 as of, from
so: 4 very 5 quite 9 extremely
so much: 4 a lot, many 6 highly 7 greatly
starter: 3 for, how, who 4 what, when, whom 5 which
Ever After (1998 film)
cast: Drew Barrymore, Patrick Godfrey, Anjelica Huston, Dougray Scott
Everage: 4 Dame, Edna
ever and __: 4 anon 5 again
Everdur: 5 alloy
component: 6 copper 7 silicon 9 manganese
Everest: 3 mtn. 4 peak 5 mount 8 mountain
conqueror: 6 Norgay 7 Hillary
locale: 4 Asia 5 Nepal, Tibet 6 Thibet, Xizang 7 Sitsang 9 Himalayas
Everett: 4 Chad, city, town 5 Betty 6 Rupert, Sloane
locale: 10 Washington
Everett, Betty
song: Let It Be Me (1964)
The Shoop Shoop Song (1964)
__ Everett Horton: 6 Edward
Everett, Rupert: 5 actor
film: Dance With a Stranger (1985)
A Midsummer Night's Dream (1999)
My Best Friend's Wedding (1997)
The Next Best Thing (2000)
__ Ever Fall in Love: 3 If I
everglades: 5 marsh, swamp
Everglades: 4 park
inhabitant: 4 ibis 5 egret
locale: 3 Fla. 7 Florida
evergreen: 3 fir, yew 4 atle, pine, wood 5 athel, boldo, cacao, erica, furze, hakea, olive, pinon, plant, thuja, thuya, toyon 6 alerce, balsam, laurel, longan, loquat, lungan, spruce 7 arbutus, cypress, juniper 8 gardenia 9 sapodilla 10 arborvitae
African ~: 4 akee
Chilean ~: 5 maqui
forest: 5 taiga
genus: 5 picea
like an ~: 4 piny 5 firry, piney
New Zealand ~: 5 kauri
oak: 4 holm, ilex
shrub: 3 box, kat, qat 4 khat 5 erica, gorse, hakea, heath, holly, maqui, pyxie, salal, toyon 6 aucuba, dahoon, kalmia, myrtle, nardin, privet 7 arbutus, boxwood, juniper, mahonia, nandina, skimmia 8 camellia, cassiope, rosemary 9 firethorn, sugarbush
Evergreen State: 4 Wash. 10 Washington
Everhart: 5 Angie
everlasting: 6 always, eterne 7 abiding, endless, eternal, undying 8 almighty, constant, enduring, immortal, infinite, timeless, unending 9 ceaseless, deathless, perennial, permanent, perpetual, unceasing
Everlasting Love (1974 song) artist: Carl Carlton
Everlasting Love, An (1978 song)
artist: Andy Gibb
everlastingly: 5 no end
Everlasting Mercy, The author: John Masefield
Everlasting Piece, An (2000 film)
cast: Anna Friel, Barry McEvoy, Pauline McLynn, Brian O'Byrne
director: Barry Levinson
Everlovin' (1961 song) artist: Ricky Nelson
Everly Brothers: 3 Don, duo 4 Phil
song: All I Have to Do Is Dream (1958)
Bird Dog (1958)
Bye Bye Love (1957)
Cathy's Clown (1960)
Crying in the Rain (1962)
Devoted to You (1958)
Ebony Eyes (1961)
I Kissed You (1959)
Let It Be Me (1960)
Problems (1958)
So Sad (1960)
That's Old Fashioned (1962)
Wake Up Little Susie (1957)
Walk Right Back (1961)
When Will I Be Loved (1960)
evermore: 6 always 9 endlessly, eternally, from now on 10 enduringly, henceforth, unendingly
__ Ever Need Is You: 4 All I
ever-present: 7 chronic 9 chronical 10 ubiquitous
Evers: 6 Johnny, Medgar 7 Charles
everse: 9 overthrow
Evers, Johnny: 3 Cub
__ ever so humble...: 4 Be it
evert: 6 refute 7 reverse
Evert, Chris: 7 netster 9 tennis pro
milieu: 5 court
every: 3 all, per 4 each 5 whole
any and ~: 3 all
bit: 4 to a T 5 fully 6 wholly 7 exactly, totally 10 throughout
eighth day: 5 octan
ender: 3 day, man, one 4 body 5 place, thing, where
evening: 7 nightly
inch: 5 fully 6 wholly 7 totally, utterly 8 entirely 10 completely, thoroughly
in prescriptions: 3 omn.
make ~ effort: 6 strive 8 struggle
morning: 5 daily 7 diurnal, regular, routine 9 quotidian
now and then: 6 seldom 8 periodic, sporadic 9 sometimes 10 occasional
other: 9 alternate
show ~ sign of: 4 seem 6 appear
which way: 5 messy, mussy 6 hectic, untidy 7 chaotic, haywire, jumbled, lawless, riotous, tangled 8 anarchic, confused, pell-mell 10 anarchical, disjointed, disordered, disorderly, topsy-turvy, tumultuous
win ~ game: 5 sweep 7 clean up
with ~ option: 4 full, rich 5 flush, tight 6 loaded, packed 7 crowded, replete, stuffed 8 brimming, cram-full 9 chock-full, jam-packed 10 wall-to-wall
12 mos.: 4 yrly. 6 yearly
24 hours: 4 a day 5 daily
60 minutes: 5 horal 6 hourly
every __: 3 bit, day 4 inch 5 other
every __ and then: 3 now
every __ in a while: 4 once
every __ jack: 3 man
every __ son: 7 mother's
every __ way: 5 which
Every __ has his day: 3 dog
Every __ of My Heart: 4 Beat
Every __ Way But Loose: 5 Which
Every __ You Take: 6 Breath
Every Beat of My Heart (1961 song)
artist: Gladys Knight and the Pips
everybody: 3 all 4 y'all 5 world 9 one and all
opposite: 5 no one
Everybody Does It (1949 film)
cast: Linda Darnell, Paul Douglas, Celeste Holm
Everybody Hurts (1993 song) artist: R.E.M.
Everybody Loves a Clown (1965 song)
artist: Gary Lewis and the Playboys
Everybody Loves a Lover (1958 song)
artist: Doris Day
Everybody Loves Me But You (1962 song) artist: Brenda Lee
Everybody Loves Raymond (CBS sitcom)
cast: Peter Boyle (Frank Barone)
Brad Garrett (Robert Barone)
Patricia Heaton (Debra Barone)
Doris Roberts (Marie Barone)
Ray Romano (Ray Barone)
dog: 7 Shamsky
Everybody Loves Somebody (1964 song) artist: Dean Martin
Everybody Ought to Have a __: 4 Maid
Everybody Plays the Fool (song)
artist: Aaron Neville, Main Ingredient
Everybody's All-American (1988 film)
cast: Timothy Hutton, Jessica Lange, Dennis Quaid
director: Taylor Hackford
Everybody (song) artist: Backstreet Boys, Tommy Roe
Everybody's Somebody's Fool (1960 song) artist: Connie Francis
Everybody's Talkin' (1969 song) artist: Nilsson
Everybody Wants to Rule the World (1985 song) artist: Tears for Fears
Every Breath You Take (1983 song)
artist: Police, Sting
everyday: 5 lowly, plain, stock, typic, usual 6 common, normal, vulgar, wonted 7 average, diurnal, general, generic, humdrum, mundane, natural, prosaic, regular, routine, trivial, typical 8 frequent, habitual, informal, ordinary, orthodox, standard 9 customary, generical, prosaical, quotidian 10 accustomed, pedestrian, prevailing, uninspired, widespread
not ~: 4 rare
Everyday People (1969 song) artist: Sly and the Family Stone
Every Day's A Holiday (1937 film)
cast: Charles Butterworth, Edmund Lowe, Mae West
Every Heartbeat (1991 song) artist: Amy Grant
Every hero becomes __ at last: 5 a bore
Every Kinda People (1978 song) artist: Robert Palmer
__ Every Little Star: 5 I Told

Every Little Step (1989 song) artist: Bobby Brown
Every Little Thing She Does Is Magic (1981 song) artist: Police
every man __: 4 jack
Every Man in His Humour author: Ben Jonson
every now and __: 4 then 5 again
every once __ while: 3 in a
everyone: 3 all 4 y'all 5 world 6 public
in music: 5 tutti
Everyone But Thee and Me author: Ogden Nash
Everyone Says I Love You (1996 film)
cast: Alan Alda, Woody Allen, Goldie Hawn, Julia Roberts
director: Woody Allen
Every Rose Has Its Thorn (1988 song) artist: Poison
every so __: 5 often
everything: 3 all 5 whole, works 6 the lot 8 the works, universe 9 aggregate
counting ~: 5 in all 6 in toto, wholly 7 totally 10 altogether, completely
despite ~: 10 regardless
else: 4 rest
in French: 4 tout 5 toute
in Spanish: 4 todo 5 todos
take ~: 3 hog 7 possess 10 monopolize
everything __ place: 5 in its
Everything (1989 song) artist: Jody Watley
Everything I Own (1972 song) artist: Bread
Everything Is Beautiful (1970 song) artist: Ray Stevens
Everything's Coming Up Roses composer: 5 Styne 8 Sondheim
Everything She Wants (1985 song) artist: George Michael
Everything that Rises Must Converge author: Flannery O'Connor
Everything That Touches You (1968 song) artist: Association
Everything to Gain author: 6 Carter
Everything Your Heart Desires (1988 song) artist: Daryl Hall and John Oates
everywhere: 7 all over, overall 9 all around 10 far and wide, high and low, near and far, pole to pole, throughout, ubiquitous
look ~: 4 comb, rake, seek, sift, sort 5 probe, scour, sweep 6 forage, search 7 examine, inspect, ransack, rummage
prefix: 4 omni-
every which __: 3 way
Every Which Way But Loose (1978 film)
beast: 5 Clyde, orang
cast: Beverly D'Angelo, Clint Eastwood, Geoffrey Lewis, Sondra Locke
Every Woman in the World (1980 song) artist: Air Supply
__ Every Woman Knows: 4 What
__ Eve, The: 4 Lady
Evian: 3 spa 5 water
alternative: 4 Naya 7 Perrier 8 Aquafina 9 Arrowhead
see also French
Évian-__-Bains, France: 3 Les
evict: 4 boot, oust 5 eject, expel 6 banish, bounce, put out, remove 7 boot out, dismiss, exclude, kick out, shut off, shut out, toss out, turn out 8 dislodge, displace, force out, throw out 9 eliminate 10 dispossess
eviction: 9 dismissal, exclusion, expulsion
eviction __: 6 clause, notice
evidence: 4 clew, clue, data, give, hint, lead, look, mark, show, sign 5 basis, proof, prove, token, trace 6 denote, evince, record, reveal 7 confirm, display, exhibit, grounds, signify, symptom, witness 8 document, indicate, manifest 9 affidavit, reference, testimony 10 deposition, illustrate, indication, smoking gun
combustion ~: 3 ash 5 ashes, flame, smoke
crime scene ~: 3 DNA 5 print
hear ~: 3 try 4 deem, rule 5 gauge, judge 6 assess, decide, decree, deduce, settle, size up 7 discern, examine, mediate 8 appraise, consider, evaluate, moderate, sentence 9 arbitrate, determine
in ~: 7 obvious
minimal ~: 5 shred
offer ~: 5 prove, quote, swear 6 adduce, attest 7 testify 8 attest to
__ evidence: 5 king's 6 direct, queen's, state's 7 hearsay
evident: 4 open, real 5 clear, lucid, naked, overt, plain, vivid 6 cogent, marked, patent 7 express, glaring, obvious, outward, seeming, visible 8 apparent, clear-cut, distinct, explicit, luminous, manifest, palpable, tangible 9 axiomatic, graspable, prominent 10 noticeable, observable, pronounced, spelled out, undeniable
be ~: 4 look, loom, show 5 pop up 6 appear, crop up, emerge, happen, show up, turn up 7 surface 8 look as if, look like, spring up
make ~: 5 prove
__-evident: 4 self
evidently: 8 markedly 9 doubtless, obviously, outwardly, seemingly 10 apparently, manifestly, officially, ostensibly
Evigan: 4 Greg
evil: 3 bad, ill, low, sin 4 base, dark, foul, harm, mean, ugly, vice, vile 5 cruel, nasty, wrong 6 guilty, horrid, infamy, malice, malign, no good, poison, sinful, unholy, unkind, wicked 7 badness, baleful, baneful, beastly, corrupt, crooked, demonic, devilry, harmful, hateful, heinous, hideous, hurtful, immoral, impiety, lawless, malefic, outrage, satanic, Stygian, unclean, vicious 8 atrocity, baseness, criminal, daemonic, damnable, demoniac, depraved, devilish, deviltry, diabolic, enormity, fiendish, foulness, ignominy, infamous, iniquity, meanness, mischief, sinister, spiteful, vileness, villainy, wrongful 9 demonical, depravity, diabolism, execrable, indecency, injurious, loathsome, malicious, malignity, miscreant, monstrous, nefarious, offensive, rancorous, repugnant, revolting, satanical, turpitude, vandalism 10 corruption, diabolical, immorality, inexpiable, iniquitous, maleficent, malevolent, misconduct, opprobrium, perfidious, pernicious, perversity, sinfulness, traitorous, villainous, virtueless, wantonness, wickedness, wrongdoing
combining form: 4 male-
do ~: 9 misbehave
encourage in ~: 4 abet 6 incite 7 collude 9 instigate
ender: 4 doer 5 doing
eye: 3 hex 4 jinx, look 5 curse, glare, scowl 7 sorcery
free from ~: 5 purge 6 purify 8 exorcise, exorcize
in French: 3 mal
look: 4 leer
one: 4 ogre 5 baddy, demon, devil, ghoul, Satan 6 baddie, daemon, daimon, diablo 7 Lucifer 9 archfiend
repeller: 5 charm, spell 6 amulet 7 periapt 8 talisman
speak ~ of: 4 slur 5 smear 6 defame, impugn, malign, smirch, vilify 7 asperse, put down, rip into, run down, slander 8 backbite, badmouth, belittle, besmirch, tear down, throw mud 9 criticize, denigrate, deprecate, disparage, fling dirt 10 calumniate, depreciate, speak ill of, throw mud on
ways: 4 hoax 5 guile, wiles 7 con game, cunning, knavery, roguery 8 deviltry, flimflam, mischief, trickery, villainy 9 chicanery 10 dishonesty, subterfuge, wrongdoing
evil __: 3 eye
__ evil: 5 king's 6 social
Evil __: 4 Ways 5 Woman
__ Evil: 5 See No
evildoer: 4 perp 5 devil, felon, fiend, Satan 6 bad guy, sinner 7 hellion, villain 8 criminal, gangster 9 miscreant 10 lawbreaker
evildoing: 3 sin 4 vice 7 outrage 8 iniquity
Evil Empire: 4 USSR
evil-minded: 4 mean 5 catty, nasty, petty, snide 6 ornery, wicked 7 harmful, hateful, hostile, hurtful, jealous, vicious 8 fiendish, vengeful, venomous 9 green-eyed, malicious 10 bad-natured, malevolent, pernicious, vindictive
evil-smelling: 4 rank 5 funky 6 rancid
...evil that __ do...: 3 men
Evil Ways (1970 song) artist: Santana
Evil Woman (1975 song) artist: ELO
evince: 4 have, show 5 argue, prove 6 reveal, unfold 7 display, exhibit, reflect, signify 8 evidence, indicate, manifest, proclaim 9 make clear, make plain 10 illustrate
Evita (1996 film): 7 musical
cast: Antonio Banderas, Madonna, Jonathan Pryce
composer: 4 Rice 11 Lloyd Webber
director: Alan Parker
role: 3 Che 4 Juan 5 Perón
evocative: 8 arousing, kindling, stirring 9 awakening, remindful 10 rekindling, suggestive
evoke: 4 draw 6 arouse, call up, elicit, induce, invite, recall, summon 7 conjure, extract, suggest 8 bring out, occasion 9 call forth, conjure up, draw forth, stimulate 10 bring forth
evolution: 6 change, growth 7 process 8 progress 9 expansion, flowering, formation, gestation, unfolding 10 maturation, perfection, transition
Evolution: 3 car 4 auto 10 Mitsubishi
evolutionary
rung on the ~ ladder: 3 ape, man 5 human 6 apeman
evolutionary __: 7 biology
evolve: 4 come, emit, grow 5 ripen 6 change, mature, mutate, unfold 7 advance, develop, give off, perfect, shape up, work out 8 progress 9 come about, formulate, originate
into: 6 become 8 emerge as
evolving: 5 early 7 initial, ongoing 8 germinal, immature 9 embryonic, incipient
Evonne: 9 Goolagong
rival: 5 Chris
evonymus: 5 shrub
Évora: 4 city, town
locale: 8 Portugal
Évreux: 4 city, town
locale: 6 France
Évry: 4 city, town
locale: 6 France
Ev'rybody's Got __ But Me: 5 a Home
__ Ev'ry Mountain: 5 Climb
Ev'ry Time __ Goodbye: 5 We Say
evulse: 3 pry 4 cull, mine, pull, take, yank 5 evoke, glean, leach, pluck, wrest, wring 6 derive, elicit, obtain, remove, select, siphon, uproot 7 distill, draw out, extract, weed out 8 bring out
E.W.: 7 Scripps
Ewa: 4 city, town
locale: 6 Hawaii
Ewan: 8 McGregor
Ewbank, Weeb: 5 coach
sport: 8 football
ewe: 3 she 6 female 7 bleater
baby: 4 lamb
covering: 4 wool
homophone: 3 yew, you
mate: 3 ram
milieu: 3 lea 5 field, grass 6 meadow 7 pasture 9 grassland
sound: 3 baa, maa 5 bleat
ewe __: 4 lamb
ewe-__: 4 neck
Ewe: 8 language
home: 4 Togo 5 Ghana 6 Africa
Ewell: 3 Tom
ewer: 3 jug 5 basin 6 vessel 7 pitcher 8 oenochoe 9 container
adjunct: 4 bowl 5 basin 6 vessel
use a ~: 4 pour
__ E. Westlake: 6 Donald
Ewing: 2 J.R. 3 Pam 4 city, Gary, Jock, Lucy, town 5 Bobby, Ellie 6 Valene 7 Patrick
concern: 3 oil
J.R. ~ foe: 5 Cliff 6 Barnes
locale: 9 New Jersey
Ewing, Patrick org.: 3 NBA
Ewings, The author: John O'Hara
Ewok: 5 alien
ally: 4 Jedi
home: 5 Endor
Ew-w-w!: 3 ick, ugh 5 gross, yecch
ex: 6 former 7 divorcé 8 divorcée, previous
ex __: 3 int., lib., off. 4 ante, lege, more, post, voto 5 animo, curia, facie, facto, parte, store 6 gratia, libris, nihilo, rights 7 officio
ex __ facto: 4 post
ex-: 4 late, past 8 outgoing
exacerbate: 4 sink, slip, sour 5 add to, decay, slide 6 worsen 7 enflame, inflame 8 compound 9 aggravate, infuriate, intensify 10 degenerate, exasperate, retrogress
exact: 3 tax 4 fine, firm, just, levy, nice, same, true 5 clear, force, fussy, level, right, rigid, seize, sound, stiff, valid, wrest, wring 6 actual, coerce, compel, dead-on, demand, direct, extort, impose, proper, severe, strict, wrench 7 call for, careful, command, correct, express, factual, finicky, inflict, literal, perfect, precise, refined, regular, require, right on, solicit 8 absolute, accurate, clear-cut, definite, distinct, faithful, finiking, finnicky, flawless, inerrant, methodic, on target, on the dot, rigorous, specific, straight, thorough, truthful, unerring, verbatim 9 definable, demanding, errorless, faultless, identical, on the nose, unbending, veracious 10 impeccable, infallible, insist upon, methodical, meticulous, nailed down, on the money, particular, scrupulous, unmistaken
retribution: 6 avenge 7 get even 9 retaliate
exact __: 7 science
exacta: 3 bet 5 wager
locale: 3 OTB 5 track

player: 6 better, bettor 7 gambler, wagerer 8 gamester
exacting: 4 firm, hard 5 bossy, cruel, fussy, harsh, picky, rigid, stern, stiff, tight, tough 6 severe, strict, taxing, trying 7 austere, careful, exigent, finicky, hard-won, onerous, precise, prudent, Spartan, weighty 8 captious, cautious, critical, despotic, exigeant, finiking, finnicky, hard-line, rigorous, thorough, tiresome 9 assiduous, attentive, demanding, difficult, draconian, imperious, judicious, observant, stringent, unbending, unfeeling, unsparing 10 burdensome, despotical, enervating, fastidious, inflexible, iron-fisted, meticulous, nitpicking, no-nonsense, oppressive, particular, scrupulous, tyrannical, unamenable
exaction: 3 fee, tax 4 duty, levy, toll 6 assess, charge, custom, excise, impose, impost, tariff 10 collection
exactitude: 5 right, rigor, truth 7 clarity 8 accuracy, fidelity, veracity 9 precision 10 conformity, factuality
exactly: 2 ay, da, ja, sí 3 aye, due, oui, pat, yea, yep, yes, yup 4 fine, just, okay, sure, to a T, yeah 5 good-o, natch, plumb, quite, right, roger, sharp, smack, spang, truly, uh-huh 6 agreed, aright, dead-on, gladly, good-oh, indeed, just so, rather, righto, surely, you bet, yowzah 7 for sure, go ahead, indeedy, mais oui, quite so, ten-four 8 all right, as you say, directly, for a fact, of course, on the dot, straight, thumbs up, verbatim, very well 9 be my guest, certainly, darn right, literally, literatim, naturally, on the nose, precisely, sure thing, you betcha, you said it 10 absolutely, by all means, definitely, for certain, on the money, positively, sure enough, that's right, unerringly
in Latin: 10 ad litteram
not ~: 5 about, kinda, sorta 6 in a way, kind of, sort of
exactness: 4 care 5 right, rigor 8 accuracy, fidelity, veracity 9 austerity, precision 10 definitude, perfection, regularity, strictness
exaggerate: 3 lie, pad 4 puff 5 add to, boast, boost, color, fudge 6 blow up, expand, overdo, puff up 7 amplify, build up, enlarge, inflate, lay it on, magnify, stretch 8 go too far, misquote, overplay, overrate 9 aggravate, dramatize, embellish, embroider, emphasize, fabricate, intensify, misreport, overstate 10 caricature
exaggerated: 4 tall 5 campy, hammy, undue 6 lavish, too-too 8 overdone, strained
exaggeration: 3 fib 4 hype, puff, rhet., tale, yarn 7 blarney, stretch 8 rhetoric, travesty
comic ~: 4 camp 5 farce
exalt: 4 hail, laud, lift 5 adore, bless, boost, crown, deify, ensky, extol, honor, raise 6 esteem, extoll, lift up, praise, puff up, revere, salute, uplift 7 acclaim, advance, applaud, build up, commend, dignify, elevate, enhance, ennoble, flatter, glorify, idolize, inflate, lionize, magnify, promote, worship 8 enshrine, enthrone, eulogize, heighten, inshrine, inthrone, sanctify 9 celebrate, recommend, reverence 10 aggrandize, compliment, panegyrize
exaltation: 5 glory, honor, kudos 6 eulogy, homage, praise, salute 7 acclaim, ecstasy, hosanna, plaudit, rapture, tribute 8 accolade, encomium, euphoria, flattery, good word 9 adoration, animation, elevation, extolment, laudation, loftiness, panegyric, promotion, reverence, transport, upgrading, uplifting 10 apotheosis, excitement, idolzation, joyousness, jubilation
exalted: 4 high 5 grand, great, lofty, noble, noted, royal 6 august, divine, lordly, superb 7 eminent, gleeful, praised, sublime 8 elevated, empyreal, empyrean, glorious, imposing, inspired, majestic, rarefied, superior 9 dignified, high-flown, honorable, top-drawer, unrivaled 10 majestical, unrivalled
exam: 4 oral, quiz, test 5 final 7 checkup, midterm, midyear 8 physical 9 true-false 10 ultrasound
base: 4 text 6 course 8 textbook
British ~: 6 A level, tripos
choice: 4 true 5 false
coll. senior's ~: 3 GRE 4 GMAT, LSAT, MCAT
for immigrants: 5 TOEFL
format: 4 test 5 essay, paper 9 true/false
for would-be teachers: 3 NTE
future doctor's: 4 MCAT
H.S. ~: 3 SAT 4 PSAT
medical ~: 3 ECG, EEG, EKG, MRI 4 x-ray 8 physical
prepare for an ~: 4 cram 5 learn, study 6 master
score: 4 mark, rank 5 grade 6 rating
take an ~: 3 sit
__ exam: 3 bar 4 oral 6 dental
examination: 4 look, oral, quiz, scan, test 5 assay, audit, check, final, probe, proof, study, trial 6 review, survey 7 battery, checkup, enquiry, inquest, inquiry, midterm, perusal, pop quiz, reading 8 analysis, checking, grilling, once-over, scrutiny 9 going-over
combining form: 4 -opsy
conduct an ~: 5 delve, probe 8 research
IRS ~: 3 aud. 5 audit
quick ~: 4 peek 7 look-see
visual: 4 gaze, leer, peek, scan, seek 5 sight, study, watch 6 aspect, gander, glance, review, survey 7 display, exhibit, glimpse, look-see, viewing 8 once-over, scrutiny 9 beholding 10 inspection
__ examination: 6 direct
examine: 3 eye, see, spy, try, vet 4 case, comb, quiz, read, scan, sift, test, view 5 assay, audit, check, grill, judge, plumb, probe, prove, query, study, sum up, think, touch, weigh 6 browse, go into, go over, handle, look at, peer at, peruse, ponder, reason, review, sample, screen, search, survey, winnow 7 analyze, canvass, collate, compare, dig into, dissect, explore, inspect, observe 8 appraise, check out, consider, factor in, look into, look over, overhaul, pick over, pore over, question 9 catechize, criticize, delve into, go through, interview, pick apart 10 scrutinize
carefully: 4 look, pore
__-examine: 5 cross 6 direct
examiner: 6 censor, tester 7 analyst, auditor, quizzer 8 reviewer 9 inspector 10 accountant, inquisitor, questioner
future ~: 5 augur, sibyl 6 medium, oracle 7 diviner, palmist, prophet, psychic 8 haruspex 9 theurgist 10 forecaster, foreteller, soothsayer
__ examiner: 4 bank, mine 5 trial
example: 4 case, noun 5 gauge, ideal, light, model, piece 6 sample 7 display, epitome, paragon, pattern, problem, warning 8 citation, instance, paradigm, specimen, standard 9 archetype, precedent, prototype 10 embodiment, stereotype
follow the ~ of: 3 ape 4 copy 5 equal, mimic, rival 6 mirror 7 emulate, imitate, pattern, reflect 9 take after
for ~: 3 say, viz. 4 thus 5 to wit 6 such as
give an ~: 4 cite, name 5 offer, quote 7 specify 8 point out, spell out 9 enumerate
helpful ~: 6 lesson, sermon 7 precept
starter: 7 counter
__ example: 3 for 4 as an 5 set an
exanimate: 6 bummed 7 defunct, extinct 8 dejected, downcast, lifeless 9 bummed-out 10 dispirited, spiritless
ex animo: 9 sincerely
exarch: 6 bishop
exasperate: 3 get, ire, vex 4 gall, rile, roil, tire, wear 5 anger, annoy, chafe, grate, peeve, pique, upset, weary 6 bother, enrage, madden, nettle, offend, put out, rankle, tee off 7 agitate, enflame, incense, inflame, provoke 8 acerbate, irritate 9 aggravate, displease, infuriate, make waves 10 exacerbate
exasperated: 3 hot, mad 4 ired, sore 5 angry, cross, fed up, huffy, irate, livid, testy, tired, wroth 6 fuming, ireful, raging, raving, red-hot 7 enraged, furious, ranting 8 choleric, wrathful 9 indignant, resentful, splenetic
sound ~: 4 sigh
exasperating: 6 trying 7 naughty 8 tiresome 9 annoyance, vexatious
exasperation: 3 ire 4 care, fury, rage 5 anger, pique, upset, wrath 7 umbrage 8 vexation 9 annoyance
exclamation: 6 enough, sheesh 8 honestly
Excalibur: 5 hotel, sword
locale: 5 Vegas 8 Las Vegas
Excalibur (1981 film)
cast: Helen Mirren, Nigel Terry, Nicol Williamson
director: John Boorman
excavate: 3 dig 4 grub, mine, sink 5 delve, dig up, gouge, scoop 6 burrow, deepen, dig out, hollow, quarry, tunnel 7 unearth 8 gouge out, scoop out 9 hollow out, undermine
excavated: 5 empty 6 sunken 7 concave 8 indented 9 depressed 10 scooped out
excavation: 3 dig, pit 4 hole, mine 5 ditch, gouge 6 burrow, cavity, dugout, hollow, quarry, trench 7 foxhole 9 shoveling 10 depression, unearthing
mine ~: 5 stope
excavator: 5 miner 6 dredge 7 backhoe
find: 3 ore 4 gold 5 relic, shard 6 fossil
Excedrin: 9 analgesic
alternative: 3 APF 4 Cope 5 Advil, Aleve, Bayer 6 Anacin, Datril, Motrin 7 Ecotrin, Tylenol 8 Bufferin, St. Joseph, Vanquish 9 Ascriptin
exceed: 3 cap, top 4 beat, best, pass 5 break, outdo, tower 6 better, go past, outrun 7 eclipse, outpace, overrun, run over, surpass 8 go beyond, outclass, outshine, outstrip, outweigh, overrate, overstep, surmount 9 rise above, transcend 10 put to shame, tower above
the limit: 5 speed
exceeding: 4 more 5 above, undue 8 superior
exceedingly: 4 most, much, very 5 madly, no end, quite 6 ever so, highly, hugely, really 7 awfully, greatly 8 terribly
excel: 3 ace, cap, top 4 lead, lick, pass 5 outdo, shine, trump 6 do well 7 surpass 8 go to town, outclass, outshine, outstrip, outweigh, stand out 9 transcend 10 overshadow
in: 6 master
Excel: 3 car 4 auto 7 Hyundai
excellence: 5 merit, value, worth 6 virtue 7 quality 8 goodness, nobility 9 greatness, supremacy 10 classicism, perfection, superbness
artistic ~: 5 vertu, virtu
standard of ~: 3 par 5 ideal 9 beau idéal
__ excellence: 3 par
Excellency: 5 title
excellent: 3 ace, A-OK, def, rad, top 4 aces, A-one, boss, braw, cool, dece, fine, gear, good, keen, neat, nice, okay, phat, tops, tuff 5 crack, dandy, ducky, grand, great, legit, marvy, moral, neato, nifty, nobby, noble, prime, primo, sharp, slick, solid, super, swell 6 bang on, bang-up, bonzer, bosker, choice, divine, dreamy, far-out, gnarly, golden, goodly, groovy, lovely, peachy, proper, select, slap-up, spot on, superb, terrif, tiptop, unreal, whizzo, wicked, worthy 7 amazing, awesome, capital, corking, ethical, optimum, perfect, premium, ripping, skookum, stellar, sublime, supreme, vintage 8 all right, dazzling, enviable, especial, eximious, fabulous, five-star, four-star, frabjous, glorious, heavenly, jim-dandy, laudable, peerless, pleasant, pleasing, skillful, slam-bang, smashing, splendid, standout, sterling, stickout, superior, terrific, top-level, top-notch, very good, wondrous 9 admirable, agreeable, beautiful, bodacious, brilliant, certified, covetable, desirable, Endsville, estimable, exemplary, exquisite, fantastic, first-rate, high-grade, hunky-dory, marvelous, masterful, matchless, priceless, reputable, sollicker, sovereign, topflight, unrivaled, wonderful, wunderbar 10 acceptable, attractive, beneficial, creditable, first-class, hotsy-totsy, invaluable, jack-a-dandy, out of sight, peachy-keen, phenomenal, remarkable, stupendous, super-duper, tremendous, unrivalled, world-class
in hip-hop: 3 rad 4 phat
more ~: 5 finer 6 better, fitter 7 greater 8 improved, stronger, superior, upgraded, worthier
player: 3 ace, pro 4 whiz 6 expert, master, talent 8 virtuoso 10 specialist
excellent adventure
participant: 3 Ted 4 Bill
excellent instrument: 3 pen
excellently: 4 well
Excellent Woman author: Barbara Pym
Excelsior: 5 motto 6 ballet
composer: 7 Marenco
Excelsior Springs: 3 spa 4 city, town
locale: 8 Missouri
except: 3 ban, bar, but 4 less, omit, save 5 debar, minus 6 all but, reject, unless 7 barring, besides, lacking, rule out, short of, without 8 disallow, leave out, omitting, pass over 9 apart from, aside from, excluding, other than, outside of, rejecting 10 leaving out
exception: 5 quirk 6 oddity 7 anomaly, barring, variant 8 omission 9 allowance, anomalism, condition, debarment, departure, deviation, exclusion, expulsion, privilege, rejection, variation 10 difference
take ~: 5 demur 6 differ 7 dissent, protest, quarrel

take ~ to: 4 mind 5 cavil 6 object, oppose, resent 8 question 9 challenge, deprecate
without ~: 3 all 5 every 6 always, to a man, wholly 8 entirely
exceptional: 3 ace, def, odd, rad 4 aces, A-one, boss, braw, cool, dece, eery, fine, gear, keen, neat, nice, phat, rare, tuff 5 dandy, ducky, eerie, grand, great, marvy, neato, nobby, prime, slick, super, swell, weird 6 atypic, bang on, bang-up, banner, bonzer, bosker, choice, divine, dreamy, far-out, freaky, gnarly, groovy, lovely, peachy, quirky, select, signal, single, slap-up, spot on, superb, terrif, tiptop, unique, unreal, whizzo, wicked 7 amazing, awesome, bizarre, capital, corking, deviant, notable, oddball, offbeat, perfect, premium, ripping, skookum, special, stellar, strange, sublime, uncanny, unusual 8 aberrant, abnormal, advanced, atypical, dazzling, especial, eximious, fabulous, five-star, four-star, frabjous, freakish, glorious, heavenly, isolated, jim-dandy, peculiar, singular, skillful, slam-bang, smashing, splendid, standout, sterling, stickout, superior, terrific, top-level, top-notch, uncommon, very good, wondrous 9 anomalous, bodacious, divergent, eccentric, Endsville, excellent, exemplary, exquisite, fantastic, first-rate, high-grade, hunky-dory, irregular, marvelous, recherché, sollicker, top-flight, unheard of, wonderful 10 first-class, hotsy-totsy, jack-a-dandy, out of sight, peachy-keen, phenomenal, prodigious, remarkable, stupendous, super-duper, unorthodox
exceptionally: 4 much, very 5 extra 6 highly, rarely 7 greatly
excerpt: 4 cite, clip, part, pick 5 glean, quote 6 choose, select 7 extract, passage, pick out, portion 8 citation, fragment, pericope 9 quotation, selection, sound bite
excerpts: 8 analecta, analects
excess: 4 glut, hype, much, orgy, rest 5 flood, slack, waste 7 backlog, license, nimiety, overage, padding, remnant, residue, surfeit, surplus, too much 8 leftover, overflow, overkill, overload, plethora 9 decadence, profusion, redundant, remainder 10 immoderacy, indulgence, lavishness, oversupply, redundancy, sybaritism
baggage: 4 load 6 weight 9 unwelcome
fill to ~: 4 cloy, sate 5 stuff 9 overstuff
in ~: 5 spare
indulge to ~: 4 cloy, glut 5 gorge, stuff 7 surfeit 8 overfill 10 gormandize
in French: 4 trop
in ~ of: 4 over 7 besides 8 more than
excess-__ tax: 7 profits
excessive: 3 big 4 high, long, over, rank, rich 5 gross, heavy, large, steep, stiff, ultra, undue 6 costly, garish, lavish, wanton 7 glaring, intense, onerous, profuse, radical, rampant, sky-high, too many, too much 8 enormous, needless, overdone, overmuch, prodigal, terrific 9 boundless, expensive, exuberant, indulgent, limitless, luxuriant, out of hand, overblown, overboard, plethoric, redundant, unbounded 10 dissipated, exorbitant, immoderate, inordinate, outrageous, profligate, undeserved, untempered
combining form: 3 sur- 4 macr- 5 macro-
make ~ demands on: 3 tax
prefix: 4 over- 5 hyper-, ultra-
take ~ pride: 4 brag 5 boast, gloat

talker: 6 gossip, magpie, yakker 7 windbag 8 prattler 10 chatterbox
excessively: 3 too 4 oh so, very 5 madly, quite, super 6 overly, unduly 7 awfully 8 to a fault
exchange: 4 deal, mart, sell, swap, swop, talk 5 bandy, shift, trade 6 barter, cash in, deal in, invert, market, redeem, rotate, seesaw, switch 7 dealing, replace, reverse, shuffle, shuttle, wrangle 8 commerce, flip-flop, take back, treasury 9 interplay, liquidate, take turns, tit for tat, transpose 10 buy and sell, conversion, quid pro quo, substitute
blows: 3 box 4 duel, spar, swat 5 argue, brawl, brush, fight, punch, run-in, whack 6 attack, battle, bicker, combat, go at it, oppose, rumble, take on, tussle 7 assault, contend, contest, mix it up, quarrel, scuffle, vie with, wage war, wrangle, wrestle 8 do battle 9 altercate, slug it out, square off 10 fisticuffs, tangle with
chips: 6 cash in, redeem
currency ~ abbr.: 3 USD
futures ~ for short: 4 Merc
give in ~: 3 pay 5 repay
letters: 3 OTC
medium of ~: 4 bill, cash, coin 5 dough, funds, money 6 dinero, moolah, specie 7 cabbage 8 currency 9 banknotes 10 green stuff
of a sort: 5 Q and A 7 inquiry
of ideas: 4 chat, talk 6 confab, dialog, parley, powwow 8 colloquy, dialogue 9 discourse, tête-à-tête 10 conference, discussion
premium: 4 agio
start of an ~: 3 tit
stock ~: 4 mart 6 market
verbal ~: 4 quip, talk 7 jesting, joshing, kidding, ribbing, teasing 8 chitchat, repartee 9 small talk, table talk
words: 3 gab, rap, yak, yap 4 chat, talk 5 prate, speak 6 banter, gossip, parley 7 prattle 8 converse, dialogue 9 tête-à-tête, touch base 10 chew the fat, conference
exchange __: 4 rate, vows 7 student
__ exchange: 3 ion 4 base, post 5 stock 7 foreign, forward
__ Exchange: 3 Key 4 Curb
exchangeable: 8 tradable 9 swappable 10 commutable, reciprocal, returnable, switchable
__ exchanger: 4 heat
exchequer: 4 fisc 5 purse 6 coffer 8 treasury, war chest
excise: 3 cut, tax 4 dele, duty, levy, trim, X out 5 elide, erase 6 censor, cut off, cut out, delete, exsect, impost, lop off, remove, resect, tariff 7 blot out, expunge, exscind, scissor 8 cross out, exaction 9 eradicate, expurgate, surcharge 10 blue-pencil, scissor out, scratch out
excision: 3 cut 7 removal 8 deletion 9 resection
combining form: 4 -tomy 6 -ectomy
excitability: 6 temper
excitable: 4 edgy 5 antsy, fiery, itchy, jumpy, nervy, tense, testy 6 feisty, touchy, uneasy 7 anxious, jittery, keyed up, nervous, peevish, restive, uptight 8 agitated, restless, skittish, troubled, volatile 9 alarmable, concerned, emotional, hotheaded, ill at ease, impatient, impetuous, impulsive, irascible, mercurial, sensitive 10 high-strung, hot-blooded, hysterical, intolerant, passionate, short-fused
excitant: 4 spur
excite: 3 get 4 abet, fire, grab, move, prod, rile, send, stir, wake, whet 5 hop up, liven, pique, prime, rev up, rouse, spark, touch, upset, waken, worry 6 arouse, awaken, incite, kindle, ruffle, stir up, thrill, tickle, turn on, wake up, whip up, work up 7 agitate, animate, delight, disturb, enflame, enliven, enthuse, ferment, fluster, inflame, inspire, juice up, provoke, quicken, thrills 8 energize, enspirit, inspirit, interest, intrigue, motivate 9 electrify, encourage, fascinate, galvanize, instigate, stimulate, titillate, transport 10 invigorate
excited: 3 ape, hot, mad 4 agog, edgy, high, warm 5 afire, amped, astir, eager, het up, hyper, jumpy, manic, tense, upset, wired 6 aflame, burbly, fervid, gung-ho, hectic, jangly, joyful, joyous, on edge, piqued 7 burning, fervent, fired up, frantic, keyed up, nervous 8 animated, feverish, fluttery, frenetic, frenzied, in a tizzy, inspired, jubilant, maniacal, skittish, up in arms 9 delirious, ebullient, exuberant, hot to trot, rapturous, wrought up 10 breathless, in an uproar, passionate
about: 4 into 5 up for 7 taken by 8 obsessed, turned on
answer: 6 I do I do
cry: 5 whoop
get ~: 4 flip, rave 5 go ape, hop up, key up 6 arouse, tingle 7 bristle, enthuse
get too ~ over: 4 gush 5 drool 7 enthuse
not ~: 5 blasé, bored, jaded, weary 7 unmoved 9 apathetic 10 nonchalant, world-weary
state: 3 fit 4 flap, stew 6 dither, lather, tumult 9 commotion, confusion
__ Excited: 4 I'm So
excitedly in music: 7 agitato
excitement: 3 ado 4 buzz, fire, fuss, heat, jazz, kick, life, stir, to-do 5 fever, furor, hoo-ha, kicks, mania, punch, shock, spice, tizzy 6 action, dither, fervor, flurry, frenzy, hoopla, hoorah, hooray, hubbub, hurrah, hurray, raptus, tumult 7 emotion, ferment, jollies, turmoil 8 activity, fervency, interest 9 adventure, agitation, animation, commotion, confusion, eagerness, intensity, melodrama, sensation 10 ebullience, enthusiasm, exaltation, exuberance, hullabaloo, impatience, incitement, motivation
exclamation: 3 ooh, yow 4 arra, oh oh 5 arrah, blimy, hoo-ha 6 blimey, hoo-hah
full of ~: 4 agog, keen 5 aboil, eager 7 psyched 9 expectant 10 breathless
show ~: 4 rave 6 bubble 7 delight, enthuse, rejoice, sparkle 10 effervesce
exciter, atom: 5 maser
exciting: 5 heady, juicy, kicky 6 hectic, moving, yeasty 7 zestful 8 dramatic, electric, readable, romantic 9 arresting, emotional, glamorous, thrilling 10 impressive, in an uproar, intoxicant, rip-roaring
not ~: 4 blah, drab, dull, flat, tame 5 banal, bland, ho-hum, tripe, vapid 6 boring 7 fustian, insipid, languid 8 lifeless, sluggish 9 apathetic, lethargic, wearisome 10 dullsville, flavorless, lackluster, monotonous, spiritless
excl.
not: 4 incl.
exclaim: 3 cry 4 call, howl, roar, yell 5 blurt, shout, utter, whoop 6 bellow, cry out, holler 7 call out 8 burst out, shout out
...exclaim __ drove out of sight: 4 as he
exclamation: 2 ah, aw, eh, ha, hi, ho, oh, ow, uh 3 aah, ack, aha, arf, bah, bam, boo, boy, brr, cry, duh, fie, gee, grr, haw, heh, hey, huh, ick, nix, och, oho, olé, oof, ooh, pah, pow, rah, rot, say, tsk, tut, ugh, why, wow, yah, yay, yea, yes, yow, yum, zzz 4 ahem, ahoy, alas, amen, arra, bosh, ciao, darn, dear, drat, ecce, egad, evoe, good, gosh, ha-ha, hail, heck, help, hush, jeez, mush, nuts, oh-oh, okay, oops, ouch, oyes, oyez, pfft, pfui, phew, phoo, pish, poof, pooh, posh, ptui, rats, roar, scat, shoo, ta-da, ta-ta, tush, uh-oh, uh-uh, well, wham, whee, whew, yeah, yell, yeow, yipe, yo-ho, yuck 5 achoo, alack, arrah, avast, banco, bingo, blimy, brava, bravo, egads, faugh, fudge, golly, goody, great, hallo, hello, hillo, ho-hum, hooey, hoo-ha, howdy, hullo, humph, huzza, later, nerts, nertz, peace, phfft, prost, pshaw, right, salud, scram, shame, shout, shush, skoal, sooey, sorry, ta-dah, te-hee, uh-huh, voilà, whoof, whoop, yecch, yipes, zooks, zowie 6 ahchoo, begone, behold, bellow, blimey, by Jove, clamor, crikey, cripes, encore, enough, eureka, giddap, goodie, good-oh, gotcha, hachoo, halloa, halloo, hallow, haw-haw, hilloa, holler, hoo-hah, hoorah, hooray, hotcha, hot dog, hulloo, hurrah, hurray, huzzah, indeed, jiminy, ka-boom, la-de-da, la-di-da, l'chaim, outcry, phooey, presto, prosit, ptooey, rather, righto, shalom, sheesh, sholom, shucks, tee-hee, thanks, touché, tsk tsk, tut-tut, whammo, whizzo, whoops, yippee, yoicks, yoo-hoo, yum-yum, zounds 7 attaboy, big deal, brother, by jingo, caramba, cheerio, gangway, giddyap, giddyup, goldarn, goldurn, good-bye, heave ho, heigh-ho, holy cow, horrors, hosanna, hushaby, jeepers, jimminy, kerchoo, l'chayim, lehayim, Odzooks, rubbish, whoopee, whoopie 8 alley-oop, all right, attagirl, by cracky, farewell, for shame, Gadzooks, gracious, holy moly, honestly, lackaday, lah-di-dah, lechayim, scramola, welladay, wellaway, whatever 10 hallelujah
acceptance: 3 def, rad 4 cool, fine, good, neat, nice, okay, phat 5 dandy, ducky, great, neato, super 6 dreamy, far-out, gnarly, groovy, peachy, terrif, wicked 7 amazing, awesome, stellar 8 terrific 9 bodacious, fantastic, hunky-dory, marvelous 10 out of sight, peachy-keen, super-duper
acclamation: 4 hail 5 hallo 6 hurrah, huzzah
admiration: 5 great 6 good-oh, touché
affectation: 6 la-de-da, la-di-da 8 lah-di-dah
affirmation: 3 yay, yea, yes 4 yeah 6 rather
agreement: 3 boy 4 amen, okay 5 uh-huh 6 by Jove, good-oh 7 by jingo
alert: 7 gangway
allergy: 5 achoo 6 ahchoo, hachoo 7 kerchoo
amazement: 6 crikey
amusement: 4 ha-ha 5 te-hee 6 haw-haw, tee-hee
anger: 7 caramba, goldarn, goldurn

annoyance: 3 bah, duh, fie, tsk, tut 4 heck 6 tsk tsk, tut-tut
anticipatory ~: 4 oh oh
apology: 5 sorry
appoval: 6 hotcha
appreciation: 5 great, huzza 6 hoorah, hooray, hurrah, hurray, huzzah, thanks
approbation: 5 huzza 6 hoorah, hooray, hurrah, hurray, huzzah
approval: 2 da, ja, sí 3 aye, boy, olé, oui, yay, yea, yep, yes, yup 4 amen, fine, good, okay, what, yeah 5 brava, bravo, good-o, goody, great, natch, roger, uh-huh, zowie 6 by Jove, encore, gladly, goodie, good-oh, indeed, rather, righto, whizzo, you bet, yowzah 7 attaboy, by jingo, go ahead, indeedy, mais oui, quite so, ten-four 8 all right, as you say, attagirl, of course, thumbs up, to be sure, very much, very well 9 be my guest, certainly, darn right, naturally, sure thing, you betcha, you said it 10 absolutely, by all means, definitely, sure enough, that's right
assent: 3 yes 4 yeah 5 right 6 rather, righto
assistance: 4 help
astonishment: 4 jeez, whew 5 zowie 6 by Jove, crikey, cripes 7 by jingo, caramba, holy cow 8 holy moly
attention: 3 hey, say 4 ahem, ahoy, ecce, help, yo-ho 5 hello 6 behold, yoo-hoo
attentiveness: 5 uh-huh
aversion: 3 ack, ick, ugh 4 yuck 5 yecch
awe: 3 boy, gee 4 gosh 5 golly, hello 6 jiminy 7 jeepers, jimminy
baccarat: 5 banco
bewilderment: 3 hey, huh 7 holy cow
blast: 6 ka-boom
boredom: 5 ho-hum 7 heigh-ho
Brit's: 4 I say 5 blimy 6 blimey, good-oh, rather, righto, whizzo 7 cheerio
campy ~: 3 oof 5 zowie
canine: 3 arf, grr
cartoon brawl ~: 3 oof
casino: 5 banco
chagrin: 4 oh-oh, oops, uh-oh 6 whoops
chasing-away: 4 scat, shoo 5 scram 6 begone 8 scramola
church: 7 hosanna
collision: 4 wham 6 whammo
concern: 4 alas, oh-oh, uh-oh 5 alack
confirmation: 5 uh-huh
confusion: 3 hey, huh
contempt: 3 aha, bah, boo, boy, huh, pah, tsk, tut, yah 4 pfui, phoo, pish, pooh, posh, tush 5 faugh, ho-hum, humph, pshaw, shame 6 phooey, tsk tsk, tut-tut 8 for shame
courtroom: 4 oyes, oyez
cowboy: 5 howdy 6 giddap 7 giddyap, giddyup
defiance: 3 yah 4 nuts 5 nerts, nertz
delight: 3 aah 4 good, whee 5 goody 6 goodie, hotcha, hot dog
derision: 3 aha, fie, yah 4 ha-ha, nuts 5 hello, nerts, nertz, te-hee 6 haw-haw, la-de-da, la-di-da, tee-hee 7 big deal 8 lah-di-dah
disagreement: 3 rot 4 bosh, uh-uh 7 rubbish
disappearance: 4 poof
disappointment: 4 darn, drat, jeez, rats 5 fudge, zooks 6 shucks, zounds 7 brother, horrors, Odzooks 8 Gadzooks
disapproval: 3 boo, fie, och 4 nuts, pooh, posh, uh-uh 5 hooey, nerts, nertz, pshaw 7 big deal
disbelief: 3 huh, pah 4 pooh, posh, rats, what 5 hooey, humph, pshaw, zooks 6 zounds 7 Odzooks 8 Gadzooks, honestly
discomfort: 2 ow 3 ack, ick, oof, ugh, yow 4 ouch, phew, yeow, yuck 5 yecch
discovery: 6 eureka
disdain: 3 bah, pah, tsk, tut 4 egad, pooh, posh, tush 5 egads, pshaw, shame 6 tsk tsk, tut-tut 8 for shame
disgust: 3 ack, fie, huh, ick, pah, rot, ugh, yah 4 bosh, darn, drat, heck, nuts, pfui, phew, phoo, pooh, posh, rats, yech, yuck 5 faugh, fudge, nerts, nertz, pshaw, yecch, zooks 6 phooey, shucks, zounds 7 brother, goldarn, goldurn, Odzooks, rubbish 8 Gadzooks
dismay: 2 ow 3 yow 4 alas, oops, ouch, whew, yeow 5 alack 6 crikey, whoops 7 caramba, horrors 8 gracious, honestly
displeasure: 2 ow 3 boy, yow 4 ouch, yeow
dissatisfaction: 4 uh-uh
distaste: 3 ack, ick, rot, ugh 4 bosh, yuck 5 yecch 7 rubbish
distress: 4 dear
dog: 3 arf, grr 4 bark
dog team: 4 mush
doubt: 3 hah 5 humph
driving-away: 4 scat, shoo 5 scram 6 begone 8 scramola
ecstatic ~: 5 whoop, zowie
elation: 5 hello
embarrassment: 4 oops 6 whoops
Emeril: 3 bam
emphasis: 3 gee 4 gosh 5 golly 8 by cracky
encouragement: 3 olé, rah 5 huzza 6 hoorah, hooray, hurrah, hurray, huzzah 7 attaboy 8 alley-oop, attagirl
enjoyment: 3 yum 6 yum-yum
exasperation: 6 enough, sheesh 8 honestly
excitement: 3 oho, ooh, yow 4 arra, evoe 5 arrah, blimy, hoo-ha, huzza, whoof, wowee 6 blimey, hoo-hah, hoorah, hooray, hurrah, hurray, huzzah, yippee 7 heigh-ho, whoopee, whoopie
exhaustion: 4 phew
exhortation: 8 alley-oop
explosion: 3 pow 6 ka-boom
face-slapper's ~: 5 fresh
failure: 4 pfft 5 phfft
fanfare: 4 ta-da 5 ta-dah
farewell: 4 ciao, ta-ta 5 later, peace 6 shalom, sholom 7 cheerio, good-bye 8 farewell
fencing: 6 touché
fight ~: 3 oof
fizzling: 4 pfft 5 phfft
food: 3 yum 5 yummy 6 yum-yum
fox hunting: 5 hallo, hillo, hullo 6 halloa, halloo, hallow, hilloa, hulloo, yoicks
French ~: 5 voilà
fright: 3 boo 4 yipe 5 yipes
frustration: 6 sheesh
fumbler's ~: 4 oops
Furby ~: 4 whee
gratitude: 6 thanks
Greek: 4 evoe
greeting: 4 hail 5 hello, howdy 6 shalom, sholom
grief: 4 alas 5 alack
Hebrew: 6 l'chaim 7 l'chayim, lehayim 8 lechayim
hippie ~: 5 peace 6 far out
hog-calling: 5 sooey
horror: 3 ack, ick, ugh 4 yuck 5 yecch
horse: 3 haw 6 giddap 7 giddyap, giddyup
Iditarod: 4 mush
impact: 3 pow 4 wham 6 whammo
impatience: 3 tsk, tut, yah 4 phew, pish, pooh, posh, tush 5 pshaw, shame 6 enough, tsk tsk, tut-tut 8 for shame
indifference: 8 whatever
interrogation: 3 huh 4 what
Irish: 3 och 4 aroo, arra, orra 5 arrah, orrow
irony: 3 aha 6 indeed 7 big deal
joy: 3 aah, yay, yea, yes, yow 4 evoe, whee, yeah 5 huzza 6 hoorah, hooray, hot dog, hurrah, hurray, huzzah, yippee 7 whoopee, whoopie 8 all right
klutz's ~: 4 oh oh
Latin: 4 ecce
laughter: 4 ha-ha 5 te-hee 6 haw-haw, tee-hee
magician: 5 voilà 6 presto
Mass: 7 hosanna 10 hallelujah
melancholy: 7 heigh-ho
mockery: 3 aha
nautical: 4 ahoy 5 avast 7 heave ho
near-miss ~: 4 whew
old-time ~: 4 egad 5 egads, mercy, pshaw 6 zounds
pain: 2 ow 3 yow 4 ouch, yeow, yipe 5 yipes
palindromic ~: 3 aha, hah, oho, wow
parting: 4 ciao, ta-ta 5 later, peace 6 shalom, sholom 7 cheerio, good-bye 8 farewell
pig-calling: 5 sooey
pity: 4 alas 5 alack 8 lackaday
pleasure: 3 gee, hey, ooh, wow, yes 4 gosh, yeah 5 golly, zowie 6 whizzo, yippee 7 whoopee, whoopie 8 all right
praise: 5 brava, bravo 6 encore 7 hosanna
pretension: 6 la-de-da, la-di-da 8 lah-di-dah
puzzlement: 3 gee 4 gosh 5 golly 6 jiminy 7 jeepers, jimminy
quiet: 4 hush 5 shush 7 hushaby
regret: 3 och 4 alas, rats 5 alack, sorry 6 shucks 7 Odzooks 8 Gadzooks, lackaday
rejection: 4 heck, pfui, phoo 6 phooey
relief: 4 phew, whew 8 gracious
reproach: 3 tch, tsk, tut 4 pfui, phoo, tush, well 6 phooey, tsk tsk, tut-tut
repugnance: 3 ack, ick, ugh 4 yuck 5 yecch
sailor: 4 ahoy 5 avast 7 heave ho
satisfaction: 3 ooh, yum 5 uh-huh, voilà 6 yum-yum
scaring-away: 4 scat, shoo 5 scram 6 begone 8 scramola
Scottish: 3 och
silence: 4 hush 5 quiet, shush 7 hushaby
sneezing: 5 achoo 6 ahchoo, hachoo 7 kerchoo
snoring: 3 zzz
sorrow: 4 alas 5 alack 8 lackaday, welladay, wellaway
Spanish: 5 salud 6 arriba
spitting: 4 ptui 6 ptooey
startling: 3 boo 5 whoop
success: 5 voilà
suddenness: 5 bingo
support: 3 yay, yea
surprise: 3 aah, aha, gee, hey, huh, och, oho, say, why, wow, yow 4 arra, dear, egad, gosh, jeez, my my, oops, phew, uh-oh, well, yipe 5 arrah, blimy, egads, golly, hello, hoo-ha, whoof, wowie, yipes 6 blimey, by Jove, crikey, cripes, hoo-hah, indeed, jiminy, whoops 7 brother, by jingo, caramba, goldarn, goldurn, heavens, heigh-ho, holy cow, horrors, jeepers, jimminy 8 by cracky, gracious, holy moly
taunting: 3 oho
teen ~: 3 rad
telephone: 5 hello 8 greeting 10 salutation
toast: 5 prost, salud, skoal 6 l'chaim, prosit 7 cheerio, l'chayim, lehayim 8 lechayim
triumph: 3 aha, olé 5 hoo-ha, voilà 6 eureka, gotcha, hoo-hah, yippee 7 whoopee, whoopie
trouble: 4 help, oh-oh, uh-oh 5 yipes
understanding: 4 okay 5 right 6 righto
unhappiness: 4 alas 5 alack 8 lackaday
Valley Girl ~: 5 oh wow
warning: 3 grr, nix 4 ahem, oh-oh, uh-oh 7 gangway
weariness: 4 blah 5 ho-hum 7 heigh-ho 10 dullsville
Western ~: 5 howdy, wahoo
winter: 3 brr
wistful ~: 4 ah me, alas 5 oh gee
with a drum roll: 4 ta-da 5 ta-dah
wonder: 3 boy, gee, wow 4 gosh 5 golly, hello 6 jiminy, whizzo 7 jeepers, jimminy

exclamation ___: 4 mark 5 point
exclude: 3 ban, bar 4 omit, oust, shun, shut, skip, tabu, veto 5 block, debar, eject, evict, expel, spurn 6 bounce, delete, disbar, exempt, forbid, ignore, outlaw, pass on, rebuff, reject, remove 7 disdain, dismiss, embargo, keep out, lock out, prevent, rule out, say no to, shut off, shut out 8 count out, disallow, drive out, force out, get rid of, leave out, pass over, preclude, prohibit, throw out, turn down 9 blackball, blacklist, cast aside, eliminate, foreclose, freeze out, interdict, ostracize, proscribe, repudiate 10 disinherit, monopolize
prefix: 3 dis-, for-
excluded: 5 apart 6 exempt 9 nonliable, unwelcome
excluding: 3 bar 6 except 7 besides 9 apart from, aside from
none: 3 all 5 fully, whole 6 entire, solely, wholly 7 totally, utterly 8 complete, entirely, everyone 9 everybody 10 completely, everything
exclusion: 3 ban, bar 4 skip, tabu 6 ouster 7 boycott, embargo, lockout, ousting, refusal, removal 8 ejection, eviction, omission 9 blackball, debarment, debarring, discharge, dismissal, exception, expulsion, interdict, occlusion, ostracism, rejection 10 preclusion, prevention, relegation, separation, suspension
reason: 4 no ID
___ exclusion principle: 5 Pauli
exclusive: 4 posh, sole 5 elite, ritzy, scoop, smart, swank, swish 6 classy, closed, deluxe, inside, modish, narrow, select, single, swanky, unique 7 private, special, stylish 8 clannish, cliquish, personal, singular, snobbish, unshared 9 sectarian, undivided 10 individual, particular, privileged, restricted, segregated, upper-crust
group: 4 club 5 elect, elite 6 clique
of: 5 minus 6 except 7 besides, without 8 omitting 9 apart from, aside from, other than 10 leaving out

exclusively: 3 all 4 only 5 alone 6 purely, solely, wholly 8 entirely
excogitate: 9 hammer out, speculate 10 deliberate
excommunicate: 3 ban, bar 4 oust 5 eject, expel 6 banish 7 cast out 9 ostracize, proscribe
excommunication, grounds for: 6 heresy
ex-con: 7 parolee
excoriate: 4 damn, flay, gall, skin, zing 5 abuse, chafe, roast, scold, strip 6 abrade, assail, attack, berate, rebuke, scathe, scrape, vilify 7 censure, condemn, lambast, reprove, scourge, upbraid 8 chastise, denounce, lambaste, reproach, strip off, tear into 9 castigate, criticize
excrete: 4 pass 5 expel, sweat 6 remove 8 perspire, throw off
excruciate: 4 rack 5 abuse 6 harrow 7 agonize, torment, torture 8 maltreat, mistreat
excruciating: 5 acute, sharp 6 severe 7 intense, painful, racking, searing 8 grueling, piercing, stabbing 9 torturous
exculpate: 5 clear 6 acquit, pardon 7 absolve, forgive, release 9 discharge, exonerate, vindicate
exculpation: 4 plea 5 alibi, reply, story 6 answer, excuse, reason, retort 7 defense 8 response 9 rejoinder
excurse: 6 ramble
excursion: 3 run 4 hike, ride, tour, trip, turn 5 drive, jaunt, sally 6 cruise, junket, outing, picnic, ramble, safari, travel 7 journey 9 round trip, wandering 10 digression, expedition
Excursion: 3 SUV 4 Ford
excursionist: 8 wayfarer
__ excursion module: 5 lunar
excursive: 7 aimless 8 rambling 9 desultory, wandering 10 digressive, tangential
excusable: 6 venial 7 tenable 9 allowable, not too bad, plausible 10 condonable, defensible, forgivable, pardonable, reasonable, remittable, vindicable
excuse: 4 call, free, plea, tale 5 alibi, clear, I can't, let go, remit, spare, story 6 acquit, cop-out, exempt, let off, pardon, reason, wink at 7 absolve, condone, defense, evasion, forgive, justify, pretext, release, warrant 8 bear with, occasion, overlook, pretense, tolerate 9 rationale, vindicate, whitewash 10 sour grapes
  like a poor ~: 4 lame, thin, weak 6 feeble 10 inadequate
  me: 5 sorry 6 whoops
  (oneself): 6 absent
excused: 4 free 5 spare 6 exempt, let off 7 cleared 8 absolved, excluded, released 10 off the hook, privileged
Excuse me!: 3 say 4 ahem, oops 6 yoo-hoo
Excuse me?: 3 huh 4 what
excusez-__: 3 moi
__ exeat: 4 bene
exec: 3 CEO 4 boss, veep 6 bigwig, gerent, leader, top dog, veepee 7 captain, manager 8 director, higher-up, kingfish, official, superior 9 authority, big cheese, commander 10 head honcho
  account ~: 3 rep
  business: 3 mgt. 4 mgmt. 10 management
  car: 4 limo
  corp. ~: 2 GM, VP 3 CEO, CFO, COO, dir., mgr., mgt. 4 mgmt., mngr., pres., prez, veep 5 admin., treas. 6 veepee
  deg.: 3 MBA
  helper: 4 aide, asst., secy. 5 steno 9 assistant, secretary
  magazine ~: 6 editor 9 publisher
  schedule: 6 agenda
exec. __: 3 dir.
__ exec.: 4 acct.
execrable: 3 low 4 evil, foul, grim, poor, ugly, vile 5 awful, curst, lousy, seamy, woful 6 crumby, crummy, cursed, dismal, horrid, odious, rotten, woeful 7 accurst, baleful, baneful, beastly, doleful, ghastly, hateful, heinous, satanic 8 accursed, devilish, dreadful, God-awful, grievous, horrible, horrific, inferior, infernal, shameful, stinking, terrible, wretched 9 abhorrent, appalling, atrocious, defective, frightful, insidious, loathsome, miserable, monstrous, nefarious, obnoxious, offensive, repellant, repellent, repulsive, revolting, satanical 10 abominable, confounded, deplorable, despicable, detestable, disastrous, disgusting, horrendous, virtueless
execrate: 4 hate 5 abhor 6 detest, loathe 7 despise, dislike 9 abominate, blaspheme
execration: 4 hate 6 hatred 9 blasphemy, damnation, profanity 10 abhorrence
execute: 5 apply, stage 6 effect, finish, fulfil 7 achieve, fulfill, perform, pull off, put over 8 bring off, carry out, complete, dispense, transact 9 discharge, implement 10 accomplish, administer, consummate, effectuate, mastermind, perpetrate, put through, take care of
  as vengeance: 5 wreak
  perfectly: 4 nail
executed: 4 done 7 wrought
  deftly ~: 4 neat 5 clean, nifty 6 clever
execution: 5 doing 6 action 9 discharge, enactment, operation, rendering, technique, treatment 10 completion, expression, fulfilling
Executioner's Song, The author: Norman Mailer
executive: 3 CEO 4 boss 5 brass, chief, mogul 6 gerent, honcho, leader, ruling, top dog, tycoon 7 captain, headman, manager, officer 8 big wheel, brass hat, director, governor, higher-up, kingfish, managing, official, overseer, superior 9 authority, commander, directing, governing, key player, organizer 10 government, head honcho, leadership, management, managerial, supervisor
  department heads: 5 board 7 Cabinet, council 8 advisors 9 committee 10 brain trust, counselors
  extra: 4 perc, perk 5 bonus
executive __: 4 park 5 class, order 7 council, officer, session
__ executive: 5 chief 7 account
Executive: 3 car 4 auto 7 Pontiac
Executive __: 5 Suite 7 Mansion
executive-branch dept.: 3 Agr., NSA, NSC, OMB
Executive Decision (1996 film)
  cast: Halle Berry, Kurt Russell, Steven Seagal
__ executive officer: 5 chief
executives: 4 head 5 board, brass, panel, suits 6 bosses, regime 7 cabinet, council 8 top brass, trustees 9 authority, committee, directors, employers, overseers, syndicate 10 management
Executive Suite (1954 film)
  cast: June Allyson, William Holden, Barbara Stanwyck
  director: Robert Wise
executor: 5 agent 7 trustee 8 guardian, watchdog 9 custodian
  concern: 4 heir, will 6 estate
exedra: 4 seat 5 bench, chair
exegesis: 7 remarks 8 analysis, critique, treatise 9 criticism, editorial 10 commentary, exposition
exemplar: 4 hero, type 5 gauge, ideal, light, model 6 lesson 7 epitome, paragon, pattern 8 original, paradigm, specimen, standard 9 archetype, precedent, prototype 10 embodiment, touchstone
exemplary: 3 def, rad 4 aces, A-one, boss, braw, cool, dece, fine, gear, good, keen, neat, nice, phat, pure, tuff 5 clean, dandy, ducky, grand, great, ideal, marvy, model, moral, neato, nobby, prime, slick, super, swell 6 bang on, bang-up, bonzer, bosker, choice, divine, dreamy, far-out, gnarly, groovy, lovely, peachy, slap-up, spot on, superb, terrif, tiptop, unreal, whizzo, wicked, worthy 7 amazing, awesome, capital, classic, corking, perfect, ripping, skookum, stellar, sublime, upright 8 dazzling, especial, eximious, fabulous, five-star, four-star, frabjous, glorious, heavenly, innocent, jim-dandy, laudable, slam-bang, smashing, splendid, standout, sterling, stickout, superior, terrific, top-level, topnotch, very good, virtuous, wondrous 9 admirable, blameless, bodacious, classical, Endsville, estimable, excellent, exquisite, faultless, first-rate, guiltless, high-grade, honorable, hunky-dory, just right, marvelous, righteous, sollicker, top-flight, unrivaled, wholesome, wonderful 10 creditable, first-class, hotsy-totsy, inculpable, jack-a-dandy, out of sight, peachy-keen, phenomenal, remarkable, stupendous, super-duper, unrivalled
  combining form: 4 arch-
exempli __: 5 causa 6 gratia
exemplification: 4 case 6 sample 8 instance, occasion, specimen 9 precedent, situation 10 occurrence
exemplify: 4 cite 6 depict, embody, imbody, typify 7 display 8 stand for 9 elucidate, enlighten, epitomize, interpret, personify, represent, symbolize 10 illuminate, illustrate
exempt: 4 free 5 clear, spare 6 excuse, immune, let off 7 absolve, cleared, exclude, excused, forgive, release, relieve 8 absolved, excluded, released 9 nonliable, not liable 10 off the hook, privileged, vindicated
  (from): 4 free 6 spared
__-exempt: 3 non, tax
exemption: 5 right 7 liberty, license, release 9 acquittal, condition, discharge, franchise, privilege 10 absolution
exercise: 3 irk, jog, try, use, vex 4 gall, have, toil, walk, work 5 annoy, apply, chafe, drill, labor, put in, sport, teach, theme, train, upset, wield, worry 6 action, bother, chin-up, effort, employ, get fit, lesson, resort, ritual, tone up, tune up 7 agitate, disturb, exploit, keep fit, operate, perturb, provoke, trouble, utilize, workout 8 activity, aerobics, distress, limber up, movement, practice, pump iron, put forth, rehearse, training 9 isotonics, operation 10 daily dozen, discipline, employment, gymnastics, isometrics, recitation, recreation
  attire: 6 shorts, sweats, T-shirt 7 leotard, tank top 9 sweatband
  floor ~: 5 event
  judgment: 4 deem, feel, hold, rate, view 5 think 6 assume, reckon, regard 7 believe, imagine, presume, suppose, surmise 8 consider
  martial arts ~: 4 kata
  meditation ~: 4 yoga
  need: 3 mat 5 bench, water 7 barbell, mirrors, trainer 8 dumbbell, Nautilus 9 treadmill
  one's franchise: 4 pick, vote 5 elect 6 choose, opt for, select, vote in 7 vote for 10 decide upon
  place: 3 gym, spa 4 club, YMCA, YWCA 10 health club
  result: 4 ache 5 speed 6 growth 7 agility, fitness 8 leanness, strength, wiriness
  target: 3 abs 4 flab, hips, neck, pecs 5 delts, quads, thigh 6 biceps, calves, glutes 7 triceps 8 forearms, shoulder 9 spare tire 10 hamstrings, midsection
  training ~: 5 drill 8 maneuver
  workout: 3 dip 4 curl 5 press, shrug, sit up, squat 6 chin-up, push-up 7 routine 10 bench press
exercise __: 4 bike 5 price 7 bicycle
__ exercise: 5 field, floor 7 aerobic
exercised: 9 concerned 10 distressed
exercises: 5 drill 9 athletics, maneuvers
exert: 3 ply 4 push 5 apply, spend, sweat, wield 6 employ, put out, strain, strive 7 trouble, try hard, utilize 8 put forth, put to use 9 make use of 10 put forward
  minimal effort: 5 coast, glide, slide 6 cruise
  oneself: 3 try 4 moil, push, work 5 labor 6 bother, strain, strive 8 bust a gut, endeavor, go all out, struggle
  pressure: 6 extort, lean on 7 squeeze
exertion: 4 dint, toil, work 5 labor, pains, sweat 6 action, effort, energy, strain 7 travail, trouble 8 activity, endeavor, hard work, industry, striving, struggle 9 diligence
Exeter: 4 city, town
  locale: 5 Devon 7 England
exeunt __: 5 omnes
ex facto: 8 actually
exfoliate: 4 molt, peel, shed 5 flake 8 flake off, laminate, scale off, throw off
ex-GI: 3 vet
  garb: 5 mufti 7 civvies
  org.: 3 VFW
exhalation: 3 air, gas 4 odor, sigh 5 steam, vapor 6 breath 8 emission 9 effluvium, emanation
exhale: 4 blow, emit, puff, sigh 6 let out 7 blow out, breathe, give off, respire 10 breathe out
Exhale (1995 song) artist: Whitney Houston
exhaust: 3 eat, sag, sap, tax, use 4 flag, jade, lose, milk, poop, tire, wane, wear 5 bleed, blunt, drain, eat up, empty, spend, use up, weary 6 finish, impair, reduce, run out, shrink, soften, unload, weaken 7 burn out, consume, deflate, deplete, fatigue, play out, poop out, suck dry, tire out, vitiate, wear out 8 bleed dry, enervate, enfeeble, evacuate, overwork, run out of, squander, wear down 9 attenuate, dissipate, effluvium, indispose, prostrate, run ragged, tucker out, undermine 10 debilitate, devitalize, run through
  emanation: 4 fume
  opposite: 6 intake
exhaust __: 3 fan 4 pipe 5 trail 6 system
exhausted: 3 dry, out 4 bare, beat, gone, limp, weak, worn 5 all in, empty,

faint, spent, tired, trite, weary, wiped **6** barren, bushed, dished, effete, sapped, vacant, winded **7** all gone, at an end, drained, far-gone, gulping, haggard, run-down, worn out **8** care-worn, dog-tired, frazzled, out of gas **9** bone-weary, dead tired, destitute, enervated, infertile, prostrate, washed-out **10** breathless, dissipated, knocked out, prostrated, squandered
exhausting: **4** hard **5** tough **6** tiring, uphill **7** arduous, hard-won, onerous, tedious **8** grueling, tiresome **9** demanding, difficult, fatiguing, laborious, murderous, strenuous **10** enervating
exhaustion: **6** anemia **7** anaemia, fatigue, frazzle **9** emptiness, lassitude, tiredness, weariness **10** absorption, bankruptcy, enervation, feebleness
exclamation ~: **4** phew **6** I'm beat
exhaustive: **3** big **4** A to Z, full **5** total, uncut, whole **6** all-out, entire, global, minute **7** in-depth, plenary **8** complete, detailed, profound, sweeping, thorough, whole hog **9** extensive, full-blown, full-dress, full-range, full-scale, intensive, out-and-out, searching, unreduced **10** definitive, soup to nuts, unabridged
exhaustively: **4** A to Z, hard **7** in depth
exhibit: **3** air **4** bare, bear, have, leak, look, show, wear **5** array, exude, sight, sport **6** detail, evince, expose, flaunt, lay out, parade, reveal, unmask, unveil **7** bespeak, display, divulge, feature, lay bare, let slip, present, produce, reflect, roll out, show off, signify, trot out, uncover **8** disclose, evidence, manifest, register, showcase, specimen **9** advertise, make clear, make known, make plain, promenade, put on view **10** illustrate, make public, wave around
exhibition: **4** expo, fair, show **5** array, scene, sight **6** airing, museum **7** display, pageant, showing **9** fireworks, spectacle **10** appearance, exposition
hall: **5** salon **7** gallery **8** pavilion
exhibition __: **4** game
exhibitionist: **7** showoff
exhilarate: **4** buoy, lift, send **5** boost, cheer, elate, flush, liven, pep up, rouse **6** buoy up, lift up, perk up, revive, thrill, uplift **7** animate, boost up, cheer up, delight, enliven, gladden, refresh, satisfy **8** enspirit, inspirit **9** encourage, make happy, stimulate **10** invigorate
exhilarated: **4** high **5** happy **8** inspired
exhilarating: **4** racy **5** brisk, heady **6** yeasty **7** bracing **8** electric, exciting, stirring **10** refreshing
exhilaration: **3** joy **4** glee **5** bliss, gusto **6** gaiety, gayety **7** delight, elation, rapture **8** euphoria, felicity, optimism **9** happiness **10** ebullience
exhort: **3** bid **4** goad, prod, spur, urge, warn **5** press **6** advise, charge, incite, preach, prompt **7** beseech, caution, counsel, entreat **8** admonish, call upon, harangue, persuade, press for **9** encourage, recommend
exhortation: **4** talk **6** charge, sermon, speech, urging **7** caution, counsel, goading, warning **8** entreaty, harangue
exclamation: **3** eat **5** order **8** alley-oop
exhume: **5** dig up **7** unearth **8** disinter
exigency: **3** jam, law **4** lack, need, pass, want **5** pinch **6** crisis, plight, scrape **7** dilemma, urgency **8** distress, hardship, pressure, quandary, zero hour **9** emergency, necessity, requisite **10** difficulty, occurrence
exigent: **4** dire **5** acute, grave **6** urgent **7** burning, crucial, hurry-up, instant **8** critical, exacting, pressing **9** clamorous, demanding, important **10** imperative, oppressive
exiguity: **4** lack, need **6** dearth **7** absence, deficit, paucity, poverty **8** scarcity, shortage, sparsity **9** depletion, shortfall, shrinkage **10** deficiency, inadequacy, meagerness, scantiness, slightness
exiguous: **4** poor, thin **5** small, spare **6** meager, minute, paltry, scanty, skimpy, slight, sparse **7** limited, slender, tenuous **10** inadequate, negligible
exiguousness: **4** lack, need, want **6** dearth **7** absence, paucity, poverty **8** scarcity, shortage, sparsity **9** scantness **10** deficiency, inadequacy, meagerness
exile: **4** oust **5** expel **6** banish, deport, pariah, punish, uproot **7** cast out, outcast, refugee, turn out **8** deportee, diaspora, displace, drive out, Napoleon, relegate, renegade **9** dismissal, expulsion, ostracism, ostracize, proscribe, transport **10** banishment, expatriate
site: **4** Elba **8** St. Helena
Exiles author: James Joyce
Exile, The author: Pearl S. Buck
eximious: **3** def, rad **4** aces, A-one, boss, braw, cool, dece, fine, gear, keen, neat, nice, phat, tuff **5** dandy, ducky, grand, great, marvy, neato, nobby, prime, slick, super, swell **6** bang on, bang-up, bonzer, bosker, choice, divine, dreamy, far-out, gnarly, groovy, lovely, peachy, slap-up, spot on, superb, terrif, tiptop, unreal, whizzo, wicked **7** amazing, awesome, capital, corking, perfect, ripping, skookum, stellar, sublime **8** dazzling, especial, fabulous, five-star, four-star, frabjous, glorious, heavenly, jim-dandy, slam-bang, smashing, splendid, standout, sterling, stickout, superior, terrific, top-level, topnotch, very good, wondrous **9** bodacious, Endsville, excellent, exemplary, exquisite, first-rate, high-grade, hunky-dory, marvelous, sollicker, top-flight, wonderful **10** first-class, hotsy-totsy, jack-a-dandy, out of sight, peachy-keen, phenomenal, remarkable, stupendous, super-duper
exist: **2** be **3** are, lie **4** fare, go on, last, live, stay **5** abide, dwell, get by, occur **6** endure, remain, reside **7** breathe, subsist, survive **8** continue, get along
did not ~: **5** wasn't
didst ~: **4** wert
does not ~: **4** isn't
do not ~: **5** aren't
ender: **3** ent **4** ence
generally: **7** prevail
in great numbers: **4** teem **5** crowd, swarm, swell **6** abound, infest, thrive **8** flourish, overflow
just ~: **4** loaf **7** go to pot, subsist **8** go to seed, languish, stagnate, vegetate
naturally: **5** dwell **6** inhere **7** inhabit
existed: **3** was **4** been, were
existence: **4** esse, life **5** being **6** entity, living **7** reality **8** lifetime, presence, survival **9** actuality, animation, endurance, real world **10** occurrence, permanence
bring into ~: **4** cast, form, make, rear **5** beget, breed, hatch, order, set up, spawn, train **6** cook up, create, effect, father, invent, mature **7** arrange, bring up, compose, concoct, develop, outline, pioneer, produce, think up, turn out **8** assemble, conceive, engineer, generate, initiate **9** actualize, construct, establish, fabricate, hammer out, originate, take shape **10** give life to, mastermind
combining form: **3** ont- **4** onto-
come into ~: **5** begin, start **6** grow up, spring **9** originate
in ~: **4** live **5** alive **6** actual, living, viable **7** organic, working **9** breathing, conscious
in French: **3** vie
in Latin: **4** esse
span of ~: **4** days, life **5** years **6** course, period **8** lifetime
existent: **4** live **5** alive **6** actual, living **8** physical **9** something **10** unimagined
Existential Essays author: Colin Wilson
existentialist, French: **4** Gide **5** Camus, Genet **6** Sartre
existing: **4** real **5** alive **6** actual, extant, living **8** standing **10** unimagined
not ~: **6** irreal
exit: **2** go **4** door, gate, quit, vent **5** adieu, go out, leave, scram, split **6** beat it, decamp, depart, egress, emerge, exodus, get out, go away, outlet, refuge, retire, way out **7** doorway, getaway, goodbye, head out, leaving, move out, off-ramp, opening, passage, pull out, push off, retreat, take off, turnoff, walk out **8** farewell, hatchway, hightail, porthole, shove off, slip away, withdraw **9** departure, disappear, egression, take a hike **10** evacuation, fire escape, passageway, retirement, shuffle off, withdrawal
mine ~: **4** adit
poll participant: **5** voter
quickly: **3** hie, lam **4** flee **5** lam it
exit __: **3** tax **4** poll, ramp **5** pupil
Exit: **4** sign **8** road sign
Exit Laughing author: Irvin S. Cobb
exit-ramp
sight: **5** diner, motel **10** gas station
word: **3** Slo
Exit the King author: Eugène Ionesco
__ Exit to Brooklyn: **4** Last
Exit to Eden author: Anne Rice
__ ex machina: **4** deus
Ex-Mrs. Bradford, The (1936 film)
cast: Jean Arthur, James Gleason, William Powell
exo-
opposite: **4** endo-, ento-
exobiology: **7** science
exocarp: **4** peel
exocrine __: **5** gland
exodus: **4** exit **6** egress, flight, hegira, hejira **7** leaving, retreat **8** trekking **9** defection, departure, desertion, egression, migration **10** emigration, evacuation, relocation, resettling, withdrawal
Exodus: **4** film, song **5** novel
artist: Ferrante and Teicher
author: Leon Uris
cast: Lee J. Cobb, John Derek, Peter Lawford, Sal Mineo, Paul Newman, Ralph Richardson, Eva Marie Saint
character: **5** Aaron, Moses **6** Joshua
director: Otto Preminger
feast of the ~: **5** seder
follower: **3** Lev. **5** Levit. **9** Leviticus
food: **5** manna
idol: **4** calf
mountain: **5** Horeb, Sinai
preceder: **3** Gen. **7** Genesis
role: **3** Ari
verb: **5** shalt
Exodus Theme (1961 song) artist: Mantovani
Exon: **5** James
exonerate: **5** clear, remit **6** acquit, let off, pardon **7** absolve, forgive, release **9** allow to go, disburden, discharge, exculpate, vindicate, whitewash
exonerated: **10** off the hook, vindicated
exorbitance: **4** glut, orgy, posh **5** frill, ritzy, waste **6** excess, luxury, wealth **7** nimiety, surfeit, surplus **8** elegance, hedonism, opulence, overflow, plethora, splendor **9** affluence, decadence, profusion **10** high living, immoderacy, indulgence, lavishness, prosperity, redundancy
exorbitant: **4** dear, high, rich, tall **5** large, pricy, steep, stiff, undue **6** costly, pricey **7** extreme **9** excessive, expensive, overboard **10** at a premium, high-priced, immoderate, inordinate, out of sight, outrageous
interest: **5** usury
exorcise: **5** expel, purge, rid of **6** purify, remove **7** cast out, dismiss **8** drive out
exorcism: **4** rite **5** spell **6** ritual **8** ejection
target: **5** demon **6** daemon, daimon
Exorcist, The (1973 film)
cast: Linda Blair, Ellen Burstyn, Lee J. Cobb, Jason Miller, Max von Sydow
director: William Friedkin
role: **5** Regan
exordium: **5** onset, start **6** advent, outset **7** kickoff, leadoff, preface, prelude **8** foreword, preamble **9** inception
exoteric: **4** open **5** outer **6** public **7** outside, outward **8** external
exotic: **3** odd **4** rare **5** alien **6** arcane, scanty, scarce **7** curious, foreign, new wave, strange, unknown, unusual **8** imported, romantic, uncommon **9** fantastic, glamorous, recherché **10** avant-garde, hard to find, outlandish, unfamiliar
name meaning ~: **7** Barbara
expand: **3** enl., pad, wax **4** boom, grow, open, rise **5** add on, add to, bloat, boost, build, bulge, plump, splay, swell, widen **6** beef up, blow up, bulk up, deepen, dilate, extend, fan out, fatten, gather, let out, puff up, pump up, spread, unfold **7** amplify, augment, balloon, bolster, broaden, build up, burgeon, develop, distend, drag out, enlarge, fill out, inflate, magnify, open out, prolong, radiate, stretch, thicken, upsurge **8** bourgeon, elongate, escalate, flesh out, heighten, increase, lengthen, multiply, mushroom, protract **9** branch out, diversify, elaborate, embellish, expatiate, get bigger, intumesce, outspread, spread out **10** aggrandize, exaggerate, grow larger, liberalize
a compressed file: **5** unzip
expanded __: **4** code **5** metal **7** plastic
expanse: **4** area, belt, land, room **5** field, orbit, range, reach, realm, scope, sheet, space, sweep, tract, width **6** extent, length, radius, region, spread **7** acreage, breadth, stretch, surface **8** clearing **9** immensity, largeness, magnitude, territory
of land: **4** land, lots **5** acres, tract
sandy ~: **5** beach **6** desert, Sahara
treeless ~: **5** pampa
vast ~: **3** sea **5** ocean
expansion: **5** boost, space **6** growth, length, spread **7** buildup **8** addition, dilation, increase, swelling **9** diffusion, evolution, extension, inflation, unfolding, unfurling **10** distension, elongation, maturation, prosperity
expansion __: **3** bit **4** bolt, card, slot, team, wave **5** attic, joint **7** chamber

expansive: **3** big **4** free, open, vast, wide **5** ample, broad, gushy, large, roomy **6** genial, lavish **7** affable, gushing **8** effusive, far-flung, friendly, outgoing, sociable, spacious, sweeping, thorough **9** capacious, extensive, garrulous, inclusive, resilient, talkative **10** bigmouthed, commodious, gregarious, loquacious, stretching, unreserved, voluminous, widespread
view: **5** vista
expatiate: **5** speak, spout **6** expand, ramble, recite **7** amplify, descant, discant, enlarge **8** perorate **9** discourse, elaborate, explicate, prerorate **10** dissertate
expatiation: **4** talk **7** descant, discant, monolog **9** discourse, monologue
expatriate: **5** exile, expel **6** banish, deport, émigré **7** outcast, refugee **8** deportee, displace, emigrant, relegate **9** ostracize, proscribe, transport
expect: **4** hope, look, rely, wait **5** await, think, trust **6** assume, bank on, intend, reckon, rely on **7** believe, count on, hope for, look for, presume, propose, require, suppose, surmise, suspect, wait for **8** theorize, watch for **9** count upon **10** anticipate, hang out for, understand
lead to ~: **7** promise
like you'd ~: **5** usual **6** as ever, normal **7** typical
too much: **8** overrate
expectancy: **4** hope **8** suspense **9** assurance **10** assumption, confidence, conjecture, impatience, likelihood, prediction
__ expectancy: **4** life
expectant: **4** agog, atip **5** alert, eager, ready **6** gravid, on edge **7** anxious, hopeful **8** enceinte, pregnant, watchful **9** confident, presuming **10** breathless, in suspense, optimistic
expectation: **4** hope **5** hunch, trust **6** belief **7** outlook, thought **8** optimism, prospect **9** prognosis
contrary to ~: **5** oddly
in ~ of: **5** until
of the worst: **9** pessimism
Expectation __: **4** Week **6** Sunday
__ Expectations: **5** Great
expectations, like some: **5** unmet
expected: **3** due **5** typic, usual **6** coming, likely **7** regular, typical **8** oncoming, probable, upcoming
as ~: **4** duly **5** on cue **8** of course
is ~ to: **5** ought **6** should
not as ~: **5** oddly
result: **3** par **4** norm
sooner than ~: **5** early **9** in advance, premature
expecting: **6** gravid **8** enceinte, pregnant **9** confident
be ~: **4** wait **5** await **8** watch for **10** anticipate
expectorate: **4** spit
expediency: **5** means, shift, worth **6** agency, device, method, resort, tactic **7** benefit, fitness, utility **8** prudence, resource, strategy **9** advantage, diplomacy, readiness
with ~: **4** fast **5** apace **7** quickly, rapidly, swiftly **8** in no time, speedily **9** hurriedly, posthaste
expedient: **3** fit **4** meet, plan **5** means, shift, trick **6** agency, device, method, refuge, resort, tactic, timely, useful **7** fitting, measure, politic, prudent, sleight, stopgap, vehicle **8** artifice, recourse, resource, strategy, suitable **9** advisable, desirable, effective, judicious, makeshift, necessary, opportune, practical, pragmatic, stratagem **10** beneficial, convenient, instrument, jury-rigged, profitable, seasonable, substitute, subterfuge, time-saving, worthwhile
expedite: **4** ease, push, rush **5** hurry, speed **6** assist, hasten, step up **7** forward, further, quicken, speed up **9** fast-track **10** accelerate, facilitate
expedition: **4** tour, trek, trip **5** haste, hurry, jaunt, quest, sally, speed **6** junket, outing, safari, search, travel, voyage **7** caravan, crusade, journey **8** alacrity, campaign, celerity, dispatch, rapidity, velocity **9** cavalcade, excursion, explorers, fleetness, quickness, readiness, swiftness **10** enterprise, promptness, travellers
need: **5** scout
sponsor: **3** NGS
__ expedition: **7** fishing
Expedition: **3** SUV **4** Ford
expeditious: **4** fast **5** brisk, fleet, hasty, quick, rapid, swift **6** flying, prompt, racing, snappy, speedy **7** express, hurried, instant **8** punctual **9** breakneck **10** double-time
expeditiously: **3** PDQ **4** fast, soon **5** apace **6** presto **7** fleetly, rapidly, swiftly **8** in a flash, in a jiffy, in no time, pell-mell, promptly **9** forthwith, instantly, like a shot, posthaste
expeditiousness: **5** haste **8** celerity, dispatch
expel: **3** ban, bar, can, rid **4** boot, dump, emit, fire, oust, rout, spew, spue, vent **5** chase, egest, eject, empty, evict, exile, exude, issue, purge, shoot, spout **6** banish, deport, punish, remove **7** boot out, cashier, cast out, diffuse, dismiss, drum out, emanate, exclude, excrete, extrude, give off, kick out, radiate, turn out **8** disgorge, displace, drive out, exorcise, exorcize, force out, get rid of, jettison, relegate, throw off, throw out **9** blackball, discharge, eliminate, order to go, ostracize, send forth **10** dispossess, expatriate
expend: **3** pay, use **4** lose **5** drain, put in, spend, use up **6** finish, lavish, lay out, outlay, pay out **7** consume, deplete, fork out, play out **8** disburse, shell out, squander **9** dissipate **10** run through
expendable: **6** excess **7** useless **8** needless, unneeded **10** disposable, unrequired
one: **4** pawn
expenditure: **3** use **4** cost **5** outgo, price **6** charge, outlay, upkeep **7** payment
acknowledgment: **3** rct. **7** receipt
monthly ~: **4** rent
__ expenditure: **3** tax **7** capital
expense: **3** fee, tax **4** cost, fare **5** debit, outgo, price, value **6** amount, charge, damage, outlay, tariff, towage **7** damages, payment, payroll **8** overhead
at the ~ of yours truly: **4** on me
bear the ~: **3** pay **5** treat
incidental ~: **3** tip
office ~: **4** rent **5** lease **8** overhead
receipt: **3** vou. **7** voucher
spare the ~ of: **5** grant, offer **6** afford, bestow, impart, render **7** furnish, provide
expense __: **7** account
__ expense: **4** at no **7** accrued, spare no
expenses: **5** outgo **6** outlay, upkeep **8** overhead
after ~: **3** net
cut ~: **4** save **5** skimp
estimate ~: **6** budget, ration **8** allocate **9** apportion
keep ~ low: **4** save **6** scrape, scrimp **8** conserve, roll back **9** economize **10** cut corners
net plus ~: **5** gross
__-expenses-paid: **3** all
expensive: **4** dear, high, posh, rich **5** fancy, pricy, ritzy, steep, stiff, swank **6** costly, deluxe, lavish, pricey, swanky **7** sky-high, upscale **8** precious, splendid, valuable **9** big-ticket, excessive, luxurious, priceless, sumptuous **10** at a premium, exorbitant, high-priced, out of sight, overpriced
auto: **3** BMW **5** Caddy, Lexus, Rolls **7** Ferrari, Lincoln, Porsche, Town Car **8** Cadillac, Maserati, Mercedes
not as ~: **4** less
Expensive People author: Joyce Carol Oates
experience: **3** see **4** face, have, know, live, meet, view **5** enjoy, event, savor, share, skill, stand, taste **6** fall on, record, sample, suffer, wisdom **7** episode, know-how, receive, sustain, undergo, witness **8** exposure, fall upon, incident, intimacy, maturity, meet with, practice, stand for, training **9** actuality, adventure, awareness, encounter, get to know, go through, happening, knowledge, seasoning **10** background, empiricism, occurrence, upbringing
bad ~: **4** drag **6** bummer **9** nightmare
combining form: **7** empirio- **8** empirico-
gain ~: **3** see **5** glean, learn, study **6** absorb, master, pick up, soak up, take in **7** catch on, find out **8** discover, pore over **9** ascertain, brush up on, get word of **10** apprentice, get down pat, understand
units of ~: **5** sensa
experience __: **5** table **7** meeting
experienced: **3** ace, old **4** deft, ripe, wise **5** adept, slick **6** adroit, au fait, expert, mature, nimble, versed **7** capable, knowing, learned, skilled, trained, veteran, worldly **8** broken-in, dextrous, familiar, graceful, masterly, prepared, seasoned, skillful **9** competent, dexterous, efficient, masterful, qualified **10** proficient
less ~: **5** newer
not ~: **3** raw **4** naif **5** naive
old-style: **5** verst **6** verste, werste
one: **3** pro, vet **6** old pro **7** old hand
Experience keeps __ school: **5** a dear
experiential: **7** empiric, factual **9** empirical, practical, pragmatic
experiment: **3** try **4** test **5** essay, prove, study, trial **6** sample, tryout **7** attempt, venture **8** rehearse, trial run **9** procedure, rehearsal, shakedown, speculate **10** dissection, enterprise, futz around
atomic ~: **5** A test, N test
combining form: **7** empirio- **8** empirico-
room: **3** lab
__ experiment: **7** control, thought
experimental: **4** beta, test **5** novel, pilot, trial **8** unproved **9** tentative
animal: **3** rat **6** lab rat **9** guinea pig
experimental __: **7** theater, theatre
experimentalize: **4** test
Experimental Novel, The author: Emile Zola
experimentation: **8** research
Experiment in Autobiography author: H.G. Wells
Experiment in Terror (1962 film)
cast: Glenn Ford, Ross Martin, Stefanie Powers, Lee Remick
director: Blake Edwards
__ Experiment, The: **6** Harrad
expert: **3** ace, apt, dab, pro, wiz **4** able, deft, good, guru, sage, whiz **5** adept, crack, great, handy, maven, mavin, ready, savvy, sharp, slick **6** adroit, artist, au fait, critic, facile, master, nimble, old pro, pundit, savant, source, versed, wizard **7** adviser, advisor, capable, hotshot, knowing, learned, old hand, prodigy, skilled, trained, veteran **8** dextrous, graceful, masterly, schooled, seasoned, skillful, superior, virtuoso **9** authority, black belt, competent, dexterous, efficient, evaluator, masterful, practiced, qualified, unrivaled **10** master hand, proficient, specialist, unrivalled, well-versed
combining form: **7** -meister
ender: **3** -ise
group: **5** panel
in England: **3** dab
expert __: **6** system **7** witness
expertise: **3** art, job **4** ease **5** craft, forte, knack, savvy, skill **6** aplomb **7** ability, aptness, faculty, fluency, know-how, mastery, prowess **8** artistry, deftness **9** adeptness, dexterity, expertise, knowledge **10** competence, department, efficiency, profession, virtuosity
field of ~: **4** area, turf **5** niche
expertly: **4** neat, well **8** worthily
expiate: **5** atone, purge **6** purify, remedy **7** rectify, redress **8** atone for **9** make up for **10** make amends, recompense
expiation: **6** amends, ransom, remedy **7** penance, redress **8** righting **9** atonement, indemnity **10** reparation
expiration: **3** end **5** close **6** ending, finish **9** cessation, departure **10** completion, conclusion
avoid ~: **5** renew
expiration __: **4** date
expire: **3** end **4** quit, stop **5** cease, close, lapse **6** elapse, run out **7** succumb **8** conclude **9** terminate **10** breathe out
expired: **3** out **4** over **6** lapsed, no more, run out **7** elapsed **10** terminated
not ~: **5** valid
expiry: **3** end **5** close **6** ending, finish **9** cessation, departure **10** completion, conclusion
explain: **4** show, tell **5** argue, brief, clear, gloss, prove, solve, state, teach **6** answer, decode, defend, define, recite, record, refine, set out, unfold **7** analyze, clarify, clear up, justify, resolve **8** annotate, construe, decipher, describe, simplify, spell out, untangle **9** adumbrate, elaborate, elucidate, expound on, interpret, make clear, put across, translate **10** account for, illuminate, illustrate, understand
away: **5** gloze **8** minimize **9** gloss over
further: **3** add, say **5** sum up **6** reckon **7** include, throw in **8** figure in **9** enumerate, interject
in Britain: **4** rede
explain __: **4** away
explanation: **3** key **4** plea **5** alibi, basis, cause, gloss, light **6** answer, excuse, reason **7** account, comment, defense, meaning, preface **8** exegesis, solution **9** narration, rationale, statement
seeker's query: **3** why
start of an ~: **4** look
__-explanatory: **4** self
explanatory note: **7** comment
expletive: **5** curse **7** epithet **8** cuss oath, cuss word **9** swear word
delete an ~: **5** bleep **6** censor
mild ~: **3** boy **4** drat, durn, egad, heck **5** egads, golly, pshaw
explicable: **7** soluble **9** countable **10** calculable
explicate: **6** unfold **8** describe **9** bring home, elucidate, expatiate, expound

on, interpret, make clear, make plain, translate **10** illustrate
explication: 5 essay, paper, prose, theme, tract **6** reason, report, thesis **8** critique, exegesis, treatise **9** discourse, monograph, rationale, reasoning, statement **10** annotation, commentary, discussion, exposition
explicit: 4 firm, open, real **5** clear, lucid, plain, sharp, vivid **6** actual, cogent, direct, formal, honest, in view, patent, public **7** evident, exposed, express, graphic, obvious, precise, visible **8** absolute, apparent, clear-cut, concrete, definite, distinct, emphatic, manifest, palpable, positive, readable, specific, tangible, unhidden, unsubtle, unveiled **9** downright, graphical, graspable, outspoken **10** definitive, observable, point-blank, spelled out, unshrouded, well-marked
explicitly: 5 plain, to wit **9** expressly, purposely **10** definitely, point-blank
explicitness: 7 clarity **8** accuracy, lucidity **9** certainty, precision **10** directness, exactitude
explode: 3 pop **4** blow, boom, fire, rage, rave, roar **5** belie, blast, burst, erupt, go off, shoot, sound **6** blow up, debunk, go boom, refute, set off **7** confute, flare up, shatter, smolder, thunder **8** backfire, detonate, disprove, dynamite, have a fit, mushroom, shoot off, smoulder **9** blow a fuse, discharge, discredit, fulminate, shoot down **10** hit the roof, invalidate, prove wrong
exploit: 3 act, tap, use **4** coup, deed, feat, gest, gull, milk, soak, work **5** abuse, apply, doing, geste, stunt, trick **6** action, employ, handle, misuse, play on, prey on, rip off **7** develop, harness, utilize **8** cash in on, escapade, exercise, play upon, profit by **9** adventure, victimize **10** manipulate
daring ~: 4 gest **5** geste, stunt
exploitable: 4 easy **6** usable **7** useable
exploitation: 5 abuse, using **6** misuse
exploited: 7 put upon **8** economic, monetary **9** for-profit **10** commercial, marketable, mercantile, profitable
exploits
in Latin: 8 res geste
tale of heroic ~: 4 saga
exploration: 5 probe, quest **7** enquiry, inquiry
exploratory mission: 5 probe, recon
explore: 2 do **4** hike, roam, rove, seek, sift, tour, view **5** assay, plumb, probe, range, scout **6** forage, go into, search, survey, travel **7** dig into, examine, pioneer, ransack, rummage **8** look into, research, traverse **9** delve into, range over **10** knock about, scrutinize
explorer: 5 diver, scout **7** pioneer **8** traveler, vagabond, wanderer **10** adventurer, pathfinder
Africa ~: 4 Park **5** Baker, Speke **6** Burton **7** Johnson, Stanley **11** Livingstone
Antarctic ~: 4 Byrd, Ross **5** Scott **6** Mawson **8** Amundsen **10** Shackleton
Arctic ~: 3 Rae **4** Ross **5** Davys, Peary **6** Bering, Nansen, Nobile **7** Barents **9** Rasmussen
Australia ~: 6 Mawson **8** Flinders **9** Vancouver
British ~: 3 Rae **4** Cook, Ross **5** Baker, Cabot, Davys, Drake, Parry, Scott, Speke **6** Baffin, Burton, Hudson, Mawson **7** Dampier, Gilbert, Hawkins, Markham, Raleigh, Stanley **8** Flinders, Franklin **9** Frobisher, Vancouver **10** Shackleton
Canada ~: 6 Joliet **7** Cartier, Gilbert, Jolliet **9** Champlain
Caribbean ~: 7 Hawkins **8** Columbus
China ~: 4 Polo
circumnavigation ~: 4 Gray **5** Drake **8** Magellan
Danish ~: 6 Bering **9** Rasmussen
Dutch ~: 6 Tasman **7** Barents
Easter Island ~: 9 Heyerdahl
Florida ~: 11 Ponce de León
French ~: 5 Salle **7** Cartier **8** Cousteau **9** Champlain, David-Neel
German ~: 7 Wegener
Greenland ~: 7 Ericson
Guiana ~: 7 Raleigh
India ~: 6 da Gama
Italian ~: 4 Polo **7** Nobilei **8** Columbus, Vespucci
Mars ~: 5 probe
Mexico ~: 4 Peck **6** Cortés
Mississippi River ~: 6 Joliet **7** Jolliet, La Salle
Mount Everest ~: 6 Norgay **7** Hillary
need: 3 map **6** octant **7** compass, sextant
New Zealand ~: 6 Tasman
North America ~: 5 Cabot **6** Hudson **8** Columbus
Northwest Passage ~: 5 Parry **6** Baffin **7** Gilbert **8** Franklin **9** Frobisher
Norwegian ~: 6 Nansen **7** Ericson **8** Amundsen **9** Heyerdahl
objective: 5 trade
Pacific Ocean ~: 6 Balboa **9** Vancouver
Peru ~: 7 Pizarro
Portuguese ~: 6 Cabral, da Gama **8** Magellan
Rocky Mountains ~: 4 Pike
Scottish ~: 4 Park, Ross **11** Livingstone
South America ~: 4 Peck **5** Cabot **6** Cabral **8** Vespucci
South Seas ~: 4 Cook **5** Davys **6** Tasman **7** Dampier, Johnson **9** Heyerdahl, Vancouver
Spanish ~: 6 Balboa, Cortés **7** Pizarro **8** Coronado **11** Ponce de León
Swedish ~: 5 Hedin
Tibet ~: 5 Hedin **9** David-Neel
underground ~: 5 caver **9** spelunker
underwater ~: 5 Beebe **8** Cousteau
Venetian ~: 4 Polo
Viking ~: 4 Eric, Leif **7** Ericson
Virginia ~: 7 Raleigh
Western: 4 Gray **5** Clark, Lewis **6** Balboa **7** Fremont **8** Coronado
Explorer: 3 SUV **4** Ford **5** Scout **8** Boy Scout
org.: 3 BSA
explorers, ancient: 5 Norse **7** Vikings
explosion: 3 pop **4** bang, boom, roar **5** blast, burst, crack, noise, salvo, spirt, spurt **6** blowup, firing, report **7** blowout, flare-up, tantrum **8** backfire, eruption, outbreak, outburst, upheaval **9** discharge **10** combustion, concussion, demolition, detonation, percussion
cause: 5 spark
outlawed ~: 5 A test, N test
explosive: 3 TNT **4** ammo, bomb, live, mine **5** nitro, shell **6** amatol, charge, unsafe **7** grenade, missile **8** dynamite, munition, volatile **9** booby trap, dangerous, detonator, ebullient, fireworks, fulminant, gunpowder, hazardous, impetuous, pineapple, unsettled **10** ammunition, convulsive, detonative, propellant
ingredient: 5 niter
sign: 6 danger, hazard
small ~ sound: 4 poof
sound: 3 pow **4** bang, blam, boom, 'wham **5** blast **6** kaboom
explosive __: 5 rivet **7** forming, welding
__ explosive: 3 low **4** high **7** plastic
expo: 4 fair, show **10** World's Fair
Expo: 3 van **4** NLer **10** baseballer, Mitsubishi
rival: 3 Cub, Met, Red **4** Twin **5** Angel, Astro, Brave, Giant, Padre, Rocky, Royal, Tiger **6** Brewer, Dodger, Indian, Marlin, Oriole, Philly, Pirate, Ranger, Red Sox, Yankee **7** Blue Jay, Mariner **8** Athletic, Cardinal, Devil Ray, White Sox
exponent: 5 power, urger **6** backer **7** booster, support **8** advocate, champion, defender, endorser, partisan, promoter **9** proponent, supporter
algebraic ~: 5 index
exponential __: 4 horn **5** curve
export: 4 ship **7** send off, ship out, smuggle **10** ship abroad
Export-__ Bank: 6 Import
exporter: 8 merchant
exports: 5 cargo, goods **7** freight, tonnage **8** shipment
Expos: 4 nine, team
home: 8 Montreal
1990s manager: 4 Alou
org.: 3 MLB, NLE
sport: 8 baseball
expose: 3 air, ope **4** bare, leak, nail, news, show, slur **5** admit, catch, strip **6** betray, debunk, denude, detect, let out, refute, reveal, show up, unfold, unmask, unveil **7** display, divulge, exhibit, lay bare, lay open, let slip, show off, uncover, unearth, weather **8** bring out, disclose, disprove, give away, ridicule, smell out, smoke out **9** discredit, make known, put on view **10** make public
to the atmosphere: 6 aerate
exposé: 5 story **6** baring **7** scandal, tell-all **9** unmasking, unveiling **10** confession, disclosure, revelation, unbosoming, uncovering
Exposé
members: Curless, Jarado, Bruno
song: Come Go With Me (1987)
I'll Never Get Over You (1993)
Let Me Be the One (1987)
Point of No Return (1987)
Seasons Change (1987)
Tell Me Why (1989)
What You Don't Know (1989)
When I Looked at Him (1989)
exposed: 3 raw **4** bare, nude, open **5** clear, naked, outer, plain, prone **6** at risk, drafty, in view, liable, on view, patent, public **7** in peril, obvious, subject, visible **8** apparent, clear-cut, explicit, helpless, in danger, manifest, unhidden, unveiled **9** on display, unguarded **10** accessible, observable, unshielded, unshrouded, vulnerable
combining form: 4 gymn- **5** gymno-
exposition: 4 fair, show **5** essay, paper, prose, theme, tract **6** reason, report, thesis **7** display **8** critique, exegesis, treatise **9** construal, criticism, discourse, discovery, editorial, monograph, rationale, reasoning, spectacle, statement, voice-over **10** annotation, commentary, conception, county fair, discussion, exhibition, literature, production
ex post __: 5 facto
expostulate: 3 say **6** reason **7** protest
expostulation: 6 rebuke
exposure: 4 leak, risk **5** peril **6** airing, baring, danger, espial **7** display **8** betrayal, jeopardy **9** detection, divulging, liability, unmasking **10** experience, revelation, uncovering
measure: 3 rad, rem **5** curie
to injury: 4 risk **5** peril **6** hazard, menace **8** jeopardy
exposure __: 4 dose **5** index, meter
__ exposure: 4 time **6** double
expound: 5 orate, solve, state, teach **7** clarify, comment, lecture, present **8** proclaim, set forth, spell out **9** interpret, talk about **10** promulgate
on: 4 tell **5** state **6** detail, relate, report, unfold **7** explain, write up **8** describe, set forth **9** chronicle, elucidate, explicate, make clear
expounder: 5 agent **6** backer **7** apostle, booster, paladin, sponsor **8** advocate, champion, crusader, promoter **9** proponent, supporter
Expo '67 site: 6 Canada, Quebec **8** Montreal
Expo '98 site: 6 Lisbon **8** Portugal
express: 3 air, put, say **4** aver, fast, look, mail, show, sign, talk, tell, vent **5** brisk, clear, couch, exact, fleet, hasty, opine, plain, quick, rapid, speak, spell, state, swift, train, utter, vivid, voice **6** act out, assert, cogent, convey, denote, direct, embody, flying, formal, imbody, phrase, proper, racing, relate, reveal, speedy **7** add up to, breathe, certain, declare, deliver, evident, forward, hurried, instant, nonstop, obvious, precise, purport, reflect, signify, special **8** apparent, clear-cut, definite, describe, distinct, emphatic, explicit, indicate, manifest, palpable, proclaim, register, set forth, specific, vocalize **9** breakneck, enunciate, graspable, personify, predicate, represent, symbolize, verbalize **10** articulate, considered, definitive, deliberate, double-time, individual, particular, spelled out, unmediated, well-marked
ability to ~ oneself: 5 oracy
alternative: 5 local
freely: 4 vent **6** unload
grief: 3 cry, rue, sob **4** keen, moan, pine, sigh, wail, weep **6** lament, sorrow
jubilance: 4 hoot, yell **5** cheer, shout **6** holler, hurrah, scream, shriek **7** exclaim
one's preference: 4 vote **6** choose
train: 3 ltd. **7** limited
express __: 4 lane **5** rifle, train
__ express: 3 air **4** pony
Express __: 4 Mail
__ Express: 4 Nova, Ohio, Pony **6** Berlin, Orient **7** Federal
expressed: 4 oral, said **5** vocal **6** spoken, verbal
expression: 3 mug **4** face, grin, look, mien, pout, term, word **5** idiom, smile, smirk, sneer, token **6** phrase, slogan, speech, visage **7** grimace, wording **8** language, locution **9** assertion, character, elocution, eloquence, execution, narration, rendition, statement, utterance **10** commentary, definition, embodiment, indication, intonation
__-expression: 4 self
Expressionism, prefix with: 3 neo
expressionless: 5 blank, stony **6** glassy, stolid, stoney, vacant, wooden **7** deadpan, neutral, vacuous **8** fisheyed
expressive: 4 rich **5** showy, vivid, vocal **6** fluent, lively, loving, moving **7** graphic, lyrical, soulful, telling **8** artistic, colorful, dramatic, eloquent, emphatic, poignant, spirited, stirring, striking, touching **9** brilliant, energetic, graphical, ingenious, pictorial, reveal-

ing **10** articulate, artistical, indicative, meaningful, passionate, responsive, revelatory, suggestive, thoughtful
expressiveness: 4 brio, fire **6** warmth **7** emotion, passion, rapture **8** lyricism, rhapsody **9** intensity
expressly: 6 namely, wholly **8** for a fact **9** decidedly, on purpose, pointedly, precisely, purposely, specially **10** absolutely, apparently, definitely, distinctly, especially, explicitly, far and away, manifestly, positively
expressway: 2 rd. **3** fwy., hwy., tpk. **4** belt, pike, road, tnpk. **7** freeway, highway, parkway, thruway **8** turnpike **10** interstate, throughway
like an ~: 5 laned
Express Yourself (1989 song) artist: Madonna
exprobate: 3 rag **4** flay **5** chide, scold **6** berate, preach, punish, rank on, rebuke, tirade **7** censure, declaim, lecture, reprove, tell off **8** admonish, harangue, moralize **9** reprimand, sermonize
expropriate: 4 take **5** annex, seize, usurp **6** assume **7** deprive, impound, preempt **8** take over **10** commandeer
expulse: 4 oust **8** relegate **9** ostracize
expulsion: 4 cast **5** exile, purge **6** ouster **7** ousting, removal **8** ejection, eviction **9** banishing, debarment, discharge, dismissal, exception, exclusion, extrusion, ostracism **10** banishment, deportment, driving out, evacuation, forcing out, keeping out, relegation, suspension
expunge: 3 cut, zap **4** dele, X out **5** clean, erase, purge **6** cancel, delete, efface, excise, remove, revoke, rub off, rub out **7** abolish, blot out, destroy, scissor, take out, wipe out **8** white out **9** eradicate, sponge out, strike out **10** annihilate, blue-pencil, obliterate
don't ~: 4 stet
expurgate: 3 cut **4** dele, edit **5** bleep, erase, purge **6** censor, delete, excise **7** cleanse, clean up, scissor **8** bleep out, sanitize **10** blue-pencil, bowdlerize
expurgated: 3 cut **7** partial, refined, sketchy **10** incomplete
exquisite: 3 def, rad **4** aces, A-one, boss, braw, cool, dece, fine, gear, keen, neat, nice, phat, rare, tuff **5** acute, dandy, ducky, grand, great, marvy, neato, nobby, prime, slick, super, swell **6** bang on, bang-up, bonzer, bosker, choice, dainty, divine, dreamy, far-out, gnarly, groovy, lovely, peachy, select, slap-up, spot on, subtle, superb, terrif, tiptop, unreal, whizzo, wicked **7** amazing, awesome, capital, corking, elegant, for show, intense, perfect, ripping, skookum, stellar, sublime **8** charming, dazzling, delicate, especial, esthetic, ethereal, eximious, fabulous, five-star, four-star, frabjous, glorious, gorgeous, heavenly, jim-dandy, luscious, piercing, poignant, precious, slam-bang, smashing, splendid, standout, sterling, stickout, superior, tasteful, terrific, top-level, topnotch, very good, wondrous **9** admirable, beautiful, bodacious, delicious, Endsville, excellent, exemplary, faultless, first-rate, high-grade, hunky-dory, marvelous, masterful, matchless, sollicker, thrilling, top-flight, unrivaled, virtuosic, wonderful **10** attractive, consummate, delectable, fastidious, first-class, hotsy-totsy, immaculate, impeccable, jack-a-dandy, meticulous, ornamental, out of sight, peachy-keen, phenomenal, remarkable, stupendous, super-duper, unrivalled
exquisiteness: 5 class, grace, merit, style, value, worth **6** beauty, luxury **7** finesse, glamour **8** artistry, delicacy, elegance, fineness, radiance **9** fragility, lightness, propriety **10** daintiness, loveliness, refinement
exsanguine: 3 wan **4** pale **5** pasty **6** anemic, sallow **7** anaemic
exscind: 4 X out **5** erase **6** censor, cut out, delete, lop off, remove **7** blot out, expunge **8** cross out **9** expurgate **10** scissor out, scratch out
exsect: 6 cut out, excise, remove
ex-senior: 4 alum, grad **7** alumnus **8** graduate
exsert: 9 thrust out
exsiccate: 5 parch **6** dry out **9** anhydrate, dehydrate
__ Ex's Live in Texas: 5 All My
ex-soldiers' org.: 3 VFW
ext.
not ~: 3 int.
extant: 4 left **5** alive, in use **6** living, modern, with us **7** current, not lost, ongoing, present **8** existing, up-to-date **9** remaining, surviving
Extasy, The author: John Donne
extemporaneous: 4 snap **5** ad hoc, ad-lib **6** casual **7** offhand
performance: 6 improv
extempore: 5 ad-lib **6** vamped **7** offhand **8** informal **9** impromptu, whipped up **10** improvised, informally, off-the-cuff, unscripted
extemporize: 5 ad-lib **6** wing it **7** toss off
extend: 3 add, jut, lie, pad, run **4** give, grow, lend **5** add to, award, boost, build, grant, offer, range, reach, renew, swell, widen **6** bestow, deepen, dilate, expand, impart, ramble, sprawl, spread, unfold **7** augment, broaden, carry on, compass, develop, drag out, draw out, enlarge, hold out, magnify, pervade, present, proffer, prolong, stretch **8** continue, elongate, escalate, go beyond, heighten, increase, lengthen, multiply, overhang, protract, protrude, reach out, stick out **9** branch out, hold forth, keep going, spread out, string out **10** aggrandize, strengthen, stretch out, supplement
(above): 5 tower
a lease: 5 relet
along: 7 overlap
a subscription: 5 renew
outward: 3 jut **4** lean, poke **5** bulge **7** poke out, project **8** overhang, protrude, stand out, stick out
over: 4 span **5** cross, reach **6** bridge **8** go across
throughout: 4 fill **7** pervade
extended: 4 long, more, open, wide **5** broad **7** lengthy **8** drawn-out, far-flung, sweeping, very long **9** capacious, elongated, spread out **10** large-scale
not ~: 5 terse
note, in music: 5 longa
extended __: 4 play **5** order **6** family
extended __ insurance: 4 term
extension: 3 arm **4** limb, loan, size, span, wing **5** add-on, annex, delay, phone, reach, scope, sweep **6** branch, growth, radius, spread **7** adjunct **8** addendum, addition, appendix, increase, widening **9** accession, accessory, appendage, expansion, inflation **10** attachment, broadening, continuity, dilatation, distension, elongation, perpetuity, projection, stretching, supplement
building ~: 3 ell **4** wing **5** annex
extension __: 4 bolt, cord, rule, tube **5** agent, field **6** course, ladder
extensive: 3 big **4** full, good, huge, long, open, rife, vast, wide **5** ample, broad, great, hefty, large, roomy **7** blanket, copious, full-out, immense, lengthy, massive, sizable **8** far-flung, handsome, pandemic, profound, sizeable, spacious, sweeping, thorough, whole-hog **9** boundless, capacious, elaborate, expansive, full-dress, full-scale, important, inclusive, pervasive, prevalent, universal, unlimited, wholesale, worldwide **10** commodious, exhaustive, large-scale, protracted, soup to nuts, voluminous, wall to wall, widespread
extensively: 4 a lot **7** in depth, largely **10** far and wide
extensiveness: 6 length **7** breadth **9** amplitude
extent: 4 area, bulk, deal, land, size, span, time **5** ambit, gamut, limit, point, range, reach, scale, scope, space, sweep, tract, width **6** amount, bounds, degree, leeway, length, radius, spread, volume **7** breadth, compass, expanse, horizon, measure, stretch **8** distance, duration, latitude **9** amplitude, dimension, immensity, incidence, largeness, magnitude, territory **10** dimensions
comparative ~: 5 ratio
greatest ~: 3 end, max, rim **4** brim, edge **5** brink, limit **6** fringe, height, period **7** ceiling, extreme, maximum **8** confines, end point **9** outskirts, parameter, perimeter, periphery **10** bottom line, boundaries
horizontal ~: 7 breadth
linear ~: 4 span **5** orbit, range **6** course, length, radius **7** breadth, expanse, measure, purview, section, segment **8** diameter, distance, longness **9** longitude
of great ~: 4 vast
of variation: 5 range
to a great ~: 4 much **6** ever so **7** largely **8** markedly
to a greater ~: 4 more
to any ~: 3 any **4** ever **5** at all
to a smaller ~: 4 less **5** fewer, lower, minor **7** limited, reduced, without **8** inferior **9** excepting, secondary, shortened **10** diminished
to some ~: 3 any **5** quite **6** in a way, in part, kind of, partly, rather, sort of **8** slightly **9** partially
to the ~ that: 5 until **7** as far as
extenuate: 5 gloze **6** lessen **7** forgive, lighten **8** decrease, diminish, downplay, minimize, mitigate, moderate, palliate **9** attenuate **10** debilitate
extenuated: 4 lean, long, thin **5** gaunt, lanky, rangy **6** gangly, meager, skinny, twiggy **7** scrawny, slender, stringy **8** beanpole, rawboned **9** beanstalk
extenuation: 4 plea **9** softening **10** mitigation
exterior: 4 face **5** front, outer, shell **6** facade, veneer **7** outdoor, outside, outward, surface **10** peripheral
combining form: 3 epi- **4** ecto-
exterminate: 3 rid **5** erase **6** ravage, remove, rub out, uproot **7** abolish, blot out, destroy, wipe out **8** stamp out **9** liquidate
exterminator
company: 5 Orkin
do an ~ job: 5 spray **8** fumigate
target: 3 ant, rat **4** pest **5** roach
extern: 2 dr., MD **6** doctor **9** physician
external: 5 outer **7** foreign, outside, outward, surface, visible **8** exoteric, outlying, skin-deep **10** peripheral
combining form: 2 ex- **3** ect-, exo- **4** ecto-
in anatomy: 5 ectal
external __: 3 ear **6** degree, galaxy **7** storage
externalize: 3 air **8** manifest **9** personify
extinct: 4 gone, late, lost **5** kaput, passé **6** bygone **7** archaic, defunct **8** obsolete, outmoded, vanished **9** exanimate
become ~: 4 fade **6** die off, die out, vanish
bird: 3 moa **4** dodo
not ~: 4 left **5** alive **6** extant, living **7** current, ongoing **9** remaining, surviving
reptile: 8 dinosaur
wild ox: 4 urus
extinction: 4 doom, ruin **10** desolation
extinguish: 3 end, out **4** kill **5** abate, douse, dowse, erase, outen, quash, quell, snuff **6** efface, put out, quench, ravage, squash, stifle **7** abolish, blot out, blow out, destroy, eclipse, obscure, put down, silence, smother, squelch, turn off, wipe out **8** snuff out, stamp out, suppress **9** eliminate, eradicate, extirpate, suffocate, terminate **10** annihilate, obliterate
__ extinguisher: 4 fire
extinguishing, needing: 6 ablaze
extirpate: 3 rid **4** rase, raze **5** erase, pluck, purge, quash **6** cut out, efface, pull up, remove, uproot **7** abolish, blow out, destroy, extract, pull out, root out, wipe out **8** demolish **9** eliminate, eradicate **10** annihilate, deracinate, extinguish
extol: 4 hail, laud, tout **5** bless, cry up, deify, ensky, exalt, honor **6** esteem, praise, puff up, salute, talk up **7** acclaim, applaud, commend, flatter, glorify, worship **8** eulogize, hand it to, sanctify **9** brag about, celebrate, publicize, recommend **10** compliment, panegyrize
extolment: 5 glory, honor, kudos, paean **6** eulogy, homage, praise **7** acclaim, hosanna, rapture, tribute **8** accolade, citation, encomium, plaudits **9** adoration, elevation, laudation, loftiness, panegyric, promotion, reverence **10** apotheosis, compliment, exaltation, exultation, idolzation
extort: 3 pry **4** levy, milk **5** bleed, bully, exact, force, gouge, mulct, screw, wrest, wring **6** coerce, wrench **7** squeeze, swindle **9** blackmail, shake down
extortion: 5 force, graft, theft **6** racket **7** squeeze, swindle **8** coercion, thievery, venality **9** blackmail, shakedown **10** compulsion, corruption, oppression, protection
extortionate: 5 undue **8** exacting, usurious **9** excessive, expensive, out-of-line, rapacious **10** avaricious, exorbitant, outrageous
extra: 4 left, more, over, part, perc, perk, plus, role, supe, supp. **5** added, bonus, fresh, frill, gravy, minor, other, spare **6** backup, doubly, margin, player, second, unused **7** adjunct, further, premium, reserve, residue, surplus, trivial **8** addendum, addition, dividend, leftover, markedly, needless, optional, picayune, residual, trifling, unneeded **9** accessory, ancillary, auxiliary, in reserve, lagniappe, newspaper, redundant, unusually **10** additional, attachment, especially, noticeably, remarkably, supplement, uncommonly, unconsumed
effort: 5 oomph

give a little ~: 6 slap on, tack on, toss in 8 increase
prefix: 5 super-
something ~: 5 bonus, frill, gravy 6 encore 8 addition
valuable ~: 4 perk 5 bonus, lucre 6 reward 8 dividend
extra __: 5 cover, large, point
extra __ attraction: 5 added
extra-__ olive oil: 6 virgin
Extra: 10 chewing gum
alternative: 5 Orbit 7 Dentyne, Trident 8 Carefree, Chiclets, Freedent 10 Doublemint, Juicy Fruit
extra-base hit: 5 homer 6 double, triple 7 home run
__ extra cost: 4 at no
extract: 3 get, pry, tax 4 cite, clip, copy, cull, draw, milk, mine, pull, take, text, yank 5 educe, elute, evoke, glean, leach, pluck, quote, wrest, wring 6 avulse, decoct, derive, elicit, evulse, flavor, liquid, liquor, nectar, obtain, recall, remove, select, siphon, syphon, uproot 7 distill, draw out, excerpt, jerk out, passage, portion, squeeze, summary, weed out 8 bring out, citation, jerk away, solution 9 decoction, extirpate, flavoring, quotation 10 distillate
__ extract: 4 beef, malt 5 liver 7 vanilla
extraction: 5 birth, roots, stock 6 origin, strain 7 descent, lineage, pulling, removal 8 ancestry, avulsion, evulsion, pedigree, wresting, wringing 9 etymology, evocation, forebears, genealogy, parentage, uprooting, wrenching 10 derivation, separation, withdrawal
extractor: 6 gadget, juicer
extracts: 6 pieces 7 sayings 8 analecta, analects, excerpts, passages 9 citations 10 quotations, selections
extradite: 3 bag, get, nab 4 grab 5 catch, grasp, seize 6 arrest, collar, detain, pick up, take in 7 capture 9 apprehend, surrender
extra-long: 4 maxi
__ extra mile: 5 go the
extramundane: 9 spiritual
extraneous: 5 outer 7 foreign, outside 9 extrinsic, inapropos, pointless, redundant, unrelated 10 accidental, additional, immaterial, inapposite, incidental, irrelevant, out of place, peripheral
extraordinarily: 4 very 6 highly, rarely 9 unusually
extraordinary: 3 ace, def, odd, rad 4 aces, A-one, boss, braw, cool, dece, eery, fine, gear, keen, neat, nice, phat, rare, tuff 5 dandy, ducky, eerie, grand, great, marvy, neato, nobby, prime, queer, slick, super, swell, weird 6 atypic, bang on, bang-up, bonzer, bosker, choice, divine, dreamy, far-out, freaky, gnarly, groovy, lovely, peachy, quirky, signal, slap-up, spot on, superb, terrif, tiptop, unique, unreal, whizzo, wicked 7 amazing, awesome, bizarre, capital, corking, deviant, intense, magical, oddball, offbeat, perfect, ripping, skookum, special, stellar, strange, sublime, uncanny, unusual 8 aberrant, abnormal, atypical, dazzling, especial, eximious, fabulous, five-star, four-star, frabjous, freakish, glorious, heavenly, historic, jim-dandy, peculiar, singular, slam-bang, smashing, splendid, standout, sterling, stickout, striking, superior, terrific, top-level, topnotch, towering, uncommon, very good, wondrous 9 anomalous, arresting, bodacious, divergent, eccentric, Endsville, excellent, exemplary, exquisite, fantastic, first-rate, high-grade, hunky-dory, irregular, marvelous, memorable, sollicker, top-flight, unearthly, unnatural, wonderful 10 first-class, hotsy-totsy, jack-a-dandy, out of sight, peachy-keen, phenomenal, remarkable, stupendous, super-duper, unorthodox
name meaning ~: 4 Myra
not ~: 5 usual
person: 6 genius
thing: 3 pip 4 oner 5 doozy 6 doozie
extraordinary __: 3 ray 4 wave 7 jubilee
__ extraordinary: 5 envoy
extrapolate: 7 project
extrasensory: 7 psychic 10 telepathic
extraterrestrial: 5 alien 7 Martian 8 Venusian
extraterrestrial life, science of: 10 exobiology
Extra, The author: Hal Porter
extravagance: 5 frill, waste 6 excess, luxury
extravagant: 4 high, rank, rich, wild 5 campy, fancy, large, outré, steep, stiff, undue 6 absurd, costly, lavish, wanton 7 opulent, profuse, rampant, ruinous 8 prodigal, romantic, wasteful 9 excessive, luxuriant, luxurious, sumptuous 10 immoderate, profligate, rhetorical
be ~: 5 spend 7 splurge
extravagantly: 4 very 6 unduly 7 largely
extravaganza: 4 gala, play 5 event 6 parade 7 pageant 9 spectacle
extreme: 3 end, far, nth, ult. 4 dire, high, last, rank, rare 5 brink, gross, limit, outré, polar, rough, sharp, sheer, steep, stiff, ultra, undue, utter, verge 6 arrant, far-out, fringe, mortal, severe, strong, utmost 7 drastic, fanatic, glaring, intense, outside, profuse, radical 8 advanced, farthest, flagrant, furthest, profound, remotest, terminal, terrible, terrific, ultimate, uncommon 9 desperate, draconian, egregious, fanatical, fantastic, nth degree, outermost 10 exorbitant, immoderate, inordinate, irrational, outrageous, undeserved, untempered
combining form: 4 arch-
other ~: 8 opposite
to the ~: 4 very
unction: 4 rite
extreme __: 7 unction
extremely: 3 far, too 4 most, much, oh so, over, very, well 5 madly, no end, quite, super 6 ever so, highly, hugely, overly, plenty, rarely, unduly, vastly 7 acutely, awfully, greatly, notably, only too, utterly 8 insanely, markedly, overmuch, powerful, severely, terribly 9 eminently, immensely, in a big way, intensely, radically, unusually, violently 10 incredibly, remarkably, strikingly, thoroughly, uncommonly
in music: 5 assai, molto
prefix: 5 ultra-
Extreme Machines network: 3 TLC
Extreme Prejudice actor: 5 Nolte
__ Extremes: 5 I Go to
extremes, go to: 6 overdo
extremist: 3 rad 5 ultra 6 zealot 7 diehard, fanatic, radical 8 agitator, ultraist 9 sectarian
group: 4 cult, sect 7 faction
'70s ~ grp.: 3 SLA
extremity: 3 arm, end, leg, rim, tip, toe 4 butt, claw, edge, foot, hand, limb, need, pole, tail 5 brink, digit, verge 6 apogee, border, finger, margin, member, plight, strait, tipoff 8 boundary 9 acuteness, adversity, appendage, emergency, requisite
extricate: 4 free, save 5 clear, loose, untie 6 loosen, redeem, rescue, unbind 7 bail out, deliver, recover, release 8 dislodge, liberate, untangle 9 disburden, disengage 10 disinvolve
extrication: 6 escape 9 salvation
extrinsic: 5 alien, outer 6 exotic 7 foreign, outside, strange, unusual 9 redundant, unrelated 10 additional, immaterial, inapposite, incidental, irrelevant, out of place, peripheral, unfamiliar
extrovert: 5 mixer 8 outgoing 9 character
extrude: 4 emit 5 eject, expel 8 force out, press out, stick out
exuberance: 3 pep, zip 4 élan, glee, life, zest, zing 5 ardor, gusto, juice, spark, verve, vigor 6 bounce, energy, fervor, pepper, plenty, spirit 7 abandon 8 buoyance, buoyancy, hilarity, lushness, plethora, richness, vitality 9 abundance, affluence, animation, eagerness, élan vital, happiness, plenitude, profusion 10 ebullience, enthusiasm, excitement, friskiness, get up and go, lavishness, liveliness, luxuriance
exclamation: 6 yippee 7 whoopee, whoopie
exuberant: 3 gay 4 high, lush, rank, rich 5 aglow, eager, zingy, zippy 6 ardent, bouncy, fecund, hearty, lavish, lively, yeasty 7 buoyant, chipper, copious, excited, fertile, fulsome, gushing, liberal, opulent, profuse, rampant, teeming, zestful, zinging 8 abundant, animated, cheerful, effusive, fruitful, grooving, prodigal, prolific, spirited, vigorous 9 bountiful, ebullient, energetic, excessive, luxuriant, plenteous, plentiful, sparkling, sprightly, vivacious 10 frolicsome, passionate, rollicking
be ~: 9 walk on air
make ~: 4 gush, rave, send 5 elate, psych 6 excite, fire up, thrill, work up 7 enthuse, impress 8 interest 9 electrify 10 bubble over, effervesce
yell: 5 wahoo, yahoo 6 yippee 7 whoopee
exudate: 4 ooze
exudation: 4 ooze 8 effluent, emission 9 discharge, emanation
exude: 4 drip, emit, flow, leak, ooze, reek, seep, shed, spew, spue 5 bleed, drain, egest, eject, expel, issue, spout, sweat 6 effuse 7 cast out, diffuse, display, emanate, exhibit, flow out, give off, ooze out, project, radiate, secrete, send out, trickle 8 perspire, throw off 9 discharge, give forth, percolate, send forth
exult: 4 brag, crow 5 cheer, gloat, glory, revel 7 delight, rejoice, triumph 8 jubilate 9 celebrate, make merry, walk on air 10 effervesce, jump for joy
exultance: 7 triumph
exultant: 4 glad 5 happy, merry 6 blithe, cheery, elated, jovial, joyful, joyous, upbeat 7 gleeful, pleased, tickled 8 blissful, cheerful, cheering, ecstatic, euphoric, jubilant, mirthful, reveling, thrilled 9 delighted, gladdened, overjoyed, rejoicing 10 flying high, triumphant
be ~: 5 preen 9 walk on air
cry: 3 aha, oho 5 huzza, whoof, wowee 6 at last, hoorah, hooray, hurrah, hurray, huzzah, yippee 7 heigh-ho, whoopee, whoopie
exultation: 3 joy 4 glee 5 glory 7 delight, elation, triumph 8 euphoria, reveling 9 happiness, jubilance, merriment, rejoicing, transport 10 joyousness, jubilation
exuviate: 4 molt, shed
Exxon
bad news for ~: 5 spill
it merged with ~: 5 Mobil
old name for ~: 4 Esso
rival: 4 Arco 5 Amoco, Shell 6 Conoco
Exxon Valdez: 5 oiler 6 tanker
E.Y.: 7 Harburg
Eyak: 6 Indian 7 Amerind
eyas: 4 hawk
__ Eyck: 6 Jan van
Eydie: 5 Gorme
husband: 5 Steve
eye: 3 orb, see 4 glom, leer, look, ogle, scan, tail, view 5 organ, sight, stare, study, watch 6 gape at, gawk at, gaze at, goggle, leer at, look at, notice, peek at, peeper, peer at, regard, size up, survey, take in, vision 7 examine, glimpse, inspect, measure, oversee, stare at 8 appraise, check out, glance at, look upon 9 flirt with 10 get a load of, needle hole, perception, rubberneck, scrutinize
ailment: 3 sty 4 stye
apple of one's ~: 3 pet 5 pearl 7 darling 8 favorite
bat an ~: 4 wink 5 blink
bat of an ~: 4 jiff 5 jiffy 6 minute, second
be a private ~: 3 spy 4 espy, find, spot 5 dig up, hit on 6 detect, expose, unmask 7 make out, uncover 8 discover, pinpoint, smell out 9 ascertain, stumble on, track down
black ~: 4 blot, slur 5 mouse, odium, stain 6 bruise, insult, shiner 7 slander
bull's ~: 4 mark 8 specific
camera ~: 4 lens
catch the ~: 8 stand out
cock the ~: 6 squint
color: 4 blue, gray, grey 5 brown, green, hazel
combining form: 4 ocul-, opto- 5 oculo- 8 ophthalm- 9 ophthalmo-
cover: 3 lid 4 wool
doctor: 7 oculist
drop: 4 tear
eagle ~: 5 stare, vigil, watch 6 acuity 7 lookout 8 scrutiny
ender: 3 cup, let, lid 4 ball, bolt, brow, hole, hook, lash, lift, shot, sore, spot, wash, wear, wink 5 glass, liner, patch, piece, shade, sight, stalk, teeth, tooth 6 bright, strain 7 dropper, glasses, witness
evil ~: 3 hex 4 jinx, look 5 curse, glare 7 sorcery
eye for an ~: 7 revenge 8 reprisal 9 vengeance
fish ~: 4 gaze
give a black ~: 4 slur 5 libel, shame, smear 6 defame, vilify 8 mistreat
give the ~: 4 ogle 5 stare
give the evil ~: 5 scowl
glad ~: 4 wink
hook and ~: 8 fastener
in a pig's ~: 5 never
inflammation: 6 iritis
insect ~ lens: 5 facet
in the wink of an ~: 4 anon, soon 7 quickly 9 momentary
irritant: 4 mote
it colors the ~: 4 iris
it has an ~: 5 storm
jaundiced ~: 4 bias 6 enmity 7 bigotry 8 aversion 9 antipathy 10 chauvinism, fanaticism, favoritism, narrowness, partiality
keep an ~ on: 4 boss, mark, mind, tend 5 guard, scout, study, watch

6 advert, attend, detect, direct, follow, look at, manage, notice 7 baby-sit, discern, monitor, observe, oversee 8 chaperon, shepherd 9 look after, supervise 10 administer, ride herd on, scrutinize
layer: 4 uvea
look in your ~: 3 ray 4 beam 5 gleam, glint 6 glance 7 glimmer, glisten, sparkle, twinkle
makeup: 4 kohl 5 liner 6 shadow 7 mascara
mind's ~: 6 memory
muscle: 6 rectus
my ~: 5 no way 8 forget it
nerve: 5 optic
network: 3 CBS 5 CBS-TV
not bat an ~: 8 keep cool 9 stay loose
of an ~ layer: 5 uveal
offend the ~: 5 clash
of the ~: 5 optic
of the storm: 4 calm, lull 6 center
opener: 5 shock
opening: 4 slit
part: 4 iris, lens, uvea 5 white 6 cornea
partner: 4 hook
private ~: 3 tec 4 dick 6 shamus 7 gumshoe 9 detective
protector: 3 lid 4 lash 5 visor, vizor
public ~: 9 spotlight
run one's ~ over: 4 skim
see eye to ~: 4 gybe, jibe 5 agree 6 accede, accord, assent, comply, concur 7 approve, consent, go along 8 coincide 9 acquiesce, harmonize
shadow: 4 kohl
shape: 6 almond
signal: 4 wink 5 blink
starter: 3 big, red 4 buck, dead, fish, frog, moon, pink, shut, wall 5 watch 6 golden, silver
the bull's-eye: 3 aim 5 aim at, point 6 target
to a poet: 3 orb
to the ~: 7 outward 9 outwardly 10 ostensibly
turn a blind ~ to: 8 overlook
watchful ~: 5 vigil 7 lookout 8 guidance, tutelage, wardship 9 oversight
weather ~: 5 vigil, watch
wink of the ~: 4 jiff 5 jiffy, trice 6 moment 7 eyewink, instant
with an ~ out: 4 wary 5 alert, awake, ready, sharp 7 all ears, careful, heedful, mindful, on guard 8 cautious, keen-eyed, vigilant, watchful 9 attentive, expectant, observant, wide-awake 10 on one's toes, perceptive
eye __: 4 bath, lens 5 chart, drops, point, rhyme 6 appeal, doctor, shadow, socket, splice 7 contact, dialect
eye-__: 6 minded 7 filling, opening, popping
eye-__ coordination: 4 hand
__ eye: 4 evil, glad 5 black, bull's, eagle, mind's, naked, screw, third 6 gimlet, pineal, public 7 batting, harness, private, weather
__-eye: 3 red 4 cat's 5 bird's, clear, crab's, white 6 tiger's
Eye __: 5 Guess
Eye __ Needle: 5 of the
Eye __ Tiger: 5 of the
eyeball: 3 spy 4 face, leer, peer, view 5 check, stare 6 assess, regard, verify 7 observe, witness 8 look hard
bender: 5 op art
covering: 6 cornea
eyebrow: 4 hair
shape: 3 arc, bow 4 arch 5 curve 8 crescent
eyebrow __: 6 pencil
__ eyebrows: 5 raise
eye-catching: 4 bold 8 gorgeous, striking, stunning
__-eyed: 3 bug, cat, doe, dry, pie 4 blue, cold, dewy, hawk, lynx, moon, open, sloe, wide, wild 5 Argus, auger, beady, blear, clear, cross, eagle, misty, sharp, stalk, teary, young 6 almond, bleary, bright, gimlet, glassy, goggle, googly, squint, starry
__ Eyed Girl: 5 Brown
__-Eyed Jacks: 3 One
__-eyed monster: 5 green
__ Eye dog: 6 Seeing
__-eyed pea: 5 black
eyed starter: 3 bog, pop 4 cock, moon, wall
__-eyed Susan: 5 black, brown
eyeful: 4 load 5 sight, views 6 beauty, looker, pretty, vision 7 dazzler, stunner 8 good look, knockout
get an ~: 3 see 4 gaze 7 observe
eyeglass: 4 lens 5 loupe
eyeglasses: 5 specs 8 bifocals, cheaters, horn-rims, pince-nez 10 spectacles
part: 4 lens 5 frame
support: 3 ear
taped ~ wearer: 4 nerd, nurd
__-eye gravy: 3 red
Eye Guess: 8 game show
host: Bill Cullen
... __ eye in the house: 4 a dry
Eye in the Sky (1982 song) artist: Alan Parsons Project
__ Eye Is on the Sparrow: 3 His
eyelash: 4 hair 6 cilium
by an ~: 4 just 6 barely, hardly 8 narrowly, scarcely
flutter: 3 bat 4 wink 5 blink 6 twitch 9 nictitate
__ eyelash: 5 bat an
eyelashes
bat ~: 5 flirt
__ eyelashes: 5 false
Eyeless in Gaza author: Aldous Huxley
eyelet: 4 loop 7 grommet 8 peephole 10 buttonhole
eyelid: 6 winker 7 blinker
combining form: 7 blephar- 8 blepharo-
feature: 4 lash
inflammation: 3 sty 4 stye
eyeliner: 4 kohl 6 makeup
site: 3 lid
__ eye movement: 5 rapid
Eye of newt and __ frog: 5 toe of
Eye of the Needle (1981 film)
cast: Ian Bannen, Kate Nelligan, Donald Sutherland
director: Richard Marquand
Eye of the Tiger (1982 song) artist: Survivor
eyeopener: 4 news 5 shock 6 coffee 8 pick-me-up, surprise 10 revelation
eyepiece: 4 lens
eyer: 5 flirt, ogler 6 viewer 7 witness 8 observer, surveyor 9 spectator 10 peeping Tom
eyes: 5 sight 9 baby blues
all ~: 6 enrapt 9 attentive 10 fascinated
big ~: 6 hunger
cover the ~: 7 obscure 9 blindfold, obfuscate
easy on the ~: 4 fair 6 lavish, lovely 8 dazzling, gorgeous, handsome, imposing, stunning 9 beautiful, exquisite, ravishing, sumptuous 10 attractive
feast for the ~: 6 beauty, vision 7 dazzler, stunner 8 knockout
feast one's ~: 3 eye, spy 4 gaze, look, ogle, peer, view 5 sight, stare, watch 6 behold, look at, regard 7 examine, eyeball, inspect, observe 8 look upon 10 scrutinize
food with ~: 4 spud
have ~ for: 4 itch, like, pant, pine, want, wish 5 covet, crave, fancy, go for, yearn 6 desire, hanker, hunger, obsess, pursue, thirst 7 long for 8 aspire to, languish
having ~ in verse: 5 orbed
keep one's ~ peeled: 5 stare, watch
lay ~ on: 3 spy 4 espy, view 5 stare
like some ~: 4 evil 5 beady, teary
make ~ at: 3 eye 4 leer, ogle 5 flirt, stare, tease 7 eyeball 8 coquette
open one's ~: 4 wake 5 edify, teach, waken 6 awaken 8 disabuse, illumine
pull the wool over one's ~: 3 con, lie, rob, sap 4 bilk, butt, dupe, have, hoax, jerk, prey, trap 5 cheat, fraud, shaft, trick 6 delude, fleece, lead on, outwit, rip off, rope in, suck in, take in 7 beguile, buffalo, chicane, deceive, defraud, mislead, swindle, two-time, wheedle 8 bulldoze, flimflam, hoodwink, inveigle, outsmart, sucker in 9 bamboozle, disinform, scapegoat
raise, as ~: 6 cast up
rivet one's ~: 5 focus 6 fixate, obsess, zero in 9 preoccupy
roll the ~: 4 leer, look, ogle 5 stare 6 goggle
scrunch the ~: 6 squint
shut one's ~ to: 6 ignore, wink at 9 disregard
with ~ open: 4 wary 5 awake 7 mindful 8 vigilant, watchful
eyes __: 4 left 5 right
eyes-__: 4 only
__ eyes: 3 all 4 make 5 snake 6 goo-goo, sheep's
Eyes __ Shut: 4 Wide
__ Eyes: 3 Sad 4 Dark, Lyin', Sexy 5 Angel, Banjo, Ebony, Green, Irish, Naked, Short, These, Tiger 6 Hungry 7 Private, Spanish
__ eyes for: 4 have
eyeshade: 5 visor, vizor
eyeshot: 3 ken 4 peek, view 5 sight 10 visibility
eyesight: 6 vision 10 perception
Eyes of Darkness, The author: Dean Koontz
Eyes of Laura Mars (1978 film)
cast: Rene Auberjonois, Brad Dourif, Faye Dunaway, Tommy Lee Jones
director: Irvin Kershner
__ eyes on: 3 lay 4 clap
eyes-only: 6 secret
eyesore: 4 mess 5 sight 6 blight, fright, litter 7 blemish
__-eye steak: 3 rib
Eyes Wide Shut (1999 film)
cast: Tom Cruise, Nicole Kidman, Sydney Pollack, Marie Richardson
director: Stanley Kubrick
Eyes Without a Face (1984 song)
artist: Billy Idol
eyeteeth
give one's ~ (for): 4 pant 5 yearn
__ Eye, The: 6 Bluest, Cosmic, Savage
eye-to-brain link: 6 nerves
eye to eye, seeing: 5 at one
eyetooth: 6 canine
__-eye view: 5 bird's, worm's
eyewash: 3 gas, rot 4 blah, bosh, bull, bunk, guff, jazz, jive, pooh, tosh 5 bilge, fudge, hokum, hooey, prate, stuff, trash, tripe 6 bunkum, bushwa, drivel, footle, gabble, gammon, gibber, havers, hot air, humbug, jabber, jargon, kibosh, piffle 7 baloney, blarney, blather, blether, boloney, bushwah, flannel, flubdub, fustian, garbage, inanity, rubbish, twaddle 8 buncombe, claptrap, falderal, falderol, flimflam, flummery, folderal, folderol, nonsense, slipslop, tommyrot, trumpery 9 banana oil, gibberish, goofiness, kidstakes, moonshine, poppycock, rigmarole 10 applesauce, balderdash, bilge water, codswallop, double-talk, flapdoodle, galimatias, Jabberwock, mumbo jumbo, rigamarole, taradiddle
acid: 5 boric 7 boracic
natural ~: 4 tear
eyewear, piece of: 4 lens
eyewink: 4 jiff 5 flash, jiffy, trice 6 moment 7 instant
eyewitness: 3 see 4 seer, view 5 watch 6 looker, viewer 7 observe, watcher, witness 8 beholder, looker-on, observer, onlooker 9 bystander, firsthand, spectator
words: 4 I saw
eyot: 3 ait, cay 6 island
eyra: 3 cat 5 felid 6 feline, jaguar 7 wildcat 10 jaguarundi
relative: 4 lion, lynx, puma 5 chita, liger, ounce, tiger, tigon 6 bobcat, cheeta, chetah, cougar, margay, ocelot, serval, tiglon 7 bay lynx, caracal, cheetah, leopard, panther 9 catamount
Eyre: 4 Jane, lake
locale: 9 Australia
eyrie: 4 nest
dweller: 5 eagle 6 eaglet
eyrir: 5 money
E.Z.C.: 6 Judson
Ezekiel follower: 6 Daniel
Ezer, father of: 7 Ephraim
E-Z formula: 3 ABC
Ezio: 5 Pinza
Ezio composer: 6 Handel
Ezra: 5 Pound, Stone 6 Benson 7 Cornell
follower: 3 Neh. 8 Nehemiah
preceder: 10 Chronicles
EZ Streets star: 4 Olin
Ezzard: 7 Charles

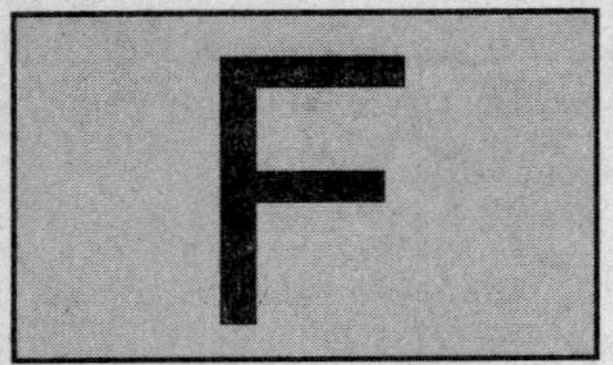

__ + 4: 3 ZIP
4 Clowns (1970 film)
cast: Charley Chase, Buster Keaton, Laurel and Hardy
director: Robert Youngson
4 for Texas (1963 film)
cast: Ursula Andress, Anita Ekberg, Dean Martin, Frank Sinatra
director: Robert Aldrich
4-H participant: 5 youth
__ 4 Love: 3 All
4/1 activity: 5 prank
__-4-One: 3 All
4 P.M. song: Sukiyaki (1994)
4 Seasons of Loneliness (1997 song) artist: Boyz II Men
4th-qtr. follower: 2 OT
__ 5: 7 Jackson
5 Against the House (1955 film)
cast: Brian Keith, Guy Madison, Kim Novak
director: Phil Karlson
5 Fingers (1952 film)
cast: Danielle Darrieux, James Mason, Michael Rennie
director: Joseph L. Mankiewicz
5K: 4 race
5th Avenue: 5 candy **9** chocolate
alternative: 4 Mars, Twix **5** Clark, Heath **6** Kit Kat, Mounds, PayDay, Reese's, Zagnut **7** Krackel, Oh Henry **8** Baby Ruth, Hershey's, Milky Way, Snickers **9** Almond Joy, Mr. Goodbar **10** NutRageous
14
creature with ~ legs: 6 isopod
__-14: 6 carbon
15 Minutes (2001 film)
cast: Avery Brooks, Edward Burns, Robert De Niro, Kelsey Grammer, Melina Kanakaredes
director: John Herzfeld
40 __ and a Mule: 5 Acres
__ 40: 3 Top
40-decibel unit: 4 sone
42nd Parallel, The
author: John Dos Passos
trilogy: 3 USA
42nd Street (1933 film)
cast: Warner Baxter, George Brent, Bebe Daniels, Ruby Keeler, Dick Powell
director: Lloyd Bacon
45
player: 5 phono
surface: 5 A-side, B-side, side A, side B
45 __: 3 RPM
__ .45: 4 Colt
45-rpm, long: 2 EP
__ 48: 5 Lower
48HRS. (1982 film)
cast: Eddie Murphy, Nick Nolte, Annette O'Toole
director: Walter Hill
49-day period in Judaism: 4 omer
49er
div.: 3 NFC
org.: 3 NFL
rival: 3 Jet, Ram **4** Bear, Bill, Colt, Lion **5** Brown, Chief, Eagle, Giant, Raven, Saint, Texan, Titan **6** Bengal, Bronco, Cowboy, Falcon, Jaguar, Packer, Raider, Viking **7** Charger, Dolphin, Panther, Patriot, Redskin, Seahawk, Steeler **8** Cardinal **9** Buccaneer
sport: 8 football
50 Ways to Leave Your Lover (1976 song) artist: Paul Simon
55 Days at Peking (1963 film)
cast: Ava Gardner, Charlton Heston, David Niven, Flora Robson
director: Nicholas Ray
__ 57: 5 Heinz
400: 5 elite
magazine: 6 Forbes
name: 5 Astor
401(k)
alternative: 4 ESOP
cousin: 5 Keogh
486: 3 CPU
500 Hats of Bartholomew Cubbins, The author: Dr. Seuss
500 Miles Away From Home (1963 song) artist: Bobby Bare
1400: 5 two p.m.
1492
caravel: 4 Niña **5** Pinta **10** Santa Maria
departure harbor: 5 Palos
1521
conqueree: 5 Aztec
1588 loser: 6 Armada
1598 edict site: 6 Nantes
5,000 Nights at the Opera author: 4 Bing
5280 feet: 4 mile
f __: 5 value
f-__: 4 hole, stop **6** number
F: 3 key **4** clef, elem., mark **5** false, grade **6** E sharp, letter **7** element **8** fluorine **10** Fahrenheit
avoid an ~: 4 pass
in phonetic alphabet: 7 Foxtrot
in physics: 5 farad
measure: 3 deg. **6** degree
9 for ~: 4 at. no.
worth an ~: 3 bad **5** awful, lousy **6** woeful **8** dreadful, horrible, terrible **9** atrocious **10** abominable, horrendous
F __: 4 clef, star **5** layer, Troop **6** region
F __ foxtrot: 4 as in
F. __ Abraham: 6 Murray
F. __ Bailey: 3 Lee
F. __ Fitzgerald: 5 Scott
'F' __ Fugitive: 5 Is for
fa: 4 note
follower: 3 sol **4** so la **5** sol la **6** so la ti **7** sol la ti
preceder: 2 mi **4** re mi **6** do re mi
fa-__: 4 la-la
__-fa: 3 sol
FAA
concern: 3 saf. **6** safety
department: 3 DOT
part: 3 Fed. **5** Admin. **7** Federal **8** Aviation
fab: 3 def, rad **4** aces, A-one, boss, braw, cool, dece, epic, fine, gear, keen, neat, nice, phat, tops, tuff **5** boffo, dandy, ducky, grand, great, marvy, neato, nobby, prime, primo, slick, super, swell **6** bang on, bang-up, bonzer, bosker, choice, divine, dreamy, far-out, gnarly, groovy, lovely, peachy, slap-up, spot on, superb, terrif, tiptop, unreal, whizzo, wicked **7** amazing, awesome, boffola, capital, corking, perfect, ripping, skookum, stellar, sublime **8** dazzling, dynamite, especial, eximious, five-star, four-star, frabjous, glorious, heavenly, jim-dandy, mythical, slam-bang, smashing, splendid, standout, sterling, stick-out, striking, superior, terrific, top-level, topnotch, very good, wondrous **9** bodacious, Endsville, excellent, exemplary, exquisite, fantastic, first-rate, high-grade, hunky-dory, imaginary, legendary, marvelous, sollicker, thrilling, top-drawer, top-flight, unrivaled, wonderful, wunderbar **10** astounding, first-class, hotsy-totsy, incredible, jack-a-dandy, miraculous, out of sight, outrageous, peachy-keen, phenomenal, remarkable, stupendous, super-duper, tremendous, unrivalled
Fab: 9 detergent
alternative: 3 All, Biz, Era, Yes **4** Bold, Dash, Gain, Surf, Tide, Wisk **5** Cheer, Dreft, Purex **6** Calgon, Dynamo, Oxydol **7** Octagon **9** Ivory Snow
Fab __: 4 Four
Fabares, Shelley: 7 actress
film: Clambake (1967)
Girl Happy (1965)
Spinout (1966)
song: Johnny Angel (1962)
spouse: Mike Farrell
TV: Coach, The Donna Reed Show
Fabergé
glaze: 6 enamel
object: 3 egg
Fab Four
name: 4 John, Paul **5** Ringo, Starr **6** George, Lennon **8** Harrison **9** McCartney
see also Beatles
Fabian: 4 pope **6** singer **7** pontiff
last name: Forte
song: Hound Dog Man (1959)
Tiger (1959)
Turn Me Loose (1959)
Fabius Maximus: 5 Roman
fable: 4 myth, tale, yarn **5** conte, story **6** apolog, legend **7** fiction, parable, recital **8** allegory, apologue **9** fairy tale, folk story
author: 4 Esop **5** Aesop
ending: 5 moral
figure: 3 ant, fox **4** hare **8** tortoise
moral ~: 6 apolog **8** apologue
fabled: 5 noted **6** famous, unreal **7** storied **8** mythical **9** legendary **10** fictitious
fables: 4 lore
__ Fables: 6 Aesop's, Flower, Modern
Fables for Our Time author: James Thurber
Fables in Slang author: George Ade
Fabray: 3 Nan **7** Nanette
fabric: 3 aba, net, rep **4** abba, duck, felt, ikat, lace, lamé, lawn, leno, mesh, poly, repp, silk, wool **5** baize, batik, blend, chino, cloth, crape, crash, crepe, denim, dhoti, dhuti, Dynel, fiber, frisé, gauze, gazar, Honan, Kasha, kente, khaki, Kodel, linen, lisle, lisse, loden, moire, ninon, nylon, pekin, piqué, plaid, plush, rayon, satin, scrim, serge, stuff, suede, surah, tammy, terry, toile, tweed, twill, voile, wigan **6** alpaca, Angora, armure, barege, battik, Bengal, bouclé, burlap, camaca, camaka, camoca, canvas, chally, chintz, coburg, cotton, coutil, crepon, Dacron, damask, dhooti, dimity, faille, fleece, gloria, jersey, linsey, madras, make-up, merino, mohair, moreen, muslin, oxford, plissé, pongee, poplin, ratiné, samite, sateen, saxony, stamin, tammie, tartan, tricot, tussah, tusseh, tusser, tussor, tussur, velour, velvet, vicuña, wadmal **7** batiste, brocade, buckram, bunting, cambric, challie, challis, charvet, Cheviot, chiffon, dhootie, drugget, duvetyn, épinglé, estamin, etamine, fishnet, flannel, foulard, fustian, galatea, gingham, Gore-Tex, grogram, hickory, jaconet, kashmir, khaddar, mockado, Mogador, nankeen, netting, oilskin, organdy, organza, ottoman, paisley, percale, sarsnet, satinet, silesia, spandex, tabaret, tabinet, taffeta, textile, ticking, tiffany, tussore, velours, Viyella, worsted **8** algerine, barathea, bayadere, Burberry, canotier, cashmere, casimere, casimire, Celanese, chambray, chenille, corduroy, cretonne, diamante, homespun, Indienne, jacquard, marcella, marocain, material, Milanese, moleskin, moquette, nainsook, oilcloth, organdie, paduasoy, popeline, prunella, prunelle, prunello, sanglier, sarcenet, sarsenet, shalloon, shantung, tabbinet, tarlatan, Venetian, whipcord, wild silk **9** astrakhan, Bengaline, bombazeen, bombazine, calamanco, cassimere, charmeuse, cothamore, crinoline, flannelet, framework, gabardine, georgette, Glen plaid, grenadine, grosgrain, henrietta, horsehair, matelassé, Naugahyde, paramatta, percaline, polyester, sailcloth, satinette, sharkskin, silkaline, structure, velveteen **10** balbriggan, broadcloth, Irish tweed, marseilles, peau de soie, seersucker, tattersall
acid-washed ~: 5 denim
ancient silk ~: 6 byssus
attachment: 4 snap **6** button, Velcro, zipper
bit of ~: 3 rag **5** scrap **6** swatch
blouse ~: 4 silk
border: 3 hem **4** seam **6** edging, fringe
camel hair ~: 3 aba **4** abba
canvas ~: 5 wigan **9** sailcloth
carpet ~: 5 frisé, plush
coarse ~: 3 aba **4** abba **5** chino, denim **6** burlap, linsey
coat ~: 5 serge **6** saxony **8** Burberry **9** cothamore
corded ~: 3 rep **4** repp
cotton ~: 3 rep **4** duck, lawn, repp **5** baize, chino, crape, crepe, dhoti, dhuti, khaki, piqué, plush, scrim, terry, toile, voile **6** canvas, chally, chintz, damask, dhooti, dimity, gloria, madras, moreen, muslin, oxford, pongee, poplin, sateen, wadmal **7** buckram, bunting, cambric, challie, challis, dhootie, duvetyn, etamine, flannel, foulard, fustian, galatea, gingham, jaconet, khaddar, nankeen, oilskin, organdy, percale, satinet, silesia, ticking, tiffany, Viyella **8** Burberry, chambray, corduroy, Indienne, marcella, moleskin, nainsook, oilcloth, organdie, shantung, tarlatan **9** crinoline, flannelet, gabardine, paramatta, percaline, sailcloth, satinette, silkaline, velveteen **10** balbriggan, marseilles, seersucker
crepe ~: 8 marocain
crinkled ~: 5 crape, crepe, lisse
curtain ~: 4 lace, leno **5** ninon, voile **6** chintz, dimity, moreen **7** tabaret **8** cretonne
delicate ~: 4 lace **5** tulle
dress ~: 5 crash, voile **6** coburg, dimity
durable ~: 5 chino, denim, khaki
elastic ~: 5 Lycra **7** spandex
embossed ~: 9 matelassé
feature: 3 nap **4** pile, wale
feltlike ~: 5 baize
filmy ~: 5 gauze, lisse, tulle
flax ~: 5 linen **7** fustian
fold: 6 crease
fuzz: 3 nap **4** lint

gather ~: 5 shirr
gauzy ~: 3 net 4 leno 5 lisse, tulle
glazed ~: 4 cire 5 tammy 6 chintz, tammie
glossy ~: 4 lamé, silk 5 ramee, ramie, satin 6 sateen 7 taffeta 8 diamante
goat ~: 3 aba 4 abba 5 Kasha 7 kashmir 8 cashmere
gown ~: 4 lamé, silk 5 satin, tulle
hand-dyed ~: 5 batik 6 battik
heavy ~: 4 wool 5 denim, loden 6 burlap, canvas, crepon 8 cretonne
hose ~: 5 lisle, nylon
lightweight ~: 5 voile
linen ~: 4 lawn 5 toile 6 canvas, damask 7 cambric 8 chambray, marcella 10 seersucker
looped ~: 5 frise
measure: 3 ell 4 bolt, yard 6 denier
mesh ~: 3 net 4 leno 5 gauze 7 fishnet, netting, tiffany 8 tarlatan
metallic ~: 4 lamé
mohair ~: 7 grogram 8 sanglier
muslin ~: 4 mull
napped ~: 5 baize 7 flannel
natural ~: 4 silk, wool 6 cotton
nonwoven ~: 4 felt 5 suede
nylon ~: 5 satin, tulle 6 gloria, jersey, tricot, velvet 7 chiffon, organza, taffeta 8 Milanese 9 grenadine, sailcloth
open ~: 3 net 4 lace, leno, mesh 5 scrim, tulle
pattern: 4 dots 5 twill
patterned ~: 5 plaid, print 6 madras, tartan 7 gingham
poplin-like ~: 9 Bengaline
puckered ~: 6 plisse
quilted ~: 5 cloky 6 cloque
rayon ~: 3 rep 4 repp 5 moire, piqué, satin, surah, tulle, voile 6 chally, faille, jersey, pongee, poplin, velvet 7 challie, challis, charvet, chiffon, duvetyn, foulard, Mogador, organza, ottoman, silesia, taffeta 8 Celanese, chenille, marocain, Milanese, popeline, shantung 9 grenadine, sharkskin 10 seersucker
reversible ~: 6 damask
ribbed ~: 3 rep 4 cord, repp 5 pique, twill 6 faille, poplin, tricot 7 épinglé 8 corduroy 9 grosgrain
sheer ~: 4 lawn, leno 5 gauze, ninon, toile, voile 6 barege, dimity 7 batiste, chiffon 9 georgette
sheet ~: 4 pima 6 cotton
shirt ~: 4 pima, silk 5 nylon 6 cotton, Madras 9 polyester
silk ~: 3 rep 4 repp 5 crape, crepe, gazar, Honan, moire, pekin, piqué, plush, satin, surah, tulle, voile 6 armure, camaca, camaka, camoca, damask, faille, gloria, jersey, pongee, poplin, samite, tricot, tussah, tusseh, tusser, tussor, tussur, velvet 7 charvet, chiffon, duvetyn, foulard, grogram, Mogador, organza, ottoman, sarsnet, tabaret, tabinet, taffeta, tussore 8 chambray, chenille, marocain, Milanese, paduasoy, popeline, sarcenet, sarsenet, tabbinet 9 charmeuse, grenadine 10 peau de soie
silklike ~: 5 ramee, ramie
silky ~: 6 fleece
soft ~: 6 chally 7 challie, challis
striped ~: 7 gingham 8 bayadere
suit ~: 4 wool 5 serge, tweed, twill
summer ~: 5 linen, voile
sweater ~: 4 wool 5 Orlon
synthetic ~: 4 poly 5 Arnel, Dynel, Kodel, Lycra, nylon, Orlon, rayon 6 Ban-Lon, Dacron 7 Gore-Tex, spandex 9 gabardine, polyester
taffeta ~: 6 faille
tie ~: 4 repp, silk 7 charvet, Mogador
tie-dyed ~: 4 ikat 5 batik 6 battik
towel ~: 5 crash, terry
transparent ~: 5 toile
twill ~: 5 chino, denim, serge 6 coburg, coutil, oxford 7 Cheviot, estamin, foulard, hickory, nankeen, silesia, Viyella 8 canotier, casimere, casimire, moleskin, prunella, prunelle, prunello, shalloon, Venetian 9 bombazeen, bombazine, cassimere, gabardine, henrietta, paramatta, sharkskin 10 broadcloth
upholstery ~: 5 frise 6 damask, velour 7 tabaret, velours 8 moquette 9 horsehair, Naugahyde
veil ~: 3 net 6 barege
velvet ~: 5 panne
velvetlike ~: 6 velour 7 mockado, velours 8 moquette
vinyl ~: 9 Naugahyde
waterproof ~: 5 loden 7 Gore-Tex, oilskin 8 oilcloth
wavelike ~: 5 moire
wax-glazed ~: 4 cire
whitener: 6 bluing 7 blueing
wool ~: 3 rep 4 felt, repp 5 baize, Kasha, khaki, plush, serge, tweed, voile 6 alpaca, Angora, armure, chally, damask, gloria, jersey, kersey, merino, mohair, moreen, poplin, saxony, stamin, tartan, tricot, vicuña, wadmal 7 bunting, challie, challis, Cheviot, drugget, duvetyn, flannel, grogram, paisley, tabinet, Viyella, worsted 8 algerine, homespun, marocain, shalloon, tabbinet, Venetian, whipcord 9 astrakhan, calamanco, grenadine, henrietta, paramatta 10 Irish tweed
wool-like ~: 7 satinet 9 satinette
worker: 4 dyer
worker's concern: 6 dye lot
worsted ~: 5 serge 6 wadmal 7 estamin, etamine 8 casimere, casimire, sanglier, Venetian 9 cassimere, gabardine, sharkskin
woven ~: 4 knit, mesh, wool 5 linen 8 barathea
wrinkle-resistant ~: 5 Orlon 6 Dacron
see also material

fabricate: 4 fake, make 5 build, draft, erect, feign, forge, frame, fudge, put up, shape, weave 6 cook up, create, devise, invent, make up, whip up 7 compose, concoct, falsify, fashion, imagine, prepare, produce, trump up, turn out 8 assemble, simulate 9 construct, establish, formulate, structure 10 brainstorm, exaggerate
fabricated: 4 fake, made, sham 5 bogus, false, phony, put-on 6 ersatz, made-up, phoney, pseudo, unreal 8 mythical, spurious 9 imitation, synthetic, unfounded, unnatural 10 artificial, fictitious, fraudulent
fabrication: 3 fib, lie 4 fake, hoax, myth, tale, yarn 5 rumor, story 6 deceit 7 fiction, forgery, product, untruth 8 assembly, creation, pretense 9 structure
fabricator: 4 liar 5 maker 6 framer 7 builder, creator, devisor, drafter 9 assembler
Fabric, Bent song: Alley Cat (1962)
fabrics, like some: 5 sheer 6 fleecy 7 natural 9 synthetic
fabric softener: 5 Downy 6 Bounce 7 Snuggle 9 Cling Free 10 Final Touch
Fabrizi: 4 Aldo
fabulist: 3 Ade 4 Esop, liar 5 Aesop 9 George Ade
fabulous: 3 def, rad 4 aces, A-one, boss, braw, cool, dece, epic, fine, gear, keen, neat, nice, phat, tops, tuff 5 boffo, dandy, ducky, grand, great, marvy, neato, nobby, prime, primo, slick, super, swell 6 bang on, bang-up, bonzer, bosker, choice, divine, dreamy, far-out, gnarly, groovy, lovely, peachy, slap-up, spot on, superb, terrif, tiptop, unreal, whizzo, wicked 7 amazing, awesome, boffola, capital, corking, perfect, ripping, skookum, stellar, sublime 8 dazzling, especial, eximious, five-star, four-star, frabjous, glorious, heavenly, jim-dandy, mythical, slam-bang, smashing, splendid, standout, sterling, stickout, striking, superior, terrific, top-level, topnotch, very good, wondrous 9 bodacious, Endsville, excellent, exemplary, exquisite, fantastic, first-rate, high-grade, hunky-dory, imaginary, legendary, marvelous, sollicker, thrilling, top-drawer, top-flight, unrivaled, wonderful, wunderbar 10 astounding, first-class, hotsy-totsy, incredible, jack-a-dandy, miraculous, out of sight, outrageous, peachy-keen, phenomenal, remarkable, stupendous, super-duper, tremendous, unrivalled
Fabulous Baker Boys, The (1989 film)
cast: Beau Bridges, Jeff Bridges, Michelle Pfeiffer
director: Steve Kloves
facade: 3 act 4 mask, pose, sham, wall 5 cloak, decoy, front, guise, put-on, shell 6 veneer 7 outside, surface 8 disguise, exterior, pretense 9 semblance 10 appearance, false front, masquerade
face: 3 air, mug 4 defy, font, line, look, meet, puss, risk, show, side 5 brave, front, guide, nerve, plane, pride, shell 6 accost, aspect, engage, give on, kisser, take on, veneer, visage 7 display, encrust, eyeball, front on, grimace, incrust, outside, profile, surface 8 boldness, confront, cope with, exterior, features, laminate, overlook 9 encounter, front onto, impudence, semblance, stand up to, withstand 10 appearance, effrontery, experience, expression, look toward, reckon with, turn toward
about ~: 4 turn 5 U-turn 6 switch 8 reversal 9 one-eighty
boldly: 4 dare, defy 5 brave 8 confront 9 stand up to
card: 4 jack, king 5 honor, queen
combining form: 6 -hedron, prosop- 7 prosopo-
cover: 4 mask, veil 6 domino
down: 4 defy 6 oppose 9 challenge
ender: 4 down 5 cloth, plate
fall flat on one's ~: 4 fail, flop
familiar ~: 6 patron 7 devotee, habitué, visitor 8 customer 10 frequenter
fly in the ~ of: 4 dare, defy 6 oppose 7 disobey
for ~ value: 5 at par
get in one's ~: 5 annoy 6 accost, bother 8 confront 9 challenge
in Spanish: 4 cara
it has a ~: 5 clock, watch
lacking ~ value: 5 no par
loss of ~: 5 shame, stain, taint 6 stigma 8 disgrace, dishonor, ignominy 9 abashment, disrepute
make a ~: 3 mug 4 moue 5 scowl, smirk, sneer, wince
make a long ~: 4 mope, pout, sulk 5 brood
off: 5 argue, brawl, clash, fight, scrap 6 bicker, debate 7 contend, dispute, mix it up, quarrel, wrangle 8 squabble 9 lock horns
on the ~ of it: 9 evidently, outwardly, seemingly 10 apparently, ostensibly
part: 3 ear, eye, jaw, lip 4 chin, hair, nose 5 cheek, mouth, naris 6 dimple 7 eyebrow, eyelash, nostril 8 philtrum
put on a happy ~: 4 beam, grin 5 smile
red in the ~: 6 ablush
see face to ~: 5 greet 7 run into 8 bump into, confront 9 run across
shape: 4 oval 5 ovate, ovoid, round 8 elliptic 10 elliptical
show one's ~: 5 pop in, visit 6 appear, arrive, attend, blow in, drop in, emerge, roll in, turn up 7 check in, clock in, punch in, turn out 8 breeze in
slap in the ~: 4 slam, slur 5 smear 6 rebuke, slight 7 affront, obloquy, offense, repulse 9 aspersion, cheap shot, rejection 10 backbiting, defamation, detraction, opprobrium
slapper's shout: 5 fresh
starter: 3 dog 4 bold, club, pale, type 5 black, dough, inter, light, white
take at ~ value: 4 rely 5 bet on, trust 6 accept, assume, bank on, commit, credit, expect, lean on, look to, rely on 7 believe, consign, count on, entrust, presume, suppose, swear by 8 depend on, rely upon
the day: 4 rise, wake 5 arise, awake, get up 6 awaken
up to: 5 admit 8 confront, cope with, deal with 10 meet head on
vertical ~: 4 crag, hill 5 bluff, cliff 8 mountain 9 precipice
wear a long ~: 4 fret, moon, pine, pout, sulk 5 brood, droop 6 grieve, lament
with a long ~: 4 glum, mopy 5 mopey
with a straight ~: 7 for real 9 seriously, sincerely
face __: 3 bow 4 card, down, gear, mask, time, up to 5 angle, cloth, facts, towel, value 6 powder
face-__: 3 off 4 down, lift, nail 6 harden, saving
__ face: 4 baby, left, long, lose, save 5 about, beach, false, make a, poker, right, smile 6 smiley 7 working
__-face: 5 about, kissy, volte
Face __ Manchu, The: 4 of Fu
__ Face: 4 Baby 5 Angel, Funny
Face Behind the Mask, The (1941 film)
cast: Evelyn Keyes, Peter Lorre
faced
combining form: 6 -hedral
starter: 4 bare 5 shame
__-faced: 3 pie, red, sad, two 4 baby, bald, bold, full, lean, long, moon, open, rock 5 glass, hairy, horse, Janus, pasty, pitch, poker, round, steel, stone, stony, white 6 brazen, double, quarry, rubber, smooth 7 freckle
__-faced lie: 4 bald
facedown: 5 prone
__-faced sandwich: 4 open
__-Faced Woman: 3 Two
Face in the Crowd, A (1957 film)
cast: Tony Franciosa, Andy Griffith, Walter Matthau, Patricia Neal, Lee Remick

director: Elia Kazan
face in the misty light, The: 5 Laura
face-lift
give a ~: 5 fix up, rehab, renew 6 revamp, update 7 remodel, restore, touch up 8 overhaul, renovate, spruce up 9 modernize, refurbish
___ Face Nelson: 4 Baby
face-off: 5 set-to, start 6 launch 7 opening 9 beginning, inception
Face/Off (1997 film)
cast: Joan Allen, Nicolas Cage, John Travolta
director: John Woo
Face of Fear, The author: Dean Koontz
Face of Fire (1959 film)
cast: Bettye Ackerman, Cameron Mitchell, James Whitmore
director: Albert Band
___ face of it: 5 on the
face powder mineral: 4 talc
Faces (1968 film)
cast: Lynn Carlin, John Marley, Gena Rowlands
director: John Cassavetes
___ Faces Life: 6 Portia
___ Faces of Eve, The: 5 Three
facet: 4 side 5 phase, plane, thing 6 aspect 7 element, feature, respect, surface 9 attribute
face that launched a thousand ships, The: 5 Helen
face the ___: 5 music
___ Face the Music and Dance: 4 Let's
Face the Nation (CBS news)
former host: 5 Stahl
facetious: 4 flip 5 comic, droll, funny, silly, witty 6 jocose, joking, jovial 7 amusing, comical, jesting, jocular, joshing, kidding, playful, satiric, waggish 8 farcical, flippant, humorous 9 frivolous, laughable, ludicrous, sarcastic, satirical, sprightly, whimsical 10 indecorous, irreverent, nonserious, ridiculous
be ~ with: 3 kid 4 twit 5 tease
facetiously: 5 in fun 7 as a joke, as a lark 8 for a joke
facetiousness: 3 wit 5 humor 6 comedy, levity 8 jocosity 10 jocularity
face-to-face: 6 direct, head-on, openly 7 vis-à-vis 8 directly, opposite 10 unmediated
see ~: 4 meet
face-up: 6 supine
facial: 7 mudpack
expression: 4 grin 5 scowl, smile, smirk 7 grimace
feature: 3 ear, eye, jaw, lip 4 chin, hair, nose 5 beard, cheek, mouth 6 dimple, eyelid 7 eyebrow, eyelash 8 philtrum
see also face
facial ___: 5 angle, index, nerve 6 tissue
___ facie: 5 prima
facile: 3 ace, pat 4 able, deft, easy, glib 5 adept, handy, light, quick, vocal 6 adroit, expert, fluent, simple, smooth 7 flowing 8 dextrous, skillful 9 dexterous 10 child's play, effortless, elementary, proficient
facileness: 4 ease
facilitate: 3 aid 4 ease, help 5 favor, speed 6 assist, enable, grease, smooth 7 further, lighten, make for, promote, speed up 8 expedite, simplify
facilitation: 3 aid 4 help 6 assist 10 assistance
facilities: 4 gear 9 equipment
facility: 3 art 4 bent, ease 5 knack, skill, touch 6 office, talent 7 ability, amenity, faculty, fluency, freedom, knowhow, prowess, sleight 8 aptitude, capacity, hang of it 9 dexterity, eloquence, readiness, technique 10 adroitness, capability, efficiency, green thumb, smoothness
health-care ~: 8 hospital 9 infirmary 10 dispensary
facing: 5 front 6 across, lining, toward, veneer 7 against, coating, towards 8 covering, opposite 10 decoration
Facing the Flag author: Jules Verne
facsimile: 4 copy, stat, twin 5 clone, ditto, image, mimeo, model, Xerox 6 double, ectype 7 replica 8 knockoff, likeness 9 duplicate, look-alike, miniature, photocopy, Photostat 10 carbon copy, dead ringer, transcript
fact: 5 datum, given, known, thing, truth 6 gospel, truism, verity 7 finding, reality 9 actuality, certainty, certitude, principle 10 particular, phenomenon
assumed as ~: 5 given 9 axiomatic 10 postulated, understood
contrary to ~: 5 false 6 untrue 9 incorrect 10 fabricated, fallacious, fictitious, inaccurate
due to the ~ that: 7 whereas
ending: 3 oid, ory
establish as ~: 5 prove 6 verify 7 certify, confirm, warrant 8 document, validate 9 ascertain, determine
for a ~: 3 yes 4 amen, sure 5 quite, truly 6 and how, easily, indeed, really, simply, surely, to a tee 7 exactly, flat out, in truth, right on 9 assuredly, certainly, decidedly, doubtless, expressly, hands down, in reality, on the nose 10 absolutely, by all means, definitely, positively
in spite of the the ~ that: 6 albeit, though 8 although 10 even though
not based on ~: 6 untrue 7 invalid 8 spurious 9 erroneous, unfounded 10 fallacious, groundless
numerical ~: 4 stat
old-style: 5 sooth
state as ~: 4 aver, avow 5 posit
take as ~: 6 accept, assume 7 believe, suppose, surmise 9 postulate
fact ___: 6 finder
fact-___ mission: 7 finding
___ facta: 4 bene
fact-finding: 8 research
faction: 3 set 4 band, bloc, camp, cell, clan, club, crew, cult, part, ring, sect, side, team, wing 5 cabal, cadre, crowd, group, junto, lobby, party, split 6 caucus, circle, clique, schism, strife 7 coterie, discord, in-group 8 disunity, intrigue, offshoot 9 coalition 10 disharmony, dissension, persuasion
factional: 8 partisan 9 divergent, sectarian, sectional
factious: 6 unruly 7 defiant, wayward 8 contrary, disloyal, indocile, mutinous, perverse, stubborn 9 alienated, bellicose, dissident, insurgent, obstinate 10 disorderly, rebellious, refractory
factitious: 4 fake, mock, sham 5 bogus, faked 8 affected 9 contrived, insincere, pretended, simulated, unnatural 10 artificial, fictitious
___ facto: 4 ipso
facto, de: 4 real 5 truly 6 actual, really 8 actually 9 actuality, in reality 10 unimagined
fact of ___: 4 life
factor: 4 part 5 agent, cause, piece, thing 6 agency, detail, medium 7 element, feature, portion, quality, steward 9 appointee, component, gobetween 10 ingredient, instrument
in: 5 weigh 6 assess 7 analyze, examine 8 appraise, consider, evaluate
pivotal ~: 3 key 5 hinge 7 fulcrum
supporting ~: 4 crux, root 5 basis, cause 6 motive, reason 7 footing, grounds, premise, pretext 8 evidence 9 criterion, principle 10 assumption, foundation
___ factor: 4 load, risk, unit 5 chill, fudge, noise 6 common, filter, Rhesus, safety 7 culture
factorage: 7 percent 10 commission
___ Factor, The: 5 Delta, Hades 7 Sot-Weed, Tangent
factory: 4 mill, shop 5 forge, plant 6 office 7 foundry 8 business
built in a ~: 3 mfd.
converted ~ space: 4 loft
figure: 3 mgr. 7 foreman, manager
group: 5 union
make in a ~: 3 mfr.
modernize a ~: 5 refit
owners' org.: 3 NAM
period: 5 shift
right from the ~: 3 new 5 fresh 8 brand-new
second: 5 irreg. 9 irregular
store: 6 outlet
work: 3 mfg.
factory ___: 4 ship 5 price 6 outlet 7 trawler
factotum: 4 aide 5 agent, do-all 6 drudge, lackey, slavey 7 lacquey 8 handyman 9 gal Friday, man Friday 10 girl Friday
facts: 4 data, dope, info, poop 5 proof, score, truth 7 details, lowdown, reality 8 material 9 knowledge 10 brass tacks
absorb ~: 4 cram 5 learn 6 soak up, take in 7 drink in 8 memorize
alter ~: 3 lie 5 fudge
bare ~: 7 outline
___ facts: 4 bare, face
Facts in the Case of M. Valdemar, The author: Edgar Allan Poe
Facts of Life, The (1960 film)
cast: Lucille Ball, Bob Hope, Ruth Hussey
Facts of Life, The (NBC sitcom)
cast: Mindy Cohn (Natalie Green) Kim Fields (Tootie Ramsey) Nancy McKeon (Jo Polniaczek) Charlotte Rae (Edna Garrett) Lisa Whelchel (Blair Warner)
factual: 4 just, real, true 5 exact, frank, legit, right, valid 6 actual, honest, kasher, kosher, square 7 correct, empiric, genuine, precise, upright 8 absolute, accurate, concrete, credible, flawless, positive, straight, truthful, unbiased, unerring, verified 9 authentic, empirical, errorless, unadorned, veracious, veritable 10 forthright, historical, on the level, scrupulous, unmistaken
factuality: 5 right, truth 8 accuracy, fidelity, veracity 9 precision 10 exactitude
factually: 5 truly
factum: 5 truth
facula: 7 sunspot
faculties: 4 mind, wits 5 sense 6 brains, reason, wisdom 8 judgment, lucidity, sagacity, sapience 9 intellect 10 perception
with full ~: 4 sane 5 sober, sound 8 composed, rational, sensible 9 collected, judicious, practical, pragmatic, temperate 10 controlled
faculty: 4 bent, gift, head 5 flair, knack, power, profs, sense, skill, staff, touch 6 talent 7 ability, aptness, know-how 8 aptitude, capacity, facility, hang of it, instinct, penchant, teachers 9 academics, dexterity, endowment, lecturers, personnel 10 adroitness, capability, efficiency, green thumb, proclivity, professors, propensity
head: 4 dean
member: 4 prof 7 teacher 8 lecturer 9 professor 10 instructor
Faculty, The (1998 film)
cast: Jordana Brewster, Josh Hartnett, Salma Hayek, Elijah Wood
Facundo author: Domingo Sarmiento
fad: 3 bug 4 mode, pogs, rage 5 craze, mania, style, thing, trend, vogue 7 in thing, lambada, novelty, pet rock 8 hot pants, Hula-Hoop, lava lamp, mood ring 9 streaking 10 dernier cri
doll: 5 troll
Fadayev, Aleksandr: 6 writer 7 Russian
faddish: 3 hip, hot, mod, new, now 4 chic 5 smart 6 latest, modish, red-hot, trendy, with-it 7 à la mode, current, dashing, in vogue, popular, stylish 8 last-word, up-to-date 9 happening 10 all the rage
___-faddle: 6 fiddle
fade: 3 die, dim, dip, ebb 4 coif, flag, melt, pale, pass, thin, tire, wane, wear, wilt 5 abate, decay, peter, waste, weary 6 blanch, bleach, blench, die out, hairdo, lessen, recede, vanish, weaken, whiten, wither 7 becloud, decline, decolor, die down, dwindle, relapse, tail off, thin out, wash out 8 coiffure, decrease, dissolve, etiolate, evanesce, get tired, languish, melt away, peter out, slack off, taper off, tone down, trail off 9 attenuate, disappear, evaporate, fizzle out 10 decolorize
ender: 3 out 4 away
in: 4 loom 6 appear, emerge
Fade Away (1981 song) artist: Bruce Springsteen
faded: 3 dim 4 dark, drab, dull, pale, weak 5 dusky, faint, fuzzy, light, mirky, murky, seedy, stale, tacky 6 bleary, blurry, shabby 7 shadowy 9 colorless, washed-out 10 indistinct, lackluster, lusterless
fade-in: 4 shot
fade-out technique: 4 iris
Fadiman: 7 Clifton
fading: 4 weak 5 decay 9 on the wane
away: 3 ebb 5 decay 6 ebbing 7 abating 8 decaying 9 abatement
faerie: 3 elf 6 sprite
Faerie Queene, The: 4 epic, poem
author: Edmund Spenser
character: 3 Ate, Una 4 Alma, Atin, Jove, Lucy 5 Aldus, Amyas, Colin, Diana, Dolon, Druon, Error, Furor, Guyon, Irena, Talus, Venus 6 Abessa, Adonis, Amavia, Amidas, Amoret, Belgae, Briana, Burbon, Coelia, Duessa, Elissa, Faunus, Medina, Merlin, Munera, Panope, Poeana, Serena, Timias 7 Acrasia, Aladine, Argante, Despair, Fidelia, Melissa, Perissa, Proteus 8 Calidore, Clarinda, Gloriana
division: 5 canto
Faeroe Islands
capital: 8 Tórshavn
locale: 3 Atl. 8 Atlantic
Fagin: 5 crook 10 pickpocket
Fahd, King: 4 Arab
faith: 5 Islam
Fahey: 4 Jeff, John
Fahr.: 4 temp.
not ~: 3 Cel.

Fahrenheit: 6 Daniel 7 Gabriel
measure: 3 deg. 6 degree
Fahrenheit 451: 4 film 5 novel
author: Ray Bradbury
cast: Julie Christie, Cyril Cusack, Oskar Werner
director: François Truffaut
Fahrenheit, Gabriel: 6 German 9 physicist
fail: 2 go 3 die, lag, sag 4 bomb, bust, flop, flub, fold, lose, miss, muff, sell, sink, tire, wane, wilt 5 close, decay, flunk, peter, yield 6 blow it, desert, fizzle, go bust, shrink, slight, weaken 7 abandon, conk out, decline, default, forsake, founder, go kaput, go under, go wrong, let down, lose out, mistake, neglect, poop out, relapse, wash out 8 backfire, collapse, fall down, fall flat, flounder, go astray, languish, lay an egg, peter out 9 backslide, break down, fall short, fizzle out, go belly up, strike out 10 be defeated, disappoint, go bankrupt, go downhill, run aground
bound to ~: 5 no-win
don't ~: 3 win 7 succeed
ender: 3 ure
prefix: 3 for-
to do: 4 miss, omit, shun, skip, snub 5 evade, scorn, shirk, spurn 6 bypass, forget, ignore, pass by 7 let pass, neglect 8 brush off, let slide, overlook, pass over 9 disregard, gloss over
to keep: 5 use up, waste 6 divest, mislay 7 forfeit 8 misplace, squander 9 dissipate 10 run through
to keep up: 4 drag, flag, poke 5 dally, tarry, trail 6 dawdle, falter, linger, loiter 7 fall off, slacken 8 hang back, lose time, straggle 10 dillydally, lose ground
without ~: 6 indeed, really, surely 9 certainly 10 absolutely, by all means, definitely, infallibly, invariably, positively
fail-__: 4 safe, soft
__-fail: 4 pass
failed
in French: 6 manqué
to: 5 didn't
failing: 3 shy 4 flaw, vice, weak 5 decay, fault, guilt, lapse, short 6 defect, foible, poorly, skimpy 7 decline 8 drawback, weakness 9 blind spot, deficient, worsening 10 deficiency, faultiness, inadequacy, inadequate, inefficacy
grade: 2 ef
that: 4 else 9 otherwise
faille: 4 silk 6 fabric 7 taffeta
fail-safe: 4 sure 7 certain 8 inerrant, reliable, unerring 9 foolproof, goofproof 10 infallible, undoubtful
Fail-Safe: 4 film 5 novel
author: 7 Burdick, Wheeler
cast: Henry Fonda, Walter Matthau, Fritz Weaver
director: Sidney Lumet
fails to be: 4 ain't, isn't
failure: 3 bum, dog, dud 4 bomb, bust, flop, loss, miss, muff, rout, ruin, slip 5 crash, lapse, lemon, loser, slump, smash, wreck 6 bungle, defeat, fiasco, turkey 7 also-ran, debacle, default, misstep, reverse, tragedy, undoing, washout 8 collapse, downfall, shortage 9 breakdown, defaulter, oversight 10 bankruptcy, inadequacy, insolvency, misfortune, nonpayment, nonsuccess
exclamation: 4 pfft 5 phfft
prefix: 3 mis-
to act, in law: 6 laches
fain: 5 ready 6 gladly
Fain: 5 Sammy 6 Ferris
faineance: 5 sloth 6 acedia, torpor 7 inertia, languor, laxness 8 idleness, laziness, otiosity 9 indolence, torpidity 10 stagnation
fainéant: 4 logy 6 torpid 7 shirker 8 indolent, slothful 9 do-nothing, goldbrick, shiftless 10 ne'er-do-well
faint: 3 dim, low, wan 4 dull, hazy, pale, slim, soft, tire, weak, wilt 5 bated, dizzy, faded, fuzzy, light, muted, piano, plotz, quail, queer, quiet, swoon, tired, vague, wispy, woozy 6 far off, feeble, go limp, hushed, sickly, silent, slight, subtle, weaken 7 distant, languid, muffled, obscure, outside, pass out, slender, starved, subdued, syncope, tenuous, unclear, wispish 8 blackout, collapse, cowardly, dampened, deadened, keel over, languish, lifeless, listless, murmured, starving, timorous, unlikely 9 enervated, exhausted, toned down, whispered 10 ill-defined, indistinct, turned down
become ~: 3 die, dim, ebb 4 fade, melt, pale, wane 6 die out, fizzle, recede, vanish 7 die away, dwindle, slacken, subside, tail off 8 diminish, evanesce, fade away, melt away, peter out, slack off, taper off, trail off 9 attenuate, fizzle out
feeling ~: 5 woozy
heart: 8 cold feet, timidity 9 cowardice
fainthearted: 4 meek, weak 5 cowed, mousy, timid, wimpy 6 afraid, craven, mousey, scared, trepid, yellow 7 abashed, alarmed, anxious, chicken, daunted, fearful, gutless, nervous, panicky, spooked, wimpish 8 cowardly, fearsome, hesitant, recreant, timorous 9 petrified, spineless, terrified, tremulous 10 frightened
faintheartedness: 4 fear
fainting: 6 aswoon
faintly: 6 hardly 7 lightly, scantly 8 scarcely, slightly
fair: 3 due 4 even, expo, just, mart, mild, nice, okay, okeh, okey, open, show, so-so, tidy 5 balmy, bazar, blond, bonny, clean, clear, equal, legal, legit, light, right, sound, sunny, white 6 bazaar, blonde, bonnie, bright, circus, comely, decent, fiesta, honest, in play, lawful, likely, lovely, market, medium, modest, not bad, pretty, proper, serene, square 7 average, clement, condign, ethical, logical, upright 8 adequate, all right, balanced, carnival, deserved, festival, gorgeous, handsome, mediocre, middling, moderate, ordinary, passable, rightful, sporting, straight, sunshiny, tolerant, unbiased 9 beautiful, cloudless, equitable, honorable, impartial, objective, palatable, righteous, temperate, tolerable, tow-haired, towheaded, unclouded, uncolored, unnotable, unslanted 10 aboveboard, acceptable, attractive, enchanting, evenhanded, exhibition, exposition, legitimate, on the level, pretty good, principled, reasonable, scrupulous
amount: 4 half, some
and square: 4 even, just 6 honest
don't play ~: 5 cheat
ender: 3 way 4 lead 5 water 6 ground, leader
local ~: 5 feria
mark: 3 cee
name meaning ~: 9 Guinevere
not ~: 4 foul 5 dirty, shady 6 biased, skewed, unjust 7 corrupt, crooked, partial 8 partisan, stinking 9 dishonest 10 subjective
offering: 4 ride
play: 6 equity 7 justice 8 equality
religious ~ of India: 4 mela
shake: 6 chance 9 equitable 10 likelihood
to middling: 4 okay, so-so 8 mediocre, moderate 9 tolerable
fair __: 3 off, sex 4 ball, copy, game, play 5 catch, shake, trade 6 dinkum 7 housing
fair-__: 6 haired, minded, spoken
fair-__ agreement: 5 trade
fair-__ boy: 6 haired
fair-__ friend: 7 weather
fair-__ law: 5 trade
fair-__ value: 6 market
__ fair: 3 fun 5 craft 6 county, world's
__ fair...: 4 All's
Fair __: 4 Deal
__ Fair: 4 All's 5 State 6 Vanity, World's
Fair, A.A., real first name: 4 Erle
fair and __: 6 square
Fair as __, when only one...: 5 a star
Fairbanks: 4 city, town 5 Chuck 7 Charles, Douglas
locale: 6 Alaska
newspaper: 9 News-Miner
road to ~: 5 Alcan
Fairbanks Jr., Douglas: 5 actor
film: Angels Over Broadway (1940)
Chances (1931)
The Corsican Brothers (1941)
Gunga Din (1939)
It's Tough to Be Famous (1932)
Joy of Living (1938)
The Life of Jimmy Dolan (1933)
Little Caesar (1930)
Morning Glory (1933)
The Narrow Corner (1933)
Our Modern Maidens (1929)
Outward Bound (1930)
The Prisoner of Zenda (1937)
The Rage of Paris (1938)
Sinbad the Sailor (1947)
State Secret (1950)
Success at Any Price (1934)
Union Depot (1932)
The Young in Heart (1938)
spouse: Joan Crawford
Fairbanks Sr., Douglas: 5 actor
film: The Black Pirate (1926)
The Iron Mask (1929)
The Mark of Zorro (1920)
Mr. Robinson Crusoe (1932)
The Thief of Bagdad (1924)
spouse: Mary Pickford
Fairborn: 4 city, town
locale: 4 Ohio
Fairchild: 6 Morgan
Fair Deal monogram: 3 HST
__-faire: 6 savoir 7 laissez
Fairest of the Fair, The composer: 5 Sousa
Fairfax: 4 city, town
locale: 8 Virginia
Fairfield: 4 city, town
locale: 4 Conn., Ohio 10 California
fairground: 5 field
employee: 5 carny 6 carney
prize: 4 doll 6 kewpie 8 goldfish
fair-haired: 3 pet 5 blond 6 blonde, chosen 7 darling, favored, popular 9 fortunate, preferred 10 privileged
one's nickname: 5 Sandy 7 blondie
fair-haired __: 3 boy
fair-hiring letters: 3 EEO, EOE 4 EEOC
fair lance, name meaning: 6 Rowena
Fairland: 4 city, town
locale: 8 Maryland
Fairlane: 3 car 4 auto, Ford 10 automobile
Fair Lawn: 4 city, town
locale: 9 New Jersey
Fairleigh Dickinson: 6 school
athletes: 7 Knights
locale: 7 Teaneck 9 New Jersey
fairly: 5 clean, quite 6 enough, kind of, pretty, rather, sort of 8 by rights, somewhat 10 moderately, more or less
good: 4 so-so 6 decent, not bad 7 average 8 adequate, all right, bearable, mediocre, middling, moderate, ordinary, passable 9 tolerable 10 acceptable, admissible, reasonable, sufficient
in Latin: 9 pari passu
well: 4 so-so 9 tolerably 10 acceptably, adequately
Fair Maid of Perth, The composer: 5 Bizet
fair-market __: 5 price, value
fair-minded: 4 just, sane 7 neutral 9 impartial, unslanted
Fairmont: 3 car 4 auto, city, Ford, town 10 automobile
locale: 3 W. Va. 9 Minnesota
fairness: 5 honor, right 6 equity 7 decency, honesty, justice, probity 8 equality 9 balminess, good faith, integrity 10 moderation
Fair Oaks: 4 city, town
locale: 10 California
Fair Penitent, The author: 4 Rowe
fair-skinned: 5 light
fairs, like state: 6 annual
__ Fair, The: 4 Holy 5 Horse
fair-trade __: 3 law
Fairuza: 4 Balk
fairway
see golf
Fairweather: 4 peak 5 mount 8 mountain
locale: 6 Alaska
fair-weather friend: 4 user 5 phony
Fairwood: 4 city, town
locale: 10 Washington
fairy: 3 elf, fay, imp 4 peri, pixy 5 pixie 6 sprite 7 brownie 10 leprechaun
concern: 5 tooth
ender: 4 land
godmother: 5 donor 6 backer, patron 10 benefactor
Irish ~: 4 shee, sidh 5 sidhe
like a ~: 3 fey 4 tiny 5 elfin, teeny 6 elfish, elvish, teensy 9 sprightly
story: 4 lore, myth, tale 5 fable 6 legend 7 fantasy, fiction 8 allegory, delusion, folktale 9 falsehood, invention
tale: 4 yarn 5 story 7 romance
fairy __: 4 lamp, lily, ring, tale, wand 5 glove, green, stone, story 6 shrimp 9 godmother
__ fairy: 5 tooth
__-fairy: 4 airy
fairyland: 9 unreality
Fairy-Land author: Edgar Allan Poe
fairy-slipper: 5 plant 6 flower
fairy tale
character: 3 elf, imp 4 nixy, ogre, pixy 5 giant, gnome, nixie, pixie, troll 6 goblin, kobold, sprite 7 brownie, gremlin, monster 9 hobgoblin 10 leprechaun
locale: 3 hut 6 castle, forest
word: 4 ever, once 5 after 7 happily
fairy-tale: 8 fanciful, mythical, romantic
Fairytale (1974 song) artist: Pointer Sisters
__ Fairy Tales: 6 Grimm's
fais-__: 4 dodo
__ fait: 5 tout à
fait accompli: 4 fact 5 given 7 reality 9 actuality, certainty

fait, au: 4 deft 5 slick 6 adroit, expert, nimble, posted, proper, versed 7 abreast, capable, skilled, trained 8 decorous, dextrous, graceful, informed, masterly, seasoned, skillful 9 competent, dexterous, efficient, masterful, qualified 10 conversant, proficient, well-versed
faites ___ jeux: 3 vos
faith: 3 rel. 4 sect 5 creed, dogma, piety, stock, tenet, trust 6 belief, credit, fealty, virtue 7 loyalty 8 credence, doctrine, fidelity, reliance, religion, theology 10 allegiance, confidence, conviction, dependance, dependence, persuasion, principles
articles of ~: 5 canon, creed, dogma 6 belief, tenets 8 doctrine, ideology, religion 9 teachings 10 persuasion, principles
bad ~: 5 fraud 6 deceit, dupery 7 perfidy 8 betrayal, quackery 9 deception, duplicity, hypocrisy, treachery 10 dishonesty, disloyalty
break ~: 4 sell 7 sell out 8 go back on
colleague: 4 hope 7 charity
good ~: 5 honor, truth 6 candor 7 decency, honesty, probity 8 fairness, veracity 9 frankness, integrity, sincerity
have ~: 7 believe
in good ~: 5 truly 7 frankly 8 candidly, for keeps, heartily, honestly 9 earnestly, genuinely, seriously, sincerely 10 aboveboard, truthfully
keeping the ~: 6 upbeat 7 hopeful, wishful 8 aspiring, sanguine, trusting 9 confident, expectant 10 optimistic
keep the ~: 7 abide by 8 adhere to, carry out
lack of ~: 5 doubt 8 distrust, mistrust, wariness 9 disbelief, misgiving, suspicion 10 skepticism
lose ~: 7 despair 10 give up hope
name meaning ~: 4 Vera
take on ~: 5 trust 6 accept, assume 7 believe
unquestioning, as ~: 8 mindless 9 oblivious, senseless
see also religion
faith ___: 4 cure 6 healer
___ faith: 3 bad 4 good 5 act of 6 animal
Faith: 4 Ford, Hill 5 Evans, Percy 7 Daniels, Popcorn
Faith (1987 song) artist: George Michael
___ faith and credit: 4 full
faithful: 4 fast, good, holy, just, nice, true 5 exact, liege, loyal, right, sound 6 ardent, devout, loving, steady, trusty 7 careful, correct, devoted, dutiful, literal, precise, sincere, staunch 8 accurate, constant, hard-core, obedient, reliable, resolute, true-blue, virtuous, yeomanly 9 allegiant, authentic, dedicated, honorable, realistic, steadfast, unfailing 10 convincing, dependable, unwavering
be ~: 6 adhere
keep ~ to: 4 heed, obey 6 adhere, follow 7 abide by, conform, fulfill, observe, respect, stand by 8 carry out 9 discharge, stick with 10 comply with
___ Faithful: 3 Old
Faithfull: 8 Marianne
faithfully: 9 honorably 10 unerringly
faithfulness: 5 honor, right, troth, trust 6 fealty, virtue 7 loyalty 8 devotion, fidelity
faithless: 5 false 6 fickle, rotten, untrue 7 corrupt, unloyal 8 cheating, disloyal, forsworn, recreant, two-faced 9 deceitful, dishonest, insincere, skeptical, two-timing 10 capricious, changeable, inconstant, perfidious, traitorous, unfaithful, unreliable, untruthful
Faithless (2000 film) director: Liv Ullmann
faithlessness: 6 deceit 7 perfidy, sellout, treason 8 betrayal 9 deception, desertion, duplicity, treachery, two-timing 10 disloyalty, infidelity
Faith No More song: Epic (1990)
Faith of Our Fathers: 4 hymn
Faith, Percy: 9 conductor
song: Theme From A Summer Place (1960)
___ fait rien: 4 ça ne
fajita: 9 appetizer
fake: 3 bad, lie, rig 4 copy, faux, hoax, imit., juke, mock, sham 5 actor, bluff, bogus, cheat, color, decoy, false, feign, forge, fraud, fudge, phony, pseud, put on, quack, quasi, setup, spoof 6 affect, assume, ersatz, forged, invent, phoney, play at, poseur, pseudo, unreal 7 assumed, bluffer, charade, falsify, feigned, forgery, pretend, trump up 8 affected, disguise, hoodwink, imposter, impostor, invented, simulate, spurious 9 charlatan, concocted, contrived, deception, deceptive, dissemble, fabricate, falsified, falsifier, hypocrite, imitation, imposture, improvise, insincere, invention, mare's nest, pretended, pretender, simulated, synthetic 10 artificial, fabricated, factitious, fictitious, fraudulent, mountebank, unreliable
in ice hockey: 4 deke
it: 3 act 4 pose, sham 5 ad-lib, feign 6 affect 7 playact, posture, pretend, show off 8 simulate 9 improvise, put on airs 10 grandstand, masquerade, put on an act
not ~: 4 real 5 legit 6 actual, square 7 genuine 8 bona fide, truthful 9 authentic 10 legitimate
out: 4 deke, fool, hoax 5 bluff, outdo, trick 6 outwit 7 pretend 8 outsmart
prove ~: 6 debunk 9 shoot down
fake ___: 3 fur, out 4 book
fake-book notation: 5 chord 6 chords, melody
faked: 4 mock 5 put-on, set-up 6 pseudo 8 spurious 9 impromptu 10 artificial, factitious, fictitious
fake-ID user: 4 teen 5 minor 10 adolescent
faker: 5 fraud, phony, pseud, quack 6 forger, phoney 8 imposter, impostor 9 charlatan, falsifier, hypocrite, pretender 10 mountebank
fakery: 4 sham 6 deceit 8 flimflam, pretense
Fakin' It (1967 song) artist: Simon and Garfunkel
fakir: 5 Hindu 6 beggar, Hindoo, Moslem, Muslim 7 ascetic, dervish 9 mendicant, religious
income: 4 alms
Fala: 3 dog, pet 7 Scottie
owner: 3 FDR 9 Roosevelt
falafel: 5 snack
bean: 4 fava
bread: 4 pita
Falana: 4 Lola
falcate: 6 curved, hooked 8 crescent
Falco, Edie: 7 actress
film: Judy Berlin (2000)
Laws of Gravity (1991)
Sunshine State (2002)
TV: The Sopranos, Oz
falcon: 4 bird, hawk 5 saker 6 lanner, merlin, tercel 7 kestrel 9 peregrine 10 bird of prey
cover a ~'s eyes: 4 seel
feature: 3 neb 4 beak, claw
home: 4 nest
hunter: 5 Spade
leash: 4 lune
like a ~: 6 hooded
relative: 4 kite 8 caracara
strap: 4 jess
young: 4 eyas
___ falcon: 5 saker 7 prairie
Falcon: 3 car 4 auto, Ford 10 automobile, footballer
rival: 3 Jet, Ram 4 Bear, Bill, Colt, Lion 5 Brown, Chief, Eagle, Giant, Niner, Raven, Saint, Texan, Titan 6 Bengal, Bronco, Cowboy, Jaguar, Packer, Raider, Viking 7 Charger, Dolphin, Panther, Patriot, Redskin, Seahawk, Steeler 8 Cardinal 9 Buccaneer
Falcon Crest (CBS drama)
cast: Ana Alicia (Melissa)
Abby Dalton (Julia Cumson)
Robert Foxworth (Chase Gioberti)
Margaret Ladd (Emma Channing)
Lorenzo Lamas (Lance Cumson)
David Selby (Richard Channing)
Susan Sullivan (Maggie Gioberti)
Jane Wyman (Angela Channing)
valley: 7 Tuscany
Falconer author: John Cheever
falconry: 5 sport
leash: 4 lune
Falcons: 4 team 6 eleven
home: 7 Atlanta
org.: 3 NFC, NFL
sport: 8 football
___ Falcon, The: 7 Maltese
falderal: 3 gas, rot 4 blah, bosh, bull, bunk, guff, jazz, jive, pooh, tosh 5 bilge, fudge, hokum, hooey, prate, stuff, trash, tripe 6 bunkum, bushwa, drivel, footle, gabble, gammon, gibber, havers, hot air, humbug, jabber, jargon, kibosh, piffle 7 baloney, blarney, blather, blether, boloney, bushwah, eyewash, flannel, flubdub, fooling, fustian, garbage, hogwash, inanity, rubbish, twaddle 8 buncombe, claptrap, flimflam, flummery, nonsense, slipslop, tommyrot, trumpery 9 banana oil, gibberish, kidstakes, moonshine, poppycock, rigmarole 10 applesauce, balderdash, bilge water, codswallop, double-talk, flapdoodle, galimatias, Jabberwock, mumbo jumbo, rigamarole, taradiddle
Faldo, Nick: 6 golfer
milieu: 5 links 6 course
org.: 3 PGA
Faline: 4 deer, toon
friend: 5 Bambi
Falkberget, Johan: 6 writer 9 Norwegian
Falkenburg, Jinx spouse: Tex McCrary
Falkirk: 4 city, town
locale: 8 Scotland
Falklands: 4 isls. 5 isles 7 islands
Falk, Peter: 5 actor
film: ... All the Marbles (1981)
The Brink's Job (1978)
The Cheap Detective (1978)
Cookie (1989)
The Great Race (1965)
The In-Laws (1979)
It's a Mad Mad Mad Mad World (1963)
Lakeboat (2001)
Luv (1967)
Made (2001)
Murder by Death (1976)
Pressure Point (1962)
Robin and the Seven Hoods (1964)
TV: Columbo
fall: 3 cut, dip, ebb, sag, set 4 dive, drip, drop, ease, flag, flop, lull, plop, rain, ruin, sink, slip, thud, tilt, trip, wane 5 abate, crash, lapse, let up, lower, occur, pitch, reach, slide, slope, slump, spill, swoop, thump, yield 6 autumn, defeat, give up, go down, happen, header, lessen, plunge, recede, relent, season, topple, tumble 7 cascade, crumble, decline, descend, descent, drop off, dwindle, founder, give way, plummet, stumble, subside, succumb, tail off, tip over 8 collapse, decrease, diminish, downturn, drop down, keel over, lowering, moderate, nosedive 9 abatement, backslide, come about, dwindling, hairpiece, lessening, overthrow, perdition, plump down, reduction, surrender, take place 10 come to pass, diminution, hit the dirt
apart: 3 rot 6 go awry 8 collapse, disunite 9 break down, decompose
asleep: 3 nap, nod 4 doze, rest 5 droop 6 catnap, drowse, snooze 7 drop off 8 drift off
at the feet of: 6 grovel
back: 3 ebb 5 lapse 6 recede, retire 7 regress, relapse, retreat 8 withdraw 10 lose ground
back on: 3 use 6 employ, look to, resort, take to 8 call upon, resort to, retire to 9 count upon, make use of, retreat to 10 withdraw to
back (on): 5 count 6 depend
behind: 3 lag 5 trail
cause of a ~: 6 hubris, hybris
clumsily: 4 trip
color: 4 rust
cousin: 3 wig 6 toupee
do a ~ chore: 4 rake
down: 4 fail 7 give way 8 collapse 10 disappoint
down on: 4 fail 6 sadden 7 sell out 8 embitter, imbitter 10 disappoint, disenchant
ender: 3 off, out 4 back, fish 5 board
event: 5 frost
fader: 3 tan
flat: 4 bomb, bust, fail, flop, lose, miss, slip, trip 5 crash, flunk 6 blow it, falter 7 blunder, founder, go under, go wrong, misfire, misstep, stumble, wash out 8 collapse, flounder, lay an egg 9 strike out
flower: 3 mum 5 aster
for: 3 buy 4 love 7 swallow
forward: 5 pitch
from grace: 3 err, sin 5 lapse, stray 7 do wrong, offense 8 iniquity 9 backslide 10 transgress
from the sky: 4 hail, rain, snow 5 sleet
gathering: 4 crop 6 leaves
guy: 3 sap 4 butt, dupe, lamb, prey 5 chump, patsy, raker 6 pigeon, sucker 9 scapegoat
heir to: 3 get, own 4 gain 6 obtain 7 acquire, inherit, receive, succeed 8 come into, take over
ill with: 3 get 5 catch
in: 4 come, sink 6 arrive 8 collapse, come down 9 break down 10 fraternize
into place: 4 form, jell 5 click
in with: 4 join, meet 5 enter 6 sign on, sign up 7 run into 8 bump into, chance on, come upon, take part 9 accompany, encounter, run across 10 chance upon, come across
let ~: 4 drop, shed 5 spill

let ~ between the cracks: 4 omit 6 forget, ignore 7 neglect 8 overlook 9 disregard
like a ~ day: 5 brisk, crisp
month: 3 Dec., Nov., Oct., Sep. 4 Sept. 7 October 8 December, November 9 September
off: 3 dip, ebb, lag 4 curb, drop, flag, slip, slow 5 erode, lower, slide, slump 6 lessen, reduce, shrink, worsen 7 curtail, cut down, dwindle, regress 8 diminish, peter out, slow down 10 degenerate
off the wagon: 5 drink, lapse 7 regress 9 backslide
on: 5 go for 6 assail, attack 7 assault, run into 8 meet with 10 experience
on one's knees: 7 bow down, worship 9 genuflect, prostrate 10 pay tribute
opposite: 4 rise
out: 5 scrap, sleep 7 quarrel, wrangle 8 squabble
over: 4 trip 5 swoon 7 pass out
planting: 4 bulb
preceder: 4 trip 5 pride
protection: 3 net
rise and ~: 4 toss 6 billow, rhythm
short: 4 fail, lack, lose, miss 7 let down
sign: 5 Libra 7 Scorpio 11 Sagittarius
silent: 5 quiet 6 shut up 7 be quiet 8 pipe down 9 keep still
sound of a ~: 5 splat
starter: 3 dew, ice, pit 4 dead, down, even, foot, land, prat, rain, snow, wind 5 night, short, water
through: 4 fail, flop 6 fizzle 7 founder, misfire 8 collapse
to: 7 get busy
upon: 4 raid 5 lunge 6 pounce, strike
worker: 5 raker
fall __: 3 for, guy, off, out 4 away, back, down, flat, foul, line, upon, wind 5 apart, front, short, under 6 behind 7 through, webworm
fall __ bed: 4 into 5 out of
fall __ grace: 4 from
fall __ line: 4 into 5 out of
fall __ on: 4 back
fall __ the cracks: 7 through
fall __ to: 4 back, prey
fall __ upon: 4 back
fall __ wayside: 5 by the
fall-__ position: 4 back
__ fall: 3 ash 4 free
Falla: 4 peak 5 mount 8 mountain
locale: 10 Antarctica
fallacious: 3 bad 5 false, not so, phony, wrong 6 faulty, phoney, untrue 7 inexact, invalid, unsound 8 deluding, delusive, delusory, illusive, illusory, mistaken, specious, spurious 9 beguiling, deceitful, deceiving, deceptive, erroneous, illogical, incorrect, sophistic, unfounded 10 fictitious, fraudulent, ill-founded, inaccurate, irrational, misleading, reasonless, ungrounded, unreasoned
fallacy: 5 error 6 deceit 7 falsity, sophism, untruth 8 delusion, illusion 9 casuistry, deception, sophistry 10 invalidity
Falla, Manuel de: 7 Spanish 8 composer
work: The Three-Cornered Hat
Fallbrook: 4 city, town
locale: 10 California
fall by the __: 7 wayside
__ fall down: 3 All
fallen: 4 flat 6 ruined, shamed 9 collapsed, disgraced, prostrate 10 dishonored
angel: 5 devil, Satan 6 Belial, diablo 7 evil one, Lucifer 9 Beelzebub
starter: 4 chap, chop 5 crest
fall from __: 5 grace
Fall From Grace author: Andrew Greeley
Fall Guy, The (ABC adventure)
cast: Douglas Barr (Howie Munson) Lee Majors (Colt Seavers) Markie Post (Terri) Heather Thomas (Jody Banks)
fallibility: 7 errancy 8 humanity
fallible: 5 human 6 broken, errant, erring, faulty, flawed, marred 7 damaged, unsound 8 careless, impaired 9 defective, imperfect 10 unreliable
falling: 4 down 7 descent
apart: 5 shaky 7 rickety, run-down 8 decrepit 9 crumbling 10 ramshackle, tumbledown
for anything: 4 naif 5 green, naive 6 simple, unwary 8 gullable, gullible, trusting 9 accepting, believing, credulous 10 uncritical
keep from ~: 4 hold, lift, prop 5 boost, brace, carry, shore, stake 6 assist, buoy up, hold up, prop up 7 bolster, fortify, shore up, support 8 buttress 9 reinforce, stabilize, undergird 10 strengthen
like ~ off a log: 4 easy, snap 6 facile, picnic, simple 7 no sweat 8 no bother 9 no problem, no trouble 10 child's play, effortless, elementary
sound: 4 plop
falling __: 4 band, door, down, star 5 apart 6 action, rhythm 7 weather
falling __ log: 4 off a
Falling (1963 song) artist: Roy Orbison
Falling in Love (1984 film)
cast: Robert De Niro, Harvey Keitel, Meryl Streep
director: Ulu Grosbard
Falling in Place author: Ann Beattie
falling-off: 4 wane 5 slump 7 decline 8 decrease
falling-out: 3 row 4 feud, fuss, rift, spat, tiff 5 clash, fight, run-in 6 breach 7 dispute, quarrel, wrangle 9 imbroglio 10 difficulty
minor ~: 4 spat, tiff 5 scrap 8 squabble
__ falling, The: 5 sky is
Fallin' in Love (1975 song) artist: Hamilton, Joe Frank & Reynolds
__ Fall in Love: 4 Let's 5 When I
fall into __: 3 bed 4 line 5 a trap
falloff: 3 dip 4 drop 5 slide, slump 7 decline 8 contract, decrease, slowdown 9 abatement
Fall of Hyperion, The poet: 5 Keats
Fall of Moondust, A author: Arthur C. Clarke
Fall of the House of Usher, The author: Edgar Allan Poe
Fall of the Roman Empire, The (1964 film)
cast: Stephen Boyd, Sir Alec Guinness, Sophia Loren, James Mason
director: Anthony Mann
fall on __ ears: 4 deaf
Falloppio: 8 Gabriele
fallout: 6 effect, result 7 outcome 9 aftermath
fall out of __: 3 bed 4 line
fallow: 4 idle 6 barren, unused, yellow 7 dormant, sterile 8 inactive, unfarmed, unplowed, unseeded, untilled 9 unplanted
lie ~: 4 idle 8 languish, stagnate
Fall River: 4 city, town
locale: 4 Mass.
Falls: 4 Mesa 5 Angel 6 Iguaçu 7 Iguassú, Kalambo, Niagara 8 Victoria, Yosemite
__ Falls Conference: 6 Seneca
__ Falls, Idaho: 4 Twin
__ Falls, NY: 5 Glens
Fall, The author: Albert Camus
fall through the __: 6 cracks
Falmouth: 4 city, port, town
locale: 4 Mass.
false: 4 fake, foul, mock, sham 5 bogus, lying, not so, phony, wrong 6 ersatz, faulty, forged, hollow, made-up, off-key, phoney, pseudo, tricky, unreal, untrue 7 assumed, corrupt, crooked, devious, feigned, in error, inexact, invalid, plastic, unloyal, unsound 8 affected, cooked-up, delusive, disloyal, forsworn, guileful, improper, libelous, mistaken, mythical, recreant, specious, spurious, strained, suborned, two-faced 9 concocted, contrived, deceitful, deceptive, disguised, dishonest, erroneous, faithless, illogical, imaginary, incorrect, insincere, pretended, simulated, synthetic, trumped-up, two-timing, unfounded, unnatural 10 artificial, fabricated, fallacious, fictitious, fraudulent, groundless, ill-founded, inaccurate, inconstant, mendacious, misleading, perfidious, substitute, traitorous, unfaithful, ungrounded, unreliable, untruthful
accusation: 4 slur 5 smear 6 bum rap 7 calumny
appearance: 3 act 4 mask 5 guise 10 camouflage
at times: 3 ans. 6 answer
bear ~ witness: 3 lie 5 libel 7 perjure 9 dissemble
claim: 4 hoax 5 frame, smear 6 canard
combining form: 5 pseud- 6 pseudo-
declare ~: 4 deny 5 rebut 6 impugn, reject 7 disavow, gainsay 8 disclaim, renounce 9 repudiate 10 contradict, controvert
friend: 5 enemy, Judas, knave, snake 7 traitor 8 betrayer, informer 9 informant
front: 3 act 4 airs, mask, pose, sham, show 5 bluff, guise 6 facade 8 disguise
give a ~ impression: 4 hoke 5 belie 6 lead on
god: 4 Baal, idol 10 juggernaut
handle: 5 alias 6 anonym 7 moniker, pen name 9 pseudonym, stage name 10 nom de plume
move: 4 trip 5 boner 7 misstep, mistake
notion: 4 myth 7 fantasy 8 delusion, illusion
play ~: 4 sell 7 sell out 8 go back on
put on a ~ front: 3 lie 7 cover up, deceive, mislead 9 misdirect, misinform 10 steer wrong
report: 3 lie 4 tale 5 libel, smear 7 calumny, slander, untruth 10 imputation
show ~: 5 belie, rebut 6 debunk, refute 7 confute 10 prove wrong
witness: 4 liar
false __: 3 rib 4 aloe, card, cast, dawn, face, move, pond, step 5 alarm, color, front, fruit, start, teeth, topaz 6 acacia, aralia, arrest, bottom, colors, indigo, ipecac, memory, mildew 7 horizon, vampire, witness
falsehood: 3 fib, lie 4 myth, sham, tale 5 rumor, story 6 canard, deceit, dupery 7 fiction, untruth, whapper, whopper 8 pretense 9 deception, duplicity, fairy tale, half-truth, invention, mendacity 10 dishonesty, distortion, imputation
False Memory author: Dean Koontz
__ false move...: 3 One
falseness: 3 lie 6 deceit 9 desertion, improbity 10 disloyalty, infidelity
False Prophet author: Faye Kellerman
__-false test: 4 true
falsetto: 4 male 6 singer
sing ~: 5 yodel, yodle
falsification: 3 lie 4 hoax 7 forgery 8 pretense
falsified: 3 bad 5 wrong 7 corrupt, crooked 8 doctored 9 erroneous, incorrect 10 fraudulent
falsifier: 4 liar 5 faker, fraud 6 forger
falsify: 3 lie, rig 4 fake, hoke 5 color, forge, fudge, twist 6 deacon, doctor, invent, juggle, suborn 7 distort, perjure, phony up 8 disguise, misquote, misstate 9 dissemble, embroider, fabricate
falsity: 3 fib, lie 4 sham 5 error, fraud 6 canard, deceit, dupery 7 fallacy, perfidy, untruth 9 deception, duplicity, mendacity, treachery 10 dishonesty, inaccuracy, infidelity, invalidity
Falstaff: 3 Sir 4 John 5 opera
composer: 5 Elgar, Verdi
friend: 3 Hal
like ~: 5 heavy, obese, stout 6 portly, rotund, stocky 8 thickset 9 corpulent 10 abdominous
quaff: 3 ale
role: 4 Anne, Ford, Page 5 Caius 6 Fenton, Pistol 7 Quickly 8 Bardolph, Nannetta
setting: 7 England, Windsor
song: 4 aria
where ~ premiered: 5 Milan
falter: 3 lag, sag 4 bomb, bust, flop, halt, limp, lose, reel, slip, trip 5 flunk, lurch, quail, waver 6 blow it, boggle, bumble, hobble, linger, recoil, teeter, topple, totter, wabble, weaken, wobble 7 blunder, founder, go under, go wrong, misstep, scruple, stagger, stammer, stumble, stutter, wash out 8 be unsure, fall flat, flounder, hang back, hesitate, lay an egg 9 hem and haw, strike out, vacillate
faltering: 4 lame, puny, weak 5 frail, shaky, wimpy 6 anemic, atonic, effete, feeble, fickle, flabby, flimsy, infirm 7 anaemic, fragile, halting, wimpish 8 delicate, helpless, hesitant, pithless, wavering 9 doddering, hesitancy, ill at ease, irregular, powerless, tentative, uncertain 10 ambivalent, hesitation, incoherent, indecisive, irresolute, vulnerable, weak-willed, wishy-washy
falteringly, move: 6 totter 7 stagger
Faltermeyer: 6 Harold
Faludi: 5 Susan
Falwell: 5 Jerry
fam.
see family
Fam and Yam author: Edward Albee
Famatina: 4 peak 5 mount 8 mountain
locale: 5 Andes 9 Argentina
fame: 4 mark, name, note 5 éclat, glory 6 credit, renown, repute 7 acclaim, laurels, stardom, success 8 eminence, prestige 9 celebrity, notoriety, spotlight 10 importance, notability, popularity, prominence, reputation
attain ~: 6 arrive
Fame (TV drama)
cast: Debbie Allen (Lydia Grant) Cynthia Gibb (Holly Laird) Carlo Imperato (Danny Amatullo) Nia Peeples (Nicole Chapman) Gene Anthony Ray (Leroy Johnson)

Fame and Fortune (1960 song) artist: Elvis Presley
famed: 5 great, noted 7 eminent, notable, storied 8 glorious, historic, laureate, renowned 9 legendary, prominent 10 celebrated, preeminent
Fame (song) artist: David Bowie, Irene Cara
familial: 6 lineal 9 ancestral 10 affiliated
familia member: 3 tía, tío 4 niña, niño 5 madre, padre 7 hermana, hermano
familiar: 3 old 4 cosy, cozy, dull, mate 5 aware, close, cozey, cozie, known, nervy, thick, usual 6 chatty, chummy, common, friend, genial, posted, social, versed, vulgar, wise to 7 abreast, affable, cordial, general, natural, popular, relaxed, routine 8 amicable, friendly, habitual, informal, informed, intimate, ordinary, sociable 9 au courant, cognizant, customary, easygoing, prevalent, well-known 10 accustomed, acquainted, buddy-buddy, conversant, dullsville, palsy-walsy, proverbial
be ~ with: 4 know 9 recognize
face: 6 patron 7 devotee, habitué, regular, visitor 8 customer 10 frequenter
get ~: 6 orient
less ~: 5 newer
not ~: 5 alien 7 foreign, strange, unknown, unusual 10 outlandish
not yet ~ with: 5 new to
too ~: 4 dull, flat 5 banal, corny, hokey, stale, tired, trite, vapid 6 common, jejune, old hat 7 clichéd, insipid, prosaic, routine 8 bromidic, ordinary, shopworn, timeworn 9 hackneyed 10 pedestrian, uninspired, unoriginal, warmed-over
with: 4 onto, upon 6 at home, used to 10 conversant, proficient, well-versed
familiarity: 4 ease 5 grasp, sense 6 déjà vu 7 freedom, liberty, license, mastery 8 intimacy, openness
familiarize: 5 enure, inure 6 ground, inform, orient 8 accustom, acquaint, initiate
Familiar Quotations author: John Bartlett
famille member: 4 fils, mère, père 5 frère, oncle, soeur, tante
family: 3 ilk, kin 4 clan, kids, kind, line, race, sort 5 brood, class, folks, group, house, stock, young 6 lineal, litter, origin, people, strain 7 kindred, kinfolk, lineage, progeny 8 kinfolks, kinsfolk 9 household, offspring, posterity, relatives 10 hereditary
member: 2 ma, pa 3 bro, dad, kin, mom, pop, rel., sis 4 aunt, gram 6 cousin, father, gramps, mother, sister 7 brother, grandma, grandpa 8 relative
room item: 2 TV 3 VCR 5 TV set
vehicle: 3 car 4 auto 5 sedan
family ___: 3 man 4 fare, hour, name, plan, room, time, tree 5 Bible, court, leave, style 6 circle, doctor, values
___ family: 5 birth, first, heath, joint, royal 7 blended, nuclear
___-family: 6 single
Family (ABC drama)
cast: Meredith Baxter-Birney (Nancy Maitland)
James Broderick (Doug Lawrence)
Gary Frank (Willie Lawrence)
Kristy McNichol (Buddy Lawrence)
Sada Thompson (Kate Lawrence)
Family ___: 3 Man 4 Feud, Plot, Ties 6 Affair, Circle, Circus
Family ___, A: 6 Affair 7 Fortune
Family ___, The: 3 Man, Way 6 Circle, Moskat 7 Arsenal, Reunion
___ Family: 4 Holy 5 Mama's, Poppy, We Are
Family Affair (CBS sitcom)
cast: Sebastian Cabot (Mr. French)
Kathy Garver (Cissy)
Anissa Jones (Buffy)
Brian Keith (Bill Davis)
Johnnie Whitaker (Jody)
dog: 6 Oliver
Family Affair (1971 song) artist: Sly and the Family Stone
Family Affair, A (1937 film)
cast: Lionel Barrymore, Spring Byington, Mickey Rooney
director: George B. Seitz
Family Arsenal, The author: Paul Theroux
Family Business (1989 film)
cast: Matthew Broderick, Sean Connery, Dustin Hoffman
director: Sidney Lumet
Family Circle, The author: André Maurois
Family Circus, The: 5 comic 7 cartoon
artist: Bil Keane
cat: 8 Kittycat
character: 3 Bil 4 Thel 5 Billy, Dolly, Jeffy
dog: 3 Sam 5 Barfy
mischief-maker: 5 Not Me
Family Feud: 8 game show
host: Richard Dawson, Ray Combs, Louie Anderson, Richard Karn
Family Fortune, A author: Weidman
Family Man (1983 song) artist: Hall and Oates
Family Man, The (2000 film)
cast: Nicolas Cage, Don Cheadle, Téa Leoni
director: Brett Ratner
Family Moskat, The author: Isaac Bashevis Singer
Family of Charles IV artist: 4 Goya
Family Plot (1976 film)
cast: Karen Black, Bruce Dern, William Devane, Barbara Harris
director: Alfred Hitchcock
Family Reunion, The author: T.S. Eliot
___ Family Robinson: 5 Swiss
___ Family Singers: 5 Trapp
family-size: 3 big 5 giant, jumbo, large
___ Family, The: 3 Abe 5 Hogan, Royal 6 Addams 7 Aldrich
Family Ties (NBC sitcom)
cast: Justine Bateman (Mallory Keaton)
Meredith Baxter-Birney (Elyse Keaton)
Michael J. Fox (Alex P. Keaton)
Michael Gross (Steve Keaton)
Tina Yothers (Jennifer Keaton)
___ Family Values: 6 Addams
Family Way, The (1966 film)
cast: Hywel Bennett, Hayley Mills, John Mills
famine: 4 lack, need, want 6 dearth 7 paucity, poverty
opposite: 5 feast
relief: 4 food
famine-stricken: 5 unfed
famish: 6 starve
famished: 5 empty, unfed 6 hungry 7 peckish, starved 8 edacious, esurient, ravenous, starving 9 insatiate, voracious
famishment: 6 hunger 7 edacity 8 appetite, voracity 9 appetence, esurience
Famke: 7 Janssen
famous: 4 star 5 great, known, noted 6 fabled, signal 7 eminent, leading, notable, popular, salient, storied 8 glorious, historic, immortal, laureate, renowned 9 acclaimed, legendary, memorable, notorious, prominent, topflight, well-known 10 celebrated, noteworthy, preeminent, proverbial, publicized, remarkable
become ~: 6 arrive 7 succeed
person: 4 lion, star 7 notable 9 celebrity, dignitary
___-famous: 5 world
___ Famous: 6 Almost
Famous Amos: 6 cookie
alternative: 7 Archway, Keebler, Nabisco 8 Sunshine 9 Mrs. Fields 10 Peak Freans
famous army, name meaning: 6 Luther
famously: 4 well 7 greatly
famous spear, name meaning: 5 Roger
famous warrior, name meaning: 6 Ludwig 8 Aloysius
fan: 3 nut 4 buff 5 fiend, freak, hound, lover, whiff 6 addict, adorer, blower, cooler, maniac, rooter, unfold 7 admirer, air-cool, cool off, devotee, groupie, support 8 adherent, disciple, follower, partisan 9 propeller, spectator, strike out, supporter 10 aficionado, enthusiast, ventilator
be a ~: 4 root
club focus: 4 idol
combining form: 5 rhipi- 6 rhipid- 7 rhipido- 8 flabelli-
creation: 6 breeze
disenchanted ~: 5 booer
display: 4 wave
ender: 3 dom, jet 4 fare, tail, wort 5 light
jazz ~: 3 cat 6 bopper, hepcat
like a ~ belt: 4 taut 5 tight
mag: 4 zine
noise: 3 rah 5 cheer
opposite: 5 hater
out: 6 expand, spread, unfold 7 scatter 8 disperse
part: 5 blade, grill, motor
setting: 3 low 4 high 5 on low 6 medium
sound: 4 whir 5 whirr
fan ___: 3 out 4 belt, club, mail, palm, roof, worm 5 delta, vault 6 letter, window
fan-___: 3 tan 6 tailed
___ fan: 3 sea 4 tail 7 ceiling, exhaust
Fan
home: 5 Gabon, Gabun 6 Africa 8 Cameroon
fanatic: 3 bug, nut 5 bigot, crank, demon, fiend, freak 6 addict, daemon, daimon, maniac, zealot 7 devotee, groupie, radical, touched, zealous 8 activist, inflamer, militant, partisan, ultraist 9 demagogue, extremist, sectarian 10 aficionado, enthusiast
ender: 3 ism
feeling: 4 zeal
fanatical: 3 mad 4 avid, wild 5 crazy, fiery, manic, rabid, ultra 6 crazed, fervid, gung-ho, raving 7 burning, extreme, fervent, intense, radical, rampant, zealous 8 dogmatic, frenzied, obsessed, wild-eyed 9 credulous, emotional, obsessive, obstinate, possessed 10 dogmatical, headstrong, immoderate, intolerant, prejudiced
fanatically: 4 very 7 greatly, rabidly 9 extremely, zealously
fanaticism: 4 zeal 6 frenzy 8 zealotry 9 contumacy, extremism, injustice, intensity, monomania, obstinacy, prejudice 10 chauvinism, dedication, enthusiasm, narrowness, partiality
fancied: 5 liked, loved 7 desired 9 imaginary, preferred
fancier: 5 liker 6 rooter 7 admirer, devotee 8 follower
fanciful: 4 tall 5 ideal 6 dreamy, irreal, quaint, unreal 8 baseless, delusive, illusive, illusory, quixotic 9 dreamlike, fairy-tale, idealized, imaginary, vagarious, visionary, whimsical 10 capricious, chimerical, fictitious, improbable, quixotical
fanciness: 4 chic 5 swank, vogue
fancy: 3 yen 4 chic, fine, haut, idea, lacy, like, love, posh, rich, urge, want, whim, will, wish 5 adore, covet, crave, dream, enjoy, favor, gaudy, haute, jazzy, quirk, ritzy, showy, swank, taste, think 6 chichi, choice, deluxe, desire, dressy, flashy, flossy, frilly, glitzy, lavish, liking, ornate, prefer, reckon, relish, spiffy, swanky, vagary 7 adorned, believe, caprice, care for, chimera, dream of, dream up, elegant, for show, imagine, impulse, opulent, passion, picture, realize, suppose, surmise, think up, thought, wish for 8 chimaera, crotchet, daydream, envisage, envision, fondness, penchant, pleasure, yearn for, yearning 9 decorated, elaborate, expensive, hankering, intricate, luxuriant, luxurious, obsession, pipe dream, sumptuous, visualize 10 conceive of, custom-made, decorative, ornamental, ornamented, partiality, preference, propensity, woolgather
affair: 2 do 4 ball, bash, gala 7 banquet, shindig 8 function, wingding
Dan: 4 dude 5 swell 10 jack-a-dandy
digs: 5 manor 6 estate 7 chateau, mansion 10 plantation
display: 4 ritz
dress: 6 finery 9 caparison
fabric: 4 lamé, silk 5 satin
flight of ~: 6 revery 7 reverie
not ~: 5 bleak, plain, stark 6 barren, severe 7 austere 9 unadorned
passing ~: 3 fad 4 rage, urge, whim 5 craze, mania, quirk 6 notion, vagary 7 caprice, impulse 8 crotchet
tickle one's ~: 5 amuse, cheer 6 divert, please, tickle 7 delight 9 entertain, titillate
fancy ___: 3 Dan 4 dive, fern 5 dress 6 diving
fancy-___: 4 free 5 pants
___ fancy: 7 passing
Fancy ___!: 4 that
Fancy Dress Party, The author: Albert Moravia
Fancy Feast: 7 cat food
alternative: 5 Amore 6 Figaro, Purina 7 Whiskas 8 Friskies 10 Chef's Blend
Fancy Free: 6 ballet
choreographer: 7 Robbins
composer: 9 Bernstein
Fancy Pants (1950 film)
cast: Lucille Ball, Bruce Cabot, Bob Hope
Fancy that!: 3 gee
fandangle: 5 frill 9 adornment 10 decoration
fandango: 5 dance
instrument: 6 guitar
kin: 6 bolero 9 malaguena
fandom: 9 followers
fane: 6 church, temple
Faneuil Hall locale: 6 Boston
fanfare: 3 ado 4 pomp 5 blare, éclat, noise, tusch 6 hoopla, hoorah, hooray, hurrah, hurray, parade 7 tan-

tara **8** ballyhoo, flourish **9** publicity
verbal ~: 4 ta-da **5** ta-dah
Fanfare for Fred composer: PDQ Bach
Fanfare for the Common Cold composer: PDQ Bach
Fanfare for the Common Man composer: Aaron Copland
fanfaron: 6 gascon **7** boaster, fanfare **8** blowhard, braggart **9** big talker
fanfaronade: 6 hot air **7** big talk, bluster, bombast, bravado **8** boasting, bragging **9** gasconade
fang: 5 tooth **7** incisor
__ Fang: 5 White
Fang home: 5 Gabon, Gabun **6** Africa **8** Cameroon
fanion: 4 flag
Fannie: 5 Flagg, Hurst **6** Farmer
Fannie __: 3 Mae
Fanny: 5 Brice **6** Burney, Kemble
Fanny (1961 film)
cast: Charles Boyer, Leslie Caron, Maurice Chevalier
director: Joshua Logan
Fanny and Alexander (1983 film)
director: Ingmar Bergman
Fanny author: Erica Jong
Fanny's First Play author: George Bernard Shaw
fanon: 4 cape **5** orale **7** maniple
Fanon: 6 Frantz
__ fan palm: 5 dwarf **7** Chinese
fans: 6 circle **8** groupies **9** entourage, followers, following
Fanshawe author: Nathaniel Hawthorne
Fansler: 4 Kate
Fanta: 9 soft drink
alternative: 3 TAB **4** Nehi **6** Fresca, Sprite **8** Diet Rite, Dr Pepper **9** Canada Dry **10** Mello Yello, Royal Crown **11** Mountain Dew
fantabulous: 3 def, rad **4** aces, A-one, boss, braw, cool, dece, fine, gear, keen, neat, nice, phat, tuff **5** dandy, ducky, grand, great, marvy, neato, nobby, prime, slick, super, swell **6** bang on, bang-up, bonzer, bosker, choice, divine, dreamy, far-out, gnarly, groovy, lovely, peachy, slap-up, spot on, superb, terrif, tiptop, unreal, whizzo, wicked **7** amazing, awesome, capital, corking, perfect, ripping, skookum, stellar, sublime **8** dazzling, especial, eximious, five-star, four-star, frabjous, glorious, heavenly, jim-dandy, slam-bang, smashing, splendid, standout, sterling, stickout, superior, terrific, top-level, topnotch, very good, wondrous **9** bodacious, Endsville, excellent, exemplary, exquisite, first-rate, high-grade, hunky-dory, marvelous, sollicker, top-flight, wonderful **10** first-class, hotsy-totsy, jack-a-dandy, out of sight, peachy-keen, phenomenal, remarkable, stupendous, super-duper
fantail: 4 bird **6** pigeon **7** warbler
fan-tan: 4 game **6** sevens **8** card game
fantasia: 5 music
Fantasia
creature: 4 faun
dancer: 5 hippo
hippo's wear in ~: 4 tutu
fantasist: 7 dreamer **8** escapist, idealist **10** daydreamer
fantasize: 4 moon **5** dream **7** imagine, picture **8** daydream, envision **10** wool-gather
fantastic: 3 odd **4** A-one, eery, huge **5** crazy, eerie, great, super, weird **6** absurd, atypic, exotic, far-out, freaky, groovy, irreal, quirky, superb, unreal **7** awesome, bizarre, deviant, extreme, massive, oddball, offbeat, strange, surreal, uncanny, unusual **8** aberrant, abnormal, atypical, enormous, fabulous, freakish, peculiar, romantic, splendid, terrific, uncommon **9** anomalous, delicious, different, divergent, eccentric, excellent, fictional, first-rate, grotesque, humongous, imaginary, irregular, laughable, ludicrous, marvelous, monstrous, whimsical, wonderful, wunderbar **10** artificial, capricious, chimerical, far-fetched, fictitious, first-class, incredible, irrational, monumental, outlandish, out of sight, phenomenal, prodigious, ridiculous, stupendous, tremendous, unfamiliar, unorthodox
trip the light ~: 4 step **5** dance, party, rumba, tango, waltz **6** cha-cha, rhumba **7** cut a rug
Fantasticks, The (2000 film)
cast: Joel Grey, Jean Louisa Kelly, Joe McIntyre, Brad Sullivan
character: 4 Matt **5** Luisa **7** El Gallo
composer: 5 Jones **7** Schmidt
director: Michael Ritchie
Fantastic Mr. Fox author: Roald Dahl
Fantastic Voyage (1966 film)
cast: Stephen Boyd, Edmond O'Brien, Donald Pleasence, Raquel Welch
director: Richard Fleischer
route: 5 aorta
Fantastic Voyage (1994 song) artist: Coolio
Fantastik: 7 cleaner
alternative: 5 Brite, Lysol **6** Top Job **7** Lestoil, Mr. Clean, Pine Sol **9** Step Saver
fantasy: 4 myth **5** dream **6** mirage, revery, vision **7** chimera, figment, reverie, romance **8** chimaera, daydream, delusion, illusion **9** dreamland, fairy tale, invention, pipe dream, unreality **10** apparition
ender: 4 land
Fantasy (1995 song) artist: Mariah Carey
Fantasy Island (ABC drama)
cast: Ricardo Montalban (Mr. Roarke) Hervé Villechaize (Tattoo)
prop: 3 lei
sighting: 5 plane
Fante home: 5 Ghana **6** Africa
Fan, The (1996 film)
cast: Ellen Barkin, Robert De Niro, Wesley Snipes
director: Tony Scott
__ fan tutte: 4 Cosi
fanzine: 3 mag
FAO __: 7 Schwarz
far: 3 off **4** much, very **5** miles, quite **6** remote, way off **7** distant, extreme, foreign, greatly, outside **8** a long way, outlying, very much **9** a ways away, decidedly, extremely **10** out of reach
afield: 4 away, awry **5** amiss **6** astray **9** off course **10** off the mark
and away: 5 truly **6** easily, surely **8** of course **9** certainly, decidedly, doubtless, expressly, obviously **10** absolutely, by all means, definitely, positively, undeniably
and wide: 6 afield **7** broadly, largely **10** everywhere
apart: 3 few **4** rare **6** meager, scarce, seldom, sparse **7** limited, unusual **8** isolated, sporadic, uncommon **9** irregular, scattered, spasmodic, uncrowded **10** infrequent, occasional, sporadical, unfrequent
as ~ as: 4 up to **5** until
away: 6 remote **7** oversea **8** overseas
by ~: 6 easily **7** clearly, plainly **8** very much **9** hands down, obviously
combining form: 3 tel- **4** tele-, telo-
cry: 7 long way **8** distance
cry from: 6 unlike
down: 4 deep **6** buried **9** cavernous
ender: 4 away **6** seeing **7** sighted
few and ~ between: 4 rare, thin **5** scant **6** scanty, scarce, skimpy, sparse, spotty **7** unusual **8** uncommon **9** scattered **10** hard to find, infrequent
go ~: 4 last **5** get on **7** advance, succeed **8** get ahead, progress
go as ~ as: 5 reach
gone: 3 mad **6** in love **7** charmed, smitten **8** beguiled, besotted, obsessed **9** bewitched, possessed **10** captivated, crazy about, enraptured, fascinated, infatuated, spellbound
go so ~: 6 gather, take it **7** presume, suppose, surmise
go too ~: 4 hype **6** overdo, pile on **7** belabor, lay it on, stretch **8** overplay **9** overstate **10** exaggerate
look ~ and wide: 5 scour
near and ~: 7 all over **9** all around **10** everywhere
not ~: 4 near, nigh **5** close, handy **6** at hand, nearby **7** close by **8** adjacent, next door, proximal **9** alongside **10** convenient, near-at-hand
on the ~ side of: 6 across **7** athwart
partner: 4 away, near, wide
point: 3 end
push too ~: 3 tax **4** task, tire, wear **6** impose, strain, weaken **7** oppress, wear out **8** overload, overtask, overwork **9** weigh down **10** overburden
so ~: 3 yet, YTD **5** as yet, by now **6** to date **7** till now, up to now **8** hitherto, until now **10** heretofore
thus ~: 8 until now
far __: 3 cry **5** piece
far __ from me: 4 be it
far-__: 3 off, out **4** gone **5** famed, flung, point **7** fetched
__ far: 4 thus
...far __ can see: 3 as I
Far __: 4 East, West **7** Eastern, Islands, Tortuga, Western
Far __, The: 4 Side **5** Field **7** Country
Far __ the Madding Crowd: 4 From
Faracy: 9 Stephanie
Faraday __: 4 cage **6** effect, shield
Faraday, Michael: 9 physicist, scientist
far and __: 4 away, near, wide
Far and Away (1992 film)
cast: Tom Cruise, Thomas Gibson, Nicole Kidman
director: Ron Howard
Far and Near author: Pearl S. Buck
farandole: 5 dance
faraway: 4 lost **6** yonder **7** distant, foreign, strange, unknown **8** outlying
far be it __ me: 4 from
...far beyond those of __ men: 6 mortal
farce: 4 camp, joke, play, sham **5** drama, humor, put-on **6** comedy, parody, satire **7** burlesk, charade, mockery **8** nonsense, ridicule, travesty **9** absurdity, burlesque, slapstick **10** buffoonery, caricature
farceur: 3 wag, wit **4** zany **5** clown, comic, joker **7** pierrot **8** comedian, funnyman, kibitzer
farcical: 4 rich **5** droll, funny, silly **6** jocose **7** amusing, comical, jocular, satiric, waggish **8** humorous **9** facetious, laughable, ludicrous, satirical, whimsical **10** ridiculous
Far Country, The (1955 film)
cast: Corinne Calvet, Ruth Roman, James Stewart
director: Anthony Mann
fardel: 6 bundle, burden
fare: 2 do, go **4** diet, eats, food, grub, live, meal, meat, menu, pass, ride, toll **5** exist, get by, get on, meals, price, rider **6** charge, income, manage, tariff **7** aliment, cuisine, edibles, expense, make out, passage, proceed, rations, turn out, victual, vittles **8** eatables, get along, progress, victuals **9** passenger **10** gastronomy, provisions, sustenance
bill of ~: 4 menu **5** carte, table
bland ~: 3 pap
carrier: 3 cab **4** hack, taxi **7** taxicab
counter: 5 meter
ender: 4 well
reduced ~: 4 diet
starter: 3 air, car, fan, war **4** work **5** field, thoro **8** thorough
thee well: 3 bye **4** ciao, ta ta **5** adieu, adios, aloha, later, peace **6** bye-bye, shalom, sholom, so long **7** cheerio, goodbye **8** sayonara **9** Abyssinia
well: 7 prosper **8** hit it big
fare-__: 6 beater
fare-__-well: 3 you **4** thee
__ fare: 3 air **6** family
Far East
see Asia
Farentino: 5 James **6** Debrah
Farentino, James
spouse: Elizabeth Ashley, Debrah Farentino, Michele Lee
farer: 7 voyager **8** traveler, vagabond
starter: 3 sea, way **5** space
__ fare-thee-well: 3 to a
farewell: 3 bye **4** ciao, exit, ta ta **5** adieu, adios, aloha, congé, later, leave, peace **6** bye-bye, congée, shalom, sholom, so long **7** cheerio, goodbye, parting, sendoff **8** sayonara **9** Abyssinia, departure **10** separation
bid ~: 4 wave
in French: 5 adieu
in Hawaiian: 5 aloha
in Italian: 4 ciao
in Latin: 3 ave **4** vale
in Spanish: 5 adios
farewell __: 7 address
__ Farewell: 4 Cape
Farewell, My Lovely author: Raymond Chandler
Farewell Symphony composer: 5 Haydn
Farewell to Arms, A: 4 film **5** novel
author: Ernest Hemingway
cast: Gary Cooper, Helen Hayes, Adolphe Menjou
character: 5 Piani **6** Ettore **7** Moretti
director: Frank Borzage
farfalle: 5 pasta **7** bow ties, noodles
alternative: 4 orzo, ziti **5** penne **7** lasagna, lasagne, pastina, ravioli **8** bucatini, couscous, linguine, linguini, macaroni, rigatoni **9** agnolotti, angelhair, cavatelli, manicotti, spaghetti **10** cannelloni, fettuccini, tortellini, vermicelli
__ far, far better...: 5 It is a
__ farfel: 5 matzo **6** matzah, matzoh
far-fetched: 4 tall **7** dubious **8** strained **9** fantastic, illogical, recondite, unnatural **10** improbable, incredible, suspicious
Far Field, The author: Theodore Roethke
far-flung: 3 big **4** vast, wide **5** broad, roomy **6** global, remote **7** distant

8 extended, outlying, spacious, sweeping 9 capacious, expansive, extensive 10 large-scale, widespread
Far From Heaven (2002 film)
cast: Patricia Clarkson, Dennis Haysbert, Julianne Moore, Dennis Quaid
director: Todd Haynes
Far From Over (1983 song) artist: Frank Stallone
Far From the Madding Crowd: 4 film 5 novel
author: Thomas Hardy
cast: Alan Bates, Julie Christie, Peter Finch, Terence Stamp
character: 3 Jan, Oak 4 Troy 5 Liddy, Lydia
director: John Schlesinger
Fargo: 4 city, town 5 Donna
locale: 4 N. Dak.
Fargo (1996 film)
cast: Steve Buscemi, William H. Macy, Frances McDormand, Harve Presnell
director: Joel Coen
__ Fargo: 5 Wells
Fargo, Donna
song: Funny Face (1972)
The Happiest Girl in the Whole U.S.A. (1972)
far-gone: 4 shot, worn 5 spent, tired, weary 6 bushed, dished, used up 7 drained, wearied, worn out 8 depleted, dog-tired, fatigued, tired out, weakened 9 enervated, exhausted 10 dissipated
Far Hills NJ org.: 4 USGA
Faribault: 4 city, town
locale: 9 Minnesota
farina: 4 meal 5 flour, grain 6 cereal, starch
Farina: 6 Dennis
farinaceous: 5 mealy 6 floury
faring starter: 3 sea, way
Farley: 5 Chris, Mowat 6 Walter 7 Granger
farm: 4 land, plow, till, work 5 abode, croft, dairy, plant, ranch, rural 6 grange, spread 8 property 9 cultivate, homestead, sharecrop 10 plantation
animal: 3 ant, cow, ewe, hen, hog, pig, ram, sow, tom 4 boar, calf, foal, goat, lamb, mare, mule 5 chick, horse, piggy, swine 6 heifer, piggie, pullet 7 chicken
animals: 4 oxen 5 stock 6 cattle
baby: 4 calf, foal, lamb 5 chick 6 piglet
barrier: 4 rail
basket: 4 skep
building: 4 barn, shed, silo
bundle: 5 sheaf
call: 5 sooey
connection: 4 yoke
dept.: 3 Agr.
do a ~ job: 3 hoe, sow 4 plow, reap 6 ensile
enclosure: 3 pen, sty 6 corral, pigpen, pigsty
ender: 4 land, yard 5 house, stead, woman, women
equipment maker: 5 Deere
fat ~: 3 spa 6 resort
feed: 4 mash 6 forage
fit to ~: 6 arable 7 fertile 8 plowable, tillable 10 cultivable
gate: 5 stile
give birth on the ~: 4 yean 5 calve
horse: 6 dobbin
implement: 3 hoe 4 fork, plow 5 churn 6 harrow
machine: 4 trac 5 baler, sower 7 tractor
mother: 3 ewe, hen, sow 4 mare
package: 4 bale
product: 4 corn, crop, eggs, milk, oats 5 wheat 6 barley 7 sorghum
show: 4 fair
small ~: 5 croft
soil: 4 dirt, land, loam 5 earth
sound: 3 baa, moo 4 oink 6 heehaw
South American ~: 5 finca
trough: 6 feeder
unit: 4 acre, bale
vehicle: 4 cart, dray, wain 5 wagon
water supply: 4 well
worker: 4 hand
farm __: 3 out 4 belt, club, hand, team 6 system
__ farm: 3 ant, fat, fur 4 bird, dirt, fish, tank, tree, work 5 dairy, stock, strip, stump, truck 6 county, oyster
...farm, __: 5 E-I-E-I-O
Farm __: 3 Aid 6 Bureau
__ Farm: 6 Animal 7 Junior's, Maggie's
farmed, not: 6 fallow
farmer: 4 Abel, hick 5 sower 6 cheese, grower, plower, reaper, rustic, tiller 7 hayseed, planter 8 gardener 9 harvester 10 agronomist, cornhusker, cultivator
addr.: 3 RFD
concern: 4 soil
friend: 4 rain
group: 4 co-op 6 Grange
in Dutch: 4 Boer
name meaning ~: 5 Bauer 6 George 7 Granger
need: 3 hoe 4 plow, rake, seed
often: 4 hoer 5 sower
org.: 3 ADA
place: 4 dell
wake-up call: 4 crow
farmer __: 6 cheese
farmer __ dell: 5 in the
__ farmer: 4 dirt 6 tenant
Farmer: 4 Gary 5 James 6 Fannie 7 Frances
Farmer in the Dell, The: 4 song
character: 3 cat, rat 4 wife 5 nurse 6 cheese
syllables: 4 hi-ho
Farmer, James org.: 4 CORE
farmers' __: 6 market
Farmers' Allminax humorist: 4 Shaw
Farmer's Almanac fare: 6 trivia 7 weather 8 forecast
Farmers Branch: 4 city, town
locale: 5 Texas
Farmer's Daughter, The (1947 film)
cast: Ethel Barrymore, Joseph Cotten, Loretta Young
__ Farmers of America: 6 Future
Farmer Takes a Wife, The author: Marc Connelly
farmhand: 5 baler 6 worker 7 laborer
farming: 3 agr. 7 growing, reaping, seeding, tillage 8 agronomy 9 geoponics, threshing 10 harvesting
agency: 4 USDA
combining form: 4 agri-, agro-
deg.: 3 MSA 4 M.Agr.
major: 5 aggie
science of ~: 11 agriculture
unfit for ~: 3 dry 4 arid, sere 5 dusty 6 barren, desert, torrid 7 bone-dry, parched 9 waterless
__ farming: 4 tank 5 ocean, strip 7 dryland
Farmington: 4 city, town
locale: 9 New Mexico
Farmington Hills: 4 city, town
locale: 8 Michigan
farmland: 3 lea, ley 4 soil 5 field
Mayan ~: 5 milpa
unit: 4 acre
farmlike: 5 rural 6 rustic 7 bucolic 8 pastoral
farmstead: 4 land 5 ranch 6 estate 7 acreage 8 hacienda 10 plantation
Farm, The artist: 4 Miró
__ far niente: 5 dolce
Farnsworth, Richard: 5 actor
film: Anne of Green Gables (1985)
The Grey Fox (1982)
Into the Night (1985)
Misery (1990)
Resurrection (1980)
The Straight Story (1999)
Farnum: 6 Dustin 7 William
faro: 4 game 8 card game
Faro: 4 city, town
locale: 6 Canada
Faroes: 4 isls. 5 isles 7 islands
far-off: 4 away 5 faint 6 dreamy, remote 7 distant, unknown 8 outlying
Far Off Place, A: 4 book, film
author: Laurens Van der Post
cast: Ethan Randall, Maximilian Schell, Reese Witherspoon
Faron: 5 Young
Farouk's father: 4 Fuad
far-out: 3 def, hip, odd, rad, wow 4 aces, A-one, boss, braw, camp, cool, dece, fine, gear, keen, neat, nice, phat, tuff, wild 5 dandy, ducky, grand, great, marvy, neato, nifty, nobby, prime, slick, super, swell, ultra, wacko, weird 6 bang on, bang-up, bonzer, bosker, choice, divine, dreamy, gnarly, groovy, lovely, peachy, slap-up, spot on, superb, terrif, tiptop, unique, unreal, whizzo, wicked 7 amazing, awesome, bizarre, capital, corking, extreme, like wow, oddball, offbeat, perfect, radical, ripping, skookum, stellar, strange, sublime, surreal 8 dazzling, especial, eximious, fabulous, five-star, four-star, frabjous, freakish, glorious, heavenly, isolated, jim-dandy, slam-bang, smashing, splendid, sterling, superior, terrific, top-level, topnotch, ultimate, very good, wondrous 9 bodacious, eccentric, Endsville, excellent, exemplary, exquisite, fantastic, first-rate, high-grade, hunky-dory, marvelous, sollicker, top-flight, unrivaled, wonderful 10 avant-garde, first-class, hotsy-totsy, jack-a-dandy, peachy-keen, phenomenal, remarkable, stupendous, super-duper, unorthodox, unrivalled
Farquhar, George: 7 British 10 playwright
Farr: 5 Jamie 7 Felicia
farrago: 4 hash, mess 6 jumble, medley 7 mélange 8 mishmash 9 potpourri 10 hodgepodge, miscellany, salmagundi
Farragut: 5 David 7 admiral
org.: 3 USN
Farrah: 7 Fawcett
ex: 3 Lee
Farrar: 8 Margaret 9 Geraldine
__ Farrar: 4 Brat
Farrar, Geraldine: 4 diva 6 singer 7 soprano
specialty: 5 opera
far-reaching: 3 big 4 deep, vast, wide 5 broad, roomy 7 general 8 pandemic, profound, spacious, sweeping 9 capacious, expansive, extensive, momentous, wholesale 10 widespread
view: 5 sweep, vista 8 panorama
Farrell: 4 Mike 5 Colin, Terry 6 Eileen, Glenda, Sharon 7 Charles, Suzanne
Farrell, Charles: 5 actor
film: Old Ironsides (1926)
Seventh Heaven (1927)
Street Angel (1928)
Sunny Side Up (1929)
TV: My Little Margie
Farrell, Eileen: 6 singer 7 soprano
specialty: 5 opera
Farrell, Glenda: 7 actress
film: The Disorderly Orderly (1964)
I Am a Fugitive From a Chain Gang (1932)
Kissin' Cousins (1964)
Life Begins (1932)
Little Caesar (1930)
Farrell, James T.: 6 author, writer
work: Studs Lonigan
Farrell, Mike spouse: Shelley Fabares
Farrell, Suzanne: 6 dancer 8 danseuse 9 ballerina
Farrelly: 5 Bobby, Peter
Farr, Felicia: 7 actress
film: 3:10 to Yuma (1957)
Charley Varrick (1973)
Kiss Me, Stupid (1964)
Kotch (1971)
The Last Wagon (1956)
spouse: Jack Lemmon
farrier: 5 smith
did a ~ job: 4 shod
item: 4 rasp, shoe 5 anvil 9 horseshoe
tool: 4 rasp
Farr, Jamie feature: 4 nose
farrow: 3 pig 6 litter
Farrow: 3 Mia 4 John, Tisa
Farrow, John: 8 director
film: Alias Nick Beal (1943)
The Big Clock (1948)
Five Came Back (1939)
His Kind of Woman (1951)
Hondo (1953)
The Saint Strikes Back (1939)
Wake Island (1942)
Farrow, Mia: 7 actress
film: Alice (1990)
Another Woman (1988)
Broadway Danny Rose (1984)
Crimes and Misdemeanors (1989)
The Great Gatsby (1974)
Hannah and Her Sisters (1986)
Husbands and Wives (1992)
A Midsummer Night's Sex Comedy (1982)
The Purple Rose of Cairo (1985)
Radio Days (1987)
Rosemary's Baby (1968)
Secret Ceremony (1968)
See No Evil (1971)
Shadows and Fog (1992)
Zelig (1983)
spouse: André Previn, Frank Sinatra
TV: Peyton Place
farseeing: 4 keen, wise 6 astute, shrewd 7 prudent 8 cautious, discreet, watchful 9 astucious, prescient 10 longheaded
Far Side, The: 5 comic 7 cartoon
animal: 3 cow
artist: Gary Larson
farsighted: 4 wise 6 shrewd 7 prudent 8 rational, sensible 9 judicious, prescient, provident, sagacious 10 coolheaded, discerning, perceptive
farsightedness: 6 vision
Farsi speaker: 5 Irani
farther: 4 more 5 other 6 yonder 7 outside
ender: 4 most
__ farther: 4 go no
farthest: 3 ult. 4 last 6 utmost 7 extreme, outside 8 ultimate 9 uttermost
point: 3 end 5 brink, limit 6 apogee, border, fringe 7 extreme 8 frontier 9 extremity, periphery
farthing: 4 coin 5 money
Far Tortuga author: Peter Matthiessen

fasces: **4** rods **5** staff **6** bundle
fascia: **4** band, belt **8** hair band
fascinate: **4** bait, draw, grip, lure, take **5** charm, rivet, tempt **6** absorb, allure, appeal, arrest, dazzle, disarm, enamor, engage, entice, excite, ravish, thrill **7** attract, beguile, bewitch, delight, enchant, engross, enthral, inthral **8** enthrall, entrance, interest, inthrall, intrigue, transfix **9** captivate, enrapture, hypnotize, infatuate, mesmerize, overpower, overwhelm, spellbind, stimulate, tantalize, titillate, transport **10** intoxicate
fascinated: **4** agog, rapt **6** enrapt **7** all eyes, far gone, smitten **8** held fast **9** attentive, attracted, bewitched, delighted, enchanted, engrossed, entranced, impressed **10** captivated, enraptured, enthralled, hypnotized, infatuated, interested, mesmerized, spellbound, tantalized, titillated, transfixed
  be ~ with: **4** love
  by: **4** into **6** in love **10** crazy about
fascinating: **5** juicy **7** amazing, lovable, winning, winsome **8** inviting, loveable, magnetic, readable, romantic, striking, tempting **10** magnetical
Fascinating Rhythm composer: **8** Gershwin
fascination: **4** lure, pull **5** charm, magic, mania, spell **6** allure, appeal, hang-up, wonder **7** charism, lovable, romance **8** charisma, loveable, mystique **9** immersion, magnetism, obsession
Fascination (song) artist: Human League, Jane Morgan
fascinator: **5** scarf
fascism: **7** tyranny **9** autocracy, brutality, despotism **10** oppression
fashion: **3** cut, fit, ton, way **4** chic, form, kind, look, make, mode, mold, rage, sort, vein, work **5** adapt, build, craft, draft, erect, forge, frame, model, retro, shape, stamp, style, trend, usage, vogue **6** adjust, cook up, create, custom, design, devise, figure, invent, make up, manner, method, tailor **7** costume, dream up, in thing, pattern, prepare, produce **8** assemble, contrive, demeanor, practice **9** construct, etiquette, fabricate, sculpture **10** convention, dernier cri, stereotype
  accessory: **3** bag, boa, tie, wig **5** scarf
  after a ~: **6** in a way **7** somehow
  brief ~: **3** fad
  British ~ plate: **4** toff
  figure: **5** model **8** designer **9** couturier
  in ~: **3** hot **4** chic **5** smart, swank **6** dapper, dressy, modish, swanky, trendy **7** à la mode, current, dashing, elegant, popular, stylish, voguish **8** up-to-date **9** au courant **10** all the rage
  initials: **3** YSL **4** DKNY
  in this ~: **4** thus **6** like so, thusly **7** that way
  item: **3** bag, tie, wig **5** A-line, scarf, skirt **6** blouse
  latest ~: **10** dernier cri
  length: **4** maxi, midi, mini
  mecca: **5** Paris
  name: **4** Dior, Oleg **5** Karan, Klein, label **6** Lauren **7** Cassini, Versace
  out of ~: **3** old **5** dated, passé **6** démodé, old hat **7** has-been **8** obsolete **9** hackneyed, out-of-date
  plate: **3** fop **4** dude **5** dandy **7** coxcomb
  plate opposite: **5** frump
fashion __: **5** plate **9** statement
__ fashion: **3** in a **4** high **6** after a **7** Bristol
fashionable: **3** hep, hip, hot, mod, new, now **4** chic, posh, tony **5** class, natty, sharp, sleek, smart, swank, swell, swish, toney, vogue **6** chichi, classy, dressy, flossy, modish, rakish, snappy, swanky, trendy, with it **7** à la mode, current, dashing, elegant, genteel, in style, in vogue, popular, stylish, voguish **8** handsome, up-to-date **10** all the rage
  group: **6** jet set
__-fashioned: **3** new, old **4** full
__ Fashioned Love Song: **5** An Old
fashioner: **5** maker **7** creator, deviser, planner **8** designer, engineer, inventer, inventor **9** architect, contriver **10** mastermind, originator
Fashions (1934 film)
  cast: Bette Davis, William Powell
fast: **3** PDQ, set **4** firm, held, lewd, sure, true **5** apace, brisk, close, fixed, fleet, glued, hasty, loose, loyal, quick, rapid, sharp, swift, tight **6** ardent, firmly, flying, presto, pronto, racing, rakish, secure, snappy, speedy, stable, steady, strong, sudden **7** abiding, abstain, cursory, dashing, express, fixedly, fleetly, hastily, hurried, instant, quickly, raffish, rapidly, staunch, swiftly, tightly **8** attached, constant, faithful, fastened, fleeting, flitting, full tilt, go hungry, in a flash, in a jiffy, in no time, keep from, promptly, resolute, securely, spanking, speedily, true blue, unbroken, uncurbed **9** breakneck, hurriedly, immovable, immovably, like a shot, posthaste, steadfast **10** double-time, harefooted, hypersonic, in high gear, profligate, supersonic, ultrasonic, unwavering
  and loose: **4** rash, wild **5** hasty **6** amoral, unruly, unwise **7** corrupt, immoral **8** careless, feckless, headlong, heedless, reckless **9** corrupted, foolhardy, imprudent, negligent **10** incautious, indiscreet
  approaching: **4** near, nigh **5** close **6** at hand, coming, in view **7** brewing, in store, looming, pending **8** imminent, in the air, on the way **9** impending, in the wind
  break ~: **3** eat
  car: **2** GT **5** racer **6** hot rod
  combining form: **5** tachy-
  ender: **4** back, ball
  exit: **3** lam
  flyer: **3** jet, SST
  follower: **6** Easter
  food: **4** nosh **5** snack
  get no place ~: **3** lag **4** drag, flag, idle, limp, loaf, loll, plod, poke **5** dally, delay, tarry **6** dabble, dawdle, diddle, loiter **7** fall off, fritter, slacken **8** hang back, straggle **9** waste time **10** dillydally, lose ground, mess around, wait around
  get there ~: **3** run **4** dash, rush, tear, whiz, zoom **5** hurry, speed, whisk **6** hasten, scurry **7** scamper
  go ~: **3** fly, hie, run, zip **4** dash, race, tear, zoom **5** hurry, scoot, speed **6** hot-rod, hurtle, hustle, sprint
  go too ~: **4** rush, tear, whiz, zoom **5** speed **6** barrel
  held ~: **4** rapt **7** charmed, gripped **8** absorbed, beguiled, immersed **9** delighted, engrossed, entranced **10** captivated, enraptured, enthralled, fascinated, hypnotized, spellbound
  hold ~: **5** cling, seize, stick **6** adhere, cohere **7** enchain
  hold ~ to: **4** obey **6** follow **7** abide by, observe, respect **10** comply with
  in music: **5** mosso
  make ~: **3** fix, peg, tie **4** bind, lock, moor, nail **5** hitch, latch, rivet, truss
  not as ~: **6** slower
  one: **4** hoax **5** cheat, fraud **6** dupery, humbug **7** swindle **8** trickery **9** deception
  on one's feet: **5** agile, fleet
  on the uptake: **3** apt **5** adept, savvy, sharp, smart **6** adroit, astute, bright, clever, cogent, gifted, shrewd **7** capable **8** incisive **9** observant
  partner: **5** loose
  pull a ~ one: **3** con **4** fool **5** cheat, outdo, trick **6** delude, outwit **7** deceive, defraud, mislead, swindle **8** flimflam, hoodwink, outsmart **9** bamboozle
  starter: **5** stead
  talk: **4** bull, bunk, jive **5** prate **6** banter, hot air, humbug, patter **7** baloney, blarney, blather **8** malarkey **9** banana oil **10** applesauce, balderdash
  time: **4** Lent
  too ~: **4** rash **5** brash, hasty **6** abrupt, madcap **8** careless, headlong, heedless, pell-mell, reckless, slapdash **9** foolhardy, impetuous, impulsive
  traveler: **7** bad news
fast __: **3** day, ice, one **4** buck, food, lane, time **5** break, track **6** asleep, dollar, motion, worker **7** forward
fast __ get-out: **5** as all
fast-__: **3** cut **4** talk **5** count **6** moving
__ fast: **4** make
__ fast!: **5** Not so
__ fast and loose: **4** play
Fast and the Furious, The (2001 film)
  cast: Jordana Brewster, Vin Diesel, Michelle Rodriguez, Paul Walker
  director: Rob Cohen
fastball: **4** heat **5** pitch **6** heater
Fast Break (1979 film)
  cast: Gabe Kaplan, Harold Sylvester, Mike Warren
  director: Jack Smight
fast-breeder __: **7** reactor
Fast Car (1988 song) artist: Tracy Chapman
Fast Eddie: **6** Felson
  need: **3** cue **5** chalk, stick
  portrayer: Paul Newman
  shot: **5** carom, massé
fasten: **3** fix, peg, pin, set, sew, tag, tie, zip **4** band, belt, bind, bolt, bond, clip, do up, glue, hook, join, knot, lace, link, lock, moor, nail, seal, shut, snap, tack, tape, weld, yoke **5** affix, annex, brace, chain, clamp, clasp, close, hitch, infix, latch, leash, paste, rivet, screw, stick, tie up, truss, zip up **6** adhere, anchor, append, attach, batten, begird, buckle, button, cement, cleave, clinch, cohere, couple, hook on, hook up, lace up, secure, solder, staple, tether **7** connect, mortice, mortise, tie down, tighten **8** button up **9** stabilize, thumbtack
  again: **5** repeg, repin, retie, rezip
  at sea: **4** lash **5** belay
  securely: **4** bolt, moor **5** rivet, tie up **6** batten
fastened: **4** fast, firm **5** tight **6** secure
fastener: **3** nut, tie **4** bolt, bond, brad, hook, lock, nail, snap, stud, T-nut **5** catch, clamp, clasp, latch, rivet, screw, T-bolt, U-bolt **6** buckle, button, cap nut, Velcro **7** bracket **10** attachment, hook and eye
  door ~: **4** bolt, hasp, hook **5** latch
  metal ~: **4** bolt, brad, nail **5** screw, U-bolt
  needing two nuts: **5** U-bolt
__ fastener: **3** zip **4** snap **5** press, slide
fasteners: **8** hardware
fastening: **3** tie **4** link, lock **5** clasp, latch **8** vinculum **10** attachment, connection
Faster __ speeding bullet: **5** than a
Faster!: **4** c'mon **5** hurry
faster, make: **6** hasten **7** quicken, speed up
Fastest Gun Alive, The (1956 film)
  cast: Jeanne Crain, Broderick Crawford, Glenn Ford
  director: Russell Rouse
fast food: **4** bite **5** snack
  drink: **4** cola, soda **5** shake
  fare: **3** sub **4** hero, taco **5** chile, chili, frank, fries, pizza **6** Big Mac, burger, chilli, hot dog, wiener **7** Whopper
  place: **3** KFC **4** deli **5** Arby's **6** Subway, Wendy's **7** Blimpie **8** Pizza Hut **9** McDonald's, Roy Rogers **10** Burger King
  symbol: **4** arch
Fast, Howard: **6** author, writer
  work: April Morning
    Citizen Tom Paine
    The Crossing
    The Dinner Party
    The Establishment
    Freedom Road
    The Immigrants
    The Legacy
    Max
    The Naked God
    The Pledge
    The Second Generation
    Spartacus
fastidious: **4** neat, nice, prim, tidy, trim **5** chary, fussy, kempt, picky **6** choosy, dainty, prissy, spruce **7** bookish, careful, choosey, finical, finicky, groomed, mincing, orderly, precise, prudent, prudish, refined **8** cautious, exacting, finiking, finnicky, precious, rigorous, thorough, well-kept **9** assiduous, attentive, demanding, difficult, disgusted, exquisite, judicious, observant, shipshape, squeamish, stickling **10** meticulous, particular, scrupulous
fastidiousness: **4** care **9** diligence, exactness, precision
fasting period: **4** Lent
Fastlove (1996 song) artist: George Michael
fast-moving object: **4** blur
fastness: **4** fort, keep **5** speed, tower **6** castle, refuge **7** bastion, bulwark, citadel, rampart, redoubt **8** fortress, garrison, presidio **10** stronghold
__ fast one: **5** pull a
fast-talk: **4** snow
fast-talking: **4** glib, oily **5** slick **6** artful, prolix, smooth **8** slippery **10** loquacious
Fast Times at Ridgemont High (1982 film)
  cast: Phoebe Cates, Jennifer Jason Leigh, Sean Penn, Judge Reinhold, Ray Walston
  director: Amy Heckerling
fast-track: **4** push **5** speed **6** hasten **7** quicken, speed up **8** expedite **10** accelerate, facilitate
fast-tracker: **5** comer
fat: **4** gras, rich, soft, suet **5** lardy, lipid, obese, plump, pudgy, stout, thick **6** grease, lipids, paunch, portly, rotund, stocky, stubby **7** weighty **8** splendid **10** abdominous

avoider of rhyme: 5 Sprat
cat: 5 mogul, nabob 6 tycoon 7 big shot, Pooh-bah 9 moneybags, plutocrat 10 man of means
cats: 4 rich 5 haves
chew the ~: 3 gab, jaw, rap, yak 4 chat, talk 5 speak 8 converse
combining form: 3 lip- 4 adip-, lipo-, sebi-, sebo- 5 adipo-, lipar-, stear-, steat- 6 liparo-, stearo-, steato-
cook in ~: 3 fry
farm: 3 spa 6 resort
full of ~: 4 oily 5 lardy, suety 6 greasy 7 buttery
in French: 4 gras
low in ~: 4 lean
margarine ~: 5 olein 6 oleine
mouth: 7 tattler 10 taleteller, tattletale
starter: 6 butter, marrow
fat __: 3 cat, lip 4 cell, city, farm, meat, pine 6 chance
fat __ land, the: 5 of the
fat __ the fire, the: 4 is in
fat-__: 4 free 6 witted 7 soluble
__-fat: 3 low
Fat __: 4 City
Fata __: 7 Morgana
Fatagaga collagist: 3 Arp
Fatal Attraction (1987 film)
cast: Anne Archer, Glenn Close, Michael Douglas
director: Adrian Lyne
role: 4 Alex
Fatal Cure author: Robin Cook
fatale, femme: 4 vamp 5 flirt, siren, vixen
fat-cat: 7 wealthy
Fat chance!: 3 hah, nah, naw, nay, nix, non 4 nein, nope, nyet, uh-uh 5 I won't, ixnay, never, nohow, no way 6 no deal, noways, nowise 7 I refuse 8 forget it, I will not, negative, negatory 9 by no means, I think not 10 count me out, not a chance, thumbs down
Fat City (1972 film)
cast: Jeff Bridges, Stacy Keach
director: John Huston
fate: 3 lot 4 luck 5 karma 6 chance, kismat, kismet 7 destiny, fortune, outcome, portion 8 fortuity, Lady Luck 10 divine will, foreordain, providence
Greek goddess of ~: 5 Moira
Norse ~ goddess: 3 Urd 4 Norn
tragic ~: 4 doom, ruin 8 downfall 9 cataclysm, ruination
fated: 5 bound 6 doomed 8 destined, impelled 9 necessary 10 inevitable, in the cards, in the stars
__-fated: 3 ill
fateful: 6 tragic 7 crucial, direful, doomful, ominous, ruinous 8 critical, decisive, eventful, tragical 9 important, momentous 10 calamitous, disastrous, portentous
Fate Is the Hunter author: Ernest K. Gann
Fates: 4 trio 9 threesome
one of the ~: 6 Clotho 7 Atropos 8 Lachesis
fat-free: 4 skim 7 skimmed
__ Fat Greek Wedding: 5 My Big
__ Fatha Hines: 4 Earl
fathead: 3 ass, oaf, sap 4 boob, clod, dolt, fool 5 chump, clown, cluck, dummy, dunce, joker, ninny, patsy 6 dimwit, lubber, lummox, nitwit, sucker, turkey 7 buffoon, dingbat, dullard, half-wit, jackass 8 dumbbell, numskull 9 birdbrain, harebrain, lamebrain, numbskull, simpleton
__ fat hen: 4 a big
father: 2 pa 3 dad, man, pop 4 curé, draw, male, papa, sire 5 beget, daddy, padre, pappy, poppa, spawn, title 6 cleric, create, curate, old man, origin, parent, parson, pastor, priest, source 7 founder, kinsman 8 ancestor, begetter, forebear, inventer, inventor, minister, preacher, relative, reverend 9 clergyman, confesser, confessor, patriarch, propagate, religious, reproduce 10 originator
brother: 3 unc, unk 5 uncle
combining form: 4 patr- 5 patri-, patro-
ender: 4 hood, land, less
expectant ~ supply: 5 cigar
first ~: 4 Adam
in Arabic: 3 abu
in French: 4 père
in Spanish: 5 padre
related on ~'s side: 6 agnate
starter: 3 god 4 fore, step 5 grand
father __: 5 image 6 figure
father-__: 5 in-law
__ father: 3 den 4 city, room 5 birth 6 church, desert, foster
Father __: 4 Time 5 Brown, Goose 6 Figure, Murphy
Father __ Best: 5 Knows
Father __ Bride: 5 of the
Father __ Sarducci: 5 Guido
__ Father: 3 Our 4 Holy
Father (1998 song) artist: LL Cool J
Father Brown (1954 film)
cast: Peter Finch, Joan Greenwood, Sir Alec Guinness
director: Robert Hamer
Father Christmas: 5 Santa 6 St. Nick 9 Saint Nick 10 Santa Claus, St. Nicholas
Father Figure (1988 song) artist: George Michael
Father Goose (1964 film)
cast: Leslie Caron, Cary Grant, Trevor Howard
Father Goose author: L. Frank Baum
fatherhood: 9 parentage, paternity
Fatherhood author: 5 Cosby
father-in-__: 3 law
Father Knows Best (CBS/NBC/ABC sitcom)
cast: Lauren Chapin (Kathy Kitten Anderson)
Elinor Donahue (Betty Princess Anderson)
Billy Gray (Bud Anderson)
Jane Wyatt (Margaret Anderson)
Robert Young (Jim Anderson)
fatherland: 4 home 5 roots
fatherless one: 3 Eve 4 Adam
fatherly: 4 kind 8 parental, paternal 10 protective
Father Murphy (NBC drama)
cast: Moses Gunn (Moses Gage)
Merlin Olsen (John Murphy)
father of fame, name meaning: 9 Cleopatra
father of light, name meaning: 5 Abner
father of many, name meaning: 7 Abraham
father of peace, name meaning: 7 Absalom
Father of the Bride (1950 film)
cast: Joan Bennett, Elizabeth Taylor, Spencer Tracy
director: Vincente Minnelli
Father of the Bride (1991 film)
cast: Diane Keaton, Steve Martin, Martin Short
director: Charles Shyer
role: 5 Ellie
Fathers and Sons author: Ivan Turgenev
Father's Day
gift: 3 tie 5 razor, shirt
month: 3 Jun. 4 June
father's joy, name meaning: 7 Abigail
Father's Little Dividend (1951 film)
cast: Joan Bennett, Elizabeth Taylor, Spencer Tracy
director: Vincente Minnelli
Father Time feature: 5 beard 6 scythe
__ Father, who art...: 3 Our
fathom: 3 get, ken, see 4 know 5 gauge, grasp, plumb, solve 6 divine, figure, follow, intuit 7 cognize, discern, make out, resolve, six feet 8 perceive 9 apprehend, figure out, penetrate 10 appreciate, comprehend, understand
hard to ~: 6 arcane, occult 8 esoteric, mystical 9 recondite 10 mysterious
Fathom (1967 film)
cast: Tony Franciosa, Clive Revill, Raquel Welch
fathomable: 5 lucid 8 knowable, luminous
fathomless: 4 deep, vast 7 abysmal 8 profound 9 cavernous, unsounded 10 bottomless, unknowable
fatidic: 6 mantic 7 Delphic 8 Delphian, oracular, sibyllic 9 prescient, prophetic, sibylline, vaticinal, visionary 10 portentous, prognostic
fatigue: 3 sag, sap 4 bore, bush, flag, jade, poop, sink, tire, wane, wear 5 blunt, drain, weary 6 anemia, fizzle, impair, overdo, reduce, shrink, soften, strain, weaken 7 anaemia, boredom, burnout, conk out, deplete, exhaust, frailty, languor, poop out, tire out, vitiate, wear out 8 debility, enervate, enfeeble, knock out, languish, overtire, peter out, puniness, weakness, wear down 9 attenuate, fragility, lassitude, prostrate, tiredness, tucker out, undermine, weariness 10 debilitate, devitalize, enervation, exhaustion, feebleness
sign of ~: 4 sigh, yawn
yield to ~: 3 sag 4 flag 5 droop, slump 6 slouch
fatigue __: 4 life 5 limit, ratio 7 clothes
__ fatigue: 6 battle, combat
fatigued: 4 beat, worn 5 all in, drawn, spent, tired, weary, wiped 6 aweary, done in, droopy, sleepy, wasted 7 haggard, languid, run-down, worn out 8 careworn, dog-tired, out of gas 9 played out, washed-out 10 knocked out
fatigues: 3 ODs 5 drabs 6 khakis 7 uniform
fatiguing: 4 hard 5 stiff 6 trying 7 tedious 8 tiresome 9 laborious 10 enervating, exhausting
Fatima husband: 3 Ali
Fat Man: 5 A-bomb
Fat Man and Little Boy (1989 film)
cast: Bonnie Bedelia, John Cusack, Paul Newman, Dwight Schultz
director: Roland Joffé
Fatman's partner: 4 Jake
Fats: 6 Domino, Waller 7 Navarro
__ Fats: 9 Minnesota
fatsia: 4 tree 5 shrub
family: 7 genseng, ginseng
fatten: 4 feed 5 bloat, plump, stuff, swell 6 beef up, enrich, expand 7 broaden, build up, distend, fill out, thicken 8 increase, overfeed, round out
fattening: 4 rich 7 caloric
fatty: 4 oily, rich 5 lardy 6 lipoid 7 adipose 8 lipoidal
acid: 3 DHA 5 oleic
not ~: 4 lean
substance: 5 lipid, sebum 6 lipide
fatty __: 3 oil 4 acid
Fatty: 8 Arbuckle
fatuitous: 5 inane, silly 6 absurd 7 asinine, foolish 10 ridiculous
fatuity: 5 folly 6 lunacy 7 foolery 8 nonsense 9 absurdity, asininity, silliness
fatuous: 4 dull, soft 5 corny, crazy, dense, empty, hokey, inane, jerky, passé, sappy, silly, stale, trite, vapid, wacky 6 absurd, common, doting, jejune, old hat, screwy, whacky 7 asinine, clichéd, foolish, humdrum, idiotic, prosaic, puerile, unsound, witless 8 bromidic, cockeyed, mindless, outdated, outmoded, specious 9 brainless, hackneyed, illogical, ludicrous, prosaical, senseless, untenable 10 boneheaded, chimerical, groundless, ridiculous, uninspired, unoriginal, weak-minded
fatuus, ignis: 6 mirage 7 chimera, eidolon, fantasm, figment 8 chimaera, delusion, phantasm 9 obsession
Faubourg St. Honore artist: 4 Erté
faucet: 3 tap 4 bibb 5 valve 6 spigot 7 petcock 8 stopcock
problem: 4 drip, leak 7 trickle
Faulkner, William: 6 writer 8 Nobelist
work: Absalom, Absalom!
As I Lay Dying
The Bear
Go Down, Moses
The Hamlet
Light in August
The Marble Faun
The Reivers
Requiem for a Nun
Sanctuary
Sartoris
Soldier's Pay
The Sound and the Fury
fault: 3 sin 4 blot, flaw, miss, onus, rift, slip, vice 5 blame, error, guilt, lapse, shift, speck, wrong 6 accuse, defect, foible, miscue, slip-up 7 blemish, blunder, failing, misdeed, mistake, offense 8 drawback, peccancy, trespass, weakness 9 criticize, oversight 10 deficiency, inaccuracy, misconduct, negligence, wrongdoing
activity: 5 quake, seism 6 tremor
at ~: 5 wrong 6 guilty, liable 7 to blame 8 blamable, culpable, mistaken 9 blameable 10 in the wrong
be at ~: 3 err 5 act up 7 do wrong, go wrong 8 go astray 9 misbehave 10 transgress
ender: 6 finder
find ~: 3 hit, nag, pan 4 carp 5 blame, cavil, gripe, knock, nag at, scold 6 accuse, jibe at, pick at 7 cavil at, censure, condemn, grumble, nitpick, put down, quarrel, quibble 8 complain 9 criticize, make a fuss, pick apart, pull apart, reprehend, shoot down 10 vituperate
hold at ~: 5 blame, decry, scold 6 accuse, charge, finger, indict, rebuke 7 censure, condemn, reprove, upbraid 8 denounce, reproach 9 criticize, implicate, reprimand 10 denunciate, take to task, vituperate
to a ~: 6 unduly 7 too much 8 overmuch
fault __: 4 line, zone 5 block, plane, scarp 7 breccia
__ fault: 3 to a 4 foot 5 comma 6 double, ground, normal, strike, thrust 7 gravity, reverse
faultfinder: 4 prig 5 momus, shrew 6 carper, censor, chider, critic, grouch 7 caviler 8 quibbler 9 nitpicker, termagant 10 fussbudget
faultfinders: 4 momi
faultfinding: 7 carping, fretful, peevish

8 captious, critical, fretsome, petulant
faultiness: 4 flaw 6 defect 7 failing 10 inadequacy, inefficacy
faultless: 3 pat 4 just, nice, pure 5 clean, exact, ideal, model, right, sound 7 correct, perfect, sinless 8 absolute, accurate, flawless, inerrant, innocent, peerless, spotless, unbroken, unerring, unmarred 9 blameless, crimeless, errorless, exemplary, exquisite, foolproof, guilt-free, guiltless, stainless, undamaged, unspotted, unsullied, virtuosic 10 consummate, immaculate, impeccable, inculpable, infallible
faultlessness: 8 accuracy 9 precision 10 exactitude
faults, crust between: 5 horst
__ fault with: 4 find
faulty: 3 bad 4 awry, lame, poor, thin, weak 5 amiss, false, leaky, lousy, wrong 6 broken, erring, feeble, flawed, marred, skimpy, untrue 7 botched, cracked, damaged, halting, ill-done, in error, inexact, invalid, lacking, limited, sketchy, unsound, wanting 8 fallible, impaired, mistaken, slipshod, specious 9 defective, deficient, erroneous, illogical, imperfect, imprecise, incorrect, sophistic, untenable 10 fallacious, inaccurate, inadequate, not working, out of order
most ~: 5 worst
faun: 5 satyr 9 libertine
fauna: 6 beasts 7 animals
category: 4 aves
collection: 3 zoo
counterpart: 5 flora
devoid of ~: 5 bleak, stark 6 barren 8 desolate, lifeless
regional ~ and flora: 5 biota
__ Faun, The: 6 Marble
Fauntleroy __: 4 suit
Fauntleroy, Little Lord name: 5 Errol
Fauré, Gabriel: 6 French 8 composer
Faust: 4 play 5 opera
author: 6 Goethe
composer: 6 Gounod
Faustino: 5 David
Faust Symphony composer: 5 Liszt
__ Faustus: 6 Doktor
faut, comme il: 5 right 6 decent, proper 7 correct, fitting 8 decorous
Fauvist painter: 4 Dufy 7 Matisse 9 Raoul Dufy
faux: 4 fake, imit., mock 9 imitation 10 artificial
faux __: 3 pas
faux-__: 4 naïf
faux pas: 4 slip, trip 5 boner, error, gaffe, lapse, wrong 6 bêtise, boo-boo, howler, slip-up 7 blooper, blunder, misstep, mistake 9 gaucherie, indecorum 10 infraction
follower: 4 oops
make a ~: 3 err 4 flub, goof, muff, slip, trip 5 botch, lapse, stray 6 bungle, foul up, fumble, mess up, slip up 7 blunder, go wrong, louse up, misstep, stumble 8 go astray
fava __: 4 bean
Favaloro: 4 René
favonian: 4 wind
favor: 3 aid 4 back, boon, egis, gift, good, help, lean, like, spur, turn 5 aegis, fancy, go for, grace, spoil, token, vogue 6 accept, assist, choose, esteem, oblige, opt for, pamper, prefer, regard, reward 7 approve, backing, benefit, cater to, endorse, indorse, indulge, memento, present, promote, respect, root for, service, smile on, support 8 advocate, approval, courtesy, good turn, goodwill, keepsake, kindness, side with, stand for 9 approbate, approve of, benignity, patronize, privilege, recommend, smile upon, subscribe 10 admiration, estimation, facilitate, indulgence, lean toward, popularity, settle upon
curry ~: 3 woo 5 court 8 fawn over 9 get next to, insinuate, shine up to 10 ingratiate
in ~: 3 aye, yes 7 popular
in ~ of: 3 for, pro 6 all for, likely 9 payable to 10 supporting
not in ~ of: 3 con 4 anti
one side: 4 limp
out of ~: 5 in bad 7 scorned, shunned, unloved 8 despised, detested, disliked, unvalued, unwanted 9 unpopular, unwelcome
return the ~: 5 repay 7 pay back, requite
win the ~ of: 6 enamor, endear 7 attract
__ favor: 3 por 5 curry, party
favorable: 3 fit 4 good, kind, nice, ripe, rosy 5 happy, right 6 aidful, benign, bright, golden, kindly, timely, useful 7 benefic, helpful, hopeful, welcome 8 amicable, friendly, pleasant, positive, remedial, salutary, suitable 9 agreeable, approving, assenting, benignant, congenial, effectual, fortunate, healthful, indulgent, laudatory, opportune, promising, receptive, welcoming, well-timed, wholesome 10 auspicious, beneficial, benevolent, charitable, commending, convenient, gratifying, heartening, productive, propitious, prosperous, reassuring, seasonable, successful, supportive, worthwhile
mention: 4 plug, puff, rave
most ~: 4 best 7 optimal, optimum
favorably: 4 well 5 right 8 very well 9 agreeably, cordially, helpfully, receptive, willingly 10 generously, graciously, positively, profitably, swimmingly
favored: 3 pet 5 blest, elite, lucky 6 chosen 7 darling, on a roll, popular 9 fortunate, on a streak, preferred 10 auspicious, fair-haired, felicitous, fortuitous, privileged
be ~ with: 3 own 4 have 5 boast, enjoy 7 possess
treatment: 4 bias 9 advantage, privilege, seniority 10 preference
__-favored: 3 ill 4 hard
__-favored-nation: 4 most
favoring: 3 for, pro 7 lenient 10 indulgence
favorite: 3 pet 4 idol, main, star 6 choice, likely 7 darling, dearest, popular 8 especial 9 best-loved, number one, preferred 10 honeybunch, preference
place: 5 haunt
thing: 3 pet
favorite __: 3 son
__ favorite: 6 odds-on
favorites, play: 4 side
__ Favorite Sport?: 4 Man's
favoritism: 4 bias 6 liking 8 inequity, nepotism 9 injustice, prejudice 10 friendship, partiality, preference, unfairness
show ~: 4 root, side
Favre, Brett: 2 QB
sport: 8 football
Fawcett, Farrah spouse: Lee Majors
__ Fawkes Day: 3 Guy
Fawlty Towers: 5 hotel 6 sitcom
creator: 6 Cleese
network: 3 BBC
fawn: 3 tan 4 deer, dote 5 brown, color, cower, crawl, kotow, toady 6 animal, cringe, kowtow 7 lay it on 8 yearling 9 yellowish
over: 3 woo 5 adore, court, toady 6 stroke 7 adulate, flatter, kotow to 8 butter up, kowtow to, make up to, play up to 9 truckle to
parent: 3 doe 4 stag
relative: 3 bay, dun, tan 4 bole, ecru, foxy, nude, seal 5 amber, beige, camel, cocoa, hazel, khaki, mocha, sepia, tawny, umber 6 auburn, bister, bistre, bronze, coffee, copper, ginger, russet, sienna, sorrel, suntan, walnut 7 biscuit, caramel, dogwood 8 chestnut, cinnamon, mahogany 9 butternut, chocolate
Fawn: 4 Hall
fawner: 5 toady 6 flunky, jackal, lackey, yes man 7 flunkey, lacquey 8 adulator, bootlick, courtier, hanger-on, kowtower, servitor, truckler 9 flatterer, sycophant 10 bootlicker
fawners: 6 claque
fawning: 4 oily 6 abject, menial 7 servile, slavish 8 unctuous 9 adulatory, spineless 10 obsequious
fax: 4 copy, send 5 repro 6 ectype 7 deliver, message 8 telecopy, transmit 9 duplicate
ancestor: 5 telex
button: 4 send
header: 4 from
fax __: 5 modem
Faxa __: 3 Bay
fay: 3 elf, imp 4 peri, pixy 5 fairy, gnome 6 sprite 7 brownie 10 leprechaun
Fay: 4 Wray 6 Weldon 7 Bainter, Vincent
Faye: 5 Alice 6 Herbie 7 Dunaway, Emerson 9 Kellerman
Faye, Alice: 7 actress
film: Alexander's Ragtime Band (1938)
In Old Chicago (1938)
On the Avenue (1937)
Poor Little Rich Girl (1936)
Sing, Baby, Sing (1936)
Tin Pan Alley (1940)
Wake Up and Live (1937)
Week-end in Havana (1941)
You Can't Have Everything (1937)
spouse: Phil Harris, Tony Martin
__ Faye Bakker: 5 Tammy
Fayette: 4 city, town
locale: 8 Kentucky
Fayetteville: 4 city, town
athletes: 10 Razorbacks
locale: 3 Ark. 4 N. Car. 8 Arkansas
Faylen: 5 Frank
faze: 3 vex 4 hurt, stun 5 abash, appal, daunt, get to 6 appall, bother, dismay, heckle, puzzle, rattle, ruffle 7 confuse, depress, fluster, inhibit, nonplus, perplex, perturb, shake up, unnerve 8 confound, frighten, irritate 9 discomfit, dumbfound, embarrass, give pause, take aback 10 discompose, disconcert
fazed: 5 upset 6 shaken 7 abashed, nervous 8 agitated, unstrung 9 flustered 10 confounded
FBI: 4 agcy. 6 agency
British ~: 3 CID
counterpart: 3 CIA
datum: 5 crime
department: 7 Justice
high-tech ~ tool: 3 DNA
letters in an ~ file: 3 aka
member: 3 agt., Fed 4 G-man 5 agent
part: 3 Bur., Fed., Inv. 6 Bureau 7 Federal
'70s ~ sting: 6 Abscam
FBI Story, The (1959 film)
cast: Murray Hamilton, Vera Miles, James Stewart
director: Mervyn LeRoy
FBI, The (ABC drama)
cast: Philip Abbott (Arthur Ward) Efrem Zimbalist Jr. (Inspector Lewis Erskine)
__ F.B. Morse: 6 Samuel
__ F. Buckley Jr.: 7 William
FCC: 4 agcy. 6 agency
concern: 2 TV 5 radio 8 airwaves
part: 3 Fed. 4 Comm. 7 Federal 10 Commission
__ F. Cody: 7 William
FDA: 4 agcy. 6 agency
department: 3 HHS
figure: 3 RDA
part: 4 Drug, Food 5 Admin.
FDIC: 4 agcy. 6 agency
part: 3 Dep., Fed., Ind. 7 Deposit, Federal 9 Insurance
FDR: 3 Dem. 4 pres.
org.: 3 NRA, PWA, REA, RFC, SSA, TVA, WPA
successor: 3 HST
see also Roosevelt
Fe: 4 elem., iron 5 metal 7 element
26 for ~: 4 at. no.
__ Fe: 5 Santa
fealty: 5 faith, honor 6 homage 7 loyalty 8 devotion, fidelity 10 allegiance
fear: 4 funk 5 alarm, angst, avoid, dread, panic, quail, qualm, worry 6 dismay, fright, horror, phobia, stress, terror, unease 7 anxiety, bugaboo, concern, jitters, respect, shudder, suspect, willies 8 cold feet, distress, fret over, mistrust, timidity 9 cowardice, misgiving, reverence, trepidity 10 insecurity
combining form: 4 phob- 5 phobo- 6 -phobia
ender: 4 some
fill with ~: 3 cow 5 alarm, daunt, scare
for ~ that: 4 lest 9 perchance
hide in ~: 5 cower, quail, quake 6 cringe, recoil, shrink 7 tremble
overcome with ~: 3 cow 4 faze 5 bully 6 dismay, menace 7 terrify, unnerve 8 paralyze 10 demoralize, intimidate, scare stiff
respectful ~: 3 awe
show ~: 3 hie, run 5 cower, quail, quake, wince 6 cringe, recoil, shrink 7 tremble
Fear __ Out: 7 Strikes
__ Fear: 4 Cape 5 Storm 6 Mortal, Primal, Sudden
fearer combining form: 5 -phobe
fearful: 3 shy 4 dire, eery, grim 5 awful, eerie, funky, jumpy, leery, mousy, pavid, timid, weird 6 afraid, craven, gun-shy, mousey, phobic, scared, trepid, uneasy, yellow 7 alarmed, anxious, baleful, chicken, daunted, ghastly, hideous, jittery, macaber, macabre, nervous, ominous, panicky, quivery, spooked, uptight, wimpish, worried 8 cowardly, dreadful, fearsome, grievous, hesitant, horrible, horrific, recreant, sheepish, shocking, skittish, terrible, terrific, timorous 9 appalling, atrocious, concerned, diffident, flinching, frightful, ill-omened, monstrous, nerveless, petrified, shrinking, spineless, terrified, tremulous, weak-kneed 10 disquieted, formidable, frightened, horrendous, horrifying, petrifying, solicitous, tremendous
fearfulness: 5 alarm, dread, panic 6 fright, phobia, terror 7 anxiety

8 timidity 9 cowardice, trepidity 10 faint heart
__-fearing: 3 God
fearing combining form: 6 -phobic
Fear Inside, The (1992 film)
cast: Christine Lahti, Dylan McDermott, Jennifer Rubin
Fear in the Night director: 5 Shane
fearless: 4 bold, game 5 brave, cocky, gutsy, nervy, stout 6 awless, brassy, daring, gritty, heroic, plucky, spunky 7 assured, aweless, dashing, defiant, doughty, gallant, impavid, leonine, staunch, valiant 8 heroical, intrepid, resolute, spirited, stalwart, unafraid, valorous 9 audacious, confident, dauntless, dreadless, unabashed, undaunted 10 courageous, mettlesome, undismayed
be ~: 4 dare
Fearless (1993 film)
cast: Jeff Bridges, Rosie Perez, Isabella Rossellini
director: Peter Weir
Fearless Fosdick creator: 4 Capp
fearlessness: 4 grit 5 nerve, pluck, valor 6 mettle 7 bravery, heroism, prowess 8 audacity
Fear Nothing author: Dean Koontz
fearnought: 4 coat 6 jacket 8 overcoat
Fear of Fifty author: Erica Jong
Fear of Flying author: Erica Jong
fears, allay: 5 quell 6 assure 10 conciliate
fearsome: 4 dire 5 funky, scary, timid 6 scared, trepid, unsafe 7 abashed, alarmed, anxious, chicken, daunted, nervous, panicky, spooked 8 cowardly, hesitant, timorous 9 frightful, illomened, petrified, terrified 10 frightened
Fear Strikes Out (1957 film)
cast: Karl Malden, Norma Moore, Anthony Perkins
director: Robert Mulligan
feasible: 3 fit 4 sane 5 utile 6 doable, likely, viable 7 earthly, fitting 8 credible, possible, probable, suitable, workable 9 plausible, potential, practical, thinkable 10 achievable, attainable, imaginable, realizable, reasonable
make ~: 3 let 6 enable, permit 7 empower, license, qualify 9 authorize
feasibly: 5 maybe 7 perhaps 8 possibly 9 perchance
feast: 3 eat 4 dine, fete, gala, luau, meal 5 party, Seder 6 dinner, regale, repast, spread 7 banquet, blowout, holiday, holy day 8 clambake, potlatch 9 celebrate, festivity, luxuriate, Pentecost
British ~: 3 ale
day: 7 jubilee
eyes on: 3 spy 4 view 5 sight, watch 6 behold, look at, regard 7 examine, inspect 8 look upon
for the eyes: 6 beauty, vision 7 dazzler, stunner 8 knockout
Hawaiian ~: 4 luau
Jewish ~: 5 Seder
love ~: 5 agape
on: 3 eat 4 love 5 adore, eat up, fancy, favor, savor 6 devour 7 consume, put away, scarf up 8 gobble up, wolf down 9 polish off, scarf down
one's eyes: 4 gaze, look, ogle, peer, view 5 stare 6 behold 7 observe 10 scrutinize
opposite: 6 famine
upon: 3 eat 7 indulge 9 delight in, luxuriate
feast __: 3 day
feast __ famine: 3 or a
__ feast: 4 love 7 movable
Feast
of Lights observer: 3 Jew
of Lots: 5 Purim
of Lots book: 6 Esther
Feast at Solhaug, The author: Henrik Ibsen
Feast of __: 4 Lots 5 Ashes, Fools, Weeks 6 Booths, Lights
Feast of All Saints author: Anne Rice
Feast of Ashes choreographer: 5 Ailey
Feast of Saint __: 5 Agnes
Feast of St. Nicholas, The artist: 5 Steen
feast one's __ on: 4 eyes
feat: 3 act 4 coup, deed 5 geste, stunt, thing 6 action, effort, stroke 7 exploit, triumph, victory 8 conquest 9 adventure 10 attainment
feather: 5 penna, pinna, plume, quill 6 fletch, pinion, pompon 7 plumule 8 plumelet
barb: 4 herl
bird's flight ~: 5 remex
birds of a ~: 7 cohorts, cronies 10 colleagues
combining form: 3 pen- 4 pinn-, pter-, ptil- 5 penni-, penno-, pinni-, ptero-, ptilo- 7 pinnati-
cut: 2 do 9 hairstyle
ender: 3 bed 4 bone, edge, head 5 brain 6 stitch, weight
full ~: 6 finery 8 glad rags 9 caparison
in one's cap: 4 fame 5 award, badge, glory, honor, kudos, medal, prize 6 credit, praise, renown, reward, trophy 7 acclaim, laurels, triumph, victory 8 accolade, citation, gold star, prestige 10 decoration
light as a ~: 4 airy, soft 5 wispy 6 creamy, dainty, flossy, slight 7 wispish 8 gossamer 10 weightless
neck ~: 6 hackle, heckle 7 hatchel
one's nest: 4 save 6 do well, make it, thrive 7 advance, develop, make out, prosper, succeed, triumph 8 conserve, flourish, go places, grow rich, hit it big, make good, progress
part: 5 shaft 6 rachis 7 rhachis
starter: 3 pin
stiff ~: 5 alula, quill
stole: 3 boa
feather __: 3 bed, key 4 palm, shot, star, worm 5 grass, tract 6 duster 7 banding
__ feather: 3 gay, sea 5 water, white 6 flight, sickle 7 contour
Feather: 5 falls 9 waterfall
locale: 10 California
featherbed: 4 idle, laze, loll 5 dog it, shirk 6 dawdle 7 goof off, slacken 8 lollygag, malinger, slack off 9 goldbrick 10 fool around
featherbrain: 3 ass, oaf, sap 4 boob, clod, dolt, fool 5 chump, clown, cluck, dummy, dunce, joker, ninny, patsy 6 dimwit, lummox, nitwit, sucker, turkey 7 buffoon, bungler, dingbat, dullard, fathead, half-wit, jackass, pinhead, saphead 8 bonehead, dumbbell, meathead, numskull 9 blockhead, numbskull, simpleton 10 dunderhead, nincompoop
featherbrained: 4 daft, dopy, soft, zany 5 daffy, dippy, dizzy, dopey, empty, giddy, goofy, inane, nutty, sappy, silly, wacky 6 absurd, jejune, simple, unwise, whacky 7 asinine, comical, doltish, fatuous, flighty, foolish, puerile, vacuous, witless 8 anserine, anserous, childish, farcical, ignorant, immature, mindless, trifling 9 brainless, dim-witted, fatuitous, foolhardy, frivolous, half-baked, illogical, ill-suited, imprudent, laughable, ludicrous, nitwitted, pointless, senseless 10 addlepated, boneheaded, cockamamie, half-witted, ill-advised, irrational, ridiculous
feathered: 5 plumy
feathered friend
see bird
Feathered Serpent, The author: 5 O'Dell
featherheaded: 4 daft, dopy, soft, zany 5 daffy, dippy, dizzy, dopey, empty, giddy, goofy, inane, nutty, sappy, silly, wacky 6 absurd, jejune, simple, unwise, whacky 7 asinine, comical, doltish, fatuous, flighty, foolish, puerile, vacuous, witless 8 anserine, anserous, childish, farcical, ignorant, immature, mindless, trifling 9 brainless, dim-witted, fatuitous, foolhardy, frivolous, half-baked, illogical, ill-suited, imprudent, laughable, ludicrous, nitwitted, pointless, senseless 10 addlepated, boneheaded, cockamamie, half-witted, ill-advised, irrational, ridiculous
feather in one's __: 3 cap
feather one's __: 4 nest
feathers: 4 down, tuft 5 fluff 7 plumage
cover with ~: 6 fledge
drop ~: 4 molt, shed 5 moult
fuss and ~: 3 ado 4 stir 5 furor 6 bother, bustle, clamor, flurry, hoopla, hubbub, rumpus, tumult, uproar 7 fanfare, trouble, turmoil 8 activity, busyness 9 commotion, confusion 10 difficulty, excitement, hullabaloo
partner: 3 tar 4 fuss
ruffle ~: 3 irk, vex 4 miff 5 annoy, peeve 6 bother, nettle 8 irritate
starter: 5 horse
trim ~: 5 preen
tuft of ~: 3 ear
__ feathers: 3 ice 5 frost
__ Feathers: 5 Horse 6 Pigeon
featherweight: 4 soft 5 light, wispy 6 creamy, dainty, flossy, slight 7 wispish 8 gossamer 9 lightsome
weapon: 3 jab 4 fist 5 punch
see also boxing
feathery: 4 soft 5 light, wispy 6 creamy, dainty, flossy, slight 7 wispish 8 gossamer 9 lightsome 10 weightless
flower: 8 tamarisk
palm: 5 assai
scarf: 3 boa
feats, flaunt one's: 4 brag 5 boast, spout, vaunt 7 lay it on, show off, swagger, talk big 9 gasconade
feature: 4 have, item, star 5 facet, movie, phase, point, story, thing, think, trait 6 aspect, column, detail, factor, play up, regard, stress, virtue 7 article, display, earmark, element, exhibit, point up, quality, realize, show off 8 hallmark, headline, landmark, property, showcase 9 attribute, component, emphasize, headliner, highlight, lineament, main event, specialty, spotlight, underline 10 accentuate, ingredient, particular, underscore
feature __: 4 film 5 story
feature-__: 6 length
__ feature: 4 main 6 double, triple
features: 3 mug, pan 4 face, mien, puss 5 looks 6 nature, visage 10 appearance, lineaments
featuring: 9 promoting 10 displaying, headlining, presenting
Feb.: 2 mo.
see also February
febrero: 3 mes 7 Spanish 8 February
febrile: 3 hot 7 boiling, pyretic 8 feverish, roasting 9 scorching
February: 2 mo. 5 month
birthstone: 8 amethyst
follower: 3 Mar. 5 March
like a ~ day: 5 brisk, crisp, nippy
plea: 6 be mine
preceder: 3 Jan. 7 January
sign: 4 Fish 6 Pisces 8 Aquarius
14 figure: 4 Amor, Eros 5 Cupid
February 5: 5 nones
FEC: 4 agcy. 6 agency
part: 3 Fed. 4 Comm., Elec. 7 Federal 8 Election 10 Commission
Fécamp: 4 city, town
locale: 6 France
feckless: 4 lazy 5 inept 6 futile 7 aimless, unready, useless 8 carefree, reckless 9 shiftless, uncareful, worthless 10 unbothered, unthinking
one: 5 idler, rogue, scamp 6 rascal 8 scalawag 9 do-nothing, reprobate 10 ne'er-do-well
fecund: 4 rich 7 fertile, teeming 8 fruitful, prolific 9 exuberant, luxuriant 10 productive
__ Fecunditatis: 4 Mare
fecundity: 8 richness 9 abundance, fertility 10 luxuriance
fed.: 4 natl.
agency: 3 ATC, ATF, BEP, BLS, CDC, CIA, DEA, DOD, DOT, EPA, FAA, FBI, FCC, FDA, FEC, FTC, GAO, GPO, GSA, HHS, HUD, INS, IRS, NEA, NIH, NPS, NRC, NSA, NSC, NSF, NWS, OMB, SBA, SEC, SSA, SSS 4 CPSC, EEOC, FDIC, FEMA, NASA, NLRB, NOAA, NTSB, OSHA, USCG, USDA, USIA, USPS 6 Amtrak
agent: 4 G-man, narc, nark, T-man 5 narco
airport monitor: 3 FAA
airport service: 3 ATC
arts sponsor: 3 NEA
auditor: 3 GAO
building agcy.: 3 HUD
clean-up org.: 3 EPA
collection org.: 3 IRS
employee: 3 agt. 5 agent
grant giver: 3 NSF
hush-hush group: 3 NSA
inspector: 4 USDA
lender: 3 SBA
medical detectives: 3 CDC
meteorology agcy.: 3 NWS
money overseer: 3 OMB
pension org.: 3 SSA
press: 3 GPO
stipend: 3 SSI
watchdog org.: 3 EPA, FDA
wellness org.: 3 NIH
__-fed: 4 clip, corn, well 5 spoon, stall 6 bottle
Fed: 4 G-man, Ness, T-man 5 agent
Fed. __: 5 Res. Bd., Res. Bk.
__-fed beef: 4 corn
Fedders alternative: 5 Rheem, Sears, Trane 6 Lennox 7 Carrier, Kenmore 9 Friedrich
federal: 6 public, united 8 national
agent: 4 G-man, narc, nark, T-man
deficit: 4 debt
issuance: 4 bond 5 T-bill, T-bond, T-note
make a ~ case of: 6 overdo
federal __: 4 case 5 court
Federal __: 4 Hill 5 party 7 Express

Federal __ Bank: 4 Land 7 Reserve
Federal __ Board: 7 Reserve
Federal __ Commission: 5 Power, Trade
Federal __ note: 7 Reserve
Federal __ System: 7 Reserve
Federal Chamber of Deputies locale: 6 Mexico
__ federalism: 3 new 5 world
Federalist __: 5 Party
Federal Reserve __: 4 Bank, note 5 Board 6 System
Federal Theater Project sponsor: 3 WPA
Federal Way: 4 city, town
locale: 10 Washington
federate: 4 band 5 merge, unify 6 league 7 conjoin
federation: 4 bloc, gild, ring 5 guild, state, union 6 league 7 academy 8 alliance 9 anschluss, coalition, syndicate 10 trade union
__ Federation: 7 Russian
Federico: 7 Fellini
in English: 9 Frederick
Federico __ Lorca: 6 García
Federko, Bernie
milieu: 3 ice 4 rink 5 arena
org.: 3 NHL
FedEx
rival: 3 DHL, UPS
send by ~: 4 rush 8 expedite
units: 3 lbs.
won't deliver to it: 5 P.O. box
Fedor: 4 tsar
fedora: 3 hat 6 topper 8 snap-brim
fabric: 4 felt
feature: 6 crease
Fedora highlight: 4 aria
__-fed press: 3 web
fed up: 3 low 4 sick 5 jaded, tired, vexed, weary 6 ireful 9 disgusted
fed-up one's shout: 6 enough
fee: 3 pay, tip 4 ante, bite, cost, dues, fine, levy, rate, toll, wage 5 price, wages 6 charge, income, salary, tariff, tipoff 7 charges, expense, payment, percent, premium, stipend, tuition 8 retainer 9 emolument, reckoning, surcharge 10 assessment, commission, honorarium, recompense
hourly ~: 4 rate
payer: 6 client, patron 8 customer
usage ~: 3 tax 4 duty, levy 6 charge, impost, tariff, towage 10 assessment
fee __: 4 tail 6 simple
fee-__-service: 3 for
__ fee: 4 user 5 green, legal 6 greens 7 advance, capping, finder's, license
Fee __ foe fum: 3 fie
feeble: 3 low, wan 4 lame, limp, poor, puny, sick, slim, tame, thin, weak 5 dotty, faint, frail, lousy, slack, timid, unfit, wimpy, woful 6 anemic, atonic, effete, faulty, flabby, flimsy, infirm, paltry, sickly, simple, skimpy, slight, tender, woeful 7 anaemic, fragile, lacking, languid, mawkish, slender, wimpish 8 decrepit, delicate, helpless, pathetic, pithless, weakened 9 enervated, faltering, nerveless, powerless, spineless, unhealthy 10 inadequate, pathetical, vulnerable
in a ~ manner: 5 wanly
make ~: 6 weaken 8 enervate 9 attenuate 10 debilitate, devitalize
feeble-minded: 3 dim 4 daft, slow 5 dense, thick 6 oafish, simple 9 brainless, dimwitted, nitwitted 10 half-witted
feebleness: 6 anemia 7 anaemia, fatigue, frailty, malaise 8 debility, puniness, weakness 9 fragility, frailness, inability, infirmity, lassitude 10 effeteness, enervation, etiolation, exhaustion, flimsiness, inadequacy, incapacity, infirmness, sickliness, unwellness
feed: 3 hay 4 corn, fuel, grub, keep, live, meal, oats, slop, tend 5 cater, grain, grass, graze, serve, stoke, straw 6 barley, fatten, fodder, forage, foster, signal, silage, supply 7 aliment, augment, bolster, cater to, nourish, nurture, provide, support, sustain, victual, vittles 8 chow down 9 encourage, pasturage, provender 10 strengthen, take care of
animal ~: 4 bran, mash 6 fodder, forage
chicken ~: 4 mash 6 change 8 pittance
don't ~: 6 famish, starve
ender: 3 bag, lot 4 back, hole 5 stock, stuff 7 through
lines to: 3 cue 6 prompt
off one's ~: 3 ill 4 sick 6 ailing, laid up, unwell
on: 3 eat 6 devour 7 consume
(on): 4 prey
the fire: 4 fuel, stir 5 stoke
the kitty: 4 ante 5 wager 6 chip in, kick in
too well: 4 cloy, glut, sate 5 gorge, stuff 7 surfeit 8 overfill 10 gormandize
feed __: 3 bag 5 grain
__ feed: 3 red 4 bird 7 chicken, gravity, tractor
__-feed: 4 hand 5 creep, float, spoon, stall 6 bottle
Feed __, starve...: 5 a cold
feedback: 5 input, reply 6 answer 7 comment 8 reaction, rebuttal, response 9 criticism 10 evaluation
give ~: 5 react, reply 6 answer 7 respond 9 get back to
nonverbal ~: 5 vibes
feedback __: 4 loop
feedbag
don the ~: 3 eat, sup
morsel: 3 oat
feeder: 5 river 6 trough 8 waterway 9 confluent, tributary
sound: 4 peep 5 chirp, tweet
feeder __: 4 line, road
__ feeder: 4 bird 5 creep, sheet, snake 6 bottom, filter
feeding __: 3 cup 6 frenzy
feeding combining form: 6 -trophy
feed the __: 5 kitty
Fee, fi, foe, __!: 3 fum
fee-for-__: 7 service
feel: 3 air, paw, see 4 aura, deem, hold, love, mood, tone 5 flair, frisk, grope, react, savor, sense, think, touch 6 finger, flavor, handle, intuit 7 believe, discern, presume, suppose, surmise, suspect, texture, undergo 8 ambiance, ambience, consider, perceive, theorize 9 semblance, sensation 10 atmosphere, conjecture, have a hunch, impression, manipulate
don't ~ so good: 3 ail 4 ache
in one's bones: 4 know
feel __: 3 for, out 4 like, up to
feel-__: 4 good
feeler: 4 hint, palp 5 offer, organ 6 palpus, sensor 7 advance, antenna, inquiry 8 overture, proposal, tentacle 10 invitation, suggestion
animal ~: 4 palp 6 palpus
put out a ~: 5 probe 7 inquire
feeling: 3 air 4 aura, idea, mood, soul, view 5 guess, heart, hunch, sense 6 belief, notion, pathos, spirit, theory 7 emotion, impulse, opinion, passion, posture, texture, thought 8 attitude, instinct, judgment, reaction 9 affection, awareness, intuition, semblance, sensation, sensitive, sentiment, suspicion, undertone 10 conviction, impression, perception
bored ~: 5 blahs 6 apathy
combining form: 5 patho-, -pathy 8 esthesio- 9 aesthesio-
down: 3 low, sad 4 blue, glum 5 moody, mopey 6 broody, dreary, gloomy, morose, somber, woeful 7 doleful, unhappy 8 dejected, downcast, mournful, troubled 9 depressed, heartsick, miserable, plaintive, saturnine, sorrowful 10 despondent, dispirited, melancholy
eerie ~: 6 déjà vu
faint: 5 woozy
fellow ~: 4 pity 6 lenity 7 charity 8 clemency, easiness, humanity, kindness, lenience, mildness, patience, softness, sympathy 9 tolerance 10 compassion, generosity, gentleness, indulgence, moderation, tenderness
fervid ~: 5 ardor
for the unfortunate: 6 warmth 7 empathy 8 sympathy 10 compassion, kindliness, tenderness
friendless: 7 forlorn 8 forsaken, isolated, lonesome
funny ~: 5 hunch 7 portent 9 suspicion
good: 3 fit 4 fine, hale, well 5 happy, hardy, husky, sound 6 hearty, robust, strong 7 chipper, healthy, up to par 8 blooming, thriving, vigorous 9 in the pink 10 able-bodied
good ~: 3 joy 4 ease, glee 6 relief, solace, thrill 7 comfort 8 sympathy 9 happiness, well-being
guilty: 5 sorry 6 rueful 7 ashamed 8 contrite, penitent 9 chastened, regretful, repentant 10 apologetic, remorseful
guilty ~: 5 shame
gut ~: 5 hunch 8 bad vibes, instinct 9 suspicion
gut-wrenching ~: 4 fear 5 dread 7 anxiety
happy ~: 3 joy 4 glee 5 bliss, cheer, mirth 6 gaiety 7 delight, ecstasy, elation, jollity 8 euphoria, gladness 9 merriment 10 exultation, joyfulness, joyousness, jubilation
harsh ~: 4 gall, hate 5 spite, venom 6 enmity, grudge, hatred, malice, rancor, spleen 7 cruelty, ill will, umbrage 8 acrimony, bad blood, contempt 9 animosity, antipathy, hostility, vengeance 10 resentment
haunted-house ~: 4 fear 5 alarm, angst, panic 6 fright, horror, terror
have a ~: 5 sense, smell 6 intuit 7 believe
ho-hum ~: 5 ennui 6 tedium, torpor 7 boredom, languor 8 lethargy 9 lassitude
ill ~: 4 bile, hate 5 odium, pique, scorn, spite, venom, wrath 6 animus, enmity, grudge, hatred, malice, rancor, spleen 7 discord, disdain, disgust, dudgeon, umbrage 8 acerbity, acrimony, aversion, bad blood, distaste, loathing 9 animosity, antipathy, harshness, hostility, malignity, mordacity, revulsion, vengeance, virulence 10 abhorrence, antagonism, bitterness, execration, repugnance, resentment
impervious to ~: 5 aloof, stoic 6 stolid 7 unmoved 9 apathetic, impassive
intense ~: 5 ardor
intensity of ~: 4 heat 5 ardor 6 fervor 7 passion 10 fervidness
lack of ~: 8 numbness
longing ~: 4 ache, pang 7 craving 9 hankering
negative ~: 3 ire 4 fury, hate, rage 5 anger, odium, pique, scorn, spite, wrath 6 animus, choler, enmity, malice, rancor 7 disdain, disgust, dislike, dudgeon, ill will, offense, outrage, umbrage 8 acrimony, aversion, distaste, loathing, vexation 9 agitation, animosity, antipathy, hostility, petulance, revulsion 10 abhorrence, antagonism, execration, irritation, repugnance, resentment
no pain: 4 numb 5 tipsy
no stress: 6 at ease 7 content, relaxed 8 carefree, composed, tranquil
not ~ well: 3 ill 4 sick 6 ailing, queasy
of unease: 4 fear 5 alarm, angst, panic 6 dismay, fright, horror, phobia, terror 10 foreboding
one's oats: 5 happy, jolly, merry 6 frisky, impish, lively 7 coltish, naughty, playful, puckish, teasing, waggish 8 mirthful, prankish, skittish, sportive 9 fun-loving, lightsome, sprightly, vivacious, whimsical 10 frolicsome, rollicking
remove ~: 4 dull 6 benumb, deaden
restless ~: 4 itch 7 craving 8 yearning 9 hankering
scared ~: 4 fear 5 alarm, angst, dread, panic 6 fright, horror, terror 7 anxiety
shared ~: 5 unity 7 empathy, rapport 8 affinity, sympathy
sinking ~: 7 portent
sore: 4 achy 5 angry
tender ~: 4 pity 5 heart, mercy 6 lenity 7 charity, empathy, quarter 8 clemency, kindness, lenience, sympathy 9 sentiment, tolerance 10 compassion, condolence, humaneness
the strain: 5 tense
vindictive ~: 3 ire 4 bile, fury, hate, rage 5 anger, wrath 6 rancor, spleen 7 dudgeon, outrage, umbrage 8 acrimony, vexation 10 resentment
walking-on-air ~: 3 joy 7 ecstasy, elation, rapture 8 euphoria, gladness 9 happiness
warm ~: 4 love 5 ardor 8 fondness 9 adoration, affection 10 tenderness
without ~: 4 numb 9 insensate
with strong ~: 5 hotly
world-weary ~: 6 apathy, tedium 7 boredom, languor 9 lassitude
feeling no __: 4 pain
feeling one's __: 4 oats
feelings: 8 sympathy
evoke good ~: 6 endear
feign ~: 3 act 5 emote 7 playact
hard ~: 5 anger 6 grudge, hatred 7 offense
have hard ~: 6 resent
hurt one's ~: 6 insult, offend 7 torment 8 distress
reveal one's ~: 4 avow, tell 5 admit, allow, let on 6 fess up 7 concede, confess, divulge 8 disclose 9 make known
wounded ~: 5 pique 6 insult 7 affront, offense, outrage, umbrage 9 indignity 10 resentment
Feelings (1975 song) artist: Morris Albert

feel in one's __: 5 bones
Feelin' Stronger Every Day (1973 song) artist: Chicago
feel no __: 4 pain
feel one's __: 4 oats
Feel So Good (1997 song) artist: Mase
Feels So Good (1978 song) artist: Chuck Mangione
__-feely: 6 touchy
feet: 5 meter
cold ~: 4 fear 5 alarm, panic 8 timidity 9 cowardice 10 faint heart
dead on one's ~: 5 tired
drag one's ~: 3 lag 4 idle, laze, loaf 5 amble, dally, mosey, stall, tarry 6 dawdle, linger, loiter, put off 7 saunter 8 lollygag, obstruct, straggle 9 waste time 10 dillydally
5280 ~: 4 mile
fall at the ~ of: 5 kneel 6 grovel 9 prostrate
fast on one's ~: 5 agile, fleet
get back on one's ~: 7 rebound, recover
get cold ~: 5 quail, waver 6 falter, wobble 8 hang back, hesitate 9 hem and haw, vacillate
get off one's ~: 3 lie, sit 4 loll, rest 5 relax 6 lounge, repose, sprawl 7 recline 10 stretch out
get one's ~ wet: 4 ford, open, wade 5 begin, slosh, start 6 launch, paddle, splash, tackle 7 kick off, lead off 8 commence, get going, set forth 9 enter into, strike out 10 inaugurate, plunge into
get to one's ~: 4 rise, wake 5 arise, awake, stand, waken 6 awaken, jump up, wake up 7 stand up
give one's ~ a rest: 3 sit 5 relax
have cold ~: 5 cower, quail, quake 6 cringe, falter, flinch, recoil, shrink 7 tremble 10 chicken out
having cold ~: 5 jumpy, timid 6 afraid, craven, scared, yellow 7 chicken, daunted, fearful, panicky, spooked, wimpish 8 cowardly, fearsome, recreant, sheepish, timorous 9 nerveless, spineless, terrified, tremulous 10 frightened
having no ~: 6 apodal 7 apodous
kiss the ~ of: 5 adore, deify, honor 6 admire, dote on, revere 7 cherish, glorify, idolize, worship 8 venerate
lay at one's ~: 4 give 5 offer 6 tender 7 present, propose
leave one's ~: 3 hop 4 jump, leap 5 bound
light on one's ~: 4 deft, spry 5 agile, lithe 6 nimble 7 lissome 8 graceful, spirited, vigorous 9 energetic, vivacious
off one's ~: 3 ill 4 sick 6 ailing, infirm, laid up, sickly, unwell 7 unsound 9 afflicted, bedridden 10 indisposed
on one's ~: 5 erect 6 arisen 8 standing
put back on one's ~: 4 cure, heal, mend 5 treat
put one's ~ up: 4 laze, loaf, loll, rest 5 relax 6 repose, unwind 7 lay back, lie down, recline, sit back, take ten 8 take five 10 settle back, take a break, take it easy
put on one's ~: 4 help 5 boost 6 assist, buck up 7 bolster, support, sustain 10 facilitate
six ~: 6 fathom
sweep off one's ~: 4 lure 5 besot, charm, tempt 6 allure, entice, rope in 7 attract, beguile, bewitch, enchant 8 entrance 9 captivate, fascinate, infatuate
three ~: 4 yard
three ~ plus: 5 meter, metre
walk on bare ~: 3 pad
__ feet: 4 cold, flat 5 board
__-feet: 5 crow's
feet of __: 4 clay
Feiffer, Jules: 10 cartoonist
feign: 3 act 4 fake, mock, pose, seem, sham 5 bluff, put on 6 affect, assume, fake it, invent, play at 7 imitate, phony up, pretend, profess 8 disguise, make as if, simulate 9 dissemble, fabricate
feelings: 3 act 7 playact
feigned: 4 fake, mock, sham 5 bogus, false, phony, put-on 6 ersatz, forged, phoney, pseudo, unreal 7 assumed 8 affected, spurious 9 imitation, insincere, pretended, synthetic, unnatural 10 artificial, fictitious, fraudulent
feijoa: 5 shrub
relative: 5 ramee, ramie 6 myrtle
__ Fein: 4 Sinn
Feinstein: 6 Dianne 7 Michael
org.: 3 Sen. 6 Senate
Feinstein, Michael: 6 singer 7 pianist
feint: 4 deke, hoax, juke, ploy, ruse, sham, trap, wile 5 bluff, dodge, fraud, trick 6 deceit, device, dupery, gambit, humbug 7 gimmick, pretext, snow job, swindle 8 artifice, pretense 9 chicanery, deception, imposture 10 subterfuge
fencer's ~: 5 appel
rink ~: 4 deke
feist: 3 cur, dog 4 mutt 5 canid 6 canine 7 mongrel
feistiness: 4 grit, guts 5 heart, moxie, nerve, pluck, spunk 6 daring, mettle 7 bravado 8 audacity, chutzpah, gumption, tenacity, true grit 9 fortitude, gutsiness, toughness 10 pluckiness
feisty: 4 game 5 alive, onery, peppy, surly, tough 6 active, bubbly, fretty, frisky, lively, ornery, plucky, spunky, touchy, unruly 7 defiant, naughty, scrappy, waspish, wayward, zestful 8 contrary, snappish, spirited, stubborn 9 difficult, excitable, irascible, irritable, splenetic, truculent 10 high-strung, hot-blooded, out of sorts, pugnacious, rebellious, unamenable
not ~: 4 tame
Feldman: 5 Corey, Marty 6 Morton
Feldman, Marty: 5 actor 8 comedian
film: Silent Movie (1976)
Yellowbeard (1983)
Young Frankenstein (1974)
in Young Frankenstein: 4 Igor
Feldon: 7 Barbara
Feldshuh: 5 Tovah
feldspar: 7 mineral
mineral: 7 granite
opalescent ~ gem: 9 moonstone
Felicia: 4 Farr
Feliciano, José song: Light My Fire (1968)
felicitate: 9 recommend 10 compliment
__ Félicité, Que.: 3 Ste.
felicitous: 3 apt, fit 4 just 5 blest, happy, lucky, right 6 timely 7 apropos, blessed, charmed, favored, fitting, germane, on a roll 8 apposite, relevant 9 befitting, fortunate, on a streak, opportune, pertinent, well-timed 10 applicable, auspicious, convincing, fortuitous, propitious, seasonable, well-chosen
felicity: 3 joy 4 glee 5 bliss, mirth 7 delight, ecstasy, elation, rapture 8 elegance, euphoria, pleasure 9 enjoyment, happiness, merriment, well-being 10 ebullience, jubilation
Felicity: 7 Huffman, Kendall
Felicity (WB drama)
cast: Scott Foley (Noel Crane)
Keri Russell (Felicity Porter)
Scott Speedman (Ben Covington)
feline: 3 cat, pet, sly 4 eyra, lion, lynx, puma, puss, wily 5 catty, chita, fossa, kitty, liger, ounce, tabby, tiger, tigon 6 bobcat, calico, cheeta, chetah, cougar, jaguar, kitten, margay, ocelot, serval, sneaky, tiglon 7 bay lynx, caracal, catlike, cheetah, cunning, leonine, leopard, panther, Siamese 8 Garfield, lynxlike, sneaking, stealthy 9 catamount, grimalkin 10 jaguarundi
Africa: 4 lion 5 chita 6 cheeta, chetah, serval 7 caracal, cheetah, leopard
Asia: 4 lion 5 chita, ounce, tiger 6 cheeta, chetah 7 cheetah, leopard
attractor: 6 catnip
Central America: 6 margay
drink like a ~: 5 lap up
forest ~: 4 lynx
hybrid: 5 liger, tigon 6 tiglon
India: 7 caracal
like a ~: 5 furry
Mexico: 6 ocelot
nemesis: 6 canine
nocturnal: 6 serval
North America: 4 lynx, puma 6 cougar 7 panther 9 catamount
often: 5 pawer
play with like a ~: 5 paw at
sound: 3 mew 4 meow 5 miaou, miaow, miaul
South America: 4 puma 6 cougar, margay, ocelot 7 panther
spotted: 5 ounce 6 jaguar, ocelot, serval 7 leopard
striped: 5 tiger
tawny: 4 puma 6 cougar 7 panther
tropical: 4 eyra 10 jaguarundi
see also cat
Felipe: 4 Alou
brother of ~: 5 Jesus, Matty
in English: 6 Philip
son of ~: 6 Moises
see also Spanish
__ Felipe: 3 San
Felipes, six: 5 reyes
felis: 3 cat
felis __: 3 leo
felis pardalis: 6 ocelot
Felix: 3 cat 4 pope 5 Bloch, Silla, Ungar, Unger 6 Salten 7 pontiff 8 Hoffmann
creator: 4 Neil
like ~: 4 neat, tidy 7 orderly 10 fastidious
roomie: 5 Oscar
Felix Holt author: George Eliot
Feliz __ Nuevo!: 3 Año
fell: 2 ax 3 axe, hew 4 chop, down, hack, moor, slid, ugly 5 level 7 cut down, inhuman, saw down 8 backslid, chop down, declined, dreadful, inhumane, pull down, went down 9 bring down, collapsed, knock down, plummeted, prostrate, shoot down, throw down 10 strike down
Fell: 6 Norman
__ Fell: 3 If I 5 A Tear
fella
see fellow
__ Fell, A: 4 Tear 7 Blossom
Fell, Dr. Gideon creator: 4 Carr
felled: 4 hewn
feller: 2 he 3 boy, bud, cat, egg, guy, lad, man, sir 4 bean, chap, dude, gent, male 5 bloke, buddy 6 mister, person 7 brother 9 gentleman
tree ~: 3 saw 5 axman 6 axeman
see also fellow
Feller, Bob: 6 hurler, Indian 7 pitcher
Fellini, Federico: 7 Italian 8 director
film: 81/2 (1963)
Amarcord (1974)
The Clowns (1971)
I Vitelloni (1953)
La Dolce Vita (1960)
La Strada (1954)
Roma (1972)
film composer: 4 Rota
__ Fell on Alabama: 5 Stars
__ Fell Out of Heaven: 5 A Star
fellow: 2 he 3 boy, bud, cat, egg, guy, him, lad, man, sir 4 beau, chap, dude, gent, male, peer 5 bloke, buddy, equal, hubby 6 cohort, mister, person, suitor 7 compeer, comrade 8 coworker, lecturer, roommate 9 associate, companion, professor 10 reciprocal
ender: 3 man, men 4 ship
feeling: 4 pity 6 lenity 7 charity 8 clemency, easiness, humanity, kindness, lenience, mildness, patience, softness, sympathy 9 tolerance 10 compassion, generosity, gentleness, indulgence, moderation, tenderness
fraternal ~: 3 Elk 4 Lion 5 Moose
funny ~: 3 wag, wit 4 hoot
in Australia: 4 mate
in England: 4 mate
in France: 8 monsieur
in Germany: 4 Herr
in Spain: 5 señor
Jamaican ~: 3 mon
regular ~: 3 Joe
starter: 3 bed 6 school
that ~: 3 him
unnamed ~: 3 bub, him, mac
young ~: 3 boy, kid, lad, tad 4 tike, tyke 5 sprig 6 shaver
fellow __: 7 feeling, servant
__ fellow: 3 old 4 good
__ Fellow: 3 Odd
Fellowes: 10 Rockcliffe
fellow's
that ~: 3 his
fellowship: 4 club, gild 5 amity, grant, guild 6 league 7 company, coterie, society, subsidy 8 alliance, sodality 9 allowance, communion 10 affability, kindliness
__ Fellow, The: 5 Quare
__-fellow-well-met: 4 hail
__ fell swoop: 5 at one, in one
felon: 3 con 4 perp 5 crook, lifer, thief 6 outlaw, rascal, robber 7 burglar, convict 8 arsonist, assassin, criminal, evildoer, internee, jailbird, kidnaper, offender, prisoner, yardbird 9 kidnapper, miscreant, purloiner 10 delinquent, lawbreaker, malefactor
aid a ~: 4 abet
certain ~: 4 yegg 5 lifer 8 arsonist
computer ~: 6 hacker
released ~: 5 ex-con
felonious: 4 tabu 5 taboo, wrong 6 banned, guilty 7 illegal, illicit 8 criminal, improper, outlawed, unlawful, verboten, wrongful 9 forbidden 10 prohibited
felony: 5 arson, crime, wrong 7 assault, battery, offense, robbery, treason 8 burglary 10 grand theft, kidnapping
Felson: 5 Eddie 9 Fast Eddie
felt: 5 cloth 6 fabric 8 material
combining form: 3 pil- 4 pilo-
deeply ~: 5 inner 8 visceral 9 emotional
hat: 3 fez 6 fedora
imitation ~: 5 baize
starter: 5 heart
surface: 3 nap

felt __: 3 pen 4 side 6 marker
felt-tip: 3 pen
felucca: 4 boat, ship 5 craft 6 vessel
fem.: 6 gender
flier: 3 WAF
neither masc. nor ~: 4 neut.
not ~: 4 masc., neut.
title: 3 Mrs.
female: 3 cow, dam, doe, ewe, gal, hen, her, Mrs., pen, she, sow 4 aunt, girl, lady, lass, maid, miss, wife 5 filly, madam, woman 6 Amazon, damsel, gender, lassie, madame, maiden, matron, missis, missus, mother, sister 7 womanly 8 daughter, ladylove 9 inamorata, matriarch, muliebral
brazen ~: 5 hussy 7 Jezebel
campus ~: 4 coed
combining form: 3 gyn- 4 gyne-, gyno-, -gyny 5 gynec-, thely- 6 gyneco-, -gynous
palindromic ~: 3 Ada, Ava, Eve, Lil, Nan 4 Anna 6 Hannah
relative: 3 mom 4 aunt, mama 5 mamma, momma, niece 6 mother 7 grandma 9 great-aunt 10 grand-niece
young ~: 3 kid 4 girl, lass, maid, teen 5 minor 6 damsel, lassie, maiden 8 Fraülein, teenager
Female (1933 film)
cast: George Brent, Ruth Chatterton
director: Michael Curtiz
FEMA part: 3 Fed., Mgt. 4 Agcy., Emer., Mgmt. 6 Agency 7 Federal 9 Emergency 10 Management
feminine: 6 gender 7 womanly 8 lady-like 9 muliebral
accessory: 5 purse 7 handbag 10 pocketbook
principle: 3 yin 5 anima
pronoun: 3 her, she 4 hers 7 herself
suffix: 3 -ess, -ina, -ine 4 -enne, -etta, -ette, -euse, -trix
feminine __: 5 rhyme 6 ending 7 caesura
Feminine Mystique, The author: Betty Friedan
feminist
cause: 3 ERA
grp.: 3 NOW
monogram: 3 ECS, SBA
femme: 10 Parisienne
canonized ~: 3 ste.
fatale: 4 vamp 5 flirt, siren, vixen
unmarried ~: 4 mlle.
femme __: 6 fatale
femoral __: 6 artery
__ femoris: 6 biceps
femur: 4 bone 9 thighbone
joiners: 4 ilia
locale: 3 leg 5 thigh
neighbor: 5 tibia
-tibia connector: 4 knee 7 kneecap, patella
fen: 3 bog 4 mire, sink 5 marsh, money, swamp 6 morass, muskeg 8 quagmire
100 ~: 4 yuan
fence: 3 buy, hem, pen 4 coop, duel, rail, sell, wall 5 bound, dodge, hedge, limit, parry 6 corral, girdle, paling, picket, robber 7 barrier, confine, defense, enclose, inclose, pickets, railing, rampart 8 encircle, palisade, restrict, separate, sidestep, simulate, stockade, surround 9 barricade 10 equivocate
alternative: 5 hedge
defense: 4 barb
get off the ~: 3 act, opt 6 choose, decide
go over the ~: 6 defect, desert, run out 7 abscond
in: 3 pen 6 define 7 impound 8 surround
material: 4 wire, wood 6 picket
off: 7 enclose, inclose, shut off, shut out 9 partition
on the ~: 4 torn 5 fluid, shaky, timid 6 fickle, unsure 7 dubious, neutral, not sure 8 detached, doubtful, hesitant, lukewarm, volatile, waffling, wavering 9 dithering, spineless, tentative, uncertain, undecided, unsettled, weak-kneed 10 ambivalent, changeable, hesitating, hot-and-cold, indecisive, irresolute, nonaligned, of two minds, wishy-washy
opening: 4 gate
part: 4 pale, post, rail
sit on the ~: 5 waver 7 abstain, quibble 8 hesitate 9 pussyfoot
steps: 5 stile
sunken ~: 4 ha-ha
supplier: 5 thief 7 burglar
fence-__: 3 off 6 sitter 7 mending
__ fence: 4 rail, rock, snow, sunk, worm 5 on the, snake, spite 6 dogleg, paling, picket 7 Cyclone
fenced
area: 3 pen, sty 4 coop 6 corral
in: 4 pent 8 confined, cooped up 9 corralled
not ~: 4 open 8 unclosed 10 accessible
fence inspector, name meaning: 7 Hayward
__ Fence Me In: 4 Don't
fencer: 8 Olympian 9 swordsman
__ fences: 4 mend
Fences: 4 play 5 drama
author: August Wilson
character: 3 Jim 4 Bono, Cory, Rose, Troy 5 Lyons 6 Maxson 7 Gabriel, Raynell
__ Fences: 6 Picket
fence-sit: 5 hedge, waver 6 dither, waffle 7 abstain, whiffle 8 hesitate, straddle 9 hem and haw, vacillate
fence-sitting response: 5 maybe 7 perhaps 8 possibly 9 it could be, it might be
fence-straddling: 8 hesitant, wavering 9 undecided 10 indecisive, irresolute, wishy-washy
fencing: 5 sport 7 hedging 9 enclosure, swordplay
area: 5 piste
art of ~: 4 épée
hit: 5 punto
Japanese ~: 5 kendo
match: 4 duel
move: 4 volt 5 appel, feint, lunge, parry 6 remise, thrust 7 riposte
shout in ~: 7 en garde
sword part: 6 foible
term: 4 épée, foil 5 feint, lunge, parry, piste, saber 6 foible, rapier, remise, thrust, touché 7 en garde, riposte
weapon: 4 épée, foil 5 blade, saber, sword
fend: 6 shield 8 get along 9 safeguard
off: 5 avert, avoid, deter, dodge, evade, parry, repel, stave 6 offend, rebuff, sicken 7 deflect, disgust, repulse 8 alienate 9 force back
(off): 4 hold, ward 5 drive
fend __: 3 off
fend __ oneself: 3 for
fender: 6 bumper, shield 8 auto part, mudguard 10 wheel guard
crumpled ~: 6 damage
flaw: 4 ding
in Britain: 4 wing
material: 6 chrome
fender __: 4 pile 6 bender
Fender: 3 Leo 6 Freddy
fender-bender: 4 dent 5 crash, wreck 6 mishap, pileup 7 smashup 8 accident 9 collision
Fender, Freddy
song: Before the Next Teardrop Falls (1975)
Wasted Days and Wasted Nights (1975)
fenestra: 6 window
feng __: 4 shui
Fenice: 4 font 8 typeface
__ Fenimore Cooper: 5 James
__ Fe, NM: 5 Santa
Fenn: 4 John 8 Sherilyn
fennec: 3 fox 5 canid 6 animal, canine
relative: 3 dog 4 wolf 5 dhole, dingo 6 corsac, coydog, coyote, jackal
fennel: 4 herb 5 plant, spice 9 flavoring, seasoning
unit: 5 stalk
__ fennel: 3 dog 4 wild 5 giant, sweet
Fenn, John: 7 chemist 8 Nobelist
fenny: 5 boggy 6 marshy, swampy
Fenrir, father of: 4 Loki
fenugreek: 5 spice
Fenway Park: 5 arena
locale: 6 Boston
nickname: 3 Yaz
team: 3 Sox 5 Bosox 6 Red Sox
Feodor: 5 Lynen 9 Chaliapin
in English: 8 Theodore
fer
not ~: 4 agin
feral: 4 wild 5 rabid 6 animal, brutal, fierce, savage 7 beastly, bestial, untamed, vicious 8 ravenous, unbroken 9 barbarous, rapacious, raptorial, unbridled
not ~: 4 tame
Ferber, Edna: 6 writer
collaborator: Kaufman
work: Cimarron
Come and Get It
Dawn O'Hara
Dinner at Eight
Giant
The Girls
Great Sun
Ice Palace
A Kind of Magic
One Basket
A Peculiar Treasure
The Royal Family
Saratoga Trunk
Show Boat
So Big
Stage Door
Ferde: 5 Grofé
fer-de-lance: 5 snake, viper
Fer-de-Lance author: Rex Stout
Ferdinand: 3 Rey 4 Cohn, Foch 6 Marcos 7 Buisson, Porsche 8 Magellan, Zeppelin 9 de Lesseps
in Spanish: 8 Fernando
land: 5 Spain
wife: 6 Imelda
Ferdinand the Bull creator: 4 Leaf
Ferenc: 6 Molnár
Fergie: 5 Sarah 7 Jenkins
ex: 4 Andy 6 Andrew
former sister-in-law: 4 Anne
Ferguson: 3 Jay 4 city, town 5 Sarah 7 Jenkins, Maynard
locale: 8 Missouri
opponent: 6 Plessy
Ferguson, Maynard: 9 trumpeter
genre: 4 jazz
feria: 4 fair 7 Spanish
ferine: 5 rabid 6 savage 7 beastly, untamed 8 unbroken 9 unbridled
ferity: 7 cruelty 8 savagery 10 inhumanity
Ferlin: 5 Husky
Ferlinghetti, Lawrence: 6 author, writer
novel: 3 Her
fermata: 4 hold 5 pause
Fermat's __ theorem: 4 last
ferment: 3 row 4 brew, flap, foam, mess, mold, stew, stir, to-do 5 chaos, froth, furor, rouse, storm, yeast 6 bedlam, clamor, excite, flurry, frenzy, hubbub, incite, mayhem, outcry, rumble, seethe, simmer, stir up, tumult, unrest, uproar, work up 7 anarchy, distill, enflame, inflame, provoke, rampage, smolder, turmoil 8 brouhaha, disarray, disquiet, smoulder, upheaval, uprising 9 agitation, commotion, confusion, imbroglio, intensity 10 excitement, turbulence
combining form: 3 zym- 4 zymo-
in a ~: 5 astir 8 bustling
fermentation
byproduct: 6 alegar
science of ~: 7 zymurgy
fermented: 4 hard, sour 9 alcoholic
beverage: 3 ale 4 beer 5 cider, lager
mash: 4 wort
milk drink: 5 kefir
palm sap: 4 arak 6 arrack
partly ~ grape juice: 4 stum
fermenting: 5 barmy, foamy 6 frothy, yeasty
fungi: 5 yeast
tank: 3 vat
Fermi, Enrico: 7 Italian 8 Nobelist 9 physicist
concern: 4 atom
fermion: 8 particle
fermium: 5 metal 7 element
fern: 4 nito 5 plant 6 osmund 7 bracken, osmunda, wall rue, woodsia 8 moonwort, polypody, staghorn 9 rock brake 10 cliff brake, fiddlehead, houseplant, maidenhair, pepperwort, spleenwort, Venus's-hair
combining form: 6 pterid- 7 pterido-
future ~: 5 spore
leaf: 5 frond
spore cluster: 5 sorus
spore clusters: 4 sori
stalk: 5 stipe
fern __: 3 bar 4 seed
__ fern: 3 lip, oak 4 ball, bead, deer, lady, male, seed, tree, wall, wood 5 beech, chain, cloak, fancy, grape, holly, marsh, royal, sword, tuber 6 Alice's, basket, Boston, bottle, dagger, meadow, shield 7 bladder, boulder, brittle, buckler, Clayton, crested, fragile, Goldie's, ostrich, parsley, walking
Fernand: 5 Léger
Fernández: 4 city, town
locale: 6 Mexico
Fernando: 3 Rey 5 Lamas, Tatis 7 Arrabal, Bujones 10 Valenzuela
in English: 9 Ferdinand
see also Spanish
Fernando (1976 song) artist: ABBA
__ Fernando Valley: 3 San
Ferndale: 4 city, town
locale: 8 Michigan
FernGully...The __ Rainforest: 4 Last
Fernie: 4 city, town
locale: 6 Canada
Fernwood 2-Night star: 4 Mull 5 DeVol 7 Willard
ferocious: 4 grim, mean, wild 5 cruel, harsh, nasty, rabid, rough 6 animal, brutal, fierce, lupine, savage, unkind, wanton 7 beastly, brutish, callous, hurtful, inhuman, tigrish, untamed, vicious, violent, wolfish 8 barbaric, fiendish, inhumane, pitiless, ravenous, ruthless, sadistic, tigerish, unbroken, vehement, vengeful 9 barbarous, cutthroat, frightful, merciless, monstrous,

predatory, rapacious, truculent, unbridled, unpitying, voracious, vulturous **10** implacable, relentless, sanguinary, unmerciful, vindictive
not ~: **4** meek, mild, tame **5** mousy, quiet **6** broken, docile, gentle, mellow **7** passive, pliable **8** lamblike, sheepish, yielding **9** compliant, easygoing, tractable **10** submissive
ferociously: **4** hard
ferocity: **4** fury, heat, rage **7** cruelty **8** savagery, violence, wildness **9** barbarity, brutality **10** fierceness, inhumanity
symbol of ~: **4** lion **5** tiger
Ferrante: **6** Arthur
Ferrante & Teicher: **8** pianists
song: Exodus (1960)
Theme from The Apartment (1960)
Tonight (1961)
Ferrara: **4** Abel, city, town
family name: **4** Este
locale: **5** Italy
Ferrare: **8** Cristina
Ferrari: **3** car **4** auto, Dino, Enzo **10** automobile
model: **3** GTO **4** Enzo **6** Modena **7** Mondial **9** Maranello **10** Testarossa
Ferraro: **9** Geraldine
Ferré: **7** Rosario
Ferrell: **8** Conchata
Ferrer: **3** Mel **4** José **6** Miguel
Ferrer, José: **5** actor
film: The Caine Mutiny (1954)
Cyrano de Bergerac (1950, AA)
The Great Man (1956)
A Midsummer Night's Sex Comedy (1982)
Miss Sadie Thompson (1953)
Moulin Rouge (1952)
Ship of Fools (1965)
State Fair (1962)
Whirlpool (1949)
spouse: Rosemary Clooney, Uta Hagen
Ferrer, Mel: **5** actor
film: The Brave Bulls (1951)
Green Mansions (1959)
Lili (1953)
The Longest Day (1962)
Lost Boundaries (1949)
Rancho Notorious (1952)
The Secret Fury (1950)
The Sun Also Rises (1957)
spouse: Audrey Hepburn
Ferré, Rosario: **6** writer **11** Puerto Rican
ferret: **3** pet **4** root **5** snoop **6** animal, mammal, search, weasel **7** ransack
female: **4** jill
male: **3** hob
out: **3** pry **4** find, seek, spot **5** dig up, scour, scout, trace **6** locate, search **7** unearth **8** discover **9** ascertain, determine, penetrate, track down
(out): **4** hunt **6** search
relative: **4** mink **5** fitch, otter, ratel, sable, skunk, stoat, tayra **6** badger, ermine, marten **7** foumart, polecat **8** carcajou, foulmart, kolinsky, muishond **9** wolverine
young: **3** kit
ferrety: **6** prying, snoopy **8** invasive **9** intrusive
ferric: **4** iron **6** steely **8** metallic
compound: **4** rust
deficiency: **6** anemia **7** anaemia
mineral: **8** hematite
ferric __: **5** oxide
ferriferous rock: **3** ore
Ferrigno: **3** Lou
role: **4** Hulk
Ferris Bueller's Day Off (1986 film)
cast: Matthew Broderick, Jeffrey Jones, Alan Ruck, Mia Sara
director: John Hughes
Ferris wheel: **4** ride
cry: **4** whee
operator: **5** carny **6** carney
ferrite: **4** iron
ferrous: **4** iron **6** steely **8** metallic
ferrous __: **5** oxide **7** sulfate, sulfide
Ferruccio: **6** Busoni
ferry: **3** lug, ply, tow **4** bear, boat, cart, pack, take, tote **5** carry **6** convey, packet **7** shuttle **8** transfer **9** chauffeur, transport
ender: **4** boat
locale: **5** river
operate a ~: **3** ply
operator: **5** plier, plyer, poler
slip: **4** dock, pier **5** berth
Ferry Cross the Mersey (1965 song)
artist: Gerry and the Pacemakers
Ferry Pass: **4** city, town
locale: **7** Florida
__ Ferry, WV: **7** Harpers
fertile: **4** lush, rich **5** loamy **6** arable, fecund **7** teeming **8** abundant, creative, fruitful, original, prolific **9** bountiful, exuberant, inventive, luxuriant, plenteous, plentiful **10** generative, productive
area: **5** oasis
Fertile Crescent
country: **4** Irak, Iraq
river: **6** Tigris **9** Euphrates
fertility: **8** richness **9** abundance, fecundity **10** luxuriance
god: **4** Baal
goddess: **4** Isis
fertilize: **5** mulch **6** enrich **7** compost **8** fructify **9** cultivate, germinate, pollinate, propagate
__-fertilize: **5** cross
fertilizer: **5** humus **7** compost **9** plant food
brand: **5** Ortho
clay ~: **4** marl
ingredient: **4** urea **5** niter, nitre
ferule: **4** whip **6** cudgel **9** truncheon
fervency: **4** brio, élan, zeal **5** ardor, gusto, verve, vigor **6** energy, spirit **7** passion **8** vivacity **9** eagerness **10** enthusiasm, excitement, heartiness
fervent
see fervid
fervently: **5** hotly, madly **6** wildly **7** greatly **8** ardently **9** furiously, intensely, like crazy, seriously **10** recklessly
fervid: **3** hot **4** avid, keen, warm **5** eager, fiery, itchy **6** ablaze, ardent, devout, hearty, heated, hectic, loving, red-hot, strong, torrid **7** amatory, burning, devoted, earnest, excited, flaming, glowing, intense, serious, sincere, valuing, zealous **8** animated, enthused, hopped up, vehement, wild-eyed **9** amatorial, emotional, fanatical, heartfelt, impetuous **10** hot-blooded, inspirited, passionate
fervor: **4** fire, heat, love, lust, soul, zeal, zest **5** ardor, flame, gusto, oomph, verve, vigor **6** desire, warmth **7** ardency, emotion, passion **8** alacrity, delirium, devotion, keenness, strength, vitality **9** animation, eagerness, inner fire, intensity, monomania, sincerity **10** conviction, devoutness, enthusiasm, excitement, exuberance, heartiness, liveliness
fescue: **5** grass
roll out the ~: **3** sod
__ fescue: **3** red **5** sheep **6** meadow
fess (up): **3** own **4** give
Fess: **6** Parker
fess up: **3** bow, let, own **4** avow, fold, quit **5** admit, agree, allow, grant, let on, yield **6** accede, accept, accord, cave in, reveal **7** concede, tell all **9** come clean, recognize, surrender **10** capitulate, understand
fest: **2** do **4** ball, bash, fete, gala **5** blast, party **6** affair **7** shindig **8** function, wingding
follower: **3** oon
starter: **3** fun, gab **4** slug, song, talk
festal: **3** fun, gay **4** gala **5** happy, jolly, merry **6** joyful, joyous, lively **7** special **8** cheerful **9** convivial
fester: **3** irk, rot, vex **4** gall **5** chafe **6** rankle **7** smolder **8** irritate, smoulder, stagnate
Fester: **5** uncle
Morticia, to ~: **5** niece
festina __: **5** lente
Festiva: **3** car **4** auto, Ford **10** automobile
festival: **4** fair, fete, gala **6** fiesta, gaiety, gayety **7** holiday, jubilee, revelry **8** carnival, jamboree
Afro-American ~: **6** Kwanza **7** Kwanzaa
Celtic harvest ~: **6** lammas
English country ~: **3** ale
Greek ~: **5** delia
Hindu ~: **4** holi **6** Dewali, Divali, Diwali
Jewish ~: **5** Purim
Moslem ~: **6** Bairam
Old English ~: **6** lammas
outdoor ~: **6** kermis
preceder: **3** eve
showing: **4** film **5** movie
spring ~: **6** Easter
Vietnamese ~: **3** Tet
Festival in Cannes (2002 film)
cast: Anouk Aimée, Greta Scacchi, Maximilian Schell
director: Henry Jaglom
festivals, Roman: **4** ludi
festive: **3** gay **4** gala **5** happy, jolly, merry **6** cheery, jocund, jovial, joyful, joyous, lively **7** gleeful, special **8** jubilant, mirthful **9** convivial
occasion: **4** fete **5** party **6** affair
festivity: **2** do **3** fun, hop **4** ball, bash, fete, gala, prom **5** blast, dance, feast, mirth, party, revel, roast **6** affair, fiesta, gaiety, gayety **7** blowout, jollity, jubilee, pageant, revelry, shindig, triumph **8** clambake, function, goings-on, hilarity, jamboree, pleasure, wingding **9** amusement, happiness, joviality, merriment, revelment **10** joyfulness, masquerade, recreation
festoon: **4** deck, hang, swag, trim **5** adorn, crown, drape **6** bedeck, wreath **7** garland, garnish **8** decorate, ornament **9** embellish **10** decoration
festoso: **3** gay **5** happy, merry **6** bright, jovial, joyful **7** gleeful **8** cheerful, mirthful
festuca: **5** grass
feta: **5** Greek **6** cheese
Fet, Afanasy: **4** poet **7** Russian
fetch: **3** get **4** draw, earn, take, tote **5** bring, carry, go for, go get, shlep **6** convey, elicit, escort, obtain, schlep, shlepp **7** bring in, deliver, produce, realize, schlepp, sell for **8** retrieve **9** transport
something to ~: **5** stick
up: **4** halt, stop **5** brake **6** arrive
__-fetched: **3** far
fetching: **6** comely, lovely, pretty **7** lovable, winning, winsome **8** adorable, alluring, charming, gorgeous, handsome, loveable, pleasing, stunning, tempting **9** covetable, desirable **10** attractive
Fetchit: **6** Stepin
fete: **2** do **4** ball, bash, fest, gala **5** bazar, big do, event, feast, honor, party, roast **6** bazaar, fiesta, soiree **7** banquet, blowout, jubilee, lionize, shindig **8** clambake, festival, function, wingding **9** celebrate, entertain, festivity
fête champêtre: **4** meal **5** feast **6** repast, spread **7** banquet
feterita: **5** grain
fetid: **4** foul, olid, rank **5** stale **6** frowsy, frowzy, rancid, rotten, smelly, stinky, strong **7** noisome, noxious, odorous, reeking, squalid, unclean **8** inedible, mephitic, stinking **10** malodorous
fetidness: **4** odor, reek **5** smell, stink **6** stench **7** malodor **9** redolence
fetish: **3** obi **4** juju **5** charm, mania, obeah, quirk, thing **6** amulet, grigri **8** fixation, greegree, gris-gris **9** obsession
fetlock: **5** joint
neighbor: **4** hoof
fetor: **4** reek **5** smell, stink
__ Fe Trail: **5** Santa
fetter: **3** tie **4** bind, bond, curb, gyve, hold **5** chain, leash, tie up **6** hamper, hand up, hinder, hobble, hogtie, pinion **7** confine, enchain, manacle, repress, shackle, trammel **8** encumber, handcuff, handicap, restrain, restrict **9** hamstring, restraint
fetters: **5** bonds, irons **6** chains **7** bondage **8** shackles, trammels **9** captivity, handcuffs
fettle: **4** form, trim **5** shape, state **6** health, kilter **7** fitness, spirits **8** wellness **9** condition
in fine ~: **4** hale, trim, well **5** hardy, right, sound **6** robust **7** healthy
fettuccine: **5** pasta **7** noodles
alternative: **4** orzo, ziti **5** penne **7** lasagna, lasagne, pastina, ravioli **8** bucatini, couscous, farfalle, linguine, linguini, macaroni, rigatoni **9** agnolotti, angelhair, cavatelli, manicotti, spaghetti **10** cannelloni, tortellini, vermicelli
topper: **5** pesto
fettuccine __: **7** Alfredo
__ feu: **5** grand, petit
__-feu: **5** pot-au
Feuchtwanger, Lion: **6** author, German, writer **10** playwright
feud: **3** row **4** spat **5** brawl, claim, clash, fight **6** battle, bicker, debate, enmity, fracas, go at it, grudge, strife **7** contend, discord, dispute, quarrel, rivalry, rupture, wrangle **8** argument, bad blood, conflict, disunity, friction, squabble, vendetta **9** bickering, discaccord, have words, hostility **10** antagonism, bone to pick, contention, difference, disharmony, dissension, falling-out, litigation
__ feud: **5** blood
__ Feud: **6** Family
feudal: **8** medieval **9** mediaeval
bigwig: **4** lord **5** baron, liege, mesne, thane, thegn
defense: **4** moat
holding: **4** fief **6** castle
Japanese ~ lord: **6** daimio, daimyo
tenure: **5** feoff
term of respect: **4** sire
territorial division: **4** vill
warrior: **5** ninja
worker: **4** esne, serf **5** liege **6** corvée **7** subject
feuder perhaps: **4** clan
feuding: **6** at odds, battle, debate **7** dis-

pute, dissent, rivalry **8** conflict, friction **9** hostility, on the outs **10** disharmony, dissidence, opposition
Feuerbach, Ludwig: **6** German **11** philosopher
__-feuille: **5** mille
feuilletée: **6** pastry
fever: **4** ague, heat **5** craze **6** frenzy, lather **7** passion, pyrexia **9** intensity **10** excitement
chills and ~: **4** ague
combining form: **5** febri-, pyret- **6** pyreto-
ender: **3** few **4** weed, wort
gold ~: **7** avarice
having spring ~: **6** draggy **7** languid **8** sluggish **9** lethargic
run a ~: **3** ail
running a ~: **3** ill **4** sick **6** ailing, unwell **10** indisposed
fever __: **4** heat, tree, twig **5** pitch
__ fever: **3** hay **4** buck, gold, run a **5** cabin **6** spring, yellow **7** Potomac
Fever (2001 film)
cast: Bill Duke, Teri Hatcher, David O'Hara, Henry Thomas
director: Alex Winter
__ Fever: **5** Night **6** Boogie, Jungle, Pac-Man **9** White Line
Fever, A author: John Donne
Fever author: Robin Cook
feverish: **3** hot, ill **4** sick **6** heated, hectic **7** burning, excited, febrile, frantic, furious, keyed up, pyretic **8** agitated, frenetic, frenzied, restless **10** in an uproar
feverishness: **4** heat, zeal
Fever (song) artist: McCoys, Peggy Lee
février: **4** mois **5** month **6** French **8** February
few: **6** scarce **7** handful, not many, pronoun **9** hardly any **10** infrequent, occasional, scattering, smattering, sprinkling
a ~: **4** some **7** several **8** one or two **10** two or three
and far between: **4** rare, thin **5** scant **6** scanty, scarce, skimpy, sparse, spotty **7** unusual **8** uncommon **9** scattered **10** hard to find, infrequent
combining form: **4** olig- **5** oligo-, pauci-
give or take a ~: **5** about
hoist a ~: **4** swig, tope **5** drink, quaff **6** guzzle, imbibe
in a ~ cases: **6** rarely, seldom **9** sometimes
in a ~ minutes: **4** anon, soon **5** later **7** erelong, shortly **8** directly **9** presently **10** before long
known by ~: **4** deep **6** mystic, occult **8** esoteric, mystical **9** recondite **10** mysterious
more than a ~: **4** many **5** loads **6** a lot of, divers, gobs of, lots of, myriad, umteen, untold **7** a host of, a slew of, copious, heaps of, no end of, piles of, profuse, scads of, umpteen **8** a bunch of, abundant, an army of, manifold, numerous, oodles of, scores of, umpsteen **9** a passel of, bountiful, countless **10** zillions of
of ~ words: **4** curt **5** brief, crisp, pithy, short, terse **6** snappy **7** brusque, clipped, concise, laconic **8** succinct **9** trenchant **10** aphoristic, to the point
org. for a ~ good men: **4** USMC
starter: **5** fever
Few __ Men, A: **4** Good
few and __ between: **3** far
__ Few Dollars More: **4** For a
fewer: **4** less
fewest: **5** least
Few Figs From Thistles, A author: Edna St. Vincent Millay
Few Good Men, A (1992 film)
cast: Kevin Bacon, Tom Cruise, Demi Moore, Jack Nicholson, Kiefer Sutherland
director: Rob Reiner
Few Green Leaves, A author: Barbara Pym
fewness: **4** lack **6** dearth **7** paucity **8** scarcity, shortage, sparsity **10** deficiency, inadequacy, meagerness
__ few rounds: **3** go a
fey: **5** elfin **6** impish **7** magical, pixyish, playful, puckish, strange **8** pixieish **9** enchanted, fairylike, visionary, whimsical
Feydeau, Georges: **6** French **10** playwright
Feynman __: **5** graph **7** diagram
Feynman, Richard: **8** Nobelist **9** physicist
fez: **3** cap, hat
Fez: **4** city, town
city near ~: **6** Meknes
locale: **3** Mor. **7** Morocco
section of ~: **6** Casbah, Kasbah
FFA study: **3** agr.
fff: **4** loud **6** loudly
ffolkes (1980 film)
cast: James Mason, Roger Moore, Anthony Perkins
director: Andrew V. McLaglen
FHA: **4** agcy. **6** agency, lender
department: **3** HUD
loan: **4** mtge. **8** mortgage
part: **3** Fed. **5** Admin. **14** Federal. Housing
__-fi: **3** sci
fiancé: **3** man **4** beau, love **7** beloved **8** intended **9** betrothed, inamorato
fiancée: **4** love **5** woman **7** beloved **8** intended **9** betrothed, inamorata
fiasco: **3** dud **4** bomb, bust, flop, loss, mess **6** defeat, mishap, turkey **7** blunder, debacle, failure, misstep, stumble, washout **8** disaster, downfall **10** nonsuccess
fiat: **5** edict, irade, order, ukase **6** decree, dictum, firman **7** command, dictate, mandate **9** ordinance
fiat __: **3** lux **5** money
Fiat: **3** car **4** auto **7** Italian **10** automobile
fib: **3** lie **4** tale **5** story **6** dupery, invent **7** falsity, untruth **8** white lie **9** deception, falsehood, fish story, invention, mendacity **10** inveracity, taradiddle
fibber: **4** liar
admission: **5** I lied
Fibber McGee and Molly: **9** radio show
fibbing: **5** lying **10** mendacious, untruthful
fiber: **3** nap **4** fuzz, hair, hemp, yarn **5** nylon, Orlon, sisal **6** Dacron, fabric, nature, strand, thread **7** essence, quality, tendril **8** filament, strength **9** substance
agave ~: **5** istle, ixtle, sisal
carpet ~: **4** kemp **5** istle, ixtle
coconut-husk ~: **4** coir
cordage ~: **4** hemp **5** istle, ixtle, sisal
ender: **4** fill **5** board, glass, scope
hemp ~: **5** abaca, oakum
hemplike ~: **4** sunn **5** sisal
moral ~: **4** grit, guts, will **5** pluck, spine, spunk, valor **6** mettle, spirit **7** bravery, courage **8** backbone, firmness, tenacity **9** fortitude, toughness **10** resolution
rope ~: **4** bast, coir, hemp, jute **5** abaca, istle, ixtle, oakum, sisal
source: **3** oat **4** bean, bran, flax **6** cereal, legume
strong ~: **6** Kevlar
see also fabric
fiber __: **3** pen **5** optic **6** bundle, optics
__ fiber: **4** bast, pulu **5** algin, nerve **6** carbon, muscle, olefin **7** acrylic, dietary, optical, Tampico
Fiber __: **3** One
fiberglass bundle: **4** batt
fiber of the gods: **6** alpaca
Fiber One: **6** cereal
competitor: **3** Kix **4** Life, Trix **5** Kashi, Quisp, Total **6** Kaboom, Muesli, Oreo O's, Pablum, Smacks **7** All-Bran, Crispix, Harmony, Hunny B's, Mueslix, Oat Bran, Pokemon **8** Boo Berry, Cheerios, Corn Chex, Corn Pops, Rice Chex, Special K, Uncle Sam, Wheaties **9** Alpha Bits, Apple Zaps, Grape Nuts, Honey Comb, Just Right, Wheat Chex **10** Apple Jacks, Bran Flakes, Cap'n Crunch, Cocoa Puffs, Froot Loops, Mini-Wheats, Nutri-Grain, Puffed Rice, Quaker Oats, Smart Start **11** Cocoa Blasts, Cookie Crisp, Golden Crisp, Lucky Charms, Puffed Wheat, Sweet Crunch, Waffle Crisp
fiber-optics pulse: **5** laser
fiber-rich cereal: **4** bran **10** bran flakes, raisin bran
Fiber 7 Flakes: **6** cereal
competitor: **3** Kix **4** Life, Trix **5** Kashi, Quisp, Total **6** Kaboom, Muesli, Oreo O's, Pablum, Smacks **7** All-Bran, Crispix, Harmony, Hunny B's, Mueslix, Oat Bran, Pokemon **8** Boo Berry, Cheerios, Corn Chex, Corn Pops, Fiber One, Rice Chex, Special K, Uncle Sam, Wheaties **9** Alpha Bits, Apple Zaps, Grape Nuts, Honey Comb, Just Right, Wheat Chex **10** Apple Jacks, Bran Flakes, Cap'n Crunch, Cocoa Puffs, Froot Loops, Mini-Wheats, Nutri-Grain, Puffed Rice, Quaker Oats, Smart Start **11** Cocoa Blasts, Cookie Crisp, Golden Crisp, Lucky Charms, Puffed Wheat, Sweet Crunch, Waffle Crisp
Fibiger, Johannes: **8** Nobelist
fibril: **4** hair **8** filament
fibrous: **3** raw **4** ropy **5** ropey, tough **7** stringy
fibula: **4** bone
combining form: **6** perono-
locale: **3** leg
neighbor: **5** tibia
FICA
ID: **3** SSN
org.: **3** SSA
fiche: **9** microfilm
Fichte, Johann: **6** German **11** philosopher
fichu: **4** cape **5** scarf
fickle: **5** light, moody **6** uneven **7** erratic, flighty, mutable, unloyal, wayward **8** hesitant, skittish, ticklish, unstable, unsteady, variable, volatile, wavering **9** arbitrary, faithless, faltering, frivolous, lightsome, mercurial, uncertain, vagarious, whimsical **10** ambivalent, capricious, changeable, coquettish, inconstant, irresolute, unfaithful, unreliable, weak-willed, wishy-washy
be ~: **4** vary **6** change **9** hem and haw
fiction: **3** lie **4** myth, tale, yarn **5** drama, fable, genre, novel, prose, rumor, story **6** legend **7** romance, untruth, western **9** fairy tale, falsehood, fish story, invention, narrative, potboiler **10** inveracity
genre: **4** play, pulp **5** drama, novel **6** comedy, Gothic **7** mystery, romance, tragedy, western **8** whodunit **9** fairy tale
inferior ~: **5** bilge, trash **6** drivel **7** garbage
like pulp ~: **5** lurid
opposite: **4** fact
__ fiction: **4** pulp **7** science
__ Fiction: **4** Pulp
fictional
see fictitious
fictitious: **4** fake, sham **5** bogus, faked, false, phony, put-on **6** ersatz, fabled, fantom, forged, made-up, phoney, pseudo, unreal, untrue **7** assumed, feigned, phantom **8** cooked-up, fanciful, imagined, mythical, spurious **9** concocted, deceptive, dishonest, fantastic, imaginary, imitation, pretended, simulated, synthetic, trumped-up **10** apocryphal, artificial, chimerical, fabricated, factitious, fallacious, fraudulent, improvised, misleading
name: **5** pseud. **9** pseudonym
fictitious __: **5** force **6** person
ficus: **3** fig **4** tree **5** shrub **6** banian, banyan
relative: **3** fig **4** upas **5** ramon **6** antiar, fustic **8** mulberry **10** breadfruit
fiddle: **3** toy **4** play, poke **6** dabble, monkey, putter, string, tamper, tinker, violin **8** fool with **9** muck about **10** mess around, play around
around: **4** idle, laze, loaf, loll **5** dally, relax, shirk **6** dawdle, linger **7** goof off, hang out **8** lollygag, malinger, slack off **9** goldbrick
ender: **4** head **6** sticks
famous ~: **5** Amati, Strad
stick: **3** bow
with: **3** rig **5** alter **6** adjust **7** correct **8** overhaul
(with): **3** toy **4** fool, mess, play **6** monkey, tamper, tinker
see also violin
fiddle __: **3** bow **4** away **7** pattern
fiddle-__: **5** de-dee **6** faddle, footed
__ fiddle: **4** bass, bull, nun's **6** second
fiddle-de-dee
see fiddle-faddle
fiddle-faddle: **3** gas, rot **4** blah, bosh, bull, bunk, guff, jazz, jive, pooh, tosh **5** bilge, fudge, hokum, hooey, prate, stuff, trash, tripe **6** bunkum, bushwa, drivel, footle, gabble, gammon, gibber, havers, hot air, humbug, jabber, jargon, kibosh, piffle **7** baloney, blarney, blather, blether, boloney, bushwah, eyewash, flannel, flubdub, fustian, garbage, hogwash, inanity, rubbish, twaddle **8** buncombe, claptrap, falderal, falderol, flimflam, flummery, folderal, folderol, nonsense, slipslop, tommyrot, trumpery **9** banana oil, gibberish, kidstakes, moonshine, poppycock, rigmarole **10** applesauce, balderdash, bilge water, codswallop, double-talk, flapdoodle, galimatias, Jabberwock, mumbo jumbo, rigamarole, taradiddle
Fiddle-faddle!: **3** bah **4** drat, pooh, rats **5** pshaw, shoot **6** darn it
Fiddle-Faddle composer: Leroy Anderson
fiddlehead: **4** fern
fiddler __: **4** crab **6** beetle
fiddler crab: **3** uca
Fiddler of Dooney, The author: William Butler Yeats
Fiddler on the Roof (1971 film): **7** musical
cast: Norma Crane, Leonard Frey,

Topol
character: 5 Chava, Golde, Hodel, Lazar, Motel, Tevye, Yente 6 Mielka 7 Perchik, Tzeitel
composer: 4 Bock 7 Harnick
director: Norman Jewison
setting: 6 Russia, shtetl 8 Anatevka
violinist: Isaac Stern
fiddlers' king: 4 Cole
Fiddlesticks!: 3 bah 4 drat, pooh, rats 5 pshaw, shoot 6 darn it
__ fide: 4 bona, mala
fide, bona: 4 good, just, real, true 5 legit, right, valid 6 actual, honest, kasher, kosher, lawful 7 genuine, literal, regular, sincere 8 official, rightful, verified 9 authentic, heartfelt, veritable
Fidel: 6 Castro
brother: 4 Raul
friend: 3 Che
home: 4 Cuba 6 Habana, Havana
see also Spanish
__ Fideles: 6 Adeste
Fidelio: 5 opera
composer: 9 Beethoven
role: 5 Rocco 7 Leonore 8 Fernando, Jacquino 9 Florestan
setting: 5 Spain 6 prison 7 Seville
song: 4 aria
__ Fidelis: 6 Semper
fidelity: 4 love 5 faith, piety, rigor, troth 6 fealty, homage, lealty 7 honesty, loyalty, realism 8 accuracy, devotion 9 constancy, exactness, fixedness, integrity, precision 10 allegiance, exactitude, factuality, observance
model of ~: 4 Enid
pledge of ~: 5 troth
__ fidelity: 4 high
fidget: 4 stir 6 jitter, squirm
fidgets: 6 nerves, unrest 7 anxiety, jitters, malaise, willies 8 disquiet, edginess 10 impatience, inquietude, uneasiness
fidgety: 5 antsy, hyper, itchy, jumpy, tense 6 jangly, on edge, uneasy 7 jittery, nervous, restive 8 fluttery, restless, skittish 9 unsettled 10 high-strung
fidla: 6 string, zither
origin: 7 Ireland
Fidler: 5 Jimmy
fido: 4 coin
Fido: 3 dog, pet 6 bowwow, canine
command to ~: 3 beg, sic, sit 4 down, heel, stay 5 fetch, sit up
pal: 4 Spot 5 Rover
see also dog
Fidrych: 4 Mark 5 Tiger 6 hurler 7 pitcher
fiduciary __: 4 bond, duty
Fie!: 3 bah 5 shame
Fiedler: 4 John 6 Arthur
Fiedler, Arthur: 9 conductor
group: 10 Boston Pops
fief
see feudal
field: 3 job, lea, ley, lot, sod 4 area, land, park, walk 5 arena, array, catch, gamut, green, orbit, patch, plain, range, realm, scope, space, sward, topic, tract, veldt, world 6 answer, career, domain, ground, handle, meadow, métier, region, sphere, swarth 7 acreage, compass, diamond, element, entries, expanse, grounds, pasture, purview, reply to, runners, section, stadium, terrain, tillage 8 business, cropland, cup of tea, deal with, entrants, farmland, gridiron, nominees, play area, precinct, province, retrieve, vineyard, vocation 9 avocation, bailiwick, grassland, ranchland, specialty, territory 10 applicants, candidates, department, discipline, fairground, occupation, playground, profession, walk of life
combining form: 4 agro-
day: 4 bash 5 binge, fling, revel, spree 6 junket 10 recreation
divider: 5 fence, hedge
ender: 4 fare, work 5 stone, strip 6 worker
home ~: 4 turf
house: 3 gym 9 gymnasium
of honor event: 4 duel
of reference: 3 run 4 area, play, span, sway, view 5 ambit, gamut, orbit, range, reach, realm, scale, scope, space, sweep, width 6 extent, margin, radius, sphere 7 breadth, compass, expanse, horizon, purview, subject 8 confines, latitude 9 amplitude, dimension
of view: 3 ken 5 range, reach, scope, sight, vista 7 compass, eyeshot, horizon, purview
partner: 5 track 6 stream
rice ~: 5 paddy
starter: 3 air, mid 4 back, down, mine 6 battle
the question: 5 reply 6 answer 7 respond
unit: 4 acre
worker: 5 agent, baler 6 farmer
field __: 3 bed, day, pea 4 army, coil, corn, crop, goal, hand, lark, lens, line, mint, stop, trip 5 event, grade, guide, house, mouse, poppy, trial 6 hockey, jacket, magnet, ration, theory 7 captain, cricket, current, glasses, marshal, officer, spaniel, sparrow, winding
field-__: 4 test 5 strip
field-__ microscope: 3 ion
__ field: 3 gas, ice, oil, old 4 coal, gold, left, open, root, skew 5 force, prime, right, short 6 broken, center, flying, scalar, vector, visual 7 landing, ordered, playing
Field: 5 Betty, Sally 6 Eugene, Rachel 7 Chelsea 8 Marshall
__ Field: 6 Ebbets 7 Wrigley
Field and __: 6 Stream
Fieldcrest product: 5 linen, sheet, towel
__ fielder: 4 left 5 right 6 center
Fielder: 4 Cook 5 Cecil
fielder's __: 6 choice
fieldfare: 4 bird
Fielding: 5 Helen, Henry
Fielding, Henry: 6 author, writer 7 British 10 playwright
work: Amelia
Tom Jones
Tom Thumb
field mouse
predator: 3 cat, owl
field of __: 4 fire, view 5 force, honor 6 vision
Field of Dreams (1989 film)
cast: Kevin Costner, James Earl Jones, Burt Lancaster, Ray Liotta, Amy Madigan
director: Phil Alden Robinson
setting: 4 Iowa
Field of Ice, The author: Jules Verne
Field of Thirteen author: Dick Francis
Fields: 2 W.C. 3 Kim 4 Shep 5 Debbi, Ernie, Totie 6 Gracie 7 Dorothy
vaudeville partner: 5 Weber
__ Fields: 3 Mrs. 6 London 7 Elysian
Field, Sally: 7 actress
film: Absence of Malice (1981)
The End (1978)
Forrest Gump (1994)
Hooper (1978)
Mrs. Doubtfire (1993)
Murphy's Romance (1985)
Norma Rae (1979, AA)
Not Without My Daughter (1991)
Places in the Heart (1984, AA)
Punchline (1988)
Smokey and the Bandit (1977)
Soapdish (1991)
Stay Hungry (1976)
Steel Magnolias (1989)
Surrender (1987)
TV: The Flying Nun
__ Fields, The: 7 Killing
Fields, The author: Conrad Richter
Fields, W.C.: 5 actor 8 comedian
costar: 3 Mae 4 West 5 Leroy
film: The Bank Dick (1940)
The Big Broadcast of 1938 (1938)
David Copperfield (1935)
If I Had a Million (1932)
International House (1933)
It's a Gift (1934)
The Man on the Flying Trapeze (1935)
Million Dollar Legs (1932)
Mississippi (1935)
Mrs. Wiggs of the Cabbage Patch (1934)
My Little Chickadee (1940)
Never Give a Sucker an Even Break (1941)
The Old-Fashioned Way (1934)
Poppy (1936)
Six of a Kind (1934)
Tillie and Gus (1933)
You Can't Cheat an Honest Man (1939)
You're Telling Me (1934)
foil: Baby Leroy
persona: 3 sot 5 souse
__ Field, The: 3 Far 5 Onion
__ field theory: 7 quantum, unified
fieldwork: 5 redan
fiend: 3 fan, imp, nut 4 ogre 5 beast, brute, demon, devil, freak, knave, rowdy 6 addict, daemon, daimon, diablo, maniac, meanie, savage, zealot 7 dastard, devotee, fanatic, monster, villain 8 evildoer 9 barbarian, hellhound 10 aficionado, enthusiast
ender: 3 ish
starter: 4 arch
fiendish: 4 evil, mean 5 cruel, harsh, nasty 6 animal, brutal, fierce, savage, unkind, wanton, wicked 7 beastly, brutish, callous, demonic, hellish, hurtful, inhuman, satanic, vicious 8 barbaric, daemonic, demoniac, devilish, diabolic, infernal, inhumane, obsessed, pitiless, ruthless, sadistic, vengeful 9 atrocious, cutthroat, demonical, ferocious, malicious, merciless, monstrous, nefarious, possessed, satanical, truculent 10 diabolical, maleficent, vindictive
fiendishness: 6 malice 7 cruelty, tyranny 8 ferocity, savagery 9 barbarism, brutality, harshness
Fiennes: 5 Ralph 6 Joseph
Fiennes, Ralph: 5 actor
film: The Avengers (1998)
The English Patient (1996)
The Prince of Egypt (1998)
Quiz Show (1994)
Red Dragon (2002)
Schindler's List (1993)
fierce: 4 mean, wild 5 angry, cruel, feral, harsh, nasty, rough, sharp 6 animal, ardent, bitter, brutal, heated, lupine, raging, raving, savage, severe, stormy, strong, unkind, wanton 7 beastly, brutish, callous, enraged, furious, hurtful, inhuman, intense, lawless, tigrish, untamed, vicious, violent 8 barbaric, fiendish, grueling, inhumane, menacing, piercing, pitiless, ruthless, sadistic, terrific, tigerish, vehement, vengeful, venomous 9 agonizing, barbarous, cutthroat, desperate, ferocious, merciless, monstrous, truculent, turbulent, unpitying 10 formidable, passionate, relentless, tumultuous, unpeaceful, vindictive
emotion: 5 wrath
something ~: 5 madly 6 wildly 7 rabidly 9 excitedly, furiously, intensely, violently 10 frenziedly
stare: 5 glare
Fierce Creatures (1997 film)
cast: John Cleese, Jamie Lee Curtis, Kevin Kline
fiercely: 4 hard 5 gonzo, madly 6 keenly 7 like mad 8 insanely 9 viciously 10 vehemently
fierceness: 4 fury, zeal 5 ardor 8 ferocity, violence 9 brutality, intensity
fieriness: 4 heat 9 vehemence 10 enthusiasm
Fiero: 3 car 4 auto 7 Pontiac 10 automobile
Fierstein: 6 Harvey
fiery: 3 hot 5 lurid, proud, spicy 6 ablaze, aflame, ardent, fervid, heated, spicey, torrid 7 blazing, boiling, burning, fervent, flaming, fiery, intense, peppery, violent 8 choleric, in flames, spirited, vehement, white-hot 9 emotional, excitable, fanatical, hotheaded, irritable, scorching 10 hot-blooded, passionate, sweltering
particle: 5 ember, spark 6 cinder
stack: 4 pyre
Fiesque composer: 4 Lalo
fiesta: 4 bash, fair, fete, gala 5 party 6 gaiety, gayety 7 holiday, jubilee, revelry 8 festival 9 festivity
Fiesta: 3 car 4 auto, Ford, Olds 8 Bowl game 10 Oldsmobile
Fiesta __: 4 Bowl, ware
Fiesta Bowl
letters: 4 NCAA
locale: 4 Ariz. 5 Tempe 7 Arizona
fiesta de __: 5 toros
Fie, thou dishonest __!: 5 Satan
fife: 4 wind 8 woodwind 10 instrument
accompaniment: 4 drum 5 taber, tabor 6 tabour
Fife: 6 Barney
Fifi: 6 D'Orsay
dog often named ~: 6 poodle
see also French
fifteen
comb. form: 8 pentadec- 9 pentadeca-
fifth
anniversary gift: 4 wood
columnist: 5 snake 7 traitor 8 quisling, turncoat
combining form: 5 quint- 6 quinti-
in a series: 5 part V
name meaning ~: 7 Quentin
person: 4 Seth
fifth __: 5 force, wheel 6 column, estate
Fifth __: 3 Ave. 6 Avenue
Fifth __, The: 3 Son 6 Column, Monkey 7 Element
Fifth Avenue: 3 car 4 auto 8 Chrysler 10 automobile
store: 4 Saks
__ Fifth Avenue: 4 Saks
Fifth Column, The author: Ernest Hemingway
Fifth Dimension
members: Davis, Larue, McCoo, McLemore, Townson
song: Aquarius/Let the Sunshine In (1969)
I Didn't Get to Sleep at All (1972)
If I Could Reach You (1972)
One Less Bell to Answer (1970)

Stoned Soul Picnic (1968)
Up, Up and Away (1967)
Wedding Bell Blues (1969)
Fifth Element, The (1997 film)
cast: Ian Holm, Milla Jovovich, Gary Oldman, Bruce Willis
cat: **7** Sweetie
director: Luc Besson
fifth-grader: **5** 'tween
Fifth Monkey, The (1990 film)
cast: Vera Fischer, Ben Kingsley, Mika Lins
Fifth of Beethoven, A (1976 song)
artist: Walter Murphy
fifth-rate: **4** poor **5** awful, lousy **6** cheesy, crumby, crummy **8** inferior
Fifth Republic nation: **6** France
Fifth Son, The author: Elie Wiesel
Fifties, The author: David Halberstam
fifty
minutes past: **5** ten of, ten to
percent: **4** half
Fifty __ Frenchmen: **7** Million
fifty-fifty: **4** even, luck **5** equal **6** even-up **10** compromise, likelihood
go ~: **5** halve, share, split
Fifty-four-forty or __: **5** Fight
Fifty Million Frenchmen: **7** musical
song: **5** Paree
songwriter: **6** Porter
fig: **4** iota, tree, whit **5** fruit, shrub **8** least bit **9** fruit tree
bar: **6** cookie
ender: **4** wort
relative: **4** upas **5** ficus, ramon **6** antiar, fustic **8** mulberry **10** bread-fruit
tree: **2** bo **5** bodhi, ficus, papal, pipal **6** banian, banyan, peepul
fig __: **4** leaf, wasp
fig.: **2** no. **4** stat.
three-D ~: **3** sph.
__ fig: **4** Java, wild **5** moldy **6** Indian, Smyrna **7** Barbary, weeping
Figaro: **3** cat **6** barber **7** cat food
alternative: **5** Amore **6** Purina **7** Whiskas **8** Friskies **10** Chef's Blend, Fancy Feast
love: **6** Rosina
tune: **4** aria
Figgis, Mike: **8** director
film: Leaving Las Vegas (1995)
Stormy Monday (1988)
Timecode (2000)
fight: **3** box, row, vie, war **4** bout, buck, claw, defy, duel, feud, fray, fuss, riot, spar, tiff, tilt, to-do **5** argue, brawl, brush, clash, match, melee, mix-up, rebel, repel, run-in, scrap, set-to, siege, sport, trial, valor **6** action, affray, attack, barney, battle, bicker, combat, debate, defend, fracas, go at it, hassle, oppose, racket, resist, rumble, strife, strive, take on, tumult, tussle **7** assault, carry on, contend, contest, dispute, grapple, lawsuit, lay into, mix it up, protest, quarrel, rivalry, scuffle, vie with, wage war, wrangle, wrestle **8** argument, campaign, conflict, do battle, object to, skirmish, squabble, struggle, tug-of-war **9** altercate, challenge, duke it out, encounter, have words, hostility, imbroglio, light into, militancy, pugnacity, scrimmage, square off, wrangling **10** aggression, buckle down, contention, dissension, donnybrook, engagement, falling-out, fisticuffs, free-for-all, make a stand, opposition, put up a fuss, resistance, tangle with, tournament
back: **5** react, rebel, reply **6** mutiny, resist **7** respond
ender: **5** truce
ending: **2** KO **3** TKO
exclamation: **3** oof, pow
for: **6** defend **8** champion, keep safe
(for): **3** vie
knight ~: **4** duel, list **6** charge, combat **7** contest, tourney **10** tournament
minor ~: **4** spat, tiff
off: **5** repel **6** defeat **7** repulse
over: **3** sue **5** argue **6** defend **7** contest **8** litigate, question
poster word: **6** versus
put up a ~: **6** resist **7** dissent **8** struggle
ready to ~: **5** armed **7** hawkish, martial, warlike **8** militant **9** bellicose, combative **10** aggressive, pugnacious
rigged ~: **5** setup
site: **4** ring **5** arena **8** coliseum
starter: **3** cat, dog, gun **4** bull, cock, fire, fist **5** prize
train for a ~: **4** spar
unit: **3** rnd. **5** round
verbal ~: **4** spat **5** fight, set-to **6** debate **7** dispute, polemic, quarrel, rhubarb **8** argument, polemics, squabble **9** bickering, encounter **10** war of words
verbally: **5** argue, claim, plead **6** appeal, bicker, debate, dicker, haggle, oppose, reason **7** contend, dispute, dissent, protest, quarrel, quibble, wrangle **8** disagree, hash over, maintain, squabble **9** lock horns **10** controvert, deliberate
with: **4** meet **6** assail, attack, engage, take on **7** assault
fight __: **3** off **5** it out, shy of
fight __ and nail: **5** tooth
__ fight: **3** sea **5** proxy
fighter: **3** pug **5** boxer **6** knight **7** bruiser, soldier, warrior **8** crusader, pugilist **9** aggressor, assailant, combatant, contender, disputant, gladiator, mercenary **10** antagonist, competitor, contestant
dirty ~: **5** biter
org.: **3** WBA, WBC
starter: **3** gun, jet **4** bull, fire **5** prize
__ fighter: **3** jet **4** club, tank **6** escort, street **7** freedom
__-fighter: **5** crime
Fighter of the Century award-winner: **3** Ali
__ Fighters: **3** Foo
fight fire __ fire: **4** with
Fight for Your Right (1987 song)
artist: Beastie Boys
fighting: **3** war **4** at it **5** angry, at war **6** battle, combat, strife **7** hawkish, hostile, martial, warfare, warlike **8** conflict, militant, violence **9** bellicose, combative **10** aggressive, fisticuffs, pugnacious, resistance
combining form: **5** -machy
force: **4** army, navy **5** troop **6** armada **7** marines
in ~ trim: **4** wiry **5** tough **6** strong
fighting __: **4** cock, fish **5** chair, words **6** chance
Fighting __: **5** Angel, Irish **6** French, Illini, Tigers
Fighting Angel author: Pearl S. Buck
__ fighting fish: **7** Siamese
Fighting Irish: **3** NDU **9** Notre Dame
Fighting Seabees, The (1944 film)
cast: Susan Hayward, Dennis O'Keefe, John Wayne
__ Fighting Ships: **5** Jane's
Fighting Tigers: **3** LSU
__ fightin' words!: **5** Them's
fight it __: **3** out
__ fight no more forever: **5** I will
fight-or-__ response: **6** flight
fights
site of many ~: **5** Vegas **8** Las Vegas
where some ~ are aired: **5** pay TV
Fight the Power (1975 song) artist: Isley Brothers
fight tooth and __: **4** nail
figment: **5** dream **6** fantom **7** chimera, fantasy, phantom **8** chimaera, creation, daydream, delusion, illusion **9** invention
Fig Newtons: **6** cookie
alternative: **4** Oreo **7** Droxies **9** Chips Ahoy! **10** Lorna Doone
__ Figs From Thistles: **4** A Few
figurant: **6** dancer
figuration: **6** sketch **7** outline
figurative: **8** symbolic **9** pictorial **10** denotative, emblematic, metaphoric, signifying
language: **7** imagery, similes **9** allusions, metaphors
figure: **3** add, bod, sum **4** body, doll, form, line, mull, rate **5** add up, build, count, digit, frame, gauge, price, quote, shape, sum up, tally, thing, torso, total, tot up **6** assess, cipher, decide, do sums, emblem, fathom, number, ponder, reckon, settle, sketch, statue, symbol, worthy **7** anatomy, chassis, compute, contour, diagram, dope out, fashion, integer, measure, notable, numeral, outline, pattern, predict, presume, profile, suppose, work out **8** appraise, estimate, keep tabs, physique, portrait, quantity, ruminate, standard, tabulate **9** calculate, celebrity, character, determine, dignitary, enumerate, keep score, make sense, personage, quotation, speculate
action ~: **3** toy **4** doer, doll **5** GI Joe
ballpark ~: **5** guess **8** estimate **9** appraisal **10** assessment, guesstimate
bottom-line ~: **3** net, sum **5** count, score, tally, total **6** amount **9** aggregate, reckoning
combining form: **3** eid- **4** eido-
do ~ eights: **5** skate
ender: **4** head
geometric ~: **4** rect. **5** rhomb, solid **6** circle, square **7** hexagon, octagon, rhombus **8** pentagon, triangle **9** rectangle, trapezoid
in: **3** add **4** form
of speech: **5** idiom, image, trope **6** simile **8** metaphor
on: **4** plan **5** hatch **6** devise **7** concoct, plan for **8** block out, envisage **10** prepare for
out: **2** do **3** get, see **4** find **5** crack, learn, solve, think **6** decode, deduce, fathom, reason, reckon **7** analyze, discern, unravel **8** decipher, evaluate **9** determine, penetrate, speculate **10** understand
(out): **4** suss, work
preliminary ~: **3** est. **8** estimate
public ~: **4** name, star **5** celeb **7** big name, notable **8** eminence, luminary, somebody **9** celebrity, dignitary, personage, superstar
starter: **5** trans
three-D ~: **4** cone, cube **5** solid **6** sphere **7** pyramid
figure __: **3** out **5** eight **6** skater **7** skating
__ figure: **3** lay **4** cut a **5** noise, stick, Venus **6** father, mother, public, school
__-figure: **3** red **5** black **6** double
figure eight
half: **3** ess
where to do a ~: **3** ice **4** rink
figurehead: **4** tool **5** front **6** puppet **9** nonentity, straw boss **10** mouthpiece
spot: **4** prow
figure of __: **6** speech
figures: **3** nos. **4** data **5** count, tally
check the ~: **5** readd
figure skater: **3** Ito **4** Kwan, Witt **5** Baiul, Heiss, Henie, Kulik **6** Button, Hamill, Hughes **7** Boitano, Cousins, Fleming **8** Albright, Hamilton, Lipinski **9** Midori Ito, Yamaguchi **10** Carol Heiss, Dick Button, Sonja Henie
British: **7** Cousins
German: **4** Witt
Japanese: **9** Midori Ito
jump: **4** axel, lutz
Norwegian: **10** Sonja Henie
Russian: **5** Kulik
Ukrainian: **5** Baiul
figure skating: **5** sport
figurine: **4** doll, idol **5** model **6** Hummel **9** statuette
Hawaiian ~: **4** tiki
material: **4** jade, lava, onyx
figuring: **6** adding **8** addition, counting, tallying **9** ciphering, reckoning **10** arithmetic
figwort: **5** plant, shrub **6** flower
Fiji: **4** isls. **5** isles **6** nation **7** country, islands
capital: **4** Suva
island: **3** Gau **4** Koro **6** Ovalau **7** Kandavu, Taveuni **8** Viti Levu **9** Vanua Levu
money: **4** cent **6** dollar
neighbor: **5** Samoa, Tonga
Fijian: **10** Melanesian
golfer: **10** Vijay Singh
fila: **7** threads
filament: **4** hair **5** cilia, fiber, fibre, floss, kapok, twine **6** cobweb, fibril, strand, string, thread **7** tendril **8** fibrilla, gossamer
filbert: **3** nut **4** tree **5** hazel, shrub
cousin: **5** pecan
filch: **3** cop, rob **4** crib, glom, lift, take **5** pinch, poach, swipe **6** pilfer, pocket, rip off, snitch, thieve **7** purloin, ransack **8** embezzle, scrounge
filcher: **5** crook, thief **7** burglar **9** purloiner
filching: **5** theft **8** burglary, thievery
file: **3** row **4** hone, line, rasp, slot, sort, tier, tool, walk, whet **5** grate, grind, index, order, queue, train **6** abrade, docket, folder, record, scrape, series, smooth, string **7** arrange, catalog, dossier, put away, rub down, sharpen, suspend **8** classify, register **9** catalogue, portfolio **10** categorize, emery board, pigeonhole, procession
a claim: **3** sue **8** litigate
as a complaint: **5** lodge
away: **4** drop, save **5** defer, delay, shunt, table **6** ignore, put off, shelve **8** lay aside **10** pigeonhole
(by): **5** march
coarse ~: **4** rasp
holder: **6** folder **7** dossier **9** portfolio
in single ~: **4** arow
label: **3** tab, XYZ **4** misc., name
partner: **4** rank
rank and ~: **5** crowd, plebs **6** masses, people, proles, public, rabble **9** hoi polloi, plebeians
subject: **4** case
suit: **9** go to court
target: **4** nail
unit: **6** drawer
file __: **4** band, card **5** clerk, dance **6** folder, server **7** cabinet, footage
__ file: **4** nail **5** round **6** Indian, master, single **7** rat-tail, spindle, tickler

__-file: 4 flat 5 cross, end-of
filé: 6 powder 9 thickener
filer: 5 clerk 8 taxpayer 10 manicurist
files: 6 annals, record 7 archive, records 8 archives 10 chronicles
  like some ~: 6 coarse
__-Files: 4 The X
filet: 3 cut 4 bone, lace 5 steak 6 debone 10 tenderloin
filet __: 4 lace 6 mignon
Filet-__: 5 O-Fish
__ File, The: 6 Odessa
filet mignon: 4 meat 5 steak
filet of __: 4 sole
filial: 5 sonly 6 loving 7 devoted, dutiful, sonlike 8 obedient 10 daughterly, respectful
filibeg: 4 kilt 5 skirt
filibuster: 3 gab 5 delay, run on, stall, tarry 6 impede, speech 8 footdrag, lose time 9 hindrance, talkathon 10 opposition, vocalizing
filigree: 3 web 4 lace, lacy 7 lattice 10 decoration
filigreed: 4 lacy 6 frilly
filing month: 3 Apr. 5 April
filings, metal: 5 swarf
Filipino: 4 Moro 8 language
Filippo: 5 Lippi
fill: 3 mob 4 cram, jade, lade, load, pack, plug, sate 5 crowd, gorge, imbue, spend, steep, stock, stuff 6 load up, make up, occupy, plug up, pump up, supply, top off 7 congest, inflate, jam-pack, pervade, process, satiate, satisfy, surfeit 8 brim over, capacity, flesh out, permeate 9 overstuff, replenish
  a position: 4 hire 6 employ, engage, retain, sign on, sign up, take on
  in: 3 sub 4 post, tell, temp, warn 5 brief, enter, prime, ready 6 act for, advise, double, inform, notify 7 apprise, apprize, prepare, replace 8 complete, flesh out, pinch-hit, round off, round out 9 alternate, change off, interject, share with 10 substitute
  in (for): 3 sub 5 cover 10 substitute
  out: 3 pad, wax 4 grow 5 swell 6 blow up, expand, fatten, mature, puff up 7 enlarge 8 complete, round off 10 supplement
  starter: 4 land, over 5 fiber
  the bill: 3 fit 4 suit 5 cater, serve 6 please 7 qualify, satisfy
  the hold: 4 lade, load, stow 5 lay in
  the tank: 4 fuel 5 gas up
  thing to ~ out: 4 form 5 blank
  to excess: 4 cloy, cram, heap, jade, sate 5 stuff
  to overflowing: 4 load, pack, pile 5 amass, mound 6 lavish 9 stockpile
  up: 4 fuel, lade 5 gorge 6 inpour 7 recruit
  up on: 3 eat
fille: 4 girl 6 French
  friend: 4 amie
  parent: 4 mère, père
__ fille: 5 jeune
filled: 3 fed 4 rife 5 laden 6 loaded 7 crowded, fraught, replete, teeming 8 abundant, brimming 9 abounding, chock-full
  not ~ in: 5 blank, clean, empty 6 vacant 8 unmarked
filled __: 4 gold, milk
__-filled: 4 gold
filled-out: 5 beefy, burly, buxom, obese, plump, pudgy, pursy, round, stout, tubby 6 chubby, chunky, fleshy, portly, rotund, stocky 9 corpulent 10 overweight
__-filled room: 5 smoke
filler: 6 insert 8 stuffing
  conversation ~: 2 er, um 4 I see 5 I mean
fillet: 3 cut 4 bone, fish, meat 5 strip 6 debone, ribbon 10 hair ribbon
  comb. form: 4 taen- 5 taeni- 6 taenio-
  narrow ~: 6 listel
fill-in: 4 temp 7 stopgap 9 alternate, surrogate 10 jury-rigged, substitute
filling: 4 rich, weft 5 beefy, inlay 6 vitals 7 amalgam, batting, caloric, innards, padding, wadding 8 contents, stuffing
filling __: 3 out 7 station
filling station freebie, once: 3 air, map
fillip: 3 tap 4 flip, goad, poke, prod, push, snap, spur 5 egg on, flick, tonic 6 arouse, prompt, strike 8 get going 9 stimulate 10 incitement
Fillmore, Millard: 9 president
  former occupation: 6 lawyer
  home: 7 Buffalo, New York
  wife: 7 Abigail 8 Caroline
fill one's __: 5 shoes
fill the __: 4 bill
fill to the __: 4 brim
filly: 4 foal, mare 5 horse 6 animal, equine, female
  food: 4 oats
  parent: 4 mare 8 stallion
film: 3 pic 4 cine, mist, rust, scum, show, skin, veil, wash 5 flick, layer, movie, scale, sheet, shoot 6 cinema, patina, patine, powder, record, talkie 7 coating, picture 8 membrane 9 celluloid, photoplay 10 photograph, production
  big shot: 5 mogul
  cast-of-thousands ~: 4 epic
  combining form: 4 cine-
  container: 3 can
  crew member: 4 grip, tech 6 editor, gaffer 7 best boy 8 stunt man
  developing abbr.: 3 enl.
  developing compound: 6 amidol
  ender: 3 dom 4 card, goer 5 going, maker, strip 6 making 7 setting
  feat: 5 stunt
  fragment: 4 clip
  light: 5 klieg
  performers' org.: 3 SAG
  processing site: 3 lab
  rating org.: 4 MPAA
  session: 5 shoot
  specification: 3 ASA 5 speed
  studio: 3 Fox, MGM 6 Disney 7 Miramax, New Line 8 Columbia 9 Paramount, Universal 10 Dreamworks, Warner Bros.
  unit: 4 reel, take
film __: 4 clip, gate, noir, pack 5 badge, speed 7 library
__ film: 3 art 4 disc, disk, roll, thin 5 pilot, sheet, sound 6 safety 7 feature, nitrate
filmgoer, G-rated: 5 minor
filmmaker: 6 auteur 8 director
films: 3 pix 6 cinema
  like some ~: 4 gory 6 G-rated, R-rated
filmy: 4 fine, thin 5 gauzy, light, sheer, wispy 6 limpid 7 chiffon, wispish 8 cobwebby, delicate, ethereal, finespun, gossamer 10 cobweblike, diaphanous
  fabric: 5 gauze, lisse, tulle
Filofax: 3 log 5 diary 7 daybook, journal 8 calendar
fils: 3 son 6 French
  parent: 4 mère, père
filter: 4 leak, ooze, seep, sift 5 clean, drain, leach, sieve, unmix 6 osmose, purify, refine, screen, strain, winnow 7 distill, trickle 8 auto part, permeate, purifier, separate 9 penetrate, percolate
  in: 4 seep 8 permeate 9 penetrate, percolate
  like some ~ s: 5 linty
  spotlight ~: 3 gel
filter __: 3 bed 5 paper 6 factor, feeder
filth: 4 crud, dirt, gunk, mire, muck, smut 5 grime, trash 6 grunge, refuse 7 garbage 8 impurity 9 pollution, profanity, vulgarity 10 corruption, defilement, impurities
filthy: 4 foul, lewd, ugly, vile 5 black, dirty, germy, grimy, mangy, muddy, nasty, sooty 6 cruddy, crumby, crummy, fouled, grubby, grungy, impure, mangey, ribald, rotten, smutty, soiled, sordid, vulgar 7 corrupt, profane, smudged, squalid, stained, tainted, unclean, unswept 8 befouled, begrimed, maculate, polluted, slovenly, stagnant, unwashed 9 blackened, loathsome, low-minded, lubricous, tarnished 10 bedraggled, besmirched, despicable, germ-ridden, insanitary, scurrilous, unsanitary
  lucre: 4 pelf
  make ~: 4 foul, soil 5 dirty, spoil, stain, sully, taint 6 befoul, defile 7 corrupt, pollute, vitiate 9 desecrate 10 adulterate
filthy __: 4 rich 5 lucre
filtrate: 4 ooze, seep 5 leach 9 percolate
filum: 6 thread
fin: 4 bill, five, limb 5 fiver, pinna 6 dorsal 7 airfoil, ventral 8 five-spot, pectoral
  change for a ~: 4 ones 7 singles
  combining form: 6 pteryg- 7 pterygo-
  ender: 4 back, fish
  starter: 3 bow 4 lobe, tail 6 thread
fin __: 3 ray 4 keel 5 whale
__ fin: 4 skid, swim, tail 6 caudal, dorsal, pelvic 7 adipose, ventral
finagle: 4 plot 5 cheat, trick 6 outwit, scheme, wangle 7 connive, finesse, swindle, wheedle 8 contrive, engineer, freeload, intrigue, maneuver, outsmart, scrounge 9 machinate 10 manipulate
final: 3 end, net, ult. 4 exam, last, test 6 ending, latest, latter, utmost 7 closing, parting, supreme 8 absolute, crowning, decisive, definite, eventual, terminal, ultimate 9 finishing, last-ditch 10 concluding, conclusive, definitive, overriding, peremptory, unarguable, undisputed
  ender: 3 ist, ity
  make ~: 5 close, sew up 6 clinch 8 finalize 10 consummate
  not ~: 6 unfirm 9 provisory, tentative, uncertain, undecided, unsettled 10 indecisive, unfinished
  not ~ in law: 4 nisi
  reckoning: 3 end 6 result, upshot 7 outcome 9 punch line 10 bottom line, conclusion, denouement, resolution, settlement
  starter: 4 semi 7 quarter
  tend to ~ details: 5 mop up
  word: 4 amen
final __: 3 cut 5 cause
Final __: 4 Four 5 Touch
Final Analysis (1992 film)
  cast: Kim Basinger, Richard Gere, Eric Roberts, Uma Thurman
  director: Phil Joanou
Final Countdown, The (1980 film)
  cast: Kirk Douglas, Charles Durning, James Farentino, Katharine Ross, Martin Sheen
  director: Don Taylor
  dog: 7 Charlie
finale: 3 end 4 coda, last 5 close, grand 6 climax, ending, epilog, windup, wrap-up 7 last act 8 curtains, end piece, epilogue, last gasp, terminus 10 conclusion, denouement, resolution
__ finale: 5 grand
Final Four
  event: 4 semi 5 round, semis
  org.: 4 NCAA
final frontier, The: 5 space
finalize: 4 jell, seal 5 sew up, tie up 6 clinch, decide, settle, wind up, wrap up 7 work out 8 complete, conclude, nail down, round off, round out 10 consummate
finally: 3 yet 4 last 6 at last, lastly 7 forever, for good 8 after all, in the end 10 eventually, for all time, ultimately
finals
  prelim: 4 semi 5 semis
  prepare for ~: 4 cram 5 study 6 bone up, review
Final Touch alternative: 5 Downy 6 Bounce 7 Snuggle 9 Cling Free
finance: 4 back, fund 5 endow, stake 6 defray, pay for 7 banking, sponsor, support 8 bankroll, maintain 9 budgeting, economics, subsidize 10 capitalize, investment, underwrite, Wall Street
  company: 6 lender
  degree: 3 MBA
  govt. ~ org.: 3 OMB
  world ~ org.: 3 IMF
finance __: 4 bill 6 charge 7 company
__ finance: 4 high
financer: 6 backer, friend, patron 7 sponsor 9 supporter 10 benefactor
finances: 5 means, money, purse 6 income 8 monetary
  science of ~: 9 economics
financial: 6 fiscal 8 economic, monetary 9 budgeting, pecuniary 10 commercial
  aid: 5 grant 6 credit 7 alimony, backing, pension, subsidy, support 8 donation 9 allowance, endowment, patronage 10 assistance, fellowship, honorarium
  aid criterion: 4 need 5 merit 6 income
  analysis tool: 5 chart, graph
  asset: 4 bond, cash 5 stock
  average: 3 Dow 5 S and P
  crisis: 5 panic
  estimate: 5 quote 9 quotation
  hedger: 3 arb
  item: 5 asset 6 credit
  market: 3 OTC 4 AMEX, NYSE 5 Comex
  officer: 2 tr. 5 treas. 9 treasurer
  plan: 6 budget
  publication: 3 WSJ 6 Forbes 7 Barron's, Fortune
  records: 5 books
  reserve: 6 buffer 7 cushion
  resources: 5 means, purse 10 pocketbook
  service: 6 escrow
  standing: 5 worth 8 net worth
  transaction: 4 loan
  U.S. ~ capital: 3 NYC
  wiz: 3 CPA 4 acct. 10 accountant
financial __: 3 aid 7 planner
financier: 5 baron 6 backer, banker, broker, tycoon 7 magnate, sponsor 8 investor 9 moneybags 10 bankroller, capitalist, grubstaker, speculator
Financier, The author: Theodore Dreiser
financing: 5 funds 7 capital, funding 9 patronage 10 investment

__ financing: 3 APR 4 debt 6 bridge 7 deficit
finback: 5 minke, whale 8 cetacean
relative: 3 orc, sei 6 beluga, narwal 7 cowfish, dolphin, grampus, narwhal, rorqual 8 narwhale, porpoise
finca: 5 ranch
finch: 4 bird 5 junco, serin, tarin, twite 6 canary, linnet, siskin, towhee, whidah, whydah 7 bunting, redpoll, sparrow, waxbill 8 grosbeak 9 grassquit, seedeater
color: 4 gold 5 green 6 yellow
home: 4 nest
relative: 9 crossbill
starter: 3 haw 4 bull, gold 5 green
__ finch: 4 Java, pine, rosy 5 grass, house, zebra 6 purple, weaver
Finch, Peter: 5 actor
film: Far From the Madding Crowd (1967)
Father Brown (1954)
Flight of the Phoenix (1966)
Network (1976, AA)
The Nun's Story (1959)
The Pumpkin Eater (1964)
The Story of Robin Hood and His Merrie Men (1952)
Sunday, Bloody Sunday (1971)
The Trials of Oscar Wilde (1960)
Windom's Way (1957)
find: 3 get 4 espy, gain, meet, rule, spot 5 dig up, judge, prove, scour, sight, trace 6 attain, collar, corral, detect, locate, look up, notice, obtain, strike, supply, turn up 7 achieve, acquire, bargain, discern, good buy, hit upon, make out, observe, procure, recover, rout out, run into, scare up, scout up, uncover, unearth 8 arrive at, bump into, chance on, come upon, discover, great buy, identify, perceive, pinpoint, rustle up, scout out, smell out, smoke out 9 ascertain, calculate, detection, determine, discovery, encounter, ferret out, figure out, light upon, recognize, run across, stumble on, track down 10 chance upon, come across, happen upon
again: 7 get back, recover
archaeologist's ~: 4 abri, bone, ruin 5 mound, relic, ruins, shard, sherd, stela, stele 6 fossil
be unable to ~: 6 mislay 7 misfile 8 misplace
fault: 3 hit, nag, pan 4 carp 5 blame, cavil, gripe, knock, nag at, scold 6 accuse, jibe at, pick at 7 cavil at, censure, condemn, grumble, nitpick, put down, quarrel, quibble 8 complain 9 criticize, make a fuss, pick apart, pull apart, reprehend, shoot down 10 vituperate
hard to ~: 4 rare 6 exotic, scanty, scarce 8 uncommon
in flagrante delicto: 5 catch
obnoxious: 4 hate 6 loathe 7 despise 8 execrate 9 abominate
out: 3 see 4 hear, seek, tell 5 catch, glean, learn, solve 6 verify 7 unearth 8 discover 9 ascertain, determine, establish, get word of 10 understand
(out): 4 hunt
the key to: 5 crack 6 decode, fathom, unlock 7 clear up, explain, hit upon, unravel, work out 8 decipher, get right, untangle 9 figure out, interpret, puzzle out 10 account for
try to ~: 4 hunt, seek 5 trace, track, trail 6 gun for, pursue 7 fish for, go after, hunt for, look for, scout up 8 quest for, run after, scout out, sniff out 9 track down
underground ~: 3 oil 4 coal 7 mineral 9 petroleum
find __: 3 out
find __ with: 5 fault
fin-de-__: 6 siècle
__ finder: 4 fact 5 depth, range
finders __: 7 keepers
finder's __: 3 fee
finder starter: 4 path, view 5 fault, water
finding: 4 fact 6 decree, result, ruling 7 verdict 8 decision, judgment 9 deduction, discovery 10 conclusion, resolution
Finding Forrester (2000 film)
cast: F. Murray Abraham, Sean Connery, Anna Paquin
director: Gus Van Sant
__-finding mission: 4 fact
Finding Nemo (2003 film)
character: 4 Dory, Gill 5 Bruce, Crush, Nigel, Peach 6 Marlin
voice cast: Albert Brooks, Willem Dafoe, Ellen DeGeneres, Geoffrey Rush
Finding the Sun author: Edward Albee
Findlay: 4 city, town 5 Maude
locale: 4 Ohio
Findley, Timothy: 6 writer 8 Canadian
__ Finds Andy Hardy: 4 Love
fine: 3 A-OK, aye, def, end, fee, oke, oui, rad, tax, top, yea, yep, yes, yup 4 aced, aces, A-one, boss, braw, cool, dece, dock, gear, good, jake, keen, lacy, levy, luxe, mild, neat, nice, okay, okeh, okey, phat, soft, sure, thin, tuff, well, yeah 5 acute, dandy, ducky, exact, fancy, filmy, gauzy, good-o, grand, great, legit, marvy, moral, mulct, natch, neato, nobby, noble, prime, primo, quite, right, roger, sharp, sheer, slick, smart, sunny, super, swell, uh-huh 6 agreed, amerce, bang on, bang-up, bonzer, bosker, choice, dainty, deluxe, divine, dreamy, far-out, gladly, gnarly, good-oh, groovy, indeed, just so, lovely, narrow, ornate, peachy, pretty, proper, punish, rather, righto, select, slap-up, spot on, subtle, superb, surely, terrif, tiptop, unreal, whizzo, wicked, you bet, yowzah 7 amazing, awesome, capital, corking, damages, elegant, ethical, exactly, forfeit, fragile, go ahead, indeedy, mais oui, netlike, penalty, perfect, powdery, precise, quite so, refined, ripping, skookum, slender, stellar, sublime, suits me, ten-four 8 all right, as you say, becoming, dazzling, delicate, distinct, especial, esthetic, eximious, fabulous, five-star, four-star, frabjous, glorious, gossamer, handsome, heavenly, jim-dandy, laudable, masterly, of course, penalize, pleasant, pleasing, skillful, slam-bang, smashing, spanking, splendid, standout, sterling, stickout, superior, tasteful, terrific, thumbs up, top-level, topnotch, top-rated, very good, very well, wondrous 9 admirable, agreeable, be my guest, bodacious, certainly, darn right, Endsville, excellent, exemplary, exquisite, first-rate, gilt-edged, high-grade, hunky-dory, marvelous, masterful, naturally, okey-dokey, precisely, reputable, sensitive, sollicker, sure thing, top-drawer, topflight, wonderful, wunderbar, you betcha, you said it 10 absolutely, acceptable, amercement, assessment, beneficial, by all means, cobweblike, creditable, definitely, diaphanous, first-class, forfeiture, good enough, hotsy-totsy, jack-a-dandy, out of sight, peachy-keen, phenomenal, positively, punishment, remarkable, reparation, stupendous, super-duper, sure enough, swimmingly, that's right, world-class
al ~: 8 to the end
alternative: 4 jail
check the ~ print: 4 pore, read 5 study 8 pore over
combining form: 4 lept- 5 lepto-
in ~ fettle: 4 hale, trim, well 5 hardy, right, sound 6 robust 7 healthy
medieval ~: 4 wite
not ~: 3 raw 4 rude 5 crude, rough, tacky 6 coarse, common, rustic 8 plebeian 9 inelegant, tasteless 10 uncultured
point: 6 detail, nicety, nuance 9 punctilio
print: 5 terms 7 details, proviso, strings 9 condition, provision 10 conditions
punish by ~: 5 mulct 6 amerce 8 penalize
set a ~: 4 levy 6 assess, impose
fine __: 3 art 4 arts, comb, nail 5 print 6 bouche
fine-__: 3 cut 4 draw, spun, tune 5 drawn, grain 7 grained
fine-__ comb: 5 tooth 7 toothed
Fine: 5 Larry 6 Sylvia
Fine __, A: 4 Mess 7 Madness, Romance
Fine __ Cannibals: 5 Young
Fine!: 4 okay, sure 6 you bet
__ Fine: 5 He's So, I Feel
__-Fine: 3 My-T
__ Fine Day: 3 One
fine kettle of fish: 4 mess
Fine Madness, A (1966 film)
cast: Sean Connery, Jean Seberg, Joanne Woodward
director: Irvin Kershner
fineness: 4 luxe 6 virtue 7 texture 8 delicacy, grandeur 10 refinement
unit: 5 karat
Fine Old Conflict, A author: Jessica Mitford
finer: 6 better 8 superior
make ~: 6 better, enrich 7 enhance, improve, sweeten 9 embellish 10 supplement
Fine Romance, A composer: 4 Kern 6 Fields
Finer Things, The (1987 song) artist: Steve Winwood
finery: 5 array, silks 6 attire, satins 7 clothes, formals, jewelry, regalia 8 frippery, glad rags 9 adornment, caparison, trappings 10 Sunday best
eschewing ~: 5 plain
finespun: 4 lacy 5 filmy, gauzy, light, sheer 6 subtle 7 refined, tissuey 8 cobwebby, delicate, gossamer 9 gauzelike 10 diaphanous
finesse: 3 art 4 tact, wile 5 bluff, craft, guile, savvy, skill, trick 6 acumen, jockey, polish, wangle 7 ability, beguile, finagle, gimmick, know-how, mastery 8 artifice, artistry, delicacy, maneuver, subtlety, urbanity 9 adeptness, dexterity, diplomacy, smartness, stratagem 10 adroitness, artfulness, cleverness, competence, craftiness, discretion, manipulate, refinement
Finesse: 7 shampoo
alternative: 4 Flex, Pert 5 Prell, Suave, Wella 7 Pantene
finest: 3 top 4 best 5 cream 9 top-drawer, topflight
__ Finest Hour: 5 Their
fine-tooth __: 4 comb
fine-tune: 4 edit, hone 5 alter, tweak 6 adjust 8 modulate 9 calibrate
finfoot: 4 bird
Fingal's __: 4 Cave
finger: 4 feel, make, name, pick 5 blame, digit, pinky, point, rat on, thumb, touch 6 dactyl, give up, handle, member, pilfer, pinkie, turn in 7 pointer, specify, toy with 8 identify, pinpoint 9 appendage, designate, implicate, recognize 10 manipulate
combining form: 6 dactyl-, digiti- 7 dactylo-
crook a ~: 6 beckon, entice, invite, signal, summon
ender: 3 tip 4 nail, pick 5 board, print, spell 7 breadth
food: 6 canapé 9 antipasto, appetizer
in the ribs: 3 jab 4 poke, prod 5 nudge 6 tickle
lay a ~ on: 5 touch
lift a ~ for: 4 help
opposite: 3 toe
part: 4 nail 7 cuticle, knuckle
point a ~ at: 5 blame 6 accuse, charge
problem: 6 agnail
put one's ~ on: 4 find 5 place 6 locate, recall 7 find out, specify 8 discover, identify, remember 9 bring back
put the ~ on: 4 name 6 betray, give up, tattle
put the ~ (on): 3 rat 4 tell 6 inform, snitch
shake a ~: 3 wag
sound: 4 snap
starter: 4 fore, lady
wrap around one's little ~: 3 use 6 misuse 7 control 10 manipulate
finger __: 3 man 4 bowl, food, gate, hole, mark, post, wave 5 grass, paint 6 puppet 7 reading
__ finger: 4 ring 5 index, lift a, third 6 little, middle 7 trigger
Finger __: 5 Lakes
fingerboard ridge: 4 fret
__-fingered: 5 light 6 sticky
__-fingered fastball: 5 split
__ Finger Exercise: 4 Five
finger-in-door reaction: 2 ow 3 yow 4 ouch, yeow
__ finger in the pie: 5 have a
Finger Lake: 5 Keuka 6 Cayuga, Owasco, Seneca 10 Canadaigua 11 Skaneateles
fingernail: 4 claw 5 talon 6 ungual, unguis
base: 4 lune
crescent: 6 lunula, lunule
in Spanish: 3 uña
polish: 5 glaze, paint 6 enamel 7 lacquer, varnish
finger-paint: 3 dab 4 daub 5 smear
Finger Poppin' Time (1960 song)
artist: Hank Ballard and the Midnighters
__ fingerprint: 3 DNA 6 latent 7 genetic
fingerprint line: 5 ridge, whorl
fingers
get one's ~ on: 3 bag, nab 4 grab, grip, take 5 catch, grasp, seize, snare, steal 6 secure, snatch 7 acquire, plunder, receive 8 glom on to 9 lay hold of
keep one's ~ crossed: 4 hope, wish 5 dream 6 aspire, expect 7 look for 10 anticipate
middle ~: 5 medii
slip through one's ~: 4 flee, skip 6 escape, run off, run out 7 abscond, bail out, duck out, get away, make off, run away, slip off 8 slip away 9 break away, steal away 10 fly the coop
starter: 6 butter

tap one's ~: 4 drum
work one's ~ to the bone: 5 slave
__ fingers: 5 green 6 sticky
Fingers (1978 film)
cast: Jim Brown, Tisa Farrow, Harvey Keitel
director: James Toback
__ Fingers: 6 Vienna
Fingers, Rollie: 6 hurler 7 pitcher
fingertip: 3 pad
fingertips
at one's ~: 4 near 5 ready
have at one's ~: 4 know 5 grasp 6 fathom 7 cognize 10 comprehend
use one's ~: 4 feel 5 touch
Fingertips-Pt. 2 (1963 song) artist: Stevie Wonder
finger-to-lips sound: 3 shh
finger wave: 4 coif 6 hairdo 8 coiffure
fini: 4 done, over 5 ended, kaput 6 sewn up 7 all over, settled, through 8 achieved 9 concluded
finial: 3 cap, epi, top
Finian's Rainbow (1968 film)
cast: Fred Astaire, Petula Clark, Tommy Steele
composer: 4 Lane 7 Harburg
director: Francis Ford Coppola
finicky: 4 neat 5 exact, fussy, picky 6 choosy, dainty, prissy 7 careful, choosey, mincing, precise, prudent, prudish 8 captious, cautious, critical, exacting, precious, rigorous, thorough 9 assiduous, attentive, demanding, difficult, judicious, observant, querulous, squeamish 10 fastidious, meticulous, nitpicking, particular, scrupulous
cat on TV: 6 Morris
eater: 3 cat
finis: 3 end 4 last 6 ending, windup 7 through 10 conclusion
finish: 2 do, go 3 end, wax, zap 4 best, coat, do in, gild, halt, last, quit, rout, ruin, slay, stop, wrap 5 cease, close, crown, drain, empty, end up, glaze, gloss, mop up, sew up, sheen, shine, spend, stain, use up 6 clinch, defeat, devour, enamel, ending, expend, finale, fulfil, luster, patina, patine, polish, refine, result, run out, settle, smooth, veneer, windup, wrap up 7 abolish, achieve, adjourn, break up, closing, closure, coating, consume, deplete, destroy, execute, exhaust, fulfill, get done, lacquer, last act, perfect, perform, play out, resolve, surface, varnish, wipe out, work out 8 complete, conclude, curtains, dispatch, hang it up, pack it in, round off, round out, shut down, surcease, terminus, transact, vaporize 9 cessation, culminate, discharge, dispose of, go through, polish off, terminate 10 accomplish, call it a day, completion, conclusion, consummate, denouement, desistance, expiration, get through, go the route, put through, refinement, resolution, run through
a course: 3 eat
ahead of: 6 defeat
at: 4 abut 5 verge 8 border on
behind: 6 lose to
dull ~: 3 mat 5 matte
first: 3 win 4 best 7 succeed, triumph
in the money: 3 win 4 show 5 place
last: 4 lose
line: 4 tape, wire
off: 3 eat, end 4 do in 5 eat up, mop up, use up 8 abrogate, close out, surcease 9 liquidate 10 annihilate
perfectly: 3 ace
photo ~: 3 mat, tie 4 stat 5 gloss, matte
second: 4 fail, lose 5 place 9 fall short
starter: 5 photo
third: 4 lose, show
finish __: 4 coat, line
__ **finish:** 5 photo 7 English, Holland
finish'd: 3 o'er
finished: 3 out 4 done, gone, lost, over, past, thru 5 empty, kaput, spent, suave, tired, total, whole 6 done in, entire, undone, urbane 7 all over, decided, elegant, plenary, through, wrecked 8 complete, cultured, flawless, over with, realized, thorough, washed-up 10 devastated, exhaustive
with: 5 rid of
__-finished: 4 half
finishing: 4 last 5 final 6 sequel 10 completion, definitive
finishing __: 4 coat, nail 5 touch 6 school
Finish What Ya Started (1988 song)
artist: Van Halen
Finisterre: 4 cape
finite: 6 mortal 7 limited 9 definable 10 measurable
finite __: 4 verb 6 clause 7 decimal
finito: 4 done, over 5 ended, kaput 6 sewn up 7 all over, settled, through 8 achieved 9 concluded
finjan: 3 cup 4 zarf, zurf
fink: 3 rat 4 nark, sing 5 namer, snake 6 canary, snitch, tattle, weasel 7 stoolie, tattler, tipster, traitor 8 fat mouth, informer, squealer, turncoat 9 miscreant 10 taleteller, tattletale
be a ~: 5 rat on 6 squeal, tattle, turn in 7 sell out
on: 4 name 6 betray, give up, tattle, turn in
starter: 3 rat
__ **Fink:** 4 Mike, Ratt 6 Barton
Finkel: 6 Fyvush
Finland: 4 gulf 6 nation 7 country
bath: 5 sauna
capital: 8 Helsinki
city: 4 Oulu 5 Espoo, Lahti, Turku, Vaasa 6 Kuopio, Vantaa 7 Tampere 8 Helsinki 9 Jyväskylä
combining form: 5 Fenno-
conductor: 7 Salonen
former money: 5 penni 6 markka
Gulf of ~ feeder: 4 Neva
islands: 5 Aland
lake: 4 Nasi 5 Enare, Inari 6 Saimaa
legislature: 9 Eduskunta
money: 4 euro
native: 4 Lapp
neighbor: 6 Norway, Russia, Sweden
Nobelist in Chemistry: 8 Virtanen
Nobelist in Literature: 9 Sillanpöö
phone maker: 5 Nokia
poet: 8 Runeberg
port: 4 Pori 5 Vaasa 8 Helsinki
runner: 5 Nurmi 10 Paavo Nurmi
to Finns: 5 Suomi
writer: 4 Kivi 5 Canth 8 Haavikko 9 Sillanpää
Finlandia composer: 8 Sibelius
Finlayson: 5 James
Finley: 7 Charlie 8 Charlie O.
Finley Peter __: 5 Dunne
__ **Finn:** 4 Huck 6 Mickey 7 Phineas
finnan __: 6 haddie 7 haddock
finnan haddie: 4 fish
__-finned: 4 soft 5 spiny
Finnegans Wake
author: James Joyce
character: 3 ALP, Ann, HCE 4 Anna, Jaun, Shem, Yawn 5 Chuff, Dolph, Glugg, Jerry, Kevin, Shaun 6 Isobel 8 Humphrey 9 Earwicker 10 Plurabelle
last word: 3 the
Finney: 4 Jack 6 Albert
Finney, Albert: 5 actor
film: Erin Brockovich (2000)
Murder on the Orient Express (1974)
Saturday Night and Sunday Morning (1960)
Scrooge (1970)
Shoot the Moon (1982)
Tom Jones (1963)
Two for the Road (1967)
Under the Volcano (1984)
Wolfen (1981)
Finney, Jack: 6 author, writer
work: Assault on a Queen
The Body Snatchers
From Time to Time
Good Neighbor Sam
Time and Again
Finn Hill: 4 city, town
locale: 10 Washington
Finn, Huck: 4 teen
craft: 4 raft
father: 3 Pap
__-Finnic: 4 Ugro
Finnic language: 4 Mari
Finnish: 8 language
see also Finland
__-Finnish War: 5 Russo
Finno-__: 5 Ugric 6 Ugrian
Finno-__ War: 5 Russo
fino: 6 sherry
Finsen, Niels: 8 Nobelist 9 physician, scientist
finspot: 4 fish
Finsteraarhorn: 3 Alp
Finsterwald: 3 Dow 6 golfer
Fiona: 5 Apple 10 Hutchinson
Fionnula: 8 Flanagan
fiord: 3 bay 4 cove, gulf 5 bight, cliff, firth, frith, inlet
locale: 4 Oslo 6 Norway
Fiore: 6 Robert
Fiorello: 9 La Guardia
Fiorello! author: Jerome Weidman
Fiorentino, Linda: 7 actress
film: The Desperate Trail (1994)
Dogma (1999)
The Last Seduction (1994)
Men in Black (1997)
Fiorucci: 4 Elio
fir: 4 tree 6 balsam 7 conifer 9 evergreen
kin: 4 pine 6 spruce 7 hemlock 8 tamarack
product: 4 cone
__ **fir:** 3 red 5 grand, Nikko, noble, white 6 alpine, balsam, Nootka, Oregon, silver 7 Douglas, lowland
Firbank, Ronald: 6 author, writer 7 British
fire: 2 ax 3 axe, can, rid, zip 4 boot, brio, dash, drop, élan, fury, hurl, oust, sack, send, stir, zeal, zing 5 ardor, blaze, drive, eject, expel, flame, gusto, heave, let go, light, liven, pitch, rally, rouse, salvo, shell, shoot, sling, spark, verve, vigor 6 arouse, attack, energy, excite, fervor, flames, hearth, incite, launch, lay off, let fly, set off, spirit, stir up, volley 7 animate, barrage, burning, cashier, dismiss, drum out, enflame, enliven, explode, inferno, inflame, inspire, passion, provoke, sniping, turn out 8 afflatus, detonate, displace, enspirit, fervency, ignition, inspirit, lyricism, motivate, pink-slip, shelling, touch off, vivacity 9 animation, cannonade, discharge, eagerness, electrify, fusillade, galvanize, impassion, intensity, scorching, terminate 10 combustion, enthusiasm, excitement, heartiness, intoxicate, liveliness
add fuel to the ~: 4 spur, stir 5 rouse 6 whip up, work up 7 agitate 9 stimulate
aftermath: 3 ash
antiaircraft ~: 4 flak 5 flack
artillery ~: 5 salvo 7 barrage 9 cannonade, fusillade
at: 6 strafe
(at): 5 snipe
back: 5 rebut, reply 6 answer, retort 7 counter, respond 9 rejoinder
ball of ~: 3 sun 4 star 6 dynamo 7 hustler 8 tireless 9 ambitious, energetic
be on ~: 4 burn 5 blaze 7 smolder
bit of ~: 5 spark
breathe ~: 4 boil, fume, rage, stew 5 storm 6 see red, seethe 7 smolder 10 hit the roof
breather: 6 dragon
breathing ~: 3 hot, mad 5 angry, irate, livid, riled, surly, vexed, wroth 6 fuming, ireful, piqued, raging, red-hot 7 angered, annoyed, berserk, boiling, enraged, furious, steamed 8 incensed, inflamed, provoked, up in arms, volcanic, worked up, wrathful 9 indignant, irritated, seeing red, ticked off 10 infuriated
calm the ~: 4 damp
catch ~: 4 burn 6 ignite, kindle, set off 8 enkindle 10 incinerate
ceremonial ~: 4 pyre
chief: 7 marshal
combining form: 3 pyr- 4 igni-, pyro-
crime: 5 arson
destroy, as by ~: 3 gut
dog name: 4 Spot
ender: 3 arm, box, bug, dog, fly, man, men 4 ball, base, bird, boat, bomb, brat, clay, damp, lock, plug, side, trap, wall, weed, wood, work 5 board, brand, break, brick, drake, fight, flood, guard, house, light, place, power, proof, stone, storm, water 7 cracker, fighter
escape: 4 exit 6 ladder
feed the ~: 4 fuel, stir
fighter: 4 rain 5 water
from ~: 7 igneous
goddess: 6 Birgit
got the ~ going again: 5 relit
hang ~: 4 pend
hanging ~: 6 put off 7 abeyant, delayed, pending 9 postponed, undecided, unsettled 10 in abeyance, up in the air
indicator: 5 smoke
inner ~: 3 vim 4 zeal, zest 5 ardor, drive, oomph, verve 6 fervor 7 longing, passion 8 ambition 9 intensity 10 fanaticism, initiative
iron in the ~: 3 gig, job 4 task 5 chore 7 project, venture 8 activity 10 assignment
light a ~ under: 4 goad, stir 5 rouse, spark 6 arouse, bestir, excite, incite, stir up, wake up, whip up, work up 7 animate, inspire, provoke 8 motivate 9 galvanize, stimulate
no ball of ~: 5 idler, sloth 7 laggard, slacker
off: 3 lob 4 cast, hurl, send, toss 5 chuck, fling, heave, pitch, shoot, throw 6 launch, let fly, propel
offshoot: 6 cinder
on ~: 3 hot 6 ablaze, aflame, flambé 7 burning
open ~: 5 blast, shoot 7 bombard
playing with ~: 5 risky 8 perilous, reckless
play with ~: 4 dare, risk 9 take a risk
pottery: 4 bake
prepare to ~: 3 aim 4 cock
pull out of the ~: 4 save 5 spare

6 rescue
put on the ~: 4 heat, warm 6 heat up, warm up
ready to ~: 5 armed 6 cocked, loaded
residue: 3 ash 4 soot
rod: 5 poker
safety activity: 5 drill
set ~ to: 3 lit 5 light 6 kindle
sign: 5 Aries
signal: 4 bell, gong 5 alarm
starter: 3 fox, gun 4 back, camp, drum, spit, wild 5 brush, cross, flint, match, shell, spark 8 kindling
tend a ~: 4 poke 5 stoke
truck: 6 engine
truck adjunct: 5 siren
up: 3 rev 4 boil, goad, heat, rile, spur, wake 5 anger, pique, rouse, start, waken 6 arouse, enrage, incite, kindle, thrill 7 actuate, enflame, enliven, enthuse, incense, inflame, inspire, outrage 9 galvanize, impassion, instigate, stimulate 10 accelerate
upon: 5 beset, blast, blitz, shell, shoot 6 attack, strike 7 barrage, besiege, bombard 9 broadside, cannonade
with many irons in the ~: 4 at it, busy 6 active, hectic, lively 7 on the go, swamped 8 bustling, immersed 9 engrossed
fire __: 3 ant, hat, off, pot, red 4 area, away, boss, clay, code, door, hose, iron, line, opal, pink, sale, ship, sign, wall 5 alarm, chief, drill, point, tower, truck 6 beetle, blight, cherry, engine, escape, screen, temple 7 balloon, brigade, company, control, curtain, gilding, hydrant, marshal, setting, station, support
fire-__: 4 cure, plow 5 eater 6 polish
fire-__ red: 6 engine
__ fire: 3 red, sea 4 hang, slow 5 brush, catch, cross, crown, Greek, quick, set on, under, watch 6 liquid 7 council, hostile, Kentish
__-fire: 4 sure 5 cease, rapid 6 center 7 central
Fire __ Time, The: 4 Next
__ Fire: 4 Cold, I'm on, Sure 5 Under 7 Chicago, Eternal
Fire and Ice author: 5 Frost
Fire and Rain (1970 song) artist: James Taylor
firearm: 3 gat, gun, Uzi 4 heat 5 piece, rifle 6 heater, musket, pistol, roscoe, weapon 7 handgun, shotgun 8 revolver
lobby: 3 NRA
part: 6 barrel, breech
fireball: 3 sun 6 bolide, dynamo 7 zealous 8 live wire 9 lightning
Fireball, The (1950 film)
cast: Pat O'Brien, Mickey Rooney
director: Tay Garnett
Firebird: 3 car 4 auto 7 Pontiac 10 automobile
Firebird, The: 6 ballet
composer: 10 Stravinsky
firebox innards: 5 alarm
firebrand: 7 hellion, hothead, radical 8 agitator, flambeau, inflamer, ultraist 9 demagogue 10 incendiary
firebrat: 3 bug 6 insect
firebug: 4 pyro 5 torch 8 arsonist 10 incendiary, pyromaniac
crime: 5 arson
firecracker
noise: 3 pop 4 bang 5 burst, crack 9 explosion
part: 4 fuse
__ Firecracker: 4 Miss
__-fired: 3 all, gas 4 hell 7 biscuit
firedamp: 3 gas 7 coal gas
firedog: 7 andiron
FireDome: 3 car 4 auto 6 De Soto 10 automobile
fired up: 3 lit 4 avid, keen 5 eager, wired 6 aflame, gung-ho, rah-rah, yeasty 7 demonic, excited, zealous 8 daemonic, inspired 9 demonical
again: 5 relit
fire-eating: 4 bold 5 brave, gutsy 9 combative, undaunted 10 courageous
fire-engine __: 3 red
fire escape sign: 4 Exit
fire-extinguishing agent: 5 halon
Firefall song: You Are the Woman (1976)
firefighter
concern: 5 arson
need: 3 axe 4 foam, hose 6 helmet, ladder
often: 5 hoser
volunteer ~: 4 vamp
Fireflies author: Rabindranath Tagore
FireFlite: 3 car 4 auto 6 De Soto 10 automobile
firefly: 3 bug 6 beetle, insect
like a ~: 3 lit 5 aglow 6 bright
output: 4 glow 5 glint
Firefly: 3 car, Geo 4 auto 10 automobile
Firefly Summer author: Maeve Binchy
Fire From Heaven author: Mary Renault
__ Fire Girl: 4 Camp
Firehouse author: David Halberstam
Fire in the Ashes author: Theodore H. White
Fire Lake (1980 song) artist: Bob Seger
Fire Next Time, The author: James Baldwin
Firenza: 3 car 4 auto, Olds 10 automobile, Oldsmobile
Firenze: 4 city, town 8 Florence
locale: 5 Italy 6 Italia
river: 4 Arno
fireplace: 5 ingle, stove 6 hearth 9 inglenook 10 hearthside
fuel: 3 log 4 wood 6 gas log
part: 3 hob 4 flue, vent 5 grate 6 ashpit
receptacle: 6 ashcan, ashpan
remnant: 3 ash 5 ember
site: 5 cabin, lodge 6 chalet 7 cottage
tool: 5 poker
vent: 6 airway 7 chimney 10 smokeshaft
firepower: 4 arms, guns 6 rifles 7 weapons 8 matériel, ordnance, weaponry 9 munitions
provide ~ to: 3 arm 7 fortify 8 embattle
fire-retardant acid: 5 boric 7 boracic
fireside: 4 home 5 abode, ingle 6 casual, hearth, low-key, social 7 amiable, cordial, domicil 8 domicile, dwelling, friendly, home life, informal, laid-back, sociable 9 easygoing, homestead, inglenook, residence 10 family life, habitation, hearthside
fireside __: 4 chat
Fire (song) artist: Arthur Brown, Ohio Players, Pointer Sisters
Firestarter: 4 film 5 novel
author: Stephen King
cast: Drew Barrymore, George C. Scott, Martin Sheen
director: Mark L. Lester
Firestone: 3 Roy 6 Harvey
FireSweep: 3 car 4 auto 6 De Soto 10 automobile
firethorn: 5 shrub
relative: 4 rose, sloe 6 kerria, spirea 7 bramble, jetbead, spiraea 8 hardhack, ninebark, photinia 9 raspberry
__ fire to: 3 set
firewater: 6 liquor, whisky 7 alcohol, spirits, whiskey 9 aqua vitae, inebriant
fireweed: 5 plant 6 flower
__ fire with fire: 5 fight
firewood: 4 fuel 8 kindling
amount: 4 cord, rick 6 armful
chopping ~: 5 chore
hauler: 4 cart
make ~: 3 cut, hew 4 chop
make ~ smaller: 5 resaw
season ~: 3 age, dry
firework: 6 fizgig
revolving ~: 5 wheel
fireworks: 4 rage, show 5 noise 6 hoopla, thrill 7 dispute 9 explosive, sparklers 10 exhibition
compound in ~: 5 niter
igniter: 4 punk 6 amadou
name: 6 Grucci
reaction to ~: 3 awe, ooh
time: 4 July 5 night
firing: 8 kindling 9 discharge, explosion
on all cylinders: 4 sane
rocket ~: 7 liftoff
firing __: 3 pin 4 line 5 glass, range
firkin: 3 keg, tub 4 cask 6 barrel 9 butter tub, container
firm: 2 co. 3 set 4 bent, corp., fast, hard, iron, snug, sure, taut, true 5 bossy, cruel, dense, exact, fixed, house, loyal, picky, rigid, rocky, solid, sound, stern, stiff, stony, tight, tough 6 agency, all-out, bolted, braced, flinty, harden, intent, nailed, outfit, rooted, secure, severe, stable, static, steady, steely, stoney, strict, strong, sturdy, tone up, welded 7 abiding, adamant, al dente, austere, certain, compact, company, concern, decided, diehard, hard-set, riveted, secured, settled, Spartan, staunch, stiffen 8 anchored, business, cemented, concrete, constant, decisive, definite, despotic, embedded, emphatic, employer, enduring, exacting, explicit, fastened, forceful, hardened, hardline, hellbent, immobile, implicit, ironclad, obdurate, positive, reliable, resolute, rigorous, soldered, stubborn, unmoving 9 assertive, condensed, demanding, draconian, immovable, immutable, impliable, inelastic, nonporous, obstinate, permanent, screwed in, stabilize, steadfast, stringent, tightened, unbending, unsparing 10 adamantine, compressed, conclusive, consistent, deep-rooted, despotical, determined, enterprise, foursquare, hard-bitten, hard-packed, impervious, inflexible, invariable, ironfisted, iron-willed, motionless, no-nonsense, oppressive, peremptory, persistent, purposeful, stationary, tyrannical, unchanging, unflagging, unshakable, unswerving, unwavering, unyielding
control: 4 grip 5 grasp 6 clench, clinch 7 command, mastery
ender: 4 ware
expanding ~: 5 hirer
foundation: 4 rock
high-tech ~: 6 dot-com
make ~: 3 fix, pin, tie 4 bind, bond, gird, lock, nail, root, weld 5 brace, build, plant, rivet, shore, steel 6 anchor, cement, enroot, fasten, harden, secure, tone up 7 bolster, build up, fortify, implant, shore up, stiffen, tighten, toughen 8 buttress, entrench, nail down, rigidify, solidify 9 reinforce, stabilize 10 straighten, strengthen
not ~: 4 soft, weak 5 boggy, saggy, slack, unset 7 flaccid 8 yielding
stand ~: 6 insist, resist 7 persist 9 persevere, withstand
up: 3 gel, set 4 jell, tone 6 anneal, harden 8 nail down, solidify 9 stabilize 10 strengthen
__ firm: 3 CPA 6 member
firmament: 3 sky 5 azure, skies 6 heaven 7 heavens 8 empyrean
in the ~: 5 above, aloft 6 high up, on high
firman: 4 fiat 5 edict, order, ukase 6 decree, dictum 7 command, mandate 9 directive, manifesto 10 injunction
firma, terra: 4 land, soil 5 earth 6 ground
firmer __: 5 gouge 6 chisel
firmly: 4 fast, hard 5 tight 8 severely 9 immovably, like a rock
firmness: 4 will 5 nerve, valor 6 fixity 7 courage, density, purpose, resolve 8 backbone, decision, hardness, obduracy, rigidity, solidity, strength, tenacity 9 assurance, certainty, constancy, fixedness, obstinacy, stability, willpower 10 conviction, durability, moral fiber, resolution
exemplar of ~: 4 vise
lacking ~: 4 limp, soft 6 droopy, flabby, floppy, pliant 7 flaccid, pliable 8 drooping
lose ~: 3 sag
Firm of Girdlestone, The author: Arthur Conan Doyle
Firm, The (1993 film)
cast: Tom Cruise, Gene Hackman, Jeanne Tripplehorn
director: Sydney Pollack
dog: 7 Hearsay
__ firmus: 6 cantus
firn: 4 névé, snow
Firpo, Luis: 5 boxer
first: 4 A-one, base, head, main, tops 5 ahead, chief, front, least, older, prime 6 choice, maiden, rather, select, superb, top dog, utmost, victor, virgin 7 forward, in front, initial, leading, lead-off, opening, optimal, optimum, pioneer, premier, primary, ranking, supreme, to start 8 champion, dominant, earliest, foremost, greatest, headmost, in the van, original, primeval, topnotch, top-rated, virginal 9 beginning, immediate, in advance, inaugural, inceptive, initially, number one, numero uno, paramount, primaeval, primarily, primitive, principal, prototype, uttermost 10 aboriginal, beforehand, consummate, originally, preeminent, primordial, super-duper
combining form: 4 arch-, prot- 5 arche-, archi-, proto-
in music: 5 primo
starter: 4 head
first __: 3 aid, off 4 base, dark, down, gear, lady, lien, mate, name, post 5 class, floor, light, night, thing, water 6 cousin, estate, family, fruits, papers, person, strike 7 baseman, edition, officer, quarter, reading
first-__: 4 born, come, foot, hand, line, rate, time 5 class, timer 6 degree, string, termer
first-__ cover: 3 day
first-__ kit: 3 aid
first-__ mail: 5 class
first-__ movie: 3 run
__ first: 6 double, safety
First __: 4 Lady, Lord, Love 5 Alert, Blood, Cause, Class, World 6 Empire, Flight, Knight, Reader 7 Chamber, Nighter

First __ Club, The: 5 Wives
First __ Ever I Saw..., The: 4 Time
First __, first...: 5 in war
First __ I see tonight...: 4 star
First __ Sin, The: 6 Deadly
First __, The: 4 Noel, Time 5 Night 6 Circle, Legion
First __ War: 5 World 6 Balkan
first aid
- **giver:** 3 EMT
- **item:** 4 tape 5 gauze, iodin, sling 6 eyecup, ice bag, iodine 7 ice pack
- **job:** 3 cut 4 gash
- **plant:** 4 aloe

first-aid __: 3 kit
First Amendment lobbyist: 4 ACLU
first and __: 3 ten 4 last
first baseman
- **famous ~:** 3 Who
- **Hall of Fame ~:** 4 Foxx, Mize 5 Anson, Perez, Terry 6 Cepeda, Gehrig, Murray, Sisler 7 Leonard, McCovey 8 Cap Anson 9 Bill Terry, Greenberg, Killebrew, Lou Gehrig, Tony Perez 10 Jimmie Foxx, Johnny Mize

First Blood (1982 film)
- **cast:** David Caruso, Richard Crenna, Brian Dennehy, Sylvester Stallone
- **director:** Ted Kotcheff

firstborn: 5 elder, older 6 eldest, oldest, senior
- **name meaning ~:** 6 Winona

First Cause, the: 4 Lord
First Circle, The author: Aleksandr Solzhenitsyn
first-class: 3 top 4 A-one, best, fine, good, tops 5 crack, dandy, elite, grand, great, prime, primo, sharp, slick, super, swell 6 choice, deluxe, goodly, grade A, lavish, select, tiptop, worthy 7 capital, private, stellar, supreme 8 fabulous, five-star, four-star, splendid, sterling, superior, topnotch, very good 9 excellent, fantastic, important, topflight, unrivaled, wunderbar 10 unrivalled
first-class __: 4 mail
__ first class: 6 airman 7 private
First Class song: Beach Baby (1974)
First Daughter
- **1960s ~:** 8 Caroline 4 Luci 5 Julie, Lynda 6 Tricia
- **1970s ~:** 3 Amy 5 Susan
- **1980s~:** 7 Maureen
- **1990s ~:** 7 Chelsea
- **2000s ~:** 5 Jenna 7 Barbara

first-day __: 5 cover
First Deadly Sin, The: 4 film 5 novel
- **author:** Lawrence Sanders
- **cast:** David Dukes, Faye Dunaway, Frank Sinatra

first-degree, in math: 5 monic
First Dog
- **1940s:** 4 Fala
- **1960s:** 3 Her, Him
- **1990s:** 5 Buddy 6 Millie

first-down yardage: 3 ten
first-family member: 3 Eve 4 Abel, Adam, Cain, Seth
First Flight author: Maxwell Anderson
first-grade lesson: 4 ABCs 8 alphabet
first-grader's shout: 4 me me
firsthand: 6 direct 8 intimate, original 9 immediate 10 eyewitness, unmediated
First Knight (1995 film)
- **cast:** Sean Connery, Richard Gere, Julia Ormond
- **director:** Jerry Zucker

First Lady of Song: 4 Ella
First Legion, The (1951 film)
- **cast:** Lyle Bettger, Charles Boyer, William Demarest
- **director:** Douglas Sirk

first-line players: 5 A-team
First Love (1939 film)
- **cast:** Deanna Durbin, Robert Stack
- **director:** Henry Koster

__ first-name basis: 3 on a
First Nighter: 9 radio show
First Night, The (1998 song) artist: Monica
First Noel, The: 5 carol
first-of-month payment: 4 rent
__, first-out: 6 last-in 7 first-in
first-pitch preceder: 6 anthem
first-place medal: 4 gold
first-quality: 5 prime
- **not ~:** 3 irr. 5 irreg. 9 irregular

first-rate: 3 ace, def, exc., rad, top 4 aces, A-one, best, boss, braw, cool, dece, fine, gear, good, jake, keen, neat, nice, phat, tops, tuff 5 boffo, class, crack, dandy, ducky, grand, great, marvy, neato, nobby, prime, primo, prize, slick, super, swell 6 bang on, bang-up, bonzer, bosker, choice, class A, classy, divine, dreamy, far-out, gnarly, goodly, groovy, lovely, peachy, select, slap-up, spot on, superb, terrif, tiptop, unreal, whizzo, wicked, worthy 7 amazing, awesome, boffola, capital, corking, perfect, ripping, skookum, stellar, sublime, supreme 8 dazzling, especial, eximious, fabulous, five-star, four-star, frabjous, glorious, heavenly, jim-dandy, slam-bang, smashing, splendid, standout, sterling, stickout, superior, terrific, top-level, topnotch, very good, wondrous 9 bodacious, Endsville, excellent, exemplary, exquisite, fantastic, high-grade, hunky-dory, marvelous, masterful, sollicker, topflight, unrivaled, wonderful, wunderbar 10 hotsy-totsy, jack-a-dandy, out of sight, peachy-keen, phenomenal, remarkable, stupendous, super-duper, unrivalled
first-sight phenomenon: 4 love
First State: 3 Del. 8 Delaware
first-string players: 5 A-team
First Time Ever I Saw Your Face, The (1972 song) artist: Roberta Flack
first-timer: 4 tyro 6 newbie, rookie 7 trainee 8 beginner, initiate, newcomer 10 tenderfoot
First Wives Club, The (1996 film)
- **cameo role:** 5 Ivana
- **cast:** Goldie Hawn, Diane Keaton, Bette Midler, Maggie Smith
- **dog:** 5 Roach
- **members:** 4 exes
- **setting:** 3 NYC 9 Manhattan

First World __: 3 War
first-year
- **cadet:** 4 pleb 5 plebe
- **law student:** 4 one L
- **student:** 5 frosh 8 freshman

__ first you don't...: 4 If at
firth: 3 bay 4 gulf 5 fiord, fjord, inlet, mouth
Firth: 5 Colin, Peter
__ Firth: 5 Moray 6 Solway
Firth of __: 3 Tay 4 Lorn 5 Clyde, Forth
Firth of Clyde
- **island:** 5 Arran
- **port:** 3 Ayr
- **river to the ~:** 4 Doon

Firth of Lorn port: 4 Oban
Firth of Tay port: 6 Dundee
fisc: 6 coffer 8 treasury 9 exchequer
fiscal: 8 economic, monetary 9 budgetary, financial, pecuniary
- **beneficiary:** 5 payee
- **period:** 2 yr. 3 qtr. 4 year 7 quarter
- **plan:** 6 budget

fiscal __: 4 plan, year 5 agent 6 period, policy
Fischer: 4 Hans 5 Bobby, Edwin, Ernst 6 Edmond 7 Hermann
Fischer, Bobby forte: 5 chess
Fischer-Dieskau: 6 German 8 baritone, Dietrich
- **forte:** 6 lieder

Fischer, Edmond: 8 Nobelist
Fischer, Edwin: 5 Swiss 7 pianist
Fischer, Ernst: 7 chemist 8 Nobelist
Fischer, Hans: 7 chemist 8 Nobelist
Fischer, Hermann: 7 chemist 8 Nobelist
'F' Is for Fugitive author: Sue Grafton
fish: 3 ayu, cat, cod, dab, eel, fry, gar, ged, ide, ihi, koi, orf, ray, sey, tai 4 barb, bass, blay, boce, boga, bret, brit, carp, cero, char, chub, chum, coho, cusk, dace, dory, drum, dupe, fugu, game, goby, hake, hiku, huss, jack, jocu, lija, ling, loro, mado, mapo, masu, meat, mero, mola, opah, orfe, parr, pega, peto, pike, pogy, pout, quab, raad, rudd, ruff, sama, scad, sesi, shad, skil, sole, spet, tope, tuna, ulua 5 akule, angle, betta, bleak, bolti, bream, brill, chiro, chopa, cisco, cobia, coney, danio, elver, grope, grunt, guasa, guppy, hilsa, jurel, loach, lotte, manta, moray, pargo, perch, porgy, sargo, saury, scrod, seine, shark, skate, smelt, smolt, snook, sprat, tench, tetra, torsk, trawl, troll, trout, tunny, wahoo 6 aimara, anabas, barbel, beluga, beshow, bichir, bigeye, blenny, bonaci, bonito, bowfin, burbot, caplin, caribe, conger, cuchia, cunner, darter, entrée, grilse, groper, gunnel, hapuku, hilsah, inanga, louvar, maigre, marlin, medaka, minnow, mullet, nonnat, piraña, Pisces, plaice, plakat, pollan, puffer, puneca, remora, roughy, saithe, salele, salema, salmon, saurel, savola, schrod, search, sennet, shiner, sucker, tandan, tarpon, tautog, testar, tetard, tiñosa, tomcod, turbot, weever, wrasse, zander 7 alewife, alfiona, anchovy, bacalao, barbudo, bloater, bluefin, cabezon, capelin, cavalla, corbina, corvina, crappie, croaker, eelpout, escolar, finspot, fly-cast, garlopa, garpike, gourami, graysby, grindle, grouper, grunion, gudgeon, gurnard, gwyniad, haddock, halibut, helleri, herring, inconnu, lamprey, lingcod, margate, mojarra, mooneye, nibbler, oldwife, opaleye, pigfoot, piranha, pollack, pollock, pomfret, pompano, ronquil, rummage, sand dab, sardine, scalare, sculpin, sea bass, snapper, sockeye, sterlet, sweeper, tilapia, torpedo, walleye, whapuku, whiting, wolf-eel 8 albacore, anableps, arapaima, baysmelt, bigmouth, bloodfin, bluegill, bluehead, brisling, bullhead, cabrilla, card game, characin, chimaera, crevalle, dragonet, flathead, flounder, gambusia, gilthead, grayling, halfbeak, halfmoon, hiwi hiwi, John Dory, mackerel, manta ray, medregal, menhaden, mulloway, nannygai, palometa, pearleye, pilchard, sea bream, sea horse, sea raven, skipjack, stingray, sturgeon, tommycod, topsmelt, trevally, tubenose, wrymouth 9 amberjack, argentine, barracuda, barreleye, blue shark, Dover sole, eelblenny, feel about, greenling, grenadier, lake trout, martinico, mudminnow, neon tetra, pikeperch, red mullet, sand lance, schnapper, sea urchin, spikedace, surfperch, swordtail, threadfin, topminnow, tubesnout, whitebait, yellowfin 10 bitterling, blanquillo, brook trout, brown trout, coelacanth, pikeblenny, red snapper, sandroller, silverside, squaretail, tiger shark, troutperch, whale shark, white cloud, white shark, yellow jack, yellowtail
- **Africa:** 5 bolti 6 anabas, bichir 7 tilapia 8 characin 10 coelacanth
- **alternative:** 4 fowl
- **appendage:** 6 barbel
- **appetizer:** 3 lox 7 ceviche
- **aquarium ~:** 3 orf 4 barb, orfe 5 danio, guppy, platy, tetra 6 medaka 7 gourami, helleri, scalare 8 bloodfin 9 neon tetra, swordtail
- **Arizona ~:** 9 spikedace
- **Asia:** 5 betta, loach, tench 6 anabas 7 gourami, sterlet
- **Atlantic:** 3 cod, sey 4 cero, cusk, hake, jack, mapo 5 lotte, porgy, saury, snook 6 gunnel, saithe, tarpon, tautog, tomcod 7 cavalla, croaker, graysby, haddock, halibut, herring, margate, pollack, pollock, pomfret, torpedo, whiting 8 mackerel, sea raven, wrymouth 9 amberjack
- **Australian:** 4 mado 6 groper, roughy, tandan 8 mulloway, nannygai, trevally 9 schnapper
- **bag-shaped ~ trap:** 4 fyke
- **bait:** 4 lure, worm 5 sprat
- **bait ~:** 4 chub, dace
- **balancer:** 3 fin
- **basslike ~:** 4 boga 5 snook 6 salele
- **big ~:** 6 lunker
- **bin for salting ~:** 5 kench
- **blackish ~:** 5 sable
- **boned ~:** 5 filet
- **bottom-feeding ~:** 7 eelpout
- **Brazil:** 5 piaba 8 arapaima
- **breakfast ~:** 3 lox
- **bright:** 4 opah 5 tetra
- **bring in a ~:** 3 net 4 land
- **by jigging:** 3 dib
- **California:** 7 alfiona, finspot, grunion, sculpin 8 halfmoon 10 yellowtail
- **canned ~:** 4 tuna 6 salmon 8 sardines
- **Caribbean ~:** 10 yellow jack
- **catcher:** 3 net 4 hook 5 seine
- **cave-dwelling ~:** 3 eel
- **Central American:** 7 helleri 9 swordtail
- **chunk-light ~:** 4 tuna
- **clean a ~:** 3 gut 5 scale
- **cold-water ~:** 5 smelt
- **collation:** 5 sushi 7 sashimi
- **combining form:** 5 pisci- 6 ichthy- 7 ichthyo-
- **cut:** 6 fillet
- **cyprinoid ~:** 3 ide
- **deep-sea ~:** 8 pearleye 9 barreleye, grenadier
- **deli ~:** 4 chub
- **delicacy:** 3 roe
- **dish:** 3 roe 5 sushi 6 caviar, kipper 7 ceviche, gravlax, sashimi 8 lutefisk, matelote 9 carbonado
- **eellike ~:** 6 cuchia, gunnel
- **eggs:** 3 roe 6 caviar
- **elongated:** 3 eel 4 ling
- **emulate ~:** 4 swim
- **ender:** 3 eye, gig, net 4 bowl, hook, meal, pond, tail, wife 5 plate 6 monger
- **Europe:** 3 dab, ide 4 blay, boce, dace, dory, ling, rudd, ruff 5 bleak, brill, guasa, loach, pargo, perch, tench 6 barbel, beluga, maigre, turbot, weever, zander 7 gudgeon,

pigfoot **8** John Dory, pilchard **10** bitterling
eye: 4 gaze
fierce ~: 5 shark
fighting ~: 5 betta
filet ~: 4 sole
finder: 5 sonar
finless ~: 3 eel
flat ~: 3 ray
food: 4 alga, bait
food ~: 3 cod, ide **4** bass, hake, mahi, scup, shad, sole, tuna **5** jurel, trout **6** bonaci, bonito
for: 4 seek **5** probe **6** pursue
(for): 4 hunt **5** grope **6** search
freshen a ~ tank: 6 aerate
freshwater ~: 3 gar, ide **4** bass, carp, chub, dace, pike, rudd **5** bream, cisco, loach, perch, roach, tench, trout **6** darter
fry: 4 meal **6** picnic
game ~: 4 bass, cero, tuna, ulua **5** trout, wahoo **6** marlin, tarpon **7** cavalla, walleye **9** barracuda
ganoid ~: 3 gar **6** bowfin **7** grindle
go ~: 8 card game, kids' game
Great Lakes ~: 4 chub **5** cisco, smelt **7** bloater
group: 5 shoal **6** school
haul: 4 take **5** catch
Hawaii: 4 ulae, ulua **5** akule, moano **8** mahimahi
herringlike ~: 4 pogy, shad **7** anchovy, mooneye
holder: 5 creel **6** kettle
how to pack ~: 5 in ice
illegally: 5 poach
India: 5 danio, hilsa **6** cuchia, hilsah
Japan: 3 ayu, koi, tai **4** fugu, masu **5** cobia **6** medaka
kettle of ~: 3 fix, jam **4** spot **5** snarl **6** fiasco, muddle, pickle, plight, scrape, tangle **7** dilemma, problem, screwup, trouble, turmoil **8** bad scene **9** deep water, mare's nest
lake ~: 4 bass **5** trout
leftover: 5 spine
like ~: 5 finny, scaly
like a cold ~: 5 aloof **6** chilly **7** distant **8** detached **9** apathetic, impassive **10** unfriendly, unsociable
like a ~ hook: 5 sharp **6** barbed **7** pointed
long ~: 3 eel
long-jawed ~: 3 gar
lung: 4 gill
lure a ~: 3 dap
marinated ~ appetizer: 7 ceviche
Mediterranean: 5 porgy **6** nonnat **7** anchovy **8** gilthead
Mexico: 7 garlopa **8** anableps
net: 5 seine, trawl
New England: 5 scrod **6** schrod
New Zealand: 3 ihi **4** hiku **6** hapuku, inanga **7** whapuku **8** hiwi hiwi
oil acid: 3 DHA
one way to ~: 5 troll
out of water: 6 misfit **7** oddball **8** maverick
Pacific ~: 5 sargo **6** beshow, bigeye, tomcod **7** cabezon, corbina, corvina, halibut, herring, nibbler, opaleye, pomfret, ronquil, sand dab, wolf-eel **8** baysmelt, flathead, palometa, topsmelt, tubenose **9** greenling, surfperch, tubesnout
parrot ~: 4 loro
part: 4 gill
Philippine ~: 9 martinico
plate: 5 scale
predator: 3 ern **4** bear, erne
prepare ~: 4 bone **6** debone, fillet
puffer ~: 4 fugu
rainbow ~: 5 smelt
raw ~: 5 sushi
relish: 4 alec
sardine ~: 5 sprat
sauce: 4 alec
scaleless ~: 3 eel
science of: 11 ichthyology
scored and broiled ~: 9 carbonado
Scotland: 3 ged
shadlike ~: 7 alewife **8** menhaden
sharp-snouted ~: 5 saury
sharp-toothed ~: 5 moray
silvery ~: 4 blay, mola **5** bleak, bream, smelt **6** shiner **7** grunion, mojarra, mooneye **8** baysmelt, bloodfin, topsmelt **9** argentine
smallmouth ~: 4 bass
smoked ~: 6 kipper, salmon **7** herring
snakelike ~: 3 eel **5** moray **7** lamprey
sound: 4 plop
South America: 6 aimara **7** piranha, scalare **8** bloodfin, characin
spear: 3 gig
Sri Lanka: 5 danio
starter: 3 bat, box, cat, cod, cow, dog, fin, gar, hag, hog, mud, oar, pig, pin, pup, rat, red, saw, sun **4** bait, bill, blow, blue, boar, bone, cave, coal, craw, deal, fall, file, flat, frog, goat, gold, gray, grey, king, lady, lion, lump, lung, milk, monk, moon, numb, pipe, rock, rose, sail, sand, star, stud, suck, tile, toad, weak **5** angel, black, blind, cling, cramp, devil, frost, glass, globe, goose, jelly, jewel, sable, shell, snake, snipe, spade, spear, stock, stone, swell, sword, trunk, viper, white **6** angler, archer, butter, candle, damsel, dollar, guitar, lizard, mutton, needle, paddle, parrot, ribbon, rudder, shrimp, silver, tongue **7** rooster, surgeon, trigger **8** squirrel
stew: 8 matelote
story: 3 fib **4** tale, yarn **7** fiction
story teller: 6 fibber **8** deceiver
striped ~: 4 bass
sushi ~: 3 eel
Tasmania: 6 inanga
trap: 3 net **4** weir
troll for ~: 5 drail
tropical ~: 3 pet **4** loro, mola, opah, scad **5** chiro, manta, moray, tetra **6** louvar, salema, tiñosa, wrasse **9** barracuda **10** pikeblenny, squaretail
try for a ~: 4 cast
unhatched ~: 3 egg
unicorn ~: 4 unie
warm-water game ~: 5 cobia
West Indies: 6 bigeye
white ~: 5 scrod **6** schrod
with a charge: 3 eel
young ~: 3 fry
fish __: 3 fry, out **4** bowl, cake, crow, duck, farm, fork, hawk, meal, pole **5** flake, flour, knife, louse, slice, stick, story, wheel **6** doctor, ladder, tackle, warden **7** culture
fish __ bait: 5 or cut
fish __ fowl: 3 nor
fish __ of water: 3 out
fish-__: 7 bellied
__ fish: 3 pan, tin **4** bony, cold, food, game, tuna **5** clown, green, pilot, rough, sport, trash **6** basket, bottom, flying, ground **7** anemone, bellows, buffalo, gefilte, jawless, rainbow, walking
Fish: 4 Phil, sign **6** Pisces **7** Stanley **8** Hamilton
month: 3 Feb., Mar. **5** March **8** February
successor: 3 Ram
the ~: 4 sign **5** dance **6** Pisces
__ Fish: 6 Rumble **7** Passion
fish-and-chips quaff: 3 ale
Fishburne, Laurence: 5 actor
film: Boyz N the Hood (1991)
The Matrix (1999)
Othello (1995)
School Daze (1988)
What's Love Got to Do With It (1993)
Fish Called Wanda, A (1988 film)
cast: John Cleese, Jamie Lee Curtis, Kevin Kline, Michael Palin
director: Charles Crichton
fisher: 5 pekan **6** angler, marten
starter: 4 king
Fisher: 3 Bud, Ham, M.F.K. **4** Fred, Gail, Toni **5** Eddie, Joely **6** Carrie **7** Dorothy, Frances, Stevens, Terence
rival: 4 Aiwa, Sony **7** Marantz, Pioneer
Fisher-__: 5 Price
Fisher, Carrie: 7 actress
film: The 'burbs (1989)
The Empire Strikes Back (1980)
Garbo Talks (1984)
Hannah and Her Sisters (1986)
Return of the Jedi (1983)
Shampoo (1975)
Soapdish (1991)
Star Wars (1977)
When Harry Met Sally ... (1989)
mother: Debbie Reynolds
spouse: Paul Simon
Fisher, Dorothy: 6 author, writer
Fisher, Eddie
daughter: Carrie, Joely
song: Cindy, Oh Cindy (1956)
Count Your Blessings (1954)
Dungaree Doll (1955)
Heart (1955)
I Need You Now (1954)
Oh! My Pa-pa (1953)
spouse: Debbie Reynolds, Connie Stevens, Elizabeth Taylor
__ Fisher Hall: 5 Avery
Fisher King, The (1991 film)
cast: Jeff Bridges, Amanda Plummer, Mercedes Ruehl, Robin Williams
director: Terry Gilliam
fisherman: 5 eeler **6** angler, seiner **7** trawler, troller **8** piscator
at times: 5 lurer **6** baiter
Newfoundland ~: 6 banker
see also fishing
fisherman's __: 4 bend, knot, ring **7** platter
Fisherman's __: 5 Wharf
fisherman's bend: 4 knot
Fisher, M.F.K.: 6 author, writer
subject: 4 food
Fisher-Price product: 3 toy
Fishers: 4 city, town
locale: 7 Indiana
__ Fishers, The: 5 Pearl
fisheye __: 4 lens
fishhook: 4 gaff
attachment: 5 snell
part: 4 barb
__ fishin': 4 gone
fishing: 5 sport
boat: 4 dory **5** smack **6** lugger, whaler **7** coaster, trawler
bob ~ bait: 3 dib
boot: 5 wader
Dutch ~ boat: 6 dogger
expedition: 6 search **8** research
float: 4 cork **6** bobber, dobber
footwear: 5 wader
garment: 5 oiler
gear: 3 bob, net, rod **4** lure, reel **6** fly rod
gear name: 5 Orvis
grounds off the Shetlands: 4 Haaf
guide: 5 gilly **6** gillie
hope: 4 bite
line: 5 troll
line material: 3 gut
lure: 3 fly, jig **4** plug **5** spoon, troll **6** dry fly
need: 3 net, rod **4** bait, line, lure, reel **5** creel, seine
net: 5 seine, trawl
reel, in Britain: 4 pirn
reel part: 5 spool
Scottish ~ boat: 6 baldie
spot: 4 lake, pier, pond **5** creek, wharf **6** stream
start ~: 4 cast
take: 4 haul **5** catch **6** keeper
fishing __: 3 rod **4** line, pole, trip, worm **5** banks, smack **6** ground
__ fishing: 3 ice **4** spin
__-fishing: 3 fly
Fish Magic artist: 4 Klee
fishnet: 6 fabric
fiber: 5 olona
fishnets: 7 hosiery
like ~: 5 meshy
__ fish nor fowl: 7 neither
fish or __ bait: 3 cut
fish out of __: 5 water
__ fish out of water: 5 like a
__ fish sandwich: 4 tuna
fish sauce, literally: 6 catsup **7** ketchup
fish story: 3 lie **4** tale
teller: 4 liar
fishtail: 3 wag **4** palm, skid **9** oscillate
fishtank need: 6 filter
fish-to-be: 3 ova, roe
__ fish to fry: 5 other
fishwife: 5 scold, shrew **6** virago **7** needler **9** henpecker, Xanthippe
fishy: 5 queer **7** dubious, suspect **9** unethical **10** incredible, suspicious
Fisk, Carlton: 7 catcher
gear for ~: 4 mitt
Fiske, John: 11 philosopher
fission: 7 parting **8** dividing, division **9** severance, splitting
experiment: 5 A-test
fission __: 4 bomb
__ fission: 6 binary **7** nuclear
fissionable: 6 atomic **8** atomical
material: 4 atom
fissure: 3 cut **4** hole, leak, reft, rent, rift, slit, tear, vent **5** break, chasm, chink, cleft, crack, gorge, split **6** breach, cranny, ravine **7** crevice, opening, rupture **8** crevasse, fracture **10** interstice
fist: 4 duke, grab, grip, hand **5** clasp, grasp, seize **6** clench, clutch, import
ender: 5 fight
hit without a ~: 4 knee, slap
make a ~: 6 clench
material: 4 iron
product: 3 jab **4** sock **5** punch **6** one-two **8** haymaker, uppercut **10** roundhouse
shake a ~ at: 8 threaten
__ fist: 6 mailed **7** monkey's
F.I.S.T. (1978 film)
cast: Peter Boyle, Melinda Dillon, Sylvester Stallone, Rod Steiger
director: Norman Jewison
__-fisted: 3 ham, two **4** hard **5** close, tight **6** narrow
fistfight: 4 bout **5** scrap **6** tussle
memento: 6 bruise, fat lip, shiner **8** black eye
prelude, perhaps: 5 shove
Fistful of Dollars (1964 film): 5 oater
cast: Clint Eastwood
director: Sergio Leone
fistic: 10 pugilistic
fisticuff: 4 bang, blow, shot **5** clout, punch, smack, thump, whack **6** pummel

fisticuffs: **4** bout **5** fight **6** boxing **7** quarrel **8** pugilism
fists, fight with: **3** box
fit: **2** go **3** apt, arm, rig, set, tic **4** able, good, gybe, hale, jibe, just, lean, meet, sane, suit, tiff, trim, well **5** adapt, agile, agree, alter, apply, burly, clock, equip, hardy, match, mount, prime, ready, right, serve, shape, sound, spasm, spate, spell, spirt, spurt, throe, throw, toned, tough, try on **6** adjust, attack, become, belong, brawny, change, concur, decent, dither, edge in, frenzy, modify, proper, robust, rugged, seemly, square, strong, tailor, timely, up to it, usable, useful, worthy **7** apropos, capable, conform, correct, fashion, furnish, healthy, in shape, livable, measure, provide, qualify, seizure, tantrum, useable **8** accouter, accoutre, adequate, apposite, athletic, decorous, dovetail, eligible, feasible, laughter, liveable, muscular, outbreak, outburst, paroxysm, powerful, prepared, regulate, relevant, rightful, stalwart, suitable, vigorous **9** advisable, competent, expedient, favorable, harmonize, hysterics, interlock, in the pink, opportune, qualified, reconcile, strapping, up to snuff, wholesome **10** able-bodied, applicable, compatible, conniption, convenient, correspond, felicitous, go together, propitious, reasonable, well-suited
as seen ~: **4** duly
be ~ for: **4** suit **6** beseem **7** behoove
check for ~: **5** try on
cut to ~: **4** trim **5** adapt **6** tailor
for a queen: **5** regal, royal **9** luxurious
get ~: **3** jog **6** tone up **7** work out **8** exercise
have a ~: **4** boil, flip, fume, rage, rant, rave **5** erupt, freak, panic, steam, storm **6** blow up, lose it **7** explode, run riot, run wild **8** boil over, freak out, run amuck **9** go berserk, overreact **10** hit the roof
in: **2** go **4** gybe, jibe **5** blend, chime, yield **6** belong, cohere, relate **7** conform **9** make sense
in with: **2** go **4** gybe, jibe, mesh **5** agree, blend **6** accord, attune, belong, square **7** conform **8** dovetail **9** correlate, harmonize **10** coordinate, correspond
keep ~: **3** run **8** exercise
make ~: **4** suit **5** adapt, alter, amend **6** adjust, recast, remold, revamp, revise, tailor **7** correct, reshape **8** fine-tune, renovate
of temper: **3** ire, pet **4** huff, pout, rage, snit **5** blast, blaze, flash, scene, storm, surge **6** access, attack, flurry, frenzy, outcry, tirade **7** flare-up, tantrum, torrent **8** eruption, outbreak, outburst, paroxysm, upheaval **9** discharge, explosion, hysterics **10** conniption, outpouring
out: **3** rig **4** garb, gear, wear **5** array, dress, equip, ready **6** attire, clothe, gear up, get set **7** appoint, bedrape, furnish, prepare, provide **8** accouter, accoutre **9** caparison, provision
(out): **4** turn
physically ~: **4** trim **5** sound **6** robust **7** healthy
render ~: **10** capacitate
see ~: **5** deign **6** please **10** condescend
starter: **5** retro
to be tied: **3** mad **4** wild **5** angry, irate, livid, vexed **6** fuming, heated, piqued, raging, red-hot **7** boiling, enraged, furious, intense, steamed, violent **8** incensed, up in arms, wrathful **9** bummed-out, indignant **10** hysterical, infuriated
to farm: **6** arable **7** fertile **8** plowable, tillable **10** cultivable
together: **4** gybe, jibe, mesh, nest **6** hook up
up: **3** rig **4** deck **5** dress, equip **6** attire, bedeck, clothe, rig out, supply **7** deck out, furnish **8** accouter, accoutre **9** caparison
fit __: **4** to a T **6** to a tee, to kill
fit __ fiddle: **3** as a
fit __ king: **4** for a
fit __ T: **3** to a
fit __ tee: **3** to a
fit __ tied: **4** to be
__ fit: **5** drive, force, hissy, press
fit as a __: **6** fiddle
fitch: **6** weasel
relative: **4** mink **5** otter, ratel, sable, skunk, stoat, tayra **6** badger, ermine, ferret, marten **7** foumart, polecat **8** carcajou, foulmart, kolinsky, muishond **9** wolverine
Fitch: **3** Val **4** John
Fitchburg: **4** city, town
locale: **9** Wisconsin
Fitch, Val: **8** Nobelist **9** physicist
fit for __: **5** a king **6** a queen
fit for combining form: **6** -worthy
fitful: **5** jerky, jumpy, moody **6** patchy, uneven **8** off and on, restless, unstable, unsteady, variable **9** desultory, irregular, spasmodic, uncertain **10** capricious
fitfully: **8** off and on **9** piecemeal
fitness: **3** vim **4** dint, form, thew, trim **5** brawn, force, might, power, shape, thews, vigor **6** energy, fettle, health, muscle **7** aptness, muscles, potence, potency, stamina, utility **8** adequacy, aptitude, strength, vitality, wellness **9** condition, congruity, endurance, fortitude, hardiness, propriety, puissance, readiness, relevancy **10** brute force, competence, consonance, expediency, pertinence
center: **3** gym, spa **4** YMCA
equipment: **3** wts. **7** weights **8** Nautilus **9** dumbbells, treadmill
pro: **7** trainer
suffix: **7** -ability, -ibility
fits
by ~ and starts: **6** spotty **9** gradually, piecemeal
where one ~ in: **5** niche
fits and __: **6** starts
fitted: **8** suitable **9** qualified **10** tailor-made
out: **5** armed, ready
fitter: **6** better, tailor **8** clothier **9** couturier **10** dressmaker
__ fitter: **3** gas **4** pipe **5** steam
fitting: **3** apt, due, pat **4** good, just, meet, part, well **5** happy, piece, right **6** cogent, decent, proper, seemly, timely **7** adjunct, apropos, condign, correct, fixture, germane **8** apposite, becoming, decorous, deserved, feasible, relevant, rightful, suitable **9** accessory, advisable, agreeable, component, deserving, expedient, opportune, pertinent, praisable **10** adjustment, applicable, attachment, compatible, felicitous
measurement: **5** waist **6** inseam
not ~: **5** unapt **9** ill-suited **10** inapposite, malapropos, out of place, unsuitable
place: **5** niche
starter: **4** form, pipe **5** steam
tightly: **4** snug
use a ~ room: **5** try on
fitting __: **4** room
__ fitting: **3** gas **4** pipe **5** curve
__-fitting: **5** close, loose
fittingly: **4** well **5** right **9** correctly **10** adequately
fittings: **4** gear **8** fixtures, hardware **9** equipment
Fittipaldi, Emerson: **5** racer **9** auto racer
milieu: **5** track
fit to __: **4** a tee, kill
fit to be __: **4** tied
Fitzcarraldo (1982 film)
cast: Claudia Cardinale, Klaus Kinski
Fitzgerald: **4** Ella, Tara **5** Barry, Zelda **6** F. Scott, Pegeen **9** Geraldine
forte: **4** scat
Fitzgerald, Barry: **5** actor
film: And Then There Were None (1945)
Going My Way (1944, AA)
The Naked City (1948)
The Quiet Man (1952)
Tonight's the Night (1954)
Welcome Stranger (1947)
FitzGerald, Edward: **4** poet **7** British
translated him: **4** Omar **7** Khayyám
Fitzgerald, F. Scott: **6** author, writer
first name: Francis
wife: Zelda
work: The Great Gatsby
The Last Tycoon
Tales of the Jazz Age
Tender Is the Night
This Side of Paradise
Fitzgerald, Geraldine: **7** actress
film: A Child Is Born (1940)
Dark Victory (1939)
Flight From Destiny (1941)
The Last American Hero (1973)
Nobody Lives Forever (1946)
O.S.S. (1946)
The Pawnbroker (1965)
So Evil My Love (1948)
The Strange Affair of Uncle Harry (1945)
Three Strangers (1946)
Watch on the Rhine (1943)
Wilson (1944)
Fitzwater: **6** Marlin
five: **3** fin **6** number **7** respite
combining form: **4** pent- **5** penta- **6** quinqu- **7** quinque-
dollars: **3** fin
high ~: **8** greeting
in dice: **6** cinque
in French: **4** cinq
in German: **4** fünf
in Italian: **6** cinque
in Portuguese: **5** cinco
in Spanish: **5** cinco
o'clock shadow: **7** stubble
one of ~: **5** sense, sight, smell, taste, touch **7** hearing
take ~: **4** rest **5** break, pause, relax **6** recess, rest up **8** intermit
to Mohs: **7** apatite
five __: **6** senses
five __ rummy: **7** hundred
five __ shadow: **6** o'clock
five-__: **4** spot, star **6** finger, gaited
five-__ chili: **3** way **5** alarm
five-__ fire: **5** alarm
five-__ plan: **4** year
five-__ transmission: **5** speed
__ five: **4** hang, take **6** nine to
__-five: **4** high
Five __: **7** Corners, Nations
Five __ in a Balloon: **5** Weeks
Five __ More: **7** Minutes
Five __ Named Moe: **4** Guys
Five __ Pieces: **4** Easy
Five __ Pips, The: **6** Orange
__ Five: **3** Big **4** Jive, Take **5** Count
five-alarmer: **4** fire **5** blaze
Five Americans song: Western Union (1967)
five-and-__: **3** ten **4** dime
five-and-ten: **5** store **8** emporium
Five Came Back (1939 film)
cast: Lucille Ball, Wendy Barrie, Chester Morris
director: John Farrow
five-card stud: **4** game **8** card game
five-centime piece: **3** sou
Five Civilized __: **6** Tribes **7** Nations
Five Corners (1988 film)
cast: Jodie Foster, Tim Robbins, John Turturro
director: Tony Bill
Five Days in Paris author: Danielle Steel
five-digit number: **3** zip **7** zip code
Five Easy Pieces (1970 film)
cast: Susan Anspach, Karen Black, Fannie Flagg, Jack Nicholson
director: Bob Rafelson
Five Families author: Oscar Lewis
Five Finger Exercise author: Peter Shaffer
five-franc coin: **3** écu
Five Graves to Cairo (1943 film)
cast: Anne Baxter, Akim Tamiroff, Franchot Tone
director: Billy Wilder
Five Guys Named __: **3** Moe
Five Heartbeats, The (1991 film)
cast: Harry J. Lennix, Leon, Robert Townsend, Michael Wright
director: Robert Townsend
five hundred __: **5** rummy
five-in-a-row game: **4** keno **5** bingo, pente
Five Minutes More composer: **4** Cahn **5** Styne
Five Nations: **6** Cayuga, Mohawk, Oneida, Seneca **8** Onandaga
foe: **5** Huron
__ Five-O: **6** Hawaii
five o'clock shadow: **5** beard **7** stubble
Five Orange Pips, The author: Arthur Conan Doyle
fiver: **3** fin **4** bill
change for a ~: **4** ones
part: **3** dol. **4** buck **6** dollar
fivesome: **7** quintet **9** quintette
five-spot: **3** fin
Five Stairsteps song: O-o-h Child (1970)
five-star: **3** def, rad, top **4** aces, A-one, boss, braw, cool, dece, fine, gear, keen, neat, nice, phat, tuff **5** dandy, ducky, grand, great, marvy, neato, nobby, prime, slick, super, swell **6** bang on, bang-up, bonzer, bosker, choice, divine, dreamy, far-out, gnarly, groovy, lovely, peachy, slap-up, spot on, superb, terrif, tiptop, unreal, whizzo, wicked **7** amazing, awesome, capital, corking, general, perfect, ripping, skookum, stellar, sublime **8** dazzling, especial, eximious, fabulous, frabjous, glorious, heavenly, jim-dandy, slambang, smashing, splendid, standout, sterling, stickout, superior, terrific, top-level, topnotch, very good, wondrous **9** bodacious, Endsville, excellent, exemplary, exquisite, first-rate, high-grade, hunky-dory, marvelous, sollicker, topflight, unrivaled, wonderful, wunderbar **10** first-class, hotsy-totsy, jack-a-dandy, out of sight, peachy-keen, phenomenal, remarkable, stupendous, super-duper, unrivalled
monogram: **3** DDE
name: **3** Ike **4** Omar
Five Star Final (1931 film)

cast: 6 Marian Marsh, Edward G. Robinson, H.B. Warner
director: Mervyn LeRoy
___-Five Theses: 6 Ninety
Five thousand years ___...: 5 agone
five-way ___: 5 chile, chili
Five Weeks in a Balloon author: Jules Verne
Five Women author: 5 Jaffe
Five W's, one of the: 3 who, why 4 what, when 5 where
five-year ___: 4 plan
fix: 3 jam, lay, peg, pin, rig, set, tie 4 bind, bond, cook, cure, glue, lock, make, mend, mess, moor, nail, nuke, plot, rank, root, site, spay, spot, stop, tack, tune, vamp, weld 5 align, aline, amend, bribe, debug, embed, emend, focus, frame, imbed, limit, lodge, paste, patch, place, plant, price, prove, ready, right, rig up, rivet, see to, set up, solve, stamp, stare 6 adjust, anchor, arrest, assess, attach, buy off, cement, corner, decide, define, doctor, enroot, fasten, get set, harden, instal, instil, juggle, locate, make up, ordain, pickle, plight, punish, remedy, repair, replan, revamp, revise, scrape, secure, settle, square, tamper, tinker, tune up, wangle, whip up 7 agree on, arrange, correct, corrupt, dilemma, engrain, implant, imprint, ingrain, install, instill, patch up, pay back, prepare, rebuild, rectify, resolve, restore, specify, stay put, stiffen, tighten, touch up, work out 8 arrive at, conclude, entrench, get ready, hot water, make fast, maneuver, nail down, overhaul, position, put right, quagmire, quandary, regulate, rigidify, set right, solidify, solution 9 deep water, determine, do justice, establish, formalize, inculcate, microwave, plan ahead, preordain, reconcile, stabilize, sterilize, thumbtack, tight spot 10 difficulty, manipulate, prearrange, recompense, straighten, tamper with
a hole: 4 mend 5 patch 6 repair
clumsy ~: 5 kluge 6 kludge
firmly: 3 tie 4 etch, glue, moor, nail 5 embed, imbed, rivet 6 anchor, attach, fasten, secure 7 enchain, engrain, ingrain 8 bolt down, make fast
get a ~ on: 6 locate 8 identify, pinpoint 9 determine
in a ~: 5 stuck 7 stymied, trapped, up a tree 8 besieged, cornered, strapped, troubled 10 up the creek
in the mind: 4 etch 5 learn 8 remember
something to ~: 5 wagon
starter: 5 trans
up: 4 mend, redo, tidy, vamp 5 primp, renew 6 adjust, better, doctor, enrich, instal, polish, reform, revamp, supply 7 arrange, correct, enhance, furbish, furnish, install, mollify, provide, rectify, restore, sharpen 8 ornament, renovate 9 meliorate, reconcile, refurbish 10 ameliorate
upon: 4 pick 5 elect, favor 6 choose, opt for, prefer, select 9 single out
(upon): 6 decide
___ fix: 5 quick 7 running
Fix: 4 Paul
fixate: 4 dote 5 focus 6 obsess, zero in 7 stick on 9 preoccupy, stabilize
(on): 6 center
fixation: 5 craze, mania, thing 6 fetich, fetish, hang-up 7 complex 9 monomania, obsession
fixative: 3 gum 4 bond, glue 5 paste 6 cement 7 stickum 8 adhesive, mucilage
fixe
idée ~: 5 mania, thing 9 obsession
___ fixe: 4 idée, prix 5 blanc
fixed: 3 set 4 fast, firm, sure 5 given, right, rigid, solid, staid, stiff, tight, usual 6 frozen, glassy, intent, narrow, rooted, secure, stable, static, steady, strong 7 abiding, adamant, certain, decided, focused, limited, precise, rebuilt, regular, uniform 8 absolute, absorbed, constant, definite, enduring, immobile, implicit, ironclad, methodic, prepared, resolute, standing, stubborn 9 definable, good as new, immovable, ingrained, iron-jawed, permanent, steadfast, tenacious, unbending, unmovable, unpliable 10 back on-line, deep-seated, definitive, gridlocked, inflexible, invariable, mechanical, methodical, motionless, persistent, prevailing, purposeful, stationary, unchanging, unflagging, unwavering, unyielding
at ~ intervals: 6 cyclic, hourly, weekly, yearly 7 monthly, regular 8 cyclical, periodic 9 recurrent, recurring
become ~: 5 lodge 6 freeze, harden 7 stiffen 8 rigidify
for: 3 set 6 all set 8 geared up
(for): 5 ready
idea: 3 bug 6 hang-up 7 craving 9 monomania, obsession
look: 4 gaze 5 stare
not ~: 5 fluid 7 mutable 8 flexible, variable 9 adaptable, malleable, mercurial, unsettled 10 changeable, indefinite
order: 4 plan 5 setup 6 method, scheme, system 7 pattern, process, routine 8 practice 9 mechanism, operation, procedure, structure, technique
points: 4 loca, loci
routine: 3 rut 4 rote 7 rat race 8 monotony 9 treadmill
fixed ___: 3 oil 4 cost, idea, sign, star 5 asset, price, trust 6 charge 7 capital
fixed-___: 4 wing 5 price 6 income, length
fixed-___ mortgage: 4 rate
fixedly: 4 fast, hard 8 intently, steadily 9 immovably
fixedness: 7 loyalty 8 devotion, fidelity, firmness 9 adherence, certainty, constancy, diligence, eagerness, endurance, fortitude, frequency, integrity, stability 10 allegiance, attachment, continuity, doggedness, permanence, regularity, resolution, steadiness, trustiness, uniformity
fixer: 5 agent 6 broker 7 liaison 8 diplomat, mediator, repairer 9 go-between, moderator, repairman 10 negotiator
fixer-___: 5 upper
Fixer, The author: Bernard Malamud
fixing: 7 binding, curbing 8 limiting 9 confining 10 adjustment
___ fixing: 4 gold 5 price
Fixing ___: 5 a Hole
fix-it ___: 4 shop
Fix-it, Mr.: 8 handyman, repairer 9 repairman
fixity: 8 firmness 9 constancy, stability 10 permanence
fix one's ___: 5 wagon
fixture: 4 lock 7 fitting 9 accessory, appliance, component
fixtures: 4 gear 8 fittings, hardware, plumbing, supplies 9 apparatus, equipment, machinery, trappings 10 facilities
fixup: 6 repair
Fixx: 3 Jim 5 James
fizgig: 8 firework
fizz: 4 foam, hiss, soda 5 drink, froth 6 bubble, bubbly 7 bubbles, hissing, seltzer, sparkle 8 beverage, bubbling, club soda 9 champagne 10 effervesce, tonic water
add ~ to: 6 aerate
ingredient: 3 gin
lacking ~: 4 flat 5 still
___ fizz: 5 royal 6 golden, silver
fizzle: 3 die 4 fail, flop 6 sizzle 7 fatigue, founder, go kaput, misfire, sparkle, sputter 8 collapse
out: 4 fade, fail 8 languish, trail off
fizzler: 3 dud 4 bomb, bust, flop 7 failure, washout
fizzling sound: 4 pfft 5 pffft, phfft
fizzy: 5 foamy 6 bubbly
drink: 4 cola, soda 7 seltzer 8 club soda, root beer 10 tonic water
remedy: 5 Bromo
Fjall: 3 cow 4 bull 6 bovine, cattle
F-J connector: 3 GHI
fjord: 3 arm, bay 4 cove, gulf 5 basin, bight, firth, frith, inlet 7 estuary
country, to its people: 5 Norge
locale: 3 Nor. 4 Norw., Oslo 6 Norway
___ Fjord: 3 Lim 4 Oslo 7 Breidha
F-K connector: 4 GHIJ
___ F. Kennedy: 4 John 6 Robert
FL
see Florida
Fla.
it borders ~: 3 Ala., Atl.
living in ~ maybe: 3 ret. 4 retd.
time: 3 EDT, EST
see also Florida
flab: 6 tissue 9 spare tire
flabbergast: 4 daze, stun 5 abash, amaze, floor, shock, throw 6 boggle, puzzle 7 astound, nonplus, stagger, stupefy 8 astonish, blow away, bowl over, confound, surprise 9 dumbfound, overwhelm 10 disconcert
flabbergasted: 4 agog
flabbiness: 5 atony 6 atonia
flabby: 3 lax 4 limp, puny, soft, weak 5 baggy, frail, loose, slack, unfit, wimpy 6 anemic, atonic, droopy, effete, feeble, flimsy 7 anaemic, flaccid, fragile, untoned, wimpish 8 delicate, drooping, helpless, pithless, toneless 9 faltering, powerless 10 out of shape, vulnerable
become ~: 6 go soft
flaccid: 3 lax 4 limp, soft, weak 5 baggy, loose, slack 6 droopy, flabby, floppy 7 hanging, sagging, untoned 8 dangling, drooping
flack: 8 promoter 9 publicity 10 press agent
concern: 5 image
Flack, Roberta
song: The Closer I Get to You (1978)
Feel Like Makin' Love (1974)
The First Time Ever I Saw Your Face (1972)
Killing Me Softly With His Song (1973)
Set the Night to Music (1991)
Tonight, I Celebrate My Love (1983)
Where Is the Love (1972)
flacon: 5 flask 6 bottle 9 container
flag: 3 ebb, lag, sag, sap, std., tab 4 fade, fall, hail, iris, jack, jade, name, sign, sink, tire, wane, wilt 5 abate, alert, blunt, droop, peter, plant, slump, trail, weary 6 banner, burgee, colors, emblem, ensign, flower, impair, loiter, pennon, reduce, shrink, signal, soften, weaken 7 decline, deplete, exhaust, fall off, fatigue, pennant, thin out 8 bookmark, enervate, enfeeble, get tired, gonfalon, languish, Old Glory, peter out, standard, streamer, taper off, tricolor, wave down 9 attenuate, banderole, undermine, Union Jack 10 debilitate, devitalize, Jolly Roger
American ~ color: 3 red 4 blue 5 white
blue ~: 5 plant 6 flower
country with a five-sided ~: 5 Nepal
down: 4 hail
ender: 3 man, men 4 pole, ship 5 staff, stick, stone
feature: 4 star 6 stripe
holder: 4 pole
maker: 4 Ross 9 Betsy Ross
military ~: 6 colors, ensign
nation with a green ~: 5 Libya
pirate ~ emblem: 5 skull 10 crossbones
raise a red ~: 4 warn 5 alert 6 tip off 7 caution
red ~: 6 caveat
roll up a ~: 4 furl
show a white ~: 9 surrender
small ~: 6 fanion, guidon
symbol on Pakistan's ~: 4 lune
wave a red ~: 6 enrage 7 caution 8 forewarn
waver: 4 gale, wind 5 jingo 7 patriot
white ~: 5 pause, truce 7 respite 9 armistice, cease-fire, surrender 10 moratorium, submission
yacht ~: 6 burgee
flag ___: 4 rank, seat, smut 7 officer, station
flag-___: 5 waver 6 waving
___ flag: 3 red 4 blue, code, mail 5 black, green, guest, house, pilot, prize, sweet, water, white 6 powder, prayer, racing, yellow 7 crimson, protest
Flag ___: 3 Day
___ Flag: 5 Black
Flag Day grp.: 3 VFW
flagellate: 4 flog, lash, whip 5 birch, strap 6 switch 7 scourge 9 horsewhip
flagellation: 7 lashing 8 birching, flogging, whipping 9 scourging, strapping, switching
flagellum: 5 organ
Flagg: 6 Fannie
flagging: 3 ebb 4 lazy, limp, weak 5 seedy, tired, weary 6 wilted 10 knocked out
flagitious: 4 vile 7 heinous 8 unlawful 9 nefarious
flag of ___: 5 truce
flagon: 3 jug 5 crock, flask 6 bottle, carafe 7 amphora 8 decanter
filler: 3 ale 4 wine
flagpole: 4 mast, pole 5 staff
run up the ~: 4 test 5 hoist, raise
topper: 5 eagle
flagpole ___: 6 sitter
flagrancy: 6 horror 8 atrocity, enormity 9 grossness, immensity, magnitude
flagrant: 4 open, rank 5 awful, gross, utter 6 arrant, brazen, patent 7 blatant, extreme, glaring, heinous, obvious, rampant 8 dreadful, grievous, shameful, shocking, striking, unsubtle 9 atrocious, barefaced, egregious, flaunting, monstrous, nefarious, out-and-out, shameless 10 noticeable, outrageous, scandalous
flagrante delicto
find in ~: 4 nail 5 catch
in ~: 9 red-handed
Flagstad, Kirsten: 6 singer 7 soprano
specialty: 5 opera
flagstaff: 4 pole

Flagstaff: **4** city, town
locale: **7** Arizona
flagstone: **4** slab
lay ~ s: **4** pave
..._ flag was still there: **3** our
Flaherty, Robert: **8** director
film: Elephant Boy (1937)
Man of Aran (1934)
Nanook of the North (1922)
flail: **3** hit, tan **4** bash, beat, club, flap, flog, hurt, slug, sock **5** knock, smack, smite **6** batter, pommel, pummel, strike, thrash, thwack, writhe **7** scourge **9** cast about, horsewhip, truncheon
flair: **3** zip **4** bent, chic, dash, élan, feel, gift, head, nose, turn **5** éclat, forte, knack, oomph, style, taste, touch, verve **6** glamor, pizazz, splash, talent **7** ability, aptness, faculty, glamour, know-how, panache, promise **8** aptitude, artistry, elegance, hang of it **9** endowment, ingenuity **10** green thumb
Flair: **3** pen **7** felt tip
flak: **3** rap **6** outcry **7** dissent, protest **8** friction **9** criticism **10** complaints, opposition
flak _: **4** suit, vest **6** jacket
flake: **3** bit **4** chip, ditz, kook, peel, zany **5** scale **6** maniac, sliver, weirdo **7** oddball, peel off, shaving, speckle **8** laminate, splinter **9** character, exfoliate, screwball **10** desquamate
combining form: **5** lepid-, -lepis **6** lepido-
off: **4** molt, peel, shed **9** exfoliate
starter: **4** snow
flakes: **4** snow, soap **6** cereal **8** dandruff
_ flakes: **4** corn, soap
flaky: **3** odd, off **4** daft, zany **5** batty, dizzy, goofy, kooky, nutty, wacky, weird **6** absurd, kookie, screwy, whacky **7** erratic, jocular, oddball **8** aberrant, peculiar **9** eccentric, laminated, senseless **10** irrational, off-the-wall, unreliable
not ~: **4** sane, wise **5** lucid, sober, sound **6** steady **7** logical, prudent **8** balanced, rational, sensible, together **9** practical, pragmatic, realistic **10** reasonable, thoughtful
flam: **4** hoax, ruse **7** swindle **9** deception
flambé: **5** afire, burnt **6** burned, on fire **7** ignited
flambeau: **4** link **5** brand, torch **9** firebrand
Flamborough: **4** city, town
locale: **6** Canada **7** Ontario
flamboyant: **3** big **4** loud **5** gaudy, jazzy, showy, swank, vivid **6** flashy, florid, ornate, rococo, snazzy, swanky **7** dashing, flowery, splashy **8** splendid **9** bombastic, brilliant, elaborate, glamorous, grandiose, luxuriant **10** peacockish, rhetorical, theatrical
flame: **2** jo **3** joe, pet **4** baby, beau, burn, dear, fire, glow, jill, love, zeal **5** amour, angel, ardor, blaze, chéri, color, cooky, cutey, cutie, deary, ducky, e-mail, flare, flash, honey, leman, light, lover, lovey, novia, novio, shine, sugar, swain, sweet, wooer **6** bon ami, chérie, cookie, dautie, dearie, fervor, orange, steady, sweets **7** beloved, darling, dearest, dear one, flare up, passion, pigsney, reddish, schatzi, squeeze, sweetie, tootsie **8** chou-chou, cutie pie, dowsabel, dulcinea, ladylove, lovebird, macushla, paramour, precious, snookums, sugar pie, sweetums, truelove **9** bonne amie, boyfriend, coruscate, dreamboat, inamorata, inamorato, petit chou, valentine **10** girlfriend, heartthrob, honeybunch, incandesce, mavourneen, pilot light, sweetheart, sweetie pie, turtledove
color: **3** red **4** blue **6** orange, yellow
ender: **3** out **5** proof **7** thrower
fancier: **4** moth
name meaning ~: **6** Brenda
relative: **5** henna **7** pumpkin, saffron **8** hyacinth **9** tangerine **10** terra cotta
up: **4** fume **6** get hot, see red, seethe
flame _: **4** cell, tree **5** color **6** azalea, stitch
_ flame: **3** old
_ Flame: **4** Blue **5** My Old **7** Eternal
Flame and Shadow author: Sara Teasdale
Flame and the Arrow, The (1950 film)
cast: Robert Douglas, Burt Lancaster, Virginia Mayo
flamenco: **5** dance **7** alegras
Flame of New Orleans, The (1941 film)
cast: Bruce Cabot, Marlene Dietrich, Roland Young
director: René Clair
Flame Over India (1959 film)
cast: Lauren Bacall, Herbert Lom, Kenneth More
director: J. Lee Thompson
Flame rival: **4** Blue, King, Star, Wild **5** Bruin, Devil, Flyer, Oiler, Sabre, Shark **6** Canuck, Coyote, Ranger **7** Capital, Panther, Penguin, Red Wing, Senator **8** Canadien, Islander, Predator, Thrasher **9** Avalanche, Blackhawk, Hurricane, Lightning, Maple Leaf **10** Blue Jacket, Mighty Duck
flames: **4** fire **5** blaze **8** wildfire
felonious ~: **5** arson
in ~: **5** afire, fiery **6** ablaze **7** burning
Flames: **3** six **4** team
home: **7** Calgary
milieu: **3** ice **4** rink
org.: **3** NHL
sport: **6** hockey
Flame, The (1988 song) artist: Cheap Trick
flaming: **3** hot, red **5** afire, fiery, livid, lurid **6** ablaze, alight, ardent, fervid, red-hot, torrid **7** fervent, flaring, intense, zealous **9** brilliant **10** combustion, infuriated, passionate
Flaming _: **4** Star **7** Feather
Flaming Feather (1951 film)
cast: Sterling Hayden, Barbara Rush, Forrest Tucker
director: Ray Enright
flamingo: **4** bird, pink
kin: **5** stork
relative: **4** nude **5** melon **6** damask, salmon **7** apricot **9** carnation
Flamingo Kid, The (1984 film)
cast: Richard Crenna, Matt Dillon, Hector Elizondo, Jessica Walter
director: Garry Marshall
Flamingo Road (1949 film)
cast: Joan Crawford, Sydney Greenstreet, Zachary Scott
director: Michael Curtiz
Flaming Star: **4** film, song
artist: Elvis Presley
cast: Barbara Eden, Steve Forrest, Elvis Presley
director: Don Siegel
flammable: **8** burnable **9** ignitable **10** incendiary
gas: **6** ethane **8** dimethyl
_ Flam Man, The: **4** Flim
flan: **7** custard, dessert, pudding
ingredient: **3** egg **4** yolk
like ~: **4** eggy
Flanagan: **5** Tommy **6** Edward, Father **8** Fionnula
Flanders: **2** Ed **3** Ned
language: **7** Flemish
locale: **7** Belgium, Holland
medieval capital: **5** Lille
town: **5** Aalst, Alost
Flanders _: **5** poppy
_ Flanders: **4** Moll
_ Flanders, A: **5** Dog of
Flanders, Ed: **5** actor
film: MacArthur (1977)
True Confessions (1981)
TV: St. Elsewhere
flange: **3** lip, rib, rim **4** brim, edge, ring **5** bezel, ridge **6** collar **8** shoulder
flank: **4** meat, side **5** skirt, steak **6** haunch
combining form: **5** lapar- **6** laparo-
muscle: **5** psoas
muscles: **5** psoae, psoai
flank _: **5** speed, steak
flanker _: **4** back
flanking: **4** side **7** lateral **8** sideward, sideways, sidewise
flannel: **3** gas, rot **4** blah, bosh, bull, bunk, guff, jazz, jive, pooh, tosh **5** bilge, cloth, fudge, hokum, hooey, prate, stuff, trash, tripe **6** bunkum, bushwa, drivel, fabric, footle, gabble, gammon, gibber, havers, hot air, humbug, jabber, jargon, kibosh, piffle **7** baloney, blarney, blather, blether, boloney, bushwah, eyewash, flubdub, fustian, garbage, hogwash, inanity, rubbish, twaddle **8** buncombe, claptrap, falderal, falderol, flimflam, flummery, folderal, folderol, material, nonsense, slipslop, tommyrot, trumpery **9** banana oil, gibberish, kidstakes, moonshine, poppycock, rigmarole **10** applesauce, balderdash, bilge water, codswallop, double-talk, flapdoodle, galimatias, Jabberwock, mumbo jumbo, rigamarole, taradiddle
feature: **3** nap
fiber: **4** wool **6** cotton
in America: **9** washcloth
item: **3** PJs **5** shirt **7** pajamas **9** nightgown
flannel _: **4** cake **5** plant
_ flannel: **6** Canton, cotton, outing **7** Viyella
flannels: **5** pants **6** slacks **8** trousers
Flannery: **5** Susan **7** O'Connor
flap: **3** ado, bat, ear, tab, tag, wag **4** beat, fold, fuss, lobe, loll, riot, spat, stew, stir, to-do, wave **5** flail, furor, lapel, panic, shake, swing, tizzy, valve **6** billow, dither, flurry, fracas, hassle, hubbub, lather, pother, ruckus, thrash, tumult, uproar **7** agitate, aileron, bluster, clutter, ferment, flutter, overlap, scandal, turmoil, twitter, wrangle **8** argument, brouhaha, conflict, rowdydow, squabble **9** agitation, commotion, confusion, encounter **10** hullabaloo
airplane ~: **6** elevon
cap ~: **6** earlap
ender: **4** jack **6** doodle
gummed ~: **4** seal
one's gums: **3** gab, gas, jaw, rap, yak, yap **4** blab, chat, gush, talk **5** prate, run on, speak, spout **6** babble, gabble, gibber, jabber, natter, parley, yammer **7** blabber, blather, chatter, maunder, prattle, twaddle **8** converse, ramble on, spout off **9** go on and on **10** yakkety-yak
starter: **3** ear
tent ~: **3** fly
flap _: **4** door **5** hinge, valve
_ flap: **3** mud **5** split **6** Fowler **7** landing
flapdoodle: **3** gas, rot **4** blah, bosh, bull, bunk, guff, jazz, jive, pooh, tosh **5** bilge, fudge, hokum, hooey, prate, stuff, trash, tripe **6** bunkum, bushwa, drivel, footle, gabble, gammon, gibber, havers, hot air, humbug, jabber, jargon, kibosh, piffle **7** baloney, blarney, blather, blether, boloney, bushwah, eyewash, flannel, flubdub, fustian, garbage, hogwash, inanity, rubbish, twaddle **8** buncombe, claptrap, falderal, falderol, flimflam, flummery, folderal, folderol, nonsense, slipslop, tommyrot, trumpery **9** absurdity, banana oil, gibberish, kidstakes, moonshine, poppycock, rigmarole **10** applesauce, balderdash, bilge water, codswallop, double-talk, galimatias, Jabberwock, mumbo jumbo, rigamarole, taradiddle
flapjack: **4** cake **7** hotcake, pancake **10** battercake
acronym: **4** IHOP
in French: **5** crepe
mix: **6** batter
order: **5** stack
flapper dance: **10** Charleston
flapping: **7** beating, darting **8** flitting
stopped ~: **3** lit **4** alit
flaps, let down the: **4** slow
flare: **3** lip **4** boil, snap **5** blaze, flame, gleam, light, shine, spark, splay, torch, widen **6** beacon, signal, spread **7** blaze up, broaden, flicker, shimmer **8** outburst
send up a ~: **4** warn **5** alert **6** signal
up: **4** boil, rage, rave, rise **5** blaze, flame **6** ignite **7** bristle, explode, surface
warning ~: **5** fusee, fuzee
_ flare: **5** solar
flare-up: **4** gust **5** blaze **7** offense, tantrum **8** outbreak, outburst **9** explosion, hysterics
flaring: **3** hot **5** afire, fiery, lurid **6** ablaze, aflame, heated **7** blazing, burning, flaming
flash: **3** ray **4** beam, bolt, élan, jiff, look, snap, tick, wink, zoom **5** blaze, blink, burst, éclat, flame, gleam, glint, jiffy, light, scoop, shine, shoot, spark, speed, telex **6** dazzle, flaunt, glance, minute, moment, pizazz, recall, regard, second, signal, thrill **7** display, flicker, glimmer, glimpse, glisten, glitter, impulse, instant, lighten, radiate, reflect, release, shimmer, show off, sparkle, twinkle **8** outbreak, outburst, shoot out, telegram **9** container, coruscate, fulgurate, lightning, recollect, sensation **10** incandesce
ender: **3** gun **4** back, cube, over **5** board, light
flood: **5** spate **8** overflow
gone in a ~: **9** momentary
in a ~: **3** PDQ **4** fast **5** apace **6** presto **7** fleetly, hastily, quickly, rapidly, swiftly **8** pell-mell, speedily **9** forthwith, hurriedly, instantly, like a shot, on the spot, posthaste
news ~: **6** notice **8** bulletin, dispatch **10** communiqué, revelation
of lightning: **4** bolt
on: **6** recall **9** recognize, recollect
on and off: **5** blink
producer: **4** bulb **6** camera
flash _: **4** bulb, burn, card, lamp, tube **5** flood, point **6** memory **7** picture, welding
flash _ pan: **5** in the
flash-_: **4** lock **6** freeze **7** forward
_ flash: **3** in a, red **4** blue, news, open **5** green **6** bounce **7** bounced
Flash: **6** Gordon

Flashdance (1983 film)
cast: Jennifer Beals, Michael Nouri, Lilia Skala
director: Adrian Lyne
dog: 5 Grunt
role: 4 Alex
song: 6 Maniac
Flashdance ... What a Feeling (1983 song) artist: Irene Cara
Flash Gordon: 6 serial
foe: 4 Ming
locale: 5 Mongo
star: 6 Crabbe 9 Middleton
Flash Gordon (1980 film)
cast: Melody Anderson, Sam J. Jones, Topol
flashiness: 4 ritz 5 glitz, style
flashing: 5 light 6 ablaze, bright 8 meteoric 9 momentary
flash in the __: 3 pan
flashlight, British: 5 torch
flashy: 3 lit 4 bold, loud 5 aglow, fancy, gaudy, jazzy, ritzy, shiny, showy, swank, tacky 6 ablaze, brazen, bright, florid, frilly, garish, glitzy, lavish, ornate, rakish, snazzy, swanky, tawdry, tinsel, vulgar 7 beaming, blatant, blazing, fulgent, glaring, glowing, lambent, opulent, radiant, shining 8 colorful, dazzling, gleaming, glittery, luminous, lustrous 9 brilliant, decorated, elaborate, flaunting, glamorous, luxurious, sparkling, sumptuous, tasteless 10 flamboyant, ornamented, theatrical
one: 4 dude 5 sport
flask: 4 vial 5 phial 6 beaker, bottle, carafe, flacon, flagon 7 canteen 9 container
drink from a ~: 4 swig 5 snort 6 guzzle, imbibe
__ flask: 5 Dewar 6 powder, Reform
flat: 3 pad 4 arid, blah, co-op, drab, dull, even, home, mild, poor, room, shoe, tame, two-D 5 abode, banal, bland, condo, empty, flush, ho-hum, house, level, matte, needy, plane, prone, stale, suite, trite, vapid 6 boring, draggy, dreary, fallen, jejune, off-key, planar, rental, smooth, supine, walk-up 7 blowout, habitat, housing, insipid, lodging, lowland, planate, prosaic, regular, shallow, tedious, unwaxed 8 absolute, complete, lifeless, outright, puncture, quarters, sea-level, tiresome, unlively, unsalted 9 apartment, colorless, container, penniless, pointless, prosaical, prostrate, recumbent, residence, tasteless 10 absolutely, dullsville, flavorless, horizontal, lackluster, lusterless, monotonous, pedestrian, spiritless, unelevated, unexciting, uninspired, warmed-over
area: 5 pampa, plain, plane, shelf 7 prairie
broke: 4 poor 8 deprived 9 destitute, penniless, penurious
cause: 4 nail, tack 5 glass, shard
combining form: 4 plan-, plat- 5 plani-, plano-, platy-
container: 4 tray 5 plate 7 platter
dweller: 6 lessee, lodger, renter, roomer, tenant 7 boarder 8 occupant, resident
ender: 3 bed, car, top 4 boat, feet, fish, foot, iron, land, ware, ways, wise, work, worm 5 bread 6 bottom, footed, lander
fall ~: 4 bomb, bust, fail, flop, lose, miss, slip, trip 5 crash, flunk 6 blow it, falter 7 blunder, founder, go under, go wrong, misfire, misstep, stumble, wash out 8 collapse, flounder, lay an egg 9 strike out
finish: 3 mat 5 matte
fix a ~: 5 patch 6 repair
fixer's tool: 4 jack
in nothing ~: 3 PDQ 4 fast 5 apace 6 presto 7 fleetly, hastily, quickly, rapidly, swiftly 8 pell-mell, promptly, speedily 9 forthwith, hurriedly, instantly, like a shot, posthaste
lack: 3 air
leave ~: 4 jilt, quit 6 desert
lying ~: 5 level, prone 6 face up, supine 8 face down 9 recumbent 10 horizontal
make ~: 4 even 5 level 8 straight
not ~: 5 foamy, hilly, on key, sharp, steep
nothing ~: 6 minute, moment, second
on one's back: 6 beaten, laid up 7 forlorn 8 helpless 9 abandoned, destitute, powerless 10 friendless
out: 5 plain, swift, total, utter 7 hastily, rapidly, swiftly, totally 8 absolute, decisive, for a fact, promptly, specific, whole hog 9 decidedly, full blast, no mistake 10 conclusive, definitive, positively, thoroughly, unarguable
payment: 4 rent
sign: 5 to let
tire: 8 puncture
flat __: 3 bug, out 4 arch, back, bond, feet, knot, race, sour, tire 5 light 6 sennit, silver
flat __ board: 3 as a
flat __ pancake: 3 as a
flat-__: 3 out, saw 4 file, knit 6 footed, rolled 7 earther, grained
flat-__ boat: 6 bottom
flat-__ plotter: 3 bed
flat-__ press: 3 bed
__ flat: 3 mud 4 fall, salt, wing 5 adobe, tidal 6 alkali, double, French, granny 7 service
flat as a __: 5 board 7 pancake
flatbed __: 5 truck 7 trailer
flatboat: 3 ark 4 scow 5 barge
flat-bottomed boat: 4 dory, junk, punt, raft, scow 5 barge
flatfish: 3 dab 4 sole 5 brill 6 plaice, turbot 7 halibut, sand dab 8 flounder 9 Dover sole
flatfoot: 3 cop 6 copper 7 officer
flat-footed: 4 open 5 frank 6 candid, direct 7 unready 10 forthright, unprepared
flathead: 4 fish 5 screw 7 catfish
Flathead: 5 tribe 6 Indian 7 Amerind, Chinook
flatland: 5 plain, plane, table
South American ~: 5 pampa
Flatliners (1990 film)
cast: Kevin Bacon, William Baldwin, Julia Roberts, Kiefer Sutherland
director: Joel Schumacher
flatness: 3 rut 5 ennui 6 tedium 7 boredom 8 banality, dullness, monotony, vapidity 10 insipidity, uniformity
flat on one's __: 4 back
flats: 5 pumps, shoes 7 loafers, sandals 8 sneakers
flat-tasting: 4 blah 5 bland 7 insipid 10 flavorless
flatten: 2 KO 3 lay 4 deck, even, kayo, rase, raze, ruin 5 crush, floor, grade, level, plane, press, smash, wreck 6 abrade, debunk, ground, lay low, smooth, spread, squash, unfold 7 deflate, depress, even out, iron out, mow down, roll out, trample, unbuild 8 beat down, bulldoze, compress, demolish, knock out, level out, puncture 9 knock down, prostrate, spread out
flatter: 4 coax, hail, laud, puff, suit 5 adorn, exalt, extol, honor, toady 6 become, cajole, extoll, fawn on, praise, puff up, salute, stroke 7 acclaim, adulate, applaud, commend, enhance, glorify, lay it on, wheedle 8 beautify, blandish, bootlick, butter up, decorate, fawn over, gush over, inveigle, kowtow to, make up to, ornament, play up to, soft-soap, suck up to 9 embellish, glamorize, shine up to, sweet-talk 10 complement, compliment, look good on, overpraise, panegyrize
in a way: 4 copy 7 imitate
oneself: 4 brag 5 boast, pride
flatterer: 5 toady 6 fawner, flunky, lackey, yes man 7 booster, flunkey, lacquey 8 adulator, courtier, kowtower, servitor 9 sycophant
flatterers: 6 claque
flattering: 4 oily 7 candied 8 specious 9 laudatory
flattery: 3 oil 5 honor, kudos 6 homage, praise, salute 7 acclaim, blarney, coaxing, palaver, plaudit, puffery, tribute 8 accolade, cajolery, encomium, good word, stroking 9 adulation, laudation, panegyric, wheedling 10 compliment, exaltation
Flattery: 4 cape
locale: 10 Washington
flat-tire cause: 4 nail, tack 5 glass, shard
Flatt, Lester: 9 guitarist
partner: Earl Scruggs
flattop: 4 coif, mesa 6 hairdo 7 frigate, warship 8 coiffure, man-of-war 9 hairstyle 10 battleship
flatware: 4 fork 5 knife, spoon 6 silver
Flaubert, Gustave: 6 author, French, writer
character: 4 Emma
homeland: France
work: Madame Bovary
flaunt: 4 show 5 boast, flash, strut 6 dangle, parade 7 display, exhibit, show off, trot out 8 brandish, flourish, proclaim 9 advertise, brag about, broadcast, promenade 10 grandstand, wave around
one's feats: 4 brag 5 boast, spout, vaunt 7 lay it on, show off, swagger, talk big 9 gasconade
flaunting: 5 gaudy 6 flashy 7 blatant, fustian 8 flagrant
flautist: 5 piper
Flava __ Ear: 4 in Ya
flavor: 3 air 4 feel, hint, lime, mint, odor, salt, tang, tone, zest, zing 5 lemon, pep up, sapor, savor, spice, style, taste 6 infuse, orange, pepper, relish, season, spirit 7 essence, extract, quality, vanilla 8 infusion, licorice, overtone, sapidity, sourness, tartness 9 character, chocolate, Rocky Road, saltiness, seasoning, spiciness, sweetness, undertone 10 bitterness, strawberry
cool ~: 4 mint
enhancer: 3 MSG 4 herb, salt 5 spice
half a ~: 5 tutti 6 frutti
have the ~: 5 smack
sharp ~: 3 nip, zip 4 bite, kick, tang, zest, zing 6 relish 8 piquancy, pungency 9 spiciness
flavor __ month: 5 of the
flavored: 5 tinct
highly ~: 5 spicy, tangy, zesty 6 savory, strong 7 peppery, piquant, pungent, zestful
flavorful: 4 rich 5 sapid, spicy, tangy, tasty, yummy, zesty 6 savory, spicey, toothy 7 piquant, pungent 8 luscious 9 ambrosial, delicious, enjoyable, nectarous, palatable, toothsome 10 appetizing, delectable
flavoring: 4 herb, zest 5 sauce, spice 6 fennel, relish 7 essence, extract 9 condiment, seasoning
sans ~: 5 basic, plain 7 regular 8 straight 9 unadorned
flavorless: 4 blah, dull, flat 5 bland, vapid 6 watery 7 insipid 8 unsalted, unsavory 9 savorless, tasteless
flavorsome: 4 rich 5 sapid, spicy, tangy, tasty, yummy, zesty 6 savory, spicey, toothy 7 piquant, pungent 8 luscious 9 ambrosial, delicious, enjoyable, nectarous, palatable, toothsome 10 appetizing, delectable
flaw: 3 bug 4 blot, kink, scar, spot, typo, vice, wart 5 crack, error, fault, speck 6 defect, foible, glitch 7 blemish, failing, pitfall, scratch 8 drawback, weakness 9 deviation 10 deficiency, faultiness, inadequacy
minor ~: 4 dent, nick
__ flaw: 6 tragic
flawed: 3 irr. 5 irreg. 6 broken, faulty, impure, marred 7 damaged, lacking, unsound 8 fallible, impaired 9 defective, deficient, erroneous, imperfect, incorrect, sophistic, untenable
flawless: 4 good, just, nice, perf., pure 5 clean, exact, ideal, model, right, sound, valid 7 correct, factual, optimum, perfect, precise 8 absolute, accurate, finished, inerrant, peerless, spotless, unbroken, unerring, unmarred 9 faultless, foolproof, just right, undamaged, unsullied, untouched, virtuosic 10 consummate, immaculate, impeccable, infallible
flawlessly: 3 pat 4 to a T 6 to a tee 9 perfectly
flawlessness: 6 purity 9 precision 10 perfection
flax: 5 plant 6 flower
dampen ~: 3 ret
ender: 4 seed
fabric: 5 linen 7 fustian
name meaning ~: 5 Linus
pod: 4 boll
starter: 4 toad
flax __: 4 lily
flaxen: 3 tow 4 tawn 5 blond, color, sandy 6 blonde, golden, yellow 7 aureate 8 xanthous 9 yellowish
relative: 4 buff, corn, gold, lime, rust, sand 5 brass, coral, cream, lemon, maize, ocher, ochre, peach, rusty, straw 6 canary, chammy, citron, crocus, shammy, shamoy 7 apricot, chamois, citrine, jasmine, mustard, nankeen, old gold, saffron 8 daffodil, primrose 9 champagne, goldenrod, jessamine
flaxen-haired: 4 fair 5 blond 6 blonde
flaxlike fiber: 5 ramee, ramie
flay: 3 pan 4 lash, pare, peel, skin, slam, whip 5 blast, roast, strip 6 attack, berate, fleece, jump on, rip off 7 chew out, defraud, lambast, lecture, swindle 8 lambaste, strip off 9 castigate, criticize, excoriate, fustigate, light into, shoot down, skin alive
flea: 3 bug 4 pest 5 biter 6 chigoe, hopper, insect, jigger, vermin 7 chigger
ender: 3 bag, pit 4 bane, bite
genus: 5 tunga
in one's ear: 3 tip 4 clue, hint 6 tip-off 7 glimmer, inkling, whisper 10 glimmering, suggestion
market: 5 bazar 6 bazaar
market stipulation: 4 as is
market transaction: 6 resale
flea __: 6 beetle, circus, collar, market

flea-__: 6 bitten 7 flicker
__ flea: 3 cat, dog 4 sand 5 beach, water 6 chigoe, jigger
Flea __ Ear, A: 5 in Her
fleabag: 5 hotel 9 flophouse
like a ~: 5 dingy, ratty, seedy 6 crummy, shabby, shoddy, sordid 7 squalid 8 decrepit
flea in one's __: 3 ear
Flea, The author: John Donne
flèche: 5 spire 7 steeple 8 pinnacle
fleck: 3 bit, dab, dot 4 mark, mote, snip, spot 5 point, speck 6 dapple, mottle 7 speckle, stipple 8 particle
flecked: 6 dotted 7 dappled, mottled, spotted 8 freckled, spangled, speckled, stippled
flection: 3 bow 4 bend, fold 5 angle
Fledermaus: 3 bat
__ Fledermaus: 3 Die
__-fledged: 4 full
fledgling: 4 tiro, tyro 5 chick, owlet, young 6 cygnet, eaglet, newbie, novice, rookie 7 budding, learner, new hand, recruit, trainee 8 beginner, duckling, neophyte, nestling 9 greenhorn, youngster 10 apprentice, catechumen, tenderfoot
comment: 5 cheep
home: 4 nest
flee: 2 go 3 fly, lam, run 4 bail, blow, bolt, jump, scat, skip 5 break, elope, elude, evade, lam it, leave, scoot, scram, skirr, split 6 beat it, bug out, cut out, decamp, depart, desert, escape, get out, go AWOL, hasten, run off, skidoo 7 abscond, get away, go south, make off, retreat, run away, scamper, scatter, skip out, take off, vamoose 8 cheese it, clear out, fugitate, run for it, skip town, slip away, turn tail, withdraw 9 cut and run, disappear, hotfoot it, scurry off, skedaddle 10 break loose, fly the coop, get clear of, hightail it, make tracks, scamper off, take flight
from: 4 duck, shun 5 avoid, dodge, evade, shirk 6 bypass, eschew 7 abstain 10 circumvent
to a J.P.: 5 elope 6 run off 8 slip away
unable to ~: 5 at bay, treed 7 trapped 8 cornered 9 powerless
F. Lee __: 6 Bailey
fleece: 2 do 3 abb, con, rob 4 bilk, burn, clip, coat, flay, gull, hoax, milk, nick, pelt, pile, rook, ruin, take, wool 5 bleed, cheat, cozen, fluff, gouge, mulct, shaft, shear 6 denude, fabric, hustle, prey on, rip off, rope in 7 deceive, defraud, plunder, swindle 8 flimflam, hoodwink 9 bamboozle, victimize 10 overcharge
product: 4 yarn
source: 3 ewe, ram 5 llama, sheep 6 alpaca, vicuna
__ Fleece: 6 Golden
fleeced: 5 burnt, shorn 6 burned
fleece-seeking ship: 4 Argo
fleecing: 4 scam 5 bunco, theft 8 thievery
fleecy: 4 soft 5 downy, furry, nappy, plush, wooly 6 fluffy, woolly 7 squishy, velvety 8 cushiony, woollike 9 sheeplike
fleeing: 3 run 7 in a rush, retreat 8 on the run
fleer: 4 grin, jeer, mock 5 scoff, smirk, sneer 6 deride, heehaw 7 escapee, grimace 8 ridicule 9 make fun of, poke fun at 10 horselaugh
Fleer rival: 5 Topps
fleet: 4 fast, navy, spry 5 agile, brisk, hasty, quick, rapid, swift 6 argosy, armada, convoy, flying, nimble, racing, snappy, speedy, sudden 7 brigade, express, hurried, instant 8 flitting, flotilla, meteoric 9 breakneck 10 double-time, harefooted, hypersonic, supersonic, ultrasonic
initials: 3 USN, USS
member: 3 cab 4 boat, ship, taxi
of the ~: 3 nav. 5 naval
VIP: 3 adm. 7 admiral
worker: 4 hack 6 cabbie 7 trucker
fleet __: 7 admiral
Fleet __: 6 Street
__ Fleet: 5 Jo Van
fleet-footed: 5 agile
fleeting: 4 fast 5 brief, short 6 little 7 cursory, passing 8 meteoric, temporal 9 ephemeral, fugacious, momentary, temporary, transient 10 evanescent, short-lived, transitory, unenduring
fleetly: 3 PDQ 4 fast, soon 5 apace 6 presto 7 hastily 8 in a flash, in a jiffy, in no time, pell-mell 9 forthwith, hurriedly, instantly, like a shot, posthaste
fleetness: 5 haste, hurry, speed 8 alacrity, celerity, dispatch, rapidity, velocity 9 quickness, swiftness 10 expedition, promptness, speediness
Fleet's In, The (1942 film)
cast: Eddie Bracken, William Holden, Dorothy Lamour
Fleet Street: 5 press
Fleetwood: 3 car 4 auto, Mick 8 Cadillac
Fleetwood Mac
members: Nicks, McVie, Buckingham
song: Big Love (1987)
Don't Stop (1977)
Dreams (1977)
Go Your Own Way (1977)
Hold Me (1982)
Little Lies (1987)
Sara (1979)
Tusk (1979)
You Make Loving Fun (1977)
Fleetwoods
song: Come Softly to Me (1959)
Mr. Blue (1959)
Tragedy (1961)
Fleischer: 3 Max, Nat 7 Richard
Fleischer, Richard: 8 director
film: 10 Rillington Place (1971)
20,000 Leagues Under the Sea (1954)
Armored Car Robbery (1950)
Bandido (1956)
Barabbas (1962)
Compulsion (1959)
Crack in the Mirror (1960)
Doctor Dolittle (1967)
Fantastic Voyage (1966)
Follow Me Quietly (1949)
The Narrow Margin (1952)
The New Centurions (1972)
See No Evil (1971)
So This Is New York (1948)
These Thousand Hills (1959)
Tora! Tora! Tora! (1970)
Violent Saturday (1955)
Fleischmann's: 4 oleo 9 margarine
alternative: 6 Parkay, Shedd's 7 Promise 8 Imperial
Fleisher: 4 Leon
Flem: 6 Snopes
Fleming: 3 Art, Ian 4 Eric 5 Peggy, Renée 6 Andrew, Rhonda, Victor 9 Alexander
valve: 5 diode
__ Fleming: 5 Rhoda
Fleming, Alexander: 3 Sir 8 Nobelist
Fleming, Ian: 6 author, writer 7 British
alma mater: 4 Eton
character: Bond, Oddjob
homeland: England
work: Casino Royale
Chitty Chitty Bang Bang
Diamonds Are Forever
Dr. No
For Your Eyes Only
From Russia, With Love
Goldfinger
Live and Let Die
The Living Daylights
The Man With the Golden Gun
Moonraker
Octopussy
On Her Majesty's Secret Service
The Spy Who Loved Me
Thunderball
A View to a Kill
You Only Live Twice
Fleming, Peggy: 6 skater
Fleming, Renée: 6 singer 7 soprano
specialty: 5 opera
Fleming, Rhonda: 7 actress
film: Alias Jesse James (1952)
Cry Danger (1951)
The Great Lover (1949)
Gunfight at the O.K. Corral (1957)
Home Before Dark (1958)
Out of the Past (1947)
Pony Express (1953)
While the City Sleeps (1956)
Fleming, Victor: 8 director
film: Bombshell (1933)
Captains Courageous (1937)
Dr. Jekyll and Mr. Hyde (1941)
Gone With the Wind (1939, AA)
Red Dust (1932)
Test Pilot (1938)
Tortilla Flat (1942)
Treasure Island (1934)
The Way of All Flesh (1927)
The Wizard of Oz (1939)
Flemish: 8 language
cartographer: 8 Mercator
medieval ~ capital: 5 Lille
painter: 6 Rubens 7 Bruegel, van Dyck, van Eyck 8 Brueghel
poet: 7 Gezelle
Flemish __: 4 bond 5 giant 6 scroll
Flemish Feast in an Inn artist: 5 Steen
flesh: 4 pulp, skin 6 muscle 8 humanity 9 humankind
and blood: 3 kin 4 aunt, life, soul 5 being, uncle 6 cousin, family, sister 7 brother, kinfolk, sibling 8 relation, relative
combining form: 3 cre- 4 creo-, kreo-, sarc- 5 creat-, sarco- 6 creato-
in the ~: 4 here 6 bodily
like the ~ proverbially: 4 weak
make one's ~ crawl: 5 chill, panic, scare, spook 7 horrify, petrify, terrify 8 frighten 9 terrorize
out: 3 pad 4 fill 5 color 6 expand, fill in 7 inflate
press the ~: 5 lobby, stump 8 campaign, politick 10 shake hands
starter: 5 horse
thorn in the ~: 4 pain, pest 6 bother, gadfly, hassle 8 irritant, nuisance 9 annoyance
flesh __: 3 fly 5 color, wound
__ flesh: 5 goose, in the
Flesh (1932 film)
cast: Wallace Beery, Ricardo Cortez, Karen Morley
director: John Ford
flesh and __: 5 blood
Flesh and Blood author: Jonathan Kellerman
Flesh and Fantasy (1943 film)
cast: Charles Boyer, Edward G. Robinson, Barbara Stanwyck
Flesh and the Devil (1927 film)
cast: Greta Garbo, John Gilbert, Lars Hanson
fleshiness: 7 obesity 9 adiposity, bulkiness, plumpness, pudginess, stoutness 10 corpulence, portliness
fleshy: 4 soft 5 beefy, fubsy, heavy, obese, plump, pudgy, pursy, stout 6 chubby, portly, pyknic, rotund, stocky, zaftig, zoftig 7 adipose, paunchy, weighty 8 roly-poly, sensuous 9 corpulent, filled-out 10 overweight, well-padded
fruit: 4 pepo, pome 5 papaw
root: 5 tuber
fletch: 5 plume 7 feather
Fletch (1985 film)
cast: Joe Don Baker, Chevy Chase, Tim Matheson
director: Michael Ritchie
Fletcher: 6 Knebel, Louise, Markle 9 Christian, Henderson
Fletcher, Jessica doctor friend: 4 Seth
Fletcher, Louise Oscar: One Flew Over the Cuckoo's Nest
fleur-de-__: 3 lis, lys
fleur-de-lis: 4 iris 5 plant 6 emblem, flower
__-fleuve: 5 roman
__ Flew Over the Cuckoo's Nest: 3 One
flex: 3 bow, sag 4 arch, bend, curl, kink, loop 5 crook, curve, hunch, slump, stoop, yield 6 camber, slouch
ender: 4 time
one's muscles: 8 threaten
flex __: 5 point
Flex: 7 shampoo
alternative: 4 Pert 5 Prell, Suave, Wella 7 Finesse, Pantene
flexed, easily: 5 lithe
flexibility: 4 give, play 6 leeway, spring 7 freedom, pliancy
flexible: 3 lax 4 easy, kind, limp, mild, open, soft, wiry 5 fluid, lithe, loose, slack 6 aidful, clayey, gentle, kindly, limber, lissom, pliant, spongy, supple 7 clayish, clement, elastic, helpful, liberal, lissome, plastic, pliable, ruthful, sparing, springy 8 bendable, laid-back, merciful, moldable, obedient, obliging, placable, tolerant, yielding 9 adaptable, assuasive, compliant, easygoing, forgiving, indulgent, lightsome, lithesome, malleable, resilient, tractable, versatile 10 adjustable, forbearing, permissive, unexacting, unhardened
not ~: 4 firm 5 fixed, rigid, stern, stiff 6 flinty, mulish, steely, strict 7 adamant 8 hard-line, indurate, ironclad, obdurate, resolute, stubborn 9 hidebound, obstinate, pigheaded, steadfast, stringent 10 bullheaded, implacable
Flexible Flyer: 4 sled
flexor: 6 biceps, muscle
flexuous: 4 wavy 5 snaky 6 curved, zigzag 7 sinuous, turning, winding 8 twisting 10 circuitous, convoluted, meandering
flexure: 3 arc, bow 4 bend, fold, turn 5 angle, crook, elbow 7 bending, curving 9 curvature, sinuosity
flibbertigibbet: 3 oaf 4 ditz, fool, jerk 5 dummy, dunce, ninny, snoop, yenta 6 gossip, lubber, nitwit 7 dullard, jackass, meddler 8 busybody, quidnunc 9 blockhead, simpleton 10 nincompoop
flic: 3 cop 6 French 9 policeman
flick: 3 dab, pat, pic, tap 4 film, lick,

show, snap, tick, wink **5** movie, oater, throw, touch, whisk **6** fillip **7** picture **10** tearjerker
minor ~: **6** B movie
something to ~: **5** wrist
see also film, movie
Flicka: **4** mare **5** horse
Flick, Elmer: **6** Indian **10** outfielder
flicker: **3** ray **4** lick, wink **5** blink, flare, flash, gleam, shake, shine, spark, waver **7** glimmer, glisten, glitter, shimmer, sparkle, twinkle **9** luminesce
ender: **4** tail
__-flicker: **4** flea
flickering: **6** spotty, uneven **7** erratic, glowing, lambent **8** sporadic **9** irregular, spasmodic
flicks: **3** pix **6** cinema
__ fliegende Holländer: **3** Der
flier: **2** ad **3** ace **5** pilot **6** airman, insert, raffle **7** aviator, leaflet, war hero **8** aeronaut, circular, handbill, pamphlet
see also airline, bird
flies
as the crow ~: **6** direct, in a row, linear, unbent **7** unbowed **8** directly, straight **10** unswerving
catch ~: **4** shag, yawn
no ~ on: **3** hip **5** alert, sharp, smart **7** knowing **9** wide-awake **10** perceptive
to spiders: **4** diet, fare, prey
Flies, The author: Jean-Paul Sartre
flight: **3** lam, run **4** trip **6** escape, exodus, hegira, hejira, voyage **7** fleeing, getaway, journey, retreat, running, shuttle, soaring **8** aviation, movement, stairway, stampede **9** departure **10** volitation
abbr.: **3** arr., dep., ETA, ETD
advisory team: **3** ATC
board: **4** sked **5** sched. **8** schedule
crew member: **3** nav. **4** capt. **5** pilot **7** captain **9** navigator
delayer: **3** fog **4** snow **5** storm **8** blizzard
dir.: **3** ENE, ESE, NNE, NNW, SSE, SSW, WNW, WSW
ender: **6** worthy
in ~: **5** aloft **8** on the run **9** on the wing
inducer: **4** fear
of fancy: **6** revery **7** reverie
part: **5** riser, stair
path: **6** ascent
pertaining to ~: **4** aero
prefix: **3** aer- **4** aero-
put to ~: **4** rout **5** panic, repel **7** overrun, repulse, scatter **8** chase out, stampede
record: **3** log
regulator: **3** FAA
route: **3** arc
science of ~: **11** aeronautics
sudden ~: **3** lam **6** escape **7** getaway
support: **5** newel
take ~: **2** go **3** run **4** bolt, flee, wing **6** decamp, escape **7** abscond, retreat **8** fugitate, withdraw **9** disappear
top-~: **4** A-one
unit: **4** step
word: **4** mach
flight __: **3** bag, cap, pay **4** deck, line, path, plan, suit **5** arrow, nurse, strip **6** leader **7** control, feather, officer, surgeon
__ flight: **4** free, take, test **5** put to, space **6** direct **7** capital, contact, nonstop
__-flight: **3** top
__ Flight: **5** First, Night
flight-accident investigators: **4** NTSB
Flight From Destiny (1941 film)
cast: Geraldine Fitzgerald, Jeffrey Lynn, Thomas Mitchell
flightiness: **5** mirth **6** levity **8** hilarity, nonsense **9** frivolity, merriment
flightless bird: **3** emu, moa **4** dodo, emeu, rhea **7** penguin
Flight of the Phoenix (1966 film)
cast: Richard Attenborough, Peter Finch, James Stewart
director: Robert Aldrich
flighty: **4** wild, zany **5** dizzy, giddy, light, moody, silly **6** fickle, giggly **7** aimless, wayward **8** flippant, skittish, volatile **9** frivolous, lightsome, mercurial, vagarious **10** capricious
flimflam: **2** do **3** con, gas, gyp, rot **4** bilk, blah, bosh, bull, bunk, burn, dupe, fool, guff, gull, hoax, hose, jazz, jive, nick, pooh, rook, scam, sham, take, tosh **5** bilge, bunco, cheat, fraud, fudge, hokum, hooey, pluck, prate, shaft, stuff, trash, trick, tripe **6** bunkum, bushwa, chisel, deceit, drivel, dupery, fakery, fleece, footle, gabble, gammon, gibber, havers, hot air, humbug, jabber, jargon, kibosh, piffle, rip off, take in **7** baloney, beguile, blarney, blather, blether, boloney, bushwah, deceive, defraud, eyewash, flannel, flubdub, fustian, garbage, hogwash, inanity, knavery, rubbish, swindle, twaddle **8** buncombe, claptrap, falderal, falderol, flummery, folderal, folderol, nonsense, pettifog, slipslop, tommyrot, trickery, trumpery **9** bamboozle, banana oil, deception, four-flush, gibberish, imposture, kidstakes, moonshine, poppycock, rigmarole, unethical, victimize **10** applesauce, balderdash, bilge water, codswallop, double-talk, flapdoodle, galimatias, Jabberwock, mumbo jumbo, rigamarole, taradiddle
guy: **5** cheat, quack, shark **6** bilker, con man **7** grifter, hustler, scammer **8** swindler **9** defrauder
Flim Flam Man, The (1967 film)
cast: Sue Lyon, Michael Sarrazin, George C. Scott
director: Irvin Kershner
flim-flammed, easily: **5** naive
flimsy: **4** lame, poor, puny, slim, soft, thin, weak **5** frail, gauzy, light, shaky, sheer, slack, tinny, wimpy **6** anemic, atonic, cheesy, effete, feeble, flabby, meager, sleazy, slight, unfirm, wabbly, wobbly **7** anaemic, chiffon, fragile, rickety, shallow, tenuous, trivial, unsound, wimpish **8** baseless, decrepit, delicate, gossamer, helpless, pithless, wretched **9** breakable, faltering, frangible, powerless, rinky-dink **10** cobweblike, diaphanous, improbable, inadequate, jerry-built, nondurable, ramshackle, tumbledown, vulnerable
Flin __, Manitoba: **4** Flon
flinch: **4** balk, jump **5** baulk, cower, quail, start, wince **6** blanch, blench, cringe, recoil, shrink **7** shy away **8** draw back, withdraw **10** shrink back
from: **4** hate **6** detest, loathe **7** despise
flinching: **3** coy, shy **4** meek **5** chary, timid **7** abashed, bashful, fearful **8** hesitant, sheepish **9** blenching, diffident, reluctant, shrinking, unassured, withdrawn
flinders: **6** pieces **7** slivers **9** fragments, splinters
Flinders: **5** range **6** Petrie **7** Matthew
locale: **9** Australia
Flinders, Matthew: **8** explorer
Flin Flon: **4** city, town
locale: **6** Canada **8** Manitoba
fling: **2** go **3** lob, peg, sow, try **4** cast, hurl, lark, send, shot, slam, stab, toot, toss **5** binge, chuck, crack, dance, heave, pitch, shoot, sling, spree, throw, trial, whack, whirl **6** effort, gamble, launch, let fly, propel **7** attempt, deliver, liaison, project, rampage, romance, scatter, splurge, venture **8** catapult
dirt: **4** slur **5** libel, smear, sully, taint **6** defame, impugn, malign, vilify **7** asperse, slander, traduce **8** besmirch, throw mud **9** disparage **10** calumniate
have a ~: **5** binge, revel, spree **6** cavort, frolic, gambol **7** carouse, roister, rollick **8** cut loose **9** celebrate, make merry, whoop it up
take a ~: **4** risk **6** gamble, hazard **7** venture **9** speculate
flint: **4** rock **5** silex, stone **6** quartz, silica **7** adamant, lighter, mineral
ancient ~: **6** eolith
creation: **5** spark
ender: **4** head, lock
starter: **3** gun **4** skin
successor: **5** match
tool: **5** burin
work with ~: **4** knap
flint __: **4** corn **5** glass
Flint: **4** city, town
locale: **8** Michigan
flinthead: **4** bird
flintlock: **3** arm, gun **5** fusil, rifle **6** musket
Flintstones, The (ABC sitcom)
boss: Slate
cast: Bea Benaderet (Betty Rubble)
Mel Blanc (Barney Rubble)
Don Messick (Bamm Bamm Rubble)
Alan Reed (Fred Flintstone)
Jean Vander Pyl (Wilma Flintstone, Pebbles Flintstone)
pet: Dino
setting: Bedrock
flinty: **4** firm, hard **5** cruel, rigid, rocky, stern, stony, tough **6** steely, stoney **7** hard-set, ice-cold **8** indurate, obdurate **9** impliable, unpitying **10** inflexible, iron-willed, unmerciful, unyielding
flip: **3** lob **4** cast, pert, rave, rude, snap, toss **5** chuck, crack, drink, fresh, go ape, nervy, pitch, sassy, saucy, throw **6** awless, brazen, cheeky, go wild, invert, jaunty, lose it, snippy, tumble **7** aweless, go crazy, uncivil **8** beverage, cocktail, coiffure, go postal, have a fit, impolite, impudent, insolent, snippety **9** blow a fuse, facetious, frivolous, go bananas, go berserk, go bonkers, hairstyle, out of line **10** hit the roof, irreverent, nonserious, somersault
a coin: **6** choose
coin ~ choice: **5** heads, tails
ender: **4** book
ingredient: **3** egg **4** wine **6** liquor, nutmeg
one's lid: **4** rage **8** freak out
over: **5** adore, enjoy, upend **10** appreciate
(over): **6** go wild
side: **6** option **7** reverse **8** opposite **9** inversion **10** antithesis
talk: **3** lip **4** guff, sass
through: **4** read, scan, skim **6** browse **8** look over
(through): **4** leaf, page
flip __: **4** side **5** a coin, chart
flip-__: **4** flap, flop
flip-__ circuit: **4** flop
Flip: **6** Wilson **8** Phillips
flip chart holder: **5** easel
flip-flop: **4** shoe **5** hedge, shift, thong, U-turn, waver **6** change, invert **7** quibble, reverse, whiffle **8** apostasy, exchange, footwear, reversal, variance **9** about-face, back-pedal, inversion, transpose, turnabout **10** conversion, turnaround
flip one's __: **3** lid, wig
flippancy: **4** sass **5** cheek, humor **6** levity **8** pertness **9** cockiness, freshness, frivolity, impudence, lightness, sauciness **10** cheekiness, disrespect, impishness, jocoseness, volatility
flippant: **4** pert, rude **5** fresh, nervy, sassy, saucy, smart **6** awless, brassy, brazen, cheeky, impish, jaunty, snippy **7** aweless, flighty, uncivil **8** impolite, impudent, insolent, snippety **9** facetious, out of line **10** irreverent
be ~ with: **3** kid **4** josh **5** tease
flippantly: **6** mildly **7** lightly **8** casually **10** carelessly, heedlessly
flipped: **4** amok **5** amuck, manic **7** berserk, bonkers, frantic, haywire, unglued **8** frenetic, frenzied, maniacal **9** delirious **10** bewildered
out: **6** raging, raving **9** wrought-up
flipper: **3** oar **5** pinna **6** paddle
Flipper (NBC adventure)
cast: Luke Halpin (Sandy Ricks)
Brian Kelly (Porter Ricks)
Tommy Norden (Bud Ricks)
pelican: Pete
title character: **7** dolphin
flip-up __: **5** visor
flirt: **3** toy **4** eyer, minx, vamp, wink **5** dally, ogler, tease, toyer, vixen **6** coquet, lead on, masher, trifle **7** toy with, trifler **8** coquette **9** libertine **10** make eyes at, trifle with
weapon: **5** hanky **6** hankie
with: **3** eye **4** ogle **6** gaze at, look at **7** stare at
flirtation: **4** idyl **5** idyll **7** romance **9** dalliance
flirtatious: **3** coy **7** playful, teasing
gesture: **4** wink
flit: **3** fly, gad, hie, rip, run, zip **4** dart, dash, race, rush, sail, skip, tear, whiz, zoom **5** drift, glide, hover, hurry, leave, scoot, shake, speed, steal, sweep, whisk **6** barrel, gallop, hasten, hustle, move it, rocket, scurry **7** floor it, flutter, hop to it, quicken, scamper **8** gad about, hurry off, step on it, volitate **9** hotfoot it, shake a leg, skedaddle **10** get a move on, hightail it
by: **5** glide **6** elapse
flitter: **4** hang **5** float, hover, shake
flitting: **4** fast **5** brief, fleet, quick, rapid, short **7** beating, darting **8** flapping **9** ephemeral, momentary, temporary, transient **10** evanescent, shortlived, transitory, unenduring
flivver: **3** car **4** auto **5** crate **6** jalopy **10** automobile, rattletrap
part: **5** choke
Flix: **7** channel
alternative: **3** AMC, HBO, IFC, SHO, TMC **5** Bravo, Starz **6** Encore **7** Cinemax **8** Showtime, Sundance
offering: **4** film **5** movie
Flo: **5** Hyman **8** Ziegfeld
boss: **3** Mel
coworker: **4** Vera **5** Alice
Flo __ Award: **5** Hyman
Flo-__: **2** Jo
__-Flo: **3** Sta
float: **3** bob **4** boat, buoy, hang, sail, skim, swim, waft, wash **5** drift, glide, hover, range **6** wander **8** beverage,

levitate, volplane 10 underwrite
don't ~: 4 sink
fishing ~: 4 cork 6 bobber, dobber
ingredient: 4 soda 5 syrup 8 ice cream
nautical ~: 7 caisson
place: 6 parade 7 pageant
to the top: 4 rise
float __: 4 bowl 5 a loan, glass, valve 6 bridge, switch 7 chamber
__ float: 4 back, bull, life, milk 5 prone
floatability: 8 buoyance, buoyancy
floater: 4 loan 5 tramp 7 release, vagrant 8 outsider, wanderer
flume ~: 3 log
pond ~: 3 pad
floating: 4 asea 5 aswim, at sea, awash, light, loose 6 adrift 7 buoyant, movable, unfixed 8 ecstatic, moveable, shifting, variable 9 lightsome, unsettled
platform: 4 boat, raft 5 barge
floating __: 3 rib 4 dock, gang, vote 5 heart, point, stock 6 island, policy, screed, supply
__-floating: 4 free
Floating City, A author: Jules Verne
floating island: 7 dessert
Float like a butterfly boxer: 3 Ali
__ Floats: 4 Hope
floaty: 7 buoyant
flock: 3 mob 4 army, bevy, herd, host, mass, meet, pack, pile 5 brood, bunch, covey, crowd, drove, group, laics, laity, press, stock, swarm, troop 6 gaggle, gather, huddle, legion, parish, rabble, throng 7 collect, company 8 assemble, assembly, converge 9 gathering, multitude 10 collection, congregate, worshipers
area: 4 nave
far from the ~: 4 lost 6 astray
funds from the ~: 5 tithe
hangout: 3 lea, ley 5 field 6 meadow 7 pasture
leader: 3 ram
leave the ~: 5 stray
member: 3 ewe 4 lamb 5 sheep 6 layman
of fowl: 5 skein
of mallards: 4 sute
of the ~: 4 laic 6 laical 7 secular 8 temporal
priest's ~: 4 fold 5 laity 6 parish
sound: 3 baa, maa 5 bleat
together: 3 mob 4 band, gang, herd 5 bunch, crowd, group, rally, swarm, troop 6 gather, muster, throng 7 cluster, collect, convene 8 assemble 9 aggregate 10 congregate
Flockhart: 7 Calista
flocks: 4 lots 5 hosts, loads, scads 6 crowds, droves, hoards, oodles, scores, swarms 7 legions, throngs 8 millions 9 livestock
floe: 3 ice 8 ice sheet
flog: 3 hit, tan 4 beat, belt, cane, drub, hurt, hype, lash, lick, sell, whip, whup 5 flail, smite, spank, whack, whomp 6 cudgel, larrup, paddle, punish, strike, thrash 7 lambast, promote, scourge, trounce 8 lambaste 9 castigate, horsewhip, publicize 10 flagellate
flogging: 6 hiding 7 lashing, tanning 8 flailing, whipping 9 switching, thrashing 10 punishment
flood: 4 glut, gush, load, pour, rain, rush, soak, spew, spue, tide 5 crowd, drown, flush, light, shock, spate, surge, swamp, swarm 6 bounty, deluge, drench, engulf, excess, ingulf, inrush, myriad, onrush, stream 7 cascade, congest, freshet, surplus, torrent 8 brim over, downpour, drencher, inundate, irrigate, overflow, plethora, submerge 9 abundance, avalanche, cataclysm, overwhelm, profusion 10 inundation, outgushing, outpouring, oversupply
control: 3 dam 4 dike 5 levee 10 embankment
control initials: 3 TVA
ender: 3 lit 4 gate 5 light, water
follower: 5 light
protect from ~: 4 dike 6 embank
residue: 3 mud
stage: 3 ebb 5 crest
survivor: 3 Ham 4 Noah, Shem 7 Japheth
the market: 4 glut 10 oversupply
flood __: 4 lamp, tide, wall 5 plain 7 control
__ flood: 5 flash
Flood: 4 Curt
flooded: 5 awash 6 packed 7 crowded, replete 8 brimming
floodgate: 4 door 5 hatch
floods, site of annual: 4 Nile
Flood, The author: Günter Grass
floodwater, like: 5 silty
flooey: 4 awry 5 amiss, askew
floor: 3 awe 4 deck, jolt, kayo, stun 5 addle, amaze, level, nadir, quota, shock, story, stump, throw, upset 6 baffle, bottom, cellar, defeat, lay low, puzzle 7 astound, confuse, conquer, flatten, landing, mystify, nonplus, perplex, stagger, startle, stupefy, unnerve 8 astonish, basement, bewilder, blow away, bowl over, confound, knock out, low point, surprise 9 dumbfound, knock down, mezzanine, overwhelm, prostrate, underside
access: 5 stair
bottom ~: 6 cellar 8 basement
cleaner: 3 vac 5 broom 6 mopper, vacuum 7 sweeper
clean the ~: 3 mop 5 sweep 6 vacuum
covering: 3 mat, rug, wax 4 lino, tile 6 carpet 8 linoleum
do the ~: 3 wax
ender: 5 board 6 walker
fix a ~: 5 repeg
hit the ~ hard: 5 stomp
in French: 5 étage
installer: 5 tiler
it: 3 fly, hie, rip, run, zip 4 dart, dash, flit, race, rush, tear, zoom 5 hurry, scoot, speed 6 barrel, gallop, hasten, hustle, rocket, scurry 7 quicken, scamper 9 get moving, shake a leg, skedaddle 10 get a move on, get hopping
mark: 5 scuff
model: 4 demo
mop the ~ with: 4 beat, rout
plan: 5 chart 6 design, layout, sketch 7 diagram, drawing, outline 9 blueprint, visual aid
space: 4 area
support: 4 beam, stud 5 joist 6 header
take the ~: 4 talk 5 orate, speak, spout 6 recite 7 lecture 9 hold forth, sermonize, speechify
top ~: 4 loft 5 attic 6 garret
walk the ~: 4 pace
floor __: 3 pan 4 lamp, loom, plan, show 5 model, price 6 broker, leader, pocket, sample, trader 7 furnace, manager
floor-__: 4 work 6 length, manage 7 through
__ floor: 3 fly, sea 4 deep 5 blind, first, plank 6 ground, second 7 selling
floorboards
like some ~: 6 creaky
sound: 5 creak
flooring
material: 5 vinyl
piece: 4 tile 5 board, plank
flooring __: 3 saw 4 brad
__ flooring: 7 parquet
floor model warning: 4 as is
floor plan: 6 design, layout 7 drawing
designation: 3 den, lav. 4 bdrm., door 5 attic 6 closet 7 bedroom, kitchen 8 basement, bathroom, lavatory 10 family room, living room
floor-show unit: 3 act
floors, like some: 4 waxy
flop: 3 dog, dud, sag 4 bomb, bust, drop, fail, fall, loll, lose, loss, play, slip, trip 5 droop, flunk, lemon, loser, slump 6 blow it, bounce, dangle, defeat, falter, fiasco, fizzle, mishap, sprawl, topple, tumble, turkey, turn in 7 blunder, debacle, failure, fizzler, founder, go kaput, go under, go wrong, misstep, stumble, washout 8 backfire, collapse, disaster, downfall, fall flat, flounder, lay an egg, plop down 9 strike out 10 nonsuccess
ender: 5 house, sweat
inclined to ~: 5 loppy 6 droopy
opposite: 3 hit 5 smash 6 winner 7 sellout, success, triumph 9 sensation
sound: 4 pfft 5 pffft, phfft
flop-__: 5 eared
__ flop: 5 belly
__-flop: 4 flip
flophouse: 5 hotel 7 fleabag
floppy: 4 disk, limp 5 baggy, slack 6 droopy 7 flaccid, hanging, sagging 8 dangling, diskette 10 ill-fitting
alternative: 5 CD-ROM
contents: 4 data
prepare a ~: 6 format
user: 2 PC 3 Mac 4 mini 5 micro 6 laptop 8 computer, notebook
floppy __: 4 disk
Flopsy brother: 5 Mopsy, Peter
Floptical __: 4 disk
flora: 6 plants 9 plant life 10 vegetation
fauna and ~: 5 biome, biota
migration: 6 ecesis
study: 6 botany
Flora: 5 Nwapa 6 Robson
flora and __: 5 fauna
floral: 7 botanic, flowery, verdant 8 blossomy
see also flower
__ Flor and Her Two Husbands: 4 Dona
Florence: 4 city, town 6 Kelley 7 Ballard, Harding 8 Chadwick, Eldridge, Lawrence 9 Henderson
locale: 5 Italy 7 Alabama 8 Kentucky 10 California
palace: 5 Pitti
river: 4 Arno
town near ~: 5 Lucca, Prato, Siena
Florence __-Joyner: 8 Griffith
Florentine: 5 onion
poet: 5 Dante
Florentine __: 6 stitch
Florentine, The (2000 film)
cast: Hal Holbrook, Michael Madsen, Mary Stuart Masterson, Christopher Penn
Flores: 3 Sea
locale: 9 Indonesia
florescence: 3 bud 5 bloom 6 flower 7 blossom 9 flowerage, flowering 10 blossoming
floret: 3 bud 5 bloom 7 blossom
Florey: 6 Howard, Robert
Florey, Howard: 8 Nobelist
Florian: 5 saint
floribunda: 4 rose 5 plant 6 flower
florid: 3 red 5 flush, ruddy, showy 6 blowsy, blowzy, flashy, ornate, rococo 7 baroque, blowsed, blowzed, flushed 8 colorful, reddened, rubicund, sanguine 9 beet-faced, elaborate, luxuriant 10 decorative, flamboyant, ornamented, rhetorical
Florida: 5 state
acquisition: 3 tan
bay: 5 Tampa 8 Biscayne 9 Apalachee, Pensacola
capital: Tallahassee
city: 4 Leto, Ojus 5 Brent, Davie, Largo, Miami, Ocala, Ocoee, Tampa 6 Apopka, De Land, Eustis, Naples, Oviedo, St. Pete, Stuart, Sunset, Weston, Wright 7 Brandon, Captiva, Deltona, Dunedin, Hialeah, Holiday, Jupiter, Kendall, Key West, Lantana, Margate, Miramar, Norland, Orlando, Palm Bay, Perrine, Sanford, Sanibel, St. Cloud, Sunrise, Tamarac, Tamiami 8 Aventura, Bellview, East Lake, Lakeland, Lakeside, Oak Ridge, Palm City, Pinewood, Sarasota, Ybor City 9 Boca Raton, Bradenton, Cape Coral, Carol City, Egypt Lake, Englewood, Ferry Pass, Fort Myers, Hollywood, Homestead, Immokalee, Kissimmee, Lake Worth, Melbourne, Mount Dora, Northdale, North Port, Palm Coast, Pensacola, Pine Hills, Plant City, Rockledge, Vero Beach 10 Bal Harbour, Boca del Mar, Citrus Park, Clearwater, Cocoa Beach, Cooper City, Dania Beach, Fort Pierce, Golden Gate, Greenacres, Hallandale, Land O'Lakes, Lauderhill, Miami Beach, Miami Lakes, North Miami, Palm Harbor, Panama City, Plantation, Port Orange, Spring Hill, Titusville, University, Warrington, Wellington, Winter Park 11 Delray Beach
conference: 3 SEC
county: 3 Bay, Lee 4 Clay, Dade, Gulf, Lake, Leon, Polk 5 Duval, Pasco 6 Citrus, De Soto, Glades, Orange, Sumter 7 Alachua, Flagler, Osceola, Volusia 8 Sarasota 9 Miami-Dade
explorer: 11 Ponce de Leon
footballer: 5 Gator, 'Nolee 8 Seminole
golf course: 5 Doral
Indian: 5 Miami 8 Mikasuki, Seminole
islands off ~: 7 Bahamas
islet: 3 cay, key
key: 3 isl. 4 isle, West 5 Largo 6 island 8 Biscayne, Longboat
lake: 10 Okeechobee
national park: 8 Biscayne 10 Everglades
neighbor: 7 Alabama, Georgia
one way to ~: 6 Amtrak
port: 5 Miami, Tampa 9 Pensacola
pro team: 4 Bucs, Heat 7 Jaguars, Marlins 8 Dolphins, Panthers 9 Lightning 10 Buccaneers
school: 7 Stetson
state gem: 9 moonstone
state mammal: 7 panther
state marine mammal: 7 manatee
state reptile: 9 alligator
state saltwater fish: 8 sailfish
state saltwater mammal: 8 porpoise
state shell: 10 horse conch
state tree: 8 palmetto
state wildflower: 9 coreopsis
theme park: 5 Epcot

Florida __: 4 Keys, moss, room 6 Strait 7 Current
Floridablanca: 4 city, town
locale: 8 Colombia
Florida State athletes: 5 'Noles 9 Seminoles
Florida State conference: 3 ACC
Florida Strait, city on the: 6 Havana
floridness: 9 euphemism, inflation, pomposity
florilegium: 8 analecta, analects
florin: 4 coin 5 Dutch, money 6 gilder, gulden 7 guilder
Florin: 4 city, town
locale: 10 California
Florissant: 4 city, town
locale: 8 Missouri
florist
need: 3 pot 4 vase
offering: 3 bud 5 bloom, roses 7 bouquet
floristics: 6 botany
Florsheim offering: 4 shoe
Flory, Paul: 7 chemist 8 Nobelist
floss: 4 fuzz 8 corn silk, filament 9 adornment
__ floss: 5 candy 6 dental
flossing advocates' org.: 3 ADA
flossy: 4 chic 5 downy, fancy, fuzzy, silky, slick 6 dressy, fluffy, frilly, satiny, silken, smooth 7 stylish, velvety, voguish 8 feathery, gossamer 9 gossamery, gussied up
flotation __: 6 device
flotilla: 4 navy 5 fleet, group 6 argosy, armada 10 naval force
flotsam: 5 lagan, ligan 6 debris, jetsam, jetsom 8 wreckage
partner: 6 jetsam, jetsom
flotsam and __: 6 jetsam
flounce: 4 toss 5 frill, strut, sweep 6 fringe, prance, ruffle
flounder: 3 dab 4 bomb, bust, fail, fish, flop, keel, lose, sink, slip, sole, toss, trip 5 botch, flunk, grope, lurch, pitch, slosh, waver 6 blow it, falter, fumble, muddle, plaice, plunge, squirm, totter, wallow 7 blunder, founder, go under, go wrong, misstep, stumble, wash out 8 fall flat, hesitate, lay an egg, struggle 9 cast about, feel about, hit bottom, strike out
in water: 6 splash
floundering: 4 asea 5 at sea, gawky, inept 6 clumsy, gauche, klutzy, oafish 7 awkward, gawkish, halting, unhandy 8 bumbling, bungling, cloddish, tactless, ungainly 9 all thumbs, graceless, lumbering, maladroit, stumbling, unskilled 10 blundering, left-handed, ungraceful, unskillful
Floundering (1994 film)
cast: John Cusack, Ethan Hawke, James LeGros
flour: 4 meal, mill 6 farina, powder
coat with ~: 6 dredge
combining form: 6 aleuro-
container: 3 bag 4 sack
make ~: 5 grind
Mexican corn ~: 4 masa
mixture: 5 dough 6 batter
process ~: 4 sift
product: 4 cake, roll 5 bread
sack weight: 5 ten lb.
sifter: 5 sieve
source: 3 oat, rye, soy 5 grist, wheat
flour __: 4 mill 6 beetle
__ flour: 3 soy 4 cake, clay, corn, fish, rock 5 bread 6 gluten, graham, patent
flourish: 2 go 3 win 4 boom, curl, dash, élan, grow, live, rise, show, wave 5 bloom, sweep, swing, swish, vaunt, verve, wield 6 abound, dangle, do well, flaunt, hack it, make it, pan out, paraph, spiral, stroke, thrive 7 blossom, burgeon, develop, display, fanfare, luck out, make out, prevail, prosper, succeed, swagger, tantara, triumph, work out 8 bourgeon, brandish, curlicue, curlycue, get ahead, go places, hit it big, make good, mushroom 9 luxuriate, make it big 10 decoration, strengthen
printing ~: 5 serif, swash 6 paraph
trumpet ~: 5 tusch 7 fanfare, tantara
flourishing: 4 hale, lush, rank, well 5 palmy 6 golden, robust 7 healthy, roaring, verdant, well-off 8 blooming, fruitful, thriving, vigorous 9 luxuriant 10 prosperous
floury: 5 mealy 7 powdery 8 granular
flout: 4 defy, gibe, jibe, mock 5 rebel, scoff, scorn, sneer, spurn 6 deride, ignore, insult, oppose, resist, revolt 7 disobey, scoff at, violate 9 disregard, go against, repudiate
flow: 3 run 4 gush, leak, move, ooze, pass, pour, purl, roll, rush, seep, stem, thaw, tide, wash 5 drift, exude, glide, issue, river, slide, spate, spirt, spurt, surge, swell, trend 6 abound, course, elapse, influx, liquid, motion, onrush, rhythm, series, spread, spring, squirt, stream 7 cascade, current, emanate, glide by, passage, process, trickle 8 fluidity, kinetics, movement, sequence, unfreeze 9 arise from, circulate, discharge, emanation, originate 10 continuity, outpouring, passageway
back: 3 ebb 4 fade, wane 5 abate 6 recede 7 dwindle, subside 8 slack off 9 retrocede
cash ~: 6 income 7 revenue 8 receipts
combining form: 4 -rhea, rheo- 5 -rrhea
ebb and ~: 4 flux, tide, wash 5 swing 6 billow 7 current 9 fluctuate, oscillate
(from): 5 arise 6 derive, result, spring 7 emanate, proceed 9 originate
go with the ~: 4 cope, roam, rove 5 agree, drift, get by, glide, mosey, yield 6 assent, give in, make do, manage, ramble, wander 7 make out, meander, saunter 9 acquiesce
heavy ~: 4 gush 5 flood, spate 6 stream 7 torrent 9 waterfall 10 inundation, outpouring
let ~: 4 open
measure: 3 amp, gph, gpm 5 cusec 6 ampere
opposite: 3 ebb
out: 4 spew, spue 5 bleed, drain, exude, spirt, spurt 6 effuse
outward ~: 3 ebb 4 tide 6 efflux, reflux 9 abatement, discharge, recession
over: 4 brim, well 5 spill
slowly: 4 ooze, seep 5 leach
starter: 3 air, mud 4 over, work
stop the ~: 3 dam 4 stem 5 block, check 6 arrest, cut off, stanch 8 hold back
together: 3 mix 4 join, meld 5 blend, merge, unify, unite 7 combine 8 converge 9 integrate
volcano ~: 4 lava 5 magma
flow __: 5 chart, sheet 7 breccia, diagram
__ flow: 3 ash 4 cash, gene 7 Couette, laminar, plastic
__ Flow: 5 Scapa
flow-chart command: 4 go to
flower: 3 mum 4 boom, flag, flax, glad, iris, lily, pink, posy, rose, sego 5 agave, aster, bloom, bluet, broom, camas, cream, daisy, elite, lehua, lilac, lotus, pansy, peony, phlox, plant, poppy, prime, stock, tulip, vetch, viola, yucca 6 acacia, annual, arnica, azalea, betony, cactus, camass, cosmos, crocus, dahlia, heyday, heydey, indigo, lupine, mallow, mature, maypop, mimosa, mullen, myrtle, orchid, oxalis, salvia, smilax, spirea, teasel, teazel, teazle, thrift, violet, yarrow, zinnia 7 aconite, anemone, arbutus, begonia, berseem, blossom, bulrush, burgeon, calypso, catalpa, cattail, comfrey, cowslip, day lily, dog rose, dogwood, figwort, foxtail, freesia, fuchsia, gentian, heather, hogweed, jasmine, jonquil, lobelia, mayweed, mullein, petunia, produce, prosper, ragwort, rambler, saffron, saguaro, spiraea, tea rose, thistle, trefoil, vanilla, verbena, veronia 8 aconitum, ageratum, amaranth, arethusa, asphodel, best part, bluebell, blue flag, boltonia, bourgeon, camellia, camomile, clematis, cyclamen, daffodil, dianthus, duckweed, erigeron, fireweed, foxglove, gardenia, geranium, gladiola, gloxinia, harebell, hawkweed, hawthorn, hepatica, hibiscus, hyacinth, japonica, laburnum, larkspur, lavender, magnolia, marigold, mosspink, moss rose, oleander, ornament, pilewort, primrose, rain lily, reed mace, rockrose, snowball, snowdrop, sweet pea, tamarisk, tidytips, trillium, tuberose, viburnum, wild rose, wistaria, wisteria 9 amaryllis, arrowhead, artichoke, bee target, bloodroot, buttercup, calendula, calla lily, candytuft, carnation, celandine, chamomile, cineraria, cockscomb, colicroot, columbine, corydalis, dandelion, edelweiss, eglantine, fairy lily, forsythia, gladiolus, goldenrod, ground ivy, groundsel, hollyhock, horehound, horsemint, hydrangea, impatiens, jessamine, mayflower, monkshood, narcissus, ohia lehua, Oswego tea, perennial, portulaca, pussy-toes, pyrethrum, rafflesia, redfescue, rudbeckia, safflower, santonica, snowberry, snow plant, sunflower, swamp pink, tiger lily, water lily, wolfsbane, woundwort 10 aspidistra, bitterroot, bluebonnet, bluebottle, buttonbush, coneflower, cornflower, damask rose, delphinium, Easter lily, fleur-de-lis, floribunda, frangipani, gaillardia, goatsbeard, heliotrope, Indian pipe, marguerite, mignonette, mock orange, motherwort, nasturtium, oxeye daisy, pennyroyal, periwinkle, poinsettia, ranunculus, snapdragon, stamen site, sweetbriar, sweetbrier, wallflower, zephyr lily
ancient Egyptian sacred ~: 5 lotus
aquatic ~: 5 lotus 8 duckweed 9 arrowhead, water lily
arrangement: 4 posy 5 spray 7 bouquet, nosegay
arranging: 3 art
bearded ~: 4 iris
bell-shaped ~: 5 tulip
blue ~: 4 flag, flax, iris 5 camas 6 camass, indigo, lupine, violet 7 aconite, gentian, veronia 8 aconitum, ageratum, boltonia, harebell, larkspur 9 columbine, ground ivy, hydrangea 10 cornflower, delphinium, periwinkle
brown ~: 7 bulrush, cattail 8 reed mace 10 aspidistra
bulbous ~: 4 glad 5 tulip
Central America: 6 dahlia
child: 5 hippy 6 hippie 8 bohemian, longhair
clove-scented ~: 4 pink
cluster: 5 ament, umbel 6 catkin
combining form: 4 anth-, flor- 5 antho-, flori-
corsage ~: 3 mum
cut ~: 4 stem
daisylike ~: 5 aster
dark-centered ~: 9 sunflower
desert ~: 5 agave, yucca 7 saguaro
display: 5 spray 7 bouquet, corsage
fall ~: 3 mum 5 aster
fragrant ~: 4 lily, pink, rose 5 lilac, stock 7 jasmine, tea rose 8 dianthus, gardenia, hyacinth, lavender, magnolia, moss rose, tuberose 9 carnation, jessamine, narcissus 10 damask rose, Easter lily, frangipani, heliotrope, mock orange, wallflower
funnel-shaped ~: 6 azalea
garden ~: 4 glad, iris, rose 5 aster, phlox, tulip, viola 6 azalea
garland: 3 lei
girl, often: 5 niece
green ~: 6 smilax 7 figwort 8 pilewort 10 mignonette
Hawaiian: 5 lehua
in ~: 6 abloom
in a Buddhist mantra: 5 lotus
in French: 5 fleur
in full ~: 4 ripe 6 bloomy, mature 7 matured 8 blooming
in Italian: 5 fiore
lavender ~: 4 lily 6 orchid, thrift 8 trillium, wistaria, wisteria 9 candytuft
lily-family ~: 5 yucca
location: 3 bed, pot, urn 4 vase 6 garden
meadow ~: 5 bluet
new ~: 3 bud
nursery rhyme ~: 4 posy
oak-tree ~: 5 ament 6 catkin
of chivalry: 6 knight
of forgetfulness: 5 lotus
oil: 4 atar, otto 5 athar, attar, ottar
orange ~: 5 poppy, tulip 6 cosmos 7 day lily 8 hawkweed, marigold 9 calendula 10 nasturtium, wallflower
orchidlike ~: 4 iris
pansylike ~: 5 viola
parasol-like ~: 5 umbel
part: 4 stem 5 petal, sepal, stalk 6 anther, carina
pink ~: 4 lily 5 lotus, peony 6 cosmos, lupine, mallow, mimosa, spirea, thrift 7 arbutus, begonia, dog rose, dogwood, freesia, rambler, spiraea, tea rose 8 arethusa, asphodel, camellia, geranium, hawthorn, larkspur, moss rose, oleander, tamarisk, wild rose 9 amaryllis, candytuft, corydalis, eglantine, hollyhock, hydrangea, mayflower, snowberry, water lily 10 bitterroot, bluebottle, cornflower, damask rose, delphinium, poinsettia, sweetbriar, sweetbrier
pink and white ~: 8 dianthus
pinkish-purple ~: 8 fireweed
potential ~: 4 seed
prickly ~: 6 teasel, teazel, teazle 7 thistle
purple ~: 3 mum 4 flag, iris 5 lilac, tulip, vetch 6 betony, crocus, maypop, orchid, violet 7 figwort, heather, saffron, thistle 8 boltonia, erigeron, foxglove, hepatica, hyacinth, lavender, wistaria, wisteria 9 candytuft, cockscomb, monkshood, wolfsbane 10 bluebottle, coneflower, cornflower, heliotrope, motherwort, pennyroyal

purple-red ~: **7** fuchsia **8** amaranth, cyclamen
rayed ~: **5** aster
red ~: **3** mum **4** lily **5** lehua, peony, poppy, tulip **6** cosmos, salvia **7** day lily, rambler **8** camellia, geranium, japonica, marigold, oleander, rockrose, tamarisk **9** amaryllis, candytuft, cockscomb, hollyhock, ohia lehua, Oswego tea, snow plant, woundwort **10** gaillardia, nasturtium, poinsettia
red-orange ~: **9** tiger lily
sepals: **5** calyx
showy ~: **3** mum **4** flag, iris, lily, rose **5** canna, lehua, lotus, pansy, peony, phlox, poppy, tulip **6** azalea, dahlia, orchid, salvia **7** day lily, fuchsia **8** hibiscus **9** calla lily, hollyhock, ohia lehua, tiger lily **10** delphinium, poinsettia, snapdragon
signature: **4** odor **5** aroma, scent **7** bouquet **9** fragrance
spring ~: **6** crocus
stalk: **4** stem **5** scape
starlike ~: **5** aster
starter: **3** cup, day, may, sun **4** ball, bell, cone, corn, foam, mist, moon, star, twin, wall, wand, wild, wind **5** bunch, globe, shell, straw **6** cuckoo **7** passion
thorny ~: **4** rose
top: **6** corona
varicolored ~: **4** glad, rose **5** canna, pansy, phlox, stock, viola **6** azalea, dahlia, oxalis, zinnia **7** anemone, comfrey, lobelia, petunia, verbena **8** clematis, gladiola, gloxinia, hibiscus, rain lily, sweet pea **9** carnation, cineraria, fairy lily, gladiolus, impatiens, portulaca, pyrethrum **10** floribunda, frangipani, snapdragon, zephyr lily
visitor: **3** bee
white ~: **3** mum **4** flag, iris, lily **5** camas, daisy, lilac, lotus, peony, poppy, tulip, yucca **6** camass, crocus, lupine, mallow, maypop, myrtle, spirea, thrift, violet, yarrow **7** aconite, arbutus, catalpa, dog rose, dogwood, freesia, hogweed, jasmine, jonquil, mayweed, rambler, saguaro, spiraea **8** aconitum, ageratum, asphodel, boltonia, camellia, erigeron, gardenia, hawthorn, hepatica, hyacinth, larkspur, magnolia, oleander, rockrose, snowball, snowdrop, tamarisk, trillium, tuberose, viburnum, wistaria, wisteria **9** arrowhead, bloodroot, calla lily, candytuft, colicroot, edelweiss, horehound, hydrangea, jessamine, mayflower, narcissus, pussy-toes, water lily **10** bluebottle, buttonbush, cornflower, delphinium, Easter lily, fleur-de-lis, goatsbeard, Indian pipe, marguerite, mock orange, oxeye daisy, poinsettia, ranunculus, spider lily
white and yellow ~: **8** camomile **9** calla lily, chamomile
willow ~: **5** ament **6** catkin
with a face: **5** pansy
with a white spathe: **5** calla **8** arum lily
world's largest ~: **9** rafflesia
wormwood ~: **9** santonica
wreath: **3** lei **4** haku **7** garland
yellow ~: **3** mum **4** flag, iris, lily **5** broom, tulip **6** acacia, arnica, cosmos, crocus, mullen, orchid, violet, yarrow **7** berseem, cowslip, day lily, freesia, jonquil, mullein, ragwort, tea rose **8** asphodel, daffodil, hyacinth, laburnum, marigold, primrose, rockrose, tidytips **9** buttercup, calendula, celandine, colicroot, corydalis, dandelion, forsythia, goldenrod, groundsel, horsemint, narcissus **10** goatsbeard, marguerite, nasturtium, ranunculus, wallflower
yellow-rayed ~: **9** coreopsis, owl's claws, rudbeckia, sunflower **10** coneflower, gaillardia

flower __: **3** bed, box, bud, bug, fly **4** girl, head **5** child, power **6** beetle
__ flower: **3** cut, ray, wax **4** coat, disk, musk, rock **5** state, tunic **6** basket, calico, monkey, tassel **7** balloon, pinxter, popcorn, trumpet
__-flower: **5** satin **6** sulfur **7** blanket, peacock, pelican
Flower: **4** toon **5** skunk
Flower __ Song: **4** Drum
__ Flower: **6** Cactus
flower bed: **4** plot **6** garden
covering: **5** humus, mulch **7** compost
foundation: **4** soil
smooth the ~: **4** rake
Flower Drum Song (1961 film): **7** musical
cast: Nancy Kwan, James Shigeta, Jack Soo, Miyoshi Umeki
composer: **7** Rodgers **11** Hammerstein
director: Henry Koster
flowered combining form: **7** -anthous, -florous
Flower Fables author: Louisa May Alcott
flowering: **5** prime **6** abloom, growth, spring **8** blooming, progress **9** evolution
flowering __: **4** flax, moss **5** maple, plant **6** quince **7** dogwood
Flowering Judas author: Katherine Anne Porter
Flowering Peach, The author: Clifford Odets
flowerless plant: **4** fern, moss
Flower Mound: **4** city, town
locale: **5** Texas
Flower Petal Gown sculptor: **4** Erté
flowerpot locale: **4** sill **5** ledge, shelf
flowers: **6** posies
encourage larger ~: **6** disbud
gather ~: **4** pick **5** pluck
goddess of ~: **5** Flora
in German: **5** rosen
in Italian: **5** fiori
like some ~: **6** abloom, annual **9** perennial
raise ~: **6** garden
ring of ~: **3** lei
Flowers: **7** Wayland
Flowers for Algernon author: **5** Keyes
Flowers in the __: **5** Attic
Flowers of Evil, The author: Charles Baudelaire
Flower Song: **4** aria
Flowers on the Wall (1965 song) artist: Statler Brothers
flowery: **5** showy **6** floral, ornate, rococo **7** pompous, stilted, verbose **9** elaborate, luxuriant, overblown **10** flamboyant, ornamented, rhetorical
language: **7** bombast **8** rhetoric **9** eloquence
name meaning ~: **6** Anthea **8** Florence
necklace: **3** lei
perfume: **4** atar, otto **5** athar, attar, ottar
recess: **5** bower
Flow Gently, Sweet __: **5** Afton
flowing: **4** soft **6** active, facile, legato, liquid, smooth **7** current, running **8** graceful, readable **9** emanation, plentiful **10** integrated
of ~ water: **5** lotic
rock: **4** lava **5** magma
together: **7** meeting **9** confluent **10** convergent
__ flowing with milk and honey: **5** A land
__-flown: **4** high
Floyd: **3** Ray **4** King **6** Cramer, Mutrux **9** Patterson
__ Floyd: **4** Pink
Floyd, Ray: **6** golfer
milieu: **5** links **6** course
org.: **3** PGA
Floy Joy (1972 song) artist: Supremes
fl. oz., one-sixth: **3** tsp.
flu: **3** bug **6** grippe **7** ailment
cause: **5** virus
down with the ~: **3** ill **4** sick **6** ailing, unwell **10** indisposed
have the ~: **3** ail **4** ache
like some ~: **5** viral
shot: **4** hypo
symptom: **4** ache, ague **5** chill, cough, fever
__ flu: **4** blue **5** Asian, swine **8** Hong Kong
flub: **3** err **4** boot, fail, goof, miss, muff, slip **5** boner, botch, error, fluff, lapse **6** blow it, boggle, bungle, foozle, foul up, fumble, goof up, mess up, slip-up **7** blunder, mistake, screwup **9** mishandle, mismanage
__ Flubber: **5** Son of
flubdub: **3** gas, rot **4** blah, bosh, bull, bunk, guff, jazz, jive, pooh, tosh **5** bilge, fudge, hokum, hooey, prate, stuff, trash, tripe **6** bunkum, bushwa, drivel, footle, gabble, gammon, gibber, havers, hot air, humbug, jabber, jargon, kibosh, piffle **7** baloney, blarney, blather, blether, boloney, bushwah, eyewash, flannel, fustian, garbage, hogwash, inanity, rubbish, twaddle **8** buncombe, claptrap, falderal, falderol, flimflam, flummery, folderal, folderol, nonsense, slipslop, tommyrot, trumpery **9** banana oil, gibberish, kidstakes, moonshine, poppycock, rigmarole **10** applesauce, balderdash, bilge water, codswallop, double-talk, flapdoodle, galimatias, Jabberwock, mumbo jumbo, rigamarole, taradiddle
fluctuate: **4** lick, sway, vary, yo-yo **5** pulse, range, shake, shift, swing, waver **6** change, seesaw, teeter **7** vibrate **9** alternate, hem and haw, oscillate, vacillate **10** ebb and flow
fluctuating: **5** fluid, shaky **6** spotty, uneven, zigzag **7** erratic, mutable, protean, varying **8** floating, periodic, unstable, unsteady, variable **9** mercurial, uncertain, vagarious **10** changeable
fluctuation: **4** sway **5** shift **6** bounce, change, motion **8** variance **9** variation, vibration **10** undulation
flue: **4** duct, pipe, tube, vent **6** airway **7** air duct, channel, chimney **10** air passage, smokeshaft, smokestack
material: **3** ash **4** soot
part: **6** damper
flue __: **4** pipe, stop
fluency: **4** ease **5** grace **8** facility, fluidity **9** eloquence, liquidity, readiness **10** smoothness
fluent: **4** easy, glib **5** vocal **6** facile, liquid, smooth **8** eloquent, graceful, readable, skillful **9** talkative **10** articulate, effortless, expressive, loquacious, well-spoken, well-versed
fluff: **3** err, nap **4** down, flub, fuzz, lint, muff, slip **5** error **6** bobble, fleece, fumble, miscue, slipup **7** blooper, blunder, misstep, mistake, stumble **8** feathers **9** eiderdown
cluster: **4** tuft
full of ~: **5** linty
up: **5** plump, tease, whisk
fluffy: **4** airy, soft **5** downy, furry, fuzzy, light, nappy, plush **6** creamy, fleecy, flossy, napped **7** squishy, velvety **8** cushiony **9** lightsome
Fluffy: **3** cat, pet **6** feline
flügelhorn: **4** wind **10** instrument
cousin: **6** cornet **7** trumpet
fluid: **3** liq., oil, sap, tea **4** ooze, soft **5** juice, runny, water **6** coffee, liquid, liquor, mobile, molten, nectar, serous, smooth, watery **7** aqueous, erratic, mutable, protean, running **8** flexible, shifting, solution, unstable, variable, wavering **9** adaptable, liquefied, malleable, mercurial, revocable, uncertain, unsettled **10** changeable, indefinite
body ~: **5** blood, humor, lymph, serum
container: **3** sac
not ~: **3** set **4** firm **5** fixed, solid **6** secure, stable, static **8** constant, definite **10** definitive, unchanging
of blood ~: **6** serous
plant ~: **3** sap **5** juice, latex, serum
rock: **4** lava
fluid __: **4** dram **5** drive, ounce **6** drachm
__ fluid: **5** brake **6** serous **7** cutting, lighter, working
fluidity: **4** ease, flow, flux **7** fluency **9** liquidity **10** smoothness
unit: **3** rhe
fluidize: **4** melt, thaw **7** defrost, liquefy, liquify **8** dissolve **10** deliquesce
fluid-ounce fraction: **5** minim
fluids, medical: **4** sera
fluke: **4** luck, tail **5** quirk **6** hazard **8** accident, fortuity **9** mischance **10** fortuitous, lucky break
Fluke (1995 film)
cast: Matthew Modine, Eric Stoltz, Nancy Travis
fluky: **3** odd **6** chance, random **7** oddball **9** hit-or-miss, unplanned **10** contingent, fortuitous, unexpected
flume: **5** chute **6** ravine, sluice, trough **7** channel, conduit **8** spillway **10** water slide
floater: **3** log
flummery: **3** gas, pap, rot **4** blah, bosh, bull, bunk, guff, jazz, jive, pooh, tosh **5** bilge, fudge, gruel, hokum, hooey, prate, stuff, trash, tripe **6** bunkum, bushwa, drivel, footle, gabble, gammon, gibber, havers, hot air, humbug, jabber, jargon, kibosh, piffle **7** baloney, blarney, blather, blether, boloney, bushwah, custard, dessert, eyewash, flannel, flubdub, fustian, garbage, hogwash, inanity, malarky, oatmeal, pudding, rubbish, twaddle **8** buncombe, claptrap, falderal, falderol, flimflam, folderal, folderol, malarkey, nonsense, slipslop, tommyrot, trumpery **9** amphigory, banana oil, gibberish, kidstakes, moonshine, poppycock, rigmarole **10** applesauce, balderdash, bilge water, blancmange, codswallop, double-talk, flapdoodle, galimatias, Jabberwock, mumbo jumbo, rigamarole, taradiddle
flummox: **4** fool, stun **5** addle **6** puzzle, rattle **7** confuse **8** confound
flummoxed: **4** asea, lost **5** at sea **7** baffled, out of it, puzzled **8** confused **9** mystified, perplexed **10** bewildered
__-flung: **3** far

__ Flung up to Heaven: 5 A Song
flunk: 4 bomb, bust, fail, flop, lose, slip, trip 6 blow it, falter 7 blunder, founder, go under, go wrong, misstep, stumble, wash out 8 fall flat, flounder, lay an egg 9 strike out
don't ~: 4 pass
letter: 2 ef 3 eff
flunky: 4 aide, pawn, tool 5 gofer, groom, toady, valet 6 butler, fawner, gopher, helper, jackal, lackey, menial, minion, yes man 7 footman, lacquey, servant 8 adulator, courtier, follower, henchman, hireling, kowtower, retainer, servitor, truckler 9 assistant, flatterer, sycophant, underling 10 bootlicker, handshaker, hatchet man
fluorescent: 4 bulb, lamp, tube 5 light
lamp filler: 5 argon
paint: 6 Day-Glo
fluoride: 4 salt
__ fluoride: 6 benzyl, silver, sodium 7 calcium, chromic, lithium
Fluorigard: 9 mouthwash
alternative: 3 Act 4 Plax 5 Scope 6 Signal 7 Lavoris 9 Listerine
fluorine: 3 gas 7 element, halogen
source of ~: 8 fluorite
fluorite: 7 mineral
rare white ~: 8 cryolite
to Mohs: 4 four
fluoroscope: 4 x-ray
flurries: 4 snow 6 powder, precip
flurry: 3 ado 4 blow, flap, fuss, gust, puff, rush, snow, stir, to-do 5 furor, haste, hurry, spasm, spirt, spurt, upset, whirl 6 action, breeze, bustle, hoopla, pother, rattle, ruffle, tumult 7 confuse, disturb, ferment, fluster, nonplus, perturb, turmoil, unhinge 8 bewilder, brouhaha, outburst, unsettle 9 commotion, confusion 10 discompose, disconcert, excitement
flush: 4 even, flat, full, glow, hand, rich, tint, wash 5 blush, clean, flood, level, rinse, scour, spurn 6 arouse, drench, florid, lavish, loaded, monied, redden, smooth 7 animate, cleanse, enthuse, inspire, moneyed, opulent, redness, wealthy, well-off 8 abundant, affluent, generous, in clover, inundate, prodigal, rosiness, squarely, well-to-do 9 abounding, ruddiness, well-fixed 10 exhilarate, in the dough, in the money, intoxicate, privileged, propertied, prosperous, well-heeled
game: 4 stud 5 poker
out: 4 hunt 5 chase, clean, erase, expel, purge, rinse, trace, track 6 ambush, banish, pursue, uproot 7 cleanse 8 exorcise 9 eliminate, overthrow
flush __: 4 girt, left 5 right
__ flush: 5 royal 6 monkey 8 straight
__-Flush: 4 Sani
flushed: 3 red 4 pink, rosy, warm 5 livid, ruddy 6 florid 8 blushing, rubicund, sanguine
__-flusher: 4 four
Flushing Meadows
locale: 3 NYC 4 Ashe, Shea 6 Queens 7 New York
sport: 6 tennis 8 baseball
team: 4 Mets
fluster: 4 faze 5 abash, addle, get to, mix up, shake, spook, throw, upset 6 bother, excite, flurry, lather, muddle, rattle, ruffle, stir up, work up 7 agitate, confuse, disturb, nonplus, perplex, perturb, unhinge, unnerve 8 befuddle, bewilder, confound, disquiet, psych out, unsettle 9 discomfit, embarrass, frustrate, give a turn 10 discompose, disconcert
flustered: 5 fazed 7 nervous 8 unstrung 9 unsettled 10 bewildered, distraught
flute: 4 fife, kink, wind 5 crimp, nguru, quena, titzu 6 crease, fujara, groove 7 shiwaya, talinka, tonette 9 corrugate
architectural ~: 5 stria
combining form: 3 aul- 4 aulo-
cousin: 4 oboe 7 piccolo
play a ~: 4 blow 5 trill
player: 5 piper
__ flute: 4 alto 6 fipple
Flute-Player, The role: 5 Elena
__ Flute, The: 3 Tin 5 Magic
Flutie, Doug: 2 QB
sport: 8 football
fluting: 5 crimp, stria 6 crease, groove 7 channel
flutist: 4 Mann 6 Galway, Rampal 10 Herbie Mann
flutter: 3 bat, fly, wag 4 bate, beat, flap, flit, fuss, lick, stir, wave, wink 5 blink, drift, hover, shake, throb, waver 6 ripple, ruffle, rustle, shiver, teeter, thrill, tremor, twitch 7 pulsate, tremble, vibrate 8 volitate 9 palpitate, toss about
flutter __: 4 kick, mill 5 wheel
fluttering sound: 5 trill
fluttery: 5 tense 6 jangly
flux: 3 run 4 rush, thaw, tide 6 change, liquid, motion, unrest 7 process, torrent 8 fluidity, kinetics, movement 10 alteration, ebb and flow, mutability, transition
magnetic ~ unit: 5 gauss, tesla
flux __: 4 gate 5 valve 7 density, linkage
fly: 2 go 3 bug, hie, rip, run, zip 4 bolt, dart, dash, flap, flee, flit, gnat, go by, lure, move, pest, race, ride, rush, sail, skim, skip, soar, tear, whiz, wing, zoom 5 break, dance, glide, hover, hurry, leave, midge, pop up, scoot, skirr, speed, sweep, swoop, whisk, zip by 6 ascend, aviate, barrel, decamp, dobson, elapse, escape, gallop, hasten, hustle, insect, move it, pass by, rocket, run off, scurry, skidoo, spring, travel, tsetse, tzetze, wing it, zipper 7 abscond, floor it, flutter, get away, hop to it, journey, make off, quicken, run away, scamper, skip out, take off, vamoose 8 clear out, glossina, hightail, levitate, make time, slip away, step on it, take wing, volation, volitate, volplane 9 barnstorm, cut and run, disappear, go swiftly, hotfoot it, make haste, shake a leg, skedaddle, steal away 10 bluebottle, get a move on, get hopping, hightail it
advance on a ~ ball: 5 tag up
African: 6 tsetse, tzetze 8 glossina
alone: 4 solo
artificial ~: 4 herl, lure
at: 3 hit 6 assail, attack, pounce 7 assault, lay into 9 light into, pitch into
(at): 4 have 6 strike 7 lash out
by: 4 flow, pass 6 elapse 8 slip away, tick away 9 transpire
cast a ~: 4 fish 5 angle
catcher: 3 web 5 honey
close a ~: 5 zip up
combining form: 3 myi- 4 myio- 5 musci-
down: 5 light, swoop 6 alight
eater: 4 frog
ender: 3 boy, way 4 away, boat, leaf, trap 5 blown, paper, sheet, speck, wheel, whisk 6 weight 7 catcher
fishing ~: 4 lure
fling a ~: 4 cast
go ~ a kite: 5 scram, split 6 beat it, begone 7 buzz off, get lost, take off 9 take a hike
half a ~: 3 tse
high: 4 soar
hit a ~: 4 loft, swat
house ~: 4 pest 8 irritant
in: 4 land 5 light 6 alight
in the face of: 4 dare, defy 6 oppose 7 disobey
in the ointment: 3 rub 4 flaw, kink, snag 5 catch, hitch, snafu 6 defect, kicker 7 problem 8 drawback
Japanese: 3 hae
let ~: 3 lob 4 cast, fire, hurl, send, toss 5 chuck, fling, heave, pitch, shoot, sling, throw 6 launch, propel 7 fire off
low: 4 buzz
off the handle: 4 rage, rant, snap 5 freak, go ape
on the ~: 7 hastily, quickly, swiftly 8 in a hurry, in motion, speedily 9 hurriedly
open: 4 gush 5 burst, erupt 7 explode
pop ~: 5 bloop 6 looper
starter: 3 bar, day, gad, may, med, saw 4 blow, deer, fire, gall, shad, shoo 5 catch, green, horse, house, stone, white 6 butter, damsel, dobson, dragon
swatter material: 4 mesh
the coop: 4 flee, skip 6 decamp, escape 7 abandon, abscond, go south 8 fugitate, jump bail 9 break away
tier: 6 angler 9 fisherman
to a spider: 4 prey
trajectory: 3 arc
trap: 3 web 5 mouth 6 cobweb
when donkeys ~: 5 nohow, no way 8 forget it 9 fat chance 10 impossible, not a chance
without an engine: 5 glide
fly __: 3 ash, net, rod 4 ball, book, high, line, loft, rail 5 block, floor, front, sheet 6 agaric 7 casting, gallery, swatter
fly __ face of: 5 in the
fly __ ointment: 5 in the
fly __ teeth of: 5 in the
fly __ the handle: 3 off
fly-__: 4 cast, over 7 fishing
__ fly: 3 bee, bot, dry, dun, let, pop, wet 4 blow, deer, frit, heel, tent, true 5 black, crane, drake, flesh, fruit, horse, March, on the, screw, shore 6 flower, hackle, pomace, robber, spider, stable, tsetse, tzetze, warble 7 cluster, harvest, Hessian, soldier, syrphid, tachina, vinegar
__, fly!: 4 Shoo
Fly: 5 river
constellation: 5 Musca
River locale: 9 New Guinea
Fly __ an Eagle: 4 Like
Fly __ the Moon: 4 Me to
Fly (1997 song) artist: Sugar Ray
__ Fly Away: 3 I'll 4 Let's
flyboy: 3 ace 5 pilot 6 airman 7 aviator 8 aeronaut
org.: 4 USAF
fly-by-__: 4 wire 5 night
fly-by-night: 5 shady 6 shifty 9 transient, trustless, unethical 10 improvised, short-lived, unreliable
fly-cast: 4 fish
fly casting: 5 sport
flycatcher: 4 bird 5 pewee 6 chebec 7 elaenia, elepaio 8 kingbird, kiskadee
relative: 9 sharpbill
__ flycatcher: 5 alder, least, silky 6 tyrant, willow 7 Acadian
flyer: 3 ace 4 bill 5 pilot, wager 6 airman, gamble 7 aviator, handout, leaflet, war hero 8 brochure, circular, handbill, pamphlet 9 broadside, navigator
fast ~: 3 SST
take a ~: 4 risk 6 gamble 7 venture
see also airline, bird
__ Flyer: 5 Radio
Flyer rival: 4 Blue, King, Star, Wild 5 Bruin, Devil, Flame, Oiler, Sabre, Shark 6 Canuck, Coyote, Ranger 7 Capital, Panther, Penguin, Red Wing, Senator 8 Canadien, Islander, Predator, Thrasher 9 Avalanche, Blackhawk, Hurricane, Lightning, Maple Leaf 10 Blue Jacket, Mighty Duck
Flyers: 3 six 4 team
milieu: 3 ice 4 rink
org.: 3 NHL
sport: 6 hockey
flyers, frequent: 6 jet set
fly-fish: 3 dap
fly-fishing: 5 sport
flying: 4 fast, high 5 aloft, avian, brisk, fleet, hasty, quick, rapid, swift, volar 6 aerial, elated, racing, speedy, travel, volant 7 express, hurried, instant, soaring 8 airborne, aviation, in the air, volitant 9 breakneck, galloping, momentary, on the wing 10 double-time, hypersonic, navigation, supersonic, ultrasonic, volitation
colors: 7 success, triumph, victory
emulate a ~ saucer: 5 hover
formation: 3 vee 7 echelon
go ~: 4 soar 6 aviate
high: 3 gay 4 glad 5 happy, merry, sunny 6 blithe, chirpy, elated, golden, joyful, joyous, upbeat 7 beaming, buoyant, chipper, content, gleeful, glowing, pleased, radiant, tickled 8 blissful, carefree, cheerful, ecstatic, exultant, gladsome, groovimg, jubilant, laughing, sanguine, thrilled, unbeaten 9 contented, delighted, fortunate, gratified, lightsome, overjoyed 10 optimistic, successful, triumphant, unbothered
in heraldry: 6 volant
machine: 4 giro 6 copter 8 autogiro
saucer: 3 UFO
with ~ colors: 4 fine, well 5 great 6 easily 7 handily 8 adroitly, smoothly, very well 9 hands down 10 skillfully, swimmingly
woe: 6 jet lag
flying __: 3 fox, jib 4 boat, bomb, bond, fish, frog, kite, mare, moor, wing 5 field, filly, jenny, lemur, mouse, robin, shear, squad, start 6 boxcar, bridge, carpet, circus, colors, column, doctor, dragon, lizard, saucer, tackle 7 gangway, gurnard, machine
__ flying: 4 send 7 contact
Flying __: 4 Home 6 Finish, Tigers 7 Dustbin, Machine
Flying __, The: 3 Nun 6 Deuces, Saucer
Flying __ to Rio: 4 Down
Flying Cloud: 3 car, Reo 4 auto
__ flying colors: 4 with
Flying Deuces, The (1939 film)
cast: Oliver Hardy, Stan Laurel
Flying Down to Rio (1933 film)
cast: Fred Astaire, Dolores Del Rio, Ginger Rogers
studio: 3 RKO
Flying Dutchman, The: 4 boat, ship 5 opera
character: 4 Erik, Mary 5 Senta 6 Daland
composer: 6 Wagner
setting: 6 Norway
Flying Finish author: Dick Francis
Flying Finn, The: Paavo Nurmi

Flying Fortress: 5 plane 6 bomber
crew: 6 airmen
Flying Grasshopper ingredient: 5 vodka
Flying Hero Class author: Thomas Keneally
Flying High star: 4 Lahr
Flying Leathernecks, The (1951 film)
cast: Jay C. Flippen, Robert Ryan, John Wayne
director: Nicholas Ray
Flying Machine song: Smile a Little Smile for Me (1969)
Flying Nun, The (ABC sitcom)
cast: Sally Field (Sister Bertrille)
Alejandro Rey (Carlos Ramirez)
Madeleine Sherwood (Mother Superior)
setting: convent, Puerto Rico
Flying Tigers (1942 film)
cast: John Carroll, Anna Lee, John Wayne
fly in the ___ of: 4 face 5 teeth
fly into ___: 5 a rage
Fly Like an Eagle (song) artist: Seal, Steve Miller Band
Fly Me to the ___: 4 Moon
Flynn: 3 Joe 5 Errol 7 Raymond
___ Flynn Boyle: 4 Lara
Flynn, Errol: 5 actor
film: Adventures of Don Juan (1949)
The Adventures of Robin Hood (1938)
Captain Blood (1935)
The Charge of the Light Brigade (1936)
The Dawn Patrol (1938)
Desperate Journey (1942)
Dive Bomber (1941)
Dodge City (1939)
Edge of Darkness (1943)
Gentleman Jim (1942)
Kim (1950)
Objective, Burma! (1945)
The Prince and the Pauper (1937)
The Private Lives of Elizabeth and Essex (1939)
San Antonio (1945)
The Sea Hawk (1940)
The Sisters (1938)
They Died With Their Boots On (1941)
spouse: Lili Damita
___ Fly Now: 5 Gonna
fly off the ___: 6 handle
flypaper: 4 lure
___-fly pie: 4 shoo
___ fly rule: 7 infield
flyspeck: 3 dot 4 iota, mote, spot 5 point
fly the ___: 4 coop
Fly, The (1958 film)
cast: David Hedison, Patricia Owens, Vincent Price
Fly, The (1986 film)
cast: Geena Davis, Jeff Goldblum
Fly, The (1961 song) artist: Chubby Checker
flytrap: 3 web 5 plant
feature: 5 hinge
___ flytrap: 5 Venus
___ Fly With Me: 4 Come
Fm: 4 elem. 7 element, fermium
100 for ~: 4 at. no.
FM: 4 band 5 radio
celeb: 2 DJ 6 deejay
choice: 3 sta., stn. 7 station
part: 4 Freq. 9 Frequency 10 Modulation
F. Murray ___: 7 Abraham
FNMA: 4 agcy. 6 agency
concern: 4 loan
part: 3 Fed., Nat. 4 Assn., Mtge., Natl. 7 Federal 8 Mortgage, National
f-number: 4 stop
foal: 4 colt 5 filly, horse 6 animal, equine
food: 3 hay 4 oats 6 fodder
like a ~: 5 leggy
parent: 3 dam 4 mare, sire
foam: 4 fizz, head, suds, surf, wave 5 froth, spray, spume 6 aerate, bubble, burble, gurgle, lather, seethe, simmer 7 bubbles, ferment 9 whitecaps 10 effervesce, frothiness
at the mouth: 4 rage, rave 6 see red, seethe 8 freak out
preceder: 5 styro
foam ___: 5 glass, metal 6 rubber
___ foam: 3 sea 7 plastic
foam-ball brand: 4 Nerf
foamed ___: 5 metal 7 plastic
foaming: 4 wild 5 soapy, sudsy 6 bubbly, frothy, yeasty 7 furious, lathery 8 agitated 9 turbulent
at the mouth: 4 wild 5 manic, rabid, upset 6 raging 7 frantic, unglued 8 agitated, frenzied, maniacal, unstrung, vehement 9 bummed-out, fanatical 10 freaked out, hysterical
foamy: 5 barmy, soapy, sudsy 6 frothy, yeasty 7 fizzing, lathery 8 burbling, unrinsed 10 carbonated, fermenting
fob: 5 chain
(off): 4 palm
fob ___: 3 off
___ fob: 5 watch
FOB
not ~: 3 COD
part: 4 Free 5 Board
focal: 7 central, pivotal 10 overriding
point: 3 hub 4 node, pith 6 center 8 cynosure 9 highlight
points: 4 loca, loci
focal ___: 4 area 5 plane, point, ratio 6 length
focalize: 5 unify 6 center 8 converge
Foch: 4 Nina 9 Ferdinand
Foch, Nina: 7 actress
film: The Dark Past (1948)
My Name Is Julia Ross (1945)
Spartacus (1960)
The Ten Commandments (1956)
The Undercover Man (1949)
fo'c's'le: 4 deck
say ~: 5 elide
focus: 3 fix, hub, nub 4 core, join, knub, look, meet, pith 5 angle, heart, level, merge, nexus, slant, stare, think, train, unite 6 adjust, center, direct, fixate, gather, home in, hone in, target, zero in, zoom in 7 keynote 8 assemble, converge, cynosure, look hard, polestar 9 highlight, spotlight, substance 10 centralize, ground zero
centers of ~: 4 loca, loci
in ~: 5 clear, sharp 8 viewable
lose ~: 4 blur 5 blear, cloud, muddy
main ~: 4 gist 5 tenor, theme, topic
on: 6 look at, take up, tend to 7 address 8 consider, deal with, mull over 10 take care of, think about
out of ~: 4 hazy 5 fuzzy 6 bleary, blurry 10 indistinct
perhaps: 4 zoom
focus ___: 5 group
___ focus: 4 back, deep, soft
___-focus: 4 auto
Focus: 3 car 4 auto, Ford 10 automobile
song: Hocus Pocus (1973)
Focus (2001 film)
cast: Meat Loaf Aday, Laura Dern, William H. Macy, David Paymer
focused: 4 rapt 5 fixed 6 intent 7 engaged, riveted 8 absorbed, hellbent, immersed 9 attentive, engrossed, wrapped up
Fo, Dario: 6 writer 7 Italian 8 Nobelist
fodder: 3 hay 4 corn, feed, food, grub, oats 5 grain, straw 6 clover, forage, leaves, silage, stalks 7 sorghum 10 cornstalks
___ fodder: 6 cannon
Fodor, Eugene: 9 violinist
foe: 4 anti, side 5 enemy, rival 7 invader, nemesis 8 attacker, opponent 9 adversary, aggressor, assailant, combatant, ill-wisher 10 antagonist, challenger, competitor, opposition
foehn: 4 wind
foeman: 4 anti, side 5 enemy, rival 7 invader, nemesis 8 attacker, opponent 9 adversary, aggressor, assailant, combatant, ill-wisher 10 antagonist, challenger, competitor, opposition
foetid: 4 foul, olid, rank 5 stale 6 frowsy, frowzy, rancid, rotten, smelly, stinky, strong 7 noisome, noxious, odorous, reeking, squalid, unclean 8 inedible, mephitic, stinking 10 malodorous
fog: 3 dim 4 blur, daze, haze, mist, smog, soup 5 brume, cloud, muddy, smaze, spray, vapor 6 muddle 7 becloud, confuse, obscure, pea soup, steam up 8 haziness, moisture 9 murkiness, obfuscate, pea-souper
ender: 3 bow, dog 4 horn 5 bound
in a ~: 4 asea, hazy, lost 5 at sea, dazed 7 out of it, puzzled 8 confused 9 perplexed, spaced out 10 bewildered
like ~: 3 wet 5 dense, misty
starter: 5 petti
up: 4 blur
fog ___: 3 gun 4 bank, drip 5 light 6 forest, signal
___ fog: 3 dry, ice 4 tule 5 black, steam 6 frozen, ground
___ Fog: 6 London
Fog author: Carl Sandburg
fogbow: 3 arc 6 seadog
Fogelberg, Dan
song: Hard to Say (1981)
Leader of the Band (1981)
Longer (1980)
Same Old Lang Syne (1980)
Fogel, Robert: 8 Nobelist 9 economist
Fogerty: 4 John
fogey: 4 dodo 6 codger, geezer 7 diehard 8 mossback 10 fuddy-duddy
___ fogey: 3 old
foggy: 3 wet 4 hazy 5 fuzzy, mirky, misty, murky, thick, vague 6 blurry, steamy 7 blurred, brumous, clouded, obscure, sunless, unclear 8 confused, nebulous, obscured, overcast, socked in 9 unfocused 10 indistinct
become ~: 4 blur 5 bedim, blear, cloud 6 muddle
Foggy ___: 6 Bottom
Foggy Day, A
city: 6 London
composer: 8 Gershwin
Fogo: 7 volcano
locale: 6 Africa 9 Cape Verde
Fog, The (1980 film)
cast: Adrienne Barbeau, Jamie Lee Curtis, Hal Holbrook, Janet Leigh
director: John Carpenter
fogy: 4 dodo 6 codger, geezer 7 diehard 8 mossback 10 fuddy-duddy
___ fogy: 3 old
fogyish: 5 fusty, passé, stale 6 stodgy 7 archaic, diehard 8 obsolete, outdated 9 old-school, out-of-date 10 antiquated
___ foi: 5 bonne
foible: 4 flaw, kink, vice 5 fault, lapse, quirk 6 defect, oddity 7 failing, frailty 8 bad habit, gambling, weakness 9 mannerism
foie gras: 5 liver 10 goose liver
foil: 4 beat, dash, defy, stop, wrap 5 avert, blade, cheat, check, cross, elude, metal, patsy, shake, stimy, stump, stymy, sword 6 baffle, bollix, defeat, hamper, outwit, rapier, scotch, stymie, thwart 7 buffalo, counter, prevent, ward off 8 contrast, laminate, outflank, preclude, shake off 9 frustrate, get around, hamstring, undermine 10 antithesis, circumvent, complement, counteract, disappoint
alternative: 4 épée 5 saber, sabre, Saran
kitchen ~: 5 Alcoa 8 Reynolds
like a ~: 5 blunt
material: 3 tin 5 metal 8 aluminum
starter: 3 air, jet 6 cinque 7 counter
use a ~: 5 fence
___ foil: 3 tin 4 gold 6 chaton, silver
Foiled again!: 3 bah
foist: 6 impose 7 force on, palm off, pass off 9 insinuate
Fokine: 6 Michel
Fokker: 5 plane 7 Anthony 8 airplane, warplane
foe: 4 Spad
folate: 3 vit. 7 vitamin 8 B vitamin
fold: 3 lap, pen, ply 4 bend, bust, fail, flap, give, ruck, tire, tuck, wrap 5 close, crimp, laity, plait, pleat, ridge, ruche, yield 6 crease, dog-ear, double, fess up, go bust, parish, pucker, relent, rumple, submit, wrap up 7 concede, crinkle, disband, dog's-ear, enclose, envelop, flexure, go broke, go under, inclose, plicate, succumb, wrinkle 8 collapse, flection, shut down 9 corrugate, surrender 10 capitulate, double over
anatomical ~: 5 plica 6 dewlap
cloth ~: 5 plait, pleat 6 crease
coat ~: 5 lapel
combining form: 5 ptych- 6 ptycho-
dweller: 3 ewe 4 lamb 5 sheep
in: 3 add
leave the ~: 4 roam 5 stray 6 depart, wander
over: 4 tuck
page ~: 6 dog-ear
starter: 3 pin 4 bill, gate, mani, many 5 blind, sheep 6 center 7 several
up: 2 go 4 bust, shut 5 close, yield
fold-___: 4 down
foldaway: 3 bed, cot
folder: 4 file 6 jacket, packet 7 dossier 8 pamphlet 9 portfolio
change the ~: 6 refile
words: 5 I'm out
___ folder: 4 file
folderol: 3 gas, rot 4 blah, bosh, bull, bunk, guff, jazz, jive, pooh, tosh 5 bilge, fudge, hokum, hooey, prate, stuff, trash, tripe 6 bunkum, bushwa, drivel, footle, gabble, gammon, gibber, havers, hot air, humbug, jabber, jargon, kibosh, piffle 7 baloney, blarney, blather, blether, boloney, bushwah, eyewash, flannel, flubdub, fustian, garbage, hogwash, inanity, rubbish, twaddle 8 buncombe, claptrap, flimflam, flummery, nonsense, slipslop, tommyrot, trumpery 9 banana oil, gibberish, kidstakes, moonshine, poppycock, rigmarole 10 applesauce, balderdash, bilge water, codswallop, double-talk, flapdoodle, galimatias, Jabberwock, mumbo jumbo, rigamarole, taradiddle
folding: 7 compact 8 portable
art: 7 origami

folding ___: 4 door, rule 5 chair, money, table
folds
arrange in ~: 5 drape, plait, pleat
Folengo, Teofilo: 4 poet 7 Italian
Foley: 3 Red, Tom 4 Axel 5 James 6 Thomas
Foley, James: 8 director
film: After Dark, My Sweet (1990)
At Close Range (1986)
Glengarry Glen Ross (1992)
Folgers: 6 coffee
alternative: 5 Sanka, Yuban 7 Melitta, Nescafé, Savarin 9 Hills Bros.
foliage: 4 leaf 5 frond 6 leaves 7 herbage, leafage, verdure 8 greenery 10 vegetation
destroy ~: 6 denude
full of ~: 5 dense, leafy 6 in leaf
folic acid: 3 vit. 7 vitamin 8 B vitamin
Folies Bergère
dance: 6 cancan
locale: 5 Paris 6 France
Folies Bergère (1935 film)
cast: Maurice Chevalier, Merle Oberon, Ann Sothern
director: Roy Del Ruth
folio: 4 leaf, page
folio ___: 5 verso
foliole: 4 leaf
folium: 5 layer 6 lamina
folk: 5 music, stock 6 humans, people, public 7 lineage 8 relative 10 population
ender: 3 mot, way 4 lore, moot, mote, tale, ways
hero: 4 icon, idol 9 celebrity
history: 4 lore 5 tales 6 fables 7 legends 9 tradition 10 traditions
like ~ songs: 4 anon., trad.
music instrument: 5 banjo
starter: 3 kin, men 4 work 5 towns, women 6 gentle
story: 4 tale 5 fable 6 legend 9 tradition
wisdom: 3 saw 5 adage, gnome, maxim, moral 6 byword, dictum, saying, slogan, truism 7 epigram, proverb 8 aphorism, apothegm 9 platitude 10 apophthegm
folk ___: 3 art 4 mass, rock, song, tale 5 dance, music, story 6 singer 7 singing, society
folk dance: 3 jig 4 hora, jota, reel
Hungary: 7 csardas, czardas
Portugal: 4 fado
Serbia: 4 kolo
Ukraine: 5 gopak, hopak
Folkestone: 4 port
locale: 7 England
Folketing locale: 7 Denmark
folkie: 4 Arlo, Baez, Joni 5 Dylan 6 Seeger 7 Guthrie 8 Bob Dylan, Joan Baez 10 Pete Seeger
instrument: 6 guitar
folklore: 4 myth 6 legend 7 culture
being: 3 elf 4 ogre 5 gnome, troll
folks: 3 kin 4 clan, ones 6 family, humans, people 7 parents 9 relatives
different ~: 4 rest 6 others
___ folks: 4 just
___ Folks: 3 Li'l 7 Oldtown
___ Folks at Home: 3 Old
Folks That Live on the Hill, The
author: Kingsley Amis
folksy: 4 cosy, cozy, homy 5 cozey, cozie, homey, plain 6 casual, earthy, low-key, modest, rustic, simple 7 natural 8 down-home, homespun, informal 10 unaffected, unassuming
folktale: 4 myth 5 story 6 legend 10 fairy story
folkways: 5 ethos, mores 6 custom, values 7 culture, customs, manners, society 9 ethnology, tradition
Follett, Ken: 6 author, writer
figure: 3 spy
work: Code to Zero
A Dangerous Fortune
Eye of the Needle
The Hammer of Eden
Hornet Flight
Jackdaws
The Key to Rebecca
Lie Down With Lions
The Man From St. Petersburg
The Modigliani Scandal
Night Over Water
On Wings of Eagles
Paper Money
The Pillars of the Earth
A Place Called Freedom
The Third Twin
Triple
follicle: 3 sac
___ follicle: 4 hair
Follies: 7 musical
composer: 8 Sondheim
___ Follies: 3 Ice
Follies fellow: Flo Ziegfeld
follow: 3 dig, dog, get, pan, see, tag 4 copy, grok, heed, mind, obey, tail 5 act on, adopt, bow to, catch, chase, ensue, grasp, mimic, segue, spy on, stalk, trace, track, trail, watch 6 absorb, accept, bend to, comply, dangle, do like, fathom, fulfil, go next, happen, mirror, pursue, result, rotate, take in 7 abide by, act upon, agree to, catch on, defer to, emulate, fulfill, go after, imitate, make out, monitor, observe, pattern, proceed, realize, reflect, replace, respect, succeed 8 adhere to, carry out, come next, displace, join with, listen to, live up to, practice, run after, supplant 9 accompany, apprehend, arise from, come after, conform to, consent to, cultivate, eventuate, grow out of, supersede, supervene, take after, track down 10 appreciate, comply with, comprehend, happen next, hold fast to, keep in step, toe the line, understand
as advice: 4 heed, obey 5 act on
closely: 3 ape, dog 5 hound, stalk 7 emulate, imitate
don't ~: 4 lead 9 supervise 10 show the way
(from): 4 come 5 arise
one's nose: 3 gad 4 roam, rove 6 ramble 7 meander, traipse 9 gallivant
orders: 4 heed, mind, obey 5 act on, bow to 6 accept, bend to, listen, submit 7 abide by, agree to, defer to, observe, stick to 8 adhere to, carry out 9 conform to, consent to, truckle to 10 comply with, keep in step, toe the line
secretly: 4 tail 5 spy on 6 shadow
the example of: 3 ape 4 copy 5 equal, mimic, rival 6 mirror 7 emulate, imitate, pattern, reflect 9 take after
through: 2 do 4 go on, last 6 attain, effect, finish, linger 7 carry on, deliver, execute, get done, persist, realize, succeed 8 bring off, carry out, complete, continue, plug away 9 discharge, keep going 10 accomplish, bring about, consummate, tough it out
up: 5 probe 6 pursue 8 check out, look into
follow ___: 3 out 4 shot, suit 5 along 7 through
follower: 3 fan, nut 4 buff, tail 5 freak, pupil, sheep 6 addict, cohort, helper, minion, rooter 7 acolyte, admirer, apostle, convert, copycat, devotee, fancier, flunkey, groupie, servant 8 adherent, believer, courtier, disciple, henchman, imitator, partisan, retainer, servitor, sidekick 9 attendant, layperson, proselyte, supporter, worshiper 10 aficionado
(suffix): 3 -ist, -ite
followers: 6 fandom, school 7 fan club 9 entourage
whom ~ follow: 3 ldr. 6 leader
___ Follow Him: 5 I Will
following: 4 cult, fans, next, then 5 after, later 6 behind, circle, coming, latter, public, school, serial 7 cortege, coterie, ensuing, later on, patrons, pursuit 8 groupies, in back of, regulars 9 adherents, afterward, attendant, clientele, deducible, entourage, hangers-on, imitative, in pursuit, patronage, posterior, presently, proximate, resulting 10 coming next, consequent, dependents, henceforth, in search of, sequential, subsequent, succeeding, successive, supporters, thereafter
and the ~: 5 et seq.
and those ~: 6 et seqq.
closely: 6 at heel
not ~: 4 lost 5 ahead, prior 7 earlier 10 beforehand
prefix: 3 epi-
that: 4 next, then 5 later 9 thereupon 10 afterwards
the ~ ones: 4 seqq.
Following the Equator author: Mark Twain
follow one's ___: 4 nose
follows
as ~: 4 thus
it ~ that: 4 ergo, then, thus 5 hence 9 therefore
Follows: 5 Megan
Follow That Dream: 4 film, song
artist: Elvis Presley
cast: Arthur O'Connell, Elvis Presley
follow the ___: 6 leader
Follow the Boys (1944 film)
cast: Marlene Dietrich, George Raft, Orson Welles
Follow the Fleet (1936 film)
cast: Fred Astaire, Ginger Rogers, Randolph Scott
composer: Irving Berlin
director: Mark Sandrich
studio: 3 RKO
follow the leader: 4 game
player: 4 aper
follow-through: 3 end 6 ending 10 conclusion, resolution
follow-up: 3 seq. 6 sequel
folly: 6 idiocy, lunacy 7 fatuity, foolery, inanity, madness 8 daftness, nonsense, rashness 9 absurdity, craziness, dottiness, frivolity, goofiness, silliness 10 imprudence
curse one's ~: 3 rue 6 bemoan, bewail, lament, regret, repent
___ Folly: 7 Seward's, Talley's
___ folly to be wise: 3 'tis
Folsom: 4 city, town
locale: 10 California
Folsom Prison Blues (1968 song)
artist: Johnny Cash
Fomalhaut: 4 star
foment: 4 abet, brew, spur 5 hop up, impel, raise, rouse 6 arouse, foster, incite, kindle, stir up, whip up, work up 7 aggress, agitate, enflame, inflame, promote, provoke, stirs up 8 engender 9 encourage, impassion, instigate, stimulate
anew: 5 resow
fomenter: 8 agitator, inflamer 9 demagogue
Fon: 8 language
locale: 5 Benin 6 Africa
fond: 4 warm 6 caring, doting, loving, tender 7 adoring, amatory, amorous, kissing, valuing 8 friendly, intimate, parental, romantic 9 amatorial
ardently ~: 4 gaga 5 giddy 7 smitten
au ~: 6 wholly 7 in depth, totally 8 from A to Z, in detail, whole hog 9 to the full 10 completely, thoroughly, to the limit
be ~ of: 4 like, love 5 adore, enjoy, go for 6 dote on, revere 7 care for, cherish, idolize, worship 8 hold dear, treasure
be too ~: 4 dote
gesture: 3 hug 4 kiss 6 caress
of: 6 keen on 7 stuck on, sweet on 9 partial to 10 cherishing, in love with
(of): 8 enamored
overly ~ one: 5 doter
Fonda: 4 Jane 5 Henry, Peter 7 Bridget
Fonda, Bridget: 7 actress
film: Aria (1987)
City Hall (1996)
Doc Hollywood (1991)
It Could Happen to You (1994)
The Road to Wellville (1994)
Scandal (1989)
A Simple Plan (1998)
Single White Female (1992)
Fonda, Henry: 5 actor
film: 12 Angry Men (1957)
Advise & Consent (1962)
The Best Man (1964)
A Big Hand for the Little Lady (1966)
Blockade (1938)
The Cheyenne Social Club (1970)
Drums Along the Mohawk (1939)
Fail-Safe (1964)
Fort Apache (1948)
The Fugitive (1947)
The Grapes of Wrath (1940)
How the West Was Won (1962)
Jesse James (1939)
Jezebel (1938)
The Lady Eve (1941)
The Longest Day (1962)
Madigan (1968)
The Magnificent Dope (1942)
The Male Animal (1942)
Mister Roberts (1955)
My Darling Clementine (1946)
Once Upon a Time in the West (1968)
On Golden Pond (1981, AA)
The Ox-Bow Incident (1943)
The Return of Frank James (1940)
Sex and the Single Girl (1964)
Spawn of the North (1938)
The Story of Alexander Graham Bell (1939)
Tales of Manhattan (1942)
There Was a Crooked Man ... (1970)
The Tin Star (1957)
Too Late the Hero (1970)
The Trail of the Lonesome Pine (1936)
Warlock (1959)
Welcome to Hard Times (1967)
The Wrong Man (1957)
Young Mr. Lincoln (1939)
You Only Live Once (1937)
Yours, Mine and Ours (1968)
spouse: Margaret Sullavan
Fonda, Jane: 7 actress
film: Agnes of God (1985)
Any Wednesday (1966)

Barbarella (1968)
Barefoot in the Park (1967)
California Suite (1978)
Cat Ballou (1965)
The China Syndrome (1979)
Coming Home (1978, AA)
The Electric Horseman (1979)
Julia (1977)
Klute (1971, AA)
Nine to Five (1980)
Old Gringo (1989)
On Golden Pond (1981)
Period of Adjustment (1962)
Stanley & Iris (1990)
Steelyard Blues (1973)
Sunday in New York (1963)
They Shoot Horses, Don't They? (1969)
spouse: Tom Hayden, Ted Turner, Roger Vadim
fondant: 5 candy **6** bonbon **10** confection
Fonda, Peter: 5 actor
film: 92 in the Shade (1975)
Dirty Mary Crazy Larry (1974)
Easy Rider (1969)
Futureworld (1976)
The Hired Hand (1971)
The Limey (1999)
Nadja (1994)
Outlaw Blues (1977)
Split Image (1982)
Ulee's Gold (1997)
title role: 4 Ulee
Fond du Lac: 4 city, town
locale: 3 Wis. **4** Wisc. **9** Wisconsin
__ fond farewell: 4 bid a
fondle: 3 pat, paw **5** touch **6** caress, cosset, stroke
fondness: 4 love **5** fancy, taste **6** desire, liking, regard, relish **7** passion **8** affinity, appetite, devotion, penchant, soft spot, weakness **9** affection **10** attachment, endearment, partiality, preference
fondu: 4 bend
fondue: 3 dip **6** cheese **9** appetizer
Fonseca: 4 gulf
locale: 7 Pacific
font: 4 City, Elan, face, pica, root, Saga, Skia, type, Zeal **5** Abadi, agate, Aldus, Arial, Basel, basin, Bembo, Boton, Dante, Delta, Devin, Didot, Dutch, elite, Emona, Gamma, Goudy, Imago, Kabel, Kalix, Norma, pearl, print, Romic, Sabon, Savoy, Swiss, Times, Weiss, Wilke **6** Aldine, Amasis, Apollo, Auriol, Avenir, Batang, Bodoni, Bulmer, Caslon, Catull, Caxton, Cerigo, Cooper, Corona, Cosmos, Delima, Dialog, Esprit, Fenice, Futura, Gareth, Geneva, Glypha, Gothic, Guardi, Joanna, Legacy, loving, Lucida, Maxima, Melior, Minion, Modern, Monaca, Myriad, Nofret, Odense, Optima, Orator, origin, Praxis, Quorum, Romana, Serifa, source, Syndor, Syntax, Tahoma, Utopia, Zurich **7** Amerigo, Barmeno, Bauhaus, Bergamo, Berling, Bookman, Calisto, Candida, Centaur, Century, Courier, Cremona, Cushing, Diotima, Electra, Formata, Korinna, Leawood, Matisse, Memphis, Origami, Pacella, Panache, Peignot, Photina, Plantin, Poetica, Present, Sassoon, Shannon, Spartan, Tiepolo, Tiffany, Univers, Vectora, Verdana, Walbaum **8** Broadway, Caecilia, Cantoria, Carniola, Compacta, Concorde, Fournier, Frutiger, Galliard, Garamond, Giovanni, Hadriano, Meridien, Minister, Novarese, Palatino, Perpetua, Playbill, Rockwell, Slimbach, Souvenir, typeface, wellhead **9** Helvetica **10** Avant Garde, Times Roman, wellspring
baptismal ~: 5 laver
widths: 3 ems, ens
Fontaine: 3 Fox **4** Joan **5** Frank
Fontaine, Joan: 7 actress
film: The Bigamist (1953)
Casanova's Big Night (1954)
The Constant Nymph (1943)
A Damsel in Distress (1937)
The Devil's Own (1966)
Frenchman's Creek (1944)
From This Day Forward (1946)
Gunga Din (1939)
Ivanhoe (1952)
Jane Eyre (1944)
Letter From an Unknown Woman (1948)
Rebecca (1940)
Suspicion (1941, AA)
This Above All (1942)
Voyage to the Bottom of the Sea (1961)
sister: Olivia de Havilland
spouse: Brian Aherne
Fontana: 4 city, town
locale: 10 California
Fontane: 7 Theodor
Fontane __: 7 Sisters
Fontane, Theodor: 4 poet **6** German, writer
Fontanne, Lynn spouse: Alfred Lunt
Fonteyn, Margot: 4 Dame **6** dancer **8** danseuse **9** ballerina
attire: 4 tutu
fulcrum: 3 toe
fontina: 6 cheese
Foochow: 4 city, port
locale: 5 China
food: 4 chow, diet, dish, eats, fare, fuel, grub, meal, meat, mess, need **5** board, bread, table, viand **6** edible, fodder, intake, ration, snacks, viands **7** aliment, cookery, cooking, cuisine, edibles, goodies, rations, support, victual, vittles **8** supplies, victuals **9** groceries, nutriment, nutrition, provender **10** gastronomy, provisions, sustenance
additive: 3 dye, MSG
chain bottom: 4 alga
Chinese ~: 4 pu pu **6** lo mein, mei fun, won ton **7** chow fun, egg roll, pea pods **8** bean curd, chop suey, chow mein, dumpling, snow peas, spare rib **9** fried rice, roast pork **10** egg foo yung, moo shu pork, Peking duck, spring roll
combining form: 4 sito-
ender: 5 stuff
exclamation: 3 yum **6** yum-yum
label stat: 4 nt. wt. **5** net wt.
starter: 3 sea
store: 4 deli **6** market **7** grocery
supply ~: 5 cater
thickener: 4 agar **8** agar-agar
wrap: 4 foil **5** cello **10** cellophane
food __: 3 web **4** bank, fish, mill **5** chain, court, grain, stamp **6** coupon, vessel **7** pyramid, science, service, vacuole
__ food: 4 baby, fast, junk, soul **5** plant **6** ethnic, finger, frozen, health, rabbit **7** comfort, natural
Food and __ Administration: 4 Drug
__ food cake: 5 angel **6** devil's
Food, Glorious Food musical: 6 Oliver!
foodie: 7 epicure, gourmet **10** gastronome
food processor: 6 enzyme **9** Cuisinart
setting: 4 chop **5** purée
__ Foods: 4 Best **7** General
food storage brand: 4 Glad **5** Hefty **6** Ziploc **8** Reynolds **9** Saran Wrap
foodstuff: 4 meat **6** viands **7** aliment, produce, victual **8** victuals
foofaraw: 3 ado **4** riot, to-do **5** hoo-ha **6** hoopla
fool: 3 ass, con, kid, nit, oaf, sap **4** boob, bozo, clod, dolt, dope, dupe, gink, goof, gowk, gull, hoax, jerk, jive, joke, juke, loon, scam, simp, snow, trap, twit, yo-yo, zany **5** bluff, booby, cheat, chump, clown, cluck, cozen, dummy, dunce, hocus, joker, let on, loser, ninny, patsy, put on, schmo, spoof, stump, trick **6** delude, dimwit, galoot, jester, lead on, lubber, lummox, nitwit, outfox, pigeon, putter, rope in, schmoe, stooge, sucker, suck in, take in, turkey **7** beguile, buffoon, bungler, chicane, coxcomb, deceive, dessert, dingbat, dullard, fake out, fathead, flummox, fribble, galloot, halfwit, jackass, mislead, pierrot, pinhead, pretend, saphead, swindle, two-time **8** bonehead, dumbbell, flimflam, hoodwink, meathead, numskull, pettifog, pushover **9** bamboozle, birdbrain, blockhead, disinform, four-flush, harebrain, harlequin, ignoramus, lamebrain, numbskull, schlemiel, simpleton, victimize **10** dunderhead, nincompoop, noodlehead, silly billy
around: 4 futz, joke, loaf, play **5** dally **6** cavort, dabble, dawdle, frolic, gambol, linger, monkey, trifle **7** goof off **9** misbehave, waste time
away: 3 sap **4** laze **5** drain, trash **6** burn up **7** deplete, fribble, play out **8** squander **9** dissipate
away time: 4 idle, laze, loaf, loll **5** dally, dream, shirk, stall **6** dawdle, loiter, lounge **7** hang out **8** malinger, slack off **9** goldbrick **10** dillydally, knock about
ender: 5 hardy, proof
make a ~ of: 6 outwit **8** outsmart, ridicule
month: 3 Apr. **5** April
no ~: 5 truly **6** really **7** for real
nobody's ~: 4 keen **5** savvy, sharp, slick, smart **6** adroit, artful, astute, brainy, bright, clever, crafty, shrewd **7** knowing **8** lynx-eyed **9** observant, on the ball **10** discerning, insightful, perceptive
old ~: 4 coot
old-style: 4 mome
play for a ~: 3 con, use **4** bilk, dupe, gull, hoax, rook, snow, take **5** cheat, trick **6** delude, entrap, outwit, rip off, take in **7** deceive, defraud, ensnare, fake out, finagle, mislead, snooker, swindle **8** flimflam, hoodwink, outsmart, sucker in **9** bamboozle, victimize **10** manipulate
play the ~: 5 amuse, clown
starter: 3 tom
(with): 3 toy **4** play **6** fiddle, monkey, tinker **9** interfere **10** mess around
fool __: 3 hen **4** away **6** around
__ fool: 5 April
Fool __ As I, A: 4 Such
Fool __ Hill, The: 5 on the
__ Fool: 3 I'm a **5** Henry, She's a **7** Nobody's
Fool #1 (1961 song) artist: Brenda Lee
foolable: 4 naif **5** green, naive **6** unwary **7** artless **8** gullible, lamblike, trustful, trusting, wide-eyed **9** credulous, guileless
__ Fool Believes: 5 What a
Fooled Around and Fell in Love (1976 song) artist: Elvin Bishop
fooled by, not: 4 onto
foolery: 3 fun **4** jest **5** antic, caper, folly **6** antics **7** fatuity **8** jocosity, zaniness **9** silliness
starter: 3 tom
foolhardiness: 5 haste **8** temerity
foolhardy: 3 mad **4** bold, rash, wild **5** brash, hasty, risky, silly **6** daring, madcap, unwise **8** headlong, heedless, reckless **9** audacious, breakneck, daredevil, desperate, idiotical, impetuous, imprudent, uncareful, venturous **10** headstrong, ill-advised, incautious, out on a limb
exploit: 5 stunt
Fool (If You Think It's Over) (1978 song) artist: Chris Rea
fooling: 3 fun **7** hijinks, mockery **8** falderal, falderol, folderol, nonsense **9** high jinks, horseplay **10** buffoonery
no ~: 5 frank **6** candid, honest, really **7** earnest **8** honestly **9** sincerely **10** forthright, on the level
foolish: 3 mad **4** daft, dopy, dumb, idle, soft, wild, zany **5** balmy, daffy, dense, dippy, dizzy, dopey, dotty, goofy, goony, goosy, inane, kooky, nutty, sappy, silly, wacky **6** absurd, gooney, goosey, kookie, madcap, obtuse, simple, stupid, unwise, whacky **7** asinine, doltish, fatuous, puerile, vacuous, witless **8** headless, ill-spent, mindless **9** brainless, dim-witted, fatuitous, frivolous, half-baked, imprudent, insensate, lightsome, ludicrous, misguided, senseless **10** cockamamie, half-witted, ill-advised, incautious, indiscreet, irrational, ridiculous, sophomoric, unprofound, unthinking, weak-minded
not ~: 4 sage, wise **5** canny, sharp, smart **6** astute, clever, shrewd **7** careful, logical, politic, prudent, sapient, tactful **8** rational, sensible **9** judicious, provident, sagacious **10** discerning, insightful, perceptive, reasonable
render ~: 5 besot
talk: 3 yap **4** guff, yaup, yawp **5** trash **6** drivel **7** blather, blether
__-foolish: 5 pound
Foolish __: 4 Beat **5** Games, Heart, Wives
Foolish Beat (1988 song) artist: Debbie Gibson
Foolish Games (1997 song) artist: Jewel
Foolish Little Girl (1963 song) artist: Shirelles
foolishness: 3 gas, rot **4** blah, bosh, bull, bunk, guff, jazz, jive, pooh, tosh **5** apery, bilge, folly, fudge, hokum, hooey, prate, stuff, trash, tripe **6** bunkum, bushwa, drivel, footle, gabble, gammon, gibber, havers, hot air, humbug, idiocy, jabber, jargon, kibosh, levity, lunacy, piffle **7** baloney, blarney, blather, blether, boloney, bushwah, eyewash, fatuity, flannel, flubdub, fustian, garbage, hogwash, inanity, rubbish, twaddle **8** buncombe, claptrap, falderal, falderol, flimflam, flummery, folderal, folderol, nonsense, slipslop, tommyrot, trumpery **9** banana oil, gibberish, kidstakes, moonshine, poppycock, rigmarole **10** applesauce, balderdash, bilge water, codswallop, double-talk, flapdoodle, galimatias, Jabberwock, mumbo jumbo, rigamarole, taradiddle
__ Foolish Things: 5 These
Fool Killer, The (1965 film)
cast: Edward Albert, Dana Elcar, Anthony Perkins

Fool me ___, shame...: 4 once
Fool me twice, shame ___: 4 on me
Fool on the Hill (song), The artist: Beatles, Sergio Mendes
foolproof: 4 safe, sure 7 certain, perfect 8 fail-safe, flawless, inerrant, reliable, sure-fire, unerring 9 faultless 10 infallible, undoubtful
fool's ___: 3 cap 4 gold 6 errand 8 paradise
Fools author: Neil Simon
fool's-cap feature: 4 bell
___ Fools' Day: 3 All 5 April
Fools Die author: Mario Puzo
fools ender: 3 cap
___ fool's errand: 3 on a
___ Fools Fall in Love: 5 Why Do
fool's gold: 6 pyrite 10 iron pyrite
fool's paradise: 6 revery 7 reverie 8 delusion
Fools Rush In (1963 song) artist: Ricky Nelson
Fool Such As I, A (1959 song) artist: Elvis Presley
Fool There Was, A star: 4 Bara
Fool to Cry (1976 song) artist: Rolling Stones
foot: 3 dog, pad, paw, pes 4 base, hoof, iamb, unit 5 nadir, socle 6 bottom, dactyl, member, plinth, podium, reckon, tootsy 7 anapest, spondee, tootsie, trotter 8 ambulate, anapaest, pedestal 9 extremity, underside 10 foundation
anatomical ~: 3 pes
ancestor: 5 cubit
animal ~: 3 paw 4 hoof
athlete's ~: 5 tinea
bone: 5 talus 6 tarsus
bones: 4 tali 5 tarsi
classical metric ~: 5 paeon
combining form: 3 ped-, pod- 4 -pede, pedi-, pedo-, podo-
covering: 4 shoe, sock 5 socks 9 stockings
division: 4 inch
ender: 3 age, boy, man, men, pad, way 4 ball, bath, fall, gear, hill, hold, long, mark, note, pace, path, race, rest, rope, slog, sore, step, wall, wear, work 5 board, cloth, loose, print, stalk, stall, stone, stool 6 bridge, lights, locker
go on ~: 4 hoof, walk 5 leg it 6 hoof it
grind under ~: 7 trample
it: 4 hike, trek, walk 5 march 6 stroll 9 take a walk
lever: 5 pedal
of the ~: 5 podal
one on ~: 3 ped. 6 walker 10 pedestrian
part: 3 pad, toe 4 arch, heel, inch, sole 6 big toe, instep
pedal: 5 lever 7 treadle
poetic ~: 4 iamb 6 dactyl 7 anapest, pyrrhic, spondee, trochee 8 anapaest
problem: 4 gout 6 bunion
put one's ~ down: 4 step, walk 5 tread 6 demand, insist 7 protest 9 stand firm
rabbit's ~: 5 charm 6 amulet 8 talisman
set ~ in: 5 enter, get to, reach 6 come to 8 arrive at
shoot oneself in the ~: 3 err 4 flub, goof 5 gum up 6 blow it, bungle, foul up, fumble, goof up, mess up 7 blunder, louse up 9 mishandle, mismanage
soldier: 2 GI 3 pvt. 5 grunt 7 private, recruit, veteran, warrior
starter: 3 hot, web 4 bare, crow, flat, fore 5 Black, colts, goose, light, pussy, splay, under 6 tender
support: 6 insole
the bill: 3 pay 5 spend, treat 6 defray
width: 3 AAA, EEE 4 AAAA, EEEE
wiper: 3 mat
foot ___: 4 line, race, rule 5 brake, fault, level, score 6 doctor, warmer 7 soldier
foot ___ door: 5 in the
foot-___: 3 ton 5 pound 6 candle 7 lambert
___ foot: 3 bar, bun, ice, pad, web 4 ball, claw, club, cord, duck, hoof, lead, tern, tube 5 board, drake, front, melon, snake, spade, stump, under, whorl 6 cloven, French, runner, scroll, square, trifid 7 bracket, presser, rabbit's, slipper, Spanish
___-foot: 3 cat 4 acre 5 cock's, crow's, first 6 second, single
___ Foot: 3 Big
___ footage: 4 file 5 stock
footage, square: 4 area
football: 4 game 5 sport
area: 7 end zone 8 midfield, sideline
boo-boo: 6 fumble
charge: 5 blitz
conference: 3 AFC, NFC 4 Amer., Natl. 8 American, National
defunct ~ grp.: 3 AFL
equipment: 6 helmet
fastener: 5 lacer
field: 4 grid 5 arena 8 gridiron
filler: 3 air
flag ~ team: 5 eight, octad
formation: 6 huddle
foul: 4 clip, hold
game duration: 4 hour
Hall of Fame coach: 4 Levy, Noll 5 Allen, Brown, Grant, Halas, Neale, Shula 6 Ewbank, Landry 7 Gillman 8 Bud Grant, Don Shula, Lombardi, Marv Levy 9 Chuck Noll, Paul Brown, Tom Landry 10 Sid Gillman, Weeb Ewbank
Hall of Fame player: 4 Huff, Lary, Lott, Page 5 Brown, Ditka, Groza, Jones, Olsen, Shell, Swann 6 Butkus, Casper, Csonka, Grange, Greene, Harris, Hirsch, Nevers, Payton, Refnro, Sayers, Taylor, Thorpe 7 Alworth, Dorsett, Gifford, Hampton, Hornung, Largent, Sam Huff, Simpson 8 Alan Page, Art Shell, Campbell, Jim Brown, Lou Groza, Nagurski, Nitschke, Stenerud, Yale Lary 9 Dickerson, Jim Thorpe, Joe Greene, Lynn Swann, Marchetti, Mel Renfro, Mike Ditka, O.J. Simpson, Red Grange 10 Buoniconti, Dan Hampton, Dave Casper, Dick Butkus, Gale Sayers, Robustelli, Ronnie Lott, Stallworth
Hall of Fame quarterback: 5 Baugh, Fouts, Kelly, Starr 6 Blanda, Dawson, Graham, Griese, Tittle, Unitas 7 Luckman, Montana 8 Bradshaw, Dan Fouts, Jim Kelly, Staubach, Y.A. Tittle 9 Bart Starr, Bob Griese, Jurgensen, Len Dawson, Tarkenton 10 Joe Montana, Otto Graham, Sammy Baugh, Sid Luckman
Hall of Fame site: 4 Ohio 6 Canton
honor: 6 All-Pro
huddle phrase: 5 on two
infraction: 7 holding, offside 8 clipping
job: 5 coach
kick: 4 punt
kind of ~: 4 Nerf
like arena ~: 6 indoor
maneuver: 4 rush, snap 5 blitz, block, sneak 6 end run 7 hand-off, reverse 8 drop kick, pitch-out
official: 3 ref 5 zebra 7 referee 8 linesman
part: 4 lace
pass: 4 bomb 6 aerial, looper, spiral 7 lateral
path: 3 arc
play: 3 run 4 down, pass, punt, rush 6 end run
political ~: 5 issue 7 problem
position: 2 LB, LG, LT, RB, RG, RT 3 end, LFB, LHB, OLB, RFB, RHB 4 back 5 guard 6 center, tackle 7 flanker, lineman 8 fullback, halfback 9 left guard 10 right guard 11 quarterback
pro team: 4 Jets, Rams 5 Bears, Bills, Colts, Lions 6 Browns, Chiefs, Eagles, eleven, Giants, Niners, Ravens, Saints, Texans, Titans 7 Bengals, Broncos, Cowboys, Falcons, Jaguars, Packers, Raiders, Vikings 8 Chargers, Dolphins, Panthers, Patriots, Redskins, Seahawks, Steelers 9 Cardinals 10 Buccaneers
reference: 8 playbook
relative: 5 rugby
score: 2 TD 4 goal 6 safety 9 field goal
season: 4 fall 6 autumn
setback: 4 loss 8 turnover
shaped like a ~: 5 ovate, ovoid
shirt: 6 jersey
shoe part: 5 cleat
shutout line score: 4 OOOO
stadium: 4 bowl
stand: 3 tee
star: 4 Moon, Rote 5 Elway, Favre, Kosar, Simms, Smith 6 Aikman, Barber, Flutie, Marino 7 Esiason, Sanders 8 Kyle Rote 9 Dan Marino, John Elway, Phil Simms 10 Brett Favre, Doug Flutie, Testaverde, Tiki Barber, Troy Aikman, Warren Moon
starter: 7 kickoff
stat: 3 int., TDs, yds. 5 yards 6 points 7 tackles
team: 6 eleven
term: 3 end, ref 4 back, bomb, down, gain, goal, pass, punt, rush, sack, snap 5 blitz, block, sneak, spike, zebra 6 aerial, All-Pro, center, end run, fumble, huddle, onside, punter, safety, spiral, tackle 7 convert, end zone, flanker, hand-off, holding, kickoff, lateral, lineman, offside, penalty, pigskin, quarter, referee, reverse, time-out 8 clipping, crossbar, drop kick, fullback, goal line, goalpost, halfback, halftime, hang time, hash mark, linesman, midfield, pitch-out, playbook, receiver, sideline, turnover
tiebreaker: 2 OT 8 overtime
yardage: 4 gain
yell: 3 rah
1-pt. ~ play: 3 PAT
2-pt. ~ play: 3 saf. 6 safety
3-pt. ~ play: 2 FG 9 field goal
6-pt. ~ play: 2 TD 9 touchdown
15 min. of ~: 3 qtr. 7 quarter
___ football: 4 flag 5 arena, touch
footballer
former pro ~: 5 LA Ram
Foot Book, The author: Dr. Seuss
foot-bridge in German: 4 steg
foot-drag: 4 loaf 5 dally, delay, stall, tarry 6 dawdle 8 obstruct 10 dillydally, equivocate, filibuster
foot-dragger: 7 holdout
foot-dragging: 4 lazy, poky 7 gradual, halting, impeded, lagging, languid, loafing 8 crawling, creeping, dallying, dawdling, delaying, dilatory, drawn-out, hesitant, plodding, slothful, sluggish, stalling, toddling 9 leisurely, lethargic, prolonged, snaillike, unhurried 10 deliberate, protracted
Foote: 6 Horton, Shelby
___-footed: 3 fin, web 4 flat, slow, sure, wing 5 fleet, heavy, light, loose 6 fiddle
footed combining form: 6 -podous
footfall: 4 step
___ foot forward: 4 best
footgear
see footwear
foothold: 4 base, grip 6 anchor 7 support 8 lodgment, purchase 9 beachhead 10 bridgehead, foundation
foot-in-___: 5 mouth
___ foot in: 3 set
footing: 4 base, hold, rank 5 basis, grade, plane, stage, state, terms 6 status 7 quality, station, support 8 position, purchase, standing 9 situation 10 foundation
equal ~: 3 par
lose one's ~: 4 fall, slip, trip
on an equal ~: 4 even, fair 5 level 6 square 7 uniform 8 balanced, matching 10 fifty-fifty
foot in the ___: 4 door
footle: 3 gas, rot 4 blah, bosh, bull, bunk, guff, jazz, jive, pooh, tosh 5 bilge, fudge, hokum, hooey, prate, stuff, trash, tripe 6 babble, bunkum, bushwa, drivel, gabble, gammon, gibber, havers, hot air, humbug, jabber, jargon, kibosh, piffle 7 baloney, blarney, blather, blether, boloney, bushwah, eyewash, flannel, flubdub, fustian, garbage, hogwash, inanity, prattle, rubbish, twaddle 8 buncombe, claptrap, falderal, falderol, flimflam, flummery, folderal, folderol, nonsense, slipslop, tommyrot, trumpery 9 asininity, banana oil, gibberish, kidstakes, moonshine, poppycock, rigmarole, silliness 10 applesauce, balderdash, bilge water, codswallop, double-talk, flapdoodle, galimatias, Jabberwock, mumbo jumbo, rigamarole, taradiddle
foot-leg connector: 5 ankle
footless: 4 apod 6 apodal 7 apodous
footless bird in heraldry: 7 martlet
footlet: 3 Ped 7 hosiery
Footlight Parade (1933 film)
cast: Joan Blondell, James Cagney, Ruby Keeler, Dick Powell
director: Lloyd Bacon
footlights: 5 stage 7 theater, theatre
Footlight Serenade (1942 film)
cast: Betty Grable, Victor Mature, John Payne, Jane Wyman
footlike part
combining form: 4 -pode 6 -podium
footlocker: 5 trunk
footloose: 4 free 8 carefree, restless, vagabond
one: 5 rover
Footloose (1984 film)
cast: Kevin Bacon, John Lithgow, Lori Singer, Dianne Wiest
director: Herbert Ross
role: 3 Ren
Footloose (1984 song) artist: Kenny Loggins
footman: 5 valet 6 flunky, lackey 7 flunkey, lacquey
attire: 6 livery
footnote: 7 comment, mention 8 annotate 10 annotation
abbr.: 3 vid. 4 et al., ibid., idem 5 et seq., op. cit. 6 loc. cit.
make a ~: 4 cite
phrase: 6 et alia, et alii

user: 5 citer
word: 6 ibidem
__-foot oil: 5 neat's
__ foot on: 3 set
footpad: 5 thief 7 brigand 10 highwayman
footpath: 4 lane, walk 5 track, trail 7 walkway
foot-pound relative: 3 erg 5 joule
footprint: 4 clew, clue, step 5 spoor, trace, track 10 impression
footprints: 5 track, trail
footrace end: 4 tape
footrest: 4 rail 5 stool 7 hassock, ottoman
footsie, play: 5 flirt
footstep: 4 pace 5 tread 6 stride
combining form: 4 ichn- 5 ichno-
Footsteps (1960 song) artist: Steve Lawrence
footstool: 4 seat 7 hassock, ottoman
foot the __: 4 bill
footway: 4 lane, path 5 trail
footwear: 3 pac 4 boot, cack, clog, geta, mule, pump, shoe 5 heels, sabot, sling, spike, stogy, thong, wader 6 bootee, bootie, brogan, brogue, buskin, chukka, galosh, gillie, kiltie, loafer, oxford, patten, rubber, sandal, stogie, wedgie 7 chopine, ghillie, gumboot, high-low, jodhpur, ski boot, slipper, sneaker, wingtip 8 balmoral, flip-flop, moccasin, plimsoll, sneakers, Top-Sider 9 ankle boot, high heels, Mary Janes, sling-back, spike heel 10 clodhopper, wellington, white bucks
ankle-length ~: 6 chukka 7 high-low, jodhpur
baby ~: 6 bootee, bootie
backless ~: 4 mule 5 thong 8 flip-flop
calf-length ~: 7 gumboot
canted ~: 6 wedgie
canvas ~: 7 sneaker 8 plimsoll, Top-Sider
casual ~: 10 white bucks
deerskin ~: 8 moccasin
divided-toe ~: 5 thong 8 flip-flop
dressy ~: 5 heels 9 high heels 10 spike heels
golfer ~: 6 kiltie
heavy ~: 5 stogy 6 stogie 10 clodhopper
heelless ~: 8 moccasin
Indian ~: 8 moccasin
infant ~: 6 bootee, bootie
knee-length ~: 10 wellington
knitted ~: 6 bootee, bootie
ladies ~: 8 balmoral
leather ~: 8 Top-Sider 10 wellington
light ~: 7 slipper
liner ~: 3 pac
low-cut ~: 4 pump 6 gillie, oxford, sandal 7 ghillie, slipper 9 ankle boot
low-heeled ~: 6 brogue 9 Mary Janes
moccasinlike ~: 6 loafer
open-backed ~: 5 sling 9 sling-back
oxford ~: 10 white bucks
perforated pattern ~: 7 wingtip
plastic ~: 7 ski boot
provided ~ to: 4 shod
rubber ~: 7 gumboot, sneaker 8 Top-Sider
rubber-soled ~: 8 plimsoll
shiny ~: 9 Mary Janes
slip-on ~: 6 loafer
soft-soled ~: 4 cack
stiff ~: 7 ski boot
strapless ~: 4 pump
sturdy ~: 4 boot 6 oxford
suede ~: 6 chukka
thick-soled ~: 4 clog 5 sabot 6 buskin, chopin, patten 7 chopine
tongueless ~: 6 gillie 7 ghillie
walking ~: 8 balmoral
waterproof ~: 4 boot 5 wader 6 galosh, rubber
wooden ~: 4 geta 5 sabot
work ~: 6 brogan
see also boot, shoe
__ foo yung: 3 egg
foozle: 3 err 4 flub, goof, muff, slip 5 botch 6 bungle, foul up, fumble, goof up, mess up 7 blunder, louse up 9 mishandle, mismanage
fop: 4 dude 5 blade, dandy, swell 7 coxcomb, peacock, preener 8 macaroni, popinjay 9 maccaroni, pretty boy 10 jack-a-dandy
like a ~: 4 vain 9 conceited
foppish: 5 dandy 6 la-de-da, la-di-da 8 lah-di-dah
for: 3 aye, pro 5 since 6 behind 7 because, through, whereas 8 favoring 9 being that, endorsing, in favor of, in honor of, in place of 10 inasmuch as, in behalf of, on behalf of, supporting, supportive
for __: 3 fun 4 free, good, life, love, real, rent, sure 5 a song, a time, keeps, short 7 certain, example, openers
for __ by owner: 4 sale
for __ intents and purposes: 3 all
for __ it's worth: 3 all 4 what
for __ life: 4 dear
for __ matter: 4 that
for __ measure: 4 good
for __ or for worse: 6 better
for __ or money: 4 love
for __ out loud: 6 crying
for __ the world: 3 all
for-__: 6 profit
__ for: 3 ask, gun, opt, pop 4 call, fall, feel, go in, look, make, pass, pull, send, take, what 5 put in, shoot, speak, stand, vouch 6 spring 7 account, bargain
__-for: 7 uncared, unhoped
...for __, for poorer: 6 richer
...for __ of woman born: 4 none
For __: 3 You 5 Annie, A' That, Kicks
For __ a jolly...: 3 he's
For __ be Queen...: 4 I'm to
For __ Dollars More: 4 a Few
For __ Eyes Only: 4 Your
For __ in My Life: 4 Once
For __ is the Kingdom...: 5 thine
For __ jolly...: 4 he's a
For __ know...: 4 all I
For __ Know: 5 All We
For __ My Gal: 5 Me and
For __ of a nail...: 4 want
For __ Sake: 5 Pete's 7 Heaven's
For __ the Bell Tolls: 4 Whom
For __ us a child is born: 4 unto
For __ We Know: 3 All
For __-With Love and Squalor: 4 Esme
__ For: 5 To Die
for a __: 4 song 6 wonder
For a __ Dollars More: 3 Few
__ for Adano: 5 A Bell
__ for a Day: 4 King, Lady 5 Queen
__ for a fall: 4 ride
For a Few Dollars More (1966 film)
cast: Clint Eastwood, Lee Van Cleef
director: Sergio Leone
__ for Africa: 3 USA
forage: 3 hay 4 comb, feed, hunt, raid, root, seek 5 prowl, scour 6 browse, fodder, ravage, search 7 aliment, explore, look for, plunder, ransack, rummage 8 scrounge 9 cast about
food: 3 hay 6 rustle
grass: 5 sorgo 6 sorgho 7 setaria
plant: 3 ers 5 emmer, ervil, vetch 6 clover, cowpea
plant of Asia: 3 urd
store ~: 6 ensile
__ for a Heavyweight: 7 Requiem
Foraker: 4 peak 5 mount 8 mountain
locale: 6 Alaska
__ for a king: 3 fit
__ for alarm: 5 cause
__ for Alibi: 3 A Is
for all __ and purposes: 7 intents
__-for-all: 4 free
for all one is __: 5 worth
__ for All Seasons: 4 A Man
for all the __: 5 world
For All We Know (1971 song) artist: Carpenters
__ for a loop: 5 knock, throw
foramen: 4 pore 7 opening, orifice
Foran: 4 Dick
For Annie author: Poe
__ for apple: 3 A is
__ for apples: 3 bob
__ for a rainy day: 4 save
for argument's __: 4 sake
__ for a ride: 4 take
For A' That author: Robert Burns
foray: 4 raid, trip 5 sally, storm 6 attack, inroad, maraud, ravage, sortie 7 assault, descent, overrun, venture 8 invasion 9 incursion, irruption
make a ~: 7 plunder
Foray: 4 June
Forbach: 4 city, town
locale: 6 France
forbear: 4 omit, shun 5 avoid, forgo, remit, spare 6 desist, eschew, forego, relent, resist 7 abstain, back off, decline, refrain 8 keep back, keep from, renounce, withhold 9 sacrifice 10 desist from, progenitor
__ for bear: 6 loaded
forbearance: 4 pity 5 mercy 6 lenity, pardon 8 clemency, kindness, lenience, patience 9 restraint, tolerance 10 temperance
forbearing: 3 lax 4 easy, kind, meek, mild, soft 5 loose 6 chaste, gentle, kindly 7 clement, lenient, patient, ruthful, sparing 8 flexible, laid-back, merciful, parental, placable, tolerant 9 assuasive, compliant, easygoing, forgiving, indulgent 10 charitable, living with, permissive, thoughtful, unexacting
forbears: 7 kinfolk, lineage 8 kinfolks, kinsfolk
Forbes: 3 mag 5 Bryan, Steve 6 Esther 7 Malcolm 8 magazine
alternative: 7 Barron's, Fortune
Forbes, Bryan: 8 director
film: I Am a Dancer (1973)
King Rat (1965)
The L-Shaped Room (1963)
Séance on a Wet Afternoon (1964)
The Slipper and the Rose (1976)
The Stepford Wives (1975)
Whistle Down the Wind (1961)
The Wrong Box (1966)
forbid: 3 ban, bar, nix 4 deny, halt, stop, tabu, veto, warn 5 block, debar, say no, taboo 6 abjure, censor, enjoin, hinder, impede, outlaw, reject 7 embargo, exclude, forfend, inhibit, prevent, rule out 8 disallow, forefend, obstruct, preclude, prohibit, restrain, restrict 9 foreclose, forestall, interdict, proscribe
forbiddance: 3 ban 4 veto 7 boycott, embargo 8 sanction 9 exclusion
forbidden: 4 tabu 5 taboo 6 banned, vetoed 7 illegal, illicit 8 criminal, improper, outlawed, smuggled, unlawful, verboten, wrongful 9 felonious, off-limits 10 closed-down, contraband, not allowed, prohibited, proscribed
thing: 4 no-no 5 taboo
forbidden __: 5 fruit
Forbidden __: 4 City 6 Planet
Forbidden City: 4 Lasa 5 Lassa, Lhasa
occupant: 3 emp. 7 emperor
forbidden fruit: 5 apple
locale: 4 Eden
Forbidden Paradise star: 5 Negri
Forbidden Planet (1956 film)
cast: Anne Francis, Leslie Nielsen, Walter Pidgeon
director: Fred M. Wilcox
forbidding: 4 dark, dour, grim, ugly 5 gaunt, stern, tough 6 odious, severe, strict 7 hostile, ominous, refusal 8 daunting, menacing, sinister 9 abhorrent, glowering, offensive, repellent, repulsive 10 censorship, off-putting, unfriendly, unpleasant
look: 5 glare, scowl 6 glower
__ for Bonzo: 7 Bedtime
__ for Burglar: 3 B Is
force: 3 pry, ram, vim 4 army, bind, cram, crew, dint, drag, fury, gist, goad, kick, make, push, soul, thew 5 agent, brawn, brunt, cadre, clout, corps, draft, drive, exact, jimmy, might, order, power, press, punch, seize, sinew, squad, staff, thews, troop, twist, vigor, wring 6 coerce, compel, demand, detail, duress, effort, energy, enjoin, extort, impact, impose, insist, legion, muscle, oblige, propel, reduce, spirit, stress, thrust, wrench 7 assault, brigade, command, dragoon, fitness, gravity, impetus, impulse, inflict, muscles, oppress, pin down, potence, potency, require, sandbag, squeeze, stamina, violate, voltage 8 bust open, coercion, division, dynamism, efficacy, emphasis, gumption, keep down, momentum, obligate, pressure, regiment, salesmen, shanghai, soldiers, squadron, stimulus, strength, validity, vitality 9 authority, battalion, beefiness, blackmail, break open, conscript, constrain, crack open, endurance, extortion, fortitude, hardiness, huskiness, influence, intensity, operation, puissance, stoutness, strong-arm, substance, toughness, will power 10 browniness, compulsion, detachment, horsepower, importance, mightiness, oppression, pressurize, robustness, sturdiness
at full ~: 5 amain
back: 5 repel 6 defeat, put off, rebuff 7 fend off, repulse, ward off 8 drive off 9 drive away
be in ~: 4 hold, rule 5 stand
brute ~: 3 vim 4 dint, thew 5 brawn, might, power, thews, vigor 6 energy, muscle 7 fitness, muscles, potence, potency, stamina 8 strength, violence, vitality 9 beefiness, endurance, fortitude, hardiness, huskiness, puissance, stoutness, toughness 10 browniness, mightiness, robustness, sturdiness
destructive ~: 4 bane 7 scourge
down: 4 sink 7 depress 8 submerge
driving ~: 4 birr, urge 6 engine 7 impetus
fighting ~: 3 GIs 4 army, navy 5 fleet 6 armada 7 cavalry, marines, sailors 8 military, soldiers
forward: 5 impel
get by ~: 3 pry 5 bully, exact, gouge, usurp, wrest, wring 6 coerce, extort, wrench 7 squeeze 9 blackmail, shake down
hostile ~: 3 foe 5 enemy 7 invader, villain 8 attacker, opponent 9 adversary, assailant, combatant, other side 10 antagonist, opposition

hypothetical ~: 4 odyl 5 odyle
in: 3 jam 6 insert, thrust 7 intrude, squeeze 9 interject, interpose, interrupt
in ~: 5 valid 6 active, at work 7 working 9 effective, operative
lacking ~: 4 limp, weak 6 effete, feeble 8 weakened 9 enervated, powerless
life ~: 3 Tao 6 spirit
main ~: 5 brunt
mystical ~: 5 karma 6 kismet
naval ~: 6 argosy 8 flotilla
obtain by ~: 3 pry 5 bully, exact, gouge, usurp, wrest, wring 6 coerce, extort, wrench 7 squeeze 9 blackmail, shake down
(on): 5 foist
open: 3 pry 5 jimmy, lever 7 crowbar
out: 4 oust, pump 5 eject, evict, expel 6 depose 7 dismiss, exclude, extrude 8 dislodge, displace, supplant
physical ~: 4 main
starter: 3 per 4 work 7 counter
strike with ~: 3 hit, ram 4 beat, push, slam 5 smash 6 batter, hammer
take by ~: 5 usurp, wrest, wring 6 extort, ravish, wrench
taken by ~ old-style: 4 reft
task ~: 6 detail 9 committee 10 detachment
tour de ~: 4 coup, feat 5 stunt 7 classic, exploit, triumph
unit: 4 dyne 6 newton
upon: 4 vent 5 visit, wreak 6 impose 7 inflict, unleash 8 carry out 9 knock down 10 bring about, perpetrate
vital ~: 4 soul 5 anima, being 6 energy, psyche, spirit 8 vivacity
with great ~: 4 hard 7 harshly, heavily 8 brutally, fiercely, intently 9 earnestly, intensely, violently, zealously 10 gruelingly, powerfully, rigorously, vehemently, vigorously
work ~: 5 labor, staff 9 personnel
force ___: 3 cup, fit 4 play, pump 5 field 7 majeure
force-___: 3 out 5 draft
___ force: 3 air 4 gale, life, task, weak, work 5 color, fifth, labor, third, vital 6 police, strike, strong 7 buoyant, landing, Lorentz
___-force: 3 ton 4 main 5 pound
___ Force: 3 Air 5 Brute 6 Magnum 7 Driving
forced: 5 bound, stiff 7 labored, stilted 8 affected, coercive, grudging, impelled, strained 9 contrived, insincere, laborious, mandatory, stringent, unnatural, unwilling 10 artificial, begrudging, compulsive, compulsory, obligatory, unobliging
is ~ to: 4 must
forced ___: 4 sale 5 march 6 coding
forceful: 4 bold, firm, hale, iron, wiry 5 beefy, burly, hardy, hefty, hunky, husky, lusty, nervy, stout, tough 6 active, all-out, brawny, cogent, hearty, mighty, potent, robust, rugged, sinewy, steely, stocky, strong, sturdy, virile 7 doughty, drastic, driving, dynamic, intense, telling, violent 8 athletic, decisive, dominant, emphatic, indurate, muscular, positive, powerful, puissant, resolute, stalwart, striking, vehement, vigorous 9 assertive, Atlantean, effective, energetic, herculean, insistent, masterful, strapping, stringent, trenchant, well-built 10 able-bodied, commanding, conclusive, iron-willed, passionate, persuasive, red-blooded, take-charge, unswerving, unwavering
one: 6 dynamo
forcefulness: 5 power, punch, vigor 6 energy, weight
forceless: 4 meek, weak 5 timid 6 feeble 8 cowardly 10 irresolute, submissive
force of ___: 5 habit
___ Force One: 3 Air
force one's ___: 4 hand
forceps: 4 tool 6 pliers
forces
furnish new ~ to: 5 reman
join ~: 4 pool 5 merge, unite 6 club up, gang up, league 9 cooperate 10 assist with
science of ~: 9 mechanics
___ forces: 5 armed
___ Forces: 7 Special
Force, The
champion of ~: 4 Jedi
dark side of ~: 4 evil
Forché, Carolyn: 4 poet
forcible: 6 strong 7 telling, violent 8 striking
forcibly: 4 hard 7 greatly 8 mightily, severely, strongly 9 intensely
___ for Columbine: 7 Bowling
___ for Corpse: 3 C Is
For crying ___ loud!: 3 out
ford: 4 span, wade 5 cross 8 go across 10 wade across
Ford: 3 car, LTD 4 auto, Doug, John, Lita, Paul 5 Betty, Faith, Frick, Glenn, Henry 6 Anitra, Eileen, Gerald, Whitey 7 Mercury, Richard, Wallace 8 Harrison 10 automobile
alternative: 4 Olds 5 Buick, Caddy, Chevy 7 Pontiac 8 Cadillac, Chrysler 9 Chevrolet 10 Oldsmobile
contemporary: 6 Edison
make: 7 Lincoln, Mercury
model: 3 LTD 5 Cobra, Edsel, Focus, Pinto, Probe, Ranch, 'Stang, T-Bird, Tempo, Tudor 6 Aspire, Bronco, Custom, Del Rio, Escape, Escort, Falcon, Fiesta, Futura, Model A, Model B, Model T, Squire, Taurus, Torino 7 Contour, Festiva, Galaxie, Grabber, Granada, Mustang 8 Aerostar, Explorer, Fairlane, Fairmont, Mainline, Maverick, Parklane, Skyliner, Sunliner, Victoria, Windstar 9 Econoline, Excursion, Town Sedan 10 Customline, Expedition, Ranch Wagon 11 Thunderbird
Ford ___ better idea: 4 has a
Ford ___ Ford: 5 Madox
___ for Danger: 5 Green
___ for Danny Fisher, A: 5 Stone
___ Ford Coley: 4 John
___ Ford Coppola: 7 Francis
Ford, Doug: 6 golfer
___ for Deadbeat: 3 D Is
for dear ___: 4 life
Ford Explorer: 3 SUV
Ford, Ford Madox: 6 writer 7 British
Ford, Gerald: 9 president
alma mater: 8 Michigan
birth name: 10 Leslie King
birthplace: 3 Neb. 4 Nebr. 5 Omaha
child: 4 Jack 5 Susan 6 Steven 7 Michael
former occupation: 6 lawyer
home: 8 Michigan
middle name: 7 Rudolph
opponent: 6 Carter
running mate: 4 Dole
vacation spot: 4 Vail
V.P.: 3 NAR 11 Rockefeller
wife: 5 Betty
Ford, Glenn: 5 actor
film: 3:10 to Yuma (1957)
The Adventures of Martin Eden (1942)
The Big Heat (1953)
Blackboard Jungle (1955)
The Courtship of Eddie's Father (1963)
Cowboy (1958)
Dear Heart (1964)
The Desperadoes (1943)
Experiment in Terror (1962)
The Fastest Gun Alive (1956)
The Gazebo (1959)
Gilda (1946)
Interrupted Melody (1955)
Jubal (1956)
The Man From Colorado (1948)
The Man From the Alamo (1953)
Pocketful of Miracles (1961)
The Sheepman (1958)
Smith! (1969)
The Teahouse of the August Moon (1956)
Texas (1941)
Trial (1955)
The Undercover Man (1949)
spouse: Eleanor Powell
Fordham: 6 school
athletes: 4 Rams
locale: 5 Bronx 7 New York
Ford, Harrison: 5 actor
film: Air Force One (1997)
Blade Runner (1982)
Clear and Present Danger (1994)
The Devil's Own (1997)
The Empire Strikes Back (1980)
The Frisco Kid (1979)
The Fugitive (1993)
Indiana Jones and the Last Crusade (1989)
Indiana Jones and the Temple of Doom (1984)
The Mosquito Coast (1986)
Patriot Games (1992)
Presumed Innocent (1990)
Raiders of the Lost Ark (1981)
Regarding Henry (1991)
Return of the Jedi (1983)
Sabrina (1995)
Six Days Seven Nights (1998)
Star Wars (1977)
What Lies Beneath (2000)
Witness (1985)
Working Girl (1988)
spouse: Melissa Mathison
Ford, Henry son: 5 Edsel
___ for dinner?: 5 What's
Ford, John: 8 director
film: 3 Bad Men (1926)
3 Godfathers (1948)
Airmail (1932)
Cheyenne Autumn (1964)
Donovan's Reef (1963)
Dr. Bull (1933)
Drums Along the Mohawk (1939)
Flesh (1932)
Fort Apache (1948)
Four Men and a Prayer (1938)
Four Sons (1928)
The Fugitive (1947)
The Grapes of Wrath (1940, AA)
Hangman's House (1928)
How Green Was My Valley (1941, AA)
How the West Was Won (1962)
The Hurricane (1937)
The Informer (1935, AA)
The Iron Horse (1924)
Judge Priest (1934)
The Last Hurrah (1958)
The Long Gray Line (1955)
The Long Voyage Home (1940)
The Lost Patrol (1934)
The Man Who Shot Liberty Valance (1962)
Mary of Scotland (1936)
Mister Roberts (1955)
Mogambo (1953)
My Darling Clementine (1946)
The Prisoner of Shark Island (1936)
The Quiet Man (1952, AA)
Rio Grande (1950)
The Searchers (1956)
Sergeant Rutledge (1960)
She Wore a Yellow Ribbon (1949)
Stagecoach (1939)
Steamboat 'Round the Bend (1935)
The Sun Shines Bright (1953)
They Were Expendable (1945)
Wagon Master (1950)
Wee Willie Winkie (1937)
The Whole Town's Talking (1935)
Young Cassidy (1965)
Young Mr. Lincoln (1939)
Ford Madox ___: 4 Ford 5 Brown
fordo: 7 destroy
___ Ford Range: 5 Edsel
Ford, Tennessee Ernie
song: Ballad of Davy Crockett (1955)
Sixteen Tons (1955)
Ford, Whitey: 6 hurler, Yankee 7 pitcher
fore: 3 bow 4 head 5 front
at the ~: 5 ahead 7 in front
be at the ~: 4 lead
combining form: 6 antero-
ender: 4 lady, word 6 father 7 quarter
opposite: 3 aft
starter: 5 there, where 6 hereto 7 thereto 8 hereunto 9 thereunto
fore-___: 5 check 7 topmast, topsail
___ fore: 5 to the
___ for Each Other: 4 Made
fore and ___: 3 aft
forearm: 7 prepare
bone: 4 ulna 6 radius
bones: 5 radii, ulnae
of a ~ bone: 5 ulnar
forebear: 6 father, mother 9 ascendant, matriarch, patriarch, precursor 10 antecedent, originator, procreator, progenitor
forebears: 5 roots, stock 7 descent, lineage 8 ancestry, heritage, pedigree 9 ancestors, bloodline, genealogy 10 extraction, family tree
forebode: 7 betoken, portend, predict, presage, promise 8 prophesy, threaten
foreboding: 4 care, omen, sign 5 dread, qualm 6 augury, threat 7 anxiety, ominous, portent, presage, warning 8 bad vibes, disquiet, mistrust, prophecy, sinister 9 misgiving, prenotion 10 prediction, prognostic
forecast: 3 tip 4 look, sign 5 augur, hunch 6 augury, tip-off 7 betoken, outlook, predict, presage, project 8 estimate, prophecy, prophesy 9 adumbrate, prognosis 10 anticipate, prediction, projection
agcy.: 4 NOAA
aid: 5 radar
letters: 3 THI
line: 5 front 6 isobar 8 isotherm
weather ~: 3 dry, fog, hot, icy, wet 4 cold, cool, damp, fair, gale, hail, haze, mild, rain, warm 5 clear, humid, sleet, storm, sunny 6 cloudy
forecaster: 4 seer 5 augur, sibyl 6 oracle 7 diviner, prophet 9 predictor 10 soothsayer
foreclose: 3 bar 5 block, debar, deter 6 forbid, hinder, impede, refuse, reject 7 exclude, lock out, prevent, shut out 8 blockade, obstruct, preclude
forefather: 8 ancestor 9 precursor 10 antecedent, progenitor
forefathers: 5 roots 7 kinfolk 8 kinfolks, kinsfolk

forefend: 4 stop 5 avert, block, debar 6 enjoin, forbid 7 prevent 8 stave off 9 interdict
forefoot: 3 paw
forefront: 3 van 4 head, lead 8 vanguard
forego: 4 lead 7 precede 9 surrender
foregoing: 4 past 5 above, prior 6 former 7 earlier 8 anterior, previous 9 precedent, preceding 10 antecedent
foregone: 4 past 5 prior 6 former 7 earlier 8 previous
foreground: 5 front
forehead: 4 brow 5 front
feature: 5 ridge 6 furrow
Hindu's ~ mark: 5 tilak
insect ~: 5 frons
slapper's comment: 3 duh
foreign: 3 far 5 alien 6 exotic, remote 7 distant, faraway, outside, oversea, strange, unknown 8 external, imported, offshore, overseas 9 nonnative, peregrine 10 extraneous, immaterial, irrelevant, outlandish, unexplored, unfamiliar
affairs: 8 politics 9 diplomacy 10 statecraft
agent: 3 spy
like some ~ words: 3 fem. 4 masc., neut. 6 neuter 8 feminine 9 masculine
matter: 5 taint 8 impurity
merchandise: 6 import
name meaning ~: 7 Barbara
not ~: 6 native 8 domestic, internal 9 home-grown 10 indigenous
representative: 5 envoy 6 consul, legate 8 delegate, diplomat, emissary, minister 10 ambassador
foreign __: 3 aid, car 4 bill 6 legion, office, policy 7 affairs, mission, service
foreign-__: 4 born, flag
Foreign Affair, A (1948 film)
cast: Jean Arthur, Marlene Dietrich, John Lund
director: Billy Wilder
Foreign Affairs author: Alison Lurie
Foreign Correspondent (1940 film)
cast: Laraine Day, Herbert Marshall, Joel McCrea
director: Alfred Hitchcock
foreigner: 5 alien 6 émigré, gaijin 7 refugee, visitor 8 newcomer, outsider, stranger 9 immigrant, outlander
name meaning ~: 7 Wallace
Foreigner
song: Cold As Ice (1977)
Double Vision (1978)
Feels Like the First Time (1977)
Hot Blooded (1978)
I Don't Want to Live Without You (1988)
I Want to Know What Love Is (1984)
Say You Will (1987)
Urgent (1981)
Waiting for a Girl Like You (1981)
foreign exchange
cost: 4 agio
listing: 3 yen 4 euro, peso 5 pound, zloty
foreknowledge: 3 ESP 4 sign 6 vision 8 prophecy 10 prescience
foreland: 4 cape, head 5 point 10 promontory
foreleg: 4 calf, shin
forelimb: 4 wing
foreman: 4 boss 7 manager 8 director, superior 10 supervisor
deck ~: 4 bo's'n 5 bosun
group: 4 jury
Foreman, George: 5 boxer
foe: 3 Ali
match: 4 bout 5 fight
milieu: 4 ring 5 arena
punch: 3 jab 4 left 5 right 8 uppercut
stat: 2 KO 3 TKO
foremost: 3 top 4 A-one, arch, best, head, lead, main, tops 5 chief, first, front, prime 6 mainly, master, top dog, urgent 7 central, highest, leading, premier, primary, supreme 8 above all, champion 9 essential, number-one, paramount, primarily, principal, prominent, topflight, worthiest 10 preeminent
combining form: 4 prot- 5 proto-
member: 4 dean 5 doyen
forenoon: 2 a.m. 4 morn 7 morning
forensic: 4 moot 5 legal 8 judicial, juristic 9 debatable, dialectic, juridical, polemical 10 juristical, rhetorical
site: 3 lab
foreordain: 4 doom, fate 7 destine 9 destinate, determine 10 prearrange, predestine
foreordained: 5 bound, fated 6 doomed 8 destined 10 inevitable
forepart: 3 bow 4 head, prow 5 front 8 anterior
__ for error: 6 margin
forerunner: 5 pacer 6 augury, herald, leader, parent 7 portent 8 ancestor, original 9 announcer, harbinger, initiator, messenger, precursor, prototype 10 antecedent, antecessor, indication, originator, progenitor, prognostic
foresail: 3 jib
foresee: 5 think 7 predict 8 envisage, envision, prophesy 10 anticipate, reckon with
foreseeable: 4 near
foreshadow: 4 bode, hint, mean 5 augur 7 betoken, portend, predict, presage, promise 8 prophesy, threaten 9 adumbrate, prefigure
foreshadowing: 4 sign 6 threat 7 portent 9 prophetic
foreshow: 4 bode, mean, omen, warn 5 augur 6 herald 7 auspice, betoken, point to, portend, predict, presage, promise, signify 8 antecede, prophesy 9 adumbrate, prefigure 10 vaticinate
foresight: 6 vision, wisdom 9 canniness, provision 10 discretion, enterprise, leadership, perception, precaution, prescience, providence
foresighted: 5 canny 6 shrewd 7 prudent 9 provident 10 discerning
For Esme-With Love and Squalor
author: J.D. Salinger
forest: 4 park, wood 5 Arden, grove, wilds, woods 6 nature, timber 8 Sherwood, wildwood, woodland 9 backwoods 10 timberland, wilderness
clearing: 5 glade
combining form: 3 hyl- 4 hylo-
commodity: 4 pulp
creature: 3 doe 4 bear, deer, fawn, hare, hart, lynx, stag 6 badger
crown: 6 canopy
deity: 3 Pan
floor: 5 humus
growth: 4 moss 6 lichen
like a ~ floor: 5 ferny
like some ~ s: 4 lush 5 firry, piney
like the earth in a ~: 5 rooty
national ~: 4 Gila, Inyo, Pike 5 Boise, Delta, Dixie, Huron, Modoc, Ocala, Ozark, Routt, Tahoe, Teton, Tonto, Twain, Uinta, Wayne 6 Apache, Ashley, Carson, Cibola, Custer, De Soto, Helena, Kaibab, Lassen, Marion, Ochoco, Oconee, Oglala, Ottawa, Pawnee, Pisgah, Plumas, Sabine, Salmon, Shasta, Sierra, Sumter, Umpqua, Winema 7 Angeles, Arapaho, Bighorn, Bridger, Caribou, Challis, Chugach, Conecuh, Fremont, Hoosier, Houston, Klamath, Lincoln, Malheur, Nicolet, Olympic, Osceola, Payette, Pinchot, San Juan, Santa Fe, Sequoia, Shawnee, Siuslaw, Targhee, Tongass, Trinity, Wasatch 8 Angelina, Bankhead, Cherokee, Chippewa, Coconino, Colville, Croatoan, Crockett, Eldorado, Fishlake, Flathead, Gallatin, Hiawatha, Humboldt, Kootenai, Manistee, Nez Perce, Okanogan, Ouachita, Prescott, Sawtooth, Shoshone, Superior, Tombigee, Tuskegee, Uwharrie 9 Allegheny, Bienville, Deschutes, Kisatchie, Roosevelt, Talladega, Wenatchee
nymph: 5 dryad
old-style: 5 weald
rain ~: 5 biome, selva 6 jungle
ranger, at times: 5 guide
region: 5 taiga
sprite: 3 elf
unit: 4 tree
way: 4 lane, path 8 footpath
forest __: 5 green 6 ranger 7 reserve
__ forest: 3 fog 4 rain 7 gallery
Forest: 8 Whitaker
Forest __: 7 Service
__ Forest: 3 New 4 Wake 5 Black, Lee De 6 Epping 7 Argonne, Waltham 8 Sherwood
forestage: 5 apron
forestall: 4 stop 5 avert, deter, parry 6 forbid, hinder, thwart 7 obviate, prevent, rule out, ward off 8 obstruct, preclude 9 frustrate 10 anticipate, get ahead of
forestalling: 4 veto
__ Forest cake: 5 Black
forested: 5 woody 6 silvan, sylvan, wooded, woodsy 8 arboreal
Forester: 3 car 4 auto 6 Subaru
Forester, C.S.: 6 writer 7 British
first name: Cecil
work: The African Queen
Sink the Bismarck!
forester tool: 3 axe 7 hatchet
Forest Hills: 4 city, town
locale: 6 Canada 8 Michigan 10 Nova Scotia
Forest of __: 4 Dean 5 Arden
forestry: 7 science
study: 5 trees
tool: 3 axe
__ Forest, The: 5 Cloud 7 Emerald
foretaste: 6 hansel 7 handsel, warning 10 anticipate
foretell: 3 see 4 bode, look, mean, warn 5 augur, spell 6 divine 7 betoken, portend, predict, presage 8 prophesy, soothsay 9 adumbrate 10 anticipate
foreteller: 4 seer 5 augur 10 soothsayer
foretelling: 5 vatic 6 augury, occult, oracle, vision 8 mystical, oracular, prophecy 9 prescient, prophetic, sibylline 10 auspicious, divination, portentous, prophesying
forethought: 4 care 7 caution 10 precaution
foretoken: 4 bode, omen, sign 5 augur 6 augury, herald 7 portend, portent, presage, promise, warning 9 harbinger, prefigure
foretop ender: 4 mast, sail 7 gallant
forever: 4 ages 5 etern 6 always, eterne 7 finally, lasting 8 eternity 9 endlessly, eternally 10 enduringly, unendingly
and a day: 3 eon 4 aeon, ages 8 long time
in verse: 5 etern 6 eterne
lasting ~: 6 eonian
now and ~: 8 immortal, timeless, unending 9 perpetual
take ~: 4 drag 5 dally, stall, tarry 6 dawdle 10 dillydally
forever __ day: 4 and a
Forever __: 5 Amber, Young 6 Female
Forever __ Girl: 4 Your
__ Forever: 6 Batman
Forever Amber (1947 film)
cast: Linda Darnell, Richard Greene, Cornel Wilde
director: Otto Preminger
forever and __: 4 a day
Forever and a Day (1943 film)
cast: Edmund Goulding, Cedric Hardwicke, Frank Lloyd
director: René Clair
Forever and Ever singer: 6 Ed Ames
Forever author: Judy Blume
Forever Female (1953 film)
cast: Paul Douglas, William Holden, Ginger Rogers
director: Irving Rapper
Forever (song) artist: Kiss, Little Dippers, Mariah Carey
Forever Young (1992 film)
cast: Jamie Lee Curtis, Mel Gibson, Elijah Wood
director: Steve Miner
Forever Young (1988 song) artist: Rod Stewart
Forever Your Girl (1989 song) artist: Paula Abdul
__ for Evidence: 3 E Is
forewarn: 3 tip 5 alert 6 advise, inform, tip off 7 apprise, apprize, caution, portend, presage 8 admonish, prophesy, threaten
forewarning: 4 omen, sign 5 alarm 6 advice, augury, caveat 7 caution, portent, presage 9 foretoken, predictor
foreword: 5 intro, proem 6 prolog 7 preface, prelude 8 exordium, overture, preamble, prologue
__ for Fears: 5 Tears
forfeit: 4 cede, drop, dump, fine, lose, pawn, sell, shed 5 chuck, ditch, forgo, yield 6 forego, give up 7 abandon, forsake, penalty 8 forswear, get rid of, give over, hand over, jettison, part with, throw out 9 cast aside, dispose of, foreswear, sacrifice, surrender, throw away 10 punishment, relinquish
ender: 3 ure
Forfeit author: Dick Francis
forfeited: 4 lost
forfeits: 4 game 8 card game
game with ~: 3 loo
variety: 3 loo
forfeiture: 4 cost, fine, loss 5 mulct 7 penalty
forfend: 6 forbid 7 obviate, prevent, rule out 8 preclude, prohibit
__ for Fire: 5 Quest
__ for Five: 5 Table 6 Dinner
__ for Fugitive: 3 F Is
forgather: 4 meet 5 group 6 muster 7 convene 8 assemble 10 congregate, rendezvous
forge: 4 fake, form, make, mint, mold, push 5 build, craft, draft, erect, frame, lunge, put up, shape, shove, stove 6 beetle, charge, create, design, devise, pirate, plunge, smithy, thrust 7 develop, factory, falsify, fashion, foundry, furnace, phony up, produce 8 assemble, simulate, smithery 9 construct, establish, fabricate, formulate, give shape, hammer out, ironworks, steamroll, strong-arm
ahead: 5 march 7 advance, recover 8 continue, progress 9 go forward

need: 4 fire 5 anvil
site of Vulcan's ~: 4 Etna 5 Aetna
worker: 5 smith 10 blacksmith
__ forge: 4 drop
forged: 4 fake, mock, sham 5 bogus, false, phony, put-on 6 ersatz, phoney, pseudo, unreal 7 assumed, feigned 8 spurious 9 imitation, simulated, synthetic 10 artificial, fabricated, fictitious, fraudulent
__ Forge, PA: 6 Valley
forger: 5 faker, fraud 8 imitator, swindler 9 falsifier
forgery: 4 copy, fake, sham 5 phony 6 phoney 9 imitation
forget: 4 lose, miss, omit, skip 5 leave 6 ignore, slight 7 let slip, neglect 8 discount, overlook, pass over, space out, write off 9 disregard 10 draw a blank
about: 4 drop, skip 8 write off
don't ~: 8 remember
forgive and ~: 6 make up, settle 9 reconcile 10 make amends, shake hands
hard to ~: 6 catchy
it: 2 no 3 nah, naw, nay, nix, non 4 nein, nope, nyet, uh-uh 5 I won't, ixnay, never, nohow, no sir, no way 6 no deal, no dice, no soap, noways, nowise 7 I refuse 8 I will not, negative, negatory, no matter 9 by no means, fat chance, I think not, never mind 10 count me out, not a chance, thumbs down
one's lines: 4 go up 5 choke, fluff 6 freeze 7 go blank 10 draw a blank
where it is: 4 lose 6 mislay 7 misfile 8 misplace
forget-__: 5 me-not
Forget __: 3 Him 5 Paris
forgetful: 3 lax 5 slack 6 remiss 7 unaware 8 careless, mindless 9 airheaded, amnemonic, negligent, oblivious, unheedful, unmindful, unwitting 10 abstracted, distracted, neglectful, out to lunch, ungrateful
forgetfulness: 5 lapse 7 amnesia, neglect
flower of ~: 5 lotus
river of ~: 5 Lethe
Forget Him (1963 song) artist: Bobby Rydell
forget-me-not: 5 plant 6 flower
Forget Paris (1995 film)
cast: Billy Crystal, Joe Mantegna, Debra Winger
director: Billy Crystal
forgivable: 6 venial 9 allowable, excusable, tolerable 10 pardonable
forgive: 4 pity 5 purge, remit, spare 6 acquit, excuse, exempt, let off, pardon, wink at 7 absolve, condone, let it go, let pass, release 8 allow for, bear with, laugh off, overlook, reprieve, take back 9 exculpate, exonerate, extenuate
and forget: 6 make up, settle 9 reconcile 10 make amends, shake hands
don't ~ and forget: 6 avenge
...__ forgiven!: 5 all is
forgiveness: 5 grace, mercy 6 lenity, pardon 7 amnesty, quarter 8 clemency, immunity, reprieve 9 remission
ask ~: 5 atone 6 repent
__ forgive those...: 4 as we
forgiving: 3 lax 4 easy, kind, mild, soft 5 loose 6 gentle, kindly, tender 7 clement, lenient, patient, ruthful 8 flexible, laid-back, merciful, placable, tolerant 9 assuasive, brotherly, compliant, easygoing, indulgent 10 charitable, forbearing, permissive, unexacting

__ for Glory: 5 Bound
forgo: 4 cede, drop, dump, miss, quit, sell, shed, shun, skip 5 chuck, ditch, spare, waive, yield 6 abjure, eschew, give up, pass on, pass up, resist, sit out 7 abandon, abstain, forbear, forsake, refrain 8 abdicate, get rid of, hand over, jettison, keep from, leave out, part with, renounce, sign away, swear off, throw out 9 cast aside, dispose of, do without, sacrifice, surrender, throw away 10 desist from, relinquish
a right: 5 waive 6 give up 8 sign away 10 relinquish
__ for Godot: 7 Waiting
forgoing: 5 sober, staid
for good __: 7 measure
For goodness sake!: 4 oh my
forgotten: 4 gone, lost, past 5 passé 6 buried, bygone, erased, lapsed 7 omitted 8 out of use 9 abandoned, blown over, repressed 10 blanked out, blotted out, left behind, suppressed, unrecalled
be ~: 4 pass 7 subside 8 blow over
something ~: 5 lapse 8 omission 9 oversight
Forgotten, The author: Faye Kellerman
__ for granted: 4 take
__ for Gumshoe: 3 G Is
For heaven's __!: 4 sake
for here, not: 4 to go
__ for her eyes, with...: 3 E is
For He's a Jolly Good Fellow end: 4 deny
__: For Hire: 7 Spenser
__ for Hollywood: 6 Hooray
__ for Homicide: 3 H Is
__ for Innocent: 3 I Is
forint: 5 money
__ for it: 3 ask
__ for Judgment: 3 J Is
fork: 4 part, turn 5 split 6 bisect, branch, divide, ramble, recess 7 diverge, utensil 8 disburse, separate, shell out 9 bifurcate, branch off, implement, tableware, tributary 10 divergence, silverware
ender: 4 ball, lift
like a ~: 5 tined 7 pronged
over: 3 pay 4 cede, deal, give 5 relay, remit, spend, yield 6 expend, pay out, render 7 cough up, deliver 8 shell out 9 surrender 10 relinquish
part: 4 tine 5 prong
partner: 5 knife
shape: 3 wye
site: 4 road 5 river
starter: 3 hay 5 pitch
use a ~: 3 eat, sup 4 chew, dine 5 feast 7 consume, partake
__ fork: 4 fish 5 salad 6 dinner, oyster, sucket, tuning 7 carving, dessert
forkball: 5 pitch
forked: 5 split, tined 6 cloven, zigzag 7 furcate, pronged 8 furcated 9 bifurcate, lightning
speak with ~ tongue: 3 fib, lie 4 dupe 5 bluff, fudge, guile 6 delude 7 deceive, falsify, mislead 8 misspeak 9 dissemble, misinform
__ for keeps: 4 play 7 playing
forkful: 4 bite
For Kicks author: Dick Francis
__ for Killer: 3 K Is
forklift: 5 truck
forks: 4 ware 9 tableware 10 dinnerware, silverware
Forlani, Claire: 7 actress
film: Antitrust (2001)
Meet Joe Black (1998)
Mystery Men (1999)
__ for Lawless: 3 L Is

__-for-leather: 4 hell
__ for Lefty: 7 Waiting
__ for Life: 4 Lust, Zest
for life in Latin: 7 ad vitam
__ for Living: 6 Design
forlorn: 3 low, sad 4 blue, down, mopy 5 alone, drear, gaunt, mopey 6 abject, bereft, dismal, dreary, gloomy, lonely, tragic 7 doleful, hangdog, in a funk, pitiful, unhappy, wistful 8 deprived, deserted, desolate, downcast, forsaken, helpless, homesick, hopeless, lonesome, pitiable, tragical, wretched 9 cheerless, depressed, desperate, heartsick, miserable, woebegone 10 despairing, despondent, lugubrious
feeling: 7 despair
forlorn __: 4 hope
__ for Love: 3 All 6 Hooray, Lookin'
For Love of __: 3 Ivy
For Love of the Game (1999 film)
cast: Kevin Costner, Kelly Preston, John C. Reilly
director: Sam Raimi
for love or __: 5 money
form: 3 bod, ilk 4 body, brew, cast, kind, make, mode, mold, rear, rite, sort, trim, type 5 blank, build, class, erect, forge, found, frame, model, order, setup, shape, stamp, state, style, teach, thing, torso, train, usage 6 appear, beetle, cook up, create, custom, design, devise, fettle, figure, health, invent, make up, manner, mature, medium, method, ritual, scheme, school, sketch, system 7 anatomy, arrange, bring up, compose, concoct, conduct, contour, decorum, develop, dream up, educate, fashion, fitness, liturgy, outline, pattern, process, produce, profile, shape up, turn out, variety 8 assemble, behavior, block out, ceremony, complete, comprise, conceive, contrive, document, figure in, generate, instruct, likeness, organize, physique, practice, protocol, symmetry 9 character, construct, establish, etiquette, framework, give shape, hammer out, lineament, originate, paperwork, placement, propriety, semblance, structure, take shape, tradition 10 appearance, bring about, constitute, convention, embodiment, observance, regulation, silhouette
a gully: 4 flow, gush 5 erode
a judgment: 3 fix 4 rule 6 choose, decide 7 appoint 8 finalize, sentence 9 determine, establish, negotiate
a notion: 5 think 6 ideate
assume the ~ of: 6 become 8 turn into
a union: 4 bond, join, yoke 5 marry, merge 7 combine, make one 9 integrate 10 tie the knot
bad ~: 8 improper, unseemly 9 graceless 10 indecorous, indelicacy, indelicate, out of order, unsuitable
combining form: 5 -morph 6 morpho-
derived ~: 7 variant
ending: 3 ula 5 ative
fill out a ~: 5 apply
good ~: 7 manners 8 protocol 9 propriety
in its original ~: 5 uncut 6 intact 8 complete 10 unabridged
pertaining to ~: 5 modal
qualification ~: 4 exam, test
return to ~: 5 rally 7 get well, rebound, recover 8 snap back 10 bounce back, convalesce, recuperate, spring back
starter: 3 ovi, uni
take ~: 4 jell 5 shape 8 incubate
vague ~: 4 blob, glob, lump, mass, spot 5 smear 6 smudge 7 splotch
without ~: 5 vague 8 nebulous 9 amorphous, shapeless 10 indefinite
form __: 4 drag, nail, stop, word 5 class, genus 6 letter
__ form: 3 art 4 life, slip 5 bound, dance, entry 6 binary, racing, sonata, speech 7 clipped, derived, ternary
__-form: 4 free, wave
__ forma: 3 pro
formable: 7 ductile, plastic, pliable 9 malleable, shapeable
formal: 4 ball, gown, prim 5 aloof, dance, legal, staid, stiff 6 dressy, lordly, polite, proper, ritual, solemn, stodgy, strict, stuffy, tuxedo 7 bookish, correct, courtly, express, nominal, orderly, regular, stately, stilted 8 academic, affected, decorous, explicit, highbred, ladylike, literary, official, reserved, starched 9 dignified, unbending 10 ceremonial, liturgical, methodical, prescribed, systematic
act: 4 rite 6 ritual 8 ceremony
address: 3 sir 4 ma'am 5 madam
affair: 4 ball, fete, meal, prom 5 feast, levee, party 6 repast, spread 7 banquet
agreement: 4 pact 6 accord, treaty 7 charter, compact, concord 8 contract, protocol 9 concordat 10 convention
attire: 3 tux 4 gown, tuck 5 tails 6 tuxedo 7 cutaway 8 black tie, white tie
ender: 4 wear
greeting: 3 bow 6 curtsy
opposite: 6 casual
overly ~: 4 prim 5 stiff
starter: 4 semi
wear of old: 4 toga
__ for Malice: 3 M Is
formalist: 4 prig 6 purist 7 fusspot, puritan 8 bluenose 9 nitpicker 10 fuddy-duddy
formalistic: 8 academic 9 pedagogic 10 scholastic
formalities: 6 ritual 7 decorum, red tape 8 ceremony, protocol 9 etiquette, politesse, propriety
formality: 4 pomp, rite 6 custom, ritual, starch 7 decorum, liturgy, p's and q's, reserve 8 ceremony, protocol 9 academism, austerity, etiquette, gentility, politesse, procedure, propriety, solemnity, tradition 10 classicism, convenance, convention, observance, solemnness, stereotype
formalize: 3 fix 4 name 5 shape 6 define, settle 7 specify 8 nail down, restrict, spell out 9 establish
formals: 6 finery 7 regalia 9 trappings
Forman, Milos: 8 director
film: Amadeus (1984, AA)
Man on the Moon (1999)
One Flew Over the Cuckoo's Nest (1975, AA)
Ragtime (1981)
Taking Off (1971)
__ for Man, so stealthily betrayed: 4 Alas
format: 4 look, plan 5 array, setup, shape 6 layout, makeup, scheme 7 arrange, pattern 8 organize 9 structure 10 appearance, dimensions
Formata: 4 font 8 typeface
formation: 6 design, layout, makeup

7 deposit, genesis 8 creation, grouping 9 evolution, synthesis 10 conception, embodiment, generation, production
 combining form: 6 -plasty 7 -poiesis
__ formation: 4 back 6 flight
formative: 6 pliant 8 immature, moldable, original 9 inventive, malleable, sensitive
 years: 5 teens, youth
__ for Me: 3 You 4 Good, Send
For Me and My Gal (1942 film)
 cast: Judy Garland, Gene Kelly, George Murphy
 director: Busby Berkeley
__-formed: 3 ill
former: 3 old 4 late, past 5 olden, older, prior 6 bygone, bypast, whilom 7 ancient, earlier, old-time, one-time, quondam 8 anterior, foregone, old-style, outgoing, previous 9 erstwhile, foregoing, preceding
 combining form: 6 proter- 7 protero-
 opposite: 6 latter
formerly: 3 ago, nee 4 erst, once, then 6 before 7 already, earlier, long ago 8 until now 9 at one time, in the past 10 beforetime, heretofore, originally, previously
form-fitting: 4 firm, snug, taut 5 rigid, stiff
formic acid producer: 3 ant
formicary: 4 nest
 dweller: 3 ant 5 emmet 6 ergate
Formicidae member: 3 ant
formidability: 5 brawn, clout, might, power, punch, sinew, vigor 6 muscle 7 potency, prowess 8 strength, vitality 9 puissance 10 brawniness
formidable: 4 dire, grim, hard, ugly 5 awful, great, heavy, rough, stiff, tough 6 fierce, knotty, mighty, potent, rugged, sticky, strong, thorny, trying, uphill 7 arduous, awesome, fearful, mammoth, onerous, serious 8 colossal, daunting, dreadful, grueling, horrible, horrific, imposing, menacing, powerful, shocking, terrible, terrific, toilsome 9 ambitious, appalling, dangerous, demanding, difficult, dismaying, effortful, frightful, herculean, laborious, strenuous 10 impressive, iron-willed, oppressive, petrifying, staggering, terrifying, tremendous
__-forming: 4 acid 5 habit
formless: 4 soft 9 amorphous, shapeless 10 unfinished
Formosa: 3 isl., str. 4 isle 6 island, strait, Taiwan
 island near ~: 4 Mazu 5 Matsu 6 Quemoy
Formosus: 4 pope 7 pontiff
__ for Mr. Goodbar: 7 Looking
__ for Mrs. Pollifax: 5 A Palm
formula: 3 law 4 milk, rule 5 usage 6 method, recipe 7 liturgy, precept, routine, theorem 8 equation 9 blueprint, principle, procedure 10 directions, stereotype
 catcher: 3 bib
formula __: 4 unit 6 weight
__ formula: 4 wing 5 Hero's 6 Euler's, Frenet 7 Kekulé's
Formula __: 3 One
Formula 409: 7 cleaner
 alternative: 5 Brite, Lysol 6 Top Job 7 Lestoil, Mr. Clean, Pine Sol 9 Fantastik, Step Saver
Formula One car: 5 racer
formulate: 3 map, put 4 draw, make, plan 5 build, couch, draft, forge, frame, hatch, write 6 codify, cook up, create, define, derive, detail, devise, draw up, evolve, invent, make up, map out, phrase 7 compose, concoct, develop, dream up, prepare, set down, think up, work out 8 conceive, contrive, legalize, organize, tabulate, theorize 9 construct, establish, fabricate, originate
formulation: 3 ism 4 idea 6 belief, system, theory, thesis 7 concept, opinion, premise, surmise, theorem, thought 8 argument, creation, doctrine, position 9 postulate, rationale 10 assumption, conception, conjecture, hypothesis, philosophy, principium
__ for Murder: 5 Dial M
__ for My Baby: 3 One
__ for news: 4 nose
__ for Noose: 3 N Is
__-for-nothing: 4 good
For Once in My Life (1968 song)
 artist: Stevie Wonder
__ for one...: 3 All
__ for One More: 4 Room
__ for oneself: 4 fend
__ for one's money: 4 a run
__ for One Year, A: 5 Widow
__ for Outlaw: 3 O Is
__ for Peace: 5 Atoms
__ for Peril: 3 P Is
For Pete's __!: 4 sake
For Pete's Sake (1974 film)
 cast: Estelle Parsons, Michael Sarrazin, Barbra Streisand
 director: Peter Yates
__-for-profit: 3 not
__ for Quarry: 3 Q Is
__ for Red October, The: 4 Hunt
Forrest: 4 Gump 5 Gregg, Steve 6 Nathan, Sawyer, Tucker 8 Frederic
Forrestal: 5 James
__ Forrester: 7 Finding
Forrest, Frederic: 5 actor
 film: Adventures of Huckleberry Finn (1985)
  The Conversation (1974)
  Hammett (1983)
  Music Box (1989)
  Rain Without Thunder (1992)
  The Rose (1979)
  Valley Girl (1983)
  Whatever (1998)
  When the Legends Die (1972)
Forrest Gump (1994 film)
 cast: Sally Field, Tom Hanks, Haley Joel Osment, Gary Sinise, Robin Wright
 character: 3 Dan 5 Bubba, Jenny
 director: Robert Zemeckis
 locale: 3 Ala., Nam 7 Alabama, Vietnam
for richer, for __: 6 poorer
forsake: 4 cede, drop, dump, fail, jilt, quit, sell, shed 5 chuck, ditch, forgo, leave, spare, spurn, yield 6 abjure, betray, defect, desert, disown, forego, give up, maroon, reject, strand 7 abandon, cast off, disavow, discard, forfeit, scuttle 8 disclaim, forswear, get rid of, give up on, go back on, hand over, jettison, part with, renounce, run out on, swear off, throw out 9 cast aside, dispose of, foreswear, repudiate, surrender, throw away, throw over, walk out on 10 relinquish
forsaken: 4 left, lone, lorn 5 alone, stark 6 jilted, lonely 7 cast off, forlorn, given up, ignored, in a funk, outcast, rundown, spurned, unloved 8 derelict, deserted, desolate, disowned, helpless, isolated, marooned, solitary, untended 9 abandoned, renounced 10 repudiated
 child: 4 waif
 starter: 3 god
forsaker: 7 heretic, runaway, traitor 8 apostate, betrayer, defector, deserter, renegade, turncoat 10 iconoclast, schismatic
forsaking: 8 apostasy 9 defection, desertion, sundering
__ for Sale: 4 Love 6 Beauty, Heroes
for sale by __: 5 owner
__ for Scandal, The: 6 School
__-for-service: 3 fee
For shame!: 3 fie, tsk, tut 4 my my 6 tsk tsk
__ for size: 5 try on
__ for sore eyes, a: 5 sight
Forssmann, Werner: 8 Nobelist
__ for St. Cecilia's Day: 3 Ode
Forster: 2 E.M. 6 Robert
Forster, E.M.: 6 author, writer 7 British
 work: Howards End
  A Passage to India
  A Room With a View
__ for Strings: 6 Adagio
__ for Success: 5 Dress
__ for Superman!: 4 a job
For sure!: 5 oh yes 6 you bet
forswear: 3 lie 4 cede, drop, dump, jilt, sell, shed 5 chuck, ditch, forgo, leave, spurn, yield 6 abjure, desert, disown, eschew, forego, give up, maroon, pass up, recall, recant, reject 7 abandon, cast off, disavow, forfeit, forsake, perjure, retract 8 disclaim, get rid of, hand over, jettison, part with, renounce, run out on, throw out, withdraw 9 cast aside, dispose of, repudiate, surrender, throw away, walk out on 10 relinquish
forswearing: 6 denial 8 apostasy 9 disavowal, rejection 10 refutation
forsworn: 5 false 6 untrue 7 unloyal 8 disloyal 9 deceitful, faithless, two-timing 10 unfaithful
Forsyte Saga, The
 author: John Galsworthy
 character: 3 Jon, Val 4 June, Mont 5 Belby, Boris, Fleur, Holly, Irene, James, Jolly 6 Dartie, Jolyon, Philip, Soames 7 Annette, Lamotte, Swithin, Timothy 8 Bosinney, Winifred
 dog: 9 Balthasar
 novel: In Chancery, To Let
Forsyth: 4 Bill 9 Frederick
Forsythe, John: 5 actor
 film: ... And Justice for All (1979)
  Escape From Fort Bravo (1953)
  The Glass Web (1953)
  In Cold Blood (1967)
  It Happens Every Thursday (1953)
  Scrooged (1988)
  Topaz (1969)
  The Trouble With Harry (1955)
 TV: Bachelor Father, Charlie's Angels, Dynasty
forsythia: 5 plant, shrub 6 flower
 relative: 5 lilac, olive 7 jasmine 9 jessamine
fort: 4 post 5 redan 6 castle, refuge 7 citadel, defense, rampart, redoubt 8 fastness, garrison, presidio 9 acropolis 10 stronghold
 Alabama: 6 Rucker
 Alaska: 10 Richardson
 Arizona: 8 Huachuca
 California: 3 Ord 5 Irwin
 Colorado: 6 Carson
 ditch: 4 moat
 El Paso: 5 Bliss
 ender: 5 night
 Georgia: 6 Gordon 7 Benning 9 McPherson
 gold ~: 4 Knox
 hold the ~: 4 stay 6 defend, remain, uphold 7 carry on, stand by 8 maintain
 Kansas: 5 Riley
 Kentucky: 4 Knox 8 Campbell
 Louisiana: 4 Polk
 Maryland: 5 Meade 7 Detrick, McHenry
 New Jersey: 3 Dix 8 Monmouth
 New York: 4 Drum 8 Hamilton
 Niagara: 4 Erie
 North Carolina: 5 Bragg
 Oklahoma: 4 Sill
 opening: 4 gate
 South Carolina: 7 Jackson
 Texas: 5 Bliss 10 Sam Houston
 Virginia: 3 Lee 6 Eustis, Monroe
 Washington: 5 Lewis
Fort __: 3 Dix, Lee, Ord 4 Drum, Erie, Hood, Knox, Mims, Myer, Polk, Sill 5 Bliss, Boise, Bragg, Henry, Irwin, Lewis, Meade, Meigs, Riley 6 Apache, Carson, Casper, Devens, Eustis, Gordon, McNair, Monroe, Orange, Rucker, Sumter 7 Belvoir, Benning, Detrick, Jackson, Kearney, Laramie, McHenry, Pickens, Pulaski, Stewart
Fort __ Dam: 4 Peck
Fort __, FL: 5 Myers
Fort __ Houston: 3 Sam
Fort __, IN: 5 Wayne
Fort __, Ont.: 4 Erie
Fort __, WI: 5 McCoy
Fort __ Wood: 7 Leonard
Fortaleza: 4 city, port, town
 locale: 5 Ceara 6 Brazil
Fort Apache (1948 film): 5 oater
 cast: John Agar, Pedro Armendariz, Ward Bond, Henry Fonda, Shirley Temple, John Wayne
 director: John Ford
Fort Apache, The Bronx (1981 film)
 cast: Danny Aiello, Edward Asner, Paul Newman
 director: Daniel Petrie
Fortas: 3 Abe
 forte: 3 law
__ for tat: 3 tit
Fort Bliss site: 6 El Paso
Fort Bragg: 4 city, town
 locale: 4 N. Car. 10 California
Fort Collins: 4 city, town
 athletes: 4 Rams
 locale: 3 Col. 8 Colorado
 school: 3 CSU
Fort Courage group: 6 F Troop
Fort-de-France: 4 city, town
 locale: 10 Martinique
Fort Dodge: 4 city, town
 locale: 4 Iowa
forte: 3 job 4 gift, loud 5 flair, noisy, thing 6 loudly, métier, talent 7 blaring, booming, jarring, pealing, rackety, raucous, reboant, roaring 8 crashing, long suit, piercing, plangent, rumbling, sonorous, strength, strident, turned up 9 big-voiced, clamorous, deafening, expertise, specialty 10 boisterous, resounding, stentorian, strepitous, strong suit, thundering, uproarious, vociferous
 opposite: 5 piano
__ forte: 5 mezzo
Fort Erie: 4 city, town
 locale: 6 Canada 7 Ontario
forth: 3 out 4 away 5 ahead, along 6 onward 7 onwards, outward
 ender: 4 with 5 right 6 coming
 starter: 5 hence 6 thence
__ forth: 3 put, set 4 call, hold, send 5 and so, bring
for that __: 6 matter
forthcoming: 3 TBA 4 near, nigh 5 on tap 6 at hand, future 7 awaited, in store, pending 8 gracious, oncoming 9 proximate

for the __: 4 best 5 birds, nonce 6 asking 7 present
for the __ being: 4 time
for the __ of it: 3 fun 4 heck
for the __ of Pete: 4 love
for the __ part: 4 most
__ for the books: 3 one
For the Boys (1991 film)
cast: James Caan, Bette Midler, Patrick O'Neal, George Segal
director: Mark Rydell
grp.: 3 USO
__ for the buck: 4 bang
__ for the Common Man: 7 Fanfare
__ for the course: 3 par
for the fun __: 4 of it
for the heck __: 4 of it
__ for the Holidays: 4 Home
For the life __,...: 4 of me
For the Love of Benji director: 4 Camp
For the Love of Money (1974 song) artist: O'Jays
__ for the Memory: 6 Thanks
__ for the mill: 5 grist
__ for the million things...: 3 M is
__ for the Misbegotten: 5 A Moon
__ for the money...: 3 One
for the most __: 4 part
__ for the only one I see: 3 O is
__ for the poor: 4 alms
__ for the Prosecution: 7 Witness
__ for the ride: 5 along
__ for the road: 3 one
__ for the Road: 3 Two
__ for the Seesaw: 3 Two
__ for the show: 3 Two
__ for the Silver Lining: 4 Look
__ for the tears...: 3 T is
for the time __: 5 being
for the time being in Latin: 10 pro tempore
__ for the Tsar: 5 A Life
for this, literally: 5 ad hoc
__ for Three Oranges, The: 4 Love
forthright: 4 bold, open 5 bluff, blunt, frank, legit, plain, vocal 6 candid, direct, honest, infelt, square 7 factual, forward, natural, sincere, up-front, upright 8 credible, definite, directly, like it is, out-front, straight, truthful 9 outspoken, veracious 10 aboveboard, flat-footed, foursquare, freespoken, from the hip, on the level, scrupulous, unmediated, unreserved, unreticent
be ~: 4 aver, avow 6 affirm, assert 7 declare 8 proclaim, speak out 10 asseverate
not ~: 3 sly 4 foxy, wily 5 cagey, slick, snaky 6 covert, crafty, impish, secret, shifty, sneaky, tricky 7 crooked, cunning, devious, evasive, furtive, roguish 8 delusive, guileful, stealthy 9 conniving, deceitful, deceptive, designing, dishonest, insidious
forthrightly: 6 openly 8 directly 10 foursquare
forthwith: 3 now, PDQ 4 anon, ASAP, soon 5 apace, today 6 at once, presto 7 fleetly, hastily, quickly, rapidly, swiftly 8 directly, in a flash, in a jiffy, in no time, pell-mell, promptly, right now, right off, speedily 9 at present, hurriedly, instantly, like a shot, posthaste, presently, right away, summarily 10 at this time, here and now, this minute
fortification: 4 keep, wall 5 redan, tower 6 buffer, castle 7 barrier, bastion, buildup, bulwark, citadel, defense, outpost, rampart 8 garrison, presidio, stockade
slope: 5 talus
fortified: 5 armed 6 secure, sturdy
place: 7 bastion, bulwark, citadel, parapet, rampart 8 fortress 10 breastwork, stronghold
fortify: 3 arm, man 4 gird, lace, prop, tone 5 brace, build, rally, ready, renew, rouse, shore, steel 6 anneal, arouse, beef up, enrich, harden, prop up, step up, temper, tone up 7 bolster, brace up, build up, bulwark, burgeon, develop, empower, enhance, enliven, hearten, prepare, protect, punch up, refresh, restore, shore up, stiffen, support, sustain, toughen 8 bourgeon, buttress, embattle, embolden, energize, imbolden, indurate, vitalize 9 intensify, reinforce 10 invigorate, strengthen, supplement
fortifying: 4 cool 5 brisk, crisp, fresh 7 bracing, healthy, rousing 8 vigorous 10 energizing, refreshing
__ for time: 4 play
Fortín: 4 city, town
locale: 6 Mexico 8 Veracruz
__ for Tinhorns: 5 Fugue
__ fortis: 4 aqua
fortis, opposite of: 5 lenis
fortitude: 3 vim 4 dint, grit, guts, thew 5 brawn, force, heart, might, moxie, nerve, pluck, power, spine, spunk, thews, valor, vigor 6 energy, mettle, muscle, spirit, starch, virtue 7 bravery, courage, fitness, heroism, muscles, potence, potency, prowess, stamina 8 backbone, boldness, decision, patience, strength, tenacity, true grit, valiance, valiancy, vitality 9 beefiness, braveness, composure, constancy, endurance, fixedness, gutsiness, hardihood, hardiness, huskiness, puissance, stoutness, tolerance, toughness 10 brawniness, brute force, confidence, mightiness, moral fiber, resolution, robustness, sturdiness
Fort Knox: 4 city, town 8 treasury
filler: 4 gold 6 ingots 7 bullion
locale: 3 Ken. 8 Kentucky
Fort Lauderdale: 4 city, town
locale: 3 Fla. 7 Florida
Fort Lee: 4 city, town
locale: 9 New Jersey
Fort Leonard __: 4 Wood
Fort Lewis: 4 city, town
locale: 4 Wash. 10 Washington
Fort MacMurray: 4 city, town
locale: 6 Canada 7 Alberta
Fort Myers: 4 city, town
city near ~: 6 Naples
locale: 3 Fla. 7 Florida
fortnighter: 3 bag 7 luggage 8 suitcase
fortnight, half a: 4 week
fortnights, two: 5 month
__ for Tomorrow: 6 Search
__ for Tots: 4 Toys
Fort Peck __: 3 Dam
Fort Pierce: 4 city, town
locale: 3 Fla. 7 Florida
Fortran: 8 language
alternative: 3 Ada, APL, SQL 4 Alef, html, Icon, Java, LISP, Logo, Orca, Perl 5 Algol, Basic, Cecil, COBOL, Dylan, SISAL 6 Delphi, Eiffel, Erlang, Oberon, Pascal, Prolog, Sather, Scheme, Snobol
developer: 3 IBM
fortress: 4 aery, eyry, keep 5 aerie, eyrie, tower 6 castle, refuge 7 bastion, chateau, citadel, defense, redoubt 8 fastness, garrison, presidio 9 acropolis 10 stronghold
Crusades ~: 5 Haifa
defense: 4 moat
extension: 5 redan
mountain ~: 4 aery, eyry 5 aerie, eyrie
North African ~: 6 Casbah, Kasbah
__ Fortress: 6 Flying
Fortress Around Your Heart (1985 song) artist: Sting
__ for trouble: 3 ask 6 asking
Fort Sam __: 7 Houston
Fort Sill
locale: 4 Okla. 8 Oklahoma
Fort Smith: 4 city, town
locale: 3 Ark. 8 Arkansas
fortuitous: 3 odd 5 blest, fluke, fluky, lucky 6 chance, flukey, random 7 blessed, charmed, favored, oddball, on a roll 9 arbitrary, haphazard, on a streak, opportune, unplanned 10 accidental, auspicious, contingent, felicitous, incidental, unforeseen, unintended
fortuitously: 7 luckily 8 by chance
fortuity: 4 luck 5 event, fluke 6 chance, hazard 7 fortune 8 accident, long shot
Fortuna Foothills: 4 city, town
locale: 7 Arizona
fortunate: 4 good, well 5 blest, happy, lucky 6 chance, in luck 7 blessed, charmed, favored, helpful, hopeful, on a roll, wealthy, well-off 8 affluent, enviable, well-to-do 9 favorable, on a streak, opportune, promising 10 auspicious, convenient, fair-haired, felicitous, flying high, profitable, propitious, prosperous, successful, triumphant, victorious
fortune: 3 hap, lot, wad 4 fate, luck, mint, pile 5 karma, means 6 chance, cookie, estate, kismat, kismet, oracle, riches, wealth 7 destiny, portion, success 8 fortuity, gold mine, opulence, opulency, treasure 9 abundance, affluence 10 prosperity, providence
good ~: 4 luck 5 break, fluke 7 godsend, welfare 8 blessing, windfall 9 well-being 10 lucky break, prosperity
holder: 6 cookie
ill ~: 3 woe 5 trial 6 misery, mishap 7 bad luck, tragedy, travail, trouble 8 bad break, calamity, disaster, distress, hardship 9 adversity, hard times, mischance, tough luck 10 affliction, hard knocks
partner: 4 fame
sharer: 6 coheir
soldier of ~: 4 merc 9 mercenary 10 adventurer
fortune __: 6 cookie, hunter, teller
Fortune Cookie, The (1966 film)
cast: Jack Lemmon, Walter Matthau
director: Billy Wilder
Fortune 500 firm: 3 AOL, CVS, Dow, IBM, NCR, UPS 4 Nike 5 Aetna, Aflac, Alcoa, Apple, Avnet, Chubb, Cigna, Cisco, Exxon, FedEx, Heinz, Intel, Kmart, Kodak, Lilly, Loews, Lowe's, Merck, Qwest, Sears, Sysco, Tyson, Xerox 6 Abbott, Altria, Amazon, Boeing, Clorox, Costco, Disney, DuPont, Hilton, Hormel, Humana, Kroger, Lauder, Mattel, Nextel, Oracle, Pfizer, Sprint, Target, Unocal, Viacom 7 Aramark, Bank One, Best Buy, Borders, Cinergy, ConAgra, Corning, Gannett, Harrah's, Hershey, Kellogg, Keyspan, Lexmark, MetLife, PepsiCo, Rite Aid, Safeway, Sara Lee, Staples, Tenneco, Toys R Us, Verizon, Visteon, Wal-Mart 8 Allstate, Auto Zone, Coca-Cola, Gillette, Goodrich, J.C. Penney, Marriott, Motorola, Navistar, Raytheon, Wachovia, Walgreen 9 BellSouth, Brunswick, Citigroup, Fannie Mae, Home Depot, Honeywell, McDonald's, Microsoft, Office Max, Starbucks, State Farm, Whirlpool 10 Albertson's, Freddie Mac, McGraw-Hill, Radio Shack, Wells Fargo
fortuneless: 4 poor 5 broke 8 dirt poor, strapped 9 destitute, insolvent, penniless 10 stone-broke, straitened
Fortune rival: 6 Forbes 7 Barron's
Fortunes of Richard Mahony author: Dorothy Richardson
Fortunes song: You've Got Your Troubles (1965)
fortune-teller: 4 seer 5 augur, sibyl 6 medium, oracle, reader 7 adviser, advisor, diviner, palmist, prophet, psychic
reading: 4 palm 5 tarot 6 I Ching 10 tarot cards
words: 4 I see
fortune-telling: 6 augury 8 prophecy 9 astrology, palmistry 10 prediction
Fort Walton Beach: 4 city, town
locale: 3 Fla. 7 Florida
Fort Washington: 4 city, town
locale: 8 Maryland
Fort Wayne: 4 city, town
clock setting: 3 EST
county: 5 Allen
locale: 3 Ind. 7 Indiana
__ for Two: 3 Tea 7 Trouble
Fort Worth: 4 city, town
county: 7 Tarrant
locale: 3 Tex. 5 Texas
river: 7 Trinity
school: 3 TCU
forty: 8 twoscore
one of the back ~: 4 acre
taking ~ winks: 6 asleep
winks: 3 nap 4 doze, rest 5 sleep 6 catnap, snooze 7 slumber
forty __: 5 winks
forty-__: 5 niner
__ forty: 4 back
forty-five: 3 gun 6 pistol 7 firearm 8 revolver
Forty Miles of Bad Road (1959 song) artist: Duane Eddy
Forty Modern Fables author: George Ade
forty-niner: 5 miner
quest: 4 gold 6 riches
stakeout: 4 mine 5 claim
Forty-Second Street composer: 5 Dubin 6 Warren
Forty Thieves foe: 3 Ali
forum: 4 talk 5 arena, court, organ 6 debate, powwow 8 assembly, colloquy, tribunal 9 symposium 10 conference
Forum: 5 arena
garb: 4 toga 5 tunic
language: 5 Latin
official: 5 edile 6 aedile 7 senator
site: 4 Rome
__ for Us: 5 A Time
For want of __...: 5 a nail, a shoe
forward: 3 aid, out 4 abet, back, bold, gear, head, help, mail, pert, post, rude, send, ship 5 ahead, along, brash, early, first, fresh, front, hurry, nervy, pushy, relay, remit, route, sassy, saucy, speed, unshy 6 better, brassy, brazen, cheeky, convey, daring, foster, hasten, incite, onward, second, unruly, wilful 7 advance, athlete, consign, deliver, express, freight, further, in front, leading, nurture, promote, restive, support, willful 8 advanced, anterior, assuming, champion, dispatch, expedite, immodest, impudent, indocile, into view, transfer, transmit 9 advancing, assertive, audacious, barefaced,

bumptious, encourage, in advance, intrusive, obtrusive, officious, pigheaded, premature, shameless, transport **10** accelerate, aggressive, forthright, precocious
bring ~: 3 lay **6** adduce **7** advance, produce
come ~: 5 offer **7** advance **8** progress **9** volunteer
drive ~: 5 impel
go ~: 4 gain, push **5** march **6** hasten, move on **7** achieve, advance, further, improve, press on, proceed, shape up **8** continue, escalate, get ahead, progress **10** accelerate, accomplish, forge ahead, gain ground, move onward, shoot ahead
jerk ~: 4 jump **5** heave, lunge, pitch
lean ~: 4 bend **5** stoop **7** bow down
look ~ to: 4 wait **5** await **6** expect **8** envision, see ahead, watch for
not ~: 3 coy, shy **4** meek **5** quiet, timid **6** demure, modest **7** bashful **8** backward, reserved, reticent, retiring, sheepish, skittish **9** diffident, shrinking, withdrawn **10** unassuming
push ~: 4 goad, move, prod, spur, urge **5** boost, drive, press, sally, shove, speed **6** attack, incite, induce, prompt, propel, stir up **7** actuate, inspire **8** motivate **9** influence, instigate, stimulate **10** accelerate
put ~: 3 lay **4** move, pose **5** offer, raise **6** assert, submit, turn in **7** advance, declare, present, produce, propose, suggest, support **8** propound **9** introduce, postulate, recommend, volunteer
rush ~: 5 lunge, lurch, pitch, surge **6** charge
starter: 5 hence **6** thence **8** straight
urge ~: 4 goad, move, poke, prod, push, spur **5** drive, press, shove **6** compel, incite, induce, prompt, propel, thrust, turn on **7** inspire, quicken **8** mobilize, motivate, persuade, pressure, railroad **9** instigate
forward __: 4 dive, pass **7** echelon
forward-__: 7 looking
__ forward: 3 put, set **4** come, fast **5** bring, carry, power **6** center, inside **7** outside
__-forward: 5 flash
__ Forward: 5 Pay It **6** Spring
__ forwarding: 4 call
forward-looking dept.: 5 R and D
forwardness: 5 brass, cheek, nerve **6** hutzpa **7** chutzpa, hutzpah, license **8** audacity, boldness, chutzpah, temerity **9** brashness, impudence, insolence **10** effrontery
forward pass in football: 6 aerial
__ forward to: 4 look
For what __ worth...: 3 it's
For What It's Worth (1967 song)
artist: Buffalo Springfield
For Whom the Bell Tolls: 4 film **5** novel
author: Ernest Hemingway
cast: Ingrid Bergman, Gary Cooper, Katina Paxinou, Akim Tamiroff
character: 4 Golz **5** André, Maria, Marty, Pablo, Pilar **6** Andrés, Eladio, Karkov, Rafael **7** Anselmo
director: Sam Wood
setting: 5 Spain
for whose benefit in Latin: 7 cui bono
__ for you!: 4 Good
__ for You: 3 All **4** Just **5** Crazy, I'd Lie, I Do It, I Feel
For You (1964 song) artist: Ricky Nelson
For You I Will (1997 song) artist: Monica
For Your Eyes Only: 4 film, song **5** novel
artist: Sheena Easton
author: Ian Fleming
cast: Roger Moore, Topol
director: John Glen
__ for Your Life: 3 Run
For Your Love (song) artist: Peaches and Herb, Yardbirds
__ for your thoughts: 5 penny
Fosbury, Dick: 10 high jumper
Foscolo, Ugo: 4 poet **6** writer **7** Italian
foss: 4 moat
Foss: 5 Lukas
fossa: 3 cat, pit **6** feline
fosse: 4 dike, moat **6** trench **7** foxhole
Fosse, Bob: 8 director
film: All That Jazz (1979)
Cabaret (1972, AA)
Lenny (1974)
Sweet Charity (1969)
forte: 5 dance
spouse: Gwen Verdon
Fossey, Dian subject: 3 ape **7** gorilla
fossil: 3 old **5** amber, copal, relic **7** crinite **8** ammonite, calamite, obsolete **9** belemnite, coprolite, encrinite, nummulite, protoavis, stone lily, trilobite **10** fuddy-duddy, graptolite
combining form: 3 -ite **4** -lite, -lyte **5** oryct- **6** orycto-
Ethiopian ~ site: 5 Hadar
fuel: 3 gas, oil **4** coal
impression: 4 fern
repository: 3 bog, tar **5** amber, copal, resin **6** tar pit
fossil __: 3 gum **4** fuel
__ fossil: 5 guide, index, trace **6** living
Fossil: 5 watch **10** wristwatch
alternative: 4 Ebel, Rado **5** Casio, Elgin, Lorus, Omega, Rolex, Seiko, Timex **6** Bulova, Movado, Pulsar, Swatch **7** Citizen **8** Longines, Tag Heuer, Tourneau
fossilize: 3 age **6** ossify **7** petrify **8** indurate
fossil tracks, science of: 9 ichnology
Foss, Lukas: 9 conductor
foster: 4 abet, back, feed, keep, rear, tend **5** boost, breed, nurse, raise, spark **6** arouse, defend, enroot, foment **7** advance, develop, forward, further, nourish, nurture, promote, protect, shelter, sponsor, support, sustain **8** champion, minister **9** cultivate, encourage, patronize **10** speak up for, take care of
child: 4 ward **7** adoptee
foster __: 3 son **4** care, home **5** child **6** father, mother, parent, sister **7** brother
Foster: 3 Hal, Meg **4** Phil, Rube **5** Jodie **6** Brooks, Norman **7** Preston, Stephen
fosterage: 8 adoption, espousal **10** acceptance
Foster City: 4 town
locale: 10 California
__ Foster Dulles: 4 John
Foster Grants: 6 shades **10** sunglasses
Foster, Jodie: 7 actress
alma mater: 4 Yale
film: The Accused (1988, AA)
Anna and the King (1999)
Backtrack (1989)
Carny (1980)
Contact (1997)
Five Corners (1988)
Freaky Friday (1977)
The Hotel New Hampshire (1984)
Little Man Tate (1991)
Maverick (1994)
Nell (1994)
Panic Room (2002)
The Silence of the Lambs (1991, AA)
Sommersby (1993)
Stealing Home (1988)
Taxi Driver (1976)
Foster, Stephen: 8 composer
song: Beautiful Dreamer
De Camptown Races
Jeanie With the Light Brown Hair
Oh! Susanna
Old Black Joe
Old Dog Tray
Old Folks at Home
Uncle Ned
Foucault, Jean: 9 physicist
Foucault's Pendulum author: Umberto Eco
foudre: 4 cask
fouetté: 4 spin
foul: 3 ill **4** base, blue, evil, grim, lewd, poor, rank, soil, ugly, vile **5** awful, dirty, error, false, fetid, grimy, gross, lousy, nasty, shady, smear, stain, sully, taint, woful **6** breach, clog up, coarse, crud up, crumby, crummy, defile, dismal, filthy, foetid, grungy, horrid, impure, no fair, odious, rancid, rotten, smelly, smudge, smutty, sordid, stinky, stormy, tangle, unfair, unjust, vulgar, wicked, woeful **7** abusive, accurst, baleful, baneful, beastly, begrime, besmear, blacken, corrupt, crooked, doleful, ghastly, hateful, heinous, low blow, noisome, noxious, odorous, offense, pollute, profane, reeking, squalid, sullied, tainted, tarnish, unclean, unswept, vicious **8** accursed, besmirch, dreadful, Godawful, grievous, horrible, indecent, infamous, inferior, mephitic, polluted, shameful, stagnant, stinking, terrible, unsavory, unwashed, wretched **9** abhorrent, appalling, atrocious, defective, dishonest, egregious, execrable, frightful, inclement, insidious, loathsome, low-minded, miserable, monstrous, nefarious, notorious, offensive, repellent, repugnant, repulsive, revolting, violation **10** abominable, despicable, detestable, disastrous, disgusting, horrendous, indelicate, infraction, iniquitous, insanitary, maleficent, malodorous, scandalous, undeserved, unpleasant, villainous
caller: 3 ref, ump **6** umpire **7** referee
language: 4 oath **5** curse **7** cursing, cussing **8** cussword, swearing **9** obscenity, profanity, swearword **10** execration, expletives
mood: 4 snit
not ~: 4 fair, just **6** proper **7** ethical **8** rightful **9** honorable **10** acceptable
odor: 4 reek **5** smell, stink **6** stench **9** effluvium
play: 4 harm **5** wrong **6** dupery, murder **8** inequity, violence
ring ~: 4 butt, knee
spot: 3 sty **5** hovel, sewer **6** pigpen, pigsty **8** pesthole
up: 3 err, mar **4** flub, goof, muff, ruin **5** botch, cross, misdo **6** blight, blow it, boggle, bollix, bungle, derail, foozle, injure, jumble, muddle **7** blunder, confuse, disturb **8** confound, obstruct **9** mishandle, mismanage **10** complicate, disconcert
(up): 3 mix **4** mess, trip
foul __: 3 tip **4** ball, line, play, pole, shot **6** matter
foulard: 3 tie **5** ascot **6** cravat, fabric **7** necktie **8** neckwear **10** four-in-hand
fouled: 5 dirty, grimy, sooty **6** filthy, grubby, grungy, soiled **8** maculate, slovenly **10** unsanitary
foulmart: 6 weasel
relative: 4 mink **5** fitch, otter, ratel, sable, skunk, stoat, tayra **6** badger, ermine, ferret, marten **7** polecat **8** carcajou, kolinsky, muishond **9** wolverine
foulmouthed: 4 lewd **5** dirty, filty **6** ribald, smutty, vulgar **7** obscene, profane **8** indecent **10** scurrilous
foulness: 4 evil **5** stink **9** indecency, pollution **10** corruption
Foul Play (1978 film)
cast: Chevy Chase, Goldie Hawn, Burgess Meredith, Dudley Moore
director: Colin Higgins
dog: 7 Chaucer
foul-smelling: 4 olid, rank **5** acrid, fetid **6** foetid
foul-up: 4 goof, slip **5** boner, snafu **6** muddle **9** mare's nest
foumart: 6 weasel
relative: 4 mink **5** fitch, otter, ratel, sable, skunk, stoat, tayra **6** badger, ermine, ferret, marten **7** polecat **8** carcajou, kolinsky, muishond **9** wolverine
found: 4 base, form **5** begin, build, endow, erect, plant, set up, start **6** create, launch **7** pioneer, start up, support **8** commence, generate, get going, initiate, organize **9** establish, institute, originate **10** constitute, inaugurate
a perch: 3 lit, sat **4** alit
as ~: 6 in situ
at this place: 6 herein
be ~: 5 occur **6** appear, crop up, show up, turn up **9** take place
by chance: 5 lit on
nowhere to be ~: 4 away, AWOL, gone, lost **6** absent **7** far away, missing **8** vanished
opposite: 4 lost
starter: 4 dumb
found __: 3 art **4** poem **5** money **6** object
foundation: 3 bed **4** ABCs, base, core, foot, root, seat **5** basis, cause, start, stays **6** bottom, corset, ground, makeup, museum, origin **7** academy, bedrock, charity, footing, grounds, support **8** backbone, creation, foothold, occasion, training, validity **9** authority, criterion, endowment, framework, institute, principle, underside **10** brass tacks, derivation, groundwork, hypothesis, settlement, substratum
exec: 3 dir. **4** pres. **8** director **9** president
firm ~: 4 rock
garment: 5 stays **6** corset, girdle
lay the ~: 5 begin, set up, start **6** launch **7** develop, kick off, prepare **8** commence **9** establish, institute, introduce, originate **10** inaugurate
material: 6 cement **8** concrete
support a ~: 6 bestow, donate **10** contribute
without ~: 8 baseless **10** groundless
__ Foundation: 4 Ford **6** Hillel
foundational: 7 radical
Foundation author: Isaac Asimov
Foundations song: Build Me Up Buttercup (1969)
founded: 3 est. **4** estd. **5** estab.
__-founded: 3 ill **4** well
founder: 4 bomb, bust, fail, fall, flop, lose, sink, slip, trip **5** flunk, wreck **6** blow it, falter, father, fizzle, go down **7** blunder, creator, go under, go wrong, misstep, pioneer, stagger, stumble, succumb, wash out **8** col-

lapse, designer, fall flat, flounder, lay an egg, submerge **9** architect, break down, hit bottom, initiator, organizer, strike out **10** benefactor, originator
foundered: 7 aground **8** marooned, stranded **10** high and dry
founders' __: 4 type **6** shares
Founders __: 3 Day
Founding __: 7 Fathers
foundling: 4 waif, ward **5** stray **6** orphan **10** ragamuffin
foundry: 4 mill **5** forge, plant **6** office **7** factory **9** ironworks
do ~ work: 6 anneal
form: 4 mold
material: 5 metal, steel
refuse: 4 slag
sound: 5 clang
fount: 4 fund, mine, well **5** store **6** origin **7** bubbler **10** wellspring
fountain: 3 jet **4** mine, well **5** spirt, spout, spurt, store **6** geyser, origin, source, spring, stream **8** wellhead **9** reservoir **10** wellspring
coin count: 5 three
coin in a ~: 4 cent, euro, lira
ender: 4 head
fare: 4 Coke, cola, cone, malt, soda **5** Pepsi, shake **6** frappe
freebie: 5 straw
New England soda ~: 3 spa
Rome ~: 5 Trevi
sound: 6 gurgle
fountain __: 3 pen **5** grass, plant
__ fountain: 3 ink **4** soda **5** Trevi, water
fountainhead: 4 germ, well **5** birth, maker **6** father, mother, origin, source, spring **7** builder, creator **10** wellspring
Fountainhead, The: 4 film **5** novel
author: Ayn Rand
cast: Gary Cooper, Raymond Massey, Patricia Neal
director: King Vidor
Fountain Hills: 4 city, town
locale: 7 Arizona
Fountain of Age, The author: Betty Friedan
Fountain of Youth site: 6 Bimini
Fountain Overflows, The author: Rebecca West
Fountain, Pete: 11 clarinetist
genre: 4 jazz **9** Dixieland
Fountains of Paradise, The author: Arthur C. Clarke
Fountain Valley: 4 city, town
locale: 10 California
four: 7 quartet
a.m.: 7 wee hour
combining form: 4 tetr- **5** quadr-, tetra- **6** quadri-, quadru-, quater-, tessar- **7** tessara-, tessera-
divide into ~: 7 quarter
ender: 4 some, teen **5** score
in French: 6 quatre
in German: 4 vier
in Italian: 7 quattro
in Japanese: 3 shi
in Portuguese: 6 quatro
in Spanish: 6 quatro
often: 3 par
three or ~: 4 a few, some **7** several
to Mohs: 8 fluorite
four __: 4 bits, o'cat
four __ cat: 3 old
four __ kind: 3 of a
four-__: 3 way **4** a-cat, spot, star **5** color, cycle **6** bagger, banger, handed, legged, stroke **7** channel, flusher, striper
four-__ bed: 6 poster
four-__ clover: 4 leaf
four-__ fire: 5 alarm
four-__-floor: 5 on-the
four-__ harmony: 4 part
four-__ highway: 4 lane
four-__ word: 6 letter
__ four: 5 front, petit
__-four: 3 ten **5** two-by
Four __: 4 Aces, Lads, Sons, Tops **5** Preps, Walls **7** Corners, Friends, Seasons
Four __ in a Jeep: 5 Jills
Four __ in Three Acts: 6 Saints
__ Four: 3 Fab **5** Final
Four Aces
song: Love Is a Many-Splendored Thing (1955)
Melody of Love (1955)
Mister Sandman (1954)
Four Apostles painter: 5 Durer
four-bagger: 5 homer **7** home run
fourberie: 6 deceit **8** intrigue, trickery, venality **9** chicanery, deception, improbity, mendacity, treachery **10** corruption, dishonesty, hanky-panky, subterfuge
__ fourché: 5 queue
Four Corners state: 4 Utah **7** Arizona **8** Colorado **9** New Mexico
Four Daughters (1938 film)
cast: Lola Lane, Priscilla Lane, Rosemary Lane, Claude Rains
director: Michael Curtiz
__-four-dollar question: 5 sixty
four-door: 3 car **4** auto **5** sedan **10** automobile
alternative: 5 coupé
Four Feathers, The (1939 film)
cast: John Clements, Ralph Richardson, C. Aubrey Smith
director: Zoltan Korda
Four Feathers, The (2002 film)
cast: Wes Bentley, Djimon Hounsou, Kate Hudson, Heath Ledger
director: Shekhar Kapur
Four Feathers, The author: A.E.W. Mason
four-flush: 5 bluff **6** take in **9** disinform, dissemble
fourflusher: 4 fake, sham **5** faker, fraud, knave, quack, rogue **6** rascal **7** bluffer, cheater **8** deceiver, imposter, impostor, swindler **9** pretender
four-footed: 9 quadruped
specialist: 3 DVM, vet
__-four-forty or Fight: 5 Fifty
Four Friends (1981 film)
cast: Jim Metzler, Jodi Thelen, Craig Wasson
director: Arthur Penn
fourgon: 3 van **5** wagon **7** tumbril
Four-H __: 4 Club
Four Horsemen of the Apocalypse, The (1921 film)
cast: Alan Hale, Rudolph Valentino
Four Horsemen, one of the: 3 War **5** Death **6** Famine **10** Pestilence
Four-H part: 4 head **5** hands, heart **6** health
Four Hundred Blows, The (1959 film)
director: François Truffaut
Fourier, Jean: 9 physicist
four-in-hand: 3 tie **5** ascot **6** cravat **7** foulard, necktie **8** neckwear
Four in the Morning (1985 song)
artist: Night Ranger
Four Jills in __: 5 a Jeep
Four Lads
song: Moments to Remember (1955)
No, Not Much! (1956)
Put a Light in the Window (1957)
Standing on the Corner (1956)
There's Only One of You (1958)
Who Needs You (1957)
four-lane __: 7 highway
four-leaf clover purpose: 4 luck
four-letter
use ~ words: 4 cuss **5** swear **9** blaspheme
word: 4 cuss, oath **5** curse **9** expletive, profanity
words: 7 cursing, cussing **8** swearing **9** blasphemy, profanity
word substitute: 5 bleep
four-letter __: 4 word
Four Men and a Prayer (1938 film)
cast: Richard Greene, George Sanders, Loretta Young
director: John Ford
four-minute __: 4 mile
Four Musketeers, The (1975 film)
cast: Richard Chamberlain, Oliver Reed, Raquel Welch
director: Richard Lester
Fournier: 4 font **8** typeface
four of __: 5 a kind
four-on-the-__: 5 floor
four-page sheet: 5 folio
four-part __: 7 harmony
fourpence: 5 groat
fourpenny __: 4 nail
four-petaled flower in heraldry: 10 quatrefoil
fourposter: 3 bed
topping: 6 canopy
Four Poster, The (1952 film)
cast: Rex Harrison, Lilli Palmer
director: Irving Reis
Four Preps
song: 26 Miles (1958)
Big Man (1958)
Four Quartets: 4 poem
author: 7 T.S. Eliot
fours
go on all ~: 5 crawl, creep, slink **7** clamber, slither, wriggle
not on all ~: 5 erect **7** upright **8** standing, straight, vertical
plus ~: 5 pants **8** breeches, knickers, trousers
__ fours: 3 all **4** plus **5** on all
Four Saints in Three Acts
composer: 7 Thomson
librettist: 5 Stein
fourscore: 6 eighty
Fourscore and seven years __: 3 ago
Four Seasons: 5 hotel
alternative: 4 Omni **5** Hyatt **6** Hilton, Westin **7** Wyndham **8** Marriott, Radisson, Sheraton **10** DoubleTree **11** Crowne Plaza
leader: Frankie Valli
song: Big Girls Don't Cry (1962)
Bye, Bye, Baby (1965)
Candy Girl (1963)
C'mon Marianne (1967)
Dawn (1964)
December 1963 (1976)
I've Got You Under My Skin (1966)
Let's Hang On (1965)
Rag Doll (1964)
Ronnie (1964)
Save It for Me (1964)
Sherry (1962)
Stay (1964)
Tell It to the Rain (1966)
Walk Like a Man (1963)
Who Loves You (1975)
Working My Way Back to You (1966)
Four Seasons, The (1981 film)
cast: Alan Alda, Carol Burnett, Len Cariou, Sandy Dennis, Rita Moreno, Jack Weston
director: Alan Alda
Four Seasons, The composer: 7 Vivaldi
__-four seven: 6 twenty
four-sharp key: 6 E major
four-sided figure: 4 rect. **6** square **7** rhombus **9** rectangle, trapezoid
foursome: 4 team **6** tetrad **7** quartet
member: 6 golfer
__ foursome: 5 mixed **6** Scotch
Four Sons (1928 film)
cast: Earle Foxe, James Hall, Margaret Mann
director: John Ford
foursquare: 4 firm **5** frank **6** candid, direct **8** resolute, resolved **9** outspoken, steadfast **10** forthright, from the hip, unwavering, unyielding
four-star: 3 def, rad **4** aces, A-one, best, boss, braw, cool, dece, fine, gear, keen, neat, nice, phat, tops, tuff **5** dandy, ducky, grand, great, marvy, neato, nobby, prime, slick, super, swell **6** bang on, bang-up, bonzer, bosker, choice, divine, dreamy, far-out, gnarly, grade A, groovy, lovely, peachy, slap-up, spot on, superb, terrif, tiptop, unreal, whizzo, wicked **7** amazing, awesome, capital, corking, perfect, ripping, skookum, stellar, sublime **8** dazzling, especial, eximious, fabulous, frabjous, glorious, heavenly, jim-dandy, slam-bang, smashing, splendid, standout, sterling, stickout, superior, terrific, top-level, topnotch, very good, wondrous **9** bodacious, Endsville, excellent, exemplary, exquisite, first-rate, high-grade, hunky-dory, marvelous, sollicker, topflight, unrivaled, wonderful **10** first-class, hotsy-totsy, jack-a-dandy, out of sight, peachy-keen, phenomenal, remarkable, stupendous, super-duper, unrivalled
review: 4 rave
four-striper: 7 captain, officer, skipper **9** commander
Four Strong Winds singer: 4 Bare
Fourteen Hours (1951 film)
cast: Richard Basehart, Barbara Bel Geddes, Paul Douglas
director: Henry Hathaway
__ Fourteen Points: 7 Wilson's
fourth: 4 part **7** portion, quarter **8** fraction
combining form: 5 quart- **6** tetart- **7** tetarto-
in a series: 5 delta
man: 4 Seth
person: 4 Abel
fourth __: 4 gear, wall **6** estate
fourth-__: 4 rate **5** class
Fourth Deadly Sin, The author: Lawrence Sanders
fourth-down option: 4 kick, pass, punt
Fourth Hand, The author: John Irving
fourth hitter in baseball: 7 clean-up
Fourth of July: 4 date **7** holiday
item: 4 flag, punk **8** sparkler
sound: 4 bang
fourth-quarter follower: 2 OT **8** overtime
fourth-rate: 4 poor **5** lousy **6** cheesy, crumby, crummy **8** inferior
Four Tops
leader: Levi Stubbs
song: Ain't No Woman (1973)
Baby I Need Your Loving (1964)
Bernadette (1967)
I Can't Help Myself (1965)
It's the Same Old Song (1965)
Keeper of the Castle (1972)
Reach Out I'll Be There (1966)
Standing in the Shadows of Love (1966)
Four Walls (1957 song)
artist: Jim Lowe, Jim Reeves
Four Weddings and a Funeral (1994 film)
cast: Hugh Grant, Andie MacDowell, Kristin Scott Thomas

director: Mike Newell
four-wheel __: 5 drive
four-wheeler: 6 go-cart, go-kart
Four Zoas, The author: William Blake
Fouts, Dan: 2 QB
sport: 8 football
fowl: 3 hen 4 bird, duck, game, meat, nene, smew, swan, teal 5 biddy, birds, brant, capon, drake, ducks, eider, geese, goose, Pekin, poult, quail, Rouen, scaup, skein, snipe 6 bantam, Brahma, Cayuga, chukar, grouse, Houdan, peahen, pullet, scoter, Sussex, turkey 7 chicken, Cornish, Dorking, gadwall, graylag, Leghorn, mallard, peacock, pintail, pochard, poultry, redhead, rooster, sea duck, widgeon 8 Araucana, curassow, garganey, gray duck, Langshan, mandarin, musk duck, oldsquaw, pheasant, Shanghai, shoveler, surf duck, woodcock, wood duck 9 black duck, broadbill, Dominique, goldeneye, goosander, greenhead, merganser, Orpington, partridge, ruddy duck, snow goose, sprigtail, Wyandotte 10 bufflehead, canvasback, surf scoter, tufted duck, wild turkey
abode: 4 coop, nest 5 roost
fill a ~: 5 stuff
place: 5 roost
sound: 5 cluck 6 cackle
starter: 3 bat, pea, sea 4 moor, wild 5 water
__ fowl: 4 game 5 scrub 6 guinea, jungle, mallee 7 prairie
fowler: 6 hunter
Fowler: 6 Robert 7 William
Fowler, William: 8 Nobelist 9 physicist
Fowles, John: 6 author, writer 7 British
work: The Aristos
The Collector
The Ebony Tower
The French Lieutenant's Woman
The Magus
Mantissa
fox: 3 fur, top 5 canid, grape, ready, trick 6 animal, canine, corsac, fennec, mammal, outwit 7 deceive 8 outflank, outsmart
African ~: 6 fennec
baby ~: 3 kit
ender: 4 fire, hole, tail, trot 5 glove, hound
female ~: 5 vixen
flying ~: 6 kalong
home: 3 den 4 lair 6 burrow
hunter coat: 5 pinks
hunter cry: 4 hark 5 hallo, hillo, hullo 6 halloa, halloo, hallow, hilloa, hulloo, yoicks
like a ~: 3 sly 4 wily 5 cagey 6 crafty, shrewd 7 cunning 8 guileful
like the ~ hunting set: 5 horsy 6 horsey
male: 3 dog
prey: 3 hen 7 chicken
relative: 3 dog 4 wolf 5 dhole, dingo 6 corsac, coydog, coyote, fennec, jackal
scent: 5 spoor
sound: 4 bark
sour fruit: 5 grape
tail: 5 brush
Uncle Remus ~: 4 Br'er
young: 3 cub, kit, pup
fox __: 4 bolt, trot 5 brush, grape, snake 6 hunter 7 hunting, sparrow, terrier
__ fox: 3 dog, kit, red, sea 4 blue, Cape, gray, grey 5 black, cross, white 6 Arctic, flying, silver
Fox: 3 car, net 4 auto 5 James, tribe 6 Edward, George, Indian, Mulder, Nellie, Nelson, studio 7 Amerind, Matthew, network 8 Fontaine, language, Samantha 10 automobile, Volkswagen
comedy series: 5 MAD TV
competitor: 3 ABC, CBS, MGM, NBC, UPN 5 ABC-TV, CBS-TV, NBC-TV 6 Disney 7 Miramax, New Line 8 Columbia 9 Paramount, Universal 10 DreamWorks, Warner Bros.
creation: 4 film 5 movie
documentary: 4 Cops
sitcom: 3 Roc
__ Fox: 4 Br'er 6 Little
Fox and His Friends (1975 film) director: Rainer Werner Fassbinder
Fox and the Grapes, The
source: 4 Esop 5 Aesop
Fox and the Hound, The director: 4 Rich
Foxes of Harrow, The author: Frank Yerby
__ Foxes, The: 6 Little
Foxfire author: Anya Seton, Joyce Carol Oates
foxglove: 5 plant 6 flower 7 blossom
Foxglove Saga, The author: Auburon Waugh
foxhole: 3 pit 4 foss 5 ditch, fosse 6 dugout, trench 9 earthwork 10 depression, excavation
deepen a ~: 5 redig
entrée: 4 Spam
Foxhound: 3 dog 5 canid 6 canine
foxiness: 5 craft, wiles 8 keenness
Fox in Socks author: Dr. Seuss
Fox, James: 5 actor
film: Isadora (1968)
King Rat (1965)
The Remains of the Day (1993)
The Servant (1963)
Thoroughly Modern Millie (1967)
Those Magnificent Men in Their Flying Machines (1965)
The Whistle Blower (1986)
Fox, Michael J.: 5 actor
film: Back to the Future (1985)
Back to the Future Part II (1989)
Back to the Future Part III (1990)
Bright Lights, Big City (1988)
Doc Hollywood (1991)
Life With Mikey (1993)
The Secret of My Success (1987)
Stuart Little (1999)
Teen Wolf (1985)
film (voice): Atlantis: The Lost Empire (2001)
spouse: Tracy Pollan
TV: Family Ties, Spin City
Fox, Samantha
song: I Wanna Have Some Fun (1988)
Naughty Girls (1988)
Touch Me (1986)
foxtail: 5 grass, plant 6 flower
fox terrier: 3 dog 5 canid 6 canine
Fox, The (1968 film)
cast: Sandy Dennis, Keir Dullea, Anne Heywood
director: Mark Rydell
__ Fox, The: 6 Desert
fox trot: 5 dance
Foxwoods: 6 casino
Foxworth: 6 Robert
Foxworthy: 4 Jeff
Foxx: 4 Inez, Redd 5 Jamie 6 Jimmie
Foxx, Inez song: Mockingbird (1963)
foxy: 3 sly 4 arch, sexy, wily 5 brown, canny, sharp, slick 6 adroit, artful, astute, clever, crafty, pretty, shifty, shrewd, tricky 7 cunning, devious, furtive, knavish, reddish, vulpine 8 alluring, guileful, scheming, slippery 9 astucious, conniving, deceitful, deceptive, glamorous, insidious, sagacious, yellowish
in a ~ fashion: 5 slyly
relative: 3 bay, dun, tan 4 bole, ecru, fawn, nude, seal 5 amber, beige, camel, cocoa, hazel, khaki, mocha, sepia, tawny, umber 6 auburn, bister, bistre, bronze, coffee, copper, ginger, russet, sienna, sorrel, suntan, walnut 7 biscuit, caramel, dogwood 8 chestnut, cinnamon, mahogany 9 butternut, chocolate
Foxy __: 4 Loxy 5 Brown
Foxy Brown star: 5 Grier
Foy: 5 Eddie
foyer: 4 hall 5 lobby 7 ingress 8 anteroom, corridor 9 concourse, vestibule
spread: 3 rug 6 carpet
__ Foyle: 5 Kitty
__-Foy, Que.: 3 Ste.
Foyt, A.J.: 5 racer 9 auto racer
contemporary: 5 Unser
milieu: 5 track
Fozzie: 4 bear 6 Muppet
friend: 6 Kermit
Fr: 4 elem. 7 element 8 francium
87 for ~: 4 at. no.
Fr.
see France
Fra: 4 monk 5 title 8 Angelico 9 religious
Fra __ Lippi: 5 Lippo
frabjous: 3 def, rad 4 aces, A-one, boss, braw, cool, dece, fine, gear, keen, neat, nice, phat, tuff 5 dandy, ducky, grand, great, marvy, neato, nobby, prime, slick, super, swell 6 bang on, bang-up, bonzer, bosker, choice, divine, dreamy, far-out, gnarly, groovy, lovely, peachy, slap-up, spot on, superb, terrif, tiptop, unreal, whizzo, wicked 7 amazing, awesome, capital, corking, perfect, ripping, skookum, stellar, sublime 8 dazzling, especial, eximious, fabulous, five-star, four-star, glorious, heavenly, jim-dandy, slam-bang, smashing, splendid, standout, sterling, stickout, superior, terrific, top-level, topnotch, very good, wondrous 9 bodacious, Endsville, excellent, exemplary, exquisite, first-rate, high-grade, hunky-dory, marvelous, sollicker, top-flight, unrivaled, wonderful 10 first-class, hotsy-totsy, jack-a-dandy, out of sight, peachy-keen, phenomenal, remarkable, stupendous, super-duper, unrivalled
fracas: 3 ado, row 4 feud, flap, fray, riot, tilt, to-do 5 brawl, brush, clash, fight, melee, mix-up, noise, run-in, scrap, set-to 6 affray, battle, mayhem, racket, rumpus, tumult, uproar 7 dispute, quarrel, rhubarb, ruction, scuffle, wrangle 8 brouhaha, conflict, disorder, skirmish, squabble 9 bickering, confusion, scrimmage 10 donnybrook, free-for-all
fraction: 2 pt. 3 bit, cut 4 bite, half, part, unit 5 chunk, fifth, ninth, piece, ratio, share, sixth, slice, tenth, third 6 eighth, fourth, morsel, trifle 7 modicum, one-half, portion, quarter, section, segment, seventh 8 division, fragment, one-fifth, one-ninth, one-sixth, one-tenth, one-third 9 one-eighth, one-fourth, two-fifths, two-ninths, two-thirds 10 five-ninths, five-sixths, four-fifths, four-ninths, nine-tenths, one-quarter, one-seventh, proportion
term: 3 LCD
__ fraction: 4 mole 6 common, proper, simple, vulgar 7 complex, decimal, packing, partial
fractional: 5 light 7 divided, partial 9 dispersed, piecemeal, sectional, segmented 10 incomplete
prefix: 4 demi-, hemi-, nano-, semi- 5 centi-, milli-
fractious: 4 mean 5 cross, huffy, onery, surly, testy 6 crabby, ornery, snappy, touchy, unruly, wilful 7 fretful, grouchy, naughty, peevish, waspish, willful 8 captious, fretsome, perverse, petulant, snappish, stubborn 9 crotchety, difficult, insurgent, irascible, irritable, querulous, splenetic 10 disorderly, intolerant, out of sorts, refractory, unamenable
fracture: 3 gap 4 bust, rend, rent, rift, rive, snap 5 break, burst, cleft, crack, crash, laugh, smash, split 6 breach, injury, regale, schism, sunder 7 fissure, rupture, shatter 8 cleavage, splinter
detector: 4 X-ray
glacier ~: 4 gulf, rift 5 chasm 7 crevice
treat a ~: 3 set
__ fracture: 5 vowel 6 closed, simple, stress 8 compound
fractured: 4 torn 6 broken 7 cracked
__ Fra Diavolo: 7 lobster
Fra Diavolo composer: 5 Auber
Fraggle Rock dog: 8 Sprocket
fragile: 4 fine, puny, slim, thin, weak 5 frail, sheer, wimpy 6 anemic, atonic, dainty, effete, feeble, flabby, flimsy, slight, tender 7 anaemic, brittle, crumbly, friable, rickety, slender, unsound, wimpish 8 decrepit, delicate, helpless, pithless 9 breakable, faltering, frangible, powerless 10 nondurable, vulnerable
fragility: 6 anemia 7 anaemia, fatigue, frailty 8 debility, delicacy, puniness, weakness 9 frailness, infirmity 10 feebleness, flimsiness, unwellness
fragment: 3 bit 4 bite, chip, clip, iota, part, snip, whit, wisp 5 break, burst, chunk, crash, crumb, piece, relic, scrap, shard, share, sherd, shred, slice, smash, split, trace 6 gobbet, morsel, sample, shiver, sliver, snatch 7 crumble, excerpt, flinder, granule, modicum, oddment, portion, remnant, section, shatter, split up 8 clipping, disunify, disunite, fraction, landmark, molecule, particle, splinter 9 come apart 10 come undone
fragmentary: 3 odd 5 light 7 oddball, partial 9 piecemeal
fragmentation: 4 rent, rift 5 break, cleft, crack, split 6 schism 7 discord 8 cleavage, disunion, division, fracture 9 dichotomy 10 divergence
Fragments author: Edward Albee
Fragonard: 4 Jean
fragrance: 4 atar, balm, nose, odor, otto 5 aroma, athar, attar, ottar, scent, smell, spice 7 bouquet, cologne, perfume 9 redolence
hint of ~: 5 whiff
without ~: 8 odorless 9 unscented
YSL ~: 5 Opium
fragrant: 5 balmy, olent, spicy, sweet 6 savory, spicey 7 odorous, perfumy 8 aromatic, perfumed, redolent 9 ambrosial, delicious 10 delectable
compound: 5 ester
flower: 4 lily, pink, rose 5 lilac, phlox, stock 7 jasmine, tea rose 8 dianthus, gardenia, hyacinth, lavender, magnolia, moss rose, tuberose 9 carnation, jessamine, narcissus 10 damask rose, Easter lily, frangipani, heliotrope, mock orange, wallflower

hardly ~: 4 olid
herb: 4 mint
make ~: 5 cense
oil: 4 atar, otto 5 athar, attar, ottar
ointment: 4 nard
plant: 5 thyme
resin: 4 tolu 5 elemi 6 balsam
root: 5 orris
shrub of Asia: 4 gumi
tree: 3 fir 4 pine 5 aloes, cedar 6 storax
vine of Hawaii: 5 maile
__ fraîche: 5 crème
fraidy-cat: 4 wimp 5 sissy 6 coward, craven 7 chicken, cowards, dastard, quitter, wimpish 8 poltroon, recreant 9 jellyfish
frail: 4 puny, sick, weak 5 reedy, wimpy 6 anemic, atonic, dainty, effete, feeble, flabby, flimsy, infirm, mortal, slight, tender 7 anaemic, brittle, fragile, invalid, rickety, tenuous, unsound, wimpish 8 delicate, helpless, pithless 9 breakable, faltering, frangible, powerless, unhealthy 10 vulnerable
not ~: 3 fit 4 hale 5 hardy, sound, stout, tough 6 brawny, robust, rugged, sinewy, strong, sturdy, virile 7 healthy 8 athletic, muscular, thriving, vigorous 9 strapping 10 able-bodied
something ~: 4 wisp
frailness: 10 unwellness
frailty: 4 vice 5 lapse 6 anemia, foible 7 anaemia, fatigue 8 debility, delicacy, puniness, weakness 9 fragility, infirmity 10 feebleness, flimsiness, insecurity
fraise: 5 scarf 10 strawberry
Frakes, Jonathan spouse: Genie Francis
Fra Lippo Lippi: 4 poem
author: Robert Browning
frame: 3 fix, map, mat, rim 4 body, cage, case, edge, form, make, mold, plan, plot, rack, tidy, trim 5 build, couch, draft, erect, forge, hatch, model, mount, pin on, set up, shape, shell, stage, stand 6 border, bum rap, casing, cook up, design, devise, draw up, encase, figure, fringe, incase, indite, invent, make up, map out, phrase, timber 7 anatomy, arrange, chassis, compose, concoct, dream up, enclose, fashion, inclose, lattice, outline, prepare, produce, project 8 assemble, block out, conceive, contrive, mounting, organize, physique, scaffold, skeleton, trimming 9 construct, enclosure, fabricate, formulate, implicate, structure 10 constitute
a photo again: 5 remat
bed ~: 5 stead
car ~: 7 chassis
cartoon ~: 3 cel 4 cell
door ~: 4 sash
ender: 4 work
film ~: 3 cel 4 cell 5 slide
fireplace ~: 5 grate
insert: 4 lens 5 photo 7 picture 8 painting
of mind: 4 mood, vein 5 humor, state 6 spirit, temper 7 outlook, posture 8 attitude 9 mentality
of reference: 4 idea, side, view 5 angle, light, slant, stand 6 aspect, stance, system 7 horizon, opinion, outlook, posture 8 attitude, position 9 viewpoint 10 estimation, philosophy, standpoint
picture ~ juncture: 5 miter, slant 8 diagonal
ship ~: 4 hull
spacecraft ~: 6 gantry
starter: 3 air 4 main
structural ~: 5 truss
weaver's ~: 4 slay, sley 6 sleigh
window ~: 4 sash 6 casing
__ frame: 3 box, web 4 cant, cold, full, open, ring, time 5 rigid 6 Balkan, braced, freeze, hopper, Oxford 7 balloon, drawing, gallows, Harvard, masking, warping, western, winding
__-frame: 6 freeze
__ Framed Roger Rabbit: 3 Who
Frame, Janet: 6 author, writer
framer: 5 maker 7 builder, creator, devisor, drafter, planner 8 composer 9 assembler 10 fabricator
frames: 5 specs 7 glasses 10 spectacles
in a game: 3 ten
frame-up: 4 plot 6 racket, scheme 10 conspiracy
framework: 4 core, form, grid, plan, sash 5 cadre, setup, shell 6 casing, fabric, nature, scheme 7 chassis, outline, setting 8 skeleton 9 bare bones, structure 10 background, foundation
metal ~: 5 grate
part: 5 truss
framing __: 6 chisel, square
Framingham: 4 city, town
locale: 4 Mass.
framing need: 3 mat
Frampton, Peter
song: Do You Feel Like We Do (1976)
I'm in You (1977)
Show Me the Way (1976)
Fram rival: 3 STP
Fran: 5 Healy 7 Allison 8 Drescher, Lebowitz 9 Tarkenton
partner: 5 Kukla, Ollie
franc: 4 coin 5 money
part of a ~: 3 sou
replacement: 4 euro
__ franca: 6 lingua
Franca: 4 city, town
locale: 6 Brazil
__ française: 3 à la
__ Française: 7 Comédie
France: 5 Nuyen, repub. 6 nation 7 Anatole, country 8 republic
ancient ~: 4 Gaul
appetizer: 9 escargots, macédoine
astronomer: 7 Laplace 8 Lagrange
ballet dancer: 6 Béjart
bay: 6 Biscay
biologist: 6 Carrel
bovine: 6 Aubrac, Herens, Salers, Vosges 7 Alberes 8 Limousin 9 Charolais
cap: 5 beret
capital: 5 Paris
car: 5 Simca 7 Peugeot, Renault
card game: 6 belote 7 belotte
cathedral city: 5 Reims 6 Rheims
cheese: 4 Brie 5 banon 7 gervais, Gruyère 9 Camembert, Port Salut, Roquefort 10 Neufchâtel 11 Pont l'Évêque
chemist: 4 Lehn 5 Curie 6 Perrin 7 Moissan, Pasteur 9 Berthelot, Gay-Lussac, Lavoisier
city: 3 Dax, Pau 4 Agde, Agen, Albi, Ales, Auch, Bron, Caen, Evry, Issy, laon, Lens, Loos, Lyon, Metz, Nice, Orly, Rezé, Riom, St. Lô 5 Arles, Arras, Blois, Bondy, Brest, Cenon, Cergy, Creil, Dijon, Douai, Dreux, Gagny, Laval, Lille, Lomme, Lunel, Lyons, Mâcon, Massy, Melun, Muret, Nancy, Nîmes, Niort, Ornes, Paris, Reims, Rodez, Rouen, Sedan, Tours, Tulle, Vichy 6 Amiens, Angers, Anglet, Annecy, Bastia, Bezons, Calais, Cannes, Cholet, Clichy, Colmar, Denain, Dieppe, Drancy, Épinal, Ermont, Evreux, Fécamp, Fréjus, Grigny, Guéret, Hyéres, Istres, Le Mans, Meudon, Millau, Nantes, Nevers, Pantin, Pessac, Poissy, Rennes, Rheims, Roanne, Sevran, Sèvres, St. Malo, Tarbes, Toulon, Troyes, Vannes, Vanves, Verdun, Vertou, Vesoul, Voiron, Yerres 7 Ajaccio, Alençon, Avignon, Bayonne, Belfort, Béziers, Castres, Chablis, Draveil, Dunkirk, Forbach, Le Havre, Limoges, Orléans, Roubaix, St.-Denis, Talence, Taverny, Valence, Vierzon 8 Biarritz, Bordeaux, Chartres, Grenoble, Poitiers, Soissons, St.-Mihiel, Toulouse 9 Cherbourg, Marseille, St.-Étienne 10 Marseilles, Strasbourg
combining form: 5 Gallo- 6 Franco-
conductor: 5 Morel, Münch 6 Boulez 7 Monteux 9 Leibowitz, Rosenthal
couturier: 4 Dior
dance: 5 gavot 6 branle, cancan 7 bourrée, favotte 9 cotillion, farandole, passepied, quadrille
department: 3 Ain, Lot, Var 4 Aube, Aude, Cher, Eure, Gard, Gers, Jura, Nord, Oise, Orne, Tarn 5 Aisne, Doubs, Drôme, Indre, Isère, Loire, Marne, Meuse, Rhone, Somme, Yonne 6 Allier, Ariège, Cantal, Creuse, Landes, Loiret, Lozère, Manche, Nièvre, Sarthe, Savoie, Vendée, Vienne, Vosges 7 Ardèche, Aveyron, Bas-Rhin, Corrèze, Côte-d'Or, Essonne, Gironde, Hérault, Mayenne, Moselle 8 Ardennes, Calvados, Charente, Dordogne, Haut-Rhin, Morbihan, Val-d'Oise, Vaucluse, Yvelines 9 Finistère, Puy-de-Dôme 10 Deux-Sèvres, Haute-Corse, Haute-Loire, Haute-Marne, Haute-Saône, Loir-et-Cher, Val-de-Marne 11 Eure-et-Loire
dialect: 6 Creole
diplomat: 5 Perse
director: 4 Tati 5 Vadim 6 Renoir 8 Truffaut 10 Jean Renoir, Roger Vadim
entomologist: 5 Fabre
essayist: 5 Péguy 7 Reverdy, Rolland, Romains
existentialist: 4 Gide
explorer: 5 Salle 6 Joliet 7 Cartier, Jolliet 8 Cousteau 9 Champlain, David-Neel
film award: 5 César
flutist: 6 Rampal
former colony: 4 Chad, Laos, Mali, Togo 5 Benin, Gabon, Haiti, Niger 6 Acadia, Canada, Guinea 7 Algeria, Morocco, Senegal, Tunisia, Vietnam 8 Cambodia, Cameroon, Djibouti 9 Louisiana 10 Ivory Coast, Madagascar, Mauritania
gulf: 5 Lions 6 St. Malo
historian: 5 Taine 9 Froissart
humanist: 8 Rabelais
impressionist: 5 Degas, Manet, Monet
journalist: 7 Prévost
lake: 6 Geneva
land measure: 6 arpent
language: 6 Basque
legislature: 5 sénat
mathematician: 6 Pascal 7 Laplace 8 Lagrange
mathemetician: 6 Pascal
medieval ~ poem: 3 lai
money: 3 écu, sol, sou 4 euro 5 franc, liard, livre, louis, obole, oboli 6 decime, obolus, teston 7 centime, testoon 8 louis d'or, napoleon
mountain: 4 Jura 6 Ecrins, Mézenc, Vosges 8 Cévennes, Pyrenees 9 Mont Blanc, Puy-de-Dôme, Savoy Alps
natural historian: 6 Buffon, Cuvier 7 Lamarck
neighbor: 5 Italy, Spain 6 Monaco 7 Andorra, Belgium, Germany 10 Luxembourg
Nobelist in Chemistry: 4 Lehn 7 Moissan 11 Joliot-Curie
Nobelist in Economics: 6 Allais, Debreu
Nobelist in Literature: 4 Gide 5 Camus, Perse, Simon 6 du Gard, France, Sartre 7 Bergson, Mauriac, Mistral, Rolland 9 Prudhomme
Nobelist in Medicine: 5 Jacob, Lwoff, Monod 6 Carrel, Richet 7 Dausset, Laveran, Nicolle 11 Metchnikoff
Nobelist in Peace: 5 Passy 6 Briand, Cassin 7 Balluet, Buisson, Jouhaux, Renault 9 Bourgeois 10 Schweitzer
Nobelist in Physics: 4 Néel 5 Curie 6 Perrin 7 Kastler 8 de Gennes, Lippmann 9 Becquerel, de Broglie, Guillaume
org.: 4 NATO
Oscar: 5 César
painter: 3 Arp 4 Dufy 5 Corot, Degas, Léger, Manet, Monet 6 Braque, Ingres, Renoir, Seurat, Tanguy, Tissot 7 Bonheur, Cézanne, Duchamp, Gauguin, Matisse, Utrillo 8 Dubuffet 9 Delacroix
palace: 6 Elysée
philosopher: 4 Weil 5 Taine 6 Pascal, Sartre 7 Bergson 8 Maritain, Rousseau, Voltaire
physicist: 4 Néel 5 Curie 6 Ampère, Franck, Perrin 7 Coulomb, Fourier, Fresnel, Kastler, Réaumur 8 de Gennes, Foucault, Lippmann 9 Becquerel, de Broglie, Gay-Lussac, Guillaume 11 Joliot-Curie
playwright: 5 Camus, Genet, Hardy, Jarry, Sagan 6 Gréban, Grévin, Musset, Racine, Sardou, Scribe 7 Anouilh, Feydeau, Garnier, Ionesco, Molière, Régnard, Rolland, Romains, Rostand, Sedaine 8 Salacrou, Sarraute 9 Corneille
poem: 6 dizain
poet: 4 Char 5 Bodel, Jacob, Jouve, Marot, Péguy, Perse, Scève 6 Breton, Desnos, Éluard, France, Grévin, Musset, writer 7 Boileau, Chénier, Heredia, Michaux, Mistral, Prévert, Queneau, Régnier, Reverdy, Rimbaud, Ronsard 8 Chartier, Soupault 9 Corneille, Deschamps, Desportes, Froissart, Lamartine, Prudhomme 10 Baudelaire
port: 4 Caen, Nice, Sète 5 Brest 6 Calais, Cannes, Dieppe, St. Malo, Toulon 7 Dunkirk, Le Havre 8 Bordeaux, Boulogne 9 Cherbourg, Marseille 10 La Rochelle, Marseilles
provincial: 5 style
region: 5 Corse, Savoy 6 Alsace, Artois, Centre 8 Auvergne, Bretagne, Brittany, Limousin, Lorraine, Normandy, Picardie 9 Aquitaine, Bourgogne 10 Rhône-Alpes

resort: 3 Pau 4 Midi, Nice 5 Evian 6 Cannes, Dinard, Menton, St. Malo 7 Riviera 8 Biarritz, St. Tropez 9 Deauville, Le Touquet, Trouville
revolutionary: 5 Marat
river: 3 Lot, Lys 4 Aire, Aube, Aude, Cher, Eure, Ille, Leie, Oise, Orne, Yser 5 Aisne, Doubs, Isère, Loire, Marne, Meuse, Rhone, Saône, Sarre, Seine, Selle, Somme, Yonne 6 Allier, Escaut 7 Garonne, Moselle 8 Dordogne
rocket: 6 Ariane
royal house: 5 Capet 6 Valois 7 Bourbon, Orleans
royal name: 5 Henry, Louis 6 Philip 7 Charles
saint: 5 Denis, Denys, Giles 6 Ansgar, Fiacre 7 Bernard, Louis IX 8 Lawrence 9 Genevieve, Joan of Arc 10 Bernadette
scientist: 5 Curie, Fabre 6 Ampère, Buffon, Carrel, Cuvier, Franck, Pascal, Perrin 7 Coulomb, Fourier, Fresnel, Lamarck, Laplace, Pasteur, Réaumur 8 Foucault, Lagrange 9 Berthelot, Gay-Lussac, Lavoisier
sculptor: 3 Arp 5 Rodin 8 Dubuffet
shrine: 7 Lourdes
silk center: 4 Lyon 5 Lyons
site of Roman ruins in ~: 5 Arles
skier: 5 Killy
soprano: 4 Pons 5 Calvé 7 Crespin
southern ~ wind: 7 mistral
take ~ leave: 4 flee
tennis pro: 7 Lacoste
Tour de ~: 4 race
Tour de ~ entrant: 5 biker
underground: 6 Maquis
vowel sound: 5 nasal
water: 3 eau 5 Evian, Vichy
waterfall: 8 Gavarnie
wine: 4 Moët 5 Gamay, Mâcon, Médoc, Tavel, Yquem 6 claret, Graves 7 aligoté, Chablis, Musigny, Pommard, Vouvray 8 Bordeaux, Cabernet, Muscadet, Sancerre 9 Champagne, Meursault 10 Beaujolais, Chambertin, Montrachet
wine region: 5 Loire, Médoc, Rhone
writer: 3 Sue 4 Aymé, Gary, Gide, Hugo, Loti, Sade, Sand, Weil, Zola 5 Butor, Camus, Dumas, Duras, Giono, Green, Hémon, Perse, Renan, Sagan, Simon, Taine, Verne 6 Aragon, Balzac, Barrès, Belloc, Boulle, Céline, Cixous, Daudet, du Gard, France, Guitry, Lesage, Marcel, Pascal, Proust, Sartre 7 Anouilh, Aubigné, Bergson, Bourget, Claudel, Cocteau, Colette, Duhamel, Mauriac, Maurois, Mérimée, Mistral, Prévost, Queneau, Rolland, Romains, Scudéry, Simenon 8 Bataille, Beauvoir, Bernanos, Cendrars, d'Aubigné, Flaubert, Goncourt, Gringore, Huysmans, Maritain, Perrault, Proudhon, Rabelais, Rousseau, Sarraute, Stendhal, Voltaire 9 Giraudoux, Montaigne, Prudhomme 10 La Fontaine, Maupassant, Oldenbourg 11 Montesquieu, Sainte-Beuve
see also French
___ France: 3 Air, New 5 Ile de 7 Marie de
France, Anatole: 4 poet 6 author, French, writer 8 Nobelist
work: The Bloom of Life
L'Etui de nacre
Penguin Island
The Red Lily
Thaïs
France: An Ode author: Samuel Taylor Coleridge
Frances: 3 Dee 4 Alda 6 Bavier, Farmer, Fisher, Harper 7 Perkins, Willard 8 Goodrich 9 Lockridge, McDormand 10 Sternhagen
Frances (1982 film)
cast: Jessica Lange, Sam Shepard, Kim Stanley
Francesca: 7 Cabrini
Francesco: 5 Berni 6 Arrivi 9 Borromini
in English: 7 Francis
Francesco Rinaldi: 10 pasta sauce
alternative: 4 Ragu 5 Prego 6 Prince 8 Classico 10 Newman's Own 11 Aunt Millie's
Frances Hodgson ___: 7 Burnett
Franchi: 6 Sergio
sister: Dana Valery
franchise: 4 vote 5 right 6 agency, ballot, patent, permit, voting 7 charter, liberty 8 election, suffrage 9 authority, exemption, privilege
exercise one's ~: 4 vote 5 elect
exerciser: 5 voter
Franchise Affair, The author: Josephine Tey
franchisee: 6 dealer, seller, vendor 8 merchant, retailer
Franchot: 4 Tone
Franciosa: 4 Tony 7 Anthony
Franciosa, Tony: 5 actor
film: Across 110th Street (1972)
Career (1959)
A Face in the Crowd (1957)
Fathom (1967)
A Hatful of Rain (1957)
The Long Hot Summer (1958)
Period of Adjustment (1962)
Rio Conchos (1964)
The Story on Page One (1959)
spouse: Shelley Winters
TV: The Name of the Game
Francis: 3 Fry, Kay 4 Anne, Dick, mule 5 Aston, Bacon, Cleve, Crick, Drake, Genie, Missy 6 Arlene, Baring, Connie, Galton, Marion, Ouimet, Xavier 7 de Sales, Lederer, Parkman, Poulenc, Quarles 8 Beaufort
imitate ~: 4 bray
in Italian: 9 Francesco
in Spanish: 9 Francisco
Francis ___ Coppola: 4 Ford
Francis ___ Key: 5 Scott
Francis, Anne: 7 actress
film: Bad Day at Black Rock (1955)
Blackboard Jungle (1955)
Forbidden Planet (1956)
The Satan Bug (1965)
TV: Honey West
Francis, Arlene spouse: Martin Gabel
Franciscan: 5 friar
founder's home: 6 Assisi
org.: 3 OFM
Francisco: 4 Goya 6 Franco, Madero 7 Pizarro 8 Coronado
in English: 7 Francis
Francisco ___ de Goya: 4 José
___ Francisco: 3 San
Francis, Connie
song: Among My Souvenirs (1959)
Breakin' in a Brand New Broken Heart (1961)
Don't Break the Heart That Loves You (1962)
Everybody's Somebody's Fool (1960)
Frankie (1959)
Lipstick on Your Collar (1959)
Mama (1960)
Many Tears Ago (1960)
My Happiness (1958)
My Heart Has a Mind of Its Own (1960)
Second Hand Love (1962)
Stupid Cupid (1958)
Together (1961)
Vacation (1962)
When the Boy in Your Arms (1961)
Where the Boys Are (1961)
Who's Sorry Now (1958)
___ Francisco River: 3 Sao
Franciscus: 5 James
Francis de Sales: 5 saint
Francis, Dick: 6 writer 7 British
former job: jockey
homeland: England
locale: 5 Ascot
work: 10 Lb. Penalty
Banker
Blood Sport
Bolt
Bonecrack
Break in
Comeback
Come to Grief
The Danger
Dead Cert
Decider
Driving Force
The Edge
Enquiry
Field of Thirteen
Flying Finish
Forfeit
For Kicks
High Stakes
Hot Money
In the Frame
Knockdown
Longshot
Nerve
Odds Against
Proof
Rat Race
Reflex
Risk
Second Wind
Shattered
Slay Ride
Smokescreen
Straight
To the Hilt
Trial Run
Twice Shy
Whip Hand
Wild Horses
Francis Ford ___: 7 Coppola
Francis, Genie spouse: Jonathan Frakes
Francis, Kay: 7 actress
film: Confession (1937)
First Lady (1937)
Girls About Town (1931)
Guilty Hands (1931)
In Name Only (1939)
Jewel Robbery (1932)
One Way Passage (1932)
Raffles (1930)
Trouble in Paradise (1932)
When the Daltons Rode (1940)
Francis of ___: 5 Paula, Sales 6 Assisi
Francis of Assisi: 5 saint
Francis Scott ___: 3 Key
Francistown: 4 city
locale: 8 Botswana
Francis X. ___: 7 Bushman
Francis Xavier: 5 saint
francium: 5 metal 7 element
Franck: 5 César, James
Franck, James: 8 Nobelist 9 physicist, scientist
Franco: 4 John, Nero 6 Harris 7 Corelli 9 Francisco, Sacchetti 10 Modigliani, Zeffirelli
François: 5 Jacob 6 Villon 7 Boucher, Mauriac 8 Duvalier, Rabelais, Truffaut 9 Mitterand
see also French
___-François Champollion: 4 Jean
Françoise: 5 Sagan
see also French
François le Champi author: George Sand
Franco, John: 3 Met 6 hurler 7 pitcher
francolin: 4 bird
Franconia: 4 city, town
locale: 8 Virginia
Franco-Prussian ___: 3 War
frangible: 4 weak 5 frail 6 flimsy 7 brittle, crumbly, fragile, rickety, unsound 8 delicate 9 breakable 10 nondurable
frangipane: 6 pastry
ingredient: 3 egg 5 cream, sugar 6 almond
frangipani: 4 tree 5 plant, shrub 6 flower
relative: 5 orris 7 dogbane, karanda 8 oleander
frank: 4 meat, open 5 bluff, blunt, brusk, legit, naked, plain, vocal, weeny 6 abrupt, candid, direct, honest, hot dog, infelt, simple, square, weenie, wiener, wienie 7 artless, brusque, factual, genuine, natural, sincere, upfront, upright 8 credible, impolite, outfront, straight, tactless, truthful 9 downright, guileless, ingenuous, outspoken, unfeigned, unguarded, veracious 10 aboveboard, flat-footed, forthright, foursquare, free-spoken, from the hip, indelicate, on the level, point-blank, scrupulous, to the point, unaffected, unreserved, unreticent
be ~: 5 level
ender: 6 pledge 7 incense
too ~: 9 impolitic, unguarded 10 indiscreet
see also frankfurter, hot dog
Frank: 2 Oz 4 Anne, Bank, Cady, Gary, Ilja 5 Baker, Beard, Capra, DeVol, Libby, Lloyd, Mills, O'Hara, Perry, Yerby, Zappa 6 Bidart, Bonner, Borman, Burnet, Chance, Coraci, Faylen, Howard, Ifield, Lawton, McHugh, Melvin, Morgan, Norris, Sutton, Tanana, Thomas, Tuttle, Whaley 7 Borzage, Gifford, Gorshin, Herbert, Kellogg, Launder, Loesser, Lovejoy, McCourt, O'Connor, Shorter, Sinatra, Tashlin 8 Crosetti, Fontaine, Gilbreth, Langella, Marshall, Robinson, Sargeson, Stallone, Sullivan, Wedekind 9 Slaughter
comics partner: 6 Ernest
daughter: 4 Tina 5 Nancy
ex: 3 Ava, Mia 5 Nancy
in German: 5 Franz
outlaw brother: 5 Jesse
pal: 4 Dean 5 Sammy
Frank & ___: 5 Ollie
Frank ___ Wright: 5 Lloyd
Frank, Anne hideout: 5 attic
___ Frank Baum: 5 Lyman
Franken: 2 Al
Franken Berry: 6 cereal
competitor: 3 Kix 4 Life, Trix 5 Kashi, Quisp, Total 6 Kaboom, Muesli, Oreo O's, Pablum, Smacks 7 All-Bran, Crispix, Harmony, Hunny B's, Mueslix, Oat Bran, Pokemon 8 Boo Berry, Cheerios, Corn Chex, Corn Pops, Fiber One, Rice Chex, Special K, Uncle Sam, Wheaties 9 Alpha Bits, Apple Zaps, Grape Nuts, Honey Comb, Just Right, Wheat Chex 10 Apple Jacks, Bran Flakes, Cap'n Crunch, Cocoa Puffs, Froot Loops, Mini-Wheats, Nutri-Grain, Puffed Rice, Quaker Oats,

Smart Start **11** Cocoa Blasts, Cookie Crisp, Golden Crisp, Lucky Charms, Puffed Wheat, Sweet Crunch, Waffle Crisp
Frankenheimer, John: 8 director
film: All Fall Down (1962)
Birdman of Alcatraz (1962)
Black Sunday (1977)
The Gypsy Moths (1969)
The Iceman Cometh (1973)
The Manchurian Candidate (1962)
Seconds (1966)
Seven Days in May (1964)
The Train (1965)
The Young Savages (1961)
The Young Stranger (1957)
Frankenstein
assistant: 4 Igor
milieu: 3 lab
monster name: 4 Adam
Frankenstein (1931 film)
cast: Mae Clarke, Colin Clive, Boris Karloff
__ Frankenstein: 5 Son of, Young
Frankenstein (1973 song) artist: Edgar Winter Group
Frankenstein author: Mary Shelley
Frankenstein Meets the Wolf Man (1943 film)
cast: Lon Chaney Jr., Patric Knowles, Bela Lugosi, Ilona Massey
Frankfort: 4 city, town **7** capital
campus: 3 KSU
locale: 3 Ken. **8** Kentucky
Frankfurt: 4 city, town
city near ~: 5 Hanau, Mainz
locale: 7 Germany
river: 4 Main, Oder, Odra
frankfurter: 3 dog **4** meat **5** Kahn's, weeny **6** Armour, hot dog, weenie, wiener, wienie **8** Ball Park **10** Oscar Mayer
accompaniment: 3 bun **5** chili, kraut, works **6** relish **7** mustard **10** sauerkraut
covering: 4 skin **6** casing
see also hot dog
Frankfurter: 5 Felix **6** German
Frankie: 5 Carle, Laine, Lymon, Valli **6** Avalon, Frisch
Frankie (1959 song) artist: Connie Francis
Frankie and Johnny (1966 film)
cast: Donna Douglas, Sue Ane Langdon, Harry Morgan, Elvis Presley
director: Frederick de Cordova
Frankie and Johnny (1991 film)
cast: Hector Elizondo, Nathan Lane, Al Pacino, Michelle Pfeiffer
director: Garry Marshall
Frankie and Johnny (1966 song)
artist: Elvis Presley
Frank, Ilja: 8 Nobelist **9** physicist
frankincense: 5 resin **8** olibanum **9** fragrance
partner: 4 gold **5** myrrh
Frankish: 8 language
Franklin: 3 Ben **4** Carl, city, John, town **5** Adams, Cover, Miles **6** Aretha, Bonnie, Kameny, Pierce, Sidney **8** Benjamin, Pangborn **9** Roosevelt, Schaffner
bill: 5 C-note
cousin: 5 Teddy **8** Theodore
Eleanor, to ~: 4 wife
flier: 4 kite
invention: 3 DST
locale: 9 Tennessee, Wisconsin
mother: 4 Sara
note: 3 cee
opponent: 3 Alf **6** Thomas **7** Wendell
Franklin __: 5 stove
Franklin __ Roosevelt: 6 Delano
Franklin, Aretha
nickname: The Queen of Soul
song: Baby I Love You (1967)
Bridge Over Troubled Water (1971)
Chain of Fools (1967)
Day Dreaming (1972)
Freeway of Love (1985)
The House That Jack Built (1968)
I Knew You Were Waiting (1987)
I Never Loved a Man (1967)
I Say a Little Prayer (1968)
A Natural Woman (1967)
Respect (1967)
Rock Steady (1971)
Since You've Been Gone (1968)
Spanish Harlem (1971)
Think (1968)
Until You Come Back to Me (1973)
Who's Zoomin' Who (1985)
Franklin, Carl: 8 director
film: Devil in a Blue Dress (1995)
High Crimes (2002)
One False Move (1992)
One True Thing (1998)
Franklin Gothic: 4 font
franklinite: 7 mineral
Franklin, John: 8 explorer
Franklin, Miles: 6 writer **10** Australian
Franklin P. __: 5 Adams
Franklin, Sidney: 8 director
film: The Barretts of Wimpole Street (1934)
The Good Earth (1937)
The Guardsman (1931)
Private Lives (1931)
Reunion in Vienna (1933)
Smilin' Through (1932)
Franklin Square: 4 city, town
locale: 7 New York
Frank Lloyd __: 6 Wright
frankly: 5 truly **6** openly, simply **8** directly, straight **9** sincerely **10** point-blank
Frankly, my dear... sayer: 5 Rhett
Frank, Melvin: 8 director
film: Above and Beyond (1952)
Buona Sera, Mrs. Campbell (1969)
Court Jester (1956)
The Facts of Life (1960)
Knock on Wood (1954)
The Prisoner of Second Avenue (1975)
A Touch of Class (1973)
Frank Mildmay, or the Naval Officer
author: Frederick Marryat
frankness: 6 candor **7** honesty, naiveté **8** veracity **9** good faith, innocence, sincerity
Franks
king: 6 Clovis
of the ~: 5 Salic
Frank's Campaign author: Horatio Alger
Frann: 4 Mary
Franny and Zooey
author: J.D. Salinger
cat: 9 Bloomberg
__, Fran & Ollie: 5 Kukla
Frans: 4 Hals **9** Sillanpää
frantic: 3 mad **4** wild **5** hyper, manic, upset, wired **6** hectic **7** burning, demonic, excited, keyed up, unglued **8** agitated, daemonic, feverish, frenetic, frenzied, in a tizzy, maniacal, vehement, worked up **9** at wits' end, delirious, demonical, desperate, last-ditch **10** corybantic, distraught, distressed, flipped out, hysterical, in an uproar, infuriated
frantically: 4 hard **5** madly **7** like mad
Frantz: 5 Fanon
Franz: 4 Boas **5** Haydn, Kafka, Kline, Lehár, Liszt **6** Arthur, Dennis, Eduard, Waxman, Werfel **7** Klammer **8** Schubert
in English: 5 Frank
see also German
Franz __ Haydn: 6 Joseph
Franz __ Land: 5 Josef
Franz, Dennis: 5 actor
film: American Buffalo (1996)
City of Angels (1998)
TV: NYPD Blue
frap: 4 bind, wrap
frappé: 4 iced **5** drink, shake **6** frozen **7** chilled, dessert **9** milkshake
Frascati: 4 wine **5** white
origin: 5 Italy
Fraser: 4 Dawn **5** Neale, river **7** Antonia, Brendan
Fraser, Antonia: 6 author, writer **7** British
spouse: Harold Pinter
Fraser, Brendan: 5 actor
film: Bedazzled (2000)
Blast From the Past (1999)
Dudley Do-Right (1999)
Encino Man (1992)
George of the Jungle (1997)
Gods and Monsters (1998)
Mrs. Winterbourne (1996)
The Mummy (1999)
School Ties (1992)
Still Breathing (1998)
Fraser, Dawn: 7 swimmer
Fraser, Neale: 7 netster **9** tennis pro
milieu: 5 court
Frasier (NBC sitcom)
cast: Peri Gilpin (Roz Doyle)
Kelsey Grammer (Dr. Frasier Crane)
Jane Leeves (Daphne Moon)
John Mahoney (Martin Crane)
David Hyde Pierce (Dr. Niles Crane)
dog: Eddie
Niles' wife: Maris
setting: Seattle, Washington
frat
see fraternity
frater: 3 bro, pal **4** chum, mate **5** buddy, crony **6** friend **7** comrade
fraternal: 4 true **5** loyal **6** caring **7** devoted, related **9** brotherly
group: 4 BPOE, Elks, IOOF **5** Lions, Lodge **7** Kiwanis **10** Odd Fellows
fraternal __: 4 twin **7** society
fraternity: 3 set **4** clan, club **5** house, order, union **7** academy, coterie **8** quarters
delivery: 3 keg
fee: 4 dues
house alternative: 4 dorm
inspection: 4 rush
letter: 2 mu, nu, pi, xi **3** chi, eta, phi, psi, rho, tau **4** beta, iota, zeta **5** alpha, delta, gamma, kappa, omega, sigma, theta **6** lambda **7** epsilon, omicron, upsilon
one in a ~: 3 mem. **6** member **7** brother
opposite: 3 sor. **8** sorority
party: 4 stag **5** mixer
party attire: 4 toga **5** sheet
quarters: 5 house
recruit: 5 frosh **8** freshman
wear: 3 pin
fraternity __: 5 house
Fraternity __: 3 Row
fraternize: 3 mix **6** fall in, hobnob, mingle **7** consort, hang out **9** associate, socialize
Fratianne, Linda: 6 skater
__ fratres: 5 orate
fratricide victim: 4 Abel
frau: 3 Mrs. **5** title, woman **6** German
husband: 4 Herr
fraud: 3 con, job **4** fake, hoax, ruse, scam, sham **5** cheat, crook, faker, feint, guile, phony, put-on, quack, rogue, shark, sting, theft, trick **6** bad guy, deceit, dupery, forger, hoaxer, humbug, hustle, phoney, racket, rascal, rip-off, robber **7** bluffer, chicane, con game, falsity, fast one, sharper, sharpie, snow job, swindle **8** artifice, bad faith, deceiver, flimflam, imposter, impostor, swindler, thievery, trickery **9** charlatan, chicanery, deception, duplicity, falsifier, hypocrisy, hypocrite, imposture, improbity, mare's nest, pretender, racketeer, treachery **10** corruption, hanky-panky, hocus-pocus, imposition, mountebank, plagiarism, subterfuge
check for ~: 5 audit **6** go over **7** examine, inspect **9** go through **10** scrutinize
ending: 5 ulent
monitoring agcy.: 3 FTC
obtain by ~: 5 grift
fraudulence: 6 deceit **7** falsity **8** cheating, pretense **9** chicanery, duplicity, imposture, treachery **10** dishonesty, subterfuge
fraudulent: 4 fake, mock, sham **5** bogus, false, phony, put-on **6** ersatz, forged, phoney, pseudo, shifty, unreal **7** assumed, corrupt, crooked, devious, feigned **8** criminal, spurious, thieving, thievish **9** deceitful, deceptive, dishonest, falsified, imitation, simulated, swindling, synthetic, underhand **10** artificial, fabricated, fallacious, fictitious
not ~: 4 good **5** legit, valid **6** kosher, lawful **7** genuine **9** authentic
fraught: 5 heavy, laden, risky **6** filled **7** replete, stuffed **8** brimming **9** bristling
Fraülein: 4 girl, lass, maid, miss **5** title **6** damsel, German, lassie, maiden **7** colleen **8** señorita **9** young lady **10** young woman
Fraunhofer, Joseph von: 9 physicist, scientist
Frawley, William: 5 actor
film: Huckleberry Finn (1939)
The Lemon Drop Kid (1934)
The Lemon Drop Kid (1951)
Miracle on 34th Street (1947)
Roxie Hart (1942)
TV: I Love Lucy, My Three Sons
TV wife: Vivian Vance
fray: 3 row, rub **4** riot, tear, wear **5** brawl, clash, fight, melee, mix-up, scrap, set-to, shred, storm **6** action, barney, battle, combat, fracas, ragged, ruckus, rumble, rumpus, tussle **7** contest, frazzle, quarrel, scuffle, unravel, wear out **8** brouhaha, conflict, skirmish, slugfest **9** encounter, imbroglio **10** donnybrook, engagement, free-for-all
above the ~: 5 aloof
ready for the ~: 5 armed
frayed: 4 worn **5** tatty **6** ragged, shabby **10** threadbare
Frayn, Michael: 6 writer **7** British **10** playwright
work: Alphabetical Order
Copenhagen
Donkey's Years
Headlong
A Landing on the Sun
Look, Look
Make and Break
Noises Off
Now You Know
Spies
Sweet Dreams
The Trick of It
Frazer: 3 Dan **5** James

Frazier: 3 Joe 4 Walt 6 Marvis
Frazier, Joe: 5 boxer
foe: 3 Ali
milieu: 4 ring
Frazier, Walt
milieu: 5 court
org.: 3 NBA
sport: 10 basketball
frazzle: 4 fray, poop, tear 5 shred 7 poop out, remnant, tire out, wear out 8 knock out 9 prostrate, tucker out 10 come undone, enervation, exhaustion
worn to a ~: 4 beat 5 jumpy, tired, weary, wired 6 bushed, dished, done in 7 drained, run-down, uptight, wound up 8 dog-tired, fatigued, in a tizzy, unnerved 9 enervated, exhausted, played out 10 distressed
frazzled: 4 worn 6 ragged 9 exhausted, prostrate
freak: 3 bug, fan, nut, odd 4 buff, rage, rave 5 fiend, go ape 6 addict, lose it, mutant, zealot 7 admirer, anomaly, devotee, fanatic, flip out, go crazy, monster, oddball, unhinge, unusual 8 follower, have a fit, mutation 9 go berserk 10 aberration, aficionado, enthusiast
out: 4 rave 5 go ape, upset 6 go nuts, lose it 8 have a fit
(out): 3 wig
out on: 3 dig 4 like 5 enjoy, savor 6 relish 10 appreciate
freak __: 3 out
__ freak: 7 control
freaked out: 3 hot, mad 4 ired, sore 5 cross, huffy, irate, livid, manic, riled, upset, wroth 6 fuming, ireful, raging, raving, red-hot 7 bananas, furious, lunatic, ranting 8 choleric, maniacal, wrathful 9 indignant, resentful, splenetic, wrought-up
freakish: 3 odd 4 eery, wild 5 eerie, outré, weird 6 atypic, far-out, quirky, way-out 7 bizarre, deviant, erratic, oddball, offbeat, strange, surreal, unusual 8 aberrant, abnormal, atypical, peculiar, uncommon 9 anomalous, divergent, eccentric, fantastic, grotesque, irregular, monstrous, unnatural 10 outlandish, unorthodox
freak of __: 6 nature
__ Freak On: 5 Get Ur
Freaky Friday (1977 film)
cast: John Astin, Jodie Foster, Barbara Harris
__ Freans: 4 Peek
Frears, Stephen: 8 director
film: Dangerous Liaisons (1988)
The Grifters (1990)
Hero (1992)
High Fidelity (2000)
The Hi-Lo Country (1998)
My Beautiful Laundrette (1985)
Prick Up Your Ears (1987)
The Snapper (1993)
Freberg: 4 Stan
Fréchette, Louis: 4 poet 8 Canadian
freckle: 3 dot 4 spot 5 speck 7 lentigo
freckle-__: 5 faced
freckled: 6 dotted 7 dappled, flecked, mottled, spotted 8 speckled
Freckle Juice author: Judy Blume
Fred: 3 Ebb 4 Lynn, Ward 5 Allen, Clark, Dryer, Hoyle, Mertz, Niblo 6 Grandy, Gwynne, Noonan, Piscop, Rogers, Savage, Stolle, Waring 7 Astaire, Couples, McGriff 8 Friendly, Newmeyer, Schepisi 9 de Cordova, MacMurray, Zinnemann 10 Flintstone
dancing partner: 3 Cyd 6 Barrie, Ginger
pet: 4 Dino
sister: 5 Adele
to Pebbles: 3 Dad
wife: 5 Wilma
Fred __: 6 Basset
Freda: 5 Payne
Fred and His Playboy Band, John song: Judy in Disguise (1967)
freddie: 5 dance
Freddie: 5 Patek 6 Prinze 7 Mercury
Freddie __: 3 Mac
Freddie and the Dreamers song: I'm Telling You Now (1965)
Freddie's Dead (1972 song) artist: Curtis Mayfield
Freddy: 6 Cannon, Fender 8 Reynolds
street: 3 Elm
Frederic: 5 Cohen 6 Dannay 7 Forrest, Manning 9 Remington
Frédéric: 5 Passy 6 Chopin 7 Mistral 9 Bartholdi
Frederica von __: 5 Stade
Frédéric Joliot-__: 5 Curie
Frederick: 4 city, town 5 Loewe, North, Rolfe, Soddy 6 Church, Delius, Reines, Sanger 7 Banting, Forsyth, Hopkins, Marryat, Olmsted, Robbins 8 Douglass
in German: 9 Friedrich
in Italian: 8 Federico
locale: 8 Maryland
Fredericksburg: 6 battle
winner: 3 Lee
Frederick the __: 5 Great
Fredericton: 4 city, town
locale: 6 Canada
Frederik: 4 Pohl
Fredo: 8 Corleone
Fredric: 5 March
Fredro, Aleksander: 6 Polish, writer 10 playwright
free: 3 big, rid 4 idle, open, save, undo, wild 5 clear, let go, loose, saved, spare, spell, unjam, unled, unpin, untie 6 acquit, excuse, exempt, gratis, lavish, let off, let out, liquid, loosen, pardon, parole, public, purify, ransom, redeem, rescue, spring, unbind, uncage, unhand, unpaid, untied, unused, unwind, vacant 7 absolve, as a gift, at large, bail out, deliver, dismiss, escaped, liberal, lighten, manumit, off-duty, pro bono, release, relieve, rescued, through, unbound, unchain, unleash, untaken, untwine 8 absolute, at no cost, costless, cut loose, detached, generous, informal, let loose, liberate, not in use, prodigal, released, reprieve, separate, set loose, unbarred, unburden, unfetter 9 at leisure, at liberty, available, disburden, discharge, disengage, expansive, extricate, footloose, leisurely, liberated, nonliable, on one's own, on the cuff, out of work, outspoken, unchained, uncoerced, unengaged, unhitched, unimpeded, unshackle, unsparing, voluntary 10 autonomous, bighearted, democratic, disengaged, emancipate, for nothing, liberalize, munificent, off the hook, on the house, on the loose, permissive, privileged, self-ruling, unattached, unconfined, unemployed, unfettered, unhampered, unhindered, unoccupied, unreserved, unreticent, unshackled, vindicated
ender: 3 dom, man, men, way 4 boot, born, form, hand, hold, load 5 board, lance, mason, stone, style, wheel 6 handed, holder, lancer, loader, martin 7 hearted, masonry, thinker 8 standing, wheeling
from: 5 rid of
(from): 6 exempt, immune 7 absolve
from evil: 5 purge 6 purify 8 exorcise, exorcize
from (prefix): 3 dis-
go ~: 4 walk 6 get out
hand: 5 swing 6 leeway 7 bigness, largess 8 largesse, latitude 10 generosity, liberality
home ~: 10 in the clear
not ~: 4 busy 6 costly 7 engaged 8 occupied
of: 6 beyond 7 lacking
(of): 3 rid 6 devoid, divest
set ~: 5 clear, let go, loose, unpen, untie 6 loosen, ransom, redeem, rescue, unbind, unhand 7 absolve, manumit, release 8 liberate 9 discharge 10 unhindered
space: 4 play, room 6 leeway 9 elbowroom
starter: 4 care, germ 5 hands
ticket: 4 comp, pass 11 Annie Oakley
time: 4 ease 6 recess, repose 7 holiday, leisure, liberty 8 vacation 9 idle hours 10 recreation, relaxation, sabbatical
up: 3 let 4 open 8 liberate
will: 6 choice, option 8 volition
work ~: 4 undo 5 untie 6 unbind 7 release, unhitch, unloose 9 disengage
free __: 3 air, bid 4 city, fall, gold, hand, jazz, kick, list, port, rein, ride, will, zone 5 agent, beach, goods, house, lance, liver, lunch, press, reach, rider, sheet, space, throw, trade, verse, world 6 ascent, charge, church, diving, energy, flight, safety, school, silver, socage, speech, spirit, weight 7 balloon, coinage, company, radical, thought
free __ bird: 3 as a
free-__: 4 form 5 blown, bored, range 6 handed, living, spoken 7 cutting, hearted, swimmer
free-__-all: 3 for
free-__ zone: 4 fire 5 trade
__ free: 3 for, set 4 home
__-free: 3 ice, tax 4 duty, post, rent, scot 5 fancy, heart 7 carrier
Free __: 4 Bird, Kirk, Ride 5 Willy 6 French
Free-__ Party: 4 Soil
__ Free: 4 Born
free and __: 4 easy 5 clear
Free and Accepted __: 6 Masons
free and easy: 3 lax 5 homey, light, loose 6 breezy, casual, folksy, mellow 7 lenient, offhand, patient, relaxed 8 informal, laid back, outgoing, tolerant 9 indulgent, leisurely 10 forbearing, nonchalant, off-the-cuff, openminded, permissive, unaffected
free as __: 5 a bird
Free as a Bird (1995 song) artist: Beatles
freebie: 4 comp, gift, pass 7 handout, premium 8 giveaway
office ~: 4 perc, perk, plus 5 bonus 7 benefit 8 dividend 10 perquisite
restaurant ~: 4 roll, salt 5 bread, jelly, sugar, syrup, water 6 catsup, napkin, pepper 7 catchup, ketchup, mustard 8 doggy bag 9 bowser bag, doggie bag
Freebie and the __: 4 Bean
Free Bird (1975 song) artist: Lynyrd Skynyrd
freeboot: 4 loot, raid, sack 5 spoil, strip 6 harrow, maraud, pirate, ravage 7 despoil, pillage, plunder, ransack 8 prey upon 9 depredate, devastate 10 lay waste to
freebooter: 6 looter, pirate, raider, viking 7 brigand, corsair 8 marauder, pillager 9 buccaneer, plunderer, privateer
__-free call: 4 toll
Freed: 4 Alan, Herb 6 Arthur
__ free delivery: 5 rural
Freedent: 3 gum 10 chewing gum
alternative: 5 Extra, Orbit 7 Dentyne, Trident 8 Carefree, Chiclets 10 Doublemint, Juicy Fruit
freedman: 4 laet
freedom: 3 lib. 5 leave, power, range, right, scope 6 laxity, leeway, parole, rescue, safety 7 abandon, ability, leisure, liberty, license, passage, release 8 autarchy, autonomy, facility, immunity, latitude, security 9 democracy, elbowroom, privilege, salvation, tolerance 10 indulgence, liberation, permission, redemption
combining form: 8 eleuther- 9 eleuthero-
from care: 4 ease 5 peace 8 calmness, serenity 9 composure
in Swahili: 5 uhuru
of movement: 4 room 5 range, scope 6 leeway 8 latitude 9 elbowroom
freedom __: 5 march, rider 7 fighter
freedom __ city: 5 of the
freedom __ press: 5 of the
freedom __ seas: 5 of the
Freedom: 5 apple
relative: 4 crab, Gala, Lodi, Rome 5 Mutsu 6 Empire, Ida Red, medlar, Pippin, russet 7 Baldwin, Bramley, costard, Liberty, Spartan, Wealthy, Winesap 8 Cortland, Jonathan, McIntosh 10 Rome Beauty
__ Freedom: 3 Cry 5 Sweet
Freedom (1985 song) artist: George Michael
freedom of __: 6 choice, speech 8 religion
Freedom of Choice artist: 4 Devo
Freedom of Information __: 3 Act
freedom of the __: 4 city, seas 5 press
Freedom Road
actor: 3 Ali
author: Howard Fast
__ Freedoms: 4 Four
__ Free Europe: 5 Radio
Free Fallin' (1989 song) artist: Tom Petty and the Heartbreakers
Free Fall in Crimson author: John D. MacDonald
free-floating: 6 adrift 7 aimless 8 goalless, unmoored 10 unanchored
free-flowing: 6 lavish 7 fulsome, gushing, profuse 8 effusive 9 expansive
free-for-all: 3 row 4 fray, riot 5 brawl, fight, furor, melee, mix-up, scrap, storm 6 affray, barney, battle, fracas, racket, tussle 7 ruction, scuffle 8 brouhaha, scramble, struggle 10 donnybrook
__-free gasoline: 4 lead
free-handed: 6 giving 7 liberal 8 generous 9 unselfish 10 benevolent, charitable, munificent, ungrudging, unstinting
free-hearted: 4 open 7 liberal 8 generous 10 ungrudging, unreserved
Freeh, Louis org.: 3 FBI
freehold: 4 land, plot 5 tract 6 parcel 8 property
Freehold: 4 city, town
locale: 9 New Jersey
freeholder: 8 landlord
name meaning ~: 8 Franklin
freeing: 7 release 8 delivery 9 discharge
freelance: 4 work 8 non-staff
assignment: 3 job

instructor: 5 tutor
payment: 3 fee
freelancer: 5 indie 6 jobber, writer
encl.: 4 SASE
Free Lance, The composer: 5 Sousa
freeload: 3 beg, bum 5 cadge, leech, mooch 6 sponge 7 finagle, wheedle 8 scrounge 9 panhandle
freeloader: 5 leech 6 cadger, sponge 7 sponger 8 deadbeat, parasite
freely: 5 ad lib 6 at will, gladly 7 lightly, readily 9 naturally, voluntary
freeman: 5 ceorl
Freeman: 4 Joan, Mona 5 Bobby, Ernie 6 Crofts, Gosden, Morgan 8 Kathleen
Freeman, Morgan: 5 actor
film: Amistad (1997)
The Bonfire of the Vanities (1990)
Bopha! (1993)
Clean and Sober (1988)
Deep Impact (1998)
Desert Blue (1999)
Driving Miss Daisy (1989)
Glory (1989)
Hard Rain (1998)
High Crimes (2002)
Hurricane Streets (1998)
Kiss the Girls (1997)
Lean on Me (1989)
Nurse Betty (2000)
Outbreak (1995)
Robin Hood: Prince of Thieves (1991)
Se7en (1995)
The Shawshank Redemption (1994)
The Sum of All Fears (2002)
Unforgiven (1992)
free on ___: 5 board
Freeport: 4 city, town
locale: 7 New York 8 Illinois
Free Press: 5 paper 9 newspaper
locale: 7 Detroit 8 Winnipeg
freer: 6 savior 7 saviour 9 liberator
___-free refrigerator: 5 frost
Freer Gallery display: 3 art
Free Ride (1973 song) artist: Edgar Winter Group
freesia: 4 irid 5 plant 6 flower
Free song: All Right Now (1970)
Free Soul, A (1931 film)
cast: Lionel Barrymore, Clark Gable, Norma Shearer
free-spoken: 4 open 5 blunt, frank, vocal 6 candid 8 out-front 9 ingenuous 10 forthright, from the hip, unreserved
___ Free State: 5 Congo, Irish 6 Orange
freestone: 5 fruit, peach
freestyle: 8 swimming
freethinker: 5 pagan 7 heathen, infidel, radical
religion: 5 deism
freethinking: 7 radical 8 doubting, maverick 9 quizzical, skeptical 10 avant-garde, rebellious
Freetown: 4 city, port 7 capital
locale: Sierra Leone
free-trade ___: 4 zone
freeway: 4 road 5 route 6 artery 10 interstate
clogger: 3 car, van 4 auto, semi 5 truck 7 traffic 10 automobile
enter a ~: 5 merge
feature: 4 exit, lane, ramp 8 entrance, rest stop
problem: 3 jam 4 smog 6 detour 8 accident
system, to tourists: 4 maze
see also highway
Freeway (1996 film)
cast: Brooke Shields, Kiefer Sutherland, Reese Witherspoon
Freeway of Love (1985 song) artist: Aretha Franklin
freewheel: 5 coast, glide
Free Willy (1993 film)
animal: 4 orca 5 whale
cast: Michael Madsen, Lori Petty, Jason James Richter
director: Simon Wincer
Free Your Mind (1992 song) artist: En Vogue
freeze: 3 ice 4 cool, halt, numb, stop 5 chill, frost, ice up, pause, store 6 arrest, benumb, harden, hold up, ossify, shelve, shiver 7 congeal, ice over, process, stiffen, suspend, terrify, thicken 8 glaciate, paralyse, paralyze, preserve, prohibit, solidify, stop cold 9 cessation, stabilize 10 inactivate, stand still, suspension
combining form: 4 cryo-
deep ~: 6 ice age
out: 3 ban, bar 4 stop 5 block 6 bounce, enjoin 7 dismiss, exclude 8 blockade, disallow, obstruct, prohibit, restrain 9 barricade, discharge 10 disqualify
over: 5 ice up
starter: 4 anti
(to): 5 stick
up: 5 panic
freeze ___: 3 out 4 on to 5 frame 7 etching
freeze-___: 3 dry 4 etch 5 dried, frame
___ freeze: 3 dry 4 deep, land
___-freeze: 5 flash, quick, sharp
Freeze!: 4 halt, stop 6 hold it 8 don't move
Freeze foe, Mr.: 6 Batman
Freeze-Frame (1982 song) artist: J. Geils Band
freezeout: 4 game 8 card game
freezer: 6 cooler, icebox
name: 5 Amana 6 Maytag 7 Kenmore 9 Whirlpool
product: 3 ice 7 ice cube
freezer ___: 4 burn
freezing: 3 icy, raw 4 cold 5 chill, gelid, nippy, polar 6 arctic, biting, bitter, chilly, frigid, frosty, wintry 7 chilled, glacial, ice-cold, numbing, shivery, wintery 8 piercing, Siberian
temperatures: 5 teens
freezing ___: 4 rain 5 point 7 drizzle
Fregonese: 4 Hugo
Frehley: 3 Ace
Freia: 8 asteroid
freight: 4 haul, load, send, ship 5 cargo, goods 6 lading 7 forward, imports, payload, traffic 8 carriage, contents, shipment 9 wagonload
agcy.: 3 ICC
bearing ~: 5 heavy, laden 6 packed
carrier: 3 van 4 semi 5 barge, train, truck 6 boxcar, coaler 8 railroad
hopper: 4 hobo
weight: 3 lbs., ton 4 tons 5 pound 6 pounds
freight ___: 3 car, ton 5 agent, house, train 6 engine
___ freight: 3 air 4 dead, hop a
freighter: 4 boat, ship 6 vessel 7 steamer 9 transport
destination: 3 POC 4 port 10 port of call
Freight Train Blues artist: 5 Acuff
___ Freischütz: 3 Der
Fréjus: 4 city, town
locale: 6 France
Fremont: 4 city, town
locale: 8 Nebraska 10 California
Frémont, John C.: 8 explorer
French: 4 lang. 5 bread, Nicki 6 course, Gallic, Harold, Victor 7 Marilyn, Stewart 8 dressing, language
door part: 4 sash
fries: 4 side 8 side dish
fries in Britain: 5 chips
Resistance center: 4 Lyon 5 Lyons
Revolution figure: 5 Marat
speaking nation: 4 Chad, Mali, Togo 5 Benin, Gabon, Gabun, Haiti, Niger 6 Canada, Guinea, Rwanda 7 Algeria, Burundi, Comoros, Morocco, Reunion, Senegal, Tunisia, Vanuatu 8 Cameroon, Dominica, Sjibouti 9 Mauritius 10 Ivory Coast, Madagascar, Mauritania, Saint Lucia, Upper Volta 11 Switzerland
see also France, French words
French ___: 3 bed, dip, fry, kid 4 Alps, arch, bean, chop, cuff, door, flat, foot, harp, heel, horn, roll, roof, rose, seam 5 bread, chalk, Congo, curve, drain, fries, India, leave, pitch, roast, Shore, Sudan, toast, twist, Union 6 endive, Guiana, Guinea, pastry, polish, Suites, system, window 7 Academy, bulldog, cruller, Morocco, Oceania, pancake, Quarter 8 dressing
French ___ Indies: 4 West
French ___ soup: 5 onion
French-___: 3 cut 5 style 6 polish
French-___ potatoes: 5 fried
___ French: 3 law, Old 4 Free 6 Middle, Modern, Norman
French and Indian ___: 3 War
French Chef, The: Julia Child
French Connection, The (1971 film)
cast: Gene Hackman, Tony Lo Bianco, Fernando Rey, Roy Scheider
cop: 4 narc, nark
director: William Friedkin
highlight: 5 chase
inspiration: 4 Egan
setting: 3 NYC 7 New York
French, Daniel Chester: 6 artist 8 sculptor
French Equatorial ___: 6 Africa
French Foreign ___: 6 Legion
French Guiana
capital: 7 Cayenne
Indian: 6 Galibi
neighbor: 6 Brazil 8 Suriname
___ French hens...: 5 three
French Indochina part: 4 Anam, Laos 5 Annam 6 Tonkin 7 Vietnam 8 Cambodia
French Leave author: P.G. Wodehouse
French Lieutenant's Woman, The: 4 film 5 novel
author: John Fowles
cast: Jeremy Irons, Leo McKern, Hilton McRae, Meryl Streep
director: Karel Reisz
Frenchman
name meaning ~: 7 Frances, Francis
Frenchman's Creek (1944 film)
cast: Joan Fontaine, Basil Rathbone
director: Mitchell Leisen
French, Nicki song: Total Eclipse of the Heart (1995)
French onion: 4 soup
French Open: 6 tennis 7 tourney
seven-time ~ champ: 5 Evert
French Polynesia
capital: 7 Papeete
island: 3 Hao 4 Anaa, Eïao, Rapa, Reao, Ua Pu 5 Tahaa 6 Hatutu, Hiva Oa, Mooréa, Rurutu, Tahiti, Tubuai, Ua Huka 7 Huahine, Makatéa, Raïatéa, Tahuata 8 Fakarava, Fatu Hiva, Nuku Hiva, Raevavae, Rangiroa, Rimatara 9 Mangareva
islands: 7 Austral, Gambier, Society, Tuamotu 9 Marquesas
French Powder Mystery, The author: Ellery Queen
French Quarter director: 4 Kane
French Revolution
calendar month: Brumaire, Floréal, Frimaire, Fructidor, Germinal, Messidor, Nivôse, Pluviôse, Prairial, Thermidor, Vendémiaire, Ventôse
figure: 5 Marat
French roast: 6 coffee
French's: 7 mustard
alternative: 7 Gulden's 10 Grey Poupon
French Sudan today: 4 Mali
French Suites composer: 4 Bach
French toast: 5 bread 9 breakfast
French Toast Crunch: 6 cereal
competitor: 3 Kix 4 Life, Trix 5 Kashi, Quisp, Total 6 Kaboom, Muesli, Oreo O's, Pablum, Smacks 7 All-Bran, Crispix, Harmony, Hunny B's, Mueslix, Oat Bran, Pokemon 8 Boo Berry, Cheerios, Corn Chex, Corn Pops, Fiber One, Rice Chex, Special K, Uncle Sam, Wheaties 9 Alpha Bits, Apple Zaps, Grape Nuts, Honey Comb, Just Right, Wheat Chex 10 Apple Jacks, Bran Flakes, Cap'n Crunch, Cocoa Puffs, Froot Loops, Mini-Wheats, Nutri-Grain, Puffed Rice, Quaker Oats, Smart Start 11 Cocoa Blasts, Cookie Crisp, Golden Crisp, Lucky Charms, Puffed Wheat, Sweet Crunch, Waffle Crisp
French twist: 4 coif 6 hairdo 8 coiffure
French West ___: 6 Africa, Indies
French White House: 6 Élysée
French Without Tears author: Terrence Rattigan
French words
a: 3 une
academy: 5 école
according to the custom: 7 à la mode
adverb: 3 ici, mal, que 4 tres 5 quand
affirmative: 3 oui
after: 5 après
ait: 3 île
all together: 7 en masse
among: 5 entre
are: 4 êtes
area: 4 aire
arm: 4 bras
article: 3 les, une
aunt: 5 tante
back: 3 dos
badly: 3 mal
be: 4 être
below: 4 à bas
between: 5 entre
between ourselves: 9 entre nous
beverage: 3 thé, vin 4 café, lait
black: 4 noir 5 noire
born: 3 née
brainstorm: 4 idée
bread: 4 pain
by the way: 9 en passant
cabbage: 4 chou
cake: 6 gateau
carefree: 9 sans souci
cat: 4 chat 5 tigre
cheer: 4 vive
cleric: 4 abbé
coffee: 4 café
color: 4 bleu, brun, noir 5 blanc, jeune, noire, rouge 7 blanche
conjunction: 2 et 3 que
count: 5 comte
customary: 7 de règle
dance: 3 bal 5 valse
day of the week: 5 jeudi, lundi, mardi 6 samedi 8 dimanche, mercredi, vendredi
dear: 4 cher

decadent: 11 fin de siècle
denial: 3 non
dessert: 5 glacé
direction: 3 est, sud 4 nord 5 ouest
distance: 5 metre 9 kilomètre
donkey: 3 ane
down with: 4 à bas
duke: 3 duc
earth: 5 terre
east: 3 est
eight: 4 huit
eleven: 4 onze
enjoy your meal: 10 bon appétit
entrée: 4 roti, veau
evil: 3 mal
exclamation: 3 zut 5 voilà 8 zut alors
failed: 6 manqué
fashionable society: 9 beau monde
fat: 4 gras
father: 4 père
fine arts: 9 beaux arts
five: 4 cinq
flower: 3 lis
four: 6 quatre
fourteen: 8 quatorze
friend: 3 ami 4 amie
golden: 3 d'or
good: 3 bon
goodbye: 5 adieu 8 au revoir
greeting: 5 salut 7 bon jour, bon soir
harm: 3 mal
head: 4 tête
health: 5 santé
hearsay: 7 oui-dire
Help!: 4 à moi
here: 3 ici
hers: 3 ses
high: 4 haut 5 haute
hint: 3 mot
his: 3 ses
holy: 5 sacre
holy woman: 3 ste. 6 sainte
hook: 4 croc
ill: 3 mal
in: 4 dans
inexpensive: 9 bon marché
infinitive: 4 être
in harmony: 9 en rapport
interrogative: 4 quel, quoi 5 quand
in the home of: 4 chez
into: 4 dans
island: 3 île
key: 3 clé 4 clef
kind: 3 bon
king: 3 roi
lady: 3 mme. 6 madame
land: 5 terre
latest fashion: 10 dernier cri
legislature: 5 sénat
life: 3 vie
lily: 3 lis
love: 5 amour
love letter: 10 billet doux
low: 3 bas
maid: 5 bonne
May: 3 mai
me: 3 moi
milk: 4 lait
mine: 4 à moi
miss: 4 Mlle.
mister: 8 monsieur
model of excellence: 9 beau idéal
monk: 5 frère
month: 3 mai 4 août, juin, mars 5 avril 7 février, janvier, juillet, octobre 8 décembre, novembre 9 septembre
mother: 4 mère
Mrs.: 3 Mme.
Ms.: 4 Mlle.
my: 3 mes, moi
naked: 9 au naturel
name: 3 nom
nine: 4 neuf
ninny: 3 ane
no: 3 non
noon: 4 midi
not: 3 pas
nothing: 4 rien
notice: 4 avis
notion: 4 idée
noun: 3 nom
number: 2 un 3 dix, six 4 cent, cinq, deux, huit, neuf, onze, sept 5 douze, mille, seize, trois, vingt 6 quatre, quinze, treize, trente 8 quarante, quatorze, soixante 9 cinquante
obligatory: 9 de rigueur
obsession: 8 idée fixe
one: 2 un
on foot: 5 à pied
opinion: 4 avis
our: 3 nos
pancake: 5 crepe
pet peeve: 9 bête noire
possessive: 3 mes, ses, tes, toi 5 notre
precipitation: 5 neige, pluie
prejudice: 9 parti pris
preposition: 3 des 4 avec, dans, sans 5 entre
priest: 4 abbé
pronoun: 3 lui, mes, moi, qui, ses, soi, tes, toi, une 4 à moi, elle, nous, tien, vous 5 notre
pseudonym: 10 nom de plume
queen: 5 reine
rabble: 8 canaille
rain: 5 pluie
reason to exist: 11 raison d'être
relative: 4 mère, père 5 frère, oncle, soeur, tante 7 cousine
right?: 9 n'est-ce pas?
salt: 3 sel
school: 5 école, lycée
sea: 3 mer
seasickness: 8 mal de mer
season: 3 été 5 hiver 7 automne 9 printemps
see you soon: 8 à bientôt
seven: 4 sept
she: 4 elle
silk: 4 soie
since: 3 des
snow: 5 neige
so-called: 9 soi-disant
social error: 7 faux pas
soft: 3 bas
soldier: 5 poilu
some: 3 des
so much the better: 9 tant mieux
so much the worse: 7 tant pis
soul: 3 âme
spoken: 3 dit
state: 4 état
step: 3 pas
stocking: 3 bas
street name starter: 3 rue 5 rue de
student: 5 élève
summer: 3 été
tea: 3 thé
ten: 3 dix
that's life: 9 c'est la vie
the: 3 les
theater: 4 cine
thirteen: 6 treize
three: 5 trois
toast: 5 salut
to be: 4 être
too much: 6 de trop
to the left: 7 à gauche
to the point: 7 à propos
treason: 11 lèse majesté
turnabout: 9 volte-face
twelve: 5 douze
two: 4 deux
uncommon: 9 recherché
upon: 3 sur
up-to-date: 9 au courant
veal: 4 veau
very: 4 tres
vineyard: 3 cru
water: 3 eau
well-versed: 6 au fait
when: 5 quand
wine: 3 vin
with: 4 avec
without: 4 sans
woman: 5 femme
word: 3 mot
year: 2 an 5 année
yes: 3 oui 7 mais oui
you: 4 vous
your: 3 tes, toi 5 votre

Freneau, Philip: 4 poet

frenetic: 3 mad 5 hyper, wired 6 hectic 7 excited, frantic, keyed up, unglued, zealous 8 agitated, feverish, frenzied, in a tizzy, maniacal, worked up 9 at wits' end, delirious 10 corybantic, distraught, distressed, flipped out, in an uproar

frenetically: 7 like mad

Freni, Mirella: 6 singer 7 soprano
specialty: 5 opera

frenum locale: 6 tongue

frenzied: 3 mad 4 amok, wild 5 amuck, hyper, irate, manic, rabid, wired 6 ablaze, heated, hectic, raging 7 burning, demonic, excited, frantic, hog-wild, keyed up, unglued 8 agitated, daemonic, feverish, frenetic, in a furor, in a tizzy, maniacal, white-hot, wild-eyed, worked up 9 at wits' end, delirious, demonical, desperate, fanatical, last-ditch, possessed, unscrewed, wrought-up 10 corybantic, distraught, distressed, flipped out, hysterical, in an uproar, infuriated, passionate

frenzy: 3 fit, row 4 fury, fuss, rage, to-do 5 fever, furor, mania, panic, spasm, tizzy 6 lather, madden, ruckus, rumble, rumpus 7 ferment, mad rush, passion, rampage, ruction, turmoil 8 delirium, hysteria, outburst, paroxysm 9 agitation, vehemence 10 excitement, fanaticism
vent with ~: 7 unleash

__ frenzy: 7 feeding

Frenzy (1972 film)
cast: Jon Finch, Barry Foster, Barbara Leigh-Hunt
director: Alfred Hitchcock

Freon: 3 gas 7 coolant

freq.
not: 3 occ.

frequency: 5 pitch 9 abundance, constancy, fixedness, iteration, pulsation 10 commonness, prevalence, recurrence, regularity, repetition
unit: 2 Hz 3 kHz, mHz 5 hertz 9 kilocycle, kilohertz, megahertz

frequency __: 4 band 5 curve 7 polygon

__ frequency: 3 low 4 gene, high 5 audio, video 6 allele, medium 7 angular

frequent: 4 many 5 haunt, usual, visit 6 common, resort 7 generic, profuse, regular, routine 8 everyday, habitual, iterated, manifold, numerous, ordinary, periodic, repeated, unwaning 9 a good many, continual, customary, generical, hang out at, patronize, prevalent, recurrent 10 hang around, persistent, reiterated, widespread

frequent __: 5 flier, flyer

frequent-__ miles: 5 flier, flyer

frequented spot: 5 haunt 7 hangout, retreat

frequenter: 6 patron 7 habitué, regular

frequently: 3 oft 4 much 5 often 6 mostly 7 as a rule, usually 8 ofttimes 9 generally, many a time, many times, regularly, sometimes, very often 10 habitually, oftentimes, ordinarily, repeatedly
not ~: 6 seldom

frère: 4 monk 6 French 7 brother
mère's ~: 5 oncle

Frère Jacques word: 4 vous

Fresca: 4 soda 9 soft drink
alternative: 3 TAB 4 Nehi 5 Fanta 6 Sprite 8 Diet Rite, Dr Pepper 9 Canada Dry 10 Mello Yello, Royal Crown 11 Mountain Dew

Freschetta: 5 pizza
alternative: 5 Jeno's, Tony's 6 Ellio's 7 Celeste, Totino's 8 DiGiorno 9 Tombstone

fresco: 3 art 5 mural 8 painting 10 watercolor
base: 5 gesso 7 plaster
do a ~: 5 paint
opposite: 5 secco

fresh: 3 new, raw 4 airy, anew, bold, cool, dewy, flip, good, keen, late, mint, more, naif, orig., pert, pure, rosy, rude, spry, wise 5 added, alert, brisk, clean, clear, crisp, extra, green, hardy, lippy, naive, nervy, novel, other, ruddy, sassy, saucy, sharp, smart, sweet, vital, windy, young 6 active, awless, bouncy, brazen, breezy, bright, callow, cheeky, chilly, clever, daring, latest, lively, modern, modish, recent, red-hot, rested, snippy, unused, virgin 7 artless, aweless, bracing, chipper, current, forward, glowing, healthy, just out, like new, offbeat, revived, uncivil, unfaded, unjaded, untried, unusual, updated, verdant 8 brand-new, creative, flippant, impolite, impudent, insolent, inspired, neoteric, original, snippety, undimmed, unsoiled, unversed, unwilted, up-to-date, vigorous, virginal, youthful 9 energetic, ingenious, inventive, out of line, sparkling, sprightly, unskilled, unspoiled, untainted, untouched, untrained, unwearied 10 additional, bright-eyed, fortifying, innovative, irreverent, newfangled, refreshing, ungracious
air: 5 ozone 7 outside 8 outdoors
get ~: 4 sass 8 mouth off, talk back 10 answer back
not ~: 3 old 5 stale, trite 6 canned, frozen
talk: 3 lip 4 guff, sass 5 cheek, mouth, sauce 9 impudence, insolence, sauciness
with ~ vigor: 5 newly

fresh __: 3 air 4 gale 5 water 6 breeze

fresh __ daisy: 3 as a

Fresh __: 3 Air

Fresh __ of Bel Air: 6 Prince

Fresh (1985 song) artist: Kool and the Gang

fresh as a __: 5 daisy

freshen: 3 air 4 perc, perk, wake 5 renew, rouse, waken 6 aerate, air out, purify, revive 7 cleanse, enliven, refresh, restore 8 spruce up 9 deodorize, ventilate 10 invigorate, revitalize
up: 4 wash

__ freshener: 3 air 6 breath

freshet: 5 flood, spate 6 stream 10 inundation

freshly: 4 anew, just 5 newly 6 lately 8 recently

freshman: 4 pleb, year 5 plebe, pupil 6 newbie, novice, rookie 7 student 8 beginner 9 collegian, greenhorn, undergrad

see also college
Freshman, The (1990 film)
cast: Marlon Brando, Matthew Broderick, Penelope Ann Miller, Maximilian Schell
director: Andrew Bergman
freshness: 3 lip 4 glow, sass 5 bloom, sauce, shine, vigor, youth 7 novelty, sparkle 9 cleanness, clearness, flippancy, greenness, innocence 10 brightness, callowness, uniqueness
check for ~: 5 sniff
lose ~: 4 wilt 5 droop, go bad, spoil 6 wither 7 shrivel
words on a ~ label: 5 use by
freshness __: 4 date
Fresh Prince of Bel Air (NBC sitcom)
cast: James Avery (Philip Banks) Will Smith (Will Smith)
freshwater
fish: 3 gar, ide 4 bass, carp, chub, dace, pike, rudd 5 bream, cisco, loach, perch, roach, tench, tetra, trout 6 darter
mussel: 4 clam, unio 5 naiad
Fresnay: 6 Pierre
Fresnel, Augustin: 9 physicist, scientist
Fresnillo: 4 city, town
locale: 6 Mexico 9 Zacatecas
Fresno: 4 city, town
athletes: 8 Bulldogs
locale: 10 California
newspaper: 3 Bee
school: 3 FSU
Fresno State conference: 3 WAC
__ Fresnos, TX: 3 Los
fret: 3 irk, nag, vex 4 fume, fuss, goad, mope, pine, rile, stew 5 annoy, brood, harry, mourn, peeve, pique, sweat, worry 6 bother, harass, nettle, offend, pother, rankle, repine, ruffle 7 agonize, anguish, disturb, provoke, torment, trouble 8 disquiet, distress, irritate 9 displease
over: 4 fear 5 dread, worry 8 mistrust
fret __: 3 saw
fretful: 4 edgy 5 cross, fussy, huffy, jumpy, onery, tense, testy, whiny 6 crabby, cranky, ornery, touchy, uneasy, whiney 7 carping, peevish, prickly, restive, worried 8 captious, caviling, critical, fluttery, petulant, restless, snappish 9 crotchety, fractious, impatient, irritable, querulous, splenetic 10 irritating, out of sorts
fretfulness: 4 care 6 nerves, temper 7 anxiety, chagrin 8 disquiet
fretting, stop: 5 relax 8 calm down
fretty: 4 edgy 5 cross, huffy, surly, testy 6 crabby, feisty, grumpy, ornery, snappy, touchy 7 grouchy, waspish 8 snappish 9 crotchety, irritable 10 out of sorts
fretwork: 7 lattice 9 adornment 10 decoration
Freud: 4 Anna 6 Lucian 7 Clement, Sigmund
contemporary: 4 Jung 5 Adler
stage: 4 oral
topic: 2 id 3 ego 5 dream
see also German
Freud (1962 film)
cast: Montgomery Clift, Larry Parks, Susannah York
director: John Huston
Freudian __: 4 slip
Freud, Sigmund: 6 author, writer 8 Austrian 12 psychiatrist
contemporary: Adler, Jung
work: The Ego and the Id
The Interpretation of Dreams
Totem and Taboo
Frewer: 4 Matt
Frey, Glenn
group: The Eagles
song: The Heat Is On (1985)
You Belong to the City (1985)
Freytag, Gustav: 6 author, German, writer 10 playwright
Fri.: 3 day
follower: 3 Sat.
man ~: 4 asst.
preceder: 3 Thu. 4 Thur. 5 Thurs.
to Sat.: 4 yest.
see also Friday
__ Fria: 4 Agua
friable: 5 crisp, light, loamy, short 6 crispy, crusty 7 brittle, fragile, powdery
friar: 4 abbé, monk 5 padre 6 priest 7 brother, recluse 8 monastic 9 Carmelite, Dominican, mendicant, religious 10 Franciscan, monastical
Hindu ~: 5 sadhu
home: 4 cell 5 abbey 8 cloister 9 monastery
Friar __: 4 Tuck 5 Minor
__ Friar: 4 Gray 5 Black, White
friar's __: 5 chair 7 lantern
Friars Club event: 5 roast
friary: 5 abbey 8 cloister 9 monastery
fribble: 3 toy 4 fool, play 5 waste 6 geegaw, gewgaw, trifle 7 trinket 8 fool away, gimcrack 9 bagatelle, frivolity 10 gamble away
Fribourg, from: 5 Swiss
fricassee: 3 fry 4 cook, meat
Frick: 4 Ford
collection: 3 art
Fricke: 5 Janie
Fricker, Brenda Oscar: My Left Foot
friction: 3 rub 4 feud, flak, wear 5 clash, flack 6 ruckus, rumpus, strife 7 chafing, discord, dispute, grating, quarrel, rasping, rivalry, rubbing, trouble 8 abrasion, bad blood, conflict, grinding, scraping, traction 9 animosity, bickering, hostility, wrangling 10 antagonism, contention, discontent, disharmony, dissension, irritation, opposition, resentment, resistance
combining form: 5 tribo-
easer: 3 lub., oil 9 lubricant
friction __: 3 saw 4 head, pile, tape 5 drive, layer, match 6 clutch 7 gearing, welding
frictionless: 6 smooth
Frid: 8 Jonathan
Frida: 5 Kahlo
Frida (2002 film)
cast: Antonio Banderas, Salma Hayek, Ashley Judd, Alfred Molina, Geoffrey Rush
director: Julie Taymor
Friday: 3 cop, Joe, man, sgt. 4 Webb 8 sergeant
man ~: 4 aide, hand 6 deputy, helper 8 adjutant, factotum 9 assistant, secretary 10 lieutenant
partner: 5 Smith 6 Gannon
quest: 5 facts
__ Friday: 3 gal, guy, man 4 girl, Good 6 Freaky
Friday Foster star: 5 Grier
__ Friday's: 3 T.G.I.
Friday the __ Slept Late: 5 Rabbi
Friday the 13th (1980 film)
cast: Kevin Bacon, Harry Crosby, Adrienne King, Betsy Palmer
prop: 3 axe
role: 5 Jason
__ Frideric Handel: 6 George
fridge: 6 cooler, icebox 9 appliance
see also refrigerator
Fridley: 4 city, town
locale: 9 Minnesota
Fridtjof: 6 Nansen
__-fried: 3 pan 4 deep, stir
Fried __ Tomatoes: 5 Green
Fried, Alfred: 8 Nobelist
Friedan, Betty: 6 author, writer
work: The Feminine Mystique
The Fountain of Age
It Changed My Life
Life So Far
The Second Stage
Fried Green Tomatoes (1991 film)
cast: Kathy Bates, Mary Stuart Masterson, Mary-Louise Parker, Jessica Tandy
director: Jon Avnet
Fried Green Tomatoes... author: 5 Flagg
Friedkin, William: 8 director
film: The Birthday Party (1968)
The Boys in the Band (1970)
The Brink's Job (1978)
The Exorcist (1973)
The French Connection (1971, AA)
The Night They Raided Minsky's (1968)
Rules of Engagement (2000)
spouse: Lesley-Anne Down, Sherry Lansing, Jeanne Moreau
Friedman: 5 Kinky 6 Jerome, Milton
Friedman, Bruce Jay: 6 author, writer
work: Scuba Duba
Stern
Tokyo Woes
Friedman, Jerome: 8 Nobelist 9 physicist, scientist
Friedman, Milton: 8 Nobelist 9 economist
__-fried potatoes: 3 pan 4 home 6 French
Friedrich: 6 Engels, Hebbel 7 Bergius, Froebel, Rückert 9 Nietzsche, Serturner
alternative: 5 Rheem, Trane 6 Lennox 7 Carrier, Fedders
collaborator: 4 Karl
in English: 9 Frederick
__-fried steak: 7 chicken
Friel, Brian: 5 Irish 10 playwright
home: 4 Eire
Friels: 5 Colin
friend: 3 bro, pal 4 ally, beau, chum, mate 5 amigo, buddy, crony 6 backer, cohort, frater, patron 7 compeer, comrade, consort, partner 8 advocate, alter ego, familiar, intimate, neighbor, playmate, roommate, sidekick, soulmate 9 associate, classmate, colleague, companion, confidant, proponent, soulmates, supporter 10 benefactor, bosom buddy, compatriot, connection, schoolmate, well-wisher
in French: 3 ami 4 amie
in Spanish: 5 amiga, amigo
starter: 3 boy 4 girl
friend __ court: 5 of the
Friend: 6 Quaker
pronoun: 3 thy 4 thee, thou 5 thine
friend in ___, A: 4 need
friendless: 4 lone 5 alone 6 lonely 8 lonesome, solitary 9 abandoned, alienated, estranged 10 ostracized, unattached
feeling ~: 6 lonely 7 forlorn 8 forsaken, isolated, lonesome
friendliness: 5 amity 6 comity, warmth 7 welcome 8 goodness, goodwill, open arms
express ~: 5 smile
friendly: 4 fond, good, homy, kind, nice, warm 5 close, homey, sweet, thick 6 allied, benign, chatty, chummy, clubby, decent, genial, hearty, kindly, loving, polite, social 7 affable, amiable, cordial, helpful, likable, lovable 8 amicable, familiar, gracious, intimate, loveable, outgoing, peaceful, pleasant, sociable 9 attentive, congenial, convivial, expansive, favorable, peaceable, receptive, welcoming 10 beneficial, benevolent, buddy-buddy, gregarious, hospitable, neighborly, personable, solicitous
skies flier: 6 United
friendly __: 4 fire
__-friendly: 3 eco 4 user
Friendly: 4 Fred
Friendly Islands: 5 Tonga
Friendly Persuasion: 4 film, song
artist: Pat Boone
cast: Gary Cooper, Marjorie Main, Dorothy McGuire, Anthony Perkins
director: William Wyler
music: Dimitri Tiomkin
Friendly's: 8 ice cream
alternative: 4 Edy's 7 Breyer's 9 Good Humor 10 Dairy Queen, Haagen Dazs, Turkey Hill
friend of the __: 5 court 6 family
Friend or __?: 3 foe
friends
and neighbors: 4 kith
be ~ with: 4 know
group: 6 circle, clique
make ~: 4 bond 7 connect
see old ~: 5 reune
__ friends: 5 among
Friends (NBC sitcom)
cast: Jennifer Aniston (Rachel Green)
Courteney Cox (Monica Geller)
Lisa Kudrow (Phoebe Buffay)
Matt LeBlanc (Joey Tribbiani)
Matthew Perry (Chandler Bing)
David Schwimmer (Ross Geller)
Friends (1989 song) artist: Jody Watley
Friends and Lovers (1986 song)
artist: Gloria Loring
Friends follower: 6 Romans
friendship: 4 bond, love 5 amity, peace, unity 6 accord, comity, warmth 7 concord, empathy, harmony, rapport, society, support 8 affinity, alliance, devotion, goodwill, intimacy, sodality 9 affection, agreement, closeness, coalition, good vibes 10 amiability, attachment, attraction, consonance, favoritism, partiality, solidarity
Friendship composer: 6 Porter
Friends of __ Coyle, The: 5 Eddie
Friends of Distinction
song: Grazing in the Grass (1969)
Love or Let Me Be Lonely (1970)
Friends of Eddie Coyle, The (1973 film)
cast: Peter Boyle, Richard Jordan, Robert Mitchum
director: Peter Yates
Friendswood: 4 city, town
locale: 5 Texas
__ Friend, The: 3 Boy 4 Girl
...friend who never made __: 4 a foe
fries: 4 side 8 side dish
future ~: 4 spud 5 tater 6 potato
partner: 6 burger 9 hamburger
topping: 6 catsup 7 ketchup
__ fries: 4 home 6 French, German 7 cottage, country
Friesland Museum site: 5 Emden
Frietchie: 7 Barbara
frigate: 4 boat, ship 7 carrier, cruiser, flattop, gunboat 8 corvette, man-of-war 9 destroyer 10 battleship
Frigga: 5 Norse 7 goddess
husband: 4 Odin 5 Othin
son of ~: 5 Baldr 6 Balder
fright: 4 fear, funk, mess, scar 5 alarm, dread, panic, scare, shock, sight 6 dismay, horror, terror 7 eyesore,

startle **9** terrorize, trepidity
exclamation: **4** yipe **5** yikes, yipes
sound of ~: **4** gasp
fright __: **3** wig
__ fright: **4** mike **5** stage
frighten: **3** awe, cow **4** faze **5** alarm, appal, chill, daunt, deter, haunt, panic, repel, scare, shake, shock, spook, unman **6** appall, dismay, menace, rattle **7** horrify, petrify, startle, terrify, unhinge, unnerve **8** disquiet, scare off, threaten, unstring **9** give a turn, give pause, terrorize **10** discomfort, disconcert, discourage, intimidate, scare stiff
frightened: **5** funky, jumpy, pavid, shaky, timid **6** afeard, afraid, aghast, gun-shy, scared, trepid, yellow **7** afeared, anxious, chicken, fearful, jittery, nervous, panicky, shivery, spooked, uptight, worried **8** cowardly, fearsome, hesitant, in a panic, recreant, timorous **9** petrified, spineless, terrified, tremulous **10** terrorized
frightening: **4** eery, grim **5** awful, dread, eerie, lurid, scary **6** creepy, horrid, spooky **7** dreaded, fearful, ghastly, hideous, macaber, macabre, ominous **8** alarming, chilling, daunting, dreadful, fearsome, gruesome, horrible, menacing, terrible **9** unearthly
exclamation: **3** boo
vision: **8** bad dream **9** nightmare
frightful: **4** dire, foul, gory, grim, poor, ugly **5** awful, dread, gross, hairy, lousy, lurid, scary, woful **6** crumby, crummy, dismal, grisly, horrid, morbid, odious, rotten, spooky, woeful **7** accurst, baleful, baneful, beastly, doleful, dreaded, fearful, ghastly, heinous, hideous, macaber, macabre, ominous, ungodly, vicious **8** accursed, alarming, chilling, daunting, dreadful, fearsome, God-awful, grievous, gruesome, horrible, inferior, menacing, shameful, stinking, terrible, terrific, wretched **9** abhorrent, appalling, atrocious, defective, execrable, ferocious, insidious, loathsome, miserable, monstrous, offensive, repellant, repellent, revolting, unsightly **10** abominable, despicable, detestable, disastrous, disgusting, formidable, horrendous, petrifying, unpleasant
combining form: **4** dino-
Fright Night (1985 film)
cast: Amanda Bearse, William Ragsdale, Chris Sarandon
frigid: **3** icy, raw **4** cold, cool **5** aloof, chill, gelid, nippy, polar, stiff **6** arctic, biting, bitter, chilly, frosty, frozen, wintry **7** chilled, distant, glacial, ice-cold, numbing, passive, shivery, wintery **8** freezing, hibernal, indurate, loveless, Siberian **9** below zero **10** insociable, unagitated
time: **6** ice age
Frigid: **4** Zone
ender: **4** aire
Frigidaire alternative: **5** Amana, Norge **6** Bendix, Maytag, Tappan **7** Admiral, Jenn-Air, Kenmore **8** Hotpoint **9** Magic Chef, Whirlpool **10** Kelvinator, KitchenAid
frigidity: **4** cold **5** chill **7** iciness **8** coldness, gelidity **10** frozenness
__ Frigoris: **4** Mare
frijol: **4** bean **6** legume
frijoles refritos, make: **5** refry
frill: **4** trim **5** dodad, extra **6** doodad, luxury, ruffle **7** amenity, flounce, garnish **8** froufrou, gimcrack, ornament, trimming **9** adornment, fandangle **10** decoration
not a ~: **9** necessity, requisite **10** obligation **11** requirement
frills, cut the: **8** simplify
frilly: **4** lacy **5** fancy, gaudy, showy **6** chichi, dressy, flashy, flossy, glitzy, lavish, ornate **7** adorned, opulent **9** decorated, elaborate, gussied up, luxurious, sumptuous **10** decorative, ornamental, ornamented
trim: **5** jabot, ruche
Friml: **6** Rudolf **8** composer
fringe: **3** hem **4** brim, edge, trim **5** brink, frame, limit, skirt, verge **6** border, edging, margin, ricrac, suburb **7** extreme, flounce **8** rickrack, surround, trimming **9** outskirts, perimeter, periphery **10** borderline
benefit: **4** boon, perc, perk, plus **5** bonus **6** reward
beyond the ~: **5** outré **7** bizarre, offbeat **8** freakish **10** outlandish
combining form: **6** thysan- **7** thysano-
on a golf course: **5** apron
fringe __: **4** area, tree **7** benefit
fringed item: **5** shawl **6** surrey
frippery: **6** finery, geegaw, gewgaw **7** clothes, jewelry **9** adornment **10** decoration, Sunday best
Frisbee: **3** fad, toy **4** disc, disk
company: **5** Wham-o
Frisch: **3** Max **4** Karl **5** Frank **6** Ragnar **7** Frankie
Frisch, Frankie: **8** Cardinal
Frisch, Max: **5** Swiss **6** writer
Frisch, Ragnar: **8** Nobelist **9** economist
Frisco: **4** city, town
see also San Francisco
Frisco Kid, The (1979 film)
cast: Harrison Ford, Gene Wilder
director: Robert Aldrich
frisé: **6** fabric **8** material
bichon ~: **3** dog, pet **6** canine
Frise __: **7** aileron
frisk: **3** hop **4** feel, jump, lark, leap, play, romp, skip **5** caper, check, dance, touch **6** bounce, cavort, frolic, gambol, prance, search **7** inspect, pat down, rollick **9** shake down
Friskies: **7** cat food
alternative: **5** Amore **6** Figaro, Purina **7** Whiskas **10** Chef's Blend, Fancy Feast
friskiness: **3** pep, zip **4** élan, zest, zing **5** spark, verve **6** bounce, fervor **7** abandon, devilry, hijinks, knavery **8** buoyancy, deviltry, mischief, vitality **9** high jinks, rascality **10** ebullience, enthusiasm, exuberance, liveliness, tomfoolery
frisky: **4** spry **5** peppy, zesty, zippy **6** active, bouncy, feisty, jaunty, lively **7** coltish, playful, romping, zestful **8** spirited, sporting, sportive **9** gamboling, kittenish **10** frolicsome, rollicking
__ frites: **6** pommes
Frito: **4** nosh **5** snack **8** corn chip
Frito-__: **3** Lay
frittata: **6** omelet **8** omelette
base: **3** egg
fritter: **4** cake, laze **5** spend **6** churro, lavish, loiter, pastry, putter, trifle **9** throw away, while away
away: **3** sap **4** idle, loaf **5** drain, trash, use up, waste **6** burn up, linger, loiter, lounge **7** consume, deplete, fribble, play out **8** squander **9** dissipate
__ fritter: **4** corn
fritto __: **5** misto
fritz
go on the ~: **5** act up
on the: **5** kaput **6** blooey, blooie, broken **7** damaged **9** defective, disrepair **10** broken-down, out of order
Fritz: **4** Lang **5** Busch, Haber, Loewe, Pregl **6** Leiber, Reiner, Weaver **7** Lipmann, Mondale **8** Kreisler
comics brother: **4** Hans
see also German
Fritzi to Nancy: **4** aunt
frivol: **5** waste **6** trifle **7** deplete **8** squander **9** bagatelle, dissipate **10** triviality
frivolity: **4** glee, jest **5** folly, mirth **6** gaiety, gayety, levity, whimsy **7** abandon, fribble, gayness, whimsey **8** dallying, nonsense, trifling, zaniness **9** diversion, flippancy, giddiness, lightness, puerility, silliness **10** triviality, volatility
frivolous: **4** flip, idle, vain **5** empty, giddy, inane, light, petty, silly **6** fickle, giggly, madcap, yeasty **7** flighty, foolish, puerile, shallow, trivial **8** childish, ill-spent, juvenile, skittish, trifling **9** arbitrary, facetious, pointless, senseless, whimsical **10** coquettish, nonserious, unprofound
be ~ with: **3** rib **4** jest, josh **5** tease
in a ~ way: **4** idly
novel: **5** fluff
frizz: **4** curl, kink **5** crimp **8** make wavy
Frizzell: **5** David, Lefty
frizzle: **4** curl, sear **6** scorch, sizzle
frizzy: **5** curly, fuzzy, kinky **6** permed
top: **4** Afro
fro: **4** away, back **6** hairdo **8** backward
move to and ~: **3** wag **4** sway, wave **5** waver
__ fro: **5** to and
Frobe: **4** Gert
Frobisher: **3** bay **6** Martin
Frobisher, Martin: **7** British **8** explorer
frock: **4** coat, gown **5** dress, smock **6** jacket, kirtle, ordain **7** clothes, garment, instate **10** Sunday best
wearer: **4** monk **5** friar, padre **6** priest **7** brother
frock __: **4** coat
Fröding, Gustaf: **4** poet **7** Swedish
Frodo: **6** hobbit **7** Baggins
uncle: **5** Bilbo
froe: **4** tool **7** cleaver
frog: **5** ranid **6** anuran, hopper, Kermit, peeper **7** crapaud, croaker, tadpole **8** polliwog, pollywog **9** amphibian
combining form: **4** rani- **7** batrach- **8** batracho-
cousin: **4** newt, toad
dish: **4** legs
ender: **3** eye, man, men **4** fish **5** mouth **6** hopper
feature: **4** wart
genus: **4** rana
in one's throat: **4** rasp **7** scratch
like a ~: **5** warty **6** croaky
pad: **4** lily
snack: **3** fly
sound: **5** croak **6** ribbit
starter: **4** bull, leap
tree ~: **4** hyla
young: **7** tadpole **8** polliwog, pollywog
frog __: **4** kick, lily, spit **7** sticker
__ frog: **4** bell, rain, tree, true, wood **6** chorus, flying, horned, robber, tailed **7** barking, cricket, leopard
Frog and the Ox, The source: **4** Esop **5** Aesop
froggy: **5** husky, raspy **6** croaky, hoarse **7** grating, throaty **8** croaking, gravelly, guttural
froghopper: **3** bug **6** insect
frogman: **5** diver
gear: **4** mask, tank **5** scuba, spear **6** oxygen **7** goggles, wet suit
Frogmen, The (1951 film)
cast: Dana Andrews, Gary Merrill, Richard Widmark
director: Lloyd Bacon
frogmouth: **4** bird
Frogner Park city: **4** Oslo
Frogs and __...: **6** snails
frogskin: **4** bill, buck **6** dollar **7** smacker **8** banknote, simoleon **9** greenback
frogskins: **3** oof **4** cash, gelt, jack, kail, kale, loot, peag, pelf **5** bread, dough, funds, lucre, moola, mopus, pesos, rhino, sewan **6** dinero, do-re-mi, mammon, mazuma, moolah, seawan, silver, specie, wampum, wealth **7** cabbage, capital, lettuce, ooftish, scratch, shekels **8** bankroll, cold cash, currency, hard cash **9** long green **10** green stuff
Frogs, The author: Aristophanes
__-froid: **4** sang **5** chaud
Froissart, Jean: **4** poet **6** author, French **9** historian
frolic: **3** fun, joy **4** lark, play, romp, trip **5** antic, caper, dance, frisk, jaunt, mirth, prank, revel, sport, spree **6** cavort, gaiety, gambol, gayety, junket, prance **7** carouse, have fun, hijinks, rollick **8** escapade **9** amusement, have a ball, high jinks, joviality, make merry, merriment, whoop it up **10** fool around, recreation, shenanigan, skylarking
ender: **4** some
frolicking: **6** at play
frolicsome: **3** fun, gay **4** spry **5** antic, jolly, merry **6** frisky, impish, jaunty, jovial, lively **7** coltish, gleeful, jesting, jocular, playful, roguish **8** sporting, sportive **9** exuberant, gamboling, hilarious, kittenish, sprightly, vivacious **10** rollicking
from: **4** as of **5** off of **6** born in **8** starting
in German: **3** von
starter: **5** there, where
from __: **4** A to Z **7** scratch
from __ one: **4** year
from __ to nuts: **4** soup
from __ to post: **6** pillar
from __ to riches: **4** rags
from __ to stern: **4** stem
from __ worse: **5** bad to
from __ Z: **3** A to
__ from: **4** hail **5** apart, aside
...from __ shining...: **5** sea to
From __ day forward: **4** this
From __ Moment On: **4** This
From __ shining...: **5** sea to
From __ to Eternity: **4** Here
From __ With Love: **6** Russia
From __ You: **4** Me to
from A __: **3** to Z
From a Distance (1990 song) artist: Bette Midler
__ from afar: **4** come **7** worship
__ from Alabama...: **5** I come
__ From Aloes, A: **6** Lesson
__ From a Mall: **6** Scenes
__ From a Marriage: **6** Scenes
Froman: **4** Jane
from bad to __: **5** worse
From Bauhaus to Our House author: Tom Wolfe
From Bed to Worse author: Robert Benchley
__ From Brazil, The: **4** Boys
__ From Brooklyn, The: **3** Kid
__ from Chelsea: **5** Elsie
From Death to Morning author: Thomas Wolfe
Frome: **5** Ethan
From Far, From Eve and Morning author: A.E. Housman
__ from grace: **4** fall
from head __: **5** to toe
__ From Heaven: **3** Far **5** A Gift **7** Pennies

From Hell (2001 film)
cast: Johnny Depp, Heather Graham, Ian Holm
from here ___: 4 on in 5 on out
From Here to Eternity: 4 film 5 novel
author: James Jones
cast: Montgomery Clift, Deborah Kerr, Burt Lancaster, Donna Reed, Frank Sinatra
director: Fred Zinnemann
___ From Ipanema, The: 4 Girl
___ From Laramie, The: 3 Man
Frommer: 6 Arthur
Fromm, Erich: 6 author, writer
work: The Art of Loving
Man For Himself
___ From Muskogee: 4 Okie
___, from New York...: 4 Live
from one's ___: 5 heart
...___ from our sponsor: 5 a word
from pillar to ___: 4 post
from rags to ___: 6 riches
From Russia With Love: 4 film 5 novel
author: Ian Fleming
cast: Pedro Armendariz, Daniela Bianchi, Sean Connery, Bernard Lee, Lotte Lenya, Lois Maxwell, Robert Shaw
director: Terence Young
___ From Snowy River, The: 3 Man
from soup to nuts: 5 gamut
from stem to ___: 5 stern
___ From Syracuse, The: 4 Boys
from the ___: 5 get-go, heart
from the ___ up: 6 ground
From the ___ of Montezuma: 5 halls
from the beginning in Latin: 5 ab ovo 8 ab initio 9 ab origine
___ from the blue: 4 bolt
___ from the Bridge: 5 A View
From the Corner of His Eye author: Dean Koontz
___ From the Crypt: 5 Tales
From the Earth to the Moon author: Jules Verne
___ from the hip: 5 shoot
___ from the horse's mouth: 5 right
___ From the Madding Crowd: 3 Far
from the outside in Latin: 7 ab extra
___ from the past: 5 blast
___ From the Portuguese: 7 Sonnets
___ from the rooftops: 5 shout
From the Terrace: 4 film 5 novel
author: John O'Hara
cast: Myrna Loy, Paul Newman, Joanne Woodward
director: Mark Robson
___ From the Underground: 5 Notes
___ From the Vienna Woods: 5 Tales
From this ___ forward: 3 day
From This Moment On (1998 song)
artist: Shania Twain
From This Moment on composer: 6 Porter
___ From U.N.C.L.E., The: 3 Man
___ from under: 3 out
From where ___...: 4 I sit
from which in Latin: 4 a quo
from within in Latin: 7 ab intra
from year ___: 3 one
frond: 4 leaf 5 blade, bract 7 foliage
holder: 4 fern, palm, stem
frondeur: 5 rebel 8 agitator, renegade, resister 9 insurgent 10 subversive
front: 3 act, bow, van 4 face, fore, head, lead, look, mask, meet, mien, pose, show, side 5 blind, cover, first, guise, put-on 6 border, facade, face on, facing, give on, veneer 7 air mass, bearing, cover-up, display, forward, leading, obverse, outside, pretext 8 advanced, anterior, demeanor, disguise, exterior, forehead, foremost, forepart, headmost, overlook, presence, vanguard 9 beginning, coalition, semblance 10 appearance, figurehead, foreground, masquerade, pretension
be in ~: 4 lead
boat ~: 3 bow 4 prow
combining form: 4 fore- 6 antero-
ender: 3 age, ier 4 ward 5 wards
false ~: 3 act 4 airs, mask, pose, sham, show 5 bluff, guise 6 facade 8 disguise
for: 7 endorse, promote 8 nominate 9 recommend 10 put forward
in ~: 4 best, tops 5 afore, ahead, first 6 onward 7 forward, leading, onwards, optimal, supreme 8 peerless 9 at the fore, nonpareil, paramount, unequaled, unrivaled 10 preeminent, unrivalled
in ~ of: 6 before 7 prior to 9 preceding
in ~ of (prefix): 3 pre-, pro- 4 ante-, fore-
man: 5 scout 7 bird-dog 8 outrider
money: 7 advance
neither ~ nor back: 4 side
office: 9 directors 10 executives, management
on: 4 face, look 8 overlook
out-~: 5 frank, on top, plain 6 candid, direct, honest, square 7 sincere, winning 8 boastful, exultant, straight, truthful, unbeaten 9 guileless, honorable, in the lead, veracious 10 forthright, on the level
put on a false ~: 3 lie 7 cover up, deceive, mislead 9 misdirect 10 steer wrong
put up a ~: 3 lie 4 pose, sham 7 pretend 9 misinform
starter: 3 bow 4 lake 5 beach, break, ocean, river, shore, store, water 6 battle
front ___: 4 desk, dive, door, foot, four, line, nine, page, room 5 bench, court, money 6 burner, loader, matter, office, runner, window
front-___: 3 end 4 line, load, rank 5 drive
front-___ drive: 5 wheel
___ front: 3 bow, fly, ice, out, sea 4 cold, drop, fall, home, warm, wave, yoke 5 block, false, oxbow, polar, shirt, shock, slant, swell 6 united 7 people's, popular
___-front: 3 out
Front ___ Farrell: 4 Page
frontal: 6 head-on 10 face-to-face
frontal ___: 4 bone, lobe 5 gyrus 7 cyclone
___-frontal: 4 full
front and ___: 6 center
front-end job: 9 alignment, alinement
Frontera: 4 city, town
locale: 6 Mexico 7 Tabasco 8 Coahuila
frontier: 4 edge 5 brink, limit 6 border, remote, sticks 7 boonies, outback 8 boundary 9 backwoods, boondocks 10 hinterland
adventurer: 5 scout
dwelling: 5 cabin
establishment: 3 bar, inn 6 saloon 7 barroom 10 blacksmith, restaurant
outpost: 4 fort
transportation: 5 buggy, horse, stage 8 carriage 10 stagecoach
Frontier: 3 car 4 auto 6 Nissan
___ Frontier: 3 New 5 On the
Frontier Marshal (1939 film)
cast: Nancy Kelly, Cesar Romero, Randolph Scott
director: Allan Dwan
frontiersman: 5 Boone 7 pioneer, settler 8 colonist, Crockett, emigrant 9 immigrant 10 inhabitant
fronting: 6 toward 7 towards 8 opposite
fronton: 5 court
basket: 5 cesta
sport: 7 jai alai
front page
box: 3 ear
item: 4 news 5 event, title
word: 5 extra
front-page: 3 big 6 of note 7 notable 9 important, momentous 10 meaningful, noteworthy
Front Page Farrell: 9 radio show
Front Page, The: 4 play
author: Ben Hecht
character: 5 Hildy 6 Mollie
Front Page, The (1931 film)
cast: Mary Brian, Adolphe Menjou, Pat O'Brien
director: Lewis Milestone
Front Page, The (1974 film)
cast: Carol Burnett, Jack Lemmon, Walter Matthau
director: Billy Wilder
front-runner: 4 star 6 choice, leader 7 darling 8 favorite 9 number one
Front, The (1976 film)
cast: Woody Allen, Herschel Bernardi, Zero Mostel
director: Martin Ritt
front-wheel ___: 5 drive
Froot Loops: 6 cereal
competitor: 3 Kix 4 Life, Trix 5 Kashi, Quisp, Total 6 Kaboom, Muesli, Oreo O's, Pablum, Smacks 7 All-Bran, Crispix, Harmony, Hunny B's, Mueslix, Oat Bran, Pokemon 8 Boo Berry, Cheerios, Corn Chex, Corn Pops, Fiber One, Rice Chex, Special K, Uncle Sam, Wheaties 9 Alpha Bits, Apple Zaps, Grape Nuts, Honey Comb, Just Right, Wheat Chex 10 Apple Jacks, Bran Flakes, Cap'n Crunch, Cocoa Puffs, Mini-Wheats, Nutri-Grain, Puffed Rice, Quaker Oats, Smart Start 11 Cocoa Blasts, Cookie Crisp, Golden Crisp, Lucky Charms, Puffed Wheat, Sweet Crunch, Waffle Crisp
frosh: 4 pleb 5 plebe 7 student
see also college, freshman
frost: 3 nip 4 cold, cool, hoar, rime 6 freeze, whiten 8 coldness 9 crispness
again: 5 reice
combining form: 4 crym- 5 crymo-
covered: 3 icy 4 rimy 5 hoary
ender: 3 bit 4 bite, fish, line, work 6 bitten
kin: 3 dew
melt the ~: 5 deice
over: 5 ice up
remover: 6 deicer
starter: 4 hoar 5 perma
victim: 3 bud
frost ___: 5 grape, heave, point, smoke 6 flower
frost-___ refrigerator: 4 free
___ frost: 5 black, white 6 silver 7 killing
...frost ___ the punkin: 4 is on
Frost: 4 Jack 5 David, Sadie 6 Robert
Frost ___: 4 Belt
Frost at Midnight author: Coleridge
frostbitten: 4 numb
Frost, David: 3 Sir
frosted: 3 icy 5 glacè, white 6 pearly
Frosted ___-Wheats: 4 Mini
Frosted Flakes: 6 cereal
competitor: 3 Kix 4 Life, Trix 5 Kashi, Quisp, Total 6 Kaboom, Muesli, Oreo O's, Pablum, Smacks 7 All-Bran, Crispix, Harmony, Hunny B's, Mueslix, Oat Bran, Pokemon 8 Boo Berry, Cheerios, Corn Chex, Corn Pops, Fiber One, Rice Chex, Special K, Uncle Sam, Wheaties 9 Alpha Bits, Apple Zaps, Grape Nuts, Honey Comb, Just Right, Wheat Chex 10 Apple Jacks, Bran Flakes, Cap'n Crunch, Cocoa Puffs, Froot Loops, Mini-Wheats, Nutri-Grain, Puffed Rice, Quaker Oats, Smart Start 11 Cocoa Blasts, Cookie Crisp, Golden Crisp, Lucky Charms, Puffed Wheat, Sweet Crunch, Waffle Crisp
Frosted Mini-Wheats: 6 cereal
competitor: 3 Kix 4 Life, Trix 5 Kashi, Quisp, Total 6 Kaboom, Muesli, Oreo O's, Pablum, Smacks 7 All-Bran, Crispix, Harmony, Hunny B's, Mueslix, Oat Bran, Pokemon 8 Boo Berry, Cheerios, Corn Chex, Corn Pops, Fiber One, Rice Chex, Special K, Uncle Sam, Wheaties 9 Alpha Bits, Apple Zaps, Grape Nuts, Honey Comb, Just Right, Wheat Chex 10 Apple Jacks, Bran Flakes, Cap'n Crunch, Cocoa Puffs, Froot Loops, Mini-Wheats, Nutri-Grain, Puffed Rice, Quaker Oats, Smart Start 11 Cocoa Blasts, Cookie Crisp, Golden Crisp, Lucky Charms, Puffed Wheat, Sweet Crunch, Waffle Crisp
frosting: 5 glaze, icing 7 topping 8 covering
apply ~: 3 ice
Frost, Robert: 4 poet
contemporary: 5 Auden
work: The Axe-Helve
Birches
Canis Major
The Death of the Hired Man
Fire and Ice
The Gift Outright
The Hill Wife
Hyla Brook
In a Poem
In a Vale
Into My Own
A Late Walk
Mending Wall
The Most of It
Mowing
Not to Keep
Once by the Pacific
The Oven Bird
Pan With Us
A Peck of Gold
The Road Not Taken
Stopping by Woods on a Snowy Evening
Storm Fear
To E.T.
Tree at My Window
The Tuft of Flowers
The Witch of Coos
frosty: 3 icy, raw 4 cold, cool, iced 5 chill, gelid, nippy, polar 6 arctic, biting, bitter, chilly, frigid, frozen, wintry 7 chilled, glacial, ice-cold, numbing, shivery, wintery 8 freezing, Siberian
Frosty accessory: 4 pipe
froth: 4 barm, fizz, foam, head, scum, suds, surf 5 spray, spume 6 aerate, bubble, burble, gurgle, lather, seethe, simmer 7 bubbles, ferment, slobber 10 effervesce
up: 4 boil, fizz, foam 6 bubble, gurgle, simmer 7 blister 9 percolate 10 effervesce
frothy: 5 barmy, foamy, light, soapy, sudsy 6 beaten, bubbly, yeasty 7 foaming, lathery 8 untaxing 10 fermenting

froufrou: 5 frill 6 gewgaw 7 trinket 8 ornament 9 adornment 10 decoration
Froward: 4 cape
locale: 5 Chile
frown: 4 lour, pout, sulk 5 glare, lower, scowl 6 glower 7 grimace
upon: 4 mind, veto 5 shame 6 object, oppose, refuse 7 censure, run down, scoff at 8 belittle, reproach, turn down 9 criticize, discredit, disparage
frowned on: 4 tabu 5 taboo 10 not allowed
frowning: 5 angry, stern, surly 6 morose, sullen 8 lowering, scowling 9 glowering
frowzy: 4 rank 5 dirty, dowdy, fetid, fusty, moldy, musty, stale 6 foetid, frumpy, rancid, shabby, sloppy, smelly, stinky, unneat, untidy 7 noisome, unkempt 8 slovenly 10 bedraggled, disheveled, malodorous
frozen: 3 icy, raw 4 cold, iced, numb 5 at bay, chill, fixed, gelid, glacé, nippy, polar, stiff 6 arctic, biting, bitter, chilly, frappé, frigid, frosty, rooted, wintry 7 chilled, glacial, ice-cold, numbing, shivery, stopped, wintery 8 freezing, immobile, Siberian 9 immovable, petrified, suspended, unpliable 10 motionless, stock-still
dessert: 3 ice 5 bombe 6 frappé, gelati, gelato 7 sherbet 8 ice cream
fall: 4 snow 5 sleet
not ~: 5 fresh
rain: 4 hail 5 sleet
region: 6 icecap
water: 3 ice 6 icicle
frozen __: 3 fog 4 food 6 assets, yogurt 7 custard, pudding
__-frozen: 4 deep
Frozen (1998 song) artist: Madonna
frozen-faced: 5 rocky, stony 6 flinty, stoney 7 deadpan 8 hardened, ruthless 9 heartless, merciless 10 inflexible
fructify: 4 bear 5 bloom, fruit 7 blossom 9 fertilize
fructose: 5 sugar
glucose, to ~: 6 isomer
frug: 5 dance
frugal: 5 chary, light, spare 6 Lenten, skimpy 7 careful, prudent, sparing, thrifty 8 ungiving 9 penny-wise, provident 10 abstemious, economical, unwasteful
be ~: 4 save 5 reuse, skimp, stint 6 scrape 9 economize
one: 5 saver
too ~: 4 mean, near 5 cheap, tight 6 greedy, stingy 7 miserly 9 penurious
Frugal Gourmet, The: Jeff Smith
frugality: 6 thrift 7 economy 9 parsimony, scrimping 10 abstinence, moderation, providence, stinginess
fruit: 3 fig, nut, pay 4 akee, bael, crop, date, kaki, kiwi, lime, pear, plum, pome, sloe, sorb, ugli 5 acorn, apple, berry, cacao, cubeb, drupe, grape, guava, lemon, mamey, mango, maqui, melon, nopal, olive, papaw, peach, prune, salal 6 annona, banana, casaba, cherry, citron, citrus, dahoon, durian, jujube, loquat, maypop, orange, papaya, pawpaw, pomelo, profit, quince, raisin, result, return, reward, sapota, tangor, tomato 7 acerola, apricot, atemoya, avocado, benefit, bilimbi, cassaba, chayote, coconut, cumquat, currant, genipap, harvest, kumquat, marasca, outcome, produce, product, pumpkin, results, saguaro, satsuma, tangelo 8 barberry, bayberry, bergamot, bilberry, canistel, cowberry, dewberry, dogberry, doom palm, doum palm, eggfruit, fructify, hawthorn, mandarin, may apple, mirliton, mulberry, pitahaya, plantain, rambutan, sea grape, shaddock, sweetsop, tamarind, teaberry 9 bearberry, blueberry, carambola, cherimoya, cranberry, freestone, hackberry, jackfruit, love apple, manzanita, muscadine, muskmelon, nectarine, persimmon, pineapple, raspberry, sapodilla, tangerine, tomatillo 10 blackberry, breadfruit, calamondin, clingstone, cloudberry, elderberry, gooseberry, granadilla, grapefruit, loganberry, mangosteen, strawberry, watermelon
acid: 6 citric
Asia: 6 durian, loquat 7 bilimbi 8 rambutan, tamarind 9 carambola
autumn ~: 4 pear
bananalike ~: 8 plantain
banned ~ spray: 4 Alar
banyan ~: 3 fig
basket for dried ~: 5 frail
bear ~: 5 bloom, ripen 6 thrive, unfold 7 blossom, prosper 8 fructify
berrylike ~: 5 cubeb
black ~: 5 olive
blue ~: 7 genipap
bog ~: 9 cranberry
bramble ~: 10 blackberry
breakfast ~: 5 melon 6 banana
brown ~: 3 fig
cactus ~: 5 nopal 7 saguaro 8 pitahaya
candlemaking ~: 8 bayberry
carambola ~: 9 star fruit
Caribbean ~: 8 eggfruit
cashew family ~: 5 mango
center: 4 core
Central America: 8 eggfruit 9 sapodilla
chayote ~: 8 mirliton
cherrylike ~: 7 acerola 9 hackberry
chicle-yielding ~: 9 sapodilla
Chile: 5 maqui
China: 6 loquat
chocolate ~: 5 cacao
citrus: 4 lime 5 lemon 6 citron, orange 7 kumquat 8 shaddock 9 tangerine 10 grapefruit
combining form: 4 -carp 5 carpo-, fruct- 6 fructi-
compote ~: 4 pear
concoction: 5 salad
cookie ~: 3 fig
covering: 4 peel, rind, skin
cucumber-shaped ~: 7 bilimbi
cupped ~: 5 acorn
desert ~: 4 date
dish: 3 pie
downy ~: 5 peach
dreamy ~ of Greek myth: 5 lotus
dried ~: 5 prune 6 raisin
drink: 3 ade 5 cider, juice, punch 6 frappé 7 limeade 8 lemonade
dry ~: 3 nut 5 regma
East Indian ~: 5 cubeb 10 mangosteen
egg-shaped ~: 5 mango 8 may apple 10 granadilla
egg-sized ~: 4 kiwi
elm family ~: 9 hackberry
ender: 3 age 4 cake, wood
fancier: 3 Eve 4 Adam
flaw: 6 bruise
fleshy ~: 4 pepo, pome 5 papaw
fuzzy ~: 4 kiwi 5 peach
Georgia ~: 5 peach
gingerbread-flavored ~: 8 doom palm, doum palm
grapefruitlike ~: 8 shaddock
green ~: 5 grape, olive 9 cherimoya 10 gooseberry
hair: 6 villus
hairs: 5 villi
hard ~: 6 quince
holder: 4 stem
India: 4 bael 5 cubeb 10 mangosteen
innards: 4 pulp
Italy: 8 bergamot
Jamaica: 4 akee
Japanese persimmon ~: 4 kaki
juicy ~: 5 berry, mango, melon 6 orange 8 tamarind 10 mangosteen
leathery ~: 5 cacao
lemonlike ~: 6 cedrat, citron
like fake ~: 3 wax 5 waxed
like some ~: 5 acerb, pulpy, tangy
melonlike ~: 5 papaw
Mexico: 7 chayote 8 eggfruit 9 sapodilla, tomatillo
musky ~: 9 muscadine
oblong ~: 5 mango
orchard ~: 4 pear 5 apple
oval ~: 8 rambutan
Pacific Coast: 5 salal 9 manzanita
Pacific islands ~: 10 breadfruit
palm ~: 4 date
pear-shaped ~: 3 fig 4 bael 7 chayote
prepare ~: 4 core, pare, peel 6 deseed
prickly ~: 6 durian 8 hawthorn 10 gooseberry
problem: 3 rot
producer: 4 tree
product: 3 jam 5 cider, jelly, juice
pulpy ~: 5 drupe
purple ~: 4 sloe 8 mulberry 10 elderberry
red ~: 7 saguaro 8 hawthorn, rambutan 9 cranberry 10 loganberry
ribbed ~: 5 cacao
ripener: 6 ethene
rose ~: 3 hip
rot: 4 blet
rowan ~: 4 sorb
sandy beach ~: 8 sea grape
service tree ~: 4 sorb
shrub ~: 5 berry 6 annona 8 barberry 9 bearberry, blueberry
single-seeded ~: 5 akene, drupe 6 achene
slot-machine ~: 5 lemon 6 cherry
sour ~: 4 lime, sloe 5 lemon 7 bilimbi
Spain: 4 pina
starter: 3 egg 4 jack 5 bread, grape
stewed ~: 5 grunt, sauce
sticky ~: 3 fig 4 date
summer ~: 4 plum 5 melon
tart ~: 4 sloe 5 berry 9 cranberry
thick pod ~: 8 tamarind
thick rind ~: 6 citron
tree: 3 fig 4 palm, pear, sorb 5 apple, papaw 6 annona, orange
tropical ~: 3 fig 4 akee, date, ugli 5 guava, mango, melon 6 banana, papaya 7 genipap 8 sea grape, sweetsop 9 cherimoya
vine ~: 5 melon 7 chayote
waxy ~: 8 bayberry
West Indies: 5 mamey 6 annona 7 acerola
white ~: 8 bayberry 9 cherimoya
wild ~: 10 blackberry
wild grape ~: 9 muscadine
wintergreen ~: 8 teaberry
wrinkly ~: 4 ugli
yellow ~: 4 bael 5 guava 6 dahoon, loquat, papaya, quince 8 may apple, sweetsop 9 carambola, jackfruit 10 cloudberry
fruit __: 3 bat, cup, fly, jar 4 tree 5 knife, ranch, sugar
__ fruit: 3 hen, key 4 bear, star, true 5 false, spore, stone 6 fleshy, simple 7 miracle
__ Fruit: 5 Juicy 7 Strange
fruit cup: 7 dessert 9 appetizer
morsel: 4 pear 6 cherry, orange
fruited combining form: 7 -carpous
__ fruitfly: 7 Mexican
fruitful: 4 rich 6 fecund, useful 7 copious, fertile, profuse, teeming 8 abundant, blooming, prolific 9 exuberant, inventive, lucrative, luxuriant, plenteous, plentiful, rewarding, well-spent 10 beneficial, blossoming, productive, profitable, successful, worthwhile
fruitfulness: 6 bounty, plenty, wealth 8 opulence 9 abundance, affluence, fecundity, profusion 10 luxuriance
fruition: 6 result 7 harvest, success 8 maturity, ripeness 10 attainment, completion, perfection
at ~: 4 ripe
bring to ~: 5 ripen 7 realize 8 complete
fruit juice: 8 beverage
fruit-juice name: 5 Mott's
fruitless: 4 idle, vain 5 empty, no-win 6 barren, futile, hollow, in vain 7 inutile, sterile, useless 8 gainless 9 for naught, infertile, pointless, thankless, to no avail 10 profitless, to no effect, unavailing, unprolific
fruitlessly: 6 in vain
Fruit of the Loom
product: 4 sock 5 brief, short 6 T-shirt
rival: 5 Hanes
fruits: 4 crop 7 harvest, produce
science of ~: 8 pomology
__ fruits: 5 first
fruit salad: 6 medals
Fruits of the Earth, The author: André Gide
Fruity Pebbles: 6 cereal
competitor: 3 Kix 4 Life, Trix 5 Kashi, Quisp, Total 6 Kaboom, Muesli, Oreo O's, Pablum, Smacks 7 All-Bran, Crispix, Harmony, Hunny B's, Mueslix, Oat Bran, Pokemon 8 Boo Berry, Cheerios, Corn Chex, Corn Pops, Fiber One, Rice Chex, Special K, Uncle Sam, Wheaties 9 Alpha Bits, Apple Zaps, Grape Nuts, Honey Comb, Just Right, Wheat Chex 10 Apple Jacks, Bran Flakes, Cap'n Crunch, Cocoa Puffs, Froot Loops, Mini-Wheats, Nutri-Grain, Puffed Rice, Quaker Oats, Smart Start 11 Cocoa Blasts, Cookie Crisp, Golden Crisp, Lucky Charms, Puffed Wheat, Sweet Crunch, Waffle Crisp
frumpy: 4 drab 5 dowdy, tacky 6 blowsy, frowsy, frowzy, shabby, unneat 7 unkempt 8 slovenly 9 unstylish 10 bedraggled
frustrate: 3 nip 4 balk, dash, defy, foil, mock, stop 5 avert, baulk, block, cheat, cross, elude, stimy, stump, stymy 6 arrest, blight, defeat, hamper, hang up, hinder, hogtie, impede, negate, outwit, resist, scotch, stymie, thwart 7 counter, fluster, inhibit, nonplus, nullify, prevent, redress, ward off 8 handcuff, obstruct, outflank, preclude, sabotage 9 discomfit, displease, forestall, hamstring, interfere, tantalize, undermine 10 circumvent, counteract, disappoint, disconcert, discourage, dishearten, neutralize
frustrated: 9 inhibited, resentful, up the wall 10 embittered
sound: 4 sigh 6 sheesh
frustration: 6 defeat 7 chagrin, failure, setback 8 headache

frustule: 5 shell 8 seashell
Frutiger: 4 font 8 typeface
___-frutti: 5 tutti
fry: 4 cook, heat, sear 5 brown, sauté, singe 6 rebuke, sizzle 7 cookout, frizzle 8 pan-broil 9 fricassee
  ender: 3 pan
  fish ~: 4 meal 6 picnic
  small ~: 3 boy, tad, tot 4 fish 5 child, kiddy, youth
fry ___: 4 cook
___ fry: 4 fish 5 small 6 French
___-fry: 3 pan 4 deep, stir 6 batter 7 chicken
Fry: 7 Francis, Stephen
Fry, Christopher: 7 British 10 playwright
  work: The Lady's Not for Burning
Frye, David: 4 aper
Frye, Deacon show: 4 Amen
___ fryer: 4 deep
fryer, Cantonese: 3 wok
frying
  medium: 3 oil 4 lard 6 Crisco
  pan: 3 wok 6 vessel 7 skillet
frying ___: 3 pan
frypan: 3 wok 6 spider 7 skillet 8 cookware, gridiron
F. Scott: 10 Fitzgerald
Fs, get: 4 fail
F-sharp alias: 5 G flat
FSU conference: 3 ACC
ft.: 4 lgth., meas.
  3280.8 ~: 2 km. 3 kil.
  6 ~ at sea: 3 fth.
Ft. ___, FL: 5 Myers
Ft. ___, IN: 5 Wayne
FTC part: 3 Fed. 4 Comm. 5 Trade 7 Federal 10 Commission
FTO: 3 car 4 auto 10 Mitsubishi
F Troop (ABC sitcom)
  cast: Ken Berry (Capt. Wilton Parmenter)
    Melody Patterson (Wrangler Jane)
    Larry Storch (Cpl. Randolph Agarn)
    Forrest Tucker (Sgt. Morgan O'Rourke)
  Indians: Hekawi
  location: Fort Courage
  structure: 4 fort, tipi 5 tepee 6 teepee
ft./sec. measure: 3 vel. 8 velocity
Ft. Worth campus: 3 TCU
___ fu: 4 kung
Fu ___: 6 Manchu
Fuad successor: 5 Faruk 6 Farouk
fubsy: 5 beefy, obese, plump, pudgy, pursy, stout 6 chubby, fleshy, portly, pyknic, rotund, stocky, zaftig, zoftig 7 adipose, paunchy 8 roly-poly 9 corpulent 10 overweight
fuchsia: 3 red 4 pink 5 color, plant, shrub 6 flower, purply 8 purplish
  relative: 4 rose, ruby, rust, wine 5 brick, coral, grape, poppy, rusty, sandy 6 cerise, cherry, claret, garnet, maroon 7 carmine, crimson, magenta, pimento, scarlet, sultana, vermeil 8 amaranth, cardinal, dubonnet, geranium, rubicund 9 carnation, cranberry, vermilion 10 strawberry
Fuchu: 4 city, town
  locale: 5 Japan
fucoid: 7 seaweed
Fudd: 5 Elmer
fuddle: 6 muddle, puzzle 7 confuse, nonplus, perplex 8 bewilder 9 inebriate
fuddle-___: 6 duddle
fuddled: 5 at sea, dazed, dizzy, tipsy 6 addled 7 rattled 8 confused 10 bewildered, confounded, taken aback
fuddy-duddy: 4 dodo, fogy, poop, prig, prim 5 fogey 6 fossil, geezer, square 9 formalist 10 fussbudget
fudge: 3 gas, lie, pad, rot 4 blah, bosh, bull, bunk, drat, fake, guff, jazz, jive, pooh, tosh 5 bilge, candy, cheat, color, dodge, evade, hedge, hokum, hooey, prate, slant, snack, stuff, trash, tripe 6 bunkum, bushwa, doctor, drivel, footle, gabble, gammon, gibber, havers, hot air, humbug, jabber, jargon, kibosh, piffle 7 baloney, blarney, blather, blether, boloney, bushwah, dessert, distort, eyewash, falsify, flannel, flubdub, fustian, garbage, hogwash, inanity, pretend, quibble, rubbish, twaddle 8 buncombe, claptrap, falderal, falderol, flimflam, flummery, folderal, folderol, nonsense, slipslop, tommyrot, trumpery 9 banana oil, chocolate, embellish, embroider, fabricate, gibberish, kidstakes, moonshine, overstate, poppycock, rigmarole, sweetmeat 10 applesauce, balderdash, bilge water, codswallop, confection, double-talk, exaggerate, flapdoodle, galimatias, Jabberwock, mumbo jumbo, rigamarole, taradiddle, understate
  flavor: 5 maple, mocha
  like ~: 5 gooey
  Oh ~ !: 3 bah, rot 4 pooh, tosh 5 pshaw 6 phooey
fudge ___: 6 factor, ripple, sundae
___ fudge: 7 vanilla
Fudge-a-mania author: Judy Blume
fudge ripple: 8 ice cream
  alternative: 5 lemon, mocha, peach 6 banana, coffee, Jamoca, toffee 7 caramel, coconut, vanilla 8 cinnamon, hazelnut 9 bubblegum, chocolate, pineapple, pistachio, raspberry, rocky road, rum raisin 10 blackberry, cheesecake, Neapolitan, peppermint, strawberry
Fuego: 7 volcano
  locale: 9 Guatemala
fuel: 3 gas, LNG, oil 4 coal, coke, feed, food, logs, peat, wood 5 gas up, juice, LP gas, stoke 6 energy, ethane, fill up, hexane, incite, kindle, petrol, tank up 7 coal gas, gasohol, impetus, nourish, propane, stoke up 8 dimethyl, energize, firewood, gasoline, kerosene, kindling, matériel, stimulus 10 ammunition, natural gas, propellant, sustenance
  additive: 6 deicer
  add ~ to the fire: 4 spur, stir 5 rouse, stoke 6 whip up, work up 7 agitate 9 stimulate
  alternative ~: 4 wind 6 ethane 7 gasohol 8 dimethyl, sunlight
  auto ~ mixer: 4 carb 10 carburetor
  bottled ~: 5 LP gas
  camper's ~: 3 LPG
  car ~: 3 gas 8 gasoline
  carrier: 4 tank 5 oiler 6 coaler
  cartel: 4 OPEC
  efficiency abbr.: 3 EPA, mpg
  fireplace ~: 4 logs, wood
  fossil ~: 3 gas, oil 4 coal
  funny-car ~: 5 nitro
  furnace ~: 4 coal, coke
  gas: 6 butane, ethane 8 dimethyl
  heating ~: 3 gas, oil 4 coal
  indicator: 5 gauge 8 gas gauge
  industrial ~: 4 coal, coke
  lamp ~: 3 oil 8 kerosene
  lighter ~: 6 butane
  measure: 6 gallon, octane
  organic ~: 6 biogas
  plane ~: 5 avgas
  rocket ~: 3 LOX
  rocket ~ ingredient: 5 nitro
  source: 4 peat
  starter: 3 syn
  train ~: 4 coal
  truck ~: 6 diesel
fuel ___: 3 oil, rod 4 cell 7 economy
___ fuel: 3 hog 6 diesel, fossil 7 nuclear
Fuentes: 5 Daisy 6 Carlos
Fuentes, Carlos: 6 author, writer 7 Mexican
  work: Aura
    The Hydra Head
    The Old Gringo
Fuentes del Valle: 4 city, town
  locale: 6 Mexico
fugacious: 8 fleeting, volatile 9 ephemeral
Fuga Meshuga composer: PDQ Bach
Fugard, Athol: 6 writer 10 playwright 12 South African
  work: The Abbess
    The Blood Knot
    Boesman and Lena
    Captain's Tiger
    The Cell
    The Coat
    Hello and Goodbye
    The Island
    The Last Bus
    A Lesson From Aloes
    Nongogo
    Playland
    The Road to Mecca
    Tsotsi
    Valley Song
Fugger: 5 Jakob
fuggy: 5 stale 7 airless
___ fugit: 6 tempus
fugitate: 3 fly, run 4 bail, blow, bolt, flee, skip 5 leave, scoot, scram, split 6 bug out, cut out, decamp, depart, escape, run off, skidoo 7 abscond, get away, make off, run away, scamper, skip out, vamoose 8 turn tail 9 cut and run, hotfoot it, skedaddle 10 fly the coop, make tracks, take flight
fugitive: 5 rover 6 outlaw 7 at large, escapee, outcast, passing, runaway 8 criminal, renegade, temporal, volatile 9 momentary, temporary, transient 10 transitory
Fugitive, The (1947 film)
  cast: Pedro Armendariz, Dolores Del Rio, Henry Fonda, J. Carrol Naish
  director: John Ford
Fugitive, The (1993 film)
  cast: Harrison Ford, Tommy Lee Jones, Sela Ward
  director: Andrew Davis
Fugitive, The (ABC drama)
  cast: David Janssen (Richard Kimble)
    Barry Morse (Lt. Philip Girard)
  narrator: William Conrad
Fugitive Trail, The author: Zane Grey
fugu: 4 fish 10 puffer fish
  locale: 5 Japan
fugue: 5 music
  composer: 4 Bach
  part: 6 answer
  relative: 5 canon
___ fugue: 6 double, triple
Fugue for Tinhorns composer: 7 Loesser
___ Fugue, The: 5 Art of
fujara: 4 wind 5 flute 10 instrument
  origin: 8 Slovakia
Fuji: 4 city, film, town 6 camera 7 volcano
  alternative: 4 Agfa 5 Canon, Kodak, Leica, Nikon 6 Konica, Pentax, Rollei 7 Minolta, Olympus, Vivitar, Yashica 8 Polaroid
  flow: 4 lava
  like ~: 5 snowy
  locale: 4 Asia 5 Japan 6 Honshu
  neighbor: 5 Asama
  opening: 6 crater
Fujian: 8 province
  capital: 6 Fuzhou
  locale: 5 China
  port: 4 Amoy
Fujimi: 4 city, town
  locale: 5 Japan
Fujimori land: 4 Peru
Fujisawa: 4 city, town
  locale: 5 Japan
Fukaya: 4 city, town
  locale: 5 Japan
Fukui: 4 city, town 7 Kenichi
  locale: 5 Japan
Fukui, Kenichi: 7 chemist 8 Nobelist
Fukuoka: 4 city, town
  locale: 5 Japan
Fukuyama: 4 city, town
  locale: 5 Japan
___-ful: 5 chock
Fula home: 4 Chad, Mali 6 Africa 7 Nigeria, Senegal 8 Cameroon 10 Mauritania
Fulani ___: 6 Empire
Fulani home: 4 Chad, Mali 6 Africa 7 Nigeria, Senegal 8 Cameroon 10 Mauritania
Fu la sorte dell' armi: 4 duet
fulcrum: 4 axis 5 hinge, pivot 6 center
  it turns on a ~: 5 lever
  oar ~: 5 thole
Fulda tributary: 4 Eder
fulfill: 2 do 4 heed, meet, mind, obey 5 bow to, crown, serve 6 accept, attain, bend to, effect, enrich, finish, follow, redeem, supply 7 abide by, achieve, agree to, delight, execute, gratify, observe, perform, realize, respect, satisfy, succeed, suffice 8 adhere to, carry out, complete, conclude, listen to, make good 9 conform to, consent to, discharge, implement 10 accomplish, complement, comply with, consummate, effectuate, make good on
  an obligation: 5 pay up 6 square 7 satisfy 10 remunerate
fulfilled: 7 content 9 compassed, completed, concluded, delighted, gladdened, gratified, perfected, performed, satisfied 10 actualized, dispatched
  be ~: 5 occur 6 happen 8 come true
  not ~: 5 unmet
fulfilling: 9 effectual, execution, rewarding 10 gratifying
___-fulfilling prophecy: 4 self
fulfillment: 3 end 5 kicks 8 exercise, fruition 10 perfection
Fulgencio: 7 Batista
fulgent: 3 lit 5 aglow, shiny 6 ablaze, bright, flashy 7 beaming, blazing, glowing, lambent, radiant, shining 8 dazzling, gleaming, luminous, lustrous 9 brilliant, sparkling
Fulghum: 6 Robert
fulgurate: 3 run, zip 4 bolt, dart, dash, race, rush, tear, whiz, zoom 5 flash, hurry, scoot, speed 6 hasten, scurry, sprint 7 scamper
fuliginous: 5 sooty
full: 3 all, big, fed, SRO 4 deep, rich, wide 5 ample, awash, broad, flush, laden, large, plump, puffy, round, sated, thick, total, whole 6 all-out, choate, cloyed, entire, gorged, imbued, jammed, loaded, minute, packed, utmost 7 brimful, copious, crammed, crowded, glutted, maximum, orotund, plenary, profuse, replete, rounded, stuffed, teeming 8 absolute, abundant, affluent, brimming, bursting, complete, detailed, generous, implicit, integral, itemized,

livelong, occupied, resonant, satiated, sonorous, thorough, whole-hog **9** abounding, bounteous, extensive, inclusive, jam-packed, plenteous, plentiful, satisfied, surfeited, undivided, unlimited **10** at capacity, blow-by-blow, exhaustive, sufficient, unabridged, voluminous
amount: **3** all **4** body **5** total, whole **8** entirety, the works, totality **9** aggregate
at ~ gallop: **4** fast **5** apace **7** hastily, quickly, rapidly, swiftly **8** pell-mell, speedily **9** posthaste
blast: **6** in toto, wholly **7** flat out, totally, utterly **8** entirely **9** to the hilt **10** completely, thoroughly, to the limit
ender: **4** back
feather: **6** finery **8** glad rags
growth: **5** prime **8** majority **9** adulthood
having a ~ plate: **4** busy
in ~: **5** uncut **6** wholly **7** totally **8** as a whole, entirely **10** completely, thoroughly, to the limit
in ~ flower: **6** mature **7** matured **8** blooming
in music: **6** grosso
not at ~ power: **5** on low
of fat: **4** oily **6** greasy **7** buttery
of fun: **5** jolly, merry **8** sporting, sportive
of ginger: **4** game **5** peppy **6** active, frisky, lively, spunky **7** scrappy **8** spirited
of holes: **5** leaky **6** flawed, porous, ragged
of jeopardy: **4** iffy **5** dicey, hairy **6** chancy, daring, touchy, tricky, unsafe **7** fraught, parlous, unsound **8** perilous, ticklish **9** dangerous, daredevil, desperate, foolhardy, hazardous, uncertain **10** touch-and-go
of substance: **4** rich **5** meaty, pithy **7** weighty **8** profound
of (suffix): **3** -ose
of vigor: **4** hale **5** alert, perky, zippy **6** active, bubbly, feisty, lively, potent, robust, strong, sturdy, virile **7** dashing, dynamic, healthy, vibrant, zestful **8** animated, muscular, powerful, spirited **9** energetic, sprightly, strenuous, vivacious
of vim: **4** go-go, spry **5** alert, alive, brisk, lusty, peppy, perky, vital, zesty, zingy, zippy **6** active, bright, bubbly, feisty, frisky, lively **7** dashing, dynamic, healthy, piquant, playful, vibrant, zinging **8** animated, skittish, spirited, vigorous, youthful **9** energetic, sparkling, sprightly, vivacious
poke ~ of holes: **6** riddle **8** puncture
range: **4** A to Z **5** gamut, sweep **7** breadth **8** spectrum
supply: **7** satiety, surfeit **8** plethora **9** plenitude **10** saturation
tilt: **4** fast **5** swift **7** rapidly, swiftly
turn: **5** orbit **6** circle **10** revolution
type of ~ house: **6** aces up
with ~ faculties: **4** sane **5** sound **8** composed, rational, sensible **9** collected, judicious, practical, pragmatic, temperate **10** controlled
full __: **4** moon, sail, stop, tilt, time, word **5** blast, blood, dress, frame, house, marks, rhyme, speed, swing, twist **6** circle, cousin, gainer, nelson **7** binding, powered, trailer
full __ air: **5** of hot
full __ and credit: **5** faith
full-__: **3** cut **4** bore, line, size, term **5** blown, dress, faced, grain, grown, power, scale, sized, timer **6** bodied, length, rigged **7** blooded, figured, fledged, frontal, mouthed, service
full-__ press: **5** court
__-full: **4** cram, half **5** chock, choke, chuck
Full __ ahead!: **5** speed, steam
Full __ and Empty Arms: **4** Moon
Full __ Jacket: **5** Metal
Full __, The: **5** Monty
fullback: **7** athlete, gridder **10** footballer
attempt: **4** gain, goal **5** carry
full-blooded: **5** hardy, sound **6** hearty, robust, unmixt, virile **7** unmixed **8** powerful, purebred, vigorous
full-blown: **4** aged **6** all-out, mature **9** unlimited **10** exhaustive
full-bodied: **4** rich **6** mellow, potent, robust, strong
full-court __: **5** press
full-dress: **4** A to Z **5** total **6** all-out, entire, minute **7** in-depth **8** complete, detailed, profound, sweeping, thorough **9** extensive, intensive, out-and-out, searching **10** definitive, exhaustive
Fuller: **3** Roy **4** Loie **5** Bobby **6** Alfred, Robert, Samuel **7** Charles **8** Margaret
Fuller __: **5** Brush
Fuller, Bobby song: I Fought the Law (1966)
Fuller, Margaret: **6** writer
Fuller, R. Buckminster: **8** engineer **9** architect
creation: **4** dome
first name: Richard
Fuller, Roy: **4** poet **7** British
Fullerton: **4** city, town
locale: **10** California
full faith and __: **6** credit
full-flavored: **4** good, nice, rich **5** spicy, tangy, tasty, yummy **6** savory, spicey **7** piquant **8** luscious, pleasing, tempting **9** ambrosial, delicious, palatable, toothsome **10** appetizing, delectable
full-fledged: **5** adult, of age, prime, whole **6** all-out, mature **7** ripened
full-grown: **3** big **4** ripe **5** adult, of age, prime **6** mature **7** ripened
Full House (ABC sitcom)
cast: Candace Cameron (D.J. Tanner)
David Coulier (Joey Gladstone)
Lori Loughlin (Becky Donaldson)
Ashley and Mary-Kate Olsen (Michelle Elizabeth Tanner)
Bob Saget (Danny Tanner)
John Stamos (Jesse Cochran)
Jodie Sweetin (Steph Tanner)
dog: **5** Comet
full-length: **5** uncut **8** complete
Full Metal Jacket (1987 film)
cast: Adam Baldwin, Vincent D'Onofrio, Matthew Modine
director: Stanley Kubrick
setting: **3** Hué, Nam **7** Vietnam
Full Moon and __ Arms: **5** Empty
Full Moon High (1981 film)
cast: Adam Arkin, Elizabeth Hartman, Ed McMahon
fullness: **7** breadth, satiety **8** maturity
full of __: **4** life **5** beans **7** baloney **8** malarkey
full of __ air: **3** hot
full of combining form: **3** -ous
Full of Life (1956 film)
cast: Richard Conte, Judy Holliday
director: Richard Quine
full-out: **5** total **9** extensive, unlimited
full-range: **4** A to Z **5** whole **10** exhaustive
full-scale: **6** all-out **9** extensive, unlimited **10** exhaustive
full-size: **4** ripe **5** adult, grown **6** mature **7** grown-up, ripened
full speed __: **5** ahead
full-strength: **4** neat, pure **8** straight **9** undiluted
fully: **3** all **4** well **5** in all, plumb, quite **6** bodily, in toto, openly, wholly **7** in depth, totally, utterly **8** entirely, from A to Z, outright, whole hog **9** all the way, every inch, inside out, perfectly, to the hilt **10** altogether, completely, thoroughly, to the teeth
fulmar: **4** bird, gull
fulminate: **4** boil, fume, lash, rage, rail **5** decry, knock **6** berate, vilify **7** censure, condemn, declaim, explode, protest, put down, smolder, thunder, upbraid **8** bloviate, denounce, detonate, smoulder **9** castigate **10** animadvert, denunciate, intimidate, vituperate
fulmination: **4** rant **5** abuse **6** screed, sermon, tirade **7** censure, ranting **8** diatribe, harangue, jeremiad, outburst **9** invective, philippic **10** revilement
fulsome: **4** oily **7** profuse **8** effusive **9** exuberant, overblown
Fulton: **5** Sheen **6** Eileen, Robert
Fulton, Robert power: **5** steam
fumarole: **4** hole, vent
fumble: **3** err **4** drop, flub, goof, miss, muff **5** botch, fluff, grope **6** bobble, boggle, bollix, bumble, bungle, foozle, mess up, slip-up **7** blunder, botch up, louse up **8** flounder, hesitate, misfield **9** feel about, mishandle, mismanage
fumbler: **2** ox **3** oaf **4** clod, lout **5** klutz
exclamation: **4** oops
fumbling: **5** crude, green, inept, unapt **6** clumsy, gauche, klutzy, oafish **7** awkward **8** bumbling, bungling, cloddish, inexpert **9** all thumbs, incapable, maladroit **10** amateurish, hesitation, unskillful
fume: **3** gas **4** boil, burn, fret, pout, rage, rant, rave, reek, stew **5** chafe, smoke, steam **6** blow up, see red, seethe, simmer **7** bristle, flame up, smolder **8** have a fit, smoulder **9** fulminate
fumes: **3** gas **5** vapor **9** effluvium
fumet: **4** soup
fumigant: **8** cleanser **9** germicide **10** antiseptic
fumigate: **6** purify **9** disinfect, sterilize
fumigation target: **4** ants **7** roaches **8** termites
fuming: **3** hot, mad **4** ired, sore, stew **5** angry, cross, huffy, irate, livid, riled, smoky, upset, wroth **6** ablaze, galled, ireful, peeved, raging, red-hot **7** enraged, furious, steamed **8** choleric, incensed, inflamed, maddened, outraged, volcanic, wrathful **9** indignant, irritated, resentful, splenetic **10** freaked out, infuriated
one: **5** rager
over: **5** mad at
fumy: **5** gassy, smoky **7** miasmic **8** aeriform, vaporous, volatile **9** effluvial
fun: **3** joy **4** kick, lark, play, romp **5** happy, humor, kicks, kicky, merry, mirth, sport **6** festal, frolic, gaiety, gayety, joking, laughs, thrill **7** amusing, foolery, hijinks, jesting, jollies, jollity, pastime, revelry **8** clowning, good time, jocosity, laughter, nonsense, pleasant, pleasure **9** amusement, convivial, diversion, diverting, enjoyable, enjoyment, festivity, high jinks, horseplay, merriment, sprightly **10** buffoonery, frolicsome, jocularity, liveliness, recreation, relaxation, tomfoolery
a lot of ~: **4** hoot, howl, kick **5** blast
ender: **4** fest, ster
for ~: **6** in jest **7** as a joke
full of ~: **5** jolly, merry **8** sporting, sportive
good clean ~: **4** lark **6** frolic
have ~: **5** enjoy **6** frolic, regale **7** carouse
having ~: **3** gay **5** happy, jolly, merry **6** elated, genial, joyful, joyous **7** buoyant, chipper, content, gleeful, playful **8** cheerful, laughing, mirthful **9** contented, convivial, vivacious
in ~: **7** as a lark **8** for a joke, jokingly **9** playfully, teasingly **10** humorously
make ~ of: **3** kid, rag **4** bait, gibe, jape, jeer, jibe, jive, mock, razz, twit **5** fleer, mimic, taunt, tease **6** banter, deride, go like **7** lampoon, laugh at, run down, scoff at **8** ridicule
no ~: **3** sad **5** bleak **6** dismal, dreary, gloomy, somber **7** joyless **8** hopeless **9** cheerless, dejecting **10** depressing, lugubrious, melancholy
poke ~ at: **3** kid, rag, rib **4** jeer, mock, ride, twit **5** fleer, roast, scoff, taunt, tease **6** deride, needle **7** put down **8** ridicule
say in ~: **3** kid **4** fool, gibe, jape, jest, joke, josh **5** clown, crack **9** kid around
fun __: **4** fair **5** house
__ fun: **3** for
Fun (1993 film)
cast: Renee Humphrey, William R. Moses, Alicia Witt
Funafuti: **4** city, town **7** capital
locale: **6** Tuvalu
funambulist: **7** acrobat
fun and __: **5** games
__ fun at: **4** poke
function: **2** do, go **3** act, job, run, use **4** duty, fest, fete, gala, goal, part, role, task, work **5** party, place, sense, serve **6** affair, behave, object, office, sphere **7** concern, mission, operate, perform, purpose, service, utility **8** activity, business, capacity, practice, province **9** festivity, gathering, objective, operation, reception **10** department, occupation
(as): **4** work **5** serve
ender: **5** ality
find another ~ for: **5** reuse
starter: **3** mal
(suffix): **3** -ive, -ure
VCR ~: **6** delete
function __: **3** key **4** word **5** space
__ function: **3** set **4** beta, loss, onto, step, trig, wave, work **5** delta, Dirac, Gibbs, vital **6** Bessel, entire, latent, linear, proper, vector **7** inverse
functional: **5** handy, utile **6** usable, useful **7** useable **8** operable **9** operative, practical
functional __: **4** load **5** group, shift, yield **6** change
functionary: **5** agent **8** official **10** bureaucrat
functioned as: **3** was
functioning: **4** live **5** alive **6** active, in gear **7** running, working **9** mechanism, operative
not ~: **4** dead **5** kaput **6** broken, busted, faulty **7** haywire **9** defective **10** broken-down, inoperable, on the blink, on the fritz, out of order
or not: **4** as is
well: **5** right, sound **7** running **8** accurate **9** effective, in the pink, up to snuff **10** unimpaired

fund: **4** back, mine, pool **5** endow, fount, hoard, kitty, money, stake, stock, store **6** defray, enable, pay for, source, supply **7** finance, reserve, sponsor, support **8** bankroll, treasury **9** endowment, grubstake, patronize, reservoir, subsidize **10** capitalize, repository, storehouse, underwrite
rainy day ~: **7** nest egg, reserve, savings
fund-___: **6** raiser **7** raising
___ fund: **4** load **5** hedge, index, money, slush, trust **6** growth, mutual, no-load **7** imprest, pension, sinking, welfare
fundamental: **3** key, law **4** main, root, rule **5** axiom, basal, basic, major, prime, vital **6** bottom, innate, staple **7** central, crucial, initial, minimal, organic, primary, radical, theorem **8** cardinal, integral, rudiment, standard, ultimate **9** necessary, necessity, principle, requisite
fundamental ___: **3** law **4** bass, note, star, tone, unit
fundamentally: **5** per se **6** au fond, wholly **7** at heart **9** primarily, virtually
fundamentals: **4** ABCs, text **6** basics **8** alphabet
funded ___: **4** debt
funding: **7** capital **9** endowment, financing, patronage
fund-raiser: **3** PTA **4** gala **5** bazar, bingo, drive **6** appeal, bazaar, raffle **7** benefit **8** bake sale, cake sale, telethon
suffix: **4** thon
funds: **3** nut, oof **4** cash, gelt, jack, kail, kale, loot, peag, pelf, pool **5** bills, bread, bucks, dough, lucre, means, money, moola, mopus, pesos, purse, rhino, sewan **6** assets, budget, dinero, do-re-mi, mammon, mazuma, monies, moolah, seawan, silver, specie, wampum, wealth **7** backing, cabbage, capital, dollars, lettuce, nest egg, ooftish, profits, revenue, savings, scratch, shekels **8** bankroll, cold cash, currency, hard cash, proceeds, smackers **9** affluence, banknotes, financing, frogskins, long green, resources, simoleons **10** collateral, greenbacks, green stuff
emergency ~ source: **3** ATM
household ~: **6** budget **9** piggy bank
in need of ~: **5** broke **6** busted **7** pinched
research ~: **5** grant **9** endowment **10** fellowship
source: **4** loan **6** backer
Fundy: **3** bay
locale: **6** Canada
___ Funèbre: **6** Marche
funereal: **6** solemn, somber **7** serious **10** lugubrious
Fun, Fun, Fun (1964 song) artist: Beach Boys
car: **5** T-bird
fungicide: **5** zineb **6** captan
fungo ___: **3** bat
fungus: **3** cep **4** koji, mold, rust, smut **5** ergot, morel, mould, mucor, plant, slime, yeast **6** agaric, blewit, lichen, mildew, torula **7** amanita, blewitt, blueleg, bluette, boletus, candida, chytrid, truffle **8** basidium, blue mold, botrytis, death cap, gray mold, mushroom, pig's ears, puffball, snow mold **9** bread mold, earth star, matsu-take, slime mold, sooty mold, sparassis, stinkhorn, toadstool, wheat rust
alga and ~: **6** lichen
combining form: **3** myc- **4** myco- **6** -mycete
grain ~: **4** smut
pouch: **3** sac
science of ~: **8** mycology
spore-case clusters: **5** telia
spores: **5** oidia
spore sac: **5** ascus **6** aecium
fungus ___: **3** bug **4** gnat, root **5** stone
___ fungus: **3** cup, ear, sac **4** club, gill, pore **5** coral, house, jelly, lower, stone, tooth **6** cellar **7** bracket, panther
fun-house figure: **5** ghost, spook, witch
Funhouse, The author: Dean Koontz
Funicello, Annette: **7** actress
costar: **6** Avalon
film: Back to the Beach (1987)
Beach Blanket Bingo (1965)
Beach Party (1963)
Bikini Beach (1964)
Muscle Beach Party (1964)
Pajama Party (1964)
The Shaggy Dog (1959)
song: O Dio Mio (1960)
Tall Paul (1959)
TV: Mickey Mouse Club
funicular ___: **7** railway
Fun in Acapulco (1963 film)
cast: Ursula Andress, Elvis Presley, Alejandro Rey
director: Richard Thorpe
___ Fun in the Summertime: **3** Hot
funk: **4** fear **5** gloom, panic, scare, slump, smell **6** fright, stench, terror **7** bad mood, sadness **8** doldrums **9** trepidity **10** depression, heavy heart, melancholy, woefulness
be in a ~: **4** fret, moon, mope, pine, pout, sulk **5** brood **6** lament
go into a ~: **4** fret, mope, sulk **5** worry **7** agonize **8** languish **10** introspect
in a ~: **4** blue, down, lorn **6** gloomy, morose **7** forlorn, joyless, unhappy **8** dejected, desolate, downcast, forsaken, wretched **9** cheerless, depressed, miserable **10** despondent, devastated, melancholy
put into a ~: **6** bum out, deject, sadden **7** depress **8** dispirit, distress **10** discourage, dishearten
___ Funk: **5** Grand
Funkdafied (1994 song) artist: Da Brat
___ Funk Railroad: **5** Grand
funky: **3** hip, sad **4** rank **5** campy, weird **6** afraid, earthy, modish, quirky, scared, smelly, stinky **7** fearful, noisome, offbeat, sensual, soulful, stylish **8** fearsome, mournful **9** blues-like, terrified **10** frightened, melancholy
Funky Broadway (1967 song) artist: Wilson Pickett
funky chicken: **5** dance
Funky Cold Medina (1989 song)
artist: Tone Loc
funky pigeon: **5** dance
fun-loving: **5** jolly, merry **7** playful **9** convivial, kittenish **10** rollicking
funnel: **6** convey, hopper **7** channel **8** transmit **10** smokestack
combining form: **5** choan- **6** choano-
funnel ___: **4** cake **5** cloud
funnel-shaped: **5** conic **7** conical
flower: **6** azalea
funnier than, be: **3** top
funnies: **6** comics, strips
funniness: **3** wit **4** gags **5** farce, humor, jests, jokes **6** comedy, joking, levity, whimsy **7** jesting **8** clowning, drollery, raillery **9** amusement **10** buffoonery, comicality, jocularity, tomfoolery, wisecracks
react to ~: **4** howl, roar **5** laugh **6** giggle, titter **7** chuckle, crack up
funny: **3** odd, wry **4** rich, zany **5** antic, comic, droll, jolly, light, queer, silly, weird, witty, wrong **6** absurd, har-har, ironic, jocose, quaint **7** amusing, bizarre, comical, curious, jesting, jocular, oddball, playful, riotous, risible, strange, unusual, waggish **8** farcical, humorous, mirthful, peculiar, puzzling **9** diverting, facetious, hilarious, laughable, ludicrous, priceless, slapstick, whimsical **10** gut-busting, hysterical, perplexing, ridiculous, suspicious, uproarious
act ~: **5** amuse
business: **5** antic, caper, humor, trick **6** levity **7** hijinks **8** mischief, trickery **9** high jinks
fare: **5** farce, humor **6** comedy, satire **9** burlesque, slapstick
feeling: **5** hunch **7** portent **9** suspicion
person: **3** wag **4** card, hoot, riot, zany **5** clown, comic **6** scream **8** comedian
thing: **4** howl, joke, quip, riot **5** crack **6** gasser, hot one, scream
very ~: **4** rich **6** absurd **7** amusing, comical **8** farcical, humorous **9** diverting, hilarious, laughable, ludicrous **10** gut-busting, ridiculous, rollicking, uproarious
funny ___: **3** car **4** bone, book **5** money, paper
___ funny!: **4** Very
Funny ___: **4** Face, Girl, Lady
Funny!: **4** ha-ha
funny bone locale: **5** elbow
Funny Face (1957 film): **7** musical
cast: Fred Astaire, Audrey Hepburn, Kay Thompson
composer: **8** Gershwin
director: Stanley Donen
setting: **5** Paris **6** France
Funny Face (1972 song) artist: Donna Fargo
Funny Girl (1968 film)
cast: Omar Sharif, Barbra Streisand
composer: **5** Styne **7** Merrill
director: William Wyler
song: **6** People
song subject: **4** Rose **5** Sadie
subject: Fanny Brice
funnyman: **3** wag, wit **4** card **5** clown, comic, cutup, joker **6** jester, kidder, scream **7** buffoon, farceur, gagster, punster **8** comedian, humorist, quipster **9** prankster
___ funny, McGee!: **5** T'aint
___ Funny That Way: **4** She's
Funny Thing Happened..., A: **7** musical
composer: **8** Sondheim
Funny Way of Laughin' (1962 song)
artist: Burl Ives
___ fun of: **4** make
Funt: **5** Allen, Peter
command: **5** smile
need: **6** camera
Fun With Dick and Jane (1977 film)
cast: Jane Fonda, Ed McMahon, George Segal
dog: **4** Spot
___ fuoco: **3** con
fur: **3** fox **4** coat, down, fuzz, hair, mink, pelt, skin, wolf, wool **5** lapin, otter, sable, stole **6** beaver, coyote, ermine, kit fox, marten, nutria, pelage, rabbit, racoon, red fox **7** blue fox, garment, karakul, krimmer, leopard, minever, miniver, raccoon **8** bearskin, sea otter **9** astrakhan, sheepskin, silver fox **10** chinchilla
in heraldry: **4** vair **8** tincture
lose ~: **4** shed
magnate: **5** Astor
piece: **3** boa **4** pelt, wrap **5** stole
rabbit ~: **4** cony **5** coney, lapin
fur ___: **4** coat, farm, seal
___ fur: **4** fake
Für ___: **5** Elise
furbelow: **6** ruffle **8** nicknack, ornament **10** decoration, knickknack
furbish: **4** buff **5** adorn, clean, fix up, glaze, renew, shine **6** polish **7** burnish, gussy up, improve, restore **8** brighten, decorate, renovate, spruce up
Furby: **3** toy
exclamation: **4** whee
maker: **6** Hasbro
furcate: **5** forky **6** forked
Furchgott, Robert: **8** Nobelist
Für Elise composer: **9** Beethoven
furfuraceous: **5** scaly
Furies: **5** Dirae **7** Erinyes **9** Eumenides
one of the ~: **6** Alecto **7** Megaera **9** Tisiphone
Furie, Sidney J.: **8** director
film: The Boys (1961)
The Boys in Company C (1978)
Hit! (1973)
Lady Sings the Blues (1972)
Furillo: **3** cop **4** Carl
___ Furioso: **7** Orlando
furioso opposite: **5** dolce
furious: **3** hot, mad **4** ired, sore, wild **5** angry, cross, huffy, irate, livid, riled, upset, vexed, wroth **6** ablaze, fierce, fuming, heated, hectic, ireful, peeved, piqued, raging, raving, red-hot, savage, stormy **7** boiling, enraged, foaming, intense, rampant, ranting, steamed, violent **8** blustery, choleric, feverish, incensed, inflamed, maddened, outraged, up in arms, vehement, white-hot, worked up, wrathful **9** bummed-out, indignant, irritated, rapacious, resentful, seeing red, splenetic, turbulent, wrought up **10** freaked out, hopping mad, hysterical, in an uproar, passionate
be ~: **4** boil, burn, fume, rage, rave **5** steam **6** blow up, see red, seethe **7** smolder **9** fulminate
make ~: **3** ire **5** peeve **6** enrage, madden
one: **5** raver
with: **5** mad at
furiously: **4** hard **5** madly **7** like mad **9** fervently, like crazy, viciously **10** vehemently
furl: **4** roll, wind **6** curl up, roll up, wrap up **10** wind around
furlong: **6** length **7** measure
eight ~ s: **4** mile
fraction: **4** foot, yard
Furlong, Edward: **5** actor
film: American Heart (1993)
American History X (1998)
Animal Factory (2000)
Before and After (1996)
Detroit Rock City (1999)
The Grass Harp (1995)
Little Odessa (1994)
Terminator 2: Judgment Day (1991)
furlough: **3** axe, can **4** boot, drop, oust, pass, sack **5** leave, let go, R and R **6** bounce, layoff **7** cashier, dismiss, drum out, liberty, release **8** get rid of, pink-slip, vacation **9** discharge, terminate **10** shore leave
furnace: **4** kiln **5** forge, stove **6** boiler, burner, cupola, heater
button: **5** reset
duct: **4** flue **6** leader
feed a ~: **4** fuel **5** stoke
fleck: **3** ash
fuel: **4** coal
like a ~: **3** hot **5** fiery **6** torrid **7** blazing, intense
part: **6** damper
room: **6** cellar **8** basement

unit: 3 BTU
worker: 5 firer 6 stoker
__ furnace: 3 arc, gas 5 blast, floor, solar 6 Scotch 7 cyclone, holding
Furness: 5 Betty
furnish: 3 fit, rig 4 gear, give, lend 5 array, cater, endow, equip, fix up, offer, stock, yield 6 afford, bestow, clothe, fit out, gear up, instal, invest, outfit, purvey, render, rig out, supply 7 advance, appoint, deck out, install, prepare, produce, provide, satisfy, turn out 8 accouter, accoutre, decorate, dispense 9 provision 10 administer
Furnished Room, The author: O. Henry
furnishings: 4 gear 5 décor, goods 8 equipage, fittings, fixtures
__ furnishings: 4 home
furniture: 3 bed 4 crib, desk, sofa 5 bench, chair, chest, couch, hutch, stool, table 6 buffet, bureau, glider, rocker, settee 7 cabinet, commode, dresser, highboy, rolltop, seating, sofa bed 8 bookcase, credenza, cupboard, love seat, recliner, wardrobe 9 appliance, davenport, equipment, secretary, sideboard 10 breakfront, possession
bedroom ~: 5 chest, table 6 bureau 8 credenza, end table 10 breakfront, cedar chest, chiffonier, night table
buildup: 4 dust
chain: 4 Ikea
den ~: 4 desk, sofa 6 settee 8 bookcase
detail: 5 inlay
dining-room ~: 5 hutch, table 7 cabinet 8 credenza 10 breakfront
feature: 3 leg, wax 5 stain 6 finish, polish 8 baluster
living-room ~: 4 sofa 5 table 7 ottoman
material: 4 wood 6 bamboo, wicker
measurement: 5 width
mover: 3 van 5 truck, U-Haul
nursery ~: 4 crib 6 cradle 8 bassinet
office ~: 4 sofa 5 couch, divan, table 6 lounge, settee 7 cabinet, rolltop 8 credenza 9 davenport, secretary, sectional 10 escritoire
ornament: 5 acorn 6 finial
patio ~: 5 chair, table 6 chaise 8 umbrella
porch ~: 6 glider
protector: 4 tarp 5 doily, stain 6 doyley 7 Formica 9 slipcover, tarpaulin 10 upholstery
school ~: 4 desk
set: 5 suite 8 ensemble
style: 4 Adam 6 Empire 7 modular 8 colonial, Sheraton
trim: 5 skirt
wheel: 6 caster
wood: 3 koa, oak 4 acle, pine, teak 5 alder, cedar, ebony, maple 6 cherry, gaboon 8 mahogany
worker: 5 caner
__ furniture: 5 patio
furniture leg decoration: 3 ear
furniture polish: 6 Behold, Endust, Pledge 10 Liquid Gold, Old English
furor: 3 ado, row 4 flap, fuss, rage, stir, to-do 5 scene, stink, storm 6 bustle, flurry, frenzy, hoopla, hubbub, ruckus, squall, tumult, uproar 7 ferment, tempest, turmoil 8 brouhaha, paroxysm 9 agitation, commotion, hue and cry, maelstrom, sensation, vehemence, whoop-de-do 10 excitement, free-for-all, hullabaloo, hurly-burly
in a ~: 4 wild 5 manic, rabid 6 crazed, raging 7 berserk 8 frenzied, unhinged 9 ferocious 10 hysterical
Furphy, Joseph: 6 author, writer 10 Australian
furrier offering: 3 fox 4 mink, pelt, wrap 5 otter, sable, stole 6 ermine 9 silver fox 10 chinchilla
furrow: 3 cut, row, rut 4 knit, line, plow, seam 5 ditch, gouge, plica, ridge, score 6 crease, groove, gutter, hollow, pucker, rabbet, rimple, sulcus, trench, trough 7 channel, crinkle, wrinkle 9 corrugate 10 depression
narrow ~: 5 stria
furry: 4 soft 5 downy, fuzzy, hairy, nappy, plush 6 fleecy, fluffy, shaggy 7 hirsute, squishy, unshorn, velvety 8 cushiony
Furst: 7 Stephen
Fürth: 4 city, town
locale: 7 Germany
further: 3 aid, and, too, yet 4 also, ease, else, help, more, push, then 5 added, again, boost, extra, lobby, other, speed 6 assist, back up, better, beyond, foster, hasten, incite, second, to boot, yonder 7 advance, benefit, besides, elevate, forward, nurture, promote, support 8 advocate, champion, expedite, increase, likewise, moreover 9 cultivate, encourage, go forward 10 accelerate, additional, facilitate
ender: 4 more, most
in time: 4 anon 5 after, later 8 eventual 9 afterward 10 thereafter
say ~: 3 add
without ~ ado: 3 now, PDQ 6 at once 8 promptly, right now 9 forthwith, right away
__ further: 4 go no
__ further ado: 7 without
Further Adventures of Nils, The author: Selma Lagerlöf
furtherance: 3 aid 6 course 7 advance, support
in ~ of: 3 for 10 supporting
furthermore: 3 and, too, yet 4 also, plus 5 again 6 as well, to boot 7 besides 8 likewise
furthermost: 3 top 4 last 5 final, prime 6 all-out 7 extreme, highest, leading, maximal, supreme 8 absolute, farthest, greatest, ultimate 9 sovereign 10 preeminent
furthest: 4 last 7 extreme, outmost, outside 8 ultimate 9 uttermost
from the hole, in golf: 4 away
point: 3 end 4 edge 5 limit 7 extreme 8 boundary 9 extremity
furtive: 3 sly 4 foxy, wily 6 artful, covert, crafty, hidden, masked, secret, shifty, slinky, sneaky, tricky, unseen, veiled 7 cloaked, cunning, elusive, elusory, evasive, private, sub rosa 8 guileful, hush-hush, obscured, scheming, secluded, shrouded, skulking, slinking, sneaking, stealthy 9 concealed, deceitful, disguised, insidious, secretive, underhand 10 undercover, under wraps, unreliable
glance: 4 peek, peep
in a ~ manner: 5 slyly
one: 5 skunk, snake, sneak 6 rascal, weasel 9 scoundrel
org.: 3 CIA
whisper: 3 pst 4 psst
furtively: 7 asquint, on the QT, sub rosa 8 on the sly, secretly
Furtwängler, Wilhelm: 6 German 9 conductor
fury: 3 ire 4 fire, heat, rage 5 anger, force, storm, wrath 6 frenzy, temper 7 outrage, passion, rampage, umbrage 8 acrimony, asperity, ferocity, rabidity, savagery, violence 9 intensity, vehemence 10 fierceness, resentment, turbulence, unkindness
fill with ~: 6 enrage
Fury: 3 car 4 auto 6 Alecto 7 Megaera 8 Plymouth 9 Tisiphone 10 automobile
Fury (1936 film)
cast: Walter Abel, Sylvia Sidney, Spencer Tracy
director: Fritz Lang
__ Fury: 5 Black, Son of 7 Blanche, Captain
Fury, The (1978 film)
cast: John Cassavetes, Kirk Douglas, Carrie Snodgress
director: Brian De Palma
furze: 5 gorse, shrub 7 bramble
like a ~: 5 spiny
Fusco Brothers, The dog: 4 Axel
Fusco, Paul role: 3 ALF
fuscous: 4 gray, grey 5 dusky 8 browning
fuse: 3 mix, wed 4 bond, join, meld, melt, thaw, weld, wick 5 blend, merge, smelt, stick, unify, unite 6 cement, cohere, mingle, solder 7 combine, lighter 8 coalesce, intermix 9 commingle, integrate 10 amalgamate, synthesize
blow a ~: 4 flip, rage, rave 5 storm 6 see red 7 explode 10 hit the roof
problem: 5 short
short ~: 6 temper 9 surliness
unit: 3 amp 6 ampere
with a short ~: 9 excitable
fuse __: 3 box
__ fuse: 5 blow a, short
fusee: 5 flare, match 7 lighter
fuselage: 4 body 7 chassis
Fushun: 4 city, town
locale: 5 China
fusil: 3 gun 6 musket, weapon 9 flintlock
fusile: 6 melted, molten 7 founded
fusillade: 4 fire 5 burst, salvo, storm 6 volley 7 barrage 9 discharge
fusilli: 5 pasta 7 noodles
alternative: 4 orzo, ziti 5 penne 7 lasagna, lasagne, pastina, ravioli 8 bucatini, couscous, farfalle, linguine, linguini, macaroni, rigatoni 9 agnolotti, angelhair, cavatelli, manicotti, spaghetti 10 cannelloni, fettuccini, tortellini, vermicelli
fusion: 5 blend, union, unity 7 mixture 9 admixture, composite, synthesis
target: 4 atom
fusion __: 4 bomb 7 reactor
__ fusion: 4 cell, cold 7 nuclear
__-fusion: 4 jazz
fuss: 3 ado, nag, row 4 flap, fret, kick, spat, stew, stir, to-do, wail 5 fight, furor, hoo-ha, noise, scene, stink, storm, whine 6 bother, bustle, clamor, flurry, frenzy, grouse, hassle, hoohah, hoopla, hubbub, kickup, lather, pother, racket, ruckus, rumpus, strife, tumult, unrest, uproar 7 clutter, dispute, fanfare, flutter, grumble, quarrel, scuffle, trouble, turmoil, whimper 8 activity, argument, busyness, complain, disorder, squabble 9 agitation, bellyache, bickering, commotion, complaint, confusion, objection 10 difficulty, excitement, falling out, hullabaloo
ender: 3 pot 6 budget
kick up a ~: 3 cry 4 yell 5 gripe, groan, shout, whine 6 holler, shriek, yammer 7 grumble, protest, screech 8 complain 9 bellyache, raise Cain
make a ~: 4 balk, beef, carp, kick, mind, moan, rail, rant, sigh, wail, weep, yell 5 act up, baulk, cavil, demur, fight, gripe, groan, growl, mourn, whine 6 clamor, grouch, grouse, holler, mutter, repine, squawk, squeal, yammer 7 grumble, protest, quarrel, trouble, whimper 8 complain, sound off 9 bellyache, find fault
over dress: 5 preen, primp, prink
with one's hair: 5 groom, preen
without ~: 6 calmly
fussbudget: 4 prig 5 biddy 8 quibbler, stickler 9 nitpicker 10 fuddy-duddy
fusspot: 9 formalist
fussy: 4 nice, prim 5 exact, picky 6 choosy, dainty, ornate, prissy 7 bookish, careful, choosey, finical, finicky, fretful, mincing, nervous, precise, prudent, prudish 8 cautious, critical, exacting, finiking, finnicky, fretsome, pedantic, rigorous, thorough 9 assiduous, attentive, demanding, difficult, judicious, observant, querulous, squeamish, stickling 10 fastidious, meticulous, nitpicking, particular, pedantical, scrupulous, unamenable
dresser: 3 fop 5 dandy 7 coxcomb 8 popinjay 10 jack-a-dandy
fustanella: 5 skirt
fustet: 4 tree
relative: 5 mango, sumac 6 cashew, mastic, sumach 9 pistachio
fustian: 3 gas, rot 4 blah, bosh, bull, bunk, guff, jazz, jive, pooh, rant, smug, tosh, vain 5 bilge, cocky, fudge, hokum, hooey, prate, stuff, trash, tripe, tumid 6 bunkum, bushwa, drivel, fabric, footle, gabble, gammon, gibber, havers, hot air, humbug, jabber, jargon, kibosh, piffle 7 baloney, blarney, blather, blether, boloney, bushwah, eyewash, flannel, flubdub, garbage, haughty, hogwash, inanity, orotund, pompous, rubbish, stuck-up, twaddle, verbose 8 arrogant, boastful, buncombe, claptrap, falderal, falderol, flimflam, flummery, folderal, folderol, inflated, nonsense, puffed up, rhetoric, slipslop, snobbish, tommyrot, trumpery 9 banana oil, big-headed, bombastic, conceited, egotistic, flaunting, gibberish, goofiness, grandiose, high-flown, kidstakes, moonshine, poppycock, rigmarole 10 applesauce, balderdash, bilge water, codswallop, double-talk, empty words, flapdoodle, galimatias, Jabberwock, mumbo jumbo, pontifical, rigamarole, taradiddle
fustic: 3 dye 4 tree 7 dyewood
relative: 3 fig 4 upas 5 ficus, ramon 6 antiar 18 breadfruit. mulberry
fustigate: 5 cavil, roast, scold 6 attack, berate, punish, rail at 7 condemn, lay into 8 backbite, badmouth, chastise, denounce 9 criticize, disparage, light into, reprehend 10 denunciate
fusty: 4 rank 5 moldy, musty, passé, stale 6 frowsy, frowzy, rancid 7 archaic, fogyish 8 mildewed, obsolete, outdated, out of use 9 old-school, out-of-date 10 antiquated, malodorous
futhark: 8 alphabet
character: 4 rune
like ~: 5 runic
futile: 4 idle, null, vain 5 no use, no-win 6 hollow, in vain, otiose, stupid 7 sterile, useless 8 feckless, hopeless, nugatory 9 for naught, fruitless, pointless, thankless, to no avail, valueless, worthless 10 for nothing, profitless, unavailing
futilely: 6 vainly 9 uselessly

futon: 3 bed 6 daybed 7 sofa bed 8 mattress
futtock: 6 timber
Futuna: 4 isls. 5 isles 7 islands
Futura: 3 car 4 auto, font, Ford 8 typeface 10 automobile
Futuramic: 3 car 4 auto, Olds 10 automobile, Oldsmobile
future: 4 time, to be 5 later 6 coming, offing 7 by and by, destiny 8 eventual, imminent, intended, tomorrow, ulterior, upcoming 9 commodity, impending, potential 10 subsequent, unrealized
at a ~ time: 3 yet 5 later 7 someday 10 eventually, ultimately
examiner: 4 seer 5 augur, sibyl 6 medium, oracle 7 diviner, palmist, prophet, psychic 8 haruspex 9 theurgist 10 forecaster, foreteller, soothsayer
generations: 4 seed 5 heirs, issue 7 progeny 8 children 9 posterity
groom: 4 beau 6 fiancé 8 intended 9 betrothed
in the ~: 3 yet 4 anon, soon, then 5 after, ahead, hence, later 7 by and by, later on, someday 8 evermore, sometime 9 afterward, hereafter 10 before long, eventually, ultimately
life: 9 hereafter, next world 10 afterworld
save for ~ use: 7 lay away
sign of the ~: 4 omen 6 augury, herald 7 portent, presage 9 foretoken, harbinger
future __: 5 shock, tense 7 perfect
future __, the: 5 is now
Future __ of America: 7 Farmers
Future Indefinite author: Noël Coward
Future Is in Eggs, The author: Eugène Ionesco
futures market: 4 Merc 5 COMEX
item: 3 oil, rye 4 corn, eggs, gold, hogs, lard, lead, oats, zinc 5 cocoa, sugar, wheat 6 barley, cattle, coffee, copper, cotton, lumber, onions, silver 7 plywood 8 crude oil, flaxseed, gasoline, platinum, potatoes 9 pork belly 10 heating oil, natural gas, soybean oil
Futureworld (1976 film)
cast: Yul Brynner, Blythe Danner, Peter Fonda, Arthur Hill
futurity __: 4 race 6 stakes
futz around: 4 idle 8 lollygag, slack off 9 waste time 10 experiment
fuze: 7 lighter 9 detonator
see also fuse
Fuzhou: 4 city, port
locale: 5 China
fuzz: 3 cop, fur, nap 4 down, hair, lint 5 beard, fiber, floss, fluff, kapok 6 copper, police 8 whiskers 9 detective
full of ~: 5 linty
fuzzy: 3 dim 4 dark, hazy 5 blear, downy, dusky, faded, faint, foggy, furry, hairy, linty, mirky, misty, muddy, murky, muted, nappy, vague, wooly 6 bleary, blurry, flossy, fluffy, frizzy, napped, woolly 7 blurred, frizzly, hirsute, obscure, shadowy, unclear, unshorn 9 equivocal, imprecise, unfocused 10 ill-defined, indefinite, indistinct, inexplicit, out of focus, unexplicit, unspecific
fruit: 4 kiwi 5 peach
make ~: 4 blur, roil, veil 5 bedim, befog 7 becloud, obscure
warm ~: 6 praise 10 compliment
fuzzy __: 3 set 4 math 5 logic
Fuzzy: 7 Zoeller
fuzzy-headed: 3 mad 4 daft, dopy, idle, soft, wild, zany 5 balmy, daffy, dense, dippy, dizzy, dopey, dotty, goofy, goosy, inane, kooky, nutty, sappy, silly, wacky 6 absurd, goosey, kookie, madcap, obtuse, simple, stupid, unwise, whacky 7 asinine, doltish, fatuous, foolish, puerile, vacuous, witless 8 mindless 9 brainless, dim-witted, fatuitous, frivolous, half-baked, imprudent, insensate, lightsome, ludicrous, misguided, senseless 10 cockamamie, half-witted, ill-advised, incautious, indiscreet, irrational, ridiculous, sophomoric, unthinking
Fuzzy-Wuzzy
author: Rudyard Kipling
Soudan, to ~: 3 'ome
Fuzzy-Wuzzy __ bear: 4 was a
Fuzzy-Wuzzy __ fuzzy...: 5 wasn't
F.W.: 7 de Klerk 9 Woolworth
fwy. cousin: 3 tpk.
F/X (1986 film)
cast: Bryan Brown, Brian Dennehy, Diane Venora
FYI, part of: 3 for 4 your 11 information
Fyodor: 4 czar, tsar 7 Gladkov, Sologub 9 Chaliapin
in English: 8 Theodore
Fyvush: 6 Finkel
F1 neighbor: 3 ESC
F-16: 5 Viper
counterpart: 3 MiG
home: 3 AFB
__ F. Zanuck: 6 Darryl

g-___: 3 cal. 4 suit
g.: 4 gram, meas.
___-g: 4 zero
G: 3 key 4 clef, thou 6 letter, rating 8 thousand
analogue: 6 E minor
Anglo-Saxon ~: 4 yogh
assign a: 4 rate
a thousand ~ s: 3 mil 7 million
flat: 4 note 8 black key
in phonetic alphabet: 4 Golf
one ~: 4 thou 7 gravity
rater: 4 MPAA
sharp: 5 A flat
G ___: 4 clef, star
G ___ go: 4 as in
G-___: 3 man, men 4 suit 5 Clefs, rated
G. ___ Liddy: 6 Gordon
___.G: 5 Kenny, Sally, super 6 Warren 7 vitamin
'G' ___ Gumshoe: 5 Is for
Ga: 4 elem. 7 element, gallium
31 for ~: 4 at. no.
Ga.
airline based in ~: 3 DAL
neighbor: 3 Ala., Fla. 8 N. Car. Tenn.
zone: 3 EDT, EST
see also Georgia
gab: 3 jaw, rap, say, yak, yap 4 blab, chat, chin, talk, yack 5 prate, run on, speak 6 confer, drivel, gibber, gossip, jabber, natter, parley, patter, pop off, rattle, yammer 7 blabber, blather, blether, chatter, palaver, prattle, schmoos 8 babbling, chitchat, converse, ramble on, rattle on, schmoose, schmooze 9 table talk, touch base 10 chew the fat, chew the rag, yackety-yak, yakkety-yak
ender: 4 fest
gift of ~: 8 rhetoric 9 eloquence, loquacity, wittiness 10 volubility
line of ~: 5 pitch, spiel 6 patter
starter: 6 baffle
gabardine: 5 twill 6 fabric 8 material
gabber: 10 motormouth
gabbing: 5 noisy 8 babbling
gabble: 3 gas, rap, rot, yak 4 blah, bosh, bull, bunk, guff, jazz, jive, pooh, talk, tosh 5 bilge, fudge, hokum, hooey, prate, stuff, trash, tripe 6 babble, bunkum, bushwa, cackle, drivel, footle, gammon, gibber, gossip, havers, hot air, humbug, jabber, jargon, kibosh, piffle, rattle 7 baloney, blarney, blather, blether, boloney, bushwah, chatter, eyewash, flannel, flubdub, fustian, garbage, hogwash, inanity, prattle, rubbish, twaddle 8 buncombe, chitchat, claptrap, falderal, falderol, flimflam, flummery, folderal, folderol, nonsense, ramble on, slipslop, tommyrot, trumpery 9 banana oil, gibberish, kidstakes, moonshine, poppycock, rigmarole, table talk 10 applesauce, balderdash, bilge water, codswallop, double-talk, flapdoodle, galimatias, Jabberwock, mumbo jumbo, rigamarole, taradiddle
gabbro: 7 mineral
gabby: 4 long 5 wordy 6 chatty, prolix 7 diffuse, lengthy, unterse, verbose, voluble 8 grasping, rambling 9 bombastic, garrulous, talkative 10 big-mouthed, discursive, long-winded, loquacious, palaverous
Gabby: 5 Hayes 8 Hartnett
Gabe: 4 Dell 6 Kaplan
Gabel, Martin spouse: Arlene Francis
Gabès: 4 gulf
locale: 7 Tunisia
gable
house with a ~: 6 A-frame
topper: 6 finial
gable ___: 3 end 4 roof, wall 6 window
Gable, Clark: 5 actor
film: Boom Town (1940)
The Call of the Wild (1935)
China Seas (1935)
Command Decision (1948)
Dancing Lady (1933)
A Free Soul (1931)
Gone With the Wind (1939)
Hold Your Man (1933)
The Hucksters (1947)
Idiot's Delight (1939)
It Happened One Night (1934, AA)
Manhattan Melodrama (1934)
The Misfits (1961)
Mogambo (1953)
Mutiny on the Bounty (1935)
Possessed (1931)
Red Dust (1932)
Run Silent, Run Deep (1958)
San Francisco (1936)
Soldier of Fortune (1955)
Strange Cargo (1940)
Strange Interlude (1932)
Teacher's Pet (1958)
Test Pilot (1938)
Too Hot to Handle (1938)
spouse: Carole Lombard
Gabler: 5 Hedda
___ Gables, FL: 5 Coral
Gabon: 6 nation 7 country
capital: 10 Libreville
money: 5 franc
neighbor: 5 Congo 8 Cameroon
people: 3 Fan 4 Fang 6 Pangwe 7 Pahouin
gaboon: 4 tree 5 viper 6 okoume
Gabor: 3 Eva 5 Jolie, Magda 6 Dennis, Zsa Zsa
Gabor, Dennis: 8 Nobelist 9 physicist
Gaborone: 4 city, town 7 capital
locale: 8 Botswana
Gabor, Zsa Zsa spouse: George Sanders
Gabriel: 4 Dell 5 angel, Byrne, Fauré, Okara, Peter, saint 6 Marcel 8 Lippmann 9 archangel 10 Fahrenheit
Gabriel ___ Márquez: 6 García
Gabriela: 7 Mistral 8 Carteris, Sabatini
see also Spanish
___ Gabriel Borkman: 4 John
___ Gabriel, CA: 3 San
Gabriele: 9 D'Annunzio, Falloppio
Gabriel Hounds, The author: Mary Stewart
Gabriella
see Italian
Gabrielle: 3 Roy 5 Anwar
Gabriel Leyva Solano: 4 city, town
locale: 6 Mexico 7 Sinaloa
___ Gabriel Mountains: 3 San
Gabriel Over the White House (1933 film)
cast: Walter Huston, Karen Morley, Franchot Tone
director: Gregory La Cava
Gabriel, Peter
song: Big Time (1987)
Sledgehammer (1986)
___ Gabriel Rossetti: 5 Dante
Gaby: 8 Hoffmann, Sabatini
Gaby–A True Story (1987 film)
cast: Norma Aleandro, Robert Loggia, Liv Ullmann
gad: 4 flit, roam, rove 5 drift 6 cruise, ramble, wander 7 meander, saunter 8 ambulate, wanderer 9 gallivant, run around 10 knock about, window-shop
ender: 3 fly 5 about
Gad
brother of ~: 3 Dan 4 Levi 5 Asher, Judah 6 Joseph, Reuben, Simeon 7 Zebulun 8 Benjamin, Issachar, Naphtali
parent of ~: 5 Jacob 6 Zilpah
sister of ~: 5 Dinah
son of ~: 3 Eri 5 Haggi
gadabout: 4 goer 5 nomad, rover 7 rambler 8 runagate, traveler, vagabond, wanderer, wayfarer 9 jet-setter, transient, wayfaring
___-Gadda-Da-Vida: 3 In-a
Gaddis, William: 6 author, writer
gadfly: 3 bug 4 pest 6 critic, insect 8 irritant, nuisance, provoker 9 annoyance
gadget: 4 tool 5 dodad, gismo, gizmo, pager, thing 6 device, doodad, whosis, widget 7 gimmick, machine, novelty, trinket, utensil 9 apparatus, appliance, can opener, doohickey, implement, invention, machinery, mechanism 10 instrument
kitchen ~: 5 corer, dicer, parer, ricer, timer 6 baster, beater, grater
gadid: 3 cod 7 codfish
gadolinium: 5 metal 7 element
Gadsden: 4 city, town
locale: 7 Alabama
Purchase boundary river: 4 Gila
gadwall: 4 bird, duck, fowl
relative: 4 smew, teal 5 eider, Pekin, Rouen, scaup 6 Cayuga, scoter 7 mallard, pintail, pochard, redhead, sea duck, widgeon 8 garganey, gray duck, mandarin, musk duck, oldsquaw, shoveler, surf duck, wood duck 9 black duck, broadbill, goldeneye, goosander, greenhead, merganser, ruddy duck, sprigtail 10 bufflehead, canvasback, surf scoter, tufted duck
Gadzooks!: 4 egad, oath 5 egads 6 zounds
Gaea
daughter of ~: 4 Ceto, Rhea, Thia 5 Aetna, Dione, Pheme 6 Creusa, Phoebe, Tethys, Themis 7 Eurybia 9 Charybdis, Mnemosyne
father of ~: 5 Chaos
husband of ~: 6 Uranus
lover of ~: 4 Zeus 6 Pontus, Uranus 7 Oceanus 8 Tartarus 10 Hephaestus
son of ~: 4 Anax, Ceto 5 Arges, Argus, Arion, Coeus, Crius, Manes, Mimas, Orion, Titan 6 Agrius, Caerus, Cronos, Cronus, Hyllus, Leitus, Nereus, Phlyus, Pontus, Typhon, Uranus 7 Antaeus, Brontes, Cecrops, Clytius, Iapetus, Oceanus, Phorcus, Thaumas 8 Hyperion, Steropes
Gael: 4 Celt, Scot 6 Greene 10 Highlander
garb: 4 kilt
republic: 4 Eire 7 Ireland
Gaelic: 4 Erse, Manx 8 language
people: 5 Irish
___ Gaelic: 5 Irish, Scots 6 Scotch
Gaels school: 4 Iona
Gaetano: 9 Donizetti
gaff: 4 boom, hook, spar 7 javelin
stand the ~: 4 cope, last 5 brook 6 endure, hang on, keep on, stay on 7 carry on, hold out, outlast, survive, weather 9 put up with 10 get through, stick it out
gaff ___: 3 rig 4 sail 7 topsail
gaffe: 4 goof, slip 5 boner, error, lapse 6 boo-boo, howler, slip-up 7 blooper, blunder, faux pas, misstep, mistake 8 solecism 9 gaucherie, indecorum
golf ~: 4 baff, hook 5 slice
make a ~: 3 err 6 slip up 7 blunder
vocal ~: 4 flub, gaff, goof 5 error, gaffe, lapse 7 blooper, misstep
gaffer: 4 hick, rube 6 rustic 9 graybeard
workplace: 3 set 10 soundstage
gag: 3 tie 4 cork, hush, jape, jest, joke, quip, stop 5 caper, crack, humor, prank, quiet, trick 6 muffle, muzzle, shut up, stifle 7 hot foot, repress, silence, squelch 8 mischief, one-liner, pretense, restrain, silencer, suppress, throttle 9 April fool, keep still, tongue-tie, wisecrack, witticism 10 shenanigan
response, informally: 4 laff
starter: 5 lolly
gag ___: 3 law 4 line, rule 5 order 6 reflex
___ gag: 5 sight 7 running
gaga: 4 daft 5 crazy, dizzy, dotty, giddy, goony, loopy 7 bananas, bonkers, bug-eyed, smitten 8 lovesick 9 bewitched 10 infatuated, out to lunch
be ~ over: 5 adore
Gagarin: 4 Yuri 9 cosmonaut
follower: 5 Titov
gage: 4 bond, pawn 5 glove, token, trial 6 pledge, surety 7 deposit, hostage 8 gauntlet, security 9 challenge
green ~: 4 plum
___ gage: 4 ring 5 broad 7 marking
gaggle: 3 set 5 flock, geese
noise: 4 honk
Gag me with a spoon!: 3 ugh
Gagny: 4 city, town
locale: 6 France
gags: 9 funniness 10 jocoseness
gagster: 3 wag 5 clown, joker 6 amuser 8 funnyman 9 leg-puller
Gahagan, Helen
role: 3 She
spouse: Melvyn Douglas
Gahan: 6 Wilson
Gahanna: 4 city, town
locale: 4 Ohio
___ Gaieties, The: 7 Garrick
gaiety: 3 fun, joy 4 glee 5 cheer, humor, mirth, revel, sport 6 fiesta, frolic 7 elation, gayness, jollity, rapture, revelry, sparkle 8 buoyance, buoyancy, festival, gladness, hilarity, pleasure, radiance, radiancy, vivacity 9 animation, festivity, frivolity, geniality, good humor, happiness, jocundity, joviality, lightness, merriment 10 blitheness, brightness, ebullience, joyousness, liveliness, risibility
gaijin: 9 foreigner
Gai-Jin author: James Clavell
Gail: 3 Max 5 Davis 6 Borden, Devers, Fisher, Godwin, O'Grady, Sheehy 7 Patrick, Russell 8 Goodrich
Gaillard ___: 3 Cut
gaillardia: 5 plant 6 flower
gaily: 6 gladly 7 merrily
gain: 3 bag, get, net, win 4 earn, find, have, land, make, mend, plus, reap, sake 5 annex, avail, boost, lucre, reach, score, seize 6 accept, attain, garner, gather, growth, look up, obtain, output, perk up, pick up, profit, rack up, return, secure, snatch, spoils 7 accrual, achieve, acquire, advance, benefit, bring in, buildup, capture, harvest, improve, inherit, procure, prosper, realize, receive, recover, recruit, revenue, triumph 8 addition, earnings, get ahead, increase, interest, proceeds, progress, purchase, receipts, winnings 9 accretion, go forward,

increment **10** accomplish, accumulate, annexation, appreciate, attainment, percentage, prosperity, recuperate
altitude: **4** go up, rise **5** climb **6** ascend
a victory: **4** beat, earn, sway, take **5** score, upset **7** achieve, conquer, edge out, prevail, realize, succeed, triumph, trounce **8** overcome **9** overwhelm
ender: **3** say **4** said
entry: **4** come **6** arrive, show up
experience: **3** see **5** glean, study **6** absorb, master, pick up, soak up, take in **7** catch on, find out **8** discover, pore over **9** ascertain, brush up on **10** apprentice, get down pat, understand
ground: **6** pick up **7** advance **8** get ahead, progress **9** go forward
on: **5** reach **7** catch up, close in **8** approach, do better, overtake **9** catch up to
time: **5** dally, delay, stall **6** put off **8** postpone **9** temporize
unlawfully: **3** rob **5** steal **6** thieve **8** shoplift
weight: **4** grow **5** swell, widen **6** expand, fatten, spread **7** broaden, enlarge, fill out, thicken
with difficulty: **5** wrest
gain ___: **4** time **6** ground
___ gain: **5** brain **7** capital
Gain: **9** detergent
alternative: **3** All, Biz, Era, Fab, Yes **4** Bold, Dash, Surf, Tide, Wisk **5** Cheer, Dreft, Purex **6** Calgon, Dynamo, Oxydol **7** Octagon **9** Ivory Snow
gainer: **4** dive
place: **4** pool
___ gainer: **4** full, half
Gaines: **4** Bill
mag: **3** MAD
Gaines, Ernest J.: **6** author, writer
Gainesville: **4** city, town
athletes: **6** Gators
locale: **7** Florida, Georgia
neighbor: **5** Ocala
gainful: **6** useful **8** salutary **9** lucrative, rewarding **10** beneficial, productive, profitable, well-paying, worthwhile
employment: **3** job **4** post, work **8** position
gainly: **8** graceful
gainsay: **4** deny **5** belie **6** impugn, negate, oppose, refute **7** disavow, dispute **8** disclaim **9** disaffirm, repudiate **10** contradict, contravene, controvert, disconfirm
gainsaying: **6** denial **7** opposed **8** negation, negative, opposing
Gainsborough, Thomas: **6** artist **7** British, painter
homeland: **7** England
work: **3** oil **7** Blue Boy **8** portrait
gains, ill-gotten: **4** loot, pelf **5** booty, grift, lucre
gainst: **6** contra **7** counter **8** contrary, opposite **9** opposed to
gait: **3** jog, run **4** clip, lope, pace, rate, step, trot, walk **5** amble, march, speed, strut, tread **6** canter, gallop, stride **8** carriage, galopade, rapidity **9** gallopade
antelope ~: **4** stot
horse's ~: **4** lope, pace, trot **6** canter, gallop
gaiter: **4** spat **5** putty **6** puttee, puttie **7** gambado, legging
Gaithersburg: **4** city, town
locale: **8** Maryland
Gaius: **7** Macenas **9** Petronius
garment: **4** toga
Gajdusek, Carleton: **8** Nobelist
gal: **3** she **4** lady, lass **5** woman **6** female, madame, person
Friday: **4** asst. **6** helper **9** assistant
gunsel's ~: **4** moll
of song: **3** Sal
palindromic ~: **3** Ada, Ava, Eve, Lil, Nan **4** Anna **6** Hannah
partner: **3** guy
see also woman
gal ___: **3** pal **6** Friday
gal.
fraction: **2** oz., pt., qt.
Gal.
follower: **3** Eph.
gala: **2** do **3** hop **4** ball, bash, fest, fete, prom **5** big do, blast, dance, feast, party, revel, roast, showy **6** affair, festal, fiesta, soiree **7** benefit, blowout, festive, jubilee, pageant, shindig, special **8** clambake, festival, function, jamboree, wingding **9** convivial, festivity **10** fund-raiser
wear: **3** tux **4** gown **5** tails **6** tuxedo
Gala: **5** apple
relative: **4** crab, Lodi, Rome **5** Mutsu **6** Empire, Ida Red, medlar, Pippin, russet **7** Baldwin, Bramley, costard, Freedom, Liberty, Spartan, Wealthy, Winesap **8** Cortland, Jonathan, McIntosh **10** Rome Beauty
galactic
distance unit: **4** lt. yr. **9** light year
time period: **3** age, eon **4** aeon
galactic ___: **4** pole, year **5** plane **6** circle, nebula **7** cluster, equator
galago: **6** mammal **7** primate **8** bush baby
relative: **3** ape **4** saki, titi **5** chimp, drill, jocko, lemur, loris, magot, orang, potto, shrew **6** aye-aye, baboon, Bandar, gelada, gibbon, grivet, guenon, howler, langur, macaco, monkey, rhesus, uakari, vervet **7** colobus, gorilla, guereza, hoolock, macaque, sapajou, siamang, tamarin, tarsier **8** capuchin, mandrill, mangabey, marmoset, talapoin **9** orangutan **10** Barbary ape, chimpanzee, orangutang
galah: **4** bird
Galahad: **3** Sir **4** hero
garb: **5** armor
go against ~: **4** list, tilt **5** joust
like ~: **4** pure **6** chaste, devout **8** spotless, virtuous **9** exemplary, lily-white, stainless, uncorrupt
mother: **6** Elaine
weapon: **5** lance
___ Galahad: **3** Kid, Sir
Galan: **4** peak **5** mount **8** mountain
locale: **5** Andes **9** Argentina
Galant: **3** car **4** auto **10** Mitsubishi
___ galante: **4** fête
Galápagos: **4** isls. **5** isles **7** islands
beast: **6** iguana
Gala Performance artist: **4** Erté
Galarraga, Andres sport: **8** baseball
galatea: **6** fabric **8** material
Galatea: **4** moon **6** Nereid
lover of ~: **4** Acis
parent of ~: **5** Doris **6** Nereus
planet: **7** Neptune
Galati: **4** city, town
locale: **7** Romania, Rumania **8** Roumania
Galatia capital: **6** Angora, Ankara
Galatians follower: **9** Ephesians
galax: **9** coltsfoot **10** beetleweed
Galaxie: **3** car **4** auto, Ford **10** automobile
galaxy: **6** cosmos **8** Milky Way **10** star system
starter: **4** meta
unit: **4** star **6** planet
___ galaxy: **4** ring **5** radio **6** spiral **7** Seyfert
Galaxy Quest (1999 film)
cast: Tim Allen, Alan Rickman, Sigourney Weaver
Galba: **5** Roman **6** Caesar
garment: **4** toga
predecessor: **4** Nero
see also Latin
Galbraith, J.K. subj.: **4** econ.
gale: **4** blow, gust, wind **5** blast, noser, storm **6** squall **7** cyclone, tempest **9** windstorm
out of the ~: **4** alee
gale ___: **5** force **7** warning
___ gale: **4** line **5** fresh, sweet, whole **6** strong
Gale: **4** Zona **5** Storm **6** Gordon, Sayers **7** Dorothy, Garnett
dog: **4** Toto
Gale ___ Hurd: **3** Ann
Galeao Airport locale: **3** Rio
galena: **3** ore, PbS **7** lead ore, mineral
Galena: **4** city, town
locale: **8** Illinois
Galeras: **7** volcano
locale: **8** Colombia
Galesburg: **4** city, town
locale: **8** Illinois
Gale, Zona: **6** author, writer
work: Miss Lulu Bett
Galibi: **6** Indian **7** Amerind
Galilean tetrarch: **5** Herod
Galilee: **3** sea
locale: **6** Israel **7** Mideast
town: **4** Acre, Cana
___ Galilee: **5** Man of, Sea of
Galileo: **5** probe **7** Galilei **10** astronomer
home: **4** Pisa **5** Italy
launcher: **4** NASA
galimatias: **3** gas, rot **4** blah, bosh, bull, bunk, guff, jazz, jive, pooh, tosh **5** bilge, fudge, hokum, hooey, prate, stuff, trash, tripe **6** bunkum, bushwa, drivel, footle, gabble, gammon, gibber, havers, hot air, humbug, jabber, jargon, kibosh, piffle **7** baloney, blarney, blather, blether, boloney, bushwah, eyewash, flannel, flubdub, fustian, garbage, hogwash, inanity, rubbish, twaddle **8** buncombe, claptrap, falderal, falderol, flimflam, flummery, folderal, folderol, nonsense, slipslop, tommyrot, trumpery **9** banana oil, gibberish, kidstakes, moonshine, poppycock, rigmarole **10** applesauce, balderdash, bilge water, codswallop, double-talk, flapdoodle, Jabberwock, mumbo jumbo, rigamarole, taradiddle
Gal in ___, A: **6** Calico
Galina: **7** Ulanova
___ gal in Kalamazoo: **5** I got a
gall: **3** bug, get, irk, vex **4** bait, bile, burn, pain, rage, rile, roil, wear **5** anger, annoy, brass, chafe, cheek, crust, grate, harry, nerve, peeve, pique, sauce, scuff, spite, upset, venom **6** abrade, bother, fester, harass, offend, plague, pother, put out, rancor, rankle, ruffle, scrape **7** bedevil, disturb, dudgeon, enflame, hauteur, inflame, provoke, torment, trouble **8** audacity, boldness, chutzpah, exercise, irritate, temerity **9** aggravate, arrogance, brashness, displease, excoriate, impudence, insolence, sauciness **10** bitterness, brazenness, effrontery, exasperate, irritation, resentment
bladder neighbor: **5** liver
combining form: **4** chol- **5** chole-, cholo-
ender: **3** fly, nut **5** stone **7** bladder
starter: **3** nut
gall ___: **4** gnat, mite, wasp **5** midge **7** bladder
___ gall: **3** oak **5** crown, glass **6** Aleppo
Gallagher: **5** Helen, Peter **7** Gateley
partner: **5** Shean
Gallagher, Peter: **5** actor
film: The Player (1992)
sex, lies, and videotape (1989)
To Gillian on Her 37th Birthday (1996)
Watch It (1993)
While You Were Sleeping (1995)
Galla home: **5** Kenya **6** Africa **8** Ethiopia
gallant: **4** bold, game, kind **5** brave, grand, gutsy, lofty, nervy, noble, suave, swain, wooer **6** awless, daring, gritty, heroic, kindly, knight, plucky, polite, spunky, urbane **7** aweless, courtly, dashing, defiant, doughty, heedful, impavid, mindful, stately, staunch, tactful, valiant **8** fearless, glorious, gracious, heroical, highbred, intrepid, knightly, obliging, resolute, splendid, stalwart, unafraid, valorous, well-bred **9** attentive, audacious, courteous, dauntless, dignified, dreadless, honorable, inamorato, libertine, sensitive, undaunted, unfearful, unfearing, unselfish **10** chivalrous, courageous, jack-a-dandy, thoughtful, undismayed
country ~: **5** swain
starter: **3** top **7** foretop
Gallant ___; The: **5** Hours **7** Seventh
Gallant Hours, The (1960 film)
cast: James Cagney, Ward Costello, Dennis Weaver
Gallant Lords of Bois-Dori, The
author: George Sand
Gallant, Mavis: **6** author, writer **8** Canadian
gallantry: **4** tact **5** heart, honor, nerve, pluck, poise, valor **6** daring, mettle **7** bravery, courage, heroism, prowess **8** audacity, boldness, civility, courtesy, nobility, urbanity, valiance, valiancy **9** deference, derring-do **10** attentions, politeness, resolution
Gallant Seventh, The composer: **5** Sousa
Gallatin: **4** city, town **6** Albert
locale: **9** Tennessee
Gallaudet communication: **3** ASL
galled: **5** angry, irate, riled, vexed **6** fuming, piqued **7** annoyed, steamed **8** incensed **9** indignant, irritated, ticked off
Gallegos, Rómulo: **6** author, writer **10** Venezuelan
galleon: **4** boat **6** argosy, vessel **8** sailboat
cargo: **3** oro
need: **4** boom, mast, pole, post, spar **6** mizzen, timber **8** flagpole
worker: **5** rower
gallery: **4** hall, loge, tier **5** salon **6** arcade, loggia, lyceum, museum **7** balcony, hearers, ingress **8** audience, showroom **9** listeners, mezzanine, onlookers, witnesses **10** spectators
display: **3** art **5** easel, op art
gallery ___: **4** wire **5** strip **6** forest
___ gallery: **3** fly **4** long **5** press **6** peanut, rogue's **7** winning
___ Gallery: **5** Night
gallet: **4** chip **5** spall, stone
galley: **4** boat, ship **5** proof **6** bireme **7** kitchen, trireme **8** sailboat **10** manuscript
ancient ~: **6** bireme **7** trireme
directive: **4** dele, stet

glitch: 4 typo 7 erratum 8 misprint
implement: 3 oar
space in a ~: 4 quad 6 em quad, en quad
stall a ~: 6 becalm
worker: 3 oar 5 rower 6 editor, writer 8 redactor
galley ___: 5 proof, slave
galleys, work on: 4 edit
Gallia ___ omnis...: 3 est
Galliano flavoring: 5 anise
galliard: 5 dance
Galliard: 4 font 8 typeface
Gallic: 6 French
Gallico: 4 Paul
Galli-Curci, Amelita: 6 singer 7 soprano
specialty: 5 opera
___ Gallienne: 5 Eva Le
Galligan: 4 Zach
gallimaufry: 4 hash, olio, stew 6 jumble, medley, ragout 7 farrago, mélange, mixture 8 mishmash 9 potpourri 10 hodgepodge, miscellany, salmagundi
Gallinas: 4 cape
locale: 5 S. Amer. 8 Colombia
galling: 6 bitter 7 onerous 8 abrasive, worrying 10 irritating
gallinipper: 3 bug 6 insect
gallinule: 4 bird
Gallipoli: 9 peninsula
cape: 6 Helles
locale: 6 Turkey
Gallipoli (1981 film)
cast: Mel Gibson, Bill Kerr, Mark Lee
director: Peter Weir
Gallipoli author: Alan Moorehead
gallium: 5 metal 7 element
gallivant: 3 gad 4 roam, rove 5 drift, jaunt, range, stray, tramp 6 cruise, ramble, trapes, wander 7 meander, traipse 8 ambulate, gad about 9 run around 10 knock about
gallivanting: 6 errant, roving 7 roaming 9 wandering
Gallo: 4 Bill 5 Julio 6 Ernest
gallon: 4 meas. 7 measure
fraction: 2 oz., pt., qt. 4 pint 5 ounce, quart
___ gallon: 4 wine 7 British
___-gallon: 4 half
___-gallon hat: 3 ten
gallop: 3 fly, hie, rip, run, zip 4 bolt, dart, dash, flit, gait, pace, race, ride, rush, step, tear, zoom 5 hurry, scoot, speed 6 barrel, canter, hasten, hustle, move it, rocket, scurry, sprint 7 floor it, hop to it, quicken, scamper 8 step on it 9 go swiftly, hotfoot it, shake a leg, skedaddle 10 get a move on, hightail it
at full ~: 4 fast 5 apace 7 hastily, quickly, rapidly, swiftly 8 pell-mell, speedily 9 posthaste
ender: 3 ade
relative: 3 jog 4 trot 6 canter
___ gallop: 3 at a
galloper: 5 horse
galloping: 5 rapid, swift 6 flying, speedy 9 whirlwind
Galloping Gourmet, The: Graham Kerr
Galloway: 3 cow, Don 4 bull 6 bovine, cattle
gallows ___: 5 bitts, frame, humor
Gallup: 4 city, town 6 George
activity: 4 poll
colleague: 5 Roper 6 Harris
locale: 9 New Mexico
galoot: 2 ox 3 ape, lug, oaf 4 bozo, dolt, goon, lout 5 klutz 6 big ape, codger, lubber 7 bumpkin, jackass, Palooka 9 eccentric, harebrain
galop: 5 dance, music
ender: 3 ade
galore: 4 much 5 à gogo, amply 7 all over, aplenty, liberal, profuse, to spare 9 in a big way, in bunches 10 in quantity
galosh: 4 boot, shoe 6 rubber 8 footwear, overshoe
relative: 4 boot 5 wader 8 overshoe
___ Gal Sunday: 3 Our
Galsworthy, John: 6 author, writer 7 British 8 Nobelist 10 playwright
group founded by: PEN
heroine: 5 Irene
work: The Forsyte Saga To Let
Galt: 4 city, town
locale: 10 California
Galton, Francis: 10 geneticist
galumph: 4 plod 5 stump 6 lumber
galumphing: 6 clumsy 7 awkward 9 ponderous 10 cumbersome
Galvani: 5 Luigi
galvanic ___: 4 cell, pile 6 couple 7 battery
galvanization material: 4 zinc
galvanize: 4 fire, jolt, move, prod, spur, stir, wake, zinc 5 hop up, pique, prime, rouse, shock, spark, waken 6 arouse, awaken, excite, fire up, thrill 7 animate, enliven, inspire, provoke, quicken, startle 8 dynamize, energize, enspirit, inspirit, motivate 9 electrify, encourage, impassion, stimulate 10 invigorate
galvanized ___: 4 iron 5 steel
galvanometer measure: 3 amp 7 current
Galveston: 3 bay 4 city, port, town
locale: 5 Texas
Galveston ___: 3 Bay 4 plan
Galveston (1969 song) artist: Glen Campbell
Gálvez, Manuel: 6 author, writer 9 Argentine
Galway: 4 city, town 5 James 7 Kinnell
island group: 4 Aran 5 Arans
locale: 4 Eire, Erin 7 Ireland
Galway, James: 5 Irish 7 flutist 8 flautist
gam: 4 limb 5 shank, visit 7 meeting
Gam: 4 Rita
gama: 5 grass
Gamal ___ Nasser: 5 Abdel
Gamalama: 7 volcano
locale: 4 Asia 9 Indonesia
Gamay: 3 red 4 wine 5 grape 7 red wine
origin: 6 France
relative: 5 pinot, Tokay 6 Merlot 7 Catawba, Concord, Niagara 8 Cabernet, malvasia, muscatel 9 muscadine, Sauvignon, zinfandel 10 Chardonnay
gambado: 4 jump, spat 6 gaiter, puttee 7 legging
Gambia: 5 river 6 nation 7 country
bovine: 5 N'dama
capital: 6 Banjul
language: 7 Malinke
money: 5 butut 6 dalasi
neighbor: 7 Senegal
gambit: 4 plan, plot, ploy, ruse, trap, wile 5 feint, shift, trick 6 device 7 gimmick, sleight 8 artifice, maneuver, strategy 9 stratagem
Gambit: 8 game show
host: Wink Martindale
Gambit (1966 film)
cast: Michael Caine, Herbert Lom, Shirley MacLaine
director: Ronald Neame
gamble: 3 bet, lay 4 dare, dice, play, risk, shot, stab 5 flier, fling, flyer, stake, wager 6 chance, hazard 7 venture 8 chance it, long shot, make book 9 speculate 10 go for broke, jeopardize, take a flyer
away: 4 blow, lose 5 waste 6 misuse 7 fribble 8 squander 9 dissipate 10 run through
badly: 4 lose
on: 5 trust 7 believe
(on): 4 bank, rely 5 count 6 depend
gambled: 7 at stake
gambler: 5 sport 6 better, bettor, punter, risker 7 plunger, wagerer 8 gamester 9 bookmaker, risk-taker 10 adventurer, speculator
consideration: 4 edge, odds 7 chances 8 handicap
cube: 3 die
loss: 5 shirt
mecca: 3 OTB 4 Reno 5 Tahoe, Vegas 6 casino, Nevada 8 Las Vegas
need: 4 luck 5 stake
pass: 5 no bet
pot: 5 chips, kitty
Gambler, The (1978 song) artist: Kenny Rogers
Gambler, The author: Fyodor Dostoyevsky
gambling
establishment: 5 house 6 casino
game: 3 loo 4 faro, keno 5 beano, bingo, craps, lotto, monte, poker 6 fan-tan 7 lottery 8 baccarat 9 blackjack, twenty-one
stake: 4 ante
gambling ___: 3 den 5 house
gambol: 4 joke, lark, play, romp, skip 5 caper, dance, frisk, revel, sport, spree 6 cavort, frolic, prance, spring 7 carry on, roister, rollick 8 recreate 9 have a ball, whoop it up 10 fool around
gamboling: 6 frisky, lively 7 coltish, playful 8 sportive 10 frolicsome
gambrel ___: 4 roof 5 stick
gambusia: 4 fish
game: 3 gin, job, lay, loo, tag, toy, uno, war 4 bold, Clue, faro, keno, lame, Myst, play, ploy, Pong, pool, prey, Risk, ruse, skat, stud 5 beano, bingo, brave, chess, craps, darts, eager, event, ghost, gutsy, hardy, jacks, Jotto, lotto, match, monte, nervy, omber, Pedro, pente, pitch, poker, prank, ready, rummy, shogi, skeet, Sorry, spoof, sport, stake, tarok, trade, trick, wager, whist 6 awless, belote, Boggle, bridge, casino, daring, écarté, euchre, fan-tan, feisty, go fish, gritty, hearts, heroic, hockey, Pac-Man, plucky, quarry, quoits, racket, spunky, squash, Tetris 7 aweless, belotte, canasta, Careers, contest, cricket, croquet, curling, defiant, doughty, gallant, marbles, old maid, Othello, pachisi, pastime, pinball, pursuit, seven-up, snooker, staunch, tenpins, valiant, venison, willing 8 amenable, baccarat, baseball, charades, checkers, cribbage, disposed, dominoes, draughts, escapade, fearless, football, heroical, intrepid, leapfrog, mah-jongg, Monopoly, ninepins, pachinko, parchesi, parchisi, peekaboo, resolute, ringtoss, Scrabble, skittles, softball, spirited, sporting, sportive, stalwart, Stratego, strategy, unafraid, valorous, vocation 9 amusement, audacious, blackjack, dauntless, diversion, dodgeball, dreadless, specialty, tic-tac-toe, twenty-one, undaunted, unfearful, unfearing, water polo 10 chuck-a-luck, courageous, Donkey Kong, jackstraws, livelihood, mettlesome, post office, profession, recreation, ring-a-levio, tetherball, tournament, undismayed, volleyball
African board ~: 3 bao
animal: 3 elk 4 deer 5 moose, rhino
anybody's ~: 5 close 10 nip and tuck
ball ~: 5 bocce, bocci, lotto, rugby 6 squash 7 jai alai 9 situation
beat the ~: 3 win 7 triumph
be ~ for: 5 allow 6 accede
bird: 4 fowl 5 quail 6 grouse 8 pheasant
board ~: 4 Clue, keno, Risk 5 chess, pente, shogi, Sorry 7 Careers, Othello 8 checkers, Monopoly, Scrabble, Stratego
board square: 5 start
card ~: 3 gin, loo, uno, war 4 faro, jass, skat, stud 5 beano, monte, omber, Pedro, poker, rummy, tarok, whist 6 belote, bridge, casino, écarté, euchre, fan-tan, go fish, hold 'em 7 belotte, canasta 8 baccarat 9 blackjack, twenty-one
center: 4 mall 6 arcade 7 gallery
computer ~: 4 Doom, Myst, Pong 6 Pac-Man, Tetris 10 Donkey Kong
computer ~ maker: 3 NES 4 Sega 5 Atari 7 Genesis 8 Nintendo
con ~: 4 hoax, lure, scam 5 bunco, dodge, fraud, sting 6 dupery, humbug, racket 7 knavery 8 trickery 9 deception 10 illegality
counting ~: 3 nim
cry: 4 I win
dice ~: 5 craps 7 Yahtzee 8 Monopoly 10 backgammon
dish: 5 salmi 6 salmis
ender: 4 cock, some, ster 6 keeper
factor: 4 luck 5 skill
fish: 4 bass, cero, tuna, ulua 5 trout, wahoo 6 marlin, tarpon 7 cavalla, walleye 9 barracuda
five-in-a-row ~: 4 keno 5 bingo, pente
(for): 3 hot 5 ready
gambling ~: 3 loo 4 faro, keno 5 beano, bingo, craps, lotto, monte, poker 6 écarté, fan-tan 8 baccarat 9 blackjack, twenty-one
get in the ~: 4 ante 6 ante up
go after ~: 4 hunt 5 chase, stalk, track 6 forage
item: 3 die 4 cube 5 board
kids' ~: 3 tag, war 4 I spy 5 catch, jacks, potsy, t-ball 6 Cootie, go fish 9 hopscotch
knocking ~: 3 gin 5 rummy
lawn ~: 4 polo 5 bocci, roque 6 tennis
little ~: 4 plot, trap 5 cabal 6 racket, scheme 8 intrigue 9 coalition, collusion, treachery 10 complicity, connivance, conspiracy, disloyalty
make ~ of: 3 rag 4 gibe, jeer, jibe, mock 5 taunt, tease 7 scoff at 8 ridicule
mallet ~: 4 polo 5 roque 7 croquet
name in ~ shows: 3 Pat 4 Alex, Merv
name of the ~: 5 point 7 meaning, reality
net ~: 6 hockey, tennis 8 Ping-Pong 9 badminton
New Year's ~: 4 Bowl 8 Rose Bowl 10 Cotton Bowl, Orange Bowl
numbers ~: 4 keno 5 beano, bingo, lotto 7 lottery
one: 5 trier
opener: 3 bet 4 ante 5 stake, wager
outdoor ~: 4 golf, polo 6 tennis 7 croquet 8 baseball, football, softball
park: 3 zoo
participant: 4 side, team 6 player
piece: 3 man 4 pawn 6 domino
plan: 4 idea, plan, ruse 5 model

6 design, scheme 8 scenario, strategy, time line 9 blueprint
  play the ~: 5 yield 6 accept 7 conform, go along 9 cooperate 10 keep in step, toe the mark
  pub ~: 4 pool 5 darts 9 billiards
  punting ~: 5 rugby 6 soccer 8 football
  racket ~: 6 squash, tennis 8 Ping-Pong 9 badminton
  run a ~ on: 2 do 3 con 4 bilk, burn, clip, dupe, fool, gull, hoax, rook, scam, snow 5 cheat, gouge, hocus, set up, shaft, sting, trick 6 fleece, hustle, rip off, rope in, take in 7 deceive, defraud, fake out, swindle 8 flimflam, hoodwink 9 bamboozle, four-flush, shake down, victimize
  shell ~: 5 cheat 7 swindle 8 trickery 9 collusion
  starter: 3 end 4 ball
  still in the ~: 4 live 5 alive
  take out of the ~: 5 bench
  unit: 3 set
  what the ~ may be: 5 afoot
  win every ~: 5 sweep 7 clean up
  with a jackpot: 7 lottery
  word ~: 5 ghost, Jotto 6 Boggle 8 Scrabble
game __: 3 law 4 bird, fish, fowl, park, plan, room, show 5 point 6 theory, warden
game, __, match: 3 set
__ game: 3 big, con, end, war 4 ball, bowl, card, draw, fair, long, love, mind, mug's, skin, word 5 board, no-hit, Ponzi, shell, short, small, video 6 arcade, badger, middle, parlor, pepper, rubber 7 numbers, perfect, singing, waiting, zero-sum
__ Game: 4 Skin 5 He Got 6 Wicked 7 All-Star
Game Boy man: 5 Mario
  rival: 4 Sega
__ game in town, the: 4 only
game is __, The: 5 afoot
gamekeeper: 6 warden
gamelan instrument: 4 gong
gameness: 4 grit 5 nerve, pluck, spunk 6 mettle
game of __: 5 skill 6 chance
games: 5 sport 9 athletics, merriment 10 recreation
  companion: 3 fun
  ender: 3 man, men
  play ~: 3 toy 6 manage, trifle 8 maneuver 9 machinate 10 manipulate
  Roman ~: 4 ludi
  six ~: 3 set
  war ~: 5 drill
__ games: 3 war 4 mind, play
Games __ Play: 6 People
__ Games: 4 Mind 6 Nemean, Summer, Winter 7 Foolish, Olympic, Patriot, Pythian 8 Goodwill
Games for the Superintelligent author: 4 Fixx
game show
  group: 5 panel
  name: 3 Pat 4 Alex, Wink 5 Vanna
  sound: 4 ding 6 buzzer
  winnings: 3 car 4 cash, loot, trip 5 prize 6 cruise
  worker: 2 MC 4 host 5 emcee, model
__-game show: 3 pre
Game Show Network program: 5 Lingo
gamesmanship, practice: 5 psych
gamesome: 6 jaunty
Games People Play author: 5 Berne
Games People Play (song) artist: Alan Parsons Project, Joe South, Spinners
gamester: 6 better, bettor 7 gambler
  emulate a ~: 3 bet, lay 4 ante, play, risk 5 hedge, stake, wager 6 gamble, hazard, parlay 8 make book 9 challenge
gamete: 3 egg 4 germ, seed 8 germ cell
  source: 5 monad
Game, The (1997 film)
  cast: Carroll Baker, Michael Douglas, Sean Penn
__ Game, The: 3 Gin, War 4 Name 5 Lion's, Match 6 Circle, Crying, Dating, Dinner, Mating, Pajama
Game, The author: A.S. Byatt
gamin: 3 imp, kid 4 waif 6 urchin 10 jackanapes, ragamuffin
gaming __: 5 table
gamma: 5 Greek 6 letter
  follower: 5 delta
  preceder: 4 beta
gamma __: 3 ray 4 iron 5 decay 6 camera
Gamma: 4 font 8 typeface
gamma ray product: 3 ion
gammon: 3 gas, ham, rot, win 4 beat, blah, bosh, bull, bunk, guff, jazz, jive, pooh, tosh 5 bilge, fudge, hokum, hooey, prate, stuff, trash, tripe 6 bunkum, bushwa, drivel, footle, gabble, gibber, havers, hot air, humbug, jabber, jargon, kibosh, piffle 7 baloney, blarney, blather, blether, boloney, bushwah, eyewash, flannel, flubdub, fustian, garbage, hogwash, inanity, rubbish, twaddle 8 buncombe, claptrap, falderal, falderol, flimflam, flummery, folderal, folderol, nonsense, slipslop, tommyrot, trumpery 9 banana oil, gibberish, kidstakes, moonshine, poppycock, rigmarole, smoked ham 10 applesauce, balderdash, bilge water, codswallop, double-talk, flapdoodle, galimatias, Jabberwock, mumbo jumbo, rigamarole, taradiddle
gamophobe fear: 7 wedlock 8 marriage 9 matrimony
Gamow, George: 9 physicist, scientist
gamp: 6 brolly 8 umbrella
Gam, Rita spouse: Sidney Lumet
gamut: 4 A to Z, span 5 field, range, reach, scale, scope, sweep 6 extent 7 breadth, compass 8 panorama, spectrum 9 full-range
...gamut of emotions from __: 4 A to B
gamy: 4 rank 6 rancid, risque 7 corrupt, tainted 10 malodorous
Gance: 4 Abel
gander: 2 he 4 bird, look, male, peek, peep, view 5 goose 6 glance 7 glimpse 8 once-over
  take a ~: 3 eye 4 look, scan, view
Gandhi: 6 Indira 7 Mahatma 8 Mohandas
Gandhi (1982 film)
  cast: Candice Bergen, Edward Fox, John Gielgud, Ben Kingsley
  director: Richard Attenborough
Gandhi __: 3 cap
Gandhi, Indira father: 5 Nehru
Gandhi, Mahatma: 5 Hindu 6 Hindoo
  associate: 5 Nehru
  foe: 3 Raj
  home: 5 India
Gandolfini, James: 5 actor
  film: Angie (1994)
    The Man Who Wasn't There (2001)
    Terminal Velocity (1994)
  TV: The Sopranos
__ Gandolfo: 6 Castel
gandy __: 6 dancer
ganef: 5 crook, rogue, thief 6 rascal 8 chiseler, swindler 9 scoundrel
  job: 5 heist
gang: 3 lot, mob, set 4 band, clan, club, crew, herd, Jets, pack, ring, team 5 bunch, covey, crowd, group, hands, horde, junto, posse, squad, troop 6 clique, league, muster, outfit, rabble, Sharks, troupe 7 cluster, company, coterie, in-group, society 9 syndicate 10 assemblage
  around: 4 herd, meet 5 bunch, crowd, flock, group, rally, swarm 6 gather, muster 7 bunch up, collect, compile, convene, hang out 8 assemble 9 forgather 10 congregate, rendezvous
  ender: 3 way 4 land, plow, ster 5 plank, punch 6 buster
  member: 4 goon, hood 5 biker, tough
  see the old ~: 5 reune 6 remeet
  territory: 4 turf
  up: 5 group 8 assemble 10 join forces
  up on: 4 rush 5 blitz 6 attack 7 assault 8 overcome
  weapon: 3 gat 4 shiv 5 knife
gang __: 3 saw 4 hook, plow, up on 5 drill 6 switch
__ gang: 4 deck, iron, road 5 black, chain, press 7 section
__ Gang: 3 Our 5 Andy's, Chain
...gang aft __: 5 agley
__ gangbusters: 4 like
Ganges: 5 river
  city on the ~: 5 Patna 7 Benares
  dress: 4 sari 5 saree
  locale: 5 India
  river to the ~: 5 Jumna 6 Yamuna
gangland girl: 4 moll
ganglia: 6 nerves
gangling: 4 lank, lean, long, tall, thin 5 lanky, leggy, rangy 6 meager, skinny 7 awkward, spindly, stringy 8 rambling, rawboned 10 long-legged
__ ganglion: 5 basal 6 spinal
gangly: 4 lank, lean, slim, tall, thin, wiry 5 lanky, rangy, spare 6 dainty, meager, skinny, slight, slinky, svelte, twiggy 7 awkward, gracile, scraggy, scrawny, slender, spidery, spindly, willowy 9 sylphlike
Gang of __: 4 Four
gangplank: 4 ramp 6 access
  use the ~: 6 debark
gangsta __: 3 rap
Gangsta Lean (1993 song) artist: D.R.S.
Gangsta's Paradise (1995 song) artist: Coolio
gangster: 4 goon, hood, thug 5 crook, tough 6 bandit, gunsel, outlaw 7 brigand, hoodlum, mobster, ruffian 8 evildoer, hooligan, tough guy 9 desperado, racketeer
  ender: 3 dom
  girl: 4 moll
gangsters: 3 mob 5 Mafia 9 syndicate 10 underworld
__ Gang, The: 7 Capital, Grissom
gangway: 4 ramp, walk 5 aisle 7 ingress
gankogui: 5 bells 10 percussion
  origin: 6 Africa
gannet: 4 bird 5 booby, solan 7 seabird 8 sea goose
Gannon University locale: 4 Erie
ganoid fish: 3 gar 6 bowfin 7 grindle
Gant: 3 Ron 6 Eugene
gantline: 4 rope
Gant, Ron sport: 8 baseball
Gantry: 5 Elmer
Ganymede: 4 moon
  parent of ~: 4 Tros 9 Callirhoe
  planet: 7 Jupiter
gaol: 4 jail 6 prison 7 bastile 8 bastille
Gaolao: 3 cow 4 bull 6 bovine, cattle
gaoler: 5 guard 6 jailer, warden 7 turnkey
GAO part: 3 Gen., Off. 5 Acctg. 6 Office 7 General 10 Accounting
Gao Xingjian: 6 writer 8 Nobelist
gap: 4 gulf, hole, lull, open, pass, rest, rift, vent, void, yawn 5 break, chasm, cleft, crack, gorge, gulch, gully, lapse, pause, space, split 6 breach, cavity, cesura, cranny, divide, gulley, hiatus, hollow, lacuna, ravine, recess, vacuum 7 caesura, crevice, interim, opening, respite, vacancy, vacuity 8 aperture, cleavage, distance, division, fracture, interval, omission, weakness 9 clearance, disparity, interlude 10 difference, divergence, interspace, interstice, passageway, separation
  bridge the ~: 3 aid 6 assist 8 tide over 9 help along 10 see through
  filler: 4 shim
  generation ~: 4 gulf 5 break, split 10 alienation
  in time: 4 stay 5 delay, hitch, pause, stall 6 holdup 7 respite, setback 8 interval, reprieve, slowdown, stoppage 9 deferment, extension, interlude 10 standstill, suspension
  narrow the ~: 4 gain, near 5 close 7 catch up, close in 8 approach, overtake
  starter: 4 stop
__ gap: 3 air 4 wind 5 spark, water 6 dollar, gender 7 missile, seismic
gape: 3 see 4 gawk, gaze, look, open, peer, rift, yawn 5 split, stare 6 goggle, marvel 10 separation
  at: 3 eye 4 view 5 watch
  make ~: 3 awe 4 daze, rock, stun 5 amaze, floor 6 bemuse, boggle, dazzle, thrill 7 astound, nonplus 8 astonish, blow away, bowl over, confound, transfix 9 dumbfound, take aback
gaper: 4 clam
gaping: 4 awed, open, vast, wide 5 broad 6 amazed, astare, rictus 7 yawning 8 wide open 9 cavernous 10 slack-jawed
  hole: 3 maw 5 abyss, chasm
gar: 4 fish 8 billfish 10 needlefish
  ender: 4 fish, pike
garage: 4 shop 5 depot 6 hangar
  bus ~: 4 barn
  do ~ work: 4 lube 5 align, aline
  item: 4 jack, tool 5 gizmo 6 gadget 7 machine, vehicle 9 implement
  occupant: 3 bus, car 4 auto
  sale sign: 4 as is, sold
  sign: 4 Exit, Park 5 Enter
garage __: 4 band, sale
garage-__ opener: 4 door
Garagiola: 3 Joe
Garamond: 4 font 8 typeface
Garand: 3 gun 5 rifle 6 weapon
garb: 4 duds, gear, gown, rags, wear 5 array, cover, drape, dress, getup, habit, robes 6 attire, clothe, enrobe, fit out, livery, outfit, rig out, suit up, tog out 7 apparel, bedrape, clothes, costume, deck out, garment, raiment, threads, toggery, uniform 8 accouter, accoutre, clothing, covering, ensemble, garments, glad rags 9 trappings, vestments 10 canonicals, habiliment, Sunday best
  ender: 3 age
  see also clothing, garment
garbage: 3 gas, rot 4 blah, bosh, bull, bunk, guff, jazz, jive, junk, pooh, tosh 5 bilge, dregs, dross, filth, fudge, hokum, hooey, offal, prate, scrap, stuff, swill, trash, tripe, waste 6 bunkum, bushwa, debris, drivel, footle, gabble, gammon, gibber, havers, hot air, humbug, jabber, jargon, kibosh, litter, piffle,

refuse, rubble 7 baloney, blarney, blather, blether, boloney, bushwah, eyewash, flannel, flubdub, fustian, hogwash, inanity, malarky, residue, rubbish, twaddle 8 buncombe, claptrap, detritus, falderal, falderol, flimflam, flummery, folderal, folderol, leavings, malarkey, nonsense, slipslop, tommyrot, trumpery 9 banana oil, gibberish, kidstakes, moonshine, poppycock, rigmarole, scrapings, sweepings 10 applesauce, balderdash, bilge water, codswallop, double-talk, flapdoodle, galimatias, Jabberwock, mumbo jumbo, rigamarole, taradiddle
collector: 6 ashman
disposal button: 5 reset
holder: 4 dump 5 barge 6 ashcan 8 landfill, trash can
pickup place: 4 curb
taking out the ~: 3 job 4 duty, task 5 chore 9 housework
garbage __: 3 bin, can
garbanzo: 4 bean 6 legume
garbed: 4 clad 6 decent
Garber: 7 Matthew
garble: 4 slur, warp 5 color, mix up, slant, twist 6 doctor, jumble 7 confuse, distort 8 misquote, scramble
Garbo, Greta: 7 actress, Swedish
film: Anna Christie (1930)
Anna Karenina (1935)
The Atonement of Gosta Berling (1924)
Camille (1937)
Conquest (1937)
Flesh and the Devil (1927)
Grand Hotel (1932)
The Kiss (1929)
Mata Hari (1932)
Ninotchka (1939)
Queen Christina (1933)
Torrent (1926)
Two-Faced Woman (1941)
A Woman of Affairs (1928)
what ~ wanted to be: 5 alone
Garbo Talks (1984 film)
cast: Anne Bancroft, Carrie Fisher, Catherine Hicks, Ron Silver
director: Sidney Lumet
Garcia: 4 Andy, Gary 5 Jerry 6 Sergio
García: 4 city, town
locale: 6 Mexico 9 Nuevo León
Garcia, Andy: 5 actor
film: Black Rain (1989)
Dead Again (1991)
The Godfather Part III (1990)
Hero (1992)
Just the Ticket (1999)
Ocean's Eleven (2001)
The Untouchables (1987)
When a Man Loves a Woman (1994)
García Lorca, Federico: 4 poet 6 author 7 Spanish
__ García Márquez: 7 Gabriel
Garcia, Sergio: 6 golfer
milieu: 5 links 6 course
org.: 3 PGA
garçon: 6 server, waiter
Garda: 4 lago, lake
locale: 5 Italy
Gard capital: 5 Nîmes
__-garde: 5 avant 7 arrière
garde, avant: 6 exotic 8 original
garden: 3 bed, dig, hoe 4 plot, till, weed, yard 5 court, patch 7 outdoor 8 outdoors 9 cultivate, flower bed
access: 4 gate 7 postern
area: 3 bed 4 path, plot 5 arbor, patch
bane: 4 weed
Biblical ~: 4 Eden
climber: 3 ivy
combining form: 4 -etum
container: 3 pod 4 hull, husk 5 shuck 6 jacket 8 seed case 10 integument
crawler: 4 worm
dweller: 3 Eve 4 Adam 5 brink
feature: 3 row 4 maze, rock 5 arbor 6 gazebo
flower: 4 glad, iris, lily, rose 5 aster, bloom, peony, phlox, tulip, viola 6 azalea, hybrid
hazard: 3 bur 5 brier, spine, thorn 7 bramble, prickle, spicule, sticker
lead up the ~ path: 7 deceive
like an unkempt ~: 5 weedy
material: 4 loam, soil 5 earth
of Eden: 6 utopia
pest: 4 coon, mole, slug 5 aphid, aphis 6 earwig 7 raccoon
products brand: 5 Ortho
spray: 5 zineb 6 fogger
tool: 3 hoe 4 hose, rake 5 edger, spade 6 dibble
variety: 5 usual 8 ordinary, standard
veggie: 3 pea 4 beet, cuke, kail, kale 5 chard 6 carrot, tomato
work in the ~: 3 hoe, sow 4 rake, seed, weed 5 spade
garden __: 3 pea 4 city, sage 5 cress, party, salad 6 center 7 webworm
garden-__: 7 variety
__ garden: 3 tea 4 bear, beer, knot, rock, roof, sunk 5 truck 6 alpine, market, sunken, winter 7 botanic, cutting, kitchen, victory
Garden: 3 MSG 4 Mary
org.: 3 NBA
__ Garden: 4 Rose 5 Olive 6 Covent, Savage, Secret
Gardena: 4 city, town
locale: 10 California
Garden City: 4 town
locale: 7 New York
gardener: 6 farmer, grower 9 caretaker 10 cultivator
at times: 4 hoer 5 hoser, raker
concern: 4 lawn, soil 5 plant, shrub
first ~: 4 Adam
purchase: 4 bulb, lime, seed 5 humus 6 barrow
sci.: 4 hort.
tool: 3 hoe 4 hose, rake 5 edger, spade 6 dibble
Garden Grove: 4 city, town
locale: 10 California
gardenia: 4 tree 5 plant, shrub 6 flower 9 evergreen
relative: 5 ixora 6 coffee, madder 8 cinchona 9 bouvardia
Gardenia, Vincent: 5 actor
film: Bang the Drum Slowly (1973)
Cold Turkey (1971)
Death Wish (1974)
Little Murders (1971)
Little Shop of Horrors (1986)
Moonstruck (1987)
Garden, Mary: 6 singer 7 soprano
specialty: 5 opera
Garden of __, The: 4 Eden 5 Allah
Garden of Earthly Delights, A author: Joyce Carol Oates
Garden of Earthly Delights artist: 5 Bosch
Garden of the Finzi-Continis, The (1971 film)
cast: Helmut Berger, Dominique Sanda
director: Vittorio De Sica
__ Garden of Verses, A: 6 Child's
Garden Party (1972 song) artist: Ricky Nelson
Garden Party, The
author: Katherine Mansfield, Václav Havel
__ Gardens: 3 Kew 5 Busch 6 Tivoli
__ Gardens of Babylon: 7 Hanging
Gardens of Stone (1987 film)
cast: James Caan, Anjelica Huston, James Earl Jones, Mary Stuart Masterson, D.B. Sweeney
director: Francis Ford Coppola
Garden State
see New Jersey
__ Garden, The: 5 Assam, Chalk, Troll 6 Secret
garden-variety: 5 plain, stock 6 common 7 average, humdrum, prosaic 9 prosaical
Gardiner: 8 Reginald
Gardner: 3 Ava, Rea 4 city, Erle, John, peak, town 5 McKay, mount 8 mountain
locale: 10 Antarctica
word in many ~ titles: 4 Case
Gardner, Ava: 7 actress
film: 55 Days at Peking (1963)
The Barefoot Contessa (1954)
The Killers (1946)
The Life and Times of Judge Roy Bean (1972)
Mogambo (1953)
The Night of the Iguana (1964)
On the Beach (1959)
Seven Days in May (1964)
Show Boat (1951)
The Snows of Kilimanjaro (1952)
The Sun Also Rises (1957)
spouse: Mickey Rooney, Artie Shaw, Frank Sinatra
Gardner, Erle Stanley: 6 author, writer
character: Della, Perry, Mason, Street, Burger
pseudonym: A.A. Fair
Gardner, John: 4 poet 6 author, writer
work: Grendel
Gare de __: 4 l'Est
Gareloi: 7 volcano
locale: 6 Alaska
Gare Saint-Lazare painter: 5 Monet
Gareth: 4 font 8 typeface
Garfield: 3 cat, pet 4 city, John, town 5 Allen, comic, James, strip 6 feline
cat: 6 Arlene
Garfield (comic strip)
artist: Jim Davis
character: 3 Jon 4 Odie 6 Arlene
Garfield County, seat of: 4 Enid
Garfield Heights: 4 city, town
locale: 4 Ohio
Garfield, James: president
assassin: 7 Guiteau
had one: 5 beard
home: 4 Ohio
middle name: 5 Abram
opponent: 7 Hancock
V.P.: 6 Arthur
wife: 8 Lucretia
Garfield, John: 5 actor
film: Air Force (1943)
Body and Soul (1947)
The Breaking Point (1950)
Castle on the Hudson (1940)
Daughters Courageous (1939)
Force of Evil (1948)
Gentleman's Agreement (1947)
Humoresque (1946)
Nobody Lives Forever (1946)
Out of the Fog (1941)
The Postman Always Rings Twice (1946)
Pride of the Marines (1945)
The Sea Wolf (1941)
Tortilla Flat (1942)
We Were Strangers (1949)
Garfunkel, Art song: All I Know (1973)
Garfunkel partner: 5 Simon
garganey: 4 bird, duck, fowl
relative: 4 smew, teal 5 eider, Pekin, Rouen, scaup 6 Cayuga, scoter 7 gadwall, mallard, pintail, pochard, redhead, sea duck, widgeon 8 gray duck, mandarin, musk duck, oldsquaw, shoveler, surf duck, wood duck 9 black duck, broadbill, goldeneye, goosander, greenhead, merganser, ruddy duck, sprigtail 10 bufflehead, canvasback, surf scoter, tufted duck
Gargantua: 5 giant
Gargantua and Pantagruel author: François Rabelais
gargantuan: 3 big 4 cast, huge, vast 5 giant, great, jumbo, large 7 hulking, immense, mammoth, massive, sizable, titanic 8 colossal, enormous, gigantic, king-size, oversize, sizeable, towering, whapping, whopping 9 difficult, herculean, humongous, leviathan, monstrous, overlarge 10 monumental, prodigious, stupendous, super-duper, tremendous
Gargan, William: 5 actor
film: Black Fury (1935)
Cheers for Miss Bishop (1941)
She Gets Her Man (1945)
Strange Impersonation (1946)
Sweepings (1933)
They Knew What They Wanted (1940)
You Only Live Once (1937)
gargoyle: 4 ogre 7 monster
garibaldi: 5 shirt
Garibaldi: 8 Giuseppe
birthplace: 4 Nice
garish: 4 loud 5 cheap, crude, gaudy, showy, tacky 6 flashy, tawdry, tinsel, vulgar 7 blatant, glaring, kitschy 8 overdone 9 excessive, tasteless
light: 4 neon
garishness: 5 glare
garland: 3 lei 4 swag 6 anadem, reward, wreath 7 chaplet, coronet, festoon
Garland: 4 city, Judy, town 6 Hamlin 7 Beverly
locale: 5 Texas
Garland, Beverly: 7 actress
film: Pretty Poison (1968)
Where the Red Fern Grows (1974)
TV: My Three Sons
Garland, Hamlin: 6 author, writer
Garland, Judy: 6 singer 7 actress
costar: 4 Lahr 5 Haley 6 Bolger, Rooney
film: A Child Is Waiting (1963)
The Clock (1945)
Easter Parade (1948)
For Me and My Gal (1942)
Girl Crazy (1943)
The Harvey Girls (1946)
In the Good Old Summertime (1949)
Judgment at Nuremberg (1961)
Life Begins for Andy Hardy (1941)
Love Finds Andy Hardy (1938)
Meet Me in St. Louis (1944)
Pigskin Parade (1936)
The Pirate (1948)
A Star Is Born (1954)
Summer Stock (1950)
The Wizard of Oz (1939)
Ziegfeld Follies (1946)
Ziegfeld Girl (1941)
spouse: Vincente Minnelli, David Rose
garlic: 5 bread, spice 6 allium 9 condiment, seasoning
California ~ center: 6 Gilroy
cousin: 4 leek 5 onion 7 shallot
-flavored mayonnaise: 5 aioli
prepare: 5 mince
segment: 5 clove
garlic __: 4 salt 5 bread, chive 7 mustard

__ garlic: 5 giant, hedge
Garlits, Don: 5 racer 9 auto racer
milieu: 5 track
garlopa: 4 fish
garment: 3 aba, alb, fur, tog 4 abba, cape, coat, garb, gown, kilt, maxi, mini, robe, sack, sari, suit, toga, tutu, vest, wear 5 A-line, apron, cloak, dress, frock, getup, jeans, oiler, pants, parka, robes, saree, shawl, shirt, skirt, skort, smock, stole, tunic 6 anorak, attire, blouse, bodice, caftan, halter, jumper, kaftan, kimono, kirtle, livery, outfit, things, tights 7 apparel, chemise, costume, dashiki, leotard, raiment 8 camisole, covering, trousers 9 housecoat, trappings, underwear
African ~: 4 bubu 5 kanzu 6 boubou 7 dashiki
alter a ~: 3 hem 6 take in 7 take out
ancient Greek ~: 6 chiton, peplos, peplus 7 chlamys
attachment: 3 tag
clerical ~: 5 Rabat
draped ~: 4 sari 5 saree
fastener: 4 snap 5 patte 6 button, Velcro, zipper
fisherman's ~: 5 oiler
foundation ~: 5 stays 6 corset, girdle
Indian: 4 sari 5 lungi, saree 6 lungee, lungyi
insert: 5 godet
judicial ~: 4 gown, robe
loose ~: 3 aba 4 abba, robe, sack 5 cloak 6 jumper
Mideast: 3 aba 4 abba, haik, izar 5 burga, burka, haick 6 burkha, chadar, chador, jubbah 7 bourkha, chaddar, chuddar
outer ~: 3 fur 4 coat, robe 5 cloak, parka, stole 6 anorak, jacket 8 raincoat
part: 4 pouf, tuck, vent, yoke 5 bosom, waist 6 revere, revers
Polynesian ~: 5 pareo, pareu 8 lava-lava
Roman: 4 toga 5 stola
size: 2 XL 3 med. 5 large, lge.. sm., small 10 extra large
Turkish ~: 6 caftan, kaftan
under a chasuble: 3 alb
upper ~: 6 jerkin 9 waistcoat
Victorian ~: 6 girdle
with a hood: 4 cowl
woman's ~: 5 dress, middy, skirt, skort 6 blouse, bodice
worker: 6 hemmer, tailor
see also clothes, clothing
garment __: 3 bag
garments: 4 duds, garb, gear, togs, wear 5 array, dress, get-up, robes 6 attire, livery, outfit 7 apparel, clothes, raiment, threads 8 wardrobe 10 habiliment, Sunday best
Garn: 4 Jake 7 senator 9 astronaut
Garneau, Hector: 4 poet 8 Canadian
garner: 3 get, net, win 4 cull, earn, gain, hold, keep, reap, save 5 amass, cache, glean, hoard, lay by, lay up, put by, store 6 corral, gather, retain, roll up, save up 7 acquire, bring in, collect, compile, deposit, harvest, lay away, put away, store up 8 assemble, cumulate, hang onto, hold onto, maintain, put aside, scrape up, stow away 9 stockpile 10 accumulate
Garner: 4 John 5 James 6 Erroll 9 John Nance
Garner, Erroll: 7 pianist 8 composer
genre: 4 jazz
Garner, James: 5 actor
film: The Americanization of Emily (1964)
Boys' Night Out (1962)
Duel at Diablo (1966)
The Great Escape (1963)
Marlowe (1969)
Maverick (1994)
Murphy's Romance (1985)
My Fellow Americans (1996)
Sayonara (1957)
Skin Game (1971)
Space Cowboys (2000)
Sunset (1988)
Support Your Local Gunfighter (1971)
Support Your Local Sheriff (1969)
The Thrill of It All (1963)
Victor/Victoria (1982)
The Wheeler Dealers (1963)
TV: Maverick, The Rockford Files
garnet: 3 gem, red 5 color 6 pyrope 7 mineral 9 almandine, demantoid
month: 7 January
relative: 4 rose, ruby, rust, wine 5 brick, coral, grape, poppy, rusty, sandy 6 cerise, cherry, claret, maroon 7 carmine, crimson, fuchsia, magenta, pimento, scarlet, sultana, vermeil 8 amaranth, cardinal, dubonnet, geranium, rubicund 9 carnation, cranberry, vermilion 10 strawberry
synthetic ~: 3 yag
garnet __: 4 jade 5 paper
Garnett: 3 Tay 4 Gale
Garnett, Tay: 8 director
film: Bataan (1943)
Cause for Alarm (1951)
Cheers for Miss Bishop (1941)
China Seas (1935)
The Cross of Lorraine (1943)
The Fireball (1950)
Joy of Living (1938)
Mrs. Parkington (1944)
One Way Passage (1932)
The Postman Always Rings Twice (1946)
She Couldn't Take It (1935)
Slave Ship (1937)
Soldiers Three (1951)
Stand-In (1937)
Trade Winds (1938)
The Valley of Decision (1945)
__ garni: 7 bouquet
garnierite: 3 ore
Garnier, Robert: 6 French 10 playwright
garnish: 3 top 4 deck, gild, lard, lime, trim 5 adorn, aspic, caper, cress, frill, grace, lemon, olive 6 attach, bedeck, set off 7 enhance, festoon, gussy up, parsley, spiff up 8 beautify, decorate, ornament, spruce up, trimming 9 adornment, embellish 10 decoration
garnished: 9 decorated, elaborate 10 ornamented
Garofalo, Janeane: 7 actress
film: Bye Bye, Love (1995)
Clay Pigeons (1998)
Cop Land (1997)
The Independent (2001)
The Minus Man (1999)
Mystery Men (1999)
Reality Bites (1994)
The Truth About Cats and Dogs (1996)
Wet Hot American Summer (2001)
Garonne: 5 river
city on the ~: 8 Bordeaux, Toulouse
locale: 6 France
river to the ~: 3 Lot
__-Garonne: 5 Haute, Lot-et
__-garou: 4 loup
Garoua: 4 city, town
locale: 8 Cameroon
garpike: 4 fish
garret: 4 loft 5 attic 6 dormer 7 atelier, mansard 8 top floor
Garret: 6 Hobart
Garrett: 3 Pat 4 Brad, Leif, Wang 5 Betty 6 Morris
Garrett, Betty: 7 actress
film: My Sister Eileen (1955)
On the Town (1949)
spouse: Larry Parks
TV: Laverne & Shirley
Garrett, Leif song: I Was Made for Dancin' (1978)
Garrick: 5 David, Utley
Garrick Gaieties, The: 7 musical
songwriter: 4 Hart 7 Rodgers
garrison: 4 base, camp, fort, post 6 casern, occupy 7 caserne, citadel, defense, station 8 barracks, fastness, fortress 10 encampment, stronghold
garrison __: 3 cap 5 house, state
Garrison: 3 Jim 7 Keillor
Garroway: 4 Dave, host 5 emcee
signoff: 5 peace
Garr, Teri: 7 actress
film: The Black Stallion (1979)
Close Encounters of the Third Kind (1977)
Dumb & Dumber (1994)
Head (1968)
Mr. Mom (1983)
Oh, God! (1977)
Tootsie (1982)
Young Frankenstein (1974)
garrulity: 8 babbling 9 jabbering, loquacity, prattling, prolixity, verbosity, wordiness 10 blathering, chattering, chattiness, volubility
garrulous: 4 glib, long 5 gabby, talky, windy, wordy 6 chatty, prolix 7 diffuse, gushing, lengthy, unterse, verbose, voluble 8 babbling, rambling 9 bombastic, expansive, gossiping, prattling, talkative 10 bigmouthed, chattering, discursive, long-winded, loquacious, motormouth, palaverous
Garry: 5 Moore 6 Maddox 7 Trudeau 8 Kasparov, Marshall 9 Shandling
__ Garry Shandling's Show: 3 It's
Garson: 5 Greer, Kanin
Garson, Greer: 7 actress
film: Blossoms in the Dust (1941)
Goodbye, Mr. Chips (1939)
Julia Misbehaves (1948)
Julius Caesar (1953)
Madame Curie (1943)
Mrs. Miniver (1942, AA)
Mrs. Parkington (1944)
Pride and Prejudice (1940)
Random Harvest (1942)
Sunrise at Campobello (1960)
The Valley of Decision (1945)
garter __: 5 snake 6 stitch
garter tosser: 5 groom
Garth: 6 Brooks, Jennie
Garver: 5 Kathy
Garvey: 5 Steve 6 Marcus
Garvey, Steve sport: 8 baseball
Gary: 4 city, Cole, Hart, town 5 Busey, Ewing, Frank, Lewis, Numan, Owens, Sandy 6 Becker, Carter, Cooper, Farmer, Garcia, Grimes, Larson, Oldman, Player, Romain, Sinise, Snyder, Wright 7 Coleman, Collins, Glitter, Merrill, Puckett 8 Burghoff, Graffman, Lockwood, Lorraine
locale: 3 Ind. 7 Indiana
Gary __ and the Playboys: 5 Lewis
Gary __ and the Union Gap: 7 Puckett
Gary, Romain: 6 author, French, writer
Gary U.S. __: 5 Bonds
Garza García: 4 city, town
locale: 6 Mexico 9 Nuevo León
gas: 3 air, rot, yak 4 blah, bosh, bull, bunk, fuel, fume, guff, jazz, jive, neon, pooh, tosh 5 argon, bilge, ethyl, fluid, Freon, fudge, fumes, hokum, hooey, mouth, ozone, prate, radon, speak, steam, stuff, trash, tripe, vapor, xenon 6 bunkum, bushwa, corona, drivel, ethane, ethene, footle, gabble, gammon, gibber, havers, helium, hot air, humbug, jabber, jargon, kibosh, oxygen, petrol, piffle, yammer 7 baloney, blarney, blather, blether, bluster, boloney, bombast, bushwah, chatter, eyewash, flannel, flubdub, fustian, garbage, hogwash, inanity, krypton, methane, premium, regular, rubbish, tankful, twaddle, utility 8 buncombe, chlorine, claptrap, falderal, falderol, firedamp, flimflam, flummery, fluorine, folderal, folderol, high-test, hydrogen, idle talk, nitrogen, nonsense, road sign, slipslop, tommyrot, trumpery, unleaded 9 banana oil, effluvium, gibberish, great time, kidstakes, moonshine, poppycock, rigmarole, wordiness 10 anesthetic, applesauce, balderdash, bilge water, codswallop, double-talk, exhalation, flapdoodle, fossil fuel, galimatias, Jabberwock, mumbo jumbo, rigamarole, taradiddle, yackety-yak
appliance: 5 grill, range, stove 8 barbecue
asset: 6 octane
bill unit: 5 therm 6 therme
combining form: 3 aer-, atm- 4 aero-, mano-
company: 4 util. 7 utility
consumption fig.: 3 mpg
ender: 3 bag 5 house, light, tight, works
fill with ~: 4 fuel 6 aerate
gauge reading: 4 full, half 5 empty 8 half-full
guzzler: 3 car 4 auto, heap 5 crate 6 jalopy, wheels 7 clunker, vehicle 9 limousine 10 automobile
holder: 4 main, pump, tank
inert ~: 4 neon 5 argon, radon, xenon 7 krypton
in physics: 5 state
meter: 5 gauge 9 indicator
natural ~: 8 resource
natural ~ component: 6 ethane 8 dimethyl
noble ~: 4 neon 5 argon, radon, xenon 7 krypton
old ~ brand: 4 Esso 7 Flying A 8 Sinclair
out of ~: 4 beat, worn 5 empty, weary 7 worn-out 8 fatigued 9 enervated, exhausted 10 knocked out
pump ~: 4 fill, fuel 6 fill up, refuel, tank up
quantity: 3 gal. 6 gallon
run out of ~: 3 sag 4 drop, flag, fold, tire, yawn 5 stall, weary 6 fizzle 7 dwindle, poop out 8 collapse
station former freebie: 3 air, map
step on the ~: 4 rush 5 hurry, spank 7 speed up 10 accelerate
word on old ~ pumps: 5 ethyl
see also gasoline
gas __: 3 jet, law, log, tax 4 coal, main, mask, pump, tank, tube, well 5 black, field, meter, pedal, plant, range 6 burner, engine, fitter, liquor, mantle 7 bladder, fitting, furnace, guzzler, station, turbine
gas-__: 5 fired 7 guzzler
__ gas: 3 air 4 blue, coal, tear 5 ideal, inert, marsh, noble, out of, swamp, water 6 leaded 7 bottled, natural, perfect, Pintsch 8 unleaded
__-gas: 3 bio
gasbag: 4 bore 8 blowhard 9 blusterer 10 chatterbox

gascon: 7 boaster, showoff 8 blowhard, braggart, fanfaron 9 know-it-all, swaggerer
ender: 3 ade
gasconade: 4 brag 5 boast, pride 6 hot air 7 bluster, bombast, bravado, talk big 8 boasting
gash: 3 cut 4 hurt, rent, rift, slit, stab, tear 5 gouge, score, slash, slice, wound 6 incise, injury, lesion 7 scratch 8 incision, lacerate 10 interspace, laceration
gashed: 4 torn 7 incised 9 lacerated
Gasherbrum: 4 peak 5 mount 8 mountain
locale: 4 Asia 9 Himalayas
gasify: 8 vaporize
Gaskell, Elizabeth Cleghorn: 6 author, writer 7 British
gasket: 4 ring, seal 5 O-ring
blow a ~: 4 rage, rant 5 freak, go ape
gaslight: 7 lantern
Gaslight (1944 film)
cast: Ingrid Bergman, Charles Boyer, Joseph Cotten
director: George Cukor
Gaslight __: 3 era
gasohol: 4 fuel
gasoline: 4 fuel 5 petro 6 diesel, hi-test, no-lead, petrol 7 premium, regular 8 high-test
additive: 4 lead 5 ethyl
dispenser: 4 pump
measure: 6 gallon
name: 4 Gulf, Hess 5 Amoco, Exxon, Shell, Sohio 6 Sunoco 7 Chevron
platform: 6 island
rating: 6 octane
see also gas
Gasoline __: 5 Alley
gasp: 4 pant, puff, sigh 6 breath, inhale, wheeze 7 breathe 10 inhalation
comics ~: 3 ulp
last ~: 3 end 6 finale, windup, wrap-up 10 conclusion
Gaspar and others: 4 Magi
gasping: 7 gulping
Gaspra: 8 asteroid
gasser: 4 joke, riot 6 scream 9 wisecrack 10 rib-tickler
Gasser, Herbert: 8 Nobelist
Gassman, Vittorio spouse: Shelley Winters
Gas-s-s-s (1970 film)
cast: Robert Corff, Bud Cort, Cindy Williams
director: Roger Corman
Gass, William H.: 6 author, writer
gassy: 4 fumy 6 chatty 7 bloated, miasmic 8 aeriform, boastful, vaporous, volatile 9 bombastic, effluvial
Gastein: 5 falls 9 waterfall
locale: 7 Austria
Gasteyer: 3 Ana
gasthaus: 3 inn 6 German
Gastonia: 4 city, town
locale: 4 N. Car.
gastric __: 4 mill 5 juice
gastronome: 6 foodie 7 epicure, gourmet 8 gourmand 9 epicurean
gastronomy: 4 fare, food, menu 5 table 6 dishes 7 cookery, cooking, cuisine
gastropod: 4 slug 5 murex 6 limpet
gat: 3 gun, rod 5 piece 6 heater, pistol, roscoe 7 firearm
gata: 5 shark
Gatam, grandfather of: 4 Esau
gate: 3 way 4 door, exit, take 5 entry, lucre, stile, torii, valve 6 access, egress, portal, profit, wicket 7 barrier, doorway, ingress, postern, revenue, turnout 8 earnings, entrance, entryway, proceeds, receipts 9 threshold, turnstile 10 attendance
closer: 3 bar 4 bolt, hasp, hook, lock 5 catch, latch 7 padlock
design: 5 grill 6 grille
ender: 3 way 4 fold, post 5 crash, house 6 keeper
figure: 3 att. 4 take 10 attendance
give the ~: 4 oust 5 spurn
make it through the ~: 5 get in
squeaker: 5 hinge, pivot
starter: 4 tail, toll 5 flood, South, water
starting ~: 4 post
gate __: 3 leg 5 array 6 theory
gate-__: 7 crasher
gate-__ table: 3 leg 6 legged
__ gate: 3 NOR, NOT, sea 4 film, flux, head, lich, lych, moon, NAND, ring, tide 5 logic, sound, waste, water 6 finger, pencil, roller 7 decuman, kissing, penning
__ Gate: 4 Iron 5 China 6 Golden
gâteau: 4 cake 6 French
__ Gate Bridge: 6 Golden
gate-crasher: 7 invader 8 intruder 10 trespasser
gatehouse: 5 lodge
gatekeeper: 5 guard, usher 6 porter, sentry 7 lookout, monitor 8 sentinel
gateleg __: 5 table
gater starter: 4 tail
Gates: 4 Bill 5 Larry 7 Horatio 8 McFadden
__ Gates: 4 Iron 6 Pearly
Gates fo the Forest, The author: Elie Wiesel
Gates of Heaven (1978 film) director: Errol Morris
Gates of the Arctic: 4 park
locale: 6 Alaska
gateway: 3 ent. 4 arch 5 lobby 6 portal 7 ingress, postern 8 entrance
Japanese ~: 5 torii
Gateway: 2 PC 8 computer
rival: 3 IBM 4 Dell, Sony 5 Apple 7 Toshiba
Gateway Arch: 8 landmark
architect: 8 Saarinen
locale: 7 St. Louis 8 Missouri
gather: 3 wax 4 band, call, cull, draw, earn, gain, grow, herd, join, levy, loom, mass, meet, pick, pile, pull, rake, reap, rise, save, take, tuck 5 amass, bring, build, bunch, crowd, flock, focus, glean, group, hoard, infer, merge, pluck, raise, rally, reune, scoop, sop up, stock, swarm, swell, think, troop, unite 6 accrue, assume, corral, deduce, derive, draw in, expand, garner, huddle, ingest, load up, muster, obtain, osmose, pick up, pile up, pucker, rake in, reason, reckon, rustle, select, soak up, suck up, summon, take in, take it, throng 7 acquire, believe, bunch up, cluster, collate, collect, compile, convene, convoke, drink in, enlarge, harvest, imagine, marshal, pick out, predict, presume, procure, receive, recruit, reunite, round up, scare up, stack up, suppose, surmise, suspect, swallow 8 assemble, conclude, converge, heighten, hold on to, increase, mobilize, muster up, rustle up, scrape up 9 aggregate, intensify, stockpile 10 accumulate, assimilate, congregate, rendezvous, understand
fabric: 5 shirr
flowers: 4 pick, snip 5 pluck
garment: 4 tuck 5 plait, pleat
leaves: 4 rake 6 rake up 7 clean up
on a surface: 4 sorb 6 adsorb
resources: 6 enlist, enroll, muster 7 procure, round up 8 mobilize
roses: 3 cut 4 clip
starter: 4 wool
gatherer: 7 hoarder, pack rat 9 collector
__-gatherer: 6 hunter
gathering: 3 bee, mob, tea 4 band, bash, be-in, bevy, body, crop, fete, heap, herd, levy, mass 5 bunch, crowd, drove, flock, group, horde, mixer, party, rally, roast, swarm, troop 6 affair, caucus, huddle, klatch, love-in, muster, parley, powwow, rabble, throng 7 cluster, company, council, harvest, meeting, reunion, roundup, session, turnout 8 assembly, audience, clambake, conclave, congress, ensemble, function, imminent, jamboree, luncheon, visitors 9 aggregate, concourse, impending, listeners, reception, stockpile 10 assemblage, attendance, collection, concursion, conference, confluence, convention, cumulation, delegation
combining form: 4 -fest
dust: 4 idle
place: 5 haunt, lobby, venue
social ~: 3 bee 5 salon 6 affair, soiree
starter: 4 news, wool
Gathering __, The: 5 Storm
...gathering nuts __: 5 in May
Gathering of Eagles, A (1963 film)
cast: Rock Hudson, Mary Peach, Rod Taylor
director: Delbert Mann
Gathering Storm, The author: Winston Churchill
...gathers no __: 4 moss
Gather Together in My Name author: Maya Angelou
__-gatherum: 6 omnium
Gatineau: 4 city, town
locale: 6 Canada, Québec
gating starter: 4 tail
Gatlin: 4 Rudy 5 Larry, Steve
Gatlin Brothers: 4 trio
Gatling: 3 gun 7 Richard
descendant: 3 Uzi
__ gato: 5 una de
gato, big: 5 tigre
gator: 6 animal 7 reptile
cousin: 4 croc 9 crocodile
home: 4 moat 5 swamp
Gator
ender: 3 ade
Gatorade: 5 drink 9 soft drink
Gator Bowl site: 3 Fla. 7 Florida
__ Gatos, CA: 3 Los
Gatsby: 3 Jay
portrayer: 4 Ladd 7 Redford
__ Gatsby, The: 5 Great
Gattaca (1997 film)
cast: Ethan Hawke, Jude Law, Uma Thurman
director: Andrew Niccol
GATT successor: 5 NAFTA
Gatún: 4 lake
locale: 6 Panama
Gatwick: 7 airport
locale: 7 England
Gaua: 7 volcano
locale: 4 Asia 7 Vanuatu
gauche: 4 left 5 crude, gawky, inapt, inept, rough, wrong 6 clumsy, coarse, oafish, rustic, wooden 7 awkward, gawkish, ill-bred, unadept, uncouth 8 bumbling, fumbling, ignorant, tactless, unsubtle 9 graceless, ham-handed, impolitic, inelegant, maladroit 10 outlandish, unbecoming, uncultured, unpolished, unskillful
__ gauche: 4 main, rive
gaucherie: 4 muff 5 gaffe 7 blunder, crudity, faux pas
gaucho: 6 cowboy, herder 7 cowpoke 8 horseman, wrangler 10 equestrian
gear: 4 bola 5 reata
home: 3 Arg. 5 pampa 6 pampas 9 Argentina
roundup: 5 rodeo
see also Spanish
gauchos: 5 pants 8 knickers, trousers
gaud: 4 bead 6 geegaw, gewgaw 7 trinket 9 bagatelle
Gaudí: 7 Antonio
gaudiness: 5 glitz 6 kitsch 7 glitter
gaudy: 4 loud, neon 5 fancy, showy, tacky, vivid 6 bright, flashy, frilly, garish, glitzy, ornate, shoddy, tawdry, tinsel, vulgar 7 glaring, kitschy, splashy 8 colorful 9 flaunting, tasteless 10 flamboyant
not ~: 4 drab
gauge: 4 dial, make, mark, norm, test 5 basis, check, count, guide, judge, meter, model, plumb, scale, tally, value, weigh 6 assess, fathom, figure, number, reckon, screen, size up 7 compute, example, measure, pointer, project 8 appraise, check out, estimate, evaluate, exemplar, gas meter, keep tabs, quantify, standard 9 ascertain, barometer, benchmark, calculate, calibrate, criterion, determine, guideline, indicator, yardstick 10 touchstone
auto ~: 3 odo 4 tach 8 odometer 10 tachometer
reading: 5 level 6 status 8 altitude 9 elevation
__ gauge: 3 air, bit, lee, sea 4 line, rain, ring, snow, tide, wind, wire 5 broad, water 6 feeler, McLeod, narrow, strain, vacuum 7 weather
Gauguin, Paul: 6 artist, French 7 painter
half a ~ book title: 3 Noa
Gaul
ancient people of ~: 4 Remi
city: 5 Lyons 6 Alesia
language: 8 Frankish
today: 6 France
Gauls, to Romans: 3 foe 5 enemy
gaunt: 4 bony, grim, lank, lean, thin 5 bleak, boney, drawn, lanky, spare 6 dismal, dreary, ill-fed, meager, skinny 7 angular, forlorn, haggard, scraggy, scrawny, sterile 8 angulose, angulous, desolate, rawboned 9 emaciated 10 forbidding
gauntlet: 4 gage, test 5 glove, trial 9 challenge
throw down the ~: 4 dare, defy 9 challenge 10 make a stand
Gauntlet, The (1977 film)
cast: Clint Eastwood, Pat Hingle, Sondra Locke
director: Clint Eastwood
gaur: 5 bovid 6 bovine
relative: 3 yak 4 anoa, arna, urus, zebu 5 bison, gayal, takin 6 mithan, muskox 7 aurochs, banteng, banting, beefalo, buffalo, carabao, cattalo, kouprey, tamarao, tamarau, timarau
Gauri Sankar: 4 peak 5 mount 8 mountain
locale: 4 Asia 5 China, Nepal 9 Himalayas
Gauss: 4 Karl
Gaussian __: 5 curve, image 7 integer
Gautama: 6 Buddha 10 Shakyamuni
birthplace: 7 Lumbini
cousin: 6 Ananda
enemy: 4 Mara
horse: 7 Kantaka
lifesaver: 6 Sujata
meditation spot: 6 bo tree
mother: 9 Queen Maya
son: 6 Rahula
wife: 9 Yasodhara

Gautier: 4 Dick 9 Théophile
gauze: 4 mesh 5 weave 6 fabric 7 chiffon 8 gossamer
  fabric: 3 net 4 leno 5 lisse, tulle 6 cotton
  like ~: 4 wove 5 woven
gauzy: 4 fine, lacy, thin 5 filmy, light, lucid, sheer 6 flimsy 8 delicate, finespun, gossamer 10 cobweblike, diaphanous, see-through
Gavarnie: 5 falls 9 waterfall
  locale: 6 France 8 Pyrenees
Gave __ through the night...: 5 proof
gavel: 6 hammer, mallet, tapper
  title: 3 sir 5 madam 9 your honor
  user: 5 chair, judge 8 chairman
  user demand: 5 order
gavel-down word: 4 gone, sold
gavial: 4 croc 6 animal 7 reptile 9 crocodile
Gavilan: 3 Kid
Gavin: 4 John, Muir 7 MacLeod, Maxwell
Gavin, John: 5 actor
  film: Imitation of Life (1959)
    Midnight Lace (1960)
    Psycho (1960)
    Romanoff and Juliet (1961)
    Spartacus (1960)
    A Time to Love and a Time to Die (1958)
Gaviscon: 7 antacid
  alternative: 4 Tums 6 Maalox, Pepcid, Riopan, Zantac 7 Gelusil, Lactaid, Mylanta, Rolaids 11 Alka-Seltzer, Pepto-Bismol
gavotte: 5 dance, music
__ Gavotte: 5 Ascot
__-Gavras: 5 Costa
Gavrilo: 7 Princip
Gawain: 3 Sir 6 knight
  need: 5 armor, lance
gawd: 4 oath
gawk: 3 see 4 gape, gaze, look, ogle, peer 5 stare 6 goggle 10 rubberneck
  at: 3 eye 4 view
gawker: 5 ogler 10 rubberneck
gawking: 6 astare
gawky: 4 lank, thin 6 clumsy, gauche, klutzy, oafish, wooden 7 awkward, loutish, unadept, uncouth 8 bumbling, bungling, lubberly, ungainly 9 all thumbs, graceless, lumbering, maladroit, stumbling, unskilled 10 leadfooted, unskillful
gawp: 4 ogle 5 stare
Gaxton: 7 William
gay: 5 happy, jolly, light, merry, riant, sunny, vivid, witty 6 blithe, bouncy, bright, cheery, chirpy, festal, jocund, jovial, joyful, joyous, lively, rakish 7 chipper, festive, gleeful, jocular, radiant, raffish, romping 8 animated, carefree, cheerful, debonair, giggling, jubilant, laughing, mirthful, sporting, sportive 9 convivial, debonaire, exuberant, lightsome, sprightly, vivacious 10 debonnaire, flying high, frolicsome, rollicking
  blade: 4 dude 5 swell 10 jack-a-dandy
  in music: 7 festoso
  starter: 4 nose
Gay: 4 John 6 Brewer, Talese
Gay __: 5 Paree 7 Divorce
__ Gay: 5 Enola
gayal: 5 bovid 6 bovine, mammal
  relative: 3 yak 4 anoa, arna, gaur, urus, zebu 5 bison, takin 6 muskox 7 aurochs, banteng, banting, beefalo, buffalo, carabao, cattalo, kouprey, tamarao, tamarau, timarau
Gay Divorcee, The (1934 film): 7 musical
  cast: Fred Astaire, Edward Everett Horton, Ginger Rogers
  director: Mark Sandrich
  music: Cole Porter
Gaye: 4 Nona 6 Marvin
Gaye, Marvin
  song: Ain't Nothing Like the Real Thing (1968)
    Ain't That Peculiar (1965)
    Got to Give It Up (1977)
    How Sweet It Is to Be Loved by You (1964)
    If I Could Build My Whole World Around You (1967)
    I Heard it Through the Grapevine (1968)
    I'll Be Doggone (1965)
    Inner City Blues (1971)
    Let's Get It On (1973)
    Mercy Mercy Me (1971)
    Pride and Joy (1963)
    That's the Way Love Is (1969)
    Too Busy Thinking About My Baby (1969)
    Trouble Man (1972)
    What's Going On (1971)
    You're All I Need to Get By (1968)
    Your Precious Love (1967)
__ Gay Hamilton: 4 Lisa
__ Gay Harden: 6 Marcia
Gayheart: 4 Lucy
Gay, John: 4 poet 7 British 10 playwright
  work: The Beggar's Opera
Gay, John work: The Beggar's Opera
Gayle: 7 Crystal 9 Hunnicutt
Gayle, Crystal
  sister: Loretta Lynn
  song: Don't It Make My Brown Eyes Blue (1977)
    You and I (1982)
Gaylord: 5 Mitch, Perry 6 Nelson 7 Ravenal
Gay-Lussac, Joseph: 7 chemist 9 physicist, scientist
Gaynes: 6 George
gayness: 3 joy 4 glee 5 mirth 6 gaiety, levity 7 jollity, revelry 8 hilarity, laughter 9 frivolity, happiness, lightness, merriment
Gay Nineties: 3 era
  like the ~: 6 gaslit
Gaynor: 5 Janet, Mitzi 6 Gloria
Gaynor, Gloria
  song: I Will Survive (1979)
    Never Can Say Goodbye (1974)
Gaynor, Janet: 7 actress
  film: Seventh Heaven (1927, AA)
    Small Town Girl (1936)
    A Star Is Born (1937)
    State Fair (1933)
    Street Angel (1928)
    Sunny Side Up (1929)
    Sunrise (1927)
    The Young in Heart (1938)
Gaynor, Mitzi: 7 actress
  film: The Joker Is Wild (1957)
    Les Girls (1957)
    South Pacific (1958)
Gay Purr-ee composer: 5 Arlen 7 Harburg
gaz.: 2 bk. 3 ref.
Gaza: 5 strip
  grp.: 3 PLO
  resident: 4 Arab
gazar: 6 fabric 8 material
gaze: 3 see 4 gape, gawk, look, peek, peep, peer, view 5 stare, watch 6 regard 7 fish eye 10 rubberneck
  at: 3 eye, see 4 leer, ogle 5 watch 6 behold, regard 9 flirt with
  crystal ~: 4 scry
  dreamily: 4 moon 5 yearn 9 fantasize 10 woolgather
  starter: 4 star
  wide-eyed: 4 gape 5 stare 6 goggle, marvel, wonder
gazebo: 5 kiosk 8 pavilion 9 belvedere
Gazebo, The (1959 film)
  cast: Glenn Ford, Carl Reiner, Debbie Reynolds
gazehound: 3 dog 5 canid 6 canine
gazelle: 3 goa 5 ariel, loper 6 animal, mammal 8 antelope
  gait: 4 stot
  relative: 3 gnu, kob 4 guib, kudu, oryx, puku, topi 5 addax, bongo, chiru, eland, goral, korin, nyala, oribi, saiga, serow 6 chammy, dik-dik, duiker, impala, koodoo, lechwe, nilgai, rhebok, shammy, shamoy 7 blaubok, blesbok, chamois, defassa, gemsbok, gerenuk, grysbok, nylghai, nylghau, sassaby 8 blesbuck, bontebok, bushbuck, gemsbuck, reedbuck, steenbok, steinbok 9 blackbuck, pronghorn, sitatunga, springbok, waterbuck 10 hartebeest, wildebeest
gazer: 9 spectator
  crystal ~: 4 seer 5 sibyl 7 psychic
  starter: 4 star
__ gazer: 7 crystal
gazette: 5 paper 7 journal 8 magazine 9 newspaper
Gazette: 5 paper 9 newspaper
  locale: 8 Montreal
gazetteer: 4 book 9 reference
  abbr.: 3 isl., mts., str. 4 N. Lat., terr.
  data: 4 area
gazing: 6 astare
  starter: 4 star
gazpacho: 4 sopa, soup
  ingredient: 3 oil 4 cuke 5 onion 6 garlic, tomato 7 vinegar 8 cucumber
  like ~: 4 cold, cool 7 chilled
Gazzara, Ben: 5 actor
  film: Anatomy of a Murder (1959)
    The Bridge at Remagen (1969)
    Convicts 4 (1962)
    Opening Night (1977)
    Saint Jack (1979)
    The Spanish Prisoner (1998)
    The Strange One (1957)
    They All Laughed (1981)
    The Thomas Crown Affair (1999)
    The Young Doctors (1961)
  spouse: Janice Rule
  TV: Run for Your Life
G.B.
  part of ~: 3 Eng. 4 Brit., Scot.
Gbari home: 6 Africa 7 Nigeria
Gbe: 8 language
__ G. Biv: 3 Roy
GBS: 4 Shaw
  home: 3 Ire.
__ G. Carroll: 3 Leo
Gd: 4 elem. 7 element 10 gadolinium
  64 for ~: 4 at. no.
Gdansk: 4 city, port, town 6 Danzig
  locale: 6 Baltic, Poland
gds.: 4 mdse.
  producer: 3 mfr.
Ge: 4 elem. 7 element 9 germanium
  32 for ~: 4 at. no.
GE
  part of ~: 3 Gen. 4 Elec.
  subsidiary: 3 NBC, RCA 5 NBC-TV
gear: 3 cog, def, kit, low, rad, rig 4 aces, A-one, boss, braw, cool, dece, duds, fine, garb, keen, neat, nice, phat, rags, suit, togs, tuff, wear 5 adapt, array, dandy, dress, drive, ducky, equip, goods, grand, great, habit, marvy, neato, nobby, prime, robes, slick, stuff, super, swell, thing, tools 6 adjust, attire, bang on, bang-up, bonzer, bosker, choice, divine, dreamy, far-out, fit out, gnarly, groovy, lovely, outfit, peachy, pinion, slap-up, spot on, superb, tackle, tailor, terrif, tiptop, unreal, whizzo, wicked 7 amazing, apparel, awesome, baggage, capital, clothes, corking, costume, effects, forward, furnish, harness, luggage, perfect, prepare, reverse, rigging, ripping, skookum, stellar, sublime, threads 8 accouter, accoutre, clothing, cogwheel, covering, dazzling, equipage, especial, eximious, fabulous, fittings, five-star, four-star, frabjous, garments, glorious, heavenly, jim-dandy, material, slam-bang, smashing, splendid, sprocket, standout, sterling, stickout, superior, terrific, top-level, topnotch, very good, wondrous 9 apparatus, bodacious, caparison, Endsville, equipment, excellent, exemplary, exquisite, first-rate, highgrade, hunky-dory, machinery, marvelous, sollicker, top-flight, trappings, wonderful 10 belongings, first-class, hotsy-totsy, instrument, jack-a-dandy, out of sight, peachy-keen, phenomenal, remarkable, stupendous, Sunday best, super-duper
  element: 5 tooth
  ender: 3 box 5 shift, wheel
  starter: 4 foot, head
  up: 7 prepare
gear __: 3 box 4 down, pump 5 lever, ratio, train
__ gear: 3 low, sun 4 back, bull, face, high, idle, mess, ring, spur, worm 5 bevel, chain, first, idler, miter, speed, third, valve 6 bottom, fourth, hypoid, planet, second, spiral 7 annular, helical, landing, lantern, running, tumbler
gears: 8 workings 9 machinery, mechanism
  change ~: 5 shift
  like ~: 6 cogged
  what ~ do: 4 lock, mesh 5 catch 6 engage
__ gears: 5 shift 6 switch
gearshift: 3 box
  position: 3 low 4 park 5 first, third 6 second 7 neutral, reverse
  sequence: 5 PRNDL
gear-tooth cutter: 3 hob
Geary: 7 Anthony, Cynthia
Geb, child of: 4 Isis 6 Osiris
Geber, father of: 3 Uri
gecko: 5 tokay 6 animal, lizard 7 reptile
  cousin: 5 skink
G.E. College Bowl: 8 game show
  host: Allen Ludden, Robert Earle
ged: 4 fish
Gedrick: 5 Jason
gee: 3 wow 4 gosh, thou 5 golly 6 cripes, jiminy 7 jimminy
  follower: 5 aitch
  one-tenth of a ~: 3 cee
  opposite: 3 haw
  preceder: 2 ef
Gee __!: 4 whiz
geebung: 4 tree 5 shrub
geegaw: 5 curio 6 bauble, doodad, trifle 7 trinket 8 gimcrack, ornament 9 bagatelle 10 knickknack
gee-gee: 5 horse 6 equine
geek: 4 dolt, nerd, nurd, tech, wonk 5 dweeb 6 techie, tekkie, weirdo 7 buffoon, egghead, oddball 9 eccentric
  computer ~: 4 guru, nerd, hurd
geeky: 5 nerdy, unhip
Geelong: 4 city, port, town
  locale: 9 Australia
Geena: 5 Davis

geep: 4 goat 5 sheep
relative: 4 ibex, tahr, thar 5 argal, shapu, urial 6 Angora, aoudad, argali, bharal, merino 7 bighorn, burrhel, markhor, mouflon 8 cimarron, markhoor, moufflon
Geer, Will: 5 actor
film: Brother John (1970)
Jeremiah Johnson (1972)
The Reivers (1969)
Salt of the Earth (1953)
TV: The Waltons
___ Gees: 3 Bee
geese: 4 fowl 5 birds 7 poultry
group: 5 flock, skein 6 gaggle
like some ~: 4 wild
Geeson: 4 Judy
geezer: 4 coot, cuss, fogy 5 fogey 6 codger 9 eccentric, graybeard 10 fuddy-duddy
query: 2 eh
Geffen: 5 David
gefilte ___: 4 fish
Gehrig: 3 Lou 4 Yank 6 Yankee 9 Iron Horse
contemporary: 4 Ruth 5 Combs 6 Dickey 7 Lazzeri 8 DiMaggio
Gehringer: 7 Charlie
___ gehts?: 3 Wie
Geiberger: 2 Al 5 Brent
Geiberger, Brent: 6 golfer
milieu: 5 links 6 course
org.: 3 PGA
Geiger counter, set off a: 4 emit
Geiger, Hans: 6 German 9 physicist
Geils: 6 Jerome
Geils Band, J.
song: Centerfold (1981)
Freeze-Frame (1982)
Geisel pen name: 5 Seuss
geisha: 5 woman 8 Japanese
accessory: 3 fan, obi
garb: 6 kimono
purse: 4 inro
serving: 3 cha, tea 4 sake
zither: 4 koto
Geissler tube illuminant: 4 neon
gel: 3 set 4 clot, goop 6 firm up, harden 7 colloid, congeal, stiffen, thicken 8 coalesce, solidify 9 coagulate, semi-solid, take shape
lab ~: 4 agar 8 agar-agar
___ gel: 6 silica
gelada: 6 baboon, mammal 7 primate
relative: 3 ape 4 saki, titi 5 chimp, drill, jocko, lemur, loris, magot, orang, potto, shrew 6 aye-aye, baboon, Bandar, galago, gibbon, grivet, guenon, howler, langur, macaco, monkey, rhesus, uakari, vervet 7 colobus, gorilla, guereza, hoolock, macaque, sapajou, siamang, tamarin, tarsier 8 bush baby, capuchin, mandrill, mangabey, marmoset, talapoin 9 orangutan 10 Barbary ape, chimpanzee, orangutang
Gelasius: 4 pope 7 pontiff
gelastic: 9 laughable, ludicrous
gelate: 3 set 4 clot, jell 6 curdle, harden 7 clabber, clobber, congeal, stiffen, thicken 8 solidify 9 coagulate
gelatin: 5 Jell-O 7 dessert
Chinese ~: 4 agar 8 agar-agar
move like ~: 5 shake 6 jiggle, shimmy, wiggle 7 wriggle
shaper: 4 mold
substitute: 4 agar 8 agar-agar
gelatinize: 3 set 4 jell 7 congeal, stiffen, thicken 8 solidify 9 coagulate
gelatinous: 4 soft 5 thick 7 jellied, viscose, viscous 9 glutinous, jelly-like 10 coagulated
gelato: 3 ice 7 dessert 8 ice cream
alternative: 6 sundae 7 parfait, spumone, spumoni, tortoni 8 snowball
Gelbart: 5 Larry
Gelber, Jack: 6 author, writer
Gelbvieh: 3 cow 4 bull 6 bovine, cattle
Gelderland commune: 3 Ede
gelding: 5 horse 6 equine
Geldof: 3 Bob
gelée: 3 goo 5 aspic
Geleon father: 3 Ion
Gelett: 7 Burgess
gelid: 3 icy 4 cold, cool, rimy 5 chill 6 arctic, bitter, chilly, frigid, frosty, frozen, wintry 7 glacial, ice-cold, wintery 8 freezing
period: 6 ice age
gelidity: 4 cold 5 chill 9 frigidity
Gellar, Sarah Michelle: 7 actress
film: I Know What You Did Last Summer (1997)
Scooby-Doo (2002)
spouse: Freddie Prinze Jr.
TV: Buffy the Vampire Slayer
Geller: 3 Uri 5 Bruce
gelling agent: 4 agar 8 agar-agar
Gell-Mann, Murray: 8 Nobelist 9 physicist
Gelsey: 8 Kirkland
gelt: 3 oof 4 cash, jack, kail, kale, loot, peag, pelf 5 bills, bread, bucks, dough, funds, lucre, money, moola, mopus, pesos, rhino, sewan 6 dinero, do-re-mi, mammon, mazuma, moolah, seawan, silver, specie, wampum, wealth 7 cabbage, capital, dollars, lettuce, ooftish, scratch, shekels 8 bankroll, cold cash, currency, hard cash, smackers 9 banknotes, frogskins, long green, simoleons 10 greenbacks, green stuff
Gelusil: 7 antacid
alternative: 4 Tums 6 Maalox, Pepcid, Riopan, Zantac 7 Lactaid, Mylanta, Rolaids 8 Gaviscon 11 Alka-Seltzer, Pepto-Bismol
gem: 3 ice 4 jade, onyx, opal, rock, ruby, sard 5 agate, angel, balas, beaut, beryl, bijou, boule, coral, dandy, honey, jewel, paste, pearl, prize, stone, topaz 6 baguet, bauble, garnet, jasper, muffin, zircon 7 cat's-eye, diamond, emerald, jewelry, kunzite, paragon, peridot, sardine, sardius 8 amethyst, baguette, cabochon, marquise, ornament, rara avis, sapphire, sparkler, treasure 9 amazonite, briolette, carnelian, moonstone, nonpareil, tiger's-eye, turquoise 10 aquamarine, birthstone, bloodstone, rhinestone, tourmaline
amethyst ~: 8 hyacinth
artificial ~: 5 paste
bed: 5 bezel
beryl ~: 7 emerald 9 morganite 10 aquamarine
blue ~: 7 azurite, euclase 8 sapphire 9 turquoise 10 aquamarine, tourmaline
brown ~: 7 zoisite 10 staurolite
carved ~: 5 cameo
chalcedony ~: 4 onyx, sard
clear ~: 6 zircon 7 peridot 9 tanzanite 10 tourmaline
corundum ~: 4 ruby 5 topaz 8 sapphire
ender: 5 stone
feldspar ~: 9 moonstone
garnet ~: 6 pyrope 9 almandine
green ~: 4 jade 7 emerald, euclase, peridot 8 nephrite 9 demantoid, hiddenite 10 tourmaline
holder: 5 prong
jade ~: 8 nephrite
like some ~ s: 3 set 5 unset
milky ~: 4 opal
mount a ~: 3 set 6 collet
nephrite ~: 4 jade
opaque ~: 9 turquoise
orange ~: 4 sard 5 balas 7 sardine, sardius
oyster ~: 5 pearl
pink ~: 7 zoisite
quartz ~: 7 citrine 8 amethyst
red ~: 4 ruby 5 balas 6 garnet, pyrope, spinel 8 spinelle 9 rhodolite, rubellite 10 ruby spinel
shape: 4 oval, pear 5 round
silica ~: 4 opal
silicate ~: 6 circon, garnet 9 rhodolite 10 tourmaline
surface: 4 face 5 culet, facet, plane
tool: 3 dop 5 loupe
tourmaline ~: 9 rubellite
unfaceted ~: 4 opal 5 pearl
unit: 2 ct. 5 carat
violet ~: 8 amethyst
white ~: 8 sardonyx
yellow ~: 7 citrine
gem ___: 4 clip, jade
Gem ___: 5 State
Gemayel: 4 Amin
Gemini: 3 duo, two 4 sign 5 Twins 6 Castor, Pollux
astronaut: 5 Scott, White, Young 6 Aldrin, Borman, Cernan, Conrad, Cooper, Gordon, Lovell 7 Collins, Grissom, Schirra 8 McDivitt, Stafford 9 Armstrong
follower: 4 crab 6 Cancer
month: 3 Jun., May 4 June
mother: 4 Leda
org.: 4 NASA
predecessor: 6 Taurus
successor: 6 Cancer
Gemini Contenders, The author: Robert Ludlum
Gemini Dream (1981 song) artist: Moody Blues
Gemma: 4 star
gemologist: 7 jeweler 8 lapidary
gemology: 7 science
gems: 6 bijoux, jewels 7 jewelry 9 heirlooms, valuables
___ Gems: 6 Screen
gemsbok: 6 animal, mammal 8 antelope
relative: 3 gnu, kob 4 guib, kudu, oryx, puku, topi 5 addax, bongo, chiru, eland, goral, korin, nyala, oribi, saiga, serow 6 chammy, dik-dik, duiker, impala, koodoo, lechwe, nilgai, rhebok, shammy, shamoy 7 blaubok, blesbok, chamois, defassa, gazelle, gerenuk, grysbok, nylghai, nylghau, sassaby 8 blesbuck, bontebok, bushbuck, reedbuck, steenbok, steinbok 9 blackbuck, pronghorn, sitatunga, springbok, waterbuck 10 hartebeest, wildebeest
Gem State: 5 Idaho
gemstone
see gem
gen.: 3 DDE, ldr., off. 5 R.E. Lee
Gen-___: 3 X'er
Gen.
follower: 4 Exod.
___ Gen.: 3 Att., Maj. 4 Atty., Brig., Comp., Surg.
Gena: 8 Rowlands
Gena ___ Nolin: 3 Lee
gendarme: 6 French 7 officer 9 policeman
what a ~ upholds: 3 loi
gender: 3 fem., sex 4 male, masc., neut. 6 female, neuter 8 feminine 9 masculine
not restricted by ~: 4 coed
suffix: 3 -ess 4 -enne, -ette
gender ___: 3 gap 4 role 6 bender
gender-___: 7 neutral
gene: 6 allele
component: 3 DNA, RNA
determinant: 5 trait
locate a ~: 3 map
sites: 4 loca, loci
gene ___: 4 flow, pool 7 mapping, therapy
___ gene: 3 HLA, Hox 6 marker 7 jumping
___ gêne: 4 sans
Gene: 4 Mako, Saks 5 Autry, Barry, Evans, Kelly, Krupa 6 Markey, Nelson, Pitney, Shalit, Siskel, Tunney, Upshaw, Wilder 7 Cornish, Hackman, Littler, Rayburn, Raymond, Sarazen, Simmons, Tierney, Vincent 8 Chandler, Lockhart 9 McDaniels
genealogy: 5 class, roots 7 descent, lineage 8 ancestry, pedigree 9 bloodline, forebears, parentage 10 derivation, extraction
carving: 5 totem
subject:: 3 fam., lin. 4 desc., tree 6 family 7 lineage 8 ancestor, pedigree 10 descendant
word: 3 née 4 born
Gene Anthony ___: 3 Ray
general: 3 lax 4 rank, rife, wide 5 broad, loose, total, typic, usual, vague 6 common, global, leader, normal, public 7 blanket, diffuse, inexact, liberal, officer, overall, plenary, popular, regular, routine, typical 8 accepted, catholic, everyday, familiar, habitual, ordinary, sweeping 9 all-around, customary, imprecise, inclusive, panoramic, pervasive, prevalent, universal, worldwide 10 collective, indefinite, prevailing, undetailed, unspecific, widespread
address: 3 sir
appearance: 3 air 6 facies
assistant: 3 ADC 4 aide 8 adjutant
combining form: 3 cen- 4 caen-, ceno-, coen- 5 caeno-, coeno-
command: 6 at ease
condition: 5 state 6 repair, status
denial: 5 no sir
designation: 4 star
idea: 4 core, crux, gist, meat, pith 5 heart, point, tenor 6 kernel, marrow, thrust, upshot 7 essence, purport 9 substance
in ~: 6 mainly 7 as a rule, overall, usually 8 as a whole, normally 9 routinely 10 by and large, on the whole, ordinarily
org. with a secretary ~: 4 NATO 5 the UN
practitioner: 3 doc 5 medic 6 doctor, medico 8 sawbones 9 physician
public: 3 mob 4 folk, herd 5 world 6 masses, people, rabble 7 society 8 populace, riffraff 9 bourgeois, citizenry, hoi polloi, multitude, plebeians
sense: 4 gist, tone, vein 5 drift, tenor, theme, trend 6 burden, intent 7 essence, meaning, purport 9 substance
store: 4 mart 6 market, outlet 8 emporium
transport: 4 jeep
general ___: 4 rule 5 staff, store 6 orders, strike 7 average, officer, partner
general ___ of relativity: 6 theory
general-___: 7 purpose
___ general: 5 major 6 consul 7 one-star, surgeon, two-star 8 attorney, five-star,

four-star **9** brigadier, three-star **10** lieutenant
___-general: 5 agent, vicar
General ___: 5 Court, Foods, Mills **6** Motors, Seeger **8** Electric
General ___ Army: 5 of the
General ___ chicken: 4 Tso's
___ General: 7 Estates
General Died at Dawn, The (1936 film)
cast: Madeleine Carroll, Gary Cooper, Akim Tamiroff
director: Lewis Milestone
General Escobedo: 4 city, town
locale: 6 Mexico **9** Nuevo León
General Foods brand: 5 Sanka
General Hospital (ABC): 9 soap opera
extra: 2 RN **5** nurse
generalist: 8 polymath
generality: 4 rule **9** half-truth, principle
generalization: 3 law **6** reason
generalize: 6 reason **9** establish, postulate, speculate
generalized: 5 vague
generally: 3 oft **5** about, often **6** mainly, mostly **7** as a rule, at large, chiefly, largely, roughly, usually **8** all in all **9** on average, popularly, primarily, regularly, routinely, typically **10** altogether, by and large, frequently, habitually, on the whole, ordinarily
General Mills
cereal: 3 Kix **4** Trix **5** Total **6** Kaboom **7** Harmony **8** Boo Berry, Cheerios, Corn Chex, Fiber One, Rice Chex, Wheaties **9** Wheat Chex **10** Cocoa Puffs **11** Cookie Crisp, Lucky Charms
General Motors: 8 carmaker **9** automaker
birthplace: 5 Flint
brand: 3 Geo **4** Olds, Opel **5** Buick, Chevy **6** Saturn **7** Pontiac **8** Cadillac **9** Chevrolet **10** Oldsmobile
general-obligation ___: 4 bond
General of the ___: 4 Army **6** Armies
Generals and Majors artist: 3 XTC
General's Daughter, The (1999 film)
cast: James Cromwell, Timothy Hutton, Madeleine Stowe, John Travolta
director: Simon West
General's Daughter, The author: Nelson Demille
General Seeger author: Ira Levin
generalship: 5 skill **7** tactics
General, The (1927 film)
cast: Buster Keaton, Marion Mack
General William Booth Enters Into Heaven author: Vachel Lindsay
generate: 4 form, make **5** breed, cause, found, hatch, set up, spawn, yield **6** create, effect, induce, whip up, work up **7** achieve, develop, perform, produce, trigger **8** engender, initiate, multiply **9** institute, introduce, originate, propagate, send forth **10** accomplish, bring about, give rise to
generated (from), be: 4 stem
generation: 3 age, day, era **4** span, time **5** epoch, years **6** period **7** bearing **8** age group, breeding, creation, spawning **9** begetting, beginning, formation, offspring **10** production
gap: 4 gulf, rift **5** break, split **10** alienation
generation ___: 3 gap
Generation ___: 3 X-er
___ Generation: 4 Beat, Lost
generations, future: 4 seed **5** heirs, issue **7** kinfolk, progeny **8** children, kinfolks, kinsfolk **9** posterity
generative: 7 fertile **8** original, prolific
generator: 5 motor **6** dynamo, engine, origin
___ generator: 3 ion **4** wind **5** motor, spark
generic: 5 usual **6** common **7** blanket, grouped, routine **8** catholic, everyday, frequent, ordinary **9** unbranded **10** collective, nonbranded, widespread
___ generis: 3 sui **6** alieni
generis, sui: 6 unique **10** unexampled
generosity: 5 mercy **6** lenity, virtue **7** charity, largess **8** free hand, goodness, goodwill, kindness, largesse, lenience, nobility **9** greatness, nobleness, profusion, readiness **10** almsgiving, liberality
generous: 3 big **4** free, full, kind, much, nice, tidy **5** ample, flush, large, lofty, noble, roomy, sweet **6** decent, giving, kindly, lavish, loving, plenty **7** copious, helpful, liberal, profuse **8** abundant, handsome, merciful, princely, prodigal, spacious, sporting, sportive **9** bounteous, bountiful, capacious, luxuriant, plenteous, plentiful, unselfish, unsparing **10** altruistic, beneficent, benevolent, bighearted, charitable, free-handed, hospitable, humanistic, munificent, openhanded, thoughtful, ungrudging, unstinting
be ~: 4 give **5** share **6** donate, lavish
name meaning ~: 6 Kareem
not ~: 4 mean **5** cheap, close, tight **6** greedy, narrow, skimpy, stingy **7** miserly, sparing, thrifty **8** grasping **9** penurious
one: 5 donor, sport
words: 4 on me
generous ___ fault: 3 to a
generously: 7 largely **9** favorably **10** handsomely
Genesee: 5 river
locale: 7 New York
genesis: 4 dawn, rise, seed **5** basis, birth, cause, onset, roots, start, sunup **6** advent, day one, origin, outset, source, spring **7** coinage, dawning, infancy, morning, opening, sunrise, trigger **8** babyhood, creation, daybreak, daylight, nascence, nascency **9** beginning, emergence, formation, inception, invention, square one **10** beginnings, brainchild, break of day, conception, derivation, first light, foundation, generation, initiation
starter: 4 meta **6** embryo
Genesis (Bible book)
bird: 4 dove
follower: 6 Exodus
fruit: 5 apple
locale: 4 Eden, Edom **5** Sodom **6** Ararat, Goshen
name: 3 Eve, Ham **4** Abel, Adam, Cain, Enos, Esau, Noah, Seth, Shem **5** Isaac, Jacob, Sarah **7** Abraham
to Deuteronomy: 4 Tora **5** Torah
vessel: 3 ark
Genesis (music group)
album: 6 Abacab
leader: Phil Collins
song: I Can't Dance (1992)
In Too Deep (1987)
Invisible Touch (1986)
Land of Confusion (1986)
That's All! (1983)
Throwing It All Away (1986)
Tonight, Tonight, Tonight (1987)
___ Genesis: 4 Sega
Genesis author: Delmore Schwartz
Genesius: 5 saint
genet: 3 cat **6** animal, mammal
genetic: 6 inbred, innate, racial **9** ancestral **10** hereditary
enzyme: 5 DNAse, RNAse
factor: 5 trait
material: 3 DNA, RNA **4** mRNA
product: 5 clone
product combining form: 7 Franken-
starter: 4 meta
genetic ___: 3 map **4** code, load **5** drift **6** coding, marker **7** fallacy
geneticist: 5 Crick **6** cloner, Galton, Watson
genetics: 7 science
study: 8 heredity
Genet, Jean: 6 French **10** playwright
work: The Balcony
The Maids
Miracle of the Rose
Our Lady of the Flowers
The Screens
Geneva: 4 city, font, lake, town **8** typeface
lake: 5 Leman
locale: Switzerland
river: 5 Rhone
Geneva ___: 4 gown **5** bands, cross
Geneva Convention concern: 3 POW, war
Genevieve: 3 Ste. **5** saint **6** Bujold, sainte
___ Genevieve, MO: 3 Ste.
Genghis Khan
follower: 5 horde, Tatar **6** Mongol
genial: 4 kind, mild, nice, warm **5** close, happy, jolly, merry, suave, sunny **6** benign, blithe, cheery, chirpy, chummy, clubby, gentle, hearty, jocund, jovial, joyful, joyous, kindly, smooth, upbeat **7** affable, amiable, chipper, cordial, likable, lovable **8** amicable, cheerful, familiar, friendly, gracious, intimate, likeable, loveable, outgoing, pleasant, sociable **9** agreeable, convivial, easygoing, expansive **10** benevolent, buddy-buddy, hospitable, neighborly, solicitous
geniality: 6 gaiety, gayety, warmth **7** amenity **9** good cheer, happiness, joviality, pleasance, sunniness **10** affability, amiability, cheeriness, cordiality, good nature, heartiness, kindliness
genie: 3 jin **4** djin, jinn **5** djinn, Jafar, jinni **6** djinni, spirit
home: 4 lamp
offering: 4 wish
portrayer: 4 Eden
summon a ~: 3 rub
Genie: 7 Francis
Genie in a Bottle (1999 song) artist: Christina Aguilera
genip: 4 tree
relative: 4 akee **6** lichee, litchi, longan, lungan **7** genipap, leechee **9** soapberry
genipap: 5 fruit
Genitrix author: François Mauriac
genius: 3 ace **4** gift, head, mind, soul, whiz **5** brain, knack, smart **6** acumen, marvel, master, spirit, talent, wisdom, wizard **7** egghead, prodigy, prowess **8** afflatus, artistry, Einstein, highbrow, longhair, virtuoso **9** intellect **10** astuteness, brilliance, mastermind
group: 5 Mensa
stroke of ~: 4 coup, feat **7** exploit, triumph
Genius, The author: Theodore Dreiser
genl.: 3 off.
employer: 3 USA **4** USAF
Genn: 3 Leo
Gennaro: 5 Peter
in English: 6 Gerald
___ Gennaro: 3 San
Genoa: 3 jib **4** city, gulf, port, town **6** salami
locale: 5 Italy
genoise: 4 cake
genome mapping company: 6 Celera
___ Genome Project: 5 Human
genomic ___: 3 DNA
Genova: 4 city, town
locale: 5 Italy
genre: 3 ilk **4** kind, sort, type **5** brand, class, group, order, style **6** school **7** fiction, variety **8** category **9** character
book ~: 4 biog. **5** drama, farce, how-to, sci-fi **7** fiction **9** biography
fiction ~: 4 pulp **6** Gothic **7** romance
film ~: 5 drama, sci-fi **6** action, comedy, horror
music ~: 3 bop **4** folk, funk, glam, rock **5** bebop, disco, R and B, swing **6** gospel, grunge, hip-hop
genro: 4 male **5** elder
gens du ___: 5 monde
gent: 3 guy, him, nob **4** chap, dude, male **5** bloke **6** feller, fellow, mister, squire
genteel: 4 nice, prim **5** civil, haute, noble **6** la-de-da, la-di-da, polite, prissy, proper, urbane **7** courtly, elegant, prudish, refined, stilted, stylish **8** cultured, highborn, highbred, ladylike, lah-di-dah, mannerly, polished, well-bred **9** courteous **10** chivalrous, cultivated
___-genteel: 6 shabby
gentian: 5 plant **6** flower
gentian ___: 6 violet
___ gentian: 5 green, horse **6** bottle, closed, yellow **7** fringed
gentility: 6 polish **7** amenity, culture, decorum **8** breeding, civility, courtesy, elegance, niceties, noblesse **9** blue blood, etiquette, formality, high birth, propriety **10** politeness, refinement, upper class, upper crust
gentle: 3 lax **4** calm, cool, easy, kind, meek, mild, nice, soft, tame **5** balmy, light, loose, lowly, muted, noble, quiet, sweet, timid **6** benign, decent, docile, genial, humane, hushed, irenic, kindly, mellow, placid, polite, sedate, serene, smooth, soothe, subdue, tender **7** affable, amiable, clement, gradual, lenient, pacific, patient, pliable, ruthful, sparing, subdued, tactful **8** dovelike, flexible, gracious, harmless, highborn, humanize, irenical, ladylike, laid-back, lamblike, maternal, merciful, moderate, parental, peaceful, placable, pleasant, tolerant, tranquil, untaxing, well-bred **9** agreeable, assuasive, compliant, courteous, easygoing, forgiving, indulgent, leisurely, peaceable, sensitive, temperate, tractable **10** altruistic, benevolent, forbearing, permissive, unagitated, unexacting, unhardened
ender: 3 man, men **4** folk **5** woman, women **6** people, person
make ~: 6 mellow, soften **8** civilize, humanize
not ~: 4 mean, rude **5** cruel, harsh, rigid, rough, sharp, stern **6** brutal, savage, severe, unkind **7** abusive, austere **8** pitiless, ruthless **9** heartless, merciless **10** hard-boiled, oppressive, relentless
one: 4 lamb
runner: 5 loper
slope: 4 rise **6** glacis **9** acclivity
touch: 3 hug, pat **6** caress, cuddle, stroke **7** embrace, snuggle
gentle ___: 3 art **5** craft **6** breeze, reader
gentle ___ lamb: 3 as a
Gentle ___: 3 Ben **5** Giant
Gentle ___ Mind: 4 on My

gentle as ___: **5** a lamb
Gentle Ben: **4** bear
like ~: **4** tame **6** ursine
Gentle Giant (1967 film)
cast: Clint Howard, Vera Miles, Dennis Weaver
gentleman: **3** guy, him, sir **4** male **5** noble **6** feller **7** grown-up **9** patrician
country ~: **3** esq. **7** esquire
friend: **4** beau **5** flame, lover, swain, wooer **6** steady, suitor **7** admirer, gallant **8** paramour **9** inamorato
gentleman's ~: **5** valet **6** butler **7** servant
in German: **4** herr
in India: **3** sri
in Portuguese: **3** dom **6** senhor
in Spanish: **3** don **5** señor
no ~: **3** cad **4** heel, rake, roué
that ~ 's: **3** his
gentleman ___: **6** caller, friend
gentleman ___ road: **5** of the
gentleman-___: **6** farmer
___ gentleman: **7** country, perfect
Gentleman ___: **3** Jim
gentleman-at-___: **4** arms
Gentleman Is a Dope, The composer: **7** Rodgers **11** Hammerstein
Gentleman Jim (1942 film)
cast: Jack Carson, Errol Flynn, Alexis Smith
director: Raoul Walsh
gentlemanly: **4** kind **5** civil, noble **6** polite, urbane **7** genteel, refined, tactful **8** gracious, mannerly, obliging, pleasant, well-bred **9** courteous **10** respectful, thoughtful
Gentleman's Agreement (1947 film)
author: Laura Z. Hobson
cast: John Garfield, Celeste Holm, Dorothy McGuire, Gregory Peck
director: Elia Kazan
gentlemen: **3** he's **6** messr.'s
Gentlemen, ___ your engines: **5** start
___ Gentlemen Marry Brunettes: **3** But
___ Gentlemen of Verona: **3** Two
Gentlemen Prefer Blondes (1953 film): **7** musical
author: Anita Loos
cast: Charles Coburn, Marilyn Monroe, Jane Russell
director: Howard Hawks
songwriter: **5** Robin, Styne
gentleness: **5** mercy **6** lenity **8** clemency, lenience, morality **9** balminess
Gentle on My Mind (1968 song) artist: Glen Campbell
gentlewoman: **4** lady **5** madam, noble **6** female **9** patrician
gently: **4** easy, soft **5** light **8** gingerly
gentry: **5** elite, lords **7** society **8** nobility, patroons **10** haute monde, landowners, upper class, upper crust
Gentry, Bobbie song: Ode to Billy Joe (1967)
genu: **4** knee **5** Latin
genuflect: **4** bend **5** kneel, knell **7** bow down, worship **9** pay homage **10** pay tribute
genuine: **4** auth., good, pure, real, sure, true **5** frank, legit, naïve, pucka, pukka, right, solid, valid **6** actual, candid, honest, infelt, kasher, kosher, proved, proven **7** artless, earnest, factual, for real, natural, serious, sincere, up-front **8** absolute, accurate, bona fide, innocent, original, positive, verified **9** authentic, certified, guileless, heartfelt, intrinsic, realistic, unfeigned, veracious, veritable **10** legitimate, true-to-life, unaffected, unimagined
not ~: **4** imit., sham **5** acted, phony **6** irreal, phoney, pseudo **9** imitation
pass off as ~: **5** foist **7** palm off
genuineness: **4** fact **5** truth **7** honesty, reality **8** validity, veracity **9** sincerity
genus: **4** kind, sort, type **5** brand, class, order, style, taxon **7** variety **8** category
gen-Xer's parent: **6** boomer
Geo: **3** car **4** auto **5** Chevy, Metro, Storm **7** Tracker **9** Chevrolet **10** automobile
model: **5** Metro, Prizm, Storm **6** Sprint **7** Firefly, Tracker
geode: **4** rock **5** stone **7** mineral
cavity: **3** vug **4** vugg, vugh
geodesic ___: **4** dome, line
geodesy: **7** science
geodetic ___: **6** survey
geoduck: **4** clam **7** bivalve, mollusk
Geoffrey: **4** Rush **5** Beene, Lewis **7** Chaucer **9** Wilkinson
Geoffrion, Bernie
milieu: **3** ice **4** rink **5** arena
nickname: Boom Boom
org.: **3** NHL
geog.: **3** sci. **7** science
___ geog.: **4** phys.
geographer: **5** Hedin **6** Strabo **9** Pausanias
geographic
datum: **4** area **9** elevation
feature: **4** hill, isle, mesa, peak **5** butte, islet, river **6** canyon, island, stream, valley **8** mountain
region: **5** biome
geographic ___: **4** mile **5** range
Geographos: **8** asteroid
geography: **6** layout **7** science **10** topography
abbr.: **2** mt. **3** alt., Atl., isl., lat., mtn., Pac., riv., str., ter. **4** sq mi., terr.
study: **5** Earth
geol.: **3** sci.
geologic ___: **4** time
geological
formation: **4** dome, mesa **5** butte, fault **6** folium, geyser
period: **3** eon, era **4** aeon **5** epoch, stade **7** stadial
sample: **4** core
suffix: **3** -ite **4** -lite, -lith, -zoic
Geological ___: **6** Survey
geologist, British: **5** Lyell
___ geology: **6** marine, mining
geom.: **3** sci. **4** math.
term: **2** sq. **3** ang., cir., ctr., sph., sqr.
geomancer: **7** prophet
geometric ___: **4** mean **5** ratio **6** series
geometry: **4** math
assignment: **5** proof
corner: **5** angle **6** vertex
Father of ~: **6** Euclid
figure: **3** cir. **4** cone, rect. **5** prism, rhomb, solid, torus **6** circle **7** hexagon, nonagon, octagon, rhombus **8** heptagon, pentagon, triangle **9** rectangle, trapezoid
line: **3** arc **4** axis, side **5** x-axis, y-axis, z-axis
measure: **3** vol. **4** area **6** volume
points: **4** loca, loci
suffix: **3** -gon
symbol: **2** pi
___ geometry: **5** plane, solid **6** affine **7** conical
geophysics: **7** science
study: **5** earth
geophyte: **5** plant
geoponics: **7** farming, science
Georg: **3** Ohm **5** Hegel, Solti **6** Kaiser, Wittig **7** Bednorz, Büchner **8** Telemann
Georg ___ Brown: **7** Sanford
George: **3** Ade, Boy, Fox, Pal **4** Bush, Kell, lake, Olah, Raft, Sand, Wald, Will **5** Allen, Baker, Boole, Brent, Brett, Burns, Cates, Cohan, Cukor, Dewey, Eliot, Gamow, Gobel, Grosz, Halas, Innes, Jones, Lucas, Meade, Mikan, Minot, Monck, Moore, Owens, Peele, saint, Segal, Snell, Susan, Szell, Takei, Wendt, Wythe **6** Abbott, Archer, Arliss, Beadle, Benson, Blanda, Carlin, Crabbe, Custer, Dallas, Gallup, Gaynes, Gervin, Gladys, Handel, Inness, Jessel, Jetson, McAfee, McCrae, Miller, Murphy, O'Brien, Orwell, Palade, Patton, Porter, Putnam, Reeves, Romney, Seaton, Sidney, Sisler, Stefan, Stokes, Strait, Stubbs, Tobias **7** Akerlof, Axelrod, Barbara, Chapman, Clinton, Clooney, Dzundza, Eastman, Foreman, Gissing, Herbert, Hurrell, Kennedy, Lazenby, Lindsey, Maharis, Mallory, McManus, Michael, O'Hanlon, Peppard, Phyllis, Pollock, Sanders, Seferis, Stevens, Stigler, Thomson, Waggner, Wallace, Whipple **8** Bancroft, Berkeley, Chakiris, Farquhar, Gershwin, Goethals, Grinnell, Grizzard, Hamilton, Harrison, Herriman, Macready, Marshall, McGinnis, McGovern, Meredith, Plimpton, Shearing **9** Bredehorn, Hitchings, McClellan, Santayana, Thorogood, Vancouver **10** Balanchine, Montgomery, Stephenson, Washington
brother: **3** Ira
couldn't tell it: **4** a lie
Gracie, to ~: **4** wife **6** costar **7** partner
in German: **6** Jürgen
in Italian: **7** Giorgio
in Russian: **4** Yuri
in Spanish: **5** Jorge
Martha, to ~: **4** wife
opponent: **4** Bill, Ross
predecessor: **3** Ron
successor: **4** Bill
who was a she: **4** Sand **5** Eliot
W.'s brother: **3** Jeb
George ___: **3** III
George ___ Carver: **10** Washington
George ___ Custer: **9** Armstrong
George ___ Handel: **8** Frideric
George ___ Hill: **3** Roy
George ___ Jungle: **5** of the
George ___ Shaw: **7** Bernard
___ George: **8** Gorgeous
George A. ___: **6** Romero
___ George Apley, The: **4** Late
George Armstrong ___: **6** Custer
George B. ___: **5** Seitz **9** McClellan
George Bernard ___: **4** Shaw
George C. ___: **5** Scott
___ George do it: **3** let
George Gordon ___ Byron: **4** Noel
George I mother: **4** Anne
George, Lloyd contemporary: **5** Lenin
George M!: **7** musical
star: **4** Grey **6** Peters
subject: **5** Cohan
George of the Jungle (1997 film)
cast: Brendan Fraser, Leslie Mann
George of the Jungle elephant: **4** Shep
George P. ___: **5** Marsh **6** Putnam **8** Cosmatos
George, Phyllis spouse: Robert Evans
George Roy ___: **4** Hill
Georges: **4** Pire **5** Bizet, Sorel **6** Braque, Cuvier, Danton, Enesco, Köhler, Seurat **7** Charpak, Duhamel, Feydeau, Rouault, Simenon **8** Bataille, Bernanos, Lemaître **10** Clemenceau
see also French
Georges ___: **4** Bank, Cinq
George S. ___: **6** Patton **7** Kaufman
George, Saint
emulate: **4** slay
foe: **6** dragon
Georges de ___: **6** Buffon, La Tour
George, Stefan: **4** poet **6** German
___ George's War: **4** King
Georgetown: **4** city, port **7** capital
athletes: **5** Hoyas
conference: **7** Big East
educator: **6** Jesuit
locale: **2** D.C. **5** Texas **6** Guyana **7** Caymans **10** Washington
georgette: **6** fabric **8** material
Georgette ___: **5** crepe
George V's wife: **4** Mary
George W. ___: **4** Bush
George Washington ___: **5** Cable **6** Bridge, Carver
George Washington ___ here: **5** slept
Georgia: **5** Engel, Gibbs **7** O'Keeffe
Georgia (country)
capital: **7** Tbilisi
city: **5** Redan **6** Batumi **7** Kutaisi, Rustavi, Tbilisi
it's south of ~: **4** Iran
mountains: **8** Caucasus
neighbor: **6** Russia, Turkey **7** Armenia **10** Azerbaijan
once: **3** SSR
river: **4** Rion **5** Rioni
Georgia (state)
capital: **7** Atlanta
city: **4** Rome **5** Macon **6** Albany, Athens, Clarke, Dalton, Duluth, Newnan, Plains, Smyrna, Tucker **7** Atlanta, Augusta, Candler, Griffin, MacAfee, Roswell **8** Columbus, Dunwoody, Kennesaw, La Grange, Mableton, Marietta, Martinez, Norcross, Richmond, Savannah, Valdosta **9** East Point **10** Alpharetta, Hinesville, Statesboro
conference: **3** SEC
county: **4** Bibb, Cobb, Dade **5** Dooly, Glynn, Lamar, Macon, Peach, Rabun, Troup, Upson **6** De Kalb, Elbert, Fulton, Lanier, Oconee, Schley, Sumter, Toombs, Twiggs
fruit: **5** peach
he went down to ~: **5** devil
Indian: **5** Creek
neighbor: **7** Alabama, Florida **9** Tennessee
nickname: **10** Peach State
river: **5** Coosa
state crop: **6** peanut
state fossil: **10** shark tooth
state game bird: **8** bobwhite
state gem: **6** quartz
state insect: **8** honeybee
state marine mammal: **10** right whale
state mineral: **10** staurolite
state tree: **7** live oak
state wildflower: **6** azalea
university: **5** Emory
University of ~ site: **6** Athens
Georgia ___: **3** Boy **4** pine, Tech
Georgia ___ Mind: **4** on My
Georgia-___: **7** Pacific
Georgia Boy author: Erskine Caldwell
___ Georgia Brown: **5** Sweet
Georgia Dome: **5** arena
Georgian: **3** bay **5** style
Georgia on My Mind (1960 song)
artist: Ray Charles
Georgia Peach: Ty Cobb
Georgia Tech
conference: **3** ACC
grad: **4** engr. **8** engineer
locale: **7** Atlanta
georgic: **4** idyl **5** idyll, rural

Georgina: **4** city, town
locale: **6** Canada **7** Ontario
Georg Sanford ___: **5** Brown
Georgy Girl: **4** film, song
artist: Seekers
cast: Alan Bates, James Mason, Lynn Redgrave
geothermal spout: **6** geyser
Gephardt: **4** Dick **7** Richard
gephyrophobe fear: **7** bridges
Ger.: **4** lang., Teut.
neighbor: **3** Aus., Pol. **4** Aust.
see also Germany
Gera: **4** city, town
locale: **7** Germany
Geraint: **3** Sir **6** knight
wife: **4** Enid
Gerald: **4** Ford **6** Levert **7** Edelman, McRaney
in Italian: **7** Gennaro
Gerald ___ Horst: **3** Ter
Geraldine: **4** Page **6** Brooks, Farrar **7** Chaplin, Ferraro **10** Fitzgerald
portrayer: **4** Flip
Geraldo: **6** Rivera
colleague: **4** Phil **5** Oprah
geranium: **3** red **5** color, plant **6** flower
relative: **4** rose, ruby, rust, wine **5** brick, coral, grape, poppy, rusty, sandy **6** cerise, cherry, claret, garnet, maroon **7** carmine, crimson, fuchsia, magenta, pimento, scarlet, sultana, vermeil **8** amaranth, cardinal, dubonnet, rubicund **9** carnation, cranberry, vermilion **10** strawberry
___ geranium: **3** ivy **4** fish, mint, rose, show, wild **5** fancy, lemon, zonal **6** cactus, jungle, nutmeg **7** feather
Gerard: **3** Gil **6** Debreu
in German: **7** Gerhard
Gerard ___ Borch: **3** Ter
Gerard ___ Hopkins: **6** Manley
Gérard: **9** Depardieu
Gerard, Gil spouse: Connie Sellecca
Gerardus: **6** 't Hooft **8** Mercator
gerbil: **3** pet **6** animal, mammal, rodent
female: **3** doe
male: **4** buck
relative: **3** rat **4** cavy, degu, jird, paca, vole **5** coypu, gundi, mouse, xerus **6** agouti, beaver, gopher, jerboa, marmot, murine **7** hamster, lemming, muskrat, viscacha **8** chipmunk, cricetid, dormouse, squirrel, tuco-tuco **9** chickaree, groundhog, guinea pig, porcupine, woodchuck **10** chinchilla, prairie dog
young: **3** pup
gerent: **4** boss, czar, emir, exec, head, khan, king, lord, rani, shah, suit **5** chief, mogul, pasha, queen, rajah, royal, ruler **6** caliph, dynast, kaiser, leader, mikado, prince, satrap, shogun, sultan, top dog **7** czarina, emperor, empress, manager, monarch, pharaoh, viceroy **8** dictator, director, governor, maharani, official, oligarch, overlord, overseer, princess, suzerain **9** chieftain, commander, executive, maharajah, potentate, sovereign, straw boss **10** supervisor
gerenuk: **8** antelope
relative: **3** gnu, kob **4** guib, kudu, oryx, puku, topi **5** addax, bongo, chiru, eland, goral, korin, nyala, oribi, saiga, serow **6** chammy, dikdik, duiker, impala, koodoo, lechwe, nilgai, rhebok, shammy, shamoy **7** blaubok, blesbok, chamois, defassa, gazelle, gemsbok, grysbok, nylghai, nylghau, sassaby **8** blesbuck, bontebok, bushbuck, gemsbuck, reedbuck, steenbok, steinbok **9** blackbuck, pronghorn, sitatunga, springbok, waterbuck **10** hartebeest, wildebeest
Gere, Richard: **5** actor
film: Chicago (2002)
The Cotton Club (1984)
Days of Heaven (1978)
Final Analysis (1992)
First Knight (1995)
The Jackal (1997)
Looking for Mr. Goodbar (1977)
An Officer and a Gentleman (1982)
Pretty Woman (1990)
Primal Fear (1996)
Runaway Bride (1999)
Sommersby (1993)
Unfaithful (2002)
Yanks (1979)
spouse: Cindy Crawford, Carey Lowell
Gerhard: **6** Domagk, Groote **8** Herzberg
in English: **6** Gerard
___ Gerhardt: **6** Jennie
Gerhardus: **8** Mercator
Geri: **9** Halliwell
geriatric: **3** old **4** aged **5** aging **6** ageing **7** ancient, elderly, wizened **8** grizzled **9** getting on, senescent, up in years
germ: **3** bud, bug **4** cell, root, seed **5** spark, strep, virus **6** embryo, gamete, kernel, origin, source **7** essence, keynote, microbe, nucleus **8** pathogen, rudiment **9** bacterium, beginning
cell: **4** seed **5** spore **6** gamete
combining form: **6** bacter- **7** bacteri- **8** bacterio-
ender: **4** free
fighter: **4** drug **5** serum **7** vaccine
germ ___: **4** cell **5** layer, plasm **6** theory
___ germ: **5** wheat
Germaine: **5** Greer
German: **4** Teut. **6** Teuton **7** Deutsch **8** Berliner, language, Teutonic **9** Hamburger
see also Germany
German ___: **3** ivy **5** fries, lapis, Ocean **6** Africa, silver **7** measles, Requiem
___ German: **3** Low **4** East, High, West
germane: **3** apt **5** ad rem **6** proper, timely **7** apropos, fitting, logical, on point, related **8** apposite, material, on target, relative, relevant, suitable **9** pertinent **10** applicable, felicitous, to the point
not ~: **5** inapt **10** extraneous, immaterial, irrelevant, out of place
not ~ to: **6** beside
German East ___: **6** Africa
Germania author: Tacitus
Germanic
god: **3** Tiu
goddess: **4** Norn
invader: **4** Goth, jute
___-Germanic: **4** Indo **5** Celto **6** Celtic
germanium: **5** metal **7** element
Germann: **4** Greg
German Requiem composer: **6** Brahms
German shepherd: **3** dog **5** canid **6** canine
in Britain: **8** Alsatian
German silver: **5** alloy
component: **4** zinc **6** copper, nickel
Germantown: **4** city
locale: **4** Penn. **8** Maryland **9** Tennessee
German words
a: **3** ein **4** eine **5** einem, einer, eines
above: **4** über
ago: **3** vor
and: **3** und
article: **3** das, dem, den, der, die, ein **4** eine
before: **3** vor
beyond: **4** über
cordial: **6** kümmel
count: **4** graf
east: **3** ost
eat: **5** essen
eleven: **3** elf
exclamation: **3** ach **6** himmel
from: **3** von
goblin: **6** kobold
I: **3** ich
league: **4** bund
me: **3** mir
mister: **4** herr
mouse: **4** maus
my: **4** mein **5** meine
near: **4** nahe
nine: **4** neun
no: **4** nein
old one: **4** alte
one: **3** ein **4** eins
our: **5** unser
over: **4** ober, über
possessive: **4** mein **5** meine
preposition: **3** aus, bei, mit, von **4** ober, ohne, über
pronoun: **3** ich, mir, sie, uns **4** mein **5** einer, meine, unser
roses: **5** rosen
salad: **5** salat
salt: **4** salz
sausage: **5** wurst
son: **4** sohn
song: **4** lied
songs: **6** lieder
star: **5** stern
state: **5** staat
the: **3** das, der, die
three: **4** drei
toast: **5** prost
us: **3** uns
with: **3** mit
without: **4** ohne
you: **3** sie
Germany: **6** nation **7** country **8** republic
archaeologist: **10** Schliemann
astronomer: **6** Kepler
auto: **2** VW **3** BMW **4** Audi, Opel **6** Beetle **8** Mercedes **10** Volkswagen
bacteriologist: **4** Koch
ballet dancer: **5** Jooss
biologist: **8** Weismann
botanist: **4** Cohn
bovine: **4** Glan **6** Angeln **8** Gelbvieh
camera: **5** Leica
canal: **4** Kiel
capital: **6** Berlin
cheese: **8** bierkäse
chemist: **4** Hahn, Kuhn **6** Bunsen, Müller, Nernst
city: **3** Aue, Ulm **4** Bonn, Gera, Hamm, Jena, Kiel, Köln, Unna **5** Baden, Düren, Emden, Essen, Fürth, Gotha, Hagen, Halle, Herne, Mainz, Neuss, Pirna, Riesa, Trier, Worms **6** Aachen, Berlin, Bremen, Dessau, Erfurt, Kassel, Lübeck, Munich, Siegen, Treves, Witten **7** Bottrop, Coblenz, Cologne, Dresden, Hamburg, Hanover, Koblenz, Krefeld, Leipsic, Leipzig, München, Münster, Potsdam, Rostock **8** Augsburg, Bayreuth, Chemnitz, Dortmund, Duisburg, Mannheim, Nürnberg, Solingen, Würzburg **9** Frankfurt, Karlsruhe, Magdeburg, Nuremberg, Offenbach, Oldenburg, Osnabrück, Stuttgart, Wiesbaden, Wolfsburg, Wuppertal **10** Düsseldorf, Heidelberg, Oberhausen
coal region: **4** Saar
composer: **4** Bach **6** Schütz
conductor: **4** Foss **5** Busch, Masur **6** Rudolf, Walter **8** Damrosch **9** Klemperer **11** Furtwängler
dance: **7** ländler
engraver: **5** Dürer
environmentalist: **5** Green
essayist: **4** Mann
figure skater: **4** Witt
first ~ president: **5** Ebert
former money: **3** pfg. **4** mark **5** taler **6** heller, thaler **7** pfennig **8** kreutzer **9** rix-dollar
former region: **4** Saxe **5** Lippe **6** Alsace
former ~ ruler: **6** kaiser
geophysicist: **7** Wegener
golfer: **6** Langer
gun: **5** Luger
historian: **8** Schiller
industrial region: **4** Ruhr, Saar
John: **4** Hans **6** Johann
journalist: **8** Remarque
legislature: **9** Bundesrat, Bundestag
liqueur: **6** kümmel
magazine: **5** Stern
mathematician: **5** Gauss **6** Kepler
money: **4** euro
mountain range: **3** Erz **4** Harz, Rhön
natural historian: **4** Baer
neighbor: **6** France, Poland **7** Austria, Belgium, Denmark **10** Luxembourg
Nobelist in Chemistry: **4** Hahn, Kuhn **5** Alder, Bosch, Diels, Eigen, Haber, Huber **6** Michel, Nernst, Wittig **7** Bergius, Buchner, Fischer, Ostwald, Wallach, Wieland, Windaus, Ziegler **9** Butenandt, von Baeyer, Zsigmondy **10** Staudinger **11** Deisenhofer, Willstötter
Nobelist in Economics: **6** Selten
Nobelist in Literature: **4** Böll, Mann **5** Grass, Hesse, Heyse **6** Eucken **7** Mommsen **9** Hauptmann
Nobelist in Medicine: **4** Koch **5** Lynen, Neher **6** Domagk, Köhler, Kossel, Lorenz **7** Ehrlich, Sakmann, Spemann, Warburg **8** Meyerhof **9** von Frisch **10** von Behring
Nobelist in Peace: **6** Brandt, Quidde **10** Stresemann
Nobelist in Physics: **4** Paul, Wien **5** Bothe, Braun, Hertz, Ruska, Stark **6** Binnig, Franck, Jensen, Planck **7** Bednorz, Dehmelt, Röntgen, von Laue **8** Einstein, Ketterle **9** Mössbauer, von Lenard **10** Heisenberg **11** von Klitzing
novelist: **4** Mann **5** Hesse
org.: **4** NATO
painter: **5** Dürer, Ernst **7** Holbein
philosopher: **8** Spengler **9** Nietzsche
physicist: **3** Ohm **4** Born **5** Hertz, Ruska, Stern **6** Binnig, Nernst, Planck **8** Einstein, Roentgen **9** Kirchhoff **10** Fahrenheit, Fraunhofer, Heisenberg
pianist: **5** Bülow
plane: **5** Stuka
playwright: **4** Holz **5** Sachs **6** Brecht, Grabbe, Hebbel, Kaiser **7** Büchner, Freytag, Gutzkow, Horvath **8** Gryphius, Schiller **9** Hauptmann, Sudermann, Zuckmayer
poet: **4** Holz **5** Brant, Celan, Heine, Hesse, Rilke, Sachs, Storm **6** Brecht, Dehmel, George, Hebbel, Mörike **7** Fontane, Rückert **8** Brentano, Chamisso, Gryphius, Schiller, Schlegel **9** Nietzsche
port: **4** Kiel **5** Emden **6** Bremen **7** Hamburg, Münster, Rostock **8** Cuxhaven
reformer: **6** Luther

region: 3 Bav. 4 Prus. 5 Baden, Hesse 6 Saxony 7 Bavaria, Prussia 8 Saarland 9 Rhineland
river: 3 Ems 4 Eder, Eger, Elbe, Isar, Main, Naab, Oder, Odra, Ohre, Oste, Ruhr 5 Fulda, Rhine, Weser
scientist: 3 Ohm 4 Baer, Born, Cohn, Hahn, Koch, Kuhn 5 Gauss, Hertz, Ruska, Stern 6 Binnig, Bunsen, Kepler, Müller, Nernst, Planck 7 Wegener 8 Einstein, Roentgen, Weismann 9 Kirchhoff 10 Fahrenheit, Fraunhofer, Heisenberg, Schliemann
silver: 6 albata
socialist: 4 Marx
soprano: 6 Berger 7 Lehmann
spa: 3 Ems 5 Baden 6 Bad Ems
speed skater: 4 Enke
sub: 5 U-boat
swimmer: 4 Otto 5 Ender
valley: 4 Ruhr, Saar 5 Mosel
violinist: 6 Mutter
wine: 4 hock, Sekt 7 Auslese, cabinet, Moselle 8 cold duck 10 Hochheimer
wine region: 5 Rhine
writer: 4 Benn, Böll, Mann, Marx 5 Arnim, Grass, Grimm, Hesse, Heyse, Raabe, Zweig 6 Döblin, Goethe, Heinse, Jünger, Kleist, Luther, Walser 7 Fontane, Freytag, Gutzkow, Hoffman, Johnson, Novalis, Richter, Wieland 8 Borchert, Remarque, Spengler, Wedekind 10 Schliemann
WWII naval base: 5 Emden
___ Germany: 4 East, West
germfree: 4 pure 5 clean 6 axenic, washed 7 aseptic, sterile 8 hygienic, pristine, sanitary, unsoiled 10 antiseptic, immaculate
germicide: 8 cleanser, fumigant 10 antiseptic
germinal: 5 early 8 evolving 9 embryonic
Germinal author: Emile Zola
germinate: 3 bud 4 grow 5 begin, bloom, shoot 6 sprout 7 blossom, burgeon, develop 8 bourgeon, take root, vegetate 9 fertilize, originate, pullulate
germination: 6 growth
germ-related: 5 viral
germ-ridden: 5 dirty 6 filthy, soiled 7 tainted 9 unhealthy 10 unsanitary
germs: 7 bacilli 8 bacteria, microbes 9 pathogens
absence of ~: 7 asepsis
germy: 5 dirty 6 filthy, septic 7 unclean 8 infected 10 unsanitary
not ~: 4 pure 5 clean 7 aseptic, sterile 8 purified, sanitary 10 sterilized, uninfected
Gernreich: 4 Rudi
Gernsback, Hugo: 6 writer
genre: sci-fi
Geronimo: 5 chief 6 Apache, Indian
Gerontion poet: 5 Eliot
Gerrit: 6 Graham
Gerry: 5 Adams 6 Cooney, Goffin 7 Ferraro, Marsden 8 Elbridge, Mulligan, Rafferty
Gerry and the Pacemakers
song: Don't Let the Sun Catch You Crying (1964)
Ferry Cross the Mersey (1965)
How Do You Do It? (1964)
gerrymander: 3 fix, rig 10 manipulate, tamper with
Gershon: 4 Gina
Gershwin, George: 8 composer
brother: 3 Ira
colleague: 4 Kern 5 Arlen 6 Berlin, Levant
heroine: 4 Bess
musical: Crazy for You
Funny Face
Girl Crazy
Lady, Be Good!
La La Lucille
Let 'Em Eat Cake
Of Thee I Sing
Oh, Kay!
Pardon My English
Porgy and Bess
Primrose
Strike Up the Band
Tip-Toes
portrayer: 4 Alda
song: Bess, You Is My Woman
Bidin' My Time
But Not for Me
Clap Yo Hands
Could You Use Me?
Delishious
Do Do Do
Do It Again
Embraceable You
Fascinating Rhythm
A Foggy Day
Funny Face
How Long Has This Been Going On?
I Got Plenty o' Nuthin'
I Got Rhythm
I'll Build a Stairway to Paradise
Isn't It a Pity?
It Ain't Necessarily So
I've Got a Crush on You
I Was Doing All Right
Let's Call the Whole Thing Off
Liza
Love Is Here to Stay
Love Is Sweeping the Country
Love Walked In
The Man I Love
Maybe
Mine
My Cousin in Milwaukee
My One and Only
Nice Work if You Can Get It
Nobody but You
Of Thee I Sing
Oh, Lady Be Good
Rialto Ripples
Somebody Loves Me
Someone to Watch Over Me
Soon
Strike Up the Band
Summertime
Swanee
Sweet and Low-Down
'S Wonderful
That Certain Feeling
They All Laughed
They Can't Take That Away From Me
Who Cares
Wintergreen for President
A Woman Is a Sometime Thing
work: An American in Paris
Concerto in F
Cuban Overture
Rhapsody in Blue
Second Rhapsody
Gert: 5 Frobe
Gertrude: 4 Berg 5 Elion, saint, Stein 6 Ederle 8 Lawrence
friend: 5 Alice
son: 6 Hamlet
Gertz: 4 Jami
Gerulaitis: 5 Vitas 7 netster 9 tennis pro
gerund end: 3 ing
gervais: 6 cheese
Gervin, George
milieu: 5 court
org.: 3 NBA
sport: 10 basketball
gest: 7 exploit
___ gestae: 3 res
gestation: 6 growth 9 evolution, gravidity, pregnancy 10 incubation, maturation
stage: 5 fetus 6 foetus
geste: 4 deed, feat 7 exploit 9 adventure
___ Geste: 4 Beau
gesticulate: 4 sign, wave 6 beckon, motion, signal
gesture: 3 bow, nod 4 beck, mime, sign, wave, wink 5 shrug, V sign 6 action, beckon, curtsy, motion, salute, signal 7 curtsey 8 laughter, movement 9 pantomime 10 indication
affectionate ~: 3 hug 4 kiss 6 caress
Buddhist ~: 5 mudra
flirtatious ~: 4 wink
of approval: 3 nod, vee 5 V sign
of greeting: 4 wave
peace ~: 3 vee 5 V sign
polite ~: 3 bow 6 curtsy 7 curtsey
gesturing performer: 4 mime 5 clown, mimer, mimic
gesundheit evoker: 5 achoo 6 ahchoo, hachoo, sneeze 7 kerchoo
get: 3 bag, bug, buy, cop, dig, irk, nab, net, see, vex, win 4 burn, coax, draw, earn, find, gain, gall, grab, hail, have, kids, know, land, make, nail, reap, rile, snag, stir, sway, take, trap, urge 5 amuse, anger, annex, annoy, bring, catch, fetch, glean, grasp, learn, peeve, pique, press, reach, ready, score, seize, sense, solve, upset 6 absorb, accept, access, affect, arouse, arrest, attain, become, bother, buy out, collar, come by, defeat, derive, effect, elicit, enlist, excite, fathom, follow, garner, induce, line up, nettle, obtain, outwit, pick up, prompt, rack up, rankle, secure, snap up, stir up, wangle 7 abscond, achieve, acquire, agitate, bring in, build up, buy into, capture, chalk up, contact, enflame, ensnare, extract, harvest, impress, inherit, insnare, nonplus, perturb, procure, progeny, provoke, realize, receive, scare up, wheedle, win over 8 come to be, contract, convince, invest in, irritate, perceive, persuade, pull down, purchase, receipts, retrieve, rustle up 9 aggravate, apprehend, catch on to, extradite, figure out, influence, intercept, lay hold of, overpower 10 accomplish, appreciate, comprehend, exasperate, fall heir to, understand
across: 5 speak 6 convey, effect 9 bring home, elucidate, make clear 10 illustrate
a fix on: 6 locate 8 identify, localize 9 determine
ahead: 3 win 4 gain, grow 5 go far 6 make it, pan out, thrive 7 advance, luck out, make out, prevail, prosper, triumph, work out 8 flourish, go places, grow rich, hit it big, make good, progress 9 go forward 10 gain ground
a hold of: 4 call, meet 5 phone, reach 6 talk to 7 contact, liaison, speak to 8 approach 9 check with, telephone, touch base
a kick out of: 3 dig, use 4 like 5 enjoy, go for 6 relish 8 flip over, thrill to 9 delight in, get high on, indulge in
a load of: 3 eye, see, spy 4 look, peek, peep, peer, view 5 watch 6 behold, glance, listen, look at, notice, regard 7 glimpse, observe, witness 10 sneak a look
a loan: 6 borrow
a loan on: 4 pawn 6 pledge
along: 2 do 3 mix 4 fare, fend, live 5 agree, exist 6 make do, manage 7 make out, subsist 8 go places
a move on: 2 go 3 fly, hie, rip, run, zip 4 dart, dash, flit, race, rush, stir, tear, zoom 5 hurry, scoot, spank, speed 6 barrel, gallop, hasten, hustle, rocket, scurry 7 floor it, hop to it, quicken, scamper, speed up 8 step on it 9 hotfoot it, shake a leg, skedaddle 10 hightail it
an A on: 3 ace
an earful: 4 heed 6 listen, take in 7 receive 8 discover, listen in, listen to 9 eavesdrop 10 understand
an eyeful: 3 see 4 gaze 7 observe
angry: 4 fume, snap 6 rear up, see red
around: 4 foil, pass, shun 5 avoid, dodge, elude, evade, shirk, skirt, visit 6 bypass, outwit 8 outsmart, overcome 9 circulate, negotiate, prevail on, socialize 10 circumvent
as far as: 5 reach
a shot: 4 snap 10 photograph
at: 5 annoy, bribe, imply, reach 6 access, locate, obtain 7 suggest 8 intimate 9 influence, insinuate
a tan: 3 sun 4 bask 8 sunbathe
a taste of: 3 try 6 sample
away: 2 go 3 fly 4 exit, flee 5 break 6 depart, escape 8 fugitate, run for it, withdraw 10 break loose
away from: 5 elude, evade, leave 8 shake off, throw off
back: 5 reply 6 avenge, recoup, redeem, regain 7 rebound, reclaim, recover, respond, salvage 8 retrieve 9 reacquire, recapture
back at: 5 react, repay 7 revenge 9 pay in kind, retaliate
behind: 4 back, hype, plug, push 6 hype up, second, talk up 7 approve, endorse, indorse, promote, support 8 sanction 9 encourage, guarantee, subscribe 10 rally round
better: 3 age 4 heal, mend 5 rally 6 look up, pick up 7 rebound, recover 10 recuperate
bigger: 3 wax 4 grow 6 expand
bored: 4 tire
boring: 4 pale, pall
bushed: 4 flag, tire
busy: 3 act 4 move 6 fall to, jump in, tackle 7 hop to it, pitch in 9 take steps 10 buckle down
but good: 4 nail
by: 2 do 4 cope, fare, live, pass 5 exist 6 hack it, make do, manage 7 make out, qualify, satisfy, suffice, survive
by force: 3 pry 5 exact, usurp, wrest, wring 6 extort, wrench
by trickery: 4 gull 5 cheat, mulct 6 extort, fleece 7 defraud, swindle
clear of: 4 duck, flee, lose 5 avoid, dodge, elude, evade, skirt 6 escape 7 fend off 8 sidestep 10 circumvent
cold feet: 5 quail, waver 6 falter, wobble 8 hang back, hesitate 9 hem and haw, vacillate
coverage for: 6 ensure, insure 7 protect, warrant 9 indemnify
cozy: 6 curl up, nestle 7 snuggle
cracking: 3 hie 4 rush 5 begin, start 6 go to it 7 pitch in 8 commence
crowned: 4 rule 5 reign 6 accede
dark: 5 laten 7 becloud
darker: 5 laten
dirty: 4 soil
done: 3 end 4 cook 5 mop up 6 finish 7 achieve 10 put through

down: 4 duck, land 5 light 6 alight, boogie 7 jump off 8 dismount
down on one knee: 3 woo
down pat: 5 learn 6 master 9 ascertain
down to basics: 6 lay out 7 explain 8 simplify, spell out 9 make plain
down to brass tacks: 6 detail 7 account, itemize, specify 9 make clear, stipulate
down to business: 5 start 7 shape up
duded up: 5 groom, preen, primp, prink
due to ~: 5 in for
established: 6 locate, settle 8 make good, take root
even: 5 repay, spite 6 avenge 7 pay back, requite, revenge 9 retaliate
excited: 4 flip 5 go ape 6 arouse, tingle 7 bristle, enthuse
extra life from: 5 reuse
fail to ~: 4 miss
familiar: 6 orient
fat: 4 gain 6 thrive
fit: 6 tone up 8 exercise
fresh: 4 sass 8 mouth off, talk back 10 answer back
F's: 4 fail
go ~: 5 bring, fetch 6 obtain 8 retrieve
going: 4 move, open, roll 5 begin, crank, found, rouse, start 6 fillip, launch, let rip, set off, set out 7 kick off, lead off, pitch in, speed up 8 commence, initiate, organize, set about, set forth 9 enter upon, originate 10 inaugurate
gratis: 5 leech 8 freeload, scrounge
hard to ~ to: 3 dim 4 dull, slow 5 dense, thick 6 obtuse, simple, stolid 9 pigheaded
help from: 6 lean on
hep: 6 wise up
higher: 4 rise, soar 6 ascend, move up 7 take off
high on: 4 like, love 5 enjoy, savor 6 relish 9 delight in 10 appreciate
hitched: 3 wed 5 elope, marry 10 tie the knot
hold of: 4 grab, have 5 catch, grasp, reach 6 locate, obtain 7 acquire, possess, receive 8 come into 9 ascertain
hopping: 3 fly, hie, run, zip 4 dart, dash, move, rush, tear 5 hurry, scoot 6 bustle, hasten, hustle, scurry 7 floor it, quicken 8 step on it 9 make haste, shake a leg 10 lose no time, make tracks
horizontal: 4 laze
hot: 7 flame up
in: 4 come 5 enter, reach 6 arrive, show up
in a dragnet: 3 nab 4 bust, grab, nail, trap 5 catch, pinch, seize 6 arrest, collar, corner, pick up, pull in, snatch 7 capture 9 apprehend
in a sting: 6 entrap
in line: 4 wait
in one's face: 5 annoy 6 accost, bother 8 confront 9 challenge
in one's hair: 3 bug, irk, vex 4 gall, rile 5 annoy, peeve, pique 6 madden, nettle, pester, plague, ruffle 7 provoke, tick off 8 irritate 9 aggravate 10 exasperate
in one's head: 5 grasp, learn, study 6 absorb, master, pick up, soak up 7 find out 8 discover, memorize 10 understand
in return: 4 earn, gain, reap 5 clear 6 derive, garner, profit, secure, take in 7 bring in, collect, harvest, receive 8 gather in
in shape: 3 jog 4 hone, tone 5 train 7 rebound, recover, work out
in someone's hair: 3 irk 4 rile 5 peeve, upset
in sync: 6 attune 10 coordinate
in the act: 7 partake
in the game: 4 ante
in the way of: 4 clog 5 deter 6 hamper, hinder, impair, impede, impose 8 handicap, obstruct
into: 3 don 6 absorb, access 7 enthuse
(into): 4 seep
into a dither: 4 fret, fuss, stew 5 sweat, worry 7 agonize
into line: 4 heed, obey 6 comply, follow, submit 7 conform, observe
into mischief: 5 act up, cut up 8 go astray 9 misbehave 10 fool around, roughhouse
in touch: 5 reach 7 contact, respond
in with: 9 associate, cultivate, insinuate, shine up to 10 ingratiate
it: 3 dig, see 7 catch on, realize 10 comprehend, understand
it together: 4 plan 5 set up 7 arrange 8 organize 10 coordinate
just ~ by: 6 eke out, make do 7 squeeze
larger: 3 wax 4 grow 5 build, swell, widen 6 dilate, expand 7 augment, broaden, develop, fill out, magnify 8 increase
licked: 4 lose
lost: 2 go 4 scat 5 scram, split, stray 6 beat it, begone, bug off, wander 7 push off 8 withdraw 10 go fly a kite
lower: 3 ebb 4 drop, wane 6 lessen, recede 7 decline, dwindle, retreat, subside, tail off 8 decrease, diminish, fall back, slack off
mad: 5 anger 6 blow up, rear up 10 hit the roof
melodramatic: 3 act 5 emote 7 carry on, overact
misty: 3 cry, sob 4 weep 7 blubber 9 shed tears
money: 6 cash in, redeem 9 liquidate
money for: 4 sell
more out of: 5 reuse
moving: 3 hie 4 roll, stir 5 speed, start 6 bestir 7 speed up 8 hightail, run along
next to: 3 woo 7 flatter, promote 8 butter up 9 cultivate, shine up to 10 curry favor
no place fast: 3 lag 4 drag, flag, idle, limp, loaf, loll, plod, poke 5 dally, delay, tarry 6 dabble, dawdle, diddle, loiter 7 fall off, fritter, slacken 8 hang back, straggle 9 inch along, poke along, waste time 10 dillydally, lose ground, mess around, wait around
nosy: 3 ask, pry
off: 6 alight, debark 7 descend, detrain 8 dismount 9 disembark
off one's chest: 3 say 4 tell 5 spill 6 relate, unload 7 confess, confide, recount, tell all, unbosom 8 unburden
off one's feet: 3 sit 4 loll, rest 6 lounge, repose, sprawl 7 recline 10 stretch out
off the fence: 3 act, opt 6 choose, decide
off the ground: 5 begin
off the hook: 4 save 5 spare 6 rescue
off the point: 5 drift, stray 6 ramble, wander 7 deviate, digress, diverge 8 divagate
off the stage: 4 exit
off the track: 5 stray 6 derail, ramble 7 digress
older: 3 age
on: 3 age, bug 4 bait, fare, ride, wear 5 agree, board, go far, mount, taunt 6 harass, thrive 7 make out, proceed 8 progress
on a horse: 6 gallop, travel 7 journey
on a soapbox: 5 orate 6 preach 7 address, declaim, lecture 8 harangue, proclaim
on board: 6 embark
one's act together: 5 rally
one's dander up: 3 ire, irk 4 rile 5 anger, peeve 7 bristle
one's feet wet: 4 ford, open, wade 5 begin, slosh, start 6 launch, paddle, splash, tackle 7 kick off, lead off 8 commence, get going, set forth 9 enter into, strike out 10 inaugurate, plunge into
one's fingers on: 3 bag, nab 4 grab, grip, take 5 catch, grasp, seize, snare, steal 6 secure, snatch 7 acquire, plunder, receive 8 glom on to 9 lay hold of
one's goat: 3 irk, vex 4 miff, rile 5 anger, peeve, upset 6 enrage, rankle
one's hands on: 3 get 4 grab, have 5 catch, seize, snare 6 obtain 7 acquire, possess, receive 9 latch onto
one's just deserts: 4 earn, rate 5 merit 7 deserve 10 have coming
one's second wind: 5 rally
on it: 5 hop to
on one's case: 3 bug, nag 4 carp, harp 6 badger 9 find fault
on one's feet: 5 stand
on one's nerves: 3 irk 4 rile 5 grate, peeve, upset
on the bandwagon for: 4 back 5 boost 7 espouse, promote, sponsor, support 8 advocate, champion
on the horn: 4 buzz, call, dial, ring 5 phone 6 call up, dial up, ring up 7 contact 9 telephone
on the wagon: 4 quit
on with it: 7 proceed
organized: 4 plan, plot 5 chart, frame, set up 6 lay out, map out 7 outline, prepare, project, propose, work out 8 engineer, rough out, schedule, think out 9 formulate 10 mastermind
out: 2 go 4 exit, flee, quit 5 be off, break, issue, leave, scram, split 6 beat it, begone, decamp, depart, escape 7 bail out, buzz off, publish, run away, skiddoo, take off, vamoose 8 evacuate, hightail, withdraw 9 broadcast, skedaddle, take a hike 10 hightail it
out from under: 6 recoup 7 recover 8 liberate
out of: 4 doff, duck, peel, shed 5 avoid, dodge, elude, evade, shake, shirk, strip 6 escape 7 disrobe, slip off, take off 8 sidestep
out of bed: 4 rise, wake 5 arise, rouse, waken
out of here: 2 go 5 leave, scram 6 move it 7 vamoose 8 run along, shove off 9 move along, take a hike 10 hit the road
out of line: 4 defy, riot, rise 5 act up, rebel 6 mutiny, oppose, resist, revolt, rise up 7 disobey, dissent, protest 9 make waves, misbehave
out of sight: 4 hide 6 lie low 9 take cover
out of the way: 4 duck 5 dodge 8 sidestep
out to ~: 5 after
over: 7 recover 9 negotiate
past: 4 beat 5 clear, outdo, steer 6 detour 8 maneuver, outstrip, overtake 9 negotiate
pleasure from: 3 dig 4 like, love, want 5 adore, enjoy, fancy, go for, savor 6 desire, dote on, relish 9 delight in, indulge in 10 appreciate, be mad about
promoted: 4 rise
psyched: 7 enthuse
ready: 3 fix 4 gird, pack, prep 5 brace, groom, ready, ripen 6 gear up 7 prepare, psych up 8 mobilize 10 square away
real: 6 come on
revenge on: 3 fix 5 set up 6 punish 7 pay back
rid of: 2 ax 3 axe, can, end, zap 4 boot, cede, drop, dump, junk, lose, oust, sack, sell, shed, toss 5 chuck, ditch, drain, eject, erase, expel, forgo, let go, purge, scrap, yield 6 banish, bounce, forego, give up, lay off, remove, unload 7 abandon, cashier, discard, dismiss, drum out, exclude, forfeit, forsake, release, wipe out 8 exorcise, exorcize, forswear, furlough, hand over, jettison, part with, pink-slip, shake off, stamp out, throw out, unburden 9 cast aside, discharge, eliminate, foreswear, liquidate, surrender, terminate, throw away 10 do away with, relinquish
rid (of): 6 divest
rid of knots: 4 undo 6 loosen 8 untangle
right: 5 solve 6 unlock 7 explain, unravel, work out 8 decipher 9 figure out, puzzle out
satisfaction from: 3 dig 4 like 5 boast, eat up, enjoy, go for, savor 6 dote on, wallow 7 revel in 8 flip over, thrill to 9 delight in 10 appreciate
set: 3 fix 4 prep 5 equip, prime, ready 6 fit out, gear up, warm up 7 arrange, prepare 8 mobilize, organize, rehearse 10 pave the way, square away
sidetracked: 5 stray 6 ramble, wander 7 digress, meander
situated: 3 set 5 dwell, lodge, perch, roost 6 locate, orient, settle
sleepy: 3 nod 4 doze, tire 5 droop 6 drowse
slippery: 5 ice up 6 freeze
smaller: 6 lessen, reduce, shrink 7 dwindle, shrivel 8 contract, diminish
smart: 4 sass 5 learn 8 mouth off 9 give lip to
soft: 4 melt, thaw 6 loosen, warm up 7 defrost 8 unfreeze 10 deliquesce
somewhere: 6 arrive
started: 4 move 5 crank 7 proceed, take off 8 turn over
steamed up: 4 boil, burn, fume, stew 5 froth 6 see red, seethe, simmer 7 bristle, smolder
straight A's: 5 excel
stuck: 4 mire 5 lodge 6 fixate, wallow
support for, as an idea: 4 sell
tangled: 3 mat 4 knot 5 snarl, twist
the ball rolling: 5 begin, cause, start 8 commence
the best of: 3 win 5 one-up, trump, unarm, upset, worst 6 defeat, master, outwit, subdue 7 conquer 8 outsmart, overcome 9 overpower
the gold: 3 win
the goods on: 3 pin 4 nail, trap

the hang of: 3 see 5 learn 6 master
the hard way: 3 pry 5 wring 6 extort, wrench
the impression: 4 feel 5 think 6 divine, intuit, pick up, reason 7 believe, discern 8 perceive 10 understand
the job done: 4 work 6 hack it
the jump on: 5 outdo 7 prevail, surpass 8 dominate, outstrip
the knack of: 5 grasp, learn 6 pick up 7 excel in
the lead out: 3 hie 4 move, rush, tear 5 erase, hurry 6 hasten
the lowdown: 5 learn
the message: 3 see 4 hear 8 perceive
the punch line: 4 grin, howl, roar 5 laugh 6 giggle, guffaw 7 chortle, chuckle, crack up, snicker, snigger
there: 4 land 5 light, reach 6 arrive, attend, blow in, make it, pull in, roll in, show up, sign in, turn up 7 check in, clock in, fetch up, hit town 8 breeze in 9 disembark, touch down 10 drop anchor
there fast: 3 run, zip 4 dash, rush, tear, whiz, zoom 5 hurry, speed, whisk 6 hasten, scurry 7 scamper
the same answer: 5 agree
the show on the road: 5 begin 6 launch 7 lead off 8 commence
the upper hand: 4 beat, bury, drub, rout, stun 5 cream, crush, drown, quell, smash, total, trash, upset, waste 6 defeat, subdue 7 clobber, conquer, oppress, put away, stagger, take out, torpedo, trounce 8 bear down, blow away, bulldoze, overcome, roll over, shellack, suppress, vanquish 9 overthrow, subjugate 10 take care of
the word: 4 hear 5 learn
the wrong idea: 3 err 7 presume 8 misjudge 9 underrate
through: 5 reach, solve 6 endure, finish 7 survive, weather 8 complete 10 accomplish
through one's head: 5 grasp, learn 7 discern 9 recognize 10 appreciate, comprehend, understand
through to: 5 reach, touch 8 register
tired: 4 fade, flag, jade 5 droop, weary 8 languish, peter out, slow down
to: 3 irk 4 faze, rile 5 anger, annoy, bribe, eat at, peeve, reach, upset 6 access, affect, attain, bother, pester, rattle, tamper 7 agitate, contact, fluster, trouble, unnerve 8 arrive at, distress, unsettle 9 aggravate, influence 10 disconcert
together: 4 mass, meet 5 amass, merge, rally, troop, unite 6 confer 7 combine, compile, convene 9 socialize 10 rendezvous
to know: 3 see 4 hear, meet, read 5 dig up, glean, grasp, greet, learn, reach, study 6 link up, master, peruse, pick up, take in, turn up 7 connect, contact, discern, find out, run into, uncover, unearth, welcome 8 approach, deal with, discover, pore over, smoke out 9 ascertain, catch on to, determine, encounter, forgather 10 experience, rendezvous, understand
too excited over: 4 gush 7 enthuse
to one's feet: 4 rise, wake 5 arise, awake, stand, waken 6 awaken, jump up, wake up 7 stand up
too personal: 3 pry, spy 5 snoop, stare 6 butt in, horn in, meddle 7 intrude, obtrude, wiretap 8 question 9 interfere
to the bottom of: 5 plumb, solve 6 fathom 9 penetrate
to the top: 3 win 5 score 6 arrive 7 achieve, make out, prosper, succeed 8 carry off, flourish, go places, make good 10 accomplish, do all right
to work: 5 begin, start 6 embark, set off, set out 7 lead off, proceed 8 commence, set about, set forth
try to ~ answers: 3 ask 4 pump, quiz 5 grill, query 7 canvass, consult, inquire, request
under one's skin: 3 ire, irk, vex 4 rile 5 annoy, pique, upset
under way: 4 open, sail, send 5 begin, speed, start 6 launch, set off, set out 7 kick off, lead off, proceed 8 commence, initiate, set forth 9 enter upon, originate, strike out 10 inaugurate
up: 4 rise, stir, wake 5 arise, awake, hatch, rouse, stand, waken 6 awaken, outfit 7 costume, roll out, turn out 8 lose a lap 10 hit the deck
up and go: 3 pep, vim 4 exit, life, push, snap 5 drive, leave, oomph, vigor 6 bounce, energy, starch 8 ambition, gumption, vitality, vivacity 10 exuberance
upright: 5 stand
upset: 4 burn, fume, lose, pout, stew 6 blow up, seethe, simmer 7 bristle, smolder
used to: 5 adapt, enure, inure 6 attune 7 break in 8 accustom, cope with 9 acclimate, reconcile
vibes: 4 feel, know, mind, read 5 grasp, smell 6 absorb, divine, intuit, notice, pick up, reason, take in 7 believe, catch on, discern, observe, realize 8 perceive 9 apprehend 10 anticipate, get the idea, have a hunch, understand
well: 4 heal, mend 5 rally 6 recoup 7 rebound, recover 10 recuperate
wind of: 4 hear 5 learn, scent, smell 6 pick up 7 find out 8 discover 9 ascertain
wise: 9 smarten up

get __: 3 off, out, set 4 away, back, down, even, into, over, to it, wise 5 about, after, ahead, along, going, ready, rid of, there 6 across, around 7 nowhere, through
get __ a good thing: 4 in on
get __ at: 4 back
get __ deal: 4 a raw
get __ for: 5 a feel
get __ for effort: 3 an A, an E
get __ for one's money: 4 a run
get __ good thing: 5 in on a
get __ holding the bag: 4 left
get __ in one's stomach: 5 a knot
get __ in one's throat: 5 a lump
get __ in the face: 5 a slap
get __ it: 4 with
get __ lease on life: 4 a new
get __ line: 4 into
get __ of: 3 rid 4 hold, wind 5 a hold, a load
get __ of one's own medicine: 5 a dose
get __ on: 5 a bead, a jump, a move
get __ one's skin: 5 under
get __ on the right foot: 3 off
get __ on the wrist: 5 a slap
get __ on the wrong foot: 3 off
get __ out of: 5 a bang, a kick, a rise
get __ shape: 4 into
get __ start: 5 a late
get __ stick: 5 on the
get __ the act: 4 into
get __ the ground floor: 4 in on
get __ the right foot: 5 off on
get __ the wrong foot: 5 off on
get __ to: 6 around
get __ to cases: 4 down
get __ together: 5 it all
get __ trouble: 4 into
get __ up: 4 a leg
get __ with: 4 away, even
get __ writing: 4 it in
get-__ card: 4 well
get-__-go: 5 up-and
Get __: 3 Off 4 a Job, Back, Down, Here, It On 5 Crazy, Happy, Ready, Smart 6 Carter, Closer, Shorty
Get __!: 4 on it, real 5 a grip, a life, Bruce
Get __ back!: 5 off my
Get __ behind me...: 4 thee
Get __ it!: 4 with
Get __ of that!: 5 a load
Get __ of yourself!: 5 a hold
Get __ the Church...: 4 Me to
Get __ up: 4 a leg
Get __ Ya-Ya's Out!: 3 Yer
geta: 4 clog, shoe 8 footwear
get a __: 5 leg up
get a __ lease on life: 3 new
get a __ of: 4 load
get a __ on: 4 bead, move 6 handle, wiggle
get a __ out of: 4 bang
get a __ up: 3 leg
Get a __: 3 Job
Get a __!: 4 grip, life
Get a __ of that!: 4 load
Get a __ on!: 4 move
Get a Job: 4 oldy 5 oldie 6 doo-wop
syllable: 3 sha
Get a Job (1958 song) artist: Silhouettes
Get a Leg Up (1991 song) artist: John Cougar Mellencamp
Get a load of that!: 4 look
get an __ effort: 4 A for, E for
get a new __ on life: 5 lease
get around __: 4 to it
getaway: 3 lam 4 exit, tour 5 break 6 escape, flight 8 breakout 9 departure 10 decampment
make a ~: 3 fly, run 4 bolt, flee, flit, skip 5 elude, evade 6 decamp, escape 7 abscond 8 jump bail, shake off 9 cut and run, disappear, skedaddle 10 fly the coop, hightail it
weekend ~: 5 B and B
Get away!: 4 shoo
Getaway, The (1972 film)
cast: Ben Johnson, Ali MacGraw, Steve McQueen
director: Sam Peckinpah
Get Back (1969 song) artist: Beatles
__ Get By: 3 I'll
Get Carter (2000 film)
cast: Rachael Leigh Cook, Alan Cumming, Miranda Richardson, Sylvester Stallone
director: Stephen Kay
Get Closer (1976 song) artist: Seals and Crofts
Get Crazy (1983 film)
cast: Gail Edwards, Malcolm McDowell, Daniel Stern
get down to __: 5 cases
Get Down Tonight (1975 song) artist: KC and the Sunshine Band
get-go: 5 onset, start 9 square one
Get going!: 4 move 6 move it
Get Happy composer: 5 Arlen 7 Koehler
Get Here (1991 song) artist: Oleta Adams
...get her poor dog __: 5 a bone
get in __ ground floor: 5 on the
get in one's __: 3 way 4 face, hair
get in on the __ floor: 6 ground
__ Get in the Way: 5 Words
get into __: 4 line
get into the __: 3 act
get it __ together: 3 all
Get it?: 3 dig, see
__ Get It for You Wholesale: 4 I Can
get left holding the __: 3 bag
Get lost!: 4 scat, shoo 5 scoot, scram, split 6 beat it, begone, bug off
Get Me to the Church on Time composer: 5 Loewe 6 Lerner
Get off my __!: 4 case
Get Off My Cloud (1965 song) artist: Rolling Stones
get off on the __ foot: 5 right, wrong
get one's __: 4 goat 6 number
get one's __ in a row: 5 ducks
get one's __ in the door: 4 foot
get one's __ into: 5 teeth
get one's __ together: 3 act
get one's __ up: 7 hackles
get one's ducks in a __: 3 row
get one's foot in the __: 4 door
get one's teeth __: 4 into
get on one's __: 6 nerves
get on one's __ horse: 4 high
get on the __: 5 stick
Get on the Bus (1996 film)
cast: Ossie Davis, Charles S. Dutton
director: Spike Lee
__ get-out: 3 all
Get Outta My Dreams... (1988 song) artist: Billy Ocean
Get real!: 4 as if, c'mon
Get Shorty: 4 film 5 novel
author: Elmore Leonard
cast: Danny DeVito, Gene Hackman, Rene Russo, John Travolta
director: Barry Sonnenfeld
__ Gets in Your Eyes: 5 Smoke
Get Smart (NBC/CBS sitcom)
cast: Don Adams (Maxwell Smart, Agent 86)
Barbara Feldon (Agent 99)
Edward Platt (The Chief)
foe: 4 KAOS 9 Siegfried
robot: Hymie
__ Get Started: 5 I Can't
__-getter: 4 vote
get the __: 4 gate, hook 5 point 7 message
get the __ of: 4 best, hang
get the __ of it: 5 worst
get the __ on: 4 drop, jump
get the __ on the road: 4 show
get the __ out: 4 lead
Get thee __ nunnery: 3 to a
get the lead __: 3 out
get the show on the __: 4 road
get the worst __: 4 of it
__ get this straight...: 5 Let me
Gettin' __ Wit It: 5 Jiggy
getting
means of ~ there: 4 belt, lane, path, pike, road, ship 5 guide, route, trail 6 access, artery, avenue, detour, street 7 channel, freeway, highway, parkway, passage, roadway, thruway, viaduct 8 shortcut, turnpike 9 boulevard, itinerary 10 expressway, throughway
nowhere: 6 in a rut
on: 4 aged 5 aging 6 ageing 7 ancient, elderly, wizened 8 grizzled 9 geriatric, senescent, up in years
warm: 4 near 5 close 7 close by
getting __ years: 4 on in 7 along in
Getting Closer (1979 song) artist: Paul McCartney

Getting It Right (1989 film)
cast: Helena Bonham Carter, Peter Cook, Lynn Redgrave
director: Randal Kleiser
__ Getting to Be a Habit...: 5 You're
Getting to Know You: 4 song, tune
composer: 7 Rodgers 11 Hammerstein
singer: 4 Anna
Getting Up and Going Home author: Robert Anderson
Gettin' Jiggy Wit It (1998 song) artist: Will Smith
Gett Off (1991 song) artist: Prince
get-together: 3 bee, mtg. 4 gala, sess. 5 mixer, party, rally 6 caucus, huddle, powwow 7 meeting, reunion, session 8 assembly, function
Getty: 5 J. Paul 6 Gordon 7 Estelle 9 Balthazar
product: 3 gas, oil
rival: 4 Gulf 5 Amoco, Exxon, Mobil, Shell 6 Texaco 7 Chevron
Gettysburg: 6 battle
addresser: 3 Abe 7 Lincoln
general: 3 Lee 5 Meade
locale: 4 Penn.
soldier: 3 reb
Gettysburg (1993 film)
cast: Tom Berenger, Jeff Daniels, Martin Sheen
Gettysburg Address ender: 5 Earth
get under one's __: 4 skin
getup: 3 rig 4 garb, suit, togs 5 array, dress, robes 6 attire, livery, outfit 7 apparel, clothes, costume, garment, turnout 8 clothing, garments 9 trappings 10 Sunday best
get-up-and-go: 3 pep, vim, zip 4 life, push, zest, zing 5 drive, moxie, oomph, vigor 6 energy, hustle 8 gumption, vitality 9 élan vital 10 enterprise, initiative
having no ~: 4 dull, idle, lazy, logy 5 inert, slack, tired 7 languid, loafing, out of it, passive 8 dilatory, feckless, flagging, indolent, lifeless, slothful, sluggish 9 apathetic, lethargic, sedentary, shiftless 10 slow-moving
Get Ur Freak On (2001 song) artist: Missy Elliott
get-well __: 4 card
Get Yer __ Out: 5 Ya-Ya's
__ Get You Into My Life: 5 Got to
__ Get Your Gun: 5 Annie
Getz, Stan
genre: 4 jazz
instrument: 3 sax 9 saxophone
song: Desafinado (1962)
The Girl From Ipanema (1964)
gewgaw: 3 toy 4 gaud 5 dodad 6 bangle, bauble, doodad, trifle 7 fribble, trinket 8 frippery, gimcrack, kickshaw, nicknack, ornament 9 adornment, bagatelle, brummagem, plaything 10 decoration, knickknack
Gewürztraminer: 4 wine 5 white
origin: 6 France 7 Germany
geyser: 3 jet 5 spirt, spurt 6 gusher, spring 8 fountain, water jet 9 hot spring
Gezelle, Guido: 4 poet 7 Flemish
G-factor: 6 weight
G. Gordon __: 5 Liddy
Ghalib, Mirza: 4 poet, Urdu
Ghana: 6 nation 7 country
capital: 5 Accra, Akkra
city: 4 Tema 5 Accra, Akkra 6 Kumasi, Obuasi, Tamale
export: 5 cocoa
fabric: 5 kente
language: 3 Ewe, Gbe, Twi 4 Tshi 7 Ashanti
money: 4 cedi 6 pesewa
neighbor: 4 Togo 10 Ivory Coast
Nobelist in Peace: 5 Annan
people: 3 Ewe 4 Akan 5 Fante 6 Asante 7 Ashanti
poet: 8 Anyidoho
river: 5 Volta
writer: 5 Aidoo, Armah 7 Awoonor
__ ghanouj: 4 baba
__ G. Harding: 6 Warren
ghastly: 3 wan 4 ashy, foul, gory, grim, pale, poor 5 ashen, awful, lousy, lurid, weird, woful 6 crumby, crummy, dismal, grisly, horrid, morbid, odious, pallid, rotten, woeful 7 accurst, baleful, baneful, beastly, doleful, fearful, heinous, hideous, macaber, macabre 8 accursed, dreadful, ghoulish, God-awful, grievous, gruesome, horrible, inferior, shameful, shocking, stinking, terrible, wretched 9 abhorrent, appalling, atrocious, defective, execrable, frightful, insidious, loathsome, miserable, offensive, repellent, revolting, unearthly 10 abominable, despicable, detestable, disastrous, disgusting, horrendous, horrifying, petrifying, terrifying
Ghats: 5 range 9 mountains
locale: 4 Asia 5 India
Ghent: 4 city, town
locale: 7 Belgium
river: 3 Lys 4 Leie 7 Schelde, Scheldt
gherkin: 6 pickle, veggie 9 vegetable
Gherman: 5 Titov
ghetto: 4 slum 6 barrio, region 7 quarter 9 inner city
__ Ghetto: 5 In the
Ghetto Supastar (1998 song) artist: Mya
ghibli: 4 wind
ghillie: 4 shoe 8 footwear
ghost: 4 game, soul 5 shade, spook, umbra, write 6 author, fantom, spirit, wraith 7 banshee, banshie, eidolon, fantasm, phantom, specter 8 illusion, phantasm, presence, word game 10 apparition, substitute
costume: 5 sheet
do a ~ job: 5 haunt
ender: 4 weed 5 write 6 writer
German ~: 6 kobold
white as a ~: 3 wan
word: 3 boo
ghost __: 4 crab, moth, town, word 5 dance, image, story 6 shrimp, writer
ghost __ chance: 3 of a
Ghost (1990 film)
cast: Whoopi Goldberg, Demi Moore, Patrick Swayze
director: Jerry Zucker
Ghost __, The: 4 Ship 6 Writer
__ Ghost: 4 Holy
Ghost and Mrs. Muir, The (1947 film)
cast: Rex Harrison, George Sanders, Gene Tierney
director: Joseph L. Mankiewicz
Ghost Breakers, The (1940 film)
cast: Richard Carlson, Paulette Goddard, Bob Hope
Ghostbusters: 4 film, song
artist: Ray Parker Jr
cast: Dan Aykroyd, Bill Murray, Harold Ramis, Sigourney Weaver
director: Ivan Reitman
goo: 5 slime
role: 4 Egon
Ghostbusters II (1989 film)
cast: Dan Aykroyd, Bill Murray, Harold Ramis, Sigourney Weaver
director: Ivan Reitman
Ghost Catchers (1944 film)
cast: Chic Johnson, Ole Olsen
director: Edward Cline
Ghost Goes West, The actor: 5 Donat
Ghostley: 5 Alice
ghostlike: 3 wan 4 eery, pale 5 eerie, weird 6 spooky 7 eidolic, haunted, macaber, macabre, uncanny 8 spectral 9 invisible, spiritual, unearthly 10 immaterial, phantasmal, wraithlike
ghostly: 10 unphysical
ghost of a __: 6 chance
Ghost of Christmas __: 4 Past 7 Present
Ghost of the Buffaloes, The author: Vachel Lindsay
Ghosts: 4 play
author: Henrik Ibsen
character: 5 Helen 6 Alving, Oswald, Regina
Ghosts of Mississippi (1996 film)
cast: Alec Baldwin, Whoopi Goldberg, Craig T. Nelson, James Woods
director: Rob Reiner
Ghost, The author: Danielle Steel
Ghost World (2001 film)
cast: Thora Birch, Steve Buscemi, Brad Renfro
director: Terry Zwigoff
Ghost Writer, The author: Philip Roth
ghoul: 5 demon 6 daemon, daimon 7 monster 8 bogeyman 9 archfiend, hobgoblin
greeting: 3 boo
ghoulish: 4 sick 6 creepy, morbid 7 ghastly, macaber, macabre 9 unearthly
G.I.: 3 NCO, PFC, pvt., rct. 4 Yank 5 grunt 6 airman 7 dogface, draftee, private, recruit, soldier, veteran, warrior
address: 3 APO
captured ~: 3 POW
clothing: 3 ODs 5 drabs 6 khakis
command: 4 halt 6 at ease
cop: 2 MP
doing ~ kitchen duty: 4 on KP
female: 3 WAC 4 WAAC
group: 4 unit 5 troop 7 brigade 8 division 9 battalion
hangout: 3 USO
ID: 2 SN 6 dogtag
Joe: 3 toy 4 doll
Joe maker: 6 Hasbro
meal: 3 MRE 4 mess, Spam 7 K-ration
money: 5 scrip
1950's ~ ally: 3 ROK
need: 4 ammo
offender: 4 AWOL
org. for former ~ s: 3 VFW
part of ~: 4 govt. 5 issue
source, once: 3 SSS
supplier: 2 PX
unaccounted-for ~: 3 MIA
see also army, military, soldier
G.I. __: 3 Joe 4 Bill, Jane 5 Blues
Gia: 5 Scala
Giacconi, Riccardo: 8 Nobelist 9 physicist
Giacobbe in English: 5 Jacob
Giacomo: 7 Puccini 8 Casanova 9 Meyerbeer
Giacosa, Giuseppe: 7 Italian 10 playwright
collaborator: Puccini
Giaever, Ivar: 8 Nobelist 9 physicist
Gia Lan Airport site: 5 Hanoi
Giambattista: 4 Vico 6 Basile, Marino
Giancarlo: 8 Esposito, Giannini
Gian Carlo __: 7 Menotti
Gianlorenzo: 7 Bernini
Gianni: 7 Versace
in English: 6 Johnny
Giannini: 2 A.P. 9 Giancarlo
Giannini, Giancarlo: 5 actor
film: Hannibal (2001)
The Innocent (1976)
Seven Beauties (1976)
Swept Away ... (1975)
giant: 3 big 4 huge, ogre, tall, vast 5 Atlas, great, jumbo, large, titan, whale 6 Amazon, Bunyan, witigo 7 Goliath, hulking, immense, mammoth, massive, monster, sizable, titanic, windigo 8 behemoth, colossal, colossus, enormous, gigantic, king-size, oversize, sizeable, towering, whapping, whopping 9 cyclopean, herculean, humongous, leviathan, monstrous, overlarge 10 family-size, gargantuan, monumental, Paul Bunyan, prodigious, stupendous, tremendous
Biblical ~: 7 Goliath
fictional ~: 9 Gargantua 10 Pantagruel
mental ~: 3 ace 4 whiz 5 brain 6 genius 7 egghead, prodigy, thinker 8 Einstein, highbrow, virtuoso 10 mastermind
of Greek myth: 4 Rhea, Thia 5 Argus, Atlas, Coeus, Crius, Dione, Orion 6 Cronus, Phoebe, Tethys, Themis, Typhon 7 Cyclops, Eurybia, Iapetus, Oceanus 8 Hyperion 9 Menoetius, Mnemosyne 10 Epimetheus, Polyphemus, Prometheus
of Norse myth: 4 Norn, Ymer, Ymir 5 Jotun
red ~: 4 Mira, star 5 S star 7 Antares
syllable: 3 fee, fie, fum
to Jack: 3 foe
giant __: 4 cane, clam, crab, kelp, reed, star 5 otter, panda, snail, squid, steps 6 fennel, fulmar, garlic, hornet, lizard, petrel, powder, slalom 7 hogweed, ragweed, redwood, scallop, sequoia
__ giant: 3 red 4 blue 7 Flemish
Giant: 4 film, NLer 5 NFLer, novel 10 baseballer, footballer
author: Edna Ferber
cast: Carroll Baker, James Dean, Rock Hudson, Elizabeth Taylor
composer: 7 Tiomkin
director: George Stevens
Hall of Famer: 3 Ott 4 Mays 5 Rusie, Terry 6 Cepeda, McGraw, Mel Ott 7 Hubbell, McCovey 8 Marichal 9 Amos Rusie, Bill Terry, Mathewson 10 John McGraw, Willie Mays
ranch: 5 Reata
rival: 3 Cub, Jet, Met, Ram, Red 4 Bear, Bill, Colt, Expo, Lion, Twin 5 Angel, Astro, Brave, Brown, Chief, Eagle, Niner, Padre, Raven, Rocky, Royal, Saint, Texan, Tiger, Titan 6 Bengal, Brewer, Bronco, Cowboy, Dodger, Falcon, Indian, Jaguar, Marlin, Oriole, Packer, Philly, Pirate, Raider, Ranger, Red Sox, Viking, Yankee 7 Blue Jay, Charger, Dolphin, Mariner, Panther, Patriot, Redskin, Seahawk, Steeler 8 Athletic, Cardinal, Devil Ray, White Sox 9 Buccaneer
__ Giant: 5 Green 6 Gentle, Jersey, Little
Giant Raft author: Jules Verne
Giants: 4 nine, team 6 eleven
home: 7 New York
org.: 3 MLB, NFC, NFL, NLW
sport: 8 baseball, football
giant-screen technology: 4 Imax
Giants in the Earth
author: Ole Rölvaag
character: 3 Ole 4 Hans, Holm 5 Beret, Peder, Seier, Sofie
__ giant slalom: 5 super

Giauque, William: **7** chemist **8** Nobelist
Giausar: **4** star
gib: **3** cat **6** tomcat
Gib.: **3** str.
Gibb: **4** Andy **5** Barry, Robin **7** Cynthia, Maurice
  brother: **6** Bee Gee
Gibb, Andy
  song: Desire (1980)
    Don't Throw It All Away (1978)
    An Everlasting Love (1978)
    I Just Want to Be Your Everything (1977)
    Shadow Dancing (1978)
    Thicker Than Water (1977)
Gibb, Barry song: Guilty (1980)
gibber: **3** gab, yak **4** rant **6** babble, footle, gossip, prater **7** blather, blether, chatter, palaver, prattle **8** chit-chat, ramble on **9** table talk
gibberish: **3** gas, rot **4** blah, bosh, bull, bunk, guff, jazz, jive, pooh, tosh, wind **5** Babel, bilge, fudge, hokum, hooey, prate, stuff, trash, tripe **6** babble, bunkum, bushwa, drivel, footle, gabble, gammon, gibber, havers, hot air, humbug, jabber, jargon, kibosh, piffle **7** baloney, blarney, blather, blether, boloney, bushwah, chatter, eyewash, flannel, flubdub, fustian, garbage, hogwash, inanity, palaver, prattle, rubbish, twaddle **8** babbling, buncombe, claptrap, falderal, falderol, flimflam, flummery, folderal, folderol, language, nonsense, slipslop, tommyrot, trumpery **9** banana oil, kidstakes, moonshine, poppycock, rigmarole **10** applesauce, balderdash, bilge water, codswallop, double-talk, empty words, flapdoodle, galimatias, hocus-pocus, Jabberwock, mumbo jumbo, rigamarole, taradiddle
gibbon: **6** animal, mammal **7** primate
  Malay ~: **3** lar
  relative: **3** ape **4** saki, titi **5** chimp, drill, jocko, lemur, loris, magot, orang, potto, shrew **6** aye-aye, baboon, Bandar, galago, gelada, grivet, guenon, howler, langur, macaco, monkey, rhesus, uakari, vervet **7** colobus, gorilla, guereza, hoolock, macaque, sapajou, siamang, tamarin, tarsier **8** bush baby, capuchin, mandrill, mangabey, marmoset, talapoin **9** orangutan **10** Barbary ape, chimpanzee, orangutang
Gibbon, Edward: **6** writer **7** British **9** historian
Gibbons: **5** Leeza **6** Cedric
Gibbs: **5** Marla, Terri **7** Georgia
Gibbs, Georgia
  nickname: Her Nibs
  song: Dance With Me Henry (1955)
    Tweedle Dee (1955)
gibe: **3** dig, dis, jab, rag **4** barb, hoot, jape, jeer, jest, mock, quip, slam, slap, slur, snub, twit **5** abuse, agree, decry, flout, libel, roast, scoff, scorn, sneer, spurn, swipe, taunt, tease **6** defame, deride, dump on, heckle, impugn, jibe at, malign, offend, rebuff, slight, vilify **7** affront, asperse, calumny, catcall, degrade, disdain, mockery, obloquy, offense, putdown, rank out, sarcasm, slander, traduce **8** belittle, brickbat, contempt, denounce, derision, ridicule, scoffing, vilipend **9** aspersion, cheap shot, contumely, denigrate, discredit, disparage, humiliate, make fun of **10** calumniate, defamation, disrespect, opprobrium
giblets part: **5** heart, liver **7** gizzard
G.I. Blues (1960 film)
  cast: Elvis Presley, Juliet Prowse
  director: Norman Taurog
Gibraltar: **4** city, port, town **6** colony, strait
  denizen: **3** ape **10** Barbary ape
  landmark: **4** rock
  locale: **6** Iberia
  neighbor: **5** Spain **7** Morocco
  port near ~: **4** Adra **5** Cadiz, Ceuta
__ Gibraltar: **6** Rocket, Rock of
Gibran, Kahlil: **4** poet **6** writer **8** Lebanese
  work: The Prophet
Gibson: **3** Bob, Don, Mel **4** Hoot, Josh, Kirk **5** Henry **6** Althea, Debbie, desert, Thomas **7** Deborah, William
Gibson __: **4** girl **6** Desert
Gibson, Althea: **7** netster **9** tennis pro
  milieu: **5** court
Gibson, Bob: **6** hurler **7** pitcher **8** Cardinal
Gibson, Debbie
  song: Foolish Beat (1988)
    Lost in Your Eyes (1989)
    Only in My Dreams (1987)
    Out of the Blue (1988)
    Shake Your Love (1987)
Gibson, Don song: Oh Lonesome Me (1958)
Gibson, Josh: **7** catcher, slugger
Gibson, Mel: **5** actor
  film: Air America (1990)
    Bird on a Wire (1990)
    The Bounty (1984)
    Braveheart (1995, AA)
    Conspiracy Theory (1997)
    Forever Young (1992)
    Gallipoli (1981)
    Hamlet (1990)
    Lethal Weapon (1987)
    Lethal Weapon 2 (1989)
    Lethal Weapon 3 (1992)
    Lethal Weapon 4 (1998)
    Mad Max (1979)
    Mad Max 2 (1981)
    The Man Without a Face (1993)
    Maverick (1994)
    The Patriot (2000)
    Ransom (1996)
    Tequila Sunrise (1988)
    We Were Soldiers (2002)
    What Women Want (2000)
    The Year of Living Dangerously (1983)
Gibson, William: **6** author, writer
gibus: **3** hat
giddiness: **6** levity **8** nonsense **9** frivolity
giddy: **4** gaga, wild **5** ditzy, dizzy, light, silly **6** awhirl, giggly, punchy **7** flighty **8** euphoric, skittish, unstable, volatile **9** brainless, frivolous, impulsive, lightsome, slaphappy **10** capricious, inconstant, nonserious
  be ~: **4** reel, swim **5** swirl
Gide, André: **6** author, French, writer **8** Nobelist
  work: The Counterfeiters
    The Fruits of the Earth
    If It Die
    Strait Is the Gate
Gideon: **5** judge
  product: **5** Bible
Gideon author: Paddy Chayefsky
Gideon's __: **7** Trumpet
Gidget (1959 film)
  cast: James Darren, Sandra Dee, Cliff Robertson
Gielgud, John: **3** Sir **5** actor
  film: Arthur (1981, AA)
    Becket (1964)
    The Elephant Man (1980)
    Gandhi (1982)
    Julius Caesar (1953)
    Murder on the Orient Express (1974)
    A Portrait of the Artist as a Young Man (1979)
    Richard III (1955)
    Time After Time (1985)
  role: **4** Lear
Gifford, Frank sport: **8** football
Gifford, Kathie Lee spouse: Frank Gifford
gift: **3** tip **4** alms, bent, boon, dole, head, nose, turn **5** award, bonus, favor, flair, forte, goody, grant, knack, power, skill, token, treat **6** bounty, genius, goodie, legacy, reward, talent, tipoff **7** ability, aptness, benefit, bequest, charity, faculty, freebee, freebie, godsend, handout, largess, premium, present, proffer, subsidy **8** aptitude, bestowal, capacity, courtesy, donation, giveaway, gratuity, instinct, kickback, largesse, offering, penchant, souvenir **9** allowance, endowment, lagniappe **10** green thumb
  acknowledge a ~: **5** thank
  as a ~: **4** free **6** gratis **8** costless **10** for nothing, on the house
  baby shower ~: **7** bootees, booties
  card word: **3** for **4** from
  container: **3** box **7** package
  ender: **4** ware
  Father's Day ~: **3** tie **5** razor, shirt
  feature: **3** bow
  giver: **5** donor
  make a ~: **5** grant, offer **6** bestow, confer, donate **8** bequeath **10** contribute
  name meaning ~: **4** Dora **6** Nathan
  naughty child's Christmas ~: **4** coal
  of gab: **8** rhetoric **9** eloquence, loquacity, wittiness **10** volubility
  of the Magi: **4** gold **5** myrrh **12** frankincense
  prepare a ~: **4** do up, tape, wrap
  receiver: **5** donee
  recipient's question: **5** for me
  reveal a ~: **4** open **5** unbox
  small ~: **5** favor, goody, token, treat **7** memento **8** keepsake, surprise
  temporary ~: **4** loan **6** credit **7** advance **9** extension
  time: **4** yule **8** birthday **9** Christmas **10** Father's Day, Mother's Day
  wrap: **5** paper **6** tissue
gift __: **3** tax **4** wrap **5** of gab **7** voucher
Gift __ Magi, The: **5** of the
__ Gift: **4** It's a
gifted: **3** apt **4** able **5** blest, smart **6** adroit, brainy, clever **7** skilled **8** creative, talented **9** brilliant, ingenious, inventive, promising, versatile **10** precocious, proficient
  one: **3** wiz **4** whiz **6** genius
...giftie __ us..., the: **3** gie
Gift of a Cow, The author: Premchand
gift of God
  name meaning ~: **7** Dorothy, Matthew **8** Dorothea, Matthias, Theodore **9** Nathaniel
Gift of the Magi, The
  author: O. Henry
  character: **3** Jim **5** Della
  device: **5** irony
  gift: **3** fob **5** combs
Gift Outright, The author: Robert Frost
Gift, The (2000 film)
  cast: Cate Blanchett, Katie Holmes, Keanu Reeves
  director: Sam Raimi
Gift, The author: Danielle Steel
Gifu: **4** city, town
  locale: **5** Hondo, Japan **6** Honshu
gig: **3** job **4** boat, show, work **7** booking, calling, concert, javelin, recital, rowboat **10** engagement
  do a ~: **4** play **6** appear **7** perform
Gig: **5** Young
gigantic: **3** big **4** huge, vast **5** giant, great, jumbo, large **6** mighty **7** hulking, immense, mammoth, massive, monster, sizable, titanic **8** colossal, enormous, king-size, oversize, sizeable, terrific, towering, whapping, whopping **9** cyclopean, herculean, humongous, monstrous, overlarge, whalelike **10** gargantuan, monumental, prodigious, stupendous, tremendous
giggle: **4** ha-ha, he-he **5** laugh, te-hee **6** cackle, guffaw, heehee, teehee, titter **7** break up, chortle, chuckle, crack up, snicker, snigger **8** laughter
giggling: **3** gay **5** happy, merry **7** gleeful **8** cackling, cheerful, laughing, laughter, mirthful **9** chuckling, tittering **10** snickering, sniggering
giggly: **5** dizzy, giddy, silly **6** jejune **7** flighty **8** immature **9** frivolous
Gigi: **7** Perreau
Gigi (film, novel)
  author: Colette
  cast: Leslie Caron, Maurice Chevalier, Hermione Gingold, Louis Jourdan
  composer: **5** Loewe **6** Lerner
  director: Vincente Minnelli
__ Gigio: **4** Topo
__ Gigolo: **5** Just a
Gigot (1962 film)
  cast: Gabrielle Dorziat, Jackie Gleason, Katherine Kath
  director: Gene Kelly
Gig, The (1985 film)
  cast: Andrew Duncan, Cleavon Little, Wayne Rogers
gigue: **5** dance
G.I. Jane (1997 film)
  cast: Anne Bancroft, Demi Moore, Viggo Mortensen
  director: Ridley Scott
Gijón: **4** city, town
  locale: **5** Spain
Gil: **5** Evans **6** Gerard, Hodges, Morgan **7** Bellows **10** Scott-Heron
Gil __: **4** Blas
Gila: **5** Golan, river
  monster: **6** animal, lizard **7** reptile
  monster's home: **6** desert **7** Arizona
  river locale: **7** Arizona **9** New Mexico
Gilbert: **3** Rod **4** Cass, John, Ryle, Sara, town **5** Cates, Lewis **6** Parker, Roland, Stuart, Walter **7** Melissa **8** Humphrey **9** Gottfried, O'Sullivan
Gilbert __: **7** Islands
Gilbert __ Chesterton: **5** Keith
Gilbert and __ Islands: **6** Ellice
Gilbert, Cass: **9** architect
Gilbert, John: **5** actor
  film: The Big Parade (1925)
    Downstairs (1932)
    Flesh and the Devil (1927)
    He Who Gets Slapped (1924)
    La Bohème (1926)
    The Merry Widow (1925)
    Queen Christina (1933)
    A Woman of Affairs (1928)
Gilbert, Lewis: **8** director
  film: Alfie (1966)
    Carve Her Name With Pride (1958)
    Cast a Dark Shadow (1955)
    A Cry From the Streets (1959)
    Damn the Defiant! (1962)
    Educating Rita (1983)
    Moonraker (1979)
    Shirley Valentine (1989)
    Sink the Bismarck! (1960)
    The Spy Who Loved Me (1977)
    You Only Live Twice (1967)

Gilbert, Melissa spouse: Bruce Boxleitner
Gilberto: **6** Astrud
Gilbert, Rod
milieu: **3** ice **4** rink **5** arena
org.: **3** NHL
Gilberts: **4** isls. **5** isles **7** islands
Gilbert, Walter: **7** chemist **8** Nobelist
Gilbert, William S.: **3** Sir **6** author, writer **7** British **8** lyricist **10** playwright
partner: Arthur Sullivan
work: The Gondoliers
The Grand Duke
HMS Pinafore
Iolanthe
The Mikado
Patience
The Pirates of Penzance
Princess Ida
Ruddigore
The Sorcerer
Trial by Jury
Utopia, Ltd.
The Yeoman of the Guard
Gil Blas author: Alain Lesage
Gilbreth: **5** Frank **9** Elizabeth
gild: **4** deck **5** adorn **6** aurify, bedeck, finish **7** aureate, dress up, encrust, enhance, garnish, incrust, overlay, varnish **8** beautify, brighten, decorate, ornament **9** embellish, embroider
Gilda: **6** Radner
Gilda (1946 film)
cast: Glenn Ford, Rita Hayworth, George Macready
director: Charles Vidor
gilded: **4** doré, rich **6** ornate
Gilded ___, The: **3** Age **4** Lily
Gilded Lily, The (1935 film)
cast: Claudette Colbert, Fred MacMurray, Ray Milland
director: Wesley Ruggles
Gilder, Nick song: Hot Child in the City (1978)
Gildersleeve: **5** nabob
like: **5** great
nickname: **4** Mort
___ Gildersleeve, The: **5** Great
gilding: **4** trim **9** adornment **10** decoration
___ gilding: **3** oil **4** fire **5** honey **6** parcel **7** amalgam
gild the ___: **4** lily
Gilead: **4** peak **5** mount **8** mountain
balm of ~: **5** resin **6** balsam
locale: **4** Asia **6** Jordan **7** Mideast
Gilels, Emil: **7** pianist, Russian
Giles: **5** saint **6** Warren
Giles Goat-Boy author: John Barth
___-Giles system: **4** Wade
Gilford, Jack: **5** actor
film: Catch-22 (1970)
Cocoon (1985)
The Daydreamer (1966)
Save the Tiger (1973)
They Might Be Giants (1971)
gilguy: **4** rope
gill: **5** organ **8** breather
combining form: **7** branchi- **8** branchio-
cousin: **4** lung
ender: **3** net
starter: **4** blue
gill ___: **3** bar, box, net **4** arch, book, slit **5** cleft, pouch, raker **6** fungus
gill-___: **6** netter
Gill: **5** Vince **6** Johnny **7** Brendan
Gillan: **3** Ian
Gillespie, Dizzy: **9** trumpeter
genre: **3** bop **4** jazz **5** bebop
Gillespie partner: **5** Tibbs
Gillette: **4** King **5** Anita, razor
alternative: **3** Bic **6** Schick
model: **4** Atra
Gilley, Mickey cousin: Jerry Lee Lewis, Jimmy Swaggart
Gilliam: **3** Stu **5** Terry
Gilliam, Terry: **5** actor **8** comedian
film: The Adventures of Baron Munchausen (1989)
Brazil (1985)
The Fisher King (1991)
Monty Python's The Meaning of Life (1983)
Time Bandits (1981)
Twelve Monkeys (1995)
Gillian: **8** Anderson
Gilliat: **6** Sidney
gillie: **4** shoe **8** footgear, footwear
Gillies, Clark
milieu: **3** ice **4** rink **5** arena
org.: **3** NHL
Gilligan home: **3** hut **4** isle
Gilligan's Island (CBS sitcom)
boat: **6** Minnow
cast: Jim Backus (Thurston Howell III)
Bob Denver (Gilligan)
Alan Hale (Skipper)
Russell Johnson (The Professor)
Tina Louise (Ginger Grant)
Natalie Schafer (Lovey Howell)
Dawn Wells (Mary Ann Summers)
feature: **6** lagoon
Gillis: **5** Dobie
Gillman, Sid: **5** coach
sport: **8** football
gills
eight ~: **5** quart
four ~: **4** pint
green around the ~: **3** ill **6** queasy, queazy
one with ~: **4** fish
stuff to the ~: **7** satiate
___ gills: **5** to the
Gill, Vince spouse: Amy Grant
Gilman: **6** Alfred **7** Dorothy **9** Charlotte
Gilman, Alfred: **8** Nobelist
Gilman, Charlotte: **6** author, writer
Gilmore, Artis
milieu: **5** court
org.: **3** NBA
sport: **10** basketball
Gilpin: **4** Peri
Gilroy: **4** city, town
locale: **10** California
gilt: **3** sow **5** color **6** golden **8** gold leaf **10** decoration
gilt-___: **4** edge **5** edged
gilt-edged: **4** A-one, fine **5** elite **7** optimum
gilthead: **4** fish
Gimbel rival: **4** Macy
...gimble in the ___: **4** wabe
gimcrack: **5** frill **6** bauble, geegaw, gewgaw, tawdry **7** fribble, trinket **8** nicknack **9** bagatelle **10** decoration, knickknack
gimel: **6** Hebrew, letter
follower: **5** dales, dalet **6** daleth
preceder: **3** bes, bet **4** beth
gimlet: **3** awl **4** tool **5** drink **8** beverage, cocktail
cousin: **5** auger
ingredient: **3** gin **4** lime **5** vodka
use a ~: **4** bore, ream **5** drill, gouge **6** pierce **8** puncture
gimme: **4** putt **5** tap-in
gimme ___: **3** cap
Gimme a break!: **4** c'mon **6** sheesh
Gimme a Break (NBC sitcom)
cast: Nell Carter (Nell Harper)
Dolph Sweet (Carl Kanisky)
Gimme Shelter (1970 film)
cast: Melvin Belli, Jefferson Airplane, Rolling Stones
gimmick: **4** lure, ploy, ruse, wile **5** dodge, feint, gizmo, stunt, trick **6** deceit, device, dupery, gadget, gambit, scheme **7** finesse, sleight **8** artifice, maneuver, strategy **9** deception, imposture, mechanism, stratagem **10** motivation
adman ~: **5** promo, tie-in
gin: **4** game, trap **5** crank, drink, rummy, snare **6** liquor **7** machine, schnaps **8** beverage, card game, schnapps, windlass
bathtub ~: **5** hooch **6** hootch
drink: **5** sling **6** Gibson, gimlet, rickey **7** martini
flavoring: **4** sloe
lover: **3** sot
mill: **3** bar, pub **6** saloon, tavern **7** barroom **8** taphouse
partner: **5** tonic
product: **6** cotton
use a ~: **6** deseed
gin ___: **4** fizz, mill **5** block, joint, rummy **6** rickey
___ gin: **4** pink, sloe **6** cotton **7** bathtub
Gina: **7** Gershon **8** Thompson
see also Italian
Gina (1962 song) artist: Johnny Mathis
gin and ___: **5** tonic
___ gin fizz: **4** sloe **5** Ramos
Ging: **4** Jack
ginger: **4** zest **5** brown, color, spice, taste **7** reddish **9** yellowish
ale: **5** mixer **8** beverage **9** soft drink
ender: **4** root, snap **5** bread
full of ~: **4** game **5** peppy **6** active, feisty, frisky, lively, spunky **7** scrappy **8** spirited
like ~: **3** hot **5** fiery, spicy, zesty, zippy **6** spicey **7** pungent **8** fragrant
relative: **3** bay, dun, tan **4** bole, ecru, fawn, foxy, nude, seal **5** amber, beige, camel, cocoa, hazel, khaki, mocha, sepia, tawny, umber **6** auburn, bister, bistre, bronze, coffee, copper, russet, sienna, sorrel, suntan, walnut **7** biscuit, caramel, dogwood **8** chestnut, cinnamon, mahogany **9** butternut, chocolate
ginger ___: **3** ale, jar **4** beer, lily, snap
___ ginger: **4** wild **5** white **6** canton **7** Jamaica
Ginger: **6** Rogers
partner: **4** Fred
predecessor: **5** Adele
___ ginger ale: **7** pale-dry
gingerbread: **4** cake, palm, trim **6** geegaw, gewgaw **8** ornament
gingerbread ___: **4** palm, plum **5** house
Ginger Bread (1958 song) artist: Frankie Avalon
Gingerbread Lady, The author: Neil Simon
gingerly: **6** gently **7** lightly **9** carefully **10** cautiously
Ginger Pye author: **5** Estes
gingersnap: **5** cooky **6** cookie
gingery: **5** spicy **6** spicey **8** spirited
gingham: **5** cloth **6** fabric **8** material
alternative: **6** calico
gingiva: **3** gum
Gingold: **8** Hermione
Gingrich: **4** Newt
Gin & Juice (1994 song) artist: Snoop Doggy Dogg
gink: **4** fool
ginkgo: **4** tree
Ginnie ___: **3** Mae
Ginny Fizz: **4** Wade
Gino: **8** Vannelli **9** Marchetti
gin rummy: **4** game **8** card game
Ginsberg: **4** poet, Ruth **5** Allen
Ginsberg, Allen: **4** poet
friend: Kerouac
genre: Beat
work: Howl
ginseng: **4** herb
relative: **3** ivy, udo **4** nard **6** fatsia
___ ginseng: **5** dwarf
Ginza
light: **4** neon
locale: **5** Japan, Tokio, Tokyo
money: **3** sen, yen
Ginzburg, Natalia: **6** writer **7** Italian
Gioacchino: **7** Rossini
giocoso: **8** jokingly **10** humorously
Giono, Jean: **6** author, French, writer
Giorgio: **6** Armani **7** Bassani, Moroder
in English: **6** George
___, Giorgio: **3** Yes
Giorgos: **7** Seferis
___ giorno!: **4** Buon
Giotto: **6** artist **7** Italian, painter **8** sculptor
contemporary: **5** Dante
place to see ~ paintings: **6** Assisi
Giovanna in English: **4** Jane, Joan
Giovanni: **3** Don **4** font **5** Nikki **6** Ribisi **7** Bellini, Belzoni, Pascoli, Pontano, Tiepolo **8** typeface **9** Boccaccio **10** Palestrina
in English: **4** John
see also Italian
___ Giovanni: **3** Don
Giovanni's Room author: James Baldwin
Gipper portrayer: **6** Reagan
Gir: **3** cow **4** bull **6** bovine, cattle
giraffe: **6** animal, mammal
cousin: **5** okapi
favorite tree: **6** acacia
feature: **4** neck
female: **3** cow
home: **3** zoo **5** veldt **6** Africa
male: **4** bull
young: **4** calf
___ Girardeau, MO: **4** Cape
girasol: **4** opal
Giraudoux, Jean: **6** French, writer
gird: **3** tie **4** band, belt, hoop, loop, ring, tone, wind **5** brace, build, equip, hem in, ready, shore, steel **6** anneal, beef up, bind up, circle, harden, prop up, secure, temper, tone up **7** bolster, brace up, build up, burgeon, develop, empower, enclose, enhance, fortify, inclose, prepare, shore up, stiffen, support, toughen **8** bourgeon, buttress, cincture, encircle, energize, indurate, surround, vitalize **9** encompass, enwreathe, intensify, reinforce **10** invigorate, strengthen
girded: **5** armed
girder: **4** beam, I-bar **5** brace, H-beam, I-beam, joist, L-beam, T-beam **6** rafter, timber
fastener: **4** weld **5** rivet
material: **5** steel
___ girder: **3** box **4** hull **5** plate **6** flitch **7** lattice
girdle: **4** band, belt, cord, loop, ring, sash **5** fence, stays **6** corset **8** cincture, lingerie, surround **9** encompass, enwreathe, waistband
gird one's ___: **5** loins
girl: **3** kid **4** lass, maid, teen **5** minor, missy, woman **6** damsel, female, lassie, maiden **7** sapling **8** daughter, fraülein, juvenile, ladylove, teenager **9** inamorata, young lady, youngster **10** adolescent, bobbysoxer, demoiselle, young woman
baby ~ clothes color: **4** pink
ender: **3** ish **6** friend
Friday: **4** asst. **9** assistant
name meaning ~: **4** Cora **7** Colleen
starter: **3** bar, bat, cow **4** atta, copy, news, play, show **5** choir, paper, sales **6** school
see also girlfriend

girl __: 4 talk 5 guide, scout 6 Friday, wonder
__ girl: 3 bar, bat, bus, old 4 ball, copy, show 5 altar, cover, Teddy 6 chorus, flower, Gibson, office, pompom, script 7 glamour, working
__ girl!: 4 Atta, It's a
Girl __: 3 Shy 4 on TV 5 Crazy, Happy, Scout 7 Watcher
Girl __, A: 5 Like I
Girl __ Golden West: 5 of the
Girl __ Help It, The: 4 Can't
Girl __ Ipanema, The: 4 From
Girl __ Marry, The: 5 That I
Girl __, The: 6 Friend 7 Hunters
__ Girl: 3 Bad, Hey 4 City, Rich, That 5 Black, Candy, China, Cover, Funny, Just a, Party, The It, Young 6 Barbie, Bobby's, Georgy, Island, Single, Surfer, Uptown, Valley, Whirly 7 Diamond, Jessie's, Working
Girl, a Guy, and __, A: 4 a Gob
__ Girl Blue: 6 Little
Girl Can't __ It, The: 4 Help
Girl Crazy (1943 film): 7 musical
cast: Judy Garland, Mickey Rooney
composer: 8 Gershwin
director: Norman Taurog
__ Girl Friday: 3 His
girlfriend: 2 jo 3 pet 4 baby, date, dear, jill, love 5 amour, angel, cooky, cutey, cutie, deary, ducky, flame, honey, leman, lover, lovey, novia, sugar, sweet, woman 6 chérie, cookie, dautie, dearie, steady, suitor, sweets 7 admirer, beloved, darling, dearest, dear one, pigsney, schatzi, squeeze, sweetie, tootsie 8 chou-chou, cutie pie, dowsabel, dulcinea, intimate, ladylove, lovebird, macushla, paramour, precious, snookums, sugar pie, sweetums, truelove 9 bonne amie, companion, dreamboat, inamorata, petit chou, valentine 10 confidante, heartthrob, honeybunch, mavourneen, sweetheart, sweetie pie, turtledove
in French: 4 amie
Girlfriends (1978 film)
cast: Melanie Mayron, Anita Skinner, Eli Wallach
director: Claudia Weill
Girl From 10th Avenue, The (1935 film)
cast: Colin Clive, Bette Davis, Ian Hunter
Girl From Ipanema, The (1964 song)
artist: Stan Getz
Girl From Missouri, The (1934 film)
cast: Lionel Barrymore, Jean Harlow, Franchot Tone
Girl Happy (1965 film)
cast: Shelley Fabares, Elvis Presley
girlhood: 5 youth
Girl Hunters, The author: Mickey Spillane
Girl I'm Gonna Miss You (1989 song)
artist: Milli Vanilli
Girl, Interrupted (1999 film)
cast: Angelina Jolie, Brittany Murphy, Winona Ryder
cat: 4 Ruby
director: James Mangold
__ Girl in Town: 3 New
girlish: 5 young 8 juvenile, youthful 10 adolescent
__ Girl Is Like a Melody, A: 6 Pretty
Girl Is Mine, The (1982 song)
artist: Michael Jackson, Paul McCartney
Girl Like I, A author: Anita Loos
Girl Like You, A (1967 song) artist: Rascals
__ Girl Marries: 5 When a
Girl Most Likely, The (1957 film)
cast: Tommy Noonan, Jane Powell, Cliff Robertson
director: Mitchell Leisen
__-girl network: 3 old
Girl of the Golden West composer: 7 Puccini
Girl on TV (1999 song) artist: LFO
girls
for boys and ~: 4 coed 6 unisex
girl's
that: 4 hers
Girls __ Out: 4 Nite
Girls __ Want to Have Fun: 4 Just
__ Girls: 3 Bad, Les 5 Cover, Spice 6 Summer 7 Buffalo, Naughty, Soldier, Working
Girls About Town (1931 film)
cast: Kay Francis, Joel McCrea
director: George Cukor
__ Girls and a Sailor: 3 Two
__ Girls Are Easy: 5 Earth
girls' club: 4 YWCA, YWHA
Girl Scouts founder: 3 Low
__ Girls Don't Cry: 3 Big
Girls! Girls! Girls! (1962 film)
cast: Elvis Presley, Stella Stevens
director: Norman Taurog
Girls, Girls, Girls (1987 song) artist: Mötley Crüe
Girls Just Want to Have Fun (1984 song) artist: Cyndi Lauper
__ Girls, The: 6 Golden, Harvey
Girls, The author: Edna Ferber
Girl, 20 author: Kingsley Amis
Girl That I Marry, The composer: 6 Berlin
__ Girl, The: 4 Lost 7 Country, Goodbye, Roaring, Russian
__ Girl Wants: 5 What a
Girl With the Hatbox, The star: 4 Sten
Girl You Know It's True (1989 song) artist: Milli Vanilli
Girl, You'll Be a Woman Soon (1967 song) artist: Neil Diamond
giro: 8 aircraft
Girolamo: 10 Fracastoro, Savonarola
Gironde, river to the: 7 Garonne
Gironella, José Maria: 6 author, writer 7 Spanish
Giroux partner: 6 Farrar, Straus
__ girt: 4 drop 5 belly, flush
Girtab: 4 star
girth: 4 band, bulk, size 5 cinch, waist, width 8 encircle
girtline: 4 rope
girt starter: 3 sea
G.I.'s: 4 unit 5 troop 6 grunts 8 infantry
Giscard D'Estaing: 6 Valéry
Gisele: 9 MacKenzie
'G' Is for Gumshoe author: Sue Grafton
Gish: 7 Dorothy, Lillian 8 Annabeth
Gish, Annabeth: 7 actress
film: Beautiful Girls (1996)
Desert Bloom (1986)
Double Jeopardy (1999)
Mystic Pizza (1988)
Gish, Lillian: 7 actress
film: The Birth of a Nation (1915)
Broken Blossoms (1919)
Intolerance (1916)
La Bohème (1926)
The Night of the Hunter (1955)
Orphans of the Storm (1922)
The Scarlet Letter (1926)
Way Down East (1920)
The Whales of August (1987)
The Wind (1928)
gismo: 5 dodad, gizmo 6 doodad, gadget, thingy, whosis, widget 7 doodads 9 doohickey, invention 10 instrument
Gissing, George: 6 author, writer 7 British
gist: 3 nub 4 body, core, crux, idea, knub, meat, pith 5 drift, force, heart, point, sense, tenor, theme 6 center, kernel, marrow, spirit, thrust, upshot 7 essence, keynote, meaning, purport, summary 8 main idea 9 main point, substance
git: 4 scat, shoo 5 scram 6 beat it 7 amscray, vamoose 9 skedaddle
git-__-git: 5 up-and
Gitano: 5 jeans, pants 6 denims
Gitarzan (1969 song) artist: Ray Stevens
Gitchee __: 5 Gumee
git-go: 5 start 6 day one, origin, outset 9 beginning, inception
gittern: 6 guitar, string
origin: 7 England
Giuliani: 4 Rudy 7 Rudolph
Giuseppe: 5 Belli, Verdi 6 Parini 7 Giacosa, Mazzini 8 Fiorelli 9 Garibaldi
in English: 6 Joseph
see also Italian
give: 3 pay, put, sag, tip 4 cede, fold, hand, lend, mete, play, show, will 5 allow, apply, award, endow, grant, issue, offer, relax, remit, serve, spare, spend, stage, utter, yield 6 accord, afford, ante up, assign, bestow, cave in, commit, confer, convey, credit, devote, donate, extend, fork up, hand in, heap on, impart, lavish, lay out, pony up, ration, relent, render, supply, tender 7 concede, consign, crumple, deal out, deliver, dish out, display, divvy up, dole out, furnish, hand out, lay upon, let have, mete out, offer up, pass out, present, produce, proffer, provide 8 bequeath, collapse, disburse, dispense, engender, evidence, fork over, hand down, hand over, heap upon, indicate, manifest, minister, set forth, shell out, transfer, turn over 9 looseness, parcel out, subscribe, surrender, vouchsafe 10 administer, contribute, distribute, elasticity, lavish upon, relinquish, resilience
a bad name: 7 asperse, slander 8 backbite
a black eye: 4 slur 5 libel, shame, smear 6 defame, vilify
a boost to: 4 help 6 assist 7 further, promote
a break: 4 save 5 spare, spell
a Bronx cheer: 4 jeer, mock 5 sneer, taunt
a darn: 4 care, heed, mind 5 sweat, worry 6 bother, object, regret, tend to 8 remember 9 make a fuss, watch over
a deposition: 4 avow 6 allege, assert, attest 7 certify, declare
a face-lift: 5 fix up, rehab, renew 6 revamp, update 7 remodel, restore, touch up 8 overhaul, renovate, spruce up 9 modernize, refurbish
a going-over: 7 lecture
a hand: 4 abet, clap 6 assist 7 bail out, relieve
a handle: 3 dub 8 christen
a hand to: 6 deal in 7 applaud
a hard time: 3 irk, nag, vex 5 tease, upset 6 harass 7 torment
a jingle: 4 call, dial 5 phone 6 ring up 9 touch base
a job to: 4 hire 6 employ, engage, sign on, take on
a lecture: 4 talk 5 edify, orate, speak, spout, teach, tutor 6 advise, inform 7 address, declaim, deliver, educate, expound, instill 8 initiate, instruct 9 discourse, hold forth, inculcate, interpret, pound into, sermonize
a leg up: 3 aid 4 help 5 boost, hoist 6 assist, succor 9 encourage
a lift to: 3 aid 5 cheer, elate, raise 6 assist, pick up 7 enliven 8 reassure
a little extra: 3 add 6 slap on, tack on, toss in 8 increase
a medal to: 4 cite 5 honor 8 decorate
an account: 4 tell 6 recite, relate 7 narrate
a name to: 3 dub, tag 4 call, term 5 label, title 7 baptize 8 christen
an audience: 4 hear 6 listen
and take: 4 swap, swop 5 bandy, share, trade 8 exchange
an edge to: 4 hone, whet 5 grind 7 sharpen
an encore performance: 5 rerun
an example: 4 cite, name 5 offer, quote 7 specify 8 point out, spell out 9 enumerate
an opinion: 3 say 5 speak, state, voice 6 assert, remark 7 chime in, observe 8 maintain, propound
an oration: 4 talk 5 speak, spout 7 declaim 9 hold forth, speechify
an ovation: 4 clap 5 cheer, honor 6 praise 7 acclaim, applaud
an overview: 5 sum up 6 digest 7 outline 8 condense 9 synopsize
a party: 6 regale 7 splurge 9 entertain
a party for: 4 fete 5 honor 7 lionize 9 celebrate, entertain
a pep talk: 4 urge 6 charge, exhort 9 encourage
a piece of one's mind: 5 scold 6 berate 7 lecture 8 admonish
a pink slip: 2 ax 3 axe, can 4 fire, sack 6 lay off
a poor review to: 3 pan
a poser to: 5 throw 6 baffle, puzzle 7 buffalo, mystify, perplex 8 confound
approval: 6 accede
a rain check: 5 defer, delay 6 put off 7 suspend 8 postpone
a reading: 6 recite, render 7 narrate 9 dramatize, interpret
a reason for: 4 show 6 defend 7 clarify, clear up, explain, justify 8 spell out 9 expound on, make clear
a recital: 4 play, sing 5 dance 7 perform
as an example: 4 cite
a talk: 5 orate, speak 6 preach 7 address, declaim, deliver, expound, lecture 9 discourse, hold forth
a talking-to: 5 scold 6 berate
a thumbs-up to: 4 laud, rate 7 approve 9 recommend
a tip to: 4 warn 5 alert 6 advise, clue in, fill in, inform 7 apprise, let know 8 acquaint, forewarn
attention: 4 heed 6 listen, regard
a turn: 5 alarm, scare, shake, shock, spook, throw 6 dismay, rattle 7 fluster, startle, unnerve 8 affright, frighten, surprise, unsettle 9 take aback 10 disconcert, intimidate
authority to: 4 name 6 assign, charge, commit, depute, invest, ordain 7 appoint, consign, empower, entrust, intrust, license 8 accredit, delegate, deputize, hand over, relegate, turn over 9 authorize, designate 10 commission
away: 4 blab, leak, sell 5 let on, spill 6 betray, expose, reveal, tattle 7 divulge, sell out, uncover 8 disclose

a wide berth to: **4** shun **5** avoid, elude, evade, scorn, skirt **6** eschew **8** flee from, sidestep **10** circumvent, recoil from, shrink from
back: **5** repay **6** refund, return **7** reflect, replace, restore
birth to: **4** bear, have **5** begin, breed, spawn **6** create **7** deliver **8** engender, generate, initiate **9** originate **10** bring forth
confidence to: **6** affirm, assure **7** hearten
consent: **2** OK **3** let **4** okay **5** agree, allow, grant, yield **6** accede, accord, assent, cave in, comply, concur, permit **7** concede **9** acquiesce, cooperate **10** come around
cover: **6** shield
credence to: **7** believe
don't ~ up: **4** keep, save **5** amass, cache, hoard, stock **6** insist, retain **8** withhold **10** accumulate
ear to: **4** care, hear, heed, mind, obey **6** attend, follow, listen, notice **7** abide by, observe **8** consider **10** bear in mind, be guided by, take care of, toe the line
emphasis: **6** accent, play up, stress **7** bracket, feature, point up **9** highlight, italicize, punctuate, reinforce, underline **10** accentuate, underscore
ender: **4** away, back
evidence: **5** swear **6** attest **7** testify, witness
expression to: **4** vent **5** voice
feedback: **5** react, reply **6** answer **7** respond **9** get back to
forth: **3** say **4** emit, shed **5** exude **7** deliver, reflect
ground: **6** retire **7** retreat **8** withdraw
grounds for: **5** prove **7** justify, testify, warrant
guns to: **7** fortify
heed to: **4** mind **6** harken, listen
in: **3** bow **4** melt **5** yield **6** accede, assent, comply, relent, submit **7** consent, succumb **9** acquiesce, lighten up, surrender **10** capitulate
incentive: **4** fire, goad, move, prod, spur, urge, whet **5** goose, impel, prime, rouse, spark, tempt **6** arouse, bestir, excite, induce, prompt, propel, stir up **7** inspire, quicken **8** energize, motivate, persuade **9** galvanize, stimulate
in return: **3** pay **6** avenge, reward **7** get even, requite **9** retaliate
insight to: **5** edify **7** clarify **8** instruct **9** elucidate
in to: **5** humor, spoil **6** coddle, cosset, dote on, pamper, pander **7** gratify, indulge
it a whirl: **3** try **4** test **7** attempt
it to: **4** beat, whip **5** pound
joy to: **5** elate
just deserts: **5** spite **6** avenge **7** get even, hit back, pay back, requite **9** get back at, stick it to
leave: **2** OK **3** let **4** okay **5** allow, grant **6** accede, free up, permit **7** approve, concede, endorse, license **8** sanction **9** authorize **10** say the word
lessons to: **5** edify, teach, train **8** instruct
life to: **4** form, sire **5** beget, breed, build, erect, forge, found, hatch, model, shape, spawn, start **6** author, create, design, devise, effect, father **7** compose, develop, dream up, fashion, imagine, produce, think up **8** conceive, engender, engineer, generate, occasion, organize **9** actualize, construct, establish, institute, originate **10** mastermind
lip to: **4** sass **8** get smart, mouth off, talk back **10** answer back
little: **4** save **5** skimp **6** scrape, scrimp, slight **8** conserve, roll back, withhold **9** economize **10** cut corners
money for: **3** buy
no choice: **5** force **6** coerce, compel
no ground: **5** force, order, press **6** demand, insist **8** pressure **9** stand firm
not about to ~: **4** firm **5** rigid, solid, tight, tough **6** flinty, secure, stable, steely, sturdy **7** adamant, diehard, staunch **8** hard-line, hellbent, resolute, stubborn **9** obstinate, steadfast, unbending **10** determined, inflexible, unshakable, unswerving, unwavering, unyielding
notice: **4** quit, warn **5** leave **6** resign
not ~ the time of day: **3** cut **4** shun, snub **5** spurn **6** ignore, rebuff, slight **8** brush off
odds: **3** fix, lay **6** gamble **8** make book **9** speculate
off: **4** beam, emit, send, spew, spue **5** eject, expel, exude, issue, yield **6** evolve, exhale **7** cast out, diffuse, emanate, radiate, release, secrete **9** discharge, send forth
off an odor: **4** reek **5** smell, stink
off light: **4** glow **5** gleam, shine
on: **4** face **5** front **8** overlook
one's blessing: **5** agree **6** concur, permit **7** approve, consent **9** acquiesce **10** condescend
one's consent: **2** OK **4** okay, okeh, okey
one's feet a rest: **5** relax
one's stamp of approval: **2** OK **4** okay, pass **5** bless **6** ratify **7** certify, confirm, consent, endorse, license **8** sanction, validate **9** authorize, sign off on
one's word: **3** vow **4** aver **5** swear **6** assure, attest **7** promise
orders: **4** boss, head, lead, rule, tell **5** steer **6** advise, charge, enjoin, govern, manage **7** command, dictate, oversee, preside **8** dominate **9** officiate, prescribe, supervise **10** administer, mastermind, ride herd on, run the show
or take: **6** nearly **7** roughly **9** virtually
out: **4** deal, dole, emit, mete, tell, tire, wilt **5** allot, grant, issue, share **6** assign, ration, reveal **7** radiate, release **8** dispense, proclaim **9** apportion
over: **4** quit **5** yield **7** forfeit **8** dedicate, leave off
partner: **4** take
pause: **3** cow **4** faze **5** alarm, daunt, deter, shake **6** bemuse, dismay **7** overawe, unnerve **8** bewilder, dispirit, frighten **10** demoralize, discourage, dishearten, intimidate
permission: **3** let **5** allow, grant **6** accede, enable, permit **7** approve, certify, endorse, license **8** sanction **9** authorize
pleasure to: **5** amuse, elate **7** gratify
power to: **6** enable **7** entitle, license **9** authorize
prominence: **6** play up **7** feature **9** publicize, spotlight
proof: **4** aver **5** prove, swear **6** assure, attest, depone, verify **7** bear out, certify, confirm, declare, stand by, testify, warrant, witness **8** vouch for
quarter: **4** pity **5** spare **6** relent
quarters to: **4** rent **5** board, house, lodge, put up **6** billet, harbor, take in **7** shelter **9** entertain
refuge: **4** hide, save **6** foster, harbor, rescue, shield **7** protect, shelter **8** insulate **9** look after, safeguard
rise to: **5** beget, breed, cause, spawn **6** effect, induce, prompt **7** inspire, produce, trigger **8** engender, generate, occasion **10** bring about
shape: **4** cast, form, mold **5** forge, model **6** design, sculpt **7** fashion, whittle
shelter: **4** hide **5** house **6** harbor, shield **7** conceal, protect
slack: **6** relent
stars to: **4** rate **6** size up **8** classify, evaluate
support: **4** abet **5** endow **6** assist
testimony: **5** swear, vouch **6** assert, depone, depose **7** certify, declare, warrant, witness
thanks: **5** bless **6** praise **10** appreciate
the boot to: **2** ax **3** axe, can **4** fire, oust, sack **6** depose **7** dismiss
the brush: **4** snub **6** slight
the bum's rush to: **4** boot **6** bounce **7** boot out, cast out, kick out, turn out **8** throw out **9** chase away
the business to: **3** bug, nag, rag **4** haze, ride **5** harry, hound **6** badger, harass, hassle, heckle, needle, plague **8** browbeat
the cold shoulder: **4** snub **5** spurn **6** ignore, rebuff, slight
the evil eye: **5** scowl
the eye to: **4** ogle **5** stare
the gate: **4** oust **5** spurn
the go-ahead: **2** OK **4** okay **5** agree, allow **6** accede, enable **7** approve, endorse, indorse
the high sign: **3** tip **4** warn **5** alert **6** advise, signal, tip off **7** caution **8** forewarn
the impression: **4** look, seem **5** imply, sound **6** appear **7** suggest **8** intimate, resemble **9** insinuate, sound like **10** appear to be
the lie to: **4** deny **5** rebut **6** differ, impugn, negate, refute **7** confute, counter, dispute, gainsay **8** disprove **9** overthrow
the low-down: **3** cue, tip **4** leak, talk, tell, warn **5** brief, spill, steer **6** advise, impart, let out, reveal, tip off **7** caution, confide, divulge, lay bare **8** disclose
the meaning of: **6** define **7** explain **8** spell out **9** interpret
the nod: **4** okay **5** admit, adopt, allow, go for **6** accept, assent, comply, concur **7** consent, include, sign off, welcome **8** sanction, stand for **9** recognize
the once-over: **3** eye **4** ogle, peek, scan, skim **6** survey **7** inspect **8** check out
the raspberry: **3** boo **4** hiss, hoot, jeer, mock **5** fleer, taunt **6** deride, heckle **7** catcall **9** make fun of
the runaround: **5** stimy, stymy **6** stymie
the rundown: **5** brief **6** fill in, inform, report, update **7** apprise
the show away: **4** blab, leak, talk **5** spill **6** tattle
the slip: **4** foil, lose **5** avoid, dodge, elude, evade, leave **8** shake off, throw off
the third degree: **4** pump, quiz **5** grill **8** question
the word: **6** advise
the wrong idea: **4** dupe, fool, gull, hoax, scam, snow **5** bluff, cheat, put on, shaft, trick **6** delude, lead on, rope in, suck in, take in **7** confuse, deceive, defraud, mislead **8** hoodwink, inveigle, misguide, throw off **9** disinform, misinform **10** lead astray
thumbs-down: **3** nix, pan **4** rate, veto **6** refuse, refute, reject
thumbs-up: **2** OK **4** okay **6** accept **7** approve
too much: **4** cloy, glut, sate **5** gorge **7** surfeit
twenty lashes: **4** cane, drub, flog, whip **5** flail **6** larrup **7** scourge
unwanted advice: **6** kibitz, meddle
up: **4** bail, cede, drop, dump, fall, kick, lose, name, quit, sell, shed, stop **5** cease, chuck, ditch, forgo, spare, waive, yield **6** comply, eschew, fess up, forego, lay off, relent, resign, vacate **7** abandon, bail out, concede, discard, forfeit, forsake, lay down, let go of, refrain, sell out **8** abdicate, forswear, get rid of, hand over, jettison, leave off, part with, renounce, say uncle, sign away, squeal on, throw out **9** cast aside, dispose of, foreswear, lose heart, sacrifice, surrender, throw away **10** capitulate, relinquish
up hope: **7** despair **9** lose heart
up on: **4** drop, quit **5** ditch **7** abandon, discard, forsake, scuttle **8** write off **9** back out of, pull out of
voice to: **3** air **4** talk, vent **5** speak, utter **7** pour out
walking papers: **3** axe, can **4** fire
way: **3** sag **4** fall, move, snap **5** budge, burst, defer, split, yield **6** buckle, cave in, relent, retire, tumble, weaken **7** crumble, crumple, succumb **8** collapse, fall down, withdraw **9** lighten up **10** come undone
what for: **3** rag **4** flay, rail, ream **5** abuse, baste, chide, scold **6** assail, berate, jump on, preach, rail at, rebuke, vilify **7** bawl out, censure, chasten, chew out, lecture, reprove, tell off, upbraid **8** admonish, chastise, denounce, lace into, lambaste, reproach, sail into, tear into **9** castigate, criticize, dress down, excoriate, fulminate, light into, reprehend, reprimand **10** denunciate, tongue-lash, vituperate
words to: **3** say **4** tell **5** speak, utter, voice **6** assert **7** express **8** proclaim **9** enunciate, verbalize **10** articulate
work to: **4** hire **6** employ, engage, sign on, take on
wrong information: **3** lie **7** cover up, deceive, mislead **8** misguide, misstate **9** misdirect, misinform **10** lead astray, steer wrong

give __: **3** off, out, way **4** a rap, away, back, it to, over **5** a damn, a darn, a hang, a hoot, an ear, chase, it a go **6** ground
give __ berth to: **5** a wide
give __ for one's money: **4** a run
give __ go: **3** it a
give __ of confidence: **5** a vote
give __ rein to: **4** free, full
give __ shot: **3** it a
give __ time: **5** a hard
give __ to: **4** rise, vent **5** a hand, birth
give __ to Cerberus: **4** a sop
give __ try: **3** it a
give __ up: **4** a leg
give __ whirl: **3** it a

Give __ a Chance: 5 Peace
Give __ break!: 3 me a, us a
Give __ day...: 6 us this
Give __. Don't pollute: 5 a hoot
Give __ rest!: 3 it a
Give __ Sailor: 3 Me a
Give __ Simple Life: 5 Me the
give a __: 4 darn, hang, hoot 5 leg up
give a __ berth to: 4 wide
give a __ up: 3 leg
Give a __ Horse He Can Ride: 4 Man a
Give all thou __: 5 canst
give an __: 3 ear
give and __: 4 take
give-and-take: 6 banter 10 reciprocal
Give a Rouse author: Robert Browning
giveaway: 4 gift, sign, slip 7 freebee, freebie, premium 8 betrayal 10 disclosure
give a wide __ to: 5 berth
giveback: 6 refund 10 concession
Give 'Em Hell, Harry! (1975 film) cast: James Whitmore
give free __ to: 4 rein
give full __ to: 4 rein
Give it __!: 4 a try 5 a rest, a shot 6 a whirl
Give me __!: 4 five
Give Me Love (1973 song) artist: George Harrison
Give Me One Reason (1996 song) artist: Tracy Chapman
Give Me the Night (1980 song) artist: George Benson
Give me your __...: 5 tired
Give My Regards to Broadway composer: 5 Cohan
given: 3 apt, set 4 fact 5 axiom, fixed 6 liable, stated 7 assumed, nominal, premise, settled 9 axiomatic, postulate, specified 10 agreed upon, understood
be ~: 7 receive
that: 2 if 8 assuming, provided 9 providing, subject to, supposing 10 in the event
(to): 6 liable, likely 10 accustomed
to (suffix): 3 -ose
given __: 4 name
__-given: 3 God
Givens, Robin spouse: Mike Tyson
__ Given Sunday: 3 Any
give one's __: 3 all
give or take: 5 about
Give Peace a Chance (1969 song) artist: John Lennon
giver: 5 donor 6 backer 7 donator, grantor 9 supporter 10 benefactor
no ~: 5 miser
verdict ~: 5 panel, peers 8 tribunal 9 veniremen
Giverny artist: 5 Monet
giver opposite: 5 taker
__ gives?: 4 What
...gives us __ the right: 5 to see
give the __: 3 axe, eye 4 gate, slip 5 lie to, shake
give the __ his due: 5 devil
give the __ to: 3 lie 4 slip
give-up: 6 refund
__ Give Up the Ship: 4 Don't
giving: 4 good, kind 7 largess, liberal, plastic 8 generous, gracious, largesse 9 unselfish 10 charitable, free-handed, humanistic, munificent, openhanded, ungrudging
one: 5 donor
starter: 3 mis
__-giving: 4 life
Giving Him Something He Can Feel (1992 song) artist: En Vogue
Giving You the Best That I Got (1988 song) artist: Anita Baker

Giza: 4 city, town
locale: 5 Egypt
river: 4 Nile
gizmo: 4 tool 5 dodad, thing 6 device, doodad, gadget, thingy, whosis, widget 7 gimmick, machine, novelty, whatsis 9 apparatus, doohickey, invention 10 instrument
gizzard: 3 maw 4 craw 5 belly, organ 6 gullet 7 stomach
Gjellerup, Karl: 4 poet 6 author, Danish, writer 8 Nobelist
Gjetost: 6 cheese
Gk.
see Greek
G.K.: 10 Chesterton
glabella: 4 bone
locale: 4 face
glabrous: 4 bald 5 naked, shorn, stark 6 shaven 8 hairless
glacé: 4 iced 6 frozen, glazed 7 candied 8 lustrous, slippery
__ glacés: 7 marrons
glacial: 3 icy, raw 4 cold, cool, mean, slow 5 aloof, chill, gelid, nasty, nippy, onery, polar, surly 6 arctic, biting, bitter, chilly, frigid, frosty, frozen, ornery, remote, wintry 7 hateful, hostile, ice-cold, wintery 8 contrary, freezing, inimical, piercing, spiteful 9 bellicose, malicious, withdrawn 10 malevolent, pugnacious, unagitated, unfriendly
glacial __: 4 meal, milk 5 drift, epoch 6 period
glaciate: 3 ice 6 freeze
glacier: 3 ice
Alaskan ~: 4 Muir
basin: 3 cwm
era: 6 ice age
field: 4 firn, névé
fracture: 4 gulf, rift 5 abyss, chasm 7 crevice
hill: 4 paha
ice pinnacle: 5 serac
in a ~ 's path: 5 stoss
marking: 5 stria
mass: 4 berg 7 iceberg
polar ~: 6 icecap
ridge: 4 kame 5 arete, esker
ridges: 4 osar
glacier __: 4 lily 5 table
Glacier: 4 park
locale: 7 Montana
Glacier Bay: 4 park
locale: 6 Alaska
sight: 4 berg
glacis: 4 bank, hill, rise 5 grade 6 ascent 7 hillock, incline, upgrade 8 gradient, hillside 9 acclivity, elevation
glad: 5 happy, merry, plant, ready 6 blithe, cheery, elated, flower, jovial, joyful, joyous, upbeat 7 content, crowing, gleeful, pleased, radiant, tickled 8 blissful, cheerful, ecstatic, euphoric, exultant, jubilant, mirthful, thrilled 9 delighted, gratified, lightsome, overjoyed, rejoicing 10 flying high, rollicking
be ~: 5 enjoy, exult 7 delight, rejoice 9 celebrate
ender: 4 some
I'm ~ that's over: 4 whew
make ~: 5 cheer, elate, liven 6 lift up, please, thrill 7 content, delight, gratify, hearten, lighten, overjoy, satisfy 9 enrapture 10 exhilarate, intoxicate
rags: 4 garb, togs 5 array 6 finery 9 caparison
glad __: 3 eye 4 hand, rags
Glad: 4 wrap
alternative: 5 Hefty, Saran 6 Ziploc 8 Reynolds

Glad All Over (1964 song) artist: Dave Clark Five
gladden: 5 cheer, elate, liven 6 divert, please, thrill, turn on 7 cheer up, console, delight, enliven, gratify, happify, hearten, lighten, satisfy 8 brighten, enspirit, inspirit 9 encourage 10 exhilarate
gladdened: 4 rapt 5 happy 6 joyous 7 charmed, gleeful, radiant 8 blissful, ecstatic, exultant, jubilant 9 delighted, delirious, enchanted, entranced, fulfilled, gratified, overjoyed, rhapsodic 10 captivated
glade: 5 space 8 clearing
Glade alternative: 6 Wizard 7 Airwick, Renuzit 8 Stick-Ups
glades starter: 4 ever
gladiator: 3 pug 5 boxer 7 fighter, warrior 8 pugilist 9 combatant
item: 3 net 5 sword 6 shield
venue: 4 Rome 5 arena
see also Latin
Gladiator (2000 film)
cast: Russell Crowe, Joaquin Phoenix, Oliver Reed
director: Ridley Scott
setting: 4 Rome 5 arena
gladiatorial: 7 warlike 8 militant
Gladiator, The composer: 5 Sousa
gladiolus: 4 irid 5 plant 6 flower
base: 4 corm
Gladkov, Fyodor: 6 writer 7 Russian
gladly: 2 ay, da, ja 3 aye, oui, yea, yep, yes, yup 4 fain, fine, lief, okay, sure, yeah 5 gaily, gayly, good-o, lieve, natch, quite, right, roger, uh-huh 6 agreed, freely, good-oh, indeed, just so, rather, righto, surely, warmly, you bet, yowzah 7 exactly, go ahead, happily, indeedy, mais oui, quite so, readily, ten-four 8 all right, as you say, cheerily, heartily, joyfully, joyously, of course, thumbs up, very well 9 be my guest, certainly, darn right, naturally, precisely, sure thing, willingly, you betcha, you said it 10 absolutely, by all means, cheerfully, definitely, positively, sure enough, that's right, with relish
gladness: 3 joy 4 glee 5 bliss, cheer, mirth 6 gaiety, gayety 7 rapture 8 pleasure 9 happiness, jocundity, lightness 10 risibility
name meaning ~: 7 Letitia
gladsome: 5 happy 6 blithe 8 cheering, pleasant, pleasing 10 flying high
Gladstone: 4 city, town 7 William
Disraeli, to ~: 5 rival
locale: 8 Missouri
prep school: 4 Eton
Gladstone __: 3 bag
Gladys: 6 Cooper, George, Knight
glair: 8 egg white
surroundings: 4 yolk
glairy: 7 viscose, viscous
glam: 5 glitz 8 alluring 10 enchanting
Glamis title: 5 thane, thegn
glamor
see glamour
glamorize: 4 deck 5 adorn, array 6 bedeck 7 dress up, enhance, flatter 8 beautify, prettify 9 embellish, smarten up
glamorous: 4 foxy, sexy 5 kicky, swank 6 classy, exotic, flashy, lovely, swanky 7 elegant 8 alluring, charming, dazzling, exciting, magnetic, romantic 10 attractive, bewitching, enchanting, entrancing, flamboyant, glittering, magnetical
in London: 5 dishy
not ~: 5 plain, stark
woman: 3 fox 5 siren 9 temptress
Glamorous Life, The (1984 song) artist: Sheila E.

glamour: 5 charm, flair, glitz, spell, style 6 allure, appeal, beauty 7 charism, glitter, romance 8 charisma, mystique 9 good looks, magnetism 10 attraction, loveliness
glamour __: 3 boy 4 girl, puss 5 stock
Glamour: 3 mag 8 magazine
founder: 4 Nast
rival: 4 Elle 5 Vogue
Glan: 3 cow 4 bull 6 bovine, cattle
glance: 4 gaze, leaf, lick, look, peek, peep, skip, view 5 carom, flash, gleam, glint, graze, sight, sweep 6 aperçu, bounce, careen, carrom, gander, look-in, regard, squint 7 deflect, glimmer, glimpse, glisten, look-see, rebound, shimmer, sparkle, twinkle 8 ricochet 10 reflection, sneak a look
at: 3 eye 4 skim 5 watch 6 advert, browse 10 get a load of
at a ~: 6 easily 7 quickly 9 right away 10 apparently
off: 5 graze, parry 6 bounce, divert 7 deflect 8 ricochet
over: 4 scan, skim 6 peruse
quick ~: 4 peep 6 gander 7 glimpse, look-see
(through): 5 thumb
__ glance: 3 at a
gland: 5 liver 6 spleen, thymus 7 adrenal, thyroid 8 pancreas, salivary 9 endocrine, pituitary
combining form: 4 aden- 5 adeno-
ending: 4 ular
sac: 6 acinus
sweat ~: 4 pore 6 outlet 7 opening, orifice
__ gland: 4 salt, silk 5 lymph, preen, renal, scent, sweat 6 pineal, thymus 7 adrenal, carotid, Cowper's, parotid, thyroid
glare: 5 blaze, frown, light, lower, scowl, shine, stare 6 dazzle, glower, goggle 7 evil eye, glisten, glitter 8 radiance, radiancy 9 dirty look 10 brilliance, garishness, incandesce
protector: 5 visor, vizor
glaring: 4 open, rank 5 gaudy, gross, lurid, overt, showy, stark, utter, vivid 6 arrant, astare, brazen, crying, flashy, garish, patent, strong 7 blatant, blazing, evident, extreme, obvious, visible 8 apparent, blinding, flagrant, grievous, manifest, shocking, unsubtle 9 audacious, barefaced, egregious, excessive, nefarious, obtrusive, prominent 10 noticeable, outrageous
Glaser, Donald: 8 Nobelist 9 physicist
Glasgow: 4 city, port, town 5 Ellen
locale: 8 Scotland
river: 5 Clyde
Glasgow, Ellen: 6 author, writer
Glashow, Sheldon: 8 Nobelist 9 physicist
glasnost initials: 4 USSR
Glaspell, Susan: 6 author, writer
work: Alison's House
glass: 3 cup 4 lens, pane 5 drink 6 beaker, bottle, goblet, jigger, mirror 7 crystal, snifter, trinket, tumbler 9 reflector
champagne ~: 5 flute
combining form: 4 hyal-, vitr- 5 hyalo-, vitri-, vitro-
container: 3 jar 4 pony, tube, vial 5 ampul, cruet, flask, phial, pipet 6 ampule, beaker, bottle, goblet, jigger 7 ampoule, pipette, snifter, tumbler 8 test tube
create ~: 4 blow
eel: 5 elver
ender: 3 ine 4 fish, ware, work, wort 5 maker 6 making
fitted with ~: 5 paned

fragment: **5** shard, sherd **6** cullet
imperfection: **5** stria
looking ~: **6** mirror
made of ~: **6** hyalin **7** hyaline
optical ~: **4** lens **5** loupe **6** ocular **7** monocle **8** eyepiece **9** magnifier
oven: **4** lehr
partly fused ~: **4** frit **5** fritt
sound: **4** ting
source: **4** sand
starter: **3** eye, spy **4** hour, wine **5** fiber **7** weather
test-tube ~: **5** Pyrex
treat ~: **6** anneal, temper **7** toughen
volcanic ~: **8** obsidian
window ~: **4** pane **5** sheet
glass __: **3** eel, jaw **4** gall, tank, wool **5** block, brick, snake **6** blower, cutter, lizard **7** ceiling, curtain
glass-__: **5** faced
__ glass: **3** art, cut **4** Amen, bell, case, dram, foam, hand, joey, lace, lead, lime, milk, muff, opal, pier, ruby, shot, spun, wire **5** broad, cameo, cased, cover, crown, flint, float, green, milch, opera, plate, satin, sheet, thumb, water **6** aurene, bonnet, bottle, cheval, firing, ground, leaded, liquid, mosaic, object, Pomona, quartz, rolled, safety, silica, studio **7** antique, Burmese, burning, cupping, figured, flashed, looking, optical, overlay, parfait, peloton, pilsner, pressed, soluble, stained, Steuben, Tiffany
Glass: **3** Ron **6** Carter, Philip
Glass __: **4** Bell **5** Tiger
Glass __, The: **3** Key, Web **4** Harp, Lake **5** House, Onion
Glass Bead Game, The author: Hermann Hesse
Glass Bell author: Anaïs Nin
Glass Bottom Boat, The (1966 film)
cast: Doris Day, Arthur Godfrey, Rod Taylor
director: Frank Tashlin
dog: **8** Vladimir
glass cleaner: **6** Windex
glassed-in: **5** paned
glassed-in __: **6** shower
glasses: **4** spex **5** specs **6** frames, shades **7** goggles **8** bifocals, cheaters, contacts, horn rims, pince-nez, stemware **9** lorgnette, tableware, trifocals **10** spectacles
big name in ~: **4** Lomb **6** Bausch, Pearle
hoist ~: **5** drink, honor, toast **6** pledge
rose-colored ~: **4** hope **8** idealism, optimism **10** positivism
starter: **3** eye, sun
__ glasses: **4** nose **5** field, opera **6** granny **7** aviator, musical, reading
Glass House, The (2001 film)
cast: Bruce Dern, Diane Lane, Leelee Sobieski
director: Daniel Sackheim
Glass Key, The: **5** novel
author: Dashiell Hammett
character: **3** Ned **4** Farr, Opal, Shad **5** O'Rory **6** Madvig
Glass Key, The (1935 film)
cast: Edward Arnold, Claire Dodd, George Raft
Glass Key, The (1942 film)
cast: Brian Donlevy, Alan Ladd, Veronica Lake
Glass Lake, The author: Maeve Binchy
glassmaking: **5** craft
material: **4** sand **5** borax, ceria, silex
rod: **5** punty **6** pontil
Glassmanor: **4** city, town
locale: **8** Maryland
Glass Menagerie, The: **4** film, play
author: Tennessee Williams
cast: Karen Allen, John Malkovich, Joanne Woodward
character: **3** Tom **5** Laura **6** Amanda **9** Wingfield
director: Paul Newman
Glass of Blessings author: Barbara Pym
Glass Plus alternative: **6** Windex
Glass Web, The (1953 film)
cast: John Forsythe, Edward G. Robinson
glassy: **3** icy **4** cold, dull, void **5** blank, clear, dazed, empty, fixed, lucid, shiny, sleek, slick **6** hyalin, smooth, vacant, vitric **7** crystal, hyaline **8** lifeless, lustrous, polished, slippery, vitreous **9** burnished, lubricous **10** mirror-like, poker-faced, reflective
it may be ~: **5** stare
glassy-eyed: **4** dull **6** vacant, wooden **8** lifeless
Glassy Sea, The author: **5** Engel
Glastonbury __: **5** chair
Glaswegian: **4** Scot
glatt __: **6** kosher
Glavine, Tom: **6** hurler **7** pitcher
glaze: **4** coat **5** color, cover, gloss, icing, sheen, shine, sirup, syrup **6** enamel, finish, luster, patina, patine, polish, smooth **7** burnish, coating, encrust, furbish, incrust, lacquer, overlay, varnish **8** covering, frosting **9** sugarcoat
base: **4** frit **5** fritt
__ glaze: **4** lead, salt **7** oilspot
glazed: **3** icy **5** glacé, slick **6** glossy, smooth **8** lustrous, slippery
fabric: **4** cire **5** tammy **6** chintz, tammie
food: **5** donut **8** doughnut
glazier need: **4** pane **5** putty
Glazunov: **9** Aleksandr, Alexander
Glazunov, Alexander ballet: Raymonda
gleam: **3** ray **4** beam, glow, wink **5** flare, flash, glint, gloss, light, sheen, shine, spark **6** glance, luster **7** flicker, glimmer, glisten, glitter, lighten, radiate, shimmer, sparkle, twinkle **8** radiance, radiancy **9** coruscate, irradiate, luminesce, scintilla **10** brightness, brilliance, effulgence, incandesce, luminosity
gleaming: **3** lit **5** aglow, lucid, shiny **6** ablaze, ashine, bright, flashy, glossy **7** fulgent, lambent, radiant **8** luminous, lustrous, spotless **9** brilliant, refulgent
glean: **3** get **4** cull, pick, reap, sift **5** amass, infer, learn **6** deduce, derive, garner, gather, obtain, pick up, select, winnow **7** collect, excerpt, extract, find out, harvest, pick out, salvage **8** conclude, discover, scrape up **9** ascertain, get to know **10** accumulate
gleaning: **4** crop
Gleason: **5** James **6** Jackie
Gleason, Jackie: **5** actor **8** comedian
costar: **4** Kean **6** Carney, MacRae **7** Meadows **8** Randolph
film: Gigot (1962)
The Hustler (1961)
Nothing in Common (1986)
Requiem for a Heavyweight (1962)
Smokey and the Bandit (1977)
Soldier in the Rain (1963)
TV: The Honeymooners, The Life of Riley
glee: **3** joy **4** song **5** cheer, mirth **6** gaiety, gayety **7** delight, elation, gayness, jollity **8** euphoria, felicity, gladness, hilarity, laughter, pleasure **9** frivolity, happiness, jocundity, joviality, lightness, merriment **10** exuberance, exultation, joyfulness, joyousness, jubilation, liveliness, risibility
cry of ~: **3** hah, yay **4** I win, whee **5** whoop **6** gotcha
fill with ~: **5** elate
for ~ clubs: **5** lyric **6** choral
name meaning ~: **4** Hoyt
show ~: **4** beam, grin **5** smile **7** sparkle
with ~: **5** gaily, gayly
glee club: **6** chorus **7** singers **8** ensemble **9** vocalists
member: **4** alto, bass **5** tenor **7** soprano **8** baritone
gleeful: **3** gay **4** boon, glad **5** happy, jolly, merry, riant **6** blithe, cheery, elated, jocund, jovial, joyful, joyous, upbeat **7** exalted, festive, jocular, pleased, tickled **8** blissful, cheerful, ecstatic, euphoric, exultant, giggling, grooving, jubilant, laughing, mirthful, thrilled **9** delighted, gladdened, lightsome, overjoyed, rejoicing **10** flying high, frolicsome, triumphant
gleek: **4** game **8** card game
Gleem: **10** toothpaste
alternative: **3** Aim **5** Crest, Topol **7** Close-Up, Colgate, Viadent **9** Aquafresh, Mentadent, Pepsodent, Rembrandt, Sensodyne **10** Pearl Drops, Ultra Brite **11** Tom's of Maine
glen: **4** dale, dell, vale **5** combe, coomb, gorge **6** coombe, dingle, valley
Glen: **4** John **8** Campbell
plaid: **6** fabric **7** pattern **8** material
Glen __: **5** check, plaid **6** Burnie
__ Glen: **3** Tam **7** Watkins
Glen Burnie: **4** city, town
locale: **8** Maryland
Glen Cove: **4** city, town
locale: **7** New York **10** Long Island
Glenda: **7** Farrell, Jackson
Glendale: **4** city, town
locale: **7** Arizona **10** California
Glendale Heights: **4** city, town
locale: **8** Illinois
Glendora: **4** city, town
locale: **10** California
Glendora (1956 song) artist: Perry Como
Glen Ellyn: **4** city, town
locale: **8** Illinois
Glengarry: **3** cap, hat
Glengarry Glen Ross: **4** film, play
author: David Mamet
cast: Alan Arkin, Alec Baldwin, Ed Harris, Jack Lemmon, Al Pacino, Kevin Spacey
director: James Foley
Glen, John: **8** director
film: For Your Eyes Only (1981)
Licence to Kill (1989)
The Living Daylights (1987)
Octopussy (1983)
A View to a Kill (1985)
Glenmont: **4** city, town
locale: **8** Maryland
Glenn: **4** Ford, Frey, John **5** Close, Gould, Scott **6** Miller **7** Corbett, Curtiss, Seaborg **8** Medeiros **9** Yarbrough
Glenne: **6** Headly
Glenn, John: **7** senator **9** astronaut
state: **4** Ohio
Glenn Miller Story, The (1954 film)
cast: June Allyson, Charles Drake, James Stewart
director: Anthony Mann
Glenn, Scott: **5** actor
film: The Hunt for Red October (1990)
Personal Best (1982)
The Right Stuff (1983)
The Silence of the Lambs (1991)
Silverado (1985)
Training Day (2001)
Urban Cowboy (1980)
Glenview: **4** city, town
locale: **8** Illinois
Gless: **6** Sharon
glib: **3** pat **4** oily **5** slick, suave, vocal **6** artful, facile, fluent, prolix, smooth **7** offhand, verbose, voluble **8** eloquent, slippery **9** garrulous, insincere, rehearsed, talkative **10** articulate, effortless, loquacious, rhetorical
talk: **4** jive
glide: **3** fly, run, ski **4** flit, flow, move, roll, sail, scud, skee, skid, skim, slip, soar, waft **5** coast, drift, float, skate, slide, slink, sneak, steal, sweep, waltz **6** chassé, stream **7** slither **8** levitate, volitate, volplane
ballroom ~: **6** chassé
by: **4** flow, pass **6** elapse, roll on
downward: **5** sweep, swoop
on snow: **3** ski **4** skee
(through): **6** breeze
glide __: **4** path **5** angle, plane, slope
glider: **4** seat **8** aircraft
locale: **5** lanai, porch **7** veranda **8** verandah
on a ~: **5** aloft
use a ~: **3** fly **4** lift, soar
wood: **5** balsa
__ glider: **4** hang **5** pygmy, sugar
__ gliding: **4** hang
glim: **4** lamp **5** light **7** lantern
glimmer: **3** ray **4** glow, hint, wink **5** blink, flash, gleam, glint, light, shine, speck, trace **6** glance **7** flicker, glisten, glitter, inkling, shimmer, sparkle, twinkle, vestige **9** coruscate, luminesce, scintilla, suspicion **10** suggestion
glimmer __: **3** ice
glimmering: **4** hint, idea **5** shiny **6** ashine **7** inkling
glimpse: **3** eye, see, spy **4** espy, look, peek, peep, spot, view **5** flash, sight, watch **6** aperçu, descry, detect, gander, glance, notice, peek at, peer at, squint, take in **7** discern, look-see, make out **8** check out, discover **10** get a load of, sneak a look
Glinda: **5** witch
Glinka, Mikhail: **7** Russian **8** composer
work: A Life for the Tsar
Russlan and Ludmilla
glint: **3** ray **5** flash, gleam, gloss, light, sheen, shine, spark **6** glance, luster **7** glimmer, glisten, glitter, inkling, shimmer, sparkle, twinkle **9** scintilla
glinty: **8** lustrous **9** sparkling
glissade: **4** slip, step **5** slink **7** slither
Glissant, Édouard: **6** writer **10** Martinican
glisten: **4** glow **5** flash, glare, gleam, glint, shine **6** glance **7** flicker, glimmer, glitter, shimmer, sparkle, twinkle **9** coruscate, luminesce **10** incandesce
glistening: **5** shiny, sleek **6** ashine, glossy **8** lustrous, slippery **9** refulgent
glitch: **3** bug **4** flaw, kink, snag, typo **5** error, hitch, snafu **6** defect, mishap **7** erratum, misfire, problem, setback **9** hindrance **10** deficiency
galley ~: **4** typo **7** erratum **8** misprint
glitter: **3** ray **4** beam, glow, show, wink **5** blink, flash, glare, gleam, glint, glitz, light, sheen, shine, spark **6** glamor, luster, tinsel **7** flicker, glamour, glimmer, glisten, radiate, shimmer, spangle, sparkle, twinkle **8** radiance, radiancy, splendor **9** coruscate, gaudiness, irradiate, luminesce, pageantry, showiness **10** brightness, brilliance
glitter __: **3** ice
Glitter: **4** Gary

glitterati: **5** elite **6** celebs, jet set
glittering: **5** beady, shiny **6** aglint, bright, flashy, tawdry **7** radiant **8** dazzling, splendid **9** brilliant, glamorous, refulgent
  fabric: **4** lamé **8** diamante
glitz: **4** glam **5** shine **6** glamor **7** glamour, glitter, sparkle **9** gaudiness, showiness **10** flashiness
glitzy: **5** fancy, gaudy, showy **6** flashy, frilly, lavish, ornate, tawdry **7** opulent **9** decorated, elaborate, luxurious, sumptuous **10** ornamented
  sign: **4** neon
Glo-__: **4** Coat
__-Glo: **3** Day
gloaming: **3** e'en **4** dusk **7** evening **8** twilight **9** nightfall
gloat: **4** brag, crow **5** boast, exult, preen, revel, savor **7** rub it in, swagger, triumph **9** whoop it up
  (in): **6** wallow
  over: **5** savor **6** relish **9** rejoice in
gloating: **4** smug **5** proud **8** arrogant, puffed-up **10** complacent
glob: **3** wad **4** bead, blob, hunk, lump, mass **5** chunk, clump **6** dollop **8** mountain
  ender: **3** ule
global: **4** intl. **5** total, world **7** earthly, general, overall **8** catholic, far-flung, sweeping **9** all around, spherical, universal, worldwide **10** exhaustive
  speck: **3** isl. **4** isle **5** islet **6** island
global __: **7** village, warming
Global: **5** mover
  rival: **6** Allied, United
Global Positioning __: **6** System
globe: **3** map, orb **4** ball **5** Earth, world **6** planet, sphere
  ender: **4** fish, trot **6** flower
Globe: **5** paper **9** newspaper
  locale: **6** Boston
Globe __: **7** Theatre
Globe and Eagle composer: **5** Sousa
Globe and Mail: **5** paper **9** newspaper
  locale: **7** Toronto
globefish: **6** puffer
globelike: **5** round **9** spherical
globetrot: **4** roam, tour **5** range **6** wander **7** journey
globetrotter: **5** rover **7** pilgrim, tourist **8** gadabout, traveler, wanderer, wayfarer **9** jet-setter, sightseer
  woe: **6** jet lag
__ Globetrotters: **6** Harlem
globetrotting: **6** roving, travel **7** on the go, roaming **8** voyaging **9** on the move, wandering, wayfaring **10** jet-setting, journeying
globular: **5** round **6** rotund **7** bulbous, orotund, rounded **9** spherical **10** ball-shaped
globule: **4** ball, bead, blob, drop, tear **5** round **6** bubble, sphere **7** dewdrop, driblet **8** spheroid, spherule, teardrop
__ globulin: **4** beta **5** alpha, gamma
glockenspiel: **4** lyra
  component: **5** chime
glögg ingredient: **4** wine
glom: **3** eye **4** lift **5** filch, grasp, seize, steal, swipe **6** pilfer
  on to: **5** catch, grasp **6** attain
  (onto): **4** grab **5** latch
Glomma: **5** river
  locale: **6** Norway
gloom: **3** woe **4** dark, funk, mirk, murk, pall **5** blues, dolor, grief, night, shade **6** misery, shadow, sorrow **7** anguish, despair, dimness, malaise, sadness **8** darkness, distress, doldrums, glumness, the blues **9** adumbrate, blackness, bleakness, dejection, heartache, murkiness, obscurity, pessimism **10** depression, desolation, dreariness, heavy heart, infelicity, loneliness, melancholy, somberness, woefulness
  partner: **4** doom
gloominess: **5** shade **7** dim view, sadness **8** glumness **9** pessimism **10** depression, desolation, heavy heart, loneliness, woefulness
__ gloom of night...: **3** nor
gloomy: **3** bad, dim, dun, low, sad **4** blue, dark, dour, down, glum, gray, grey, grim, lour, ugly **5** black, bleak, drear, dusky, grave, heavy, leady, livid, loury, mirky, moody, murky, sorry, sulky, surly, unlit, woful **6** broody, cloudy, crabby, dismal, dreary, leaden, lowery, moping, mopish, morbid, morose, somber, sullen, woeful **7** doleful, forlorn, hangdog, in a funk, joyless, obscure, ominous, shadowy, unhappy, way down **8** darkened, dejected, desolate, downbeat, downcast, hopeless, liverish, lonesome, lowering, negative, overcast, troubled, wretched **9** bummed out, cheerless, depressed, heartsick, lightless, mirthless, miserable, saddening, saturnine, sorrowful, tenebrous, unhopeful, unlighted, woebegone **10** chapfallen, depressing, despondent, dispirited, lugubrious, melancholy, oppressive, out of sorts, tenebrific
  atmosphere: **4** pall
  be ~: **4** mope
  make ~: **6** dampen, darken, deject, sadden, shadow **7** depress, obscure **8** dispirit **9** bring down **10** demoralize, discourage, dishearten
  one: **3** Gus **4** mope **5** moper **7** killjoy **9** pessimist, worrywart
Gloomy __: **3** Gus
Gloomy Dean, The: **4** Inge
glop: **3** goo **4** gunk, mess, muck, mush, ooze **5** slime **6** dollop
gloppy: **7** jellied
gloria: **4** halo **6** fabric **8** material
Gloria: **4** hymn **5** Henry **6** Bunker, Gaynor, Loring, Stivic, Stuart **7** De Haven, Estefan, Grahame, Steinem, Swanson **10** Vanderbilt
  mom: **5** Edith
Gloria in Excelsis __: **3** Deo
Gloria Patri ending: **4** amen
Gloria (song) artist: Laura Branigan, Shadows of Knight
glorification: **5** honor **6** eulogy **7** hosanna **8** encomium
glorify: **4** hail, laud, sing, tout **5** adore, bless, deify, ensky, exalt, extol, grace, honor **6** admire, extoll, praise, revere, salute **7** acclaim, applaud, commend, elevate, flatter, idolize, lionize, magnify, worship **8** canonize, enthrone, eulogize, inthrone, sanctify, venerate **9** celebrate, recommend **10** aggrandize, compliment, panegyrize
gloriole: **4** aura, halo, ring **5** glory **6** circle, corona, nimbus **7** aureola, aureole **8** radiance, radiancy
gloriosa __: **4** lily
glorious: **3** def, rad **4** aces, A-one, boss, braw, cool, dece, fine, gear, keen, neat, nice, phat, tuff **5** dandy, ducky, famed, grand, great, marvy, neato, nobby, noble, noted, palmy, prime, proud, slick, super, swell **6** august, bang on, bang-up, bonzer, bosker, choice, divine, dreamy, famous, far-out, gnarly, golden, groovy, heroic, lovely, peachy, slap-up, spot on, superb, terrif, tiptop, unreal, whizzo, wicked **7** amazing, awesome, capital, corking, eminent, exalted, gallant, honored, perfect, radiant, ripping, shining, skookum, stellar, sublime **8** dazzling, especial, esteemed, eximious, fabulous, five-star, four-star, frabjous, gorgeous, heavenly, heroical, idolized, jim-dandy, lustrous, majestic, renowned, slam-bang, smashing, splendid, standout, sterling, stickout, superior, terrific, top-level, topnotch, very good, wondrous **9** beautiful, bodacious, brilliant, Endsville, excellent, exemplary, exquisite, first-rate, high-grade, hunky-dory, marvelous, memorable, sollicker, top-flight, unrivaled, venerable, well-known, wonderful, wunderbar **10** celebrated, delightful, first-class, hotsy-totsy, incredible, jack-a-dandy, majestical, out of sight, peachy-keen, phenomenal, remarkable, stupendous, super-duper, triumphant, unrivalled
  starter: **4** vain
glory: **4** fame **5** éclat, exult, honor, kudos, revel, state **6** credit, honors, praise, renown, wallow **7** dignity, laurels, majesty, rapture, rejoice, triumph **8** eminence, gloriole, grandeur, jubilate, nobility, prestige, splendor **9** celebrity, greatness, sublimity **10** exaltation, exultation, importance, reputation
  starter: **4** vain
__ glory: **7** morning
Glory (1989 film)
  cast: Matthew Broderick, Cary Elwes, Morgan Freeman, Denzel Washington
  director: Edward Zwick
Glory __: **4** Days, Road
__ Glory: **3** Old **7** Morning
glory day, name meaning: **6** Dagmar
Glory Days (1985 song) artist: Bruce Springsteen
Glory of Love (1986 song) artist: Peter Cetera
Glory of the Yankee Navy, The composer: **5** Sousa
Glory Road author: Bruce Catton
glory ruler, name meaning: **8** Roderick
glory wolf, name meaning: **4** Rolf
gloss: **3** rub **4** buff, coat, lick, note **5** color, glaze, gleam, glint, input, paint, sheen, shine **6** enamel, finish, luster, makeup, polish, remark, smooth, veneer **7** burnish, comment, explain, lacquer, shimmer, touch up, varnish **8** annotate **9** comment on, elucidate, interpret, silkiness, translate, whitewash **10** annotation, brightness, brilliance
  over: **4** coat, omit **5** elide, gloze, mince **7** neglect **8** leave out, palliate, play down, shrug off **9** underplay, whitewash
  put a ~ on: **3** rub, wax **4** buff **5** shine **6** polish **7** burnish
__ gloss: **3** lip
glossa: **6** tongue
glossary: **4** list **5** lexis, vocab. **7** lexicon **10** vocabulary
glossy: **5** light, nitid, photo, print, shiny, silky, sleek, slick **6** bright, glazed, satiny, silken, smooth **8** gleaming, lustrous, magazine, polished **9** brilliant, burnished, lubricous **10** glistening, photograph
  material: **5** satin **6** enamel, sateen **7** taffeta
  not ~: **3** mat **5** matte **10** lusterless
glottal __: **4** stop
glottis starter: **3** epi
Gloucester: **4** city, port, town
  cape: **3** Ann
  king: **4** Lear
  locale: **4** Mass. **6** Canada **7** England, Ontario
Gloucestershire: **6** county
  city: **6** Stroud
  locale: **7** England
  neighbor: **4** Avon
Gloucs: **6** county
  locale: **7** England
glove: **4** gage, mitt **8** gauntlet
  alternative: **4** muff
  boxing ~ of ancient Rome: **6** cestus
  game: **6** boxing
  hand in ~: **4** deep **5** close, solid, thick, tight **6** allied, chummy, united **7** unified **8** friendly, in league **10** buddy-buddy, palsy-walsy
  insert: **4** hand
  material: **3** kid **5** latex **7** leather
  part: **4** palm **5** thumb **6** finger
  starter: **3** fox
  wearer: **5** boxer **8** pugilist
glove __: **3** box **4** silk **7** leather
__ glove: **3** kid **4** golf **5** fairy **6** boxing, velvet
glove-box item: **3** map **6** deicer **10** flashlight
Glover: **4** John **5** Danny **6** Savion **7** Crispin
Glover, Danny: **5** actor
  film: Angels in the Outfield (1994)
    Bat*21 (1988)
    Bopha! (1993)
    The Color Purple (1985)
    Grand Canyon (1991)
    Lethal Weapon (1987)
    Lethal Weapon 2 (1989)
    Lethal Weapon 3 (1992)
    Lethal Weapon 4 (1998)
    Places in the Heart (1984)
    Silverado (1985)
    To Sleep With Anger (1990)
Glover, John: **5** actor
  film: The Chocolate War (1988)
    Gremlins 2 The New Batch (1990)
    Last Embrace (1979)
    Scrooged (1988)
__ gloves: **3** kid
glow: **4** aura, burn, tint **5** flame, flush, gleam, light, sheen, shine, spark, sweat **6** luster, redden, thrill **7** glimmer, glisten, glitter, light up, radiate, shimmer, sparkle, twinkle **8** lambency, perspire, radiance, radiancy **9** freshness, luminesce **10** brightness, brilliance, complexion, effulgence, luminosity, refulgence
  ender: **4** worm
  enjoy the ~: **4** bask
  make ~: **5** shine **6** polish **7** burnish, cheer up, light up **8** brighten, illumine **10** illuminate
  starter: **3** air **5** after, night **7** counter
glow __: **4** lamp, plug
Glow-__: **4** Worm
glower: **4** look, pout, sulk **5** frown, glare, scowl, stare
glowing: **3** lit, red **4** avid, keen, rosy, warm **5** eager, fresh, happy, light, lit up, ruddy, shiny, sunny, vivid **6** ablaze, ardent, ashine, bright, fervid, flashy, sweaty **7** fervent, fulgent, lambent, radiant, vibrant, zealous **8** blooming, ecstatic, luminous, lustrous, sanguine, splendid **9** adulatory, brilliant, laudatory, refulgent, rhapsodic **10** flickering, flying high, passionate
  bit: **5** ember, spark
  name meaning ~: **7** Candace, Candice
glowworm: **3** bug **6** insect
gloxinia: **5** plant **6** flower
gloze: **7** justify **8** minimize, palliate

9 extenuate, gloss over, underplay
Gluck: 4 Alma 6 Louise 9 Christoph
Gluck, Alma: 7 soprano
spouse: Efrem Zimbalist
Gluck, Christoph ballet: Don Juan
glückliche Reise: 5 adieu
Glück, Louise: 4 poet
glucose: 5 sugar
to lactose: 6 isomer
glue: 3 fix, gum 4 bond, join, tack 5 affix, epoxy, paste, resin, stick 6 adhere, attach, cement, cohere, Elmer's, fasten 7 stickum 8 adhesive, fixative, mucilage
combining form: 4 coll- 5 collo-
glue ___: 3 gun 4 cell
___ glue: 3 bee 5 Super 6 casein, marine
glued: 4 fast 8 watchful 9 attentive
gluey: 5 gummy, pasty, tacky 6 clayey, sticky, viscid 7 clayish, viscose, viscous 8 adhesive, cohesive 9 glutinous
glum: 3 low, sad 4 blue, dark, dour, down, grim, mopy, ugly 5 moody, mopey, sulky, surly, woful 6 broody, crabby, dismal, dreary, gloomy, moping, morose, solemn, somber, sullen, woeful 7 doleful, joyless, roubled, unhappy 8 brooding, dejected, downbeat, downcast, liverish, lowering 9 bummed-out, cheerless, depressed, heartsick, miserable, saturnine, sorrowful, woebegone 10 chapfallen, despondent, dispirited, melancholy
not ~: 5 happy, jolly, merry, sunny 6 blithe, bouncy, bright, cheery, chirpy, jovial, joyful, joyous 7 chipper, festive, gleeful 8 animated, carefree, cheerful, jubilant, laughing, mirthful 9 convivial, sprightly, vivacious 10 flying high
Glumdalclitch: 5 giant
glumness: 3 woe 5 blues, dumps, gloom, mopes 7 despair, sadness 8 cynicism, doldrums 9 dejection, moodiness, pessimism 10 depression, gloominess, heavy heart, low spirits, melancholy
gluon: 8 particle
glut: 4 cloy, cram, load, sate 5 flood, gorge, stuff, weary 6 excess 7 congest, engorge, nimiety, satiate, satiety, satisfy, surfeit, surplus 8 inundate, overfeed, overfill, overload, plethora, saturate 9 overstock, plenitude, profusion, repletion 10 gormandize, inundation, oversupply, saturation
gluten ___: 5 bread, flour
gluten source: 4 corn 5 grain, wheat
glutinous: 4 ropy 5 gluey, gummy, ropey, slimy 6 sticky, viscid 7 viscose, viscous 10 gelatinous
glutted: 3 fed 4 full 5 blasé, sated 7 replete 8 satiated
glutton: 3 hog, pig 5 eater 6 gorger 7 gobbler 8 gourmand 9 overeater
delight: 5 feast 6 buffet
gluttonize: 5 gorge 10 gormandize
gluttonous: 5 piggy 6 greedy, piggie 7 gorging, hoggish, lustful, piggish, starved 8 covetous, edacious, ravenous 9 epicurean, insatiate, rapacious, voracious 10 insatiable, omnivorous, quenchless
gluttony: 3 sin 7 edacity, license 8 voracity
glyceride: 5 ester, olein 6 oleine
glycerin: 5 ester
starter: 5 nitro
Glyn, Elinor: 6 author, writer 7 British
Glynis: 5 Johns
Glynn: 6 Turman
Glynnis: 7 O'Connor
glyph: 10 pictograph
prefix for ~: 5 petro
Glypha: 4 font 8 typeface
gm.: 2 wt. 4 meas.
GM: 4 boss 8 carmaker 9 automaker
former ~ rival: 3 AMC
home: 4 Mich.
part: 3 gen., mgr. 6 Motors 7 General
workers' org.: 3 UAW
see also General Motors
G-man: 3 agt., fed 4 narc, nark 5 agent 8 FBI agent
GMA rival: 5 Today
GMAT: 4 exam, test
GMC: 3 van 5 truck
model: 5 Jimmy, Yukon 6 Denali, Safari, Savana 7 Vandura 8 Suburban 9 Starcraft
G Men (1935 film)
cast: James Cagney, Ann Dvorak
G-mez Palacio: 4 city, town
locale: 6 Mexico 7 Durango
gnar: 5 growl, snarl
gnarl: 4 bump, knot, knur, lump, spur 5 growl, snarl 6 deform, knot up 7 contort, distort 8 swelling
gnarled: 5 lumpy, rough 6 knobby 7 knurled
gnarly: 3 def, rad 4 aces, A-one, bent, boss, braw, cool, dece, fine, gear, keen, neat, nice, phat, tuff 5 dandy, ducky, grand, great, marvy, neato, nobby, prime, slick, super, swell 6 bang on, bang-up, bonzer, bosker, choice, divine, dreamy, far-out, groovy, lovely, peachy, slap-up, spot on, superb, terrif, tiptop, unreal, whizzo, wicked 7 amazing, awesome, capital, corking, perfect, ripping, skookum, stellar, sublime, twisted 8 dazzling, especial, eximious, fabulous, five-star, four-star, frabjous, glorious, heavenly, jim-dandy, slambang, smashing, splendid, standout, sterling, stickout, superior, terrific, toplevel, topnotch, very good, wondrous 9 bodacious, Endsville, excellent, exemplary, exquisite, first-rate, highgrade, hunky-dory, marvelous, sollicker, top-flight, wonderful 10 first-class, hotsy-totsy, jack-a-dandy, out of sight, peachy-keen, phenomenal, remarkable, stupendous, super-duper
gnash: 5 chomp, grate, grind, snarl
gnat: 3 bug, fly 4 pest 5 biter, midge, punky 6 insect, punkie 7 no-see-um
combining form: 5 culic- 6 culici-
group: 5 swarm
like a ~: 5 pesky, pesty 10 bothersome
___ gnat: 4 gall 5 black 6 fungus 7 buffalo
gnatcatcher: 4 bird
gnaw: 3 eat 4 bite, chew 5 champ, chomp, eat at, munch, tease 6 crunch, nibble 9 eat away at, masticate
at: 4 bite 5 worry 6 bother, plague 7 corrode
on: 4 bite 5 eat at 9 masticate
gnawed away: 5 erose
gneiss: 7 mineral
GNMA: 6 lender
concern: 4 loan 8 mortgage
part of ~: 3 Gov., Nat. 4 Assn., Govt., Mtge., Natl. 8 Mortgage, National
gnocchi: 7 noodles
gnome: 3 elf, fay, saw 4 rule 5 moral, troll 6 byword, dictum, goblin, kobold, midget, sprite 7 gremlin, proverb 8 aphorism, laconism 10 leprechaun
Gnome-Mobile, The (1967 film)
cast: Walter Brennan, Richard Deacon, Karen Dotrice, Matthew Garber
gnomic: 5 terse 9 axiomatic 10 synopsized
G-note: 4 thou
GNP: 4 stat
part: 3 Nat. 4 Natl., Prod. 5 Gross 7 Product 8 National
topic: 4 econ. 9 economics
gnu: 6 animal, mammal 8 antelope 10 wildebeest
milieu: 3 zoo 5 veldt 6 Africa
relative: 3 kob 4 guib, kudu, oryx, puku, topi 5 addax, bongo, chiru, eland, goral, korin, nyala, oribi, saiga, serow 6 chammy, dik-dik, duiker, impala, koodoo, lechwe, nilgai, rhebok, shammy, shamoy 7 blaubok, blesbok, chamois, defassa, gazelle, gemsbok, gerenuk, grysbok, nylghai, nylghau, sassaby 8 blesbuck, bontebok, bushbuck, gemsbuck, reedbuck, steenbok, steinbok 9 blackbuck, pronghorn, sitatunga, springbok, waterbuck 10 hartebeest, wildebeest
go: 3 fit, fly, hie, pep, try, zip 4 bear, exit, fail, fare, flee, game, gybe, jibe, mesh, move, part, pass, push, quit, shot, snap, stab, take, test, time, turn, work, zest 5 abide, agree, allow, be off, blend, break, brook, crack, drive, fit in, fling, lam it, leave, match, mosey, occur, oomph, reach, refer, scram, split, stand, verve, vigor, whack, whirl, zip by 6 attend, beat it, belong, bug out, decamp, depart, elapse, embark, endure, energy, escape, finish, fold up, get out, happen, move it, pan out, pass by, permit, pop off, push on, repair, run off, set off, set out, spirit, suffer, thrive, travel, vanish 7 abscond, advance, attempt, blend in, carry on, conform, crumble, develop, get away, get lost, head out, hop to it, journey, make off, make out, migrate, move off, move out, operate, perform, persist, potence, potency, proceed, pull out, push off, ride off, run away, skip out, step out, stomach, succeed, take off, turn out, vamoose 8 collapse, continue, dovetail, evacuate, flourish, function, hightail, run along, set forth, shove off, slip away, tick away, tolerate, vitality, vivacity, withdraw 9 animation, consent to, disappear, eventuate, harmonize, move along, put up with, steal away, take a hike, take a turn, transpire 10 assist with, correspond, get a move on, green light, hightail it, hit the road, sally forth, shuffle off, step lively, take flight
aboard: 4 ship 6 embark 7 emplane, entrain, set sail, ship out 9 leave port
about: 6 tackle 8 shoulder 9 undertake
abroad: 4 tour 6 travel 8 sightsee, vacation
across: 4 ford, span 5 reach 6 bridge 7 connect, stretch 8 pass over, traverse
adrift: 3 err
a few rounds: 4 spar 5 fight
after: 4 seek 5 chase, ensue, set at, trail 6 assail, attack, follow, have at, pursue, rebuke, strive 7 succeed 9 track down
after game: 4 hunt 5 chase, stalk, track 6 forage
against: 4 foil 5 flout 6 hinder, offset, oppose, thwart 7 infract, obviate, prevent, redress 9 frustrate 10 contravene, counteract, neutralize
against the grain: 3 bug, get, irk, try, vex 4 gall, rile 5 annoy, peeve, pique, upset 6 bother, nettle, offend, rankle, ruffle 7 grate on, provoke 8 irritate 9 aggravate 10 exasperate
ahead: 2 ay, da, ja 3 aye, oui, yea, yep, yes, yup 4 fine, lead, okay, pass, sure, yeah 5 begin, good-o, natch, quite, right, roger, start, uh-huh 6 agreed, gladly, good-oh, indeed, just so, rather, righto, set off, set out, surely, you bet, yowzah 7 advance, exactly, indeedy, lead off, mais oui, proceed, quite so, ten-four 8 all right, as you say, of course, set forth, thumbs up, very well 9 be my guest, certainly, darn right, naturally, precisely, sure thing, you betcha, you said it 10 absolutely, by all means, definitely, positively, sure enough, that's right
ahead of: 4 lead 7 precede, presage 8 antecede 9 introduce
ahead with: 5 act on 6 follow
aimlessly: 4 rove
all out: 3 try 5 speed 6 strain, strive 8 struggle
allow to ~: 4 free 5 loose 6 acquit, let off, pardon, parole 7 cashier, dismiss, release, set free 8 liberate 9 discharge, exonerate, muster out, terminate
all systems ~: 5 ready 8 prepared
all the way: 4 last 6 endure, hold on, linger 7 carry on, survive 8 continue, plug away 9 hang tough, keep going, persevere, stand firm 10 tough it out
along: 5 agree, say OK 6 accede, assent, behave, comply, concur, say yes 7 approve, consent 8 join with 9 accompany, acquiesce, cooperate, play along 10 assist with
along with: 4 obey 5 abide, humor, yield 6 accept, relent, second 7 agree to, approve, endorse, indorse, indulge, support 8 overlook, tolerate 9 subscribe
ape: 4 flip, rage, rant, rave, snap 5 crack, freak 6 lose it 8 freak out
around: 4 spin, turn, wind 5 orbit, skirt 6 bypass, circle, rotate 7 revolve
as far as: 5 reach
ashore: 4 land 6 arrive, debark 9 disembark
astray: 3 err, sin 4 fail 6 derail, ramble, wander 9 backslide, misbehave
at: 6 assail, attack
at it: 4 feud 5 brawl, fight 6 battle, tussle 7 grapple, mix it up, quarrel
at top speed: 3 run 4 dash, race, rush, tear, whiz 5 scoot 6 gallop, scurry, sprint, streak 7 scamper
away: 4 exit 5 leave, scram, split 6 beat it, decamp, depart, recede, retire, skidoo, vacate, vanish 7 head out, pull out, skiddoo 8 run along, separate, shove off 10 shuffle off
away from: 4 drop, quit 5 leave 6 desert 7 abandon, forsake 8 run out on 9 throw over, walk out on
AWOL: 4 flee 6 desert 7 abscond 9 play hooky
awry: 3 err 9 break down, fall apart
back: 4 turn 6 recede, return, revert 7 regress, retreat, revisit 9 weasel out
back and forth: 3 wag 4 jolt, reel, rock, roll, sway, toss, yo-yo 5 hedge, hover, lurch, pitch, shake, shift, swing, waver 6 careen, dither,

jiggle, jounce, seesaw, teeter, waffle, wobble **7** vibrate **8** fence-sit, hesitate, straddle **9** alternate, fluctuate, hem and haw, oscillate, pussyfoot, vacillate
back on: **3** lie **4** deny **5** belie, renig **6** betray, cop out, renege **7** disavow, forsake, retract **9** play false, repudiate **10** break faith
back on one's word: **5** unsay **6** recant, renege **7** retract **9** weasel out, worm out of
backwards: **7** reverse **8** flip-flop
bad: **3** rot **4** turn **5** decay, spoil
ballistic: **4** flip, rage, rant, snap, vent **5** freak **6** lose it
bananas: **4** flip, rage, rant, rave, snap **6** lose it
bankrupt: **4** bust, fail, fold, sink
before: **7** precede **8** antecede, run ahead
belly-up: **4** fail, fold **6** topple
berserk: **4** flip, rage, riot, snap **5** freak, panic **6** lose it **7** rampage, run wild **8** have a fit
beyond: **3** top **4** pass **5** break **6** exceed, extend **7** overlap, overrun, run over, surpass **8** overstep **9** cut across, transcend
bonkers: **4** flip, rant, rave, snap **5** crack **6** lose it
boom: **5** erupt **7** explode, thunder **8** detonate **9** discharge
by: **3** fly **4** pass, snub **6** elapse, roll on
by air: **3** fly **6** aviate, fly out
by shanks' mare: **4** slog, walk **5** leg it, march **6** foot it, hoof it, trudge
cause to ~: **6** betake
come and ~: **5** recur **9** alternate, oscillate
counter to: **4** defy **5** flout, rebel **6** ignore **7** disobey, violate **9** disregard **10** contravene
crazy: **4** flip, rage, rant, rave, snap **5** freak **7** rampage
don't ~: **4** bide, stay **6** loiter
don't ~ together: **3** jar **5** clash **6** jangle
down: **3** dip, ebb, set **4** dive, drop, fall, lose, sink, wane **5** abate, slide, slump, swoop **6** plunge, topple **7** descend, founder, plummet, subside **9** hit bottom, surrender
downhill: **4** fail, sink **5** slide, slump **6** worsen **7** decline **10** degenerate
down the tubes: **4** fail
easy: **5** let up, relax **10** take it slow
easy on: **4** pity **5** spare **6** relent **7** absolve, release **9** lighten up
far: **4** last **5** get on **7** advance, succeed **8** get ahead, progress
fast: **3** fly, hie, run, zip **4** race, tear, zoom **5** speed **6** hot rod, hurtle, hustle
fifty-fifty: **5** share, split
first: **4** head, lead **5** guide, usher **7** conduct, lead off, pioneer, precede **9** spearhead **10** trail-blaze
fish: **4** game **8** card game
fly a kite: **5** scram, split **6** beat it, begone **7** buzz off, get lost, take off **9** take a hike
for: **3** opt, vie **4** like, love, okay **5** admit, adopt, adore, allow, crave, elect, enjoy, favor, fetch **6** accept, admire, assent, attack, choose, comply, desire, fall on, have at, leap at, prefer, ratify, relish, revere **7** cherish, idolize, include, realize, welcome, worship **8** fall upon, hold dear, treasure **9** put up with, recognize, sign off on **10** concur with, give the nod
(for): **7** contend
for a ride: **6** travel
for broke: **4** dare, risk **6** gamble, hazard, strain, strive **7** serious **9** persevere
force to ~: **4** send **5** exile
for it: **3** try **4** dare **6** tackle **9** persevere
forth: **5** leave, sally, split **7** advance, head out
for the gold: **3** dig, run, vie **4** mine, race **5** rival **6** battle, strive **7** compete, contend
for the jugular: **3** vie **7** compete, contend **8** bear down
forward: **4** gain, push **5** march **6** hasten, move on **7** achieve, advance, further, improve, press on, proceed, shape up **8** continue, escalate, get ahead, progress **10** accelerate, accomplish, forge ahead, gain ground, move onward, shoot ahead
from pillar to post: **3** gad **4** roam, rove **5** drift **6** ramble, wander
furtively: **4** lurk, slip **5** creep, prowl, skulk, slink, snake, sneak, steal **6** crouch **7** slither
get: **5** bring, fetch **6** obtain **8** retrieve
get up and ~: **3** pep, vim **4** life, push, snap **5** drive, leave, oomph, vigor **6** bounce, energy, starch **8** ambition, gumption, vitality, vivacity **10** exuberance
great guns: **5** excel **8** flourish
hand over hand: **5** climb, scale **6** ascend, shinny **7** clamber
have a ~ at: **3** try **5** essay **6** take on **7** address, attempt
have another ~: **5** retry
headlong: **4** rush, trip **6** careen
head over heels: **4** fall, slip **5** lurch **6** plunge, sprawl, topple, tumble **7** stumble
head to head: **3** pit, vie **4** play **5** fight, match, rival **6** oppose, take on **7** compete, contend **8** struggle **9** challenge
hellbent for leather: **6** careen, hasten, hurtle **7** rampage **8** stampede
here and there: **3** gad **4** roam, rove, trek **5** drift, range **6** ramble, travel, wander **7** explore, journey, meander, traipse **9** bat around, bum around, gallivant, run around **10** knock about
hog-wild over: **5** enjoy
hungry: **6** starve
in: **5** enter **6** arrive
in advance: **5** usher **6** herald **7** precede, presage **8** antecede, run ahead **10** anticipate
in search of: **4** seek **5** quest **6** aspire, gun for, pursue **7** hunt for, long for, look for **8** yearn for **9** track down
into: **4** sift **5** enter, probe, treat **6** choose, select **7** discuss, examine, explore, touch on **9** touch upon, undertake
(into): **5** delve
into a funk: **4** fret, mope, sulk **5** brood, worry **7** agonize **8** languish **10** introspect
into detail: **4** list **5** brief, gloss **6** lay out **7** analyze, clarify, explain, itemize, specify **8** annotate, describe, spell out **9** blueprint, elaborate, elucidate, enumerate, expound on, make clear, put across
into hysterics: **4** flip, rant, snap **8** get angry
in with: **4** pool **5** share
kaput: **3** die **4** fail, flop, fold **6** fizzle **7** conk out **8** backfire **9** break down
let ~: **2** ax **3** axe, can **4** axed, boot, drop, fire, free, miss, omit, oust, sack, weep **5** clear, fired, freed, loose, relax, spare, throw, untie, waive, yield **6** acquit, bounce, canned, excuse, ignore, lay off, let off, loosen, relent, sprang, spring, sprung, unhand, untied **7** abandon, cashier, dismiss, drum out, forgive, manumit, neglect, release, set free **8** cut loose, furlough, get rid of, liberate, overlook, pink-slip, released **9** discharge, disengage, dismissed, liberated, sacrifice, surrender, terminate, turn loose **10** discharged, relinquish
let it ~: **6** excuse, pardon **8** laugh off, overlook
let ~ of: **4** drop, dump, shed **5** ditch, spurn **6** give up, unload **7** abandon, discard, toss out **8** renounce **9** eighty-six, repudiate, throw away **10** relinquish
let oneself ~: **5** relax, unlax **6** rest up, unwind **7** lay back, sit back **8** loosen up, slack off **9** hang loose **10** settle back, take it easy
let's ~: **4** c'mon
like: **3** ape **4** copy, echo, mime, mock **5** mimic **7** imitate **9** make fun of, pantomime **10** caricature
like a shot: **3** fly, hie, rip, run **4** race, rush, whiz **5** hurry, speed **6** hurtle, streak
limp: **3** sag **4** wilt **5** droop, faint, swoon **6** weaken **7** crumple, pass out, shrivel **8** black out, keel over
make ~: **7** operate
make a ~ of it: **6** thrive
native: **5** adapt **7** blend in **9** integrate **10** assimilate
near: **8** approach
next: **6** follow **7** succeed
off: **4** ring **5** burst, erupt, leave, spoil **6** depart **7** explode **8** detonate
off-course: **3** err, yaw, zag **4** roam, rove, skid, slue, tack, turn, veer **5** drift, lurch, range, slide, stray, swing **6** divert, ramble, swerve, wander **7** deflect, deviate, digress, diverge, maunder, meander **8** sideslip, straggle
off on a tangent: **5** stray **6** ramble, wander **7** digress
on: **3** add **4** last **5** exist, reach, spout **6** endure, happen, resume **7** persist **8** continue **9** persevere
on about: **4** gush, rail, rant, rave **6** stress **7** belabor, enthuse **8** harangue **10** effervesce, hammer home, rhapsodize
on a diet: **4** lose **6** reduce **8** slim down **10** lose weight
on a jag: **5** spree **7** splurge
on all fours: **5** crawl, creep, slink **7** clamber, slither, wriggle
on and on: **3** yak **4** rant, rave **5** drone, spout **6** babble, jabber, ramble
on a spree: **5** binge, revel **7** carouse
on bended knee: **3** beg, sue **4** urge **5** crawl **7** beseech, declare, entreat, implore **8** petition **9** importune **10** supplicate
one better: **3** top **5** outdo **7** surpass
(one's way): **4** wend
on foot: **4** hoof, walk **5** leg it
on stage: **3** act **5** enter **7** perform
on strike: **5** rebel **6** resist, revolt **7** protest
on the ~: **4** busy, spry **6** active **8** restless, tireless **9** traveling, wayfaring
on the air: **6** report **7** network **8** announce, televise **9** advertise, broadcast, publicize **10** make public
on the fritz: **5** act up
on the lam: **4** bolt, flee **6** bug out
on the road: **4** tour
on the wagon: **4** quit, stop **6** eschew **7** abstain, refrain **8** renounce **9** do without
on with: **6** pick up, resume **7** persist, proceed **8** continue, maintain, return to **9** persevere **10** recommence
order to ~: **4** fire, mail, oust, post, send, ship **5** exile, expel, route **6** assign, banish, deport, direct, put out **7** cast out, consign, turn out **8** dispatch, displace, drive out, transfer **9** dismissal, ostracize, transport **10** expatriate
out: **3** ebb **4** date, exit **5** leave **6** egress, recede **9** socialize
out of business: **4** fail, fold **6** fold up
out of control: **4** yell **5** erupt, freak, storm **6** blow up, careen, rail at, scream **7** explode, rampage, run wild **8** boil over, have a fit, run amuck **9** blow a fuse, go berserk **10** hit the roof, kick up a row
out on a limb: **5** guess **6** hazard **7** venture
out with: **3** see **4** date **5** court
out with a whimper: **6** fizzle
over: **4** read **5** audit, cross, study **6** pan out, review **7** examine, inspect, iterate, rectify **8** practice, question, rehearse, traverse **9** reiterate
over again: **5** recap **6** repeat **9** reiterate
over and over: **3** nag **6** harp on, repeat, stress **7** iterate **9** emphasize, reiterate
over big: **3** wow **5** score **6** please, thrill, turn on **7** impress **8** blow away **9** electrify
over lightly: **4** leaf, scan, skim **6** riffle **8** glance at
over the fence: **5** vault **6** defect, desert, escape, run out **7** abscond
over the hill: **3** lam **4** bolt, flee **6** desert, run off **7** abscond, bail out, run away **8** break out
over the wall: **3** run **4** bolt, flee, jump, leap, skip **5** bound **6** desert, run off, run out **7** abscond, bail out, get away, make off, run away **8** cut loose, slip away, turn tail **9** cut and run, steal away **10** fly the coop
partner: **4** come, stop **5** get up
partners: **5** unite **6** hook up, team up **9** affiliate, associate **10** join up with
past: **4** omit, skip **6** exceed **9** overshoot
pell-mell: **4** bolt, race, rush, tear, whiz, zoom **5** lunge, speed **6** charge, hurtle
pfft: **4** fail
pitapat: **4** beat **5** pound, throb **7** flutter **9** palpitate
places: **3** win **4** rise **6** hack it, make it, pan out, thrive **7** advance, luck out, make out, prevail, prosper, succeed, triumph, work out **8** flourish, get ahead, get along, hit it big, make good **10** do all right
postal: **4** flip, rage, rant, snap
preceder: **6** get set
public with: **3** air **4** bare, leak, talk **5** admit, spill, voice **6** betray, expose, report, reveal **7** divulge, publish **8** disclose, give away **9** broadcast, make known
quickly: **3** hie, run **4** race, rush, zing **5** scoot, skirr, speed **6** hustle
raring to ~: **4** avid, keen **5** eager, itchy, ready **6** all set, on edge **9** hot to trot **10** inspirited

ready to ~: 3 set 6 at hand 7 in store 9 available 10 obtainable
refuse to ~: 4 balk, stop 5 baulk, demur 6 recoil
see: 5 visit
separate ways: 4 fork, part 5 leave, split 7 break up, disband, diverge, pull out, scatter, split up 10 say goodbye
slowly: 4 ease, inch, plod 5 crawl, creep
smoothly: 3 fly 4 flow, sail, skim, soar 5 coast, drift, float, glide, slide, sweep 6 cruise
so far: 6 gather, take it 7 suppose, surmise
soft: 4 melt, thaw 6 relent 8 languish
sour: 4 ruin, turn 5 addle, spoil, taint 6 curdle, mildew 7 acidify
south: 4 bolt, flee, quit 5 split 6 beat it, decamp, defect, escape 7 abscond, make off, pull out, skip out, vamoose 9 cut and run, disappear, skedaddle, steal away 10 fly the coop, hightail it, make a break
stale: 3 rot 4 mold, rust, tire 5 decay 7 crumble 8 stagnate
steady with: 3 pin, see, woo 4 date
stealthily: 5 slink, steal 7 slither
straight: 6 reform 7 shape up
swiftly: 3 fly, run 4 bolt, dart, flee 5 hurry, scoot, scram 6 gallop, hasten, scurry, sprint, streak 7 scamper
the distance: 4 last 6 endure, finish, strive 7 persist 8 keep at it
through: 4 sift 5 audit, brave, rifle, spend, use up 6 endure, finish, lavish, misuse, search, suffer 7 consume, examine, inspect, ransack, receive, undergo 8 permeate, rehearse, squander 9 penetrate, withstand 10 experience
through one's head: 5 occur 6 dawn on
through the roof: 4 grow, rise, soar 5 mount, surge 6 ascend 7 burgeon, mount up 8 escalate, increase 9 intensify 10 appreciate
to: 4 join 5 reach, visit 6 attend, resort 7 head for
to bat for: 3 aid 4 back, help 6 assist, defend 7 endorse, indorse, stick by, support 8 advocate, champion 10 rally round, speak up for
to bed: 3 lie 6 retire, turn in 7 sack out 10 hit the sack
to court: 3 sue 6 appeal 7 contest, dispute 8 file suit, litigate 9 prosecute
toe-to-toe: 5 fight
to extremes: 6 overdo
together: 3 fit 4 gybe, jibe, suit 5 agree, blend, click, match, rhyme 6 belong 9 accompany
to it: 5 begin, start 7 pitch in
to law: 3 sue, try 6 accuse, appeal, indict, summon 7 arraign, contest, dispute 8 file suit, litigate 9 fight over, prosecute 10 put on trial
too far: 4 hype 6 overdo, pile on 7 belabor, lay it on, stretch 8 overplay 9 overstate 10 exaggerate
too fast: 4 tear, whiz, zoom 5 speed 6 barrel
to pieces: 3 rot 5 panic 7 crumble 8 collapse, languish 9 break down 10 degenerate
to pot: 4 rust 5 spoil 8 vegetate
to press: 7 let roll
to see: 5 pop in, visit 6 attend, call on, drop by, look up, stop in, travel 7 sojourn, swing by 8 pay a call, stay with
to seed: 3 rot 4 rust 5 decay 8 stagnate, vegetate
to sleep: 3 nap 4 rest 6 retire, turn in 7 lie down, sack out 8 abdicate 9 hit the hay 10 hit the sack
to the dogs: 4 sink 5 decay 7 decline 9 fall apart 10 degenerate
to the mat for: 4 back 5 stake, vouch 7 endorse, promote, sponsor, support, warrant 8 champion 9 get behind 10 underwrite
to town: 5 excel 7 prosper
touch and ~: 6 unsafe, unsure, urgent 8 perilous 9 debatable, uncertain
toward: 7 advance, make for 8 approach
under: 4 bomb, bust, fail, flop, fold, lose, sink, slip, trip 5 close, flunk 6 blow it, falter, perish 7 blunder, founder, misstep, stumble, succumb, wash out 8 fall flat, flounder, lay an egg, submerge 9 hit bottom, strike out
undercover: 3 spy 4 hide 6 hole up, lie low
underground: 6 hole up, lie low 7 descend
underwater: 3 dip 4 dive, swim 5 drown, scuba 6 fall in 7 capsize, descend, founder, immerse 8 submerge 9 scuba-dive, shipwreck
unused: 4 stay 6 remain
up: 4 incr., rise, shin, soar 5 arise, climb, mount, scale 6 ascend, aviate 8 escalate
up against: 4 abut, defy, face 6 combat 8 confront, struggle
up in smoke: 4 burn, fail 6 ignite
up to: 8 approach, draw near 10 move toward
well: 5 blend 6 pan out, result 7 succeed, turn out
whole hog: 4 jump, leap, push, rush, sink 6 hurtle, plunge
wild: 4 flip, rave 5 crack
with: 3 see 4 date, take 6 belong, escort 9 accompany
(with): 7 conform
without: 4 miss, want 5 avoid 6 eschew
with the flow: 4 cope, roam, rove 5 adapt, agree, drift, get by, glide, mosey, yield 6 assent, give in, manage, ramble, wander 7 make out, meander, saunter 9 acquiesce
wrong: 3 err 4 bomb, bust, flop, lose, slip, trip 5 flunk, misdo, stray 6 blow it, falter 7 blunder, founder, misstep, stumble, wash out 8 fall flat, flounder, lay an egg 9 misbehave, strike out
go ___: 3 ape, far, for, off, out 4 at it, away, bust, down, fish, into, over, to it, with 5 about, after, ahead, along, Dutch, for it, in for, to pot, under, wrong 6 around, native, places, postal 7 against, bananas, begging, belly-up, through
go ___ a kite: 3 fly
go ___ better: 3 one
go ___ board: 5 by the
go ___ broke: 3 for
go ___ detail: 4 into
go ___ diet: 3 on a
go ___ dogs: 5 to the
go ___ flames: 4 up in
go ___ for: 5 to bat
go ___ guns: 5 great
go ___ half-cocked: 3 off
go ___ hog: 5 whole
go ___ hotcakes: 4 like
go ___ it: 3 for
go ___ kite: 4 fly a
go ___ length: 4 on at
go ___ mat: 5 to the
go ___ of one's way: 3 out
go ___ of style: 3 out
go ___ on: 4 back 5 light
go ___ one's way: 5 out of
go ___ saying: 7 without
go ___ smoke: 4 up in
go ___ style: 5 out of
go ___ the deep end: 3 off
go ___ the gold: 3 for
go ___ the hammer: 5 under
go ___ the line: 4 down
go ___ the motions: 7 through
go ___ the roof: 7 through
go ___ the window: 3 out
go ___-up: 5 belly
go ___ wall: 5 to the
go ___ way: 5 a long
go ___ wayside: 5 by the
go ___ with: 3 out 6 public
go-___: 3 fer 4 cart, kart, slow 5 ahead, devil, train 6 getter 7 between
___ go: 3 let 5 on the
___ go!: 4 Let's 5 Way to
___-go: 3 get, git
Go ___: 4 Fish, Home, West
Go ___ It on the Mountain: 4 Tell
Go ___ Little Girl: 4 Away
Go ___, Moses: 4 Down
Go ___, young man: 4 West
Go ___ Your Dance: 4 Into
Go ___ your father: 3 ask
Go, ___!: 4 team
goa: 6 mammal 7 gazelle 8 antelope
relative: 3 gnu, kob 4 guib, kudu, oryx, puku, topi 5 addax, bongo, chiru, eland, korin, nyala, oribi, saiga, serow 6 chammy, dik-dik, duiker, impala, koodoo, lechwe, nilgai, rhebok, shammy, shamoy 7 blaubok, blesbok, chamois, defassa, gemsbok, gerenuk, grysbok, nylghai, nylghau, sassaby 8 blesbuck, bontebok, bushbuck, gemsbuck, reedbuck, steenbok, steinbok 9 blackbuck, pronghorn, sitatunga, springbok, waterbuck 10 hartebeest, wildebeest
go a ___ way: 4 long
Goa: 5 state
garment: 4 sari 5 saree
locale: 5 India
goad: 3 egg, nag 4 fret, prod, push, spur, urge 5 annoy, bully, drive, egg on, force, hop up, hound, impel, liven, pique, prick, rouse, taunt, tease, worry 6 arouse, badger, bother, coerce, exhort, fillip, fire up, harass, incite, needle, nettle, noodge, prompt, propel, stir up, whip up 7 impetus, impulse, provoke, quicken 8 catalyst, embolden, imbolden, irritate, motivate, stimulus, talk into 9 encourage, impassion, incentive, instigate, stimulate 10 cattle prod, incitement, inducement, motivation
___ go again!: 5 Here I 6 Here we
go-ahead: 2 OK 3 nod 4 okay, word 5 leave 6 assent, permit, signal 7 consent, license, mandate, warrant 8 approval, sanction 9 clearance 10 green light, permission
give the ~: 2 OK 3 nod 4 okay 5 agree, allow, clear 6 accede, enable 7 approve
Go ahead!: 5 shoot, try me
Go ahead...___ my day!: 4 make
goal: 3 aim, end, job, obj. 4 hope, mark 5 cause, dream, point, score 6 design, intent, object, reason, target 7 meaning, mission, purpose 8 ambition, function 9 intention, objective, touchdown 10 aspiration, ground zero
lofty ~: 6 vision
set a lofty ~: 4 hope, wish 5 dream 6 aspire
ultimate ~: 6 end-all
goal ___: 4 kick, line, post 6 crease
___ goal: 5 field 6 career
Goalby, Bob: 6 golfer
goalie: 6 player 7 athlete 9 netkeeper
concern: 4 puck
feat: 4 save
fool the ~: 4 deke
game: 6 hockey
get past the ~: 5 score
milieu: 3 ice, net 4 rink 6 crease
org.: 3 NHL
protection: 4 mask
goalless: 6 adrift
go a long ___: 3 way
goal-oriented: 5 telic
goals
like some ~: 5 lofty, unmet
goanna: 6 animal 7 reptile
go-anywhere vehicle: 3 ATV
goat: 4 geep, ibex, meat, tahr, thar 5 bovid, patsy 6 Angora, animal, butter, lecher, mammal, target 7 markhor 8 easy mark, markhoor, omnivore 9 Capricorn, livestock
antelope: 5 goral, serow
Asian ~: 4 ibex, tahr, thar 7 markhor 8 markhoor
assault like a ~: 4 butt
baby: 3 kid 8 yeanling
bear a ~: 4 yean
cheese: 4 feta 6 chevre 7 chevret, crottin
combining form: 5 capri-
ender: 4 fish, skin 6 sucker
fabric: 3 aba 4 abba 5 Kasha 7 kashmir 8 cashmere
feature: 5 beard
female: 3 doe 5 nanny
foot: 4 hoof
get one's ~: 3 irk, vex 4 miff, rile 5 anger, peeve, upset 6 enrage, rankle
hybrid ~: 4 geep
male: 4 buck 5 billy
meat: 6 chevon
noise: 3 maa 4 blat 5 bleat
old ~: 4 roué 9 libertine 10 profligate
relative: 5 sheep
starter: 5 scape
goat ___: 3 god 6 cheese
___ goat: 5 billy, nanny 6 Angora, Nubian 7 Kashmir 8 Cashmere
___ go at: 5 have a
Goat: 4 sign 7 January 8 December 9 Capricorn
follower: 11 Water Bearer
month: 3 Dec., Jan. 7 January 8 December
predecessor: 6 Archer
___ Goat-Boy: 5 Giles
goatee: 4 hair, tuft 5 beard 8 whiskers
get rid of a ~: 4 snip 5 shave
site: 4 chin
goatfish: 5 moana 6 mullet
goat-footed deity: 3 Pan 5 satyr
goatish: 6 caprid 7 caprine, hircine, lustful 9 lubricous 10 libidinous
___ go at it: 5 have a
goatsbeard: 4 weed 5 plant 6 flower
goatskin: 3 kid 5 mocha, suede 6 galyak 7 leather 8 cordovan
Goat Song author: Frank Yerby, Franz Werfel
goatsucker: 4 bird 8 nightjar 9 nighthawk
relative: 5 potoo 9 frogmouth
Go away!: 4 scat, shoo 5 scram 6 beat it
Go Away Little Girl (song) artist: Steve Lawrence, Donny Osmond

gob: **3** tar, wad **4** hunk, lump, mass, pile, salt, swab, swob **5** bunch, chunk, clump **6** dollop, sailor, sea dog, seaman **7** crewman, jack tar, mariner, matelot, matelow, portion, swabbie **8** deckhand, mouthful, seafarer **10** bluejacket
see also nautical, sailor
Gobat, Charles: **8** Nobelist
gobbet: **3** bit **4** lump, mass **5** piece **8** fragment
gobble: **3** eat **4** bolt, cram, gulp, wolf **5** gorge, scarf, stuff **6** devour, guzzle, inhale, suck up **7** put away, scarf up, swallow **8** wolf down **9** grab a bite, scarf down **10** gormandize
up: **3** eat, use **4** wolf **5** eat up **6** devour, obtain **7** consume, engorge, feast on
gobbledegook: **3** gas, rot **4** blah, bosh, bull, bunk, guff, jazz, jive, pooh, tosh **5** bilge, fudge, hokum, hooey, prate, stuff, trash, tripe **6** bunkum, bushwa, drivel, footle, gabble, gammon, gibber, havers, hot air, humbug, jabber, jargon, kibosh, piffle **7** baloney, blarney, blather, blether, boloney, bushwah, eyewash, flannel, flubdub, fustian, garbage, hogwash, inanity, rubbish, twaddle **8** buncombe, claptrap, falderal, falderol, flimflam, flummery, folderal, folderol, nonsense, slipslop, tommyrot, trumpery **9** banana oil, gibberish, kidstakes, moonshine, poppycock, rigmarole **10** applesauce, balderdash, bilge water, codswallop, double-talk, flapdoodle, galimatias, Jabberwock, mumbo jumbo, rigamarole, taradiddle
gobbler: **3** tom **4** male **5** eater **6** turkey **7** glutton
Gobel: **6** George
go-between: **3** agt. **5** agent, envoy, fixer, proxy **6** broker, deputy, factor **7** arbiter, liaison, referee **8** attorney, emissary, mediator **9** appointee, messenger, middleman, negotiant **10** arbitrator, connection, interagent, interceder, matchmaker, negotiator, peacemaker
be a ~: **6** liaise
Gobi: **6** desert
like the ~: **3** dry **4** arid **5** sandy
site: **4** Asia **8** Mongolia
goblet: **3** cup **5** glass, grail, mazer **7** chalice, snifter **8** stemware **9** wineglass
part: **4** stem
Scottish ~: **4** tass
sound: **4** ting
goblin: **3** elf, imp **4** nixy, pixy **5** demon, gnome, nixie, ouphe, pixie, spook **6** daemon, daimon, kobold, sprite **7** brownie, bugbear, gremlin
German ~: **6** kobold
greeting: **3** boo
in Scandinavian folklore: **5** nisse
starter: **3** hob
__ go bragh: **4** Erin
gobs: **4** a lot, lots, much, peck, slew **5** ocean
of: **4** many **6** divers, myriad, umteen, untold **7** copious, profuse, umpteen **8** abundant, manifold, numerous, umpsteen **9** bountiful, countless, quite a few
goby: **4** fish
go-by: **6** rebuff
go by the __: **5** board **7** wayside
god: **5** deity, maker **6** daemon **8** divinity
bellicose ~: **4** Ares, Mars
combining form: **3** the- **4** theo-
Egyptian ~: **3** Bes, Set **4** Ptah, Seth **5** Horus, Sebek, Thoth **6** Amon-Ra, Anubis, Osiris **7** Taueret
ender: **3** son **4** head, send **5** child **6** father, mother, parent **8** children, daughter, forsaken
goat-footed ~: **5** satyr
Greek ~: **3** Pan **4** Ares, Eros, Zeus **5** Hades **6** Aeolus, Apollo, Charon, Helios, Hermes, Hypnos, Icarus **8** Cerberus, Dionysus, Poseidon **10** Hephaestus
Hindu ~: **4** Agni, Kama, Siva, Soma, Yama **5** Indra, Shiva, Surya **6** Brahma, Varuna, Vishnu **7** Ganesha, Hanuman, Krishna
in Latin: **3** deo
Islamic ~: **5** Allah
Japanese ~: **5** Inari
love ~: **4** Amor, Eros **5** Cupid
Norse ~: **4** Frey, Loki, Odin, Thor **5** Aegir, Njord, Othin **6** Balder **7** Forseti
Phoenician ~: **4** Baal
Roman ~: **3** Dis **4** Mars **5** Cupid, Janus, Pluto **6** Apollo, Saturn, Vulcan **7** Bacchus, Jupiter, Mercury, Neptune **8** Silvanus
solar ~: **4** Aten, Aton
starter: **4** demi
sylvan ~: **3** Pan **5** satyr
tutelary ~: **3** lar
Vedic ~: **4** Agni, Kama, Siva, Soma, Yama **5** Indra, Shiva, Surya **6** Brahma, Varuna, Vishnu **7** Ganesha, Hanuman, Krishna
woodland ~: **5** satyr
__ god: **3** sun, tin **4** goat **5** earth, Greek
God: **4** Lord **5** Allah, Jahve, Jahwe, Yahve, Yahwe **6** Jahveh, Jahweh, Yahveh, Yahweh **7** Creator, Jehovah **8** Almighty, divinity
ender: **5** speed
God __: **5** bless, knows
God __ America: **5** Bless
God __ Co-Pilot: **4** Is My
God __ the Queen: **4** Save
God-__: **3** man **5** awful, given **7** fearing
__ God: **5** act of, man of, Son of
__ God!: **5** Thank
God and Mammon author: François Mauriac
God and Man at __: **4** Yale
Godard: **7** Jean-Luc
Godavari: **5** river
God-awful: **4** foul, grim, poor **5** awful, lousy, woful **6** crumby, crummy, dismal, horrid, odious, rotten, woeful **7** accurst, baleful, baneful, beastly, doleful, ghastly **8** accursed, dreadful, grievous, horrible, inferior, shameful, stinking, terrible, wretched **9** abhorrent, appalling, atrocious, defective, execrable, frightful, insidious, loathsome, miserable, offensive, revolting **10** abominable, despicable, detestable, disastrous, horrendous, lamentable
God Bless America composer: **6** Berlin
God bless us __ one: **5** every
God bless you
preceder: **5** achoo **6** ahchoo, hachoo, sneeze **7** kerchoo
__ God Brown, The: **5** Great
godchild: **4** ward
__ God Created Woman: **3** And
Goddard: **4** Mark **6** Robert **8** Paulette
Goddard, Paulette: **7** actress
film: The Cat and the Canary (1939)
The Ghost Breakers (1940)
The Great Dictator (1940)
Hold Back the Dawn (1941)
Kitty (1945)
Modern Times (1936)
Nothing but the Truth (1941)
Reap the Wild Wind (1942)
So Proudly We Hail! (1943)
The Young in Heart (1938)
spouse: Charles Chaplin, Burgess Meredith, Erich Maria Remarque
Goddard, Robert: **9** physicist, rocketeer
Godden: **5** Rumer
goddess: **5** deity **8** divinity
Egyptian ~: **3** Mut, Nut **4** Bast, Isis, Maat **6** Hathor **7** Sekhmet **8** Nephthys
Greek ~: **3** Eos **4** Hebe, Hera, Iris, Nike **5** Aeaea, Circe, Kirke **6** Athena, Athene, Hecate, Hekate, Hestia, Medusa, Selene **7** Artemis, Demeter **9** Aphrodite **10** Persephone
Hindu ~: **4** Devi, Kali, Usha **5** Durga, Ushas **7** Lakshmi, Parvati **9** Sarasvati
in Latin: **3** dea
Japanese ~: **9** Amaterasu
Norse ~: **3** Hel **5** Freya, Frigg
Roman ~: **3** Ops **4** Juno **5** Ceres, Diana, Flora, Venus, Vesta **6** Aurora **7** Fortuna, Minerva
Vedic ~: **4** Devi, Kali, Usha **5** Durga, Ushas **7** Lakshmi, Parvati **9** Sarasvati
goddesses
Greek ~: **6** Furies, Gorgon, Graces
Norse ~: **5** Norns
Goddess, The (1958 film)
cast: Lloyd Bridges, Steven Hill, Kim Stanley
Godeberta: **5** saint
go-devil: **4** sled
God exists, name meaning: **5** Jesse
Godey's Lady's Book editor: **4** Hale
godfather: **3** don
Godfather Part III, The (1990 film)
cast: Andy Garcia, George Hamilton, Diane Keaton, Joe Mantegna, Al Pacino, Talia Shire, Eli Wallach
director: Francis Ford Coppola
Godfather Part II, The (1974 film)
cast: John Cazale, Robert De Niro, Robert Duvall, Diane Keaton, Al Pacino, Talia Shire, Lee Strasberg
director: Francis Ford Coppola
Godfather, The: **4** film **5** novel
author: Mario Puzo
cast: Marlon Brando, James Caan, John Cazale, Robert Duvall, Diane Keaton, Al Pacino, Talia Shire
composer: **4** Rota
director: Francis Ford Coppola
God-fearing: **5** pious **6** devout **9** religious
godforsaken: **6** lonely, remote **8** deserted, desolate, stranded **9** miserable
Godfrey: **5** Peter **6** Arthur **9** Cambridge **10** Hounsfield
in German: **9** Gottfried
__ Godfrey: **5** My Man
Godfrey, Arthur: **4** host **5** emcee
instrument: **3** uke **7** ukulele
God gave, name meaning: **8** Jonathan
God-given: **6** innate
godhood: **8** divinity
God in Ruins, A author: Leon Uris
Go directly to __: **4** Jail
God is high, name meaning: **8** Jeremiah
God is light, name meaning: **5** Uriah
God is salvation, name meaning: **6** Joshua
God is with us, name meaning: **7** Emanuel
Godiva: **4** Lady **5** rider
God judges, name meaning: **6** Daniel
God Knows author: Joseph Heller
godless: **5** pagab **7** impious, profane **9** atheistic
godlike: **6** deific, divine **8** almighty **9** celestial **10** omnipotent
make ~: **5** adore, deify, exalt, extol **7** elevate, glorify, worship **8** sanctify, venerate **10** consecrate
godliness: **4** zeal **5** piety **8** divinity **10** devoutness
godly: **4** holy **5** pious **6** deific, devout, divine, sacred **7** angelic, saintly **9** ambrosial, angelical, pietistic, religious, righteous
God Makers, The author: Frank Herbert
godmother
fairy ~: **5** donor **6** backer, patron **10** benefactor
often: **4** aunt **8** relative
__ godmother: **5** fairy
go down in __: **6** flames
Go Down, Moses author: William Faulkner
go down the __: **4** line
godparent: **7** sponsor
Godplayer author: Robin Cook
God Rest Ye Merry, Gentlemen: **4** noel **5** carol
gods
in Latin: **3** dei
Norse ~: **5** Aesir, Vanir
Roman household ~: **5** Lares **7** Penates
God's __: **4** acre, Word **5** penny **6** plenty **7** country
God Said, 'HA!' (1999 film) cast: Julia Sweeney
Gods and Monsters (1998 film)
cast: Lolita Davidovich, Brendan Fraser, Ian McKellen, Lynn Redgrave
God Save the Queen: **6** anthem
God's Country (1985 film) director: Louis Malle
God-Seeker, The author: Sinclair Lewis
godsend: **4** boon, gift, luck **7** benefit **8** blessing, surprise, windfall **10** lucky break
God shed His grace on __: **4** thee
God's Little Acre: **4** film **5** novel
author: Erskine Caldwell
cast: Tina Louise, Aldo Ray, Robert Ryan
director: Anthony Mann
Gods Must Be Crazy, The (1981 film)
cast: Sandra Prinsloo, Marius Weyers
character: **4** Xixo
director: Jamie Uys
Gods of the Lightning author: Maxwell Anderson
God's Other Son author: **4** Imus
Godspeed: **5** adieu
God strengthens, name meaning: **7** Ezekiel
__ God's Wife, The: **7** Kitchen
Godthab: **4** city, town
locale: **9** Greenland
Godunov: **5** Boris **9** Alexander
see also Russian
Godunov, Boris: **4** czar, tsar
God will hear, name meaning: **7** Ishmael
Godwin Austen: **3** mtn. **4** peak **5** mount **8** mountain
locale: **4** Asia
Godwin, Gail: **6** author, writer
godwit: **4** bird **9** shorebird
Godzilla: **7** monster **8** dinosaur
foe: **5** Rodan **6** Mothra
setting: **5** Japan, Tokio, Tokyo
Godzilla (1998 film)
cast: Hank Azaria, Matthew Broderick, Maria Pitillo, Jean Reno
director: Roland Emmerich
Godzilla's Revenge director: **5** Honda
Goen: **3** Bob

Goeppert-Mayer, Maria: **8** Nobelist **9** physicist
goer: **7** habitué **8** attendee, gadabout, traveler
starter: **4** film, play **5** movie **7** theater, theatre
__ **goes!:** **4** Here
__ **Goes On:** **4** Life
__ **Goes On, The:** **4** Beat
...goes out like __**:** **5** a lamb
__ **goes there?:** **3** Who
__ **Goes to College:** **5** Bonzo
__ **Goes Visiting:** **4** Pooh
Goethals, George: **8** engineer
Goethe, Johann Wolfgang von: **4** poet **6** author, German, writer
work: The Erl-King
Faust
goethite: **3** ore
gofer: **4** aide, page **5** grunt **6** flunky, helper, lackey **7** flunkey, lacquey **8** henchman **9** assistant, errand boy, messenger
job: **6** errand
sports ~: **5** caddy **6** bat boy, caddie
Goffin: **5** Gerry
go fish: **4** game **8** card game
alternative: **3** war **7** old maid
Go fly __**!:** **5** a kite
go for __**:** **4** a dip **5** a spin, broke **7** the gold
Gog and __**:** **5** Magog
__ **go gentle...:** **5** Do not
go-getter: **4** doer **5** mover, tiger **6** dynamo **7** hustler **8** live wire
no ~: **5** sloth
goggle: **3** eye **4** gape, gawk, leer, look, ogle **5** glare, stare **6** marvel
box: **2** TV **5** TV set **10** television
goggle-eyed: **6** astare **7** staring
Gogi: **5** Grant
__ **go, girl!:** **3** You
go-go: **5** pushy, zippy **6** active, lively **7** buzzing, driving, dynamic, jumping **9** energetic **10** aggressive
music: **5** disco
go-go __**:** **6** dancer
gogo, à: **6** galore
Gogol, Nikolai: **6** writer **7** Russian
work: Dead Souls
Diary of a Madman
The Inspector General
The Overcoat
Taras Bulba
Go-Go's
leader: Belinda Carlisle
song: Vacation (1982)
We Got the Beat (1982)
go great __**:** **4** guns
Go Home (1985 song) artist: Stevie Wonder
Goiânia: **4** city, town
locale: **6** Brazil
go in __**:** **3** for **4** with
Goin' __ **My Head:** **5** Out of
going: **7** current, parting, running, working **9** departure
around: **5** faddy **6** trendy **7** current, popular **9** in the news **10** widespread
away: **6** easily **9** departure
easy on: **3** lax **4** mild, soft **6** benign, gentle, humane **7** clement, lenient, liberal, sparing **8** allowing, excusing, merciful, obliging, tolerant, yielding **9** condoning, forgiving, indulgent, pampering, pardoning **10** charitable, permissive
get ~: **4** move, open, roll **5** begin, crank, found, rouse, start **6** fillip, launch, let rip, set off, set out **7** kick off, lead off, pitch in, speed up **8** commence, initiate, organize, set about, set forth **9** enter upon, originate **10** inaugurate
is ~ to: **4** will
keep ~: **5** run on **6** extend, hold on, push on **7** persist, subsist, sustain **8** maintain, progress, protract, tide over **9** persevere **10** perpetuate
keep one ~: **3** aid **6** assist **9** help along **10** see through
nowhere: **4** lost **6** adrift, in a rut **9** pointless
on: **5** afoot **6** serial **7** present **8** underway **10** in progress
on and on: **5** gabby, windy, wordy **6** chatty, prolix, turgid **7** gushing, lengthy, tedious, verbose, voluble **8** babbling, inflated, rambling **9** bombastic, garrulous, jabbering, talkative **10** bigmouthed, blathering, long-winded, loquacious
set ~: **6** launch
starter: **3** sea **4** easy, film, play **5** dance, movie, ocean **6** church **7** concert, theater, theatre **8** thorough
strong: **5** palmy **7** booming, healthy, roaring, rolling **8** thriving **9** advancing, doing well **10** prospering, prosperous, successful
going __**:** **3** ape **4** rate **5** train **7** concern
going- __**:** **4** over
__ **going:** **3** get
__**-going:** **4** easy **6** steady
Going __**:** **4** Home, Solo **5** My Way
Going __**,...:** **4** once
Going Back to Cali (1988 song) artist: LL Cool J
Going, going, __**:** **4** gone
Going Hollywood (1933 film)
cast: Bing Crosby, Marion Davies, Fifi D'Orsay
director: Raoul Walsh
Going Home (1971 film)
cast: Robert Mitchum, Brenda Vaccaro, Jan-Michael Vincent
Going in Style (1979 film)
cast: George Burns, Art Carney, Lee Strasberg
director: Martin Brest
Going My Way (1944 film)
cast: Bing Crosby, Barry Fitzgerald, Ris' Stevens
director: Leo McCarey
__ **going on?:** **5** What's
going-over: **6** rebuke **7** lecture **9** rehearsal **10** upbraiding
Going Solo author: Roald Dahl
goings-on: **6** action, doings, events **7** revelry **8** business, occasion, partying **9** festivity **10** happenings
Going to a Go-Go (1966 song) artist: Miracles
...going to St. Ives, __**...:** **4** I met
Going to the Territory author: Ralph Ellison
Goin' Out of My Head (1964 song)
artist: Little Anthony and the Imperials
Goin' Out of My Head... (1968 song)
artist: Lettermen
Goin' South (1978 film)
cast: Christopher Lloyd, Jack Nicholson, Mary Steenburgen
director: Jack Nicholson
go into __**:** **6** detail
__ **go, into the...:** **5** Off we
go it __**:** **5** alone
goiter treatment: **5** iodin **6** iodine
go-kart: **5** racer
Golan: **4** Gila **7** Menahem
Golan Heights locale: **3** Isr. **6** Israel
Gola, Tom
milieu: **5** court
org.: **3** NBA
sport: **10** basketball
gold: **5** medal, metal, money **6** riches, wealth, yellow **7** bullion, element, laurels **8** treasure **9** valuables
alloy: **8** electrum
Biblical kingdom of ~: **5** Ophir
black ~: **3** oil
braid: **5** orris
coat with ~: **4** gild **5** plate
combining form: **3** aur- **4** auri- **5** chrys- **6** chryso-
compound: **6** aurate
container: **3** pan, pot **4** mint
containing ~: **5** auric **6** aurous
digger: **5** miner
ender: **4** fish **5** brick, field, finch, smith, stone **6** beater, thread
fabric: **4** lamé
fever: **5** greed **7** avarice
get the ~: **3** win
go for the ~: **3** dig, run, vie **4** mine, race **5** rival **6** battle, strive **7** compete, contend
in Spanish: **3** oro
item: **3** bar **5** ingot, medal
leaf: **4** gilt
measure: **2** ct., kt. **3** pwt. **5** carat, karat
medalist: **4** hero **5** first **6** victor, winner **8** champion
mine: **4** lode **5** cache, stock, store **6** source, supply, wealth **7** bonanza, cash cow, deposit, fortune, reserve **8** windfall **10** mother lode
oak leaf wearer: **3** maj. **5** major
old ~: **5** amber, color, tawny **6** yellow **7** saffron
old ~ coin: **4** rial **5** dobla, ducat, krone, mohur, riyal **6** aureus
ore: **9** sylvanite
partner: **5** myrrh **12** frankincense
record: **3** hit **5** smash **7** success, triumph **9** sensation
relative: **4** buff, corn, lime, rust, sand **5** blond, brass, coral, cream, flaxy, lemon, maize, ocher, ochre, peach, rusty, straw **6** blonde, canary, chammy, citron, crocus, flaxen, shammy, shamoy **7** apricot, chamois, citrine, jasmine, mustard, nankeen, saffron, xanthic **8** daffodil, primrose **9** champagne, jessamine
seek ~: **3** dig, pan
solid ~: **7** optimum **8** splendid **9** marvelous
source: **3** ore **4** lode, mine, seam, vein **6** pocket, streak **7** stratum
star: **5** award, prize **6** trophy **7** laurels
the ~: **7** triumph, victory
gold __**:** **4** bond, dust, foil, lamé, leaf, mine, note, rush, star **5** basis, fever, field, medal, plate, point, stick **6** beetle, bronze, digger, fixing, orange **7** beating, bullion, reserve
gold- __**:** **6** filled, plated
__ **gold:** **3** old **4** free **5** black, Dutch, fool's, paper, pot of, Talmi, white **6** filled, good as, liquid, mosaic, rolled
Gold: **5** Missy **6** Andrew, Ernest, Tracey **7** Herbert
Gold __**:** **5** Coast
Gold __**, The:** **3** Bug **4** Rush **5** Coast
__ **Gold:** **4** Inca, Rold **5** Irish, Ulee's **6** Desert
Golda: **4** Meir
colleague: **4** Abba **5** Moshe
Gold, Andrew song: Lonely Boy (1977)
Goldberg: **4** Rube **6** Arthur, Whoopi
Goldbergs, The actress: **4** Berg
Goldberg Variations composer: **4** Bach
Goldberg, Whoopi: **7** actress
film: Boys on the Side (1995)
The Color Purple (1985)
Corrina, Corrina (1994)
Deep End of the Ocean (1999)
Ghost (1990, AA)
Ghosts of Mississippi (1996)
How Stella Got Her Groove Back (1998)
Kingdom Come (2001)
The Long Walk Home (1990)
Moonlight and Valentino (1995)
The Player (1992)
Rat Race (2001)
Sister Act (1992)
Soapdish (1991)
TV: Star Trek: The Next Generation, Hollywood Squares
Goldblum, Jeff: **5** actor
film: Between the Lines (1977)
The Big Chill (1983)
Earth Girls Are Easy (1989)
The Fly (1986)
Independence Day (1996)
Into the Night (1985)
Jurassic Park (1993)
The Lost World: Jurassic Park (1997)
Nine Months (1995)
spouse: Geena Davis
goldbrick: **3** veg **4** loaf **5** dog it, idler, shirk **6** loafer, lounge, truant **7** goof-off, shirker, slacker **8** fainéant, loiterer, malinger, parasite, slack off **9** do-nothing, lazybones **10** ne'er-do-well
in Britain: **5** sculk, skulk
goldbricking: **4** lazy
Goldbrick Variations composer: PDQ Bach
gold bronze: **5** alloy
component: **3** tin **4** lead, zinc **6** copper
Gold Bug, The author: Edgar Allan Poe
__ **Gold Cadillac, The:** **5** Solid
gold-chained actor: **3** Mr. T
Gold Coast: **5** Ghana
capital: **5** Accra, Akkra
tribe: **4** Akra
Gold Coast, The author: Nelson Demille
goldcup: **5** shrub
family: **10** nightshade
Gold Diggers of 1933 (1933 film)
cast: Joan Blondell, Ruby Keeler, Aline MacMahon
director: Mervyn LeRoy
Gold Diggers of 1935 (1935 film)
cast: Adolphe Menjou, Dick Powell, Gloria Stuart
director: Busby Berkeley
golden: **4** A-one, dore, gilt **5** auric, flaxy, happy, lucky, wheat **6** aurous, blonde, bright, flaxen, joyful, joyous, yellow **7** aureate, shining **8** blissful, glorious, precious, valuable **9** brilliant, excellent, favorable, opportune, promising **10** auspicious, delightful, flying high, propitious
age: **6** heyday
ager: **5** elder **6** senior
ager grp: **4** AARP
aster: **5** plant **6** flower
brown: **5** hazel
calf: **10** juggernaut
cowrie: **5** shell **8** seashell
egg producer: **5** goose
ender: **3** eye, rod **4** seal
in French: **3** d'or
name meaning ~: **5** Gilda
oldie: **4** song, tune **6** melody
rule word: **4** unto **6** others
touch man: **5** Midas
golden __**:** **3** age, lab **4** ager, aloe, buck, calf, club, fizz, gram, mean, mole, oldy, rose, rule **5** aster, chain, eagle, goose, oldie, perch, stars, syrup, years **6** oriole, plover, shiner,

wattle 7 currant, hamster, jubilee, ragwort, section, thistle, warbler, wedding
golden-__: 5 brown
golden-__ corn: 5 eared
Golden: 4 city, town 5 Harry
locale: 8 Colorado
Golden __: 3 Boy 4 Bull, Gate, Horn 5 Bough, Horde, Years 6 Fleece 7 Earring, Gophers, Jubilee
Golden __ Bridge: 4 Gate
Golden __, The: 3 Ass 4 Bear, Boat, Bowl, Hind, Seal 5 Girls 6 Apples, Legend 7 Harvest
Golden __ Warriors: 5 State
Golden Apples of the Sun, The author: Ray Bradbury
Golden Apples, The author: Eudora Welty
Golden Arches: 9 McDonald's
favorite: 6 Big Mac
Golden Bear: 8 Nicklaus
Golden Bears: 4 U. Cal., UCLA
Golden Boat, The author: Rabindranath Tagore
Golden Bowl, The (2001 film)
cast: Kate Beckinsale, Nick Nolte, Uma Thurman
director: James Ivory
Golden Bowl, The author: Henry James
Golden Boy: 7 musical
author: Clifford Odets
character: 3 Joe, Tom 4 Moon 5 Eddie, Lorna, Moody
songwriter: 7 Strouse
Golden Calf, The artist: 4 Erté
Golden Cockerel, The: 5 opera
Golden Crisp: 6 cereal
competitor: 3 Kix 4 Life, Trix 5 Kashi, Quisp, Total 6 Kaboom, Muesli, Oreo O's, Pablum, Smacks 7 All-Bran, Crispix, Harmony, Hunny B's, Mueslix, Oat Bran, Pokemon 8 Boo Berry, Cheerios, Corn Chex, Corn Pops, Fiber One, Rice Chex, Special K, Uncle Sam, Wheaties 9 Alpha Bits, Apple Zaps, Grape Nuts, Honey Comb, Just Right, Wheat Chex 10 Apple Jacks, Bran Flakes, Cap'n Crunch, Cocoa Puffs, Froot Loops, Mini-Wheats, Nutri-Grain, Puffed Rice, Quaker Oats, Smart Start 11 Cocoa Blasts, Cookie Crisp, Lucky Charms, Puffed Wheat, Sweet Crunch, Waffle Crisp
Golden Delicious: 5 apple
relative: 4 crab, Gala, Lodi, Rome 5 Mutsu 6 Empire, Ida Red, medlar, Pippin, russet 7 Baldwin, Bramley, costard, Freedom, Liberty, Spartan, Wealthy, Winesap 8 Cortland, Jonathan, McIntosh 10 Rome Beauty
Golden Eagles: 9 Marquette
golden-eared __: 4 corn
Golden Earring song: Twilight Zone (1983)
goldeneye: 4 bird, duck, fowl 8 whistler
relative: 4 smew, teal 5 eider, Pekin, Rouen, scaup 6 Cayuga, scoter 7 gadwall, mallard, pintail, pochard, redhead, sea duck, widgeon 8 garganey, gray duck, mandarin, musk duck, oldsquaw, shoveler, surf duck, wood duck 9 black duck, broadbill, goosander, greenhead, merganser, ruddy duck, sprigtail 10 bufflehead, canvasback, surf scoter, tufted duck
GoldenEye (1995 film)
cast: Joe Don Baker, Pierce Brosnan, Judi Dench, Famke Janssen
golden fizz: 5 drink 8 beverage, cocktail
ingredient: 3 gin 4 soda 5 vodka 7 egg yolk 10 lemon juice
Golden Fleece
land: 7 Colchis
princess: 5 Medea
seeker: 5 Jason
ship: 4 Argo
source: 5 Aries
Golden Gate: 4 park, town 6 bridge
Golden Gate Bridge, county north of the: 5 Marin
Goldengirl actress: 5 Anton
Golden Girls, The (NBC sitcom)
cast: Bea Arthur (Dorothy Zbornak)
Estelle Getty (Sophia Petrillo)
Rue McClanahan (Blanche Devereaux)
Betty White (Rose Nylund)
setting: 5 Miami 7 Florida
Golden Globe: 5 award
Golden Grahams: 6 cereal
competitor: 3 Kix 4 Life, Trix 5 Kashi, Quisp, Total 6 Kaboom, Muesli, Oreo O's, Pablum, Smacks 7 All-Bran, Crispix, Harmony, Hunny B's, Mueslix, Oat Bran, Pokemon 8 Boo Berry, Cheerios, Corn Chex, Corn Pops, Fiber One, Rice Chex, Special K, Uncle Sam, Wheaties 9 Alpha Bits, Apple Zaps, Grape Nuts, Honey Comb, Just Right, Wheat Chex 10 Apple Jacks, Bran Flakes, Cap'n Crunch, Cocoa Puffs, Froot Loops, Mini-Wheats, Nutri-Grain, Puffed Rice, Quaker Oats, Smart Start 11 Cocoa Blasts, Cookie Crisp, Golden Crisp, Lucky Charms, Puffed Wheat, Sweet Crunch, Waffle Crisp
golden-haired: 4 fair 5 blond, light, sandy 6 blonde, flaxen 9 towheaded
Golden Harvest, The author: Jorge Amado
Golden Hind: 4 boat, ship
captain: 5 Drake
Golden Horde member: 5 Tatar
Golden Hurricanes school: 5 Tulsa
Golden Jubilee composer: 5 Sousa
Golden Legend, The author: Henry Wadsworth Longfellow
Golden Nugget locale: 5 Vegas
golden retriever: 3 dog 5 canid 6 canine
goldenrod: 5 plant 6 flower, yellow
relative: 4 buff, corn, gold, lime, rust, sand 5 aster, blond, brass, coral, cream, flaxy, lemon, maize, ocher, ochre, peach, rusty, straw 6 blonde, canary, chammy, citron, crocus, flaxen, shammy, shamoy 7 apricot, chamois, citrine, jasmine, mustard, nankeen, saffron, xanthic 8 daffodil, primrose 9 champagne, jessamine
__ Golden Slippers: 5 Oh Dem
Golden Spike state: 4 Utah
Golden State
see California
Golden Temple worshiper: 4 Sikh
Golden Valley: 4 city, town
locale: 9 Minnesota
Golden Years (1976 song) artist: David Bowie
goldfinch: 4 bird
Goldfinger: 4 film, song 5 Auric, novel
artist: Shirley Bassey
author: Ian Fleming
cast: Honor Blackman, Sean Connery, Shirley Eaton, Gert Frobe, Bernard Lee, Lois Maxwell, Harold Sakata
director: Guy Hamilton
goldfish: 3 pet 4 carp
at a carnival: 5 prize
relative: 4 dace
Goldfish, The artist: 4 Klee
Goldie: 4 Hawn
cohort of yore: 3 Dan 4 Alan, Arte, Lily, Ruth
goldilocks: 5 plant
Golding, William: 6 writer 7 British 8 Nobelist
work: Lord of the Flies
Goldman: 4 Emma 7 William
Goldman __: 5 Sachs
Goldmark: 5 Peter
gold-medal position: 5 first
Goldoni, Carlo: 7 Italian 10 playwright
Goldovsky, Boris: 9 conductor
gold piece, ten-dollar: 5 eagle
Gold Rush
figure: 5 miner, niner
implement: 6 cradle
locale: 6 Alaska, Juneau 10 California
Gold Rush, The (1925 film) cast: Charles Chaplin
Goldsboro: 4 town
locale: 4 N. Car.
Goldsboro, Bobby
song: Honey (1968)
See the Funny Little Clown (1964)
Watching Scotty Grow (1971)
Goldsmith: 5 Jerry 6 Oliver
Goldsmith, Oliver: 6 author, writer 7 British
work: The Deserted Village
She Stoops to Conquer
The Vicar of Wakefield
Goldstein, Joseph: 8 Nobelist
Goldthwait: 6 Bobcat
Goldwater: 5 Barry
Goldwyn: 4 Tony 6 Samuel
colleague: 5 Mayer
__-Goldwyn-Mayer: 5 Metro
Goldwyn's Folly: 4 Sten
Goldwyn, Tony: 5 actor
film: The 6th Day (2000)
An American Rhapsody (2001)
Kiss the Girls (1997)
The Pelican Brief (1993)
A Walk on the Moon (1999)
film (voice): Tarzan (1999)
golem: 5 droid, robot 9 automaton
Goleta: 4 city, town
locale: 10 California
golf: 4 game 5 sport
alert: 4 fore
area: 3 tee 5 apron, green, rough 6 fringe 7 fairway
bad shot in ~: 4 baff
baff a ~ ball: 4 loft
ball feature: 6 dimple
ball material: 6 balata
ball position in ~: 3 lie
bet in ~: 6 Nassau
club: 4 iron, wood 5 cleek, wedge 6 driver, mashie, putter 7 brassie, niblick
club part: 3 toe 4 head, hose, sole 5 hosel, shaft 6 flange
coup: 3 ace 5 eagle
course: 5 links
course feature: 6 dogleg
course material: 3 sod 4 lawn, turf 5 grass, sward
course piece: 3 sod 5 divot
cup: 5 Ryder
distance a ~ ball rolls: 3 run
do ~ course work: 5 resod
easy ~ shot: 5 tap in
Florida ~ course: 5 Doral
furthest from the hole, in ~: 4 away
gear: 3 tee 4 ball, club, iron, wood 5 cleek, spoon, visor, vizor, wedge 6 driver
get ready to play ~: 5 tee up
gofer: 5 caddy 6 caddie
goof: 4 hook 5 shank, slice
group: 8 foursome
half the ~ course: 3 out 4 nine
hazard: 4 sand, trap 6 bunker
hole edge: 3 lip
hole in one: 3 ace
instructor: 3 ace, pro
locale: 5 green, links, rough 6 hazard
match-play ~ score: 5 one up
motion: 6 waggle
official: 7 starter
org.: 3 PGA 4 LPGA, USGA
position: 3 lie
score: 3 ace, par 5 bogey, bogie, eagle 6 birdie
shoe feature: 5 cleat
shot: 4 chip, putt 5 drive, pitch
target: 3 cup, pin 4 hole
term: 3 ace, cup, lie, par, tee 4 away, baff, chip, club, draw, fade, fore, hook, iron, loft, putt, wood, yips 5 apron, bogey, caddy, cleek, divot, dormy, drive, eagle, gimme, green, halve, honor, hosel, links, pitch, pro-am, rough, slice, wedge 6 birdie, bunker, caddie, dimple, dogleg, dormie, driver, duffer, fringe, hazard, marker, mashie, Nassau, putter, stroke, stymie, waggle 7 address, brassie, fairway, niblick, starter 8 approach, backspin, best ball, duck hook, foursome, handicap, mulligan, sand trap
vehicle: 4 cart
woe: 4 hook 5 slice 6 bad lie, stymie 8 duck hook
golf __: 3 bag, tee 4 ball, cart, club 5 glove, links, widow 6 course
__ golf: 6 midget 9 miniature
Golf: 2 VW 3 car 4 auto 10 Volkswagen
Golf Begins at Forty author: 5 Snead
golfer: 3 Els, Pak 4 Aoki, Berg, Daly, Ford, Hoch, Kite, Lema, Love, Lyle, Mann, Mize, Toms, Wall, Webb, Weir, Wood 5 Aaron, Baugh, Beman, Boros, Burke, Coody, Duval, Estes, Faldo, Floyd, Hagen, Hogan, Irwin, Jones, Lopez, Pavin, Price, Rawls, Singh, Smith, Snead, Stacy, Suggs, Woods 6 Alcott, Archer, Armour, Brewer, Caponi, Carner, Casper, Daniel, Garcia, Goalby, Harmon, Haynie, Hinkle, Janzen, Keiser, Langer, Mallon, Miller, Morgan, Nelson, Norman, O'Meara, Ouimet, Palmer, Picard, Player, Rankin, Sluman, Sutton, Watson, Wright 7 Art Wall, athlete, Azinger, Couples, Demaret, Guldahl, Inkster, Littler, Masters, Mediate, Sarazen, Se Ri Pak, Sheehan, Stadler, Stewart, Tom Kite, Trevino, Venturi, Wadkins, Woosnam, Zoeller 8 Crenshaw, Doug Ford, Ernie Els, Isao Aoki, John Daly, Nicklaus, Olazabal, Ray Floyd, Sam Snead, Tony Lema, Zaharias 9 Amy Alcott, Bob Goalby, Gay Brewer, Geiberger, Gil Morgan, Hal Sutton, Lee Janzen, Lon Hinkle, Meg Mallon, Mickelson, Nick Faldo, Nick Price, Patty Berg, Scott Hoch, Sorenstam, Stevenson, Tom Watson 10 Baker-Finch, Beth Daniel, Corey Pavin, Deane Beman, Gary Player, Greg Norman, Ian Woosnam, Jeff Sluman, Judy Rankin, Ken Venturi, Laura Baugh, Lee Trevino, Mark O'Meara, Middlecoff, Tiger Woods, Vijay Singh 11 Ballesteros
at times: 4 teer
Australian ~: 6 Norman 9 Stevenson 10 Baker-Finch
average, to a ~: 3 par
bad ~: 6 duffer, hacker

British ~: **5** Faldo
Fijian ~: **5** Singh
German ~: **6** Langer
Japanese ~: **4** Aoki
Korean ~: **3** Pak
nickname: **3** Sam **5** Arnie, Tiger
South African ~: **3** Els **5** Price **6** Player
Spanish ~: **6** Garcia **11** Ballesteros
Swedish ~: **9** Sorenstam
Welsh ~: **7** Woosnam
Golgi __: **4** body
Golgi, Camillo: **8** Nobelist
Goliath: **5** giant, he-man
hometown: **4** Gath
to David: **3** foe **5** enemy
Golightly: **5** Holly
Golino, Valeria: **7** actress
film: Big Top Pee-wee (1988)
Hot Shots! (1991)
The Indian Runner (1991)
Rain Man (1988)
golly: **3** gee, wow **4** gosh **6** my gosh, my oh my **7** gee whiz, jeepers **8** well well
__ Golly, Miss Molly: **4** Good
Go, Lovely Rose author: Edmund Waller
__ Go Lover: **5** Let Me
__-go-lucky: **5** happy
Goma: **5** Bantu
Gombrowicz, Witold: **6** author, Polish, writer
Gomeisa: **4** star
Gomel: **4** city, town
locale: **7** Belarus
Gomer: **4** Pyle
cousin: **6** Goober
grandfather of ~: **4** Noah
husband of ~: **5** Hosea
rank: **3** PFC
Gomer Pyle, U.S.M.C. (CBS sitcom)
cast: Jim Nabors (Pvt. Gomer Pyle)
Frank Sutton (Sgt. Vince Carter)
Gomez: **5** Lefty **6** Addams
cousin: **3** Itt
uncle: **6** Fester
wife: **4** Tish **8** Morticia
see also Spanish
Gomez, Lefty: **6** Yankee **7** pitcher
Gomorrah neighbor: **5** Sodom
Gompers: **6** Samuel
-gon
starter: **4** deca, hexa, nona, octa, poly **5** penta **6** dodeca
Gonaïves: **4** gulf
locale: **5** Haiti
Gonâve __: **4** Gulf **6** Island
__ Gonçalo, Brazil: **3** Sao
Goncharov, Ivan: **6** writer **7** Russian
Goncourt: **5** Jules **6** Edmond
Goncourt, Edmond: **6** author, French, writer
Goncourt, Jules: **6** author, French, writer
Gondar's province: **6** Amhara
gondola: **4** boat
maneuver a ~: **4** pole
place: **5** canal **6** Venice
worker: **5** poler
gondola __: **3** car **4** back
__ Gondola: **3** In a
Gondoliers, The
composer: **7** Gilbert **8** Sullivan
role: **4** Inez, Luiz **5** Tessa
gone: **3** off, out **4** away, AWOL, left, lost, over, past, quit, shot, worn **5** ended, moved, not in, spent, split **6** absent, lapsed, passed, run off, used up **7** defunct, dried up, eaten up, elapsed, extinct, lacking, missing, sold out, worn-out **8** decamped, departed, depleted, finished, obsolete, vamoosed, vanished **9** destroyed, dissolved, elsewhere, exhausted, forgotten, out of here, traveling, withdrawn **10** by the board, cleared out, dissipated, on vacation
all ~: **3** out **5** empty, spent **9** exhausted **10** dissipated, squandered
astray: **4** lost **7** mislaid, missing **9** misplaced
bad: **3** off **4** rank, sour **6** rancid, rotten, turned **7** curdled **8** vinegary
be ~: **4** flit, quit **5** leave, split **6** beat it, cut out, defect, go away **7** drop out, head out, make off, pull out, push off, ride off, ship out, skip out, walk out **8** check out, clear out, light out, run along, shove off, slip away, step down **9** disappear, take a hike **10** give notice
by the boards: **3** out **5** dated, fusty, hoary, passé, stale **6** démodé, old hat **7** archaic, outworn **8** obsolete, outdated, outmoded **9** forgotten, moss-grown, out-of-date **10** antiquated, superseded
days ~ by: **4** once, past **5** of old **6** before
far ~: **3** mad **6** in love **7** charmed, smitten **8** beguiled, besotted, obsessed **9** bewitched, possessed **10** captivated, crazy about, enraptured, fascinated, infatuated, spellbound
haywire: **5** kaput **10** broken-down, on the blink, on the fritz, out of order, out of whack
in a flash: **9** momentary
long ~: **3** ago **4** late, over, yore **6** former **7** old-time, one-time **8** finished, obsolete **9** forgotten, out-of-date, preceding, yesterday **10** historical, out of style, yesteryear
starter: **3** dog
to seed: **4** soft **5** passé, ratty **9** enervated **10** dissipated
__ gone: **3** all, far **4** real
Gone __ the Wind: **4** With
Gone (1957 song) artist: Ferlin Husky
__ Gone A-Hunting: **6** Daddy's
Gone Are the Days (1963 film)
cast: Ossie Davis, Ruby Dee
goner: **8** lame duck **9** lost cause
like a ~: **4** lost, sunk **6** doomed, ruined, undone **7** done for **8** luckless
name: **3** mud
Goneril
father: **4** Lear
sister: **5** Regan **8** Cordelia
Gone Till November (1998 song) artist: Wyclef Jean
Gone With the Wind: **4** film **5** novel
author: Margaret Mitchell
cast: Olivia de Havilland, Clark Gable, Leslie Howard, Victor Jory, Evelyn Keyes, Vivien Leigh, Hattie McDaniel, Butterfly McQueen, Thomas Mitchell
character: **5** Ellen, Frank, India, Mammy, O'Hara, Rhett **6** Ashley, Butler, Gerald, Wilkes **7** Charles, Kennedy, Melanie, Suellen **8** Hamilton, Pittypat, Scarlett **10** Bonnie Blue
director: Victor Fleming
music: Max Steiner
setting: **4** Tara **7** Atlanta, Georgia
gonfalon: **4** flag **6** banner, ensign
gong: **3** kin **4** bell, peal, ring, toll **5** chime, clang, knell **6** jangle, jingle, kenong, tam-tam **7** resound **10** percussion
Góngora, Luis de: **4** poet **7** Spanish
Gong Show, The: **8** game show
host: Chuck Barris
regular: **4** Farr
Gonna Fly Now (1977 song) artist: Bill Conti
film: **5** Rocky
__ Gonna Give You Up: **5** Never
Go Now! (1965 song) artist: Moody Blues
Gonzaga: **6** school **10** university
athletes: **4** Zags **8** Bulldogs
locale: **7** Spokane **10** Washington
Gonzales: **6** Pancho, Speedy
see also Spanish
Gonzales, Pancho: **7** netster **9** tennis pro
milieu: **5** court
Gonzales, Speedy: **4** toon **5** mouse
gonzo: **7** bizarre **9** eccentric
goo: **4** glop, gunk, muck, ooze **5** paste, slime **6** liquid **8** baby talk
goober: **6** peanut
goober __: **3** pea
Goober: **4** Pyle
cousin: **5** Gomer
Goobers: **5** candy
good: **2** OK **3** ace, apt, fit, rad, use **4** able, aces, boss, fine, kind, meet, neat, nice, okay, okeh, okey, pure, real, sake, tidy, well **5** adept, avail, bully, crack, favor, fresh, great, legal, legit, licit, loyal, moral, prime, primo, pucka, pukka, right, smart, solid, sound, tasty, valid, yummy **6** adroit, benign, chaste, choice, clever, decent, edible, expert, giving, honest, humane, kasher, kindly, kosher, lawful, polite, proper, savory, seemly, stable, toothy, up to it, useful, virtue, worthy **7** benefit, capable, capital, correct, dutiful, eatable, ethical, fitting, genuine, healthy, helpful, honesty, likable, orderly, probity, saintly, sizable, skilled, upright, welcome, welfare **8** accurate, adequate, all right, becoming, bona fide, dextrous, esculent, faithful, flawless, friendly, gracious, innocent, interest, mannerly, merciful, morality, obedient, obliging, orthodox, pleasant, pleasing, positive, reliable, salutary, sizeable, skillful, splendid, sterling, suitable, talented, very well, virtuous **9** admirable, advantage, agreeable, allowable, authentic, blameless, competent, covetable, delicious, desirable, dexterous, efficient, estimable, excellent, exemplary, extensive, favorable, first-rate, fortunate, guiltless, healthful, honorable, incorrupt, lucrative, marvelous, okey-dokey, opportune, palatable, qualified, rectitude, reputable, righteous, shipshape, sprightly, unspoiled, untainted, up to snuff, well-being, wholesome, wonderful **10** acceptable, admissible, altruistic, auspicious, beneficent, beneficial, benevolent, charitable, comestible, convenient, creditable, dependable, first-class, gratifying, inculpable, in the rules, law-abiding, legitimate, proficient, respectful, salubrious, satisfying, upstanding, usefulness, worthwhile
as ~ as: **6** almost, nearly **7** equal to **8** rivaling **9** virtually **10** tantamount
as ~ as won: **5** on ice **7** assured **10** guaranteed
as new: **5** fixed **6** healed **8** repaired, restored **9** unspoiled
at a ~ clip: **5** apace
be ~ enough: **2** do **4** pass, suit, work **5** avail, get by, serve **6** answer **7** content, deliver, qualify, satisfy, suffice **10** hit the spot
be ~ for: **3** aid **4** help, suit **5** edify, serve **6** assist **7** benefit, enhance, further, improve **9** agree with
be on ~ terms with: **4** know
between prime and ~: **6** choice
bit: **4** some **5** quite **6** rather
breeding: **6** polish **7** conduct, culture, decorum, manners, p's and q's **8** behavior, courtesy, urbanity **9** etiquette, politesse **10** deportment, politeness, refinement
buddy: **3** bro, pal **4** CBer **5** crony
but ~: **4** a lot, very **5** mucho **6** highly, hugely, plenty **9** decidedly **10** thoroughly
buy: **4** deal, find **5** cheap **6** on sale **7** bargain, cut-rate **9** dirt cheap, low-priced **10** economical, marked down
cheer: **8** optimism **9** geniality, happiness
citizen: **5** voter **7** patriot
clean fun: **6** frolic
combining form: **2** eu- **4** bene- **5** agath- **6** agatho-
condition: **5** order **6** health, kilter **7** fitness
create ~ will: **6** endear
deal: **4** lots **5** steal **6** plenty **7** bargain
deed: **8** kindness **10** kindliness
eating: **4** fare, menu **7** cuisine
ender: **3** bye **4** will **7** hearted
enough: **4** fine **8** very well **9** tolerable
fairly ~: **2** OK **4** fair, so-so **6** decent, not bad **7** average **8** adequate, all right, bearable, mediocre, middling, moderate, ordinary, passable **9** tolerable **10** acceptable, admissible, reasonable, sufficient
faith: **5** honor, truth **6** candor **7** decency, honesty, probity **8** fairness, veracity **9** frankness, integrity, sincerity
feeling: **4** ease **6** relief, solace, thrill **7** comfort **8** sympathy **9** happiness, well-being
feeling ~: **3** fit **4** fine, hale, well **5** happy, hardy, husky, sound **6** hearty, robust, strong **7** chipper, healthy, up to par **8** blooming, thriving, vigorous **9** in the pink **10** able-bodied
find ~: **4** like
for ~: **6** at last **7** finally, forever **8** after all, in the end **10** eventually, ultimately, unendingly
for growing: **7** fertile **8** plowable, tillable
form: **7** manners **8** protocol **9** propriety
for ~ measure: **4** free **6** gratis **7** as a gift **8** as a bonus **9** as an extra **10** in addition, on the house
for nothing: **3** bad **4** evil **6** abject, dismal, rotten **7** pitiful **8** wretched **9** miserable, worthless **10** deplorable, despicable, detestable
for something: **5** handy, utile **6** useful **9** practical
fortune: **4** luck **7** welfare **9** well-being **10** prosperity
full of ~ cheer: **5** merry
general ~: **4** weal
get but ~: **4** nail
grade: **5** B plus
guy: **4** hero
habits: **6** ethics, morals **7** decency, virtues **9** integrity, rectitude **10** principles
hand: **5** flush **8** straight **10** royal flush
have a ~ time: **5** enjoy, party, revel **6** cavort **7** carouse, skylark **8** cut loose, live it up **9** celebrate, make merry, whoop it up
humor: **3** joy **5** mirth **6** gaiety, gayety **9** happiness

in a ~ mood: 5 happy, jolly, riant 6 cheery 7 chipper 8 cheerful, sanguine
in ~ condition: 3 fit 4 neat, well 5 hardy, right, sound 7 healthy 9 untouched
in ~ faith: 5 truly 7 frankly 8 candidly, for keeps, heartily, honestly 9 earnestly, genuinely, seriously, sincerely 10 aboveboard, truthfully
in French: 3 bon
in Italian: 4 bene
in Latin: 4 bene
in ~ shape: 3 fit 4 neat, tidy, trim 5 hardy, sound 6 robust, spruce 7 healthy 8 vigorous
in ~ taste: 6 decent, seemly, snappy 8 tasteful
in the ~ old days: 4 once, past 6 before 7 earlier, long ago, time was, way back 8 back when, formerly, years ago 10 previously
in ~ time: 4 anon, soon 5 early 6 prompt, timely 7 by and by, erelong, shortly 8 punctual 9 presently 10 beforehand, before long
judgment: 5 sense 6 sanity, wisdom
least ~: 5 worst
life: 6 luxury 7 comfort, leisure 9 affluence 10 bed of roses, prosperity
look: 6 eyeful
look ~ on: 3 fit 4 suit 6 become 7 flatter
looks: 4 plus 5 class 6 beauty 7 glamour 8 elegance 9 advantage 10 loveliness
make ~: 3 pay, win 5 atone, pay up, repay 6 arrive, do well, fulfil, hack it, pan out, pay for, recoup, redeem, refund, settle, thrive 7 deliver, fulfill, luck out, pay back, prevail, prosper, realize, recover, rectify, satisfy, succeed, triumph, work out 8 atone for, flourish, get ahead, go places, hit it big, square up 9 indemnify, reimburse 10 accomplish, do all right, recompense
make ~ on: 5 repay 6 fulfil, remedy 7 correct, fulfill, realize 8 carry out, set right 10 accomplish
manners: 5 couth 8 civility, courtesy 9 propriety
many: 8 frequent, numerous
name: 3 rep 5 asset, honor, worth 6 credit, esteem, regard, repute 8 prestige, standing 9 character 10 reputation
name meaning ~: 6 Agatha, Bonnie
nature: 6 gaiety, warmth 9 geniality, joviality, pleasance, sunniness 10 affability, amiability, cheeriness, cordiality, kindliness
no ~: 4 evil, junk 5 lousy 7 useless 10 virtueless
not ~: 3 bad 4 evil, poor
not as ~: 5 worse
not ~ enough: 7 lacking, wanting 8 inferior 9 deficient, half-baked, imperfect 10 inadequate, incomplete
not feel ~: 3 ail 4 hurt
not in ~ humor: 4 dour, glum, ugly 5 cross, gruff, huffy, irate, sulky, surly, testy 6 crabby, cranky, gloomy, grumpy, morose, ornery, sullen 7 grouchy, hostile, peevish 8 frowning, growling, perverse, snappish 9 crotchety, irritable 10 out of sorts, ungracious
old days: 4 past, yore 7 earlier, history, long ago 8 back when 9 yesterday 10 yesteryear
on ~ terms: 4 kind 5 close, thick 6 chummy, clubby, genial, kindly 7 affable, amiable, cordial 8 amicable, friendly, intimate, outgoing, peaceful, sociable 9 convivial 10 benevolent, buddy-buddy, neighborly, solicitous
on the ~ side of: 6 in with
opinion: 6 esteem, regard 7 respect 8 approval, prestige 10 reputation
point: 4 plus 5 asset 6 virtue
pretty ~: 4 fair, so-so, tidy
prospects: 4 hope 7 promise
public ~: 4 weal
put in a ~ word for: 4 laud, plug 8 champion 9 recommend
put in ~ shape: 4 tidy 5 fix up 6 neaten 10 straighten
relations: 5 amity, peace 6 comity 7 concord, harmony 8 goodwill 10 cordiality, fellowship, friendship
review: 4 rave
right arm: 8 backbone, linchpin
sense: 3 wit 5 logic 10 discretion
showing ~ judgment: 4 sane, wise 5 lucid, sober, sound 6 steady 7 logical, prudent 8 all there, balanced, moderate, rational, sensible, together 9 judicious, practical, pragmatic, realistic 10 discerning, fair-minded, reasonable, thoughtful
spirits: 4 glee 5 cheer, mirth 6 gaiety, levity 7 elation, jollity, rapture 8 euphoria, gladness, hilarity 9 happiness, joviality, merriment, well-being 10 enthusiasm, exuberance, joyfulness
stretch of ~ luck: 3 run
stroke of ~ fortune: 4 luck 5 break, fluke 7 godsend 8 blessing, windfall 10 lucky break
taste: 4 tact 5 taste 7 culture
time: 3 fun 4 lark, romp 5 blast
times: 3 fun, ups 10 prosperity
to eat: 4 rich 5 spicy, tasty, yummy 6 delish, savory, toothy 8 heavenly, luscious 9 delicious, flavorful, palatable, succulent, toothsome 10 appetizing, delectable
too ~ for: 10 unworthy of
too much of a ~ thing: 4 glut 5 flood 6 excess 7 surfeit, surplus 8 overload 10 indulgence, oversupply
turn: 5 favor 8 kindness 10 kindliness
very ~: 3 def, rad 4 aces, A-one, boss, braw, cool, dece, fine, gear, keen, neat, nice, phat, tuff 5 dandy, ducky, grand, great, marvy, neato, nifty, nobby, prime, slick, super, swell 6 bang on, bang-up, bonzer, bosker, choice, divine, dreamy, far-out, gnarly, groovy, lovely, peachy, slap-up, spot on, superb, terrif, tip-top, unreal, whizzo, wicked 7 amazing, awesome, capital, corking, perfect, ripping, skookum, stellar, sublime 8 dazzling, especial, eximious, fabulous, five-star, four-star, frabjous, glorious, heavenly, jim-dandy, slam-bang, smashing, splendid, standout, sterling, stickout, superior, terrific, top-level, topnotch, wondrous 9 bodacious, Endsville, excellent, exemplary, exquisite, first-rate, high-grade, hunky-dory, marvelous, sollicker, top-flight, unrivaled, wonderful 10 first-class, hotsy-totsy, jack-a-dandy, out of sight, peachy-keen, phenomenal, remarkable, stupendous, super-duper, unrivalled
vibes: 4 bond 5 unity 6 accord 7 concord, empathy, harmony, rapport 8 affinity 9 agreement, communion 10 friendship
vision: 8 keenness
will: 5 unity 7 harmony 8 kindness 9 readiness, tolerance 10 friendship
wishes: 7 benison, devoirs, regards 8 blessing 10 salutation
with ~ grace: 6 freely, gladly, warmly 7 happily, readily 8 cheerily, heartily 9 willingly 10 cheerfully
with ~ heart: 4 bold 5 brave 6 daring, gritty, plucky, spunky 7 doughty, gallant, valiant 8 intrepid, valorous 9 dauntless 10 courageous
with tools: 4 able 5 adept, handy 6 adroit 7 skilled 8 skillful
with words: 3 pat 4 glib, oily 5 slick, suave 6 artful, facile, fluent, smooth 7 voluble 8 eloquent, slippery 10 articulate, loquacious
word: 4 plug 5 honor, kudos 6 homage, praise, salute 7 acclaim, plaudit, tribute 8 accolade, encomium, flattery 9 laudation, panegyric, reference 10 compliment, exaltation

good __: 3 day, egg, Joe, use 4 life, luck, news, time, word 5 as new, buddy, cheer, faith, humor, looks, night, ol' boy, speed, title, usage, vibes 6 fellow, morrow, nature 7 evening, morning, offices
good __ boy: 3 old, ole
good __ days: 3 old
good __ nothing: 3 for
good __ was had by all, A: 4 time
good-__: 3 bye 5 sized 7 hearted, looking, natured
good-__ Charlie: 4 time
__ good: 3 for 4 make 5 to the
__-good: 4 feel
Good __: 4 Book, News 5 for Me, Thing, Times 6 Enough, Friday
Good __!: 4 idea 5 grief
Good __ Hard to Find, A: 5 Man is
Good __ Hunting: 4 Will
Good __, Miss Molly: 5 Golly
Good __, The: 3 Son 4 Deed, Life 5 Earth, Fairy, Fight 6 Doctor, Morrow, Mother
Good __, Vietnam: 7 Morning
Goodacre, Jill spouse: Harry Connick Jr.
Goodall: 4 Jane
subject: 3 ape
good and __: 5 ready
Good and __: 6 Fruity, Plenty
Good and Fruity: 4 nosh 5 candy, snack
Good and Plenty: 4 nosh 5 candy, snack
good as __: 4 gold
Good as Gold author: Joseph Heller
Good Book: 5 Bible
__ Good Boy Does Fine: 5 Every
goodbye: 4 ciao, exit, ta-ta 5 adieu, adios, aloha, later, leave, peace, see ya 6 bye-bye, shalom, so long 7 cheerio, parting 8 au revoir, farewell, sayonara, toodle-oo 9 Abyssinia, departure
in French: 5 adieu
in Hawaiian: 5 aloha
in Italian: 4 ciao
in Latin: 3 ave 4 vale
in Spanish: 5 adios
kiss ~: 3 rid 4 lose 5 eject, spend 7 abandon, forsake 8 forswear 9 foreswear
say ~: 4 part 5 leave 6 go home
silent ~: 4 wave
Goodbye Again (1961 film)
cast: Ingrid Bergman, Yves Montand, Anthony Perkins
director: Anatole Litvak
Goodbye, Columbus: 4 film 7 novella
author: Philip Roth
cast: Richard Benjamin, Jack Klugman, Ali MacGraw
director: Larry Peerce
Goodbye Cruel World (1961 song)
artist: James Darren
Goodbye Girl, The (1977 film)
cast: Quinn Cummings, Richard Dreyfuss, Marsha Mason
director: Herbert Ross
Goodbye, Janette author: Harold Robbins
Goodbye, Mr. Chips: 4 film 5 novel
author: James Hilton
cast: Robert Donat, Greer Garson, Paul Henreid
director: Sam Wood
Goodbye, My Fancy (1951 film)
cast: Joan Crawford, Frank Lovejoy, Robert Young
Goodbyes All We Got Left singer: 5 Earle
Goodbye (song) artist: Night Ranger, Spice Girls
Good-Bye to All That author: Robert Graves
Goodbye to Berlin author: Christopher Isherwood
Goodbye to Love (1972 song) artist: Carpenters
Goodbye Yellow Brick Road (1973 song) artist: Elton John
__ Good Care of My Baby: 4 Take
__ good cheer!: 4 Be of
Good Christian Men, Rejoice: 5 carol
__ good conscience: 5 in all
good deed
doer: 4 hero 8 Boy Scout
org.: 3 BSA
__ good deed: 3 do a
Good Deed, The author: Pearl S. Buck
Good Doctor, The author: Neil Simon
Good Earth, The: 4 film 5 novel
author: Pearl S. Buck
cast: Walter Connolly, Paul Muni, Luise Rainer
character: 3 Liu 4 O-Lan 5 Ching 6 Nung En 7 Nung Wen 8 Wang Lung
director: Sidney Franklin
sequel: 4 Sons
Gooden, Dwight: 6 hurler 7 pitcher
nickname: 3 Doc
Good enough!: 4 okay 6 It'll do
Good Enough (1992 song) artist: Bobby Brown
Goodeve: 5 Grant
__ good example: 4 set a
Good Fairy, The (1935 film)
cast: Herbert Marshall, Frank Morgan, Margaret Sullavan
director: William Wyler
__ good faith: 5 act in
__ Good Feeling: 5 Era of
GoodFellas (1990 film)
boss: 3 don
cast: Lorraine Bracco, Robert De Niro, Ray Liotta, Joe Pesci, Paul Sorvino
director: Martin Scorsese
group: 5 Mafia
Goodfellow: 3 AFB 5 Robin
Good for Me (1992 song) artist: Amy Grant
good-for-nothing: 3 bum, cad, low 4 heel, punk 5 brute, churl, crook, fiend, idler, knave, leech, loser, louse, quack, rogue, rowdy, scamp, snake, sorry 6 bad boy, bad egg, bad guy, con man, crummy, loafer, rascal, rotter, varlet, weasel 7 bounder, goof-off, ignoble, laggard, lowlife, moocher, shirker, shyster, slacker, stinker, useless, varmint, wastrel 8 blighter, bootless, chiseler, deadbeat, derelict, fainéant, feckless, inferior, layabout,

parasite, picaroon, prodigal, recreant, scalawag, slugabed, sluggard, spalpeen, swindler, unworthy, wretched **9** charlatan, do-nothing, goldbrick, lazybones, miserable, no-account, reprobate, scallawag, scallywag, scoundrel, valueless, worthless **10** malingerer, mountebank, ne'er-do-well, scapegrace
good for what __ you: **4** ails
good friend, name meaning: **6** Godwin
__ Good Friends: **4** Such
good gift, name meaning: **6** Eudora
Good Golly, Miss Molly (1958 song)
artist: Little Richard
Good grief!: **4** egad, oh my **5** egads
good-hearted: **4** kind **6** kindly **8** generous, gracious **9** unselfish
Good Hearted Woman (1976 song)
artist: Willie Nelson
Good Hope: **4** cape
locale: **3** RSA **6** Africa
Good Housekeeping award: **4** seal
Good Humor: **8** ice cream
alternative: **4** Edy's **7** Breyer's **9** Friendly's **10** Dairy Queen, Haagen Dazs, Turkey Hill
good-humored: **4** easy, mild **5** funny, sweet **7** affable **8** amicable, cheerful, pleasant
goodie: **3** yay **4** gift **5** candy, cooky, snack, sweet, treat **6** cookie **7** present
goodies: **4** eats, food, loot **5** snack **6** reward **8** junk food
Gooding: **4** Cuba, Omar
Gooding Jr., Cuba: **5** actor
film: As Good as It Gets (1997)
Boyz N the Hood (1991)
Instinct (1999)
Jerry Maguire (1996, AA)
Losing Isaiah (1995)
Men of Honor (2000)
Pearl Harbor (2001)
Rat Race (2001)
What Dreams May Come (1998)
Good Intentions poet: **4** Nash
Good job!: **5** bravo
Good King Wenceslas: **5** carol
Good Life, The (1963 song) artist: Tony Bennett
__ good light: **3** in a
__, Good-Lookin': **3** Hey
good-looking: **4** cute, fair, nice **5** bonny **6** bonnie, comely, dreamy, lovely, pretty **7** winsome **8** alluring, gorgeous, handsome, striking, stunning **9** ravishing **10** attractive
guy: **4** hunk **6** Apollo
Good Lord!: **4** egad **5** egads
Good Lovin' (1966 song) artist: Rascals
Good Luck Charm (1962 song) artist: Elvis Presley
Good Luck, Miss Wyckoff author: William Inge
good-luck piece: **5** charm **6** amulet, scarab **8** talisman
goodly: **3** big **4** tidy **5** ample, large, prime **6** choice, select **7** quality, sizable **8** sizeable, superior, topnotch **9** excellent, first-rate, top-drawer **10** first-class
number: **4** gobs, lots, many, tons **5** heaps, horde, piles, scads **6** divers, legion, myriad, oodles, plenty, scores, throng, untold **7** jillion, no end of, umpteen **8** numerous **9** abundance, countless, multitude, thousands, uncounted
part of: **4** most
Goodman: **3** Ace **4** Dody, John **5** Benny, Ellen **6** Dickie
Goodman, Benny: **11** clarinetist
genre: **4** jazz
instrument: clarinet
portrayer: **5** Allen
__ Goodman Brown: **5** Young
Good Man is Hard to Find, A author: Flannery O'Connor
Goodman, John: **5** actor
film: Always (1989)
Arachnophobia (1990)
The Babe (1992)
Barton Fink (1991)
The Big Lebowski (1998)
Blues Brothers 2000 (1998)
Bringing Out the Dead (1999)
Coyote Ugly (2000)
King Ralph (1991)
Matinee (1993)
One Night at McCool's (2001)
Punchline (1988)
Sea of Love (1989)
film (voice): The Emperor's New Groove (2000)
Monsters, Inc. (2001)
TV: Roseanne
good man, name meaning: **7** Evander
__ good measure: **3** for
__ Good Men: **4** A Few
Good Morning America alternative: **5** Today
Good Morning, America author: Carl Sandburg
Good Morning, Dearie: **7** musical
songwriter: **4** Kern
Good Morning, Midnight author: Jean Rhys
Good Morning, Miss Dove (1955 film)
cast: Jennifer Jones, Robert Stack
director: Henry Koster
Good Morning Starshine (1969 song)
artist: Oliver
show: **4** Hair
Good Morning, Vietnam (1987 film)
cast: Forest Whitaker, Robin Williams
director: Barry Levinson
Good Morrow, The author: John Donne
Good Mother, The (1988 film)
cast: Ralph Bellamy, Diane Keaton, Liam Neeson, Jason Robards
director: Leonard Nimoy
good-natured: **4** easy, kind, mild, nice **5** jolly, sweet **6** genial, jovial, kindly, polite **7** affable, amiable, cordial, helpful, lenient, likable **8** friendly, gracious, obliging, sociable, tolerant **10** personable
one: **5** sport
Good Neighbor __: **3** Sam **6** Policy
Good Neighbor Sam (1964 film)
cast: Jack Lemmon, Edward G. Robinson, Romy Schneider
goodness: **4** oh my, oh no, pity **5** heart, honor, merit, right, worth **6** dear me, my word, oh dear, virtue **7** decency, honesty, probity **8** kindness, morality **9** integrity, rectitude **10** excellence, generosity, humaneness, kindliness
honest to ~: **5** truly **6** actual, indeed, really
my ~: **4** gosh **6** dear me **7** heavens
__ goodness: **5** thank
Good News (1947 film)
cast: June Allyson, Peter Lawford
director: Charles Walters
Goodnight __: **5** Irene **6** Ladies **7** Tonight
Good night, __: **4** Chet **5** David
Goodnight (1965 song) artist: Roy Orbison
Goodnight girl: **5** Irene
Goodnight Tonight (1979 song) artist: Paul McCartney
good-o: **3** aye, oui, yea, yep, yup **4** fine, okay, sure, yeah **5** natch, quite, right, roger, uh-huh **6** agreed, gladly, indeed, just so, rather, righto, surely, you bet, yowzah **7** exactly, go ahead, indeedy, mais oui, quite so, ten-four **8** all right, as you say, of course, thumbs up, very well **9** be my guest, certainly, darn right, naturally, precisely, sure thing, you betcha, you said it **10** absolutely, by all means, definitely, positively, sure enough, that's right
good ol' __: **3** boy
Good Queen __: **4** Bess
Goodrich: **2** B.F. **4** Gail **7** Frances
Goodrich, Gail
milieu: **5** court
org.: **3** NBA
sport: **10** basketball
goods: **4** gear, line, load, loot, mdse, ware **5** booty, cargo, order, proof, skill, stock, stuff, wares **6** assets, estate, lading, spoils, tackle, things, wealth **7** effects, freight, imports, produce, product **8** chattels, material, property **9** knowledge, materials, resources, trappings, vendibles, wagonload **10** belongings, right stuff
custodian of ~: **6** bailee
deliver the ~: **7** perform
delivery of ~: **7** receipt
get the ~ on: **3** pin **4** nail, trap
move ~: **4** hawk, push, sell, vend **5** pitch, trade **6** barter, handle, hustle, market, peddle, retail, unload **7** auction, promote, traffic **9** wholesale
sell a bill of ~: **2** do **3** con, rob **4** bilk, burn, clip, dupe, fool, gull, have, hoax, nick, rook, scam, take, trim **5** cheat, cozen, fraud, gouge, mulct, pluck, set up, shaft, stiff, sting, trick **6** diddle, extort, fleece, hustle, outwit, rip off, sucker **7** deceive, defraud, finagle, sandbag, swindle **8** flimflam, hoodwink, outsmart **9** bamboozle, four-flush, shake down, victimize **10** run a game on
stolen ~: **4** loot, swag **5** booty **6** spoils **7** plunder
stolen ~ outlet: **5** fence
the ~: **4** dope, info, news, word **7** lowdown
thrown overboard: **5** lagan, ligan
transfer illegal ~: **4** push **7** bootleg, smuggle
yard ~: **5** cloth, stuff **6** fabric **8** material, textiles
goods __: **4** yard **5** train, wagon **6** engine
__ goods: **3** dry **4** case, free, gray, grey, hard, soft, wash, yard **5** brown, dress, piece, white **7** capital, durable
Good Seasons: **8** dressing
alternative: **8** Wish-Bone **9** Seven Seas
__ Good Ship Lollipop: **5** On the
good-sized: **3** lge. **4** tidy **5** ample, large
Goodson: **4** Mark
good-tasting: **5** tasty, yummy **6** savory **8** luscious, tempting **9** ambrosial, delicious, flavorful, palatable, succulent, toothsome **10** appetizing, delectable
good-tempered: **4** calm, easy, kind, mild, warm **5** sunny, sweet **6** breezy, genial, gentle, mellow, placid, serene **7** affable, amiable, equable, lenient, patient, relaxed **8** amenable, carefree, obliging, outgoing, peaceful, pleasant, tolerant, tranquil **9** easygoing, forgiving, indulgent, peaceable **10** forbearing, unexacting
Good, the Bad, and the Ugly, The: **4** film, song **5** oater **7** western
artist: Hugo Montenegro
cast: Clint Eastwood, Lee Van Cleef, Eli Wallach
director: Sergio Leone
Good Thing (song) artist: Fine Young Cannibals, Paul Revere and the Raiders
__ good time: **5** all in
good-time Charlie: **5** sport
Good Time Charlie's Got the Blues (1972 song) artist: Danny O'Keefe
Good Times (CBS sitcom)
cast: John Amos (James Evans)
Esther Rolle (Florida Evans)
Jimmie Walker (J.J. Evans)
catchword: Dynomite
setting: Chicago, Illinois
Good Times (1979 song) artist: Chic
__ good to be true: **3** too
__ good turn: **3** do a
Good Vibrations (song) artist: Beach Boys, Marky Mark and the Funky Bunch
good victory, name meaning: **6** Eunice
good walk spoiled, A: **4** golf
goodwill: **5** amity, favor **6** comity **7** charity, concord, rapport **8** altruism **9** sincerity, tolerance **10** cordiality, friendship, generosity
...good will __: **5** to men
Goodwill Games venue: **5** track
Good Will Hunting (1997 film)
cast: Ben Affleck, Matt Damon, Minnie Driver, Robin Williams
director: Gus Van Sant
setting: **3** MIT
Goodwin: **3** Kia
...good witch __ bad witch?: **3** or a
Good work!: **4** nice **5** bravo
goody: **4** gift **5** bonus, candy, cooky, snack, treat **6** cookie, tidbit
often: **4** oldy **5** oldie
two-shoes: **4** prig **5** prude **7** puritan **9** nice Nelly
Goody!: **3** yay, yea, yum **5** oh boy
Goodyear: **4** city, town **7** Charles
craft: **5** blimp
home: **5** Akron
locale: **7** Arizona
goody-goody: **4** prig, prim **5** moral, pious, prude **6** prissy **7** prudish, puritan **8** priggish, virtuous **9** nice Nelly
Goody Goody (1957 song) artist: Frankie Lymon and the Teenagers
goody-two-shoes: **4** prim **5** sissy **6** demure, proper, stuffy **7** prudish **8** overnice, precious **9** sissified, squeamish, Victorian **10** fastidious, tight-laced
Goody Two Shoes singer: **3** Ant
gooey: **4** icky, oozy **5** gummy, slimy, tacky, thick **6** creamy, sticky, viscid **7** maudlin, mawkish, viscose, viscous **8** adhesive
stuff: **4** glob, glop, ooze **5** slime
goof: **3** err **4** flub, slip, type **5** boner, botch, error, gaffe, lapse, mix up, snafu, wrong **6** blow it, boo-boo, bungle, foozle, foul up, fumble, mess up, slip up **7** blunder, clinker, erratum, jackass, louse up, mistake, screw up **9** indecorum, mishandle, mismanage
data-entry ~: **4** typo
ender: **4** ball **5** proof
off: **3** veg **4** idle, laze, loll **5** coast, dog it, relax, shirk, slack, tarry **6** dawdle, linger, lounge, putter **7** hang out, slacken **8** lallygag, lollygag, malinger **9** bum around **10** featherbed, fool around, mess around
off, in Britain: **5** sculk, skulk
up: **4** flub **5** botch **6** blow it, boggle, bungle, foozle, mess up **7** blunder **9** mishandle, mismanage
goof-__: **3** off

__ go of: 5 make a
goofball: 4 bozo, nerd, nurd 5 dufus 6 doofus 7 bungler, jackass
go off __-cocked: 4 half
goofiness: 3 rot 4 bosh, bull, guff, jazz, jive 5 folly, hokum, hooey, tripe 6 bunkum, bushwa, drivel, humbug 7 baloney, bushwah, eyewash, fustian, hogwash, inanity, rubbish, twaddle 8 claptrap, nonsense, tommyrot 9 absurdity, banana oil, moonshine, poppycock, rigmarole, silliness 10 applesauce, balderdash, bilge water, mumbo jumbo, rigamarole, taradiddle, tomfoolery
goof-off: 5 idler 6 loafer 7 slacker 8 loiterer 9 do-nothing, goldbrick, lazybones 10 ne'er-do-well
goofproof: 4 safe, sure 8 fail-safe, reliable 10 dependable
goofs: 6 errata
goof-up: 5 lapse 7 mistake
goofy: 4 loco, zany 5 daffy, dippy, ditzy, dotty, flaky, goosy, inane, kooky, nutty, silly, wacky 6 absurd, flakey, kookie, screwy, whacky 7 comical, foolish 10 ridiculous, weak-minded
__ goo gai pan: 3 moo
Google: 6 Barney 7 Web site
 specialty: 6 search
googly-__: 4 eyed
googol, suffix for: 4 plex
goo-goo: 8 baby talk
 make ~ eyes at: 4 ogle 5 flirt 8 check out
Goo Goo Dolls
 song: Iris (1998)
  Name (1995)
  Slide (1998)
Goolagong, Evonne: 7 netster 9 tennis pro
 milieu: 5 court
goon: 3 ape 4 boor, hood, thug 5 rowdy, tough 6 galoot, gunsel, lummox 7 bruiser, galloot, gorilla, hoodlum, ruffian 8 gangster, hooligan, tough guy 9 roughneck
goon __: 5 squad
go on __: 5 a diet, a tear 6 record
Go on...: 3 and
go one __: 6 better
gooney: 4 bird 5 silly 9 albatross
Goonies 'R' Good Enough, The (1985 song) artist: Cyndi Lauper
Go On With the Wedding (1956 song)
 artist: Patti Page
goony: 3 mad 4 bird, gaga 5 sappy, silly, wacky 6 absurd, madcap 7 foolish 9 half-baked, ludicrous, senseless 10 ridiculous
goop: 3 gel, tar 4 gunk 6 liquid
goopy: 5 yucky 7 viscose, viscous
goosander: 4 duck, fowl
 relative: 4 smew, teal 5 eider, Pekin, Rouen, scaup 6 Cayuga, scoter 7 gadwall, mallard, pintail, pochard, redhead, sea duck, widgeon 8 garganey, gray duck, mandarin, musk duck, oldsquaw, shoveler, surf duck, wood duck 9 black duck, broadbill, goldeneye, greenhead, merganser, ruddy duck, sprigtail 10 bufflehead, canvasback, surf scoter, tufted duck
goose: 4 bird, dolt, fowl, lift, meat, nene, poke, prod, push, spur 5 biped, brant, ninny, pique, raise, silly 6 dimwit, Embden, honker, outwit 7 graylag, greylag, jackass, pinhead 8 motivate, outsmart 9 harebrain, simpleton 10 nincompoop
 arctic ~: 5 brant
 cousin: 4 swan
 down garment: 4 vest
 egg: 3 nil, zip 4 nada, none, null, zero 5 zilch, zippo 6 cipher, naught, nought 7 nothing
 eggs: 3 OOO 4 OOOO 5 OOOOO
 ender: 4 fish, foot, neck 5 berry
 formation: 3 vee
 genus: 5 anser
 group: 5 flock 6 gaggle
 have ~ bumps: 6 shiver, thrill
 Hawaiian ~: 4 nene
 male: 6 gander
 sea ~: 5 solan 6 gannet
 snow ~ genus: 4 chen
 something for the ~: 5 sauce
 sound: 4 honk, yang 6 cackle
 young: 7 gosling
goose __: 3 egg 4 skin, step 5 bumps, flesh, grass 6 grease 7 pimples
__ goose: 4 blue, pied, snow, wild 5 brant, brent, solan 6 Canada, golden, magpie
Goose: 5 Tatum 6 Goslin 7 Gossage
Goose __: 3 Bay
__ Goose: 6 Father, Mother, Spruce
Goose and Tomtom author: David Rabe
gooseberry: 5 fruit, shrub
 Chinese ~: 4 kiwi
 Hawaiian ~: 4 poha
 wild ~: 8 dogberry
gooseberry __: 5 gourd 6 garnet
__ gooseberry: 3 sea 4 cape 6 Ceylon 7 Chinese, English
gooseberry fool: 7 dessert
goose bumps
 have ~: 6 tingle
 raising ~: 4 eery 5 eerie, scary, weird 6 creepy, occult, spooky 7 ghostly, macabre, uncanny 9 unearthly 10 mysterious
Goosebumps
 author: R.L. Stine
 like ~: 4 eery 5 eerie
__-goose chase: 4 wild
Goose Creek: 4 city, town
 locale: 4 S. Car.
goosefoot plant: 5 orach 6 orache
gooseneck __: 4 lamp
goosenecker: 9 spectator
__-goosey: 6 loosey
Goossens, Eugene: 9 conductor
goosy: 4 daft 5 balmy, daffy, dotty, goofy, inane, kooky, nutty, sappy, silly, wacky 6 simple 7 asinine, foolish, witless 9 brainless, half-baked, senseless 10 half-witted
go out of __: 5 style
go out of one's __: 3 way
go out the __: 6 window
go out with __: 5 a bang
GOP: 5 party 10 Republican
 birthplace: 5 Ripon
 elephant creator: 4 Nast
 member: 3 Rep.
 opponent: 3 Dem.
 org.: 3 RNC
 part of ~: 3 Old 5 Grand, Party
gopak: 5 dance
gopher: 6 animal, mammal, rodent
 gig: 6 errand
 relative: 3 rat 4 cavy, degu, jird, paca, vole 5 coypu, gundi, mouse, xerus 6 agouti, beaver, gerbil, jerboa, marmot, murine 7 hamster, lemming, muskrat, visacha 8 chipmunk, cricetid, dormouse, squirrel, tuco-tuco 9 chickaree, groundhog, guinea pig, porcupine, woodchuck 10 chinchilla, prairie dog
gopher __: 4 ball, wood 5 plant, snake 6 turtle
__ gopher: 6 pocket 7 striped
__ Gophers: 6 Golden
Gopher State: 4 Minn. 9 Minnesota
gor: 4 oath
goral: 8 antelope
 relative: 3 gnu, kob 4 guib, kudu, oryx, puku, topi 5 addax, bongo, chiru, eland, korin, nyala, oribi, saiga, serow 6 chammy, dik-dik, duiker, impala, koodoo, lechwe, nilgai, rhebok, shammy, shamoy 7 blaubok, blesbok, chamois, defassa, gazelle, gemsbok, gerenuk, grysbok, nylghai, nylghau, sassaby 8 blesbuck, bontebok, bushbuck, gemsbuck, reedbuck, steenbok, steinbok 9 blackbuck, pronghorn, sitatunga, springbok, waterbuck 10 hartebeest, wildebeest
Gorbachev: 5 Raisa 7 Mikhail 8 Nobelist
 realm: 4 USSR
 see also Russian
Gorcey: 3 Leo 7 Bernard
Gordian knot: 5 poser
 undoer's reward: 4 Asia
Gordie: 4 Howe
Gordimer, Nadine: 6 writer 8 Nobelist 12 South African
Gordius
 problem for ~: 4 knot
 son of ~: 5 Midas
__ Gordo: 5 Cerro
Gordon: 4 Gale, Jump, Ruth 5 Barry, Flash, Gekko, Keith, Parks, Scott 6 Dexter, MacRae, Stuart 7 Douglas, Jenkins, Michael 9 Lightfoot
Gordon __: 6 setter
Gordon, Dexter: 11 saxophonist
 genre: 4 jazz
Gordon, Flash: 4 hero
 alma mater: 4 Yale
 milieu: 5 space
 partner: 4 Dale
__ Gordon, GA: 4 Fort
Gordon, Gale: 5 actor
 film: Speedway (1968)
 TV: Here's Lucy, Our Miss Brooks, The Lucy Show
Gordon, Ruth: 7 actress
 film: Abe Lincoln in Illinois (1940)
  Dr. Ehrlich's Magic Bullet (1940)
  Harold and Maude (1972)
  Maxie (1985)
  Rosemary's Baby (1968, AA)
  Whatever Happened to Aunt Alice? (1969)
 spouse: Garson Kanin
Gordy: 5 Berry
gore: 4 stab 5 panel, stick 6 empale, gusset, impale, pierce 9 penetrate
Gore: 2 Al 5 Vidal 6 Lesley, Tipper 7 Michael
 interest: 4 ecol. 7 ecology
Gore, Lesley
 song: It's My Party (1963)
  Judy's Turn to Cry (1963)
  She's a Fool (1963)
  You Don't Own Me (1964)
Goren, Charles forte: 6 bridge
Gore-Tex: 6 fabric 8 material
Gorey: 6 Edward
gorge: 3 eat, gap 4 bolt, cloy, fill, glen, glut, gulf, gulp, hole, pass, rift, sate, wolf 5 abyss, binge, cañon, chasm, cleft, dig in, gulch, stuff 6 arroyo, canyon, devour, fill up, gobble, guzzle, hollow, pig out, ravine, valley 7 consume, fissure, Olduvai, overeat, satiate, satisfy, surfeit 8 crevasse 10 gluttonize, gormandize
gorged: 3 fed 4 full 7 replete
Gorge of the __: 3 Aar 4 Aare
gorgeous: 4 cute, fair, rich 5 bonny, plush, showy 6 bonnie, comely, lavish, lovely, pretty 7 elegant, sublime, winsome 8 adorable, alluring, dazzling, fetching, glorious, handsome, imposing, pleasing, splendid, striking, stunning 9 beautiful, exquisite, luxurious, ravishing, sumptuous 10 attractive
 one: 4 hunk 6 Adonis, Apollo 8 knockout
Gorgeous __: 6 George
gorgeousness: 6 dazzle 7 glitter 8 splendor
gorger: 7 glutton
gorget: 6 wimple
gorging: 7 hoggish 9 voracious 10 gluttonous
Gorgon: 3 hag 6 Medusa
 mother: 4 Ceto
Gorgonzola: 6 cheese
gorilla: 3 ape 4 goon, thug 5 biped 6 animal 7 primate
 like a ~: 5 apish, hairy
 relative: 4 saki, titi 5 chimp, drill, jocko, lemur, loris, magot, orang, potto, shrew 6 aye-aye, baboon, Bandar, galago, gelada, gibbon, grivet, guenon, howler, langur, macaco, monkey, rhesus, uakari, vervet 7 colobus, guereza, hoolock, macaque, sapajou, siamang, tamarin, tarsier 8 bush baby, capuchin, mandrill, mangabey, marmoset, talapoin 9 orangutan 10 Barbary ape, chimpanzee, orangutang
 small ~: 6 apelet
__ gorilla: 7 lowland
Gorilla at Large (1954 film)
 cast: Anne Bancroft, Lee J. Cobb, Cameron Mitchell
Gorillas in the Mist (1988 film)
 cast: Bryan Brown, Julie Harris, Sigourney Weaver
 director: Michael Apted
__ Goriot: 4 Père
Gorki: 4 city, town 5 Maxim 6 Maksim
 locale: 6 Russia
 river: 3 Oka 5 Volga
Gorky: 5 Maxim 6 Maksim 7 Arshile, Russian
Gorky Park (1983 film)
 cast: Brian Dennehy, William Hurt, Lee Marvin
 director: Michael Apted
Gorman: 5 Cliff
gormandize: 3 eat 4 cloy, glut, sate 5 binge, gorge, stuff 6 devour, gobble 7 overeat, satiate, surfeit 10 gluttonize
gormandizer: 5 eater 7 glutton, gobbler
Gorme, Eydie
 song: Blame It on the Bossa Nova (1963)
 spouse: Steve Lawrence
__-go-round: 5 merry
gorp: 5 snack 8 trail mix
 eater: 5 hiker
gorse: 4 whin 5 brush, furze, shrub 7 bramble
 like a ~: 5 spiny 7 prickly
 locale: 4 moor
Gorshin: 5 Frank
Gortner: 6 Marjoe
gory: 3 raw, red 5 lurid 6 bloody, grisly 7 ghastly, graphic, macabre, violent 8 gruesome 9 frightful 10 horrifying
Gosden, Freeman role: 4 Amos
Gosdin: 4 Vern
Gosford Park (2001 film)
 cast: Bob Balaban, Alan Bates, Kristin Scott Thomas
 director: Robert Altman
gosh: 3 gee, wow 4 oath, oh my 5 golly 6 jiminy 7 heavens, jeepers, jimminy 10 my goodness
 preceder: 3 omi

goshawk: 4 bird
Goshen: 4 city, town
  locale: 7 Indiana
___ Goshen!: 5 Land o'
gosling: 4 bird
  parent: 5 goose 6 gander
Goslin, Goose: 10 outfielder
gospel: 4 fact 5 dogma, genre, music, truth 6 truism, verity 8 doctrine 9 actuality
  take as ~: 3 buy 6 accept, credit, rely on 7 believe, swallow, swear by
gospel ___: 4 side 5 music, truth
Gospel: 4 John, Luke, Mark 5 truth 7 Matthew, the Word
Gospels follower: 4 Acts
Gossage, Goose: 6 hurler 7 pitcher
gossamer: 3 web 4 airy, fine, lacy, thin 5 filmy, gauze, gauzy, light, sheer, wispy 6 flimsy, flossy 7 netlike, tenuous, weblike 8 delicate, ethereal, feathery, filament, finespun 9 lightsome 10 cobweblike, diaphanous
Gossett: 3 Lou 5 Louis
Gossett Jr., Louis Oscar: An Officer and a Gentleman
gossip: 3 gab, jaw, mud, wag, yak, yap 4 blab, buzz, chat, chin, dirt, dish, dope, info, poop, talk, word 5 juice, prate, rumor, snoop, story, yenta 6 babble, earful, gabble, gibber, latest, ramble, report, rumors, tattle, yakker 7 babbler, blather, blether, chatter, hearsay, meddler, palaver, prattle, scandal, schmoos, tattler, whisper 8 busybody, chitchat, dish dirt, fat mouth, idle talk, prattler, quidnunc, schmoose, schmooze 9 loose talk, small talk, table talk 10 backbiting, chatterbox, chew the rag, dirty linen, noise about, taleteller, tattletale
  column subject: 4 item, star 5 actor, celeb 7 actress, notable 8 luminary 9 celebrity, headliner, personage
  ender: 6 monger
  like a ~ 's tongue: 4 awag
  like some ~: 4 idle
  spread ~: 3 gab, yak 5 bandy
  tidbit: 4 item, tale 5 on dit, rumor
Gossip From the Forest author: Thomas Keneally
gossiping: 5 prate 9 garrulous 10 scandalous
gossipmonger: 5 yenta 7 meddler 8 busybody, quidnunc
gossipy: 5 abuzz, juicy, newsy 6 blabby, chatty 9 talkative 10 bigmouthed, loquacious
Gosta Berlings Saga author: Selma Lagerlöf
Got ___ O' Livin' To Do: 4 a Lot
Got ___ There: 4 to Be
Got ___ With an Angel: 5 a Date
Göta: 5 canal, river
  locale: 6 Sweden
___ Got a Brand New Bag: 5 Papa's
___ Got a Crush on You: 3 I've
Got a Date With an ___: 5 Angel
___ Got a Friend: 5 You've
___ Got a Gal in Kalamazoo: 3 I've
Got a Hold of Me (1984 song) artist: Christine McVie
Gotama ___: 6 Buddha
___ Got a Name: 3 I've
___ Got a Secret: 3 I've
___ Got a Way: 4 She's
gotcha: 3 aha, hah, oho 4 I see, trap 7 mistake
Go, team!: 3 rah, yay, yea
Göteborg: 4 city, port, town
  locale: 6 Sweden
Go Tell ___ Rhody: 4 Aunt
Go Tell ___ the Mountain: 4 It on
Go Tell It on the Mountain author: James Baldwin
Go Tell the Spartans (1978 film)
  cast: Burt Lancaster, Craig Wasson
  director: Ted Post
___ Got Five Dollars: 3 I've
Goth: 9 barbarian
  foe: 5 Roman
  kin: 3 Hun
  target: 4 Rome
Gotha: 4 city, town
  locale: 7 Germany
Gotham
  see New York City
Gotham City (1997 song) artist: R. Kelly
Gothamite: 4 NYer 9 New Yorker
gothic: 5 crude 8 barbaric 9 barbarous
Gothic: 4 font 5 style 6 quaint 8 medieval, typeface 9 mediaeval
  architectural feature: 5 gable, ogive 6 flèche 8 gargoyle
Gothic ___: 4 arch 5 armor, novel
go through the ___: 4 roof 7 motions
___ got it!: 3 I've
Got it!: 4 I dig, I see
Got it?: 3 See
Gotland: 3 isl. 4 isle 6 island
  locale: 6 Baltic, Sweden
___ Got Mail: 5 You've
Got me!: 6 I dunno
Got My Mind Set on You (1987 song) artist: George Harrison
___ Got Noboby: 5 I Ain't
go to ___: 3 pot 4 seed, town 5 press, waste 6 pieces
go to ___ for: 3 bat
go-to-___: 7 meeting
go to one's ___: 4 head
go to the ___: 3 mat 4 dogs, wall
___ Got Sixpence: 3 I've
___ Gotta Be Me: 3 I've
___ Gotta Crow: 3 I've
___ gotta do what...: 5 A man's
___ Gotta Have It: 4 She's
___-gotten gains: 3 ill
Götterdämmerung: 5 opera
  composer: 6 Wagner
  role: 4 Norn 5 Hagen 7 Gunther, Gutrune 8 Alberich 9 Siegfried, Waltraute 10 Brünnhilde
  setting: 5 Rhine 7 Germany
Gottfried: 4 Benn 5 Brian 6 Keller 7 Gilbert
  in English: 7 Godfrey
  in Lohengrin: 4 swan
  sister: 4 Elsa
___ Got the Sun in the Morning: 3 I've
___ Got the Whole World...: 3 He's
___ Got the World on a String: 3 I've
Gottlieb: 4 Mark 7 Daimler
Got to Be There (1971 song) artist: Michael Jackson
Got to Get You Into My Life (song) artist: Beatles, Earth, Wind & Fire
Got to Give It Up (1977 song) artist: Marvin Gaye
___ Got Tonight: 4 We've
___ Got You Under My Skin: 3 I've
gouache: 3 art 5 paint 7 picture
Gouda: 4 city, town 6 cheese
  kin: 4 Edam
  locale: 7 Holland 11 Netherlands
Goudy: 4 font 8 typeface
gouge: 3 cut, dig, pit, rut 4 bilk, bore, gash, hole, nick, rook 5 cheat, notch, scoop, score 6 burrow, chisel, dredge, extort, fleece, furrow, groove, shovel, trench, tunnel 7 channel, defraud, swindle 8 excavate 9 victimize 10 excavation, overcharge, run a game on
  out: 4 bore, rout 8 excavate
___ gouge: 6 firmer, paring
gouging, interest: 5 usury
goulash: 3 mix 4 stew 6 jumble 7 mélange, mixture 8 mishmash 9 casserole, potpourri 10 hodgepodge
Gould: 3 Jay 5 Glenn, Shane 6 Harold, Morton 7 Chester, Elliott
Gould, Chester character: 4 Dick, Tess 5 Tracy 9 Trueheart
___ Gould Cozzens: 5 James
Gould, Elliott: 5 actor
  film: Bob & Carol & Ted & Alice (1969)
    Bugsy (1991)
    Capricorn One (1978)
    Little Murders (1971)
    MASH (1970)
    The Silent Partner (1978)
  spouse: Barbra Streisand
Gould, Glenn: 7 pianist 8 Canadian, musician
Goulding: 3 Ray 6 Edmund
Goulding, Edmund: 8 director
  film: Claudia (1943)
    The Constant Nymph (1943)
    Dark Victory (1939)
    The Dawn Patrol (1938)
    Everybody Does It (1949)
    Forever and a Day (1943)
    Grand Hotel (1932)
    The Great Lie (1941)
    Mister 880 (1950)
    Nightmare Alley (1947)
    The Old Maid (1939)
    The Razor's Edge (1946)
    Riptide (1934)
    We're Not Married (1952)
Gould, Jay railroad: 4 Erie
Gould, Shane: 7 swimmer
Goulet, Robert spouse: Carol Lawrence
go under the ___: 6 hammer
Gounod: 7 Charles
  contemporary: 4 Lalo 5 Bizet
  opera: 5 Faust
Goupil, Rene: 5 saint
go up in ___: 5 smoke 6 flames
gourami: 3 pet 4 fish 6 anabas
___ gourami: 7 kissing
gourd: 4 pepo 5 melon 6 ipu ipu, noggin, veggie 7 shekere 8 calabash 9 vegetable
  kin: 6 squash 7 pumpkin
  musical instrument: 5 guiro
  sponge ~: 5 loofa, luffa 6 loofah
___ gourd: 3 rag, wax 4 sour 5 white 6 bitter, bottle, teasel
gourde: 5 money
gourmand: 5 diner, eater 7 epicure, glutton 10 gastronome
gourmandism: 7 cookery, cuisine 8 gluttony 10 gastronomy
gourmandize: 3 eat 4 dine 5 feast
gourmet: 6 foodie 7 epicure 9 bon vivant 10 gastronome
  treat: 6 luxury 8 ambrosia, delicacy
govern: 3 run 4 curb, head, lead, rule, sway, tame 5 pilot, reign, steer 6 direct, handle, head up, manage, subdue 7 command, conduct, contain, control, dictate, oversee, preside 8 dominate, hold sway, regulate, restrain, rule over 9 determine, officiate, reign over, supervise 10 administer, predispose
governable: 8 obedient 9 compliant, malleable, tractable 10 manageable, submissive
governed: 5 ruled, under 7 subject 9 subject to 10 answerable, controlled
  be ~ by: 4 obey
governess: 4 amah, ayah, nana 5 nanny, nurse 6 duenna, nannie 8 tutoress 9 nursemaid
  fictional ~: 4 Anna, Eyre 7 Poppins
  like ~ novels: 6 Gothic
governing: 4 main 5 major, prime 7 leading, primary 9 executive, number one, paramount, principal 10 preeminent
  body: 5 board, panel 7 council 8 trustees 9 directors 10 commission, executives, management
___-governing: 4 self 7 nonself
government: 4 rule 5 power, state, taxer, union 6 regime 7 command, control 8 dominion, politics, Uncle Sam 9 authority, direction, dominance, executive, restraint, supremacy 10 domination, management, presidency, regulation, statecraft, Washington
  agent: 4 G-man, narc, nark, T-man
  bite: 3 tax
  combining form: 5 -archy, -cracy
  head: 2 p.m. 4 pres. 9 president
  local ~ unit: 2 tp. 3 twp. 8 township
  of ~: 5 polit. 9 political
  official: 5 envoy 6 consul, legate 8 delegate, diplomat, emissary, minister 10 ambassador
  official in India: 5 dewan, diwan
  provisional ~: 5 junta
  rules of ~: 3 law 10 due process
  rules, to some: 4 maze 6 jungle, morass 7 red tape 9 labyrinth
  seat of ~: 7 capital
  security: 5 E bond, T-bill, T-bond, T-note
  veteran: 3 pol
  see also govt.
government-in-___: 5 exile
governor: 4 boss, head 5 chief, ruler 6 gerent, leader, master, top dog, warden 7 manager 8 director, official 9 executive, organizer 10 supervisor
  Algerian ~: 3 dey
governor ___: 7 general
Governors ___: 6 Island
govt.
  agcy.: 3 ATF, BEP, BLS, CDC, CIA, DEA, DOD, DOT, EPA, FAA, FBI, FCC, FDA, FEC, FTC, GAO, GPO, GSA, HHS, HUD, INS, IRS, NEA, NIH, NPS, NRC, NSA, NSC, NSF, NWS, SBA, SEC, SSA, SSS 4 CPSC, EEOC, FDIC, FEMA, NASA, NLRB, NOAA, NTSB, OSHA, USCG, USDA, USIA, USPS 6 Amtrak
  agency: 3 bur. 4 dept.
  agt.: 3 Fed
  assistance fund: 3 SSI
  bank underwriter: 4 FDIC
  document: 3 lic.
  employee: 3 agt.
  '40s ~ agcy.: 3 OPA
  flight regulator: 3 FAA
  investigation grp.: 3 ATF
  investigator: 4 G-man, T-man
  lender: 3 FHA 4 FNMA, GNMA
  local ~ unit: 3 twp.
  meteorology agcy.: 3 NWS
  news source: 4 USIA
  -owned: 4 natl.
  purchasing org.: 3 GSA
  representative: 3 amb.
  research sponsor: 3 NSF
  seed-money agency: 3 SBA
  shortwave service: 3 VOA
  spending watchdog: 3 GAO, OMB
  training program: 4 CETA
  undercover group: 3 NSA
Gowdy: 4 Curt
Gower: 4 John 8 Champion
  wife: 5 Marge
Gower, John: 4 poet 7 British
Go West (1940 film)
  cast: Chico Marx, Groucho Marx, Harpo Marx

Go West, Young Man (1936 film)
cast: Randolph Scott, Mae West, Warren William
director: Henry Hathaway
go whole __: 3 hog
go without __: 6 saying
go-with-the-flow: 6 pliant 7 pliable 8 flexible, moldable 9 adaptable, malleable, tractable
gowk: 3 sap 4 clod, dolt, dope, fool 5 cluck, dummy, dunce, klutz, ninny 6 dimwit, lummox, nitwit 7 dullard, half-wit 8 dumbbell, lunkhead 9 blockhead, simpleton 10 dunderhead, nincompoop
gown: 4 garb, robe 5 dress, frock, habit, tunic 6 formal, kimono, kirtle 7 costume, garment
fabric: 4 lamé, silk 5 satin, tulle
like some ~ s: 6 beaded, dressy
occasion: 4 prom
part: 5 train
renter: 3 snr. 6 senior
Roman ~: 5 stola
starter: 5 night
__ gown: 3 tea 6 bridal, Geneva 7 evening, hostess 8 dressing, hospital
Goya, Francisco: 6 artist, etcher 7 painter, Spanish
locale: 5 Prado
Go Your Own Way (1977 song) artist: Fleetwood Mac
Gozzi, Carlo: 7 Italian 10 playwright
gp.: 3 org. 4 assn.
GP: 2 dr., MD 3 doc 6 doctor 9 physician
exam for future ~ s: 4 MCAT
expertise: 4 anat.
horse ~: 3 DVM
org.: 3 AMA
reference: 3 PDR
GPA part: 3 avg. 5 grade, point 7 average
GPO
concern: 3 ltr. 4 mail
part: 6 Office 8 Printing 10 Government
GQ: 3 mag 8 magagine
Gr.
see Greece
grab: 3 get, nab 4 fist, glom, grip, hook, land, nail, snag, snap, take, tear, trap 5 catch, clasp, grasp, pluck, seize, usurp 6 arrest, clinch, clutch, collar, corral, engage, jump at, kidnap, obtain, please, regale, snap up, snatch, tackle 7 acquire, capture, ensnare, enthral, grapple, impress, insnare, inthral, latch on, possess, procure, receive, seizure 8 enthrall, glom on to, interest, inthrall, intrigue, take over 9 apprehend, extradite, get hold of, latch onto, lay hold of, stimulate, titillate 10 confiscate, lay hands on, usurpation
a bite: 3 eat 4 nosh 5 lunch, snack 6 gobble, nibble 7 munch on, put away, scarf up 8 chow down, wolf down 9 have a meal, scarf down
a chair: 3 sit 4 park 5 perch 8 plop down
a plane: 6 hijack 8 highjack
away: 3 nab 4 snag 6 abduct, kidnap, snatch 7 capture
bag: 3 mix 7 mixture 9 patchwork
smash and ~: 4 loot 5 rifle 7 plunder
some z's: 4 doze 5 sleep 6 catnap, drowse, nod off, snooze 7 drop off, slumber
the check: 3 buy 5 treat 6 pay for, pick up
grab __: 3 bag, bar 4 line, rope
grab __ to eat: 5 a bite
Grabbe, Christian: 6 German 10 playwright
grabber: 5 cleat, proof, talon 6 pliers 7 mystery
Grabber: 3 car 4 auto, Ford 10 automobile
grabbiness: 5 greed 7 avarice 8 cupidity, rapacity
grabby: 6 greedy 7 selfish 9 mercenary 10 avaricious
Grable, Betty: 5 pinup 7 actress
film: Coney Island (1943)
Down Argentine Way (1940)
Footlight Serenade (1942)
How to Marry a Millionaire (1953)
I Wake Up Screaming (1941)
Moon Over Miami (1941)
Mother Wore Tights (1947)
The Nitwits (1935)
Song of the Islands (1942)
Springtime in the Rockies (1942)
Tin Pan Alley (1940)
Wabash Avenue (1950)
A Yank in the RAF (1941)
spouse: Jackie Coogan, Harry James
grabs, up for: 4 iffy, open 6 chancy, unsure 7 anyone's, to be had 9 ambiguous, available, uncertain, unsettled 10 accessible, indefinite, obtainable, unoccupied, unresolved
grab the __ by the horns: 4 bull
grace: 4 deck 5 adorn, balon, charm, favor, honor, mercy, poise, style 6 allure, ballon, beauty, bedeck, pardon, polish, prayer, set off 7 culture, dignify, elevate, enhance, fluency, garnish, glorify, quarter, smile on 8 beautify, blessing, breeding, clemency, decorate, elegance, kindness, lenience, leniency, ornament, reprieve, urbanity 9 embellish, lightness, smile upon, tolerance 10 invocation, loveliness, refinement, suppleness
coup de ~: 4 blow 5 ender 9 final blow
embodiment of ~: 4 swan
fall from ~: 3 err, sin 5 lapse, stray 7 do wrong, offense 8 iniquity 9 backslide 10 transgress
follower: 5 dig in
lack of ~: 9 gaucherie
name meaning ~: 3 Ann 4 Anna, Anne 6 Hannah
say ~: 4 pray 6 invoke
starter: 3 dis 5 scape
under pressure: 4 cool, tact 5 poise 6 aplomb 7 dignity 8 presence 9 assurance, composure, diplomacy, sang-froid 10 confidence, equanimity
with good ~: 6 freely, gladly, warmly 7 happily, readily 8 cheerily, heartily 9 willingly 10 cheerfully
word: 4 amen 5 bless
grace __: 3 cup 4 note 6 period
__ grace: 6 saving
Grace: 4 Mark 5 Jones, Kelly, Moore, Paley, Slick 6 Aglaia, Bumbry, Thalia 7 Van Owen 8 Coolidge 9 Metalious, Mirabella 10 Euphrosyne
ender: 4 land
__ & Grace: 4 Dale, Will
Grace Abounding author: John Bunyan
graceful: 4 airy, deft, neat, nice, trim 5 agile, clean, light, lithe, slick 6 adroit, au fait, dainty, expert, fluent, gainly, limber, lissom, lovely, nimble, poised, pretty, smooth, supple, svelte 7 capable, elegant, flowing, lissome, refined, shapely, skilled, tactful, trained, willowy 8 artistic, delicate, dextrous, esthetic, masterly, seasoned, skillful, tasteful 9 aesthetic, competent, dexterous, efficient, lightsome, lithesome, masterful 10 artistical, proficient, statuesque
combining form: 5 habro-
one: 4 peri, swan 5 sylph 6 impala
Graceland: 6 estate
locale: 4 Tenn. 7 Memphis 9 Tennessee
name: 4 Aron 5 Elvis
graceless: 4 rude 5 crude, gawky, inept, rough, stiff, unapt 6 clumsy, clunky, coarse, gauche, klutzy, oafish 7 awkward, boorish, corrupt, gawkish, loutish, unadept, uncouth 8 barbaric, bumbling, bungling, improper, ungainly, unpoised 9 all thumbs, barbarian, barbarous, inelegant, lumbering, maladroit, ponderous, shameless, stumbling, tasteless, unskilled 10 indecorous, outlandish, uncultured, unmannered, unskillful
one: 2 ox 3 lug, oaf 4 boor, clod, lout 5 klutz 6 lummox 7 bumbler, bungler, fumbler, palooka 8 meathead 10 stumblebum
Grace, Mark sport: 8 baseball
...grace of God __: 3 go I
graces
social ~: 7 manners 9 propriety
Grace Under Fire (ABC sitcom) cast: Brett Butler (Grace Kelly)
Grace Van __: 4 Owen
gracias: 6 thanks 7 spasibo 8 thank you
response: 6 de nada
Gracie: 5 Allen 6 Fields 7 Charlie
to George: 4 wife 6 costar 7 partner
Gracie __: 7 Mansion
gracile: 4 lank, lean, slim, thin, wiry 5 lanky, spare 6 dainty, gangly, skinny, slight, slinky, svelte, twiggy 7 scraggy, scrawny, slender, spidery, willowy 8 gangling 9 sylphlike
gracious: 3 big 4 good, kind, nice, warm 5 civil, noble, suave 6 benign, decent, genial, gentle, giving, kindly, polite, tender, urbane 7 affable, amiable, clement, cordial, courtly, dutiful, gallant, heedful, lenient, mindful, refined, sparing, stately, tactful, willing 8 amenable, amicable, debonair, friendly, highbred, ladylike, likeable, mannerly, merciful, obliging, pleasant, pleasing, sociable, yielding 9 agreeable, attentive, compliant, congenial, courteous, debonaire, favorable, indulgent, sensitive, tractable, unselfish 10 altruistic, beneficent, benevolent, bighearted, charitable, chivalrous, debonnaire, diplomatic, hospitable, neighborly, propitious, respectful, submissive, thoughtful
be ~: 5 bless, smile, thank 6 praise
Gracious!: 4 egad, oh no 5 egads
graciousness: 5 heart 8 kindness, sympathy 10 compassion
grackle: 3 daw 4 bird
call: 3 caw 5 croak 6 squawk
__ grackle: 5 rusty 6 common, purple 7 bronzed
grad: 4 alum 6 reuner 7 alumnus, student
achievement: 3 deg. 6 degree
degree: 2 MS 3 Ed.D., MFA, Ph.D
future ~: 2 jr., sr. 3 jnr., snr. 6 junior, senior
sch. exam: 3 GRE 4 GMAT, LSAT
school major: 3 law 4 math
tech ~: 2 EE, IE, ME 4 engr.
gradation: 4 rank, step 5 level, order, scale, shade, stage 6 degree, series 8 sequence 9 variation 10 difference, divergence, succession
grade: 3 bee, cee, dee 4 hill, mark, ramp, rank, rate, sift, sort, step, tier, tilt 5 A plus, B plus, class, C plus, D plus, level, pitch, score, slant, slope, stage 6 A minus, assort, B minus, C minus, degree, divide, D minus, glacis, league, rating, screen, status 7 echelon, flatten, footing, incline, measure, quality, station, stratum, variety 8 category, classify, evaluate, graduate, standard 9 acclivity
A: 4 best 5 prime 8 four-star, topnotch 9 egg rating, topflight 10 first-class, milk rating
adjuster: 4 plus 5 minus
bad ~: 2 ef 5 D plus 6 D minus
good ~: 5 A plus, B plus
junior-high ~: 5 ninth 6 eighth 7 seventh
make the ~: 3 win 4 pass 5 ace it, cut it, score 6 arrive, hack it, pan out, thrive 7 luck out, prevail, prosper, qualify, satisfy, succeed, triumph, work out 8 flourish, get ahead, go places 9 measure up 10 pass muster
middling ~: 5 C plus 6 C minus
not make the ~: 4 bomb, fail, flop, fold 7 lose out 8 fall flat 9 fall short
range: 4 elhi
receive a high ~ on: 3 ace
starter: 4 down 5 retro
steak ~: 5 prime 6 choice
up to ~: 8 adequate, suitable 10 acceptable, sufficient
grade __: 4 line 5 point 6 school
grade __ average: 5 point
__ grade: 3 pay 5 field 6 ruling 7 company
__-grade: 3 low 4 high
Grade: 3 Lew
Grade A product: 4 eggs, milk
grade-schooler: 3 kid 5 child 9 youngster
gradient: 4 ramp, rise, tilt 5 pitch, slant, slope 6 glacis 7 incline 9 acclivity, declivity
grad-to-be: 2 sr. 3 snr. 6 senior
gradual: 4 poky, slow 6 draggy, gentle, steady 7 halting, impeded, lagging, languid 8 bit by bit, crawling, creeping, dawdling, dilatory, dragging, drawn-out, hesitant, plodding, slothful, sluggish, toddling 9 by degrees, leisurely, lethargic, piecemeal, prolonged, snaillike, unhurried 10 deliberate, protracted, step-by-step
decrease: 5 slump 7 decline, falloff 8 downturn, slowdown 9 downtrend 10 slackening
gradually: 8 bit by bit 9 by degrees, leisurely, piecemeal, regularly 10 constantly, inch by inch, moderately, step by step
graduate: 4 alum, pass, rank, sort 5 grade, group, order 6 alumna, doctor, master 7 alumnus, arrange, mark off, promote, student 8 bachelor, classify 9 calibrate, diplomate 10 measure out
assistant: 7 teacher 8 lecturer 10 instructor
deg.: 3 DDS, LLD, MBA, MFA, MPA, Sc.D.
garb: 3 cap 4 gown
work: 5 paper 6 thesis 9 discourse 10 exposition
graduate __: 5 nurse 6 school
Graduate, The (1967 film)
cast: Anne Bancroft, William Daniels, Murray Hamilton, Dustin Hoffman, Katharine Ross
character: 3 Ben 6 Elaine
director: Mike Nichols
hotel: 4 Taft

graduation: **5** event **8** ceremony, sequence
month: **4** June
Grady: **3** Don
Graeco-___: **5** Roman
Graf: **4** Hans **6** Steffi
rival: **5** Seles
see also German
Graf ___: **4** Spee
Graff: **5** Ilene
Graffias: **4** star
graffiti: **7** doodles, marring **9** scribbles **10** defacement
apply ~: **3** mar **5** spray **6** deface
artist's addition: **5** beard **6** goatee
to some: **3** art
Graffman, Gary: **7** pianist
Graf, Hans: **9** conductor
Graf, Steffi spouse: Andre Agassi
graft: **3** bud **4** cion, join, loot **5** bribe, scion, shoot **6** boodle, payoff, payola, racket, splice, spoils **7** bribery, implant, jobbery **8** kickback, venality **9** extortion, hush money **10** corruption, transplant
recipient: **4** host, tree **5** plant
___ graft: **4** root, whip **5** crown, inlay
grafted, in heraldry: **4** enté
grafter: **6** rascal, robber
Grafton, Sue: **6** author, writer
sleuth: Kinsey Millhone
work: 'A' Is for Alibi
'B' Is for Burglar
'C' Is for Corpse
'D' Is for Deadbeat
'E' Is for Evidence
'F' Is for Fugitive
'G' Is for Gumshoe
'H' Is for Homicide
'I' Is for Innocent
'J' Is for Judgment
'K' Is for Killer
'L' Is for Lawless
'M' Is for Malice
'N' Is for Noose
'O' Is for Outlaw
'P' Is for Peril
'Q' Is for Quarry
graham ___: **5** flour, wafer **7** cracker
Graham: **4** Bill, Hill, Kerr, Nash, Otto, town **5** Billy, Larry **6** Gerrit, Greene, Martha, Parker **7** Chapman, Heather, Sheilah, Stedman **9** Katharine
___ Graham Bell: **9** Alexander
Graham, Billy: **3** rev. **8** reverend
Graham, Bob state: **3** Fla. **7** Florida
Grahame: **6** Gloria **7** Kenneth
Grahame, Gloria: **7** actress
film: The Bad and the Beautiful (1952, AA)
The Big Heat (1953)
The Greatest Show on Earth (1952)
In a Lonely Place (1950)
Oklahoma! (1955)
Sudden Fear (1952)
Grahame, Kenneth: **6** author, writer **7** British
character: **4** Mole, Toad **5** Otter
work: The Wind in the Willows
Graham, Heather: **7** actress
film: Austin Powers: The Spy Who Shagged Me (1999)
Boogie Nights (1997)
Bowfinger (1999)
From Hell (2001)
Lost in Space (1998)
Sidewalks of New York (2001)
Graham, Otto: **2** QB
sport: **8** football
Graig: **7** Nettles
grail: **3** cup **6** goblet, trophy **7** chalice
seeker: **6** knight
___ Grail: **4** Holy
grain: **3** bit, dot, jot, oat, rye **4** atom, bran, corn, drop, feed, iota, malt, masa, milo, mite, mote, oats, ragi, rice, seed, whit **5** crumb, durra, durum, grits, kasha, ounce, raggy, scrap, shred, spark, speck, stone, trace, wheat **6** barley, bulgur, cereal, farina, fodder, groats, hegari, hominy, kernel, millet, morsel, raggee, tittle **7** basmati, einkorn, minimum, modicum, polenta, scruple, smidgen, smidgin, sorghum, texture **8** cornmeal, couscous, feterita, molecule, particle, semolina, smidgeon, wild rice **9** brown rice, buckwheat, scintilla, white rice
beard: **3** awn **6** arista
bearded, as ~: **5** awned
bundle: **5** sheaf, shock, stack
cereal ~: **3** oat, rye **4** corn **5** wheat **6** barley
chaff: **5** palea
combining form: **4** cocc-, sito- **5** cocci-, cocco-, grani-
disease: **4** smut **5** ergot
ear: **5** spica
gather ~: **4** reap
go against the ~: **3** bug, get, irk, try, vex **4** gall, rile **5** annoy, peeve, pique, upset **6** bother, nettle, offend, rankle, ruffle **7** grate on, provoke **8** irritate **9** aggravate **10** exasperate
goddess of ~: **5** Ceres
grinder: **4** mill **5** quern
ground ~: **4** meal **5** flour, grist
holder: **3** bin **4** crib, silo **5** barge
husks: **4** bran **5** chaff
implement: **5** flail
like some ~: **4** oaty **5** oaten
prefix: **5** multi-
sorghum: **4** milo **5** doura, durra, kafir **6** dourah, hegari
spike: **3** ear
store ~: **6** ensile
unprocessed ~: **5** grist
whiskey ~: **3** rye **4** corn
grain ___: **6** growth **7** alcohol, refiner, sorghum
___ grain: **3** end **4** feed, food **6** pollen **7** quarter
___-grain: **4** fine, full **5** whole
___-Grain: **5** Nutri
___-grained: **4** fine, flat **5** close, cross **6** coarse
___ grain of salt: **5** with a
grains: **6** powder
60 ~: **4** dram
grainy: **6** coarse, gritty **7** powdery **8** gravelly **9** unrefined
gram: **4** unit **8** chickpea
starter: **4** deca, deka, echo, kilo, logo, mono, sono, tele **5** audio, cable, milli, penta
grama: **5** grass
Grambling: **6** school **7** college
athletes: **6** Tigers
locale: **9** Louisiana
Gramm: **3** Lou **4** Phil
gramma: **5** grass
grammar: **6** syntax **9** structure **10** morphology
abbr.: **3** inf., obj. **4** neut., poss. **5** irreg.
case: **6** dative
concern: **4** word **5** usage **6** custom **7** diction, lexicon, wording **8** phrasing
connector: **6** copula
do a ~ task: **5** parse
Lat. ~ case: **3** abl., acc.
no-no: **4** ain't
subject: **4** noun, verb **6** adverb **7** article, pronoun **9** adjective
grammar ___: **6** school
grammatical ___: **6** gender **7** meaning
Grammer: **5** Billy **6** Kelsey
Grammer, Kelsey: **5** actor
film: 15 Minutes (2001)
TV: Cheers, Frasier
Grammy: **5** award
category: **3** pop, rap **4** jazz **5** album, R and B
org.: **5** NARAS
gramp's
son: **2** pa **3** dad **6** father
wife: **4** gran, nana
grampus: **3** orc **5** whale **8** cetacean
family: **3** gam
relative: **3** sei **5** whale **6** beluga, narwal **7** cowfish, dolphin, finback, narwhal, rorqual **8** narwhale, porpoise
grams
28.35 ~: **5** ounce
1000 ~: **4** kilo
gran: **4** nana
Gran ___: **5** Chaco **7** Canaria
Gran ___ Omologato: **7** Turismo
Granada: **3** car **4** auto, city, Ford, town
city near ~: **4** Jaen
locale: **5** Spain
granadilla: **5** fruit
___ granadilla: **5** giant **6** purple, yellow
Granatelli: **4** Andy
Granby: **4** city, town
locale: **6** Canada, Québec
gran casa: **4** drum **8** bass drum
grand: **3** def, fab, rad **4** aces, A-one, boss, braw, cool, dece, epic, fine, gear, keen, lush, main, neat, nice, phat, posh, rich, thou, tuff **5** chief, dandy, ducky, G-note, great, large, lofty, marvy, neato, nobby, noble, noted, piano, prime, proud, regal, royal, slick, super, swank, swell, swish **6** august, bang on, bang-up, bonzer, bosker, choice, cosmic, deluxe, divine, dreamy, epical, far-out, finale, gnarly, groovy, heroic, lavish, lordly, lovely, peachy, scenic, slap-up, solemn, spot on, superb, swanky, terrif, tiptop, unreal, whizzo, wicked **7** amazing, awesome, capital, corking, elegant, eminent, exalted, gallant, highest, Homeric, leading, massive, opulent, perfect, pompous, ripping, skookum, stately, stellar, sublime, supreme **8** cosmical, dazzling, elevated, especial, eximious, fabulous, five-star, four-star, frabjous, glorious, heavenly, heroical, imperial, imposing, jim-dandy, kinglike, majestic, palatial, scenical, slam-bang, smashing, splendid, standout, Steinway, sterling, stickout, superior, terrific, top-level, topnotch, very good, wondrous **9** admirable, ambitious, beautiful, bodacious, dignified, Endsville, excellent, exemplary, exquisite, first-rate, high-grade, hunky-dory, luxurious, marvelous, principal, sollicker, sumptuous, top-flight, unrivaled, wonderful, wunderbar **10** first-class, hotsy-totsy, impressive, jack-a-dandy, majestical, monumental, out of sight, peachy-keen, phenomenal, preeminent, remarkable, statuesque, stupendous, super-duper, unrivalled
achievement: **4** coup
adventure: **4** epic, saga, tale, yarn **5** story **6** legend **9** chronicle
combining form: **3** meg- **4** mega- **5** megal- **6** megalo-
design: **6** scheme **8** game plan, scenario, strategy
display: **4** pomp, show **5** state **7** fanfare, panoply **8** ceremony, heraldry **9** pageantry
ender: **3** dad, kid, sir, son **4** aunt, baby, sire **5** child, daddy, niece, stand, uncle **6** father, master, mother, nephew, parent **7** stander **8** daughter
occasion: **4** ball, bash, fete, gala, prom **5** feast, party **6** affair, fiesta **7** blowout, jubilee, pageant, shindig **8** festival, wingding
opening: **5** debut **7** kickoff **8** premiere
slam: **5** homer **7** success, triumph, victory **9** landslide
thousand ~: **3** mil **7** million
view: **5** sight, sweep, vista **7** horizon, scenery **8** panorama, prospect **9** landscape
grand ___: **3** feu, fir **4** chop, coup, duke, jeté, jury, slam, tier, tour **5** duchy, juror, march, opera, piano, prize, theft, vizir **6** finale, rounds, vizier **7** drapery, duchess, larceny, marshal, opening, passion, quarter
grand ___ homer: **4** slam
grand ___ man: **3** old
grand-___: **5** scale **7** slammer
___ grand: **4** baby **6** parlor **7** concert
Grand: **5** Canal, river
Canal locale: **5** Italy **6** Venice
city on the ~: **7** Lansing
river locale: **8** Michigan
Grand ___: **3** Cru, Pre **4** Bank, Funk, Lama, Prix, Turk **5** Banks, Canal, Hotel, Manan, Mufti, Teton **6** Bahama, Canary, Canyon, Cayman, Kabuki, Master, Prixes **7** Guignol, Marnier
Grand ___ Dam: **6** Coulee
Grand ___ Island: **6** Bahama
Grand ___, MI: **6** Rapids
Grand ___ National Park: **5** Teton
Grand ___, ND: **5** Forks
Grand ___, NS: **3** Pré
Grand ___ of the Republic: **4** Army
Grand ___ Opry: **3** Ole
Grand ___ Party: **3** Old
Grand ___ Plaza: **4** Army
Grand ___ Railroad: **4** Funk
Grand ___ Suite: **6** Canyon
Grand Alliance, The author: Winston Churchill
Grandbois, Alain: **4** poet **8** Canadian
Grand Canal worker: **5** poler
Grand Canyon: **4** park **5** gorge
emotion: **3** awe
feature: **3** rim
locale: **4** Ariz. **7** Arizona
transport: **5** burro **6** copter
Grand Canyon (1991 film)
cast: Danny Glover, Kevin Kline, Steve Martin, Mary McDonnell
director: Lawrence Kasdan
Grand Canyon State
see Arizona
Grand Canyon Suite composer: **5** Grofé
Grand Cayman: **3** isl. **4** isle **6** island
Grand Central: **3** sta., stn. **7** station
locale: **3** NYC **7** New York **9** Manhattan
___-grandchild: **5** great
grandchildren, watch the: **3** sit
Grand Coulee: **3** dam
locale: **10** Washington
granddaughter: **5** woman **7** kinsman
___-granddaughter: **5** great
Grand Duke's father: **4** czar, tsar, tzar
Grand Duke, The
composer: **7** Gilbert **8** Sullivan
grande ___: **4** dame
___ Grande: **3** Rio **4** Casa
grandee: **3** don **4** rank **5** title
___ Grande, FL: **4** Boca
Grande Prairie: **4** city, town
locale: **6** Canada **7** Alberta
grander: **6** better **8** superior
Grande-Terre: **3** isl. **4** isle **6** island
locale: **10** Guadeloupe

grandeur: **4** pomp **5** glory, state, style **7** dignity, majesty **8** elegance, eminence, fineness, nobility, opulence, opulency, richness, splendor **9** celebrity, elevation, greatness, largeness, loftiness, magnitude, sublimity **10** augustness, brilliance, kingliness
grandfather: **3** kin, man **4** male **7** kinsman **8** ancestor
grandfather ___: **5** clock **6** clause
___-grandfather: **5** great
grandfathered: **6** exempt
grandfatherly: **4** kind **10** protective
Grand Forks: **4** city, town
  locale: **4** N. Dak.
Grand Funk
  song: Bad Time (1975)
    The Loco-Motion (1974)
    Some Kind of Wonderful (1974)
    We're an American Band (1973)
Grand Hotel: **4** film **5** novel
  author: Vicki Baum
  cast: John Barrymore, Wallace Beery, Joan Crawford, Greta Garbo
  character: **4** Otto
  director: Edmund Goulding
  studio: **3** MGM
___ Grand Hotel: **3** MGM
Grand Illusion (1937 film)
  cast: Pierre Fresnay, Jean Gabin, Erich von Stroheim
  director: Jean Renoir
grandiloquence: **7** bombast, fustian **8** rhetoric **9** pomposity
grandiloquent: **5** lofty, tumid, windy **6** florid, lavish, turgid **7** flowery, fustian, orotund, pompous, stilted, swollen, verbose **8** elevated, inflated **9** overblown
  be ~: **4** talk **5** orate, speak, spout **6** preach **7** address, declaim, lecture **8** harangue, sound off **9** discourse, hold forth, sermonize, speechify
grandiose: **4** epic **5** large, lofty, noble, showy **6** august, cosmic, epical, heroic, lordly **7** fustian, orotund, pompous, splashy, stately, utopian **8** affected, cosmical, heroical, imposing, splendid **9** ambitious, bombastic, egotistic, high-flown, luxurious, monstrous **10** euphuistic, flamboyant, impressive, monumental, rhetorical, theatrical, unfeasible
Grand Island: **4** city, town
  locale: **8** Nebraska
Grand Junction: **4** city, town
  locale: **8** Colorado
grandly: **9** in a big way
grandma: **4** nana
Grandma Moses: **4** Anna
Grand Marnier: **5** drink **8** beverage
Grand Marquis: **3** car **4** auto, Merc **7** Mercury **10** automobile
Grandma's ___: **3** Boy
Grandmaster ___: **5** Flash
grandmother: **3** kin **5** woman **6** female **7** kinsman **8** ancestor
  first ~: **3** Eve
grandmother ___: **5** clock
___-grandmother: **5** great
grandmotherly: **4** kind **5** sweet **6** loving **9** indulgent **10** bighearted, protective, solicitous
___ Grand Night for Singing: **4** It's a
grand old ___: **3** man
Grand Old ___: **5** Party
grand old name: **4** Mary
Grand Ole ___: **4** Opry
Grandpa: **5** Jones
  emulate ~: **4** dote
grandparent: **5** doter **6** adorer **7** kinsman **8** relative
  of a ~: **4** aval
___-grandparent: **5** great
Grand Prairie: **4** city, town
  locale: **5** Texas
Grand Prix: **3** car **4** auto **7** Pontiac
  competitor: **5** racer
  site: **6** Le Mans
Grand Rapids: **4** city, town
  county: **4** Kent
  locale: **8** Michigan
grand slam: **5** homer **7** home run
grandson: **4** cion **5** scion **7** kinsman **10** descendant
  maybe: **3** III
___-grandson: **5** great
grandstand: **4** brag, pose, show **5** boast, strut **6** fake it, hot dog **7** show off, swagger **8** flaunt it, showboat **9** bleachers
  level: **4** tier
  maneuver: **4** wave
  sound: **4** hoot, roar, yell **5** shout **6** scream
grandstand ___: **4** play
grandstander: **3** ham **6** hotdog **9** daredevil
Grand Teton: **4** park
  locale: **7** Wyoming
Grand Tour
  locale: **3** Eur. **6** Europe
___-granduncle: **5** great
Grandview: **4** city, town
  locale: **8** Missouri
Grandview, U.S.A. (1984 film)
  cast: Jamie Lee Curtis, C. Thomas Howell, Jennifer Jason Leigh, Patrick Swayze
  director: Randal Kleiser
Grand Ville: **3** car **4** auto **7** Pontiac
Grandy: **4** Fred
Gran Fury: **3** car **4** auto **8** Plymouth
grange: **4** farm **9** homestead
Granger: **4** city, town **6** Farley **7** Stewart
  locale: **7** Indiana
Grange, Red sport: **8** football
Granger, Farley: **5** actor
  film: Hans Christian Andersen (1952)
    I Want You (1951)
    The Purple Heart (1944)
    Rope (1948)
    Side Street (1949)
    Strangers on a Train (1951)
    They Live by Night (1949)
Granger, Stewart: **5** actor
  film: Beau Brummel (1954)
    Blanche Fury (1948)
    King Solomon's Mines (1950)
    North to Alaska (1960)
    Scaramouche (1952)
    The Secret Invasion (1964)
    The Secret Partner (1961)
    Soldiers Three (1951)
    Waterloo Road (1944)
    Young Bess (1953)
  spouse: Jean Simmons
Grani: **5** horse, steed **6** equine
Granicus: **5** river
  locale: **6** Turkey
granite: **4** gray, grey, rock **6** aplite **7** mineral
  ender: **4** ware
  in ~: **3** set
  quarry locale: **5** Barre
Granite: **4** peak **5** mount **8** mountain
  locale: **7** Montana **10** California
Granite City: **4** city, town
  locale: **8** Illinois
granitelike: **4** hard **8** indurate
Granit, Ragnar: **8** Nobelist
granny: **4** knot, nana **5** nanna **9** matriarch
  companion: **5** gramp **6** gramps
  daughter: **4** aunt **5** aunty
  garment: **5** shawl **6** bonnet
granny ___: **4** flat, knot **5** dress **7** glasses
Granny Dan author: Danielle Steel
Granny Smith: **4** pome **5** apple
  relative: **4** crab, Gala, Lodi, Rome **5** Mutsu **6** Empire, Ida Red, medlar, Pippin, russet **7** Baldwin, Bramley, costard, Freedom, Liberty, Spartan, Wealthy, Winesap **8** Cortland, Jonathan, McIntosh **10** Rome Beauty
granola: **6** cereal
  like ~: **4** oaty **5** chewy, oaten
___ grano salis: **3** cum
Gran Paradiso: **3** alp
Gran Sport: **3** car **4** auto **5** Buick
grant: **3** let, own **4** alms, avow, cede, dole, gift, give, lend, send **5** admit, allot, allow, award, endow, let on, offer, spare, waive, yield **6** accede, accept, accord, afford, assume, bestow, bounty, confer, convey, donate, extend, fess up, permit, render, reward, supply **7** agree to, backing, bequest, charity, concede, confess, funding, give out, handout, license, pension, present, provide, stipend, subsidy, suppose **8** allocate, bestowal, donation, gratuity, largesse **9** allotment, allowance, authorize, consent to, endowment, give leave, patronage, privilege, recognize, subscribe, vouchsafe **10** allocation, contribute, fellowship
  a mortgage: **4** lend, loan
  applicant: **5** asker
  criterion: **4** need **5** merit
  entry to: **5** admit, greet, let in **6** accept **7** include, receive, welcome
  fed. ~ giver: **3** NSF
  permission: **3** let **5** agree, allow, yield **6** permit **7** approve, concede, empower, entitle, license **8** sanction **9** acquiesce, authorize
  recipient: **5** donee
grant-___: **5** in-aid
___ grant: **4** land **5** block **6** action
Grant: **3** Amy, Bud, Lee, Lou **4** Cary, Earl, Eddy, Gogi, Hugh, Show, Wood **5** Kirby, Shaud **6** Tinker **7** Goodeve, Kathryn, Ulysses **8** Jennifer, Ulysses S., Williams
  colleague: **5** Meade
  feature: **5** beard
  foe: **3** Lee **5** R.E. Lee
Grant, Amy
  song: Baby Baby (1991)
    Every Heartbeat (1991)
    Good for Me (1992)
    The Next Time I Fall (1986)
    That's What Love Is for (1991)
  spouse: Vince Gill
Grant, Bud: **5** coach
  sport: **8** football
Grant, Cary: **5** actor
  film: Arsenic and Old Lace (1944)
    The Awful Truth (1937)
    The Bachelor and the Bobby-Soxer (1947)
    The Bishop's Wife (1947)
    Blonde Venus (1932)
    Bringing Up Baby (1938)
    Charade (1963)
    The Eagle and the Hawk (1933)
    Father Goose (1964)
    The Grass Is Greener (1960)
    Gunga Din (1939)
    His Girl Friday (1940)
    Holiday (1938)
    Houseboat (1958)
    I'm No Angel (1933)
    Indiscreet (1958)
    In Name Only (1939)
    I Was a Male War Bride (1949)
    The Last Outpost (1935)
    Monkey Business (1952)
    Mr. Blandings Builds His Dream House (1948)
    Mr. Lucky (1943)
    My Favorite Wife (1940)
    Night and Day (1946)
    None but the Lonely Heart (1944)
    North by Northwest (1959)
    Notorious (1946)
    Only Angels Have Wings (1939)
    Operation Petticoat (1959)
    Penny Serenade (1941)
    People Will Talk (1951)
    The Philadelphia Story (1940)
    Room for One More (1952)
    She Done Him Wrong (1933)
    Suspicion (1941)
    Sylvia Scarlett (1935)
    The Talk of the Town (1942)
    The Toast of New York (1937)
    To Catch a Thief (1955)
    Topper (1937)
    Walk, Don't Run (1966)
  spouse: Dyan Cannon, Barbara Hutton
___-grant college: **3** sea **4** land
granted: **3** yes **5** legal **6** indeed, though **8** very well **9** axiomatic
  permission ~: **3** aye, oui, yea, yep, yes, yup **4** fine, okay, sure, yeah **5** uh-huh **6** agreed, gladly, surely **7** go ahead, mais oui, ten-four **8** all right, of course, thumbs up, very well **9** be my guest, certainly **10** by all means, sure enough
  take for ~: **5** posit **6** assume **7** believe, presume, suppose **9** postulate
  taken for ~: **5** given, tacit **6** unsaid **7** assumed **8** implicit, unspoken, unstated, unvoiced **9** axiomatic **10** understood
grantee: **4** heir **7** heiress, legatee **9** inheritor
Grant, Gogi
  song: Suddenly There's a Valley (1955)
    The Wayward Wind (1956)
Grant, Hugh: **5** actor
  film: About a Boy (2002)
    Bridget Jones's Diary (2001)
    Four Weddings and a Funeral (1994)
    Impromptu (1991)
    Nine Months (1995)
    Notting Hill (1999)
    Sense and Sensibility (1995)
    Small Time Crooks (2000)
grant-in-___: **3** aid
granting: **2** if **8** provided
  that: **3** tho **6** though
Grant, Kathryn: **7** actress
  film: The 7th Voyage of Sinbad (1958)
    Gunman's Walk (1958)
    The Guns of Fort Petticoat (1957)
    The Phenix City Story (1955)
  spouse: Bing Crosby
Grantland: **4** Rice
Grant, Lee Oscar: Shampoo
Grant, Lou: **5** Asner
  emulate ~: **4** edit
  wife: **4** Edie
Grant Moves South author: Bruce Catton
grantor: **5** angel, donor, giver **6** backer, patron **8** altruist, bestower **9** supporter **10** benefactor
Grant's ___: **4** Tomb
Grants Pass: **4** city, town
  locale: **6** Oregon
Grant Takes Command author: Bruce Catton

Grant, Ulysses S.: 9 president
alma mater: 4 USMA 9 West Point
former occupation: 7 general, soldier
home: 4 Ohio
middle name: 7 Simpson
opponent: 7 Greeley, Seymour
publisher: 5 Twain
real first name: 5 Hiram
V.P.: 6 Colfax, Wilson
wife: 5 Julia
granular: 5 mealy 6 gritty 7 powdery 8 gravelly
snow: 4 firn, névé
granulate: 4 mill 5 crush, grate, grind 6 powder 7 atomize, crumble 9 comminute, pulverize, triturate
granulated: 6 gritty 8 gravelly
granulated ___: 5 sugar
granule: 3 bit 4 bead, mite 5 crumb, speck 6 pellet 8 fragment, particle
Granville: 5 Hicks 6 Bonita
grape: 3 fox, red 4 fern 5 color, fruit, gamay, pinot, skunk, Tokay 6 Merlot, Muscat, purple, purply 7 Catawba, Concord, Niagara 8 Cabernet, Grenache, malvasia, muscatel, purplish 9 muscadine, Sauvignon, zinfandel 10 Chardonnay
brandy: 4 marc
disease: 6 coleur
ender: 4 shot, vine 5 fruit
partly fermented ~ juice: 4 stum
pit: 6 acinus
plant: 4 vine
product: 4 wine
purchase: 5 bunch 7 cluster
relative: 4 rose, ruby, rust, wine 5 brick, coral, poppy, rusty, sandy 6 cerise, cherry, claret, garnet, maroon 7 carmine, crimson, fuchsia, magenta, pimento, scarlet, sultana, vermeil 8 amaranth, cardinal, dubonnet, geranium, rubicund 9 carnation, cranberry, vermilion 10 strawberry
seeker of fable: 3 fox
stuffed ~ leaf: 5 dolma
tartar: 5 argal, argol
valley: 4 Napa
wild ~ fruit: 9 muscadine
grape ___: 3 ivy 4 fern, Nehi 5 stake, sugar
___ grape: 3 fox, sea 5 frost 6 Oregon, pigeon, summer 7 African, Concord
Grape ___: 4 Nuts
grapefruit: 4 tree 6 citrus
hybrid: 4 ugli 7 tangelo
league locale: 3 Fla. 7 Florida
like ~ juice: 6 acidic
relative: 4 lime, ugli 5 lemon, navel 6 orange, pomelo, tangor 7 kumquat, satsuma, Seville, tangelo 8 bergamot, mandarin, shaddock, Valencia 9 tangerine 10 calamondin
serving: 4 half
topper: 5 sugar 6 cherry
grapefruit ___: 6 league
Grapefruit author: 3 Ono
grapefruitlike fruit: 8 shaddock
Grape Nuts: 6 cereal
competitor: 3 Kix 4 Life, Trix 5 Kashi, Quisp, Total 6 Kaboom, Muesli, Oreo O's, Pablum, Smacks 7 All-Bran, Crispix, Harmony, Hunny B's, Mueslix, Oat Bran, Pokemon 8 Boo Berry, Cheerios, Corn Chex, Corn Pops, Fiber One, Rice Chex, Special K, Uncle Sam, Wheaties 9 Alpha Bits, Apple Zaps, Honey Comb, Just Right, Wheat Chex 10 Apple Jacks, Bran Flakes, Cap'n Crunch, Cocoa Puffs, Froot Loops, Mini-Wheats, Nutri-Grain, Puffed Rice, Quaker Oats, Smart Start 11 Cocoa Blasts, Cookie Crisp, Golden Crisp, Lucky Charms, Puffed Wheat, Sweet Crunch, Waffle Crisp
grapes
crush ~: 5 stomp, tramp, tread
first cultivator of ~: 6 Oeneus
like sour ~: 6 acidic
sour ~: 6 excuse, reason 9 rationale
___ grapes: 4 sour
Grapes of Wrath, The: 4 film 5 novel
author: John Steinbeck
cast: John Carradine, Jane Darwell, Henry Fonda
character: 3 Ivy, Tom 4 Casy, Ella, Joad, Noah, Okie 5 Aggie, Sairy 6 Feeley, Ruthie
director: John Ford
grapevine: 4 buzz, talk 5 rumor 6 report 7 hearsay
combining form: 5 ampel- 6 ampelo-
product: 4 buzz, news, tale, talk, word 5 rumor 6 canard, earful, gossip, report 7 hearsay, whisper
Grapevine: 4 city, town
locale: 5 Texas
graph: 3 map 4 draw, grid, plot 5 chart, table 7 diagram 8 bar chart, pie chart 9 visual aid
draw points on a ~: 4 plot
ender: 3 -ite
line: 4 axis 5 x-axis, y-axis, z-axis
points: 4 loca, loci
starter: 3 iso, odo, oro 4 auto, logo, para, tele 5 mimeo, phono, photo 6 corona, shadow
statistical ~: 5 ogive
graph ___: 5 paper 6 theory
___ graph: 3 bar, pie 6 circle, linear 7 Feynman
graphic: 4 gory 5 clear, lucid, lurid, vivid 6 lively, visual 7 drawing, precise, telling 8 colorful, definite, detailed, distinct, eloquent, explicit, incisive, luculent, readable, stirring, striking, viewable 9 pictorial, realistic, trenchant 10 expressive
starter: 3 geo 4 ideo, xero 5 ortho, photo
graphic ___: 4 arts 5 novel 6 accent, design 7 granite
graphical ___ interface: 4 user
___ graphics: 6 vector
graphite: 6 carbon 7 mineral 8 plumbago
remover: 6 eraser
grapnel: 4 hook 5 hitch
grapple: 4 cope, grab, hook, lock 5 clash, fight, grasp, seize 6 battle, go at it, snatch, tackle, take on, tussle 7 contend, scuffle, vie with, wrestle 8 do battle, struggle 9 lay hold of, pitch into, titillate
with: 4 face 9 withstand
(with): 4 deal
grapple ___: 4 shot 5 plant 6 ground
grappling ___: 4 hook, iron
graptolite: 6 fossil
gras: 3 fat 6 French
___ gras: 4 foie
___ Gras: 5 Mardi
Grasmere: 4 lake
locale: 7 England
grasp: 3 dig, get, ken, see, wit 4 fist, glom, grab, grip, have, hold, hook, keep, know, land, lock, snap, take, wits 5 ahold, catch, clasp, learn, reach, seize, sense 6 absorb, acumen, attain, clench, clinch, clutch, collar, corral, fathom, follow, handle, intuit, master, pick up, secure, snatch, take in 7 catch on, cognize, command, compass, grapple, make out, mastery, purview, reading, realize 8 clutches, glom on to, judgment, perceive, relate to 9 apprehend, awareness, get hold of, handclasp, knowledge, lay hold of, penetrate 10 appreciate, comprehend, perception, understand
hard to ~: 4 deep, eely 6 arcane 8 slippery
graspable: 5 clear, lucid, plain, vivid 6 cogent 7 evident, express, obvious 8 apparent, distinct, explicit, luminous, manifest, palpable 10 spelled out
grasp at ___: 6 straws
grasping: 4 avid 5 gabby, itchy, tight 6 greedy, stingy 7 miserly, selfish, wishful 8 covetous, desirous, ravenous, ungiving 9 mercenary, penurious, rapacious, voracious 10 avaricious
sort: 5 taker
grass: 3 lea, ley, sod 4 feed, lawn, turf, yard 5 Bahia, plant, sward 6 bamboo, fescue, meadow, swarth, zoysia 7 pasture, verdure 10 vegetation
African ~: 4 teff 6 kikuyu, napier 7 esparto
Asian cereal ~: 4 ragi 5 raggy 6 raggee
bamboolike ~: 4 cane
cereal ~: 3 oat, rye 4 rice 5 grain, wheat
change the ~: 5 resod
clump: 4 tuft
cutter: 5 mower
cut the ~: 3 mow 4 trim
eat ~: 4 feed 5 graze
eater: 3 cow
ender: 4 land 5 roots 6 hopper
European ~: 7 esparto
fodder ~: 5 sorgo 6 sorgho
forage ~: 7 setaria
for thatching: 5 cogon
fungus: 4 smut
genus: 3 poa, zea
Indian ~: 4 kans 7 vetiver 8 khus-khus
invader: 4 weed
lawn ~: 6 fescue, redtop, zoysia 7 festuca
leaf of ~: 5 blade
like ~ in the morning: 3 wet 4 damp, dewy 5 moist
like tall ~: 5 reedy
marsh ~: 4 reed
Mexican basket ~: 5 otate
moor ~: 4 nard
of temperate regions: 5 brome
pasture ~: 5 grama 6 fescue, redtop 7 festuca
path: 5 swath 6 swathe
prickly ~: 7 sandbur
rye ~: 6 darnel
scatter ~: 3 ted
second ~ crop: 5 rowen
snake in the ~: 5 knave, rogue, sneak 7 traitor 8 turncoat 9 scoundrel
sod ~: 5 Bahia
stalk: 4 cane, reed
starter: 3 cut, eel, rib, rye 4 bent, blue, crab, knot, wire, worm 5 bunch, lemon 6 carpet, hopper, pepper, ripple 7 sparrow
swamp ~: 5 sedge
tropical ~: 5 Bahia, cogon 6 bamboo 7 Bermuda
grass ___: 3 bug, rug 4 carp, pink, sack, tree 5 cloth, court, finch, roots, skirt, snake, snipe, stain, style 6 hockey, shears, skiing, sponge 7 sorghum
___ grass: 3 boo, cut, elk, nut, oat, rie, rye 4 barn, bear, bent, bird, club, cord, crab, deer, dune, gama, hair, holy, June, kans, salt, star, tape, wire, worm 5 Bahia, beach, bunch, camel, cloud, couch, goose, grama, heath, lemon, marsh, Means, mondo, panic, quack, quick, spear, Sudan, sweet, sword, witch 6 Aleppo, alkali, Bahama, bottom, canary, carpet, cotton, Dallis, fescue, finger, guinea, kikuyu, manila, marram, meadow, napier, needle, pampas, quitch, rescue, Rhodes, scurvy, scutch, switch, twitch 7 Bermuda, buffalo, esparto, feather, heather, Johnson, orchard, pangola, quaking, timothy, tussock
Grass: 4 poem 6 Günter
author: Carl Sandburg
Grass ___, The: 4 Harp
grass-animal name: 4 Chia
Grass author: Carl Sandburg
Grass, Günter: 6 German, writer 8 Nobelist
work: The Call of the Toad
Cat and Mouse
Dog Years
The Flood
The Rat
The Tin Drum
Grass Harp, The: 4 book, film
author: Truman Capote
cast: Piper Laurie, Walter Matthau, Sissy Spacek
director: Charles Matthau
grasshopper: 3 bug 5 drink 6 insect, locust 8 beverage, cocktail
colleague: 3 ant
ingredient: 5 cream
sound: 5 chirr, churr, trill 6 chirre
young: 5 nymph
grasshopper ___: 3 pie 6 engine 7 sparrow
Grasshopper, The (1970 film)
cast: Jacqueline Bisset, Jim Brown, Joseph Cotten
director: Jerry Paris
Grass Is Always Greener Over the Septic Tank, The author: Erma Bombeck
Grass Is Greener, The (1960 film)
cast: Cary Grant, Deborah Kerr, Robert Mitchum
director: Stanley Donen
grassland: 3 lea, ley, sod 4 veld 5 campo, field, green, llano, plain, sward, veldt 6 meadow, pampas, swarth 7 lowland, pasture, prairie, savanna, verdure 8 savannah
Grassle: 5 Karen
Grasso: 4 Ella
grassquit: 4 bird
Grass Roots
song: Let's Live for Today (1967)
Midnight Confessions (1968)
Sooner or Later (1971)
grass-roots musician: 5 folky 6 folkie
grass skirt
accessory: 3 lei
dance: 4 hula
___ Grass, The: 5 Sea of
grassy: 5 green 7 emerald, verdant 9 verdurous
area: 4 lawn, yard 5 campo, llano, sward 6 meadow, swarth
border: 5 verge
___ grata: 3 non 7 persona
grata, persona non: 3 bum 5 tramp 6 pariah 7 outcast 8 derelict 9 miscreant, reprobate
grate: 3 irk, jar, rub, vex 4 file, gall, rasp, rile 5 annoy, chafe, clash, creak, gnash, grind, mince, peeve, pique, shred 6 abrade, hearth, nettle, powder, rankle, scrape 7 enflame, inflame, lattice, provoke, scratch 8 gridiron, irritate, levigate 9 aggra-

vate, granulate, pulverize 10 exasperate
contents: 3 ash 5 ember 6 cinder
on: 3 vex 4 rasp, rile 6 bother
residue: 3 ash 5 ember 6 cinder
grated cheese: 6 Romano 8 Parmesan
grateful: 7 obliged 8 beholden, indebted, relieved, thankful
feel ~ to: 3 owe 10 appreciate
Grateful Dead
label: 6 Arista
leader: Jerry Garcia
song: Touch of Grey (1987)
gratefulness: 6 thanks
__ gratia: 3 Dei 7 exempli
__ Gratia Artis: 3 Ars
__ gratias: 3 deo
gratification: 3 joy 4 kick 5 pride 6 luxury 7 comfort, rapture
__ gratification: 7 instant
gratified: 4 glad 5 happy, proud 6 joyful, joyous 7 content 8 jubilant, relieved, thankful 9 contented, delighted, fulfilled, gladdened 10 complacent, flying high
be ~ by: 4 like
not ~: 5 unmet
gratify: 4 sate 5 cheer, humor 6 coddle, divert, fulfil, oblige, pamper, pander, please, regale, thrill, tickle 7 appease, cater to, content, delight, fulfill, gladden, hearten, indulge, satiate, satisfy 8 give in to 9 delectate, entertain, make happy
gratifying: 4 good 5 sweet 6 lovely 7 welcome 8 pleasant, pleasing, readable, tasteful 9 agreeable, covetable, delicious, desirable, enjoyable, favorable, indulgent, luxurious, rewarding 10 delectable, delightful, fulfilling, satisfying
grating: 4 grid 5 grill, gruff, harsh, noisy, raspy, rough, roupy 6 grille, hoarse, off-key, shrill 7 irksome, jarring, lattice, rasping, raucous 8 abrasion, annoying, friction, grinding, guttural, jangling, scraping, strident, worrying 9 cacophony, dissonant, unmusical 10 discordant, irritating, stridulent, unpleasant
noise: 5 creak 6 squeak, squeal
gratis: 4 free 7 as a gift 8 costless 9 on the cuff 10 for nothing, on the house
get ~: 3 bum 5 leech 8 freeload, scrounge
provide ~: 4 comp
gratitude: 5 thanx 6 thanks 10 obligation
gratuitous: 5 undue 6 unpaid 7 unasked 8 baseless, mindless, needless 9 causeless, unfounded, uninvited, unmerited, voluntary 10 chargeless, for nothing, groundless, inordinate, reasonless, unasked-for, undeserved, unprovoked
gratuity: 3 tip 4 gift, perc, perk, toke 5 bonus, grant, token 6 reward 7 present, stipend 8 donation, largesse, offering 9 emolument, lagniappe, sweetener
Grauman: 3 Sid
Grau, Shirley Ann: 6 author, writer
grave: 3 bad, sad 4 dire, dour, grim, ugly 5 acute, heavy, major, sober, staid, tempo, vault 6 accent, gloomy, incise, severe, solemn, somber, urgent 7 crucial, exigent, heinous, learned, ominous, onerous, pensive, serious, subdued, weighty 8 critical, exigeant, grievous, perilous 9 desperate, hazardous, momentous, ponderous, unsmiling 10 inexpiable, portentous, thoughtful

faster than ~: 5 largo
gravel: 4 grit, rock 5 stone 7 pebbles 8 detritus
gravelly: 5 harsh, raspy, rocky, roupy, sandy, stony 6 froggy, grainy, gritty, hoarse, pebbly, stoney 7 rasping, shingly, throaty 8 croaking, granular, guttural 10 granulated, laryngitic
voice: 5 grate 7 scratch
gravely: 8 for keeps, severely, terribly 9 seriously
graven: 6 carved 7 incised 8 sculpted
image: 4 idol
graven __: 5 image
Gravenstein: 5 apple
relative: 4 crab, Gala, Lodi, Rome 5 Mutsu 6 Empire, Ida Red, medlar, Pippin, russet 7 Baldwin, Bramley, costard, Freedom, Liberty, Spartan, Wealthy, Winesap 8 Cortland, Jonathan, McIntosh 10 Rome Beauty
Graves: 4 wine 5 Peter 6 Robert
origin: 6 France
Graves, Peter: 5 actor
brother: James Arness
film: Airplane! (1980)
Black Tuesday (1954)
TV: Fury, Mission: Impossible
Graves, Robert: 4 poet 6 author, writer 7 British
work: Good-Bye to All That
I, Claudius
The White Goddess
graveyard __: 5 shift, watch
gravid: 8 enceinte, pregnant 9 expectant, expecting, with child
gravidity: 9 gestation
graving __: 4 dock 5 piece
gravitate: 4 lean, tend 5 trend 7 conduce, incline
(toward): 4 lean, tend 5 verge
gravitational __: 4 lens, mass, wave 5 field 6 radius
graviton: 8 particle
gravity: 4 heft, one G 5 force 6 import, moment, weight 7 concern, urgency 8 severity 9 acuteness, heaviness 10 importance
defy ~: 4 lift
respond to ~: 3 sag 4 drop, fall, sink 6 plunge, topple 7 plummet
gravity __: 3 dam 4 cell, feed, wave, wind 5 clock, fault, hinge, meter
__ gravity: 4 zero
gravity-powered vehicle: 4 luge, pung, sled 6 sleigh 8 toboggan
Gravity's Rainbow author: Thomas Pynchon
gravy: 3 jus 4 perc, perk 5 bonus, lucre, money, sauce 6 juices, profit, reward 7 jobbery, revenue 8 dividend 9 condiment
dip in ~: 3 sop
flaw: 4 lump
holder: 4 boat
ingredient: 4 roux 5 broth, flour, liver 6 giblet
like bad ~: 5 lumpy
train: 7 success
gravy __: 4 boat 5 train
__ gravy: 3 pan 4 beef, dish, milk 6 giblet, red-eye 7 chicken
Gravy (for My Mashed Potatoes) (1962 song) artist: Dee Dee Sharp
gray: 3 age, ash, old 4 ashy, drab, dull, hoar, pale 5 ashen, color, dingy, dusky, hoary, mirky, mousy, murky, shade, smoky 6 cloudy, gloomy, leaden, mousey, shadow, somber 7 clouded, granite, neutral, peppery, silvery, sunless 8 darkened, gunmetal, lowering, overcast 9 cinereous

become ~: 3 age
bluish ~: 5 merle, pearl, slate 8 platinum
brownish ~: 4 drab 5 beige, putty, taupe 7 fuscous 8 charcoal
color: 3 ash 4 ashy, dove, drab, opal 5 beige, dusty, merle, pearl, putty, slate, steel, taupe 6 silver 7 grizzly 8 charcoal, gunmetal, platinum
combining form: 4 poli- 5 glauc-, polio- 6 glauco-
cover the ~ again: 5 redye
ender: 3 lag 4 fish, mail 5 beard
matter: 4 head, mind 5 brain 9 mentality
name meaning ~: 5 Lloyd
use the ~ matter: 5 think 6 ideate
yellowish ~: 4 drab 5 putty
gray __: 3 fox, jay, urn 4 area, body, card, duck, iron, mold, pine, wolf 5 birch, goods, power, scale, skate, trout, whale 6 market, matter, mullet, parrot 7 catbird, snapper
__ gray: 3 ash 4 iron, navy 5 cadet, pearl, steel 6 Oxford, silver 7 African
Gray: 3 Asa 4 Erin 5 Billy, Dobie, Linda, Simon 6 Coleen, Harold, Robert, Thomas 8 Spalding
monogram: 3 CSA
subject: 4 anat. 7 anatomy
work: 3 ode 5 elegy
Gray __: 4 Lady 5 Friar 7 Panther
__ Gray: 4 Lucy 6 Duncan
Gray, Asa: 8 botanist 9 scientist
grayback: 4 bird
gray battle, name meaning: 8 Griselda
graybeard: 4 sage 6 codger, gaffer, geezer 7 old-time 9 patriarch, venerable
Gray, Dorian
what ~ didn't do: 3 age
gray duck: 4 fowl
relative: 4 smew, teal 5 eider, Pekin, Rouen, scaup 6 Cayuga, scoter 7 gadwall, mallard, pintail, pochard, redhead, widgeon 8 garganey, mandarin, oldsquaw, shoveler 9 broadbill, goldeneye, goosander, greenhead, merganser, sprigtail 10 bufflehead, canvasback, surf scoter
gray-haired: 4 aged 5 hoary 6 senior 7 elderly, wizened 8 grizzled 9 venerable
grayish: 3 wan 4 ashy, pale 5 livid 6 pallid 7 cindery 9 colorless
color: 3 dun 4 ecru, nude, sage 5 Alice, beige, flaxy, loden, lovat, sepia, slate 6 chammy, flaxen, indigo, oyster, reseda, shammy, shamoy 7 celadon, chamois 8 mulberry
graylag: 4 bird, fowl 5 goose
genus: 5 anser
relative: 4 nene 5 brant 9 snow goose
__ Gray Line, The: 4 Long
grayling: 4 fish
Gray, Robert: 8 explorer
graysby: 4 fish
Gray, Simon: 7 British 10 playwright
Grayson: 4 Dick 7 Kathryn
Grayson, Dick to Bruce Wayne: 4 ward
Grayson, Kathryn: 7 actress
film: Anchors Aweigh (1945)
Kiss Me Kate (1953)
Rio Rita (1942)
Show Boat (1951)
Two Sisters From Boston (1946)
The Vanishing Virginian (1942)
Gray, Thomas: 4 poet 7 British
alma mater: 4 Eton
work: Elegy Written in a Country Churchyard

graywacke: 7 mineral
Graz: 4 city, town
locale: 7 Austria
graze: 3 eat, rub 4 chew, feed, kiss, lick, rake, skim, skin, skip, wear, wing 5 brush, chafe, shave, touch 6 abrade, browse, glance, nibble, scrape 7 scratch 9 glance off, masticate
grazer: 3 cow, ewe 4 bull, calf, goat, herd, lamb 5 sheep
Graziano, Rocky: 5 boxer
foe: 4 Zale
milieu: 4 ring
grazie: 6 thanks 7 Italian, spasibo 8 thank you
response: 5 prego
grazing area: 3 lea, ley 4 veld 5 range, veldt
Grazing in the Grass (song) artist: Friends of Distinction, Hugh Masekela
Gr. Br.: 5 the UK
locale: 3 Eur.
part: 3 Eng. 4 Scot.
grease: 3 fat, lub., oil, sop 4 lard, lube 5 bribe 6 buy off, payoff, reward 7 jobbery, rake-off 8 kickback, leverage 9 drippings, lubricant, lubricate 10 facilitate, recompense
a palm: 5 bribe, get to 6 buy off, pay off, suborn 7 corrupt 9 lubricate
combining form: 4 sebi-, sebo-
deposit: 4 crud 5 filth, grime
elbow ~: 4 toil, work 6 effort 8 exertion
ender: 4 wood 5 paint, proof
remove ~: 5 defat
the wheels: 4 ease 6 smooth 8 expedite 10 facilitate
use elbow ~: 3 ply 4 buff 5 apply, scour, scrub, sweat, wield 6 employ, polish, strain 7 trouble, utilize 8 put forth
wool ~: 5 suint
grease __: 3 cup, gun 4 wool 5 paint 6 monkey, pencil
__ grease: 4 axle 5 elbow, goose
Grease: 4 film, song
artist: Frankie Valli
cast: Eve Arden, Stockard Channing, Jeff Conaway, Didi Conn, Olivia Newton-John, John Travolta
character: 5 Sandy
director: Randal Kleiser
prop: 4 comb
Grease __ word: 5 is the
greasepaint: 6 makeup 7 pancake 9 cosmetics 10 foundation, maquillage
greasy: 4 oily 5 lardy, slick, slimy 8 slippery, unctuous 9 lubricous 10 lubricated, lubricious, oleaginous
residue: 4 gunk, ooze 5 grime, slime
Greasy: 5 Neale
greasy spoon: 4 café 5 diner 6 eatery 10 restaurant
patron: 5 eater
sign: 4 eats
great: 3 ace, big, def, rad 4 aces, A-one, boss, braw, cool, dece, fine, gear, good, huge, keen, neat, nice, okay, phat, star, tall, tops, tuff, vast 5 adept, ample, bulky, dandy, ducky, famed, giant, grand, jumbo, large, legit, lofty, marvy, mondo, moral, neato, nifty, nobby, noble, noted, prime, primo, slick, stiff, super, swell 6 adroit, august, bang on, bang-up, bonzer, bosker, choice, divine, dreamy, epical, expert, famous, far-out, gnarly, groovy, heroic, lovely, mortal, peachy, proper, signal, slap-up, spot on, strong, superb, terrif, tip-top, unreal, whizzo, wicked 7 amazing, awesome, capital, corking, emi-

nent, ethical, exalted, hulking, immense, intense, mammoth, massive, notable, perfect, ripping, sizable, skookum, stellar, sublime, titanic **8** abundant, all right, colossal, dazzling, elevated, enormous, especial, eximious, fabulous, five-star, four-star, frabjous, gigantic, glorious, heavenly, heroical, infinite, jim-dandy, king-size, laudable, masterly, oversize, peerless, pleasant, pleasing, profound, renowned, sizeable, skillful, slam-bang, smashing, spacious, splendid, standout, sterling, stickout, superior, terrific, top-level, topnotch, top-rated, towering, very good, whapping, whopping, wondrous **9** admirable, agreeable, bodacious, dignified, Endsville, excellent, exemplary, exquisite, extensive, fantastic, first-rate, Herculean, high-grade, honorable, humongous, hunky-dory, important, marvelous, memorable, monstrous, overlarge, prominent, reputable, sollicker, superstar, top-drawer, topflight, unlimited, unrivaled, virtuosic, wonderful, wunderbar **10** acceptable, beneficial, celebrated, consummate, creditable, first-class, formidable, gargantuan, high-minded, hotsy-totsy, impressive, incredible, jack-a-dandy, monumental, noteworthy, out of sight, peachy-keen, phenomenal, prodigious, remarkable, stupendous, super-duper, swimmingly, tremendous, unrivalled, voluminous, world-class
combining form: **3** meg- **4** macr-, magn-, mega- **5** macro-, magni-, megal- **6** megalo-
ender: **4** coat **7** hearted
in music: **6** grosso
name meaning ~: **5** Grant
not ~: **4** fair, okay, so-so
prefix: **4** maxi-, mega- **5** macro-
great ___: **3** ape, auk, toe **4** guns, helm, pace, seal, skua **5** gross, wheel **6** circle, laurel, primer **7** basinet, bustard, council, lobelia, ragweed
great ___ heron: **4** blue **5** white
great ___ owl: **4** gray **6** horned
great ___ shark: **4** blue **5** white
great-___: **4** aunt **5** niece, uncle **6** nephew
Great ___: **3** Day, Dog, Sun, War **4** Ajax, Bear, Dane, Rift, Week, Year **5** Abaco, Basin, Lakes, Mogul, Power, Scott, White **6** Circle, Divide, Plains, Schism, Spirit, Sunday **7** Britain, Russian, Smokies, Society
Great ___ Bay: **5** South
Great ___ Brown, The: **3** God
Great ___ Desert: **4** Salt **5** Sandy
Great ___ Detective, The: **5** Mouse
Great ___ Hope, The: **5** White
Great ___ Lake: **4** Salt **5** Slave
Great ___ Mountains: **5** Smoky
Great ___ of China: **4** Wall
Great ___ of Fire: **5** Balls
Great ___ Pepper, The: **5** Waldo
Great ___ Reef: **7** Barrier
Great ___ Robbery, The: **5** Train
Great ___ Spot: **3** Red
Great ___, The: **3** Lie, Man **4** Race **5** Brain, Lover **6** Caruso, Escape, Gatsby, Shadow **7** Garrick, McGinty
Great ___ Valley: **4** Rift
Great ___ Way: **5** White
Great American Novel, The author: **4** Roth
great-aunt: **3** kin **5** woman **7** kinsman **9** kinswoman
Great Australian ___: **5** Bight
Great Balls of Fire (1957 song) artist: Jerry Lee Lewis
Great Barrier Island: **4** Otea
Great Barrier Reef essentially: **5** coral
Great Basin: **4** park **6** desert
language: **5** Piute **6** Paiute
locale: **3** Nev. **6** Nevada
Great Bear: **4** lake
locale: **6** Canada
Great Beyond, The artist: **3** R.E.M.
great blue ___: **5** heron, shark
Great Britain: **4** isls. **5** isles **7** islands
see also England
Great Caesar's ___!: **5** ghost
Great Caruso, The (1951 film)
cast: Ann Blyth, Mario Lanza
director: Richard Thorpe
Great Circle author: Conrad Aiken
Great Commoner, The: **4** Pitt
Great Compromiser, The: **4** Clay
Great Dane: **3** dog **5** canid **6** canine
Great Day in Harlem, A (1994 film)
cast: Dizzy Gillespie, Milt Hinton, Marian McPartland
director: Jean Bach
Great Dictator, The (1940 film)
cast: Charles Chaplin, Paulette Goddard, Jack Oakie
director: Charles Chaplin
Great Dividing ___: **5** Range
Great Eight: **3** car **4** auto **6** Hudson
greater: **3** lgr. **4** more **5** major **6** better, larger **8** superior
become ~: **3** wax **4** grow **6** accrue, expand, mature **7** augment, enlarge, magnify **8** escalate, increase, multiply
in seniority: **5** elder, older **9** first-born
make ~: **3** pad **4** feed, hike **5** add to, boost, swell, widen **6** beef up, expand, extend, jack up **7** amplify, augment, build up, develop, enhance, enlarge, inflate, magnify, scale up **8** heighten, increase, lengthen **9** intensify **10** aggrandize, strengthen, supplement
part: **4** bulk, mass **8** majority **9** plurality
than: **4** over **5** above **6** beyond **8** superior **9** exceeding, upwards of **10** surpassing
Greater ___ York: **3** New
Greater Sundas: **4** isls. **5** isles **7** islands
Great Escape, The (1963 film)
cast: Sir Richard Attenborough, Charles Bronson, James Coburn, James Garner, David McCallum, Steve McQueen, Donald Pleasence
director: John Sturges
greatest: **3** top **4** A-one, arch, best, most, tops **5** first, major, prime **6** utmost **7** leading, maximum, optimum, primary, supreme, topmost **8** champion, ultimate **9** marvelous, principal, topflight, uppermost, uttermost **10** preeminent
extent: **3** end, max, rim **4** brim, edge, most **5** brink, limit **6** fringe, height, period **7** ceiling, extreme, maximum **8** confines, end point **9** outskirts, parameter, perimeter, periphery **10** bottom line, boundaries
greatest common ___: **6** factor **7** divisor
greatest hits album phrase: **6** best of
Greatest Love of All (1986 song)
artist: Whitney Houston
Greatest Show on Earth, The (1952 film)
cast: Gloria Grahame, Charlton Heston, Betty Hutton, Dorothy Lamour, James Stewart, Cornel Wilde
director: Cecil B. DeMille
Greatest Story Ever Told, The (1965 film)
cast: Carroll Baker, Jose Ferrer, Van Heflin, Charlton Heston, Angela Lansbury, Sidney Poitier, Claude Rains, Telly Savalas, Max von Sydow, John Wayne, Shelley Winters, Ed Wynn
director: Cecil B. DeMille
Greatest, The: **3** Ali
Great Expectations: **5** novel
author: Charles Dickens
character: **3** Pip **4** Abel **5** Biddy, Clara **6** Pirrip **7** Estella
Great Expectations (1946 film)
cast: Valerie Hobson, Bernard Miles, John Mills
director: David Lean
Great Expectations (1998 film)
cast: Anne Bancroft, Chris Cooper, Ethan Hawke, Gwyneth Paltrow
Great Falls: **4** city, town
locale: **7** Montana
Great Forest, The artist: **5** Ernst
Great Garrick, The (1937 film)
cast: Brian Aherne, Olivia de Havilland, Edward Everett Horton
director: James Whale
Great Gatsby, The: **4** film **5** novel
author: F. Scott Fitzgerald
cast: Karen Black, Bruce Dern, Mia Farrow, Robert Redford
character: **3** Jay, Tom **4** Nick **5** Baker, Daisy, Meyer **6** George, Jordan, Myrtle, Wilson **8** Buchanan, Carraway **9** Wolfshiem
Great Gildersleeve, The: **9** radio show
Great God Brown, The author: Eugene O'Neill
greathearted: **3** big **5** noble **6** heroic, humane **7** gallant, valiant **8** generous **9** unselfish **10** benevolent, charitable, high-minded
Great Impostor, The (1961 film)
cast: Tony Curtis, Karl Malden, Raymond Massey, Edmond O'Brien
director: Robert Mulligan
Great Lake: **4** Erie **5** Huron **7** Ontario **8** Michigan, Superior
canals: **3** Soo
cargo: **3** ore
fish: **4** chub, coho **5** cisco, cohoe, smelt **6** salmon **7** bloater
Indian: **4** Cree, Erie **5** Miami
native language: **6** Ojibwa **7** Ojibway **8** Chippewa
of a ~: **5** Erian
port: **6** Duluth
state: **4** Ohio **8** Michigan
when the ~ s were formed: **6** ice age
Great Leap Forward proponent: **3** Mao
Great Lie, The (1941 film)
cast: Mary Astor, George Brent, Bette Davis
Great Lover, The (1949 film)
cast: Rhonda Fleming, Bob Hope, Roland Young
director: Alexander Hall
greatly: **3** far **4** a lot, most, much, very, well **5** quite **6** highly, hugely, vastly **7** largely, notably **8** famously, markedly, mightily, terribly, very much **9** eminently, extremely, fervently, glaringly, immensely, intensely, like crazy, supremely **10** abundantly, enormously, ever so much, incredibly, powerfully, remarkably, strikingly
Great Man, The (1956 film)
cast: José Ferrer, Dean Jagger, Keenan Wynn
director: José Ferrer
Great Man Votes, The (1939 film)
cast: John Barrymore, Peter Holden, Virginia Weidler
director: Garson Kanin
Great McGinty, The (1940 film)
cast: Brian Donlevy, Akim Tamiroff
director: Preston Sturges
Great Mosque locale: **5** Mecca
Great Muppet Caper, The (1981 film)
director: Jim Henson
Great Nebula locale: **5** Orion
Great Neck: **4** city, town
locale: **7** New York **10** Long Island
greatness: **4** note, size **5** glory, honor **7** dignity **8** eminence, enormity, grandeur, nobility **9** abundance, amplitude, celebrity, immensity, intensity, loftiness, magnitude, sublimity **10** excellence, generosity, importance, prominence, worthiness
Great Opposer, The: **5** Borah
Great Outdoors, The (1988 film)
cast: Dan Aykroyd, Annette Bening, John Candy
Great Pacificator, The: **4** Clay
Great Plains
dwelling: **4** tipi **5** tepee **6** teepee
Indian: **3** Kaw, Oto **4** Crow, Otoe **5** Caddo, Kansa, Kiowa, Osage **6** Dakota, Pawnee, Quapaw, Siouan **7** Arapaho **8** Arapahoe, Cheyenne, Comanche, Kickapoo **9** Blackfoot
Great Pretender, The (1955 song)
artist: Platters
Great Pyramid site: **4** Giza **5** Egypt
Great Pyrenees: **3** dog **5** canid **6** canine
Great Race, The (1965 film)
cast: Tony Curtis, Peter Falk, Jack Lemmon, Natalie Wood
composer: **7** Mancini
director: Blake Edwards
Great Railway Bazaar, The author: Paul Theroux
Great Red ___: **4** Spot
Great Rift Valley locale: **5** Kenya
Great Salt: **6** desert
locale: **4** Utah
Great Salt Lake: **6** desert
locale: **4** Utah
river to the ~: **4** Bear
Great Sandy: **6** desert
locale: **6** Arabia **9** Australia
Great Seal
bird: **5** eagle
word on the ~: **4** ordo **5** novus
Great Shadow, The author: Arthur Conan Doyle
Great Slave: **4** lake
locale: **6** Canada
Great Smoky Mountains: **4** park **5** range
locale: **9** Tennessee
Great South ___: **3** Bay
Great Sun author: Edna Ferber
Great Train Robbery, The: **4** film **5** novel
cast: Sean Connery, Lesley-Anne Down, Donald Sutherland
director: Michael Crichton
Great Trek participant: **4** Boer
great-uncle: **3** kin **7** kinsman **8** relative
Great Victoria: **6** desert
locale: **8** Victoria
Great Waldo Pepper, The (1975 film)
cast: Robert Redford, Susan Sarandon, Bo Svenson
director: George Roy Hill
Great Wall
dynasty: **3** Qin **4** Chin
locale: **4** Asia **5** China
Great weeds do grow ___: **5** apace
great white ___: **5** heron, shark
Great White ___: **3** Way **6** Father
Great White Hope, The (1970 film)
cast: Jane Alexander, Lou Gilbert, James Earl Jones

director: Martin Ritt
Great White North: 6 Canada
great white relative: 4 mako
Great White Way light: 4 neon
great work in Latin: 10 magnum opus
Great Ziegfeld, The (1936 film)
cast: Myrna Loy, William Powell, Luise Rainer
director: Robert Z. Leonard
Greaves, R.B. song: Take a Letter Maria (1969)
Gréban, Arnoul: 6 French 10 playwright
grebe: 4 bird 5 diver 8 dabchick, didapper 9 helldiver
Grecian: 9 classical
Grecian __: 4 bend 7 profile
Greco: 4 José 5 Buddy
Greco-Roman alternative: 4 sumo
Greco-Roman wrestling: 5 sport
GRE cousin: 4 LSAT
Greece: 5 Ellas 6 Hellas, nation 7 country
capital: 6 Athens
cheese: 4 feta
city: 6 Athens, Edessa, Patros 7 Piraeus 8 Iráklion, Peiraeus
combining form: 5 Greco- 6 Graeco- 7 Helleno-
conductor: 11 Mitropoulos
food: 4 feta, gyro, lamb 5 olive 8 moussaka, olive oil
former money: 5 lepta 6 drachm, lepton 7 drachma 9 didrachma
from ~: 6 Balkan
guerrilla: 6 klepht
gulf: 6 Aegina, Patras 7 Laconia, Saronic 8 Messinia, Salonika
infantry: 6 evzone
island: 3 Cos, Ios, Kos 4 Milo 5 Corfu, Crete, Delos, Leros, Melos, Milos, Naxos, Paros, Samos, Thera, Thira, Zante 6 Candia, Euboea, Lemnos, Lesbos, Patmos, Skiros, Skyros 8 Santorin 9 Santorini
islands: 6 Ionian
language: 5 Koine 8 Hellenic
leftist coalition: 3 EAM
legislature: 5 boule
letter: 2 mu, nu, pi, xi 3 chi, eta, phi, psi, rho, tau 4 beta, iota, zeta 5 alpha, delta, gamma, kappa, omega, sigma, theta 6 lambda 7 epsilon, omicron, upsilon
liqueur: 4 ouzo
money: 4 euro
mountain: 4 oros, Ossa 5 Athos 6 Pindus 7 Olympus
mountains: 4 Oeta 6 Pindus
musical note: 4 nete
neighbor: 6 Turkey 7 Albania 8 Bulgaria 9 Macedonia
Nobelist in Literature: 6 Elytis 7 Seferis
org.: 4 NATO
peninsula: 5 Morea
political movement: 6 enosis
port: 5 Aulis, Corfu, Pilos, Pylos 6 Patras, Rhodes 7 Piraeus 8 Peiraeus
river: 4 Arta
saint: 5 Cyril
sea: 5 Egean 6 Aegean, Ionian
township: 4 deme
tycoon: 3 Ari 7 Onassis
underground: 4 ELAS
verb form: 6 aorist
volcano: 9 Santorini
vowel: 3 eta 4 iota 5 omega 7 omicron, upsilon
wine: 7 malmsey, retsina
Greece (ancient)
architect: 6 Scopas
architectural style: 5 Ionic
astronomer: 10 Hipparchus 11 Aristarchus 12 Eratosthenes
author: 4 Esop 5 Aesop, Homer
boat: 6 galley
carved image: 6 xoanon
carved images: 5 xoana
chorus part: 5 epode
city: 4 Arta, Elea 5 Argos, Pella, polis, siris, Tegea 6 Tiryns 7 Eleusis
clan: 6 phyles
colonnade: 4 stoa
colony: 4 Elea 5 Cumae, Ionia 6 Aeolia, Aeolis
dialect: 5 Doric, Ionic 6 Aeolic
district: 6 Phocis
dreamy fruit of ~ myth: 5 lotus
drinking cup: 5 cylix, kylix
drinking horns: 5 rhyta
epic: 5 Iliad 6 Aeneid 7 Odyssey
exclamation: 4 evoe
garment: 5 tunic 6 chiton, peplos, peplus 7 chlamys
geographer: 6 Strabo 9 Pausanias
god: 3 Pan 4 Ares, Eros, Zeus 5 Hades, theos, Titan 6 Aeolus, Apollo, Charon, Helios, Hermes, Hypnos, Icarus 8 Cerberus, Dionysus, Poseidon 10 Hephaestus
goddess: 3 Ate, Eos 4 Hebe, Hera, Iris, Nike 5 Aeaea, Circe, Kirke 6 Athena, Athene, Hecate, Hekate, Hestia, Medusa, Selene 7 Artemis, Demeter 9 Aphrodite 10 Persephone
goddesses: 6 Furies, Gorgon, Graces
goddess of discord: 4 Eris
goddess of fate: 5 Moira
goddess of peace: 5 Irene
goddess of wisdom: 6 Athena, Athene
god of love: 4 Eros
god of ridicule: 5 Momus
hero struggle: 4 agon
instrument: 4 lyre
jug: 4 olpe
magistrate: 6 archon
marketplace: 5 agora
mathematician: 10 Pythagoras
messenger of the gods: 4 Iris
money: 4 mina, obol 6 stater, talent
personification of the sea: 6 Pontos, Pontus
philosopher: 8 Plotinus, Socrates 10 Pythagoras
physician: 5 Galen
playwright: 8 Menander 9 Aeschylus, Euripides, Sophocles 12 Aristophanes
poet: 6 Ritsos 9 Simonides 11 Homer Pindar 15 Sappho Aeschylus
provincial governor: 6 eparch
queen of the gods: 4 Hera
region: 6 Achaea, Actium, Attica
rhetorician: 6 Zoilus
sanctuary: 5 secos, sekos
scientist: 6 Strabo 9 Pausanias 10 Archimedes, Hipparchus 11 Aristarchus 12 Eratosthenes
sculptor: 5 Myron 6 Scopas
stanza: 5 epode
statue: 4 Kore
storyteller: 4 Esop 5 Aesop
strongman: 5 Atlas
temple: 4 naos 6 hieron
temple detail: 4 anta
theater: 5 odeon, odeum
theaters: 4 odea
tribe: 6 phyles
underworld river: 4 Styx 5 Lethe
valley: 5 Nemea
verse form: 4 epos
war god: 4 Ares
weight: 5 oboli 6 obolus
wine pitcher: 4 olpe
writer: 5 Plato 6 Zoilus 8 Plotinus, Plutarch, Xenophon
greed: 4 lust 6 hunger 7 avarice, avidity, edacity 8 cupidity, rapacity, venality, voracity 9 esurience, gold fever 10 grabbiness
exemplar of ~: 5 Midas
Greed (1925 film)
cast: Chester Conklin, Jean Hersholt, ZaSu Pitts
director: Erich von Stroheim
greedy: 4 avid 5 itchy, piggy, tight 6 grabby, hungry, piggie, stingy 7 craving, hoggish, lustful, miserly, piggish, selfish, swinish, thirsty 8 covetous, edacious, esurient, grasping, ravenous, ungiving 9 mercenary, penurious, predatory, rapacious, voracious 10 avaricious, gluttonous, insatiable, possessive, skinflinty
be ~: 4 envy, want 5 covet 7 burn for 8 begrudge
one: 3 hog, pig 5 harpy, taker
person's demand: 5 gimme
Greek: 5 Attic 6 Cretan 7 Hellene, Spartan 8 language 9 classical
group: 4 frat 8 sorority 10 fraternity
see also Greece
Greek __: 3 god 4 fire, rite 5 cross, salad 6 Church 7 calends, kalends, Revival
__ Greek: 3 New 4 Late 6 Middle, Modern
Greek alphabet:
1st - alpha
2nd - beta
3rd - gamma
4th - delta
5th - epsilon
6th - zeta
7th - eta
8th - theta
9th - iota
10th - kappa
11th - lambda
12th - mu
13th - nu
14th - xi
15th - omicron
16th - pi
17th - rho
18th - sigma
19th - tau
20th - upsilon
21st - phi
22nd - chi
23rd - psi
24th - omega
Greek/Roman god equivalents:
Aphrodite - Venus
Apollo - Apollo
Ares - Mars
Artemis - Diana
Athena - Minerva
Ceres - Demeter
Cronos - Saturn
Dionysus - Bacchus
Eos - Aurora
Eros - Amor, Cupid
Hades - Pluto
Helios - Sol
Hephaestus - Vulcan
Hera - Juno
Hermes - Mercury
Hestia - Vesta
Irene - Pax
Persephone - Proserpina
Poseidon - Neptune
Rhea - Ops
Zeus - Jupiter, Jove
Greeks Had a Word for Them, The (1932 film)
cast: Joan Blondell, Ina Claire, Madge Evans
Greek Tycoon, The
model: 3 Ari 7 Onassis
Greeley: 4 city, town 6 Andrew, editor, Horace
direction: 4 west
emulate ~: 4 edit
locale: 8 Colorado
Greeley, Andrew: 6 author, writer
character: Ryan, McGrail
work: The Bishop at Sea
The Cardinal Sins
Cardinal Virtues
Fall From Grace
Irish Eyes
Irish Gold
Irish Lace
Irish Love
Irish Mist
Irish Stew!
Irish Whiskey
A Midwinter's Tale
Patience of a Saint
Rite of Spring
Wages of Sin
White Smoke
green: 3 new, pea, raw 4 aqua, jade, lawn, lime, lush, naif, Nile, park, sick 5 field, fresh, kelly, leafy, loden, moola, naive, olive, plaza, young 6 boyish, callow, common, grassy, in leaf, moolah, simple, tender 7 emerald, envious, jealous, puerile, verdant 8 fumbling, gullable, gullible, ignorant, immature, inexpert, innocent, juvenile, unartful, untested, unversed, unwilted, youthful 9 beardless, credulous, grassland, ingenuous, sprouting, untrained, unworldly, vegetable 10 chartreuse, ecological, unpolished, unseasoned, unskillful
around the gills: 3 ill 6 queasy, queazy
beverage: 3 tea 5 hyson
bluish ~: 4 aqua, cyan, jade, Nile 5 beryl 6 myrtle 9 turquoise 10 aquamarine
brownish ~: 5 breen, olive
card holder: 5 alien 7 refugee 8 emigrant, newcomer 9 foreigner, immigrant 10 noncitizen
cheese: 7 sapsago
color: 3 pea 4 aqua, cyan, jade, lime, Nile, sage 5 beryl, breen, kelly, loden, olive, virid 6 myrtle, reseda 7 avocado, celadon, emerald, verdant 9 pistachio, turquoise 10 aquamarine, chartreuse
combining form: 4 verd- 5 chlor-, verdo- 6 chloro-
cover: 5 baize
ender: 3 fly, way 4 back, belt, gage, head, horn, mail, room, sand, sick, side, wood 5 brier, finch, heart, house, shank, stone, sward 6 grocer, market, swarth 7 grocery
feature: 3 pin 4 flag, hole
fix the ~: 5 resod
flower: 6 smilax 7 figwort 8 pilewort 10 mignonette
fruit: 4 pear 5 grape, olive
gage: 4 plum
gemstone: 4 jade
give the ~ light: 2 OK 4 okay 5 agree, allow 6 accede, enable 7 endorse, indorse
grayish ~: 4 sage 5 lovat 6 reseda 7 celadon
in heraldry: 4 vert
light: 2 go, OK 3 yes 4 okay, word 5 leave 6 assent, permit, signal 7 go-ahead, license, mandate, war-

rant **8** approval, sanction **9** clearance **10** acceptance
not ~: **4** ripe **6** mature **7** ripened, skilled **8** seasoned **10** well-versed
one: **4** tyro **6** novice, rookie **7** recruit, trainee **8** beginner, neophyte, newcomer **9** fledgling **10** apprentice, tenderfoot
opposite: **3** tee
org.: **3** PGA
shoot for the ~: **4** chip **5** slice
shot: **4** putt
spot: **5** oasis **6** garden
starter: **4** ever **6** winter
stuff: **3** oof **4** cash, gelt, jack, kail, kale, loot, peag, pelf **5** bills, bread, bucks, dough, funds, lucre, moola, mopus, pesos, rhino, sewan **6** dinero, do-re-mi, mammon, mazuma, moolah, seawan, silver, specie, wampum, wealth **7** cabbage, capital, dollars, lettuce, ooftish, scratch, shekels **8** bankroll, cold cash, currency, hard cash, smackers **9** banknotes, frogskins, simoleons
thumb: **4** gift **5** flair, knack, touch **6** talent
turn ~ over: **4** envy **5** covet **8** begrudge
vegetable: **3** pea **4** kail, kale **5** chard, cress **7** cabbage, lettuce, parsley, spinach
village ~: **4** park **5** plaza **6** common, square
yellowish ~: **3** pea **4** jade, sage **5** olive **9** pistachio **10** chartreuse
green ___: **3** bag, fee, pea, sea, tea **4** bass, bean, card, corn, crab, fish, flag, gram, line, mold, soap **5** algae, earth, flash, glass, heron, light, onion, osier, power, snake, stuff, thumb **6** dragon, monkey, pepper, plover, turtle **7** fingers, gentian, vitriol
green-___ monster: **4** eyed
___ green: **3** pea, sap, sea **4** bice, jade, lime, long, moss, Nile, sage, zinc **5** apple, beryl, fairy, kelly, loden, olive, Paris, salad **6** biscay, bottle, chrome, cobalt, forest, hunter, Kendal, myrtle **7** bowling, cadmium, emerald, Hooker's, Lincoln, Niagara, putting
___-green: **4** blue, leek **5** grass
Green: **2** Al **3** Guy **4** city, Paul, town **5** Henry, Hetty, Mitzi, Nigel, range **6** Johnny, Julien
land: **4** Eire, Erin **7** Ireland
locale: **4** Ohio **7** Vermont
Green ___: **3** Bay, Day **4** Card, Eyes **5** Acres, Beret, Giant, Grass, Paper, party, River, Stamp **6** Onions
Green ___ and Ham: **4** Eggs
Green ___ Packers: **3** Bay
Green ___, The: **3** Hat, Man, Ray **4** Door, Mile **6** Hornet, Ripper
___ Green: **6** Gretna
Greenacres: **4** city, town
locale: **7** Florida
Green Acres (CBS sitcom)
cast: Eddie Albert (Oliver Douglas)
Pat Buttram (Mr. Haney)
Mary Grace Canfield (Ralph Monroe)
Eva Gabor (Lisa Douglas)
Tom Lester (Ed Dawson)
Sid Melton (Alf Monroe)
Alvy Moore (Hank Kimball)
cow: Eleanor
dog: **6** Mignon **7** Cynthia
pig: Arnold
structure: **4** barn
Green, Adolph collaborator: **6** Comden
Green, Al
song: Call Me (1973)
Here I Am (1973)
I'm Still in Love With You (1972)
Let's Stay Together (1971)
Look What You Done for Me (1972)
Put a Little Love in Your Heart (1988)
Sha-La-La (1974)
You Ought to Be With Me (1972)
Green, Alfred E.: **8** director
film: Colleen (1936)
Dangerous (1935)
Disraeli (1929)
Ella Cinders (1926)
The Girl From 10th Avenue (1935)
It's Tough to Be Famous (1932)
The Jackie Robinson Story (1950)
The Jolson Story (1946)
The Narrow Corner (1933)
A Thousand and One Nights (1945)
Top Banana (1954)
Union Depot (1932)
___ Green Apples: **6** Little
Greenaway: **4** Kate **5** Peter
greenback: **4** bill, buck **5** money **6** dollar **7** smacker **8** banknote, frogskin, simoleon
greenbacks: **3** oof **4** cash, gelt, jack, kail, kale, loot, peag, pelf **5** bread, dough, funds, lucre, money, moola, mopus, pesos, rhino, sewan **6** dinero, do-re-mi, mammon, mazuma, moolah, seawan, silver, specie, wampum, wealth **7** cabbage, capital, dollars, lettuce, ooftish, scratch, shekels **8** bankroll, cold cash, currency, hard cash
Greenbaum, Norman song: Spirit in the Sky (1970)
Green Bay: **4** city, port, town
city near ~: **6** Antigo
locale: **9** Wisconsin
quarterback: **5** Starr
team: **7** Packers
green bean: **6** legume, veggie **9** vegetable
Greenbelt: **4** city, town
locale: **8** Maryland
Green Beret: **6** marine **7** soldier
like the ~ s: **5** elite
org.: **4** USMC
Greenberg, Hank: **5** Tiger **7** slugger
Greenberg, Uri Zvi: **4** poet **6** Hebrew
Greenbrier: **3** car **4** auto **5** Chevy **9** Chevrolet **10** automobile
Green Card (1990 film)
cast: Gérard Depardieu, Andie MacDowell, Bebe Neuwirth
director: Peter Weir
Greene: **3** Bob, Joe **4** Gael **5** Ellen, Lorne **6** Graham, Robert, Shecky **7** Mean Joe, Michele, Richard
costar: **6** Landon **7** Blocker, Roberts
Green Eggs and Ham
author: Dr. Seuss
character: **3** Sam **6** Sam-I-Am
Greene, Graham: **6** author, writer **7** British
work: Brighton Rock
A Gun for Sale
The Heart of the Matter
Our Man in Havana
The Third Man
Greene, Joe sport: **8** football
Greene, Lorne song: Ringo (1964)
Greene, Robert: **6** author, writer **7** British
greenery: **7** foliage, verdure
bit of ~: **5** plant, sprig
chew the ~: **5** graze
conceal with ~: **6** embosk
urban ~: **4** lawn **6** common, square **7** reserve **8** preserve
green-eyed: **7** envious, jealous **9** invidious, malicious **10** suspicious
monster: **4** envy
Green-Eyed Lady (1970 song) artist: Sugarloaf
Greenfield: **4** city, town
locale: **9** Wisconsin
Greenfields (1960 song) artist: Brothers Four
greenfinch: **4** bird
Green for Danger (1946 film)
cast: Sally Gray, Trevor Howard, Alastair Sim
director: Sidney Gilliat
Green Gables girl: **4** Anne
greengage: **4** plum
relative: **4** sloe **6** cherry, damson **9** myrobalan
Greengard, Paul: **8** Nobelist
Green Giant
competitor: **5** Libby **6** Libby's **8** Birdseye, Del Monte
___ Green Giant: **5** Jolly
Green Grass (1966 song) artist: Gary Lewis and the Playboys
Green Grass of Wyoming, The author: Mary O'Hara
Green, Green Grass of Home (1967 song) artist: Tom Jones
Green Hat, The author: Michael Arlen
greenhead: **4** duck, fowl
relative: **4** smew, teal **5** eider, Pekin, Rouen, scaup **6** Cayuga, scoter **7** gadwall, mallard, pintail, pochard, redhead, sea duck, widgeon **8** garganey, gray duck, mandarin, musk duck, oldsquaw, shoveler, surf duck, wood duck **9** black duck, broadbill, goldeneye, goosander, merganser, ruddy duck, sprigtail **10** bufflehead, canvasback, surf scoter, tufted duck
Green, Henry: **6** author, writer **7** British
Green Hills of Africa author: Ernest Hemingway
greenhorn: **4** babe, lamb, naif, tiro, tool, tyro **5** newie **6** intern, novice **7** amateur, dabbler, interne, learner, new hand, recruit **8** beginner, freshman, neophyte, newcomer, putterer **9** fledgling, simpleton **10** apprentice, dilettante, tenderfoot, uninitiate
like a ~: **3** new
social ~: **4** nerd
Green Hornet, The: **9** radio show
greenhouse: **7** nursery
area: **6** hotbed
do a ~ chore: **5** repot
like a ~: **5** humid, moist **6** steamy
greenhouse ___: **3** gas **6** effect
Greening of America, The author: **5** Reich
greenish color: **4** aqua, cyan, lime, Nile, teal **5** hazel, lemon **6** acacia, citron, cobalt, sallow **7** luteous, peacock **8** cerulean **9** champagne, robin's-egg, turquoise **10** aquamarine
Green, Julien: **6** author, French, writer
Greenland: **3** isl., sea **4** isle **6** island
air base: **5** Thule
bay: **6** Baffin
bovine: **6** muskox
capital: **7** Godthab
explorer: **7** Ericson
garb: **5** parka **6** anorak
native: **5** Inuit **6** Eskimo, Innuit, Inupik
sea: **8** Labrador
settlement: **4** Etah
sight: **5** fiord, fjord **6** icecap
Greenland ___: **3** Sea **4** spar **5** whale **7** Current
green leaf, name meaning: **7** Phyllis
___ Greenleaf Whittier: **4** John
green light
give the ~: **2** OK **3** let **4** okay **5** allow, clear **6** enable **7** approve
greenling: **4** fish
Green Mansions: **4** film **5** novel
author: W.H. Hudson
cast: Lee J. Cobb, Sessue Hayakawa, Audrey Hepburn, Anthony Perkins
character: **4** Abel, Rima, Runi **5** Nuflo
director: Mel Ferrer
Green Man, The author: Kingsley Amis
Green Mare, The author: **4** Ayme
Green Mile, The (1999 film)
author: Stephen King
cast: Michael Clarke Duncan, Tom Hanks, Bonnie Hunt
director: Frank Darabont
Green Mountain
Boy: **5** Allen, Ethan
locale: **7** Vermont
range: **6** Hoosac
greenness: **5** youth **7** naiveté, verdure **8** verdancy, viridity **9** credulity, freshness, innocence **10** callowness, immaturity
Greenock: **4** city, port, town
locale: **8** Scotland
greenockite: **3** ore **7** mineral
Green Onions (1962 song) artist: Booker T. and the MGs
Green Pastures, The
author: Marc Connelly
character: **4** Lawd
Green, Paul: **6** author, writer
Greenpeace concern: **4** ecol., nuke **5** A-test **7** ecology
Green Ray, The author: Jules Verne
Green Ripper, The author: John D. MacDonald
Green River (1969 song) artist: Creedence Clearwater Revival
greenroom: **6** lounge
greens: **5** salad **6** veggie **7** produce **10** rabbit food, vegetables
ender: **6** keeper
game: **4** golf
greens ___: **3** fee
___ greens: **5** salad **6** turnip **7** collard
Greensboro: **4** city, town
locale: **4** N. Car.
greenshank: **4** bird
greenskeeper's job, do a: **3** mow **6** aerate
Greenspan, Alan: **9** economist
org.: **3** Fed, FRS
spouse: Andrea Mitchell
subj.: **3** GNP **4** econ. **7** economy
green-stamp company: **5** S and H
Greenstreet, Sydney: **5** actor
costar: **5** Lorre
film: Background to Danger (1943)
Casablanca (1942)
Christmas in Connecticut (1945)
Flamingo Road (1949)
The Hucksters (1947)
The Maltese Falcon (1941)
The Mask of Dimitrios (1944)
Three Strangers (1946)
The Woman in White (1948)
greensward: **3** sod **4** lawn, turf
Green Tambourine (1967 song) artist: Lemon Pipers
___ Green Tomatoes: **5** Fried
Greenville: **4** city, town
athletes: **7** Pirates
city near ~: **6** Easley
college: **3** ECU **5** Thiel
locale: **5** Texas
___ Green Was My Valley: **3** How
Green Wave: **6** Tulane
Greenway: **6** Aurora
Greenwich: **4** city, town **5** Ellie
locale: **4** Conn. **7** England
river: **6** Thames
Greenwich ___: **4** Time **7** Village

Greenwich ___ Time: 4 Mean
Greenwich Village
  neighbor: 4 Soho 7 Tribeca
  sch.: 3 NYU
green with ___: 4 envy
Greenwood: 3 Lee 4 city, Joan, town
  locale: 7 Indiana
greeny: 3 cub 6 novice 7 recruit, trainee 8 beginner, neophyte 10 apprentice, tenderfoot
Greer: 3 Hal 4 Jane 6 Garson 8 Germaine
Greer, Germaine: 6 author, writer
Greer, Jane: 7 actress
  film: Big Steal (1949)
    Man of a Thousand Faces (1957)
    Out of the Past (1947)
    Run for the Sun (1956)
    Station West (1948)
    They Won't Believe Me (1947)
greet: 3 bow, hug, nod, see 4 hail, meet 5 let in, nod to, see in, shake 6 accost, herald, salaam, salute, wave to 7 embrace, receive, usher in, welcome 8 high-five 9 recognize
  the day: 4 wake 5 arise, awake, get up, waken 6 awaken
  the moon: 3 bay 4 howl 7 ululate
  the villain: 3 boo 4 hiss, jeer 8 sibilate
  warmly: 3 hug 5 ask in
greeting: 2 hi 3 hey, nod 4 ciao, hail, hiya, oh hi 5 aloha, hello, howdy 6 curtsy, halloa, how now, salaam, salute, shalom, sholom 7 bon jour, regards, welcome 8 high five 9 reception 10 how do you do, pleasantry, salutation
  Australian: 4 g'day
  British: 4 'ello 5 hullo
  formal ~: 3 bow 6 curtsy
  French: 5 salut
  gesture: 3 nod 4 wave
  Hawaiian ~: 5 aloha
  hippie ~: 5 peace
  Indian ~ in oaters: 3 how
  infant: 4 dada, mama
  Maori ~: 5 hongi
  nautical: 4 ahoy
  reunion ~: 3 hug
  warm ~: 3 hug 4 kiss 7 embrace
  Zen ~: 6 gassho
greeting card
  feature: 4 poem 5 rhyme, verse 8 doggerel
  like some ~ verses: 4 zany 5 corny, inane, mushy, sappy, silly 6 drippy, slushy, sticky 7 maudlin, mawkish 8 overdone
  word: 4 Noel, yule 5 happy
greetings: 7 regards, tidings 8 respects
Greetings (1968 film)
  cast: Robert De Niro, Gerrit Graham
  director: Brian De Palma
Greetings ___...: 4 from
Greetings org.: 3 SSS
Greg: 4 Lake 6 Evigan, Gumbel, LeMond, Maddux, Morris, Norman 7 Germann, Kinnear 8 Louganis, Luzinski, Mullavey
  TV wife: 6 Dharma
___ & Greg: 6 Dharma
gregarious: 6 clubby, social 7 affable, cordial 8 friendly, outgoing, sociable 9 convivial, expansive 10 hospitable, personable
  type: 5 mixer 6 joiner 7 mingler 9 extrovert 10 socializer
Gregg: 4 John 6 Allman 7 Forrest
grego: 4 coat 6 jacket
Gregor: 6 Mendel
Gregorian
  chant notation: 4 neum 5 neume
  cycle: 4 year
  preceder: 6 Julian
  tune: 5 chant
Gregorian ___: 4 mode 5 chant, water 8 calendar
Gregory: 4 Dick, Peck, pope 5 Corso, Hines, saint 6 Abbott, Horace, La Cava, Martin, Ratoff, Sierra 7 Cynthia, pontiff 8 Harrison
Gregory, Horace: 4 poet
Gregory of ___: 5 Nyssa, Tours
___ Gregson Wagner: 7 Natasha
greige: 6 undyed 10 unbleached
Greist, Kim: 7 actress
  film: Brazil (1985)
    Homeward Bound: The Incredible Journey (1993)
    Manhunter (1986)
___ gré, mal gré: 3 bon
gremlin: 3 elf, imp 4 bogy 5 gnome 6 goblin, kobold, sprite 8 barghest 9 hobgoblin
Gremlin: 3 AMC, car 4 auto 10 automobile
Gremlins (1984 film)
  cast: Hoyt Axton, Phoebe Cates, Zach Galligan
  director: Joe Dante
  dog: 6 Barney
Gremlins 2 The New Batch (1990 film)
  cast: Phoebe Cates, Zach Galligan, John Glover
  director: Joe Dante
Grenache: 5 grape
Grenada: 4 isle 6 island, nation 7 country
  capital: 9 St. George's
  money: 4 cent 6 dollar
  org.: 3 OAS
grenade: 4 bomb, frag 5 shell 9 explosive
___ grenade: 4 hand, tear 5 rifle
grenades: 4 ammo 9 munitions 10 ammunition
grenadier: 4 fish
grenadine: 5 syrup 6 fabric 8 material
Grenadines: 4 isls. 5 isles 7 islands
  locale: 9 Caribbean
Grendel: 4 ogre
  ancestor: 4 Cain
Grendel author: John Gardner
Grenoble: 4 city, town
  city near ~: 4 Lyon 5 Lyons
  department: 5 Isère
  locale: 6 France
  river: 5 Isère
Greschner, Ron spouse: Carol Alt
Gresham: 4 city, town
  locale: 6 Oregon
Gresham's ___: 3 law
Greta: 5 Garbo 7 Scacchi
Gretchen: 3 Mol
  in English: 8 Margaret
Grete: 5 Waitz
Gretel
  brother: 6 Hansel
  see also German
Gretna: 4 city, town
  locale: 9 Louisiana
Gretna Green, go to: 5 elope
Gretzky, Wayne
  emulate ~: 5 skate
  milieu: 3 ice 4 rink 5 arena
  nine-time award: 3 MVP
  org.: 3 NHL
  quest: 4 goal
  workplace: 3 ice 4 rink
Grévin, Jacques: 4 poet 6 author, French 10 playwright
grey: 3 ash 4 ashy, drab, hoar 5 ashen, dingy, hoary, smoky 6 cloudy, gloomy, leaden, somber 7 silvery, sunless 8 lowering, overcast 9 cinereous
  ender: 3 hen, lag 5 hound
  see also gray
Grey: 3 Nan 4 Earl, Jane, Joel, Lita, Zane 8 Jennifer, Virginia
Grey ___: 6 Poupon
___ Grey: 5 Agnes
Grey Cup grp.: 3 CFL
___ Grey Goose, The: 3 Ole
greyhound: 3 dog 5 pooch, racer 6 canine
Greyhound: 3 bus
  alternative: 6 Amtrak
  get off the ~: 5 debus
greyhound racing: 5 sport
greyish: 3 wan 4 ashy, pale 5 ashen, livid, pasty, waxen 6 pallid
Grey, Jane: 4 Lady
Grey, Joel Oscar: Cabaret
greylag: 4 bird
Grey Poupon: 7 mustard
  alternative: 7 French's, Gulden's
Greystoke: 4 lord 6 Tarzan
  playmate: 3 ape
Greystoke... (1984 film)
  cast: Ian Holm, Christopher Lambert, Andie MacDowell, Ralph Richardson
  director: Hugh Hudson
___ Grey tea: 4 Earl
Grey, Zane: 6 writer
  genre: western
  work: Arizona Ames
    Arizona Clan
    Black Mesa
    Call of the Canyon
    Code of the West
    Desert Gold
    The Desert of Wheat
    The Dude Ranger
    The Fugitive Trail
    Knights of the Range
    The Last of the Plainsmen
    The Last Trail
    The Last Wagon Train
    The Lone Star Ranger
    Lost Pueblo
    The Man of the Forest
    The Maverick Queen
    The Mysterious Rider
    Nevada
    The Rainbow Trail
    Riders of the Purple Sage
    Robbers' Roost
    Rogue River Feud
    Shadow on the Trail
    The Spirit of the Border
    Stranger From the Tonto
    Sunset Pass
    The Thundering Herd
    To the Last Man
    The Trail Driver
    Twin Sombreros
    Under the Tonto Rim
    The U.P. Trail
    Valley of Wild Horses
    West of the Pecos
    Wildfire
    Wild Horse Mesa
    Wyoming
GRF: 4 Ford
  predecessor: 3 RMN
  successor: 3 JEC
grid: 5 graph 6 matrix 7 grating, lattice, network 9 framework, grillwork
  ender: 4 iron, lock
  see also football, gridiron
grid ___: 4 bias, leak, road 7 circuit, current
gridder
  see football, gridiron
griddle: 3 pan 4 cook
  ender: 4 cake
  hot off the ~: 3 new 5 fresh
griddlecake: 8 flapjack
gridiron: 5 field, grate 6 frypan 7 stadium
  action: 4 fake, juke, kick, pass, play, punt 5 blitz, catch, sneak 6 end run, fumble, huddle, tackle 7 penalty 9 field goal, touchdown
  arbiter: 3 ref 5 zebra 7 referee
  defunct ~ grp.: 4 USFL
  gear: 3 tee 6 helmet
  group: 3 AFC, NFC, NFL, sqd. 4 line, NCAA 5 squad 6 huddle
  honor: 6 All-Pro
  injury site: 4 knee
  no-no: 4 clip
  opportunity: 4 down
  position: 2 FB, HB, LG, LH, LT, RB, RG, RT 3 ctr., end, RFB, RHB 5 guard 6 back. QB, center, tackle 8 fullback, halfback
  quota: 6 eleven
  setback: 4 loss
  stat: 2 TD 3 int. 9 touchdown
  two ~ periods: 4 half
  unit: 4 yard
  see also football
gridlock: 3 cog, jam 5 jam-up 6 holdup, logjam 7 impasse, traffic 8 blockage, prohibit, stoppage 9 stalemate 10 bottleneck, congestion, standstill, traffic jam
  unit: 3 car 4 auto
gridlocked: 5 fixed, stuck 6 packed, static 7 stalled, stopped 8 immobile 9 congested
Grieco: 7 Richard
grief: 3 rue, woe 4 ache, dole, pain 5 agony, dolor, gloom, trial, worry 6 lament, misery, regret, sorrow 7 anguish, despair, emotion, remorse, sadness, trouble 8 distress, hardship, mourning, troubles, vexation 9 dejection, heartache, suffering 10 affliction, depression, desolation, heartbreak, heavy heart, loneliness, melancholy, woefulness
  come to ~: 4 fail 5 abort 7 founder, misfire 8 miscarry
  exclamation: 4 alas 5 alack
  express ~: 3 cry, rue, sob 4 keen, moan, pine, sigh, wail, weep 5 mourn 6 lament, sorrow
  feel ~ for: 4 pity 10 sympathize
Grief author: Elizabeth Barrett Browning
grief-stricken: 3 sad 4 down 6 morose 7 hurting, unhappy 8 dejected, overcome, troubled 9 plaintive, woebegone
  be ~: 3 cry, sob 4 wail, weep 5 mourn 6 lament 9 break down, shed tears
Grieg, Edvard: 8 composer
  home: 4 Oslo 6 Norway
  work: Holberg Suite
    Peer Gynt
Grier: 3 Pam 5 Rosey 9 Roosevelt
Griese, Bob: 2 QB
  sport: 8 football
grievance: 4 beef, hurt 5 gripe, score, stink, wrong 6 bygone, grouse, grudge, injury, matter, plaint, squawk 7 affront, protest 8 big stink, distress, hardship, inequity, jeremiad 9 annoyance, ax to grind, bellyache, complaint, indignity, injustice, objection 10 affliction, difficulty, resentment
grieve: 3 rue 4 ache, hurt, moan, mope, pain, pine, wail, weep 5 bleed, brood, crush, mourn, upset, wound 6 bemoan, bewail, injure, lament, regret, sadden, sorrow, suffer 7 afflict, agonize, trouble 8 distress, languish 10 feel sorrow, take it hard
  for: 4 pity 6 bemoan, bewail
grieving: 3 sad 4 hurt, sore 5 sorry, tears, woful 6 lament, sorrow, woeful

7 doleful, injured, keening, unhappy 8 mourning 9 heartsick, sorrowful 10 despondent
grievous: 3 sad 4 dire, foul, grim, poor, ugly 5 awful, grave, gross, heavy, lousy, sorry, tough, woful 6 bitter, crumby, crummy, dismal, horrid, mortal, odious, rotten, severe, taxing, tragic, unfair, woeful 7 accurst, baleful, baneful, beastly, doleful, fearful, ghastly, glaring, harmful, heinous, hurtful, onerous, painful, piteous, pitiful, serious, weighty 8 accursed, damaging, dolorous, dreadful, flagrant, God-awful, horrible, inferior, mournful, shameful, shocking, stinking, terrible, tragical, wretched 9 abhorrent, agonizing, appalling, atrocious, defective, egregious, execrable, frightful, harrowing, ill-omened, injurious, insidious, loathsome, miserable, monstrous, offensive, plaintive, revolting, sorrowful, upsetting 10 abominable, calamitous, deplorable, despicable, detestable, disastrous, disturbing, horrendous, lamentable, oppressive, outrageous, unbearable, villainous
Grievous Sin author: Faye Kellerman
Griffey Jr., Ken sport: 8 baseball
Griffin: 4 city, Merv, town 5 Dunne 6 Archie
locale: 7 Georgia
Griffith: 2 D.W. 4 Andy, Hugh, Park 5 Clark, Emile 7 Melanie
Griffith, Andy: 5 actor
film: A Face in the Crowd (1957)
Hearts of the West (1975)
No Time for Sergeants (1958)
TV: Matlock, The Andy Griffith Show
Griffith, D.W.: 8 director
film: America/The Fall of Babylon (1924)
The Birth of a Nation (1915)
Broken Blossoms (1919)
Intolerance (1916)
Orphans of the Storm (1922)
Way Down East (1920)
rival: 4 Ince
Griffith, Emile: 5 boxer
milieu: 4 ring
Griffith, Hugh: 5 actor
film: Ben-Hur (1959, AA)
The Counterfeit Traitor (1962)
Start the Revolution Without Me (1970)
Tom Jones (1963)
Griffith-Joyner, Florence: 6 runner
Griffith, Melanie: 7 actress
film: Another Day in Paradise (1998)
Body Double (1984)
The Bonfire of the Vanities (1990)
Crazy in Alabama (1999)
Lolita (1997)
Nobody's Fool (1994)
Pacific Heights (1990)
Paradise (1991)
Shining Through (1992)
Stormy Monday (1988)
Working Girl (1988)
mother: Tippi Hedren
spouse: Antonio Banderas, Steven Bauer, Don Johnson
__ griffon: 7 Belgian
grifter: 5 cheat, shark 6 con man 7 hustler 8 swindler
brainchild: 4 scam
Grifters, The (1990 film)
cast: Annette Bening, John Cusack, Anjelica Huston
director: Stephen Frears
grig: 3 eel
home: 6 eelery
trap: 6 eelpot
Grignard, Victor: 7 chemist 8 Nobelist
Grigny: 4 city, town
locale: 6 France
grigri: 5 charm 6 amulet, fetich, fetish
grill: 3 ask 4 cook, heat, pump, quiz, sear, test 5 broil, query, roast, toast 6 sizzle 7 brasier, brazier, examine, hibachi, lattice, torture 8 barbecue, question 9 catechize, interview, lunchroom 10 restaurant, rotisserie
ender: 3 age 4 room, work
partner: 3 bar
remnant: 3 ash 5 ember 6 cinder
site: 4 yard 5 patio
treat: 3 rib 5 cabob, frank, kabab, kabob, kebab, kebob, steak 6 burger, hot dog 7 chicken
__ grill: 3 gas 5 mixed 8 barbecue
grille: 7 grating 8 auto part 10 cowcatcher
material: 6 chrome
protector: 3 bra
Grillparzer, Franz: 8 Austrian 10 playwright
grillwork: 4 grid
grilse: 4 fish
grim: 3 bad 4 dark, dire, dour, foul, glum, poor 5 awful, bleak, cruel, gaunt, grave, harsh, lousy, lurid, mirky, murky, no-win, sorry, stark, stern, sulky, woful 6 crumby, crummy, dismal, dogged, gloomy, grisly, horrid, morbid, morose, odious, rotten, savage, severe, somber, strict, sullen, tragic, woeful 7 accurst, austere, baleful, baneful, beastly, doleful, fearful, ghastly, hangdog, hideous, inhuman, macaber, macabre, ominous, serious, unhappy 8 accursed, dreadful, God-awful, grievous, gruesome, hopeless, horrible, inferior, inhumane, lowering, resolute, ruthless, shameful, sinister, stinking, terrible, tragical, wretched 9 abhorrent, appalling, atrocious, cheerless, defective, depressed, execrable, ferocious, frightful, insidious, loathsome, merciless, miserable, offensive, revolting, unpitying, woebegone 10 abominable, deplorable, depressing, despicable, detestable, disastrous, forbidding, formidable, horrendous, implacable, iron-willed, lamentable, relentless, unpleasant, unyielding
not ~: 4 pink, rosy 6 bright, upbeat 7 glowing, hopeful 8 cheerful, pleasing, sanguine 9 favorable, promising 10 auspicious, optimistic
grimace: 3 mug 4 face, moue, pout 5 fleer, frown, scowl, smirk, sneer, snoot, wince 10 contortion, expression
word said with a ~: 2 ow 3 yow 4 ouch, yeow
grimalkin: 3 cat 5 felid, kitty, tabby 6 feline
grime: 4 crud, dirt, gunk, muck, smut, soil, soot 5 filth 6 grunge, smooch, smudge, smutch 8 impurity
remover: 4 soap 8 cleanser 9 detergent
Grimes: 4 Gary 5 Tammy 6 Martha 8 Burleigh
__ Grimes: 5 Peter
Grimes, Tammy: 7 actress
daughter: Amanda Plummer
spouse: Christopher Plummer
Grimley: 2 Ed
Grimm: 5 Jacob 7 Wilhelm
character: 3 elf 4 ogre 5 gnome, troll
Grimm, Jacob: 6 author, German, writer
Grimm, Wilhelm: 6 author, German, writer
Grimsby: 4 city, town
locale: 6 Canada 7 Ontario
grimy: 4 foul 5 dingy, dirty, dusty, messy, mucky, muddy, smoky, sooty 6 filthy, fouled, grubby, grungy, soiled, sordid 7 muddied, smeared, smudged, squalid, stained, tainted, unclean, unswept 8 befouled, maculate, polluted, slovenly, unwashed 9 blackened, tarnished 10 bedraggled, besmirched, lusterless, unsanitary
grin: 4 beam 5 fleer, laugh, smile, smirk, sneer 6 simper 9 say cheese 10 expression
and bear it: 4 cope, take 5 stick 6 adjust, submit 7 stomach 8 overlook
like some ~ s: 6 boyish, impish
Grin, Aleksandr: 6 author, writer 7 Russian
Grin and Bear It senator: 5 Snort
Grinch: 4 ogre 6 meanie
creator: 5 Seuss
dog: 3 Max
victim: 3 Who
grind: 3 job, rub, rut 4 chew, edge, file, grit, hone, mash, mill, plod, rasp, task, toil, wear, whet, wonk, work 5 annoy, chore, crush, gnash, grate, hound, labor, mince, munch, pound, slave, study, sweat, usual 6 abrade, crunch, harass, pestle, plague, powder, scrape, smooth, tedium 7 atomize, crumble, crumple, drudger, oppress, rat race, routine, sharpen, slavery, torment, travail, trouble 8 drudgery, hard work, keep down, levigate, struggle, tireless 9 comminute, granulate, grunt work, lucubrate, persecute, pulverize, triturate, tyrannize 10 livelihood
against: 3 bug, irk, rub, vex 4 gall, wear 5 annoy, chafe, erode, grate 6 abrade, bother, harass, nettle, scrape 7 enflame, incense, inflame, provoke 8 exercise, irritate 10 exasperate
an ax: 4 edge, file, hone, whet 5 strop 7 sharpen
away: 4 plod, read, toil, work 5 labor, slave, study 6 drudge 9 lucubrate
ax to ~: 6 agenda 9 grievance, obsession
daily ~: 3 job, rut 4 work 5 labor 6 groove 7 routine
down: 4 wear 5 erode
ender: 5 stone
underfoot: 5 crush, worst 6 defeat 7 flatten, trample
__ grind: 4 drip
grinder: 4 hero, mill 5 hoagy, molar, tooth 6 hoagie, pestle 8 sandwich
__ grinder: 4 meat 5 organ
grinding: 4 hard 7 grating, onerous, raucous 8 abrasive, friction 10 oppressive
in need of ~: 4 dull 5 blunt
machine: 5 lathe
substance: 5 emery
tooth: 5 molar
Grinding It Out author: 4 Kroc
grindle: 4 fish, tuna 6 bowfin
Gringore, Pierre: 6 author, French, writer
Grinnell: 6 George
grip: 3 ken 4 case, fist, grab, hold, keep, lock, snap, take, vise 5 ahold, brace, catch, cinch, clamp, clasp, grasp, rivet, seize 6 arrest, clench, clinch, clutch, engage, snatch, valise 7 command, embrace, enchant, engross, enthral, inthral, mastery, squeeze, tighten 8 clutches, enthrall, entrance, foothold, interest, inthrall, suitcase, traction 9 fascinate, handclasp, handshake, hypnotize, lay hold of, mesmerize, spellbind, stagehand 10 perception, possession
loosen one's ~: 4 free 5 let go 6 unhand 7 release, set free 9 disengage
starter: 4 hand
tight ~: 3 hug 4 lock 6 clinch, clutch 7 bear hug, squeeze
__ grip: 3 key 6 pistol
__ grip!: 4 Get a
__-Grip: 4 Poli
gripe: 3 nag 4 beef, carp, crab, kick, moan, pain, pang, sulk 5 groan, peeve, whine 6 charge, grouch, grouse, kvetch, mutter, plaint, repine, squawk, yammer 7 grumble, protest, quibble 8 complain 9 annoyance, bellyache, complaint, find fault, grievance, make a fuss
about nothing: 3 nag 4 carp 5 cavil, whine 6 bicker, grouse 7 nitpick, quibble 8 pettifog
griper: 5 grump 6 grouch, kvetch, moaner 7 crybaby 8 grumbler 10 malcontent
grippe: 3 bug, flu 5 virus 9 influenza
gripped: 4 rapt 8 held fast, obsessed, ravished 10 spellbound
gripper: 4 vise 5 cleat, tongs 6 C-clamp, pliers
gripping: 6 moving 8 readable 9 thrilling
grips with, come to: 4 face 6 handle, tackle 8 cope with, deal with 9 encounter 10 meet head on
gris-gris: 5 charm 6 amulet, fetish
Grisham, John: 6 author, writer
profession: 3 law
work: The Brethren
The Chamber
The Client
The Firm
The Partner
The Pelican Brief
The Rainmaker
Runaway Jury
Street Lawyer
Testament
A Time to Kill
Gris, Juan: 6 artist 7 painter, Spanish
grisly: 4 gory, grim, ugly 5 awful, livid, lurid 6 horrid, morbid 7 ghastly, hideous, macaber, macabre 8 dreadful, gruesome, horrible, shocking, terrible 9 appalling, frightful 10 abominable, horrendous, horrifying, petrifying, terrifying
Gris-Nez: 4 cape
locale: 6 France
Grissom: 3 Gus 6 Virgil 9 astronaut
Grissom Gang, The (1971 film)
cast: Irene Dailey, Kim Darby, Scott Wilson
director: Robert Aldrich
grist ender: 4 mill
grist for the __: 4 mill
gristly: 5 tough 7 stringy
grit: 4 guts, sand 5 grind, heart, moxie, nerve, pluck, spine, spunk, valor 6 daring, gravel, mettle, powder, spirit, starch 7 bravery, courage, prowess, resolve, stamina 8 abrasive, backbone, gameness, gumption, tenacity, valiance, valiancy 9 endurance, fortitude, gutsiness, hardiness, toughness, willpower 10 confidence, doggedness, durability, feistiness, moral fiber, pluckiness, spunkiness
one's teeth: 5 steel 6 clench
true ~: 4 guts 5 pluck, spunk 9 fortitude
__ Grit: 4 True
grits: 5 grain 6 cereal
prepare ~: 4 boil

__ grits: **4** corn **6** hominy
gritty: **4** bold, game **5** brave, gutsy, hardy, nervy, sandy, tough **6** awless, daring, dogged, grainy, heroic, plucky, spunky **7** aweless, defiant, doughty, gallant, powdery, staunch, valiant **8** abrasive, fearless, granular, gravelly, heroical, indurate, intrepid, resolute, sandlike, scratchy, spirited, stalwart, unafraid, valorous **9** audacious, dauntless, dreadless, steadfast, tenacious, undaunted, unfearful **10** courageous, determined, granulated, lusterless, mettlesome, undismayed, unflagging
__-gritty: **5** nitty
grivet: **6** mammal **7** primate
 relative: **3** ape **4** saki, titi **5** chimp, drill, jocko, lemur, loris, magot, orang, potto, shrew **6** aye-aye, baboon, Bandar, galago, gelada, gibbon, guenon, howler, langur, macaco, monkey, rhesus, uakari, vervet **7** colobus, gorilla, guereza, hoolock, macaque, sapajou, siamang, tamarin, tarsier **8** bush baby, capuchin, mandrill, mangabey, marmoset, talapoin **9** orangutan **10** Barbary ape, chimpanzee, orangutang
Grizabella: **3** cat
 creator: **5** Eliot
Grizzard: **5** Lewis **6** George
grizzle: **6** whiten
grizzled: **3** old **4** aged **5** aging, hoary **6** ageing **7** ancient, elderly, wizened **9** geriatric, getting on, senescent, up in years **10** gray-haired
Grizzlies: **4** five, team
 home: **7** Memphis
 org.: **3** NBA
 sport: **10** basketball
grizzly: **4** bear, gray, grey **5** ursid
 home: **3** den **4** lair
 relative: **3** ash **4** dove, drab **5** beige, dusty, merle, pearl, putty, slate, taupe **6** silver **8** charcoal, gunmetal, platinum
 young ~: **3** cub
Grizzly rival: **3** Cav, Mav, Net, Sun **4** Buck, Bull, Hawk, Heat, Jazz, King, Spur **5** Knick, Laker, Magic, Pacer, Sixer, Sonic **6** Celtic, Hornet, Nugget, Piston, Raptor, Rocket, Wizard **7** Clipper, Warrior **8** Cavalier, Maverick **10** SuperSonic, Timberwolf
Grk.: **4** lang.
gro.
 fraction: **3** doz.
groan: **3** nag **4** carp, crab, howl, moan, sigh **5** creak, gripe, whine **6** grouse, kvetch, lament, mutter, plaint, repine, sorrow, squawk, yammer **7** grumble, screech **8** complain, vocalize **9** bellyache, make a fuss
 about: **4** moan **6** bemoan, bewail, lament, regret **7** deplore
groaner: **3** pun
groat: **4** coin **5** money **9** fourpence
groats: **4** oats **5** grain, kasha, wheat **6** cereal
__ G. Robinson: **6** Edward
Groce, Larry song: Junk Food Junkie (1976)
grocer: **6** dealer, seller, vendor **8** merchant, purveyor, retailer **10** shopkeeper
groceries: **4** food **10** essentials, provisions
 remove the ~: **5** unbag
grocery: **3** mkt. **4** mart **6** bodega, market **9** food store
 bags: **6** armful
 bars: **3** UPC
 box fig.: **5** net wt.
 buy: **3** can, ham, pop, tea, tin **4** beef, chop, eggs, food, kail, kale, meat, milk, rice, salt **5** limes, pasta, pears, roast, sugar, viand **6** apples, cereal, lemons **7** cookies, oranges **9** detergent
 chain letters: **3** IGA
 coupon value: **5** cents
 holder: **3** bag, box, jar **4** case **5** quart **6** bottle, carton
 list abbr.: **3** doz.
 need: **4** bags **5** scale
 section: **4** deli, lane **5** aisle, dairy
 starter: **5** green
 trip: **6** errand
grocery __: **4** cart **5** store
Grodin, Charles: **5** actor
 film: 11 Harrowhouse (1974)
  Heart and Souls (1993)
  The Heartbreak Kid (1972)
  Ishtar (1987)
  It's My Turn (1980)
  King Kong (1976)
  The Lonely Guy (1984)
  Midnight Run (1988)
  Seems Like Old Times (1980)
grody: **5** dirty, seedy **6** sleazy **8** slovenly
Grody __ max!: **5** to the
Groening: **4** Matt
 parent: **5** Homer, Marge
Grofé, Ferde: **8** composer
 work: Grand Canyon Suite
  Hollywood Suite
  Mark Twain Suite
  Mississippi Suite
  New England Suite
grog: **3** ale **5** booze, drink, quaff **6** liquor **7** alcohol, spirits **8** beverage **10** intoxicant
 ingredient: **3** rum
 shop: **6** tavern **7** barroom **8** taphouse
groggy: **5** dazed, dizzy **6** sleepy **9** heavy-eyed, somnolent
grogram: **6** fabric **8** material
Groh: **5** David
grok: **3** dig **5** enjoy **6** follow **8** relate to **9** empathize **10** appreciate, comprehend
Grolier's: **3** enc. **4** ency. **5** encyc.
grommet: **6** eyelet
Gromyko: **6** Andrei
groom: **4** clip, comb, hand, male, mate, prep, tend, tidy, wash **5** brush, clean, curry, drill, preen, prime, primp, ready, train, tutor, vower **6** flunky, lackey, spouse, tidy up **7** educate, equerry, flunkey, husband, lacquey, nurture, prepare, shape up, spiff up **8** benedict, horseman, neaten up, newlywed, prettify, pretty up, spruce up **9** make ready, smarten up
 acquisition: **5** in-law
 area: **6** stable
 buy: **4** band, ring
 future ~: **4** beau **6** fiancé **8** intended **9** betrothed
 of India: **4** sice, syce **5** saice
 partner: **5** bride
 response: **3** I do
 starter: **5** bride
 wear: **3** tux **4** tuck **10** cummerbund
groomed: **4** tidy **5** natty, sleek, slick, smart **6** all set, dapper, primed, spruce **10** fastidious, immaculate
__-groomed: **4** well
grooming aid: **4** comb
groove: **3** cut, rut, sit **4** dado, kerf, line, rote, slot **5** canal, crimp, ditch, flute, gouge, habit, notch, ridge, score, track, trail **6** crease, furrow, gutter, hollow, incise, rabbet, trench **7** channel, fluting, rapport, routine **8** accustom, habitude **9** corrugate **10** daily grind, depression, interspace
 barrel ~: **5** croze
 bowstring ~: **4** nock
 carpenter ~: **4** dado
 shaft ~: **6** keyway
 sliding door ~: **5** regle
 small ~: **4** nurl **5** knurl, stria
Groovin' (1967 song) artist: Rascals
grooving: **5** happy, merry, peppy, perky **6** joyful **7** gleeful **8** animated, carefree, cheerful, jubilant, laughing, mirthful **9** energetic, exuberant, sprightly **10** flying high, optimistic
groovy: **3** def, fab, rad **4** aces, A-one, boss, braw, cool, dece, fine, gear, keen, neat, nice, phat, tuff **5** dandy, ducky, grand, great, marvy, neato, nifty, nobby, prime, slick, super, swell **6** bang on, bang-up, bonzer, bosker, choice, divine, dreamy, far out, gnarly, lovely, peachy, slap-up, spot on, superb, terrif, tiptop, unreal, whizzo, wicked **7** amazing, awesome, capital, corking, perfect, ripping, skookum, stellar, sublime **8** dazzling, especial, eximious, fabulous, five-star, four-star, frabjous, glorious, heavenly, jim-dandy, slam-bang, smashing, splendid, standout, sterling, stickout, superior, terrific, top-level, topnotch, very good, wondrous **9** bodacious, Endsville, excellent, exemplary, exquisite, fantastic, first-rate, high-grade, hunky-dory, marvelous, sollicker, top-flight, wonderful **10** first-class, hotsy-totsy, jack-a-dandy, out of sight, peachy-keen, phenomenal, remarkable, stupendous, super-duper
Groovy Kind of Love (song), A artist: Mindbenders, Phil Collins
grope: **3** paw **4** feel, fish **5** probe, touch **6** fumble, search **8** flounder **9** cast about, feel about
groper: **4** fish **5** pawer
Gropius, Walter: **6** German **9** architect
Grosbard, Ulu: **8** director
 film: Deep End of the Ocean (1999)
  Falling in Love (1984)
  Straight Time (1978)
  The Subject Was Roses (1968)
  True Confessions (1981)
grosbeak: **4** bird **8** cardinal, hawfinch
 beak: **3** neb, nib
__ grosbeak: **4** blue, pine **7** evening
groschen: **5** money
gros de __: **5** Tours **7** Londres
grosgrain: **5** cloth **6** fabric **8** material
gross: **3** all, big, low, raw, sum **4** earn, foul, huge, icky, lewd, loud, make, rank, rude, sick, ugly **5** awful, bulky, crass, crude, heavy, large, nasty, sheer, stark, total, utter, whole, yucky **6** coarse, entire, patent, profit, ribald, rotten, scuzzy, take in, unmeet, vulgar **7** blatant, boorish, bring in, extreme, glaring, hateful, heinous, hideous, loutish, massive, obvious, sizable, uncouth, weighty **8** abnormal, apparent, complete, degraded, dreadful, enormous, entirety, flagrant, grievous, horrible, improper, indecent, manifest, outright, pull down, receipts, shameful, shocking, sizeable, sum total, terrible, totality, unsavory, unseemly, unsubtle, unwieldy, wretched **9** aggregate, appalling, downright, egregious, excessive, frightful, grotesque, inelegant, loathsome, low-minded, lubricous, monstrous, nefarious, offensive, out-and-out, repellant, revolting, tasteless, unrefined, unsightly, unwieldly **10** abominable, disgusting, immoderate, indecorous, indelicate, inordinate, lascivious, outrageous, overweight, scurrilous, uncultured, uninviting, unpleasant
 fraction: **5** dozen
 not ~: **3** net **6** profit **8** take-home
 out: **5** appal, repel **6** appall, offend, revolt, sicken **7** disgust
gross __: **3** out, ton **6** income, profit, weight **7** anatomy, revenue, tonnage
Gross: **4** Arye, Mary, Milt **5** Henry **7** Michael
Gross!: **3** ick, ugh **4** yech, yuck **5** yecch
Gross Anatomy (1989 film)
 cast: Christine Lahti, Matthew Modine, Daphne Zuniga
gross domestic __: **7** product
Grosse __: **3** Ile
Grosse __, MI: **6** Pointe
Grosse Pointe Blank (1997 film)
 cast: Alan Arkin, Dan Aykroyd, Joan Cusack, John Cusack, Minnie Driver
Grosset partner: **6** Dunlap
Grossglockner: **3** alp
gross national __: **7** product
grossness: **8** enormity, ribaldry **9** bawdiness, brutality, crudeness, indecency, vulgarity
grosso: **4** full **5** great
__ Grosso: **4** Mato **5** Matto
Gros Ventre: **5** tribe
grosz: **5** money
Grosz: **6** George
groszy, 100: **5** zloty
Grote: **5** Jerry, Reber
grotesque: **3** odd **4** eery, ugly, wild **5** antic, eerie, gross, weird **6** absurd **7** bizarre, hideous, strange, surreal **8** aberrant, freakish **9** distorted, fantastic, ludicrous, malformed, misshapen, monstrous, unnatural, whimsical **10** outlandish, ridiculous
grotto: **4** cave, cove **5** antre, bower **6** alcove, cavern, recess **7** hideout
grotty: **5** dirty, seedy **8** wretched
grouch: **4** carp, crab, moan **5** churl, crank, gripe, growl, grump, shrew, whine **6** griper, grouse, kvetch, moaner, mutter, whiner **7** grouser, growler, grumble **8** complain, grumbler, sorehead, sourball, sourpuss **9** bellyache, make a fuss **10** bellyacher, complainer, crosspatch, curmudgeon, malcontent
 look: **5** scowl
grouchiness: **4** bile **6** spleen, temper
Groucho: **3** wit **4** host, Marx **5** emcee
 brother: **5** Chico, Gummo, Harpo, Zeppo
 cap: **5** beret
 glance from ~: **4** leer
 specialty: **3** pun **5** ad-lib
grouchy: **4** sour **5** cross, gruff, moody, onery, rough, sulky, surly, testy **6** crabby, cranky, crusty, fretty, grumpy, ireful, morose, ornery, snappy, touchy **7** bearish, huffish, kvetchy, peevish, waspish **8** choleric, churlish, growling, grumpish, liverish, petulant, snappish **9** crotchety, fractious, irascible, irritable, querulous, splenetic **10** out of sorts
 be ~: **4** bark, vent **5** growl, grunt, snarl **7** grumble **8** complain
ground: **3** bed, sod **4** base, dirt, land, root, site, soil, turf, zone **5** basis, coach, earth, field, level, lower, patch, teach, train, tutor, venue **6** bottom, inform, keep in, punish, reason, region, school, sphere **7** confine, flatten, powdery, premise, prepare, qualify, support, terrain, topsoil **8** acquaint, initiate, instruct, restrict **9** landscape, principle, pulverize, underside

10 foundation, real estate, terra firma
break ~: 4 plow 5 begin 7 kick off
breaker: 3 hoe 5 spade
breaking new ~: 5 fresh, novel 6 clever 7 unusual 8 creative, inspired, original, singular 9 ingenious, inventive 10 innovative
breeding ~: 6 hotbed
combining form: 3 geo- 5 chame- 6 chamae-
cover: 3 sod 4 lawn, snow, tarp 5 ajuga, grass, mulch, plant, sedum
cover ~: 3 fly, hie, run 4 rush 5 speed 6 travel 8 progress
ender: 3 hog, nut, out 4 ball, mass, side, sill, work 5 cover, speed, swell, water 6 keeper, stroke 7 breaker 8 breaking
gain ~: 6 pick up 7 advance 8 get ahead, progress 9 go forward
get off the ~: 5 begin, start
give ~: 6 retire 7 retreat 8 withdraw
give no ~: 5 force, order, press 6 demand, insist 8 pressure 9 stand firm
giving no ~: 8 stubborn
grain: 4 meal 5 flour, grist
happy hunting ~: 6 heaven, utopia 7 Arcadia, Elysium 9 Shangri-la
high ~: 4 hill, rise 5 knoll, ridge 7 plateau 8 eminence, mountain 9 acclivity, elevation 10 prominence
hit the ~: 3 lit 4 alit, fell, land 5 light 6 alight
hold one's ~: 4 stay 6 adhere, endure, remain, take it 7 persist, stay put
leave the ~: 3 fly 4 rise, soar 5 arise, climb, vault 6 ascend, rocket 7 balloon, take off 8 levitate
lose ~: 3 lag 4 slip 5 slide 7 regress 8 fall back
near the ~: 3 low 5 below 7 beneath 8 crouched, low-lying
on slippery ~: 4 iffy 5 dicey, hairy, risky 6 chancy, daring, touchy, tricky, unsafe 7 fraught 8 ticklish 9 dangerous, desperate, foolhardy, hazardous 10 precarious, touch-and-go
on solid ~: 6 ashore
piece of ~: 3 lot 4 area 5 field, range, tract 7 section, terrain
plan: 3 map 5 chart, draft 6 design, layout, scheme, sketch, survey 7 diagram, outline, program, rundown 8 proposal, scenario 9 blueprint, framework, rough idea 10 rough draft
rising ~: 4 bank, hill 5 slope 7 incline 8 gradient
rule: 6 policy 7 precept 9 guideline
run into the ~: 6 overdo 7 belabor, overuse 8 overplay
starter: 4 back, camp, fair, play 5 above, below 6 battle
stomping ~: 4 turf 5 haunt 6 domain, locale, region, sphere 7 hangout, quarter 8 locality 9 territory
toward the ~: 3 low 4 down 5 below 10 underneath
wet ~: 3 bog 5 marsh
zero: 4 goal 5 focus 6 target 8 bull's-eye 9 objective
ground __: 3 fog, ice, ivy, log, owl, pea, rod, row 4 bait, ball, bass, beam, coat, crew, dove, fish, loop, pine, pink, plan, plum, rent, rule, wave, ways, wire, zero 5 alert, cable, cedar, cloth, color, cover, fault, floor, glass, layer, level, plane, plate, robin, rules, shark, sheet, sloth, state, track, water 6 beetle, cherry, sluice, stroke, tackle 7 control, hemlock, station
__ ground: 3 low 4 gain, give, hard, high, home, lose, soft 5 break, cover, spoil 6 common, middle, teeing 7 etching, fishing, grapple, hunting, neutral, proving, vantage
__-ground: 5 air-to, white 6 figure, hollow 7 dumping
groundbreaking: 3 new 5 novel 7 radical
grounded: 6 ashore 7 learned 8 stranded
nautically: 6 neaped
__-grounded: 4 well
grounder, botched: 5 error
groundhog: 6 animal, digger, mammal, rodent
relative: 3 rat 4 cavy, degu, jird, paca, vole 5 coypu, gundi, mouse, xerus 6 agouti, beaver, gerbil, gopher, jerboa, marmot, murine 7 hamster, lemming, muskrat, visacha 8 chipmunk, cricetid, dormouse, squirrel, tuco-tuco 9 chickaree, guinea pig, porcupine, woodchuck 10 chinchilla, prairie dog
Groundhog Day (1993 film)
cast: Chris Elliott, Andie MacDowell, Bill Murray
director: Harold Ramis
Groundhog Day month: 3 Feb. 8 February
grounding: 8 training 9 education 10 background, upbringing
groundless: 4 idle, null 5 empty, false, inane, silly, wacky, wrong 6 absurd, screwy, wanton, whacky 7 fatuous, unsound 8 baseless, cockeyed, needless, specious 9 causeless, illogical, imaginary, senseless, unfounded, untenable 10 bottomless, chimerical, gratuitous, ungrounded, unprovoked
ground-level: 3 low 4 flat 5 short 10 unelevated
__-ground missile: 5 air-to
groundnut: 5 tuber 6 veggie 9 vegetable
ground-round serving: 5 patty 6 pattie
grounds: 3 lot, why 4 area, call, land, lees, park, root 5 basis, cause, dregs, field, proof, realm, tract 6 campus, domain, estate, motive, reason, sphere 7 acreage, country, deposit, habitat, premise, pretext, residue, terrain 8 district, environs, evidence, leavings, occasion, premises, property, sediment, validity 9 rationale, settlings, territory, testimony, wherefore 10 foundation, legitimacy, real estate
ender: 6 keeper
for a suit: 4 tort 5 abuse, crime, libel, smear, wrong 6 attack 7 calumny, slander 10 defamation
give ~ for: 5 incur, prove 7 justify, testify
house and ~: 5 manor, ranch 6 estate 8 premises, property 10 plantation
school ~: 4 quad 6 campus
__ grounds: 6 parade
groundsel: 4 weed 5 plant 6 flower
groundskeeper
at times: 5 mower, raker
concern: 5 shrub
groundswell: 5 flood, surge 6 onrush 10 outpouring
ground-to-__: 3 air
__-ground wheat: 5 stone
groundwood __: 4 pulp
groundwork: 3 bed 4 base 5 basis 7 support 8 research, training 10 background, foundation, substratum
lay the ~: 4 plan 5 draft, found, frame, set up, shape, start 6 create, draw up, launch 7 develop, pioneer, prepare, provide 8 initiate 9 establish, formulate, institute, introduce, spearhead 10 anticipate, trailblaze
group: 3 lot, org., set 4 assn., band, bevy, bloc, body, clan, clot, club, crew, cult, gang, herd, link, lump, mass, pack, pool, rank, sect, sort, team, tier, type, unit 5 batch, bunch, chain, class, clump, corps, covey, crowd, flock, genre, order, party, posse, squad, suite, troop 6 assort, bundle, cartel, circle, clique, clutch, corral, divide, family, gang up, gather, huddle, league, legion, muster, outfit, parcel, passel, school, series, throng 7 arrange, battery, brigade, bunch up, cluster, collect, combine, company, consort, coterie, faction, marshal, platoon, round up, scare up, society, species 8 assemble, assembly, category, classify, ensemble, flotilla, graduate, organize, separate 9 aggregate, associate, coalition, committee, concourse, forgather, gathering, syndicate 10 assemblage, assortment, categorize, collection, concursion, congregate, contingent, cumulation, distribute, pigeonhole
ender: 5 think
in golf: 8 foursome
group __: 4 work 6 theory 7 annuity
__ group: 3 age, Lie, rap 4 peer, soil, user 5 blood, focus, point, space, study, youth 6 acetyl, affine, battle, breath, factor, simple, status, Trojan 7 Abelian, acrylyl, control, linkage, primary, support, torsion
grouped: 5 joint 6 mutual 7 generic, unified 8 combined, communal, compiled, conjoint 9 assembled, composite, concerted, generical 10 collective, cumulative
grouper: 4 fish, mero 5 guasa
groupie: 3 fan, nut 4 buff 7 admirer, devotee, fanatic 8 follower, hanger-on 9 sycophant 10 aficionado
need: 4 hero, icon, idol 7 darling, pop star 8 luminary 9 celebrity, superstar
grouping: 4 tier 5 class 6 league 7 bracket 8 category, division, sequence 9 formation
symbol: 5 paren.
Group, The (1966 film)
author: Mary McCarthy
cast: Candice Bergen, Joan Hackett, Elizabeth Hartman
director: Sidney Lumet
groupthink: 4 talk 10 conference, discussion
grouse: 4 beef, bird, carp, crab, fowl, fuss, moan, sulk 5 cavil, gripe, groan, whine 6 grouch, kvetch, mutter, plaint 7 grumble, protest 8 complain, game bird 9 bellyache, complaint, grievance, make a fuss, ptarmigan, sprigtail
female ~: 6 gorhen
relative: 5 poult, quail, snipe 6 chukar, peahen, turkey 7 peacock, peafowl 8 curassow, moorfowl, pheasant, woodcock 9 partridge 10 guinea fowl, jungle fowl, wild turkey
__ grouse: 3 red 4 blue, sage, sand, wood 5 black, dusky, hazel, sooty 6 ruffed, spruce 7 prairie
grouser: 6 grouch, kvetch 8 sorehead
grousing: 7 peevish 9 grumbling, querulous
grout: 6 cement, filler, mortar 7 plaster
user: 5 tiler
grouty: 5 sulky, surly, testy
grove: 4 mott, park, wood 5 copse, motte, stand, woods 6 bosket, forest, timber 7 bosquet, coppice, orchard
__ grove: 5 sugar 6 orange
Grove City: 4 city, town
locale: 4 Ohio
grovel: 3 beg 5 cower, crawl, kotow, toady 6 cringe, kowtow 7 eat crow 8 bootlick 9 prostrate
Grove, Lefty: 6 hurler 7 pitcher
groveler: 5 toady 6 lackey 7 lacquey 8 kowtower 9 sycophant
groveling: 6 abject, menial 7 servile, slavish 8 cringing, toadying, toadyish 9 kowtowing 10 obsequious, submissive
__ Grove, NJ: 5 Penns
Grover: 9 Cleveland 10 Washington
vice president: 5 Adlai
Grover __ Alexander: 9 Cleveland
Groves of Academe, The author: Mary McCarthy
Groveton: 4 city, town
locale: 8 Virginia
__ Grove Village, IL: 3 Elk
grow: 3 age, sow, wax 4 rise, till 5 add to, bloat, bloom, build, mount, plant, raise, ripen, shape, swell, widen 6 accrue, beef up, deepen, dilate, evolve, expand, extend, gather, mature, spread, spring, sprout, step up, thrive, unfold 7 accrete, advance, amplify, augment, balloon, broaden, build up, burgeon, develop, enlarge, fill out, inflate, magnify, mount up, prosper, quicken, recover, stretch 8 bourgeon, escalate, flourish, get ahead, heighten, increase, incubate, lengthen, maturate, multiply, progress, snowball, vegetate 9 branch out, germinate, increment, luxuriate, propagate 10 accumulate, appreciate, burst forth, gain weight, liberalize, supplement
accustomed: 5 adapt, inure 6 adjust, harden, orient 7 conform 9 acclimate, reconcile 10 assimilate, come around
dim: 4 fade 6 darken 7 blacken
dull: 4 fade, pale
into: 4 turn 7 advance 8 progress
larger: 3 wax 5 widen 6 expand
older: 3 age 4 grow 6 mature 7 develop
on: 6 accept, affect 9 influence
out of: 5 arise, issue 6 derive, emerge, follow, result 7 proceed 9 arise from, originate
profusely: 4 riot 5 bloom 6 abound, thrive 7 burgeon, run riot 8 flourish 9 luxuriate
rapidly: 4 boom 5 swell 6 thrive 7 burgeon, explode, shoot up 8 flourish, mushroom
rich: 4 gain 5 get on, score 6 arrive, batten, do well, profit 7 burgeon, make out, prosper, succeed 8 flourish, get ahead, go places, hit it big, make good 9 make money
smaller: 3 ebb 4 wane 6 lessen, narrow, shrink 7 decline, deflate, drop off, dwindle 8 contract, decrease, diminish
stronger: 5 rally, train 6 arouse, perk up, pick up, revive 7 get well, improve, rebound, recover, shape up 8 come back 9 get better 10 bounce back, come around, recuperate, rejuvenate, turn around
together: 4 knit, mend 7 entwine
up: 5 arise 6 appear, mature 7 develop 9 come of age 10 burst forth
weary: 4 flag, jade, pall, tire 8 peter out

white: **4** fade **6** blanch, bleach **8** etiolate
grow __: **4** into, lamp **5** light
grower: **6** farmer **7** planter **8** gardener **10** agronomist, cultivator
starter: **4** wine, wool
growing: **5** alive, young **7** farming, ongoing, rampant **8** blooming, thriving
business: **4** farm
early: **4** rath **5** rathe
good for ~: **6** arable **7** fertile **8** plowable, tillable
medium: **4** dirt, loam, soil **5** earth **6** ground **7** topsoil
org.: **3** UFW
out: **5** enate
room: **4** acre
season: **3** spr. **6** spring
together: **9** confluent
vigorously: **4** rank, wild **7** rampant **8** prolific **9** exuberant, luxuriant **10** junglelike
years: **5** teens, youth **7** boyhood **8** girlhood **9** childhood **10** immaturity, pubescence
growing __: **5** pains, point
growing-__ mortgage: **6** equity
Growing Pains (ABC sitcom)
cast: Kirk Cameron (Mike Seaver) Tracey Gold (Carol Seaver) Joanna Kerns (Maggie Seaver) Jeremy Miller (Ben Seaver) Alan Thicke (Dr. Jason Seaver)
Growing Up in New Guinea author: Margaret Mead
growl: **4** bark, gnar, howl, moan, roar, roll, snap **5** gnarl, gnarr, grunt, snarl **6** bellow, grouch, mutter, rumble **7** grumble, thunder **8** complain **9** make a fuss **10** vituperate
source: **5** belly, tummy **7** stomach
growler: **6** grouch, kvetch **7** pitcher
grow like __: **5** a weed
growling: **5** gruff, surly, testy **6** grumpy, ornery, touchy **7** bearish, grouchy, peevish, uncivil **8** snappish **9** irascible, irritable, querulous **10** out of sorts
grown: **3** big **5** adult **6** mature **8** full-size **9** full-sized
starter: **4** home, moss
together: **6** adnate
up: **3** big **4** ripe **5** adult, of age **6** mature **9** developed
grown-__: **3** ups
__-grown: **4** full **5** shade
__ Grown Accustomed to Her Face: **3** I've
grown-up: **3** man **4** lady **5** adult, woman **6** mature, mister, person **9** gentleman
__ grow on: **5** one to
__ Grows in Brooklyn: **5** A Tree
growth: **4** boom, gain, hike, incr., life, rise **5** boost, surge, swell **6** upping, waxing **7** accrual, advance, buildup, process, stature, success **8** increase, progress, widening **9** beefing up, evolution, expansion, extension, flowering, gestation, sprouting **10** incipience, maturation, production, prosperity, transition
combining form: **3** aux- **4** auxo- **6** auxamo-, -trophy
full ~: **5** prime **8** majority, maturity **9** adulthood
new ~: **4** twig, wand **5** shoot, sprig
rapid ~ environment: **3** den **4** nest **6** cradle, hotbed
rings: **6** annuli
season's ~: **4** crop **5** yield **7** harvest
slow ~: **5** stunt
spell: **4** boom **5** spirt, spurt
underground ~: **5** radix, tuber **7** radicle, rhizome
unwelcome ~: **4** weed
growth __: **4** cone, fund, ring **7** company
__ growth: **3** old **5** grain **6** second
__ Grow Too Old to Dream: **5** When I
__ Grow Up: **5** I Won't, When I
Groza, Lou sport: **8** football
nickname: **3** Toe
grp.: **3** org. **4** assn. **5** assoc.
grub: **3** bug, dig **4** chow, eats, fare, feed, food, meal, meat, nosh, plod, root, slog, toil, wonk **5** delve, labor, larva, scour, shove, slave, snack **6** burrow, drudge, fodder, insect, search, uproot **7** aliment, edibles, rations, rummage, uncover, unearth, victual, vittles **8** excavate, scrounge, victuals **9** provender **10** provisions, sustenance
ender: **5** stake
grownup ~: **6** beetle
grub __: **3** hoe, saw **4** beam
Grub __: **6** Street
grubber starter: **5** money
grubby: **5** dirty, grimy, messy, muddy, nasty, seedy, sooty, tacky **6** filthy, fouled, grungy, soiled, sordid, unneat **7** smudged, stained, tainted, unkempt, unswept **8** befouled, begrimed, maculate, polluted, slovenly, unwashed **9** blackened, tarnished **10** besmirched, unsanitary
grubstake: **4** fund **7** funding, sponsor **9** guarantee, subsidize
grubstaker: **7** sponsor **9** financier, guarantor **10** benefactor
grudge: **4** feud **5** score, spite, stint, venom **6** animus, enmity, hatred, malice, rancor **7** dislike, ill will, umbrage **8** bad blood **9** animosity, antipathy, grievance **10** bitterness, resentment
bear a ~: **6** resent
carrying a ~: **3** mad **4** sore **6** bitter
have a ~ against: **4** hate **5** spite **6** detest **7** despise
__ grudge: **5** bear a
grudging: **4** sour **6** forced, stingy **7** jealous **8** ungiving **9** reluctant, unwilling **10** unfriendly, unobliging, vindictive
gruel: **7** oatmeal **8** flummery, porridge
oatmeal ~: **6** burgoo
grueling: **4** hard **5** hairy, harsh, rough, stiff, tough **6** brutal, fierce, severe, taxing, thorny, trying, uphill **7** arduous, hard-won, onerous, racking **8** crushing, toilsome **9** demanding, difficult, herculean, laborious, punishing, strenuous, torturous **10** enervating, exhausting, formidable, oppressive
gruesome: **4** gory, grim, vile **5** awful, lurid **6** creepy, grisly, horrid, morbid **7** ghastly, hideous, macaber, macabre, squalid **8** horrible, horrific, shocking, terrible **9** appalling, frightful, monstrous, repugnant **10** abominable, disgusting, horrendous, horrifying, petrifying, terrifying
gruff: **4** curt, rude **5** blunt, brusk, harsh, husky, raspy, rough, short, surly **6** abrupt, coarse, crabby, croaky, crusty, grumpy, hoarse, ireful, morose, snappy, snippy, sullen **7** bearish, boorish, brusque, grating, grouchy, loutish, raucous, throaty, uncivil **8** churlish, growling, grumpish, guttural, impolite, inurbane, snippety, tactless **9** truculent **10** ill-humored, unfriendly, ungracious, unmannerly
sound ~: **4** bark, snap, yell **5** growl, snarl **6** bellow
grumble: **4** bark, beef, carp, crab, fuss, kick, moan, mope, pule, snap **5** gripe, groan, growl, snarl, whine **6** grouch, grouse, kvetch, mumble, murmur, mutter, repine, rumble, snivel, squawk, yammer **7** protest **8** complain **9** bellyache, complaint, find fault, make a fuss
grumbler: **4** bear, crab **5** shrew **6** chider, griper, grouch, kvetch, moaner **7** crybaby, grouser **8** sourball **9** termagant **10** bellyacher, curmudgeon
grumbling: **7** carping **8** grousing, petulant **9** grouching, irritable, muttering, nattering, querulous **10** discontent
Grumman: **5** Leroy
grump: **4** bear, crab, mope, sulk **5** crank **6** grouch, whiner **8** complain, sorehead, sourball, sourpuss **10** bellyacher, complainer, curmudgeon, malcontent
Grumpier Old Men (1995 film)
cast: Ann-Margret, Jack Lemmon, Sophia Loren, Walter Matthau, Burgess Meredith
grumpiness: **4** bile **5** spite, venom **6** rancor, spleen, temper **8** acrimony
grumpy: **5** cross, gruff, huffy, moody, onery, sulky, surly, testy **6** crabby, cranky, fretty, ornery, sullen, touchy **7** bearish, bilious, griping, grouchy, huffish, kvetchy, peevish, pettish, prickly, waspish **8** churlish, growling, liverish, petulant, snappish **9** crotchety, grumbling, irritable, querulous, splenetic, truculent **10** out of sorts
be ~: **4** fret, mope, sulk **5** brood, chafe **6** kvetch
expression: **5** frown, glare, scowl **7** grimace **9** dirty look
mood: **4** huff, snit, stew **5** pique **6** temper
Grumpy: **5** dwarf
colleague: **3** Doc **5** Dopey, Happy **6** Sleepy, Sneezy **7** Bashful
Grumpy Old Men (1993 film)
cast: Ann-Margret, Jack Lemmon, Walter Matthau, Burgess Meredith
__ Grundy: **3** Mrs.
grunge: **4** dirt **5** filth, grime, trash **7** rubbish
grungy: **3** bad **4** foul, vile **5** dirty, grimy, messy, sooty **6** cruddy, filthy, fouled, grubby, shoddy, sloppy, soiled, trashy, unneat **7** rundown, smudged, stained, tainted, unkempt, unswept **8** befouled, begrimed, maculate, polluted, slovenly, untended, unwashed, wretched **9** blackened, tarnished **10** besmirched, disgusting, disheveled, unsanitary
grunion: **4** fish **10** silverside
grunt: **4** fish, hand, oink, snap **5** croak, gofer, growl, sargo **6** gopher, mutter **7** dessert, laborer, soldier **9** reckoning
sound: **3** oof, ugh
work: **4** moil, toil **5** grind, labor, sweat **7** travail **8** drudgery
grunt __: **4** work
grunter: **3** hog, pig **5** swine
grunts: **3** GIs **8** dogfaces, infantry, soldiers
gruntwork: **3** job
Grusin: **4** Dave
Gruyère: **6** cheese
coat: **4** rind
Gryphius, Andreas: **4** poet **6** German **10** playwright
grysbok: **6** animal, mammal **8** antelope
relative: **3** gnu, kob **4** guib, kudu, oryx, puku, topi **5** addax, bongo, chiru, eland, goral, korin, nyala, oribi, saiga, serow **6** chammy, dikdik, duiker, impala, koodoo, lechwe, nilgai, rhebok, shammy, shamoy **7** blaubok, blesbok, chamois, defassa, gazelle, gemsbok, gerenuk, nylghai, nylghau, sassaby **8** blesbuck, bontebok, bushbuck, gemsbuck, reedbuck, steenbok, steinbok **9** blackbuck, pronghorn, sitatunga, springbok, waterbuck **10** hartebeest, wildebeest
GSA part: **3** Gen. **4** Serv. **5** Admin. **7** General **8** Services
GSO: **4** aide, asst.
Gstaad: **6** resort
gear: **3** ski **4** skee
locale: **4** Alps **11** Switzerland
G-String Murders, The author: **3** Lee
G-suit buyer: **4** NASA
GT: **3** car
like a ~: **6** sporty
maker: **4** Opel
Gt. Brit.
locale: **3** Eur.
part of ~: **3** Eng., Ire. **4** Scot.
GTE: **2** co.
employee: **4** oper.
rival: **3** ITT
GTI: **2** VW **3** car **4** auto **10** automobile, Volkswagen
GTO: **3** car **4** auto **7** Ferrari, Pontiac
like a ~: **6** sporty
part of ~: **4** Gran **7** Turismo
G.T.O. (1964 song) artist: Ronny & the Daytonas
GTV: **3** car **4** auto **9** Alfa Romeo **10** automobile
GTX: **3** car **4** auto **8** Plymouth **10** automobile
guacamole: **3** dip **9** appetizer
partner: **4** chip
source: **7** avocado
guacharo: **4** bird
Guadalajara: **4** city, town
locale: **6** Mexico **7** Jalisco
see also Spanish
Guadalcanal: **3** isl. **4** isle **6** island
island near ~: **4** Savo
Guadalcanal Diary (1943 film)
cast: William Bendix, Richard Conte, Lloyd Nolan, Anthony Quinn
director: Lewis Seiler
Guadalquivir: **5** river
city on the ~: **7** Córdoba, Seville
locale: **5** Spain
Guadalupe: **4** city, town **5** range
city on the ~: **7** San Jose
locale: **6** Mexico **9** Nuevo León, Zacatecas
see also Spanish
Guadalupe __: **4** palm **7** Hidalgo
Guadalupe Mountains: **4** park
locale: **5** Texas
Guadeloupe: **3** isl. **4** isle **6** island
capital: **10** Basse-Terre
writer: **5** Condé
Guadiana: **5** river
locale: **5** Spain **8** Portugal
Guam: **3** ter. **4** isle, terr. **6** island
capital: **5** Agana
Guamúchil: **4** city, town
locale: **6** Mexico **7** Sinaloa
guan: **4** bird
Guanabara: **3** bay
locale: **3** Rio **6** Brazil
guanaco: **6** animal, mammal
like the ~: **6** Andean
relative: **5** camel, llama **6** alpaca, vicuna **8** Bactrian **9** dromedary
Guanajuato: **4** city, town **5** state
city: **4** León **5** Silao **6** Celaya, Marfil, Romita **7** Abasolo, Allende, Octopan, Pacueco, Pénjamo, Yuriria **8** Acámbaro, Cortazar, Irapuato, Moroleón, Tarimoro **9** Comonfort, Salamanca, San Felipe, Uriangato, Villagrán
locale: **6** Mexico
Guangzhou: **4** city, town
locale: **5** China

Guantanamera (1966 song) artist: Sandpipers
Guantánamo: 3 bay 4 city, town 5 Gitmo
locale: 4 Cuba
Guaporé: 5 river
locale: 6 Brazil 7 Bolivia
guar __: 3 gum
guar.: 4 cert.
Guaraldi, Vince: 7 pianist
genre: 4 jazz
guarana: 5 shrub
guarani: 5 money
Guarani: 6 Indian 7 Amerind
__-Guarani: 4 Tupi
guarantee: 3 ice, vow 4 aver, bond, oath, pawn, seal, word 5 cinch, swear, vouch 6 affirm, assure, attest, avouch, cosign, ensure, insure, pledge, secure, surety 7 certify, confirm, endorse, indorse, promise, protect, sponsor, warrant 8 attest to, contract, make sure, reassure, security, vouch for, warranty 9 agreement, answer for, assurance, certainty, get behind, grubstake, insurance, stipulate, sure thing, testament, undertake 10 collateral, commitment, stand up for, underwrite
the outcome: 3 peg, rig 5 frame, set up 6 buy off, cement, doctor 8 nail down 9 formalize, plan ahead, preordain 10 manipulate, prearrange, tamper with
with no ~: 4 as is
guaranteed: 4 sure 5 on ice 7 certain, for sure 8 definite, in the bag, positive, sure-fire 9 certified, confirmed, protected, warranted 10 conclusive, sure enough
guaranteed __: 4 bond 5 stock 6 income
guarantor: 6 backer, patron 7 sponsor 10 grubstaker
guaranty: 4 egis, pawn 6 pledge 7 warrant 8 warranty
guard: 4 egis, mind, save, tend 5 aegis, armor, cover, watch 6 attend, buffer, convoy, defend, embank, ensure, escort, gaoler, keeper, patrol, picket, police, screen, secure, sentry, shield, warden 7 athlete, baby-sit, bouncer, bulwark, defense, lookout, observe, protect, rampart, shelter, soldier, support, ward off, watcher 8 chaperon, defender, preserve, security, sentinel, shepherd, treasure, watchman 9 accompany, chaperone, look after, protector, safeguard, supervise 10 doorkeeper, gatekeeper, protection
against: 5 avoid 6 beware 8 watch out
against (prefix): 3 par- 4 para-
be on ~: 4 mind 5 watch 6 patrol 7 look out
cry: 4 halt, stop 6 freeze
drop one's ~: 3 nap
ender: 3 ant 4 rail, room 5 house
keep ~: 5 watch 6 defend, picket, police 7 protect
off ~: 4 rash 6 unwary 7 unalert 8 careless, heedless, reckless, unawares 9 negligent, unmindful 10 incautious, not careful, unthinking, unvigilant, unwatchful
old ~: 7 veteran 8 warhorse
on ~: 4 wary 5 alert, awake, leery 7 heads-up, heedful, wakeful 8 keen-eyed, prepared, vigilant, watchful
put on ~: 4 warn 5 alarm, alert, awake, scare 6 arouse, clue in, inform, notify, tip off 7 apprise, caution, forearm, prepare 8 acquaint, forewarn
route: 6 rounds
starter: 3 mud, van 4 body, fire, life, safe 5 black 6 splash
throw off ~: 4 stun 5 shake 7 astound, nonplus, stagger 8 astonish, bowl over, surprise 9 discomfit, dumbfound, take aback 10 disconcert
guard __: 3 dog, pin 4 band, cell, duty, hair, ring
__ guard: 3 off, old, rat 4 home, nose, rear, roof, shin, snow 5 color, honor, point, stand, stock, watch 6 bumper, cattle, middle, palace, splash 7 advance, provost
__ Guard: 3 Old, Red 5 Coast, Right, Swiss
__-guard cutter: 5 coast
guarded: 4 cagy, safe, wary 5 cagey, canny, chary, leery 6 unsure 7 careful, dubious, prudent 8 cautious, discreet, doubtful, doubting, hesitant, vigilant, watchful 9 skeptical, uncertain 10 suspicious
guardedness: 10 weather eye
guardhouse: 4 brig, jail 6 lockup, prison
Guardi: 4 font 8 typeface
guardian: 5 angel 6 escort, keeper, parent, savior, sitter 7 curator, paladin, saviour, sponsor 8 Cerberus, chaperon, defender, executor, overseer, sentinel, shepherd, watchdog 9 attendant, chaperone, custodian, preserver, protector 10 baby sitter, doorkeeper, supervisor
charge: 4 ward 5 child, minor 6 orphan 7 adoptee, protege
spirit: 3 Lar 5 angel 6 daemon, genius
spirits: 5 Lares
guardian __: 5 angel
Guardian Angel cap: 5 beret
guardianship: 4 care, egis, ward 5 aegis, trust, watch 7 custody, keeping 9 oversight 10 protection
Guarding Tess (1994 film)
cast: Nicolas Cage, Shirley MacLaine, Austin Pendleton
Guardino, Harry: 5 actor
film: Dirty Harry (1972)
The Enforcer (1976)
Madigan (1968)
Pork Chop Hill (1959)
Guard of Honor author: James Gould Cozzens
__ Guards: 4 Foot, Life 5 Horse
Guardsman, The (1931 film)
cast: Lynn Fontanne, Alfred Lunt, Roland Young
__ Guardsmen: 5 Royal
Guare, John: 6 author, writer
work: The House of Blue Leaves
Lydie Breeze
Marco Polo Sings a Solo
Rich and Famous
Six Degrees of Separation
Guarneri kin: 5 Amati, Strad
Guarujá: 4 city, town
locale: 6 Brazil
Guarulhos: 4 city, town
locale: 6 Brazil
guasa: 4 fish
Guasave: 4 city, town
locale: 6 Mexico 7 Sinaloa
Guatemala: 6 nation 7 country
ancient city of ~: 5 Tikal
capital: 9 Guatemala
city: 5 Cobán, Mixco, Zunil 6 Flores, Jalapa, Salamá, Sololá, Zacapa 7 Cuilapa
garment: 6 huipil
Indian: 3 Mam 4 Maya
lake: 6 Izabal, Yzabal 7 Atitlán
money: 6 quezal 7 quetzal
native language: 5 Mayan
neighbor: 3 Mex. 6 Belize, Mexico 8 Honduras 10 El Salvador
Nobelist in Literature: 8 Asturias
Nobelist in Peace: 3 Tum
org.: 3 OAS
river: 5 Hondo
volcano: 5 Fuego, Tacan 6 Pacaya
writer: 8 Asturias
see also Spanish
guava: 4 tree 5 fruit, shrub
relative: 6 myrtle 7 cajeput 10 eucalyptus
Guayaquil: 4 city, gulf, port, town
locale: 7 Ecuador
Guaymas: 4 city, port, town
locale: 6 Mexico, Sonora
guayule: 4 bush 5 shrub
Guber: 5 Peter
Gucci: 4 Aldo
guck: 4 dirt 5 slime 6 sludge
gudgeon: 4 fish 6 socket
Gudrun husband: 4 Atli
Guelph: 4 city, town
locale: 6 Canada 7 Ontario
guemal: 4 deer 6 mammal
relative: 3 elk, roe 4 axis, pudu, shou, sika 5 moose 6 chital, hangul, sambar, sambur, thamin, wapiti 7 brocket, caribou, muntjac, muntjak, sambhar, sambhur 8 reindeer 9 barasingh
guenon: 6 mammal 7 primate
relative: 3 ape 4 saki, titi 5 chimp, drill, jocko, lemur, loris, magot, orang, potto, shrew 6 aye-aye, baboon, Bandar, galago, gelada, gibbon, grivet, howler, langur, macaco, monkey, rhesus, uakari, vervet 7 colobus, gorilla, guereza, hoolock, macaque, sapajou, siamang, tamarin, tarsier 8 bush baby, capuchin, mandrill, mangabey, marmoset, talapoin 9 orangutan 10 Barbary ape, chimpanzee, orangutang
guerdon: 5 prize 6 reward, trophy 10 remunerate
Guéret: 4 city, town
locale: 6 France
guereza: 6 mammal 7 primate
relative: 3 ape 4 saki, titi 5 chimp, drill, jocko, lemur, loris, magot, orang, potto, shrew 6 aye-aye, baboon, Bandar, galago, gelada, gibbon, grivet, guenon, howler, langur, macaco, monkey, rhesus, uakari, vervet 7 colobus, gorilla, hoolock, macaque, sapajou, siamang, tamarin, tarsier 8 bush baby, capuchin, mandrill, mangabey, marmoset, talapoin 9 orangutan 10 Barbary ape, chimpanzee, orangutang
Guernica: 5 mural
artist: 7 Picasso
guernsey: 5 shirt
Guernsey: 3 cow 4 bull, isle 6 bovine, cattle, island
exclamation: 3 moo
neighbor: 4 Sark
Guernsey __: 4 lily
guerra opposite: 3 paz
guerre, nom de: 4 name 5 alias 6 anonym 8 cognomen 9 pseudonym
Guerrero: 5 Pedro, state 7 Mexican
city: 5 Taxco, Tlapa 6 Atoyac, Coyuca, Iguala, Tecpan, Tixtla 7 Arcelia, Chilapa 8 Acapulco, Huitzuco, Ometepec, Petatlán, Zumpango 10 Altamirano, Teloloapan
guerrilla: 3 huk 6 Contra, klepht 7 soldier 8 partisan 9 warmonger
1970's ~ grp.: 3 SLA
guerrilla __: 7 warfare
guess: 3 est., say 4 call, shot, stab 5 dance, hunch, infer, judge, opine, think 6 assess, assume, belief, deduce, divine, notion, reckon, theory 7 daresay, feeling, imagine, opinion, predict, presume, suppose, surmise, suspect, thought, venture 8 estimate, judgment, theorize 9 reckoning, speculate, suspicion, take a shot 10 assumption, conjecture, hypothesis, prediction, projection
ender: 4 work
word: 5 about
words: 4 or so
__-guess: 6 second 7 another
Guess __!: 5 again
Guess __?: 3 who 4 what
__ Guess: 3 Eye
Guess? competitor: 6 Gitano
Guess Who
song: American Woman (1970)
Clap for the Wolfman (1974)
Laughing (1969)
No Time (1970)
Share the Land (1970)
These Eyes (1969)
Guess Who's Coming to Dinner (1967 film)
cast: Katharine Hepburn, Sidney Poitier, Spencer Tracy
director: Stanley Kramer
guesswork: 7 surmise 9 suspicion 10 conjecture
guest: 6 caller, client, lodger, renter, roomer, tenant 7 boarder, company, invitee, visitor 8 customer 9 partygoer, sojourner, transient 10 vacationer
be a ~ at: 5 visit 6 attend
be my ~: 3 aye, oui, yea, yep, yes, yup 4 fine, okay, sure, yeah 5 good-o, natch, quite, right, roger, uh-huh 6 agreed, gladly, good-oh, indeed, just so, rather, righto, surely, you bet, yowzah 7 exactly, go ahead, indeedy, mais oui, quite so, ten-four 8 all right, as you say, of course, thumbs up, very well 9 certainly, darn right, naturally, precisely, sure thing, you betcha, you said it 10 absolutely, by all means, definitely, positively, sure enough, that's right
combining form: 3 xen- 4 xeno-
ender: 5 house
paying ~: 5 liver 6 lodger, patron
room: 3 den
starter: 5 house
take in a ~: 5 greet 6 invite 7 receive, welcome
unwanted ~: 3 ant, bug, fly, nag 4 bore, drag, drip, flea, gnat, pain, pest, pill 5 creep, mouse 6 drop-in, insect 7 termite 8 headache, housefly, mosquito, nuisance 9 cockroach
guest __: 4 flag, room 6 worker
guest-__: 4 rope, shot
Guest: 2 C.Z. 3 Val 5 Edgar 6 Judith 8 Cornelia
__ Guest: 4 Be My
Guest, Christopher spouse: Jamie Lee Curtis
guesthouse: 3 inn 5 lodge 6 hostel 7 auberge
Guest in the House (1944 film)
cast: Anne Baxter, Ralph Bellamy, Aline MacMahon
guest of __: 5 honor
Guest of Reality author: Pär Lagerkvist
guests: 7 callers, company 8 assembly, visitors
desirable ~: 5 A-list

have ~: 4 fete, host 5 eat in, put up 6 regale 9 entertain, make merry, socialize
where honored ~ sit: 4 dais 6 podium 7 rostrum 8 platform
Guest, Val: 8 director
film: The Creeping Unknown (1956)
The Day the Earth Caught Fire (1962)
When Dinosaurs Ruled the Earth (1970)
Where the Spies Are (1965)
Guevara: 3 Che 7 Ernesto
guff: 3 gas, lip, rot 4 blah, bosh, bull, bunk, jazz, jive, pooh, sass, tosh 5 bilge, fudge, hokum, hooey, mouth, prate, sauce, stuff, trash, tripe 6 bunkum, bushwa, drivel, footle, gabble, gammon, gibber, havers, hot air, humbug, jabber, jargon, kibosh, piffle 7 baloney, blarney, blather, blether, boloney, bushwah, eyewash, flannel, flubdub, fustian, garbage, hogwash, inanity, malarky, rubbish, twaddle 8 backtalk, buncombe, claptrap, falderal, falderol, flimflam, flummery, folderal, folderol, malarkey, nonsense, slipslop, tommyrot, trumpery 9 banana oil, gibberish, goofiness, impudence, insolence, kidstakes, loquacity, moonshine, poppycock, rigmarole 10 applesauce, balderdash, bilge water, codswallop, double-talk, effrontery, flapdoodle, galimatias, Jabberwock, mumbo jumbo, rigamarole, taradiddle
guffaw: 4 ha-ha, hoot, howl, laff, roar 5 laugh 6 cackle, giggle, haw-haw, heehaw, titter 7 break up, chortle, chuckle, crack up, snicker, snigger 8 laughter 10 belly laugh, horse laugh
E-mail ~: 3 LOL
Guggenheim: 5 Peggy
Gughe: 4 peak 5 mount 8 mountain
locale: 6 Africa 8 Ethiopia
Gugino, Carla: 7 actress
film: The Center of the World (2001)
Judas Kiss (1999)
Spy Kids (2001)
Guglielmo: 7 Marconi
in English: 7 William
__ Guiana: 5 Dutch 6 French 7 British
Guiana explorer: 7 Raleigh
Guiana Indian: 6 Arawak
guib: 6 mammal 8 antelope
relative: 3 gnu, kob 4 kudu, oryx, puku, topi 5 addax, bongo, chiru, eland, goral, korin, nyala, oribi, saiga, serow 6 chammy, dik-dik, duiker, impala, koodoo, lechwe, nilgai, rhebok, shammy, shamoy 7 blaubok, blesbok, chamois, defassa, gazelle, gemsbok, gerenuk, grysbok, nylghai, nylghau, sassaby 8 blesbuck, bontebok, bushbuck, gemsbuck, reedbuck, steenbok, steinbok 9 blackbuck, pronghorn, sitatunga, springbok, waterbuck 10 hartebeest, wildebeest
guidance: 3 aid 4 hand, help 6 advice 7 conduct, control, warning 8 training, tutelage 9 direction, education, influence 10 assistance, counseling, leadership, management, regulation
lacking ~: 5 unled
guide: 3 aid 4 face, guru, head, helm, help, lead, menu, show, take, warn 5 bible, bring, edify, gauge, index, pilot, point, refer, route, scout, shape, steer, swing, teach, train, tutor, usher 6 advise, attend, beacon, convoy, direct, docent, escort, handle, jockey, leader, lead in, lead to, manage, manual, mentor, pundit, school, Sherpa 7 adviser, advisor, channel, conduct, control, counsel, go first, monitor, pattern, pioneer, support, teacher, usher in 8 chaperon, cicerone, handbook, instruct, landmark, lodestar, navigate, paradigm, regulate, shepherd, workbook 9 abecedary, accompany, attendant, chaperone, companion, conductor, counselor, directory, enlighten, indicator, influence, vade mecum 10 instructor, lead the way, pathfinder, show the way, trailblaze
ender: 4 book, line, post, word
group: 4 tour
naval ~: 10 lighthouse, watchtower
to a chair: 4 seat 5 usher
tour ~: 3 map 6 docent
guide __: 3 dog 4 left, rail, rope, word 5 right 6 center, fossil
__ guide: 4 girl 5 field, honey, light
guidebook: 5 bible 6 manual 8 Baedeker 9 itinerary, vade mecum
guided __: 4 tour, wave 7 missile
guided by, be: 4 heed 6 follow
Guide for the Married Man, A (1967 film)
cast: Walter Matthau, Robert Morse, Inger Stevens
director: Gene Kelly
guideline: 4 rule 5 bylaw, gauge 6 policy 7 precept 8 standard 9 direction, parameter 10 ground rule
guidepost: 4 sign 5 pylon
guiding: 5 polar 9 sovereign
light: 4 guru 6 beacon 8 cynosure, lodestar, polestar 10 apotheosis
principle: 3 saw 5 adage, axiom, credo, maxim, moral, motto, tenet 6 belief, byword, dictum, saying, slogan, war cry 7 epigram, precept, proverb 8 aphorism 9 battle cry, platitude, watchword
Guiding Light, The (CBS): 4 soap 9 soap opera
character: 4 Nola
Guido: 4 Reni 7 Gezelle 10 Cavalcanti
high note: 3 e la
in English: 3 Guy
see also Italian
Guido __: 7 d'Arezzo
guidon: 4 flag
Guidry, Ron: 6 hurler 7 pitcher
__ Guignol: 5 Grand
guild: 4 club 5 order, union 6 league 7 society 8 congress 10 federation, fellowship, trade union
ender: 4 hall
medieval ~: 5 hansa, hanse
__ guild: 5 trade
Guildenstern friend: 6 Hamlet
guilder: 4 coin 5 money 6 florin
guile: 3 art, lie 4 jive, ruse 5 craft, fraud, wiles 6 acumen, deceit, dupery 7 cunning, finesse, knavery, slyness 8 artifice, trickery, wiliness 9 chicanery, deception, dirty pool, duplicity, smartness, treachery 10 artfulness, cleverness, craftiness, dishonesty, trickiness
guileful: 3 sly 4 cagy, foxy, wily 5 cagey, canny, false, lying, slick, snaky 6 artful, crafty, shifty, shrewd, sneaky, subtle, tricky 7 crooked, cunning, devious, furtive, vulpine 8 delusive, slippery 9 deceitful, deceptive, dishonest, insidious, insincere, underhand 10 mendacious, untruthful
guileless: 4 naif, open, pure 5 frank, naive 6 callow, candid, honest, infelt, simple 7 artless, genuine, natural, sincere 8 innocent, lamblike, out-front, truthful, unartful 9 childlike, ingenuous, unguarded, unstudied 10 aboveboard, unaffected
one: 4 lamb, naif
guilelessness: 6 candor 7 naiveté 8 openness 9 credulity, innocence 10 simplicity
Guillaume: 6 Robert 7 Charles
in English: 7 William
see also French
Guillaume, Charles: 8 Nobelist 9 physicist
Guillaume, Robert: 5 actor
film: Lean on Me (1989)
TV: Benson, Soap
Guillemin, Roger: 8 Nobelist
guillemot: 4 bird 5 murre
kin: 3 auk
Guillén, Jorge: 4 poet 7 Spanish
Guillén, Nicolás: 4 poet 5 Cuban
Guillermin, John: 8 director
film: The Bridge at Remagen (1969)
The Day They Robbed the Bank of England (1960)
King Kong (1976)
Shaft in Africa (1973)
The Towering Inferno (1974)
Waltz of the Toreadors (1962)
Guillermo: 5 Vilas
in English: 7 William
guilt: 3 sin 4 onus 5 blame, fault, lapse, shame, wrong 6 infamy 7 failing, misstep, offense, remorse 8 disgrace, dishonor, iniquity 9 liability 10 misconduct, repentance
admission of ~: 6 I did it 8 mea culpa
admit ~: 9 apologize, beg pardon 10 make amends
guilt __: 4 trip
guiltiness: 9 collusion 10 complicity, connivance, conspiracy
guiltless: 4 good, pure 5 clean, clear 7 sinless 8 innocent, spotless, unsoiled, virtuous 9 blameless, crimeless, exemplary, faultless, righteous, unsullied, untainted 10 exculpated, immaculate, impeccable, inculpable, in the clear
Guilt of Janet Ames, The (1947 film)
cast: Sid Caesar, Melvyn Douglas, Rosalind Russell
director: Henry Levin
guilty: 4 evil 5 wrong 6 liable, sinful, unholy, wicked 7 at fault, verdict 8 blamable, criminal, culpable 9 blameable, convicted, felonious, red-handed 10 delinquent, iniquitous, in the wrong
feel ~: 3 rue 6 regret, repent
feeling ~: 5 sorry 6 rueful 7 ashamed 8 contrite, penitent 9 chastened, regretful, repentant 10 apologetic, remorseful
find ~: 3 hit, rap 4 damn, defy, hiss 5 blame, chide, decry, knock, sneer 6 outlaw, punish, rail at 7 censure, condemn, convict, deplore, dislike, reprove, upbraid 8 denounce, penalize, reproach, sentence 9 castigate, criticize, deprecate, excoriate, fulminate, imprecate, proscribe, reprehend 10 come down on, vituperate
not ~: 7 sinless 8 innocent 9 acquitted, blameless, faultless, untainted 10 inculcable, inculpable, in the clear
one: 4 perp 5 crook, felon 8 criminal
guilty __: 5 as sin
__ guilty: 5 plead
Guilty (1980 song)
artist: Barbra Streisand, Barry Gibb
Guilty by Suspicion (1991 film)
cast: Annette Bening, Robert De Niro, George Wendt, Patricia Wettig
director: Irwin Winkler
Guilty Hands (1931 film)
cast: Lionel Barrymore, Madge Evans, Kay Francis
director: W.S. Van Dyke
Guilty Pleasures author: Lawrence Sanders
Guinan: 5 Texas
guinea: 4 coin 5 money
guinea __: 3 hen, pig 4 fowl, worm 5 grass 6 grains
Guinea: 4 gulf 6 nation 7 country
bovine: 5 N'dama
capital: 7 Conakry
city: 6 Kankan 7 Conakry, Konakri
coin: 4 syli
Gulf of ~ port: 5 Lagos
Gulf of ~ republic: 5 Ghana
neighbor: 4 Mali 7 Liberia, Senegal 10 Ivory Coast
people: 6 Kpelle 7 Malinka, Malinke 8 Mandingo, Mandinka
river to the Gulf of ~: 5 Niger
Guinea __: 4 corn 6 pepper 7 Current
__ Guinea: 3 New 6 French 7 Spanish
Guinea-Bissau: 6 nation 7 country
capital: 6 Bissau
money: 4 peso
neighbor: 7 Senegal
guinea fowl: 4 fowl
relative: 5 poult, quail, snipe 6 chukar, grouse, peahen, turkey 7 peacock 8 curassow, pheasant, woodcock 9 partridge 10 wild turkey
young ~: 4 keat, keet
guinea pig: 3 pet 4 cavy 6 animal, mammal, rodent 7 subject
female: 3 doe, sow
home: 3 lab 4 cage
male: 4 buck
relative: 3 rat 4 degu, jird, paca, vole 5 coypu, gundi, mouse, xerus 6 agouti, beaver, gerbil, gopher, jerboa, marmot, murine 7 hamster, lemming, muskrat, visacha 8 chipmunk, cricetid, dormouse, squirrel, tuco-tuco 9 chickaree, groundhog, porcupine, woodchuck 10 chinchilla, prairie dog
young: 3 pup
Guinevere lover: 8 Lancelot 9 Launcelot
Guinier: 4 Lani
Guinness: 4 Alec 5 drink 7 brewery 8 beverage
brew: 3 ale 5 stout
Guinness, Alec: 3 Sir 5 actor
film: All at Sea (1958)
The Bridge on the River Kwai (1957, AA)
Captain's Paradise (1953)
Damn the Defiant! (1962)
Doctor Zhivago (1965)
The Fall of the Roman Empire (1964)
Father Brown (1954)
The Horse's Mouth (1958)
Kind Hearts and Coronets (1949)
The Ladykillers (1955)
The Lavender Hill Mob (1951)
Lawrence of Arabia (1962)
The Man in the White Suit (1951)
The Mudlark (1950)
Murder by Death (1976)
Oliver Twist (1948)
The Prisoner (1955)
The Promoter (1952)
The Quiller Memorandum (1966)
Scrooge (1970)
Star Wars (1977)
The Swan (1956)
Times of Glory (1960)
Guinness Book
entry: 4 feat
suffix: 3 est
superlative: 4 most

guipure: 4 lace
Güiraldes, Ricardo: 4 poet 6 author, writer 9 Argentine
guise: 4 look, mask, mien, pose, role, show, veil 5 cloak, cover, front, shape 6 aspect, attire, facade, outfit 7 costume, posture, pretext 8 demeanor, likeness, pretense 9 semblance 10 appearance, camouflage, complexion, false front, masquerade
starter: 3 dis
Guisewite: 5 Cathy
guitar: 5 Dobro, Strat 6 cither, cuatro, ramkie, string 7 cittern, gittern, machete
adjunct: 3 amp 4 capo, pick
ancestor: 4 lute
cousin: 3 uke 5 banjo
diagram: 5 chord
effect: 4 wawa 6 wah wah
ender: 3 ist 4 fish
like a loud ~: 5 amped
part: 4 fret, neck 5 waist
play a ~: 5 pluck, strum, thrum
sound: 5 twang
___ guitar: 5 slide, steel 7 Spanish
Guitar: 6 Bonnie
guitarist: 4 Byrd, King, Paul 5 Charo, Flatt 6 Atkins, B.B. King 7 Clapton, Diddley, Hendrix, Les Paul, Segovia 8 Ritenour 9 Bo Diddley 10 Chet Atkins, Montgomery
blues ~: 4 King 7 Diddley
jazz ~: 4 Byrd 10 Montgomery
Spanish ~: 5 Charo 7 Segovia
Guitarist, The artist: 5 Manet
Guiteau: 7 Charles
Guitry, Sacha: 6 author, French, writer 10 playwright
Gujarat ___: 6 States
Gujarat garment: 4 sari 5 saree
gulag: 6 prison 7 Russian
Gulag Archipelago, The author: Aleksandr Solzhenitsyn
Gulager: 3 Clu
gulch: 3 gap 4 rift, wadi, wady 5 cañon, gorge, gully 6 arroyo, canyon, coulee, gulley, ravine, trench 7 channel
___-gulch: 3 dry
Guldahl, Ralph: 6 golfer
gulden: 5 Dutch, money 6 florin
Gulden's: 7 mustard
alternative: 7 French's 10 Grey Poupon
gules: 3 red 5 color
gulf: 3 bay, gap, pit 4 cove, hole, rift, void 5 abyss, bayou, bight, cañon, chasm, cleft, depth, fiord, firth, fjord, frith, gorge, gully, inlet, sound, split 6 breach, canyon, gulley, hiatus, lacuna, lagoon, ravine 7 vacuity 8 crevasse 10 profundity
Adriatic: 6 Venice 7 Trieste 8 Quarnero
Aegean: 5 Izmir, Saros 6 Africa, Guinea 7 Argolis, Saronic 8 Salonika
Argentina: 8 San Jorge 9 San Matias
Atlantic: 6 Guinea, Mexico 8 San Jorge 9 San Matias
Baltic: 4 Riga 6 Danzig 7 Bothnia, Finland
Canada: 7 Boothia 10 St. Lawrence
Caribbean: 6 Darien, Gonâve 7 San Blas 8 Gonaïves, Honduras
Central America: 6 Panama 7 Fonseca 8 Honduras
Chile: 5 Penas
China: 5 Bohai, Pohai 8 Liaodong, Liaotung
Costa Rica: 8 Papagayo
Ecuador: 9 Guayaquil
English Channel: 6 St. Malo
France: 5 Lions 6 St. Malo
Greece: 6 Aegina, Patras 7 Laconia, Saronic 8 Messinia, Salonika
Haiti: 6 Gonâve 8 Gonaïves
Indian Ocean: 6 Mannar
Ionian: 4 Arta 6 Patras 7 Corinth, Laconia, Lepanto, Taranto 8 Messinia
Italy: 5 Genoa 6 Venice 7 Taranto, Trieste
Ivory Coast: 6 Guinea
Mediterranean: 5 Gabès, Lions, Sidra
Mexico: 8 Campeche
Mideast: 4 Aden, Oman, Suez 5 Akaba, Aqaba, Sidra 7 Arabian, Persian
Myanmar: 8 Martaban
New Guinea ~: 5 Papua
Pacific: 5 Davao, Papua, Penas 6 Alaska 7 Fonseca 8 Papagayo 9 Guayaquil 10 California
Panama: 7 San Blas
Philippines: 5 Davao, Panay
Poland: 6 Danzig
Red Sea: 4 Suez
Russia: 8 Taganrog
Scandinavia: 7 Bothnia
Sea of Azov: 8 Taganrog
South America: 9 Guayaquil
South China Sea: 4 Siam 6 Tonkin 8 Thailand
Spain: 5 Cádiz
Tunisia: 5 Gabès
Turkey: 5 Izmir
Tyrrhenian Sea: 5 Gaeta
Venezuela: 5 Paria 9 Maracaibo
Yugoslavia: 8 Quarnero
Gulf: 3 gas 8 gasoline
rival: 5 Amoco, Exxon, Getty, Mobil 6 Sunoco 7 Chevron
Gulf ___: 3 Oil, War 5 Coast 6 States, Stream
___ Gulf: 5 Davao, Dulce 6 Gonâve 7 Arabian, Persian, Saronic
Gulf Coast
city: 5 Tampa 6 St. Pete 8 Sarasota
Gulf of ___: 4 Aden, Arta, Oman, Oran, Riga, Siam, Suez 5 Akaba, Aqaba, Cadiz, Lions, Papua, Saros, Sidra, Tunis 6 Alaska, Cambay, Guinea, Mexico, Panama 7 Argolis, Bothnia, Corinth, Finland, Fonseca, Lepanto
Gulf of Aden
country: 5 Yemen
vessel: 3 dau, dow 4 dhow
Gulf of Bothnia
river to the ~: 3 Dal, Ume 4 Oulu
Gulf of Cádiz, river to the: 8 Guadiana
Gulf of California
river to the ~: 5 Yaqui 8 Colorado
Gulf of Finland, river to the: 4 Neva
Gulf of Guinea
capital: 5 Accra, Akkra
island: 7 Sao Tomé
Gulf of Mexico
bay: 5 Tampa 6 Mobile 9 Galveston, Pensacola
city: 5 Tampa
river to the ~: 5 Pearl 6 Pánuco, Sabine 8 Suwannee 9 Rio Grande
Gulf of Tonkin, river to the: 3 Red
Gulf of Trieste, river to the: 6 Isonzo
Gulfport: 4 city, port, town
locale: 4 Miss.
neighbor: 6 Biloxi
Gulf Stream, The painter: 5 Homer
Gulf War
ally: 5 Saudi, Syria
city: 5 Basra, Busra 6 Busrah
figure: 4 amir, emir 5 ameer, emeer
foe: 4 Irak, Iraq
missile: 4 Scud
participant: 4 Arab
gull: 3 con, gyp, mew, mug, sap 4 bilk, bird, dupe, fool, hoax, mark, prey, rook, take 5 cheat, chump, cozen, hocus, mulct, patsy, sting, trick 6 fleece, fulmar, outwit, pigeon, rope in, sea mew, sucker, take in, target, victim 7 deceive, defraud, exploit, jackass, mislead, seabird, swindle 8 flimflam, hoodwink, outsmart 9 bamboozle, four-flush, kittiwake, scapegoat, schlemiel, shorebird, victimize
ender: 4 wing
genus: 5 larus
like a ~: 6 larine
perch: 4 buoy
relative: 4 skua, tern
___ gull: 3 mew, sea 5 ivory 6 little 7 herring
gullet: 3 cut, maw 4 craw, crop 5 ditch 6 ravine, throat, trench 7 channel, gizzard, pharynx 9 esophagus 10 oesophagus
gullibility: 7 naiveté 9 credulity, greenness
gullible: 4 easy, naif 5 green, naive 6 simple, stupid 8 innocent, trusting 9 credulous
not ~: 3 sly 4 foxy, wary, wily, wise 5 acute, cagey, canny, quick, slick, smart 6 astute, clever, crafty, shrewd 7 careful, cunning, guarded, knowing, prudent 8 cautious, watchful
person: 3 sap 4 butt, dupe, fool, mark, tool 5 chump, patsy, yokel 6 pigeon, sucker 8 pushover
Gullible's Travels author: Ring Lardner
Gulliver's Travels: 5 novel 6 satire
author: Jonathan Swift
character: 5 Yahoo
land: 6 Laputa
Gullstrand, Allvar: 8 Nobelist
gully: 3 gap 4 gulf, rift, wadi, wady 5 cañon, chasm, ditch, gulch 6 arroyo, canyon, ravine, trench, trough 7 channel, culvert 8 crevasse
form a ~: 4 flow, gush, wash 5 erode
in Britain: 4 sike, syke
___ gully: 5 hully
gullywasher: 4 rain 5 flood, spate, storm 6 deluge, precip 7 monsoon, torrent 8 downpour, drencher 9 rainstorm 10 cloudburst
gulp: 3 eat 4 bolt, chug, pant, puff, swig, wolf 5 choke, drink, gorge, quaff, scarf, swill 6 breath, devour, englut, gobble, guzzle, imbibe, inhale 7 breathe, consume, draught, scarf up, swallow 8 chug-a-lug, mouthful, wolf down 9 knock back, scarf down 10 inhalation
big ~: 4 belt, swig 7 swallow
down: 4 bolt, chug 6 ingest 7 engorge
empty in one ~: 5 swill 6 guzzle
___ Gulp: 3 Big
gulping: 6 winded 7 anxious, gasping, panting 9 exhausted 10 breathless
Gulu: 4 city, town
locale: 6 Uganda
gum: 4 bond, glue, seal, tree 5 paste, resin 6 cement, clog up 7 Bazooka, gingiva 8 adhesive, fixative, mucilage
arabic: 6 acacia
arabic tree: 5 babul
art ~: 6 eraser
by ~: 4 oath
ender: 4 ball, drop, shoe, wood
like some ~: 5 minty
non-elastic ~: 6 balata
resin: 4 kino 5 myrrh 6 copalm
source: 4 guar 6 chicle
starter: 6 bubble
tree denizen: 3 bee 5 drone
up: 3 jam 4 muff 5 botch, snarl, spoil 6 bungle 9 mishandle, mismanage
up the works: 3 err 4 flub, mess, slip 5 botch, fluff 6 boggle, bumble, bungle, fumble, mess up, slip up 7 blunder, stumble 9 mishandle, mismanage
use ~: 4 chew 5 erase 9 masticate
gum ___: 4 band, thus, tree 5 elemi, plant, print, resin 6 acacia, arabic, dammar, eraser, guaiac, myrtle 7 benzoin, elastic
gum ___ works: 5 up the
___ gum: 3 bee, red 4 blue, guar, kino, silk, sour 5 black, ester, karri, kauri, sweet, water, white 6 bubble, chicle, cotton, fossil, karaya, spirit, yellow 7 British, chewing, xanthan
___-gum: 3 dad
Gumball Rally, The (1976 film)
cast: Raul Julia, Tim McIntire, Michael Sarrazin
director: 4 Bail
Gumbel: 4 Greg 6 Bryant
gumbo: 4 soup, stew 6 bisque, patois
ingredient: 4 file, ocra, okra, okro 5 thyme
like ~: 5 Cajan, Cajun
gumboot: 4 shoe 8 footwear
Gum Drop (1955 song) artist: Crew-Cuts
gumdrops: 5 candy, sweet 10 confection
___-gummed: 3 dad
Gummo: 4 Marx
brother of ~: 5 Chico, Harpo, Zeppo 7 Groucho
gummy: 4 icky 5 gluey, gooey, muddy, thick 6 clayey, sticky, viscid 7 clayish, jellied, viscose, viscous 8 adhesive 9 glutinous
Gump: 3 Min 4 Andy 7 Forrest, Worsley
dog: 4 Buck
Gumps, The
cat: 4 Hope
dog: 4 Buck
gumption: 4 grit, guts, push 5 drive, force, moxie, nerve, pluck, spine, spunk 6 energy, hustle, starch 7 bravery, courage 8 industry 9 ingenuity 10 enterprise, feistiness, get up and go, initiative, shrewdness
gums: 3 ula
be good to your ~: 5 brush, floss
combining form: 3 ulo- 6 gingiv- 7 gingivo-
flap one's ~: 3 gab, gas, jaw, rap, yak, yap 4 blab, chat, gush, talk 5 prate, run on, speak, spout 6 babble, gabble, gibber, jabber, natter, parley, yammer 7 blabber, blather, chatter, maunder, prattle, twaddle 8 converse, ramble on, spout off 9 go on and on 10 yakkety-yak
gumshoe: 2 PI 3 tec 4 dick, lurk 5 sneak, snoop 6 shamus 9 detective
quest: 4 clue 5 proof
gum up the ___: 5 works
gun: 3 aim, cap, gat, man, men, pop, rev, rod, Uzi 4 ammo, bang, blow, boat, Bren, Colt, draw, fire, hand, kick, load, lock, play, room, shot, Sten, thug, wale 5 aim at, chase, fight, flash, flint, Luger, metal, piece, point, proof, rifle, round, salvo, shoot, sight, skeet, smith, spray, stock, taser, vroom 6 ack ack, barrel, Bertha, breech, cannon, cotton, muzzle, powder, pursue, report, runner, search 7 barrage, fighter, notable, slinger 8 air rifle 9 Big Bertha, dignitary, equalizer, flintlock, forty-five 10 accelerate, six-shooter
jumping the ~: 7 too soon 8 too early 9 overhasty 10 half-cocked

gun __: **3** dog, for **4** brig, crew, deck, moll, room **6** camera, tackle **7** control
gun-__: **3** shy **6** toting
__ gun: **3** air, big, cap, fog, jet, ray, top, zip **4** Bren, bull, burp, dust, flit, glue, heat, pump, riot, Sten, stun **5** hired, Lewis, Maxim, spear, spray, Tommy, water **6** Bofors, grease, minute, Quaker, rocket, squirt, staple, swivel **7** Gatling, harpoon, machine, morning, smoking
__-gun: **3** six
__ Gun: **3** Top
Guna: **4** peak **5** mount **8** mountain
  locale: **6** Africa **8** Ethiopia
gunboat: **7** frigate, warship **8** man-of-war **10** battleship
Guncrazy (1992 film)
  cast: Drew Barrymore, Billy Drago, James LeGros
  director: Tamra Davis
gundi: **6** animal, mammal, rodent
  relative: **3** rat **4** cavy, degu, jird, paca, vole **5** coypu, mouse, xerus **6** agouti, beaver, gerbil, gopher, jerboa, marmot, murine **7** hamster, lemming, muskrat, visacha **8** chipmunk, cricetid, dormouse, squirrel, tuco-tuco **9** chickaree, groundhog, guinea pig, porcupine, woodchuck **10** chinchilla, prairie dog
Gunfight at the O.K. Corral (1957 film): **5** oater **7** western
  cast: Kirk Douglas, Rhonda Fleming, John Ireland, Burt Lancaster, Jo Van Fleet
  director: John Sturges
gunfighter dare: **4** draw
Gunfighter, The (1950 film)
  cast: Millard Mitchell, Gregory Peck, Helen Westcott
  director: Henry King
__ Gun for Hire: **4** This
Gunga Din: **4** film, poem
  author: Rudyard Kipling
  cast: Douglas Fairbanks Jr., Joan Fontaine, Cary Grant, Sam Jaffe, Victor McLaglen
  director: George Stevens
  setting: **5** India
  studio: **3** RKO
gung-ho: **4** avid, into, keen, warm **5** can-do, eager **6** ardent, rah-rah, red-hot **7** anxious, excited, fired up, keyed up, zealous **8** enthused, spirited **9** fanatical, hot to trot **10** inspirited, passionate
  quality: **3** pep, zip **4** élan, fire, push, zeal, zest **5** drive, gusto, oomph, punch, verve **6** energy, fervor, relish, spirit **7** passion **8** alacrity, dispatch, interest, keenness **9** animation, assiduity, diligence, eagerness, intensity, readiness **10** ebullience, enterprise, enthusiasm, exuberance, heartiness, initiative
Gung Ho (1986 film)
  cast: Michael Keaton, Gedde Watanabe, George Wendt
  director: Ron Howard
gunk: **3** goo **4** blob, crud, dirt, glop, goop, muck, ooze **5** grime, slime **8** sediment
gunky: **4** icky, oozy **5** muddy, thick **6** sticky
gunman: **6** sniper **7** shooter **9** desperado
Gunman's Walk (1958 film)
  cast: Kathryn Grant, Van Heflin, Tab Hunter
gunmetal: **4** gray, grey **5** alloy, color
  component: **3** tin **4** zinc **6** copper
  relative: **3** ash **4** dove, drab **5** beige, dusty, merle, pearl, putty, slate, taupe **6** silver **7** grizzly **8** charcoal, platinum
Gunn: **3** Ben **4** Thom **5** Moses, Peter
Gunnar: **6** Ekelöf, Myrdal, Nelson
gunnel: **4** fish **6** blenny **7** railing
gunner: **7** soldier
  need: **4** ammo
gunning for: **5** after
Gunn, Moses: **5** actor
  film: Aaron Loves Angela (1975)
    Heartbreak Ridge (1986)
    Remember My Name (1978)
    Shaft (1971)
    Shaft's Big Score! (1972)
  TV: Father Murphy
Gunn, Peter: **3** tec **6** sleuth **7** gumshoe **9** detective **10** private eye
  girlfriend: **4** Edie
Gunn, Thom: **4** poet **7** British
gunny-__: **3** bag
gunny ender: **4** sack
gunnysack: **3** bag **4** poke
  material: **4** jute **6** burlap
gunpowder: **3** tea **9** explosive **10** ammunition
  chemical: **5** niter
  holder: **3** keg
  igniter: **5** spark
Gunpowder __: **4** Plot
guns: **4** arms **7** battery **8** materiel, weaponry **9** artillery, firepower, munitions
  alternative: **6** butter
  get new ~: **5** rearm
  give ~ to: **3** arm **7** fortify
  go great ~: **5** excel **8** flourish
  sticking to one's ~: **3** set **4** firm **5** dug in **6** dogged, steely, strong **7** adamant, decided, do-or-die **8** hard-line, locked in, resolute, stubborn **9** iron-jawed, steadfast, tenacious **10** unswayable, unyielding
  stick to one's ~: **6** insist **7** persist **9** persevere
__ guns: **5** great
__ Guns: **5** Young
gunsel: **4** goon, thug **5** tough **7** hoodlum, mobster **8** criminal, gangster, hooligan **9** racketeer
  gal: **4** moll
  gig: **5** heist
gun-shy: **5** balky, chary, timid **6** afraid, scared **7** chicken, dubious, fearful, nervous **8** hesitant **9** reluctant **10** frightened
Gun Shy (2000 film)
  cast: Sandra Bullock, Liam Neeson, Oliver Platt
gunslinger: **6** outlaw **9** desperado
  command: **4** draw **5** reach
  unit: **5** notch
Gunslinger, The author: Stephen King
Gunsmoke (CBS western)
  bartender: **3** Sam
  cast: James Arness (Matt Dillon)
    Amanda Blake (Kitty Russell)
    Ken Curtis (Festus Haggen)
    Burt Reynolds (Quint Asper)
    Milburn Stone (Doc Adams)
    Dennis Weaver (Chester Goode)
  deputy: **5** Newly
  setting: Dodge City, Kansas
Guns N' Roses
  leader: Axl Rose
  song: Don't Cry (1991)
    November Rain (1992)
    Paradise City (1989)
    Patience (1989)
    Sweet Child o' Mine (1988)
    Welcome to the Jungle (1988)
Guns of August, The: **4** book, film
  author: Barbara Tuchman
  director: Nathan Kroll
Guns of Fort Petticoat, The (1957 film)
  cast: Hope Emerson, Kathryn Grant, Audie Murphy
Guns of Navarone, The (1961 film)
  cast: David Niven, Gregory Peck, Anthony Quinn
  composer: **7** Tiomkin
  director: J. Lee Thompson
gunter: **4** sail
Günter: **5** Grass **6** Blobel
  see also also German
__ Gun, The: **5** Naked **6** Bofors
Gunther __-Williams: **5** Gebel
Gunther, John: **6** author, writer
  work: Death Be Not Proud
    Inside Africa
    Inside Asia
    Inside Australia
    Inside Europe Today
    Inside Russia Today
    Inside South America
    Inside U.S.A.
Gunton: **3** Bob
gunwale: **7** railing
  pin: **5** thole
__ Gun Will Travel: **4** Have
Guofeng: **3** Hua
guppy: **3** pet **4** fish
__-gurdy: **5** hurdy
Gurganus, Allan: **6** author, writer
  work: Oldest Living Confederate Widow Tells All
gurgle: **3** coo, lap **4** foam, purl **5** froth **6** babble, bubble, murmur, ripple, splash
Gurkha land: **5** Nepal
Gurla Mandhata: **4** peak **5** mount **8** mountain
  locale: **4** Asia **5** China, Tibet **9** Himalayas
__ Gurley Brown: **5** Helen
gurnard: **4** fish
Gurnee: **4** city, town
  locale: **8** Illinois
gurney: **3** cot **4** cart **9** stretcher
guru: **4** lama, sage, seer, tech **5** guide, Hindu, maven, mavin, rishi, swami, swamy, tutor **6** cleric, expert, Hindoo, leader, master, mentor, pundit, techie, tekkie **7** teacher **9** abecedary, authority, preceptor **10** specialist, technician
  discipline: **4** yoga
  home: **6** ashram, asrama
  student: **5** chela
  title: **4** yogi **5** yogin
Gus: **4** Kahn **5** Meins **7** Grissom, Van Sant
  gloomy ~: **4** mope **5** moper **9** pessimist, worrywart
Gus (1976 film)
  cast: Edward Asner, Gary Grimes, Don Knotts
gush: **3** jet, run, yak **4** emit, flow, go on, pour, rave, rush, spew, spue, wash **5** burst, drool, emote, erupt, flood, issue, prate, river, spate, spirt, spout, spurt, surge, swell **6** babble, deluge, effuse, jabber, rattle, spring, stream **7** blabber, blather, blether, cascade, chatter, emanate, enthuse, pour out, prattle, run over, torrent **8** outbreak, outburst, overflow, well over **9** discharge, emanation, pour forth, send forth, spillover, upwelling **10** bubble over, outpouring
  over: **6** praise **7** adulate, flatter, lionize
gusher: **6** geyser **7** oil well
  go for a ~: **5** drill **7** wildcat
gushing: **4** oily **5** wordy **6** hearty **7** mawkish, unterse, verbose **8** effusive **9** ebullient, emanation, expansive, exuberant, garrulous **10** pleonastic, unreserved
gushy: **7** maudlin, mawkish **8** effusive **9** expansive
  writing: **4** slop
gusset: **4** gore **5** plait, pleat **6** insert
gussied up: **4** chic **5** natty **6** chichi, dapper, flossy, spiffy **7** adorned, duded up
gussy up: **4** deck, doll **5** adorn, preen, primp, prink **7** furbish, garnish **8** decorate, emblazon **9** embellish, embroider, refurbish
gust: **4** blow, gale, puff, rush, waft, wind **5** blast, burst, draft, storm, whiff **6** breeze, flurry, squall **7** cyclone, flare-up, outrush **8** eruption, outburst
Gustafson, Ralph: **4** poet **8** Canadian
Gustafsson, Lars: **4** poet **7** Swedish
Gustav: **5** Hertz, Holst **6** Mahler **7** Freytag **9** Kirchhoff **10** Stresemann
Gustave: **4** Doré **5** Klimt **7** Courbet **8** Flaubert
__ Gustav Jung: **4** Carl
Gustavus __: **8** Adolphus
gusto: **3** pep, vim, zip **4** brio, élan, fire, zeal, zest, zing **5** ardor, savor, spice, taste, verve **6** fervor, relish, spirit **7** delight, passion **8** appetite, fervency, pleasure **9** eagerness, enjoyment **10** enthusiasm, exuberance
  with ~: **7** eagerly, readily
gusty: **5** windy **6** breezy, stormy
gut: **3** tum **4** sack **5** belly, clean, empty, inner, rifle, strip, tummy **6** innate, inside, paunch, ravage **7** abdomen, destroy, pillage, plunder, ransack, stomach **8** clean out, decimate, potbelly, visceral **9** depredate, emotional, intuitive **10** deep-seated, midsection
  ender: **6** bucket
  feeling: **5** hunch **8** bad vibes, instinct **9** suspicion
  section: **5** ileum
  starter: **3** cat, rot **4** hind
__ gut!: **4** Sehr
gut-busting: **4** rich **5** funny **7** comical, riotous **8** humorous **9** hilarious, priceless **10** hysterical, uproarious
Gutenberg: **8** Johannes
  partner: **4** Fust
Gutenberg __: **5** Bible
Gutenberg Galaxy, The author: Marshall McLuhan
Guthrie: **2** A.B. **4** Arlo, city, town **5** Janet, Woody **6** Tyrone **7** Carlene
  locale: **8** Oklahoma
Guthrie, A.B.: **6** author, writer
  genre: western
  work: The Way West
Guthrie, Arlo
  father: Woody
  song: Alice's Restaurant (1967)
    The City of New Orleans (1972)
gutless: **6** craven, yellow **7** wimpish **8** cowardly **9** spineless
guts: **4** grit **5** heart, moxie, nerve, pluck, spice, spine, spunk, valor **6** daring, mettle, spirit, starch **7** bravery, courage, innards, insides, prowess, stamina, viscera **8** audacity, backbone, boldness, gumption, strength, tenacity, true grit, vitality **9** endurance, fortitude, substance **10** durability, feistiness, moral fiber, resolution
gutsy: **4** bold, game **5** brave, nervy **6** awless, brazen, daring, gritty, heroic, plucky, spunky, strong **7** assured, aweless, defiant, doughty, gallant, impavid, staunch, valiant **8** fearless, heroical, intrepid, resolute, spirited, stalwart, unafraid, valorous **9** audacious, dauntless, dreadless, undaunted, unfearful **10** courageous, iron-willed, mettlesome, undismayed

one: 4 hero
gutta percha: 3 gum
alternative: 6 balata
source: 5 latex 9 sapodilla
Guttenberg, Steve: 5 actor
film: 3 Men and a Baby (1987)
Bedroom Window (1987)
Cocoon (1985)
Diner (1982)
Short Circuit (1986)
Surrender (1987)
gutter: 4 duct 5 chute, ditch, drain, least 6 cullis, furrow, groove, sluice, trench, trough 7 channel, conduit, culvert 9 rainspout
ender: 5 snipe
site: 4 eave
guttersnipe: 4 waif 5 gamin 6 beggar
guttural: 3 low 4 deep 5 gruff, harsh, husky, raspy, velar 6 hoarse 7 grating, rasping, throaty 8 gravelly
sound: 5 grunt
gut-wrenching
feeling: 4 fear 5 angst, dread 7 anxiety
Gutzkow, Karl: 6 German, writer 10 playwright
Gutzon: 7 Borglum
guy: 2 he 3 bud, cat, him, lad, man, sir 4 chap, dude, gent, josh, male, twit 5 bloke, buddy, fella, hubby, taunt, tease 6 feller, fellow, mister, person 7 brother 9 gentleman
bad ~: 4 ogre 6 meanie 7 villain
in Australia: 4 mate
in Britain: 4 mate
partner: 3 gal 4 doll
that ~: 3 him
tough ~: 4 hood 7 hoodlum
typical ~: 3 Joe 7 Joe Blow 9 Joe Doakes 10 Joe Six-Pack
see also man
guy __: 6 Friday
__ guy: 4 fall, lazy, wise
Guy: 5 Buddy, Green 6 Fawkes, Kibbee 7 Jasmine, Lafleur, Laroche, Madison, Ritchie 8 Hamilton, Lombardo, Mitchell, Williams
in Italian: 5 Guido
Guyana: 6 nation 7 country
city: 10 Georgetown
Indian: 6 Arawak
money: 4 cent 6 dollar
native language: 6 Arawak
neighbor: 6 Brazil 8 Suriname 9 Venezuela
org.: 3 OAS
waterfall: 8 Kaieteur
writer: 6 Harris
Guy de __: 10 Maupassant
Guy Fawkes Day month: 3 Nov. 8 November
Guy Mannering author: Walter Scott
guys: 3 hes
bad ~: 4 them 5 enemy
just for ~: 4 stag
Guys __ Dolls: 3 and
__ Guys: 4 Wise 5 Tough
Guys and Dolls: 4 play 7 musical
locale: 4 Cuba 6 Havana 7 New York
role: 3 Sky 5 Sarah 6 Nathan 7 Detroit 8 Adelaide 9 Masterson
song: 5 Sue Me
songwriter: 7 Loesser
Tony winner: 4 Alda
Guys and Dolls (1955 film)
cast: Vivian Blaine, Marlon Brando, Stubby Kaye, Jean Simmons, Frank Sinatra
director: Joseph L. Mankiewicz
source: Damon Runyon
__ Guys Don't Dance: 5 Tough
guy's, that: 3 his
__ Guy, The: 4 Fall, Tall 5 Cable, Other 6 Lonely
Guzmán: 4 city, town
locale: 6 Mexico 7 Jalisco
Guzmán, Martin Luis: 6 author, writer 7 Mexican
guzzle: 3 eat 4 bolt, chug, gulp, swig, tope, wolf 5 drink, gorge, quaff, scarf, slurp, swill 6 devour, englut, gobble, imbibe, inhale, tipple 7 consume, scarf up, swallow 8 chugalug, wolf down 9 hoist a few, knock back, scarf down
Guzzle, King land: 3 Moo
guzzler: 3 sot 4 lush 5 souse, toper 7 tippler
comment: 3 hic
gas ~: 3 car 4 heap 5 crate 6 jalopy 7 clunker 9 limousine 10 automobile
__ guzzler: 3 gas
Gwari home: 6 Africa 7 Nigeria
Gwen: 6 McCrae, Verdon
Gwendolyn: 6 Brooks 7 Bennett
Gwenn, Edmund: 5 actor
film: The Hills of Home (1948)
Life With Father (1947)
Miracle on 34th Street (1947, AA)
Mister 880 (1950)
Mister Scoutmaster (1953)
Pride and Prejudice (1940)
Them! (1954)
The Trouble With Harry (1955)
The Walking Dead (1936)
A Woman of Distinction (1950)
Gweru: 4 city, town
locale: 8 Zimbabwe
Gwinnett: 6 Button
GWTW
see Gone With the Wind
GWU locale: 4 Wash.
Gwyn: 4 Nell
Gwyneth: 7 Paltrow
former boyfriend: 4 Brad
mother: 6 Blythe
role: 4 Emma
gwyniad: 4 fish
Gwynne: 4 Fred
Gwynn, Tony sport: 8 baseball
Gyllenhaal: 7 Stephen
gym: 3 spa 5 arena 6 lyceum, phys. ed. 10 field house, health club, hippodrome
apparatus: 5 horse
black belt: 4 dojo
compartment: 6 locker
event: 3 hop 4 gala, prom 5 dance
exercise: 5 shrug, sit-up
gear: 3 wts. 7 weights 8 Nautilus
iteration: 3 rep
muscles: 3 abs 5 delts, quads 6 biceps 7 triceps
output: 5 sweat 6 effort
site: 4 YMCA, YMHA, YWCA, YWHA
surface: 3 mat
teacher deg.: 3 BPE
wear: 5 shoes 6 shorts, sneaks, sweats, T-shirt 7 leotard, tank top 8 sneakers
gym __: 4 shoe, suit 6 shorts
__ gym: 6 jungle
gymnasium
see gym
gymnast: 6 Korbut, Retton, turner 7 acrobat, athlete, tumbler, vaulter 8 Comaneci 9 aerialist 10 Olga Korbut
competition: 4 meet
concern: 4 form, tone 9 condition
device: 4 beam 5 horse
goal: 3 ten
like a ~: 4 spry 5 agile, lithe 9 lithesome
maneuver: 4 flip 5 nip-up, split, vault 6 aerial
need: 3 mat 5 rosin
gymnastics: 5 sport 7 workout 8 exercise, tumbling, vaulting 10 aerobatics
Gymnopédies composer: 5 Satie
gynephobe fear: 5 women
Gynt, Peer
creator: 5 Ibsen
mother: 3 Ase
Gyor: 4 city, town
locale: 7 Hungary
gypsum: 7 mineral, plaster
to Mohs: 3 two
gypsy: 5 nomad, rover 7 migrant, nomadic, outcast 8 bohemian, traveler, vagabond, wanderer 9 journeyer, migratory
language: 6 Romani, Romany 7 Rommany
male ~: 3 rom
revenge: 5 curse
Spanish ~: 6 gitano
gypsy __: 3 cab 4 moth 5 scale, winch 7 capstan, setting
Gypsy (1962 film): 7 musical
cast: Karl Malden, Rosalind Russell, Natalie Wood
composer: 5 Styne 8 Sondheim
director: Mervyn LeRoy
dog: 8 Chow Mein
Gypsy __: 3 Man 5 Woman 7 Rose Lee
Gypsy __, The: 5 Baron, Moths
Gypsy Girl artist: 4 Hals
Gypsy Man (1973 song) artist: War
Gypsy Moths, The (1969 film)
cast: Gene Hackman, Deborah Kerr, Burt Lancaster
director: John Frankenheimer
Gypsys, Tramps & Thieves (1971 song) artist: Cher
Gypsy Woman (song) artist: Brian Hyland, Crystal Waters
__ Gyra: 5 Spyro
gyrate: 4 jink, roll, spin, turn 5 dance, shake, twirl, wheel, whirl 6 circle, rotate 7 revolve, shudder 9 pirouette
gyration: 4 gyre, roll, spin 5 swirl, twirl, whirl 6 spiral 7 rolling 8 rotation, spinning, swirling, twirling, wheeling, whirling 9 pirouette, swiveling 10 revolution
gyre: 4 ring 5 wheel 6 circle, vortex
gyrene: 6 Marine 7 soldier
gyrfalcon: 4 bird
gyro: 5 Greek 8 sandwich
need: 4 lamb, pita, spit
gyroscope: 5 rotor 10 stabilizer
cousin: 3 top
imitate a ~: 4 spin 6 rotate
part: 4 axis
Gyumri: 4 city, town
locale: 7 Armenia
gyve: 5 chain 6 fetter 7 shackle, trammel

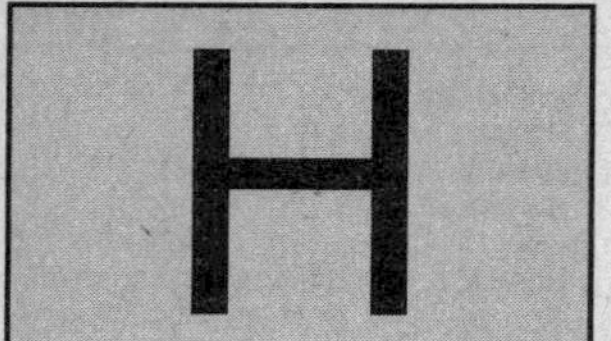

H: 3 eta 4 elem. 6 letter 7 vitamin 8 hydrogen
in phonetic alphabet: 5 Hotel
1 for ~: 4 at. no.
position: 6 eighth
H __ hat: 4 as in
H-__: 4 beam, bomb, hour, Town 5 hinge
H. __: 3 Res.
H. __ Brown: 3 Rap
H. __ Haggard: 5 Rider
H. __ Perot: 4 Ross
H. __ Smith: 5 Allen
'H' __ Homicide: 5 Is for
__-ha: 3 hoo
Ha!: 3 oho 4 I bet
__ Haag: 3 Den
Haagen Dazs: 8 ice cream
alternative: 4 Edy's 7 Breyer's 9 Friendly's, Good Humor 10 Dairy Queen, Turkey Hill
Haakon VI son: 4 Olaf, Olav
Haarlem: 4 city, town
locale: 7 Holland
Haas: 5 Lukas
Haavelmo, Trygve: 8 Nobelist 9 economist
Haavikko, Paavo: 6 author, writer 7 Finnish
hab. __: 4 corp.
Habakkuk: 4 book
follower: 9 Zephaniah
preceder: 5 Nahum
habanera: 5 dance
habeas corpus: 4 writ 5 trial
haberdasher: 6 tailor 8 clothier 9 outfitter
deparment: 4 men's
offering: 3 hat, tie 4 sock 5 scarf, shirt 6 bowtie, cravat 7 necktie
Haber, Fritz: 7 chemist 8 Nobelist
habile: 4 deft 5 adept 6 adroit, clever 7 skilled 8 masterly, skillful 9 dexterous, ingenious, inventive, masterful 10 proficient, well-versed
habiliment: 4 garb, gear 5 dress, getup, habit 6 attire, outfit, things 7 apparel, clothes 8 clothing 9 machinery, trappings, vestments 10 Sunday best
__ habilis: 4 homo
habit: 3 rut, way 4 bent, garb, gear, gown, rote, wont 5 dress, quirk, trait, usage 6 attire, custom, groove, livery, praxis 7 apparel, costume, routine, uniform 8 accouter, accoutre, penchant, practice, tendency, vestment 9 addiction, mannerism 10 canonicals, convention, habiliment, propensity
bad ~: 4 vice 6 foible
be in the ~ of: 4 tend
in the ~: 7 grooved 10 accustomed
in the ~ of: 6 likely, used to 8 disposed, inclined
kick the ~: 4 quit, stop 5 cease 6 desist, lay off 8 renounce
part: 4 veil
riding ~: 4 togs
wearer: 3 nun
__ habit: 6 riding
habitable: 7 livable 8 liveable
habitant: 7 denizen, resider 8 indigene, resident
habitat: 3 pad 4 co-op, digs, flat, home, nest, site, turf 5 abode, condo, house, place, range, roost 6 domain, locale, medium 7 domicil, element, grounds, housing, lodging, shelter, terrain 8 domicile, dwelling, quarters 9 apartment, biosphere, residence, territory
establishment in a new ~: 6 ecesis
prefix: 3 eco-
habitation: 7 lodging, mansion 8 fireside, quarters 9 occupancy, residence
elevated ~: 4 aery, eyry 5 aerie, eyrie
habits: 4 ways 6 praxes 8 behavior 10 ins and outs
good ~: 6 ethics, morals 7 decency, virtues 8 morality 9 integrity, rectitude 10 principles
habitual: 5 typic, usual 6 common, normal, steady, wonted 7 chronic, general, natural, regular, routine, typical 8 accepted, constant, everyday, familiar, frequent, knee-jerk, ordinary, orthodox, repeated, standard, unwaning 9 automatic, chronical, confirmed, continual, customary, ingrained, practiced, prevalent, recurrent, unabating 10 accustomed, deep-seated, inveterate, mechanical, methodical, persistent, prevailing, systematic
manner: 3 way
habitually: 3 oft 5 often 7 usually 9 generally, many a time, naturally 10 frequently
habituate: 5 enure, haunt, inure, train 6 adjust, harden 7 break in 8 accustom, indurate 9 acclimate, condition 10 discipline
habituated: 7 abiding 8 enduring 9 confirmed, ingrained 10 deep-rooted, deep-seated, inveterate
habitude: 4 wont 5 usage 6 custom, groove 7 routine 8 practice 9 tradition
habitué: 4 goer, user 6 addict, patron 7 devotee, visitor 8 customer 10 frequenter
Hachinohe: 4 city, port, town
locale: 5 Japan 6 Honshu
Hachioji: 4 city, town
locale: 5 Japan
hacienda: 4 casa 5 house, ranch 6 estate 7 mansion 9 farmstead 10 plantation
material: 5 adobe
room: 4 sala
Hacienda __, CA: 3 Hts.
Hacienda Heights: 4 city, town
locale: 10 California
hack: 3 axe, cab, cut, hew, rip 4 chop, fell, jade, maim, ride, take, taxi 5 cabby, cough, horse, labor, mince, slash, slice, split 6 cabbie, cabmen, common, driver, drudge, equine, jackal, mangle 7 pickaxe, plodder, scissor, taxicab, vehicle 8 hireling, inferior, mutilate 9 detractor, transport 10 second-rate
ender: 3 saw 4 work 5 berry 6 butter
it: 4 pass 5 get by 6 manage, thrive 7 make out, prosper, qualify, succeed 8 flourish, go places, make good 9 measure up 10 do all right, make the cut, pass muster
off: 2 ax 3 axe 5 sever 7 cut down 8 chop down
rider: 4 fare
hack __: 5 board, house 6 hammer 7 license
Hack: 6 Wilson 7 Shelley
hackberry: 4 tree 5 fruit, shrub
cousin: 3 elm 7 zelkova
family: 3 elm
Hackensack: 4 city, town
locale: 9 New Jersey
hacker: 4 user 6 golfer 10 cyber-crook
creation: 4 code 5 virus
headache: 3 bug
like a ~: 5 nerdy
purchase: 2 PC 4 disk 8 computer
Hackett: 4 Joan 5 Bobby, Buddy 6 Albert
Hackett, Joan: 7 actress
film: The Group (1966)
Support Your Local Sheriff (1969)
The Terminal Man (1974)
Will Penny (1968)
Hackford, Taylor: 8 director
film: The Devil's Advocate (1997)
Dolores Claiborne (1995)
Everybody's All-American (1988)
An Officer and a Gentleman (1982)
Proof of Life (2000)
hackie: 5 cabby 6 cabbie, driver 9 cab driver 10 taxi driver
hacking __: 4 coat 6 jacket
hackle: 3 cut 6 mangle
hackles: 4 hair 5 anger
raise one's ~: 3 bug, get, irk, try, vex 4 fret, gall, miff, rile 5 annoy, chafe, grate, harry, peeve, pique 6 abrade, bother, harass, hector, needle, nettle, pester, plague, rankle, ruffle 7 disturb, provoke 8 irritate 9 aggravate, displease
where ~ rise: 4 nape
hackly: 5 rough 6 jagged, uneven 9 irregular
Hackman, Gene: 5 actor
film: Absolute Power (1997)
All Night Long (1981)
Bat*21 (1988)
Behind Enemy Lines (2001)
the birdcage (1995)
Bite the Bullet (1975)
Bonnie and Clyde (1967)
Cisco Pike (1972)
Class Action (1991)
The Conversation (1974)
Crimson Tide (1995)
Downhill Racer (1969)
Enemy of the State (1998)
The Firm (1993)
The French Connection (1971, AA)
Get Shorty (1995)
The Gypsy Moths (1969)
Heartbreakers (2001)
Heist (2001)
Hoosiers (1986)
I Never Sang for My Father (1970)
Mississippi Burning (1988)
Night Moves (1975)
No Way Out (1987)
The Poseidon Adventure (1972)
Postcards From the Edge (1990)
Prime Cut (1972)
The Quick and the Dead (1995)
Riot (1969)
The Royal Tenenbaums (2001)
Scarecrow (1973)
Superman (1978)
Superman II (1980)
Twice in a Lifetime (1985)
Twilight (1998)
Under Fire (1983)
Unforgiven (1992, AA)
Wyatt Earp (1994)
film (voice): Antz (1998)
hackney: 5 coach, horse 6 equine 8 carriage
hackneyed: 3 old 4 dull, worn 5 banal, corny, hokey, moldy, musty, passé, stale, stock, tired, trite, vapid 6 common, jejune, old hat 7 clichéd, fatuous, humdrum, prosaic, worn-out 8 bromidic, outdated, outmoded, timeworn, well-used 9 moth-eaten, out-of-date, played out, prosaical, quotidian 10 antiquated, dullsville, overworked, pedestrian, threadbare, uninspired, unoriginal
expression: 6 cliché
hacksaw: 4 tool
Hacky Sack company: 5 Wham-o
Had __ and couldn't keep her: 5 a wife
__ Had a Hammer: 3 If I
__ Had a Million: 3 If I
Hadano: 4 city, town
locale: 5 Japan
Hadar: 4 star
__ had a secret love: 5 Once I
Haddam: 4 city, town
locale: 4 Conn.
__ haddie: 6 finnan
haddock: 3 cod 4 fish 5 scrod 6 schrod
__ haddock: 6 finnan
__ had 'em: 4 Adam
Hades: 3 Dis 4 hell 5 abyss, limbo, Orcus, Pluto 7 Avernus, inferno 9 perdition 10 lower world, underworld
brother of ~: 4 Zeus 8 Poseidon
dog: 8 Cerberus
entrance: 6 Averno
equivalent: 5 Pluto
parent of ~: 4 Rhea 6 Cronos, Cronus
place enroute to ~: 6 Erebus
river: 4 Styx 5 Lethe
sister of ~: 4 Hera 6 Hestia 7 Demeter
wife of ~: 10 Persephone
Hades Factor, The author: Robert Ludlum
__ had it!: 3 I've
hadj: 4 trek, trip 10 pilgrimage
__ had my way...: 3 If I
hadn't, wish you: 3 rue
Hadrian: 5 Roman 6 Caesar
Hadriano: 4 font 8 typeface
Hadrian's Wall, south of: 6 Anglia
hadron: 8 particle
component: 5 quark
Haeckel, Ernst: 11 philosopher
Haedus I: 4 star
Hafey: 5 Chick
Hafez: 4 poet 7 Al-Assad, Persian
Haffner Symphony composer: 6 Mozart
Hafiz: 4 poet 7 Persian
hafnium: 5 metal 7 element
haft: 6 handle
hag: 5 crone, harpy, witch 6 beldam, gorgon 7 beldame 8 harridan
assembly: 5 coven
ender: 4 fish
Hagar: 5 Sammy
Hägar the Horrible: 5 comic 10 comic strip
daughter: 4 Honi
dog: 5 Snert
wife: 5 Helga
Hagen: 3 Uta 4 city, Jean, town 5 Earle 6 Walter
locale: 7 Germany
Hagen, Jean: 7 actress
film: The Asphalt Jungle (1950)
Carbine Williams (1952)
The Shaggy Dog (1959)
Singin' in the Rain (1952)
TV: The Danny Thomas Show
Hagen, Uta spouse: José Ferrer
Hagen, Walter: 6 golfer
milieu: 5 links 6 course
org.: 3 PGA
won four of these: 4 PGAs
Hagerstown: 4 city
locale: 8 Maryland
Hagerty, Julie: 7 actress
film: Airplane! (1980)
Lost in America (1985)
A Midsummer Night's Sex Comedy (1982)
Noises Off (1992)
What About Bob? (1991)
haggadah time: 5 seder 8 Passover
Haggai: 4 book
follower: 9 Zechariah
preceder: 9 Zephaniah
haggard: 3 wan 4 lean, pale, thin, worn

5 drawn, gaunt, spare, tired 6 ill-fed, peaked 7 starved, worn-out 8 care-worn, fatigued, starving, weakened, worn-down 9 emaciated, exhausted
Haggard: 5 Merle, Rider 6 H. Rider
Haggard, H. Rider: 6 author, writer 7 British
character: 6 Ayesha
first name: Henry
work: Allan Quatermain
Ayesha
King Solomon's Mines
Nada the Lily
She
Haggerty: 3 Dan
haggle: 5 argue 6 barter, bicker, dicker 7 bargain, quarrel, wrangle 9 have words, negotiate 10 horse-trade
point: 5 price
hagiology subject: 3 ste., sts. 5 saint
Hagiwara Sakutaro: 4 poet 8 Japanese
Hagler, Marvin: 5 boxer
milieu: 4 ring
Hagman, Larry: 5 actor
costar: 4 Eden
film: Stardust (1975)
Up in the Cellar (1970)
mother: Mary Martin
TV: Dallas, I Dream of Jeannie
Hague, The: 4 city, town 7 capital
locale: 7 Holland 11 Netherlands
__-hah: 3 hoo
ha-ha: 5 laugh 6 cackle, giggle, guffaw, titter 7 break up, chortle, chuckle, crack up 8 laughter
Hahn: 4 Otto 6 Hilary
Hahn, Hilary: 9 violinist
Hahn, Otto: 7 chemist 8 Nobelist
hai: 3 yes 8 Japanese
__ H'ai: 4 Bali
Haid: 7 Charles
Haida: 5 tribe 6 Indian 7 Amerind 8 language
Haifa: 4 city, port, town
locale: 3 Isr. 6 Israel
port north of ~: 4 Acre
Haig: 2 Al 9 Alexander
former command: 4 NATO
Haight-Ashbury city: 6 Frisco
haiku: 4 poem 5 verse 6 poetry
birthplace: 5 Japan
kin: 5 tanka
hail: 3 ave, get, ice 4 flag, laud, rain 5 cheer, exalt, extol, greet, hallo, hillo, honor, hullo, huzza, salvo, storm 6 accost, call to, extoll, halloa, halloo, hallow, hilloa, hoorah, hooray, hulloo, hurrah, hurray, huzzah, praise, salute, shower, signal, summon, yell to 7 acclaim, applaud, approve, barrage, call for, commend, flatter, glorify, torrent, welcome, yell for 8 flag down, greeting, wave down 9 recognize 10 compliment, panegyrize, salutation
ender: 5 stone, storm
(from): 4 come 9 originate
in Latin: 3 ave
something to ~: 3 cab 4 taxi 7 taxicab
hail __: 4 a cab, from
hail-__-well-met: 6 fellow
__ hail: 3 all 4 soft 6 within
Hail __: 4 Mary
Hail __ Chief: 5 to the
Hail __ pass: 4 Mary
Hail, Caesar!: 3 ave
Haile Selassie: 9 Ras Tafari
Hailey, Arthur: 6 author, writer
work: Airport
Detective
The Evening News
The Final Diagnosis
Hotel
In High Places
The Moneychangers
Overload
Runway Zero-Eight
Strong Medicine
Wheels
hail-fellow well met: 5 mixer 7 mingler 9 extrovert 10 socializer
Hail Mary __: 4 pass, play
Hail Mary counter: 6 rosary
Hail the Conquering Hero (1944 film)
cast: Eddie Bracken, Ella Raines
director: Preston Sturges
Haim: 5 Corey
Haines: 4 city, town 5 Randa
locale: 6 Alaska
Haines, Randa: 8 director
film: Children of a Lesser God (1986)
Dance With Me (1998)
The Doctor (1991)
Haing: 4 Ngor
Haiphong: 4 city, town
locale: 3 Nam 7 Vietnam
hair: 3 bun, fur, mop, wig 4 fuzz, lock, mane, pelt 5 beard, fiber, locks, pilus, tress 6 cilium, goatee, strand, toupee 7 bristle, cowlick, eyebrow, eyelash, minimum, tresses 8 coiffure, filament, sideburn, whiskers 9 moustache
adornment: 3 bow
animal ~: 3 fur 4 coat
appliance: 5 drier, dryer 6 blower
application: 3 dye, gel 5 frost, spray
arrange ~: 4 comb, do up 5 tease
band: 6 fascia
by a ~: 6 barely 8 narrowly
cause of a bad ~ day: 4 wind
color: 3 dye, red 4 gray, grey, tint 5 black, blond, brown, henna, rinse, trait, white 6 auburn, blonde 8 brunette
combining form: 3 pil- 4 pili-, pilo- 5 chaet-, crini-, trich- 6 chaeto-, -tricha, tricho-
covering: 3 hat, net
curl one's ~: 5 alarm, scare, spook 7 horrify, terrify 8 frighten
cut ~: 5 layer, shave
cutter: 5 razor 6 barber
dryer setting: 5 on low
ender: 3 cut, dos, pin 4 ball, line, worm 5 brush, cloth, piece, spray, style, weave 6 cutter, spring, streak 7 breadth, dresser 8 splitter
facial ~: 5 beard 8 mustache, whiskers 9 moustache
foundation: 5 scalp
fuss with one's ~: 5 groom, preen, primp
gel amount: 4 glob
get in one's ~: 3 bug, irk, vex 4 gall, rile 5 annoy, peeve, pique, upset 6 madden, nettle, pester, plague, ruffle 7 provoke, tick off 8 irritate 9 aggravate 10 exasperate
having ~ like horses: 5 maned
in one's ~: 5 pesky 7 irksome 8 annoying 9 obnoxious, vexatious 10 bothersome, irritating, nettlesome
interwoven ~: 5 braid, plait, queue 7 pigtail 8 ponytail
let one's ~ down: 4 undo 5 unpin 6 relate 8 unburden
like some ~: 4 wavy 5 curly, silky 6 frizzy
long ~: 3 mop 4 mane
lose ~: 4 bald, molt, shed 5 moult
microscopic ~: 6 cilium
neck ~: 7 hackles
problem: 4 knot 5 snarl 6 tangle
quality: 4 body 6 luster
quantity: 4 curl, hank, lock, tuft, wisp 5 shock, tress
remover: 4 Nair, Neet 10 depilatory
ribbon: 6 fillet
root ~: 6 fibril
shirt: 7 penance 9 penitence 10 contrition
shirt wearer: 6 atoner
shop: 5 salon
short ~: 7 bristle, whisker
splitter: 4 part
spray name: 5 Adorn
starter: 4 long, wire 5 cross, horse, short
style: 2 DA, do 3 bob, bun, cut, 'fro 4 Afro, burr, coif, conk, fade, flip, perm, pouf, puff, punk, shag, updo 5 bangs, braid, butch, queue, twist 6 braids, marcel, Mohawk, plaits 7 beehive, chignon, crew cut, flattop, natural, pageboy, topknot, upsweep 8 bouffant, brush cut, coiffure, cold wave, cornrows, ducktail, Dutch bob, pigtails, pin curls, pixie cut, ponytail, razor cut, ringlets 9 headdress, permanent, pompadour, poodle cut, scalp lock, spit curls 10 cornbraids, dreadlocks, feather cut, finger wave, Psyche knot
stylist, at times: 4 dyer
transplanted ~: 4 plug
treat ~: 3 dye, set 4 tint 5 rinse, tease
where ~ rises: 4 nape
with no ~ out of place: 4 neat, tidy 5 natty, sleek, slick, smart 6 dapper, spruce 7 orderly 8 spotless 9 shipshape
hair __: 3 net 4 cell, seal 5 grass, shirt, space, spray, style 6 stroke 7 stylist, trigger
hair __ dog: 5 of the
hair-__: 6 raiser 7 raising
__ hair: 3 big, by a 4 root 5 angel, crepe, guard, Pele's, turn a 6 angel's, camel's
Hair: 7 musical
character: 3 Hud 4 Woof 6 Berger, Claude, Crissy, Sheila 7 Jeannie
lyricist: 4 Rado
producer: 4 Papp
song: 3 Air
Hair (1969 song) artist: Cowsills
__ hair coat: 6 camel's
haircream holder: 4 tube
Haircut author: Ring Lardner
__ hair day: 3 bad
hairdo: 2 DA 3 bob, bun, cut, 'fro 4 Afro, coif, conk, fade, flip, perm, pouf, puff, punk, shag, updo 5 bangs, braid, butch, queue, twist 6 braids, marcel, Mohawk, plaits 7 beehive, chignon, crew cut, flattop, natural, pageboy, topknot, upsweep 8 bouffant, brush cut, coiffure, cold wave, cornrows, ducktail, Dutch bob, pigtails, pin curls, pixie cut, ponytail, razor cut, ringlets 9 headdress, permanent, pompadour, poodle cut, scalp lock, spit curls 10 cornbraids, dreadlocks, feather cut, finger wave, Psyche knot
feature: 4 part 5 roach, swirl
like a punk ~: 5 spiky
hairdresser: 6 barber 7 friseur, stylist 8 coiffeur
at times: 4 dyer
haired: 6 pilose, pilous
starter: 4 long, wire 5 short
__-haired: 4 fair 5 white
__-haired boy: 4 fair
__-haired terrier: 4 wire
hairless: 4 bald 5 pelon, shorn 6 shaved, shaven, smooth 7 egghead 8 glabrate, glabrous
__ hairless: 7 Mexican
hairnet: 5 snood
hair of the __: 3 dog
...hair on my __...: 6 chinny
hairpiece: 3 rug, wig 4 fall 6 toupee
hairpin: 6 bodkin
curve: 3 zag, zig
hair-raising: 4 eery 5 eerie, scary 6 creepy 7 fearful 8 chilling, exciting 9 thrilling, unearthly
hairs
ender: 7 breadth
fruit ~: 5 villi
split ~: 5 cavil 6 niggle 7 nitpick, quibble 8 pettifog
starter: 5 cross
use the cross ~: 3 aim 5 sight
__ hairs: 5 cross, split
hairsplitting: 4 fine 7 carping 8 caviling, finespun, pedantic 10 pedantical
Hairspray (1988 film)
cast: Sonny Bono, Ruth Brown, Divine
director: John Waters
hairstyle
see hairdo
hairy: 4 hard 5 bushy, furry, fuzzy, pilar, risky, rough, scary, tough 6 chancy, comate, pilose, pilous, shaggy, sticky, unsafe 7 bearded, bristly, hirsute, parlous, pileous, unshorn 8 critical, grueling, perilous, unshaven 9 dangerous, difficult, frightful, hazardous, uncertain, whiskered 10 abominable, jeopardous, precarious, touch-and-go
combining form: 4 dasy-
no longer ~: 5 shorn
one: 3 ape
Hairy Ape, The author: 6 O'Neill
hairy-chested: 5 macho, manly 6 virile 9 masculine
hairy one, Biblical: 4 Esau
Haiti: 6 nation 7 country
city: 6 Delmas 9 Carrefour
gulf: 6 Gonâve 8 Gonaïves
island off ~: 6 Gonâve
language: 6 Creole, French
money: 3 gde. 6 gourde
org.: 3 OAS
practice: 5 vodun 6 voodoo
rum: 5 tafia 6 taffia
Haje: 9 Khrystyne
hajj destination: 5 Mecca
Haj, The author: Leon Uris
haka: 5 dance
hake: 4 fish
hakea: 4 tree 5 shrub 9 evergreen
Hakeem: 8 Olajuwon
Hakodate: 4 city, town
locale: 5 Japan
Hal: 5 Ashby, Chase, David, Greer, Leroy, March, Roach, Smith 6 Foster, Linden, Porter, Prince, Salwen, Sutton, Walker, Wallis 7 Hartley, Ketchum, Needham 8 Holbrook, McIntyre, Williams 9 Newhouser 10 Fittipaldi
halala: 4 coin
Halas, George: 5 coach
sport: 8 football
halberd, medieval: 5 vouge
Halberstam, David: 6 author, writer
subject: 6 Jordan 7 Vietnam 8 baseball
work: The Amateurs
The Best and the Brightest
The Breaks of the Game
The Fifties
Firehouse
October 1964
Playing for Keeps
The Powers That Be
The Reckoning
Summer of '49
War in a Time of Peace
halcyon: 4 bird, calm 5 happy, palmy,

quiet **6** joyful, serene **7** at peace **8** carefree, peaceful, tranquil **10** harmonious, untroubled
Haldan: 8 Hartline
Haldane: 7 Richard
Haldeman: 2 H.R.
Haldimand: 4 city, town
locale: 6 Canada **7** Ontario
hale: 3 fit **4** iron, trim, well, wiry **5** beefy, burly, hardy, hefty, hunky, husky, lusty, right, sound, stout, tough, whole **6** brawny, hearty, mighty, potent, robust, rugged, sinewy, steely, stocky, strong, sturdy, virile **7** doughty, healthy, in shape, up to par **8** athletic, forceful, indurate, muscular, powerful, puissant, stalwart, vigorous **9** Atlantean, energetic, Herculean, in the pink, strapping, well-built **10** able-bodied, red-blooded
partner: 6 hearty
Hale: 4 Alan **5** Irwin **6** Nathan, Philip **7** Barbara
hero: 5 Nolan
Haleakala: 4 park **6** crater
locale: 4 Maui **6** Hawaii
Hale, Barbara: 7 actress
film: Jolson Sings Again (1949)
Lady Luck (1946)
The Window (1949)
son: William Katt
TV: Perry Mason
Hale-Bopp: 5 comet
__ Hale Broun: 7 Heywood
__ Halen: 3 Van
Hale, Nathan: 3 spy
alma mater: 4 Yale
Halen, Eddie Van spouse: Valerie Bertinelli
haleness: 6 health
ha-Levi: 5 Judah
Haley: 4 Alex, Bill, Jack
costar: 4 Lahr **6** Bolger **7** Garland
Haley __ Osment: 4 Joel
Haley, Alex: 6 author, writer
ancestor: Kinte
work: The Autobiography of Malcolm X
Roots
Haley and His Comets, Bill
song: Burn That Candle (1955)
Rock Around the Clock (1955)
See You Later, Alligator (1956)
Shake, Rattle and Roll (1954)
Haley Jr., Jack spouse: Liza Minnelli
half: 5 piece **6** handle, moiety **9** bisection
ender: 3 way **4** back, time, tone **5** pence, penny **6** cocked **7** hearted
in music: 5 mezzo
prefix: 4 demi-, hemi-, semi-
half __: 3 pay **4** bath, boot, buck, cent, deck, dime, hose, note, pint, rest, size, sole, step, tide, tone **5** blood, board, crown, eagle, hitch, rhyme, shell, snipe, story, title, twist **6** dollar, gainer, nelson, relief, sister, volley **7** binding, brother, cadence, leather
half-__: 3 wit **4** full, hour, inch, life, mast, mile, moon, note, pint, sole, turn **5** baked, pound, right, truth **6** asleep, cocked, gallon, joking
half-__ over: 4 seas
__ half: 5 other **6** better **7** shelter
Half __ Bay, CA: 4 Moon
Half __ is better...: 5 a loaf
__ half a mind to: 4 have
half-and-half
amount: 2 pt. **4** pint
part: 4 milk **5** cream
half-asleep: 4 dozy, logy **5** tired **6** drowsy **9** heavy-eyed
half-awake: 4 dozy, logy **5** tired **6** drowsy **9** heavy-eyed
halfback: 7 athlete, gridder **10** footballer
move: 4 juke **5** feint **6** end run
__ half bad: 3 not
half-baked: 4 daft **5** batty, goony, goosy, silly **7** foolish, shallow, vacuous, wanting, witless **9** brainless, senseless **10** boneheaded, dilettante, ill-advised, indiscreet, sophomoric, unfinished, weak-minded
halfbeak: 4 fish
half-cocked
see half-baked
__ half-cocked: 5 go off
half-cup: 4 gill
half dollar: 4 coin **5** money
word: 3 God **4** unum **5** trust **6** States, United **7** America, liberty **8** pluribus
half-done: 7 sketchy **10** incomplete, unfinished
half-gainer: 4 dive
half-goat, half-man: 3 Pan **4** faun **5** satyr
half-grown: 5 young **6** callow **8** immature **10** adolescent, developing
halfhearted: 4 cold, cool, tame **5** tepid **7** passive **8** grudging, hesitant, listless, lukewarm
Half Heaven - Half Heartache (1963 song) artist: Gene Pitney
half-hour at sea: 4 bell
Half-Lives author: Erica Jong
halfmoon: 4 fish
half-moon: 3 arc **4** lune
Half Moon: 4 boat, ship
captain: 6 Hudson
half-note feature: 4 stem
half-off event: 4 sale
halfpenny: 4 coin **5** money **6** bawbee
half-pint: 3 boy, kid, lad **4** runt **5** child, sprig, youth **6** peewee **8** juvenile **9** stripling, youngster
serving: 3 ale **4** beer **5** stout
half-price: 5 cheap **6** on sale **7** cut-rate, low-cost, reduced **10** economical, marked down, reasonable
half-seas __: 4 over
half-serpent, half-woman: 5 lamia
halftime entertainer: 4 band
Half Time rapper: 3 Nas
halftone: 5 print
Halftrack: 4 Amos **7** general
half-truth: 4 myth **9** falsehood **10** generality
half turn in ballet: 7 déboulé
halfway: 3 mid **4** mean **5** midst **6** almost, in part, median, middle, nearly, partly **7** partial **9** partially
meet ~: 7 mediate **9** arbitrate, negotiate, reconcile **10** conciliate
point: 6 center, median, middle
__ halfway: 4 meet
halfway house program: 5 rehab
half-wit: 3 ass, nit, oaf, sap **4** boob, bozo, clod, dolt, dope, fool, gowk, zany **5** chump, clown, cluck, dummy, dunce, joker, ninny, patsy **6** dimwit, lummox, sucker, turkey **7** buffoon, dingbat, dullard, fathead, jackass, pinhead, saphead **8** bonehead, dumbbell, meathead, numskull **9** birdbrain, blockhead, harebrain, lamebrain, numbskull, simpleton **10** dunderhead
half-witted: 5 goosy, silly, thick **6** simple **7** foolish **8** headless **10** weak-minded
Haliburton, Thomas: 6 author, writer **8** Canadian
halibut: 4 fish, sole
Halifax: 4 city, port, town
clock setting: 3 AST
locale: 6 Canada **10** Nova Scotia
newspaper: 4 News **6** Herald
school: 9 Dalhousie
halite: 7 mineral **8** rock salt
melter: 4 snow
halitosis: 9 bad breath
cause: 5 onion **6** garlic
fighter: 5 Scope **9** Listerine
hall: 5 foyer, lobby, odeon, odeum **6** lyceum, museum, palace **7** gallery, ingress, mansion, passage, theater, theatre, walkway **8** anteroom, ballroom, corridor **9** classroom, concourse, dormitory, residence, vestibule **10** auditorium, passageway, schoolroom
activity: 5 study
concert ~: 5 odeon, odeum, venue **7** theater, theatre
dance ~: 5 disco
decker: 5 holly
dining ~: 4 mess
ender: 3 way **4** mark
entrance ~: 5 foyer, lobby **9** vestibule
exhibition ~: 5 salon **8** pavilion
in Spanish: 4 sala
lecture ~: 6 lyceum **10** auditorium
mess ~: 10 dining room
of justice: 5 court
preceder: 4 town
starter: 4 gild **5** dance, guild, White
hall __: 4 tree **7** monitor
__ hall: 4 beer, city, mess, moot, pool, town **5** bingo, dance, music, study **6** dining, hiring **7** borough
Hall: 3 Edd, Jon **4** Fawn **5** Annie, Daryl, Huntz, Jerry, Monty, Peter **6** Deidre, Donald **7** Arsenio, Juanita **8** Bartlett **9** Alexander, Radclyffe
partner: 5 Oates
__ Hall: 4 City **5** Annie, Seton **6** Nassau **7** Faneuil, Kingdom, Tammany
Hall, Alexander: 8 director
film: Bedtime Story (1941)
The Doctor Takes a Wife (1940)
Goin' to Town (1935)
The Great Lover (1949)
Here Comes Mr. Jordan (1941)
Let's Do It Again (1953)
Little Miss Marker (1934)
Louisa (1950)
There's Always a Woman (1938)
This Thing Called Love (1941)
Hallam, Arthur: 4 poet **7** British
Hallandale: 4 city, town
locale: 7 Florida
Hall and Oates
song: Adult Education (1984)
Did It in a Minute (1982)
Everything Your Heart Desires (1988)
Family Man (1983)
I Can't Go For That (1981)
Kiss on My List (1981)
Maneater (1982)
Method of Modern Love (1985)
One on One (1983)
Out of Touch (1984)
Private Eyes (1981)
Rich Girl (1977)
Sara Smile (1976)
Say It Isn't So (1983)
She's Gone (1976)
You Make My Dreams (1981)
Hall, Arsenio: 2 MC **4** host **5** emcee
Hall, Donald: 4 poet
Halle: 4 city, town **5** Berry
locale: 7 Germany
river: 5 Saale
hallelujah: 4 amen, pean **5** huzza, paean, shout **6** hoorah, hooray, hurrah, hurray, huzzah **7** hosanna **8** alleluia
Hallelujah, __ Bum: 3 I'm a
Hallelujah, Baby!: 7 musical
songwriter: 5 Styne
Hallelujah, I'm a Bum (1933 film)
cast: Madge Evans, Al Jolson, Frank Morgan
director: Lewis Milestone
H. Allen __: 5 Smith
Halley, Edmund: 10 astronomer
Halley's __: 5 comet
Halliwell: 4 Geri **6** Leslie
Hall, Jerry spouse: Mick Jagger
Hall, Jon: 5 actor
film: Cobra Woman (1944)
The Hurricane (1937)
Kit Carson (1940)
San Diego, I Love You (1944)
The Tuttles of Tahiti (1942)
hallmark: 4 seal, sign **5** badge, brand, stamp, trait **6** emblem, symbol **7** feature **8** property, sure sign **9** indicator **10** indication
Hallmark __: 5 Cards
Hall, Monty: 2 MC **4** host **5** emcee
offering: 4 deal
hallo: 3 cry **4** call, hail, yell **5** shout **6** call to, cry out **7** address, exclaim **8** greeting **9** call out to **10** salutation
Hall of __: 4 Fame **5** Famer
Hall of Fame
baseball ~ executive: 5 Frick, Giles, Veeck **6** Barrow, Landis, Rickey, Yawkey **7** Johnson **8** Chandler, Griffith, MacPhail, Spalding **9** Bill Veeck, Ford Frick, Tom Yawkey **10** Ban Johnson
baseball ~ manager: 4 Mack **5** Lopez, Selee **6** Alston, Hanlon, Harris, McGraw, Weaver **7** Al Lopez, Huggins, Lasorda, Stengel **8** Anderson, Durocher, McCarthy **9** McKechnie, Ned Hanlon **10** Connie Mack, Earl Weaver, Frank Selee, John McGraw
baseball ~ player: 3 Day, Fox, Ott **4** Babe, Bell, Cobb, Dean, Doby, Fisk, Ford, Foxx, Hoyt, Mays, Mize, Rice, Ruth, Ryan, Wynn, Yogi **5** Aaron, Anson, Banks, Bench, Brett, Brock, Carew, Combs, Doerr, Evers, Flick, Gomez, Grove, Irvin, Kiner, Klein, Lemon, Paige, Perez, Reese, Rixey, Roush, Rusie, Smith, Spahn, Terry, Vance, Waner, Wheat, Young, Yount **6** Bender, Carter, Cepeda, Cronin, Cuyler, Dihigo, Feller, Foster, Frisch, Gehrig, Gibson, Goslin, Hunter, Kaline, Koufax, Lajoie, Mantle, Mel Ott, Morgan, Murray, Musial, Niekro, Palmer, Seaver, Sisler, Snider, Sutton, Ty Cobb, Wagner, Wilson **7** Appling, Ashburn, Averill, Bunning, Carlton, Collins, Cy Young, Fingers, Hornsby, Hubbell, Jackson, Jenkins, Johnson, Lazzeri, Leon Day, Mathews, McCovey, Medwick, Puckett, Rizzuto, Roberts, Ruffing, Sam Rice, Schmidt, Speaker, Stearns, Traynor, Vaughan, Waddell, Wilhelm **8** Al Kaline, Aparicio, Babe Ruth, Bob Lemon, Boudreau, Cap Anson, Clemente, Cochrane, DiMaggio, Drysdale, Edd Roush, Lou Brock, Marichal, Marquard, Robinson, Rod Carew, Stargell, Williams, Winfield **9** Alexander, Amos Rusie, Bill Terry, Bob Feller, Bob Gibson, Dandridge, Dizzy Dean, Don Sutton, Early Wynn, Eppa Rixey, Greenberg, Hank Aaron, Jim Palmer, Joe Cronin, Joe Morgan, Killebrew, Larry Doby, Lou Gehrig, Mathewson, Mazeroski, Nap Lajoie, Nellie Fox, Newhouser, Nolan Ryan, Paul Waner, Radbourne, Slaughter, Tom Seaver, Tony Perez, Waite Hoyt, Yogi Berra, Zack Wheat **10** Bobby Doerr, Campanella, Charleston,

Chuck Klein, Dazzy Vance, Duke Snider, Earle Combs, Elmer Flick, Ernie Banks, Gary Carter, Hack Wilson, Jim Bunning, Jimmie Foxx, Joe Medwick, Josh Gibson, Kiki Cuyler, Lefty Gomez, Lefty Grove, Lloyd Waner, Monte Irvin, Ozzie Smith, Phil Niekro, Pie Traynor, Ralph Kiner, Red Ruffing, Robin Yount, Rube Foster, Stan Musial, Whitey Ford, Willie Mays 11 Yastrzemski
baseball ~ umpire: 4 Klem 6 Chylak, Conlan 7 Barlick, Hubbard 8 Bill Klem 9 Al Barlick
football ~ coach: 4 Levy, Noll 5 Allen, Brown, Grant, Halas, Neale, Shula 6 Ewbank, Landry 7 Gillman 8 Bud Grant, Don Shula, Lombardi, Marv Levy 9 Chuck Noll, Paul Brown, Tom Landry 10 Sid Gillman, Weeb Ewbank
football ~ player: 4 Huff, Lary, Lott, Page 5 Brown, Ditka, Groza, Jones, Olsen, Shell, Swann 6 Butkus, Casper, Csonka, Grange, Greene, Harris, Hirsch, Nevers, Payton, Refnro, Sayers, Taylor, Thorpe 7 Alworth, Dorsett, Gifford, Hampton, Hornung, Largent, Sam Huff, Simpson 8 Alan Page, Art Shell, Campbell, Jim Brown, Lou Groza, Nagurski, Nitschke, Stenerud, Yale Lary 9 Dickerson, Jim Thorpe, Joe Greene, Lynn Swann, Marchetti, Mel Renfro, Mike Ditka, O.J. Simpson, Red Grange 10 Buoniconti, Dan Hampton, Dave Casper, Dick Butkus, Gale Sayers, Robustelli, Ronnie Lott, Stallworth
football ~ quarterback: 5 Baugh, Fouts, Kelly, Starr 6 Blanda, Dawson, Graham, Griese, Tittle, Unitas 7 Luckman, Montana 8 Bradshaw, Dan Fouts, Jim Kelly, Staubach, Y.A. Tittle 9 Bart Starr, Bob Griese, Jurgensen, Len Dawson, Tarkenton 10 Joe Montana, Otto Graham, Sammy Baugh, Sid Luckman
Hall of Famer: 5 great
basketball ~: 3 Iba, Yow 4 Bing, Bird, Daly, Gola, Reed, Rupp, West 5 Barry, Brown, Cousy, Hayes, Issel, Lucas, Mikan, Olson 6 Baylor, Cowens, Erving, Gervin, Holman, Kay Yow, Knight, Lanier, Malone, McAdoo, Meyers, Monroe, Pettit, Thomas, Twyman, Unseld, Walton, Wooden 7 Bellamy, Bradley, Frazier, Hank Iba, Holzman, Johnson, Russell, Schayes, Tom Gola, Wilkens 8 Auerbach, Bob Cousy, Dan Issel, Dave Bing, Goodrich, Havlicek, Heinsohn, Maravich, Petrovic, Thurmond 9 Ann Meyers, Archibald, Bob Knight, Bob Lanier, Bob McAdoo, Bob Pettit, Chuck Daly, Jerry West, Larry Bird, Lute Olson, Nat Holman, Rick Barry, Robertson, Wes Unseld 10 Adolph Rupp, Bill Walton, Carnesecca, Dave Cowens, Earl Monroe, Elvin Hayes, Jack Twyman, Jerry Lucas, John Wooden, Larry Brown, Red Holzman, Willis Reed 11 Abdul-Jabbar, Chamberlain, DeBusschere
hockey ~: 3 Orr 4 Howe, Hull, Park 5 Bossy 6 Dionne, Mikita, Parent, Plante, Potvin 7 Federko, Gilbert, Gillies, Gretzky, Lafleur, Langway, Lemieux, Richard, Sawchuk, Worsley 8 Bathgate, Bobby Orr, Brad Park, Esposito, Trottier 9 Bobby Hull, Geoffrion, Mike Bossy 10 Gordie Howe, Guy Lafleur, Rod Gilbert, Stan Mikita
hallow: 5 bless, honor 6 anoint, devote, revere 7 respect 8 dedicate, enshrine, inshrine, sanctify, venerate 10 consecrate
hallowed: 4 holy 5 blest 6 sacred, solemn 7 beloved 9 inviolate
place: 6 church, shrine 9 sanctuary
Halloween
activity: 5 prank 6 booing
animal: 3 bat, cat
decor: 5 skull 6 cobweb 7 pumpkin
like ~: 4 eery 5 eerie, scary
month: 3 Oct. 7 October
option: 5 treat, trick
reaction: 6 fright
sound: 3 boo 4 moan
treat: 5 candy
wear: 3 wig 4 mask, wart 5 fangs, ghost, sheet, spook 6 goblin
Halloween (1978 film)
cast: Jamie Lee Curtis, Nancy Loomis, Donald Pleasence
director: John Carpenter
Halloween H20 (1998 film)
cast: Adam Arkin, Jamie Lee Curtis, Josh Hartnett, Michelle Williams
director: Steve Miner
Hallow ender: 3 een
__ Hallows' Eve: 3 All
Hall, Radclyffe: 6 author, writer 7 British
halls of ivy: 6 school 7 academy, college
Hallström: 5 Lasse
hallucinate: 7 imagine 8 daydream
hallucination: 5 dream 6 fantom, mirage, vision 7 phantom 8 delusion 9 nightmare
hallucinatory: 6 unreal 8 fanciful, illusory 9 fantastic, imaginary
__ Hall University: 5 Seton
hallux: 3 toe 6 big toe
hallway: 5 aisle, lobby 7 ingress, passage 8 corridor 9 vestibule
halo: 4 aura, ring 6 circle, corona, gloria, nimbus 7 aureola, aureole 8 gloriole
combining form: 7 stephan- 8 stephano-
halogen: 6 iodine 7 bromine 8 astatine, chlorine, fluorine
compound: 6 iodate
suffix: 3 ide, ine
halogen __: 4 lamp
Halpin: 4 Luke
Halsey: 4 Bull 5 Brett 7 admiral, William
org.: 3 USN
Hals, Frans: 5 Dutch 6 artist 7 painter
halt: 3 bar, end 4 kill, lame, limp, quit, rest, stay, stop, wait 5 block, brake, break, cease, check, close, letup, lie to, pause, stall, tie up, truce, waver 6 arrest, becalm, cesura, cool it, cutoff, desist, dither, falter, finish, forbid, freeze, hiatus, hold up, lay off, loiter, period, pull up, recess, remain, stifle, tackle, thwart, wind up, wrap up 7 adjourn, break up, caesura, fetch up, impasse, prevent, refrain, squelch, stammer, stumble, suspend, ward off 8 break off, conclude, deadlock, hesitate, hold back, intermit, knock off, leave off, obstruct, pack it in, paralyse, paralyze, prohibit, shut down, stoppage, surcease 9 cessation, close down, intercept, interlude, interrupt, terminate, vacillate 10 call it a day, knock it off, standstill, suspension
at sea: 5 avast
Halt!: 4 whoa 5 avast
caller: 6 sentry
halted: 5 still 6 at rest, static 8 stagnant, unmoving 10 motionless
halter: 3 top 4 curb, rein 5 check, shirt 6 blouse, bodice, bridle, tether 7 control, harness, trammel 9 restraint
halter __: 3 top
halting: 4 poky, slow 6 clumsy, draggy, faulty 7 awkward, gradual, impeded, labored, lagging, languid, unadept 8 bumbling, dilatory, drawn-out, hesitant, slothful, sluggish, toddling, unsteady, wavering 9 faltering, imperfect, leisurely, lethargic, maladroit, prolonged, snaillike, stumbling, tentative, uncertain, unhurried 10 deliberate, indecisive, protracted
haltingly: 7 loathly 8 bit by bit
speak ~: 6 mumble 7 sputter, stumble, stutter
Haltom City: 4 town
locale: 5 Texas
Halton Hills: 4 city, town
locale: 6 Canada 7 Ontario
halvah: 4 nosh 5 candy, snack
ingredient: 6 sesame
halve: 5 split 6 bisect, divide 7 divvy up, split up
halved: 5 in two
halves
go ~: 5 share 6 divide
two ~: 4 buck 5 whole 6 dollar, single 7 one-spot, smacker 8 simoleon
halyard: 4 line
ham: 4 meat 5 actor 6 emoter, gammon, hotdog, player 7 actress, cold cut, overact, showoff 10 prosciutto
alternative: 3 BLT 4 tuna 8 tuna fish 9 roast beef 10 corned beef
baked ~ insert: 5 clove
cut: 4 hock
device: 5 radio
ender: 4 burg, ster 6 burger, string, strung
it up: 3 act 4 play 5 emote 7 overact, perform 8 overplay
mate: 3 rye 4 eggs 5 Swiss
place: 4 deli 5 stage 7 theater, theatre
prepare ~: 4 cure 5 glaze, mince, slice
product: 4 Spam
relative: 4 pork
salad ingredient: 4 mayo 6 pickle
source: 3 pig 5 swine 6 porker
theft: 5 scene
word: 4 over 5 roger
ham __: 4 it up 5 on rye
ham-__: 6 fisted, handed
__ ham: 5 daisy 6 picnic, Polish, spiced 7 country 8 Virginia
Ham: 6 Fisher
brother of ~: 4 Shem 7 Japheth
father of ~: 4 Noah
son of ~: 3 Put 4 Cush 5 Egypt 6 Canaan
Hama: 4 city, town
locale: 5 Syria
hamadryad: 5 nymph
hamaki: 4 belt
Hamal: 4 star
ham and __: 4 eggs 6 cheese
Haman nemesis: 6 Esther
hamate: 4 bone 9 wrist bone 10 hook-shaped
Hambletonian gait: 4 trot
Hamburg: 4 city, port, town
city north of ~: 4 Kiel
locale: 7 Germany
river: 4 Elbe
hamburger: 4 meat 5 patty 6 pattie 8 sandwich
holder: 3 bun
topping: 5 onion 6 catsup, pickle, relish, tomato 7 ketchup, lettuce
Hamburger: 6 German
Hamburger __: 6 Helper
Hamden: 4 city, town
locale: 4 Conn.
Hamel: 3 Ray 8 Veronica
Hamelin visitor: 3 rat 5 piper
Hamer: 5 Rusty 6 Robert
ham-handed: 6 clumsy, gauche 7 unadept
one: 3 oaf 5 klutz, pawer 6 galoot, lummox 7 botcher, bungler, fumbler 8 stumbler
Hamhung: 4 city, town
locale: 10 North Korea
Hamill: 4 Mark, Pete 7 Dorothy
Hamill, Dorothy: 6 skater
maneuver: 4 axel, lutz, spin 5 camel
milieu: 3 ice 4 rink
Hamill, Mark: 5 actor
film: The Big Red One (1980)
The Empire Strikes Back (1980)
Return of the Jedi (1983)
Star Wars (1977)
Hamilton: 3 Guy, Roy 4 city, Emma, Fish, John, Neil, Russ, town 5 Edith, Linda, Luske, river, Scott, Smith 6 Donald, George, Jordan, Murray 7 Lisa Gay 8 Margaret 9 Alexander
athletes: 7 Raiders
bill: 3 ten
-Burr meeting: 4 duel
foe: 4 Burr
locale: 3 Ont. 4 Ohio 6 Canada 7 Bermuda, Ontario 9 New Jersey 10 New Zealand
River locale: 8 Labrador
school: 7 Colgate 8 McMaster
Hamilton Beach competitor: 5 Oster
Hamilton, Donald: 6 author, writer
spy: Matt Helm
Hamilton, Emma: 4 Lady
Hamilton, George: 5 actor
film: Angel Baby (1961)
The Godfather Part III (1990)
Home From the Hill (1960)
Love at First Bite (1979)
The Man Who Loved Cat Dancing (1973)
The Power (1968)
The Victors (1963)
Your Cheatin' Heart (1964)
Hamilton, Guy: 8 director
film: The Best of Enemies (1961)
The Colditz Story (1957)
The Devil's Disciple (1959)
Diamonds Are Forever (1971)
Goldfinger (1964)
Live and Let Die (1973)
The Man With the Golden Gun (1974)
The Mirror Crack'd (1980)
The Ringer (1952)
A Touch of Larceny (1959)
Hamilton, Joe Frank & Reynolds
song: Don't Pull Your Love (1971)
Fallin' in Love (1975)
Hamilton, Linda spouse: James Cameron
Hamilton, Murray: 5 actor
film: The FBI Story (1959)
The Graduate (1967)
Jaws (1975)
The Spirit of St. Louis (1957)
Hamilton, Neil: 5 actor
film: America/The Fall of Babylon (1924)
One Sunday Afternoon (1933)
The Sin of Madelon Claudet (1931)
Tarzan and His Mate (1934)
What Price Hollywood? (1932)
TV: Batman
__ Hamilton, NY: 4 Fort
Hamilton, Scott: 6 skater

maneuver: 4 axel, lutz, spin 5 camel
milieu: 3 ice 4 rink
___ Hamilton Woman: 4 That
Hamish in English: 5 James
Hamite: 6 Berber, Nimrod
hamlet: 3 vil. 4 burg, dorp, town 5 place, thorp 6 suburb, thorpe 7 village 8 Dogpatch 9 community 10 settlement
old-style: 5 thorp 6 thorpe
Hamlet: 4 Dane, play 5 drama 7 tragedy
aromatic plant: 3 rue
author: William Shakespeare
catch: 3 rub
character: 5 Osric 6 Hamlet 7 Horatio, Laertes, Ophelia 8 Bernardo, Claudius, Gertrude, Polonius, Reynaldo 9 Francisco, Marcellus 10 Fortinbras 11 Rosencrantz 12 Guildenstern
emulate ~: 6 avenge
exclamation: 3 fie 4 alas
father: 5 ghost
language: 6 Danish
opener: 4 Act I
phrase: 4 to be
prop: 5 arras, skull
quintet: 4 acts
to Gertrude: 3 son
what ~ smelled: 4 a rat
Hamlet (1948 film)
cast: Eileen Herlie, Laurence Olivier, Basil Sydney
director: Laurence Olivier
Hamlet (1990 film)
cast: Alan Bates, Helena Bonham Carter, Glenn Close, Mel Gibson, Ian Holm, Paul Scofield
director: Franco Zeffirelli
Hamlet, The author: William Faulkner
Hamlin: 5 Harry 7 Garland, Vincent 8 Hannibal
Hamlin, Harry
spouse: Lisa Rinna, Nicollette Sheridan
Hamlisch, Marvin: 8 composer
song: The Entertainer (1974)
Hamm: 3 Mia 4 city, town
locale: 4 Ruhr 7 Germany
Hammarskjöld, Dag: 7 Swedish 8 diplomat, Nobelist
predecessor: 3 Lie
successor: 6 U Thant
hammer: 3 hit, ram 4 bang, beat, bone, club, drub, lash, nail, pelt, slam, tool, whip 5 gavel, knock, pound, pulse, smite, stamp, whack, whomp 6 batter, beetle, defeat, mallet, pommel, pummel, sledge, strike, thrash, wallop 7 clobber, lambast, trounce 8 lambaste
drop the ~: 4 fire 5 shoot
ender: 4 head, lock
head: 3 tup
heavy ~: 4 mall, maul
home: 7 belabor, dwell on 9 go on about
hurler: 4 Thor
in: 5 embed, imbed
into: 5 drill 7 impress, ingrain 9 inculcate
judge's ~: 5 gavel
locale: 3 ear
obliquely: 3 toe
out: 4 form 5 forge 9 construct, establish, negotiate 10 accomplish, bring about, excogitate
part: 4 claw, peen
partner: 4 claw 5 tongs 6 chisel, sickle
sound: 3 bam
starter: 4 jack, trip 6 sledge, yellow
stirrup and ~ partner: 5 anvil
target: 4 gong, nail
throw: 5 event
hammer ___: 4 mill, pond 5 throw
___ hammer: 3 air, war 4 bush, claw, drop, hack, pole, tack, tilt 5 steam, water 6 patent 7 lathing
Hammer: 2 M.C. 3 Jan 4 Mike 6 Armand
hammer and ___: 5 tongs 6 sickle
hammerhead: 4 bird 5 shark
feature: 4 claw
relative: 4 mako
Hammerin' Hank: 5 Aaron
Hammer, Jan song: Miami Vice Theme (1985)
hammerkop: 4 bird
Hammer, Mike: 3 tec 6 shamus, sleuth 7 gumshoe 9 detective 10 private eye
hammer-on-thumb cry: 2 ow 3 yow 4 ouch, yeow
hammers are thrown, where: 4 meet
Hammerstein II, Oscar: 8 lyricist
collaborator: 4 Kern 7 Rodgers, Romberg
musical: Allegro
Carousel
Flower Drum Song
The King and I
Me and Juliet
Oklahoma!
Pipe Dream
Show Boat
The Sound of Music
South Pacific
Hammett (1983 film)
cast: Peter Boyle, Frederic Forrest, Marilu Henner
director: Wim Wenders
Hammett, Dashiell: 6 author, writer
dog: 4 Asta
first name: Samuel
friend: 7 Hellman, Lillian
sleuth: 3 Sam 4 Nick, Nora 5 Spade 7 Charles
work: The Continental Op
The Dain Curse
The Glass Key
The Maltese Falcon
The Thin Man
hammock
rigging: 5 clews
use a ~: 3 lie 4 bask, idle, laze, loaf, loll, rest 5 relax 6 dawdle, lounge, repose 7 goof off 10 take it easy
weave: 3 net
Hammond: 4 city, town 5 Peter 6 Albert
locale: 7 Indiana
product: 3 map 5 atlas, organ
hammy: 5 stagy 6 stagey 8 affected, overdone 10 theatrical
ham on ___: 3 rye
hamper: 3 bin, tie 4 bind, clog, curb, foil, load, rein, slow, snag, stop 5 block, brake, check, cramp, crimp, delay, leash, limit, stall, stimy, stymy, tie up 6 baffle, basket, dampen, fetter, hang up, hinder, hobble, hogtie, hold up, hurdle, impede, rein in, retard, slow up, stymie, thwart 7 confine, inhibit, prevent, shackle, trammel 8 encumber, entangle, handicap, obstruct, preclude, prohibit, restrain, restrict, sabotage, slow down, straiten 9 container, frustrate, hamstring, weigh down 10 receptacle
contents: 4 wash 7 laundry
in the ~: 5 dirty 7 unclean
Hampshire: 3 pig 5 sheep, Susan, swine 6 county
city: 6 Havant
locale: 7 England
Hampton: 3 Dan 4 city, town 5 James 6 Lionel
locale: 8 Virginia
Hampton ___, VA: 5 Roads
Hampton Court feature: 4 maze
Hampton, Dan sport: 8 football
Hampton Inn: 5 motel
alternative: 7 Days Inn 9 Ramada Inn 10 Comfort Inn, Econo Lodge, Holiday Inn, Quality Inn, Red Roof Inn, Travelodge 11 Best Western
Hampton, Lionel: 12 vibraphonist
genre: 4 jazz
Hampton Roads: 6 battle
locale: 8 Virginia
Hamptons route: 4 LIRR
hamster: 3 pet 6 animal, mammal, rodent
female: 3 doe
home: 4 cage
kin: 6 gerbil
male: 4 buck
relative: 3 rat 4 cavy, degu, jird, paca, vole 5 coypu, gundi, mouse, xerus 6 agouti, beaver, gerbil, gopher, jerboa, marmot, murine 7 lemming, muskrat, visacha 8 chipmunk, cricetid, dormouse, squirrel, tuco-tuco 9 chickaree, groundhog, guinea pig, porcupine, woodchuck 10 chinchilla, prairie dog
young: 3 pup
hamstring: 4 foil, maim 5 block, check, cramp 6 fetter, hamper, hang up, hinder, hobble, hogtie, hold up, impair, impede, thwart 7 disable, inhibit, prevent, shackle 8 encumber, handicap, obstruct, restrain, restrict 9 frustrate
site: 3 leg 5 thigh
Hamsun, Knut: 6 writer 8 Nobelist 9 Norwegian
Han: 4 Solo 5 river 6 Indian 7 Amerind, dynasty
city on the ~: 5 Seoul
River locale: 5 China, Korea
Hana: 4 city, town 10 Mandlikova
locale: 4 Maui 6 Hawaii
Hancock: 4 John 6 Herbie
Hancock, Herbie: 7 pianist
genre: 4 jazz
hand: 3 paw 4 aide, duke, fist, give, help, lift, mitt, peon, serf, side, span, unit 5 boost, clerk, grunt, labor, leg up, offer, reach, slave, yield 6 assist, helper, jobber, member, relief, sailor, tender, worker 7 artisan, crewman, employe, jack tar, laborer, ovation, present, proffer, servant, support, tribute 8 applause, donation, employee, guidance, hireling, kindness 9 attendant, extremity 10 apprentice, assistance, crewperson, roustabout, wage earner, working man
a line: 10 ingratiate
and glove: 6 allied, united 7 unified 8 friendly, in league
at ~: 4 near, nigh 5 close, ready 6 nearby, next to, usable 7 close-by, in store, looming, present, useable 8 adjacent, imminent, next door 9 available, bordering, impending, proximate, ready to go 10 accessible, convenient, in the cards, obtainable
at ~ , poetically: 4 nigh 5 anear
at the ~ of: 3 per 7 through
back: 6 return
be at ~: 4 loom
big ~: 5 kudos 6 praise 7 ovation, plaudit 8 accolade, applause, cheering 9 standing O
by ~: 8 manually
clenched ~: 4 fist
combining form: 5 chiro- 6 cheiro-
covering: 4 mitt, muff 5 glove 6 mitten
dab ~: 8 skillful
deck ~: 6 sailor 7 jack tar
done by ~: 6 manual
down: 4 give, will 5 leave, relay 6 impart, pass on, render 7 deliver 8 bequeath, transmit
empty ~ , literally: 6 karate
ender: 3 bag, car, gun, off, out, saw, set 4 ball, bill, book, cart, clap, cuff, fast, grip, held, hold, made, maid, pick, rail, sell, some, work, wove 5 blown, clasp, craft, print, shake, spike, stand, woven 6 barrow, cuffed, maiden, spring 7 breadth, crafted, wringer, writing 8 kerchief
extend one's ~ to: 5 greet
field ~: 4 peon
follower: 5 shake
free ~: 5 swing 6 leeway 7 bigness, largess 8 largesse, latitude 10 generosity, liberality
get the upper ~: 4 beat, best, bury, drub, rout, stun 5 cream, crush, drown, quell, smash, total, trash, upset, waste 6 defeat, subdue 7 clobber, conquer, oppress, put away, stagger, take out, torpedo, trounce 8 bear down, blow away, bulldoze, dominate, overcome, roll over, shellack, suppress, vanquish 9 overpower, overthrow, subjugate 10 take care of
give a ~ to: 3 aid 4 abet, clap, help 6 assist, deal in, step in 7 applaud, bail out, pitch in, relieve, sustain 9 cooperate
go ~ over hand: 5 climb, scale 6 ascend, shinny 7 clamber
hand in ~: 7 jointly 8 together
have a ~ in: 5 share, split 6 divide 7 split up 9 partake of
have the upper ~: 4 boss, head, lead, rule 5 reign 6 direct, govern, manage 7 command, control, dictate, prevail, triumph 8 overrule 9 subjugate, tyrannize 10 monopolize, run the show
helping ~: 5 break, leg up, start
hide in the ~: 4 palm
hired ~: 6 jobber, worker 7 employe 8 employee 9 jobholder
holder: 5 wrist
hold out one's ~: 3 beg 5 cadge, hit up, mooch 8 freeload 9 impetrate, mendicate, panhandle 10 supplicate
in: 4 give 5 offer 6 pass on, render, submit, tender 7 deliver, present 8 turn over
in ~: 7 secured
in glove: 4 deep 5 close, solid, thick, tight 6 chummy 10 buddy-buddy, palsy-walsy
in hand: 7 jointly 8 together
iron ~: 5 rigor 7 cruelty, tyranny 8 coercion, hardness, severity 9 austerity, autocracy, brutality, despotism, harshness, sternness 10 oppression, severeness, strictness
items on ~: 5 these
it to: 4 laud 5 extol 6 admire, praise 7 applaud, commend 10 compliment
keep on ~: 4 have, save 5 carry, stock, store 9 inventory
matter at ~: 3 job 5 theme, topic 7 subject
menacing ~: 4 fist
milieu: 4 farm 5 ranch
motion: 4 clap, wave 5 wring
new ~: 4 babe, lamb, naif, tiro, tyro 6 intern, novice 7 learner, recruit 8 beginner, freshman, neophyte 9 fledgling, greenhorn 10 tenderfoot

off: 4 send 5 relay 7 forward 8 transmit
old ~: 3 ace, pro, vet 4 whiz 5 adept 6 expert, master, wizard 7 hotshot, veteran 8 virtuoso 10 specialist
on: 4 send 5 relay 7 forward 8 transmit
on ~: 4 here 5 ready, there 6 with us 7 present 9 available
one is dealt: 3 lot 4 life
on the other ~: 3 but, yet 4 else 5 if not 7 however 9 otherwise
out: 4 deal, dole, give, mete 5 allot, award, issue, spend 6 assign, bestow, divide, donate, ration 7 divvy up 8 disburse, dispense 10 contribute, distribute
out of ~: 5 rowdy 6 unruly, wanton 7 rampant 9 excessive, unbridled, unchecked
over: 3 pay 4 cede, drop, dump, give, pass, sell, shed 5 chuck, ditch, forgo, relay, waive, yield 6 forego, fork up, give up, render, resign, supply, turn in 7 abandon, commend, consign, cough up, deliver, drop off, entrust, forfeit, forsake, intrust, present 8 delegate, forswear, get rid of, jettison, part with, relegate, shell out, transfer, turn over 9 cast aside, dispose of, foreswear, surrender 10 relinquish
part: 4 palm 5 digit, thumb 6 finger
poker ~: 4 pair 5 flush 6 aces up 7 ace high, two pair 8 straight 9 full house 10 royal flush
pork belly, in ~: 6 actual
ranch ~: 5 groom 6 cowboy, drover 8 buckaroo, wrangler
right ~: 6 dexter
seek the ~ of: 3 woo 5 court 6 pursue
set one's ~ to: 4 sign
sleight of ~: 5 magic, trick 9 dexterity
starter: 3 cow, off 4 back, deal, dock, fore, free, long, over 5 first, short, stage, third, under 6 before, behind, second
stock on ~: 3 inv. 9 inventory
take a ~: 6 butt in, step in 7 barge in, mediate 9 intercede, intervene
take by the ~: 4 lead 5 guide, steer, usher 6 assist, direct, escort, lead in 7 bolster, conduct 9 encourage
throw in one's ~: 4 quit 5 yield 6 submit 7 concede 9 surrender
tip one's ~: 4 show, tell 6 expose, reveal 7 divulge, lay bare, lay open, uncover 8 disclose 9 make known
truck: 5 dolly 6 barrow
try one's ~: 5 essay 7 attempt, venture 9 have a go at, take a shot
up: 6 fetter 7 inhibit 8 encumber
upper ~: 4 edge 7 control, victory 9 advantage, authority, dominance
with an iron ~: 4 hard 6 firmly 7 harshly, roughly, sternly 8 severely, strictly 10 rigorously
wringer: 4 ruer
wringer word: 4 alas
hand ___: 3 axe, log, off, out 4 down, horn, it to, lens, over, tool 5 brake, drill, glass, level, mower, organ, press, screw, tight, truck 6 letter, puppet, scroll, signal 7 grenade
hand ___ fist: 4 over
hand-___: 4 feed, held, knit, ride, walk, wash 5 blown, carry 6 tailor 7 deliver, launder, running
___ hand: 3 bow, dab, old, pat 4 deck, farm, free, glad, hour, iron, lone, text, whip 5 cap in, court, elder, field, hat in, hired, lend a, out of, right, round, sweep, upper 6 bridle, eldest, master, minute, second 7 helping, Italian, running, section
___-hand: 3 law 4 glad, left 5 first, hat-in
Hand: 6 Rollin 7 Learned
___ Hand: 4 Slow, Whip 5 Black
Handa: 4 city, town
locale: 5 Japan
hand and ___: 4 foot 5 glove
handbag: 4 tote 5 pouch, purse 6 clutch 8 carryall, reticule 10 pocketbook
like some ~ s: 6 beaded
part: 5 strap
handball: 4 game 5 sport
need: 4 wall 5 glove
handbill: 5 flier, flyer 6 dodger 7 leaflet 8 brochure, circular 9 broadside, throwaway
handbook: 4 text 5 bible, guide 6 manual, primer 8 Baedeker 9 companion, directory, vade mecum 10 compendium
handcart: 6 barrow
handclasp: 4 grip 5 grasp, shake 7 squeeze
___-hand coordination: 3 eye
handcrafted: 8 homemade
hand-cream ingredient: 4 aloe
handcuff: 4 bind, bond, iron 5 chain, run in 6 fetter, hinder, impede, pinion, thwart 7 enchain, inhibit, manacle, shackle 8 restrain, restrict 9 frustrate
holder: 5 wrist
handcuffed: 8 helpless 9 powerless
handcuffs: 5 irons 6 chains 7 fetters 8 manacles, shackles, trammels 9 bracelets
___ handcuffs: 6 golden 7 Chinese
hand-dyed fabric: 5 batik 6 battik
handed
down: 10 bequeathed, hereditary
starter: 3 off 4 back, bare, even, iron, open
___-handed: 3 ham, one, red, two 4 four, free, hard, high, left, sure 5 clean, empty, heavy, light, right, short, three 6 single, steady
___-handedly: 4 high 6 single
Handel, George Frideric: 6 German 8 composer
work: Admeto
Alcina
Arianna
Atalanta
Berenice
Esther
Ezio
Hercules
Israel in Egypt
Jephtha
Joshua
Messiah
Nero
Orlando
Ottone
Rinaldo
Samson
Saul
Semele
Serse
Solomon
Susanna
Teseo
Theodora
Tolomeo
Water Music
Xerxes
___-hander: 4 left 5 right
___ Hand for the Little Lady: 4 A Big
handful: 3 few 4 lump, some 6 strong 7 several 10 scattering, smattering, sprinkling
a ~ of: 5 scant 6 meager, paltry 7 limited 8 one or two
maybe: 4 brat
more than a ~: 4 gobs, lots, many, much, tons 5 heaps, piles, scads 6 oodles, plenty, scores 7 copious, umpteen 8 abundant, numerous 9 bountiful, multitude, thousands
Handful of Dust, A author: Evelyn Waugh
handgun: 5 Luger 6 pistol 7 firearm 8 revolver
see also gun
Handi-___: 5 Wipes
handicap: 4 edge, odds 5 block, limit, minus, tie up 6 burden, fetter, hamper, hinder, hogtie, hurdle, impede, impost, points 7 barrier, inhibit, oppress, penalty, prevent 8 drawback, encumber, hold back, obstacle, penalize, restrain, restrict, weakness 9 advantage, detriment, hamstring, head start, hindrance, liability 10 impairment, impediment, incapacity, limitation
in boxing: 8 glass jaw
handicapper hangout: 3 OTB 5 track
handicraft: 4 work 10 production
gaudy ~: 6 kitsch
handicraftsman: 7 artisan 9 carpenter
handily: 4 neat 6 deftly, easily, nimbly 7 capably 8 adroitly, facilely, very well 10 swimmingly
hand in ___: 5 glove
___ hand in: 5 have a
handiness: 5 skill 7 ability 9 dexterity, readiness 10 adroitness, cleverness, nimbleness, usefulness
Hand in Glove author: Ngaio Marsh
Hand in My Pocket (1995 song) artist: Alanis Morissette
Handi-Wipes, like: 5 moist
handiwork: 4 work 5 doing 7 product 8 creation
do ~: 3 tat
Handke, Peter: 6 author, writer 8 Austrian
handkerchief
dance: 9 siciliano
material ~: 6 cotton, Madras
place: 5 purse 6 pocket
handle: 3 ear, ply, run, try, use 4 ansa, bail, feel, haft, half, hilt, hold, knob, meet, name, sell, take, tend, test, work 5 alias, carry, check, crank, field, grasp, guide, helve, see to, serve, stand, steer, stock, strap, title, touch, trade, treat, wield 6 byname, deal in, direct, employ, finger, govern, holder, jockey, manage, pick up, retail, tiller 7 command, conduct, control, examine, exploit, moniker, operate, preside, process, support, surname, survive, trade in, utilize, work out 8 cognomen, cope with, deal with, dominate, maneuver, monicker, nickname, receipts, regulate, stand for, transact 9 negotiate, officiate, sobriquet, supervise, traffic in 10 administer, manipulate, reckon with, take care of
an order: 4 fill, lade, load, pack 6 make up, supply 7 process, satisfy
archeologist's ~: 4 ansa
as questions: 5 field 7 reply to
badly: 5 abuse
capably: 5 wield
easy to ~: 3 yar 4 yare
ender: 3 bar
false ~: 5 alias 7 moniker, pen name 9 pseudonym, stage name 10 nom de plume
fly off the ~: 4 rage, rant, snap 5 freak, go ape
gently: 4 baby 6 caress
give a ~: 3 dub 4 name 8 christen
hard to ~: 5 bulky, spiny 7 awkward 10 cumbersome
having a ~: 5 eared 6 ansate
knife ~: 4 grip, haft, hilt
long ~: 5 shaft
problems: 4 cope
roughly: 3 paw 4 mall, maul 5 paw at 6 misuse 8 mistreat
starter: 3 man, mis, pan 5 stick
sword ~: 4 hilt
tool ~: 4 haft 5 helve, shaft, snath 6 snathe
word above a ~: 4 pull, push
___ Handle a Woman: 5 How to
___ handle on: 4 get a 5 have a
handler: 5 agent 8 promoter
starter: 3 pan 5 stick
___ handler: 7 baggage
handle with ___: 4 care
handle with ___ gloves: 3 kid
Handle With Care (1977 film)
cast: Candy Clark, Paul LeMat, Ann Wedgeworth
director: Jonathan Demme
Handlin: 5 Oscar
handling: 3 use 5 usage 7 conduct, running 9 oversight, treatment 10 employment, management, regulation
rough ~: 5 abuse 6 misuse
___ handling: 4 ball 7 special
hand-lotion ingredient: 4 aloe
___ Hand Luke: 4 Cool
Hand-Made Fables author: George Ade
handmaiden: 6 female 7 servant 9 attendant
Handmaid's Tale, The author: Margaret Atwood
___-hand man: 5 right
hand-me-down: 3 rag 4 used 6 reused 8 preowned
hand-me-downs: 4 togs 7 apparel, clothes, raiment, threads 8 garments
Hand of Bridge, A composer: 6 Barber
___ Hand of God, The: 4 Left
Hand of God, The sculptor: 5 Rodin
Handöl: 5 falls 9 waterfall
locale: 6 Sweden
___ hand on: 4 lay a
hand-operated: 6 manual
handout: 3 tip 4 alms, dole, gift 5 flyer, grant 6 notice, tipoff 7 charity, freebee, freebie, present, release 8 brochure, bulletin, circular, pamphlet 9 broadside, publicity, throwaway 10 free sample, propaganda
seek a ~: 3 beg 5 cadge
hand over ___: 4 fist
handpick: 4 cull, take 5 elect 6 choose, select 8 nominate 9 designate, single out
handpicked: 6 choice, select 9 preferred
handrail: 4 post 8 banister
ballet ~: 3 bar 5 barre
post: 5 newel
___ Hand Rose: 6 Second
hands: 4 crew, gang, help, team 5 corps, squad, staff, troop 6 outfit 7 company
can't lay one's ~ on: 8 misplace
clean ~: 7 probity 9 innocence
down: 5 by far 6 easily 8 for a fact, very well 9 no contest 10 absolutely, positively, swimmingly, undeniably
get one's ~ on: 3 get 4 find, grab, have 5 catch, seize, snare 6 collar, locate, obtain, snatch 7 acquire, possess, procure, receive 9 latch onto
good with one's ~: 6 adroit
it has ~ and a face: 5 clock, watch
join, as ~: 4 grip
laying on of ~: 8 blessing

move on one's ~ and knees: 4 inch 5 crawl, creep, slink, sneak, steal 7 clamber, slither, wriggle
putty in one's ~: 8 yielding 9 malleable, tractable
shake ~: 3 run 4 meet 5 agree, greet, reach 6 make up 7 receive
shake ~ on: 4 seal 5 close 6 clinch, settle 7 confirm 8 finalize
shaking ~: 6 custom, ritual 9 formality 10 convention
show of ~: 4 vote
sit on one's ~: 7 abstain
speak with one's ~: 4 sign
use one's ~: 4 mime, wave 6 beckon, signal 7 gesture 9 pantomime
wash one's ~ of: 6 disown 7 abandon, bail out, disavow, forsake 8 forswear, renounce 9 foreswear, repudiate
win ~ down: 5 sweep 7 conquer, prevail, succeed, triumph, trounce 8 blow away, dominate, vanquish, walk over
with ~ on hips: 6 akimbo
with ~ tied: 5 at bay 8 helpless 9 powerless
hands-__: 4 down
hands-__ policy: 3 off
__ hands: 5 clean, shake 6 change, strike 7 dishpan
__ Hands: 5 Dirty 6 Guilty
Hands (1998 song) artist: Jewel
Hands Across the Sea composer: 5 Sousa
Hands Across the Table (1935 film)
cast: Ralph Bellamy, Carole Lombard, Fred MacMurray
director: Mitchell Leisen
handsel: 9 foretaste
handshake: 4 grip 5 clasp 6 clench 7 welcome
__ handshake: 6 golden
handshaker: 5 toady 6 lackey, minion, yes man 7 flunkey 9 candidate, jobhunter, sycophant 10 politician
Hands off!: 3 hey
handsome: 4 cute, fair, fine, tidy 5 ample, bonny, hunky, large, sharp 6 bonnie, comely, dapper, lavish, lovely, pretty 7 elegant, liberal, sizable, stylish, winsome 8 abundant, adorable, alluring, becoming, cleancut, fetching, generous, gorgeous, pleasing, princely, sizeable, striking, stunning, tasteful 9 beautiful, bounteous, bountiful, extensive, plentiful, ravishing, unsparing 10 attractive, munificent
dark and ~ companion: 4 tall
name meaning ~: 7 Kenneth
one: 4 hunk 6 Adonis, Apollo
Handsome __ handsome does: 4 is as
handsomely: 4 well 9 liberally 10 abundantly, generously
handsomeness: 5 charm 6 beauty, glamor 7 glamour 8 elegance 9 good looks
__ hands on deck!: 3 all
Hands to Heaven (1988 song) artist: Breathe
Hand That Rocks the Cradle, The (1992 film)
cast: Ernie Hudson, Rebecca De Mornay, Annabella Sciorra
director: Curtis Hanson
__ Hand, The: 5 Hired 6 Fourth, Mummy's
hand-to-__: 5 mouth
Hand to Hold on to (1982 song) artist: John Cougar Mellencamp
handwrite: 3 pen 4 sign 8 inscribe 9 autograph
handwriting: 6 scrawl, script 7 writing 8 printing
feature: 5 slant
on the wall: 4 omen, sign 7 portent, warning
see the ~ on the wall: 7 predict
handwriting-on-the-wall book: 6 Daniel
handy: 4 able, deft, easy, near 5 adept, close, of use, ready, utile 6 adroit, expert, nearby, nimble, useful, wieldy 7 capable, close by, helpful, skilled 8 adjacent, dextrous, portable, prepared, skillful 9 available, dexterous, efficient, practical, versatile 10 accessible, beneficial, convenient, functional, proficient, time-saving
come in ~ for: 3 aid
ender: 3 man
to: 4 near
handy-__: 4 andy 5 dandy
Handy: 2 W.C.
Handycam maker: 4 Sony
handyman: 5 do-all 6 jobber 7 Mr. Fix-it 8 factotum
do a ~ job: 3 fix 6 repair 7 restore 8 renovate
need: 4 tool, vise 6 pliers, wrench
handyman's __: 7 special
Handy Man (song) artist: James Taylor, Jimmy Jones
Hanes competitor: 3 BVD 5 Leggs 6 Jockey
Haney: 5 Carol
Hanff: 6 Helene
Hanford: 4 city, town
locale: 10 California
hang: 4 pend, stay, wait 5 drape, float, hover, pin up, swing 6 dangle, depend 7 festoon, suspend 8 levitate
about: 4 stay 6 dangle
a left: 4 turn
around: 4 bide, laze, loll, lurk, stay, wait 5 abide, haunt, tarry 6 dangle, dawdle, linger, loiter, lounge, remain 8 frequent 9 associate, socialize 10 hover about
around for: 5 await 6 expect
back: 3 lag 4 poke 5 trail 6 boggle, falter, loiter, shrink 8 hesitate
(by): 5 stand, stick
don't ~ onto: 4 lose
down: 3 lop, sag 5 droop, trail 6 dangle
ender: 3 dog, out, tag 4 nail, over
fire: 4 pend
five: 4 surf
get the ~ of: 3 see 4 know 5 learn 6 master
in: 3 try 4 last, stay, take 5 abide 6 be cool, endure 7 persist, sustain 8 continue 9 persevere, withstand
in the breeze: 3 air, dry 6 air-dry
it up: 4 quit, stop 6 finish, resign
let it all ~ out: 4 bare 6 reveal, unveil 7 divulge, lay bare 8 disclose, manifest 9 make known 10 make public
loose: 4 loll 5 relax
loosely: 3 lop 5 drape, droop
of it: 5 flair, knack, skill, trick 6 method 7 ability, faculty, knowhow, mastery 8 facility 9 technique
on: 4 last 5 cling, pivot, stand 6 adhere, endure, linger 7 outlast, subsist 8 stand for 9 be patient 10 stick it out
(on): 4 rest 6 depend
one's hat: 4 live 5 dwell 6 locate, reside
on one's words: 6 listen
onto: 4 hold, keep, save 5 amass, cache, hoard, put by, store 6 garner, retain, save up 7 put away 8 maintain, put aside 10 accumulate
open: 4 gape, yawn
out: 3 mix 4 idle, laze, loaf, stay 5 haunt 6 linger, loiter, mingle, remain 7 consort, goof off 9 pal around, socialize 10 congregate, fraternize, wait around
out at: 5 haunt, visit 8 frequent 9 patronize
out one's shingle: 6 settle
out with: 3 mix 6 hobnob, mingle 9 socialize 10 fraternize
over: 4 loom 5 sling 8 threaten
(over): 4 arch
starter: 4 over 5 strap
suspended: 5 float, hover
ten: 4 surf
the lip: 4 mope, pout, sulk 5 brood
together: 4 ally 5 unite 6 cleave, cohere, hook up, pair up 7 combine, partner 8 assemble, coalesce 9 cooperate, integrate 10 close ranks, join forces
tough: 6 take it 7 persist 9 persevere, withstand
up: 4 clog, slow 5 block, spite, stimy, stymy 6 cut off, detain, hamper, hobble, hold up, impede, retard, shelve, stymie 7 ring off, set back 8 hold over, obstruct, restrict, slow down 9 frustrate, hamstring 10 bottleneck, disconnect
hang __: 3 out, ten 4 back, fire, five, it up, on to, time 5 a left, loose, tough 6 around, glider 7 gliding
hang __ balance: 5 in the
__ hang: 5 care a, give a
__-hang: 5 cliff
Hang __ Index: 4 Seng
hang a __: 4 left 5 right
hangar: 4 shed 6 garage 7 shelter
tenant: 3 jet 4 bird 5 blimp, plane
Hangchow: 3 bay
locale: 5 China
hangdog: 3 sad 4 blue, down, grim 5 mopey 6 abject, broody, gloomy, woeful 7 doleful, forlorn 8 dejected, downcast 9 bummed-out, cheerless, depressed, long-faced, plaintive, sorrowful, woebegone 10 chapfallen, despondent, dispirited, melancholy
look: 4 pout
Hang 'em High (1968 film)
cast: Ed Begley, Clint Eastwood, Pat Hingle, Inger Stevens
director: Ted Post
Hang 'Em High (1968 song) artist: Booker T. and the MGs
hanger
material: 4 wire 7 plastic
place: 6 closet
starter: 5 cliff, crape, paper, strap
support: 3 rod
__ hanger: 3 ape 4 coat
hanger-on: 5 leech 6 fawner, jackal, lackey, sponge 7 lacquey, sponger 8 henchman, kowtower 9 sycophant
hangers-on: 5 suite 6 circle 7 coterie, retinue 8 groupies 9 entourage, following, retainers 10 attendants
hang glide: 4 soar
hang gliding: 5 sport
finished ~: 3 lit 4 alit
Hang in __!: 5 there
hanging: 4 limp 5 baggy, loose, slack 6 droopy, floppy 7 drapery, flaccid, pendant, pendent, pending 8 overhead 9 pendulous, suspended
back: 3 shy 5 balky, chary 7 fearful 8 hesitant, wavering 9 reluctant, skeptical, tentative 10 wishy-washy
by a thread: 5 risky 6 unsafe 9 uncertain
fire: 6 put off 7 abeyant, delayed, pending 9 postponed, undecided, unsettled 10 in abeyance, up in the air
in the balance: 6 at risk
keep ~: 5 tease, worry 6 entice, lead on 7 torment 8 interest 9 fascinate, frustrate, tantalize, titillate
leave ~: 4 jilt, quit 6 desert, maroon 7 abandon, forsake
loose: 6 at ease 7 relaxed 8 carefree, composed, tranquil
loosely: 4 alop
on every word: 4 rapt
starter: 5 paper, strap
together: 5 sound
tough: 3 set 7 adamant 8 stalwart
wall ~: 5 arras, litho, pin-up, tapis 6 cobweb, sconce 8 tapestry
hanging __: 3 lie 4 post, step, wall 5 stile 6 scroll, valley
__ hanging: 4 wall
Hanging __ of Babylon: 7 Gardens
Hanging Tree, The (1959 film)
cast: Gary Cooper, Karl Malden, Maria Schell
director: Delmer Daves
Hanging Up (2000 film)
cast: Diane Keaton, Lisa Kudrow, Walter Matthau, Meg Ryan
director: Diane Keaton
hang in the __: 7 balance
Hangin' Tough (1989 song) artist: New Kids on the Block
hang-loose: 9 easygoing
Hangman, The author: Pär Lagerkvist
Hang on!: 4 whoa
__ Hang On: 4 Let's
Hang on Sloopy (1965 song) artist: McCoys
hangout: 3 bar 4 dive, nest, site, spot 5 haunt, joint, place 6 resort 7 purlieu 10 rendezvous
hangover: 6 clamor, uproar 7 anguish 8 distress 10 uneasiness
have a ~: 4 ache
remedy: 5 Bromo
Hangover Square (1945 film)
cast: Laird Cregar, Linda Darnell, George Sanders
hangs
where one ~ one's hat: 3 pad 4 home 5 house 7 lodging 8 domicile, dwelling 9 residence
__ Hangs High, The: 5 Noose
hang-tough: 5 stern 10 relentless
hangul: 4 deer
relative: 3 elk, roe 4 axis, pudu, shou, sika 5 moose 6 chital, guemal, huemul, sambar, sambur, thamin, wapiti 7 brocket, caribou, muntjac, muntjak, sambhar, sambhur 8 reindeer 9 barasingh
hang-up: 3 rub 4 snag 5 block, delay, hitch, mania, quirk, thing 6 phobia 7 complex, problem 8 fixation, obstacle 9 obsession 10 difficulty, impediment, inhibition
Hangzhou: 3 bay 4 city, town
locale: 5 China
hank: 4 coil, knot, loop, roll 5 piece, skein, twist 6 length
Hank: 3 Iba 4 Snow 5 Aaron, Bauer 6 Azaria 7 Ballard, Ketcham, Locklin 8 Williams 9 Greenberg
hanker: 4 ache, itch, long, need, pine, sigh, want, wish 5 yearn 7 long for 8 languish, yearn for
for: 4 like, seek, want 5 covet, crave
hankering: 3 yen 4 ache, achy, itch, love, urge, want, will, wish 5 fancy, letch 6 desire, hunger, hungry, pining, thirst 7 craving, longing 8 appetite, yearning 9 adoration, affection 10 aspiration, attachment
Hanks: 3 Tom 5 Nancy

Hanks, Tom: 5 actor
film: Apollo 13 (1995)
Bachelor Party (1984)
Big (1988)
The Bonfire of the Vanities (1990)
The 'burbs (1989)
Cast Away (2000)
Dragnet (1987)
Forrest Gump (1994, AA)
The Green Mile (1999)
Joe Versus the Volcano (1990)
A League of Their Own (1992)
The Man With One Red Shoe (1985)
The Money Pit (1986)
Nothing in Common (1986)
Philadelphia (1993, AA)
Punchline (1988)
Road to Perdition (2002)
Saving Private Ryan (1998)
Sleepless in Seattle (1993)
Splash (1984)
that thing you do! (1996)
Turner & Hooch (1989)
Volunteers (1985)
You've Got Mail (1998)
film (voice): Toy Story (1995)
spouse: Rita Wilson
TV: Bosom Buddies
hanky
place: 5 purse **6** pocket
use a ~: 4 wipe
hanky-panky: 5 antic, cheat, fraud **6** dupery **7** knavery **9** chicanery, dalliance, deception, fourberie **10** dishonesty, subterfuge, tomfoolery
Hanky Panky (song) artist: Madonna, Tommy James and the Shondells
Hanna: 4 city, Mark, town **7** William
locale: 6 Canada **7** Alberta
Hanna-Barbera dog: 5 Astro
Hannah: 4 Page **5** Adams, Daryl, Moore **6** Arendt, Glasse
like ~'s heart: 4 hard
son of ~: 6 Samuel
Hannah and Her Sisters (1986 film)
cast: Woody Allen, Michael Caine, Mia Farrow, Carrie Fisher, Barbara Hershey, Lloyd Nolan, Maureen O'Sullivan, Daniel Stern, Max von Sydow, Dianne Wiest
director: Woody Allen
Hannah, Daryl: 7 actress
film: Legal Eagles (1986)
The Pope of Greenwich Village (1984)
The Real Blonde (1998)
Roxanne (1987)
Splash (1984)
Steel Magnolias (1989)
A Walk to Remember (2002)
Wall Street (1987)
Wildflowers (1999)
Hannibal: 6 Hamlin, Lecter
crossed them: 4 Alps
where ~ was defeated: 4 Zama
Hannibal (2001 film)
cast: Giancarlo Giannini, Anthony Hopkins, Ray Liotta, Julianne Moore
director: Ridley Scott
Hannigan, Miss charge: 5 Annie
Hanoi: 4 city, town **7** capital
Hilton resident: 3 POW
locale: 7 Vietnam
New Year in ~: 3 Tet
Hanover: 4 city, town
athletes: 8 Big Green
locale: 7 Germany
school: 9 Dartmouth
__ Hanover: 4 Bret
Hanover Park: 4 city, town
locale: 8 Illinois
Hans: 3 Arp **4** Blix, Graf **5** Bethe, Henze, Krebs, Sachs **6** Geiger **7** Brinker, Conried, Dehmelt, Driesch, Fischer, Holbein, Memling, Oersted, Spemann
in English: 4 John
see also German
Hans __ Bülow: 3 von
Hansberry, Lorraine: 6 author, writer
work: A Raisin in the Sun
To Be Young, Gifted and Black
Hans Brinker author: Mary Mapes Dodge
Hans Christian Andersen (1952 film)
cast: Farley Granger, Jeanmarie, Danny Kaye
director: Charles Vidor
role: 4 Doro, Otto **5** Niels
Hanseatic League
member: 4 Hamm **5** Halle **6** Lubeck
Hansel
see German
Hansel and Gretel: 5 opera
need: 4 oven
setting: 6 forest
Hansel & Gretel & Ted & Alice composer: P.D.Q. Bach
Hänsel und Gretel: 5 opera
Hansen: 5 Patti
hansom: 3 cab
relative: 6 chaise
Hanson: 4 Lars **6** Curtis, Howard
members: Isaac, Taylor, Zac
song: I Will Come to You (1997)
MMMBop (1997)
Hanson, Curtis: 8 director
film: The Arousers (1970)
Bedroom Window (1987)
The Hand That Rocks the Cradle (1992)
L.A. Confidential (1997)
The River Wild (1994)
Wonder Boys (2000)
Hans von __: 5 Bülow, Ohain
Hants: 6 county
locale: 7 England
Hanukkah
pancake: 5 latke
prayer: 6 Hallel
top: 7 dreidel
Hanya: 4 Holm
haole: 7 tourist **8** Hawaiian
gift for a ~: 3 lei
greeting: 5 aloha
hap: 3 lot **4** luck **6** chance **7** fortune **8** accident **10** occurrence
ender: 6 hazard
starter: 3 may
__ Hap-Hap-Happy Day: 4 It's a
haphazard: 5 loose **6** casual, chance, random **7** aimless, cursory, erratic, offhand **8** careless, pell-mell, reckless, slapdash, slipshod **9** arbitrary, desultory, hit-or-miss, irregular, vagarious **10** accidental, contingent, designless, disorderly, fortuitous, incidental, nonuniform, unexpected, unintended, unthinking, unthorough, willy-nilly
haphazardly: 6 anyhow **8** at random, by chance, pell-mell **9** any old way
hapless: 5 curst, hexed, sorry, woful **6** cursed, jinxed, tragic, woeful **7** unblest, unlucky **8** ill-fated, luckless, tragical, wretched **9** miserable, unblessed, unfavored **10** ill-starred
one: 5 schmo **6** schmoe
happen: 2 go **4** come, fall, go on **5** arise, break, ensue, occur, pop up **6** appear, arrive, befall, betide, crop up, follow, pan out, result **7** come off, develop, proceed, turn out, work out **8** come over, come to be, come true **9** come about, eventuate, intervene, take place, transpire **10** come to pass, take effect
about to ~: 6 at hand, coming **7** in store, pending **8** imminent
again: 5 recur **6** repeat, return
be about to ~: 4 loom **6** impend
bound to ~: 4 sure **7** certain, cinched **8** definite, in the bag, positive **10** guaranteed, inevitable
cause to ~: 4 spur **5** incur, spark **6** incite, prompt, set off **7** produce, trigger **8** generate, motivate, touch off **9** stimulate **10** bring about
ender: 6 chance, stance
let ~: 5 allow **6** permit **8** sanction, tolerate
let it ~: 6 give in, give up, relent **7** back off **9** acquiesce **10** capitulate
make ~: 5 cause **7** realize **8** occasion **10** bring about, effectuate
next: 5 ensue **6** follow
to: 6 befall, betide **7** betides **8** come over
upon: 4 find, meet **6** locate, strike **7** run into, stumble **8** bump into **9** encounter **10** come across
with: 9 accompany
__ happened was ...: 4 What
happening: 4 case **5** afoot, event, faddy, scene, thing **6** action, actual, affair, modish **7** episode **8** accident, incident, occasion, underway **9** adventure, milestone **10** enterprise, experience, in progress, occurrence, phenomenon, proceeding
after: 5 later
chance ~: 5 fluke, quirk **8** accident, fortuity
dreadful ~: 4 blow **7** tragedy **8** calamity, disaster **10** misfortune
keep from ~: 4 foil **5** avert, block **6** stifle, stymie, thwart **7** fend off, forfend, head off, hold off, prevent, ward off **8** hold back, obstruct, stave off **9** forestall, interrupt
now: 4 live **7** current, running
sudden ~: 5 burst **7** flare-up **8** outbreak
what's ~: 6 action **8** activity
__ happening?: 5 What's
happenings: 6 doings, events **8** business, goings-on
Happenings
song: I Got Rhythm (1967)
See You in September (1966)
Happening, The (1967 song) artist: Supremes
__ happens: 4 as it
happenstance: 4 luck **5** fluke **6** chance **8** accident, fortuity
__ happen to you...: 5 It can
Happiest Day, The author: Edgar Allan Poe
Happiest Girl in the Whole U.S.A., The (1972 song) artist: Donna Fargo
happify: 5 cheer, elate **6** thrill **7** delight, gladden, hearten
happily: 4 well **6** gladly **7** luckily, with joy **9** agreeably, willingly **10** swimmingly
...happily __ after: 4 ever
happiness: 3 joy **4** glee, life, luck, play, weal **5** bliss, cheer, mirth **6** gaiety, gayety, heaven, utopia **7** comfort, delight, ecstasy, elation, emotion, gayness, rapture, success, triumph, welfare **8** euphoria, felicity, gladness, good luck, hilarity, optimism, pleasure, radiance, radiancy **9** beatitude, enjoyment, festivity, geniality, good cheer, good humor, jocundity, joviality, merriment, rejoicing, well-being **10** cheeriness, ebullience, exuberance, exultation, jubilation, prosperity
fill with ~: 5 elate
name meaning ~: 7 Gwyneth
name meaning ~ bringer: 8 Beatrice
paradigm of ~: 4 clam
sound of ~: 2 ah
Happiness (1998 film)
cast: Jane Adams, Dylan Baker, Philip Seymour Hoffman, Jon Lovitz
director: Todd Solondz
Happiness __ Warm Puppy: 3 Is a
happy: 3 apt, fun, gay **4** gaga, glad, high, warm, well **5** aglow, blest, jolly, lucky, merry, perky, ready, riant, sunny, tipsy **6** blithe, bright, cheery, chirpy, elated, festal, genial, golden, jovial, joyful, joyous, lively, timely, upbeat **7** beaming, blessed, buoyant, chipper, content, festive, fitting, gleeful, glowing, halcyon, jocular, playful, pleased, radiant, tickled **8** blissful, carefree, cheerful, ecstatic, euphoric, exultant, giggling, gladsome, groov-ing, jubilant, laughing, mirthful, sanguine, suitable, thrilled **9** contented, convivial, delighted, delirious, favorable, fortunate, gladdened, gratified, lightsome, opportune, overjoyed, promising, rejoicing, satisfied, vivacious, well-timed **10** accidental, convenient, felicitous, flying high, nonchalant, optimistic, propitious, rollicking, successful, triumphant
days: 5 toast **6** kampai
feel ~: 4 live **5** enjoy, exult, glory, revel **7** delight, rejoice, triumph **8** jubilate **9** celebrate, make merry, walk on air **10** effervesce
feeling: 3 joy **4** glee **5** bliss, cheer, mirth **6** gaiety **7** delight, ecstasy, elation, jollity **8** euphoria, gladness **9** merriment **10** exultation, joyfulness, joyousness, jubilation
hour: 7 respite
hour establishment: 3 pub **6** saloon, tavern **7** taproom **8** alehouse, taphouse
hunting ground: 6 heaven, utopia **7** Arcadia, Elysium **8** paradise **9** Shangri-la
look ~: 4 grin **5** smile
make ~: 5 cheer, elate **6** please **7** beatify, gladden, gratify, sweeten **8** brighten **10** exhilarate
medium: 7 balance **8** midpoint **10** compromise
name meaning ~: 3 Ida **5** Felix **7** Felicia
name meaning ~ friend: 5 Edwin **6** Edwina
name meaning ~ guardian: 6 Edward
name meaning ~ hall: 5 Edsel
name meaning ~ protection: 6 Edmond, Edmund
name meaning ~ spear: 5 Edgar
name meaning ~ war: 5 Edith **6** Edythe
not ~: 3 sad **4** blue **5** upset
sound: 2 ah **5** chirp
starter: 4 slap
happy __: 4 hour **6** camper, ending **7** warrior
happy __ clam: 3 as a
happy __ ground: 7 hunting
happy __ lark: 3 as a
__-happy: 7 trigger
Happy: 5 dwarf **8** Chandler
colleague: 3 Doc **5** Dopey **6** Grumpy, Sleepy, Sneezy **7** Bashful
Happy __: 4 Days, Jack, Talk **6** Trails
Happy __ Are Here Again: 4 Days
Happy __, The: 5 Organ, Years
Happy, __: 5 Texas
__ Happy: 3 Get **4** Girl, Love

Happy (1972 song) artist: Rolling Stones
happy as ___: **5** a clam, a lark
Happy Birthday ___: **5** to You
Happy Birthday, Sweet Sixteen (1961 song) artist: Neil Sedaka
Happy Birthday, Wanda June (1971 film)
cast: George Grizzard, Rod Steiger, Susannah York
director: Mark Robson
Happy Birthday writer: **4** icer
Happy Days (ABC sitcom)
cast: Tom Bosley (Howard Cunningham)
Ron Howard (Richie Cunningham)
Erin Moran (Joanie Cunningham)
Donny Most (Ralph Malph)
Marion Ross (Marion Cunningham)
Anson Williams (Potsie Weber)
Henry Winkler (Arthur Fonz Fonzarelli)
catchphrase: Sit on it
dog: **6** Spunky
hangout: Arnold's
setting: Milwaukee
Happy Days Are Here Again composer: **4** Ager
Happy Feet composer: **4** Ager
___ Happy Fella, The: **4** Most
happy-go-lucky: **5** merry **6** blithe, casual **8** carefree, cheerful
Happy Hollisters
cat: **9** White Nose
dog: **3** Zip
Happy Hooligan: **5** comic **10** comic strip
cartoonist: **5** Opper
dog: **4** Flip
happy hour: **6** recess
charge: **6** bar tab
establishment: **3** bar
order: **3** ale **4** beer, wine **5** drink, lager
perch: **5** stool
happy hunting ___: **6** ground
Happy New ___: **4** Year
Happy Organ, The (1959 song) artist: Dave Cortez
Happy Prince and Other Tales, The
author: Oscar Wilde
___ happy returns: **4** many
Happy Talk composer: **7** Rodgers **11** Hammerstein
Happy, Texas (1999 film)
cast: William H. Macy, Ally Walker, Steve Zahn
Happy Together (1967 song) artist: Turtles
Happy Trails
singer: Dale Evans, Roy Rogers
Happy Warrior, The: Al Smith
Happy Years, The (1950 film)
cast: Scotty Beckett, Darryl Hickman, Dean Stockwell
director: William Wellman
Hapsburg
see German
hapuku: **4** fish
hara-___: **4** kiri
Harald III, city founded by: **4** Oslo
Harald, King father: **4** Olaf, Olav
Haramosh Peak: **4** peak **5** mount **8** mountain
locale: **4** Asia **8** Pakistan
harangue: **3** nag **4** rant, rave, talk **5** orate, spiel, spout **6** berate, exhort, preach, raving, screed, sermon, speech, tirade **7** chew out, declaim, inveigh, lecture, monolog, oration, ranting, venting **8** bloviate, diatribe, jeremiad, perorate, spouting **9** discourse, go on about, hold forth, monologue, philippic **10** peroration, vocalizing
Harare: **4** city, town **7** capital
locale: **8** Zimbabwe
harass: **3** bug, dog, irk, nag, ply, rag, try, vex **4** bait, fret, gall, goad, pain, ride, roil, tire **5** annoy, bedog, beset, bully, chafe, get on, grind, harry, hit on, hound, nag at, press, spite, taunt, tease, upset, weary, worry **6** accost, badger, bother, hassle, heckle, hector, maraud, needle, nettle, noodge, pester, pick on, plague, pother, pursue, put out, rankle, rattle, ruffle **7** afflict, bedevil, besiege, bombard, disturb, henpeck, oppress, rip into, torment, trouble **8** aggrieve, browbeat, disquiet, distress, irritate **9** beleaguer, importune, persecute **10** discompose, intimidate
harasser: **4** pest **6** nudnik
harassment: **8** hounding **9** annoyance, badgering, bothering, pestering, provoking **10** difficulty, irritation
Harbach: **4** Otto
Harbin: **4** city, town
locale: **5** China
harbinger: **4** omen, sign **5** augur **6** augury, herald, leader, signal **7** portent, presage **9** foretoken, messenger, precursor, predictor **10** forerunner, indication
harbinger of ___: **6** spring
harbor: **3** bay **4** bear, cove, dock, hide, hold, pier, port **5** basin, berth, board, cover, haven, house, jetty, lodge, put up, wharf **6** asylum, marina, refuge, resort, secure, shield **7** conceal, domicil, landing, lodging, mooring, protect, quarter, retreat, seaport, secrete, shelter **8** domicile **9** anchorage, entertain, safeguard, sanctuary **10** protection
city: **2** pt. **3** spt. **4** port **7** seaport
ender: **3** age **6** master
enter a ~: **4** dock **5** put in
expert: **5** pilot
locale: **4** cove, dock, pier **5** inlet, jetty
machine: **6** dredge
out of the ~: **4** asea **5** at sea
sound: **4** toot
vessel: **3** hoy, tow, tug **4** boat, scow **5** barge, ferry **7** tugboat
harbor ___: **4** seal **6** master
___ harbor: **3** air **4** safe
Harbor ___: **6** Lights
___ Harbor: **3** Bar, Sag **5** Pearl
harborage: **5** haven **6** refuge **7** shelter **9** anchorage, sanctuary
Harbor Lights (1959 song) artist: Platters
___ Harbour, FL: **3** Bal
Harburg: **2** E.Y. **3** Yip
hard: **4** firm, iron, mean **5** bossy, cruel, dense, hairy, heavy, madly, picky, rigid, rocky, rough, solid, stale, stern, stiff, stony, thick, tough **6** avidly, bitter, brutal, firmly, flinty, keenly, knotty, packed, rugged, severe, steely, stoney, strict, strong, thorny, tiring, trying, unjust, unkind, uphill **7** arduous, austere, callous, eagerly, harshly, heavily, hostile, intense, labored, onerous, operose, painful, roughly, serious, sharply, Spartan, toilful, wearing **8** ardently, bitterly, brutally, concrete, despotic, doggedly, exacting, fiercely, forcibly, granitic, grinding, grueling, indurate, intently, leathery, pitiless, puzzling, resolute, rigorous, rocklike, ruthless, savagely, severely, strongly, stubborn, terrible, tiresome, toilsome, urgently, vigorous, wearying **9** alcoholic, ambitious, arduously, austerely, compacted, demanding, difficult, draconian, earnestly, fatiguing, fermented, furiously, herculean, insensate, insoluble, intensely, laborious, merciless, obstinate, onerously, painfully, realistic, recondite, seriously, stonelike, strenuous, stringent, unbending, unfeeling, unpitying, unpliable, unsparing, viciously, violently, zealously **10** adamantine, burdensome, compressed, despotical, diligently, exhausting, formidable, gruelingly, impervious, inflexible, iron-fisted, no-nonsense, oppressive, perplexing, pitilessly, powerfully, relentless, rigorously, ruthlessly, sedulously, solidified, studiously, thoroughly, tyrannical, unmerciful, unpleasant, untiringly, unyielding, vehemently, vigorously
and fast: **3** set
as nails: **5** rigid, tough **6** steely, strong **9** unbending
as rock: **7** lithoid **9** lithoidal
blow: **4** gale, gust **5** blast, storm **6** squall **7** cyclone, tempest **9** windstorm
breathe ~: **4** gasp, pant, puff **5** heave
by: **4** near, next, nigh **5** close
candy: **4** drop **5** charm, lolly
case: **4** hull, husk, thug **5** shell **8** carapace **10** integument
cash: **4** gelt, loot **5** bread, bucks, dough, funds, money, moola **6** dinero, moolah **7** capital, dollars, lettuce, scratch **8** bankroll, currency, smackers **9** banknotes, simoleons **10** green stuff
combining form: **5** scler- **6** sclera-, sclero-
come down ~: **4** pour, rain, teem
come down ~ on: **6** punish **8** admonish
don't work very ~: **4** laze **7** goof off **8** slack off
ender: **3** hat, pan, top **4** back, ball, core, edge, hack, head, line, news, tack, ware, wire, wood **5** board, bound, cover, heads, stand **6** headed **7** hearted **8** scrabble
feelings: **5** anger **6** grudge, hatred **7** offense
get the ~ way: **3** pry **5** wrest, wring **6** extort, wrench
give a ~ time to: **3** irk, nag, vex **5** tease, upset **6** harass **7** torment
hat: **5** labor **6** helmet
have ~ feelings: **6** resent
hit: **4** blow, slap
hit ~: **4** belt, slam, slug, wham **5** paste, smack, smite, whack, whomp
knocks: **3** woe **7** bad luck, travail, trouble **9** adversity, mischance, tough luck **10** misfortune
labor: **4** toil **5** sweat **7** travail **8** drudgery, exertion
look ~: **4** gape, gawk, gaze, peer **5** focus, glare, rivet, stare **7** eyeball
luck: **6** mishap **7** setback, trouble **8** bad break, calamity **9** adversity, mischance, suffering **10** misfortune
not ~: **4** easy, soft **5** mushy **6** cuddly, fleecy, fluffy, simple, spongy, supple **7** no sweat, pliable, snuggly, squishy **8** cushiony, no bother, painless **9** no problem, no trouble **10** child's play, effortless, unexacting
not yet ~: **5** unset
one working ~: **5** plier, plyer
playing ~: **7** serious
pull ~: **3** tug **4** jerk, yank **5** pluck **6** wrench
put: **8** strained
question: **5** poser **6** enigma, puzzle, riddle, teaser **7** problem, stumper **9** conundrum
requiring ~ labor: **7** arduous, onerous **8** grueling **9** strenuous **10** exhausting, oppressive
sell: **5** spiel **6** patter **8** cajolery **10** persuasion
starter: **3** die **4** blow
stuff: **4** rock **5** metal, sauce **6** liquor, whisky **7** alcohol, spirits, whiskey **9** inebriant
take it ~: **3** cry, sob **4** bawl, howl, keen, moan, mope, wail, weep **5** brood, mourn **6** bemoan, bewail, grieve, lament
think ~: **5** focus **6** fixate
time: **6** hassle, rebuff, rebuke **8** distress **9** rejection **10** upbraiding
times: **5** slump **9** adversity, recession **10** depression, woefulness
to find: **4** rare **6** exotic, scanty, scarce **8** uncommon
to get to: **3** dim **4** dull, slow **5** thick **6** obtuse, simple, stolid **9** pigheaded
to please: **5** fussy, picky **6** choosy **7** choosey, finicky **8** finiking, finnicky **9** querulous
to see: **3** dim **4** hazy **5** faint, fuzzy, murky, muzzy, vague **6** bleary, blurry, far-off, opaque **7** blurred, clouded, muddled, obscure, shadowy, unclear **8** nebulous **10** indistinct
to understand: **4** mazy **5** tough **6** knotty, opaque, sticky, thorny, tricky **7** complex, obscure, unclear **8** abstruse, baffling, puzzling **9** difficult, intricate **10** formidable, mystifying, perplexing
to use: **7** awkward **8** affected, unwieldy **9** ponderous **10** cumbersome
up: **4** poor **5** broke, needy **6** bad off, ill off, in need, in want **7** pinched **8** badly off, bankrupt, beggarly, indigent, strapped **9** desperate, destitute, insolvent, moneyless, penniless, penurious **10** down and out, pauperized, straitened
work: **4** moil, toil **5** grind, sweat **7** travail **8** drudgery, exertion, industry **10** punishment
work ~: **4** moil, push, slog, toil **5** exert, labor, slave **6** drudge, hustle, strain **9** persevere
worker: **4** doer **5** demon, grind, plier, plyer **6** daemon, daimon, dynamo **7** hustler
hard ___: **3** bop, hat, put **4** case, cash, clam, coal, copy, core, disk, head, lens, line, mass, news, rock, sell, sign, tick, time **5** candy, cider, court, drive, goods, labor, light, maple, masse, paste, peach, sauce, stuff, water, wheat **6** cheese, dinkum, ground, knocks, palate, rubber, solder **7** landing, science
hard ___ rock: **3** as a
hard ___ to crack: **3** nut
hard ___ to hoe: **3** row
hard-___: **3** hat, put, set **4** bill, boil, laid, nose, spun **5** asset, edged, knock, liner, nosed, shell, wired **6** bitten, boiled, coated, fisted, handed, ticket **7** favored, hitting, pressed, surface
hard-___ clam: **5** shell
hard-___ crab: **5** shell
___-hard: **3** die **4** blow **7** leather
Hard ___: **4** Rain **5** Candy, Times, to Get, to Say
Hard ___!: **4** alee **5** aport
Hard ___ Cafe: **4** Rock
Hard ___ Night, A: **4** Day's

hard-and-fast: **6** strict **7** binding **8** exacting **9** stringent, unbending **10** unyielding
hard-and-fast ___: **4** rule
hard as ___: **5** a rock, nails
hardback: **4** book
___ hardball: **4** play
Hardball (2001 film)
cast: John Hawkes, Diane Lane, Keanu Reeves
Hardball broadcaster: **5** MSNBC
hard-bitten: **4** firm **5** balky, rigid, sober, stern, stony, tough **6** dogged, mulish, ornery **7** adamant **8** contrary, hellbent, indurate, obdurate, resolute, stubborn **9** immovable, obstinate, pigheaded, practical, pragmatic, steadfast, tenacious, unbending **10** bullheaded, inflexible, unromantic, unshakable
hard-boiled: **5** harsh, stern, tough **7** callous **9** heartless, practical, pragmatic, realistic **10** determined, iron-willed, unromantic
Hard Candy author: Tennessee Williams
Hard Cash author: **5** Reade
hard cider: **5** drink **8** beverage
hard-copy creator: **3** ptr. **7** printer
Hard Copy network: **3** CBS **5** CBS-TV
hard-core: **5** stern **8** faithful **10** unyielding
hardcover: **4** book
part: **5** spine
Hard Day's Night A: **4** film, song
artist: Beatles
cast: George Harrison, John Lennon, Paul McCartney, Ringo Starr
director: Richard Lester
hard-driving: **5** type A **6** virile **8** vigorous
not ~: **5** type B
har-de-har-har: **5** laugh
harden: **3** dry, fix, gel, set **4** cake, clot, firm, gird, jell, tone **5** adapt, build, enure, inure, set in, shore, steel, train **6** adjust, anneal, beef up, cement, curdle, firm up, freeze, gelate, ossify, prop up, season, settle, temper, tone up **7** bolster, brace up, build up, burgeon, calcify, coarsen, congeal, develop, empower, enhance, fortify, petrify, shore up, stiffen, thicken, tighten, toughen, vitrify **8** accustom, bourgeon, buttress, energize, indurate, solidify, vitalize **9** acclimate, coagulate, habituate, intensify, reinforce, vulcanize **10** amalgamate, invigorate, strengthen
(to): **5** enure, inure
___-harden: **3** oil **4** face **5** water
Harden, Arthur: **7** chemist **8** Nobelist
hardened: **3** old, set **4** cold, firm, numb **5** cruel, set in, stiff, stony, tough **6** steely, stoney **7** callous **8** indurate, leathery, obdurate, uncaring **9** impassive, impliable, insensate, obstinate, unbending, unfeeling, unpliable **10** inveterate
starter: **4** case
Harden, Marcia Gay Oscar: Pollock
___ Harder: **5** We Try
Harder They Fall, The (1956 film)
cast: Humphrey Bogart, Rod Steiger, Jan Sterling
director: Mark Robson
writer: Budd Schulberg
Hard Habit to Break (1984 song)
artist: Chicago
hardhack: **5** shrub
relative: **4** rose, sloe **6** kerria, spirea **7** bramble, jetbead, spiraea **8** ninebark, photinia **9** firethorn, raspberry
hardheaded: **5** stern, stiff **8** stubborn **9** impliable, practical, pragmatic **10** hard-bitten, iron-willed
Hard Headed Woman (1958 song)
artist: Elvis Presley
hardhearted: **4** cold **5** cruel, stern, stony **6** stoney, unkind **7** brutish, callous, inhuman **8** obdurate, pitiless, ruthless, uncaring **9** merciless, unfeeling
Hard Hearted Hannah composer: **4** Ager
hardihood: **5** valor **7** prowess **9** fortitude **10** confidence
Hardin: **2** Ty
hardiness: **3** vim **4** dint, grit, thew, will **5** brawn, force, might, power, thews, valor, vigor **6** energy, health, muscle **7** bravery, courage, fitness, muscles, potence, potency, stamina **8** audacity, boldness, strength, tenacity, vitality **9** endurance, fortitude, puissance, tolerance **10** brute force, resolution, robustness
Harding: **3** Ann **5** Tonya **6** Warren **8** Florence
Harding, Ann: **7** actress
film: The Animal Kingdom (1932)
Holiday (1930)
The Magnificent Yankee (1950)
Mission to Moscow (1943)
Peter Ibbetson (1935)
When Ladies Meet (1933)
Harding, Warren G.: **9** president
former occupation: **9** publisher
home: **4** Ohio **6** Marion
middle name: **8** Gamaliel
opponent: **3** Cox **4** Debs
V.P.: **8** Coolidge
wife: **8** Florence
Hardison: **6** Kadeem
hard-line: **4** firm **5** bossy, cruel, picky, rigid, stern, tough **6** severe **7** austere, Spartan **8** despotic, exacting, orthodox, rigorous **9** demanding, draconian, stringent, unbending, unsparing **10** despotical, inflexible, iron-fisted, iron-willed, no-nonsense, oppressive, tyrannical, unyielding
hardliner: **4** hawk
Hard Lines poet: **4** Nash
hard-luck guy: **5** patsy
hardly: **4** just, only **6** adverb, barely, little, seldom **7** faintly, not a bit, not much, scantly **8** not at all, not often, scarcely, slightly **9** by no means, not likely
hardly ___: **4** ever
Hardly ___ is now alive...: **4** a man
___ hardly wait!: **4** I can
hardness: **5** rigor **7** density **8** firmness, iron hand, rigidity **9** harshness, stiffness, toughness **10** difficulty, inclemency, strictness
epitome of ~: **5** nails
of heart: **5** odium **6** animus, enmity, hatred, rancor **7** ill will **8** acrimony **9** animosity **10** antagonism, resentment
hard-nosed: **4** mean **5** harsh, stern, tough **6** mulish, severe, strong, wilful **7** adamant, willful **8** resolute, stubborn **9** immovable **10** headstrong, iron-willed, unyielding
not ~: **3** lax
hard nut to ___: **5** crack
hard-packed: **4** firm **5** dense, solid, thick, tight **6** jammed **7** compact, crammed, crowded **9** condensed **10** compressed
hard-place alternative: **4** rock
hard-pressed: **7** harried **8** burdened, harassed **9** oppressed, pressured **10** overloaded
Hard Rain (1998 film)
cast: Minnie Driver, Morgan Freeman, Randy Quaid, Christian Slater
Hard Road to Glory, A author: **4** Ashe
Hard Rock ___: **4** Cafe
hard row to ___: **3** hoe
hard-set: **4** firm **5** rigid, stern, stiff, tough **6** flinty, mulish, steely, strict **7** adamant **8** immobile, indurate, obdurate, resolute, stubborn **9** immovable, obstinate, pig-headed, steadfast, stringent, unbending **10** bullheaded, implacable, inflexible, unyielding
hard-shell: **4** clam, crab **5** stern **9** confirmed **10** headstrong
hard-shelled: **5** stern, stout, tough **6** feisty, robust, steely, strict, strong **7** adamant, callous, staunch **8** obdurate, resolute, rigorous, stubborn **9** merciless, obstinate, resilient, resistant, stringent, tenacious, unbending **10** courageous, formidable, pugnacious
hardship: **3** woe **4** care, toil **5** grief, rigor, trial **6** burden, misery, mishap, sorrow, strait **7** poverty, tragedy, travail, trouble **8** calamity, disaster, distress, drudgery, exigence, exigency, obstacle **9** adversity, austerity, grievance, privation, suffering **10** affliction, difficulty, discomfort, ill fortune, infelicity, misfortune, oppression
face ~: **4** cope
Hard Times (1975 film)
cast: Charles Bronson, James Coburn, Jill Ireland, Strother Martin
director: Walter Hill
Hard Times author: Charles Dickens
Hard to Get (1938 film)
cast: Olivia de Havilland, Dick Powell, Charles Winninger
director: Ray Enright
Hard to Get (1955 song) artist: Gisele MacKenzie
Hard to Kill (1990 film)
cast: Kelly LeBrock, William Sadler, Steven Seagal
hardtop: **3** car **4** auto **5** sedan **10** automobile
Hard to Say (1981 song) artist: Dan Fogelberg
Hard to Say I'm Sorry (song)
artist: Az Yet, Chicago, Peter Cetera
hardware: **3** PCs **5** metal, tools **8** fittings, fixtures, plumbing, printers, trinkets **9** computers, fasteners **10** implements
install new ~: **5** refit
item: **3** awl, nut **4** bolt, nail, tack, T-nut **5** screw, t bolt, U-bolt
hardware ___: **5** cloth, store
___ Hardware: **3** Ace
Hard Way, The (1942 film)
cast: Joan Leslie, Ida Lupino, Dennis Morgan
Hardwicke, Cedric: **3** Sir **5** actor
film: The Cross of Lorraine (1943)
The Desert Fox (1951)
Forever and a Day (1943)
The Hunchback of Notre Dame (1939)
The Invisible Man Returns (1940)
Les Miserables (1935)
The Moon Is Down (1943)
On Borrowed Time (1939)
Suspicion (1941)
The Ten Commandments (1956)
Things to Come (1936)
Valley of the Sun (1942)
Victory (1940)
Wilson (1944)
The Winslow Boy (1948)
hard-won: **5** rough, tough **6** thorny, trying, uphill **7** arduous **8** exacting, grueling, toilsome **9** difficult, effortful, laborious **10** exhausting
hardwood: **3** ash, elm, oak **4** poon, teak, tree **5** cedar, ebony, larch, lehua, maple **6** jarrah, locust, timber, wandoo **7** wallaba **8** mahogany
block: **5** rabot
Hawaiian ~: **4** ohia **5** lehua
hard-working: **4** busy, spry **5** astir, perky **6** active, lively **7** dynamic, working **8** animated, bustling, diligent, sedulous, studious, tireless **9** assiduous, dedicated, energetic, motivated, sprightly
hardy: **3** fit **4** able, game, hale, iron, well, wiry **5** beefy, burly, fresh, hefty, hunky, husky, lusty, right, solid, sound, stout, tough **6** brawny, gritty, hearty, mighty, potent, robust, rugged, sinewy, steely, stocky, strong, sturdy, virile **7** capable, doughty, healthy, staunch **8** athletic, forceful, indurate, muscular, powerful, puissant, seasoned, stalwart, vigorous **9** Atlantean, energetic, Herculean, in the pink, resilient, strapping, tenacious, well-built **10** able-bodied, courageous, iron-willed, red-blooded, unflagging
name meaning ~ bear: **7** Bernard
name meaning ~ lion: **7** Leonard
starter: **4** fool
Hardy: **3** Joe **4** Andy **5** Ollie **6** Oliver, Thomas **9** Alexandre
partner: **6** Laurel
Hardy ___: **4** Boys
Hardy, Alexandre: **6** French **10** playwright
Hardy Boys character: **4** Chet
Hardy, Thomas: **4** poet **6** author, writer **7** British
setting: Wessex
villain: **4** Alec
work: The Dynasts
Far From the Madding Crowd
Jude the Obscure
The Mayor of Casterbridge
The Return of the Native
Tess of the d'Urbervilles
The Woodlanders
hare: **3** hie **4** cony **5** coney, speed **6** animal, malkin, mammal, mawkin **7** leveret **9** lagomorph
and hounds: **4** game
combining form: **3** lag- **4** lago-
ender: **4** bell **7** brained
female: **3** doe
like a March ~: **3** mad
male: **4** buck
name meaning ~: **4** Haas
tail: **4** scut
to hounds: **4** prey
young: **7** leveret
___ hare: **3** sea **6** jugged **7** Belgian, jumping, varying
Hare
constellation: **5** Lepus
Hare ___: **7** Krishna
hare and hounds: **4** game
harebell: **5** plant **6** flower
harebrain: **2** ox **3** ass, oaf, sap **4** clod, dolt, dope, fool, jerk, loon, lout, simp **5** chump, dummy, dunce, goose, klutz, ninny **6** cuckoo, dimwit, galoot, nitwit **7** bungler, dingbat, dullard, fathead, half-wit, jackass, jughead, pinhead, tomfool **8** bonehead, dumbbell, dummkopf, numskull **9** blockhead, ding-a-ling, ignoramus, simpleton **10** dunderpate, muttonhead, nincompoop, rattlepate
harebrained: **4** rash, wild, zany **5** balmy, barmy, dizzy, giddy, inane, silly, wacky **6** absurd, madcap, whacky **7** asinine, bizarre, flighty, foolish **8** careless, heedless, mindless, reckless **9** idiotical

harefooted: **4** fast **5** fleet, quick, rapid **6** snappy, speedy
Hare Krishna offering: **5** chant
harem: **6** zenana **7** odalisk **8** seraglio **9** odalisque
jewelry: **6** anklet
members: **5** wives
one with a ~: **5** sheik **6** shaikh, sheikh
room: **3** oda **4** odah
harem __: **5** pants
hare's-foot __: **4** fern
Hargitay: **6** Mickey **7** Mariska
har-har: **5** comic, droll, funny **7** amusing, comical, risible **8** humorous **9** hilarious, laughable, ludicrous
Hari: **4** Mata **6** Rhodes
haricot: **4** bean, stew **6** legume, veggie **9** vegetable
haricot __: **4** vert
haricot bean: **6** veggie **9** vegetable
Haring: **5** Keith
hark: **4** hear, heed **6** attend, listen **9** bend an ear **10** give head to
back: **6** recall **8** look back **9** recollect, reminisce
harkening, name meaning: **6** Simeon
Harkin: **3** Tom
Hark, the Herald Angels Sing: **5** carol
Harlan: **4** John **7** Ellison
Harland: **7** Sanders
Harleian __: **7** Library
Harlem: **5** river
locale: **3** NYC **7** New York
theater: **6** Apollo
__ Harlem: **7** Spanish
Harlem Shuffle (1986 song) artist: Rolling Stones
harlequin: **4** duck, fool, zany **5** clown **6** jester, motley **7** buffoon, pierrot **10** motley fool
ender: **3** ade
harlequin __: **3** bug **4** duck, opal **5** table
Harlequin __: **7** Romance
harlequin duck: **4** fowl
relative: **4** smew, teal **5** eider, Pekin, Rouen, scaup **6** Cayuga, scoter **7** gadwall, mallard, pintail, pochard, redhead, widgeon **8** garganey, mandarin, oldsquaw, shoveler **9** broadbill, goldeneye, goosander, greenhead, merganser, sprigtail **10** bufflehead, canvasback, surf scoter
Harlequin's Carnival, The painter: **4** Miró
Harley: **3** hog **4** bike **5** cycle **10** motorcycle
alternative: **5** Honda **6** Yamaha **8** Kawasaki
partner: **8** Davidson
Harline: **5** Leigh
Harlingen: **4** city, town
locale: **5** Texas
Harlin, Renny: **8** director
film: Cliffhanger (1993)
Cutthroat Island (1995)
Deep Blue Sea (1999)
Die Hard 2 (1990)
spouse: Geena Davis
Harlow: **4** Jean **6** Shalom
Harlow, Jean: **6** blonde **7** actress
film: The Beast of the City (1932)
Bombshell (1933)
China Seas (1935)
Dinner at Eight (1933)
The Girl From Missouri (1934)
Hell's Angels (1930)
Hold Your Man (1933)
Libeled Lady (1936)
Platinum Blonde (1931)
The Public Enemy (1931)
Red Dust (1932)
Red-Headed Woman (1932)

harm: **3** ill, mar **4** beat, evil, hurt, loss, maim, pain, ruin **5** abuse, break, crack, lay up, spite, spoil, wound, wreck, wrong **6** bruise, damage, deface, defile, impair, injure, injury, malign, mess up, mishap, misuse, molest, muck up, poison **7** corrupt, offense, vitiate **8** aggrieve, breakage, disserve, foul play, ill-treat, lacerate, maltreat, mischief, mistreat, sabotage **9** adversity, detriment, mishandle, mismanage, prejudice, vandalism, vandalize **10** defacement, defilement, impairment, misfortune
cause ~ to: **3** mar **4** maim, ruin **5** abuse, spoil, stain, wound, wrong **6** batter, bruise, damage, deface, defile, impair, injure, mangle, ravage **7** corrupt, pollute, scratch, tarnish **9** undermine
free from ~: **4** safe
in French: **3** mal
protection from ~: **6** asylum, refuge, safety **7** shelter **9** sanctuary
__ harm: **4** do no **6** bodily
harmattan: **4** wind
harmed: **4** hurt **7** injured **9** aggrieved
easily ~: **9** sensitive
harmful: **3** bad, ill **4** dire, evil **5** lousy, toxic **6** costly, lethal, malign, nocent, sinful, unsafe **7** adverse, baleful, baneful, hurtful, malefic, nocuous, noisome, noxious, ruinous **8** damaging, grievous, inimical, menacing, sinister, virulent **9** injurious, malicious, pestilent, poisonous, unhealthy **10** calamitous, corrupting, disastrous, incendiary, maleficent, pernicious, subversive
not ~: **4** mild **6** benign, gentle **7** healthy **9** healthful
thing: **4** bane **5** curse **6** blight, plague, poison **7** scourge **8** calamity **9** detriment
Harmful Intent author: Robin Cook
harmfully: **3** ill **5** wrong **9** seriously
harmless: **4** kind, safe, sage, tame **6** benign, gentle, secure **8** innocent, nontoxic, reliable **9** innocuous, innoxious
make ~: **5** unarm **6** defang, defuse, defuze, dehorn, disarm **7** disable
__ harmless: **4** save
Harmon: **3** Tom **4** Anne, Mark **5** Angie, Kelly **6** Claude **9** Killebrew
Harmon, Angie spouse: Jason Sehorn
Harmon, Claude: **6** golfer
Harmonia: **5** nymph
brother of ~: **6** Deimos, Phobus
daughter of ~: **5** Agave **9** Hippolyte
husband of ~: **6** Cadmus
parent of: **4** Ares **9** Aphrodite
harmonic: **5** tonal
harmonic __: **3** law **4** mean, tone **6** motion, series
harmonica: **4** wind **10** instrument, mouth organ
maker: **6** Hohner
part: **4** reed
player: **5** Adler
harmonious: **4** calm **5** in key, on key, sweet **6** in step, in tune **7** cordial, halcyon, lyrical, melodic, musical, regular, tuneful **8** amicable, balanced, esthetic, in accord, of a piece, peaceful, sonorous, tasteful **9** accordant, according, agreeable, classical, congenial, congruent, congruous, consonant, in concert, melodious, of one mind, simpatico, symphonic, unanimous, well-tuned **10** compatible, concordant, concurrent, consistent, euphonious, like-minded, rhythmical, synchronal, true to type

make ~: **4** tune **9** reconcile
relationship: **4** sync **5** unity
sounds: **5** music
harmonium: **8** keyboard **10** instrument
harmonize: **2** go **3** fit **4** gybe, jibe, mesh, sing, tune **5** agree, blend, chime, fit in, match, synch **6** accord, attune, belong, cohere, square, tune up **7** comport, compose, conform **8** dovetail, modulate **9** chime with, cooperate, correlate, integrate, reconcile **10** coordinate, correspond, proportion
Harmon, Mark: **5** actor
film: Stealing Home (1988)
spouse: Pam Dawber
TV: Chicago Hope, St. Elsewhere
harmony: **4** calm, sync, tune **5** amity, blend, chord, music, order, peace, quiet, sound, synch, triad, unity **6** accord, comity, melody, unison **7** concert, concord, euphony, keeping, kinship, oneness, rapport **8** diapason, good will, serenity, symmetry, symphony **9** agreement, communion, congruity, consensus, good vibes, unanimity **10** conformity, friendship, proportion
be in ~: **4** gybe, jibe **5** agree
in ~: **5** at one **6** jibing **10** compatible, like-minded
name meaning ~: **4** Alan **5** Allan, Allen
one in ~: **6** agreer
part: **4** alto, bass **5** tenor **7** soprano
restore ~: **7** mediate **9** reconcile **10** conciliate
__ harmony: **5** close, vowel
Harmony: **6** cereal
competitor: **3** Kix **4** Life, Trix **5** Kashi, Quisp, Total **6** Kaboom, Muesli, Oreo O's, Pablum, Smacks **7** All-Bran, Crispix, Hunny B's, Mueslix, Oat Bran, Pokemon **8** Boo Berry, Cheerios, Corn Chex, Corn Pops, Fiber One, Rice Chex, Special K, Uncle Sam, Wheaties **9** Alpha Bits, Apple Zaps, Grape Nuts, Honey Comb, Just Right, Wheat Chex **10** Apple Jacks, Bran Flakes, Cap'n Crunch, Cocoa Puffs, Froot Loops, Mini-Wheats, Nutri-Grain, Puffed Rice, Quaker Oats, Smart Start **11** Cocoa Blasts, Cookie Crisp, Golden Crisp, Lucky Charms, Puffed Wheat, Sweet Crunch, Waffle Crisp
harm's way: **5** peril **6** danger **8** jeopardy
in ~: **6** unsafe
out of ~: **2** OK **4** safe, snug **6** secure **8** harbored, home-free, shielded **9** protected, sheltered
harness: **3** use **4** curb, gear, rein, tame, yoke **5** apply, check, hitch, strap **6** couple, employ, halter, hook up, inspan, rein in, tether **7** contain, control, exploit, utilize **8** mobilize, restrain **9** constrain
gear: **4** tack
part: **3** bit **4** curb, hame, rein **5** strap, trace **6** bridle
sharers: **4** team
harness __: **3** eye **4** race **5** hitch, horse **6** racing
harnessed: **4** tame **5** yoked
harness racing: **5** sport
gait: **4** trot
horse: **5** pacer **7** trotter
need: **5** sulky
Harney: **4** peak **5** mount **8** mountain
locale: **4** S. Dak. **10** Black Hills
Harnick: **7** Sheldon
Harold: **4** Gray, Rome, Teen, Urey **5** Arlen, Bloom, Evans, Gould, Kroto, Lloyd, Monro, Ramis **6** Baines, Becker, Clarke, French, Melvin, Pinter, Sakata, Varmus, Wilson **7** Brodkey, Kushner, Robbins, Russell **9** Macmillan
__ Harold: **6** Childe
Harold and Maude (1972 film)
cast: Bud Cort, Ruth Gordon, Vivian Pickles
director: Hal Ashby
Harold author: Edward Bulwer-Lytton
Harold in Italy composer: **7** Berlioz
__ Harold's Pilgrimage: **6** Childe
harp: **3** nag **4** carp **5** bolon **6** string **8** clarsach, complain **10** tongue-lash
cousin: **4** lyre
on: **3** nag **4** push **5** press, rub in **6** ramble, repeat, stress **7** belabor, iterate **9** emphasize, reiterate
(on): **5** dwell **6** fixate
player: **5** angel
play the ~: **5** strum
sky ~: **4** Lyra
starter: **4** auto
tuner: **5** wrest
harp __: **4** seal **5** shell
__ harp: **4** jaw's, Jew's, wind **5** mouth **6** Aeolic, French **7** Aeolian
harper: **3** nag **8** minstrel, musician
Harper: **3** Lee **4** Tess **7** Frances, Jessica, Valerie
partner: **3** Row **7** Collins
Harper (1966 film)
cast: Lauren Bacall, Julie Harris, Paul Newman, Shelley Winters
Harper, Frances: **6** author, writer
work: Iola Leroy
Harper, Frances work: Iola Leroy
__ Harper Lee: **5** Nelle
Harper's: **3** mag **8** magazine
cartoonist: **4** Nast
Harper's Bazaar: **3** mag **8** magazine
artist: **4** Erté
Harpers Ferry
event: **4** raid
locale: **3** W.Va.
Harper, Valerie: **7** actress
film: Blame It on Rio (1984)
TV: Rhoda, The Hogan Family, The Mary Tyler Moore Show
Harper Valley P.T.A. (1968 song)
artist: Jeannie C. Riley
Harpies' sister: **4** Iris
Harpo: **4** Marx
brother of ~: **5** Chico, Gummo, Zeppo **7** Groucho
harpoon: **5** lance, spear **7** javelin
harpsichord: **7** cembalo **8** keyboard **10** instrument
harpsichordist: **9** Landowska
__ Harp, The: **5** Grass
Harp Weaver and Other Poems, The
author: Edna St. Vincent Millay
harpy: **3** hag **5** shrew, vixen **6** chider, virago **8** harridan, predator **9** henpecker, termagant, Xanthippe
like a ~: **6** grabby, greedy **7** hoggish, piggish **8** covetous, edacious, esurient, grasping **9** penurious **10** avaricious, gluttonous
Harpy: **5** Aello **7** Celaeno, Ocypete, Podarge
Harrah: **4** Bill, Toby **7** William
Harrah's: **6** casino
Harrah, Toby sport: **8** baseball
Harrelson: **3** Bud **5** Woody
Harrelson, Woody: **5** actor
film: Ed TV (1999)
The Hi-Lo Country (1998)
Indecent Proposal (1993)
Kingpin (1996)
Play It to the Bone (1999)
White Men Can't Jump (1992)
TV: Cheers
harridan: **3** hag, nag **5** crone, harpy, scold, shrew **6** beldam, chider, virago

7 beldame 8 battle-ax 9 battle-axe, henpecker, termagant
harried: 5 tense 9 pressured 10 overworked
harrier: 4 bird 5 bully, racer 6 runner
Harrier: 3 dog 5 canid 6 canine
Harriet: 3 spy 6 Monroe, Nelson, Tubman 7 Lothrop 8 Hilliard, Matineau 9 MacGibbon
husband: 5 Ozzie
son: 4 Rick 5 David, Ricky
Harriet Beecher __: 5 Stowe
Harriet Craig (1950 film)
cast: Wendell Corey, Joan Crawford
Harrigan composer: 5 Cohan
Harriman: 6 Pamela 7 Averell
Harrington: 3 Eve, Pat 7 Michael
Harris: 2 Ed 3 Lou, Mel 4 Neil, Phil, Rolf 5 Bucky, Julie, Major, Steve, Yulin 6 Franco, Wilson 7 Barbara, Emmylou, Estelle, Richard, William 8 Jonathan, Thurston
Harris __: 5 Tweed
Harris, Barbara: 7 actress
film: Family Plot (1976)
Freaky Friday (1977)
Plaza Suite (1971)
The Seduction of Joe Tynan (1979)
A Thousand Clowns (1965)
Harrisburg: 4 city, town 7 capital
county: 7 Dauphin
locale: 4 Penn.
Harris, Ed: 5 actor
film: Absolute Power (1997)
The Abyss (1989)
Apollo 13 (1995)
A Beautiful Mind (2001)
Enemy at the Gates (2001)
Glengarry Glen Ross (1992)
Jacknife (1989)
Knightriders (1981)
Nixon (1995)
Paris Trout (1991)
Places in the Heart (1984)
Pollock (2000)
The Right Stuff (1983)
The Rock (1996)
State of Grace (1990)
Sweet Dreams (1985)
The Third Miracle (1999)
The Truman Show (1998)
spouse: Amy Madigan
Harris, Franco sport: 8 football
Harris, Joel Chandler: 6 author, writer
character: Remus
honorific: Brer
work: The Tar-Baby
Harris, Julie: 7 actress
film: Brontë (1983)
East of Eden (1955)
Gorillas in the Mist (1988)
Harper (1966)
The Haunting (1963)
I Am a Camera (1955)
The Member of the Wedding (1952)
Harris, Mel: 7 actress
film: K-9 (1989)
Suture (1993)
TV: thirtysomething
Harrison: 3 Rex 4 city, Ford, town 6 George 7 Gregory, Wilbert 8 Benjamin, Jennilee
in Star Wars: 3 Han
locale: 7 New York 8 Michigan
Harrison, Benjamin: 9 president
alma mater: 5 Miami
former occupation: 6 lawyer
home: 4 Ohio 7 Indiana
opponent: 9 Cleveland
V.P.: 6 Morton
wife: 8 Caroline
Harrisonburg: 4 city, town
locale: 8 Virginia
Harrison, George
song: All Those Years Ago (1981)
Give Me Love (1973)
Got My Mind Set on You (1987)
Isn't It a Pity (1970)
My Sweet Lord (1970)
What Is Life (1971)
Harrison, Gregory: 5 actor
film: Air Bud: Golden Receiver (1998)
Fraternity Row (1977)
Groove (2000)
TV: Trapper John, M.D.
Harrison, Rex: 3 Sir 5 actor
film: Anna and the King of Siam (1946)
Blithe Spirit (1945)
The Citadel (1938)
Cleopatra (1963)
The Constant Husband (1955)
Doctor Dolittle (1967)
Escape (1948)
The Four Poster (1952)
The Ghost and Mrs. Muir (1947)
Major Barbara (1941)
Midnight Lace (1960)
My Fair Lady (1964, AA)
Sidewalks of London (1938)
Storm in a Teacup (1937)
Unfaithfully Yours (1948)
The Yellow Rolls-Royce (1964)
son: 4 Noel
spouse: Lilli Palmer
Harrison, Wilbert song: Kansas City (1959)
Harrison, William Henry: 9 president
former occupation: 7 soldier
home: 4 Ohio
opponent: 8 Van Buren
V.P.: 5 Tyler
wife: 4 Anna
Harris, Phil spouse: Alice Faye
Harris, Richard: 5 actor
film: The Cassandra Crossing (1977)
Cry, the Beloved Country (1995)
Harry Potter and the Sorcerer's Stone (2001)
Hawaii (1966)
Man in the Wilderness (1971)
Robin and Marian (1976)
This Sporting Life (1963)
Unforgiven (1992)
song: MacArthur Park (1968)
Harris, Rolf song: Tie Me Kangaroo Down, Sport (1963)
Harris, Thurston song: Little Bitty Pretty One (1957)
Harris Tweed: 6 fabric 8 material
Harris, Wilson: 6 author, writer 8 Guyanese
Harrod's conveyance: 4 lift
Harrold: 7 Kathryn
harrow: 4 disk, loot, pain, rack, rake, rend, rive, sack, till 6 ravage, strike 7 agonize, anguish, break up, despoil, pillage, plunder, torment, torture 8 distress, freeboot 9 cultivate, depredate 10 excruciate
blade: 4 disc, disk
Harrow: 6 school
rival: 4 Eton
harrowing: 6 tragic 7 painful, parlous, racking 8 alarming, chilling, dolorous, grievous, terrible, tragical 9 agonizing, appalling, dangerous, murderous, torturous, traumatic 10 disturbing, petrifying, terrifying, tormenting
Harrumph!: 3 bah, tut 4 ahem 5 pshaw
harry: 3 irk, nag, rag, rob, vex 4 fret, gall, raid, ride, sack 5 annoy, hound, strip, tease, upset, worry 6 badger, bother, harass, hassle, maraud, molest, noodge, pester, plague, pother, pursue, ravage 7 afflict, bedevil, disturb, oppress, perturb, pillage, plunder, ransack, torment, trouble 8 aggrieve, distress, irritate 9 beleaguer, devastate, persecute 10 discompose
Harry: 4 Cohn, Lime 5 Caray, Carey, James 6 Chapin, Debbie, Golden, Hamlin, Hooper, Jackée, Lauder, Morgan, Truman, Warren 7 Connick, Deborah, Houdini, Langdon, Nilsson, Shearer, Simeone, Von Zell 8 Anderson, Beaumont, Blackmun, Guardino, Helmsley, Kemelman, Matinson, Reasoner 9 Belafonte, Markowitz, Martinson 10 Blackstone
successor: 3 Ike
wife: 4 Bess
Harry __ Stanton: 4 Dean
__ Harry: 3 Old 5 Dirty
Harry and Tonto (1974 film)
cast: Ellen Burstyn, Art Carney, Chief Dan George
director: Paul Mazursky
Harry in Your Pocket (1973 film)
cast: James Coburn, Michael Sarrazin, Trish Van Devere
director: Bruce Geller
__ Harry Lee: 10 Light-Horse
__ Harry Met Sally ...: 4 When
Harry Potter
cat: 5 Snowy, Tufty 6 Mr. Paws 7 Tibbles 9 Mrs. Norris
Harry Potter and the Chamber of Secrets (2002 film)
cast: Richard Griffiths, Rupert Grint, Daniel Radcliffe, Emma Watson
director: Chris Columbus
Harry Potter and the Sorcerer's Stone (2001 film)
cast: Rupert Grint, Richard Harris, Daniel Radcliffe, Emma Watson
composer: 8 Williams
director: Chris Columbus
dog: 6 Fluffy
Harry, Prince: 5 royal 7 Windsor
aunt: 4 Anne
parent: 5 Diana 7 Charles
uncle: 6 Andrew, Edward
Harsanyi, John: 8 Nobelist 9 economist
harsh: 3 bad, raw 4 acid, grim, mean, rude 5 acerb, acrid, crude, cruel, gruff, heavy, husky, nasty, noisy, raspy, rigid, rough, sharp, stark, stern, stiff, tough 6 animal, biting, bitter, brutal, coarse, craggy, fierce, hoarse, jagged, morose, off-key, rugged, savage, severe, strict, unkind, wanton, wintry 7 abusive, acerbic, arduous, austere, beastly, callous, caustic, cragged, drastic, grating, hooting, hurtful, intense, jarring, onerous, raucous, Spartan, uncivil, vicious, wintery 8 abrasive, asperous, barbaric, clashing, despotic, exacting, fiendish, gravelly, grueling, guttural, inhumane, jangling, no picnic, pitiless, punitive, rigorous, ruthless, sadistic, scathing, strident, tactless, terrific, vengeful 9 cutthroat, dissonant, draconian, ferocious, hard-nosed, heartless, implicable, inclement, merciless, monstrous, stringent, truculent, unfeeling, unmusical, unpitying, unsparing 10 astringent, despotical, discordant, hard-boiled, inexorable, iron-willed, irritating, oppressive, relentless, ungracious, unpleasant, vindictive
criticism: 4 slam 5 blast 6 attack, earful, rebuke 7 censure, lecture, obloquy, reproof 8 berating, reproach, reproval 9 aspersion, reprimand, talking-to 10 bawling-out, upbraiding
cry: 3 caw 4 yaup, yawp
feeling: 4 gall 5 spite 6 enmity, hatred, malice, rancor, spleen 7 ill will, umbrage 8 acrimony, bad blood, contempt 9 animosity, antipathy, hostility, vengeance 10 resentment
in sound: 6 shrill 7 blaring, grating, raucous 8 piercing, strident 10 clangorous, discordant, screeching
not ~: 3 lax 4 calm, kind, mild 5 balmy 6 benign, genial, gentle, kindly, placid, remiss, serene, tender 7 affable, amiable, clement, lenient, pacific, patient, subdued, tactful 8 laid-back, merciful, moderate, peaceful, tolerant, tranquil, yielding 9 easygoing, sensitive, temperate 10 neglectful, permissive
old-style: 5 asper
harshly: 4 hard 5 rough 8 severely 9 viciously
harshness: 5 rigor 6 rancor 7 cruelty, discord 8 acrimony, asperity, hardness, iron hand, violence 9 austerity 10 bitterness, coarseness, dissonance, oppression, unkindness
hart: 4 deer, stag 6 animal
mate: 4 hind
part: 6 antler
Hart: 4 Gary, Mary, Moss 5 Bobby, Corey, Crane, Doris, Larry, Roxie 6 Johnny, Lorenz 7 Bochner, Dolores, Roxanne
Hartack, Bill: 6 jockey
milieu: 5 track
__ Hart Benton: 6 Thomas
hartebeest: 4 tora 6 animal, mammal 8 antelope
relative: 3 gnu, kob 4 guib, kudu, oryx, puku, topi 5 addax, bongo, chiru, eland, goral, korin, nyala, oribi, saiga, serow 6 chammy, dikdik, duiker, impala, koodoo, lechwe, nilgai, rhebok, shammy, shamoy 7 blaubok, blesbok, chamois, defassa, gazelle, gemsbok, gerenuk, grysbok, nylghai, nylghau, sassaby 8 blesbuck, bontebok, bushbuck, gemsbuck, reedbuck, steenbok, steinbok 9 blackbuck, pronghorn, sitatunga, springbok, waterbuck 10 wildebeest
Harte, Bret: 6 author, writer
collaborator: Twain
work: Ah Sin
The Luck of Roaring Camp
The Outcasts of Poker Flat
Hartford: 4 city, town
locale: 4 Conn.
newspaper: 7 Courant
rival: 5 Aetna 7 Met Life 9 State Farm
Hartley: 2 L.P. 3 Bob, Hal 8 Mariette
__-Hartley Act: 4 Taft
Hartley, L.P.: 6 author, writer 7 British
Hartline, Haldan: 8 Nobelist
Hart, Lorenz: 8 lyricist
collaborator: 7 Rodgers
musical: Babes in Arms
The Boys From Syracuse
By Jupiter
A Connecticut Yankee
Dearest Enemy
The Garrick Gaieties
The Girl Friend
Heads Up!
Higher and Higher
I'd Rather Be Right
I Married an Angel
Jumbo
On Your Toes
Pal Joey
Peggy-Ann
Present Arms
Simple Simon
Spring Is Here
Too Many Girls

Hartman: 3 Dan 4 Lisa, Mary, Phil 5 David 9 Elizabeth
Hartman, Dan song: I Can Dream About You (1984)
Hartman, Elizabeth: 7 actress
film: The Beguiled (1970)
Full Moon High (1981)
The Group (1966)
A Patch of Blue (1965)
You're a Big Boy Now (1966)
Hartman, Lisa spouse: Clint Black
Hart, Moss: 6 author, writer
collaborator: Kaufman, Weill, Berlin, Porter
spouse: Kitty Carlisle
work: Act One
Lady in the Dark
The Man Who Came to Dinner
Once in a Lifetime
You Can't Take It With You
Hartnett: 4 Josh 5 Gabby
Hartnett, Josh: 5 actor
film: Black Hawk Down (2001)
The Faculty (1998)
Halloween H20: 20 Years Later (1998)
O (2001)
Pearl Harbor (2001)
hart's-tongue: 4 fern
Hart's War (2002 film)
cast: Colin Farrell, Terrence Howard, Bruce Willis
director: Gregory Hoblit
Hart to Hart (ABC adventure)
cast: Stefanie Powers (Jennifer Hart)
Lionel Stander (Max)
Robert Wagner (Jonathan Hart)
dog: Freeway
Hartwell, Leland: 8 Nobelist
__ Harum: 6 Procol
harum-scarum: 4 rash 5 giddy, hasty 6 daring 7 chaotic, erratic, flighty 8 careless, reckless
Harum Scarum (1965 film)
cast: Michael Ansara, Mary Ann Mobley, Elvis Presley
haruspex: 4 seer 5 augur 7 diviner, prophet 10 soothsayer
Harvard: 3 sch. 4 coll., John, peak, univ. 5 mount 7 college 8 mountain
art museum: 4 Fogg
athletes: 7 Crimson
deg.: 3 MBA
league: 3 Ivy
locale: 4 Mass. 7 Rockies, Sawatch 8 Colorado 9 Cambridge
neighbor: 3 MIT
rival: 4 Yale
student: 6 Cantab
Harvard __: 4 Yard 5 beets, chair, frame
Harvarder rival: 3 Eli
Harve: 8 Presnell
harvest: 3 get 4 crop, cull, gain, pick, reap, stow 5 amass, cache, crops, fruit, glean, hoard, pluck, stash, store, yield 6 garner, gather, output, pile up, profit 7 collect, produce, reaping 8 fruition 9 garnering, gathering 10 accumulate, vegetables
Celtic ~ festival: 6 lammas
clean up after ~: 5 glean
farm ~: 4 corn 5 wheat
festival: 6 Kwanza
goddess: 3 Ops 5 Ceres
leavings: 5 chaff
machine: 5 baler 6 reaper
time: 3 Oct. 4 fall, Sept. 6 autumn 7 October 9 September
unit: 5 sheaf 6 bushel
harvest __: 3 fly 4 home, mite, moon, tick 5 index, mouse
__ Harvest: 6 Random
harvester: 6 farmer, reaper
harvester __: 3 ant
Harvest Home author: Thomas Tryon
Harvest Poems author: Carl Sandburg
Harvey: 4 city, Paul, town 5 Wiley 6 Keitel, Korman, Penick 7 Anthony, William 8 Laurence 9 Fierstein, Firestone
locale: 8 Illinois 9 Louisiana
Harvey (1950 film)
cast: Peggy Dow, Josephine Hull, James Stewart
character: 4 Dowd, Veta 6 Elwood
director: Henry Koster
Harvey Girls, The (1946 film)
cast: Ray Bolger, Judy Garland, John Hodiak
director: George Sidney
Harvey, Laurence: 5 actor
film: The Alamo (1960)
Butterfield 8 (1960)
Darling (1965)
I Am a Camera (1955)
The Manchurian Candidate (1962)
Room at the Top (1959)
The Running Man (1963)
Summer and Smoke (1961)
The Wonderful World of the Brothers Grimm (1962)
Harvey Wallbanger: 5 drink 8 beverage, cocktail
ingredient: 5 vodka 8 Galliano
Harz: 5 range 9 mountains
locale: 6 Europe 7 Germany
has-__: 4 been
__ Has a Birthday: 6 Eeyore
has-been: 5 loser, passé 8 outdated, outmoded 9 out-of-date
Hasbro product: 5 Furby, G.I. Joe 8 Scrabble
Hasbrouck __, NJ: 3 Hts.
Hasek, Jaroslav: 5 Czech 6 author, writer
hasenpfeffer: 4 stew
__ has fleas: 5 My dog
hash: 4 mess, muss, stew 5 mince 6 jumble, litter, medley, muddle, ragout 7 farrago, mélange, mixture 8 mishmash, scramble 9 leftovers, patchwork, potpourri 10 assortment, hodgepodge, miscellany, salmagundi
house: 5 diner 6 eatery 10 restaurant
make ~: 5 mince
make a ~ of: 4 flub, goof, muff 5 botch, gum up 6 bungle, foul up, goof up, mess up 7 louse up 9 mishandle, mismanage
over: 5 argue 6 debate, review 7 discuss 10 kick around
propel ~: 5 sling
slinger: 4 chef, cook
hash __: 3 out 4 mark 5 house 6 browns
hash-__: 7 slinger
__ Hashanah: 4 Rosh
Hashemite kingdom: 6 Jordan
hashhouse
client: 5 diner, eater 7 luncher
need: 5 grill
order: 4 eggs
sign: 4 Eats
see also diner, restaurant
Hasidic: 6 Jewish
leader: 5 rabbi, rebbe
mysticism: 6 cabala, kabala 7 cabbala, kabbala
__ has it...: 5 Rumor
Haskell: 5 Eddie
__ Has Landed, The: 5 Eagle
Has Man a Future? author: Bertrand Russell
hasn't: 5 lacks, needs
Has 1,001 __: 4 uses
hasp: 4 lock 5 catch, latch 7 bracket
Hassam, Childe: 6 artist 7 painter
hassar: 4 fish 7 catfish
Hasselhoff: 5 David
Hassel, Odd: 7 chemist 8 Nobelist
hassle: 3 bug, nag, row, vex 4 flap, fuss, rile, to-do 5 annoy, fight, harry, hound, mix up, press, run-in, scrap, trial, upset, whirl, worry 6 badger, bicker, bother, burden, clamor, harass, hubbub, lather, noodge, pester, plague, stress, strife, tsuris, tumult, tussle, uproar 7 dispute, problem, quarrel, quibble, rhubarb, trouble, tsouris, turmoil, wrangle 8 argument, hard time, headache, irritant, nuisance, pressure, squabble, struggle, vexation 9 annoyance, commotion, tight spot 10 difficulty, hullabaloo
hassock: 4 pouf 5 squab 7 cricket, cushion, ottoman, taboret 8 footrest, tabouret 9 footstool
Hasso, Signe: 7 actress
film: A Double Life (1947)
The House on 92nd St. (1945)
Johnny Angel (1945)
The Seventh Cross (1944)
Thieves' Holiday (1946)
To the Ends of the Earth (1948)
Where There's Life ... (1947)
Hass, Robert: 4 poet
hasta __: 5 luego 6 mañana 7 la vista
hasta la vista: 3 bye 4 ciao, ta-ta 5 adieu, adios, aloha, later 6 bye-bye, shalom, so long 7 cheerio, goodbye 8 au revoir, farewell, sayonara, toodle-oo
hasta luego
see hasta la vista
haste: 4 dash, rush 5 hurry, press, speed 6 bustle, flurry, hustle, scurry 7 urgency 8 alacrity, celerity, dispatch, rapidity, rashness, velocity 9 briskness, fleetness, quickness, swiftness 10 expedition, impatience, promptness
in ~: 7 quickly, rapidly, swiftly 8 on the run, speedily 9 hurriedly
in great ~: 5 amain
make ~: 3 fly, hie, run, zip 4 rush 5 hurry, scoot, speed 7 quicken 8 hightail, scramble 10 get hopping
product: 5 waste
without ~: 4 slow 6 calmly, casual, lazily, slowly 7 relaxed 8 casually, laid-back 9 gradually, leisurely, unhurried
__ haste: 4 make
Haste makes waste: 5 adage
hasten: 3 fly, hie, rip, run, zip 4 bolt, dart, dash, flee, flit, push, race, rush, skip, tear, zoom 5 bound, hurry, press, scoot, shoot, speed, whisk 6 barrel, bustle, gallop, hustle, move it, rocket, scurry, sprint, step up 7 advance, floor it, forward, further, hop to it, quicken, scamper, speed up 8 dispatch, expedite, hightail, scramble, snap to it, step on it 9 go forward, go swiftly, hotfoot it, shake a leg, skedaddle 10 accelerate, get a move on, get hopping, hightail it, make tracks
hastily: 3 PDQ 4 fast, soon 5 apace, madly, quick, short 6 presto 7 briefly, flat out, rapidly, swiftly 8 chop-chop, in a flash, in a hurry, in a jiffy, in no time, on the fly, on the run, pell-mell, promptly 9 forthwith, headfirst, instantly, like a shot 10 in high gear
Hastings: 4 city, town 6 battle
locale: 6 Sussex 7 England 8 Nebraska
Hast thou __ the Jabberwock?: 5 slain
__ Has Two Faces, The: 6 Mirror
hasty: 3 lax 4 fast, rash, rush 5 blind, brash, brief, brisk, fleet, quick, rapid, swift 6 abrupt, flying, little, madcap, prompt, racing, remiss, rushed, sloppy, snappy, speedy, sudden, unwary 7 cursory, express, hurried, instant, quickie 8 careless, headlong, heedless, pell-mell, reckless, slapdash, slipshod, tactless, unsubtle 9 breakneck, desperate, foolhardy, impatient, impetuous, imprudent, impulsive, momentary, negligent, premature, unadvised, uncareful, unmindful, whirlwind 10 double-time, hypersonic, ill-advised, incautious, indiscreet, nonchalant, supersonic, unthinking
make a ~ escape: 5 lam it
retreat: 3 lam 6 escape, flight 7 getaway
hasty __: 7 pudding
__ hasty retreat: 5 beat a
hat: 3 cap, lid, tam 4 kepi, topi 5 beret, derby, gibus, miter, toque 6 beaver, bicorn, boater, bonnet, bowler, cloche, fedora, helmet, hennin, Panama, sailor, topper, trilby, turban 7 bicorne, burnous, chapeau, leghorn, petasus, pillbox, porkpie, skimmer, Stetson, tricorn 8 burnoose, coonskin, covering, headgear, jipijapa, snap-brim, sombrero, tricorne 9 sou'wester, stovepipe, sunbonnet, ten-gallon 10 pith helmet
attachment: 4 veil
bad ~: 3 cad 5 knave, scamp, skunk 6 rascal 8 picaroon, recreant, scalawag 9 reprobate, scoundrel 10 blackguard, ne'er-do-well, scapegrace
brass ~: 4 boss 6 top dog 7 manager 8 employer, superior 9 executive 10 supervisor
brimless ~: 3 tam 5 beret, toque
broad-brimmed ~: 5 terai
decoration: 5 plume
ender: 3 box, pin 4 band 5 check
felt ~: 3 fez 5 terai
flat ~: 3 tam 5 beret
French ~: 5 beret
hang one's ~: 4 live 5 dwell 6 locate, reside
hard ~: 5 labor 6 helmet
holder: 4 head
jaunty ~: 3 cap
material: 4 felt 5 straw 6 beaver
military ~: 4 kepi 5 busby, shako 6 helmet
old ~: 4 dull 5 corny, dated, dowdy, hokey, musty, passé, stale, trite, vapid 6 common, jejune 7 archaic, clichéd, fatuous, humdrum, outworn, prosaic 8 bromidic 9 hackneyed, played out, prosaical 10 antiquated, out of style, uninspired, unoriginal
part: 4 brim 5 visor, vizor 6 earlap
pass the ~: 3 beg 7 collect, solicit
Pope's ~: 5 miter
soft ~: 3 tam 5 beret
starter: 4 hard
straw ~: 6 boater
sun ~: 4 topi 5 topee
tip one's ~ to: 4 hail 5 cheer, greet, honor 6 praise, salute 7 applaud, commend 10 compliment
tipper's word: 4 ma'am
under one's ~: 6 hidden 7 private 9 concealed
where one hangs one's ~: 3 pad 4 home 5 abode, house 7 lodging 8 domicile, dwelling 9 residence
woman's ~: 5 toque 6 Breton, cloche
hat __: 4 tree 5 check, dance, trick
__ hat: 3 old, red, tin, top, war 4 fire, hard, high, iron, plug, silk 5 black,

brass, cooly, gibus, opera, straw, terai, white **6** cocked, coolie, cowboy, kettle, Panama, shovel, slouch **7** picture, pillbox, scarlet
__-hat: 4 hard, high
__ Hat: 3 Top
Hatari! (1962 film)
cast: Red Buttons, Elsa Martinelli, John Wayne
composer: 7 Mancini
director: Howard Hawks
hatch: 3 lay **4** brew, door, make, plan, plot **5** brood, cause, frame, get up, sit on, spawn **6** cook up, create, derive, design, devise, invent, make up, scheme, spring, whip up, work up **7** concoct, dream up, ingress, opening, prepare, produce, think up, trump up **8** conceive, contrive, engender, generate, incubate, trapdoor **9** floodgate, formulate, machinate, originate, reproduce **10** brainstorm, bring forth, come up with
as an idea: 4 brew, form **6** cook up, create, devise, invent, make up **7** concoct, develop, dream up
down the ~: 5 toast
ender: 3 way **4** back
starter: 3 nut **5** cross
__ hatch: 5 booby **6** escape
Hatch: 5 Orrin **6** Wilbur
hatchback: 3 car **4** auto **10** automobile
cousin: 5 sedan
hatched: 4 born
Hatcher, Teri: 7 actress
costar: 4 Cain
film: Fever (2001)
Tomorrow Never Dies (1997)
role: 4 Lane, Lois
TV: Lois & Clark
hatchery
sound: 4 peep **5** cheep, chirp, tweet
unit: 3 egg
__ hatchery: 4 fish
__ Hatches the Egg: 6 Horton
hatchet: 2 ax **3** axe **4** tool **5** hewer **8** tomahawk
aborigine ~: 4 mogo
bury the ~: 5 agree **6** make up, pardon **7** forgive **9** negotiate, reconcile
handle: 4 haft
man: 5 firer **6** flunky **8** henchman
use a ~: 3 cut, hew **4** chop
hatchet __: 3 job, man
__ hatchet: 5 broad **7** lathing
hatchetlike tool: 3 zax
hatchling: 4 baby, bird **5** chick
home: 4 nest
identifier: 5 sexer
hatchlings: 5 brood, covey
Hatch, Orrin: 7 senator
state: 4 Utah
hatchway: 4 door, exit **5** entry **6** portal **8** entrance
__-hat cymbals: 4 high
__ hat dance: 7 Mexican
hate: 4 loth **5** abhor, dread, loath, odium, scorn, spite, venom, wrath **6** animus, detest, enmity, loathe, malice, rancor, spleen **7** bigotry, contemn, deplore, despise, disdain, disgust, dislike, ill will **8** aversion, distaste, execrate, loathing **9** abominate, animosity, antipathy, deprecate, disrelish, hostility, revulsion **10** abhorrence, antagonism, execration, flinch from, repugnance, resentment
combining form: 3 mis- **4** miso-
old-style: 5 spise
opposite: 4 love
hate __: 4 mail **5** crime
hated: 7 unloved **9** unpopular
hateful: 4 cold, cool, evil, foul, mean, vile **5** awful, catty, cruel, curst, gross, lousy, nasty, onery, snide, surly **6** bitter, chilly, cursed, horrid, malign, odious, ornery, remote, unkind **7** accurst, blasted, cutting, glacial, heinous, hideous, hostile, inhuman, satanic, vicious **8** abrasive, accursed, annoying, contrary, infamous, inhumane, inimical, shocking, spiteful, terrible, venomous, virulent **9** abhorrent, bellicose, execrable, invidious, loathsome, malicious, obnoxious, offensive, rancorous, repellent, repugnant, repulsive, revolting, satanical, truculent **10** abominable, confounded, despicable, detestable, disgusting, malevolent, pugnacious, vindictive
hatefulness: 5 spite, wrath **6** malice, rancor **7** disgust
hater: 5 bigot **9** miscreant **10** misogynist
work ~: 5 drone **6** loafer, rascal, truant **7** dawdler, laggard, shirker, slacker **8** parasite **9** do-nothing, goldbrick, lazybones **10** ne'er-do-well
__-hate relationship: 4 love
Hatfield: 4 Mark
to a McCoy: 3 foe **5** enemy
Hatfields: 4 clan
Hatful of Rain, A (1957 film)
cast: Tony Franciosa, Don Murray, Eva Marie Saint
director: Fred Zinnemann
hath: 4 owns
hatha-__: 4 yoga
Hathaway: 4 Anne **5** Donny, Henry, shirt
competitor: 4 Izod
on Steve Allen's show: 3 Nye
Hathaway, Donny
song: The Closer I Get to You (1978)
Where Is the Love (1972)
Hathaway, Henry: 8 director
film: 23 Paces to Baker Street (1956)
Call Northside 777 (1948)
The Dark Corner (1946)
The Desert Fox (1951)
Diplomatic Courier (1952)
Down to the Sea in Ships (1949)
Fourteen Hours (1951)
Go West, Young Man (1936)
Home in Indiana (1944)
The House on 92nd St. (1945)
How the West Was Won (1962)
Johnny Apollo (1940)
Kiss of Death (1947)
The Lives of a Bengal Lancer (1935)
Nevada Smith (1966)
Niagara (1953)
North to Alaska (1960)
Peter Ibbetson (1935)
The Real Glory (1939)
Seven Thieves (1960)
Shepherd of the Hills (1941)
The Sons of Katie Elder (1965)
Souls at Sea (1937)
Spawn of the North (1938)
Ten Gentlemen From West Point (1942)
The Trail of the Lonesome Pine (1936)
True Grit (1969)
Wing and a Prayer (1944)
hat-in-hand type: 6 beggar **8** deadbeat **9** mendicant **10** panhandler, supplicant
Hatlo, Jimmy: 10 cartoonist
hatrack: 7 antlers
hatred: 5 odium, pique, scorn, spite, venom **6** animus, enmity, grudge, malice, phobia, rancor, spleen **7** disdain, disgust, dislike, ill will **8** acrimony, aversion, bad blood, contempt, distaste, ignominy, loathing **9** animosity, antipathy, hostility, militancy, repulsion, revulsion **10** abhorrence, antagonism, bitterness, execration, repugnance, unkindness
Hats Off to Larry (1961 song) artist: Del Shannon
hatter: 8 milliner
__ Hatter: 3 Mad
__ Hatteras, NC: 4 Cape
Hatters: 7 Stetson
__ Hat, The: 5 Green
Hattie: 8 McDaniel
__ Hattie: 6 Panama
Hattiesburg: 4 city, town
locale: 4 Miss.
school: 3 USM
hat-trick part: 4 goal
__ Hat, White Tie and Tails: 3 Top
hauberk: 5 shirt
Hauer: 6 Rutger
haughtiness: 4 airs **5** pride, scorn **6** hubris, hybris
haughty: 3 big **4** smug, vain **5** aloof, cocky, lofty, proud, regal **6** lordly, sniffy, snooty, stuffy **7** fustian, pompous, stately, stuck-up **8** arrogant, assuming, boastful, cavalier, kinglike, scornful, snobbish, superior **9** big-headed, conceited, egotistic, hubristic, imperious **10** disdainful, hoity-toity
be ~: 4 snub **7** disdain
one: 4 snob
response: 5 never, sniff
haul: 3 bag, lug, tow, tug **4** cart, drag, draw, load, loot, move, pack, pelf, pull, ship, swag, take, tote **5** booty, bring, cargo, carry, catch, heave, prize, shlep, trail, truck **6** bagful, convey, lading, schlep, shlepp **7** freight, plunder **8** cart away, transfer **9** transport
away: 3 tow **4** drag **9** transport
heist ~: 4 take **5** booty **7** plunder
in: 3 nab **4** take **6** arrest
in for the long ~: 6 stable **7** abiding, durable, lasting **8** enduring **9** permanent, unabating
long ~: 4 trek **6** battle **7** journey, odyssey **8** struggle **10** pilgrimage
off on: 4 belt, slug, swat **5** punch, smash, thump, whack **6** assail, attack, strike, wallop **7** assault, bombard, clobber, lay into **8** lace into **9** light into
on board: 4 lade, load
over the coals: 5 roast
short ~: 3 hop, run **5** jaunt **6** outing **7** day trip
starter: 3 box **4** down, keel
up: 4 heft, lift **5** boost, hoist, raise **7** elevate
haul __: 3 off
__ haul: 4 long **5** short
haulable: 7 movable **8** portable
hauler: 3 van **4** cart, dray, semi, tram, wain **5** toter, truck, wagon **7** trucker **8** teamster
British ~: 5 lorry
haul in one's __: 5 horns
haulm: 5 stalk
haul over the __: 5 coals
haunch: 3 hip **4** rump, side **5** flank, thigh
haunt: 3 bar, den, dog, vex **4** dive, lair, nest, site **5** beset, hound, joint, lodge, prowl, shade, spook, stalk, visit **6** fantom, locale, madden, obsess, plague, prey on, pursue **7** bedevil, besiege, hangout, phantom, purlieu, retreat, terrify, torment, trouble, weigh on **8** frequent, frighten, locality **9** clubhouse, habituate, hang out at, terrorize **10** hang around, rendezvous, scare stiff
haunted: 4 eery **5** eerie **7** ghostly **8** obsessed **9** possessed, unearthly
like a ~ house: 5 eerie **6** creepy, spooky **7** macabre **8** chilling
Haunted __, The: 4 Mesa **6** Palace
haunted-house
feature: 5 ghost, spook **6** cobweb
feeling: 4 fear **5** alarm, angst, dread, panic **6** fright, horror, terror
sound: 4 moan **5** creak
Haunted Palace, The author: Edgar Allan Poe
haunting: 4 eery **5** eerie, weird **6** spooky **7** nagging **9** memorable, nostalgic, obsessive, recurrent **10** persistent
Haunting, The (1963 film)
cast: Claire Bloom, Julie Harris
director: Robert Wise
Haunts (1977 film)
cast: May Britt, Cameron Mitchell, Aldo Ray
Hauppauge: 4 city, town
locale: 7 New York **10** Long Island
Hauptman, Herbert: 7 chemist **8** Nobelist
Hauptmann, Gerhart: 6 German, writer **8** Nobelist **10** playwright
haus: 5 abode, house **6** German
the lady of the ~: 4 frau
Hausa home: 5 Niger **6** Africa **7** Nigeria
Hauser: 5 Wings
haut __: 5 monde
Haut-__: 4 Rhin
hautboy: 4 oboe, reed, wind **10** instrument
haute: 4 chic **5** fancy, swank **6** chichi, classy, lavish, swanky **7** elegant, genteel, refined, stylish, voguish **9** luxurious
monde: 6 gentry, jet set **7** society, who's who **10** upper class, upper crust
haute __: 5 école, monde **7** couture, cuisine
Haute-__: 5 Loire, Marne, Saône **6** Savoie, Vienne **7** Garonne
haute couture
designer: 4 Dior
magazine: 4 Elle **5** Vogue
__ Haute, IN: 5 Terre
Hautes-__: 5 Alpes
Haute-Savoie
range: 5 Alpes
spa: 5 Evian
hauteur: 4 airs, gall **5** nerve, pride **6** vanity **7** conceit, dignity, disdain, egotism **8** audacity, contempt, elegance, noblesse **9** arrogance, pomposity **10** narcissism, self-esteem
show ~ toward: 4 snub
with ~: 5 icily
haut monde: 5 elite
Havana: 4 city, port, town **5** cigar, smoke **7** capital
castle: 5 Morro
locale: 4 Cuba
see also Spanish
Havana (1990 film)
cast: Alan Arkin, Lena Olin, Robert Redford
director: Sydney Pollack
Havana Brown: 3 cat **5** felid **6** feline
Havanese: 3 dog **5** canid **6** canine
Havant: 4 city, town
locale: 7 England **9** Hampshire
__ Havasu City: 4 Lake
Havasupai: 6 Indian **7** Amerind
have: 3 con, eat, get, own **4** bear, dupe, gain, hold, keep, land, rook, take **5** beget, carry, cheat, enjoy, grasp, ought, solve, stock, trick, wield **6** embody, endure, evince, imbody,

obtain, outfox, outwit, permit, pick up, retain, secure, suffer, take in **7** acquire, carry on, contain, deceive, deliver, exhibit, feature, include, involve, possess, procure, receive, subsume, swindle, two-time, undergo **8** comprise, engage in, exercise, hoodwink, maintain, outsmart, tolerate **9** bamboozle, encompass, get hold of, latch onto, partake of, put up with, victimize **10** experience, keep on hand, monopolize
a ball: **4** romp **5** party **9** celebrate
a bug: **3** ail
a crush on: **4** like **5** adore
a long face: **4** mope, pout
a look at: **3** eye, see
a yearning: **4** ache
bills: **3** owe
coming: **4** earn **5** merit
dinner: **3** eat, sup **5** feast
down cold: **4** know
importance: **4** rate **6** matter
literally: **6** habeas
no doubts: **4** know
relevance: **6** relate
the nerve: **4** dare
words: **5** argue **6** bicker
have __: **4** a cow, a fit **5** a ball, a care, a go at, a seat, a talk, had it, it out, words
have __ a mind to: **4** half
have __ at: **3** a go **5** a shot
have __ day: **5** an off
have __ for: **4** a yen, eyes, it in **5** a feel, a need, an eye, no use
have __ for news: **5** a nose
have __ good authority: **4** it on
have __ in: **4** a say **5** a hand
have __ in common: **4** a lot
have __ in one's bonnet: **4** a bee
have __ in one's eyes: **5** stars
have __ in the hole: **5** an ace
have __ mind to: **5** a good, half a
have __ of: **4** none
have __ of tea: **5** a spot
have __ on: **4** pity
have __ on one's shoulder: **5** a chip
have __-see: **5** a look
have __ spot for: **5** a soft
have __ to: **5** a mind
have __ to eat: **5** a bite
have __ to grind: **4** an ax **5** an axe
have __ to pick: **5** a bone
have __ to play: **5** a role
have __ to the ground: **5** an ear
have __ up one's sleeve: **5** an ace
have __ with: **4** an in, a way, done, to do **5** a word
have-__: **3** not
Have __ and safe holiday: **5** a sane
Have __ and sane holiday: **5** a safe
Have __ day!: **5** a good, a nice **6** a great
Have __ girl for you!: **5** I got a
Have __ news for you!: **4** I got
Have __ Will Travel: **3** Gun
have a __: **4** ball, go at, seat **5** heart
have a __ at: **4** shot **5** whack
have a __ for news: **4** nose
have a __ in: **4** hand
have a __ in one's bonnet: **3** bee
have a __ in the pie: **6** finger
have a __ it: **4** go at
have a __ mind to: **4** good
have a __ on: **6** handle
have a __ one's bonnet: **5** bee in
have a __ skin: **4** thin **5** thick
have a __ stand on: **5** leg to
have a __ to pick: **4** bone
have a __ with: **3** way **4** word
Have a __ day!: **4** good, nice **5** great
have a bee in one's __: **6** bonnet
have a bone to __: **4** pick
have a finger in the __: **3** pie
have a go __: **4** at it
have a good __ to: **4** mind
have an __ for: **3** eye
have an __ grind: **4** ax to **5** axe to
have an __ one's sleeve: **5** ace up
have an __ the ground: **5** ear to
have an __ to grind: **3** axe
have an __ to the ground: **3** ear
have an ax to __: **5** grind
have an ear to the __: **6** ground
Have a nice __!: **3** day
have a nose __ news: **3** for
__ Have Another Cup of Coffee: **4** Let's
Have a taste!: **5** try it
have a thick __: **4** skin
have a thin __: **4** skin
have a way __: **4** with
have a word __: **4** with
__ have been changed..., The: **5** names
__ have ears, The: **5** walls
have eyes __: **3** for
__ have eyes for: **4** only
__ Have Eyes for You: **5** I Only
Have Gun Will Travel (CBS western)
cast: Richard Boone (Paladin)
have half __ to: **5** a mind
have it __: **3** out **4** made **5** in for **7** knocked
have it in __: **3** for
Have I Told You Lately (1993 song) artist: Rod Stewart
have it on __ authority: **4** good
__ have it, the: **4** ayes
__ have it, The: **4** ayes, nays
Havel: **5** river
city on the ~: **6** Berlin **7** Potsdam
locale: **7** Germany
Havelock: **4** city, town **5** Ellis
locale: **4** N. Car.
Havel, Václav: **4** poet **5** Czech **10** playwright
work: The Garden Party
Letters to Olga
The Memorandum
haven: **4** port **5** cover, oasis **6** asylum, harbor, refuge, resort, shield **7** harbour, hideout, retreat, sanctum, shelter **9** anchorage, harborage, hermitage, sanctuary **10** ivory tower, protection, safe harbor
safe ~: **4** nest
__ haven: **3** tax **4** safe
__ Haven: **3** New **4** West **6** Winter
have no __ for: **3** use **5** words
__ Have No Bananas: **5** Yes! We
have-not: **6** beggar, pauper **8** indigent **9** mendicant
__ Have Nothing: **4** I Who
condition: **7** poverty
have no use __: **3** for
have no words __: **3** for
Havens: **6** Richie
haven't: **4** lack
Haven't Got Time for the Pain (1974 song) artist: Carly Simon
have one's __: **3** say **5** eye on **6** number
have one's __ about one: **4** wits
have one's __ court: **5** day in
have one's __ crossed: **7** fingers
have one's __ on: **3** eye
have one's __ set on: **5** heart
have one's __ tied: **5** hands
have one's fingers __: **7** crossed
have one's hands __: **4** tied
have one's heart __ on: **3** set
Haverhill: **4** city, town
locale: **4** Mass.
Haver, June spouse: Fred MacMurray
havers: **3** gas, rot **4** blah, bosh, bull, bunk, guff, jazz, jive, pooh, tosh **5** bilge, fudge, hokum, hooey, prate, stuff, trash, tripe **6** bunkum, bushwa, drivel, footle, gabble, gammon, gibber, hot air, humbug, jabber, jargon, kibosh, piffle **7** baloney, blarney, blather, blether, boloney, bushwah, eyewash, flannel, flubdub, fustian, garbage, hogwash, inanity, rubbish, twaddle **8** buncombe, claptrap, falderal, falderol, flimflam, flummery, folderal, folderol, nonsense, slipslop, tommyrot, trumpery **9** banana oil, gibberish, kidstakes, moonshine, poppycock, rigmarole **10** applesauce, balderdash, bilge water, codswallop, double-talk, flapdoodle, galimatias, Jabberwock, mumbo jumbo, rigamarole, taradiddle
Havers: **5** Nigel
haversack: **3** bag **4** pack **6** kitbag **8** knapsack **9** duffelbag
haves: **4** rich **5** elite **6** jet set **7** fat cats
one of the ~: **5** nabob **6** tycoon **7** magnate **9** plutocrat
have stars in one's __: **4** eyes
have the __ laugh: **4** last
have the __ of: **4** best
have the __ of it: **5** worst
have the __ on: **4** drop, jump **5** goods
have the last __: **5** laugh
have the worst __: **4** of it
__ have to?: **3** Do I
__ have to do!: **4** It'll
__ Have to Do Is Dream: **4** All I
__ have you: **4** what
...have you __ wool?: **3** any
Have You __ Her?: **4** Seen
Have You Ever? (1998 song) artist: Brandy
Have You Ever Really Loved a Woman? (1995 song) artist: Bryan Adams
Have You Ever Seen the Rain (1971 song) artist: Creedence Clearwater Revival
Have You Never Been Mellow (1975 song) artist: Olivia Newton-John
Have Yourself a __ Little Christmas: **5** Merry
Have You Seen Her (1971 song) artist: Chi-Lites
Have You Seen Her (1990 song) artist: M.C. Hammer
Have You Seen Your Mother, Baby? (1966 song) artist: Rolling Stones
Have you two __?: **3** met
__ Having a Baby: **4** She's
__ having fun yet?: **5** Are we
Having My Baby (1974 song) artist: Paul Anka
Havlicek, John: **5** cager
milieu: **5** court
org.: **3** NBA
sport: **10** basketball
havoc: **4** mess, ruin **5** chaos, waste **6** mayhem **7** carnage, debacle **8** calamity, disorder, shambles, wreckage **9** cataclysm, confusion, mobocracy, ruination **10** desolation
cause ~: **5** wreak, wreck
wreak ~ on: **4** loot, raid, ruin, sack **5** rifle, spoil, strip, waste, wreck **6** harrow, maraud, ravage **7** despoil, destroy, pillage, plunder, ransack **9** depredate, desecrate, devastate, vandalize
__ havoc: **3** cry **5** wreak
Havoc: **4** June
sister: **3** Lee **9** Gypsy Rose
__ 'Havoc': **3** Cry
Havoline competitor: **3** STP
Havre de Grace: **4** city, town
locale: **8** Maryland
haw: **5** dally, demur **8** hesitate **10** dilly-dally, equivocate
cousin: **2** er, uh, um
direction: **4** left
ender: **4** king **5** finch, thorn
hem and ~: **4** sway, vary **5** dodge, evade, hedge, shift, stall, waver **6** falter, waffle **7** quibble, stammer, whiffle **8** hesitate **9** fluctuate, pussyfoot, vacillate **10** equivocate
opposite: **3** gee
partner: **3** hem
__ haw: **4** pear **5** black **6** poison, possum
Haw.
once: **3** ter. **4** terr.
see also Hawaii
__ Haw: **3** Hee
Hawaii: **3** isl. **4** film, isle, saga **5** novel, state **6** island
author: James A. Michener
bird: **2** oo **4** nene, omao **5** alala, koloa, shama **7** elepaio
carving: **4** tiki
carving material: **4** lava
cast: Julie Andrews, Richard Harris, Max von Sydow
celebration: **6** Lei Day
city: **3** Ewa **4** Aiea, Hana, Hilo **6** Kailua **7** Kahului, Kaneohe, Waimalu, Waipahu **8** Honolulu, Mililani
coffee region: **4** Kona
conference: **3** WAC
County seat: **4** Hilo
dance: **4** hula **8** hula-hula
director: George Roy Hill
dish: **3** poi
dress: **6** muumuu
feast: **4** luau
first governor: **4** Dole
fish: **4** mano, ulae **5** akule, moano **8** mahimahi
flower: **5** lehua
goodbye: **5** aloha
goose: **4** nene
gooseberry: **4** poha
hardwood: **4** ohia **5** lehua
hark: **4** mano
hello: **5** aloha
honcho: **6** kahuna
honeycreeper: **4** iiwi
honey-eater: **2** oo
hors d'oeuvre: **4** pupu
instrument: **3** uke **7** ukulele
island: **4** Maui, Oahu **5** Kauai, Lanai
islet: **6** Laysan
long, in ~: **3** loa
major employer: **4** Dole
mountain: **5** Mauna
national park: **9** Haleakala
native: **6** kanaka
necklace shell: **4** puka
neckpiece: **3** lei
nickname: **10** Aloha State
not at all, in ~: **4** aole
once: **3** ter. **4** terr. **9** territory
port: **4** Hilo **8** Honolulu
region: **4** Kona
shark: **4** mano
shrub: **4** poha **5** aalii, akala, olona
state bird: **4** nene
state flower: **8** hibiscus
state gem: **10** black coral
steep slope: **4** pali
tree: **3** koa **5** kukui, lehua
tuna: **3** ahi
vine: **5** maile
volcano: **7** Kilauea **8** Mauna Loa
waterfall: **5** Akaka
wind: **4** Kona
Hawaii __: **4** time **5** Five-O
Hawaii __ College: **3** Loa
__ Hawaii: **4** Blue
Hawaiian __: **3** Eye **4** hawk, high

5 goose, Punch, shirt 6 guitar, Pidgin 7 Islands
Hawaiian Punch rival: 3 HiC
Hawaiians, The (1970 film)
cast: Geraldine Chaplin, Charlton Heston, John Phillip Law
Hawaiian Wedding Song, The (1959 song) artist: Andy Williams
Hawaii Five-O (CBS drama, song)
artist: Ventures
cast: Jack Lord (Steve McGarrett) James MacArthur (Danny Dano/Danno Williams)
setting: 4 Oahu 8 Honolulu
villain: Wo Fat
hawfinch: 4 bird
haw-haw: 5 laugh 6 guffaw
__ Haw-Haw: 4 Lord
hawing, hemming and: 8 hesitant, waffling, wavering 9 dithering, equivocal, tentative, undecided, unsettled 10 ambivalent, indecisive, irresolute, of two minds, on the fence, unresolved, up in the air, wishy-washy
hawk: 4 bird, kite, push, sell, vend 5 buteo 6 elanet, falcon, market, osprey, peddle 7 buzzard, harrier, kestrel, lookout, solicit 9 advertise, hardliner, warmonger 10 bird of prey
attack like a ~: 5 swoop 7 descend, plummet 9 sweep down
female: 3 hen
home: 4 aery, eyry, nest 5 aerie, eyrie
leash: 4 lune
male: 7 tiercel
opposite: 4 dove
relative: 5 eagle
starter: 5 Black, night
trap: 6 bownet
young: 4 eyas
hawk __: 3 owl 4 moth
hawk-__: 4 eyed
__ hawk: 3 hen, war 4 ball, duck, fish 5 marsh 6 pigeon 7 chicken, Cooper's, passage, skeeter, sparrow
Hawk: 3 car 4 auto 10 Studebaker
__ Hawk: 5 Black, Kitty 6 Baker's
Hawke: 5 Ethan 10 Youngblood
Hawke, Ethan: 5 actor
film: Alive (1993)
Dead Poets Society (1989)
Floundering (1994)
Gattaca (1997)
Great Expectations (1998)
A Midnight Clear (1992)
Reality Bites (1994)
Tape (2001)
Training Day (2001)
White Fang (1991)
spouse: Uma Thurman
hawker: 5 crier 6 pedlar, pedler, seller, vender, vendor 7 peddler 8 huckster 10 proclaimer
starter: 3 jay
talk: 5 spiel
Hawkes: 4 John 7 Chesney
Hawkes, John: 6 author, writer
Hawkeye: 5 Iowan 6 Pierce
milieu: 4 MASH
portrayer: Alan Alda, Donald Sutherland
Hawkeye State: 4 Iowa
Hawking: 7 Stephen
Hawkins: 4 Jack, John 5 Sadie 7 Coleman
Hawkins, Coleman: 11 saxophonist
genre: 4 jazz
__ Hawkins Day: 5 Sadie
Hawkins, Jack: 5 actor
film: Ben-Hur (1959)
The Bridge on the River Kwai (1957)
Crash of Silence (1953)
The Cruel Sea (1953)
Lawrence of Arabia (1962)
The Prisoner (1955)
The Small Back Room (1949)
The Third Key (1956)
Zulu (1964)
spouse: Jessica Tandy
hawkish: 7 hostile, martial, warlike 8 militant 9 bellicose, combative 10 aggressive, pugnacious
__ Hawk, NC: 5 Kitty
hawk's-__ quartz: 3 eye
Hawks: 4 five, team 6 Howard
city: 7 Atlanta
former home: 4 Omni
home: 3 Atl 7 Atlanta, Georgia
org.: 3 NBA
sport: 10 basketball
hawksbill: 6 animal 7 reptile
hawkshaw: 3 tec 6 shamus, sleuth 7 gumshoe 9 detective
Hawks, Howard: 8 director
film: Air Force (1943)
Ball of Fire (1941)
Barbary Coast (1935)
The Big Sky (1952)
The Big Sleep (1946)
Bringing Up Baby (1938)
Ceiling Zero (1935)
Come and Get It (1936)
El Dorado (1967)
Gentlemen Prefer Blondes (1953)
Hatari! (1962)
His Girl Friday (1940)
I Was a Male War Bride (1949)
Monkey Business (1952)
Only Angels Have Wings (1939)
Red River (1948)
Rio Bravo (1959)
Rio Lobo (1970)
The Road to Glory (1936)
Scarface (1932)
Sergeant York (1941)
Tiger Shark (1932)
To Have and Have Not (1944)
Twentieth Century (1934)
__ Hawk, The: 3 Sea
__ Hawk War: 5 Black
hawkweed: 5 plant 6 flower
__-Hawley: 5 Smoot
Hawn, Goldie: 7 actress
daughter: Kate Hudson
film: Bird on a Wire (1990)
Butterflies Are Free (1972)
Cactus Flower (1969, AA)
Death Becomes Her (1992)
$ (Dollars) (1971)
Everyone Says I Love You (1996)
The First Wives Club (1996)
Foul Play (1978)
The Out-of-Towners (1999)
Overboard (1987)
Private Benjamin (1980)
Seems Like Old Times (1980)
Shampoo (1975)
The Sugarland Express (1974)
There's a Girl in My Soup (1970)
Wildcats (1986)
TV: Rowan and Martin's Laugh-In
Haworth, Walter: 7 chemist 8 Nobelist
hawser: 4 line, rope 5 cable 10 anchor rope, towing rope
bend: 4 knot
hawthorn: 4 tree 5 fruit, plant 6 flower
relative: 4 pear, plum, rose 5 apple, peach 6 almond, cherry, medlar, quince 7 apricot 8 oiticica 10 blackthorn
Hawthorne: 4 city, town 5 Nigel 9 Nathaniel
locale: 10 California
Hawthorne, Nathaniel: 6 author, writer
friend: Emerson, Thoreau, Melville
town: 5 Salem
work: The Blithedale Romance
Fanshawe
The House of the Seven Gables
The Marble Faun
The Old Manse
The Scarlet Letter
Twice-Told Tales
Young Goodman Brown
Hawthorne, Nigel: 3 Sir 5 actor
film: Amistad (1997)
Demolition Man (1993)
Madeline (1998)
The Object of My Affection (1998)
The Winslow Boy (1999)
hay: 4 feed 5 straw 6 fodder, forage, redtop 7 alfalfa, timothy 9 pasturage
area: 3 mow 4 loft
ask for ~: 5 neigh
bit: 3 awn 4 wisp
bundle: 4 bale 5 stack
bundler: 5 baler
cut ~: 3 mow
ender: 3 mow 4 cock, fork, loft, rack, rick, ride, seed, wire 5 maker, stack
fever reaction: 5 achoo 6 ahchoo, hachoo 7 allergy, kerchoo
hit the ~: 5 crash, sleep 6 retire, turn in 7 sack out 9 go to sleep
pitch, as ~: 4 fork
preserve ~: 6 ensile
second ~ crop: 5 rowen
hay __: 4 rake 5 baler, fever, shock 6 doodle
__ hay: 4 make, salt 5 camel
Hay: 3 Ian 4 John
__ Hay: 5 Antic
Hayakawa: 2 S.I. 6 Sessue
Hayden: 3 Tom 6 Robert 7 Carruth, Melissa 8 Sterling
Hayden, Robert: 4 poet
Hayden, Sterling: 5 actor
film: The Asphalt Jungle (1950)
Dr. Strangelove (1964)
Flaming Feather (1951)
Johnny Guitar (1954)
The Killing (1956)
Loving (1970)
The Outsider (1979)
So Big (1953)
The Star (1952)
Suddenly (1954)
Hayden, Tom spouse: Jane Fonda
Haydn: 6 Joseph 7 Richard
Haydn, Joseph: 8 Austrian, composer
nickname: 4 Papa
work: Clock Symphony
The Creation
Drum Roll Symphony
Farewell Symphony
Military Symphony
Surprise Symphony
Toy Symphony
Hayek, Salma: 7 actress
film: The Faculty (1998)
Frida (2002)
Timecode (2000)
Wild Wild West (1999)
Hayes: 3 Bob 4 Bill, Lucy 5 Billy, Elvin, Gabby, Helen, Isaac, Woody
product: 5 modem
Hayes, Bill song: The Ballad of Davy Crockett (1955)
Hayes, Bob: 6 runner 8 sprinter
Hayes, Elvin: 5 cager
milieu: 5 court
org.: 3 NBA
sport: 10 basketball
Hayes, Helen: 7 actress
film: Airport (1970, AA)
Anastasia (1956)
Another Language (1933)
A Farewell to Arms (1932)
The Sin of Madelon Claudet (1931, AA)
What Every Woman Knows (1934)
spouse: Charles MacArthur
Hayes, Isaac song: Theme from Shaft (1971)
Hayes, Rutherford B.: 9 president
feature: 5 beard
former occupation: 6 lawyer
home: 4 Ohio 7 Fremont
middle name: 8 Birchard
opponent: 6 Tilden
V.P.: 7 Wheeler
wife: 4 Lucy
hayfork: 4 tool 9 implement
Hayley: 5 Mills
hayloft: 3 mow
locale: 4 barn
haymaker: 4 sock 5 punch 6 wallop 8 uppercut
evade a ~: 3 bob 4 duck
land a ~: 2 KO
target: 3 jaw
throw a ~: 5 swing
Haymarket Square event: 4 riot
Haymes, Dick: 6 singer
spouse: Joanne Dru, Rita Hayworth
haymow: 4 loft
Hayne, Paul: 4 poet
Haynes: 4 Todd 5 Lloyd 7 Marques
Haynie, Sandra: 6 golfer
milieu: 5 links 6 course
org.: 4 LPGA
hayrick: 5 mound
__ Hayride: 7 Mexican
Hay River: 4 city, town
locale: 6 Canada
Hays: 4 Will 6 Robert
Haysbert: 6 Dennis
hayseed: 3 oaf 4 boor, hick, rube 5 yokel 6 farmer, lummox, rustic 7 bumpkin, plowboy 9 hillbilly 10 clodhopper
haystack: 4 rick 5 mound
item: 6 needle
Haystacks painter: 5 Monet
Hayward: 4 city, town 5 Louis, Susan 6 Leland
locale: 10 California
Hayward, Leland spouse: Margaret Sullavan
Hayward, Louis: 5 actor
film: And Then There Were None (1945)
The Black Arrow (1948)
The House by the River (1950)
Ladies in Retirement (1941)
The Man in the Iron Mask (1939)
Repeat Performance (1947)
Ruthless (1948)
The Saint in New York (1938)
The Son of Monte Cristo (1940)
Hayward, Susan: 7 actress
film: Ada (1961)
The Fighting Seabees (1944)
House of Strangers (1949)
I Can Get It for You Wholesale (1951)
I'd Climb the Highest Mountain (1951)
I'll Cry Tomorrow (1955)
I Want to Live! (1958, AA)
The Lost Moment (1947)
The Lusty Men (1952)
My Foolish Heart (1949)
The President's Lady (1953)
The Saxon Charm (1948)
Smash-up, the Story of a Woman (1947)
The Snows of Kilimanjaro (1952)
Soldier of Fortune (1955)
They Won't Believe Me (1947)
Tulsa (1949)
Untamed (1955)
With a Song in My Heart (1952)
haywire: 4 amok 5 amuck 6 broken

7 **berserk**, bonkers, chaotic, flipped, unglued **8** confused **9** defective **10** broken-down, disordered, out of order, out of whack, upside-down
gone ~: 5 kaput **10** on the blink, on the fritz, out of order, out of whack
Hayworth, Rita: 7 actress
film: Angels Over Broadway (1940)
Blood and Sand (1941)
Cover Girl (1944)
Gilda (1946)
The Lady From Shanghai (1948)
The Lone Wolf Spy Hunt (1939)
Miss Sadie Thompson (1953)
My Gal Sal (1942)
Only Angels Have Wings (1939)
Pal Joey (1957)
Separate Tables (1958)
The Story on Page One (1959)
The Strawberry Blonde (1941)
Tales of Manhattan (1942)
Tonight and Every Night (1945)
You'll Never Get Rich (1941)
You Were Never Lovelier (1942)
spouse: Dick Haymes, Aly Khan, Orson Welles
hazan: 6 cantor
hazard: 3 lay **4** dare, game, luck, play, risk **5** fluke, peril, stake, wager **6** chance, danger, gamble, menace, threat **7** iceberg, imperil, pitfall, thin ice, trouble, venture **8** accident, endanger, fortuity, jeopardy, unsafety **9** adventure, hot potato, postulate, speculate, undertake **10** go for broke, impediment, insecurity, jeopardize
a guess: 5 opine **7** suppose, surmise, suspect **9** speculate
driving ~: 3 fog, ice **4** mist **5** glare, sleet
garden ~: 3 bur **5** brier, spine **7** bramble, prickle, spicule, sticker
golf ~: 4 lake, trap **5** water **6** bunker
navigation ~: 3 fog **4** berg, floe, reef **5** shoal
hazard __: 5 light
__ hazard: 5 moral **6** losing **7** winning
Hazard (1992 song) artist: Richard Marx
hazardous: 3 icy **5** dicey, grave, hairy, risky, rocky, tight **6** chancy, unsafe, wicked **7** parlous, unsound **8** insecure, perilous **9** dangerous, desperate, difficult, explosive, uncertain, unhealthy **10** precarious, touch-and-go
not ~: 4 safe
hazardous __: 5 waste
hazardousness: 7 gravity
__ Hazard Perry: 6 Oliver
haze: 3 fog **4** film, mirk, mist, murk, pall, smog **5** brume, bully, roast, taunt, vapor **6** badger, dry fog, hector, muddle, shadow **7** dimness **8** ridicule **9** fogginess, obscurity, vagueness **10** overshadow
Haze: 6 Lolita
__ Haze: 6 Purple
hazel: 3 nut **4** tree **5** acorn, brown, color, shrub **6** cobnut **7** filbert **8** nutbrown
cousin: 5 birch
ender: 3 nut
relative: 3 bay, dun, tan **4** bole, ecru, fawn, foxy, nude, seal **5** alder, amber, beige, camel, cocoa, khaki, mocha, sepia, tawny, umber **6** auburn, bister, bistre, bronze, coffee, copper, ginger, russet, sienna, sorrel, suntan, walnut **7** biscuit, caramel, dogwood **8** chestnut, cinnamon, hornbeam, mahogany **9** butternut, chocolate
tree: 6 cobnut **7** filbert
hazel __: 3 hen **6** grouse
__ hazel: 5 witch
Hazel: 4 maid **5** comic
cartoonist: 3 Key
dog: 6 Smiley
Hazel (NBC/CBS sitcom)
cast: Whitney Blake (Dorothy Baxter) Shirley Booth (Hazel Burke) Don DeFore (George Baxter)
hazelnut: 8 ice cream
alternative: 5 lemon, mocha, peach **6** banana, coffee, Jamoca, toffee **7** caramel, coconut, vanilla **8** cinnamon **9** bubblegum, chocolate, pineapple, pistachio, raspberry, rocky road, rum raisin **10** blackberry, cheesecake, Neapolitan, peppermint, strawberry
Hazel Park: 4 city, town
locale: 8 Michigan
Hazelwood: 4 city, town
locale: 8 Missouri
haziness: 3 fog **4** blur, smog
hazing target: 4 pleb **5** frosh, plebe
Hazleton: 4 city, town
locale: 4 Penn.
Hazlitt, William: 6 writer **7** British **8** essayist
hazy: 3 dim **4** soft **5** dizzy, faint, foggy, fuzzy, mirky, misty, muddy, murky, muzzy, smoky, vague **6** addled, bleary, blurry, cloudy, in a fog, opaque, steamy **7** blurred, clouded, muddled, obscure, shadowy, sunless, unclear **8** confused, nebulous, obscured, overcast **9** befuddled, equivocal, imprecise, uncertain, unfocused **10** bewildered, ill-defined, indefinite, indistinct, inexplicit, obfuscated, out of focus, unexplicit, unspecific
become ~: 4 blur
make ~: 4 blur **5** bedim, befog, blear, cloud, muddy, smear **7** becloud, obscure **9** adumbrate
Hazy __ of Winter: 5 Shade
Hazy Shade of Winter (song) artist: Bangles, Simon and Garfunkel
HBO: 7 channel
alternative: 3 AMC, IFC, SHO, TMC **4** Flix **5** Bravo, Starz **6** Encore **7** Cinemax **8** Showtime, Sundance
offering: 5 movie
receiver: 2 TV **5** TV set
H.C.: 6 Potter **7** McNeile
HCl: 4 acid
__-H Club: 4 Four
hdg.: 3 dir.
compass ~: 3 ENE, ESE, NNE, NNW, SSE, SSW, WNW, WSW
ship ~: 3 SbE
hd. of state: 3 ldr. **4** pres.
he: 3 guy, man, sir **4** chap, male, pron. **5** bloke **6** feller, fellow, gander, Hebrew, letter, mister **7** pronoun **9** gentleman
and she: 4 they
not ~: 3 she
predecessor: 6 daleth
successor: 3 vav, vaw, waw
he-__: 3 man, men
He: 3 gas **4** elem. **6** helium **7** element
2 for ~: 4 at. no.
He (song)
artist: Al Hibbler, McGuire Sisters, Righteous Brothers
He __ Game: 3 Got
He __ heavy...: 4 ain't
He __ you when you're sleeping...: 4 sees
__ & He: 3 She
H.E.: 5 Bates
head: 3 ldr., mgr., run, tip, top **4** acme, apex, bent, boss, dean, dome, foam, fore, gift, lead, main, mind, pate, peak, pres., rule, stem, suds, tend, turn **5** act on, brain, chief, crest, crown, first, flair, front, froth, guide, knack, prime, skill, skull, title **6** apogee, bigwig, climax, direct, genius, gerent, govern, height, honcho, lather, leader, legend, manage, master, noggin, noodle, origin, sconce, senior, source, summit, talent, tipoff, top dog, vertex **7** ability, act upon, captain, coconut, command, conduct, control, cranium, faculty, forward, go first, highest, latrine, leading, lead off, manager, officer, oversee, premier, supreme, topmost **8** antecede, aptitude, big wheel, capacity, chairman, champion, cocoanut, director, dominate, foreland, foremost, forepart, governor, kingfish, light out, overseer, superior, vanguard **9** braincase, chieftain, commander, forefront, intellect, mentality, organizer, president, principal, supervise **10** administer, gray matter, management, preeminent, promontory, supervisor
a ~: 3 per **4** each
and shoulders: 4 bust
away: 3 ebb **4** fade, flag, wane **5** abate **6** die out, ease up, recede, reflux **7** decline, die down, dwindle, ease off, slacken, subside, tail off **8** decrease, diminish, withdraw
bend the ~: 3 nap, nod **4** doze **6** drowse
big ~: 3 ego
bone: 3 jaw **7** maxilla **8** mandible
cavity: 5 naris, sinus **7** nostril
combining form: 6 cephal- **7** cephalo-, -cephaly **8** -cephalic **9** -cephalous
come to a ~: 5 crest **6** climax **9** culminate
cooler: 6 ice bag **7** ice pack
count: 5 tally **6** census
covering: 3 cap, hat, tam **4** cowl, hair, hood **5** scarf, shawl
crowned ~: 4 czar, king, tsar, tzar **5** ruler **7** monarch
dept. ~: 3 mgr. **4** boss **7** manager
ender: 3 man, set, way **4** ache, achy, band, fast, gear, hunt, lamp, land, line, lock, long, most, race, rest, room, sail, ship, shot, wear, wind, word, work **5** board, dress, first, light, liner, phone, piece, scarf, shake, space, stall, stand, stock, stone, water **6** cheese, hunter, master, spring, strong, waiter, worker **7** counter, hunting, quarter, scarves **8** foremost, mistress, quarters **9** quartered
for: 4 go to, move **5** steer **6** lead to, repair
(for): 3 aim **4** bear, make
for the bottom: 4 sink
for the hills: 2 go **3** fly, lam, run **4** bolt, flee **5** break, leave, scram **6** beat it, bug out, decamp, depart, desert, escape, get out **7** abscond, make off, retreat, run away, take off, vamoose **8** clear out **9** disappear, skedaddle **10** fly the coop, hightail it, hit the road
get in one's ~: 5 grasp, learn, study **6** absorb, master, pick up, soak up **7** find out **8** discover, memorize **10** understand
get through one's ~: 5 grasp, learn **7** discern, realize **9** recognize **10** appreciate, comprehend, understand
go head to ~: 3 pit, vie **4** play **5** fight, match, rival **6** oppose, take on **7** compete, contend **8** struggle **9** challenge
go ~ over heels: 4 fall, flip, slip **5** lurch **6** plunge, sprawl, topple, tumble **7** stumble
go through one's ~: 5 occur **6** dawn on
have a ~ start: 4 lead **7** precede
have in one's ~: 4 know
hit upside the ~: 3 wap **4** beat, whap, whop
honcho: 4 boss, exec, king, prex, prez **5** chief, prexy **7** manager **8** higher-up, official, overseer **9** commander, executive, key player
hurt: 4 ache
in England: 4 noll
in French: 4 tête
it's over your ~: 3 hat **4** hair, roof
lose one's ~: 4 flip **5** freak, panic **6** blow up **7** explode, flip out **8** freak out, have a fit
make one's ~ swim: 3 awe **5** amaze **6** dazzle **7** impress
meet ~ on: 8 confront, cope with, deal with, face up to
movement: 3 nod **5** shrug
off: 5 avert, catch, quell **7** inhibit, prevent **8** preclude **9** intercept, interpose
off the top of one's ~: 5 ad-lib **9** extempore, impromptu, unplanned **10** improvised, unprepared
of state: 5 ruler
of steam: 5 force
of the class: 3 ace **4** best
opposite: 3 toe **4** tail
ornament: 5 crown, tiara **6** anadem, diadem, wreath **7** coronet
out: 2 go **4** exit, move, sail **5** be off, leave, scram, split **6** beat it, be gone, decamp, depart, embark, go away, run off, set off **7** abscond, go forth, push off, retreat, ride off, take off, vamoose **8** run along, set forth, shove off, slip away, withdraw **10** shuffle off
over heels: 4 gaga **6** in love **7** smitten **8** absorbed **9** intensely **10** completely, thoroughly
over one's ~: 4 high **5** above, aloft **6** high up, on high **7** skyward **8** skywards **10** up in the air, up in the sky
part: 3 ear, eye, lip **4** chin, hair, nose, pate **5** scalp
per ~: 4 a pop, each **5** a shot **6** apiece, a throw, singly
remove ~ covering: 5 unhat
start: 4 edge, jump **5** leg up **8** handicap
starter: 3 air, big, bow, cat, egg, fat, god, hot, jar, pin, red, sap, tow, war **4** bald, bill, bone, bulk, bull, dead, drum, fore, hard, hogs, long, mast, meat, over, rail, skin, soft, sore, well **5** arrow, beach, black, block, cross, flint, green, river, snake, spear, steel, swell, thick, trail **6** barrel, bridge, bubble, copper, dragon, fiddle, figure, hammer, knight, letter, logger, mutton, shovel, shower, sleepy, spring, timber, turtle, wooden **7** chuckle, feather, knuckle, leather, thunder **8** fountain
support: 4 neck
swelled ~: 3 ego **5** pride, quirk **6** egoism, vanity **7** conceit, egotism, hauteur, swagger **8** self-love, smugness **9** arrogance, immodesty, vainglory **10** pretension, stuffiness
tilt, as the ~: 4 cock
top of a bird's ~: 6 pileus

toward: **7** make for
(toward): **4** move
trip: **6** revery, vision **7** reverie
up: **3** run **5** chair, climb **6** direct, govern **7** control, preside **8** antecede
use one's ~: **5** think **6** reason **8** cogitate **9** cerebrate
with one's ~ together: **4** sane **5** lucid, sober **8** rational
head ___: **3** dip, off, pin, sea, tax **4** cold, gate, tone, trip, wind **5** count, money, rhyme, start, table, to toe **6** margin **7** balance, lettuce
head ___ heels: **4** over
___ head: **3** pan **4** arch, dado, hard, jump **5** erase, sound **6** flower, leader **7** chapter, dragon's, erasing, pumpkin, running, stagger, swelled, talking
Head: **3** Roy **5** Edith **6** Bessie, Howard, Murray
Head (1968 film)
cast: Teri Garr, Monkees, Vito Scotti
director: Bob Rafelson
Head ___ Class: **5** of the
___ Head: **6** Lizard **7** Diamond, Sounion
headache: **4** bane, pest, task **5** worry **6** bother, hassle, megrim, misery **7** problem, trouble **8** irritant, migraine, nuisance, quagmire, vexation **9** annoyance, hindrance **10** difficulty
remedy: **3** APC **5** Advil, Bromo **6** Anacin, ice bag **7** ice pack
___ headache: **5** sinus
head and shoulders ___: **5** above
headband: **5** snood **6** diadem **7** coronet
headband cord, Arab: **4** agal
Head, Bessie: **6** writer **12** South African
headcloth: **5** scarf **8** kerchief, mantilla
headdress: **3** cap, taj **4** coif, pouf **5** scarf, tiara **6** bonnet, hairdo, turban **8** coiffure, kaffiyeh, kerchief
clerical ~: **5** miter, mitre
headed
for: **5** off to **6** toward **7** towards
starter: **3** hot, pig, red, sap, tow **4** bare, hard, long, soft **5** level, light, swell **6** mutton
___-headed: **3** red **4** cool, gray, grey, hard, long, soft, weak, wild **5** clear, empty, fuzzy, giddy, hoary, hydra, sober, wagon, white, wrong **6** bubble, Hathor, wooden, woolly
___-Headed League, The: **3** Red
___ Headed Woman: **4** Hard
Head 'em off at the ___!: **4** pass
header: **4** beam, dive, fall, trip **5** spill, title **6** plunge **7** attempt, stumble
starter: **6** double, triple
take a ~: **4** fall, risk **6** topple, tumble
headfirst: **6** rashly **7** hastily **9** hurriedly **10** heedlessly, recklessly
headgear: **3** fex, hat, tam **5** beret, crown, tiara **6** bonnet, diadem, helmet **7** homburg
heavenly ~: **4** halo
see also hat
headhunter
come-on: **5** no-fee
company: **4** agcy. **6** agency
slot: **3** job
heading: **4** name, tack, west **5** label, route, title, track **6** course, legend **7** bearing, caption **8** category, tendency **9** direction **10** trajectory
calendar ~: **3** Apr., Aug., Dec., Feb., Fri., Jan., Jul., Jun., Mar, May, Mon., Nov., Oct., Sat., Sun., Thu., Wed. **4** Sept., Thur. **5** Thurs.
ship ~: **3** ENE, ESE, NbE, NbW, NNE, NNW, SbE, SSE, SSW, WNW, WSW **4** NEbE, NebN
headland: **3** ras **4** cape, hill, mull, ness **5** bluff, point **10** prominence, promontory
headless: **6** stupid **7** aimless, foolish, idiotic, witless **8** mindless, unguided **9** brainless, idiotical, senseless **10** half-witted, leaderless, rudderless, undirected, ungoverned
headlight
holder: **5** bezel
setting: **3** dim **4** high
headline: **4** lead, news, star **5** title **6** banner, stress **7** caption, feature **8** screamer, showcase **9** emphasize, publicize
like some ~ s: **5** lurid
scream, as a ~: **5** blaze
headliner: **4** hero, name, star **7** feature
Headlines comic: **4** Leno
headlong: **4** rash **5** amain, brash, hasty, quick, swift **6** abrupt, daring, rushed, speedy, sudden **7** hurried, rushing **8** pell-mell, reckless **9** breakneck, dangerous, daredevil, desperate, foolhardy, impatient, impetuous, impulsive, uncareful, whirlwind **10** passionate
go ~: **4** rush, trip **6** careen, tumble
Headlong author: Michael Frayn
Headlong Hall author: Thomas Peacock
Headly, Glenne: **7** actress
film: Dick Tracy (1990)
Dirty Rotten Scoundrels (1988)
Making Mr. Right (1987)
Mr. Holland's Opus (1995)
What's the Worst That Could Happen? (2001)
spouse: John Malkovich
headman: **4** boss **5** chief, ruler **6** bigwig, honcho, leader, top cat, top dog **7** kingpin, manager, skipper **8** big wheel, director, kingfish **9** big cheese, commander, executive **10** supervisor
headmaster: **4** dean **8** director **9** principal
headmost: **5** chief, first, front, prime **7** leading, premier, primary, supreme **8** cardinal, foremost **9** paramount, principal
___ Head, NC: **4** Nags
head of ___: **5** state **9** household
Head of the Class (ABC sitcom)
cast: Khrystyne Haje (Simone Foster)
Howard Hesseman (Charlie Moore)
head-on: **6** direct **7** frontal **8** opposing **10** face-to-face, unmediated
strike ~: **3** ram **4** butt **5** smash **6** batter
Head over Feet (1997 song) artist: Alanis Morissette
Head Over Heels (1985 song) artist: Tears for Fears
headpiece: **3** wig **5** tiara **6** anadem
headquarters: **4** base, seat, site **6** center, office **7** address, offices, station **8** barracks **9** residence
headrest: **7** cushion
headroom: **4** room **5** space **9** allowance, clearance, open space **10** empty space
___ Headroom: **3** Max
heads
alternative: **5** tails
bump ~: **6** debate **7** wrangle **8** struggle
count ~: **3** add **4** tote **5** add up, tally, total **6** reckon, tote up
family ~: **3** mas, pas
make ~ or tails of: **3** see **6** fathom, follow, pick up **9** figure out **10** comprehend, understand
put ones' ~ together: **6** confer **10** brainstorm
up: **7** look out, warning, watch it **8** watch out **9** be careful
-up situation: **6** danger
___ heads: **4** bump **5** count
Heads ___,...: **4** I win
___ Heads: **7** Crowned, Talking
headset: **4** ears **5** phone **7** outlook
Heads I win, tails you ___: **4** lose
head-splitting: **5** forte, noisy **7** blaring, booming, jarring, pealing, rackety, raucous, reboant, roaring **8** crashing, piercing, plangent, rumbling, sonorous, strident, turned up **9** big-voiced, clamorous, deafening **10** boisterous, resounding, stentorian, strepitous, thundering, uproarious, vociferous
headstrong: **4** rash **5** brash, onery, stiff, tough **6** mulish, ornery, unruly, wilful **7** adamant, naughty, piggish, wayward, willful **8** contrary, indocile, obdurate, perverse, stubborn **9** desperate, fanatical, foolhardy, hard-nosed, hardshell, imprudent, impulsive, obstinate, pigheaded **10** bullheaded, determined, refractory, self-willed, unyielding
not ~: **5** timid
heads-up: **4** wary **5** alert, aware **7** on guard **8** vigilant, watchful **9** wide-awake **10** on one's toes, on the stick
Heads Up!: **7** musical
songwriter: **4** Hart **7** Rodgers
head to ___: **3** toe
Head to Toe (1987 song) artist: Lisa Lisa and Cult Jam
head-turner: **5** cutey, cutie
headway: **3** way **4** dent **5** space, speed **6** leeway **7** advance **8** progress
make ~: **4** sail **5** go far **7** advance, shape up
headwear
see hat
headword: **5** lemma
heady: **4** racy **5** kicky **6** strong **8** dizzying, exciting **9** thrilling **10** intoxicant
He Ain't Heavy, He's My Brother (1970 song) artist: Hollies
heal: **4** cure, knit, mend **5** nurse, treat **6** doctor, remedy **7** get well, patch up, rebound, recover, restore **8** minister **9** get better **10** convalesce, recuperate
Heald: **7** Anthony
healed: **6** better **9** good as new
healer: **3** doc **5** curer, medic **6** doctor, medico, mender, shaman **9** physician, therapist
name meaning ~: **5** Jason
org.: **3** AMA
___ healer: **5** faith
Healey: **2** Ed **4** Jeff
healing: **7** therapy **8** curative, remedial, sanative **9** on the mend, treatment **10** corrective
combining form: **5** iatro-, -iatry **7** -iatrics
sign of ~: **4** scab
substance: **4** aloe, balm **5** salve **6** arnica
waters: **3** spa
healing of God
name meaning ~: **6** Rafael **7** Raphael
health: **4** form, luck, trim **5** shape, vigor **6** fettle **7** fitness, hygiene, welfare **8** haleness, strength, wellness **9** condition, hardiness, salubrity, soundness, toast word, well-being **10** robustness
bad ~: **7** illness **8** sickness **9** infirmity
booster: **3** vit. **7** mineral, vitamin
care facility: **6** clinic **8** hospital **9** infirmary
club: **3** gym, spa **9** gymnasium
food buy: **4** bran, kelp, tofu **5** carob **8** bean curd
good ~: **4** pink, tone **5** asset, vigor
hazard: **5** radon
ill ~: **6** malady **7** ailment, disease **9** infirmity **10** affliction, unwellness
improve in ~: **4** gain, heal, mend **5** rally **6** pick up **7** get well, rebound, recover **9** come along, get better **10** bounce back, convalesce, recuperate
in good ~: **4** well **5** right, sound
in poor ~: **3** ill **4** sick **6** sickly, unwell **7** unsound
mental ~: **6** sanity
org.: **3** CDC, FDA **6** HMO. PPO
professional: **2** MD, RN **3** LPN
regain one's ~: **4** heal **7** get well, rebound, recover **8** snap back **9** get better **10** convalesce, recuperate
restore to ~: **4** cure, heal, mend **5** fix up, treat **6** doctor, remedy **7** patch up
Roman goddess of ~: **5** Salus
science of ~: **8** medicine
to your ~: **5** salud, salut, skoal, toast **6** cheers, prosit **7** l'chayim **9** happy days
health ___: **3** spa **4** care, club, code, food **7** officer
___ health: **3** ill **6** mental, public
healthful: **4** good, pure **6** benign **7** outdoor **8** curative, salutary, sanative, sanitary **9** favorable, wholesome **10** beneficial, nutritious, salubrious
healthier: **6** better
___ Health Organization: **5** World
healthy: **3** fit **4** good, hale, safe, sane, spry, tidy, trim, well **5** fresh, hardy, lusty, sound, tonic, whole **6** active, benign, robust, septic, strong, sturdy, virile **7** bracing, chipper, up to par **8** all right, athletic, blooming, hygienic, muscular, salutary, sanatory, sanitary, thriving, vigorous **9** in the pink, wholesome **10** able-bodied, beneficial, bright-eyed, fortifying, mitigative, nourishing, nutritious, salubrious, unimpaired
hue: **4** pink
looking: **4** rosy **5** ruddy
make ~: **4** cure, heal
mind: **6** sanity
more ~: **6** better
not ~: **3** ill **4** sick **6** ailing, laid up, sickly, unwell **8** below par, feverish **9** afflicted, bedridden **10** indisposed, out of shape
state: **4** weal
healthy ___ horse: **3** as a
Healthy Choice: **6** cereal
competitor: **3** Kix **4** Life, Trix **5** Kashi, Quisp, Total **6** Kaboom, Muesli, Oreo O's, Pablum, Smacks **7** All-Bran, Crispix, Harmony, Hunny B's, Mueslix, Oat Bran, Pokemon **8** Boo Berry, Cheerios, Corn Chex, Corn Pops, Fiber One, Rice Chex, Special K, Uncle Sam, Wheaties **9** Alpha Bits, Apple Zaps, Grape Nuts, Honey Comb, Just Right, Wheat Chex **10** Apple Jacks, Bran Flakes, Cap'n Crunch, Cocoa Puffs, Froot Loops, Mini-Wheats, Nutri-Grain, Puffed Rice, Quaker Oats, Smart Start **11** Cocoa Blasts, Cookie Crisp, Golden Crisp, Lucky Charms, Puffed Wheat, Sweet Crunch, Waffle Crisp
healthy-looking: **7** flushed, glowing
Heaney, Seamus: **4** poet **5** Irish **8** Nobelist
heap: **3** car, lot, wad **4** auto, carn, load, lots, lump, mass, mint, pack, peck, pile, raft **5** amass, bunch, cairn, crate, drift, hoard, mound, ocean, stack,

wreck 6 bagful, bundle, huddle, jalopy, jungle, lavish, myriad, pileup 7 buildup, bunch up, clunker, numbers, smother 8 mountain 9 abundance, aggregate, amassment, congeries, gathering, great deal, multitude, profusion, stockpile 10 accumulate, automobile, collection, cumulation, rattletrap
combining form: 5 cumul- 6 cumuli-, cumulo-
kudos on: 5 extol, honor 6 admire, praise, puff up, stroke 7 acclaim, approve, build up, commend, flatter, lionize 8 hand it to 10 compliment
on: 4 give 6 assign, bestow, confer
refuse ~: 8 junkyard
starter: 5 scrap
top of the ~: 4 acme, A-one, best 5 elite
up: 4 load, pile 5 amass, stack 10 accumulate
__ heap: 3 ash 5 scrap
heaped: 5 thick 6 jammed 7 replete 8 abundant 9 abounding, aggregate, jam-packed
heaping: 6 myriad, untold 7 endless 9 countless
heaps: 4 a lot, lots, many, much 6 oceans, oodles, plenty 10 inundation
of: 6 divers, myriad, umteen, untold 7 copious, profuse, umpteen 8 abundant, manifold, numerous, umpsteen 9 bountiful, countless, quite a few
hear: 3 try 4 heed 5 catch, learn, sense 6 descry, harken, listen, pick up, take in 7 find out, learn of, receive 8 discover, listen in, listen to 9 apprehend, ascertain, eavesdrop, get wind of, get word of 10 adjudicate, understand
cases: 3 try 5 judge
eager to ~: 7 all ears 9 attentive
ender: 3 say
fail to ~: 4 miss
not ~ of: 4 deny 5 spurn 6 ignore, oppose, rebuff, reject 7 disdain, dismiss 8 brush off, disallow 9 disregard
of: 10 learn about
out: 4 heed 6 attend, listen 9 lend an ear
so all can ~: 5 aloud 6 loudly 8 viva voce
the alarm: 4 rise, stir 5 arise, awake, get up, waken 6 awaken, bestir, wake up
ye: 4 oyes, oyez
hear __ drop: 4 a pin
hearable: 5 aloud 7 sensory 9 sensorial
__ Hear a Waltz?: 3 Do I
heard
make oneself ~: 5 shout, speak 6 assert, insist 7 declare, speak up 8 sound off, speak out
something ~: 5 sound
Heard, John: 5 actor
film: Beaches (1988)
Between the Lines (1977)
Big (1988)
Heaven Help Us (1985)
Home Alone (1990)
The Pelican Brief (1993)
Radio Flyer (1992)
The Trip to Bountiful (1985)
__ Heard That Song Before: 3 I've
hearer: 5 judge
hearers: 5 crowd 7 gallery 8 audience
Hear, hear!: 4 amen 6 I agree
hearing: 5 sense, trial 6 review, tryout 7 earshot, enquiry, inquiry, meeting, session 8 audience, audition 9 listening 10 conference, discussion, perception
combining form: 4 acou- 5 acouo-, audio-
court ~: 4 oyer
of ~: 4 otic 5 aural 6 audial
organ: 3 ear
problem: 6 earwax, otitis, otosis
within ~: 4 near 5 close 6 at hand, nearby 7 close by
hearing __: 3 aid, dog
hearing-__ dog: 3 ear
hearing impaired
device: 3 TDD
lang. for the ~: 3 ASL
__ Hear It for the Boy: 4 Let's
hearken: 4 heed, mark 6 attend, listen 7 look out, pay heed 8 take heed 9 bend an ear, lend an ear
Hearn: 5 Chick 8 Lafcadio
Hearn, Lafcadio: 6 author, writer
work: Chita
Youma
Hear no __...: 4 evil
__ Hears a Who: 6 Horton
hearsay: 4 buzz, news, talk, word 5 noise, rumor 6 gossip, report, tattle 7 scandal 9 grapevine
in French: 7 oui-dire
Hearst: 5 Patty
heart: 3 hub, nub 4 core, crux, gist, grit, guts, knub, meat, pith, seat, soul, will 5 focus, midst, moxie, nerve, organ, pluck, point, spunk, valor 6 center, inside, kernel, marrow, mettle, middle, morale, nature, recess, spirit, ticker, warmth 7 bravery, courage, emotion, essence, feeling, keynote, meaning, nucleus, prowess, purport, stamina 8 backbone, boldness, goodness, interior, kindness, sympathy 9 endurance, fortitude, gallantry, innermost, main point, sincerity, substance, valentine 10 compassion, confidence, durability, humaneness, resolution, tenderness
all ~: 4 kind 6 kindly, tender 8 merciful 10 altruistic, benevolent, charitable, personable
and soul: 4 pith 6 wholly 7 essence 8 entirely 10 completely, thoroughly
at ~: 5 truly 6 really 8 innately 9 basically, in reality
at the ~ of: 6 amidst
bleeding ~: 5 plant 6 flower
break one's ~: 4 jilt 6 bum out, sadden 7 depress, let down 8 dispirit, distress 10 disappoint, dishearten
chambers: 5 atria
chart: 3 ECG, EKG
combining form: 5 cardi- 6 -cardia, cardio- 7 -cardium
cross one's ~: 3 vow 4 avow 5 swear 6 pledge 7 promise
eat one's ~ out: 4 fret, mope 5 mourn 6 grieve, lament, sorrow
ender: 4 ache, beat, burn, felt, land, leaf, sick, wood, worm 5 break, throb 6 broken, string 7 rending, warming 8 breaking
essentially: 4 pump
faint ~: 8 cold feet, timidity 9 cowardice
hardness of ~: 5 odium 6 animus, enmity, hatred, rancor 7 ill will 8 acrimony 9 animosity 10 antagonism, resentment
have a ~: 4 care
have a broken ~: 5 mourn
have a change of ~: 6 recant 7 retract, reverse 8 pull back, withdraw 9 back-pedal
heavy ~: 3 woe 4 funk 5 blues, dolor, gloom, grief 6 misery, pathos, sorrow 7 anguish, sadness 8 distress, doldrums, glumness 9 dejection 10 depression, gloominess, melancholy
hurt: 4 ache 5 dolor, grief 6 misery 7 anguish 8 distress
in French: 5 coeur
it comes from the ~: 5 blood
know by ~: 4 cite 6 retain 8 memorize
learn by ~: 4 know 8 memorize, remember
line: 4 vein 5 aorta 6 artery
lose ~: 4 mope 5 quail 6 give up 7 despair 10 give up hope
lose one's ~ to: 4 love
name meaning ~: 4 Hugh
near to one's ~: 6 adored, prized 7 beloved, darling 8 cared for, endeared 9 cherished, treasured, worshiped
of a ~ chamber: 6 atrial
of the ~: 7 cardial
of the matter: 3 nub 4 crux, gist, knub 5 nexus, point
part: 5 valve 6 atrium 7 auricle 9 ventricle
rate: 5 pulse
set one's ~ on: 4 wish 5 yearn 6 desire
sick at ~: 3 sad 4 blue, glum 5 moody, mopey 6 gloomy, morose, woeful 7 doleful 8 dejected, dolorous, downcast, grieving, mournful, troubled 9 cheerless, depressed, miserable, saturnine, sorrowful, woebegone 10 despondent, dispirited, melancholy
starter: 3 CPR 5 green, sweet 6 purple
take ~: 6 perk up 7 cheer up 10 brighten up
take to ~: 4 heed, obey 6 follow 7 abide by, observe, respect 8 adhere to
take to one's ~: 6 endear
tug at the ~: 4 move 6 affect
where the ~ is: 4 home
with a heavy ~: 5 sadly
with all one's ~: 5 truly 8 candidly 9 sincerely
with good ~: 4 bold, game 5 brave 6 daring, gritty, plucky, spunky 7 doughty, gallant, valiant 8 intrepid, valorous 9 dauntless 10 courageous
heart __: 3 cam 4 back, rate 5 point, shell 6 cherry, urchin
heart __ matter: 5 of the
heart-__: 4 free 5 whole 7 rending
__ heart: 3 red 4 take 5 brown, have a 6 broken 7 bullock
Heart
song: Alone (1987)
Magic Man (1976)
Never (1985)
Nothin' at All (1986)
Tell It Like It Is (1980)
These Dreams (1986)
What About Love? (1985)
Who Will You Run To (1987)
Heart __ Lonely Hunter, The: 3 is a
__ Heart: 4 Dear 6 Clara's, Hungry, Purple, Sacred, Wooden 7 Burning, Captive, Foolish
Heart (1955 song) artist: Eddie Fisher
heartache: 3 woe 4 pain 5 agony, dolor, gloom, grief, worry 6 misery, regret, sorrow 7 anguish, despair, sadness, torment, trouble 8 distress, the blues 9 dejection, suffering 10 depression, desolation, loneliness, melancholy, woefulness
__ Heartache: 4 It's a
Heartaches by the Numbers (1959 song) artist: Guy Mitchell
Heartache Tonight (1979 song) artist: Eagles
heart and __: 4 soul
Heart and Soul (1983 song) artist: Huey Lewis and the News
Heart and Soul (1987 song) artist: T'Pau
Heart and Souls (1993 film)
cast: Robert Downey Jr., Charles Grodin, Alfre Woodard
director: Ron Underwood
Heart Attack (1982 song) artist: Olivia Newton-John
heartbeat: 5 pulse, throb
quickener: 6 crisis
sound: 5 thump
Heartbeat (1986 song) artist: Don Johnson
Heartbeat author: Danielle Steel
Heartbeat - It's a Lovebeat (1973 song) artist: DeFranco Family
heartbreak: 3 woe 5 agony, dolor, grief, trial 6 misery, regret, sorrow 7 anguish, despair, sadness, torment 8 distress 9 dejection, suffering 10 affliction, bitterness, depression, desolation, loneliness, woefulness
Heartbreak __: 5 Hotel, House, Ridge
Heartbreaker (song)
artist: Dionne Warwick, Jay-Z, Mariah Carey
__ Heartbreaker: 5 She's a
Heartbreakers (2001 film)
cast: Gene Hackman, Jennifer Love Hewitt, Ray Liotta, Sigourney Weaver
Heartbreak Hotel (song)
artist: Elvis Presley, Faith Evans, Kelly Price, Whitney Houston
Heartbreak House
author: George Bernard Shaw
character: 4 Addy, Dunn 5 Ellie, Hessy
heartbreaking: 3 sad 4 dire 5 sorry, woful 6 bitter, moving, tragic, woeful 7 joyless, piteous, pitiful 8 dolorous, grievous, pathetic, poignant, touching, tragical 10 lamentable, pathetical
Heartbreak Kid, The (1972 film)
cast: Eddie Albert, Charles Grodin, Cybill Shepherd
director: Elaine May
role: 5 Lenny
Heartbreak Ridge (1986 film)
cast: Clint Eastwood, Moses Gunn, Marsha Mason
director: Clint Eastwood
heartbroken: 3 sad 4 blue, down, glum 5 sorry, woful 6 gloomy, morose, somber, woeful 7 crushed, doleful, joyless, unhappy 8 dejected, dismayed, downcast, grieving, mournful, troubled, wretched 9 bummed-out, cheerless, depressed, heartsick, miserable, sorrowful, woebegone 10 chapfallen, dispirited, melancholy
one: 5 piner
heartburn: 5 agita
cause: 3 gas
remedy: 4 Tums 6 Maalox, Pepcid, Riopan, Zantac 7 Gelusil, Lactaid, Mylanta, Rolaids 8 Gaviscon 11 Alka-Seltzer, Pepto-Bismol
Heartburn (1986 film)
cast: Jeff Daniels, Jack Nicholson, Meryl Streep
director: Mike Nichols
__-hearted: 3 big 4 cold, free, good, iron, open, soft, warm 5 black, faint, false, heavy, stony, stout 6 pigeon, simple, single, tender 7 chicken
hearted starter: 4 down, free, good,

half, hard, kind, lion, open, soft 5 great, light, stone, stony, stout, whole 6 broken, tender
hearten: 4 buoy, stir 5 cheer, elate, liven, rouse, steel 6 arouse, assure, buck up, buoy up, please, solace, stir up, thrill 7 cheer up, comfort, condole, console, delight, elevate, enliven, fortify, gladden, gratify, happify, inspire, lighten 8 brighten, embolden, enspirit, imbolden, inspirit, motivate, psyche up, reassure, revivify 9 encourage 10 strengthen
heartening: 6 cheery, joyful, joyous, upbeat 7 hopeful 8 cheerful, jubilant 9 favorable 10 optimistic
heartfelt: 4 dear, deep, real, true, warm 6 ardent, devout, fervid, honest 7 earnest, fervent, genuine, sincere 8 bona fide, profound 9 unfeigned 10 passionate
Heart Full of Soul (1965 song) artist: Yardbirds
hearth: 4 fire, home 5 grate, ingle 8 fireside 9 fireplace
ender: 3 rug 4 side 5 stone
goddess: 5 Vesta
like an unswept ~: 4 ashy
residue: 3 ash 6 cinder
Roman ~ protector: 3 Lar
Roman ~ protectors: 5 Lares
tend the ~: 5 stoke
tool: 5 poker
___ hearth: 3 ore
___-hearth: 4 open
hearthside: 9 fireplace
hearthstone, use a: 5 scour
heartily: 4 well 6 avidly, gladly, warmly 8 ardently 9 cordially, sincerely, zealously
heartiness: 4 fire, zest 5 vigor 6 fervor 9 eagerness, geniality 10 cordiality
Heart in Hand (1962 song) artist: Brenda Lee
Heart is a Lonely Hunter, The author: Carson McCullers
character: 4 Biff, Jake, Mick 5 Alice 6 Portia, Spiros
heartland unit: 4 acre
heartless: 4 cold 5 cruel, harsh, stony 6 brutal, savage, stoney, unkind, wicked 7 callous, inhuman 8 pitiless, ruthless, uncaring 9 barbarous, impassive, merciless, unfeeling, unpitying 10 hard-boiled, unmerciful
one: 4 ogre 5 beast, brute 6 animal, tyrant 9 barbarian
Heartlight (1982 song) artist: Neil Diamond
heart of ___: 4 palm
Heart of a Woman, The author: Maya Angelou
Heart of Darkness author: Joseph Conrad
Heart of Dixie: 3 Ala. 7 Alabama
Heart of Glass (1979 song) artist: Blondie
Heart of Gold (1972 song) artist: Neil Young
Heart of Midlothian, The author: Walter Scott
Heart of Rock & Roll, The (1984 song) artist: Huey Lewis and the News
Heart of Stone (1965 song) artist: Rolling Stones
Heart of the Hunter, The author: Laurens Van der Post
Heart of the Matter, The author: Graham Greene
Heart of the Night (1979 song) artist: Poco
heartrending: 3 bad, sad 4 dire 5 sorry, woful 6 moving, tragic, woeful 7 doleful, pitiful 8 dolorous, grievous, pathetic, poignant, touching, tragical 9 harrowing, plaintive 10 pathetical
hearts: 4 game, suit 8 card game
at times: 5 trump
ender: 4 ease
starter: 6 lonely
two ~: 3 bid
Hearts Afire (CBS sitcom)
cast: Edward Asner (George Lahti) Markie Post (Georgie Hartman) John Ritter (John Hartman)
hearts and ___: 7 flowers
___ Hearts and Coronets: 4 Kind
___ Hearts Dance: 5 Sweet
heart's desire: 4 love, will 7 darling
heart's-ease: 5 pansy
heartsick: 3 low, sad 4 blue, down, glum 5 woful 6 aching, broody, gloomy, morose, somber, woeful 7 doleful, forlorn, joyless, unhappy 8 dejected, downcast, grieving, mournful, troubled 9 bummed out, cheerless, miserable, sorrowful, woebegone 10 chapfallen, dispirited, melancholy
be ~: 4 ache
be ~ about: 3 rue 5 mourn 6 bemoan, bewail, lament, regret
one: 5 piner
heartsickness: 3 woe 5 agony, angst, gloom, grief, worry 6 misery, sorrow 7 anguish, anxiety, despair 9 dejection 10 depression, desolation, melancholy
Hearts of the West (1975 film)
cast: Jeff Bridges, Andy Griffith, Donald Pleasence
Hearts on Fire (1981 song) artist: Randy Meisner
heartstring sound: 4 zing
heartstrings, tug on the: 4 stir
___ Hearts Were Young and Gay: 3 Our
___ Heart, The: 6 Ponder, Purple 7 Divided
heartthrob: 2 jo 3 pet 4 baby, dear, jill, love 5 amour, angel, chéri, cooky, cutey, cutie, deary, ducky, flame, honey, leman, lover, lovey, novia, novio, sugar, sweet 6 bon ami, chérie, cookie, dautie, dearie, steady, sweets 7 beloved, dearest, dear one, pigsney, schatzi, squeeze, sweetie, tootsie 8 chou-chou, cutie pie, dowsabel, dulcinea, ladylove, lovebird, macushla, paramour, precious, snookums, sugar pie, sweetums, truelove 9 bonne amie, boyfriend, dreamboat, inamorata, inamorato, petit chou, valentine 10 girlfriend, honeybunch, mavourneen, sweetie pie, turtledove
heart-to-heart: 4 chat 5 frank 6 candid, honest
heart-to-heart ___: 4 talk
Heart to Heart (1982 song) artist: Kenny Loggins
heartwarming: 4 good 9 rewarding 10 delightful, fulfilling, gratifying, satisfying
hearty: 3 fit 4 avid, hale, iron, warm, well, wiry 5 beefy, burly, eager, hardy, hefty, hunky, husky, jolly, lusty, sound, stout, tough 6 ardent, brawny, cheery, devout, fervid, genial, jovial, mighty, potent, robust, rugged, sinewy, steely, stocky, strong, sturdy, virile 7 affable, cordial, doughty, earnest, fervent, gushing, profuse, sincere, zealous 8 animated, athletic, cheerful, effusive, forceful, friendly, indurate, muscular, powerful, puissant, stalwart, vehement, vigorous 9 Atlantean, convivial, ebullient, energetic, exuberant, Herculean, strapping, unfeigned, vivacious, well-built 10 able-bodied, passionate, red-blooded, rollicking, unreserved
partner: 4 hale
Hear ye!: 4 oyes, oyez
heat: 3 fry 4 bake, boil, char, fury, race, rage, sear, warm 5 anger, ardor, broil, fever, grill, roast, scald, singe, toast 6 fervor, fire up, police, scorch, stress, summer, temper, warmth, warm up 7 firearm, hotness, passion, swelter, torrefy, torrify 8 calidity, calorify, ferocity, melt down, pressure, violence, warmness 9 carbonize, fieriness, intensity, surliness, torridity, vehemence 10 caloricity, excitement, fervidness, sultriness
body ~: 7 pyrexia
combining form: 3 pyr- 4 pyro- 5 therm- 6 calori-, thermo-, -thermy
conductor: 4 coil
dead ~: 3 tie 4 draw
emotional ~: 3 ire 4 fury, rage 5 anger, pique, wrath 6 choler, enmity 7 offense, outrage 10 antagonism
ender: 5 proof
feel the ~: 4 bask 8 sunbathe
join with ~: 4 bond, fuse, melt, weld 6 solder
measure: 3 BTU, cal., deg. 4 kcal. 6 degree 7 calorie
mind's ~: 4 zeal 5 ardor 6 fervor 7 avidity, passion
one in a ~: 4 vier 6 runner 8 sprinter
react to ~: 6 expand
shriveled from ~: 3 dry 4 sere 7 parched 10 desiccated
source: 3 sun 4 coal, fire 6 boiler
suffer from the ~: 4 wilt 5 sweat 7 shrivel, swelter
take the ~ off: 4 ease 5 allay, let up, relax 6 lessen, relent 7 lighten, slacken 8 mitigate, moderate 9 alleviate, disburden
unit: 5 therm 7 calorie
up: 4 boil, cook, nuke, warm 6 arouse 9 impassion, intensify, reinforce
heat ___: 3 gun 4 lamp, pump, sink, wave 5 devil, index 6 engine, island, shield 7 barrier, content
heat ___!, The: 4 is on
heat-___: 4 seal 5 treat
___ heat: 3 red 4 dead 5 blood, fever, solar, steam, total, white 6 bottom, canned, latent 7 Peltier, prickly, radiant
Heat: 4 five, team
home: 5 Miami
org.: 3 NBA
rival: 3 Cav, Mav, Net, Sun 4 Buck, Bull, Hawk, Jazz, King, Spur 5 Knick, Laker, Magic, Pacer, Sixer, Sonic 6 Celtic, Hornet, Nugget, Piston, Raptor, Rocket, Wizard 7 Clipper, Grizzly, Warrior 8 Cavalier, Maverick 10 SuperSonic, Timberwolf
sport: 10 basketball
Heat (1995 film)
cast: Robert De Niro, Val Kilmer, Al Pacino, Jon Voight
director: Michael Mann
Heat ___: 4 Wave
___ Heat: 3 Red 4 Body, City 5 Steam, White
Heat and the Clouds, The artist: 4 Erté
heated: 3 hot 4 warm 5 angry, fiery, irate, upset 6 ablaze, bitter, fervid, fierce, hectic, ireful, raging, stormy, torrid 7 burning, fervent, flaring, furious, intense, thermal, violent 8 feverish, frenzied, vehement, volcanic, wrathful 9 emotional, indignant 10 in an uproar, infuriated, passionate
slightly ~: 5 tepid 8 lukewarm
___-heated: 5 steam
heater: 3 gat, gun, rod 5 stove 6 boiler, pistol, roscoe 7 furnace 8 auto part, fastball, radiator
lab ~: 4 etna
pack a ~: 4 tote 5 carry
___ heater: 5 block, space, water 6 pebble
heath: 4 moor 5 plain, shrub 6 meadow 7 lowland 9 scrubland
family shrub: 5 erica, salal 6 azalea, kalmia, sorrel 7 arbutus, madrone, rhodora 8 cassiope, cowberry 9 blueberry, deerberry
genus: 5 erica
Heath: 5 candy 6 Edward, Ledger 8 candy bar 9 chocolate
alternative: 4 Mars, Twix 5 Clark 6 Kit Kat, Mounds, PayDay, Reese's, Zagnut 7 Krackel, Oh Henry 8 Baby Ruth, Hershey's, Milky Way, Snickers 9 Almond Joy, Mr. Goodbar 10 NutRageous
___ Heath: 5 Egdon
Heathcliff: 3 cat 4 toon
Heath, Edward: 2 P.M. 7 British
predecessor: 6 Wilson
successor: 6 Wilson
heathen: 5 pagan 7 infidel, profane 9 barbarian
ender: 3 dom
heather: 5 color, erica, plant 6 flower, purple 7 pinkish
relative: 4 plum, puce 5 lilac, mauve 6 dahlia, damson, orchid 7 petunia 8 amethyst, burgundy, eggplant, lavender, mulberry 9 raspberry 10 heliotrope
where ~ grows: 4 moor
Heather: 6 Graham, Thomas 7 Menzies, O'Rourke, Rattray 8 Locklear 10 Langenkamp
Heather on the Hill, The composer: 5 Loewe 6 Lerner
Heathers (1989 film)
cast: Shannen Doherty, Winona Ryder, Christian Slater
Heatherton: 3 Ray 4 Joey
Heathrow arr., former: 3 SST
heating
conduit: 4 duct
fuel: 3 oil 4 coal
unit: 5 therm 6 burner, therme
heating ___: 3 pad
heating ___-day: 6 degree
___ heating: 5 panel, solar, steam 7 central, radiant
Heat Is on, The (1985 song) artist: Glenn Frey
Heat of the Day, The author: 5 Bowen
___ heat of the moment: 5 in the
Heat of the Moment (1982 song) artist: Asia
___ Heat of the Night: 5 In the
Heat of the Night (1987 song) artist: Bryan Adams
Heaton: 8 Patricia
heat-resistant
alloy: 6 cermet 7 ceramal
material: 5 Pyrex 6 boride
___ Heat, The: 3 Big
Heat Wave composer: Irving Berlin
Heat Wave (song) artist: Linda Ronstadt, Martha & the Vandellas
heave: 3 lug, pry, tug 4 cast, fire, haul, heft, hurl, keel, lift, move, pant, puff, pull, roll, sigh, spew, spue, toss, wash, wave 5 boost, bulge, chuck, fling, hoist, lurch, pitch, raise, roust, sling, surge, swell, throw 6 billow, launch, let fly, plunge, propel, thrust,

well up **7** elevate, project **8** catapult, jettison
at sea: 5 scend
out: 4 boot, bump, rout **5** eject, evict, expel **6** banish, bounce, depose **7** cast off **8** drive off, get rid of **9** eliminate **10** dispossess
heave-ho: 4 boot **9** discharge, dismissal
give the ~: 3 axe, can **4** boot, fire, oust **6** depose
heaven: 3 sky **5** azure, bliss **6** utopia **7** Arcadia, ecstasy, Elysium, nirvana, rapture **8** empyrean, paradise **9** cloud nine, firmament, happiness, Shangri-la
ender: 4 ward **5** wards
food from ~: 5 manna
highest ~: 8 empyrean
in ~: 4 glad, over **5** above, aloft, happy, merry **6** blithe, cheery, elated, jovial, joyful, joyous, upbeat **7** gleeful, pleased, tickled **8** blissful, cheerful, ecstatic, euphoric, exultant, jubilant, mirthful, thrilled **9** delighted, ebullient, overjoyed, rapturous, rejoicing, rhapsodic
like ~: 5 above, aloft
made in ~: 5 ideal **7** perfect, utopian **9** exemplary, nonpareil
manna from ~: 4 boon **7** godsend **8** blessing, windfall
on earth: 4 Eden
opposite: 5 Hades
queen of ~: 4 Hera
search high ~: 4 comb **6** forage **7** ransack
vault of ~: 3 sky **8** empyrean
heaven ___: 5 knows
heaven ___ me: 4 help
heaven-___: 4 born, sent
___ heaven: 3 hog **5** thank **6** peanut **7** seventh
___ Heaven: 5 Cry to **7** Seventh
___ heaven and earth: 4 move
Heaven Can Wait (1943 film)
cast: Don Ameche, Charles Coburn, Gene Tierney
director: Ernst Lubitsch
Heaven Can Wait (1978 film)
cast: Warren Beatty, Dyan Cannon, Julie Christie, Jack Warden
director: Warren Beatty, Buck Henry
___ Heaven for Little Girls: 5 Thank
Heaven Help Me (1989 song)
artist: Dean Estus, George Michael
Heaven Help Us (1985 film)
cast: John Heard, Andrew McCarthy, Donald Sutherland
Heaven Help Us All (1970 song) artist: Stevie Wonder
Heaven Is a Place on Earth (1987 song) artist: Belinda Carlisle
Heaven Knows (1979 song) artist: Donna Summer
Heaven Knows, Mr. Allison (1957 film)
cast: Deborah Kerr, Robert Mitchum
director: John Huston
heavenly: 3 def, rad **4** aces, A-one, boss, braw, cool, dece, fine, gear, keen, lush, neat, nice, phat, tuff **5** dandy, ducky, grand, great, marvy, neato, nobby, prime, slick, super, sweet, swell, tasty, yummy **6** astral, bang on, bang-up, bonzer, bosker, choice, divine, dreamy, edenic, far-out, gnarly, groovy, lovely, peachy, slap-up, spot on, superb, terrif, tiptop, toothy, unreal, whizzo, wicked **7** amazing, angelic, awesome, capital, corking, darling, perfect, ripping, skookum, stellar, sublime **8** adorable, alluring, almighty, beatific, blissful, dazzling, empyreal, empyrean, especial, ethereal, eximious, fabulous, five-star, four-star, frabjous, glorious, jim-dandy, luscious, pleasant, seraphic, slam-bang, smashing, splendid, standout, sterling, stickout, stunning, superior, supernal, terrific, top-level, topnotch, very good, wondrous **9** ambrosial, angelical, beautiful, bodacious, celestial, delicious, Endsville, enjoyable, excellent, exemplary, exquisite, first-rate, good to eat, high-grade, hunky-dory, ineffable, marvelous, nectarous, rapturous, sollicker, succulent, top-flight, unrivaled, wonderful **10** delectable, delightful, entrancing, first-class, hotsy-totsy, jack-a-dandy, out of sight, peachy-keen, phenomenal, remarkable, seraphical, stupendous, super-duper, unrivalled
name meaning ~: 7 Celeste
heavenly ___: 4 hash **6** bamboo
heavenly hash: 8 ice cream
alternative: 5 lemon, mocha, peach **6** banana, coffee, Jamoca, toffee **7** caramel, coconut, vanilla **8** cinnamon, hazelnut **9** bubblegum, chocolate, pineapple, pistachio, raspberry, rocky road, rum raisin **10** blackberry, cheesecake, Neapolitan, peppermint, strawberry
Heaven Makers, The author: Frank Herbert
heavens: 3 sky **5** ether **6** aether **9** firmament **10** atmosphere
combining form: 4 uran- **5** urano-
survey the ~: 4 gaze
Heavens ___!: 5 above
Heavens!: 4 egad, gosh, oh my, oh no **5** egads, mercy **6** dear me **10** my goodness
Heaven (song) artist: Bryan Adams, Warrant
___ heaven's sake!: 3 For
heavenward: 5 above
heavier-___-air: 4 than
heavily: 4 hard
in music: 7 pesante
heaviness: 4 heft, mass **6** weight **7** boredom, gravity **8** dullness, pressure
determine the ~ of: 5 weigh
heaving sound: 5 grunt
Heaviside ___: 5 layer
heavy: 3 big, sad **4** deep, hard, huge, logy, rich **5** ample, beefy, dense, grave, gross, harsh, hefty, laden, leady, obese, prime, rough, solid, squat, stiff, stout, thick, tough **6** bad guy, broody, chunky, dismal, fleshy, gloomy, knotty, leaden, portly, severe, sleepy, solemn, stodgy, stolid, stuffy, sullen, sultry, taxing, torpid, zaftig, zoftig **7** arduous, complex, fraught, labored, languid, lumpish, massive, onerous, sensual, serious, tedious, weighty **8** abstruse, abundant, dejected, downcast, grievous, listless, profound, sluggish, tiresome, toilsome, unwieldy, weighted **9** corpulent, depressed, difficult, excessive, impassive, laborious, lethargic, momentous, ponderous, recondite, sorrowful, strenuous, unwieldly, wearisome **10** burdensome, cumbersome, despondent, enervating, formidable, melancholy, oppressive, overweight, passionate, well-padded
be ~: 5 weigh
blow: 4 welt **5** thump, whomp **6** wallop
coat: 5 parka, wamus **6** anorak, ulster, wammus, wampus
combining form: 4 bary- **5** gravi-
ender: 3 set **6** weight
fabric: 4 wool **5** denim, loden **8** cretonne
heart: 3 woe **4** funk **5** blues, dolor, gloom, grief **6** misery, pathos, sorrow **7** anguish, sadness **8** distress, doldrums, glumness **9** dejection **10** depression, gloominess, melancholy
hitter: 4 czar **5** mogul
hot and ~: 6 ardent
jacket: 5 wamus **6** ulster, wammus, wampus
knock: 4 slam, thud **5** clonk, clunk, thunk
load: 4 onus **6** burden, weight
metal: 4 iron, lead **5** armor, brass, music
not ~: 4 lean, puny, slim, thin, trim **5** light, spare **6** dainty, flimsy, gentle, scanty, skinny, slight, sparse, svelte, twiggy **7** slender, willowy **8** delicate, ethereal, feathery, gossamer **9** gossamery
sound: 4 thud, wham **5** clonk, clunk, thump, thunk
weight: 3 ton
weigh ~ upon: 5 worry **6** burden, plague, sadden **7** oppress, torment **8** distress **10** dishearten
heavy ___: 4 spar **5** chain, cream, metal, water **6** bomber, hitter, oxygen **7** cruiser, lifting, traffic
heavy-___: 4 duty **5** laden **6** footed, handed **7** bearded, hearted
___-heavy: 3 top
Heavy (1996 film)
cast: Deborah Harry, Liv Tyler, Shelley Winters
director: James Mangold
heavy-duty: 3 big **6** hearty, potent, robust, rugged, strong **7** durable **8** powerful, well-made **9** well-built
heavy-eyed: 4 dozy **5** yawny **6** drowsy, groggy, sleepy **9** somnolent **10** half-asleep
heavy-footed: 5 gawky **6** clumsy, klutzy **7** awkward, hulking **8** clunking, ungainly **9** lumbering, maladroit
heavy-handed: 4 hard **5** bossy, harsh, unfit **6** clumsy, gauche, severe **7** awkward, uncouth **8** despotic, lubberly **9** draconian, graceless, maladroit, ponderous **10** autocratic, despotical, ironfisted, oppressive, tyrannical, ungraceful
one: 3 ape, oaf **6** galoot, lummox
heavy-hearted: 3 sad **4** blue **5** sorry **7** crushed, forlorn, unhappy **8** dejected, downcast, mournful **9** depressed, long-faced, miserable, sorrowful **10** chapfallen, melancholy
be ~: 4 moan, mope, pine **5** brood, mourn **6** grieve, lament **7** agonize **8** languish
heavy hydrogen discoverer: 4 Urey
heavy-load mover: 5 dolly, truck
heavy-metal: 4 rock **5** music
heavyset: 3 big **5** squat **6** chunky, rugged, stocky, stubby
Heavy Traffic (1973 film) director: Ralph Bakshi
heavyweight: 3 big, VIP **5** biggy, boxer, hefty **6** biggie, big gun, bigwig **7** big name, big shot, massive, notable **8** big wheel, powerful, somebody, superior, wrestler **9** dignitary, important, personage, ponderous
see also boxing
___ heavyweight: 5 light
Hebb, Bobby song: Sunny (1966)
Hebbel, Friedrich: 4 poet **6** German **10** playwright
hebdomad: 4 week **6** septet
hebe: 4 tree **5** shrub
Hebe: 8 asteroid
brother of ~: 4 Ares
husband of ~: 8 Heracles
parent of ~: 4 Hera, Zeus
Hebert: 3 Jay **6** Lionel
Hébert, Anne: 4 poet **8** Canadian
hebetude: 5 sloth **6** torpor **7** languor **8** laziness, lethargy **9** indolence, torpidity
hebetudinous: 4 logy **5** heavy **6** torpid
Hebrew: 5 Isaac, Jacob **6** Danite, Jewish, Levite **7** Abraham, Solomon **8** language **9** Israelite
bushel: 4 epha, omer **5** ephah
dance: 4 hora
dry measure: 4 epha, omer **5** ephah
eve: 4 ereb, erev
exclamation ~: 6 l'chaim **7** l'chayim, lehayim **8** lechayim
feast: 5 seder
holiday: 5 Purim **8** Passover
judge: 3 Eli
king: 4 Saul **5** David **7** Solomon
law: 4 Tora **5** Torah
letter: 2 he, pe **3** bes, bet, heh, kof, mem, nun, peh, sin, tau, tav, taw, tet, vav, vaw, waw, yod **4** alef, ayin, beth, caph, heth, kaph, koph, qoph, resh, sadi, shin, teth, yodh **5** aleph, cheth, gimel, lamed, sadhe, tsade, tsadi, zayin **6** daleth, lamedh, samech, samekh
lyre: 4 asor
measure: 3 hin, kor
month: 2 Av **4** Adar, Elul, Iyar **5** Nisan, Sivan, Tevet **6** Kislev, Shevat, Tammuz, Tishri **7** Heshvan
people: 4 Sion, Zion
poet: 6 Bialik **8** Alterman **9** Greenberg
prayer: 5 shema
priest: 5 Aaron
prophet: 4 Amos, Ezra **5** Elias, Hosea, Moses
queen: 6 Esther
sacrifice: 6 corban, korban
scholar: 5 rabbi, rebbe
tribe: 3 Dan **4** Levi
underworld: 5 Sheol
writer: 5 Agnon
___ Hebrew: 3 New **5** Early **6** Modern
Hebrew National: 5 frank **6** hot dog, wiener
alternative: 5 Kahn's **6** Armour **8** Ball Park **10** Oscar Mayer
Hebrews: 4 book
follower: 5 James
preceder: 8 Philemon
Hebrides: 4 isls. **5** isles **7** islands
island: 4 Iona, Mull, Skye, Uist **5** Barra, Islay
language: 4 Erse
locale: 8 Scotland
___ Hebrides: 5 Inner, Outer
Hebrides Overture composer: 11 Mendelssohn
Hebron grp.: 3 PLO
Hecate: 8 conjurer, sorcerer
daughter of ~: 5 Aeaea, Circe, Kirke, Medea **6** Scylla **8** Apsyrtus
Heche, Anne: 7 actress
film: John Q (2002)
The Juror (1996)
Return to Paradise (1998)
Six Days Seven Nights (1998)
The Third Miracle (1999)
Volcano (1997)
Wag the Dog (1997)
Hecht, Ben: 5 actor **6** author, writer **10** playwright
film: Angels Over Broadway (1940)
Crime Without Passion (1934)
The Scoundrel (1935)
Specter of the Rose (1946)

work: Erik Dorn
The Front Page
heck: 4 darn, drat, rats 6 phooey 7 dickens 9 all get-out
Heckart, Eileen Oscar: Butterflies Are Free
Heckerling, Amy: 8 director
film: Clueless (1995)
Fast Times at Ridgemont High (1982)
Look Who's Talking (1989)
heckle: 3 boo, dis, nag, rag 4 bait, faze, gibe, hiss, jeer, jibe, mock, razz, ride, slam, slur, snub 5 abuse, annoy, decry, hound, libel, scorn, spurn, taunt 6 badger, bother, defame, deride, dump on, harass, impugn, malign, needle, noodge, offend, pester, plague, rattle, rebuff, slight, vilify 7 affront, asperse, catcall, degrade, disdain, disrupt, disturb, put down, rank out, shout at, slander, torment, traduce 8 belittle, denounce, ridicule, vilipend 9 denigrate, discomfit, discredit, disparage, humiliate 10 calumniate, disconcert, disrespect
Heckle: 4 toon 6 magpie
colleague: 6 Jeckle
heckler: 4 pest 5 booer
missile: 3 egg 6 tomato
Heckman, James: 8 Nobelist 9 economist
hectare cousin: 4 acre
hectic: 4 busy, wild 5 crazy, wooly 6 fervid, heated, rushed, woolly 7 chaotic, excited, frantic, furious, hurried, riotous 8 agitated, animated, confused, exciting, feverish, frenetic, frenzied 9 turbulent 10 boisterous, disordered, in an uproar, rip-roaring, tumultuous
hector: 3 cow, irk, nag, vex 4 haze, jeer, ride, roil 5 annoy, bully, hound, peeve, scold, tease, worry 6 badger, harass, needle, noodge, pester, pick on, plague, pother 7 bluster, henpeck, swagger 8 bludgeon, browbeat, bulldoze, bullyboy, domineer 9 persecute, strong-arm, terrorize, tyrannize 10 intimidate
Hector: 4 hero 6 Trojan 7 Babenco, Berlioz, Garneau 8 Elizondo
brother of ~: 5 Paris 6 Pammon 7 Helenus, Polites, Troilus 8 Antiphus 9 Deiphobus, Hipponous, Polydorus
home: 4 Troy
in Italian: 6 Ettore
parent of ~: 5 Priam 6 Hecuba 7 Priamus
sister of ~: 6 Creusa, Iliona 7 Laodice 8 Polyxena 9 Cassandra
slayer of ~: 8 Achilles
son of ~: 8 Astyanax
victim of ~: 6 Dolops 7 Epigeus, Trechus 8 Aesymnus, Coeranus, Oresbius, Schedius, Stichius, Teuthras 9 Anchialus, Lycophron, Menesthes, Patroclus 10 Antilochus, Periphetes
wife of ~: 10 Andromache
Hector ___ Camacho: 5 Macho
...Hector ___ a pup: 3 was
Hector Servadac author: Jules Verne
Hecuba: 6 Trojan
brother of ~: 5 Asius
daughter of ~: 6 Creusa, Iliona 7 Laodice 8 Polyxena 9 Cassandra
home: 4 Troy
husband of ~: 5 Priam 7 Priamus
son of ~: 5 Paris 6 Hector, Pammon 7 Helenus, Polites, Troilus 8 Antiphus 9 Deiphobus, Hipponous, Polydorus
Hecuba author: Euripides
Hedaya: 3 Dan
Hedda: 6 Gabler, Hopper
Hedda Gabler author: Henrik Ibsen
character: 4 Thea 5 Brack 6 Eilert 7 Tessman
hedge: 3 pen 4 bush, duck, ring 5 avoid, delay, dodge, evade, fence, fudge, hem in, skirt, stall, wager, waver 6 corral, offset, privet, screen, waffle 7 barrier, confine, enclose, inclose, shuffle, thicket, whiffle 8 boundary, flip-flop, hesitate, sidestep, surround 9 hem and haw, pussyfoot, runaround, shrubbery, stonewall, temporize, vacillate 10 equivocate
arrangement: 4 maze
cut the ~: 4 snip, trim 5 prune
ender: 3 hog, hop, row
expert: 3 arb
something to hedge: 3 bet 4 risk
trimmer: 6 shears
hedge ___: 4 fund 5 apple 6 garlic, nettle 7 sparrow
hedged in: 4 pent
hedgehog: 6 animal, mammal
cousin: 4 mole
feature: 5 spine
female: 3 sow
like a ~: 5 spiny 7 bristly, prickly
male: 4 boar
video-game ~: 5 Sonic
young: 3 pup
hedgehog ___: 5 gourd 6 cactus
hedges: 9 shrubbery
hedging one's bets: 4 sage, wary, wise 5 chary, leery 7 careful, guarded, politic, prudent 8 cautious 9 judicious, provident, sagacious, tentative
Hedin, Sven: 7 Swedish 8 explorer 10 geographer
Hedison: 5 David
He done ___ wrong: 3 her
hedonism: 6 luxury 10 indulgence, profligacy, sybaritism
hedonist: 5 pagan 8 sybarite 9 bon vivant, libertine 10 sensualist, voluptuary
hedonistic: 7 sensual 8 sensuous 9 epicurean, luxurious
He Don't Love You (1975 song) artist: Tony Orlando & Dawn
He don't plant ___: 6 taters
Hedren, Tippi: 7 actress
daughter: Melanie Griffith
-hedron starter: 5 penta-
___ he drove out of sight...: 3 ere
Hedy: 6 Lamarr
___-hee: 3 tee
heebie-jeebies: 6 nerves 7 anxiety, fidgets, jitters, willies
heed: 3 ear 4 care, hark, hear, look, mind, obey 5 bow to, study, watch 6 accept, advert, attend, bend to, concur, follow, fulfil, hollow, listen, notice, regard 7 abide by, agree to, caution, concern, defer to, fulfill, hearken, hear out, observe, respect, thought 8 adhere to, carry out, consider, listen to, listen up 9 alertness, attention, conform to, consent to, give a darn, give ear to, lend an ear, vigilance 10 bear in mind, cognizance, comply with, observance, solicitude, take note of, take notice, toe the line
don't ~: 6 ignore 7 disobey
give ~ to: 4 mind 6 listen
giving no ~: 4 deaf
take ~: 4 mark, mind, tend 5 watch 6 advert, attend, beware, harken, listen, notice 7 hearken, observe, respect 8 listen to, watch out
take ~, old-style: 4 reck
the alarm: 4 rise, wake 5 awake, get up, waken 6 awaken
heedful: 4 kind, wary 5 alert, awake, aware, canny, chary, ready 6 kindly, polite 7 careful, gallant, mindful, on guard, prudent, tactful, wakeful 8 cautious, gracious, obliging, vigilant, watchful 9 attentive, observant, regardful, sensitive, unselfish 10 meticulous, on one's toes, protective, solicitous, thoughtful
heedfulness: 7 caution, concern 9 chariness 10 precaution
heedless: 4 deaf, rash, rude 5 blind, brash, hasty, loose, nervy, slack 6 blithe, madcap, remiss, unruly, unwary, wanton 7 boorish, selfish, unaware 8 careless, impolite, listless, mindless, reckless, slovenly, tactless, uncaring 9 daredevil, foolhardy, impetuous, imprudent, incurious, negligent, oblivious, unadvised, uncareful, unguarded, unhearing, unmindful 10 incautious, indiscreet, neglectful, regardless, ungracious, unthinking
heedlessly: 7 lightly 8 absently, pellmell 9 headfirst
heedlessness: 5 haste 6 laxity 7 neglect 8 lethargy
Heeger, Alan: 7 chemist 8 Nobelist
heehaw: 4 bray 5 fleer 6 guffaw 7 snicker, snigger 8 laughter 10 horselaugh
Hee Haw (TV variety)
host: Roy Clark, Buck Owens
humor: 4 corn
mascot: 3 ass 6 donkey
radio station: KORN
heehee: 5 laugh 6 giggle, titter 7 chuckle, snicker
heel: 3 cad, cur, end, tag, tip 4 jerk, list, rear, tilt, toad, worm 5 churl, knave, louse, rogue, scamp, slant, sneak 6 bad guy, plunge, rascal, rotter 7 dastard, lowlife, recline, remnant, residue, villain 9 miscreant, reprobate, scoundrel, vulgarian 10 blackguard
Achilles ~: 8 weakness
at ~: 5 close 6 at hand, nearby
attachment: 3 tap
bring to ~: 4 tame
down at ~: 5 needy
ender: 3 tap 4 ball, post, work 5 piece
high ~: 4 pump 5 spike
light of ~: 4 fast 5 fleet, quick, rapid, swift 6 nimble, speedy
over: 3 tip 4 list 5 pitch 6 careen
partner: 3 toe 4 sole
heel ___: 3 fly 4 bone 6 breast
___ heel: 5 Cuban, Louis, spike, stack, wedge 6 French 7 Spanish, stacked
___ Heel: 3 Tar
heel-and-___: 3 toe
heeler: 3 dog, pol 5 canid 6 canine 8 politico 10 politician
___ heeler: 4 ward
heeling, nautically: 5 alist
heels: 4 shoe 8 footwear
cool one's ~: 4 wait 5 tarry 8 sit tight
dig in one's ~: 4 balk 6 refuse, resist
down at the ~: 4 poor, worn 5 broke, needy, seedy 6 bad off, hard up, ill off, in need, in want 7 pinched 8 badly off, bankrupt, beggarly, indigent, strapped 9 destitute, insolvent, moneyless, penniless, penurious 10 pauperized, straitened
go for, as the ~: 5 nip at
go head over ~: 4 fall, slip, trip 5 lurch 6 plunge, sprawl, topple, tumble 7 stumble
head over ~: 4 gaga 6 in love 7 smitten 8 absorbed 9 intensely 10 completely, thoroughly
kick up one's ~: 4 lark, romp 5 caper, jaunt, revel 6 cavort, frolic, gambol, prance 7 carouse, rollick 9 make merry, whoop it up
lay by the ~: 3 bag, nab 4 bust, grab, nail 5 catch, pinch, run in, seize 6 arrest, collar, detain, pick up, pull in, snap up, snatch 7 capture 9 apprehend
on the ~ of: 5 after 6 behind 9 following
take to one's ~: 3 fly, hie, run 4 flee 5 lam it
___ heels of: 5 on the
___ Heel State: 3 Tar
Heep: 5 Uriah
emulate: 4 fawn
Heflin: 3 Van 6 Howell
Heflin, Van: 5 actor
film: 3:10 to Yuma (1957)
Act of Violence (1949)
Airport (1970)
Battle Cry (1955)
Flight From Glory (1937)
Gunman's Walk (1958)
Johnny Eager (1941, AA)
Kid Glove Killer (1942)
Madame Bovary (1949)
Patterns (1956)
Possessed (1947)
The Raid (1954)
Shane (1953)
Woman's World (1954)
Hefner: 4 Hugh 8 Christie
Hefner, Hugh prop: 4 pipe, robe
heft: 4 bulk, lift, mass 5 heave, hoist, raise, weigh 6 haul up, import, lift up, pounds, weight 7 gravity, hoist up, raise up 9 bulkiness, heaviness, substance 10 importance
Hefti: 4 Neal
hefty: 3 big 4 hale, iron, wiry 5 ample, beefy, bulky, burly, hardy, heavy, hulky, hunky, husky, large, lusty, pudgy, solid, stout, tough 6 brawny, chubby, hearty, leaden, mighty, portly, potent, robust, rugged, severe, sinewy, steely, stocky, strong, sturdy, taxing, virile 7 doughty, hulking, massive, onerous, sizable, weighty 8 athletic, colossal, forceful, indurate, muscular, powerful, puissant, sizeable, stalwart, thumping, tiresome, unwieldy, vigorous, whapping, whopping 9 Atlantean, corpulent, extensive, Herculean, ponderous, strapping, unwieldy, well-built 10 able-bodied, burdensome, cumbersome, oppressive, overweight, red-blooded, tremendous, well-padded
chunk: 4 slab
guy: 4 hulk
Hefty: 4 wrap
alternative: 4 Glad 5 Saran 6 Ziploc 8 Reynolds
hegari: 5 grain
Hegel, Georg: 11 philosopher
hegemony: 4 rule, sway 5 power 7 command, control, primacy 8 dominion 9 supremacy 10 domination, leadership
hegira: 6 exodus, flight 7 journey
He Got Game (1998 film)
cast: Ray Allen, Milla Jovovich, Denzel Washington
director: Spike Lee
Hegyes: 6 Robert
heh: 5 laugh 6 Hebrew, letter
predecessor: 6 daleth
successor: 3 vav, vaw, waw
Heidegger, Martin: 11 philosopher
Heidelberg: 4 city, town
locale: 7 Germany
river: 6 Neckar
Heidelberg ___: 3 jaw, man

Heiden, Eric: 6 skater
Heidi: 5 Bohay, novel
  author: Johanna Spyri
  home: 4 Alps
Heidt, Horace: 10 bandleader
heifer: 3 cow 4 calf 6 animal, bovine, cattle, mammal
  dehorned ~: 5 muley 6 mulley
  hangout: 3 lea, ley 4 farm
heifers: 4 kine
Heifetz, Jascha: 9 violinist
  colleague: 5 Elman
  teacher: 4 Auer
height: 3 alt., tip, top 4 acme, apex, cusp, elev., head, hill, peak, rise, size 5 crest, crown, level, limit, pitch 6 apogee, climax, heyday, heydey, length, summit, tip-top, vertex, zenith 7 ceiling, maximum, stature 8 altitude, eminence, mountain, pinnacle, solstice, tallness, ultimate 9 dimension, elevation, largeness, loftiness, precipice 10 prominence
  combining form: 3 acr- 4 acro-, hyps- 5 hypsi-, hypso-
  enhancer: 4 lift 5 stilt
  how ~ may be measured: 5 y-axis
  name meaning ~: 3 Eli
  of fashion: 3 hem 4 rage
  of the same ~: 4 even 5 level 6 square 8 parallel
  opposite: 5 depth 6 length
  prefix: 4 alti-
  rocky ~: 3 tor 4 crag 5 cliff
  to a cager: 5 asset
__ height: 4 spot 5 slant
heighten: 3 wax 4 grow, lift, rise 5 add to, bloat, boost, build, exalt, mount, raise, rouse, swell 6 beef up, dilate, expand, extend, gather, spread 7 amplify, augment, boost up, broaden, build up, burgeon, develop, elevate, enhance, enlarge, improve, inflate, magnify, raise up, spice up 8 bourgeon, escalate, increase, multiply 9 intensify 10 accentuate, aggrandize, strengthen
__ Heights: 5 Golan 6 Shaker 7 Liberty, Pacific
heights, reach the: 4 soar 5 climb
Heimskringla: 4 saga
Hein: 3 Mel
Heine, Heinrich: 4 poet 6 German
  homeland: Germany
  work: Atta Troll
Heineken: 4 beer
  alternative: 5 Becks, Coors, Pabst 6 Amstel, Corona, Miller, Molson 7 Schlitz 8 Michelob 9 Lowenbrau 10 Ballantine
Heinie: 6 Manush
heinous: 3 bad 4 base, evil, foul 5 awful, curst, grave, gross, nasty 6 crying, cursed, odious, unholy, wicked 7 accurst, beastly, ghastly, hateful, hideous, ignoble, satanic, vicious 8 accursed, flagrant, grievous, horrible, infamous, shameful, shocking 9 abhorrent, atrocious, execrable, frightful, monstrous, nefarious, offensive, repellant, repellent, revolting, satanical 10 abominable, detestable, flagitious, horrendous, horrifying, inexpiable, iniquitous, outrageous, scandalous, villainous, virtueless
heinousness: 4 evil, vice 6 horror, infamy 7 outrage 8 atrocity, ignominy, iniquity, villainy 9 flagrancy, indecency 10 corruption, opprobrium
Heinrich: 4 Böll, Mann 5 Heine, Hertz 6 Rohrer, Schütz 7 Wieland 10 Schliemann
  in English: 5 Henry
  see also German
Heinse, Wilhelm: 6 German, writer
Heinsohn, Tom
  milieu: 5 court
  org.: 3 NBA
  sport: 10 basketball
Heinz: 6 catsup 7 ketchup
  alternative: 5 Hunt's 8 Del Monte
  product: 4 food 5 beans 7 pickles
  see also German
heir: 4 cion 5 owner, scion, sprig 7 devisee, grantee, heritor, legatee 9 inheritor, offspring, successor 10 descendant
  concern: 4 will 6 estate
  ender: 3 dom, ess 4 loom
  fall ~ to: 3 get, own 4 gain 6 obtain 7 acquire, inherit, receive, succeed 8 come into, take over
  homophone: 3 air, ere
  maybe: 3 son 5 niece 6 eldest, nephew 8 daughter
  to the throne: 6 dynast
heiress: 4 cion 5 owner, scion 7 devisee, grantee, heritor, legatee 9 inheritor, successor
Heiress, The (1949 film)
  cast: Montgomery Clift, Olivia de Havilland, Ralph Richardson
  director: William Wyler
heirloom: 5 relic 6 legacy 7 antique, bequest 8 valuable
heirs: 4 kids, seed 5 issue 7 kinfolk, progeny 8 children, kinfolks, kinsfolk 9 posterity
  proverbial ~: 4 meek
Heisenberg, Werner: 8 Nobelist 9 physicist, scientist
Heisler, Stuart: 8 director
  film: Along Came Jones (1945)
    Beachhead (1954)
    The Biscuit Eater (1940)
    Blue Skies (1946)
    The Glass Key (1942)
    Smash-up, the Story of a Woman (1947)
    The Star (1952)
    Tulsa (1949)
Heisman Trophy: 5 award
  sport: 8 football
Heiss, Carol: 6 skater
heist: 3 job, rob 4 lift 5 caper, crime, steal, swipe, theft 6 holdup, pilfer, rip-off, thieve 7 bank job, break-in, larceny, robbery, stickup 8 burglary, thievery 9 pilferage
  heister: 5 crook, ganef, thief
  stuff: 4 haul, loot, take 5 booty 7 plunder
Heist (2001 film)
  cast: Danny DeVito, Gene Hackman, Delroy Lindo
  director: David Mamet
hejira: 6 exodus, flight 7 journey, odyssey 9 migration 10 pilgrimage
__ Hejirae: 4 Anno
Hekawi: 5 tribe 7 Indians
__ He Kissed Me: 4 Then
Hekla: 7 volcano
  locale: 7 Iceland
Hel
  father of ~: 4 Loki
held: 4 fast 6 jailed 7 captive, reputed 8 obsessed 10 spellbound
  back: 5 sat on 6 pent-up 9 in reserve
  be ~ by: 8 belong to
  dear: 8 valuable
  down: 5 under 6 pinned
  fast: 4 rapt 7 charmed, gripped 8 absorbed, beguiled, immersed 9 engrossed, entranced 10 captivated, enraptured, enthralled, fascinated, hypnotized, spellbound
  in ballet: 5 tendu
  it may be ~: 4 mayo
  off: 5 at bay 6 caught 8 cornered 9 powerless
  starter: 4 hand, with
  up: 4 late 5 tardy 7 overdue 8 detained
Held, Anna spouse: Flo Ziegfeld
Helen: 4 Hunt, Kane, Mack, play 5 Hayes, Price, Reddy, saint, Trent, Wills 6 Keller, Mirren, Morgan, Shaver, Slater, Thomas 7 Gahagan, Traubel 8 Fielding, MacInnes, O'Connell, Van Slyke 9 Broderick
  abductor: 5 Paris
  attendant of ~: 7 Adraste
  author: Euripides
  brother of ~: 6 Castor, Pollux
  city: 4 Troy 5 Ilium
  daughter of ~: 8 Hermione 9 Iphigenia
  husband of ~: 5 Paris 8 Menelaus 9 Deiphobus
  in French: 6 Elaine
  in Italian: 5 Elena
  in Russian: 6 Yelena
  in Spanish: 5 Elena
  lover of ~: 7 Theseus
  parent of ~: 4 Leda, Zeus
  son of ~: 6 Aganus, Idaeus, Xuthus 7 Bunomus 8 Corythus
  suitor of ~: 4 Aias, Ajax 5 Meges, Thoas 6 Leitus, Nireus, Teucer 7 Ancaeus, Clytius, Eumelus, Machaon 8 Agapenor, Alcmaeon, Diomedes, Ialmenus, Leonteus, Menelaus, Meriones, Odysseus, Peneleus, Podarces, Prothous, Schedius, Thalpius 9 Elephenor, Eurypylus, Idomeneus, Lycomedes, Patroclus, Phidippus, Polyxenus, Sthenelus 10 Antilochus, Menestheus, Podalirius, Polypoetes, Tlepolemus
Helen __ Brown: 6 Gurley
Helen __ Douglas: 7 Gahagan
Helen __ Jackson: 4 Hunt
Helen __ Moody: 5 Wills
Helen __ Slyke: 3 Van
Helena: 4 city, town 5 falls 9 waterfall 10 Rubinstein
  locale: 7 Montana
  rival: 5 Estée
Helena __ Carter: 6 Bonham
Helene: 4 moon 5 Hanff
  planet: 6 Saturn
Hélène: 6 Cixous
  see also French
Hélène author: Emile Zola
Helene Curtis rival: 4 Avon, Pert 5 Prell
Helen Gahagan __: 7 Douglas
Helen Gurley __: 5 Brown
Helen Hunt __: 7 Jackson
Helen of __: 4 Troy
Helens, Mt. St.: 4 peak 7 volcano
  clock setting: 3 PDT, PST
  locale: 4 Wash. 10 Washington
Helenus: 4 seer
  brother of ~: 5 Paris 6 Hector
  parent of ~: 5 Priam 6 Hecuba 7 Priamus
  twin of ~: 9 Cassandra
Helen Van __: 5 Slyke
Helen Wheels (1973 song) artist: Paul McCartney
Helen Wills __: 5 Moody
Helfgott, David: 7 British, pianist
Helga: 4 toon
  daughter: 4 Honi
  husband: 5 Hägar
Helgenberger: 4 Marg
helical: 5 spiry 6 coiled, curled, spiral 7 whorled
helical __: 4 gear, rack
Helice husband: 3 Ion
helicon: 4 horn, tuba, wind 10 instrument
helicopter: 7 chopper 8 aircraft 10 whirlybird
  Army ~: 6 Apache
  like some ~ rescues: 6 air-sea
  part: 5 rotor
  sound: 4 whir 5 whirr
heliophobe fear: 3 Sun
Helios: 3 god
  daughter of ~: 3 Aex 5 Aeaea, Circe, Kirke 8 Pasiphae
  equivalent: 3 Sol
  lover of ~: 5 Aegle, Rhode 7 Clymene, Perseis
  parent of ~: 4 Thia 8 Hyperion
  sister of ~: 3 Eos 6 Selene
  son of ~: 5 Actis, Auges, Macar 6 Aeetes 7 Ochimus, Tenages, Thrinax, Triopas 8 Candalus, Phaethon 9 Cercaphus 10 Electryone
heliotrope: 5 color, plant 6 flower, purple 7 reddish
  relative: 4 plum, puce 5 lilac, mauve 6 dahlia, damson, orchid 7 heather, petunia 8 amethyst, burgundy, eggplant, lavender, mulberry 9 raspberry
heliport site, often: 4 roof
helium: 3 gas 7 element
  like ~: 5 inert
helix: 4 coil, curl 5 screw, twist, whorl 6 spiral, volute 9 corkscrew
  double ~: 3 DNA
  single ~: 3 RNA
hell: 5 abyss, Hades 6 misery, ordeal 7 anguish, inferno, torment 9 nightmare, suffering 10 underworld
  denizen: 5 demon, devil 6 daemon, daimon
  ender: 3 box, cat 4 bent, hole 5 diver, hound 6 bender
  feature: 4 fire 6 flames 7 inferno
  like ~: 6 ablaze
  like a bat out of ~: 5 manic
  like a rare day in ~: 4 cold, cool 6 chilly 8 freezing
  raise ~: 5 party 9 celebrate, make merry
  raising ~: 4 wild 5 noisy, rowdy 6 unruly 7 lawless, naughty, raucous 9 turbulent 10 boisterous, disorderly, tumultuous
  starter: 4 rake
  sure as ~: 5 truly 9 certainly, doubtless 10 absolutely, definitely, positively
  to pay: 7 censure, penalty 10 discipline, punishment
  to Sherman: 3 war
hell __: 4 week 5 to pay
hell-__: 4 bent 5 fired 6 raiser
hell-__-leather: 3 for
__ hell: 5 raise, War is
Hell __ Heroes: 5 Is for
Hell __ no fury...: 4 hath
hellbent: 4 firm 6 driven, intent 8 obsessed, resolute, resolved, stubborn 9 steadfast, tenacious 10 determined, hard-bitten, persistent, unwavering
  go ~ for leather: 4 tear 5 speed 6 careen, hasten, hurtle 7 rampage 8 stampede
  (on): 3 set
helldiver: 4 bird 5 grebe
Hellene: 5 Greek
  capital: 6 Athens
Hellenic: 8 language 9 classical
  see also Greece
heller: 5 money, rowdy 7 ruffian
helleri: 4 fish

Heller, Joseph: **6** author, writer
work: Catch-22
Closing Time
God Knows
Good as Gold
Something Happened
hell-for-__: **7** leather
He'll Have to Go (1960 song) artist: Jim Reeves
hellhound: **5** beast, brute, fiend, knave **6** savage **7** dastard, monster **9** barbarian
Hell in the Pacific (1968 film)
cast: Lee Marvin, Toshiro Mifune
director: John Boorman
hellion: **3** imp **4** brat **5** demon, rowdy **6** daemon, daimon **7** inciter, monster **8** agitator, evildoer, inflamer, recreant, renegade **9** firebrand **10** holy terror, instigator
Hell Is for Heroes (1962 film)
cast: Bobby Darin, Steve McQueen, Fess Parker
director: Don Siegel
hellish: **5** cruel, nasty **6** savage, wicked **7** accurst, demonic, satanic, vicious **8** accursed, daemonic, devilish, diabolic, fiendish, horrible, infernal, terrible **9** atrocious, barbarous, demonical, monstrous, murderous, nefarious, satanical **10** abominable, diabolical, malevolent, petrifying, unpleasant
Hellman: **5** Monte **7** Lillian
Hellman, Lillian: **6** author, writer **10** playwright
friend: Dashiell, Hammett
work: The Children's Hour
The Little Foxes
Maybe
Pentimento
Toys in the Attic
Watch on the Rhine
Hellmann's: **4** mayo **10** mayonnaise
hello: **4** ahoy, hi ya **5** aloha, howdy **7** welcome **8** greeting **9** greetings **10** salutation
Aussie ~: **4** g'day
Hawaii ~: **5** aloha
Navajo ~: **6** yateeh
returnee ~: **6** I'm home
say ~: **5** greet
silent ~: **3** nod **4** wave
warm ~: **3** hug **4** kiss **7** embrace
Hello __: **5** Again, It's Me, Walls **7** Goodbye
Hello __!: **5** Dolly
Hello __ Lou: **4** Mary
Hello __ Me: **3** It's
Hello, __!: **5** Dolly **6** Eeyore
Hello, __ Be Going: **5** I Must
Hello, __ Lovers: **5** Young
Hello, __ You: **5** I Love
Hello (1984 song) artist: Lionel Richie
Hello Again (1987 film)
cast: Corbin Bernsen, Gabriel Byrne, Judith Ivey, Shelley Long, Carrie Nye
Hello Again (1983 song) artist: Neil Diamond
Hello and Goodbye author: Athol Fugard
Hello, Dolly! (1969 film): **7** musical
cast: Michael Crawford, Walter Matthau, Barbra Streisand
director: Gene Kelly
role: **4** Levi
songwriter: **6** Herman
Hello, Dolly! (1964 song) artist: Louis Armstrong
Hello, Eeyore! author: A.A. Milne
Hello Goodbye (1967 song) artist: Beatles
Hello, I Love You (1968 song) artist: Doors
Hello It's Me (1973 song) artist: Todd Rundgren
Hello Mary Lou (1961 song) artist: Ricky Nelson
Hello Mudduh, Hello Fadduh! (1963 song) artist: Allan Sherman
__ hell or high water: **4** come
Hello Stranger (1963 song) artist: Barbara Lewis
Hello Walls (1961 song) artist: Faron Young
Hello, Young Lovers composer: **7** Rodgers **11** Hammerstein
hell's __: **5** bells
Hell's __: **5** Angel **6** Angels, Canyon **7** Kitchen
Hell's Angel: **5** biker
Hell's Angels (1930 film)
cast: John Darrow, James Hall, Jean Harlow, Ben Lyon
director: Howard Hughes
Hells Canyon state: **5** Idaho
hell to __: **3** pay
Hellzapoppin' (1941 film)
cast: Mischa Auer, Chic Johnson, Ole Olsen, Martha Raye
helm: **4** lead **5** guide, reins, steer, wheel **6** rudder, tiller **7** control
dir.: **3** ENE, ESE, NNE, NNW, SSE, SSW, WNW, WSW
position: **4** alee **8** aweather
take the ~: **5** steer **6** direct, manage **8** navigate
Helm: **4** Matt
Helmand: **5** river
locale: **4** Iran
Helmer, Nora creator: **5** Ibsen
helmet: **3** hat **4** topi **5** armet, terai **6** casque **7** hard hat **8** headgear
adornment: **5** plume **7** feather
name meaning ~: **4** Elmo
one with a ~: **5** miner
part: **5** visor, vizor
pith ~: **3** hat **4** topi **5** topee
plume: **5** crest
prickly ~: **5** shell **8** seashell
helmet __: **5** liner, shell
__ helmet: **4** pith **5** close, crash
Helm, Matt: **3** spy
Helmond, Katherine: **7** actress
film: Time Bandits (1981)
TV: Soap, Who's the Boss?
Helms: **5** Bobby, Jesse
Helms, Bobby
song: Jingle Bell Rock (1957)
My Special Angel (1957)
Helms, Jesse: **3** sen. **7** senator
Helmsley: **5** Harry, Leona
helmsman: **5** pilot **6** sailor **7** captain, jack tar, mariner, skipper **8** seafarer **9** navigator
direction: **4** alee **5** aport **8** aweather
Helmut: **4** Kohl **6** Berger **7** Schmidt
see also German
Héloïse
see French
Héloise and Abélard author: George Moore
Heloise tidbit: **4** hint
helot: **4** serf **7** bondman, villein
cousin: **4** esne
helotry: **4** yoke
he loves in Latin: **4** amat
help: **3** aid, SOS, use **4** abet, back, boon, ease, hand, lift **5** aides, asset, boost, favor, guide, hands, labor, maids, serve, slave, speed, staff, tutor **6** advice, assist, better, buck up, jobber, join in, Mayday, profit, relief, remedy, second, soothe, succor, uphold, wait on, worker **7** backing, benefit, bolster, butlers, comfort, forward, further, improve, offices, pitch in, promote, redress, relieve, servant, service, sponsor, stand by, support, sustain, utility, workers, work for **8** abetment, deputies, guidance, kindness, minister, mitigate, palliate, recourse, servants, stump for, tide over, wait upon **9** alleviate, cooperate, disburden, employees, encourage, intercede, lend a hand, patronage, smile upon, stimulate, subsidize **10** ameliorate, assistance, assistants, attendants, facilitate, go to bat for, hired hands, see through, stick up for
ask for ~, maybe: **4** pray
be of ~: **5** avail, serve
beyond ~: **4** sunk **5** kaput **6** doomed **7** done for
can't ~ but: **4** must **6** have to, should **7** ought to
ender: **4** less, mate, meet
for the needy: **4** alms **7** charity
get ~ from: **6** lean on
household ~: **4** cook, maid **5** nanny, valet **6** au pair, butler, nannie
in crime: **4** abet **7** collude
in the kitchen: **3** dry, mop **4** wash **5** clean, clear **6** sponge
name meaning ~: **4** Ezra
one beyond ~: **5** goner
oneself to: **3** nip **4** take **6** pocket
on-line ~ source: **3** FAQ
puzzle ~: **4** hint
the cause: **6** chip in, donate **10** contribute
to make up: **6** pacify, soothe **7** appease, assuage, mediate, mollify, placate, reunite, satisfy, sweeten, win over **9** arbitrate, intervene, reconcile **10** compromise, conciliate
with costs: **6** defray
with homework: **5** tutor
without ~: **5** alone **7** forlorn, unaided **8** forsaken, isolated, solitary **9** abandoned **10** unassisted
with the dishes: **3** dry **4** wipe
worthy of ~: **5** needy **8** indigent **9** destitute, penniless, penurious **10** down-and-out
help __: **3** out
__-help: **4** self
Help __ Its Way: **4** Is on
Help!: **3** SOS **4** film, song **6** Mayday
artist: Beatles
cast: George Harrison, John Lennon, Paul McCartney, Ringo Starr
director: Richard Lester
in French: **4** à moi
__ Help: **4** I Can
helper: **4** aide, ally, asst., hand, mate, page, temp **5** aides, gofer, labor **6** backer, backup, cohort, deputy, flunky, gopher, lackey, patron, second **7** abetter, abettor, acolyte, adjunct, adviser, advisor, flunkey, lacquey, partner, recruit, servant, sponsor **8** adherent, adjutant, follower, henchman **9** accessory, assistant, attendant, auxiliary, coadjutor, gal Friday, man Friday, secretary, supporter, volunteer **10** accomplice, apprentice, coadjutant, girl Friday, lieutenant
kitchen ~: **4** tool **7** utensil **9** appliance
name meaning ~: **6** Alexis
name meaning ~ of men: **9** Cassandra
office ~: **4** temp **5** clerk, gofer **6** gopher **9** assistant, gal Friday, man Friday, secretary **10** girl Friday
phrase: **5** let me
__ helper: **6** Santa's **7** mother's
__ Helper: **4** Tuna
helpful: **4** good, kind, nice **5** handy, of use, utile **6** benign, caring, decent, kindly, timely, usable, useful **7** useable **8** flexible, friendly, generous, obliging, positive, remedial, salutary, suitable, valuable **9** covetable, desirable, effectual, favorable, fortunate, operative, opportune, practical, symbiotic, unselfish **10** applicable, beneficial, benevolent, convenient, invaluable, neighborly, productive, profitable, supportive, thoughtful, timesaving, worthwhile
be ~: **3** aid **6** assist **7** pitch in
example: **5** model **6** lesson
hint: **3** tip **6** advice, tipoff **7** inkling, pointer, warning **10** suggestion
helpful __: **4** hint
helpfulness: **5** value **7** benefit **8** function **9** advantage, relevance, usability **10** assistance
helping: **4** part **5** plate, share, slice **6** ration **7** portion
hand: **5** break
helping __: **4** hand, verb
helpless: **4** puny, weak **5** at bay, frail, naked, wimpy **6** anemic, atonic, clumsy, effete, feeble, flabby, flimsy, pinned, unable **7** anaemic, exposed, forlorn, fragile, unadept, wimpish **8** delicate, forsaken, pithless, stranded, up a creek **9** abandoned, dependant, dependent, destitute, faltering, incapable, powerless, prostrate **10** handcuffed, impuissant, unequipped, vulnerable
one: **4** dupe, lamb **5** patsy **6** sucker **7** fall guy **8** easy mark, innocent, pushover
render ~: **4** bind **5** unarm **6** fetter, hamper, hobble, hogtie **8** restrain **9** hamstring
__ helpless as a kitten...: **4** I'm as
helplessness, show: **5** shrug
__ Help Lovin' Dat Man: **4** Can't
helpmate: **4** mate, wife **5** bride **6** spouse **7** husband, partner
Help Me (1974 song) artist: Joni Mitchell
helpmeet: **4** wife **6** spouse **7** husband
Help Me Make It Through the Night (1971 song) artist: Sammi Smith
Help Me, Rhonda (1965 song) artist: Beach Boys
__ Help Myself: **5** I Can't
__ Help Us: **6** Heaven
help-wanted
letters: **3** EEO, EOE, SOS
notices: **3** ads
__ help you?: **4** Can I, May I
Helsingborg: **4** city, port, town
locale: **6** Sweden
Helsingör: **4** city, port, town
locale: **7** Denmark
Helsinki: **4** city, port, town **7** capital
hot spot: **5** sauna
lake northwest of ~: **4** Nasi
locale: **7** Finland
suburb: **5** Espoo
Helsinki __: **4** Pact
helter-skelter: **5** about **6** hectic **7** chaotic **8** pell-mell, reckless **10** disorderly
helve: **6** handle
__-Helve, The: **3** Axe
Helvetica: **4** font **8** typeface
hem: **3** rim **4** edge, seam, tack, tuck **5** fence, skirt, verge **6** border, edging, fringe, margin **7** enclose, inclose **9** perimeter, periphery
and haw: **2** um **4** sway, vary **5** dodge, evade, hedge, shift, stall, waver **6** falter, waffle **7** quibble, stammer, whiffle **8** hesitate **9** fluctuate, pussyfoot, vacillate **10** equivocate
change a ~: **5** alter, lower, raise, resew
cousin: **2** er, uh, um

ender: 4 line, lock 6 stitch
in: 3 pen 4 gird, ring, wall 5 beset, bound, hedge, limit 6 begird, circle, corner 7 compass, confine, enclose, inclose 8 encircle, restrain, restrict, surround 9 constrain, encompass
make a ~: 3 sew
material: 6 edging
partner: 3 haw
prepare a ~: 5 baste, pin up
he-man: 4 hunk, stud 5 atlas, macho 6 Samson, Tarzan 7 bruiser, Goliath 8 Hercules, tough guy 10 powerhouse
like a ~: 5 macho 6 brawny, strong, virile 8 muscular, vigorous 9 masculine, strapping
no ~: 4 wimp 5 sissy, weeny 8 weakling
He-Man, sister of: 5 She-Ra
hematite: 3 ore 7 mineral
Hemet: 4 city, town
locale: 10 California
hemi-: 4 half
hemidemisemiquaver: 4 note
hemimorphite: 3 ore
Hemings: 5 Sally
Hemingway, Ernest: 6 author, writer 8 Nobelist
granddaughter: 6 Mariel 7 Margaux
nickname: Papa
work: Death in the Afternoon
A Farewell to Arms
The Fifth Column
For Whom the Bell Tolls
Green Hills of Africa
Islands in the Stream
A Moveable Feast
The Old Man and the Sea
The Snows of Kilimanjaro
The Sun Also Rises
To Have and Have Not
Hemingway, Mariel: 7 actress
film: Creator (1985)
Manhattan (1979)
Personal Best (1982)
Sunset (1988)
hemipode: 4 bird
___ Hemisphere: 7 Eastern, Western
hemlock: 4 tree 5 toxin 6 conium
home: 4 nest
poison in ~: 5 conin
relative: 3 fir 4 pine 6 spruce 8 tamarack
hemmed in: 4 pent 5 bound 6 narrow 7 cramped, limited 8 confined 10 restrained, restricted
hemmer: 6 tailor
interjection: 2 er, uh, um
hemming and hawing: 8 hesitant, waffling, wavering 9 dithering, equivocal, tentative, undecided, unsettled 10 ambivalent, indecisive, irresolute, of two minds, on the fence, unresolved, up in the air, wishy-washy
Hemmings: 5 David
hemoglobin
shortage: 6 anemia 7 anaemia
Hémon, Louis: 6 author, French, writer
hemophobe fear: 5 blood
hemp: 4 bast 5 bhang, fiber
fabric: 6 canvas
fiber: 5 abaca, oakum
Indian ~ shrub: 4 pooa 5 pooah
moisten ~: 3 ret
product: 4 rope 5 twine 6 opiate
Russian ~: 4 rine
hemplike fiber: 4 sunn 5 sisal
Hempstead: 4 city, town
athletes: 5 Pride
locale: 7 New York 10 Long Island
school: 7 Hofstra
Hemsley, Sherman sitcom: 4 Amen

hen: 3 she 4 bird, fowl 5 biddy, layer 6 bantam, female, pullet 7 brooder, clucker, Leghorn, poulard, poultry 8 busybody, poularde
act the mother ~: 4 fuss
ender: 3 bit 4 bane, coop, peck
family: 5 brood
lack: 5 teeth
like a wet ~: 3 mad 5 irate
product: 3 egg
sound: 5 cluck 6 cackle
starter: 3 pea 4 grey, moor
hen ___: 4 hawk 5 fruit, party 6 tracks 7 harrier
___ hen: 3 mud 4 fool, sage 5 hazel, heath, marsh, water 6 guinea, mother
henbane: 5 toxin 6 poison
henbit: 4 weed
hence: 4 away, ergo, then, this, thus 6 avaunt, onward, thence 7 onwards 8 from here 9 as a result, from now on, hereafter, therefore, therefrom, thereupon
ender: 5 forth 7 forward
henceforth: 6 onward, thence 7 onwards 8 evermore, from here 9 following, from now on, hereafter
henchman: 4 aide, ally, pawn 5 gofer 6 backup, cohort, deputy, flunky, gopher, helper, jackal, lackey, stooge 7 abetter, abettor, adjunct, flunkey, lacquey 8 adherent, follower, hanger-on, sidekick 9 accessory, assistant, attendant, bodyguard, coadjutor, colleague, companion, supporter 10 accomplice, apprentice, coadjutant
be a ~: 4 abet
Hench, Philip: 8 Nobelist
Henderson: 3 Joe 4 city, town 6 Arthur, Rickey, Skitch 8 Fletcher, Florence
locale: 6 Nevada 8 Kentucky
Henderson, Arthur: 8 Nobelist
Henderson, Fletcher: 7 pianist
genre: 4 jazz
Henderson, Rickey
sport: 8 baseball
theft: 4 base
Henderson the Rain King author: Saul Bellow
Hendersonville: 4 city, town
locale: 9 Tennessee
Hendrik: 7 Lorentz 10 Conscience
Hendrix, Jimi: 9 guitarist
genre: 4 rock
Hendry: 3 Ian
Hendryx: 4 Nona
henhouse: 4 coop 5 roost
sound: 5 cluck 6 cackle
Henie, Sonja: 6 skater
home: 4 Oslo 6 Norway
Henle's ___: 4 loop
Henley: 3 Don 4 Beth 5 shirt 7 William
need ~: 3 oar
participant: 5 rower
Henley ___: 5 shirt 7 Regatta
Henley, Beth: 6 author, writer 10 playwright
work: Abundance
Am I Blue
Crimes of the Heart
The Debutante Ball
Impossible Marriage
The Lucky Spot
The Miss Firecracker Contest
Henley, Don
song: All She Wants to Do is Dance (1985)
The Boys of Summer (1984)
Dirty Laundry (1982)
The End of the Innocence (1989)
Leather and Lace (1981)
Sometimes Love Just Isn't Enough (1992)

Henley-on-___: 6 Thames
Henley, William: 4 poet 7 British 10 playwright
work: Invictus
Henn: 6 Carrie
henna: 3 dye 4 tree 5 color, rinse, shrub 6 orange 7 hair dye, reddish
apply ~: 3 dye 4 tint 6 redden
apply more ~: 5 redye
relative: 5 flame 7 pumpkin, saffron 8 hyacinth 9 tangerine 10 terra cotta
user: 4 dyer
Henner, Marilu: 7 actress
film: Hammett (1983)
L.A. Story (1991)
Noises Off (1992)
role: 3 Ava 5 Nardo 6 Elaine
TV: Evening Shade, Taxi
hennin: 3 hat
Henning: 4 Doug 8 magician
Henny: 8 Youngman
hen of the woods: 6 fungus
henpeck: 3 nag 4 carp, ride 5 annoy, bully, hound, scold 6 badger, berate, bother, harass, hector, needle, noodge, pester, pick on 7 torment 8 domineer, irritate
henpecker: 3 nag 5 harpy, scold, shrew 6 beldam, chider, kvetch, ogress, virago, whiner 7 caviler, rebuker, reviler 8 fishwife, harridan, spitfire 9 termagant, Xanthippe 10 castigator, complainer
Henreid, Paul: 5 actor
film: Casablanca (1942)
Deception (1946)
Goodbye, Mr. Chips (1939)
Hollow Triumph (1948)
Joan of Paris (1942)
Now, Voyager (1942)
Rope of Sand (1949)
Henri: 7 Bergson, Matisse, Michaux, Moissan 8 Rousseau
see also French
Henri ___-Bresson: 7 Cartier
Henrich: 4 Yank 5 Tommy 6 Yankee
Henri de ___-Lautrec: 8 Toulouse
henrietta: 6 fabric 8 material
Henrik: 3 Dam 5 Ibsen
Henriksen: 5 Lance
Henry: 3 Pye 4 Buck, Clay, Dale, Ford, King, Luce, Rous 5 Adams, Bacon, Fonda, Green, Gross, James, Lawes, Levin, Moore, Percy, Silva, Taube, Tudor 6 Czerny, Draper, Gibson, Gloria, Hudson, Jaglom, Joseph, Justin, Koster, Kravis, Miller, Picard, Robert, Selick, Thomas 7 Higgins, Kendall, Mancini, Patrick, Purcell, Travers, Winkler 8 Bessemer, Clarence, Fielding, Hathaway, Maudslay, Shrapnel, Wilcoxon 9 Armstrong, Cavendish, Kissinger 10 Morgenthau
in French: 5 Henri
in German: 8 Heinrich
in Italian: 6 Enrico
in Spanish: 7 Enrique
son: 5 Edsel
Henry ___: 4 Fool, P'u Yi, VIII 6 Esmond
Henry ___ Beecher: 4 Ward
Henry ___ Lodge: 5 Cabot
Henry ___ Longfellow: 9 Wadsworth
Henry ___ Perot: 4 Ross
Henry ___ Stanley: 6 Morton
Henry ___ Thoreau: 5 David
___ Henry: 4 Fort, John 5 After
Henry Aldrich, Editor (1942 film)
cast: John Litel, Jimmy Lydon, Charles Smith
Henry and Cato author: Iris Murdoch
Henry Cabot ___: 5 Lodge
___ Henry Dana: 7 Richard
Henry David ___: 7 Thoreau

Henry Esmond author: William Makepeace Thackeray
Henry Fool (1998 film)
cast: Maria Porter, Parker Posey, Thomas Jay Ryan, James Urbaniak
director: Hal Hartley
___ Henry Harrison: 7 William
___ Henry Hoover: 3 Lou
Henry IV author: William Shakespeare
Henry James author: Rebecca West
Henry, John drove it: 5 steel
Henry, Joseph: 9 physicist
Henry & June (1990 film)
cast: Maria de Medeiros, Uma Thurman, Fred Ward
role: 3 Nin 5 Anaïs 6 Miller
Henry Morton ___: 7 Stanley
___ Henry Newman: 4 John
Henry, O.: 6 writer
real name: Porter
work: The Furnished Room
The Gift of the Magi
The Last Leaf
The Ransom of Red Chief
The Trimmed Lamp
Henry, Patrick: 6 orator
Henry the ___: 9 Navigator
Henry V: 3 Hal 9 Prince Hal
Henry V (1945 film)
cast: Leslie Banks, Robert Newton, Laurence Olivier
device: 5 irony
director: Laurence Olivier
Henry V (1989 film)
cast: Brian Blessed, Kenneth Branagh, Derek Jacobi
director: Kenneth Branagh
Henry V author: William Shakespeare
Henry VI author: William Shakespeare
Henry VI founded it: 4 Eton
Henry VIII
daughter: 5 Mary I
desire: 3 son
like ~: 5 obese, stout 6 portly, rotund 9 corpulent
wife: 4 Anne, Parr 6 Boleyn, Howard 9 Catherine
wife count: 3 six
Henry Wadsworth ___: 10 Longfellow
Henry Ward ___: 7 Beecher
Hensley: 6 Pamela
Henson, Jim: 8 director 9 puppeteer
creation: 4 Bert 5 Ernie, Oscar 6 Kermit, Muppet 7 Big Bird 9 Miss Piggy
film: The Dark Crystal (1982)
The Great Muppet Caper (1981)
Labyrinth (1986)
___ hen's teeth: 6 rare as
Henstridge, Natasha: 7 actress
film: Bounce (2000)
Species (1995)
The Whole Nine Yards (2000)
Hentoff: 3 Nat
hep: 4 cool, in on, onto, wise 5 aware, savvy 6 posted, versed, wise to, with it 7 current, knowing, mindful, tuned in 8 apprised, informed 9 cognizant, in the know, plugged in 10 conversant
ender: 3 cat
get ~: 6 wise up
to: 4 up on 9 in the know, wise about
hepatic: 5 renal
hepatic ___: 4 duct
hepatica: 5 plant 6 flower
___ Hepatica: 3 Sal
hepatologist concern: 5 liver
Hepburn, Audrey: 7 actress
film: Breakfast at Tiffany's (1961)
Charade (1963)
Funny Face (1957)
Green Mansions (1959)
How to Steal a Million (1966)
Love in the Afternoon (1957)
My Fair Lady (1964)

The Nun's Story (1959)
Robin and Marian (1976)
Roman Holiday (1953, AA)
Sabrina (1954)
They All Laughed (1981)
Two for the Road (1967)
The Unforgiven (1960)
Wait Until Dark (1967)
real first name: 4 Edda
spouse: Mel Ferrer
Hepburn, Katharine: 7 actress
costar: 5 Tracy
film: Adam's Rib (1949)
The African Queen (1951)
Alice Adams (1935)
A Bill of Divorcement (1932)
Bringing Up Baby (1938)
Desk Set (1957)
Guess Who's Coming to Dinner (1967, AA)
Holiday (1938)
Keeper of the Flame (1943)
The Lion in Winter (1968, AA)
The Little Minister (1934)
Little Women (1933)
Long Day's Journey Into Night (1962)
Love Affair (1994)
Mary of Scotland (1936)
Morning Glory (1933, AA)
On Golden Pond (1981, AA)
Pat and Mike (1952)
The Philadelphia Story (1940)
Quality Street (1937)
The Rainmaker (1956)
Rooster Cogburn (1975)
Stage Door (1937)
State of the Union (1948)
Suddenly, Last Summer (1959)
Summertime (1955)
Sylvia Scarlett (1935)
Without Love (1945)
Woman of the Year (1942)
A Woman Rebels (1936)
nickname: 4 Kate
hepcat: 4 dude 6 daddy-o 7 hipster, swinger
Hephaestus
equivalent: 6 Vulcan
lover of ~: 4 Gaea 6 Aglaia, Athena, Athene, Cabiro, Charis 7 Ocresia 8 Anticlia 9 Aphrodite
mother of ~: 4 Hera
son of ~: 5 Alcon, Cacus 6 Olenus 7 Ardalus, Cercyon 8 Cadmilus, Caeculus, Palaemon 9 Corynetes, Eurymedon, Philammon, Philottus 10 Periphetes
Hepplewhite: 5 style 6 George
hepta-: 5 seven
follower: 4 octa-, octo-
preceder: 3 hex- 4 hexa-
heptad: 4 seas 5 seven 6 dwarfs
plus one: 5 octad
heptarch: 5 ruler
Hepworth: 7 Barbara
her: 3 she 4 pron. 5 woman 6 female 7 pronoun
ender: 4 self 5 story
his and ~: 5 their
like ~: 4 poss.
not ~: 3 him
her __: 4 nibs
Her: 3 dog 6 beagle, canine
owner: 3 LBJ
predecessor: 4 Fala
Her __ Georgia Gibbs: 4 Nibs
Her __ Highness: 5 Royal 6 Serene
Her __ Too: 4 Town
Hera: 7 goddess
brother of ~: 4 Zeus 5 Hades
daughter of ~: 4 Eris, Hebe 8 Pasithea
equivalent: 4 Juno
husband of ~: 4 Zeus
lover of ~: 8 Dionysus
parent of ~: 4 Rhea 6 Cronos, Cronus
rival of ~: 4 Leda
sister of ~: 6 Hestia 7 Demeter
son of ~: 4 Ares 10 Hephaestus
__ Her About It: 4 Tell
Heracles: 8 Argonaut
child of ~: 5 Creon, Iobes, Lydus, Teles 6 Buleus, Celtus, Evenus, Everes, Glenus, Hyllus, Mentor, Nephus, Onites, Pallas 7 Agelaus, Alcaeus, Alopius, Atromus, Bucolus, Capylus, Chromis, Deicoon, Euhenus, Eumedes, Galates, Gelonus, Hippeus, Latinus, Macaria, Olympus, Ophites, Phalias, Polyaus, Scythes, Temenus, Tigasis 8 Agylleus, Anicetus, Antiades, Antileon, Antiphus, Asrybies, Astyanax, Cleolaus, Dynastes, Erythras, Euryopes, Laomedon, Laomenes, Leucites, Leucones, Lycurgus, Lyncaeus, Palaemon, Phaestus, Telephus, Tyrsenus 9 Alexiares, Amestrius, Antiochus, Archelaus, Aventinus, Ctesippus, Dexamenus, Echephron, Entelides, Erasippus, Eucycapys, Eurypylus, Leucippus, Onesippus, Patroclus, Thessalus, Thestalus, Thettalus 10 Antimachus, Archedicus, Halocrates, Hippozygus, Homolippus, Nicodromus, Oestrobles
lover of ~: 4 Auge, Eone, Lyse, Meda, Nice, Oria, Rhea 5 Erato, Exole, Hippo, Iphis, Mares, Patro 6 Aglaia, Anthea, Argele, Asopis, Certhe, Euboea, Eubote, Meline, Panope, Phialo 7 Antiope, Autonoe, Celtine, Elachia, Epilais, Eurybia, Laothoe, Lavinia, Lysippe, Nicippe, Omphale, Phyleis, Procris, Psophis, Pyrippe, Tiphyse, Xanthis 8 Anthippe, Astyoche, Chryseis, Clytippe, Deianira, Epicasta, Eurypyle, Eurytele, Hesychia, Lysidice, Menippis, Olympusa 9 Aeschreis, Astydamia, Calametis, Chalciope, Heliconis, Praxithea, Toxicrate 10 Hippocrate, Parthenope, Stratonice
parent of ~: 4 Zeus 7 Alcmena
ship: 4 Argo
twin of ~: 8 Iphicles
victim of ~: 5 Ladon, Linus, Lycus 6 Cycnus, Geryon 7 Antaeus, Busiris, Erginus, Homadus, Iphitus 8 Dercynus, Emathion, Eurytion, Ialebion 9 Polygonus, Telegonus
wife of ~: 4 Hebe 6 Megara
Heraclitus: 5 Greek 11 philosopher
__ Her Again: 4 I Saw
herald: 4 mean, omen, sign, tout 5 augur, crier, greet, robin, spell, token, usher 6 bearer, leader, signal 7 courier, declare, portend, presage, prophet, swallow, trumpet, usher in 8 announce, antecede, ballyhoo, foreshow, proclaim 9 advertise, announcer, broadcast, foretoken, harbinger, make known, messenger, precursor, publicize, town crier 10 forerunner, indication, missionary, proclaimer
Herald: 5 paper 9 newspaper
locale: 5 Miami 6 Boston 7 Calgary, Halifax
heraldry: 4 pomp 5 badge, crest 6 design, device, emblem, symbol 7 insigne 8 blazonry, ceremony, insignia, splendor 9 pageantry
heraldry terms
arrangement: 10 coat of arms
background: 5 field
band: 4 orle 5 fesse
bearing: 6 charge 8 ordinary
black: 5 sable
blue: 5 azure
border: 7 bordure
center: 9 fess point 10 fesse point
centerless: 6 voided
center point of lower half: 7 nombril
coat of arms: 5 crest 6 blazon
coat of arms panel: 9 hatchment
color: 8 tincture
device: 7 bearing
diagonal band: 4 bend
diamond: 7 lozenge
dragon: 6 wyvern
emblem: 6 device
flying: 6 volant
footless bird: 7 martlet
four-petaled flower: 10 quatrefoil
fur: 4 vair 8 tincture
gold: 2 or
green: 4 vert
horizontal band: 3 bar
horned giraffe: 10 camelopard
inverted V: 7 chevron
left: 8 sinister
lion: 7 leopard
lion-eagle: 7 griffin
looking backward: 9 regardant
lower part: 4 base
lying down: 7 dormant 8 couchant
metal: 8 tincture
narrow horizontal: 5 label 6 fillet
one of four divisions: 7 quarter
purple: 7 purpure
rearing up: 7 rampant
red: 5 gules
repeated pattern: 4 semé
ribbon with motto: 6 scroll 9 banderole
right: 6 dexter
rising: 7 issuant
shield: 4 enté 10 escutcheon
shortened diagonal band: 5 baton
side view: 7 gardant 8 guardant
silver: 6 argent
sprinkled,: 4 semé
St. Andrew's cross: 7 saltire
three-petaled flower: 7 trefoil
three-petaled iris: 10 fleur-de-lis
triangle: 5 gyron
upper right: 6 canton
walking: 7 passant
wavy: 4 onde, undé
wedge: 4 pile
white: 6 argent
wide horizontal band: 4 fess 5 fesse
wide vertical band: 4 pale
wreath: 5 torse
Herat: 4 city, town
locale: 11 Afghanistan
herb: 3 rue 4 balm, dill, mint, sage 5 anise, basil, chive, cumin, plant, thyme 6 borage, catnip, endive, fennel, lovage, savory 7 bay leaf, caraway, chervil, chicory, mustard, oregano, parsley 8 angelica, cardamom, cilantro, marjoram, rosemary, tarragon 9 coriander, flavoring, horehound, lemon balm, medicinal, seasoning, spearmint, vegetable 10 peppermint
aromatic ~: 4 dill, mint, nard, sage 5 anise, tansy, thyme 6 catnip, fennel, hyssop
Asian ~: 5 orach 6 orache
ender: 3 age, ose
European ~: 6 borage, lovage
healing ~: 6 arnica
Japanese ~: 3 udo
kitchen ~: 4 dill, sage 5 anise, basil, chive, cumin, thyme 6 fennel 7 oregano, parsley 8 cilantro, marjoram, rosemary
like a certain ~: 4 sagy 5 minty
medicinal ~: 4 sage 5 urena
perennial ~: 5 orpin 6 asarum
remedy: 5 jalap
starter: 3 cow, pot
herb __: 3 tea 5 Paris 6 bennet, doctor, Robert
__ herb: 6 bitter, willow
Herb: 4 Caen 5 Freed 6 Alpert 7 Edelman, Pennock, Shriner, Stempel, Woodley
herbage: 7 foliage, verdure 10 vegetation
dried ~: 3 hay
herbal __: 3 tea
__ Herb Brown: 5 Nacio
Herbert: 3 Lom 4 Agar, Gold, Read, Ross 5 Brown, Frank, saint, Simon 6 Gasser, George, Hoover, Victor, Wilcox, Xavier 7 Asquith, Kroemer, Marcuse, Spencer 8 Anderson, Hauptman, Marshall, Zbigniew
Herbert __ Karajan: 3 von
Herbert, Frank: 6 author, writer
genre: sci-fi
work: The Dragon in the Sea
Dune
The God Makers
The Heaven Makers
Herbert, George: 4 poet 5 Welsh
Herbert, Victor: 8 composer
org. cofounded by: 5 ASCAP
Herbert, Xavier: 6 writer 10 Australian
Herbert, Zbigniew: 4 poet 6 Polish
__ herbes: 5 fines
herbicide: 3 DDT 6 poison
target: 4 weed
Herbie: 2 VW 3 car 4 auto, Faye, Mann 7 Hancock, Love Bug 10 Volkswagen
herbivore: 5 rhino, vegan 7 gorilla
herculean: 3 big 4 hale, hard, huge, iron, vast, wiry 5 beefy, brave, burly, giant, great, hardy, hefty, hunky, husky, jumbo, large, lusty, stout, tough 6 brawny, hearty, heroic, mighty, potent, robust, rugged, sinewy, steely, stocky, strong, sturdy, virile 7 arduous, doughty, hulking, immense, mammoth, massive, onerous, sizable, titanic, valiant 8 athletic, colossal, enormous, forceful, gigantic, grueling, heroical, indurate, king-size, muscular, oversize, powerful, puissant, sizeable, stalwart, toilsome, towering, vigorous, whapping, whopping 9 Atlantean, difficult, humongous, laborious, overlarge, strapping, strenuous, well-built 10 able-bodied, courageous, formidable, gargantuan, iron-willed, monumental, prodigious, red-blooded, stupendous, tremendous
not ~: 4 puny, tiny, weak 5 frail 6 feeble 8 trifling 9 pint-sized 10 diminutive
Hercules: 4 city, hero, town 5 he-man
constellation near ~: 4 Lyra
labor site: 5 Nemea
locale: 10 California
one of twelve for ~: 5 labor
quest: 6 girdle
wife of ~: 4 Hebe
Hercules __: 6 beetle
__ Hercules: 4 Nike
Hercules... (TV adventure) cast: Kevin Sorbo (Hercules)
Herculina: 8 asteroid
herd: 3 mob 4 bevy, gang, mass, pack, tend 5 bunch, covey, crowd, drive, drove, flock, group, horde, press, rally, steer, stock, swarm, troop 6 cattle, corral, gather, huddle, people, rab-

ble, throng **7** bunch up, cluster, collect, grazers, numbers, oversee, roundup, wrangle **8** assemble, shepherd **9** gathering, livestock, multitude **10** assemblage, collection, congregate
cattle: **5** drive
ID: **5** brand
member: **3** cow **5** sheep, steer
orphan: **4** dogy **5** dogey, dogie
ride ~ on: **3** run **4** mind, tend **5** drive **6** direct **7** conduct, oversee **9** supervise, trample on, tyrannize **10** administer
sound: **3** baa, low, moo
starter: **3** cow **4** neat **5** swine
stray: **5** rogue
__ herd: **5** trail
herder: **6** collie, cowboy, gaucho **8** sheepdog
herding __: **3** dog
__ herd on: **4** ride
herds: **4** kine
herdsman: **6** cowboy, drover **7** cowpoke
constellation: **6** Boötes
first ~: **4** Abel
hut: **6** chalet
here: **6** hither, in town, on hand, with us **7** on board, on Earth, present **9** attending **10** at this time
again: **4** back
and now: **5** today **6** at once **7** quickly **8** promptly, right off **9** at present, forthwith, presently, right away **10** at this time, this minute
and there: **5** about **6** around **7** in spots **8** rambling **9** irregular, sometimes, somewhere
around ~: **6** nearby
ender: **4** into, unto, upon, with **5** about, after
from ~: **5** hence
get out of ~: **2** go **5** leave, scram **6** move it **7** vamoose **8** run along, shove off **9** move along, take a hike **10** hit the road
go ~ and there: **3** gad **4** roam, rove, trek **5** drift, range **6** ramble, travel, wander **7** explore, journey, meander, traipse **9** bat around, bum around, gallivant, run around **10** knock about
in French: **3** ici
in Latin: **3** hic
it's neither ~ nor there: **5** limbo **7** nowhere
not ~: **4** gone **5** there **6** absent **9** elsewhere
out of ~: **3** off **4** away, gone **6** yonder **9** elsewhere
partner: **3** now **5** there
see ~: **4** look, wait
the ones ~: **5** these
up to ~: **6** excess **7** satiety, surfeit **8** bellyful, plethora
here __ now: **3** and
__ here!: **4** Same **6** They're
Here __!: **3** I am, I go **4** goes, we go **5** we are
Here __ Come Again: **3** You
Here __ Mr. Jordan: **5** Comes
Here __ nothing!: **4** goes
Here __ the Judge: **5** Comes
Here __, there...: **4** a moo
Here __ the Sun: **5** Comes
hereabout: **4** near
to a poet: **5** anear
hereafter: **4** anon, soon, then **5** hence **6** in a bit, in time **7** by and by, later on, someday **8** in a while, sometime **9** after this, from now on, next world **10** afterworld, before long, eventually, henceforth, otherworld, ultimately
here and __: **3** now **5** there
Here and Now (1990 song) artist: Luther Vandross
here and there in Latin: **6** passim
hereby: **4** thus **9** as a result, in this way
Here Comes Mr. Jordan (1941 film)
cast: Evelyn Keyes, Robert Montgomery, Claude Rains
director: Alexander Hall
Here Comes Santa Claus singer: Gene Autry
Here Comes That Rain Again (1984 song) artist: Eurythmics
Here Comes the __: **3** Sun **5** Groom
Here Comes the Groom (1951 film)
cast: Bing Crosby, Franchot Tone, Jane Wyman
director: Frank Capra
Here Comes the Judge (1968 song) artist: Pigmeat Markham, Shorty Long
Here comes trouble: **4** oh-oh, uh-oh
Here Come the Co-Eds (1945 film)
cast: Bud Abbott, Lou Costello
Here Come the Warm Jets composer: **3** Eno
Here Come the Waves (1944 film)
cast: Bing Crosby, Betty Hutton, Sonny Tufts
director: Mark Sandrich
Heredia, José Maria de: **4** poet **6** French
hereditary: **5** genic **6** family, inborn, inbred, innate, lineal, racial **7** genetic **9** ancestral, genetical, ingrained, intrinsic **10** bequeathed, derivative, handed down
cause of ~ variation: **6** allele
factor: **4** gene
identification: **5** genom **6** genome
letters: **3** DNA, RNA
ruler: **4** king **6** dynast
heredity: **4** line **7** descent, lineage **8** ancestry, genetics
science of ~: **8** genetics
Hereford: **3** cow, pig **4** bull, city, town **5** swine **6** bovine, cattle, county
city: **9** Worcester
locale: **7** England
Herefordshire: **6** county
locale: **7** England
Here I Am (song) artist: Air Supply, Al Green
Here I Go Again (1987 song) artist: Whitesnake
herein: **3** enc. **8** enclosed
ender: **5** after **6** before
hereinafter: **8** evermore **9** from now on **10** henceforth
Here Is Your War author: **4** Pyle
Here it is!: **4** ta-da **5** ta-dah, voila
Herek, Stephen: **8** director
film: 101 Dalmatians (1996)
Bill & Ted's Excellent Adventure (1989)
Life or Something Like It (2002)
The Mighty Ducks (1992)
Mr. Holland's Opus (1995)
Rock Star (2001)
The Three Musketeers (1993)
Here Lies author: Dorothy Parker
__ here nor there: **7** neither
Herens: **3** cow **4** bull **6** bovine, cattle
Here on Gilligan's __: **4** isle
__ Here, Private Hargrove: **3** See
Herero home: **6** Africa, Angola **7** Namibia **8** Botswana
Here's __: **4** Lucy
Here's __!: **3** how **6** Johnny
Here's looking at you!: **5** toast
Here's Lucy (CBS sitcom)
cast: Desi Arnaz Jr. (Craig Carter)
Lucie Arnaz (Kim Carter)
Lucille Ball (Lucy Carter)
Gale Gordon (Harrison Carter)
Here's mud in your eye!: **5** toast
Here's to you!: **5** salud, skoal, toast **6** cheers
heresy: **7** dissent **9** blasphemy, rebellion, sacrilege **10** dissension
heretic: **5** rebel **7** infidel **8** agitator, forsaker, maverick, renegade **9** dissenter, dissident, protester **10** iconoclast, malcontent
heretical: **7** deviant **9** atheistic, differing, dissident, heterodox, miscreant, sectarian, skeptical **10** dissenting, idolatrous, schismatic, unorthodox
hereto: **3** yet **5** as yet **6** before **8** until now
ender: **4** fore
__ Here to Eternity: **4** From
heretofore: **3** ago, née **4** once **5** as yet, so far **6** erenow **7** already, earlier **8** formerly, hitherto, until now **9** at one time, preceding **10** previously
mentioned: **5** above
hereupon: **4** anon, soon **7** ere long, shortly **9** presently **10** before long
Here We Are (1990 song) artist: Gloria Estefan
Here With Me (1988 song) artist: REO Speedwagon
Here You Come Again (1977 song) artist: Dolly Parton
heriot: **7** tribute
heritage: **5** birth, roots **6** legacy, origin **8** ancestry, pedigree **9** tradition **10** birthright
__ Heritage: **6** Rhythm **8** American
heritor: **4** heir **7** heiress, legatee
herky-__: **5** jerky
__ Her Like a Lady: **5** Treat
herm: **4** bust
Her Majesty: **5** queen
Herman: **4** Babe, Bang, Wouk **5** Billy, Jerry, Woody **6** Keiser, Pee-wee **7** Munster **8** Melville
hermana: **6** sister **7** Spanish
father's ~: **3** tía
Herman, Jerry: **8** composer
musical: Hello, Dolly!
La Cage Aux Folles
Mack & Mabel
Mame
Hermann: **5** Broch, Hesse **6** Muller **7** Fischer **9** Sudermann **10** Staudinger
hermano: **7** brother, Spanish
father's ~: **3** tío
Herman, Pee-wee
persona: **4** nerd, nurd
Herman's Hermits
leader: Peter Noone
song: Can't You Hear My Heartbeat (1965)
Dandy (1966)
I'm Henry VIII, I Am (1965)
Just a Little Bit Better (1965)
Leaning on the Lamp Post (1966)
Listen People (1966)
Mrs. Brown You've Got a Lovely Daughter (1965)
A Must to Avoid (1966)
Silhouettes (1965)
There's a Kind of Hush (1967)
Wonderful World (1965)
Herman, Woody: **10** bandleader
genre: **4** jazz
instrument: clarinet, sax
hermeneutics: **8** exegesis
Hermes: **3** Pan
epithet: **6** Dolius **7** Pronaos **9** Acacesius, Cyllenian, Epimelius, Promachos, Spelaites
equivalent: **7** Mercury
half-brother of ~: **4** Ares
invention: **4** lyre
lover of ~: **4** Lara, Sose **5** Daira, Herse, Rhene **6** Acalle, Chione, Creusa, Peitho **7** Erythia, Thronia **8** Aglaurus, Iphthime, Penelope, Philonis, Polymele, Theobula **9** Alcidamea, Antianira, Aphrodite, Carmentis, Eupolemia
parent of ~: **4** Maia, Zeus
son of ~: **3** Pan **4** Saon **5** Bunus, Ceryx, Cydon, Lycus, Norax **6** Agreus, Arabus, Echion, Faunus, Nomius, Pharis **7** Abderus, Daphnis, Eleusis, Eudorus, Eurytus, Evander, Polybus **8** Cephalus, Myrtilus, Pronomus **9** Autolycus **10** Aethalides
hermetic: **5** tight **6** hidden, occult **7** recluse **8** profound, secluded **9** leakproof, nonporous, reclusive, recondite **10** impervious
Hermione: **7** Gingold **8** asteroid, Baddeley
hermit: **4** crab, monk **5** loner **6** cookie **7** ascetic, eremite, isolato, recluse **8** anchoret, solitary **9** anchorite, religious **10** solitarian, stay-at-home
ender: **3** age
home: **3** hut
like a ~: **5** alone **8** eremitic, solitary **9** reclusive, withdrawn **10** antisocial, cloistered, unsociable
hermit __: **4** crab **6** thrush
hermitage: **5** haven **6** refuge **7** retreat, shelter **8** cloister, hideaway **9** sanctuary, seclusion
Hermitage figure: **4** czar, tsar, tzar
hermitic: **5** alone **8** solitary **9** reclusive **10** antisocial
__ Hermits: **7** Herman's
Hermon: **4** peak **5** mount **8** mountain
locale: **4** Asia **5** Syria
Hermosillo: **4** city, town
locale: **6** Mexico, Sonora
see also Spanish
__ Her Name With Pride: **5** Carve
Hernán: **6** Cortés, Cortez
Hernando: **6** Cortés, Cortez, de Soto
see also Spanish
Hernando's Hideaway: **4** song **5** tango
composer: **4** Ross **5** Adler
Hernani author: Victor Hugo
Herndon: **4** city, town
locale: **8** Virginia
Herne: **4** city, town
locale: **7** Germany
region: **4** Ruhr
Herne, James A.: **6** author, writer **10** playwright
Herne's __, The: **3** Egg
Herne's Egg, The author: William Butler Yeats
hero: **3** sub **4** idol, lead, lion, part, role, star **5** hoagy, model, po boy **6** hoagie, savior, victor, winner **7** good guy, grinder, paragon, poor boy, saviour, torpedo, warrior **8** champion, cynosure, exemplar, lead role, luminary, male lead, sandwich **9** conqueror, headliner, lifesaver, role model, submarine, superstar **10** leading man
ender: **3** ine, ism
journey: **5** quest **6** voyage **7** crusade, mission **9** adventure **10** expedition
starter: **4** anti
trait: **4** grit, guts, will **5** moxie, nerve, pluck, valor **6** daring, mettle **7** bravery, courage **8** audacity, backbone, boldness, gumption, strength, tenacity **9** brashness, fortitude, gallantry **10** confidence
work: **4** deed
hero __: **7** worship
Hero
lover of ~: **7** Leander

Hero (1992 film)
cast: Joan Cusack, Geena Davis, Andy Garcia, Dustin Hoffman
director: Stephen Frears
Hero (1993 song) artist: Mariah Carey
Hero and Leander author: Christopher Marlowe
Herod: 4 king
kingdom: 6 Judaea
niece: 6 Salome
Herod ___: 7 Agrippa, Antipas
heroes
like some ~: 5 macho
___ Heroes: 6 Hogan's, Kelly's
Heroes for Sale (1933 film)
cast: Richard Barthelmess, Aline MacMahon, Loretta Young
director: William Wellman
heroic: 4 bold, epic, game 5 brave, grand, great, gutsy, nervy, noble, stout 6 awless, daring, epical, gritty, mighty, plucky, spunky 7 aweless, defiant, doughty, gallant, Homeric, impavid, staunch, valiant 8 fearless, glorious, immortal, intrepid, resolute, stalwart, unafraid, valorous 9 audacious, dauntless, dreadless, grandiose, herculean, undaunted, unfearful, unfearing 10 chivalrous, courageous, mettlesome, undismayed
achievement: 4 coup, deed, feat 7 exploit, triumph, victory 8 conquest
not ~: 3 shy 4 meek, weak 5 mousy, timid 6 afraid, craven, yellow 7 chicken, daunted, fearful, wimpish 8 cowardly, sheepish, timorous 9 dastardly, nerveless, spineless 10 frightened, irresolute, submissive
poem: 4 epic, epos 5 epode 6 epopee 8 epopoeia
tale: 4 edda, epic, gest, saga 5 geste
heroic ___: 3 age 4 poem 5 drama, meter, tenor, verse 6 stanza 7 couplet
___-heroic: 4 mock
heroics: 5 deeds 6 rescue 9 derring-do
Heroide composer: 5 Reger
Heroides author: 4 Ovid
heroine: 4 star
answer to a villain: 5 never
heroism: 5 pluck, valor 6 daring, rescue 7 bravery, courage, prowess 8 boldness, valiance, valiancy 9 fortitude, gallantry
heron: 4 bird 5 egret, wader 7 bittern 8 boatbill 9 marsh bird, shorebird 10 wading bird
cousin: 4 ibis 5 crane, stork
home: 4 nest 5 marsh, swamp 7 lowland, wetland 9 swampland
___ heron: 4 blue 5 green, night 6 purple
___ Her on Monday: 4 I Met
Hero of Lake Erie, The: 5 Perry
Hero's ___: 7 formula
hero-worship: 5 exalt 7 adulate, glorify, idolize, lionize
herpetology: 7 science
branch of ~: 9 ophiology
study: 7 reptile 10 amphibians
herpetophobe fear: 8 reptiles
...___ her poor dog a bone: 5 to get
Herr: 5 title 6 German, mister
Herrera, Fernando de: 4 poet 7 Spanish
Herrick, Robert: 4 poet 7 British
Herriman: 6 George
feline: Krazy Kat
herring: 4 brit, fish, shad, sild 5 sprat 6 kipper 7 sardine 8 brisling
barrel: 4 cade
ender: 4 bone
red ~: 4 ploy, ruse 5 decoy 9 diversion 10 camouflage
young ~: 4 brit 9 whitebait
___ herring: 3 red 4 lake, wolf 5 round 6 matjes 7 pickled
___ Herring: 6 Albert
herringbone: 6 coutil, fabric
herringbone ___: 4 bond, gear 5 tweed, weave 6 stitch
herringlike fish: 4 pogy, shad
Herriot, James: 3 vet 4 Scot 6 author, writer
Herrmann: 6 Edward 7 Bernard
Herrmann, Bernard: 8 composer
film score: Citizen Kane
The Day the Earth Stood Still
The Man Who Knew Too Much
Marnie
North by Northwest
Psycho
Vertigo
Herrmann, Edward: 5 actor
film: Big Business (1988)
Compromising Positions (1985)
Overboard (1987)
Reds (1981)
Take Down (1978)
Her Royal Majesty (1962 song) artist: James Darren
hers: 4 pron. 7 pronoun
his or ~ item: 5 towel
in French: 3 ses
like ~: 4 poss.
not ~: 3 his 5 yours
Herschbach, Dudley: 7 chemist 8 Nobelist
Herschel: 4 John 6 Walker 7 William 8 Bernardi
Herschel, John: 7 British 10 astronomer
Herschel, William: 3 Sir 7 British 10 astronomer
Hersey, John: 6 writer 7 British
work: A Bell for Adano
Hiroshima
The Wall
Hershey: 6 Alfred, Milton 7 Barbara
brand: 4 Rolo 6 Kit-Kat
product: 3 bar 4 kiss 9 chocolate
st.: 4 Penn.
see also Hershey's
Hershey, Alfred: 8 Nobelist
Hershey, Barbara: 7 actress
film: Beaches (1988)
Hannah and Her Sisters (1986)
Hoosiers (1986)
Lantana (2001)
Last Summer (1969)
The Last Temptation of Christ (1988)
Paris Trout (1991)
The Pursuit of Happiness (1971)
The Right Stuff (1983)
Soldier's Daughter Never Cries (1998)
The Stunt Man (1980)
Tin Men (1987)
Hershey's: 5 candy 9 chocolate
alternative: 4 Mars, Twix 5 Clark, Heath 6 Kit Kat, Mounds, PayDay, Reese's, Zagnut 7 Krackel, Oh Henry 8 Baby Ruth, Milky Way, Snickers 9 Almond Joy, Mr. Goodbar 10 NutRageous
Hershfield cartoon character: 4 Abie
Hershiser, Orel: 6 hurler 7 pitcher
Hersholt, Jean: 5 actor
film: Emma (1932)
Greed (1925)
The Student Prince in Old Heidelberg (1927)
___ Her Standing There: 4 I Saw
Hertel: 5 Peter
Hertfordshire: 6 county
city: 7 Watford
locale: 7 England
___ Her to Heaven: 5 Leave
Her Town Too (1981 song) artist: James Taylor
Herts: 6 county
locale: 7 England
Hertz: 6 Gustav 8 Heinrich 9 car rental 10 auto rental
alternative: 4 Avis 5 Alamo 6 Budget, Dollar 7 Thrifty 8 National 10 Enterprise
Hertz ___: 6 effect
Hertz, Gustav: 8 Nobelist 9 physicist
Hertz, Heinrich: 9 physicist
Hertzian ___: 4 wave
hertz starter: 4 kilo-, mega-, tera-
Hervey: 5 Allen, Irene, Jason
Hervey, Irene spouse: Allan Jones
Herzberg, Gerhard: 7 chemist 8 Nobelist
Herzegovina partner: 6 Bosnia
Herzl: 7 Theodor
Herzog: 6 Werner, Whitey
Herzog author: Saul Bellow
he's: 4 boys 5 bucks, bulls, stags 6 drakes
He's ___: 4 Mine 5 So Shy
He's ___ nowhere man: 5 a real
He's ___ Picker: 4 a Rag
He Said, She Said (1991 film)
cast: Kevin Bacon, Elizabeth Perkins, Sharon Stone
He's a Rebel (1962 song) artist: Crystals
___, He's Crazy: 4 Mama
He Sees You When You're Sleeping author: Mary Higgins Clark
He's Got the Whole World ___ Hands: 5 in His
Heshvan: 5 month 6 Hebrew
predecessor: 6 Tishri
successor: 6 Kislev
Hesiod: 4 poet 5 Greek
hesistantly: 8 bit by bit 9 piecemeal 10 step by step
hesitancy: 4 stop 5 break, doubt, pause 8 stopping 9 faltering, timidness 10 diffidence, indecision
hesitant: 3 shy 4 loth, poky, wary, weak 5 balky, chary, loath, timid 6 afraid, averse, draggy, fickle, gun-shy, scared, trepid, unsure 7 abashed, alarmed, anxious, chicken, daunted, dubious, fearful, gradual, guarded, halting, impeded, lagging, languid, nervous, panicky, spooked, uneager 8 cautious, cowardly, crawling, creeping, dawdling, delaying, dilatory, doubtful, doubting, dragging, drawn-out, fearsome, lukewarm, plodding, slothful, sluggish, timorous, toddling, wavering 9 diffident, faltering, flinching, leisurely, lethargic, petrified, prolonged, reluctant, skeptical, snaillike, tentative, terrified, uncertain, undecided, unhurried, unwilling 10 ambivalent, deliberate, frightened, indecisive, indisposed, irresolute, protracted, suspicious, uninclined, unobliging, unresolved, weak-willed, wishy-washy
remark: 5 maybe 7 perhaps 8 possibly
sounds: 2 er, uh, um
hesitate: 3 haw 4 balk, halt, wait 5 baulk, dally, defer, delay, demur, hedge, pause, waver 6 boggle, falter, fumble, linger, recoil, seesaw, shrink, totter, waffle 7 hold off, scruple, shy away, stagger, stammer, stumble, stutter, whiffle 8 flounder, hang back, hold back, pull back, question 9 hem and haw, oscillate, pussyfoot, vacillate 10 dillydally, equivocate
hesitating: 8 doubtful 9 skeptical 10 indecisive, irresolute
hesitation: 5 delay, doubt, pause, qualm 7 dubiety, scruple 8 delaying, demurral, fumbling, wavering 9 dubiosity, faltering, misgiving, stumbling 10 averseness, diffidence, indecision, reluctance, skepticism, stammering, stuttering
exclamation: 3 why
show ~: 5 waver 6 falter, wobble 9 hem and haw, vacillate
sound: 2 er, uh, um
without ~: 6 flatly 7 readily 8 directly 9 willingly
word of ~: 4 well
hesitation ___: 5 waltz
He's making ___...: 5 a list
He's Mine (song) artist: Mokenstef, Platters
Hesperia: 4 city, town 5 nymph
father of ~: 5 Atlas
locale: 10 California
hesperidium: 5 fruit
Hess: 4 Leon, Myra 6 Rudolf, Victor, Walter
___ Hess: 7 Amerada
Hess, Dame Myra: 7 British, pianist
Hesse, Hermann: 4 poet 6 German, writer 8 Nobelist
work: The Glass Bead Game
Siddhartha
Steppenwolf
Hesseman, Howard: 5 actor
film: Doctor Detroit (1983)
TV: Head of the Class, WKRP in Cincinnati
Hesse river: 4 Eder
see also German
Hessian ___: 3 fly 4 boot 7 andiron
He's So Fine (1963 song) artist: Chiffons
He's So Shy (1980 song) artist: Pointer Sisters
Hess, Victor: 8 Nobelist 9 physicist, scientist
Hess, Walter: 8 Nobelist
Hester's mark: 4 red A
Hester Street (1975 film)
cast: Mel Howard, Carol Kane, Steven Keats
director: Joan Micklin Silver
He's the Greatest Dancer (1979 song) artist: Sister Sledge
He's the Wiz and he lives ___: 4 in Oz
Hestia: 7 goddess
brother of ~: 4 Zeus 5 Hades 8 Poseidon
equivalent: 5 Vesta
mother of ~: 4 Rhea
parent of ~: 4 Rhea 6 Cronos, Cronus
sister of ~: 4 Hera 7 Demeter
Heston, Charlton: 5 actor
adversary: 3 ape
film: 55 Days at Peking (1963)
Ben-Hur (1959, AA)
The Buccaneer (1958)
El Cid (1961)
The Greatest Show on Earth (1952)
The Hawaiians (1970)
The Naked Jungle (1954)
Planet of the Apes (1968)
Pony Express (1953)
The President's Lady (1953)
The Ten Commandments (1956)
Touch of Evil (1958)
The War Lord (1965)
Will Penny (1968)
org: 3 NRA
role: 5 Moses
heterodox: 7 lawless 8 abnormal 9 dissident, heretical
heterodoxy: 9 disaccord 10 disharmony, dissension, dissidence

heterogeneity: 3 mix 7 mélange, mixture, variety 9 diversity, potpourri 10 miscellany
heterogeneous: 4 misc., mixt 5 mixed 6 motley, unlike, varied 7 diverse, various 8 assorted, multiple
heterophyte: 5 plant
heth: 6 Hebrew, letter
predecessor: 5 zayin
successor: 3 tet 4 teth
He that ___ clean hands...: 4 hath
Hetty: 5 Green
het up: 4 agog 5 afire, angry, irate, riled 7 excited 8 agitated, in a state, in a tizzy, incensed 9 in a lather, indignant, perturbed
heurige: 4 wine 5 white 9 white wine
origin: 7 Austria
heuristic: 9 inquiring 10 analytical
___ Heusen: 3 Van
hew: 2 ax 3 axe, cut 4 chop, crop, fell, hack 5 sever, shape 6 chisel, cleave, saw off 7 cut down 8 chop down, chop wood 9 sculpture
anew: 5 recut
___-hew: 5 rough
HEW
part: 4 Educ. 6 Health 7 Welfare 9 Education
successor: 3 HHS
He Walked by Night (1948 film)
cast: Richard Basehart, Scott Brady, Roy Roberts
he was, in Latin: 4 erat
hewer: 3 axe 6 axeman 7 hatchet
He Who Gets Slapped (1924 film)
cast: Lon Chaney, John Gilbert, Norma Shearer
He Will Break Your Heart (1960 song)
artist: Jerry Butler
Hewish, Antony: 8 Nobelist 9 physicist
Hewitt: 3 Don 8 Jennifer
Hewitt, Jennifer Love: 7 actress
film: Heartbreakers (2001)
I Know What You Did Last Summer (1997)
I Still Know What You Did Last Summer (1998)
TV: Party of Five
Hewlett: 7 William
Hewlett-Packard
competitor: 3 IBM 5 Epson
product: 2 PC 7 printer 8 computer
hewn: 6 felled 8 rough-cut
___-hewn: 5 rough
He wouldn't harm ___: 4 a fly 5 a flea
hex: 3 pox 4 jinx 5 charm, curse, magic, spell 6 voodoo, whammy 7 bewitch, enchant, evil eye, sorcery 10 hocus-pocus
halter: 6 amulet
sign locale: 4 barn
hex ___: 4 mark, sign
hex-: 3 six
halved: 3 tri-
predecessor: 4 pent-
successor: 4 sept-
hexa-: 3 six
plus two: 4 octa-, octo-
predecessor ~: 5 penta-
successor: 5 septi-
___ hexachloride: 6 carbon 7 benzene
hexad: 3 six 6 sextet 8 sextette
half a ~: 4 trio 5 triad 6 triple
hexade: 3 six
___ hexafluoride: 5 xenon 7 uranium
hexahedron: 3 die 4 cube
hexane: 4 fuel 7 solvent
hexapod: 3 bug 6 insect
hexed: 7 accurst, hapless 8 accursed, luckless
hexing: 5 spell
hexone: 7 solvent
hexose: 5 sugar
Hexum: 7 Jon-Erik
hey: 8 greeting
ender: 3 day
follower: 6 diddle
hey ___: 4 rube
Hey ___: 4 Girl, Jude, Mr. D.J. 5 Lover, Paula, There 6 Deanie
Hey ___ Lonely Girl: 5 There
Hey!: 3 cry, pst 4 ahoy, psst 6 listen
say ~: 4 yell
Hey, ___!: 3 you
Hey, ___ Me Over: 4 Look
heyday: 4 acme, peak, pink, time 5 prime 6 flower, height, zenith 8 pinnacle 9 golden age
Hey Deanie (1977 song) artist: Shaun Cassidy
Heyerdahl, Thor: 8 explorer 9 Norwegian
island destination: 6 Easter
transport: 3 Ra I 4 raft, Ra II 7 Kon-Tiki
word in a ~ title: 3 Aku
Hey Girl (1971 song) artist: Donny Osmond
Hey, Good ___: 6 Lookin'
___ Hey Hey Kiss Him Goodbye: 4 Na Na
Hey! Jealous Lover (1956 song) artist: Frank Sinatra
Hey Jude (1968 song) artist: Beatles
___ Hey Kid: 3 Say
Hey, kids! What time ___?: 4 is it
Hey Lover (1995 song) artist: LL Cool J
Heymans, Corneille: 8 Nobelist
Hey Mr. D.J. (1993 song) artist: Zhané
Hey Nineteen (1980 song) artist: Steely Dan
Heyrovsky, Jaroslav: 7 chemist 8 Nobelist
Heyse, Paul: 6 German, writer 8 Nobelist
Hey there!: 4 ahoy
Hey There (1954 song) artist: Rosemary Clooney
Hey There Lonely Girl (1970 song) artist: Eddie Holman
Heyward, DuBose: 6 author, writer
work: Porgy
Porgy and Bess
Heywood: 4 John 5 Broun, Eddie 6 Thomas
Heywood ___ Broun: 4 Hale
Heywood, Eddie song: Canadian Sunset (1956)
Heywood, John: 4 poet 7 British
Heywood, Thomas: 7 British 10 playwright
Hey you!: 3 pst 4 ahoy, psst
Hezekiah's mother: 3 Abi
Hezuo: 3 pig 5 swine
Hf: 4 elem. 7 element, hafnium
72 for ~: 4 at. no.
Hg: 4 elem., merc. 7 mercury
80 for ~: 4 at. no.
H.G.: 5 Wells
hgt.: 2 mt. 3 alt., mtn. 4 elev.
HGTV: 7 channel
alternative: 3 BET, CMT, MTV, PAX, TBS, TLC, TNN, TNT, USA 4 ESPN 5 A and E, C-SPAN, Style 6 Noggin, Tech TV, TV Land 7 Court TV, Ovation, SoapNet 8 Lifetime
hgwy.: 2 rt. 3 rte.
HHH: 7 Liberal 8 Humphrey
boss: 3 LBJ
he defeated ~: 3 RMN
org. cofounded by ~: 3 ADA
HHS
agency: 3 CDC, FDA, NIH, SSA
part: 5 Human 6 Health 8 Services
hi-___: 3 res 4 tech
Hi: 5 aloha, hello 6 shalom 8 greeting
say ~ to: 5 greet
wife: 4 Lois
Hi, ___!: 3 Mom
Hi-___, Hi-Lo: 4 Lili
HI
see Hawaii
Hialeah: 4 city, town
locale: 7 Florida
transaction: 5 wager
Hi and Lois: 5 comic, strip 10 comic strip
dog: 4 Dawg
kid: 3 Dot 4 Chip 5 Ditto 6 Trixie
hiatus: 3 gap 4 gulf, halt, lull, rift 5 break, lapse, pause, space 6 breach, lacuna, layoff, recess 7 interim, respite 8 interval, omission 9 cessation, interlude 10 sabbatical
Hiawatha: 4 poem 6 Indian
author: Henry Wadsworth Longfellow
boat: 5 canoe
hibachi: 7 brasier, brazier
feature: 5 grate
residue: 3 ash
Hibbert: 7 Eleanor
Hibbing: 4 city, town
locale: 9 Minnesota
Hibbler, Al
song: He (1955)
Unchained Melody (1955)
hibernal: 6 chilly, frigid, wintry 7 wintery
hibernate: 4 hide, idle, rest 5 sleep 6 hole up 8 stagnate 10 lie dormant
place to ~: 3 den 4 lair
hibernating: 6 asleep, dozing 7 dormant, napping 8 dreaming 9 sacked out, somnolent
hibernation: 5 sleep
Hibernia: 4 Eire, Erin 7 Ireland
Hibernian: 4 Celt 5 Irish
Hiberno-___: 5 Saxon 7 English
hibiscus: 4 tree 5 plant 6 flower
cousin: 4 ocra, okra, okro 6 mallow
___ hibiscus: 3 sea 7 Chinese
hic ___: 5 jacet
hic, ___, hoc: 4 haec
hiccup: 5 spasm 6 reflex 7 setback 10 difficulty
hick: 3 oaf 4 boor, rube 5 rural, yokel 6 farmer, gaffer, rustic 7 bumpkin, hayseed, plowboy 9 backwater, hillbilly 10 clodhopper, provincial
Hickey: 7 William
Hickman: 6 Darryl, Dwayne
Hickok: 4 Bill 8 Wild Bill
hickory: 3 nut 4 tree 6 fabric
tree: 5 pecan 6 hognut, pignut, walnut 9 butternut
hickory ___: 4 pine 5 cloth 6 stripe
Hickory: 4 town
locale: 4 N. Car.
___ Hickory: 3 Old
Hickory Dickory ___: 4 Dock
Hickox: 7 Douglas
Hicks: 4 John 6 Edward 9 Catherine, Granville
Hicks, Granville: 6 author, writer
Hicks, John: 8 Nobelist 9 economist
Hicksville: 4 city, town
locale: 7 New York 10 Long Island
Hidalgo: 4 city, town 5 state
city: 4 Apan 6 Tepeji, Vindho 7 Actopan, Pachuca, Sahagún, Zimapán 8 Huejutla, Progreso, Tizayuca 10 Tezontepec, Tulancingo
locale: 6 Mexico 9 Chihuahua, Michoacán
see also Spanish
hidden: 4 dark, deep, lost 5 blind, inner, leafy, perdu, privy 6 arcane, buried, covert, inward, latent, masked, mystic, occult, perdue, secret, unseen, untold, veiled 7 cloaked, clouded, covered, cryptic, furtive, obscure, on the QT, private, shadowy, unknown 8 abstruse, eclipsed, esoteric, hermetic, hush-hush, isolated, mystical, obscured, screened, secluded, shielded, shrouded, ulterior, withheld 9 concealed, cryptical, disguised, incognito, innermost, in the dark, invisible, nonpublic, out of view, potential, recondite, unexposed, unnoticed 10 cloistered, mysterious, out of sight, tucked away, undercover, underlying, under wraps, undetected, undivulged, unrevealed, unviewable
combining form: 4 adel- 5 adelo-, crypt-, krypt- 6 crypto-, krypto-
drawback: 4 snag, trap 5 catch
not ~: 5 clear, overt, plain 6 patent 7 obvious, visible 8 apparent, manifest 10 observable
supply: 5 cache, hoard, stash
wait while ~: 4 lurk
hidden ___: 3 tax 6 agenda
hiddenite: 3 gem 8 gemstone
Hidden Valley: 8 dressing
alternative: 8 Wish-Bone 9 Seven Seas 11 Good Seasons
Hidden Valley ___: 5 Ranch
hide: 4 bury, lurk, mask, pelt, skin, veil, whip, wrap 5 cache, cloak, couch, cover, cower, ditch, shade, sneak, spank, stash, store 6 closet, harbor, hole up, hush up, inhume, lie low, pocket, screen, shield, shroud 7 becloud, blot out, conceal, cover up, eclipse, envelop, harbour, leather, obscure, protect, seclude, secrete, shelter, shut off, smuggle 8 covering, disguise, ensconce, enshroud, hold back, salt away, sock away, stow away, suppress, tuck away, withhold 9 adumbrate, dissemble, hibernate, keep quiet, obfuscate, sequester, take cover, whitewash 10 camouflage, integument, interweave, keep secret
away: 4 save 5 stash, store 9 sequester
brushed ~: 5 suede
cure ~ s: 3 tan
don't ~: 5 pop in 6 appear, show up, turn up 7 turn out
ender: 3 out 4 away 5 bound
from: 5 avoid
in fear: 5 cower, quail 6 cringe, shrink 7 tremble
in the hand: 4 palm
partner: 4 hair, seek
place to ~: 4 hole, lair 5 haven 6 refuge 7 retreat, shelter 9 safe house, sanctuary
starter: 3 cow, raw 5 horse
tan a ~: 5 spank 6 punish
untanned ~: 3 kip
hide ___: 3 out 4 away
hide ___ hair: 3 nor
hide-___-seek: 5 and-go
Hide-___: 4 A-Bed
hide and seek: 4 game
cheat at ~: 4 peek
phrase: 5 not it 7 you're it
spot: 4 base
word: 5 ready
hideaway: 3 den, mew 4 aery, cave, eyry, lair, nest, nook 5 aerie, eyrie 6 asylum, burrow, corner, covert, lounge, refuge, resort 7 retreat, shelter 9 hermitage, nightclub, sanctuary, seclusion 10 ivory tower
hideaway ___: 3 bed
Hideaway author: Dean Koontz
hidebound: 5 rigid, stiff, tight 6 little, narrow 9 bourgeois, impliable,

parochial **10** inflexible, intolerant, provincial
Hide in Plain Sight (1980 film)
cast: James Caan, Jill Eikenberry
director: James Caan
hide nor ___: **4** hair
Hideo: **4** Nomo
hide one's ___: **4** head
hideous: **4** evil, grim, ugly **5** awful, gross, lurid **6** grisly, horrid, morbid, odious **7** beastly, fearful, ghastly, hateful, heinous, macaber, macabre **8** dreadful, gruesome, horrible, shocking, terrible, wretched **9** appalling, frightful, grotesque, loathsome, monstrous, offensive, repellant, repellent, repugnant, repulsive, revolting, unsightly **10** abominable, detestable, disgusting, horrendous, horrifying, petrifying, terrifying, unpleasant
hideout: **3** den **4** lair, nest, nook **5** cover, haven **6** corner, grotto, refuge **7** shelter **9** safe house, sanctuary **10** ivory tower
hider: **8** stowaway
hidey-hole: **5** cache
hiding: **7** beating, masking, secrecy, veiling **8** cloaking, covering, flogging **9** screening, seclusion, secretion, shielding, thrashing **10** out of sight
come out of ~: **4** show **6** appear, emerge **7** peep out, surface **10** break cover
nothing: **4** bare, open **5** frank, overt, plain **7** exposed, obvious **8** wide-open
place: **3** den **4** lair **5** cache, cover, haven, niche **6** recess, refuge
hie: **2** go **3** fly, rip, run, zip **4** dart, dash, flit, hare, pelt, race, rush, tear, trot, zoom **5** hurry, scoot, scram, shoot, spank, speed **6** barrel, gallop, hasten, hustle, move it, repair, rocket, run off, scurry **7** dash off, floor it, hop to it, quicken, scamper, take off, tear off **8** hightail, light out, make time, step on it **9** get moving, go quickly, hotfoot it, make haste, shake a leg, skedaddle **10** double-time, get a move on, get hopping, hightail it, make tracks
hiemal: **4** cold **6** wintry **7** wintery
hierarchy: **4** rank **5** order, scale **7** ranking **8** echelons **9** apparatus
level: **4** rank, rung
hieratic: **8** clerical, priestly **10** sacerdotal
hieroglyphics: **4** code **6** cipher **7** writing **9** ideograms **10** characters, cryptogram
Hieronymus: **5** Bosch
hi-fi: **5** phono **6** stereo **8** Victrola **10** phonograph
buy: **2** LP **3** amp **5** tuner **6** stereo
Higgins: **4** Jack **5** Henry **6** Bertie
Higgins, Bertie song: Key Largo (1982)
___ Higgins Clark: **4** Mary
Higgins, Henry creator: **4** Shaw
higgle: **6** dicker, palter **7** bargain
high: **3** big **4** dear, rank, tall **5** above, aloft, happy, light, lofty, noble, pricy, steep, stiff, tight, tipsy, upper **6** aerial, alpine, costly, elated, flying, joyful, lordly, piping, pricey, pumped, rancid, shrill, strong, treble **7** crucial, eminent, exalted, excited, extreme, psyched, soaring, soprano, stately, sublime **8** cheerful, ecstatic, elevated, hovering, piercing, powerful, towering, upraised **9** essential, excessive, expensive, exuberant, important, prominent **10** at a premium, exorbitant, malodorous, optimistic, overpriced, up in the air
abode: **4** aery, eyry **5** aerie, eyrie
aim ~: **5** dream **6** aspire
and dry: **7** aground **8** cast away, deserted, marooned, stranded **9** abandoned
and low: **7** all over **10** everywhere
and mighty: **5** lofty **7** haughty, pompous **8** arrogant, dogmatic, snobbish **10** dogmatical
ball: **3** lob **5** pop-up
beams: **7** brights
be in ~ spirits: **4** crow **5** exult **6** bubble **7** enthuse, rejoice **9** make merry **10** effervesce, jump for joy
birth: **9** blue blood, gentility **10** upper class, upper crust
blow sky ~: **5** rebut **6** refute **8** disprove **9** discredit, shoot down **10** invalidate
combining form: **3** alt- **4** alti-
command: **5** brass **10** management
country: **4** mesa **5** butte, Nepal, Tibet **6** Thibet, Xizang **7** plateau, Sitsang
degree of insight: **5** depth **6** acuity, acumen, wisdom **8** sagacity **10** astuteness
dudgeon: **3** ire **4** rage **5** anger, wrath **7** umbrage
ender: **3** boy, way **4** ball, born, bred, brow, jack, land, life, rise, road, tail **5** chair, flier, flyer, lands, light **6** binder, flying, handed, lander **7** lighter
five: **4** slap **8** greeting
fly ~: **4** soar
flying ~: **3** gay **4** glad **5** happy, merry, sunny **6** blithe, cheery, chirpy, elated, golden, joyful, joyous, upbeat **7** beaming, buoyant, chipper, content, gleeful, glowing, pleased, radiant, tickled **8** blissful, carefree, cheerful, ecstatic, exultant, gladsome, grooving, jubilant, laughing, sanguine, thrilled, unbeaten **9** contented, delighted, fortunate, gratified, lightsome, overjoyed **10** optimistic, successful, triumphant, unbothered
get ~ on: **4** like, love **5** enjoy, savor **6** relish **9** delight in **10** appreciate
give the ~ sign: **3** tip **4** warn **5** alert **6** advise, signal, tip off **7** caution **8** forewarn
ground: **4** hill, rise **5** knoll, ridge **7** plateau **8** eminence, mountain **9** acclivity, elevation **10** prominence
heel: **4** pump **5** spike
hit ~ into the air: **4** loft
hit the ~ spots: **4** skim **8** simplify
hold ~: **4** love **5** adore, honor **6** esteem
in alcohol: **4** hard
in ~ dudgeon: **5** irate
in ~ gear: **4** fast **5** apace **7** hastily, quickly, rapidly, swiftly **8** speedily **9** hurriedly
in music: **3** alt
in place names: **4** Alta
in ~ style: **3** mod **4** chic **5** natty, swank **6** classy, dapper, dressy, modish **7** à la mode, dashing, elegant, voguish
IQ: **10** braininess
jinks: **4** lark **5** caper, prank, spree **7** fooling, revelry **8** mischief **9** vandalism
jump: **5** event
leave ~ and dry: **4** jilt **6** desert, maroon, strand **8** abdicate
live ~ on the hog: **4** bask **5** revel **6** thrive **7** indulge, rollick **8** flourish **9** luxuriate
living: **6** luxury, wealth **8** opulence, splendor **9** affluence **10** prosperity
look ~ and low: **4** hunt, seek **5** scour **6** search **7** ransack, rummage
low to ~: **5** range
mark: **5** A plus
mountain: **3** alp
muckamuck: **6** honcho
name meaning ~ peace: **8** Humphrey
noon: **6** zenith **8** meridian
not ~: **3** low **4** deep, down **5** lowly
not as ~: **5** below, lower, under
note: **3** e la
old time: **4** lark **5** caper, fling, revel, spree **6** frolic, gambol, picnic **7** rollick
on ~: **4** over **5** above, aloft, lofty **8** overhead
on one's ~ horse: **6** snooty **7** haughty
opinion: **6** esteem, regard **7** respect **9** reverence **10** admiration
partner: **3** dry, low
pitched too ~: **5** sharp
place: **6** heaven **9** firmament
point: **3** top **4** acme, apex, peak **5** crest **6** climax, zenith **10** prominence
pt.: **2** mt. **3** mtn.
raise ~: **4** heft, hike, lift **5** extol **6** hike up **7** build up, elevate, ennoble, glorify, idolize, lionize, worship
rate ~: **4** like, love **5** adore, enjoy, favor, go for **6** admire, prefer, relish, revere **7** cherish, idolize **8** hold dear, venerate **10** appreciate
rating: **4** A-one, one-A
regard: **4** love **6** esteem **10** attachment
repute: **4** fame **5** éclat, glory **6** renown **7** acclaim **8** eminence, prestige **9** celebrity
roller: **7** spender **8** prodigal **10** big spender
search ~ heaven: **4** comb **6** forage **7** ransack, rummage
seas: **5** ocean
sign: **4** wink **5** alarm, alert **6** motion
society: **5** elite **6** bon ton, jet set **8** nobility
spirits: **3** joy, pep **4** élan, glee, life, mood **5** mirth **6** gaiety, gayety, levity **7** elation, jollity **8** buoyance, buoyancy, euphoria, felicity, hilarity
spot: **4** acme, apex, peak **5** attic, crest, crown, tower **6** climax, payoff, summit, zenith **8** capstone, pinnacle **10** denouement
standing: **4** note **5** glory, honor **6** esteem, renown **7** acclaim, dignity **8** eminence, prestige **9** celebrity, greatness, magnitude, reverence **10** importance, prominence
temperature: **4** heat **5** fever
time: **4** noon **5** spree **6** at last
to a ~ degree: **4** very **5** quite **6** deeply, rather, vastly **7** acutely, greatly **8** terribly **9** decidedly, extremely, seriously, supremely, unusually **10** enormously, especially, profoundly, remarkably, thoroughly, uncommonly
tops: **6** sneaks **8** sneakers
up: **5** aloft, lofty **8** elevated, towering
value: **4** perk, plum **5** bonus, price, prize **6** bounty **7** premium **8** dividend **10** perquisite
water alternative: **4** hell
high ___: **3** bar, day, hat, key, tea **4** beam, gear, jump, mass, noon, road, seas, sign, tide, time, wine, wire **5** altar, board, chest, horse, jinks, liver, place, style, table, water **6** blower, comedy, fulham, ground, jumper, priest, relief, roller, school, yellow **7** command, concept, fashion, finance, hurdles, milling, polymer, profile, society, spirits, treason
high ___ hog: **5** on the **6** off the
high ___ kite: **3** as a
high-___: **3** end, hat **4** five, rise, risk, step, tech, test **5** class, count, flown, grade, level, power, speed, toned **6** energy, handed, income, minded, necked, octane, priced, strung, ticket **7** colored, density, pitched, powered, rolling, tension, voltage, wrought
high-___ act: **4** wire
high-___ cymbals: **3** hat
high-___ district: **4** rent
high-___ lipoprotein: **7** density
high-___ mark: **5** water
high-___ poker: **3** low
high-___ sneakers: **3** top
___ high: **3** fly **4** ride **6** Azores **7** Bermuda, Pacific
___-high: **3** ace, sky **4** hole, knee, type **5** waist
High ___: **3** Tor **4** Mass, Noon, Wall **5** Court, Hopes, on You, Tatra **6** Church, Crimes, Enough, German, Sierra, Stakes **7** Anxiety, Holiday, Rollers, Society
High ___ Day: **4** Holy
High ___ Drifter: **6** Plains
High ___ Shoes: **6** Button
High ___ the Mighty, The: **3** and
___ High: **3** How, Sky **4** Aces **6** Cooley **7** Natural
high-altitude: **4** tall **6** alpine **8** towering
high and ___: **3** dry, low **6** mighty
high-and-mighty: **4** vain **5** proud **6** stuffy **8** cavalier, snobbish, superior
High and the Mighty, The (1954 film)
cast: Laraine Day, Robert Stack, Claire Trevor, John Wayne
composer: **7** Tiomkin
director: William Wellman
writer: **4** Gann
High Anxiety (1977 film)
cast: Mel Brooks, Madeline Kahn, Harvey Korman, Cloris Leachman
director: Mel Brooks
high as ___: **5** a kite
highball: **5** drink **8** beverage, cocktail, libation **10** intoxicant
ingredient: **3** rye
highborn: **5** noble, royal **6** gentle **7** genteel **9** patrician **10** upper-class
unfit for the ~: **4** non-U
highboy: **5** chest **7** dresser **9** furniture
highbred: **5** noble, royal **6** august, formal, polite **7** courtly, elegant, gallant, genteel, refined **8** cultured, decorous, gracious, polished **9** dignified **10** chivalrous, respectful
highbrow: **3** ace **4** sage, snob, whiz **5** brain, snoot **6** august, brainy, genius, proper, savant **7** bookish, egghead, elegant, elitist, erudite, learned, prodigy, refined, scholar, stately, thinker **8** academic, cerebral, cultured, decorous, Einstein, longhair, studious, virtuoso **9** dignified, intellect, scholarly **10** mastermind
highbrows: **5** elite **8** literati **10** illuminati, upper-crust
High Button Shoes: **7** musical
songwriter: **5** Styne
high-caliber: **8** superior
highchair: **4** seat
hazard: **5** spill
part: **4** tray
user: **3** tot **6** infant
high-class: **4** A-one, best, chic, luxe, posh, rich **5** elite, ritzy **6** choice, deluxe **7** stylish, supreme, voguish **8** ladylike, superior

High Crimes (2002 film)
cast: Morgan Freeman, Ashley Judd, Amanda Peet
__ High Dam: 5 Aswan
higher: 4 more 5 upper 6 senior
get ~: 4 rise, soar 6 ascend, move up 7 take off
make ~: 4 hike 5 boost, raise 6 jack up 7 elevate 8 increase
of ~ rank: 6 senior 8 superior
prefix: 5 super-, supra-
than: 4 over, past 5 above 6 beyond 9 upwards of
higher-__: 3 ups
Higher __: 4 Love 6 Ground
Higher and Higher: 7 musical
songwriter: 4 Hart 7 Rodgers
Higher and Higher (song) artist: Jackie Wilson, Rita Coolidge
Higher Ground (1973 song) artist: Stevie Wonder
Higher Love (1986 song) artist: Steve Winwood
higher-quality: 6 better
higher-up: 4 boss, exec 5 chief 6 honcho, leader, top dog 7 big shot, manager 8 big wheel, kingfish, overseer, superior 9 authority, executive 10 head honcho, supervisor
highest: 3 nth, top, ult. 4 A-one, best, head, most, tops 5 chief, grand, prime 6 utmost 7 leading, maximum, optimum, premier, primary, supreme, topmost 8 foremost, ultimate 9 principal, sovereign, uppermost, uttermost
of the ~ order: 6 curule
point: 3 tip, top 4 acme, apex, peak 5 crest, crown, limit 6 apogee, summit, zenith 7 maximum 8 pinnacle 10 prominence
prefix: 4 arch-
highest __ factor: 6 common
highest-quality: 4 A-one, best, tops 5 first, primo
__-High-Everything-Else: 4 Lord
highfalutin: 6 august 7 pompous, stately 8 affected, mannered
manner: 4 airs
type: 4 snob
high-five: 5 greet
exchange a ~: 5 exult
slapper: 4 palm
sound: 4 slap
high-flown: 5 lofty, showy 6 ornate 7 exalted, fustian, pompous, stilted 8 inflated 9 bombastic, grandiose 10 rhetorical
__ high gear: 4 into
__ High German: 3 New, Old 6 Middle
high-grade: 3 def, rad 4 aces, A-one, boss, braw, cool, cull, dece, fine, gear, keen, neat, nice, phat, tops, tuff 5 dandy, ducky, grand, great, marvy, neato, nobby, prime, slick, super, swell 6 bang on, bang-up, bonzer, bosker, choice, divine, dreamy, far-out, gnarly, groovy, lovely, peachy, slap-up, spot on, superb, terrif, tiptop, unreal, whizzo, wicked 7 amazing, awesome, capital, corking, perfect, ripping, skookum, stellar, sublime 8 dazzling, especial, eximious, fabulous, five-star, four-star, frabjous, glorious, heavenly, jim-dandy, slam-bang, smashing, splendid, standout, sterling, stickout, superior, terrific, top-level, topnotch, very good, wondrous 9 bodacious, Endsville, excellent, exemplary, exquisite, first-rate, hunky-dory, marvelous, sollicker, top-flight, wonderful 10 first-class, hotsy-totsy, jack-a-dandy, out of sight, peachy-keen, phenomenal, remarkable, stupendous, super-duper
high-handed: 5 proud 6 lordly 8 despotic 9 arbitrary, imperious 10 despotical, peremptory
high-handedness: 7 cruelty, tyranny 8 coercion 9 autocracy, despotism 10 oppression
high-hat: 4 snob, snub 5 scorn, snoot 6 stuffy 7 cymbals 8 snobbish, superior 10 percussion
look: 5 sneer
high-hatter: 4 snob 5 snoot
high-heel: 4 shoe 8 footwear
High Holy __: 3 Day
High Hopes (1959 song) artist: Frank Sinatra
animal: 3 ant, ram
composer: 4 Cahn 9 Van Heusen
high-income: 8 well-paid 9 lucrative 10 profitable
high-IQ club: 5 Mensa
high jump: 5 event, sport
high jumper: 6 Brumel 7 Fosbury
highland: 4 hill 7 plateau
Highland: 4 city, town
locale: 7 Indiana 10 California
see also Scotland
__ Highland: 4 West 6 Scotch
Highlander: 3 SUV 4 Celt, Gael, Scot 6 Toyota
Highlander (1986 film)
cast: Sean Connery, Roxanne Hart, Christopher Lambert
Highland fling: 5 dance
Highland Park: 4 city, town
locale: 8 Illinois, Michigan
highlands: 5 peaks 9 mountains
like the ~: 5 hilly
Highlands
see Scotland
high-level: 7 crucial 8 critical, historic 9 big-league, important, momentous, paramount
highlight: 4 peak 5 focus, light 6 accent, play up, stress 7 feature, point up 8 best part 9 emphasize, punctuate, spotlight, underline 10 accentuate, focal point, illuminate, illustrate, underscore
hockey ~: 5 fight
highlighted, be: 8 stand out
highlights: 5 recap 6 wrap-up 7 summary 8 synopsis
high-low: 4 game, shoe 5 poker 8 card game, footwear
high-low-jack: 4 game 8 card game
alias: 5 pitch 7 seven-up 9 old sledge
highly: 4 a lot, much, very, well 5 mucho, quite 6 deeply, hugely, plenty, vastly 7 but good, greatly 8 terribly, very much, very well 9 decidedly, extremely, immensely 10 profoundly, remarkably, thoroughly, to the quick
highly-wrought: 4 posh 5 fancy, plush, showy, swank 6 flashy, frilly, glitzy, lavish, ornate, swanky 7 elegant, opulent 8 splendid 9 decorated, elaborate, intricate, luxurious, sumptuous 10 decorative, munificent, ornamented
high-minded: 4 just 5 great, lofty, moral, noble 6 honest 7 ethical, liberal, refined, stately, upright 8 elevated, knightly, virtuous 9 honorable 10 chivalrous
high-mindedness: 6 ethics, purity, virtue 7 decency, honesty, probity 8 fairness, morality, nobility 9 character, integrity, rectitude 10 generosity, temperance
high-muck-a-muck: 3 VIP 4 boss, king 5 mogul, nabob
Highness: 5 title
__ Highness: 3 Her 4 Your 8 Royal. His
High Noon (1952 film): 5 oater 7 western
cast: Lloyd Bridges, Gary Cooper, Katy Jurado, Grace Kelly, Thomas Mitchell
composer: 7 Tiomkin
director: Fred Zinnemann
singer: 5 Laine
high-occupancy __: 7 vehicle
__ high off the hog: 3 eat
high on the __: 3 hog
high-pH substance: 3 lye 6 alkali
high-pitched: 5 fluty, reedy, sharp 6 shrill 8 piercing
sound: 4 ting 5 whine 6 squawk, squeak
High Plains Drifter (1973 film): 5 oater
cast: Verna Bloom, Clint Eastwood, Marianna Hill
director: Clint Eastwood
High Point: 4 city, town
locale: 4 N. Car.
high-powered: 5 type A 6 active, mighty, potent, robust 7 driving, dynamic, intense, pushing 8 forceful, hustling, vigorous 9 attacking, energetic 10 aggressive, compelling
not ~: 5 type B
High Pressure (1932 film)
cast: Evelyn Brent, Frank McHugh, William Powell
director: Mervyn LeRoy
high-priced: 4 dear, rich 5 steep, stiff 6 costly 8 precious, valuable 9 expensive 10 at a premium, exorbitant
high-principled: 4 true 6 honest 7 ethical 8 reliable, virtuous 9 veracious
high-priority: 7 crucial 8 critical, pressing
high-profile: 3 big 4 star 5 famed 6 famous 7 eminent, popular 8 renowned 9 important, prominent, well-known 10 celebrated
high-quality: 5 prime 6 grade A 9 excellent
high-ranking: 5 noble 6 august 7 eminent
one: 6 aristo
high-rise: 5 lofty, tower 8 building
locale: 3 urb 4 city
support: 4 I-bar
unit: 5 condo 9 apartment
high-risk: 4 spec
High Rollers: 8 game show
host: Alex Trebek
high school
class: 3 alg., art, bio., Eng., gym, mus., sci. 4 chem., math, shop, trig 5 music 6 home ec 7 algebra, biology, English, history, physics, science 8 geometry 9 chemistry
dance: 3 hop 4 prom
equiv.: 3 GED
keepsake: 2 yb. 8 yearbook
misfit: 4 geek, nerd, nurd 7 egghead
safety org.: 4 SADD
school student: 10 adolescent
sport: 4 golf 5 track 6 soccer, tennis 7 bowling 8 baseball, football, lacrosse 9 wrestling 10 basketball
student: 4 teen 5 minor
__ high school: 6 junior, senior
High School Cadets, The composer: 5 Sousa
High School Confidential (1958 song) artist: Jerry Lee Lewis
High Sierra (1941 film)
cast: Humphrey Bogart, Alan Curtis, Ida Lupino
director: Raoul Walsh
dog: 4 Pard
Highsmith, Patricia: 6 author, writer
work: Strangers on a Train The Talented Mr. Ripley
High Society (1956 film): 7 musical
cast: Bing Crosby, Celeste Holm, Grace Kelly, Frank Sinatra
composer: Cole Porter
director: Charles Walters
high-speed number: 4 Mach
high-spirited: 5 alive, peppy, vital 6 frisky, jaunty, lively, snappy 7 dashing, dynmaic, vibrant 8 animated, vigorous 9 energetic, vivacious
__ High Stadium: 4 Mile
High Stakes author: Dick Francis
__ high standard: 4 set a
high-strung: 4 edgy 5 hyper, itchy, jumpy, tense, wired 6 feisty, jangly, uneasy 7 anxious, fidgety, jittery, keyed up, nervous, restive, shook up, uptight 8 agitated, fluttery, restless, shaken up, skittish, stressed, troubled 9 concerned, excitable, ill at ease, impatient, irascible, irritable, sensitive, unrestful 10 all shook up
hightail it: 2 go 3 fly, hie, lam, rip, run, zip 4 bolt, dart, dash, flee, flit, race, rush, scat, tear, zoom 5 hurry, scoot, scram, speed 6 barrel, decamp, gallop, get out, hasten, hustle, rocket, scurry 7 abscond, go south, make off, quicken, scamper, take off 8 shove off 9 get moving, make haste, shake a leg, skedaddle 10 get a move on
high-tech: 6 modern 10 electronic
company: 6 dot-com
memo: 3 fax 5 E-mail
high-temperature: 3 hot
high-test: 3 gas 8 gasoline
__ High the Moon: 3 How
high-toned: 4 chic, tony 5 moral, put on, ritzy, suave, toney 6 classy, la-de-da, la-di-da, urbane 7 elegant, ethical 8 affected, lah-di-dah 9 honorable, insincere, uncorrupt 10 aboveboard
Hightower: 7 Rosella
highty-__: 6 tighty
high-water mark: 4 acme, apex, peak 5 crest 6 apogee, summit, zenith 8 meridian, pinnacle
highway: 3 way 4 pike, road 5 route 6 artery 7 freeway, ingress, thruway 8 main road, toll road, turnpike 10 expressway, interstate, throughway
abbr. on ~ overpasses: 3 max
agcy.: 3 DOT
alert: 5 flare, fusee, fuzee
ancient ~: 3 via
crosser, maybe: 4 deer
enter a ~: 5 merge
feature: 4 exit, lane, ramp 6 stripe 8 shoulder
fee: 4 toll
hanging: 4 sign
hazard: 3 ess
headache: 3 jam 5 delay, tie up 8 accident, slowdown 10 bottleneck, congestion, traffic jam
improve a ~: 5 widen
like some ~ s: 5 laned
Maine-to-Florida ~: 5 US one
marker: 4 cone 5 pylon
material: 3 tar 7 asphalt 8 concrete
Minneapolis-to-Fargo ~: 5 US ten
noisemaker: 4 horn
sight: 3 car 4 auto, semi 5 truck
sign: 3 SLO 4 eats, Exit, hill, slow
starter: 5 super
stop: 5 diner, motel
US-to-Alaska ~: 5 Alcan
worker: 5 paver
see also road
highway __: 6 patrol 7 robbery
__ highway: 4 belt, data, dual 5 king's 6 queen's 7 divided
__ Highway: 5 Alcan 6 Alaska, Powwow 7 Thieves', Ventura
highwayman: 4 thug 5 thief 6 bandit,

looter 7 brigand, footpad 8 marauder
Highwayman, The: 4 poem
author: Alfred Noyes
heroine: 4 Bess
Highway to Heaven (NBC drama)
cast: Victor French (Mark Gordon) Michael Landon (Jonathan Smith)
High Window, The author: Raymond Chandler
high-wire
garb: 6 tights
insurance: 3 net
high-wire __: 3 act
Higuchi Ichiyo: 4 poet **6** writer **8** Japanese
hi-hat: 7 cymbals **10** percussion
Hi, Hi, Hi (1972 song) artist: Paul McCartney
Hi-Ho competitor: 4 Ritz
Hi, honey, __!: 6 I'm home
hijack: 3 rob **4** take **5** seize, steal, usurp **6** kidnap **7** plunder **8** take over **10** commandeer
Hijack (1975 song) artist: Herbie Mann
hijacker: 5 thief **6** bandit, robber **9** kidnapper
hijinks: 3 fun **5** caper **6** frolic **7** fooling **9** horseplay
hike: 2 up **4** jack, jump, lift, rise, roam, trek, trip, walk **5** add to, boost, jaunt, leg it, march, raise, tramp, tromp **6** foot it, growth, jack up, jerk up, junket, mark up, pull up, ramble, stroll, trudge, wander **7** amplify, augment, elevate, explore, journey, magnify **8** addition, backpack, increase, progress **9** excursion, inflation **10** hit the road
starter: 5 hitch
take a ~: 2 go **4** blow, exit, part, quit **5** leave **6** begone, get out **8** light out, withdraw **10** go fly a kite
__ hike: 5 take a
Hiken: 3 Nat
hiker: 6 center **10** backpacker, pedestrian
need: 3 map **4** pack **5** trail **8** backpack
path: 5 trail
snack: 4 gorp **7** berries
Hikmet, Nazim: 4 poet **7** Turkish
hiku: 4 fish
Hilaire: 6 Belloc
hilarious: 4 rich **5** funny, jolly, merry **6** har-har, jovial **7** comical **8** humorous **9** convivial, laughable, priceless, very funny **10** frolicsome, gut-busting, ridiculous, rollicking, uproarious
one: 4 riot **6** scream
__ Hilarious: 5 Missa
hilarity: 3 joy **4** glee **5** cheer, mirth, revel **6** comedy, gaiety, gayety, levity **7** gayness, jollity, revelry **8** jocosity, laughter, partying **9** festivity, happiness, jocundity, joviality, jubilance, merriment **10** exuberance, joyfulness, recreation
Hilary: 4 Hahn, pope **5** saint, Swank **7** pontiff
Hilda: 8 asteroid **9** Doolittle
__-Hilda: 5 Broom
Hildebrand: 5 saint
Hildegarde: 4 Neff
Hilfiger: 5 Tommy
Hi-Lili, __: 4 Hi-Lo
hill: 3 tor **4** dune, mesa, rise **5** bluff, butte, cliff, grade, knoll, mound, ridge, slope, stack **6** barrow, glacis, height, upland **7** incline, rampart, upgrade **8** eminence, headland, highland, landmark **9** acclivity, elevation **10** high ground, prominence, promontory
arctic ~: 5 pingo
bottom: 4 foot
broad-topped ~: 4 loma
builder: 3 ant
companion: 4 dale
crest: 4 brow
ender: 3 ock, top **4** side **5** billy, crest
glacial ~: 4 paha
go over the ~: 3 lam **4** bolt, flee **6** desert, escape, run off **7** abscond, bail out, run away **8** break out
hollow: 6 corrie
isolated ~: 4 mesa **5** butte **9** tableland **10** prominence
king of the ~: 5 on top
large ~: 8 mountain
name meaning ~: 4 Tara
of beans: 6 trifle
over the ~: 3 old **5** passé **7** ancient, fogyish **9** out-of-date **10** antiquated, out of style
rolling ~: 4 wold
rounded ~: 4 knob **5** morro
sand ~: 4 dune
Scottish ~: 4 brae
slope: 4 side
small ~: 4 dune **5** knoll, mound
starter: 3 ant **4** down, foot, mole
hill __: 4 myna **5** climb, mynah **7** station
Hill: 3 Dan, Joe, Sam **5** Anita, Benny, Faith **6** Arthur, Bunker, Graham, Lauryn, Steven, Walter **7** Capitol, Rowland **9** Archibald, Blueberry
group: 6 Senate
Hill __ Blues: 6 Street
__ Hill: 3 Dru, Nob, Sam **4** Boot **6** Beacon, Breed's, Bunker **7** Capitol, Federal, Mission, Notting, Silbury
__-Hill: 6 McGraw
__ hill and dale: 3 o'er
Hill, Archibald: 8 Nobelist
Hillary: 5 Waugh **6** Brooke, Edmund **7** Clinton
to Bill: 4 wife
Hillary Clinton, __ Rodham: 3 née
Hillary, Edmund: 3 Sir **8** explorer
emulate ~: 5 climb
locale: 5 Nepal **7** Everest
__ Hillbillies, The: 7 Beverly
hillbilly: 3 oaf **4** hick, rube **5** yokel **6** rustic **7** bumpkin, hayseed
parent: 3 maw, paw
hill-builder, small: 3 ant **5** emmet
__ Hillel: 4 Beth
Hiller: 5 Wendy **6** Arthur
Hiller, Arthur: 8 director
film: The Americanization of Emily (1964)
Author! Author! (1982)
The Babe (1992)
The Hospital (1971)
The In-Laws (1979)
The Lonely Guy (1984)
Love Story (1970)
The Out-of-Towners (1970)
Outrageous Fortune (1987)
Plaza Suite (1971)
Popi (1969)
Silver Streak (1976)
Teachers (1984)
W.C. Fields and Me (1976)
The Wheeler Dealers (1963)
Hillerman: 4 John
Hiller, Wendy: 4 Dame **7** actress
film: I Know Where I'm Going! (1945)
Major Barbara (1941)
A Man for All Seasons (1966)
Murder on the Orient Express (1974)
Pygmalion (1938)
Sailor of the King (1953)
Separate Tables (1958, AA)
Sons and Lovers (1960)
Hill, Faith
song: Breathe (1999)
It's Your Love (1997)
This Kiss (1998)
spouse: Tim McGraw
Hill, George Roy: 8 director
film: Butch Cassidy and the Sundance Kid (1969)
The Great Waldo Pepper (1975)
Hawaii (1966)
The Little Drummer Girl (1984)
A Little Romance (1979)
Period of Adjustment (1962)
Slap Shot (1977)
Slaughterhouse-Five (1972)
The Sting (1973, AA)
Thoroughly Modern Millie (1967)
The World According to Garp (1982)
The World of Henry Orient (1964)
Hilliard: 4 city, town
locale: 4 Ohio
Hillis, Margaret: 9 conductor
Hill, Lauryn song: Doo Wop (1998)
__ Hill, NC: 6 Chapel
hillock: 4 rise **5** knoll, mound, ridge **6** glacis **7** hummock **9** acclivity, elevation **10** prominence
hill of __: 5 beans
hills: 8 outdoors
chain of ~: 5 ridge
head for the ~: 2 go **3** fly, run **4** bolt, flee **5** break, leave, scram **6** beat it, bug out, decamp, depart, desert, escape, get out **7** abscond, make off, retreat, run away, take off, vamoose **8** clear out **9** disappear, skedaddle **10** fly the coop, hightail it, hit the road
like the ~: 3 old
old as the ~: 6 creaky **7** ancient **9** venerable **10** antiquated
Hills: 5 Carla
__ Hills: 5 Black **6** Holmby, Valdai **7** Beverly, Nilgiri, Vindhya
Hills Beyond, The author: Thomas Wolfe
Hillsboro: 4 city, town
locale: 6 Oregon
Hills Bros.: 6 coffee
alternative: 5 Sanka, Yuban **7** Folgers, Melitta, Nescafe, Savarin
__ Hills Cop: 7 Beverly
hillside: 5 slope **6** glacis **9** acclivity
detritus: 5 scree
Hillside: 4 city, town
locale: 9 New Jersey
__ Hills 90210: 7 Beverly
Hills of Home, The (1948 film)
cast: Donald Crisp, Tom Drake, Edmund Gwenn
__ Hills of Rome: 5 Seven
Hill, Steven: 5 actor
film: The Goddess (1958)
TV: Law & Order, Mission: Impossible
Hill Street Blues (NBC drama)
cast: Michael Conrad (Sgt. Phil Esterhaus)
Charles Haid (Off. Andy Renko)
Veronica Hamel (Joyce Davenport)
Ken Olin (Det. Harry Garibaldi)
Daniel J. Travanti (Capt. Frank Furillo)
Michael Warren (Off. Bobby Hill)
character: 3 cop
producer: MTM
Hill Street Blues Theme, The (1981 song) artist: Mike Post
Hill, The (1965 film)
cast: Harry Andrews, Sean Connery, Ian Hendry
director: Sidney Lumet
hilltop: 5 crest **7** outdoor
sight: 5 vista **8** panorama **9** landscape
Hilltoppers
song: Marianne (1957)
Only You (1955)
Hill, Walter: 8 director
film: 48HRS. (1982)
The Driver (1978)
Hard Times (1975)
The Long Riders (1980)
Red Heat (1988)
Streets of Fire (1984)
Trespass (1992)
The Warriors (1979)
Hill Wife, The author: Robert Frost
hilly: 6 rugged, uneven **7** rolling
not ~: 4 flat **5** level **6** planar **7** planate
Hilo: 4 city, port, town
locale: 6 Hawaii
Hi-Lo Country, The (1998 film)
cast: Patricia Arquette, Billy Crudup, Sam Elliott, Woody Harrelson
director: Stephen Frears
hilsa: 4 fish
hilt: 4 haft **6** handle
to the ~: 5 fully **6** wholly **7** totally **8** entirely **9** all the way **10** completely
__ hilt: 5 to the **6** basket
Hilton: 5 hotel, James, Nicky **6** Conrad
alternative: 4 Omni **5** Hyatt **6** Westin **7** Wyndham **8** Marriott, Radisson, Sheraton **10** DoubleTree **11** Crowne Plaza, Four Seasons
__ Hilton: 5 Hanoi
Hilton Head Island: 4 city, town
locale: 4 S. Car.
Hilton-Jacobs: 8 Lawrence
Hilton, James: 6 author, writer **7** British
work: Goodbye, Mr. Chips
Lost Horizon
Random Harvest
hilum extension: 4 aril
him: 3 guy, man, sir **4** gent, male, poem **6** fellow **7** pronoun **9** gentleman
author: e.e. cummings
ender: 4 self
not ~: 3 her
__ Him: 4 Tell **5** Run to **6** Forget
Him (1980 song) artist: Rupert Holmes
Himalayan: 3 cat **5** felid **6** feline
Himalayas: 5 range
aromatic ~ plant: 4 nard
bovine: 3 yak **5** takin
cedar: 6 deodar **7** deodara
city: 4 Lasa **5** Lassa, Lhasa
country: 3 Nep. **5** India, Nepal, Tibet **6** Bhutan, Thibet, Xizang **7** Sitsang
goat: 4 tahr, thar
home: 4 Asia
legend: 4 yeti
mountain: 3 Api **4** Mana **5** Kabru, Kamet **6** Cho Oyu, Kangto, Lhotse, Makalu, Nunkun, Nuptse, Trisul **7** Everest, Manaslu, Pyramid, Trisuli **8** Anapurna, Baruntse, Chamlang, Changtzu, Dunagiri, Pauhunri, Tent Peak **9** Ama Dablam, Annapurna, Badrinath, Nanda Devi, Nepal Peak, Sia Kangri **10** Chomo Lhari, Dhaulagiri, Himalchuli, Kula Kangri
river from the ~ to the Ganges: 5 Jumna
sheep: 6 bharal **7** burrhel
Himalchuli: 4 peak **5** mount **8** mountain
locale: 4 Asia **5** Nepal **9** Himalayas
Himalia: 4 moon **5** nymph
planet: 7 Jupiter
Himeji: 4 city, town
locale: 5 Japan
Himes, Chester: 6 author, writer
work: Cotton Comes to Harlem
If He Hollers Let Him Go
Hi, Mom! (1970 film)
cast: Robert De Niro, Allen Garfield, Lara Parker
director: Brian De Palma

Him or Me—What's It Gonna Be? (1967 song) artist: Paul Revere and the Raiders
Him With His Foot in His Mouth
  author: Saul Bellow
hind: 3 doe, roe **4** back, deer, rear **6** animal, rustic **7** peasant, red deer **8** rearmost **9** aftermost
  ender: 3 gut **4** most **5** brain, sight **7** quarter **8** quarters
  mate: 4 hart, stag
  on one's ~ legs: 5 erect
  part: 6 breech
  rise on the ~ legs: 4 rear
hind __: 4 wing **5** shank
__ hind: 3 red **4** rock
__ Hind: 6 Golden
Hindemith, Paul: 6 German **8** composer
Hindenburg: 4 Paul
Hindenburg __: 4 line
hinder: 3 bar, dam, jam, tie **4** clog, curb, rein, slow, stay, stem, stop **5** block, box in, brake, check, cramp, crimp, cross, debar, delay, deter, embar, limit, stall, stimy, stunt, stymy, tie up **6** arrest, burden, cumber, dampen, detain, fetter, forbid, hamper, hobble, hogtie, hold up, impair, impede, oppose, rein in, resist, retard, slow up, stymie, thwart **7** confine, inhibit, occlude, prevent, set back, trammel **8** encumber, handcuff, handicap, hold back, obstruct, preclude, prohibit, restrain, sabotage, slow down, straiten **9** foreclose, forestall, frustrate, hamstring, interdict, interrupt, posterior, prejudice **10** bottleneck, counteract, disconcert, discourage
  in law: 5 debar
hindered: 4 slow
Hindi: 5 Indic **8** language
  cousin: 4 Urdu
  king, in ~: 4 raja
  see also Hindu
hindmost: 4 back, last, rear **6** latter **9** posterior
  part: 4 back, rear
hindrance: 3 bar, rub **4** care, clog, curb, drag, load, snag, wall **5** block, brake, catch, check, delay, hitch, minus **6** burden, glitch, hurdle, kicker **7** baggage, barrier, setback, trammel **8** drawback, handicap, headache, obstacle, weakness **9** albatross, cumbrance, detention, deterrent, detriment, impedance, liability, millstone, restraint **10** constraint, difficulty, filibuster, impediment, inhibition, limitation
hindsight: 6 recall **10** retrospect
  phrase: 6 if only
  word: 6 coulda, woulda **7** shoulda
Hindu: 4 guru, Jain, Sikh **5** faker, fakir, faqir, Jaina, swami, swamy **6** faquir **7** Brahmin
  aphorism: 5 sutra
  archeological site: 6 Ellora
  ascetic: 4 yogi **5** faker, fakir, faqir, sadhu, swami, swamy, yogin **6** faquir
  caste: 4 jati **5** Sudra, Varna
  class: 5 caste
  Creator: 6 Brahma
  Destroyer: 5 Shiva
  devotion: 6 bhakti
  discipline: 4 yoga
  doctrine: 6 dharma
  emotion: 4 rasa
  eon: 4 yuga
  festival: 6 Dewali, Divali, Diwali
  forehead mark: 5 tilak
  garb: 4 sari **5** saree
  god: 4 Agni, Kama, Mara, Siva, Soma, Yama **5** Indra, Shiva, Surya **6** Brahma, Varuna, Vishnu **7** Ganesha, Hanuman, Krishna
  goddess: 4 Devi, Kali, Usha **5** Durga, Ushas **7** Lakshmi, Parvati **9** Sarasvati
  god of love: 4 Kama
  hero of a ~ epic: 4 Rama
  holy work: 4 Veda
  honcho: 4 raja **5** nawab, rajah
  language: 3 Skr, Skt. **4** Skrt. **5** Vedic **8** Sanskrit
  leader: 5 Nehru **6** Gandhi
  loincloth: 5 dhoti, dhuti **6** dhooti **7** dhootie
  lute: 5 sarod, sitar
  mantra: 2 om **3** aum
  melody: 4 raga
  monarchy: 5 Nepal
  monk: 5 sadhu
  month: 4 Magh
  nectar of the gods: 6 amrita **7** amreeta
  noble: 4 raja, rani **5** rajah, ranee
  of a ~ philosophy: 5 yogic
  of ~ scripture: 5 Vedic
  pilgrimage place: 4 Gaya, Puri
  Preserver: 6 Vishnu
  religious society: 5 samaj
  retreat: 6 ashram, asrama
  sacred river: 6 Ganges
  sage: 4 guru **5** rishi
  sentiment: 4 rasa
  shirt: 5 kurta
  soul: 4 atma **5** atman
  spring festival: 4 holi
  teacher: 4 guru **5** swami, swamy
  temple: 6 ashram
  title: 3 sri **4** babu, shri **5** baboo
  village chief: 5 patel
  worship: 4 puja
Hinduism: 3 rel. **8** religion
Hindu Kush: 5 range
  locale: 4 Asia **11** Afghanistan
Hindustani: 8 language
  derivative: 4 Urdu
Hines: 4 Earl **6** Connie, Duncan, Jerome **7** Gregory
__ Hines: 6 Duncan
Hines, Earl Fatha: 7 pianist
  genre: 4 jazz
Hines, Gregory: 5 actor **6** dancer
  film: The Cotton Club (1984)
    The Preacher's Wife (1996)
    Renaissance Man (1994)
    Tap (1989)
    The Tic Code (2000)
  milieu: 3 tap
Hines, Jerome: 4 bass **5** basso
Hinesville: 4 city, town
  locale: 7 Georgia
hinge: 4 base, knee, rest **5** elbow, joint, pivot **6** depend, swivel **7** fulcrum **8** junction, juncture
  anatomical ~: 4 knee **5** elbow **7** knuckle
  door ~ site: 4 jamb **5** jambe
  (on): 4 rely, rest, turn **6** depend
hinge __: 5 joint
__ hinge: 3 pew **4** butt, flap **5** piano **6** rising **7** gravity, liftoff
hinged fastener: 4 hasp
Hinge of Fate, The author: Winston Churchill
Hingis, Martina: 7 netster **9** tennis pro
  milieu: 5 court
Hingle, Pat: 5 actor
  film: The Carey Treatment (1972)
    The Gauntlet (1977)
    Hang 'em High (1968)
    Running Wild (1973)
    Splendor in the Grass (1961)
    The Strange One (1957)
    Sudden Impact (1983)
Hinkle, Lon: 6 golfer
  milieu: 5 links **6** course
  org.: 3 PGA
Hinky __ Parlay Voo: 5 Dinky
hinny: 6 animal, equine, mammal
  mother: 3 ass
  opposite: 4 mule
Hino: 4 city, town
  locale: 5 Japan
Hinshelwood, Cyril: 7 chemist **8** Nobelist
hint: 3 cue, tip **4** clew, clue, lead, lick, seem, sign, talk, tang, tint, warn, wind, wisp **5** imply, infer, let on, point, scent, shade, spark, taste, tinge, token, touch, trace, whiff **6** breath, feeler, flavor, little, prompt, remind, shadow, streak, tipoff, trifle **7** connote, glimmer, inkling, make out, pointer, portend, promise, soupçon, suggest, symptom, vestige, warning, whisper **8** allude to, allusion, evidence, indicate, innuendo, intimate, mnemonic, overtone, reminder, spoonful **9** adumbrate, indicator, insinuate, reference, scintilla, suspicion, undertone **10** foreshadow, glimmering, imputation, indication, intimation, sprinkling, suggestion
  at: 4 mean **5** imply **6** advert, allude, broach **7** connote, mention, purport, suggest **8** allude to, intimate, lead up to
  give a ~: 3 tip **5** let on, steer
  helpful ~: 6 advice, tipoff **7** inkling, pointer, warning **10** suggestion
  in French: 3 mot
__ hint: 5 drop a, take a
hinted at: 5 tacit **7** implied **8** unvoiced **9** intimated
hinter ender: 4 land **5** lands
hinterlands: 4 bush **5** wilds **6** inland, sticks **7** country **8** frontier **9** backwater, backwoods
Hinton, S.E.: 6 author, writer
  names: 5 Susan **6** Eloise
  work: Big David, Little David
    The Outsiders
    The Puppy Sister
    Rumble Fish
    Taming the Star Runner
    Tex
    That Was Then, This Is Now
hip: 3 hot, mod **4** chic, cool, in on, wise **5** aware, faddy, funky, joint, savvy, smart **6** astute, chichi, far-out, haunch, modish, posted, trendy, versed, wise to, with it **7** current, in style, in vogue, knowing, mindful, stylish, tuned in, voguish **8** apprised, informed **9** astucious, cognizant, in the know, plugged in **10** all the rage, conversant
  about: 4 onto
  be ~: 5 swing
  bone: 6 pelvis
  boot: 8 overshoe
  combining form: 4 coxa- **5** ischi-, ischo-
  cow's ~ joint: 5 thurl
  ender: 4 bone, ster
  follower: 6 hooray
  from the ~: 4 open **5** bluff, blunt, frank, plain **6** candid, direct, honest **7** up-front **8** like it is, straight, truthful **9** outspoken **10** aboveboard, forthright, foursquare, free-spoken, unreserved
  joint: 4 coxa
  muscle: 5 psoas
  muscles: 5 psoae, psoai
  neighbor: 5 thigh
  of the ~ bone: 5 iliac
  part: 6 haunch
  swiveler: 5 Elvis
  talk: 4 jive
  to: 7 aware of
hip __: 4 boot, roof **5** joint
hip-__: 3 hop **7** huggers
__ hip: 4 rose
hipbones: 4 ilia
Hip hip __!: 6 hooray
hip-hop: 3 rap **5** music
  excellent, in ~: 3 def, rad **4** phat
Hip Hop Hooray (1993 song) artist: Naughty by Nature
hiphuggers: 5 pants **6** slacks **8** trousers
Hipparchus: 5 Greek **10** astronomer
hippety-hop: 4 jump, leap, skip **5** bound **6** spring
hippie: 8 bohemian, longhair
  adornment: 4 ankh
  ender: 3 dom
  gathering: 4 be-in **6** love-in
  gesture: 5 V sign
  greeting: 5 peace
  home: 3 pad
  money: 5 bread
  phrase: 5 dig it **6** far out
hippocras: 4 wine
Hippocratic __: 4 oath
hippodrome: 4 ring **5** arena **7** theater, theatre **8** coliseum **9** colosseum, gymnasium
hippo ender: 5 drome **6** campus
Hippolyte: 5 Taine **6** Amazon
  parent of ~: 4 Ares **8** Harmonia
Hippolytus: 4 pope **7** pontiff
Hippolytus author: Euripides
hippophobe fear: 6 horses
hippopotamic: 3 big
hippopotamus: 5 beast **6** animal, mammal
  female: 3 cow
  hangout: 5 river
  home: 3 zoo **6** Africa
  male: 4 bull
  young: 4 calf
Hippopotamus, The poet: 5 Eliot
Hippo Regius: 4 city, port, town
  locale: 6 Annaba **7** Algeria
hippy: 3 big **4** wide **5** broad
  dance: 4 hula
__ hips: 4 rose
hipster: 3 cat **6** hepcat
  address: 6 daddy-o
  no ~: 4 nerd, nurd
hips, with hands on: 6 akimbo
Hip to Be Square (1986 song) artist: Huey Lewis and the News
Hirakata: 4 city, town
  locale: 5 Japan
Hiram: 6 Powers, Walker
Hiram, King home: 4 Tyre
hircine: 7 goatish **8** goatlike
hire: 3 pay **4** book, rent, take **5** lease, price, put on **6** employ, engage, enlist, line up, retain, sign on, sign up, take on **7** charter **9** put to work, situation **10** commission
  opposite: 6 lay off
hired
  car: 3 cab **4** limo, taxi **7** taxicab **9** limousine
  gun: 4 goon, thug
  hand: 6 jobber, worker **7** employe **8** employee **9** jobholder
  just ~: 3 new, raw **5** green **9** untrained
hired __: 3 gun **4** hand
Hired Hand, The (1971 film)
  cast: Verna Bloom, Peter Fonda, Warren Oates
  director: Peter Fonda
Hired Wife (1940 film)
  cast: Brian Aherne, Virginia Bruce, Rosalind Russell
  director: William A. Seiter

hireling: **4** hack, hand, tool **5** labor, venal **6** flunky **7** employe, flunkey, laborer, servant **8** employee **9** mercenary
hirer: **4** boss **7** manager **8** employer, superior **10** supervisor
Hires: **4** soda **5** drink **8** beverage, root beer **9** soft drink
 rival: **4** Dad's
hiring __: **4** hall
hiring fairness agcy.: **3** OEO
Hirobumi: **3** Ito
Hirosaki: **4** city, town
 locale: **5** Japan
Hiroshima: **4** city, port, town
 locale: **5** Japan
 river: **3** Ota
Hiroshima, __ Amour: **3** Mon
Hiroshima author: John Hersey
Hirsch: **4** Judd **5** Elroy **9** Crazylegs
Hirsch, Crazylegs sport: **8** football
Hirschfeld: **2** Al
 daughter: **4** Nina
Hirsch, Judd: **5** actor
 film: Ordinary People (1980)
  Running on Empty (1988)
  Teachers (1984)
 TV: Taxi
hirsute: **5** furry, fuzzy, hairy, pilar **6** pilose, pilous, shaggy **7** bearded, unshorn **8** unshaven **9** whiskered
Hirt, Al: **9** trumpeter
 song: Java (1964)
his: **4** pron. **7** pronoun
 and hers: **5** their **6** theirs
 Honor: **5** judge, mayor **6** jurist **10** magistrate
 in French: **3** ses
 like: **4** poss.
 not ~: **4** hers **5** yours
 or hers item: **5** towel
his __: **4** nibs
His __ Friday: **4** Girl
His __ Highness: **5** Royal
His __ on the Sparrow: **5** Eye Is
Hi, sailor!: **4** ahoy
his and __: **4** hers
His Eye __ the Sparrow: **4** Is On
'H' Is for Homicide author: Sue Grafton
His Girl Friday (1940 film)
 cast: Ralph Bellamy, Cary Grant, Rosalind Russell
 director: Howard Hawks
His Kind of Woman (1951 film)
 cast: Robert Mitchum, Vincent Price, Jane Russell
 director: John Farrow
His Latest Flame (1961 song) artist: Elvis Presley
His Master's Voice company: **3** RCA
Hispanic: **6** Latina, Latino
 neighborhood: **6** barrio
 nickname: **4** Paco
 see also Spanish
Hispaniola: **4** boat, isle, ship **6** island
 part: **5** Haiti **6** Dom. Rep.
hispid: **5** spiny **7** bristly
hiss: **3** boo **4** fizz, jeer, razz, spit, whiz **5** decry **6** deride, heckle, sizzle, wheeze **7** catcall, condemn, whisper, whistle **8** ridicule, sibilant, sibilate **9** sibilance **10** sibilation
Hiss: **5** Alger
hisser: **5** snake **7** serpent
hissing: **4** fizz
hissy fit: **4** snit
hist.: **4** subj.
Histoire de Ma Vie author: George Sand
Historiae author: Tacitus
historian: **6** Nevins, Shirer, Sparks **7** Parkman **8** annalist, recorder **9** archivist **10** chronicler **11** Schlesinger
 British ~: **6** Gibbon
 English ~: **7** Toynbee, Walpole **8** Runciman, Strachey
 French ~: **5** Taine **9** Froissart
 German ~: **8** Schiller
 military: **5** Foote **6** Catton **7** Ambrose, Weigley
 natural ~: **3** Ray **4** Baer **6** Buffon, Cuvier, Darwin, Gesner **7** Agassiz, Lamarck, Wallace
 Roman ~: **4** Livy **7** Sallust, Tacitus **9** Suetonius
 Scottish ~: **7** Carlyle
 tribal ~: **5** griot
 Welsh ~: **7** Nennius
 word: **3** ago **6** before
historic: **5** famed **6** famous **7** notable **8** renowned **9** important, memorable, momentous, red-letter, well-known **10** celebrated, monumental, remarkable
 event: **5** first
 org.: **3** DAR
 starter: **3** pre
historical: **4** past **6** actual **7** factual **8** archival **9** authentic, classical, important **10** chronicled, documented, unimagined, verifiable
 of an ~ time: **4** eral
 period: **3** age, era **6** decade
 piece: **3** bio
 records: **6** annals **7** archive **9** chronicle
 sight: **5** ruins **6** marker **8** landmark, monument
 souvenir: **5** relic **7** antique **8** artifact
historical __: **5** novel **6** method, school **7** geology, present
history: **3** ago **4** life, past **5** genre, story **6** annals, record, report **7** account **9** chronicle, narrative, olden days, posterity, recountal **10** background, literature, upbringing
 ancient ~: **4** over, past, yore **8** years ago **9** olden days **10** yesteryear
 bit of ~: **5** relic
 book verb: **3** did, was **4** were
 case ~: **4** file **6** record, report **7** dossier **8** document, specimen **10** background
 class fixture: **5** globe
 family ~: **4** line **5** birth, blood, roots, stock **6** origin, strain **7** descent, lineage **8** ancestry, heredity, heritage, pedigree **9** genealogy **10** derivation, extraction
 folk ~: **4** lore **5** tales **7** legends **9** tradition
 homework: **5** essay
 Muse of ~: **4** Clio
 oral ~: **4** myth **5** sagas, tales **7** beliefs, customs, legends, sayings **8** folklore **10** traditions
 oral ~ keeper: **5** griot
 personal ~: **3** bio **6** memoir, résumé **7** memoirs, profile
 segment: **3** era
 teacher's question: **4** when
 work ~: **4** vita **6** résumé
__ history: **4** case, life, oral **7** ancient, natural
History Is Made at Night (1937 film)
 cast: Jean Arthur, Charles Boyer, Leo Carrillo
 director: Frank Borzage
History of Mr. Polly, The author: H.G. Wells
History of New York, A author: Washington Irving
History of Rome author: **4** Livy
History of the Standard Oil Company author: Ida Tarbell
__ History of Time, A: **5** Brief
History of Western Philosophy, A author: Bertrand Russell
histrionic: **5** stagy **6** stagey **7** emotive **8** dramatic, thespian **9** bombastic, emotional **10** theatrical
 episode: **5** scene **7** tantrum **8** outburst
histrionics: **6** acting **9** dramatics **10** stagecraft
hit: **2** KO **3** jab, jag, pop, ram, rap, win **4** bang, bash, beat, belt, blow, bump, butt, cane, clip, club, cuff, drub, flog, hurt, kayo, lace, lash, lick, mall, maul, pelt, slam, slap, sock, swat, verb **5** abuse, brain, clout, crack, flail, fly at, homer, knock, lunge, occur, pound, punch, reach, serve, shoot, smack, smash, solve, swipe, thump, touch, whack, wound **6** attain, batter, berate, buffet, cudgel, defame, double, hammer, impact, larrup, malign, murder, single, strike, stroke, thrash, thwack, triple, wallop, winner **7** censure, clobber, condemn, lambast, offense, put down, rough up, sellout, success, triumph, victory **8** arrive at, arrive in, bang into, bludgeon, come upon, denounce, lambaste, reaction, uppercut **9** castigate, collision, crash into, criticize, denigrate, knock into, sensation, sideswipe, smash into **10** bestseller, calumniate, crunch into, gold record
 abbr.: **3** SRO
 a fly, perhaps: **3** bat
 a high ball: **3** fly **4** loft
 alternative: **4** walk
 and rebound: **5** carom **6** carrom
 a sour note: **5** clash **6** jangle, rattle
 back: **5** react, reply **6** answer, resist **7** counter, revenge **9** retaliate
 below the belt: **4** knee
 between infield and outfield: **5** bloop
 big ~: **3** win **5** homer, smash **6** winner **7** home run, success, triumph, victory
 bottom: **4** fall, sink **6** go down, plunge **7** founder, go under **8** flounder, submerge
 box-office ~: **4** boff **5** boffo, smash **7** boffola, success
 broadside: **3** ram
 extra-base ~: **5** homer **6** double, triple **7** home run **9** grand slam
 fail to ~: **4** miss
 hard: **4** pelt, slam, slug, wham **5** paste, smack, smite, whack, whomp
 in baseball: **5** homer **6** double, single, triple **7** home run
 it big: **6** arrive, do well **7** make out, prosper, succeed, triumph **8** fare well, flourish, get ahead, go places, make good
 it off: **4** jibe **5** agree, click **9** harmonize
 lightly: **3** tap **5** touch
 like a ton of bricks: **3** jar **4** jolt, kayo, stun **5** shock **6** bedaze **7** astound, flummox, horrify, nonplus, outrage, stagger, stupefy, terrify **8** astonish, bewilder, blow away, bowl over, knock out, unsettle **9** dumbfound, overpower, overwhelm, take aback **10** discompose
 list: **5** chart
 location, often: **5** side A
 make a ~: **5** score **7** succeed, triumph
 make ~ the ceiling: **5** anger **6** madden, offend **7** incense, outrage **9** infuriate
 old-style: **4** smit
 on: **6** detect **7** solicit, think of **8** smell out **9** run across
 on the noggin: **4** conk
 opposite: **4** flop **6** turkey
 or miss: **6** random
 out: **5** blast **6** assail, attack **7** censure **9** light into
 outfield ~: **3** fly
 pinch ~: **7** replace
 precisely: **4** nail
 ready to ~: **5** at bat
 send: **5** e-mail
 soft ~: **4** bunt
 softly: **4** bump **5** nudge
 starter: **4** mega
 the big time: **6** arrive, thrive **7** prosper, succeed
 the books: **4** cram, read **5** study **6** master
 the brakes: **4** slow **6** ease up, hold up, rein in **7** ease off **8** hold back, moderate, slow down **10** decelerate
 the bricks: **2** go **4** exit, move **5** leave **6** beat it, depart, go away, move on **7** make off, pull out, push off, take off **8** shove off, slip away **10** shuffle off
 the ceiling: **4** rage, rant, snap **5** freak **6** seethe
 the deck: **4** wake **5** arise, awake, get up, waken
 the dirt: **4** fall **5** slide **6** topple
 the floor hard: **5** stamp
 the ground: **3** lit **4** alit, fall, fell, land **5** light **6** alight, landed
 the hay: **5** crash, sleep **6** retire, turn in **7** sack out
 the high spots: **4** skim **8** simplify
 the horn: **4** blow, honk
 the jackpot: **3** win **5** score **7** prosper, succeed
 the + key: **3** add
 the low spots: **4** slum
 the mall: **4** shop **6** browse
 the road: **2** go **4** blow, hike, rove, scat, tour, walk, went **5** leave, scram, start **6** beat it, decamp, depart, set off, set out **7** push off, take off **8** hightail, set forth
 the roof: **4** flip, rage, rant, rave, snap **5** storm **6** blow up, bridle, get mad, see red **7** explode **9** blow a fuse, throw a fit
 the sack: **5** sleep **6** retire, turn in
 the skids: **4** fail, sink **7** decline
 the sky: **3** fly **4** soar **6** aviate
 the slopes: **3** ski **4** skee
 the spot: **6** please **7** satisfy, suffice
 the switch: **4** kill, stop **5** douse, light **6** kindle, turn on **7** turn off **8** activate **9** throw open
 the track: **3** jog, run **4** trot
 the trail: **3** run **4** tour **5** start **6** depart, set off, set out **7** take off **8** campaign, set forth
 town: **4** come **5** get in, pop up, reach **6** arrive **8** get there
 up: **3** beg **7** request, solicit **8** question **9** impetrate
 upon: **4** find **5** catch, solve **6** locate, turn up **7** uncover **8** discover **9** encounter, run across
 upside the head: **3** wap **4** whap, whop
hit __: **4** home, upon **5** a snag, it big, it off **6** parade **7** batsman
hit __ note: **5** a sour
hit-__: **6** or-miss
__ hit: **3** leg **4** base **5** pinch, smash **7** infield, one-base, scratch, two-base
__-hit: **4** king **5** pinch **6** switch
Hit! (1973 film)
 cast: Paul Hampton, Richard Pryor, Billy Dee Williams
 director: Sidney J. Furie

hit a __: **4** snag
Hitachi: **2** TV **4** city, town **5** TV set **10** television
alternative: **3** JVC, NEC, RCA **4** Sony **6** Quasar, Zenith **7** Emerson, ProScan, Toshiba **8** Magnavox, Sylvania **9** Panasonic
locale: **5** Japan
hit-and-__: **3** run **4** miss
hitch: **3** rub, tie, tug **4** bind, hook, join, kink, knot, limp, link, moor, ride, snag, term, tour, yank, yoke **5** block, catch, delay, pause, snafu, spell, strap, tie up **6** attach, couple, fasten, glitch, hang-up, holdup, hook on, hook up, inspan, kicker, mishap, secure, splice, tether **7** conjoin, connect, grapnel, harness, problem, setback, trouble **8** drawback, make fast, obstacle, sentence **9** hindrance **10** difficulty, impediment, thumb a ride, tour of duty
do another ~: **4** reup
ender: **4** hike
on: **4** join, link, yoke **5** annex, unite **6** attach, cohere, couple, hook up **7** combine, conjoin, connect
without a ~: **6** easily **7** handily **10** swimmingly
hitch __: **5** a ride
__ hitch: **4** half **5** clove **6** double, Magnus, timber **7** harness, rolling, weaver's
Hitchcock, Alfred: **3** Sir **8** director
designer: **4** Head
film: The 39 Steps (1935)
The Birds (1963)
Blackmail (1929)
Dial M for Murder (1954)
Family Plot (1976)
Foreign Correspondent (1940)
Frenzy (1972)
The Lady Vanishes (1938)
Lifeboat (1944)
The Man Who Knew Too Much (1934, 1956)
Marnie (1964)
Mr. and Mrs. Smith (1941)
North by Northwest (1959)
Notorious (1946)
Psycho (1960)
Rear Window (1954)
Rebecca (1940)
The Ring (1927)
Rope (1948)
Sabotage (1936)
Saboteur (1942)
Shadow of a Doubt (1943)
Spellbound (1945)
Strangers on a Train (1951)
Suspicion (1941)
To Catch a Thief (1955)
Topaz (1969)
Torn Curtain (1966)
The Trouble With Harry (1955)
Vertigo (1958)
The Wrong Man (1957)
Young and Innocent (1937)
performance: **5** cameo
wife: **4** Alma
hitched
get ~: **3** wed **5** marry **10** tie the knot
get ~ in a hurry: **5** elope
hitchhike: **4** ride **5** dance, thumb
hitchhiker: **5** rider, tramp **7** drifter **8** traveler, vagabond **9** passenger
need: **4** lift **5** thumb
site: **4** berm **5** berme
words to a ~: **5** get in, hop in
Hitchin' a Ride (1970 song) artist: Vanity Fare
hitching __: **4** post
hitching area: **5** altar **6** chapel

Hitchings, George: **8** Nobelist
Hitchy-__: **3** Koo
Hitch your wagon to __: **5** a star
Hite: **5** Shere
hi-tech: **6** modern **10** electronic
hither: **4** here **8** over here
come ~: **6** allure **10** attraction, enticement
ender: **4** most, ward **5** wards
move ~ and thither: **3** gad **4** roam **6** ramble, wander **7** meander, traipse **8** ambulate, nomadize **9** bum around, gallivant, globe-trot
partner: **3** yon
__-hither: **4** come
hither and __: **3** yon **7** thither
hitherto: **3** yet **5** so far **6** before, ere now, of late **7** thus far **8** until now **9** at one time, to this day **10** heretofore, previously
unknown: **5** fresh, novel **7** offbeat **8** original **9** different **10** innovative, newfangled
hit it __: **3** big, off
hitless stretch: **5** slump
Hit Me With Your Best Shot (1980 song) artist: Pat Benatar
hit one's __: **6** stride
hit-or-miss: **5** fluky **6** casual, chance, flukey, random **7** aimless **8** slipshod, sporadic **9** haphazard, irregular, makeshift **10** improvised, nonuniform, sporadical, unthorough, willy-nilly
__ Hit Parade: **4** Your
hitter: **7** batsman
bull's-eye ~: **4** dart **5** arrow **6** archer
chance: **5** at bat
heavy ~: **5** mogul **7** bigshot
pinch ~: **3** sub **9** surrogate **10** substitute
problem: **5** slump
stat: **2** HR **3** RBI
__ hitter: **4** pull **5** heavy, pinch **6** switch
hit the __: **3** hay **4** deck, road, roof, sack, silk, spot, wall **5** books **7** ceiling, jackpot
hit the __ on the head: **4** nail
hit the __ running: **6** ground
hit the __ spots: **4** high
Hit the __ Jack: **4** Road
hit the high __: **5** spots **6** points
Hit the Ice (1943 film)
cast: Bud Abbott, Lou Costello
Hit the road!: **3** git **4** scat, shoo **5** scram **6** beat it
Hit the Road Jack (1961 song) artist: Ray Charles
hitting: **5** at bat
__-hitting: **4** hard
__-Hittite: **4** Indo
Hiva Oa: **3** isl. **4** isle **6** island
locale: **9** Marquesas, Polynesia
hive: **4** nest **6** apiary **8** vespiary
group: **5** swarm
resident: **3** bee **5** drone, queen
sound: **3** hum **4** buzz **5** drone
hives: **4** rash **5** uredo
Hive, The author: **4** Cela
hiwi hiwi: **4** fish
Hi-yo Silver, __!: **4** away
H.J. __: **3** Res. **5** Heinz
Hjalmar: **7** Bergman **9** Söderberg
H.L.: **7** Mencken
HLA __: **4** gene **7** antigen
__ H. Macy: **7** William
HMO: **8** WellCare **10** BlueChoice
alternative: **3** PPO
concern: **8** wellness
employee: **2** Dr., MD, RN **3** doc **5** nurse **6** doctor
part: **3** org. **5** maint. **6** health
requirement: **5** copay
Hmong: **4** Miao **8** language

H.M. Pulham, Esq. (1941 film)
cast: Ruth Hussey, Hedy Lamarr, Robert Young
director: King Vidor
HMS part: **3** her, his **4** ship **8** majesty's
H.M.S. Pinafore
character: **4** Dick, Hebe **5** Ralph **7** Deadeye
composer: **7** Gilbert **8** Sullivan
fleet: **5** navee
ho-__: **3** dad, hum
__ ho!: **4** Land **5** Heave
__-ho: **4** gung **5** heave, heigh
Ho: **3** Don **4** elem. **7** element, holmium
home, once: **5** Hanoi
67 for ~: **4** at. no.
Ho __: **7** Chi Minh
HO __: **5** gauge
hoactzin: **4** bird
Hoad, Lew: **7** netster **9** tennis pro
milieu: **5** court
hoagie: **3** sub **4** hero **5** po' boy **7** grinder **8** sandwich **9** submarine
ingredient: **3** ham **4** mayo, tuna **5** onion **6** cheese, pepper, pickle, tomato, turkey **7** chicken, lettuce **9** roast beef
where to get a ~: **4** deli
Hoagland, Edward: **6** author, writer
hoagy: **9** See hoagie
Hoagy: **10** Carmichael
__-ho and a bottle...: **4** Yo-ho
hoar: **4** rime **5** frost
like ~: **3** icy
hoard: **4** fund, heap, hold, keep, mass, mine, pile, save, stow **5** amass, buy up, cache, lay by, lay up, put by, stack, stash, stock, store, trove **6** garner, gather, obtain, pile up, retain, save up, scrimp, supply, wealth **7** collect, harvest, lay away, put away, reserve **8** conserve, gather up, hang onto, hold onto, maintain, put aside, salt away, sock away, stow away, treasure, treasury **9** abundance, amassment, inventory, stash away, stockpile **10** accumulate, collection, cumulation
private ~: **5** cache, stash **7** reserve **9** stockpile
hoarder: **5** miser, saver **7** pack rat **8** gatherer
cry: **4** mine, more
hoards: **4** lots, tons **5** loads, scads **6** droves, oodles, scores **7** throngs **8** billions, millions
hoarfrost: **4** rime
hoariness: **9** antiquity
hoarse: **5** gruff, harsh, husky, raspy, rough, roupy **6** croaky, croupy, froggy **7** breathy, cracked, grating, raucous, throaty **8** croaking, gravelly, guttural **10** laryngitic
sound ~: **4** frog, rasp **5** croak
hoary: **3** old **4** dull, gray, grey **5** musty, passé, white **7** ancient, antique, revered **8** grizzled, out of use, time-worn, well-used **9** out-of-date, venerable, venerated, weathered **10** antiquated, dullsville, gray-haired
hoatzin: **4** bird
hoax: **2** do **3** con, lie **4** dupe, fake, flam, fool, gull, quiz, rook, ruse, scam, sham, snow **5** cheat, dodge, feint, fraud, hocus, prank, put on, set up, spoof, sting, trick **6** canard, deceit, delude, dupery, fleece, humbug, hustle, outwit, rope in, scheme, take in **7** chicane, con game, deceive, defraud, fake out, fast one, knavery, mislead, snow job, swindle **8** artifice, flimflam, hoodwink, outsmart, trickery **9** bamboozle, deception, disinform, four-flush, imposture, mare's nest, victimize **10** imposition, run a game on, subterfuge
like a ~: **4** fake **5** bogus, false, phony **6** unreal, untrue **8** delusive **9** concocted, contrived **10** fabricated, untruthful
pull a ~: **5** bluff, cheat, feign, put on **7** deceive, mislead, pretend
hoaxer: **5** fraud **6** Barnum
hob: **3** elf, peg
ender: **3** nob **4** nail **6** goblin
game: **6** quoits
Hoban, James: **9** architect
Hobart: **4** city, town **6** Garret
locale: **7** Indiana **9** Australia
river: **7** Derwent
Hobbes, Thomas: **7** British **11** philosopher
hobbit
community: **5** Shire
foe: **3** orc
like ~ feet: **5** furry
Hobbit, The
author: J.R.R. Tolkien
character: **5** Bilbo **7** Baggins, Gandalf
hobble: **3** lag **4** bind, curb, limp **5** cramp, leash, skirt **6** dodder, falter, fetter, hamper, hang up, hinder, hogtie, impede, linger, tether **7** trammel **8** restrict **9** hamstring
hobble __: **5** skirt
hobbledehoy: **2** ox **3** lug, oaf **4** boob, boor, clod, dolt, fool, jerk, lout, rube, yo-yo **5** chump, churl, dunce, ninny **6** duffer, galoot, lummox, nitwit **7** botcher, bumbler, bungler, dullard, fathead, fumbler, jackass, saphead, tomfool **8** bonehead, lunkhead, meathead **9** birdbrain, blockhead, blunderer, schlemiel, simpleton **10** dunderhead, stumblebum
Hobbs: **4** city, town
locale: **9** New Mexico
hobby: **3** bag **7** pastime, pursuit **8** activity, interest, sideline **9** avocation, diversion, specialty **10** recreation
ender: **3** ist **5** horse
shop buy: **3** kit **5** model
hobgoblin: **3** elf, imp **5** bogey, bogie, bogle, ghoul **6** boggle, sprite **7** brownie, bugbear, gremlin
Hobie Cat need: **4** wind
hobnob: **3** mix **5** party **6** mingle **7** consort, schmoos **8** schmoose, schmooze **9** associate, pal around, rub elbows, socialize **10** chum around, fraternize
hobo: **3** bum, vag **5** nomad, tramp **6** beggar **7** drifter, migrant, outcast, vagrant **8** derelict, traveler, vagabond, wanderer **9** sundowner, transient **10** ragamuffin
blanket: **6** bindle
dinner: **4** stew
home: **5** shack **6** jungle
transport: **4** rail **6** boxcar
Hoboken: **4** city, port, town
locale: **9** New Jersey
Hobson: **5** Laura **7** Valerie
Hobson-__: **6** Jobson
Hobson, Laura Z.: **6** author, writer
work: Gentleman's Agreement
Hobson, Laura Z. work: Gentleman's Agreement
Hobson's choice: **4** bind **5** horse
Hobson, Valerie: **7** actress
film: Blanche Fury (1948)
Bride of Frankenstein (1935)
Contraband (1940)
Great Expectations (1946)
Kind Hearts and Coronets (1949)
The Rocking Horse Winner (1949)
The Spy in Black (1939)
__ hoc: **4** post **5** quoad **7** propter
Hoc __ in votis: **4** erat
Hoccleve, Thomas: **4** poet **7** British

___ hoc, ergo propter hoc: 4 post
Hochheimer: 4 wine
origin: 7 Germany
Ho Chi Minh ___: 4 City 5 Trail
Ho Chi Minh City: 4 city, port, town
locale: 7 Vietnam
river: 6 Saigon
Ho Chi Minh Trail
locale: 3 Nam 4 Laos
Hoch, Scott: 6 golfer
milieu: 5 links 6 course
org.: 3 PGA
hock: 4 debt, pawn, wine 5 ankle 6 pledge 9 Rhine wine
be in ~: 3 owe
ender: 4 shop
get out of ~: 6 cash in, redeem
horse's ~: 5 ankle
in ~: 6 pawned 7 obliged 8 beholden, indebted 9 obligated
origin: 7 Germany
starter: 3 ham 5 holly
hockey: 4 game 5 sport
area: 4 cage, goal 6 crease
birthplace: 6 Canada
Boston team: 6 Bruins
Buffalo team: 6 Sabres
Calgary team: 6 Flames
Edmonton team: 6 Oilers
extra period: 2 OT 8 overtime
gear: 3 net 4 puck 5 stick
Hall of Famer: 3 Orr 4 Howe, Hull, Park 5 Bossy 6 Dionne, Mikita, Parent, Plante, Potvin 7 Federko, Gilbert, Gillies, Gretzky, Lafleur, Langway, Lemieux, Richard, Sawchuk, Worsley 8 Bathgate, Bobby Orr, Brad Park, Esposito, Trottier 9 Bobby Hull, Geoffrion, Mike Bossy 10 Gordie Howe, Guy Lafleur, Rod Gilbert, Stan Mikita
highlight: 5 brawl, fight
Houston team: 5 Aeros
infraction: 5 icing
locale: 4 rink 5 arena
Los Angeles team: 5 Kings
Philadelphia team: 6 Flyers
player: 4 wing 6 center, goalie, iceman
ploy: 4 deke
prize: 3 cup 10 Stanley Cup
protection: 3 pad 4 mask
San Jose team: 6 Sharks
shutout line score: 3 OOO
sportscaster cry: 5 score
stat: 4 goal 6 assist
surface: 3 ice
team: 3 six 4 Wild 5 Blues, Kings, Stars 6 Bruins, Devils, Flames, Flyers, Oilers, Sabres, Sharks 7 Canucks, Coyotes, Rangers 8 Capitals, Panthers, Penguins, Red Wings, Senators 9 Avalanche, Canadiens, Islanders, Lightning, Predators, Thrashers 10 Blackhawks, Hurricanes, Maple Leafs
Winnipeg team: 4 Jets
hockey ___: 5 skate, stick
___ hockey: 3 ice 4 road 5 field, grass 6 roller, street
___-Hockey: 3 Nok
Hockney: 5 David
hocus: 4 dupe, fool, gull, hoax 5 trick 6 take in 7 deceive 8 hoodwink
hocus-pocus: 3 hex 5 fraud, magic, spell, trick 6 dupery 7 sorcery 9 chicanery, conjuring, deception, gibberish, imposture, rigmarole 10 dishonesty, imposition, invocation, mumbo jumbo, open sesame
hod: 7 carrier 9 container
___ hod: 4 coal
Hodding: 6 Carter
___ Hodesh: 4 Rosh
Hodge: 2 Al
hodgepodge: 3 mix 4 hash, mess, misc., olio 6 jumble, litter, medley 7 clutter, farrago, goulash, mélange, mixture 8 mishmash, mixed bag, pastiche, shambles 9 confusion, patchwork, potpourri 10 assortment, collection, cumulation, miscellany, salmagundi
Hodges: 3 Gil 4 Mike 5 Eddie
Hodges, Gil sport: 8 baseball
Hodges, Mike: 8 director
film: Black Rainbow (1991)
Croupier (1999)
Flash Gordon (1980)
Pulp (1972)
The Terminal Man (1974)
Hodgkin, Alan: 8 Nobelist 12 biophysicist
Hodgkin, Dorothy: 7 chemist 8 Nobelist
___ Hodgson Burnett: 7 Frances
Hodiak, John: 5 actor
film: Battleground (1949)
A Bell for Adano (1945)
The Harvey Girls (1946)
Marriage Is a Private Affair (1944)
Night Into Morning (1951)
Sunday Dinner for a Soldier (1944)
Trial (1955)
Ho, Don: 6 singer 8 Hawaiian
hoe: 3 dig 4 till, tool 6 garden 9 cultivate 10 cultivator
cousin: 4 rake 6 harrow
ender: 4 cake, down
long row to ~: 4 task 5 grind 6 burden
starter: 4 back
target: 4 clod, weed
___ hoe: 4 back, grub 6 rotary 7 scuffle
hoedown: 5 dance
date: 3 gal
instrument: 6 fiddle
prop: 3 hay 4 bale
hoeing, in need of: 5 weedy
Hoek: 3 Ren
Hoff: 3 Syd
Hoffa: 5 Jimmy 8 Portland
Hoffa (1992 film)
cast: Armand Assante, Danny DeVito, Jack Nicholson, J.T. Walsh
director: Danny DeVito
Hoffa, Portland spouse: Fred Allen
Hoffer, Eric: 6 author, writer
Hoffman: 3 E.T.A. 5 Abbie 6 Dustin 7 Malvina, William
Hoffman, Dustin: 5 actor
film: Agatha (1979)
All the President's Men (1976)
American Buffalo (1996)
Billy Bathgate (1991)
Family Business (1989)
The Graduate (1967)
Hero (1992)
Hook (1991)
Ishtar (1987)
Kramer vs. Kramer (1979, AA)
Lenny (1974)
Little Big Man (1970)
Marathon Man (1976)
Midnight Cowboy (1969)
Outbreak (1995)
Papillon (1973)
Rain Man (1988, AA)
Sleepers (1996)
Sphere (1998)
Straight Time (1978)
Straw Dogs (1971)
Tootsie (1982)
Wag the Dog (1997)
Hoffman Estates: 4 city, town
locale: 8 Illinois
Hoffman, E.T.A.: 6 author, German, writer
Hoffmann: 4 Gaby 5 Cecil, Felix, Roald
Hoffmann, Roald: 7 chemist 8 Nobelist
Hoffman, William play: 4 As Is
Hofmann, Josef: 6 Polish 7 pianist
Hofstadter: 6 Robert 7 Richard
Hofstadter, Robert: 8 Nobelist 9 physicist
Hofstra: 10 university
athletes: 5 Pride
locale: 7 New York 9 Hempstead 10 Long Island
Hofu: 4 city, town
locale: 5 Japan
hog: 3 pig, sow 4 bike, boar 5 cycle, shoat, shote, shott, swine 6 animal, barrow, Harley, oinker, porker, tusker 7 glutton, grunter, peccary, possess 8 dominate 9 razorback 10 monopolize, motorcycle
call: 5 sooey
ender: 3 tie 4 back, fish, wash, weed
feed: 4 mast, slop 5 swill
go whole ~: 4 jump, leap, push, rush, sink 6 hurtle, plunge
home: 3 pen, sty 4 farm
in ~ heaven: 5 happy 6 cheery, elated, joyful, joyous 7 gleeful 8 blissful, ecstatic, euphoric, exultant, jubilant 9 ebullient, overjoyed
live high on the ~: 4 bask 5 revel 6 thrive 7 indulge, rollick 8 flourish 9 luxuriate
love: 3 mud
rider: 5 biker
starter: 4 sand, wart 5 hedge 6 ground
whole ~: 5 fully 7 flat out, in depth, totally 8 entirely, from A to Z, in detail 9 inside out, up-and-down 10 completely, thoroughly, to the limit
young ~: 5 shoat, shote, shott
see also pig
hog ___: 4 fuel, plum 5 Latin, score 6 heaven, peanut, sucker
hog-___: 3 tie 4 wild 6 backed
___ hog: 3 sea 4 bush, musk, road
___-hog: 5 whole
Hogan: 3 Ben 4 Hulk, Paul
Hogan, Ben: 6 golfer
milieu: 5 links 6 course
org.: 3 PGA
rival: 5 Snead
Hogan Family, The (NBC/CBS sitcom)
cast: Jason Bateman (David Hogan)
Sandy Duncan (Sandy Hogan)
Valerie Harper (Valerie Hogan)
Jeremy Licht (Mark Hogan)
Hogan, Hulk: 8 wrestler
hogan material: 3 sod
Hogan, Paul spouse: Linda Kozlowski
Hogan's ___: 4 Goat 6 Heroes
Hogan's Heroes (CBS sitcom)
cast: John Banner (Sgt. Schultz)
Robert Clary (Cpl. LeBeau)
Bob Crane (Col. Hogan)
Richard Dawson (Cpl. Newkirk)
Ivan Dixon (Sgt. Kinchloe)
Larry Hovis (Sgt. Carter)
Werner Klemperer (Col. Klink)
group: 4 POWs
setting: stalag, Germany
Hogarth, William: 6 artist 7 British, painter
subject: 4 rake
hogback: 5 ridge, spine
Hogg: 3 Ima 5 James
hoggish: 6 greedy 7 gorging, lustful, piggish, porcine, selfish, swinish 9 rapacious 10 avaricious, gluttonous
hoggishness: 5 greed 7 avarice, avidity 8 cupidity, gluttony, rapacity, venality 9 esurience
Hogg, James: 4 poet 8 Scottish
hognose: 5 adder, snake
hognut: 4 tree 7 hickory
hogs: 5 stock 9 livestock
ender: 4 head
slopping the ~: 5 chore
hogshead: 3 keg, tub 4 cask, unit 6 barrel
hogtie: 4 bind 6 fetter, hamper, hinder, hobble, impede, pinion, thwart 7 confine, contain, inhibit, shackle, truss up 8 encumber, handicap, restrain 9 constrain, frustrate, hamstring 10 immobilize
hogwash: 3 gas, rot 4 blah, bosh, bull, bunk, guff, jazz, jive, pooh, tosh, wind 5 bilge, fudge, hokum, hooey, prate, stuff, swill, trash, tripe 6 bunkum, bushwa, drivel, dupery, footle, gabble, gammon, gibber, havers, hot air, humbug, jabber, jargon, kibosh, piffle, refuse 7 baloney, blarney, blather, blether, boloney, bushwah, eyewash, flannel, flubdub, fustian, garbage, inanity, malarky, rubbish, twaddle 8 buncombe, claptrap, falderal, falderol, flimflam, flummery, folderal, folderol, malarkey, nonsense, slipslop, tommyrot, trumpery 9 banana oil, deception, gibberish, goofiness, kidstakes, moonshine, poppycock, rigmarole 10 applesauce, balderdash, bilge water, codswallop, double-talk, empty words, flapdoodle, galimatias, Jabberwock, mumbo jumbo, propaganda, rigamarole, taradiddle
hogweed: 5 plant 6 flower
hog-wild: 5 manic, rabid 7 berserk 8 frenzied, maniacal 10 hysterical
go ~ over: 5 eat up, enjoy, lap up
Hohe Tauern: 4 Alps 5 range
locale: 7 Austria
ho ho: 5 laugh
Ho Ho: 4 cake, nosh 5 snack
ho-hum: 4 blah, drab, dull, flat, mild, so-so 5 bland 6 boring, stuffy 7 insipid, mundane, nowhere, prosaic, routine, tedious 8 tiresome 9 prosaical, wearisome 10 dullsville, lackluster, monotonous, unexciting
feeling: 5 ennui 6 apathy, tedium, torpor 7 boredom, languor 8 lethargy 9 lassitude
same old ~: 3 rut 7 rat race, routine 9 treadmill
hoick shouter: 6 hunter
hoi polloi: 3 mob 4 ruck 6 masses, people, public, rabble 8 populace, riffraff
one of the: 5 prole 6 worker
hoist: 4 heft, lift, rear 5 boost, crane, heave, raise, sling 6 haul up, lift up, pick up, tackle, uphold, uplift, uprear 7 derrick, elevate, upheave, upraise
a few: 4 tope 5 drink 6 imbibe
chain: 3 tye
device: 5 crane, sling, winch
glasses: 5 drink, honor, toast 6 pledge
marina ~: 5 davit
hoist by one's own ___: 6 petard
hoisted, nautically: 5 atrip
hoity-toity: 5 proud 6 la-de-da, la-di-da, uppity 7 haughty, pompous 8 arrogant, lah-di-dah, snobbish 9 conceited, hubristic 10 disdainful
act ~: 5 snoot
group: 5 elite 6 gentry, jet set 7 society 8 old money 10 blue bloods, glitterati, main liners, upper crust
one: 4 snob 5 snoot 7 elitist 8 highbrow 9 swellhead
HoJo rival: 4 IHOP
hoke: 4 mock 5 alter 6 jazz up 7 deceive, falsify, phony up 10 manipulate

hokey: **4** dull, mock **5** banal, corny, passé, phony, stale, trite, vapid **6** common, jejune, old hat, phoney **7** clichéd, fatuous, humdrum, mawkish, prosaic **8** bromidic, cornball, outdated, outmoded, shopworn **9** contrived, hackneyed, prosaical **10** uninspired, unoriginal

hokey-___: **5** pokey

Hokkaido: **3** isl. **4** isle **6** island
  city: **5** Otaru **6** Ebetsu, Kitami **7** Kushiro, Obihiro, Sapporo **8** Hakodate
  islands off ~: **5** Kuril
  locale: **4** Asia **5** Japan
  native: **4** Ainu
  volcano: **3** Usu **4** Akan **6** Oshima

hokum: **3** gas, rot **4** blah, bosh, bull, bunk, guff, jazz, jive, pooh, tosh **5** bilge, fudge, hooey, prate, stuff, trash, tripe **6** bunkum, bushwa, drivel, dupery, footle, gabble, gammon, gibber, havers, hot air, humbug, jabber, jargon, kibosh, piffle **7** baloney, blarney, blather, blether, boloney, bushwah, eyewash, flannel, flubdub, fustian, garbage, hogwash, inanity, malarky, rubbish, twaddle **8** buncombe, claptrap, falderal, falderol, flimflam, flummery, folderal, folderol, malarkey, nonsense, slipslop, tommyrot, trumpery **9** banana oil, deception, gibberish, goofiness, kidstakes, moonshine, poppycock, rigmarole **10** applesauce, balderdash, bilge water, codswallop, double-talk, flapdoodle, galimatias, Jabberwock, mumbo jumbo, rigamarole, taradiddle

Holbein, Hans: **6** artist, German **7** painter

Holberg, Ludvig: **6** Danish, writer

Holberg Suite composer: **5** Grieg

Holbrook: **3** Hal **4** city, town
  locale: **7** New York **10** Long Island

Holbrook, Hal: **5** actor
  film: All the President's Men (1976)
    Capricorn One (1978)
    The Florentine (2000)
    The Fog (1980)
    Judas Kiss (1999)
    Magnum Force (1973)
    Waking the Dead (2000)
    Wall Street (1987)
  spouse: Dixie Carter
  TV: Evening Shade

Holcroft Covenant, The author: Robert Ludlum

hold: **3** den, hug, own, tie **4** aver, avow, bear, deem, feel, grip, have, jail, keep, last, prop, save, seat, stay, take, view, vise **5** amass, apply, brace, cache, carry, claim, clasp, grasp, hoard, house, judge, press, put by, seize, sense, shore, stand, store, think, tie up, wield **6** absorb, accept, adhere, affirm, allege, arrest, assert, assume, clench, clinch, clutch, coop up, cork up, cradle, cuddle, defend, detain, endure, enfold, fetter, garner, handle, harbor, immure, infold, lock up, nelson, occupy, reckon, regard, remain, retain, save up, shelve, tenure **7** believe, bolster, carry on, conduct, confine, contain, control, convene, embrace, enclose, fermata, footing, harbour, impound, inclose, include, observe, operate, persist, possess, presume, put away, receive, repress, reserve, shore up, squeeze, stay put, support, suspect, sustain **8** bottle up, buttress, continue, dominion, hang onto, imprison, location, maintain, purchase, put aside, restrain, set aside, stand for, transfix, underpin **9** influence, persevere **10** accumulate, monopolize, possession
  a brief for: **6** defend, second **7** approve, endorse, indorse, support **8** champion, sanction, side with
  a meeting: **3** sit **4** call, meet **5** rally **6** confer, gather, muster, summon **7** convene, convoke **8** assemble **10** congregate
  a powwow: **6** confer, huddle, parley **7** commune, palaver **8** converse **10** deliberate
  a reading: **5** drill **6** review **8** practice, rehearse **9** go through **10** run through
  as an opinion: **4** deem, feel, view **5** think **6** assume, reckon, regard **7** believe, presume, suppose, surmise **8** consider
  at bay: **5** parry, repel **7** fend off, repulse, ward off **8** stave off
  at fault: **5** blame **6** accuse, finger **7** censure, condemn, reprove **8** denounce, reproach **9** criticize, implicate, reprimand **10** take to task
  back: **3** dam **4** curb, halt, hide, save, slow, stay, stem, stop **5** check, demur, deter, leash, stint, tarry **6** arrest, bridle, detain, hinder, impede, refuse, rein in, slow up **7** confine, contain, control, inhibit, prevent, prolong, repulse, reserve, trammel **8** handicap, hesitate, restrain, slow down, stave off, suppress, withhold **9** constrain, keep at bay **10** discourage, keep a lid on, keep in line
  back a year: **4** fail **5** flunk
  catch ~ of: **3** nab **4** grab, hook, land, nail, snag **5** seize **6** arrest, collar, corral, snap up, snatch **7** capture, ensnare **9** apprehend, latch onto
  contents: **5** cargo, goods **7** freight,. tonnage **8** shipload
  dear: **4** like, love **5** adore, go for, honor, prize, value **6** esteem, revere **7** care for, cherish, idolize, worship **8** remember, stand for, treasure **9** care about
  dominion: **4** rule **5** reign **6** direct, govern **7** command, control, oversee
  don't ~: **5** let go
  down: **3** pin **6** anchor, manage **7** inhibit **8** restrict
  down a job: **4** earn, work
  ender: **3** all, out **4** back, fast, over
  fast: **5** cling, seize, stick **6** adhere, cohere **7** enchain
  fast to: **6** follow **7** abide by **10** comply with
  filler: **5** lader
  fill the ~: **4** load, stow **5** lay in
  fondly: **3** hug **4** love **5** press **6** caress, cosset, cuddle, dandle, nestle, nuzzle **7** embrace, snuggle, squeeze
  for later: **4** keep, save
  for ransom: **6** abduct, hijack, kidnap, pirate
  forth: **4** talk **5** offer, orate, speak, spout **6** extend, recite **7** advance, declaim, lecture, narrate, proffer **8** bloviate, harangue, perorate **9** discourse
  gently: **3** hug **6** cradle
  get ~ of: **4** call, grab, have, meet **5** catch, phone, reach **6** locate, obtain, talk to **7** acquire, contact, liaison, possess, receive, speak to **8** approach, come into **9** ascertain, check with, telephone, touch base
  hard to ~: **4** eely
  in: **7** contain, repress, tighten **8** bottle up, suppress
  in check: **4** keep, rein **6** govern
  in contempt: **5** sneer, spurn
  in custody: **6** detain, immure, intern **8** imprison
  in music: **7** fermata
  in trust: **6** escrow
  in view: **3** eye, see, spy **4** espy, spot **5** watch **7** discern **8** perceive **10** get a load of
  it: **4** stop **5** cease
  it down: **4** hush **5** quiet **6** hush up, muffle, muzzle, stifle **7** repress **8** restrain, suppress
  it ~ s water: **3** cup **4** vase
  it won't ~ water: **3** net **5** sieve **8** colander
  lay ~ of: **3** get, nab **4** grab, grip, jerk, land, pull, snag, stop, take **5** catch, clasp, grasp, seize, twist, usurp, wrest **6** clinch, clutch, snatch **7** capture, grapple **8** come into
  like a sword: **5** wield
  loosen one's ~: **4** free **5** let go, untie **6** let off **7** release, set free **9** disengage
  low: **4** hate **5** abhor **6** detest, loathe **7** despise, dislike **8** execrate **9** abominate
  off: **5** delay, parry, repel, stall **6** offend, put off, rebuff, refuse, shelve, sicken **7** adjourn, disgust, prevent, repulse, suspend **8** alienate, hesitate, postpone
  (off): **4** fend
  off for: **5** await
  office: **5** serve **6** act for **7** serve as **8** speak for **9** represent **10** administer
  on: **4** bide, wait **5** abide, cling, stick **6** endure **7** persist, stand by **8** continue **9** keep going, persevere **10** stay a while
  on ~: **8** inactive
  one's attention: **5** rivet **6** absorb, arrest **7** bewitch, engross **8** enthrall, transfix **9** captivate, enrapture, fascinate, preoccupy
  one's ground: **4** stay **5** stick **6** adhere, endure, remain, take it **7** persist, stay put
  one's horses: **4** rein, wait
  one's own: **4** cope **5** get by **6** manage **7** make out
  one's tongue: **6** shut up **7** keep mum, silence **8** be silent
  on to: **4** cull, keep, save **5** amass, cache, hoard, lay by, put by, stack, store **6** accrue, detain, garner, gather, pile up, rack up, retain, save up **7** collect, compile, possess, procure, put away, shelter, store up **8** assemble, maintain, put aside, salt away **9** aggregate, stockpile **10** accumulate
  other views: **6** differ **7** dissent **8** disagree
  out: **5** offer, reach **6** endure, extend, refuse, resist **7** present, proffer, survive **9** withstand
  out one's hand: **3** beg **5** cadge, hit up, mooch **8** freeload **9** impetrate, mendicate, panhandle **10** supplicate
  over: **5** defer, delay **6** detain, hang up, hold up, put off, shelve **7** prolong **8** postpone, protract
  place in the ~: **4** fill, lade, pack, stow
  prepare to ~ out: **5** dig in
  put on ~: **5** defer, table **6** recess, shelve **7** suspend **8** postpone
  rapt: **5** charm **6** absorb, engage **7** enchant, engross, immerse **8** enthrall, entrance **9** fascinate, preoccupy
  responsible: **5** blame, thank **6** assign
  sacred: **5** exalt **6** hallow **8** enshrine, inshrine, sanctify **10** consecrate
  scoreless: **5** skunk
  something to ~: **4** mayo
  spellbound: **5** charm **7** enchant **8** enthrall, entrance, transfix **9** captivate, fascinate, hypnotize, mesmerize
  starter: **3** toe **4** foot, free, hand, root, with **5** choke, house, lease, stoke **6** strong **8** strangle
  sway: **4** head, rule **5** reign **6** direct, govern, manage **7** command, control, prevail **8** dominate, overrule
  take ~: **3** fix **5** set in **6** enroot
  take ~ of: **3** bag, nab **4** bust, grab, grip, nail, snag **5** catch, grasp, pinch, seize, snare **6** abduct, arrest, collar, detain, hijack, obtain, secure, snap up, snatch, tackle **7** capture, impound, overrun, procure, receive **8** carry off **9** apprehend, overwhelm **10** commandeer, confiscate
  the attention of: **4** grab, grip, lure **5** catch, rivet, tempt **6** absorb, divert, engage, entice, occupy **7** attract, engross, impress, involve **8** enthrall, interest **9** entertain, fascinate, tantalize, titillate
  the deed to: **3** own **7** possess
  the fort: **4** stay **6** defend, remain, uphold **7** carry on, stand by **8** maintain
  the phone: **4** wait **6** cool it **7** stand by **8** mark time, sit tight
  the reins: **4** rule **5** guide, reign **6** direct, govern **7** command, control, oversee
  the scepter: **4** rule **5** reign **6** govern **7** command
  tight: **5** clamp, clasp, cling **6** clench **7** squeeze
  to: **6** pursue **7** abide by, believe **8** obligate
  to keep: **6** redeem
  up: **3** rob **4** halt, last, prop, rein, slow, wear **5** block, brace, delay, laten, raise, steal, waive **6** detain, endure, freeze, hamper, hinder, impede, rein in, retard, shelve, thwart, verify, waylay **7** bolster, display, set back, support, suspend **8** blockade, encumber, obstruct, postpone, prohibit **9** hamstring, interrupt, recommend, stonewall, undergird
  up to ridicule: **4** mock, twit **5** sneer, taunt **6** dump on, insult **7** disdain, lampoon, put down **8** belittle, satirize **9** burlesque **10** caricature
  water: **4** wash **5** add up **6** cohere **9** make sense
  with: **5** grant **6** accept, affirm **7** believe **10** set store by
  wrestling ~: **4** lock **6** nelson

hold ___: **3** off, out **4** back, down, over, sway, with **5** at bay, forth, water **6** button

___ hold: **4** take **5** lower

hold a ___ to: **6** candle

holdall: **3** bag **6** duffel, kitbag **8** backpack, knapsack

Hold Back the Dawn (1941 film)
  cast: Charles Boyer, Olivia de Havilland, Paulette Goddard
  director: Mitchell Leisen

hold 'em: **4** game **5** poker **8** card game

Holden: **3** Ron **4** Eben **7** William

Holden, William: **5** actor
  film: Apartment for Peggy (1948)
    Boots Malone (1952)
    Born Yesterday (1950)

The Bridge on the River Kwai (1957)
The Bridges at Toko-Ri (1955)
The Counterfeit Traitor (1962)
The Country Girl (1954)
The Dark Past (1948)
Escape From Fort Bravo (1953)
Executive Suite (1954)
The Fleet's In (1942)
Forever Female (1953)
Invisible Stripes (1939)
Love Is a Many Splendored Thing (1955)
The Man From Colorado (1948)
Network (1976)
Our Town (1940)
Picnic (1955)
Rachel and the Stranger (1948)
Sabrina (1954)
S.O.B. (1981)
Stalag 17 (1953, AA)
Sunset Blvd. (1950)
Texas (1941)
The Towering Inferno (1974)
The Wild Bunch (1969)
Wild Rovers (1971)

holder: 3 urn 4 rack, vase 5 owner, stein 6 handle, tenant 7 bracket 8 occupant, oven mitt 9 container 10 proprietor, receptacle
starter: 3 gas, job, pen, pot 4 bond, card, copy, free, land 5 house, lease, place, share, stake, stock, title 6 candle, office, policy
Hold Her Tight (1972 song) artist: Osmonds
holding: 4 land 5 asset, title 6 tenure 7 keeping, logical 8 monopoly 9 occupancy, ownership
be in a ~ pattern: 4 pend, wait
company: 4 corp. 6 cartel
one left ~ the bag: 4 dupe, goat 5 chump, patsy 6 sucker, victim 7 cat's-paw, fall guy 9 scapegoat
pattern: 5 delay
starter: 4 with 5 share, stock
holding __: 3 pen 4 sway, tank 7 company, furnace, pattern
Holding On (1988 song) artist: Steve Winwood
Holding Out for a Hero (1984 song) artist: Bonnie Tyler
holdings: 5 means 6 assets, estate, wealth 7 effects 8 property 9 resources 10 belongings, securities
vast ~: 5 realm 6 empire 7 kingdom 8 dominion 9 territory
Hold it!: 3 hey 4 stop, whoa
Hold Me Now (1984 song) artist: Thompson Twins
Hold Me (song) artist: Fleetwood Mac, K.T. Oslin
Hold Me Tight (1968 song) artist: Johnny Nash
Hold My Hand (song) artist: Don Cornell
artist: Hootie and the Blowfish
__ hold of: 3 get
__ Hold of Me: 4 Got a
Hold on!: 3 hey 4 stop, whoa 6 one sec
Hold On (1990 song) artist: En Vogue
artist: Wilson Phillips
Hold on a __!: 3 sec
hold one's __: 3 own 5 peace 6 ground, horses, tongue
Hold On! I'm a Comin' (1966 song) artist: Sam and Dave
Hold on Tight (1981 song) artist: ELO
Hold On to the Nights (1988 song) artist: Richard Marx
holdout: 4 mule
Holdridge: 3 Lee 6 Cheryl
holds barred, no: 8 absolute, straight 9 limitless
Hold That Blonde star: 4 Lake
Hold That Co-ed (1938 film)
cast: John Barrymore, George Murphy, Marjorie Weaver
Hold That Ghost (1941 film)
cast: Bud Abbott, Lou Costello
director: Arthur Lubin
hold the __: 3 bag 4 fort, line, mayo 5 phone
Hold the Line (1978 song) artist: Toto
holdup: 3 jam, job 4 snag, wait 5 crime, delay, heist, hitch, theft 7 mugging, problem, robbery, setback, stickup, trouble 8 burglary, gridlock, lateness, stoppage, thievery 10 bottleneck, difficulty, impediment
man: 5 thief 6 mugger, robber
Hold What You've Got (1965 song) artist: Joe Tex
Hold your __!: 4 fire 6 horses
Hold Your Man (1933 film)
cast: Stuart Erwin, Clark Gable, Jean Harlow
director: Sam Wood
Hold You Tight (1991 song) artist: Tara Kemp
hole: 3 gap, jam, pit, rip 4 cave, gulf, lair, leak, nook, sink, slit, slot, spot, tear, vent, void, well 5 abyss, break, chasm, crack, ditch, gorge, gouge, niche, space 6 breach, burrow, cavern, cavity, cranny, crater, hollow, kennel, lacuna, locale, pickle, plight, pocket, recess, refuge, trench, tunnel 7 chamber, crevice, dungeon, fissure, opening, orifice, vacuity 8 aperture, locality, puncture, quagmire 9 concavity, sanctuary 10 depression, excavation, interspace, interstice, standstill
air ~: 4 vent
be in the ~: 3 owe
black ~ once: 4 star
combining form: 5 -trema
finish a ~: 4 putt
fix a ~: 4 darn, mend 5 patch 6 repair
furthest from the ~ in golf: 4 away
gaping ~: 3 maw 5 abyss, chasm
in one: 3 ace 7 triumph
in the ground: 3 pit 4 cave, well 6 cavern, crater
in the head: 5 mouth, naris, sinus 7 nostril
in the wall: 4 vent 6 outlet, refuge 7 hideout, retreat, shelter 8 hideaway 9 sanctuary
make a ~: 3 dig 4 bore 5 drill, gouge 6 burrow, dredge 8 excavate 9 hollow out
make a new ~: 5 redig
maker: 3 awl 4 moth 5 auger, borer 6 gimlet
needle ~: 3 eye
one in the ~: 4 ower
out: 4 putt
pipe ~: 4 leak 5 crack, drain
put another ~ in the cask: 5 retap
shoelace ~: 6 eyelet
start a ~: 5 tee up
starter: 3 arm, eye, fox, key, man, pin, pot 4 blow, bolt, bore, feed, hell, knee, knot, loop, peep, pest, port, post, sink, worm 5 chuck, cubby, hawse, stoke, thumb, touch 6 button, pigeon
subpar ~: 6 birdie
Swiss cheese ~: 3 eye
up: 4 hide, wait 5 lodge 6 lie low 7 conceal, hide out 9 hibernate 10 lie dormant
water ~: 4 pond, well
watering ~: 3 bar, pub 4 pond, well 5 haunt, oasis 6 bistro, lounge, saloon, tavern
wear a ~ in the rug: 4 pace
widen a ~: 4 ream
hole __: 3 saw 4 card 5 in one
hole __ wall: 5 in the
__ hole: 3 air, bog, dry 4 gunk, mill, shot, weep 5 black, blind, floss, glory, in the, judas, namma, ozone, sound, water, white 6 culver, finger, gnamma, kettle, limber, linnet, stroke 7 coronal, lubber's
__-hole: 3 top 4 bolt 5 bogey, hidey
__ Hole: 7 Jackson
hole in __: 3 one
__ hole in one's pocket: 5 burn a
hole in the __: 4 wall
__ Hole of Calcutta: 5 Black
holes
cheese with ~: 5 Swiss
18 ~: 5 round
full of ~: 5 leaky, mothy 6 flawed, porous, ragged
in ~: 6 ragged 8 tattered 9 motheaten 10 threadbare
poke full of ~: 6 refute, riddle 8 puncture 9 perforate
holey: 5 leaky 6 porous 9 moth-eaten
Holguín: 4 city, town
locale: 4 Cuba
holiday: 4 rest, stay, tour 5 break, event, feast, leave, visit 6 fiesta, recess 7 jubilee, leisure, liberty, time off 8 festival, vacation 10 recreation
annual ~: 6 Fourth
Asian ~: 3 Tet
cheer: 3 nog
Christian: 6 Advent, Easter
exhibit: 6 crèche
extravaganza: 6 parade
helper: 3 elf
Italian ~: 5 festa
Jewish: 5 Purim 8 Passover 9 Yom Kippur
Jewish ~ dinner: 5 seder
Jewish ~ eve: 4 ereb, erev
month: 3 Dec. 8 December
month without a ~: 6 August
preceder: 3 eve
purchase: 3 fir
quaff: 6 eggnog
quick ~: 5 jaunt
season: 4 Noel, Xmas, yule
song: 4 noel 5 carol
suitable for a ~: 6 festal
take a ~: 4 loaf, rest, slow 5 break, pause, relax 6 unwind 8 recreate, slack off, slow down, vacation
visitor: 5 Santa 6 St. Nick 10 Santa Claus
word: 5 happy
see also Christmas
__ holiday: 4 bank 5 legal, Roman 7 busman's
Holiday: 3 car 4 auto, city, Olds, town 6 Billie 10 automobile, Oldsmobile
locale: 7 Florida
Holiday (1930 film)
cast: Mary Astor, Ann Harding, Edward Everett Horton
Holiday (1938 film)
cast: Cary Grant, Katharine Hepburn, Doris Nolan
director: George Cukor
Holiday __: 3 Inn 5 on Ice 6 Affair
__ Holiday: 4 High 5 Roman 6 Johnny 7 Bugler's, Thieves'
Holiday (1983 song) artist: Madonna
Holiday Affair (1949 film)
cast: Wendell Corey, Janet Leigh, Robert Mitchum
Holiday in Mexico (1946 film)
cast: Ilona Massey, Roddy McDowall, Walter Pidgeon
director: George Sidney
Holiday Inn: 5 motel
alternative: 4 HoJo 7 Days Inn 9 Ramada Inn 10 Comfort Inn, Econo Lodge, Hampton Inn, Quality Inn, Red Roof Inn, Travelodge 11 Best Western
Holiday Inn (1942 film)
cast: Fred Astaire, Bing Crosby, Marjorie Reynolds
composer: Irving Berlin
director: Mark Sandrich
holier-than-thou: 4 smug 6 stuffy 7 pompous, stuck-up 8 arrogant, snobbish, superior 9 conceited
holiness: 5 piety 8 divinity, sanctity
Holiness, his: 4 pope 7 pontiff
Holland: 3 Tom 4 city, Neth., town 5 Brian, Eddie 11 Netherlands
born in ~: 5 Dutch
locale: 8 Michigan
Holland __ Cruises: 7 America
hollandaise: 5 sauce
Hollander, Lorin: 7 pianist 9 conductor
holler: 3 cry, yap 4 bawl, call, hoot, howl, rant, rave, roar, wail, yell, yelp, yowl 5 cheer, go ape, shout, storm, whoop 6 bellow, clamor, scream, shriek, squawk, squeal 7 bluster, carry on, declaim, exclaim, screech, sing out, ululate 8 bloviate, complain, freak out, shout out 9 make a fuss, raise Cain 10 hit the roof, vociferate
hollering: 5 noisy
Hollerith __: 4 card, code
__ hollers,...: 4 If he
Holley, Robert: 8 Nobelist
Holliday: 3 Doc 4 Judy 5 Polly 8 Jennifer
pal: 4 Earp
Holliday, Judy: 7 actress
film: Adam's Rib (1949)
Bells Are Ringing (1960)
Born Yesterday (1950, AA)
Full of Life (1956)
It Should Happen to You (1954)
The Marrying Kind (1952)
Phffft! (1954)
The Solid Gold Cadillac (1956)
Holliday, Polly role: 3 Flo
Hollies
song: The Air That I Breathe (1974)
Bus Stop (1966)
Carrie-Anne (1967)
He Ain't Heavy, He's My Brother (1970)
Long Cool Woman (1972)
Stop Stop Stop (1966)
Holliman: 4 Earl
Hollings: 6 Ernest
Hollis: 5 Stacy
Hollister: 4 city, town
locale: 10 California
hollow: 3 gap, pit, rut 4 dell, dent, dull, heed, hole, idle, sink, vain, vale, void 5 basin, cleft, empty, false, gorge, muted, niche, notch, scoop, tubal 6 absent, cavity, cranny, crater, dig out, dimple, dingle, furrow, futile, groove, pocket, recess, sunken, untrue, vacant, valley 7 concave, muffled, useless, vacuity 8 empty out, excavate, lifeless, scoop out, sinkhole, unfilled 9 cup-shaped, deceitful, depressed, excavated, fruitless, illogical, insincere, pointless, worthless 10 artificial, depression, excavation, unreliable
not: 5 solid
out: 3 dig 6 burrow 8 excavate 9 undermine
place: 4 cave, hole 5 ditch, gorge 6 cavern, cavity, crater, trench, tunnel 7 chamber 10 depression
secluded ~: 4 dell
small ~: 4 dent 6 areola, areole
sound: 5 clunk, thunk

hollow __: 3 sea 4 back, tile 5 newel
Hollow __, The: 3 Men 5 Hills
__ Hollow: 6 Sleepy
Holloway: 7 Stanley 8 Sterling
Holloway, Stanley: 5 actor
film: The Beggar's Opera (1953)
Brief Encounter (1945)
The Lavender Hill Mob (1951)
My Fair Lady (1964)
The Titfield Thunderbolt (1953)
The Way Ahead (1944)
Hollow Hills, The author: Mary Stewart
Hollow Men, The author: T.S. Eliot
Hollow Triumph (1948 film)
cast: Joan Bennett, Eduard Franz, Paul Henreid
holly: 4 tree 5 shrub
ender: 4 hock
feature: 5 berry
genus: 4 ilex
sea ~: 6 eryngo
season: 4 Xmas, Yule
shrub: 4 ilex 5 yapon 6 yaupon 8 inkberry
holly __: 3 oak 4 fern
__ holly: 3 sea 7 English
Holly: 4 Near 5 Buddy 6 Hunter, Lauren 7 Palance
Holly __: 4 Holy
Holly and the Crickets, Buddy
song: Oh, Boy! (1957)
Peggy Sue (1957)
That'll Be the Day (1957)
hollyhock: 5 plant 6 flower
__ hollyhock: 3 sea 4 wild
Holly Holy (1969 song) artist: Neil Diamond
__-Holly Johnson: 4 Lynn
Holly, Lauren: 7 actress
film: Beautiful Girls (1996)
Dragon: The Bruce Lee Story (1993)
Dumb & Dumber (1994)
spouse: Jim Carrey
hollylike tree: 4 holm
Hollywood: 4 city, town
clashers: 4 egos
figure: 3 rep 4 star 5 actor, agent, celeb 8 director, producer 9 celebrity
industry: 6 cinema, movies
locale: 7 Florida 10 California
magnate: 4 Cohn 5 Mayer 7 Goldwyn
publicity frame: 5 still
release: 5 movie
studio: 3 Fox, MGM, RKO 6 Warner 8 Columbia 9 Paramount
walk-on: 5 extra
workplace: 3 set 6 studio 10 soundstage
Hollywood __: 3 bed 5 Suite 6 Ending, Nights 7 Argyles
Hollywood __ of Fame: 4 Walk
__ Hollywood: 3 Doc 5 Going
Hollywood Argyles song: Alley-Oop (1960)
Hollywood Boulevard
crosser: 4 Vine
embedment: 4 star
Hollywood Ending (2002 film)
cast: Woody Allen, Téa Leoni, Debra Messing, Treat Williams
director: Woody Allen
__ Hollywood Goodby: 4 Kiss
Hollywood Nights (1978 song) artist: Bob Seger
Hollywood Squares, The: 8 game show
answer: 5 agree 8 disagree
former regular: 3 Cox 5 Lynde 6 Weaver
host: Peter Marshall, John Davidson, Tom Bergeron
non-win: 3 OOX, OXO, OXX, XOO, XOX, XXO
ploy: 5 bluff
star complement: 4 nine
win: 3 OOO, XXX
Hollywood Suite composer: 5 Grofé
Hollywood Swinging (1974 song)
artist: Kool and the Gang
Holm: 3 Ian 5 Hanya 7 Celeste, Eleanor
Holman: 3 Nat 4 Hunt 5 Eddie
Holman, Eddie song: Hey There Lonely Girl (1970)
Holman, Nat
milieu: 5 court
org.: 3 NBA
sport: 10 basketball
Holm, Celeste: 7 actress
film: All About Eve (1950)
Champagne for Caesar (1950)
Come to the Stable (1949)
Everybody Does It (1949)
Gentleman's Agreement (1947, AA)
High Society (1956)
Road House (1948)
Still Breathing (1998)
The Tender Trap (1955)
Tom Sawyer (1973)
Holmes: 5 Clint, Katie, Larry 6 Oliver, Rupert 8 Sherlock
O.W. ~ carriage: 4 shay
Holmes, Clint song: Playground in My Mind (1973)
Holmes, Larry: 5 boxer
milieu: 4 ring
Holmes, Oliver Wendell: 4 poet
work: The Autocrat of the Breakfast-Table
The Chambered Nautilus
Elsie Venner
Old Ironsides
The Wonderful One-Hoss Shay
Holmes, Rupert
song: Escape (1979)
Him (1980)
Holmes, Sherlock: 6 sleuth 9 detective
adverb for ~: 5 afoot
clue: 3 ash
colleague: 6 Watson
creator: 5 Doyle
foe: 8 Moriarty
girl: 5 Elsie
home: 6 London 7 Baker St.
landlady: 6 Hudson
portrayer: 8 Rathbone
prop for ~: 4 pipe
quest: 4 clew, clue
task for ~: 4 case
Holm, Ian: 3 Sir 5 actor
film: Another Woman (1988)
The Bofors Gun (1968)
Dance With a Stranger (1985)
The Fifth Element (1997)
From Hell (2001)
Greystoke: The Legend of Tarzan, Lord of the Apes (1984)
Hamlet (1990)
The Homecoming (1973)
Joe Gould's Secret (2000)
A Severed Head (1971)
holmium: 7 element
holm oak: 4 ilex, tree
Holocaust documentary: 5 Shoah
hologram maker: 5 laser
holographic __: 4 will
holography tool: 5 laser
Holstein: 3 cow 4 bull 6 bovine, cattle
comment: 3 moo
home: 4 barn
part: 5 udder
holster item: 3 gun, rod 5 piece 6 pistol, roscoe, weapon 7 firearm 8 revolver 9 forty-five
Holst, Gustav work: The Planets
Holt: 3 Tim 8 Victoria
Holt, Laura partner: 6 Steele
Holtz: 3 Lou
Holub, Miroslav: 4 poet 5 Czech
holy: 5 blest, godly, pious 6 devout, divine, sacred, solemn 7 angelic, blessed, sainted, saintly 8 faithful, hallowed, numinous, reverent, seraphic 9 angelical, celestial, inviolate, religious, righteous, spiritual 10 inviolable, sacrosanct, sanctified, seraphical
combining form: 4 hagi-, hier- 5 hagio-, hiero-
ender: 3 day 5 stone
name meaning ~: 4 Olga 5 Helga
terror: 3 imp 4 brat
holy __: 3 cow, day, oil, war 4 cats, moly 5 bread, grass, Moses, synod, water 6 clover, orders, terror 7 thistle
Holy __: 3 Ark, Joe, One, See 4 City, Lamb, Land, Rood, Week, Writ, Year 5 Bible, Cross, Ghost, Grail 6 Family, Father, Island, Mother, Office, Spirit 7 Apostle, Trinity
Holy __!: 3 cow 4 moly 5 smoke 6 Toledo 8 mackerel
Holy __ Empire: 5 Roman
Holy __, The: 3 War 4 Fair
__ Holy: 5 Holly
Holy Ark locale: 4 shul 5 schul 9 synagogue
Holy cow!: 3 gee, wow 4 egad, gosh, yipe 5 egads, yikes, yipes
Holy Cross
athletes: 9 Crusaders
locale: 4 Mass. 9 Worcester
__ Holy Day: 4 High
Holy Fair, The author: Robert Burns
Holy Father: 4 pope 7 pontiff
Holyfield, Evander: 5 boxer
milieu: 4 ring
rival: 5 Tyson
Holy Innocents' __: 3 Day
Holy Land: 4 Sion, Zion 5 Judea 6 Judaea
Holy mackerel!: 3 gee, wow 4 egad 5 egads, golly
Holy Matrimony (1943 film)
cast: Laird Cregar, Gracie Fields, Monty Woolley
Holyoke: 4 city, town
locale: 4 Mass.
Holy One: 4 Lord
Holy Roman Empire founder: 4 Otto
Holy smoke!: 3 gee, wow 4 egad, oath 5 egads, golly
Holy Toledo!: 3 gee, wow 4 egad 5 egads, golly
Holy War, The author: John Bunyan
holy-water basin: 4 font 5 stoup
Holy Week ends it: 4 Lent
Holz, Arno: 4 poet 6 German 10 playwright
Holzman, Red: 5 coach
milieu: 5 court
org.: 3 NBA
sport: 10 basketball
homage: 4 pean 5 honor, kudos, paean 6 esteem, fealty, praise, regard, salute 7 acclaim, loyalty, plaudit, respect, tribute, worship 8 accolade, devotion, encomium, fidelity, flattery, good word 9 adoration, adulation, deference, laudation, obeisance, panegyric, reverence 10 admiration, allegiance, exaltation
pay ~ to: 4 hail 5 exalt, honor 6 attend, praise, revere, salute 7 glorify 9 genuflect
Homage to Clio author: W.H. Auden
Homage to Mistress Bradstreet...
author: John Berryman
Homage to Picasso painter: 4 Gris
Homage to the Square: 5 op art
hombre: 4 game 8 card game
Hombre (1967 film)
cast: Richard Boone, Fredric March, Paul Newman
director: Martin Ritt
homburg: 3 hat 7 chapeau 8 headgear
alternative: 6 fedora
__ Homburg: 3 Bad
home: 3 hut, pad 4 base, co-op, digs, flat, land, nest, site, soil, turf 5 abode, cabin, condo, house, joint, local, lodge, manor, place, roost, villa 6 castle, hearth, locale, palace, refuge 7 address, chez moi, cottage, domicil, habitat, housing, lodging, mansion, shelter 8 bungalow, crash pad, domestic, domicile, dwelling, fireside, interior, internal, locality, lodgment, property, quarters 9 apartment, dormitory, household, residence, townhouse 10 birthplace, fatherland, native land
ender: 3 boy 4 body, bred, land, made, port, room, sick, spun, town, ward, work 5 bound, buyer, grown, maker, owner, stead, wards 6 coming, making 7 builder, stretch 8 steading
in French: 6 maison
in Spanish: 4 casa
large ~: 6 castle, estate, palace 7 mansion
lofty ~: 4 aery, eyry 5 aerie, eyrie
not ~: 3 out 4 away
on the range: 5 ranch
site: 4 plot
see also house
home __: 3 row, run 4 base, brew, free, keys, page, port, rule 5 fries, front, guard, plate, range, scrap, stand, study, truth, video 6 center, ground, office, screen 7 mission
home __ loan: 6 equity
home __ potatoes: 5 fried
home-__: 4 brew, care 5 style
__ home: 3 hit 5 bring, motor, not at, solar 6 foster, mobile, second, strike, tumble 7 harvest, leisure, stately, tourist
__-home: 4 down
Home __: 5 Alone, Depot
Home __ Baker: 3 Run
Home __ Brave: 5 of the
Home __ Range: 5 on the
Home __ the Holidays: 3 for
Home, __!: 5 James
__ Home: 5 Going, I'll Be 6 Coming, Daddy's, Flying 7 Harvest
Home Again host: 4 Vila
__ Home Alabama: 5 Sweet
Home Alone (1990 film)
cast: Macaulay Culkin, John Heard, Catherine O'Hara, Joe Pesci, Daniel Stern
composer: 8 Williams
director: Chris Columbus
kid: 5 Kevin
Home Alone 2... (1992 film)
cast: Macaulay Culkin, Catherine O'Hara, Joe Pesci, Daniel Stern
director: Chris Columbus
Home Before Dark (1958 film)
cast: Rhonda Fleming, Dan O'Herlihy, Jean Simmons
director: Mervyn LeRoy
homebody: 5 loner 7 recluse 9 introvert
homeboy: 3 pal
homebuyer option: 5 condo
homecoming: 6 return 7 arrival
attend ~: 5 reune
celebrant: 4 alum, grad 6 alumna 7 alumnus
Homecoming, The: 4 film, play
author: Harold Pinter
cast: Cyril Cusack, Ian Holm

director: Peter Hall
home delivery terr.: 3 rte.
home-district
some ~ appropriations: 4 pork
home equity __: 4 loan
Home for the Holidays (1954 song)
artist: Perry Como
home-free: 4 safe
home fries: 8 potatoes
Home From the Hill (1960 film)
cast: George Hamilton, Robert Mitchum, Eleanor Parker, George Peppard
director: Vincente Minnelli
homegirl: 3 pal 4 chum 5 amiga, crony 6 friend
homegrown: 5 local 6 native 8 domestic 10 indigenous, provincial
Homegrown (1998 film)
cast: Hank Azaria, Kelly Lynch, Billy Bob Thornton
home heating need: 3 gas, oil
Homeier: 2 G.V. 4 Skip
Home Improvement (ABC sitcom)
cast: Tim Allen (Tim Taylor)
Debbe Dunning (Heidi)
Patricia Richardson (Jill Taylor)
setting: Detroit
show: Tool Time
Home in Indiana (1944 film)
cast: Walter Brennan, Jeanne Crain, June Haver
director: Henry Hathaway
__ home is his castle: 5 A man's
homeland: 4 soil 5 roots 7 country
homeless: 5 stray 6 exiled, lonely 7 vagrant 8 derelict, indigent, stranded, unhoused, vagabond
one: 4 waif 5 gamin, stray 6 pauper 7 vagrant
homelike: 4 cozy, snug 5 comfy 7 livable 8 intimate
home-loan org.: 3 FHA 4 FNMA, GNMA
homemade: 5 crude, rough 6 rustic, simple 9 inelegant, makeshift 10 amateurish
liquor: 4 jake 5 hooch 6 hootch 9 moonshine
homemaker, at times: 4 cook 5 sewer 6 duster, ironer, washer
home of the brave: 3 USA
Home on the Range beast: 4 deer 7 buffalo 8 antelope
homeowner
new ~: 6 lienee
paper: 4 deed
payment: 4 mtge. 8 mortgage
pride: 4 lawn 5 grass 8 backyard
__-home pay: 4 take
homer: 3 hit, run 6 dinger 7 triumph 9 grand slam 10 four-bagger
hitter's run: 4 trot
king: 5 Aaron
trying for a ~: 5 at bat
two-run ~ requirement: 5 one on
Homer: 4 city, poet, town 5 Greek 7 Simpson, Winslow
instrument: 4 lyre
locale: 6 Alaska
opus: 4 epic, epos 5 Iliad 7 Odyssey
partner: 6 Jethro
wife: 5 Marge
see also Greek
Homeric: 4 epic 5 grand 6 heroic 8 heroical 9 classical 10 monumental
Homeric __: 6 simile
Homeric Greek: 6 Argive
home ruler, name meaning: 5 Henry
home run
see homer
Home Run __: 5 Baker
Homer, Winslow: 6 artist 7 painter
home: 5 Maine
__ Homes and Gardens: 6 Better
home security device: 5 alarm
Home Shopping Network rival: 3 QVC
homesick: 7 forlorn 8 lonesome
homesite: 3 lot
HOMES part: 4 Erie 5 Huron 7 Ontario 8 Michigan, Superior
homespun: 5 plain 6 fabric, folksy, rustic, simple 8 ordinary 10 provincial, unpolished
homestead: 4 farm, soil 5 ranch 6 estate, grange, settle 8 fireside
Homestead: 4 city, town
locale: 7 Florida
Homestead Act
measure: 4 acre
offering: 4 land
homesteader: 5 liver 6 nester, sooner 7 pioneer, settler 8 colonial, colonist, squatter
tract: 5 claim
Home, Sweet Home
composer: 5 Payne
starter: 3 mid
__ home the bacon: 5 bring
Home to Harlem author: 5 McKay
__ home to roost: 4 come
home video format: 3 DVD, VHS 4 Beta
__ Homeward, Angel: 4 Look
Homeward Bound... (1993 film)
cast: Kim Greist, Robert Hays, Jean Smart
cat: 5 Sassy
Homeward Bound (1966 song) artist: Simon and Garfunkel
Homewood: 4 city, town
locale: 7 Alabama
homework: 4 task 6 lesson 10 assignment
do ~: 5 study 9 grind away
do elementary-school ~: 3 add
English ~: 5 essay, theme
help with ~: 5 tutor
homey: 4 cosy, cozy, nice, snug, warm 5 comfy, cozey, cozie 6 casual, earthy, folksy, rustic, simple 7 livable, natural, relaxed 8 friendly, informal, inviting, liveable, pleasant 9 household 10 unaffected
homilize: 5 orate 6 preach
homily: 3 ser. 4 talk 6 cliché, lesson, saying, sermon, speech 7 oration 8 teaching 9 discourse 10 admonition, vocalizing
homing __: 6 device, pigeon
hominy: 4 samp 5 grain, grits
__ hominy: 3 lye 5 pearl
homme: 3 man 6 French
homme d'__: 4 état
homme du __: 5 monde
__ homo: 4 ecce
Homo __: 7 erectus, habilis, sapiens
Homo erectus: 5 biped
homogeneous: 4 akin, even, like 5 alike 6 allied 7 cognate, kindred, of a kind, similar, uniform 8 constant, parallel 9 analogous, unanimous 10 comparable, equivalent
homogenize: 3 mix 5 blend 9 integrate 10 amalgamate, assimilate
homogenized product: 4 milk
homogenous: 6 on a par 9 analogous, identical, unvarying 10 comparable, consistent, homologous, true to type
Homolka, Oscar: 5 actor
film: Ball of Fire (1941)
The Code of Scotland Yard (1946)
I Remember Mama (1948)
Mission to Moscow (1943)
Sabotage (1936)
homologize: 6 absorb 9 integrate 10 assimilate
homologous: 4 like 5 equal 9 analogous 10 equivalent, homogenous
homo sapiens: 3 man 5 biped, human 6 people
Homs: 4 city, town
locale: 5 Syria
homunculus: 5 dwarf, pigmy, pygmy 6 midget, pee-wee 7 manikin 8 mannikin 9 miniature
hon: 3 luv 4 babe, dear 5 deary, sugar, toots 6 dearie 7 darling, pet name, sweetie 8 snookums 10 endearment, sweetheart, sweetie pie
Honan: 6 fabric, pongee
honcho: 3 VIP 4 boss, head, jefe, king, lord, prex, prez 5 chief, Mr. Big, nabob, prexy, wheel 6 bigwig, kahuna, top dog 7 bigshot, headman 8 director, higher-up, kingfish, overseer, superior 9 big kahuna, commander, executive, organizer
head ~: 8 higher-up 9 key player
Hond.
neighbor: 3 Nic. 4 Guat.
see also Honduras
Honda: 3 car 4 auto 6 import 8 Soichiro 10 automobile
model: 3 CRV 5 Acura, civic, Pilot 6 Accord, Del Sol 7 Element, Odyssey, Prelude 8 Passport
rival: 4 Ford
Hondo: 5 river
locale: 6 Belize, Mexico 9 Guatemala
Hondo (1953 film): 5 oater
cast: Ward Bond, Geraldine Page, John Wayne
director: John Farrow
Honduras: 4 gulf 6 nation 7 country
Indian: 4 Maya 5 Lenca 7 Miskito
money: 7 lempira
native: 4 Maya
neighbor: 9 Guatemala, Nicaragua 10 El Salvador
org.: 3 OAS
town in ~: 4 Tela
see also Spanish
__ Honduras: 7 British
hone: 4 file, whet 5 grind, strop, train 6 refine 7 improve, perfect, sharpen 8 fine-tune, oilstone, practice, rehearse 9 acuminate, whetstone
in: 5 focus
honed: 4 keen 5 edged, sharp 9 sharpened
Honegger: 6 Arthur
contemporary of ~: 5 Satie
honest: 4 even, fair, good, just, open, true 5 blunt, frank, legit, moral, naïve, plain, right 6 actual, candid, decent, direct, proper, simple, square, trusty, worthy 7 artless, ethical, factual, genuine, serious, sincere, unfaked, upfront, upright, veridic 8 bona fide, credible, explicit, innocent, out front, reliable, straight, truthful, unbiased, virtuous 9 downright, guileless, heartfelt, honorable, impartial, ingenuous, objective, reputable, righteous, unfeigned, unslanted, veracious, veridical 10 aboveboard, believable, evenhanded, forthright, from the hip, high-minded, inviolable, law-abiding, legitimate, on the level, point-blank, reasonable, scrupulous, unaffected, upstanding
be ~: 5 level 6 face it
to goodness: 5 truly 6 indeed, really
Honest __: 3 Abe 4 John
Honest!: 5 no lie 6 I swear
honestly: 5 clean, right, truly 6 openly, really, simply 8 directly 9 honorably, sincerely 10 point-blank, virtuously
honestness: 5 truth 6 ethics, virtue 7 probity 8 morality, veracity 9 character, integrity, principle, rectitude
honest-to-__: 3 God
honest-to-goodness: 4 real, true 5 legit, plumb, valid 6 actual, kasher, kosher, proven, really 7 certain, factual, for real, genuine 8 absolute, accurate, bona fide, straight 9 authentic, confirmed, downright, heartfelt, in reality, out-and-out, seriously, sincerely 10 definitely
honesty: 4 good 5 honor, right 6 candor, ethics, virtue 7 loyalty, probity 8 fairness, fidelity, goodness, morality, openness, veracity 9 bluntness, frankness, good faith, integrity, rectitude, sincerity 10 candidness, trustiness
exemplar of ~: 3 Abe 7 Lincoln
of dubious ~: 5 shady 7 corrupt, crooked, devious 8 slippery, unsavory 9 notorious, unethical
Honesty __ best policy: 5 is the
Honesty (1979 song) artist: Billy Joel
honey: 2 jo 3 gem, luv, pet 4 baby, bear, beau, dear, doll, jill, love 5 amour, angel, chéri, cooky, cutey, cutie, deary, ducky, flame, jewel, leman, lover, lovey, novia, novio, peach, prize, sugar, sweet 6 bon ami, chérie, cookie, dautie, dearie, steady, sweets 7 beloved, darling, dearest, dear one, jobbery, pigsney, schatzi, squeeze, sweetie, tootsie 8 chou-chou, cutie pie, dowsabel, dulcinea, ladylove, lovebird, macushla, paramour, precious, snookums, sugar pie, sweetums, truelove 9 bonne amie, boyfriend, dreamboat, inamorata, inamorato, petit chou, valentine 10 endearment, girlfriend, heartthrob, honeybunch, mavourneen, sweetheart, sweetie pie, turtledove 19 turtledove bonne amie
badger: 5 ratel
color: 4 gold 5 amber
drink: 4 mead
ender: 3 bee, dew 4 comb, moon 5 berry, eater 6 suckle 7 creeper
factory: 4 comb, hive 6 apiary
land of milk and ~: 6 utopia 7 Arcadia, Erehwon 8 paradise 9 Shangri-la
like ~: 5 sweet 6 sticky
maker: 3 bee
source: 6 clover
honey __: 3 ant, bee, bun 4 bear, palm 5 eater, guide 6 badger, locust 7 buzzard, gilding, mustard, stomach
Honey __: 4 Cone, Fitz 5 Chile
Honey __ Cheerios: 3 Nut
__-Honey: 4 Bit-o
Honey (1968 song) artist: Bobby Goldsboro
Honey (1997 song) artist: Mariah Carey
Honey and Salt author: Carl Sandburg
honeybee: 3 bug 6 insect
name meaning ~: 7 Melissa
honeybunch
see honey
Honey Bunches of Oats: 6 cereal
competitor: 3 Kix 4 Life, Trix 5 Kashi, Quisp, Total 6 Kaboom, Muesli, Oreo O's, Pablum, Smacks 7 All-Bran, Crispix, Harmony, Hunny B's, Mueslix, Oat Bran, Pokemon 8 Boo Berry, Cheerios, Corn Chex, Corn Pops, Fiber One, Rice Chex, Special K, Uncle Sam, Wheaties 9 Alpha Bits, Apple Zaps, Grape Nuts, Just Right, Wheat Chex 10 Apple Jacks, Bran Flakes, Cap'n Crunch, Cocoa Puffs, Froot Loops, Mini-Wheats, Nutri-Grain, Puffed Rice, Quaker Oats, Smart Start 11 Cocoa Blasts, Cookie Crisp,

Golden Crisp, Lucky Charms, Puffed Wheat, Sweet Crunch, Waffle Crisp
Honey Chile (1967 song) artist: Martha & the Vandellas
honeycomb: 6 pierce **9** penetrate
material: 3 wax
unit: 4 cell
honeycomb __: 4 work **5** tripe
Honey Comb: 6 cereal
competitor: 3 Kix **4** Life, Trix **5** Kashi, Quisp, Total **6** Kaboom, Muesli, Oreo O's, Pablum, Smacks **7** All-Bran, Crispix, Harmony, Hunny B's, Mueslix, Oat Bran, Pokemon **8** Boo Berry, Cheerios, Corn Chex, Corn Pops, Fiber One, Rice Chex, Special K, Uncle Sam, Wheaties **9** Alpha Bits, Apple Zaps, Grape Nuts, Just Right, Wheat Chex **10** Apple Jacks, Bran Flakes, Cap'n Crunch, Cocoa Puffs, Froot Loops, Mini-Wheats, Nutri-Grain, Puffed Rice, Quaker Oats, Smart Start **11** Cocoa Blasts, Cookie Crisp, Golden Crisp, Lucky Charms, Puffed Wheat, Sweet Crunch, Waffle Crisp
Honeycomb (1957 song) artist: Jimmie Rodgers
Honey Cone song: Want Ads (1971)
honeycreeper: 4 bird, iiwi
honeydew: 5 fruit, melon
kin: 6 casaba **7** cassaba
honey Dijon: 8 dressing
Honeydrippers song: Sea of Love (1984)
honeyeater: 3 tui **4** bird **9** friarbird
honey-eating bird: 2 oo **3** iao
honeyed: 5 sweet **6** sugary **7** candied **9** adulatory **10** saccharine
Honey Fitz daughter: 4 Rose
Honey, I Blew Up the Kid (1992 film)
cast: Rick Moranis, Robert Oliveri, Marcia Strassman
Honey, I Shrunk the Kids (1989 film)
cast: Matt Frewer, Rick Moranis, Marcia Strassman
honeymoon __: 5 suite **6** bridge
Honeymooners, The (CBS sitcom)
cast: Art Carney (Ed Norton) Jackie Gleason (Ralph Kramden) Audrey Meadows (Alice Kramden) Joyce Randolph (Trixie Norton)
dog: 5 Lucky
laugh: 3 har
prop: 6 icebox
setting: 7 New York **8** Brooklyn
Honeymoon Festivel, The author: **5** Engel
Honeymoon in Bali (1939 film)
cast: Madeleine Carroll, Allan Jones, Fred MacMurray
Honeymoon in Vegas (1992 film)
cast: James Caan, Nicolas Cage, Sarah Jessica Parker
director: Andrew Bergman
honeymoon locale: 5 Aruba **6** Hawaii **7** Niagara
Honey Nut Cheerios: 6 cereal
competitor: 3 Kix **4** Life, Trix **5** Kashi, Quisp, Total **6** Kaboom, Muesli, Oreo O's, Pablum, Smacks **7** All-Bran, Crispix, Harmony, Hunny B's, Mueslix, Oat Bran, Pokemon **8** Boo Berry, Cheerios, Corn Chex, Corn Pops, Fiber One, Rice Chex, Special K, Uncle Sam, Wheaties **9** Alpha Bits, Apple Zaps, Grape Nuts, Just Right, Wheat Chex **10** Apple Jacks, Bran Flakes, Cap'n Crunch, Cocoa Puffs, Froot Loops, Mini-Wheats, Nutri-Grain, Puffed Rice, Quaker Oats, Smart Start **11** Cocoa Blasts, Cookie Crisp, Golden Crisp, Lucky Charms, Puffed Wheat, Sweet Crunch, Waffle Crisp
Honey Nut Clusters: 6 cereal
competitor: 3 Kix **4** Life, Trix **5** Kashi, Quisp, Total **6** Kaboom, Muesli, Oreo O's, Pablum, Smacks **7** All-Bran, Crispix, Harmony, Hunny B's, Mud & Bugs, Mueslix, Oat Bran, Pokemon **8** Boo Berry, Cheerios, Corn Chex, Corn Pops, Fiber One, Rice Chex, Special K, Uncle Sam, Wheaties **9** Alpha Bits, Apple Zaps, Grape Nuts, Just Right, Wheat Chex **10** Apple Jacks, Bran Flakes, Cap'n Crunch, Cocoa Puffs, Froot Loops, Mini-Wheats, Nutri-Grain, Puffed Rice, Quaker Oats, Smart Start **11** Cocoa Blasts, Cookie Crisp, Golden Crisp, Lucky Charms, Puffed Wheat, Sweet Crunch, Waffle Crisp
honeysuckle: 5 plant **6** flower
shrub: 5 elder **6** abelia **8** snowball
__ honeysuckle: 3 fly **4** bush, wild **5** coral **6** yellow **7** Jamaica, trumpet
Honeysuckle Rose (1980 film)
cast: Dyan Cannon, Amy Irving, Willie Nelson
honey-tongued: 4 glib, oily **5** slick, suave **6** artful, facile, smooth **8** eloquent **9** garrulous
Honey West ocelot: 5 Bruce
Hong Kong: 4 isls. **5** isles **7** islands
boat: 4 junk
locale: 4 Asia **5** China
money: 4 cent **6** dollar
neighbor: 5 Macao, Macau
river: 5 Pearl
Hong Kong __: 3 flu
honi __ qui mal y pense: 4 soit
Honiara: 4 city, town **7** capital
locale: 8 Solomons
honied: 5 sweet
honk: 4 beep, blow, bray, toot, yang **5** blare, blast, noise **6** tootle
honker: 4 horn **5** goose **8** motorist
honkers: 5 geese, skein **6** gaggle
Honk if you... locale: 6 bumper
Honky Cat (1972 song) artist: Elton John
honky-tonk: 3 bar **5** joint, music **6** tavern **8** taphouse **9** nightclub
Honkytonk Man (1982 film)
cast: Clint Eastwood, Kyle Eastwood, John McIntire
director: Clint Eastwood
Honky Tonk Women (1969 song)
artist: Rolling Stones
Honolulu: 4 city, port, town
athletes: 8 Warriors
greeting: 5 aloha
locale: 4 Oahu **6** Hawaii
newspaper: 10 Advertiser
shindig: 4 luau
suburb: 4 Aiea
honor: 4 fete, hail, laud, name, palm, sing **5** adore, award, bless, crown, endue, exalt, extol, glory, grace, indue, kudos, medal, merit, prize, raise, toast **6** admire, credit, esteem, extoll, fealty, hallow, homage, praise, regard, renown, revere, reward, salute, trophy, virtue **7** acclaim, adulate, applaud, commend, decency, dignify, dignity, ennoble, flatter, glorify, honesty, laurels, lionize, loyalty, magnify, observe, plaudit, probity, respect, tribute, worship **8** accolade, decorate, eminence, encomium, eulogize, fairness, flattery, good name, goodness, good word, live up to, look up to, morality, nobility, ornament, prestige, venerate, veracity **9** adoration, adulation, celebrate, celebrity, character, deference, gallantry, greatness, integrity, laudation, liquidate, panegyric, privilege, recognize, rectitude, reverence, sincerity **10** admiration, compliment, consecrate, decoration, exaltation, panegyrize, veneration
an IOU: 3 pay **5** pay up, repay **6** refund, settle **7** pay back **8** make good, settle up, square up **9** reimburse **10** remunerate
battle of ~: 4 duel
card: 3 ace, ten **4** king
in ~ of: 3 for **5** after
name meaning ~: 4 Nora
place of ~: 4 dais
put on the ~ system: 5 trust
sense of ~: 6 ethics, morals, values **7** probity **8** morality **9** character, integrity, rectitude **10** conscience, principles
with a title: 3 dub **6** knight
with insults: 5 roast
word of ~: 3 vow **4** oath, word **6** pledge **7** promise
honor __: 4 camp, card, roll **5** guard, point, trick **6** bright, system **7** society
honor __ thieves: 5 among
honor-__: 5 bound
__ honor: 4 your
Honor: 8 Blackman
his ~: 5 judge, mayor **6** jurist **10** magistrate
Honor __ Father: 3 Thy
__ Honor: 5 Men of **6** Secret, Silent **7** Prizzi's
honorable: 4 fair, good, just, true **5** clean, great, moral, noble, right, sound **6** august, decent, honest, trusty, worthy **7** eminent, ethical, exalted, gallant, notable, sincere, upright **8** elevated, esteemed, faithful, knightly, reliable, sterling, straight, truthful, unsoiled, virtuous **9** dignified, estimable, exemplary, high-toned, reputable, righteous, venerable **10** chivalrous, creditable, high-minded, scrupulous, upstanding
honorable __: 7 mention
honorably: 4 well **5** right **7** morally **8** honestly, properly **9** carefully, ethically, uprightly **10** dependably, faithfully, virtuously
honorarium: 3 fee, pay **7** payment, subsidy **9** allowance, emolument
honorary: 6 unpaid **7** nominal, titular **10** unsalaried
honorary __: 5 canon **6** degree, member
honor-bound: 6 liable **7** obliged **8** beholden, indebted **9** obligated
Honoré: 6 Balzac **7** Daumier
honored: 5 noted, proud **7** storied, welcome **8** glorious, laureate **9** venerable **10** preeminent
where ~ guests sit: 6 podium **7** rostrum **8** platform
__-honored: 4 time
honored by God, name meaning: **7** Timothy
honorific: 5 title **7** address
female ~: 4 ma'am **5** madam
Japanese ~: 3 san
honoris __: 5 causa
Honorius: 4 pope **7** pontiff
__ honor, I will do my...: 4 On my
honors: 5 glory, kudos, prize **6** esteem, laurel, praise **7** acclaim, laurels
confer ~: 5 award
do the ~: 7 present, preside **9** officiate
honors __: 5 of war **6** course
__ honors: 5 do the **6** simple
honor society
concern: 3 GPA
letter: 3 phi **4** beta **5** kappa
Honor Thy Father author: 6 Talese
Honourable Schoolboy, The author: John le Carré
Honshu: 3 isl. **4** isle **6** island
cape: 3 Oma
city: 3 Ise, Ito, Ome, Ota, Tsu, Ube, Uji, Yao **4** Ageo, Anjo, Fuji, Gifu, Hino, Hofu, Iida, Kobe, Kofu, Kure, Mito, Nara, Noda, Otsu, Seto, Soka, Tama, Toda, Ueda, Zama **5** Abiko, Akita, Aomon, Asaka, Chiba, Chofu, Daito, Ebina, Fuchu, Fukui, Handa, Ikeda, Ikoma, Iruma, Itami, Iwaki, Izumi, Kioto, Kiryu, Kyoto, Minoo, Niiza, Ogaki, Omiya, Osaka, Oyama, Sakai, Suita, Tokio, Tokyo, Urawa, Yaizu **6** Akashi, Aomori, Atsugi, Fujimi, Fukaya, Hadano, Himeji, Kadoma, Kuwana, Matsue, Misato, Mitaka, Nagano, Nagoya, Numazu, Sakado, Sakata, Sakura, Sayama, Sendai, Sukuka, Toyama, Toyota, Yamato, Yonago **7** Hitachi, Ibaraki, Isesaki, Iwakuni, Kashiwa, Katsuta, Kawagoe, Kodaira, Komatsu, Machida, Matsudo, Mishima, Morioka, Nagaoka, Niigata, Odawara, Okayama, Okazaki, Shimizu, Takaoka, Tottori, Tsukuba **8** Ashikaga, Fujisawa, Fukuyama, Hachioji, Hirakata, Hirosaki, Ichihara, Ichikawa, Kakogawa, Kanazawa, Kawasaki, Koriyama, Maebashi, Neyagawa, Shizuoka, Tokuyama, Toyonaka, Wakayama, Yamagata, Yokohama, Yokosuka **9** Hiroshima
lake: 3 Omi
locale: 4 Asia **5** Japan
port: 3 Ito, Ube **4** Kobe, Kure **5** Akita, Aomon, Chiba, Osaka
river: 3 Ota
volcano: 4 Fuji **5** Asama, Azuma, Oyama **6** Bandai, Chokai, Ontake **7** Adatara
Honus: 6 Wagner
hoo-__: 3 hah
__-hoo: 3 boo, yoo
hooch: 3 liq **5** booze, sauce **6** red-eye, whisky **7** bootleg, spirits, whiskey **9** moonshine **10** bathtub gin, intoxicant
holder: 3 jug
maker: 5 still
slug of ~: 4 belt
__ & Hooch: 6 Turner
hood: 3 ape **4** cowl, goon, mask, punk, thug, yegg **5** tough **6** outlaw **7** brigand, capuche, mobster, ruffian **8** gangster, hooligan, tough guy
combining form: 8 calyptri-, calyptro-
ender: 4 mold, wink
garment with a ~: 4 cowl **5** parka
in Britain: 3 yob **6** bonnet
it's under the ~: 5 motor **6** engine **10** power train
starter: 3 boy, god, man **4** baby, girl, lady **5** adult, angel, child, monks, saint, state **6** father, knight, matron, mother, parent, priest, sister **7** brother **8** bachelor **9** woman. wife
weapon: 3 gat **4** shiv **5** piece **6** roscoe
wearer: 4 monk **5** cobra, friar, viper
'hood: 4 area **8** vicinity
man in the ~: 5 mista
Hood: 2 mt. **3** mtn. **4** peak **5** Darla, mount **6** Thomas **8** mountain
locale: 6 Oregon **8** Cascades

___ Hood: 4 Fort 5 Mount, Robin
hooded: 9 cucullate
garment: 5 capot, grego, parka 6 anorak, capote, duffle
hooded ___: 3 top 4 crow, seal 7 warbler
hoodlum: 3 ape 4 goon, punk, thug 5 rowdy, tough 6 gunsel, outlaw, vandal 7 brigand, mobster, ruffian 8 criminal, gangster, hooligan 9 miscreant, racketeer 10 delinquent
Hoodlum Priest, The (1961 film)
cast: Keir Dullea, Larry Gates, Don Murray
director: Irvin Kershner
hoodoo: 4 jinx 5 curse, magic 7 bad luck 10 witchcraft
Hood, Robin
colleague: 4 Will 7 Scarlet 8 Scarlett 9 Alan-a-Dale, Friar Tuck 10 Allan-a-Dale, Little John
girlfriend: 10 Maid Marian
portrayer: 5 Errol
quaff: 3 ale
weapon: 3 bow 5 arrow
Hoods (1999 film)
cast: Joe Mantegna, Joe Pantoliano, Kevin Pollak
hood-shaped petal: 5 galea
Hood, Thomas: 4 poet 7 British
___ Hood, TX: 4 Fort
hoodwink: 3 con, gyp 4 bilk, burn, dupe, fake, fool, gull, have, hoax, nick, scam, snow, take 5 cheat, cozen, hocus, lie to, trick 6 befool, delude, euchre, fleece, lead on, outwit, suck in, take in 7 beguile, buffalo, deceive, defraud, mislead, pretend, swindle, two-time 8 outsmart, pettifog 9 bamboozle, disinform, four-flush, victimize
hoodwinking: 4 hoax, scam 5 fraud, guile, put-on, sting, trick 6 deceit, dupery, humbug, racket, rip-off 7 fast one, swindle 8 flimflam, trickery 9 chicanery, duplicity, imposture 10 hocus-pocus
hooey: 3 gas, rot 4 blah, bosh, bull, bunk, guff, jazz, jive, pooh, tosh, wind 5 bilge, fudge, hokum, prate, stuff, trash, tripe 6 bunkum, bushwa, drivel, footle, gabble, gammon, gibber, havers, hot air, humbug, jabber, jargon, kibosh, piffle 7 baloney, blarney, blather, blether, boloney, bushwah, eyewash, flannel, flubdub, fustian, garbage, hogwash, inanity, rubbish, twaddle 8 buncombe, claptrap, falderal, falderol, flimflam, flummery, folderal, folderol, nonsense, rhetoric, slipslop, tommyrot, trumpery 9 banana oil, gibberish, goofiness, kidstakes, moonshine, poppycock, rigmarole 10 balderdash, bilge water, codswallop, double-talk, flapdoodle, galimatias, Jabberwock, mumbo jumbo, rigamarole, taradiddle
hoof: 4 foot, step 6 unguis 8 ambulate
it: 4 walk 5 dance 8 tap-dance
worker: 5 shoer
___ hoof: 5 on the 6 cloven
hoofbeat: 4 clop
hoofed animal: 3 pig 5 horse, tapir
hoofer: 6 dancer 7 Astaire, O'Connor 9 Gene Kelly, tap dancer
Hooft, Gerardus 't: 8 Nobelist 9 physicist
Hooghly: 5 river
locale: 5 India
hoo-ha: 3 ado, din 4 fuss, stir, to-do 5 noise, tizzy 6 clamor, outcry, racket, ruckus, rumpus, uproar 8 foofaraw 9 commotion, maelstrom 10 excitement, hullabaloo, hurly-burly
hook: 3 bag, net 4 barb, bend, draw, gaff, grab, land, lift, lock, lure, trap, turn 5 angle, catch, curve, grasp, hitch, latch, punch, snare, swipe, tempt 6 allure, arrest, collar, enmesh, entice, entrap, fasten, immesh, inmesh, locate, pilfer, pull in, rope in, secure, tackle, Velcro 7 attract, capture, deceive, engross, ensnare, enthral, graplin, grapnel, grapple, insnare, inthral, win over 8 appeal to, convince, crotchet, entangle, enthrall, fastener, grapline, interest, inthrall, intrigue, inveigle, persuade 9 grapeline, stimulate, titillate 10 inducement
alternative: 3 jab 5 clasp
and eye: 5 latch 8 fastener
attachment: 4 bait, worm 5 snell
by ~ or by crook: 7 somehow, someway 8 someways
cheap ~: 4 nail
combining form: 3 onc- 4 onch-, onci-, onco- 5 oncho- 6 ancylo-, ankylo- 7 anchylo-
deliverer: 4 fist
destination, often: 5 rough
ender: 4 nose, worm
fishing ~: 4 gaff
get off the ~: 4 save 5 spare 6 rescue
grab with a ~: 4 gaff
in French: 4 croc
leaded ~: 5 drail
let off the ~: 5 unpeg 6 exempt 7 absolve 9 exonerate
off the ~: 4 free 6 exempt 7 cleared 9 acquitted 10 exonerated, vindicated
on: 3 add, tie 4 link, yoke 5 affix, hitch 6 attach, couple, fasten 7 connect
opposite: 5 slice
partner: 3 eye 6 ladder
prepare a ~: 4 bait
starter: 3 eye, pot, sky 4 bill, fish 6 button, tenter
target: 3 jaw
trolling ~: 5 drail
up: 3 tie 4 bind, dock, join, link, pair, yoke 5 annex, hitch, unite 6 attach, cohere, couple, fasten, instal, plug in 7 combine, conjoin, connect, harness, hitch on, install 8 assemble 9 affiliate 10 go partners
up again: 5 rerig
up with: 4 join, meet 5 marry, unite 10 amalgamate
hook ___: 4 bolt, shot 5 check
hook, ___ and sinker: 4 line
___ hook: 3 big, dog 4 boat, boot, bush, cant, deck, duck, gang, meat, rave, slip 5 bench, cabin, dough, gorge, kirby, latch, on the, screw, spoon 6 keeper, safety, sproat 7 crochet, pelican, pigtail, pruning
___-hook: 3 sky
Hook (1991 film)
cast: Dustin Hoffman, Bob Hoskins, Julia Roberts, Robin Williams
character: 3 Pan 4 Nana, Smee 5 Peter 6 pirate 10 Tinker Bell
director: Steven Spielberg
hookah: 4 pipe 9 water pipe
Hook, Captain
alma mater: 4 Eton
nemesis: 3 Pan 4 croc 5 Peter
sidekick: 4 Smee
hooked: 7 crooked 8 aquiline, obsessed 9 dependant, dependent, possessed 10 spellbound
anatomical part: 5 uncus
on: 4 into
up: 6 allied, banded, linked, united 7 unified 8 in league 9 in cahoots, plugged in 10 affiliated, integrated
hooked ___: 3 rug
Hooked on a Feeling (song) artist: B.J. Thomas, Blue Swede
Hooker: 6 Joseph 7 John Lee
Hooke, Robert: 7 British 9 physicist
Hooke's ___: 3 law
hook, line and ___: 6 sinker
Hook of Holland: 4 port
Hooks: 3 Jan 5 Kevin 6 Robert
___ Hooks: 5 Use No
hook-shaped: 6 hamate
Hook, Sidney: 11 philosopher
Hook, The (1963 film)
cast: Nick Adams, Kirk Douglas, Robert Walker Jr.
director: George Seaton
hookup: 3 tie 4 bond, link 6 scheme, system 7 circuit, liaison, linkage, linking, network 8 assembly, coupling, junction, juncture, vinculum 10 connecting, connection
hooky: 7 absence
play ~: 4 skip 6 go AWOL 7 abscond
playing ~: 4 AWOL 6 absent 7 missing
hooligan: 4 goon, hood, punk, thug 5 rogue, rowdy, tough 6 bad guy, bandit, gunsel, outlaw, rascal 7 hoodlum, mobster, ruffian 8 criminal, gangster, tough guy 10 delinquent, jackanapes
in Britain: 3 yob
hoolock: 6 animal, mammal 7 primate
relative: 3 ape 4 saki, titi 5 chimp, drill, jocko, lemur, loris, magot, orang, potto, shrew 6 aye-aye, baboon, Bandar, galago, gelada, gibbon, grivet, guenon, howler, langur, macaco, monkey, rhesus, uakari, vervet 7 colobus, gorilla, guereza, macaque, sapajou, siamang, tamarin, tarsier 8 bush baby, capuchin, mandrill, mangabey, marmoset, talapoin 9 orangutan 10 Barbary ape, chimpanzee, orangutang
hoop: 3 rim, toy 4 band, gird, loop, ring 5 skirt, wheel 6 basket, circle, wicket 7 earring 8 encircle, surround
edge: 3 rim
ender: 4 ster
group: 3 NBA 4 NCAA, WNBA
hanger: 3 net
like a ~: 4 oval 5 round 6 curved 8 circular
site: 3 ear
see also basketball
hoop ___: 4 back, iron, pine 5 skirt, snake
hoop-___: 4 de-do
___ hoop: 5 chime, truss 7 futtock
___-hoop: 5 cock-a 7 quarter
___-Hoop: 4 Hula
Hoop Dreams (1994 film) director: Steve James
Hooper: 4 Tobe 5 Harry
Hooper (1978 film)
cast: Sally Field, Burt Reynolds, Jan-Michael Vincent
director: Hal Needham
Hooperman dog: 6 Bijoux
hooper's concern: 6 barrel
hoopla: 3 ado 4 buzz, fuss, hype, stir, to-do 5 drama, furor 6 action, bustle, flurry, hubbub, lather, racket, ruckus, rumpus 7 buildup, emotion, fanfare, puffery 8 activity, ballyhoo, brouhaha, foofaraw, jamboree 9 commotion, fireworks, promotion, publicity 10 excitement, hullabaloo
Hoople: 4 Amos 5 Major
cry: 4 egad
hoopoe: 4 bird
home: 4 nest
hoops: 5 b-ball 7 baskets 10 basketball
hoopster: 5 cager
hooray: 3 olé, rah, yay 5 cheer 6 hot dog, yippee
for me: 4 ta-da 5 ta-dah
Hooray ___ Hollywood: 3 for
Hooray for ___: 4 Love
Hooray for Hazel (1966 song) artist: Tommy Roe
Hooray for Love (1935 film)
cast: Gene Raymond, Bill Robinson, Ann Sothern
director: Walter Lang
hoosegow: 3 can, jug, pen 4 cell, coop, jail, poky, stir 5 clink, pokey 6 cooler, lockup
Hoosier
see Indiana
Hoosier Poet, The: 5 Riley
Hoosiers (1986 film)
cast: Gene Hackman, Barbara Hershey, Dennis Hopper
hoot: 3 cry 4 bray, gibe, howl, jeer, jibe, kick, mock, roar, twit, yell 5 scorn, shout, whoop 6 deride, guffaw, holler, revile, scream, squawk 7 catcall, laugh at 8 particle, ridicule 10 rib-tickler, vociferate
and holler: 4 rant, rave, yell 5 go ape, storm 6 bellow 7 bluster, carry on, declaim 8 bloviate, freak out 9 raise Cain 10 hit the roof
at: 4 jeer, mock 5 scorn 6 deride
give a ~: 4 care, mind
hoot ___: 3 owl
___ hoot: 5 care a, give a
Hoot: 6 Gibson
hoot and ___: 6 holler
hootch: 5 booze 7 alcohol 9 moonshine
hootchy-kootchy: 5 dance
hooter: 3 owl
Hootie and the Blowfish
song: Hold My Hand (1994)
Let Her Cry (1995)
Only Wanna Be With You (1995)
hooting: 4 loud 5 harsh, noisy 9 clamorous
Hoover: 3 dam, vac 4 city, town 6 J. Edgar, vacuum 7 Herbert
competitor: 5 Kirby, Oreck 6 Eureka 10 Electrolux
locale: 7 Alabama
Hoover Dam
city near ~: 5 Vegas 8 Las Vegas
lake: 4 Mead
locale: 3 Nev. 6 Nevada
Hoover, Herbert: 9 president
alma mater: 8 Stanford
birthplace: 4 Iowa
former occupation: 8 engineer
former specialty: 6 mining
opponent: 5 Smith
V.P.: 6 Curtis
wife: 3 Lou
Hoover, J. Edgar
employee: 4 G-man
org.: 3 FBI
hooves, like some: 10 cloven. shod
hop: 4 gala, jump, leap, skip, tour, trip, verb 5 bound, dance, frisk, jaunt 6 bounce, hurdle, junket, spring 8 jump over, leap over 9 festivity
ballet ~: 9 temps levé
ender: 4 sack 6 scotch
off: 4 land 6 alight 7 descend 8 dismount
on: 5 board, catch 7 enplane, entrain
out of bed: 4 wake 5 arise, awake, get up, waken 6 awaken, wake up
over: 4 jump 5 bound 6 hurdle
starter: 3 bar, car, day 4 bell 5 hedge
to: 2 go 3 act, fly, hie, rip, run, zip 4 dart, dash, flit, move, race, rush, tear, zoom 5 scoot, speed 6 barrel, gallop, hasten, hustle, move it, rocket, scurry 7 get busy, pitch in,

quicken, scamper **9** shake a leg, skedaddle **10** get a move on
up: **4** goad, spur, stir **5** rouse, waken **6** arouse, bestir, excite, foment, incite, vivify **7** enliven, inflame, inspire, provoke **8** energize, inspirit, motivate **9** galvanize, instigate, stimulate **10** invigorate
hop __: **4** to it **6** clover
hop, __ and a jump: **4** skip
hop-__-thumb: **3** o'-my
__ hop: **3** bad **4** sock **5** bunny, lindy
__-hop: **3** hip, jet, job **4** bell **5** table **6** island
Hop __: **4** Sing **5** on Pop
Hop __!: **4** to it
__ Hop: **5** At the
Hopalong Cassidy star: **4** Boyd
hope: **4** goal, look, wish **5** dream **6** aspire, desire, expect, intent, resort, virtue **7** believe, longing, look for, promise, propose, purpose, thought **8** ambition, daydream, optimism, prospect, yearning **9** intention **10** anticipate, aspiration, expectancy, woolgather
companion: **5** faith **7** charity
ender: **3** ful **4** less **5** fully
for: **4** need, want, wish **5** crave **6** aspire, desire, expect **7** dream of **8** aspire to **10** anticipate
(for): **4** long, pine, wish **5** yearn
give false ~: **6** lead on
give up ~: **7** despair **9** lose heart
name meaning ~: **5** Nadia
Roman goddess of ~: **4** Spes
(to): **4** mean **6** aspire
trace of ~: **5** gleam
hope __: **5** chest
hope __ hope: **7** against
__ hope: **5** ray of, white **7** forlorn
Hope: **2** A.D. **3** Bob **5** Davis, Lange **7** Anthony
costar: **6** Crosby, Lamour
Hope __: **6** Floats **7** diamond
__ Hope: **5** Ryan's **7** Chicago
Hope, A.D.: **4** poet **10** Australian
Hope and Glory (1987 film)
cast: David Hayman, Sarah Miles, Derrick O'Connor
director: John Boorman
Hope, Bob: **5** actor **8** comedian
film: Alias Jesse James (1952)
Beau James (1957)
The Big Broadcast of 1938 (1938)
Casanova's Big Night (1954)
The Cat and the Canary (1939)
Caught in the Draft (1941)
The Facts of Life (1960)
Fancy Pants (1950)
The Ghost Breakers (1940)
The Great Lover (1949)
The Lemon Drop Kid (1951)
Let's Face It (1943)
Monsieur Beaucaire (1946)
My Favorite Blonde (1942)
My Favorite Brunette (1947)
My Favorite Spy (1951)
Never Say Die (1939)
Nothing but the Truth (1941)
The Paleface (1948)
The Princess and the Pirate (1944)
Road to Bali (1952)
The Road to Hong Kong (1962)
Road to Morocco (1942)
Road to Rio (1947)
Road to Singapore (1940)
Road to Utopia (1945)
Road to Zanzibar (1941)
The Seven Little Foys (1955)
Son of Paleface (1952)
Star Spangled Rhythm (1942)
Where There's Life ... (1947)
sponsor: **3** USO **8** Chrysler
Hope/Crosby
destination: **3** Rio **4** Bali **6** Utopia **7** Morocco **8** Hong Kong, Zanzibar **9** Singapore
locale: **4** road
Hope Floats (1998 film)
cast: Sandra Bullock, Harry Connick Jr., Gena Rowlands
director: Forest Whitaker
hopeful: **4** rosy **5** lucky **6** bright, likely, timely, upbeat **7** nominee, wishful **8** aspiring, desirous, possible, sanguine, trustful, trusting **9** applicant, candidate, confident, expectant, favorable, fortunate, inspiring, job-hunter, opportune, presuming, promising, well-timed **10** auspicious, beneficial, contestant, convenient, heartening, inspirited, optimistic, propitious
be ~: **4** rely **5** trust **6** assume, bank on **7** believe, count on, entrust, presume **8** depend on, gamble on, rely upon
hopefulness: **8** optimism
Hope Is the Thing With Feathers: **4** poem
author: **9** Dickinson
hopeless: **4** dark, grim, lost, vain **5** black, bleak, inept, no use, no-win, woful **6** abject, dismal, futile, gloomy, tragic, woeful **7** forlorn, useless **8** ill-fated, reckless, tragical, wretched **9** desperate, for naught, in despair, miserable, saddening **10** depressing, impossible, infeasible, irremedial, out of reach, unavailing, unfeasible, up the creek
case: **5** goner
Hopelessly Devoted to You (1978 song) artist: Olivia Newton-John
hopelessness: **7** despair, sadness **9** pessimism
__ Hopes: **4** High
hopes, dash: **6** dismay, thwart **7** let down **10** disappoint, dishearten
Hopewell: **4** city, town
locale: **8** Virginia
Hop-Frog author: Edgar Allan Poe
Hopi: **5** tribe **6** Indian **7** Amerind **8** language
prayer stick: **4** paho
sunken chamber: **4** kiva
hoping: **10** optimistic
__ hoping!: **5** Here's
Hopkin, Mary song: Those Were the Days (1968)
Hopkins: **2** Bo **5** Johns, Telma **6** Miriam **7** Anthony **9** Frederick
Hopkins, Anthony: **3** Sir **5** actor
film: 84 Charing Cross Road (1987)
Amistad (1997)
The Bounty (1984)
Bram Stoker's Dracula (1992)
The Elephant Man (1980)
Hannibal (2001)
Howards End (1992)
Instinct (1999)
The Mask of Zorro (1998)
Meet Joe Black (1998)
Nixon (1995)
Red Dragon (2002)
The Remains of the Day (1993)
The Road to Wellville (1994)
Shadowlands (1993)
The Silence of the Lambs (1991, AA)
Titus (1999)
Hopkins, Frederick: **8** Nobelist **10** biochemist
__ Hopkins Gallaudet: **6** Thomas
Hopkins, Gerard Manley: **4** poet **7** British
__ Hopkins Joyce: **5** Peggy
Hopkinsville: **4** city, town
locale: **8** Kentucky
hop-o'-my-__: **5** thumb
Hop on Pop author: Dr. Seuss
hopped up: **4** avid **5** angry, eager, hyper **6** fervid, on edge, stormy **7** anxious, burning, furious **8** vehement
hopper: **3** bin, 'roo **4** flea, frog, toad **6** funnel, rabbit **7** coal car **8** kangaroo **9** container **10** receptacle
filler: **4** coal
starter: **4** clod, frog, leaf, tree **5** grass
hopper __: **3** car **4** vent **5** barge, frame, light **6** dredge, window
__ hopper: **3** job **4** sand
Hopper: **5** Hedda **6** Dennis, DeWolf, Edward **7** William
Hopper, Dennis: **5** actor
film: Backtrack (1989)
Black Widow (1987)
Blue Velvet (1986)
Colors (1988)
Easy Rider (1969)
Hoosiers (1986)
Paris Trout (1991)
Red Rock West (1993)
Rumble Fish (1983)
Speed (1994)
True Romance (1993)
Waterworld (1995)
spouse: Michelle Phillips
Hopper, Edward: **6** artist **7** painter
Hopper, Hedda trademark: **3** hat
Hoppe, Willie game: **4** pool **9** billiards
hopping
animal: **4** hare **6** rabbit **8** kangaroo
be ~ mad: **4** boil, burn, fume, rage, rave, stew **6** blow up, see red, seethe
get ~: **3** fly, hie, run, zip **4** dart, dash, move, rush, tear **5** hurry, scoot **6** bustle, hasten, hustle, scurry **7** floor it, quicken **8** step on it **9** make haste, shake a leg **10** make tracks
mad: **4** sore **5** angry, cross, huffy, irate, livid, vexed **6** ireful **7** furious **9** irritated
hopple: **6** tether
hops
beverage: **3** ale **4** beer **5** stout **6** porter
kiln: **4** oast
stem: **4** bine
hopscotch: **4** game **5** potsy **6** wander
Hopscotch (1980 film)
cast: Ned Beatty, Glenda Jackson, Walter Matthau, Sam Waterston
director: Ronald Neame
hop, skip __ jump: **4** and a
hor.
not ~: **4** vert.
hora: **5** dance
Horace: **4** Mann, poet **5** Heidt, odist, Roman **7** Greeley, Gregory, McMahon, Walpole **8** satirist
author: George Sand, Pierre Corneille
contemporary: **4** Ovid
work: Ars Poetica
Epodes
Odes
Satires
Horae Lyricae author: Isaac Watts
Horae, one of the: **4** Dike **5** Irene **7** Eunomia
__ hora es?: **3** Qué
horal: **6** hourly
horas, 24: **3** día
Horatian __: **3** ode
Horatio: **4** Dane **5** Alger, Gates **6** Nelson
horde: **3** mob **4** army, bevy, gang, herd, host, many, mass, pack **5** crowd, crush, drove, loads, press, swarm, tribe, troop **6** legion, myriad, rabble, throng **7** legions, numbers **9** gathering, multitude
member: **3** Hun
__ Horde: **6** Golden
hordeolum: **3** sty
Horeb: **4** peak **5** mount **8** mountain
horehound: **4** herb **5** candy, plant **6** flower
Horgan, Paul: **6** author, writer
horizon: **5** range, reach, scope, vista **6** extent **7** compass, purview, setting **9** viewpoint
be on the ~: **6** impend **8** forebode, threaten
fall below the ~: **3** set
on the ~: **4** afar, nigh **5** ahead **8** imminent
__ horizon: **4** gyro **5** event, false, radio **7** visible
Horizon: **3** car **4** auto **8** Plymouth
__ Horizon: **4** Lost
horizontal: **4** flat **5** level, plane, prone **6** smooth **8** straight **9** accumbent, prostrate, recumbent
band: **6** fascia
bar: **4** rail **5** event
extent: **5** scope **7** breadth
get ~: **4** laze
opposite: **4** vert. **8** vertical
supporter: **4** beam **5** joist **6** rafter **8** crossbar **10** crosspiece
horizontal __: **3** bar **5** union
horizontally: **4** flat **6** across **10** side to side
Hormel
competitor: **6** Armour
product: **4** Spam
Hormisdas: **4** pope **7** pontiff
hormone: **4** ACTH **5** auxin, kinin **6** estrin, ligand **7** insulin
combining form: **5** kinin-
producer: **5** gland
Hormuz: **3** str. **6** strait
nation on the Strait of ~: **4** Iran
horn: **4** tuba **5** bugle, cornu, pager, phone **6** antler, beeper, claxon, cornet, honker, klaxon **7** helicon, trumpet **8** auto part, trombone **9** euphonium, telephone **10** cornucopia, sousaphone
accessory: **4** mute **6** damper
big ~: **4** tuba **9** euphonium **10** sousaphone
blow one's own ~: **4** brag, crow **5** boast, vaunt **7** talk big
combining form: **4** -corn **5** cerat-, kerat- **6** cerato-, kerato-
crescent-moon ~: **4** cusp
effect: **6** wah-wah
ender: **4** beam, bill, book, pipe, pout, tail, worm, wort **6** blende
English ~: **3** cor **4** reed
get on the ~: **4** buzz, call, dial, ring **5** phone **6** call up, dial up, ring up **7** contact **9** telephone
Greek drinking ~: **6** rhyton
harsh ~: **6** claxon, klaxon
hit the ~: **4** blow, honk
in: **3** pry **5** crash, enter **6** impose, meddle, tamper **7** intrude, obtrude **8** trespass **9** insinuate, interfere, interpose, interrupt, intervene
in Latin: **5** cornu
man with a ~: **5** Harpo **6** Al Hirt, Alpert **7** Satchmo **9** Armstrong, Harpo Marx
nautical: **6** typhon
orchestra ~: **4** alto
play the ~: **4** blow, toot
rims: **7** glasses **8** cheaters **10** spectacles
sound: **4** beep, honk
sound the ~: **4** beep, blow, honk, toot
starter: **3** big, fog, ink, leg, sax, tin

4 buck, bull, long, shoe 5 green, prong, short, stink
horn __: 5 chair, poppy, shell 6 silver, timber
horn-__: 3 mad 4 rims 6 spread
horn-__ glasses: 6 rimmed
__ horn: 3 air 4 alto, bass, bull, hand, long, post, ram's 5 mossy, tenor 6 basset, French, powder, saddle 7 English, hunting
__ Horn: 4 Cape 6 Dorset, Golden, Trader
hornbeam: 4 tree 5 shrub
relative: 5 alder, birch, hazel
hornbill: 4 bird
home: 4 nest
hornblende: 7 mineral
Hornblower, Horatio: 7 captain
milieu: 3 sea 5 ocean
wife: 5 Maria
Horn Blows at Midnight, The (1945 film)
cast: Jack Benny, Dolores Moran, Alexis Smith
director: Raoul Walsh
__-horn coral: 5 stag's
Horne: 4 Lena 5 James 7 Marilyn
solo: 4 aria
horned __: 3 owl 4 frog, lark, pout, toad 5 poppy, viper, whiff 6 lizard, scully
Horned Frogs' sch.: 3 TCU
horned giraffe in heraldry: 10 camelopard
Horne, Lena: 6 singer
film: Cabin in the Sky (1943) Stormy Weather (1943) Ziegfeld Follies (1946)
Horne, Marilyn: 4 diva 5 mezzo 6 singer 7 soprano
specialty: 4 aria 5 opera
Horner: 3 Bob 4 Jack 5 James
Horner, Jack: 5 eater
last words: 3 am I
treat: 3 pie
hornet: 3 bug 4 pest, wasp 6 insect 7 stinger
home: 4 nest
kin: 4 wasp
Hornet: 3 AMC, car 4 auto 6 Hudson
Hornet rival: 3 Cav, Mav, Net, Sun 4 Buck, Bull, Hawk, Heat, Jazz, King, Spur 5 Knick, Laker, Magic, Pacer, Sixer, Sonic 6 Celtic, Nugget, Piston, Raptor, Rocket, Wizard 7 Clipper, Grizzly, Warrior 8 Cavalier, Maverick 10 SuperSonic, Timberwolf
Hornets: 4 five, team
home: 9 Charlotte
org.: 3 NBA
sport: 10 basketball
hornet's nest: 3 ado, fix 4 mess, stir 5 furor 6 clamor, pickle, rumpus, scrape, tumult, uproar 7 travail, trouble, turmoil 8 quagmire, quandary
__ Hornet, The: 5 Green
Horney: 5 Karen
hornless: 7 acerous
cattle: 5 muley 6 mulley
horn of __: 6 plenty
hornpipe: 4 wind 5 dance, music 6 alboka 8 clarinet
horn-rims: 7 glasses 8 cheaters 10 eyeglasses
horns
Greek drinking ~: 5 rhyta
lock ~: 5 argue, clash 6 debate 7 compete, contend, quarrel, wrangle 8 conflict, struggle 9 have words, square off
Hornsby: 5 Bruce 6 Rogers
nickname: 5 Rajah
Hornsby and the Range, Bruce
song: Mandolin Rain (1987) The Valley Road (1988) The Way It Is (1986)
hornswoggle: 3 con 4 dupe, fool, gull, have, snow 5 cheat 6 suck in, take in 8 hoodwink 9 bamboozle
Hornung, Paul sport: 8 football
hornworm: 3 bug 6 insect
horologist: 7 jeweler 10 watchmaker
horology: 7 science
study: 4 time
horoscope: 5 chart 8 forecast 10 prediction
do a ~: 4 cast
__ horoscope: 5 natal
Horovitz, Israel: 10 playwright
Horowitz, Vladimir: 7 pianist
horrendous: 4 foul, grim, poor 5 awful, lousy, scary, woful 6 crumby, crummy, dismal, grisly, horrid, odious, rotten, unholy, woeful 7 accurst, baleful, baneful, beastly, doleful, fearful, ghastly, heinous, hideous, ungodly 8 accursed, dreadful, God-awful, grievous, gruesome, horrible, inferior, shameful, stinking, terrible, wretched 9 abhorrent, appalling, atrocious, defective, execrable, frightful, insidious, loathsome, miserable, monstrous, offensive, revolting 10 abominable, despicable, detestable, disastrous, petrifying
horrible: 4 dark, dire, foul, grim, poor, ugly, vile 5 awful, cruel, dread, gross, lousy, lurid, nasty, woful 6 crumby, crummy, dismal, grisly, odious, rotten, woeful 7 accurst, baleful, baneful, beastly, doleful, dreaded, fearful, ghastly, heinous, hellish, hideous, macaber, macabre, satanic, squalid, ungodly 8 accursed, dreadful, God-awful, grievous, gruesome, inferior, shameful, shocking, stinking, terrible, terrific, wretched 9 abhorrent, appalling, atrocious, defective, execrable, frightful, insidious, loathsome, miserable, monstrous, nefarious, obnoxious, offensive, repellent, revolting, satanical 10 abominable, despicable, detestable, disastrous, formidable, horrendous, outrageous, petrifying, scandalous, terrifying, unpleasant
horrid: 4 dire, evil, foul, grim, ugly, vile 5 awful, nasty, yucky 6 grisly, morbid, odious 7 ghastly, hateful, hideous, noisome, satanic, squalid, ungodly, vicious 8 dreadful, gruesome, terrible 9 appalling, atrocious, frightful, offensive, repugnant, revolting, satanical, unsightly 10 abominable, detestable, disgusting, petrifying, unpleasant
horrific: 4 dire 5 awful, weird 7 fearful 8 dreadful, gruesome, shocking, terrific 9 appalling, execrable 10 formidable
horrified: 6 aghast
horrify: 5 alarm, appal, chill, scare, shake, shock 6 appall, offend, revolt 7 disgust, petrify, terrify 8 affright, frighten, unstring 9 terrorize 10 scandalize, scare stiff
horrifying: 4 gory 5 lurid, scary 6 grisly 7 fearful, ghastly, heinous, hideous 8 gruesome, shocking, terrible 9 appalling, atrocious, monstrous 10 deplorable, petrifying
horripilating: 4 eery 5 eerie, scary 6 creepy, spooky 7 bizarre, macabre, strange, uncanny 8 haunting 9 grotesque
Horro: 3 cow 4 bull 6 bovine, cattle
Horrocks: 4 Jane
horror: 4 fear 5 alarm, dread 6 fright, phobia, terror 7 monster 8 aversion, enormity 9 revulsion, trepidity 10 abhorrence, repugnance
cause ~: 5 appal 6 appall 7 horrify, terrify 8 frighten 9 terrorize
exclamation: 2 oy 3 ack, ick, ugh 4 yuck 5 yecch
like ~ films: 4 eery, gory 5 eerie
horror __: 4 film 5 movie, story
Horrors!: 3 ugh 4 oh my, oh no
horror-struck: 6 aghast, scared 7 shocked, stunned 8 appalled 10 speechless
hors d'__: 4 état 6 oeuvre
hors de __: 6 combat
hors d'oeuvre: 4 whet 5 snack, taste 6 canapé, caviar 7 caviare 9 appetizer
garnish: 5 caper
Hawaiian ~: 4 pupu
spread: 4 pâté 5 liver
horse: 3 bay, cob, dun, nag, pet 4 Arab, barb, colt, foal, hack, jade, mare, moke, plug, pony, roan 5 bronc, filly, mount, neddy, pacer, paint, pinto, steed 6 animal, bronco, cayuse, dapple, dobbin, equine, gee-gee, hunter, jumper, mammal, Morgan, mudder, sorrel, tarpan 7 Arabian, bobtail, broncho, charger, courser, cow pony, gelding, hackney, mustang, palfrey, piebald, trooper, trotter 8 bangtail, buckskin, chestnut, claybank, destrier, eohippus, galloper, palomino, polo pony, Shetland, skewbald, stallion 9 appaloosa, broodmare, Percheron 10 Clydesdale, Indian pony, Lippizaner
agile ~: 7 cow pony
ailment: 5 colic
ancestor: 8 eohippus
and wagon: 3 rig
ankle: 4 hock
Arabian-descended ~: 7 mustang
Arabian-related ~: 4 barb
armor: 5 barde
around: 4 joke, play 5 act up, caper 6 cavort, gambol
Australian ~: 4 moke 5 neddy, waler
Austrian ~: 10 Lippizaner
back the wrong ~: 4 fail, lose
bi-colored ~: 7 piebald 8 skewbald
blanket: 5 manta
brake: 4 rein
carriage ~: 7 hackney
cavalry ~: 7 charger, trooper
charley ~: 4 kink 5 cramp, crick, spasm
chestnut: 6 conker
clip a ~ mane: 5 roach
color: 3 bay, dun 5 pinto 8 chestnut
combining form: 4 hipp- 5 hippo- 6 -hippus
command: 3 gee, haw 4 whoa 6 giddap 7 giddyap, giddyup
could eat a ~: 7 starved 8 ravenous, starving
dark ~: 8 opponent, underdog 9 candidate 10 competitor, contestant
doctor: 3 DVM, vet
draft ~: 9 Percheron 10 Clydesdale
dressage ~: 10 Lippizaner
eat like a ~: 5 chomp, gorge 10 gormandize
ender: 3 fly, man, men 4 back, hair, hide, mint, play, race, shoe, tail, weed, whip 5 flesh, laugh, leech, power, woman, women 6 racing, radish 8 feathers
farm ~: 6 dobbin
father: 4 sire, stud
female: 3 dam 4 mare 5 filly
foot: 4 hoof
fresh team of ~ s: 5 relay
gear: 3 bit 4 rein 6 bridle, halter, saddle
genus: 5 equus
get on a ~: 4 ride 6 gallop, travel 7 journey
golden coat ~: 8 palomino
grayish-brown ~: 3 dun
groom a ~: 5 curry
group of ~ s: 4 span, team
guiding rope: 5 longe
hair: 4 mane
handicap: 6 impost
handler: 5 groom
harness racing ~: 5 pacer 7 trotter
height measure: 4 hand
high-spirited ~: 5 steed
hock: 5 ankle
home: 4 barn 6 corral, stable
horse sport: 4 polo 6 racing
Indian ~: 6 cayuse
in horse racing: 3 dam 4 mare, sire 5 filly, pacer 6 maiden, mudder 7 trotter
jump: 6 curvet
jumping ~: 6 hunter
laugh: 4 howl, roar 6 guffaw
left, to a ~: 3 haw
leg part: 6 gaskin
like a ~: 5 maned 6 hoofed
male ~: 8 stallion
marking: 5 blaze
meal: 3 hay 4 feed, oats 6 fodder
noise: 4 clop 5 neigh, snort 6 whinny
of a different color: 3 new 5 novel
old ~: 3 nag 4 hack, jade, moke, plug
on one's high ~: 7 haughty 8 up in arms
opera: 5 drama, oater
pace: 4 gait, lope, pace, trot 6 canter, gallop
part of a ~ collar: 4 hame
player hangout: 3 OTB 5 track
race: 4 pace, trot 5 derby
ranch ~: 7 cow pony
range ~: 6 cayuse
reddish-brown ~: 3 bay 6 sorrel 8 chestnut
relative: 3 ass 4 mule 5 burro, kiang, zebra 6 donkey, onager, quagga 7 jackass 8 chigetai 9 dziggetai
restrainer: 5 trave
rider: 6 jockey 10 equestrian
right, to a ~: 3 gee
rump: 5 croup
saddle ~: 4 hack, pony 5 mount, steed 7 hackney, palfrey 9 Appaloosa
sense: 5 savvy 6 acumen, brains, reason, wisdom 7 insight 8 judgment, prudence, sagacity 9 ingenuity, reasoning, sharpness 10 astuteness, perception, shrewdness
short-legged ~: 3 cob
small ~: 4 pony 8 polo pony 10 Indian pony
soldier: 6 lancer
soldiers: 7 cavalry
sometimes: 5 loper
spotted ~: 5 paint, pinto 6 dapple
starter: 3 saw, sea, war 4 cock, fire, pack, race, stud, work 5 hobby 7 clothes
steppes ~: 6 tarpan
stocky ~: 3 cob
stopper: 4 whoa
stubborn ~: 6 balker
swift ~: 4 Arab, barb 7 Arabian, courser
tend the ~: 5 brush, groom
thick-set ~: 3 cob
tie a ~: 5 hitch 6 tether
tooth: 4 tush
trade: 4 deal 9 negotiate
trainer's aid: 4 whip
TV talking ~: 4 Mr. Ed
where ~ races start: 4 gate
white mane ~: 8 palomino
wild ~: 5 bronc 6 bronco, brumby,

ladino, tarpan **7** broncho, mustang
young: 4 colt, foal **5** filly
see also horses and riders
horse __: 3 fly **4** balm, bean, clam, corn, race, rake, show, tail **5** block, brass, conch, laugh, opera, sense, trade **6** around, collar, marine, nettle, parlor, pistol, racing, trader **7** gentian, stinger
horse __ different color: 3 of a
horse-__: 5 coper, faced **6** collar **7** trading
__ horse: 3 cow, sea **4** cart, dark, dawn, dray, high, iron, long, pole, post, salt, side **5** coach, light, paint, river, stake, stock, trial, wheel, white **6** pommel, saddle, Trojan **7** Arabian, charley, cutting, harness, painted, quarter, rocking, shaving, walking
__ horse!: 4 Get a
__ Horse: 4 Dark **5** Crazy **6** Little, Winged, Wooden
horse and __: 4 cart **5** buggy
horse-and-buggy: 3 era **5** passé **8** obsolete, outmoded
users: 5 Amish
__ horseback: 5 man on
horse chestnut tree: 7 buckeye
horse doctor, name meaning: 8 Marshall
horse-donkey offspring: 5 hinny
horse-drawn
carriage: 6 calash, fiacre, hansom **7** caleche
vehicle of India: 5 tonga
horsefeathers: 3 gas, rot **4** blah, bosh, bull, bunk, guff, jazz, jive, pooh, tosh **5** bilge, fudge, hokum, hooey, prate, stuff, trash, tripe **6** bunkum, bushwa, drivel, footle, gabble, gammon, gibber, havers, hot air, humbug, jabber, jargon, kibosh, piffle **7** baloney, blarney, blather, blether, boloney, bushwah, eyewash, flannel, flubdub, fustian, garbage, hogwash, inanity, rubbish, twaddle **8** buncombe, claptrap, falderal, falderol, flimflam, flummery, folderal, folderol, nonsense, slipslop, tommyrot, trumpery **9** banana oil, gibberish, kidstakes, moonshine, poppycock, rigmarole **10** applesauce, balderdash, bilge water, codswallop, double-talk, flapdoodle, galimatias, Jabberwock, mumbo jumbo, rigamarole, taradiddle
Horsefeathers!: 3 bah **5** nerts, nertz, pshaw
Horse Feathers (1932 film)
cast: Chico Marx, Groucho Marx, Harpo Marx, Zeppo Marx, Thelma Todd
director: Norman Z. McLeod
horsehair: 6 fabric
__-Horse Harry Lee: 5 Light
Horsehead: 6 Nebula
horsehide: 4 ball **8** baseball
Horse in the Gray Flannel Suit, The (1968 film)
cast: Diane Baker, Lloyd Bochner, Dean Jones
horselaugh: 6 guffaw
horseless carriage: 3 car **4** auto **7** vehicle **10** automobile
horse lover, name meaning: 6 Philip
horseman: 5 groom, rider **6** cowboy, gaucho, hussar, jockey, knight, lancer, ostler **7** Cossack, cowgirl, dragoon, equerry, hostler **8** buckaroo, cavalier **10** cavalryman, equestrian
Hungarian ~: 6 hussar
Mexican ~: 6 charro
Horseman of the Apocalypse: 3 War **5** Death **6** Famine **10** Pestilence
Horseman Pass By author: Larry McMurtry
horsemen, army: 3 cav. **7** cavalry
horsemint: 5 plant **6** flower
horse of a different __: 5 color
horseplay: 3 fun **5** prank, sport **6** antics, capers, pranks **7** fooling, hijinks **8** clowning
like ~: 5 rowdy
horsepower: 5 drive, force, power, punch, vigor **6** effort, energy, muscle **7** impetus, potency, voltage **8** dynamism, strength **9** toughness
booster: 5 turbo
coiner: 4 Watt
fraction: 4 watt
__ horsepower: 5 brake, shaft **6** boiler
horse protection
name meaning ~: 8 Rosamond, Rosamund
horse-pulled vehicle: 4 cart, dray **5** buggy **8** carriage
horse race: 4 pace **5** Derby **7** Belmont **9** Preakness
horse racing: 5 sport
announcer: 6 caller
area: 4 rail **5** track **7** paddock
bet: 4 show **5** place **6** exacta, parlay **8** perfecta, quinella, trifecta
devotee: 8 railbird
horse: 3 dam **4** mare, sire **5** filly, pacer **6** maiden, mudder **7** trotter
measure: 4 mile **6** length **7** furlong
term: 3 dam, win **4** mare, nose, odds, show, sire, tout, turf **5** filly, groom, pacer, place, purse, silks, sulky **6** caller, exacta, length, maiden, mudder, odds-on, parlay, sloppy **7** furlong, inquiry, paddock, scratch, stretch, trotter **8** blinkers, dead heat, long shot, perfecta, post time, quinella, railbird, trifecta
tie: 8 dead heat
winnings: 5 purse
worker: 5 groom
horseradish: 5 spice **6** relish **9** condiment
horses: 5 stock **9** livestock
group of ~: 4 team
hold one's ~: 4 wait
play the ~: 3 bet
__ Horses: 4 Wild **5** Crazy
Horses and Men author: Sherwood Anderson
horses and riders
Achilles: 7 Xanthus
Alexander the Great: 10 Bucephalus
Autry, Gene: 8 Champion
Bellerophon: 7 Pegasus
Ben-Hur: 5 Rigel **6** Altair **7** Antares **9** Aldebaran
Caligula: 9 Incitatus
Cisco Kid: 6 Diablo
Custer, George: 8 Comanche
Evans, Dale: 10 Buttermilk
Grant, Ulysses S.: 10 Cincinnati
Lee, Robert E.: 9 Traveller
Lone Ranger: 6 Silver
Mix, Tom: 4 Tony
Muhammad: 7 Alborak
Napoleon: 7 Marengo
Odin: 8 Sleipner, Sleipnir
Quixote, Don: 9 Rocinante, Rosinante
Rogers, Roy: 7 Trigger
Rogers, Will: 8 Soapsuds
Sigurd: 5 Grani
Tonto: 5 Scout
Turpin, Dick: 9 Black Bess
Wellington, Duke of: 10 Copenhagen
horseshoe: 5 charm **6** amulet
place: 4 hoof
projection: 4 calk
sound: 4 clop
horseshoe __: 4 arch, back, crab **6** magnet
__ Horseshoe: 6 Golden
Horseshoe Falls locale: 6 Canada
horseshoer: 5 smith **7** farrier **10** blacksmith
horseshoes: 4 game **5** sport
game like ~: 6 quoits
play ~: 4 toss
score: 6 leaner, ringer
sound: 5 clang
horseshoe-shaped fastener: 5 U-bolt
horse's mouth: 6 expert, origin, source **9** authority **10** originator
Horse's Mouth, The (1958 film)
cast: Sir Alec Guinness, Renee Houston, Kay Walsh
director: Ronald Neame
Horse's Mouth, The author: 4 Cary
horse's neck: 5 drink **8** beverage, cocktail
ingredient: 6 whisky **9** ginger ale, lemon peel
horsetail: 4 rush **5** plant
__ Horse, The: 4 Iron, Pale **6** Wooden
__-horse town: 3 one
horse-trade: 4 deal **6** haggle
horsewhip: 4 flog, lash, whip **5** flail **7** scourge **10** flagellate
Horse Whisperer, The: 4 film **5** novel
author: Nicholas Evans
cast: Sam Neill, Robert Redford, Kristin Scott Thomas, Dianne Wiest
director: Robert Redford
Horse With No Name, A (1972 song)
artist: America
Horse Without a Head, The (1963 film)
cast: Jean-Pierre Aumont, Herbert Lom, Leo McKern
director: Don Chaffey
horsewoman: 5 rider **6** jockey
Horsley: 3 Lee
Horst: 5 Louis **7** Störmer **8** Buchholz
horsy: 6 equine
Hortense: 8 Calisher
horticultural art: 6 bonsai
horticulture: 6 botany **7** science
study: 6 fruits, plants **7** gardens **10** vegetables
horticulturist: 8 gardener
mixture: 5 mulch
topic: 6 botany
Horton: 5 Foote, Peter, Smith **6** Johnny, Robert **9** Who hearer
creator: 5 Seuss
Horton, Edward Everett: 5 actor
film: The Gay Divorcee (1934)
The Great Garrick (1937)
Holiday (1930)
Lady on a Train (1945)
Lost Horizon (1937)
San Diego, I Love You (1944)
Summer Storm (1944)
Top Hat (1935)
The Way to Love (1933)
Horton Hatches the Egg author: Dr. Seuss
Horton Hears a Who author: Dr. Seuss
Horton, Johnny
song: The Battle of New Orleans (1959)
North to Alaska (1960)
Sink the Bismarck (1960)
Horus: 3 god **8** Egyptian
parent of ~: 4 Isis **6** Osiris
Horvath, Odon von: 6 German **10** playwright
Horvitz, Robert: 8 Nobelist
Hosain, Attia: 6 Indian, writer
hosanna: 4 hymn, laud, pean **5** paean **6** praise **8** hallejah **10** exaltation, hallelujah
hose: 4 pipe, tube **5** cheat, socks, water **6** drench, nylons, siphon, syphon, tights, tubing **7** anklets, argyles, legwear, mislead, wet down **8** flimflam, footwear, lingerie, wash down **9** stockings
plastic: 3 PVC
use a ~: 3 wet **4** wash **5** douse, dowse, spray, water
see also hosiery
__ hose: 4 fire, half **5** panty, trunk **7** support
Hosea: 4 book **7** Prophet
follower: 4 Joel
in the Douay Bible: 4 Osee
preceder: 6 Daniel
wife of ~: 5 Gomer
hosiery: 4 sock, tabi **5** socks **6** anklet, argyle, bootee, bootie, nylons **7** anklets, footlet, woolens **8** crew sock, fishnets, knee-high, knee-sock, stocking, tube sock **9** ankle sock, kneehighs, stockings **10** bobbysocks, thigh-highs
brand: 4 Peds **5** L'eggs
fabric: 5 lisle, nylon
filler: 3 leg **4** foot
holder: 6 garter
item: 6 anklet
Japanese ~: 4 tabi
like some ~: 5 meshy, sheer
measure: 6 denier
mishap: 3 run **4** kink, snag
part: 3 toe **4** heel
shade: 4 ecru, nude **5** taupe
hosing: 5 abuse **6** con job **7** calumny **8** reproach **10** debasement, impugnment
Hoskins, Bob: 5 actor
film: Cousin Bette (1998)
Hook (1991)
The Long Good Friday (1981)
Mermaids (1990)
Nixon (1995)
Sweet Liberty (1986)
Who Framed Roger Rabbit (1988)
role: 4 Smee
Hosni: 7 Mubarak
hosp.
see hospital
hospice: 5 lodge **6** hostel, imaret **9** infirmary
hospitable: 4 kind, open, warm **6** genial, kindly, social **7** cordial **8** amenable, amicable, friendly, generous, gracious, obliging, sociable **9** bountiful, convivial, courteous, receptive, welcoming **10** accessible, charitable, gregarious, neighborly, open-minded, responsive
be ~: 4 host **5** ask in, ask up **6** invite
not ~: 5 aloof, stony **6** chilly, frosty **7** hostile **10** unfriendly
hospital: 6 clinic **7** sick bay **9** infirmary **10** sanatorium
amt.: 2 cc.
Brit. ~ coverage: 3 NHI
cart: 6 gurney
delivery: 4 baby
device: 2 IV
do a animal ~ job: 4 spay
employee: 2 dr., MD, RN **3** EMT, LPN **5** nurse **6** intern **7** interne, orderly **8** resident
extension: 4 wing
facility: 2 ER, IC, OR **3** CCU, ICU, MRI **4** ward **5** pre-op
furniture: 3 bed
popular ~ name: 5 Mercy
reference: 3 PDR **5** chart
routine: 6 rounds
scourge: 5 staph
sign: 5 quiet
supply: 4 sera **5** blood, drugs, serum **8** medicine
test: 3 ECG, EEG, EKG

wear: 4 gown
hospital __: 3 bed 4 ship 5 light, train 6 corner
__ hospital: 5 field
__ Hospital: 7 General
hospital-cornered: 4 neat
hospitality: 5 cheer 6 warmth 7 welcome 8 kindness
recipient: 5 guest
show one's ~: 9 entertain
hospitality __: 4 room 5 suite
hospitalization: 9 treatment
hospitalize: 5 lay up 7 confine
Hospital Sketches author: Louisa May Alcott
Hospital, The (1971 film)
cast: Barnard Hughes, Diana Rigg, George C. Scott
director: Arthur Hiller
hoss: 5 mount 6 cayuse
Hoss: 9 Radbourne 10 Cartwright
brother: 3 Joe 4 Adam 9 Little Joe
father: 3 Ben
host: 2 MC 3 mob 4 army, mass, raft, slew 5 array, bunch, cater, crowd, emcee, flock, horde, ocean, owner, press, swarm, troop 6 anchor, keeper, legion, myriad, throng 7 manager, numbers, receive 8 hotelier 9 entertain, innkeeper, moderator, multitude, profusion 10 proprietor
a party: 5 throw
counterpart: 5 guest
ender: 3 age, ess
generous ~: 5 sater
music-show ~: 2 DJ, VJ 6 deejay, veejay
of: 6 divers, myriad, umteen, untold 7 copious, profuse, umpteen 8 abundant, manifold, numerous, umpsteen 9 bountiful, countless, quite a few
play ~: 5 ask in, emcee, see in, treat 9 entertain
preference: 5 A-list
request: 4 RSVP
roast ~: 2 MC 5 emcee, Friar
hostage: 4 gage, pawn 6 surety 7 captive 8 internee, leverage, prisoner, security
taker: 6 captor
take ~ s: 6 abduct
Hostage, The author: Brendan Behan
hostel: 3 inn 4 khan 5 hotel, lodge 6 bethel 7 hospice, lodging, shelter 8 lodgment 10 guesthouse
Turkish ~: 6 imaret
__ hostel: 5 elder, youth
hosteler: 9 innkeeper
hostelry: 3 inn 5 hotel, lodge 6 tavern 7 lodging
hostess
bar ~: 5 B-girl
Japanese ~: 6 geisha
Washington ~: 5 Mesta
Hostess with the Mostes': 5 Mesta
hostile: 3 icy, ill 4 cold, cool, hard, mean 5 angry, catty, chill, enemy, nasty, onery, stony, surly 6 averse, bitter, chilly, malign, ornery, stoney, sullen 7 adverse, glacial, hateful, hawkish, martial, ominous, opposed, scrappy, warlike 8 clashing, contrary, fighting, inimical, militant, opposing, spiteful, venomous, viperous, virulent 9 bellicose, malicious, oppugnant, rancorous, resentful, truculent, vitriolic, withdrawn 10 forbidding, jingoistic, malevolent, pugnacious, unamicable, unfriendly, unsociable
be ~ to: 4 hate 5 abhor 6 detest, loathe
in a ~ manner: 5 icily
look: 5 glare
make ~: 9 disaffect 10 antagonize
one: 3 foe 5 enemy
reaction: 4 flak 5 flack 6 outcry 7 dissent, protest 9 criticism
to: 3 con 6 down on 8 opposing 10 at odds with
hostilities: 3 war 7 warfare 8 fighting
begin ~: 5 set on, storm 6 attack, invade, strike 7 set upon
break in ~: 5 truce 9 cease-fire
engaged in ~: 5 at war
hostility: 3 ire, war 4 feud, hate 5 anger, fight, spite, venom 6 animus, battle, enmity, hatred, malice, rancor, spleen 7 discord, dislike, ill will, tension 8 aversion, bad blood, conflict, distaste, friction, meanness 9 animosity, antipathy, nastiness, virulence 10 abhorrence, aggression, antagonism, bitterness, contention, opposition, resentment
feel ~ toward: 4 hate 5 scorn 6 detest, loathe 7 deplore, despise, dislike 8 execrate 9 abominate
hostler: 8 horseman
Host, vessel containing the: 3 pix, pyx
hot: 3 hip, mad, red 4 ired, live, sore, warm 5 angry, cross, eager, fiery, huffy, irate, livid, lucky, riled, sharp, spicy, wroth, zesty 6 ardent, baking, erotic, fervid, fuming, heated, ireful, on fire, peeved, piping, piqued, raging, raving, spicey, steamy, stolen, stormy, strong, sultry, sweaty, toasty, torrid, touchy, trendy, tropic 7 blazing, boiling, burning, enraged, excited, faddish, febrile, fervent, flaming, flaring, furious, intense, in vogue, on a roll, peppery, piquant, popular, pungent, ranting, searing, sensual, smoking, summery, sweltry, thermal, violent, zealous 8 agitated, broiling, choleric, feverish, incensed, in demand, inflamed, maddened, outraged, ovenlike, parching, roasting, scalding, sizzling, spirited, steaming, tropical, up-to-date, valuable, vehement, wrathful 9 au courant, calescent, impetuous, indignant, irascible, irritable, irritated, lubricous, on a streak, resentful, scorching, splenetic 10 all the rage, blistering, equatorial, freaked out, infuriated, lascivious, marketable, much-wanted, passionate, sweltering
air: 3 gas, rot 4 blah, bosh, bull, bunk, guff, jazz, jive, pooh, talk, tosh 5 bilge, fudge, hokum, hooey, mouth, prate, steam, stuff, trash, tripe 6 bunkum, bushwa, drivel, footle, gabble, gammon, gibber, havers, humbug, jabber, jargon, kibosh, piffle 7 baloney, blarney, blather, blether, bluster, boloney, bombast, bushwah, eyewash, flannel, flubdub, fustian, garbage, hogwash, inanity, malarky, rubbish, twaddle 8 babbling, buncombe, claptrap, falderal, falderol, flimflam, flummery, folderal, folderol, malarkey, nonsense, rhetoric, slipslop, tommyrot, trumpery 9 banana oil, gasconade, gibberish, kidstakes, loquacity, moonshine, poppycock, rigmarole 10 applesauce, balderdash, bilge water, codswallop, double-talk, flapdoodle, galimatias, Jabberwock, mumbo jumbo, rigamarole, taradiddle
and heavy: 6 ardent
and humid: 5 muggy 6 steamy, sultry, sweaty
baseball's ~ corner: 5 third
blow ~ and cold: 4 sway, vary 5 hedge, shift, waver 6 falter 9 fluctuate, vacillate
blowing ~ and cold: 6 fickle 7 erratic, flighty, mutable 8 variable, volatile 9 impulsive, mercurial, undecided 10 capricious, changeable, inconstant
combining form: 6 thermo-
crime: 5 arson
cuisine: 4 Thai 5 Hunan
diggety: 3 wow 5 huzza, oh boy, super 6 hoorah, hooray, hurrah, hurray, huzzah
drink: 3 tea 4 grog 5 cocoa, glogg, mocha, toddy 6 coffee
ender: 3 bed, box, dog 4 cake, foot, head, line, shot, spot 5 house 6 headed
foot: 3 gag 5 prank 8 mischief
(for): 4 game 5 ready
full of ~ air: 5 gassy, windy, wrong 9 talkative
goods: 4 loot 6 spoils 7 plunder
in ~ water: 7 trapped, up a tree 9 on the spot 10 on the ropes
lead: 3 tip 4 clew, clue
not ~: 4 cold, mild, warm 5 tepid 8 lukewarm, moderate, pleasant 9 temperate
not so ~: 4 cool, mild, sick, so-so 5 tepid
off the press: 3 fad, new 5 fresh 6 recent
on: 9 wild about
one: 4 riot 6 scream
pepper: 3 aji 5 chile, chili 6 chilli
pot: 4 stew
potato: 6 hazard
property: 8 valuable
red ~: 5 spicy, zesty 7 peppery, piquant, pungent 8 seasoned
rocks: 3 ice 4 lava 5 magma 6 basalt, pumice, scoria 8 obsidian
run ~ and cold: 4 yo-yo 5 hedge 6 dither, seesaw, waffle, wobble 8 straddle 9 hem and haw, pussyfoot, vacillate
sauce: 4 mole 7 Tabasco
sauce quality: 4 tang, zest, zing 5 punch, spice
spot: 3 spa, sun 4 hell, kiln, oven 5 sauna 6 boiler, desert
spring: 3 spa 4 bath 6 geyser, resort
stuff: 4 fire, lava 5 anger, chile, chili, salsa 6 chilli
time: 4 July 6 August, Jul. Aug., summer 7 dog days
tip: 4 clue, lead
toddy spice: 5 clove
topic: 5 issue 7 problem 8 argument
to trot: 4 avid 5 eager 6 gung ho 7 anxious, excited 10 raring to go
trend: 3 fad 4 rage 5 craze, mania, vogue 7 in thing
tub: 3 spa 5 sauna 7 Jacuzzi 9 whirlpool
under the collar: 4 sore 5 angry, het up, irate, riled, upset
water: 3 fix 4 bind 6 pickle 7 problem, trouble 9 deep water 10 difficulty
hot __: 3 air, bed, cap, dog, pot, rod, tea, tub, war 4 cake, comb, lick, line, pack, pink, seat, shoe, shot, spot, tear, type, well 5 light, metal, money, pants, plate, sauce, stuff, toddy, water 6 button, corner, pepper, potato, rodder, spring, switch, tamale
hot __ bun: 5 cross
hot __ oven: 4 as an
hot __ pistol: 3 as a
hot __ sundae: 5 fudge
hot __ the collar: 5 under
hot __ trail: 5 on the
hot-__: 4 draw, roll, wire, work 5 press, short 6 button, dipped, dogger 7 blooded
hot-__ bottle: 5 water
hot-__ league: 5 stove
__ hot: 6 piping
__-hot: 3 red 5 white
Hot __: 4 Boyz, Legs, Line 5 Money, Stuff, Water 6 Butter, Wheels 7 Blooded, Diggity
Hot __!: 5 Shots
Hot __ Houlihan: 4 Lips
Hot __ in the Summertime: 3 Fun
Hot __ National Park: 7 Springs
Hot __, The: 4 Rock
hot-air ballooning: 5 sport
__, Hot and Blue!: 3 Red
hot-and-cold: 9 impulsive 10 indecisive, irresolute
__ hot and cold: 4 blow
hot and sour: 4 soup
hot as a __: 6 pistol
hotbed: 3 den 4 nest 5 nidus 6 cradle 7 nursery
hot-blooded: 5 fiery, lusty 6 ardent, feisty, fervid, torrid 7 fervent, lustful 8 spirited 9 emotional, excitable, impetuous, impulsive 10 passionate
Hot Blooded (1978 song) artist: Foreigner
Hot Boyz (1999 song)
artist: Eve, Missy Elliott, Nas, Q-Tip
hot buttered __: 3 rum
hotcake: 5 bread 8 flapjack
place: 4 IHOP
Hot Child in the City (1978 song)
artist: Nick Gilder
__ Hot Chili Peppers: 3 Red
Hotchner: 2 A.E.
hot chocolate: 8 beverage
hot cross bun: 6 pastry
time: 4 Lent
Hot cross buns, __ penny, two...: 4 one a
Hot Diggity (1956 song) artist: Perry Como
hot dog: 3 ham 4 brag, meat 5 Coney, frank, huzza, Kahn's, weeny 6 Armour, hoorah, hooray, hurrah, hurray, huzzah, weenie, wiener 7 showoff 8 Ball Park, stuntman 9 daredevil 10 grandstand, Oscar Mayer
covering: 4 skin 6 casing
expand, as a ~ dog: 5 plump
length, perhaps: 4 foot
partner: 3 bun 5 chile, chili, kraut, works 6 catsup, chilli, onions, relish 7 ketchup, mustard 10 sauerkraut
place: 5 stand 8 ballpark
hotel: 3 inn 4 Omni, Ritz 5 Hyatt, lodge, Penta, Plaza, Savoy 6 Hilton, hostel, resort, tavern, Westin 7 auberge, fleabag, lodging, pension, Wyndham 8 hostelry, lodgment, Marriott, Radisson, Sheraton 9 flophouse, roadhouse 10 DoubleTree 11 Crowne Plaza, Four Seasons
canine ~: 5 pound 6 kennel 7 shelter 8 doghouse
employee: 4 maid 5 valet 7 bellhop, bellman 9 concierge
ender: 3 ier 6 keeper
feature: 2 TV 3 bed, gym 4 safe 5 Bible, lobby, TV set 6 atrium, canopy 7 dresser 10 night table
features: 5 atria
floating ~: 4 ship 5 liner 10 cruise ship
group: 5 chain
Las Vegas ~: 3 MGM 7 Aladdin
lobby locale: 4 desk
London ~: 5 Savoy
New York City ~: 5 Plaza
offering: 3 bed 5 rooms, suite
Paris ~: 4 Ritz

patron: 5 guest 6 lodger
pest: 6 bedbug
price: 4 rate 8 rack rate
restriction: 6 no pets
seedy ~: 7 fleabag 9 flophouse
sign: 3 Ice 4 Exit
supply: 5 linen 6 sheets 7 bedding
unit: 2 rm. 4 room
visit: 4 rest, stay 7 holiday, respite, sojourn 8 stopover, vacation
youth ~: 6 hostel
Hotel (ABC drama)
cast: James Brolin (Peter McDermott) Connie Sellecca (Christine Francis)
Hotel __ Hampshire, The: 3 New
__ Hotel: 5 Grand
Hôtel __ Invalides: 3 des
Hotel California (1977 song) artist: Eagles
hôtel de __: 5 ville
Hotel Happiness (1962 song) artist: Brook Benton
hotelier: 4 host 8 landlord 9 innkeeper
Hotel New Hampshire, The: 4 film 5 novel
author: John Irving
cast: Beau Bridges, Jodie Foster, Rob Lowe
director: Tony Richardson
hotfoot: 4 hike, walk 5 prank
it: 3 fly, hie, rip, run, zip 4 bolt, dart, dash, flee, flit, race, rush, tear, zoom 5 scoot, speed 6 barrel, gallop, hasten, hustle, rocket, scurry 7 quicken, scamper 9 shake a leg, skedaddle 10 get a move on
reaction: 4 yeow
hot fudge __: 6 sundae
Hot Fun in the Summertime (1969 song) artist: Sly and the Family Stone
hothead: 8 inflamer 9 demagogue, firebrand
hotheaded: 4 rash, wild 5 brash, fiery, irate 6 madcap, touchy 7 violent 8 reckless, volatile 9 excitable, unadvised 10 ill-advised, incautious, passionate
hotheadedness: 6 temper
Hot l Baltimore, The author: Lanford Wilson
Hot Lead and Cold Feet (1978 film)
cast: Jim Dale, Darren McGavin, Karen Valentine
Hot Legs (1978 song) artist: Rod Stewart
hot-line situation: 6 crisis
Hot Lips: 5 nurse 8 Houlihan
portrayer: 4 Swit 9 Kellerman
Hot Money author: Dick Francis
hot on the __: 5 trail
hot pepper: 5 spice
Hotpoint: 9 appliance
alternative: 5 Amana, Norge 6 Bendix, Maytag, Tappan 7 Admiral, Jenn-Air, Kenmore 9 Magic Chef, Whirlpool 10 Frigidaire, Kelvinator, KitchenAid
hot pot: 4 stew
Hot Rock, The (1972 film)
cast: Ron Leibman, Robert Redford, George Segal
director: Peter Yates
hot rod: 3 car 4 auto, rush 5 motor, racer, speed 8 dragster 9 racing car 10 speed demon
part: 4 carb
propellant: 5 nitro
hotshot: 3 ace, VIP, wiz 4 smug, whiz 5 adept, biggy, comer 6 biggie, bigwig, dynamo, expert, wizard 7 old hand 8 cocksure, virtuoso 9 celebrity, personage
Hot Shots! (1991 film)
cast: Cary Elwes, Valeria Golino, Charlie Sheen
director: Jim Abrahams
Hot Springs: 3 spa 4 city, park, town
locale: 3 Ark. 8 Arkansas
hotspur: 9 daredevil
hot-stove __: 6 league
Hot Stuff (1979 song) artist: Donna Summer
__ Hot Summer, The: 4 Long
hotsy-totsy: 3 def, rad 4 aces, A-one, boss, braw, cool, dece, fine, gear, keen, neat, nice, phat, tuff 5 dandy, ducky, grand, great, marvy, neato, nobby, prime, slick, super, swell 6 bang on, bang-up, bonzer, bosker, choice, divine, dreamy, far-out, gnarly, groovy, lovely, peachy, slap-up, spot on, superb, terrif, tiptop, unreal, whizzo, wicked 7 amazing, awesome, capital, corking, perfect, ripping, skookum, stellar, sublime 8 dazzling, especial, eximious, fabulous, five-star, four-star, frabjous, glorious, heavenly, jim-dandy, slam-bang, smashing, splendid, standout, sterling, stickout, superior, terrific, top-level, topnotch, very good, wondrous 9 bodacious, Endsville, excellent, exemplary, exquisite, first-rate, high-grade, hunky-dory, marvelous, sollicker, top-flight, wonderful 10 first-class, jack-a-dandy, out of sight, peachy-keen, phenomenal, remarkable, stupendous, super-duper
hot-tempered: 5 angry, cross, fiery, huffy, irate, onery, surly, testy 6 crusty, ornery, touchy 7 bearish, grouchy, peevish, peppery 8 choleric, liverish, snappish 9 irascible, irritable, querulous, splenetic 10 ill-humored
Hottentot tongue: 4 Nama
hot to __: 4 trot
__ hot to handle: 3 too
hot under the __: 6 collar
hot-water __: 6 bottle
hot-weather
quencher: 3 ade
stat: 3 THI
wear: 6 shorts 7 cut-offs 8 bermudas
Houdan: 4 fowl 7 chicken
relative: 6 Bantam, Brahma, Sussex 7 Cornish, Dorking, Leghorn 8 Araucana, Langshan, Shanghai 9 Dominique, Orpington, Wyandotte
Houdini: 5 Harry
Houdini (1953 film)
cast: Tony Curtis, Janet Leigh
Houk: 5 Ralph
Houlihan: 5 major, nurse 7 Hot Lips 8 Margaret
Houma: 4 city, town
locale: 9 Louisiana
hound: 3 bug, dog, dun, fan, mut, nag, ply, vex 4 bait, goad, mutt, prod, ride, tail 5 annoy, bedog, beset, canid, chase, grind, harry, haunt, stalk 6 addict, badger, bark at, basset, beagle, bother, bowwow, canine, harass, hassle, heckle, hector, noodge, pester, plague, pursue 7 admirer, basenji, bird dog, bombard, coon dog, henpeck, mongrel, oppress, provoke, redbone, torment 8 distress, run after 9 importune, keep after, persecute 10 intimidate
for payment: 3 dun 9 keep after
hotel: 6 kennel
name: 4 Fido, Spot 5 Rover
quarry: 3 fox 4 duck, hare 7 raccoon
sound: 3 yip 4 woof
starter: 3 elk, fox 4 boar, buck, chow, coon, deer, gaze, grey, hell, news, stag, wolf 5 blood 6 sleuth
trail: 5 scent, spoor, track
hound __: 3 dog
__ hound: 4 rock 5 media, Plott 6 Afghan, basset, Ibizan, Orion's, Walker 7 entered, gazelle, pharaoh 9 autograph
Hound __ Baskervilles, The: 5 of the
Hound Dog (1956 song) artist: Elvis Presley
Hound-Dog Man: 4 film, song
artist: Fabian
cast: Fabian, Carol Lynley, Arthur O'Connell, Stuart Whitman
director: Don Siegel
hounding: 6 bother 9 annoyance 10 harassment, irritation
__ hounding: 4 rock
Hound of the Baskervilles, The: 4 film 5 novel
author: Arthur Conan Doyle
cast: Nigel Bruce, Richard Greene, Basil Rathbone
locale: 4 moor
hounds, ride to: 4 hunt
hound's-tooth __: 5 check
Hounsfield, Godfrey: 8 Nobelist
hour: 4 sext, time 5 nones, prime, terce 6 matins, moment, tierce 7 complin, set time, vespers 8 compline
afternoon: 3 one, two 4 five, four 5 one p.m., three, two p.m. 6 five p.m., four p.m. 7 three p.m.
canonical ~: 4 sext 5 matin, nones, terce 7 worship
ender: 4 long 5 glass
evening ~: 3 six, ten 4 nine 5 eight, seven, six p.m. 6 nine p.m. 7 eight p.m., seven p.m.
happy ~: 6 recess 7 respite
happy ~ establishment: 3 pub 6 saloon, tavern 7 taproom 8 alehouse, taphouse
in French: 5 heure
in Spanish: 4 hora
man of the ~: 4 hero, star 6 victor, winner 8 luminary
morning ~: 3 six, ten 4 nine 5 eight, seven, six a.m., ten a.m. 6 eleven, nine a.m. 7 eight a.m., seven a.m. 8 eleven a.m.
nearing the ~: 5 ten of, ten to 6 five of, five to
prime-time ~: 3 ten 4 nine 5 eight, ten p.m. 6 nine p.m. 7 eight p.m.
rush ~: 7 traffic
sound the ~: 4 peal, toll 5 chime
TV news ~: 3 six, ten 5 six p.m., ten p.m. 6 eleven 8 eleven p.m.
vacant ~: 6 recess 8 free time 9 spare time 10 recreation, relaxation
wee ~: 3 one, two 4 four, morn 5 night, one a.m., three, two a.m. 6 four a.m. 7 morning, three a.m.
witching ~: 8 midnight
zero ~: 4 D-day 6 crisis 7 due date 8 deadline, exigence, exigency, juncture 9 countdown, crossroad, emergency
hour __: 4 hand 5 angle 6 circle
hour-__: 4 long
__ hour: 4 rush, zero 5 happy, lunch 6 coffee, credit, family 7 amateur, working
__-hour: 3 man, off 4 half, watt, work 5 clock, lumen, woman 6 ampere
Hour Before Daylight, An author: 6 Carter
hourglass: 5 timer 9 timepiece 10 timekeeper
figure feature: 5 waist
filler: 4 sand
part: 4 neck
Hour Glass, The author: William Butler Yeats
hourly: 5 horal, often 8 periodic
hour-minute divider: 5 colon
__ Hour Photo: 3 One
hours
after ~: 4 late 5 night 9 nighttime
enter the wee ~: 5 laten
every 24 ~: 4 a day 5 daily, horal 7 diurnal
from now: 5 after, later 6 in time 7 by and by 8 in a while 9 afterward 10 thereafter
idle ~: 4 ease, rest 6 repose 7 holiday, leisure, time off 8 free time, vacation 9 spare time
in the wee ~: 5 early
wee ~: 9 nighttime
while away the ~: 4 idle, laze, loaf, loll 5 dally 6 dawdle, loiter 8 kill time, malinger, slack off 9 bum around, goldbrick, sit around, waste time 10 dillydally, fool around, knock about, take it easy
__ hours: 5 small 6 little, office 7 bankers'
__-hours: 5 after
Hours of Idleness author: Byron
Hours, The (2002 film)
cast: Nicole Kidman, Julianne Moore, Meryl Streep
director: Stephen Daldry
__ Hours, The: 7 Gallant
__ Hour With You: 3 One
Housatonic: 5 river
locale: 4 Conn., Mass.
house: 3 hut, pad 4 clan, coop, digs, firm, flat, hold, home 5 abode, admit, cabin, condo, lodge, place, put up, ranch, roost, shack, Tudor 6 A-frame, billet, castle, chalet, encase, family, harbor, incase, outfit, shield, take in 7 address, Cape Cod, company, concern, contain, cottage, council, domicil, dynasty, habitat, harbour, lineage, mansion, quarter, shelter, station, vacancy 8 audience, bungalow, business, crash pad, domicile, dressing, dwelling, hacienda, lodgment, property, quarters 9 apartment, monastery, residence, structure 10 parliament, split-level
addition: 3 ell 4 wing 5 annex
and grounds: 5 manor, ranch 6 estate 8 property 10 plantation
away from the ~: 5 not in 9 elsewhere
big ~: 4 jail 5 manor 6 castle, estate, lockup, prison
big ~ resident: 3 con 5 crook, felon, lifer 7 convict 8 criminal, jailbird, prisoner, yardbird 10 lawbreaker
bird ~: 4 nest 6 aviary 9 enclosure
boarding ~: 5 hotel 7 lodging 8 lodgment
bring down the ~: 3 wow 5 amaze, level 6 topple 7 delight, flatten 8 bulldoze, demolish, entrance
clean ~: 5 purge, sweep
cleaner, in England: 4 char
country ~: 5 cabin, lodge, villa 6 chalet
covering: 5 paint 6 siding, stucco
dish of the ~: 9 specialty
drawing: 4 plan 6 layout
ender: 3 boy, fly, man, men, sat, sit, top 4 boat, coat, hold, keep, leek, maid, mate, room, ware, wife, work 5 bound, break, broke, dress, guest, plant, train, wares, wives 6 broken, holder, keeper, lights, master, mother, wifely, worker 7 husband, keeping, painter, sitting, warming 8 cleaning, wifelike
enlarge the ~: 5 add on

feature: 3 den 4 deck, door, hall, lawn, roof, stud, wall, yard 5 alarm, attic, gable, patio, porch 6 cellar, garage, screen, siding, stairs, window 7 bedroom, ceiling, kitchen, library, mailbox 8 backyard, basement, doorbell, driveway 10 living room, smoke alarm, welcome mat
field ~: 9 gymnasium
fix up an old ~: 5 rehab
fly: 8 irritant
hash ~: 5 diner 6 eatery 10 restaurant
haunted ~ feature: 5 ghost 6 cobweb
high ~: 4 aery, eyry 5 aerie, eyrie
ice ~: 4 iglu 5 igloo
in French: 6 maison
in Spanish: 4 casa
inspection concern: 5 radon
instant ~: 6 prefab
it may be on the ~: 5 drink
keep ~: 6 settle 7 clean up
large ~: 6 castle, estate, palace 7 chateau, mansion
level a ~: 4 rase, raze
like a ~ afire: 6 wildly 7 eagerly 8 fiercely 9 furiously 10 vigorously
like a haunted ~: 5 eerie, scary 6 creaky, creepy, spooky 7 macabre 8 chilling
manor ~: 7 chateau
movie ~: 5 odeon, odeum 7 theater, theatre 10 auditorium
not a new ~: 6 resale
of correction: 3 pen 4 jail, poky, stir 6 prison 7 slammer
of worship: 4 shul 5 schul 6 bethel, church 9 cathedral
on the ~: 4 free 6 gratis, unpaid 7 as a gift 8 costless 10 for nothing
opera ~: 5 odeon, odeum 7 theater, theatre 10 auditorium
opera ~ section: 3 row
out of the ~: 7 outdoor 8 alfresco, exterior
paper: 4 deed
pet: 3 cat, dog 4 bird, fish 6 canary, parrot 8 parakeet
public ~: 3 bar, inn, pub 5 lodge 6 saloon, tavern 7 barroom
room in a Roman ~: 6 atrium
rooming ~: 3 inn 5 hotel 7 lodging
safe ~: 6 asylum 7 hideout, retreat 9 sanctuary
shader: 3 elm, oak 4 tree
site: 3 lot 4 plot 5 tract 6 parcel
small ~: 3 hut 5 bower, cabin, hovel, hutch, shack 6 cabana, chalet, lean-to, shanty 7 cottage 8 bungalow
starter: 3 ale, bug, dog, fun, gas, hot, ice, mad, pot, tea 4 alms, bath, bird, boat, brew, bunk, chop, club, deck, doll, farm, fire, flop, gate, jail, long, play, poor, road, spec, toll, town, ware, work 5 block, court, glass, green, guard, guest, light, pilot, power, rough, round, smoke, state, steak, store, sugar, sweat, wheel 6 barrel, coffee, custom, mother, porter, school, spring, summer 7 charter, meeting, packing, station 8 boarding, clearing, counting
style: 5 ranch, Tudor 6 A-frame 7 Cape Cod 10 split-level
tree ~: 4 nest
upper ~: 6 Senate
wing: 3 ell
woman of the ~: 4 ma'am, wife 6 missis, missus
work: 5 chore
wrecker: 5 razer
see also home
house ___: 4 call, crow, dick, flag, mark, moss, rule, seat, wren 5 agent, brand, finch, mouse, music, of God, organ, party, place, snake 6 arrest, doctor, fungus, martin, sitter 7 counsel, cricket, curtain, manager, painter, slipper, sparrow, surgeon, trailer
house-___: 7 raising
___ house: 3 art, big, fun, pit, row, sod 4 acid, base, doss, free, full, hack, hash, joss, long, mast, meat, open, post, safe, show, tied, town, tree, wire 5 block, chart, clean, coach, dower, field, frame, grind, lower, manor, movie, on the, opera, panel, ranch, shaft, solar, storm, third, tract, Tudor, upper, Wendy 6 bastel, bastle, bridge, cadent, coffee, custom, duplex, engine, johnny, mother, parish, parlor, public 7 angular, chapter, country, customs, freight, galerie, halfway, lodging, meeting, octagon, rooming, station 8 discount
House
counterpart: 6 Senate
divider: 5 aisle
eye on the ~: 5 CSPAN
member: 3 rep.
vote: 3 nay, yea
House ___: 5 Calls, of Wax, Party
House ___, A: 7 Divided
House ___ a Home, A: 5 Is Not
House ___ Rising Sun: 5 of the
House ___ Seven Gables, The: 5 of the
___ House: 3 Our 4 Full, Hull, In My, Open, Road, This 5 Blair, Bleak, Brick, Crazy, Noble, White 6 Animal, Iggie's, Random 7 Alison's, Crowded, Maxwell
___ House, A: 5 Doll's
___ house afire: 5 like a
House at Pooh Corner, The author: A.A. Milne
House Beautiful topic: 5 decor
houseboat: 4 junk
Houseboat (1958 film)
cast: Cary Grant, Martha Hyer, Sophia Loren
director: Melville Shavelson
housebound, make: 5 ice in
housebreak: 5 train
housebreaker: 5 crook, thief 6 robber 7 burglar, prowler 8 criminal, picklock, pilferer 9 plunderer
housebroken: 4 tame
House by the River, The (1950 film)
cast: Lee Bowman, Louis Hayward, Jane Wyatt
director: Fritz Lang
House Calls (1978 film)
cast: Richard Benjamin, Art Carney, Glenda Jackson, Walter Matthau
housecat: 3 pet 5 tabby
housecleaning: 5 purge
housecoat: 4 robe 6 duster, kimono 7 garment
___ House cookies: 4 Toll
House Divided, A author: Pearl S. Buck
housefly: 3 bug 4 pest 6 insect
genus: 5 Musca
houseguest, be a bad: 6 impose
household: 4 clan, home, homy 5 homey 6 family, ménage 8 domestic, ordinary 9 customary
animal: 3 cat, dog, pet 4 bird, fish
appliance: 2 TV 3 vac, VCR 4 iron, oven 5 drier, dryer, stove, TV set, waxer 6 fridge, vacuum, washer
appliance brand: 5 Amana, Norge 6 Bendix, Maytag, Tappan 7 Admiral, Jenn-Air, Kenmore 8 Hotpoint 9 Magic Chef, Whirlpool 10 Frigidaire, Kelvinator, KitchenAid
chore: 4 wash 7 ironing, laundry
funds: 6 budget
help: 4 maid 5 nanny 6 au pair, nannie
member: 3 cat, dad, dog, mom, pet, sis
name: 7 notable 8 somebody 9 celebrity
new ~ member: 3 pup 4 baby 5 puppy 6 infant, kitten
pest: 3 ant 5 roach
Roman ~ god: 3 Lar
Roman ~ gods: 5 Lares
servant: 4 mozo
see also home, house
household ___: 3 art, god 4 word 5 goods 6 income, knight, troops 7 ammonia, cavalry, effects
householder: 5 liver 6 tenant 8 occupant, resident
Household Saints (1993 film)
cast: Vincent D'Onofrio, Lili Taylor, Tracey Ullman
House in Paris, The author: 5 Bowen
House Is Not ___, A: 5 a Home
housekeeper: 4 maid 7 servant 8 domestic
at times: 6 ironer
___ housekeeper: 6 live-in 7 sleep-in
___ Housekeeping: 4 Good
housekeeping, set up: 5 dwell
Houseman, John Oscar: The Paper Chase
house of ___: 3 God 5 cards, study 6 prayer 7 worship
House of ___: 3 Wax 4 Dior, Keys 5 Lords, Peers, Usher 7 Commons
House of ___, The: 4 Fear
House of Blue Leaves, The author: John Guare
House of Commons locale: 6 Canada
House of Dark Shadows (1970 film)
cast: Jonathan Frid, Grayson Hall, Kathryn Leigh Scott
House of Dust author: Conrad Aiken
House of Fear, The (1945 film)
cast: Nigel Bruce, Basil Rathbone
director: Roy William Neill
House of Five Talents, The author: Louis Auchincloss
House of Games (1987 film)
cast: Lindsay Crouse, Joe Mantegna, Mike Nussbaum
director: David Mamet
House of Lancaster symbol: 4 rose 7 red rose
House of Life, The author: Dante Gabriel Rossetti
House of Lords member: 3 sir 4 peer 5 baron
House of Mirth, The author: Edith Wharton
House of Rothschild (1934 film)
cast: George Arliss, Boris Karloff, Loretta Young
House of Seven Gables, The (1940 film)
cast: Margaret Lindsay, Vincent Price, George Sanders
House of Strangers (1949 film)
cast: Richard Conte, Susan Hayward, Edward G. Robinson
director: Joseph L. Mankiewicz
House of the Dead, The author: Fyodor Dostoyevsky
House of the Rising Sun (song) artist: Animals, Frijid Pink
House of the Seven Gables, The: 4 film 5 novel
author: Nathaniel Hawthorne
cast: Vincent Price, George Sanders
character: 5 Maule 6 Phoebe, Venner
director: Joe May
site: 5 Salem
House of the Spirits, The author: Isabel Allende
House of Thunder, The author: Dean Koontz
House of Usher (1960 film)
cast: Mark Damon, Myrna Fahey, Vincent Price
director: Roger Corman
House of Wax (1953 film)
cast: Phyllis Kirk, Frank Lovejoy, Vincent Price
director: Andre de Toth
House of Wax role: 4 Igor
House of York symbol: 4 rose 9 white rose
House on 92nd St., The (1945 film)
cast: Signe Hasso, Lloyd Nolan
director: Henry Hathaway
House on Haunted Hill (1958 film)
cast: Richard Long, Vincent Price
House on Hope Street, The author: Danielle Steel
House on the Hill, The author: Cesare Pavese
___ House on the Prairie: 6 Little
houseplant: 4 aloe, fern 5 areca 6 coleus
tend to a ~: 5 repot, unpot, water
Houser: 5 Jerry
___ House roll: 6 Parker
___ House Rules, The: 5 Cider
House That Jack Built, The (1968 song) artist: Aretha Franklin
___ House, The: 3 Big, Red 5 Glass 6 Russia, Summer 7 Doctor's
housetop: 4 roof
sight: 4 vane
housewares name: 4 Ekco
housewarming gift: 5 plant
House Without a Key, The hero: 4 Chan
housework: 5 chore 6 sewing 7 cooking, dusting, ironing, laundry, mopping, washing 8 cleaning, sweeping 9 bed-making, vacuuming 10 homemaking, laundering
do ~: 3 mop, sew 4 cook, dust, iron, wash 5 clean, sweep 7 launder
housing: 3 pad 4 coop, digs, flat, home 5 abode, condo, roost 6 billet, castle 7 domicil, habitat, mansion, shelter 8 covering, crash pad, domicile, dwelling, quarters 9 apartment, residence
development: 5 tract
housing ___: 5 start 6 estate 7 project
___ housing: 4 bell, fair, open 5 tract 6 public
Housman: 2 A.E. 8 Laurence
Housman, A.E.: 4 poet 7 British
first name: Alfred
work: From Far, From Eve and Morning
The Lent Lily
Loveliest of Trees
On the Idle Hill of Summer
On Wenlock Edge
A Shropshire Lad
To an Athlete Dying Young
When I Was One-and-Twenty
With Rue My Heart Is Laden
Houssay, Bernardo: 8 Nobelist
Houston: 3 Sam 4 city, Matt, port, town 5 Cissy, David 6 Thelma 7 Whitney
athletes: 4 Owls 7 Cougars
county: 6 Harris
former ~ hockey player: 4 Aero
locale: 3 Tex. 5 Texas
newspaper: 9 Chronicle
org.: 4 NASA
school: 3 TSU 9 Rice. Rice U.
team: 6 Astros, Texans 7 Rockets
Houston-to-Dallas dir.: 3 NNW
Houston, Whitney
hometown: Newark

song: All the Man That I Need (1991)
Could I Have This Kiss Forever (2000)
Count on Me (1996)
Didn't We Almost Have It All (1987)
Exhale (1995)
Greatest Love of All (1986)
Heartbreak Hotel (1999)
How Will I Know (1985)
I Believe in You and Me (1996)
I Have Nothing (1993)
I'm Every Woman (1993)
I'm Your Baby Tonight (1990)
It's Not Right But It's Okay (1999)
I Wanna Dance With Somebody (1987)
I Will Always Love You (1992)
Love Will Save the Day (1988)
Miracle (1991)
My Love Is Your Love (1999)
One Moment in Time (1988)
Saving All My Love for You (1985)
So Emotional (1987)
Where Do Broken Hearts Go (1988)
You Give Good Love (1985)
spouse: Bobby Brown
Houyhnhnms subject: 5 Yahoo
HOV __: 4 lane
hovel: 3 hut, sty **4** dump, shed **5** house, shack **6** lean-to, pigpen, pigsty, shanty **7** cottage, piggery, rathole
hover: 3 fly **4** flit, hang, loom, wait **5** float, pause, poise **6** impend, linger, loiter, remain **7** flitter, flutter **8** levitate, volitate **9** vacillate **10** wait around
about: 5 haunt **7** bedevil **8** frequent **9** habituate **10** hang around
ender: 5 craft
hovercraft: 3 ACV **4** boat
hovering: 4 high **5** above **8** elevated
hovering __: 3 act **6** accent, vessel
Hovhaness: 4 Alan
Hovis: 5 Larry
how: 6 the way **9** in what way
and ~: 6 surely, you bet **8** for a fact, of course **9** certainly, you said it **10** absolutely, positively
do you do: 4 ciao, hail **5** aloha, hello, howdy **7** bon jour, welcome **8** greeting
ender: 4 ever **6** soever
find ~ many: 5 count
in French: 3 que **5** comme **7** combien, comment
in Spanish: 4 cómo
knows ~: 3 can
no ~: 3 nah, naw, nay, nix, non **4** ever, nein, nope, nyet, uh-uh **5** at all, I won't, ixnay, never **7** I refuse **8** forget it, I will not, negative, negatory, not at all **9** fat chance, I think not **10** count me out, not a chance, thumbs down
now: 2 hi **4** ciao **5** aloha, hello **6** shalom **7** bon jour
others see us: 9 depiction **10** appearance, conception, impression, perception, projection
so: 3 why
starter: 3 any **4** some
things are: 7 reality **9** condition, situation
how __: 4 come **6** and why
how __ do: 5 do you
how __ that: 5 about
__ how!: 3 And **5** Here's
__-how: 4 know
How __!: 4 true
How __?: 4 come
How __ Be Sure: 4 Can I
How __, brown cow: 3 now
How __ doing?: 3 am I
How __ Got Her Groove Back: 6 Stella
How __ Has This Been Going On?: 4 Long
How __ Is the Ocean: 4 Deep
How __ Is Your Love: 4 Deep
How __ it is!: 5 sweet
How __ love thee?: 3 do I
How __ Me Now: 5 U Like
How __ the little busy bee...: 4 doth
How __ the Moon: 4 High
How __ the War: 4 I Won
How __ things?: 3 are
How __ Want It: 3 Do U
How __ Was My Valley: 5 Green
How __ We Know: 6 Little
How __ you!: 4 dare
How __ you?: 3 are **5** about
How about that!: 3 gee **4** gosh
How Am I Supposed to Live Without You (1989 song) artist: Michael Bolton
Howard: 3 Ken, Moe, Ron **4** duck, Duff, Fast, Keel, Koch **5** Adina, Clint, Curly, Dietz, Frank, Hawks, Jones, Rance, Ronny, Shemp, Stern, Temin, Zieff **6** Arliss, Carter, Cosell, Florey, Hanson, Hughes, Leslie, Morris, Sidney, Trevor **7** da Silva, Lindsay, Nemerov, Rollins **8** Hesseman
athletes: 5 Bison
locale: 10 Washington
Howard K. __: 5 Smith
Howard, Leslie: 5 actor
film: The Animal Kingdom (1932)
Berkeley Square (1933)
Gone With the Wind (1939)
Intermezzo (1939)
It's Love I'm After (1937)
Of Human Bondage (1934)
Outward Bound (1930)
The Petrified Forest (1936)
Pygmalion (1938)
Romeo and Juliet (1936)
The Scarlet Pimpernel (1935)
Smilin' Through (1932)
Spitfire (1942)
Stand-In (1937)
role: 5 Romeo **6** Ashley, Wilkes
Howard, Ron: 5 actor **8** director
film: American Graffiti (1973)
Apollo 13 (1995)
Backdraft (1991)
A Beautiful Mind (2001, AA)
Cocoon (1985)
The Courtship of Eddie's Father (1963)
Ed TV (1999)
Far and Away (1992)
Gung Ho (1986)
How the Grinch Stole Christmas (2000)
The Music Man (1962)
Night Shift (1982)
The Paper (1994)
Parenthood (1989)
Ransom (1996)
The Shootist (1976)
Splash (1984)
Willow (1988)
role: 4 Opie **6** Taylor
TV: Andy Griffith Show, Happy Days
Howards End: 4 film **5** novel
author: E.M. Forster
cast: Helena Bonham Carter, Anthony Hopkins, Vanessa Redgrave, Emma Thompson
character: 4 Bast, Evie, Paul, Ruth **5** Annie, Helen, Henry, Juley, Tibby **6** Wilcox **7** Charles, Leonard **8** Margaret, Schlegel
director: James Ivory
Howard, Sidney: 6 author, writer **10** playwright
work: Lute Song
They Knew What They Wanted
__ Howard Taft: 7 William
Howard, Trevor: 5 actor
film: The Adventuress (1946)
Brief Encounter (1945)
Father Goose (1964)
Green for Danger (1946)
Operation Crossbow (1965)
Outcast of the Islands (1951)
Run for the Sun (1956)
Ryan's Daughter (1970)
Sons and Lovers (1960)
The Stranger's Hand (1954)
Von Ryan's Express (1965)
How Are Things in Glocca __?: 5 Morra
How awful!: 4 alas **6** oh dear
howbeit: 3 yet **8** although
How Bizarre (1997 song) artist: OMC
How Can I Be Sure (1967 song) artist: Rascals
How Can We Be Lovers (1990 song) artist: Michael Bolton
How Can You Mend a Broken Heart (1971 song) artist: Bee Gees
How'd __?: 4 it go
How Deep Is the Ocean composer: Irving Berlin
How Deep Is Your Love (song) artist: Bee Gees, Dru Hill, Redman
How disgusting!: 3 ick, ugh **5** yecch
how do __: 5 you do
How do __ thee?: 5 I Love
How does that __ you?: 4 grab
How Does That Grab You, Darlin'? (1966 song) artist: Nancy Sinatra
How Do I Live (1997 song) artist: LeAnn Rimes, Trisha Yearwood
How do I love thee?: 4 poem
author: 8 Browning
How Do I Make You (1980 song) artist: Linda Ronstadt
How do you __ relief?: 5 spell
how-do-you-do, fine: 6 plight
How Do You Do It? (1964 song) artist: Gerry and the Pacemakers
How do you like them __?: 6 apples
howdy: 5 aloha, hello **7** bon jour, welcome **8** greeting
say ~: 5 greet **7** welcome
Howdy __: 5 Doody
__ Howdy Doody Time: 3 It's
Howdy Symphony composer: PDQ Bach
Howe: 5 Elias **6** Gordie
on Cheers: 5 Alley
Howe, Gordie
milieu: 3 ice **4** rink **5** arena
org.: 3 NHL
Howell: 5 Lovey **6** Heflin **8** Thurston
partner: 4 Bell
Howells, William Dean: 6 writer
work: The Rise of Silas Lapham
however: 3 but, tho, yet **5** still **6** though, withal **8** after all **9** per contra **10** all the same, for all that
How Great Thou __: 3 Art
How Green Was My Valley (1941 film)
cast: Donald Crisp, Anna Lee, Roddy McDowall, Maureen O'Hara, Walter Pidgeon
character: 3 Huw **4** Beth, Davy, Ivor, Owen **5** Ianto, miner **6** Gwilym, Iestyn, Marged **7** Bronwen, Ceinwen
director: John Ford
How High the __: 4 Moon
Howie: 6 Mandel, Meeker, Morenz
How Important Can It Be? (1955 song) artist: Joni James
howitzer: 3 arm, gun **4** arty. **6** cannon **9** artillery
need: 4 ammo
nickname: 6 Bertha
howl: 3 bay, cry, sob **4** bark, bawl, hoot, keen, moan, riot, roar, sigh, wail, weep, yell, yelp, yowl **5** groan, growl, laugh, shout, storm, whine, whoop **6** bellow, clamor, guffaw, holler, lament, outcry, scream, shriek, squeal **7** blubber, exclaim, ululate **9** caterwaul **10** take it hard, vociferate
Howland: 3 isl. **4** Beth, isle **6** island
Howl author: Allen Ginsberg
howler: 4 slip **5** error, gaffe **6** animal, coyote, mammal, monkey **7** blunder, faux pas, mistake, primate **10** inaccuracy
relative: 3 ape **4** saki, titi **5** chimp, drill, jocko, lemur, loris, magot, orang, potto, shrew **6** aye-aye, baboon, Bandar, galago, gelada, gibbon, grivet, guenon, langur, macaco, rhesus, uakari, vervet **7** colobus, gorilla, guereza, hoolock, macaque, sapajou, siamang, tamarin, tarsier **8** bush baby, capuchin, mandrill, mangabey, marmoset, talapoin **9** orangutan **10** Barbary ape, chimpanzee, orangutang
Howlin' __: 4 Wolf
howling: 4 wild **6** stormy **8** laughter **9** turbulent
Howling, The (1981 film)
cast: Dennis Dugan, Patrick Macnee, Dee Wallace
director: Joe Dante
How Little We Know (1956 song) artist: Frank Sinatra
How Long (1975 song) artist: Ace, Pointer Sisters
How Long Has This Been Going On? composer: 8 Gershwin
How'm I doin'? asker: 4 Koch **6** Ed Koch
How now! __?: 4 a rat
How're you? response: 4 fine **6** I'm fine
How's __?: 6 tricks
How sad!: 4 alas **5** alack
Howser: 4 Dick **6** Doogie
How Sheba Sings the Song author: Maya Angelou
How silly of me!: 3 duh
How soothing!: 3 aah
How Stella Got Her Groove Back (1998 film)
cast: Angela Bassett, Taye Diggs, Whoopi Goldberg
How sweet __!: 4 it is
How Sweet It Is (song) artist: James Taylor, Marvin Gaye
How's Your Glass? author: Kingsley Amis
How the Grinch Stole Christmas: 4 book, film
author: Dr. Seuss
cast: Christine Baranski, Jim Carrey, Bill Irwin, Jeffrey Tambor
director: Ron Howard
dog: 3 Max
How the Other Half Lives author: Jacob Riis
How the Other Half Loves author: Alan Ayckbourn
How the West Was Won (1962 film): 5 oater
cast: Carroll Baker, Henry Fonda, Carolyn Jones, Gregory Peck, George Peppard, Robert Preston, Debbie Reynolds, James Stewart, Eli Wallach, John Wayne, Richard Widmark
director: John Ford, Henry Hathaway, George Marshall
how-to: 4 book
part: 4 step

How to __ a Million: 5 Steal
How to Kill Your Neighbor's Dog (2001 film)
cast: Kenneth Branagh, Robin Wright Penn, Lynn Redgrave
How to Make an American Quilt (1995 film)
cast: Maya Angelou, Anne Bancroft, Ellen Burstyn, Winona Ryder
How to Marry a Millionaire (1953 film)
cast: Lauren Bacall, Betty Grable, Marilyn Monroe
director: Jean Negulesco
How to Murder Your Wife (1965 film)
cast: Jack Lemmon, Virna Lisi, Terry-Thomas
director: Richard Quine
How to Save Your Own Life author: Erica Jong
How to Steal a Million (1966 film)
cast: Charles Boyer, Audrey Hepburn, Peter O'Toole
director: William Wyler
How to Succeed... (1967 film): 7 musical
cast: Michele Lee, Robert Morse, Rudy Vallee
composer: 7 Loesser
How to Write a Blackwood Article
author: Edgar Allan Poe
How was __ know?: 3 I to
How Will I Know (1985 song) artist: Whitney Houston
hoy: 4 boat 5 barge, craft, vessl
hoya: 4 vine 5 plant, shrub
Hoyas: 10 Georgetown
hoyden: 4 bold, rude, snip, wild 5 rowdy 6 tomboy, unruly 10 boisterous
Hoyle: 4 Fred 6 Edmond
according to ~: 5 legal, legit, licit, valid 6 kosher, lawful 7 correct 8 bona fide, orthodox 9 allowable 10 admissible, authorized, meticulous, on the level, scrupulous
Hoyt: 5 Axton, Waite 7 Wilhelm
Hoyt, Waite: 6 hurler 7 pitcher
H.P.: 9 Lovecraft
HP product: 2 PC 3 ptr. 6 laptop 7 printer 8 computer
HQ: 4 base
hr.
see hour
H.R.: 8 Haldeman
Hrabal, Bohumil: 5 Czech 6 writer
H. Rap __: 5 Brown
Hrbek: 4 Kent
H&R Block staffer: 3 CPA
HRE part: 3 Emp., Rom. 4 Holy 5 Roman 6 Empire
HRH: 3 VIP 4 king 5 queen
award from ~: 3 OBE
part of ~: 3 Her, His 5 Royal 8 Highness
H. Rider __: 7 Haggard
H. Ross __: 5 Perot
H.S.
course: 2 PE 3 alg., bio., Eng., mus., sci. 4 biol., chem., geog., hist., math.
dropout's certificate: 3 GED
exam: 3 SAT 4 PSAT
head: 4 prin.
keepsake: 2 yb.
organization: 3 PTA
part of ~: 3 sch.
proficiency test: 3 GED
safety advocate: 4 SADD
student: 2 jr., sr. 3 jnr., snr.
see also high school
Hsing-Hsing: 5 panda
HSN: 8 shopping
alternative: 3 QVC 7 ShopNBC
HST: 3 Dem. 4 pres. 6 Truman
defeated him: 3 AES
predecessor: 3 FDR
successor: 3 DDE
see also Truman
ht.: 3 alt. 4 elev.
H2O: 5 water
html: 8 language
alternative: 3 ADA, APL, SQL 4 Alef, Icon, Java, LISP, Logo, Orca, Perl 5 Algol, Basic, Cecil, COBOL, Dylan, SISAL 6 Delphi, Eiffel, Erlang, Oberon, Pascal, Prolog, Sather, Scheme, Snobol 7 Fortran
http
see Internet, Web
__ Huachuca, AZ: 4 Fort
Huajuapan: 4 city, town
locale: 6 Mexico, Oaxaca
Hua Kuo-__: 4 Feng
Huamantla: 4 city, town
locale: 6 Mexico 8 Tlaxcala
Huandoy: 4 peak 5 mount 8 mountain
locale: 4 Peru 5 Andes
Huang He: 5 river
locale: 5 China
Huangpu, city on the: 8 Shanghai
Huascarán: 4 peak 5 mount 8 mountain
locale: 4 Peru 5 Andes
Huastec: 6 Indian 7 Amerind
Huatabampo: 4 city, town
locale: 6 Mexico, Sonora
Huatusco: 4 city, town
locale: 6 Mexico 8 Veracruz
Huauchinango: 4 city, town
locale: 6 Mexico, Puebla
hub: 4 core, seat 5 focus, heart, Mecca, midst 6 center, kernel, middle 7 nucleus 8 polestar 10 focal point
ender: 3 cap
in the ~ of: 6 amidst
of activity: 3 ctr. 6 center
wheel ~: 4 nave
hub-and-__: 5 spoke
Hubba __: 5 Bubba
hubba-hubba: 6 clamor, uproar 10 hullabaloo
Hubba-hubba!: 3 wow 6 oo-la-la
Hubbard: 3 Cal, Kin 4 peak 5 mount 6 Elbert 8 mountain
Hubbard __: 6 squash
Hubbard, Mother: 5 dress
like ~: 3 old
like ~'s cupboard: 4 bare
pet: 3 dog
quest: 4 bone
Hubbell, Carl: 5 Giant 6 hurler 7 pitcher
teammate: 3 Ott
hubble-__: 6 bubble
Hubble: 9 telescope
component: 4 lens
Hubble, Edwin: 10 astronomer
hubbly: 5 rough 6 coarse, uneven
hubbub: 3 ado, din 4 flap, fuss, stir, to-do 5 babel, furor, noise, whirl 6 bedlam, clamor, hassle, hoopla, hoorah, hooray, hurrah, hurray, jangle, lather, pother, racket, ruckus, rumpus, tumult, uproar 7 clangor, clutter, dispute, ferment, ruction, turmoil 8 brouhaha, disorder, rowdydow 9 commotion, confusion, hue and cry, maelstrom 10 clattering, excitement, hullabaloo, hurly-burly
hubby: 3 guy 4 mate 6 fellow, mister, spouse 7 husband
partner: 4 wife 6 missus
hubcap: 8 auto part
Hubei capital: 5 Wuhan
Hubel, David: 8 Nobelist
Huber Heights: 4 city, town
locale: 4 Ohio
Huber, Robert: 7 chemist 8 Nobelist
Hubert: 5 Booth, saint, Selby 7 van Eyck 8 Givenchy, Humphrey 9 Cornfield
comics wife: 5 Trudy
in Italian: 6 Uberto
Hubley: 6 Season
hub-rim connector: 5 spoke
hubris: 5 brass, cheek, nerve, pride 6 vanity 8 audacity, chutzpah 9 arrogance, cockiness, loftiness, pomposity 10 pretension
source: 3 ego
hubristic: 4 smug, vain 5 proud 6 snooty 7 haughty, pompous, stuck-up 8 arrogant, egoistic, snobbish 9 conceited, imperious 10 hoity-toity
hubs: 4 loca, loci
huck ender: 4 ster
huckleberry: 5 fruit, shrub
relative: 5 heath, salal 6 azalea, kalmia 7 arbutus, rhodora 8 cassiope, cowberry 9 blueberry, deerberry
__ huckleberry: 3 box 4 blue, bush 5 black, dwarf
Huckleberry Finn: 4 film 5 novel
author: Mark Twain
cast: Walter Connolly, William Frawley, Mickey Rooney
character: 3 Jim, Pap, Tom 9 Aunt Polly, Tom Sawyer
hucklebuck: 5 dance
huckster: 5 crier 6 barker, hawker, vender, vendor 10 mountebank, proclaimer
Hucksters, The (1947 film)
cast: Clark Gable, Sydney Greenstreet, Deborah Kerr
director: Jack Conway
Hud (1963 film)
cast: Melvyn Douglas, Patricia Neal, Paul Newman
cinematographer: 4 Howe
director: Martin Ritt
Oscar-winner: 4 Neal
HUD
agency: 3 FHA
part: 4 Dept. 5 Urban 7 Housing 10 Department
place: 7 Cabinet
Huddersfield: 4 city, town
locale: 7 England 9 Yorkshire
huddle: 4 heap, herd, mass, meet, mess, talk 5 bunch, chaos, crowd, flock, group 6 confab, confer, crouch, gather, hunker, jumble, nestle, parley, powwow, shrink, throng 7 bunch up, cluster, consult, meeting, palaver, session, snuggle 8 assemble, assembly, converge, disarray, disorder 9 confusion, gathering, touch base 10 assemblage, conference, discussion
count: 6 eleven
ender: 5 break
up: 6 crouch, cuddle, curl up, nestle 7 snuggle
...huddled __ yearning...: 6 masses
Hudibras author: Samuel Butler
Hudson: 2 W.H. 3 bay, car, riv. 4 auto, city, Kate, Rock, town 5 Ernie, Henry, river 8 Rochelle 10 automobile
competitor: 3 Reo 6 De Soto
locale: 4 Ohio
model: 4 Wasp 6 Big Boy, Hornet 7 Rambler 8 Super Six, Traveler 9 Commodore, Pacemaker 10 Great Eight, Terraplane
1920s ~ car: 5 Essex
Hudson __: 3 Bay 4 seal 6 Strait
Hudson Bay: 3 sea
locale: 6 Canada
river to ~: 6 Nelson, Thelon 9 Churchill
tribe: 4 Cree
Hudson, Henry: 7 British 8 explorer
Hudson, Kate: 7 actress
film: About Adam (2001)
Almost Famous (2000)
Desert Blue (1999)
The Four Feathers (2002)
mother: Goldie Hawn
Hudson River
canal: 4 Erie
city on the ~: 4 Troy 5 Nyack 6 Albany
locale: 7 New York
river to the ~: 6 Mohawk
sch.: 4 USMA
Hudson, Rock: 5 actor
film: All That Heaven Allows (1955)
The Ambassador (1984)
Battle Hymn (1957)
Bend of the River (1952)
Captain Lightfoot (1955)
Come September (1961)
Darling Lili (1970)
A Gathering of Eagles (1963)
Giant (1956)
Ice Station Zebra (1968)
The Last Sunset (1961)
The Lawless Breed (1952)
Lover Come Back (1961)
Magnificent Obsession (1954)
The Mirror Crack'd (1980)
Pillow Talk (1959)
Pretty Maids All in a Row (1971)
Seconds (1966)
Send Me No Flowers (1964)
Something of Value (1957)
The Tarnished Angels (1958)
Written on the Wind (1956)
TV: McMillan and Wife
Hudson's Bay __: 7 blanket, Company
Hudson, W.H.: 6 writer 7 British
work: Green Mansions
Hudson, W.H. work: Green Mansions
Hudsucker Proxy, The (1994 film)
cast: Jennifer Jason Leigh, Paul Newman, Tim Robbins
director: Joel Coen
hue: 3 dye 4 cast, tint, tone 5 color, shade, tinct, tinge 6 chroma 7 pigment 8 tincture
and cry: 3 ado, din, row 5 alarm, furor, stink 6 clamor, hubbub, uproar 9 commotion 10 hullabaloo
partner: 3 cry
unbleached ~: 3 tan 5 brown
use a new ~: 5 redye
without ~: 3 wan 4 ashy, drab, dull, pale 5 ashen, faded, mousy, waxen, white 6 dreary, mousey 8 blanched, bleached 9 colorless, washed-out 10 achromatic
see also color
Hué: 4 city, town
city near ~: 6 Danang
locale: 3 Nam 7 Vietnam
was its capital: 4 Anam 5 Annam
hued: 5 vivid 7 vibrant 8 colorful 9 chromatic
Huejutla: 4 city, town
locale: 6 Mexico 7 Hidalgo
huemul: 4 deer
relative: 3 elk, roe 4 axis, pudu, shou, sika 5 moose 6 chital, hangul, sambar, sambur, thamin, wapiti 7 brocket, caribou, muntjac, muntjak, sambhar, sambhur 8 reindeer 9 barasingh
Hues Corporation song: Rock the Boat (1974)
Huetamo: 4 city, town
locale: 6 Mexico 9 Michoacán
Huey: 4 Long 5 Lewis 6 Newton
brother: 5 Dewey, Louie
Donald Duck, to ~: 4 unca
huff: 3 pet 4 pant, puff, rage, snit, stew, tiff 5 pique, snort, tizzy 7 bad mood, umbrage 10 irritation, resentment

and puff: 4 blow, gasp, pant

be in a ~: 4 mope, sulk 5 brood, grump, scowl 6 resent

in a ~: 3 hot, mad 4 curt, ired, sore 5 angry, cross, irate, livid, moody, onery, riled, short, sulky, surly, testy, upset, vexed, wroth 6 crabby, crusty, fuming, grumpy, ireful, ornery, peeved, piqued, put out, raging, raving, red-hot, snappy, stewed, sullen, touchy 7 angered, annoyed, enraged, fretful, furious, nettled, peevish, pettish, ranting, waspish 8 choleric, fretsome, grumpish, incensed, inflamed, maddened, offended, outraged, petulant, provoked, snappish, wrathful 9 crotchety, fractious, indignant, irascible, irritable, irritated, querulous, resentful, splenetic 10 freaked out, infuriated, out of sorts

Huff: 3 Sam

huffer, fictional: 4 wolf 10 Big Bad Wolf

huffiness: 3 ire 4 snit 5 anger, wrath 6 dander, temper 9 pugnacity, short fuse, surliness

huffish: 4 curt 5 cross, testy 6 crabby, cranky, grumpy, snappy, touchy 7 grouchy, peevish, waspish 8 bullying, grumpish, insolent, snappish 9 irascible, irritable 10 blustering, out of sorts, swaggering

Huffman: 8 Felicity

Huff, Sam sport: 8 football

huffy: 3 hot, mad 4 curt, ired, sore 5 angry, cross, irate, livid, moody, onery, riled, short, sulky, surly, testy, upset, vexed, wroth 6 crabby, crusty, fuming, grumpy, ireful, ornery, peeved, piqued, put out, raging, raving, red-hot, snappy, stewed, sullen, touchy 7 angered, annoyed, enraged, fretful, furious, in a snit, nettled, peevish, pettish, ranting, waspish 8 choleric, fretsome, grumpish, incensed, inflamed, maddened, offended, outraged, petulant, provoked, snappish, wrathful 9 crotchety, fractious, indignant, irascible, irritable, irritated, querulous, resentful, splenetic 10 freaked out, infuriated, out of sorts

hug: 4 hold, lock, love 5 clasp, crush, greet, press, touch 6 caress, clench, clinch, clutch, cradle, cuddle, enfold, infold, nestle 7 cling to, embrace, envelop, snuggle, squeeze, welcome 8 greeting 9 hold close, keep close

love letter ~ s: 3 OOO

partner: 4 kiss

__ hug: 4 bear 5 bunny

huge: 3 big 4 vast 5 bulky, giant, great, gross, heavy, jumbo, large, massy, mondo 6 cosmic, mighty 7 hulking, immense, mammoth, massive, monster, oceanic, outsize, sizable, titanic 8 colossal, cosmical, enormous, gigantic, king-size, oversize, sizeable, spacious, terrific, towering, whapping, whopping 9 cavernous, cyclopean, extensive, fantastic, herculean, humongous, leviathan, monstrous, overlarge, oversized, ponderous, walloping 10 gargantuan, monumental, overweight, prodigious, stupendous, tremendous

amount: 4 lots, slew 5 scads 6 oodles, scores

poetically: 5 enorm

prefix: 4 mega-

seem ~: 4 loom 5 tower

hugely: 4 much, very 5 quite 6 highly, vastly 7 awfully, but good, greatly 9 extremely, in a big way 10 incredibly, thoroughly

hugeness: 4 size 8 enormity 9 amplitude, immensity, largeness, magnitude 10 infinitude

huggable: 6 cuddly 7 snuggly 10 cuddlesome

hugger-mugger: 4 mask, mess, veil 5 chaos, cloak, mussy 6 covert, jumble, muddle, secret 7 conceal, jumbled, muddled, secrecy 8 balled-up, confused, disarray, disorder, fouled-up 9 concealed, confusion 10 disorderly, in disarray, in disorder, keep secret, undercover

__-huggers: 3 hip

Huggies: 6 diaper

alternative: 4 Luvs 7 Drypers, Pampers

hugging: 6 in love, tender 7 amorous 8 romantic 10 passionate

Huggins: 3 Roy 6 Miller 7 Charles, William

Huggins, Charles: 8 Nobelist

Huggins, William: 10 astronomer

Hugh: 5 Capet, Downs, Grant 6 Hefner, Laurie, O'Brian, Wilson 7 Jackman, Lofting, Marlowe, Walpole 8 Beaumont, Griffith, Masekela 9 McElhenny 10 MacDiarmid

in Italian: 3 Ugo

Hughes: 3 Ken, Ted 4 John, Rudd 5 Jimmy, Sarah 6 Howard 7 Barnard 8 Langston

Hughes, Howard

spouse: Terry Moore, Jean Peters

Hughes, John: 8 director

film: The Breakfast Club (1985)
Ferris Bueller's Day Off (1986)
Planes, Trains & Automobiles (1987)
She's Having a Baby (1988)
Sixteen Candles (1984)
Uncle Buck (1989)
Weird Science (1985)

Hughes, Langston: 6 author, writer

collaborator: Hurston

work: Ask Your Mama
The Big Sea
Dream Deferred
Ennui
I, Too
I Wonder As I Wander
Jazzonia
Mule Bone
Po' Boy Blues
Sea Calm

Hughes, Sarah: 6 skater

Hughes, Ted: 4 poet 7 British

spouse: Sylvia Plath

Hughie: 8 Jennings

Hugli, city on the: 8 Calcutta

Hugo: 4 Ball 5 award, Black 6 Victor 7 De Vries, Grotius 9 Fregonese, Gernsback 10 Montenegro

contemporary: 5 Dumas

see also French

Hugo, Victor: 6 author, French, writer

work: Hernani
The Hunchback of Notre Dame
Les Misérables

__ Huguenots: 3 Les

Huguenot stronghold: 4 Caen

Huh?: 4 what

huia: 4 bird

Huilango: 4 city, town

locale: 6 Mexico

Huimanguillo: 4 city, town

locale: 6 Mexico 7 Tabasco

huipil: 6 blouse

huisache: 5 shrub

huit: 5 eight 6 French

follower: 4 neuf

preceder: 4 sept

Huitzilopochtli worshiper: 5 Aztec

Huitzuco: 4 city, town

locale: 6 Mexico 8 Guerrero

Huixquilucan: 4 city, town

locale: 6 Mexico

Huixtla: 4 city, town

locale: 6 Mexico 7 Chiapas

hula: 5 dance

accessory: 3 lei

skirt material: 5 grass

strings: 3 uke

where to see a ~: 4 luau

hula __: 5 skirt

Hula __: 4 Bowl, Hoop

Hula Hoop: 3 fad

company: 5 Wham-o

hula-hula: 5 dance

Hulce, Tom: 5 actor

film: Amadeus (1984)
Black Rainbow (1991)
Dominick and Eugene (1988)
Parenthood (1989)
Those Lips, Those Eyes (1980)

hulk: 4 boat, loom 5 tower, wreck 9 shipwreck

like a ~: 5 beefy, bulky, burly, hefty, husky 6 brawny 7 massive 9 strapping

Hulk: 5 Hogan

hulking: 3 big 4 huge, vast 5 beefy, bulky, burly, giant, great, hefty, jumbo, large, stout 6 clumsy, sturdy 7 immense, mammoth, massive, sizable, titanic, weighty 8 colossal, enormous, gigantic, imposing, king-size, muscular, oversize, sizeable, towering, ungainly, unwieldy, whapping, whopping 9 Herculean, humongous, lumbering, overlarge, ponderous, strapping, unwieldly, whalelike 10 cumbersome, gargantuan, monumental, prodigious, stupendous, tremendous

hull: 3 bur, pod 4 body, husk, peel, rind, skin 5 cover, crust, frame, shell, shuck, strip 6 bottom, casing 8 covering 10 integument

appendage: 3 fin

caulking: 5 oakum

interior: 4 hold

outer ~ of a trimaran: 3 ama

part: 3 rib 4 keel, wale 5 bilge

hull __: 6 girder 7 balance

__ hull: 6 convex 7 planing

Hull: 4 city, port, town 5 Bobby, Isaac 7 Cordell 9 Josephine

locale: 6 Canada, Québec

Hull __: 5 House

hullabaloo: 3 ado, cry, din, row 4 flap, to-do 5 babel, furor, hoo-ha, mania, melee, noise, scene, whirl 6 bedlam, clamor, hassle, hoopla, hubbub, jangle, lather, outcry, pother, racket, ruckus, rumpus, tumult, uproar 7 clatter, ruction, turmoil 8 brouhaha, disorder, rowdydow 9 hue and cry 10 clattering, excitement, hubba-hubba

Hull, Bobby

milieu: 3 ice 4 rink 5 arena

org.: 3 NHL

Hull, Cordell: 8 Nobelist

Hull, Josephine Oscar: Harvey

hully gully: 5 dance

Hulme heroine: 3 nun

Hulot portrayer: 4 Tati

Hulse, Russell: 8 Nobelist 9 physicist

hum: 3 pur 4 buzz, purr, roll, sing, whir, whiz, zoom 5 croon, drone, sound, whirr 6 bustle, intone, mantra, mumble, murmur 7 mantram, operate, vibrate, whisper 9 bombinate, undertone

ender: 3 bug 4 drum

human: 4 body, soul, warm 5 being, biped, child, woman 6 mortal, person 7 primate 8 fallible, naked ape 9 character, Cro-Magnon, earthborn, earthling, incarnate 10 altruistic, error-prone, individual

act ~: 3 err

being: 4 life, soul 5 wight 6 person 10 individual

combining form: 5 homin- 6 homini- 7 anthrop- 8 anthropo-

dynamo: 4 doer 7 hustler 8 go-getter, live wire

ending: 3 oid

genus: 4 homo

it's ~: 5 to err

race: 3 man 4 life 5 Earth, world 6 people 7 mankind

resources: 5 staff 6 people 7 workers 9 employees, personnel, work force

rights org.: 3 ADL 4 ACLU 5 NAACP

score: 5 nails 6 digits

human __: 4 race 5 being, error 6 nature, rights 7 ecology

Human __: 5 Beinz, Touch 6 League, Nature

Human __ Project: 6 Genome

Human __, The: 5 Beast 6 Comedy

__ humana: 3 vox

Human Beast, The author: Emile Zola

Human Comedy, The: 5 novel

author: Honoré de Balzac, William Saroyan

character: 4 Bess 5 Homer, Katey, Tobey 6 Lionel

Human Comedy, The (1943 film)

cast: Jackie Jenkins, Frank Morgan, Mickey Rooney

Human Concretion artist: 3 Arp

humane: 4 good, kind, mild 5 noble 6 benign, caring, gentle, kindly, tender 7 clement, ethical, lenient, sparing 8 merciful, tolerant 9 unselfish 10 altruistic, benevolent, charitable, reasonable

org.: 4 SPCA 5 ASPCA

humane __: 7 society

humaneness: 5 heart 8 goodness 10 compassion

__ humani generis: 6 amicus

human-interest __: 5 story

__ humanism: 7 secular

humanist

British ~: 4 More

French ~: 8 Rabelais

humanistic: 6 giving 7 liberal 8 generous 9 classical, unselfish 10 benevolent, bighearted, charitable

humanitarian: 4 good, kind 6 giving, kindly 7 liberal 8 altruist, do-gooder, generous, merciful 9 unselfish

concern: 5 needy

no ~: 5 miser, piker 7 Scrooge 8 tightwad 9 skinflint 10 cheapskate, pinchpenny

__-humanité: 4 lèse

humanities: 4 arts 10 literature

class: 3 soc. 9 sociology

deg.: 3 LHD

humanity: 5 flesh, mercy, world 6 lenity, people 7 charity, society 8 kindness, lenience 9 tolerance

humanize: 4 ease 6 gentle, mellow, soften, temper 8 civilize

humankind: 5 flesh, world 7 society 9 community

Human Nature (2001 film)

cast: Patricia Arquette, Miranda Otto, Tim Robbins

Human Nature (1983 song) artist: Michael Jackson

__ humano: 4 jure

Humanoids From the Deep (1980 film)

cast: Doug McClure, Vic Morrow, Ann Turkel

Human Resources worker: 5 hirer

humans: 4 folk 5 folks 6 people

Human Touch (1992 song) artist: Bruce Springsteen
humanum __ errare: **3** est
Humbard: **3** Rex
Humber: **5** river
locale: **7** England
source ~: **4** Ouse **5** Trent
Humberstone, H. Bruce: **8** director
film: Charlie Chan at the Opera (1936)
If I Had a Million (1932)
I Wake Up Screaming (1941)
Sun Valley Serenade (1941)
Three Little Girls in Blue (1946)
Wonder Man (1945)
humble: **3** low, shy **4** base, mean, meek, poor, puny, snub, sunk **5** abase, abash, lower, lowly, plain, shame, small, timid **6** abject, common, debase, demean, demote, demure, meager, measly, menial, modest, paltry, reduce, shabby, simple, squash, subdue **7** bashful, chasten, conquer, deflate, degrade, ignoble, lowborn, mortify, pitiful, put down, scrubby, servile, unknown **8** cast down, contrite, inferior, ordinary, plebeian, pull down, reserved, retiring, take down, vanquish, wretched, yielding **9** bring down, denigrate, diffident, discredit, embarrass, humiliate, miserable **10** inglorious, put to shame, respectful, soft-spoken, unassuming
abode: **5** hovel, shack **6** lean-to, shanty
not ~: **4** vain **5** cocky, proud **7** fustian, haughty, stuck-up **8** arrogant, boastful, cocksure, egoistic, puffed up **9** bigheaded, conceited **10** egocentric, swaggering
oneself: **4** sink **5** crawl, kneel, stoop **6** grovel
humble __: **3** pie **5** abode, plant
humbled: **7** abashed, ashamed **8** penitent **9** awestruck, regretful **10** remorseful
meal for the ~: **4** crow
humbleness: **7** modesty, reserve **8** humility
__ humble pie: **3** eat
Humboldt: **3** bay **5** river **7** current
city on the ~: **4** Elko
river locale: **6** Nevada
Humboldt's Gift author: Saul Bellow
humbug: **3** con, gas, rot **4** blah, bosh, bull, bunk, cant, guff, hoax, jazz, jive, pooh, ruse, scam, sham, tosh **5** bilge, bluff, feint, fraud, fudge, hokum, hooey, prate, put-on, quack, sting, stuff, trash, tripe **6** babble, bunkum, bushwa, deceit, drivel, footle, gabble, gammon, gibber, havers, hot air, hustle, jabber, jargon, kibosh, piffle **7** baloney, blarney, blather, blether, boloney, bushwah, con game, eyewash, fast one, flannel, flubdub, fustian, garbage, hogwash, inanity, rubbish, snow job, swindle, twaddle **8** artifice, buncombe, claptrap, falderal, falderol, flimflam, flummery, folderal, folderol, nonsense, slipslop, snake oil, tommyrot, trumpery **9** banana oil, empty talk, gibberish, goofiness, hypocrite, imposture, kidstakes, moonshine, poppycock, rigmarole, silliness **10** applesauce, balderdash, bilge water, codswallop, double-talk, empty words, flapdoodle, galimatias, Jabberwock, mumbo jumbo, rigamarole, subterfuge, taradiddle
__, humbug!: **3** Bah
Humbug!: **3** bah **5** pshaw
humdify: **6** dampen
humdinger: **3** pip **4** lulu, oner **5** beaut, dandy, doozy, prize **6** beauty, doozie, pistol **7** whapper, whopper
humdrum: **4** arid, blah, drab, dull, tame **5** banal, bland, corny, hokey, passé, prosy, stale, trite, unfun, vapid **6** boring, common, dreary, jejune, old hat **7** clichéd, fatuous, insipid, mundane, nowhere, prosaic, routine, tedious **8** bromidic, dragging, everyday, mediocre, monotony, ordinary, outdated, outmoded, plodding, tiresome **9** hackneyed, ponderous, prosaical, wearisome **10** dullsville, enervating, monotonous, pedestrian, uneventful, uninspired, unoriginal
Hume: **4** Brit, John **5** David **6** Cronyn
Hume, David: **8** Scottish **11** philosopher
Hume, John: **8** Nobelist
humeral __: **4** veil
humerus: **4** bone **7** arm bone
neighbor: **4** ulna
opposite: **5** femur
humid: **3** wet **4** damp, dank, dewy **5** close, moist, muggy, soggy, undry **6** clammy, hydric, steamy, sticky, sultry, sweaty **7** wettish **8** tropical **10** equatorial, sweltering
humidifier
output: **5** vapor
part: **5** grill **6** grille
humidify: **3** wet **4** damp, soak **5** water **6** dampen **7** moisten **8** saturate, sprinkle **10** moisturize
humidity: **7** swelter, wetness **8** dampness, dankness, dewiness, moisture **9** mugginess, sogginess **10** clamminess, steaminess, stickiness, sultriness
react to ~: **4** wilt
humidor: **3** box **9** container **10** receptacle
item: **5** cigar, claro **6** corona, Havana
humiliate: **3** rip **4** gibe, jeer, jibe, mock, sink, slam, slur, snub, sunk **5** abase, abash, abuse, break, decry, libel, lower, scorn, shame, spurn, taunt **6** debase, defame, demean, demote, deride, dump on, heckle, humble, impugn, insult, malign, offend, rebuff, reduce, slight, squash, subdue, vilify **7** affront, asperse, chasten, deflate, degrade, disdain, mortify, put down, rank out, run down, slander, traduce **8** belittle, cast down, denounce, disgrace, dishonor, pull down, ridicule, take down, vilipend **9** bring down, denigrate, discomfit, discredit, disparage, embarrass, shoot down **10** calumniate, dishearten, disrespect, put to shame
humiliated: **5** small **6** abject **7** abashed
humiliating: **4** base, vile **6** odious **8** humbling, infamous, shameful **9** degrading **10** belittling, derogatory, mortifying
humiliation: **3** dig **4** barb, gibe, jibe, slam, slap, slur, snub **5** abuse, libel, scorn, shame, taunt **6** rebuff, slight **7** affront, calumny, catcall, disdain, mockery, obloquy, offense, put-down, slander, undoing **8** contempt, disgrace, dishonor, ignominy, ridicule **9** abashment, cheap shot, contumely **10** disrespect, opprobrium
humility: **7** modesty **8** docility, meekness, timidity **9** lowliness, servility **10** demureness, submission
eschew ~: **4** brag, crow **5** boast, exult, gloat, vaunt **6** hotdog **7** bluster, show off, swagger, talk big **8** showboat **9** gasconade **10** grandstand
hummable: **6** catchy
hummer: **4** bird
Hummer: **7** vehicle
humming: **4** busy **5** abuzz **6** murmur
hummingbird
color of some ~ throats: **4** ruby
emulate a ~: **4** dart **5** hover, whirr
home: **4** nest
relative: **5** swift
sound: **5** whirr
Hummingbird (1955 song) artist: Les Paul and Mary Ford
hummock: **4** rise **5** knoll, mound **7** hillock
humongous: **3** big **4** huge, vast **5** giant, great, jumbo, large, massy **7** hulking, immense, mammoth, massive, sizable, titanic **8** colossal, enormous, gigantic, king-size, oversize, sizeable, towering, whapping, whopping **9** fantastic, Herculean, overlarge **10** gargantuan, monumental, prodigious, stupendous, tremendous
prefix: **4** mega-
quantity: **3** sea **4** lots, raft **5** ocean, scads **6** oodles
humor: **3** fun, joy, wit **4** baby, gags, mood, tone, vein **5** farce, jests, jokes, spoil **6** banter, coddle, comedy, gaiety, gayety, joking, levity, makeup, nature, pamper, permit, please, spirit, temper, whimsy **7** cater to, gratify, indulge, jesting, kidding, mollify, whimsey **8** badinage, clowning, drollery, give in to, raillery, tolerate **9** amusement, flippancy, funniness **10** buffoonery, comicality, jocoseness, jocularity, tomfoolery, wisecracks, witticisms
bodily ~: **4** bile **5** blood **6** choler, phlegm **8** jocosity **9** silliness
country ~: **4** corn
dry ~: **4** salt
ending: **3** ous
good ~: **3** joy **5** mirth **6** gaiety, gayety **9** happiness
ill ~: **6** spleen **7** bad mood **9** testiness **10** crabbiness, crankiness, grumpiness, irritation, touchiness
like some ~: **5** crude **6** coarse, earthy, folksy
not in good ~: **4** dour, glum, ugly **5** cross, gruff, huffy, irate, sulky, surly, testy **6** crabby, cranky, gloomy, grumpy, morose, ornery, sullen **7** grouchy, hostile, peevish **8** frowning, growling, perverse, snappish **9** crotchety, irritable **10** out of sorts, ungracious
overwhelm with ~: **4** slay
response: **4** ha-ha
sardonic ~: **5** irony **7** sarcasm
sense of ~: **3** wit **9** wittiness **10** cleverness
without ~: **5** drily, dryly
__ humor: **3** ill **4** good **5** black **7** aqueous, gallows
Humoresque (1946 film)
cast: Joan Crawford, John Garfield, Oscar Levant
director: Jean Negulesco
humoring: **7** coaxing, lenient **8** cajolery **9** wheedling **10** indulgence
humorist: **3** wag, wit **4** card, zany **5** clown, comic, cutup, joker **8** comedian, jokester, quipster, satirist **9** jokesmith **10** comedienne
humorless: **5** sober, staid **6** solemn, somber, stuffy **7** deadpan, serious **9** unamusing **10** no-nonsense, unhumorous
humorous: **4** camp, joky, nice, rich, zany **5** campy, comic, droll, funny, jokey, light, merry, silly, witty **6** harhar, ironic, jocose, jovial **7** amusing, comical, jesting, jocular, joshing, playful, waggish **8** farcical, humorous **9** facetious, hilarious, laughable, ludicrous, priceless, whimsical **10** capricious, gut-busting
dryly ~: **3** wry **5** droll **8** sardonic
in music: **5** buffa, buffo
remark: **3** gag, mot, pun **4** gibe, jest, joke, quip **5** crack **6** bon mot, zinger **8** one-liner **9** wisecrack, witticism
humorously: **5** in fun **7** as a joke, as a lark
in music: **7** giocoso
__ Humorum: **4** Mare
hump: **4** arch **5** bulge, mound **8** mountain, swelling **9** elevation **10** projection, protrusion
ender: **4** back
humpback: **5** whale
home: **3** sea **5** ocean **8** high seas
humpback __: **5** whale **6** salmon
humped animal: **4** zebu **5** camel **8** Bactrian **9** dromedary
Humperdinck, Engelbert
song: After the Lovin' (1976)
Release Me (1967)
Humphrey: **6** Bogart, Hubert, Muriel **7** Gilbert
in Italian: **8** Onofredo
Humphry: **4** Davy
Humpty Dumpty: **3** egg
like ~: **4** ooid, oval **5** obese, ovate, ovoid, round
Humpty Dumpty sat __ wall: **3** on a
humus: **3** mor **4** soil **5** mulch **7** compost **10** fertilizer
Humvee forerunner: **4** jeep
Hun: **6** Vandal **7** invader, ravager **8** marauder **9** barbarian
king: **4** Atli
Huna: **3** bay
locale: **7** Iceland
Hunan: **7** cuisine
like ~: **3** hot **5** spicy
pan: **3** wok
hunch: **4** arch, bend, flex, idea **5** cower, guess, slump, squat, stoop **6** augury, crouch, hunker, notion, theory **7** feeling, inkling, portent, surmise **8** forecast, instinct **9** intuition, suspicion **10** assumption, conjecture, gut feeling, impression, prediction
have a ~: **4** feel **5** sense **6** intuit **7** predict, suspect **9** determine, speculate **10** anticipate
__ hunch: **3** on a
Hunchback of Notre Dame, The (1939 film)
cast: Cedric Hardwicke, Charles Laughton, Thomas Mitchell
director: William Dieterle
Hunchback of Notre Dame, The (1923 film) cast: Lon Chaney
Hunchback of Notre Dame, The
author: Victor Hugo
Hunches in Bunches author: Dr. Seuss
hundred: **6** centum **7** century
combining form: **4** cent-, hect-, hekt- **5** centi-, hecto-, hekto-
DC ~: **6** Senate
dollars: **5** C-note, C-spot **8** Franklin
ender: **6** weight
one in a ~: **4** cent
percent: **3** all **5** fully **6** in full, in toto, purely, wholly **7** cap-a-pie, totally, utterly **8** entirely, from A to Z **9** all the way, every inch, to the hilt **10** absolutely, completely, thoroughly, to the limit
sawbucks: **4** one G **5** G-note
years: **7** century **9** centenary
Hundred __ War: **5** Years'
Hundred __ Woods: **4** Acre

__ Hundred and One Dalmatians: 3 One
__ Hundred Men and a Girl: 3 One
Hundred Pounds of Clay, A (1961 song) artist: Gene McDaniels
__ hundred rummy: 4 five
hundred's __: 5 place
Hundred Secret Senses, The author: Amy Tan
hundredth: 9 centenary
combining form: 4 cent- 5 centi-
part: 3 pct. 7 percent
hundredth's __: 5 place
Hundred Years' __: 3 War
__ Hundred Years of Solitude: 3 One
Hundred Years' War winner: 6 France
hung __: 4 jury
Hungaria composer: 5 Liszt
Hungarian: 8 language
Hungarian __: 7 goulash, pointer
__-Hungarian Empire: 6 Austro
Hungarian Rhapsodies composer: 5 Liszt
Hungary: 6 nation 7 country
airline: 5 MALEV
capital: 8 Budapest
cellist: 7 Starker
cheese: 8 Liptauer
city: 4 Eger, Gyor, Pécs, Raab 5 Tokay 6 Szeged 7 Miskolc 8 Budapest, Debrecen
composer: 5 Lehár
conductor: 5 Solti, Szell 6 Dorati, Reiner 7 Ormandy
dance: 7 csardas, czardas
Danube, in ~: 4 Duna
horseman: 6 hussar
jam: 6 lekvar
lake: 7 Balaton
language: 5 Ugric
money: 5 pengo 6 filler, forint
mountain: 5 Kekes
neighbor: 3 Aus., Rom., Ukr. 4 Aust. 7 Austria, Croatia, Romania, Ukraine 8 Slovakia, Slovenia 10 Yugoslavia
Nobelist in Chemistry: 8 de Hevesy
Nobelist in Literature: 7 Kertész
Nobelist in Medicine: 12 Szent-Györgyi
org.: 4 NATO
poet: 6 József
river of ~: 4 Eger, Raab, Raba 5 Tisza
saint: 7 Stephen 9 Elizabeth
sheepdog: 4 puli 6 kuvasz
sheepdogs: 5 pulik
violinist: 4 Auer 7 Joachim, Szigeti
wine: 5 tokay
writer: 6 Molnár
__-Hungary: 7 Austria
hunger: 3 yen 4 itch, long, need, sigh, want, wish 5 greed, yearn 6 desire, thirst 7 craving, edacity, longing 8 appetite, cupidity, languish, munchies, voracity, yearning 9 appetence, eagerness, esurience, hankering, indigence 10 famishment, sweet tooth
cause ~: 6 famish
end one's ~: 3 eat
feeling of ~: 4 pang
for: 4 need, want
(for): 4 long, pant, pine 5 crave
reveal one's ~: 5 drool 8 salivate
symbol of voracious ~: 3 maw
__ hunger: 4 from
hungering: 7 longing, starved 8 starving
hunger strike, go on a: 4 fast
hungrily, eat: 4 wolf 6 devour, gobble, inhale 7 scarf up 9 scarf down
hungry: 5 eager, empty, itchy, unfed 6 greedy 7 longing, starved, thirsty, wishful 8 covetous, desirous, edacious, esurient, famished, ravenous, starving, unfilled 9 ambitious, hankering, insatiate, voracious
go ~: 4 fast 6 starve
no longer ~: 4 full 5 sated 6 gorged 7 glutted, stuffed 8 satiated 9 surfeited
hungry __ bear: 3 as a
Hungry __: 4 Eyes, Jack 5 Heart
__ Hungry: 4 Stay
Hungry (1966 song) artist: Paul Revere and the Raiders
Hungry Eyes (1987 song) artist: Eric Carmen
Hungry Heart (1980 song) artist: Bruce Springsteen
__ hungry I could...: 4 I'm so
Hungry Like the Wolf (1983 song) artist: Duran Duran
hung up: 4 late 5 tardy 7 overdue, puzzled, worried 8 detained, obsessed
__-hung window: 6 double, single
hunk: 3 gob, wad 4 clod, glob, lump, mass, part, slab, stud 5 batch, block, chunk, clump, he-man, macho, piece, scrap, slice, solid, wedge 6 Apollo, looker, morsel, nugget 7 portion, section 8 beefcake, quantity
asset: 3 bod
of junk: 3 dud 5 crate, lemon
hunker down: 3 sit 4 bend, duck 5 hunch, squat, stoop 6 crouch, huddle
__ Hunk O' Love: 4 A Big
Hunkpapa: 5 tribe 6 Indian 7 Amerind
hunky: 4 hale, iron, wiry 5 beefy, burly, hardy, hefty, husky, lusty, stout, tough 6 brawny, hearty, mighty, potent, robust, rugged, sinewy, steely, stocky, sturdy, virile 7 doughty 8 athletic, forceful, handsome, indurate, muscular, powerful, puissant, stalwart, vigorous 9 Atlantean, Herculean, strapping, well-built 10 able-bodied, red-blooded
hunky-dory: 3 A-OK, def, rad 4 aces, A-one, boss, braw, cool, dece, fine, gear, jake, keen, neat, nice, phat, rosy, tuff 5 dandy, ducky, grand, great, marvy, neato, nobby, prime, slick, super, swell 6 bang on, bang-up, bonzer, bosker, choice, divine, dreamy, far-out, gnarly, groovy, lovely, peachy, slap-up, spot on, superb, terrif, tiptop, unreal, whizzo, wicked 7 amazing, awesome, capital, corking, perfect, ripping, skookum, stellar, sublime 8 dazzling, especial, eximious, fabulous, five-star, four-star, frabjous, glorious, heavenly, jim-dandy, slambang, smashing, splendid, standout, sterling, stickout, superior, terrific, top-level, topnotch, very good, wondrous 9 admirable, agreeable, bodacious, Endsville, excellent, exemplary, exquisite, first-rate, high-grade, marvelous, sollicker, top-flight, wonderful 10 acceptable, first-class, hotsy-totsy, jack-a-dandy, out of sight, peachy-keen, phenomenal, remarkable, stupendous, super-duper
Hunley: 5 Leann
Hunnicutt: 5 Gayle
Hunny B's: 6 cereal
competitor: 3 Kix 4 Life, Trix 5 Kashi, Quisp, Total 6 Kaboom, Muesli, Oreo O's, Pablum, Smacks 7 All-Bran, Crispix, Harmony, Mueslix, Oat Bran, Pokemon 8 Boo Berry, Cheerios, Corn Chex, Corn Pops, Fiber One, Rice Chex, Special K, Uncle Sam, Wheaties 9 Alpha Bits, Apple Zaps, Grape Nuts, Honey Comb, Just Right, Wheat Chex 10 Apple Jacks, Bran Flakes, Cap'n Crunch, Cocoa Puffs, Froot Loops, Mini-Wheats, Nutri-Grain, Puffed Rice, Quaker Oats, Smart Start 11 Cocoa Blasts, Cookie Crisp, Golden Crisp, Lucky Charms, Puffed Wheat, Sweet Crunch, Waffle Crisp
hunt: 4 look, rake, root, seek 5 chase, probe, prowl, quest, scour, stalk, trace, track, trail 6 chivvy, forage, prey on, pursue, search 7 dragnet, look for, pursuit, ransack, rummage, seek out 8 run after, scout out, scrounge 9 chase down, come after, track down
and peck: 4 type
for: 4 seek, shop 6 look up, pursue 7 scout up 8 run after, scout out
(for): 3 dig 4 fish 5 quest 6 forage
goddess: 5 Diana
illegally: 5 poach
in the dark: 5 grope 6 fumble 9 feel about
on the ~: 9 piratical, predatory, raptorial, vulturous 10 predacious
(out): 4 find 6 ferret
partner: 4 peck
scavenger ~: 4 game
starter: 3 man 4 head
hunt __: 3 box 5 board, table 6 button
__ hunt: 4 drag 5 still, witch
__-hunt: 3 job
Hunt: 3 Tim 5 Helen, Leigh, Linda, Peter 6 Bonnie, Holman, Marsha, Walter
__ Hunt: 3 Man, Sea 4 Wild 5 Mouse
hunt and __: 4 peck
hunted: 4 mark, pawn, prey 5 patsy 6 pigeon, quarry, target, victim
hunter: 3 dog 5 canid, Diana, horse, jager, Orion, yager 6 canine, equine, jaeger, nimrod, seeker 7 Actaeon, pursuer, quester, shikari, stalker, tracker 8 Atalanta, Atalante, searcher, shikaree 9 Elmer Fudd, sportsman
attire: 3 cap 4 camo, topi, vest 5 topee
Biblical ~: 4 Cain, Esau
bird ~: 6 fowler
cabin: 5 lodge
cartoon ~: 4 Fudd 5 Elmer
conger ~: 5 eeler
fox ~ coat: 5 pinks
fox ~ cry: 4 hark, toho 5 hallo, hillo, hoick, hullo 6 halloa, halloo, hallow, hilloa, hulloo, yoicks
guide: 5 gilly 6 gillie 7 ghillie
mark: 4 game, prey 6 quarry
mythical ~: 5 Orion
need: 3 lic. 4 ammo 5 decoy, rifle 6 waders 7 license
org.: 3 NRA
post: 5 blind, stand
starter: 3 pot 4 head
track: 5 spoor
hunter __: 5 green 6 trials
__ hunter: 3 fox 5 white 6 bounty 7 fortune
__-hunter: 3 job 4 demi
Hunter: 3 Ian, Kim, Tab, Tim 4 Bill, Evan, peak, Ross, Tylo 5 Holly, mount 6 Nimrod, Rachel 7 Alberta, Catfish, Jeffrey 8 mountain
peak locale: 7 New York 9 Catskills
Hunter (NBC drama)
cast: Fred Dryer (Rick Hunter) Stepfanie Kramer (Dee Dee McCall)
employer: L.A.P.D.
__ Hunter, Black Heart: 5 White
Hunter, Catfish: 6 hurler 7 pitcher
Hunter, Evan: 6 author, writer
pseudonym: Ed McBain
real last name: Lombino
work: The Blackboard Jungle
Hunter Gets Captured..., The (1967 song) artist: Marvelettes
Hunter, Holly: 7 actress
film: Always (1989)
Broadcast News (1987)
Copycat (1995)
Living Out Loud (1998)
Miss Firecracker (1989)
O Brother, Where Art Thou? (2000)
The Piano (1993, AA)
Raising Arizona (1987)
Hunter, Ian: 5 actor
film: Appointment in London (1953)
The Girl From 10th Avenue (1935)
The Long Voyage Home (1940)
Strange Cargo (1940)
Hunter, Jeffrey: 5 actor
film: Dreamboat (1952)
The Great Locomotive Chase (1956)
King of Kings (1961)
A Kiss Before Dying (1956)
The Last Hurrah (1958)
No Down Payment (1957)
Sailor of the King (1953)
The Searchers (1956)
Sergeant Rutledge (1960)
Seven Angry Men (1955)
Hunter, Kim: 7 actress
film: Escape From the Planet of the Apes (1971)
Planet of the Apes (1968)
The Seventh Victim (1943)
Stairway to Heaven (1946)
A Streetcar Named Desire (1951, AA)
When Strangers Marry (1944)
The Young Stranger (1957)
Hunter, Rachel spouse: Rod Stewart
hunter's __: 4 moon, pink, robe 5 sauce
__ Hunters, The: 4 Girl 7 Mammoth
Hunter, Tab: 5 actor
film: The Arousers (1970)
Battle Cry (1955)
Damn Yankees (1958)
Gunman's Walk (1958)
That Kind of Woman (1959)
song: Young Love (1957)
__ Hunter, The: 4 Deer
Hunt for Red October, The (1990 film)
cast: Alec Baldwin, Sean Connery, Scott Glenn
device: 5 sonar
director: John McTiernan
Hunt, Helen: 7 actress
film: As Good as It Gets (1997, AA)
Cast Away (2000)
The Curse of the Jade Scorpion (2001)
Mr. Saturday Night (1992)
Pay It Forward (2000)
Trancers (1985)
Twister (1996)
The Waterdance (1992)
What Women Want (2000)
spouse: Hank Azaria
TV: Mad About You
hunting: 5 sport
happy ~ ground: 6 heaven, utopia 7 Arcadia, Elysium 8 paradise 9 Shangri-la
hunting __: 3 box 4 case, horn 5 chair, knife, sword, watch 6 ground 7 leopard
__ hunting: 3 fox, job 4 deer, duck
Huntingdonshire: 6 county
locale: 7 England
Hunting of the Snark, The author: Lewis Carroll
Huntington: 4 town
locale: 7 New York 10 Long Island
Huntington Beach: 4 city, town

locale: 10 California
Huntington Park: 4 city, town
locale: 10 California
__ Hunt Jackson: 5 Helen
Hunt, Leigh: 4 poet 7 British
friend: Shelley, Keats
work: Abou Ben Adhem
Huntley: 4 Chet
colleague: 8 Brinkley
Hunt, Linda Oscar: The Year of Living Dangerously
__ Hunt of the Sun, The: 5 Royal
Hunts: 6 county
locale: 7 England
Hunt's: 6 catsup 7 ketchup
alternative: 5 Heinz 8 Del Monte
Huntsville: 4 city, town
locale: 3 Ala., Tex. 5 Texas 7 Alabama
Hunt, Tim: 8 Nobelist
Huntz: 4 Hall
milieu: 6 Bowery
Hunucmá: 4 city, town
locale: 6 Mexico 7 Yucatán
Huon Gulf, port on: 3 Lae
Hupmobile: 3 car 4 auto 10 automobile
contemporary: 3 Reo
Huppert, Isabelle: 7 actress
film: Bedroom Window (1987)
Coup de Torchon (1981)
Entre Nous (1983)
__-Hur: 3 Ben
Hurd: 7 Gale Ann
hurdle: 3 bar, hop, rub 4 jump, leap, lick, snag 5 bound, clear, minus, vault 6 hamper, spring 7 barrier, hop over 8 blockage, drawback, handicap, jump over, leap over, obstacle, overcome, surmount, weakness 9 barricade, detriment, hindrance, liability 10 difficulty, impediment
hurdler: 5 racer 6 runner 7 athlete
__ hurdles: 3 low 4 high
hurdy-gurdy: 8 keyboard 10 instrument
Hurdy Gurdy Man (1968 song) artist: Donovan
hurl: 3 lob, peg 4 cast, fire, pelt, send, slam, toss 5 chuck, fling, heave, pitch, shoot, sling, throw 6 launch, let fly, propel 7 deliver, project 8 catapult, jettison
hurler: 7 catapul, pitcher
stat.: 3 ERA
hurley: 4 club
Hurley: 3 Liz 9 Elizabeth
Hurley, Elizabeth: 7 actress
film: Austin Powers: International Man of Mystery (1997)
Austin Powers: The Spy Who Shagged Me (1999)
Bedazzled (2000)
Permanent Midnight (1998)
hurling: 4 game 5 sport
hurly-burly: 3 ado 4 flap, stir, to-do 5 chaos, furor, hoo-ha 6 bedlam, clamor, hubbub, pother, racket, ruckus, rumpus, squall, tumult, uproar 7 turmoil 8 brouhaha, upheaval 9 commotion, confusion 10 hullabaloo
Hurlyburly author: David Rabe
Hurok: 3 Sol
Huron: 4 lake 5 tribe 6 Indian 7 Amerind
locale: 4 S. Dak. 6 Canada
neighbor: 4 Erie
hurrah: 3 cry, olé, rah, yay 4 hail, viva, vive, yell 5 bravo, cheer, huzza, whoop 6 banzai, hooray, hot dog, hubbub, huzzah, yippee 7 fanfare, way to go 9 commotion 10 boola boola, excitement, halleluhah, hot diggety
in Spanish: 3 olé
__ Hurrah, The: 4 Last
hurray preceder: 3 hip
hurricane: 4 blow, wind 5 storm 7 cyclone, lantern, monsoon, tempest, tornado, twister, typhoon
center: 3 eye
every other ~: 3 her, him
lamp part: 4 wick
like a ~ center: 4 calm 5 quiet 6 placid, serene 8 tranquil
remains: 6 debris, rubble
track: 4 path
water-wall: 5 surge
1960: 5 Donna
1964: 4 Dora
1970: 5 Celia
1972: 5 Agnes
1975: 6 Eloise
1992: 5 Iniki 6 Andrew
1999: 4 Gert 6 Bertha
zone: 5 coast 9 shoreline
hurricane __: 4 deck, lamp 7 lantern, warning
hurricane-__ wind: 5 force
Hurricane rival: 4 Blue, King, Star, Wild 5 Bruin, Devil, Flame, Flyer, Oiler, Sabre, Shark 6 Canuck, Coyote, Ranger 7 Capital, Panther, Penguin, Red Wing, Senator 8 Canadien, Islander, Predator, Thrasher 9 Avalanche, Blackhawk, Lightning, Maple Leaf 10 Blue Jacket, Mighty Duck
Hurricanes: 3 six 4 team
home: 4 N. Car. 7 Raleigh
milieu: 3 ice 4 rink
org.: 3 NHL
school: 5 Miami
sport: 6 hockey
Hurricane, The (1937 film)
cast: Mary Astor, Jon Hall, Dorothy Lamour
director: John Ford
Hurricane, The (1999 film)
cast: Liev Schreiber, Deborah Kara Unger, Denzel Washington
director: Norman Jewison
hurried: 4 fast, rush 5 brief, brisk, fleet, hasty, quick, rapid, short, swift 6 abrupt, flying, hectic, racing, rushed, speedy, sudden 7 cursory, express, instant, rushing 8 headlong, pell-mell, slapdash 9 breakneck, impetuous 10 double-time, hypersonic, in an uproar, supersonic
hurriedly: 3 PDQ 4 fast 5 apace, madly, short 6 presto 7 briefly, fleetly, hastily, in haste, rapidly, swiftly 8 in a flash, in a jiffy, in no time, on the fly, on the run, pell-mell 9 forthwith, headfirst, instantly, like a shot, posthaste 10 in high gear
leave ~: 4 dart, zoom 5 split 6 decamp 7 take off, vamoose
hurriedness: 3 zip 4 rush 5 haste, speed 6 hustle 8 alacrity, celerity, dispatch, rapidity, scramble, velocity 9 hastiness 10 expedition
hurry: 3 fly, hie, rip, run, zip 4 dart, dash, flit, move, pelt, race, rush, tear, trot, whiz 5 drive, haste, press, scoot, smoke, speed, whisk 6 barrel, bustle, flurry, gallop, hasten, hustle, rocket, scurry, step up 7 be quick, floor it, forward, quicken, scamper, urgency 8 alacrity, celerity, dispatch, expedite, hightail, make time, pressure, rapidity, stampede, step on it, velocity 9 fleetness, go swiftly, make haste, quickness, shake a leg, swiftness 10 accelerate, expedition, get a move on, make tracks, promptness, speediness
in a ~: 7 hastily, quickly, rapidly, swiftly 8 speedily
leave in a ~: 3 hie, run 4 bolt, flee, flit 6 decamp 9 bundle off
old-style: 5 sessa
hurry __ wait: 5 up and
hurry-__: 6 scurry, skurry
__ hurry: 3 in a 4 in no
Hurry!: 4 ASAP, c'mon, stat 6 come on, let's go
Hurry on Down author: John Wain
hurry-scurry: 3 ado 4 dash, fuss, rush, to-do 5 furor, haste, hasty 6 flurry, rushed 7 chaotic, flutter, hurried 8 agitated, confused, pell-mell 9 agitation, confusion
hurry-up: 4 dire, rush 5 acute 6 urgent 7 burning, crucial, exigent 8 pressing 9 important 10 compelling
hurry up and __: 4 wait
Hurst: 4 city, town 6 Fannie
locale: 5 Texas
Hurst, Fannie: 6 author, writer
work: Imitation of Life
Hurst, Fannie work: Imitation of Life
Hurston, Zora Neale: 6 author, writer
collaborator: Hughes
work: Dust Tracks on a Road
Mule Bone
Their Eyes Were Watching God
hurt: 3 ail, cut, hit, ill, mar, vex 4 ache, belt, blow, burn, faze, flog, gash, harm, kick, lash, loss, maim, mall, maul, miff, nick, ouch, pain, pang, scar, slap, slug, sore, stab, tear, whip, yeow, zing 5 abuse, break, burnt, crack, cramp, cut up, flail, lay up, pinch, pique, prick, punch, smart, spank, spite, spoil, sting, throb, upset, whack, wound, wreck, wrong 6 aching, batter, boo-boo, bruise, burned, damage, grazed, grieve, harmed, impair, injure, injury, in pain, lament, lean on, maimed, marred, mauled, mess up, miffed, nicked, offend, pained, piqued, pommel, pummel, punish, rankle, sadden, struck, suffer, tender, torn up, trauma 7 afflict, bruised, contuse, corrupt, crushed, damaged, injured, offense, rough up, scraped, scratch, slander, torment, torture, trample, trouble, unhappy, vitiate, wounded 8 aggrieve, battered, buffeted, busted up, contused, distress, grieving, impaired, insulted, lacerate, maltreat, mischief, offended, soreness 9 affronted, aggrieved, contusion, detriment, displease, disturbed, grievance, indignant, lacerated, miserable, prejudice, resentful, scratched, suffering, undermine 10 affliction, discomfort, distressed, laceration, resentment, traumatize
easily ~: 6 touchy 8 skittish 9 sensitive 10 vulnerable
for: 4 lack, miss, need, want 5 covet, crave 6 desire
heart ~: 5 dolor, grief 6 misery 7 anguish 8 distress
reaction: 2 ow 3 yow 4 ouch, yeow
small ~: 6 boo-boo, bruise 7 scratch
Hurt: 4 John 7 William 8 Mary Beth
Hurt __: 5 So Bad
hurtful: 3 bad, ill 4 evil, mean 5 cruel, harsh, nasty, sharp, snide, toxic 6 aching, animal, bitter, brutal, fierce, lethal, malign, nocent, savage, unkind, wanton 7 baneful, beastly, callous, cutting, harmful, nocuous, noisome, noxious, vicious 8 abrasive, barbaric, damaging, fiendish, grievous, inhumane, inimical, pitiless, ruthless, sadistic, sinister, spiteful, vengeful 9 cutthroat, dangerous, ferocious, injurious, insulting, malicious, merciless, monstrous, poisonous, truculent, upsetting 10 afflictive, maleficent, pernicious, unmerciful, vindictive
hurting: 3 sad 4 achy, sore 6 in pain, misery, somber 7 painful, unhappy 8 wretched 9 irritated, miserable, sorrowful 10 lamentable
for: 7 lacking
Hurting Each Other (1972 song)
artist: Carpenters
Hurt, John: 5 actor
film: Alien (1979)
Captain Corelli's Mandolin (2001)
Contact (1997)
The Elephant Man (1980)
Nineteen Eighty-Four (1984)
Rob Roy (1995)
Scandal (1989)
Second Best (1994)
White Mischief (1988)
hurtle: 3 ram 4 bolt, dart, jerk, jump, race, rush, tear, whiz, zoom 5 crash, lunge, shoot, speed 6 careen, charge, plunge 7 collide 8 catapult, leapfrog
Hurt, Mary Beth: 7 actress
film: Six Degrees of Separation (1993)
The World According to Garp (1982)
__ Hurts: 4 Love
Hurt So Bad (song) artist: Lettermen, Linda Ronstadt, Little Anthony and the Imperials
Hurts So Good (1982 song) artist: John Cougar Mellencamp
__ Hurt, The: 3 Big
Hurt, William: 5 actor
film: The Accidental Tourist (1988)
Altered States (1980)
The Big Chill (1983)
Body Heat (1981)
Broadcast News (1987)
Children of a Lesser God (1986)
The Doctor (1991)
Gorky Park (1983)
Kiss of the Spider Woman (1985, AA)
Lost in Space (1998)
Michael (1996)
One True Thing (1998)
Second Best (1994)
Smoke (1995)
Hus: 3 Jan
husband: 4 keep, male, save 5 groom, hubby, store 6 mister, retain, spouse 7 consort, partner 8 benedict, helpmate, helpmeet 9 other half 10 bridegroom, married man
and wife: 3 duo 4 pair
first ~: 4 Adam
former: 2 ex 7 divorcé
mate: 4 wife 6 missus
starter: 5 house
to-be: 6 fiancé 8 intended 9 betrothed
husbandless: 5 unwed 6 single 8 eligible 9 unmarried 10 unattached
__ husbandry: 6 animal
Husbands and Wives (1992 film)
cast: Woody Allen, Blythe Danner, Judy Davis, Mia Farrow, Juliette Lewis, Liam Neeson, Sydney Pollack
director: Woody Allen
hush: 3 gag 4 calm, lull, mute, stop 5 pause, peace, quiet, shush, still 6 muffle, muzzle, shut up, silent, soothe, stifle 7 cover up, secrecy, silence 8 pipe down, quietude, suppress 9 keep still, quiet down, stillness, voiceless 10 hold it down
money: 5 bribe, graft 6 payoff 7 jobbery 8 kickback 9 blackmail
up: 4 hide 5 quash, quell 6 concel, stifle 7 cover up, smother, squelch 8 palliate, suppress 9 keep quiet 10 hold it down, keep secret

hush __: **5** money, puppy
Hush!: **3** shh **5** bag it **6** shut up, stow it
Hush (1968 song) artist: Deep Purple
hushed: **3** low **4** calm **5** faint, piano, quiet **6** gentle, silent **7** subdued **8** tranquil **9** noiseless, secretive, soundless **10** untroubled
tone: **6** murmur **7** whisper
up: **3** mum **4** calm **5** quiet **6** placid, silent **7** muffled, quieted, stilled **8** becalmed **9** quiescent **10** unspeaking
hush-hush: **5** close, privy **6** covert, hidden, masked, secret, unseen, veiled **7** furtive, private, silence, sub rosa **8** obscured, secluded, secretly, shrouded, stealthy **9** nonpublic, underhand **10** classified, restricted, undercover, under wraps
Hush ... Hush, Sweet Charlotte: **4** film, song
artist: Patti Page
cast: Mary Astor, Victor Buono, Joseph Cotten, Bette Davis, Olivia de Havilland, Bruce Dern, Cecil Kellaway, Agnes Moorehead
director: Robert Aldrich
Hush Puppies mascot: **6** basset
Husing: **3** Ted
husk: **3** bur, pod **4** aril, bark, bran, case, hull, peel, rind, skin **5** chaff, shell, shuck, strip **7** outside **8** covering **10** integument
husker concern: **3** ear **4** corn
huskiness: **3** vim **4** dint, roup, thew **5** brawn, force, might, power, thews, vigor **6** energy, muscle **7** fitness, muscles, potence, potency, stamina **8** vitality **9** endurance, fortitude, puissance **10** brute force
husking __: **3** bee
husky: **3** big, dog **4** deep, hale, iron, well, wiry **5** beefy, burly, canid, gruff, hardy, harsh, hefty, hunky, lusty, raspy, rough, roupy, solid, stout, thick, tough **6** brawny, canine, chubby, chunky, croaky, hearty, hoarse, mighty, portly, potent, robust, rugged, sinewy, steely, stocky, strong, sturdy, virile **7** doughty, rasping, raucous, sizable, sled dog, throaty **8** athletic, croaking, forceful, guttural, indurate, muscular, powerful, puissant, scratchy, sizeable, stalwart, thickset, vigorous **9** Atlantean, corpulent, Herculean, strapping, well-built **10** able-bodied, red-blooded, well-padded
command: **4** mush
group: **4** team
hangout: **5** Yukon **6** Alaska
load: **4** sled
Husky, Ferlin song: Gone (1957)
huss: **4** fish
hussar: **7** dragoon **8** horseman
blade: **5** saber
Hussein: **5** Waris
Hussein, King: **4** Arab **9** Jordanian
Husserl, Edmund: **6** German **11** philosopher
Hussey: **4** Ruth **6** Olivia
Hussey, Ruth: **7** actress
film: The Facts of Life (1960)
H.M. Pulham, Esq. (1941)
The Lady Wants Mink (1953)
Louisa (1950)
Northwest Passage (1940)
The Philadelphia Story (1940)
The Uninvited (1944)
hussy: **4** minx **7** Jezebel **8** spitfire
hustings: **5** stump **8** campaign
hustle: **3** fly, hie, mob, rip, rob, run, zip **4** dart, dash, flit, hoax, push, race, rush, scam, sell, tear, work, zoom **5** cheat, dance, fraud, haste, hurry, scoot, shove, spank, speed **6** barrel, bustle, dupery, fleece, gallop, hasten, humbug, move it, rocket, scheme, scurry **7** floor it, hop to it, quicken, request, scamper, solicit, swindle **8** activity, celerity, dispatch, gumption, hightail, shoulder, step on it, struggle, work hard **9** bundle off, deception, go quickly, hotfoot it, shake a leg, skedaddle **10** enterprise, get a move on, get hopping, get-up-and-go, hightail it
and bustle: **4** to-do **5** hoo-ha **6** clamor, flurry, hoopla, hubbub, tumult, uproar **7** ferment, turmoil **8** activity, brouhaha, foofaraw **9** commotion **10** excitement, hullabaloo
do the ~: **5** dance, disco
partner: **6** bustle
hustler: **4** doer **5** cheat, shark **6** bilker, con man, dynamo **7** busy bee, grifter, scammer **8** go-getter, live wire, swindler **9** defrauder **10** ball of fire
Hustler, The (1961 film)
cast: Jackie Gleason, Piper Laurie, Paul Newman, George C. Scott
director: Robert Rossen
prop: **3** cue **4** rack
Hustle, The (1975 song) artist: Van McCoy
phrase: **4** do it
Huston: **4** John **6** Walter **8** Anjelica
Huston, Anjelica: **7** actress
film: The Addams Family (1991)
Addams Family Values (1993)
The Dead (1987)
Enemies, A Love Story (1989)
Ever After (1998)
Gardens of Stone (1987)
The Grifters (1990)
Manhattan Murder Mystery (1993)
Prizzi's Honor (1985, AA)
The Royal Tenenbaums (2001)
The Witches (1990)
Huston, John: **8** director
film: The African Queen (1951)
The Asphalt Jungle (1950)
Beat the Devil (1954)
Casino Royale (1967)
Chinatown (1974)
The Dead (1987)
Fat City (1972)
Freud (1962)
Heaven Knows, Mr. Allison (1957)
In This Our Life (1942)
Key Largo (1948)
The Life and Times of Judge Roy Bean (1972)
The List of Adrian Messenger (1963)
The Maltese Falcon (1941)
Man in the Wilderness (1971)
The Man Who Would Be King (1975)
The Misfits (1961)
Moby Dick (1956)
Moulin Rouge (1952)
Myra Breckinridge (1970)
The Night of the Iguana (1964)
Prizzi's Honor (1985)
The Red Badge of Courage (1951)
The Treasure of the Sierra Madre (1948, AA)
Under the Volcano (1984)
The Unforgiven (1960)
We Were Strangers (1949)
Wise Blood (1979)
spouse: Evelyn Keyes
Huston, Walter: **5** actor
film: American Madness (1932)
And Then There Were None (1945)
The Beast of the City (1932)
The Devil and Daniel Webster (1941)
Dodsworth (1936)
Edge of Darkness (1943)
Gabriel Over the White House (1933)
Kongo (1932)
Law and Order (1932)
The Light That Failed (1939)
Mission to Moscow (1943)
The Outlaw (1943)
The Ruling Voice (1931)
Star Witness (1931)
The Treasure of the Sierra Madre (1948, AA)
Yankee Doodle Dandy (1942)
hut: **4** digs, dump, home, shed **5** bower, cabin, house, hovel, hutch, lodge, shack **6** billet, cabana, chalet, lean-to, shanty, wikiup **7** cottage, quonset, rathole, shelter, wickiup, wickyup **8** bungalow
follower: **3** one, two
ice ~: **4** iglu **5** igloo
Mexican ~: **5** jacal
Quonset ~: **8** barracks
sayer: **2** QB **11** quarterback
Shetland Islands ~: **4** skeo
__ hut: **6** Nissen **7** Quonset
__ Hut: **5** Pizza
hutch: **3** bin, box, cot, hut, pen **4** cage, coop **5** cabin, chest, shack **7** cabinet, confine, cottage **8** cupboard **9** container, enclosure, furniture
display: **5** china **6** dishes **8** ceramics
Hutchence: **7** Michael
Hutchinson: **4** city, town **5** Fiona
locale: **6** Kansas
Hutchins, Will: **5** actor
film: Clambake (1967)
The Shooting (1967)
TV: Sugarfoot
Hutch portrayer: **4** Soul
Hutt like Jabba the: **5** heavy, obese **9** corpulent **10** overweight, well-padded
Hutton: **2** E.F. **3** Jim **5** Betty **6** Ina Ray, Lauren, Robert **7** Barbara, Timothy
Hutton, Barbara spouse: Cary Grant
Hutton, Betty: **7** actress
film: Annie Get Your Gun (1950)
The Greatest Show on Earth (1952)
Here Come the Waves (1944)
Incendiary Blonde (1945)
Let's Face It (1943)
The Miracle of Morgan's Creek (1944)
The Perils of Pauline (1947)
Hutton, Brian G.: **8** director
film: The First Deadly Sin (1980)
Kelly's Heroes (1970)
Where Eagles Dare (1969)
The Wild Seed (1965)
Hutton, Jim: **5** actor
film: Period of Adjustment (1962)
Walk, Don't Run (1966)
Who's Minding the Mint? (1967)
TV: Adventures of Ellery Queen
Hutton, Timothy: **5** actor
film: Beautiful Girls (1996)
City of Industry (1997)
Daniel (1983)
Deterrence (2000)
Everybody's All-American (1988)
The General's Daughter (1999)
Iceman (1984)
Ordinary People (1980, AA)
The Temp (1993)
spouse: Debra Winger
Hutu
foe: **4** Tusi **5** Tussi, Tutsi **6** Watusi **7** Watutsi
home: **6** Africa
Huxley: **6** Aldous, Andrew, Julian, Thomas
Huxley, Aldous: **6** writer **7** British
alma mater: Eton, Oxford
work: Antic Hay
Brave New World
Crome Yellow
Eyeless in Gaza
Point Counter Point
Huxley, Andrew: **7** British **8** Nobelist
Huxley, Julian: **3** Sir **7** British **9** biologist
book: **4** Ants
Huxley, Thomas: **7** British **9** biologist
Huxtable: **3** Ada **4** Rudy, Theo **5** Clair, Cliff **6** Denise **7** Vanessa
Huxtable, Cliff portrayer: **3** Cos **5** Cosby
Huygens, Christiaan: **5** Dutch **9** physicist **10** astronomer
Huysmans, Joris: **6** author, French, writer
huzzah: **3** cry, rah **4** hail, viva, vive, yell **5** bravo, cheer, shout **6** banzai, hoorah, hooray, hot dog, hurrah, hurray, yippee **7** way to go **8** accolade **10** boola boola, halleluhah, hot diggety
in Spanish: **3** olé
__ H. White: **8** Theodore
hwy.: **2** rd. **3** rte., tpk.
designer: **2** CE
intersection: **3** jct.
offense: **3** DWI
safety org.: **4** MADD
sign abbr.: **3** alt.
strip: **2** ln.
Hy: **8** Averback
hyacinth: **3** gem **5** color, plant **6** flower, orange **7** reddish **8** gemstone
home: **3** bed
relative: **5** flame, henna **7** pumpkin, saffron **9** tangerine **10** terra cotta
__ hyacinth: **4** wild, wood **5** grape, water
Hyakutake: **5** comet
hyaline: **5** clear **6** glassy **9** glasslike
hyalite: **4** opal **7** mineral
Hyams: **5** Leila, Peter
Hyams, Peter: **8** director
film: 2010 (1984)
Capricorn One (1978)
Timecop (1994)
Hyannis: **4** city, town
course: **3** cod **5** scrod **6** schrod
locale: **4** Mass. **7** Cape Cod
Hyatt: **5** hotel
alternative: **4** Omni **6** Hilton, Westin **7** Wyndham **8** Marriott, Radisson, Sheraton **10** DoubleTree **11** Crowne Plaza, Four Seasons
Hyatt __: **7** Regency
hybrid: **3** cur, mix **4** mule **5** cross, liger, plant, tigon **6** tiglon **7** amalgam, beefalo, cattalo, mixture, mongrel **8** assorted **9** composite, cross-bred, immixture
bovine: **6** catalo **7** beefalo
cat: **5** liger, tigon
combining form: **4** noth- **5** notho-
tangerine ~: **4** Ugli
tree: **7** plumcot **8** limequat
hybrid __: **3** tea **4** chip, corn **5** vigor
hybridize: **3** mix **5** cross **10** interbreed
Hyde, Mr., like: **4** evil
Hyde Park
initials: **3** FDR
locale: **6** London **7** England, New York
__ Hyde Pierce: **5** David
Hyderabad: **4** city, town
dress: **4** sari **5** saree
locale: **5** India
river: **5** Indus
sovereign: **5** Nizam

Hyde-White, Wilfrid: **5** actor
film: My Fair Lady (1964)
On the Double (1961)
Two Way Stretch (1960)
hydra: **5** polyp
hydra-___: **6** headed
Hydra: **7** monster, serpent
neighbor: **3** Leo **5** Libra **6** Antlia
number of heads: **4** nine
Hydra Head, The author: Carlos Fuentes
hydrangea: **5** plant, shrub **6** flower
___ hydrangea: **4** wild **6** peegee **7** oak-leaf
hydrant: **3** tap **4** plug **5** valve
hookup: **4** hose
___ hydrant: **4** fire
___ hydrate: **4** lime **6** barium, terpin **7** calcium, chloral
hydraulic ___: **3** ram **4** lift, pile **5** brake, fluid, motor, press **6** cement, mining, radius
hydraulic ___ converter: **6** torque
hydraulics: **7** science
study: **7** liquids
hydriad: **5** nymph
hydro: **10** power plant, water power
hydro-___: **3** ski
hydrocarbon: **4** amyl **5** arene, hexyl, tolan **6** alkane, butane, butene, cetane, ethane, hexane **8** dimethyl
ending: **3** -ane, -ene, -yne
radical: **5** alkyl
hydrochloric: **4** acid
hydrodynamics: **7** science
study: **7** liquids
hydroelectric: **5** power
org.: **3** TVA
project: **3** dam
hydrofluoric ___: **4** acid
hydrofoil: **4** boat, ship **5** craft **6** vessel
hydrogen: **3** gas **7** element
hydrogen ___: **3** ion **4** bomb, bond **6** iodide **7** bromide, sulfide
___ hydrogen: **5** heavy **6** active, atomic
hydrogeology: **7** science
hydrographic: **6** marine **7** oceanic, pelagic **8** maritime, nautical
hydrokinetics: **7** science
hydrology: **7** science
study: **5** water
hydrolyzed vegetable ___: **7** protein
hydromassage facility: **3** spa
hydrometer scale: **5** Baume
hydrophobe fear: **5** water
hydrophobia: **5** lyssa **6** rabies
hydrophyte: **4** alga
hydroplane: **4** boat, skim **5** craft **6** vessel
part: **5** float
hydrostatics: **7** science
hydrous: **3** wet **6** liquid, watery **7** aqueous
hydroxide: **3** ion **4** base **6** alkali **7** antacid
potassium ~: **3** KOH
sodium ~: **4** NaOH
solution: **3** lye
___ hydroxide: **6** barium, cobalt, copper, cupric, sodium **7** calcium, lithium
Hydrox rival: **4** Oreo
hydroxyl: **3** ion
compound: **4** enol
Hydrus neighbor: **5** Mensa
hyena: **4** Lena **6** animal, mammal
kin: **6** jackal
___ hyena: **5** brown **7** spotted, striped
Hyéres: **4** city, town
locale: **6** France
Hyer, Martha: **7** actress
film: Battle Hymn (1957)
Bikini Beach (1964)
The Delicate Delinquent (1957)
Houseboat (1958)
The Sons of Katie Elder (1965)
hyetal: **5** rainy **7** pluvial, showery **8** pluvious
Hygiea: **8** asteroid
hygiene: **6** health **10** sanitation
___ hygiene: **4** oral **6** dental
hygienic: **5** clean **6** washed **7** aseptic, healthy, sterile **8** germ-free, pristine, sanitary, spotless, unsoiled **9** wholesome **10** antiseptic, immaculate, salubrious
___ hygienist: **6** dental
Hyginus: **4** pope **7** pontiff
hygric: **3** wet **4** damp **5** humid, moist **6** watery
hyla: **8** tree frog, tree toad **9** amphibian
Hyla Brook author: Robert Frost
Hyland: **5** Brian, Diana
Hyllus, wife of: **4** Iole
Hyman: **3** Flo, Mac **4** Dick **5** Earle **8** Rickover
___ Hyman Award: **3** Flo
Hyman, Dick: **7** pianist
genre: **4** jazz
hymenopteran: **3** bee **6** insect
hymn: **3** ode **4** laud, lied, pean, poem, song **5** carol, dirge, motet, music, paean, psalm **6** anthem, choral, praise **7** chorale, hosanna **8** canticle, evensong
accompaniment: **5** organ
ender: **4** book
finale: **4** amen
of praise: **3** ode **4** pean **5** paean
opening: **6** adeste
singers: **5** choir, flock, laity
hymnal: **4** book
___ Hymn of the Republic, The: **6** Battle
Hymn to Apollo: **4** poem
author: Shelley
Hymn to Intellectual Beauty author: Percy Bysshe Shelley
Hymn to Proserpine author: Algernon Swinburne
Hynde: **8** Chrissie
hyoid: **4** bone
locale: **6** tongue
hyoshigi: **10** clap sticks, percussion
origin: **5** Japan
hype: **4** plug, puff, push, tout **5** lobby **6** hoopla, overdo, talk up **7** advance, buildup, promote, puffery, trumpet **8** ballyhoo, plugging **9** advertise, get behind, promotion, publicity, publicize, reinforce **10** propaganda
bit of ~: **4** plug **5** blurb, promo
up: **4** plug, push, stir, tout **5** rouse **6** arouse, bestir, incite **7** animate, enliven, inspire, promote, push for **8** ballyhoo, inspirit, motivate, vitalize **9** publicize, stimulate
hyped up: **5** zippy **6** lively **7** dynamic, kinetic, orotund, pompous **8** animated, inflated **9** bombastic, energetic, overblown **10** immoderate
hyper: **5** manic, tense, wired **6** jangly, lively **7** anxious, excited, fidgety, frantic, keyed up **8** fluttery, frenetic, frenzied, hopped up, restless, tireless, vehement **9** sprightly **10** high-strung, overactive, unwearying
not ~: **4** calm **5** staid **6** sedate **7** relaxed
hyperbaric ___: **7** chamber
hyperbola: **3** arc **5** curve
hyperbole: **5** trope **7** big talk **8** rhetoric **10** distortion
hyperbolize: **7** ham it up, overact **9** overstate **10** exaggerate
hypercritical: **7** carping **8** captious, exacting **9** squeamish
hypercriticize: **4** carp **5** cavil **7** nitpick, quibble **8** pettifog **10** split hairs
Hyperion: **4** moon **5** giant, Titan
daughter of ~: **3** Eos
parent of ~: **4** Gaea **6** Uranus
planet: **6** Saturn
sister of ~: **4** Thia
son of ~: **6** Helios
Hyperion author: Keats, Longfellow
hyperon: **8** particle
hyperphysical: **6** occult **8** ethereal **9** unearthly
hypersensitive: **6** touchy **7** waspish **8** allergic
hypersensitivity: **7** allergy
hypersonic: **4** fast **5** brisk, fleet, quick, rapid, swift **6** flying, speedy **9** breakneck
hypertrophic: **3** big
hyperventilate: **4** gasp, pant
___ hyphen: **4** soft
hyphen cousin: **4** dash **6** em dash, en dash
Hypnos: **3** god
domain: **5** sleep
parent of ~: **3** Nyx **6** Erebus
son of ~: **8** Morpheus
hypnosis: **6** stupor, trance **8** numbness **9** mesmerism
hypnotic: **6** sleepy **8** magnetic, mesmeric, sedative **9** soporific **10** anesthetic, magnetical
state: **6** trance
hypnotism: **5** spell **9** magnetism
hypnotist: **9** mesmerist
word: **5** sleep
hypnotize: **4** grip, vamp **5** charm **6** dazzle **7** bewitch, enchant, enthral, inthral **8** enthrall, entrance, inthrall, transfix **9** captivate, fascinate, magnetize, mesmerize, spellbind
Hypnotize (1997 song) artist: Notorious B.I.G.
hypnotized: **4** rapt **5** under **8** held fast **10** fascinated
hypo: **4** shot **6** needle **7** syringe **9** injection
bulb: **5** ampul **6** ampule **7** ampoule
contents: **4** sera
user: **2** dr., MD, RN **5** nurse **6** doctor
hypocrisy: **4** cant, sham **5** fraud **6** deceit, dupery **7** mockery **8** bad faith, pretense, quackery **9** casuistry, deception, duplicity, imposture, phoniness **10** dishonesty, imposition, lip service, pharisaism, pretension, sanctimony
hypocrite: **4** fake **5** cheat, faker, fraud, knave, phony, quack **6** con man, humbug, phoney, poseur, rascal **7** bluffer, two-face **8** deceiver, imposter, impostor, two-timer **9** charlatan, con artist, pretender **10** backslider, dissembler
hypocritical: **4** oily **5** false, phony **6** phoney **7** canting **8** affected, recreant, two-faced
act ~: **3** lie **7** deceive, mislead, pretend **8** simulate **9** dissemble, misinform
hypodermic: **6** needle **7** syringe
amt.: **2** cc.
hypotenuse: **4** side
hypothesis: **4** idea **5** guess, posit **6** belief, theory, thesis **7** concept, opinion, premise, surmise, thought **8** proposal **9** apriority, deduction, postulate, principle, rationale, reasoning **10** antecedent, assignment, assumption, conclusion, conjecture, contention, derivation, foundation, philosophy, suggestion
___ hypothesis: **4** Gaia, null **7** nebular, working
hypothesize: **5** guess, posit **6** assume **7** explain, presume, suppose, surmise, think up **8** theorize **9** postulate, predicate, speculate **10** conjecture, put forward
hypothetical: **4** moot **5** ideal **6** unreal **7** assumed, guessed **8** abstract, academic, possible, supposed **10** indefinite, intangible
hyrax: **4** cony **5** coney **6** animal, dassie, mammal
Hyser: **5** Joyce
hyson: **3** tea **8** green tea
hysteria: **5** panic, shock, storm **6** frenzy, nerves **8** delirium
Hysteria (1988 song) artist: Def Leppard
hysterical: **3** mad **4** wild **5** funny, irate, rabid **6** crazed, raging, raving **7** berserk, frantic, furious, hog-wild, nervous **8** frenzied, unnerved, vehement, wild-eyed **9** delirious, emotional, excitable, possessed, spasmodic **10** convulsive, distracted, distraught, ridiculous, uproarious
something ~: **4** hoot, howl, riot **5** laugh **6** scream
hysterics: **3** fit **4** rage **7** tantrum **8** outburst **10** conniption
go into ~: **4** rant, rave **7** run amok
Hyundai: **3** car **4** auto **10** automobile
headquarters: **5** Korea
model: **6** Accent, Scoupe, Sonata **7** Elantra, Santa Fe, Tiburon
rival: **3** Kia **6** Daewoo
Hywel: **7** Bennett

i
topper: 3 dot 6 tittle
I: 3 one 4 elem. 5 vowel 6 iodine, letter
53 for ~: 4 at. no.
Greek ~: 4 iota
in German: 3 ich
in Latin: 3 ego
in phonetic alphabet: 5 India
trouble: 3 ego 6 egoism 7 egotism
I __: 3 Ran, Spy 4 Know, Will, Wish 5 Am Sam, Ching, Got Id, Hate U, Swear 6 Gotcha 7 Believe, Dreamed
I __!: 3 say 5 dunno
I __ a crook: 5 am not
I __ a dream: 4 have
I __ a Happy Tune: 7 Whistle
I __ a Kick Out of You: 3 Get
I __ a Little Prayer: 3 Say
I __ Always Love You: 4 Will
I __ a Male War Bride: 3 Was
I __ America Singing: 4 Hear
I __ a Mystery: 4 Love
I __ a Name: 3 Got
I __ Anyone Till You: 5 Hadn't
I __ a Parade: 4 Love
I __ a Piano: 4 Love
I __ a Place: 4 Know
I __ a Rainy Night: 4 Love
I __ Around: 3 Get
I __ As I Wander: 6 Wonder
I __ a Song Coming On: 4 Feel
I __ a Symphony: 4 Hear
I __ a Tear: 5 Cried
I __ a Teenage Werewolf: 3 Was
I __ a thing to wear!: 6 haven't
I __ at the office: 4 gave
I __ at the Stars: 3 Aim
I __ Bad, and That Ain't Good: 5 Got It
I __ bad moon...: 4 see a
I __ Be Around: 5 Wanna
I __ been a contender!: 6 coulda
I __ Being a Girl: 5 Enjoy
I __ Be Loved By You: 5 Wanna
I __ Camera: 3 Am a
I __ Care: 4 Don't 6 Should
I __ Dance: 4 Can't, Won't
I __ Dancer: 3 Am a
I __ differ!: 5 beg to
I __ Doing All Right: 3 Was
I __ Dreamin': 4 Like
I __ Extremes: 4 Go to
I __ Fine: 4 Feel
I __ Follow Him: 4 Will
I __ for Animals: 5 Brake
I __ for You: 4 Do It, Feel 5 Cried
I __ Found Someone: 7 Finally
I __ Fugitive...: 3 Am a
I __ gal in Kalamazoo: 4 got a
I __ Get It for You Wholesale: 3 Can
I __ Get Next to You: 4 Can't 5 Wanna
I __ Get No Satisfaction: 4 Can't
I __ Get Started: 4 Can't
I __ Go for That: 4 Can't
I __ Got Nobody: 4 Ain't
I __ Grow Up: 4 Won't
I __ Have Danced All Night: 5 Could
I __ Have Eyes for You: 4 Only
I __ Help: 3 Can
I __ Help It: 4 Can't
I __ Help Myself: 4 Can't
I __ Her Again: 3 Saw
I __ Her Standing There: 3 Saw
I __ Hold Your Hand: 5 Wanna
I __ idea!: 5 had no
I __ Ideas: 3 Get
I __ Ike: 4 Like
I __ I Love You: 5 Think
I __ in You: 7 Believe
I __ iodine: 4 as in
I __ It: 4 Dood, Like
I __ It Through the Grapevine: 5 Heard
I __ I Were in Love Again: 4 Wish
I __ kick from champagne: 5 get no
I __ Kick Out of You: 4 Get a
I __ Know: 5 Gotta
I __ Know What Time It Was: 5 Didn't
I __ Letter to My Love: 5 Sent a
I __ lineman for the county: 3 am a
I __ Little Prayer: 4 Say a
I __ Love: 4 Am In, Feel, Need
I __ Lucy: 4 Love
I __ Made for Dancin': 3 Was
I __ Made to Love Her: 3 Was
I __ Male War Bride: 4 Was a
I __ man with seven wives: 4 met a
I __ Men: 4 Hate
I __ Music: 4 Hear, Love
I __ my case!: 4 rest
I __ Mystery: 5 Love a
I __ My Sugar in Salt Lake City: 4 Lost
I __ my way: 5 did it
I __ my wits' end!: 4 am at
I __ Name: 4 Got a
I __ no kick from champagne...: 3 get
I __ Not Be Moved: 5 Shall
I __ of Jeannie: 5 Dream
I __ of You: 3 Beg
I __ Parade: 5 Love a
I __ Paris: 4 Love
I __ Piano: 5 Love a
I __ Pieces: 4 Go to
I __ Place: 5 Know a
I __ Plenty o' Nuthin': 3 Got
I __ Pretty: 4 Feel
I __ Promised You a Rose Garden: 5 Never
I __ Rainy Night: 5 Love a
I __ reason why not: 5 see no
I __ return: 5 shall
I __ Rhapsody: 5 Hear a
I __ Rhythm: 3 Got
I __ Right to Sing the Blues: 5 Gotta
I __ Rock: 3 Am a
I __ Rock and Roll Music: 3 Dig
I __ Russia $1200: 3 Owe
I __ Said: 3 Am...I
I __ Sang for My Father: 5 Never
I __ saw...: 5 came I
I __ Say No: 5 Cain't
I __ See Clearly Now: 3 Can
I __ See for Miles: 3 Can
I __ Song Coming On: 5 Feel a
I __ Song Go...: 4 Let a
I __ Stop Loving You: 4 Can't
I __ Stung: 3 Got
I __ Survive: 4 Will
I __ Symphony: 5 Hear a
I __ Teenage Were-wolf: 4 Was a
I __ tell a lie: 6 cannot
I __ That Emotion: 6 Second
I __ the Body Electric: 4 Sing
I __ the Earth Move: 4 Feel
I __ thee late a rosy: 4 sent
I __ the Law: 6 Fought
I __ the Light: 3 Saw
I __ the Line: 4 Walk
I __ the Nightlife: 4 Love
I __ the Sheriff: 4 Shot
I __ the Songs: 5 Write
I __ the Stars: 5 Aim at
I __ the Sun in the Morning: 3 Got
I __ Three Lives: 3 Led
I __ to Be Happy: 4 Want
I __ to Be in Pictures: 5 Ought
I __ to Cook Book: 4 Hate
I __ to differ!: 3 beg
I __ to Hold Your Hand: 4 Want
I __ to Live!: 4 Want
I __ to Pieces: 4 Fall
I __ to the Trees: 4 Talk
I __ to Walk You Home: 4 Want
I __ to You: 4 Turn 6 Belong
I __ Trouble: 4 Love
I __ vacation!: 5 need a
I __ Walrus: 5 Am the
I __ Wanna Cry: 4 Don't
I __ Wanna Stop: 4 Just
I __ Want to Be Right: 4 Don't
I __ Want to Celebrate: 4 Just
I __ We're Alone Now: 5 Think
I __ Why the Caged Bird Sings: 4 Know
I __ Write a Book: 5 Could
I __ You: 3 Got 4 Love, Miss, Need, Want 5 Beg of, Thank 6 Kissed
I __ You Babe: 3 Got
I __ You Knocking: 4 Hear
I __ you one!: 3 owe
I __ Your Love Tonight: 4 Need
I __ you so!: 4 told
I __ You Truly: 4 Love
I, __: 3 Too 4 Tina 5 Robot
I-__: 3 bar 4 beam
'I' __ Innocent: 5 Is for
...I __ a puddy tat!: 3 taw
...I __ not want: 5 shall
Ia.
see Iowa
Iacocca: 3 Lee 4 Lido
lacta __ alea: 3 est
lacta est __: 4 alea
Iago: 6 ensign 7 villain 8 Venetian
emulate ~: 3 lie 6 betray
in English: 5 James
wife of ~: 6 Emilia
I agree!: 3 yep 4 amen 5 ditto, me too
Iain in English: 4 John
I Ain't __ Nobody: 3 Got
I Ain't Gonna Stand for It (1981 song) artist: Stevie Wonder
I Ain't Marching Anymore singer: 4 Ochs
I Almost Lost My Mind (1956 song) artist: Pat Boone
I Am __: 5 a Rock
I Am, __: 5 I Said
__ I Am: 4 Here, What
__-I-Am: 3 Sam
I Am a Camera (1955 film)
cast: Julie Harris, Laurence Harvey, Shelley Winters
I Am a Fugitive From a Chain Gang (1932 film)
cast: Glenda Farrell, Paul Muni
director: Mervyn LeRoy
I Am a Rock (1966 song) artist: Simon and Garfunkel
iamb: 4 foot
relative: 6 dactyl 7 anapest, pyrrhic, spondee, trochee
iambic
pentameter: 4 rime 5 meter, rhyme
I am here in Latin: 5 adsum
I Am...I Said (1971 song) artist: Neil Diamond
Iams: 7 dog food
alternative: 4 Alpo 5 Nutro 6 Purina 8 Eukanuba 10 Ken-L Ration
I Am Sam (2001 film)
cast: Sean Penn, Michelle Pfeiffer, Dianne Wiest
I am the __ of the sphere...: 5 owner
I Am Woman (1972 song) artist: Helen Reddy
-ian
cousin: 3 ist, ite 4 ster
Ian: 3 Hay 4 Holm 5 Janis, Smith, Wolfe 6 Bannen, Gillan, Hendry, Hunter, McEwan, Wilmut 7 Fleming, McShane, Paisley, Woosnam, Ziering 8 Anderson, McKellen, Whitcomb 9 Charleson, Dalrymple 10 Baker-Finch, Ballantine, Carmichael, McNaughton, Richardson
in English: 4 John
I and Thou author: 5 Buber
Ian, Janis song: At Seventeen (1975)
Iapetus: 4 moon 5 giant, Titan
parent of ~: 4 Gaea 6 Uranus
planet: 6 Saturn
son of ~: 5 Atlas 10 Prometheus
Iasi: 4 city, town
locale: 7 Romania, Rumania 8 Roumania
__ I a stinker?: 4 ain't
iatric: 7 medical 8 curative, remedial, sanative 9 medicinal
iatrophobe fear: 7 doctors
Ibadan: 4 city, town
locale: 7 Nigeria
Ibagué: 4 city, town
locale: 8 Colombia
Iba, Hank: 5 coach
milieu: 5 court
org.: 3 NBA
sport: 10 basketball
I-bar: 4 beam
Ibaraki: 4 city, town
locale: 5 Japan
Ibarguren, Eva, née: 5 Perón
Ibb: 4 city, town
locale: 5 Yemen
Ibbetson: 5 Peter
I-beam: 4 beam 6 cursor
material: 5 steel
projection: 6 flange
i before e except after c: 4 rule
I beg of you: 6 please
I Beg of You (1958 song) artist: Elvis Presley
I beg to differ!: 5 not so
I beg your pardon: 4 ahem
I Believe __: 5 in You
I Believe I Can Fly (1996 song) artist: R. Kelly
I believe in Latin: 5 credo
I Believe in You and Me (1996 song) artist: Whitney Houston
I Believe singer: 5 Laine
Iberia: 7 airline 9 peninsula
part of ~: 5 Spain 6 España 8 Portugal
river: 4 Ebro, Miño 5 Douro, Minho, Tagus
see also Portugal, Spain
Iberian: 3 pig 5 swine
Ibert: 7 Jacques
I bet!: 3 Hah
ibex: 4 goat 6 animal, mammal
relative: 4 geep, tahr, thar 6 Angora 7 markhor 8 markhoor
Ibibio: 8 language
home: 6 Africa 7 Nigeria
ibid.: 4 same
relative: 5 op. cit.
ibis: 4 bird 5 wader 10 wading bird
relative: 5 stork 9 spoonbill
__ ibis: 4 wood 6 sacred
Ibiza: 4 isle 6 island
Ibizan __: 5 hound 7 Podenco
Ibizan Hound: 3 dog 5 canid 6 canine
__, I Blew Up the Kid: 5 Honey
IBM: 2 co., PC 7 Big Blue, company 8 computer
early ~ computer model: 2 AT, XT
headquarters: 6 Armonk 7 New York
motto: 5 Think
part of ~: 3 Bus., Int. 4 Intl. 8 Business, Machines
rival: 3 DEC, Mac, NCR, NEC 5 Apple, Epson
Ibn: 4 Saud, Sina 7 al-'Arabi, Kahldun 8 Battutah, Taymiyah 9 al-Haytham
what ~ means: 5 son of
Ibn Saud: 4 Arab
Ibo: 8 language
home: 6 Africa 7 Nigeria
Ibsen, Henrik: 5 Norse 9 dramatist, Norwegian 10 playwright

character: 3 Ase 4 Nora
home: 4 Oslo
work: Brand
Catiline
A Doll's House
Emperor and Galilean
An Enemy of the People
The Feast at Solhaug
Ghosts
Hedda Gabler
John Gabriel Borkman
The Lady From the Sea
Lady Inger of Osteraad
The League of Youth
Little Eyolf
Love's Comedy
The Master Builder
Olaf Liljekrans
Peer Gynt
Pillars of Society
The Pretenders
Rosmersholm
St. John's Night
The Vikings at Helgeland
The Warrior's Barrow
When We Dead Awaken
The Wild Duck
ibuprofen: 5 NSAID
brand: 5 Advil
dose: 6 caplet
target: 4 ache, pain 5 cramp 8 headache, soreness
I burn, literally: 4 Etna 5 Aetna
Ica: 4 city, town
locale: 4 Peru
Icahn: 4 Carl
I Cain't Say No composer: 7 Rodgers 11 Hammerstein
I call 'em like I __: 5 see 'em
I came: 4 veni
I Can __ for Miles: 3 See
I Can Dream, __?: 5 Cant I
I Can Get It for You Wholesale: 4 film 5 novel
author: Jerome Weidman
cast: Dan Dailey, Susan Hayward, Sam Jaffe
I Can Help (1974 song) artist: Billy Swan
__ I can help it!: 5 Not if
I Can Never Go Home Anymore (1965 song) artist: Shangri-las
I cannot __ lie: 5 tell a
I Can Read With My Eyes Shut author: Dr. Seuss
I Can See Clearly Now (1972 song) artist: Johnny Nash
I Can See for Miles (1967 song) artist: Who
I can't __ satisfaction: 5 get no
I can take __!: 5 a hint
I Can't Dance (1992 song) artist: Genesis
I Can't Get Next to You (1969 song) artist: Temptations
I Can't Go for That (1981 song) artist: Hall and Oates
I can't hear you!: 6 louder 7 speak up
I Can't Help It (1980 song) artist: Olivia Newton-John
I Can't Help Myself (1965 song) artist: Four Tops
I Can't Make You Love Me (1992 song) artist: Bonnie Raitt
I Can't Sleep Baby (1996 song) artist: R. Kelly
I Can't Stand It (1981 song) artist: Eric Clapton
I Can't Stay Mad at You (1963 song) artist: Skeeter Davis
I Can't Stop Loving You (1962 song) artist: Ray Charles
I Can't Tell You Why (1980 song) artist: Eagles
I Can't Wait (1986 song) artist: Nu Shooz, Stevie Nicks
__ I care!: 4 As if
Icarian __: 3 Sea
Icarus: 8 asteroid
emulate ~: 3 fly 4 soar
parent of ~: 7 Dedalus 8 Daedalus, Naucrate
Icarus Agenda, The author: Robert Ludlum
ICBM: 4 MIRV 5 Atlas, Titan 7 Polaris
part of ~: 5 Inter 7 Missile 9 Ballistic
ICC concern: 3 trk.
ice: 3 gem 4 do in, floe, hail 5 chill, cinch, cubes, quiet, rocks, sew up 6 clinch, cooler, ensure, freeze, gelato, sorbet 7 dessert, glacier, jewelry 8 cool down, diamonds, glaciate 9 guarantee, sparklers 10 permafrost
break the ~: 5 begin, start 6 embark, launch 8 commence
coated with ~: 4 rimy 5 gelid
crystals: 6 frazil
cut some ~: 4 rate 5 count, weigh 6 matter
ender: 3 box, cap, man, men 4 berg, boat, fall 5 blink, bound, house, maker, scape 7 breaker
glacial ~: 4 firn 5 serac
house: 4 iglu 5 igloo
in German: 3 Eis
like ~: 4 cold 5 gelid, slick 6 frosty
liquor over cracked ~: 4 mist
mass: 4 berg, calf, floe 7 glacier
melter: 3 tea 4 rain, salt
on ~: 6 secure 7 assured, certain, chilled 8 confined, in the bag, put aside 9 in reserve 10 guaranteed, in abeyance, undoubtful
on thin ~: 5 risky 6 unsafe 8 perilous 9 uncertain 10 precarious
out: 3 ban 4 thaw 7 boycott
palace: 4 rink 5 arena
pellets: 4 hail 5 sleet
perhaps: 4 numb
put on ~: 5 chill, delay, table 6 assure, shelve 7 confine, suspend 8 sentence
thin ~: 5 glaze 6 danger, hazard
tool: 3 awl 4 pick, tong 5 borer, tongs
travel on ~: 5 skate
unit: 4 cube
without ~: 4 neat 8 straight
ice __: 3 age, bag, cap, fog, jam, out, run 4 beer, blue, cave, cube, dock, drag, floe, foot, milk, pack, pick, rain, show 5 apron, chest, cream, field, front, plant, point, sheet, shelf, skate, storm, tongs, water 6 anchor, bucket, hockey, island, skater, tongue 7 dancing, fishing, flowers, needles, pellets, rampart, station
ice-__: 4 cold, free 7 scoured
__ ice: 3 bay, dry 4 ball, blue, fast, pack, raft, rime, slob, snow 5 black, brash, clear, cream, cut no, drift, glare, glaze, sheet, shelf, water 6 anchor, bottom, broken, ground, rafted, rotten 7 camphor, glimmer, glitter, pancake
Ice __: 3 Age 4 Cube 6 Palace 7 Capades, Castles, Follies
Ice __ Zebra: 7 Station
__ Ice: 3 Dry 7 Vanilla
Ice Age (2002 film)
voice cast: Denis Leary, John Leguizamo, Ray Romano
iceberg: 6 hazard 7 lettuce
extremity: 3 tip
form an ~: 5 calve
iceboating: 5 sport
iceboat necessity: 4 sail
Icebound author: Dean Koontz
icebox: 6 cooler, fridge 7 freezer
visit: 4 nosh, raid
icebreaker: 4 boat, ship 5 craft 6 vessel
Ice Brothers author: Sloan Wilson
__ ice cap: 5 polar
Ice Capades
move: 4 axel, lutz
workplace: 4 rink 5 arena
Ice Castles (1979 film)
cast: Robby Benson, Colleen Dewhurst, Lynn-Holly Johnson
director: Donald Wrye
ice-cold: 5 algid, aloof, chill, gelid, polar, stony 6 arctic, bitter, brumal, flinty, frigid, frosty, frozen, stoney, wintry 7 cutting, glacial, wintery 8 freezing, Siberian 9 unfeeling
ice cream: 4 Edy's 5 dairy, treat 6 gelati 7 Breyer's, dessert 9 Friendly's, Good Humor 10 Dairy Queen, Haagen Dazs, Turkey Hill
British ~ cone: 6 cornet
choice: 4 pint 6 flavor, gallon 10 half gallon
flavor: 5 lemon, mocha, peach 6 almond, banana, coffee, Jamoca, toffee 7 caramel, coconut, vanilla 8 cinnamon, hazelnut 9 bubblegum, chocolate, pineapple, pistachio, raspberry, rocky road, rum raisin 10 blackberry, cheesecake, Neapolitan, peppermint, strawberry
have ~: 3 eat 4 lick, nosh
holder: 4 cone 5 stick
ingredient: 4 agar 5 sugar 7 berries, guar gum 8 agar-agar
Italian ~: 6 gelati, gelato 7 spumone, spumoni, tortoni
pattern: 5 swirl
serving: 3 dip 4 glob 5 scoop
treat: 4 cone, malt, soda 5 bombe, float, shake 6 frappe, sundae
variety: 6 gelati, gelato, sundae 7 parfait, spumone, spumoni, tortoni 8 snowball
ice cream __: 3 pop 4 cone, soda, suit 5 chair, scoop 6 parlor, social, supper
__ ice cream: 4 soft 6 French
ice cream soda: 8 beverage
Ice Cube music: 3 rap
iced: 4 cold 5 glacé 6 frappé, frosty, frozen 10 on the rocks
dessert: 4 cake 6 frappe
drink: 3 tea 6 cooler
ice dancing: 5 sport
iced tea addition: 4 mint 5 lemon
ice fishing: 5 sport
jig: 5 tip up
tool: 5 auger
Ice Follies venue: 4 rink 5 arena
ice hockey: 4 game 5 sport
area: 4 cage, rink 6 crease 7 red line 8 blue line
commit an ~ infraction: 4 knee
coup: 8 hat trick
fake: 4 deke
gear: 4 mask, puck 5 stick
infraction: 5 icing
machine: 7 Zamboni
need: 3 net 4 puck 5 arena
position: 4 wing 6 center, goalie
starter: 7 face-off
stat: 5 goals 6 points 7 assists
team: 3 six
term: 4 cage, deke, goal, puck, rink, wing 5 icing, stick 6 assist, center, crease, goalie, period 7 face-off, penalty, red line, time-out, Zamboni 8 blue line, hat trick, slap shot
see also hockey, NHL
Ice Ice Baby (1990 song) artist: Vanilla Ice
Iceland: 3 isl. 4 isle 6 island, nation 7 country
bay: 4 Faxa, Huna
capital: 9 Reykjavík
legislature: 7 Althing
letter: 3 edh
locale: 3 Eur. 6 Europe
money: 5 aurar, eyrir, krona
moss: 6 lichen
Nobelist in Literature: 7 Laxness
of ~ poetry: 5 eddic
org.: 4 NATO
prose: 4 edda, saga
volcano: 5 Hekla 6 Krafla
Iceland __: 4 moss, spar
Icelandair competitor: 3 KLM, SAS
Iceland Fisherman, An author: 4 Loti
Icelandic: 8 language
relative: 6 Danish
iceless: 4 neat 8 straight
Ice Maiden, The: 5 Evert 10 Chris Evert
iceman: 5 NHLer 10 jewel thief
Iceman (1984 film)
cast: Lindsay Crouse, Timothy Hutton, John Lone
director: Fred Schepisi
Iceman Cometh, The: 4 film, play
author: Eugene O'Neill
cast: Fredric March, Lee Marvin, Robert Ryan
director: John Frankenheimer
Iceni: 5 tribe
Ice Palace author: Edna Ferber
__ ices: 7 Italian
__ Ice Shelf: 4 Ross 5 Amery, Ronne 6 Larsen
ice-show venue: 4 rink 5 arena 8 coliseum
ice skating: 5 sport
figure: 5 eight
move: 4 axel, lutz
see also skating
Ice Station Zebra (1968 film)
cast: Ernest Borgnine, Jim Brown, Rock Hudson, Patrick McGoohan
director: John Sturges
Ice Storm, The (1997 film)
cast: Joan Allen, Kevin Kline, Christina Ricci, Sigourney Weaver
director: Ang Lee
Ice-T specialty: 3 rap
Ich __: 4 Dien
Ich __ dich: 5 liebe
Ich __ ein Berliner: 3 bin
Ichabod: 4 poem 5 Crane
author: John Greenleaf Whittier
grandfather of ~: 3 Eli
like ~: 4 bony 5 boney
__ I Change My Mind: 3 Can
Ichihara: 4 city, town
locale: 5 Japan
Ichikawa: 4 city, town
locale: 5 Japan
Ichiro: 6 Suzuki
ichnology: 7 science
ichorous: 6 liquid
ichthyoid: 3 eel
ichthyology: 7 science
study: 4 fish
ichthyophobe fear: 4 fish
icicle site: 4 eave
iciness: 4 cold 5 chill 9 frigidity
icing: 5 glaze 7 topping 8 frosting
add ~ to: 3 top
design: 4 rose 5 swirl
icing __ cake: 5 on the
Ici on __ français: 5 parle
ick: 3 ugh 4 yuck 5 gross
opposite: 3 yum 5 yummy 9 delicious
icky: 3 bad 5 gooey, gross, gummy, gunky, nasty, slimy, sweet, yucky 6 sticky, viscid 8 slovenly, unsavory 9 repellant, repellent, repugnant, repulsive, revolting 10 disgusting, uninviting, unpleasant
stuff: 3 goo 4 glob, gook, muck 5 slime

I, Claudius
  author: Robert Graves
  character: 4 Nero 5 Aelia, Julia, Livia, Macro 8 Claudius
  garment: 4 toga
  network: 3 BBC, PBS
I Come as a Thief author: Louis Auchincloss
icon: 4 idol 5 image 6 emblem, statue, symbol 7 mandala, picture 8 likeness 10 simulacrum
  element: 3 dot 5 pixel
  figure: 5 orans, orant 6 orante
Icon: 8 language
  alternative: 3 ADA, APL, SQL 4 Alef, html, Java, LISP, Logo, Orca, Perl 5 Algol, Basic, Cecil, COBOL, Dylan, SISAL 6 Delphi, Eiffel, Erlang, Oberon, Pascal, Prolog, Sather, Scheme, Snobol 7 Fortran
I Concentrate on You composer: 6 Porter
iconic: 6 sacred 10 emblematic
iconoclast: 5 rebel 7 heretic, radical 8 bohemian, forsaker, maverick, renegade 9 dissenter, protester 10 malcontent
iconoclastic: 7 radical 8 renegade
  I conquered: 4 vici
Icosa-, half of: 4 deca-
icosahedron's
  one of an ~ twenty: 4 face
I could ___ horse!: 4 eat a
I could ___ unfold...: 5 a tale
I Could Fall in Love (1995 song)
  artist: Selena
I Could Fall in Love singer: 6 Selena
I Could Have Danced All Night composer: 5 Loewe 6 Lerner
I Could Never Take the Place of Your Man (1987 song) artist: Prince
I couldn't care ___!: 4 less
I Couldn't Live Without Your Love (1966 song) artist: Petula Clark
I Could Write a Book composer: 4 Hart 7 Rodgers
I Cried ___: 5 a Tear
I cried all the way to the ___: 4 bank
I Cried a Tear (1958 song) artist: LaVern Baker
ICU
  amount: 2 cc.
  apparatus: 2 IV
  part of ~: 4 Care, Unit 9 Intensive
  worker: 2 dr., MD, RN 3 LPN 5 nurse 6 doctor
icy: 3 raw 4 cold, rimy 5 algid, aloof, chill, gelid, hoary, nippy, polar, slick, stony 6 arctic, biting, bitter, chilly, frigid, frosty, frozen, glassy, glazed, remote, steely, stoney, wintry 7 distant, frosted, glacial, hostile, numbing, shivery, wintery 8 chilling, detached, freezing, loveless, reserved, slippery 9 hazardous, lubricous, undaunted, unfeeling 10 insociable, unamicable, unfriendly
  treat an ~ road: 4 salt, sand
id: 4 that 6 libido
  counterpart: 3 ego
  est: 3 viz. 6 namely, that is
I'd ___ Be Right: 6 Rather
I'd ___ You to Want Me: 4 Love
ID: 3 SSN, tag 5 badge 6 dogtag, papers 8 passport
  abbr.: 3 NMI
  ask for an ~: 4 card
  card datum: 3 DOB, hgt. 4 addr. 6 height 7 address
  means of ~: 3 DNA
  see also Idaho
ID ___: 3 tag 4 card
___ ID: 5 photo 6 caller
Ida: 4 peak 5 mount, Wells 6 Cantor, Lupino 7 Tarbell 8 asteroid, Kaminska, Kavafian, McKinley, mountain
  daughter: 5 Rhoda
  Mt. ~ locale: 5 Crete 6 Candia
Ida, ___ as Apple Cider: 5 Sweet
Ida.
  neighbor: 3 Nev., Wyo. 4 Mont., Oreg., Wash.
  see also Idaho
___-Ida: 3 Ore
Idaho: 4 spud 5 state, tater 6 potato
  city: 5 Boise, Nampa 6 Moscow 7 Ketchum 8 Caldwell, Lewiston, Meridian 9 Pocatello, Sun Valley, Twin Falls
  county: 3 Ada, Gem 5 Boise, Latah, Teton 6 Oneida
  Indian: 7 Bannock, Kutenai 8 Sahaptin
  like ~: 6 inland
  mountain: 5 Borah 6 Tetons 7 Wasatch
  neighbor: 4 Utah 6 Canada, Nevada, Oregon 7 Montana, Wyoming 10 Washington
  nickname: 8 Gem State
  river: 5 Boise, Snake
  school: 10 Boise State
  senator: 5 Borah
  start of ~ motto: 4 esto
  state flower: 7 syringa
  state gem: 10 star garnet
  state horse: 9 Appaloosa
  state tree: 9 white pine
  waterfall: 8 Shoshone
Idaho Statesman: 5 paper 9 newspaper
  locale: 5 Boise
Ida Red: 5 apple
  relative: 4 crab, Gala, Lodi, Rome 5 Mutsu 6 Empire, medlar, Pippin, russet 7 Baldwin, Bramley, costard, Freedom, Liberty, Spartan, Wealthy, Winesap 8 Cortland, Jonathan, McIntosh 10 Rome Beauty
Ida, Sweet as ___ Cider: 5 Apple
I'd be happy to!: 3 yes 4 fine, okay, sure 5 great, swell
I'd Be Surprisingly Good for You musical: 5 Evita
I'd Climb the Highest Mountain (1951 film)
  cast: Rory Calhoun, Susan Hayward, William Lundigan
  director: Henry King
I'd Do Anything for Your Love (1993 song) artist: Meat Loaf
ide: 4 fish
idea: 4 gist, plan, seed, text, view 5 fancy, hunch, point, theme, thing 6 belief, intent, motive, notion, reason, scheme, theory, thesis, vision 7 conceit, concept, feeling, inkling, opinion, purport, purpose, surmise, thought 8 game plan, instinct, proposal, scenario 9 intention, leitmotif, suspicion, viewpoint 10 brainchild, brainstorm, conception, conviction, glimmering, hypothesis, impression, perception, philosophy, reflection, suggestion
  bad ~: 3 pap 5 folly
  central ~ in music: 4 tema 5 motif
  entertain an ~: 4 muse 5 study 6 ponder 7 reflect 8 cogitate, consider, meditate, mull over, ruminate 9 think over 10 deliberate, introspect
  exchange: 4 chat, talk 6 confab, dialog, parley, powwow 8 colloquy, dialogue 9 discourse, tête-à-tête 10 conference, discussion
  fixed ~: 3 bug 5 mania 6 hang-up 7 craving 9 monomania, obsession
  get the ~: 3 see 5 sense 7 realize
  get the wrong ~: 3 err 7 presume 8 misjudge 9 underrate
  give the wrong ~: 4 dupe, fool, gull, hoax, scam, snow 5 bluff, cheat, put on, shaft, trick 6 delude, lead on, rope in, suck in, take in 7 confuse, deceive, defraud, mislead 8 hoodwink, inveigle, misguide, throw off 9 disinform, misinform 10 lead astray
  have the same ~: 4 jibe 5 agree, match 6 concur 8 coincide 9 harmonize
  main ~: 4 core, crux, gist, meat, pith 5 heart, motif, point, tenor 6 kernel, marrow, thrust, upshot 7 essence, keynote, purport 9 substance
  man: 6 pundit 7 thinker 8 theorist
  rough ~: 4 clew, clue 6 sketch 7 outline 10 ground plan
  source: 4 germ, Muse, seed 5 spark 6 kernel
  sudden ~: 4 whim 5 fancy 7 caprice, impulse 8 crotchet
  whole ~: 6 motive, reason 7 purpose 9 rationale
idea ___: 3 man
___ idea: 3 big 5 fixed
ideal: 4 best 5 cause, dream, model, right, typic 6 edenic, unreal, utmost, vision 7 eidolon, epitome, example, nonsuch, optimal, optimum, paragon, perfect, supreme, typical, utopian 8 absolute, abstract, exemplar, fanciful, flawless, nonesuch, paradigm, standard, ultimate, unproved 9 archetype, beautiful, exemplary, faultless, just right, nonpareil, principle, prototype, role model 10 apotheosis, archetypal, chimerical, consummate, intangible, perfection, touchstone
  beau ~: 5 model 7 paragon 8 paradigm
  ender: 3 ism, ist 5 istic
  state: 6 utopia 10 perfection
ideal ___: 3 gas 4 type 5 point
___ ideal: 3 ego 4 beau 5 beaux, prime 7 maximal
Ideal Husband, An author: Oscar Wilde
idealist: 7 dreamer, utopian 8 escapist, optimist, romantic
  need: 5 cause 7 crusade
idealistic: 6 dreamy 7 utopian 8 quixotic, romantic 9 unworldly, visionary 10 quixotical, unfeasible
ideality: 8 illusion 9 unreality 10 conception
idealized: 5 lofty 7 utopian 8 fanciful, quixotic 9 visionary 10 starry-eyed, unworkable
ideally: 6 at best 8 in theory 9 in thought
ideal of ___ reason: 4 pure
ideals: 6 morals, values 8 morality, standard
___ Ideal, The: 4 Beau
idea of ___ reason: 4 pure
idea of pure ___: 6 reason
ideas
  exchange of ~: 4 chat, talk 6 confab, dialog, parley, powwow 8 colloquy, dialogue 9 discourse, tête-à-tête 10 conference, discussion
  open to new ~: 7 pliable 8 amenable, tolerant 9 acceptive, receptive, sensitive 10 hospitable, responsive
  presentation of ~: 5 input
  share ~: 10 brainstorm
___ Ideas: 4 I Get
ideate: 4 plan 5 opine, think 6 cook up, ponder 7 dream up, imagine, picture 8 conceive, daydream, theorize 10 brainstorm, conceive of
___ idée: 5 bonne
idée fixe: 5 mania, thing 9 obsession
idem: 7 as above
___ idem: 5 alter 6 semper
Identi-___: 3 Kit
identical: 4 even, like, same, twin 5 alike, equal, exact, level 6 cloned 7 similar, uniform 8 matching, selfsame 9 congruent, duplicate, lookalike 10 carbon copy, dead ringer, equivalent, homogenous, synonymous, tantamount, two of a kind
  not ~: 5 other 6 unlike 7 unalike, unequal 8 distinct, separate 9 different, unrelated 10 dissimilar
  to: 6 same as
  twin: 5 sosie
identical ___: 4 twin 5 rhyme
identification: 3 tag 4 make, name, pass 5 badge, label 6 dog tag 8 labeling, passport, password
identification ___: 3 tag 4 card 6 thread
identified: 5 known
  wrongly ~: 8 mistaken 9 incorrect 10 inaccurate
identifier: 5 brand, theme
identify: 3 peg, see, tab, tag 4 find, know, link, mark, name, spot, tell 5 label, place, smell 6 detect, finger, select 7 analyze, catalog, make out, pick out 8 bookmark, classify, diagnose, discover, pinpoint, point out, smell out 9 catalogue, determine, establish, preordain, recognize, single out 10 button down, categorize
  a caller: 5 trace
  with: 4 pity 6 be into 8 relate to
identity: 3 ego 4 self 8 likeness 9 character, integrity 10 uniqueness
  a question of ~: 3 who
  assumed ~: 5 cover 8 disguise
identity ___: 4 card 6 crisis, matrix 7 element
___ Identity, The: 6 Bourne
ideogram: 6 symbol 8 logogram 9 character 10 hieroglyph
ideology: 3 ism 4 line 5 credo, creed, dogma, tenet 6 belief, system 7 beliefs 10 philosophy, principles
Ides of March, The author: Thornton Wilder
ides precursor: 5 nones
I'd hate to break up ___: 4 a set
Idi ___ Dada: 4 Amin
___ I Did for Love: 4 What
I didn't do it: 5 not me 6 denial
I Didn't Get to Sleep at All (1972 song) artist: Fifth Dimension
___ I didn't know!: 4 As if
I didn't need a ___...: 5 shove
I Dig Rock and Roll Music (1967 song) artist: Peter, Paul and Mary
idiocy: 5 folly 6 lunacy 7 fatuity, inanity
idiom: 3 phr. 4 cant, jive, word 5 argot, lingo 6 jargon, patois, phrase, slogan, speech, tongue 7 dialect 8 language, localism, locution, parlance 10 expression, vernacular
idiomatic: 5 slang 6 common, vulgar 8 informal, regional 9 dialectal 10 colloquial, vernacular
idiosyncrasy: 3 tic, way 4 kink 5 habit, quirk, trait 6 foible, manner, oddity 7 feature 8 crotchet 9 mannerism
idiosyncratic: 3 odd 5 queer 6 quaint 7 oddball, offbeat, strange 8 peculiar
idiot: 3 ass, sap 4 bozo, dodo, dope, fool, jerk, zany 5 booby, ninny 6 dimwit, lummox 7 bungler, jackass, pinhead 8 bonehead, numskull 9 blockhead, numbskull
  box: 2 TV 4 tube 5 TV set 10 television

idiot ___: 3 box 4 card 5 board, light
idiot-___: 5 proof
idiotic: 4 daft 5 batty, daffy, inane, sappy, silly 6 absurd, simple, stupid 7 asinine, fatuous, foolish 8 headless, mindless 9 fatuitous, foolhardy, senseless
idiot's delight: 4 game 8 card game
Idiot's Delight: 4 film, play
author: Robert E. Sherwood
cast: Edward Arnold, Clark Gable, Norma Shearer
director: Clarence Brown
Idiots First author: Bernard Malamud
Idiot, The author: Fyodor Dostoyevsky
Iditarod: 4 race
conveyance: 4 sled
cry: 4 mush
locale: 4 Nome 6 Alaska
puller: 3 dog 5 husky
idle: 3 lag, lax, veg 4 free, laze, lazy, loaf, logy, loll, moon, mope, poke, rest, vain 5 amble, dally, empty, inert, mosey, not on, relax, slack, spend, stall, still, tarry 6 asleep, at rest, dawdle, draggy, fallow, futile, hollow, lay off, linger, loiter, lounge, otiose, torpid, unused 7 aimless, dormant, foolish, goof off, hang out, inutile, jobless, laid off, loafing, not used, off-duty, passive, resting, saunter, sitting, slacken, trivial, unsound, useless, vacuous 8 baseless, ill-spent, inactive, indolent, kill time, lollygag, malinger, mark time, misspent, not in use, slack off, slothful, sluggish, stagnant, stagnate, straggle, untilled, vagabond, vegetate 9 at leisure, do-nothing, for naught, frivolous, fruitless, hibernate, in neutral, lethargic, loitering, out of work, pointless, sedentary, senseless, shiftless, unfounded, unhelpful, valueless, waste time, worthless 10 dillydally, disengaged, groundless, irrelevant, mothballed, motionless, not serious, not working, on the shelf, stationary, take it easy, unavailing, unemployed, unoccupied
be ~: 3 sit 4 loaf 5 relax
hours: 4 ease, rest 6 repose 7 holiday, leisure, time off 8 free time, vacation 9 spare time
make ~ conversation: 3 gab, yak 4 chat, chin
not ~: 4 busy 7 working 8 occupied
talk: 3 gab, gas, yap 4 wind 5 bilge, mouth, prate 6 babble, cackle, gossip 8 babbling, chitchat 9 loquacity
idle ___: 4 gear 5 wheel 6 pulley 7 chatter
Idle, Eric: 5 actor 8 comedian
film: The Adventures of Baron Munchausen (1989)
And Now for Something Completely Different (1972)
Dudley Do-Right (1999)
Monty Python's The Meaning of Life (1983)
film (voice): Quest for Camelot (1998)
idleness: 4 ease 5 sloth 6 acedia, torpor 7 inertia, languor 8 laziness, lethargy, otiosity 9 faineance, indolence, lassitude, torpidity 10 inactivity, stagnation
idler: 3 bum 5 drone, sloth 6 loafer, rascal, truant 7 dawdler, goof-off, laggard, shirker, slacker 8 layabout, parasite, slugabed, sluggard 9 do-nothing, goldbrick, lazybones, no-account 10 ne'er-do-well
bane: 3 job 4 work
opposite: 4 doer 6 dynamo
Idler, The author: Samuel Johnson
I'd Lie for You (1995 song) artist: Meat Loaf
I'd Like to Teach the World to Sing (1971 song)
artist: Hillside Singers, New Seekers
idling: 9 in neutral
I'd Love You to Want Me (1972 song) artist: Lobo
idly: 4 easy 7 lightly 8 by chance, casually 9 leisurely
___ idly by: 5 stand
I do: 3 vow
say ~: 3 wed 4 mate
sayer: 4 wife 5 bride, groom 7 husband 10 bridegroom
site: 5 altar
___ I Do: 3 But 4 Deed 6 What'll
I Do, I Do, I Do, I Do, I Do (1976 song) artist: ABBA
___ I doin'?: 4 How'm
___ I Do Is Dream of You: 3 All
I Do It for You (1991 song) artist: Bryan Adams
idol: 4 baal, hero, icon, ikon, joss, star, tiki 5 eikon 6 shrine 7 beloved, darling, pop star 8 false god, favorite, figurine, folk hero, loved one, luminary, megastar 9 celebrity, role model, sacred cow, superstar 10 golden calf, juggernaut
Biblical ~: 4 Baal, calf
Chinese ~: 4 joss
Cockney ~: 3 'ero
Hawaiian ~: 4 tiki
worshiper: 5 pagan 7 heathen
___ idol: 4 teen 7 matinée, Moorish
idolator: 5 pagan
idolatrous: 5 pagan 6 loving 9 heretical
idolatry: 5 honor 6 esteem, homage 7 respect, worship 8 devotion 9 adoration, reverence 10 admiration, veneration
Idol, Billy
song: Cradle of Love (1990)
Eyes Without a Face (1984)
Mony Mony (1987)
To Be a Lover (1986)
idolize: 4 like, love 5 adore, deify, exalt, go for 6 admire, dote on, esteem, revere 7 care for, cherish, glorify, lionize, worship 8 canonize, dote upon, hold dear, look up to, treasure, venerate 9 care about
idolized: 7 beloved 8 glorious, precious
Idomeneo composer: 6 Mozart
I do not ___ for any crown...: 3 ask
I don't believe it: 4 bosh, nuts 5 my eye 6 phooey 7 baloney
I Don't Have the Heart (1990 song) artist: James Ingram
___ I Don't Have You: 5 Since
I don't know gesture: 5 shrug
I Don't Know How to Love Him (1971 song) artist: Helen Reddy
I Don't Need You (1981 song) artist: Kenny Rogers
I don't think so!: 3 nah 4 nope
I Don't Wanna Cry (1991 song) artist: Mariah Carey
I Don't Wanna Fight (1993 song) artist: Tina Turner
I Don't Wanna Go on With You Like That (1988 song) artist: Elton John
I Don't Wanna Live Without Your Love (1988 song) artist: Chicago
I Don't Want ___ the World on Fire: 5 to Set
I don't want to: 3 nah 4 nope
I Don't Want to Be Right (1972 song) artist: Luther Ingram
I Don't Want to Live Without You (1988 song) artist: Foreigner
I Don't Want to Miss a Thing (1998 song) artist: Aerosmith
I Don't Want to Walk Without You, Baby composer: 5 Styne 7 Loesser
I Don't Want Your Love (1988 song) artist: Duran Duran
I doubt it: 4 game 8 card game
I'd Rather Be Right: 7 musical
author: George S. Kaufman
role: 3 FDR
songwriter: 4 Hart 7 Rodgers
star: 5 Cohan
I'd Really Love to See You Tonight (1976 song) artist: England Dan and John Ford Coley
I Dream of Jeannie (NBC sitcom)
cast: Bill Daily (Capt. Roger Healey)
Barbara Eden (Jeannie)
Larry Hagman (Capt. Tony Nelson)
dog: 10 Djinn Djinn
I Drove All Night (1989 song) artist: Cyndi Lauper
Idu author: Flora Nwapa
...I'd've Baked ___: 5 a Cake
idyll: 4 poem 5 verse 7 bucolic, eclogue, georgic, romance 8 pastoral 9 bucolical 10 flirtation
idyllic: 6 poetic, serene 8 pastoral, poetical, romantic
locale: 3 lea, ley 4 Eden
Idylls of the King: 4 epic, poem
author: Alfred Tennyson
character: 3 Kay 4 Bors, Enid, Mark 5 Balan, Balin, Isolt, Uther, Ynoil 6 Arthur, Elaine, Gareth, Gawain, Merlin, Modred, Pellam, Vivien, Ygerne 7 Ettarre, Galahad, Geraint, Gorloïs, Lavaine, Lynette, Pelleas 8 Bedivere, Lancelot, Tristram 9 Guinevere, Launcelot, Percivale
I-80: 3 rte. 5 route 7 highway 10 Interstate
city on ~: 4 Elko, Gary, Reno 5 Omaha 6 Moline 7 Chicago, Oakland, Teaneck 8 Cheyenne 9 Cleveland, Davenport, Des Moines, South Bend
runs through it: 3 Cal., Ill., Ind., Neb., Nev., Wyo. 4 Iowa, Nebr., Ohio, Penn., Utah 5 Calif. 6 Nevada 7 Indiana, Wyoming 8 Illinois, Nebraska 9 New Jersey 10 California
i.e.: 3 viz. 5 id est, to wit 6 namely, that is
I eat what ___: 4 I see
I Enjoy Being a Girl composer: 7 Rodgers 11 Hammerstein
Ieoh Ming ___: 3 Pei
I, Etcetera author: Susan Sontag
___ I Ever Need Is You: 3 All
if: 3 yet 4 conj. 5 altho, doubt, maybe 6 in case, though 7 whether 8 although, granting, provided 9 condition, given that, providing, qualifier, supposing 10 for all that
all goes right: 6 at best
as ~: 4 like, that 5 quasi 8 just like 9 presuming, seemingly, so to speak 10 supposedly
even ~: 3 tho 5 altho 6 albeit, though 8 although
it were not for: 7 besides, without 8 omitting 9 apart from, aside from, excluding
look as ~: 4 seem 6 appear
make as ~: 3 act 4 pose 5 feign 7 pretend 8 simulate
not: 3 but 4 else 9 otherwise
not for: 3 but 6 except
so: 4 then 10 in that case
if ___ be: 4 need
if ___ comes to shove: 4 push
___ if: 4 what
If ___: 4 I May 5 I Fell, It Die, You Go
If ___ a Bell: 5 I Were
If ___ a Carpenter: 5 I Were
If ___ a Hammer: 4 I Had
If ___ a Million: 4 I Had
If ___ Answers: 4 a Man
If ___ a Rich Man: 5 I Were
If ___ be so bold...: 4 I may
If ___ Came True: 6 Dreams, Wishes
If ___ Could Read My Mind: 3 You
If ___ Fall in Love: 5 I Ever
If ___ Had a Brain: 5 I Only
If ___ Hammer: 5 I Had a
If ___ Have You: 5 I Can't
If ___ I See You Again: 4 Ever
If ___ I Would Leave You: 4 Ever
If ___ King of the Forest: 5 I Were
If ___ Knew Susie: 3 You
If ___ Love Me: 3 You
If ___ make it there...: 4 I can
If ___ Million: 5 I Had a
If ___ My Druthers: 4 I had
If ___ My Way: 4 I Had
If ___ Street Could Talk: 5 Beale
If ___ the Circus: 4 I Ran
If ___ the Zoo: 4 I ran
If ___ Tuesday...: 3 It's
If ___ were horses...: 6 wishes
If ___ Would Leave You: 5 Ever I
If ___ you...: 5 I were
If ___ You: 4 I Had
If ___ Your Woman: 5 I Were
If ___ you were coming...: 5 I knew
if all ___ fails: 4 else
___ I Fall in Love: 4 When
I Fall to Pieces (1961 song) artist: Patsy Cline
I Fall to Pieces singer: 5 Cline
If Anyone Falls (1983 song) artist: Stevie Nicks
If author: Rudyard Kipling
last word: 3 son
If Beale Street Could Talk author: James Baldwin
___ if by land...: 3 One
IFC: 7 channel
alternative: 3 AMC, HBO, SHO, TMC 4 Flix 5 Bravo, Starz 6 Encore 7 Cinemax 8 Showtime, Sundance
If Dreams Came True (1958 song) artist: Pat Boone
Ife: 4 city, town
locale: 7 Nigeria
I Feel Fine (1964 song) artist: Beatles
I Feel for You (1984 song) artist: Chaka Khan
I Feel Love (1977 song) artist: Donna Summer
I Feel Pretty: 4 song, tune 5 waltz
composer: 8 Sondheim 9 Bernstein
I Feel So Bad (1961 song) artist: Elvis Presley
I Feel the Earth Move (1971 song) artist: Carole King
___ I Fell for You: 5 Since
If Ever ___ You Again: 4 I See
If Ever I Would Leave You composer: 5 Loewe 6 Lerner
If Ever You're in My Arms Again (1984 song) artist: Peabo Bryson
iffy: 5 risky, rocky 6 chancy, unsure 7 dubious, in doubt 8 doubtful, not final, variable 9 ambiguous, debatable, tentative, uncertain, undecided, unsettled 10 improbable, indefinite, precarious, unresolved, up for grabs, up in the air
If He Hollers Let Him Go author: Chester Himes
If He Walked Into My Life show: 4 Mame
If I ___: 4 Fell
If I ___ a Million: 3 Had
If I ___ Care: 5 Didn't
If I ___ Hammer: 4 Had a

If I __ King of the Forest: 4 Were
If I __ Rich Man: 5 Were a
If I __ the World: 5 Ruled
If I __ you...: 4 were
If I Can Dream (1968 song) artist: Elvis Presley
__ if I can help it!: 3 Not
If I Can't Have You (1978 song) artist: Yvonne Elliman
If I Could Build My Whole World Around You (1967 song) artist: Marvin Gaye, Tammi Terrell
If I Could Reach You (1972 song) artist: Fifth Dimension
If I Could Turn Back Time (1989 song) artist: Cher
If I Could Turn Back Time singer: 4 Cher
Ifield: 5 Frank
If I Give My Heart to You (1954 song) artist: Doris Day
If I Had a Hammer (song) artist: Peter, Paul and Mary, Trini Lopez
If I Had a Million (1932 film) cast: Gary Cooper, W.C. Fields, George Raft
If I Loved You composer: 7 Rodgers 11 Hammerstein
If I May (1955 song) artist: Nat King Cole
I Finally Found Someone (1996 song) artist: Barbra Streisand, Bryan Adams
If I Only Had a Brain composer: 5 Arlen 7 Harburg
If I Only Had the Nerve singer: 4 Lahr
If I Ran the Circus author: Dr. Seuss
If I Ran the Zoo author: Dr. Seuss
If I rest, I __: 4 rust
If I Ruled the World (1965 song) artist: Tony Bennett
If I Ruled the World rapper: 3 Nas
If it __ been for you...: 5 hadn't
If it __ broke...: 4 ain't
If It Die author: André Gide
If It Makes You Happy (1996 song) artist: Sheryl Crow
If it quacks like __...: 5 a duck
If it should rain, we'll __: 5 let it
If It's Tuesday, This Must Be Belgium (1969 film) cast: Ian McShane, Mildred Natwick, Suzanne Pleshette
If I've told you __,...: 4 once
If I Were __: 5 a Bell
If I Were __ Man: 5 a Rich
If I Were a Carpenter (1966 song) artist: Bobby Darin
If I Were King (1938 film) cast: Ronald Colman, Frances Dee, Basil Rathbone
director: Frank Lloyd
If I Were King of the Forest composer: 5 Arlen 7 Harburg
singer: 4 Lahr
If I Were Your Woman (1970 song) artist: Gladys Knight and the Pips
If Morning Ever Comes author: Anne Tyler
__ Ifni, Morocco: 4 Sidi
If Not for You (1971 song) artist: Olivia Newton-John
I forbid in Latin: 4 veto
I forgive you: 5 it's OK
I Fought the Law (1966 song) artist: Bobby Fuller
I Found Someone (1988 song) artist: Cher
if push __ to shove: 5 comes
ifs: 6 hedges 8 provisos
no ~ ands or buts: 6 really 7 exactly 9 precisely 10 absolutely, definitely, positively
If (song) artist: Bread, Janet Jackson
If the __ fits...: 4 shoe
If This __ Love: 4 Isn't
If This Is It (1984 song) artist: Huey Lewis and the News
If Tomorrow Comes author: Sidney Sheldon
If We Only Have Love composer: 4 Brel
If wishes __ horses...: 4 were
if worst __ to worst: 5 comes
if you __: 4 dare 6 please
If You Asked Me to (1992 song) artist: Celine Dion
If You Can Want (1968 song) artist: Miracles
If You Could Read My Mind (1971 song) artist: Gordon Lightfoot
If You Don't Know Me by Now (song) artist: Harold Melvin and the Blue Notes, Simply Red
If You Go (1994 song) artist: Jon Secada
If You Go Away composer: 4 Brel
If You Had My Love (1999 song) artist: Jennifer Lopez
If You Knew Susie: 4 song, tune
refrain: 6 oh oh oh
singer: 6 Cantor
If You Leave Me Now (1976 song) artist: Chicago
If You Love Me (song) artist: Brownstone, Olivia Newton-John
If You Love Somebody... (1985 song) artist: Sting
If You Really Love Me (1971 song) artist: Stevie Wonder
If you're ever in __: 4 a jam
If You're Ready (1973 song) artist: Staple Singers
If You Talk in Your Sleep (1974 song) artist: Elvis Presley
Igbo home: 6 Africa 7 Nigeria
I Get __: 5 Ideas
I Get a Kick Out of You composer: 6 Porter
I Get Around (song) artist: Beach Boys, Tupac
I get it: 3 aha, oho
__ I Get It Right: 3 'Til
I Get Lonely (1998 song) artist: Blackstreet, Janet Jackson
__ I Get to You, The: 6 Closer
I Get Weak (1988 song) artist: Belinda Carlisle
Iggie's House author: Judy Blume
Iggy: 3 Pop
I give up!: 5 uncle 6 enough, no more
Iglesias, Enrique
father: Julio
song: Bailamos (1999)
Iglesias, Julio song: To All the Girls I've Loved Before (1984)
igloo: 3 hut 4 dome 5 abode
dweller: 3 Esk. 5 Inuit 6 Eskimo, Innuit, Inupik
igloo-shaped auto: 5 Pacer
Ignacy: 8 Krasicki 10 Paderewski
Ignarro, Louis: 8 Nobelist
Ignatius: 5 saint
Ignatius of __: 6 Loyola
Ignatow, David: 4 poet
igneous rock: 4 lava, sima 6 basalt, gabbro 7 pumices 8 obsidian
source: 5 magma 7 volcano
ignis fatuus: 6 mirage 7 chimera, eidolon, fantasm, figment 8 chimaera, delusion, phantasm 9 obsession
ignitable: 9 flammable 10 incendiary
ignite: 4 burn, lick 5 light, shoot, spark, start 6 kindle, set off, turn on 7 enflame, flare up, inflame, light up, trigger 8 enkindle, set afire, touch off 9 catch fire, set ablaze, set aflame, set alight, set on fire 10 illuminate, incinerate
ignited: 3 lit 6 ablaze, flambé
again: 5 relit
igniter: 5 flint, spark
fireworks ~: 4 punk 6 amadou
ignition: 4 fire 7 lighter 10 combustion
awaiting ~: 4 dark 5 unlit
rocket ~: 7 liftoff
ignition __: 4 coil 5 point 6 system
ignition system part: 3 cam 5 choke
ignoble: 3 low 4 base, mean, ugly, vile 5 lowly, seamy, small 6 abject, coarse, common, craven, humble, menial, modest, shabby, sordid, vulgar 7 caddish, corrupt, heinous, miserly, servile, squalid 8 baseborn, degraded, infamous, inferior, ordinary, plebeian, shameful, unworthy, wretched 9 dastardly, low-minded 10 despicable, inglorious, outrageous, villainous
ignominious: 5 shady, sorry 6 abject, shoddy 7 ignoble 8 infra dig, shameful, unworthy 10 despicable
ignominy: 4 evil 5 odium, shame 6 hatred, infamy 8 contempt, disgrace, dishonor 9 disrepute, ill repute 10 opprobrium, virtueless, wickedness
ignoramus: 3 nit, oaf, sap 4 boob, clod, dolt, dope, dupe, fool, jerk, loon, simp, twit 5 clown, cluck, dummy, dunce, joker, klutz, ninny, patsy 6 dimwit, lubber, lummox, nitwit, stooge, sucker, turkey 7 buffoon, bungler, dullard, fathead, halfwit, jackass 8 bonehead, dumbbell, numskull 9 barbarian, birdbrain, blockhead, harebrain, ignoramus, lamebrain, schlemiel, simpleton 10 dunderhead, nincompoop, noodlehead
ignorance: 5 youth 7 naiveté 8 darkness 9 blindness, crudeness, denseness, disregard, innocence, nescience, vagueness 10 callowness, illiteracy, incapacity, obtuseness, simplicity
in an adage: 5 bliss
in Buddhism: 7 samsara
liberation from ~: 7 nirvana
sign of ~: 5 shrug
sound of ~: 3 duh
Ignorance __ excuse: 4 is no
ignorant: 3 raw 4 dark, naif 5 green, naive, silly, thick, young 6 gauche, simple, stupid, unread 7 lowbred, out of it, shallow, unaware 8 innocent, untaught 9 backwater, in the dark, unadvised, unknowing, unlearned, unmindful, untrained 10 uneducated, unfamiliar, uninformed, unschooled
not ~: 4 sage 5 smart 6 brainy 7 erudite, learned 8 cerebral 9 in the know, scholarly
of right and wrong: 6 amoral
ignore: 4 defy, miss, omit, shun, skip, snub 5 avoid, elide, evade, flout, rebel, scorn, skirt, spurn 6 bypass, forget, oppose, pass by, pass up, rebuff, refuse, reject, resist, revolt, slight, wink at 7 blink at, disobey, exclude, forsake, let go by, neglect, rule out, tune out, violate 8 brush off, discount, file away, laugh off, lay aside, overlook, overrule, pass over, pooh-pooh, shrug off, sneeze at 9 disregard 10 work around
ignoring: 6 rebuff 7 despite 9 disregard, in spite of
__ I Go Again: 4 Here
Igor: 4 aide, Tamm 6 prince, Ulanov 8 Moiseyev, Sikorsky 9 Markevich 10 Stravinsky
I got __ in Kalamazoo: 4 a gal
I Got __: 5 a Name
I Got a Feeling (1958 song) artist: Ricky Nelson
I Got a Name (1973 song) artist: Jim Croce
I Gotcha (1972 song) artist: Joe Tex
I Got Id (1995 song) artist: Pearl Jam
I Go to Extremes (1990 song) artist: Billy Joel
I Go to Pieces (1965 song) artist: Peter and Gordon
I Got Plenty o' Nuthin' composer: 8 Gershwin
I Got Rhythm: 4 song, tune
composer: 8 Gershwin
last word: 4 more
I Got Stung (1958 song) artist: Elvis Presley
I Gotta Know (1960 song) artist: Elvis Presley
I Gotta Right to Sing the Blues composer: 5 Arlen 7 Koehler
I got the __ the morning...: 5 sun in
I Got the Feelin' (1968 song) artist: James Brown
I Got the Sun in the Morning composer: 6 Berlin
I Got You (1965 song) artist: James Brown
I Got You Babe singer: 4 Bono, Cher 5 Sonny
__ I Grow to Old to Dream: 4 When
__ I Grow Up: 4 When
Iguaçu: 5 falls 9 waterfall
locale: 6 Brazil
Iguala: 4 city, town
locale: 6 Mexico 8 Guerrero
iguana: 3 pet 6 animal, lizard 7 reptile
cousin: 5 agama, anole
fare: 6 insect
iguanodon: 8 dinosaur
Iguassú: 5 falls, river 9 waterfall
locale: 6 Brazil
I Guess That's Why They Call It the Blues (1983 song) artist: Elton John
__ I had heard of Lucy Gray: 3 Oft
I Had Trouble Getting to Solla Sollew author: Dr. Seuss
I hate __ to pieces!: 6 meeces
I Hate Men composer: 6 Porter
I Hate Myself for Loving You (1988 song) artist: Joan Jett and the Blackhearts
I hate to break up __: 4 a set
I Hate U (1995 song) artist: Prince
I have __ walked...: 5 often
I have a dream
monogram: 3 MLK
speaker: 4 King
I Have a Rendezvous with Death author: Alan Seeger
__ I Have Fears: 4 When
I have half __ to...: 5 a mind
I have no __!: 4 idea
I have not __ begun to fight: 3 yet
I Have Nothing (1993 song) artist: Whitney Houston
I haven't __!: 5 a clue
__ I Have to Do Is Dream: 3 All
I Hear America Singing author: Walt Whitman
I Hear a Symphony (1965 song) artist: Supremes
I Heard a Rumour (1987 song) artist: Bananarama
I Heard It Through the Grapevine (song) artist: Gladys Knight and the Pips, Marvin Gaye
ihi: 4 fish
Ihimaera, Witi: 5 Maori 6 author, writer
I Honestly Love You (1974 song) artist: Olivia Newton-John
IHOP: 5 chain 6 eatery 10 restaurant
freebie: 5 sirup, syrup
order: 2 OJ 5 stack 8 pancakes

part of ~: 4 Intl. 5 House
rival: 4 HoJo 6 Denny's
II: 3 two 9 the Second
__ II: 5 Rocky 7 Richard
Iida: 4 city, town
locale: 5 Japan
III: 5 three 8 the Third
father: 2 jr.
__ III: 5 Rambo, Rocky 7 Richard
__ II Men: 4 Boyz
I intended __: 5 an ode
'I' Is for Innocent author: Sue Grafton
__ II Society: 6 Menace
Ijaw home: 6 Africa 7 Nigeria
Ijo home: 6 Africa 7 Nigeria
Ijssel: 5 river
attraction: 4 dike
locale: 7 Holland 11 Netherlands
town on the: 4 Edam
Ijsselmeer: 4 lake
locale: 7 Holland 11 Netherlands
I Just Called to Say I Love You (1984 song) artist: Stevie Wonder
I Just Can't Help Believing (1970 song) artist: B.J. Thomas
I Just Can't Stop Loving You (1987 song) artist: Michael Jackson
I Just Fall in Love Again (1979 song) artist: Anne Murray
I Just Want to Be Your Everything (1977 song) artist: Andy Gibb
ikat: 6 fabric 8 material
__ ikat: 4 warp, weft 6 double
Ike: 3 DDE, gen. 6 Pappas, Turner 7 Clanton, general
alma mater: 4 Army, USMA
colleague of ~: 3 Hap 4 Doug, Omar
command: 3 ETO 4 NATO
ex: 4 Tina
like ~: 4 bald
Mamie, to ~: 4 wife
opponent: 5 Adlai
see also Eisenhower
__ Ike: 5 Alibi, I Like
ikebana: 3 art
chrysanthemum, in ~: 4 kiku
home: 5 Japan
Ikeda: 4 city, town
locale: 5 Japan
Ikhnaton's river: 4 Nile
I Kid You Not author: 4 Paar
Ikiru (1952 film) director: Akira Kurosawa
__ I Kissed You: 3 'Til
I Kissed You (1959 song) artist: Everly Brothers
Ikkesh, son of: 3 Ira
I knew it!: 3 aha
I Knew You Were Waiting (1987 song) artist: Aretha Franklin, George Michael
__ I Know: 3 All 6 Nobody
I Know a Place (1965 song) artist: Petula Clark
I Know What I Like (1987 song) artist: Huey Lewis and the News
I Know What You Did Last Summer (1997 film)
cast: Sarah Michelle Gellar, Jennifer Love Hewitt, Ryan Phillippe, Freddie Prinze Jr.
I Know Why the Caged Bird Sings author: Maya Angelou
Ikoma: 4 city, town
locale: 5 Japan
Ikons, The author: Lawrence Durrell
Il __ della rosa: 4 nome
IL *see* Illinois
__ I lay me...: 3 Now
île: 6 Tahiti 10 Martinique
Ile-de-France river: 4 Oise
Ile de la Cité site: 5 Seine
I Led Three Lives (TV adventure)
cast: Richard Carlson (Herbert Philbrick)
Ile du __: 6 Diable
I Left My Heart in San Francisco (1962 song) artist: Tony Bennett
Ilene: 5 Graff
Iles __ Société: 4 de la
ileus: 5 colic
ilex: 4 tree 5 holly, shrub 7 holm oak
__ il faut: 5 comme
ILGWU: 5 union
chapter: 3 lcl. 5 local
do an ~ job: 3 sew 6 stitch
members: 5 labor
part of ~: 3 Int. 4 Intl. 5 Union 6 Ladies 7 Garment, Workers
Ilhéus: 4 city, town
locale: 6 Brazil
Ilia: 5 Kulik
iliac __: 6 artery
iliac starter: 5 sacro
Iliad: 4 epic, epos, poem 6 epopee 8 epopoeia
author: 5 Homer
character: 4 Aias, Ajax, Ares, Hera, Iris, Zeus 5 Dolon, Eneas, Helen, Paris, Priam 6 Aeneas, Apollo, Athena, Athene, Hector, Hecuba, Nestor, Teucer, Thetis, Trojan 7 Antenor, Briseis, Calchas, Glaucus, Helenus, Machaon, Priamus 8 Achilles, Chryseis, Diomedes, Melelaus, Odysseus, Pandarus, Poseidon, Sarpedon 9 Agamemmon, Aphrodite, Cassandra, Deiphobus, Patroclus, Polydamus 10 Andromache, Hephaestus
locale: 4 Troy
Iliamna: 4 lake 7 volcano
locale: 6 Alaska
Ilie: 7 Nastase
Iliescu: 3 Ion
__ I Lie to You?: 5 Would
I like __, except for meals: 4 eels
I Like __: 3 Ike 4 Beer
I Like Dreamin' (1976 song) artist: Kenny Nolan
I Like It Here author: Kingsley Amis
I Like It Like That (song) artist: Chris Kenner, Dave Clark Five
I like your __: 5 style
I Like Your Kind of Love (1956 song) artist: Andy Williams
ilium: 4 bone
locale: 3 hip 6 pelvis
Ilium: 4 Troy 5 Troia
feature: 5 tower
__ I Live: 5 How Do, Where
ilk: 4 form, kind, sort, type 5 brand, class, genre, stamp 6 family, nature, stripe 7 variety 8 category 9 character
of that ~: 4 akin 7 related, similar
Ilka: 5 Chase
ill: 3 bad, low 4 evil, foul, harm, hurt, sick 5 badly, rocky, wrong 6 ailing, infirm, injury, laid up, malady, malice, misery, peaked, poorly, queasy, queazy, unwell, wicked 7 adverse, badness, disease, harmful, hostile, hurtful, invalid, laid low, not well, ruinous, trouble, unsound 8 below par, calamity, damaging, diseased, feverish, inimical, sickness, sinister 9 adversely, afflicted, bedridden, depravity, harmfully, in a bad way, infirmity, injurious, malicious, miserable, unhealthy 10 affliction, indisposed, iniquitous, malevolent, misfortune, out of sorts, wickedness
at ease: 4 edgy 5 antsy, itchy, jumpy, tense 6 on edge 7 abashed, anxious, awkward, jittery, keyed up, nervous, restive, uptight, worried 8 agitated, restless, skittish, troubled 9 concerned, disturbed, excitable, faltering, unrelaxed, unsettled 10 disquieted, high-strung, out of place, suspicious
be ~ with: 3 get 4 have 5 catch 7 develop 8 contract
combining form: 3 dys-, mal-, mis-
feel ~: 3 ail
feeling: 4 bile, hate 5 odium, pique, scorn, spite, venom, wrath 6 animus, enmity, grudge, hatred, malice, rancor 7 discord, disdain, disgust, dudgeon, umbrage 8 acerbity, acrimony, aversion, bad blood, distaste, loathing 9 animosity, antipathy, harshness, hostility, malignity, mordacity, revulsion, vengeance, virulence 10 abhorrence, antagonism, bitterness, execration, repugnance, resentment
fortune: 7 bad luck 9 adversity
health: 6 malady 7 ailment, disease 8 sickness 9 infirmity 10 affliction, unwellness
humor: 3 ire 4 bile 6 spleen, temper 7 bad mood 8 acerbity 9 surliness, testiness 10 crabbiness, crankiness, grumpiness, irritation, touchiness
in French: 3 mal
less ~: 6 better
looking ~: 3 wan 4 ashy, pale 5 ashen
make ~: 5 repel, upset 6 infect, offend, poison, revolt, sicken 7 afflict
not ~: 4 ably, well 6 robust 7 adeptly, capably, healthy 8 expertly, properly 9 in the pink
off: 5 broke, needy 6 hard up, in need, in want 7 pinched 8 bankrupt, beggarly, indigent, strapped 9 destitute, insolvent, moneyless, penniless, penurious 10 down and out, pauperized, straitened
of ~ repute: 5 shady 8 infamous, shameful, unsavory 9 dishonest, notorious, unethical 10 scandalous
once: 5 amort
repute: 5 odium, shame 6 infamy 7 obloquy 8 disfavor, disgrace, dishonor, ignominy 9 disesteem, notoriety 10 opprobrium
speak ~ of: 5 abase 6 malign, vilify 7 asperse, run down 8 backbite 10 calumniate, villainize
treatment: 4 harm 5 abuse
will: 4 hate 5 odium, spite, venom 6 animus, enmity, grudge, hatred, malice, rancor 8 acrimony, aversion, bad blood 9 animosity, antipathy, hostility, nastiness 10 antagonism, resentment, unkindness
(with): 4 down
ill __: 4 will, wind 5 humor 6 health, nature, temper
ill-__: 3 off, use 4 bred 5 being, fated, kempt, spent, timed, treat 6 boding, fitted, formed, housed, judged, omened, shapen, sorted, suited, wisher 7 advised, defined, favored, founded, natured, starred
ill-__ gains: 6 gotten
Ill.
neighbor: 3 Ind., Ken., Wis. 4 Wisc.
see also Illinois
I'll __: 4 Wait 5 Get By
I'll __ at Your Wedding: 5 Dance
I'll __ By: 3 Get
I'll __ 4 Ya: 6 Tumble
I'll __ Manhattan: 4 Take
I'll __ monkey's uncle!: 3 be a
I'll __ my hat!: 3 eat
I'll __ Smile Again: 5 Never
I'll __ Tomorrow: 3 Cry
I'll __ You Halfway: 4 Meet
I'll __ Your Side: 4 Be by
I'll __ You There: 4 Take
ill-advised: 4 rash 5 brash, hasty, silly, wrong 6 madcap, stupid, unwary, unwise 7 foolish 8 improper, mistaken, reckless 9 foolhardy, half-baked, hotheaded, impolitic, imprudent, misguided, overhasty 10 incautious, indiscreet, ungrounded
I'll Always Love You (1988 song) artist: Taylor Dayne
Illampu: 4 peak 5 mount 8 mountain
locale: 5 Andes 7 Bolivia
I'll be!: 3 wow 4 gosh 5 golly
I'll Be (1997 song)
artist: Foxy Brown, Jay-Z
I'll Be __ for Christmas: 4 Home
I'll Be Around (1972 song) artist: Spinners
I'll Be Doggone (1965 song) artist: Marvin Gaye
ill-behaved: 3 bad 6 bratty, unruly
I'll Be Home (1956 song) artist: Pat Boone
I'll Be Home for Christmas (1998 film)
cast: Jessica Biel, Adam LaVorgna, Sean O'Bryan, Jonathan Taylor Thomas
I'll be loving you, __: 6 always
I'll Be Loving You (1989 song) artist: New Kids on the Block
I'll Be Missing You (1997 song) artist: Faith Evans, Puff Daddy
I'll Be Seeing You author: Mary Higgins Clark
I'll be there __ long: 3 ere
I'll Be There for You (song)
artist: Bon Jovi, Mary J. Blige, Method Man
I'll Be There (song) artist: Escape Club, Jackson 5, Mariah Carey
I'll Be With You in __ Blossom Time: 5 Apple
I'll Be Your Shelter (1990 song) artist: Taylor Dayne
ill-boding: 4 dire 7 ominous 8 sinister
ill-bred: 3 low 4 rude 5 crude 6 gauche 7 bearish, boorish, caddish, loutish, raffish, uncivil, uncouth 8 impolite, impudent, inurbane, unpoised 9 ungallant 10 indecorous, unladylike, unmannerly
I'll Build a Stairway to Paradise composer: 8 Gershwin
Ill, city on the: 10 Strasbourg
ill-considered: 3 mad 4 luny, rash, wild, zany 5 crazy, hasty, inane, loony, sappy, silly, wacky, weird 6 absurd, looney, madcap, unwise, whacky 7 bizarre, fatuous, foolish, lunatic 9 fantastic, foolhardy, half-baked, imprudent, ludicrous, premature, senseless, unguarded 10 outrageous, ridiculous
I'll Cry Tomorrow (1955 film)
cast: Richard Conte, Susan Hayward, Jo Van Fleet
director: Daniel Mann
subject: Lillian Roth
ill-defined: 3 dim 4 hazy 5 faint, fuzzy, loose, vague 9 imprecise, unfocused 10 indistinct, inexplicit
ill-disposed: 6 averse, down on 7 adverse, against, hostile 8 spiteful 9 malicious 10 unfriendly
ill-done: 3 bad 4 poor 5 awful, lousy, sorry, wrong 6 faulty, woeful 8 dreadful, slipshod, terrible 9 atrocious, deficient, imperfect, incorrect, miserable, third-rate 10 inadequate
I'll do that!: 5 Let me
Ille: 5 river
locale: 6 France

Illeana: 7 Douglas
grandfather: 6 Melvyn
...I'll eat __!: 5 my hat
illegal: 4 tabu 5 shady, taboo, wrong 6 banned 7 bootleg, crooked, illicit, sub rosa, wildcat 8 criminal, outlawed, smuggled, unlawful, verboten, wrongful 9 felonious, forbidden, unethical 10 actionable, contraband, indictable, not allowed, prohibited, proscribed, unlicensed
act: 3 sin 5 bribe, crime, usury 6 bag job 9 smuggling
inducement: 5 graft 6 grease, payoff, payola 8 kickback 9 hush money
make ~: 3 ban 6 forbid, outlaw
transfer ~ goods: 4 push 7 bootleg
illegal __: 5 alien
illegality: 5 theft, wrong 6 racket 7 con game, misdeed, offense, swindle 8 cheating, thievery 9 violation 10 corruption, dishonesty, infraction
lure into ~: 6 entrap
illegible: 7 obscure, scrawly, unclear 8 scrawled 10 indistinct, unreadable
render ~: 5 smear
illegitimate: 3 bad 5 bogus 8 spurious, unlawful, wrongful
__ Ille Pooh: 6 Winnie
ill-fated: 4 poor 5 curst 6 cursed, doomed, jinxed, ruined, tragic 7 accurst, hapless, ominous, unblest, unhappy, unlucky 8 accursed, blighted, hopeless, luckless, tragical 9 unblessed, unfavored 10 disastrous, portentous
ill-favored: 4 ugly 9 unwelcome
ill-fed: 4 bony 5 gaunt 7 haggard, scrawny 9 emaciated
ill-fitting: 5 baggy, loose 6 floppy 7 sagging
ill-founded: 5 false, wrong 7 invalid, unsound 8 baseless 9 erroneous 10 fallacious, unreasoned
I'll Get By (1992 song) artist: Eddie Money
I'll get right __!: 4 on it
ill-gotten gains: 4 pelf 5 booty, grift, lucre
I'll Have to Say I Love You in a Song (1974 song) artist: Jim Croce
ill-humored: 4 dour 5 cross, gruff, moody, nasty, surly 6 crusty, morose, sullen 7 bilious, vicious, waspish 8 choleric, petulant, snappish 9 irritable, splenetic 10 out of sorts
be ~: 4 mope, pout, sulk 5 brood, gripe 6 grouse
one: 4 crab 5 crank, grump 6 grouch 8 sorehead, sourpuss 10 curmudgeon, malcontent
illiberal: 5 close 6 little, narrow, skimpy, stingy 7 insular, miserly 8 ungiving 9 bourgeois 10 intolerant
illiberality: 4 bias 6 racism 7 bigotry 9 injustice, prejudice 10 chauvinism, narrowness, partiality, unfairness
illicit: 4 tabu 5 dirty, taboo, wrong 6 banned 7 bootleg, illegal, lawless 8 criminal, improper, not legal, outlawed, unlawful, verboten, wrongful 9 felonious, forbidden 10 contraband, indictable, prohibited, unlicensed
scheme: 3 con 5 bunco 6 racket
Illimani: 4 peak 5 mount 8 mountain
locale: 7 Bolivia
illimitable: 3 big 4 vast 7 abysmal, endless 8 infinite 9 limitless, unlimited
Illini: 4 team
conference: 6 Big Ten
locale: 6 Urbana
Illinois: 5 river, state 6 Indian 7 Amerind
Benedictine College site: 5 Lisle
city: 4 Iola, Pana, Zion 5 Alton, Cairo, Elgin, Lisle, Niles, Olney, Pekin 6 Aurora, Berwyn, Cicero, Darien, De Kalb, Dolton, Galena, Gurnee, Harvey, Joliet, Macomb, Moline, Normal, Peoria, Quincy, Skokie, Urbana 7 Addison, Batavia, Burbank, Chicago, Decatur, Lansing, Lombard, Maywood, Oak Lawn, Oak Park, O'Fallon, Roselle, Wheaton 8 Bartlett, Bellwood, Danville, Elk Grove, Elmhurst, Evanston, Freeport, Glenview, Kankakee, MacHenry, Palatine, Rockford, Waukegan, Westmont, Wheeling, Wilmette 9 Algonquin, Belvidere, Champaign, Galesburg, Glen Ellyn, Loves Park, Mundelein, Oak Forest, Park Ridge, St. Charles, Villa Park, Woodridge, Woodstock 10 Belleville, Blue Island, Carbondale, Charleston, Des Plaines, East Moline, East Peoria, Lake Forest, Naperville, Northbrook, Orland Park, Park Forest, Rock Island, Romeoville, Schaumburg, Streamwood, Tinley Park
conference: 6 Big Ten
neighbor: 4 Iowa 7 Indiana 8 Kentucky, Missouri 9 Wisconsin
school: 6 DePaul, Loyola 7 Bradley
state fish: 8 bluegill
state flower: 6 violet
state mineral: 8 fluorite
state state bird: 8 cardinal
state tree: 8 white oak
illiteracy: 9 ignorance
illiterate: 6 simple, unread 9 benighted, inerudite, unlearned, untutored 10 solecistic, uneducated, unlettered, unschooled
Illiterate Digest, The author: Will Rogers
ill-judged: 9 impolitic, imprudent 10 incautious
ill-kempt: 5 messy, tatty 6 ragged
I'll leave it __ you: 4 up to
ill-lit: 3 dim 4 dark 5 dingy, murky 7 obscure, shadowy
ill-looking: 3 wan 4 ashy, pale 5 ashen
Ill-Made Knight, The author: T.H. White
ill-mannered: 4 loud, rude 5 crude, rough, surly, tacky 6 bratty, coarse, gauche, vulgar 7 boorish, caddish, loutish, lowbred, uncivil, uncouth 8 churlish, impolite, impudent, insolent
one: 2 ox 3 ass, cad, oaf 4 boob, boor, clod, goon, hick, lout, rube 5 brute, churl, clown, looby, yahoo, yokel 6 galoot, lummox, rustic 7 buffoon, bumpkin, hayseed, palooka, peasant 9 barbarian, vulgarian 10 philistine
ill-matched: 6 uneven, unfair 7 unequal 8 lopsided, one-sided
I'll Meet You Halfway (1971 song) artist: Partridge Family
ill-natured: 4 mean, sour 5 catty, nasty, onery, sulky, surly 6 crabby, ornery, sullen, touchy, unkind 7 bearish, peevish, vicious 8 churlish, perverse, petulant, spiteful 9 crotchety, dyspeptic, irritable, malicious 10 malevolent, unfriendly, unpleasant
illness: 3 bug 5 spell, upset, virus 6 malady 7 ailment, disease, malaise, trouble 8 disorder, sickness 9 complaint, condition, infirmity 10 affliction, invalidism, unwellness
overcome ~: 5 rally 6 revive 7 get well, rebound, recover, shape up 9 get better 10 bounce back, come around, recuperate, turn around
Illness as Metaphor author: Susan Sontag
illnesses, like some: 5 viral
I'll Never __ Again: 5 Smile
I'll Never Fall in Love Again (song) artist: Dionne Warwick, Tom Jones
I'll Never Find Another You (1965 song) artist: Seekers
I'll Never Forget What's 'is Name (1967 film)
cast: Oliver Reed, Orson Welles
I'll Never Love This Way Again (1979 song) artist: Dionne Warwick
ill-off: 4 poor 5 broke, needy 6 bad off, busted, hard up, in need, in want 7 pinched 8 badly off, bankrupt, beggarly, dirt poor, homeless, indigent, strapped 9 destitute, insolvent, moneyless, penniless, penurious 10 down and out, pauperized, straitened
illogical: 3 mad 5 false, inane, nutty, sappy, silly, wacky 6 absurd, faulty, hollow, screwy, whacky 7 fatuous, invalid, unsound 8 cockeyed, mistaken, specious 9 casuistic, incorrect, pointless, senseless, sophistic, untenable 10 fallacious, far-fetched, groundless, irrational, irrelevant, off-the-wall, unreasoned
ill-omened: 4 dire 6 cursed, doomed, jinxed, tragic, woeful 7 baleful, drastic, fearful, ruinous, unlucky 8 alarming, fearsome, grievous, luckless, terrible 10 calamitous, disastrous
I'll Remember (1994 song) artist: Madonna
I'll say!: 4 amen 6 sure is
ill-smelling: 4 gamy 5 funky, gamey 6 frowsy, frowzy
ill-spent: 4 idle 5 empty 7 foolish, trivial, unsound 8 wasteful 9 frivolous, pointless, valueless
ill-starred: 5 curst 6 cursed, jinxed, tragic 7 hapless, unblest, unhappy, unlucky 8 luckless, tragical 9 unblessed, unfavored 10 disastrous
ill-suited: 5 inapt, silly, unapt, unfit, wrong 8 improper, untimely 10 irrelevant, nongermane, unbecoming, unsuitable
I'll Take Manhattan author: Judith Krantz
I'll take that as __: 3 a no 4 a yes
I'll Take You There (1972 song) artist: Staple Singers
...I'll tell __ lies: 5 you no
ill-tempered: 3 hot, mad 4 ired, mean, sore, sour 5 acerb, angry, cross, huffy, irate, livid, moody, nasty, riled, surly, testy, waspy, wroth 6 crabby, feisty, fuming, grumpy, ireful, morose, peeved, raging, raving, red-hot, snappy, touchy 7 annoyed, bearish, bilious, enraged, furious, grouchy, huffish, ranting, vicious, waspish 8 choleric, churlish, grumpish, incensed, inflamed, maddened, outraged, spiteful, wrathful 9 indignant, irritated, resentful, splenetic 10 freaked out, infuriated
person: 4 ogre 5 shrew 6 virago
ill-timed: 8 improper 10 out of joint
ill-treat: 4 harm, mall, maul 5 abuse, wrong 6 injure, misuse 8 aggrieve 9 manhandle, persecute
I'll Tumble 4 Ya (1983 song) artist: Culture Club
illume: 5 light 7 lighten 8 brighten
illuminate: 5 color, edify, light, shine, solve 6 ignite, inform, kindle 7 clarify, clear up, explain, lighten, light up 8 brighten 9 bring home, dramatize, elucidate, enlighten, exemplify, highlight, interpret, irradiate, make clear, spotlight 10 account for, floodlight, illustrate, incandesce
illuminated: 3 lit 5 aglow, light, lit up, shiny 6 ablaze, bright, flashy, gaslit 7 beaming, blazing, fulgent, glowing, lambent, radiant, shining, well-lit 8 dazzling, gleaming, luminous, lustrous 9 brilliant, sparkling
from below: 5 uplit
illuminati: 5 elite 8 literati 9 aesthetes, highbrows 10 upper-crust
illumination: 3 ray 4 beam, info, rays 5 beams, flame, flash, gleam, light 6 flames, gleams, lights 7 flashes
gas: 4 neon
source: 4 lamp 5 flare, light 6 beacon 10 flashlight
unit: 3 lux 4 phot, watt
units: 5 luces
illumine: 5 edify, light, shine 7 clarify, light up, radiate 8 brighten, instruct 9 elucidate, irradiate
illus.: 4 diag., pict.
ill-use: 4 harm 6 injure 8 aggrieve, maltreat, mistreat 9 brutalize
illusion: 4 myth 5 dream, ghost, magic, trick 6 mirage, vision 7 chimera, fallacy, fantasy, figment, mistake 8 chimaera, daydream, disguise, ideality 9 deception, dreamland, misbelief, nightmare, unreality 10 apparition
__ illusion: 7 optical, Zollner
__ Illusion: 5 Grand
illusionist: 8 conjurer, magician
illusive: 6 subtle 9 imaginary
illusory: 6 dreamy, fantom, irreal, unreal 7 phantom 8 apparent, fanciful 9 deceitful, deceptive, imaginary, visionary 10 chimerical, fallacious, ostensible, subjective
illustrate: 4 draw, etch, limn, show 5 paint, teach 6 adduce, depict, embody, evince, imbody, lay out, mirror, sketch, typify, unfold 7 clarify, clear up, display, exhibit, explain, get over, picture, point up, portray 8 describe, evidence, indicate, manifest, stand for 9 bring home, delineate, elucidate, embellish, emphasize, epitomize, exemplify, explicate, get across, highlight, interpret, make clear, make plain, personify, represent, spotlight, symbolize 10 allegorize, illuminate
illustrated: 7 graphic 9 decorated, graphical
__ Illustrated: 6 Sports 8 Classics
Illustrated Man, The author: Ray Bradbury
illustration: 3 art 4 case, icon, logo 5 chart, image, light, model, photo, plate, table 6 design, figure, sample, sketch 7 analogy, cartoon, drawing, etching, example, pattern, picture, tableau 8 citation, halftone, instance, painting, sampling, snapshot, specimen, vignette
illustrative: 5 typic 6 sample 7 graphic, typical 8 symbolic 9 graphical
illustrator: 4 Erté, Kent 5 Abbey 6 Potter 8 Rockwell
illustrious: 4 star 5 famed, grand, great, lofty, noble, noted, proud 6 famous, mighty, signal 7 eminent, exalted, notable, sublime 8 esteemed, glorious, immortal, laureate, renowned, splendid 9 legendary, memorable, well-known 10 preeminent
illustriousness: 5 glory 6 renown 8 eminence, nobility, prestige
I'll Wait (1984 song) artist: Van Halen
ill wind nobody blows good, An: 4 oboe

ill-wisher: 3 foe 5 enemy, rival 6 foeman 7 defamer, invader, nemesis, opposer, traitor, villain 8 attacker, betrayer, opponent, saboteur 9 adversary, assailant, combatant, detractor, other side, terrorist 10 antagonist, competitor
ilmenite: 3 ore 7 mineral
Il mio tesoro: 4 aria
Il nome della rosa author: Umberto Eco
ILO
  headquarters: 6 Geneva
  part of ~: 3 Int., Org. 4 Intl. 5 Labor
Iloilo: 4 city, port, town
  locale: 5 Panay
  town near ~: 4 Oton
Ilona: 6 Massey 7 Stoller
Ilorin: 4 city, town
  locale: 7 Nigeria
___ I Lost, The: 4 Love
___ I Lost You: 4 When
I Love ___: 4 Lucy 5 Paris 6 Louisa
I Love a Mystery: 9 radio show
I Love a Parade composer: 5 Arlen 7 Koehler
I Love a Piano composer: 6 Berlin
I Love a Rainy Night (1980 song) artist: Eddie Rabbitt
___ I Love Her: 3 And
I Love How You Love Me (song) artist: Bobby Vinton, Paris Sisters
I love in Latin: 3 amo
I Love Lucy (CBS sitcom)
  cast: Desi Arnaz (Ricky Ricardo) Lucille Ball (Lucy Ricardo) William Frawley (Fred Mertz) Vivian Vance (Ethel Mertz)
  dog: 4 Fred 5 Butch
  producer: 5 Arnaz 6 Desilu
I Love Music (1975 song) artist: O'Jays
I Love Paris composer: 6 Porter
I Love Rock 'n Roll (1982 song) artist: Joan Jett and the Blackhearts
I Loves You, Porgy singer: 4 Bess
___ I Love, The: 3 Man, One
I Love the Nightlife (1978 song) artist: Alicia Bridges
I Love to ___: 5 Laugh, Rhyme, Singa
I Love Trouble (1948 film)
  cast: Janet Blair, Franchot Tone
I Love Trouble star: 5 Nolte 7 Roberts
___ I Love You?: 5 Why Do
___, I Love You: 4 Baby 5 Hello
I Love You Again (1940 film)
  cast: Myrna Loy, Frank McHugh, William Powell
  director: W.S. Van Dyke
I Love You, Alice B. Toklas (1968 film)
  cast: Peter Sellers, Leigh Taylor-Young, Jo Van Fleet
I Love You Because (1963 song) artist: Al Martino
I Love You More and More Every Day (1964 song) artist: Al Martino
Il pendolo di Foucault author: Umberto Eco
Il Penseroso author: John Milton
Ilsa: 6 Laszlo
  love: 4 Rick
Ilse: 9 Aichinger
Il Trovatore: 5 opera
  composer: 5 Verdi
  prop: 5 anvil
  role: 4 Inez, Ruiz 7 Leonora, Manrico
  setting: 6 Aragon, Biscay
Ilya in English: 6 Elijah
Ilyich: 4 Ivan
I'm ___: 4 a Man, Easy, Free 5 in You, Ready, Sorry, Yours 7 Alright, Walking
I'm ___ as Fast as I Can: 7 Dancing
I'm ___ Baby Tonight: 4 Your
I'm ___ boy!: 4 a bad
I'm ___ Cowhand: 5 an Old
I'm ___ Get You Sucka: 5 Gonna
I'm ___ in Love: 3 Not
I'm ___ in Love With You: 5 Stone
I'm ___ it!: 4 agin
I'm ___ Lisa: 3 Not
I'm ___ Mood for Love: 5 in the
I'm ___ Rappaport: 3 Not
I'm ___ Sentimental Over You: 7 Getting
I'm ___ sit right down...: 5 gonna
I'm ___ VIII, I Am: 5 Henry
I'm ___ Wild About Harry: 4 Just
I'm ___ Woman: 5 Every
I'm ___ You Now: 7 Telling
I'm ___ your tricks!: 4 onto
I.M.: 3 Pei
Ima: 4 Hogg
I'm a ___: 5 Loser
I'm a Believer (1966 song) artist: Monkees
iMac: 5 Apple 8 computer
  alternative: 2 PC
___, I'm Adam: 5 Madam
I Made It Through the Rain (1980 song) artist: Barry Manilow
image: 4 copy, icon, ikon, mold 5 eikon, model 6 double, effigy, mirror, notion, symbol, vision 7 concept, picture, realize, replica, thought 8 likeness, metaphor, portrait 9 adumbrate, depiction, facsimile, photocopy, semblance 10 appearance, conception, dead ringer, embodiment, envisaging, impression, perception, photograph, projection, reflection, simulacrum
  combining form: 3 eid-, typ- 4 eido-, icon-, ikon-, typo- 5 eicon-, icono-, idolo-, ikono- 6 eicono-, eidolo-
  computer-screen ~: 3 gif, jpg, tif 4 icon, jpeg 6 bitmap
  crude ~: 6 effigy
  darkroom: 3 neg. 8 negative
  form an ~: 5 think 6 ideate
  graven ~: 4 baal, idol
  Greek carved ~: 6 xoanon
  holy ~: 4 icon, ikon 5 eikon
  indistinct ~: 4 blur
  maker: 5 flack, PR man 6 camera, mirror 8 promoter
  mental ~: 4 idea 6 memory, vision 7 thought
  mirror ~: 4 refl. 10 reflection
  radar ~: 3 pip 4 blip
  reverse ~: 3 neg. 8 negative
  spitting ~: 4 copy, twin 5 clone, match 6 double 7 picture 8 likeness 9 duplicate, look-alike 10 dead ringer
  starter: 5 after
  the very ~ of: 4 like
___ image: 4 body 5 ghost, spit 'n 6 father, graven, latent, mirror 7 counter, inverse, virtual
___-image: 4 self 5 micro
image-orthicon ___: 4 tube
imager: 3 MRI 6 artist
imagery: 7 similes 9 allusions, imagining, metaphors, picturing
Images (1972 film)
  cast: Rene Auberjonois, Susannah York
  director: Robert Altman
___ Image, The: 7 Sharper
imaginable: 6 doable, likely, viable 7 earthly 8 credible, feasible, possible, workable 9 plausible, potential, practical, thinkable 10 achievable, attainable, believable, calculable, convincing, supposable
imaginably: 5 maybe 7 perhaps 8 probably
imaginary: 5 false 6 dreamy, irreal, made-up, unreal 7 assumed, fancied 8 abstract, delusive, fabulous, fanciful, illusive, illusory, invented, mythical, notional, quixotic, spectral, supposed 9 deceptive, dreamed-up, dreamlike, fantastic, fictional, legendary, pretended, trumped-up, visionary, whimsical 10 apocryphal, chimerical, fictitious, groundless, phantasmal, phantasmic, quixotical
  not ~: 4 real 5 solid 6 actual 7 genuine 8 concrete, existing, tangible 9 authentic, corporeal
imaginary ___: 4 axis, part, unit 6 number
Imaginary ___: 5 Lover 7 Friends
Imaginary Friends author: Alison Lurie
imagination: 4 myth 5 fancy 6 vision 7 fantasy, insight 8 artistry, daydream, ideality
  figment of the ~: 6 fantom 7 phantom 8 illusion
  product of the ~: 4 idea 5 dream 6 notion 7 thought
imaginative: 5 novel, slick, vivid 6 clever, dreamy, mental, poetic 7 cunning, fertile, fictive, offbeat, utopian 8 artistic, creative, fanciful, inspired, original, poetical, quixotic 10 artistical, quixotical
  be ~: 4 coin 6 create, design, devise, make up 7 compose, concoct, dream up, fashion, think up 8 conceive, contrive 9 fabricate, formulate
imagine: 3 see 4 deem, take 5 dream, fancy, guess, infer, think 6 assume, cook up, create, deduce, devise, gather, ideate, invent, make up, reckon, take it 7 believe, dream of, dream up, picture, presume, pretend, realize, suppose, surmise, suspect, think of, think up 8 conceive, conclude, daydream, envisage, envision, theorize 9 conjure up, fabricate, fantasize, think of as, visualize 10 brainstorm, conjecture, understand, woolgather
  old-style: 4 ween
Imagine ___!: 4 that
imagined: 6 unreal, unseen 9 vicarious 10 fictitious
Imagine singer: 3 Ono 6 Lennon
imagining: 7 imagery 8 daydream 10 conception, envisaging
I'm agin it!: 3 naw
imagist: 4 poet
imago: 3 bug 5 adult 6 insect
  future ~: 4 pupa 5 pupae
Imago: 4 font 8 typeface
I'm a Little ___: 6 Teapot
I'm Alive artist: 3 ELO
I'm all ears!: 6 Do tell
I'm Alright (1980 song) artist: Kenny Loggins
imam: 5 calif, kalif, title 6 caliph, cleric, kaliph, khalif
  deity: 5 Allah
  text: 5 Koran, Quran
I'm a Man (1965 song) artist: Yardbirds
I'm a man of means ___ means...: 4 by no
Imamu ___ Baraka: 5 Amiri
Iman: 5 model 10 supermodel
  spouse: David Bowie
imaret: 3 inn 5 serai 7 hospice
Imari ___: 4 ware
I Married an Angel: 7 musical
  songwriter: 4 Hart 7 Rodgers
I Married a Witch (1942 film)
  cast: Robert Benchley, Veronica Lake, Fredric March
  director: René Clair
I'm a Stranger Here Myself author: Alden Nowlan, Ogden Nash
___ I'm-a Want You: 4 Baby
I'm a Woman (1975 song) artist: Maria Muldaur
Imax: 7 theater, theatre
imbalance: 6 nerves 9 disparity 10 inequality
imbed: 5 lodge, plant 6 anchor 7 implant
imbibe: 3 sip 4 belt, chug, down, gulp, swig, take, tope 5 drink, quaff 6 absorb, guzzle, ingest, tipple 7 consume, put away, swallow 8 toss back 9 hoist a few
imbiber: 3 sot 7 tippler
  bill: 3 tab 6 bar tab
imbricate: 3 lap 7 overlap
___ Imbrium: 4 Mare
imbroglio: 3 row 4 fray, maze, riot, spat 5 brawl, fight, mix-up, run-in 6 crisis 7 dispute, ferment, quarrel 8 argument, brouhaha, disorder, quagmire, squabble 9 bickering, confusion, soap opera 10 complexity, difficulty, falling-out
I'm broke-it's ___: 3 oke
imbrue: 4 soak, soil 5 dirty, douse, dowse, drown, souse, stain, sully, taint 6 defile, drench, infuse, stains 7 immerse, implant, suffuse 8 permeate, saturate
Imbruglia: 7 Natalie
imbue: 4 fill 5 bathe, color, infix, steep, teach, tinge 6 charge, drench, infuse, instil, invest 7 breathe, engrain, implant, ingrain, inspire, instill, pervade, suffuse 8 permeate, saturate 9 inculcate
  with spirit: 6 ensoul, insoul
imbued: 4 full 5 awash 6 loaded 7 teeming 8 brimming 9 chock-full
I'm Coming Home (1974 song) artist: Spinners
I'm Coming Out (1980 song) artist: Diana Ross
I'm Dancing as Fast as I Can author: David Rabe
I'm Easy (1976 song) artist: Keith Carradine
Imelda: 6 Marcos 8 Filipina
  obsession: 5 shoes
I met ___ with...: 4 a man
I'm Every Woman (song) artist: Chaka Khan, Whitney Houston
IMF, part of: 3 Int. 4 Fund, Intl. 8 Monetary
I'm Free (song) artist: Kenny Loggins, Who
I'm game!: 4 fine, let's, okay, sure
I'm glad that's over: 4 phew, whew
I'm Goin' Down (1985 song) artist: Bruce Springsteen
I'm Gonna Be Strong (1964 song) artist: Gene Pitney
I'm Gonna Get You Sucka (1988 film)
  cast: Bernie Casey, Antonio Fargas, Keenen Ivory Wayans
  director: Keenen Ivory Wayans
I'm Gonna Love You Just... (1973 song) artist: Barry White
I'm Gonna Make You Love Me (1968 song)
  artist: Supremes, Temptations
I'm Gonna Make You Mine (1969 song) artist: Lou Christie
I'm Henry VIII, I Am (1965 song) artist: Herman's Hermits
___, I'm home!: 5 Honey
I'm in Love Again (1956 song) artist: Fats Domino
I'm innocent!: 5 Not me
imitate: 3 ape 4 copy, echo, mock, sham 5 ditto, feign, mimic, spoof 6 assume, be like, borrow, do like, follow, go like, mirror, parody, parrot,

pass as, repeat, send up **7** act like, burlesk, emulate, pattern, portray, pretend, reflect **8** make like, parallel, simulate **9** burlesque, duplicate, personate, replicate **10** borrow from, caricature
imitation: **4** copy, dupe, echo, fake, faux, mock, sham **5** apery, aping, bogus, clone, ditto, phony, put-on **6** acting, double, ersatz, forged, parody, phoney, pseudo, ringer, unreal **7** assumed, feigned, forgery, mimicry, mockery, replica, takeoff **8** knockoff, likeness, spurious, travesty **9** duplicate, imposture, parroting, photocopy, semblance, simulated, synthetic, unnatural **10** artificial, carbon copy, caricature, fabricated, fictitious, fraudulent, impression, patterning, reflection, simulacrum, simulation
in ~ of: **3** à la **4** like
not an ~: **4** orig. **8** original
suffix: **3** -een, -ine **4** -ette
Imitation author: Edgar Allan Poe
Imitation of Life: **4** film **5** novel
author: Fannie Hurst
cast: Sandra Dee, John Gavin, Lana Turner
director: Douglas Sirk
Imitations of Horace author: Alexander Pope
imitative: **4** hack **5** apish **6** copied, echoic, ersatz, pseudo **7** copycat, mimetic **8** simulant **9** deceptive, emulative, following, mimicking, simulated **10** derivative, reflective, secondhand, threadbare, unoriginal
behavior: **5** apery
imitator: **3** ape **4** aper, echo **5** mimic, phony **6** copier, epigon, forger, monkey, parrot, phoney, shadow **7** copycat, epigone **8** emulator, follower, imposter, impostor **10** plagiarist
I'm Just a Singer (1973 song) artist: Moody Blues
I'm Just Wild About Harry composer: **5** Blake **6** Sissle
I'm Leaving It Up to You (1974 song) artist: Donny and Marie Osmond
I'm listening: **4** go on **8** continue
I'm Livin' in Shame (1969 song) artist: Supremes
I'm Losing You (1999 film)
cast: Rosanna Arquette, Salome Jens, Frank Langella, Andrew McCarthy
I'm Losing You (song) artist: Rod Stewart, Temptations
immaculate: **4** neat, pure **5** clean, snowy, white **6** chaste, decent, virgin, washed **7** aseptic, groomed, perfect, sinless **8** flawless, germ-free, hygienic, innocent, pristine, sanitary, spotless, unbroken, unmarred, unsoiled, virginal, virtuous **9** blameless, errorless, exquisite, faultless, guiltless, incorrupt, stainless, taintless, undamaged, undefiled, unspoiled, unsullied, untouched **10** antiseptic, impeccable, unpolluted
immalleable: **4** hard **5** stiff, stony
immanent: **7** central **8** intimate **9** innermost
Immanuel: **4** Kant, Lord
immaterial: **4** airy **6** dreamy, mental **7** foreign, ghostly, trivial **8** bodiless, ethereal, spectral **9** asomatous, celestial, disbodied, dreamlike, inapropos, no big deal, spiritual, unearthly **10** discarnate, extraneous, impalpable, inapposite, insensible, intangible, irrelevant, unembodied, unphysical, wraithlike
immature: **3** kid, raw **4** baby, rash, weak **5** crude, early, green, silly, small, young **6** boyish, callow, giggly, jejune, larval, little, tender, unripe, unwise **7** babyish, kiddish, puerile **8** childish, juvenile, underage, untested, youthful **9** beardless, childlike, dependent, embryonic, formative, half-grown, infantile, unsettled **10** adolescent, sophomoric, unfinished, unseasoned
immaturity: **5** youth **6** nonage **7** rawness **9** childhood, greenness, puerility **10** unripeness
immeasurable: **4** huge, much, vast **5** great, large **6** cosmic, myriad **7** abysmal, endless, immense **8** infinite, unending **9** boundless, countless, limitless, unlimited **10** gargantuan
time: **3** eon **4** aeon
void: **5** abysm, abyss
immeasurably: **5** by far **7** greatly
immediacy: **7** urgency **8** nearness, priority, vicinity **9** closeness, proximity **10** importance, precedence
immediate: **4** near **5** close, first, quick **6** direct, nearby, prompt, recent, snappy, speedy, sudden, urgent **7** current, instant, present, primary **8** adjacent, pressing, proximal **9** firsthand, intuitive, paramount, proximate **10** contiguous, convenient, imperative, near-at-hand, time-saving
area: **8** premises, presence, vicinity
needing ~ attention: **4** dire **5** acute **6** urgent **7** crucial, exigent, serious **8** critical, pressing **9** desperate, important **10** compelling, imperative
to a poet: **5** anear
vicinity: **5** midst **8** nearness **9** closeness, proximity
immediate __: **6** family **7** annuity
Immediate Family (1989 film)
cast: Glenn Close, Kevin Dillon, Mary Stuart Masterson, James Woods
immediately: **3** now, PDQ **4** anon, ASAP, stat **5** right, today **6** at once, pronto **7** rapidly, readily **8** directly, hereupon, in a flash, in a jiffy, in a trice, on the dot, promptly, right now, right off **9** at present, forthwith, on the spot, presently, right away, summarily **10** at this time, here and now, this minute
immemorial: **3** old **5** olden **6** age-old **7** ageless, ancient
__ immemorial: **4** time
immense: **3** big **4** huge, vast **5** broad, bulky, giant, great, jumbo, large, massy, super **6** cosmic, mighty **7** hulking, mammoth, massive, sizable, titanic **8** colossal, cosmical, enormous, gigantic, king-size, oversize, sizeable, spacious, terrific, towering, whapping, whopping **9** boundless, extensive, Herculean, humongous, limitless, monstrous, overlarge, unbounded, unlimited, whalelike **10** gargantuan, monumental, prodigious, stupendous, tremendous
immensely: **4** a lot, much, over **5** no end **6** highly, vastly **7** awfully, greatly **9** extremely, in a big way **10** incredibly
enjoy ~: **5** eat up, lap up, savor
immensity: **4** bulk, mass, size **5** space, width **6** extent **7** bigness, breadth, expanse, measure **8** enormity, hugeness, infinity, vastness **9** amplitude, bulkiness, greatness, largeness, magnitude **10** infinitude
immerse: **3** dip **4** bury, busy, dunk, sink, soak, wash **5** bathe, douse, dowse, drown, rinse, souse, steep **6** absorb, drench, embrue, engage, engulf, imbrue, ingulf, obsess, occupy, plunge, wallow **7** baptize, engross, involve **8** interest, inundate, saturate, submerge **9** preoccupy
immersed: **4** busy, deep, rapt **6** buried, intent, sunken, tied up **7** bound up **8** consumed, held fast **9** submerged, wrapped up **10** spellbound
immersion: **3** dip **7** bathing, dipping, dousing, ducking, dunking, sousing **8** infusion, plunging **9** attention **10** absorbtion, absorption, saturating, saturation, submerging
immersion __: **4** coil, foot, lens **6** heater
immesh: **6** tangle **8** tangle up
immigrant: **5** alien **7** pioneer **8** colonist, newcomer, stranger **9** foreigner
course: **3** ESL
exam: **5** TOEFL
island: **5** Ellis
Immigrants, The author: Howard Fast
immigration concern: **5** quota
imminent: **4** near, nigh **5** close **6** at hand, coming, future, in view, nearby **7** brewing, in store, looming, nearing, pending **8** adjacent, in the air, oncoming, on the way, upcoming **9** bordering, gathering, impending, in the wind, proximate **10** coming soon, convenient, in the cards, in the works
be ~: **4** loom **6** impend **8** overhang, threaten
to a poet: **5** anear
imminently: **4** anon, soon **6** any day
immix: **4** meld, pool **5** blend, merge **6** mingle **7** combine **9** commingle, integrate **10** interweave
immixture: **5** blend **6** hybrid **7** amalgam **9** composite, synthesis
immobile: **4** firm **5** fixed, inert, rigid, stiff, still **6** frozen, nailed, rooted, static **7** hard-set, riveted **8** anchored, stagnant **9** steadfast **10** gridlocked, inexorable, motionless, stationary, stock-still
immobilize: **3** pin **5** stick **6** hogtie **7** petrify **8** paralyse, paralyze **9** overpower
immobilized: **3** set **6** frozen, rooted **7** riveted **9** paralytic **10** motionless
immoderacy: **4** glut **6** excess **7** surfeit **8** plethora **9** profusion
immoderate: **4** wild **5** gross, loose, steep, ultra, undue **6** lavish, wanton, wonton **7** drastic, extreme, hyped up, profuse, radical, ruinous, violent **8** dizzying, prodigal, ultraist, wasteful **9** egregious, excessive, expensive, fanatical, irregular, luxurious, overblown, unbridled, unthrifty **10** exorbitant, inordinate, profligate, unbalanced, untempered
immoderately: **3** too **4** very **6** overly, unduly **7** largely **8** to a fault
immoderation: **6** excess, luxury **7** license
immodest: **4** bold, lewd, racy, rank **5** lofty, nasty **6** brazen, coarse, risqué **7** forward **8** impudent, indecent, shameful, unseemly **9** barefaced, conceited, shameless, unashamed **10** big-talking, indelicate, suggestive
immodesty: **5** pride **7** conceit **9** indecency **10** narcissism
Immokalee: **4** city, town
locale: **7** Florida
immoral: **3** bad **4** base, evil, lewd, vile **5** loose, nasty, wrong **6** sinful, smutty, unfair, unholy, wicked **7** corrupt, lustful, profane, vicious **8** depraved, improper, indecent, shameful, unchaste, wrongful **9** corrupted, debauched, dishonest, dissolute, low-minded, lubricous, miscreant, nefarious, shameless, unethical **10** dissipated, indelicate, iniquitous, lascivious, licentious, profligate, villainous, virtueless
act: **3** sin
sort: **3** cad **4** rake, roué **7** bounder **9** libertine **10** profligate
Immoralist, The author: **4** Gide
immorality: **3** sin **4** evil, vice **5** wrong **8** iniquity, venality **9** depravity **10** corruption, degeneracy
immortal: **6** famous, heroic **7** eminent, eternal, undying **8** almighty, heroical, laureate, timeless, unending **9** deathless, legendary, perennial, permanent, perpetual **10** celebrated, monumental
name meaning ~: **7** Ambrose
Immortal Beloved (1994 film)
cast: Gary Oldman, Isabella Rossellini
director: Bernard Rose
immortalize: **5** deify **7** lionize **8** preserve **10** perpetuate
immovable: **3** set **4** fast, firm, iron **5** dug in, fixed, rigid, stuck **6** frozen, rooted, secure, static, steady **7** adamant, diehard, hard-set **8** locked in, obdurate, resolute, stubborn **9** dead set on, hard-nosed, immutable, impassive, obstinate, quiescent, steadfast **10** hard-bitten, inexorable, inflexible, invariable, motionless, set in stone, stationary, unshakable, unwavering, unyielding
immovably: **4** fast **6** firmly **7** fixedly, tightly **8** securely
immune: **6** exempt **8** free from **9** protected, resistant **10** impervious, privileged, vaccinated
immune __: **5** serum **6** system **7** complex
immune-system element: **5** T-cell
immunity: **6** refuge, safety **7** freedom, liberty, license **8** security **9** privilege **10** protection
give ~ to: **6** excuse, exempt, let off
__ immunity: **3** use **6** active, native **7** natural, passive
immunization
agents: **4** sera
device: **6** jet gun
letters: **3** DPT
immunize: **9** inoculate, vaccinate
immunological starter: **4** sero
immunologist: **4** Salk **5** Sabin
immunology adjective: **5** viral
immure: **4** hold, jail **6** detain, entomb, intern, lock up, punish, shut in, shut up, wall in, wall up **7** close in, close up, confine, enclose, impound, inclose, seclude **8** imprison
immured: **4** pent **6** pent up
immurement: **10** internment
immutable: **4** firm **6** stable **8** constant **9** immovable, permanent, perpetual, steadfast **10** changeless, inflexible, invariable, sacrosanct, unchanging, undecaying
I'm No Angel (1933 film)
cast: Edward Arnold, Cary Grant, Mae West
director: Wesley Ruggles
I'm not __ complain: **5** one to
I'm not half the __ used to be: **4** man I
I'm not kidding: **5** no lie, truly **6** no joke, really **7** for real **9** seriously
I'm Not Lisa (1975 song) artist: Jessi Colter
Imogene: **4** Coca
cohort: **3** Sid
I'm OK—You're OK author: **6** Harris
I'm on Fire (1985 song) artist: Bruce Springsteen
I'm outta here: **3** bye **4** ciao, ta-ta **5** adieu, later **6** so long **7** goodbye

imp: **3** elf, fay **4** brat, pixy, puck, tike, tyke **5** child, cutup, demon, devil, fairy, fiend, gamin, pixie, scamp **6** bad boy, daemon, daimon, goblin, rascal, sprite, urchin **7** brownie, gremlin, hellion **8** devilkin **9** hobgoblin **10** holy terror, jackanapes
imp. __: **3** gal.
impact: **3** hit, jar **4** bang, blow, jolt **5** brunt, clash, crash, crush, force, knock, punch, shock, smash, thump, touch **6** affect, crunch, effect, jounce, strike, wallop **7** contact, smash-up **8** bang into **9** aftermath, collision, crash into, influence, rear-ender **10** concussion, impression, percussion
  on: **4** sway **5** alter **6** affect **9** influence
  sound: **3** bam, pow **4** wham **5** kapow, smack, splat **6** whammo
impact __: **4** zone **6** crater, wrench
Impact (1949 film)
  cast: Brian Donlevy, Ella Raines
  director: Arthur Lubin
__ Impact: **4** Deep **6** Sudden
impair: **3** mar, sag, sap **4** flag, harm, hurt, maim, tear, tire, wane **5** blunt, break, crack, spoil, wreck **6** damage, debase, deface, dilute, hinder, impair, injure, lessen, mangle, ravage, reduce, riddle, shrink, soften, weaken **7** corrupt, deplete, depress, devalue, disable, exhaust, fatigue, shatter, vitiate **8** enervate, enfeeble **9** attenuate, devaluate, hamstring, make worse, prejudice, undermine **10** adulterate, debilitate, devitalize
impaired: **4** hurt, sick, torn **5** rusty **6** broken, faulty, flawed **7** injured, lacking, unsound **8** fallible **9** defective, deficient, imperfect
impairment: **4** harm, loss, wear **5** abuse, decay **6** damage, injury **8** breakage, handicap, weakness **9** deformity, detriment **10** disability
impala: **6** animal, mammal **8** antelope
  relative: **3** gnu, kob **4** guib, kudu, oryx, puku, topi **5** addax, bongo, chiru, eland, goral, korin, nyala, oribi, saiga, serow **6** chammy, dikdik, duiker, koodoo, lechwe, nilgai, rhebok, shammy, shamoy **7** blaubok, blesbok, chamois, defassa, gazelle, gemsbok, gerenuk, grysbok, nylghai, nylghau, sassaby **8** blesbuck, bontebok, bushbuck, gemsbuck, reedbuck, steenbok, steinbok **9** blackbuck, pronghorn, sitatunga, springbok, waterbuck **10** hartebeest, wildebeest
Impala: **3** car **4** auto **5** Chevy **9** Chevrolet
Impalas song: Sorry (1959)
impale: **4** gore, stab **5** lance, spear, spike, stick **6** pierce, skewer, thrust **7** spindle, stick on, torture **8** puncture, transfix **9** penetrate **10** run through
Impaler, The: **4** Vlad
impalpable: **8** bodiless **9** imprecise, invisible **10** immaterial, indistinct, insensible, intangible, unapparent
impart: **4** give, lend, send, tell **5** allow, break, lends, teach **6** accord, afford, bestow, confer, convey, extend, inform, infuse, instil, pass on, recite, relate, render, report, reveal **7** breathe, confide, divulge, instill, mention, provide **8** advise of, announce, describe, disclose, hand down, transmit, vocalize **9** inculcate, make known **10** contribute
  knowledge: **4** show **5** brief, coach, drill, edify, guide, teach, train, tutor **6** advise, ground, inform, school **7** educate, explain, instill, lecture **8** instruct **9** catechize, enlighten, inculcate, interpret
impartial: **4** even, fair, just, open **5** equal, sober **6** candid, honest, square **7** neutral **8** balanced, detached, moderate, rational, unbiased, unskewed **9** equitable, objective, unbigoted, uncolored, unslanted **10** evenhanded, fair-minded, impersonal, on-the-fence, open-minded, reasonable
  not ~: **6** biased, myopic, skewed, unfair, unjust **7** bigoted **10** intolerant
impartiality: **6** equity **7** justice **8** fairness
impartially: **5** right
impartible: **8** catching **10** contagious
impassable: **6** closed **7** blocked **9** closed off **10** invincible, obstructed
impasse: **4** halt **6** corner, logjam, plight **7** dead end **8** cul-de-sac, deadlock, gridlock, quagmire, quandary, standoff **9** stalemate **10** blind alley, difficulty, standstill
  at an ~: **5** mired, stuck
__ impasse: **4** at an
impassion: **4** fire, goad, spur, stir, wake **5** awake, rouse, spark **6** arouse, awaken, bestir, fire up, foment, heat up, incite, kindle, stir up, wake up, whip up, work up **7** actuate, agitate, animate, enliven, inflame, inspire, provoke **8** enkindle, inspirit, motivate, vitalize **9** galvanize, stimulate
impassioned: **3** hot, mad **4** keen **5** fiery, vivid **6** ablaze, ardent, fervid, fierce, hearty, heated, loving, moving, red-hot, torrid **7** amorous, blazing, burning, earnest, excited, fervent, fired up, flaming, furious, glowing, intense, rousing, violent, zealous **8** animated, romantic, stirring, vehement **10** hot-blooded
impassive: **4** calm, cold, cool **5** aloof, blank, inert, quiet, staid, stoic, stony **6** at ease, bovine, low-key, mellow, placid, sedate, serene, stolid, stoney, wooden **7** amiable, at peace, callous, equable, languid, pacific, relaxed, stoical, unmoved **8** amicable, carefree, composed, hardened, laid-back, listless, peaceful, taciturn, tranquil **9** apathetic, bloodless, collected, easygoing, heartless, immovable, lethargic, nerveless, quiescent, temperate, unexcited, unfeeling, unruffled, unstirred **10** impervious, insensible, nonchalant, phlegmatic, poker-faced, spiritless, unaffected, unagitated, unreactive, untroubled
impassivity: **8** lethargy, stoicism
impatience: **5** haste **6** temper **7** anxiety, fidgets **8** edginess, rashness **9** agitation, annoyance, eagerness, hastiness, shortness, surliness, vehemence **10** excitement, expectancy, snappiness, uneasiness
  sign of ~: **4** honk
impatiens: **5** plant **6** flower
impatient: **4** curt, edgy, rash **5** antsy, brusk, eager, hasty, itchy, quick, testy, type A, weary **6** abrupt, on edge, uneasy **7** anxious, brusque, chafing, fretful, restive **8** fretsome, headlong, petulant, restless **9** demanding, excitable, impetuous, indignant, irascible, irritable, straining **10** breathless, high-strung, intolerant, solicitous
  how the ~ stand: **6** akimbo
  not ~: **4** calm **5** type B **6** serene
  one: **6** chafer
  one's query: **4** when
  remark: **3** tsk, tut, yah **4** c'mon, phew, pish, pooh, posh, tush **5** pshaw, shame **6** enough, let's go, move it, tsk tsk, tut-tut **8** for shame
impavid: **4** bold **5** brave, gutsy, nervy, stout **6** daring, heroic, plucky **7** doughty, gallant, valiant **8** fearless, heroical, intrepid, unafraid, valorous **9** dauntless, undaunted **10** courageous
impeach: **3** tax **6** accuse, charge, indict **8** denounce, question **9** inculpate
impeachment: **5** blame, trial **7** lawsuit
impeccable: **3** A-OK **4** pure **5** clean, exact, sound **7** correct, perfect, precise, sinless **8** absolute, accurate, flawless, inerrant, innocent, reliable, unerring, unflawed, unsoiled **9** blameless, errorless, exquisite, faultless, guiltless, incorrupt, stainless, virtuosic **10** consummate, immaculate, infallible
impecunious: **4** poor **5** broke, needy **6** bad off, busted, hard up, ill-off, in need, in want **7** pinched **8** badly off, bankrupt, beggarly, dirt poor, homeless, indigent, strapped **9** destitute, insolvent, moneyless, penniless, penurious **10** down and out, pauperized, straitened
impecuniousness: **4** need, want **7** beggary, poverty
impedance: **3** jam **4** clog **8** blockage, obstacle **9** hindrance, occlusion **10** bottleneck, congestion
impede: **3** bar, dam, jam **4** clog, curb, plug, rein, slow, stop **5** block, brake, check, choke, cramp, cross, dam up, delay, deter, stimy, stunt, stymy, tie up **6** bother, cut off, dampen, detain, forbid, hamper, hang up, hinder, hobble, hogtie, hold up, rein in, retard, slow up, stop up, stymie, thwart **7** congest, disrupt, inhibit, occlude, prevent, set back, trammel **8** close off, encumber, entangle, handcuff, handicap, hold back, obstruct, preclude, prohibit, restrain, restrict, slow down, straiten **9** foreclose, frustrate, hamstring, interdict, interfere, interrupt, stonewall **10** complicate, discourage, filibuster
  legally: **5** estop
impeded: **4** poky, slow **6** draggy **7** gradual, halting, lagging, languid **8** crawling, creeping, dawdling, dilatory, dragging, drawn-out, hesitant, plodding, slothful, sluggish, toddling **9** leisurely, lethargic, snaillike **10** deliberate
impediment: **3** bar, rub **4** clog, curb, dike, drag, kink, snag, wall **5** block, check, cramp, delay, hitch, minus, thorn **6** burden, hang-up, hazard, holdup, hurdle, kicker **7** barrier, red tape, setback, shackle, trammel **8** blockade, blockage, drawback, handicap, obstacle, weakness **9** barricade, detention, deterrent, detriment, hindrance, liability, millstone, restraint, roadblock, stricture **10** bottleneck, dead weight, difficulty, inhibition
impedimenta: **4** gear **5** goods, stuff **6** things **7** baggage, luggage **8** equipage, materiel, supplies **9** equipment, trappings
impel: **4** cast, goad, make, move, poke, prod, push, spur, urge **5** boost, drive, egg on, press, shove, speed, throw **6** arouse, compel, foment, incite, induce, prompt, propel, stir up, thrust, turn on **7** actuate, inspire, press on, quicken **8** activate, mobilize, motivate, persuade, pressure, railroad **9** constrain, determine, influence, instigate, preordain, stimulate **10** accelerate, pressurize
impelled: **5** bound, fated **6** driven, forced **7** obliged **8** destined, required
impelling: **6** moving, urgent **8** forceful **10** persuasive
impend: **4** hang, loom, near **5** await, hover **6** menace **8** overhang, threaten
impending: **4** near, nigh **5** close **6** at hand, coming, future, nearby **7** brewing, in store, looming, nearing, ominous, pending **8** adjacent, imminent, lowering, menacing, oncoming, upcoming **9** dangerous, gathering, in the wind, proximate **10** convenient, inevitable, in the cards, in the works, portending
impenetrable: **4** firm, hard **5** dense, mirky, murky, solid, thick, tight **6** arcane, mystic, opaque, unseen **7** compact, obscure **8** abstruse, airtight, baffling, hardened, hermetic **10** fathomless, mysterious
impenitent: **8** indurate
imperative: **4** must **5** acute, state, vital **6** urgent **7** binding, burning, crucial, exigent, mandate **8** critical, exigeant, pressing, required **9** clamorous, essential, immediate, important, mandatory, necessary, necessity, requisite, strategic **10** autocratic, compulsory, obligatory, peremptory
Imperato: **5** Carlo
Imperatriz: **4** city, town
  locale: **6** Brazil
imperceptible: **4** slow, tiny, weak **5** faint, small, teeny **6** hidden, little, minute, slight, subtle, teensy, unseen **7** gradual, trivial
imperceptibly: **6** hardly **8** scarcely, slightly
imperceptive: **3** dim **5** crass, dense, thick **6** obtuse **8** mindless
imperfect: **3** bad, irr. **4** poor, sick **5** amiss, rough, tense **6** broken, faulty, flawed, marred, patchy **7** damaged, halting, ill-done, inexact, sketchy, unsound, wanting **8** below par, fallible, impaired, slipshod **9** defective, deficient, irregular **10** disfigured, inadequate, incomplete, unfinished
imperfect __: **5** rhyme, stage **6** fungus
imperfection: **3** bug, mar **4** blot, dent, flaw, kink, spot, tear, vice, wart **5** fault, stain, taint **6** defect, foible, glitch **7** blemish, failing, frailty, problem **8** drawback, weakness
Imperfect Sympathies writer: **4** Elia
imperial: **5** beard, grand, noble, regal, royal **6** kingly, lordly **7** emperor, empress, queenly, stately **8** despotic, imposing, kinglike, majestic, princely, splendid **9** dignified, monarchal, queenlike, sovereign **10** autocratic, despotical, majestical, tyrannical
  volute: **5** shell **8** seashell
imperial __: **4** jade, moth **5** eagle **6** bushel, gallon
Imperial: **3** car **4** auto, oleo **8** Chrysler **9** margarine **10** automobile
  alternative: **6** Parkay, Shedd's **7** Promise
Imperial Beach: **4** city, town
  locale: **10** California
Imperial Woman author: Pearl S. Buck
imperil: **4** risk **5** stake **6** hazard, menace **8** endanger, threaten **10** compromise, jeopardize
imperiled: **6** at risk **7** at stake **9** on the line **10** in jeopardy
imperilment: **4** risk **6** hazard **8** jeopardy
imperious: **3** big **5** bossy, proud, stern **6** kingly, lordly **7** haughty, pompous **8** arrogant, assuming, despotic, dogmatic, dominant, exacting, kinglike

9 arbitrary, demanding, dignified, hubristic, insistent, tyrannous 10 aggressive, autocratic, commanding, despotical, dogmatical, high-handed, iron-willed, oppressive, peremptory, tyrannical
imperiousness: 7 tyranny 9 autocracy, despotism 10 absolutism, oppression
imperishable: 7 abiding, eternal, lasting, undying 8 immortal, unfading 9 deathless, perennial, permanent, perpetual 10 changeless, undecaying
imperium: 5 power
impermanence: 9 mortality
impermanent: 5 brief, short 6 fickle, mortal 7 passing 8 fleeting, flitting, temporal, unstable 9 ephemeral, momentary, temporary, transient 10 evanescent, perishable, short-lived, transitory, unenduring
impermeable: 4 firm, hard, numb, safe 5 solid, thick, tight 6 immune 8 airtight, hermetic 9 impassive, nonporous, resistant, unstirred 10 unaffected, waterproof, watertight
impersonal: 4 cold, cool 6 remote 7 neutral 8 abstract, detached 9 colorless, equitable, impartial, objective, uncolored, unslanted 10 poker-faced, unagitated, unfriendly
pronoun: 3 one
impersonate: 2 do 3 ape 4 play, pose 5 enact, mimic 6 assume, mirror, parody, pose as 7 act like, dress as, imitate, portray, pretend 8 double as, make like
impersonation: 4 copy, role 5 apery 6 acting
impersonator: 4 aper 5 mimic 8 imitator 9 look-alike
silent ~: 4 mime 5 mimer
impertinence: 3 lip 4 gall, guff, sass 5 cheek, crust, mouth, nerve, sauce 6 hutzpa, insult 7 chutzpa, hutzpah 8 audacity, back talk, boldness, chutzpah, pertness, rudeness, temerity
impertinent: 4 bold, flip, pert, rude, wise 5 brash, fresh, lippy, nervy, sassy, saucy, smart 6 brassy, brazen, cheeky 7 foreign, forward, off-base, uncivil, uncouth 8 arrogant, flippant, impolite, impudent, insolent 9 obtrusive, offensive, officious
one: 4 snip
imperturbability: 6 aplomb 8 patience, presence, stoicism
imperturbable: 4 calm, cool, even 5 sober, stoic 6 assure, placid, sedate, serene, steady 7 assured, equable, patient, stoical 8 composed, tranquil 9 nerveless, unruffled
impervious: 4 firm, hard, numb, safe 5 solid, thick, tight 6 immune 8 airtight, hermetic 9 impassive, nonporous, resistant, unstirred 10 unaffected, waterproof, watertight
to feeling: 4 numb 5 aloof, stoic 6 stolid 7 unmoved 9 apathetic, impassive
impetrate: 3 ask, beg 5 cadge, hit up, mooch, plead 6 appeal, demand 7 beseech, entreat, implore, solicit 9 importune, mendicate, panhandle
impetration: 4 plea 6 appeal, demand 8 entreaty
impetuosity: 4 élan 5 haste 6 fervor 7 abandon 8 rashness 9 brashness, eagerness, hastiness, incaution 10 abruptness
impetuous: 3 hot 4 rash, wild 5 blind, brash, eager, hasty, quick 6 abrupt, fervid, sudden, unwary 7 dashing, hurried, rampant, rushing 8 headlong, heedless 9 desperate, emotional, excitable, explosive, foolhardy, impatient, impulsive, unbridled, unplanned, whirlwind 10 boisterous, hot-blooded, incautious, passionate, unexpected, unthinking
impetuously: 8 pell-mell 9 headfirst
impetus: 4 birr, fuel, goad, road, spur, urge 5 drive, force 6 reason, spring, thrust 7 advance 8 catalyst, momentum, progress, stimulus 9 incentive 10 horsepower, incitement, motivation
impiety: 3 sin 4 evil 9 blasphemy, profanity, sacrilege 10 disrespect, wickedness
impinge: 6 affect
upon: 5 touch 6 adjoin
impingement: 4 raid 5 foray 6 inroad 7 advance 8 invasion, trespass 9 incursion
impious: 6 unholy 7 godless, profane, ungodly, wayward 8 agnostic, apostate, diabolic 9 atheistic 10 diabolical, irreverent
impish: 3 fey, sly 5 elfin 6 bratty, elfish, elvish, jaunty, wicked 7 naughty, pixyish, playful, puckish, waggish 8 devilish, flippant, pixieish, prankish, rascally, sporting, sportive 10 frolicsome
act: 5 prank
one: 3 elf 4 pixy 5 pixie 6 sprite
impishness: 4 sass 5 cheek 8 mischief 9 flippancy, impudence, rascality, sauciness 10 cheekiness, tomfoolery
implacability: 4 hate 5 odium, spite 6 animus, enmity, hatred, malice, rancor 7 ill will 8 acrimony, bad blood 9 animosity, antipathy, hostility 10 bitterness, resentment
implacable: 4 grim, iron 5 cruel, rigid, stern 6 deadly, severe 7 hard-set, piggish 8 pitiless, ruthless, vengeful 9 ferocious, merciless, pigheaded, rancorous, unbending, unpitying 10 inexorable, inflexible, ironfisted, relentless, unyielding, vindictive
implant: 3 fix, set, sow 4 bury, root 5 embed, graft, imbed, imbue, infix, lodge, plant, set in, teach, train 6 embrue, enroot, imbrue, infuse, inject, insert, instil 7 engrain, impress, imprint, ingrain, inspire, instill 9 inculcate, influence, interject, interpose, pound into
tissue: 5 graft
implausible: 4 lame, tall, thin, weak 5 fishy 6 far-out, flimsy 7 dubious, suspect 8 doubtful, unlikely
implement: 2 ax 3 axe, hoe, mop, oar, saw, use 4 file, fork, plow, rake, tool 5 agent, apply, churn, corer, dicer, drill, flail, knife, means, parer, ricer, spoon, thing, whisk 6 agency, beater, device, effect, engine, fulfil, gadget, harrow, invoke, slicer 7 execute, fulfill, hayfork, machine, perform, realize, utensil, vehicle 8 carry out, dispense 9 actualize, apparatus, appliance, equipment 10 bring about, effectuate, instrument
ancient stone ~: 6 amgarn
combining form: 4 -labe
farm ~: 3 hoe 4 fork, plow, rake 5 churn, flail 6 harrow
kitchen ~: 5 corer, dicer, parer, ricer, whisk 6 beater, slicer
wherry ~: 6 paddle
see also tool
implementation: 8 exercise
implements: 3 kit 6 tackle 8 hardware 9 machinery
impliable: 4 firm 5 harsh, rigid, stern, stiff, stony 6 dogged, flinty, mulish, steely 7 adamant, piggish, starchy 8 hardened, obdurate, pitiless, resolute, stubborn 9 hidebound, obstinate, pigheaded, unbending 10 hardheaded, inflexible, unbendable, unyielding
implicate: 4 mire 5 blame, frame, rat on 6 accuse, charge, draw in, finger, tangle 7 connect, involve 8 entangle 9 associate, inculpate, insinuate 10 compromise, stigmatize
implication: 4 hint 5 drift, sense 7 meaning, purport 8 allusion, innuendo, overtone 9 reference, undertone
implicit: 4 firm, full 5 fixed, tacit, total 6 latent, silent, subtle, unsaid 7 certain, virtual 8 absolute, complete, connoted, definite, hinted at, indirect, inferred, inherent, unspoken, unvoiced 9 alluded to, intimated, potential, steadfast, suggested, unuttered 10 insinuated, undeclared, understood, unshakable
implicitly: 8 in effect 9 basically, in essence, so to speak, virtually
implied: 5 tacit 6 latent, silent, subtle, unsaid 7 certain, virtual 8 connoted, hinted at, indirect, inferred, inherent, unspoken, unvoiced 9 alluded to, intimated, potential, suggested, unuttered 10 insinuated, undeclared, understood
implied __: 7 consent
implode: 5 break, burst, smash, wreck 7 shatter
imploration: 4 plea 6 appeal 8 entreaty
implore: 3 ask, beg, sue 4 pray, urge 5 plead, press 6 adjure, appeal, demand, invoke 7 beseech, entreat, solicit 8 petition 9 impetrate, importune 10 supplicate
implosion: 5 burst 6 inrush
imply: 3 say 4 hint, mean, seem 5 get at, let on, point, spell 6 advert, allude, denote, entail, hint at 7 betoken, connote, involve, make out, purport, signify, suggest 8 indicate, intimate, lead up to, stand for 9 insinuate, predicate 10 presuppose
Imp of the Perverse, The author: Edgar Allan Poe
impolite: 4 flip, pert, rude 5 blunt, brash, brusk, crude, frank, fresh, gruff, nervy, rough, sassy, saucy, short 6 abrupt, awless, brazen, candid, cheeky, coarse, oafish, snippy 7 aweless, boorish, brusque, ill-bred, loutish, lowbred, selfish, uncivil, uncouth 8 churlish, flippant, heedless, impudent, insolent, inurbane, snippety, tactless, unsubtle 9 out of line, outspoken, ungallant, unrefined 10 indecorous, indelicate, mannerless, ungracious, unmannerly, unthinking
look: 4 leer, ogle 5 sneer, stare
one: 4 boor, lout 5 ogler 6 starer
sound: 3 boo, hic 4 burp, jeer 5 belch 7 catcall 10 Bronx cheer
impolitic: 5 brash, unapt 6 gauche, unwise 8 tactless, unsubtle 9 ill-judged, imprudent, maladroit, misguided, unguarded 10 ill-advised, indiscreet
imponderable: 7 elusive, elusory 8 baffling, puzzling 10 mysterious
imponderous: 5 light, wispy 6 slight
import: 4 fist, heft 5 drift, point, sense, spell, value, worth 6 effect, moment, stress, thrust, weight 7 bearing, gravity, meaning, message, purport, purpose, signify 8 emphasis, Infiniti 9 intention, magnitude, substance
car: 3 BMW, Kia 4 Audi, Saab 5 Honda, Rolls, Volvo 6 Jaguar, Subaru, Suzuki 10 Mitsubishi, Rolls-Royce
importance: 4 fame, heft, note, pith, rank 5 force, glory, value, worth 6 effect, esteem, moment, status, stress, weight 7 concern, gravity, stature 8 eminence, emphasis, interest, position, prestige, priority, salience 9 attention, greatness, immediacy, influence, magnitude, relevance, substance 10 denotation, notability, precedence, prominence, reputation, usefulness
be of ~ old-style: 4 reck
have ~: 4 rate 5 count 6 matter
of no ~: 4 moot 5 minor, petty, small 6 little 7 trivial
person of ~: 3 VIP 4 lion 5 biggy, nabob 6 biggie, bigwig 7 magnate 8 luminary 9 plutocrat
person of no ~: 4 geek, nerd 5 dweeb 6 nobody 7 nebbish 9 nonentity
__ importance: 4 of no
Importance of Being Earnest, The author: Oscar Wilde
important: 3 big, key 4 dear, high 5 acute, great, major, vital 6 needed, of note, staple, urgent 7 burning, crucial, earnest, eminent, exigent, fateful, hurry-up, notable, pivotal, primary, salient, serious, special, weighty 8 cardinal, critical, decisive, exigeant, historic, material, pregnant, pressing, relevant, required, valuable 9 big-league, essential, extensive, front-page, high-level, mandatory, memorable, momentous, necessary, operative, paramount, ponderous, principal, prominent, right-hand, something, strategic, top-drawer, well-known 10 celebrated, first-class, historical, imperative, impressive, meaningful, monumental, noteworthy, portentous, preeminent, remarkable, upper-class, worthwhile
be ~: 4 rate 5 weigh 6 matter
deem ~: 5 value 10 set store by
event: 8 landmark 9 milestone
less ~: 5 lower, minor 9 auxiliary, secondary 10 derivative, incidental, peripheral
most ~: 4 head 5 chief, grand 8 above all 9 principal, uppermost
most ~ part: 3 nub 4 body, core, crux, gist, knub, meat, pith 5 basis, heart, point 6 kernel, thrust 7 essence, keynote 10 bottom line
most ~ (prefix): 4 arch-
not ~: 4 mere, moot 5 minor, petty, small 6 little 7 trivial
one: 3 VIP 4 lion 5 biggy, nabob 6 biggie, bigwig 7 magnate 8 luminary 9 plutocrat
point: 6 factor 7 concern
time: 3 age, era 5 epoch
work: 4 opus 6 oeuvre 10 magnum opus
__-important: 3 all 4 self
imported: 6 exotic 7 foreign
imports: 5 cargo, goods 7 freight
importunate: 9 obtrusive
importune: 3 beg, dun, nag, sue, woo 4 coax, pray, urge 5 beset, court, hound, plead, press, tease, worry 6 appeal, badger, demand, harass, insist, pester, plague, work on 7 beseech, besiege, entreat, implore, solicit 9 impetrate 10 supplicate
impose: 3 lay, put, set, tax 4 levy, loom 5 exact, foist, force, order 6 assess, charge, compel, decree, demand, enjoin, meddle 7 be pushy, command, dictate, foist on, inflict, intrude, lay down, obtrude, presume 8 horn in on

9 establish, force upon, incommode, institute, prescribe, stipulate 10 administer, ask too much, promulgate, thrust upon
on: 5 wrong 6 lumber, put out 7 trouble
__-imposed: 4 self
imposed on, easily: 4 meek 5 timid
imposing: 3 big 5 grand, large, lofty, noble, proud, regal, royal, showy 6 august, lordly, mighty, solemn 7 awesome, exalted, hulking, massive, stately, sublime 8 gorgeous, imperial, kinglike, majestic, palatial, stirring, striking, towering 9 dignified, grandiose, luxurious, sumptuous 10 commanding, formidable, impressive, majestical, monumental, statuesque
residence: 5 manor, villa 6 castle, estate 7 mansion
imposition: 3 con, tax 4 drag, hoax, levy, onus, pain 5 fraud, trick 6 burden, demand 8 artifice 9 deception, hypocrisy, intrusion, restraint 10 constraint, craftiness, hocus-pocus
impossible: 3 out 5 never, no how, no way, no-win 6 absurd, can't be 7 useless, utopian 8 hopeless 9 ludicrous, offensive, visionary 10 impassable, incredible, infeasible, outrageous, unfeasible, unworkable
dream: 5 quest
make ~: 4 veto 8 preclude, prohibit
__ Impossible: 3 It's
__: Impossible: 7 Mission
Impossible Marriage author: Beth Henley
impost: 3 tax 4 duty, levy, toll 6 custom, excise, tariff 7 tribute 8 taxation, usage fee
Imposters, The (1998 film)
cast: Alfred Molina, Oliver Platt, Lili Taylor, Stanley Tucci
impostor: 4 fake, sham 5 actor, cheat, faker, fraud, mimic, phony, quack 6 con man, phoney, poseur 7 bluffer 8 imitator, swindler 9 charlatan, hypocrite, pretender 10 mountebank
__ Impostor, The: 5 Great
imposture: 3 con 4 fake, hoax, ploy, ruse, sham, wile 5 cheat, feint, fraud, phony, put-on, spoof, trick 6 deceit, dupery, humbug, phoney 7 gimmick, snow job, swindle 8 artifice, flimflam, maneuver, pretense, trickery 9 deception, hypocrisy, imitation, stratagem 10 hocus-pocus, masquerade, pretension, subterfuge
impound: 3 pen 4 cage, hold, keep, take 5 seize 6 coop up, immure, intern, shut in, shut up 7 confine, enclose, fence in, inclose, interne 8 imprison, restrain, sentence 10 confiscate
impoverish: 4 bust, ruin, sink, undo 5 break, drain 6 beggar, reduce 7 deplete 8 bankrupt, straiten 9 pauperize
impoverished: 4 flat, poor 5 broke, needy, sorry 6 bad off, barren, bereft, hard up, ill-off, in need, in want, ruined 7 drained, pinched 8 badly off, bankrupt, beggarly, depleted, indigent, strapped 9 destitute, insolvent, miserable, moneyless, penniless, penurious 10 down and out, pauperized, straitened
impoverishment: 4 need 6 penury 7 poverty 8 exigency, exiguity, hardship 9 indigence, privation 10 insolvency
impractical: 4 wild 5 crazy 6 absurd, dreamy, insane, unreal 7 useless, utopian 8 abstract, chimeric, quixotic, romantic 9 visionary 10 chimerical, quixotical, ridiculous
impracticality: 5 folly
imprecate: 4 damn 5 curse 7 condemn
imprecation: 3 ban 4 jinx, oath 5 curse 6 darn it, hoodoo, prayer, whammy 7 evil eye 8 anathema
imprecise: 3 lax, off 4 hazy 5 fuzzy, loose, rough, vague 6 cloudy, faulty, untrue 7 general, inexact 8 careless, nebulous 9 ambiguous, incorrect 10 ill-defined, impalpable, inaccurate, indefinite, indistinct, inexplicit, uncritical, unspecific
impregnable: 4 firm 6 secure, strong
impregnate: 4 soak 5 souse, steep, tinge 8 permeate, saturate 9 percolate, transfuse
Impresario author: 5 Hurok
impress: 3 awe, get 4 dent, etch, grab, mark, move, sway 5 amaze, brand, draft, infix, print, stamp, touch 6 affect, arouse, dazzle, emboss, instil, strike, thrill 7 engrain, engrave, enthuse, implant, ingrain, inspire, instill, recruit 8 blow away, inscribe, interest, knock out, persuade, register, shanghai 9 conscript, drive home, emphasize, go over big, inculcate, influence, prevail on 10 hammer into, predispose
impressed: 7 touched 8 affected 9 engrossed 10 fascinated, interested
more than ~: 4 awed 5 in awe 6 amazed 7 floored, shocked
not ~: 5 stoic 6 awless 7 aweless
impressible: 4 soft 7 plastic, pliable 8 moldable 9 malleable
impression: 3 air 4 cast, dent, feel, idea, mark, mold, show, view 5 brand, hunch, image, print, sense, spoor, stamp, track 6 aperçu, belief, effect, impact, memory, notion, parody, result, send-up 7 concept, feeling, inkling, opinion, outline, pattern, reading, takeoff, thought 8 reaction, stamping 9 engraving, footprint, imitation, influence, sensation, suspicion 10 appearance, atmosphere, conception, conjecture, conviction, depression, estimation, masquerade, perception
get the ~: 4 feel 5 sense, think 6 divine, intuit, pick up, reason 7 believe, discern 8 perceive 10 understand
give a false ~: 4 hoke 5 belie 6 delude
give the ~: 4 look, seem 5 imply, sound 6 appear 7 suggest 8 intimate, resemble 9 insinuate, sound like 10 appear to be
have the ~: 4 feel 5 think 7 believe
lasting ~: 4 scar
make an ~: 5 score, stamp 8 register
wrong ~: 5 error 7 mistake
__ impression: 5 first
impressionable: 7 plastic 9 malleable 10 responsive
impressionist: 3 ape 4 aper 5 mimic
Impressionist: 5 Degas, Manet, Monet 6 Renoir 7 Cassatt, Utrillo
starter: 3 neo
Impression: Sunrise artist: 5 Monet
impressive: 4 cool, deep 5 grand, great, noble, socko 6 august, epical, lavish, lordly, mighty, moving, potent, scenic, solemn, superb 7 awesome, massive, notable, rousing, salient, stately, telling 8 dramatic, eloquent, exciting, imposing, majestic, palatial, powerful, profound, scenical, splendid, stirring, striking, stunning, touching, towering, well done 9 absorbing, affecting, ambitious, arresting, effective, grandiose, important, inspiring, luxurious, momentous, monstrous, sumptuous, thrilling 10 believable, commanding, convincing, formidable, majestical, monumental, remarkable
group: 5 array
not ~: 4 puny 5 dinky 10 second-rate
Impressive!: 3 gee, wow 5 golly
impressiveness: 4 pomp 5 glory 7 majesty 8 elegance, grandeur, opulence, splendor 10 brilliance
imprest: 4 loan
Impreza: 3 car 4 auto 6 Subaru
imprimatur: 4 seal
imprint: 3 fix 4 etch, mark, name 5 infix, print, stamp, track 6 emblem, offset, symbol 7 engrain, engrave, implant, ingrain 8 inscribe 9 signature, trademark
imprison: 4 cage, hold, jail, shut 5 embar 6 arrest, closet, detain, immure, intern, lock in, lock up, punish, remand, shut in, shut up 7 confine, impound, interne, put away 8 restrain, sentence, stockade
imprisoned: 4 pent 6 jailed 7 captive
imprisonment: 6 arrest, chains 7 custody 9 restraint 10 internment
improbable: 4 iffy, lame, rare, slim, tall, thin, weak 6 flimsy, remote 7 dubious 8 doubtful, fanciful, unlikely 9 legendary, not likely, uncertain, unheard of 10 far-fetched, incredible
improbity: 5 fraud 7 scandal 9 falseness 10 dishonesty, misconduct, wrongdoing
impromptu: 5 ad hoc, ad-lib, faked 6 casual, sudden, vamped, winged 7 offhand, stopgap 9 dashed-off, extempore, thrown-off, tossed-off, whipped-up 10 improvised, jury-rigged, off the cuff, unprepared, unscripted
Impromptu (1991 film)
cast: Judy Davis, Hugh Grant, Mandy Patinkin
director: James Lapine
improper: 4 lewd, racy, tabu 5 false, gross, inapt, nasty, taboo, unapt, undue, unfit, wrong 6 banned, risqué, smutty, unfair, unmeet, vulgar 7 awkward, bad form, illicit, ill-time, immoral, naughty, off-base 8 criminal, indecent, outlawed, unlawful, unseemly, untimely, untoward, verboten, wrongful 9 erroneous, felonious, forbidden, graceless, ill-suited, incorrect, inelegant, irregular, low-minded, shameless, tasteless, unethical, unfitting 10 discordant, ill-advised, inaccurate, indecorous, indelicate, irrelevant, malapropos, out of order, prohibited, scandalous, suggestive, unbecoming, undeserved, unsuitable
thing: 4 no-no 5 taboo
improperly: 3 too 5 amiss 6 overly, unduly 8 unfairly, unjustly 10 unsuitably
influence ~: 5 bribe, get at, get to
impropriety: 4 nono 5 fault, gaffe 7 license 9 gaucherie
improve: 3 age 4 edit, gain, help, hone, lift, mend, redo, rise 5 amend, boost, build, emend, raise, rally 6 adjust, better, enrich, look up, perk up, pick up, profit, purify, refine, reform, revamp, revise, step up, update, work up 7 advance, augment, benefit, build up, correct, develop, elevate, enhance, furbish, perfect, promote, recruit, rectify, restore, shape up, sharpen, spice up, touch up, upgrade 8 beautify, heighten, increase, overhaul, polish up, progress, regulate 9 cultivate, go forward, meliorate, modernize 10 ameliorate
an edge: 4 hone, whet 5 strop
in health: 4 gain, heal, mend 5 rally 6 pick up 7 get well, rebound, recover 9 come along, get better 10 bounce back, convalesce, recuperate
upon: 3 top 4 beat, best 5 outdo 6 better, exceed 7 eclipse, outpace, surpass 8 go beyond, outclass, outshine, outstrip, surmount 9 transcend 10 outperform, overshadow, tower above
improved partner: 3 new
improvement: 4 gain, rise 5 rally 6 growth 7 advance, buildup, headway, upgrade, upswing 8 comeback, increase, progress, recovery, revision
show ~: 4 gain, mend 5 rally 6 look up, pick up 7 advance, shape up 8 progress 9 come along, get better 10 recuperate
__-improvement: 4 self
__ Improvement: 4 Home
improvidence: 5 waste 7 neglect 8 rashness, temerity
improvident: 6 lavish, unwise, wanton 8 careless, prodigal, wasteful 9 excessive 10 immoderate, profligate
improving: 6 better 8 cosmetic 9 on the mend
improvisation: 5 ad-lib 6 acting
improvise: 3 rig 4 fake, vamp 5 ad-lib 6 devise, fake it, invent, make up, wing it 7 concoct, dash off, dream up, think up 8 contrive, knockoff 10 brainstorm
improvised: 5 ad hoc, ad-lib 6 vamped 7 offhand, stopgap 9 extempore, hit-or-miss, impromptu, makeshift, patchwork, unstudied, whipped up 10 fictitious, fly-by-night, jury-rigged, unprepared, unscripted
arrangement: 6 lashup
bit: 4 riff 5 ad-lib
improv offering: 3 gag 4 joke, quip, skit 5 ad-lib, comic 6 comedy 8 comedian, one-liner
imprudence: 4 slip 5 folly 8 rashness
imprudent: 3 lax, mad 4 rash, wild 5 brash, crazy, hasty, loose, silly, slack, unapt, wrong 6 madcap, remiss, sloppy, unwary, unwise 7 foolish 8 careless, heedless, reckless, slipshod, tactless 9 foolhardy, ill-judged, impolitic, misguided, negligent, overhasty, unadvised, uncareful, unguarded, unmindful 10 headstrong, ill-advised, incautious, indiscreet, nonchalant, unthinking
one: 3 oaf, sap 4 boob, clod, dolt, dope, dupe, fool, jerk, loon, twit 5 clown, cluck, dummy, dunce, joker, ninny, patsy 6 dimwit, lummox, nitwit, stooge, sucker, turkey 7 buffoon, bungler, dullard, fathead, halfwit, jackass 8 bonehead, dumbbell, numskull 9 birdbrain, blockhead, ignoramus, lamebrain, schlemiel, simpleton 10 dunderhead, nincompoop
impudence: 3 lip 4 face, gall, guff, sass 5 brass, cheek, crust, mouth, nerve, sauce 6 insult 8 audacity, back talk, boldness, chutzpah, defiance, pertness, rudeness, temerity 9 assurance, flippancy, insolence 10 confidence, disrespect, effrontery, impishness
impudent: 4 bold, flip, pert, rude, wise 5 brash, cocky, crude, fresh, lippy, nervy, rough, sassy, saucy, smart

6 arrant, awless, brashy, brassy, bratty, brazen, cheeky, coarse, daring, mouthy, snippy, vulgar 7 aweless, blatant, forward, ill-bred, uncivil 8 cocksure, flippant, immodest, impolite, insolent, overbold, snippety 9 audacious, barefaced, boldfaced, bumptious, officious, out-of-line, shameless, unabashed 10 irreverent, smartmouth, ungracious, unmannerly
be ~: 4 sass 8 talk back
one: 4 brat, snip 5 whelp 9 minx. hussy
impugn: 3 tar, tax, zap 4 deny, gibe, jeer, jibe, mock, slam, slur, snub, zing 5 abuse, blast, cross, decry, knock, libel, query, scorn, smear, spurn, taunt, trash 6 assail, attack, charge, defame, deride, dump on, heckle, malign, negate, offend, oppose, rebuff, refute, slight, vilify 7 affront, asperse, censure, degrade, disavow, disdain, dispute, gainsay, put down, rank out, rip into, run down, slander, traduce 8 backbite, belittle, denounce, question, ridicule, vilipend 9 blaspheme, challenge, criticize, denigrate, disaffirm, discredit, disparage, humiliate, stick it to 10 calumniate, come down on, contradict, contravene, disrespect
impugnment: 5 abuse, libel 6 attack, hosing 7 affront, assault, calumny, obloquy, slander 8 derision, diatribe, outburst, reproach, scolding 9 aspersion, criticism, invective 10 assailment, backbiting, defamation, upbraiding
impuissant: 4 weak 6 unable 8 helpless 9 incapable, powerless
impulse: 3 yen 4 bent, goad, itch, spur, urge, whim 5 drive, fancy, flash, force, nisus 6 desire, motive, vagary 7 abandon, caprice, feeling, passion, resolve 8 instinct, momentum, stimulus, tendency 9 actuation 10 incitement, motivation
transmitter: 4 axon 5 axone
__ impulse: 4 on an 5 act on, nerve, total
Impulse: 3 car 4 auto 5 Isuzu
Impulse (1990 film)
cast: George Dzundza, Jeff Fahey, Theresa Russell
director: Sondra Locke
impulsion: 5 drive 6 thrust 10 constraint, motivation
impulsive: 4 rash 5 brash, giddy, hasty, moody 6 abrupt, madcap, sudden 7 offhand, rampant 8 careless, headlong, knee-jerk 9 automatic, daredevil, emotional, excitable, impetuous, intuitive, mercurial, momentary, unguarded, vagarious, whirlwind 10 capricious, changeable, headstrong, hot-and-cold, hot-blooded, incautious, passionate, unexpected, unprompted, unthinking
Impulsive (1990 song) artist: Wilson Phillips
impulsively: 6 rashly 7 hastily 9 headfirst, hurriedly 10 heedlessly, recklessly
impulsiveness: 5 brass, haste
impunity: 9 exemption, indemnity
impure: 4 foul, lewd, vile 5 dirty 6 coarse, filthy, flawed, rancid, sordid 7 admixed, alloyed, corrupt, debased, defiled, diluted, profane, squalid, sullied, tainted, unclean 8 maculate, polluted, shameful, unchaste, vitiated 9 lubricous, unrefined 10 insanitary, licentious
make ~: 4 foul 5 dirty, sully, taint 6 debase, defile, poison 7 corrupt, degrade, pollute, vitiate 10 adulterate
impurity: 4 dirt 5 dross, filth, grime, stain, taint 6 poison 8 lewdness 9 infection, lubricity, pollutant, pollution 10 corruption, defilement
remove ~: 4 sift 5 clean 6 refine
imputable: 5 due to 7 owing to 8 blamable 9 blameable
imputation: 3 lie 4 blot, hint, slur, spot 5 abuse, blame, brand, curse, libel, smear, stain, taint 6 charge, smirch, stigma 7 blemish, calumny, censure, slander, tarnish, untruth 8 allusion, brickbat, citation, innuendo, reproach 9 aspersion, falsehood, invective 10 accusation
impute: 3 lay, tax 5 blame 6 accuse, adduce, allude, assign, attach, charge, credit 7 ascribe, make out, qualify 8 accredit 9 attribute, chalk up to, inculpate, insinuate
(to): 6 credit
Imre: 4 Nagy 7 Kertész
__ I'm Ready: 3 Yes
I'm Ready for Love (1966 song) artist: Martha & the Vandellas
__ Imroth: 4 Anna
I'm Sitting on Top of the World (1926 song) artist: Al Jolson
I'm So Excited (1982 song) artist: Pointer Sisters
I'm So Into You (1993 song) artist: SWV
I'm So Lonesome... (1966 song) artist: B.J. Thomas
I'm Sorry (song) artist: Brenda Lee, John Denver, Platters
I'm so sorry!: 4 alas 5 alack
I'm Still __: 4 Here
I'm Still in Love With You (song) artist: Al Green, New Edition
I'm Stone in Love With You (1972 song) artist: Stylistics
I'm Telling You Now (1965 song) artist: Freddie and the Dreamers
I'm That Kind of Guy (1989 song) artist: LL Cool J
I'm the Only One (1994 song) artist: Melissa Etheridge
...__ I'm told: 4 or so
Imus: 3 Don 4 Fred
medium: 5 radio
I'm Walkin' (1957 song) artist: Fats Domino, Ricky Nelson
__ I'm With You: 4 When
I'm Wondering (1967 song) artist: Stevie Wonder
I'm working __!: 4 on it
I'm Your Angel (1998 song) artist: Celine Dion, R. Kelly
I'm Your Baby Tonight (1990 song) artist: Whitney Houston
I'm Your Boogie Man (1977 song) artist: KC and the Sunshine Band
I'm Your Man (1985 song) artist: George Michael
__, I'm yours: 6 Take me
__ I'm Yours: 4 Baby
I'm Yours (1965 song) artist: Elvis Presley
in: 3 mod, now, tip 4 link, tony 5 faddy, funky, swish, toney, vogue 6 access, amidst, at home, chi-chi, entrée, latest, modish, tipoff, trendy, within 7 a la mode, current, liaison, popular, stylish, voguish 8 up-to-date 9 advantage, incumbent 10 all the rage
any way: 4 ever 5 at all
a while: 4 anon, soon 5 later
concert: 5 as one, at one 8 together
front: 5 ahead, first 7 leading
in French: 4 dans
one piece: 5 whole 6 entire, intact
perpetuity: 4 ever 7 forever 9 eternally
the ball park: 4 near 5 close 7 close by
the center: 4 amid 5 among 6 amidst, mongst 7 amongst
with: 4 amid 5 among 6 amidst, mongst 7 amongst
in __: 3 fun, tow, two 4 a bit, a box, a fog, a jam, a pet, a row, a rut, a sec, a way, esse, full, gear, half, hand, luck, part, play, situ, sync, time, toto, turn, vain 5 a bind, a daze, a hole, a rage, a rush, a snit, a spot, a stew, a walk, a word, brief, force, front, limbo, order, phase, print, shape, short, spots, stock, store, style, synch, tears, truth 6 camera, cement, charge, clover, common, detail, effect, person, public, spades, stages, tandem, unison 7 advance, earnest, essence, extenso, general, harness, passing, private, reality, reserve
in __ act: 5 on the
in __ and starts: 4 fits
in __ case: 3 any
in __ conscience: 4 good
in __ course: 3 due
in __ day and age: 4 this
in __ ear...: 3 one
in __ event: 3 any
in __ eye: 5 a pig's
in __ feather: 4 fine, good, high
in __ fell swoop: 3 one
in __ fettle: 4 fine
in __ finish: 5 at the
in __ for: 4 line
in __ gear: 4 high
in __ good conscience: 3 all
in __ land: 4 la-la
in __ light: 4 a bad 5 a good
in __ of: 4 case, lieu, view 5 favor, light, place, spite, terms 6 excess 7 advance, default
in __ of fact: 5 point
in __ of fire,...: 4 case
in __ of trouble: 5 a heap
in __ only: 4 name
in __ order: 5 short
in __ parentis: 4 loco
in __ part: 4 good
in __ probability: 3 all
in __ quo: 5 statu
in __ res: 6 medias
in __ secret: 3 on a
in __ shakes: 3 two
in __ signo vinces: 3 hoc
in __ swing: 4 full
in __ that: 5 order
in __ the money: 5 it for
in __ time: 4 good
in __ to: 5 order 6 regard
in __ veritas: 4 vino
in __ water: 3 hot 4 deep
in __ way: 3 the 4 a bad 5 harm's
in __ words: 5 other
in-__: 3 box, law 4 goal, home, joke, kind 5 crowd, depth, group, house 6 basket 7 between, migrant, migrate, service
in-__-face: 4 your
in-__ movie: 6 flight
in-__ skating: 4 line
in.: 4 meas.
__ in: 3 all, cut, did, dig, eat, get, hem, key, lay, log, pay, pop, run, set, sit, tie 4 blow, butt, call, cash, cave, chip, clue, come, done, draw, drop, fall, fill, give, hang, horn, kick, lock, pile, plug, pull, rein, rope, send, shut, sign, sock, stay, step, suck, take, tuck, tune, turn, wade, work, zero, zoom 5 barge, break, bring, build, check, chime, close, count, phase, pitch, rub it, sleep, stand, throw, trade, write 6 breeze, factor, figure, listen, muster, strike 7 rejoice
__-in: 3 run, sit, tap 4 cave, fade, iris, lead, love, shoo 5 carry 6 circle
...in __ tree: 5 a pear
In: 4 elem. 6 indium 7 element
49 for ~: 4 at. no.
In __: 4 Neon 5 a Poem, a Vale, My Bed 6 Dreams 7 Country, Society
In __?: 5 or out
In __ and out...: 6 one ear
In __ Arizona: 3 Old
In __ beginning...: 3 the
In __ Blood: 4 Cold
In __ Color: 6 Living
In __ eye!: 5 a pig's
In __ is truth: 4 wine
In __ of Folly: 6 Praise
In __ Our Life: 4 This
In __ Still Felt: 3 Joy
In __ Trust: 5 God We
In __ We Trust: 3 God
In __ Yet Green: 6 Memory
__ In: 5 Let 'Em, Let Me
IN
see Indiana
in a __: 3 box, jam, row, rut, sec, way 4 bind, jiff, rush, snit, spot, stew, word 5 flash, jiffy, sense, state, tizzy, trice, while 6 dither, minute, pickle 7 fashion
in a __ age: 5 coon's
in a __ eye: 4 pig's
in a __ light: 3 bad 4 good
in a __ of speaking: 6 manner
Ina: 5 Balin, Souez 6 Claire 9 Coolbrith
Ina __ Hutton: 3 Ray
In-a-__-Da-Vida: 5 Gadda
in a bad __: 5 light
In a beautiful __-green boat: 3 pea
inability: 9 ineptness, unfitness 10 disability, feebleness, inadequacy, inaptitude, incapacity, inefficacy, ineptitude
__ in a blanket: 3 pig
__ in Able: 3 A as
__ in a Blue Dress: 5 Devil
__ in a blue moon: 4 once
__ in a Bottle: 4 Time 5 Genie 7 Message
__ in Acapulco: 3 Fun
inaccessible: 4 away 5 aloof 6 far-off, remote 7 distant, elusive, elusory, far away 10 impassable
inaccuracy: 3 lie 4 slip, tale, typo 5 error, fault 6 defect, howler 7 blunder, erratum, falsity, mistake 9 deception
inaccurate: 3 lax 4 wide 5 false, wrong 6 all wet, erring, faulty, untrue, way off 7 in error, inexact, off-base, unsound 8 improper, mistaken, slipshod, specious 9 defective, erroneous, imprecise, incorrect 10 apocryphal, discrepant, fallacious, ungrounded, unreliable
be ~: 3 err 7 go wrong
inaccurately: 5 wrong
in a coon's __: 3 age
In a cowslip's bell __: 4 I lie
inaction: 7 default, languor 8 lethargy 9 inertness, lassitude 10 standstill
inactivate: 4 stop 6 freeze, shelve 7 shut off, suspend 9 interrupt
inactive: 3 lax, old, ret. 4 calm, down, idle, lazy, logy, slow 5 inert, quiet, slack, still 6 asleep, at rest, draggy, fallow, latent, on hold, otiose, sleepy, static, torpid 7 abeyant, dormant, languid, passive, retired 8 indolent, slothful, sluggish, stagnant 9 lethargic, quiescent, sedentary, somnolent 10 disengaged, motionless, on the shelf, unemployed, unoccupied, unrealized

be ~: 4 laze, loaf, rest 5 relax
element: 4 neon 5 argon 7 krypton
not ~: 4 busy 5 astir 6 lively 8 bustling, in motion
inactivity: 4 ease, rest 5 sloth 6 repose, stasis, torpor 7 inertia, languor, latency, slumber 8 abeyance, dullness, idleness, laziness, lethargy 9 inertness, lassitude 10 depression, quiescence
period of ~: 4 calm, lull 6 hiatus, layoff, recess, stasis 7 respite, timeout 8 downtime 9 interlude
__ in a day's work: 3 all
inadequacy: 4 flaw, lack, need 6 dearth, defect 7 absence, deficit, failing, failure, paucity, poverty 8 drawback, scarcity, shortage, sparsity, underage, weakness 9 inability, inaptness, shortfall, unfitness 10 deficiency, faultiness, feebleness, incapacity, inefficacy, ineptitude, meagerness, scantiness, skimpiness
inadequate: 3 bad, low, shy 4 lame, poor, puny, slim, thin, weak 5 light, lousy, scant, short, small, sorry, unfit, woful 6 faulty, feeble, flimsy, meager, scanty, scarce, skimpy, sparse, stingy, unable, woeful 7 failing, ill-done, lacking, limited, miserly, pitiful, sketchy, slender, stinted, wanting 8 beggarly, exiguous, pathetic 9 defective, deficient, imperfect, incapable, spineless, too little 10 bush-league, incomplete, pathetical, unequipped
inadmissible: 8 improper, untimely 9 unethical, unwelcome 10 out of order
inadvertence: 4 goof, miss, slip 5 lapse 6 laxity, slip-up 7 mistake, neglect 8 omission
inadvertent: 6 chance 8 careless, heedless 9 negligent, unwitting
inadvertently: 8 absently, by chance
say ~: 5 blurt 8 blurt out
inadvisability: 5 folly
inadvisable: 5 folly 6 unwise 8 improper 9 unadvised
In-a-Gadda-Da-Vida (1968 song)
artist: Iron Butterfly
__ in a Gilded Cage: 5 A Bird
In a Gondola author: Robert Browning
__ in a good word: 3 put
__ in a Harem: 4 Lost
in-a-hurry
letters: 3 PDQ 4 ASAP
word: 3 now 4 fast, stat 7 quickly
__-in-aid: 5 grant
__ in Alabama: 5 Crazy
__ in a Lifetime: 4 Once 5 Twice
in all __ conscience: 4 good
In a Lonely Place (1950 film)
cast: Humphrey Bogart, Gloria Grahame, Frank Lovejoy
director: Nicholas Ray
__ in a Manger: 4 Away
__ in America: 4 Lost, Made, Only 6 Living
__ in a million: 3 one
inamorata: 2 jo 3 pet 4 baby, dear, girl, jill, love 5 amour, angel, cooky, cutey, cutie, deary, ducky, flame, honey, leman, lover, lovey, novia, sugar, sweet 6 adorer, chérie, cookie, dautie, dearie, female, steady, sweets 7 beloved, darling, dearest, dear one, fiancée, pigsney, schatzi, squeeze, sweetie, tootsie 8 chou-chou, cutie pie, dowsabel, dulcinea, ladylove, lovebird, macushla, mistress, paramour, precious, snookums, sugar pie, sweetums, truelove 9 bonne amie, dreamboat, petit chou, valentine 10 girlfriend, heartthrob, honeybunch, mavourneen, sweetheart, sweetie pie, turtledove
inamorato: 2 jo 3 pet 4 baby, beau, dear, love 5 amour, angel, chéri, cooky, cutey, cutie, deary, ducky, flame, honey, leman, lover, lovey, novio, Romeo, spark, sugar, swain, sweet, wooer 6 adorer, bon ami, cookie, dautie, dearie, fiancé, steady, suitor, sweets 7 admirer, beloved, dearest, dear one, gallant, pigsney, pursuer, schatzi, squeeze, sweetie, tootsie 8 chou-chou, cutie pie, dowsabel, ladylove, lovebird, macushla, paramour, precious, snookums, sugar pie, sweetums, truelove 9 boyfriend, dreamboat, petit chou, valentine 10 heartthrob, honeybunch, mavourneen, sweetheart, sweetie pie, turtledove
in an __: 6 uproar 7 instant
__ in a name?: 5 What's
in and of __: 6 itself
In and Out of Love (1967 song) artist: Supremes
inane: 4 daft, dopy 5 balmy, batty, crazy, daffy, dippy, dizzy, dopey, empty, goofy, goosy, kooky, nutty, sappy, silly, vapid, wacky 6 absurd, jejune, kookie, screwy, simple, stupid, unwise, vacant, whacky 7 asinine, fatuous, foolish, idiotic, insipid, inutile, puerile, shallow, unsound, vacuous, witless 8 cockeyed, mindless, specious 9 fatuitous, frivolous, idiotical, illogical, laughable, ludicrous, pointless, senseless, untenable, worthless 10 amphigoric, cockamamie, groundless, nonserious, off the wall, pedestrian, ridiculous, unprofound, weak-minded
inanga: 4 fish 5 smelt
inanimate: 5 inert, still 8 lifeless, listless 9 insensate, quiescent, unfeeling 10 insentient, motionless, spiritless, unreactive
inanition: 6 torpor 7 languor, vacuity 8 lethargy
inanity: 3 gas, rot 4 blah, bosh, bull, bunk, guff, jazz, jive, pooh, tosh 5 bilge, folly, fudge, hokum, hooey, prate, stuff, trash, tripe 6 bunkum, bushwa, drivel, footle, gabble, gammon, gibber, havers, hot air, humbug, idiocy, jabber, jargon, kibosh, lunacy, piffle 7 baloney, blarney, blather, blether, boloney, bushwah, eyewash, flannel, flubdub, fustian, garbage, hogwash, rubbish, twaddle 8 buncombe, claptrap, falderal, falderol, flimflam, flummery, folderal, folderol, futility, nonsense, slipslop, tommyrot, trumpery, zaniness 9 absurdity, banana oil, gibberish, goofiness, inutility, kidstakes, kookiness, moonshine, poppycock, rigmarole, silliness 10 applesauce, balderdash, bilge water, codswallop, double-talk, flapdoodle, galimatias, Jabberwock, mumbo jumbo, rigamarole, taradiddle, tomfoolery
in any __: 3 way 4 case 5 event
__-in apartment: 4 walk
In a pig's eye: 5 never, no how, no way
In a Poem author: Robert Frost
__ in a poke: 3 pig 4 a pig
inappeasable: 4 hard 5 rigid 7 adamant 8 pitiless, vengeful
__ in apple: 3 A as
inapplicable: 5 unapt 8 improper 9 different, unrelated
inapposite: 5 inapt, unapt, unfit, wrong 7 off-base 8 unsuited 10 extraneous, immaterial, irrelevant, nongermane
inappreciable: 3 wee 4 tiny 5 minor, small, teeny 6 little, minute, slight, teensy 7 trivial 8 trifling
...in apprehension how like __: 4 a god
inappropriate: 3 bad 5 inapt, silly, unapt, undue, unfit, wrong 6 unwise 8 improper, mistaken, unseemly, untimely, untoward 9 ill-suited 10 irrelevant, out of order, unsuitable
inappropriately: 3 bad 5 afoul, amiss, badly, wrong 6 astray, rotten 7 wrongly 10 improperly
inapropos: 5 unapt 9 unrelated 10 extraneous, immaterial, irrelevant, out of place
inapt: 4 non-U 5 unfit, wrong 6 clumsy, gauche, unmeet 7 awkward, unhandy 8 improper, unfacile, unseemly, untimely 9 ill-suited, maladroit, unfitting, unskilled 10 inapposite, indecorous, irrelevant, malapropos, nongermane, out of place, unbecoming, unsuitable
Ina Ray: 6 Hutton
inarguable: 4 true 7 certain 8 absolute, concrete, decisive, definite, positive 10 conclusive, undisputed
Inari: 4 lake
locale: 7 Finland
__ in arms: 7 comrade
__ in Arms: 5 Babes 6 Rabble
inarticulate: 3 mum, shy 5 muted, quiet 6 silent 7 bashful 8 nonvocal, reserved, reticent, taciturn, wordless 9 clammed up 10 tongue-tied
inarticulately, say: 6 mumble, mutter
__ in a rut: 5 stuck
inasmuch as: 3 for 5 since 7 because 9 therefore
__ in a teacup: 5 storm 7 tempest
__ in a teapot: 7 tempest
inattention: 6 laxity, slight 7 neglect 9 oversight
inattentive: 3 lax 4 lazy 5 blind, bored, slack 6 asleep, remiss, sloppy 7 faraway, unaware 8 careless, heedless, listless, mindless, reckless 9 negligent, unmindful
be ~: 3 nod 4 doze 5 sleep
one's response: 3 huh 4 what
inaudible: 4 weak 5 quiet 9 noiseless, soundless 10 indistinct
inaugural: 5 first 6 maiden 7 initial, leading, pioneer, premier 9 beginning, inceptive, induction 10 initiation
inaugurate: 4 open 5 begin, build, enter, found, set up, start, usher 6 induct, instal, launch 7 break in, install, instate, kick off, lead off, usher in 8 commence, dedicate, get going, initiate 9 enter upon, establish, institute, introduce, originate 10 commission
inauguration: 4 rise 5 debut, start 6 launch, origin 7 opening 8 starting
need: 4 oath 5 Bible
Inauguration __: 3 Day
inauspicious: 4 dire 5 curst 6 cursed, jinxed 7 baleful, baneful, hapless, ominous, unblest, unlucky 8 ill-fated, ill-timed, luckless, sinister, untimely 9 unblessed, unfavored 10 ill-starred, portentous
In a Vale author: Robert Frost
__ in aviary: 3 A as
__ in a while: 4 once
in bad faith in Latin: 8 mala fide
__-in-bag: 4 boil
__-in-Bay: 3 Put
in-between: 4 amid 5 among 6 amidst, mongst 7 amongst
state: 5 limbo
__ in Black: 3 Men
__ in Bloom: 4 Love
__ in Blue Jeans: 5 Venus
__ in B Minor: 4 Mass
inboard-outboard: 5 motor
__ in Bohemia, A: 7 Scandal
__ in bond: 7 bottled
__ in Boots: 4 Puss
inborn: 6 innate, native, rooted 7 chronic, natural 9 chronical, ingrained, intrinsic, intuitive 10 congenital, connatural, deep-seated, hereditary, indigenous
inbred: 6 native, rooted 7 genetic 8 inherent 9 genetical, ingrained, instilled, intrinsic 10 deep-seated, hereditary, indigenous
__ in Budapest: 3 Zoo
inbue: 5 embed, infix 7 engrain, implant, ingrain, instill 9 inculcate
__ in Bunches: 7 Hunches
Inca: 6 Andean, Indian, Kechua 7 Amerind, Kechuan, Quechua, Quichua 8 Quechuan 9 Atahualpa
city: 5 Cusco, Cuzco
counting device: 5 quipu
language: 6 Kechua 7 Kechuan, Quechua, Quichua 8 Quechuan
territory: 4 Peru 5 Andes
Incahuasi: 4 peak 5 mount 8 mountain
locale: 5 Andes, Chile 9 Argentina
incalculable: 4 huge, iffy, vast 5 great 6 chancy, myriad, unsure, untold 7 endless 8 enormous, infinite 9 limitless, priceless, uncertain, unlimited
__ in Calico: 4 A Gal
incandesce: 4 burn, glow 5 blaze, flame, flash, glare, gleam, light, shine 7 glisten, shimmer, sparkle, twinkle 9 coruscate 10 illuminate
incandescence: 3 ray 4 beam, fire, glow 5 blaze, flame, flash, light, sheen, shine 6 luster 7 shimmer, sparkle, twinkle 8 radiance, radiancy, splendor
incandescent: 5 aglow, lucid 6 ablaze, bright, lucent 7 beaming, burning, fulgent, glowing, lambent, radiant, shining 8 luminous, lustrous
incandescent __: 4 lamp
incant: 3 say 5 chant 6 recite
incantation: 3 hex 5 chant, charm, magic, spell 6 voodoo 7 sorcery 8 wizardry 10 hocus pocus
incapable: 5 unapt, unfit 6 unable 8 fumbling, helpless 9 powerless, unskilled 10 impuissant, inadequate, unequipped, unskillful
is ~ of: 4 can't 6 cannot
incapacious: 6 narrow 7 cramped, limited 9 confining 10 compressed, contracted, restricted
incapacitate: 4 maim 5 lay up, wreck 6 hogtie 7 disable 8 paralyse, paralyze, sabotage
incapacitated: 5 unfit 6 unable 9 paralytic, powerless
incapacity: 8 handicap, weakness 9 ignorance, inability 10 disability, feebleness, inadequacy
incarcerate: 4 hold, jail 5 embar, seize 6 arrest, coop up, detain, immure, intern, lock up, punish, shut up 7 confine, impound, interne, put away 8 imprison, sentence
incarcerated: 4 pent 7 captive
incarceration: 6 arrest, chains, prison 7 custody
incarnate: 5 human 8 embodied, physical 9 personify 10 in the flesh, manifested
incarnation: 5 tulku 6 avatar 7 rebirth
__ in Casablanca, A: 5 Night
__ in case: 4 just

incautious: 3 lax 4 bold, rash, wild 5 brash, hasty 6 madcap, remiss, sloppy, unwary 7 foolish, unalert 8 careless, heedless, off-guard, reckless, slipshod 9 desperate, foolhardy, hotheaded, ill-judged, impetuous, imprudent, impulsive, negligent, unadvised, uncareful, unguarded, unmindful 10 ill-advised, indiscreet, neglectful, nonchalant, regardless, unthinking, unvigilant, unwatchful
incautiously: 9 any old way
incautiousness: 5 haste
Incaviglia: 4 Pete
inc. cousin: 3 LLC, ltd.
Ince: 6 Thomas
incendiarism: 5 arson 9 pyromania
incendiary: 7 firebug, harmful 8 arsonist, inflamer 9 dangerous, demagogic, demagogue, firebrand, flammable, ignitable, insurgent, seditious 10 pyromaniac, subversive
Incendiary Blonde (1945 film)
cast: Betty Hutton, Charlie Ruggles
incense: 3 ire, irk 4 rile, roil 5 anger, aroma, chafe, egg on, peeve, pique, scent, smell, smoke, steam 6 bum out, burn up, enrage, fire up, madden, nettle 7 bouquet, enflame, inflame, outrage, perfume, provoke 8 irritate 9 displease, infuriate 10 exasperate
resin: 5 myrrh
starter: 5 frank
Incense and Peppermints (1967 song)
artist: Strawberry Alarm Clock
incensed: 3 hot, mad 4 ired, sore 5 angry, cross, het up, huffy, irate, livid, riled, upset, wroth 6 ablaze, fuming, galled, ireful, raging, raving, red-hot 7 enraged, furious, ranting, steamed 8 choleric, up in arms, white-hot, wrathful 9 indignant, resentful, splenetic, wrought up 10 infuriated
be ~: 4 boil, burn, fume, rage, stew 5 steam, storm 6 see red, seethe, simmer 7 bristle, smolder
incentive: 4 bait, goad, lure, spur 5 bonus, drive, spark 6 carrot, come-on, motive, reason 7 impetus 8 catalyst, stimulus 9 rationale, stimulant 10 allurement, enticement, incitement, inducement, motivation, persuasion, temptation
give ~: 4 fire, goad, move, prod, spur, urge, whet 5 goose, impel, prime, rouse, spark, tempt 6 arouse, bestir, excite, induce, prompt, propel, stir up 7 inspire, quicken 8 energize, motivate, persuade 9 galvanize, stimulate
incentive __: 3 pay 4 wage
incept: 3 eat 6 take in 7 receive
inception: 4 dawn, rise 5 birth, git-go, onset, start 6 advent, origin, outset, source 7 genesis, kickoff, leadoff, opening 8 creation, entrance, exordium 9 beginning, threshold 10 derivation, initiation, provenance
inceptive: 5 early, first 7 initial, nascent, pioneer 8 earliest, original 9 beginning, inaugural, incipient 10 archetypal, innovative
incertitude: 7 dubiety 8 mistrust 9 dubiosity, suspicion
incessant: 6 steady 7 chronic, endless, eternal, lasting, nonstop, running, undying 8 constant, enduring, tireless, unbroken, unending, unwaning 9 ceaseless, chronical, continual, perennial, perpetual, unabating, unceasing 10 continuous, monotonous, persistent, relentless
incessantly: 4 ever 5 no end, on end
inch: 3 bit, lag 4 unit 5 crawl, creep, sidle 6 trifle 7 modicum
by inch: 6 slowly 8 bit by bit 9 gradually
ender: 4 meal, worm
every ~: 5 fully 6 wholly 7 totally, utterly 8 entirely 10 completely, thoroughly
fraction: 3 mil
multiple: 4 foot, mile, yard
inch __: 5 along, plant
inch-__: 5 pound
__ inch: 5 cubic, every 6 column, miner's, square
__-inch: 4 acre, half 5 water
__ in Charge: 7 Charles
__-in-cheek: 6 tongue
inches
nine ~: 4 span
20 ~: 5 cubit
36 ~: 4 yard
39+ ~: 5 meter, metre
__ in chief: 6 editor, tenant
__ Inch Nails: 4 Nine
inchoate: 8 unformed, unshaped 9 amorphous 10 incomplete
Inchon: 4 city, port, town
city near ~: 5 Seoul
locale: 10 South Korea
incidence: 4 area, rate 5 range, scope 6 extent 7 compass 10 occurrence
incident: 4 case 5 event, scene, thing 6 affair, matter 7 episode, related 8 activity, occasion 9 adventure, attendant, happening 10 experience, occurrence, phenomenon
unpleasant ~: 6 bummer, downer
incidental: 3 odd 4 side 5 minor, stray 6 casual, chance, random 7 related, trivial 9 ancillary, attendant, haphazard, secondary 10 accidental, concurrent, contingent, extraneous, fortuitous, occasional, subsidiary, synchronal
expense: 3 tip
incidental __: 5 music
incidentally: 3 BTW 7 by the by 8 by the way 9 in passing
Incident at Oglala (1992 film) director: Michael Apted
Incident at Vichy author: Arthur Miller
Incident, The (1967 film)
cast: Beau Bridges, Tony Musante, Martin Sheen
__ Incident, The: 5 Ox-Bow 7 Bedford
__ in Cincinnati: 4 WKRP
incinerate: 3 ash 4 burn 5 torch 6 ignite 7 combust
incinerator: 6 boiler, burner 7 furnace
debris: 3 ash
incipience: 4 dawn, rise 5 debut, onset, start 6 growth, origin, outset 9 ascension, beginning, emergence
incipient: 7 budding, initial 9 beginning, embryonic, inceptive 10 commencing, developing, elementary, initiatory
incise: 3 cut 4 bite, etch, gash, nick, slit 5 carve, grave, lance, notch, score, slash, slice 6 chisel, sculpt 7 cut into, engrave, scratch 9 sculpture
incised: 3 cut 4 slit 5 cleft, split 6 carved, cloven, etched, gashed, graven, nicked 7 cut into, grooved, notched, slashed 8 engraved, sculpted
incision: 3 cut 4 gash, slit, stab 5 slash 10 laceration
combining form: 4 -tomy
incisive: 4 acid, keen 5 acerb, acute, sharp, terse 6 biting, bright, clever, gnomic, severe 7 acerbic, caustic, cutting, graphic, mordant, pointed, precise, pungent, satiric 8 definite, piercing, profound, sardonic, scathing 9 graphical, sarcastic, satirical, trenchant
incisiveness: 5 irony 6 acuity, acumen, satire 7 acidity, sarcasm 8 accuracy, judgment, keenness
incisor: 4 fang 5 biter, tooth
elongated ~: 4 tusk
neighbor: 5 molar 6 canine
Incitatus: 5 horse, steed 6 equine
rider: 8 Caligula
incite: 3 set 4 abet, bait, coax, fire, fuel, goad, move, prod, push, spur, stir, urge 5 cause, drive, egg on, hop up, impel, key up, raise, rouse, spark, tempt, wreak 6 arouse, ask for, excite, exhort, fire up, foment, induce, kindle, prompt, set off, stir up, urge on, whip up, work up 7 actuate, aggress, agitate, animate, enflame, ferment, forward, further, inflame, inspire, promote, provoke, psych up, quicken, trigger 8 engender, enspirit, inspirit, motivate, persuade 9 encourage, impassion, influence, instigate, stimulate 10 cause a riot
incitement: 3 jog 4 call, goad, itch, jolt, poke, prod, push, spur, urge 5 drive, prick 6 desire, fillip, motive, thrust 7 dictate, impetus, impulse 8 stimulus 9 annoyance, awakening, incentive 10 excitement, inducement, invitation
inciter: 7 demagog, hellion 8 agitator, inflamer 9 demagogue
incivility: 4 sass 6 insult 7 crudity 8 rudeness 9 indecency, insolence 10 disrespect, effrontery
inclemency: 4 cold 5 rigor 7 cruelty, rawness 8 hardness, severity 9 austerity
inclement: 3 bad, raw 4 cold, foul, wild 5 cruel, harsh, nasty, rainy, rough 6 bitter, rugged, savage, severe, stormy, unkind, wintry 7 callous, wintery 8 pitiless, rigorous, ruthless 9 draconian, merciless, turbulent, unfeeling, unpitying 10 tyrannical, unmerciful
weather: 4 rain 5 sleet, storm 7 showers 8 blizzard 9 rainstorm
inclination: 3 set 4 bend, bent, bias, cant, lean, list, tilt, will, wish 5 angle, fancy, grade, pitch, slant, slope, taste, trend 6 animus, liking 7 impulse, leaning, opinion 8 affinity, aptitude, attitude, gradient, penchant, pleasure, tendency, weakness 9 appetence, readiness, sentiment 10 partiality, proclivity, propensity
strong ~: 3 yen 4 itch, urge 7 craving, impulse 8 appetite, yearning 9 hankering
inclinatory: 4 awry 5 askew, atilt 6 canted, skewed, uneven 7 crooked, leaning, tilting 8 cockeyed, lopsided, one-sided, unsteady 10 off-balance, unbalanced
incline: 3 dip, tip 4 bend, bias, cant, hill, lean, list, ramp, rise, sway, tend, tilt, turn 5 chute, grade, level, pitch, ready, slant, slope, verge, way up 6 ascent, glacis 7 descent, dispose 8 gradient, motivate, persuade 9 acclivity, declivity, gravitate, prejudice 10 predispose
toward: 4 like, want 6 prefer
upward, nautically: 6 steeve
__ incline: 4 on an
inclined: 3 apt 4 bent, wont 5 atilt, bevel, leant, prone, ready 6 aslant, aslope, liable, likely 7 tending, willing 8 disposed, prepared
at sea: 5 alist
be ~: 4 lean, tend 5 slope
favorably ~: 7 partial
highly ~: 5 steep 6 abrupt
not ~: 5 balky, loath 6 averse 7 opposed, uneager 8 hesitant 9 reluctant, unwilling 10 indisposed
to (suffix): 3 -ish
inclined __: 5 plane
incl., not: 4 excl.
__-in closet: 4 walk
include: 3 add 4 bear, have, hold, okay, take 5 admit, adopt, allow, carry, co-opt, count, cover, go for, let in 6 append, assent, comply, deal in, embody, entail, imbody, insert, number, take in 7 build in, contain, embrace, enclose, inclose, involve, subsume, welcome 8 allow for, comprise, stand for 9 consist of, encompass, interject, put up with, recognize, sign off on 10 concur with, constitute, give the nod
don't ~: 4 drop, omit, shun, skip, snub 5 avoid, scorn 6 bypass, forget, pass by, pass up, reject 7 neglect 8 leave out, overlook 9 disregard
included
not ~: 3 out 5 apart 6 absent
with: 4 amid 5 among, one of 6 amidst, mongst 7 amongst
including: 3 and 4 also, plus, with 8 as well as, counting 9 along with 10 containing
not ~: 4 sans 7 without
inclusion: 9 belonging, comprisal, insertion 10 admittance
inclusive: 4 full, wide 5 broad, total 6 entire 7 blanket, general, overall, plenary 8 catchall, catholic, sweeping, umbrella 9 all-around, ball-of-wax, expansive, extensive 10 ecumenical, wall-to-wall
abbr.: 3 etc.
make more ~: 5 widen 6 expand, spread 7 augment, broaden, enlarge
pronoun: 3 our 4 ours
__-inclusive: 3 all
inclusiveness: 5 scope, width 7 breadth
incognita, terra: 6 enigma
incognito: 6 hidden, masked, secret 7 bearded, unknown 8 nameless 9 anonymous, concealed, disguised, unexposed 10 in disguise, undercover
incognizant: 4 deaf 7 napping, unaware 8 careless, heedless, off-guard
incoherent: 6 silent 8 rambling 9 delirious, faltering, wandering 10 breathless, discordant, disjointed, disordered, incomplete, irrational, maundering, stammering, stuttering, tongue-tied
incohesive: 5 messy 7 aimless, chaotic, jumbled, muddled 8 confused 10 disjointed, disordered
In Cold Blood: 4 book, film
author: Truman Capote
cast: Robert Blake, John Forsythe, Scott Wilson
income: 3 fee, job, pay, rev. 4 alms, cash, fare, rent, tips, wage 5 lucre, means, money, wages, yield 6 living, payoff, profit, return, salary 7 annuity, revenue, royalty 8 cash flow, dividend, earnings, finances, proceeds, receipts 9 emolument, resources, royalties 10 IRS concern, livelihood
after taxes: 3 net
in French: 5 rente
investor ~: 3 div., int. 6 return 8 dividend, interest
opposite: 5 outgo 8 spending
source: 3 job 6 living 10 livelihood
income __: 3 tax 4 bond 7 account
income-__ return: 3 tax

__ income: 3 net 4 real 5 gross 6 earned 7 accrued, psychic
__-income: 3 low 4 high 5 fixed 6 middle
incomer: 8 outsider, stranger 9 outlander
incommensurate: 6 uneven 7 unequal 8 lopsided 9 disparate, divergent 10 dissimilar, mismatched, unbalanced
incommode: 6 bother, burden, impose, put out 7 disturb, trouble 9 disoblige 10 discommode
incommodious: 4 boxy, tiny 5 teeny 6 narrow, teensy 7 cramped, irksome, unhandy, unroomy 8 confined
__ in common: 6 tenant 7 nothing, tenancy
incommunicable: 5 privy 7 private 8 eyes-only, personal
incommunicado: 6 cut off, hidden 7 shut off 8 isolated, secluded, shielded 10 cloistered, tucked away
incommunicative: 3 mum, shy 4 curt, dumb, mute 5 brief, quiet, short, terse 6 silent 7 evasive, laconic 8 reserved, reticent, taciturn
incomparable: 4 best 5 ideal 6 unique 7 perfect, supreme 8 peerless, superior, ultimate, uncommon 9 matchless, priceless, unequaled 10 preeminent
incomparably: 5 by far 7 greatly
incompatibility: 6 rancor, strife, tussle 7 discord, dispute, dissent 8 bad blood, conflict, disunity, friction 9 antipathy, hostility 10 antagonism, contention, disharmony, dissension, dissonance, opposition
incompatible: 5 alien 6 motley, unlike 8 clashing, contrary 9 different, disparate, dissonant 10 discordant, dissimilar, mismatched
incompetence: 7 failure 8 weakness
incompetent: 3 raw 5 gawky, inapt, inept, unapt, unfit 6 clumsy, klutzy, oafish, unable 7 amateur, awkward, bungler, gawkish, useless 8 bumbling, bungling, feckless, helpless, inexpert, ungainly 9 all thumbs, graceless, lumbering, maladroit, stumbling, unskilled 10 unskillful
be ~: 9 mishandle, mismanage
incomplete: 6 broken 7 lacking, partial, sketchy, wanting 8 half-done 9 defective, deficient, imperfect 10 expurgated, fractional, inadequate, incoherent, unexecuted, unfinished
incompletely: 4 part 6 in part 8 somewhat
incomprehensible: 5 Greek, vague 6 arcane, opaque 7 cryptic, obscure, unclear 8 abstruse, baffling, nebulous, puzzling 9 confusing, cryptical, enigmatic, limitless, unlimited 10 fathomless, indistinct, perplexing
incompressible: 4 firm, hard 5 dense, solid, tight 7 compact
incomputable: 4 vast 6 untold 7 endless, immense, no end of 8 infinite
inconceivable: 8 hopeless, unlikely 9 marvelous, unheard-of 10 impossible, infeasible, out of reach
inconclusive: 4 weak 5 shaky 6 unsure 7 tenuous 10 inadequate
Inconel: 5 alloy
component: 4 iron 6 nickel 8 chromium
incongruity: 6 oddity 7 anomaly, illogic, paradox 8 conflict, variance
incongruous: 3 odd 4 rich 5 alien, inapt, wrong 6 absurd, ironic, unlike 7 unsound 8 improper, rambling, untimely 9 ill-suited, ludicrous, senseless 10 irrelevant, unsuitable
incongruousness: 5 irony
inconnu: 4 fish 8 stranger
inconsequential: 4 idle, null, punk, puny, tiny 5 dinky, light, minor, petty, scrub, small 6 frilly, measly, paltry, scanty, two-bit 7 nominal, trivial 8 picayune, trifling 9 valueless, worthless
inconsiderable: 4 slim, tiny 5 light, minor, small 6 little, minute, scanty, slight 7 nominal, trivial 8 trifling
inconsiderate: 4 rude 5 brash, crass, hasty, nervy, rough, short 6 madcap, shabby, unkind, wanton 7 boorish, selfish 8 careless, impolite, inurbane, reckless, tactless 9 negligent, thankless, unadvised
inconsideration: 6 laxity 7 laxness, neglect 8 omission 9 oversight 10 negligence, remissness
inconsistency: 7 anomaly, paradox 8 conflict, contrast, oxymoron, variance
inconsistent: 5 silly 6 at odds, fickle, spotty, unlike 7 erratic 8 contrary, opposite, unstable, variable 9 up-and-down
be ~: 4 sway, vary, yo-yo 5 swing, waver 9 fluctuate, hem and haw, oscillate, vacillate 10 ebb and flow, equivocate
inconsolable: 3 sad 4 blue, glum 5 woful 6 gloomy, morose, somber, woeful 7 doleful, forlorn, joyless, unhappy 8 dejected, desolate, downcast, troubled, wretched 9 bummed out, cheerless, desperate, heartsick, miserable, prostrate, sorrowful, woebegone 10 chapfallen, dispirited, melancholy
inconspicuous: 6 hidden, unseen 9 unnoticed 10 unobserved
inconstancy: 8 weakness
inconstant: 5 false, giddy 6 fickle, uneven, untrue 7 erratic, mutable, unloyal, wayward 8 disloyal, ticklish, unstable, unsteady, variable, volatile 9 faithless, irregular, mercurial, two-timing, uncertain, unsettled 10 capricious, changeable, nonuniform, perfidious, traitorous
incontestable: 4 real, sire, true 5 final, fixed, plain, solid 7 certain, evident, for sure 8 absolute, airtight, decisive, definite, positive 9 axiomatic
incontestably: 5 by far 9 going away, hands down
incontinent: 6 amoral 7 corrupt, immoral 8 depraved 9 corrupted, dissolute 10 licentious, lubricious, profligate
incontrovertible: 4 sure, true 5 clear 7 assured, certain, decided, settled 8 accurate, definite, in the bag, positive, resolved, surefire 10 conclusive, determined, guaranteed
inconvenience: 4 snag 5 trial 6 bother, hamper, hassle, put out 7 put upon, trouble 8 headache 9 liability
inconvenient: 3 bad 5 messy 7 awkward, unhandy 8 annoying, untimely, unwieldy 9 unwieldly
more than ~: 6 odious
Inconvenient Woman, An author: 5 Dunne
incorporate: 3 mix 4 fuse, have, join, link, pool 5 add to, annex, blend, co-opt, cover, merge, tie in, unite, weave 6 absorb, digest, embody, gather, imbody 7 combine, contain, embrace, include, subsume 8 coalesce, comprise, gather up 10 synthesize
incorporated: 4 mixt 5 mixed 6 united 9 municipal
incorporation: 3 mix 5 blend, union 6 merger 7 mixture
in corpore __: 4 sano
incorporeal: 6 unreal 7 ghostly 8 bodiless, spectral 9 spiritual, unworldly
incorrect: 3 bad, off 5 false, not so, wrong 6 erring, faulty, flawed, untrue, way off 7 ill-done, inexact, unsound 8 improper, mistaken, specious 9 erroneous, illogical, imprecise, unfitting 10 fallacious, inaccurate, ungrounded, unreliable, unsuitable
be ~: 3 err 4 flub, goof, slip 5 botch, lapse, stray 6 bungle, foul up, mess up, slip up 7 blunder, deviate, go wrong, louse up, stumble 8 go astray
marks ~: 3 xes
prefix: 3 mis-
incorrectly: 5 amiss, badly, wrong
incorrigible: 6 unruly, wicked 7 problem, wayward 8 indocile, indurate 9 scoundrel, shameless 10 rebellious
incorrupt: 4 good, pure 5 loyal, moral, noble 6 chaste, heroic, worthy 8 reliable 9 untouched 10 immaculate, impeccable
incorruptibility: 5 honor 6 virtue 7 honesty, loyalty, probity 8 morality, nobility
incorruptible: 4 fair, just, pure 5 moral 6 honest 7 upright 8 reliable, straight, virtuous 9 unselfish
In Country (1989 film)
cast: Joan Allen, Emily Lloyd, Bruce Willis
director: Norman Jewison
setting:: 3 Nam 7 Vietnam
__ in court: 3 day
incr.: 3 enl.
increase: 2 up 3 add, enl., wax 4 boom, bump, gain, grow, hike, jump, leap, rise, whet 5 add to, boost, build, mount, raise, revup, run up, surge, swell, widen 6 accrue, deepen, expand, extend, fatten, gather, growth, jack up, jerk up, mark up, pick up, spread, step up, thrive, upturn, waxing 7 accrual, advance, amplify, augment, broaden, buildup, burgeon, develop, enhance, enlarge, further, improve, inflate, magnify, mount up, prolong, promote, prosper, quicken, recover, scale up, upgrade, upsurge, upswing 8 addition, bourgeon, escalate, heighten, lengthen, multiply, mushroom, progress, protract, snowball, swelling, widening 9 accretion, branch out, crescendo, expansion, extension, increment, inflation, intensify, luxuriate, propagate, pullulate, reinforce 10 accumulate, aggrandize, appreciate, broadening, burgeoning, cumulation, escalation, prosperity, strengthen, supplement
combining form: 3 aux- 4 auxo- 6 auxamo-
suddenly: 4 zoom 5 spike, surge, swell
__ increase: 4 on an 5 on the
Increase: 6 Mather
increased: 3 new 4 more 5 ran up, upped 10 additional
by: 3 and 4 plus
increaser, name meaning: 6 Joseph
incredible: 5 fishy, great 6 absurd, unreal 7 amazing, awesome, surreal, suspect, uncanny 8 fabulous, glorious, unlikely 9 fantastic, ineffable, marvelous, untenable, wonderful 10 astounding, far-fetched, impossible, improbable, marvellous, outlandish, prodigious, ridiculous, superhuman
Incredible!: 3 wow 5 great, super
Incredible Hulk, The (CBS sci-fi)
cast: Bill Bixby (David Banner) Lou Ferrigno (The Hulk)
Incredible Journey, The
cat: 3 Tao
dog: 5 Luath 6 Bodger, Chance, Shadow
Incredible Shrinking Man, The (1957 film) cast: April Kent, Grant Williams
incredibly: 4 very 6 hugely, vastly 7 greatly 8 markedly, mightily, very much 9 extremely, immensely, intensely 10 abundantly, enormously, powerfully, remarkably, strikingly
incredulity: 5 doubt 6 wonder 8 distrust, mistrust, surprise, unbelief 9 suspicion
exclamation: 6 indeed, really 8 is that so 9 no kidding
incredulous: 5 leery 7 cynical, dubious 8 doubting 9 quizzical, skeptical
increment: 4 bump, gain, grow, rise, step 5 add to, boost, build, raise 6 profit, step up 7 augment, build up 8 addition, escalate, increase 9 accession, accretion, accrument 10 annexation, supplement
incrementally: 6 slowly 8 bit by bit
increscent: 9 on the rise 10 augmenting, cumulative, increasing
incriminate: 3 tax 4 name 5 blame, frame, rat on 6 accuse, charge, finger, give up, indict 8 denounce
incriminated: 6 guilty
incrimination: 5 blame, guilt
in crowd: 4 clan 5 elite 6 clique, jet set
'In' Crowd, The (1975 song) artist: Ramsey Lewis
incrust: 3 set, tar 4 coat, face, gild, line, pave, tile 5 adorn, cover, glaze, inlay, japan, paint, plate 6 cement, emboss, enamel, stucco, veneer 7 lacquer, overlay, plaster, varnish 8 decorate, ornament 9 embellish, whitewash
incrustation: 4 crud, scab 5 scale, shell 6 casing 7 coating 8 covering
Inc. subject: 2 co. 7 company
incubate: 4 grow 5 brood, hatch, sit on 6 mature 7 develop, gestate, nurture 8 take form
incubation __: 6 period
incubation site: 4 nest
incubus: 4 onus 5 demon, fiend 6 daemon, daimon, spirit 9 archfiend, nightmare
inculcate: 3 fix, sow 5 drill, edify, imbue, infix, plant, teach 6 impart, infuse, instil 7 engrain, implant, impress, ingrain, instill 8 drum into, instruct 9 brainwash, break down, establish, pound into 10 hammer into
inculpable: 4 good 5 clean, moral 6 chaste 7 upright 8 innocent, spotless, virtuous 9 blameless, exemplary, faultless, guiltless 10 in the clear
inculpate: 3 tax 6 accuse, charge, impute, indict 7 arraign, impeach 9 implicate 10 take to task
incult: 4 rude, wild 6 coarse 7 boorish 9 unrefined
incumbency: 5 reign 6 regime, tenure
incumbent: 2 in 5 lying 6 inside 7 binding, in power, leaning, resting 8 lounging, occupant, official, reposing 10 inhabitant, politician
incur: 3 owe 4 draw 5 run up 6 afford 7 acquire, bring on, provoke 8 contract
incurable: 7 chronic 9 unfixable 10 inveterate, remediless
incuriosity: 5 ennui 6 apathy 7 boredom 8 coolness, lethargy 9 jadedness, lassitude, weariness

incurious: 4 cool 5 aloof, bored, jaded 8 heedless 10 nonchalant, unagitated
incursion: 4 raid 5 foray 6 attack, inroad 7 assault, descent 8 invasion 9 intrusion, irruption, onslaught 10 aggression
incus: 4 bone 5 anvil
locale: 3 ear
incuse: 5 stamp 8 hammer in
In days ___...: 5 of old
indebted: 4 owed 5 bound 6 in hock, liable 7 obliged 8 beholden, grateful, thankful 9 obligated 10 answerable, honor-bound
be ~: 3 owe 5 owe to, thank 10 appreciate
one: 4 ower
indebtedness: 3 due 5 debit, debts 7 arrears, default, deficit 9 liability
indecency: 4 evil 7 crudity 8 foulness, lewdness, ribaldry, vileness 9 bawdiness, grossness, immodesty, indecorum, obscenity, vulgarity 10 coarseness, incivility, indelicacy
indecent: 3 low 4 base, blue, foul, lewd, racy, rude, vile 5 crude, dirty, gross, nasty, wrong 6 coarse, earthy, ribald, risqué, smutty, unmeet, vulgar, wicked, X-rated 7 immoral, obscene, profane, uncouth 8 immodest, improper, off-color, shameful, unseemly 9 low-minded, shameless 10 indecorous, indelicate, lascivious, scurrilous, suggestive, unbecoming
Indecent Obsession, An author: Colleen McCullough
Indecent Proposal (1993 film)
cast: Woody Harrelson, Demi Moore, Robert Redford
director: Adrian Lyne
indecipherable: 3 dim 4 dark, hard 5 perdu, run-on, tough, vague 6 arcane, erased, hidden, knotty, perdue, secret, tricky, veiled 7 blotted, blurred, complex, cramped, cryptic, obscure, puzzing, smudged, tangled, unclear 8 abstract, abstruse, baffling, esoteric, involved, nebulous 9 cryptical
indecision: 5 doubt, qualm 7 dubiety 8 weakness 9 dubiosity, hesitancy 10 hesitation
sound of ~: 2 er, uh, um
indecisive: 4 weak 5 shaky, timid 6 unfirm, unsure 7 aimless, halting 8 doubtful, hesitant, lukewarm, waffling, wavering 9 astraddle, faltering, tentative, uncertain, undecided, unsettled, weak-kneed 10 borderline, changeable, hesitating, hot-and-cold, indefinite, irresolute, of two minds, on the fence, wishy-washy
be ~: 3 hem 5 waver 6 teeter 9 vacillate
indecorous: 4 base, rank, rude, vile 5 bawdy, crass, crude, gross, inapt, nasty, rough, unapt 6 coarse, common, ribald, risqué, unmeet, vulgar 7 boorish, ill-bred, loutish, lowbred, naughty, uncivil, uncouth 8 churlish, impolite, improper, indecent, inurbane, unseemly 9 facetious, graceless, tasteless, unrefined 10 indelicate
be ~: 5 act up 9 misbehave
indecorum: 4 goof, slip 5 boner, gaffe, lapse 6 slip-up 7 bad move, blunder, faux pas, misstep, stumble 8 bad taste, rudeness 9 indecency
indeed: 2 ay, da, ja, sí, so 3 aye, nay, oui, yea, yep, yes, yup 4 amen, fine, okay, sure, yeah 5 good-o, natch, oh yes, quite, right, roger, truly, uh-huh 6 agreed, gladly, good-oh, it is so, just so, rather, really, righto, surely, verily, you bet, yowzah 7 exactly, for real, go ahead, granted, in truth, mais oui, quite so, ten-four 8 actually, all right, as you say, for a fact, of course, thumbs up, to be sure, very much, very well 9 be my guest, certainly, darn right, in reality, naturally, precisely, sure thing, you betcha, you said it 10 absolutely, admittedly, by all means, definitely, positively, sure enough, that's right, undeniably
old-style: 5 pardi, pardy 6 pardie, perdie
___, indeed!: 3 yes
indefatigability: 3 vim 4 grit, guts 5 might, moxie, power, vigor 6 energy, mettle 7 prowess, stamina 8 vitality 9 endurance, fortitude, gutsiness, hardiness 10 durability, resilience
indefatigable: 5 hardy 8 sedulous, tireless, untiring 9 laborious 10 unflagging
In Defense of Women author: H.L. Mencken
indefinite: 3 lax 4 hazy, iffy, wide 5 broad, fluid, fuzzy, ideal, loose, vague 6 chancy, unsure 7 dubious, general, inexact, unclear, unfixed, unknown 8 abstract, confused, doubtful, nebulous 9 ambiguous, boundless, equivocal, imprecise, limitless, shapeless, tentative, uncertain, undecided, undefined, unlimited, unsettled 10 borderline, indecisive, indistinct, inexplicit, unexplicit, unresolved, unspecific, up for grabs, up in the air
amount: 3 any, few 4 many, some
answer: 5 maybe 7 perhaps 8 possibly, probably 9 it could be, it might be, perchance 10 imaginably
combining form: 4 myri- 5 myrio-
indefinite ___: 6 number 7 article, pronoun
___ Indefinite: 4 Time 6 Future
indefinitely: 4 ever 7 forever, sine die
indelible: 3 ink 7 lasting 8 enduring 9 ingrained, memorable, permanent 10 inerasable, unerasable
indelicacy: 7 bad form, crudity 8 bad taste, ribaldry, rudeness 9 indecency 10 coarseness, smuttiness
indelicate: 3 low 4 base, blue, foul, lewd, racy, rude, vile 5 bawdy, brusk, crass, crude, frank, gross, nasty, rough, salty, spicy 6 abrupt, candid, coarse, earthy, risqué, smutty, spicey, unmeet, vulgar, wicked 7 brusque, immoral, obscene, uncouth 8 immodest, impolite, improper, indecent, inurbane, off-color, tactless, unseemly 9 inelegant, offensive, outspoken, tasteless, ungallant, untactful 10 indecorous, outrageous, suggestive, unbecoming, unblushing
indemnify: 3 pay 5 atone, repay 6 ensure, insure, refund, return, reward, secure 7 certify, endorse, indorse, pay back, satisfy, warrant 8 make good 9 reimburse 10 compensate, make amends, recompense, remunerate
indemnity: 3 pay 6 pardon 7 damages, redress, warrant 8 impunity 9 expiation, insurance, jury award, privilege 10 commission, protection
___ indemnity: 6 double
indent: 5 notch 6 recess 9 serration
indentation: 3 cut, dip, pit, rut 4 bowl, dent, gash, hole, nick, sink 5 basin, cleft, niche, notch, score, stamp 6 cavity, crater, dimple, groove, hollow, recess 7 scallop, scollop 8 sinkhole
shoreline ~: 3 bay 4 cove, gulf 5 basin, bayou, bight, fiord, firth, fjord, inlet 6 lagoon 7 estuary
indented: 6 sunken 7 concave 8 serrated 9 depressed
indenture: 3 tie 4 bind, bond, deal, deed 5 lease 7 compact, enslave, enthral, inthral, slavery, voucher 8 contract, document, enthrall, inthrall 9 agreement
indentured ___: 7 servant
indentured one: 4 esne, serf
independence: 7 freedom, liberty, license 8 autarchy, autonomy, home rule, latitude, self-rule
Independence: 4 city, town
initials: 3 HST
locale: 8 Missouri
Independence ___: 3 Day 4 Hall
___ Independence: 5 War of
Independence Day (1996 film)
cast: Jeff Goldblum, Mary McDonnell, Bill Pullman, Randy Quaid, Will Smith
director: Roland Emmerich
dog: 6 Boomer
foe: 2 ET 5 alien
Independence Day time: 4 July 6 fourth, summer 9 the fourth
Independence Hall st.: 4 Penn.
independent: 4 free, rich 5 apart, proud, rebel 6 closed, strong 7 private, unaided, wealthy 8 maverick, opposite, separate, unallied 9 sovereign, unrelated, voluntary
make ~: 4 wean
of ~ means: 4 rich 5 flush 6 loaded 7 moneyed, opulent, upscale, wealthy, well-off 8 affluent, thriving, well-to-do 10 in the chips, in the money, privileged, prosperous, successful, well-heeled
one: 5 loner 6 hermit
independent ___: 5 audit, axiom 6 clause
independently: 4 solo 5 alone, apart, per se, unled 6 singly 7 unaided 9 by oneself 10 unassisted
Independent, The (2001 film)
cast: Janeane Garofalo, Jerry Stiller
Independent Woman (2000 song)
artist: Destiny's Child
in-depth: 5 total 8 complete, thorough 9 full-dress, intensive, searching 10 exhaustive, soup to nuts
indescribable: 4 huge, vast 6 untold 7 immense 9 boundless
indestructible: 5 hardy 7 durable, lasting, undying 8 immortal 9 permanent 10 changeless
Buddhist symbol of the ~: 5 vajra
indeterminate: 4 gray, grey, wide 5 broad, loose, mousy, vague 6 mousey, unsure 7 dubious, general, inexact, unclear, unfixed, unknown 8 confused, doubtful, nebulous, possible 9 uncertain 10 unresolved
amount: 3 any, few 4 many, some
index: 4 clew, clue, DJIA, file, list, mark, sign, sort 5 guide, order, table, token 6 docket, roster, symbol, the Dow 7 arrange, pointer 8 classify, tabulate 9 benchmark, catalogue, directory, inventory 10 indication, tabulation
entry: 2 pg. 4 name, page 5 title
starter: 3 sub
index ___: 3 set 4 card, case, fund 5 crime, plate 6 finger, fossil, number
___ index: 4 bond, card, heat 5 color, nasal, price, stock, thumb 6 facial, Miller, misery, skelic 7 aridity, cranial, gnathic, harvest, orbital
___-indexed: 5 cross
indexing, word ignored in: 3 the
index of ___ indicators: 7 leading
India: 3 ink 6 nation 7 country
aborigine: 4 Gond
actor: 4 Sabu
antelope: 5 sasin
bay: 6 Bengal
bovine: 3 Gir 4 arna, Rath, Siri, zebu 5 Dajal, Dangi, Deoni, gayal, Malvi, Rathi 6 Channi, Gaolao, Mewati, Nagori, Nimari, Ongole, Ponwar, Rojhan 7 Bachaur, Brahman, Brahmin, Sahiwal
British rule: 3 raj
Buddhist king of ~: 5 Asoka
butter: 4 ghee
bwana, in ~: 5 saheb, sahib
camel: 4 oont
capital: 8 New Delhi
caste: 4 ahir
city: 4 Agra, Puna 5 Delhi, Mandi, Patan, Patna, Poona, Simla, Surat, Thana 6 Bhopal, Bombay, Ellora, Imphal, Indore, Jaipur, Kanpur, Madras, Mumbai, Pattan 7 Chennai, Jodhpur, Kolkata 8 Calcutta, New Delhi 9 Bangalore, Hyderabad
coat: 6 achkan, banian, banyan
conductor: 5 Mehta 10 Zubin Mehta
court: 6 adalat 7 adawlut
court officials: 5 omlah
criminal: 6 dacoit, dakoit
crocodile: 6 gavial
cymbals: 3 tal
dance: 6 kathak
deer: 4 axis 6 chital, sambar, sambur 7 sambhar, sambhur 9 barasingh
desert: 4 Tahr, Thar, Tuhr
district: 3 Goa 5 Daman
dog: 5 dhole
drum: 5 tabla
estate: 5 taluk 7 talooka
export: 3 tea
fabric: 6 Madras 7 khaddar
feline: 7 caracal
forage crop: 3 urd
garment: 4 sari 5 lungi, saree 6 lungee, lungyi
Gateway to ~: 6 Bombay
gesture: 5 mudra
goat: 7 markhor 8 markhoor
government official: 5 dewan, diwan
grass: 7 vetiver 8 khus-khus
groom: 4 sice, syce 5 saice
invader: 5 Arian, Aryan
island: 3 Diu
language: 4 Pali, Tulu, Urdu 5 Hindi, Oriya, Tamil, Vedic 6 Telegu, Telugu 8 Sanscrit, Sanskrit 10 Hindustani
legislature: 6 Sansad
location: 4 Asia
maid: 4 ayah
memorial tower: 5 minah
millet: 5 doura, durra 6 dourah
mister: 3 sri 4 shri 5 saheb, sahib
Mogul capital: 4 Agra
money: 3 pie 4 anna, pice 5 mohur, paisa, rupee
mountain: 4 Mana 5 Ghats, Kamet 6 Trisul 7 Trisuli 8 Cardamom, Dunagiri, Pauhunri 9 Badrinath, Himalayas, Nanda Devi
music: 4 raga, tala 5 filmi
musket: 6 jingal 7 gingall
mystic: 5 faker, fakir, faqir 6 faquir
native: 4 Sikh 5 Hindu, Nahal, Parsi, Tamil 6 Hindoo, Lepcha
neighbor: 5 Burma, China, Nepal 6 Bhutan 8 Pakistan 10 Bangladesh
Nobelist: 3 Sen 5 Raman 6 Tagore
nursemaid: 3 ama 4 amah
pants: 7 shalwar, shulwar
peasant: 4 ryot
peninsula: 6 Deccan
police club: 5 lathi 6 lathee

port: 4 Puri 6 Bombay, Cochin, Madras 8 Calcutta 10 Chittagong
primate: 4 lori 6 Bandar, rhesus 7 hoolock
reception: 6 durbar
religion: 4 Jain 5 Jaina 8 Hinduism
religious fair: 4 mela
river: 5 Indus, Jumna, Purna, Sarda 6 Ganges
riverbank steps: 4 ghat 5 ghaut
ruler: 4 raja, rana, rani 5 mogul, ranee
scarf: 5 rumal
sea: 7 Arabian
servant: 4 maty 5 matee
shawl: 5 pattu
shirt: 4 pooa 5 kurta, pooah 6 banian, banyan, khurta
shrub: 4 sola, sunn 5 cubeb 7 karanda
silkworm: 4 eria
sir: 5 saheb, sahib
sitarist: 7 Shankar
social stratum: 5 caste
soldier: 5 Sepoy
soup: 3 dal
spice: 5 curry
stable worker: 4 sice, syce 5 saice
state: 3 Goa 5 Assam, Bihar 6 Kerala, Orissa, Sikkim 7 Gujurat, Haryana, Manipur, Mizoram, Tripura 8 Nagaland
statesman: 5 Nehru 6 Gandhi 7 Shastri
story: 5 katha
stringed instrument: 4 vina 5 sitar, veena
temple: 4 rath 5 ratha
tree: 2 bo 3 bel 4 bael, pich, poon, teak 5 bodhi, ebony, mahua, mahwa, mohwa, mowra, papal, pipal 6 banian, banyan, deodar, mowrah, nutmeg, peepul 7 deodara, karanda, soursop 8 cinnamon
vehicle: 5 tonga 6 gharri, gharry
water container: 4 lota 5 lotah
weasel: 5 ratel
weight: 3 ser 4 tola
writer: 3 Rao 5 Anand, Desai, Iqbal, Mehta 6 Hosain, Moraes, Tagore 7 Bharati, Narayan, Rushdie 8 Kalidasa 9 Premchand 10 Markandaya

India __: 3 ink 4 silk 5 paper, print, wheat 6 chintz, rubber 7 drugget

__ India: 3 Air 6 French, Song of, Star of 7 British, Farther

__ India Company: 4 East

Indian: 3 Fox, Han, Kaw, Oto, Sac, Ute 4 ALer, Cree, Crow, Cuna, Erie, Eyak, Hopi, Inca, Iowa, Maya, Otoe, Pima, Pomo, Sauk, Seri, Tama, Taos, Tewa, Tiwa, Tupi, Yana, Yuma, Zuni 5 Ahtna, Asian, brave, Brulé, Caddo, Carib, Creek, Haida, Huron, Kansa, Kaska, Kiowa, Lenca, Lipan, Maidu, Makah, Miami, Miwok, Modoc, ocean, Omaha, Osage, Otomi, Piute, Ponca, Sioux, Taino, Teton, Unami, Washo, Wintu, Yaqui 6 Abnaki, Ahtena, Apache, Arawak, Aymara, Cayuga, Cayuse, Dakota, Feller, Galibi, Jivaro, Kechua, Laguna, Lengua, Lumbee, Mandan, Micmac, Mohave, Mohawk, Mojave, Munsee, Navaho, Navajo, Nootka, Oglala, Ojibwa, Oneida, Ottawa, Paiute, Papago, Patwin, Pawnee, Pequot, Plains, Pueblo, Quapaw, Salish, Santee, Seneca, Tanana, Toltec, Wintun, Yahgan, Yakima, Yokuts 7 Abenaki, Arapaho, Arikara, Atakapa, Bannock, Chibcha, Chilcat, Chilkat, Chinook, Choctaw, Chumash, Guarani, Huastec, Kechuan, Klamath, Koyukon, Kutchin, Kutenai, Mahican, Mazatec, Miskito, Mohegan, Mohican, Naskapi, Nipmuck, Ojibway, Quechua, Quichua, San Blas, Shawnee, Takelma, Tanaina, Tlingit, Washita, Wichita, Wyandot, Yankton, Yavapai, Yucatec, Zapotec 8 Arapahoe, Cahuilla, Caingang, Cherokee, Cheyenne, Chippewa, Comanche, Delaware, Hunkpapa, Illinois, Iroquois, Kickapoo, Kwakiutl, Malecite, Maricopa, Mikasuki, Missouri, Muskogee, Nez Percé, Onondaga, Ouachita, Puyallup, Quechuan, Sahaptin, Seminole, Squamish, Tarascan, Wabanaki, Wahpeton 9 Blackfoot, Chickasaw, Havasupai, Jicarilla, Karankawa, Menominee, Mescalero, Nanticoke, Penobscot, Saulteaux, Suquamish, Tehuelche, Tiger Lily, Tsimshian, Tuscarora, Wahpekute, Wampanoag, Winnebago, Wyandotte 10 Adirondack, Araucanian, Assiniboin, Athabaskan, Bellabella, Bellacoola, Chiricahua, Miniconjou, Potawatomi, Tarahumara
beads: 5 sewan
boat: 5 canoe
carving: 5 totem
corn: 5 maize
corn genus: 3 zea
dwelling: 4 tipi 5 hogan, tepee 6 teepee
fish: 5 danio, hilsa 6 cuchia, hilsah
footwear: 3 moc
friend: 5 netop
fruit: 4 bael
grass: 4 kans
greeting, in oaters: 3 how
Hall of Famer: 4 Doby, Wynn 5 Flick, Lemon 6 Feller, Lajoie 7 Speaker 8 Bob Lemon, Boudreau 9 Bob Feller, Early Wynn, Larry Doby, Nap Lajoie 10 Elmer Flick
horse: 6 cayuse
language family: 5 Numic
on the ~: 4 asea 5 at sea
paintbrush: 5 plant 6 flower
palindromic ~: 3 Oto
pipe: 5 plant 6 flower
pony: 6 cayuse
rival: 3 Cub, Met, Red 4 Expo, Twin 5 Angel, Astro, Brave, Giant, Padre, Rocky, Royal, Tiger 6 Brewer, Dodger, Marlin, Oriole, Philly, Pirate, Ranger, Red Sox, Yankee 7 Blue Jay, Mariner 8 Athletic, Cardinal, Devil Ray, White Sox
subdivision: 5 tribe
summer phenomenon: 4 haze
Territory, today: 4 Okla. 8 Oklahoma

Indian __: 3 fig, red 4 bean, club, corn, file, hemp, Lake, meal, pipe, poke, rice, silk, wolf 5 agent, bison, bread, cobra, cress, lotus, Ocean 6 agency, almond, balsam, Desert, Empire, jujube, mallow, millet, Mutiny, Outlaw, Runner, summer, turnip, yellow 7 currant, mustard, pudding, sanicle, warrior

Indian __ Call: 4 Love

Indian __, The: 6 Runner 7 Fighter

__ Indian: 6 Digger, Plains, wooden 7 Buffalo

__-Indian: 5 Anglo, Paleo

Indiana: 5 Jones, state 6 Robert
basketballer: 5 Pacer
city: 4 Gary 5 Paoli 6 Carmel, Goshen, Hobart, Kokomo, Marion, Muncie 7 Elkhart, Fishers, Granger, Hammond, La Porte, Munster, Portage 8 Anderson, Columbus, Highland, Lawrence, Richmond 9 Fort Wayne, Greenwood, Lafayette, Mishawaka, New Albany, South Bend 10 Crown Point, Evansville, Terre Haute, Valparaiso
county: 4 Cass, Owen, Vigo 5 Parke 6 Jasper, Starke 7 Elkhart, La Porte
humorist: 3 Ade
Indian: 5 Miami
neighbor: 4 Ohio 8 Illinois, Kentucky, Michigan
school: 3 NDU 6 Goshen, Purdue 9 Ball State, Notre Dame
Standard Oil of ~ today: 5 Amoco
state bird: 8 cardinal
state flower: 5 peony
state river: 6 Wabash
state stone: 9 limestone

Indiana __: 4 Moon 6 ballot

__, Indiana: 5 Eerie

Indiana author: George Sand

Indiana Jones and the Last Crusade (1989 film)
cast: Sean Connery, Alison Doody, Denholm Elliott, Harrison Ford
director: Steven Spielberg

Indiana Jones and the Temple of Doom (1984 film)
cast: Kate Capshaw, Harrison Ford
director: Steven Spielberg

Indianapolis: 4 city, town
city near ~: 6 Kokomo
county: 6 Marion
newspaper: 4 Star
pro team: 5 Colts
river: 5 White

Indianapolis 500 winners:
2004 - Buddy Rice
2003 - Gil de Ferran
2002 - Helio Castroneves
2001 - Helio Castroneves
2000 - Juan Montoya
1999 - Kenny Brack
1998 - Eddie Cheever Jr.
1997 - Arie Luyendyk
1996 - Buddy Lazier
1995 - Jacques Villeneuve
1994 - Al Unser Jr.
1993 - Emerson Fittipaldi
1992 - Al Unser Jr.
1991 - Rick Mears
1990 - Arie Luyendyk
1989 - Emerson Fittipaldi
1988 - Rick Mears
1987 - Al Unser
1986 - Bobby Rahal
1985 - Danny Sullivan
1984 - Rick Mears
1983 - Tom Sneva
1982 - Gordon Johncock
1981 - Bobby Unser
1980 - Johnny Rutherford
1979 - Rick Mears
1978 - Al Unser
1977 - A.J. Foyt
1976 - Johnny Rutherford
1975 - Bobby Unser
1974 - Johnny Rutherford
1973 - Gordon Johncock
1972 - Mark Donohue
1971 - Al Unser
1970 - Al Unser
1969 - Mario Andretti
1968 - Bobby Unser
1967 - A.J. Foyt
1966 - Graham Hill
1965 - Jim Clark
1964 - A.J. Foyt
1963 - Parnelli Jones
1962 - Rodger Ward
1961 - A.J. Foyt
1960 - Jim Rathmann

Indiana, Robert: 6 artist 9 pop artist
painting: 4 Love

Indiana University
athletes: 8 Hoosiers
conference: 6 Big Ten
locale: 4 Gary 6 Kokomo 8 Richmond 9 Fort Wayne, New Albany, South Bend

Indian Fighter, The (1955 film)
cast: Kirk Douglas, Elsa Martinelli, Walter Matthau
director: Andre de Toth

Indian Head: 4 cent, coin 5 penny

Indian in the Cupboard, The (1995 film)
cast: Lindsay Crouse, Litefoot, Hal Scardino
director: Frank Oz

Indian Lake (1968 song) artist: Cowsills

Indian Ocean
archipelago: 7 Comoros
bay: 6 Bengal 7 Delagoa
gulf: 6 Mannar
island: 5 Cocos 6 Comoro 8 Sri Lanka 9 Christmas, Mauritius 10 Madagascar, Seychelles
port: 6 Durban
river to the ~: 4 Juba, Tana 5 Tsana 6 Murray, Rovuma, Ruvuma 7 Limpopo, Zambezi
seaman: 6 lascar 7 lashkar
vessel: 3 dau, dow 4 dhow
wind: 7 monsoon

Indianola: 4 city
locale: 4 Iowa

Indian Outlaw (1994 song) artist: Tim McGraw

Indian pony: 5 horse 6 equine

Indian pudding: 7 dessert

Indian Reservation (1971 song) artist: Paul Revere and the Raiders

Indian Runner: 4 duck, fowl
relative: 4 smew, teal 5 eider, Pekin, Rouen, scaup 6 Cayuga, scoter 7 gadwall, mallard, pintail, pochard, redhead, sea duck, widgeon 8 garganey, gray duck, mandarin, musk duck, oldsquaw, shoveler, surf duck, wood duck 9 black duck, broadbill, goldeneye, goosander, greenhead, merganser, ruddy duck, sprigtail 10 bufflehead, canvasback, surf scoter, tufted duck

Indian Runner, The (1991 film)
cast: Valeria Golino, David Morse, Viggo Mortensen
director: Sean Penn

Indians: 3 ten 4 team
home: 9 Cleveland
org.: 3 ALC, MLB
sport: 8 baseball

Indian Summer (1993 film)
cast: Alan Arkin, Matt Craven, Diane Lane

__ Indian Too: 4 I'm an

Indic: 4 Pali, Urdu 5 Hindi 7 Bengali 8 Sanscrit, Sanskrit 9 Sinhalese
language (abbr.): 3 Skr., Skt. 4 Skrt.

indicate: 3 nod, peg, tab, tag 4 bode, give, hint, look, mark, mean, show, sign, wave 5 argue, augur, imply, let on, point, prove, spell 6 advert, attest, denote, evince, record, reveal, signal 7 add up to, bespeak, betoken, connote, display, express, pin down, point to, portend, promise, purport, reflect, signify, specify, suggest 8 announce, bookmark, evidence, intimate, manifest, pinpoint, point out, register, stand for 9 adumbrate, designate, predicate, symbolize, underline 10 illustrate

indication: 3 cue 4 clew, clue, hint, lead, mark, omen, sign, tick, wisp 5 index, proof, token, trace, track 6 augury, herald, signal, symbol 7 auspice, gesture, inkling, portent, presage, symptom, vestige, warning 8 bad vibes, evidence, hallmark, mnemonic, reminder 9 attribute, direction, harbinger, reference, signifier, testimony 10 denotation, directions, expression, forerunner, intimation, prognostic, suggestion

indicative: 7 augural 8 denotive 9 testatory 10 auspicious, denotative, diagnostic, emblematic, evidential, exhibitive, expressive, prognostic, suggestive

___ indicative: 7 Present

indicator: 4 clew, clue, dial, hint, mark, omen, sign 5 gauge, guide, meter, token 6 beacon, signal, symbol 7 pointer, warning 8 gas meter, hallmark 9 predictor 10 prediction

___ indicator: 4 ball, bank, slip, turn, wind 5 climb, drift, speed 6 flight 7 leading

indict: 3 sue, tax 4 name 5 blame 6 accuse, charge 7 arraign, censure, impeach 8 denounce 9 castigate, criminate, inculpate, prosecute

indictable: 7 illegal, illicit 8 criminal, unlawful 10 chargeable

indictment: 5 blame, trial 6 charge 7 lawsuit 9 detention, statement 10 accusation, allegation

Indienne: 6 fabric 8 material

___ Indies: 4 East, West

indifference: 5 ennui 6 apathy, laxity, slight, torpor 7 boredom, disdain, neglect 8 coldness, coolness, lethargy, stoicism 9 jadedness

exclamation: 8 whatever

show ~: 5 shrug

indifferent: 3 icy, lax 4 cold, cool, deaf, lazy, logy, so-so 5 aloof, blasé, blind, stoic, stony, tepid 6 amoral, chilly, remote, stolid, stoney 7 callous, distant, glacial, languid, neutral, stoical 8 careless, detached, feckless, heedless, listless, lukewarm, mediocre, middling, ordinary, pitiless, scornful, uncaring 9 lethargic, negligent, tolerable, untouched, withdrawn 10 regardless

indifferently: 7 lightly 8 absently, casually, sloppily 10 carelessly, heedlessly

indigence: 4 lack, need, want 6 hunger, misery, penury 7 beggary, poverty, straits 8 distress 9 neediness, privation 10 bankruptcy

indigene: 5 local 6 native 7 citizen, dweller 8 habitant 9 aborigine 10 compatriot, countryman, inhabitant

indigenous: 4 wild 5 local 6 ethnic, inborn, inbred, innate, native 7 connate, endemic, natural 8 domestic, inherent, internal, regional 9 endemical, homegrown, inherited, primitive 10 aboriginal, congenital, connatural, unacquired

indigent: 4 poor 5 broke, needy, sorry 6 bad off, beggar, busted, hard up, ill-off, in need, in want, pauper 7 have-not, pinched 8 badly off, bankrupt, beggarly, deprived, homeless, strapped 9 destitute, insolvent, miserable, moneyless, penniless, penurious 10 down and out, pauperized, straitened

indigestion: 3 gas 5 agita

___ indigestion: 4 acid

indignant: 3 hot, mad 4 hurt, ired, sore 5 angry, cross, het up, huffy, irate, livid, riled, upset, wroth 6 fuming, galled, heated, ireful, miffed, peeved, piqued, raging, raving, red-hot 7 annoyed, boiling, enraged, furious, in a huff, ranting, steamed 8 burned up, choleric, incensed, inflamed, maddened, outraged, up in arms, wrathful 9 impatient, irritated, resentful, seeing red, splenetic, wrought up 10 displeased, freaked out, infuriated, intolerant

be ~: 4 boil, burn, fume, rage, rave 5 storm 6 blow up, see red, seethe 7 bristle, smolder 10 hit the roof

indignation: 3 ire 4 fury, rage 5 anger, pique, wrath 6 animus 7 offense, outrage, umbrage 9 annoyance

indignity: 3 cut 4 snub 6 insult 7 affront, offense 9 blasphemy, contumely, grievance 10 disrespect, opprobrium

indigo: 3 dye 4 anil, blue 5 color, plant 6 flower 7 grayish

relative: 4 anil, cyan, navy, Nile, teal 5 Alice, azure, slate 6 cobalt, raisin, violet 7 peacock 8 cerulean, sapphire 9 turquoise 10 aquamarine, periwinkle

indigo ___: 4 bird, blue 5 snake 7 bunting

___ Indigo: 4 Mood

Indio: 4 city, town

locale: 10 California

Indira: 6 Gandhi

attire: 4 sari 5 saree

father: 5 Nehru

son: 5 Rajiv

see also India

indirect: 4 side 5 snaky, tacit 6 sneaky, subtle, zigzag 7 devious, implied, sinuous, virtual 8 circular, tortuous 9 underhand, vicarious 10 collateral, meandering, roundabout, secondhand

indirect ___: 3 tax 4 cost 5 labor, proof 6 object 7 address, primary

indirectly: 7 sideway 8 sideways, sidewise 10 secondhand

let know ~: 4 hint 5 let on 6 allude, hint at 7 suggest 8 intimate, lead up to 9 insinuate

indiscernable: 3 dim 5 vague 6 cloudy, hidden, minute, slight 7 gradual, obscure, shadowy, unclear 8 nebulous

indiscreet: 4 rash 5 brash, hasty 6 stupid, unwary, unwise 7 foolish 8 careless, heedless, reckless, tactless 9 half-baked, impolitic, imprudent, misguided, unadvised, unguarded 10 headstrong, ill-advised, incautious

be ~: 4 blab, blat, tell 5 blurt 6 gossip, let out, reveal, squeal, tattle 7 divulge, let slip 8 disclose, give away

Indiscreet (1958 film)

cast: Ingrid Bergman, Cary Grant

director: Stanley Donen

role: 4 Anna

indiscretion: 4 goof, slip, trip 5 error, fault, folly, gaffe, guilt, lapse 6 bumble, foul-up, miscue, slip-up 7 faux pas, misstep, mistake, stumble 8 rashness

indiscriminate: 6 motley, random, wanton 9 wholesale

___ in Disguise: 4 Judy 5 Devil

indispensable: 3 key, nec. 5 basal, basic, major, vital 6 needed, urgent 7 crucial, needful, pivotal, primary 8 cardinal, integral, material, must-have, required 9 important, mandatory, necessary, requisite

thing: 4 must, need 8 must-have 9 essential, necessity, requisite 10 imperative, obligation, sine qua non

indispose: 3 ail 4 lame, maim 5 lay up, upset 6 sicken, weaken 7 disable, exhaust 8 enervate, enfeeble, paralyse, paralyze, sideline 10 discourage, dishearten

indisposed: 3 ill, low, shy 4 loth, sick 5 loath 6 afraid, ailing, averse, infirm, laid up, poorly, queasy, queazy, sickly, unwell 7 not well, out of it, uneager, unsound 8 below par, diseased, hesitant 9 afflicted, bedridden, reluctant, unwilling 10 out of sorts, uninclined

be ~: 3 ail

indisposition: 3 ill 6 malady 7 ailment, illness 8 distaste, headache, migraine, sickness, weakness 10 hesitation

indisputable: 4 real, sure, true 5 clear, plain 6 actual 7 certain, evident, obvious 8 absolute, accurate, airtight, decisive, in the bag, positive

indisputably: 6 easily 7 clearly 9 going away, hands down, literally

indissoluble: 4 firm 5 fixed, solid 6 stable, steady 7 abiding, binding, lasting 8 constant, enduring

indistinct: 3 dim 4 dark, hazy, pale, thin 5 dusky, faded, faint, foggy, fuzzy, light, mirky, misty, murky, muted, vague 6 arcane, bleary, blurry, cloudy, silent 7 bleared, blurred, cryptic, obscure, shadowy, unclear 8 abstruse, confused, darkened, nebulous, puzzling 9 ambiguous, confusing, cryptical, enigmatic, equivocal, hard to see, illegible, imprecise, inaudible, shapeless, uncertain, unfocused 10 ill-defined, impalpable, indefinite, inexplicit, out of focus, perplexing, unreadable

image: 4 blur

make ~: 4 blur, fade 5 befog, blear, cloud, fog up 7 becloud

indistinctness: 3 fog 4 blur, daze, haze, murk 5 blear, cloud, smear 6 muddle, smudge

indistinguishable: 4 akin, same 5 alike, equal 7 the same 8 fungible 9 identical 10 equivalent, synonymous

___ in Distress, A: 6 Damsel

indite: 3 pen 5 couch, draft, frame, write 6 enjoin, record 7 compose 8 inscribe

indium: 5 metal 7 element

49 for ~: 4 at. no.

indiv.: 4 pers., sing.

individual: 3 man, one, own 4 body, lone, self, sole, soul 5 alone, being, child, human, party, thing, woman 6 entity, mortal, person, proper, signal, single, unique 7 express, oddball, private, special, unalike, unusual, various 8 creature, discrete, distinct, especial, peculiar, personal, separate, singular, solitary, specific, specimen 9 character, different, exclusive, personage, singleton, something 10 dissimilar, human being, particular, respective

item: 4 unit 5 piece 6 detail, entity, module 7 article, element, section, segment

unspecified ~: 3 one 6 anyone

individual ___: 6 medley 7 liberty

individualist: 5 loner, rebel 6 egoist

individuality: 4 soul 6 makeup, nature 8 identity

individualize: 4 name 6 detail 7 itemize, pin down, specify 9 stipulate

individually: 4 a pop, each 5 alone, apart 6 apiece, singly, solely 8 one by one 9 piecemeal

individuals: 4 folk 5 folks 6 people

indivisible: 3 one 5 solid, whole 6 atomic, single 8 atomical

literally, ~: 4 atom

Ind. neighbor: 3 Ill., Ken. 4 Mich.

see also Indiana

Indo-___: 5 Aryan 7 Hittite, Iranian, Malayan, Pacific

Indochina

country: 4 Laos 5 Burma 7 Myanmar, Vietnam 8 Cambodia, Thailand

language: 3 Lao 4 Thai 10 Vietnamese

native: 3 Tai 4 Laos, part, Thai 7 Vietnam 8 Cambodia, Thailand

___ Indochina: 6 French

indocile: 3 bad 4 wild 6 mulish, unruly, wilful 7 forward, opposed, restive, willful 8 contrary, factious, obdurate, perverse, stubborn 9 obstinate, pig-headed, resistant 10 headstrong, rebellious, refractory, self-willed

indoctrinate: 5 drill, imbue, infix, plant, teach, train 6 ground, infuse, instil, school 7 educate, implant, instill, program 8 initiate, instruct 9 prejudice

Indo-European: 5 Arian, Aryan

language: 5 Oscan

language family: 6 Italic

Indo-Iranian: 5 Arian, Aryan

indolence: 5 sloth 6 acedia, apathy, stupor, torpor 7 inertia, languor 8 dullness, hebetude, idleness, laziness, lethargy, loginess, otiosity 9 faineance, inertness, torpidity 10 stagnation

___ Indolence: 5 Ode on

indolent: 3 lax 4 idle, lazy, logy, slow 5 inert, slack 6 asleep, draggy, otiose, torpid 7 dormant, languid, passive 8 careless, dallying, fainéant, inactive, listless, slothful, sluggish 9 apathetic, do-nothing, leisurely, lethargic, negligent, sedentary, shiftless 10 disengaged, neglectful

be ~: 4 idle, laze, loaf, loll 5 dally, shirk 6 dawdle, loiter, lounge 7 goof off, hang out 8 kill time, lallygag, malinger, slack off, vegetate 9 bum around, do nothing, goldbrick, lie around, waste time 10 dillydally, fool around, knock about

indomitability: 4 grit, will 5 heart, moxie, nerve, pluck, spunk, valor 6 daring, mettle, spirit, starch 7 bravery, courage, heroism, prowess, resolve 8 audacity, backbone, boldness, firmness, gumption, rashness, temerity, tenacity

indomitable: 4 bold, firm, game 5 brave, gutsy, nervy, stoic, stout 6 awless, daring, dogged, gritty, heroic, mighty, plucky, spunky 7 aweless, defiant, doughty, gallant, staunch, stoical, valiant 8 fearless, heroical, intrepid, resolute, stalwart, unafraid, untiring, valorous 9 audacious, dauntless, dreadless, obstinate, undaunted, unfearful 10 courageous, unflagging

Indonesia: 4 isle 6 island, nation 7 country

bay: 6 Sarera

boat: 4 prao, prau, proa

bovine: 4 anoa

capital: 7 Jakarta 8 Djakarta

city: 5 Ambon, Bogor, Depok, Medan 6 Malang, Manado, Padang 7 Bandung, Jakarta, Mataram 8 Bengkulu, Djakarta, Semarang, Surabaya

export: 3 tea

island: 4 Bali, Biak, Java, Laut, Nias, Roti, Savu, Sawu 5 Ceram, Rotti, Spice, Sumba, Timor 6 Borneo, Butung, Lombok, Madura, Serang 7 Celebes, Sumatra 8 Krakatoa, Moluccas, Sulawesi

islands: 3 Aru 4 Aroe, Arru, Leti 5 Letti

money: 3 sen

native: 3 Ata 5 Malay

neighbor: 8 Malaysia

org.: 4 OPEC

primate: 5 orang 7 tarsier

sea: 5 Timor
until 1949: 3 ter. 4 terr. 9 territory
volcano: 5 Kelut, Raung 6 Dukono, Merapi, Semeru, Slamet 7 Kerinci 8 Gamalama
indoor: 8 enclosed
indoor __: 4 pool 6 soccer 8 plumbing
indoors: 6 within 8 enclosed 9 sheltered
In Dreams (1963 song) artist: Roy Orbison
In Dreams star: 3 Rea
In Dubious Battle author: John Steinbeck
indubitable: 4 sure, true 5 right 6 actual 7 assured, certain, for sure, genuine 8 absolute, definite, positive 9 veritable
indubitably: 2 ay, da, ja, sí 3 aye, oui, yea, yep, yes, yup 4 fine, okay, sure, yeah 5 good-o, natch, quite, right, roger, uh-huh 6 agreed, easily, gladly, good-oh, indeed, just so, rather, really, righto, surely, you bet, yowzah 7 exactly, for sure, go ahead, indeedy, mais oui, quite so, ten-four 8 all right, as you say, of course, thumbs up, very well 9 be my guest, certainly, darn right, naturally, precisely, sure thing, you betcha, you said it 10 absolutely, by all means, definitely, positively, sure enough, that's right
induce: 3 get, put 4 coax, lead, lure, move, spur, sway, urge 5 bring, cause, evoke, impel, lobby, tempt 6 ask for, cajole, effect, incite, kindle, lead to, prompt 7 actuate, bring on, procure, produce, provoke, wheedle, win over 8 convince, engender, generate, inveigle, motivate, occasion, persuade 9 influence, instigate, prevail on, sweet-talk 10 bring about, give rise to, predispose
inducement: 4 bait, goad, hook, lure, spur, urge 5 bribe, cause, prize 6 carrot, come-on, motive, reason, reward 8 occasion, stimulus 9 incentive, sweet talk 10 attraction, enticement, incitement, invitation, temptation
illegal ~: 5 bribe, graft 6 grease, payoff, payola 8 kickback 9 hush money
induct: 5 admit, draft, enrol 6 enlist, enroll, instal 7 install, instate, receive, recruit, swear in 8 initiate, shanghai 9 conscript 10 inaugurate
induction: 5 logic 6 reason 8 judgment 9 accession, beginning, corollary, enrolment, inaugural, inference, reception 10 conclusion, conjecture, deducement, enrollment, initiation, ordination
motor pioneer: 5 Tesla
org.: 3 SSS
unit: 5 gauss
induction __: 4 coil 5 motor 7 furnace, heating
in due __: 6 course
indulge: 4 baby, dote 5 favor, humor, revel, spoil, treat 6 coddle, cosset, dandle, dote on, pamper, pander, permit, please 7 cater to, delight, gratify, immerse, satiate, satisfy, yield to 8 dote upon, give in to, tolerate 9 luxuriate, spoon-feed
don't ~ in: 4 duck, shun, skip, snub 5 avoid, dodge, evade, scorn 6 bypass, eschew, ignore 8 sidestep
in: 2 do 4 like, play 9 partake of
oneself: 4 bask 5 enjoy, revel 6 wallow 7 delight 9 luxuriate
something to ~: 3 yen 4 urge, whim
to excess: 4 cloy, glut, sate 5 gorge, stuff 7 surfeit 8 overfill 10 gormandize
indulgence: 4 orgy 5 favor, leave 6 excess, lenity, luxury 7 babying, freedom, license 8 coddling, courtesy, favoring, hedonism, humoring, kindness, latitude, lenience, leniency, patience, spoiling 9 allowance, attention, endurance, enjoyment, pampering, privilege, satiation, tolerance 10 concession, debauchery, partiality, profligacy, sybaritism, toleration
brief ~: 5 binge, fling, spree
indulgent: 3 lax 4 easy, kind, mild, soft 5 loose 6 doting, gentle, kindly 7 clement, lenient, liberal, ruthful, sparing 8 flexible, gracious, laid-back, merciful, parental, placable, tolerant 9 assuasive, compliant, dissolute, easygoing, excessive, favorable, forgiving, luxurious 10 charitable, forbearing, gratifying, permissive, unexacting, unhardened, voluptuous
be ~: 4 baby, dote 5 cater, spoil 6 coddle
indurate: 3 set 4 bony, cold, gird, hale, hard, iron, tone, wiry 5 beefy, boney, build, burly, enure, hardy, hefty, hunky, husky, inure, lusty, rigid, rocky, shore, steel, stony, stout, tough, train 6 anneal, beef up, brawny, flinty, frigid, gritty, harden, hearty, mighty, ossify, potent, prop up, robust, rugged, season, sinewy, steely, stocky, stoney, strong, sturdy, temper, tone up, virile 7 bolster, brace up, build up, burgeon, calcify, callous, develop, doughty, empower, enhance, fortify, hard-set, petrify, shore up, stiffen, toughen, vitrify 8 accustom, athletic, bourgeon, buttress, concrete, energize, forceful, granitic, hardened, muscular, obdurate, powerful, puissant, recusant, stalwart, stubborn, vigorous, vitalize 9 acclimate, Atlantean, condition, fossilize, habituate, Herculean, intensify, obstinate, reinforce, strapping, unfeeling, vulcanize, well-built 10 able-bodied, adamantine, caseharden, hard-bitten, impenitent, invigorate, red-blooded, strengthen
Indus: 5 river 6 valley
city on the ~: 7 Karachi
constellation near ~: 4 Grus
locale: 5 Tibet 6 Thibet, Xizang 7 Kashmir, Sitsang 8 Cashmere, Pakistan
river to the ~: 5 Kabul 6 Sutlej
industrial: 8 economic 9 automated, technical 10 mechanical, mechanized, vocational
industrial __: 4 arts, park 5 store, union 6 design, estate, school
industrialist: 3 mfr. 4 boss, czar 5 baron, mogul 6 tycoon 7 builder, magnate 8 producer
industrious: 4 busy 5 eager 6 active, intent, lively 7 dynamic, earnest, on the go, operose, zealous 8 diligent, sedulous, spirited, studious, tireless 9 assiduous, laborious, motivated
be ~: 4 work 8 plug away
insect: 3 ant, bee
name meaning ~: 5 Emily 6 Amelia
industry: 3 job, mfg. 4 care, toil, work, zeal 5 labor, trade, vigor 6 action, effort, energy 8 activity, business, commerce, exertion, gumption, hard work 9 assiduity, diligence 10 enterprise
captain of ~: 3 CEO 4 czar, exec 5 baron, mogul 6 tycoon 7 magnate 9 executive
watchdog org.: 4 OSHA
__ industry: 7 cottage, primary
Industry is its motto: 4 Utah
indweller: 6 native 7 citizen, denizen 8 resident 10 inhabitant
indwelling: 9 ingrained, intrinsic 10 congenital, connatural
Indy: 4 race 8 auto race
sound: 5 vroom 6 varoom
trouble: 5 crash
Indy 500: 4 race
sound: 5 vroom 6 varoom
...in earth, __ is in heaven: 4 as it
inebriant: 4 beer 5 booze, drink, sauce, stock 6 liquor 7 alcohol, liqueur, potable 9 alcoholic, aqua vitae, firewater, hard stuff, moonshine 10 intoxicant
inebriate: 3 sot 4 stew 5 addle, besot, charm, crock, elate, souse, stone 6 fuddle, muddle, pickle, thrill 7 animate, bewitch, enchant, pollute, stupefy 8 befuddle, enspirit, entrance, inspirit
inebriated: 3 lit 5 drunk, tight, tipsy 9 irrigated, plastered
inebriating: 4 hard 6 strong 9 alcoholic, spiritous
inedible: 3 bad 4 sour 5 fetid, moldy, yucky, yukky 6 foetid, putrid, rotten, spoilt, turned 7 spoiled, tainted 9 uneatable 10 disgusting
mouthful: 3 gum 10 chewing gum
inee: 6 curara, curare, poison
I Need Love singer: LL Cool J
I Need You (1972 song) artist: America
I Need You Now (1954 song) artist: Eddie Fisher
I Need Your Love Tonight (1959 song) artist: Elvis Presley
ineffable: 6 divine 8 empyreal, empyrean, ethereal, heavenly 9 celestial, spiritual 10 delightful, incredible, untellable
ineffective: 4 idle, lame, vain, weak 5 inept, unfit 6 feeble, futile, in vain, otiose, paltry 7 inutile, useless 8 feckless, nugatory 9 spineless, worthless 10 unavailing
ineffectual: 3 wan 4 idle, lame, puny, vain, weak 5 empty, inept, mousy, small 6 feeble, futile, little, mousey, paltry, unable 7 inutile, limited, useless 8 feckless, nugatory 9 pointless, powerless, spineless, worthless 10 wishy-washy
make ~: 6 defang, hogtie, weaken
one: 3 oaf 4 boob, clod, nerd, nurd, wimp 5 dweeb, klutz 7 nebbish
inefficacious: 4 idle, lame, vain, weak 5 inept 6 feeble, futile, in vain, unable 7 inutile, useless 8 bootless 9 for naught, to no avail
inefficacy: 6 defect 7 failing 8 drawback 9 inability 10 faultiness, inadequacy
inefficient: 4 lame 5 inept 6 faulty, sloppy, unable 8 careless, slipshod, wasteful 9 illogical
be ~: 3 err 4 flub, goof 6 bungle, foul up, goof up, mess up 9 mishandle, mismanage
__ in Egypt: 6 Israel
inelaborate: 5 plain 6 humble, modest, simple, slight 7 limited 9 unadorned
inelastic: 4 firm, iron 5 rigid 6 steely 9 unbending 10 inflexible
inelegant: 5 crass, crude, gross, rough, tacky 6 clumsy, coarse, gauche, vulgar 7 awkward, boorish, unadept, uncouth 8 bungling, homemade, improper, unseemly 9 graceless, makeshift, primitive, tasteless, unrefined 10 amateurish, indelicate, uncultured, ungraceful, unpolished
ineligible: 5 unfit 8 unworthy 10 unequipped, unsuitable
ineluctable: 7 crucial 8 required 9 essential, necessary 10 imperative, obligatory
inept: 3 bad 4 weak 5 dorky, nerdy, unfit 6 clumsy, gauche, klutzy, unable, unwise 7 artless, awkward, labored, unadept, unhandy, useless 8 bumbling, bungling, cloddish, feckless, fumbling, hopeless, inexpert, lubberly, tactless, ungainly 9 all thumbs, graceless, maladroit, unskilled 10 amateurish, unbecoming, undextrous, unskillful
one: 3 oaf 4 boob, clod, nerd, nurd, yo-yo 5 dweeb 7 nebbish
inequality: 9 disparity, diversity, imbalance, injustice, prejudice, variation 10 difference, unevenness, unfairness, unjustness
inequitable: 6 unfair, unjust 7 unequal
inequity: 5 abuse, wrong 6 injury 8 foul play, nepotism 9 grievance, injustice 10 favoritism, unfairness
inerasable: 7 lasting 8 enduring 9 indelible, ingrained, permanent
inerrant: 4 sure 5 exact 7 certain 8 absolute, accurate, fail-safe, flawless, reliable 9 faultless, foolproof 10 dependable, impeccable, infallible
inert: 3 lax 4 idle, lazy, logy, numb, slow 5 quiet, slack, still 6 asleep, draggy, frozen, latent, leaden, static, stolid, torpid 7 dormant, languid, out cold, passive 8 immobile, inactive, indolent, lifeless, listless, slothful, sluggish, stagnant, unmoving 9 impassive, inanimate, insensate, lethargic, not moving, quiescent, sedentary 10 disengaged, insentient, motionless, stationary, stock-still, unreactive
be ~: 4 idle, laze, loaf 5 sleep 8 languish, stagnate, vegetate
gas: 4 neon 5 argon, radon, xenon 6 helium 7 krypton
material: 6 filler
inertia: 5 sloth 6 acedia, apathy, stupor, torpor 7 languor, laxness 8 doldrums, idleness, laziness, lethargy, otiosity, slowness 9 faineance, indolence, torpidity 10 inactivity, stagnation
inertial __: 4 mass 6 system
inertness: 5 sloth 6 apathy, torpor 7 languor 8 dullness, inaction, lethargy 9 indolence, torpidity 10 inactivity
inerudite: 9 unlearned 10 illiterate, uncultured, uneducated, unschooled
inescapable: 4 sure 5 fated 7 certain, visible 8 destined 9 necessary, pervasive
Ines in English: 5 Agnes
in esse: 8 actually
inessential: 5 extra 7 surplus 8 needless 9 redundant
inestimable: 4 rare, vast 6 untold 7 endless, immense 8 infinite, manifold, peerless, precious, valuable 9 priceless
I never __ man...: 4 met a
I never __ purple cow: 4 saw a
I Never Loved a Man (1967 song) artist: Aretha Franklin
I Never Promised You a Rose Garden (1977 film)
cast: Bibi Andersson, Kathleen Quinlan
director: Anthony Page
I Never Sang for My Father: 4 film, play
author: Robert Anderson
cast: Melvyn Douglas, Gene Hackman
director: Gilbert Cates
I never saw __: 5 a moor
__ in Every Port: 5 A Girl

inevitable: 4 sure 5 fated 6 doomed 7 assured, certain, decided, decreed, settled 8 destined, eventual, in the bag, ordained 9 automatic, impending, necessary 10 compulsory, determined, for certain, inexorable, obligatory, prescribed, undeniable, undoubtful
the ~: 4 fate 5 karma 6 kismet 7 destiny
inevitably: 6 always, surely 7 for sure 9 certainly, decidedly 10 definitely, for certain, inexorably, invariably, positively
inexact: 3 lax, off 5 false, rough, wrong 6 faulty, untrue 7 general, in error, offbase, unsound 8 specious 9 erroneous, imperfect, imprecise, incorrect 10 fallacious, inaccurate, indefinite, unspecific
be ~: 3 fib, lie 5 fudge 7 deceive
phrase: 4 or so
in excelsis __: 3 deo
inexcusable: 3 bad, low 5 cruel, wrong 6 unfair, unjust 7 immoral 8 criminal, grievous, improper 9 dishonest, unethical 10 unsporting
inexhaustible: 7 endless, lasting 8 enduring, infinite, tireless, untiring 9 limitless, plentiful, unfailing
inexorable: 4 sure 5 cruel, harsh, rigid, stern, stiff, stony 6 severe, stoney 7 adamant, dead set 8 destined, immobile, ironclad, obdurate, pitiless, resolute, stubborn 9 immovable, merciless, necessary, obstinate, unbending, unmovable, unpitying 10 adamantine, compulsory, implacable, inevitable, inflexible, relentless, set in stone, unyielding
inexpedient: 4 dumb 6 stupid, unwise 7 foolish, harmful 8 untimely 9 misguided 10 ill-advised
inexpensive: 3 low 5 cheap 6 budget, low-end, modest 7 bargain, cut-rate, low-cost, nominal 8 moderate 9 dirtcheap, low-priced 10 affordable, dime a dozen, economical, reasonable
in French: 9 bon marché
inexperience: 5 youth 7 naiveté 9 greenness, ignorance, innocence
inexperienced: 3 new, raw 4 naif 5 fresh, green, inapt, inept, naive, unfit, young 6 boyish, callow, simple 7 amateur, puerile, untried, verdant 8 ignorant, immature, inexpert, innocent, unversed, youthful 9 beardless, untrained, unworldly
one: 3 pup 4 naif, tiro, tyro 5 puppy 8 untested
with: 5 new at
inexpert: 3 lay 5 crude, green, inept, unfit 6 clumsy, simple 7 awkward, unadept, unhandy 8 bumbling, bungling, fumbling 9 maladroit, unskilled, untrained, untutored 10 amateurish, blundering, left-handed, unschooled, unseasoned, unskillful
inexpiable: 3 bad 4 evil, vile 5 awful, black, grave 6 mortal, sinful, wicked 7 capital, heinous, serious
inexplicable: 3 odd 5 eerie, vague, weird 6 spooky 7 strange, uncanny 8 baffling, peculiar, puzzling
inexplicit: 4 hazy 5 fuzzy, vague 7 evasive 9 ambiguous, deceptive, enigmatic, equivocal, imprecise, uncertain 10 ill-defined, indefinite, indistinct, misleading
inexpressible: 6 silent, untold 7 amazing, strange 8 wondrous
inexpressive: 4 cold, dead, dull, flat 5 blank, stony 6 boring, stoney 7 deadpan, passive, unmoved 8 lifeless
inextinguishable: 7 endless, eternal, lasting, undying 8 immortal, timeless, unending 9 ceaseless, incessant, perennial, permanent, perpetual, unceasing
inextricable: 6 knotty 7 complex, tangled 8 baffling, involved, puzzling
Inez: 4 Foxx
in English: 5 Agnes
infallible: 4 sure, true 5 exact, right 7 certain, perfect 8 absolute, accurate, fail-safe, flawless, inerrant, reliable, surefire, unerring 9 agreeable, apodictic, effective, effectual, faultless, foolproof, unfailing 10 acceptable, dependable, impeccable, omniscient, unbeatable, undoubtful
infamous: 3 bad 4 dark, evil, foul, vile 5 shady 6 odious, rotten, wicked 7 corrupt, hateful, heinous, ignoble, vicious 8 ill-famed, shameful, shocking 9 miscreant, monstrous, nefarious, notorious, well-known 10 outrageous, villainous
infamy: 4 evil 5 guilt, odium, shame 7 obloquy, scandal 8 atrocity, contempt, disgrace, dishonor, ignominy, iniquity, villainy 9 disrepute, ill repute, notoriety 10 corruption, opprobrium, wickedness
__ Infamy: 5 Day of
infancy: 4 dawn, rise 5 birth, start 6 cradle 7 arising, genesis 8 babyhood, nascence 9 beginning, childhood, emergence 10 beginnings, conception
infant: 3 kid, tot 4 babe, baby 5 bairn, child, minor, young 6 little, rug rat, wee one 7 babyish, bambino, nascent, neonate, newborn, puerile, toddler, young 'un 8 childish, juvenile, nonvoter, original, youthful 9 little one
abandoned ~: 4 waif 9 foundling
attention-getter: 3 cry, wah 4 bawl
bed: 4 crib 6 cradle 8 bassinet
fare: 4 milk 7 formula 8 baby food
name meaning ~: 6 Thelma
sound: 3 goo 6 goo-goo, gurgle
tend to an ~: 4 burp, feed 7 baby-sit
upset: 5 colic
wear: 6 bonnet, bootee, bootie, diaper
word: 3 mom 4 dada, mama 5 mamma
infantile: 7 babyish, kiddish, puerile 8 childish, immature, juvenile
infantry: 3 GIs 4 army 6 grunts 8 dogfaces, soldiers
action: 4 fray 6 attack, battle, charge, combat 7 warfare 8 fighting, skirmish 9 encounter 10 engagement
fare: 4 Spam 7 rations
Greek ~: 6 evzone
weapon: 5 rifle 7 bayonet
infantryman: 2 GI 5 GI Joe, grunt 7 dogface, soldier
infatuate: 5 besot, charm, lover 6 allure, enamor, obsess 7 beguile, bewitch, enthral, inthral 8 enthrall, inthrall, stultify 9 captivate, fascinate
infatuated: 3 mad 4 gaga 5 crazy 6 in love, loving 7 charmed, far gone, smitten 8 beguiled, besotted, obsessed 9 bewitched, possessed 10 captivated, enraptured, enthralled, fascinated, spellbound
by: 6 mad for 8 mad about 9 far gone on 10 crazy about
infatuation: 4 love, rage 5 craze, crush, furor, mania 7 passion 8 fixation 9 obsession
Infatuation (1984 song) artist: Rod Stewart
infeasible: 7 dubious 8 doubtful, hopeless, undoable, unlikely 10 impossible, out of reach
infect: 5 spoil, taint 6 blight, defile, poison 7 corrupt, make ill, pollute, vitiate
infected: 3 ill 4 sick 5 dirty, germy 7 corrupt 10 unsanitary
become ~ with: 3 get 5 catch 7 develop 8 contract
infection: 3 bug 6 plague, poison 7 disease 8 epidemic, impurity 9 contagion
cause: 4 germ 5 staph, strep, virus
type of ~: 5 viral
infectious: 5 viral 8 catching, epidemic, virulent 9 pestilent, spreading 10 contagious, epidemical, inoculable
organism: 3 bug 4 germ 7 microbe
infelicitous: 3 sad 4 poor 5 bleak, inapt, woful 6 gauche, gloomy, pained, woeful 7 awkward, forlorn, hapless, unhappy, unlucky 8 desolate, hopeless, ill-timed, improper, pitiable, sinister, wretched
infelicity: 3 woe 5 gloom 6 misery, sorrow, trials 7 bad luck, chagrin, despair, sadness, travail 8 hardship, troubles
infelt: 5 frank 6 candid 7 earnest, genuine, sincere 8 truthful 9 guileless, unfeigned 10 forthright, on the level
infer: 4 draw, hint 5 educe, glean, guess, judge, think 6 assume, deduce, derive, gather, intuit, reason, reckon, take it 7 imagine, make out, mention, presume, suggest, suppose, surmise 8 arrive at, conclude, construe, intimate 9 ascertain, interpret, reason out, speculate 10 conjecture, presuppose, understand
ender: 4 ence 6 ential
inferable: 6 likely 9 deducible, derivable 10 consequent
inference: 5 logic 6 reason 7 surmise, thought 8 allusion, overtone 9 corollary, deduction, induction 10 assumption, conclusion, conjecture
inferential: 6 cogent 7 a priori, logical, tenable 8 analytic, methodic, rational 9 deductive 10 methodical
inferior: 3 bad, low, off 4 foul, grim, hack, junk, less, mean, poor, punk 5 awful, below, cheap, lousy, lower, lowly, minor, scrub, small, sorry, under, woful, worse 6 cheapo, cheesy, common, crumby, crummy, dismal, horrid, humble, lesser, odious, rotten, second, shoddy, two-bit, woeful 7 accurst, baleful, baneful, beastly, doleful, ghastly, ignoble, subject, wanting 8 accursed, déclassé, dreadful, el cheapo, God-awful, grievous, horrible, low-grade, mediocre, middling, ordinary, shameful, stinking, terrible, wretched 9 abhorrent, appalling, atrocious, defective, deficient, execrable, fifth-rate, frightful, insidious, loathsome, miserable, offensive, revolting, secondary, third-rate 10 abominable, despicable, detestable, disastrous, fifth-class, fourth-rate, horrendous, low-quality, second-rate, third-class
of ~ quality: 4 junk 5 cheap 7 schlock
product: 3 dog 4 junk 5 trash, tripe 7 schlock
to: 5 below, under 7 beneath 10 unworthy of
treat as ~: 5 deign, stoop 6 demean 7 stoop to 9 patronize 10 condescend, look down on, talk down to
inferiority complex coiner: 5 Adler
infernal: 4 dark, evil 5 curst, stark 6 cursed, cussed, damned, nether, savage, wicked 7 accurst, blasted, demonic, hellish, satanic 8 accursed, daemonic, damnable, devilish, diabolic, fiendish 9 demonical, execrable, monstrous, nefarious, satanical 10 diabolical, malevolent
inferno: 4 fire, hell, pyre 5 Hades 10 underworld
Inferno, The: 4 poem 5 verse
division: 5 canto
starter: 3 nel
writer: 5 Dante
inferred: 5 tacit 6 subtle, unsaid 7 implied 8 unvoiced 10 derivative, understood
infertile: 3 dry 4 sere 6 barren, desert, effete 7 sterile 8 infecund 9 exhausted, fruitless 10 unfruitful
infest: 6 abound, invade, riddle 7 overrun, pervade 10 run through
infestation: 6 blight
infested: 4 rife 5 mothy 7 overrun, profuse, rampant, replete, teeming 8 abundant, swarming 9 abounding, pervasive, prevalent
infidel: 5 pagan 7 atheist, heathen, heretic, sceptic, skeptic 8 agnostic 10 unbeliever
infidelity: 7 falsity 9 duplicity, falseness, treachery, two-timing 10 dishonesty, disloyalty, untrueness
infield
corner: 4 base, home
covering: 4 tarp
hit: 4 bunt 5 bloop
stat: 2 DP 6 assist, putout
infield __: 3 hit, out 6 single
infield __ rule: 3 fly
infielder fluff: 5 error 6 bobble
infiltrate: 3 mix 4 soak 5 crack, enter, tinge 7 creep in, get into, sneak in 8 move into, pass into, permeate, worm into 9 insinuate, interject, penetrate, percolate 10 adulterate
infiltration: 4 raid 5 foray 6 attack, breach 7 assault, osmosis, transit 8 invasion, trespass 9 onslaught
infiltrator: 3 spy 4 mole 5 agent
in fine __: 4 form 6 fettle 7 feather
infinite: 3 big 4 vast 5 great 6 cosmic, eonian, myriad, untold 7 endless, eternal, undying 8 absolute, almighty, cosmical, spacious, unending 9 boundless, countless, limitless, perpetual, unbounded, unlimited 10 innumerous, unnumbered, without end
infinite __: 6 baffle, series 7 decimal, product, regress
Infinite Plan, The author: Isabel Allende
infinitesimal: 3 wee 4 puny, tiny 5 bitty, small, teeny 6 atomic, little, minute, teensy 8 atomical, atomlike 9 itsy-bitsy, itty-bitty 10 teeny-weeny
Infiniti: 3 car 4 auto 6 import
alternative: 4 Audi 5 Lexus
infinitive __: 6 clause, phrase
__ infinitive: 5 split
infinitude: 8 enormity, hugeness, vastness 9 immensity
infinitum, ad: 5 no end 7 forever
infinity: 4 time 5 space 9 immensity, largeness, multitude
infirm: 3 ill 4 puny, sick, weak 5 anile, frail, shaky, slack 6 ailing, anemic, feeble, laid up, sickly, unwell, wabbly, wobbly 7 anaemic, invalid, languid, rickety, unsound 8 unsteady 9 afflicted, bedridden, doddering, enfeebled, faltering, powerless, unhealthy 10 indisposed
infirmary: 6 clinic 7 hospice, sick bay 8 hospital
infirmity: 3 ill 6 malady, unease 7 ailment, disease, frailty, illness, malaise

8 debility, disorder, sickness, syndrome, weakness 9 complaint, condition, fragility, frailness, ill health 10 affliction, disability, feebleness, sickliness, unwellness
__-in, first-out: 4 last 5 first
infix: 5 embed, imbed, imbue, lodge, rivet 6 fasten, infuse, inject, insert, instil 7 drive in, engrain, engrave, implant, impress, imprint, ingrain, instill 9 inculcate
in flagrante __: 7 delicto
inflame: 3 vex 4 fire, gall, rile, roil, stir 5 anger, annoy, chafe, grate, hop up, light, rouse, steam 6 arouse, enrage, excite, fire up, foment, ignite, incite, kindle, madden, rankle, whip up, work up 7 agitate, ferment, incense, inspire, provoke, steam up 8 enspirit, inspirit, irritate 9 aggravate, impassion, infuriate, instigate, stimulate 10 exacerbate, exasperate, intoxicate
inflamed: 3 hot, mad, red 4 ired, sore 5 angry, cross, huffy, irate, livid, puffy, riled, wroth 6 fuming, ireful, raging, raving, red-hot, tender 7 angered, enraged, furious, painful, ranting, swollen, violent 8 choleric, inspired, vehement, volcanic, white-hot, wrathful 9 indignant, irritated, resentful, splenetic 10 freaked out, infuriated, passionate
inflamer: 7 fanatic, hellion, hothead, inciter 8 agitator, fomenter 9 demagogue, firebrand 10 incendiary, instigator, politician
__ in flames: 4 go up
inflammation: 4 pain, rash 6 pimple 7 redness 8 swelling
joint ~: 4 gout 9 arthritis
(suffix): 4 -itis
inflate: 3 pad 4 fill, grow, puff, pump 5 bloat, boost, exalt, raise, swell, widen 6 aerate, beef up, blow up, dilate, expand, puff up, pump up 7 amplify, augment, balloon, broaden, build up, burgeon, distend, enlarge, magnify, puff out, stiffen, stretch, swell up 8 bourgeon, flesh out, heighten, increase, lengthen 9 intumesce, overstate 10 aggrandize, exaggerate
inflated: 3 big 4 vain 5 puffy, tumid, windy, wordy 6 prolix, turgid 7 fustian, hyped up, pompous, stilted, swollen, unterse, verbose 9 bombastic, high-flown, overblown 10 rhetorical
feeling: 3 ego 6 egoism 7 egotism
inflater: 4 pump
inflation: 4 hike, rise 7 buildup 8 increase, swelling 9 euphemism, expansion, extension, puffiness, recession 10 depression, distension, escalation, floridness
meas.: 3 CPI, psi
protection: 5 hedge
inflationary __: 6 spiral
inflect: 4 vary 5 alter 6 change, intone, modify 7 decline 8 modulate, vocalize 9 conjugate
inflection: 4 tone 5 pitch, voice 6 accent, timbre 8 delivery, locution, tonality 9 variation 10 intonation, modulation
inflexibility: 5 rigor 6 starch 8 firmness, tautness, tenacity 9 toughness
inflexible: 3 set 4 firm, hard, iron, taut 5 balky, bossy, cruel, fixed, onery, picky, rigid, stern, stiff, stony, tight, tough 6 dogged, flinty, mulish, narrow, ornery, severe, steely, stoney, strict, wilful, wooden 7 adamant, austere, decided, diehard, hard-set, piggish, precise, Spartan, starchy, staunch, willful 8 contrary, despotic, exacting, hard-line, ironclad, obdurate, perverse, resolute, rigorous, starched, straight, stubborn 9 demanding, draconian, hidebound, immovable, immutable, impliable, inelastic, iron-jawed, obstinate, pigheaded, steadfast, stringent, tenacious, unbending, unpliable, unsparing 10 adamantine, despotical, determined, hard-bitten, implacable, inexorable, intolerant, invariable, iron-fisted, iron-willed, nononsense, oppressive, relentless, tyrannical, unswayable, unyielding
inflict: 3 put 4 deal 5 apply, exact, force, visit, wreak 6 impose 7 deal out, deliver, mete out, subject 8 dispense 9 force upon 10 administer
infliction: 4 load 5 curse, worry 6 burden, ordeal 7 nemesis, penalty, scourge, torment, torture, trouble 8 disaster
inflictive: 5 penal 8 punitive
in-flight
announcement: 3 ETA 8 altitude
offering: 4 meal 5 drink, movie
inflorescence: 3 bud 5 bloom 6 floret, flower 7 blossom
inflow: 5 draft 6 afflux, feeder, influx 9 tributary
influence: 3 get 4 bend, bias, coax, drag, hold, lead, mold, move, pull, push, rule, sell, snow, sway, tint, turn, urge 5 act on, alter, bribe, budge, clout, force, get at, get to, guide, impel, juice, lobby, orbit, power, reach, reign, rouse, shape, slant, steer, swing, tempt 6 access, affect, agency, compel, credit, direct, effect, entrée, grow on, impact, incite, induce, manage, muscle, weight 7 act upon, channel, command, control, implant, impress, inspire, potence, potency, promote, squeeze, win over 8 dominion, grow upon, guidance, impact on, jaundice, leverage, override, overrule, persuade, pressure, prestige, purchase 9 advantage, argue into, authority, brainwash, determine, direction, dominance, instigate, magnetism, prejudice, prevail on, supremacy 10 ascendance, ascendancy, ascendence, ascendency, domination, importance, impression, leadership, manipulate, predispose, prominence, reputation
have ~: 4 rank, rate 5 count 6 matter
improperly: 5 bribe, get to
pervading ~: 4 aura 10 atmosphere
sphere of ~: 4 area 5 ambit, orbit, range 6 domain 8 dominion
try to ~: 4 coax, urge 5 lobby, press 6 lean on 8 pressure
under the ~: 3 lit 4 high 5 tight, tipsy
influential: 3 big 4 high 5 major 6 cogent, famous, moving, potent, strong 7 guiding, telling, weighty 8 dominant, powerful 9 important
one: 3 VIP 5 mover, nabob
people: 5 elite
influenza: 3 bug, flu 5 virus 6 grippe
influx: 4 flow, rush, wave 5 surge 6 inflow, stream 7 arrival, ingress, traffic 8 entrance, invasion 9 inpouring, intrusion, upwelling 10 inundation
info: 3 tip 4 data, dirt, dope, line, news, poop 5 facts, scoop 6 advice, earful, gossip, notice, report, skinny, wisdom 7 lowdown, message, tidings 8 learning, the goods 9 erudition, knowledge
info-gathering
mission: 5 recon
org.: 3 CIA, FBI
infomercial: 2 ad 5 promo
phrase: 5 try it 6 act now 7 call now
in for __ awakening: 5 a rude
inform: 3 say 4 post, sing, talk, tell, warn 5 alert, break, brief, cue in, edify, prime, spill, teach 6 advise, clue in, direct, fill in, ground, impart, notify, report, school, tip off, update 7 apprise, apprize, caution, counsel, educate, let in on, let know 8 acquaint, advise of, forewarn, instruct, relate to 9 enlighten, irradiate, touch base 10 illuminate, send word to
on: 3 rat 6 betray, finger, give up, squeal, turn in
informal: 4 cool, easy, free, homy 5 homey, loose, plain 6 breezy, casual, chatty, colloq., folksy, mellow, simple, slangy 7 natural, outdoor, relaxed, unfussy 8 down home, everyday, familiar, fireside, intimate, laid back, outgoing 9 easygoing, extempore, idiomatic 10 colloquial, off-the-cuff, unofficial
usage: 4 cant 5 argot, lingo 6 jargon, patois, pidgin 7 dialect 10 street talk, vernacular
informality: 4 ease 10 simplicity
informally: 5 ad-lib 9 extempore, on the side 10 off the cuff
informant: 3 rat 5 namer 6 canary, snitch, source, tattle 7 accuser, monitor, stoolie, tattler, tipster 8 betrayer 10 taleteller
information: 3 tip 4 data, dirt, dope, line, lore, news, word 5 facts, light, proof, scoop, thing 6 advice, earful, notice, report, tipoff, wisdom 7 lowdown, message, pointer, tidings 8 evidence, learning, material 9 testimony 10 literature
acquire ~: 4 read 5 glean, learn, study 6 absorb, pick up 7 find out
agency: 6 bureau
bit of ~: 3 tip 4 fact 5 datum
conductor: 5 nerve
digital ~ carrier: 7 databus
extract ~: 4 milk 7 debrief
give ~: 3 tip 5 brief 6 clue in, tip off
give wrong ~: 3 fib, lie 7 cover up, deceive, mislead 8 misguide, misstate 9 misdirect, misinform 10 lead astray
inside ~: 3 tip 4 dope 6 tipoff
seek ~: 3 ask 5 refer 7 enquire, inquire
seeker: 5 asker
share ~ with: 5 let in
source: 3 Net, Web 4 oper. 5 CD/ROM 7 library 8 Internet, operator 9 reference 10 dictionary
store ~: 4 file 5 enter 6 record 7 archive, catalog, put away 8 document, preserve, tabulate
unit: 3 bit 4 byte 8 gigabyte, megabyte
information __: 6 theory 7 science
Information __: 3 Age 6 Please 7 Society
Information, __!: 6 Please
informational meeting: 5 Q and A
Information, Please!: 9 radio show
Information, The author: 4 Amis
informative: 5 newsy 6 chatty, social, useful 7 gossipy, helpful 10 newsworthy
informed: 3 hep, hip 4 onto, wise 5 aware, privy, savvy 6 au fait, posted, versed, wise to, with it 7 abreast, knowing, mindful, tuned in, versant 8 familiar, profound, sensible 9 au courant, cognizant, in the know, in the loop, judicious, plugged in 10 conversant
about: 4 up on 5 hep to, hip to
be ~ of: 4 hear, know 5 learn
stay ~: 6 keep up
informer: 3 rat, spy 4 fink, nark 5 namer, sneak 6 canary, tattle 7 accuser, stoolie, tattler, tipster, traitor 8 betrayer, fat mouth 10 taleteller, tattletale
British ~: 4 nark
turn ~: 4 sing 5 rat on, spill 6 betray, expose, fink on, give up, squeal 7 sell out 8 give away
Informer, The (1935 film)
cast: Heather Angel, Preston Foster, Victor McLaglen
director: John Ford
Informer, The author: Liam O'Flaherty
infra: 5 below, under 7 beneath 8 less than 10 underneath
opposite: 5 ultra
infra __: 3 dig
infract: 3 err, sin 5 break, lapse 6 breach 7 disobey, violate 9 go against 10 contravene, transgress
infraction: 3 sin 4 foul, slip 5 crime, error, lapse, wrong 6 breach 7 faux pas, offense 8 breaking, trespass 9 injustice, veniality, violation 10 illegality
in baseball: 4 balk
in basketball: 4 foul 7 palming
in bowling: 4 foul
in football: 7 holding, offside 8 clipping
in ice hockey: 5 icing
infrangible: 4 holy 6 divine, sacred 7 blessed 8 hallowed 9 enshrined 10 sanctified
infrared
light: 4 lamp
radiation: 4 heat
infrared __: 4 star 6 galaxy
infrastructure: 4 base, root 5 basis, cadre 7 footing, support
infrequency: 6 rarity 7 fewness 8 rareness, scarcity 10 sparseness
infrequent: 3 few, occ. 4 rare 5 occas. 6 casual, meager, scarce, seldom, sparse 7 limited, several, unusual 8 far apart, isolated, sporadic, uncommon 9 irregular, scattered, spasmodic 10 occasional, sporadical
infrequently: 6 hardly, little, rarely, seldom 8 scarcely 10 hardly ever
infringe: 5 break 6 invade, meddle 7 presume, trample, violate 8 trespass 9 interrupt
on: 5 poach, usurp 6 butt in 8 displace 10 dispossess, plagiarize
infringement: 4 raid 5 drive, foray, sally 6 breach, inroad, sortie 7 evasion, ingress, misdeed, outrage, seizure 8 inequity, invasion, trespass 9 violation
__ in front!: 4 Down
in front combining form: 5 proso- 6 antero-
in full __: 5 swing
__ in full: 4 paid
infuriate: 3 ire 4 rile 5 anger 6 enrage, madden, tee off 7 enflame, incense, inflame, outrage, provoke 8 irritate 9 aggravate 10 exacerbate, exasperate
infuriated: 3 hot, mad 4 ired, sore 5 angry, cross, huffy, irate, livid, rabid, riled, upset, wroth 6 crazed, fuming, heated, ireful, raging, raving, red-hot, savage 7 enraged, flaming, frantic, furious, ranting, steamed, violent 8 agitated, choleric, frenzied, in a tizzy, incensed, inflamed, storming, white-hot, wild-eyed, wrathful 9 indignant, resentful, splenetic 10 freaked out

be ~: 4 boil, fume, rage, rave 5 steam 6 blow up, rear up, see red, seethe 7 bristle, flare up 10 get excited
infuriating: 5 pesky, pesty 7 irksome 9 vexatious 10 bothersome, nettlesome
infuriation: 3 ire 4 rage 5 anger, pique 6 choler 7 dudgeon, outrage 8 rabidity, vexation 9 petulance
infuse: 3 mix 4 brew, lade, load, soak 5 color, imbue, infix, steep 6 embrue, flavor, imbrue, impart, instil, invest 7 animate, breathe, engrain, implant, ingrain, inspire, instill, pervade 8 permeate, saturate 9 inculcate, inoculate, insinuate, introduce
infusion: 3 dip 4 bath, brew, soak 5 stain, tinge 6 flavor, liquor 8 coloring, steeping, tincture 9 immersion, injection 10 permeation, submersion
__ in G: 6 Minuet
Inga: 7 Swenson
Ingalls: 5 Laura
ingathering: 5 cache 7 harvest
__ in Gaza: 7 Eyeless
Inge: 6 Morath 7 William
Ingels, Marty spouse: Shirley Jones
ingenious: 3 apt, sly 4 deft, neat 5 canny, fresh, nifty, novel, sharp, slick, smart 6 adroit, artful, astute, brainy, bright, clever, crafty, daedal, gifted, habile, shifty, shrewd, subtle 7 cunning, knowing, unusual 8 artistic, creative, dextrous, inspired, original, readable, skillful, talented 9 astucious, brilliant, deviceful, dexterous, inventive 10 artistical, discerning, expressive, innovative, innovatory
ingénue: 4 naif, role 6 player 7 actress
like an ~: 4 naif 5 naïve 6 demure
ingenuity: 3 art, wit 4 wits 5 craft, flair, skill 6 acumen, brains, talent 7 ability 8 gumption, judgment, resource 9 dexterity, smartness 10 cleverness
__ ingenuity: 6 Yankee
ingenuous: 4 naif, open 5 frank, green, naive, plain 6 candid, honest, simple, square 7 artless, natural, sincere, unjaded, up-front 8 innocent, trustful, trusting, truthful, unartful 9 childlike, guileless, outspoken, unguarded, unstudied, unworldly 10 free-spoken, unaffected, unreserved, unschooled
ingenuousness: 7 naiveté 9 greenness
Inger: 7 Stevens
Ingersoll-__: 4 Rand
ingest: 3 eat 4 down, take 5 drink, sop up 6 absorb, devour, digest, gather, imbibe, osmose, soak up, suck up 7 consume, partake, scarf up, swallow 8 chow down, gulp down, pack away 9 scarf down 10 assimilate
opposite: 5 egest
Inge, William: 6 author, writer 9 dramatist 10 playwright
dog: 5 Sheba
nickname: The Gloomy Dean
work: Bus Stop
Christian Mysticism
Come Back, Little Sheba
The Dark at the Top of the Stairs
Good Luck, Miss Wyckoff
The Last Pad
A Loss of Roses
Picnic
Splendor in the Grass
Summer Brave
Where's Daddy?
ingle: 6 hearth 8 fireside 9 fireplace
ender: 4 nook
__ inglese: 5 zuppa
Inglewood: 4 city, town
locale: 10 California, Washington
inglorious: 5 shady 6 humble, shoddy 7 ignoble 8 shameful, unworthy
ingloriousness: 5 odium, shame 6 infamy, malice 7 lowness, treason 8 disgrace, dishonor, vileness
__ in glove: 4 hand
Ingmar: 7 Bergman
collaborator: 4 Sven
protégé: 3 Liv
-ing, noun ending in: 6 gerund
In God We __: 5 Trust
in good __: 4 part, time 7 feather
in good faith in Latin: 8 bona fide
__ in good health!: 5 Use it
__ in good stead: 5 stand
__ in good time: 3 all
ingot: 3 bar 4 slab 5 block, metal
ingrain: 3 fix 4 etch 5 embed, imbed, imbue, inbue, infix, lodge, rivet, steep, teach, train 6 infuse, inject, instil 7 implant, impress, imprint, instill 9 inculcate, insinuate, introduce, pound into 10 hammer into
ingrained: 5 fixed 6 etched, inborn, inbred, innate, rooted 7 built-in, chronic, infixed 8 habitual 9 chronical, confirmed, implanted, indelible, intrinsic 10 congenital, deep-rooted, deep-seated, habituated, hereditary, indwelling, in the blood, inveterate
activity: 5 habit
Ingram: 3 Rex 5 James 6 Luther
Ingram, James
song: Baby, Come to Me (1982)
I Don't Have the Heart (1990)
Somewhere Out There (1987)
ingratiate: 5 charm 6 endear 9 captivate, get in with, insinuate
oneself to: 3 woo 5 court, toady 6 kowtow 7 flatter, truckle 8 butter up, fawn over
ingratiating: 4 nice, oily 5 suave 6 smooth 7 candied
ingredient: 4 item, part 6 factor 7 element, feature 8 material 9 component
__ ingredient: 4 main 6 active
ingredients: 6 recipe 7 fixings 8 contents
Ingres, Jean: 6 artist, French 7 painter
inspirer: 5 Degas
ingress: 3 way 4 adit, door, gate, hall, lane, path, road 5 enter, entry, foyer, hatch, lobby, means, porch, route, stile, way in 6 access, arcade, avenue, course, entrée, influx, inroad, portal, street, wicket 7 doorway, gallery, gangway, gateway, hallway, highway, opening, passage, pathway, portico, postern, roadway, walkway 8 anteroom, aperture, approach, corridor, driveway, entrance, entryway, invasion 9 admission, boulevard, intrusion, penetrate, threshold, turnstile, vestibule 10 admittance, passageway
Ingrid: 6 Thulin 7 Bergman
daughter: 3 Pia 8 Isabella
role: 4 Ilsa 5 Golda
__ in Grouchland: 4 Elmo
in-group: 3 set 4 clan, club, gang, ring 5 cabal, crowd, elite 6 circle, clique, outfit 7 coterie, faction
ingungu: 4 drum
ingurgitate: 4 gulp 5 quaff 6 absorb, guzzle, imbibe 7 consume
inhabit: 5 dwell 6 inhere, live at, live in, locate, occupy, reside, settle, tenant 7 dwell at, dwell in, lodge in, sojourn 8 populate, reside in
inhabitable: 7 livable 8 liveable
inhabitant: 5 liver, local, voter 6 native, renter, roomer, tenant 7 citizen, denizen, dweller, resider, settler 8 colonist, indigene, occupant, resident 9 aborigine, addressee, incumbent, indweller 10 autochthon
locale: 4 digs, home 5 abode, house, place 7 lodging 8 domicile, dwelling, quarters 9 residence
of (suffix): 3 -ese, -ite, -ote
inhabitants: 4 folk 5 folks 6 people 7 country 10 population
inhalation: 4 drag, gasp, gulp, puff, toot 5 aroma, sniff, snort 6 breath 7 sniffle, snuffle 9 breathing 10 aspiration
combining form: 4 anem- 5 anemo-
involuntary ~: 3 hic
inhale: 3 eat 4 bolt, drag, gasp, gulp, puff, take 5 smell, smoke, sniff, snort, whiff 6 devour, draw in, gobble, guzzle, suck in, suck up, take in 7 breathe, consume, inspire, respire, swallow 8 wolf down 9 breathe in, scarf down 10 eat quickly, get some air
inhaler target: 6 asthma 10 congestion
__ in hand: 3 cap, hat 4 bird
__-in-hand: 4 four
__ in Harlem: 5 A Rage
inharmonious: 4 flat 5 harsh 6 atonal, off-key 7 grating, jarring, raucous 8 clashing, factious, jangling, negative, strident, tuneless 9 dissonant, unmusical
inharmoniousness: 5 clash 6 racket 7 discord 8 conflict, jangling, variance
__ in Heaven: 4 Made, Pigs 5 Tears
inhere: 4 stay 5 abide, dwell 6 belong, make up, reside 7 inhabit
inherent: 4 born 5 basic 6 inbred, innate, latent, native 7 implied, natural, organic, radical 8 implicit 9 essential, innermost, potential 10 deep-seated, indigenous
inherently: 5 per se 8 by nature, innately 9 basically
inherit: 3 get, own 4 gain 6 obtain 7 acquire, receive, succeed 8 accede to, come into, take over 10 fall heir to
inheritance: 6 devise, estate, legacy 7 bequest 8 heirloom, heritage, property 9 patrimony 10 birthright
document: 4 will
factor: 4 gene
inheritance __: 3 tax
Inheritance, The author: Louisa May Alcott
inherited: 6 native 9 ancestral 10 congenital, connatural, indigenous
inheritor: 4 cion, heir, seed 5 issue, scion 6 coheir 7 grantee, heiress, legatee, progeny 8 receiver
inheritors, Earth: 4 meek
Inheritors, The author: Harold Robbins
Inherit the Wind (1960 film)
cast: Gene Kelly, Fredric March, Spencer Tracy, Dick York
director: Stanley Kramer
role: 5 Brady, Cates 7 Bertram 8 Drummond, Hornbeck
inhibit: 3 bar 4 curb, faze, hold, slow, stop 5 avert, brake, check, cramp, delay, deter, limit, stimy, stint, stymy 6 arrest, bridle, dampen, detain, enjoin, forbid, hamper, hand up, hinder, hogtie, impede, retard, slow up, stymie 7 abolish, head off, prevent, refrain, repress, sandbag, silence, trammel 8 bottle up, handcuff, handicap, hold back, hold down, obstruct, preclude, prohibit, restrain, restrict, slow down, suppress, throttle 9 constrain, constrict, frustrate, hamstring, interdict 10 discourage, keep in line
inhibited: 6 pent-up, silent 7 hogtied 8 hampered 9 confident, repressed, withdrawn 10 frustrated
inhibition: 5 check 6 hang-up 7 scruple, trammel 8 neurosis 9 hindrance, restraint, reticence 10 constraint, impediment, prevention
inhibitions, abandon: 5 let go
in high __: 4 gear 7 feather, spirits
__ in his heaven...: 4 God's
In His Image subject: 5 clone
__ in hoary winter's night: 3 As I
in hoc __ vinces: 5 signo
inhospitable: 3 icy 4 cold, cool, mean, rude 5 aloof, brusk, nasty, onery, short, surly 6 chilly, ornery, remote, unkind 7 brusque, glacial, hateful, hostile 8 contrary, inimical, spiteful 9 bellicose, malicious, withdrawn 10 malevolent, pugnacious, unfriendly
in hot __: 5 water
__-in housekeeper: 4 live 5 sleep
inhuman: 4 fell, grim, mean 5 cruel 6 brutal, fierce, malign, savage, unkind 7 beastly, bestial, hateful, vicious 8 barbaric, devilish, fiendish, pitiless, ruthless 9 barbarian, barbarous, ferocious, heartless, monstrous, unfeeling 10 oppressive, outrageous, relentless
inhumane: 3 bad 4 fell, grim, mean 5 cruel, harsh, nasty 6 animal, brutal, fierce, malign, savage, unkind, wanton 7 beastly, bestial, callous, hateful, hurtful, vicious 8 barbaric, devilish, fiendish, pitiless, ruthless, sadistic, vengeful 9 barbarian, barbarous, cutthroat, ferocious, merciless, monstrous, truculent, unpitying 10 unmerciful, vindictive
inhumanity: 7 cruelty, outrage 8 atrocity, ferocity, savagery, violence 9 barbarism, barbarity, brutality
__ inhumanity to...: 4 man's
inhume: 4 bury, hide 5 cover 6 entomb 7 conceal, cover up
Inigo: 5 Jones
inimical: 3 icy, ill 4 cold, cool, mean 5 aloof, nasty, onery, surly 6 averse, chilly, malign, ornery, remote 7 adverse, glacial, harmful, hateful, hostile, hurtful, noxious, opposed, warlike 8 contrary, opposing, opposite, spiteful 9 bellicose, injurious, malicious, repugnant, withdrawn 10 malevolent, pugnacious, unfriendly
inimitable: 4 best, rare 6 unique 7 perfect, supreme 8 peerless, uncommon 9 matchless, nonpareil, unequaled, unmatched, unrivaled, virtuosic 10 consummate, unequalled, unexampled, unrivalled
inion: 4 bone
iniquitous: 3 bad, ill 4 base, evil, foul, vile 5 nasty 6 guilty, unholy, wicked 7 corrupt, heinous, immoral, satanic 8 unlawful 9 injurious, miscreant, nefarious, satanical 10 malevolent, villainous
iniquity: 3 sin 4 evil, vice 5 crime, guilt, wrong 6 infamy 7 devilry 8 baseness, deviltry 9 depravity, evildoing 10 corruption, immorality, miscreancy, sinfulness, wickedness, wrongdoing
__ iniquity: 5 den of
init.: 3 ltr.
__ in Italy: 6 Harold
__ in it for me?: 5 What's
initial: 2 OK 4 mark, okay, sign 5 basic, early, first, prime 6 letter, maiden, virgin 7 leading, nascent, opening, pioneer, premier, primary 8 earliest, original, virginal 9 beginning, embryonic, inaugural, inceptive, incipient 10 elementary
stage: 4 dawn 5 onset, start 6 outset 7 dawning, kickoff, opening 8 outbreak 9 beginning, inception
initialize a disk: 6 format

initially: **5** first **7** at first **9** primarily **10** at the start, originally
initiate: **3** set **4** haze, open, tiro, tyro **5** admit, begin, build, cause, coach, edify, enter, erect, found, newie, set up, start, teach, train **6** create, enlist, ground, induct, instal, invest, launch, take up **7** aggress, entrant, install, instate, kick off, lead off, learner, pioneer, receive, recruit, trigger, usher in **8** activate, ambition, beginner, commence, generate, get going, instruct, touch off **9** enlighten, enter upon, instigate, institute, introduce, originate, undertake **10** catechumen, inaugurate, lead the way, tenderfoot
initiation: **5** debut, intro, onset, start **6** origin **7** baptism, genesis, joining, opening **8** entrance **9** admission, beginning, enrolment, inaugural, inception, induction **10** conception, enrollment
initiative: **4** push, zeal **5** drive, moxie, punch, spunk, vigor **6** action, energy **8** ambition, dynamism, gumption, resource **9** eagerness **10** enterprise, enthusiasm, get-up-and-go, leadership
take the ~: **3** act **4** lead **9** spearhead, volunteer
initiator: **7** creator, founder **10** forerunner
initiatory: **5** first **6** maiden **7** opening **8** starting **9** inaugural, incipient
inject: **3** add **5** infix **6** insert, instil **7** breathe, engrain, implant, ingrain, instill **9** inoculate, insinuate, interpose, introduce, vaccinate
injected, not: **4** oral
injection: **4** hypo, shot **6** needle **8** infusion, medicine **10** medication
amt.: **2** cc.
reaction: **2** ow **4** ouch **5** wince
__ injection: **3** air **4** fuel **5** solid
__ injector: **3** jet **4** fuel
in jest: **7** as a joke **8** jokingly **9** kiddingly
In Joy Still Felt author: Isaac Asimov
injudicious: **4** dumb, rash **5** silly, wrong **6** stupid, unwise **7** foolish **8** careless, tactless **9** misguided, unadvised
injunction: **3** ban, law **4** word, writ **5** edict, order **6** decree, demand **7** command, dictate, mandate, precept, warning **8** sanction **9** directive, enjoinder **10** admonition
injure: **3** cut, mar **4** beat, harm, hurt, knee, maim, mall, maul, pain, ruin, scar, stab, tear, undo **5** abuse, break, crack, lay up, slash, spite, spoil, sting, wound, wrong **6** batter, bruise, damage, deface, foul up, grieve, impair, insult, malign, mangle, strain **7** contuse, disable, distort, slander, torture, trample, vitiate **8** aggrieve, distress, ill-treat, lacerate, maltreat, mistreat, mutilate **9** prejudice
slightly: **4** wing **6** bruise **7** scratch
injured: **3** cut **4** hurt **5** burnt, lamed, stung **6** abused, broken, burned, harmed, maimed, marred, ruined **7** cracked, damaged, grieved, libeled, mangled, misused, wounded, wronged **8** crippled, deformed, impaired, maligned, offended, traduced, vilified, weakened **9** aggrieved, blackened, enfeebled, lacerated, miserable, mutilated, slandered **10** denigrated, ill-treated, maltreated, mistreated
party: **6** sucker, victim **9** scapegoat
injurious: **3** bad, ill **4** evil **5** toxic **6** malign, nocent, unjust **7** abusive, adverse, baleful, baneful, harmful, hurtful, nocuous, noisome, noxious, ruinous **8** damaging, grievous, inimical, libelous, negative, sinister, virulent, wrongful **9** dangerous, insulting, malicious, pestilent, poisonous, unhealthy **10** calamitous, corrupting, defamatory, derogatory, disastrous, iniquitous, maleficent, pernicious, slanderous
act: **4** tort **5** wrong **9** violation
not ~: **4** safe **6** benign, gentle **8** harmless, nontoxic **9** innocuous
injury: **3** cut, ill **4** bite, burn, gash, harm, hurt, loss, nick, pain, pang, sore, welt **5** abuse, break, cramp, shock, sting, wound, wrong **6** boo-boo, bruise, damage, lesion, misuse, scrape, sprain, strain, trauma, twinge **7** affront, offense, outrage, scratch, umbrage **8** abrasion, breakage, distress, fracture, inequity, mischief, swelling **9** contusion, detriment, grievance **10** affliction, impairment, laceration, oppression
addition: **6** insult
exposure to ~: **4** risk **5** peril **6** danger, hazard, menace **8** jeopardy
minor ~: **4** welt **6** boo-boo, bruise, scrape **7** scratch **8** black eye **9** contusion
muscle ~: **4** pull, tear **6** sprain
result: **4** scab, scar
injustice: **4** bias **5** abuse, wrong **6** bum rap **7** offense, outrage **8** inequity **9** dirty deal, grievance, prejudice, violation **10** detraction, disservice, fanaticism, favoritism, inequality, infraction, negligence, oppression, partiality, unfairness, wrongdoing
do an ~: **4** harm **5** abuse **6** damage, ill-use, injure, misuse **7** torment **8** aggrieve, distress, ill-treat, maltreat, mistreat **9** mishandle, persecute
ink: **4** sign **5** India, sepia, write **7** endorse, indorse **9** publicity
debit ~: **3** red
dry ~: **5** toner
ender: **4** blot, horn, well **5** berry, stand
holder: **4** well **5** quill **8** fountain
Japanese ~: **4** sumi
red ~: **4** debt, loss **7** arrears, deficit **8** mortgage **9** arrearage, debenture, liability **10** obligation
sac: **5** organ
slinger: **6** writer **8** reporter **9** columnist **10** journalist, newswriter
source: **3** pen, soy **5** squid **7** octopus
spot: **4** blot **5** stain **6** blotch
user: **5** press **7** printer **9** newspaper
ink __: **4** ball, blot
ink-__ printer: **3** jet
__ ink: **3** red **5** India **7** Chinese
Inka __ Doo: **5** Dinka
Inkatha Party supporter: **4** Zulu
inkberry: **5** shrub
inkblot __: **4** test
inked: **3** sgd. **5** wrote **6** signed
inkle: **4** tape
material: **5** linen
inkling: **3** cue, tip **4** clew, clue, hint, idea, seed, sign, wind **5** glint, hunch, touch **6** notion, tipoff **7** glimmer **9** suspicion **10** conception, glimmering, impression, indication, intimation, suggestion
Inkster: **4** city, Juli, town
locale: **8** Michigan
Inkster, Juli: **6** golfer
milieu: **5** links **6** course
org.: **4** LPGA
Ink Truck, The author: William Kennedy
inkwell site of old: **4** desk
inky: **3** jet **4** dark, ebon **5** black, ebony, sooty **9** blackened, coal-black, lightless, unlighted **10** pitch-black
relative: **4** onyx **5** raven, sable
inky __: **3** cap
inlaid: **3** set **5** tiled **6** mosaic **7** studded **8** enameled, veneered **9** champlevé, checkered **10** ornamented
inland: **7** upriver **8** interior, internal **9** backwoods, upcountry
water: **4** lake
in-law: **6** affine **8** relative
offering: **5** dowry **6** dowery
__-in-law: **3** son **6** father, mother, parent, sister **7** brother **8** daughter
In-Laws, The (1979 film)
cast: Alan Arkin, Peter Falk
director: Arthur Hiller
inlay: **3** set **4** tile **5** embed, imbed **6** insert, mosaic, tiling **7** checker, encrust, filling, incrust, parquet **10** decoration, tessellate
elaborate ~: **4** buhl **5** boule **6** boulle
material: **5** nacre
__ in left field: **3** out
inlet: **3** bay, ria **4** cove, gulf **5** basin, bayou, bight, fiord, firth, fjord, frith, mouth **6** laguna **7** estuary **8** entrance
__ Inlet: **4** Cook
...in like __: **5** a lion
in line __: **3** for
in-line __: **7** skating
__ in line: **4** next
In Living Color segment: **4** skit
in loc. __: **3** cit.
in loco: **7** in place
__ in Love: **4** Lost **5** Blume, I'm Not, Swann, Woman, Women, You're **7** Falling
__ in Love Again: **4** Back **7** Falling
__ in Love With Amy: **4** Once
__-in maid: **4** live
inmate: **3** con **5** lifer **7** convict, patient **8** jailbird, prisoner, resident, yardbird
in medias __: **3** res
In Memoriam author: Alfred Tennyson
In Memory Yet Green author: Isaac Asimov
__ in mind: **4** bear, have, keep
inmost: **6** center, innate, secret **7** deepest **9** essential, intrinsic
__ in motion: **3** set **6** poetry
__-in-mouth: **4** foot
__-in movie: **5** drive
__ in My Arms Again: **4** Back
__ in my backyard!: **3** Not
In My Dreams (1987 song) artist: REO Speedwagon
In My Little Corner of the World (1960 song) artist: Anita Bryant
__ in my memory lock'd: **3** 'tis
In My Room (1963 song) artist: Beach Boys
__ in My Shoes: **4** Sand
inn: **3** pub **5** B and B, hotel, lodge, motel, serai **6** hostel, imaret, posada, resort, saloon, Tabard, tavern **7** auberge, lodging **8** gasthaus, hostelry, lodgment, taphouse **9** roadhouse **10** guesthouse, restaurant
ender: **6** keeper
offering: **2** rm. **4** room
Turkish ~: **5** serai **6** imaret
waterfront ~: **5** botel **6** boatel
__ inn: **5** motor
Inn: **5** river
locale: **7** Austria, Germany
__ Inn: **4** Days **5** Gray's **6** Tabard **7** Holiday, Red Roof
Inn Album, The author: Robert Browning
in name __: **4** only
In Name Only (1939 film)
cast: Kay Francis, Cary Grant, Carole Lombard
innards: **4** guts **6** bowels, vitals **7** filling, viscera **8** contents, workings **9** mechanism
innate: **3** gut **4** born **5** basic **6** inborn, inmost, native **7** genetic, natural, organic, radical **8** born with, God-given, internal **9** genetical, ingrained, innermost, intrinsic, intuitive, unlabored, unlearned **10** congenital, hereditary, indigenous
innately: **5** per se **7** at heart **8** in itself **9** in essence, naturally
inner: **3** gut **6** center, clique, hidden, middle, secret, within **7** central, private **8** interior, internal, intimate, personal, visceral **9** emotional, essential, intrinsic, nonpublic, spiritual **10** deep-rooted, deep-seated
circle: **5** elite **6** clique
city: **3** urb **4** slum **6** barrio, ghetto, region **7** quarter
combining form: **3** eso- **4** endo-, ento-
ender: **4** most, sole, wear **6** spring
in anatomy: **5** ental
motivation: **4** urge **5** ardor, drive
not ~: **5** outer **7** outward **8** exterior, external
sanctum: **6** adytum
self: **4** soul **5** anima **6** psyche
voice: **8** superego **10** conscience
inner __: **3** bar, ear, jib, man **4** city, tube **5** child **6** circle, planet **7** mission, product, sanctum
Inner __: **4** Word **5** Light **6** Circle, Temple
Inner Circles author: **4** Haig
Inner City Blues (1971 song) artist: Marvin Gaye
Inner Hebrides
cape: **5** Sleat
isle: **4** Eigg, Mull, Skye **5** Islay, Tiree, Tyree
innermost: **4** core, deep, pith **5** basic, heart, privy **6** center, depths, hidden, innate, marrow, secret, veiled **7** central, intense, organic, private **8** esoteric, immanent, inherent, intimate, personal, profound, recesses, visceral **9** out of view
part: **4** core **6** center **7** nucleus
Inner Sanctum, The: **9** radio show
Innerspace (1987 film)
cast: Kevin McCarthy, Dennis Quaid, Meg Ryan, Martin Short
director: Joe Dante
inner-tube
innards: **3** air
outsides: **4** tire
Innes: **5** Laura **7** Michael
Inness, George: **6** artist **7** painter
__ in New York: **5** A King **6** Autumn, Sunday
innie: **5** navel
opposite: **5** outie
inning: **5** frame
ender, often: **2** DP **9** strikeout
extra ~: **5** tenth
half an ~: **3** top **6** bottom
last ~ usually: **5** ninth
outs in an ~: **3** six
penultimate ~: **6** eighth
recap part: **6** no hits, no runs
unit: **3** out
__-inning stretch: **7** seventh
Innis: **3** Roy
org.: **4** CORE
Innisfail: **4** city, Eire, Erin, isle, town **7** Ireland
locale: **6** Canada **7** Ontario
Innisfree: **4** Eire, Erin, isle
innkeeper: **4** host **8** boniface, hosteler, hotelier, landlord

in Italian: 4 oste
in no __: 3 way 4 time
innocence: 5 youth 6 purity, virtue 7 naiveté, probity 9 frankness, freshness, greenness, ignorance, nescience, plainness, sincerity 10 candidness, clean hands, simplicity
remark of ~: 5 not me
__ Innocence, The: 5 Age of
innocent: 4 babe, good, lamb, naif, open, pure 5 clean, clear, green, legal, naive 6 boyish, chaste, cherub, honest, lawful, simple, victim, virgin 7 angelic, artless, genuine, natural, sincere, sinless, unjaded, upright 8 gullable, gullible, harmless, ignorant, lamblike, pristine, spotless, unartful, unsoiled, virginal, virtuous 9 angelical, blameless, childlike, exemplary, faultless, guileless, guilt-free, guiltless, ingenuous, innocuous, lily-white, not guilty, righteous, stainless, uncorrupt, unsullied, untainted, unwitting, unworldly, wholesome 10 immaculate, impeccable, inculcable, inculpable, in the clear, legitimate, unaffected, uninvolved
escapade: 4 lark 5 antic, caper, fling 6 frolic, gambol 7 rollick
find ~: 5 clear 6 acquit 9 vindicate
kid: 5 angel 6 cherub
not ~: 6 guilty, liable, sinful 7 at fault 8 culpable 10 in the wrong
innocent __ lamb: 3 as a
Innocent: 4 pope 7 pontiff
Innocent Blood (1992 film)
cast: Anthony LaPaglia, Robert Loggia
director: John Landis
Innocent Man, An (1984 song) artist: Billy Joel
Innocents Abroad, The author: Mark Twain
Innocents, The (1961 film)
cast: Deborah Kerr, Michael Redgrave
innocuous: 4 mild, safe 5 banal, bland 6 pallid 7 insipid 8 harmless, innocent, painless 9 innoxious
Inn of the Sixth Happiness, The (1958 film)
cast: Ingrid Bergman, Robert Donat, Curt Jurgens
director: Mark Robson
In nomine __: 5 patri
innovate: 4 coin 5 alter 6 change, recast 7 remodel, restyle 8 renovate 9 modernize, originate, transform
innovation: 6 change 7 coinage, newness, novelty 9 departure, deviation, discovery, invention, modernism, variation 10 alteration, conversion, new wrinkle
innovative: 3 new 4 orig. 5 fresh, novel 6 clever 7 new-wave, unusual 8 creative, inspired, original 9 deviceful, inceptive, ingenious, inventive 10 avant-garde, newfangled
innovator: 7 creator, pioneer 8 inventer, inventor
prefix: 3 neo
innoxious: 4 safe 8 harmless, nontoxic 9 innocuous
Innsbruck: 4 city, town
locale: 3 Aus. 4 Alps, Aust. 5 Tirol, Tyrol 7 Austria
see also German
Inns of __: 5 Court
innuendo: 4 hint, slur, talk 5 smear 7 whisper 8 allusion, overtone 9 aspersion, reference 10 imputation, intimation, suggestion
Innuit: 6 Eskimo
innumerable: 4 many, more 6 a lot of, divers, gobs of, legion, lots of, myriad, umteen, untold 7 a host of, a slew of, copious, heaps of, no end of, piles of, profuse, scads of, umpteen 8 a bunch of, abundant, an army of, manifold, numerous, oodles of, prodigal, scores of, umpsteen 9 a passel of, bountiful, bunches of, countless, limitless, quite a few 10 zillions of
innumerous: 4 many 6 myriad, untold 7 endless, umpteen 8 infinite 9 countless, limitless, unlimited
Ino
brother of ~: 9 Polydorus
father of ~: 6 Cadmus
husband of ~: 7 Athamas
sister of ~: 5 Agave 6 Semele
son of ~: 8 Learchus 10 Melicertes
inoculable: 8 catching 10 contagious, infectious
inoculant: 5 serum
inoculate: 6 infuse, inject, instil 7 instill 8 immunize 9 vaccinate
inoculation: 4 hypo, shot 6 needle 8 medicine
inoffensive: 4 calm, mild, safe 5 bland, clean, quiet 6 humble 7 neutral 8 friendly, harmless, innocent, pleasant, retiring
In Old Arizona: 5 oater
In Old Chicago (1938 film)
cast: Don Ameche, Alice Faye, Tyrone Power
director: Henry King
In Old Monterey: 5 oater
__ in on: 3 key, let 4 horn, look, move, zero 5 barge, close
in one __ and out...: 3 ear
in one __ swoop: 4 fell
__ in one: 4 hole
__-in-one: 3 all
in one's __: 4 book 6 pocket, tracks
in one's __ right: 3 own
__ in one's belfry: 4 bats
__ in one's bones: 4 feel
__ in one's bonnet: 4 a bee
__ in one's cap: 7 feather
__ in one's craw: 5 stick
__ in one's ear: 4 flea 5 a flea
__ in one's hair: 3 get
__ in one's horns: 4 draw, haul, pull
in one's own __: 5 right
__ in one's own juice: 4 stew
__ in one's pants: 4 ants
__ in one's side: 5 thorn
__ in one's sleeve: 5 laugh
__ in one's throat: 4 lump
__ in one's ways: 3 set
__ in on the ground floor: 3 get
__-i-noor Diamond: 3 Koh
inoperative: 4 no-go, null, void 6 broken, futile, unable, voided 7 inutile, invalid, revoked, useless 8 abortive, annulled, bootless, canceled, inactive, nugatory, reversed, set aside 10 out of order
inopportune: 5 unapt 7 adverse, awkward 8 improper, previous, untimely 9 premature
in order __: 4 that
inordinate: 5 gross, steep, undue 6 lavish, wanton 7 copious, extreme, profuse, surplus, too much 8 a bit much, dizzying, needless, overmuch, wasteful 9 excessive, expensive, irregular, redundant 10 exorbitant, gratuitous, immoderate, irrational, outrageous, undeserved, untempered
inordinately: 3 too 4 over, very 6 overly, unduly 9 extremely
inordinateness: 4 glut 6 excess 7 surplus 8 plethora 9 profusion 10 immoderacy, lavishness, sybaritism
inositol to glucose: 6 isomer
In other words: 5 id est, I mean
Inoue Yasushi: 6 writer 8 Japanese
__ in Our Time: 5 Peace
In & Out (1997 film)
cast: Joan Cusack, Matt Dillon, Kevin Kline, Tom Selleck
director: Frank Oz
Inouye, Daniel org.: 3 Sen.
__ in Paradise: 4 Ruby 5 To One 7 Trouble
__ in Paris: 5 April 6 Satori
__ in Peoria: 4 play
__-in period: 5 break
__ in Pink: 6 Pretty
__ in place: 3 run
in place in Latin: 6 in loco
__ in Plain Sight: 4 Hide
__ in point: 4 case 5 a case
in point of __: 4 fact
inpour: 6 fill up
In Praise of __: 5 Folly
In Praise of Johnny Appleseed
author: Vachel Lindsay
__ in progress: 4 work
__ in Provence: 5 A Year
input: 3 key 4 note, type 5 enter, gloss 6 advice, remark 7 comment, observe, opinion 8 critique, feedback, point out 9 criticism, editorial, interject, statement 10 discussion
inq.: 4 ques.
inquest: 5 panel 6 assize
inquietude: 5 angst 6 unrest 7 anxiety, fidgets, jitters, malaise 8 disquiet, edginess 10 discomfort
inquire: 3 ask, pry 4 quiz, seek, sift 5 apply, probe, query, scour 6 demand, meddle, wonder 7 request, solicit 8 look into, question 9 catechize
into: 4 test 5 assay, study 6 size up, try out 7 analyze, examine, explore 8 check out, evaluate 10 scrutinize
Inquirer: 5 paper 9 newspaper
inquiring: 4 nosy 5 nosey 7 curious 9 heuristic, quizzical, searching, wondering 10 analytical, interested
inquiry: 4 ques. 5 audit, check, probe, Q and A, query, quest, study 6 asking, demand, survey 7 hearing, pursuit, request 8 question, quizzing, research, scrutiny 10 inspection
judicial ~: 6 assize
make an ~: 3 ask 5 probe 8 look into
word of ~: 3 how, who, why 4 what, when 5 where
inquisition: 5 probe, trial 6 assize 7 enquiry, hearing, inquest, inquiry 8 grilling
Inquisition offense: 6 heresy
inquisitive: 4 nosy 5 nosey 6 prying, snoopy 7 big-eyed, curious 8 snooping 9 officious, quizzical
be ~: 3 ask 5 snoop 6 wonder
one: 5 asker, prier, pryer
inquisitor: 4 ogre 5 bully 6 tyrant 8 autocrat, dictator, examiner, martinet 9 oppressor 10 questioner
demand: 6 answer
__ in Red, The: 4 Lady 5 Woman
inroad: 4 raid 5 foray 7 advance, ingress, overrun 8 invasion, progress, trespass 9 incursion, intrusion, irruption, onslaught
__ in Rome...: 4 When
inrush: 5 flood 7 pouring 9 implosion
ins.
bank ~ initials: 4 FDIC, SBLI 5 FSLIC
health ~ choice: 3 HMO, PPO
payment: 4 prem.
see also insurance
INS: 4 agcy. 6 agency
part of ~: 4 Serv. 7 Service
insalubrious: 4 foul 5 dirty, fatal, toxic 6 deadly, lethal, septic, sickly 7 harmful, hurtful, jejuene, noisome, noxious, unclean 8 damaging, virulent 9 unhealthy
ins and outs: 4 ways 5 bends, turns 6 curves, habits, traits, twists 7 customs, details 8 patterns, windings
insane: 3 mad 4 daft, wild 5 manic, wacky 6 fierce, whacky 7 extreme, fatuous, foolish, meshuga, touched, unsound 8 maniacal, meshugga 9 ludicrous, possessed, senseless, unscrewed 10 moonstruck, off-the-wall
insanitary: 4 foul 5 dirty, germy 6 filthy, impure, septic 7 dirtied, noxious, unclean 8 infected, polluted, unwashed
insatiable: 4 avid 6 greedy 7 lustful 8 esurient, ravenous 9 clamorous, demanding, insistent, rapacious, voracious 10 gluttonous, quenchless
desire: 4 lust, urge 5 greed 6 fervor, hunger, thirst 7 avidity, craving 8 cupidity 9 appetence
insatiate: 6 hungry 7 piggish, starved, wolfish 8 edacious, esurient, famished, ravenous, starving 9 voracious 10 gluttonous, omnivorous
__ in Scarlet, A: 5 Study
inscribe: 3 pen 4 etch, sign 5 enter, write 6 indite, record 7 address, engrave, impress, imprint 8 register, take down 9 autograph, handwrite
inscribed rock: 5 stela, stele
inscription: 3 tag 5 label, motto, title 6 legend, record 7 caption, epitaph, heading, message 8 memorial
like some old ~ s: 5 runic
inscrutable: 5 blank 6 mystic 7 complex 8 esoteric, mystical 10 fathomless, mysterious
inseam measure: 4 lgth. 6 length
In Search of the Castaways author: Jules Verne
insect: 3 ant, bee, bot, bug, dor, fly, nit 4 flea, gnat, grub, lice, mite, moth, pest, pupa, tick, tine, wasp 5 aphid, aphis, borer, cimex, cooty, drone, emmet, imago, larva, louse, midge, roach 6 bedbug, beetle, botfly, chafer, chigoe, chinch, cicada, cocoon, cootie, dayfly, earwig, gadfly, hornet, lo moth, larvae, locust, looper, maggot, mantid, mantis, mayfly, scarab, thrips, tussah, vermin, weevil 7 ant lion, billbug, blowfly, chigger, cricket, firefly, hexapod, katydid, ladybug, no-see-um, pismire, termite, viceroy 8 armyworm, conenose, firebrat, fruit fly, glowworm, honeybee, housefly, lacewing, mealybug, mosquito, muckworm, reduviid, silkworm, stinkbug, white ant, woodworm 9 arthropod, bumblebee, butterfly, chrysalis, cockroach, corn borer, damselfly, dobsonfly, doodlebug, dorbeetle, dragonfly, earthworm, saturniid, sheep tick, tarantula, woodborer 10 bluebottle, calicoback, deathwatch, digger wasp, froghopper, iguana fare, pear thrips, rose chafer, spittlebug, treehopper, woolly bear
busy ~: 3 ant, bee
cheek: 5 bucca
combining form: 6 entomo-
covering: 6 chitin
dorsal surface: 5 notum
eater: 4 frog, toad 8 aardvark
egg: 3 nit
eye lens: 5 facet
feeler: 4 palp 6 palpus

forehead: 5 frons

home:: 4 hive, nest 5 nidus

mouth parts: 5 labra

of an ~ nest: 5 nidal

of an ~ stage: 5 pupal 6 larval

part of an ~ stinger: 5 oopod

scale ~: 6 coccid

science: 5 entom. 10 entomology

sound: 5 chirr, churr 6 chirre

stage: 4 pupa 5 imago, larva 6 instar

stinging ~: 3 bee 4 wasp 6 hornet

upper plate: 5 notum

wing part: 5 jugum

wings: 4 alae

__ insect: 3 lac, wax 4 leaf 5 scale, stick

insecticide: 3 DDT 4 deet, neem 5 mirex, spray

Insect Play, The author: Karel Capek

insects, parasitic: 4 lice

insecure: 4 weak 5 antsy, risky, shaky 6 uneasy, unfirm, unsafe, wabbly, wobbly 7 rickety, unsound 8 slippery, unstable 9 hazardous, uncertain, unsettled 10 precarious

insecurity: 4 fear, risk 5 doubt, peril 6 danger, hazard 7 anxiety, frailty, shyness 8 jeopardy, timidity, unsafety, wariness, weakness 9 misgiving, timidness 10 diffidence

insensate: 4 cold, dead, deaf, hard, numb 5 blind, inert 6 inured, zonked 7 callous, foolish, mineral, witless 8 hardened, lifeless, tuned out, uncaring 9 inanimate, unfeeling

insensibility: 4 daze 5 shock 6 stupor, trance 8 numbness

insensible: 7 unaware 8 lifeless, pitiless 9 apathetic, bloodless, impassive, unfeeling 10 immaterial, impalpable

insensitive: 4 hard, numb 5 aloof, blind, blunt, brusk, crass, stony, tough 6 abrupt, gauche, obtuse, stoney, unkind 7 boorish, brusque, callous 8 deadened, impolite, inurbane, tactless, uncaring 9 outspoken, unfeeling

one: 3 oaf 4 boor, clod 5 brute

insentient: 4 dead, numb 5 inert, under 6 zonked 7 mineral 8 comatose, deadened, lifeless 9 inanimate 10 unreactive

inseparable: 5 as one, close, solid, thick, whole 6 united 7 unified 8 attached

insert: 3 add, put, set 4 edit, root, stay, tuck 5 embed, flier, flyer, imbed, infix, inlay, place, plant, shove, stick, tenon 6 filler, gusset, inject, record 7 enclose, implant, inclose, include, obtrude, squeeze 8 shoehorn 9 enclosure, interject, interpose, introduce 10 put between, supplement

mark: 5 caret

__ in sheep's clothing: 4 wolf 5 a wolf

in short __: 5 order

__ in show: 4 best

inside: 3 gut 4 core 5 belly, heart 6 at home, bowels, center, lining, middle, secret, vitals, within 7 central, indoors, innards, private 8 deep down, esoteric, interior, internal, inwardly 9 exclusive, incumbent, protected, sheltered 10 classified, restricted, tucked away

combining form: 4 endo-, ento-

nautically: 4 alow

turn ~ out: 6 forage 7 ransack, rummage

inside __: 3 job, out 4 joke, loop 5 story, track 7 caliper, forward

__ inside: 5 Intel, on the

Inside __: 3 U.S.A. 4 Asia 6 Africa 7 Edition, Passage

Inside __ Today: 6 Europe, Russia

Inside Africa author: John Gunther

Inside Asia author: John Gunther

Inside Australia author: John Gunther

Inside Daisy Clover (1965 film)

cast: Roddy McDowall, Christopher Plummer, Robert Redford, Natalie Wood

director: Robert Mulligan

Inside Europe Today author: John Gunther

inside-out: 5 messy 7 jumbled, muddled, upended 8 inverted 10 topsy-turvy

turn ~: 5 probe, rifle, scour 6 forage, search 7 examine, inspect, ransack, rummage 9 go through 10 scrutinize

Inside, Outside author: Herman Wouk

insider: 5 shill 9 accessory 10 accomplice

former ~: 5 ex-con

signal: 4 wink

talk: 5 argot, idiom, lingo 6 jargon, patois

insider __: 7 trading

Insider, The (1999 film)

cast: Russell Crowe, Al Pacino, Christopher Plummer, Diane Venora

director: Michael Mann

Inside Russia Today author: John Gunther

insides: 4 guts 5 works 6 bowels, vitals 7 filling, viscera 8 contents, workings 9 mechanism

Inside South America author: John Gunther

Inside the Atom author: Isaac Asimov

Inside the Onion author: Howard Nemerov

Inside the Third Reich author: 5 Speer

Inside the Tornado author: 5 Moore

Inside U.S.A. author: John Gunther

insidious: 3 sly 4 foul, foxy, grim, poor, wily 5 awful, lousy, slick, snaky, woful 6 artful, crafty, crumby, crummy, dismal, horrid, odious, rotten, shifty, sneaky, subtle, tricky, woeful 7 accurst, baleful, baneful, beastly, cunning, devious, doleful, furtive, ghastly, knavish 8 accursed, dreadful, God-awful, grievous, guileful, horrible, inferior, shameful, stealthy, stinking, terrible, wretched 9 abhorrent, appalling, atrocious, dangerous, deceitful, deceptive, defective, designing, dishonest, ensnaring, execrable, frightful, loathsome, miserable, offensive, revolting, underhand 10 abominable, despicable, detestable, disastrous, horrendous, intriguing, perfidious, traitorous

insight: 3 wit 4 wits 5 depth, light, sense 6 acumen, aperçu, vision, wisdom 8 epiphany, sagacity, sapience 9 awareness, intuition, knowledge 10 horse sense, luminosity, perception, profundity

give ~ to: 5 edify, teach, train 6 advise 7 clarify 8 illumine, instruct 9 elucidate

high degree of ~: 6 acuity, acumen, wisdom 8 sagacity 10 astuteness

meditation ~: 9 vipassana

mock phrase of ~: 4 ah so

__ in sight: 5 no end

insightful: 4 keen, wise 5 acute, alert, quick, savvy, sharp, smart 6 astute, brainy, shrewd 7 knowing, sapient 8 lynx-eyed, profound 9 astucious, sagacious 10 discerning, perceptive

insignia: 4 mark 5 badge, crest, label, patch 6 device, emblem, symbol 7 earmark 8 heraldry 10 coat of arms, decoration

Insignificance (1985 film)

cast: Gary Busey, Tony Curtis, Michael Emil, Theresa Russell

director: Nicolas Roeg

insignificant: 4 idle, mere, null, punk, puny, tiny 5 dinky, light, minor, petty, scrub, small, sorry, teeny 6 casual, humble, lesser, little, meager, measly, minute, paltry, scanty, slight, teensy 7 lowborn, minimal, nominal, tenuous, trivial 8 marginal, mediocre, nugatory, picayune, piddling, trifling 9 senseless, valueless, worthless

amount: 3 dot, jot 4 iota, whit 5 minim, speck 6 trifle

most ~: 5 least

one: 4 nerd, nurd, snip, twit 5 dweeb, twerp, twirp 7 nebbish

insincere: 4 fake, glib, sham 5 false, lying, phony, slick 6 forced, hollow, phoney, shifty, tricky, unreal, untrue 7 crooked, devious, evasive, feigned, knavish, mincing, plastic, unloyal 8 affected, delusive, guileful, two-faced, unctuous 9 deceitful, deceptive, dishonest, faithless, high-toned, pretended, unnatural 10 artificial, backhanded, factitious, mendacious, perfidious, unfaithful, untruthful

be ~: 5 flirt 6 trifle 8 lollygag 10 dilly-dally, fool around

insincerity: 4 cant, jive 5 guile, hokum, lying 6 bunkum, deceit 7 perfidy 8 bad faith, betrayal, buncombe, claptrap, flattery, pretense

insinuate: 3 say 4 hint, seem, slur, worm 5 foist, get at, imply 6 advert, allude, horn in, impute, infuse, inject, slip in, worm in 7 ascribe, connote, engrain, ingrain, make out, signify, suggest, wedge in, whisper 8 allude to, intimate, lead up to, muscle in 9 get in with, implicate, interject, interpose, introduce 10 curry favor, infiltrate, ingratiate

insinuating: 4 oily 5 snide 7 pointed 8 unctuous

insinuation: 4 hint, slur, talk 7 whisper 8 innuendo 9 reference 10 imputation

insipid: 3 dry 4 arid, blah, drab, dull, flat, mild, tame, weak 5 banal, bland, empty, ho-hum, inane, plain, stale, tired, trite, vapid 6 boring, jejune 7 humdrum, maudlin, mundane, prosaic, tedious 8 lifeless, ordinary, unlively, unsavory 9 colorless, innocuous, pointless, prosaical, tasteless, wearisome 10 dullsville, flavorless, wishy-washy

become ~: 4 cloy, pall

one: 4 bore, drip, jerk, pest

insipidity: 6 anemia 7 anaemia, aridity, dryness 8 banality, dullness, flatness, limpness, monotony, thinness, vapidity, weakness

insist: 4 aver, avow, urge 5 claim, force, order, press 6 affirm, assert, demand, pester 7 command, contend, persist, protest, require, speak up 8 maintain, pressure, speak out 9 importune, persevere, stand firm 10 make a stand

ender: 3 ent 4 ence

on: 4 aver, urge 5 exact, press 6 assert, badger, demand, stress 7 require 9 challenge, emphasize, stipulate

insistence: 4 will 6 demand, stress, urging 7 goading 8 emphasis, pressure, prodding, spurring 9 assertion

insistent: 4 bent, dire 5 pushy, vocal 6 crying, dogged, urgent 7 adamant, burning 8 emphatic, forceful, pressing 9 assertive, clamorous, demanding, imperious, obstinate, pigheaded 10 continuous, insatiable, peremptory, persistent, vociferous

__ in Slang: 6 Fables

__ in smoke: 4 go up

in so __ words: 4 many

insociable: 3 icy 4 cold, cool 5 aloof, stiff 6 frigid, remote 7 distant 8 detached, reserved 10 unfriendly

In Society (1944 film)

cast: Bud Abbott, Lou Costello

__ in Socks: 3 Fox

insolence: 3 lip 4 gall, guff, sass 5 abuse, brass, cheek, mouth, nerve, pride, sauce 6 hutzpa, insult 7 chutzpa, hutzpah 8 audacity, back talk, boldness, chutzpah, contempt, defiance, pertness 9 arrogance, contumely, impudence 10 assumption, brazenness, disrespect, effrontery, incivility

insolent: 4 bold, flip, pert, rude, wise 5 brash, fresh, lofty, nervy, sassy, saucy, smart 6 awless, brassy, brazen, cheeky, snippy 7 abusive, aweless, defiant, huffish, uncivil 8 cavalier, flippant, impolite, impudent, off-based, snippety, superior 9 audacious, barefaced, insulting, offensive, out of line, shameless 10 disdainful, irreverent, ungracious

be ~: 4 sass 8 get smart, mouth off, talk back 10 answer back, disrespect

insoluble: 4 hard 6 thorny 7 obscure 8 baffling, puzzling 9 difficult 10 mysterious, mystifying, unresolved

insolvency: 4 ruin 6 penury 7 beggary, default, failure, poverty, straits 10 bankruptcy, nonpayment

insolvent: 4 poor 5 broke, needy 6 bad off, busted, hard up, ill-off, in need, in want, ruined 7 pinched 8 badly off, bankrupt, beggarly, deprived, indigent, in the red, strapped, wiped out 9 destitute, moneyless, penniless, penurious 10 down and out, foreclosed, on the rocks, out of money, pauperized, straitened

Insomnia (2002 film)

cast: Al Pacino, Hilary Swank, Maura Tierney, Robin Williams

director: Christopher Nolan

Insomnia author: Stephen King

insouciance: 8 airiness, buoyance, buoyancy, lethargy

insouciant: 8 carefree, listless 9 easy-going, unworried 10 nonchalant, unbothered, untroubled

__ in Space: 4 Lost

__ in Spain: 6 castle

__ in Spain, The: 4 Rain

inspan: 4 yoke 7 harness, hitch up

inspect: 3 eye, see, vet 4 case, comb, look, peer, scan, sift, view 5 audit, check, frisk, probe, study, touch 6 go over, patrol, peruse, review, sample, search, survey, try out 7 canvass, compare, dissect, examine, observe, oversee 8 appraise, check out, consider, evaluate, look into, look over, overhaul 9 go through, supervise 10 scrutinize

the joint: 4 look 5 spy on 6 survey 7 examine 8 check out 10 scrutinize

inspection: 4 look, scan, test, view 5 audit, check, probe, sight 6 review, search, survey 7 checkup, enquiry, inquiry, look-see, perusal, reading 8 analysis, once-over, scrutiny 9 inventory, maneuvers 10 dissection

__ inspection: 6 on-site

inspector: 5 judge 6 tester 7 auditor, checker, monitor 8 assessor, examiner, overseer, reviewer 10 supervisor

name meaning ~: 6 Conner

Inspector Gadget dog: 5 Brain
Inspector General, The
author: Nikolai Gogol
character: 4 Anna, Ivan, Luka 5 Anton, Marya
Inspector General, The (1949 film)
cast: Danny Kaye, Walter Slezak
director: Henry Koster
inspiration: 3 awe 4 idea, muse, soul, spur, whim 5 fancy, flash, hunch, spark 6 breath, motive, notion, origin, thrill, vision 7 impulse, insight, rapture, thought 8 afflatus, stimulus 10 inhalation
for a poet: 4 Muse 5 Erato
romantic ~: 4 moon, rose 5 stars
inspirational phrase: 3 saw 5 adage, axiom, maxim, motto 6 saying, slogan 7 epigram, precept, proverb 8 aphorism
inspire: 3 awe 4 fire, move, push, spur, stir, sway, urge 5 amaze, boost, flush, hop up, imbue, impel, liven, rouse, sniff, spark, touch 6 affect, arouse, ask for, bestir, buck up, excite, fire up, incite, infuse, instil, kindle, motive, perk up, prompt, stir up, strike, thrill, turn on, work up 7 actuate, animate, cheer up, elevate, enflame, enliven, hearten, implant, impress, inflame, instill, lighten, provoke, quicken, trigger 8 embolden, enspirit, imbolden, inspirit, interest, motivate, occasion, psyche up, reassure, start off 9 encourage, enhearten, galvanize, impassion, influence, irradiate, stimulate 10 give rise to, invigorate, predispose
inspired: 4 avid 5 fresh, novel 6 clever 7 aroused, exalted, excited, fired up, kindled, sparked, unusual 8 animated, creative, enthused, inflamed, original, vivified 9 energized, enkindled, enlivened, heartened, ingenious, inventive 10 innovative, reanimated, revivified
inspiring: 6 moving, poetic 7 hopeful 8 luminous, original, poetical 10 impressive, intoxicant, passionate
__-inspiring: 3 awe
inspirit: 4 fire, stir 5 cheer, hop up, rally, rouse 6 arouse, buck up, excite, incite, kindle, stir up, turn on, vivify 7 animate, console, enflame, enliven, gladden, hearten, inflame, quicken, refresh 8 embolden, energize, imbolden, motivate, psyche up, reassure, vitalize 9 encourage, enhearten, galvanize, impassion, inebriate, stimulate 10 exhilarate, intoxicate, invigorate, regenerate, strengthen
inspirited: 4 avid, keen 5 eager 6 fervid, gung ho 7 anxious, fervent, fired up, hopeful, zealous, zestful 8 sanguine 9 promising, psyched up 10 optimistic, raring to go
inspissate: 7 stiffen, thicken 9 coagulate
inst.: 3 min., sch., sec., sem. 4 acad., coll., univ.
instability: 4 flux 5 anomy 6 anomie, danger 8 neurosis, weakness
install: 3 fit, fix, lay, put, set, sit 4 seat 5 crown, embed, endue, fix up, imbed, indue, lodge, mount, place, plant, put in, set up, stick 6 hook up, induct, invest, ordain, settle 7 appoint, deposit, furnish, instate, quarter, receive, station 8 ensconce, initiate, position 9 establish, institute, introduce 10 inaugurate, put in place
in office: 4 seat 6 enseat 7 swear in
installation: 4 base, fort, post 5 setup 7 fitting, station
installment: 3 pmt. 4 part, payt. 5 issue, piece 7 chapter, episode, payment, portion, premium, section 8 division
buying: 6 credit
installment __: 4 plan
instance: 4 case, item, time 5 piece 6 detail, sample 7 example 8 occasion, sampling, specimen 9 precedent, situation 10 occurrence
for ~: 3 say 5 to wit 6 namely 10 explicitly
instant: 3 bit, sec 4 dire, fast, jiff, tick, time, wink 5 brisk, flash, fleet, hasty, jiffy, point, quick, rapid, swift, trice 6 flying, minute, moment, prompt, racing, second, snappy, speedy, urgent 7 burning, clamant, exigent, express, hurried 8 exigeant, juncture, pressing 9 breakneck, immediate, on-the-spot, twinkling 10 double-time, hypersonic, supersonic
at that ~: 4 then
replay technique: 5 slo-mo
this ~: 3 now, PDQ 4 anon, fast, soon 5 apace, quick, right, today 6 at once, presto 7 quickly, rapidly, swiftly 8 directly, in a flash, in a jiffy, in no time, outright, pell-mell, promptly, right now, right off, speedily 9 at present, forthwith, like a shot, on the spot, posthaste, presently, right away 10 double-time, here and now
instant __: 6 camera, coffee, replay
__ instant: 4 in an
instantaneous: 5 quick, rapid, swift 6 prompt 9 momentary
instantaneously: 3 now 4 anon, fast 5 apace 6 at once, presto 8 abruptly, directly, full tilt, in a jiffy, in a trice, in no time, suddenly
Instant Karma (1970 song) artist: John Lennon
instantly: 3 PDQ 4 anon, soon 5 apace, right 6 at once, presto 7 quickly, rapidly, swiftly 8 directly, in a flash, in a jiffy, in no time, outright, pell-mell, promptly, right now, right off, speedily 9 forthwith, like a shot, on the spot, posthaste, right away 10 double-time, this minute
instate: 4 seat 5 chair, crown, endue, frock, indue 6 induct, instal, invest, ordain 7 install, swear in 8 enthrone, initiate, inthrone 9 establish 10 inaugurate
in statu __: 3 quo
instead: 4 else 6 in lieu, rather 7 in place 8 on behalf 10 preferably
of: 4 over 10 rather than
instep: 4 arch
instigate: 3 set 4 abet, goad, spur, urge 5 cause, egg on, impel, raise, rouse, start 6 arouse, ask for, excite, fire up, foment, incite, induce, kindle, launch, needle, prompt, stir up, turn on, whip up, work up 7 actuate, enflame, inflame, provoke, steam up 8 engender, initiate, motivate, persuade, touch off 9 encourage, influence, make waves, stimulate 10 bring about, lead the way
instigation: 4 goad, prod, push, spur 5 cause 6 fillip, thrust, urging 7 dictate 9 incentive
instigator: 7 demagog, hellion 8 agitator, inflamer 9 demagogue
instill: 3 fix 5 imbue, infix, plant, teach 6 impart, infuse, inject 7 breathe, diffuse, engrain, engrave, implant, impress, inbreed, ingrain, inspire 8 engender, transmit 9 inculcate, inoculate, introduce, pound into
forcefully: 4 drub, drum
instinct: 4 gift, idea, nose, urge 5 hunch, knack, savvy, sense 7 faculty, feeling, impulse, know-how 8 aptitude 9 appetence, intuition 10 gut feeling, proclivity, sixth sense
having a killer ~: 5 cruel 6 brutal, savage 8 pitiless, ruthless 9 cutthroat, dog-eat-dog, ferocious
__ instinct: 3 gut 4 herd, life 6 animal
Instinct (1999 film)
cast: Cuba Gooding Jr., Anthony Hopkins, Donald Sutherland, Maura Tierney
director: Jon Turteltaub
__ Instinct: 5 Basic
instinctive: 3 gut 6 inborn, inbred, innate, native, reflex, rooted 7 natural 8 knee-jerk, visceral
feeling: 4 vibe 5 hunch, sense
institute: 4 open 5 begin, build, enact, erect, found, set up, start 6 create, impose, instal, launch, lyceum 7 academy, install, pioneer, society, usher in 8 generate, initiate 9 establish, introduce, originate, prescribe 10 come up with, foundation, inaugurate
__ Institute: 4 Salk 5 Pratt 6 Esalen
institution: 5 trust 6 museum 7 society 8 creation, localism
educational ~: 3 sch. 4 acad., coll., univ. 6 lyceum, school 7 academy, college
penal ~: 3 pen 4 jail 5 clink 6 prison 7 slammer 8 bastille, big house, hoosegow 9 calaboose
institutional: 4 cold, drab, dull, same 5 bland 7 inhuman, uniform 8 unvaried
__ in stone: 6 carved, etched
instr.: 4 prof.
__ in stride: 4 take
instruct: 3 set 4 form, show, tell 5 brief, coach, drill, edify, guide, order, teach, train, tutor 6 advise, assign, charge, clue in, direct, ground, inform, notify, school 7 apprise, apprize, break in, command, counsel, educate, lecture, nurture, require 8 acquaint, illumine, initiate 9 catechize, enlighten, inculcate, prescribe
instruction: 4 info 5 drill, order 6 charge, homily, lesson 7 command, lecture, lessons, mandate, precept, tuition 8 coaching, drilling, guidance, pedagogy, teaching, training, tutelage 9 direction, paedagogy
manual: 5 how-to 8 handbook
unit: 4 step 6 lesson
Instruction Paintings author: 3 Ono
instructions: 6 method, recipe 7 formula 9 procedure 10 directions
instructor: 4 prof 5 coach, guide, tutor 6 didact, lector, master, mentor 7 adviser, advisor, pedagog, teacher, trainer 8 educator, lecturer 9 abecedary, counselor, pedagogue, preceptor, professor
__ instructor: 5 drill
instructors: 7 faculty
instructors' org.: 3 AFT, NEA, UFT
instrument: 3 sax, uke, way 4 fife, gear, gong, harp, horn, lute, lyre, Moog, oboe, pawn, tool, tuba, viol 5 agent, banjo, bongo, bugle, cello, dodad, flute, gismo, gizmo, kazoo, labor, means, organ, paper, piano, thing, viola 6 agency, chimes, cornet, device, doodad, engine, factor, fiddle, gadget, guitar, medium, puppet, tam-tam, tom-tom, violin, zither 7 alto sax, bagpipe, bassoon, celesta, channel, clavier, cymbals, helicon, machine, maracas, marimba, musette, ocarina, panpipe, piccolo, saxhorn, trumpet, ukulele, utensil, vehicle 8 altohorn, autoharp, bass drum, bass viol, calliope, castanet, clarinet, dulcimer, mandolin, melodeon, recorder, theremin, triangle, trombone 9 accordion, alpenhorn, apparatus, appliance, balalaika, equipment, euphonium, expedient, harmonica, harmonium, implement, mechanism, saxophone, testament, vibraharp 10 clavichord, concertina, contrabass, flugelhorn, hurdy-gurdy, kettledrum, sousaphone, squeezebox, tambourine, vibraphone 11 harpsichord
combining form: 4 -labe
instrument __: 5 panel 6 flying 7 landing, station
__ instrument: 4 reed, wind 5 brass 6 flight 7 transit
instrumental: 3 key 5 music, vital 6 active, of help, useful 7 helpful, pivotal 8 involved
instrumentalist: 5 fifer 6 bugler, oboist, player 7 cellist, drummer, flutist, harpist, pianist 8 banjoist, flautist, musician 9 guitarist, trumpeter, violinist
instrumentality: 4 help, mode, tool, ways 5 means 6 agency, device, method, system 7 channel, machine, vehicle 8 resource, strategy 9 operation
instruments
guided only by ~: 5 blind
__ Instruments: 5 Texas
__ in Style: 5 Going
insubordinate: 5 onery, rebel 6 feisty, ornery, unruly 7 defiant, lawless, naughty, radical, wayward 8 contrary, factious, insolent, mutinous, stubborn 10 rebellious
be ~: 5 act up, be bad, cut up 7 carry on, go wrong 8 go astray 9 misbehave 10 fool around, transgress
insubordination: 6 heresy, mutiny, revolt 8 apostasy, audacity, contempt, defiance 9 contumacy, defection, impudence, insolence, rebellion 10 brazenness, effrontery
insubstantial: 4 airy, idle, poor, puny, slim, thin, weak 5 false, frail, light, trite 6 feeble, flimsy, porous, skimpy, slight, unreal 7 fragile, slender, tenuous, unsound 8 ethereal, illusive, illusory, skin-deep 9 transient
insufferable: 3 bad 4 hard 5 awful, lousy 7 painful 8 dreadful, horrible
one: 4 bore, drip, pain, pest, pill
insufficiency: 4 lack, need, want 5 minus 6 dearth 7 absence, beggary, deficit, paucity, poverty 8 exiguity, scarcity, shortage, sparsity 10 meagerness
insufficient: 3 shy 4 lame, poor, slim, weak 5 light, scant, short, small 6 little, meager, scanty, scarce, skimpy, sparse 7 failing, lacking, limited, sketchy, slender, unample, wanting
__ in sugar: 3 S as
insular: 6 closed, cut off, narrow 7 bigoted, limited, topical 8 confined, detached, isolated, secluded, separate 9 illiberal, parochial, sectarian 10 prejudiced, provincial, restricted
insulate: 6 shield 7 protect 8 cloister, separate 9 segregate, sequester
insulated, poorly: 6 drafty
insulation: 3 PVC 4 batt, down 5 kapok, Mylar
banned ~: 3 PCB 8 asbestos
insult: 3 cut, dig, dis 4 barb, jeer, mock, quip, slam, slap, slur, snub, zing 5 abase, abuse, crack, flout, libel, roast, scorn, shock, sneer, taunt,

wound, wrong 6 debase, deride, dump on, injure, malign, offend, rebuff, slight 7 affront, blister, degrade, disgust, epithet, low blow, mockery, obloquy, offense, outrage, provoke, put down, slander 8 black eye, derision, dishonor, rudeness 9 aspersion, cheap shot, contumely, humiliate, impudence, indignity, insolence, invective 10 antagonize, disrespect, incivility, opprobrium, scurrility, vituperate
Internet ~: 5 flame
insulted, feeling: 4 hurt 8 offended
insulting: 4 rude 5 snide 6 biting 7 abusive, hurtful, jeering, uncivil 8 derisive, insolent, inurbane 9 injurious, offensive, ungallant 10 defamatory, scurrilous
look: 4 gibe 5 smirk, sneer 7 snigger
insupportable: 4 weak 6 flawed 8 doubtful, specious 9 untenable
insuppressible: 4 wild
insurance: 5 hedge 7 backing, promise, reserve, support 8 coverage, overhead, security 9 allowance, assurance, guarantee, indemnity, provision, safeguard 10 precaution, protection
addendum: 5 rider 9 amendment
center: 5 Omaha 8 Hartford
concern: 4 loss, prem., risk 5 claim 7 premium
giant: 3 Pru 4 MONY 5 Aetna 6 Kemper, Lloyd's 7 MetLife 10 Prudential
kind of ~: 3 car 4 auto, home, life, term 5 flood 6 health
office: 6 agency
org.: 3 HMO, PPO 4 FDIC 5 FSLIC
worker: 3 CLU 5 agent 7 actuary
___ insurance: 3 car 4 auto, fire, life, term 5 flood, group, theft, title 6 dental, excess, health, keyman, marine, mutual, social 7 no-fault
insure: 5 cover, sew up 6 clinch, defend, secure, shield 7 promise, protect 8 attest to 9 guarantee, indemnify, safeguard 10 underwrite
insurgence: 6 revolt 8 defiance, uprising 9 commotion, rebellion
insurgent: 5 rebel 6 anarch 7 lawless, radical, riotous 8 agitator, factious, frondeur, mutineer, mutinous, renegade, resister 9 anarchist, fractious, revolting, seditious 10 anarchical, incendiary, malcontent, rebellious, subversive, unpeaceful
starter: 7 counter
insurmountable: 8 hopeless 10 impassable, infeasible, out of reach
insurrection: 4 coup, riot 6 mutiny, revolt, unrest 8 disorder, outbreak, sedition, uprising 9 rebellion
insurrectionist: 5 rebel 7 heretic, radical, traitor 8 agitator, mutineer, renegade 9 dissenter, dissident, insurgent 10 malcontent
insusceptible: 3 icy 4 cold, cool, hard 5 stony 6 dead to, deaf to, flinty, frigid, inured, steely, stoney 7 callous
int.
not ~: 3 ext.
where ~ may appear: 4 stmt.
Int. ___: 3 Rev.
intact: 4 mint 5 as one, solid, sound, uncut, whole 6 entire, unhurt, virgin 7 perfect, working 8 all there, complete, together, unbroken, unharmed, unmarked, virginal 9 inviolate, not broken, undamaged, uninjured, unscathed, untouched 10 in one piece, unabridged, unimpaired
intaglio: 7 carving, jewelry 9 engraving
counterpart: 5 cameo
stone: 4 onyx
intake: 4 diet, food 7 suction 8 air shaft, air valve 10 absorption
intake ___: 5 valve
intangible: 5 ideal 6 dreamy, unreal 7 elusive, elusory 8 abstract, abstruse, bodiless, ethereal 9 invisible, spiritual 10 evanescent, immaterial, impalpable, indefinite, unapparent, unphysical, unviewable
___ in tango: 3 T as
...in tears amid the ___ corn: 5 alien
integer: 2 no. 3 one, six, two 4 five, four, nine, unit 5 eight, seven, three 6 figure, number 7 numeral
integers, like some: 3 odd 4 even
Integra: 3 car 4 auto 5 Acura
integral: 3 sum 4 full 5 basic, total, vital, whole 6 choate, entire 7 organic, pivotal 8 complete 9 aggregate, elemental, essential, intrinsic, necessary, requisite, undivided
integrate: 3 mix, wed 4 fuse, join, knit, link, meld, mesh 5 blend, immix, merge, unify, unite 6 embody, imbody 7 combine, conjoin 8 coalesce, go native 9 associate, commingle, harmonize, interface, reconcile 10 amalgamate, assimilate, centralize, complement, constitute, coordinate, homogenize, proportion, synthesize
integrated: 6 joined, linked, meshed, smooth, united 7 flowing, unified 8 cohesive, complete, hooked up
integrated ___: 3 bar 6 optics 7 circuit
integration: 5 blend, union 6 fusion 7 amalgam 9 synthesis
org. promoting ~: 4 CORE 5 NAACP
integrity: 5 asset, honor, right, truth, unity 6 ethics, purity, virtue 7 honesty, loyalty, probity 8 cohesion, fairness, fidelity, goodness, identity, morality, nobility, totality, veracity 9 character, coherence, constancy, fixedness, good faith, principle, rectitude, sincerity, soundness, stability, wholeness 10 entireness, honestness, perfection, principles, simplicity
integument: 3 pod 4 aril, bark, case, hide, hull, husk, rind, skin 5 crust, shell, shuck, testa 6 casing, sheath 7 coating, outside, peeling 8 covering, envelope, membrane, pellicle
intellect: 4 head, mind, nous, sage, soul, wits 5 brain, depth, savvy, sense 6 acuity, acumen, brains, genius, pundit, reason, smarts 7 ability, egghead, scholar, thinker 8 aptitude, Einstein, highbrow, judgment, sagacity 9 ingenuity, mentality 10 profundity
intellection: 4 idea, mind 5 brain, sense 6 acumen, brains, reason, senses 7 marbles 8 judgment, lucidity, sapience 9 mentality
intellectual: 3 ace 4 nerd, nurd, sage, whiz 5 brain, smart, sound 6 brainy, genius, mental, pundit 7 bookish, egghead, erudite, learned, prodigy, scholar, thinker 8 abstract, academic, cerebral, creative, Einstein, highbrow, longhair, profound, rational, studious, virtuoso 9 scholarly 10 mastermind
intellectualize: 5 think 6 ideate, reason 8 cogitate, ruminate 9 cerebrate
intelligence: 3 wit 4 head, info, mind, news, soul, wits, word 5 brain, depth, savvy, sense, skill 6 acuity, acumen, brains, esprit, genius, reason, report, sanity, smarts, wisdom 7 ability, lowdown, message, tidings 8 aptitude, judgment, keenness, sagacity, sapience 9 mentality
org.: 3 CIA, NSA
intelligence ___: 4 test 5 agent 6 agency, bureau, office 7 officer
intelligent: 3 apt 4 able, keen, sage, sane, wise 5 quick, ready, sharp, smart, witty 6 astute, brainy, bright, clever, gifted, shrewd, strong 7 capable, knowing, liberal, logical, sapient 8 cerebral, highbrow, incisive, profound, rational, sensible, thinking 9 astucious, brilliant, ingenious, inventive, observant, sagacious 10 perceptive, reasonable
group: 5 Mensa
not ~: 3 dim 4 dull, dumb, slow 5 inane, silly 6 oafish, obtuse, simple 7 asinine, boorish, doltish, foolish, witless 8 ignorant 9 brainless, dimwitted, nitwitted, senseless 10 half-witted, illiterate, soft-headed
intelligentsia: 6 brains 7 savants 8 literati
intelligible: 4 open 5 clear, lucid, plain 6 limpid, simple 7 legible, obvious 8 coherent, distinct, knowable, luminous, readable, simplify
Intellivision rival: 5 Atari
Intel rival: 3 AMD
intemperance: 6 luxury
intemperate: 3 hot 4 wild 5 undue 6 bitter, lavish, severe, torrid, wanton 7 hoggish, lustful, piggish, raucous 8 prodigal, rigorous, tropical, uncurbed
be ~: 6 overdo 7 lay it on, run riot 8 overplay
intemperately: 3 too 4 very 6 unduly
intemperence: 4 lust 6 excess 8 gluttony, voracity
intend: 3 aim 4 mean, plan 5 aim to, essay, spell 6 aspire, design, expect 7 attempt, propose, purport, purpose, resolve, signify 8 endeavor 10 have in mind, have in view
to: 4 will 5 shall
intended: 5 meant 6 fiancé, future, wilful 7 fiancée, willful 8 plighted, promised 9 affianced, betrothed, voluntary 10 deliberate, purposeful, volitional
intense: 3 hot 4 avid, deep, hard, keen, loud, rich, warm, wild 5 acute, eager, fiery, great, harsh, lurid, sharp, type A, vivid 6 ardent, biting, bitter, devout, fervid, fierce, heated, marked, mortal, red-hot, severe, solemn, steady, strong, torrid, urgent 7 burning, cutting, dynamic, earnest, extreme, fervent, flaming, furious, soulful, vicious, violent, zealous 8 diligent, forceful, piercing, poignant, powerful, profound, stinging, strained, terrific, vehement, vigorous, wild-eyed 9 agonizing, desperate, energetic, excessive, exquisite, fanatical, innermost, steadfast, undivided 10 passionate, purposeful, unwavering
become less ~: 3 ebb 4 wane 5 abate 7 decline, subside, tail off
look: 3 eye 4 gaze, leer 5 glare, stare
not ~: 4 calm 5 type B 8 laid-back
intensely: 4 deep, hard 5 madly 6 keenly, vastly 7 greatly 8 forcibly, mightily, severely, terribly, urgently 9 extremely, fervently, like crazy, seriously 10 incredibly, powerfully, thoroughly
intensification: 5 surge, swell 6 growth, step-up, upturn, waxing 7 buildup, upsurge, upswing 8 increase, swelling, widening 9 crescendo, deepening 10 broadening, burgeoning
intensify: 4 boom, gird, rise, tone, whet 5 add to, boost, build, crank, mount, raise, revup, shore, spike, steel, swell 6 accent, anneal, beef up, deepen, gather, harden, heat up, prop up, step up, stress, temper, tone up 7 augment, bolster, brace up, build up, burgeon, develop, elevate, empower, enhance, fortify, magnify, quicken, scale up, sharpen, shore up, stiffen, toughen 8 bourgeon, brighten, buttress, compound, energize, escalate, heighten, increase, indurate, redouble, vitalize 9 aggravate, emphasize, reinforce 10 accentuate, aggrandize, exacerbate, exaggerate, invigorate, strengthen
intensity: 4 fire, fury, heat, kick, size, zeal 5 ardor, depth, fever, force, might, power, vigor 6 degree, energy, fervor, volume 7 emotion, ferment, passion, potence, potency, tension 8 devotion, emphasis, keenness, lyricism, severity, strength, violence 9 acuteness, diligence, greatness, high pitch, magnitude, sharpness, toughness, vehemence 10 enthusiasm, excitement, fanaticism, fierceness
lose ~: 3 ebb 4 wane 5 abate 7 subside
Intensity author: Dean Koontz
intensive: 4 deep 6 all-out, severe 7 in-depth 8 complete, profound, thorough, whole hog 9 demanding, full-dress, out-and-out, speeded-up 10 exhaustive
___-intensive: 5 labor 7 capital
intent: 3 aim, end, set 4 bent, firm, goal, hope, idea, keen, plan, rapt, will, wish 5 alert, bound, drift, eager, fixed, point, tenor 6 desire, motive, notion, object, spirit, target 7 dead-set, decided, earnest, engaged, focused, meaning, purport, purpose, riveted, settled 8 absorbed, ambition, decisive, hell-bent, immersed, occupied, resolute, resolved, studious, volition, watchful 9 ambitious, attentive, committed, engrossed, iron-jawed, objective, steadfast, wrapped up 10 determined, purposeful, resolution, thoughtful
malicious ~: 5 spite 6 enmity, hatred, malice, rancor 7 cruelty, ill will, revenge 8 acrimony 9 animosity, hostility, vengeance
name meaning ~: 6 Ernest
with the ~: 4 so as
intention: 3 aim, end 4 goal, hope, idea, plan, will, wish 5 angle, drift 6 animus, design, desire, import, motive, notion, object, reason, spirit, target 7 meaning, purport, purpose, resolve, thought 8 volition 10 resolution
intentional: 5 meant 6 wilful 7 advised, knowing, planned, studied, willful, willing, witting 8 designed, unforced 9 voluntary 10 purposeful
intently: 4 hard 6 firmly, keenly 7 alertly, closely, fixedly, sharply 8 steadily, urgently 9 seriously
intentness: 4 zeal 9 assiduity, attention, diligence, eagerness 10 absorption
___ intents and purposes: 5 to all 6 for all
inter ___: 3 nos 4 alia, alii 5 alios, vivos
interact: 4 talk 6 relate 7 combine, connect, network 8 converse 9 cooperate, interface, touch base
interactive: 5 joint 6 mutual, shared 8 communal, conjoint 9 concerted 10 collective, reciprocal
interactive ___: 5 novel 7 fiction
interbreed: 3 mix 5 blend, cross 6 mingle 9 hybridize
intercede: 3 aid 4 help 5 mix in 6 assist, butt in, step in 7 barge in, intrude, mediate 9 arbitrate, intervene, negotiate, reconcile, take a hand

interceder: 5 agent, envoy 7 arbiter, liaison, referee 8 emissary, mediator 9 go-between, middleman 10 arbitrator, negotiator, peacemaker
intercept: 3 get 4 curb, halt, snag, stop, take 5 block, catch, check, seize 6 ambush, arrest, cut off, tackle, waylay 7 deflect, head off, prevent 8 obstruct, overhear 9 interpose, interrupt, shortstop 10 anticipate
intercession: 3 bid 4 plea, suit 6 agency, orison, prayer 8 intreaty, petition 9 mediation 10 assistance
intercessor: 3 ref, ump 5 judge 6 umpire 7 referee 10 arbitrator
interchange: 4 swap, swop 5 bandy, trade 6 barter, rotate, switch 7 liaison 8 exchange, language 9 take turns, transpose
sight: 5 diner, motel 10 gas station
interchangeable: 4 same 5 alike 7 related 8 fungible 10 reciprocal
intercom call: 4 page
interconnect: 6 adjoin, engage, relate
interconnection: 3 web 4 link 7 network
Inter-Continental: 5 hotel
alternative: 4 Omni 5 Hyatt 6 Hilton, Westin 7 Wyndham 8 Marriott, Radisson, Sheraton 10 DoubleTree 11 Crowne Plaza, Four Seasons
intercourse: 5 trade, union 6 speech 7 contact, jobbing, rapping, talking, trading, traffic 8 colloquy, commerce
interdependent: 6 linked, mutual 7 related 10 reciprocal
interdict: 3 ban, bar 4 stop, tabu, veto 5 debar, taboo 6 censor, forbid, hinder, impede, outlaw 7 embargo, exclude, inhibit, prevent, repress 8 disallow, preclude, prohibit, restrain 9 exclusion, proscribe
interdicted: 5 taboo 7 crooked, illegal, illicit 8 criminal, unlawful, verboten 9 felonious, forbidden 10 not allowed
interdiction: 3 ban, bar 4 tabu, veto 7 embargo, refusal
interest: 4 care, gain, good, grab, grip, hook, lure, move, note, part, sake, side, stir, zest 5 amuse, catch, claim, hobby, piece, pique, right, rivet, rouse, share, snare, sport, stake, tempt, touch 6 absorb, affect, allure, arouse, arrest, behalf, divert, engage, entice, excite, matter, notice, occupy, perk up, please, points, profit, regard, return, strike, turn on 7 attract, benefit, concern, engross, enthral, enthuse, immerse, impress, inspire, inthral, involve, passion, pastime, portion, pursuit, revenue, welfare 8 activity, appeal to, dividend, enthrall, inthrall, intrigue, lifework, proceeds 9 advantage, affection, avocation, curiosity, diversion, entertain, fascinate, relevance, spotlight, stimulate, tantalize, titillate, well-being 10 absorption, attraction, enthusiasm, excitement, importance, motivation, percentage, prosperity, recreation, snoopiness
common ~: 3 tie 4 bond, link
devoid of ~: 4 blah, dull, flat 5 vapid 6 boring, jejune 7 insipid, prosaic 9 tasteless, wearisome 10 dullsville, flavorless, lackluster
excessive ~: 5 usury
factor: 3 pct. 4 rate 5 yield 7 percent
have an ~ in: 3 own 4 hold 7 possess
hold one's ~: 6 engage
in the ~ of: 3 for
lack of ~: 5 ennui 6 tedium 7 boredom
lose ~: 3 nod 4 pale, pall, tire 5 weary
paying ~: 5 owing 6 in debt
personal ~: 5 share, stake 6 behalf 10 investment
point of ~: 5 locus, scene, sight, vista 6 vision 7 display, exhibit 9 spectacle
provide at ~: 4 lend, loan
regard with ~: 4 gape, gawk, gaze 5 stare 10 rubberneck
show lack of ~: 4 doze, yawn
special ~ group: 3 soc. 5 guild, lobby 6 caucus 7 society
strong ~: 4 zeal, zest 5 ardor, mania 6 fervor, thirst 7 craving, passion 8 devotion 9 intensity, obsession 10 dedication, enthusiasm
take an ~ in: 4 like
to a usurer: 3 vig 8 vigorish
unit: 2 pt. 5 point
__ interest: 4 life 5 short 6 public, simple, vested 7 accrued, special
interested: 4 keen 5 drawn 6 caught 7 curious, liberal 9 attentive, attracted, concerned, engrossed, impressed, inquiring, observant, on the case, receptive 10 fascinated, implicated, prejudiced, responsive, stimulated
be ~: 4 care 9 give a darn
become ~: 5 sit up
be ~ in: 5 watch 6 follow, take in 7 monitor, observe 9 cultivate
too ~: 4 nosy 5 nosey 6 prying, snoopy 8 meddling, snooping 9 butting in, intrusive, obtrusive 10 meddlesome
very ~: 4 avid 5 afire 6 ardent
interesting: 5 fresh, juicy, meaty, novel 6 clever, exotic 7 curious, unusual 8 creative, gripping, inspired, inviting, magnetic, original, readable 9 ingenious, inventive, memorable 10 innovative, magnetical
not ~: 3 dry 4 blah 5 banal, ho-hum
__ interesting!: 4 Very
__-interest story: 5 human
interface: 4 link, talk 7 combine, connect, liaison 8 interact 9 integrate, touch base
interfere: 3 pry 4 nose, poke 5 mix in, snoop 6 butt in, horn in, impede, kibitz, meddle, step in, tamper 7 barge in, intrude, obtrude 8 conflict, obstruct 9 frustrate, interlope, interpose, interrupt, intervene 10 contravene, discommode, discourage
with: 5 block, cross, delay 6 hamper, hinder
(with): 4 fool, mess
interference: 8 blocking, meddling, obstacle
reception ~: 4 snow 6 static
run ~ for: 4 help 6 assist 8 advocate
interfering: 4 nosy, rude 5 pushy 8 meddling 9 intrusive, obtrusive, officious 10 meddlesome
interfold: 5 weave 6 enlace, inlace
interim: 3 gap 4 wait 5 break, letup, pause, while 6 acting, breach, hiatus, lacuna, layoff, pro tem, recess 7 stopgap, time-out 8 breather, downtime, interval, meantime 9 makeshift, temporary, tentative 10 jury-rigged, pro tempore
in the ~: 8 meantime 9 meanwhile
interior: 4 core, home, soul 5 heart, inner, midst 6 bowels, center, inland, inside, marrow, within 7 central, in-house, private 8 domestic, national
combining form: 4 endo-, ento-
destroy the ~: 3 gut
interior __: 5 angle 6 design 7 lineman, mapping
Interior Dept. agcy: 3 BLM, NPS
Interiors (1978 film)
cast: Diane Keaton, E.G. Marshall, Geraldine Page
director: Woody Allen
interject: 3 add 5 input, put in 6 fill in, insert, jump in, thrust 7 comment, force in, implant, include, intrude, throw in 9 insinuate, interpose, interrupt, introduce, punctuate, squeeze in 10 infiltrate
interjection: 2 ah, aw, eh, ha, hi, ho, oh, ow, oy, uh 3 aah, ack, aha, arf, bah, bam, boo, boy, brr, cry, duh, fie, gee, grr, haw, heh, hey, huh, ick, nix, och, oho, olé, oof, ooh, pah, pow, rah, rot, say, tsk, tut, ugh, why, wow, yah, yay, yea, yes, yow, yum, zzz 4 ahem, ahoy, alas, amen, arra, bosh, ciao, darn, dear, drat, ecce, egad, evoe, good, gosh, ha-ha, hail, heck, help, hush, jeez, mush, nuts, oh-oh, okay, oops, ouch, oyes, oyez, pfft, pfui, phew, phoo, pish, poof, pooh, posh, ptui, rats, roar, scat, shoo, ta-da, ta-ta, tush, uh-oh, uh-uh, well, wham, whee, whew, whoo, word, yeah, yell, yeow, yipe, yo-ho, yuck 5 achoo, alack, arrah, avast, banco, bingo, blimy, brava, bravo, egads, faugh, fudge, golly, goody, great, hallo, hello, hillo, ho-hum, hooey, hoo-ha, howdy, hullo, humph, huzza, later, nerts, nertz, peace, phfft, prost, pshaw, right, salud, scram, shame, shout, shush, skoal, sooey, sorry, ta-dah, tehee, uh-huh, voilà, whoof, whoop, yecch, yipes, zooks, zowie 6 ahchoo, begone, behold, bellow, blimey, by Jove, cheers, clamor, crikey, cripes, encore, enough, eureka, giddap, goodie, good-oh, gotcha, hachoo, halloa, halloo, hallow, haw-haw, hilloa, holler, hoo-hah, hoorah, hooray, hotcha, hot dog, hulloo, hurrah, hurray, huzzah, indeed, jiminy, ka-boom, la-de-da, la-di-da, l'chaim, outcry, phooey, presto, prosit, ptooey, rather, remark, righto, shalom, sheesh, sholom, shucks, tee-hee, thanks, touché, tsk tsk, tut-tut, whammo, whizzo, whoops, yippee, yoicks, yoohoo, yum-yum, zounds 7 attaboy, big deal, brother, by jingo, caramba, cheerio, gangway, giddyap, giddyup, goldarn, goldurn, good-bye, heave ho, heigh-ho, holy cow, horrors, hosanna, hushaby, jeepers, jimminy, kerchoo, l'chayim, lehayim, Odzooks, rubbish, whoopee, whoopie 8 alley-oop, all right, attagirl, by cracky, farewell, for shame, Gadzooks, gracious, holy moly, honestly, lackaday, lah-di-dah, lechayim, scramola, welladay, wellaway, whatever 10 hallelujah
palindromic ~: 3 aha, hah, oho, wow
see also exclamation
interlace: 3 mat, mix, tie 4 bind, join, knit, knot, lace 5 braid, plait, twine, weave 6 engage, enmesh, immesh, inmesh, mingle, splice, zigzag 7 combine, entwine, intwine 8 entangle
interlaced: 4 wove 5 woven
Interlaken river: 3 Aar 4 Aare
interlard: 5 admix, mix in 7 dress up, spice up
interlink: 4 join, link, mesh 5 unite 6 splice 7 connect 8 dovetail
interlock: 3 fit 4 knit, mesh 6 engage, enlace, inlace 8 dovetail
interlocution: 4 chat, talk 6 confab, gossip, parley, powwow 7 chatter, palaver, schmoos 8 chitchat, converse, schmoose, schmooze
interlocutor: 2 MC 4 host 5 emcee
interlope: 3 pry 4 nose 5 snoop 6 tamper 7 intrude 8 trespass 9 interfere
interloper: 7 invader 8 kibitzer, outsider, stranger 10 trespasser
interlude: 3 gap 4 halt, lull, rest, wait 5 break, delay, pause, space, spell 6 hiatus, recess 7 episode, liaison, respite 8 downtime, interval, stoppage
intermediary: 3 rep 4 tool 5 agent, envoy, judge, means 6 broker, buffer, medium 7 channel, liaison, vehicle 8 delegate, emissary, mediator 9 appointee, messenger, middleman 10 peacemaker
intermediate: 6 center, medium, middle 7 average, neutral 8 moderate 9 appointee
in law: 5 mesne
intermediate __: 4 card 6 school
intermesh: 6 engage 8 activate
Intermezzo (1939 film)
cast: Ingrid Bergman, Edna Best, Leslie Howard
composer: 7 Steiner
director: Gregory Ratoff
interminable: 4 dull, long 6 boring 7 endless, eternal, lengthy, nonstop, undying 8 constant, infinite, timeless, unending 9 perpetual, unlimited
interminably: 4 ever 5 no end, on end 7 forever, on and on
intermingle: 3 mix, wed 4 fuse, join, meld, mesh, pool 5 admix, blend, merge 6 mingle 7 combine 8 intermix
intermission: 4 lull, rest, stop, wait 5 break, lapse, let-up, pause, spell 6 layoff, recess 7 interim, leisure, respite, time-out 8 abeyance, breather, downtime, interval, stoppage
follower: 5 Act II 6 act two
intermit: 3 end 4 halt, stay 5 break, cease, let up, pause, recur 6 arrest, recess 7 suspend, take ten 8 take five 9 interrupt, terminate
intermittent: 6 broken, uneven 8 frequent, periodic, sporadic 9 recurrent, spasmodic 10 sporadical
intermittent __: 5 fever 7 current, showers
intermittently: 8 fitfully, off and on, on and off 9 piecemeal, sometimes
intermix: 4 fuse 5 alloy, blend, merge 6 mingle 7 shuffle 9 commingle 10 adulterate, assimilate
intermixture: 4 meld 5 alloy, blend, union 6 fusion, medley 7 amalgam, mélange, variety 8 mishmash, mixed bag 9 composite, diversity, synthesis, variation 10 assortment, collection, concoction, miscellany
intern: 3 pen 4 cage, jail, keep, stay, tyro 5 gofer, medic, pupil, seize 6 detain, doctor, gopher, immure, lock up, novice, shut in 7 confine, enclose, impound, inclose, learner, new hand, student, trainee 8 imprison, resident, restrict 9 greenhorn, new doctor, physician 10 apprentice, tenderfoot
place: 4 ward 6 clinic 8 hospital
internal: 4 home 5 civic, inner 6 inland, innate, inside, inward 8 domestic, national 10 indigenous
combining form: 3 end-, ent- 4 endo-, ento-
internal __: 3 ear 4 gear 5 audit, clock, exile, rhyme 6 energy, stress 7 revenue
Internal Affairs actor: 4 Gere
internalize
anger: 4 boil, fret, fume 5 chafe 6 seethe
internalize anger: 4 stew 6 seethe
international: 5 alien, world 6 global 7 foreign, oversea 8 offshore, overseas 9 worldwide

international __: **3** law **4** unit **5** pitch **6** candle
International __: **4** Code **5** House, Style **6** Gothic, Master, Orange
International __ Line: **4** Date
__ International: **5** First, Third **6** Fourth, Second, Vienna **7** Amnesty, Gideons
International House (1933 film)
cast: Stuart Erwin, W.C. Fields, Peggy Hopkins Joyce
interne: **5** medic **6** doctor **9** physician
internecine: **4** gory **5** civil **6** bloody, deadly, family, mortal **7** ruinous **8** domestic, familial, internal
internee: **3** con **5** felon, lifer **7** captive, convict, hostage **8** criminal, detainee, jailbird, offender, prisoner, yardbird **10** lawbreaker
Internet: **3** Web, WWW **6** the Web **10** cyberspace
access method: **5** modem, Web TV
ad: **6** banner
addict, perhaps: **4** nerd, nurd
auction site: **4** eBay
browse the ~: **4** surf
commerce: **5** e-tail **6** e-trade
company: **6** dot-com
convenience: **4** link
insult: **5** flame
large ~ database: **5** Lexis, Nexis
letters: **3** URL, www **4** html, http
mag.: **5** e-zine
messages: **5** e-mail
program: **6** applet
programming language: **4** Java
provider: **3** AOL
query: **3** FAQ
search engine: **6** Google
separator: **3** dot
software: **7** browser
start an ~ session: **5** log in, log on
suffix: **3** com, edu, gov, net, org
surfer: **4** user
surf the ~: **6** browse
internist: **2** MD **5** medic **6** doctor **9** physician
org.: **3** AMA
internment: **6** arrest **7** bondage, custody **9** captivity, detention **10** detainment, immurement
Interns, The (1962 film)
cast: Michael Callan, James MacArthur, Cliff Robertson
__ inter pares: **5** prima **6** primus
interpersonal __: **6** skills, theory
interplay: **6** banter **8** exchange **9** tit for tat **10** networking
interpolation: **3** tag **5** ad lib, aside, rider **6** insert, prefix, suffix **7** adjunct, codicil **8** addendum, addition, footnote
word ~: **6** tmesis
interpose: **3** pry **5** cut in, judge **6** butt in, edge in, horn in, inject, insert, kibitz, meddle, step in, toss in, umpire, work in, worm in **7** barge in, head off, implant, mediate, referee, wedge in **8** chisel in, muscle in, sandwich **9** arbitrate, insinuate, intercept, interfere, interject, intervene, introduce **10** contravene
interposing: **4** nosy **5** nosey **6** prying, snoopy **8** snooping **9** intrusive
interpret: **4** limn, read, take **5** enact, gloss, infer, solve, state, teach, treat **6** decode, define, depict, recite, render **7** analyze, clarify, explain, expound, perform, portray **8** annotate, construe, decipher, simplify, spell out **9** criticize, delineate, elaborate, elucidate, exemplify, explicate, represent, translate **10** commentate, illuminate, illustrate, paraphrase, understand
interpretation: **4** spin **5** grasp, light, sense, slant **6** aspect **7** insight, meaning, reading, version **8** analysis, judgment **9** rendition
Interpretation of Dreams, The
author: Sigmund Freud
interpreter: **5** guide **6** critic, editor **7** decoder, exegete, prophet **8** cicerone, dragoman, exponent
interregnum: **3** gap **4** lull, rest **5** break, letup, pause **6** hiatus, lacuna, recess **7** interim, respite **8** abeyance, half time, interval
interrelationship: **4** bond, link **6** accord **7** concord, empathy, harmony, rapport **8** affinity, goodwill, sympathy **9** communion
__ in Terris: **5** Pacem
interrogate: **3** ask **4** pump, quiz **5** grill, probe, query, roast **6** go over **7** examine **8** question, work over
interrogation: **5** Q and A, query **6** asking **7** enquiry, inquiry, pumping **8** grilling, question
interrogation __: **4** mark **5** point
interrogative
adverb: **3** how **4** when **5** where
French ~: **4** quel, quoi
pronoun: **3** who, why **4** what, whom
Spanish ~: **3** qué **4** cómo **5** quíen
interrupt: **3** cut, end **4** halt, stop **5** barge, break, check, crash, cut in, delay, sever, stall **6** arrest, bother, bust in, butt in, cut off, divide, edge in, hinder, hold up, horn in, impede, jump in **7** barge in, break in, chime in, crowd in, disjoin, disturb, intrude, prevent, refrain, suspend **8** break off, cut short, disunite, infringe, intermit, obstruct, separate **9** intercept, interfere, interject, intervene, punctuate, shortstop **10** disconnect, inactivate
__, Interrupted: **4** Girl
Interrupted Melody (1955 film)
cast: Glenn Ford, Roger Moore, Eleanor Parker
interruption: **3** gap **4** halt, rift, stop **5** break, delay, lapse, letup, pause, space, split **6** breach, cutoff, detour, hiatus, lacuna, layoff **8** abeyance, blackout, break off, division, interval, obstacle, stoppage **10** disruption
cause: **5** pager
follow without ~: **4** flow **5** segue
polite ~: **4** ahem **8** pardon me
without ~: **5** on end **8** steadily
intersect: **3** cut **4** meet **5** cross **6** bisect, divide **8** converge, traverse **9** cut across, decussate **10** crisscross
intersection: **3** hub, jct. **4** link **5** joint **6** corner **7** meeting **8** crossing, junction, juncture
divider: **6** island
kind of ~: **3** tee
sign: **4** stop, walk **5** yield **8** don't walk
interspace: **3** cut, gap **4** gash, hole, mesh, rent, slit, slot **5** crack, space, split **6** cavity, cranny, groove, lacuna **7** opening **8** aperture
intersperse: **5** strew **7** scatter **9** punctuate
interstate: **2** rd. **3** rte. **4** pike, road **5** route **7** freeway, highway **8** national **10** expressway
access: **4** ramp
enter the ~: **5** merge
interruption: **6** bypass, detour
like an: **5** laned
sight: **3** car **4** auto, semi **5** truck
sign: **3** Gas **4** Exit
stopover: **3** inn **5** lodge, motel **10** motor court, motor lodge
see also freeway, highway
interstellar dist.: **4** lt. yr.
interstice: **3** gap **4** hole, slit **5** crack, space **6** areola, areole, lacuna **7** crevice, fissure, opening **8** aperture, interval
intertwine: **4** coil, knit, lace, mesh **5** braid, plait, twist, unite, weave **6** enlace, enmesh, immesh, inlace, inmesh, tangle **7** sinuate **8** entangle
intertwined: **4** wove **5** woven **7** related
interval: **3** gap, lag **4** lull, rest, span, term, time, wait **5** break, delay, lapse, letup, pause, point, space, spell **6** breach, hiatus, lacuna, layoff, length, period, radius, season **7** timeout **8** distance, downtime
musical ~: **4** step **5** fifth, ninth, sixth, third **6** fourth, octave **7** seventh
intervals
at ~: **6** slowly **8** off and on **9** gradually, piecemeal, sometimes **10** now and then, on occasion, step by step
at fixed ~: **6** cyclic, hourly, weekly, yearly **7** monthly, regular **8** cyclical, periodic **10** periodical
intervene: **5** ensue, mix in, occur **6** butt in, divide, elapse, happen, horn in, meddle, step in **7** barge in, intrude, mediate, obtrude **8** muscle in, separate **9** arbitrate, intercede, interfere, interpose, interrupt, negotiate, reconcile, supervene, take a hand **10** come to pass, conciliate
intervening: **6** middle **7** between, halfway
in law: **5** mesne
interview: **3** ask, see **4** poll, quiz, talk **5** grill, Q and A, visit **6** depose, talk to **7** examine **8** question, sound out **9** circulate, encounter, tête-à-tête, touch base **10** cattle call, conference, discussion, engagement
Zen ~: **7** dokusan
__ interview: **4** exit
interviewer: **4** host **5** asker, press **8** enquirer, inquirer, reporter
request: **2** CV **4** vita **6** résumé
Interview With the Vampire... (1994 film)
cast: Antonio Banderas, Tom Cruise, Brad Pitt, Stephen Rea
Interview With the Vampire author: Anne Rice
interweave: **3** mix **4** hide, knit, lace, mesh, plat **5** blend, braid, cross, immix, plait, twine, twist, weave **6** enlace, inlace, mingle, relate, splice, tangle, tuck in **7** combine, entwine, intwine, wreathe **8** entangle **10** complicate
interwoven
hair: **5** plait, queue **7** pigtail **8** ponytail
intestinal: **9** abdominal
fortitude: **4** guts **5** nerve, pluck, spunk, valor **7** stamina **8** backbone, tenacity
intestine
combining form: **5** enter- **6** entero-
of the small ~: **5** ileac, ileal
part: **5** colon, ileum
in the __: **3** air, bag, end, red, way **4** dark, hole, hunt, know, loop, main, pink, soup, swim, wind, zone **5** black, cards, clear, flesh, least, money, wings, works **6** offing
in the __ boat: **4** same
in the __ luxury: **5** lap of
in the __ of: **4** name, wake **5** midst
in the __ of duty: **4** line
in the __ of luxury: **3** lap
in the __ of Morpheus: **4** arms
in the __ of time: **4** nick
in the __ run: **4** long **5** short
in the __ way: **5** worst
In the __: **5** Arena
In the __ of Fire: **4** Line
In the __ of the Night: **4** Heat **5** Still
In the __ Old Summertime: **4** Good
__ In, The: **6** Fleet's
__ in the Afternoon: **4** Love **5** Chloe, Death
__ in the air: **6** castle **7** castles
__ in the Air: **5** Music **7** Castles
In the Arena author: **5** Nixon
__ in the arm: **4** shot
__ in the Attic: **4** Toys
__ in the back: **4** stab
in the back in Latin: **6** a tergo
__ in the bag!: **3** It's
__ in the balance: **4** hang
__ in the Balance: **5** Earth
__ in the Band, The: **4** Boys
In the Bar of a Tokyo Hotel author: Tennessee Williams
In the Bedroom (2001 film)
cast: Sissy Spacek, Nick Stahl, Marisa Tomei
In the Beginning author: Chaim Potok
in the blink __ eye: **4** of an
__-in-the-bone: **4** bred
In the Boom Boom Room author: David Rabe
__ in the Boondocks: **4** Down
__-in-the-box: **4** jack
__ in the bucket: **5** a drop
__ in the bud: **3** nip **5** nip it
In the Chapel in the Moonlight (1967 song) artist: Dean Martin
__ in the City: **6** Summer **7** Thunder
In the Clap Shack author: William Styron
In the Closet (1992 song) artist: Michael Jackson
__ in the Clowns: **4** Send
__ in the cold: **3** out
__ in the Country: **4** A Day, Wild **6** A Month
__ in the Cradle: **4** Cat's
__ in the Crowd: **5** A Face
__ in the dark: **4** keep, leap, shot **7** whistle
__ in the Dark: **4** A Cry, Lady **5** A Shot, Piano **7** Dancing
__ in the Deep: **6** Asleep
__ in the Dell, The: **6** Farmer
__ in the door: **4** foot
__ in the dust: **5** leave
__ in the Earth: **6** Giants
In The Evening artist: **4** Erté
in the event __: **4** that
__ in the face: **4** blue
__ in the face of: **3** fly
__ in the Family: **3** All
__ in the fire: **4** iron **5** irons
In the Fire of Spring author: Thomas Tryon
In the Frame author: Dick Francis
In the Ghetto (1969 song) artist: Elvis Presley
In the Good Old Summertime: **4** song, tune **5** waltz
In the Good Old Summertime (1949 film)
cast: Judy Garland, Van Johnson, S.Z. Sakall
__ in the grass: **5** snake
__ in the Gray Flannel Suit, The: **3** Man **5** Horse
__ in the hand...: **5** A bird
__ in the Hat, The: **3** Cat
__ in the Head: **5** A Hole
__ in the Heart: **4** Deep **6** Places
__ in the Heart of Texas: **4** Deep
In the Heat of the Night (1967 film)
cast: Lee Grant, Warren Oates, Sidney Poitier, Rod Steiger
director: Norman Jewison
In the Heat of the Night (NBC/CBS drama)
cast: Carroll O'Connor (Bill Gillespie) Howard Rollins (Virgil Tibbs)
setting: **4** Miss. **6** Sparta

__ in the hole: 3 ace
__ in the House: 5 Guest 6 Doctor
__ in the Iron Mask, The: 3 Man
__ in the Lake, The: 4 Lady
__ in the least: 3 not
__ in the Life: 4 A Day
in the line of __: 4 duty
In the Line of Fire (1993 film)
cast: Clint Eastwood, John Malkovich, Rene Russo
director: Wolfgang Petersen
in the long __: 3 run
__ in the manger: 3 dog
__ in the market: 4 drug
In the Mecca author: Gwendolyn Brooks
In the Middle of an Island (1957 song) artist: Tony Bennett
In the Midnight Hour (1921 song) artist: Wilson Pickett
__ in the Mirror: 3 Man 5 Crack
__ in the Money: 4 We're
__ in the moon: 3 man
__ in the Morning: 4 Four 5 Early
__ in the Morning, No: 3 But
__ in the mouth: 4 down
__-in-the-mud: 5 stick
In the name of __: 5 Allah
__! In the Name of Love: 4 Stop
In the Name of the Father (1993 film)
cast: Daniel Day Lewis, Pete Postlethwaite, Emma Thompson
In the Navy (1941 film)
cast: Bud Abbott, Lou Costello, Dick Powell
director: Arthur Lubin
In the Navy (1979 song) artist: Village People
__ in the neck: 4 pain 5 a pain
__ in the new year: 4 ring
__ in the Night: 4 A Cry, Fear 5 Blues, Vigil
__ in the ocean: 4 spit
__ in the ointment: 3 fly 4 a fly
__ in the Outfield: 6 Angels
__ in the Pacific: 4 Hell
__ in the pan: 5 flash
__ in the pants: 4 kick
__ in the Park With George: 6 Sunday
In the Penal Colony author: Franz Kafka
...in the pot, __ days old: 4 nine
__-in-the-pulpit: 4 jack
__ in the RAF: 5 A Yank
__ in the Rain: 6 Crying, Singin' 7 Soldier
__ in there: 4 hang
__ in the reins: 4 draw
__ in the right direction: 5 a step
__ in the rough: 7 diamond
__-in-the-round: 7 theater, theatre
__ in the Ruins: 4 Love
__ in the Rye, The: 7 Catcher
__ in the Saddle: 4 Tall
in the same __: 4 boat 6 breath
in the same place in Latin: 4 ibid.
__ in the shade: 4 made
__ in the sky: 3 pie
__ in the Sky: 3 Eye 5 Cabin 6 Spirit
__ In The Sky With Diamonds: 4 Lucy
__ in the Stars: 4 Lost 7 Written
...__ in the state of Denmark: 6 rotten
In the Still of the Nite (1992 song) artist: Boyz II Men
__ in the Stone, The: 5 Sword
__ in the Stream: 7 Islands
__ in the street: 3 man 5 woman
__ in the Street: 7 Dancing
__ in the Streets: 5 Panic
In the Summertime (1970 song) artist: Mungo Jerry
__ in the sun: 5 place 6 a place
__ in the Sun, A: 4 Walk 5 Place 6 Raisin
__ in the teeth of: 3 fly
__ in the tooth: 4 long
__ in the Underworld: 7 Orpheus
__ in the USA: 4 Born, made
__ in the wall: 4 hole
__ in the Wall Gang: 4 Hole
__ in the water: 4 dead
__ in the Willows, The: 4 Wind
__ in the wind: 5 straw
__ in the Wind: 4 Dust 5 Voice 6 Blowin', Candle
__ in the Wine: 7 Bubbles
in the wink __ eye: 4 of an
__ in the woods: 4 babe
__-in-the-wool: 4 dyed
in the worst __: 3 way
In the Year 2525 (1969 song) artist: Zager and Evans
in-thing: 6 latest, modish, trendy 7 faddish 8 up-to-date
in this __ and age: 3 day
In This Our Life (1942 film)
cast: George Brent, Bette Davis, Olivia de Havilland
director: John Huston
intimacy: 8 affinity 9 affection, closeness 10 experience, friendship
Intimacy author: Jean-Paul Sartre
intimate: 3 bro, pal, say 4 chum, cosy, cozy, dear, deep, fond, hint, kind, mate, mean, near, pers., seem, snug, warm 5 bosom, buddy, close, cozey, cozie, crony, get at, imply, infer, inner, thick, tight 6 advert, allude, bon ami, chummy, clubby, friend, genial, hint at, inward, kindly, loving, secret, tip off 7 affable, amiable, compeer, comrade, connote, cordial, devoted, make out, mention, private, purport, signify, suggest, trusted, whisper 8 amicable, familiar, friendly, homelike, immanent, indicate, informal, lead up to, outgoing, personal, roommate, sociable 9 associate, boyfriend, companion, confidant, convivial, firsthand, innermost, insinuate, predicate 10 benevolent, bosom buddy, buddy-buddy, girlfriend, neighborly, solicitous
group: 4 club 6 circle, clique 7 coterie
intimated: 5 tacit 6 unsaid 8 hinted at, implicit, unspoken, unstated, unvoiced 9 alluded to
Intimate Exchanges author: Alan Ayckbourn
intimately: 4 well 6 dearly, fondly, warmly 7 closely, privily 8 secretly
intimation: 3 cue 4 clew, clue, hint, sign, wind, word 5 tinge, touch, trace 6 shadow 7 inkling, warning 8 allusion, innuendo, overtone 9 suspicion 10 indication, suggestion
__ in Time: 4 Just 5 Steps
__ in time..., A: 6 stitch
__ in Time of Hesitation: 5 An Ode
intimidate: 3 awe, cow 5 alarm, bully, chill, daunt, deter, hound, psych, scare, shake, spook 6 coerce, dampen, harass, hector, lean on, menace, prey on, ruffle 7 bluster, buffalo, overawe, terrify, unnerve 8 bludgeon, browbeat, bulldoze, dispirit, dissuade, domineer, frighten, prey upon, psych out, threaten, unstring 9 constrain, fulminate, give a turn, give pause, strong-arm, terrorize, trample on, tyrannize 10 discourage, dishearten, pressurize, push around, scare stiff
intimidated: 5 timid 6 afraid, trepid 7 anxious, chicken, fearful, nervous, panicky 8 cowardly, fearsome, hesitant, timorous 9 awestruck
intimidating: 5 scary 6 feared 8 menacing 9 truculent
intimidation: 3 awe 4 fear, funk 5 alarm, dread 6 dismay, fright, terror, threat 7 tyranny 8 affright, bullying, coercion, daunting, pressure
intimidator: 5 bully, tough 8 hooligan
intl. alliance: 3 OAS 4 NATO
into: 7 taken by 8 beholden, hooked on, obsessed, pursuing, turned on 9 taken with, wild about 10 crazy about, involved in, obsessed by
in French: 4 dans
starter: 4 here 5 there, where
__ into: 3 buy, dig, eat, get, lay, lit, ram, rip, run, tap 4 bump, come, grow, lace, look, plow, plug, sail, tear, wade, work 5 break, build, delve, enter, light, pitch 6 breeze, plunge, settle
__ into account: 4 take
Into each __...: 4 life
intolerable: 5 awful 7 extreme, onerous, painful, too much 8 a bit much, grievous 9 monstrous
one: 4 bore, drip, pain, pest, pill
intolerance: 4 bias 7 bigotry 8 jingoism, zealotry 9 prejudice
Intolerance (1916 film)
cast: Lillian Gish, Mae Marsh
director: D.W. Griffith
intolerant: 6 biased, narrow 7 bigoted 9 excitable, fanatical, fractious, hidebound, illiberal, impatient, indignant, irritable, jaundiced, short-fuse, unwilling 10 disdainful, inflexible, prejudiced, short-fused, xenophobic
one: 5 bigot
__ into line: 3 get 4 come, fall 5 bring
Into My Own author: Robert Frost
intonated: 4 oral 5 vocal
intonation: 4 tone 5 sound, voice 6 accent 7 cadence, cadency 8 delivery 10 expression, inflection
intone: 3 hum, say 4 sing, talk 5 carol, chant, croon, drawl, mouth, speak, utter, voice 6 murmur, recite, warble 7 inflect, whisper 8 singsong, vocalize 9 enunciate, pronounce 10 articulate
In Too Deep (1999 film)
cast: Omar Epps, LL Cool J, Nia Long, Stanley Tucci
director: Michael Rymer
In Too Deep (1987 song) artist: Genesis
__ into one's hands: 4 play
__ into one's head: 4 take
__ into one's own: 4 come
__ into play: 5 bring
__ into question: 4 call
__ into shape: 4 lick, whip
__ into the act: 3 get
__ into the ground: 3 run 5 drive
Into the Night (1985 film)
cast: Richard Farnsworth, Jeff Goldblum, Michelle Pfeiffer
director: John Landis
Into the Night host: 4 Dees
Into the Woods: 7 musical
songwriter: 8 Sondheim
__ into thin air: 6 vanish
in toto: 10 completely
intoxicant: 4 grog, kava 5 booze, drink, heady, hooch, sauce 6 hootch, liquor, rotgut 7 alcohol, liqueur, spirits 8 cocktail, demon rum, exciting, highball, libation, potation, stirring 9 aqua vitae, inebriant, inspiring, thrilling
intoxicate: 4 fire, send, stew 5 addle, besot, charm, crock, elate, flush, rouse, souse, stone 6 arouse, kindle, muddle, pickle, sozzle, thrill 7 animate, bewitch, enchant, enflame, enliven, inflame, plaster, pollute, stupefy 8 befuddle, enspirit, entrance, inspirit 9 fascinate
intoxicated: 3 lit 5 drunk, tight, tipsy
intoxicating: 5 heady 6 strong 7 rousing 8 exciting, stirring
intoxication: 6 frenzy 7 ecstasy, elation, madness 8 delirium
__ in Toyland: 5 Babes
intra __: 5 muros, vires, vitam
intractability: 7 resolve 8 defiance, firmness, hardness, rigidity, tenacity, wildness 9 obstinacy, toughness
intractable: 4 firm, grim 5 balky, tough 6 unruly, wilful 7 defiant, naughty, piggish, problem, wayward, willful 8 contrary, perverse, stubborn 9 obstinate, pigheaded, unbending
__ in trade: 5 stock
intransigence: 5 spunk 7 resolve 8 defiance, rigidity, tenacity 9 obstinacy 10 doggedness, resolution
intransigent: 4 firm 5 balky, onery, rigid 6 mulish, ornery, wilful 7 adamant, diehard, piggish, radical, willful 8 contrary, obdurate, perverse, stubborn 9 obstinate, pigheaded, tenacious, unbending 10 inflexible
intransitive __: 4 verb
intrepid: 4 bold, game 5 brave, gutsy, macho, nervy, stout 6 awless, daring, gritty, heroic, plucky, spunky, steely 7 aweless, defiant, doughty, gallant, impavid, staunch, valiant 8 fearless, heroical, resolute, spirited, stalwart, unafraid, valorous 9 audacious, confident, dauntless, dreadless, nerveless, tenacious, undaunted, unfearful, unfearing 10 courageous, mettlesome, undismayed
be ~: 4 dare, defy
one: 4 hero 5 darer 7 heroine
Intrepid: 3 car 4 auto, boat, ship 5 Dodge 10 automobile, battleship
intrepidity: 4 grit, guts, sand, will 5 blood, heart, moxie, nerve, pluck, spunk, valor 6 daring, mettle, spirit, starch 7 bravery, courage, heroism, prowess, resolve 8 audacity, backbone, boldness, defiance, firmness, gumption, rashness, temerity, tenacity
intrepidness: 4 grit 5 nerve, pluck, valor
intricacy: 4 knot 9 confusion, labyrinth 10 complexity, knottiness
intricate: 5 fancy, tough 6 daedal, knotty, tricky 7 complex, tangled 8 abstruse, involved, tortuous 9 Byzantine, difficult, elaborate, entangled 10 convoluted, perplexing
intrigue: 4 draw, grab, hook, plan, plot, pull, ruse, trap, wile 5 cabal, charm, dodge, pique, rivet 6 affair, cook up, devise, draw in, excite, lead on, racket, scheme 7 attract, collude, connive, delight, enchant, engross, faction, finagle, liaison, romance 8 artifice, conspire, contrive, interest, maneuver, trickery 9 captivate, chicanery, collusion, fascinate, machinate, stratagem, titillate 10 conspiracy
metaphorically: 3 web
Intrigue: 3 car 4 auto, Olds 10 automobile, Oldsmobile
intriguer: 5 snake 6 sharpy 7 plotter, schemer, wangler 8 finagler, slyboots
intriguing: 3 sly 4 wily 5 juicy 6 subtle 8 inviting, tempting 9 absorbing, designing, insidious 10 diplomatic, enchanting, engrossing
intrinsic: 3 own 4 born, real, true 5 basic, inner 6 inborn, inbred, inmost, innate, latent, native 7 built-in, central, genuine, natural, radical 8 integral, peculiar 9 component, elemental, essential, ingrained 10 congenital, connatural, deep-seated, hereditary, indwelling, underlying
be ~: 5 dwell 6 inhere, reside

intrinsic ___: **6** factor, parity
intrinsically: **5** per se, truly **7** at heart
intro: **3** fwd. **4** pref., vamp **5** debut **6** lead-in, prelim, prolog **7** opening, prelude **8** foreword, overture, preamble, prologue **9** beginning **10** initiation
  exclamation: **4** ta-da **5** ta-dah
introduce: **3** add, set **4** lead **5** begin, enter, offer, put in, raise, set up, start, usher **6** broach, infuse, inject, insert, instal, instil, launch, work in **7** bring up, engrain, ingrain, install, instill, kick off, lead off, pioneer, precede, preface, presage, present, propose, receive, roll out, suggest, throw in, usher in **8** antecede, bring out, commence, generate, initiate, set forth **9** establish, insinuate, institute, interject, interpose, make known, originate, recommend **10** inaugurate, pave the way, put forward
introduced to, be: **4** meet
introducer, act: **2** MC **4** host **5** emcee
introduction: **4** word **5** debut, entry, proem, start **6** access, entrée, influx, launch, lead-in, prolog **7** baptism, meeting, opening, preface, prelude **8** entrance, overture, preamble, prologue **9** reception
introductory: **3** new **5** early, first **7** initial, opening **8** original, starting **9** preceding
  material: **4** ABCs **6** basics
introit: **4** song **5** psalm **6** anthem
introspect: **4** muse **5** brood **6** ponder **7** reflect **8** meditate, ruminate
introspection: **4** look **6** musing **7** thought **10** meditation, reflection, rumination
introspective: **4** rapt **5** moody **6** musing **7** pensive **8** absorbed, occupied, ruminant **9** engrossed
introvert: **5** loner **7** brooder, isolato **8** homebody **10** narcissist, wallflower
introverted: **3** shy **5** timid **6** demure **7** bashful **8** cautious, reserved, solitary **9** withdrawn
intrude: **3** pry **4** nose, poke **5** barge, cut in, enter, poach, snoop **6** butt in, horn in, impose, meddle, push in, tamper **7** barge in, presume **8** trespass **9** intercede, interfere, interject, interlope, interrupt, intervene **10** contravene
  on: **4** raid **5** storm **6** assail, attack, invade, strike **7** assault, overrun **8** encroach, trespass
intruder: **5** alien **7** burglar, invader, meddler, prowler **8** outsider, stranger **9** aggressor **10** trespasser
intruding: **4** bold **7** forward **10** aggressive
intrusion: **6** attack, influx, inroad **7** ingress **8** invasion, overture, trespass **9** incursion **10** imposition
intrusive: **4** nosy **5** nosey, saucy **6** prying **7** ferrety, forward, salient **8** invasive, meddling **9** obtrusive, officious **10** aggressive, meddlesome
intuit: **3** see **4** feel, know **5** grasp, infer, sense **6** divine, fathom **7** realize **8** discover, perceive **9** apprehend **10** comprehend, have a hunch, understand
intuition: **3** ESP **4** vibe **5** hunch, sense **6** acumen, esprit, vision **7** feeling, insight, thought **8** instinct **10** divination, perception, sixth sense
intuitive: **3** gut **4** wise **5** acute **6** inborn, innate **7** natural **8** lynx-eyed, visceral **9** affective, automatic, emotional, immediate, impulsive **10** perceptive, subjective, understood
intumesce: **3** bag **5** belly, bloat, bulge, swell **6** blow up, expand, puff up **7** distend, enlarge, inflate **8** bubble up
Inuit: **3** Esk. **5** tribe **6** Eskimo
  abode: **4** iglu **5** igloo
  craft: **5** kayak, umiak
  outerwear: **6** anorak
inundate: **4** glut, pour, snow **5** drown, flood, flush, swamp, water **6** deluge, drench, engulf, ingulf **7** immerse, overrun, smother **8** overflow, submerge **9** overwhelm, snow under
inundation: **4** glut, tide, wave **5** flood, river, spate **6** deluge, influx, stream **7** cascade, freshet, monsoon, torrent **8** downpour, overflow **9** avalanche, cataclysm
  an ~ (of): **4** lots, tons **5** heaps **7** barrels
inurbane: **4** rude **5** crass, gruff, surly **7** boorish, ill-bred, uncivil **8** impolite, tactless, unpoised, unsubtle **9** insulting, uncourtly, ungallant **10** indecorous, indelicate, ungracious, unladylike
inure: **5** train **6** season **7** break in, coarsen, toughen **8** accustom, indurate **9** acclimate, condition, habituate, withstand **10** take effect
  (to): **5** adapt **6** harden **7** get used
inutile: **4** idle, null, vain **5** inane **6** futile **7** useless **8** bootless, unusable **9** for naught, fruitless, worthless **10** unavailing
Inuvik: **4** city, town
  locale: **6** Canada
invade: **4** loot, raid **5** blitz, crash, enter, storm **6** assail, attack, breach, infest, maraud, occupy, ravage, strike **7** assault, make war, overrun, pillage, plunder, violate **8** encroach, infringe, permeate, trespass **9** intrude on, penetrate **10** burglarize, encroach on, muscle in on, trespass on
  privacy: **3** pry **4** nose, poke **5** mix in, snoop **6** horn in, impose, kibitz, meddle, worm in **7** barge in, break in, intrude, obtrude **9** interfere, intervene
invader: **3** foe, Hun **4** germ **5** alien, enemy **6** raider, vandal **8** attacker, intruder, marauder **9** aggressor, assailant, ill-wisher **10** encroacher, interloper, trespasser
  ancient ~: **3** Hun **4** Goth, Jute, Moor **5** Horsa, Saxon, Tatar **6** Norman
invalid: **3** bad, ill **4** null, sick, void **5** false, frail, wrong **6** ailing, faulty, infirm, untrue **7** laid low, patient, unsound **8** baseless, below par, nugatory **9** erroneous, illogical, sophistic, unfounded, unhealthy, worthless **10** fallacious, ill-founded, ungrounded, unreasoned
invalidate: **3** nix **4** ruin, undo, void **5** abate, annul, quash **6** cancel, negate, offset, refute, repeal, revoke, show up **7** abolish, confute, disable, explode, nullify, rescind, reverse, vitiate **8** abrogate, disprove, dissolve, override, overrule, overturn **9** discredit, eliminate, overthrow **10** annihilate, circumduct, compensate, counteract, disqualify, neutralize, prove wrong
invalidation: **4** veto **6** denial, exposé, repeal **8** disproof, negation, overturn, rebuttal, reversal, voidance **9** discredit
invalidism: **7** frailty, illness **8** debility, sickness, weakness
invalidity: **7** fallacy, falsity, nullity, sophism **8** voidness, weakness
invaluable: **4** rare **6** worthy **7** helpful **8** precious, valuable **9** excellent, expensive, priceless
Invar: **5** alloy
  component: **4** iron **6** nickel
invariability: **5** habit **7** routine **8** evenness, fastness, firmness, habitude, monotony, sameness, solidity
invariable: **4** firm, same **5** fixed, rigid **6** smooth, stable, static **7** regular, uniform **8** constant, straight **9** immovable, immutable, perpetual, unfailing **10** changeless, consistent, inflexible, monotonous, true to type, unchanging, unrelieved, unwavering
invariably: **4** ever **6** always, as ever, surely **9** regularly **10** inevitably
invasion: **4** raid **5** foray, storm **6** attack, breach, influx, inroad **7** assault, descent, ingress **8** trespass **9** incursion, intrusion, irruption, offensive, onslaught, violation **10** occupation
  site of '44: **5** Leyte
invasion of ___: **7** privacy
Invasion of the Body Snatchers (1956 film)
  cast: Larry Gates, Kevin McCarthy, Dana Wynter
  director: Don Siegel
  prop: **3** pod
Invasion of the Body Snatchers (1978 film)
  cast: Brooke Adams, Leonard Nimoy, Donald Sutherland
Invasion of the Sea author: Jules Verne
invasive: **5** pushy **6** prying, snoopy **7** ferrety **9** intrusive
invective: **5** abuse, scorn **6** insult, tirade **7** censure, lampoon, obloquy **8** berating, diatribe, jeremiad, reproach, swearing **9** aspersion, blasphemy, contumely, philippic **10** accusation, backbiting, impugnment, imputation, revilement, scurrility
  bit of ~: **3** cut, dig **4** barb, gibe, oath **5** taunt **6** insult, needle, zinger
inveigh: **4** rail **6** revile **7** censure, protest **8** harangue
inveigle: **3** con **4** bait, coax, hook, lure, snow, trap **5** charm, decoy, shill, tempt **6** allure, cajole, disarm, entice, entrap, induce, lead on, rope in, stroke **7** beguile, ensnare, flatter, insnare, mislead, wheedle **8** blandish, maneuver, persuade **9** sweet-talk
inveiglement: **5** decoy, snare **7** coaxing
inveigler: **5** lurer **6** coaxer **7** cajoler, tempter **8** beguiler, swindler
___ in Venice: **5** Death
invent: **3** fib, lie **4** coin, fake, form, make, mint **5** feign, frame, hatch **6** cook up, create, design, devise, drum up, make up **7** concoct, dream up, falsify, fashion, imagine, pioneer, produce, think up, toss off, trump up, turn out **8** contrive, misstate, simulate **9** fabricate, formulate, improvise, originate **10** conceive of, mastermind
invented: **4** fake, made **6** unreal **8** mythical **9** imaginary, legendary
invention: **3** fib, lie **4** fake, myth, sham, tale, yarn **5** dodad, gismo, gizmo, rumor **6** deceit, design, device, doodad, gadget **7** coinage, fantasy, fiction, figment, novelty, product, untruth **8** creation, pretense, tall tale **9** apparatus, causation, discovery, falsehood, tall story **10** brainchild, conception, concoction, creativity, fairy story, innovation
  ancient ~: **5** wheel
  mother of ~: **4** idea **9** necessity
Inventions of the Monsters artist: **4** Dali
inventive: **4** orig. **5** fresh, novel, sharp, slick, smart **6** adroit, astute, brainy, bright, clever, gifted, habile, shifty **7** fertile, knowing, new wave, unusual **8** artistic, creative, dextrous, fruitful, inspired, original **9** astucious, brilliant, causative, demiurgic, deviceful, dexterous, formative, ingenious **10** artistical, avant-garde, innovative, productive
inventiveness: **3** art **8** resource **10** cleverness, creativity
inventor: **4** Bell, Eads, Land, Moog, Otis, Watt **5** Deere, maker, Morse, Nobel, Tesla, Volta **6** author, Bunsen, coiner, Diesel, Edison, father, Fulton, Geiger, Schick, Sperry, Tupper **7** builder, creator, Eastman, Gatling, Marconi, pioneer, Pullman **8** Bessemer, Bushnell, Daguerre, De Forest, designer, Foucault, Franklin, Gillette, Goodyear, Sikorsky, Zworykin **9** artificer, fashioner, Gutenberg, innovator, James Watt **10** Elisha Otis, Fahrenheit, originator
  agcy.: **4** USPO
  cry: **3** aha
  monogram: **3** TAE
  need: **4** idea **6** patent
inventory: **4** list **5** asset, hoard, index, stock, store, table, tally **6** record, roster, supply **7** account, backlog, catalog, inspect, itemize, reserve, summary **8** register, tabulate **9** catalogue, enumerate, keep count, reservoir, stock book, stockpile, summarize **10** inspection, keep on hand, tabulation
  abbr.: **3** etc., gds., SKU, UPC **4** FIFO, LIFO **8** mdse.. whse.
  in ~: **4** here **6** on hand **9** available
  place: **5** shelf **9** stockroom, warehouse
  unit: **3** SKU, UPC **4** item
inveracity: **3** fib, lie **6** deceit **7** fiction, untruth, whopper
Inver Grove Heights: **4** city, town
  locale: **9** Minnesota
Inverness: **4** cape, coat **6** jacket **8** overcoat **9** outerwear
  attraction: **4** Ness
  see also Scottish
inverse: **5** wrong **7** reverse **8** negation, opposite **10** antithesis, antithetic
inverse ___: **4** sine **5** image **6** cosine, secant **7** tangent
inversely: **9** vice versa
inversion: **4** flip **6** switch **8** flip-flop, flip side, opposite, reversal **9** about-face, one-eighty, other side, turnabout **10** antithesis
inversion ___: **5** layer **6** center **7** casting
invert: **4** flip, turn **5** upend, upset **6** upturn **7** capsize, reverse **8** exchange, flip-flop, overturn, turn over **9** transpose, turn about **10** turn around
invert ___: **4** soap **5** sugar
inverted: **7** upended **8** backward **9** inside-out **10** topsy-turvy, upside-down
inverted ___: **5** comma, pleat **7** mordent
inverted V in heraldry: **7** chevron
invest: **3** put **5** cover, crown, endow, endue, imbue, indue, put in, put up, spend, stake, steep **6** attire, charge, infuse, instal, lay out, ordain **7** buy into, empower, entrust, furnish, go in for, install, instate, intrust, license **8** accouter, accoutre, bankroll, delegate, enthrone, initiate, inthrone, purchase, salt away, sanction **9** authorize, establish
  in: **3** buy, get **6** obtain, pick up **7** acquire **8** purchase
invested: **6** at risk **7** at stake
investigate: **3** dig, pry, see, spy **4** case, comb, scan, seek, sift **5** assay, audit,

check, cover, delve, go see, probe, scout, study **6** go into, search **7** analyze, dissect, enquire, examine, explore, feel out, inquire, inspect, ransack, run down **8** check out, consider, look into, look over, question, research, see about, stake out **9** enter into
investigation: **3** inq. **5** audit, check, probe, query, quest, study, trial **6** examen, review, search, survey **7** enquiry, hearing, inquest, inquiry, legwork, probing **8** analysis, question, research, scrutiny **9** going-over
investigative report: **6** exposé
investigator: **3** spy **4** G-man, narc, nark, T-man **5** agent **6** shamus, sleuth **7** analyst, auditor, gumshoe **8** enquirer, examiner, inquirer, Sherlock
job: **4** case **5** caper
__ investigator: **7** private
investiture: **4** garb, robe **5** habit **6** attire, mantle **7** apparel, garment, raiment **8** chairing, crowning, frocking, vestment
investment: **3** buy **4** bond **5** asset, stake, stock **6** outlay **7** backing, capital, finance, venture **8** purchase **9** accession, endowment, financing, interests **10** commercial, smart money
for short: **2** CD **3** IRA, stk. **4** ESOP, REIT **5** R and D, T-bill, T-bond, T-note
insurance: **5** hedge
return: **3** int. **5** yield **6** income, profit **7** revenue **8** earnings, interest, proceeds
swindle: **5** Ponzi
world: **10** Wall Street
investment __: **4** bank **5** trust **6** banker **7** banking, casting, company
investments: **5** stock **7** savings **8** holdings **9** interests, portfolio
like venture capital ~: **5** dicey **6** chancy, daring, unsafe **9** uncertain **10** precarious
__ investment trust: **4** unit **5** fixed
investor: **4** bear, bull **5** owner **6** backer, banker **9** financier **10** capitalist
activity, for short: **4** spec
bane: **4** loss **6** red ink
concern: **3** Dow **4** risk **5** yield
good news for an ~: **5** rally
mail-in: **5** proxy
inveterate: **3** old **4** avid **6** rooted **7** abiding, chronic, settled **8** constant, enduring, habitual, hardened, lifelong **9** chronical, confirmed, customary, incurable, ingrained, long-lived, perennial, permanent, unabating, unfixable **10** accustomed, congenital, continuing, deep-rooted, deep-seated, entrenched, habituated, persistent, persisting
Invicta: **3** car **4** auto **5** Buick
Invictus author: William Henley
invidious: **4** base **6** odious **7** hateful **8** annoying, libelous **9** green-eyed, loathsome, maligning, offensive, repugnant, slighting, vilifying **10** abominable, calumnious, defamatory, detestable, detracting, detractive, detractory, scandalous, slanderous
invidiousness: **4** hate **5** odium, scorn, spite, venom **6** animus, enmity, hatred, malice, rancor, spleen **7** disdain, disgust, dislike, ill will **8** acrimony, aversion, contempt, distaste, ignominy **9** animosity, antipathy, hostility, malignity, repulsion, revulsion **10** abhorrence, antagonism, execration, repugnance, resentment
invigorant: **5** tonic **6** bracer, elixir **7** cordial **8** pick-me-up **9** stimulant
invigorate: **4** gird, stir, tone **5** brace, build, hop up, liven, pep up, raise, rally, renew, rouse, shore, steel **6** anneal, beef up, buck up, excite, harden, perk up, pick up, prop up, revive, temper, tone up, turn on, vivify **7** bolster, brace up, build up, burgeon, develop, empower, enhance, enliven, fortify, freshen, inspire, liven up, punch up, quicken, refresh, shore up, stiffen, toughen **8** bourgeon, buttress, embolden, energize, enspirit, imbolden, indurate, inspirit, vitalize **9** electrify, galvanize, intensify, reinforce, stimulate **10** exhilarate, rejuvenate, revitalize, strengthen
invigorating: **5** brisk, crisp, fresh, tonic **6** lively **7** bracing, charged, healthy, outdoor **8** curative **10** refreshing
invincibility: **5** moxie, pluck, power, valor **6** mettle **7** stamina **9** fortitude, hardiness **10** resolution
invincible: **5** stout **8** almighty **9** dauntless, unfearing **10** impassable, inviolable, unbeatable, unyielding
Invincible (1985 song) artist: Pat Benatar
Invincible Eagle, The composer: **5** Sousa
in vino __: **7** veritas
inviolability: **7** honesty, loyalty **8** holiness, sanctity, trueness
inviolable: **4** holy, safe, true **5** blest, loyal **6** honest, sacred, trusty **7** blessed **8** constant, reliable, true-blue, virtuous **10** invincible
inviolate: **4** holy, pure **5** blest, whole **6** entire, intact, sacred, unhurt **7** blessed **8** complete, hallowed, unbroken, unharmed, unmarred **10** sacrosanct
invisible: **5** perdu **6** covert, hidden, latent, minute, occult, perdue, unseen **7** ghostly **8** obscured, ulterior **9** concealed, deceptive, disguised, unseeable **10** impalpable, intangible, out of sight, tucked away, unapparent, undetected, unviewable, wraithlike
become ~: **4** fade **6** die out, vanish **7** die away **8** dissolve, evanesce, fade away, vaporize **9** disappear, dissipate, evaporate
combining form: **5** aphan- **6** aphano-
invisible __: **3** ink **5** fence, glass **6** shadow
Invisible __: **3** Man **5** Touch **6** Cities **7** Friends, Stripes
Invisible Cities author: Italo Calvino
Invisible Friends author: Alan Ayckbourn
Invisible Man
author: Ralph Ellison
setting: **3** . NYC **6** Harlem **9** Manhattan
Invisible Man Returns, The (1940 film)
cast: Nan Grey, Cedric Hardwicke, Vincent Price
director: **3** May
Invisible Man, The: **4** film **5** novel
author: H.G. Wells
cast: Una O'Connor, Claude Rains, Gloria Stuart
character: **4** Ayde, Kemp
director: James Whale
Invisible Stripes (1939 film)
cast: William Holden, George Raft
director: Lloyd Bacon
Invisible Touch (1986 song) artist: Genesis
Invisible Woman, The (1941 film)
cast: John Barrymore, Virginia Bruce
invitation: **3** bid **4** call, date, lure **5** offer **6** appeal, asking, feeler **7** request **8** overture, petition, proposal **9** challenge, prompting, rain check **10** allurement, attraction, engagement, enticement, incitement, inducement, suggestion, temptation
addendum: **3** BYO **4** BYOB, RSVP
go sans ~: **5** crash **7** barge in
word: **3** s'il **4** come, vous **5** plaît, where
invite: **3** ask, bid **4** lure, seek **5** ask in, evoke, tempt **6** ask out, beckon, call on, lead on, pick up, summon, ticket **7** attract, receive, request, welcome **8** petition **9** encourage
invited: **7** welcome
not ~: **5** unbid
invitee: **5** guest **7** visitor
invitees, top: **5** A-list
inviting: **4** cosy, cozy, homy, nice **5** homey **7** cordial, winning, winsome **8** alluring, charming, engaging, enticing, magnetic, pleasing, readable, tempting **9** appealing, beguiling **10** attractive, bewitching, delectable, delightful, intriguing, magnetical, persuasive
phrase: **6** call me
invocation: **5** grace **6** appeal, litany, prayer, speech **7** worship **8** blessing, entreaty **10** beseeching, hocus-pocus, mumbo jumbo
invoice: **3** tab **4** bill, list **9** reckoning, statement
abbr.: **3** amt. **7** ppd.. stmt.
add-on: **3** tax
stamp: **3** rcd. **4** paid **8** received
word: **3** net, pay **5** remit
invoke: **3** use **4** pray **5** apply **6** call on, pray to, summon **7** call for, conjure, enforce, entreat, implore, plead to, pray for, solicit **8** appeal to, call upon, petition, resort to, say grace **9** call forth, conjure up, implement
involuntary: **6** forced, reflex **7** natural **8** knee-jerk **9** mandatory, unwilling, unwitting
movement: **3** tic **5** start **6** shiver
noise: **3** hic **4** burp, gasp **6** hiccup **8** hiccough
involve: **4** have, mire **5** catch, cover, imply, snare, touch **6** absorb, affect, draw in, engage, enmesh, entail, immesh, inmesh, occupy **7** concern, contain, embrace, embroil, immerse, include, require **8** comprise, entangle, interest, persuade, relate to **9** implicate
involved: **4** rapt **6** active, knotty, lively, tricky **7** at stake, complex, engaged, prickly, tangled, verbose **8** abstruse, puzzling, tortuous **9** Byzantine, confusing, difficult, elaborate, intricate, recondite **10** convoluted, unsettling
become ~: **6** step in **7** mediate **9** intercede
be very ~: **6** wallow
person ~: **5** party
recently ~ with: **5** new to
with: **4** into, up to
involvement: **4** love, part, stew **5** stake **6** jumble, jungle **7** dilemma, farrago **8** interest, quandary **9** immersion, liability
__-in vote: **5** write
invulnerability: **6** safety **8** safeness, security
invulnerable: **4** safe **5** tight **6** secure
__ in wait: **3** lie
__-in-waiting: **4** lady, lord, maid
__ in war...: **5** First
inward: **6** hidden, secrêt, within **7** private **8** internal, intimate, personal **9** privately
inwardly: **6** inside, within **8** mentally, secretly **10** internally
In Which We Serve (1942 film)
cast: Noël Coward, Bernard Miles, John Mills
director: Noël Coward, David Lean
__ in Winter, The: **4** Lion
__ in with: **4** fall
__ in with both feet: **4** jump
__ in Wonderland: **4** Alex **5** Alice
__ in wood: **4** aged
INXS
member: Hutchence, Pengilly, Beers, Farriss
song: Devil Inside (1988)
Disappear (1990)
Need You Tonight (1987)
Never Tear Us Apart (1988)
New Sensation (1988)
Suicide Blonde (1990)
What You Need (1986)
__ in Ya Ear: **5** Flava
__ in years: **5** along
__ in Yonkers: **4** Lost
in-your-__: **4** face
In your dreams!: **5** no how, no way
__ in Your Eyes: **4** Lost **6** Heaven
In Your Letter (1981 song) artist: REO Speedwagon
__ in your mouth, not...: **5** Melts
In Youth I Have Known One author: Edgar Allan Poe
Io: **4** moon, moth
planet: **7** Jupiter
__-I-O: **3** E-I-E
I object!: **3** hey **4** stop **6** stop it
iodate: **4** salt
__ iodide: **6** silver, sodium
iodine: **7** element, halogen **10** antiseptic
combining form: **3** iod- **4** iodo-
compound: **6** halide
source: **4** kelp **7** seafood
__ Iodine: **6** Little
Iola: **4** city, town
locale: **6** Kansas
Iola Leroy author: Frances Harper
Iolani Palace locale: **4** Oahu **6** Hawaii **8** Honolulu
Iolanthe: **8** operetta
character: **5** Celia, Fleta, Leila **6** Willis **7** Phyllis **8** Strephon
composer: **7** Gilbert **8** Sullivan
Iolcos, ship from: **4** Argo
ion: **8** particle
chg.: **3** neg., pos.
source: **4** atom
ion __: **6** engine, rocket **7** chamber
Ion: **3** car **4** auto **6** Saturn, Tiriac **7** Iliescu
parent of ~: **6** Apollo, Creusa
son of ~: **6** Geleon **7** Argades **8** Hopletes **9** Aegicores
wife of ~: **6** Helice
Iona: **3** isl. **4** isle **6** island, school
athletes: **5** Gaels
locale: **7** New York **8** Scotland
Ion author: Euripides
Ione: **4** Skye **5** nymph **8** sea nymph
Ionesco, Eugène: **6** author, French **9** dramatist **10** playwright
homeland: Romania, France
work: Amédée
The Bald Soprano
The Chairs
Exit the King
The Future Is in Eggs
The Lesson
The New Tenant
Rhinoceros
A Stroll in the Air
Victims of Duty
Ionian: **3** sea **5** Homer **10** Heraclitus
ancient ~ city: **4** Teos
ancient ~ kingdom: **6** Epirus
Ionian __: **3** Sea **4** mode **7** Islands

Ionian Sea
gulf: 4 Arta 6 Patras 7 Corinth, Laconia, Lepanto, Taranto 8 Messenia
island: 5 Corfu, Zante
locale: 5 Italy 6 Greece
view from ~: 4 Etna 5 Aetna
Ionic: 5 order 6 column 9 classical
not ~: 5 Doric 10 Corinthian
ionize: 6 charge
I Only Have Eyes for You: 4 song, tune
composer: 5 Dubin 6 Warren
musical: 5 Dames
I Only Want to Be With You (1964 song) artist: Dusty Springfield
ionosphere
part: 6 D layer, E layer, F layer
IOOF cousin: 4 BPOE, Elks 7 Kiwanis
iota: 3 bit, dot, jot, tad 4 atom, drop, mite, mote, spot, whit 5 crumb, grain, Greek, pinch, scrap, shred, skosh, speck, straw, trace 6 letter, morsel, tittle, wee bit 7 minimum, modicum, smidgen, smidgin 8 flyspeck, fragment, molecule, particle, smidgeon 9 little bit, scintilla
follower: 5 kappa
preceder: 5 theta
IOU: 3 tab 4 chit, debt, note 6 marker 8 mortgage 9 debenture, liability
honor an ~: 3 pay 5 pay up, repay 6 settle 7 pay back 8 make good, settle up, square up 9 reimburse 10 remunerate
receive an: 4 lend, loan
signer: 4 ower
write an ~: 3 owe 6 borrow
I Ought to Be in Pictures author: Neil Simon
Iowa: 5 river, state 6 Indian 7 Amerind
athletes: 8 Hawkeyes
city: 4 Ames 5 Amana, Pella 6 Ankeny, Marion 7 Clinton, Dubuque, Ottumwa 8 Waterloo 9 Davenport, Des Moines, Fort Dodge, Mason City, Muscatine, Sioux City, Urbandale 10 Bettendorf, Burlington, Cedar Falls
conference: 6 Big Ten
crop: 4 corn
like ~: 6 inland
neighbor: 8 Illinois, Missouri, Nebraska 9 Minnesota, Wisconsin
painter from ~: 4 Wood
school: 3 Coe 5 Drake, Loras
state bird: 9 goldfinch
state flower: 8 wild rose
state rock: 5 geode
state tree: 3 oak
Iowa Baseball Confederacy, The author: W.P. Kinsella
Iowa State
athletes: 8 Cyclones
conference: 9 Big Twelve
locale: 4 Ames
I Pagliacci
composer: 11 Leoncavallo
role: 5 Beppe, Canio, Nedda, Tonio 6 Silvio
setting: 5 Italy 8 Calabria
Ipanema: 5 beach
locale: 3 Rio 6 Brazil
I pass: 5 no bet
ipecac: 4 drug
Iphegenia in Brooklyn composer: 4 Bach 7 PDQ Bach
Iphigenia
brother of ~: 7 Orestes
parent of ~: 5 Helen 9 Agamemnon
sister of ~: 7 Electra
Iphigenia in __: 5 Aulis
Iphigenia in Aulis author: Euripides
Iphigenie en Aulide author: Jean Racine
ipil: 4 tree
Ipoh: 4 city, town
locale: 8 Malaysia
__ ipsa loquitur: 3 res
ipse __: 5 dixit
ipso: 6 itself
ipso __: 4 jure 5 facto
Ipswich: 4 city, town
locale: 4 Mass. 7 England, Suffolk
ipu ipu: 5 gourd 10 percussion
origin: 9 Polynesia
IQ: 6 brains 9 mentality 10 braininess
I.Q. (1994 film)
cast: Walter Matthau, Tim Robbins, Meg Ryan
director: Fred Schepisi
Iqaluit: 4 city, town
locale: 6 Canada 7 Nunavut
Iqbal: 7 Mahomet 8 Mohammed, Muhammad
Iqbal, Muhammad: 4 poet 6 Indian
Iquique: 4 city, town
locale: 5 Chile
Ir: 4 elem. 6 indium 7 element
77 for ~: 4 at. no.
Ira: 4 Wohl 5 Levin 6 Berkow, Remsen, Thomas 7 Wolfert 8 Aldridge, Gershwin 9 Magaziner
IRA: 7 nest egg, pension 8 Roth plan 10 tax shelter
accrual: 3 int. 8 interest
alternative: 4 ESOP 5 Keogh
investment: 2 CD
legislation: 5 ERISA
offerer: 4 bank 5 S and L
part of ~: 3 Acc., Ind., Rep., Ret. 4 Acct., Army 5 Irish 7 Account
__ IRA: 3 SEP 4 Roth
irade: 4 fiat 5 edict, order, ukase 6 decree, dictum
__ Irae: 4 Dies
Iráklion: 4 city, port, town 7 seaport
locale: 5 Crete 6 Candia, Greece
Iran: 6 nation 7 Barkley, country
ancient part of ~: 4 Elam
bovine: 5 Kurdi 6 Sarabi
capital: 6 Tehran 7 Teheran
city: 3 Qom, Qum 5 Ahvaz, Ahwaz, Rasht, Resht 6 Abadan, Shiraz, Tabriz, Tehran 7 Esfahan, Mashhad, Teheran
desert: 3 Lut 9 Dasht-e Lut, Great Salt
lake: 5 Urmia
language: 4 Pers. 5 Farsi, Parsi, Tajik 6 Tadjik, Tajiki 7 Persian, Tadzhik
money: 4 kran, rial 5 dinar
mountain: 6 Elburz, Zagros
mountain dweller: 4 Kurd
neighbor: 4 Irak, Iraq 6 Turkey 7 Armenia 8 Pakistan 10 Azerbaijan
org.: 4 OPEC
religion: 5 Baha'i
royal name: 4 Reza 7 Pahlavi, Pahlevi
title: 4 imam, shah 5 imaum
Iran-Contra grp.: 3 NSC
Irani: 7 Persian 8 Bani-Sadr, Khomeini 10 Rafsanjani
ancient ~: 4 Mede 5 Alani
neighbor: 4 Turk 5 Iraqi, Saudi
__-Iranian: 4 Indo
I ran out of gas: 5 alibi 6 excuse
Irapuato: 4 city, town
locale: 6 Mexico 10 Guanajuato
Iraq: 6 nation 7 country
bovine: 5 Kurdi
capital: 6 Bagdad 7 Baghdad
city: 5 Arbil, Basra, Busra, Erbil, Irbil, Mosul 6 Arbela, Bagdad, Busrah, Kirkuk, Tikrit 7 Baghdad
desert: 6 Syrian
export: 3 oil 4 date
invaded it: 6 Koweit, Kuwait
minority: 4 Kurd
money: 4 fils 5 dinar
mountain: 6 Zagros
neighbor: 4 Iran 5 Syria 6 Jordan, Kuwait, Turkey
org.: 4 OPEC 10 Arab League
province: 5 Basra, Busra 6 Busrah
river: 6 Tigris
Iraqi: 4 Arab, Kurd 5 Asian 6 Arabic 8 language
neighbor: 4 Turk 5 Irani, Saudi
irascibility: 4 bile, gall 5 anger 6 spleen, temper 8 acerbity, asperity, edginess, ill humor, tartness
irascible: 3 hot 4 sour 5 angry, cross, huffy, moody, onery, short, surly, testy 6 crabby, cranky, crusty, feisty, ireful, ogrish, ornery, snappy, snippy, touchy 7 bearish, bristly, grouchy, huffish, ogreish, peevish, peppery, uptight, waspish 8 choleric, growling, liverish, petulant, snappish, snippety 9 excitable, fractious, impatient, irritable, querulous, sarcastic, splenetic 10 high-strung, out of sorts
irate: 3 hot, mad 4 sore 5 angry, cross, het up, huffy, livid, riled, surly, vexed, wroth 6 fuming, galled, heated, in a pet, ireful, peeved, piqued, raging, raving, red-hot, stormy, ticked 7 angered, annoyed, burning, enraged, furious, in a huff, in a snit, nettled, ranting, ruffled, steamed, teed off, violent 8 agitated, burned up, choleric, frenzied, incensed, inflamed, maddened, outraged, petulant, provoked, seething, steaming, up in arms, volatile, volcanic, worked up, wrathful 9 hotheaded, indignant, irritated, resentful, seeing red, splenetic, ticked off, wrought up 10 freaked out, hopping mad, hysterical, infuriated, pugnacious
Irazú: 7 volcano
locale: 9 Costa Rica
Irbid: 4 city, town
locale: 6 Jordan
Irbil: 4 city, town
locale: 4 Irak, Iraq
ire: 3 vex 4 fury, rage 5 anger, annoy, upset, wrath 6 burn up, choler, dander, enmity, enrage, madden, nettle, spleen, temper 7 dudgeon, incense, offense, outrage, provoke, tick off, umbrage 8 irritate 9 hostility, huffiness, infuriate, surliness 10 exasperate, irritation, resentment
Ire.: 3 isl.
I read you!: 5 roger
I Really Don't Want to Know (1971 song) artist: Elvis Presley
ired: 3 hot, mad 4 sore 5 angry, cross, huffy, riled, vexed, wroth 6 peeved, piqued 7 annoyed, boiling, enraged, furious 8 choleric, incensed, inflamed, outraged, up in arms, vehement, wrathful 9 indignant, irritated, resentful, splenetic 10 infuriated
ireful: 3 hot, mad 4 edgy, sore 5 angry, brusk, cross, fed up, gruff, huffy, irate, livid, riled, surly, testy, vexed, wroth 6 crabby, enrage, fuming, heated, peeved, raging, raving, red-hot, touchy 7 annoyed, bearish, brusque, caustic, enraged, furious, grouchy, mordant, peevish, ranting 8 choleric, incensed, inflamed, maddened, outraged, petulant, snappish, venomous, virulent, wrathful 9 indignant, irascible, irritable, irritated, resentful, splenetic, trenchant 10 aggravated, freaked out, infuriated
Ireland: 4 Eire, Erin, isle, Jill, John 5 Kathy 6 island, nation 7 country
accent: 6 brogue
ancestor: 4 Celt, Gael
ballet dancer: 8 De Valois
bay: 5 Sligo 6 Dublin, Galway
bovine: 5 Kerry 6 Dexter
capital: 6 Dublin
city: 4 Cobh, Cork 5 Ennis, Sligo 6 Dublin, Galway, Tralee 7 Donegal, Shannon, Wexford 8 Limerick 9 Waterford
combining form: 7 Hiberno-
county: 4 Cork, Mayo, Tara 5 Cavan, Clare, Kerry, Louth, Meath, Sligo 6 Antrim, Armagh, Carlow, Dublin, Galway, Offaly 7 Donegal, Kildare, Leitrim, Wexford, Wicklow 8 Kilkenny, Laoighis, Limerick, Longford, Monaghan 9 Roscommon, Tipperary, Waterford, Westmeath
dagger: 5 skean, skene
dance: 3 jig
dramatist: 4 Shaw 6 O' Casey
exclamation: 3 och 4 aroo, arra, orra 5 arrah, orrow
fairy: 4 shee, sidh 5 sidhe
flutist: 6 Galway
goddess: 6 Birgit
island: 4 Aran 6 Achill
John, in ~: 4 Sean
knife: 5 skean, skene
lake: 5 lough, Neagh
language: 4 Erse 6 Celtic, Gaelic
luck: 4 cess
lullaby syllables: 5 loo-ra, too-ra
money: 4 punt 5 penny, pound
name part: 3 Mac 4 Fitz
national symbol: 4 harp
Nobelist in Literature: 4 Shaw 5 Yeats 6 Heaney 7 Beckett
Nobelist in Peace: 4 Hume 7 Trimble 8 Corrigan, MacBride, Williams
Nobelist in Physics: 6 Walton
old Greek name for ~: 5 Ierne
old ~ script: 4 ogam 5 ogham
parliament: 4 Dail
patron: 5 St. Pat 7 Patrick
philosopher: 7 Murdoch
playwright: 4 Shaw 5 Colum, Friel, Synge, Wilde, Yeats 6 O'Casey 8 Donleavy
poet: 5 Colum, Moore, Wilde, Yeats 6 Boland, O'Grady 7 Parnell 8 MacNeice 9 Kavanaugh
poetic name: 5 Irena
port: 4 Cobh, Cork 5 Derry 6 Dublin 7 Donegal 9 Waterford
product: 5 linen 7 whiskey
rebel: 5 O'more 6 Fenian
republic: 4 Eire
river: 4 Erne, Nore 5 Boyne
saint: 5 Aidan, Kevin
sea god: 3 Ler, Lir
seat of ancient kings: 4 Tara
spirit: 4 puca 5 pooka
symbol: 4 harp
word on ~ coins: 4 Eire
writer: 5 Behan, Joyce, Moore 6 Binchy, Crofts, Heaney, O'Brien 7 Beckett, Maturin, Murdoch, O'Connor 8 Carleton, Donleavy, O'Faolain 9 Edgeworth, O'Flaherty
Ireland, Jill
spouse: Charles Bronson, David McCallum
Ireland, John: 5 actor
film: All the King's Men (1949) Gunfight at the O.K. Corral (1957) I Saw What You Did (1965) Railroaded! (1947)
I Remember It Well: 4 song, tune
composer: 5 Loewe 6 Lerner
musical: 4 Gigi

I Remember Mama (1948 film)
cast: Barbara Bel Geddes, Irene Dunne, Oscar Homolka
director: George Stevens
role: **4** Lars, Nels **5** Marta, Trina **6** Katrin
I Remember You (song) artist: Frank Ifield, Skid Row
Irene: **4** Cara, Rich, Ryan **5** Dunne, Papas, Worth **6** Castle, Hervey **7** Bordoni
equivalent: **3** Pax
in Russian: **5** Irina
parent of ~: **4** Zeus **6** Themis
Irène: **5** Jacob
Irène __-Curie: **6** Joliot
irenic: **4** mild **6** dovish, gentle **7** pacific **8** peaceful, tranquil **9** placating **10** diplomatic, mollifying, nonviolent
irid: **4** lily **7** freesia **8** gladiola **9** gladiolus
iridescence: **5** sheen, shine **6** dazzle, luster **7** glimmer, glisten, glitter, shimmer, sparkle
iridescent: **6** pearly **7** opaline **8** lustrous, nacreous **9** prismatic **10** opalescent, shimmering
gem: **4** opal
iridium: **5** metal **7** element
alloy: **7** platina
Irina
in English: **5** Irene
see also Russian
Iringa: **4** city, town
locale: **8** Tanzania
iris: **4** flag **5** plant **6** flower, sunbow **7** rainbow **10** fleur-de-lis
center: **5** pupil
combining form: **4** irid- **5** irido-
cover: **6** cornea
fragrant ~: **5** orris
locale: **3** eye
of the ~: **5** uveal
part: **4** uvea **6** areola, areole
South African ~: **4** ixia
__ iris: **4** roof **6** copper, violet **7** bearded, crested, English, Spanish
Iris: **6** Rainer **7** Murdoch **8** asteroid
parent of ~: **7** Electra, Thaumas
sister of ~: **4** Arce **5** Harpy
Iris (2001 film)
cast: Jim Broadbent, Dame Judi Dench, Kate Winslet
director: Richard Eyre
__ & Iris: **7** Stanley
Iris (1998 song) artist: Goo Goo Dolls
Iris composer: **8** Mascagni
__ I Rise: **5** Still
Irises: **3** oil **7** van Gogh **8** painting
Irish: **3** sea **4** stew **6** dander, temper **9** Hibernian
Irish __: **3** elk, jig, Sea, yew **4** boat, bull, Eyes, Gold, Lace, lord, Love, Mist, moss, Pale, stew **5** linen, tweed **6** bridge, coffee, Gaelic, potato, Rovers, setter, Spring, whisky **7** English, terrier, whiskey
Irish __ spaniel: **5** water
Irish __ State: **4** Free
__ Irish: **3** Old **6** Middle
__-Irish: **5** Anglo **6** Scotch
Irish coffee: **5** drink **8** beverage
ingredient: **7** whiskey
__ Irish Eyes Are Smiling: **4** When
Irish Eyes author: Andrew Greeley
Irish Gold author: Andrew Greeley
Irish Lace author: Andrew Greeley
Irish Love author: Andrew Greeley
Irishman: **4** Celt, Gael
Irish Mist author: Andrew Greeley
__ Irish Rose: **5** Abie's
Irish Sea
feeder: **3** Dee
island: **3** Man
river to the ~: **6** Mersey
Irish setter: **3** dog **5** canid **6** canine
Irish Spring: **4** soap
alternative: **3** Lux **4** Dial, Dove, Lava, Tone, Zest **5** Camay, Coast, Ivory, Lever **6** Boraxo, Caress, Shield **8** Lifebuoy **9** Palmolive, Safeguard
Irish Stew! author: Andrew Greeley
Irish Terrier: **3** dog **5** canid **6** canine
Irish water spaniel: **3** dog **5** canid **6** canine
Irish whiskey: **5** drink **8** beverage
Irish Whiskey author: Andrew Greeley
Irish wolfhound: **3** dog **5** canid **6** canine
irk: **3** bug, eat, get, jar, try, vex **4** bait, fret, gall, miff, pain, rile, roil, tire, wear **5** annoy, chafe, get to, grate, harry, peeve, pique, steam, upset, weary **6** abrade, bother, fester, harass, hector, madden, needle, nettle, noodge, pester, plague, put out, rankle, ruffle, tee off, work up **7** afflict, disturb, incense, perturb, provoke, tick off, trouble **8** distress, exercise, irritate **9** aggravate, displease **10** discompose, run afoul of
ender: **4** some
irked: **4** sore **5** tired **9** resentful
easily ~: **4** edgy **5** cross, huffy, moody, surly, testy **6** crabby, cranky, crusty, grumpy, ireful, morose, ornery, snappy, sullen, touchy **7** bearish, grouchy, huffish, peevish, uptight, waspish **8** captious, choleric, petulant, snappish **9** crotchety, excitable, fractious, impatient, irascible, irritable, querulous, splenetic **10** out of sorts
irksome: **4** sore **5** pesky, pesty **6** thorny, trying, vexing **7** grating, onerous, tedious **8** annoying, tiresome, worrying **9** vexatious **10** in one's hair, irritating, unpleasant
one: **3** nag **4** drip, pain, pest, pill **5** creep **6** gadfly **7** annoyer **8** headache **9** tormentor
Irkutsk: **4** city, town
locale: **6** Russia
Irlene: **8** Mandrell
sister: **6** Louise **7** Barbara
Irma: **6** Thomas **8** Rombauer
Irma la Douce (1963 film)
cast: Lou Jacobi, Jack Lemmon, Shirley MacLaine
director: Billy Wilder
I, Robot author: Isaac Asimov
IROC: **5** Chevy **6** Camaro **9** Chevrolet
I roll: **5** Volvo
iron: **4** club, cuff, firm, hale, hard, wiry **5** beefy, burly, chain, hardy, hefty, hunky, husky, lusty, mashy, metal, press, rigid, spoon, stout, tough, wedge **6** brawny, ferric, hearty, mangle, mashie, mighty, potent, robust, rugged, sinewy, smooth, steely, stocky, sturdy, virile **7** adamant, doughty, element, ferrite, ferrous, manacle, niblick, shackle **8** athletic, forceful, golf club, handcuff, indurate, muscular, obdurate, powerful, puissant, stalwart, stubborn, vigorous **9** Atlantean, Herculean, immovable, inelastic, merciless, smooth out, strapping, unbending, well-built **10** able-bodied, implacable, inflexible, red-blooded, relentless, unyielding
alloy: **5** Invar, Monel, steel **7** Elinvar, Inconel, Mumetal **8** cast iron, kamacite, Nichrome **9** Platinite **10** superalloy
alternative: **4** wood
angle ~: **4** L bar
bar of a sort: **5** U-bolt
cast ~: **5** alloy
clothes: **4** mail **5** armor
combining form: **5** ferri-, ferro-, sider- **6** sidero-
construction ~: **5** rebar
creation: **6** crease
deficiency: **6** anemia **7** anaemia
ender: **4** clad, ware, weed, wood, work **5** bound, smith, stone, works **6** handed, monger, worker
glassmaker's ~ rod: **5** punty **6** pontil
hand: **5** rigor **7** cruelty, tyranny **8** coercion, hardness, severity **9** austerity, autocracy, brutality, despotism, harshness, sternness **10** oppression, severeness, strictness
holder: **3** bag
hook: **4** gaff
horse sound: **4** chug
in German: **5** eisen
in the fire: **3** gig, job **4** task **5** chore **7** project, venture **8** activity
like ~: **6** dogged **7** adamant, durable **8** obdurate, resolute **9** obstinate, steadfast, tenacious, unbending **10** determined, relentless, unyielding
man: **5** robot **7** machine **9** automaton
number one ~: **5** cleek
on: **5** affix **6** attach
ore: **8** hematite, limonite, siderite, taconite **9** magnetite
out: **5** solve **6** smooth **7** arrange, flatten, resolve
oxide: **4** rust **9** corrosion
pigment: **4** heme **5** ocher, ochre
pump ~: **4** heft, lift **7** work out **8** exercise
pumper: **5** he-man
pumper pride: **3** bod, pec **6** biceps
pumper routine: **4** curl
pumper unit: **3** rep
source: **3** ore **5** liver
starter: **3** and, pig **4** flat, grid
use a branding ~: **4** sear
use a curling ~: **5** crimp
with ~: **6** ferric **7** ferrous
with an ~ hand: **4** hard **6** firmly **7** harshly, roughly, sternly **8** severely, strictly **10** rigorously
worker: **5** smith
work with ~: **4** weld **5** smelt **6** refine
iron __: **3** hat, man, out **4** blue, gang, gray, grey, hand, mold, rust, will **5** brick, horse, oxide, plant, putty **6** maiden, pyrite, sponge **7** curtain, pyrites, sulfate, vitriol
iron __ fire: **5** in the
iron-__: **5** jawed **6** pumper **7** hearted
__ iron: **3** box, dog, pig **4** beta, cast, fire, gray, grey, hoop, lily, long, nine, pump, tire **5** alpha, angle, cramp, delta, gamma, ingot, plane, scrap, short, steam, white **6** crance, mashie, sponge, toggle, waffle **7** channel, curling, driving, ductile, grozing, lofting, pinking, spiegel, timbale, wrought **8** branding
Iron __: **3** Age **4** Duke, Gate **5** Cross, Gates **7** Curtain
Iron __, The: **4** Heel, Mask **5** Giant, Horse **7** Curtain
__ Iron: **5** Man of **7** Pumping
Iron Age culture: **6** La Tène
__ iron bars a cage: **3** nor
Iron Butterfly song: In-a-Gadda-Da-Vida (1968)
ironclad: **3** set **4** boat, firm, ship **5** fixed, rigid, tight **6** rooted, stable, static **7** certain, settled **8** constant, definite **9** permanent **10** changeless, inexorable, inflexible, unchanging, undoubtful, unwavering
Iron Curtain, The (1948 film)
cast: Dana Andrews, June Havoc, Gene Tierney
director: William Wellman
Irondequoit: **4** city, town
locale: **7** New York
ironfisted: **4** firm, hard **5** bossy, cruel, picky, rigid, stern, tough **6** severe, strict **7** austere, Spartan **8** despotic, exacting, hard-line, rigorous, ruthless **9** demanding, draconian, merciless, stringent, unbending, unpitying, unsparing **10** despotical, implacable, inflexible, no-nonsense, oppressive, tyrannical
one: **4** czar, tsar **6** despot, tyrant **8** autocrat, dictator **9** oppressor
Iron Giant, The (1999 film)
voice cast: Jennifer Aniston, Harry Connick Jr., Vin Diesel
ironhanded: **4** firm, hard **5** bossy, cruel, picky, rigid, stern, tough **6** severe, strict **7** austere, Spartan **8** despotic, exacting, hard-line, rigorous, ruthless **9** demanding, draconian, merciless, stringent, unbending, unsparing **10** despotical, implacable, inflexible, no-nonsense, oppressive, tyrannical
Iron Heel, The author: Jack London
Iron Horse, The: **5** oater **6** Gehrig
ironic: **3** dry, wry **4** arch **5** funny **7** satiric **8** humorous, sardonic **9** sarcastic, satirical **10** unexpected
Ironic (1996 song) artist: Alanis Morissette
ironing: **5** chore **9** housework
challenge: **6** collar
obstacle: **6** button
ironing __: **5** board
iron in the __: **4** fire
iron-jawed: **3** set **5** fixed **6** intent, mulish **7** decided **8** resolute **9** unbending **10** inflexible, purposeful, unwavering, unyielding
Iron John author: **3** Bly
Ironman phase: **3** run **4** swim **7** cycling
Iron Mike: **5** Ditka
iron-on: **5** decal, patch **8** appliqué
jeans ~: **8** appliqué
iron oxide
pigment: **5** ocher, ochre
iron pyrite: **7** mineral **9** fool's gold
irons: **5** bonds, cuffs **7** fetters **8** manacles, shackles **9** bracelets, handcuffs, restraint
carrier: **5** caddy **6** caddie
game with ~: **4** golf
put in ~: **6** fetter **7** enchain, manacle, shackle, trammel **8** handcuff
with many ~ in the fire: **4** at it, busy **6** active, hectic, lively **7** on the go, swamped **8** bustling, immersed **9** engrossed
Ironside (NBC drama)
cast: Barbara Anderson (Eve Whitfield)
Raymond Burr (Robert Ironside)
Don Galloway (Ed Brown)
Don Mitchell (Mark Sanger)
employer: SFPD
__ Ironsides: **3** Old
Iron & Silk director: **3** Sun
irons in the __: **4** fire
Irons, Jeremy: **5** actor
film: Dead Ringers (1988)
Die Hard With a Vengeance (1995)
The French Lieutenant's Woman (1981)
Lolita (1997)
The Man in the Iron Mask (1998)
Moonlighting (1982)
Reversal of Fortune (1990, AA)
Stealing Beauty (1996)
Waterland (1992)
__-iron stomach: **4** cast

ironstone: 5 china **6** dishes, plates **8** ceramics **10** dinnerware

Ironweed: 4 film **5** novel
author: William Kennedy
cast: Carroll Baker, Jack Nicholson, Michael O'Keefe, Meryl Streep

iron-willed: 4 firm, grim **5** brave, cruel, gutsy, hardy, harsh, rigid, stern, stout **6** crusty, fervid, fierce, flinty, mighty, rugged, severe, steely, strong **7** austere, fervent, staunch **8** despotic, exacting, forceful, hard-line, powerful, resolute, ruthless, stubborn, vigorous **9** draconian, hard-nosed, herculean, imperious, steadfast, tenacious, unsparing **10** autocratic, bullheaded, courageous, formidable, hard-boiled, hardheaded, inflexible, relentless, unmerciful, unyielding

ironworks: 5 forge **6** smithy **7** foundry **8** smithery
device: 5 anvil

irony: 3 wit **5** trope **6** satire **7** sarcasm **10** enantiosis
exclamation: 3 aha **6** indeed **7** big deal

__ irony: 6 tragic

Iroquois: 5 Huron, tribe **6** Cayuga, Indian, Oneida **7** Amerind **8** Onondaga
enemy: 4 Erie
language: 4 Erie **5** Huron **6** Oneida

Iroquois League
member: 6 Cayuga, Mohawk, Oneida, Seneca **8** Onondaga **9** Tuscarora

irr.: 6 imperf.

irradiate: 4 beam **5** gleam, light, shine, teach **6** inform **7** glitter, inspire, lighten, light up, radiate, shimmer, sparkle **8** brighten, illumine **10** illuminate

irradiation: 3 ray **4** beam, glow, x-ray **5** light **8** radiance, radiancy

irrational: 3 mad **4** wild **5** flaky, kooky, queer, silly, wacky **6** absurd, flakey, kookie, unwise, whacky **7** extreme, foolish, unsound **8** mindless, unstable **9** arbitrary, brainless, delirious, emotional, fantastic, illogical, senseless, sophistic, unscrewed **10** cockamamie, disjointed, distraught, fallacious, incoherent, inordinate, off-the-wall, reasonless, ridiculous, unreasoned, unthinking
number: 4 surd

irrationality: 4 bosh **5** folly **6** drivel, idiocy, lunacy **7** fatuity, illogic, inanity, madness, oddness, prattle, twaddle **8** insanity, nonsense, wildness

Irrawaddy: 5 river
city on the ~: 3 Ava **9** Manadalay
locale: 5 Burma **7** Myanmar
river to the ~: 8 Chindwin

irreal: 6 dreamy **8** delusive, fanciful, illusory **9** fantastic, imaginary **10** chimerical

irreclaimable: 4 gone, lost

irreconcilable: 7 opposed **8** opposing, opposite

Irreconcilable Differences (1984 film)
cast: Drew Barrymore, Shelley Long, Ryan O'Neal
director: Charles Shyer

irrecoverable: 4 gone, lost **6** ruined **7** defunct, extinct, wrecked **8** consumed, vanished **9** destroyed **10** demolished, eradicated

irredeemable: 8 hopeless

__ irredenta: 6 Italia

irreducible: 3 net

irrefragable: 4 firm, hard, sure **5** solid **8** hardened, rocklike

irrefutable: 4 sure **5** final, valid **6** proven **7** assured, certain **8** accurate, airtight, ironclad, luculent, positive

irreg., not: 3 std. **4** perf.

irregular: 3 odd **4** eery **5** bumpy, eerie, erose, jerky, lumpy, queer, rough, weird **6** atypic, broken, casual, fitful, freaky, hackly, jagged, off-key, patchy, quirky, ragged, random, rugged, spotty, uneven, wabbly, way-out, wobbly, zigzag **7** aimless, bizarre, crooked, deviant, erratic, knurled, oddball, offbeat, strange, unalike, unequal, unusual **8** aberrant, abnormal, atypical, cockeyed, far apart, freakish, improper, lopsided, on-and-off, peculiar, periodic, rambling, shifting, sporadic, uncommon, unsteady, variable **9** amorphous, anomalous, desultory, different, dissonant, divergent, eccentric, faltering, fantastic, haphazard, hit-or-miss, malformed, off-center, recurrent, shapeless, spasmodic, unaligned, uncertain, unnatural, up-and-down, vagarious, zigzagged **10** capricious, changeable, disorderly, immoderate, inconstant, infrequent, inordinate, meandering, nonuniform, occasional, off-balance, out of order, sporadical, suspicious, unfrequent, unofficial, unorthodox, unpunctual, unreliable, willy-nilly
combining form: 4 anom- **5** anomo-
not ~: 4 even **5** level **6** smooth, stable, steady **7** uniform **8** balanced, constant, straight **9** unvarying **10** consistent, rhythmical, unwavering

irregularity: 4 blip **5** quirk **6** defect, oddity **7** anomaly, caprice, oddness, variant **9** confusion

irregularly: 6 seldom **7** by turns **8** fitfully, off and on, on and off

irrelevant: 4 idle, moot **5** inapt, unapt **6** stupid **7** foreign, strange, trivial **8** improper, untimely **9** illogical, ill-suited, inapropos, pointless, unrelated **10** extraneous, immaterial, inapposite, nongermane, not germane, out of order, out of place, unsuitable

irreligious: 5 pagan **7** godless, heathen, impious, profane, ungodly **8** undevout
one: 5 pagan **7** atheist, heathen **10** unbeliever

irremedial: 5 no-win **6** ruined, undone **8** hopeless

irremissible: 8 required **9** de rigueur, essential, mandatory **10** compulsory, imperative, obligatory

irremovable: 4 firm **5** fixed, solid **6** rooted, secure **7** riveted

irreparable: 8 hopeless

irreplaceable: 4 rare **5** vital **6** needed, unique **9** priceless

irrepressible: 6 bouncy **7** buoyant **9** mercurial, resilient

irreproachable: 4 good, pure **5** clean **8** spotless **9** guiltless

irresilient: 4 limp **5** baggy, slack **6** droopy, flabby **7** flaccid **8** drooping **10** out of shape

irresistible: 5 siren **6** cogent **8** magnetic **10** magnetical

Irresistible Forces author: Danielle Steel

irresolute: 4 torn, weak **5** timid **6** fickle, unsure **8** hesitant, lukewarm, wavering **9** faltering, spineless, tentative, uncertain, undecided, unsettled, weak-kneed **10** ambivalent, changeable, hesitating, hot-and-cold, indecisive, on the fence, weak-willed, wishy-washy
be ~: 5 waver **8** hesitate **9** vacillate

irresolution: 5 doubt **6** apathy **7** dubiety, frailty **8** softness, suspense, timidity, weakness **9** dubiosity, hesitancy **10** hesitation

irrespective: 7 despite **8** distinct, ignoring, separate

irresponsibility: 6 excess **7** license **8** audacity, boldness **10** indulgence, profligacy

irresponsible: 3 lax **4** rash, wild **5** giddy, hasty, loose, silly **6** fickle, remiss, sloppy, stupid, unwise **7** flighty **8** carefree, careless, derelict, feckless, immature, reckless, skittish, slipshod **9** imprudent, negligent, unmindful **10** incautious, nonchalant, unreliable, unthinking
one: 3 cad, cur **4** boor, heel, toad **5** knave, rogue, scamp, swine **6** rascal **9** miscreant, scoundrel, vulgarian **10** blackguard

irresponsive: 3 icy, mum **4** cold, cool, dull, mute **5** aloof, quiet **6** frigid, silent **7** languid, removed **8** detached, listless, reserved, reticent, taciturn

irretrievable: 4 gone, lost **8** past hope
one: 5 goner **9** lost cause

irreverence: 4 sass **5** sauce **7** impiety **9** profanity, sacrilege

irreverent: 4 flip **5** fresh, sassy, saucy **6** awless, cheeky, unholy **7** aweless, impious, mocking, profane, ungodly **8** derisive, flippant, impudent, insolent **9** facetious, out-of-line **10** unhallowed

irreversible: 4 lost **5** bleak **6** dismal, futile **7** useless **8** hopeless, ill-fated **9** desperate, permanent

irrevocable: 4 firm, lost, sure **5** final, fixed **7** certain, settled **8** constant, hopeless
damage: 4 ruin **7** debacle **8** calamity, disaster **9** cataclysm, perdition **10** extinction

irrigate: 3 wet **4** soak, wash **5** flood, spray, water **6** dampen, drench **7** moisten **8** sprinkle

irrigated: 3 lit **5** drunk, tipsy **6** stewed **8** besotted **10** inebriated

irrigation: 8 watering
device: 5 noria
need: 4 hose **5** water
needing ~: 3 dry **4** arid, sere **7** bone-dry, drained, parched, thirsty **9** shriveled, waterless **10** dehydrated, desiccated
project: 3 dam

irritability: 5 anger **6** choler, spleen, temper **8** acerbity, asperity, edginess, ill humor, tartness

irritable: 3 hot **4** edgy, sour **5** cross, fiery, huffy, moody, onery, raspy, surly, testy, waspy **6** crabby, crusty, feisty, fretty, grumpy, ireful, morose, ornery, snappy, snippy, sullen, touchy **7** annoyed, bearish, bristly, fretful, grouchy, huffish, nervous, peevish, peppery, prickly, waspish **8** captious, choleric, fretsome, growling, grumpish, liverish, petulant, snappish, snarling, snippety **9** crotchety, difficult, dyspeptic, fractious, grumbling, impatient, irascible, querulous, resentful, sensitive, splenetic **10** high-strung, ill-humored, ill-natured, intolerant, out of humor, out of sorts
in Britain: 5 tilty
one: 4 crab **5** crank, grump **6** grouch **8** grumbler, sourball **10** curmudgeon

irritant: 3 bur **4** bore, load, pest **5** thorn, trial **6** bother, burden, gadfly, hassle, ordeal **8** headache, nuisance, pet peeve, sore spot, vexation **9** annoyance
starter: 7 counter

irritate: 3 bug, get, ire, irk, jar, nag, rag, rub, try, vex **4** bait, burn, faze, fret, gall, goad, miff, pain, rile, roil, tire **5** anger, annoy, chafe, grate, harry, peeve, pique, sting, upset, worry **6** abrade, bother, enrage, fester, harass, madden, needle, nettle, noodge, offend, pester, pother, put out, rankle, rattle, redden, ruffle, scrape **7** affront, bedevil, disturb, enflame, henpeck, incense, inflame, perturb, provoke, torment, trouble **8** distress, embitter, imbitter **9** aggravate, displease, infuriate **10** antagonize, discomfort, discompose, exasperate

irritated: 3 hot, mad, raw, red **4** ired, sore **5** angry, cross, huffy, irate, livid, riled, tired, vexed, wroth **6** chafed, fuming, galled, ireful, pained, peeved, piqued, raging, raving, red-hot, tender **7** annoyed, burning, furious, hurting, nettled, painful, plagued, ranting **8** choleric, harassed, inflamed, pestered, smarting, wrathful **9** indignant, resentful, splenetic
state: 3 pet **4** huff, snit **5** pique

irritating: 5 acrid, harsh, pesky, pesty **6** thorny, trying, vexing **7** burning, fretful, galling, grating, irksome **8** abrasive, annoying, fretsome, nettling, tiresome, worrying **9** annoyance, difficult, offensive, vexatious **10** bothersome, in one's hair

irritation: 3 ire **4** bile, gall, huff, itch, pest, tiff **5** anger, pique, trial, worry, wrath **6** bother, choler, nerves, spleen **7** dudgeon, offense, umbrage **8** acerbity, acrimony, friction, ill humor, slow burn, vexation **9** annoyance **10** difficulty, discomfort, harassment, unkindness
cause ~: 3 irk, vex **4** gall, rile **5** annoy, chafe, clash, grate, peeve, pique **6** abrade, nettle, rankle **7** inflame, provoke **9** aggravate **10** exasperate
show ~: 4 boil, fume, rage, rant, rave **5** chafe **6** blow up, seethe

irrupt: 7 break in, burst in **8** overflow

irruption: 4 raid **5** foray, sally **6** attack, inroad, sortie **8** invasion, outbreak **9** incursion

IRS: 4 agcy. **6** agency
action: 3 aud. **5** audit
busy month: 3 Apr. **5** April
concern: 3 IRA, tax **6** income
department: 8 Treasury
employee: 3 acc., agt., aud., CPA **4** acct., T-man **5** agent
identifier: 3 SSN
part of ~: 3 Int., Rev., Svc. **4** Serv. **7** Revenue, Service **8** Internal
sheet: 4 form
web site suffix: 3 gov

IRT: 6 subway
kin: 3 BMT
locale: 3 NYC **7** New York

Irtysh: 5 river **8** Ob feeder
city on the ~: 4 Omsk
feeder: 3 Oma
locale: 5 China **6** Russia **10** Kazakhstan
river to the ~: 5 Tobol

Iruma: 4 city, town
locale: 5 Japan

Irvin: 4 Cobb **5** Monte **8** Kershner

Irvine: 4 city, town
locale: 8 Scotland **10** California
sch.: 3 UCI **4** U Cal.

Irving: 3 Amy **4** city, John, Reis, town **5** Stone **6** Berlin, Pichel, Rapper **7** Wallace **8** Cummings, Langmuir, Thalberg **10** Washington

locale: 5 Texas
snoozer: 3 Rip
Irving, Amy: 7 actress
film: Carrie (1976)
The Competition (1980)
Crossing Delancey (1988)
Honeysuckle Rose (1980)
Micki + Maude (1984)
Yentl (1983)
spouse: Steven Spielberg
Irving, Henry: 3 Sir
Irving, John: 6 author, writer
work: The Cider House Rules
The Fourth Hand
The Hotel New Hampshire
A Prayer for Owen Meany
A Son of the Circus
Trying to Save Piggy Sneed
The Water-Method Man
A Widow for One Year
The World According to Garp
Irvington: 4 city, town
locale: 9 New Jersey
Irving, Washington: 6 writer
work: A History of New York
The Legend of Sleepy Hollow
Rip Van Winkle
Irvin, Monte: 10 outfielder
Irwin: 4 Hale, Shaw 5 Allen, Corey 7 Winkler
__ Irwin, CA: 4 Fort
Irwin, Hale: 6 golfer
milieu: 5 links 6 course
org.: 3 PGA
is: 4 verb
as ~: 7 unfixed 9 unchanged 10 unimproved
in Spanish: 4 esta
it ~ so: 4 amen
like it ~: 7 reality, sincere 8 candidly, veracity 9 situation, veracious 10 forthright, from the hip, truthfully
no longer ~: 3 was
not: 4 ain't
plurally: 3 are
that ~: 3 viz. 5 id est, to wit 6 namely
__ is: 4 that
...is __ itself: 4 fear
Is __ All There Is: 4 That
Is __ Crime: 3 It a
Is __ dagger...: 5 this a
Is __ fact?: 5 that a
Is __ so?: 4 that
Isaac: 4 Hull 5 Hayes, Stern, Watts 6 Asimov, Newton, Pitman 7 Albéniz
brother of ~: 7 Ishmael
parent of ~: 5 Sarah 7 Abraham
son of ~: 4 Esau 5 Jacob
wife of ~: 7 Rebekah
Isaac __ Singer: 6 Merrit 8 Bashevis
Isaak: 5 Babel, Chris
__ Is a Battlefield: 4 Love
Isabeau composer: 8 Mascagni
Isabel: 5 Jeans, Perón 6 Jewell 7 Allende, Sanford
in English: 9 Elizabeth
see also Spanish
Isabella: 4 poem 5 queen 10 Rossellini
parent: 6 Ingrid 7 Roberto
poet: 5 Keats
spouse: Ferdinand
vessel backed by: 4 Niña 5 Pinta 10 Santa Maria
Isabella author: John Keats
Isabella d'__: 4 Este
Isabelle: 6 Adjani 7 Huppert
Isadora: 6 Duncan
Isadora (1968 film)
cast: James Fox, Vanessa Redgrave, Jason Robards
director: Karel Reisz
...is a friend __: 6 indeed
Isaiah: 6 Berlin 7 prophet
father of ~: 4 Amoz
follower: 8 Jeremiah
__ Isaiah: 6 Losing
__, I Said: 3 I Am
__ is a jealous mistress: 3 Art
Isak: 5 Karen 7 Dinesen
__ Is All Around: 4 Love
__ is a Lonely Hunter, The: 5 Heart
__ Is a Many Splendored Thing: 4 Love
Isamu: 7 Noguchi
__ is an island: 5 No man
Isao: 4 Aoki
Isar: 5 river
city on the ~: 6 Munich
locale: 7 Austria, Germany
__ is as good...: 5 A miss
__ Is a Sometime Thing, A: 5 Woman
__ is a terrible thing to waste: 5 A mind
__ Is a Tramp, The: 4 Lady
I saw: 4 vidi
...__ I saw Elba: 3 ere
I Saw Her Again (1966 song) artist: Mamas & the Papas
I Saw Her Standing There (song) artist: Beatles
I Saw Him Standing There (1988 song) artist: Tiffany
I Saw the Light (1972 song) artist: Todd Rundgren
I Saw Three Ships: 5 carol
__ I say...: 4 Do as
__ I Say: 5 What'd
I Say a Little Prayer (song) artist: Aretha Franklin, Dionne Warwick
__ I say more?: 4 Need
__ Is Beautiful: 4 Life
__ is believing: 6 seeing
__ Is Blue: 4 Love
ISBN: 2 ID
part: 2 No. 3 Int., Std. 4 Book, Intl. 6 Number
__ Is Born, A: 4 Star 5 Child
__ Is Bustin' Out All Over: 4 June
__ is but a dream: 4 life
__ Iscariot: 5 Judas
__ is cast, the: 3 die
__ is cast, The: 3 die
ischium: 4 bone
locale: 6 pelvis
Ischl: 3 spa 6 resort
locale: 7 Austria
Ise: 3 bay 4 city, town
locale: 5 Japan
I second that!: 4 amen
I Second That Emotion (1967 song) artist: Miracles
I see!: 3 aah, aha 4 ah so 5 got it, uh-huh
__ I See You, The: 4 More
__ Is Ended, The: 4 Song
__ Is Enough: 3 One 5 Eight
Isère: 5 river
city on the ~: 8 Grenoble
locale: 6 France
Isesaki: 4 city, town
locale: 5 Japan
Is ev'rybody happy? asker: 5 Lewis
Isfahan locale: 4 Iran
__ is falling, The: 3 Sky
__ is father of the man, The: 5 child
...is fear __: 6 itself
__ is forgiven: 3 all
__ is golden: 7 Silence
__ Is Green, The: 4 Corn
-ish: 4 like, near
relative: 3 -oid 5 -esque, quasi-
Ish: 8 Kabibble
I Shall Not Be Moved author: Maya Angelou
Isham: 4 Mark 5 Jones
__ Is Here: 6 Spring
__ Is Here to Stay: 4 Love
Isherwood, Christopher: 6 author, writer 7 British 10 playwright
colleague: Auden, Spender
work: The Berlin Stories
Goodbye to Berlin
Lions and Shadows
Mr. Norris Changes Trains
Sally Bowles
__ Is High, The: 4 Tide
Ishihara __: 4 test
Ishikari Bay, city on: 5 Otaru
Ishmael: 4 Reed
brother of ~: 5 Isaac
captain: 4 Ahab
descendant: 4 Arab
parent of ~: 5 Hagar 7 Abraham
son of ~: 4 Tema 5 Dumah, Hadad, Kedar, Massa 6 Adbeel, Mibsam, Mishma 7 Kedemah, Naphish 8 Zebadiah
I Shot the Sheriff (1974 song) artist: Eric Clapton
I should say __!: 3 not
__, I Shrunk the Kids: 5 Honey
Ishtar (1987 film)
beast: 5 camel
cast: Isabelle Adjani, Warren Beatty, Charles Grodin, Dustin Hoffman
director: Elaine May
__ is human: 5 To err
Isiah: 6 Thomas
Isidor: 4 Rabi
Isidore of Seville: 5 saint
Isidore the Farmer: 5 saint
isigubu: 4 drum
isinglass: 4 mica
I Sing the Body Electric author: Ray Bradbury, Walt Whitman
...__ is in Heaven: 4 as it
__ is in the fire, the: 3 fat
__ Is in the Streets: 5 A Lion
Isis
animal sacred to ~: 3 cow
brother of ~: 3 Set 6 Osiris
husband of ~: 6 Osiris
parent of ~: 3 Geb, Nut
son of ~: 5 Horus
Is It a Crime singer: 4 Sade
Is It Love (1986 song) artist: Mr. Mister
Is it soup __?: 3 yet
Is It True (1964 song) artist: Brenda Lee
__ is just...: 5 A sigh
Isla: 4 city, town
locale: 6 Mexico 8 Veracruz
Isla de __: 6 Pascua
Islam: 3 rel. 8 religion
ablution: 4 wudu
bridge to paradise: 5 sirat
center: 5 Mecca 6 Medina
coin: 5 dinar
community: 4 umma 5 ummah
decoration: 9 arabesque
doctors: 5 ulema
festival: 6 Bairam
God of ~: 5 Allah
holy book: 5 Koran, Quran
law: 5 sunna
leader: 4 amir, emir, imam 5 ameer, calif, emeer, imaum, kalif 6 caliph, kaliph, khalif
messiah: 5 mahdi
miracle: 5 miraj
month: 4 Rabi 5 Rajab, Safar 6 Jumada, Shaban 7 Ramadan, Shawwal 8 Muharram 9 Dhu al-Qa'da 10 Dhu al-Hijja
pilgrimage: 3 haj 4 hadj, hajj
prayers: 4 raka 5 salah, salat
republic: 4 Iran
sect: 5 Sunni
spirit: 3 jin 4 djin, jinn 5 djinn, jinni 6 djinni
teacher: 5 mulla
weight: 4 rotl
weights: 5 artal
see also Moslem, Muslim
Islamabad: 4 city, town 7 capital
locale: 3 Pak. 8 Pakistan
island: 3 ait, cay, Cos, key, Kos, Man, Yap 4 Aran, Bali, Cook, Cuba, Elba, eyot, Fiji, Guam, Iona, Java, Long, Maui, Milo, Oahu, Sark, Skye 5 Arran, Aruba, atoll, Capri, Cocos, Corfu, Crete, Delos, Ellis, Haiti, Hondo, Ibiza, Iviza, Kauai, Lanai, Leyte, Lundy, Luzon, Malta, Melos, Milos, Naxos, Panay, Samoa, Samos, Thera, Thira, Thule, Timor, Tonga, Wight 6 Baffin, Bahama, Bikini, Borneo, Canary, Candia, Cayman, Comoro, Cyprus, Easter, Hawaii, Hiva Oa, Honshu, Jersey, Jinmen, Kinmen, Kiushu, Kodiak, Kyushu, Lemnos, Madura, Midway, Parris, Patmos, Penang, Philae, Quemoy, Rhodes, Saipan, Savaii, Sicily, Staten, Sundas, Tahiti, Taiwan, Thanet, Tobago 7 Bahrain, Bahrein, Bali Ha'i, Bermuda, Celebes, Chinmen, Corsica, Curaçao, Formosa, Gotland, Grenada, Iceland, Ireland, Iwo Jima, Jamaica, La Palma, Liparis, Madeira, Majorca, Mindoro, Minorca, Mombasa, Mykonos, Nicobar, Norfolk, Oceania, Okinawa, Orkneys, Raiatea, Rapa Nui, Roanoke, Ryukyus, Sao Tomé, St. Croix, St. Lucia, Sumatra, Vanuatu, Wrangel 8 Alcatraz, Atlantis, Barbados, Bora Bora, Dominica, Eniwetok, Guernsey, Hokkaido, Hong Kong, Krakatoa, Mindanao, Moluccas, Pitcairn, Sakhalin, Sandwich, Santorin, Sardinia, Sri Lanka, St. Helena, St. Martin, St. Thomas, Sulawesi, Tasmania, Tenerife, Trinidad, Unalaska, Victoria, Viti Levu, Zanzibar 9 Ascension, Australia, Christmas, Ellesmere, Galápagos, Greenland, Indonesia, Innisfail, Innisfree, Manhattan, Mauritius, Nantucket, New Guinea, Rarotonga, Santorini, segregate, Singapore, St. George's, Stromboli, Teneriffe, Vancouver 10 Cape Breton, Guadeloupe, Hispaniola, Madagascar, Martinique, Montserrat, Puerto Rico, Saint Kitts, Upolu. Wight
Aegean: 3 Cos, Ios, Kea, Kos, Zea 4 Keos, Milo 5 Chios, Crete, Delos, Khios, Melos, Milos, Samos 6 Candia, Icaria, Lemnos, Lesbos, Patmos, Rhodes, Rhodos, Skiros, Skyros 7 Mykonos 8 Cyclades
Aleutian: 3 Rat 4 Adak, Atka, Attu 8 Unalaska
Atlantic: 6 Faroes 7 Iceland, Ireland 8 St. Helena 9 Ascension, Greenland
Balearic: 5 Ibiza, Iviza 7 Majorca, Menorca, Minorca
Canada: 6 Baffin 8 Victoria 9 Ellesmere, Vancouver
Canary: 6 Hierro 7 La Palma 8 Tenerife 9 Teneriffe
Caribbean: 3 BWI 4 Saba 5 Aruba 7 Bahamas, Caymans
Channel ~: 4 Sark 6 Jersey 8 Guernsey
combining form: 4 neso- 5 -nesia
coral ~: 3 cay, key
Cyclades: 3 Kea, Zea 4 Keos, Milo 5 Delos, Melos, Milos, Naxos, Paros, Thera, Thira 8 Santorin 9 Santorini
Dodecanese: 5 Leros 6 Patmos, Rhodes, Rhodos
East China Sea: 4 Mazu 5 Matsu 6 Kiushu, Kyushu

England: 3 Ely, Man 4 Sark 5 Wight 6 Jersey 8 Guernsey
Greece: 3 Cos, Ios, Kos 4 Milo 5 Corfu, Crete, Delos, Leros, Melos, Milos, Naxos, Paros, Samos, Thera, Thira, Zante 6 Candia, Euboea, Lemnos, Lesbos, Skiros, Skyros 8 Santorin 9 Santorini
Hawaiian: 4 Maui, Oahu 5 Kauai, Lanai
Hebrides: 4 Iona, Mull, Skye
Indian Ocean: 5 Cocos 6 Comoro 8 Sri Lanka 9 Christmas, Mauritius 10 Madagascar, Seychelles
Indonesia: 4 Bali, Biak, Java, Laut, Leti, Nias, Roti, Savu, Sawu 5 Banka, Ceram, Letti, Rotti, Spice, Sumba, Timor 6 Bangka, Borneo, Butung, Lombok, Madura, Serang 7 Celebes, Sumatra 8 Krakatoa, Moluccas, Sulawesi
in French: 3 île
Ionian Sea: 5 Corfu, Zante
Japan: 5 Hondo 6 Honshu, Kiushu 7 Okinawa, Shikoku 8 Hokkaido 13 Kyushu. Ryukyus
Leeward ~: 4 Saba 8 St. Martin 10 Guadeloupe, Montserrat
Malay: 5 Timor 6 Borneo, Sundas 9 Indonesia 10 East Indies
Mediterranean ~: 3 Sar. 4 Elba 5 Capri, Corfu, Crete, Malta 6 Candia, Cyprus, Sicily
nation: 5 Malta 6 Cyprus 7 Bermuda, Jamaica 8 Sri Lanka 9 Indonesia 10 New Zealand
New York: 4 Fire, Long 5 Coney, Ellis 6 Rikers, Staten 9 Manhattan
North Sea: 7 Frisian, Orkneys
Pacific: 3 Yap 4 Cook, Fiji, Guam, Niue, Reao, Savo, Truk, Wake 5 Hondo, Nauru, Palau, Samar, Samoa, Tonga, Upolu 6 Bikini, Easter, Hawaii, Hivaoa, Honshu, Midway, Saipan, Savaii, Tahiti 7 Oceania, Phoenix, Rapa Nui, Society, Vanuatu 8 Bora Bora, Eniwetok, Friendly, Gilberts, Hokkaido 9 Australia, Marquesas, Marshalls, New Guinea, Polynesia 10 Micronesia, New Zealand
Philippines: 4 Cebu, Jolo 5 Bohol, Leyte, Luzon, Panay, Samar 6 Negros 7 Mindoro 8 Mindanao, Visayans
river ~: 3 ait 4 eyot
Scotland: 4 Mull, Skye 5 Tiree, Tyree 8 Hebrides
small ~: 3 ait, cay, key 4 eyot
South China Sea: 6 Hainan, Taiwan 7 Formosa 8 Hong Kong 9 Singapore
Taiwan Strait: 4 Amoy 6 Jinmen, Kinmen, Quemoy 7 Chinmen 10 Pescadores
welcome: 3 lei 5 aloha
West Indies: 4 Cuba 5 Aruba, Haiti 6 Virgin 7 Jamaica 8 Antilles, Barbados, Windward 10 Hispaniola, Martinique, Puerto Rico
Windward ~: 7 Grenada, St. Lucia 8 Dominica 9 St. George's 10 Grenadines
see also Hawaii
island-___: 3 hop
___ island: 3 ice 4 heat 6 monkey, safety, speech 7 barrier, traffic
___ Island: 4 Fire, Goat, Holy, Long, Mare, On an, Plum, Ross, Spud, Wake 5 Baker, Banks, Block, Coney, Ellis, North, Rhode, South, Stony 6 Baffin, Chiloe, Devil's, Easter, Gonâve, Mercer, Parris, Savage, Staten, Turtle 7 Baranof, Bedloe's, Berkner, Fantasy, Howland, Hungtow, Liberty, Minicoy, Penguin, Roanoke, Sanibel, Stewart, Thunder, Valcour, Watling, Welfare
___ Island Earth: 4 This
Islander rival: 4 Blue, King, Star, Wild 5 Bruin, Devil, Flame, Flyer, Oiler, Sabre, Shark 6 Canuck, Coyote, Ranger 7 Capital, Panther, Penguin, Red Wing, Senator 8 Canadien, Predator, Thrasher 9 Avalanche, Blackhawk, Hurricane, Lightning, Maple Leaf 10 Blue Jacket, Mighty Duck
Islanders: 3 six 4 team
gear: 4 puck 5 stick
home: 7 New York
milieu: 3 ice 4 rink
org.: 3 NHL
sport: 6 hockey
___ Island, FL: 5 Marco
Island Girl (1975 song) artist: Elton John
___ Island Line: 4 Rock
___ Island, NY: 4 City 5 Coney, Ellis 6 Rikers, Staten
Island of Dr. Moreau: 4 film 5 novel
author: H.G. Wells
cast: Nigel Davenport, Burt Lancaster, Michael York
director: Don Taylor
Island of Lost Souls (1933 film)
cast: Richard Arlen, Charles Laughton, Bela Lugosi
director: Erle C. Kenton
Island of the Blue Dolphins author: 5 O'Dell
Island of the Day Before, The author: Umberto Eco
Island of the Fay, The author: Edgar Allan Poe
___ Island Red: 5 Rhode
islands: 6 Azores, Faroes 7 Bahamas, Caymans, Faeroes, Ionians, Liparis, Oceania, Orkneys, Ryukyus 8 Andamans, Antilles, Canaries, Cyclades, Gilberts, Hebrides, Leewards, Marianas, Moluccas, Sandwich, Solomons, Visayans 9 Aleutians, Antipodes, Carolines, Falklands, Indonesia, Marquesas, Marshalls, Polynesia, Prilibofs 10 East Indies, Grenadines, Pescadores, Seychelles, West Indies
___ Islands: 3 Aru, Bay, Far, Sea 4 Aran, Aroe, Arru, Cook, Fiji, Near, Truk 5 Åland, Amber, Batan, Bonin, Cocos, Egadi, Faroe, Manua, Palau, Pelew, Spice, Sunda 6 Aegean, Aeolic, Bahama, Bimini, Caicos, Canary, Cayman, Comoro, Ellice, Faeroe, Futuna, Ionian, Kurile, Lagoon, Lipari, Lubang, Orkney, Safety, Scilly, Virgin 7 Aeolian, Aldabra, Andaman, Babuyan, Basilan, Bijagos, Channel, Chatham, Diomede, Frisian, Gambier, Gilbert, Keeling, Ladrone, Leeward, Lofoten, Maldive, Mariana, Molucca, Nicobar, Phoenix, Society, Solomon, Visayan, Volcano, Western
___ Islands, AK: 3 Far 4 Near
Islands in the Stream
author: Ernest Hemingway
locale: 6 Bimini
Islands in the Stream (1983 song)
artist: Dolly Parton, Kenny Rogers
___ Island Sound: 4 Long
Island, The: 4 play 5 novel
author: Athol Fugard, Peter Benchley
___ Island With You: 4 On an
Isla Vista: 4 city, town
locale: 10 California
isle: 3 ait, cay, key 4 eyot
see also island
Isle ___ National Park: 6 Royale
___ Isle: 5 Apple 6 Garden 7 Emerald, Presque
Isle of ___: 3 Ely, Man 4 Skye 5 Capri, Pines, Wight
Isle of Man
language: 4 Manx
man: 4 Gael
Isle of Mull neighbor: 4 Iona
Isle of Wight city: 4 Ryde
Isle Royale: 4 park
locale: 8 Michigan
___ Isles: 6 Scilly 7 British
islet: 3 ait, cay, key 4 eyot 5 atoll
Isley: 6 O'Kelly, Ronald 7 Rudolph
Isley Brothers
song: Fight the Power (1975)
It's Your Thing (1969)
That Lady (1973)
Islip: 4 city, town
locale: 7 New York
ism: 5 creed, dogma, tenet 6 belief, school, system, theory 7 precept 8 doctrine, ideology, practice 9 principle 10 philosophy
Ismail: 8 Merchant
Ismail Samani: 4 peak 5 mount 8 mountain
locale: 4 Asia 10 Tajikistan
___ is me!: 3 Woe
I smell ___!: 4 a rat
___ Is Mine, The: 3 Boy 4 Girl
___ is more: 4 less
___ Is My Country: 4 This
___ is my shepherd..., The: 4 Lord
___ is my witness...: 5 As God
___ Is Not Enough: 4 Once 8 The World
___ Is Nothin' Like a Dame: 5 There
isn't: 4 ain't
Isn't ___ bit like you and me?: 3 he a
Isn't ___ Lovely?: 3 She
Isn't It a Pity (1970 song) artist: George Harrison
Isn't It a Pity? composer: 8 Gershwin
Isn't It Romantic composer: 4 Hart 7 Rodgers
___ Isn't Love: 4 If It
___ Isn't So: 5 Say It
iso-: 4 equi-, same 5 equal
isobar: 4 line
Isocrates: 5 Greek 6 orator
isogon: 6 square 9 rectangle
isolate: 5 ice in, split 6 banish, cut off, detach, enisle, maroon, shut in, strand 7 confine, seclude 8 block off, close off, separate, set apart 9 disengage, keep apart, segregate, sequester 10 disconnect, quarantine
isolated: 4 lone, only, sole 5 alone, apart, aside, quiet, stray 6 atypic, far-out, hidden, lonely, narrow, random, remote, single, unique 7 insular, private, recluse, special, strange, unusual 8 abnormal, atypical, deserted, eremitic, far apart, forsaken, lonesome, secluded, separate, solitary, sporadic 9 abandoned, anomalous, nonpublic, reclusive, untypical, withdrawn 10 infrequent, sporadical
isolation: 7 privacy, secrecy 8 solitude 9 backwoods, seclusion 10 desolation, loneliness
isolation ___: 5 booth
isolato: 5 loner 6 hermit 7 eremite, recluse 9 anchorite, introvert
isometrics: 7 regimen 8 exercise
___ Is on My Side: 4 Time
isonomy: 6 parity 7 balance 8 equality, evenness
Isonzo: 5 river
locale: 5 Italy 10 Yugoslavia
isopropyl ___: 5 ether 7 alcohol
isotonics: 7 regimen 8 exercise
ISP: 3 AOL 5 Yahoo 9 Earthlink 10 Mindspring
I 'spect I growed sayer: 5 Topsy
I Spy (NBC drama)
cast: Bill Cosby (Alexander Scott) Robert Culp (Kelly Robinson)
Israel: 4 Sion, Zion 6 nation, Putnam 7 country 8 Horovitz
airline: 4 El Al
airport: 3 Lod 9 Ben-Gurion
Biblical name for ~: 6 Beulah, Canaan
bovine: 6 Baladi
capital: 9 Jerusalem
city: 3 Lod 4 Elat, Yafo 5 Eilat, Elath, Haifa, Jaffa 6 Ashdod, Bat Yam 7 Netanya, Tel Aviv 8 Nazareth 9 Beersheba, Jerusalem
dance: 4 hora 5 horah
desert: 5 Negeb, Negev
diplomat: 4 Eban
ender: 3 ite
gun: 3 Uzi
king: 4 Ahab, Saul 5 David 7 Solomon
lake: 7 Dead Sea
language: 3 Heb. 4 Hebr. 6 Hebrew
legislature: 7 Knesset
locale: 4 Asia 7 Mideast 8 Near East
money: 5 agora 6 agorot, shekel
mountain: 5 Tabor
native: 5 sabra
neighbor: 3 Leb., Syr. 5 Egypt, Syria 6 Jordan 7 Lebanon
Nobelist in Economics: 8 Kahneman
Nobelist in Literature: 5 Agnon
Nobelist in Peace: 5 Begin, Peres, Rabin
political party: 5 Likud, Mapam
port: 4 Acre, Yafo 5 Eilat, Elath, Haifa, Jaffa
sea: 4 Dead 7 Galilee
tribe of ~: 3 Dan, Gad 4 Levi 5 Asher, Judah 6 Joseph, Reuben, Simeon 7 Zebulun 8 Benjamin, Issachar, Naphtali
violinist: 7 Perlman 8 Zukerman
writer: 2 Oz 7 Amichai 9 Appelfeld
see also Hebrew
___ Israel: 5 Eretz
Israel in Egypt composer: 6 Handel
___-Israeli relations: 4 Arab
Israelite: 3 Jew 6 Hebrew, Jewish
home: 6 Goshen
leader: 5 Moses 6 Joshua
Israel prime ministers:
2001– Ariel Sharon
1999–2001 Ehud Barak
1996–1999 Benjamin Netanyahu
1995–1996 Shimon Peres
1992–1995 Yitzhak Rabin
1986–1992 Yitzhak Shamir
1984–1986 Shimon Peres
1983–1984 Yitzhak Shamir
1977–1983 Menachem Begin
1974–1977 Yitzhak Rabin
1969–1974 Golda Meir
1963–1969 Levi Eshkol
1955–1963 David Ben-Gurion
1954–1955 Moshe Sharett
1948–1954 David Ben-Gurion
Israfel author: Edgar Allan Poe
___ is Rich: 6 Rabbit
___ Is Right, The: 5 Price
Issachar
brother of ~: 3 Dan, Gad 4 Levi 5 Asher, Judah 6 Joseph, Reuben, Simeon 7 Zebulun 8 Benjamin, Naphtali
parent of ~: 4 Leah 5 Jacob
sister of ~: 5 Dinah
Issa, Kobayashi: 4 poet 8 Japanese
Issei: 8 Japanese 9 immigrant
child: 5 Nisei

Issel, Dan
milieu: 5 court
org.: 3 NBA
sport: 10 basketball
__ is silence, The: 4 rest
__ Is Sleeping: 4 Enid
Is so! rebuttal: 4 ain't 5 am not 6 are not
__ Is Spinal Tap: 4 This
...is still ___: 5 a kiss
__ Is Strange: 4 Love
issue: 3 run 4 cion, copy, emit, flow, give, gush, kids, mint, ooze, pour, rise, seed, send, sons, spew, spue, stem, text, vent 5 eject, expel, exude, heirs, point, print, query, scion, spawn, spirt, spurt, start, topic, young 6 emerge, get out, matter, put out, ration, scions, sequel, spring, stream, upshot 7 cast out, deal out, diffuse, dish out, divvy up, dole out, edition, emanate, give off, give out, hand out, kinfolk, mete out, outflow, pass out, problem, proceed, product, progeny, publish, radiate, release, send out, subject, trickle 8 argument, bring out, children, delivery, disburse, dispatch, dispense, emission, hot topic, kinfolks, kinsfolk, magazine, overflow, printing, question, throw off, transmit 9 arise from, circulate, daughters, grow out of, inheritor, offspring, originate, posterity, send forth 10 administer, contention, descendant, dispersion, distribute, promulgate, put forward
at ~: 4 open 10 in question
avoid the ~: 5 hedge, stall 6 waffle
cloud the ~: 5 befog 7 confuse 8 confound 9 obfuscate
for short: 3 pub
(from): 4 stem 5 arise 6 result
nettlesome ~: 5 thorn
no longer an ~: 4 dead, moot
not an ~: 4 moot 8 academic
point at ~: 5 theme, topic 8 argument, question
side: 3 con, pro
special ~: 5 extra 6 annual
take ~: 5 argue, clash 6 differ, oppose 7 quarrel, quibble 8 conflict, disagree
violently: 5 eruct, erupt
__ issue: 4 debt, take 5 joint
issued, soon to be: 3 NYP
Issus: 6 battle
__ Is Sweeping the Country: 4 Love
Issy: 4 city, town
locale: 6 France
-ist: 4 doer
cousin: 3 -ite, -nik, -yer 4 -ster
Istanbul: 4 city, port, town
area: 6 Galata
city near ~: 6 Edirne
it replaced ~: 6 Angora, Ankara
locale: 4 Asia 6 Europe, Turkey
I Started a Joke (1969 song) artist: Bee Gees
Is that __?: 5 a fact
Is That All There Is (1969 song) artist: Peggy Lee
Is that so?: 6 do tell, oh yeah, really
Is that your __ answer?: 5 final
__ Is the Army: 4 This
__ Is the Gate: 6 Strait
__ Is the Love: 5 Where
__ is the Message, The: 6 Medium
__ Is the Night: 6 Tender
Is There Something I Should Know (1983 song) artist: Duran Duran
__ is the time...: 3 Now
__ is the winter...: 3 Now
Is this a dagger which ___...: 4 I see
Is this seat __?: 5 taken
Is this the end of __?: 4 Rico
isthmus: 3 Kra 4 neck, Suez 6 Panama 7 Corinth 10 land bridge
__ Is Tight: 4 Time
I Still Believe (1999 song) artist: Mariah Carey
I Still Know What You Did Last Summer (1998 film)
cast: Brandy, Jennifer Love Hewitt, Freddie Prinze Jr.
I Still See __: 5 Elisa
istle: 4 rope 5 fiber
source: 5 yucca
Istoben: 3 cow 4 bull 6 bovine, cattle
Istomin, Eugene: 7 pianist
__ Is Too Much With Us, The: 5 World
Istoro Nal: 4 peak 5 mount 8 mountain
locale: 4 Asia 8 Pakistan
__ is to say: 4 that
Istres: 4 city, town
locale: 6 France
ISU
conference: 9 Big Twelve
locale: 4 Ames
__ is up!, The: 3 jig
Isuzu: 3 car 4 auto 10 automobile
model: 5 Amigo, Axiom, Rodeo 6 Stylus 7 Impulse, Trooper 8 Ascender
__ Is Waiting, A: 5 Child
I swear!: 5 no lie 6 honest, really
__ is well: 3 All
__ Is Wild, The: 5 Joker
__ is yet to be, The: 4 best
__ Is Yet to Come, The: 4 Best
Is You __ Is You Ain't Ma Baby?: 4 Is or
__ Is Your Life: 4 This
__ Is You, The: 4 Song
it: 5 charm 6 appeal, neuter, seeker 7 charism 8 charisma
game: 3 tag
__ it: 3 bag, cut, dog, get, leg, mix 4 beat, cool, go at, go to, hoof, make, take, wing, with 5 catch, get to, go for, hop to, out of, rough, see to, watch 6 cheese
__ it!: 3 Bag, Can, Hit 4 Cool, Darn, I get, So be, Stow 5 Hop to, Prove
...it __ for thee: 5 tolls
It: 5 novel
author: Stephen King
It __ a dark...: 3 was
It __ as Well Be Spring: 5 Might
It __ a Thief: 5 Takes
It __ a Very Good Year: 3 Was
It __ Be Him: 4 Must
It __, be not afraid: 3 is I
It __ Be You: 5 Had to, Might
It __ Come Easy: 4 Don't
It __ Depends on You: 3 All
It __ Fair: 4 Isn't
It __ far far better thing...: 3 is a
It __ From Outer Space: 4 Came
It __ Happen to You: 5 Could 6 Should
It __ laugh: 4 is to
It __ Mean a Thing: 4 Don't
It __ Me Babe: 4 Ain't
It __ Necessarily So: 4 Ain't
It __ to Be Ignorant: 4 Pays
It __ to Be You: 3 Had
It __ Two: 5 Takes
It __ Very Good Year: 4 Was a
It.
see Italian
__ It: 3 Eat, Say 4 Beat, Boog, Doin', Push 5 Fakin', I Like, Makin', Touch, Watch
__ it a day: 4 call
__ It Again, Sam: 4 Play
__ it a go: 4 give
Itaguí: 4 city, town
locale: 8 Colombia
It Ain't __ Rain No Mo': 5 Gonna
It ain't a fit night out for man or __: 5 beast
It Ain't Hard To Tell rapper: 3 Nas
It Ain't Hay (1943 film)
cast: Bud Abbott, Lou Costello
director: Erle C. Kenton
It Ain't Me Babe (1965 song) artist: Turtles
It Ain't Me Babe composer: 5 Dylan
It Ain't Necessarily So composer: 8 Gershwin
It Ain't Over 'Til It's Over (1991 song) artist: Lenny Kravitz
Ital.: 4 lang.
see also Italian
Italia, city in: 4 Roma 6 Milano, Napoli, Torino 7 Firenze, Livorno, Venezia
Italian: 8 dressing, language
see also Italy
Italian __: 4 Alps, hand, ices 5 aster, bread 6 clover, sonnet, turnip 7 jasmine, pointer
Italian Symphony composer: Mendelssohn
Italian words
apology: 5 scusa
art: 4 arte
asset: 4 bene
be: 3 ser
count: 5 conte
dear: 4 cara, caro
desk: 5 stipo
earth: 5 terra
eight: 4 otto
evening: 4 sera
farewell: 4 ciao
flower holder: 4 vaso
fruit: 5 oliva
good: 4 bene
goodbye: 4 ciao
holiday: 5 festa
holy man: 5 santo
innkeeper: 4 oste
ladder: 5 scala
lady: 5 donna
land: 5 terra
love: 5 amore
monk: 3 fra
month: 5 Marzo
moon: 4 luna
my: 3 mia, mio
noble: 5 conte
number: 3 due, sei, tre, uno 4 otto
off: 3 via
one: 3 una, uno
peak: 5 monte
road: 3 via
six: 3 sei
skill: 4 arte
street: 3 via
they: 4 esse, esso
three: 3 tre
two: 3 due
way: 3 via
wine: 4 vino
see also Italy
italicize: 6 stress 7 point up 9 emphasize, underline 10 accentuate
italics: 4 type
like ~: 6 aslant 7 slanted
what ~ show: 6 accent, stress 8 emphasis 10 importance
Italics: 3 cat
italic type: 6 aldine
I Talk to the Trees composer: 5 Loewe 6 Lerner
__ it all: 5 above
__-it-all: 4 know
It All Adds Up author: Saul Bellow
__ it all hang out: 3 let
__ it all together: 3 get, put
Italo: 4 Tajo 5 Balbo, Svevo 7 Calvino 10 Montemezzi
Italy: 6 nation 7 country
ancient town: 4 Elea 5 Ostia
artist: 4 Reni 6 Giotto, Titian 7 Cellini, da Vinci, Raphael, Tiepolo 8 Angelico, del Sarto 9 Donatello 10 Botticelli, Modigliani, Tintoretto 12 Michelangelo
art patron: 4 Este
astronomer: 6 Piazzi 7 Galilei, Galileo
bass: 5 Pinza
bay: 6 Naples
bovine: 5 Oropa 8 Chianina
bowling: 5 bocce, bocci 6 boccia, boccie
brandy: 6 grappa
capital: 4 Roma, Rome
car: 4 Alfa, Fiat, Ghia 7 Bugatti, Ferrari 8 Maserati 9 Alfa Romeo
cheese: 6 Romano 7 fontina, ricotta 8 Bel Paese, Parmesan, pecorino 9 provolone 10 Gorgonzola, mascarpone, mozzarella
city: 3 Ven. 4 Asti, Atri, Bari, Enna, Iesi, Lodi, Pisa, Roma, Rome 5 Anzio, Cuneo, Eboli, Genoa, Lucca, Massa, Milan, Monza, Padua, Parma, Prato, Siena, Terni, Trent, Turin, Udine 6 Albino, Ancona, Assisi, Cesena, Genova, Milano, Modena, Naples, Napoli, Padova, Rimini, Torino, Trento, Venice, Verona 7 Bologna, Brescia, Catania, Cremona, Ferrara, Firenze, Leghorn, Livorno, Messina, Palermo, Perugia, Ravenna, Salerno, Sassari, Taranto, Trieste, Venezia 8 Cagliari, Florence, Siracusa
commune: 4 Asti, Este, Oria, Todi 5 Paola, Riesi
conductor: 4 Muti 6 Abbado 9 Mantovani, Toscanini
dance: 5 ballo, gigue 10 bergamasca, saltarello, tarantella, villanella
explorer: 4 Polo 5 Cabot 6 Nobile 7 Belzoni 8 Columbus, Vespucci
film director: 5 Leone 6 De Sica 7 Fellini 8 Pasolini
food: 5 pasta 9 antipasto
fountain: 5 Trevi
fruit: 8 bergamot
gulf: 5 Genoa 6 Venice 7 Taranto, Trieste
ice cream: 6 gelati, gelato 7 spumone, spumoni, tortoni
island off ~: 3 Sar. 4 Elba, Lido 5 Malta 6 Sicily 7 Corsica 8 Sardinia
lake: 4 Como, Orta 5 Garda 6 Albano, Averno, Lugano 8 Maggiore 9 Trasimeno
language: 5 Oscan 6 Tuscan 7 Umbrian
last queen: 5 Elena
legislature: 6 Senate
magistrate: 4 doge
money: 4 euro, lira, lire, tari 5 scudi, scudo, soldi, soldo 6 florin 9 centesimo
mountain: 6 Cadore 7 Bernina 9 Apennines, Dolomites, Mont Blanc 10 Carnic Alps, Monte Corno
neighbor: 6 France 7 Austria 8 Slovenia 9 San Marino
news agency: 4 ANSA
newspaper: 6 Avanti
Nobelist in Chemistry: 5 Natta
Nobelist in Economics: 10 Modigliani
Nobelist in Literature: 2 Fo 7 Deledda, Montale 8 Carducci 9 Quasimodo 10 Pirandello
Nobelist in Medicine: 5 Bovet, Golgi 8 Dulbecco 14 Levi-Montalcini

Nobelist in Peace: 6 Moneta
Nobelist in Physics: 5 Fermi 6 Rubbia 7 Marconi
noble house: 4 Este
org.: 4 NATO
pet form of John: 4 Gino
physicist: 5 Fermi, Volta 7 Marconi 8 Avogadro 10 Torricelli
playwright: 5 Betti, Gozzi 6 Oriani 7 Giacosa, Goldoni, Rovetta 10 Pirandello
poet: 5 Belli, Berni, Tasso 6 Marino, Oriani, Parini, Pavese 7 Ariosto, Boiardo, Colonna, Folengo, Foscolo, Montale, Morante, Pascoli, Pontano 8 Carducci, Pasolini, Petrarch 9 Boccaccio, D'Annunzio, Quasimodo, Sacchetti 10 Cavalcanti
port: 4 Bari 5 Genoa, Ostia 6 Ancona, Naples, Venice 7 Leghorn, Livorno, Marsala, Messina, Palermo, Salerno, Trieste
pottery: 6 Faenza
region: 5 Aosta, Udine 6 Apulia
river: 4 Arno, Nera, Sele 5 Adige, Oglio, The Po
royal house: 5 Savoy
saint: 5 Paolo, Pius X 7 Ambrose, Anthony, Francis, Gregory 8 Benedict 9 Catherine 10 Philip Neri
sauce: 5 pesto 6 tomato 8 marinara
scientist: 5 Fermi, Volta 6 Piazzi 7 Galilei, Galvani, Marconi 8 Avogadro 10 Torricelli
scooter: 5 Vespa
sculptor: 12 Michelangelo
sea: 6 Ionian 8 Adriatic, Ligurian 10 Tyrrhenian
shape: 4 boot
skier: 5 Tomba
soprano: 5 Freni, Patti 7 Tebaldi 8 Albanese 10 Galli-Curci, Tetrazzini
soup ingredient: 4 orzo
temple: 5 duomo
tenor: 6 Caruso 7 Corelli 9 Pavarotti
TV network: 3 RAI
violinmaker: 5 Amati 10 Stradivari
volcano: 4 Etna 5 Aetna 8 Vesuvius 9 Stromboli
waterfall: 4 Toce
wine: 5 corvo, Soave 6 Arneis, Barolo 7 Amarone, Barbera, Chianti, Marsala, Orvieto 8 Dolcetto, Frascati, spumante 9 Bardolino, lambrusco
wine measure: 4 orna
writer: 3 Eco 5 Dante, Svevo 6 Basile, Silone 7 Alberti, Alfieri, Aretino, Bassani, Calvino, Capuana, Cassola, Collodi, Deledda, Foscolo, Manzoni, Morante, Moravia, Rovetta 8 Ginzburg 18 Pico della Mirandola
Itami: 4 city, town
locale: 5 Japan
___ It a Pity?: 4 Isn't
Itar-___: 4 Tass
___ it art?: 5 But is
Itasca: 4 lake
locale: 9 Minnesota
___ it a shot: 4 give
___ It as It Lays: 4 Play
___ it a try: 4 give
I taut I ___ a puddy tat!: 3 taw
___ it away: 4 pack, take
___ It Bad: 4 I Got
___ it be?: 6 What'll
___ It Be: 3 Let
___ It Be Magic: 5 Could
___ It Be Me: 3 Let
___ it big: 3 hit 4 make
___ it by ear: 4 play
It Came From Outer Space (1953 film) cast: Richard Carlson, Charles Drake, Barbara Rush
___ It Can Be Told: 3 Now
It can't be!: 4 oh no
It Can't Happen Here author: 5 Lewis
itch: 3 yen 4 long, lust, need, urge, wish 5 yearn 6 desire, hanker, hunger, tickle, tingle 7 craving, impulse, longing, passion 8 appetite, pruritus, tingling, yearning 9 hankering, prickling 10 incitement, irritation
cause: 5 mange, tinea
combining form: 4 psor- 5 psoro-
for: 4 want 5 covet, crave
(for): 4 long, pant
scratch an ~: 5 react
It Changed My Life author: Betty Friedan
itchy: 4 avid, edgy, keen 5 antsy, eager, jumpy, tense 6 fervid, greedy, hungry, tingle, uneasy 7 anxious, burning, craving, fidgety, jittery, keyed up, longing, nervous, restive, uptight, wishful, zealous 8 agitated, covetous, crawling, desirous, grasping, restless, scratchy, skittish, stinging, ticklish, tingling, troubled, yearning 9 concerned, excitable, ill at ease, impatient 10 high-strung, raring to go
___ it close to the vest: 4 play
It Could Happen to You (1994 film) cast: Nicolas Cage, Bridget Fonda, Rosie Perez
director: Andrew Bergman
It does ___ good: 5 a body
It don't ___ thing...: 5 mean a
It Don't Come Easy (1971 song) artist: Ringo Starr
It Don't Matter to Me (1970 song) artist: Bread
-ite: 4 rock 6 native
cousin: 3 -ese, -ist 4 -ster
itea: 4 tree 5 shrub 6 willow 9 saxifrage
item: 3 net 4 part, unit 5 entry, piece, thing 6 aspect, couple, detail, entity, object, regard 7 article, element, feature, subject 8 instance, specific 9 component 10 ingredient, particular
itemize: 4 cite, list 5 count, tally 6 detail, lay out, number, recite, record, relate, report, set out 7 catalog, mention, recount, specify 8 document, set forth, spell out 9 catalogue, enumerate, inventory, keep count
itemized: 4 full 8 detailed, thorough
items: 5 goods, stuff 7 rations 8 supplies 10 provisions
___-item veto: 4 line
iterate: 3 rpt. 4 echo 5 refer, resay 6 go over, harp on, rehash, repeat, retell, stress 7 dwell on, recount, restate, run over 8 practice, rehearse, return to 9 dwell upon, emphasize, reiterate 10 underscore
iterated: 8 frequent, manifold, numerous 9 recurrent
iteration: 3 rep 9 frequency 10 repetition
___ It for Me: 4 Save
___ It Forward: 3 Pay
___ it from me: 5 far be
It Girl, The: 3 Bow 8 Clara Bow
___ it goes: 5 And so
Ithaca: 4 city, town
athletes: 6 Big Red
locale: 7 New York
school: 7 Cornell
It Had to Be You lyricist: 4 Kahn
I Thank You (1968 song) artist: Sam and Dave
It Happened at the World's Fair (1963 film) cast: Gary Lockwood, Joan O'Brien, Elvis Presley
director: Norman Taurog
It Happened One Night (1934 film) cast: Claudette Colbert, Clark Gable
director: Frank Capra
It Happened Tomorrow (1944 film) cast: Linda Darnell, Jack Oakie, Dick Powell
director: René Clair
It Happens Every Spring (1949 film) cast: Paul Douglas, Ray Milland, Jean Peters
director: Lloyd Bacon
It Happens Every Thursday (1953 film) cast: John Forsythe, Frank McHugh, Loretta Young
...I thee ___: 3 wed
I, the Jury author: Mickey Spillane
I think ___!: 3 not
I Think I Love You (1970 song) artist: Partridge Family
I Think We're Alone Now (song) artist: Tiffany, Tommy James and the Shondells
It Hit Me Like a Hammer (1991 song) artist: Huey Lewis and the News
I thought so!: 3 aha
I thought you'd never ___!: 3 ask
It Hurts to Be in Love (1964 song) artist: Gene Pitney
___ it in: 3 rub 4 pack
itinerant: 5 nomad, rover 6 arrant, errant, mobile, roving 7 drifter, migrant, nomadic, rambler, roaming, vagrant 8 rambling, stranger, traveler, vagabond, wanderer 9 journeyer, migratory, traveling, unsettled, wandering, wayfaring 10 ambulatory, journeying, travelling
itinerary: 3 rte. 4 beat, path, plan 5 route 6 course 7 circuit, journey, program 8 schedule 9 guidebook 10 travel plan
amend an ~: 5 remap
dizzying ~: 5 whirl 6 flurry
planner: 3 AAA
word: 3 via
itinerate: 4 rove 6 travel, wander
___ it in for: 4 have
___ it is: 4 like
It is ___ told...: 5 a tale
It Isn't Right (1956 song) artist: Platters
it is so: 3 yes 4 amen 5 truly 6 indeed, verily 7 right on 10 positively
It is the ___, and Juliet...: 4 east
___ it like it is: 4 tell
___ It Like That: 5 I Like
It'll be ___ day in July...: 5 a cold
___ it made: 4 have
It May Sound Silly (1955 song) artist: McGuire Sisters
...___ it Memorex?: 4 or is
It Might as Well Be Spring composer: 7 Rodgers 11 Hammerstein
It Might Be You (1983 song) artist: Stephen Bishop
It might have ___: 4 been
It must be him, ___...: 3 or I
It Must Be Him (1967 song) artist: Vikki Carr
___ it my way: 4 I did
It never ___ but it pours: 5 rains
It Never Rains... (1972 song) artist: Albert Hammond
___-it note: 4 Post
___ It Now: 3 See 4 Cool 5 I Want
Ito: 4 Yuko 5 Lance 6 Midori, Robert 8 Hirobumi
___ it off: 3 hit 5 knock
I told you so!: 3 hah, see
Ito, Midori: 6 skater
maneuver: 4 axel, spin 5 camel
milieu: 3 ice 4 rink
___ it on: 3 get, lay 4 pour 5 bring
It Only Hurts for a Little While (1956 song) artist: Ames Brothers
It'$ Only Money (1962 film) cast: Jerry Lewis, Joan O'Brien, Zachary Scott
director: Frank Tashlin
___ It on Rio: 5 Blame
___ it on the chin: 4 take
___ it on the lam: 4 take
___ it on the line: 3 lay
___ it on thick: 3 lay
I, Too author: Langston Hughes
I topper: 3 dot 6 tittle
___ it or leave it: 4 take
___ it or lose it: 3 use
___ it or not: 4 like
___ it out: 4 dish, duke, hash, have 5 check, fight, sweat, tough
___ it over: 4 lord, talk
It Pays to Be Ignorant: 9 radio show
___ it quits: 4 call
___ it rich: 6 strike
___ it rich?: 4 Isn't
___ It Romantic?: 4 Isn't
its: 6 neuter 7 pronoun
...it's ___ work we go: 5 off to
It's ___: 4 a Sin, Late, Over 5 a Gift, Magic
It's ___!: 4 a boy, a hit 5 a date, a deal, a girl, Alive
It's ___ a Long, Long Time: 4 Been
It's ___ a Paper Moon: 4 Only
It's ___ bag!: 5 in the
It's ___ country!: 5 a free
It's ___ for Me to Say: 3 Not
It's ___ in the Game: 3 All
It's ___, it's...: 5 a bird
It's ___ Kiss: 5 in His
It's ___ Late: 3 Too
It's ___ Long, Long Time: 5 Been a
It's ___ Love: 4 Only, You I, Your
It's ___ Make Believe: 4 Only
It's ___ Never: 5 Now or
It's ___ Paper Moon: 5 Only a
It's ___ point!: 5 a moot
It's ___ Rock and Roll to Me: 5 Still
It's ___ than you think: 5 later
It's ___ the Game: 5 All in
It's ___ the pale moon...: 3 not
It's ___ time!: 5 about
It's ___ to Tell a Lie: 4 a Sin
It's ___ True: 3 All
It's ___ Unusual: 3 Not
It's ___ Unusual Day: 5 a Most
It's ___-win situation!: 3 a no
It's a ___!: 3 boy 4 bird, deal, girl 5 plane
It's a ___ Tell a Lie: 5 Sin to
It's about ___!: 4 time
It's a deal!: 4 done, okay
___ it safe: 4 play
It's a Gift (1934 film) cast: W.C. Fields, Baby LeRoy
director: Norman Z. McLeod
It's a Grand Night for Singing composer: 7 Rodgers 11 Hammerstein
It's a Heartache (1978 song) artist: Bonnie Tyler
It's All ___: 4 True
It's All About Me (1998 song) artist: Mya
It's All About the Benjamins (1997 song) artist: Lil' Kim, Lox, Notorious B.I.G., Puff Daddy
It's All Coming Back to Me Now (1996 song) artist: Celine Dion
It's all in the ___: 5 wrist
It's All in the Game (1958 song) artist: Tommy Edwards
It's All in the Game composer: 5 Dawes

It's All Over Now (1964 song) artist: Rolling Stones
It's All Right (1963 song) artist: Impressions
It's all the __ to me: 4 same
It's Almost Tomorrow (1955 song) artist: Dream Weavers, Snooky Lanson
It's a Lovely Day Today composer: 6 Berlin
It's Alright singer: 3 Ono
It's Always Fair Weather (1955 film)
cast: Cyd Charisse, Dan Dailey, Gene Kelly
director: Stanley Donen, Gene Kelly
It's a Mad Mad Mad Mad World (1963 film)
cast: Edie Adams, Milton Berle, Sid Caesar, Jimmy Durante, Peter Falk, Buddy Hackett, Buster Keaton, Ethel Merman, Mickey Rooney, Dick Shawn, Phil Silvers, Spencer Tracy, Jonathan Winters
director: Stanley Kramer
It's a Man's Man's Man's World (1966 song) artist: James Brown
It's a Miracle (1975 song) artist: Barry Manilow
It's a Mistake (1983 song) artist: Men at Work
It's a Sin to Tell __: 4 a Lie
__ it's at: 5 where
It's a Wonderful Life (1946 film)
cast: Lionel Barrymore, Beulah Bondi, Thomas Mitchell, Donna Reed, James Stewart
composer: 7 Tiomkin
director: Frank Capra
role: 4 Bert, Mary 5 Billy, Ernie 6 Bailey, George, Potter, Violet 8 Clarence
studio: 3 RKO
It's a Wonderful World (1939 film)
cast: Claudette Colbert, Guy Kibbee, James Stewart
director: W.S. Van Dyke
It's been __!: 4 ages, real 5 great
It's Been a Long, Long Time composer: 4 Cahn 5 Styne
It's clear!: 3 aha 4 I see
It's cold!: 3 brr
__, It's Cold Outside: 4 Baby
It's De-Lovely composer: 6 Porter
It's Ecstasy... (1977 song) artist: Barry White
itself
by ~: 5 alone, apart, per se 6 as such 10 separately
in: 8 innately
It's Gonna Take a Miracle (1982 song) artist: Deniece Williams
It's grrrreat! growler: 4 Tony
__-it shop: 3 fix
It Should Happen to You (1954 film)
cast: Judy Holliday, Peter Lawford, Jack Lemmon
director: George Cukor
It shouldn't happen to __!: 4 a dog
It's Howdy Doody __: 4 time
It's Impossible (1970 song) artist: Perry Como
It's in the __!: 3 bag
It's in the Bag! (1945 film)
cast: Fred Allen, Binnie Barnes, Robert Benchley
It's Just a Matter of Time (1959 song) artist: Brook Benton
It's Late (1959 song) artist: Ricky Nelson
It's Love I'm After (1937 film)
cast: Bette Davis, Olivia de Havilland, Leslie Howard
director: Archie Mayo
It's Magic composer: 4 Cahn 5 Styne
__ It's Me: 5 Hello
It's My Party (1963 song) artist: Lesley Gore
It's My Turn (1980 film)
cast: Jill Clayburgh, Michael Douglas, Charles Grodin
director: Claudia Weill
It's My Turn (1980 song) artist: Diana Ross
It's no __!: 3 use
It's Not for Me to Say (1957 song) artist: Johnny Mathis
It's Not Over (1987 song) artist: Starship
It's Not Right But It's Okay (1999 song) artist: Whitney Houston
It's not the __ moon...: 4 pale
It's Not Unusual (1965 song) artist: Tom Jones
__ It Snow: 3 Let
It's Now or Never (1960 song) artist: Elvis Presley
...it's off to work __: 4 we go
It's okay with me!: 4 fine
It's only __!: 5 a game
It's Only a Paper Moon composer: 4 Rose 5 Arlen 7 Harburg
It's Only Love (1985 song) artist: Tina Turner
It's Only Make Believe (song) artist: Conway Twitty, Glen Campbell
It's Only Rock 'n Roll (1974 song) artist: Rolling Stones
It's Over (1964 song) artist: Roy Orbison
__ It's Sleepy Time Down South: 4 When
It's So Easy (1977 song) artist: Linda Ronstadt
It's So Hard to Say Goodbye... (1991 song) artist: Boyz II Men
__ It's Spinach: 4 I Say
It's Still Rock and Roll to Me (1980 song) artist: Billy Joel
It's still the same __ story...: 3 old
It Started With Eve (1941 film)
cast: Robert Cummings, Deanna Durbin, Charles Laughton
director: Henry Koster
It's the __!: 3 law
It's the end of __!: 5 an era
It's the Hard-Knock Life show: 5 Annie
It's the Same Old Song (1965 song) artist: Four Tops
It's Time to Cry (1959 song) artist: Paul Anka
__ its toll: 4 take
It's Too Late (1971 song) artist: Carole King
It's Too Soon to Know (1958 song) artist: Pat Boone
__ it straight: 4 play
It's true!: 5 no lie
It's Up to You (1962 song) artist: Ricky Nelson
itsy-bitsy: 3 wee 4 tiny 5 eensy, teeny 6 teensy 9 miniature, minuscule 10 diminutive
Itsy Bitsy Teenie Weenie... (1960 song) artist: Brian Hyland
__ It's You: 4 Baby
It's You I Love (1957 song) artist: Fats Domino
It's Your Love (1997 song) artist: Faith Hill, Tim McGraw
It's Your Thing (1969 song) artist: Isley Brothers
ITT: 2 co. 7 company
part of ~: 3 Int., Tel. 4 Intl., Tele.
rival: 3 GTE
__ it takes: 4 what
It takes __ know...: 5 one to
It takes __ o' livin'...: 5 a heap
It takes __ tango: 5 two to
It Takes a Thief (ABC drama)
cast: Malachi Throne (Noah Bain) Robert Wagner (Alexander Mundy)
__ it, the cops!: 6 Cheese
__ it the truth!: 4 Ain't
__ It Through the Rain: 5 I Made
__ it to: 3 put 4 give, hand 5 stick
__ It to Beaver: 5 Leave
__ it together: 3 get 4 keep
__ it to me!: 4 Sock
__ It to Me!: 5 Leave
__ It to the Limit: 4 Take
__ it to the Marines!: 4 Tell
__ It to Ya: 4 Wot's
itty-bitty: 3 wee 4 baby, puny, tiny 5 bitty, small, teeny, weeny 6 atomic, bantam, little, minute, peewee, petite, teensy 8 atomical, atomlike 9 miniature, pint-sized 10 diminutive, teeny-weeny, vest-pocket
__ it up: 3 ham, mix 4 camp, hang, live, pick 5 whoop
__ It Up: 3 Rip 4 Stir, Turn 5 Light, Shake 6 Living, Strike
Iturbi, José: 7 pianist, Spanish 8 composer 9 conductor
I Turn to You (2000 song) artist: Christina Aguilera
It Walks by Night author: 4 Carr
it was __ and stormy night: 5 a dark
It was __ killed the beast: 6 beauty
It was __ mistake!: 4 all a
It Was a Very Good Year (1966 song) artist: Frank Sinatra
it was in Latin: 4 erat
It was twenty years __ today...: 3 ago
__ It With Music: 3 Say
...__ it would seem: 4 or so
It Would Take a Strong Strong Man (1988 song) artist: Rick Astley
__ Itzá: 5 Petén 7 Chichén
Itzhak: 5 Rabin 7 Perlman
IU: 3 amt.
I understand!: 4 ah so 5 got it
Ivan: 4 czar, tsar, tzar 5 Bunin, Dixon, Klíma, Lendl 6 Boesky, Krylov, Passer, Pavlov 7 Reitman, Sokolov, Susanin 8 Turgenev 9 Goncharov, Karamazov, Mestrovic
in English: 4 John
son of ~ the Terrible: 6 Dmitri
see also Russian
Ivana: 5 Trump
daughter: 6 Ivanka
Ivanhoe: 4 film, hero 5 novel
author: Walter Scott
cast: Joan Fontaine, Elizabeth Taylor, Robert Taylor
character: 5 Brian, Isaac, Lucas 6 Cedric, Rowena 7 Rebecca
contest: 4 tilt
director: Richard Thorpe
weapon: 5 lance
Ivan IV composer: 5 Bizet
Ivanov author: Anton Chekhov
Ivanovna: 4 Anna
Ivanov, Vsevolod: 6 writer 7 Russian
Ivan the __: 5 Great 8 Terrible
Ivan the Terrible, Part One (1943 film)
director: Sergei Eisenstein
I've __!: 5 had it
I've __ Accustomed to Her Face: 5 Grown
I've __ a Crush on You: 3 Got
I've __ a Gal in Kalamazoo: 3 Got
I've __ a Secret: 3 Got
I've __ Be Me: 5 Gotta
I've __ Crow: 5 Gotta
I've __ Crush on You: 4 Got a
I've __ Date With an Angel: 4 Got a
I've __ Every Little Star: 4 Told
I've __ Feeling I'm Falling: 4 Got a
I've __ Gal in Kalamazoo: 4 Got a
I've __ had!: 4 been
I've __ it!: 3 had
I've __ robbed!: 4 been
I've __ Secret: 4 Got a
I've __ the World on a String: 3 Got
I've __ to London...: 4 been
I've __ Working on the Railroad: 4 Been
I've __ You Under My Skin: 3 Got
I've a feeling we're not in __ anymore: 6 Kansas
I've been __!: 3 had
I've Been Lonely Too Long (1967 song) artist: Rascals
I've Come to __ it Wealthily...: 4 Wive
I've Done Everything for You (1981 song) artist: Rick Springfield
I've found it!: 6 eureka
I've Got __ in Kalamazoo: 4 a Gal
I've Got a Crush on You composer: 8 Gershwin
I've Got a Gal in Kalamazoo composer: 6 Gordon, Warren
I've Got a Secret: 8 game show
host: Garry Moore, Steve Allen, Bill Cullen
I've Got a Tiger by the Tail (1965 song) artist: Buck Owens
I've got it!: 3 Aha
I've Got Love on My Mind (1977 song) artist: Natalie Cole
I've Gotta __: 4 Be Me, Crow
I've Gotta Be Me (1969 song) artist: Sammy Davis Jr.
I've Got the Music __: 4 in Me
I've Got the World on a String composer: 5 Arlen 7 Koehler
I've Got to Get a Message to You (1968 song) artist: Bee Gees
I've Got to Use My Imagination (1973 song) artist: Gladys Knight and the Pips
I've Got You __: 4 Babe
I've Got You Under My Skin (1966 song) artist: Four Seasons
composer: 6 Porter
I've Grown Accustomed to Her Face composer: 5 Loewe 6 Lerner
I've had __ to here!: 4 it up
I've Heard That Song Before composer: 4 Cahn 5 Styne
I've Never Been to Me (1982 song) artist: Charlene
Iverson, Allen
milieu: 5 court
org.: 3 NBA
sport: 10 basketball
Ives: 4 Burl 5 James 7 Charles
__! I've Said It Again: 5 There
Ives, Burl: 5 actor 6 singer
film: Baker's Hawk (1976)
The Big Country (1958, AA)
Cat on a Hot Tin Roof (1958)
East of Eden (1955)
Let No Man Write My Epitaph (1960)
Smoky (1946)
So Dear to My Heart (1949)
song: Funny Way of Laughin' (1962)
A Little Bitty Tear (1962)
I Vespri Siciliani heroine: 5 Elena
I've Told Every Little Star composer: 4 Kern 11 Hammerstein
Ivey: 4 Dana 6 Judith
Ivins: 5 Molly
I Vitelloni (1953 film) director: Federico Fellini
Ivo: 5 Robic 6 Andric
ivories: 4 keys 5 piano
tickle the ~: 4 play
ivory: 3 key 4 tusk 5 color, white 6 yellow 7 neutral 9 yellowish
relative: 4 bone, milk, snow 5 cream, milky 6 argent, oyster, silver

8 eggshell
source: 4 tusk 6 walrus 8 elephant
tower: 4 lair 5 haven 6 asylum, escape, refuge 7 hideout, retreat 8 hideaway 9 sanctuary
ivory ___: 3 nut 4 gull, palm 5 black, tower
Ivory: 4 soap 5 James 9 detergent
alternative: 3 Lux 4 Dial, Dove, Lava, Tone, Zest 5 Camay, Coast, Lever 6 Boraxo, Caress, Shield 8 Lifebuoy 9 Palmolive, Safeguard 11 Irish Spring
Ivory Coast: 6 nation 7 country
capital: 7 Abidjan
city: 4 Divo 5 Daloa 6 Anyama, Bouake 7 Abidjan, Korhogo
gulf: 6 Guinea
language: 4 Akan
money: 5 franc
neighbor: 4 Mali 5 Ghana 6 Guinea 7 Liberia
people: 4 Akan 6 Senufo 7 Malinka, Malinke 8 Mandingo, Mandinka
Ivory, James: 8 director
film: The Europeans (1979) The Golden Bowl (2001) Howards End (1992) Jefferson in Paris (1995) Mr. & Mrs. Bridge (1990) The Remains of the Day (1993) A Room With a View (1986) Roseland (1977) Soldier's Daughter Never Cries (1998)
Ivory Snow: 9 detergent
alternative: 3 All, Biz, Era, Fab, Yes 4 Bold, Dash, Gain, Surf, Tide, Wisk 5 Cheer, Dreft, Purex 6 Calgon, Dynamo, Oxydol 7 Octagon
ivory-towered: 5 aloof 6 remote 7 distant, removed 8 academic, detached, quixotic, retiring, secluded 10 quixotical
___ Ivory Wayans: 6 Keenen
IV overseer: 2 RN 3 LPN
measure: 2 cc.
Ivry-___-Seine: 3 sur
ivy: 4 vine 5 plant 7 creeper
clump: 3 tod
emulate ~: 5 cling, creep, stick, twine
halls of ~: 6 school 7 academy, college
like ~: 4 viny 5 twiny, vined 6 twined
place: 4 wall
poison ~ genus: 4 rhus
poison ~ relative: 5 sumac 6 sumach
___ ivy: 5 grape 6 Boston, German, ground, marine, poison 7 English, Mexican, Swedish
Ivy ___: 5 Three 6 League 7 Leaguer
Ivy League
city: 5 Phila. 6 Ithaca 7 Hanover, New York 8 New Haven 9 Cambridge, Princeton 10 Providence
school: 4 Penn., Yale 5 Brown 7 Cornell, Harvard 8 Columbia 9 Dartmouth, Princeton
team: 4 Elis 5 Bears, Lions 6 Big Red, Tigers 7 Crimson, Quakers 8 Big Green, Bulldogs
Ivy Leaguer: 3 Eli 5 Tiger, Yalie
Ivy Tree, The author: Mary Stewart
I.W.: 4 Abel
I Wake Up Screaming (1941 film)
cast: Betty Grable, Carole Landis, Victor Mature
Iwaki: 4 city, town
locale: 5 Japan
I Walk the Line (1956 song) artist: Johnny Cash
I Wandered Lonely as a Cloud: 4 poem
author: William Wordsworth
I Wanna Be Around (1963 song) artist: Tony Bennett
I Wanna Be Down (1994 song) artist: Brandy
I Wanna Dance With Somebody (1987 song) artist: Whitney Houston
___ I Wanna Do: 3 All
I Wanna Get Next to You (1977 song) artist: Rose Royce
I Wanna Go Back (1987 song) artist: Eddie Money
I Wanna Hold Your Hand (1978 film)
cast: Nancy Allen, Marc McClure
director: Robert Zemeckis
I Wanna Love You Forever (1999 song) artist: Jessica Simpson
I want ___ just like...: 5 a girl
I Want ___: 3 You 4 a Man
___ I want for Christmas...: 3 All
I want it ___!: 3 all
I Want It Now author: Kingsley Amis
I Want It That Way (1999 song) artist: Backstreet Boys
I want my ___!: 3 MTV 5 Maypo
I Want to Be Happy: 4 song, tune
composer: 6 Caesar 7 Youmans
I Want to Be Wanted (1960 song) artist: Brenda Lee
I Want to Hold Your Hand (1964 song) artist: Beatles
I Want to Know What Love Is (1984 song) artist: Foreigner
I Want to Live! (1958 film)
cast: Susan Hayward, Simon Oakland
director: Robert Wise
I Want to Walk You Home (1959 song) artist: Fats Domino
I Want You (1951 film)
cast: Dana Andrews, Farley Granger, Dorothy McGuire
director: Mark Robson
I Want You Back (song) artist: Jackson 5, 'Nsync
I Want You guy: 3 Sam 8 Uncle Sam
I Want You, I Need You, I Love You (1956 song) artist: Elvis Presley
I Want Your Love (1979 song) artist: Chic
I Want You to Be My Girl (1956 song) artist: Frankie Lymon and the Teenagers
I Want You to Want Me (1979 song) artist: Cheap Trick
I Was a Male War Bride (1949 film)
cast: Cary Grant, Ann Sheridan
director: Howard Hawks
...I was born to ___ right!: 5 set it
I Was Doing All Right composer: 8 Gershwin
I Was Made for Dancin' (1978 song) artist: Leif Garrett
I Was Made to Love Her (1967 song) artist: Stevie Wonder
___ I Was One-and-Twenty: 4 When
I Was the One (1956 song) artist: Elvis Presley
___ I Were in Love Again: 5 I Wish
I Whistle a Happy Tune composer: 7 Rodgers 11 Hammerstein
I will ___ and go now: 5 arise
I Will (1965 song) artist: Dean Martin
I Will Always Love You (1992 song) artist: Whitney Houston
I Will Come to You (1997 song) artist: Hanson
I Will Follow Him (1963 song) artist: Little Peggy March
I Will Remember You (1999 song) artist: Sarah McLachlan
I Will Survive (1979 song) artist: Gloria Gaynor
___ I win,...: 5 heads
I Wish (1976 song) artist: Stevie Wonder
I Wish It Would Rain (1968 song) artist: Temptations
I Wish It Would Rain Down (1990 song) artist: Phil Collins
I Wish I Were in Love Again composer: 4 Hart 7 Rodgers
Iwo Jima: 3 isl. 4 isle 6 battle, island
terrain: 4 sand
I Woke Up in Love This Morning (1971 song) artist: Partridge Family
I Wonder As I Wander author: Langston Hughes
I Won't ___ Day Without You: 5 Last a
I Won't Back Down (1989 song) artist: Tom Petty and the Heartbreakers
I Won't Dance composer: 4 Kern 7 Harbach 11 Hammerstein
___ I Won the War: 3 How
I Won't Hold You Back (1983 song) artist: Toto
I Would Die 4 U (1984 song) artist: Prince
I wouldn't have ___ other way!: 5 it any
I Write the Songs (1975 song) artist: Barry Manilow
Ixmiquilpan: 4 city, town
locale: 6 Mexico 7 Hidalgo
ixnay: 2 no 3 nah, naw, nay, nix, non 4 nein, nope, nyet, uh-uh 5 I won't, never, no how, noway 6 no deal, no dice, noways, nowise 7 I refuse 8 forget it, I will not, negative, negatory 9 by no means, fat chance, I think not 10 count me out, not a chance, thumbs down
ixora: 4 tree 5 shrub
relative: 6 coffee, madder 8 cinchona, gardenia 9 bouvardia
Ixtapa: 4 city, town 6 resort
locale: 6 Mexico 7 Jalisco
Ixtapaluca: 4 city, town
locale: 6 Mexico
Ixtapan: 4 city, town
locale: 6 Mexico
Ixtepec: 4 city, town
locale: 6 Mexico, Oaxaca
Ixtlán del Río: 4 city, town
locale: 6 Mexico 7 Nayarit
Iyar: 5 month 6 Hebrew
preceder: 5 Nisan 6 Nissan
successor: 5 Sivan
Iynx, mother of: 4 Echo
Izamal: 4 city, town
locale: 6 Mexico 7 Yucatán
Izar: 4 star
Izmir: 4 city, gulf, port, town
locale: 6 Turkey
Izod product: 5 shirt
Izúcar: 4 city, town
locale: 6 Mexico, Puebla
Izumi: 4 city, town
locale: 5 Japan
izzard: 3 zed
Izzy & ___: 3 Moe

J

J: 6 letter
and others: 3 Drs.
in phonetic alphabet: 6 Juliet
position of ~: 5 tenth
topper: 3 dot 6 tittle
J __ John: 4 as in
J-__: 3 bar 6 stroke
J-__ Forever!: 3 Men
J. __ Band: 5 Geils
J. __ Fulbright: 7 William
J. __ Getty: 4 Paul
J. __ Hoover: 5 Edgar
J. __ Naish: 6 Carrol
J. __ Oppenheimer: 6 Robert
'J' __ Judgment: 5 Is for
ja: 2 ay, da, sí 3 aye, oui, yea, yep, yes, yup 4 fine, okay, sure, yeah 5 good-o, natch, quite, right, roger, uh-huh 6 agreed, gladly, good-oh, indeed, just so, rather, righto, surely, you bet, yowzah 7 exactly, go ahead, indeedy, mais oui, quite so, ten-four 8 all right, as you say, of course, thumbs up, very well 9 be my guest, certainly, darn right, naturally, precisely, sure thing, you betcha, you said it 10 absolutely, by all means, definitely, positively, sure enough, that's right
opposite: 4 nein
jab: 3 hit 4 blow, gibe, jibe, knee, left, peck, poke, prod, slam, stab 5 lunge, nudge, prick, punch, right, shove, stick, taunt 6 jostle, justle, thrust, thwack 8 puncture, uppercut 9 penetrate
target: 3 jaw, yap 4 chin, jowl 5 chops, mouth
Jabalpur: 4 city, town
locale: 5 India
Jabba the Hutt, like: 5 heavy, obese 9 corpulent 10 overweight
jabber: 3 gab, gas, jaw, rap, rot, yak, yap 4 blab, blah, bosh, bull, bunk, chat, guff, gush, jazz, jive, pooh, rave, talk, tosh 5 bilge, fudge, hokum, hooey, noise, prate, run on, sound, stuff, trash, tripe 6 babble, bunkum, bushwa, drivel, footle, gabble, gammon, gibber, havers, hot air, humbug, jargon, kibosh, mutter, patter, piffle, ramble, rattle, tattle 7 baloney, blarney, blather, blether, boloney, bushwah, chatter, eyewash, flannel, flubdub, fustian, garbage, hogwash, inanity, prattle, rubbish, stammer, twaddle 8 buncombe, claptrap, falderal, falderol, flimflam, flummery, folderal, folderol, nonsense, slipslop, tommyrot, trumpery 9 banana oil, gibberish, go on and on, kidstakes, loquacity, moonshine, poppycock, rigmarole 10 applesauce, balderdash, bilge water, codswallop, double-talk, flapdoodle, galimatias, Jabberwock, mumbo jumbo, rigamarole, taradiddle
jabbering: 5 noisy, prate, wordy 6 babble 7 unterse 8 babbling 9 garrulity 10 loquacious
Jabberwocky: 3 gas, rot 4 blah, bosh, bull, bunk, guff, jazz, jive, pooh, tosh 5 bilge, fudge, hokum, hooey, prate, stuff, trash, tripe 6 bunkum, bushwa, drivel, footle, gabble, gammon, gibber, havers, hot air, humbug, jabber, jargon, kibosh, piffle 7 baloney, blarney, blather, blether, boloney, bushwah, eyewash, flannel, flubdub, fustian, garbage, hogwash, inanity, rubbish, twaddle 8 buncombe, claptrap, falderal, falderol, flimflam, flummery, folderal, folderol, nonsense, slipslop, tommyrot, trumpery 9 banana oil, gibberish, kidstakes, moonshine, poppycock, rigmarole 10 applesauce, balderdash, bilge water, codswallop, double-talk, flapdoodle, galimatias, mumbo jumbo, rigamarole, taradiddle
start of ~: 4 'Twas
word: 4 mome, 'twas, wabe 5 raths, toves 6 slithy
jabiru: 4 bird 5 stork
jaborandi: 5 shrub
family: 3 rue
relative: 7 skimmia
jabs, trade: 3 box 4 spar
__-jac: 5 shirt
jacamar: 4 bird
jacana: 4 bird 10 wading bird
jacaranda: 4 tree
family: 7 catalpa
J'Accuse author: Emile Zola
__ jacet: 3 hic
jacinth: 6 ligure
Jacinto: 9 Benavente
__ Jacinto: 3 San
jack: 3 oof 4 card, cash, fish, flag, gelt, hike, kail, kale, loot, peag, pelf, tool 5 bills, bread, bucks, dough, funds, knave, lucre, money, moola, mopus, pesos, raise, rhino, sewan 6 dinero, do-re-mi, lifter, mammon, mazuma, moolah, seawan, silver, specie, wampum, wealth 7 cabbage, capital, dollars, lettuce, ooftish, pennant, scratch, shekels 8 bankroll, cold cash, currency, face card, hard cash, smackers 9 banknotes, frogskins, long green, simoleons 10 greenbacks, green stuff
ender: 3 ass, daw, leg, pot 4 boot, stay 5 fruit, knife, light, plane, screw, shaft, snipe, stone, straw 6 hammer, rabbit 8 mackerel
in cards: 5 knave
in cribbage: 3 nob 4 nibs
locale: 5 trunk
predecessor: 3 ten
starter: 3 sea, sky 4 boot, flap, high, skip, slap 5 amber, apple, black, cheap 6 lumber 7 cracker, steeple
tar: 4 bo's'n, hand, salt, swab 5 bosun, middy 6 pirate, sailor, sea dog, seaman 7 boatman, captain, crewman, mariner, matelot, old salt, recruit, skipper 8 coxswain, deck hand, helmsman, salty dog, seafarer, water dog 9 boatswain, first mate, yachtsman 10 midshipman
up: 4 hike, lift 5 boost, raise 7 augment, elevate, enlarge, magnify 8 escalate, increase 10 accelerate, aggrandize
jack __: 3 oak, rod 4 arch, bean, pine, post, rope 5 block, chain, plane, staff, towel, truss 6 cheese, ladder, rabbit, rafter, salmon
jack-__-box: 5 in-the
jack-__-pulpit: 5 in-the
jack-__-trades: 5 of-all
__ jack: 3 wax 4 blue, door, sand 5 brace, clock, screw, taper, union 6 bumper, whisky, yellow 7 jumping, ratchet, whiskey
__-jack: 5 cheap
Jack: 3 Soo 4 Elam, Ging, Kemp, lord, Paar, Webb 5 Benny, Burke, Haley, Jones, Kelly, Kilby, Oakie, Scott, Sprat 6 Arnold, Bailey, Carson, Carter, Conway, Finney, Gelber, Horner, Kramer, Larson, Lemmon, London, Smight, Twyman, Wagner, Warden, Warner, Weston 7 Cardiff, Cassidy, Clayton, Couffer, Dempsey, Gilford, Hawkins, Higgins, Johnson, Kerouac, Klugman, LaLanne, Lambert, Palance, Valenti 8 Anderson, Buchanan, Nicklaus, Thompson 9 Albertson, Nicholson, Teagarden 10 Williamson, Youngblood
adversary: 5 giant
Jackie, to ~: 4 wife
Jack (1996 film)
cast: Diane Lane, Jennifer Lopez, Robin Williams
director: Francis Ford Coppola
Jack __: 3 Tar 4 Rose 5 Frost
Jack __ could eat...: 5 Sprat
Jack __ terrier: 7 Russell
__ Jack: 5 Happy, Saint, Union 6 Cousin, Hungry, Smilin' 7 Bulldog, Cracker, Wolfman
jack-a-dandy: 3 def, fop, rad 4 aces, A-one, boss, braw, buck, cool, dece, dude, fine, gear, keen, neat, nice, phat, toff, tuff 5 blade, blood, ducky, grand, great, marvy, neato, nobby, prime, slick, spark, super, swell 6 bang on, bang-up, bonzer, bosker, choice, divine, dreamy, far-out, gnarly, groovy, lovely, peachy, slap-up, spot on, superb, terrif, tiptop, unreal, whizzo, wicked 7 amazing, awesome, capital, corking, coxcomb, gallant, peacock, perfect, ripping, skookum, stellar, sublime 8 dazzling, especial, eximious, fabulous, fancy Dan, five-star, four-star, frabjous, gay blade, glorious, heavenly, macaroni, popinjay, slam-bang, smashing, splendid, standout, sterling, stickout, superior, terrific, top-level, topnotch, very good, wondrous 9 bodacious, Endsville, excellent, exemplary, exquisite, first-rate, high-grade, hunky-dory, maccaroni, marvelous, pretty boy, sollicker, top-flight, wonderful 10 first-class, hotsy-totsy, out of sight, peachy-keen, phenomenal, remarkable, stupendous, super-duper
jackal: 4 dupe, hack, tool 5 canid, drone, leech, slave, toady 6 animal, canine, drudge, fawner, flunky, lackey, minion, puppet, stooge, yes man 7 cat's-paw, doormat, flunkey, lacquey, wild dog 8 creature, hanger-on, henchman, parasite 10 accomplice
relative: 3 dog, fox 4 lobo, wolf 5 dhole, dingo 6 corsac, coydog, coyote, fennec
Jackal, The: 5 alias
Jackal, The (1997 film)
cast: Richard Gere, Sidney Poitier, Bruce Willis
jackanapes: 3 imp, pup 4 brat, punk 5 devil, gamin, scamp 6 monkey, rascal, smarty 7 upstart, wannabe, wise guy 8 hooligan, wiseacre
Jack and Jill prop: 4 pail
Jack and the Beanstalk
syllable: 3 fie, fum
Jack Armstrong, the All-American Boy: 9 radio show
jackass: 3 ass, mut, nit, oaf, sap 4 boob, clod, dolt, dope, fool, goof, gull, jerk, loon, moke, mutt, simp 5 burro, chump, clown, cluck, dummy, dunce, goose, idiot, joker, klutz, neddy, ninny, patsy 6 boobie, cuckoo, dimwit, donkey, equine, galoot, lummox, nitwit, sucker, turkey 7 buffoon, bungler, dingbat, dullard, fathead, galloot, half-wit, jughead, pinhead, saphead, tomfool 8 bonehead, dumbbell, dummkopf, goofball, meathead, numskull 9 birdbrain, blockhead, ding-a-ling, harebrain, ignoramus, lamebrain, numbskull, simpleton 10 dunderhead, dunderpate, muttonhead, nincompoop, rattlepate
relative: 3 ass 5 burro, horse, kiang, zebra 6 donkey, onager, quagga 8 chigetai 9 dziggetai
jackass __: 3 rig 4 bark, brig 6 gunter 7 penguin
Jack-be-nimble
like ~: 3 fit 4 spry 5 agile 6 active, limber, lively 9 sprightly
__ Jack City: 3 New
jackdaw: 4 bird
Jackée: 5 Harry
jackeroo: 6 Aussie
jacker starter: 3 sea, sky 4 high
jacket: 3 mac, Mao, pod, tux 4 case, coat, Eton, skin, tuck, wrap 5 capot, frock, grego, jemmy, jibba, loden, Nehru, parka, simar, tails, tunic, wamus 6 achkan, anorak, banian, banyan, blazer, bolero, bomber, capote, casing, coatee, duffle, duster, folder, jerkin, raglan, record, reefer, sheath, tabard, tuxedo, ulster, wammus, wampus 7 cagoule, car coat, cassock, cutaway, doublet, kuletuk, oilskin, paletot, peacoat, slicker, spencer, surcoat, surtout, topcoat, zamarra 8 benjamin, bush coat, chaqueta, covering, envelope, mackinaw, overcoat, polo coat, raincoat, sack coat 9 balmacaan, book cover, greatcoat, Inverness, petersham, redingote, sou'wester, sport coat, storm coat 10 fearnought, macfarlane, mackintosh, potato skin, protection, trench coat
arctic ~: 5 parka 6 anorak
book ~ promo: 5 blurb 6 review
British ~: 5 jemmy, tunic 9 greatcoat
Canada ~: 7 kuletuk
church ~: 7 cassock
close a ~: 3 zip 5 zip up
cowboy ~: 8 chaqueta
feature: 3 arm 4 snap 5 lapel 6 lining, peplum, zipper
formal ~: 3 tux 4 tuck 5 tails 6 tuxedo 7 cutaway
heavy ~: 5 wamus 6 anorak, ulster, wammus, wampus
hooded ~: 5 grego, parka 6 duffle
India ~: 6 achkan, banian, banyan
material: 5 suede, tweed 7 leather
medieval ~: 6 corset
Moslem ~: 5 jibba
opening: 4 slit, vent
pants and ~: 4 suit 6 outfit 8 ensemble
short ~: 5 grego 6 coatee, jerkin, reefer 8 sack coat
Spain ~: 7 zamarra
starter: 4 blue 6 strait 7 leather 8 straight
waterproof ~: 5 loden
woman's ~ of old: 5 simar
woolen ~: 8 mackinaw
yellow ~: 4 pest, wasp 6 insect
see also coat
__ jacket: 3 air, bed, Ike, Mao, pea 4 book, bush, dust, Eton, flak, life, mess 5 field, Nehru, shell, shirt, steam, water 6 battle, bomber, combat, dinner, lumber, monkey, ragged, safari, sports, yellow 7 assault, hacking, Norfolk, smoking, stadium
__ Jack Flash: 6 Jumpin'
Jack Frost: 4 rime 6 winter
work: 6 icicle
jackfruit: 5 fruit
jackhammer: 3 bit 4 bore, tool 5 auger, drill
Jackie: 4 Chan 5 Mason 6 Coogan,

Cooper, Mrs. JFK, Wilson **7** Collins, Gleason, Jackson, Kennedy, Onassis, Stewart **8** Robinson **9** DeShannon
sister: **3** Lee
to Ari: **4** wife
to Jack: **4** wife
to Roseanne: **3** sis
Jackie ___-Kersee: **6** Joyner
Jackie Brown (1997 film)
cast: Pam Grier, Samuel L. Jackson, Michael Keaton
director: Quentin Tarantino
Jackie Robinson Story, The (1950 film)
cast: Ruby Dee, Jackie Robinson
jacking
starter: **3** sea, sky **4** high **5** black
jack-in-the-box part: **3** lid
jack-in-the-pulpit: **4** arum **5** aroid, plant **6** flower
cousin: **5** calla
jackknife ___: **4** clam, dive
Jackman: **4** Hugh
Jacknife (1989 film)
cast: Kathy Baker, Robert De Niro, Ed Harris
jack-of-all-trades: **5** do-all **6** jobber **8** factotum, handyman **10** generalist
jack-o'-lantern: **7** pumpkin
feature: **4** eyes, grin, nose **5** smile
make a ~: **5** carve
jackpot: **3** pot **4** bank, pool **5** award, kitty, prize, total, whole **6** reward, stakes **8** windfall
game with a ~: **5** lotto **7** lottery
hit the ~: **3** win **5** score **7** prosper, succeed
Jack Robinson, before one can say: **4** fast, soon **7** quickly
Jack Rose: **5** drink **8** beverage, cocktail
ingredient: **9** grenadine, lime juice **10** lemon juice
Jack Russell ___: **7** terrier
jacks: **4** game
knucklebone in ~: **3** dib
Jacks: **5** Terry
___ Jacks: **5** Apple **7** One-Eyed
Jackson: **2** Bo **3** Joe, Stu **4** Alan, Anne, city, Fort, Kate, Milt, Phil, Tito, town **5** Janet, Jesse, Laura, Peter **6** Andrew, Browne, Glenda, Jackie, Joshua, La Toya, Marlon, Millie, Rachel, Rebbie, Reggie, Sherry **7** Mahalia, Maynard, Michael, Pollock, Shirley, Wilfred **8** Jermaine, Victoria **9** Stonewall
county: **5** Hinds
locale: **4** Mich., Miss., Tenn. **8** Michigan **9** Tennessee
resort near Mt. ~: **4** Vail
river: **5** Pearl
Jackson ___: **3** Day **4** Hole
___ Jackson: **4** Fort **6** Action
Jackson 5
song: ABC (1970)
Dancing Machine (1974)
Enjoy Yourself (1976)
I'll Be There (1970)
I Want You Back (1969)
The Love You Save (1970)
Mama's Pearl (1971)
Never Can Say Goodbye (1971)
Shake Your Body (1979)
State of Shock (1984)
Sugar Daddy (1971)
Jackson, Andrew: president
former occupation: **6** lawyer **7** soldier
home: **9** Hermitage, Nashville, Tennessee
opponent: **4** Clay **5** Adams
predecessor: **5** Adams
V.P.: **7** Calhoun **8** Van Buren
wife: **6** Rachel
Jackson, Anne spouse: Eli Wallach
Jackson 5
members: Jackie, Jermaine, Marlon, Michael, Randy, Tito
Jackson, Glenda: **7** actress
film: Hopscotch (1980)
House Calls (1978)
Marat/Sade (1966)
Mary, Queen of Scots (1971)
The Romantic Englishwoman (1975)
Stevie (1978)
Sunday, Bloody Sunday (1971)
A Touch of Class (1973, AA)
Turtle Diary (1985)
Women in Love (1969, AA)
Jackson, Helen Hunt: **6** author, writer
work: Ramona
Jackson, Helen Hunt work: Ramona
Jackson Hole: **4** city, town
county: **5** Teton
locale: **7** Wyoming
river: **5** Snake
Jackson, Janet
brother: **4** Tito **6** Marlon **7** Michael
sister: **6** La Toya
song: Again (1993)
All for You (2001)
Alright (1990)
Any Time, Any Place (1994)
Because of Love (1994)
The Best Things in Life... (1992)
Black Cat (1990)
Come Back to Me (1990)
Control (1986)
Doesn't Really Matter (2000)
Escapade (1990)
If (1993)
I Get Lonely (1998)
Let's Wait Awhile (1987)
Love Will Never Do (1990)
Miss You Much (1989)
Nasty (1986)
Rhythm Nation (1989)
Runaway (1995)
Scream (1995)
Someone to Call My Lover (2001)
State of the World (1991)
That's the Way Love Goes (1993)
Together Again (1997)
What's It Gonna Be (1999)
When I Think of You (1986)
You Want This (1994)
Jackson, Jesse: **3** rev. **8** reverend
onetime hairdo: **4** Afro
Jackson, Kate spouse: Andrew Stevens
Jackson, Laura: **4** poet
Jackson, Michael
album: **3** Bad **8** Thriller
brother: **4** Tito **6** Jackie, Marlon
hometown: **4** Gary
onetime do: **4** Afro
sister: **5** Janet **6** La Toya
song: Bad (1987)
Beat It (1983)
Ben (1972)
Billie Jean (1983)
Black or White (1991)
Dirty Diana (1988)
Don't Stop 'Til You Get Enough (1979)
The Girl Is Mine (1982)
Got to Be There (1971)
Human Nature (1983)
I Just Can't Stop Loving You (1987)
In the Closet (1992)
Man in the Mirror (1988)
Off the Wall (1980)
P.Y.T. (1983)
Remember the Time (1992)
Rockin' Robin (1972)
Rock With You (1979)
Say Say Say (1983)
Scream (1995)
She's Out of My Life (1980)
Smooth Criminal (1988)
Thriller (1984)
Wanna Be Startin' Somethin' (1983)
The Way You Make Me Feel (1987)
Will You Be There (1993)
You Are Not Alone (1995)
spouse: Lisa Marie Presley
trademark: glove
Jackson, Reggie: **10** outfielder
Jackson, Samuel L.: **5** actor
film: Changing Lanes (2002)
Deep Blue Sea (1999)
Die Hard With a Vengeance (1995)
Jackie Brown (1997)
The Negotiator (1998)
Pulp Fiction (1994)
Rules of Engagement (2000)
Shaft (2000)
Sphere (1998)
A Time to Kill (1996)
White Sands (1992)
XXX (2002)
Jackson, Shirley: **6** author, writer
work: The Lottery
Jackson, Stonewall: **7** general
biographer: **4** Tate
Jacksonville: **4** city, port, town
county: **5** Duval
locale: **7** Florida **8** Arkansas
pro team: **7** Jaguars
river: **7** St. Johns
Jacks, Terry song: Seasons in the Sun (1974)
jackstraws: **4** game
jack-tar: **3** gob **4** salt **6** sailor, seaman **7** mariner, swabbie **10** bluejacket
Jack Tar composer: **5** Sousa
Jack the ___ Killer: **5** Giant
Jack the Bear (1993 film)
cast: Danny DeVito, Gary Sinise
director: Michael Herskovitz
Jaclyn: **5** Smith
colleague of ~: **4** Kate **6** Farrah
Jacob: **3** cat, Max **4** Riis **5** Grimm, Irène, Smith **7** Epstein **8** François **9** Bronowski
daughter of ~: **5** Dinah
father-in-law of ~: **5** Laban
grandson of ~: **3** Eri
in Italian: **8** Giacobbe
in Russian: **5** Yakov
parent of ~: **5** Isaac **7** Rebekah
son of ~: **3** Dan, Gad **4** Levi **5** Asher, Judah **6** Joseph, Reuben, Simeon **7** Zebulun **8** Benjamin, Issachar, Naphtali
son of ~ in the Douay Bible: **4** Aser
twin of ~: **4** Esau
wife of ~: **4** Leah **6** Rachel
___ Jacob Astor: **4** John
Jacob, François: **6** French **8** Nobelist
Jacobi: **3** Lou **5** Derek
Jacob, Max: **4** poet **6** French
Jacob's ___: **4** Room **5** staff **6** ladder
Jacobsen, Jens: **6** Danish, writer
Jacobs Field player: **6** Indian
Jacobson, Dan: **6** writer **12** South African
Jacob's Room author: Virginia Woolf
Jacobsson: **4** Ulla
jacobus: **5** money
Jacobus ___ Hoff: **4** van't
Jacona: **4** city, town
locale: **6** Mexico **9** Michoacán
jaconet: **6** fabric **8** material
Jacopo: **10** Tintoretto
jacquard: **5** cloth **6** fabric **7** textile **8** material
Jacquard ___: **4** card, loom **5** weave
Jacqueline: **5** du Pré **6** Bisset, Susann **7** Cochran, Kennedy, Onassis
Jacqueline Kennedy, ___ Bouvier: **3** née
Jacques: **4** Brel, Tati **5** Ibert, Monod **6** Barzun, Grévin, Plante **7** Cartier, Prévert **8** Bergerac, Clouseau, d'Amboise, Lipchitz, Maritain, Tourneur **9** Offenbach
see also French
Jacques-___ Cousteau: **4** Yves
___ Jacques: **5** Frère
___ Jacques Rousseau: **4** Jean
Jacques-Yves: **8** Cousteau
Jacta est ___: **4** alea
Jacuzzi: **3** spa **6** hot tub
enjoy the ~: **4** soak
Jada ___ Smith: **7** Pinkett
jade: **3** gem **4** bore, cloy, fill, flag, hack, pall, tire, wear **5** color, green, horse, weary **6** bluish, equine, weaken **7** blueish, exhaust, fatigue, mineral, overtax, poop out, satiate, satisfy, surfeit, tire out, vitiate, wear out **8** enervate, gemstone, nephrite, overwork, wear down **9** tucker out, yellowish **10** debilitate, devitalize
relative: **3** pea **4** cyan, sage **5** beryl, breen, olive, virid **6** myrtle, reseda **7** avocado, celadon, emerald, verdant **9** pistachio, turquoise **10** aquamarine, chartreuse
work with ~: **5** carve **6** incise, sculpt **7** engrave
jade ___: **5** green, plant
___ jade: **3** gem **6** garnet **7** Burmese, Mexican
Jade: **6** Jagger
jaded: **4** sick, worn **5** blasé, bored, fed up, tired, weary **7** worn-out **10** world-weary
jadeite: **3** gem **8** gemstone
Jaeckel: **7** Richard
jaeger: **4** bird **6** hunter **7** seabird
relative: **4** skua **6** bonxie
Jafar: **5** genie
Jaffa: **4** city, town
locale: **6** Israel
Jaffa ___: **6** orange
Jaffe: **3** Sam **4** Rona **7** Stanley
Jaffe, Sam: **5** actor
film: The Accused (1948)
Ben-Hur (1959)
The Day the Earth Stood Still (1951)
Gunga Din (1939)
I Can Get It for You Wholesale (1951)
Lost Horizon (1937)
TV: Ben Casey
jag: **3** cut, hit, rip **4** nick, orgy, snag **5** binge, prick, spell, spree **6** bender **8** carousal, lacerate, splinter
go on a ~: **5** binge, spree **7** splurge
Jag
see Jaguar
jagged: **5** harsh, rocky, rough, sharp **6** broken, craggy, hackly, ragged, ridged, rugged, spiked, uneven, zigzag **7** cragged, notched, serrate, unlevel **8** serrated, unsmooth **9** irregular, lacerated **10** nonuniform
as a leaf: **5** erose
rock: **3** tor **4** crag **5** arête **8** pinnacle **10** escarpment
Jagged Edge (1985 film)
cast: Jeff Bridges, Glenn Close, Peter Coyote, Robert Loggia
Jagger: **4** Jade, Mick **6** Bianca
Jagger, Dean: **5** actor
film: Bad Day at Black Rock (1955)
Elmer Gantry (1960)
The Great Man (1956)
King Creole (1958)
The Proud Rebel (1958)
Sister Kenny (1946)
Smith! (1969)

Twelve O'Clock High (1949, AA)
Valley of the Sun (1942)
Western Union (1941)
When Strangers Marry (1944)

Jagger, Mick: 5 Stone
spouse: Jerry Hall
Jaglom: 5 Henry
jaguar: 3 cat **4** eyra **5** felid **6** animal, feline, mammal **7** wild cat
relative: 4 lion, lynx, puma **5** chita, liger, ounce, tiger, tigon **6** bobcat, cheeta, chetah, cougar, margay, ocelot, serval, tiglon **7** bay lynx, caracal, cheetah, leopard, panther **9** catamount
Jaguar: 3 car **4** auto **10** automobile
alternative: 3 BMW **8** Corvette
model: 3 XJS, XKE, XKR
rival: 3 Jet, Ram **4** Bear, Bill, Colt, Lion **5** Brown, Chief, Eagle, Giant, Niner, Raven, Saint, Texan, Titan **6** Bengal, Bronco, Cowboy, Falcon, Packer, Raider, Viking **7** Charger, Dolphin, Panther, Patriot, Redskin, Seahawk, Steeler **8** Cardinal **9** Buccaneer
what a ~ symbolizes: 5 class **6** cachet, status **7** station **8** position, prestige, standing **10** prominence
Jaguars: 4 team **6** eleven
org.: 3 AFC, NFL
sport: 8 football
jaguarundi: 3 cat **4** eyra **5** felid **6** animal, feline, mammal **7** wild cat
relative: 4 lion, lynx, puma **5** chita, liger, ounce, tiger, tigon **6** bobcat, cheeta, chetah, cougar, margay, ocelot, serval, tiglon **7** bay lynx, caracal, cheetah, leopard, panther **9** catamount
Jahan, Shah built here: 4 Agra
jai alai: 4 game **5** sport
ball: 6 pelota
basket: 5 cesta
cloth: 5 cinta
court: 6 cancha **7** fronton
language: 6 Basque
need: 5 cesta **6** pelota
player: 8 pelotari
sash: 4 faja
shot: 5 chula
wall: 6 rebote
jail: 3 can, jug, nab, pen **4** bars, brig, cage, cell, coop, gaol, hold, poky, stir **5** clink, joint, pinch, pokey, run in, seize **6** arrest, cooler, detain, immure, lockup, prison, punish **7** bastile, confine, dungeon, hoosgow, put away, slammer **8** bastille, big house, hoosegow, imprison, restrain, sentence, stockade **9** calaboose, captivity **10** boobyhatch, guardhouse
break ~: 6 escape **10** fly the coop
door sound: 5 clang
ender: 4 bird **5** break, house
in ~: 4 pent, sick **5** bound, close, local, on ice **6** laid up, pent-up, shut in **7** captive, insular, limited **8** confined
in Britain: 4 gaol, quod
-related: 5 penal
jailbird: 3 con **5** felon, lifer **6** inmate, outlaw, trusty **7** convict, parolee **8** internee, prisoner **9** miscreant
jailed: 4 held **7** captive **8** confined, locked up **9** in custody **10** imprisoned
jailer: 6 captor, gaoler, keeper, warden **7** turnkey
need: 3 key
jailhouse ___: 6 lawyer
Jailhouse Rock: 4 film, song
artist: Elvis Presley
cast: Elvis Presley, Judy Tyler
jailing: 4 bust **5** pinch **6** arrest, collar **7** custody **9** detention
jail-related: 8 punitive **10** corrective
Jaime: 6 Laredo **9** Escalante
in English: 5 James
see also Spanish
Jaime ___ Bauer: 3 Lyn
j'aime in Latin: 3 amo
Jainism: 8 religion
Jaipur: 4 city, town
locale: 5 India
Jaja: 4 peak **5** mount **8** mountain
locale: 4 Asia **9** New Guinea
Jakarta: 4 city, port, town **7** capital
city near ~: 5 Bogor
locale: 4 Java **9** Indonesia
river: 6 Liwung
jake: 2 OK **4** fine, okay, okeh, okey **9** copacetic, first-rate, hunky-dory
Jake: 4 Garn **6** Kasdan **7** LaMotta
Jake and the Fatman (CBS drama)
cast: William Conrad (Jason McCabe) Joe Penny (Jake Styles)
dog: 3 Max
Jake's ___: 5 Thing, Women
Jakes, John: 6 author, writer
___ Jakes, The: 3 Two
Jake's Thing author: 4 Amis
Jake's Women
actor: 4 Alda
author: Neil Simon
Jakob: 5 Dylan **10** Wassermann
Jakob the Liar (1999 film)
cast: Alan Arkin, Bob Balaban, Robin Williams
Jalam, father of: 4 Esau
Jalapa: 4 city, town
locale: 6 Mexico **8** Veracruz
jalapeño: 5 spice **6** pepper **9** seasoning
hot stuff: 5 salsa **6** pepper **7** mustard **9** condiment, seasoning
Jaleel: 5 White
Jalisco: 5 state **7** Mexican
city: 4 Tala **5** Ameca, Jamay **6** Acatic, Ajijic, Autlán, Cocula, Guzmán, Ixtapa, Sayula, Tonalá, Tuxpan **7** Arandas, Ayotlán, Chapala, El Salto, La Barca, Ocotlán, Tequila, Zapopan **8** Colotlán, El Grullo, Etzatlán, Tesistán, Tototlán, Zacoalco **9** Las Pintas **10** San Agustín, Tepatitlán, Zapotiltic **11** Encarnación, Nuevo México
neighbor: 6 Colima
see also Spanish
jalopy: 3 car **4** auto, heap **5** crate, lemon, wreck **6** junker **7** clunker, vehicle **10** automobile, rattletrap
like a ~: 5 noisy, rusty **6** beat-up
Jalostotitlán: 4 city, town
locale: 6 Mexico **7** Jalisco
Jalousie composer: 4 Gade
jalousie feature: 4 slat
Jalpa: 3 car **4** auto, city, town **10** automobile **11** Lamborghini
locale: 6 Mexico **7** Tabasco **9** Zacatecas
Jáltipan: 4 city, town
locale: 6 Mexico **8** Veracruz
jam: 3 box, fix, mob, ram **4** bind, clog, cram, hole, load, mess, pack, push, spot, stem **5** block, crowd, crush, delay, jelly, press, shove, snarl, sqush, stick, stuff, swarm, tie-up **6** corner, hinder, holdup, impede, pickle, plight, scrape, spread, squash, squish, squush, throng, thrust **7** congest, dilemma, force in, squeeze, squoosh, traffic **8** compress, deadlock, exigence, exigency, gridlock, obstruct, quagmire, quandary, slowdown, stoppage **9** conserves, deep water, impedance, multitude, overcrowd, overstuff, preserves, squeeze in, tight spot **10** bottleneck, confection, congestion, difficulty
holder: 3 jar
Hungarian ~: 6 lekvar
in: 4 pack **5** press, shove, wedge **7** bunch up **9** overcrowd
in a ~: 5 stuck **7** stymied, trapped, up a tree **8** besieged, cornered, strapped, troubled **10** up the creek
ingredient: 5 grape **6** pectin **7** apricot **10** strawberry
join a ~ session: 4 play **5** sit in
session: 7 concert
starter: 3 log
traffic ~: 4 clog **5** snarl, tie up **7** squeeze **8** blockage, clogging, crowding, gridlock, overflow **9** profusion **10** bottleneck, congestion
up: 3 dam **5** block, stick
jam ___: 3 nut **7** session
jam-___: 4 pack **6** packed
___ jam: 3 ice, in a **7** traffic
___ Jam: 5 Getto, Pearl
Jamaal: 6 Wilkes
Jamaica: 4 isle **6** island, nation **7** country
athletes: 8 Red Storm
capital: 8 Kingston
city: 8 Kingston, Portmore **10** Montego Bay
export: 3 rum **5** sugar
fellow: 3 mon
fruit: 4 akee, ugli
locale: 3 BWI **10** West Indies
money: 4 cent **6** dollar
music: 3 ska
native: 5 Rasta **6** Arawak, Creole
org.: 3 OAS
school: 3 SJU **10** Saint John's
sect member: 5 rasta
tree: 8 milkwood
writer: 7 Brodber
Jamaica ___: 3 Bay, Inn, rum **6** ginger, shorts
___-Jamal Warner: 7 Malcolm
JAMA reader: 2 dr., GP, MD
Jamay: 4 city, town
locale: 6 Mexico **7** Jalisco
jamb: 4 beam, post, side **7** upright **8** doorpost **9** doorframe, sidepiece
ending: 4 oree
place: 6 window **8** casement, fenestra
starter: 4 door
jambalaya: 5 carbo
country: 5 bayou
like ~: 6 creole
jamboree: 4 bash, gala **5** party, rally, spree **6** hoopla **7** blowout, jubilee, shindig **8** festival, wingding **9** festivity, gathering **10** convention
org.: 3 BSA
participant: 5 scout, troop
shelter: 4 camp, tent
Jamboree (1999 song)
artist: Naughty by Nature, Zhané
James: 2 P.D. **3** bay, Fox, Orr **4** Agee, Best, Bond, Caan, Coco, Cook, Daly, Dean, Dunn, Etta, Exon, Fixx, Hogg, Ives, John, Joni, Mill, Olga, Ross, Watt **5** Algar, Avery, Baker, Beard, Black, Blish, Brady, Brown, Craig, Dewar, Drury, Ensor, Foley, Frank, Harry, Henry, Hoban, Horne, Ivory, Jesse, Jones, Joule, Joyce, Keach, Mason, Meade, Noble, Purdy, Ralph, Randi, range, river, Sonny, Steve, Tobin, Tommy, Whale, Wolfe, Woods **6** Arness, Baxter, Brolin, Cagney, Coburn, Cronin, Darren, Dickey, Doohan, Franck, Frazer, Galway, Garner, Hilton, Ingram, LeGros, Levine, McGraw, Monroe, Reston, Sheila, Spader, Sumner, Taylor, Tissot, Toback, Watson, Wright **7** Baldwin, Baskett, Beattie, Belushi, Boswell, Bridges, Cameron, Clavell, Clifton, Dearden, Ellison, Gleason, Hampton, Heckman, Herriot, Madison, Merrill, Neilson, Shigeta, Shirley, Starley, Stewart, Thurber, William **8** Breasted, Buchanan, Callahan, Carville, Chadwick, Crichton, Cromwell, Garfield, Lovelock, Mirrlees, Naismith, Redfield, Schuyler, Whitmore **9** Broderick, Callaghan, Cleveland, Farentino, Finlayson, Forrestal, Goldstone, MacArthur, Patterson **10** Franciscus, Gandolfini
brother of ~: 5 Jesus
city on the ~: 8 Richmond
follower: 5 Peter
in Irish: 6 Seamus
in Scottish: 6 Hamish
in Spanish: 4 Iago **5** Diego, Jaime
preceder: 7 Hebrews
River locale: 8 Virginia
river to the ~: 10 Appomattox
James ___: 3 Bay **5** Range
James ___ Allen: 3 Van
James ___ Beek: 6 Van Der
James ___ Bennett: 6 Gordon
James ___ Carter: 4 Earl
James ___ Cooper: 8 Fenimore
James ___ Cozzens: 5 Gould
James ___ Flagg: 10 Montgomery
James ___ Garfield: 5 Abram
James ___ Heusen: 3 Van
James ___ Johnson: 6 Weldon
James ___ Jones: 4 Earl
James ___ Lowell: 7 Russell
James ___ Polk: 4 Knox
James ___ Riley: 8 Whitcomb
James ___ the Giant Peach: 3 and
James ___ Whistler: 7 McNeill
___ James: 4 Beau
___, James!: 4 Home
James A. ___: 5 Herne **8** Michener
James and the Giant Peach author: Roald Dahl
James and the Shondells, Tommy
song: Crimson and Clover (1968)
Crystal Blue Persuasion (1969)
Hanky Panky (1966)
I Think We're Alone Now (1967)
Mirage (1967)
Mony Mony (1968)
Sweet Cherry Wine (1969)
___ James Audubon: 4 John
___ James Bible: 4 King
James Buchanan ___: 4 Duke, Eads
James D. ___: 6 Watson
James Earl ___: 5 Jones
James Fenimore ___: 6 Cooper
James Gordon ___: 7 Bennett
James Gould ___: 7 Cozzens
James, Harry: 10 bandleader
instrument: trumpet
spouse: Betty Grable
James, Henry: 6 author, writer
friend: Howells
work: The Ambassadors
The American
The Aspern Papers
The Awkward Age
The Bostonians
Daisy Miller
The Europeans
The Golden Bowl
The Portrait of a Lady
The Princess Casamassima
Roderick Hudson
The Sacred Fount
The Spoils of Poynton
The Tragic Muse
The Turn of the Screw
Washington Square
What Maisie Knew
The Wings of the Dove

James II daughter: 4 Anne
James J. __: 7 Corbett
James, Joni
song: How Important Can It Be? (1955)
You Are My Love (1955)
James K. __: 4 Polk
James L. __: 6 Brooks
James M. __: 4 Cain 6 Barrie
James McNeill __: 8 Whistler
James Montgomery __: 5 Flagg
__ James Olmos: 6 Edward
Jameson: 6 Parker
James, P.D.: 6 writer 7 British
first name: Phyllis
James Range locale: 9 Australia
James Robertson __: 7 Justice
James Russell __: 6 Lowell
James T. __: 4 Kirk 7 Farrell
James the __: 4 Less 5 Great 7 Greater
James the Greater: 5 saint
Jamestown: 4 city 6 colony
locale: 7 New York 8 St. Helena, Virginia
James Van __: 5 Allen 6 Heusen 7 Der Beek
__ James Version: 4 King
__ James Waller: 6 Robert
James Weldon __: 7 Johnson
James Whitcomb __: 5 Riley
James, William: 11 philosopher
Jami: 5 Gertz
Jamie: 4 Farr, Foxx 5 Luner, Wyeth
Jamie Lee: 6 Curtis
parent: 4 Tony 5 Janet
jammed: 4 full, rife 5 close, dense, laden, thick, tight 6 heaped, loaded, packed 7 compact, crammed, crowded, replete, stuffed, teeming 8 brimming, populous, squeezed 9 chockfull, congested 10 compressed, hardpacked
jammer starter: 4 wind
jammies: 3 PJs 7 pajamas 9 nightwear, sleepwear
Jammu and __: 7 Kashmir
Jamoca: 8 ice cream
alternative: 5 lemon, mocha, peach 6 banana, coffee, toffee 7 caramel, coconut, vanilla 8 cinnamon, hazelnut 9 bubblegum, chocolate, pineapple, pistachio, raspberry, rocky road, rum raisin 10 blackberry, cheesecake, Neapolitan, peppermint, strawberry
jamoke: 3 joe, mud 4 java 6 coffee
jam-pack: 3 ram 4 cram, fill 5 crowd
jam-packed
see jammed
__-jams: 3 jim
jam-session phrase: 4 riff
jam-up: 8 gridlock 10 bottleneck
Jan: 3 Hus 5 Berry, Brady, Hooks, Kadar, Kodes, Miner, Smuts, Steen 6 De Bont, Hammer, Morris, Murray, Neruda, Peerce 7 Clayton, Kubelik, van Eyck, Vermeer 8 Smithers, Stenerud, Sterling 9 Stevenson, Tinbergen
Jan & __: 4 Dean
Jan-__ Vincent: 7 Michael
Jan.: 2 mo.
follower: 3 Feb.
from ~ 1 to now: 3 YTD
predecessor: 3 Dec.
Jana: 7 Novotna
Janácek: 4 Leos 8 composer
Jan & Dean
members: Berry, Torrence
song: Baby Talk (1959)
Dead Man's Curve (1964)
Jennie Lee (1958)
The Little Old Lady (1964)
Surf City (1963)
Jane: 3 Ace, Doe, Roe 4 Eyre, Grey 5 Brody, Child, Fonda, Greer, March, Wyatt, Wyman 6 Addams, Austen, Bowles, Curtin, Froman, Jetson, Leeves, Marple, Morgan, Pauley, Powell 7 Campion, Clayson, Darwell, Goodall, Russell, Seymour 8 Horrocks, Morrison 9 Alexander, Krakowski
creator: 5 Edgar
G.I. ~: 3 WAC
in Irish: 5 Shana
in Italian: 8 Giovanna
in Scottish: 5 Shona 6 Sheena
to Peter: 3 sis
__ Jane: 4 Baby, Lady 8 Calamity
__ & Jane: 7 Antonia
Janeane: 8 Garofalo
Jane Austen's Mafia! (1998 film)
cast: Christina Applegate, Lloyd Bridges
director: Jim Abrahams
Jane Cunningham __: 5 Croly
Jane Eyre: 4 film 5 novel
author: Charlotte Brontë
cast: Joan Fontaine, Margaret O'Brien, Orson Welles
character: 4 Reed 5 Abbot, Adele, Eliza, Grace, Maria, Poole 6 Bertha, Bessie
dog: 5 Pilot
__ Jane Grey: 4 Lady
__ Janes: 4 Mary
Jane's love: 6 apeman, Tarzan
Janesville: 4 city, town
locale: 9 Wisconsin
Janet: 4 Lynn, Reno 5 Blair, Evans, Frame, Leigh, Munro, Waldo 6 Dailey, Gaynor, Lennon 7 Guthrie, Jackson 8 Margolin
daughter of Tony and ~: 5 Jamie
sister: 6 La Toya
Janeway: 5 Eliot 7 Kathryn
jangle: 3 din, jar 4 gong, ring 5 babel, clang, clank, clash, clink, noise, sound 6 hubbub, racket, rattle, tinkle, tumult, uproar 7 clangor, clatter, discord, dispute, quarrel 8 argument 9 cacophony 10 dissonance, hullabaloo
jangled __: 6 nerves
jangling: 5 harsh 6 off-key, shrill 7 grating, jarring 8 clashing, strident 9 dissonant, unmusical 10 cacophonic, discordant, inharmonic, screeching
jangly: 4 edgy 5 drawn, hyper, jumpy, tense, wired 6 on edge 7 excited, fidgety, jittery, keyed up, nervous, uptight, wound up 8 agitated, fluttery, in a tizzy, unnerved 9 stressful, strung out, up the wall 10 high-strung
Janice: 4 Rule
Janie: 6 Fricke
Janie's Got a Gun (1989 song) artist: Aerosmith
Janine: 6 Turner
Janis: 3 Ian 5 Elsie, Paige 6 Carter, Conrad, Joplin
janitor: 6 porter 7 sweeper 8 watchdog 9 attendant, caretaker, custodian 10 doorkeeper
chore: 6 waxing 7 mopping, washing 8 cleaning, sweeping
need: 3 mop 5 Lysol
Janklow: 6 Morton
Jan-Michael: 7 Vincent
Jannings, Emil Oscar: The Way of All Flesh
Jan. 1
from ~ to now: 3 YTD
Janos: 7 Starker
Janowitz: 4 Tama
Janson Directive, The author: Ludlum
Janssen: 5 David, Famke
Janssen, David: 5 actor
TV: Harry-O, The Fugitive
Janssen, Famke: 7 actress
film: Celebrity (1998)
City of Industry (1997)
Don't Say a Word (2001)
GoldenEye (1995)
Love & Sex (2000)
Made (2001)
X-Men (2000)
Jansson, Tove: 6 writer 7 Finnish
__ Janszoon Tasman: 4 Abel
Januarius: 5 saint
January: 5 month
birthstone: 6 garnet
event: 4 sale 9 white sale
honoree's initials: 3 MLK
in Spanish: 5 enero
like a ~ day: 4 cold 5 brisk, crisp, nippy 6 frigid, frosty, frozen 8 freezing
sign: 4 Goat 8 Aquarius 9 Capricorn
to December: 4 year
warming: 4 thaw
January 5: 5 nones
Janus: 3 god 4 moon
daughter of ~: 6 Canens
planet: 6 Saturn
son of ~: 4 Fons
Janus-__: 5 faced
Janvier: 4 mois
janvier to décembre: 5 année
Janzen, Lee: 6 golfer
milieu: 5 links 6 course
org.: 3 PGA
japan: 6 enamel 7 encrust, incrust, varnish
Japan: 3 sea 5 Nihon 6 nation, Nippon 7 country
aborigine: 4 Ainu
admiral: 3 Ito
affirmative: 3 hai
airline: 3 ANA
apricot: 3 ume
art: 3 noh 6 bonsai
assassin: 5 ninja
auto: 5 Honda 6 Accord, Datsun, Nissan, Toyota
bay: 6 Sagami, Suruga
bean: 6 adzuki
bed: 3 mat 5 futon
beer: 5 Kirin
belt: 3 obi 6 hamaki
beverage: 3 tea 4 sake, saki
biologist: 6 Susumu
board game: 5 shogi
bovine: 5 Wagyu
bread: 3 pan
Buddhism of ~: 8 Mahayana
Buddhist monk of ~: 5 bonze
camera: 5 Canon, Nikon
cape: 3 Oma
capital: 5 Tokyo
capital, onetime: 3 Edo 4 Nara, Yedo 5 Yeddo
cartoon genre: 5 Anime
celery: 3 udo
city: 3 Ise, Ome, Ota, Tsu, Ube, Uji, Usa, Yao 4 Ageo, Anjo, Fuji, Gifu, Hino, Hofu, Iida, Kobe, Kofu, Kure, Mito, Naha, Nara, Noda, Oita, Otsu, Saga, Seto, Soka, Tama, Toda, Ueda, Zama 5 Abiko, Akita, Asaka, Beppu, Chiba, Chofu, Daito, Ebina, Fuchu, Fukui, Handa, Ikeda, Ikoma, Iruma, Itami, Iwaki, Izumi, Kioto, Kiryu, Kochi, Kyoto, Minoo, Niiza, Ogaki, Omiya, Omuta, Osaka, Otaru, Oyama, Sakai, Suita, Tokio, Tokyo, Urawa, Yaizu 6 Akashi, Aomori, Atsugi, Ebetsu, Fujimi, Fukaya, Hadano, Himeji, Kadoma, Kasuga, Kitami, Kurume, Kuwana, Matsue, Misato, Mitaka, Nagano, Nagoya, Numazu, Sakado, Sakata, Sakura, Sasebo, Sayama, Sendai, Sukuka, Toyama, Toyota, Yamato, Yonago 7 Fukuoka, Hitachi, Ibaraki, Isesaki, Iwakuni, Kashiwa, Katsuta, Kawagoe, Kodaira, Komatsu, Kushiro, Machida, Matsudo, Mishima, Morioka, Nagaoka, Niigata, Nobeoka, Obihiro, Odawara, Okayama, Okazaki, Sapporo, Shimizu, Takaoka, Tottori, Tsukuba 8 Ashikaga, Fujisawa, Fukuyama, Hachioji, Hakodate, Hirakata, Hirosaki, Ichihara, Ichikawa, Kakogawa, Kanazawa, Kawasaki, Koriyama, Kumamoto, Maebashi, Miuazaki, Nagasaki, Neyagawa, Shizuoka, Tokuyama, Toyonaka, Wakayama, Yamagata, Yokohama, Yokosuka 9 Hiroshima, Kagoshima
coat: 5 haori, happi
computer company: 3 NEC
conductor: 3 Oue 5 Ozawa
cooking ingredient: 4 miso
cypress: 5 **dance:** 6 bugaku, bukavu
delicacy: 4 fugu
diver: 3 ama
dog: 5 Akita
drama: 3 noh 6 kabuki
earthenware: 4 raku
elder statesman of ~: 5 genro
electronics giant: 4 Sony 5 Sanyo
emperor's title: 5 tenno
ender: 3 ese
entertainer: 6 geisha
feudal lord: 6 daimio, daimyo
first-generation ~: 5 Issei
first prime minister: 3 Ito
fish: 3 koi, tai 4 fugu, masu 5 cobia 6 medaka
food: 3 eel 5 sushi 6 rumaki 7 sashimi, tempura
footwear: 4 geta, tabi, zori
fragrant-flowered ~ shrub: 4 gumi
gateway: 5 torii
gelatin: 4 agar 8 agar-agar
god: 5 Inari 9 Amaterasu
golfer: 4 Aoki
good morning in ~: 5 ohayo
hamlet: 4 mura
historical period: 5 Meiji
honorific: 3 san
hostess: 6 geisha
immigrant: 5 Nisei
ink: 4 sumi
iris: 5 plant 6 flower
island: 5 Hondo 6 Honshu, Kiushu, Kyushu, Ryukyu 7 Okinawa, Shikoku 8 Hokkaido
islands near ~: 5 Bonin 6 Kurils
knife: 5 Ginsu
lake: 3 Omi 4 Biwa
language: 4 Ainu
legislature: 4 Diet
locale: 4 Asia 6 Orient
Mahayana school in ~: 3 Zen
martial art: 6 aikido, karate
measure: 3 sho
mercenary: 5 ninja
money: 3 sen, yen
mountain: 4 Fuji 5 Oyama 8 Fujiyama
movie monster: 5 Rodan 8 Godzilla
mushroom: 5 enoki
neighbor: 5 China
Nobelist in Chemistry: 5 Fukui 6 Noyori, Tanaka 9 Shirakawa
Nobelist in Literature: 2 Oe 8 Kawabata
Nobelist in Medicine: 8 Tonegawa
Nobelist in Peace: 4 Sato
Nobelist in Physics: 5 Esaki 6 Yukawa 7 Koshiba 8 Tomonaga
overcoat: 4 mino

painter: 6 Sesshu
partition: 6 fusuma
pasta: 5 ramen 6 larmen
perfume source: 5 rasse
persimmon: 4 kaki
physician: 8 Mori Ōgai
physicist: 5 Esaki 6 Yukawa
plum: 6 loquat
poem: 5 haiku, tanka
poet: 4 Issa 5 Basho, Buson 6 Yosano 7 Higuchi, Masaoka 8 Hagiwara 9 Shimazaki
porcelain: 5 imari
port: 4 Kobe, Kure, Naha, Oita 5 Akita, Kochi, Osaka, Otaru 6 Aomori 7 Niigata 8 Nagasaki, Yokohama 9 Amagasaki, Hiroshima, Kagoshima
radish: 6 daikon
rain, in ~: 3 ame
red snapper: 3 tai
rice cake: 5 mochi
river: 3 Ota
robe: 6 kimono, yukata
royal: 3 emp.
salmonlike fish of ~: 3 ayu
sash: 3 obi
scientist: 5 Esaki 6 Susumu, Yukawa
screen: 5 shoji
script: 4 kana
sea: 5 China, Japan 6 Inland, Sagami 9 East China
seaweed: 4 nori
shrub: 6 nardin, tobira 7 nandina
soup: 5 ramen 6 larmen
sport: 4 sumo 5 kendo
sports car: 5 Miata
spy: 5 ninja
stringed instrument: 4 koto
system of writing: 5 kanji
tangerine: 7 satsuma
temple city of ~: 5 Kioto, Kyoto, Nikko
theater: 3 noh 6 kabuki
tree: 4 kaki 6 hinoki
tub: 4 furo
vegetable: 3 udo
village: 4 mura
violinist: 6 Midori
volcano: 3 Aso, Usu 4 Akan, Fuji, Nasu 5 Asama, Azuma, Oyama, Unzen 6 Asosan, Bandai, Chokai, Ontake, Oshima 7 Adatara
war cry: 6 banzai
watch: 5 Seiko
waterfall: 5 Kegon
wine: 4 sake, saki
winter sports center: 4 Arai
writer: 4 Endo 5 Inoue 7 Abe Kobo, Higuchi, Mishima, Natsume 8 Kawabata, Mori Ōgai, Murasaki 9 Nagai Kafu, Yokomitsu 10 Dazai Osamu
yes, in ~: 3 hai
Japan ___: 3 wax 5 cedar 6 clover, Stream, tallow 7 Current
___ Japan: 5 Sea of
Japanese: 5 Asian 8 language
Japanese ___: 3 ivy, yew 4 Chin, iris, mink, newt, pear, plum, silk, wolf 5 cedar, holly, larch, maple, paper, quail 6 beetle, cherry, clover, laurel, oyster, quince, radish, spurge 7 anemone, gelatin, lacquer, lantern, spaniel
Japanese ___ ceremony: 3 tea
Japanese-American: 5 Issei, Nisei
Japanese bobtail: 3 cat 5 felid 6 feline
Japanese Chin: 3 dog 5 canid 6 canine
___-Japanese War: 4 Sino 5 Russo
jape: 3 gag, rib 4 gibe, jest, jibe, joke, mock, quip 5 antic, caper, prank, taunt 7 lampoon, waggery 8 ridicule 9 kid around, make fun of, wisecrack 10 shenanigan, tomfoolery
japery: 5 jests, jokes, quips 7 mocking
Japheth
brother of ~: 3 Ham 4 Shem
father of ~: 4 Noah
son of ~: 5 Gomer, Madai, Magog
japonica: 5 plant 6 flower
Japur: 5 river
locale: 6 Brazil 8 Colombia
jar: 3 irk, pot 4 bang, bump, jerk, jolt, kick, olla, rock, stun, thud, vase 5 clash, crash, crock, cruse, flask, grate, shake, shock, smash, sound, start, thump 6 bottle, bounce, impact, jangle, jiggle, jostle, jounce, justle, nettle, offend, rattle, scream, vessel, wallop 7 agitate, amphora, disturb, shake up, startle, tremble 8 disquiet, irritate, surprise 9 buffeting, collision, container 10 concussion, discompose
contents ~: 3 jam 4 mayo 5 jelly
oil ~: 5 cruse
starter: 5 night
top: 3 cap, lid 5 cover
___ jar: 4 bell, slop 5 cooky, fruit, mason 6 cookie, ginger, Leyden 7 battery, stirrup
Jardin des Tuileries: 4 parc
locale: 5 Paris 6 France
Jardine: 4 Alan
Jardines: 4 city, town
locale: 6 Mexico 9 Nuevo León
jardiniere: 3 pot, urn 4 vase 7 amphora, epergne
Jared: 4 Leto 6 Sparks
grandson of ~: 10 Methuselah
son of ~: 5 Enoch
jargon: 3 gas, rot 4 blah, bosh, bull, bunk, cant, guff, jazz, jive, pooh, talk, tosh 5 argot, bilge, fudge, hokum, hooey, idiom, lingo, prate, slang, stuff, trash, tripe 6 babble, bunkum, bushwa, drivel, footle, gabble, gammon, gibber, havers, hot air, humbug, jabber, kibosh, patois, patter, piffle, speech 7 baloney, blarney, blather, blether, boloney, bushwah, dialect, eyewash, flannel, flubdub, fustian, garbage, hogwash, inanity, palaver, rubbish, twaddle 8 buncombe, claptrap, falderal, falderol, flimflam, flummery, folderal, folderol, language, nonsense, parlance, shoptalk, slipslop, tommyrot, trumpery 9 banana oil, buzzwords, gibberish, kidstakes, moonshine, poppycock, rigmarole 10 applesauce, balderdash, bilge water, codswallop, double-talk, flapdoodle, galimatias, Jabberwock, mumbo jumbo, rigamarole, taradiddle, vernacular, vocabulary
suffix: 3 ese
jargonelle: 4 pear
Jarlsberg: 6 cheese
Jarmusch, Jim: 8 director
film: Dead Man (1996)
Mystery Train (1989)
Night on Earth (1991)
Stranger Than Paradise (1984)
Jaroslav: 5 Hasek 7 Seifert 9 Heyrovsky
jarrah: 4 tree 8 hardwood
Jarre: 7 Maurice
Jarreau: 2 Al
Jarrell, Randall: 4 poet 6 author, writer
Jarrett: 4 Dale 5 Keith
Jarrett, Dale: 9 auto racer
milieu: 5 track
jarring: 5 bumpy, forte, harsh, noisy, rough, shock 6 jouncy, off-key 7 blaring, booming, grating, pealing, rackety, raucous, reboant, roaring 8 crashing, jangling, piercing, plangent, rumbling, sonorous, strident, turned up 9 big-voiced, clamorous, deafening, dissonant, unmusical 10 boisterous, discordant, resounding, stentorian, strepitous, thundering, uproarious, vociferous
Jarrott: 7 Charles
Jarrow: 4 city, town
locale: 7 England
Jarry, Alfred: 6 French 10 playwright
___ Jar, The: 4 Bell
Jarvik: 6 Robert
Jascha: 7 Heifetz
jasmine: 4 vine 5 plant, shrub 6 flower, yellow
relative: 4 buff, corn, gold, lime, rust, sand 5 blond, brass, coral, cream, flaxy, lemon, lilac, maize, ocher, ochre, olive, peach, rusty, straw 6 blonde, canary, chammy, citron, crocus, flaxen, shammy, shamoy 7 apricot, chamois, citrine, mustard, nankeen, old gold, saffron, xanthic 8 daffodil, primrose 9 champagne, forsythia, goldenrod
jasmine ___: 3 tea
___ jasmine: 3 day 4 blue, Cape, rock, star 5 crape, night 6 winter, yellow 7 Arabian, Italian, Spanish
Jasmine: 3 Guy
Jason: 4 hero, Kidd, Rick 5 Biggs, Gould 6 Hervey, Miller, Patric, Sehorn 7 Bateman, Connery, Gedrick, Robards 8 Argonaut 9 Alexander, Priestley
boat: 4 Argo
daughter of ~: 7 Eriopis
father of ~: 5 Aeson
lover of ~: 6 Glauce 9 Hypsipyle
ship: 4 Argo
son of ~: 5 Argus, Medus, Thoas 6 Euneus, Medeus, Pheres 8 Deipylus, Mermerus, Tisander 9 Alcimedes, Alcimenes, Thessalus, Tisandrus
wife of ~: 5 Medea
Jason ___ Lee: 5 Scott
___ Jason Leigh: 8 Jennifer
Jason's ___: 5 Lyric
jasper: 3 gem 4 rock 5 stone 7 pottery 8 ceramics 9 stoneware
ender: 4 ware
Jasper: 5 Johns
jass: 4 game 8 card game
Jassy in Romania: 4 Iasi
jati: 5 caste, Hindu 6 Hindoo
Jaulan: 3 cow 4 bull 6 bovine, cattle
jaundice: 4 bias, mold, tint, warp 5 cloud, color, shade, shape, tinge, twist 9 influence, prejudice
jaundiced: 4 sour 6 sallow 7 partial 8 liverish, negative, partisan 9 distorted, resentful, skeptical 10 intolerant, prejudiced, suspicious, unfriendly
eye: 4 bias 6 enmity 7 bigotry 8 aversion 9 antipathy, prejudice 10 chauvinism, fanaticism, favoritism, narrowness, partiality
___ jaundiced eye upon: 5 cast a
jaunt: 3 hop, run 4 hike, ride, tour, trek, trip, turn, walk 5 drive, march, sally 6 cruise, frolic, junket, outing, picnic, ramble, safari, stroll, travel, voyage, wander 7 day trip, journey 9 adventure, excursion, gallivant 10 expedition
jaunty: 4 airy, bold, flip, pert 5 brash, cocky, natty, perky, sassy, sleek, swank 6 blithe, breezy, dapper, frisky, impish, lively, rakish, snazzy, spiffy, sporty, swanky 7 buoyant, dashing, raffish 8 animated, carefree, cheerful, debonair, flippant, gamesome, sporting, sportive 9 debonaire, sprightly, vivacious 10 debonnaire, frolicsome, rollicking, swaggering, unbothered
hat: 3 cap, tam 5 beret
Jauregui: 4 city, town
locale: 6 Mexico 9 Querétaro
java: 3 joe 5 mocha 6 coffee, jamoke
holder: 3 cup, mug, urn 7 samovar
inferior ~: 3 mud
locale: 4 café 6 bistro, eatery
type of ~: 5 decaf, latte 8 espresso
see also coffee
___ java: 5 mocha
Java: 3 sea 4 isle 6 island 8 language
alternative: 3 ADA, APL, SQL 4 Alef, html, Icon, LISP, Logo, Orca, Perl 5 Algol, Basic, Cecil, COBOL, Dylan, SISAL 6 Delphi, Eiffel, Erlang, Oberon, Pascal, Prolog, Sather, Scheme, Snobol 7 Fortran
carriage: 4 sado 5 sadoo
city: 5 Bogor 8 Semarang
coin: 3 sen
folk art of ~: 5 batik 6 battik
locale: 4 Asia
neighbor: 4 Bali 6 Borneo
ruler: 4 raja
tree: 4 upas
volcano: 5 Kelut, Raung 6 Merapi, Semeru, Slamet
work: 6 applet
Java ___: 3 fig, man, Sea 5 finch 6 cotton, Trench 7 sparrow
Java (1964 song) artist: Al Hirt
Javanese: 3 cat 5 felid 6 feline 8 language
Javari: 5 river
locale: 4 Peru 6 Brazil
Java Sea
island: 4 Laut
locale: 4 Bali
javelin: 3 gig 4 bolt, gaff, pike, pile 5 event, lance, shaft, spear, sport 7 assagai, assegai, harpoon 8 spontoon
cords: 6 amenta
Roman ~: 4 pila 5 pilum
javelin ___: 5 throw
Javelin: 3 car 4 auto 10 automobile
Javelle ___: 5 water
___ Javelle: 5 eau de
Javier ___ Cuellar: 7 Pérez de
jaw: 3 gab, say, yak, yap 4 bone, chat, chin, jowl, rail, rate, talk 5 chops, mouth, orate, scold, speak, utter 6 babble, berate, gossip, jabber, rail at, rattle, revile, yammer 7 censure, chatter, jawbone, maxilla, prattle, upbraid 8 backtalk, chitchat, mandible 9 criticize 10 chew the fat, tongue-lash, vituperate
combining form: 4 geny- 5 genyo-, gnath- 6 gnatho-
drop one's ~: 4 gape, gawk 5 stare 6 goggle, marvel
ender: 4 bone 7 breaker 8 breaking
lower ~: 4 chin, jowl 6 muzzle
place: 3 mug 4 face, puss 6 kisser
starter: 4 lock
with dropped ~: 5 agape 6 aghast, amazed 9 astounded, awestruck, stupefied, surprised 10 astonished, bewildered, dumbstruck, spellbound
___ jaw: 5 glass 7 lantern
Jawaharlal: 5 Nehru
daughter: 6 Indira
jawbone: 3 jaw 4 coax 6 rebuke 7 maxilla 8 mandible
source: 3 ass
jawbreaker: 5 candy
jawed
combining form: 8 -gnathous
tool: 4 vise 6 wrench
___-jawed: 4 iron 5 slack
Jaworski: 4 Leon
Jaws: 9 film, novel

author: Peter Benchley
boat: 4 Orca
cast: Richard Dreyfuss, Lorraine Gary, Murray Hamilton, Roy Scheider, Robert Shaw
director: Steven Spielberg
dog: 6 Pippet
setting: 5 Amity
terror: 5 shark
___ Jaw, Saskatchewan: 5 Moose
Jaws of ___: 4 Life
Jaws Theme (1975 song) artist: John Williams
jay: 4 bird 6 letter
adjective: 5 avian
ender: 3 vee 4 bird, walk 6 hawker, walker 7 walking
follower: 3 kay
home: 4 nest 6 aviary
kin: 4 crow
starter: 3 dee, vee
___ jay: 4 blue, gray, grey 5 piñon, scrub 6 Canada, pinyon
Jay: 4 John, Leno, Ward 5 Gould, North, Ricky, Roach 8 Ferguson, Sandrich 9 McInerney 10 Livingston
ender: 3 cee
Jay and the Americans
leader: Jay Black
song: Cara Mia (1965)
Come a Little Bit Closer (1964)
Let's Lock the Door (1965)
Only in America (1963)
She Cried (1962)
This Magic Moment (1969)
jaybird, like a: 5 naked
Jay C. ___: 7 Flippen
Jaye: 8 Davidson
Jaye P. ___: 6 Morgan
___ Jay Friedman: 5 Bruce
___ Jay Gould: 7 Stephen
Jayhawker: 6 Kansan
___ Jay Hawkins: 8 Screamin'
___ Jay Lerner: 4 Alan
Jaymes partner: 7 Bartles
Jayne: 7 Kennedy, Meadows 9 Mansfield
jaywalk: 5 cross
jaywalker: 10 pedestrian
warn a ~: 4 beep, honk, toot 5 blare
jazz: 3 bop, gas, rot 4 blah, bosh, bull, bunk, guff, jive, pooh, tosh, zest 5 bebop, bilge, blues, fudge, genre, hokum, hooey, music, prate, stuff, swing, trash, tripe 6 boogie, bunkum, bushwa, drivel, footle, gabble, gammon, gibber, havers, hot air, humbug, jabber, jargon, kibosh, piffle, spirit 7 baloney, blarney, blather, blether, boloney, bushwah, eyewash, flannel, flubdub, fustian, garbage, hogwash, inanity, malarky, rubbish, twaddle 8 buncombe, claptrap, falderal, falderol, flimflam, flummery, folderal, folderol, malarkey, nonsense, slipslop, tommyrot, trumpery, vivacity 9 banana oil, Dixieland, gibberish, goofiness, kidstakes, moonshine, poppycock, rigmarole 10 applesauce, balderdash, bilge water, codswallop, double-talk, excitement, flapdoodle, galimatias, Jabberwock, liveliness, mumbo jumbo, rigamarole, taradiddle
appreciate ~: 3 dig
bassist: 6 Mingus 7 Blanton 9 Pettiford
clarinetist: 4 Shaw 6 Bechet, Herman 7 Goodman 8 Fountain
dance: 4 jive 5 bebop, stomp, swing 9 jitterbug
drummer: 4 Rich, Webb 5 Krupa, Roach 6 Blakey, Puente 7 Bellson
effect: 4 wail
ensemble: 4 band 5 combo
fan: 3 cat 6 bopper, hepcat
flutist: 4 Mann
genre: 3 bop 4 scat 5 bebop, rebop, swing 6 boogie
guitarist: 4 Byrd 10 Montgomery
instrument: 3 axe, sax 4 horn 7 trumpet 8 clarinet 9 saxophone
Latin ~: 5 salsa
like some ~: 4 cool
nickname: 5 Trane 7 Satchmo
performance: 3 gig, jam, set
phrase: 4 lick, riff, vamp
pianist: 4 Monk 5 Blake, Hines, Hyman, Lewis, Tatum 6 Garner, Kenton, Morton, Simone, Waller 7 Allison, Brubeck, Hancock 8 Guaraldi, Marsalis 9 Ellington, Henderson, Strayhorn 10 McPartland
record label: 5 Verve
saxophonist: 4 Getz, Sims 5 Young 6 Barnet, Bechet, Beneke, Carter, Gordon, Herman, Kenny G, Parker 7 Coleman, Desmond, Hawkins, Rollins 8 Adderley, Coltrane, Marsalis, Mulligan
singing name: 4 Ella
trombonist: 3 Ory 6 Miller 9 Teagarden
trumpeter: 5 Davis, James 7 Nichols 8 Cheatham, Eldridge, Ferguson, Mangione, Marsalis 9 Armstrong, Gillespie 11 Beiderbecke
up: 4 hoke 7 enliven 8 decorate, emblazon, energize 9 embellish 10 supplement
vibraphonist: 5 Norvo 7 Hampton
jazz ___: 4 band, shoe 6 singer
jazz-___: 4 rock 6 fusion
___ jazz: 4 cool, free 6 modern
Jazz: 4 five, team
home: 4 Utah
org.: 3 NBA
rival: 3 Cav, Mav, Net, Sun 4 Buck, Bull, Hawk, Heat, King, Spur 5 Knick, Laker, Magic, Pacer, Sixer, Sonic 6 Celtic, Hornet, Nugget, Piston, Raptor, Rocket, Wizard 7 Clipper, Grizzly, Warrior 8 Cavalier, Maverick 10 SuperSonic, Timberwolf
sport: 10 basketball
Jazz ___: 3 Age
Jazzman (1974 song) artist: Carole King
Jazz on a Summer's Day (1959 film)
cast: Louis Armstrong, Chuck Berry, Big Maybelle
Jazzonia author: Langston Hughes
Jazz Pizzicato composer: 8 Anderson
jazzy: 5 fancy, showy, zesty, zippy 6 active, flashy, lively, snazzy, tawdry 7 stylish, zestful 8 animated, spirited, striking 9 vivacious 10 flamboyant
street: 5 Beale
J.B.: 9 Priestley
j-bar: 3 tow 4 lift 6 ski tow 7 ski lift
___ J. Blige: 4 Mary
J.C.: 5 Powys, Snead 6 Penney 7 Dithers
___ J. Cannell: 7 Stephen
J. Carrol ___: 5 Naish
___ J. Cobb: 3 Lee
___ J. Corbett: 5 James
JCS
mem.: 3 adm., CNO, gen.
part: 5 Joint, Staff 6 Chiefs
J.D.: 3 att. 4 atty., punk 5 tough 6 Cannon 8 hooligan, Salinger
forerunner: 3 LL.B.
part: 5 Juris 6 Doctor 8 juvenile 10 delinquent
-to-be's test: 4 LSAT
___ J. Dalton: 4 Lacy
jealous: 5 green 7 envious, envying, wishful 8 covetous, desirous, grudging 9 green-eyed, malicious, resentful 10 begrudging, possessive, protective, suspicious
one's cry: 5 me too
jealous mistress, Emerson's: 3 art
jealousy: 4 envy 9 suspicion 10 sour grapes
Jean: 3 Arp 4 Auel, Bach, Kerr, Rhys 5 Bodel, Borel, Corot, Fabre, Genet, Giono, Hagen, Marsh, Morel 6 Arthur, Dunant, Harlow, Ingres, Knight, Millet, Monnet, Parker, Perrin, Peters, Piaget, Racine, Renoir, Seberg, Toomer, Wyclef 7 Anouilh, Cocteau, Dausset, Fourier, Lafitte, Lamarck, Nicolet, Nidetch, Shepard, Simmons 8 Beliveau, Chrétien, Dubuffet, Foucault, Hersholt, Shepherd, Sibelius, Stafford 9 Fragonard, Froissart, Giraudoux, Negulesco, Shrimpton, Stapleton, Vander Pyl 10 de Brunhoff
in English: 4 John
see also French
Jean ___ Fontaine: 4 de La
Jean ___ Getty: 4 Paul
Jean ___ Marat: 4 Paul
Jean ___ Pyl: 6 Vander
Jean-___ Aumont: 6 Pierre
Jean-___ Belmondo: 4 Paul
Jean-___ Duvalier: 6 Claude
Jean-___ Godard: 3 Luc
Jean-___ Killy: 6 Claude
Jean-___ Picard: 3 Luc
Jean-___ Rampal: 6 Pierre
Jean-___ Sartre: 4 Paul
Jean-___ Van Damme: 6 Claude
___ Jean: 4 Blue 6 Billie
Jean (1969 song) artist: Oliver
Jean Baptiste ___: 3 Say 7 Colbert
Jean-Baptiste: 5 Lully
Jean-Claude: 5 Killy 8 Duvalier
Jeane: 5 Dixon
Jeanette: 5 Nolan 9 MacDonald
Jeanie With the Light Brown Hair
composer: 6 Foster
Jean Jacques: 8 Rousseau
___ Jean King: 6 Billie
Jean-Luc: 6 Godard, Picard
Jean-Marie: 4 Lehn 5 Le Pen
Jeanne: 3 ste. 4 Abel 5 Black, Crain 6 Lanvin, Moreau, Pruett, sainte
see also French
Jeannie: 5 Seely 6 Berlin
___ Jeannie: 6 Little
Jeannie C. ___: 5 Riley
Jeannine: 5 Riley
Jeannot: 6 Szwarc
Jean Paul: 5 Getty, Marat
Jean-Paul: 6 Sartre 8 Belmondo, Gaultier
Jean-Pierre: 5 Léaud 6 Aumont, Rampal
jeans: 4 togs 5 cords, Levi's, pants 6 chinos, denims, slacks 8 trousers 9 corduroys, dungarees, Wranglers
cut of some ~: 4 slim 5 husky
iron-on: 5 patch 8 appliqué
like ~: 6 casual
material: 5 chino, denim 8 corduroy
measurement: 5 waist 6 inseam
name: 3 Lee 4 Levi 6 Gitano
partner: 3 tee 6 T-shirt
shortened ~: 7 cutoffs
starter: 4 blue
Jeb: 4 Bush 8 Magruder
J.E.B.: 6 Stuart
Jeckle: 4 toon 6 magpie
Jed: 6 Harris 8 Clampett
daughter: 4 Elly 7 Elly May
nephew: 6 Jethro
Jeddah native: 5 Saudi
J. Edgar ___: 6 Hoover
Jedi: 6 Kenobi, Obi-Wan
ally: 4 Ewok
teacher: 4 Yoda
___-jeebies: 6 heebie
Jeep: 3 SUV 5 truck 7 vehicle
model: 6 Laredo, Sahara 8 Cherokee, Wagoneer, Wrangler
onetime ~ mfr.: 3 AMC
relative: 6 Humvee
jeepers: 3 wow 4 gosh, yipe 5 golly, yikes, yipes
Jeepers Creepers composer: 6 Warren
jeer: 3 boo 4 gibe, hiss, hoot, jibe, mock, quip, razz, slam, slur, snub, twit 5 abuse, chaff, decry, fleer, libel, scoff, scorn, sneer, snipe, spurn, taunt, whoop 6 banter, defame, deride, dump on, heckle, hector, hiss at, hoot at, impugn, jibe at, malign, offend, rail at, rebuff, slight, vilify 7 affront, asperse, catcall, degrade, disdain, laugh at, mockery, poke fun, put down, rank out, sarcasm, slander, traduce 8 belittle, denounce, ridicule, vilipend 9 denigrate, discredit, disparage, humiliate, make fun of 10 calumniate, disrespect
at: 4 mock 5 scorn, taunt 8 ridicule
jeering: 7 mocking 8 derisive, scoffing, scornful, taunting 9 insulting, sarcastic 10 disdainful, ridiculing
Jeeves: 5 valet
Jeeves author: P.G. Wodehouse
jefe: 5 chief 6 honcho, top dog 8 kingfish, superior 9 commander
Jeff: 4 Beck 5 Barry, Corey, Fahey, Lynne 6 Healey, Sluman 7 Bagwell, Bridges, Conaway, Daniels, Reardon 8 Chandler, Goldblum 9 Foxworthy
brother: 4 Beau
father: 5 Lloyd
friend: 4 Mutt
___ & Jeff: 4 Mutt
Jefferson: 4 city, Fort, town 5 Davis 6 Martha, Thomas
locale: 8 Virginia
Jefferson ___: 3 Day
___ Jefferson: 4 Fort
Jefferson Airplane
members: Slick, Kantner
song: Count on Me (1978)
Miracles (1975)
Somebody to Love (1967)
White Rabbit (1967)
Jefferson City: 4 city, town 7 capital
county: 4 Cole
locale: 8 Missouri
river: 8 Missouri
Jefferson in Paris (1995 film)
cast: James Earl Jones, Thandie Newton, Nick Nolte, Gwyneth Paltrow, Greta Scacchi
director: James Ivory
Jeffersons, The (CBS sitcom)
cast: Franklin Cover (Tom Willis)
Marla Gibbs (Florence Johnston)
Sherman Hemsley (George Jefferson)
Roxie Roker (Helen Willis)
Isabel Sanford (Louise Jefferson)
producer: 4 Lear
theme: Movin' on Up
Jefferson, Thomas: 9 president
belief: 5 deism
bill: 3 two
former occupation: 6 lawyer
hair: 3 red
home: 8 Virginia 10 Monticello
opponent: 5 Adams 8 Pinckney
predecessor: 5 Adams
sch. founded by ~: 3 U. Va.
V.P.: 4 Burr 7 Clinton
wife: 6 Martha

Jeffersontown: 4 city
  locale: 8 Kentucky
Jeffersonville: 4 city, town
  locale: 7 Indiana
Jeffers, Robinson: 4 poet 6 writer
  like ~ stallion: 4 roan
Jeffrey: 4 Lynn 5 Jones 6 Archer, Hunter, Tambor 7 Osborne 10 Katzenberg
Jeffreys, Anne: 7 actress
  film: Dillinger (1945)
    Riffraff (1947)
  TV: Topper
Jeffries: 6 Lionel
Jehan: 4 Shah
Jehoshaphat father: 3 Asa
Jehovah: 3 God 4 Lord
Jehovah's __: 7 Witness
jejune: 3 dry 4 arid, blah, dull, flat, naif, tame 5 banal, corny, empty, hokey, inane, naive, passé, silly, stale, trite, vapid 6 boring, callow, common, draggy, giggly, old hat 7 clichéd, fatuous, humdrum, insipid, kiddish, prosaic, puerile, tedious 8 bromidic, childish, immature, jevenile, juvenile, lifeless, ordinary, outdated, outmoded, tiresome 9 hackneyed, pointless, prosaical, senseless 10 pedestrian, spiritless, uninspired, unoriginal, wishywashy
  area: 6 desert
jejunum neighbor: 5 ileum
Jekyll and Hyde, like: 4 dual
Jekyll hangout: 3 lab
jell: 3 set 4 clot 5 occur 6 cohere, firm up, gelate, harden 7 congeal, stiffen, thicken 8 finalize, solidify, take form 9 coagulate, make sense, take shape 10 gelatinize
jelled: 3 set 5 stiff, thick
  garnish: 5 aspic
Jellicle Ball musical: 4 Cats
Jellicoe: 3 Ann
jellied: 5 gummy, stiff, thick 6 gloppy 9 congealed, thickened 10 coagulated, gelatinous, solidified
  appetizer: 9 macédoine
  food: 3 eel 6 jujube
Jell-O: 7 dessert, gelatin
  like freshly mixed ~: 5 unset
  shaper: 4 mold
jelly: 3 jam 5 aspic, Kraft 6 Knott's, spread, Welch's 7 Polaner, stiffen 8 Smucker's 9 conserves, preserves
  container: 3 jar, pot
  dinner ~: 5 aspic
  ender: 4 bean, fish, roll
  flavor: 5 grape, guava 7 apricot 10 strawberry
  lump of ~: 4 blob, glob 6 dollop
  roll: 4 cake 10 confection
jelly __: 4 coat, roll 5 donut 6 fungus
__ jelly: 4 comb 5 royal 7 mineral
Jelly __ Morton: 4 Roll
jellybean: 5 candy
Jelly Belly: 5 candy
  flavor: 4 pear 5 lemon, peach 6 banana, cherry 7 coconut, popcorn 8 cinnamon, jalapeño, licorice, root beer 9 blueberry, bubble gum, cream soda, lemon lime, margarita, pineapple, raspberry, tangerine 10 cantaloupe, cappuccino, grapefruit, grape jelly, green apple, piña colada, watermelon
jellyfish: 4 wimp 5 pansy, sissy 6 coward, craven, turkey 7 chicken, dastard, nebbish, quitter 8 poltroon, pushover, recreant, weakling 9 fraidy cat 10 pantywaist
  part: 5 cnida 6 pileus
  young ~: 5 polyp
jellylike: 5 shaky, thick 6 unfirm, wobbly 7 aquiver, viscous 10 gelatinous
Jellylorum: 3 cat
jelly roll: 4 cake
Jelly's __ Jam: 4 Last
Jellystone Park bear: 4 Yogi 6 Boo Boo
jelutong: 4 tree
Jemima: 4 aunt, duck
Jemima Puddleduck author: Beatrix Potter
Jemison, Mae: 9 astronaut
jemmy: 4 coat 6 jacket 8 overcoat
Jena: 4 city, town 6 battle, Malone
  locale: 7 Germany
je ne __ quoi: 4 sais
Jenkins: 5 Allen 6 Fergie, Gordon, Tamara 8 Ferguson
Jenkins, Fergie: 7 pitcher
__ Jenks Bloomer: 6 Amelia
Jenna: 6 Elfman
Jenn-Air: 5 stove 6 fridge
  alternative: 5 Amana, Norge 6 Bendix, Maytag, Tappan 7 Admiral, Kenmore 8 Hotpoint 9 Magic Chef, Whirlpool 10 Frigidaire, Kelvinator, KitchenAid
Jenner: 5 Bruce 6 Edward 10 decathlete
jennet: 3 ass 6 animal, donkey
Jenney: 7 William
Jennie: 5 Garth 6 Jerome
Jennie Gerhardt author: 7 Dreiser
Jennie Lee (1958 song) artist: Jan & Dean
Jennifer: 4 Grey, Lien, Salt 5 Beals, Grant, Jones, Lopez, Lynch, Paige, Tilly 6 O'Neill, Warnes, Warren 7 Aniston 8 Bartlett, Capriati, Connelly, Holliday, Saunders
  on WKRP: 4 Loni
Jennifer __ Hewitt: 4 Love
Jennifer __ Leigh: 5 Jason
Jennifer Lorn author: Elinor Wylie
Jennilee: 8 Harrison
Jennings: 5 Peter 6 Hughie, Waylon
  forte: 4 news
  network: 3 ABC 5 ABC-TV
__ Jennings Bryan: 7 William
jenny: 3 ass, jib 6 donkey
  cry: 4 bray 6 heehaw
__ jenny: 6 flying, silver
Jenny: 4 Lind 5 Craig, Jones 7 Agutter 8 McCarthy
Jennyanydots: 3 cat
Jenny, Jenny (1957 song) artist: Little Richard
Jeno's: 5 pizza
  alternative: 5 Tony's 6 Ellio's 7 Celeste, Totino's 8 DiGiorno 9 Tombstone 10 Freschetta
Jens: 4 Skou 6 Salome 8 Jacobsen
Jensen, J. Hans: 8 Nobelist 9 physicist
Jensen, Johannes: 6 Danish, writer 8 Nobelist
Jens, Salome: 7 actress
  film: Angel Baby (1961)
    I'm Losing You (1999)
    Seconds (1966)
Jenufa: 5 opera
  composer: 7 Janácek
jeon: 5 money
jeopardize: 4 risk 5 peril, stake 6 chance, gamble, hazard, menace 7 imperil 8 endanger, threaten 10 compromise
jeopardous: 5 hairy, risky 7 parlous 9 dangerous, unhealthy
jeopardy: 4 risk 5 peril 6 danger, hazard, menace 7 trouble 8 exposure, unsafety 9 liability 10 insecurity
  full of ~: 4 iffy 5 dicey, hairy, risky 6 chancy, daring, touchy, tricky, unsafe 7 fraught, parlous, unsound 8 perilous, ticklish 9 dangerous, daredevil, desperate, foolhardy, hazardous, uncertain 10 touch-and-go
  in ~: 6 at risk 7 at stake 9 on the line 10 endangered
  put in ~: 3 bet 4 dare, risk 5 brave, stake, wager 6 chance, gamble, hazard 7 venture 9 speculate 10 take a flyer
__ jeopardy: 6 double
Jeopardy!: 8 game show
  announcer: 5 Pardo
  clue: 6 answer
  contestant: 5 asker
  creator: 4 Merv 7 Griffin
  host: Art Fleming, Alex Trebek
  owner: 4 Sony
  staple: 6 trivia
Jephtha composer: 6 Handel
jerboa: 6 animal, mammal, rodent
  relative: 3 rat 4 cavy, degu, jird, paca, vole 5 coypu, gundi, mouse, xerus 6 agouti, beaver, gerbil, gopher, marmot, murine 7 hamster, lemming, muskrat, visacha 8 chipmunk, cricetid, dormouse, squirrel, tuco-tuco 9 chickaree, groundhog, guinea pig, porcupine, woodchuck 10 chinchilla, prairie dog
jeremiad: 6 lamant, lament, tirade 8 diatribe, harangue 9 complaint, grievance, invective, philippic
Jeremiah: 7 Johnson
  brother of ~: 6 Hanani
  father of ~: 7 Hilkiah
  preceder: 6 Isaiah
Jeremiah Johnson (1972 film)
  cast: Will Geer, Robert Redford
  director: Sydney Pollack
Jeremiah Symphony composer: 9 Bernstein
Jeremy: 5 Brett, Clyde, Irons, Licht, Piven 6 Miller 7 Bentham
  singing partner: 4 Chad
Jérez: 4 city, town
  former name: 4 Xera 5 Xeres
  locale: 6 Mexico 9 Zacatecas
Jergens: 5 Adele 6 lotion
  alternative: 4 Keri 5 Curel, Nivea 6 Aveeno 7 Eucerin, Pacquin 9 Lubriderm
Jeri: 4 Ryan
Jericho: 6 battle
  feature: 5 walls
  rose of ~: 4 posy 5 bloom, plant 6 flower 7 blossom
Jerilyn: 5 Britz
Jeritza: 5 Maria
jerk: 3 ass, cad, jar, jog, nit, oaf, sap, tic, tug 4 boor, bozo, buck, bump, dope, drip, dupe, fool, heel, jolt, lout, nerd, nurd, pull, shmo, snap, whip, yank, yo-yo 5 brute, creep, dance, dummy, dunce, dweeb, idiot, loser, lurch, ninny, pluck, quake, schmo, shake, spasm, start, twerp, twirp, twist 6 bounce, hurtle, jiggle, jounce, quiver, recoil, schmoe, shiver, snatch, thrash, thrust, turkey, twitch, wiggle, wrench, writhe 7 bumbler, dullard, jackass 8 dumbbell, preserve 9 ding-a-ling, harebrain, lay hold of, schlemiel 10 nincompoop, noodlehead
  away: 3 pry 4 tear 5 wrest 6 snatch, wrench 7 extract
  companion: 5 clean
  ender: 5 water
  forward: 4 jump 5 heave, lunge, lurch, pitch
  knee ~: 8 response
  out: 3 tug 4 pick, pull, yank 5 pluck, tweak 6 uproot 7 extract 9 extirpate
  up: 4 hike 5 boost, raise 7 elevate 8 increase
__ jerk: 4 knee, soda 5 ankle
__-jerker: 4 tear
jerkin: 4 coat, vest 6 jacket 7 doublet
Jerk, The (1979 film)
  cast: Steve Martin, Bernadette Peters
  director: Carl Reiner
jerky: 4 meat 5 bumpy 6 abrupt, fitful, uneven 7 fatuous 9 irregular, spasmodic 10 convulsive, nonuniform
  like beef ~: 5 chewy, cured, spicy
  motion: 3 bob
__-jerky: 5 herky
Jermaine: 7 Jackson
Jerne, Niels: 6 Danish 8 Nobelist
Jerome: 4 Kern 5 Geils, Hines, Karle, saint 6 Moross 7 Robbins, Weidman 8 Friedman
jerry __: 3 can
jerry-__: 5 build, built
Jerry: 4 Bock, Ford, Hall, Reed, Rees, Rice, Vale, Wald, West 5 Brown, Grote, Lewis, Lucas, Maren, mouse, Paris 6 Belson, Butler, Garcia, Herman, Houser, Leiber, Orbach, Siegel, Zucker 7 Buckner, Colonna, Falwell, Maguire, Mathers, Stiller, Van Dyke, Wallace 8 Seinfeld, Springer 9 Goldsmith, Tarkanian 10 Schatzberg
  Betty, to ~: 4 wife
  daughter: 5 Susan
  ex-partner: 4 Dean
  friend: 6 Elaine
  partner: 3 Ben
  Tom and ~ ingredient: 3 egg, rum 4 milk 5 sugar 6 brandy 10 baking soda
Jerry __ Lewis: 3 Lee
__ Jerry: 5 Mungo
jerry-built: 5 cheap, junky 6 flimsy, shoddy, unfirm 7 rickety, unsound 8 slipshod 10 ramshackle, unthorough
  structure: 3 hut 4 shed 5 shack 6 lean-to, shanty
Jerry Maguire (1996 film)
  cast: Tom Cruise, Cuba Gooding Jr., Kelly Preston, Renée Zellweger
  director: Cameron Crowe
jersey: 3 top 5 shirt 6 fabric 7 sweater 8 pullover
  fabric: 5 rayon 6 cotton
__ jersey: 5 Rugby
Jersey: 3 cow 4 bull, isle 6 bovine, cattle, island
  see also New Jersey
Jersey __: 4 City, pine 5 Giant 6 Bounce
Jersey __ Walcott: 3 Joe
__ Jersey: 3 New
Jersey Giant: 4 fowl 7 chicken
  relative: 6 Bantam, Brahma, Houdan, Sussex 7 Cornish, Dorking, Leghorn 8 Araucana, Langshan, Shanghai 9 Dominique, Orpington, Wyandotte
Jerusalem: 4 city, town 7 capital
  artichoke: 5 tuber
  hill: 4 Zion
  locale: 6 Israel
  town near ~: 3 Lod 4 Gaza 6 Bethel
Jerusalem __: 3 oak 4 date 5 cross, thorn 6 cherry 7 cricket
Jerusalem author: Selma Lagerlöf
Jerusalem Delivered: 4 epic, poem
  author: Torquato Tasso
Jerzy: 6 Neyman 8 Kosinski
Jess: 7 Willard
jessamine: 5 plant 6 flower
Jessamyn: 4 West
Jesse: 5 Helms, James, Lasky, Owens 6 Orosco, Powell 7 Jackson, Ventura 8 Bradford
  son of ~: 5 David, Eliab

Jesse (1980 song) artist: Carly Simon
Jesse James (1939 film)
cast: Henry Fonda, Tyrone Power
__ Jesse James: 5 Alias
Jessel, George: 2 MC 4 host 5 emcee
Jessi: 6 Colter
Jessica: 4 Alba, Biel 5 Lange, Tandy 6 Harper, Walter 7 Mitford, Simpson
__ Jessica Parker: 5 Sarah
Jessie: 4 Ames
Jessie __ Landis: 5 Royce
Jessye: 6 Norman
__ Jessy Raphael: 5 Sally
jest: 3 gag, kid, toy 4 gibe, jape, jibe, joke, josh, play, quip 5 caper, chaff, clown, crack, humor, laugh, prank, put on, sneer, spoof, sport, taunt, tease 6 banter, bon mot, japery 7 foolery, mockery 8 badinage, drollery, jocosity, nonsense, one-liner, raillery 9 crack wise, frivolity, kid around, wisecrack, witticism 10 crack jokes, joke around, pleasantry, rib-tickler, tomfoolery
in ~: 6 for fun
jester: 3 wag, wit 4 fool, mime, zany 5 clown, comic, cutup, joker, mimer 6 madcap 7 buffoon, pierrot 8 comedian, jokester 9 harlequin, prankster, Rigoletto
__ jester: 5 court
Jest 'Fore Christmas: 4 poem
author: Eugene Field
jesting: 3 fun 5 comic, droll, funny, humor, merry, sport, witty 6 banter, comedy, jocose, jocund, joking 7 comical, jocular, kidding, playful, roguish, waggish 8 badinage, humorous, laughing, raillery, spoofing, zaniness 9 facetious 10 frolicsome, rollicking
Jesuit: 9 clergyman 10 missionary
Jesus
brother of ~: 5 James, Joses, Judas, Matty, Simon 6 Joseph
mother of ~: 4 Mary
Jesús: 4 Alou
Jesus Christ Superstar: 7 musical
songwriter: 4 Rice 11 Lloyd Webber
Jesus to a Child (1996 song) artist: George Michael
jet: 3 MiG, SST 4 ebon, gush, inky, pour, spew, spue, zoom 5 black, color, ebony, plane, raven, sable, sooty, spirt, spout, spurt, surge, turbo 6 airbus, geyser, squirt, stream, travel 8 aircraft, airliner, airplane, Concorde, fountain, midnight 9 transport 10 pitch-black, shoot forth
ender: 3 lag 4 foil, pack, port 5 liner 7 fighter
home: 6 hangar
hop a ~: 3 fly
mil. ~ locale: 3 AFB
relative: 4 inky, onyx 5 ebony, raven, sable, sooty
route: 4 lane 6 airway 7 air lane
starter: 3 fan, ram 4 prop, twin 5 pulse, scram
trail: 4 wake
unit: 4 Mach
water ~: 5 spirt, spout, spurt 6 geyser, spritz, squirt 8 fountain
jet __: 3 gun, lag, set 4 boat, wash 5 motor, pilot, plane 6 engine, setter, stream 7 fighter
jet-__: 3 hop 5 black
__ jet: 3 gas 4 jump 5 jumbo
Jet: 2 Li 5 NFLer 10 footballer
rival: 3 Ram 4 Bear, Bill, Colt, Lion 5 Brown, Chief, Eagle, Giant, Niner, Raven, Saint, Texan, Titan 6 Bengal, Bronco, Cowboy, Falcon, Jaguar, Packer, Raider, Viking 7 Charger, Dolphin, Panther, Patriot, Redskin, Seahawk, Steeler 8 Cardinal 9 Buccaneer
Jet __: 3 Ski
__ Jet: 4 Lear
Jet (1974 song) artist: Paul McCartney
Jet Airliner (1977 song) artist: Steve Miller Band
jetbead: 5 shrub
relative: 4 rose, sloe 6 kerria, spirea 7 bramble, spiraea 8 hardhack, ninebark, photinia 9 firethorn, raspberry
jet-black: 4 dark 5 ebony 9 lightless, unlighted
Jet Blue: 7 airline
alternative: 5 Delta 6 United 8 American 9 Southwest 11 America West, Continental
jeté: 4 jump, leap 8 movement
__ jeté: 4 tour 5 grand
Jeter: 5 Derek 7 Michael
Jeter, Derek: 4 Yank 6 Yankee 9 shortstop
sport: 8 baseball
Jetfire: 3 car 4 auto, Olds 10 Oldsmobile
Jethro: 4 Tull 6 Bodine
cousin: 4 Elly 7 Elly May
son-in-law: 5 Moses
uncle: 3 Jed
__-jet printer: 3 ink
Jet Propulsion Lab org.: 4 NASA
Jets: 4 gang, team 6 eleven
foe: 6 Sharks
home: 7 New York
org.: 3 AFC, NFL
sport: 8 football
jetsam: 5 trash 6 debris 8 discards 17 throwaways. garbage
Boston Harbor ~: 3 tea
jet set: 5 elite, haves 6 fliers, flyers 7 in-crowd, society 8 well-to-do 9 beau monde 10 glitterati, haute monde, socialites, upper crust
city: 4 Nice 6 Cannes
need: 4 visa
jet-setter: 7 tourist, visitor 8 gadabout, traveler 9 passenger, sightseer 10 vacationer
jetski: 10 watercraft
Jetsons, The (sitcom)
high school: Orbit
voice cast: Mel Blanc (Mr. Spacely)
Daws Butler (Elroy Jetson)
Don Messick (Astro)
George O'Hanlon (George Jetson)
Penny Singleton (Jane Jetson)
Jean Vander Pyl (Rosie the Robot)
Janet Waldo (Judy Jetson)
Jetstar: 3 car 4 auto, Olds 10 Oldsmobile
jet stream: 4 wind
Jett: 4 Joan, Rink
Jetta: 2 VW 3 car 4 auto 10 Volkswagen
Jett and the Blackhearts, Joan
song: Crimson and Clover (1982)
I Hate Myself for Loving You (1988)
I Love Rock 'n Roll (1982)
jettison: 4 cede, drop, dump, hurl, junk, sell, shed 5 chuck, ditch, eject, expel, forgo, heave, scrap, yield 6 forego, give up, reject, unload 7 abandon, cast off, deep-six, discard, forfeit, forsake, lighten 8 forswear, get rid of, hand over, part with, throw out 9 cast aside, dispose of, foreswear, surrender, throw away 10 relinquish
jettisoned cargo: 5 lagan, ligan
jetty: 4 dock, pier, quay, slip 5 berth, wharf 6 harbor 7 harbour, landing 9 anchorage 10 breakwater
support: 6 gabion
jeu __: 7 d'esprit
jeu de __: 4 mots
jeune __: 5 fille 7 premier
Jeux d'eau composer: 5 Ravel
Jew: 9 Israelite
__ Jew: 6 Reform 8 Orthodox
jewel: 3 gem 4 rock, ruby 5 angel, bijou, honey, pearl, prize, stone, topaz 6 amulet, baguet, bangle, bauble 7 darling, diamond, emerald, trinket 8 baguette, gemstone, ladylove, ornament, sapphire, sparkler, treasure 9 solitaire 10 birthstone
ender: 4 fish, weed
thief: 6 iceman
jewel __: 3 box 4 case 5 block
__ jewel: 5 crown
Jewel: 5 Akens
song: Foolish Games (1997)
Hands (1998)
You Were Meant for Me (1996)
Jewel __ Nile, The: 5 of the
jeweler: 6 artist 8 engraver, lapidary 9 craftsman 10 gemologist, horologist, watchmaker
measure: 2 kt. 5 carat, karat
tool: 3 dop 5 loupe
jewelers' __: 5 putty, rouge
Jewell: 6 Isabel
Jewel of the East: 4 Bali
Jewel of the Nile, The (1985 film)
cast: Danny DeVito, Michael Douglas, Kathleen Turner
jewelry: 3 gem, ice, pin 4 band, gems, pins, ring 5 bands, beads, bijou, cameo, chain, charm, cross, crown, rings, stone, tiara 6 anklet, armlet, bangle, bauble, bijoux, broach, brooch, cameos, chains, charms, choker, diadem, finery, locket, tiaras, tiepin, tie tac 7 anklets, bangles, baubles, chokers, crosses, diamond, earring, lockets, pendant, tiepins, tie tack, tie tacs, trinket 8 bracelet, brooches, diamonds, earrings, frippery, gemstone, necklace, ornament, scarfpin, sparkler, stickpin, tie tacks, treasure, trinkets, wristlet 9 adornment, gemstones, lavaliere, solitaire, valuables
box: 6 casket
box opener: 4 hasp 5 catch, latch
chain: 5 Zales
fake: 5 glass, paste
fastener: 5 clasp
holder: 3 box 4 case 5 chest 6 coffer
material: 5 amber
place for a ~ clasp: 4 nape, neck
wrist ~: 5 chain 6 bangle
__ jewelry: 4 junk 7 costume
jewels: 4 gems 6 bijoux 9 valuables
deck with ~: 5 begem
set, as ~: 3 fix 5 embed, imbed, inlay
Jewels author: Danielle Steel
Jewels of Tessa Kent, The author: Judith Krantz
Jewel Song: 4 aria
Jewish: 3 Sem. 6 Hebrew, Judaic 7 Hasidic, Semitic 9 Israelite 10 Ashkenazic
bread: 6 hallah
cabala work: 5 zohar
campus ~ organization: 6 Hillel
ceremonial palm branch: 5 lulab, lulav
holiday: 5 Purim 8 Passover 9 Yom Kippur
holiday dinner: 5 seder
holiday eve: 4 ereb, erev
homeland: 4 Sion, Zion
like some ~ food: 6 kasher, kosher
month: 2 Av 4 Adar, Elul, Iyar 5 Iyyar, Nisan, Sivan, Tevet 6 Kislev, Nissan, Shevat, Tammuz, Tishri 7 Heshvan
mystic: 6 Essene
prayer: 5 shema 6 Hallel
robot of ~ folklore: 5 golem
school: 5 heder 6 cheder 7 yeshiva
sect member: 5 Hasid
seven-week period: 4 omer
snack: 5 knish
teacher: 5 rabbi, rebbe
temple: 4 shul 5 schul 9 synagogue
youth org.: 4 YMHA, YWHA
Jewish __: 3 rye
Jewison, Norman: 8 director
film: Agnes of God (1985)
... And Justice for All (1979)
The Cincinnati Kid (1965)
Fiddler on the Roof (1971)
F.I.S.T. (1978)
The Hurricane (1999)
In Country (1989)
In the Heat of the Night (1967)
Jesus Christ Superstar (1973)
Moonstruck (1987)
Only You (1994)
Other People's Money (1991)
Rollerball (1975)
Send Me No Flowers (1964)
A Soldier's Story (1984)
The Thomas Crown Affair (1968)
The Thrill of It All (1963)
Jew of Malta, The author: 7 Marlowe
jew's harp: 10 percussion
sound: 5 twang
Jezebel: 4 vamp 5 hussy
deity: 4 Baal
father of ~: 7 Ethbaal
hometown: 4 Tyre
husband: 4 Ahab
son of ~: 7 Ahaziah
Jezebel (1938 film)
cast: George Brent, Bette Davis, Henry Fonda
director: William Wyler
Jezebel singer: 5 Laine
JFK: 3 Dem. 4 pres.
abbr.: 3 arr., ETA, ETD
alternative: 3 LGA
data: 5 sched.
debater: 3 RMN
lander: 3 KLM, SST
locale: 3 NYC
predecessor: 3 DDE
regulator: 3 FAA
to RFK: 3 bro
UN ambassador: 3 AES
see also airport, Kennedy
JFK (1991 film)
cast: Edward Asner, Kevin Bacon, Kevin Costner, Tommy Lee Jones, Jack Lemmon, Walter Matthau, Laurie Metcalf, Gary Oldman, Joe Pesci, Jay O. Sanders, Sissy Spacek, Donald Sutherland
director: Oliver Stone
__ J. Fox: 7 Michael
J. Fred __: 5 Coots, Muggs
jg., lt.: 3 off.
Jhabvala, Ruth Prawer: 6 author, writer 7 British
work: Amrita
Jhelum: 5 river
locale: 7 Kashmir 8 Cashmere, Pakistan
JHS, part of: 3 sch. 4 high 6 junior, school
Jiang Qing husband: 3 Mao
Jiangsu city: 4 Wuxi 5 Wuhsi, Wusih
jiao, ten: 4 yuan
Jiaozhou: 3 bay
jib: 3 arm 4 sail 6 canvas 8 foresail
racing ~: 5 Genoa, jenny
support: 4 boom, mast, pole, post, spar 6 mizzen, timber
jib __: 4 boom 5 crane
__ jib: 3 cap 5 Genoa, inner, miter 6 flying

jibba: 4 coat 6 jacket
jibe: 2 go 3 fit 4 mesh 5 agree, crack, fit in, match, scoff, tally 6 concur, square 7 comport, conform, put-down 8 coincide, dovetail, hit it off 9 harmonize 10 correspond, go together
at: 4 gibe, jeer, mock, slam 5 cavil, scoff, scorn, smirk, sneer, taunt 6 deride 7 nitpick, put down, quibble 8 belittle, ridicule 9 deprecate, disparage, find fault 10 look down on
jicama: 3 veg. 4 root 9 vegetable
Jicarilla: 5 tribe 6 Indian 7 Amerind
Jidda: 4 city, port, town
city near ~: 5 Mecca
from ~: 5 Saudi
water: 6 Red Sea
Jif alternative: 6 Skippy 8 Peter Pan
jiff: 3 sec 5 trice 6 moment 7 instant
jiffy: 3 bit, sec 4 wink 5 flash, trice 6 breath, minute, moment, second 7 eyewink, instant 9 short time, twinkling 10 bat of an eye
in a ~: 3 PDQ 4 anon, ASAP, fast, soon 5 apace 6 presto 7 fleetly, hastily, quickly, rapidly, readily, swiftly 8 pell-mell, speedily 9 forthwith, hurriedly, instantly, like a shot, posthaste, right away
__ jiffy: 3 in a
Jiffy __: 3 Pop 4 Lube
jig: 3 bob 4 lure, ruse 5 dance, music
ender: 3 saw
ice-fishing ~: 5 tip up
sailor's ~: 8 hornpipe
jig __!, The: 4 is up
__ jig: 5 Irish
jigger: 3 tot 4 sail 5 glass 9 shot glass 10 manipulate
jigger __: 4 flea
jiggerful: 3 nip 5 drink, snort
jiggery-__: 6 pokery
jigging, fish by: 3 dib
jiggle: 3 bob, jar, jog 4 jerk, rock, toss 5 nudge, shake 6 bobble, bounce, jounce, rattle, shimmy, teeter, twitch, wiggle 7 agitate, wriggle
jiggly: 5 shaky 6 uneven, wobbly 7 rickety 8 unstable, unsteady 9 teetering 10 precarious, unbalanced
Jiggs' wife: 6 Maggie
__ Jiggy Wit It: 6 Gettin
Jig of Forslin, The author: Conrad Aiken
jigsaw: 4 tool 6 puzzle
part: 5 piece 8 fragment
jihad: 3 war 6 combat, strife 8 conflict
Jihan: 5 Sadat
Jilin: 4 city, town
locale: 5 China
jill: 2 jo 3 pet 4 baby, dear, love 5 amour, angel, chéri, cooky, cutey, cutie, deary, ducky, flame, honey, leman, lover, lovey, novia, sugar, sweet 6 cookie, dautie, dearie, steady, sweets 7 beloved, dearest, dear one, pigsney, schatzi, squeeze, sweetie, tootsie 8 chou-chou, cutie pie, dowsabel, dulcinea, ladylove, lovebird, macushla, paramour, precious, snookums, sugar pie, sweetums, truelove 9 bonne amie, dreamboat, inamorata, petit chou, valentine 10 girlfriend, heartthrob, honeybunch, mavourneen, sweetheart, sweetie pie, turtledove
Jill: 6 St. John, Whelan 7 Ireland 8 Goodacre 9 Clayburgh 10 Eikenberry
Jillette: 4 Penn
Jillian: 3 Ann
Jillie: 4 Mack
jillions: 4 a lot, many, scad 6 oodles
jilt: 4 dump 5 ditch, leave, spurn 6 desert, reject 7 abandon, discard, forsake, stand up 8 forswear, run out on 9 cast aside, foreswear, leave flat, skip out on, throw over
jim-__: 4 jams 5 dandy
Jim: 4 Dale, Fixx, Kaat, Lowe, Otto, Page, Ryun 5 Bowie, Brown, Croce, Davis, Kelly, Lange, McKay, Ringo, Seals 6 Backus, Bakker, Bishop, Bouton, Carrey, Henson, Hutton, Jordan, Langer, Lehrer, Nabors, Palmer, Parker, Reeves, Taylor, Thorpe, Varney 7 Bunning, Courier, Lonborg, McMahon, Messina, Metzler 8 Abrahams, Braddock, Caviezel, Garrison, Jarmusch, Morrison, Plunkett, Stafford 9 Broadbent, Weatherly
__ Jim: 4 Lord, Slim 5 Lucky 7 Diamond
__ Jima: 3 Iwo
__ Jim Brady: 7 Diamond
jim-dandy: 3 def, rad 4 aces, A-one, boss, braw, cool, dece, fine, gear, keen, neat, nice, phat, tuff 5 ducky, grand, great, marvy, neato, nobby, prime, slick, super, swell 6 bang on, bang-up, bonzer, bosker, choice, divine, dreamy, far-out, gnarly, groovy, lovely, peachy, slap-up, spot on, superb, terrif, tiptop, unreal, whizzo, wicked 7 amazing, awesome, capital, corking, perfect, ripping, skookum, stellar, sublime 8 dazzling, especial, eximious, fabulous, five-star, four-star, frabjous, glorious, heavenly, slam-bang, smashing, splendid, standout, sterling, stickout, superior, terrific, top-level, topnotch, very good, wondrous 9 bodacious, Endsville, excellent, exemplary, exquisite, first-rate, high-grade, hunky-dory, marvelous, sollicker, top-flight, wonderful 10 first-class, hotsy-totsy, out of sight, peachy-keen, phenomenal, remarkable, stupendous, super-duper
Jiménez: 4 city, Juan, town
locale: 6 Mexico 9 Chihuahua
Jimenez, Jose: Bill Dana
Jiménez, Juan: 4 poet 7 Spanish 8 Nobelist
Jimi: 7 Hendrix
jiminy: 3 gee, wow 4 gosh
Jiminy __: 7 Cricket
jimjams: 3 DTs 6 creeps
Jimmie: 4 Dodd, Foxx 5 Noone 6 Walker 7 Rodgers
jimmy: 3 pry 4 open 5 force, lever 7 crowbar, pry open 9 force open
card used to ~ spring locks: 4 loid
Jimmy: 3 Key, SUV 4 Baio, Dean, Page, Reed, Soul, Webb 5 Arias, Ellis, Hatlo, Hoffa, Jones, Lydon, Olsen, Smits 6 Carter, Castor, Dorsey, Fidler, Hughes, McHugh, Ruffin 7 Blanton, Breslin, Buffett, Charles, Clanton, Connors, Demaret, Durante, Rushing 8 McNichol, Piersall, Swaggart 10 McCracklin
daughter: 3 Amy
mfr.: 3 GMC
Rosalyn, to ~: 4 wife
successor: 3 Ron
Jimmy Carter Library site: 7 Atlanta
Jimmy Mack (1967 song) artist: Martha & the Vandellas
Jimmy the __: 5 Greek
jimson weed: 6 datura
Jim Thorpe - All-American (1951 film)
cast: Charles Bickford, Steve Cochran, Burt Lancaster
director: Michael Curtiz
Jinan: 4 city, town
locale: 5 China
jingle: 4 ding, gong, ring, tune 5 clang, clink, ditty, verse 6 slogan, tinkle
give a ~: 4 call, dial 5 phone 6 ring up 9 telephone, touch base
writer: 5 adman
jingle __: 4 bell 5 shell
Jingle __: 5 Bells 6 Jangle
Jingle __ Rock: 4 Bell
Jingle Bells: 4 Noel 5 carol
preposition: 3 o'er
vehicle: 6 sleigh
jingles
where ~ are heard: 3 ads
jingo: 5 bigot 7 patriot 10 chauvinist
jingoism: 10 chauvinism, flag-waving, narrowness, patriotism
jingoistic: 7 hostile, warlike 8 militant 9 bellicose, combative 10 aggressive
Jinhua: 3 pig 5 swine
Jinja: 4 city, town
locale: 6 Uganda
jink: 4 spin, turn 5 pivot, twist, whirl 6 gyrate, rotate, swivel 9 pirouette
jinks, high: 5 caper, prank, spree 7 fooling, revelry 8 mischief 9 vandalism
jinni: 5 demon, genie 6 daemon, daimon
jinx: 3 hex 5 curse, Jonah, spell 6 hoodoo, whammy 7 bad luck, bedevil, bewitch, bugaboo, evil eye, sorcery
Jinx: 10 Falkenburg
jinxed: 7 hapless, unblest, unlucky 8 ill-fated, luckless 9 ill-omened, unblessed, unfavored 10 ill-starred
Jinx, Mr.: 3 cat 4 toon
jipijapa: 3 hat 5 plant
Jiquilpan: 4 city, town
locale: 6 Mexico 9 Michoacán
Jirásek, Alois: 5 Czech 6 author, writer 10 playwright
jird: 6 animal, mammal, rodent
relative: 3 rat 4 cavy, degu, paca, vole 5 coypu, gundi, mouse, xerus 6 agouti, beaver, gerbil, gopher, jerboa, marmot, murine 7 hamster, lemming, muskrat, visacha 8 chipmunk, cricetid, dormouse, squirrel, tuco-tuco 9 chickaree, groundhog, guinea pig, porcupine, woodchuck 10 chinchilla, prairie dog
'J' Is for Judgment author: Sue Grafton
jitney: 3 bus 7 minibus, shuttle
relative: 3 cab 4 hack, taxi 7 taxicab
jitter: 5 quake, shake 6 fidget, quiver, shiver 7 shudder, tremble
jitterbug: 4 jive 5 dance
relative: 5 lindy
jitterbugger: 3 cat 6 hepcat
jitters: 4 fear 6 nerves, shakes 7 anxiety, fidgets, shivers, tension, willies 9 tightness 10 inquietude, uneasiness
jittery: 4 edgy 5 antsy, itchy, jumpy, nervy, shaky, tense, upset 6 jangly, on edge, uneasy 7 anxious, fearful, fidgety, keyed up, nervous, panicky, restive, spooked, uptight 8 agitated, cowardly, fluttery, restless, skittish, troubled 9 concerned, excitable, ill at ease, quivering, trembling, tremulous 10 frightened, high-strung
not ~: 4 calm, cool, even 5 quiet, sober, staid, tepid 6 placid, poised, remote, sedate, serene, steady, stolid 7 assured, offhand, relaxed, stoical 8 composed, detached, reserved, tranquil 9 apathetic, collected, easygoing, impassive, nerveless, unexcited, unruffled 10 nonchalant, phlegmatic, restrained, unagitated, untroubled
Jiutepec: 4 city, town
locale: 6 Mexico 7 Morelos
Jivaro: 6 Indian 7 Amerind 8 language
jive: 3 gas, kid, rot 4 blah, bosh, bull, bunk, fool, guff, jazz, josh, mock, pooh, sham, talk, tosh 5 bilge, bluff, dance, fudge, guile, hokum, hooey, idiom, music, prate, stuff, tease, trash, tripe 6 banter, bunkum, bushwa, delude, drivel, dupery, footle, gabble, gammon, gibber, havers, hot air, humbug, jabber, jargon, kibosh, patter, piffle 7 baloney, blarney, blather, blether, boloney, bushwah, deceive, defraud, eyewash, flannel, flubdub, fustian, garbage, hogwash, inanity, malarky, mislead, rubbish, twaddle 8 buncombe, claptrap, falderal, falderol, fast talk, filmflam, flimflam, flummery, folderal, folderol, malarkey, nonsense, pettifog, ridicule, slipslop, tommyrot, trumpery 9 banana oil, deception, disinform, gibberish, goofiness, jitterbug, kid around, kidstakes, make fun of, moonshine, poppycock, rigmarole, trash talk 10 applesauce, balderdash, bilge water, codswallop, double-talk, flapdoodle, galimatias, Jabberwock, mumbo jumbo, rigamarole, taradiddle
talk: 5 argot, lingo, slang 6 patois 8 parlance 10 vernacular
Jive __: 4 Five 6 Talkin'
jiver: 3 cat 6 hepcat
Jive Talkin' (1975 song) artist: Bee Gees
J.K.: 7 Rowling
JKL on a phone: 4 five
jo: 3 pet 4 baby, dear, jill, love 5 amour, angel, chéri, cooky, cutey, cutie, deary, ducky, flame, honey, leman, lover, lovey, novia, novio, sugar, sweet 6 bon ami, chérie, cookie, dautie, dearie, steady, sweets 7 beloved, dearest, dear one, pigsney, schatzi, squeeze, sweetie, tootsie 8 chouchou, cutie pie, dowsabel, dulcinea, ladylove, lovebird, macushla, paramour, precious, snookums, sugar pie, sweetums, truelove 9 bonne amie, boyfriend, dreamboat, inamorata, inamorato, petit chou, valentine 10 girlfriend, heartthrob, honeybunch, mavourneen, sweetheart, sweetie pie, turtledove
Jo: 5 March 8 Davidson, Stafford, Van Fleet 9 Mielziner
sister: 3 Amy, Meg 4 Beth
Jo __ Pflug: 3 Ann
Jo __ Worley: 4 Anne
__-Jo: 3 Flo
Joachim, Joseph: 9 Hungarian, violinist
Joad: 2 Al 3 Tom 4 Noah 6 Ruthie
Joan: 4 Baez, Chen, Jett, Miró 5 Allen, Davis, Evans, Weber 6 Benoit, Cusack, Didion, Leslie, Lunden, Rivers, Van Ark 7 Bennett, Collins, Freeman, Hackett, Osborne 8 Blackman, Blondell, Crawford, Fontaine 9 Caulfield, Greenwood, Plowright, Severance 10 Sutherland
in Italian: 8 Giovanna
Joan __ Payson: 7 Whitney
__ Joan: 5 Saint
__ Joan Hart: 7 Melissa
Joanie: 6 Somers
she played ~: 4 Erin
Jo Ann: 5 Pflug
Joanna: 4 font 5 Going, Kerns 6 Barnes, Lumley, Pacula, Pettet 7 Cassidy 8 typeface
Joanna (1983 song) artist: Kool and the Gang
Joanne: 3 Dru 7 Whalley 8 Woodward
JoAnne: 6 Carner

Jo Anne: 6 Worley
Joan of Arc: 5 saint
Joan of Lorraine author: 8 Anderson
Joanou: 4 Phil
Joaquin: 6 Miller 7 Phoenix
__ Joaquin Valley: 3 San
job: 2 do 3 act, aim, bag, bit, biz, gig, rut 4 case, deed, duty, feat, game, goal, keep, line, onus, part, post, role, slot, spot, task, toil, tour, work 5 berth, caper, chore, craft, crime, doing, drill, field, forte, fraud, grind, heist, labor, level, means, niche, place, quest, realm, score, shift, skill, stint, sweat, theft, thing, trade 6 action, affair, billet, career, charge, domain, drudge, effort, errand, holdup, income, living, matter, métier, milieu, office, outfit, racket, scheme, snatch, sphere, status, tenure 7 booking, break-in, calling, company, concern, con game, gesture, larceny, measure, mission, program, project, purpose, pursuit, rat race, robbery, routine, service, station, stickup, support, swindle, venture 8 activity, benefice, burglary, business, capacity, contract, covenant, dealings, drudgery, endeavor, exercise, exertion, function, homework, industry, lifework, measures, poaching, position, practice, province, thievery, vocation 9 adventure, bailiwick, condition, expertise, gruntwork, happening, life's work, objective, operation, procedure, salt mines, servitude, situation, specialty, workplace 10 assignment, commission, commitment, daily grind, department, discipline, employment, engagement, enterprise, initiative, line of work, livelihood, nine-to-five, obligation, occupation, plundering, profession, sustenance
  ender: 6 holder, seeker, sharer
  figuratively: 3 hat
  second story ~: 5 heist, theft
job __: 3 lot 4 bank, case, shop, work 5 order, stick 6 action, market, seeker, setter, ticket 7 costing, printer
job-__: 3 hop 4 hunt 6 hunter 7 hunting, sharing
__ job: 3 axe, bag, con, day, odd 4 desk, lube, nose, snow 5 cushy, on the 6 inside 7 hatchet
Job
  follower: 6 Psalms
  friend of ~: 7 Eliphaz
  lot: 3 woe 9 suffering
  preceder: 6 Esther
Job __: 5 Corps
__ Job: 4 Get a
job-application datum (abbr.): 3 SSN
jobber: 4 hand, help 5 agent 6 broker, dealer, worker 7 laborer, migrant 8 handyman, merchant, salesman, supplier 9 consignor, dispenser, hired hand, middleman 10 freelancer, wholesaler
jobbery: 3 cut 4 loot, swag 5 booty, graft, gravy, honey 6 boodle, grease, payoff, payola, racket, velvet 7 plunder, rake-off 8 kickback, pickings, venality 9 hush money, shakedown 10 corruption
JoBeth: 8 Williams
jobholder: 4 hand 6 worker 7 employe, laborer, staffer 8 employee 9 hired hand 10 wage earner
job-hunter: 6 seeker 7 hopeful 8 aspirant, prospect 9 applicant, candidate, contender 10 competitor, handshaker
  bio: 4 vita 6 resume
jobless: 4 idle 9 out of work 10 unemployed
__ job on: 3 do a
Jobs: 5 Steve 6 Steven
  company: 5 Apple
job safety org.: 4 OSHA
__-Jobson: 6 Hobson
job-training org.: 4 CETA
Jobyna: 7 Ralston
Jocasta
  brother of ~: 5 Creon
  daughter of ~: 6 Ismene 8 Antigone
  husband of ~: 5 Laius 7 Oedipus
  son of ~: 7 Oedipus 8 Eteocles 9 Polynices
Jochebed, son of: 5 Aaron, Moses
jock: 6 player 7 athlete 10 enthusiast
Jock: 5 Ewing 7 Mahoney
jockey: 3 Day 4 move, ride 5 Baeza, drive, guide, Krone, pilot, racer, rider, Sande, steer 6 Arcaro, direct, driver, handle, Pat Day, Pincay, strive 7 athlete, Cauthen, Cordero, finesse, Hartack 8 horseman, maneuver, navigate, scramble, Turcotte 9 Earl Sande, negotiate, Shoemaker 10 Julie Krone, manipulate
  assistance for a ~: 5 boost, leg up
  bench ~: 3 sub 5 scrub
  disc ~: 6 deejay 9 announcer
  for position: 3 pit, vie 5 rival 7 compete, contend 9 challenge
  item: 4 crop, rein, tack
jockey __: 3 box, cap 4 club
__ jockey: 4 desk, disc, disk 5 bench, video
Jockeys: 6 boxers, briefs, shorts 9 underwear
  rival: 4 BVDs 5 Hanes
Jockeys in the Rain painter: 5 Degas
jocko: 5 chimp 10 chimpanzee
  relative: 3 ape 4 saki, titi 5 drill, lemur, loris, magot, orang, potto, shrew 6 aye-aye, baboon, Bandar, galago, gelada, gibbon, grivet, guenon, howler, langur, macaco, monkey, rhesus, uakari, vervet 7 colobus, gorilla, guereza, hoolock, macaque, sapajou, siamang, tamarin, tarsier 8 bush baby, capuchin, mandrill, mangabey, marmoset, talapoin 9 orangutan 10 Barbary ape, orangutang
Jocko: 6 Conlan
jocose: 3 gay 4 camp, joky 5 comic, droll, flaky, funny, happy, jokey, jolly, merry, silly, witty 6 blithe, flakey, joking, jovial 7 amusing, comical, gleeful, jesting, joshing, playful, waggish 8 cheerful, farcical, humorous, prankish, roughish, sportive 9 facetious, laughable, ludicrous, whimsical 10 frolicsome
jocosity: 3 fun, wit 4 gags, glee 5 humor, jests, mirth 6 antics, banter, levity, whimsy 7 foolery, kidding, waggery 8 badinage, clowning, drollery, hilarity, raillery 9 flippancy, merriment 10 buffoonery, tomfoolery, wisecracks
jocu: 4 fish
jocular: 3 gay 4 camp, joky 5 comic, droll, flaky, funny, happy, jokey, jolly, merry, silly, witty 6 blithe, flakey, joking, jovial 7 amusing, comical, gleeful, jesting, joshing, playful, waggish 8 cheerful, farcical, humorous, prankish, roughish, sportive 9 facetious, laughable, ludicrous, whimsical 10 frolicsome
  sounds: 4 ha-ha
  suffix: 4 aroo, eroo
jocularity: 3 fun, wit 4 gags, glee 5 cheer, humor, jests, mirth 6 antics, banter, gaiety, gayety, levity, whimsy 7 delight, foolery, jollity, kidding, waggery 8 badinage, buoyance, buoyancy, clowning, drollery, gladness, hilarity, laughter, pleasure, raillery, sunshine 9 flippancy, happiness, joviality, merriment 10 buffoonery, tomfoolery, wisecracks
jocund: 3 gay 4 camp, joky 5 comic, droll, flaky, funny, happy, jokey, jolly, merry, silly, witty 6 blithe, cheery, flakey, genial, joking, jovial, lively 7 amusing, comical, festive, gleeful, jesting, joshing, playful, waggish 8 cheerful, farcical, humorous, prankish, roughish, sportive 9 convivial, facetious, laughable, ludicrous, whimsical 10 frolicsome
jocundity: 3 fun, wit 4 gags, glee 5 cheer, humor, jests, mirth 6 antics, banter, gaiety, gayety, levity, whimsy 7 delight, foolery, jollity, kidding, waggery 8 badinage, buoyance, buoyancy, clowning, drollery, gladness, hilarity, laughter, pleasure, raillery, sunshine 9 flippancy, happiness, joviality, merriment 10 buffoonery, tomfoolery, wisecracks
__ Jo Dean: 5 Sammy
Jodhpur: 4 city, town
  locale: 5 India
jodhpurs: 5 boots, pants, shoes 8 breeches, footwear, knickers, trousers
Jodie: 6 Foster
Jodrell __ Observatory: 4 Bank
Jody: 6 Watley 8 Reynolds, Williams
joe: 4 java 5 mocha 6 coffee, jamoke 8 beverage
  joltless ~: 5 decaf, Sanka
  like a sloppy ~: 5 spicy 6 spicey
  relative: 5 latte
joe-__ weed: 3 pye
Joe: 3 Ely, May, Tex 4 Blow, Camp, Hill 5 Clark, Dante, Flynn, Jones, Lando, Louis, Orton, Penny, Perry, Pesci, Simon, South, Torre, Walsh 6 Cocker, Cronin, Doakes, Dowell, Friday, Greene, Morgan, Morton, Namath, Niekro, Sewell 7 Frazier, Jackson, Medwick, Montana, Palooka, Paterno, Piscopo, Schmidt, Shuster 8 DiMaggio, Johnston, Mantegna, McCarthy, McIntyre, Williams 9 Berlinger, Eszterhas, Garagiola, Henderson, McGinnity, Regalbuto 10 Campanella, Cartwright, Pantoliano
Joe __: 4 Blow 6 Doakes, Miller, Public 7 College, Six-pack
Joe __ Baker: 3 Don
__ Joe: 4 good, Holy, Poor 6 little, sloppy
__ Joe Black: 4 Meet
__ Joe Cartwright: 6 Little
Joe E. __: 4 Ross 5 Brown
__ Joe Greene: 4 Mean
Joel: 4 Coen, Grey 5 Billy, Zwick 6 Barlow, McCrea 8 Spingarn 10 Schumacher
  follower: 4 Amos
  preceder: 5 Hosea
Joel, Billy
  song: Allentown (1982)
    Big Shot (1979)
    Don't Ask Me Why (1980)
    Honesty (1979)
    I Go to Extremes (1990)
    An Innocent Man (1984)
    It's Still Rock and Roll to Me (1980)
    Just the Way You Are (1977)
    The Longest Time (1984)
    A Matter of Trust (1986)
    Modern Woman (1986)
    Movin' Out (1978)
    My Life (1978)
    Only the Good Die Young (1978)
    Piano Man (1974)
    The River of Dreams (1993)
    She's Always a Woman (1978)
    She's Got a Way (1981)
    Tell Her About It (1983)
    Uptown Girl (1983)
    We Didn't Start the Fire (1989)
    You May Be Right (1980)
    You're Only Human (1985)
  spouse: Christie Brinkley
Joel Mc__: 4 Crea
__ Joel Osment: 5 Haley
Joely: 6 Fisher 10 Richardson
__ Joe McDonald: 7 Country
Joe Miller offering: 4 joke 8 joke book
joe-pye: 4 weed
__ Joe's: 4 Papa 5 Eat at 6 Sloppy
Joe Somebody (2001 film)
  cast: Tim Allen, Kelly Lynch
__ Joe Turner: 3 Big
Joe Versus the Volcano (1990 film)
  cast: Lloyd Bridges, Tom Hanks, Meg Ryan, Robert Stack
__ Joe Walcott: 6 Jersey
joey: 3 'roo 5 money 6 animal 8 kangaroo
  spot: 5 pouch
Joey: 3 Dee 5 Adams 6 Bishop, Lauren, Powers 8 Lawrence, McIntyre 10 Heatherton
__ Joey: 3 Pal
__ Joe Young: 6 Mighty
Joffe: 6 Roland
Joffrey: 6 Robert
jog: 3 run 4 bend, bump, gait, jerk, lope, pace, prod, push, stir, trot, turn 5 nudge, press, shake 6 arouse, bounce, canter, jiggle, jostle, jounce, justle, prompt, remind, spring 7 agitate, refresh, work out 8 activate, exercise 9 stimulate 10 incitement
jog __: 4 trot
jogger: 4 shoe 6 runner 7 sneaker
  brand: 4 Avia, Nike 6 Adidas, Reebok
  memory ~: 4 list, note 8 reminder
  wear: 6 sweats, T-shirt
  woe: 4 ache 5 cramp
jogging __: 4 shoe, suit 5 pants
joggle: 3 bob 4 toss 5 shake 6 bobble, bounce, jostle, jounce, juggle, justle
Johan: 5 Bojer 8 Runeberg 10 Falkberget
Johann: 6 Fichte, Goethe 7 Strauss 10 Pestalozzi
  in English: 4 John
Johann __ Bach: 9 Sebastian
Johanna: 5 Spyri
johannes: 5 money
Johannes: 5 Stark 6 Brahms, Jensen, Kepler 7 Eckhart, Fibiger 9 Gutenberg
  in English: 4 John
Johannesburg: 4 city, town
  see also South Africa
Johansen: 5 David
john: 2 WC 3 can, lav, loo 5 privy 6 lounge, toilet 7 latrine 8 bathroom, lavatory, outhouse, rest room 10 powder room
  starter: 4 demi
__-john: 5 cheap
John: 3 Doe, Dye, Gay, Hay, Jay, Pym, Rae, Ray, Woo 4 Agar, Amos, Beck, Cage, Dahl, Dall, Daly, Dean, Drew, Fenn, Ford, Glen, Hume, Hurt, Kerr, Knox, Lahr, Lone, Lund, Mott, Muir, Nash, Parr, Paul, pope, Reed, Ross, Shea, Tesh, Vane, Venn, Wain 5 Adams, Alden, Arden, Astin, Barth, Boles, Bosco, Brahm, Brown, Byner, Cabot, Candy, Clare, Davys, Deere, Derek, Dewey, Donne, Elton, Elway, Fiske, Fitch, Fleck, Gavin, Glenn, Gower, Gregg, Guare, Heard, Hicks, Hough, Jakes, James, Keats, Kerry,

Korty, Litel, Locke, Loder, Lynch, Major, Marin, McKay, McVie, Megna, Mills, Nance, Oates, O'Hara, Payne, Pople, Prine, Raitt, Saxon, Sloan, Smith, Synge, Tommy, Tyler, Waite, Wayne **6** Badham, Banner, Braine, Buchan, Bunyan, Calvin, Carson, Carver, Cazale, Ciardi, Cleese, Cullum, Cusack, Dalton, Denver, Dryden, Duigan, Eccles, Eckert, Enders, Evelyn, Farrow, Fowles, Franco, Glover, Gorrie, Graunt, Harlan, Hawkes, Hersey, Hodiak, Hughes, Huston, Irving, Kander, Karlen, Landis, Larson, Lennon, Lupton, Madden, Mayall, McAdam, McCrae, McGraw, Milius, Milton, Musker, Napier, Olerud, Pankow, Ritter, Robert, Ruskin, Sayles, Schuck, Stamos, Strutt, Sutter, Sutton, Torrey, Turner, Updike, Vernon, Walker, Warner, Waters, Wesley, Wooden **7** Ashbery, Bardeen, Belushi, Boorman, Bubbles, Chapman, Cheever, Cleland, Fiedler, Fogerty, Gardner, Gielgud, Gilbert, Goodman, Grisham, Gunther, Hancock, Harvard, Hawkins, Heywood, Ireland, Kendrew, Knowles, Le Carre, Lithgow, Macleod, Mahoney, Marston, McEnroe, Millais, Montagu, Munonye, Newbery, Newlove, Osborne, Patrick, Polanyi, pontiff, Russell, Skelton, Spencer, Stewart, Sturges, Sulston, Tyndall, Vianney, Webster, Whiting, Wyndham **8** Bartlett, Berryman, Betjeman, Boulting, Burgoyne, Cafferty, Coltrane, Crawford, Cromwell, Davidson, DeForest, DeLorean, Forsythe, Franklin, Garfield, Halliday, Hamilton, Harsanyi, Havlicek, Herschel, Houseman, Marshall, McIntire, McMartin, Newcombe, Northrop, Pershing, Phillips, Randolph, Rayleigh, Ringling, Roebling, Stockton, Suckling, Travolta, Turturro, Williams, Winthrop, Wycliffe, Zacherle **9** Barrymore, Burroughs, Carpenter, Carradine, Cleveland, Cockcroft, Constable, Cornforth, Dillinger, Harington, Hillerman, Macdonald, Malkovich, Masefield, McTiernan, Pemberton, Schneider, Sebastian, Singleton, Steinbeck **10** Barbirolli, Cassavetes, Chancellor, Chrysostom, Ehrlichman, Entwhistle, Galsworthy, Guillermin, Schrieffer, Stallworth
  follower: 4 Acts, Jude
  in French: 4 Jean
  in German: 4 Hans **6** Johann **8** Johannes
  in Irish: 4 Sean **5** Shane
  in Italian: 4 Gino **8** Giovanni
  in Russian: 4 Ivan
  in Scottish: 3 Ian **4** Iain
  in Spanish: 4 Juan
  in Welsh: 4 Evan
  preceder: 4 Luke **5** Peter
  Q. Public: 6 people
John __: 4 Bull, Dory **5** Henry, of God, Paul I **6** Paul II **7** Boyd Orr
John __ Adams: 6 Quincy
John __ Astor: 5 Jacob
John __ Audubon: 5 James
John __ Body: 6 Brown's
John __ Booth: 6 Wilkes
John __ Carr: 7 Dickson
John __ Coley: 4 Ford
John __ Copley: 9 Singleton
John __ Dulles: 6 Foster
John __ Garner: 5 Nance
John __ Hooker: 3 Lee
John __ I: 4 Paul
John __ II: 4 Paul
John __ Jones: 4 Paul
John __ Kellogg: 6 Harvey
John __ Keynes: 7 Maynard
John __ Law: 7 Phillip
John __ Lennon: 3 Ono
John __ Mellencamp: 6 Cougar
John __ Mill: 6 Stuart
John __ Neumann: 3 von
John __ Newman: 5 Henry
John __ Orr: 4 Boyd
John __ Passos: 3 Dos
John __ Sargent: 6 Singer
John __ Scotus: 4 Duns
John __ Sousa: 6 Philip
John __ Swayze: 7 Cameron
John __ Walton: 3 Boy
John __ Whittier: 9 Greenleaf
__ John: 3 Odd **4** King **6** Honest, Little **7** Brother, hopping, Prester
John Anderson My Jo: 4 poem
  author: Robert Burns
John and Yoko son: 4 Sean
Johnathon: 7 Schaech
__ John B: 5 Sloop
John Barleycorn: 4 poem
  author: Jack London
John Boyd __: 3 Orr
John Brown's Body author: 5 Benet
John Bull's Other Island author: George Bernard Shaw
John C. __: 6 Reilly **7** Calhoun, Frémont **8** McGinley
John Cameron __: 6 Swayze
John Charles __: 7 Fremont
John Cougar __: 10 Mellencamp
John D. __: 9 MacDonald
John de __: 6 Lancie
John Dickson __: 4 Carr
John Doe: 9 anonymous
__ John Doe: 4 Meet
John Dory: 4 fish
John Dos __: 6 Passos
John, Elton: 3 Sir
  collaborator: Taupin, Rice, Dee
  song: Bennie and the Jets (1974)
    Candle in the Wind (1987)
    Can You Feel the Love Tonight (1994)
    Crocodile Rock (1972)
    Daniel (1973)
    Don't Go Breaking My Heart (1976)
    Don't Let the Sun Go... (1974)
    Goodbye Yellow Brick Road (1973)
    Honky Cat (1972)
    I Don't Wanna Go on... (1988)
    I Guess That's Why... (1983)
    Island Girl (1975)
    Little Jeannie (1980)
    Lucy in the Sky With Diamonds (1974)
    Mama Can't Buy You Love (1979)
    Nikita (1986)
    The One (1992)
    Philadelphia Freedom (1975)
    Rocket Man (1972)
    Sad Songs (1984)
    Someone Saved My Life... (1975)
    Sorry Seems to Be... (1976)
    That's What Friends Are for (1985)
    Your Song (1970)
John F. __: 7 Kennedy
John Ford __: 5 Coley
John Foster __: 6 Dulles
John G. __: 8 Avildsen
John Gabriel Borkman author: 5 Ibsen
John Greenleaf __: 8 Whittier
John Hancock: 9 signature
  put one's ~ on: 3 ink **4** sign **7** endorse **9** formalize
John Hancock Building architect: 3 Pei
John Hanning __: 5 Speke
John Harvey __: 7 Kellogg
John Henry: 9 signature
  put one's ~ on: 3 ink **4** sign **7** endorse **9** formalize
John Henry __: 6 Newman
John Herschel __: 5 Glenn
John Jacob __: 5 Astor
John James __: 7 Audubon
John Kennedy __: 5 Toole
John Le __: 5 Carré
John Lee __: 6 Hooker
__ John Malkovich: 5 Being
John Maynard __: 6 Keynes
John Mc__: 5 Enroe
__ John, M.D.: 7 Trapper
John Nance __: 6 Garner
Johnnie: 3 Ray **6** Taylor **8** Whitaker
Johnny: 3 Lee **4** Cash, Depp, Gill, Hart, Kemp, Mize, Nash, Otis **5** Bench, Burke, Evers, Green, Pesky **6** Carson, Horton, Mandel, Mathis, Mercer, Miller, Rivers, Rotten, Torrio, Unitas, Winter **7** Bristol, Desmond, Maestro, Preston **8** Burnette, Crawford, Paycheck **9** Appleseed, Sheffield, Tillotson
  bandleader for ~: 3 Doc
  in Italian: 6 Gianni
  in Russian: 5 Vanya
Johnny __: 3 Reb **4** Cool **5** Angel, Eager, Suede **6** Apollo, collar, Guitar **7** Belinda, Holiday, Tremain
Johnny __ Meer: 6 Vander
Johnny __ Note: 3 One
Johnny-__-lately: 4 come
Johnny-__-spot: 5 on-the
Johnny-__-up: 4 jump
__ Johnny!: 5 Here's
Johnny Angel (1945 film)
  cast: Signe Hasso, George Raft, Claire Trevor
Johnny Angel (1962 song) artist: Shelley Fabares
Johnny Apollo (1940 film)
  cast: Dorothy Lamour, Tyrone Power
  director: Henry Hathaway
Johnny B. __: 5 Goode
Johnny Belinda (1948 film)
  cast: Lew Ayres, Charles Bickford, Agnes Moorehead, Jane Wyman
  director: Jean Negulesco
Johnny B. Goode (1958 song) artist: Chuck Berry
johnnycake: 4 pone **5** bread
Johnny-come-lately: 7 upstart **8** new-comer **9** arriviste
__ Johnny Comes Marching Home: 4 When
Johnny Cool (1963 film)
  cast: Sammy Davis Jr., Elizabeth Montgomery
Johnny Eager (1941 film)
  cast: Robert Taylor, Lana Turner
  director: Mervyn LeRoy
Johnny Guitar (1954 film)
  cast: Joan Crawford, Sterling Hayden
  director: Nicholas Ray
Johnny Mnemonic actor: 4 Ice-T
Johnny One Note composer: 4 Hart **7** Rodgers
Johnny-on-the-__: 4 spot
Johnny Reb org.: 3 CSA
Johnny Reno star: 4 Agar
Johnny's Theme composer: 4 Anka
Johnny Vander __: 4 Meer
John of __: 3 God **5** Gaunt **7** Austria **10** Capistrano
John of Capistrano: 5 saint
John of the Cross: 5 saint
John Paul: 4 pope **7** pontiff
John Paul __: 5 Jones, Young
John Paul II: 4 Pole, pope **7** pontiff
John Philip __: 5 Sousa
John Phillip __: 3 Law
John Q (2002 film)
  cast: Robert Duvall, Anne Heche, Denzel Washington, James Woods
  director: Nick Cassavetes
John Q. __: 6 Public
John Quincy __: 5 Adams
John R. __: 6 Pierce **7** Coryell
John, Robert
  song: The Lion Sleeps Tonight (1972)
    Sad Eyes (1979)
__ johns: 4 long
Johns: 5 Sammy **6** Glynis, Jasper **7** Hopkins
John's __ Wife: 5 Other
Johns Hopkins subj.: 4 anat.
__ John Silver: 4 Long
John Singer __: 7 Sargent
John Singleton __: 6 Copley
Johns, Jasper: 6 artist **7** painter
johns, long: 9 underwear
John Smith: 5 alias
Johnson: 3 Ben, Don, Kay, Osa, Tom, Uwe, Van **4** Arte, Brad, Chic, Jack, Marv, Rita **5** Betty, Celia, Magic, Rafer, Randy **6** Andrew, Betsey, Cherie, Earvin, Eyvind, Lamont, Lionel, Lyndon, Pamela, Philip, Samuel, Walter **7** Beverly, Russell **8** Lady Bird, Michelle, Nunnally **9** Lynn-Holly
  Johnson & ~ competitor: 5 Curad
Johnson, Andrew: 9 president
  home: 9 Tennessee
  wife: 5 Eliza
Johnson, Ben: 5 actor
  film: Breakheart Pass (1976)
    Dillinger (1973)
    The Getaway (1972)
    The Last Picture Show (1971, AA)
    Mighty Joe Young (1949)
    One-Eyed Jacks (1961)
    Rio Grande (1950)
    The Sugarland Express (1974)
    Terror Train (1980)
    Wagon Master (1950)
Johnson City: 4 city, town
  locale: 5 Texas **9** Tennessee
Johnson, Don: 5 actor
  film: Paradise (1991)
    Sweet Hearts Dance (1988)
    Tin Cup (1996)
  song: Heartbeat (1986)
  spouse: Melanie Griffith
  TV: Miami Vice, Nash Bridges
Johnson, Earvin: 5 Magic
  milieu: 5 court
  org.: 3 NBA
  sport: 10 basketball
Johnson, Eyvind: 6 writer **7** Swedish **8** Nobelist
Johnson, Jack: 5 boxer
  milieu: 4 ring
Johnson, James Weldon: 6 writer
Johnson, Lady Bird
  first name: 7 Claudia
  middle name: 4 Alta
Johnson, Lionel: 4 poet **7** British
Johnson, Lyndon B.: 9 president
  biographer: 4 Caro
  cabinet member: 4 Barr, Boyd, Rusk, Wood **5** Clark, Cohen, Smith, Udall, Wirtz **6** Connor, Dillon, Fowler, Hodges, O'Brien, Watson, Weaver **7** Freeman, Gardner, Kennedy **8** Clifford, McNamara **9** Gronouski **10** Celebrezze, Katzenbach, Trowbridge
  child: 4 Luci **5** Lynda
  home: 5 Texas
  opponent: 9 Goldwater
  V.P.: 8 Humphrey
  wife: 7 Claudia **8** Lady Bird
Johnson, Osa: 8 explorer
Johnson, Pamela: 6 writer **7** British

Johnson, Philip: 9 architect
Johnson, Rafer: 10 decathlete
Johnson, Randy: 3 ace 6 hurler 7 pitcher
nickname ~: 4 Unit 7 Big Unit
Johnson, Samuel: 6 writer 7 British
alma mater: Oxford
cat: 5 Hodge
friend: Boswell
work: dictionary
The Idler
Johnson, Uwe: 6 German, writer
Johnson, Van: 5 actor
film: 23 Paces to Baker Street (1956)
Battleground (1949)
Brigadoon (1954)
The Caine Mutiny (1954)
Easy to Love (1953)
Easy to Wed (1946)
Go for Broke! (1951)
In the Good Old Summertime (1949)
The Last Time I Saw Paris (1954)
Men of the Fighting Lady (1954)
Remains to Be Seen (1953)
The Romance of Rosy Ridge (1947)
Thirty Seconds Over Tokyo (1944)
Two Girls and a Sailor (1944)
The White Cliffs of Dover (1944)
Yours, Mine and Ours (1968)
Johnson, Walter: 6 hurler 7 pitcher, Senator
John's Other Wife: 9 radio show
Johnston: 3 Joe 4 city, town 7 Kristen
Johnston, Joe: 8 director
film: Honey, I Shrunk the Kids (1989)
Jumanji (1995)
Jurassic Park III (2001)
October Sky (1999)
The Rocketeer (1991)
Johnstown: 4 city
disaster: 5 flood
locale: 4 Penn.
John Stuart __: 4 Mill
John the __: 7 Apostle, Baptist
John the Apostle: 5 saint
John the Baptist: 5 saint
parent of ~: 9 Elizabeth, Zechariah
John van __: 5 Vleck
John von __: 7 Neumann
John Wilkes __: 5 Booth
Joi: 7 Lansing
Joie: 3 Lee
joie de vivre: 4 élan, zest 6 gaiety, gayety 8 pleasure
Joie de Vivre author: Emile Zola
join: 3 mix, pin, tie, wed 4 abut, band, clip, fuse, glue, go to, knit, link, lock, mate, meet, melt, nail, pair, side, weld, yoke 5 affix, blend, clamp, clasp, enrol, enter, focus, graft, hitch, marry, merge, piece, reach, stick, tenon, tie up, touch, unify, unite, verge, weave 6 adhere, append, attach, border, bridge, cement, cleave, cohere, couple, enlist, enroll, fasten, gather, hook up, link up, mingle, sign on, sign up, solder, splice, team up 7 bracket, combine, connect, entwine, hitch on, intwine 8 assemble, border on, coalesce, neighbor, pair with, register, side with, take part 9 accompany, affiliate, enter into, integrate, interlace, interlink, socialize 10 amalgamate, assist with, fall in with, hook up with, synthesize, take part in, take up with, team up with
a jam session: 5 sit in
a jury: 3 sit
as hands: 4 grip 5 clasp
at the edge: 4 abut
at the seams: 3 sew 4 tack 5 baste 6 repair, stitch
forces: 4 pool 5 merge, unite 6 club up, gang up, league 9 cooperate 10 assist with
forces (with): 6 attach
in: 4 help 6 accept, take on 7 partake, pitch in 8 deal with, take part 9 cooperate, partake of 10 contribute
(in): 4 chip 5 chime
the cast of: 5 act in
the enemy: 4 turn 6 defect, desert 7 forsake, pull out, sell out
the game: 6 ante up 8 shell out
the military: 5 serve 6 enlist, sign on, sign up 9 volunteer
the party: 4 be at 6 appear, attend, drop in, make it, show up 9 accompany
the rat race: 4 moil, slog, toil, work 5 labor, slave, sweat 6 drudge, hustle, strive 7 achieve, peg away 8 plug away 9 freelance, grind away, moonlight 10 buckle down
together: 3 fit, tie, wed 4 band, meld, pool 5 unite 6 fasten
up: 3 enl. 4 team 5 enrol, enter 6 enlist, enroll, sign on, sign up 10 rendezvous
up in space: 4 dock, link
up (with): 4 ally 5 align, aline 9 associate 10 go partners
with: 6 follow 7 go along 9 accompany
with heat: 4 bond, fuse, melt, weld 6 solder
wood: 4 nail 5 spike 6 fasten, hammer
joined: 3 wed 6 allied, linked, united 8 combined, in league 9 bracketed, connected, undivided 10 affiliated, associated
(with): 5 along 8 together
joiner: 3 and 4 link 5 clamp, miter, mixer 6 member, rabbet 7 artisan 8 vinculum 9 carpenter 10 journeyman, woodworker
cry: 5 ditto, me too
group: 4 club, frat 8 sorority 10 fraternity
joining: 4 link 5 union 7 meeting 8 assembly, marriage 9 confluent 10 contiguity, convergent
combining form: 3 gam- 4 gamo-
name meaning ~: 4 Levi
point: 4 link, seam 5 ridge 8 juncture 9 stitching 10 connection
joint: 3 bar, ell, pub, tee, tie 4 crux, dive, dump, home, jail, knee, link, mixt, node, seam, spot, stir 5 ankle, elbow, haunt, hinge, mixed, nexus, place, wrist 6 common, corner, mutual, prison, shared, splice, swivel, tavern, united, wedded 7 bracket, coowned, domicil, grouped, hangout, knuckle, related, shelter 8 abutment, combined, communal, conjunct, coupling, domicile, junction, juncture, taphouse, vinculum 9 concerted, corporate, honky-tonk, nightclub, nightspot, speakeasy 10 agreed upon, collective, connection, restaurant
after-hours ~: 7 cabaret 9 nightclub, nightspot 10 supper club
arm ~: 5 elbow, wrist
beer ~: 3 bar, pub 6 saloon, tavern
blow the ~: 2 go 4 exit, quit 5 leave 6 bow out, cut out, decamp, depart, get out 7 abscond, bail out, pull out, push off 8 check out, hang it up, knock off, light out, pack it in, run out on, shove off, skip town 9 take a hike, walk out on 10 call it a day
carpentry ~: 5 bevel, miter
combining form: 5 arthr- 6 ancylo-, ankylo-, arthro- 7 anchylo-
filler: 5 grass
get one's nose out of ~: 6 resent
half a ~: 5 tenon 7 mortise
hip ~: 4 coxa
inspect the ~: 4 case, look 5 spy on 6 survey 7 examine 8 check out 10 scrutinize
leg ~: 4 knee 5 ankle
like some ~ s: 6 creaky
metalworker's ~: 4 bond, weld 6 solder 8 juncture
miter ~ feature: 5 bevel
out of ~: 5 amiss 7 ominous, unhappy, unlucky 8 ill-timed
pelvic ~: 3 hip
plumber's ~: 3 ell, tee, wye
problem: 4 ache, gout 6 strain, twinge 8 soreness 9 arthritis, throbbing
sealer: 6 luting
sidewalk ~: 5 chink, crack 7 crevice
stem ~: 4 node 8 juncture, swelling
strengthener: 6 gusset
tenant: 3 con 5 felon 7 convict 8 prisoner
venture: 4 co-op
joint __: 3 bar, ill 5 issue, stock, stool 6 family, return, runner, tenant 7 account, session, tenancy, venture
joint __ insurance: 4 life
joint-__ company: 5 stock
__ joint: 3 gin, hip, lap 4 ball, butt, clip, jook, juke, rule, rust, slip 5 bevel, dummy, facet, hinge, miter, out of, plumb, scarf 6 bridle, Cardan, rabbet, rustic, saddle, toggle 7 beaking, fetlock, gliding, knuckle, mortise, squeeze, weather
Joint Chiefs off.: 3 adm., CNO, gen.
__-jointed: 5 loose 6 double
Join the __!: 4 club
jointly: 8 mutually, together 9 in concert 10 hand in hand
prefix: 3 col-, com-, con-
__-joint pliers: 4 slip
joints, like some: 5 stiff
Joinville: 4 city, town
locale: 6 Brazil
joist: 4 beam 6 girder, rafter, timber
JoJo (1980 song) artist: Boz Scaggs
jojoba: 3 oil 5 shrub
Jojutla: 4 city, town
locale: 6 Mexico 7 Morelos
joke: 3 gag, kid, pun, rib, yak, yok, yuk 4 fool, jape, jest, josh, lark, play, quip, yock, yuck 5 antic, caper, chaff, clown, crack, cut up, farce, humor, laugh, prank, sally, spoof, tease 6 banter, bon mot, corker, gambol, gasser, japery 7 buffoon, caprice, mockery 8 drollery, escapade, nonsense, one-liner, raillery 9 crack wise, kid around, wisecrack, witticism 10 fool around, knock-knock, pleasantry, rib tickler
as a ~: 5 in fun 6 for fun, injest 10 humorously
ender: 4 ster
enjoy a ~: 4 crow, grin, hoot, howl, roar, yuck 5 laugh, smile, snort, whoop 6 cackle, giggle, guffaw, scream, titter 7 chortle, chuckle, crack up, snicker, snigger
funny ~: 4 howl, riot 6 scream
knock-knock ~: 3 pun 8 wordplay
no ~: 4 ugly 5 heavy, tough 6 severe, urgent 7 arduous, crucial, serious, weighty 8 menacing, sobering, terrible 9 dangerous, difficult, laborious, momentous, strenuous 10 formidable
object of a ~: 4 butt, dupe 5 chump, patsy 7 fall guy
practical ~: 4 dido, hoax, jape, quiz 5 prank, sport, trick
react to a bad ~: 4 moan 5 groan, wince 6 flinch 7 grimace
response: 4 ha-ha 5 laugh 6 ha-ha-ha, I get it
response, informally: 4 laff
response to an on-line ~: 3 LOL
tell a ~: 5 amuse 6 regale
trite ~: 4 corn
writer: 6 gagman
__ joke: 6 inside 7 running
__-Joke: 5 Dial-a
joker: 3 ass, oaf, sap, wag, wit 4 boob, card, clod, dolt, fool, zany 5 chump, clown, cluck, comic, cutup, dummy, dunce, ninny, patsy, scamp 6 dimwit, gagman, jester, kidder, lummox, nitwit, person, scream, sucker, turkey 7 buffoon, dingbat, dullard, farceur, fathead, gagster, half-wit, jackass, pinhead, proviso, punster, saphead, wise guy 8 bonehead, comedian, dumbbell, funnyman, humorist, meathead, numskull, obstacle, quipster, wild card, wiseacre 9 birdbrain, blockhead, lamebrain, numbskull, prankster, provision, simpleton 10 dunderhead
at times: 4 wild
Joker foe: 5 Robin 6 Batman
Joker Is Wild, The (1957 film)
cast: Jeanne Crain, Mitzi Gaynor, Frank Sinatra
director: Charles Vidor
Joker's Wild, The: game show
host: Jack Barry, Bill Cullen, Jim Peck
Joker, The (1973 song) artist: Steve Miller Band
joke's __!, The: 4 on me 5 on you
jokester: 3 wag, wit 4 card 5 comic 6 jester 8 comedian, humorist, kibitzer, quipster
query: 5 get it
routine: 3 act
jokey: 5 funny, jolly 6 jovial 7 amusing, jocular 8 humorous 9 laughable
joking: 3 fun 5 humor, sport 6 banter, comedy, levity 7 jesting, jocular 8 badinage, raillery, zaniness 9 facetious 10 not serious
all ~ aside: 9 seriously, sincerely
__-joking: 4 half
jokingly: 5 in fun 6 injest
in music: 7 giocoso
Jolene: 7 Blalock
Jolie: 5 Gabor 8 Angelina
daughter: 3 Eva 6 Zsa Zsa
Jolie, Angelina: 7 actress
father: Jon Voight
film: The Bone Collector (1999)
Girl, Interrupted (1999, AA)
Lara Croft: Tomb Raider (2001)
Life or Something Like It (2002)
Original Sin (2001)
Pushing Tin (1999)
spouse: Billy Bob Thornton
Joliet: 4 city, town 5 Louis
locale: 8 Illinois
Joliet, Louis: 6 French 8 explorer
discovery: 4 Erie
Joliot-Curie: 5 Irène 8 Frédéric
Joliot-Curie, Frédéric: 6 French 7 chemist 8 Nobelist
Joliot-Curie, Irène: 6 French 7 chemist 8 Nobelist 9 physicist
Jolley, Elizabeth: 6 writer 10 Australian
jollies: 3 fun 5 kicks 7 thrills 8 pleasure 9 amusement 10 excitement
jollity: 3 fun 4 glee 5 mirth, revel, sport 6 gaiety, gayety 7 elation, gayness, revelry 8 buoyance, buoyancy, hilarity 9 festivity, jocundity, joviality, light-

ness, merriment **10** recreation
bit of ~: 5 laugh
jolly: 3 gay **4** boon, joky **5** funny, happy, jokey, merry, sunny **6** blithe, bouncy, bright, bubbly, cheery, chirpy, festal, genial, hearty, jocose, jocund, jovial, joyful, joyous **7** buoyant, chipper, festive, gleeful, jocular, joshing, lay it on, playful **8** carefree, cheerful, jubilant, laughing, mirthful, pleasant, sportive **9** convivial, enjoyable, full of fun, fun-loving, hilarious, sprightly, vivacious **10** frolicsome, rollicking
boat: 4 yawl
to the British: 4 very
jolly ___: 4 boat **6** jumper
Jolly ___: 5 Roger **7** balance, Rancher
Jolly ___ Giant: 5 Green
... ___ jolly good fellow: 4 he's a
jollying: 6 jovial **7** coaxing **8** cajolery **9** wheedling
Jolly Rancher: 5 candy
Jolly Roger: 4 flag
depiction: 5 skull **10** crossbones
Jolly Roger crewman: 4 Smee
Jolly Toper, The painter: 4 Hals
Jolly Trio painter: 4 Hals
Jolson, Al
contemporary: 6 Cantor, Jessel
real first name: 3 Asa
song: April Showers (1922)
California, Here I Come! (1924)
I'm Sitting on Top of the World (1926)
Let Me Sing and I'm Happy (1930)
Liza (1929)
My Mammy (1928)
Rock-a-Bye Your Baby With a Dixie Melody (1918)
Sonny Boy (1928)
Swanee (1920)
There's a Rainbow Round My Shoulder (1928)
Toot Toot Tootsie (1922)
spouse: Ruby Keeler
Jolson Sings Again (1949 film)
cast: William Demarest, Barbara Hale, Larry Parks
Jolson Story, The (1946 film)
cast: William Demarest, Evelyn Keyes, Larry Parks
jolt: 3 jar, zap **4** bang, blow, bump, daze, jerk, kick, push, rock, stun, toss **5** amaze, clash, crash, floor, punch, shake, shock, upset **6** impact, jostle, jounce, justle, rattle, recoil, trauma, wallop **7** astound, disturb, setback, shake up, stagger, startle **8** astonish, backlash, bang into, bowl over, bump into, disquiet, reversal, surprise, unstring, uppercut **9** bombshell, collision, galvanize **10** discompose, disconcert, earthquake, incitement
jolted: 5 agape **6** amazed **7** shocked, stunned **10** dumbstruck
Joltin' Joe: 8 DiMaggio
brother: 3 Dom **5** Vince
joltless joe: 5 decaf, Sanka
Jomo: 8 Kenyatta
Jon: 4 Agee, Hall, Lord, Seda **5** Amiel, Avnet, Cryer **6** Bauman, Lovitz, Peters, Secada, Tenney, Voight **7** Bon Jovi, Stewart, Vickers **8** Arbuckle, Walmsley **10** Turteltaub
Jon-___ Hexum: 4 Erik
Jonah: 4 jinx
father of ~: 7 Amittai
follower: 5 Micah
preceder: 7 Obadiah
Jonas: 4 Salk **7** Savimbi
Jonathan: 4 Frid, Lynn **5** apple, Demme, Pryce, Swift **6** Frakes, Harris, Kaplan, Larson, Penner **7** Edwards, Winters **8** Lipnicki **9** Kellerman, Silverman
father of ~: 4 Saul
grandfather of ~: 5 Moses
relative: 4 crab, Gala, Lodi, Rome **5** Mutsu **6** Empire, Ida Red, medlar, Pippin, russet **7** Baldwin, Bramley, costard, Freedom, Liberty, Spartan, Wealthy, Winesap **8** Cortland, McIntosh **10** Rome Beauty
Jonathan ___ Thomas: 6 Taylor
___ Jonathan: 7 Brother
Jonathan Livingston Seagull author: 4 Bach
Jon-Erik: 5 Hexum
Jones: 3 Joe, Tom **4** Amos, Bert, Davy, Dean, Etta, Indy, Jack, Oran **5** Allan, Bobby, Brian, Casey, Chuck, Elvin, Grace, Inigo, Isham, James, Jenny, Jimmy, Leroi, Spike **6** Anissa, Deacon, Donell, George, Howard, Quincy **7** Barnaby, Carolyn, Grandpa, Indiana, Jeffrey, Rashida, Shirley **8** Jennifer, John Paul, Parnelli
___ Jones: 3 Dow, Tom **4** Davy **5** Jesus **6** Carmen **7** Barnaby, Delilah, Lorenzo
Jones, Allan: 5 actor **6** singer
film: A Day at the Races (1937)
Honeymoon in Bali (1939)
A Night at the Opera (1935)
One Night in the Tropics (1940)
Show Boat (1936)
son: Jack
spouse: Irene Hervey
Jones, Barnaby portrayer: 5 Ebsen
Jones, Bobby: 6 golfer
milieu: 5 links **6** course
org.: 3 PGA
Jonesboro: 4 city, town
locale: 8 Arkansas
Jones, Carolyn: 7 actress
film: How the West Was Won (1962)
King Creole (1958)
Last Train From Gun Hill (1959)
spouse: Aaron Spelling
TV: The Addams Family
Jones, Casey vehicle: 5 train
Jones, Davy locker: 3 sea **5** ocean
Jones, Deacon sport: 8 football
Jones, Dean: 5 actor
film: The Horse in the Gray Flannel Suit (1968)
The Love Bug (1969)
The Shaggy D. A. (1976)
That Darn Cat! (1965)
Under the Yum Yum Tree (1963)
Jones' financial partner: 3 Dow
Jones, George spouse: Tammy Wynette
Jones, Jack
father: Allan
spouse: Jill St. John
Jones, James: 6 writer
work: From Here to Eternity
The Pistol
Some Came Running
The Thin Red Line
Viet Journal
Jones, James Earl: 5 actor
film: The Bingo Long Traveling All-Stars & Motor Kings (1976)
Coming to America (1988)
Conan the Barbarian (1982)
Convicts (1991)
Cry, the Beloved Country (1995)
Dr. Strangelove (1964)
Field of Dreams (1989)
Gardens of Stone (1987)
The Great White Hope (1970)
Jefferson in Paris (1995)
My Little Girl (1986)
A Piece of the Action (1977)
The River Niger (1976)
Sommersby (1993)
voice: The Empire Strikes Back (1980)
The Return of the Jedi (1983)
Star Wars (1977)
Jones, Jennifer: 7 actress
film: Beat the Devil (1954)
Cluny Brown (1946)
Duel in the Sun (1946)
Good Morning, Miss Dove (1955)
Love Is a Many Splendored Thing (1955)
Madame Bovary (1949)
The Man in the Gray Flannel Suit (1956)
Portrait of Jennie (1948)
Since You Went Away (1944)
The Song of Bernadette (1943, AA)
The Towering Inferno (1974)
We Were Strangers (1949)
spouse: David O. Selznick
Jones, Parnelli: 5 racer **9** auto racer
milieu: 5 track
Jones, Quincy
record label: Qwest
spouse: Peggy Lipton
___ Jones's Diary: 7 Bridget
Jones, Shirley: 7 actress
film: Carousel (1956)
The Cheyenne Social Club (1970)
The Courtship of Eddie's Father (1963)
Elmer Gantry (1960. AA)
The Music Man (1962)
Oklahoma! (1955)
spouse: Jack Cassidy, Marty Ingels
TV: The Partridge Family
___ Jones's locker: 4 Davy
Jones, Tom
homeland: Wales
song: Delilah (1968)
Green, Green Grass of Home (1967)
I'll Never Fall in Love Again (1969)
It's Not Unusual (1965)
Love Me Tonight (1969)
She's a Lady (1971)
Thunderball (1966)
What's New Pussycat? (1965)
Without Love (1970)
Jones, Tommy Lee: 5 actor
film: Batman Forever (1995)
The Betsy (1978)
The Big Town (1987)
Blue Sky (1994)
The Client (1994)
Coal Miner's Daughter (1980)
Cobb (1994)
Double Jeopardy (1999)
Eyes of Laura Mars (1978)
The Fugitive (1993, AA)
JFK (1991)
Men in Black (1997)
Men in Black II (2002)
Rules of Engagement (2000)
Space Cowboys (2000)
Stormy Monday (1988)
Under Siege (1992)
U.S. Marshals (1998)
Volcano (1997)
Jong, Erica: 6 author, writer
work: Any Woman's Blues
Fanny
Fear of Fifty
Fear of Flying
Half-Lives
How to Save Your Own Life
Loveroot
Parachutes and Kisses
Serenissima
Shylock's Daughter
___-jongg: 3 mah
Jongsong Peak: 5 mount **8** mountain
locale: 4 Asia **5** India, Nepal **6** Sikkim
Joni: 5 James **8** Mitchell
Jonker ___: 7 diamond
Jonny Quest dog: 6 Bandit
Jonquière: 4 city, town
locale: 6 Canada, Québec
jonquil: 5 plant **6** flower
Jonson, Ben: 4 poet **6** writer **7** British **10** playwright
genre: 3 ode
work: The Alchemist
Epicene
Every Man in His Humour
Tale of a Tub
To Celia
Volpone
Jonze, Spike spouse: Sofia Coppola
jook ___: 5 joint
___ & Joon: 5 Benny
Jooss, Kurt: 6 dancer **7** danseur
specialty: 6 ballet
Joplin: 4 city, town **5** Janis, Scott
locale: 8 Missouri
Joplin, Janis
nickname: Pearl
song: Me and Bobby McGee (1971)
Joplin, Scott: 8 composer
genre: 3 rag **7** ragtime
work: The Cascades
The Easy Winners
Elite Syncopations
The Entertainer
Euphonic Sounds
Maple Leaf Rag
Solace
Treemonisha
Jordan: 3 Jim **4** Neil **5** river **6** Knight, Marian, nation **7** Barbara, country, Michael, Montell, Richard, Stanley **8** Hamilton
ancient city: 5 Petra
ancient kingdom near ~: 5 Ammon
bovine: 6 Baladi
capital: 5 Amman
city: 5 Akaba, Amman, Aqaba, Irbid, Zarqa **7** Az-Zarqa
desert: 6 Syrian
former queen of ~: 4 Alia, Noor
group: 10 Arab League
lake: 7 Dead Sea
money: 4 fils **5** dinar
mountain: 4 Nebo **6** Gilead, Pisgah
neighbor: 4 Irak, Iraq **5** Syria **6** Israel **11** Saudi Arabia
once: 4 Moab
River locale: 6 Israel **7** Lebanon
river to the ~: 6 Yarmuk
sea: 4 Dead
where ~ is: 4 Asia **7** Mideast
Jordan ___: 3 arc **5** curve **6** almond, engine
___ Jordan: 3 Air
Jordana: 8 Brewster
Jordanian: 4 Arab
neighbor: 5 Saudi
Jordan, Michael
milieu: 5 court
org.: 3 NBA
sport: 10 basketball
Jor-El wife: 4 Lara
son: 5 Kal-El **8** Superman
Jorge: 5 Adoum, Amado **7** Edwards, Guillén **8** Manrique
in English: 6 George
see also Spanish
Jorge ___ Borges: 4 Luis
___ Jorge: 3 Sao
joropo: 5 dance
jorum: 4 bowl **9** punchbowl
Jory, Victor: 5 actor
film: The Capture (1950)
Gone With the Wind (1939)
The Man From the Alamo (1953)
The Miracle Worker (1962)
Papillon (1973)
Party Wire (1935)

Jo's Boys author: Louisa May Alcott
Jose ___ Olazabal: 5 Maria
José: 4 Sert 5 Greco, Limón, Martí, Rizal, Silva 6 Donoso, Ferrer, Iturbi, Orozco, Rivera 7 Canseco, Jimenez 8 Carreras, Saramago 9 Echegaray, Feliciano 10 Capablanca, Ramos-Horta
in English: 6 Joseph
see also Spanish
José ___ Duarte: 8 Napoleón
José ___ Martín: 5 de San
___ José: 3 San
Josef: 5 Krips 6 Sommer 7 Hofmann 9 Pilsudski, Skvorecky
in English: 6 Joseph
Josef ___ Sternberg: 3 von
Jose Maria: 6 Eguren 8 Arguedas, Olazabal 9 Gironella
José Napoleón ___: 6 Duarte
Joseph: 4 Kane, Papp 5 Alsop, Banks, Biden, Black, Haydn, Henry, Losey, Renan, Ruben, saint, Smith 6 Alioto, Bramah, Conrad, Cotten, Furphy, Heller, Kearns, Lister, Monier, Murray, Pevney, Stalin, Strick, Taylor, Wapner 7 Anthony, Barbera, Bologna, Bottoms, Brodsky, Fiennes, Glidden, Joachim, Rotblat, Sargent, Szigeti, Thomson, Wiseman 8 Califano, Erlanger, Lagrange, Pulitzer, Stiglitz, Wambaugh 9 Gay-Lussac, Goldstein, Priestley 10 Mankiewicz
brother of ~: 3 Dan, Gad 4 Levi 5 Asher, Jesus, Judah 6 Reuben, Simeon 7 Zebulun 8 Benjamin, Issachar, Naphtali
father of ~: 5 Jacob
in German: 5 Josef
in Italian: 8 Giuseppe
in Spanish: 4 José
mantle: 4 coat
mother of ~: 6 Rachel
sister of ~: 5 Dinah
son of ~: 4 Igal 7 Ephraim 8 Manasseh
wife of ~: 7 Asenath
Joseph ___-Lussac: 3 Gay
Joseph ___ Renan: 6 Ernest
___ Josepha Hale: 5 Sarah
Joseph and His Brothers author: Thomas Mann
Joseph and the Amazing Technicolor Dreamcoat: 7 musical
songwriter: 4 Rice 11 Lloyd Webber
Joseph Ernest ___: 5 Renan
___ Joseph Haydn: 5 Franz
Josephine: 3 Tey 4 Hull 5 Baker, Miles
Joseph of ___: 9 Arimathea, Cupertino
Joseph of Arimathea: 5 saint
Joseph of Cupertino: 5 saint
Joseph P. ___: 7 Kennedy
Josephson, Brian: 8 Nobelist 9 physicist
Joseph von ___: 10 Fraunhofer
José Ramos-___: 5 Horta
___ Josey Wales, The: 6 Outlaw
josh: 3 guy, kid, rib 4 jest, jive, joke 5 chaff, tease 6 banter 8 ridicule
Josh: 5 Logan 6 Brolin, Gibson, Mostel 7 Saviano 8 Billings, Hartnett
joshing: 5 jolly 6 banter, jovial 7 jocular 8 badinage, humorous, raillery 9 facetious, laughable
Joshua: 5 Logan 7 Jackson 8 Reynolds 9 Lederberg
father of ~: 3 Nun
follower: 6 Judges
preceder: 11 Deuteronomy
tree: 5 yucca
Joshua composer: 6 Handel
Joshua Tree: 4 park
locale: 10 California
Josiah: 5 Royce, Spode 8 Wedgwood
Josip: 4 Broz
Joslyn: 5 Allyn
___ Jo Sperber: 6 Wendie
Josquin ___ Prés: 3 des
joss: 4 idol
burn a ~ stick: 5 cense
joss ___: 5 house, stick
Joss: 5 Addie
jostle: 3 jab, jar, jog, mob 4 bump, jolt, poke, push 5 elbow, knock, nudge, shake, shove 6 joggle, jounce, stir up, thrust 7 scuffle, squeeze 8 bang into, scramble
jot: 3 bit, dot, tad 4 atom, iota, mite, mote, spot, whit 5 grain, pinch, shred, spark, speck, straw, touch, trace, write 6 doodle, tittle, trifle 7 minimum, modicum, smidgen, smidgin 8 molecule, particle, smidgeon, take down 9 little bit, scintilla
down: 3 pen 4 note 5 write 6 record 7 put down
jota: 5 dance
jot and ___: 6 tittle
jotting: 4 memo, note 8 notation, reminder 10 memorandum
Jouhaux, Léon: 6 French 8 Nobelist
joule fraction: 3 erg
Joule, James: 7 British 9 physicist
jounce: 3 bob, jar, jog 4 bump, jerk, jolt, rock 5 quake, shake 6 bobble, bounce, impact, jiggle, joggle, jostle, justle, rattle
jouncy: 5 bumpy, rocky, rough, stony 6 choppy, uneven 7 jarring 9 turbulent
jour: 3 day 5 jeudi, lundi, mardi 6 French, samedi 8 dimanche, mercredi, vendredi
bon ~: 7 welcome 8 greeting
carte du ~: 4 list, menu 10 bill of fare
early in the ~: 5 matin
time of ~: 4 nuit
___-jour: 4 abat 6 contre
Jourdan, Louis: 5 actor
film: Can-Can (1960)
Gigi (1958)
Letter From an Unknown Woman (1948)
Octopussy (1983)
Silver Bears (1978)
The Swan (1956)
The V.I.P.s (1963)
Jour de Fête star: 4 Tati
journal: 3 log, mag 4 book 5 daily, diary, organ, paper, print 6 ledger, memoir, record, review 7 account, daybook, Filofax, gazette, logbook, tabloid, writing 8 magazine, register 9 chronicle, newspaper, recountal 10 chronology, periodical
ender: 3 ese
note: 4 item 5 entry 6 record
page: 3 day
ship's ~: 3 log 4 book 5 diary 6 record 7 account, daybook, logbook
trade ~: 5 organ 6 review 8 magazine 10 instrument, periodical
VIP: 2 ed. 6 editor 9 publisher
journal ___: 3 box 6 bronze, intime
Journal: 5 paper 9 newspaper
locale: 8 Edmonton, Montreal
Journal ___ Plague Year: 5 of the
___ Journal: 4 Viet
journal bronze: 5 alloy
component: 3 tin 4 lead, zinc 6 copper
Journal-Bulletin: 5 paper 9 newspaper
locale: 10 Providence
Journal-Constitution: 5 paper 9 newspaper
locale: 7 Atlanta
journalism: 4 news 5 press 6 estate 7 writing 9 reportage, reporting
deg.: 2 MJ
___ journalism: 5 print, video 6 yellow
___ Journalism: 3 New
journalist: 5 press 6 author, scribe, writer 8 reporter, stringer 9 announcer, columnist, publicist, scrivener, wordsmith 10 ink slinger, newsperson
approach: 5 angle, pitch, slant, twist 7 opinion 9 viewpoint
credit: 6 byline
list: 6 five w's
need: 3 pad 4 copy 7 note pad
question: 3 how, who, why 4 what, when 5 where
starter: 5 photo
style: 5 gonzo
journalize: 3 log 5 write 6 record 8 take down
Journal of the Plague Year author: Daniel Defoe
Journal Sentinel: 5 paper 9 newspaper
locale: 9 Milwaukee
journey: 2 go 3 fly, run 4 hike, lift, ride, roam, rove, tour, trek, trip 5 drive, jaunt, march, quest 6 cruise, flight, hegira, hejira, junket, outing, ramble, repair, safari, travel, voyage, wander 7 caravan, migrate, odyssey, passage, proceed, push off 8 long haul, movement, navigate, progress 9 adventure, excursion, globetrot, itinerary, migration, wandering, wayfaring 10 expedition, knock about, pilgrimage
begin a ~: 2 go 4 sail 5 leave, start 6 embark, set off, set out 7 emplane, entrain, jump off, set sail, ship out 8 go aboard, set forth 9 leave port, undertake
hero's ~: 5 quest 6 voyage 7 crusade, mission 9 adventure 10 expedition
in Latin: 4 iter
over: 5 cover, cross 8 traverse
segment: 3 leg 5 stage
Journey
song: Be Good to Yourself (1986)
Don't Stop Believin' (1981)
Only the Young (1985)
Open Arms (1982)
Separate Ways (1983)
Wno's Crying Now (1981)
Journey ___ a Dustless Room: 4 into
Journey ___ Fear: 4 Into
___ Journey: 4 Dark 5 Night
Journey author: Danielle Steel
journeyer: 5 gypsy, rover 7 drifter, pilgrim, rambler, tourist, trekker, voyager 8 traveler, vagabond, wanderer, wayfarer 9 itinerant, passenger, sojourner, transient 10 adventurer
Journey for Margaret (1942 film)
cast: Fay Bainter, Laraine Day, Robert Young
journeying: 6 errant 8 vagabond 9 itinerant, on the road, wayfaring
Journey into a Dustless Room author: Nelly Sachs
Journey Into Fear (1942 film)
cast: Joseph Cotten, Dolores Del Rio, Orson Welles
Journey Into Fear author: Eric Ambler
journeyman: 6 joiner, master, worker 7 artisan 9 carpenter, craftsman
Journey of Natty ___, The: 4 Gann
Journey, The (1959 film)
cast: Yul Brynner, Deborah Kerr, Jason Robards
director: Anatole Litvak
Journey to Jericho author: 5 O'Dell
Journey to the Center of the Earth: 4 film 5 novel
author: Jules Verne
cast: Pat Boone, Arlene Dahl, James Mason
journeywork: 4 moil, toil 5 craft, labor, skill, trade 7 travail 8 drudgery
joust: 4 duel, spar, tilt 6 combat 7 compete 10 tournament
competitor: 6 knight 7 fighter, warrior 8 champion, defender, horseman
need: 5 armor, lance
ready to ~: 5 atilt
jousting: 5 atilt, sport
Jouve, Pierre-Jean: 4 poet 6 French
Jo Van ___: 5 Fleet
Jove equivalent: 4 Zeus
___ Jovi: 3 Bon 6 Jon Bon
jovial: 3 gay 4 airy, glad, joky 5 happy, jokey, jolly, merry, sunny 6 blithe, bouncy, cheery, chirpy, genial, hearty, jocose, jocund, joyful, joyous, upbeat 7 affable, amiable, buoyant, chipper, cordial, festive, gleeful, jocular, joshing, larking, pleased, tickled 8 blissful, carefree, cheerful, ecstatic, euphoric, exultant, humorous, jollying, jubilant, laughing, mirthful, pleasant, sociable, thrilled 9 congenial, convivial, delighted, facetious, hilarious, overjoyed, rejoicing 10 delightful, frolicsome, rollicking, unbothered
joviality: 4 glee 5 mirth 6 frolic, gaiety, gayety 7 elation, jollity 8 airiness, hilarity 9 festivity, geniality, happiness, jocundity, merriment 10 good nature
Jovovich: 5 Milla
jowl: 3 jaw 4 chop 5 cheek 6 dewlap, muzzle, wattle 8 mandible
cheek by ~: 4 near 5 close, dense, thick 6 beside, packed 7 crowded 8 abutting, adjacent, touching 9 congested, jam-packed 10 near-at-hand
joy: 3 fun 4 glee, kick 5 bliss, cheer, humor, mirth 6 frolic, gaiety, gayety 7 delight, ecstasy, elation, emotion, gayness, rapture, revelry, triumph 8 euphoria, felicity, gladness, hilarity, pleasure, radiance, radiancy 9 good humor, happiness, jubilance, lightness, merriment 10 ebullience, exultation, jubilation
bundle of ~: 3 tot 4 baby 6 infant 7 bambino, newborn, toddler 9 little one
causing ~: 8 cheering, gladsome, pleasant, pleasing
ender: 4 ride 5 stick
ending: 3 ful, ous
exclamation of ~: 2 ah 3 aah, yay, yea, yes, yow 4 evoe, whee, yeah 5 huzza 6 hoorah, hooray, hot dog, hurrah, hurray, huzzah, yippee 7 whoopee, whoopie 8 all right 10 hallelujah
fill with ~: 5 elate
jump for ~: 5 exult 9 celebrate
jumping for ~: 4 high 5 happy 6 elated 7 beaming, gleeful 8 ecstatic, euphoric, exultant, in heaven, jubilant 9 ebullient 10 flying high, triumphant
name meaning ~: 4 Gail 5 Alisa 6 Alissa
pride and ~: 8 treasure
sign of ~ maybe: 4 tear 8 teardrop
starter: 4 kill
wish ~ to: 4 fete 5 honor, toast 10 compliment, felicitate
with ~: 5 gaily, gayly 7 happily
joy ___: 6 buzzer
Joy: 7 Adamson 8 Leatrice 9 detergent
alternative: 4 Ajax, Dawn 7 Cascade 8 Sunlight 9 Palmolive 10 Electrasol
Joy ___ Club, The: 4 Luck
Joy ___ World: 5 to the

__ Joy: 4 Floy 5 Ode to 6 Almond
joy bringer, name meaning: 8 Beatrice
Joyce: 4 Cary, Ella 5 Hyser, James 6 DeWitt, Kilmer 8 Brothers, Randolph 9 Van Patten
Joyce __ Oates: 5 Carol
Joyce, James: 5 Irish 6 author, writer
homeland: 4 Eire, Erin
wife: 4 Nora
work: The Dubliners
Exiles
Finnegans Wake
A Portrait of the Artist as a Young Man
Ulysses
Joycelyn: 6 Elders
Joyeux __: 4 Noel
joyful: 3 gay 4 glad, high 5 blest, happy, jolly, merry, sunny 6 blithe, bright, cheery, elated, enrapt, festal, genial, golden, jovial, upbeat 7 beaming, blessed, excited, festive, gleeful, halcyon, pleased, radiant, tickled 8 blissful, cheerful, ecstatic, euphoric, exultant, grooving, jubilant, laughing, mirthful, thrilled 9 delighted, gratified, overjoyed, rapturous, rejoicing 10 enraptured, flying high, heartening, rollicking, triumphant
cry: 3 aah 4 whee 5 whoop
make ~: 7 beatify 8 enthrall 9 enrapture, transport
joyfulness: 4 glee 5 cheer 7 ecstasy 8 hilarity 9 festivity 10 enthusiasm
joyless: 3 low, sad 4 blue, cold, dark, glum, mopy 5 black, bleak, dusky, mopey, sorry, woful 6 bleary, broody, dismal, dreary, droopy, gloomy, morose, somber, woeful 7 doleful, in a funk, unhappy 8 dejected, desolate, downcast, mournful, troubled 9 bummed out, cheerless, depressed, heartsick, miserable, saddening, sorrowful, woebegone 10 chapfallen, depressing, dispirited, lugubrious, melancholy
Joy Luck Club, The: 4 film 5 novel
author: Amy Tan
cast: Kieu Chinh, Tsai Chin, France Nuyen
director: Wayne Wang
Joyner-Kersee: 6 Jackie
Joy of Living (1938 film)
cast: Alice Brady, Irene Dunne, Douglas Fairbanks Jr.
__, Joy of Man's Desiring: 4 Jesu
Joy of Signing, The subj.: 3 ASL
joyous: 3 gay 4 glad 5 blest, happy, jolly, merry, sunny 6 blithe, bright, cheery, elated, festal, genial, golden, jovial, upbeat 7 blessed, excited, festive, gleeful, pleased, radiant, tickled 8 blissful, cheerful, ecstatic, euphoric, exultant, jubilant, mirthful, sporting, sportive, thrilled 9 delighted, gladdened, gratified, lightsome, overjoyed, rapturous, rejoicing, sprightly 10 enraptured, flying high, heartening, rollicking, triumphant
joyousness: 4 glee 5 cheer, mirth 6 gaiety, gayety 7 ecstasy 8 euphoria 10 exaltation, exultation
joyride: 4 spin 5 drive, jaunt
joystick, use a: 6 aviate
Joy to the World: 4 hymn
Joy to the World (1971 song) artist: Three Dog Night
József, Attila: 4 poet 9 Hungarian
J.P.: 6 Morgan 8 Donleavy, Marquand
flee to a ~: 5 elope 6 run off 8 slip away
__ J. Pakula: 4 Alan
J. Paul: 5 Getty
JPEG alternative: 3 gif, tif
__ J. Pollard: 7 Michael
jr.
eldest, maybe: 3 III
exam: 4 PSAT
grade officer: 5 lieut.
last yr.'s ~: 2 sr. 3 snr.
next year's ~: 4 soph.
J.R.: 5 Ewing
foe: 5 Cliff 6 Barnes
parent: 4 Jock 5 Ellie
J.R.R.: 7 Tolkien
J.T.: 5 Walsh
J. Thaddeus __: 4 Toad
__ J. Travanti: 6 Daniel
Juan: 4 Gris, Ruiz 5 Benet, Perón, Rulfo 6 Boscán, Carlos 7 Jiménez 8 Cabrillo, Marichal, Montalvo
in English: 4 John
wife of ~: 3 Eva 5 Evita 6 Isabel
see also Spanish
Juan __: 6 Carlos, de Mena
__ Juan: 3 Don, San
Juana
see Spanish
__ Juana: 3 Tia
__ Juana Cruz: 3 Sor
Juan Aldama: 4 city, town
locale: 6 Mexico 9 Chihuahua
__ Juan Capistrano: 3 San
Juan Carlos: 3 rey 4 king 7 Spanish
daughter of ~: 5 Elena
Juan de Fuca __: 6 Strait
__ Juan DeMarco: 3 Don
__ Juan Hill: 3 San
Juanita: 4 Hall 5 Kreps
see also Spanish
Juan José Ríos: 4 city, town
locale: 6 Mexico 7 Sinaloa
Juárez: 4 city, town 6 Benito
locale: 6 Mexico 9 Chihuahua
see also Spanish
Juarez (1939 film) cast: Brian Aherne, Bette Davis, Paul Muni
juba: 5 dance
Juba: 5 river
locale: 7 Somalia 8 Ethiopia
Jubal: 5 Early
Jubal (1956 film)
cast: Ernest Borgnine, Glenn Ford, Rod Steiger
director: Delmer Daves
jubilance: 3 joy 4 glee 7 ecstasy, triumph 8 hilarity 10 exultation
express ~: 4 hoot, yell 5 cheer, shout, whoop 6 holler, hurrah, scream, shriek 7 exclaim
jubilant: 3 gay 4 glad 5 happy, jolly, merry, sunny 6 blithe, cheery, elated, jovial, joyful, joyous, upbeat 7 excited, festive, gleeful, pleased, tickled 8 blissful, cheerful, ecstatic, euphoric, exultant, grooving, laughing, mirthful, thrilled 9 delighted, gladdened, gratified, lightsome, overjoyed, rapturous, rejoicing 10 enraptured, flying high, heartening, triumphant
be ~: 5 exult 7 rejoice 9 celebrate
make ~: 5 elate 6 thrill, turn on 7 delight, gladden, hearten 9 inebriate 10 exhilarate, intoxicate
jubilate: 4 crow 5 exult, glory 7 delight, rejoice, triumph
jubilation: 3 joy 4 glee 7 ecstasy, elation, rapture, triumph 8 euphoria, felicity, pleasure, rhapsody 9 happiness 10 exaltation, exultation
jubilee: 2 do 4 bash, fete, gala 5 party 6 fiesta, revels 7 blowout, holiday, revelry, shindig, triumph 8 birthday, carnival, feast day, festival, jamboree, shivaree, wing-ding 9 festivity
diamond ~ number: 5 sixty
__ jubilee: 6 golden, silver 7 diamond
Jubilee: 7 musical
author: Margaret Walker
songwriter: 6 Porter
Jubilee, like cherries: 6 flambé
Juchitán: 4 city, town
locale: 6 Mexico, Oaxaca
Judah: 6 Ben-Hur, ha-Levi
brother of ~: 3 Dan, Gad 4 Levi 5 Asher 6 Joseph, Reuben, Simeon 7 Zebulun 8 Benjamin, Issachar, Naphtali
city in ~: 4 Enam, Lehi
king of ~: 3 Asa
parent of ~: 4 Leah 5 Jacob
sister of ~: 5 Dinah
Judaic: 6 Jewish
literature: 4 Tora 5 Torah
Judaism: 3 rel. 8 religion
see also Jewish
__ Judaism: 6 Reform 7 Liberal 8 Orthodox
Judas: 7 traitor 8 betrayer, turncoat
brother of ~: 5 Jesus
kiss: 9 duplicity
Judas __: 4 Kiss, tree 6 Priest
Judas Kiss (1999 film)
cast: Carla Gugino, Hal Holbrook, Alan Rickman, Emma Thompson
Judas, My Brother author: 5 Yerby
Judd: 5 Naomi 6 Ashley, Hirsch, Nelson 7 Wynonna
Judd, Ashley: 7 actress
film: Divine Secrets of the Ya-Ya Sisterhood (2002)
Double Jeopardy (1999)
Frida (2002)
High Crimes (2002)
Kiss the Girls (1997)
Ruby in Paradise (1993)
Simon Birch (1998)
mother: Naomi
sister: Wynonna
TV: Sisters
judder: 6 rattle, shimmy 7 vibrate
Jude: 3 Law 5 saint
follower: 10 Revelation
preceder: 4 John
__ Jude: 3 Hey
Judea: 8 Holy Land
king of ~: 5 Herod
Judean Plateau locale: 6 Israel
Judeo-Spanish: 6 Ladino
Jude the Obscure
author: Thomas Hardy
character: 3 Sue 4 Anny, Donn 5 Sarah 6 Fawley 8 Arabella
judge: 3 say, try 4 cadi, call, deem, find, hold, make, rank, rate, rule, view 5 bench, check, count, court, gauge, guess, infer, jurat, rater, think, trier 6 assess, critic, decide, decree, deduce, hearer, jurist, reckon, regard, settle, size up, umpire 7 arbiter, believe, discern, examine, measure, mediate, referee 8 appraise, conclude, consider, estimate, evaluate, his Honor, keep tabs, look upon, moderate, penalize, sentence 9 arbitrate, ascertain, authority, criticize, determine, evaluator, inspector, interpose, moderator, preordain, pronounce 10 arbitrator, magistrate, negotiator
address: 3 hon. 9 honorable, Your Honor
as bad: 3 pan, rap 4 bash, damn, flay, slam 5 blame, blast, decry, knock, roast, trash 6 assail, berate, impugn, oppugn, rail at 7 censure, condemn, run down 8 belittle, denounce, talk down 9 criticize, cut to bits, disparage, excoriate, find fault, frown upon, skin alive 10 come down on, disapprove
bring before a ~: 3 try
chambers: 6 camera
come before a ~: 6 appear
concern: 5 guilt, trial 8 evidence
demand: 4 cite, fiat 5 edict, order, ukase 6 charge, decree, dictum, ruling 7 booking, mandate, precept 8 sentence 9 directive 10 injunction
expertise: 3 law
job: 4 case, suit 5 trial 7 lawsuit 9 probation 10 indictment, litigation
missing ~: 6 Crater
Muslim ~: 4 cadi, kadi, qadi, qaid
need: 4 gown, jury, robe 5 gavel
Old Testament ~: 3 Eli
order: 4 hold, stay 5 defer, delay, waive 6 arrest, detain, shelve 7 adjourn, suspend 8 postpone, prohibit, reprieve
seat: 4 banc 5 bench
sports ~: 3 ref, ump 6 umpire 7 referee
tell the ~: 3 sue 5 argue, plead 6 appeal 7 declare 8 petition
__ judge: 7 circuit
Judge: 4 Mike 8 Reinhold
Judge __: 5 Dredd 6 Priest
judge advocate __: 7 general
Judge Dredd role: 4 Ilsa
Judge Not author: 4 Asch
Judge Priest (1934 film)
cast: Anita Louise, Will Rogers
director: John Ford
Judges
follower: 4 Ruth
preceder: 6 Joshua
town in ~: 4 Lehi
Judge, The author: Rebecca West
Judging Amy star: 4 Daly 9 Brenneman
judgment: 3 act, wit 4 tact, view, wits 5 grasp, guess, logic, savvy, sense, slant, stock, taste 6 acumen, belief, choice, decree, rating, reason, ruling, sanity, wisdom 7 feeling, finding, opinion, thought, verdict 8 analysis, capacity, critique, decision, estimate, position, prudence, sagacity, sapience, sentence 9 appraisal, awareness, deduction, induction, ingenuity, intellect, reasoning, sentiment, sharpness 10 assessment, astuteness, conclusion, discretion, estimation, evaluation, horse sense, perception, resolution, shrewdness
artistic ~: 5 taste
await ~: 4 pend 6 dangle 8 hang fire
breach of ~: 5 error, lapse
court ~: 4 fiat, writ 5 edict, order 6 decree, dictum, ruling 7 mandate, verdict 8 sanction 9 directive 10 injunction
exercise ~: 4 deem, hold, view 6 assess, decide, reckon, regard 7 presume, suppose, surmise
form ~: 3 fix 4 rule 6 choose, decide, settle 7 appoint 8 finalize, sentence 9 determine, establish, negotiate
pass ~: 4 jail, rule 5 assay 6 punish 7 censure, condemn, convict, put away 8 imprison, penalize, sentence
showing good ~: 4 wise 5 lucid, sober, sound 6 steady 7 logical, prudent 8 all there, balanced, moderate, rational, sensible, together 9 judicious, practical, pragmatic, realistic 10 discerning, fair-minded, reasonable, thoughtful
unfair ~: 5 frame 6 bum rap
use poor ~: 3 err 4 flub, goof, muff 5 botch 6 bungle, foul up, mess up, slip up 7 blunder, go wrong, louse up, snarl up, stumble 9 mishandle, mismanage
value ~: 4 idea, view 5 slant, stand

6 belief, notion 7 concept, feeling, opinion, outlook, thought 8 attitude, judgment, position 9 sentiment, viewpoint 10 assessment, conception, conviction, impression, persuasion, philosophy, standpoint
judgment __: 4 call, debt, note
__ judgment: 4 snap 5 value 7 consent, private, summary
Judgment __: 3 Day 4 Book
__ Judgment: 4 Last 5 Day of, Final
Judgment at Nuremberg (1961 film)
cast: Montgomery Clift, Marlene Dietrich, Judy Garland, Burt Lancaster, Maximilian Schell, William Shatner, Spencer Tracy, Richard Widmark
director: Stanley Kramer
Judgment of Paris, The composer: 4 Arne
Judi: 5 Dench
__ judicata: 3 res
judicial: 5 legal, licit 6 lawful 8 forensic
action: 4 stay 6 appeal, decree, dictum
body: 5 court
garment: 4 gown, robe
inquiry: 6 assize
make a ~ decision: 4 find, rule 5 order 6 decide, decree, ordain 7 preside, resolve 8 sentence 9 prescribe, pronounce
opening: 4 oyes, oyez
system: 3 bar 5 bench, court
writ: 6 elegit
judiciary: 3 bar 5 bench 9 courtroom
judicious: 4 just, keen, sage, sane, wise 5 canny, clean, fussy, right, smart, sober, sound 6 astute, polite, shrewd, subtle, timely 7 careful, finicky, learned, logical, politic, prudent, sapient, tactful 8 cautious, discreet, exacting, finiking, finnicky, informed, moderate, rational, rigorous, sensible, skillful, thorough 9 advisable, assiduous, astucious, attentive, cognizant, courteous, expedient, observant, provident, sagacious, selective, sensitive 10 considered, diplomatic, discerning, farsighted, fastidious, meticulous, particular, perceptive, reasonable, scrupulous, seasonable, thoughtful, well-chosen
judiciousness: 4 care 5 sense 6 sanity, wisdom 8 maturity, prudence, sobriety 9 foresight 10 astuteness, horse sense, shrewdness
Judith: 4 Ivey 5 Crist, Guest, Light 6 Krantz, Viorst, Wright 7 Rossner 8 Anderson
father of ~: 5 Beeri
husband of ~: 4 Esau
in German: 5 Jutta
Judith composer: 4 Arne
judo: 5 sport 10 martial art
attire: 2 gi 4 belt
level: 3 dan
relative: 6 aikido, karate 7 jujitsu
studio: 4 dojo
warm-up: 4 kata
Judson, E.Z.C.: 6 author, writer
pen name: Ned Buntline
subject: Cody
Judy: 5 Blume, Carne, Davis, Tyler 6 Canova, Geeson, Jetson, Rankin 7 Collins, Garland, Landers 8 Holliday
daughter: 4 Liza 5 Lorna
partner: 5 Punch
__: Judy Blue Eyes: 5 Suite
Judy's Turn to Cry (1963 song) artist: Lesley Gore
jug: 3 pot 4 brig, ewer, jail, poky, wind 5 pokey 6 bottle, flagon, lockup, prison, vessel 7 hoosgow 8 hoosegow 9 container 10 receptacle
ancient ~: 4 olpe
chemist's ~: 6 carboy
contents: 5 cider 9 moonshine
cousin: 5 cruet 6 carafe 7 pitcher
handle: 3 ear
size: 5 quart 6 gallon
jug __: 4 band, wine
__ jug: 4 Toby 6 puzzle
jugal: 4 bone
locale: 5 cheek
jug band
instrument: 5 gazoo, kazoo 8 mirliton
Juggernaut: 4 army 5 force
juggle: 3 fix, rig 5 alter 6 change, doctor, joggle 7 falsify, shuffle 10 keep in play, manipulate, tamper with
Juggler, the: 9 tarot card
jugglery: 6 dupery 8 trickery 9 chicanery, deception 10 hocus pocus
juggling: 3 art 5 skill
jughead: 3 ass, oaf, sap 4 boob, clod, dolt, dope, fool, goof, gull, jerk, loon, simp 5 chump, clown, cluck, dummy, dunce, goose, idiot, joker, klutz, ninny, patsy 6 boobie, cuckoo, dimwit, galoot, lummox, nitwit, sucker, turkey 7 buffoon, bungler, dingbat, dullard, galloot, half-wit, jackass, tomfool 8 dumbbell, dummkopf, goofball, numskull 9 birdbrain, ding-a-ling, harebrain, ignoramus, lamebrain, numbskull, simpleton 10 dunderpate, nincompoop, rattlepate
Jughead: 4 teen 5 Jones
dog: 6 Hot Dog
Jug of Wine, A poet: 4 Omar
__, Jugs & Speed: 6 Mother
jugular __: 4 vein
jugular locale: 4 neck
juice: 4 fuel 5 clout, drink, fluid, power, vigor 6 energy, gossip, liquid, nectar, thrill 7 potable, potence, potency, scandal 8 beverage, solution, strength, vitality 9 influence, stimulate, subsidize 10 exuberance, percentage
bang ~: 5 nitro
combining form: 3 opo- 4 chyl- 5 chili-, chylo-
digestive ~: 4 bile
drink: 3 ade 5 cider
extract ~: 4 ream
fermented ~: 5 cider
flavor: 4 lime 5 apple, grape, lemon, prune 6 orange
holder: 3 can, cup 5 glass 6 bottle 7 tumbler
like some ~: 5 acerb, pulpy, tangy 6 acidic
make orange ~: 4 bore
meat ~: 5 gravy
moo ~: 4 milk
moo ~ container: 5 udder
out of ~: 4 dead 8 lifeless 10 lackluster
partly fermented grape ~: 4 stum
seal in the ~: 4 sear
unfermented ~: 4 must
up: 5 liven 6 turn on, vivify 7 animate, enliven 8 activate, energize, vitalize 9 stimulate
__ juice: 3 moo, pan 7 gastric
Juice: 6 Newton
juiced: 8 squeezed
up: 5 eager, wired 6 aflame 7 excited
juiceless: 3 dry 4 arid, sere 7 bone-dry, dried up, parched, wizened 8 withered 9 shriveled 10 dehydrated, desiccated
juicer: 6 gadget 9 appliance, extractor
refuse: 4 pulp 6 pomace 9 sarcocarp
juicy: 3 wet 4 rich 5 kicky, moist, spicy, undry, vivid 6 liquid, mellow, ribald, spicey 7 gossipy, piquant 8 colorful, dripping, exciting, luscious 9 saturated, succulent, with a kick 10 intriguing, scandalous
fruit: 4 pear 5 apple, berry, melon, peach 6 orange
like ~ turkeys: 6 basted
tidbit: 4 buzz, dirt, talk, word 5 rumor 6 gossip, report 7 hearsay, scandal
Juicy Fruit: 3 gum 10 chewing gum
alternative: 5 Extra, Orbit 7 Dentyne, Trident 8 Carefree, Chiclets, Freedent 10 Doublemint
Juillet: 4 July, mois 5 month 6 French
follower: 4 Août
preceder: 4 Juin
Juilliard subject: 3 mus. 5 music
Juin: 4 June, mois 5 month 6 French
follower: 7 Juillet
preceder: 3 Mai
Juiz de Fora: 4 city, town
locale: 6 Brazil
jujitsu: 5 sport
relative: 4 judo 6 aikido, karate
juju: 4 mojo 5 charm 6 amulet, fetich, fetish
jujube: 4 date, tree 5 candy, fruit, snack
family: 9 buckthorn
__ jujube: 6 Indian 7 Chinese, cottony
juke: 4 fake, fool, ruse 5 dodge, feint
ender: 3 box
juke __: 5 joint
Juke Box Baby singer: 4 Como
jukebox part: 4 slot
Jul.: 2 mo.
follower: 3 Aug.
Jule: 5 Styne
julep: 5 drink 8 beverage
__ julep: 4 mint
Jules: 4 bass 5 Verne 6 Bordet, Dassin 7 Feiffer, Munshin, Romains 8 Goncourt, Massenet
see also French
Jules and Jim (1961 film)
cast: Jeanne Moreau, Oskar Werner
director: François Truffaut
Juli: 7 Inkster
Julia: 4 Raul 5 Child, Duffy 6 Ormond, Stiles 7 Migenes, Roberts, Sweeney 8 Phillips
brother: 4 Eric
Julia (1977 film)
cast: Jane Fonda, Vanessa Redgrave, Jason Robards
director: Fred Zinnemann
Julia (NBC sitcom)
cast: Diahann Carroll (Julia Baker) Lloyd Nolan (Morton Chegley)
Julia __-Dreyfus: 5 Louis
Julia __ Howe: 4 Ward
Julia Misbehaves (1948 film)
cast: Greer Garson, Peter Lawford, Walter Pidgeon
Julian: 4 Bond 5 Roman 6 Barnes, Huxley, Lennon, Symons 9 Schwinger
to John: 3 son
Julian __: 3 Day 4 Alps 8 calendar
Julianna: 9 Margulies
Julianne: 5 Moore 8 Phillips
Julia, Raul: 5 actor
film: The Addams Family (1991)
Addams Family Values (1993)
Compromising Positions (1985)
The Gumball Rally (1976)
Kiss of the Spider Woman (1985)
Moon Over Parador (1988)
Presumed Innocent (1990)
Romero (1989)
Tequila Sunrise (1988)
musical: 4 Nine
Julie: 5 Adams, Delpy, Krone, Moran 6 Bishop, Harris, Kavner, London, Newmar, Warner 7 Andrews, Hagerty, Walters 8 Christie
Julie __ Eisenhower: 5 Nixon
__ Julie: 4 Miss
Julien: 5 Green 8 Duvivier
julienne: 4 soup 5 broth 8 bouillon, consommé, potatoes
Juliet: 4 moon 5 lover, Mills 6 Prowse
beloved: 5 Romeo
betrothed: 5 Paris
planet: 6 Uranus
__ Juliet: 5 Me and
Juliette: 3 Low 5 Lewis 7 Binoche
julio: 3 mes 4 July 5 month 7 Spanish
follower: 6 agosto
preceder: 5 junio
Julio: 5 Gallo 8 Cortázar, Iglesias
brother: 6 Ernest
see also Spanish
Julius: 4 pope 5 Boros, Rudel 6 Caesar, Erving, LaRosa 7 Axelrod, Dithers, Nyerere, pontiff
Julius __-Jauregg: 6 Wagner
__ Julius: 6 Orange
Julius Caesar: 4 play 8 film. play
author: William Shakespeare
cast: Marlon Brando, Louis Calhern, Greer Garson, Sir John Gielgud, Deborah Kerr, James Mason, Edmond O'Brien
character: 4 Cato 5 Casca, Cinna 6 Brutus, Cicero, Lucius, Portia, Strato 7 Cassius, Flavius, Messala, Publius 8 Marullus, Pindarus, Titinius 9 Calpurnia 10 Marc Antony
costume: 4 toga
director: Joseph L. Mankiewicz
quintet: 4 acts
setting: 4 Rome 6 Senate
__ Julius Caesar: 5 Caius, Gaius
July: 5 month 9 midsummer
birthstone: 4 ruby
clock setting: 3 DST
follower: 3 Aug. 6 August
preceder: 3 Jun. 4 June
sign: 3 Leo 4 Crab, Lion 6 Cancer
was named for him: 6 Caesar
July 7: 5 nones
Jumanji (1995 film)
cast: Kirsten Dunst, Bonnie Hunt, Robin Williams
jumble: 3 mix 4 hash, mess, muss, olio, pile, stew 5 chaos, mix up, snarl, upset 6 cookie, foul up, garble, huddle, jungle, litter, medley, mess up, muddle, tangle, tumble 7 clutter, confuse, derange, disturb, farrago, goulash, mélange, mistake, mixture, rummage, shuffle, snarl up 8 confound, disarray, dishevel, disorder, entangle, mishmash, pastiche, scramble, unsettle 9 confusion, dislocate, mare's nest, patchwork, potpourri 10 assortment, complicate, disarrange, hodgepodge, miscellany, salmagundi
jumble __: 4 sale
jumbled: 5 messy, mussy 6 unneat, untidy 7 chaotic, in a mess, tangled 9 inside-out 10 disjointed, disorderly, incohesive, in disarray, out of order, topsy-turvy, upside-down
Jumblies, The: 4 poem
author: Edward Lear
vessel: 5 sieve
jumbo: 3 big 4 huge, size, vast 5 giant, great, large 6 mighty 7 hulking, immense, mammoth, massive, sizable, titanic 8 colossal, enormous, gigantic, king-size, oversize, sizeable, towering, whapping, whopping 9 cyclopean, Herculean, humongous, leviathan, overlarge 10 gargantuan, monumental, prodigious, stupendous, tremendous
mumbo ~: 3 gas, rot 4 blah, bosh, bull, bunk, guff, jazz, jive, pooh, tosh 5 bilge, fudge, hokum, hooey,

prate, stuff, trash, tripe **6** bunkum, bushwa, drivel, footle, gabble, gammon, gibber, havers, hot air, humbug, jabber, jargon, kibosh, piffle **7** baloney, blarney, blather, blether, boloney, bushwah, eyewash, flannel, flubdub, fustian, garbage, hogwash, inanity, rubbish, twaddle **8** buncombe, claptrap, falderal, falderol, flimflam, flummery, folderal, folderol, nonsense, slipslop, tommyrot, trumpery **9** banana oil, gibberish, goofiness, kidstakes, moonshine, poppycock, rigmarole **10** applesauce, balderdash, bilge water, codswallop, double-talk, empty words, flapdoodle, galimatias, hocus-pocus, invocation, Jabberwock, rigamarole, taradiddle
jumbo ___: **3** jet **4** eggs
___ jumbo: **5** mumbo
Jumbo: **7** musical
songwriter: **4** Hart **7** Rodgers
Jumna: **5** river
city on the ~: **4** Agra **5** Delhi
locale: **5** India
jump: **3** bob, hop **4** axel, buck, dive, flee, hike, jeté, leap, lutz, miss, move, omit, pass, rise, romp, skip, verb **5** avoid, boost, bound, dance, evade, frisk, lunge, lurch, spirt, spurt, start, surge, vault, wince **6** ambush, bounce, bypass, curvet, flinch, hurdle, hurtle, launch, plunge, pounce, prance, recoil, snatch, spring, twitch, upturn, waylay **7** abscond, bail out, gambado, hop over, saltate, skydive, startle, upsurge **8** capriole, increase, leapfrog, obstacle, pass over **9** advantage, barricade, head start, overshoot, parachute, saltation **10** go whole hog, hippety hop
all over: **4** flay **5** blame, chide, scold **6** attack, berate, lean on, rebuke **7** bawl out, chew out, go after, lay into, lecture, reprove, rip into, tell off, upbraid **8** admonish, lambaste **9** criticize, dress down, reprimand, tear apart **10** take to task
as a spark: **3** arc
at: **4** grab **5** catch **6** snatch
back: **5** wince
bail: **3** fly **6** run out **7** skip out **8** skip town **9** leave town **10** fly the coop
ender: **4** suit **6** master
for joy: **5** exult **7** rejoice **9** celebrate
get the ~ on: **4** best, lead **5** outdo **7** prevail, surpass **8** dominate, outstrip
high ~: **5** event **7** contest
horse ~: **6** curvet
in: **5** enter, start **6** butt in **7** burst in, get busy, pitch in **9** interject, interrupt
(in): **5** chime
into: **5** begin, enter, start **6** launch, set out, take up **7** kick off, lead off **8** commence, embark on, get going, initiate **9** undertake
long ~: **5** event **7** contest
make ~: **5** alarm, panic, scare, spook **7** disturb, startle **8** affright, frighten, surprise **9** galvanize, give a turn
off: **5** begin, start **6** alight, embark **7** detrain, get down **8** dismount
out of the way: **4** duck **5** avoid, dodge, elude, evade, parry, skirt **6** escape **8** sidestep
over: **3** hop **4** leap, skip **5** clear, vault **6** hurdle
rope: **3** toy **4** game, skip **7** pastime **9** amusement, diversion
skating ~: **4** axel, lutz
the gun: **4** rush **5** start **7** presume **10** anticipate
the line: **5** cut in
the track: **6** derail
up: **4** lift, rise **5** raise, stand **7** magnify
voltage ~: **5** surge
with a pole: **4** soar **5** bound, vault **6** hurdle, spring **8** overleap
jump ___: **3** bid, cut, jet **4** bail, ball, boot, dial, head, line, pass, rope, seat, shot, turn, wire **5** spark **6** aboard
jump ___ hoops: **7** through
jump-___: **5** shift, start
___ jump: **3** ski **4** high, long, pole **5** broad, water **6** center, double, triple **7** gelände, quantum
Jump: **6** Gordon
jumper: **3** 'roo **5** horse **6** equine, rabbit, romper **7** wallaby **8** kangaroo
Aussie ~: **3** 'roo **15** wallaby. kangaroo
Calaveras County ~: **4** frog
checkers ~: **4** king
for short: **4** para
need: **5** chute
starter: **5** smoke
jumper ___: **3** ant **5** cable
___ jumper: **4** high, long **5** broad, jolly
___-jumper: **5** claim **6** puddle
jumper cable connection: **5** anode
Jump (For My Love) (1984 song)
artist: Pointer Sisters
jump in ___ both feet: **4** with
Jumpin' ___ Flash: **4** Jack
jumping: **4** busy, go-go **5** noisy **6** lively **7** hopping **8** tireless **9** vivacious
for joy: **4** high **5** happy **6** elated **7** beaming, gleeful **8** ecstatic, euphoric, exultant, in heaven, jubilant **9** ebullient **10** flying high, triumphant
out of a plane: **4** feat **5** stunt **7** exploit
the gun: **7** too soon **8** abortive, too early **9** overhasty, premature **10** half-cocked
to conclusions: **4** rash **5** hasty **8** careless, heedless, reckless **9** foolhardy, hotheaded, impetuous, imprudent, impulsive, overhasty **10** headstrong, incautious
jumping ___: **4** bean, gene, hare, jack **5** mouse **6** spider
jumping-___ point: **3** off
___ jumping: **6** bungee
___ jumping bean: **7** Mexican
jumping-bean occupant: **4** worm
Jumpin' Jack Flash (1968 song)
artist: Rolling Stones
Jumpin' Jack flash, it's ___...: **4** a gas
Jumpin', Jumpin' (2000 song) artist: Destiny's Child
jump rope: **4** game
Jump (song) artist: Van Halen, Kris Kross
jump the ___: **3** gun
jump through ___: **5** hoops
___-jump-up: **6** Johnny
jumpy: **4** edgy **5** antsy, itchy, shaky, tense, upset, wired **6** fitful, jangly, on edge, scared, touchy, uneasy **7** alarmed, anxious, excited, fearful, fidgety, fretful, jittery, keyed up, nervous, panicky, restive, spooked, uptight **8** agitated, atremble, fluttery, fretsome, restless, skittish, timorous, troubled **9** concerned, excitable, ill at ease, quivering, trembling, tremulous, unrelaxed **10** disquieted, frightened, high-strung
in music: **4** stac. **8** staccato
Jun.: **2** mo.
follower: **3** Jul.
it ends in ~: **3** spr.
see also June
Juncal: **4** peak **5** mount **8** mountain
locale: **5** Andes, Chile **9** Argentina
junco: **4** bird **8** snowbird
junction: **4** bond, link, lock, node, seam, weld **5** hinge, joint, tie-in, union **6** corner, hookup, splice **7** linking, meeting, mortice, mortise **8** coupling, crossing, dovetail **9** concourse **10** assemblage, attachment, confluence, connection, crossroads
electrical ~: **3** wye
of a ~ point: **5** nodal
road ~: **4** fork, turn **6** branch
junction ___: **3** box
___ Junction: **6** tuxedo **9** Petticoat
Junction City: **4** city, town
locale: **6** Kansas
juncture: **4** bond, node, pass, seam, time, weld **5** hinge, joint, phase, point, stage, state, tie-in, union **6** crisis, hookup, moment, splice **7** dilemma, instant, linking, meeting, mortice, mortise **8** coupling, crossing, dovetail, occasion, quandary, zero hour **9** concourse, emergency **10** assemblage, attachment, concursion, confluence, crossroads, occurrence
at this ~: **3** now **4** here
leaf ~: **4** axil
picture frame ~: **5** bevel, miter, slant **8** diagonal
___ juncture: **4** open, plus **5** close
Jundiaí: **4** city, town
locale: **6** Brazil
June: **5** Foray, Haver, Havoc, month, Valli **6** Carter **7** Allyson, Cleaver, Collyer **8** Lockhart
award: **6** degree
birthstone: **5** pearl
bug: **3** dor **4** dorr **6** beetle
dance: **4** prom
honoree: **3** dad **4** grad **5** Daddy **6** father
like ~: **5** sixth
sign: **4** Crab **5** Twins **6** Cancer, Gemini
to Ward: **4** wife
vow: **3** I do
June ___: **3** bug **4** Moon **5** bride, grass
___ & June: **5** Henry
Juneau: **4** city, town **7** capital
locale: **6** Alaska
June Bride (1948 film)
cast: Fay Bainter, Bette Davis, Robert Montgomery
June 5: **5** nones
June Is Bustin' Out All Over composer: **7** Rodgers **11** Hammerstein
June Moon
author: George S. Kaufman, Ring Lardner
Jung: **4** Carl
rival: **5** Freud
topic: **3** ego
___ Jung: **6** Kim Dae
Jünger, Ernst: **6** German, writer
Jungfrau: **3** alp **4** peak **5** mount **8** mountain
locale: **4** Alps **6** Europe **11** Switzerland
jungle: **4** bush, heap, mass, maze **5** chaos, snarl, wilds **6** jumble, litter, region, sphere, tangle **7** clutter, society, thicket, tropics **8** disarray **9** confusion, labyrinth, mobocracy, wasteland **10** rain forest, wilderness
creature: **3** ape, boa **4** lion **5** hyena, rhino, tapir **6** hyaena
from the ~: **4** wild
home: **3** den **4** lair
knife: **4** bolo **7** machete
like a ~: **4** lush, rank, viny **9** overgrown
person: **4** Jane **6** Tarzan
sound: **3** cry, din **4** call, drum, howl, roar **5** blast, crash, growl, laugh **6** bellow, clamor, scream **7** trumpet
vine: **5** liana, liane
jungle ___: **3** gym **4** cock, fowl
Jungle ___: **3** Jim **4** Book **5** Fever
Jungle Boogie (1974 song) artist: Kool and the Gang
Jungle Book (1942 film)
cast: Sabu
director: Zoltan Korda
setting: **5** India
Jungle Books, The
author: Rudyard Kipling
character: **3** KAA **5** Akela, Baloo, Hathi **6** Buldeo, Messua, Mowgli **8** Bagheera **9** Shere Khan
Jungle Fever (1991 film)
cast: Spike Lee, Annabella Sciorra, Wesley Snipes
director: Spike Lee
jungle fowl relative: **5** poult, quail, snipe **6** chukar, grouse, peahen, turkey **7** peacock **8** curassow, pheasant, woodcock **9** partridge **10** wild turkey
___ jungle out there!: **4** It's a
Jungle Princess, The (1936 film)
cast: Dorothy Lamour, Ray Milland, Akim Tamiroff
Jungle, The
author: Upton Sinclair
character: **3** Ona **5** Jonas **6** Connor, Jurgis, Marija, Rudkus
___ Jungle, The: **5** Naked **7** Asphalt
jung opposite: **3** alt
junio: **3** mes **4** June **5** month **7** Spanish
follower: **5** julio
preceder: **4** mayo
junior: **3** boy, lad, son **4** size, year **5** lower, minor, pupil, under, young **6** lesser, little, puisne **7** student, younger **8** juvenile **9** collegian, secondary, youngster
college degree: **2** AA, AS
dress size: **4** nine
officer: **5** cadet **7** soldier
sibling: **3** sis
junior ___: **4** high, miss, prom **6** school **7** college, counsel, varsity
Junior: **6** Walker **7** Gilliam **9** Girl Scout
watch ~: **3** sit
Junior (1994 film)
cast: Danny DeVito, Frank Langella, Arnold Schwarzenegger, Emma Thompson
director: Ivan Reitman
Junior ___: **6** Bonner, League
Junior Bonner (1972 film)
cast: Ida Lupino, Steve McQueen, Robert Preston
director: Sam Peckinpah
junior high: **6** school
grade: **5** ninth **6** eighth **7** seventh
juniority: **9** childhood
Junior League wannabe: **3** deb
Junior's Farm (1974 song) artist: Paul McCartney
juniper: **4** tree **5** savin, shrub **6** savine **9** evergreen
Biblical ~: **5** retem
product: **3** gin
relative: **7** cypress **8** sandarac **10** arborvitae
tar: **4** cade
juniper ___: **3** oil, tar **5** berry
___ juniper: **7** Chinese, western
Junipero: **5** Serra
junk: **3** rid **4** boat, dump, poor **5** chaff, ditch, offal, scrap, stuff, trash, waste **6** debris, litter, no good, refuse, remove, shabby, shlock, shoddy, trashy **7** discard, garbage, rejects, rubbish, salvage, schlock, toss out,

trinket 8 castoffs, discards, get rid of, inferior, jettison, leavings, narcotic, throw out, unusable 9 dispose of, houseboat, sweepings, throw away, worthless 10 second-rate
cyberspace ~ mail: 4 spam
drawer abbr.: 4 misc.
ender: 4 yard
food: 4 eats, nosh 5 snack, sweet 6 sweets 7 goodies, munchie
hunk of ~: 3 dud 5 lemon
mail: 3 ads
pile: 8 landfill
junk __: 3 art, DNA 4 bond, call, food, mail 6 artist 7 jewelry
__ junk: 4 salt 7 Chinese
junker: 4 heap 5 crate, wreck 6 jalopy 10 rattletrap
junket: 3 hop 4 hike, ride, sail, tour, trek, trip, walk 5 drive, jaunt, sally, spree 6 airing, cruise, frolic, outing, picnic, stroll, travel, voyage 7 custard, journey, pudding, tapioca 9 excursion 10 blancmange, expedition
junkman: 6 carter
junky: 3 bad 5 cheap 6 shoddy, tawdry 7 devotee 8 slipshod 9 worthless 10 jerry-built
junkyard: 4 dump, heap 8 landfill
dog: 3 cur, mut 4 mutt 5 biter 7 mongrel 10 crossbreed
like a ~ dog: 3 bad 4 mean, ugly 5 dirty, mangy 7 lowdown, scruffy, vicious 8 churlish 9 dangerous 10 despicable, ill-natured
Juno: 3 dea 8 asteroid
brother of ~: 5 Pluto 7 Jupiter, Neptune
epithet of ~: 6 Lucina, Moneta, Regina 7 Curitis 8 Lanuvina
equivalent: 4 Hera
husband of ~: 7 Jupiter
messenger: 4 Iris
offered him a kingdom: 5 Paris
parent of ~: 3 Ops 6 Saturn
sister of ~: 5 Ceres, Vesta
son of ~: 4 Mars 6 Vulcan
Juno and the Paycock author: Sean O'Casey
junta: 4 bloc, ring 5 cabal, party 7 council 9 coalition
act: 4 fiat 5 edict, order 6 decree, dictum, rulers 7 command, dictate, mandate 9 directive, manifesto 10 injunction
action: 4 coup 5 purge 6 revolt, stroke
junto: 4 band, gang, ring 5 cabal, party 6 circle, clique 7 coterie, faction 8 alliance 9 coalition
Jupiter: 3 deo, god 4 city, Jove, town
brother of ~: 5 Pluto 7 Neptune
daughter of ~: 3 Pax 5 Diana, Venus
domain: 3 sky
equivalent: 4 Zeus
locale: 7 Florida
moon: 2 Io 4 Leda 5 Carme, Elara, Metis, Thebe 6 Ananke, Europa, Sinope 7 Himalia 8 Adrastea, Amalthea, Callisto, Ganymede, Lysithea, Pasiphae
neighbor: 4 Mars 6 Saturn
parent of ~: 3 Ops 6 Saturn
sister of ~: 4 Juno 5 Ceres, Vesta
son of ~: 4 Mars 6 Apollo 7 Bacchus, Mercury
wife of ~: 4 Juno
Jupiter's __: 4 Wife 5 Bones 7 Darling
Jupiter's-__: 5 beard
Jupiter's Bones author: Faye Kellerman
Jupiter's Darling (1955 film)
cast: Howard Keel, George Sanders, Esther Williams
Jupiter Symphony composer: 6 Mozart
Jura: 5 range 9 mountains
locale: 5 Switz. 6 Europe, France
Jurado, Katy spouse: Ernest Borgnine
jural: 3 due 5 legal, legit, licit, valid 6 kosher, lawful 8 rightful 9 allowable, canonical, statutory, warranted 10 admissible, authorized, legitimate, sanctioned
Jurassic Park: 4 film 5 novel
author: Michael Crichton
beast: 4 T-rex 5 clone 6 raptor
cast: Richard Attenborough, Laura Dern, Jeff Goldblum, Sam Neill
composer: 8 Williams
director: Steven Spielberg
preserver: 5 amber, resin
role: 5 Ellie
Jurassic Park III (2001 film)
cast: Téa Leoni, William H. Macy, Sam Neill
jurat: 5 judge 7 bailiff 10 magistrate
jure __: 6 divino, humano
__ jure: 3 suo 4 ipso 5 pleno
jure, de: 7 by right
jurel: 4 fish
Jürgen: 8 Prochnow
in English: 6 George
Jurgens: 4 Curt 6 lotion
competitor: 5 Nivea
Jurgens, Curt: 5 actor
film: The Enemy Below (1957)
I Aim at the Stars (1960)
The Inn of the Sixth Happiness (1958)
Lord Jim (1965)
The Spy Who Loved Me (1977)
This Happy Feeling (1958)
Jurgensen, Sonny: 2 QB
sport: 8 football
juridical: 5 legal 6 lawful 8 forensic
__ juris: 3 sui 6 alieni, corpus 7 nullius
jurisdiction: 4 area, rule, sway, turf 5 field, orbit, power, range, reach, reign, scope 6 bounds, domain, empire, extent, limits, sphere 7 circuit, command, compass, control, purview 8 district, dominion, hegemony, province
remove beyond legal ~: 5 eloin
jurisprudence: 3 law 10 due process
jurisprudent: 3 due 5 legal, legit, licit, valid 6 kosher, lawful, lawyer, legist, proper 7 condign 8 attorney, bona fide, mandated, official, rightful 9 allowable, barrister, canonical, counselor, solicitor, statutory, warranted 10 admissible, authorized, legal eagle, legitimate
jurist: 5 judge 6 lawyer 7 counsel, justice 8 attorney, defender, his Honor 9 barrister, counselor 10 magistrate
Moslem ~: 5 mufti
juristic: 5 legal 8 forensic 9 polemical
__ juror: 5 grand, petit, petty
jurors: 5 panel, peers 7 council
place: 3 box 5 court 9 courtroom
Juror, The (1996 film)
cast: Alec Baldwin, Anne Heche, Demi Moore
Juru: 5 river
locale: 4 Peru 6 Brazil
jury: 5 board, panel, peers 8 tribunal 9 veniremen
award: 7 damages, penalty 9 indemnity 10 reparation
complement: 5 dozen
determination: 5 guilt
grand ~ activity: 5 probe
join a ~: 3 sit
member: 4 peer 5 equal
jury __: 3 box 4 room 5 wheel
jury-__: 3 rig 6 rigged 7 packing
__ jury: 4 hung 5 grand, petit, petty, trial 6 struck 7 special
__ Jury: 4 I the
jury-rigged: 6 fill-in 7 interim, stopgap 9 contrived, expedient, impromptu, makeshift, temporary 10 improvised
jus: 5 gravy
jus __: 6 civile 7 divinum, gentium
just: 3 all, apt, but, due, fit 4 even, fair, meet, mere, only, wise 5 exact, legal, moral, newly, quite, right, sound, truly 6 actual, barely, cogent, decent, hardly, honest, kasher, kosher, lawful, merely, proper, purely, simply, square 7 by a nose, condign, correct, ethical, exactly, factual, fitting, freshly, merited, neutral, only now, precise, sincere, upright, utterly, veridic 8 accurate, actually, balanced, bona fide, deserved, entirely, faithful, flawless, narrowly, recently, reliable, rightful, squarely, straight, suitable, tolerant, unbiased, virtuous 9 authentic, befitting, equitable, errorless, faultless, honorable, impartial, judicious, objective, precisely, righteous, unbigoted, uncolored, uncorrupt, unslanted, veracious, veridical 10 aboveboard, absolutely, completely, definitely, dependable, evenhanded, fair-minded, felicitous, high-minded, legitimate, no more than, nothing but, principled, reasonable, scrupulous, upstanding
about: 4 near 6 almost, nearly
a little: 3 bit, nip, sip 4 bite, dash, dram, drop, shot 5 pinch, snort, taste 6 morsel, nibble, sample, tidbit, trifle 7 soupçon, swallow 8 mouthful, spoonful
around the corner: 4 near 5 handy 7 close by 8 adjacent 10 accessible, convenient
as: 4 as if, then, when 5 while 6 during
as soon: 6 gladly, rather 7 instead, mais oui 9 be my guest 10 by all means, preferably
barely: 4 a bit 6 hardly 8 narrowly, scarcely
beat: 4 edge 7 nose out 8 slip past
before: 4 till, up to 5 until 6 down to 7 prior to
bought: 3 new 5 fresh
deserts: 3 due 5 merit 6 reward 7 payback 10 recompense
exist: 4 loaf 7 go to pot 8 go to seed, languish, stagnate, vegetate
get one's ~ deserts: 4 earn, rate 5 merit 10 have coming
give ~ deserts: 5 spite 6 avenge 7 get even, hit back, pay back, requite, revenge 9 get back at, stick it to
hired: 3 new, raw 5 green 9 untrained
kidding: 5 in fun 7 as a lark 8 for a joke
like: 4 as if 5 quasi 9 seemingly
make it: 4 last 5 exist, get by 6 eke out, endure, hang on, manage 7 ride out, subsist, survive 8 scrape by 9 squeeze by, stay alive 10 stick it out
miss sinking, as a putt: 3 lip
more than ~ a little: 4 much, very 5 amply, quite 6 deeply, highly, hugely, unduly, vastly 7 greatly, largely, only too, rabidly 8 terribly 9 decidedly, extremely, seriously, unusually 10 enormously, incredibly, profoundly, remarkably, thoroughly, uncommonly
now: 6 lately 8 latterly, recently
once: 4 ever 5 at all
only ~: 6 little 8 narrowly, scarcely
out: 3 new 5 fresh 6 recent
picked: 5 crisp, fresh
punishment: 6 desert
right: 4 to a T 5 ideal 6 to a tee 7 optimal, perfect, utopian 8 flawless 9 correctly, exemplary, faultless, nonpareil, on the nose, perfectly, precisely 10 accurately, consummate
so: 2 ay, da, ja, sí 3 aye, oui, yea, yep, yes, yup 4 fine, okay, sure, to a T, yeah 5 good-o, natch, quite, right, roger, uh-huh 6 agreed, gladly, good-oh, indeed, rather, righto, surely, to a tee, you bet, yowzah 7 exactly, go ahead, indeedy, mais oui, quite so, ten-four 8 all right, as you say, of course, thumbs up, very well 9 be my guest, certainly, darn right, naturally, on the nose, precisely, sure thing, you betcha, you said it 10 absolutely, by all means, definitely, positively, sure enough, that's right
the same: 3 yet 5 still 6 anyhow, anyway, even so 9 at any rate
washed: 5 clean, fresh, snowy 8 dirtless, germfree, pristine, sanitary, spotless, unsoiled 9 laundered, sparkling, unsmudged, unspotted, unstained 10 immaculate
just __: 3 now 4 a bit, a dab, a tad 5 about, folks 6 in case 7 deserts
Just __: 4 a sec, do it 5 a Girl, say no
Just __ Before I Go: 5 a Song
Just __ Look: 3 One
Just __ Me: 4 Like, You 'N' 5 Shoot
Just __ of Those Things: 3 One
Just __, skip...: 4 a hop
Just __ suspected!: 3 as I
Just __ the guys: 5 one of
Just __ thought!: 3 as I
Just a __: 3 sec 6 Gigolo
Just Above My Head author: James Baldwin
Just a Little Bit Better (1965 song)
artist: Herman's Hermits
Just a Little Too Much (1959 song)
artist: Ricky Nelson
Just a minute: 4 whoa 6 hang on, hold on, one sec
Just Another Day (1992 song) artist: Jon Secada
Just Ask Your Heart (1959 song)
artist: Frankie Avalon
Just a Song Before I Go (1977 song)
artist: Crosby, Stills & Nash
Just Between You and Me (song)
artist: Chordettes, Lou Gramm
Just Do It company: 4 Nike
Just Dropped In (1968 song) artist: Kenny Rogers
juste-__: 6 milieu
__ juste: 3 mot
Just for You (1952 film)
cast: Ethel Barrymore, Bing Crosby, Jane Wyman
Just Got Paid (1988 song) artist: Johnny Kemp
justice: 5 judge, right 6 equity, jurist, virtue 7 redress 8 evenness, fairness, fair play, justness, morality 9 rectitude 10 due process, lawfulness, recompense
bring to ~: 3 try 4 hear 9 prosecute 10 adjudicate
do ~: 3 fix 4 mend 5 emend, right 6 remedy, repair, square 7 correct, realize, rectify, redress, requite, restore, succeed 9 make up for, vindicate 10 accomplish, take care of
do ~ to: 9 vindicate

hall of ~: 5 court
it seasons ~: 5 mercy
justice __ peace: 5 of the
__ justice: 5 chief, lit de 6 poetic
Justice Dept.
div.: 3 FBI
employee: 4 atty.
head: 2 AG
__ justice for all: 3 and
justice of the __: 5 peace
justicia: 4 bush 5 shrub 10 ornamental
justifiable: 4 fair 5 legal, licit, right, sound, valid 6 lawful, proper 7 logical, tenable 8 deserved, rightful, suitable 9 allowable 10 legitimate, reasonable
justification: 4 call, plea 5 alibi, basis, title 6 excuse, reason 7 defense, grounds, pretext 8 apologia, argument, occasion 9 rationale
means ~: 4 ends
__-justification: 4 self
justification by __: 5 faith, works
justified: 3 due 5 legal 8 deserved
not ~: 4 idle 5 empty, false, undue, wrong 6 unfair, wanton 7 extreme 8 baseless, needless 9 excessive, illogical, imaginary, overblown, unfounded, untenable 10 exorbitant, gratuitous, groundless, inordinate, undeserved, unprovoked
justifier: 9 apologist
justify: 5 gloze, merit, prove 6 defend, excuse, pardon, reason, uphold 7 bear out, confirm, explain, support, sustain, warrant 8 argue for, palliate, validate 9 recommend, vindicate, whitewash 10 legitimize, strengthen
__-justify: 4 cost
Justify My Love (1990 song) artist: Madonna
just in __: 4 case
Justin: 5 Henry
Justine: 7 Bateman
author: de Sade, Lawrence Durrell
Justine (1969 film)
cast: Anouk Aimée, Dirk Bogarde
director: George Cukor
Justinian __: 4 Code
Just in Time composer: 5 Green, Styne 6 Comden
justitia __: 7 omnibus
Just kidding!: 3 not
Just like __ and Bacall: 5 Bogie
Just Like Jesse James (1989 song) artist: Cher
Just Like Me (1965 song) artist: Paul Revere and the Raiders
Just Like Paradise (1988 song) artist: David Lee Roth
(Just Like) Starting Over (1980 song) artist: John Lennon
justly: 5 right, truly 6 aright 8 by rights 10 virtuously
Just My Imagination (1971 song) artist: Temptations
justness: 6 equity 7 justice 8 meetness 9 rightness 10 lawfulness, moderation
Just Once in My Life (1965 song) artist: Righteous Brothers
__ just one of those things: 5 It was
Just One of Those Things composer: 6 Porter
Just Right: 6 cereal
competitor: 3 Kix 4 Life, Trix 5 Kashi, Quisp, Total 6 Kaboom, Muesli, Oreo O's, Pablum, Smacks 7 All-Bran, Crispix, Harmony, Hunny B's, Mueslix, Oat Bran, Pokemon 8 Boo Berry, Cheerios, Corn Chex, Corn Pops, Fiber One, Rice Chex, Special K, Uncle Sam, Wheaties 9 Alpha Bits, Apple Zaps, Grape Nuts, Honey Comb, Wheat Chex 10 Apple Jacks, Bran Flakes, Cap'n Crunch, Cocoa Puffs, Froot Loops, Mini-Wheats, Nutri-Grain, Puffed Rice, Quaker Oats, Smart Start 11 Cocoa Blasts, Cookie Crisp, Golden Crisp, Lucky Charms, Puffed Wheat, Sweet Crunch, Waffle Crisp
Just say __ drugs: 4 no to
Just Shoot Me (NBC sitcom)
cast: Wendie Malick (Nina Van Horn) Laura San Giacomo (Maya Gallo) George Segal (Jack Gallo)
cat: Spartacus
magazine: Blush
Just So Stories author: Rudyard Kipling
__ just stand there: 4 Don't
Just Take My Heart (1992 song) artist: Mr. Big
just the __: 4 same
Just the __, ma'am: 5 facts
Just the Ticket (1999 film)
cast: Andy Garcia, Andie MacDowell
Just the Two of Us (1981 song) artist: Bill Withers, Grover Washington Jr.
Just the Way You Are (1984 film)
cast: Kristy McNichol, Michael Ontkean
Just the Way You Are (1977 song) artist: Billy Joel
Just this __...: 4 once
Just to Be Close to You (1976 song) artist: Commodores
Just to See Her (1987 song) artist: Smokey Robinson
Just Walking in the Rain (1956 song) artist: Johnnie Ray
__ Just Want to Have Fun: 5 Girls
Justy: 3 car 4 auto 6 Subaru
Just You 'n' Me (1973 song) artist: Chicago
Just you wait, __ 'iggins: 4 'enry
jut: 4 lean, poke 5 bulge 6 extend 7 poke out, project 8 overhang, protrude, stand out, stick out 10 projection
jute: 4 bast, rope 5 fiber
cousin: 4 hemp
fabric: 5 oakum 6 burlap
fiber resembling ~: 5 kenaf
product: 4 rope 5 twine 6 string 7 cordage
Jute invader: 5 Horsa
Jutland: 6 battle
port: 5 Arhus 6 Alborg
resident: 4 Dane
Jutta in English: 6 Judith
jutting: 7 pendant, pendent, salient 9 obtrusive, prominent
piece: 8 abutment
Juvenal: 4 poet 5 Roman 8 satirist
see also Latin
juvenescent: 5 fresh, green, young 6 boyish, callow 7 budding, girlish, growing, newborn, puerile 8 childish, immature, teenaged 9 childlike, half-grown, unfledged 10 developing
juvenile: 3 boy, kid, lad, tot 4 baby, girl, teen 5 child, green, kiddy, minor, sprig, young, youth 6 boyish, callow, infant, jejune, junior, unripe, vernal 7 babyish, budding, girlish, kiddish, puerile, sapling, teenage, toddler 8 childish, half-pint, immature, nonvoter, teenager, underage, unweaned, youthful 9 childlike, frivolous, infantile, stripling, youngster 10 adolescent, nonserious
juvenile __: 5 court 7 officer 10 delinquent
juvenility: 9 childhood 10 schooldays
Juventino Rosas: 4 city, town
locale: 6 Mexico 10 Guanajuato
juxtapose: 4 abut, meet 5 verge 6 adjoin 8 border on 9 lie beside
juxtaposed: 4 near 5 close 6 beside 8 abutting, adjacent, touching 9 adjoining, bordering, in contact 10 connecting, contiguous
juxtaposition: 7 abuttal, contact, joining, meeting 8 abutment, touching 9 adjacence, adjacency, adjoining, proximity 10 contiguity
place in ~: 6 appose
JVC: 2 TV 3 VCR 5 TV set 10 television
alternative: 3 NEC, RCA 4 Sony 6 Quasar, Zenith 7 Emerson, Hitachi, ProScan, Toshiba 8 Magnavox, Sylvania 9 Panasonic
invention: 3 VHS
J. Walter __: 8 Thompson
J W Coop (1972 film)
cast: Cristina Ferrare, Geraldine Page, Cliff Robertson
J. William __: 9 Fulbright
__ J. Wilson: 6 Sheree

K: 3 vit. **4** elem. **6** letter **7** element, vitamin **9** potassium
followers: 3 LMN **4** LMNO **5** LMNOP
in phonetic alphabet: 4 Kilo
19 for ~: 4 at. no.
preceders: 3 HIJ **4** GHIJ **5** FGHIJ
rations: 4 chow
rations successor: 3 MRE
star: 8 Arcturus **9** Aldebaran
to 12: 4 elhi **5** grade
K ___: 4 Mart, star **5** meson **6** ration
K ___ kind: 4 as in
K-___: 3 Tel **4** line **5** shell, truss **6** series
K. ___: 3 of C., of P.
'K' ___ Killer: 5 Is for
___-K: 3 pre
K-9 (1989 film)
cast: James Belushi, Mel Harris, Ed O'Neill
dog: 8 Jerry Lee
ka-___: 4 blam, boom **5** ching
Ka ___, HI: 3 Lae
Kaaba
dedicatee: 5 Allah
pilgrim: 5 hadji
Kaat, Jim sport: 8 baseball
Kabel: 4 font **8** typeface
Kabibble: 3 Ish
kabob: 9 brochette
ingredient: 4 lamb
skewer: 4 spit
kaboom: 3 pow **4** bang **5** blast, noise **6** whammo
Kaboom: 6 cereal
competitor: 3 Kix **4** Life, Trix **5** Kashi, Quisp, Total **6** Muesli, Oreo O's, Pablum, Smacks **7** All-Bran, Crispix, Harmony, Hunny B's, Mueslix, Oat Bran, Pokemon **8** Boo Berry, Cheerios, Corn Chex, Corn Pops, Fiber One, Rice Chex, Special K, Uncle Sam, Wheaties **9** Alpha Bits, Apple Zaps, Grape Nuts, Honey Comb, Just Right, Wheat Chex **10** Apple Jacks, Bran Flakes, Cap'n Crunch, Cocoa Puffs, Froot Loops, Mini-Wheats, Nutri-Grain, Puffed Rice, Quaker Oats, Smart Start **11** Cocoa Blasts, Cookie Crisp, Golden Crisp, Lucky Charms, Puffed Wheat, Sweet Crunch, Waffle Crisp
Kabru: 4 peak **5** mount **8** mountain
locale: 4 Asia **5** Nepal **9** Himalayas
kabuki: 5 drama **7** theater **8** Japanese
alternative: 3 noh
performer: 4 male
___ Kabuki: 5 Grand
Kabul: 4 city, town **5** river **7** capital
locale: 4 Asia **11** Afghanistan
native: 6 Afghan **7** Afghani
River locale: 8 Pakistan
Kabwe: 4 city, town
locale: 6 Zambia
kachina: 4 doll
creator: 4 Hopi
Kadar: 3 Jan
Kádár: 5 János
Kaddish Symphony composer: 9 Bernstein
Kadeem: 8 Hardison
Kadett: 3 car **4** auto, Opel **10** automobile
Kadiddlehopper: 4 Clem
portrayer: 7 Skelton
Kadoma: 4 city, town
locale: 5 Japan **8** Zimbabwe
Kaduna: 4 city, town
locale: 7 Nigeria
Kael: 7 Pauline
Kaélé: 4 city, town
locale: 8 Cameroon
Kaempfert: 4 Bert **9** conductor
kaffee ___: 6 klatch **7** klatsch
Kaffir: 6 Afghan **7** Afghani
kaffiyeh: 5 scarf **8** kerchief **9** headdress
cord: 4 agal
Kafkaesque: 5 weird
emotion: 5 angst
Kafka, Franz: 6 German, writer
birthplace: Prague
work: Amerika
The Castle
In the Penal Colony
The Metamorphosis
The Trial
kaftan: 4 robe
kin: 6 kimono
Kafue: 5 river
locale: 5 Congo, Zaire **6** Zambia
Kagera: 5 river
locale: 6 Africa, Uganda **8** Tanzania
Kagoshima: 4 city, port, town
locale: 5 Japan
kagu: 4 bird
Kahldun: 3 Ibn
Kahlil: 6 Gibran
Kahlo, Frida: 6 artist **7** Mexican, painter
spouse: Diego Rivera
work: The Broken Column
The Dream
My Birth
Kahn: 3 Gus **4** Otto **5** Louis **6** Albert **8** Madeline
Kahneman, Daniel: 8 Nobelist **9** economist
Kahn, Gus: 8 lyricist
song: Ain't We Got Fun
Carolina in the Morning
Chloe
Dream a Little Dream of Me
I'll See You in My Dreams
It Had to Be You
Liza
Love Me or Leave Me
Makin' Whoopee
My Baby Just Cares for Me
My Buddy
San Francisco
Toot Toot Tootsie
When Lights Are Low
Yes Sir, That's My Baby
You Stepped Out of a Dream
Kahn, Madeline: 7 actress
film: Blazing Saddles (1974)
City Heat (1984)
High Anxiety (1977)
Paper Moon (1973)
What's Up, Doc? (1972)
Young Frankenstein (1974)
TV: Cosby
Kahn's: 6 hot dog
alternative: 6 Armour **8** Ball Park **10** Oscar Mayer
Kahului: 4 city, town
locale: 4 Maui **6** Hawaii
kahuna: 3 VIP **7** big shot **9** dignitary
___ kahuna: 3 big
Kai: 7 Winding **8** Siegbahn
Kaieteur: 5 falls **9** waterfall
locale: 6 Guyana
Kailua: 4 city, town
locale: 4 Oahu **6** Hawaii
kaiser: 4 roll **5** ruler, title **6** gerent **7** monarch, Wilhelm
counterpart: 4 czar, king, tsar **7** emperor
Kaiser: 3 car **4** auto **5** Georg
Kaiser, Georg: 6 German **10** playwright
Kaiser Permanente: 3 HMO
Kai-shek: 6 Chiang
kaka: 4 bird
kakapo: 4 bird
kaki: 4 tree **5** drupe, fruit **9** persimmon
Kakkab: 4 star
kakko: 4 drum
origin: 5 Japan
Kakogawa: 4 city, town
locale: 5 Japan
Kal ___: 3 Kan
Kalahari: 6 desert
beast: 6 impala
lake north of the ~: 5 Ngami
like the ~: 3 dry **4** arid, bare, flat, sere **5** dusty **6** barren, desert **7** bone-dry, parched, thirsty **9** waterless
Kalamazoo: 4 city, town
athletes: 7 Broncos
locale: 8 Michigan
school: 3 WMU
Kalambo ___: 5 Falls
kalanchoe: 5 shrub
Kalb: 6 Marvin **7** Bernard
kale: 3 oof **4** cash, gelt, jack, loot, peag, pelf **5** bills, bread, bucks, dough, funds, lucre, money, moola, mopus, pesos, rhino, sewan **6** dinero, do-re-mi, greens, mammon, mazuma, moolah, seawan, silver, specie, veggie, wampum, wealth **7** cabbage, capital, dollars, lettuce, ooftish, scratch, shekels **8** bankroll, borecole, cold cash, colewort, currency, hard cash, smackers **9** banknotes, frogskins, long green, simoleons, vegetable **10** greenbacks, green stuff
___ kale: 3 sea **4** ruvo
Kaleidoscope author: 5 Steel
kaleidoscopic: 6 motley **7** protean, surreal **8** colorful, shifting
Kalember: 8 Patricia
___ kalends: 5 Greek
Kalevala: 4 epic
Kalidasa: 4 poet **6** Indian **10** playwright
Kalifornia (1993 film)
cast: David Duchovny, Juliette Lewis, Brad Pitt
kalimba: 5 mbira **7** marimba **10** percussion
origin: 6 Africa
Kaline: 2 Al **7** Mr. Tiger **10** outfielder
Kalispell: 4 city, town
locale: 7 Montana
Kalisz: 4 city, town
locale: 6 Poland
Kalix: 4 font **8** typeface
Kal Kan rival: 4 Alpo, Iams **6** Purina
Kallen: 5 Kitty
Kalliope: 8 asteroid
Kalmar: 4 Bert, port **5** Sound
kalmia: 5 shrub
relative: 5 heath, salal **6** azalea **7** arbutus, rhodora **8** cassiope, cowberry **9** blueberry, deerberry
kalong: 9 flying fox
kalungu: 4 drum
origin: 6 Africa
Kama: 5 river
locale: 6 Russia
Kama ___: 5 Sutra
kamacite: 5 alloy
component: 4 iron **6** nickel
Kamali: 5 Norma
Kamba home: 5 Kenya **6** Africa
Kamehameha ___: 3 Day
Kamehameha Highway locale: 4 Oahu
Kamerlingh Onnes, Heike: 5 Dutch **8** Nobelist **9** physicist
Kamet: 4 peak **5** mount **8** mountain
locale: 4 Asia **5** China, India
Kami: 6 Cotler
Kamina: 4 city
locale: 5 Congo
Kaminska: 3 Ida
Kamloops: 4 city, town
locale: 6 Canada
kampai: 5 salud, skoal, toast **6** cheers, prosit, salute **9** happy days
Kampala: 4 city, town **7** capital
former ~ kingpin: 3 Idi **4** Amin
locale: 6 Uganda
Kan.
neighbor: 2 Mo. **3** Col., Neb. **4** Colo., Nebr., Okla.
see also Kansas
___ Kan: 3 Kal
Kanab: 4 city, town
locale: 4 Utah
kanaka: 3 man **8** Hawaiian
Kanakaredes: 6 Melina
Kanaly: 5 Steve
Kananga: 4 town
Kanasín: 4 city, town
locale: 6 Mexico **7** Yucatán
Kanata: 4 city, town
locale: 6 Canada **7** Ontario
Kanawha, city on the: 10 Charleston
Kanazawa: 4 city, town
locale: 5 Japan
Kanchenjunga: 4 peak **5** mount
locale: 4 Asia **5** Nepal **6** Sikkim
Kandel, Eric: 8 Nobelist
Kander, John: 8 composer
collaborator: Fred Ebb
musical: 70, Girls, 70
The Act
Cabaret
Chicago
A Family Affair
Flora, the Red Menace
The Happy Time
Kiss of the Spider Woman
The Rink
Steel Pier
Woman of the Year
Zorba
song: All I Care About
All That Jazz
Arthur in the Afternoon
But the World Goes 'Round
Cabaret
City Lights
Class
Coffee in a Cardboard Cup
Colored Lights
Dance With Me
Dressing Them Up
Everybody's Girl
First You Dream
The Grass Is Always Greener
The Happy Time
How Lucky Can You Get
I Don't Care Much
I Don't Remember You
Isn't This Better?
Life Is
Married
Marry Me
Maybe This Time
Me and My Baby
Mein Herr
Mister Cellophane
Money
My Coloring Book
My Own Best Friend
My Own Space
New York, New York
Nowadays
Perfectly Marvelous
A Quiet Thing
Razzle Dazzle
Ring Them Bells
Roxie
Sara Lee
Sing Happy
Sometimes a Day Goes By
There Goes the Ball Game
We Can Make It
When You're Good to Mama
Where You Are
Willkommen
Yes

Kandinsky: 6 Vasily 7 Wassily
Kandinsky, Vasily: 6 artist 7 painter
colleague: 4 Klee
homeland: 6 Russia
Kandy-Kolored Tangerine... author: Tom Wolfe
Kane: 3 Bob 5 Carol, Erica, Helen 6 Joseph
last memory: 4 sled 7 Rosebud
portrayer: 6 Welles
Xanadu to ~: 6 estate
__ Kane: 7 Citizen
Kane and __: 4 Abel
Kaneohe: 3 bay 4 city, town
locale: 4 Oahu 6 Hawaii
Kanga
creator: 5 Milne
offspring: 3 Roo
kangaroo: 6 animal, hopper, jumper, mammal 9 marsupial
feature: 3 sac 5 pouch 6 pocket
female: 3 doe 5 flier, flyer
large ~: 4 euro
like a ~ court: 4 fake, mock, sham 5 bogus, false, hokey, phony 6 ersatz, parody, pseudo 8 so-called, spurious, travesty 9 pretended
male: 4 buck 6 boomer
relative: 4 euro 5 bilbi, bilby, koala 6 numbat, wombat 7 bettong, dasyure, opossum, wallaby 8 wallaroo 9 bandicoot, phalanger
small ~: 5 tungo
young ~: 4 joey
kangaroo __: 3 rat 4 vine 5 court
Kangaroo author: D.H. Lawrence
__ Kangaroo Down, Sport: 5 Tie Me
Kangto: 4 peak 5 mount 8 mountain
locale: 4 Asia 5 China, Tibet
Kanin, Garson: 6 author 8 director
film: Bachelor Mother (1939)
The Great Man Votes (1939)
My Favorite Wife (1940)
They Knew What They Wanted (1940)
Tom, Dick and Harry (1941)
spouse: Ruth Gordon
kanji alternative: 4 kana 6 romaji 8 hiragana, katakana
Kanjut Sar: 4 peak 5 mount 8 mountain
locale: 4 Asia 7 Kashmir
Kankakee: 4 city, town
locale: 8 Illinois
Kankan: 4 city, town
locale: 6 Guinea
Kannapolis: 4 city, town
locale: 4 N. Car.
Kano: 4 city, town
locale: 7 Nigeria
Kanpur: 4 city, town
locale: 5 India
kans: 5 grass
Kans.
see Kan., Kansas
Kansa: 5 tribe 6 Indian 7 Amerind
Kansan: 7 Bob Dole, Dorothy 8 Auntie Em 9 Alf Landon, Jayhawker, Jim Lehrer, Wyatt Earp 10 Mort Walker, Wizard of Oz
Kansas: 4 band 5 river, state
city: 4 Iola 5 Paola 6 Lenexa, Olathe, Salina, Topeka 7 Abilene, Emporia, Leawood, Liberal, Shawnee, Wichita 8 Lawrence 9 Dodge City, Fort Riley, Manhattan 10 Garden City, Hutchinson, Kansas City
city on the ~: 6 Topeka
conference: 9 Big Twelve
crop: 4 corn 5 wheat 7 sorghum 8 soybeans
Indian: 8 Kickapoo
like ~ in August: 5 corny
motto word: 5 astra 6 aspera
neighbor: 8 Colorado, Missouri, Nebraska, Oklahoma
pooch: 4 Toto
river: 5 Osage
river to the ~: 10 Republican
song: Dust in the Wind (1978)
state animal: 7 buffalo
state bird: 10 meadowlark
state flower: 9 sunflower
state insect: 8 honeybee
state tree: 10 cottonwood
Kansas __ Confidential: 4 City
Kansas __ steak: 4 City
Kansas City: 4 city, town
county: 4 Clay 6 Platte 7 Jackson
locale: 6 Kansas 8 Missouri
newspaper: 4 Star
pro team: 6 Chiefs, Royals
river: 8 Missouri
Kansas City (1959 song) artist: Wilbert Harrison
Kansas-Nebraska __: 3 Act
Kansas State University
athletes: 8 Wildcats
conference: 9 Big Twelve
locale: 9 Manhattan
kantele: 4 lute 6 string
origin: 7 Finland
Kant, Immanuel: 6 German 11 philosopher
Kantner: 4 Paul
Kantor: 4 Seth 6 Mickey 9 MacKinlay
Kantorovich, Leonid: 8 Nobelist 9 economist
Kanuri home: 4 Chad 5 Niger 6 Africa 7 Nigeria 8 Cameroon
kanzu: 4 robe
Kaohsiung: 4 city, port, town
locale: 6 Taiwan
kaolin: 4 clay 9 china clay, terra alba
kaon: 5 meson 8 particle
Kapell, William: 7 pianist
kaph: 6 Hebrew, letter
predecessor: 3 yod 4 yodh
successor: 5 lamed 6 lamedh
__ Kapital: 3 Das
Kapitän command: 5 U-boat
Kapitsa: 5 Pyotr
Kaplan: 4 Gabe, peak 5 Hyman, mount 8 Jonathan, mountain
locale: 10 Antarctica
kapok: 4 fuzz 5 ceiba, fiber 8 filament
kapok __: 3 oil 4 tree
Kapor: 5 Mitch
kapow: 3 bam 4 boom, slam, wham
kappa: 5 Greek 6 letter
follower: 6 lambda
preceder: 4 iota
Kappelhoff, Doris: 3 Day
Kapture: 5 Mitzi
kapuka: 4 tree
family: 7 dogwood
relative: 7 assagai, assegai, javelin
kaput: 4 beat, fini, over, shot, sunk, worn 5 broke 6 broken, done in, finito, no more, ruined, undone 7 all over, belly-up, damaged, defunct, done for, extinct, totaled, worn-out, wrecked 8 finished, obsolete, washed-up, wiped out 9 burned out, destroyed 10 beyond help, broken-down, demolished, dissipated, on the blink, on the fritz
go ~: 3 die 4 fail, flop, fold 6 fizzle 7 conk out 8 backfire 9 break down
not ~: 5 going 6 usable 7 running, working 8 operable, unbroken 9 operative
Kara __: 3 Kum, Sea
Karachi: 4 city, port, town
language: 4 Urdu
locale: 8 Pakistan
river: 5 Indus
Karajan, Herbert von: 8 Austrian 9 conductor
Karakoram: 5 range
locale: 4 Asia 7 Kashmir 8 Cashmere
karakul: 3 fur 5 sheep
Kara Kum: 6 desert
Karamazov: 4 Ivan 5 Mitya 6 Alexey, Dmitri, Fyodor 7 Alyosha
Karamzin, Nikolay: 6 writer 7 Russian
Karan: 5 Donna
karanda: 4 tree 5 shrub
family: 7 dogbane
relative: 8 oleander 10 frangipahi
Karankawa: 6 Indian 7 Amerind
__ karaoke: 5 laser
karaoke need: 4 mike
Karas, Anton instrument: zither
Kara Sea, river to the: 7 Yenisei
karate: 5 sport 10 martial art
attire: 2 gi 4 belt
belt: 5 black, brown, green, white
cousin: 4 judo 6 aikido
level: 3 dan
move: 4 chop; kick
origin: 5 Japan
studio: 4 dojo
target: 5 board
warm-up: 4 kata
karate __: 4 chop 6 sticks
Karate Kid, The (1984 film)
cast: Ralph Macchio, Pat Morita, Elisabeth Shue
director: John G. Avildsen
Kareem: 3 Lew
alma mater: 4 UCLA
Kareem __-Jabbar: 5 Abdul
Karel: 5 Capek, Reisz
Karelian __: 7 Isthmus
Karen: 5 Akers, Allen, Black, Duffy 6 Blixen, Finlay, Horney, Morley, Sillas 7 Dotrice, Grassle 8 Silkwood 9 Carpenter, Valentine
Karen __ Gorney: 4 Lynn
__ Karenina: 4 Anna
Kariba: 4 lake
locale: 6 Zambia 8 Zimbabwe
Karim of the Khans: 3 Aga
Karin: 4 Enke
Karina: 7 Lombard
Karkheh: 5 river
locale: 4 Iran
Karl: 4 Benz, Böhm, Marx, Rove 5 Barth, Gauss, Kraus 6 Czerny, Malden, Malone, Popper 7 Gutzkow, Jaspers, Scheele, Shapiro, von Baer, Ziegler 8 Baedeker, Branting, Siegbahn, Wallenda 9 Gjellerup, Lagerfeld, Menninger
in English: 7 Charles
Karle, Jerome: 7 chemist 8 Nobelist
Karlfeldt, Erik: 4 poet 7 Swedish 8 Nobelist
Karloff, Boris: 5 actor
film: Bedlam (1946)
The Black Cat (1934)
The Black Room (1935)
The Body Snatcher (1945)
Bride of Frankenstein (1935)
Charlie Chan at the Opera (1936)
The Climax (1944)
The Comedy of Terrors (1964)
Frankenstein (1931)
House of Rothschild (1934)
Isle of the Dead (1945)
The Lost Patrol (1934)
The Mummy (1932)
Night World (1932)
The Old Dark House (1932)
The Raven (1935)
The Raven (1963)
The Secret Life of Walter Mitty (1947)
Son of Frankenstein (1939)
Targets (1968)
The Walking Dead (1936)
real last name: 5 Pratt
Karlovy Vary: 3 spa 5 Czech
Karlson: 4 Phil
Karlsruhe: 4 city, town
locale: 7 Germany
Karl von __: 4 Baer 6 Frisch
karma: 3 lot 4 fate, luck, vibe 5 vibes 6 kismat, kismet 7 destiny, fortune
__ Karma: 7 Instant
Karma Chameleon (1983 song) artist: Culture Club
Karmann __: 4 Ghia
Karnak
locale: 5 Egypt
neighbor: 5 Luxor
river: 4 Nile
Temple of ~ site: 6 Thebes
Karns: 6 Roscoe
karo: 4 tree 5 shrub
Karo: 5 syrup
Karolyi: 4 Bela
kaross: 4 wrap 5 cloak
Karpov, Anatoly forte: 5 chess
Karras, Alex: 5 actor
film: Paper Lion (1968)
Victor/Victoria (1982)
spouse: Susan Clark
TV: Webster
Karrer, Paul: 7 chemist 8 Nobelist
karri: 4 tree
Karrie: 4 Webb
Karsavina: 6 Tamara
Karsh: 6 Yousuf
kart: 5 racer
Karthala: 7 volcano
locale: 6 Africa 7 Comoros
Karun: 5 river
locale: 4 Iran
Karymsky: 7 volcano
locale: 4 Asia 6 Russia
Karyn: 5 White 7 Allison
Kasai: 5 river
locale: 5 Congo 6 Angola
Kasbah
see Casbah
Kasdan: 4 Jake 8 Lawrence
Kasdan, Lawrence: 8 director
film: The Accidental Tourist (1988)
The Big Chill (1983)
Body Heat (1981)
Grand Canyon (1991)
Mumford (1999)
Silverado (1985)
Wyatt Earp (1994)
Kasem, Casey: 6 deejay 10 disc jockey
kasha: 5 grain 6 groats 9 buckwheat
Kasha: 6 fabric
Kashi: 6 cereal
competitor: 3 Kix 4 Life, Trix 5 Quisp, Total 6 Kaboom, Muesli, Oreo O's, Pablum, Smacks 7 All-Bran, Crispix, Harmony, Hunny B's, Mueslix, Oat Bran, Pokemon 8 Boo Berry, Cheerios, Corn Chex, Corn Pops, Fiber One, Rice Chex, Special K, Uncle Sam, Wheaties 9 Alpha Bits, Apple Zaps, Grape Nuts, Honey Comb, Just Right, Wheat Chex 10 Apple Jacks, Bran Flakes, Cap'n Crunch, Cocoa Puffs, Froot Loops, Mini-Wheats, Nutri-Grain, Puffed Rice, Quaker Oats, Smart Start 11 Cocoa Blasts, Cookie Crisp, Golden Crisp, Lucky Charms, Puffed Wheat, Sweet Crunch, Waffle Crisp
Kashiwa: 4 city, town
locale: 5 Japan
Kashmir: 4 wool 7 sweater
cash: 5 rupee
deer: 6 hangul
feature: 4 vale
mountain: 6 Nunkun 7 Mustagh 9 Karakoram, Sia Kangri 10 Masherbrum
river: 5 Indus

Kashmir __: 3 rug 4 goat
kashruth expert: 5 rabbi, rebbe
Kaska: 6 Indian 7 Amerind
Kaslo: 4 city, town
  locale: 6 Canada
Kasparov, Garry
  forte: 5 chess
  rival: 6 Karpov 8 Deep Blue
Kassebaum, Nancy: 6 Kansan
  father: 3 Alf 6 Landon
  formerly: 3 sen. 7 senator
Kassel: 4 city, town
  locale: 7 Germany
  river: 4 Eder 5 Fulda
Kastler, Alfred: 8 Nobelist 9 physicist
Kastner: 5 Peter
Kastor and __: 6 Pollux
Kasuga: 4 city, town
  locale: 5 Japan
kat: 5 shrub
Katahdin: 4 peak 5 mount 8 mountain
  locale: 5 Maine
katakana alternative: 4 kana 5 kanji 6 romaji 8 hiragana
Katarina: 4 Witt
Katayev, Valentin: 6 author, writer 7 Russian 10 playwright
__-Kat Club: 3 Kit
Kate: 4 Bush, Moss, Reid 5 O'Mara, Smith 6 Chopin, Hudson, Linder, Wiggen 7 Capshaw, Fansler, Jackson, Millett, Mulgrew, Pierson, Winslet 8 Nelligan 9 Greenaway 10 Beckinsale
  colleague of ~: 6 Farrah, Jaclyn
  companion: 5 Allie
  to Petruchio: 4 wife
Kate & Allie (CBS sitcom)
  cast: Jane Curtin (Allie Lowell)
    Ari Meyers (Emma McArdle)
    Susan Saint James (Kate McArdle)
Kate & Leopold (2001 film)
  cast: Hugh Jackman, Meg Ryan, Liev Schreiber
__-Kate Olsen: 4 Mary
Katey: 5 Sagal
kathak: 5 dance
Katharine: 4 Ross 6 Graham 7 Cornell, Hepburn
Katharine __ Bates: 3 Lee
Katharine __ McCormick: 6 Dexter
Katharine __ School: 5 Gibbs
Katherine: 6 Dunham 7 Cornell, Helmond 9 Mansfield
  in Irish: 7 Caitlin
Katherine __ Porter: 4 Anne
Kathie __ Gifford: 3 Lee
Kathleen: 5 Lloyd, Nolan, Noone, Raine 6 Battle, Norris, Turner 7 Freeman, Kinmont, Quinlan 8 Sullivan
Kathryn: 5 Grant 6 Murray 7 Bigelow, Grayson, Harrold
Kathryn's dancing partner: 6 Arthur
Kathy: 5 Baker, Bates, Young 6 Garver, Kinney, Lennon, Linden, Mattea, Najimy 7 Ireland 9 Whitworth
Katie: 6 Couric, Holmes, Wagner
Katie Went to Haiti composer: 6 Porter
Katina: 7 Paxinou
Katmai: 4 park, peak 5 mount 7 volcano 8 mountain
  locale: 6 Alaska
Katmandu: 4 city, town 7 capital
  like ~: 4 high 5 lofty 8 elevated
  locale: 5 Nepal
Kato to the Green Hornet: 4 aide
Katrina and the Waves song: Walking on Sunshine (1985)
Katrine: 4 loch
  locale: 8 Scotland
Katsuta: 4 city, town
  locale: 5 Japan
Katt: 5 Nicky 7 William
Katy: 6 Jurado
__-Katy: 3 K-K-K
katydid: 3 bug 6 insect

Katz, Bernard: 8 Nobelist
Katzenberg: 7 Jeffrey
katzenjammer: 6 clamor, uproar 7 anguish 8 distress, hangover 10 uneasiness
Katzenjammer Kids, The: 5 comic, strip
  artist: 5 Dirks, Knerr
  kid: 4 Hans 5 Fritz
Kauai: 3 isl. 4 isle 6 island
  locale: 6 Hawaii
  neighbor: 4 Oahu
Kaufman: 3 Bel 4 Andy 6 George, Philip
Kaufman, Andy sitcom: 4 Taxi
Kaufman, George S.: 6 author, writer 10 playwright
  collaborator: 4 Hart 6 Ferber 7 Lardner, Ryskind 8 Connelly
  middle name: Simon
  nickname: The Great Collaborator
  work: Animal Crackers
    Beggar on Horseback
    The Butter and Egg Man
    The Cocoanuts
    Dinner at Eight
    Dulcy
    I'd Rather Be Right
    June Moon
    The Man Who Came to Dinner
    Of Thee I Sing
    Once in a Lifetime
    The Solid Gold Cadillac
    Stage Door
    You Can't Take It With You
Kaufman, Philip: 8 director
  film: Henry & June (1990)
    Invasion of the Body Snatchers (1978)
    Quills (2000)
    The Right Stuff (1983)
    Rising Sun (1993)
    The Unbearable Lightness of Being (1988)
    The Wanderers (1979)
Kaunas: 4 city, town
  locale: 9 Lithuania
kauri: 4 tree
kauri __: 3 gum 4 pine 5 copal, resin
kava: 5 booze, drink, shrub 7 alcohol, potable 8 beverage 10 intoxicant
  relative: 5 cubeb 6 pepper
Kavafian: 3 Ani, Ida
Kavanaugh, Patrick: 4 poet 5 Irish
Kavi: 3 Raz
Kavir: 6 desert
Kavner, Julie: 7 actress
  film: Awakenings (1990)
    Radio Days (1987)
    This Is My Life (1992)
  TV: Rhoda, The Simpsons, The Tracey Ullman Show
Kawabata, Yasunari: 6 writer 8 Japanese, Nobelist
Kawagoe: 4 city, town
  locale: 5 Japan
Kawasaki: 4 city, town 10 motorcycle
  competitor: 5 Yamah 6 Harley
  locale: 5 Japan
kay: 6 letter
  follower: 3 ell
  preceder: 3 jay
Kay: 3 Yow 4 Lenz 5 Armen, Boyle, Kyser, Starr, Swift, Walsh 6 knight 7 Francis, Johnson, Kendall, Miniver 8 Corleone, Thompson
  title for ~: 3 Sir
__ Kay: 4 Mary
kayak: 4 boat 5 canoe, skiff
  cousin: 5 umiak 6 dugout 9 outrigger
  locale: 6 Arctic, rapids
  need: 3 oar
  user: 5 Inuit, rower 6 Eskimo, Innuit, Inupik
__ Kay Ash: 4 Mary
Kaye: 5 Danny, Sammy 6 Stubby 7 Ballard

Kaye, Danny: 5 actor 8 comedian
  film: Court Jester (1956)
    Hans Christian Andersen (1952)
    The Inspector General (1949)
    The Kid From Brooklyn (1946)
    Knock on Wood (1954)
    On the Double (1961)
    On the Riviera (1951)
    The Secret Life of Walter Mitty (1947)
    White Christmas (1954)
    Wonder Man (1945)
Kaye Lani Rae __: 5 Rafko
Kaye, Sammy instrument: clarinet, sax
kayo: 3 hit 4 deck, stun 5 floor 6 defeat 7 flatten 8 knock out
__ Kay Place: 4 Mary
Kaysville: 4 city, town
  locale: 4 Utah
Kazakhstan: 6 nation 7 country
  capital: 6 Astana
  city: 6 Astana 7 Alma-Ata
  desert: 7 Kara Kum 8 Kyzyl Kum
  lake: 8 Balkhash
  neighbor: 5 China 6 Russia 10 Kyrgyzstan, Uzbekistan
  once: 3 SSR
  range: 5 Altai
  river: 4 Ural 5 Tobol
  sea: 4 Aral
Kazan: 4 city, Elia, town 6 Lainie
  locale: 6 Russia
  republic: 5 Tatar
Kazan, Elia: 8 director
  film: America, America (1963)
    Baby Doll (1956)
    Boomerang! (1947)
    East of Eden (1955)
    A Face in the Crowd (1957)
    Gentleman's Agreement (1947, AA)
    The Last Tycoon (1976)
    On the Waterfront (1954, AA)
    Panic in the Streets (1950)
    Pinky (1949)
    Splendor in the Grass (1961)
    A Streetcar Named Desire (1951)
    A Tree Grows in Brooklyn (1945)
    Viva Zapata! (1952)
    Wild River (1960)
Kazantzakis, Nikos: 5 Greek 6 writer
  work: The Last Temptation of Christ
    Zorba the Greek
kazatsky: 5 dance 7 Russian
kazoo: 3 toy 4 wind, zobo
  play a ~: 3 hum 4 buzz 5 drone
Kazurinsky: 3 Tim
KC and the Sunshine Band
  song: Get Down Tonight (1975)
    I'm Your Boogie Man (1977)
    Keep It Comin' Love (1977)
    Please Don't Go (1979)
    Shake Your Booty (1976)
    That's the Way (1975)
    Yes I'm Ready (1979)
k.d.: 4 lang
__ K. Dick: 6 Philip
K-Doe: 5 Ernie
kea: 4 bird 6 parrot
__ Kea: 5 Mauna
Keach: 5 James, Stacy
Keach, James: 5 actor
  brother: Stacy
  film: The Experts (1989)
    The Long Riders (1980)
    The New Swiss Family Robinson (1998)
  spouse: Jane Seymour
Keach, Stacy: 5 actor
  brother: James
  film: Butterfly (1981)
    End of the Road (1970)
    Fat City (1972)
    The Killer Inside Me (1976)
    The Long Riders (1980)
    The New Centurions (1972)
    The Ninth Configuration (1980)
    Up in Smoke (1978)
  TV: Caribe, Mike Hammer, Titus
Kean: 6 Edmund
Keane: 3 Bil
Keanu: 6 Reeves
Kearney: 4 city, town
  locale: 8 Nebraska
__ Kearney: 4 Fort
Kearns: 4 city, town 6 Joseph
  locale: 4 Utah
Kearny: 4 city, town
  locale: 9 New Jersey
Keating: 5 Larry 7 Dominic
Keaton: 5 Diane 6 Buster 7 Michael
  to Allen: 6 costar
Keaton, Buster: 5 actor 8 comedian
  film: 4 Clowns (1970)
    The Cameraman (1928)
    College (1927)
    Film (1965)
    A Funny Thing Happened... (1966)
    The General (1927)
    It's a Mad Mad Mad Mad World (1963)
    Our Hospitality (1923)
    Seven Chances (1925)
    Sherlock, Jr. (1924)
    Speak Easily (1932)
    Spite Marriage (1929)
    Steamboat Bill, Jr. (1928)
    Three Ages (1923)
  nickname: The Great Stone Face
Keaton, Diane: 7 actress
  film: Annie Hall (1977, AA)
    Baby Boom (1987)
    Crimes of the Heart (1986)
    Father of the Bride (1991)
    The First Wives Club (1996)
    The Godfather (1972)
    The Godfather Part II (1974)
    The Godfather Part III (1990)
    The Good Mother (1988)
    Hanging Up (2000)
    Interiors (1978)
    The Little Drummer Girl (1984)
    Looking for Mr. Goodbar (1977)
    Love and Death (1975)
    Manhattan (1979)
    Manhattan Murder Mystery (1993)
    The Other Sister (1999)
    Play It Again, Sam (1972)
    Reds (1981)
    Shoot the Moon (1982)
    Sleeper (1973)
    Something's Gotta Give (2003)
Keaton, Elyse
  child: 4 Alex 7 Mallory
Keaton, Michael: 5 actor
  film: Batman (1989)
    Batman Returns (1992)
    Beetlejuice (1988)
    Clean and Sober (1988)
    The Dream Team (1989)
    Gung Ho (1986)
    Jack Frost (1998)
    Jackie Brown (1997)
    Mr. Mom (1983)
    Much Ado About Nothing (1993)
    Night Shift (1982)
    Out of Sight (1998)
    Pacific Heights (1990)
    The Paper (1994)
    Speechless (1994)
Keats, John: 4 poet 7 British
  contemporary: 5 Byron 7 Shelley
  like some ~ works: 4 odic
  Muse for ~: 5 Erato
  work: Endymion
    The Eve of St. Agnes
    Hyperion

Isabella
Lamia
Meg Merrilies
Ode on a Grecian Urn
Ode on Indolence
Ode on Melancholy
Ode to a Nightingale
Ode to Autumn
Ode to Psyche
On First Looking Into Chapman's Homer
To Autumn
To Homer
To Sleep
When I Have Fears

kebab: 5 spear **6** skewer **9** brochette
bed: 5 pilaf, pilau, pilaw **6** pilaff
ingredient: 4 lamb, meat
__ kebab: 5 shish
kedge: 6 anchor
Kedrova, Lila Oscar: Zorba the Greek
Keds: 6 sneaks **8** sneakers
competitor: 4 Avia, Nike **6** Adidas, Reebok **8** Converse
Keebler: 6 cookie
alternative: 7 Archway, Nabisco **8** Sunshine **9** Mrs. Fields **10** Famous Amos, Peak Freans
brand: 5 Zesta
worker: 3 elf
Keefe: 3 Tim **9** Brasselle
keel: 3 yaw **4** cant, lean, list, reel, roll, sway, toss **5** heave, lurch, pitch, swing **6** careen, wallow **8** flounder
deck just above the ~: 5 orlop
ender: 4 boat, haul
extension: 4 skeg
on an even ~: 5 level **6** smooth, stable, steady
over: 3 tip **4** fall, list **5** faint, slump, swoon **6** go limp, topple **7** capsize, pass out **8** overturn
pole: 4 mast
keel __: 4 bone, over **6** vessel
__ keel: 3 box, fin **4** bulb, drop, duct **5** bilge **7** docking
Keel: 6 Howard
keel, at right angles to: 5 abeam
keelbone, bird: 6 carina
Keeler: 4 Ruby **6** Willie
Keeler, Ruby: 6 dancer **7** actress
film: 42nd Street (1933)
Colleen (1936)
Dames (1934)
Footlight Parade (1933)
Gold Diggers of 1933 (1933)
spouse: Al Jolson
style: 3 tap
Keeler, Willie: 10 outfielder
Keel, Howard: 5 actor
film: Annie Get Your Gun (1950)
Calamity Jane (1953)
Day of the Triffids (1963)
Jupiter's Darling (1955)
Kiss Me Kate (1953)
Seven Brides for Seven Brothers (1954)
Show Boat (1951)
The War Wagon (1967)
TV: Dallas
Keeling __: 7 Islands
Keelung: 4 city, port, town
locale: 6 Taiwan
Keely: 5 Smith
keen: 3 def, mad, rad **4** able, aces, agog, A-one, avid, boss, braw, cool, dece, fine, gear, howl, moan, neat, nice, phat, sour, tuff, wail, weep **5** acute, brisk, dandy, ducky, eager, edged, fresh, grand, great, honed, itchy, marvy, mourn, neato, nifty, nobby, prime, quick, ready, sharp, slick, smart, spicy, super, swell, witty **6** ardent, astute, bang on, bang-up, bonzer, bosker, bright, choice, divine, dreamy, far-out, fervid, gnarly, groovy, gung ho, intent, lament, lively, lovely, on edge, peachy, rah-rah, shrewd, slap-up, spicey, spot on, strong, subtle, superb, terrif, tiptop, unreal, whizzo, wicked **7** amazing, anxious, athirst, awesome, capital, corking, cunning, cutting, earnest, fervent, fired up, glowing, intense, perfect, pointed, pungent, ripping, skookum, stellar, sublime, thirsty, ululate, whetted, zealous **8** animated, dazzling, deep-felt, desirous, enthused, especial, eximious, fabulous, five-star, four-star, frabjous, glorious, heavenly, incisive, jim-dandy, lynx-eyed, piercing, poignant, profound, slam-bang, smashing, spirited, splendid, standout, sterling, stickout, superior, terrific, top-level, topnotch, very good, vigilant, watchful, wondrous **9** admirable, astucious, bodacious, Endsville, excellent, exemplary, exquisite, farseeing, first-rate, high-grade, hunky-dory, judicious, marvelous, observant, sagacious, sensitive, sharpened, sollicker, sprightly, top-flight, trenchant, wonderful **10** all fired up, discerning, first-class, hotsy-totsy, insightful, inspirited, interested, jack-a-dandy, longheaded, out of sight, passionate, peachy-keen, perceptive, phenomenal, raring to go, remarkable, sharp-edged, solicitous, stupendous, super-duper, take it hard, thoughtful
be ~ on: 4 like, love **5** adore
make ~: 4 whet **5** pique, rally, rouse, strop **6** arouse, excite, kindle **7** sharpen
not ~: 4 dull, slow **5** blunt, dense **6** obtuse, stupid **7** witless **9** dimwitted
on: 6 fond of **7** stuck on, sweet on **9** partial to **10** in love with
perception: 3 wit **5** grasp **6** acuity, acumen, wisdom **7** insight **8** judgment, lucidity **9** acuteness, awareness **10** astuteness, brainpower, brilliance, cleverness, shrewdness
(to): 7 itching **9** hankering
__ keen: 6 peachy
Keenan: 4 Wynn
father: 2 Ed
Keene: 4 city, town **7** Carolyn
sleuth: 4 Drew **5** Nancy
keen-edged: 5 sharp
Keenen __ Wayans: 5 Ivory
Keener, Catherine: 7 actress
film: Being John Malkovich (1999)
Death to Smoochy (2002)
Full Frontal (2002)
Living in Oblivion (1995)
The Real Blonde (1998)
Keene's __: 6 cement
keen-eyed: 4 wary **5** acute, alert, chary, sharp **6** bright, intent **7** careful, on guard, prudent **8** cautious, discreet, hawk-eyed, lynx-eyed, on the job, vigilant, watchful **9** eagle-eyed, observant, wide-awake **10** discerning, perceptive
keening: 6 lament **7** moaning, wailing **8** grieving, mourning, threnody
keenly: 4 hard **5** madly, sharp **6** avidly **7** acutely, eagerly **8** ardently, bitterly, doggedly, fiercely, intently, strongly, urgently **9** earnestly, intensely, painfully, zealously **10** rigorously
keenness: 3 wit **4** edge, wits, zeal, zest **5** ardor, depth, sense **6** acuity, acumen, smarts, thirst, vision, wisdom **7** cogency, cunning **8** foxiness, vivacity **9** assiduity, awareness, canniness, diligence, eagerness, intensity, poignancy, readiness, sharpness, smartness **10** astuteness, cleverness, cognizance, enthusiasm, perception
keen-witted: 5 alert, quick, smart **6** bright, clever **8** animated **9** sprightly
keep: 3 hog, own, run **4** feed, grip, have, hold, mind, save, tend **5** amass, cache, carry, grasp, hoard, lay by, lay up, put by, stack, stock, store, tower **6** detain, donjon, foster, garner, intern, living, manage, occupy, pickle, prison, retain, save up, shield, upkeep **7** aliment, care for, carry on, château, citadel, conduct, control, deposit, impound, nourish, nurture, observe, operate, possess, prevent, provide, put away, refrain, reserve, respect, shelter, support, sustain **8** adhere to, conserve, fastness, fortress, hang onto, hold on to, maintain, preserve, put aside, salt away, sanctify, withhold **9** carry over, celebrate, look after, ritualize, safeguard, solemnize, watch over **10** accumulate, administer, consecrate, livelihood, minister to, provide for, stronghold, sustenance
abreast of: 6 follow **7** monitor
account: 3 log **4** file, list **5** tally **6** record, report **7** archive, catalog, itemize, jot down, journal, monitor, put down, set down **8** mark down, register, tabulate **9** catalogue, chronicle, enumerate, inventory, write down
afloat: 4 swim **7** survive, sustain
after: 3 dun, nag **5** hound
after class: 6 detain
alert: 5 watch **6** beware **7** look out
a lid on: 4 curb **5** cover, limit **6** rein in, stifle **7** conceal, contain, control, cover up, repress **8** bottle up, hold back, restrain, restrict, suppress **9** constrain, stonewall, whitewash **10** keep secret
a low profile: 4 hide, lurk **6** hole up **7** conceal **9** take cover
an eye on: 4 boss, mark, mind, tend **5** guard, scout, study, watch **6** advert, attend, detect, direct, follow, manage, notice, patrol, police **7** babysit, discern, monitor, observe, oversee **8** chaperon, shepherd **9** look after, supervise **10** administer, ride herd on, scrutinize
apart: 7 isolate, seclude **8** separate
a promise: 4 meet **6** please **7** fulfill, gratify, perform, satisfy **8** make good, reassure **9** discharge
as a bird: 6 encage
a step ahead of: 5 one up, outdo
a stiff lower lip: 4 fume, mope, pout, sulk **5** brood, frown **6** glower
a stiff upper lip: 6 bear up, hang in **8** face up to
at: 7 stick to **8** continue, stay with **9** persist in **10** see through
at bay: 5 repel **6** rebuff **7** ward off **8** hold back
at it: 4 goon, plod **5** retry
away from: 4 duck, shun, skip, snub **5** avoid, ditch, dodge, elude, evade, parry, scorn, shirk **6** beware, escape, eschew, give up, ignore, refuse, reject, shrink **7** boycott, disdain, neglect, refrain **8** forswear, renounce, shake off, sidestep, swear off **9** ostracize
back: 5 check, dam up, delay, flunk **6** detain **7** forbear, reserve **8** withhold
busy: 5 tie up **6** employ, engage, occupy
castle ~: 6 donjon **7** dungeon
clear of: 4 shun **5** avoid, elude, skirt **6** rebuff **7** neglect, ward off
close: 3 hug, pet **5** clasp, touch **6** clutch, cradle, cuddle, enfold, nestle **7** embrace, snuggle
company: 3 woo **6** hobnob **7** consort **9** socialize
company with: 3 see **4** date **5** court
don't ~: 3 can **4** fire **5** let go, throw, yield **6** unhand **7** abandon, release, set free **8** cut loose **9** discharge, sacrifice, surrender **10** relinquish
don't ~ a secret: 3 air, gab **4** blab, leak, tell **5** blurt, let on, level, spill **6** clue in, fill in, gossip, impart, inform, notify, open up, relate, report, reveal, squeal, tattle, tip off, unveil **7** apprise, breathe, divulge, find out, give out, let in on, let know, let slip, mention, recount, spit out, whisper **8** acquaint, announce, disclose, give away **9** leave word, make known **10** keep posted, let be known
don't ~ straight: 4 bend, skew, warp **5** curve, slant **6** buckle, deform **7** contort, distort
down: 3 eat **5** abuse, bully, crush, force, grind **6** ingest, pick on, sadden, saddle, subdue **7** afflict, depress, oppress, put upon, smother **8** aggrieve, browbeat, domineer, maltreat, overload, suppress **9** overpower, overwhelm, persecute, subjugate, trample on, tyrannize
ender: 4 sake
expenses low: 4 save **5** skimp **6** scrape, scrimp **8** conserve, roll back **9** economize **10** cut corners
fail to ~: 4 lose **5** use up, waste **6** divest, mislay **7** forfeit **8** misplace, squander **9** dissipate **10** run through
fail to ~ up: 3 lag **4** drag, flag, poke **5** dally, tarry, trail **6** dawdle, falter, linger, loiter **7** fall off, slacken **8** hang back, lose time, straggle **9** inch along **10** dillydally, lose ground, move slowly
faithful to: 4 heed, obey **6** adhere, follow **7** abide by, conform, fulfill, observe, respect, stand by **8** carry out **9** discharge, stick with **10** comply with
fit: 3 jog, run **7** work out **8** exercise
from: 4 curb, fast, shun **5** avoid, evade, forgo, spurn **6** abjure, eschew, pass up, refuse, resist **7** abstain, back off, forbear, inhibit, refrain **8** abnegate, leave off, renounce, restrain, withhold **9** do without, interrupt
from falling: 5 brace, stake **6** hold up **7** shore up, support **8** buttress **9** reinforce, stabilize **10** strengthen
from happening: 4 foil **5** avert, avoid, block, deter **6** stifle, stymie, thwart **7** fend off, forfend, head off, hold off, prevent, ward off **8** hold back, obstruct, stave off **9** forestall, interrupt
from leaving: 4 hold **5** delay **6** detain, hold up, impede **7** set back **8** restrain, slow down **10** buttonhole
going: 5 run on **6** extend, hold on, push on **7** persist, subsist, sustain **8** continue, maintain, progress, protract **9** persevere **10** perpetuate
guard: 5 watch **6** defend, patrol, picket, police **7** protect
hanging: 5 tease, worry **6** entice, lead on **7** torment **8** interest **9** fascinate, frustrate, tantalize, titillate
house: 4 dust **6** settle **7** clean up
in: 6 ground, stifle **7** repress **9** constrain

in a steady state: **3** fix, set **4** prop **6** freeze, secure, steady **7** balance, support **8** maintain, preserve **9** stabilize
in custody: **4** hold, jail **6** arrest, detain, immure, intern, lock up, remand **7** confine, impound, put away **8** imprison, sentence
in line: **4** curb, stem **5** check, deter, leash, limit, sit on **6** forbid, stifle, tether **7** control, curtail, inhibit, repress, squelch **8** hold back, moderate, prohibit, restrain, restrict, straiten, suppress, tone down **9** constrain, crack down
in mind: **6** recall **7** bethink **8** remember **9** entertain, recognize, recollect
in play: **6** joggle, juggle **7** shuffle
in reserve: **5** put by, store **7** put away **8** put aside
inside: **6** garage **7** enclose
in sight: **3** dog, tag **4** tail **5** spy on, stalk, trail, watch **6** pursue, shadow **8** run after **9** accompany
in step: **4** obey **6** comply, follow **7** abide by, agree to, conform **10** toe the line
in stitches: **5** amuse **9** entertain
in stock: **4** have, save **5** carry, stock, store **6** handle **9** inventory
in the loop: **4** tell, warn **5** brief **6** advise, fill in, inform, notify, tip off **7** apprise, apprize **8** forewarn **9** enlighten
in touch: **4** meet **5** reach **6** roll in, show up **7** check in, contact **9** get hold of
it down: **4** mute **6** cool it **7** silence
it won't ~ you up: **5** decaf, Sanka
nothing back: **5** level
occupied: **4** hold **5** amuse, delay, tie up **6** divert, engage, hinder, impede **8** encumber, obstruct, slow down
on: **5** abide **6** endure, pursue, remain, resume **8** continue **9** persevere
one going: **3** aid **6** assist **8** tide over **9** help along **10** see through
one's distance: **4** shun, snub **5** evade, scorn, shirk, spurn **6** bypass, ignore, rebuff, slight **7** disdain, dismiss, neglect, tune out **8** brush off, shrug off **9** disregard, pay no mind **10** disrespect, leave alone
(oneself) away: **6** absent
one's fingers crossed: **4** hope, wish **5** dream **6** aspire, expect **7** look for **10** anticipate
one's nose clean: **4** obey **6** behave **10** toe the line
one's nose to the grindstone: **4** moil, plod, toil, work **5** labor, sweat **6** drudge, strain, strive **8** work hard **9** plug along, pound away
one's shirt on: **4** bide, wait **5** abide **6** cool it, hold on **7** stand by, sweat it **8** sit tight
one who can't ~ a secret: **5** sieve
out: **3** ban, bar **4** tabu **5** debar **7** exclude, shut off
out of sight: **4** bury, hide, mask, palm, stow, veil **5** cache, cloak, couch, cover, shade, stash **6** harbor, lie low, pocket, screen, shield, shroud **7** blanket, conceal, cover up, envelop, harbour, obscure, seclude, secrete, shelter, shut off, shut out **8** disguise, ensconce, enshroud, stow away, suppress, withhold **9** adumbrate, dissemble, whitewash **10** camouflage
pace: **4** meet **5** rival **9** measure up
pace with: **3** tie **5** equal, match, rival **8** parallel
posted: **4** tell **5** ready **6** advise
quiet: **4** hide **5** quell, sit on **6** hush up, stifle **7** cover up, smother, squelch **8** suppress
repeating: **5** chant **6** intone
safe: **4** hide **5** guard **6** assure, back up, defend, foster, harbor, patrol, police, screen, secure, shield **7** fortify, protect, shelter, ward off **8** chaperon, fight for, preserve, shepherd **9** look after, safeguard, watch over **10** take care of
saying: **5** rub in **6** harp on **7** belabor
score: **3** add, sum **5** add up, count, sum up, tally, total, tot up **6** figure, number, record **7** compute **8** register **9** enumerate
secret: **4** hide, mask, veil **5** cache, cloak, couch, cover, sit on **6** hush up **7** conceal, cover up, obscure **8** disguise, suppress **10** camouflage
smiling: **5** amuse, cheer **6** divert, please, tickle **7** delight **9** entertain
starter: **3** bar **5** house
still: **3** gag **4** hush **5** choke, shush **6** muzzle, shut up, stifle **7** silence **8** pipe down
tabs: **5** gauge, judge **6** assess, figure, notice, reckon **7** account, compute, look out, measure **8** appraise, evaluate, watch out **9** calculate
the faith: **6** redeem **7** abide by, believe **8** adhere to, carry out
the wolf from the door: **4** work **7** peg away **9** grind away
time: **3** tap **4** clap
together: **3** mix, wed **4** ally, band, meet, pool **5** marry, unite **6** cleave, club up, hook up, mingle, pair up **7** partner **9** affiliate, associate, cooperate **10** close ranks, join forces
track of: **4** tend **5** track, watch **6** follow **7** monitor, oversee **9** check up on
under surveillance: **5** guard, watch **6** patrol, police **7** baby-sit, observe, protect **9** chaperone, safeguard
up: **8** continue, maintain, preserve, stay even
(up): **4** prop
up with: **3** tie **4** draw, meet **5** match, rival **9** break even
up with the times: **5** adapt **6** adjust, change, modify, revise **7** conform, remodel **8** accustom **10** assimilate, come around
waiting: **4** slow **5** delay, stall **6** detain, hang up, hinder, hold up, impede, retard **7** bog down, set back **8** postpone
within bounds: **4** curb **5** check, limit **6** temper **7** contain **8** moderate, regulate, restrain, restrict **9** constrict
keep ___: **4** at it, back, down, it up, pace, time, up on **7** smiling
keep ___ dark: **5** in the
keep ___ of: **5** track
keep ___ on: **4** tabs **5** an eye
keep ___ out for: **5** an eye
keep ___ profile: **4** a low
keep ___ to the ground: **5** an ear
keep ___ with: **7** company
Keep ___ cards and letters coming!: **5** those
keep a ___ eye open: **7** weather
keep a ___ upper lip: **5** stiff
Keep A Knockin' (1957 song) artist: Little Richard
keep an ___: **5** eye on **6** eye out
keep an ___ the ground: **5** ear to
keep a straight ___: **4** face
Keep Coming Back (1991 song) artist: Richard Marx
Keep 'Em Flying (1941 film)
cast: Bud Abbott, Lou Costello, Martha Raye
keeper: **4** host **5** guard, owner **6** jailer, warden **7** curator, steward **8** defender, guardian, overseer, watchdog **9** archivist, attendant, caretaker, custodian, protector **10** supervisor
peace ~: **7** bailiff, marshal, sheriff **9** policeman **10** law officer
starter: **3** bar, bee, inn, net, zoo **4** book, door, game, gate, goal, lock, shop, time **5** hotel, house, peace, score, store **6** greens, ground, saloon, wicket **7** grounds
___ keeper: **4** cost **6** saloon
Keeper ___ Castle: **5** of the
Keeper ___ Flame: **5** of the
Keeper of the Castle (1972 song) artist: Four Tops
Keeper of the Flame (1942 film)
cast: Katharine Hepburn, Spencer Tracy
director: George Cukor
___ keepers: **7** finders
Keepers of the House, The author: **4** Grau
keep in ___: **4** mind
keeping: **4** care, egis **5** aegis, trust **6** accord, charge, saving **7** custody, harmony, holding **8** auspices, hoarding, tutelage, wardship **9** orthodoxy, oversight, patronage, retaining, storing up **10** conformity, husbanding, observance, preserving, protection
be in ~ with: **6** follow
in: **6** arrest **7** custody **9** detention, retention **10** constraint, detainment, immurement, internment, quarantine
in ~: **5** typic **7** typical **8** suitable **9** agreeable, agreeably **10** compatible
in ~ (with): **5** along
out: **7** boycott, embargo **9** exclusion, expulsion, interdict, ostracism
out of ~: **4** rude **5** crude, gross, inapt, undue **6** coarse, off-key, vulgar **7** lowbred, uncouth **8** immodest, improper, indecent, unseemly, untoward **9** inelegant, tasteless, unrefined **10** indecorous, indelicate, malapropos, suggestive, unbecoming, unsuitable
starter: **4** book, safe, time **5** house, peace, score, store
the faith: **6** upbeat **7** hopeful **8** aspiring, sanguine, trusting **9** confident, expectant **10** optimistic
Keeping Faith author: **6** Carter
Keeping the Faith (2000 film)
cast: Anne Bancroft, Jenna Elfman, Edward Norton, Ben Stiller
keep in the ___: **4** dark
keep-in-touch device: **5** pager
Keep It Comin' Love (1977 song) artist: KC and the Sunshine Band
Keep it down!: **3** shh **4** hush **5** quiet
Keep It Together (1990 song) artist: Madonna
___ Keep Me Hangin' On: **3** You
keep one's ___: **4** cool, head, word **5** eye on, peace, place **8** distance
keep one's ___ above water: **4** head
keep one's ___ clean: **4** nose
keep one's ___ crossed: **7** fingers
keep one's ___ dry: **6** powder
keep one's ___ on: **5** shirt
keep one's ___ up: **4** chin
keep one's eyes ___: **4** open **6** peeled
Keep On, Keepin' On (1996 song) artist: MC Lyte, Xscape
Keep On Loving You (1980 song) artist: REO Speedwagon
Keep On Singing (1974 song) artist: Helen Reddy
Keep on Truckin' (1973 song) artist: Eddie Kendricks
keepsake: **5** favor, relic, token **7** memento **8** reminder, souvenir
holder: **5** attic **6** locket
keeps, for: **4** ever **6** always, grimly **7** for good, gravely, soberly **9** earnestly, eternally, seriously, sincerely **10** resolutely, unendingly
keep the ___: **5** faith, peace
keep the ___ from the door: **4** wolf
keep the ___ rolling: **4** ball
Keep the Aspidistra Flying author: George Orwell
Keep the Fire Burnin' (1982 song) artist: REO Speedwagon
Keep Their Heads Ringin' (1995 song) artist: Dr. Dre
keep up ___ the Joneses: **4** with
Keep Ya Head Up (1993 song) artist: Tupac
Keep your ___ on!: **5** shirt
Keep your ___ shut!: **3** yap **4** trap
Keep your ___ the ball!: **5** eye on
Keeshan: **3** Bob
Keeshond: **3** dog **5** canid **6** canine
Keeslar: **4** Matt
Keesler: **3** AFB
Kefauver: **3** sen. **5** Estes **7** senator
home: **9** Tennessee
kefir: **5** drink **7** Russian **8** beverage
keg: **3** bbl., tub **4** cask **6** barrel, firkin **8** hogshead **9** container
adjunct: **3** tap
contents: **3** ale **4** beer **6** powder
cousin: **3** vat
party locale: **4** frat **10** fraternity
stopper: **4** bung, cork, plug
keg ___: **5** party
___ keg: **6** powder
kegler: **6** bowler
Kegon: **5** falls **9** waterfall
locale: **5** Japan **6** Honshu
Keid: **4** star
Keighley: **7** William
Keillor: **8** Garrison
Keino, Kip: **6** Kenyan, runner **10** marathoner
Keio University city: **5** Tokio, Tokyo
Keir: **6** Dullea
Keiser, Herman: **6** golfer
Keitel, Harvey: **5** actor
film: Blue Collar (1978)
The Border (1982)
Bugsy (1991)
City of Industry (1997)
Clockers (1995)
Cop Land (1997)
Death Watch (1980)
The Duellists (1977)
Falling in Love (1984)
Fingers (1978)
The Last Temptation of Christ (1988)
Mean Streets (1973)
Monkey Trouble (1994)
Mother, Jugs & Speed (1976)
The Piano (1993)
Pulp Fiction (1994)
Red Dragon (2002)
Reservoir Dogs (1992)
Rising Sun (1993)
Shadrach (1998)
Sister Act (1992)
Smoke (1995)
Taxi Driver (1976)
Thelma & Louise (1991)
Three Seasons (1999)
The Two Jakes (1990)
U-571 (2000)
Who's That Knocking at My Door? (1968)
spouse: Lorraine Bracco
Keith: **4** Moon, Toby **5** Brian, David, Sweat **6** Coogan, Gordon, Haring,

Reddin 7 Emerson, Jarrett 8 Lockhart, Richards 9 Carradine
Keith, Brian: 5 actor
film: 5 Against the House (1955)
Joe Panther (1976)
The McKenzie Break (1970)
Moon Pilot (1962)
Nevada Smith (1966)
Nightfall (1956)
The Parent Trap (1961)
Scandalous John (1971)
Those Calloways (1965)
Tight Spot (1955)
The Yakuza (1975)
TV: Family Affair
__ Keith Kellogg: 4 Will
Keizer: 4 city, town
locale: 6 Oregon
Kekes: 4 peak 5 mount 8 mountain
locale: 6 Europe 7 Hungary
Kele: 3 pig 5 swine
kelep: 3 ant
Kell: 6 George
Kellaway: 5 Cecil
Keller: 4 city, town 5 Helen 6 Marthe 7 Charlie 9 Gottfried
locale: 5 Texas
Keller, Gottfried: 4 poet 5 Swiss
Keller, Helen: 6 writer
portrayer: 4 Duke
work: Out of the Dark
Kellerman: 4 Faye 5 Sally 8 Jonathan
Kellerman, Faye: 6 writer
character: Decker, Lazarus, Rina
spouse: Jonathan
work: Day of Atonement
False Prophet
The Forgotten
Grievous Sin
Jupiter's Bones
Milk and Honey
Moon Music
The Quality of Mercy
The Ritual Bath
Sacred and Profane
Sanctuary
Serpent's Tooth
Stalker
Stone Kiss
Kellerman, Jonathan: 6 writer
character: Alex, Delaware
spouse: Faye
work: Bad Love
Billy Straight
Blood Test
The Clinic
Devil's Waltz
Flesh and Blood
Monster
Over the Edge
Silent Partner
Time Bomb
When the Bough Breaks
Kellerman, Sally: 7 actress
film: Back to School (1986)
Brewster McCloud (1970)
Last of the Red Hot Lovers (1972)
MASH (1970)
Serial (1980)
Slither (1973)
That's Life! (1986)
Kelley: 5 Barry, Kitty 6 David E., Sheila 8 DeForest, Florence
costar: 5 Nimoy 7 Shatner
Kelley, David E. spouse: Michelle Pfeifer
Kelley, Kitty creation: 3 bio
Kellogg: 4 Lynn 5 Frank
brand: 4 Eggo
product: 6 cereal
Kellogg-__ Pact: 6 Briand
Kellogg, Frank: 8 Nobelist
Kellogg's cereal: 6 Smacks 7 All-Bran, Crispix, Hunny B's, Mueslix, Pokemon 8 Corn Pops, Special K 9 Just Right 10 Apple Jacks, Froot Loops, Mini-Wheats, Nutri-Grain, Smart Start
Kellogg's Frosted Flakes tiger: 4 Tony
kelly: 5 color, green
Kelly: 3 Jim, Ned 4 Gene, Jack, Reno, Walt 5 Brian, Grace, Lynch, Moira, Nancy, Patsy, Price 6 Emmett, Harmon 7 LeBrock, Preston 8 McGillis 9 Ellsworth, Shipwreck 10 Rutherford
Kelly, Emmett: 4 hobo 5 clown
Kelly, Gene: 5 actor 6 dancer
film: An American in Paris (1951)
Anchors Aweigh (1945)
Black Hand (1950)
Brigadoon (1954)
The Cheyenne Social Club (1970)
Christmas Holiday (1944)
Cover Girl (1944)
The Cross of Lorraine (1943)
DuBarry Was a Lady (1943)
For Me and My Gal (1942)
Gigot (1962)
A Guide for the Married Man (1967)
Hello, Dolly! (1969)
Inherit the Wind (1960)
It's Always Fair Weather (1955)
Les Girls (1957)
Marjorie Morningstar (1958)
On the Town (1949)
The Pirate (1948)
Singin' in the Rain (1952)
Summer Stock (1950)
Take Me Out to the Ball Game (1949)
The Tunnel of Love (1958)
Kelly, Grace: 7 actress
film: The Bridges at Toko-Ri (1955)
The Country Girl (1954, AA)
Dial M for Murder (1954)
High Noon (1952)
High Society (1956)
Mogambo (1953)
Rear Window (1954)
The Swan (1956)
To Catch a Thief (1955)
spouse: Prince Rainier
Kelly, Jim: 2 QB
sport: 8 football
Kelly, R.
song: Bump 'n Grind (1994)
Down Low (1996)
Gotham City (1997)
I Believe I Can Fly (1996)
I Can't Sleep Baby (1996)
I'm Your Angel (1998)
Satisfy You (1999)
You Remind Me of Something (1995)
Kelly's Heroes (1970 film)
cast: Clint Eastwood, Carroll O'Connor, Don Rickles, Telly Savalas, Donald Sutherland
Kelly, Walt cartoon: 4 Pogo
Kelowna: 4 city, town
locale: 6 Canada
kelp: 4 alga 5 algae 7 seaweed 10 health food
component: 5 algin, iodin 6 iodine
concoction: 4 agar 8 agar-agar
kelp __: 4 bass, crab
Kelp: 6 Julius
kelpie: 3 dog 5 canid 6 canine, spirit, sprite
kelpies herd them: 5 sheep
Kelsey: 5 Linda 7 Grammer
Kelton: 4 Pert
Kelut: 7 volcano
locale: 4 Asia, Java 9 Indonesia
Kelvin: 5 scale 7 William
alternative: 7 Celsius 10 Fahrenheit
Kelvinator: 6 fridge
alternative: 5 Amana, Norge 6 Bendix, Maytag, Tappan 7 Admiral, Jenn-Air, Kenmore 8 Hotpoint 9 Magic Chef, Whirlpool 10 Frigidaire, KitchenAid
Kelvin, William: 4 Lord 7 British 9 physicist
Kemal: 7 Atatürk
Kemble: 5 Fanny
__ Kemble Siddons: 5 Sarah
Kemelman: 5 Harry
Kemo Sabe: 10 Lone Ranger
companion: 5 Tonto
trademark: 4 mask
Kemp: 4 Gary, Jack, Tara 6 Johnny
Kemper __: 4 Open 5 Arena
kempt: 4 neat, tidy, trim 6 spruce 7 orderly 9 shipshape 10 fastidious
not ~: 4 torn 5 messy, ratty, seedy 6 beat-up, grubby, ragged, shabby, shoddy, untidy 7 scruffy 8 slovenly, tattered 10 bedraggled, disheveled, threadbare
__-kempt: 3 ill
Kempton: 6 Murray
ken: 4 grip 5 grasp, range, reach, sight 6 fathom 7 eyeshot, purview 9 awareness, knowledge 10 cognizance, perception, understand
Ken: 4 doll, Olin, Wahl 5 Berry, Burns, Kesey, Starr 6 Curtis, Dryden, Howard, Hughes, Murray, Norton, Osmond 7 Annakin, Auletta, Daneyko, Follett, Griffey, Maynard, Russell, Stabler, Venturi 8 Rosewall 9 Kercheval 10 Weatherwax
friend: 6 Barbie
Ken.
neighbor: 3 Ill., Ind., W. Va. 4 Tenn.
see also Kentucky
Kenai: 4 city, town
locale: 6 Alaska
Kenan & __: 3 Kel
Kenaz, grandfather of: 4 Esau
Ken Caryl: 4 city, town
locale: 8 Colorado
Kendal: 4 city, town 5 green 8 Felicity
locale: 7 England
Kendall: 3 Kay 4 city, town 5 Henry 6 Edward
locale: 7 Florida
Kendall, Edward: 8 Nobelist
Kendall, Henry: 8 Nobelist 9 physicist
kendo: 5 sport
practice ~: 5 fence
Kendrew, John: 7 chemist 8 Nobelist
Kendricks, Eddie
song: Boogie Down (1974)
Keep on Truckin' (1973)
Keneally, Thomas: 6 writer 10 Australian
work: American Scoundrel
Blood Red, Sister Rose
Bring Larks and Heroes
Flying Hero Class
Gossip From the Forest
The Playmaker
A River Town
Schindler's List
Victim of the Aurora
Woman of the Inner Sea
Kenesaw __ Landis: 8 Mountain
Kenilworth: 5 novel
author: Walter Scott
character: 3 Amy 5 Giles, Janet 6 Blount, Dickie, Dudley, Edmund, Robert, Varney 7 Richard, Robsart, Wayland 10 Tressilian
Kenilworth __: 3 ivy
Ken-L Ration: 7 dog food
alternative: 4 Alpo, Iams 5 Nutro 6 Kal Kan, Purina 8 Eukanuba
Kenmore: 9 appliance
alternative: 5 Amana, Norge 6 Bendix, Maytag, Tappan 7 Admiral, Jenn-Air 8 Hotpoint 9 Magic Chef, Whirlpool 10 Frigidaire, Kelvinator, KitchenAid
brand owner: 5 Sears
Kennebec: 5 river
city on the ~: 7 Augusta
locale: 5 Maine
Kennedy: 3 Joe, Ted, Tom 4 Burt, clan, John, Mimi, Rose 5 Bobby, Edgar, Ethel, Jayne, John F., Teddy 6 Arthur, Edward, George, Jackie, Joseph, Robert 7 Anthony, William 8 Caroline 10 Jacqueline
coin: 4 half
quote starter: 3 ask, ich
sister: 3 Pat 4 Jean 6 Eunice 8 Kathleen, Rosemary
Kennedy __: 6 Center 7 Airport
__ Kennedy: 4 Cape
Kennedy Airport loc.: 3 NYC
Kennedy, Arthur: 5 actor
film: Bend of the River (1952)
Bright Victory (1951)
Champion (1949)
The Desperate Hours (1955)
Lawrence of Arabia (1962)
The Lusty Men (1952)
The Man From Laramie (1955)
Murder, She Said (1961)
Peyton Place (1957)
Rancho Notorious (1952)
They Died With Their Boots On (1941)
The Window (1949)
Kennedy Center focus: 4 arts
Kennedy, George: 5 actor
film: Airport (1970)
Airport '77 (1977)
Bandolero! (1968)
Cool Hand Luke (1967, AA)
Dirty Dingus Magee (1970)
The Dirty Dozen (1967)
The Eiger Sanction (1975)
The Naked Gun... (1988)
Naked Gun 2 1/2... (1991)
Naked Gun 33 1/3... (1994)
Thunderbolt and Lightfoot (1974)
Kennedy, John F.: 9 president
alma mater: 6 Choate 7 Harvard
biographer: 8 Sorensen
birthplace: 4 Mass. 9 Brookline
book: Profiles in Courage
The Strategy of Peace
Why England Slept
cabinet member: 3 Day 4 Rusk 5 Udall, Wirtz 6 Dillon, Hodges 7 Freeman 8 Goldberg, McNamara, Ribicoff
child: 8 Caroline
opponent: 5 Nixon
parent: 3 Joe 4 Rose 6 Joseph
sibling: 3 Pat, Ted 4 Jean 6 Eunice, Robert 8 Kathleen, Rosemary
V.P.: 7 Johnson
wife: 6 Jackie 10 Jacqueline
Kennedy Library architect: I.M. Pei
Kennedy, Ted: 3 sen. 6 Edward 7 senator
middle name: 5 Moore
Kennedy, William: 6 author, writer
work: The Ink Truck
Ironweed
Legs
kennel: 3 den 4 hole, lair, pack 5 pound 6 burrow 7 shelter 8 doghouse
cry: 3 arf, grr, yip 4 bark, woof, yelp, yowl 5 growl
feature: 3 pen, run 4 cage
resident: 3 dog, pet, pup 5 doggy, pooch, puppy, whelp 6 canine
kennel __: 4 club
Kennelly-Heaviside __: 5 layer
Kennel Murder Case, The (1933 film)
cast: Mary Astor, William Powell
director: Michael Curtiz

Kenner: **4** city, town **5** Chris
locale: **9** Louisiana
Kennesaw: **4** city, town
locale: **7** Georgia
Kenneth: **4** Koch, Mars, More **5** Anger, Arrow, Starr, Tynan **6** Wilson **7** Branagh, Grahame, Patchen, Rexroth, Roberts, Slessor
Kennewick: **4** city, town
locale: **10** Washington
Kenny: **3** Tom **4** Ball **5** Baker, Nolan **6** Rogers **7** Loggins, Stabler **9** Elizabeth
__ Kenny: **6** Sister
Kenny G
genre: **4** jazz
instrument: alto sax **3** sax
last name: Gorelick
song: Songbird (1987)
keno: **4** game
kin: **5** lotto **7** lottery
play ~: **3** bet **5** wager **6** gamble
Kenobi: **6** Obi-Wan
Keno City: **4** city, town
locale: **6** Canada
kenong: **4** bell, gong **10** percussion
origin: **4** Java
Kenosha: **4** city, town
locale: **9** Wisconsin
Kensington __ Stone: **4** Rune
Kensington and __: **7** Chelsea
Kensit: **5** Patsy
Kent: **4** city, town **5** Clark, Hrbek, Smith **6** Arthur, county, McCord, Stacey **8** Rockwell
city: **5** Dover **7** Margate
colleague: **4** Lane **5** Olsen
locale: **4** Ohio **7** England **10** Washington
school: **3** KSU
Kent __: **5** State
__ Kentaurus: **5** Rigel, Rigil
kente: **6** fabric **8** material
kentia __: **4** palm
Kentish __: **4** fire **7** tracery
Kenton: **4** Erle, Stan
Kenton, Stan: **7** pianist
genre: **4** jazz
Kent, Rockwell: **6** artist **7** painter **11** illustrator
Kent, Stacey: **6** singer
genre: **4** jazz
Kent State University
conference: **3** MAC
locale: **4** Ohio
Kentucky: **5** river, state
city: **5** Berea, Eolia **7** Ashland, Fayette, Newburg, Paducah **8** Florence, Fort Knox, Radcliff, Richmond **9** Covington, Frankfort, Henderson, Lexington, Owensboro **10** Louisville
college: **5** Berea
conference: **3** SEC
county: **5** Boone
neighbor: **4** Ohio **7** Indiana **8** Illinois, Missouri, Virginia **9** Tennessee **12** West Virginia
pioneer: **5** Boone
state bird: **8** cardinal
state fish: **4** bass
state flower: **9** goldenrod
state fossil: **10** brachiopod
state mineral: **4** coal
state rock: **5** agate
statesman: **4** Clay
Kentucky (1938 film)
cast: Walter Brennan, Loretta Young
Kentucky __: **4** Rain **5** Derby, fried, rifle, Woman **7** colonel, Kernels, warbler, windage
Kentucky __ Movie, The: **5** Fried
Kentucky Derby: **4** race
drink: **5** julep **9** mint julep
month: **3** May
Kentucky Derby winners:
2004 - Smarty Jones
2003 - Funny Cide
2002 - War Emblem
2001 - Monarchos
2000 - Fusaichi Pegasus
1999 - Charismatic
1998 - Real Quiet
1997 - Silver Charm
1996 - Grindstone
1995 - Thunder Gulch
1994 - Go For Gin
1993 - Sea Hero
1992 - Lil E. Tee
1991 - Strike the Gold
1990 - Unbridled
1989 - Sunday Silence
1988 - Winning Colors
1987 - Alysheba
1986 - Ferdinand
1985 - Spend A Buck
1984 - Swale
1983 - Sunny's Halo
1982 - Gato del Sol
1981 - Pleasant Colony
1980 - Genuine Risk
1979 - Spectacular Bid
1978 - Affirmed
1977 - Seattle Slew
1976 - Bold Forbes
1975 - Foolish Pleasure
1974 - Cannonade
1973 - Secretariat
1972 - Riva Ridge
1971 - Canonero II
1970 - Dust Commander
1969 - Majestic Prince
1968 - Forward Pass
1967 - Proud Clarion
1966 - Kauai King
1965 - Lucky Debonair
1964 - Northern Dancer
1963 - Chateaugay
1962 - Decidedly
1961 - Carry Back
1960 - Venetian Way
1959 - Tomy Lee
1958 - Tim Tam
1957 - Iron Liege
1956 - Needles
1955 - Swaps
1954 - Determine
1953 - Dark Star
1952 - Hill Gail
1951 - Count Turf
1950 - Middleground
1949 - Ponder
1948 - Citation
1947 - Jet Pilot
1946 - Assault
1945 - Hoop Jr.
1944 - Pensive
1943 - Count Fleet
1942 - Shut Out
1941 - Whirlaway
1940 - Gallahadion
1939 - Johnstown
1938 - Lawrin
1937 - War Admiral
1936 - Bold Venture
1935 - Omaha
1934 - Cavalcade
1933 - Brokers Tip
1932 - Burgoo King
1931 - Twenty Grand
1930 - Gallant Fox
1929 - Clyde Van Dusen
1928 - Reigh Count
1927 - Whiskery
1926 - Bubbling Over
1925 - Flying Ebony
1924 - Black Gold
1923 - Zev
1922 - Morvich
1921 - Behave Yourself
1920 - Paul Jones
1919 - Sir Barton
1918 - Exterminator
1917 - Omar Khayyam
1916 - George Smith
1915 - Regret
1914 - Old Rosebud
1913 - Donerail
1912 - Worth
1911 - Meridan
1910 - Donau
1909 - Wintergreen
1908 - Stone Street
1907 - Pink Star
1906 - Sir Huon
1905 - Agile
1904 - Elwood
1903 - Judge Himes
1902 - Alan-a-Dale
1901 - His Eminence
1900 - Lieut. Gibson
1899 - Manuel
1898 - Plaudit
1897 - Typhoon II
1896 - Ben Brush
1895 - Halma
1894 - Chant
1893 - Lookout
1892 - Azra
1891 - Kingman
1890 - Riley
1889 - Spokane
1888 - MacBeth II
1887 - Montrose
1886 - Ben Ali
1885 - Joe Cotton
1884 - Buchanan
1883 - Leonatus
1882 - Apollo
1881 - Hindoo
1880 - Fonso
1879 - Lord Murphy
1878 - Day Star
1877 - Baden Baden
1876 - Vagrant
1875 - Aristides
__ Kentucky Home: **5** My Old
Kentucky Rain (1970 song) artist: Elvis Presley
Kentucky Woman (1967 song) artist: Neil Diamond
Kentwood: **4** city, town
locale: **8** Michigan
Kenya: **6** nation **7** country
anthropologist: **6** Leakey
beast: **5** zebra
capital: **7** Nairobi
city: **4** Meru **5** Nyeri **6** Kisumu, Kitale, Nakuru **7** Eldoret, Mombasa, Nairobi **8** Machakos
half a ~ rebel group: **3** Mau
lake: **6** Rudolf **7** Turkana **8** Victoria
language: **5** Masai **6** Kikuyu, Maasai
legislature: **5** Bunge
locale: **6** Africa
money: **4** cent **8** shilling
mountain: **5** Elgon
national park: **5** Tsavo
neighbor: **5** Sudan **6** Uganda **7** Somalia **8** Ethiopia, Tanzania
people: **3** Luo **5** Galla, Kamba, Masai, Nandi, Oromo **6** Dorobo, Kikuyu, Maasai, Somali **9** Wandorobo
river of ~: **4** Tana **5** Tsana, Tsavo
runner: **5** Keino
Kenyatta: **4** Jomo
Kenyon, Kathleen: **4** Dame
Keogh __: **4** plan **7** account
Keogh alternative: **3** IRA
Keokuk: **4** city
locale: **4** Iowa
kepi: **3** cap, hat, lid
feature: **5** visor, vizor
wearer: **5** poilu
Kepler, Johann: **6** German **10** astronomer
__-kept: **4** best, well
kerar: **4** lyre **6** string
origin: **8** Ethiopia
__ keratotomy: **6** radial
Kercheval: **3** Ken
kerchief: **5** curch, do-rag, scarf **6** hankie, madras **7** bandana, muffler **8** babushka, bandanna, covering, kaffiyeh, mantilla, neckwear **9** headcloth, headdress
bright ~: **6** Madras
starter: **4** hand
Kerensky successor: **5** Lenin
kerf: **3** cut **5** notch **6** groove
kerflooie: **6** broken, busted **10** broken-down, on the blink, on the fritz
Keri: **6** lotion **7** Russell
alternative: **5** Curel, Nivea **6** Aveeno **7** Eucerin, Jergens, Pacquin **9** Lubriderm
Kerinci: **7** volcano
locale: **4** Asia **7** Sumatra **9** Indonesia
Kerman: **4** city
locale: **4** Iran
Kermit: **4** frog **6** Muppet **9** Roosevelt
colleague: **4** Bert **5** Ernie, Piggy
cousin: **4** toad
creator: **3** Jim **6** Henson
street: **6** Sesame
kernel: **3** hub, nub, nut **4** core, corn, crux, germ, gist, knub, meat, pith, seed **5** grain, heart **6** center, marrow **7** essence, keynote, nucleus, nutmeat **8** key point **9** substance
combining form: **5** caryo-, karyo-
holder: **3** cob, ear
kernite: **3** ore **7** mineral
yield: **5** boron
Kern, Jerome: **8** composer
collaborator: DeSylva, Fields, Hammerstein, Harbach, Wodehouse
contemporary: **5** Arlen **6** Berlin, Porter **8** Gershwin
musical: The Cat and the Fiddle
Criss Cross
Good Morning, Dearie
Have a Heart
Leave It to Jane
Love o' Mike
Miss 1917
Music in the Air
Oh, Boy!
Oh, Lady! Lady!
Roberta
Sally
Show Boat
Stepping Stones
Sunny
Sweet Adeline
Very Good Eddie
Very Warm for May
song: All the Things You Are
All Through the Day
Bill
Can't Help Lovin' Dat Man
Dearly Beloved
Don't Ever Leave Me
A Fine Romance
The Folks Who Live on the Hill
How'd You Like to Spoon With Me?
I'm Old Fashioned
I've Told Ev'ry Little Star
I Won't Dance
The Last Time I Saw Paris
Life Upon the Wicked Stage
Long Ago (And Far Away)
Look for the Silver Lining
Lovely to Look At
Make Believe
Ol' Man River
Pick Yourself Up

She Didn't Say Yes
Smoke Gets in Your Eyes
The Song Is You
Sunny
They Didn't Believe Me
Till the Clouds Roll By
The Way You Look Tonight
Who?
Why Do I Love You?
Why Was I Born?
Yesterdays
You Are Love
You Couldn't Be Cuter
You Were Never Lovelier

Kerns: 6 Joanna
kerosene: 3 oil 7 lantern
Kerouac, Jack: 6 author, writer
character: 3 Sal 8 Paradise
colleague: Ginsberg, Corso, Snyder, Whelan
genre: Beat
hometown: Lowell
work: Bug Sur
The Dharma Bums
Doctor Sax
On the Road
Satori in Paris
Visions of Cody
kerplunk: 6 splash
Kerr: 4 Jean, John 5 Anita, Smith 6 Graham, Walter 7 Deborah
Kerr ___: 4 cell 6 effect
Kerr, Deborah: 7 actress
film: The Adventuress (1946)
The Assam Garden (1985)
Black Narcissus (1947)
Bonjour Tristesse (1958)
The Chalk Garden (1964)
The Day Will Dawn (1942)
From Here to Eternity (1953)
The Grass Is Greener (1960)
The Gypsy Moths (1969)
Heaven Knows, Mr. Allison (1957)
The Hucksters (1947)
The Innocents (1961)
The Journey (1959)
Julius Caesar (1953)
The King and I (1956)
King Solomon's Mines (1950)
Life and Death of Colonel Blimp (1943)
The Night of the Iguana (1964)
Quo Vadis? (1951)
Separate Tables (1958)
The Sundowners (1960)
Tea and Sympathy (1956)
Vacation From Marriage (1945)
role: 4 Anna
Kerrey: 3 Bob, Jim, sen. 7 senator
Kerr, Graham: 4 chef 7 gourmet
Kerri: 5 Strug
kerria: 5 shrub
relative: 4 rose, sloe 6 spirea 7 bramble, jetbead, spiraea 8 hardhack, ninebark, photinia 9 firethorn, raspberry
Kerrigan, Nancy: 6 skater
maneuver: 4 axel, Lutz, spin 5 camel
milieu: 3 ice 4 rink
Kerrville: 4 city, town
locale: 5 Texas
Kerry: 3 cow, sen. 4 bull, John 6 bovine, Butler, cattle 7 senator
Kerry ___ terrier: 4 blue
Kerry Blue terrier: 3 dog 5 canid, pooch 6 canine
kersey: 4 wool 6 fabric
kerseys: 5 pants
Kershner, Irvin: 8 director
film: The Empire Strikes Back (1980)
Eyes of Laura Mars (1978)
A Fine Madness (1966)
The Flim Flam Man (1967)
The Hoodlum Priest (1961)
Loving (1970)
The Luck of Ginger Coffey (1964)
Never Say Never Again (1983)
Up the Sandbox (1972)
Kert: 5 Larry
Kertész, Imre: 6 writer 8 Nobelist
Kerwin: 5 Brian, Lance 7 Mathews
Kesey, Ken: 6 author, writer
work: Demon Box
One Flew Over the Cuckoo's Nest
Sometimes a Great Notion
Keshia ___ Pulliam: 6 Knight
Kessel: 6 Barney
kestrel: 4 bird, hawk 6 falcon
ketch: 4 boat 5 yacht 8 sailboat
Chesapeake Bay ~: 6 bugeye
cousin: 4 yawl 6 galiot
Levantine ~: 4 saic
___ ketch: 4 bomb 6 mortar
Ketcham: 4 Hank
creation: 6 Dennis
Ketchikan: 4 city, port, town
locale: 6 Alaska
Ketchum: 3 Hal 4 city, town
locale: 5 Idaho
ketchup: 5 Heinz, Hunt's, sauce 6 relish 8 Del Monte 9 condiment
alternative: 4 mayo
noise: 4 plop 5 plunk
ketone: 6 acetol
Kett: 4 Etta
Kettering: 4 city, town
locale: 4 Ohio
Ketterle, Wolfgang: 8 Nobelist 9 physicist
kettle: 3 pan, pot, vat 6 boiler, teapot, vessel 7 caldron 8 cauldron 9 container
ender: 4 drum
handle: 4 bail
insulter: 3 pot
of fish: 3 fix, jam 4 mess, spot 5 snarl 6 fiasco, muddle, pickle, plight, scrape, tangle 7 dilemma, problem, screwup, trouble 8 bad scene 9 deep water, mare's nest
output: 5 steam, vapor
sound: 3 sss 4 ssss
starter: 3 tea
kettle ___: 3 hat 4 base, corn, hole 6 stitch
Kettle: 2 Ma, Pa
kettledrum, Spanish: 6 atabal
Keuka: 4 lake
locale: 7 New York
keV: 4 meas.
Kevin: 5 Bacon, Brown, Kline, saint, Smith, Sorbo, Tighe 6 Conway, Curran, Dobson, Nealon, Pollak, Spacey 7 Costner 8 McCarthy, Mitchell 10 Williamson
Kevlar company: 6 Dupont
Kewpie: 3 toy 4 doll 5 prize
Kewpie Doll (1958 song) artist: Perry Como
key: 3 Alt, Del, End, Esc, Ins, Tab 4 A maj., B maj., clew, clue, C maj., code, Ctrl, D maj., E maj., F maj., G maj., Home, isle, main, note, Pg Dn, Pg Up, West 5 A flat, basic, B flat, Break, C flat, chief, D flat, E flat, Enter, F flat, G flat, islet, ivory, Largo, major, Pause, pitch, Shift, vital 6 A major, A minor, answer, A sharp, B major, B minor, B sharp, C major, C minor, C sharp, Delete, D major, D minor, D sharp, E major, E minor, E sharp, F major, F minor, F sharp, G major, G minor, G sharp, Insert, island, legend, Page Up, staple, ticket 7 central, Control, crucial, pivotal, primary 8 A flat maj., B flat maj., Caps Lock, cardinal, critical, deciding, decisive, E flat maj., linchpin, lynchpin, material, Page Down, password, solution 9 Backspace, coral reef, essential, important, operative, principal, right-hand, strategic 10 A flat major, B flat major, B flat minor, E flat major 11 C sharp minor
as data: 5 input
bagpipe ~: 5 B flat
banjo ~ changer: 4 capo
black ~: 5 A flat, B flat, D flat, E flat, G flat 6 A sharp, C sharp, D sharp, F sharp, G sharp
calculator ~: 3 CLR, sin 4 sine
car ~: 7 starter
combining form: 5 clavi-, clavo-
computer ~: 3 Alt, Del, Esc, Ins, Tab 4 Ctrl, Home, Pg Dn, Pg Up 5 Enter, Shift 6 Delete, Escape, Insert, Page Up 7 Control 8 Page Down
ender: 3 pad, way 4 card, hole, note, word 5 board, noter, punch, stone 6 stroke
find the ~ to: 5 crack, solve 6 decode, fathom, unlock 7 clear up, explain, hit upon, unravel, work out 8 decipher, get right, untangle 9 figure out, interpret, puzzle out 10 account for
five-sharp ~: 6 B major
Florida ~: 4 West 5 Largo 8 Biscayne
four-sharp ~: 6 E major
guitar ~ changer: 4 capo
hit the + ~: 3 add
in: 5 enter
in ~: 7 musical, tuneful 9 melodious 10 euphonious, harmonious
in French: 4 clef
item: 6 answer
it may have a ~: 4 door 5 diary
it usually has a ~: 5 music
lacking a ~: 6 atonal
letter: 3 phi 4 beta 5 kappa
locale: 3 Fla. 7 Florida
material: 5 ebony, ivory
musical: 4 A maj., B maj., C maj., D maj., E maj., F maj., G maj. 5 A flat, B flat, C flat, E flat 6 A major, A minor, A sharp, B major, B minor, C major, C minor, D major, D minor, E major, E minor, F major, F minor, G major, G minor 8 A flat maj., B flat maj., E flat maj. 10 A flat major, B flat major, B flat minor, E flat major 11 C sharp minor
note: 5 tonic
off ~: 4 flat 5 false, sharp
on: 4 pick 6 choose, opt for, select 9 designate, single out
on ~: 5 tonal 6 in tune 9 melodious 10 harmonious
one-flat ~: 6 D minor, F major
one-sharp ~: 6 E minor, G major
partner: 4 lock
personnel: 4 core 5 cadre
player: 3 CEO, VIP 4 boss, czar 5 brass, mogul, wheel 6 honcho, leader, top dog, tycoon 7 big shot, magnate 8 big wheel, director, governor, higher-up, kingfish, top brass 9 commander, executive 10 head honcho, management
point: 3 nub 4 crux, gist, meat, pith 5 drift, heart 6 kernel, marrow, thrust, upshot 7 essence 9 substance 10 bottom line
position: 5 pivot
starter: 3 off 4 pass, turn 5 latch
three-sharp ~: 6 A major
turn the ~: 4 lock 6 fasten, secure
two-flat ~: 6 G minor
two-sharp ~: 6 B minor, D major
uncut ~: 5 blank
under lock and ~: 4 held, safe 5 bound, caged 6 in jail, jailed, secure 7 captive, guarded, immured 8 confined, locked up 9 in custody, protected 10 imprisoned
up: 4 spur 5 tense, upset 6 incite, kindle, thrill 7 actuate 9 stimulate
key ___: 4 card, case, club, grip, in on, ring, word 5 chain, fruit, light, money, plate, scarf 7 station
___ key: 3 bit, tab 4 high 5 major, minor, night, shift 6 chroma, church, master 7 feather
___-key: 3 low, off 4 card 5 color
Key: 3 Ted 5 Jimmy
Key ___: 4 deer, lime, West 5 Largo
Key ___ pie: 4 lime
keyboard: 4 Moog 5 organ, piano, synth 6 spinet 7 celesta, celeste, cembalo, clavier, klavier, orphica, Pianola, upright, vocoder 8 calliope, melodeon, melodion, theremin, virginal 9 accordion, harmonium 10 clavichord, concertina, hurdy-gurdy, instrument, squeezebox
sequence: 6 QWERTY
slip: 4 typo 7 erratum, mistake 8 misprint 10 inaccuracy
striker: 6 finger
stroke: 3 tap
use a ~: 4 type 5 enter 6 sign on 9 make music, typewrite
___ keyboard: 5 pedal
___ Keyboard: 6 Dvorak
Keydets' sch.: 3 VMI
Keye: 4 Luke
keyed
not ~: 6 atonal
up: 4 edgy 5 antsy, hyper, itchy, jumpy, tense 6 gung-ho, jangly, uneasy 7 anxious, excited, frantic, jittery, nervous, restive, uptight 8 agitated, feverish, fluttery, frenetic, frenzied, restless, skittish, troubled 9 concerned, excitable, ill at ease 10 high-strung
Keyes, Evelyn: 7 actress
film: 99 River Street (1953)
Enchantment (1948)
The Face Behind the Mask (1941)
Gone With the Wind (1939)
Here Comes Mr. Jordan (1941)
The Jolson Story (1946)
Ladies in Retirement (1941)
The Seven Year Itch (1955)
A Thousand and One Nights (1945)
spouse: John Huston, Artie Shaw
___ Key, FL: 4 Boot, Duck, Long, Vaca 5 Conch, Craig, Crawl, Shark 6 Cudjoe, Fiesta, Grassy, Indian, Knight, No Name, Pigeon, Ramrod, Siesta, Wilson 7 Big Pine, Fat Deer, Windley 8 Missouri, Rockland, Sunshine, Teatable 9 Boca Chica, Sugarloaf 10 Bahia Honda, Big Coppitt, Little Duck, Plantation, Summerland
keyhole: 4 slit, slot 7 opening 8 aperture
glance: 4 peek, peep 6 gander 7 glimpse, look-see
keyhole ___: 3 saw
Key Largo: 4 film, play, song
artist: Bertie Higgins
author: Maxwell Anderson
cast: Lauren Bacall, Lionel Barrymore, Humphrey Bogart, Edward G. Robinson, Claire Trevor
composer: 7 Steiner
director: John Huston
keyless: 6 atonal
Key lime ___: 3 pie
Keynes subject: 4 econ. 9 economics
keynote: 3 nub 4 core, crux, germ, gist, knub, pith, root 5 basis, focus, heart, orate, speak, theme 6 center, kernel, marrow, speech 7 essence 8 linchpin, lynchpin, main idea, quiddity 9 substance
keynote ___: 6 speech 7 address,

speaker
__ keypad: 7 numeric
keypad place: 2 PC 3 ATM, Mac 8 computer
__ **Keys:** 7 Florida
Keys of the Kingdom, The (1944 film)
cast: Thomas Mitchell, Gregory Peck, Vincent Price
__ **Keys to Baldpate:** 5 Seven
keystone: 5 basis, coign, quoin, wedge 6 coigne
site: 4 arch
Keystone: 6 studio
missile: 3 pie
St.: 4 Penn. 5 Penna.
Keystone __: 4 Kops 6 comedy
Keystone State
see Pennsylvania
keystroke: 3 dah, dit
__ **Key, The:** 5 Glass, Third
Key to Midnight, The author: Koontz
Key West: 4 city, port, town
locale: 7 Florida
Key West Intermezzo (1996 song)
artist: John Cougar Mellencamp
KFC: 10 restaurant
order: 6 bucket
piece: 3 leg
rival: 6 Wendy's 8 Pizza Hut 9 McDonald's 10 Burger King
kg.: 2 wt. 3 amt. 4 meas.
__ **K. Gandhi:** 8 Mohandas
__ **K. Gann:** 6 Ernest
KGB
counterpart: 3 CIA
predecessor: 4 NKVD, OGPU
successor: 3 RIS
Khabur: 5 river
locale: 5 Syria 6 Turkey
Khachaturian, Aram: 7 Russian 8 composer
work: Sabre Dance
khaddar: 6 fabric 8 material
Khafre, father of: 6 Cheops
Khaibar __: 4 Pass
khaki: 3 tan 5 brown, color 6 fabric 7 uniform 9 yellowish
like ~: 3 tan 4 drab, dull 9 colorless
relative: 3 bay, dun, tan 4 bole, ecru, fawn, foxy, nude, seal 5 amber, beige, camel, cocoa, hazel, mocha, sepia, tawny, umber 6 auburn, bister, bistre, bronze, coffee, copper, ginger, russet, sienna, sorrel, suntan, walnut 7 biscuit, caramel, dogwood 8 chestnut, cinnamon, mahogany 9 butternut, chocolate
twill: 5 chino
khakis: 5 pants 6 slacks 8 trousers
Khambatta: 6 Persis
khamsin: 4 wind
khan: 5 ruler 6 gerent, hostel
concern: 6 empire
relative: 3 aga 4 agha
Khan: 3 Aga, Aly 4 Batu 5 Chaka, Kubla, Shere 6 Kublai, Tengri 7 Genghis
Khan, Aly spouse: Rita Hayworth
Khan, Chaka
group: Rufus
song: I Feel for You (1984)
I'm Every Woman (1978)
Once You Get Started (1975)
Sweet Thing (1976)
Tell Me Something Good (1974)
Khan, Jasmine grandfather: 3 Aga
Kharkov: 4 city, town
locale: 7 Ukraine
Khartoum: 4 city, town 7 capital
locale: 5 Sudan
river: 4 Nile
Khashoggi: 5 Adnan
Khayyám, Omar: 4 poet 7 Persian
Khigh: 6 Dheigh
Khirghiz range: 4 Alai
Khmer: 8 language 9 Cambodian
capital: 6 Angkor
Khmer __: 5 Rouge
Khoikhoi
home: 6 Africa
people: 4 Nama
Khomeini: 5 Irani
khon: 5 dance
Khorana, Gobind: 8 Nobelist
__ **K. Howard:** 7 William
Khrushchev: 6 Nikita
home: 4 USSR 6 Russia
Khrystyne: 4 Haje
khurta: 5 shirt
khus-khus: 5 grass
Khuzistan capital: 5 Ahvaz, Ahwaz
Khyber __: 4 Pass 5 knife
Khyber Pass terminus: 5 Kabul 8 Peshawar
Kia: 3 car 4 auto 10 automobile
model: 3 Rio 6 Optima, Sedona, Sephia, Serona 7 Sorento, Spectra 8 Rio Cinco, Sportage
origin: 5 Korea
Kiam: 6 Victor
kiang: 6 donkey, equine
relative: 3 ass 5 burro, horse, zebra 6 onager, quagga 7 jackass 8 chigetai 9 dziggetai
Kiaochow: 3 bay
kiawe: 4 tree
Kibbee: 3 Guy
kibble: 7 dog food
kibbutz: 7 commune 10 collective
one born on a ~: 5 sabra
see also Israel
kibitz: 6 butt in, meddle 9 interpose
kibitzer: 3 wag, wit 4 card 5 clown, cutup 6 kidder 7 farceur 8 jokester, quipster
kibosh: 3 gas, rot 4 blah, bosh, bull, bunk, guff, jazz, jive, pooh, tosh 5 bilge, fudge, hokum, hooey, prate, stuff, trash, tripe 6 bunkum, bushwa, drivel, footle, gabble, gammon, gibber, havers, hot air, humbug, jabber, jargon, piffle 7 baloney, blarney, blather, blether, boloney, bushwah, eyewash, flannel, flubdub, fustian, garbage, hogwash, inanity, rubbish, twaddle 8 buncombe, claptrap, falderal, falderol, flimflam, flummery, folderal, folderol, nonsense, slipslop, tommyrot, trumpery 9 banana oil, gibberish, kidstakes, moonshine, poppycock, rigmarole 10 applesauce, balderdash, bilge water, codswallop, double-talk, flapdoodle, galimatias, Jabberwock, mumbo jumbo, rigamarole, taradiddle
put the ~ on: 3 ban, nix, zap 4 curb, halt, stop, veto 5 check, quash, quell 7 abolish, contain, put down, repress, squelch 8 cut short, suppress
kick: 3 fun, jar, joy, pep 4 bang, beef, bite, blow, boot, buck, buzz, carp, fuss, hoot, hurt, jolt, punt, quit, snap, tang, wail, zest, zing 5 force, gripe, power, punch, spark, spice, taste, verve, vigor, whine 6 give up, object, recoil, repine, thrill, twitch, wallop 7 abandon, grumble, potence, potency, protest, sparkle 8 backlash, complain, pleasure, pungency, reaction, stimulus, strength, vitality 9 complaint, enjoyment, intensity, make a fuss, sensation 10 excitement
around: 5 abuse 6 debate 7 discuss 8 cogitate, hash over, maltreat, mistreat, talk over, walk over 9 manhandle, speculate, sweat over 10 deliberate
back: 3 pay 4 loll 5 relax 7 rebound
dance with a ~: 5 conga
ender: 3 off 4 back 5 boxer, stand 6 boxing
get a ~ out of: 3 dig, use 4 like 5 enjoy, go for 6 relish 8 flip over, thrill to 9 delight in, get high on, indulge in
in: 3 pay 4 ante, open 6 ante up, donate, pony up, supply 7 present 10 contribute
in football: 4 punt
in the teeth: 4 slur 6 rebuff, rebuke 7 repulse 9 rejection
off: 4 open 5 begin, start 6 launch 7 lead off 8 commence, get going, initiate 9 enter upon, introduce, originate 10 inaugurate
oneself: 3 rue 6 lament, regret
out: 2 ax 3 axe, can 4 boot, oust 5 eject, evict, expel, roust 6 banish, bounce, deport, depose 7 dismiss 9 discharge
over the traces: 4 riot 5 rebel 6 mutiny, revolt
the habit: 4 quit, stop 5 cease 6 desist, lay off 8 renounce
up a fuss: 3 cry 4 yell 5 gripe, groan, shout, whine 6 holler, shriek, squawk, yammer 7 grumble, protest, screech 8 complain 9 bellyache, raise Cain
up one's heels: 4 lark, romp 5 caper, jaunt, revel 6 cavort, frolic, gambol, prance 7 carouse, rollick 9 celebrate, make merry, whoop it up
upstairs: 4 bump 5 boost, favor, raise 6 better, move up 7 advance, elevate, endorse, further, promote
with a ~: 3 hot 4 sour, tart 5 juicy, peppy, sharp, spicy, tangy, tasty, zesty 6 acidic, biting, lively, strong 7 acerbic, peppery, piquant, pungent 8 vinegary 9 flavorful, sparkling
kick __: 3 off, out 4 back, turn 5 about, plate, pleat, serve 6 around, boxing 7 starter
kick __ pants: 5 in the
kick __ the traces: 4 over
kick-__: 5 start
__ **kick:** 3 top 4 drop, free, frog, goal 5 place, quick 6 corner, onside 7 bicycle, dolphin, flutter, penalty
Kickapoo: 3 Fox 5 tribe 6 Indian 7 Amerind 8 language
kickback: 3 cut, oil 4 gift 5 bribe, graft, share 6 boodle, grease, payoff, payola, rebate, refund, reward 7 jobbery, percent 8 reaction, response 9 hush money 10 commission, percentage
kick boxing: 5 sport
kicker: 4 snag 5 catch, hitch, point 7 proviso 8 obstacle 9 hindrance, provision 10 difficulty, impediment
asset: 3 toe
target: 4 shin
__**-kicker:** 5 place
kicking
alive and ~: 4 spry, well 5 sound
around: 5 about 9 somewhere
back: 6 at ease 7 content, relaxed 8 carefree
game: 6 soccer 8 football
kick in the __: 4 shin 5 pants
kickoff: 5 debut, onset, start 6 advent, outset 7 opening 8 exordium 9 beginning, inception
get ready for ~: 5 tee up
prop: 3 tee
__ **Kick Out of You:** 5 I Get a
kick over the __: 6 traces
kicks: 3 fun 5 mirth 6 thrill 7 jollies 8 pleasure 10 excitement
__ **kicks:** 3 for
Kicks (1966 song) artist: Paul Revere and the Raiders
kickshaw: 6 geegaw, gewgaw, tidbit, trifle 7 trinket 9 bagatelle
kick the __: 3 can 5 habit
kickup: 3 row 4 fuss 9 commotion
kick up __: 5 a fuss
kick up one's __: 5 heels
kicky: 3 fun 5 heady, juicy 7 amusing, zestful 8 electric, exciting 9 diverting, enjoyable, glamorous, thrilling
kid: 3 boy, cub, lad, rag, rib, son, tot 4 baby, fool, girl, jest, jive, joke, josh, lass, mock, razz, teen 5 chaff, child, minor, put on, roast, sonny, sprig, suede, tease, youth 6 animal, banter, bother, deride, infant, moppet 7 leather, preteen, sapling 8 daughter, goatskin, half-pint, immature, juvenile, ridicule, teenager 9 little one, make fun of, offspring, poke fun at, stripling, youngster 10 adolescent
ammo: 3 BBs, pea
aunt's ~: 6 cousin
ball: 4 Nerf
block: 4 Lego
cereal: 3 Kix 4 Trix
colorer: 6 crayon
comment: 5 bleat
complaint: 5 mumps 7 measles
computer language: 4 Logo
cry: 5 Mommy
ender: 3 nap 4 skin
end of a ~ tune: 3 EIO 5 EIEIO
entertainer: 5 Raffi
game: 3 tag, war 5 jacks, t-ball 6 Cootie, go fish 7 old maid
in Spanish: 4 niña, niño
protest: 5 not me
query: 3 why
retort: 4 am so 5 am too, can so, did so
ride: 4 bike, pony 5 trike, wagon 6 go-cart, go-kart 7 scooter 8 tricycle 9 school bus
rotten ~: 3 imp 4 brat
sch.: 4 elem.
shooter: 5 BB gun
starter: 5 grand
stickum: 5 paste
taunt: 6 are not, did not
kid __: 5 glove, stuff 6 gloves 7 brother
kid-__: 3 vid
__ **kid:** 4 quiz, whiz 6 French 7 Dongola
Kid: 3 Ory 6 Creole 7 Gavilan, Nichols
__ **Kid:** 8 Sundance
kid-brotherish: 5 pesky, pesty 7 irksome 8 annoying 9 maddening, provoking, vexatious 10 bothersome, irritating
Kid Brother, The director: 4 Howe
kidcom: 7 cartoon
Kidd: 5 Jason 7 Captain, Michael, William
kidder: 3 wag 5 joker, tease 8 kibitzer
Kidder, Margot: 7 actress
film: 92 in the Shade (1975)
Quackser Fortune ... (1970)
Sisters (1973)
Superman (1978)
Superman II (1980)
Willie and Phil (1980)
role for ~: 4 Lane, Lois
kiddie: 3 tot
use the ~ pool: 4 wade 6 splash
kiddie __: 3 car, lit
kidding: 5 humor, sport 6 banter, japery 7 jesting 8 badinage, jocosity 9 facetious 10 jocoseness
just ~: 7 as a lark 8 for a joke
no ~: 6 honest, really
person who takes ~: 5 sport
wasn't ~: 7 meant it
__ **kidding!:** 5 You're
kiddingly: 5 in fun 6 in jest

Kiddio (1960 song) artist: Brook Benton
kiddish: 6 jejune 7 babyish, puerile 8 childish, immature, juvenile 9 childlike, infantile
Kidd, Jason
milieu: 5 court
org.: 3 NBA
sport: 10 basketball
kiddo: 3 bro 4 dude 5 buddy 6 buster
kiddy: 3 tot 4 brat 5 bairn, child 6 moppet, nipper, squirt 7 bambino, preteen 8 juvenile, small fry 9 offspring, youngster
Kid From Brooklyn, The (1946 film)
cast: Danny Kaye, Virginia Mayo, Vera-Ellen
Kid From Spain, The (1932 film)
cast: Eddie Cantor, Robert Young
director: Leo McCarey
Kid Galahad (1937 film)
cast: Humphrey Bogart, Bette Davis, Edward G. Robinson
director: Michael Curtiz
Kid Galahad (1962 film)
cast: Lola Albright, Joan Blackman, Elvis Presley, Gig Young
__ Kid in Town: 3 New
kid lit
doctor: 5 Seuss
inventor: 5 Swift 8 Tom Swift
sleuth: 4 Drew 5 Hardy
wizard: 5 Harry 6 Potter
Kidman: 3 Nic 6 Nicole
Kidman, Nicole: 7 actress
film: Batman Forever (1995)
Billy Bathgate (1991)
Days of Thunder (1990)
Dead Calm (1989)
Eyes Wide Shut (1999)
Far and Away (1992)
The Hours (2002, AA)
Malice (1993)
Moulin Rouge (2001)
The Others (2001)
Practical Magic (1998)
To Die For (1995)
spouse: Tom Cruise
Kid Millions (1934 film)
cast: Eddie Cantor, Ethel Merman, Ann Sothern
kidnap: 3 nab 4 grab 5 seize, steal 6 abduct, hijack, pirate, snatch, waylay 7 capture 8 carry off, grab away, highjack, shanghai 9 bundle off 10 spirit away
victim: 5 Helen
Kidnapped author: Stevenson
kidnapper: 5 felon 6 captor 8 abductor, hijacker
kidnapping: 6 felony 7 capture, seizure
kidney: 3 cut 4 bean, cast, kind, make, mold, sort, type 5 brand, breed, organ 7 variety 9 character, chili bean
combining form: 4 reni-, reno- 5 nephr- 6 nephro- 7 -nephron, -nephros
enzyme: 5 renin
of a ~: 5 renal
-shaped nut: 6 cashew
kidney __: 4 bean 5 vetch
kidney bean: 6 legume, veggie 9 vegetable
__ kid on the block: 3 new
kids: 3 get 4 seed 5 heirs, issue, young 6 family, scions 7 progeny 8 children 9 offspring, posterity
like bored ~: 5 antsy, itchy 7 fidgety 8 restless 9 unsettled
not for ~: 5 adult
one with ~: 4 goat 5 billy, nanny 6 father, mother, parent
tend the ~: 3 sit
__ Kids: 3 Spy 4 Rich
Kids Are Alright, The
band: 6 The Who
director: 5 Stein
__ Kids on the Block: 3 New
kidstakes: 3 gas, rot 4 blah, bosh, bull, bunk, guff, jazz, jive, pooh, tosh 5 bilge, fudge, hokum, hooey, prate, stuff, trash, tripe 6 bunkum, bushwa, drivel, footle, gabble, gammon, gibber, havers, hot air, humbug, jabber, jargon, kibosh, piffle 7 baloney, blarney, blather, blether, boloney, bushwah, eyewash, flannel, flubdub, fustian, garbage, hogwash, inanity, rubbish, twaddle 8 buncombe, claptrap, falderal, falderol, flimflam, flummery, folderal, folderol, nonsense, slipslop, tommyrot, trumpery 9 banana oil, gibberish, moonshine, poppycock, rigmarole 10 applesauce, balderdash, bilge water, codswallop, double-talk, flapdoodle, galimatias, Jabberwock, mumbo jumbo, rigamarole, taradiddle
__ Kids, The: 4 Quiz
Kid, The (1921 film)
cast: Charles Chaplin, Jackie Coogan, Edna Purviance
director: Charles Chaplin
__ Kid, The: 5 Cisco 6 Frisco, Karate
Kid, The author: Conrad Aiken
Kiefer: 10 Sutherland
to Donald: 3 son
Kieffer: 4 pear
Kiel: 4 city, port, town 5 canal 6 Martin 7 Richard
locale: 7 Germany
kielbasa: 4 meat 6 Polish 7 sausage
Kieran: 6 Culkin
Kierkegaard, Sören: 6 Danish 11 philosopher
Kiev: 4 city, town 7 capital
city near ~: 4 Lvov
locale: 7 Ukraine
river: 7 Dneiper
__ Kiev: 7 chicken
Kigali: 4 city, town 7 capital
locale: 6 Rwanda
Kigoma: 4 city, town
locale: 8 Tanzania
Kiki: 3 Dee 6 Cuyler
kikuyu: 5 grass
Kikuyu: 8 language
home: 5 Kenya 6 Africa
Kikwit: 4 city, town
kil.: 4 meas.
Kilauea: 7 volcano
city near ~: 4 Hilo
locale: 6 Hawaii
output: 4 lava
Kilborn: 5 Craig
Kilbride: 5 Percy
Kilby, Jack: 8 Nobelist 9 physicist
Kildare: 3 Jim 5 James 6 doctor
org.: 3 AMA
Kiley: 6 Steven 7 Richard
Kiley, Steven org.: 3 AMA
colleague: 5 Welby
Kilgallen: 7 Dorothy
kilij: 5 blade, sword 7 Turkish
kilim: 3 rug
Kilimanjaro: 4 peak 5 mount 8 mountain
like ~: 5 snowy, white
locale: 6 Africa 8 Tanzania
Kilkenny __: 4 cats
kill: 3 nix 4 halt, prey, slay, stop, veto 5 annul, douse, dowse, purge, quash, quell, shoot, spend 6 cancel, defeat, poison, reject, remove, repeal, revoke, scotch, squash, stifle 7 abolish, nullify, shut off, squelch, turn off, wipe out 8 prohibit, suppress 9 eighty-six, liquidate, overwhelm 10 do away with, 'extinguish, neutralize
as a bill: 4 veto
could ~ for: 4 want 5 covet, crave, fancy, yearn 6 desire 9 lust after
ender: 3 joy 4 deer
time: 4 idle, laze, loaf 5 stall 6 loiter, lounge
with kindness: 5 spoil 6 coddle, dote on, pamper 7 indulge 9 spoon-feed
kill __: 3 fee 4 shot, time
Killarney: 4 city
county: 5 Kerry
locale: 4 Eire, Erin 7 Ireland
killdeer: 4 bird 6 plover
Killebrew, Harmon: 4 Twin 7 slugger
Killeen: 4 city, town
locale: 5 Texas
killer: 5 doozy 6 doozie, slayer 8 assassin, criminal, enforcer 9 cutthroat
bug ~: 3 DDT
germ ~: 4 drug 10 antibiotic
having a ~ instinct: 5 cruel 6 brutal, savage 8 pitiless, ruthless 9 cutthroat, dog-eat-dog, ferocious, merciless
starter: 4 pain
whale: 3 orc 4 orca 7 grampus
killer __: 3 app, bee 4 bars, boat, cell 5 T cell, whale
killer-__: 6 diller
__ killer: 4 time 7 penalty
__-killer: 4 weed 5 spark
Killer McCoy (1947 film)
cast: Ann Blyth, Brian Donlevy, Mickey Rooney
Killers, The (1946 film)
cast: Ava Gardner, Burt Lancaster, Edmond O'Brien
killing: 9 landslide
make a ~: 5 score 6 profit 7 prosper
killing __: 5 frost
__ killing: 4 twin
Killing 'em Softly actress: 4 Cara
Killing Fields, The (1984 film)
cast: John Malkovich, Haing S. Ngor, Sam Waterston
director: Roland Joffe
Killing Me Softly With His Song (1973 song) artist: Roberta Flack
Killing, The (1956 film)
cast: Vince Edwards, Sterling Hayden
director: Stanley Kubrick
Killing Time author: Thomas Berger
killjoy: 5 cynic 6 downer 7 scoffer, skeptic, worrier 8 sourpuss 9 defeatist, gloomy Gus, pessimist, worrywart 10 complainer, wet blanket
Killy, Jean-Claude: 5 skier 6 French
Kilmer: 3 Val 5 Joyce
Kilmer, Joyce: 4 poet
work: Trees
Kilmer, Val: 5 actor
film: At First Sight (1998)
Batman Forever (1995)
The Doors (1991)
Heat (1995)
Pollock (2000)
The Saint (1997)
Thunderheart (1992)
Tombstone (1993)
Top Gun (1986)
Willow (1988)
spouse: Joanne Whalley
voice: The Prince of Egypt (1998)
kiln: 4 oast, oven 5 stove 7 furnace
operator: 5 firer
product: 5 brick
put in a ~: 3 dry
starter: 4 lime
use a ~: 4 bake, heat 6 season
kilocalories
1000 ~: 5 therm 6 therme
kiloelectron __: 4 volt
kilogram __: 7 calorie
kilogram-__: 5 force, meter
kilograms
.454 ~: 5 pound
1000 ~: 5 tonne
kilometers, 1.609 ~: 4 mile
kilo, Turkish: 3 oka
kilowatt-hour fraction: 3 erg 5 joule
kilowatts: 3 pwr. 5 power
Kilroy __ here: 3 was
kilt: 5 skirt 7 filibeg 8 philibeg
cousin: 5 A-line
fold: 5 plait, pleat
material: 5 plaid
wearer: 4 clan, Gael, Scot 5 piper 8 bagpiper
kilter: 4 sync, trim 5 order
out of ~: 4 awry, shot 5 amiss, atilt, kaput 6 aslant, broken, faulty, flawed 7 damaged 9 defective 10 on the blink, on the fritz, out of whack
kiltie: 4 shoe 8 footwear
Kim: 4 Andy 5 Darby, Novak, O'Hara, Wilde 6 Alexis, Carnes, Fields, Greist, Hunter, Philby 7 Delaney, Stanley 8 Basinger, Campbell, Cattrall
author: Rudyard Kipling
city in ~: 6 Lahore
Kim (1950 film)
cast: Errol Flynn, Paul Lukas, Dean Stockwell
Kim __ Jung: 3 Dae
__ Kim: 3 Lil'
Kim, Andy
song: Baby, I Love You (1969)
Rock Me Gently (1974)
Kimberly: 4 Beck 5 Elise 8 Williams
Kimberly-__: 5 Clark
Kimbrough: 7 Charles
kimchi country: 5 Korea
Kim Dae Jung: 6 Korean 8 Nobelist
Kim Il Sung opponent: 4 Rhee
kimono: 4 robe 7 garment, wrapper 8 bathrobe, lingerie, negligee, peignoir 9 housecoat
accessory: 3 obi 4 inro
fabric: 4 silk
kin: 6 caftan, kaftan
wearer: 6 geisha
kin: 3 bro, rel., sib, sis 4 aunt, gong, sibs 5 aunts, blood, folks, stock, uncle 6 cousin, family, father, mother, people, sister 7 brother, grandma, grandpa, lineage, progeny, related, sibling, similar 8 brethren, relation, relative 9 connected, great-aunt, relations, relatives 10 great-uncle
ender: 4 folk
__ kin: 6 next of 7 kissing
-kin
kin: 3 -ule
Kin: 7 Hubbard
Kinabalu: 4 peak 5 mount 8 mountain
locale: 4 Asia 6 Borneo
kind: 3 big, ilk, lax 4 easy, form, good, mild, mold, nice, soft, sort, type, warm 5 brand, breed, civil, class, close, genre, genus, loose, model, order, style, sweet 6 benign, chummy, clubby, decent, family, genial, gentle, giving, humane, kidney, loving, manner, nature, polite, tender 7 affable, amiable, bracket, clement, cordial, fashion, gallant, heedful, helpful, lenient, liberal, mindful, pattern, quality, ruthful, sparing, species, tactful, variety 8 all heart, amicable, category, fatherly, flexible, friendly, generous, gracious, harmless, intimate, ladylike, laid-back, maternal, merciful, motherly, obliging, outgoing, parental, placable, sisterly, sociable, tolerant 9 assuasive, attentive, avuncular, brotherly, character, compliant, congenial, convivial, courteous, easygoing, favorable, forgiving, indulgent, sensitive, temperate, unselfish

10 altruistic, beneficent, benevolent, bighearted, buddy-buddy, charitable, chivalrous, forbearing, hospitable, neighborly, permissive, solicitous, thoughtful, unexacting, unhardened
be ~: 4 care 10 have a heart
be so ~: 5 deign, lower, stoop 6 see fit 9 patronize 10 condescend
combining form: 4 phyl- 5 phylo-
deed: 3 aid 4 help 5 favor 7 service 8 courtesy
ender: 7 hearted
first of its ~: 3 new 5 novel 8 brand-new, original 10 avant-garde, futuristic, innovative, newfangled
in ~: 4 like, thus 8 likewise 9 similarly, tit-for-tat
in French: 3 bon
in Latin: 4 alma
make ~: 6 gentle, mellow, soften, temper 8 humanize
of: 4 a bit 5 quasi, sorta 6 fairly, in a way, pretty, rather, sort of 7 a little 8 slightly, somewhat 9 to a degree 10 moderately, more or less
of (prefix): 4 semi-
of (suffix): 3 -ish
of that ~: 4 such
one: 5 angel, donor, saint 6 backer, patron 7 sponsor 9 supporter 10 benefactor 11 underwriter
pay in ~: 6 avenge 7 get even, requite 9 get back at, retaliate
starter: 3 man 5 woman, women
that ~ of: 4 such 7 similar
two of a ~: 4 same 5 alike 9 identical 10 synonymous
wishes: 7 devoirs, regards 8 respects 9 greetings
Kind: 6 Roslyn 7 Richard
kinda: 5 sorta 6 rather, sort of
kindergarten: 5 class 6 school
break: 3 nap 4 rest 6 snooze
denizen: 3 boy, kid, tot 4 girl, tike, tyke 5 pupil 7 student
fare: 4 ABCs 6 letter 8 alphabet
game: 4 I spy
song opening: 3 ABC 4 ABCD 5 ABCDE
staple: 5 chalk, paste 6 crayon
wear: 5 smock
Kindergarten Cop (1990 film)
cast: Linda Hunt, Penelope Ann Miller, Pamela Reed, Arnold Schwarzenegger
director: Ivan Reitman
Kindertotenlieder composer: 6 Mahler
Kind & Generous (1998 song) artist: Natalie Merchant
kindhearted: 3 big, lax 4 easy, good, mild, nice, soft, warm 5 great, loose, sweet 6 benign, gentle, humane, loving, tender 7 amiable, clement, cordial, lenient, ruthful, sparing 8 amicable, flexible, friendly, generous, gracious, laid-back, merciful, obliging, placable, tolerant 9 assuasive, compliant, congenial, courteous, easygoing, forgiving, indulgent, unselfish 10 altruistic, beneficent, benevolent, charitable, forbearing, hospitable, neighborly, permissive, solicitous, thoughtful, unexacting
soul: 5 softy, sport 6 softie
Kind Hearts and Coronets (1949 film)
cast: Alec Guinness, Valerie Hobson
Kind Lady (1951 film)
cast: Ethel Barrymore, Maurice Evans, Angela Lansbury
kindle: 4 burn, fuel, lick, stir, wake, whet 5 cause, egg on, key up, light, liven, pique, raise, rally, rouse, spark, waken 6 arouse, awaken, bestir, excite, fire up, foment, ignite, incite, induce, turn on, whip up, work up 7 actuate, agitate, animate, enflame, inflame, inspire, provoke, quicken 8 activate, brighten, enspirit, inspirit, set afire, touch off 9 impassion, instigate, set alight, set fire to, stimulate 10 illuminate, intoxicate
kindliness: 4 pity 5 mercy 6 warmth 8 good deed, goodness, good turn 9 geniality 10 fellowship, good nature
kindling: 4 fuel, twig, wood 5 brush, fagot, twigs 6 firing, tinder 7 burning 8 arousing, firewood, igniting, lighting, shavings 9 awakening, driftwood, evocative, fomenting 10 combustion, quickening
kindly: 3 big, lax 4 easy, good, mild, nice, soft, warm 5 close, loose, moral, sweet 6 benign, chummy, clubby, decent, genial, gentle, humane, loving, please, polite, tender 7 affable, amiable, clement, cordial, gallant, heedful, helpful, lenient, mindful, ruthful, sparing, tactful 8 all heart, amicable, flexible, friendly, generous, gracious, intimate, laid-back, merciful, obliging, outgoing, placable, pleasant, sociable, tolerant 9 assuasive, compliant, congenial, convivial, courteous, easygoing, favorable, forgiving, indulgent, sensitive, unselfish 10 altruistic, beneficent, benevolent, buddy-buddy, charitable, forbearing, hospitable, neighborly, permissive, solicitous, thoughtful, unexacting, unhardened
__ kindly to: 4 take
kindness: 3 aid 4 hand, help, pity 5 favor, grace, heart, mercy 6 lenity, succor, virtue 7 amenity, charity, decency, service, thought 8 altruism, clemency, courtesy, good deed, goodness, good turn, good will, humanity, lenience, patience, sympathy 9 affection, tolerance 10 amiability, assistance, compassion, cordiality, generosity, indulgence, liberality, solicitude
kill with ~: 5 spoil 6 coddle, dote on, pamper 7 indulge 9 spoon-feed
__-kindness: 6 loving
Kind of a Drag (1967 song) artist: Buckinghams
__ Kind of Fool Am I?: 4 What
__ Kind of Hero: 4 Some
__ Kind of Love: 6 Groovy
Kind of Magic, A author: Edna Ferber
__ Kind of Wonderful: 4 Some
kindred: 4 akin, clan, like 5 alike, stock, tribe 6 agnate, allied, family 7 cognate, lineage, progeny, related, similar 8 parallel, relation 9 analogous, relatives 10 comparable, equivalent
kinds of, all: 4 gobs, lots, many, much, pile, tons 5 ample, heaps, loads, lotsa, no end, scads 6 barrel, galore, oodles, plenty 7 aplenty, copious 8 beaucoup, mountain, plethora 9 abundance, thousands
kine: 4 cows 5 herds 6 cattle 7 bovines, heifers 9 livestock
Kiner, Ralph: 6 Pirate 7 slugger 10 outfielder
kinetic: 7 dynamic 8 in motion 9 energetic
kinetic __: 3 art 6 energy
kinetics: 4 flow, flux 6 motion 8 movement
kinetic theory of __: 4 heat 5 gases 6 matter
kinetoscope inventor: 6 Edison
kinfolk: 4 clan, kith, seed, sons 5 folks, heirs, issue 6 family, people 7 parents, progeny 8 ancestry, brethren, children, forbears 9 ancestors, daughters, offspring, posterity, relations, relatives
king: 3 bed, HRH, rex, sov. 4 boss, card, czar, dean, male, tsar, tzar 5 chief, doyen, mogul, Mr. Big, nabob, noble, royal, ruler, title 6 dynast, gerent, leader, top dog, tycoon, victor 7 big shot, his nibs, majesty, monarch, viceroy 8 big wheel, enthrone, inthrone, tetrarch 9 honor card, potentate, sovereign 10 chess piece, head honcho
address: 4 sire
beater: 3 ace
beater, in pinochle: 3 ten
Biblical ~: 3 Asa 4 Ahab, Reba, Saul 5 Abner, David, Herod 7 Solomon
Egyptian ~: 6 Ramses 7 Rameses
ender: 3 cup, dom, let, pin 4 bird, bolt, fish, ship, side, wood 5 craft, maker 6 fisher, making
fit for a ~: 5 regal, royal 9 luxurious
greedy ~: 5 Midas
home: 6 castle, palace
Hun ~: 4 Atli
in a Steve Martin tune: 3 Tut
Indian ~: 4 raja
in French: 3 roi
in Latin: 3 rex
in Spanish: 3 rey
Jack Kent's comic-strip ~: 4 Aroo
jungle ~: 4 lion
land of Anna's ~: 4 Siam
like the ~ of beasts: 5 noble
merry ~ of nursery rhymes: 4 Cole
move: 4 jump
mythical ~ of Calydon: 6 Oeneus
name meaning ~: 5 Elroy, Leroy
neighbor: 6 bishop
Norse mythical ~: 4 Atli
nursery-rhyme ~: 4 Cole
of beasts: 4 lion
of Phrygia: 5 Midas
of the hill: 5 on top
of the road: 4 hobo 5 tramp 7 vagrant 8 vagabond, wanderer
order: 3 act 4 fiat 5 edict, ukase 6 decree, dictum, ruling 7 dictate, mandate, precept 9 manifesto
place for a ~: 4 deck
Shakespearean ~: 4 Lear
Volsunga Saga ~: 4 Atli
king __: 3 bee, rod 4 clam, crab, post, rail 5 cobra, devil, plank, snake, truss 6 closer, salmon 7 penguin, vulture
king __ hill: 5 of the
king-__: 3 hit 4 size 5 sized 7 whiting
king-__ bed: 4 size 5 sized
__ king: 3 à la, sea
King: 2 B.B. 3 Don, Sky, Tut 4 Alan, Ben E., Fahd, peak, Saul 5 David, Floyd, Henry, Larry, Mabel, mount, Perry, ranch, Vidor 6 Albert, Carole, Claude, Evelyn, Oliver, Pee Wee 7 Morgana, Solomon, Stephen 8 Gillette, mountain 10 Billie Jean
had one: 5 dream
rival: 3 Net, Sun 4 Blue, Buck, Bull, Hawk, Heat, Jazz, Spur, Star, Wild 5 Bruin, Devil, Flame, Flyer, Knick, Laker, Magic, Oiler, Pacer, Sabre, Shark, Sixer 6 Canuck, Celtic, Coyote, Hornet, Nugget, Piston, Ranger, Raptor, Rocket, Wizard 7 Capital, Clipper, Grizzly, Panther, Penguin, Red Wing, Senator, Warrior 8 Canadien, Cavalier, Islander, Maverick, Predator, Thrasher 9 Avalanche, Blackhawk, Hurricane, Lightning, Maple Leaf 10 Blue Jacket, Mighty Duck, Super-Sonic, Timberwolf
sport: 6 hockey 10 basketball
King __: 3 Rat, Tut 4 Aroo, Coal, John, Kong, Lear, Pest 5 Ralph 6 Cotton, Creole
King __ a Day: 3 for
King __ Bible: 5 James
King __ Country: 3 and
King __ Road: 5 of the
King __ spaniel: 7 Charles
King __ Stomp: 6 Porter
King __, The: 4 and I
King __ tomb: 4 Tut's
King __ Version: 5 James
King __ War: 7 George's, Philip's
King __ York, A: 5 in New
King and Country (1964 film)
cast: Dirk Bogarde, Tom Courtenay, Leo McKern
King and I, The (1956 film): 7 musical
cast: Yul Brynner, Deborah Kerr, Rita Moreno
character: 4 Anna 5 Orton 6 Lun Tha, Tuptim 7 Mongkut
composer: 7 Rodgers 11 Hammerstein
director: Walter Lang
locale: 4 Siam
King Arthur
enchantress: 5 Le Fay 6 Morgan, Vivien
father: 5 Uther
foster brother: 3 Kay
island paradise: 6 Avalon
knight: 3 Kay, Tor 4 Bors, Eric 5 Driam, Ector, Floll, Lucan, Yvain, Ywain 6 Acolon, Brunor, Ewaine, Gareth, Gawain, Hector, Lanval, Lavain, Manier, Morolt, Ryence, Sagrid, Torres 7 Belvour, Bersunt, Caradoc, Dinadam, Dodynas, Gaheris, Galahad, Geraint, Grislet, Ladynas, Lionell, Marhaus, Mordred, Pelleas, Peredur, Tristan, Wigamor 8 Agravain, Beaumans, Bevidere, Galohalt, Lancelot, Meliadus, Palamede, Percival, Tristram, Turquine, Wigalois 9 Ballamore, Brandiles, Launcelot, Pellinore
magician: 6 Merlin
palace site: 7 Camelot
queen: 9 Guinevere
quest: 9 Holy Grail
sister: 4 Anne 5 Le Fay 6 Morgan
sword: 9 Excalibur
King, B.B.: 8 bluesman 9 guitarist
first name: Riley
guitar: Lucille
King, Ben E.
song: Spanish Harlem (1961)
Stand by Me (1961)
Supernatural Thing (1975)
King, Billie Jean: 7 netster 9 tennis pro
milieu: 5 court
king can __ wrong, The: 4 do no
King, Carole
song: I Feel the Earth Move (1971)
It's Too Late (1971)
Jazzman (1974)
Nightingale (1975)
So Far Away (1971)
Sweet Seasons (1972)
King Charles __: 7 spaniel
King, Claude song: Wolverton Mountain (1962)
King Coal author: Upton Sinclair
__ King Cole: 3 Nat, Old
King Cotton composer: 5 Sousa
__ king crab: 6 Alaska 7 Alaskan
King Creole (1958 film)
cast: Dolores Hart, Dean Jagger, Carolyn Jones, Elvis Presley
director: Michael Curtiz
King David actor: 4 Gere
kingdom: 4 land 5 realm 6 domain, empire, nation 7 country, dynasty 8 monarchy
ancient ~: 4 Cush, Edom, Elam, Moab

5 Ammon, Nubia, Ophir, Sheba 6 Epirus
Anglo-Saxon ~: 5 Essex
Asian ~: 5 Nepal 6 Bhutan
N. Sea ~: 4 Holl., Neth.
of a ~: 5 regal, royal 8 dynastic, imperial, majestic
onetime Asian ~: 4 Anam 5 Annam
Polynesian ~: 5 Tonga
subdivision: 6 phylum
kingdom ___: 4 come
___ kingdom: 5 plant 6 animal 7 mineral
Kingdom ___: 4 Hall
Kingdom ___ Spiders: 5 of the
___ Kingdom: 3 New, Old 4 Wild 5 Silla 6 Hermit, Middle
Kingdom Come (2001 film)
cast: Vivica A. Fox, Whoopi Goldberg, LL Cool J, Jada Pinkett Smith
Kingdom, The composer: 5 Elgar
King, Evelyn song: Shame (1978)
King Features competitor: 3 NEA
kingfish: 4 amir, boss, czar, emir, exec, head, jefe, tsar, tzar 5 ameer, chief, emeer, ruler 6 honcho, leader, master, top dog 7 captain, headman, skipper 8 director, higher-up, top brass 9 big cheese, commander, executive, key player, top banana 10 mastermind
kingfisher: 4 bird 7 halcyon 10 kookaburra
coif: 5 crest
genus: 6 alcedo
relative: 4 tody 6 motmot
Kingfish, The: 4 Huey, Long
King for a Day (1986 song) artist: Thompson Twins
King George's ___: 3 War
King, Henry: 8 director
film: Alexander's Ragtime Band (1938)
A Bell for Adano (1945)
The Black Swan (1942)
The Bravados (1958)
Captain From Castile (1947)
Carousel (1956)
The Gunfighter (1950)
I'd Climb the Highest Mountain (1951)
In Old Chicago (1938)
Jesse James (1939)
Lloyd's of London (1936)
Love Is a Many Splendored Thing (1955)
Margie (1946)
Remember the Day (1941)
The Snows of Kilimanjaro (1952)
The Song of Bernadette (1943)
Stanley and Livingstone (1939)
State Fair (1933)
The Sun Also Rises (1957)
Tol'able David (1921)
Twelve O'Clock High (1949)
Untamed (1955)
Wait 'Til the Sun Shines, Nellie (1952)
Wilson (1944)
A Yank in the RAF (1941)
King in New York, A (1957 film)
cast: Dawn Addams, Charles Chaplin
director: Charles Chaplin
King James ___: 5 Bible 7 Version
King John author: William Shakespeare
kingklip catcher: 5 eeler
King Kong: 3 ape
author: Edgar Wallace
King Kong (1933 film)
cast: Robert Armstrong, Bruce Cabot, Fay Wray
character: 3 Ann 4 Carl 6 Darrow, Denham 9 Ann Darrow 10 Carl Denham
composer: 7 Steiner
King Kong (1976 film)
cast: Jeff Bridges, Charles Grodin, Jessica Lange
King Lear: 4 play 7 tragedy
author: Shakespeare
character: 5 Edgar, Regan 6 Edmund, Oswald 7 Goneril 8 Cordelia 10 Earl of Kent
Kurosawa's ~: 3 Ran
kinglet: 4 bird
kinglike: 5 grand, noble, regal, royal 6 august, lordly 7 haughty 8 imperial, imposing, majestic 9 imperious 10 autocratic, commanding
kingliness: 7 dignity, majesty 8 eminence, grandeur, splendor
kingly: 5 noble, regal, royal 7 leonine, stately 8 despotic, imperial, majestic 9 imperious 10 autocratic, despotical, majestical
Kingman: 4 city, Dave, town
locale: 7 Arizona
King Mark, wife of: 6 Iseult
King, Martin Luther: 8 Nobelist
title: 3 Rev. 8 Reverend
King Must Die, The author: Mary Renault
king of ___: 6 beasts
King of All Media: 5 Stern
King of Comedy, The (1983 film)
cast: Sandra Bernhard, Robert De Niro, Jerry Lewis
director: Martin Scorsese
King of Kings (1961 film)
cast: Jeffrey Hunter, Siobhan McKenna, Robert Ryan
director: Nicholas Ray
King of Marvin Gardens, The (1972 film)
cast: Ellen Burstyn, Bruce Dern, Jack Nicholson
director: Bob Rafelson
King of Pain (1983 song) artist: Police
King of Prussia: 4 town
King of Prussia, Pa.: 4 city
locale: 4 Penn.
king of the ___: 4 hill 6 forest
King of the ___: 4 Road
King of the Cowboys, The: 6 Rogers
King of the Hill (Fox sitcom)
setting: Arlen, Texas
voice cast: Mike Judge (Hank Hill) Brittany Murphy (Luanne Platter) Kathy Najimy (Peggy Hill)
King of the Road (1965 song) artist: Roger Miller
King of Torts, The: 5 Belli
King Olaf composer: 5 Elgar
King Peak locale: 5 Yukon 6 Canada
King Pest author: Edgar Allan Poe
King Philip's ___: 3 War
kingpin: 4 boss, czar, tsar 5 Mr. Big 7 headman 8 director 9 authority, commander, organizer
Kingpin (1996 film)
cast: Vanessa Angel, Woody Harrelson, Bill Murray, Randy Quaid
director: Bobby Farrelly, Peter Farrelly
King Ralph actor: 6 O'Toole 7 Goodman
King Ranch: 6 spread
locale: 5 Texas
unit: 4 acre
King Rat: 4 film 5 novel
author: James Clavell
cast: Tom Courtenay, James Fox, George Segal
king's ___: 4 blue, evil 5 color, crown, scout 6 bounty, ransom, yellow 7 English, highway, pattern, weather
king's-___ openings: 4 pawn
Kings: 3 six 4 five, team
follower: 10 Chronicles
home: 10 Los Angeles, Sacramento
milieu: 3 ice 4 rink
org.: 3 NBA, NHL
preceder: 6 Samuel
sport: 6 hockey 10 basketball
town near the Valley of the ~: 5 Luxor
Valley of the ~ locale: 5 Egypt
King's ___: 3 Men 4 mark 5 Bench 6 speech, Stilts 7 Counsel, Proctor
Kingsblood Royal author: Sinclair Lewis
Kings Canyon: 4 park
locale: 10 California
Kingsfield profession: 3 law
King's Fifth, The author: 5 O'Dell
kings, game of: 5 chess 8 checkers
Kings Go Forth (1958 film)
cast: Tony Curtis, Frank Sinatra, Natalie Wood
director: Delmer Daves
King's Henchmen, The: 5 opera
composer: Deems Taylor
kingship: 4 rule, sway 5 crown, power, reign 6 regime, throne 7 command, royalty, scepter 8 dominion, monarchy 9 accession, authority, supremacy 10 ascendance, ascendancy, ascendence, ascendency, succession
king-size: 3 big 4 huge, vast 5 giant, great, jumbo, large 7 hulking, immense, mammoth, massive, sizable, titanic 8 colossal, enormous, gigantic, sizeable, towering, whapping, whopping 9 Herculean, humongous, overlarge 10 gargantuan, monumental, prodigious, stupendous, tremendous
king-sized ___: 3 bed
Kingsley: 3 Ben 4 Amis 6 Sidney
Kingsley, Ben: 5 actor
film: Bugsy (1991)
Dave (1993)
Death and the Maiden (1994)
The Fifth Monkey (1990)
Gandhi (1982, AA)
Rules of Engagement (2000)
Schindler's List (1993)
Sexy Beast (2000)
Silas Marner (1985)
Sneakers (1992)
Species (1995)
Turtle Diary (1985)
What Planet Are You From? (2000)
Kingsmen
song: The Jolly Green Giant (1965)
Louie Louie (1963)
King Solomon's Mines: 4 film 5 novel
author: H. Rider Haggard
cast: Stewart Granger, Deborah Kerr
King Solomon's Ring author: Konrad Lorenz
Kingsolver, Barbara: 6 writer
work: The Bean Trees
Pigs in Heaven
Prodigal Summer
Small Wonder
Kings Peak: 4 peak 5 mount 8 mountain
locale: 4 Utah 6 Uintas
Kingsport: 4 city, town
locale: 9 Tennessee
Kings Row (1942 film)
cast: Robert Cummings, Ronald Reagan, Ann Sheridan
director: Sam Wood
King's Stilts author: Dr. Seuss
King, Stephen: 6 writer
enjoy ~: 4 read
genre: horror
home: Maine
like a ~ novel: 4 eery 5 eerie, scary, weird 6 creepy, spooky 7 bizarre, macabre, strange, uncanny 9 fantastic
pen name: Bachman
work: Bag of Bones
Carrie
Christine
Creepshow
Cujo
The Dark Half
The Dark Tower
The Dead Zone
Desperation
Dolores Claiborne
Dream Catcher
Firestarter
The Green Mile
The Gunslinger
Insomnia
It
Misery
Needful Things
Night Shift
Pet Sematary
The Plant
Rage
Roadwork
Rose Madder
The Running Man
Salem's Lot
The Shining
The Stand
The Talisman
The Tommyknockers
The Waste Lands
___ Kings, The: 5 Mambo
King's Thief, The (1955 film)
cast: Ann Blyth, David Niven, George Sanders
Kingston: 4 city, port, town 7 capital
athletes: 4 Rams
locale: 6 Canada 7 Jamaica, New York, Ontario
music: 3 ska
school: 3 URI 6 Queen's
Kingston ___ Thames: 4 upon
Kingston Trio
song: M.T.A. (1959)
Reverend Mr. Black (1963)
Tom Dooley (1958)
Kingston upon Hull: 4 city, town
city near: 5 Leeds
locale: 7 England
Kingstown: 4 city 7 capital
locale: 10 West Indies
Kingsville: 4 city, town
locale: 5 Texas
Kingswood: 3 car 4 auto 5 Chevy 9 Chevrolet 10 automobile
King, The: 5 Elvis, Gable 7 Presley
daughter: 4 Lisa
middle name: 4 Aron
portrayer: 3 Yul 7 Brynner
___ King, The: 3 Sun 4 Lion 5 March, Waltz 6 Fisher, Little
___-King, The: 3 Erl
King Tut's ___: 4 tomb
King William's ___: 3 War
Kinison, Sam: 5 comic 8 comedian
kink: 4 bend, coil, curl, flaw, flex, friz, knot, loop, pain, pang 5 cramp, crick, frizz, hitch, quirk, spasm, twist 6 curl up, defect, foible, glitch, tangle, twinge 7 sinuate 8 crotchet, soreness 9 stiffness 10 difficulty, impediment
kinkajou: 5 potto 6 animal, mammal
Kinks
song: All Day and All of the Night (1965)
Come Dancing (1983)
Lola (1970)
Tired of Waiting for You (1965)
You Really Got Me (1964)
kinky: 3 odd 4 wiry 5 curly, queer, weird 6 coiled, frizzy, matted 7 crimped, frizzly, knotted, oddball, tangled, twisted 8 peculiar 10 outlandish, unbalanced

Kinky: 8 Friedman
Kinmont: 8 Kathleen
__ Kinnan Rawlings: 8 Marjorie
Kinnear, Greg: 5 actor
film: As Good as It Gets (1997)
Auto Focus (2002)
Dear God (1996)
Mystery Men (1999)
Nurse Betty (2000)
Sabrina (1995)
Someone Like You (2001)
We Were Soldiers (2002)
What Planet Are You From? (2000)
You've Got Mail (1998)
Kinnell, Galway: 4 poet
Kinney: 5 Kathy, Terry
Kino: 4 city, town
locale: 6 Mexico, Sonora
kin's companion: 4 kith
Kinsella: 2 W.P. 6 Thomas
Kinsella, W.P.: 6 writer
work: Box Socials
The Iowa Baseball Confederacy
Magic Time
Shoeless Joe
Kinsey: 6 Alfred
concern: 3 sex
Kinshasa: 4 city, town 7 capital
locale: 5 Congo
locale, once: 5 Zaire
river: 5 Congo
kinship: 3 tie 5 blood 7 bearing, harmony 8 affinity, relation 9 belonging, community 10 connection, similarity
group: 4 clan 5 folks, tribe 6 family
Kinski, Klaus: 5 actor
film: Aguirre: The Wrath of God (1972)
Android (1982)
Burden of Dreams (1982)
Fitzcarraldo (1982)
The Little Drummer Girl (1984)
Nosferatu the Vampyre (1979)
Operation Thunderbolt (1977)
Kinski, Nastassja: 7 actress
film: An American Rhapsody (2001)
The Savior (1998)
Terminal Velocity (1994)
Tess (1979)
kinsman: 3 son 4 aunt 5 child, enate, niece, uncle 6 affine, agnate, cousin, father, mother, nephew, parent, sister 7 brother, cognate 8 daughter, grandson, relation, relative 9 great-aunt 10 grandchild, great-uncle, stepfather, stepmother, stepsister
Kinsman Saga, The author: 4 Bova
kinsperson: 6 sister 8 relation, relative
Kinston: 4 town
locale: 4 N. Car.
kinswoman: 4 aunt 5 enate, niece 6 affine, cousin, mother, sister 7 cognate, kinsman 8 relative 9 great-aunt
__ Kinte: 5 Kunta
Kioga: 4 lake
locale: 6 Uganda
kiosk: 5 booth, stall, stand 6 gazebo 9 bandstand, newsstand
buy: 3 mag 4 Elle, Time 8 magazine, Newsweek
Kiowa: 5 tribe 6 Indian 7 Amerind 8 language
kip: 3 bed 5 money
locale: 4 Laos
Kip: 5 Keino, Niven
Kipchoge: 5 Keino
Kipling, Rudyard: 4 poet 6 author, writer 7 British 8 Nobelist
biographer: 4 Amis
birthplace: Bombay, India
setting: 5 India
villain: 5 cobra
work: Barrack-Room Ballads
Captains Courageous
Danny Deever
Fuzzy Wuzzy
Gunga Din
If
The Jungle Book
Just So Stories
Kim
The Light That Failed
Mandalay
The Man Who Would Be King
Recessional
kipper: 3 dry 4 cure, salt 5 smoke 6 salmon 7 herring 8 preserve
__ Kippur: 3 Yom
kir: 4 wine
ingredient: 6 cassis
kir __: 6 royale
kirby: 4 hook 8 fishhook
Kirby: 4 Jack 5 Bruno, Grant 6 vacuum 7 Durward, Puckett
rival: 5 Miele, Oreck 6 Eureka, Hoover 10 Electrolux
Kirchhoff, Gustav: 6 German 9 physicist
Kirghiz: 8 language
city: 3 Osh
once: 3 SSR
range: 4 Alai
tent: 4 yurt
Kirghiz __: 6 Steppe
__-kiri: 4 hara
Kiri: 8 Te Kanawa
Kiribati: 6 nation 7 country
capital: 6 Tarawa
money: 4 cent 6 dollar
kirk: 6 church, temple 8 Scottish
Kirk: 4 Alyn, Lisa 5 Tommy 6 Gibson 7 Cameron, captain, Douglas, Phyllis
Michael Douglas, to ~: 3 son
Kirk, Captain: 3 Jim 5 James
birthplace: 4 Iowa
crew: 4 Sulu 5 McCoy, Scott, Spock, Uhura 6 Chekov, Scotty
middle name: 8 Tiberius
Kirkland: 4 city, Lane, town 5 Sally 6 Gelsey
locale: 10 Washington
Kirkpatrick: 5 Jeane
Kirkstall Abbey locale: 5 Leeds
Kirkuk: 4 city, town
locale: 4 Irak, Iraq
Kirkwood: 4 city, town
locale: 8 Missouri
Kirlian image: 4 aura
Kirman: 3 rug
kirpan: 6 dagger
kirsch: 5 drink 8 beverage
kin: 6 cognac
Kirschner: 3 Don, Mia
Kirsten: 5 Dunst 8 Flagstad
Kirstie: 5 Alley
kirtle: 4 gown 5 dress, frock 7 garment
Kirundi: 8 language
Kiryu: 4 city, town
locale: 5 Japan
Kisangani: 4 city, town
'K' Is for Killer author: Sue Grafton
kishka: 3 gut 5 derma
Kish, son of: 4 Saul
Kishwaukee, city on the: 6 De Kalb
kiskadee: 4 bird
Kiska locale: 6 Alaska
Kislev: 5 month 6 Hebrew
predecessor: 7 Heshvan
successor: 5 Tevet
kismet: 3 lot 4 fate, luck 5 karma 7 destiny, fortune, portion 10 providence
Kismet: 7 musical
character: 4 Imam, Omar
melodist: 7 Borodin
setting: 4 Irak, Iraq
kiss: 3 pet 4 buss, love, neck, peck, skim 5 candy, graze, shave, smack, touch 6 cookie, smooch 8 osculate, pucker up 10 confection, osculation, salutation
and make up: 5 yield 6 accept, pardon 7 appease, forgive, let it go, let pass, patch up, placate, reunite 8 overlook, take back 9 acquiesce, reconcile
babies: 3 run 4 gush 5 stump 6 hustle 8 campaign, politick
good-bye: 3 end, rid 4 drop, jilt, lose 5 eject, spend 6 reject 7 abandon, forsake 8 forswear 9 foreswear 10 relinquish
how dogs ~: 5 wetly
partner: 3 hug 4 ride, tell
target: 3 lip 5 cheek, mouth
the feet of: 5 adore, deify, honor 6 admire, dote on 7 glorify, idolize, worship 8 venerate 9 be stuck on, be sweet on 10 be mad about
kiss __: 3 off 7 good-bye
__ kiss: 3 air
Kiss
members: Criss, Frehley, Simmons, Stanley
song: Beth (1976)
Forever (1990)
Kiss (1986 song) artist: Prince
Kiss an Angel Good Mornin' (1971 song) artist: Charley Pride
kiss and __: 4 tell
kiss-and-__: 4 ride
Kiss and Say Goodbye (1976 song) artist: Manhattans
kissar: 4 lyre 6 string
origin: 6 Africa
Kiss Before Dying, A author: Ira Levin
Kissel: 3 car 4 auto 10 automobile
kisser: 3 mug, pan, yap 4 face, lips, puss 5 bazoo, mouth
baby ~: 3 pol 10 politician
kisses
love and ~: 7 devoirs, regards 9 greetings 10 best wishes, good wishes
symbols: 3 xes
__ Kisses: 6 Stolen 8 Hershey's
Kisses on the Wind (1989 song) artist: Neneh Cherry
Kisses Sweeter Than Wine (1957 song) artist: Jimmie Rodgers
Kiss Hollywood Good-By author: Loos
Kissimmee: 4 city, town
locale: 7 Florida
Kissin' __: 3 You 4 Time 7 Cousins
Kissin' Cousins: 4 film, song
artist: Elvis Presley
cast: Jack Albertson, Glenda Farrell, Elvis Presley
kissing: 4 fond, warm 6 loving, tender 7 amorous 8 romantic 10 passionate
kissing __: 3 kin 4 gate 6 bridge, cousin 7 gourami
Kissing a Fool (1988 song) artist: George Michael
Kissinger, Henry: 8 Nobelist
Kissin' Time (1959 song) artist: Bobby Rydell
Kiss, Kiss author: 4 Dahl
Kiss Me Deadly author: Mickey Spillane
Kiss Me Kate: 7 musical
character: 4 Lane, Lois 5 Felix, Lilli 6 Virgil
composer: 6 Porter
Kiss Me Kate (1953 film)
cast: Kathryn Grayson, Howard Keel, Ann Miller
director: George Sidney
Kiss me, my fool! sayer: 4 Bara
Kiss Me, Stupid (1964 film)
cast: Felicia Farr, Dean Martin, Kim Novak, Ray Walston
director: Billy Wilder
Kiss my grits! role: 3 Flo
kiss of __: 5 peace
Kiss of Death (1947 film)
cast: Brian Donlevy, Coleen Gray, Victor Mature
director: Henry Hathaway
Kiss of the Spider Woman: 4 film 5 novel
author: 4 Puig
cast: Sonia Braga, William Hurt, Raul Julia
Kiss on My List (1981 song) artist: Hall and Oates
Kiss, The (1929 film)
cast: Greta Garbo, Conrad Nagel
Kiss, The artist: 5 Klimt, Rodin
Kiss, The author: Danielle Steel
Kiss the Boys Goodbye author: Clare Boothe Luce
Kiss the Girls (1997 film)
cast: Cary Elwes, Morgan Freeman, Tony Goldwyn, Ashley Judd
kissy-__: 4 face
__-Kist: 4 Star
Kistler: 5 Darci
Kisumu: 4 city, town
locale: 5 Kenya
kit: 3 fox, rig, set 4 gear, pack 5 stuff, tools 6 duffel, duffle, outfit, string, tackle 7 tool set 8 knapsack, supplies, utensils 9 apparatus, container, equipment 10 implements, provisions
and caboodle: 3 all, lot 6 entire
mother: 5 vixen
sewing ~: 4 etui 5 etwee
kit __: 3 bag, fox
__ kit: 4 mess, tool 5 press 6 sewing 8 first aid
Kit: 6 Carson 7 Marlowe
Kit-__ Club: 3 Cat, Kat
__-Kit: 6 Identi
Kitaen: 5 Tawny
Kitale: 4 city, town
locale: 5 Kenya
Kitami: 4 city, town
locale: 5 Japan
kitbag: 4 pack 5 pouch 6 duffel, duffle 7 holdall 8 backpack, knapsack, rucksack 9 haversack
Kit Carson (1940 film)
cast: Dana Andrews, Lynn Bari, Jon Hall
Kit Carson's Ride author: Joaquin Miller
kitchen: 6 galley 7 canteen, cookery 8 scullery 9 cookhouse
appliance: 4 oven 5 mixer, range, stove 6 fridge, juicer 7 blender
attraction: 4 odor 5 aroma, scent, smell, whiff 9 fragrance, redolence
cloth: 5 towel
denizen of song: 5 Dinah
do a ~ chore: 4 chop, cube, dice, grat, mash, pare, peel, rice
doing ~ duty, to a GI: 4 on KP
employee: 4 chef, cook 5 baker
ender: 4 ette, ware
floor covering: 4 lino, tile 8 linoleum, oilcloth
gadget: 5 corer, parer, ricer, timer, whisk 6 baster, beater, canner, grater
garment: 4 mitt 5 apron
helper: 4 tool 6 gadget 7 utensil 9 appliance
help in the ~: 3 dry, mop 4 wash, wipe 5 clean, clear 6 sponge
herb: 4 sage 5 basil, chive, thyme
kind of ~: 5 eat-in
like the ~ sink: 5 soapy, sudsy
meas.: 3 tbs., tsp. 4 tbsp.
pest: 5 roach 6 insect
portable ~: 7 canteen 10 chuck wagon

ruin, in the ~: **4** burn, char, sear **5** singe **6** scorch **9** carbonize
spice: **4** mace **5** clove, cumin
staple: **3** oil **4** oleo, salt **5** flour, sugar, yeast **9** margarine
staple, once: **4** lard **6** grease
tear-jerker: **5** onion
topper: **3** cap, lid **5** cover
utensil: **3** pan, pot, wok **5** knife, ladle, sieve **6** boiler, cooker
utensil brand: **3** Oxo **4** Ekco
wrap: **4** foil **5** Saran
kitchen ___: **3** tea **4** sink **5** match **6** garden, midden, police **7** cabinet
___ kitchen: **4** diet, soup **6** summer **7** country, pullman, rolling
Kitchen ___, The: **4** Toto
___ Kitchen: **5** Hell's
KitchenAid: **9** appliance
alternative: **5** Amana, Norge **6** Bendix, Maytag, Tappan **7** Admiral, Jenn-Air, Kenmore **8** Hotpoint **9** Magic Chef, Whirlpool **10** Frigidaire, Kelvinator
Kitchener: **4** city, earl, town
foe: **4** Boer
locale: **6** Canada **7** Ontario
Kitchen God's Wife, The
author: Amy Tan
kite: **3** toy **4** bird **5** glede **6** elanet, letter **9** plaything **10** bird of prey
cousin: **5** stilt
end: **4** tail
go fly a ~: **5** scram, split **6** beat it, begone **7** buzz off, get lost, take off **8** scramola **9** take a hike
nemesis: **4** tree
___ kite: **3** box **5** black **6** flying
Kite, Tom: **6** golfer
milieu: **5** links **6** course
org.: **3** PGA
kith: **7** kinfolk **8** kinfolks, kinsfolk
kith and ___: **3** kin
kithara: **4** lyre **6** string
origin: **6** Greece
Kit Kat: **5** candy **8** candy bar **9** chocolate
alternative: **4** Mars, Twix **5** Clark, Heath **6** Mounds, PayDay, Reese's, Zagnut **7** Krackel, Oh Henry **8** Baby Ruth, Hershey's, Milky Way, Snickers **9** Almond Joy, Mr. Goodbar **10** NutRageous
Kits, cats, sacks and ___...: **5** wives
kitschy: **5** gaudy, tacky **6** garish
Kitt: **6** Eartha
Kitt ___ Observatory: **4** Peak
K.I.T.T.: **3** car **4** auto **10** automobile
kitten: **3** cat, pet **4** puss **5** felid, kitty, pussy **6** feline **8** pussycat
at times: **5** mewer **6** purrer
cry: **3** mew **4** meow, mewl **5** miaou, miaow, miaul
like a ~: **4** soft **5** furry, fuzzy **6** fluffy
Kitten ___ Keys: **5** on the
kittenish: **6** frisky **9** fun-loving **10** coquettish, frolicsome
kittens: **5** young **6** litter
kittiwake: **4** bird
___ Kitts and Nevis: **5** Saint
kitty: **3** cat, pet, pot **4** fund, pool, puss, till **5** cache, felid, means, money, prize, purse, stake **6** feline, kitten **7** jackpot, savings **9** grimalkin, resources
command to ~: **4** scat, shoo
comment: **3** mew **4** meow **5** miaou, miaow, miaul
delighter: **6** catnip
feed the ~: **5** wager **6** chip in, kick in
retiree's ~: **3** IRA **7** nest egg, pension
start the ~: **3** bet **4** ante **5** stake, wager **8** shell out
Kitty: **3** cat **5** Wells **6** Kallen, Kelley **7** Dukakis **8** Carlisle **10** Carruthers
Kitty (1945 film)
cast: Paulette Goddard, Ray Milland
Kitty ___: **4** Hawk **5** Foyle **6** Litter
Kitty Foyle: **4** film **5** novel
author: Christopher Morley
cast: Dennis Morgan, Ginger Rogers
director: Sam Wood
Kitty, Miss
establishment: **3** bar **6** saloon
friend: **4** Matt **6** Dillon
portrayer: **5** Blake **6** Amanda
Kitwe: **4** city, town
locale: **6** Zambia
Kivi, Aleksis: **6** writer **7** Finnish
Kivu: **4** lake
locale: **5** Zaire **6** Rwanda
Kiwanian colleague: **4** Lion
kiwi: **4** bird **5** fruit **6** ratite **7** apteryx
kin: **3** emu, moa **4** emeu
language: **5** Maori
neighbor: **4** weka
Kix: **6** Brooks, cereal
competitor: **4** Life, Trix **5** Kashi, Quisp, Total **6** Kaboom, Muesli, Oreo O's, Pablum, Smacks **7** All-Bran, Crispix, Harmony, Hunny B's, Mueslix, Oat Bran, Pokemon **8** Boo Berry, Cheerios, Corn Chex, Corn Pops, Fiber One, Rice Chex, Special K, Uncle Sam, Wheaties **9** Alpha Bits, Apple Zaps, Grape Nuts, Honey Comb, Just Right, Wheat Chex **10** Apple Jacks, Bran Flakes, Cap'n Crunch, Cocoa Puffs, Froot Loops, Mini-Wheats, Nutri-Grain, Puffed Rice, Quaker Oats, Smart Start **11** Cocoa Blasts, Cookie Crisp, Golden Crisp, Lucky Charms, Puffed Wheat, Sweet Crunch, Waffle Crisp
Kjellin: **3** Alf
Kjölen: **5** range **9** mountains
locale: **6** Europe, Norway, Sweden
KJV: **5** Bible
K-K-K-___: **4** Katy
kl.: **4** meas.
Klaatu ___ nikto: **6** barada
klaberjass: **4** game **8** card game
variant: **6** belote **7** belotte
Klamath: **5** river **6** Indian **7** Amerind
locale: **6** Oregon **10** California
Klamath ___: **4** weed **5** Lakes
Klamath Falls: **4** city, town
locale: **6** Oregon
Klammer, Franz: **5** skier
___ klatsch: **6** coffee, kaffee
Klaus: **6** Kinski
in English: **8** Nicholas
Klaus ___ Brandauer: **5** Maria
klaxon: **4** horn **5** alarm
Klee, Paul: **5** Swiss **6** artist **7** painter
colleague: **3** Arp
___ K. Le Guin: **6** Ursula
Kleiber, Erich: **8** Austrian **9** conductor
Klein: **2** A.M. **4** Anne **5** Chuck, Norma **6** bottle, Calvin, Robert **8** Lawrence
rival: **5** Beene, Blass
Klein, A.M.: **4** poet **8** Canadian
Klein, Chuck: **10** outfielder
___ kleine Nachtmusik: **4** Eine
Klein, Lawrence: **8** Nobelist **9** economist
Klein's Obsession: **5** scent **7** perfume
Kleiser: **6** Randal
Kleist, Heinrich von: **6** German, writer
Klem, Bill: **3** ump **6** umpire
Klemperer: **4** Otto **6** Werner
Klensch: **4** Elsa
beat: **5** style
kleptomaniac: **5** thief **10** shoplifter
kleptomaniacal: **8** thieving, thievish
klezmer ___: **5** music
Kliban: **7** Bernard
klieg ___: **5** light
Klíma: **4** Ivan
Klíma, Ivan: **5** Czech **6** writer
Klimt, Gustav: **6** artist **7** painter **8** Austrian
Kline: **5** Franz, Kevin **7** Richard
Kline, Kevin: **5** actor
film: The Big Chill (1983)
Cry Freedom (1987)
Dave (1993)
Fierce Creatures (1997)
A Fish Called Wanda (1988, AA)
Grand Canyon (1991)
The Ice Storm (1997)
In & Out (1997)
Life as a House (2001)
A Midsummer Night's Dream (1999)
The Pirates of Penzance (1983)
Silverado (1985)
Soapdish (1991)
Sophie's Choice (1982)
Wild Wild West (1999)
spouse: Phoebe Cates
Klinger: **3** Max **7** Maxwell
home: **4** Ohio **6** Toledo
portrayer: **4** Farr
Klingon: **5** alien
Klinker: **5** dummy, Effie
Klink rank: **7** colonel
klippe: **4** coin
klipspringer: **8** antelope
relative: **3** gnu, kob **4** guib, kudu, oryx, puku, topi **5** addax, bongo, chiru, eland, goral, korin, nyala, oribi, saiga, serow **6** chammy, dik-dik, duiker, impala, koodoo, lechwe, nilgai, rhebok, shammy, shamoy **7** blaubok, blesbok, chamois, defassa, gazelle, gemsbok, gerenuk, grysbok, nylghai, nylghau, sassaby **8** blesbuck, bontebok, bushbuck, gemsbuck, reedbuck, steenbok, steinbok **9** blackbuck, pronghorn, sitatunga, springbok, waterbuck **10** hartebeest, wildebeest
KLM: **7** airline
destination: **3** Eur., JFK, Nor.
rival: **3** SAS
Klondike: **5** river
locale: **5** Yukon
strike: **4** gold
Klondike Annie (1936 film)
cast: Victor McLaglen, Mae West
director: Raoul Walsh
Kloge and I, The author: Danielle Steel
kludge: **3** fix **5** patch **6** repair
Klug, Aaron: **7** chemist **8** Nobelist
Klugman, Jack: **5** actor
film: 12 Angry Men (1957)
Goodbye, Columbus (1969)
role: **5** Oscar **7** Madison
spouse: Brett Somers
TV: Quincy, M.E., The Odd Couple
Kluszewski, Ted: **7** slugger
Klute (1971 film)
cast: Jane Fonda, Donald Sutherland
director: Alan J. Pakula
klutz: **2** ox **3** oaf **4** dolt, gowk, lout **5** cluck, dunce, schmo **6** galoot, lubber, lummox, schmoe **7** botcher, bungler, dullard, fumbler, galloot, jackass, pinhead **8** bonehead, lunkhead, shlemiel, stumbler **9** blockhead, blunderer, harebrain, ignoramus, simpleton **10** bananahead, noodlehead
comment: **4** oh-oh, oops, uh-oh
klutzes: **4** oxes
klutzy: **5** gawky, inept, unapt **6** clumsy, gauche, oafish **7** awkward, gawkish, halting, unadept, unhandy **8** bumbling, bungling, cloddish, clownish, fumbling, lubberly, ungainly **9** all thumbs, graceless, ham-handed, inelegant, lumbering, maladroit, stumbling, unskilled **10** blundering, unskillful
km.: **4** lgth., meas.
knack: **3** art, way **4** bent, gift, head, nose, turn **5** craft, flair, savvy, skill, touch, trick **6** genius, talent **7** ability, aptness, faculty, know-how, mastery, sleight **8** aptitude, capacity, facility, hang of it, instinct **9** dexterity, expertise, technique **10** adroitness, green thumb, propensity
ender: **5** wurst
get the ~ of: **5** grasp, learn **6** master, pick up **7** excel in **9** figure out
Knack song: My Sharona (1979)
knap ender: **4** sack, weed
knapsack: **3** bag, kit **4** pack, poke **5** pouch **6** duffel, duffle, kitbag **7** holdall **8** backpack, rucksack **9** haversack, saddlebag
part: **4** lash **5** strap
knar: **4** burl, knot, node **6** nodule
knave: **3** cad, cur, dog, rat **4** card, heel, jack, toad, worm **5** brute, cheat, churl, crook, fiend, louse, phony, quack, rogue, scamp, shark, snake **6** bad boy, bad guy, bad hat, bad man, con man, phoney, rascal, varlet **7** bounder, cheater, dastard, lowlife, ruffian, sharper, sharpie, shyster, stinker, traitor, wastrel **8** betrayer, blighter, chiseler, deceiver, picaroon, recreant, scalawag, swindler **9** charlatan, hellhound, hypocrite, miscreant, pretender, reprobate, scallawag, scallywag, scoundrel, vulgarian **10** blackguard, dissembler, mountebank, ne'er-do-well, scapegrace
Knave of Hearts: **4** card
booty: **4** tart
crime: **5** theft
knavery: **4** hoax **5** blind, craft, guile, trick, wiles **7** con game, cunning, devilry, roguery **8** deviltry, evil ways, flimflam, mischief, trickery, villainy **9** chicanery, dirty pool, stratagem **10** artfulness, dishonesty, hanky-panky, subterfuge, wrongdoing
knavish: **3** low, sly **4** base, foxy, mean, wily **5** lying, nasty **6** artful, sneaky, tricky **7** corrupt, crooked, cunning, naughty, roguish, waggish **8** plotting, rascally, scheming **9** conniving, dastardly, deceitful, designing, dishonest, insidious, insincere, two-timing, unethical **10** mendacious, villainous
one: **5** rogue
knead: **3** mix, rub **4** mold, work **5** shape, twist **6** soften **7** massage **10** manipulate
kneaded: **4** mixt **5** mixed **7** blended
Knebel, Fletcher: **6** author, writer
work: Dark Horse
Night of Camp David
Seven Days in May
knee: **3** jab **4** genu **5** hinge, joint **7** patella
-ankle connector: **5** shank
be ~ deep in: **4** teem **5** swarm **6** abound, infest
bend the ~: **3** bow **7** bow down **9** genuflect, pay homage
bend the ~ to: **4** obey
combining form: **4** genu-
concealer: **4** midi **5** dress, skirt
counterpart: **5** elbow
ender: **3** cap, pad **4** hole **5** board
get down on one ~: **3** woo **7** propose
go on bended ~: **3** beg, sue **4** urge **5** crawl, plead **7** beseech, declare, entreat, implore **8** petition **9** importune **10** supplicate
jerk: **6** reflex **8** reaction, response
neighbor: **4** calf, shin **5** thigh, tibia
of the ~: **6** genual
put over one's ~: **3** tan **4** lick, whip

5 smack, spank 6 punish, thrash, wallop 8 chastise 10 paddywhack
saver: 3 rug 6 carpet, runner 9 carpeting
scrape, as the ~: 4 bark, skin 5 graze 6 abrade, scrape
knee __: 3 cop, pad 4 bend, jerk, sock 5 brace, pants, socks 6 action, rafter
knee-__: 4 deep, high 7 slapper
__ knee: 5 trick 7 cypress, lodging
__-knee: 5 knock, thick
__ Knee: 7 Claire's, Wounded
knee-ankle connector: 3 leg
__ knee bend: 4 deep
knee-bending dance: 5 limbo
knee bend, Nureyev's: 4 plie
kneecap: 4 bone 7 patella
__-kneed: 4 weak 5 knock
Knee-Deep in June: 4 poem
author: 5 Riley
knee-high: 4 flat, sock 5 short 6 midget 7 hosiery 8 sea-level 10 unelevated
kneehole: 4 desk
knee-jerk: 6 reflex 8 habitual, mindless, reaction 9 automatic, impulsive 10 mechanical, unthinking
kneel: 3 bow 4 bend 5 kotow, stoop 6 kowtow 7 bow down 8 bend down 9 genuflect, prostrate
kneeling
figure: 5 orans, orant 6 orante
site: 5 altar
kneeling __: 3 bus
knees
ask on one's ~: 5 plead
fall on one's ~: 7 bow down, worship 9 genuflect, pay homage, prostrate 10 pay tribute
move on one's hands and ~: 4 inch 5 crawl, creep, slink, sneak, steal 7 clamber, slither, wriggle
weak ~: 4 fear 8 cold feet, timidity 9 cowardice 10 faint heart
weak in the ~: 5 dazed, dizzy, faint, giddy, rocky, shaky, woozy 6 punchy, wobbly 7 reeling 8 unsteady
__ knees: 4 bee's
knee-slapper: 4 hoot, howl, joke 6 gasser, hot one, scream
knee-sock: 4 hose 7 hosiery
knell: 4 gong, peal, ring, toll 5 clang 7 pealing, ringing 9 genuflect
Knesset
language: 6 Hebrew
locale: 6 Israel
party: 5 Likud
knew homophone: 3 gnu, new
__ Knew Susie: 5 If You
__ Knew What They Wanted: 4 They
K'Nex competitor: 4 Lego
Knickerbocker Holiday: 7 musical
author: Maxwell Anderson
songwriter: 5 Weill
knickerbockers: 5 pants 8 trousers
Knickerbockers: 4 five, team
org.: 3 NBA
knickers: 5 pants 6 shorts 7 culotes, cut-offs, gauchos 8 bermudas, breeches, jodhpurs, trousers 9 plus fours
knickknack: 5 curio, dodad 6 bauble, doodad, geegaw, gewgaw, notion, trifle 7 bibelot, novelty, trinket, whatnot 8 furbelow, gimcrack, ornament 9 bagatelle, bric-a-brac, curiosity, miniature, objet d'art, plaything, show-piece
locale: 5 ledge, shelf 6 mantel, mantle 7 etagere 8 cupboard
Knick rival: 3 Net, Sun 4 Buck, Bull, Hawk, Heat, Jazz, King, Spur 5 Laker, Magic, Pacer, Sixer 6 Celtic, Hornet, Nugget, Piston, Raptor, Rocket, Wizard 7 Clipper, Grizzly, Warrior 8 Cavalier, Maverick 10 SuperSonic, Timberwolf
Knicks: 4 five, team
home: 7 New York
loc.: 3 MSG
org.: 3 NBA
sport: 10 basketball
Knievel: 4 Evel 6 Robbie 9 daredevil
knife: 4 bolo, dirk, shiv, slit, snee, stab, tool 5 blade, carve, parer, saber, sabre, slice, sword 6 cutlas, cutter, dagger, lancet, murder, pierce, scythe, sickle 7 bayonet, cleaver, cutlass, cutlery, machete, poniard, scalpel, sidearm, simitar, utensil 8 lacerate, puncture, scimitar, scimiter, stiletto 9 penetrate
African ~: 5 panga
brand of ~: 5 Xacto
eating peas with a ~: 7 faux pas
ender: 5 point
Eskimo ~: 3 ulu
game with a ~: 4 Clue
handle: 4 grip, haft
handle material: 5 nacre
Irish ~: 5 skean, skene
like a ~: 4 keen 5 edged, sharp
like an old ~: 4 dull
maker: 6 cutler
Nepalese ~: 5 kukri
part: 4 edge, hilt 5 blade 6 handle
Philippine ~: 4 bolo 6 barong
Scottish ~: 5 skean, skene
seen on TV: 5 Ginsu
starter: 3 pen 4 draw, jack 5 paper 6 pocket
use a ~: 3 cut, lop 4 chop, cube, dice, dock, gash, hack, maim, nick, pare, peel, scar, skin, slit, snip, stab, trim 5 carve, gouge, lance, mince, notch, prune, score, sever, shave, shred, slash, slice, wound 6 bisect, cleave, cut off, incise, injure, open up, scrape, sunder 7 cut away, cut back, cut down, dissect, scratch, whittle 8 lacerate, mutilate 9 split open
wielder's move: 3 cut, jab 4 stab 5 lunge, swing 6 plunge, pounce, spring, strike, thrust 8 fall upon
wound: 3 cut 4 gash, slit, stab 5 gouge, slash, slice 6 injury 7 scratch 8 incision 10 laceration
knife __: 3 box 4 edge, rest 5 pleat 6 switch
__ knife: 4 bolo, case, fish, moon 5 bowie, bread, clasp, fruit, paper, putty, steak 6 barlow, boning, butter, casing, dinner, Khyber, pallet, paring, sheath, trench 7 butcher, carving, dessert, drawing, hunting, palette
knifelike: 4 keen 5 sharp 8 piercing
make ~: 4 file, hone, whet 5 grind, strop 7 sharpen
knight: 3 dub, Kay, sir 4 male, rank 5 piece, title 6 Gawain 7 fighter, Galahad, gallant, Geraint, Mordred, soldier, warrior 8 champion, defender, horseman, Lancelot, nobleman, Percival 9 Launcelot, protector
address for a ~: 3 sir
attire: 4 mail 5 armor 6 helmet
attribute: 5 valor 6 daring, mettle 7 bravery, courage, heroism, prowess 8 boldness 9 derring-do, gallantry
award: 3 OBE
consort: 4 dame, lady
expedition: 5 quest
feat: 4 deed 7 exploit 9 adventure
fight: 4 duel, list, tilt 5 joust 6 charge, combat 7 contest, tourney 10 tournament
foe: 6 dragon
glove: 4 gage
King Arthur ~: 3 Kay, Tor 4 Bors, Eric 5 Driam, Ector, Floll, Lucan, Yvain, Ywain 6 Acolon, Brunor, Ewaine, Gareth, Gawain, Hector, Lanval, Lavain, Manier, Morolt, Ryence, Sagrid, Torres 7 Belvour, Bersunt, Caradoc, Dinadam, Dodynas, Gaheris, Galahad, Geraint, Grislet, Ladynas, Lionell, Marhaus, Mordred, Pelleas, Peredur, Tristan, Wigamor 8 Agravain, Beaumans, Bevidere, Galohalt, Lancelot, Meliadus, Palamede, Percival, Tristram, Turquine, Wigalois 9 Ballamore, Brandiles, Launcelot, Pellinore
like a jousting ~: 5 atilt
lodging: 6 castle
name meaning ~: 5 Ryder 6 Ritter
neighbor: 6 bishop
noise: 5 clank
nose guard: 5 nasal
of the road: 4 hobo 5 tramp 7 drifter 8 vagabond, wanderer
protector, perhaps: 4 pawn
quest: 5 Grail 9 Holy Grail
rescuee: 6 damsel
sci-fi ~: 4 Jedi
-to-be: 4 page
weapon: 4 mace 5 lance, sword
white ~: 4 hero 5 model 7 paragon 8 champion, cynosure, exemplar
knight-__: 6 errant
__ knight: 4 Jedi 5 white
Knight: 3 Bob, car, Ted 4 auto, Eric, Jean 5 Bobby, Wayne 6 Gladys, Jordan, Philip, Willys 7 Shirley 9 Etheridge
Knight __: 5 Rider
Knight __ Bath: 5 of the
__ Knight: 5 Black, First
Knight, Bobby: 5 coach
milieu: 5 court
org.: 4 NCAA
sport: 10 basketball
Knight, Death and the Devil engraver: 5 Durer
knighted, prepare to be: 5 kneel
Knight, Etheridge: 4 poet
Knight, Gladys
backup: 4 Pips
song: Best Thing That Ever Happened to Me (1974)
Every Beat of My Heart (1961)
If I Were Your Woman (1970)
I Heard It Through the Grapevine (1967)
I've Got to Use My Imagination (1973)
Midnight Train to Georgia (1973)
Neither One of Us (1973)
On and On (1974)
That's What Friends Are For (1985)
knighthood: 5 valor 7 bravery, courage 8 altruism, boldness, chivalry, courtesy, nobility
confer ~: 3 dub 7 entitle
initials: 3 OBE
Knight in Rusty Armour (1967 song)
artist: Peter and Gordon
knight in shining __: 5 armor
Knight, Jean song: Mr. Big Stuff (1971)
knightly: 4 true 5 noble 7 gallant 9 honorable 10 chivalrous, high-minded
Knightly Quest, The author: Tennessee Williams
Knight of the __: 4 Bath 6 Garter
__ Knight Pulliam: 6 Keshia
Knight Rider (NBC adventure)
car: K.I.T.T.
cast: William Daniels (voice of K.I.T.T.)
David Hasselhoff (Michael Knight)
Edward Mulhare (Devon Miles)
Knights __: 7 Templar
Knights __ Round Table: 5 of the
Knightsbridge store: 7 Harrod's
knights of __: 4 yore
Knights of __: 5 Labor, Malta 7 Pythias 8 Columbus
Knights of the Range author: Zane Grey
Knights, The author: Aristophanes
Knight, Ted: 5 actor
film: Caddyshack (1980)
TV: The Mary Tyler Moore Show, Too Close for Comfort
knish: 5 snack
filling: 5 kasha 6 potato
kin: 8 turnover
place: 4 deli
knit: 4 heal, join, mend, purl 5 purse, unite, weave 6 furrow, pucker, splice, stitch 7 crochet, entwine, intwine 9 integrate, interlace, interlock 10 intertwine, interweave
ender: 4 wear
one's brow: 5 frown
partner: 4 purl
shoe: 6 bootee, bootie
together: 7 related 10 interwoven
__ knit: 4 warp 5 plain 6 double
__-knit: 3 rib 4 flat, hand 5 close, tight 6 double, ribbed, single
knit one, __ two: 4 purl
__-knitted: 4 weft
knitter
material: 4 wool, yarn 5 Orlon 6 angora
need: 5 skein 6 needle
project: 5 scarf, socks 6 afghan 7 argyles, bootees, mittens, sweater
knitting __: 6 needle
__ knitting: 4 flat, warp, weft 7 filling
knob: 3 nub 4 dial, knub, knur, lump, node, nurl 5 bulge, knurl 6 button, handle, nodule 8 swelling 10 projection, protrusion
combining form: 3 tyl- 4 tylo-
ornamental ~: 4 boss
shield ~: 4 umbo
starter: 4 door
stereo ~: 4 bass 6 treble, volume
TV ~: 3 vol. 4 dial, tint, vert. 6 volume 8 vertical
violin ~: 3 peg
watch ~: 5 crown
knob __: 4 lock 5 latch 6 celery
knobby: 4 bony 5 boney, bumpy, lobed, lumpy, nodal, rough, warty 6 uneven 7 gnarled, knurled, nodular
item: 4 knee
knobcone __: 4 pine
knock: 3 dis, hit, pan, rap, tap 4 bang, bash, beat, blow, carp, clip, conk, cuff, drub, nick, ping, slam, slap, slur, swat, thud 5 abuse, clout, decry, flail, libel, pound, punch, roast, scoff, smack, swipe, thump, whack, whang 6 batter, beat up, bruise, buffet, defame, deride, hammer, impact, impugn, jostle, justle, oppugn, pommel, pummel, rattle, rebuff, strike, thrash, thwack, vilify, wallop 7 censure, condemn, lambast, protest, put-down, run down 8 badmouth, bang into, belittle, denounce, lambaste, minimize, talk down, throw mud 9 criticism, criticize, denigrate, deprecate, disparage, find fault, hammering, manhandle, reprehend 10 denunciate
about: 3 gad 4 maul, roam, rove, tour, trek 5 abuse, drift, range, tramp 6 bruise, damage, ramble, travel, wander 7 explore, journey, traipse 8 work over 9 bum around, gallivant, manhandle, run around
around: 4 beat, loaf, mall, maul, roam, rove, walk 5 pound 6 bang up,

debate, ramble, travel 7 rough up 8 mistreat 9 manhandle
back: 4 gulp 5 drink 6 guzzle, imbibe
dead: 5 amaze, amuse 6 divert, regale 8 enthrall 9 entertain
down: 4 deck, earn, fell, rase, raze, ruin 5 abase, floor, level, smash, wreak, wreck 6 defame, demean, demote, laylow, reduce, topple 7 break up, destroy, flatten, unbuild 8 bulldoze, demolish, minimize, overturn 9 devastate, dismantle, prostrate, take apart
ender: 3 off, out 4 down 5 about, wurst
flat: 5 level
for a loop: 4 daze, jolt, stun, wham 5 amaze, floor
heavy ~: 4 slam, thud 5 clonk, clunk, thump, thunk
into: 3 hit, ram 4 bump
it off: 4 halt, quit, stop 5 cease 6 at ease, desist
loose: 4 bump 5 budge 8 dislodge, shake off 9 dislocate
off: 3 end, zap 4 make, quit, slay, stop 5 cease, relax, write 6 desist, make up, murder 8 leave off, simulate, subtract 10 call it a day
on, as a door: 3 rap 5 rap at
oneself out: 3 try 4 tire, toil 6 strive
one's socks off: 3 awe, wow 6 thrill
on the noggin: 3 bop 4 bonk
out: 2 KO 3 awe, wow 4 beat, drug, kayo, slay, stun, zonk 5 floor, punch, write 6 defeat 7 delight, fatigue, flatten, frazzle, impress, stupefy 8 abrogate, languish 9 eliminate, overpower
over: 3 rob, tip 5 level, spill, upend, upset 6 topple 7 astound 8 astonish, overturn, pull down
reply to a ~: 5 enter 6 come in
senseless: 4 kayo, stun 5 floor 6 lay out 9 overpower
something to ~ on: 4 wood
starter: 4 anti
stopper: 6 octane
together: 5 build 6 cobble 7 throw up 10 jerry-build
knock __: 3 off, out 4 back, cold, down, wood 5 about, it off, rummy 6 around
knock __ a loop: 3 for
knock __ of the box: 3 out
knock-__: 4 knee 5 kneed
knock-__-drag-out: 4 down
__-knock: 4 hard
Knock __!: 5 it off
Knock __ Times: 5 Three
Knock, __ shall be opened: 5 and it
knockabout: 5 sloop 8 sailboat
knockback: 7 refusal 8 turndown
Knockdown author: Dick Francis
knock-down-drag-out: 5 melee, mix-up 7 dustups
knocked out: 4 beat 5 all in, had it, spent, tired, weary 6 bushed, done in, drowsy, pooped, punchy, sleepy, zonked 7 drained 8 dog-tired, drooping, fatigued, flagging, out of gas 9 bone-tired, dead-tired, enervated, exhausted, overtired, prostrate
knocked over: 5 fazed, upset 7 shocked, shook up, spilled, toppled, unglued 8 agitated, capsized, dismayed, overcome, unstrung 9 bummed-out 10 disordered, freaked out, in disarray, overturned, psyched out, upside-down
knock for __: 5 a loop
knocking game: 3 gin 8 gin rummy
Knockin' on Heaven's Door (1973 song) artist: Bob Dylan
Knock it off!: 3 shh 4 stop, whoa
knock-knock joke: 3 pun 8 wordplay
knockoff: 4 copy 5 clone, ditto 6 double 7 replica 8 likeness 9 duplicate, imitation
knock on __: 4 wood
Knock on __ Door: 3 Any
knock one's __ off: 5 socks
Knock on Wood (1954 film)
cast: Danny Kaye, Mai Zetterling
knockout: 5 smash 6 beauty, eraser, eyeful, looker, lovely
drink: 6 Mickey 10 Mickey Finn
gas: 5 ether
in boxing: 6 eraser
knock out __ box: 5 of the
knock rummy: 4 game 8 card game
knocks, hard: 3 woe 7 bad luck, travail, trouble 9 adversity, mischance, tough luck 10 ill fortune, misfortune
knock the __ off: 5 socks
knock the __ out of: 3 tar
Knock Three Times (1970 song) artist: Tony Orlando & Dawn
knockwurst: 4 meat 7 aliment, sausage
knoll: 4 hill, rise 5 mound, ridge 7 hillock, hummock 9 elevation 10 high ground, prominence
Knossos site: 5 Crete 6 Candia
knot: 3 tie 4 bird, burl, hank, kink, link, loop, lump, mass, node, slip, snag, tuft 5 gnarl, hitch, nodus, skein, snarl, tie up, twist, unite 6 enigma, fasten, granny, nodule, puzzle, square, tangle 7 bowline, cat's-paw, chignon, dilemma, grannie 8 ligature 9 half hitch, interlace, intricacy, labyrinth, Turk's-head 10 clove hitch, complexity, get tangled, hawser bend, perplexity, sheepshank
cotton ~: 3 nep
detail: 4 loop 5 noose
ender: 4 hole, weed 5 grass
hair ~: 3 bun
like a ~: 5 nodal
rope ~: 4 loop 5 noose, snare
rug ~: 5 sehna
starter: 3 bow, top 4 slip
thread ~: 4 burl, node
tie the ~: 3 wed 4 mate 5 marry, unite 7 espouse 10 get hitched
tree ~: 4 burl, knar, knur 5 gnarl
untie the ~: 4 free, part 5 sever 6 loosen 7 break up, divorce, split up 8 separate 10 put asunder
up: 5 gnarl, snarl
knot __: 6 garden, stitch
__ knot: 3 pin 4 flat, loop, love, mesh, reef, root 5 black, blood, Sehna, sheet, slide, sword, turle 6 anchor, barrel, granny, lovers', Psyche, single, square 7 bowline, Gordian, lubber's, netting, Persian, running, trefoil, Turkish, weaver's, Windsor
KNO3: 5 niter, nitre
knots: 4 nodi
get rid of ~: 4 comb, undo 5 untie 6 loosen 8 untangle
in ~: 4 achy 5 tense 6 tied up
where ~ get tied: 5 altar 6 shrine 9 sanctuary
Knots Landing (CBS drama)
cast: William Devane (Gregory Sumner)
Kevin Dobson (Mack MacKenzie)
Julie Harris (Lilimae Clements)
Lisa Hartman (Ciji Dunne)
Michele Lee (Karen McKenzie)
Donna Mills (Abby Cunningham)
Ted Shackelford (Gary Ewing)
Nicolette Sheridan (Paige Matheson)
Joan Van Ark (Valene Ewing)
knotted: 5 kinky 6 matted 7 snarled, tangled, twisted 8 uncombed
Knott's: 5 jelly
alternative: 5 Kraft 6 Welch's 7 Polaner 8 Smucker's
Knott's __ Farm: 5 Berry
Knotts, Don: 5 actor
film: Gus (1976)
TV: The Andy Griffith Show, Three's Company
knotty: 4 hard, mazy 5 heavy, nodal, rough, tough 6 nodous, sticky, thorny, tricky 7 complex, prickly, tangled 8 baffling, involved, puzzling, worrying 9 difficult, elaborate, intricate 10 formidable, mystifying, perplexing
question: 6 riddle
wood: 4 pine 9 evergreen
knotty __: 4 pine 7 problem, rhatany
knot-tying
org.: 3 BSA
place: 5 altar 6 chapel, church, shrine
words: 3 I do
knout: 4 lash, whip
know: 3 get, see, tie 4 bind, tell 5 grasp, learn, place, sense, taste 6 fathom, intuit, secure, tether 7 cognize, discern, realize 8 memorize, perceive 9 apprehend, recognize 10 appreciate, comprehend, experience, have in mind, understand
before you ~ it: 4 anon, soon 6 pronto
by heart: 4 cite 6 retain 8 memorize, remember
dying to ~: 4 nosy 5 nosey 6 prying, snoopy 7 curious 8 meddling 9 butting in, intrusive, obtrusive 10 meddlesome
for all we ~: 5 maybe 7 perhaps 8 feasibly, possibly, probably 9 perchance 10 imaginably
get to ~: 3 see 4 hear, meet, read 5 dig up, glean, grasp, greet, learn, reach, study 6 link up, master, peruse, pick up, take in, turn up 7 connect, contact, discern, find out, run into, uncover, unearth, welcome 8 approach, deal with, discover, pore over, smoke out 9 ascertain, catch on to, determine, encounter, forgather 10 experience, rendezvous, understand
how to: 3 can
in Scottish: 3 ken
instinctively: 4 feel 6 intuit 7 discern 10 have a hunch
in the ~: 3 hep, hip 4 onto, wise 5 aware, hep to, hip to, privy, savvy 6 astute, shrewd, versed, wise to, with it 7 knowing, learned, mindful 8 apprised, informed 9 astucious, cognizant
let ~: 3 air 4 tell 5 cue in 6 inform, tip off
let ~ indirectly: 4 hint 5 imply, let on 6 allude 7 suggest 8 intimate, lead up to 9 insinuate
old enough to ~ better: 5 adult, grown, of age 6 mature 7 grown-up
the language: 5 speak
the password: 5 enter, get in
want to ~: 3 ask 4 quiz, seek 5 grill, probe, query 7 canvass, consult, inquire
know-__: 3 all, how 5 it-all 7 nothing
__ know: 3 you 5 in the
Know __ enemy: 5 thine
__ Know: 3 I'll 4 All I 5 Do You
knowable: 4 bare 5 clear, lucid, naked, plain 6 patent 8 clear-cut, luminous, manifest, palpable, pellucid, revealed, unhidden, unmasked, unveiled 9 disclosed, learnable, uncloaked, unobscure 10 fathomable, ostensible, realizable
know-how: 3 art 5 craft, flair, knack, moxie, savvy, skill, trick 6 talent, wisdom 7 ability, command, faculty, finesse, mastery 8 aptitude, facility, hang of it, instinct 9 dexterity, expertise, technique 10 adroitness, capability, competence, efficiency, experience
has the ~: 3 can
knowing: 3 hep, hip 4 able, arch, in on, sage, wily, wise 5 aware, canny, quick, savvy, sharp, slick, smart 6 astute, brainy, bright, clever, expert, posted, shrewd, versed, wise to, with it 7 cunning, mindful, sapient, thought, tuned in, worldly 8 apprised, informed, profound, rational, sensible, sentient, skillful 9 astucious, brilliant, cognizant, competent, ingenious, inventive, plugged in, sagacious, sensitive 10 conversant, insightful, perceptive, reasonable
about: 4 onto 7 mindful 9 cognizant
combining form: 7 -gnostic 9 -gnostical
look: 4 leer, ogle 5 smirk, sneer
knowingly: 9 purposely, wittingly 10 designedly
Knowing Me, Knowing You (1977 song) artist: ABBA
__ know is what I read...: 4 all I
know-it-all: 5 cocky, maven, mavin 6 gascon, smarty 7 egghead, wise guy 8 braggart, cocksure, wiseacre 9 conceited 10 big-talking
knowledge: 3 ken, tip 4 dope, info, lore 5 facts, goods, grasp, light, sense 6 tipoff, wisdom 7 ability, insight, letters, reading, science, thought 8 learning, literacy, sapience 9 awareness, cognition, education, erudition, expertise, principle, schooling 10 experience, philosophy, refinement
anecdotal ~: 4 lore 5 myths, tales 6 fables 7 legends, sayings 10 traditions
basic ~: 4 ABCs
branch of ~: 5 ology
combining form: 5 -gnomy, -sophy 6 -gnosis
gain ~: 5 learn 6 absorb
having ~: 3 hep, hip 5 aware, privy 6 posted, wise to, with it 8 apprised, familiar, informed 9 au courant, cognizant, plugged in 10 acquainted, conversant
having private ~: 4 in on
impart ~: 4 show 5 brief, coach, drill, edify, guide, teach, train, tutor 6 advise, ground, inform, school 7 educate, explain, instill, lecture 8 instruct 9 catechize, enlighten, inculcate, interpret
mystical ~: 6 gnosis
seek ~: 3 ask 7 inquire
knowledge __: 4 base
__ Knowledge: 6 Carnal, Summer
knowledgeable: 3 ace, hep, hip 4 sage, wise 5 aware, savvy, smart 6 au fait, brainy, bright, clever, expert, posted, versed, with it 7 abreast, erudite, learned, mindful, tuned in 8 apprised, educated, informed, literate 9 cognizant, plugged in, qualified, sagacious
about: 4 upon 6 versed 8 prepared 9 cognizant
one: 5 maven, mavin 6 oracle
Knowles: 4 John 6 Patric
Knowles, William S.: 7 chemist 8 Nobelist
know like __: 5 a book
__ Know Me, Al: 3 You
__ Know Much: 4 Don't
known: 4 fact 5 noted 6 avowed, common, famous, public 7 popular 8 accepted, admitted, familiar, manifest, on the map 9 axiomatic, certified,

published **10** celebrated, identified, proverbial, recognized, understood
also ~ as: 5 alias
become ~: 5 break **6** appear, emerge **7** come out, surface **9** transpire
by few: 4 deep **6** arcane, mystic, occult **8** esoteric, mystical **9** recondite **10** mysterious
let be ~: 4 blab, tell **6** tattle
make ~: 3 air, out, say **4** bare, leak, post, show, tell **5** admit, let on, speak, utter, voice **6** advise, convey, expose, herald, impart, let out, report, reveal, spread, unfold, unmask, unveil **7** declare, display, divulge, exhibit, lay bare, let slip, mention, narrate, uncover **8** advise of, announce, disclose, proclaim **9** advertise, circulate, introduce, propagate, publicize, ventilate **10** make public, promulgate
make one's position ~: 6 assert **7** declare, speak up **8** sound off, speak out **10** stand up for
once ~ as: 3 née **4** born **8** formerly **10** heretofore, previously
widely ~: 5 great, noted **6** fabled, famous **7** eminent, leading, popular, storied **8** immortal, renowned **9** acclaimed, legendary, memorable, notorious, prominent **10** celebrated, preeminent, publicized
__-known: 4 well
know-nothing: 3 sap **4** boob, dolt, dupe, fool, gull, jerk **5** chump, dummy, dunce, stupe **7** doubter, fathead, sceptic, skeptic **8** agnostic, bonehead, dumbbell, numskull **9** numbskull
Know Nothings: 5 party
__ known then...: 4 Had I
know one's __: 4 oats **5** place **6** onions
know one's __ mind: 3 own
__ knows: 3 God **6** heaven, nobody
__ Knows Best: 6 Father
__ Knows, Mr. Allison: 6 Heaven
__ Knows My Name: 6 Nobody
__ knows, The: 6 Shadow
know the __: 5 drill, ropes, score
Know what __?: 5 I mean
Knox: 4 Fort, John **9** Alexander
Knoxville: 4 city, town
athlete: 3 Vol **9** Volunteer
its HQ is in ~: 3 TVA
locale: 9 Tennessee
Knox with the Rhythm Orchids, Buddy
song: Hula Love (1957)
Party Doll (1957)
KNP part: 4 pawn **5** king's **7** knight's
knuckle: 5 joint
down: 4 work **5** begin, start **7** get busy **8** fire away, get going
down to: 6 have at **7** address, focus on **8** engage in **10** plug away at
ender: 4 ball, bone, head
sandwich: 4 fist **5** punch
under: 3 bow **4** obey **5** defer, kotow, stoop, yield **6** comply, give in, kowtow, submit **7** concede, consent, succumb, truckle **8** say uncle **9** surrender **10** capitulate
knuckle __: 4 down **5** under **8** sandwich
knuckle-__: 6 duster
__-knuckle: 4 bare **5** white
knuckleball: 4 toss **5** pitch, throw
knucklebone in the game of jacks: 3 dib
knucklehead: 3 ass, oaf, sap **4** boob, bozo, clod, dodo, dolt, dope, fool, simp **5** chump, clown, cluck, dummy, dunce, idiot, joker, klutz, ninny, patsy, schmo, stupe **6** dimwit, lummox, nitwit, schmoe, sucker, turkey **7** buffoon, dingbat, dullard, half-wit, jackass **8** dumbbell, numskull **9** birdbrain, lamebrain, numbskull, simpleton

knuckles
rap on the ~: 5 scold **6** punish **8** admonish
__ knuckles: 5 brass
Knud: 9 Rasmussen
knur: 4 knob, knot **5** gnarl
knurl: 4 knob, lump, node **5** ridge **8** swelling
knurled: 5 bumpy, lumpy **6** knobby, uneven **7** gnarled **9** irregular
Knut: 6 Hamsun
Knute Rockne, All American (1940 film)
cast: Donald Crisp, Pat O'Brien, Ronald Reagan
role: 4 Gipp **6** Gipper
Knute successor: 3 Ara
KO: 3 hit **4** deck, stun **5** floor **6** defeat **7** flatten **8** knock out
count: 3 ten
counter: 3 ref **7** referee
org.: 3 WBA
koa: 4 tree **6** acacia
family: 6 legume
relative: 5 carob **6** cassia, cercis, locust, padauk, padouk, redbud **7** araroba, mesquit **8** mesquite, tamarind **9** poinciana
KOA: 10 campground
amenity: 6 hookup
vehicle: 2 RV
koala: 6 animal, Aussie **9** marsupial
company with a ~: 6 QANTAS
home: 9 Australia
like a ~: 5 furry
relative: 4 euro **5** bilbi, bilby **6** numbat, wombat **7** bettong, dasyure, opossum, wallaby **8** kangaroo, wallaroo **9** bandicoot, phalanger
koan: 5 poser **6** riddle **7** paradox, stumper **8** question **9** conundrum **10** puzzlement
discipline: 3 Zen
kob: 8 antelope
relative: 3 gnu **4** guib, kudu, oryx, puku, topi **5** addax, bongo, chiru, eland, goral, korin, nyala, oribi, saiga, serow **6** chammy, dik-dik, duiker, impala, koodoo, lechwe, nilgai, rhebok, shammy, shamoy **7** blaubok, blesbok, chamois, defassa, gazelle, gemsbok, gerenuk, grysbok, nylghai, nylghau, sassaby **8** blesbuck, bontebok, bushbuck, gemsbuck, reedbuck, steenbok, steinbok **9** blackbuck, pronghorn, sitatunga, springbok, waterbuck **10** hartebeest, wildebeest
Kobe: 4 city, port, town **6** Bryant
locale: 5 Hondo, Japan **6** Honshu
Kobe __: 4 beef
Koblenz: 4 city, town
locale: 7 Germany
river: 5 Mosel **7** Moselle
kobo: 5 money
Kobo: 3 Abe
kobold: 3 elf **5** gnome **6** goblin, sprite **7** gremlin
Kobuk Valley: 4 park
locale: 6 Alaska
Koch: 2 Ed **6** Howard, Robert **7** Kenneth
Kochab: 4 star
Köchel __: 6 number **7** listing
Kocher, Emil: 5 Swiss **8** Nobelist
Kochi: 4 city, port, town
locale: 5 Japan
Koch, Kenneth: 6 writer
Koch, Robert: 8 Nobelist
K-O connection: 3 LMN
Kodachrome (1973 song) artist: Paul Simon
Kodaira: 4 city, town
locale: 5 Japan
Kodak: 4 film **6** camera **10** photograph

alternative: 4 Agfa, Fuji **5** Canon, Leica, Nikon **6** Konica, Pentax, Rollei **7** Minolta, Olympus, Vivitar, Yashica **8** Polaroid
__ Kodak: 7 Eastman
Kodály, Zoltán: 8 composer **9** Hungarian
Kodel: 6 fabric **8** material
__ Kodesh: 4 Aron
Kodes, Jan: 7 netster **9** tennis pro
milieu: 5 court
Kodiak: 4 bear, city, isle, town **5** ursid **6** island
locale: 6 Alaska
young ~: 3 cub
Koehler, Ted: 8 lyricist
song: Get Happy
I Gotta Right to Sing the Blues
I Love a Parade
I've Got the World on a String
Let's Fall in Love
Stormy Weather
Koenig: 4 Mark **6** Walter
Koestler, Arthur: 6 author, writer
work: Darkness at Noon
Kofi: 5 Annan **7** Awoonor **8** Anyidoho
Kofu: 4 city, town
locale: 5 Japan
KOH: 3 lye
Kohath, father of: 4 Levi
Koh-i-__ Diamond: 4 noor
kohl: 5 paint **6** makeup, shadow **7** mascara **8** cosmetic, eyeliner **9** eye shadow **10** maquillage
site: 6 eyelid
Kohl: 6 Helmut
see also German
Köhler, Georges: 8 Nobelist
kohlrabi: 6 veggie **9** vegetable
Kohn, Walter: 7 chemist **8** Nobelist
Kohoutek: 5 comet
koi: 4 fish
Koichi: 6 Tanaka
Koine: 8 language
Kojak (CBS drama)
cast: Kevin Dobson (Bobby Crocker)
Dan Frazer (Frank McNeil)
Telly Savalas (Lt. Theo Kojak)
employer: N.Y.P.D.
trademark: lollipop
Kojak, like: 4 bald
koji: 5 yeast **6** fungus
ko-kiu: 6 string, violin
origin: 5 Japan
Kokomo: 4 city, town
locale: 7 Indiana
Ko Ko Mo (1955 song)
artist: Crew-Cuts, Perry Como
Kokomo (1988 song) artist: Beach Boys
Koko Nor: 4 lake
locale: 5 China
nowadays: 9 Qinghai Hu
Kokoschka: 5 Oskar
Ko-Ko weapon: 4 snee
Kol __: 5 Nidre
kola: 3 nut **4** tree
kolinsky: 6 weasel
relative: 4 mink **5** fitch, otter, ratel, sable, skunk, stoat, tayra **6** badger, ermine, ferret, marten **7** foumart, polecat **8** carcajou, foulmart, muishond **9** wolverine
Kolkata: 4 city, town
locale: 5 India
Kollege of Musical Knowledge leader: 5 Kyser
Kollwitz: 5 Käthe
Köln: 4 city, town **7** Cologne
locale: 7 Germany
river: 5 Rhein, Rhine
kolo: 5 dance
koloa: 4 bird

Koloski: 2 K.C.
Kolwezi: 4 city, town
locale: 5 Congo
Kolyma: 5 range, river
locale: 4 Asia **6** Russia **7** Siberia
Komatsu: 4 city, town
locale: 5 Japan
__ Kommissar: 3 Der
Komodo __: 6 dragon, lizard
Komodo dragon: 6 animal **7** reptile
Komondor: 3 dog **5** canid **6** canine
Komsomolsk-on-__: 4 Amur
Kon-__: 4 Tiki
kona __: 7 cyclone
Kona __: 5 coast **6** coffee
__ Kong: 4 Hong, King **6** Donkey
Kongo (1932 film)
cast: Walter Huston, Conrad Nagel, Lupe Velez
__ Kong, The: 5 Son of
Konica: 6 camera
alternative: 4 Fuji **5** Canon, Kodak, Leica, Nikon **6** Pentax, Rollei **7** Minolta, Olympus, Vivitar, Yashica **8** Polaroid
Konrad: 5 Bloch **6** Lorenz **8** Adenauer
Konstantin: 9 Chernenko
Kon-Tiki: 4 raft
builder: 4 Thor **9** Heyerdahl
material: 5 balsa
Museum city: 4 Oslo
starting point: 4 Peru
Konwicki, Tadeusz: 6 Polish, writer
Konya: 4 city, town
locale: 6 Turkey
koodoo: 8 antelope
relative: 3 gnu, kob **4** guib, oryx, puku, topi **5** addax, bongo, chiru, eland, goral, korin, nyala, oribi, saiga, serow **6** chammy, dik-dik, duiker, impala, lechwe, nilgai, rhebok, shammy, shamoy **7** blaubok, blesbok, chamois, defassa, gazelle, gemsbok, gerenuk, grysbok, nylghai, nylghau, sassaby **8** blesbuck, bontebok, bushbuck, gemsbuck, reedbuck, steenbok, steinbok **9** blackbuck, pronghorn, sitatunga, springbok, waterbuck **10** hartebeest, wildebeest
kook: 3 nut **4** zany **5** crank, flake, wacko **6** maniac, weirdo **7** dingbat, oddball **8** crackpot **9** character, eccentric, screwball
kookaburra: 4 bird **10** Australian
__ Kookie Byrnes: 3 Edd
Kookie, Kookie (1959 song) artist: Connie Stevens, Edd Byrnes
kooky: 3 odd **4** daft, loco, zany **5** flaky, goofy, goosy, inane, weird **6** absurd, flakey **7** bizarre, bonkers, foolish, oddball **8** peculiar, reckless **9** eccentric **10** irrational
Kool __ Dee: 3 Moe
Kool-Aid flavor: 4 lime **5** grape, lemon **6** cherry, orange **9** lemon-lime, tangerine **10** strawberry
Kool and the Gang
song: Celebration (1980)
Cherish (1985)
Fresh (1985)
Get Down on It (1982)
Hollywood Swinging (1974)
Joanna (1983)
Jungle Boogie (1974)
Ladies Night (1979)
Misled (1985)
Stone Love (1987)
Too Hot (1980)
Victory (1986)
Koontz, Dean: 6 writer
like a ~ novel: 4 eery **5** eerie
work: After the Last Race

The Bad Place
Cold Fire
Darkfall
Dark Rivers of the Heart
Demon Seed
The Door to December
Dragonfly
Dragon Tears
The Eyes of Darkness
The Face of Fear
False Memory
Fear Nothing
From the Corner of His Eye
The Funhouse
Hideaway
The House of Thunder
Icebound
Intensity
The Key to Midnight
Lightning
The Mask
Midnight
Mr. Murder
Night Chills
Nightmare Journey
One Door Away From Heaven
Phantoms
Prison of Ice
Santa's Twin
Seize the Night
The Servants of Twilight
Shadowfires
Shattered
Sole Survivor
Strangers
Tick Tock
Twilight Eyes
The Vision
The Voice of the Night
Watchers
Whispers
Winter Moon

Koopmans, Tjalling: 8 Nobelist **9** economist
Kootenay: 5 river
  locale: 5 Idaho **7** Montana
kopeck: 4 coin **5** money
  100: 6 rouble
kopecks
  100: 5 ruble
Kopell: 6 Bernie
koph: 6 Hebrew, letter
  follower: 4 resh
  preceder: 4 sadi **5** sadhe, tsade, tsadi
Kopit, Arthur: 10 playwright
Koppel: 3 Ted
  network: 3 ABC **5** ABC-TV
kora: 6 string **8** harp lute
  origin: 6 Africa
Korab: 4 peak **5** mount **8** mountain
  locale: 6 Europe **7** Albania **9** Macedonia
Korah
  father: 4 Esau
Koran: 8 holy book
  alphabet: 5 Kufic
  chapter: 4 sura **5** surah
  deity: 5 Allah
  honorific for ~ memorizers: 5 hafiz
  language: 6 Arabic
  reader: 4 imam **5** imaum
korat: 3 cat **5** felid **6** feline
Korbut, Olga: 7 gymnast, Russian
Korda: 6 Zoltan **7** Michael **9** Alexander
Korda, Alexander: 8 director
  film: The Private Life of Henry VIII (1933)
    Rembrandt (1936)
    That Hamilton Woman (1941)
    Vacation From Marriage (1945)
  spouse: Merle Oberon
Korda, Zoltan: 8 director
  film: Cry, the Beloved Country (1951)
    Drums (1938)
    Elephant Boy (1937)
    The Four Feathers (1939)
    Jungle Book (1942)
    The Macomber Affair (1947)
    Sahara (1943)
    A Woman's Vengeance (1947)
Korea
  alphabet: 6 Hangul
  apricot: 4 ansu
  automaker: 3 Kia **6** Daewoo
  Buddhism of ~: 8 Mahayana
  continent: 4 Asia
  dish: 6 kimchi **7** kimchee
  golfer: 3 Pak **7** Se Ri Pak
  river: 4 Yalu
  sea: 6 Yellow
  seaport: 6 Inchon
  soldier: 3 ROK
  TV series set in ~: 4 MASH
  see also North Korea, South Korea
Korea __: 6 Strait
__ Korea: 5 North, South
Korean: 5 Asian **8** language
Korean War
  flier: 3 MIG
  grp.: 3 WAC
kor fraction: 4 epha **5** ephah
Korhogo: 4 city, town
  locale: 10 Ivory Coast
korin: 8 antelope
  relative: 3 gnu, kob **4** guib, kudu, oryx, puku, topi **5** addax, bongo, chiru, eland, goral, nyala, oribi, saiga, serow **6** chammy, dik-dik, duiker, impala, koodoo, lechwe, nilgai, rhebok, shammy, shamoy **7** blaubok, blesbok, chamois, defassa, gazelle, gemsbok, gerenuk, grysbok, nylghai, nylghau, sassaby **8** blesbuck, bontebok, bushbuck, gemsbuck, reedbuck, steenbok, steinbok **9** blackbuck, pronghorn, sitatunga, springbok, waterbuck **10** hartebeest, wildebeest
Korinna: 4 font **8** typeface
Koriyama: 4 city, town
  locale: 5 Japan
Korman, Harvey: 5 actor **8** comedian
  film: Blazing Saddles (1974)
    High Anxiety (1977)
  TV: The Carol Burnett Show
Kornberg, Arthur: 8 Nobelist
Kornelia: 5 Ender
Korngold: 5 Erich
Korolyov: 6 Sergey
Koror: 4 city, town
  locale: 5 Palau
Korovin volcano island: 4 Atka
koruna: 5 money
  spender: 5 Czech
Kos: 3 isl. **4** isle **6** island
  locale: 6 Turkey
Kosar, Bernie: 2 QB **11** quarterback
  sport: 8 football
Koscina: 5 Sylva
Kosciusko: 4 peak **5** mount **8** mountain
  locale: 9 Australia
kosher: 2 OK **4** good, just, okay, okeh, okey, pure, real **5** jural, legal, legit, licit, moral, sound, valid **6** lawful, proper **7** allowed, factual, genuine, logical **8** accepted, bona fide, rightful **9** allowable, authentic, befitting, by the book, permitted, veritable **10** acceptable, authorized, legitimate, sanctioned
  expert: 5 rabbi, rebbe
  it's not ~: 3 ham **4** pork **6** shrimp **7** lobster
  not ~: 4 tref **5** trayf, treyf **6** pseudo **7** terefah
__ kosher: 5 glatt
Koshiba, Masatoshi: 8 Nobelist **9** physicist
Kosice: 4 city, town
  locale: 8 Slovakia
Kosinski, Jerzy: 6 author, writer
  birthplace: Lodz, Poland
  work: Being There
    Blind Date
    Cockpit
    The Painted Bird
    Passion Play
    Pinball
    Steps
Kosovo peacekeeping org.: 4 NATO
Kossel, Albrecht: 6 German **7** chemist **8** Nobelist
Kostelanetz, André: 9 conductor
  spouse: Lily Pons
Koster: 5 Henry **7** Palamas
Koster, Henry: 8 director
  film: The Bishop's Wife (1947)
    Come to the Stable (1949)
    D-Day the Sixth of June (1956)
    First Love (1939)
    Good Morning, Miss Dove (1955)
    Harvey (1950)
    The Inspector General (1949)
    It Started With Eve (1941)
    A Man Called Peter (1955)
    My Cousin Rachel (1952)
    No Highway in the Sky (1951)
    One Hundred Men and a Girl (1937)
    The Rage of Paris (1938)
    Spring Parade (1940)
    Three Smart Girls (1936)
    Three Smart Girls Grow Up (1939)
    Two Sisters From Boston (1946)
    The Virgin Queen (1955)
    Wabash Avenue (1950)
Kosygin: 7 Aleksei
Kota Kinabalu: 4 city, port, town
  locale: 6 Borneo **8** Malaysia
Kotch (1971 film)
  cast: Felicia Farr, Walter Matthau
  director: Jack Lemmon
Kotcheff, Ted: 8 director
  film: The Apprenticeship of Duddy Kravitz (1974)
    First Blood (1982)
    North Dallas Forty (1979)
    Split Image (1982)
    Switching Channels (1988)
    Who Is Killing the Great Chefs of Europe? (1978)
koto: 6 string, zither **10** instrument
  origin: 5 Japan
Kottke: 3 Leo
Kotto, Yaphet: 5 actor
  film: Across 110th Street (1972)
    Blue Collar (1978)
    Brubaker (1980)
    Live and Let Die (1973)
    Midnight Run (1988)
    The Running Man (1987)
Koufax, Sandy: 5 lefty **6** Dodger, hurler **7** pitcher
  stat: 3 ERA **4** wins **8** shutouts **10** strikeouts
kouprey: 5 bovid **6** bovine
  relative: 3 yak **4** anoa, arna, gaur, urus, zebu **5** bison, gayal, takin **6** mithan, muskox **7** aurochs, banteng, banting, beefalo, buffalo, carabao, cattalo, tamarao, tamarau, timarau
Kournikova, Anna: 7 netster **9** tennis pro
  milieu: 5 court
Koussevitzky, Serge: 9 conductor
Kovacs, Ernie spouse: Edie Adams
Kovic: 3 Ron
  portrayer: 6 Cruise
Kowalski: 6 Stella **7** Stanley
kowhai: 4 tree
Kowloon: 4 city, port, town
  locale: 8 Hong Kong
kowtow: 3 bow **4** fawn **5** bow to, cower, kneel, stoop, toady **6** cringe, grovel, submit **7** defer to, wheedle **9** be servile, prostrate, reverence
  to: 3 woo **5** court, toady **6** stroke **7** adulate, flatter, truckle **8** bootlick, butter up, fawn over
kowtower: 5 toady **6** fawner, flunky, lackey, minion, stooge, yes-man **7** doormat, flunkey **8** courtier, groveler, hanger-on **9** flatterer, sycophant **10** bootlicker **13** apple-polisher
Koyaanisqatsi (1983 film) director: Godfrey Reggio
Koyukon: 6 Indian **7** Amerind
Kozlowski, Linda spouse: Paul Hogan
KP
  item: 4 spud **5** tater **6** potato
  one on ~: 2 GI **7** private, recruit, soldier
  tool: 5 parer **6** peeler
  worker: 5 parer **6** peeler
K-P connection: 4 LMNO
Kpelle home: 6 Africa, Guinea **7** Liberia
__ K. Polk: 5 James
K-Q connection: 5 LMNOP
Kr: 4 elem. **7** element, krypton
  36 for ~: 4 at. no.
kraal: 4 stad **7** village **12** South African
Krackel: 5 candy **8** candy bar **9** chocolate
  alternative: 4 Mars, Twix **5** Clark, Heath **6** Kit Kat, Mounds, PayDay, Reese's, Zagnut **7** Oh Henry **8** Baby Ruth, Hershey's, Milky Way, Snickers **9** Almond Joy, Mr. Goodbar **10** NutRageous
Krafla: 7 volcano
  locale: 7 Iceland
Kraft: 5 jelly
  alternative: 6 Knott's, Welch's **7** Polaner **8** Smucker's
krait: 3 asp **5** snake **6** animal **7** reptile, serpent
  relative: 3 boa **5** aboma, adder, cobra, mamba, racer, viper **6** dhaman, python, taipan **7** markhor, rattler **8** anaconda, moccasin, ringhals **9** boomslang, coachwhip **10** bushmaster, copperhead, sidewinder
  weapon: 4 fang
Krakatoa: 4 isle **6** island **7** volcano
  output: 3 ash
Kraków: 4 city, town
  locale: 6 Poland
Krakowski: 4 Jane
Kramden: 5 Alice, Ralph
  collection: 4 fare
  Norton, to ~: 3 pal
  vehicle: 3 bus
Kramer: 4 Jack **5** Cosmo **7** Stanley **9** Stepfanie
Kramer, Jack: 7 netster **9** tennis pro
  milieu: 5 court
Kramer, Stanley: 8 director
  film: Bless the Beasts and Children (1972)
    The Defiant Ones (1958)
    Guess Who's Coming to Dinner (1967)
    Inherit the Wind (1960)
    It's a Mad Mad Mad Mad World (1963)
    Judgment at Nuremberg (1961)
    Not as a Stranger (1955)
    Oklahoma Crude (1973)
    On the Beach (1959)
    Ship of Fools (1965)
Kramer vs. Kramer (1979 film)
  cast: Jane Alexander, Justin Henry, Dustin Hoffman, Meryl Streep
  director: Robert Benton
Kramnik, Vladimir forte: 5 chess
kran: 5 money

Kranepool: 2 Ed
Krantz, Judith: 6 writer
work: Dazzle
I'll Take Manhattan
The Jewels of Tessa Kent
Mistral's Daughter
Princess Daisy
Scruples
Spring Collection
Till We Meet Again
Krasicki, Ignacy: 4 poet **6** Polish
Krasna: 6 Norman
Krasner, Lee spouse: Jackson Pollock
Krasny: 4 Paul
krater: 4 bowl
K-ration: 4 meal
Kraus, Karl: 6 writer **8** Austrian
Krauss: 6 Alison **7** Clemens
Krauss, Clemens: 9 conductor
Kravis: 5 Henry
Kravitz, Lenny
song: It Ain't Over 'Til It's Over (1991)
spouse: Lisa Bonet
Krazy __: 3 Kat **4** Glue
Krazy Kat: 5 comic, strip
character: 6 Ignatz **11** Offissa Pupp
Krebs: 4 Hans **5** Edwin
Krebs cycle product: 3 ATP
Krebs, Edwin: 8 Nobelist
Krebs, Hans: 6 German **8** Nobelist
Krefeld: 4 city, town
locale: 7 Germany
Kreisler, Fritz: 8 Austrian **9** violinist
__ Kreme: 6 Krispy
Kremlin Colonel ingredient: 5 vodka
Kremlin name: 5 Lenin **6** Stalin **8** Brezhnev **10** Khrushchev
Kresge, S.S. today: 5 K Mart
Kreskin claim: 3 ESP
__ Kreskin, The: 7 Amazing
Kreuk: 7 Kristin
kreutzer: 5 money
Kreutzer Sonata composer: 9 Beethoven
Krige: 5 Alice
krill: 6 shrimp
krimmer: 3 fur **4** pelt
Krimmler: 5 falls **9** waterfall
locale: 7 Austria
krin: 4 drum
origin: 6 Africa
__ Kringle: 4 Kris **5** Kriss
Krips, Josef: 8 Austrian **9** conductor
kris: 5 blade, knife
Kris: 6 Nelson **7** Kringle
Kris __: 5 Kross
Krishna: 4 shah **5** river
beloved: 5 Radha
devotee: 5 Hindu **6** Hindoo
locale: 5 India
__ Krishna: 4 Hare
Kris Kross song: Jump (1992)
__ Krispies: 4 Rice **5** Cocoa
Krispy: 7 cracker
alternative: 4 Ritz **5** Zesta **7** Cheez-It, Premium **8** Triscuit **10** Cheese Nips, Wheat Thins
Krispy __: 5 Kreme
Kriss Kringle: 5 Santa
Kristen: 5 Marta **8** Johnston
Kristi: 9 Yamaguchi
emulate ~: 5 skate
Kristin: 4 Otto **5** Davis, Kreuk
Kristin __ Thomas: 5 Scott
Kristofferson, Kris: 5 actor **6** singer
film: Alice Doesn't Live Here Anymore (1974)
Big Top Pee-wee (1988)
Blade (1998)
Blume in Love (1973)
Cisco Pike (1972)
Dance With Me (1998)
Heaven's Gate (1980)
Limbo (1999)
Lone Star (1996)
Semi-Tough (1977)
A Soldier's Daughter Never Cries (1998)
A Star Is Born (1976)
spouse: Rita Coolidge
Kristy: 7 Swanson **8** McNichol
Kroc: 3 Ray
Krock: 6 Arthur
Kroemer, Herbert: 8 Nobelist **9** physicist
Krofft: 3 Sid **5** Marty
Kroft: 5 Steve
__ Kröger: 5 Tonio
Krogh: 4 Egil **6** Schack
Krogh, Schack: 6 Danish **8** Nobelist
krona: 4 coin **5** money
fractions: 5 aurar
krone: 4 coin **5** money
word on a ~: 5 Norge
Krone, Julie: 6 jockey
milieu: 5 track
kroon: 5 money
Kropotkin: 5 Pyotr
__ Kross: 4 Kris
Kroto, Harold: 7 chemist **8** Nobelist
Krueger, Freddy street: 3 Elm
Kruger: 4 Alma, Otto, Paul
ender: 4 rand
Kruger National Park
terrain: 4 veld **5** veldt
Krugerrand: 4 coin **8** gold coin
Krull, Felix creator: 4 Mann
krummkake: 6 cookie
Krupa, Gene: 7 drummer
genre: 4 jazz
Krupp: 6 Alfred
gun: 6 Bertha **9** Big Bertha
home: 4 Ruhr **5** Essen
Krusty: 5 clown
Krylov, Ivan: 6 writer **7** Russian
krypton: 3 gas **7** element
like ~: 5 inert
kryptonite: 4 rock
KS
see Kansas
__ K. Smith: 6 Howard
KSU conference: 9 Big Twelve
kt.: 2 wt.
K.T.: 5 Oslin
K2: 3 mtn. **4** peak **5** mount **8** mountain
locale: 4 Asia **7** Kashmir
Kuala Lumpur: 4 city, town **7** capital
language: 5 Malay
locale: 8 Malaysia
Kuban: 5 river
locale: 6 Russia
Kubek: 4 Tony
Kubelik: 3 Jan **6** Rafael
Kubelik, Jan: 5 Czech **9** violinist
Kubelik, Rafael: 5 Czech **9** conductor
Kublai: 4 Khan
Kubla Khan: 4 poem
author: Samuel Taylor Coleridge
locale: 4 Asia **6** Xanadu
river: 4 Alph
Kubrick, Stanley: 8 director
film: 2001: A Space Odyssey (1968)
Barry Lyndon (1975)
A Clockwork Orange (1971)
Dr. Strangelove (1964)
Eyes Wide Shut (1999)
Full Metal Jacket (1987)
The Killing (1956)
Lolita (1962)
Paths of Glory (1957)
The Shining (1980)
Spartacus (1960)
kuchen: 4 cake **6** German **7** dessert **10** coffeecake
Kuda __: 3 Bux
kudo: 6 praise **7** tribute **8** accolade **10** compliment
kudos: 5 éclat, glory, honor, raves **6** credit, esteem, homage, honors, praise, salute **7** acclaim, big hand, laurels, plaudit, tribute **8** accolade, applause, encomium, flattery, good word, plaudits **9** laudation, panegyric **10** exaltation, popularity, prominence
heap ~ on: 4 laud **5** extol, honor **6** admire, extoll, praise, puff up, stroke **7** acclaim, applaud, approve, build up, commend, flatter, lionize **8** hand it to **10** compliment
Kudrow, Lisa: 7 actress
film: Analyze This (1999)
Hanging Up (2000)
Lucky Numbers (2000)
The Opposite of Sex (1998)
TV: Friends
kudu: 6 animal, mammal **8** antelope
relative: 3 gnu, kob **4** guib, oryx, puku, topi **5** addax, bongo, chiru, eland, goral, korin, nyala, oribi, saiga, serow **6** chammy, dik-dik, duiker, impala, lechwe, nilgai, rhebok, shammy, shamoy **7** blaubok, blesbok, chamois, defassa, gazelle, gemsbok, gerenuk, grysbok, nylghai, nylghau, sassaby **8** blesbuck, bontebok, bushbuck, gemsbuck, reedbuck, steenbok, steinbok **9** blackbuck, pronghorn, sitatunga, springbok, waterbuck **10** hartebeest, wildebeest
kudzu: 4 vine
Kuhn: 4 Walt **5** Bowie **6** Maggie **7** Richard
Kuhn, Richard: 7 chemist **8** Nobelist
Kukhoe locale: 10 South Korea
Kukla: 6 puppet
creator: 4 Burr **9** Tillstrom
friend: 4 Fran **5** Ollie **7** Allison
Kukla, Fran & Ollie (TV)
cast: Fran Allison
Burr Tillstrom
kukui: 4 tree **9** candlenut
kulak: 7 peasant, Russian
Kula Kangri: 4 peak **5** mount **8** mountain
locale: 4 Asia **5** Tibet **6** Bhutan
kuletuk: 4 coat **6** jacket **8** overcoat
Kulik: 4 Buzz, Ilia
Kulik, Ilia: 6 skater **7** Russian
Kulp: 5 Nancy
Kulthum: 3 Umm
__ Kum: 4 Kara **5** Kyzyl
Kumamoto: 4 city, town
locale: 5 Japan
Kumasi: 4 city, town
locale: 5 Ghana
Kumba: 4 city, town
locale: 8 Cameroon
Kumin, Maxine: 6 writer
kumiss: 5 drink **8** beverage
kummel: 5 drink **8** beverage
kumquat: 4 tree **5** fruit, shrub **6** citrus
cover: 4 rind
relative: 4 lime, Ugli **5** lemon, navel **6** orange, pomelo, tangor **7** satsuma, Seville, tangelo **8** bergamot, mandarin, shaddock, Valencia **9** tangerine **10** calamondin, grapefruit
shape: 4 oval
__ kumquat: 4 oval **5** round **6** marumi, nagami
Kun: 4 Béla
Kundera, Milan: 5 Czech **6** writer
work: The Unbearable Lightness of Being
kundu: 4 drum
kung __ chicken: 3 pao
kung fu: 5 sport
star: 3 Lee
Kung Fu (ABC drama)
cast: David Carradine (Caine)
kung-fu cousin: 6 karate
Kung Fu Fighting (1974 song) artist: Carl Douglas
Kungur: 4 peak **5** mount **8** mountain
locale: 4 Asia **5** China
Kunitz, Stanley: 4 poet
Kunlun: 5 range **9** mountains
locale: 4 Asia **5** China
Kunstler, William: 3 att. **4** atty. **8** attorney
forte: 3 law
org.: 3 ABA
Kunta Kinte portrayer: 4 Amos **6** Burton
Kunzel, Erich: 9 conductor
kunzite: 3 gem **8** gemstone
Kuoyu: 8 Mandarin
Kuprin, Aleksandr: 6 writer **7** Russian
Kura: 5 river
locale: 6 Turkey **7** Georgia **10** Azerbaijan
Kuralt: 7 Charles
Kurd: 5 Asian
Kurdi: 3 cow **4** bull **6** bovine, cattle
Kurdish: 8 language
home: 4 Iran
Kure: 4 city, port, town
locale: 5 Hondo, Japan **6** Honshu
Kuri: 3 cow **4** bull **6** bovine, cattle
Kurile Islands aborigine: 4 Ainu
Kurosawa, Akira: 8 director, Japanese
film: Dersu Uzala (1975)
Ikiru (1952)
Kagemusha (1980)
Ran (1985)
Rashomon (1950)
The Seven Samurai (1954)
Stray Dog (1949)
Throne of Blood (1957)
Yojimbo (1961)
kurrajong: 4 tree
Kurt: 5 Adler, Alder, Jooss, Loder, Masur, Weill **6** Cobain, Thomas **7** Neumann, Russell **8** Vonnegut, Waldheim, Wüthrich
wife: 5 Lotte
kurta: 5 shirt
Kurtz, Swoosie: 7 actress
film: Bright Lights, Big City (1988)
Dangerous Liaisons (1988)
Liar Liar (1997)
Stanley & Iris (1990)
Wildcats (1986)
TV: Sisters
Kurume: 4 city, town
locale: 5 Japan
kurus: 5 money
Kuryakin: 5 Illya
partner: 4 Solo
Kurys: 5 Diane
Kusch, Polykarp: 8 Nobelist **9** physicist
Kushiro: 4 city, town
locale: 5 Japan
__ Kush Mountains: 5 Hindu
Kushner: 4 Tony **6** Harold
Kutaisi: 4 city, town
locale: 7 Georgia
Kutchin: 6 Indian **7** Amerind
Kutenai: 6 Indian **7** Amerind
Kutuzov: 7 Mikhail
Kuvasz: 3 dog **5** canid **6** canine
Kuwait: 6 nation **7** country
capital: 10 Kuwait City
currency: 5 dinar
group: 10 Arab League
location: 6 Arabia
money: 4 fils **5** dinar
neighbor: 4 Irak, Iraq
nonvoter in ~: 5 woman
org.: 4 OPEC
ruler: 4 amir, emir **5** ameer, emeer
Kuwaiti: 4 Arab
neighbor: 5 Iraki, Iraqi, Saudi
Kuwana: 4 city, town
locale: 5 Japan
Kuznetsk __: 5 Basin
Kuznets, Simon: 8 Nobelist **9** economist

kvass: 5 drink **8** beverage
ingredient: 3 rye **6** barley
relative: 4 beer, suds **5** lager **7** brewski
kvetch: 4 carp, crab **5** gripe, groan, shrew, whine **6** carper, grouse, whiner **7** grumble, needler **8** complain **9** bellyache, henpecker **10** complainer
be a ~: 4 carp, fuss, kick, moan, pule, sigh, wail **5** cavil, gripe, groan, whine **6** grouch, grouse, murmur, snivel, squawk, yammer **7** grumble, nitpick, quibble **8** complain **9** bellyache, criticize, make a fuss
phrase: 5 oy vey
Kwa: 8 language
kwacha: 5 money
Kwai: 5 river
Kwakiutl: 6 Indian **7** Amerind
Kwame: 7 Nkrumah
Kwan: 5 Nancy **6** skater **8** Michelle
milieu: 3 ice **4** rink
Kwangju: 4 city, town
locale: 10 South Korea
Kwanzaa
fifth day of ~: 3 Nia
principle: 5 faith, unity
kwanza, where to spend: 6 Angola
Kwekwe: 4 city, town
locale: 8 Zimbabwe
Kwik-E-Mart owner: 3 Apu
__ kwon do: 3 tae
K.W.S. song: Please Don't Go (1992)
Ky.
neighbor: 3 Ill., Ind., W.Va. **4** Tenn., Virg.
see also Kentucky
kyat: 5 money
Kyd, Thomas: 7 British **10** playwright
work: The Spanish Tragedy
Kyle: 4 Rote **8** Chandler **10** MacLachlan
Kylie: 7 Minogue
Kym: 4 Sims
Kyoga: 4 lake
locale: 6 Uganda
Kyongbok Palace site: 5 Seoul
kyoodle: 3 yap **4** bark, yelp
Kyoto: 4 city, town
carrier to ~: 3 ANA, JAL
coin: 3 sen, yen
locale: 5 Hondo, Japan **6** Honshu
port near ~: 4 Kobe
Kyra: 8 Sedgwick
Kyrgyz mountains: 4 Alai
Kyrgyzstan: 6 nation **7** country
capital: 7 Bishkek
city: 3 Osh **7** Bishkek
locale: 4 Asia
mountain: 8 Tian Shan, Tien Shan **9** Trans Alai
neighbor: 5 China **10** Kazakhstan, Tajikistan, Uzbekistan
Kyrie __: 7 eleison
Kyser: 3 Kay
Kyu: 8 Sakamoto
Kyushu: 4 isle **6** island
city: 4 Oita, Saga **5** Beppu, Omuta **6** Kasuga, Kurume, Sasebo **7** Fukuoka, Nobeoka **8** Kumamoto, Miuazaki, Nagasaki **9** Kagoshima
locale: 5 Japan
volcano: 3 Aso **5** Unzen **6** Asosan
Kyzyl Kum: 6 desert
locale: 10 Kazakhstan, Uzbekistan

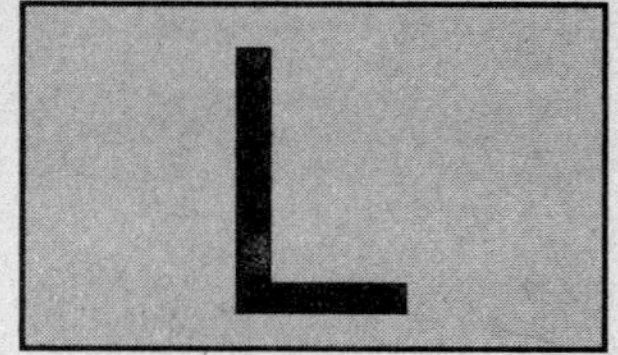

L: 6 letter
followers: 3 MNO 4 MNOP 5 MNOPQ
in phonetic alphabet: 4 Lima
preceders: 3 JKL 4 IJKL 5 HIJKL
L ___: 3 bar 4 beam, sill, wave 5 chain
L ___ Larry: 4 as in
L'___, c'est moi: 4 état
L'___ del Cairo: 3 Oca
L'___ Heurtebise: 4 Ange
L'___-midi d'un Faune: 5 après
L. ___ Baum: 5 Frank
L. ___ Hubbard: 3 Ron
___ L: 3 One 4 P and, S and
___ L.: 4 A.F. of
la: 4 note
à ~: 4 like 9 emulating 10 resembling
à ~ mode: 2 in 3 mod 4 chic, tony 5 faddy, toney 6 chi-chi, modish, trendy 7 current, in style, popular, stylish, voguish 8 up-to-date 9 in fashion 10 all the rage
preceder: 2 so 3 sol
la-___: 4 de-da, di-da
___-la: 3 tra 4 fa-la 5 tra-la 7 Shangri
La: 4 elem. 7 element 9 lanthanum
57 for ~: 4 at. no.
La ___: 3 Mer 4 La La, Vida 5 Bamba, Curée, Grâce, Ronde, Valse 6 Boheme, Strada 7 Chienne, Rondine
La ___ aux Folles: 4 Cage
La ___, Bolivia: 3 Paz
La ___ Bonita: 4 Isla
La ___, CA: 4 Mesa 5 Jolla
La ___ del Destino: 5 Forza
La ___ des Nymphes: 5 Danse
La ___ en Rose: 3 Vie
La ___ Humaine: 4 Bête
La ___, IL: 5 Salle
La ___, IN: 5 Porte
La ___ Jackson: 4 Toya
La ___ Nikita: 5 Femme
La ___ nuova: 4 vita
La ___ opera house: 5 Scala
La ___ Pacifica: 4 Casa
La ___ Rose: 5 Vie en
La ___ tar pits: 4 Brea
La ___ Vita: 5 Dolce
La ___, WI: 6 Crosse
La, ___ to follow sew: 5 a note
La-___: 4 Z-Boy
La.
neighbor: 3 Ark., Tex. 4 Miss.
see also Louisiana
L.A.
to Bakersfield dir.: 3 NNW
to Reno direction: 3 NNW
to Seattle dir.: 3 NNW
see also Los Angeles
L.A. ___: 3 Law 5 Story
Laa-Laa: 9 Teletubby
La, a note to follow ___: 3 sew
lab
animal: 3 rat 5 mouse 9 guinea pig
assistant of film: 4 Igor
course: 3 bio. 4 chem., phys. 7 biology, physics, science 9 chemistry
culture: 4 agar 8 agar-agar
discovery: 4 cure, drug 5 serum
garment: 5 smock
glassware: 4 vial 5 ampul, flask, phial, pipet 6 aludel, ampule, beaker, retort 7 ampoule 9 Petri dish, Pitot tube
heater: 4 etna
liquid: 4 acid
project: 4 test 5 assay
rat challenge: 4 maze
slide dye: 5 eosin 6 eosine
slide sighting: 6 amoeba
solution strength: 5 titer
unit: 2 cc, gr., mg. 3 mol 4 gram 9 milligram
weak, in a ~: 3 dil. 7 diluted
Lab: 3 dog, pet 5 pooch 6 canine
La Baie: 4 city, town
locale: 6 Canada, Québec
La Bamba (1987 film)
cast: Rosanna DeSoto, Esai Morales, Lou Diamond Phillips
director: Luis Valdez
La Bamba (song) artist: Los Lobos, Ritchie Valens
Laban
daughter of ~: 4 Leah 6 Rachel
father of ~: 7 Bethuel
sister of ~: 7 Rebekah
son-in-law of ~: 5 Jacob
La Barca: 4 city, town
locale: 6 Mexico 7 Jalisco
label: 3 dub, tab, tag 4 call, logo, mark, name, term 5 brand, class, decal, stamp, style, title 6 define, design, ticket 7 address, company, entitle, epithet, heading, insigne, intitle, specify, sticker, stick-on 8 bookmark, classify, describe, identify, insignia, nickname, subtitle 9 brand name, designate, trademark 10 stereotype
again: 5 retag
info: 3 UPC 4 size 5 waist 7 bar code 11 price inseam
___ label: 3 red 4 care 5 union, zebra 7 private, stick-on
La Belle ___: 5 Paree 6 Helene
La Belle Dame sans Merci: 4 poem
author: 5 Keats
La Belle et la ___: 4 Bête
LaBelle, Patti
real name: Patricia Holt
song: Lady Marmalade (1975)
New Attitude (1985)
On My Own (1986)
La Bête Humaine author: Emile Zola
labile: 7 mutable, protean 9 versatile 10 changeable
Labine: 4 Clem 6 Dodger, hurler 7 pitcher
labium: 3 lip
La Bohème: 5 opera
cafe: 5 Momus
character: 4 Mimi 6 Benoît 7 Colline, Musetta, Rodolfo 8 Marcello 9 Alcindoro, Schaunard
composer: 7 Puccini
highlight: 4 duet
musical based on ~: 4 Rent
setting: 5 Paris 6 France
La Bohème (1926 film)
cast: Renee Adoree, John Gilbert, Lillian Gish
director: King Vidor
labor: 3 act, job 4 grub, hack, hand, help, moil, plod, pull, push, task, tend, till, toil, wade, work 5 chore, drive, grind, pains, serve, slave, sweat 6 drudge, effort, energy, helper, strain, stress, strive, throes, toiler, worker 7 employe, hard hat, laborer, service, travail 8 activity, bear down, drudgery, employee, endeavor, exercise, exertion, hireling, industry, plug away, struggle 9 cultivate, diligence, grind away, gruntwork, moonlight, work force 10 apprentice, blue collar, daily grind, employment, instrument
forced ~: 7 slavery
group: 3 AFL, AFT, CIO, NEA, UAW, UFT 5 ILGWU, union 6 AFL-CIO 9 Teamsters
hard ~: 5 sweat 7 travail 8 drudgery, exertion
onetime ~ union: 3 IWW
opposite: 3 mgt. 4 mgmt. 10 management
requiring hard ~: 5 harsh, heavy 6 taxing, tiring 7 arduous, onerous 8 exacting, grinding, grueling, toilsome 9 demanding, difficult, herculean, laborious, strenuous 10 burdensome, exhausting, formidable, oppressive, overtaxing
saving device: 5 robot 7 machine
labor ___: 3 spy 5 force, union 6 market
labor ___ vincit: 5 omnia
labor-___: 6 saving
___ labor: 3 big, day 4 hard 5 child, stoop 6 direct 7 skilled
laborare ___ orare: 3 est
Labor author: Emile Zola
Labor Day: 3 Mon.
kid: 5 Virgo
month: 3 Sep. 4 Sept
telethon org.: 3 MDA
Labor Dept. org.: 4 OSHA
labored: 4 hard 5 heavy, inept, stiff 6 clumsy, forced, stodgy, uphill 7 arduous, awkward, halting, operose, stilted, studied 8 affected, overdone, strained, toilsome 9 contrived, effortful, laborious, maladroit, ponderous, strenuous, unnatural 10 artificial
laborer: 4 hand, peon 5 grunt, labor, prole, slave 6 drudge, jobber, worker 7 employe 8 employee, farmhand, hireling 9 jobholder 10 working man
medieval ~: 4 esne 5 helot 6 vassal 7 bondman, chattel, villein
unskilled ~: 4 peon 6 drudge
___ laborer: 3 day
laboring: 4 busy 6 at work 7 working 8 employed, on the job
laborious: 4 hard 5 heavy, rough, stiff, tough 6 active, forced, no joke, sticky, thorny, trying, uphill, wicked 7 arduous, hard-won, labored, onerous, operose, painful, rough go, serious, tedious, wearing 8 diligent, grueling, sedulous, strained, tireless, tiresome, toilsome 9 assiduous, demanding, difficult, effortful, fatiguing, herculean, ponderous, strenuous, wearisome 10 burdensome, enervating, exhausting, formidable, oppressive, unflagging
task: 5 chore
laboriously: 4 hard 7 wearily 8 doggedly, in detail, steadily
labor of ___: 4 love
labor omnia ___: 6 vincit
Labour: 5 party
___ Labour's Lost: 5 Love's
La Boutique fantastique: 6 ballet
composer: 7 Rossini
Labrador: 3 sea
Indian: 7 Naskapi
locale: 6 Canada
mountain: 8 Caubvick
zone: 3 AST
Labrador ___: 3 tea 4 duck 7 Current
Labrador Retriever: 3 dog, pet 5 canid, pooch 6 canine
La Brea ___ pits: 3 tar
___ Labs: 4 Bell
L'Absinthe artist: 5 Degas
laburnum: 5 plant 6 flower
labyrinth: 3 web 4 coil, knot, maze, mesh 5 skein, snarl 6 jungle, morass, puzzle, riddle, tangle 7 network, problem 9 catacombs, confusion, intricacy 10 complexity, perplexity
ender: 3 ine
locale: 5 Crete 6 Candia
Labyrinth (1986 film)
cast: David Bowie, Jennifer Connelly
director: Jim Henson
dog: 6 Merlin
labyrinthine: 4 mazy 6 daedal, knotty 7 complex, winding 8 Daedalic, involved, mazelike, puzzling, tortuous
Labyrinth of Solitude, The author: Octavio Paz
Labyrinth, The author: Edwin Muir
lac: 5 resin
La Cage Aux Folles: 7 musical
character: 4 Zaza 5 Albin
songwriter: 6 Herman
La Campagne de Rome artist: 5 Corot
La Campanella: 5 étude
La Canada Flintridge: 4 city, town
locale: 10 California
la casa, lady of: 6 señora
La Cava, Gregory: 8 director
film: Affairs of Cellini (1934)
Bed of Roses (1933)
Gabriel Over the White House (1933)
The Half-Naked Truth (1932)
My Man Godfrey (1936)
Stage Door (1937)
What Every Woman Knows (1934)
Laccadive: 4 isls. 5 isles 7 islands
lace: 3 add, hit, mix, net, tie 4 band, bind, cord, do up, mesh, plat, rope, trim 5 close, Cluny, filet, spike, strap, thong, twine 6 attach, border, edging, fabric, fasten, season, string, thread 7 Alençon, banding, crochet, entwine, fortify, intwine, netting, tatting 8 appliqué, filagree, filigree, openwork, ornament, shoelace, trimming 9 fillagree, interlace, punctuate 10 decoration, intertwine, interweave, shoestring, threadwork
apply ~: 4 edge, trim 5 adorn 6 bedeck 7 dress up 8 decorate, ornament, pretty up 9 embellish
collar: 4 ruff 5 ruche 6 bertha
ender: 4 wing
feature: 4 knot
for upholstery: 5 orris
French ~: 3 val
heavily: 4 lard
hole: 4 loop 6 eyelet
into: 4 slam 5 roast, scold 6 assail, oppugn, rave at, thwack 7 assault 9 haul off on 10 pounce upon, vituperate
(into): 4 sail, tear
like ~: 5 fancy 6 dainty, frilly 9 elaborate
make ~: 3 tat
something to ~: 5 punch
starter: 4 neck, shoe 5 inter
town: 5 Cluny 7 Alençon
up: 3 tie 4 bind 6 fasten 7 tighten
with liquor: 5 spike
work: 3 net 5 doily, frill, picot, ruche 6 doyley
yoke: 6 guimpe
lace ___: 3 bug 4 into, stay 5 glass 6 pillow
___ lace: 3 Val 5 Cluny, filet, point 6 bobbin, Breton, pillow 7 Alençon, cutwork, Mechlin, torchon
Lace
star: 5 Cates
___-laced: 6 strait
laced garment: 6 bodice
lacer: 4 tier
lacerate: 3 cut, jag, rip 4 claw, gash, harm, hurt, maim, mall, maul, open, rend, stab, tear 5 knife, lance, score, slash, wound 6 injure, mangle 7 scratch, serrate, torment 8 mutilate, puncture
lacerated: 3 cut 4 hurt, rent, slit, torn 5 split 6 gashed, jagged, ragged 7 injured, slashed
laceration: 3 cut, rip 4 gash, hurt, slit,

stab, tear **5** slash, slice, wound **6** injury, lesion, pierce **7** scratch **8** incision
laces
fix your ~: 5 retie
it has ~: 4 shoe **6** corset, girdle **7** sneaker
lacewing: 3 bug **6** insect
Lacey: 3 cop **4** city, town **7** Chabert
locale: 10 Washington
partner: 6 Cagney
La Chanson de la puce: 4 aria
__-la-Chapelle: 3 Aix
Lachesis: 4 Fate **8** asteroid
colleague: 6 Clotho **7** Atropos
mother of ~: 6 Themis
La Chienne (1931 film) director: Jean Renoir
Lachine: 4 city, town
locale: 6 Canada, Québec
Lachryma __: 7 Christi
lachrymal drop: 4 tear
lachrymose: 3 sad **5** teary, weepy, woful **6** crying, woeful **7** maudlin, sobbing, tearful **8** mournful **9** sniveling
become ~: 3 cry, sob **4** sigh, weep **6** boohoo **7** blubber **9** break down, cry a river, shed tears
lacing: 3 tie **4** cord **5** thong, twine **6** defeat, string **8** shoelace
__ la Cité: 5 île de
lack: 4 loss, miss, need, void, want **5** minus, stint **6** dearth, defect, haven't **7** absence, default, deficit, paucity, poverty, require **8** decrease, distress, exigence, exigency, exiguity, omission, run out of, scarcity, shortage, sparsity **9** depletion, fall short, indigence, necessity, privation, reduction, shortfall, shortness, shrinkage, shrinking **10** abridgment, deficiency, delinquent, have need of, inadequacy, meagerness, scantiness, slightness
combining form: 5 -penia
ender: 6 luster
of enthusiasm: 6 apathy, tedium **7** boredom, languor **8** doldrums, monotony **9** lassitude, weariness
of faith: 8 distrust, mistrust, wariness **9** disbelief, misgiving, suspicion **10** skepticism
opposite: 3 own **4** have
prefix: 3 mis-
lackadaisical: 3 lax **4** dull, idle, lazy, limp, logy, poky, slow **5** hasty, inert, moony, slack **6** draggy, dreamy, remiss, sloppy, torpid **7** gradual, halting, impeded, lagging, languid, passive **8** careless, crawling, creeping, dawdling, dilatory, dragging, drawn-out, fainéant, hesitant, indolent, laid-back, listless, plodding, romantic, slipshod, slothful, sluggish, toddling **9** apathetic, enervated, hit or miss, imprudent, incurious, leisurely, lethargic, negligent, prolonged, snaillike, unhurried, unmindful **10** abstracted, deliberate, energyless, incautious, languorous, nonchalant, protracted, spiritless, unthinking
lackadaisicalness: 5 sloth **6** torpor **8** laziness, lethargy **9** fainéance, indolence **10** stagnation
Lackaday!: 4 alas
Lackawanna: 4 city, town
locale: 7 New York
__-Lackawanna Railroad: 4 Erie
lackey: 4 page, pawn, tool **5** gofer, groom, toady **6** fawner, flunky, gopher, helper, jackal, menial, minion, puppet, stooge, yes man **7** doormat, flunkey, footman, servant, steward **8** creature, factotum, groveler, hanger-on, henchman, kowtower **9** attendant, flatterer, stableboy, sycophant, underling **10** bootlicker, handshaker
lacking: 3 shy **4** gone, poor, sans, thin, weak **5** lousy, minus, out of, short **6** absent, bereft, devoid, except, faulty, feeble, flawed, free of, in need, meager, needed, skimpy **7** missing, needing, wanting, without **8** devoid of, impaired **9** defective, deficient, penniless, subnormal **10** deprived of, inadequate, incomplete, unfinished
combining form: 3 lyo- **4** lipo-
courage: 3 shy **4** weak **5** faint, timid **6** afraid, craven, scared, yellow **7** fearful, gutless, panicky **8** cowardly, recreant, timorous **9** dastardly, nerveless, spineless, tremulous **10** frightened
empathy: 4 mean **5** cruel, rigid, rough, stern, tough **6** bitter, brutal, severe, strict, unkind **7** austere, callous, harshly, hostile **8** despotic, grueling, indurate, pitiless, rocklike, ruthless, savagely, severely, stubborn, wearying **9** difficult, insensate, merciless, obstinate, stringent, unbending, unfeeling, unsparing, viciously **10** adamantine, inflexible, pitilessly, relentless, unmerciful, unpleasant
firmness: 4 soft **6** droopy, flabby, floppy, pliant **7** flaccid, pliable **8** drooping
force: 4 limp, weak **6** effete **8** weakened **9** enervated, powerless
nothing: 4 full **5** whole **6** entire **7** perfect **8** complete, thorough **9** inclusive **10** exhaustive
suffix: 4 -free, -less
value: 3 nil, zip **4** nada, none, zero **5** zilch **6** naught **7** nothing **8** goose egg
vegetation: 3 dry **4** arid **6** fallow **7** parched, sterile **8** deserted, desolate, infecund, lifeless **9** fruitless
vigor: 4 weak, worn **6** feeble **7** worn-out
volume: 4 bony, lank, lean, puny, slim, trim **5** gaunt, lanky, reedy, wispy **6** flimsy, meager, skimpy, skinny, slight, slinky, sparse **7** haggard, scrawny, slender **8** skeletal, twiglike, wisplike **9** emaciated, paper-thin, wafer-thin
wit: 4 dull **5** vapid **7** humdrum, prosaic, tedious
Lackland: 3 AFB
lackluster: 3 dim, dry **4** arid, blah, dead, drab, dull, flat, pale, zero **5** faded, ho-hum, mousy, muted, unfun, vapid **6** barren, boring, draggy, leaden, mousey, sickly, somber **7** nothing, obscure, prosaic, vanilla **8** laid-back, lifeless, unlively **9** colorless, prosaical, unsightly, washed-out
lacks: 5 hasn't
lackwit: 4 dope **5** ninny
La classe de danse painter: 5 Degas
La Clemenza di Tito composer: 6 Mozart
Lacombe: 3 pig **5** swine
Lacombe, Lucien (1974 film) director: Louis Malle
La Confession de Claude author: Emile Zola
L.A. Confidential (1997 film)
cast: Kim Basinger, Russell Crowe, Kevin Spacey
director: Curtis Hanson
laconic: 4 curt **5** brief, brusk, crisp, pithy, short, terse, tight **6** silent **7** brusque, compact, concise **8** succinct, taciturn **10** of few words, to the point
laconism: 3 mot, saw **4** quip **5** gnome, maxim, motto **6** saying **7** brevity, epigram **8** aphorism, apothegm **9** pithiness, terseness, witticsim **10** apophthegm
Lacoste, Rene: 7 netster **9** tennis pro
milieu: 5 court
La Cousine __: 5 Bette
lacquer: 4 coat **5** glaze, gloss, layer **6** enamel, finish, veneer **7** coating, encrust, incrust, varnish **8** covering **10** lamination
black ~: 5 japan
component: 5 elemi, resin
lacquer __: 4 tree, ware
lacquerware: 4 tole
Lacrima __: 7 Christi
lacrimal __: 3 sac **4** bone, duct **5** gland
lacrosse: 4 game **5** sport
area: 3 net **4** goal
position: 6 goalie
team: 3 ten
La Crosse: 4 city, town
locale: 4 Wisc. **9** Wisconsin
Lactaid: 7 antacid
alternative: 4 Tums **6** Maalox, Pepcid, Riopan, Zantac **7** Gelusil, Mylanta, Rolaids **8** Gaviscon **11** Alka-Seltzer, Pepto-Bismol
__ Lactea: 3 Via
lactic: 4 acid **5** milky
lacto-__-vegetarian: 3 ovo
lactose: 5 sugar
glucose, to ~: 6 isomer
__-lacto-vegetarian: 3 ovo
lacuna: 3 gap **4** gulf, hole **5** blank, break, lapse, pause, space **6** cavity, cesura, hiatus **7** caesura, interim, opening **8** interval, omission **10** interspace, interstice
La Curée author: Emile Zola
lacy: 4 fine, open, thin **5** fancy, gauzy, meshy, sheer **6** dainty, frilly, ornate **7** elegant, netlike, weblike **8** delicate, filagree, filigree, finespun, gossamer, lacelike **9** filigreed, fillagree, patterned **10** diaphanous
Lacy: 6 Dalton
lad: 3 boy, cub, guy, kid, son **4** runt **5** bairn, buddy, child, minor, sprig, swain, youth **6** feller, fellow, junior **7** preteen **8** half-pint, juvenile, young man **9** schoolboy, stripling, youngster
date: 4 lass
in Spanish: 4 niño
Lad, __: 4 a Dog
Lada: 3 car **4** auto **7** Russian **10** automobile
model: 4 Niva **6** Samara
Lad: A Dog author: 7 Terhune
dog: 5 Knave
La Dame __ Camélias: 3 aux
La Danse des Nymphes artist: 5 Corot
Ladd: 4 Alan **5** Diane **6** Cheryl **8** Margaret
Ladd, Alan: 5 actor
film: All the Young Men (1960)
Appointment With Danger (1951)
The Badlanders (1958)
The Blue Dahlia (1946)
Captain Carey, U.S.A. (1950)
The Glass Key (1942)
The McConnell Story (1955)
O.S.S. (1946)
The Proud Rebel (1958)
Salty O'Rourke (1945)
Shane (1953)
This Gun for Hire (1942)
Ladd, Diane: 7 actress
daughter: Laura Dern
film: 28 Days (2000)
All Night Long (1981)
Rambling Rose (1991)
spouse: Bruce Dern
ladder: 3 run **5** scale **10** fire escape
component: 4 heel, rung, step
cousin: 5 stair
danger: 4 fall, slip **5** spill **6** topple
in Italian: 5 scala
use a ~: 4 go up **5** climb, mount, scale **6** ascend **7** clamber
ladder __: 5 track, truck **6** stitch **7** company, polymer
__ ladder: 3 sea **4** fish, jack **5** pilot **6** aerial, Jacob's **7** chicken, scaling
ladder-back: 5 chair
part: 4 slat
Ladder of Years author: Anne Tyler
Ladders to Fire
author: Anaïs Nin
laddie: 3 boy, kid, son **4** male **5** child
lade: 3 tax **4** fill, load, pack **6** burden, fill up, infuse, lumber, pile on **8** overload
la-de-da
see la-di-da
laden: 4 full, rife **5** heavy, taxed **6** filled, jammed, loaded, packed **7** charged, crammed, crowded, fraught, replete, stuffed, teeming **8** brimming, burdened, hampered, weighted **9** oppressed **10** encumbered, loaded down
__-laden: 5 heavy
lader: 9 stevedore
la-di-da: 4 posh **6** snooty, snotty, too-too **7** foppish, genteel, mincing **8** affected, mannered, snobbish **9** conceited, high-toned, unnatural **10** artificial, hoity-toity, show-offish
__ ladies dancing...: 6 eleven
Ladies' Delight, The author: Emile Zola
Ladies in Retirement (1941 film)
cast: Louis Hayward, Evelyn Keyes, Ida Lupino
director: Charles Vidor
ladies' man: 3 cad **4** dude, rake, roué **8** lothario
Ladies' Man, The (1961 film)
cast: Kathleen Freeman, Jerry Lewis, Helen Traubel
director: Jerry Lewis
Ladies Night (1979 song) artist: Kool and the Gang
Ladies of the Canyon: 4 song
name: 5 Annie, Trina **8** Estrella
singer: Joni Mitchell
lading: 4 haul, load **5** cargo, goods **6** burden, charge, weight **7** freight **8** boatload, cartload, shipment **9** truckload, wagonload
place: 4 dock, pier, port, quay **5** berth, jetty, wharf **7** landing
ladino: 5 horse **9** wild horse
ladle: 4 skim **5** scoop, spoon **6** dipper **7** dish out, utensil **8** spoon out
natural ~: 5 gourd
La Doce: 4 city, town
locale: 6 Mexico, Sonora
L.A. Doctors star: 4 Olin
Ladoga: 4 lake
locale: 6 Russia
La Dolce Vita (1960 film)
cast: Anouk Aimée, Anita Ekberg, Marcello Mastroianni
composer: Nino Rota
director: Federico Fellini
La donna è mobile: 4 aria
composer: 5 Verdi
opera: 9 Rigoletto
__ la Douce: 4 Irma
Ladrone: 4 isls. **5** isles **7** islands
__ Lads: 4 Four
lady: 3 gal, her, she **4** lass, wife **5** noble, title, woman **6** female, madame, matron, señora **7** duchess, grown-up, peeress, senhora, signora **8** baroness, countess **10** noblewoman
address for a ~: 4 ma'am **5** madam
alternative: 5 tiger
bow: 6 curtsy

ender: 3 bug 4 bird, fish, like, love, ship 6 beetle, finger
escort: 4 gent
fickle ~: 4 Luck
first ~: 3 Eve
in German: 4 frau
In Italian ~: 5 donna
in Portuguese ~: 4 dona
in Spanish: 3 sra. 4 dama, dona 6 Latina, señora
knight's ~: 4 dame
leading ~: 4 star 7 actress
malicious ~: 5 vixen
mate: 3 sir 4 lord
name meaning ~: 6 Martha
old ~ habitat: 4 shoe
painted ~: 3 bug 6 insect
palindromic ~: 3 Ada, Ava, Eve, Lil, Nan 4 Anna, ma'am 5 madam
starter: 4 fore, land 5 sales
that ~: 3 her, she 5 woman 6 female
title: 5 madam
wear: 4 flat, pump 5 frock, skirt 6 blouse, halter 7 camises, chemise 9 high heels, nightgown
young ~: 4 girl, lass, maid 5 missy 6 damsel, female 8 fraülein 9 stripling
see also woman

lady __: 4 crab, fern, palm 5 apple, tulip 6 chapel
__ lady: 4 pink 5 first, young 6 dragon 7 leading, painted
Lady: 4 dame 5 title 7 duchess 8 baroness, countess 10 grande dame, noblewoman
Lady __: 3 Day 4 Anna, Jane, Love, Luck 6 chapel, Godiva, Killer, Oracle 7 Lazarus, Madonna
Lady __ Dark: 5 in the
Lady __ Day: 4 for a
Lady __ Johnson: 4 Bird
Lady __ Lake, The: 5 in the, of the
Lady __ Memorial Trophy: 4 Byng
Lady __, The: 3 Eve 5 in Red 7 Gambles
Lady __ the Blues: 5 Sings
Lady __ the Tramp: 3 and
Lady __ Tramp, The: 3 is a
__ Lady: 3 Our 4 Dark, Gray, Kind, Moon, Pink, That 5 A Lost, Disco, First, She's a, Sweet 7 Chained, Dancing, Libeled, Phantom, Special, Valiant
__ Lady, A: 4 Lost
Lady and the __: 5 Tramp
Lady author: Thomas Tryon
Lady Baltimore: 4 cake
Lady Be __: 4 Cool, Good
Lady Be Cool (1941 film)
cast: Eleanor Powell, Ann Sothern, Robert Young
director: Norman Z. McLeod
Lady, Be Good!: 7 musical
songwriter: 8 Gershwin
ladybird: 6 beetle, insect
Lady Bird: 7 Johnson
follower: 3 Pat
middle name: 4 Alta
preceder: 6 Jackie 10 Jacqueline
son-in-law: 4 Robb 6 Nugent
spouse: 6 Lyndon
ladybug: 6 beetle, insect
food: 5 aphid
Lady Byng Trophy org.: 3 NHL
Lady Chatterley's Lover author: D.H. Lawrence
__ Lady Down: 4 Gray
Lady Eve, The (1941 film)
cast: Charles Coburn, Henry Fonda, Barbara Stanwyck
director: Preston Sturges
ladyfinger: 4 cake 6 cookie
Lady for a Day (1933 film)
cast: Guy Kibbee, May Robson, Warren William
director: Frank Capra
Lady From Dubuque, The author: Edward Albee
Lady From Shanghai, The (1948 film)
cast: Rita Hayworth, Everett Sloane, Orson Welles
director: Orson Welles
Lady From the Sea, The author: Henrik Ibsen
Lady Gambles, The (1949 film)
cast: Stephen McNally, Robert Preston, Barbara Stanwyck
Lady Godiva (1966 song) artist: Peter and Gordon
Lady Gregory collaborator: 5 Yeats
Ladyhawke (1985 film)
cast: Matthew Broderick, Rutger Hauer, Leo McKern, Michelle Pfeiffer
director: Richard Donner
lady-in-__: 7 waiting
Lady in __, The: 3 Red
Lady in a Cage (1964 film)
cast: Jeff Corey, Olivia de Havilland, Ann Sothern
director: Walter Grauman
Lady Inger of Osteraad author: Henrik Ibsen
Lady in the Dark: 7 musical
author: Moss Hart
songwriter: 5 Weill 8 Gershwin
Lady in the Lake, The author: Raymond Chandler
Lady in White (1988 film)
cast: Len Cariou, Lukas Haas, Alex Rocco
Lady Is a Tramp, The composer: 4 Hart 7 Rodgers
Lady Is Willing, The (1942 film)
cast: Marlene Dietrich, Aline MacMahon, Fred MacMurray
director: Mitchell Leisen
Lady Jane (1985 film)
cast: Helena Bonham Carter, Cary Elwes, John Wood
director: Trevor Nunn
Lady Jane (1966 song) artist: Rolling Stones
Lady Jane Grey author: 4 Rowe
Lady Killer (1933 film)
cast: James Cagney, Mae Clarke, Leslie Fenton
director: Roy Del Ruth
Ladykillers, The (1955 film)
cast: Sir Alec Guinness, Katie Johnson, Herbert Lom, Cecil Parker
Lady L actress: 5 Loren
Lady Lazarus author: Sylvia Plath
Lady Liberty's home: 3 USA 5 US of A 7 New York
ladylike: 4 kind, nice 5 civil 6 formal, gentle, polite, proper 7 correct, elegant, genteel, refined, womanly 8 cultured, decorous, feminine, gracious, polished, wellborn, well-bred 9 courteous, dignified, high-class 10 cultivated, well-spoken
ladylove: 2 jo 3 pet 4 baby, dear, girl, jill 5 amour, angel, cooky, cutey, cutie, deary, ducky, flame, honey, jewel, leman, novia, novio, sugar, sweet, woman 6 chérie, cookie, dautie, dearie, female, steady, sweets 7 beloved, darling, dearest, dear one, pigsney, schatzi, squeeze, sweetie, tootsie 8 chou-chou, cutie pie, dowsabel, dulcinea, macushla, mistress, paramour, precious, snookums, sugar pie, sweetums, truelove 9 bonne amie, dreamboat, inamorata, petit chou, valentine 10 girlfriend, heartthrob, honeybunch, mavourneen, sweetheart, sweetie pie, turtledove
Lady Love (1978 song) artist: Lou Rawls
Lady Luck: 4 fate
like ~: 6 fickle
Lady Luck (1946 film)
cast: Barbara Hale, Frank Morgan, Robert Young
director: Edwin L. Marin
Lady Madonna (1968 song) artist: Beatles
Lady Marmalade (song) artist: Christina Aguilera, Patti LaBelle
Lady of __: 5 Spain
Lady of Burlesque (1943 film)
cast: J. Edward Bromberg, Michael O'Shea, Barbara Stanwyck
director: William Wellman
__ Lady of Fatima: 3 Our
__ Lady of Guadalupe: 3 Our
__ Lady of Loreto: 3 Our
__ Lady of Lourdes: 3 Our
Lady of Shalott, The author: Alfred Tennyson
Lady of Spain, I __ you: 5 adore
lady of the __: 5 house
Lady of the Lake: 5 Ellen 6 Vivien
Lady of the Lake, The
author: Walter Scott
character: 3 Dhu
Lady on a Train (1945 film)
cast: Ralph Bellamy, Deanna Durbin, Edward Everett Horton
Lady Oracle author: Margaret Atwood
Lady or the Tiger?, The setting: 5 arena
Lady Remington alternative: 4 Nair, Neet
lady's
slipper: 5 plant 6 flower
that ~: 4 hers
tresses: 5 plant 6 flower
lady's __: 3 man 4 maid
lady's-__: 5 thumb 7 slipper, thistle, tresses
Lady Schick alternative: 4 Nair, Neet
Lady Sings the Blues (1972 film)
cast: Richard Pryor, Diana Ross, Billy Dee Williams
director: Sidney J. Furie
Lady's Not for Burning, The author: Christopher Fry
Lady (song) artist: Commodores, D'Angelo, Kenny Rogers, Little River Band, Styx
lady's-slipper: 5 plant 6 flower
Lady's Yes, The author: Elizabeth Barrett Browning
Lady Takes a Chance, A (1943 film)
cast: Jean Arthur, John Wayne, Charles Winninger
director: William A. Seiter
__ Lady, The: 6 Divine, Lonely
Lady Vanishes, The (1938 film)
cast: Margaret Lockwood, Paul Lukas, Michael Redgrave
director: Alfred Hitchcock
Lady Wants Mink, The (1953 film)
cast: Eve Arden, Ruth Hussey, Dennis O'Keefe
director: William A. Seiter
Lady Willpower (1968 song) artist: Gary Puckett and the Union Gap
Lady Windermere's Fan author: Oscar Wilde
Lae: 4 city, town
locale: 9 New Guinea
Laemmle: 4 Carl
Laertes: 4 Dane 5 Greek
father of ~: 8 Polonius
friend of ~: 6 Hamlet
sister of: 7 Ophelia
son of ~: 8 Odysseus
La Fanciulla __ West: 3 del
La Farge, Oliver: 6 writer
work: As Long as the Grass Shall Grow
The Enemy Gods
Laughing Boy
Raw Material
Lafayette: 3 car 4 auto, city, Nash, town
athletes: 8 Leopards
locale: 6 Easton 7 Indiana 8 Colorado 9 Louisiana 10 California
__ La Fayette: 3 Rue
Lafcadio: 5 Hearn
la femme: 4 elle
La Femme Nikita (1990 film) director: Luc Besson
La Femme Nikita network: 3 USA
Laffer __: 5 curve
Laffit: 6 Pincay
La Fille Perdue writer: 4 Anet
Lafitte: 4 Jean 6 pirate
see also French
Lafleur, Guy
milieu: 3 ice 4 rink 5 arena
org.: 3 NHL
La Follette: 6 Robert
La Fontaine, Henri: 8 Nobelist
model for ~: 4 Esop 5 Aesop
La Fontaine, Jean de: 6 French, writer
La Fortune des Rougons author: Emile Zola
La Forza del Destino
composer: 5 Verdi
role: 5 Carlo, Curra 6 Alvaro 7 Leonora 8 Don Carlo 9 Don Alvaro
setting: 5 Italy, Spain
__ la France!: 4 Vive
L'Africaine role: 4 Inez
lag: 3 ebb 4 drag, fail, flag, idle, inch, laze, limp, loaf, plod, poke, slow, stay, tail, tool, wane 5 amble, dally, delay, mosey, stall, tarry, trail 6 dawdle, falter, hobble, linger, loiter, lounge, put off, retard, slouch, slow up, trudge 7 fall off, saunter, shuffle, slacken 8 decrease, diminish, hang back, interval, lollygag, lose time, relegate, straggle 9 inch along, lose speed, waste time 10 dillydally, lose ground
behind: 4 drag, flag 5 dally, delay, dog it, tarry, trail 6 dawdle, linger, loiter 7 draggle 8 drop back, hang back, straggle 9 poke along 10 fall behind
starter: 3 jet 4 gray, grey
lag __: 4 bolt, line 5 screw 6 behind
__ lag: 3 jet 4 time 7 culture
Lag __: 5 b'Omer
lagan: 7 flotsam
La Gare Saint-Lazare artist: 5 Monet
L'Age d'Or (1930 film) director: Luis Buñuel
lager: 4 beer, brew 5 drink 7 pilsner 8 beverage
cousin: 3 ale
holder: 3 keg 4 cask 6 barrel
Lagerkvist, Pär: 6 writer 7 Swedish 8 Nobelist
work: Barabbas
The Dwarf
Guest of Reality
The Hangman
Pilgrim at Sea
The Sibyl
Lagerlöf, Selma: 6 writer 7 Swedish 8 Nobelist
work: The Further Adventures of Nils
Gosta Berlings Saga
Jerusalem
The Wonderful Adventures of Nils
laggard: 4 lazy, logy, poke, slow 5 idler, slack 6 loafer 7 dawdler, lounger, unready 8 dilatory, lingerer, loiterer, slowpoke 9 latecomer, lazybones, leisurely, lethargic, straggler
laggardly: 5 tardy 9 leisurely, reluctant
lagging: 4 late, lazy, poky, slow

6 behind, draggy, in back, losing 7 gradual, halting, impeded, languid, unready 8 dilatory, drawn-out, hesitant, listless, plodding, slothful, sluggish 9 leisurely, lethargic, prolonged, snaillike, unhurried 10 deliberate, protracted
La Gioconda: 5 opera
composer: 10 Ponchielli
highlight: 4 aria
name: 4 Lisa, Mona
role: 4 Enzo 5 Isepo, Laura, Zuane 6 Alvise 7 Barnaba, La Cieca
setting: 5 Italy 6 Venice
__ la giubba: 5 Vesti
lagniappe: 3 tip 4 gift, perc, perk, plus 5 bonus, extra 6 reward, tipoff 7 douceur 8 gratuity
Lago: 4 Como 5 d'Orta, Garda 8 Maggiore, Titicaca 9 Maracaibo
lagomorph: 4 hare
lagoon: 3 bay 4 gulf, lake, pond, pool 5 bayou, marsh, shoal 8 shallows
site: 4 reef 5 atoll 6 island
Lagoon: 4 isls. 5 isles 7 islands
__ Lagoon, The: 4 Blue
Lagos: 4 city, port, town
locale: 7 Nigeria
Lagos de Moreno: 4 city, town
locale: 6 Mexico 7 Jalisco
La Grâce author: Gabriel Marcel
Lagrange: 6 Joseph
La Grange: 4 city, town
locale: 7 Georgia
La Guaira: 4 port
locale: 9 Venezuela
La Guardia: 8 Fiorello
La Guardia Airport locale: 3 NYC 6 Queens 7 New York
__ la guerre!: 4 C'est
La Guerre Est Finie (1966 film)
cast: Genevieve Bujold, Yves Montand
director: Alain Resnais
laguna: 3 bay 5 inlet
Laguna: 3 car 4 auto, city, town 5 Chevy 6 Indian 7 Amerind, Renault 9 Chevrolet 10 automobile
locale: 10 California
Laguna Beach: 4 city, town
locale: 10 California
Laguna Hills: 4 city, town
locale: 10 California
Laguna Niguel: 4 city, town
locale: 10 California
lah-__: 5 di-dah
La Habra: 4 city, town
locale: 10 California
La Hague: 4 cape
Lahaina locale: 4 Maui 6 Hawaii
lah-di-dah: 4 posh 6 snooty, snotty, tootoo 7 foppish, genteel, mincing 8 affected, mannered, snobbish 9 conceited, high-toned, unnatural 10 artificial, hoity-toity, show-offish
Lahontan: 4 lake
locale: 6 Nevada 10 California
Lahore: 4 city, town
locale: 8 Pakistan
Lahr: 4 Bert, John
Lahr, Bert role: 4 lion
Lahti, Christine: 7 actress
film: The Doctor (1991)
The Fear Inside (1992)
Gross Anatomy (1989)
My First Mister (2001)
Running on Empty (1988)
Whose Life Is It Anyway? (1981)
TV: Chicago Hope
L.A. hustle: 5 dance
laic: 7 secular 8 temporal 9 layperson 10 unordained
not ~: 8 clerical, priestly 9 religious
laics: 5 flock
laid
away: 4 kept 8 reserved, retained, set aside
low: 3 ill 5 unfit 7 invalid 9 unhealthy
off: 4 idle 10 unemployed
starter: 3 way
laid-__: 4 back
__-laid: 4 deep, hard, left 5 plain, right, short, strap, twice, water 6 hawser, shroud
laid-back: 3 lax 4 calm, cool, easy, kind, mild, soft 5 loose, quiet, staid, stoic, type B 6 at ease, casual, gentle, kindly, low-key, mellow, placid, sedate, serene 7 amiable, at peace, clement, equable, languid, natural, offhand, pacific, relaxed, ruthful, sparing, stoical, unmoved 8 amicable, carefree, composed, fireside, flexible, informal, listless, merciful, peaceful, placable, sluggish, tolerant, tranquil 9 assuasive, collected, compliant, easygoing, forgiving, impassive, indulgent, leisurely, lethargic, quiescent, temperate, unexcited, unruffled 10 forbearing, lackluster, nonchalant, permissive, unaffected, unagitated, unbothered, unexacting, untroubled
not ~: 5 type B 10 aggressive
__ laid plans: 4 best
laid-up: 3 ill 4 abed, sick 5 in bed 6 ailing, infirm, sickly, unwell 7 unsound 8 confined, disabled, diseased 9 bedridden 10 indisposed
Laila: 3 Ali 6 Robins
Laine: 4 Cleo 7 Frankie
Laine, Frankie
real name: Frank LaVecchio
song: High Noon (1952)
I Believe (1953)
Jezebel (1951)
Love Is a Golden Ring (1957)
Moonlight Gambler (1956)
Mule Train (1949)
Laing: 2 R.D.
Lainie: 5 Kazan
lair: 3 den, pen 4 cave, hole, nest 5 earth, haunt 6 burrow, kennel, refuge 7 hideout, retreat, sanctum 8 cloister, hideaway 9 sanctuary 10 ivory tower
hawk's ~: 4 aery, eyry, nest 5 aerie, eyrie
Laird: 6 Cregar, Melvin
La Isla Bonita (1987 song) artist: Madonna
laissez-__: 5 aller 6 passer
laissez-faire: 9 free trade 10 neutrality
lait: 4 milk 6 French
__-lait: 4 sac-a
laity: 4 fold 5 flock 6 parish 10 worshipers
not ~: 6 clergy
place: 3 pew 4 nave
Laius
slayer of ~: 7 Oedipus
son of ~: 7 Oedipus
wife of ~: 7 Jocasta
Lajoie: 3 Nap 8 Napoleon
Lajoie, Nap: 6 Indian
La Jolla campus: 4 UCSD
La Joya: 4 city, town
locale: 6 Mexico
__ Lak' a Rose: 6 Mighty
lake: 4 loch, mere, pond, pool, tarn 5 basin, mouth 6 lagoon 8 millpond 9 reservoir
Africa: 4 Chad, Kivu, Tana 5 Assal, Mweru, Ngami, Nyasa, Tsana
Albania: 7 Scutari
Alberta: 6 Louise 9 Athabasca
Australia: 4 Eyre 7 Torrens
Banff: 6 Louise
bed mineral: 5 trona
Bern: 6 Brienz
boat: 5 canoe
Bolivia: 8 Titicaca
Botswana: 5 Ngami
bottom: 6 crater 7 benthos
Boulder Dam: 4 Mead
Buffalo: 4 Erie
California ~: 4 Mono 5 Tahoe 8 Lahontan 9 Salton Sea
Cambodia: 8 Tonle Sap
Cameroon: 4 Chad, Nios, Nyos
Canada: 4 Erie 5 Huron, Rainy 6 Louise, Simcoe 7 Nipigon, Ontario 8 Manitoba, Michigan, Superior, Winnipeg 9 Athabasca, Great Bear 10 Great Slave
Castel Gandolfo: 6 Albano
Chile: 4 Laja
China: 5 Tai Hu 7 Koko Nor 9 Qinghai Hu
Cleveland: 4 Erie
combining form: 4 limn- 5 limni-, limno-
Congo: 4 Kivu 5 Mweru 6 Albert, Mobuto 10 Tanganyika
Cornell: 6 Cayuga
denizen: 4 duck
desert ~: 6 mirage 8 illusion
dweller: 4 fish, swan 5 algae
Egypt: 6 Nasser
ender: 3 bed 4 side 5 front, shore
England: 8 Grasmere 10 Windermere
Estonia: 6 Peipus
Ethiopia: 4 Tana 5 Abaya, Tsana
feeder: 6 inflow
Finland: 4 Nasi 5 Enare, Inari 6 Saimaa
fish: 4 bass 5 trout
Florida: 10 Okeechobee
France: 6 Geneva
Geneva: 5 Leman
Guatemala: 6 Izabal, Yzabal 7 Atitlán
Hoover Dam: 4 Mead
Hungary: 7 Balaton
Iran: 5 Urmia
Ireland: 5 lough, Neagh
Israel: 7 Dead Sea
Italy: 4 Como, Orta 5 Garda 6 Albano, Averno, Lugano 8 Maggiore 9 Trasimeno
Japan: 3 Omi 4 Biwa
Jordan: 7 Dead Sea
Kazakhstan: 8 Balkhash
Kenya: 6 Rudolf 7 Turkana 8 Victoria
Lombardy: 4 Como
Maine: 9 Moosehead
maker: 3 dam
Manitoba: 8 Winnipeg
Michigan border ~: 5 Huron
Minnesota: 5 Rainy 6 Itasca
mountain ~: 4 pool, tarn 9 reservoir
Mozambique: 5 Nyasa 6 Malawi
Netherlands: 9 Zuider Zee 10 Ijsselmeer
Nevada: 4 Mead 5 Tahoe 8 Lahontan
New York: 5 Keuka 6 Cayuga, Oneida, Placid, Seneca 9 Champlain 10 Chautauqua
New Zealand: 5 Taupo
Niger: 4 Chad
Nigeria: 4 Chad
Ontario: 5 Rainy 6 Simcoe 7 Nipigon
Oregon: 6 Crater
Panama: 5 Gatún
Peru: 8 Titicaca
poetic ~: 4 mere
relative: 4 pond
Russia: 5 Onega 6 Ladoga, Peipus
Rwanda ~: 4 Kivu
Saginaw Bay ~: 5 Huron
saltwater ~: 4 Aral
Saskatchewan: 9 Athabasca
Scotland: 4 Ness 6 Lomond 8 Loch Ness 10 Loch Lomond
Scottish: 3 Awe 4 loch, Ness
Siberia: 6 Baikal
swamp ~: 5 kioga
Sweden: 5 Malar
Switzerland: 3 Zug 4 Biel 6 Bienne, Brienz
Switzerland ~: 4 Thun 6 Geneva, Lugano, Zurich 7 Lucerne 8 Maggiore 9 Neuchâtel
Tanzania: 5 Nyasa 6 Malawi 8 Victoria 10 Tanganyika
Toledo: 4 Erie
Turkey: 3 Van
Uganda: 5 Kioga, Kyoga 6 Albert, Mobuto 8 Victoria
Utah: 9 Great Salt
Venezuela: 9 Maracaibo
Vermont: 9 Champlain
Wisconsin: 9 Winnebago
world's deepest ~: 6 Baikal
Yugoslavia: 7 Scutari
Zambia: 5 Mweru 6 Kariba 9 Bangweulu
Zimbabwe: 6 Kariba
lake __: 5 trout 6 breeze, effect, salmon 7 dweller, herring
__ lake: 3 dry 4 salt 5 oxbow 6 bitter, madder
Lake: 4 Greg 5 Ricki 6 Arthur 8 Veronica
Lake __ City, AZ: 6 Havasu
Lake __, MN: 4 Elmo
Lake __ of Innisfree, The: 4 Isle
Lake __ Woods: 5 of the
__ Lake: 4 Loon 6 Crater
Lake Albert
drainer: 4 Nile
today: 6 Mobuto
__, Lake and Palmer: 7 Emerson
Lake Baikal
river from ~: 4 Lena
river to ~: 7 Selenga
Lakeboat (2001 film)
cast: Charles Durning, Peter Falk, Robert Forster, Tony Mamet
director: Joe Mantegna
Lake Chad
river to ~: 5 Chari, Shari
Lake Champlain
river to ~: 7 Ausuble
Lake Charles: 4 city, town
locale: 9 Louisiana
__ Lake City: 4 Salt
Lake Clark: 4 park
locale: 6 Alaska
Lake Elsinore: 4 city, town
locale: 10 California
Lake Erie: 6 battle
city on ~: 6 Toledo 7 Buffalo 8 Sandusky 9 Cleveland
river to ~: 6 Maumee 7 Detroit
Lake Forest: 4 city, town
locale: 8 Illinois 10 California
Lake Geneva
feeder: 5 Rhone
spa town: 5 Evian
Lake Havasu City: 4 town
locale: 7 Arizona
Lakehead University
location: 6 Canada 7 Ontario 10 Thunder Bay
Lake Huron
bay: 7 Saginaw
river to ~: 7 St. Marys
Lake in the Hills: 4 city, town
locale: 8 Illinois
Lake Isle of Innisfree, The author: William Butler Yeats
Lake Jackson: 4 city, town
locale: 5 Texas
Lakeland: 4 city, town
locale: 7 Florida
Lakeland Terrier: 3 dog 5 canid 6 canine
Lake Louise, city near: 5 Banff
Lake Magdalene: 4 city, town

locale: 7 Florida
Lake Malawi: 5 Nyasa
Lake Mead
city near: 5 Vegas 8 Las Vegas
dam: 6 Hoover
Lake Michigan
city: 4 Gary 7 Chicago
river to ~: 5 Grand
Lake Mobuto formerly: 6 Albert
Lake Nasser
dam: 5 Aswan
site: 4 Nile
__ Lake, NM: 3 Ute
Lake Nyasa formerly: 6 Malawi
Lake of Brienz river: 3 Aar 4 Aare
Lake of the __: 5 Woods
Lake Ontario
river to ~: 7 Genesee, Niagara
Lake Oswego: 4 city, town
locale: 6 Oregon
Lake Placid: 3 spa 6 resort
gear: 3 ski 4 skee
locale: 7 New York
Lake Poet concern: 5 metre
Lake Ridge: 4 city, town
locale: 8 Virginia
Laker rival: 3 Net, Sun 4 Buck, Bull, Hawk, Heat, Jazz, King, Spur 5 Knick, Magic, Pacer, Sixer 6 Celtic, Hornet, Nugget, Piston, Raptor, Rocket, Wizard 7 Clipper, Grizzly, Warrior 8 Cavalier, Maverick 10 SuperSonic, Timberwolf
Lakers: 4 five, team
home: 10 Los Angeles
org.: 3 NBA
sport: 10 basketball
Lake Rudolf: 7 Turkana
__ Lakes: 5 Great, Land o', Lower 6 Finger 7 Klamath, Saranac
Lakeshore Limited offerer: 6 Amtrak
lakeside: 5 shore
Lakeside: 4 city, town
locale: 7 Florida 10 California
Lake Stickney: 4 city, town
locale: 10 Washington
Lake Superior
city: 6 Duluth
island: 6 Royale
Lake Tahoe
city near ~: 4 Reno
tribe: 5 Washo
Lake Tanganyika explorer: 5 Speke
Lake Titicaca
city near ~: 5 La Paz
locale: 4 Peru 5 Andes 7 Bolivia
people: 6 Aymara
Lake Turkana: 6 Rudolf
Lake Tuz
city near ~: 6 Angora, Ankara
Lake, Veronica: 7 actress
film: The Blue Dahlia (1946)
The Glass Key (1942)
I Married a Witch (1942)
So Proudly We Hail! (1943)
Sullivan's Travels (1941)
This Gun for Hire (1942)
Lake Victoria
city on ~: 5 Jinja
outlet: 4 Nile
river to ~: 6 Kagera
Lakeville: 4 city, town
locale: 9 Minnesota
Lake Wobegon __: 4 Days
Lakewood: 4 city, town
locale: 4 Ohio 8 Colorado 9 New Jersey 10 California, Washington
Lake Worth: 4 city, town
locale: 7 Florida
Lakhota: 5 Sioux, Teton 10 Crazy Horse
Lakmé: 5 opera
composer: 7 Delibes
highlight: 4 aria
role: 4 Rose 5 Ellen, Hadji 6 Benson, Gérald 7 Mallika 8 Frédéric
10 Nilakantha
setting: 5 India
Lakota: 5 Sioux, Teton, tribe 10 Crazy Horse
__ la la: 3 ooh, tra
__-La-La: 3 Sha
La La La (1969 song) artist: Bobby Sherman
la-la land, in: 5 spacy 6 asleep, spacey
La La Lucille: 7 musical
songwriter: 8 Gershwin
La-La - Means I Love You (1968 song) artist: Delfonics
LaLanne: 4 Jack
place: 3 spa
L.A. Law (NBC drama)
business: 4 case 5 trial
cast: Corbin Bernsen (Arnie Becker)
Susan Dey (Grace Van Owen)
Larry Drake (Benny Stulwicz)
Richard Dysart (Leland McKenzie)
Jill Eikenberry (Ann Kelsey)
Michele Greene (Abby Perkins)
Harry Hamlin (Michael Kuzak)
Alan Rachins (Douglas Brackman)
Susan Ruttan (Roxanne Melman)
Jimmy Smits (Victor Sifuentes)
Michael Tucker (Stuart Markowitz)
Blair Underwood (Jonathan Rollins)
figure: 2 DA 3 att. 4 atty. 8 attorney
__ la Liberté, A: 4 Nous
Lalique: 4 René
Lalla Rookh author: Thomas Moore
lall kin: 4 lisp
lallygag: 4 idle, laze, loaf, loll 6 dawdle, lounge 7 fritter, goof off 8 fool away, kill time 9 do nothing, lie around
Lalo: 7 Edouard 8 Schifrin
Lalo, Édouard
work: Le Roi d'Ys
Symphonie Espagnole
lalophobe fear: 8 speaking
lam: 2 go 3 fly, run 4 bolt, flee 5 split 6 beat it, bug out, escape, flight 7 getaway, make off 9 scramming, skedaddle 10 hightail it, take flight
one on the ~: 5 fleer 7 escapee
on the ~: 4 free 5 loose 7 at large, escaped, fleeing
lama: 4 guru, monk 5 bonze 6 cleric, priest 9 religious
land: 5 Tibet 6 Thibet, Xizang 7 Sitsang
melody: 5 chant 6 mantra 7 mantram
reincarnate ~: 5 Tulku
...lama __ priest: 4 he's a
__ Lama: 5 Dalai, Grand, Tashi 7 Bainqen, Panchen
__ Lama Ding Dong: 4 Rama
__ la Mancha: 5 Man of
Lamarck: 4 Jean
La Mare au diable author: George Sand
Lamarr, Hedy: 7 actress
film: Algiers (1938)
Come Live With Me (1941)
Crossroads (1942)
H.M. Pulham, Esq. (1941)
My Favorite Spy (1951)
Samson and Delilah (1949)
Tortilla Flat (1942)
La Marseillaise: 6 anthem
Lamartine, Alphonse de: 4 poet 6 French
Lamas: 6 Carlos 7 Lorenzo 8 Fernando
Lamas, Carlos: 8 Nobelist
lamasery: 6 temple 8 cloister 9 monastery
Lamas, Fernando
spouse: Arlene Dahl, Esther Williams
La Matanza: 4 city, town
locale: 9 Argentina
__ lama..., The: 4 one-l
lamb: 3 fur 4 dupe, meat, rack 5 chump, patsy, sheep 6 animal, sucker 7 darling, fall guy 8 easy mark, innocent, pushover, yearling 9 greenhorn 10 honeybunch
bear a ~: 4 yean
cry: 3 baa, maa 5 bleat
dish: 4 chop, gyro, stew 5 cabob, gigot, kabab, kabob, kebab, kebob 6 cutlet, hot pot
like a ~: 5 ovine 6 lanose, woolly
name meaning ~: 6 Rachel
parent: 3 dam, eve, ram
pet ~: 6 cosset
place: 4 cote
seasoning: 4 mint
__ lamb: 3 ewe 5 leg of 6 spring 7 paschal, Persian
Lamb: 6 Willis 7 Charles 8 Caroline
Lamb __: 5 of God
lambada: 3 fad 4 step 5 dance
lambaste: 3 hit, pan 4 beat, flay, flog, lash, lick, pelt, slam, slap, trim, whip, zing 5 abuse, blast, cream, knock, pound, punch, roast, scold, slash, smear, smite, whack 6 assail, attack, batter, berate, cudgel, defeat, hammer, pummel, punish, rebuke, scathe, scorch, strike, thrash, thwack, wallop 7 blister, censure, clobber, lay into, overrun, rip into, scourge, shellac, smother, trounce, upbraid 8 bludgeon, denounce, lash into, shellack 9 castigate, criticize, dish it out, excoriate, lash out at, light into, reprimand 10 vituperate
Lamb, Charles: 4 Elia 6 writer 7 English 8 essayist
genre: 5 essay
work: A Chapter on Ears
A Dissertation on Roast Pig
Dream Children
Mrs. Battle's Opinions of Whist
The Superannuated Man
Tales from Shakespeare
Lamb Chop: 6 puppet
voice: 5 Lewis, Shari
lambda: 5 Greek 6 letter
follower: 2 mu 4 mu nu
preceder: 5 kappa
Lambeau: 5 Curly
lambency: 4 glow 5 light 6 luster 10 luminosity
lambent: 3 lit 5 agile, aglow, light, lucid, nitid, shiny 6 ablaze, bright, flashy 7 beaming, blazing, dancing, fulgent, glowing, playing, radiant, shining 8 dazzling, gleaming, luminous, lustrous 9 brilliant, sparkling 10 flickering
Lambert: 4 Jack 8 Constant
Lambert Field locale: 3 St. L. 7 St. Louis
Lambeth __: 4 walk 6 degree, Palace
Lambeth walk: 5 dance
lamblike: 4 meek, mild, naif, tame 5 naive 6 broken, docile, gentle, pliant, wnwary 7 artless, pacific, passive, subdued, trained 8 dovelike, innocent, obedient, trusting 9 childlike, compliant, guileless, peaceable, tractable, unworldly 10 manageable, submissive
Lamborghini: 3 car 4 auto 7 Italian 10 automobile
model: 5 Jalpa 6 Diablo 8 Countach 10 Murcielago
lambrusco: 3 red 4 wine
origin: 5 Italy
lamb's
in two shakes of a ~ tail: 3 now 4 anon, soon 6 at once, in a sec, pronto 7 hastily, quickly, rapidly, shortly 8 directly, promptly, right now, speedily 9 forthwith, in a minute, in a second, right away 10 this moment
two shakes of a ~ tail: 4 jiff 5 jiffy, trice 6 moment
lamb's __: 4 ears, tail, wool 6 tongue 7 lettuce
...lamb was __ go: 6 sure to
Lamb, Willis: 8 Nobelist 9 physicist
lame: 4 game, halt, poor, sore, thin, weak 5 stiff 6 faulty, feeble, flimsy 7 bruised, limping 8 hobbling, pathetic 9 faltering, indispose, sidelined 10 improbable, inadequate, pathetical, unsuitable
duck: 5 goner
ender: 5 brain
name meaning ~: 6 Claude 7 Claudia
lame __: 4 duck
lamé: 6 fabric 8 material
lamebrain: 3 ass, nit, oaf, sap 4 boob, clod, dodo, dolt, dope, fool, simp 5 chump, clown, cluck, dufus, dummy, dunce, joker, moron, ninny, patsy 6 dimwit, doofus, lubber, lummox, nitwit, sucker, turkey 7 buffoon, dingbat, dullard, fathead, half-wit, jackass, lunatic, pinhead, saphead 8 bonehead, dumbbell, meathead, numskull 9 blockhead, numbskull, simpleton 10 dunderhead
lamebrained: 4 daft, dumb 5 batty, crazy, daffy, dippy, dizzy, dopey, goofy, inane, kooky, nutty, sappy, silly, vapid, wacky 6 absurd, insane, jejune, screwy, stupid, unwise 7 asinine, fatuous, foolish, idiotic, insipid, puerile, witless 8 mindless 9 airheaded, brainless, half-baked, laughable, ludicrous, pointless, senseless 10 boneheaded, ridiculous
Lamech
father of ~: 5 Enoch 10 Methuselah
son of ~: 4 Noah 5 Jabal, Jubal
lamed: 6 Hebrew, letter 7 injured
predecessor: 4 kaph
successor: 3 mem
lame-duck
held a ~ session: 5 remet, resat
lamellar: 5 scaly
lament: 3 cry, rue, sob 4 alas, bawl, howl, hurt, keen, moan, mope, rain, sigh, sing, wail, weep, yell 5 bleed, brood, dirge, elegy, grief, groan, mourn, tears 6 bemoan, bewail, grieve, plaint, regret, repent, repine, sorrow 7 cry over, deplore, keening, moaning, requiem, sobbing, wailing, weep for, weeping 8 grieving, jeremiad, mourning, threnody 9 complaint, ululation 10 take it hard
poem of ~: 5 dirge, elegy 6 monody 8 threnody
with: 4 pity 7 ache for, feel for, weep for 8 bleed for 9 grieve for 10 sympathize
lamentable: 3 bad, low, sad 4 dire, grim, mean, poor 5 awful, dirty, lousy, woful 6 meager, rotten, rueful, tragic, woeful 7 doleful, hurting, piteous, pitiful, tearful 8 dolorous, God-awful, grievous, mournful, pathetic, stinking, tragical, wretched 9 miserable, plaintive, regretful, sorrowful, upsetting 10 afflictive, calamitous, deplorable, lugubrious, melancholy, pathetical
situation: 6 bummer
lamentation: 3 rue, sob, woe 4 keen, moan, sigh, wail 5 dirge, elegy, grief, tears 6 lament, plaint, regret, sorrow 7 keening, moaning, requiem, sobbing, wailing, weeping 8 grieving, jeremiad, mourning, threnody 9 complaint, ululation
Lamentations
follower: 7 Ezekiel
preceder: 8 Jeremiah

lamenting: 6 sorrow 7 tearful 9 plaintive, querulous, sniveling
la mer, land in: 3 île
La Mesa: 4 city, town
locale: 10 California
Lamia author: John Keats
lamina: 3 ply 4 coat 5 layer, plate, scale, sheet 6 folium, veneer 7 overlay, stratum 8 membrane
laminate: 4 coat, face, foil 5 flake, layer, plate, split 6 veneer 7 foliate, overlay 8 separate, stratify 9 exfoliate, overlayer
laminated: 5 flaky 6 flakey 7 layered
lamination: 4 coat 5 layer 7 coating, lacquer
La Mira: 4 city, town
locale: 6 Mexico 9 Michoacán
La Mirada: 4 city, town
locale: 10 California
lammergeier: 4 bird
Lammermoor, Lucia di, like: 3 mad
__ la mode: 4 pie à
Lamont: 6 Dozier 7 Johnson 8 Cranston
portrayer: 4 Alec
LaMotta, Jake: 5 boxer
milieu: 4 ring
Lamour, Dorothy: 7 actress
costar: 4 Hope 6 Crosby
film: The Big Broadcast of 1938 (1938)
Caught in the Draft (1941)
Dixie (1943)
The Fleet's In (1942)
The Greatest Show on Earth (1952)
The Hurricane (1937)
Johnny Apollo (1940)
The Jungle Princess (1936)
The Last Train From Madrid (1937)
A Medal for Benny (1945)
My Favorite Brunette (1947)
Pajama Party (1964)
Road to Bali (1952)
The Road to Hong Kong (1962)
Road to Morocco (1942)
Road to Rio (1947)
Road to Singapore (1940)
Road to Utopia (1945)
Road to Zanzibar (1941)
Spawn of the North (1938)
St. Louis Blues (1939)
L'Amour, Louis: 6 author 8 novelist
genre: 7 western
lamp: 5 light 6 beacon 7 lantern
dweller: 4 djin 5 djinn, genie 6 spirit
ender: 4 post 5 black, light, shade, shell 7 lighter, working
fuel: 3 oil 8 kerosene
gas: 4 neon 5 argon
old-style: 4 glim
part: 4 base, blub, harp 5 shade 6 finial
part of an oil ~: 4 wick
starter: 4 head
lamp __: 3 oil 5 shell 7 trimmer
__ lamp: 3 arc, oil, sun 4 Davy, glow, grow, heat, neon, pole, tail, time 5 Betty, blast, fairy, flash, flood, floor, Morse, pilot, table 6 Argand, bridge, quartz, safety, sodium, spirit 7 exciter, halogen, student, Tiffany
...lamp __ my feet: 4 unto
__ Lamp: 4 Lava
lampblack: 4 soot 6 carbon
lamper __: 3 eel
lampoon: 4 jape, mock, rail, skit, twit 5 put on, roast, sneer, spoof, squib 6 debunk, parody, satire, send up 7 burlesk, laugh at, mockery, pasquil, takeoff 8 pastiche, ridicule, satirize, takedown, travesty 9 burlesque, invective, make fun of 10 caricature, pasquinade
lampoonery: 6 satire 7 burlesk, sarcasm 9 burlesque 10 vaudeville
lamppost-sign abbr.: 2 rd., st. 3 ave. 4 blvd.
lamprey: 3 eel 4 fish
kin: 6 conger
lurer: 5 eeler
trap: 6 eelpot
LAN
part: 4 area 5 local 7 network
unit: 2 PC
Lana: 4 Lang, Wood 6 Turner 8 Cantrell
lanai: 5 porch 6 piazza 7 veranda 8 verandah
Lanai: 3 isl. 4 isle 6 island
locale: 6 Hawaii
neighbor: 4 Maui
lanate: 5 fuzzy, wooly 6 fleecy, lanose, woolly
La Navarraise character: 5 Anita
Lancashire: 5 chair 6 county
city: 7 Burnley
locale: 7 England
Lancaster: 4 Burt, city, town 5 House
foe: 4 York
locale: 4 Ohio 5 Texas 10 California
symbol: 4 rose 7 red rose
Lancaster, Burt: 5 actor
film: Airport (1970)
All My Sons (1948)
Atlantic City (1981)
Birdman of Alcatraz (1962)
Brute Force (1947)
The Cassandra Crossing (1977)
Cattle Annie and Little Britches (1980)
A Child Is Waiting (1963)
Come Back, Little Sheba (1952)
Crimson Pirate (1952)
Criss Cross (1949)
The Devil's Disciple (1959)
Elmer Gantry (1960, AA)
Field of Dreams (1989)
The Flame and the Arrow (1950)
From Here to Eternity (1953)
Go Tell the Spartans (1978)
Gunfight at the O.K. Corral (1957)
The Gypsy Moths (1969)
The Island of Dr. Moreau (1977)
Jim Thorpe - All-American (1951)
Judgment at Nuremberg (1961)
The Killers (1946)
Lawman (1971)
The Leopard (1963)
Local Hero (1983)
Mister 880 (1950)
The Rainmaker (1956)
Rocket Gibraltar (1988)
Rope of Sand (1949)
The Rose Tattoo (1955)
Run Silent, Run Deep (1958)
Separate Tables (1958)
Seven Days in May (1964)
Sorry, Wrong Number (1948)
Sweet Smell of Success (1957)
The Swimmer (1968)
Tough Guys (1986)
The Train (1965)
Trapeze (1956)
Ulzana's Raid (1972)
The Unforgiven (1960)
Vera Cruz (1954)
The Young Savages (1961)
Zulu Dawn (1979)
role: 5 Elmer, Moses 6 Gantry, Stroud, Thorpe
Lancaster County group: 5 Amish
lance: 4 open, slit, stab 5 spear, spike 6 empale, impale, incise, launch, pierce 7 cut open, harpoon, javelin, missile 8 lacerate 9 penetrate
carrying a ~: 5 atilt
combining form: 5 lonch- 6 loncho-
use a ~: 4 tilt 5 joust
__ lance: 3 air 4 bomb, free, sand 6 oxygen
__-lance: 3 air 5 fer-de
Lance: 3 Ito 4 Bird 5 Major 6 Kerwin 7 Alworth, Parrish 9 Henriksen
Lancelot: 3 Sir 4 hero 6 knight
colleague: 3 Kay
lover of ~: 6 Elaine
nephew: 4 Bors
Lancelot du __: 3 Lac
lancepod: 5 shrub
lancer: 4 ulan 5 uhlan 8 horseman 10 cavalryman, equestrian
__ lancer: 6 Bengal
Lancer: 3 car 4 auto 5 Dodge 10 automobile, Mitsubishi
Lancer Spy (1937 film)
cast: Dolores Del Rio, Peter Lorre, George Sanders
director: Gregory Ratoff
lancet: 5 blade, knife 7 scalpel
lancet __: 4 arch 5 clock 6 window
Lanchester, Elsa: 7 actress
film: The Beachcomber (1938)
Bride of Frankenstein (1935)
Easy Come, Easy Go (1967)
Murder by Death (1976)
Pajama Party (1964)
The Private Life of Henry VIII (1933)
Rembrandt (1936)
Witness for the Prosecution (1957)
spouse: Charles Laughton
lancinate: 4 stab 5 spear 6 impale, pierce
Lancome: 6 makeup
alternative: 4 Avon 5 Almay 6 Revlon 7 Mary Kay 8 Clinique 9 Cover Girl, Max Factor 10 Maybelline 11 Estée Lauder, Merle Norman
Lancs: 6 county
locale: 7 England
land: 3 bag, get, sod, win 4 area, dirt, dock, farm, gain, grab, have, home, hook, loam, plot, soil, trap 5 acres, beach, berth, earth, field, fly in, grasp, light, manor, perch, pilot, put in, ranch, reach, realm, shore, snare, state, steer, tract 6 alight, arrive, come in, debark, estate, extent, ground, hop off, lumber, nation, obtain, old sod, parcel, quarry, realty, reel in, region, secure, settle, wind up 7 acquire, acreage, bring in, capture, country, expanse, get down, grounds, holding, kingdom, procure, purlieu, put down, set down, sit down, stretch, terrain, tillage 8 come down, dismount, district, freehold, get there, go ashore, homeland, mainland, make land, property, province, take down 9 bring down, continent, disembark, farmstead, lay hold of, territory, touch down 10 come ashore, drop anchor, real estate, splash down, terra firma
dot of ~: 3 ait, cay, key 4 isle 5 atoll, islet 6 island
ender: 4 fall, fill, form, lady, line, lord, mark, mass, side, slip, ward 5 owner, scape, slide, wards 6 holder, locked, lubber
expanse of ~: 4 land, lots
high ~: 4 mesa 5 butte, ridge 7 plateau 8 mountain
holding: 4 park 5 manor, ranch 6 domain, estate 7 acreage 8 property 9 farmstead 10 plantation
in French: 5 terre
in Italian: 5 terra
in Latin: 5 terra
in Spanish: 6 tierra
in the ~ of Nod: 3 out 6 asleep, dozing 7 napping 8 sleeping, snoozing 9 somnolent 10 slumbering
low ~: 3 bog, fen 5 swale, swamp
measure: 3 are 4 acre 7 hectare
narrow ~: 4 isth., spit 7 isthmus
native ~: 3 sod 4 home 5 roots
never-never ~: 6 heaven 8 paradise 9 Shangri-la
no man's ~: 3 DMZ
not on ~: 4 asea 5 at sea
of milk and honey: 7 Arcadia, Erehwon 8 paradise 9 Shangri-la
on: 5 reach
on ~: 6 ashore
piece of ~: 3 lot 4 acre, plot 5 field, patch, tract 6 parcel, spread
public ~: 4 park
rich, as ~: 6 arable 7 fertile 8 farmable, tillable 10 cultivable
starter: 3 Ice, low, wet 4 crop, farm, flat, gang, head, high, home, main, Mary, moor, park, pine, Port, Saar, Scot, Thai, tide, wood 5 cloud, coast, Dixie, dream, fairy, Grace, grass, heart, march, marsh, range, Rhine, scrub, south, swamp, Swazi, table, waste 6 border, bottom, father, forest, hinter, meadow, mother, screen, timber, wonder 7 fantasy, pasture 8 vacation
take by force, as ~: 5 annex
work the ~: 3 hoe 4 farm, plow 9 cultivate
land __: 3 art 4 bank, crab, lane, lead, legs, mass, mile, rail, rain, wind 5 agent, grant, of Nod, power, snail, yacht 6 breeze, bridge, freeze, office, patent, reform 7 measure, plaster
land-__: 4 poor 7 grabber
land-__ business: 6 office
land-__ college: 5 grant
__ land: 4 la-la 5 black, crown, glebe, lotus 6 bottom, no man's
__-land: 4 soft 5 belly, crash
Land __: 4 of Oz 5 Dayak 6 O'Lakes
Land __!: 5 sakes
Land __ Midnight Sun: 5 of the
Land __ Rising Sun: 5 of the
__ Land: 3 Cop 4 Byrd, Holy, Love, Pure 5 Candy, Dixie 6 Adélie, Arnhem, Baffin, Graham, Palmer, Wilkes 7 Enderby
landau: 4 auto 8 carriage
Landau: 3 Lev 6 Martin
Landau, Lev: 8 Nobelist 9 physicist
Landau, Martin: 5 actor
film: City Hall (1996)
Ed Wood (1994, AA)
North by Northwest (1959)
Tucker: The Man and His Dream (1988)
spouse: Barbara Bain
TV: Mission: Impossible, Space 1999
Landcruiser: 3 SUV 6 Toyota
landed: 3 lit 4 alit, rich 6 ashore
Land, Edwin: 8 inventor
company: 8 Polaroid
Landers: 3 Ann, Lew 4 Judy 6 Audrey
Landers, Ann: 4 twin 9 columnist
sister: 4 Abby 7 Abigail 8 Van Buren
landfill: 4 dump 5 depot 8 junk pile, junkyard
fodder: 4 junk 5 trash, waste 6 debris, litter, refuse, rubble, scraps 7 garbage 8 oddments 9 sweepings
Landi: 6 Elissa
landing: 4 dock, pier, port, quay, slip 5 floor, jetty, stage, wharf 6 harbor, runway 7 harbour, mooring 8 airfield, airstrip, platform 9 anchorage, touchdown 10 embankment, splashdown
place: 4 dock, pier, quay 5 field, levee, perch, stair, strip 7 airport 8 stairway
landing __: 3 net, tee 4 card, flap, gear, ship 5 clerk, craft, field, force, party, stage, strip 6 strake
__ landing: 4 hard, soft 5 belly, crash, lunar 7 pancake

__ Landing: 5 Knots
Landing on the Sun, A author: Michael Frayn
Landis: 4 John 6 Carole
Landis, Carole: 7 actress
film: I Wake Up Screaming (1941)
Secret Command (1944)
Thieves' Holiday (1946)
Topper Returns (1941)
Landis, John: 8 director
film: An American Werewolf in London (1981)
The Blues Brothers (1980)
Blues Brothers 2000 (1998)
Coming to America (1988)
Innocent Blood (1992)
Into the Night (1985)
The Kentucky Fried Movie (1977)
National Lampoon's Animal House (1978)
Spies Like Us (1985)
Three Amigos! (1986)
Trading Places (1983)
__ Land is Your Land: 4 This
landlady: 5 owner 6 lessor, porter 9 caretaker, concierge, custodian
ländler: 5 dance 8 Austrian
landlord: 3 saw 5 owner 6 leaser, lessor, squire 8 hotelier 9 innkeeper 10 free-holder, proprietor
concern: 4 rent 5 lease 6 tenant
notice: 5 to let 6 no pets, vacant
Landlord of New York: 5 Astor
Landlord, The (1970 film)
cast: Pearl Bailey, Beau Bridges, Diana Sands
director: Hal Ashby
landlubber's place: 6 ashore
landmark: 4 bend, hill, mark, sign, tree 5 blaze, event, guide, ruins, stage, stone, trace 6 crisis, marker, museum 7 feature, remnant, vestige, waypost 8 fragment, memorial, milepost, monument, mountain, souvenir, specimen, survival 9 benchmark, milestone, watershed 10 promontory
Lando: 3 Joe 10 Calrissian
Land o' __!: 6 Goshen
Land o' __: 5 Lakes
land of __: 3 Nod
land of __ and honey: 4 milk
Land of __: 6 Beulah 7 Promise
Land of 1000 Dances (1966 song) artist: Wilson Pickett
Land of Confusion (1986 song) artist: Genesis
Land of Darkness, The author: Emile Zola
Land of Mist, The author: Arthur Conan Doyle
land of Nod, in the: 4 abed 6 asleep
Land of Smiles, The composer: 5 Lehár
Land of the __ Sun: 6 Rising 8 Midnight
land of the free: 3 USA
Land of the Giants dog: 7 Chipper
Land of Unlikeness author: Robert Lowell
Land O'Lakes: 4 city, town 6 butter
locale: 7 Florida
Landon: 3 Alf 7 Michael
__ Landon Kassebaum: 5 Nancy
Landon, Michael
TV: Bonanza, Highway to Heaven, Little House on the Prairie
land on one's __: 4 feet
Landor's Cottage author: Edgar Allan Poe
Landover: 4 city, town
locale: 8 Maryland
landowner: 4 heir 5 owner 6 squire 7 heiress 9 bourgeois 10 capitalist
landowners: 6 gentry 8 nobility
Landowska, Wanda: 6 Polish 14 harpsichordist
Landrace: 3 pig 5 swine
landrail: 4 bird
Landry: 3 Ali, Tom
Landry, Tom: 5 coach
sport: 8 football
Land's __: 3 End
Land sakes!: 4 egad
landscape: 3 art 4 view 5 mural, scene, vista 6 ground, nature, sketch 7 outlook, picture, scenery, terrain 8 painting, panorama, prospect 10 photograph, topography
dip: 4 dale, glen 6 dingle, valley
do a ~: 5 paint
Landscape author: Harold Pinter
landscaping
plant: 4 bush, rose 5 hedge, hosta, shrub
tool: 10 edger. mower
land's end: 6 border
Land's End: 4 cape
locale: 7 England 8 Cornwall
landslide: 3 win 4 rout 5 sweep 6 defeat 7 killing, triumph 8 conquest 9 advantage, avalanche, earthfall, grand slam, overthrow 10 clean sweep
result: 5 scree 6 debris 8 detritus
Landsteiner, Karl: 8 Nobelist
__ Land, The: 5 Waste 6 Secret
Landus: 4 pope 7 pontiff
lane: 3 way 4 path, road, walk 5 aisle, byway, track 6 airway, by-path, byroad, street 7 bikeway, footway, ingress, passage, pathway, walkway 8 air route, bike path, by-street, foot-path, side road 10 passageway, side street
add a ~ to: 5 widen 7 broaden
button: 5 reset
conversion: 5 spare
for carpoolers: 3 HOV
in the fast ~: 3 lax 4 wild 5 loose 6 rakish, wanton 7 immoral 8 depraved, swinging, uncurbed 9 ambitious, debauched, dissolute 10 lascivious, profligate
marker: 4 cone
slow ~: 5 right
__ lane: 3 air, HOV, sea 4 fast, land 6 lovers', memory 7 diamond, express, passing
Lane: 4 Abbe, Dick, Lois, Lola, Mark 5 Allen, Diane, Smith 6 Burton, Nathan 7 Charles, Christy 8 Kirkland, Rosemary 9 Priscilla
coworker: 4 Kent 5 Olsen
Lane, Abbe spouse: Xavier Cugat
Lane, Diane: 7 actress
film: The Big Town (1987)
The Cotton Club (1984)
The Glass House (2001)
Hardball (2001)
Indian Summer (1993)
Jack (1996)
A Little Romance (1979)
Murder at 1600 (1997)
My Dog Skip (2000)
The Perfect Storm (2000)
Rumble Fish (1983)
Streets of Fire (1984)
Unfaithful (2002)
A Walk on the Moon (1999)
__-lane highway: 4 four
Lane, Nathan: 5 actor
film: The birdcage (1995)
Frankie and Johnny (1991)
Life With Mikey (1993)
Mouse Hunt (1997)
film (voice): Stuart Little (1999)
Lane, Priscilla: 7 actress
film: Arsenic and Old Lace (1944)
Daughters Courageous (1939)
Four Daughters (1938)
The Meanest Man in the World (1943)
The Roaring Twenties (1939)
Saboteur (1942)
Varsity Show (1937)
__ Lane Theatre: 5 Drury
Lanfield, Sidney: 8 director
film: The Hound of the Baskervilles (1939)
The Last Gentleman (1934)
The Lemon Drop Kid (1951)
Let's Face It (1943)
The Meanest Man in the World (1943)
My Favorite Blonde (1942)
One in a Million (1936)
Sing, Baby, Sing (1936)
Station West (1948)
Wake Up and Live (1937)
Where There's Life ... (1947)
You'll Never Get Rich (1941)
Lanford: 6 Wilson
lang: 2 k.d.
lang.: 3 Eng., Ger., Grk., Heb., Lat., Swe. 4 Hebr., Ital., Port., Russ., Span. *see also* language
Lang: 4 Lana 5 Fritz 6 Andrew, Walter
Lang, Clubber portrayer: 3 Mr. T
Langdon: 5 Harry 6 Sue Ane
Lange: 3 Jim, Ted 4 Hope 7 Jessica 8 Dorothea 9 Christian
Lange, Christian: 8 Nobelist
Lange, Hope: 7 actress
film: The Best of Everything (1959)
Death Wish (1974)
Peyton Place (1957)
Pocketful of Miracles (1961)
Wild in the Country (1961)
TV: The Ghost and Mrs. Muir
Lange, Jessica: 7 actress
film: All That Jazz (1979)
Blue Sky (1994, AA)
Cape Fear (1991)
Country (1984)
Cousin Bette (1998)
Crimes of the Heart (1986)
Everybody's All-American (1988)
Frances (1982)
King Kong (1976)
Losing Isaiah (1995)
Men Don't Leave (1990)
Music Box (1989)
Rob Roy (1995)
Sweet Dreams (1985)
Titus (1999)
Tootsie (1982, AA)
Langella, Frank: 5 actor
film: Cutthroat Island (1995)
Dave (1993)
Diary of a Mad Housewife (1970)
I'm Losing You (1999)
Junior (1994)
Lolita (1997)
Those Lips, Those Eyes (1980)
The Twelve Chairs (1970)
Langenkamp: 7 Heather
Langer: 2 A.J. 3 Jim 7 Susanne 8 Bernhard
Langer, Bernhard: 6 golfer
milieu: 5 links 6 course
org.: 3 PGA
Lang, Fritz: 8 director
film: The Big Heat (1953)
The Blue Gardenia (1953)
Clash by Night (1952)
Die Nibelungen (1924)
Fury (1936)
The House by the River (1950)
M (1931)
Man Hunt (1941)
Metropolis (1926)
Ministry of Fear (1944)
Rancho Notorious (1952)
The Return of Frank James (1940)
Scarlet Street (1945)
Western Union (1941)
While the City Sleeps (1956)
The Woman in the Window (1944)
You Only Live Once (1937)
l'anglaise, à: 6 boiled
Langland, William: 4 poet
Langley: 3 AFB 4 city, peak, town 5 mount 8 mountain
locale: 6 Canada 10 California
org.: 3 CIA
school: 3 TWU
Langmuir, Irving: 7 chemist 8 Nobelist
langoustine: 5 prawn
Langshan: 4 fowl 7 chicken
relative: 6 Bantam, Brahma, Houdan, Sussex 7 Cornish, Dorking, Leghorn 8 Araucana, Shanghai 9 Dominique, Orpington, Wyandotte
Langston: 6 Hughes
__ Lang Syne: 4 Auld
Langtry: 6 Lillie
language: 3 ADA, APL, Ebo, Ewe, Fon, Fox, Gbe, Ibo, Kwa, Lao, Oto, Sac, SQL, Tai, Twi, Ute, Yao 4 Ainu, Alef, cant, Cree, Crow, Eboe, Erse, Hopi, html, Icon, Igbo, Java, Lapp, LISP, Logo, Luba, Manx, Orca, Otoe, Pali, Perl, Sama, Sauk, Shan, Taal, talk, Thai, Tshi, Tupi, Urdu, word, Xosa, Yuma, Zulu, Zuni 5 Algol, argot, Aztec, Bantu, Basic, Caddo, Carib, Cecil, COBOL, Czech, Dayak, Dutch, Dylan, Greek, Haida, Hindi, Hmong, idiom, Iraki, Iraqi, Khmer, Kiowa, Koine, Latin, lingo, Maidu, Malay, Maori, Masai, Mayan, Norse, Osage, Oscan, Piute, prose, Punic, SISAL, slang, Sotho, sound, style, Swazi, Tamil, Turki, Ugric, Uigur, Usbeg, Usbek, Uzbeg, Uzbek, voice, Welsh, Wolof, Xhosa, Yakut, Yaqui, Yurok 6 accent, Afghan, Arabic, Arawak, Aymara, Baltic, Basque, Berber, brogue, Celtic, Coptic, Creole, Dakota, Danish, Delphi, Eiffel, Erlang, French, Gaelic, German, Hebrew, Ibibio, jargon, Jivaro, Kechua, Kikuyu, Korean, Maasai, Manchu, Mbundu, Mixtec, Mohawk, Navaho, Navajo, Nepali, Oberon, Ojibwa, Oneida, Othman, Paiute, Papago, Pascal, Pashto, patois, Pawnee, Pequot, Polish, Prolog, Pushto, Pushtu, Quapaw, Romani, Romany, Sather, Scheme, Seneca, signal, Siouan, Slavic, Slovak, Snobol, Somali, speech, Tajiki, Telegu, Telugu, tongue, Tuscan, Uighur 7 Afghani, Aramaic, Arapaho, Ashanti, Bengali, Bisayan, Chinese, Chinook, dialect, diction, English, Finnish, Flemish, Fortran, Italian, Kechuan, Kirghiz, Kirundi, Kurdish, Latvian, lexicon, Malinke, Mohegan, Mohican, Montauk, Nahuatl, Ndebele, Ojibway, Ottoman, palaver, Persian, Punjabi, Quechua, Quichua, Rommany, Russian, Semitic, Serbian, Shawnee, Shilluk, Siamese, Slovene, Spanish, Swahili, Swedish, Tagalog, Tibetan, Tlingit, Turkish, Umbrian, Visayan, wording, Wyandot, Yiddish 8 Accadian, Akkadian, Albanian, Arapahoe, Armenian, Balinese, Cherokee, Cheyenne, Chippewa, Comanche, Croatian, Egyptian, Estonian, Etrurian, Etruscan, Filipino, Frankish, Hellenic, Japanese, Javanese, Kickapoo, locution, Mandarin, Nez Perce, Onondaga, parlance, Parthian, Phrygian, Quechuan, Romanian, Rumanian, Sanscrit, Sanskrit, Scythian, Slavonic, Thibetan, Thracian 9 Afrikaans, Bhutanese, Blackfoot, Bulgarian,

Castilian, discourse, Esperanto, gibberish, Hungarian, Icelandic, Mongolian, Norwegian, Provençal, Roumanian, Sasquatch, Slovenian, Suquamish, Ukrainian, utterance, Winnebago, Wyandotte **10** Algonquian, dictionary, expression, Hindustani, Macedonian, Phoenician, Polynesian, Portuguese, Singhalese, Tarahumara, vernacular, Vietnamese, vocabulary
Afghanistan: **6** Pashto, Pushto, Pushtu
Africa: **7** Swahili
Alaska Indian: **5** Haida **7** Tlingit
Amazon: **4** Tupi
ancient ~: **3** Lat. **5** Assyr., Latin, Norse, Oscan, Punic **7** Aramaic **8** Assyrian, Etruscan, Frankish, Parthian, Phrygian, Thracian
Andes: **6** Kechua **7** Kechuan, Quechua, Quichua **8** Quechuan
Angola: **6** Mbundu
Antilles: **5** Carib
artificial ~: **9** Esperanto
Assyria: **8** Accadian, Akkadian
Austria: **6** German
Babylonia: **8** Accadian, Akkadian
Bangladesh: **7** Bengali
Benin: **3** Fon, Gbe
Bolivia: **6** Aymara
Borneo: **5** Dayak
Brazil: **10** Portuguese
Burundi: **7** Kirundi
Cambodia: **5** Khmer
Canada Indian: **4** Cree **5** Haida **6** Ojibwa **7** Ojibway, Tlingit **8** Chippewa
Central America: **7** Nahuatl
Chile: **6** Aymara
China: **4** Shan **5** Hmong, Uigur **6** Manchu, Uighur **7** Chinese **8** Mandarin **9** Cantonese
coarse ~: **5** abuse
Colorado Indian: **3** Ute **4** Yuma
combining form: **4** -glot **5** glott- **6** glotto-
Connecticut Indian: **6** Pequot **7** Mohegan, Mohican
Djibouti: **6** Somali
Eastern Europe: **5** Turki, Usbeg, Usbek, Uzbeg, Uzbek **6** Slavic **7** Russian, Yiddish **8** Slavonic
Ecuador: **6** Jivaro
Egypt: **6** Coptic
Estonia: **6** Baltic
Ethiopia: **6** Somali
Finland: **4** Lapp
Gambia: **7** Malinke
Ghana: **3** Ewe, Gbe, Twi **4** Tshi **7** Ashanti
Great Basin Indian: **5** Piute **6** Paiute
Great Lakes Indian: **6** Ojibwa **7** Ojibway **8** Chippewa
Great Plains Indian: **3** Oto **4** Crow, Otoe **5** Caddo, Kiowa, Osage **6** Dakota, Pawnee, Quapaw, Siouan **7** Arapaho **8** Arapahoe, Cheyenne, Comanche, Kickapoo **9** Blackfoot
Guyana: **6** Arawak
Gypsy: **6** Romani, Romany **7** Rommany
Hungary: **5** Ugric
Inca: **6** Kechua **7** Kechuan, Quechua, Quichua **8** Quechuan
India: **4** Pali, Urdu **5** Hindi, Tamil **6** Telegu, Telugu **8** Sanscrit, Sanskrit **10** Hindustani
Iran: **6** Tajiki **7** Persian
Iraq: **6** Arabic
Ireland: **4** Erse **6** Celtic, Gaelic
Isle of Man: **4** Manx
Israel: **3** Heb. **4** Hebr. **6** Hebrew
Italy: **6** Tuscan **7** Umbrian
Japan: **4** Ainu
Kenya: **5** Masai **6** Kikuyu, Maasai
Laos: **3** Lao **5** Hmong
Louisiana: **6** Creole
Mexico: **5** Aztec, Mayan, Yaqui **6** Mixtec, Papago **7** Nahuatl, Spanish **10** Tarahumara
Middle East: **6** Arabic **7** Aramaic, Kurdish, Semitic
Netherlands: **5** Dutch
New York Indian: **6** Mohawk, Oneida, Seneca **7** Montauk **8** Onondaga **10** Algonquian
New Zealand: **5** Maori
Nigeria: **3** Ebo, Gbe, Ibo **4** Eboe, Igbo **6** Ibibio
North Africa: **6** Berber
Northwest Indian: **5** Yurok **7** Chinook **8** Nez Perce **9** Sasquatch, Suquamish
Pakistan: **4** Urdu
Peru: **6** Aymara, Jivaro **7** Spanish
Philippines: **4** Sama **7** Bisayan, Tagalog, Visayan **8** Filipino
Sarawak: **5** Dayak
Scotland: **4** Erse **6** Celtic, Gaelic
Senegal: **5** Wolof **7** Malinke
Siberia: **5** Yakut
sign ~: **3** ASL
South Africa: **4** Taal, Xosa, Zulu **5** Sotho, Swazi, Xhosa **7** Ndebele **9** Afrikaans
South America: **7** Spanish **10** Portuguese
Southeast Asia: **3** Tai, Yao **5** Malay
Southwest Indian: **4** Hopi, Zuni **5** Yaqui **6** Navaho, Navajo, Papago
Spain: **6** Basque **9** Castilian
Sri Lanka: **5** Tamil **10** Singhalese
Sudan: **7** Shilluk
suffix: **3** -ese
Suriname: **6** Arawak
Switzerland: **6** French, German **7** Italian
Tanzania: **5** Masai **6** Maasai
Thailand: **3** Lao **5** Hmong
Togo: **3** Ewe, Gbe
unit: **3** syl. **8** syllable
Vietnam: **5** Hmong
Wales: **5** Welsh **6** Celtic
Wisconsin Indian: **3** Fox, Sac **4** Sauk **9** Winnebago
written ~: **5** prose
Zaire: **4** Luba
Zimbabwe: **7** Ndebele

language __: **3** lab **4** arts
__ language: **4** body, sign, tone **5** trade, union **6** modern, mother, object, second, source, syntax, target **7** aureate, machine, natural
__-Language: **4** Sein
Language of Clothes, The author: Alison Lurie
__ languages: **7** Romance
languid: **3** wan **4** blah, dopy, dull, easy, lazy, limp, logy, poky, slow, weak **5** dopey, faint, heavy, inert, moony, tardy, tepid, weary, wimpy **6** draggy, drowsy, feeble, infirm, leaden, otiose, pining, sickly, snoozy, supine, torpid **7** gradual, halting, impeded, lagging, nebbish, warmish, wimpish **8** comatose, crawling, creeping, dawdling, dilatory, dragging, drawn-out, drooping, fatigued, hesitant, inactive, indolent, laid-back, listless, plodding, slothful, sluggish, toddling **9** apathetic, enervated, impassive, leisurely, lethargic, prolonged, snaillike, unhurried **10** deliberate, energyless, languorous, phlegmatic, protracted, spiritless
languidly: **6** lazily, slowly **8** bit by bit **9** leisurely **10** indolently, listlessly
languidness: **5** sloth **6** apathy, phlegm, stupor, torpor **7** boredom, inertia, languor **8** doldrums, dullness, hebetude, laziness, lethargy, slowness **9** inanition, indolence, lassitude, unconcern **10** drowsiness, inactivity, sleepiness, stagnation
languish: **3** ail, ebb, rot, sag **4** fade, fail, flag, long, moon, mope, pine, sigh, wilt **5** brood, droop, faint, sleep, waste, yearn **6** desire, go soft, grieve, hanker, hunger, repine, sicken, snivel, sorrow, suffer, tucker, weaken, wither **7** conk out, decline, despond, dwindle, fatigue **8** get tired, knock out, listless, stagnate, vegetate **9** fizzle out, lie fallow, waste away **10** go to pieces
languishing: **4** limp, mopy, slow, weak **5** faint **6** ebbing, fading, feeble, pining, waning **7** failing, languid, longing, wistful **8** dejected, drawn-out, drooping, flagging, listless, lovelorn **9** declining **10** despairing, despondent, melancholy
languor: **5** ennui, sloth **6** acedia, stupor, torpor **7** fatigue, inertia, latency, laxness, slumber, vacuity **8** hebetude, idleness, inaction, laziness, lethargy, loginess, otiosity, weakness **9** faineance, inanition, indolence, inertness, lassitude, tiredness, torpidity, weariness **10** inactivity, stagnation
languorous: **4** lazy **6** torpid **7** languid **8** listless, sluggish **9** enervated, lethargic
langur: **6** mammal, monkey **7** primate
relative: **3** ape **4** saki, titi **5** chimp, drill, jocko, lemur, loris, magot, orang, potto, shrew **6** aye-aye, baboon, Bandar, galago, gelada, gibbon, grivet, guenon, howler, macaco, monkey, rhesus, uakari, vervet **7** colobus, gorilla, guereza, hoolock, macaque, sapajou, siamang, tamarin, tarsier **8** bush baby, capuchin, mandrill, mangabey, marmoset, talapoin **9** orangutan **10** Barbary ape, chimpanzee, orangutang
Lang, Walter: **8** director
film: Call Me Madam (1953)
Can-Can (1960)
Cheaper by the Dozen (1950)
Claudia and David (1946)
Coney Island (1943)
Desk Set (1957)
Hooray for Love (1935)
The King and I (1956)
The Little Princess (1939)
The Magnificent Dope (1942)
The Mighty Barnum (1934)
Moon Over Miami (1941)
Mother Wore Tights (1947)
On the Riviera (1951)
Sitting Pretty (1948)
Song of the Islands (1942)
State Fair (1945)
Tin Pan Alley (1940)
Week-end in Havana (1941)
With a Song in My Heart (1952)
Langway, Rod
milieu: **3** ice **4** rink **5** arena
org.: **3** NHL
Lani: **7** Guinier
Lanier: **3** Bob **6** Sidney, Willie
Lanier, Bob
milieu: **5** court
org.: **3** NBA
sport: **10** basketball
Lanier, Sidney: **4** poet
work: The Marshes of Glynn
The Song of the Chattahoochee
The Symphony
Tiger Lilies
lank: **4** bony, lean, long, slim, tall, thin, wiry **5** boney, eager, gaunt, gawky, rangy, spare, stilt, weedy **6** dainty, gangly, meager, skinny, slight, slinky, svelte, twiggy **7** angular, gawkish, gracile, scraggy, scrawny, slender, spidery, spindly, stringy, willowy **8** angulose, angulous, beanpole, gangling, rawboned **9** beanstalk, emaciated, spindling, sylphlike **10** attenuated, broomstick, extenuated
__ Lanka: **3** Sri
lanky: **4** bony, lean, long, slim, tall, thin, wiry **5** boney, eager, gaunt, rangy, spare, stilt, weedy **6** dainty, gangly, meager, skinny, slight, slinky, svelte, twiggy **7** angular, gracile, scraggy, scrawny, slender, spidery, spindly, stringy, willowy **8** angulose, angulous, beanpole, gangling, rawboned **9** beanstalk, spindling, sylphlike **10** attenuated, broomstick, extenuated
lanner: **4** bird **6** falcon **10** bird of prey
Lanny: **4** Ross **7** Wadkins
lanolin: **3** oil
source: **4** wool **6** fleece
Lanos: **3** car **4** auto **6** Daewoo **10** automobile
lanose: **5** wooly **6** lanate, woolly
Lansbury, Angela: **7** actress
Broadway role: **4** Mame
film: Bedknobs and Broomsticks (1971)
Blue Hawaii (1961)
Court Jester (1956)
Kind Lady (1951)
The Manchurian Candidate (1962)
The Mirror Crack'd (1980)
National Velvet (1944)
The Picture of Dorian Gray (1945)
The Pirates of Penzance (1983)
The Private Affairs of Bel Ami (1947)
Remains to Be Seen (1953)
State of the Union (1948)
The World of Henry Orient (1964)
TV: Murder, She Wrote
Lansford: **6** Carney
Lansing: **3** Joi **4** city, town **6** Sherry
county: **5** Eaton **6** Ingham **7** Clinton
locale: **8** Illinois, Michigan
river: **5** Grand **8** Red Cedar
Lansing, Sherry spouse: William Friedkin
Lansky: **5** Meyer
Lanson, Snooky
show: Your Hit Parade
song: It's Almost Tomorrow (1955)
Lantana: **4** city, town
locale: **7** Florida
Lantana (2001 film)
cast: Barbara Hershey, Anthony LaPaglia, Geoffrey Rush
lantern: **4** lamp **5** light, torch **6** beacon **7** gas lamp
part: **4** wick
lantern __: **3** jaw **4** gear, ring **5** clock, shell, slide, wheel
__ lantern: **4** dark **5** magic, stone **6** battle, friar's **7** Chinese **8** Japanese
__'-lantern: **5** jack-o
Lantern, The author: Don Marquis
lanthanide: **6** cerium, erbium **7** holmium, terbium, thulium **8** europium, lutetium, samarium **9** neodymium, ytterbium **10** dysprosium, gadolinium, promethium
lanthanum: **5** metal **7** element
Lantz: **6** Walter
Lanus: **4** city, town
locale: **9** Argentina
lanyard: **4** line, rope **6** hawser **7** cordage
Lanza, Mario: **5** tenor **6** singer
specialty: **5** opera
Lanzhou: **4** city, town
locale: **5** China

province: 5 Gansu
Lao: 3 She 8 language
neighbor: 3 Tai 4 Thai
Lao-__: 3 tse, tze, tzu
__ Lao: 6 Pathet
Laodice
brother of ~: 5 Paris 6 Hector
parent of ~: 5 Priam 6 Hecuba 7 Priamus
sister of ~: 9 Cassandra
Laon: 4 city, town
locale: 6 France
Laos: 6 nation 7 country
bovine: 7 kouprey
capital: 9 Vientiane
language: 3 Lao 5 Hmong
locale: 4 Asia
money: 2 at 3 att, kip
neighbor: 5 China 7 Myanmar, Vietnam 8 Cambodia, Thailand
people: 4 Miao 5 Hmong
Lao She: 6 writer 7 Chinese
work: Rickshaw Boy
Laotian: 5 Asian
neighbor: 3 Tai 4 Thai
Lao-tzu: 4 sage 6 writer 7 Chinese 11 philosopher
way of ~: 3 Tao 6 Taoism
work: Tao Te Ching
lap: 3 leg, sip 4 fold, lave, lick, loop, purl, slap, turn, wash, wrap 5 bathe, cover, drink, orbit, plash, round, slosh, slurp, stage, swish 6 burble, circle, course, gurgle, ripple, splash, swathe 7 circuit, envelop, overlap, overlie, shingle, swaddle 8 distance, override 9 imbricate
dog: 3 pom 4 peke 6 Yorkie 7 Shih Tzu 9 Pekingese 10 Pomeranian
ender: 3 top 4 wing 5 board 6 streak
form a ~: 3 sit
in the ~ of luxury: 4 posh, rich 5 plush, ritzy, swank 6 swanky 7 upscale 8 affluent, pampered, princely 9 sumptuous, sybaritic
lose a ~: 4 rise 5 arise, get up, stand 7 stand up
of luxury: 5 means, money 6 riches, wealth 7 fortune 8 opulence 9 abundance, affluence 10 gravy train, prosperity
planetary ~: 4 year
starter: 3 dew, ear 4 ship
lap __: 3 dog 4 belt, link, robe 5 child, joint
__ lap: 4 bell, pace 5 Dutch, plain
__ Lap: 4 Phar
LaPaglia: 7 Anthony
__ la Paix: 5 Rue de
La Palma: 4 isle 6 island
locale: 8 Canaries
La Paz: 4 city, town 7 capital
locale: 6 Mexico 7 Bolivia
see also Spanish
LAPD part: 3 Los 4 Dept. 6 Police 7 Angeles 10 Department
lapel: 4 flap 6 revere, revers
attachment: 4 mike 5 ID tag 9 carnation 10 microphone
attach to a ~: 5 pin on
La Petite Fadette author: George Sand
lapidary: 6 etcher 7 jeweler 8 engraver 9 loupe user 10 gemologist
concern: 3 gem
measure: 5 carat
lapidify: 6 harden 7 petrify 9 fossilize
La Piedad: 4 city, town
locale: 6 Mexico 9 Michoacán
lapin: 3 fur 6 rabbit
lapis: 3 gem 5 azure 7 mineral, sky-blue 8 gemstone
__ lapis: 5 Swiss 6 German
lapis lazuli: 3 gem 4 blue 5 azure 7 mineral 8 gemstone
La Placa: 6 Alison
Laplace: 4 city, town 6 Pierre
locale: 9 Louisiana
Laplander: 4 Sami
__ la Plata: 5 Rio de
La Plata: 4 city, port, town
locale: 9 Argentina
La plume __ tante: 4 de ma
lap of __: 6 luxury
La Porte: 4 city, town
locale: 5 Texas 7 Indiana
La Poza: 4 city, town
locale: 6 Mexico 8 Veracruz
Lapp: 4 Sami 5 nomad 8 language
neighbor: 4 Finn
lappet: 6 wattle
lapping: 4 purl 6 murmur
sound: 5 slurp 7 swallow
La Presa: 4 city, town
locale: 10 California
L'Après-midi d'un faune composer: 7 Debussy
La Presse locale: 8 Montreal
lapsang: 3 tea
lapse: 3 die, end, err, gap, sin 4 drop, fall, flub, gaff, goof, lull, pass, sink, slip, trip 5 cease, crime, error, fault, guilt, letup, pause, slide, space 6 boo-boo, breach, bungle, elapse, expire, foible, goof-up, hiatus, lacuna, miscue, recede, return, revert, run out, slip up, weaken 7 blooper, blunder, decline, default, descend, descent, failing, failure, frailty, misstep, mistake, neglect, offense, passage, regress, relapse, screw-up, subside 8 fall back, interval, omission, shortage, trespass, weakness 9 backslide, decadence, indecorum, oversight, recession, terminate, violation, worsening 10 aberration, apostatize, degenerate, devolution, infraction, negligence, nonpayment, recidivate, regression, retrograde
lapsed: 3 ago 4 gone, lost, over, past 6 no more, run out 7 elapsed, expired 9 forgotten 10 terminated
__-lapse photography: 4 time
lapses: 6 errata
lapsus: 4 slip 5 error 7 mistake 9 oversight
lapsus __: 6 calami 7 linguae
Laptev Sea
feeder: 4 Lena
locale: 6 Russia 7 Siberia
laptop: 2 PC 8 computer, notebook
La Puente: 4 city, town
locale: 10 California
lapwing: 4 bird 5 pewit 6 peewit
La Quinta: 4 city, town
locale: 10 California
lar: 6 gibbon 7 primate
Lar: 9 Lubovitch
Lara __: Tomb Raider: 5 Croft
Lara author: Byron
Lara Croft... (2001 film)
cast: Angelina Jolie, Noah Taylor, Jon Voight
director: Simon West
Lara Flynn __: 5 Boyle
Laraine: 3 Day 6 Newman
ex: 3 Leo
Laramie: 4 city, town 5 range
athletes: 7 Cowboys
locale: 3 Wyo. 4 Colo. 7 Wyoming 8 Colorado
__ Laramie: 4 Fort
Lara's Theme composer: 5 Jarre
larboard: 4 left, port
L'Arc en Ciel artist: 4 Erté
larcenist: 5 thief
larcenous: 7 crooked 8 thieving, thievish
larceny: 4 lift 5 crime, heist, pinch, steal, theft, touch 7 robbery 8 burglary, stealing, thievery, thieving 9 pilfering 10 purloining
__ larceny: 5 grand, petit, petty
Larceny, Inc. (1942 film)
cast: Broderick Crawford, Edward G. Robinson, Jane Wyman
director: Lloyd Bacon
larch: 4 tree 7 conifer 8 hardwood, tamarack
cousin: 4 pine
product: 4 cone
lard: 3 oil 6 enrich, grease 7 garnish 9 lubricate 10 shortening
get the ~ out: 5 defat
substitute: 4 oleo
larder: 5 store 6 pantry 8 cupboard
lardhead: 3 oaf 5 looby
Lardner, Ring: 6 author, writer
work: Gullible's Travels
Haircut
June Moon
The Love Nest and Other Stories
You Know Me, Al
lardy: 3 fat 4 oily 5 fatty 6 greasy 7 buttery 8 blubbery 9 fattening
lardy-__: 5 dardy
Laredo: 3 SUV 4 city, Jeep, town 5 Jaime
locale: 5 Texas
__ Laredo, Mexico: 5 Nuevo
__ la Renta: 7 Oscar de
La Repasseuse painter: 5 Degas
lares and __: 7 penates
large: 3 big 4 full, huge, size, tidy, vast, wide 5 ample, broad, bulky, giant, grand, great, gross, hefty, hulky, jumbo, plump, roomy, super 6 chubby, goodly, mighty, portly, robust 7 booming, copious, hulking, immense, liberal, mammoth, massive, sizable, stately, titanic 8 abundant, colossal, enormous, generous, gigantic, handsome, king-size, majestic, outsized, oversize, populous, sizeable, spacious, sweeping, thumping, towering, whapping, whopping 9 capacious, cavernous, corpulent, excessive, expansive, extensive, grandiose, Herculean, humongous, overgrown, overlarge, plentiful, ponderous, prominent, well-known 10 commodious, embonpoint, exorbitant, family-size, gargantuan, majestical, monumental, overweight, prodigious, stupendous, tremendous, voluminous, well-padded
combining form: 3 meg- 4 macr-, magn-, maxi-, mega- 5 macro-, magni-, megal- 6 megalo-
name meaning ~: 5 Grant
large __: 4 cane 5 print 7 calorie
large-__: 4 type 5 print, scale 6 minded
__ large: 4 writ 5 by and 6 living
__ Large Array: 4 Very
large-bellied: 5 obese, plump, pudgy, round, tubby 6 chubby, portly, rotund 7 paunchy 9 corpulent 10 abdominous, overweight, well-padded
large-hearted: 4 good, kind, mild, nice, soft 5 noble 6 benign, decent, genial, gentle, giving, humane, loving, tender 7 clement, lenient, liberal, pitying 8 generous, gracious, merciful
largely: 4 very 5 quite 6 mainly, mostly, widely 7 as a rule, broadly, chiefly, grandly, greatly, overall 8 lavishly 9 copiously, generally, in a big way, liberally, primarily 10 abundantly, far and wide, generously, imposingly, prodigally
largemouth: 4 bass, fish
largeness: 4 area, bulk, mass, room, size 5 range, reach, scope, space, width 6 extent, height, spread, volume 7 bigness, breadth, caliber, expanse 8 capacity, fullness, grandeur, hugeness, infinity, vastness 9 amplitude, immensity, magnitude
Largent, Steve sport: 8 football
larger: 4 more 7 greater
get ~: 4 grow 5 build, swell, widen 6 dilate, expand 7 augment, broaden, develop, fill out, magnify 8 increase
on one side: 4 awry 5 askew 6 canted, uneven 7 crooked, unequal 8 cockeyed, lopsided, top-heavy 9 irregular 10 off-balance, unbalanced
part: 4 mass 8 majority
than: 5 above
than life: 4 epic 5 famed 6 famous, heroic 7 awesome 8 heroical, immortal, imposing, mythical, renowned, towering 9 legendary 10 celebrated, impressive
Larger Than Life (1999 song) artist: Backstreet Boys
large-scale: 4 mass, vast, wide 5 broad, macro 6 cosmic 7 blown-up, diffuse, sizable 8 catholic, cosmical, expanded, extended, far-flung, sizeable, sweeping 9 extensive, wholesale
largesse: 3 aid 4 alms, boon, dole, gift, perc, perk 5 bonus, grant 6 bounty, giving 7 charity, present, stipend, subsidy 8 bestowal, donation, free hand, generous, gratuity 9 emolument, endowment, sweetener 10 altruistic, benevolent, charitable, generosity, lavishness, liberality, thoughtful
largest: 3 max. 4 most 7 maximum
largo: 5 music, tempo 6 slowly
faster than ~: 5 lengo
slower than ~: 5 grave
Largo: 3 key 4 city, town
locale: 7 Florida
__ Largo: 3 Key
lariat: 4 rope 5 lasso, reata, riata 6 tether 10 cow catcher
loop: 5 noose
larine: 8 gull-like
Larissa: 4 moon
planet: 7 Neptune
lark: 3 fun 4 bird, joke, play, whim 5 antic, caper, fling, frisk, prank, revel, spree 6 cavort, frolic, gambol, picnic 7 rollick, warbler 8 songbird 9 adventure, high jinks 10 shenanigan
as a ~: 5 in fun 10 humorously
ender: 4 spur
like a ~: 5 happy
starter: 3 sky, tit 4 wood 6 meadow
Lark: 3 car 4 auto 10 automobile, Studebaker
larking: 6 jovial
larkish: 8 sporting, sportive
larklike bird: 5 pipit
__ Larks and Heroes: 5 Bring
larkspur: 5 plant 6 annual, flower
Lark, The author: Jean Anouilh
l'Arlésienne composer: 5 Bizet
Laroche: 3 Guy
La Rochefoucauld: 8 François
La Ronde author: Arthur Schnitzler
La Rondine composer: 7 Puccini
LaRosa, Julius employer: Arthur Godfrey
Larouche: 6 Lyndon
La Rouchefoucauld, François de: 6 author, French, writer
Larrocha, Alicia de: 7 pianist, Spanish
Larroquette: 4 John
larrup: 3 hit, tan, tar 4 beat, flog, swat, whap, whip 5 pound, spank, whang, whomp 6 attack, thrash
Larry: 4 Bird, Bowa, Doby, Fine, Kert, King, Mize 5 Adler, Brown, Drake, Gates, Groce, Hovis, Niven, Parks,

Verne 6 Blyden, Csonka, Gatlin, Graham, Hagman, Holmes, Peerce, Storch, Walker, Wilcox, Wilson 7 Gelbart, Mathews, Parrish 8 Linville, MacPhail, McMurtry
colleague: 3 Moe 5 Curly, Shemp
Larry __ Melman: 3 Bud
Larry King Live network: 3 CNN
Larry, Moe and Curly: 4 trio 7 Stooges
Larry Sanders Show, The network: 3 HBO
Lars: 6 Hanson 7 Onsager, Porsena 10 Gustafsson
Larsen: 3 Don
Larsen __ Shelf: 3 Ice
Larson: 4 Gary, Jack, John 8 Jonathan 9 Nicolette
Larter: 3 Ali
LaRue: 4 Lash
larus: 4 gull
larva: 3 bug 4 grub, zoea 5 nymph, redia 6 insect, maggot 7 cutworm, tadpole 8 silkworm, wriggler
crustacean ~: 4 zoea
mayfly ~: 5 nymph
successor: 4 pupa 5 imago, pupae
larval: 6 masked 8 immature
laryngitic: 5 husky, raspy, rough 6 hoarse 7 throaty 8 croaking, gravelly
larynx: 8 voice box
affliction: 5 croup
opening: 7 glottis
Lary, Yale sport: 8 football
Las __: 5 Tunas, Vegas 6 Cruces, Palmas
Las __, CO: 6 Animas
Las __ night: 5 Vegas
lasagna: 5 pasta 7 noodles
alternative: 4 orzo, ziti 5 penne 6 noodle 7 lasagne, pastina, ravioli 8 bucatini, couscous, farfalle, linguine, linguini, macaroni, rigatoni 9 agnolotti, angelhair, cavatelli, manicotti, spaghetti 10 cannelloni, fettuccini, tortellini, vermicelli
filling: 4 meat 6 cheese 7 ricotta
land of ~: 5 Italy
LaSalle: 4 Eriq
La Salle: 3 car 4 auto, city, town 10 automobile
locale: 6 Canada, Québec 7 Ontario
La Scala
highlight: 4 aria
home: 5 Milan
production: 5 opera
La Scala di __: 4 Seta
Láscar: 7 volcano
locale: 5 Chile
Lascaux: 4 cave
locale: 6 France
Las Choapas: 4 city, town
locale: 6 Mexico 8 Veracruz
lascivious: 4 blue, lewd 5 bawdy, crude, gross, nasty, randy 6 coarse, ribald, smutty, steamy, vulgar, wanton, X-rated 7 immoral, obscene, raunchy 8 indecent, off-color, unchaste, uncurbed 9 dissolute, libertine, offensive, salacious 10 licentious, profligate
Las Cruces: 4 city, town
athletes: 6 Aggies
locale: 9 New Mexico
school: 4 NMSU
la señorita: 4 ella
laser
cousin: 5 maser
crystal: 4 ruby
gas: 4 neon
output: 3 ray
part: 3 yag
radar: 5 lidar
sound: 3 zap
laser __: 4 beam, disc, disk 7 printer, surgery
Laser: 3 car 4 auto 8 Plymouth 10 automobile
La Serena: 4 city, port, town
locale: 5 Chile
laser printer
alternative: 6 ink-jet
part: 4 drum
resolution: 3 dpi
Las Guacamayas: 4 city, town
locale: 6 Mexico 9 Michoacán
lash: 3 hit, tie, wag 4 beat, bind, flay, flog, hurt, moor, whip 5 abuse, baste, pound, scold, smack, spank, strap, truss, whale 6 attack, batter, berate, buffet, cilium, hammer, pummel, punish, secure, strike, thrash 7 bawl out, belabor, blister, censure, chew out, lambast, scourge, tell off, tie down, upbraid, wear out 8 chastise, lambaste, ridicule, satirize, tear into 9 castigate, fulminate, horsewhip 10 flagellate, tongue-lash, vituperate
down a sail: 4 frap
holder: 3 lid 6 eyelid
out at: 3 hit 5 abuse, blast, chide, knock 6 assail, attack, berate, insult, rail at, rebuff, rebuke, revile, vilify 7 censure, lay into, put down, reprove, rip into, tell off 8 lambaste 9 criticize, light into, reprimand
starter: 3 eye 4 back, whip
lash __: 3 out 4 line, rail
__-lash: 6 tongue
Lash: 5 LaRue
Lasher author: Anne Rice
lashes
give twenty ~: 4 cane, drub, whip 5 flail 6 larrup 7 scourge 10 flagellate
__-lashing: 6 tongue
Lasker: 6 Albert 7 Emanuel
Lasker, Emanuel forte: 5 chess
Lasky: 5 Jesse 6 Victor
Lasorda: 5 Tommy 6 Dodger 7 manager
Las Palmas: 4 city, port, town
locale: 5 Spain
Las Pintas: 4 city, town
locale: 6 Mexico 7 Jalisco
Las Pintitas: 4 city, town
locale: 6 Mexico 7 Jalisco
lass: 3 gal, kid 4 girl, maid, miss, Scot 5 bairn, missy, woman, youth 6 damsel, female, maiden 7 colleen 8 fraülein 9 debutante, young lady, youngster 10 young woman
counterpart: 3 lad
starter: 4 wind
Lasse: 9 Hallström
Lassen: 4 peak 5 mount 7 volcano 8 mountain
locale: 8 Cascades 10 California
Lasser, Louise spouse: Woody Allen
lassie: 3 gal, kid 4 girl, maid, miss, Scot 5 bairn, missy, woman, youth 6 damsel, female, maiden 7 colleen 8 fraülein 9 debutante, young lady, youngster 10 young woman
Lassie: 3 dog 6 canine, collie
Lassie (1994 film)
cast: Thomas Guiry, Helen Slater, Jon Tenney
director: Daniel Petrie
Lassie Come Home (1943 film)
cast: Donald Crisp, Roddy McDowall, May Whitty
director: Fred M. Wilcox
lassitude: 5 ennui 6 apathy, stupor, torpor 7 boredom, fatigue, languor, laxness, malaise 8 doldrums, dullness, idleness, inaction, laziness, lethargy, weakness 9 disregard, tiredness, weariness 10 exhaustion, feebleness, inactivity, sleepiness
lasso: 4 rope, trap 5 catch, reata, riata 6 lariat, rope in
loop: 5 noose
wielder: 5 roper
last: 3 end, run 4 go on, hold, live, stay, wear 5 abide, exist, final, finis, go far, least, omega, stick 6 behind, ending, endure, finale, finish, hang on, hold up, latest, linger, lowest, newest, remain, utmost 7 closing, extreme, finally, meanest, parting, persist, subsist, supreme, survive, to sum up, weather 8 after all, at the end, continue, crowning, curtains, eventual, farthest, furthest, hindmost, in the end, previous, rearmost, remotest, swan song, terminal, trailing, ultimate 9 aftermost, antipodal, bitter end, climactic, finishing, in the rear, outermost, uttermost 10 brave it out, completion, concluding, conclusive, definitive, lattermost, most recent, stay around, stick it out, ultimately
of a series: 5 omega
last __: 4 name, post, word 5 laugh, licks, straw 6 hurrah, minute, resort 7 quarter
last __ not least: 3 but
last-__: 4 born 5 ditch
Last __: 4 Date, Days, Kiss, Song 5 Dance, Night 6 Gospel, Summer, Supper, Things 7 Embrace
Last __ Hero: 6 Action
Last __ in Paris: 5 Tango
Last __ I Saw Paris, The: 4 Time
Last __ Man, The: 5 Angry
Last __ Mohicans, The: 5 of the
Last __ of Pompeii, The: 4 Days
Last __ Plainsmen, The: 5 of the
Last __ Red Hot Lovers: 5 of the
Last __ Saw Paris, The: 5 Time I
Last __ Show, The: 7 Picture
Last __, The: 3 Bus, Pad 4 Leaf, Mile, Time 5 Panda, Party, Trail, Wagon, Waltz 6 Detail, Flight, Hurrah, Outlaw, Sunset, Tycoon, Voyage 7 Command, Emperor, Outpost, Puritan
Last __ to Brooklyn: 4 Exit
Last __ to Clarksville: 5 Train
__ Last: 6 Safety
Last Action Hero (1993 film)
cast: F. Murray Abraham, Art Carney, Arnold Schwarzenegger
director: John McTiernan
Last Act Is a Solo, The author: Robert Anderson
Last American Hero, The (1973 film)
cast: Jeff Bridges, Geraldine Fitzgerald, Valerie Perrine
cat: 8 Whiskers
Last Angry Man, The (1959 film)
cast: Paul Muni, Betsy Palmer, David Wayne
director: Daniel Mann
Last Boy Scout, The (1991 film)
cast: Chelsea Field, Damon Wayans, Noble Willingham, Bruce Willis
director: Tony Scott
Last Bus, The author: Athol Fugard
last but not __: 5 least
Last Carousel, The author: Nelson Algren
Last Chance Gulch site: 6 Helena
Last Chance to Turn Around (1965 song) artist: Gene Pitney
Last Command, The (1928 film)
cast: Evelyn Brent, Emil Jannings, William Powell
director: Josef von Sternberg
Last Dance (1978 song) artist: Donna Summer
Last Date (1960 song) artist: Floyd Cramer
Last Days author: Joyce Carol Oates
Last Days of Disco, The (1998 film)
cast: Mackenzie Astin, Kate Beckinsale, Chloë Sevigny
director: Whit Stillman
Last Days of Pompeii: 4 book, film
author: Edward Bulwer-Lytton
cast: Preston Foster, Basil Rathbone, Dorothy Wilson
character: 4 Ione 5 Burbo, Julia, Nydia 6 Diomed 7 Arbaces, Clodius, Glaucus
Last Detail, The (1973 film)
cast: Jack Nicholson, Randy Quaid
director: Hal Ashby
last-ditch: 4 wild 5 final 6 all-out 7 do-or-die, frantic, gasping 8 frenzied
Last Embrace (1979 film)
cast: John Glover, Janet Margolin, Roy Scheider
director: Jonathan Demme
Last Emperor, The (1987 film)
cast: Joan Chen, John Lone, Peter O'Toole
director: Bernardo Bertolucci
role: 4 P'u Yi
Last Enchantment, The author: Mary Stewart
Last Exit to Brooklyn author: Hubert Selby Jr.
Last Flight, The (1931 film)
cast: Richard Barthelmess, Johnny Mack Brown, Helen Chandler
Last Frontier, The: 6 Alaska
Last Gangster, The (1937 film)
cast: Edward G. Robinson, James Stewart
Last Gentleman, The (1934 film)
cast: George Arliss, Edna May Oliver
director: Sidney Lanfield
Last Good Time, The (1994 film)
cast: Armin Mueller-Stahl, Lionel Stander, Maureen Stapleton
director: Bob Balaban
Last Hurrah, The (1958 film)
cast: Dianne Foster, Jeffrey Hunter, Spencer Tracy
director: John Ford
last-in, __-out: 5 first
lasting: 3 old 6 stable 7 abiding, chronic, durable, endless, eternal, forever, undying 8 constant, enduring, lifelong, long-term, unending, unwaning 9 chronical, continual, deathless, incessant, indelible, long-lived, memorable, perennial, permanent, perpetual, unabating, unceasing 10 continuing, deep-rooted, inerasable, monumental, perdurable, persisting, unchanging
impression: 4 mark, scar 5 brand
starter: 4 ever
__-lasting: 4 long
lastingness: 4 time 6 length 9 longevity
Last Kiss (1999 song) artist: Pearl Jam
last lamenting
Donne's ~ thing: 4 kiss
Last Leaf, The author: O. Henry
lastly: 7 finally 10 ultimately
last-minute: 4 late 5 hasty 6 put off, recent 7 belated, cursory, hurried, offhand, overdue 8 careless, dilatory, slapdash, slipshod 9 haphazard 10 unpunctual
__ last minute: 5 at the
__ Last Night ...: 5 About
Last Night (song) artist: Az Yet, Mar-Keys
Last of His Tribe subject: 4 Ishi
Last of Mrs. Cheyney, The (1937 film)
cast: Joan Crawford, Robert Montgomery, William Powell
Last of Sheila, The (1973 film)
cast: Dyan Cannon, James Coburn, James Mason, Raquel Welch

director: Herbert Ross
Last of the Mohicans, The (1936 film)
cast: Heather Angel, Binnie Barnes, Randolph Scott
director: George B. Seitz
Last of the Mohicans, The (1992 film)
cast: Daniel Day Lewis, Russell Means, Madeleine Stowe
director: Michael Mann
Last of the Mohicans, The author: James Fenimore Cooper
character: 4 Cora **5** Alice, David, Gamut, Magua, Munro, Natty, Uncas **6** Bumppo, Duncan **7** Hawkeye, Heyward **12** Chingachgook
Last of the Plainsmen, The author: Zane Grey
Last of the Red Hot __: 5 Mamas
Last of the Red Hot Lovers: 4 film, play
author: Neil Simon
cast: Alan Arkin, Sally Kellerman, Paula Prentiss, Renee Taylor
director: Gene Saks
Last of the Vikings, The character: 4 Lars
Last of the Wine, The author: Mary Renault
Last one __ rotten egg!: 4 in's a **5** in is a
L.A. Story (1991 film)
cast: Marilu Henner, Steve Martin, Victoria Tennant
Last Outlaw, The (1936 film)
cast: Harry Carey, Hoot Gibson
Last Outpost, The (1935 film)
cast: Cary Grant, Claude Rains
Last Pad, The author: William Inge
Last Picture Show: 4 film **5** novel
author: Larry McMurtry
cast: Timothy Bottoms, Jeff Bridges, Ellen Burstyn, Ben Johnson, Cloris Leachman, Cybill Shepherd
director: Peter Bogdanovich
setting: 5 Texas
last-place finisher: 5 loser
Last Puritan, The author: George Santayana
La Strada (1954 film)
cast: Richard Basehart, Giulietta Masina, Anthony Quinn
director: Federico Fellini
__ last resort: 3 as a
Last Resorts, The author: 5 Amory
Last Seduction, The (1994 film)
cast: Peter Berg, Linda Fiorentino, Bill Pullman, J.T. Walsh
director: John Dahl
Last Seen Wearing author: Hillary Waugh
__ Lasts Forever: 7 Nothing
Last Song (1973 song) artist: Edward Bear
__ Last Stand: 7 Custer's
Last Summer (1969 film)
cast: Bruce Davison, Barbara Hershey, Richard Thomas
director: Frank Perry
Last Sunset, The (1961 film)
cast: Kirk Douglas, Rock Hudson, Dorothy Malone
director: Robert Aldrich
Last Supper, The: 5 mural
artist: 7 da Vinci
city: 5 Milan
cup: 5 Grail
Last Tango in Paris (1973 film)
cast: Marlon Brando, Maria Schneider
director: Bernardo Bertolucci
like: 6 X-rated
Last Temptation of Christ, The (1988 film)
cast: Willem Dafoe, Barbara Hershey, Harvey Keitel
director: Martin Scorsese
__ last theorem: 7 Fermat's
Last Time I Saw Paris, The (1954 film)
cast: Van Johnson, Donna Reed, Elizabeth Taylor
director: Richard Brooks
Last Time I Saw Paris, The composer: 4 Kern **11** Hammerstein
Last Time, The (1965 song) artist: Rolling Stones
Last Trail, The author: Zane Grey
Last Train From Gun Hill (1959 film)
cast: Kirk Douglas, Carolyn Jones, Anthony Quinn
director: John Sturges
Last Train From Madrid, The (1937 film)
cast: Lew Ayres, Dorothy Lamour, Gilbert Roland
director: James Hogan
Last Train to Clarksville (1966 song) artist: Monkees
Last Tycoon: 4 film **5** novel
author: F. Scott Fitzgerald
cast: Tony Curtis, Robert De Niro, Robert Mitchum, Jeanne Moreau
character: 4 Pete **5** Brady, Stahr, Whyte, Wylie **6** Monroe **7** Cecilia
director: Elia Kazan
Last Voyage, The (1960 film)
cast: Dorothy Malone, George Sanders, Robert Stack
director: Andrew Stone
Last Wagon, The (1956 film)
cast: Felicia Farr, Richard Widmark
director: Delmer Daves
Last Wagon Train, The author: Zane Grey
Last Waltz, The (1978 film)
cast: The $ Band, Bob Dylan, Neil Young
director: Martin Scorsese
last-word: 3 hip, mod, new, now **4** chic **5** faddy, smart **6** latest, modish, trendy, with-it **7** current, stylish **8** up-to-date **9** happening
Last Word in Lonesome __, The: 4 is Me
__ la suisse: 5 eggs à
Las Varas: 4 city, town
locale: 6 Mexico **7** Nayarit
Las Vegas: 4 city, town
area: 5 Strip
athletes: 6 Rebels **8** Wolf Pack
casino: 3 MGM **5** Luxor **6** Bally's, Sahara **7** Caesar's, Riviera **8** Harrrah's, MGM Grand **9** Excalibur, Tropicana
county: 5 Clark
devotee: 5 gamer **7** gambler
employee: 6 dealer **7** pit boss **8** croupier
gas: 4 neon
locale: 3 Nev. **6** Nevada
lure: 4 keno, slot **5** poker **6** casino **8** baccarat, roulette
newspaper: 3 Sun
school: 4 UNLV
show: 5 revue **6** review
trade show: 6 Comdex
Las Vegas __: 5 night
__ Las Vegas: 4 Diva, Viva **7** Leaving
Laszlo: 4 Ilsa **6** Victor
Lat.: 4 lang.
see also Latin
Latakia locale: 5 Syria
latch: 3 bar, dam **4** bolt, clog, cork, hasp, hook, lock, plug, seal, shut **5** block, catch, cinch, clamp, close, dam up **6** clog up, fasten, lock up, plug up, seal up, secure, stop up **7** close up, closure, padlock, seal off, shutter **8** blockade, button up, fastener, make fast, obstruct **9** fastening **10** hook and eye
door ~: 4 hasp
draw the ~: 4 open **5** unbar
ender: 3 key **6** string
onto: 4 glom, grab **5** seize **6** absorb **7** acquire, possess, procure, receive
piece: 5 U-bolt
place: 4 door, exit, gate **5** entry **6** portal **7** postern **8** entrance
sound: 4 snap **5** clack, click
starter: 3 pot **6** throat
latch __: 4 hook, onto **6** needle
__ latch: 4 knob **5** night
latchkey __: 5 child
late: 3 new, old **4** once, past, slow **5** fresh, tardy **6** behind, bygone, former, held up, hung up, modern, put off, recent, stayed **7** belated, defunct, delayed, extinct, lagging, onetime, overdue, quondam, tardily **8** advanced, deceased, departed, detained, dilatory, long gone, previous, sometime, untimely **9** erstwhile, nocturnal, not on time, postponed, preceding **10** after hours, behind time, delinquent, last-minute, unpunctual
be ~ for: 4 miss
ender: 5 comer
get ~: 6 darken
make ~: 4 keep **5** delay **6** detain, hang up, hinder, hold up, impede, retard **7** bog down, set back **8** slow down **10** buttonhole
not early or ~: 5 on cue **6** on time
of ~: 3 new **4** anew **5** newly **6** afresh **7** freshly, just now **8** hitherto, latterly, recently, until now **9** these days **10** not long ago
prefix: 3 neo-
state: 6 arrear **7** arrears
too little too ~: 6 paltry **9** deficient, half-baked, shortfall **10** inadequate
late __: 4 show, wood **6** blight, charge **7** bloomer
late-__: 5 night
Late __ Apley, The: 6 George
Late Child, The author: Larry McMurtry
latecomer: 7 dallier, dawdler, laggard, parvenu, upstart **8** newcomer, slowpoke **9** arriviste
lateen: 4 sail
lateen-rigged
craft: 3 dau, dow **4** dhow
Late George Apley, The: 4 film **5** novel
author: J.P. Marquand
cast: Vanessa Brown, Ronald Colman, Peggy Cummins
director: Joseph L. Mankiewicz
Late in the Evening (1980 song) artist: Paul Simon
lately: 3 new **4** anew **5** newly **6** afresh **7** freshly, just now **8** hitherto, latterly, recently **9** these days **10** not long ago
Lately (song) artist: Divine, Jodeci
latency: 5 sleep **6** torpor **7** languor, slumber **8** abeyance, dormancy **10** inactivity, quiescence, suspension
lateness: 4 stay **5** delay **6** holdup **8** deferral **10** suspension
late-news hour: 6 eleven
late-night
hangout: 3 bar, pub **4** dive **5** joint **6** lounge, saloon, tavern **7** barroom, gin mill, taproom **8** alehouse, grogshop, taphouse **9** roadhouse
host: 3 Jay **4** Dave, Leno **9** Letterman
hour: 3 one, two **4** four **5** one a.m., three, two a.m. **6** four a.m. **7** three a.m.
latent: 5 inert **6** covert, hidden, secret, torpid, unripe, unseen, veiled **7** abeyant, dormant, passive **8** implicit, inactive, inherent, possible, sleeping, untapped **9** concealed, intrinsic, invisible, out of view, potential, quiescent, unexposed **10** in abeyance, smoldering, suppressed, underlying, undetected, unreactive, unrealized, unviewable
latent __: 4 heat **5** image **7** content
later: 4 anon, next, then **5** after **6** future, in a bit, in time, mañana, not now, not yet **7** by and by, ensuing, goodbye **8** au revoir, eventual, farewell, in a while **9** after a bit, afterward, following, posterior, proximate **10** afterwards, before long, downstream, sequential, subsequent, succeeding, thereafter
hold for ~: 5 sit on, table
not ~: 3 now **5** ahead, today **6** at once, before **7** earlier **8** directly, previous, right now, right off **9** forthwith, in advance, on the spot, preceding, right away **10** at this time, the present, this minute
not ~ than: 4 till, up to **5** until **7** through
prefix: 4 meta-, post- **5** infra-
see you ~: 3 bye **4** ciao, ta-ta **5** adieu, adios, aloha **6** bye-bye, shalom, so long **7** cheerio, goodbye **8** au revoir, farewell, sayonara, toodle-oo
sooner or ~: 3 yet **4** anon **5** after **6** at last, in a bit, in time **7** by and by, finally, later on, someday **8** in a while, in the end, sometime **9** afterward, hereafter **10** before long, eventually, inevitably
than: 5 after **6** behind
Later!: 3 bye **4** ciao, ta-ta **5** adieu, adios, aloha, see ya **6** bye-bye, bye now, I'm gone, shalom, so long **7** cheerio, goodbye **8** au revoir, farewell, sayonara, toodle-oo
in French: 5 adieu
in Hawaiian: 5 aloha
in Italian: 4 ciao
in Latin: 3 ave **4** vale
in Spanish: 5 adios
lateral: 4 side **7** oblique, sideway **8** crabwise, edgeways, flanking, sidelong, sideward, sideways, sidewise, skirting **10** side-by-side
combining form: 5 pleur- **6** pleuro-
measurement: 4 span **5** girth, width **6** spread **7** breadth **9** broadness
starter: 3 tri, uni **5** multi
lateral __: 3 bud **4** line, pass **5** canal, chain **6** system **7** fissure, moraine
laterally: 6 beside **7** abreast, sideway **8** edgeways, edgewise, sidelong, sideways, sidewise
nautically: 5 abeam
Lateran __: 6 Palace **7** Council
__ later date: 3 at a
Late Show feature: 5 rerun
Late Show, The (1977 film)
cast: Art Carney, Bill Macy, Lily Tomlin
director: Robert Benton
latest: 3 new **4** last, news, rage **5** faddy, final, fresh, vogue **6** gossip, latter, modern, modish, newest, skinny, trendy **7** current, in vogue **8** last word, ultimate, up-to-date **10** dernier cri
full of the ~: 5 newsy
the ~: 4 dope, news, poop, word **5** scoop, today **6** modern **7** current, just out, lowdown, release **8** bulletin, contempo, up-to-date **9** headlines, news flash **10** communiqué
thing: 4 mode, rage **5** trend **7** fashion
__ latest: 5 at the
__ Latest Flame: 3 His
__ late than never: 6 better
Late Walk, A author: Robert Frost
latex: 5 paint **6** rubber
lath: 4 beam, slat **5** board, strip
lather: 4 beat, flap, foam, fuss, head,

snit, soap, stew, suds, wash, whip **5** cream, fever, froth, scrub, spume, state, storm, sweat, tizzy, yeast **6** bustle, clamor, dither, frenzy, hassle, hoopla, hubbub, tumult **7** bubbles, fluster, turmoil, twitter **8** cleanser, perspire, soapsuds **9** agitation, commotion, confusion **10** hullabaloo, turbulence
in a ~: **5** het up, upset **6** pacing **7** worried **9** perturbed **10** distraught, distressed
source: **4** soap **7** shampoo
work into a ~: **5** rouse **6** arouse, foment, incite, stir up **7** agitate, inflame, provoke **9** instigate
lathery: **5** foamy, soapy, sudsy **6** bubbly, frothy **7** foaming **8** unrinsed
lathy: **4** long, tall, thin
__ Latifah: **5** Queen
Latin: **5** Cuban **8** Bolivian, language **9** Argentine, Brazilian, caballero, Dominican
case: **6** dative
dance: **5** conga, mambo, samba, tango **6** cha-cha
forerunner: **5** Oscan
see also Spanish
Latin __: **4** Rite **5** cross **6** Church, school, square **7** America, Quarter
__ Latin: **3** dog, hog, Low, New, Old, pig **4** Late **6** Middle, Vulgar
Latina: **7** Chicana **8** señorita
see also Spanish
Latin America
see South America, Spanish
__ Latin from Manhattan: **5** She's a
Latino: **8** Hispanic
see also Spanish
Latin words
abbr.: **3** etc. **4** et al.
adverb: **3** hoc, quo
art: **3** ars
bear: **4** ursa **5** ursus
behold: **4** ecce
being: **4** esse
bird: **4** avis
birds: **4** aves
bones: **4** ossa
day: **4** diem
earth: **5** terra
eggs: **3** ova
eight: **4** octo
existence: **4** esse
god: **3** deo
goddess: **3** dea
gods: **3** dei
good: **4** bene
greeting: **3** ave
he loves: **4** amat
here: **3** hic
he was: **4** erat
I: **3** ego
I believe: **5** credo
I came: **4** veni
I conquered: **4** vici
I forbid: **4** veto
I love: **3** amo
in other words: **5** id est
in the same place: **4** ibid.
I saw: **4** vidi
it was: **4** erat
journey: **4** iter
kind: **4** alma
king: **3** rex
land: **5** terra
life: **4** esse
love: **4** amor
mass: **5** missa
monarch: **3** rex
moon: **4** luna
mouths: **3** ora
no: **3** non
one: **3** una
others: **4** alia
passage: **4** iter
phrase: **6** et alia, et alii, in esse
possessive: **3** sua
pray: **3** ora
prayer: **5** kyrie
pronoun: **3** sua **4** quis
road: **3** via **4** iter
room: **6** camera
route: **3** via
salutation: **3** ave **4** vale
she loves: **4** amat
so: **3** sic
sun: **3** sol
that is: **5** id est
therefore: **4** ergo
thing: **3** res
this: **3** hic
thus: **3** sic **4** ergo
to be: **4** esse
uncommon: **4** rara
water: **4** aqua
way: **4** iter
wings: **4** alae
without: **4** sine
you love: **4** amas
latissimus __: **5** dorsi
latitude: **3** run **4** play, room, span **5** range, reach, scope, space, sweep, swing, width **6** extent, laxity, leeway, margin, spread **7** breadth, compass, freedom, liberty, license **8** free hand **9** elbowroom, situation **10** indulgence, liberality
segment: **3** arc **6** degree, minute, second
__ latitudes: **5** horse
latitudinarian: **4** easy, fair, just **7** lenient, liberal, neutral **8** amenable, balanced, catholic, straight, tolerant, unbiased **9** equitable, impartial
latitudinous: **5** broad
latke: **7** pancake
La Tosca sculptor: **4** Erté
La Toya: **7** Jackson
sister: **5** Janet
La Traviata: **5** opera
composer: **5** Verdi
role: **5** Flora **6** Annina, Valery **7** Alfredo, Bervoix, Douphol, Gastone, Germont, Giorgio **8** Giuseppe, Violetta
song: **4** aria
La Traviata (1982 film)
cast: Plácido Domingo, Cornell MacNeil, Teresa Stratas
director: Franco Zeffirelli
latrine: **2** WC **3** can, loo **4** john **5** privy **6** lounge, toilet **8** bathroom, lavatory, men's room, outhouse, rest room, toilette **10** ladies' room, powder room
Latrobe: **4** city, town **8** Benjamin
locale: **4** Penn.
Latrobe, Benjamin: **9** architect
lats neighbors: **3** abs
Lattanzi: **4** Matt
latte: **6** coffee **8** espresso
place for a ~: **4** café **6** bistro
latten: **5** alloy **10** sheet metal
component: **4** zinc **6** copper
latter: **5** final **6** latest, modern, recent, second **7** closing **8** eventual, hindmost, rearmost **9** following, posterior **10** concluding
Latter-__ Saint: **3** day
latter-day: **6** modern, recent
latterly: **8** recently
lattermost: **4** last **6** latest **8** ultimate
lattice: **3** net, web **4** grid, mesh **5** frame, grate, grill **6** screen **7** grating, network, tracery, trellis **8** filagree, filigree, fretwork, openwork **9** fillagree, structure
ender: **4** work
piece: **4** lath
__ lattice: **5** space **7** Bravais, crystal
latticework: **4** grid, mesh **5** arbor, frame, grill **6** screen **7** grating, trellis **8** openwork
La Tulipe __: **5** Noire
Latvia: **6** nation **7** country
capital: **4** Riga
legislature: **6** Saeima
money: **3** lat
neighbor: **4** Lith. **6** Russia **7** Belarus, Estonia **9** Lithuania
once: **3** SSR
region: **6** Baltic
river: **5** Dvina
Latvian: **4** Balt, Lett **5** Rigan **8** language
laud: **4** hail, hymn, sing **5** adore, bless, boost, cry up, ensky, exalt, extol, honor **6** admire, extoll, praise, puff up, revere, salute, stroke **7** acclaim, approve, beatify, build up, commend, flatter, glorify, hosanna, lionize, magnify, worship **8** encomium, eulogize, hand it to, venerate **9** celebrate, recommend **10** compliment, panegyrize
laudable: **4** fine, nice, okay **5** great, legit, moral, noble **6** of note, proper, worthy **7** ethical, stellar **8** all right, pleasant, pleasing, splendid, superior, terrific **9** admirable, agreeable, deserving, estimable, excellent, exemplary, praisable, reputable, wonderful **10** acceptable, beneficial, creditable
laudably: **4** ably, to a T, well **6** nicely **7** adeptly, capably **8** expertly, properly, suitably, worthily **9** admirably, fittingly, perfectly **10** skillfully, splendidly, swimmingly, thoroughly
laudanum: **4** drug **7** anodyne **8** narcotic
laudation: **5** honor, kudos **6** eulogy, homage, praise, salute **7** acclaim, plaudit, tribute **8** accolade, encomium, flattery, good word **9** extolment, panegyric **10** compliment, exaltation
laudatory: **7** glowing **9** adulatory, approving, favorable, praiseful **10** eulogistic, flattering
__ laude: **3** cum
Lauder: **5** Estée, Harry **6** makeup
rival: **4** Coty **5** Arden, Arpel **6** Chanel
__ Lauderdale, FL: **4** Fort
Lauderdale Lakes: **4** city, town
locale: **7** Florida
Lauderhill: **4** city, town
locale: **7** Florida
Laudo: **4** peak **5** mount **8** mountain
locale: **5** Andes **9** Argentina
Lauer: **4** Matt
laugh: **3** yak, yok, yuk **4** crow, grin, ha-ha, howl, jest, joke, roar, yock, yuck **5** burst, mirth, scoff, smile, snort, tehee, whoop **6** cackle, giggle, guffaw, hahaha, haw-haw, heehee, scream, shriek, tee-hee, titter **7** break up, chortle, chuckle, crack up, snicker, snigger **8** fracture **9** convulsed, make merry, merriment **10** cachinnate
at: **4** hoot, jeer, mock **5** scoff, scorn, taunt **6** deride **7** lampoon, snicker, snigger **8** belittle, ridicule **9** make fun of
derisive ~: **3** hah, heh **4** he he, hoot **5** fleer, snort **6** cackle
getter: **3** wag, wit **4** card **5** clown, cutup **6** jester **7** buffoon, farceur **8** comedian, humorist, jokester, quipster
get the last ~: **7** triumph
hearty ~: **4** boff, ho ho, howl, roar **6** guffaw
make ~: **5** amuse, cheer **6** divert, regale, tickle **7** delight **9** entertain
off: **6** ignore **7** dismiss, forgive, neglect **8** overlook, ridicule, shrug off, sneeze at **9** disregard
starter: **5** horse
syllable: **3** hee
laugh __: **3** off **4** away, line, riot **5** track
laugh __ court: **5** out of
__ laugh: **4** last **5** belly, horse
laughable: **4** camp, joky, rich, riot **5** campy, comic, droll, funny, inane, jokey, nutty, silly, witty **6** absurd, harhar, jocose, scream, stupid **7** amusing, asinine, bizarre, comical, jocular, joshing, mocking, risible, unusual **8** derisive, derisory, farcical, gelastic, humorous, mirthful **9** diverting, eccentric, facetious, fantastic, hilarious, ludicrous, quizzical **10** ridiculous
Laughable Lyrics author: Edward Lear
Laugh at Me (1965 song) artist: Sonny and Cher
Laugh-In
bit: **4** skit
name: **3** Dan **4** Arte, Judy, Lily, Rick, Ruth **5** Rowan **6** Martin
laughing: **3** gay **5** happy, jolly, merry, riant, sunny **6** cheery, jovial, joyful **7** gleeful, jesting, roaring, smiling, yukking **8** cackling, cheerful, giggling, grooving, jubilant, mirthful **9** chuckling, guffawing, lightsome, tittering **10** flying high, snickering, sniggering
ender: **5** stock
matter: **3** fun, wit **4** gags **5** farce, humor, jests, jokes **6** comedy, gaiety, levity **8** drollery, raillery **10** wisecracks
no ~ matter: **3** bad, big **4** grim, ugly **5** grave, heavy, major, tough **6** urgent **7** serious, weighty **8** grievous, sobering, terrible **9** dangerous, important **10** formidable
laughing __: **3** gas **4** gull **5** hyena **6** matter **7** jackass
__ Laughing: **4** Exit **5** Enter
Laughing (1969 song) artist: Guess Who
Laughing All the Way author: **5** Howar
Laughing Boy author: Oliver La Farge
Laughing Cavalier artist: **4** Hals
laughing jackass: **4** bird **10** kookaburra
Laughing Matter, The author: William Saroyan
laughingstock: **3** ass **4** butt, dupe, fool, goat, joke **5** chump, sport **6** sucker **7** fall guy, mockery, schnook
make a ~ of: **8** ridicule
laugh in one's __: **6** sleeve
Laughlin: **3** AFB, Tom **6** Robert
Laughlin, Robert: **8** Nobelist **9** physicist
laugh out of __: **5** court
laughs: **3** fun **5** mirth **9** amusement, diversion, merriment **10** recreation
just for ~: **5** in fun **7** as a joke, as a lark **8** jokingly **10** humorously
Laugh's __, The: **4** on Me
__ laughs at probabilities: **4** Fate
laughter: **3** fit, fun, has **4** crow, glee, ha-ha, peal, roar, yuck **5** mirth, shout, snort, sound, sport **6** cackle, gaiety, giggle, guffaw, heehaw, shriek, titter **7** chortle, chuckle, crack-up, gesture, howling, snicker, snigger **8** giggling, hilarity **9** amusement, chuckling, jocundity, merriment, rejoicing
burst of ~: **4** gale, peal, roar
evoke: **5** amuse **6** tickle
exclamation: **4** ha-ha **5** te-hee **6** haw-haw, tee-hee
name meaning ~: **5** Isaac, Isaak
__ laughter: **7** Homeric
Laughter in the Rain (1974 song) artist: Neil Sedaka
Laughter on the 23rd Floor author: Neil Simon
Laughton, Charles: **5** actor

film: Advise & Consent (1962)
Arch of Triumph (1948)
The Barretts of Wimpole Street (1934)
The Beachcomber (1938)
The Big Clock (1948)
The Blue Veil (1951)
The Canterville Ghost (1944)
The Hunchback of Notre Dame (1939)
Island of Lost Souls (1933)
It Started With Eve (1941)
Les Miserables (1935)
The Man on the Eiffel Tower (1949)
Mutiny on the Bounty (1935)
The Night of the Hunter (1955)
The Old Dark House (1932)
Payment Deferred (1932)
The Private Life of Henry VIII (1933, AA)
Rembrandt (1936)
Ruggles of Red Gap (1935)
Sidewalks of London (1938)
Spartacus (1960)
The Suspect (1944)
They Knew What They Wanted (1940)
The Tuttles of Tahiti (1942)
Witness for the Prosecution (1957)
Young Bess (1953)
spouse: Elsa Lanchester
laugh up one's __: **6** sleeve
launch: **3** bow **4** boat, cast, fire, hurl, jump, open, toss **5** begin, drive, eject, fling, found, heave, lance, pitch, set up, shoot, sling, start, throw, usher **6** let fly, let rip, propel, send up, tackle **7** barrage, bombard, deliver, kick off, lead off, liftoff, pioneer, preface, project, rollout, send off, usher in **8** catapult, commence, dispatch, get going, initiate, put to sea, set about **9** discharge, enter upon, instigate, institute, introduce, originate, send forth, undertake, water taxi **10** embark upon, inaugurate
area: **3** pad
cancel a ~: **5** abort, scrub
deep-space ~: **5** probe
org.: **4** NASA
launch __: **3** pad **6** window **7** vehicle
__ launcher: **6** rocket **7** grenade
launching: **7** baptism, opening **10** conception
launching __: **3** pad
launder: **4** lave, wash **5** bathe, clean, rinse, scrub **7** cleanse, correct, deterge, rectify **8** legalize **9** disinfect
laundered: **5** clean, snowy **6** washed **8** dirtless, spotless, unsoiled **10** immaculate
launderer: **4** maid **5** valet **6** au pair **7** servant **8** domestic
Launder, Frank: **8** director
film: The Adventuress (1946)
The Belles of St. Trinian's (1953)
The Blue Lagoon (1949)
Blue Murder at St. Trinian's (1957)
The Bridal Path (1959)
Wee Geordie (1956)
laundering: **9** housework
Laundromat
fixture: **5** drier, dryer
like a ~: **6** coin-op
laundry: **4** wash **5** chore **7** washing **8** cleaning **9** housework
collection: **4** lint
cycle: **4** soak, spin **5** rinse
detergent: **3** All, Biz, Era, Fab, Yes **4** Bold, Dash, Gain, Surf, Tide, Wisk **5** Cheer, Dreft, Purex **6** Calgon, Dynamo, Oxydol **7** Octagon **9** Ivory Snow
do a ~ job: **3** dry **4** fold, iron, wash **5** wring
holder: **3** bin **6** basket, hamper
list: **6** agenda
loss, maybe: **4** sock
need: **4** soap **6** bleach **8** softener **9** detergent
problem: **5** grime, stain **6** grease
quantity: **4** load **6** bundle, hamper
worker: **6** ironer
laundry __: **4** list
__ laundry: **5** dirty
Lauper, Cyndi
song: All Through the Night (1984)
Change of Heart (1986)
Girls Just Want to Have Fun (1984)
The Goonies 'R' Good Enough (1985)
I Drove All Night (1989)
She Bop (1984)
Time After Time (1984)
True Colors (1986)
What's Going On (1987)
Laura: **4** Bush, Dern, Nyro, Tate **5** Baugh, Innes, Keene **6** Ashley, Hobson, Linney, Petrie **7** Ingalls, Jackson **8** Branigan, Esquivel, Leighton **10** San Giacomo
to George W.: **4** wife
Laura (1944 film)
cast: Judith Anderson, Dana Andrews, Vincent Price, Gene Tierney, Clifton Webb
director: Otto Preminger
Laura Bush, __ Welch: **3** née
Laura Ingalls __: **6** Wilder
Laura Lee: **4** Hope
Laura Z. __: **6** Hobson
laureate: **4** poet **5** famed, noted **6** famous **7** honored, praised **8** immortal, renowned **9** acclaimed
__ laureate: **4** poet
laurel: **3** bay **4** tree **5** title **6** wreath **7** bay tree **9** evergreen **10** blue ribbon
tree: **3** bay **7** avocado, camphor **8** cinnamon **9** sassafras
wear the ~: **3** win **6** attain **7** achieve, conquer, edge out, succeed, triumph
wreathe with ~: **4** fete, hail, laud **5** award, crown, exalt, grace, honor **6** credit, praise, reward, salute **7** acclaim, adulate, applaud, commend, dignify, ennoble **8** decorate, eulogize **9** recognize **10** compliment
laurel __: **3** oak **6** cherry
__ laurel: **3** bay, big **5** dwarf, great, sheep **6** cherry **7** English
Laurel: **4** city, Stan, town
locale: **8** Maryland
Laurel and Hardy: **3** duo **4** pair, team
Laurel Canyon (2002 film)
cast: Christian Bale, Kate Beckinsale, Frances McDormand, Natascha McElhone
director: Lisa Cholodenko
laurels: **4** fame, gold **5** award, badge, crown, glory, honor, kudos, prize **6** credit, honors, praise, renown, reward, trophy **7** acclaim, victory **8** accolade, gold star, prestige **10** decoration
Lauren: **4** Joey, Wood **5** Holly, Ralph, Tewes, Velez **6** Bacall, Chapin
rival: **4** Dior **5** Beene, Klein **6** Armani **7** Versace **9** St. Laurent
Laurence: **6** Binyon, Harvey, Sterne **7** Housman, Olivier **9** Fishburne **10** Luckinbill
Laurens: **10** van der Post
Laurentians: **5** range **9** mountains
locale: **6** Canada
Laurentides __: **4** Park
__ Laurentiis: **6** Dino De
Laurents: **6** Arthur
Laurey's aunt: **5** Eller
Lauria: **3** Dan
Laurie: **4** Hugh **5** Piper **6** London **7** Metcalf
__ Laurie: **5** Annie
Laurie, Piper: **7** actress
film: Carrie (1976)
Children of a Lesser God (1986)
The Grass Harp (1996)
The Hustler (1961)
Other People's Money (1991)
Lauritz: **8** Melchior
Lauryn: **4** Hill
Lausanne: **4** city, town
canton: **4** Vaud
Lautenberg: **3** Sen. **5** Frank **7** senator
Lauter: **2** Ed
lav
see lavatory
lava: **4** rock **5** magma **6** basalt, ejecta, pumice, scoria **7** mineral **8** obsidian, pahoehoe, rhyolite
from ~: **7** igneous
let out ~: **4** spew, spue **5** erupt
material: **3** ash **4** slag **6** basalt, scoria **8** obsidian
move like ~: **4** flow, ooze **6** spread
Lava: **4** soap
alternative: **3** Lux **4** Dial, Dove, Tone, Zest **5** Camay, Coast, Ivory, Lever **6** Boraxo, Caress, Shield **8** Lifebuoy **9** Palmolive, Safeguard **11** Irish Spring
Lava __: **4** Lamp
lavabo: **5** basin **8** washbowl
lavage: **7** washing
Lavagetto: **6** Cookie
Laval: **4** city, town
locale: **6** Canada, France, Quebec
Lava Lamp: **3** fad
lavalava: **5** pareo, pareu, skirt
lavaliere: **6** locket **7** jewelry
__-la-Vallée: **5** Marne
La Valse composer: **5** Ravel
Laval University
location: **6** Canada, Quebec
lavation: **4** bath, wash **8** ablution **9** cleansing
lavatory: **2** WC **3** can, loo **4** bath, john **5** privy **6** lounge, shower, toilet **7** latrine **8** bathroom, lavatory, men's room, outhouse, restroom, toilette, washroom **10** ladies' room, powder room
sign: **5** in use **8** occupied
lave: **3** lap **4** wash **5** bathe, clean **6** shower, wash up **7** clean up, deterge, launder, scrub up, shampoo
lavender: **5** color, mauve, plant, shrub **6** bluish, flower, purple **7** blueish
family: **4** mint
flower: **4** lily **6** orchid, thrift **8** trillium, wistaria, wisteria **9** candytuft
relative: **4** plum, puce, sage **5** lilac, mauve **6** dahlia, damson, orchid **7** heather, petunia **8** amethyst, burgundy, eggplant, mulberry, rosemary **9** raspberry **10** heliotrope
lavender __: **5** water **6** cotton
__ lavender: **3** sea **5** oil of, spike
Lavender Hill Mob, The (1951 film)
cast: Sir Alec Guinness, Stanley Holloway
director: Charles Crichton
La vendetta: **4** aria
Laveran, Charles: **8** Nobelist
LaVerne: **7** Andrews
sister: **5** Patty **6** Maxene
La Verne: **4** city, town
locale: **10** California
Laverne & Shirley (ABC sitcom)
cast: Phil Foster (Frank De Fazio)
Betty Garrett (Edna Babish)
David L. Lander (Squiggy)
Penny Marshall (Laverne De Fazio)
Michael McKean (Lenny)
Eddie Mekka (Carmine Ragusa)
Cindy Williams (Shirley Feeney)
Laver, Rod: **7** netster **9** tennis pro
contemporary: **4** Ashe
milieu: **5** court
Lavi: **6** Dahlia
La Vida author: Oscar Lewis
__ La Vida Loca: **5** Livin'
__ la vie: **4** c'est
La Vie en Rose singer: **4** Piaf
La Ville Noire author: George Sand
Lavinia author: George Sand
Lavin, Linda
spouse: Ron Leibman
TV: Alice
lavish: **4** free, give, heap, lush, much, posh, pour, rain, rich, wild **5** ample, fancy, flush, grand, haute, plush, ritzy, showy, spend, swank, waste **6** bestow, costly, deluge, expend, flashy, frilly, glitzy, lordly, ornate, pamper, plenty, shower, swanky, wanton **7** copious, fritter, liberal, opulent, profuse, replete, riotous, scatter **8** abundant, effusive, generous, gorgeous, handsome, princely, prodigal, prolific, splendid, squander, wasteful **9** bountiful, decorated, dissipate, elaborate, excessive, expansive, expensive, exuberant, go through, luxuriant, luxurious, plentiful, profusive, sumptuous, unsparing, unstinted, unthrifty **10** first-class, immoderate, impressive, inordinate, munificent, openhanded, ornamented, profligate, run through, thriftless, thrust upon, unstinting
don't ~: **5** skimp
lavishly: **9** in a big way
lavishness: **6** bounty, excess, luxury **7** largess, surplus **8** largesse, richness **10** exuberance
__ la vista: **5** hasta
La vita nuova author: **5** Dante
Lavoisier, Antoine: **7** chemist
Lavoris: **9** mouthwash
alternative: **3** Act **4** Plax **5** Scope **6** Signal **9** Listerine **10** Fluorigard
law: **3** act **4** code, rule, tabu, writ **5** axiom, canon, edict, maxim, order, power, taboo, truth **6** assize, decree, police, ruling **7** command, dictate, formula, mandate, measure, precept, statute, theorem **8** covenant, exigence, exigency, standard **9** authority, criterion, enactment, ordinance, postulate, principle **10** due process, injunction, principium, profession, regulation
according to ~: **5** licit
arm of the ~: **2** PD **6** police **7** marshal, sheriff
breach of ~: **5** crime, wrong **7** misdeed, offense **9** violation **10** misconduct, wrongdoing
break a ~: **3** sin **6** breach, offend **7** disobey, do wrong, infract, violate **8** encroach, infringe **9** disregard **10** transgress
brush with the ~: **4** bust **5** pinch, run-in **6** arrest, collar
by ~: **7** legally
church ~: **5** canon, dogma **7** precept **8** doctrine
combining form: **4** nomo-
deg.: **3** LL.B., LLD, MCL, SJD
ender: **3** man, men, yer **4** suit **5** giver, maker **6** making **7** breaker
enforcement grp.: **3** FOP, PBA
expert: **5** judge **6** legist **9** barrister
first-year ~ student: **4** one L
go to ~: **3** sue, try **6** accuse, appeal, indict, summon **7** arraign, contest,

dispute **8** file suit, litigate **9** fight over, prosecute **10** put on trial
in French: **3** loi
lay down the ~: **4** rule **5** order, scold **6** decree, demand, direct, govern, insist **7** command, control, dictate, mandate **8** bulldoze, domineer, proclaim, regulate
make into ~: **4** pass **5** enact **9** institute, legislate
outside the ~: **4** tabu **5** taboo **6** banned **7** illegal, illicit **8** criminal, improper, unlawful, verboten, wrongful **9** felonious, forbidden **10** prohibited
partner: **5** order
pertaining to ~: **5** jural
starter: **5** scoff
to Mr. Bumble: **3** ass
unwritten ~: **4** lore **5** mores, usage **8** folkways, practice **9** tradition **10** convention
within the ~: **3** due **5** clean, legal, legit, licit, valid **6** kosher, proper **8** judicial, rightful **9** allowable, canonical, statutory **10** admissible, legitimate, prescribed, sanctioned
see also law terms, legal
law __: **5** clerk, court, of war **6** French
law __ jungle: **5** of the
law-__: **4** hand **7** abiding
__ law: **3** dry, gag, gas **4** blue, case, game, Ohm's, poor, Say's **5** Bode's, canon, civil, Gauss, leash, lemon, Malus', Roman, Salic, sound, space **6** Boyle's, Bragg's, common, cosine, Curie's, Engel's, Grimm's, higher, Hooke's, Joule's, public, shield, Snell's, Stokes', sunset **7** Ampère's, blue-sky, Charles', Dalton's, dietary, Ferrel's, Hubble's, martial, medical, Mendel's, natural, Pascal's, private, Raoult's, statute, Verner's
__-law: **5** son-in **6** decree, square
Law: **4** Jude **5** Bonar
__ Law: **4** Corn, Ohm's **6** Burke's, Mosaic **7** Murphy's
law-abiding: **4** good **5** solid **6** honest **7** duteous, dutiful, orderly, upright **8** obedient, straight **9** compliant, righteous **10** upstanding
law and __: **5** order
LaWanda: **4** Page
Law and Disorder (1974 film)
cast: Ernest Borgnine, Carroll O'Connor, Ann Wedgeworth
Law and Jake Wade, The (1958 film)
cast: Patricia Owens, Robert Taylor, Richard Widmark
director: John Sturges
lawbreaker: **4** . perp **5** felon **7** runaway **8** criminal, evildoer, internee, prisoner **9** desperado **10** delinquent
lawbreaking: **5** crime **6** breach, felony **7** misdeed, offense
lure into ~: **4** hook, trap **5** decoy, set up, trick **6** entice, entrap, reel in, suck in **8** inveigle
Lawes: **5** Henry
Lawford: **3** Pat **5** Peter **8** Patricia
Lawford, Peter: **5** actor
film: Buona Sera, Mrs. Campbell (1969)
Easter Parade (1948)
Exodus (1960)
Good News (1947)
It Should Happen to You (1954)
Julia Misbehaves (1948)
The Longest Day (1962)
Ocean's Eleven (1960)
On an Island With You (1948)
Royal Wedding (1951)
spouse: Patricia Kennedy
lawful: **3** due **4** fair, good, just **5** jural, legal, legit, licit, right, ruled, valid **6** judged, kasher, kosher, passed, proper, vested **7** allowed, condign, decreed, enacted, ordered, regular **8** bona fide, bone fide, enforced, enjoined, innocent, judicial, mandated, official, ordained, rightful **9** allowable, by the book, canonical, commanded, juridical, legalized, permitted, protected, statutory, warranted **10** aboveboard, admissible, authorized, legislated, legitimate, on the level, sanctioned
lawfully: **5** right, truly **6** justly **7** validly **10** rightfully, virtuously
lawfulness: **5** order, right **7** justice **8** justness, legality, validity **10** legitimacy
lawgiver: **7** senator **10** legislator
law is __, The: **4** a ass
lawless: **3** bad **4** evil, wild **5** rowdy **6** fierce, savage, unruly **7** chaotic, illicit, radical, riotous, untamed, violent, warlike **8** anarchic, criminal, despotic, mutinous, reckless, recusant, unlawful, wrongful **9** barbarous, heterodox, insurgent, piratical, seditious, turbulent, tyrannous **10** anarchical, despotical, disordered, disorderly, infringing, nihilistic, rebellious, traitorous, ungoverned, unorthodox, unpeaceful
Lawless: **4** Lucy
Lawless Breed, The (1952 film)
cast: Julie Adams, Rock Hudson, Hugh O'Brian
director: Raoul Walsh
lawlessness: **4** riot **5** anomy, chaos, crime **6** anomie, felony, mutiny, piracy, racket, revolt **7** abandon, anarchy, bribery, license, mob rule, roguery **8** disorder, iniquity, nihilism, sedition, uprising, violence
lawmaker: **3** sen. **5** solon **7** senator **8** politico **9** statesman **10** legislator, politician
lawmaking body: **5** legis. **6** senate
lawman: **3** cop **4** Earp **6** deputy **7** sheriff **9** constable, Wyatt Earp **10** Matt Dillon
Lawman (1971 film)
cast: Lee J. Cobb, Robert Duvall, Burt Lancaster, Robert Ryan
director: Michael Winner
lawn: **3** sod **4** park, turf, yard **5** grass, green, sward **6** cotton, fabric, swarth **8** backyard **10** greensward
care brand: **5** Ortho
chemical: **4** lime **10** fertilizer
cover: **3** sod **5** grass **6** fescue, redtop, zoysia **7** festuca
do ~ work: **3** mow, sow **4** seed, weed
ender: **5** mower
equipment: **5** edger, mower
fix a ~: **3** sod **5** resod
game: **5** bocce, bocci, roque **6** boccia, boccie, tennis
item: **6** chaise
like some ~ s: **5** soddy, weedy
mowing the ~: **4** task **5** chore
pest: **4** mole
weed: **6** arnica
work on the ~ again: **5** remow
lawn __: **5** chair, party **6** tennis **7** bowling, sleeves
Lawndale: **4** city, town
locale: **10** California
lawnmower
brand: **4** Toro **5** Deere
feature: **5** blade
path: **5** swath **6** swathe
Lawnmower Man, The (1992 film)
cast: Pierce Brosnan, Jeff Fahey
law of __: **3** war **5** areas, sines **6** motion **7** cosines, nations, thought
law of __ numbers: **5** large
law of diminishing __: **7** returns
law of the __: **4** mean **6** jungle
Law of the Lash star: **5** Larue
__ law of thermodynamics: **5** first, third **6** second, zeroth
__ law of wages: **4** iron **6** brazen
Law & Order (NBC drama)
cast: George Dzundza (Det. Sgt. Max Greevey)
Angie Harmon (Abbie Carmichael)
Steven Hill (Adam Schiff)
Christopher Noth (Det. Mike Logan)
Jerry Orbach (Det. Lennie Briscoe)
Sam Waterston (Jack McCoy)
character: **2** DA
Lawrence: **2** D.H., T.E. **4** city, Joey, pope, town, Welk **5** Block, Carol, Klein, saint, Steve, Tracy, Vicki **6** Ernest, Eusden, Kasdan, Martin, Sharon, Taylor, Thomas **7** Durrell, pontiff, Sanders, Tibbett **8** Florence, Gertrude
athletes: **8** Jayhawks
city on the St. ~: **5** Laval, Sorel
locale: **6** Arabia, Kansas **7** Indiana
Lawrence __-Jacobs: **6** Hilton
Lawrence, Carol spouse: Robert Goulet
__ Lawrence College: **5** Sarah
Lawrence, D.H.: **6** author, writer **7** British
work: Birds, Beasts, and Flowers
Etruscan Places
Kangaroo
Lady Chatterley's Lover
The Lost Girl
Mornings in Mexico
Pansies
The Plumed Serpent
The Rainbow
Reflections on the Death of a Porcupine
Sea and Sardinia
Sons and Lovers
The Trespasser
Twilight in Italy
The White Peacock
Women in Love
Lawrence, Ernest: **8** Nobelist **9** physicist
Lawrence, Gertrude
Broadway role: **4** Anna
film bio: **4** Star
Lawrence of Arabia (1962 film)
cast: Sir Alec Guinness, Jack Hawkins, Arthur Kennedy, Peter O'Toole, Anthony Quayle, Anthony Quinn, Claude Rains, Omar Sharif
composer: **5** Jarre
director: David Lean
locale: **5** Aqaba **6** desert
__ Lawrence Seaway: **5** Saint
Lawrence, Steve
song: Footsteps (1960)
Go Away Little Girl (1962)
Party Doll (1957)
Portrait of My Love (1961)
Pretty Blue Eyes (1959)
spouse: Eydie Gorme
Lawrence, T.E.: **6** author, writer **7** British, soldier
work: Seven Pillars of Wisdom
Lawrence, Vicki
role: **4** Mama
song: The Night the Lights Went Out in Georgia (1973)
TV: Mama's Family, The Carol Burnett Show
Lawrenceville: **4** city, town
locale: **7** Georgia
lawrencium: **7** element
Laws of Gravity (1991 film)
cast: Edie Falco, Peter Greene, Adam Trese
director: Nick Gomez
Laws of Our Fathers, The author: Scott Turow
__-law student: **3** pre
lawsuit: **4** bill, case **5** cause, claim, fight, trial **6** action **7** contest, dispute **8** argument, replevin **9** assumpsit, court case **10** accusation, indictment, litigation
award: **5** costs **7** damages **10** reparation
beneficiary: **4** usee
cause: **4** tort **5** libel
law terms
against: **5** in rem
by word of mouth: **5** parol
country: **4** pais
eldest: **4** aine
hinder: **5** debar
husband: **3** vir
intermediate: **5** mesne
lease: **6** demise
legal: **5** licit **6** de jure
minor: **5** petit
negligence: **6** laches
not final: **4** nisi
prohibit: **5** estop
take: **5** seise
thing: **3** res
wife: **4** feme
wrongful act: **4** tort
Lawton: **4** city, town **5** Frank **6** Chiles
locale: **8** Oklahoma
Law West of the Pecos, The: **4** Bean
lawyer: **3** att. **4** atty. **5** agent **6** arguer, jurist, legist **7** adviser, advisor, counsel, pleader, proctor **8** advocate, attorney, defender **9** ABA member, barrister, counselor, solicitor **10** counsellor, legal eagle, mouthpiece, procurator
concern: **4** case, jury **6** client
deg.: **3** LL.B., LL.D.
expel a ~: **6** disbar
group: **3** ABA, bar
hire a ~: **3** sue **5** plead, press **6** accuse, appeal, indict **7** contest **8** litigate, petition **9** fight over, prosecute
holding: **6** escrow
hurdle: **4** jury **7** bar exam
title: **3** esq. **7** esquire
__ lawyer: **3** sea **5** canon, trial
Lawyer Man (1932 film)
cast: Joan Blondell, William Powell
lax: **4** easy, idle, kind, lazy, limp, mild, soft **5** broad, hasty, inert, loose, relax, slack, vague **6** asleep, casual, draggy, flabby, gentle, kindly, remiss, sloppy, torpid **7** clement, dormant, flaccid, general, inexact, lenient, passive, ruthful, slacken, sparing **8** careless, derelict, dilatory, flexible, inactive, indolent, laid-back, merciful, overeasy, placable, slipshod, slothful, sluggish, tolerant, unstrict, yielding **9** assuasive, compliant, dissolute, easygoing, forgetful, forgiving, imprecise, imprudent, indulgent, leisurely, lethargic, negligent, oblivious, sedentary, shapeless, unheedful, unmindful **10** behindhand, delinquent, disengaged, forbearing, inaccurate, incautious, indefinite, licentious, neglectful, nonchalant, permissive, regardless, unexacting, unthinking
become ~: **6** go soft
not ~: **5** harsh, rigid, stern, tough **6** severe, strict **7** careful
LAX
airport NW of ~: **3** SFO
laxity: **5** sloth **7** freedom, license, neglect **8** latitude, laziness **9** disregard, looseness, oversight, slackness, unconcern **10** negligence, remissness, sloppiness
laxly: **9** any old way
laxness: **5** sloth **6** apathy **7** inertia, languor, neglect **8** idleness, laziness, lethargy **9** fainéance, indolence, lassi-

tude, passivity, slackness, stolidity **10** negligence, remissness
Laxness, Halldór: 6 writer **8** Nobelist
lay: 3 bet, fix, put, set **4** cite, game, plan, rest, sink, site, tune **5** hatch, level, lodge, music, place, plant, quiet, stick, still, verse, wager **6** ballad, burden, charge, devise, gamble, hazard, impose, impute, instal, locate, melody, racket, saddle, set out, settle, spread **7** amateur, appease, arrange, ascribe, concoct, deposit, flatten, install, present, produce, profane, recline, secular, set down **8** contrive, encumber, inexpert, position, temporal **9** attribute, chalk up to, establish **10** put forward
a finger on: 5 touch
an egg: 4 bomb, bust, fail, flop, lose, slip, trip **5** flunk **6** blow it, falter **7** blunder, founder, go under, go wrong, misstep, stumble, wash out **8** fall flat, flounder **9** strike out
aside: 4 drop, save **5** defer, delay, shunt, table **6** ignore, put off, reject, shelve **7** abandon, discard, suspend **8** file away, renounce, salt away **9** disregard, pay no mind **10** pigeonhole, relinquish
at one's door: 3 tax **5** blame **6** accuse, charge, finger **7** censure **8** sentence **9** attribute, implicate **10** credit with
at one's feet: 4 give **5** offer **6** extend, tender **7** present, proffer, propose
away: 4 pile, save **5** amass, cache, hoard, set by, stash, store **6** garner, retain **7** deposit, reserve **8** set apart, set aside **9** economize, stockpile
back: 4 lull **5** relax, slack **6** relent **7** slacken **9** lighten up, lose speed
bare: 3 air **4** blab, leak, skin, tell **5** admit, strip **6** denude, expose, relate, reveal, show up, unfold, unmask, unveil **7** breathe, confess, divulge, exhibit, let slip, publish, uncloak, uncover **8** blurt out, disclose, unburden **9** broadcast, make known **10** make public
by: 4 keep, save, stow **5** amass, hoard, lay up, put by, stock **6** garner, load up **7** build up, procure, put away, store up **8** conserve, cumulate, hold on to, put aside, salt away, set apart, set aside **10** accumulate
by the heels: 3 bag **4** bust, grab, nail **5** catch, pinch, run in, seize **6** arrest, collar, detain, pick up, pull in, snap up, snatch **7** capture **9** apprehend
down: 3 set **4** drop **6** give up, impose, record **7** recline **8** turn over **9** prescribe, stipulate, surrender **10** relinquish
down the law: 4 rule **5** order, scold **6** decree, demand, direct, govern, insist **7** command, control, dictate, mandate **8** bulldoze, domineer, proclaim, regulate
ender: 3 man, men, off, out **4** away, back, over **5** about, woman, women **6** people, person
eyes on: 3 spy **4** espy, spot, view **5** stare
for: 4 lurk **5** prowl, sculk, set up, skulk **6** ambush, entrap, waylay **8** surprise
hold of: 3 get, nab **4** find, grab, grip, jerk, land, pull, snag, stop, take **5** catch, clasp, grasp, seize, twist, usurp, wrest **6** clinch, clutch, collar, locate, snatch **7** capture, grapple **8** come into
into: 4 whip **5** fight, fly at, set at, set on, smack **6** assail, attack, bang up, rebuke, thwack **7** assault, lambast, set upon **8** chastise, lambaste, let fly at **9** criticize, fustigate, haul off on, lash out at
it on: 4 fawn **5** boast, drool, jolly **6** cajole, overdo, pander, praise, slaver **7** blarney, flatter, talk big, wheedle **8** butter up, go too far, overplay, pile it on, softsoap **9** dish it out, embroider **10** exaggerate
low: 5 floor, level **7** flatten **9** knock down, overpower
off: 2 ax **3** axe, can, end **4** boot, drop, fire, halt, idle, oust, quit, sack, stop **5** cease, let be, let go, let up, spell **6** bounce, cool it, dehire, desist, give up **7** cashier, dismiss, drum out, release, suspend **8** get rid of, pink-slip, unemploy **9** discharge, stop doing, terminate **10** leave alone, take a break
on: 4 levy **5** apply **6** beetle **7** present **8** credit to **10** credit with
on the line: 4 risk
open: 4 tell **6** expose, unveil **7** uncover **8** endanger
out: 3 map, pay, zap **4** give, lend, plan, plot, show, stun **5** chart, put up, spend **6** assort, define, design, detail, expend, invest, sketch **7** arrange, diagram, display, exhibit, itemize, outline, program, specify **8** disburse, simplify **9** delineate **10** illustrate
over: 5 delay **8** postpone
siege to: 4 gird **5** beset, box in, hem in **6** attack, begird, circle **7** besiege, fence in **8** blockade, encircle, surround **9** beleaguer, close in on, encompass
starter: 3 way
the foundation: 5 begin, set up **6** launch **7** develop, kick off **8** commence **9** establish, institute, introduce, originate **10** inaugurate
the groundwork: 4 plan **5** draft, found, frame, set up, shape, start **6** create, draw up, launch **7** develop, provide **8** initiate **9** establish, formulate, institute, introduce, spearhead **10** anticipate, trailblaze
to: 6 attack
up: 4 harm, hurt, keep, save, shot **5** amass, hoard, lay in, store **6** garner, injure, obtain **7** confine, disable, put away, reserve **8** conserve, cumulate, preserve, salt away, set apart, set aside **9** indispose **10** accumulate, two-pointer
waste to: 4 raid, ruin, sack, undo **5** harry, smash, smite, wreck **6** ravage **7** consume, destroy, pillage, plunder, ransack **8** desolate, freeboot **9** depredate
lay __: 3 day, low, off, out **4** away, back, down, into, it on, open, over **5** an egg, aside, clerk, vicar, waste **6** figure, people, reader, rubber, sister **7** analyst, baptism, brother
lay __ land: 5 of the
lay __ on: 4 eyes
lay __ the law: 4 down
lay __ the line: 4 it on
lay __ thick: 4 it on
lay __ to: 5 claim, siege
lay-__: 3 ups
__-Lay: 5 Frito
lay a __: 6 course
layabout: 5 idler **6** truant **7** dawdler, shirker, slacker **10** ne'er-do-well
Layamon: 4 poet **7** British
lay an __: 3 egg
lay at one's __: 4 door
layaway __: 4 plan
Lay Down (1970 song)
artist: Edwin Hawkins Singers, Melanie
Lay Down Sally (1978 song) artist: Eric Clapton
lay down the __: 3 law
__ Lay Dying: 3 As I
layer: 3 bed, hen, ply **4** band, coat, film, seam, skin, slab, tier, vein **5** cover, crust, level, scale, sheet, strip **6** course, folium, lamina, pullet, streak, stripe, veneer **7** blanket, coating, lacquer, stratum **8** covering, laminate, snowfall **9** thickness **10** lamination, substratum
atmospheric ~: 5 ozone
combining form: 5 ptych- **6** ptycho-, strati-
outer ~: 4 bark, coat, hull, rind, skin **5** crust, shell **6** cortex **7** coating **8** covering **10** integument
starter: 4 mine **5** brick
thin ~: 4 film **5** sheet **6** lamina
layer __: 4 cake **5** board
__ layer: 3 air **4** germ **5** cloud, mixed, ozone **6** active, ground **7** surface
layette
item: 6 bootee, bootie **9** crib sheet, stretchie
user: 4 babe, baby **6** infant **7** neonate, newborn
laying
it on the line: 4 free, open **5** bluff, blunt, frank, plain, vocal **6** abrupt, candid, direct, square **7** sincere, upfront **8** explicit, truthful **10** forthright, from the hip, point-blank, unreserved
laying on of hands: 8 blessing
lay it __ line: 5 on the
Lay it __!: 4 on me
lay it on __: 5 thick
Layla (1972 song) artist: Eric Clapton
Lay Lady Lay (1969 song) artist: Bob Dylan
layman: 7 amateur **8** civilian **9** nonexpert
__ lay me...: 4 Now I
Layne: 5 Bobby
layoff: 3 RIF **4** lull **6** hiatus, recess **7** cutback, interim **8** furlough, interval, stoppage **9** cessation, discharge, dismissal
on ~: 8 leisured **9** unengaged
Lay off!: 6 stop it
lay of the __: 4 land
Lay of the Last Minstrel, The author: Walter Scott
lay one's __ on: 4 eyes **6** finger
lay one's __ on the table: 5 cards
layout: 3 map **4** plan, site **5** chart, draft, setup **6** design, format, scheme, spread **7** diagram, display, outline, purpose **8** proposal **9** blueprint, floor plan, formation, geography **10** ground plan
__ layout: 5 photo **7** picture
layover: 4 stay, stop **7** sojourn **8** stopover **9** overnight
layperson: 4 laic **6** laical, member, novice **7** amateur, recruit, secular **8** believer, follower, neophyte, outsider **9** proselyte **10** dilettante
lay to __: 4 rest
Layton: 4 city, town
locale: 4 Utah
Lay Your Hands on Me (song) artist: Bon Jovi, Thompson Twins
La-Z-__: 3 Boy
Lázaro Cárdenas: 4 city, town
locale: 6 Mexico **9** Michoacán
Lazar, Swifty: 5 agent
Lazarus: 4 Emma, Mell
Lazarus, Emma: 4 poet
work: By the Waters of Babylon
Dance to Death
The New Colossus
Lazarus Laughed author: Eugene O'Neill
laze: 3 lag, lie **4** bask, idle, loaf, loll, rest **5** amble, dally, mosey, relax, spend, stall, tarry, while **6** dawdle, linger, loiter, lounge, trifle, veg out **7** fritter, goof off, hang out, saunter **8** fool away, kill time, lallygag, lollygag, straggle **9** bum around, do nothing, lie around, sit around **10** dillydally, hang around, take it easy, take it slow
Lazenby: 6 George
Lazer __: 3 Tag
lazily: 9 languidly
laziness: 5 sloth **6** acedia, apathy, laxity, torpor **7** inertia, languor, laxness **8** dullness, hebetude, idleness, lethargy, otiosity **9** fainéance, indolence, lassitude, passivity, slackness, stolidity, torpidity **10** dreaminess, drowsiness, inactivity, negligence, remissness, sleepiness, stagnation, torpidness
LaZonga: 3 Mme. **6** Madame
__ lazuli: 5 lapis
lazy: 3 lax **4** dull, idle, logy, slow **5** inert, slack, tardy, tired, weary **6** asleep, draggy, drowsy, loafer, otiose, remiss, sleepy, snoozy, supine, torpid **7** dormant, laggard, lagging, languid, loafing, out of it, passive, unready **8** careless, comatose, dallying, dilatory, feckless, flagging, inactive, indolent, lifeless, slothful, sluggish, trifling **9** apathetic, do-nothing, leisurely, lethargic, loitering, sedentary, shiftless, somnolent, unhurried **10** disengaged, languorous, neglectful, slow-moving
be ~: 4 idle, loaf, loll **5** drift, evade, shirk, stall **6** dawdle, loiter, lounge, piddle, slouch, sprawl **7** hang out **8** kill time, malinger, slack off, slow down, vegetate **9** bum around, goldbrick, sit around, waste time **10** dillydally, knock about, take it easy
ender: 5 bones
in a ~ way: 4 idly
one: 5 drone, idler, sloth, Susan **6** loafer
Susan: 4 tray **6** server
lazy __: 3 guy **5** Susan, tongs
Lazy __: 5 Bones
lazybones: 4 poke **5** idler **6** loafer, slouch, truant **7** dawdler, goof-off, laggard **8** loiterer, slugabed, sluggard **9** do-nothing, goldbrick
bane: 3 job **4** work **5** labor **8** exertion
Lazy composer: 6 Berlin
__ Lazy River: 3 Up a
Lazzeri, Tony: 6 Yankee
lb.: 2 wt. **4** meas.
fraction: 2 oz.
__ l Baltimore, The: 3 Hot
LBJ: 3 Dem. **4** pres.
Library site: 6 Austin
predecessor: 3 JFK
successor: 3 RMN
see also Lyndon Johnson
LCD
cousin: 3 CRT
part of ~: 5 least **6** common, liquid **7** crystal, display, divisor
l'chayim: 5 toast **6** Hebrew
ldr.: 3 CEO, gen. **4** cmdr., pres.
platoon ~: 3 NCO
team ~: 3 mgr.
see also leader
LDS center: 4 Utah
Le __: 3 Cid **4** Mans **5** Fanal, Freak, Villi
Le __ d'Arthur: 5 Morte
Le __ de Lahore: 3 Roi
Le __ de Monte Cristo: 5 Comte

Le ___ des cygnes: 3 lac
Le ___ d'Or: 3 Coq
Le ___ du printemps: 5 Sacre
Le ___ d'Ys: 3 Roi
Le ___ et le Noir: 5 Rouge
Le ___ Field: 7 Bourget
Le ___, France: 5 Havre
Le ___ Goriot: 4 Père
Le ___ Soleil: 3 Roi
Le ___ Tho: 3 Duc
lea: 5 campo, field, grass, llano, sward, veldt 6 meadow, pampas, swarth 7 pasture, savanna, verdure 8 farmland, savannah 9 grassland 10 meadowland
cry: 3 baa, maa, moo 5 bleat
lady: 3 cow, ewe
Lea: 7 Massari, Salonga 8 Thompson
Lea & ___: 7 Perrins
leach: 4 ooze, seep 5 drain, empty 6 filter, strain 7 extract 8 filtrate, wash away 9 lixiviate, percolate
Leach: 5 Robin
Leachman, Cloris: 7 actress
film: The Beverly Hillbillies (1993)
Crazy Mama (1975)
Dillinger (1973)
High Anxiety (1977)
Kiss Me Deadly (1955)
The Last Picture Show (1971, AA)
Prancer (1989)
Young Frankenstein (1974)
TV: Phyllis, The Mary Tyler Moore Show
leachy: 6 porous, spongy 9 sievelike
Leacock: 6 Philip 7 Stephen
lead: 3 tip, top, win 4 clew, clue, draw, edge, head, helm, hero, hint, part, role, rule, sign, star, take, tend 5 actor, bring, cause, chair, excel, front, guide, leash, metal, model, outdo, pilot, point, proof, reach, spark, start, steer, usher 6 direct, escort, forego, govern, hot tip, induce, leader, manage, margin, player, prompt, squire, tether 7 actress, advance, command, conduce, conduct, control, convert, element, go ahead, go first, pioneer, plumbum, precede, presage, preside, prevail, primacy, surpass, top spot, vantage 8 antecede, dominate, evidence, foremost, headline, motivate, outstrip, persuade, premiere, priority, result in, shepherd 9 advantage, chaperone, come first, forefront, front rank, go ahead of, influence, introduce, plurality, principal, run things, spearhead, supervise, supremacy, title role, transcend 10 come before, contribute, first place, indication, mastermind, precedence, set the pace, show the way, suggestion, take charge, trail-blaze
alloy: 6 pewter 7 tinfoil 8 calamine, pot metal 9 type metal 10 gold bronze, soft solder, terne metal, Wood's metal
astray: 4 ruin 6 outwit 7 deprave, mislead 8 outsmart 9 misinform
away: 6 divert 8 distract 9 sidetrack
balloon: 3 dud 4 flop 6 fiasco 7 failure
by the nose: 4 rule, sway 6 induce 7 control 8 persuade 9 brainwash, influence, prevail on
combining form: 5 plumb- 6 plumbo-
down the aisle: 4 seat 5 guide, usher 6 escort, show in 7 conduct 9 accompany
get the ~ out: 3 hie 4 rush 5 hurry 6 hasten
hot ~: 3 tip
in: 5 usher
in the ~: 5 ahead, first, on top 7 in front, winning 8 jubilant, out front, unbeaten
into: 5 usher 9 introduce
into sin: 5 tempt 6 entice, entrap
off: 4 head, open 5 begin, start 6 launch, let rip 7 go ahead, go first, kick off 8 commence, get going, initiate 9 enter upon, introduce, originate 10 inaugurate
on: 3 toy 4 abet, bait, dupe, fool, lure 5 charm, decoy, flirt, shill, tease, tempt, trick 6 allure, delude, entice, entrap, invite, trifle 7 beguile, deceive, mislead 8 hoodwink, intrigue, inveigle 9 disinform, tantalize
pellets: 4 shot
pigment: 6 ceruse
remover: 6 eraser
role: 4 hero 7 heroine
sharer: 6 costar
slight ~: 4 edge 9 advantage, head start
source: 3 ore 6 galena 8 galenite 10 vanadinite
take the ~: 4 head, rule 5 exact, order, reign 6 direct, enjoin, govern, handle, manage 7 command, control, dictate, mandate, oversee 8 dominate, instruct 9 officiate, supervise
the way: 5 guide 7 conduct, pioneer, trigger, usher in 8 initiate 9 instigate
to: 4 make 5 cause, guide 6 induce 7 head for, provoke 8 engender, occasion, result in 10 bring about
to believe: 4 hint 5 imply, infer, let on 6 tip off 7 suggest 8 indicate, intimate 9 insinuate
to expect: 3 vow 4 bode, hint 5 augur, swear, vouch 6 assure, pledge, plight 7 betroth, declare, portend, presage, promise, warrant 8 forebode, foreshow, indicate 9 foretoken, guarantee, stipulate 10 foreshadow, take an oath
up to: 5 imply 6 hint at 7 suggest 8 intimate 9 insinuate
weight: 5 plumb
(with): 4 open
lead ___: 3 off 4 foot, line, pipe, time, tree, up to 5 azide, block, glass, glaze, oxide, screw, sheet, story, track, white 6 pencil 7 acetate, balloon, dioxide
lead ___ altar: 5 to the
lead ___ life: 5 a dog's
lead ___ nose: 5 by the
lead ___ the garden path: 4 down
lead-___: 4 time
lead-___ cinch: 4 pipe
lead-___ gasoline: 4 free
___ lead: 3 pig, red 4 land 5 black, drift, white
Lead ___: 4 Me On
Lead ___ into temptation...: 5 us not
lead a ___ life: 4 dog's
Leadbelly (1976 film)
cast: Paul Benjamin, Roger E. Mosley, Madge Sinclair
director: Gordon Parks
lead by the ___: 4 nose
lead down the ___ path: 6 garden
leaded ___: 3 gas 5 glass 7 crystal 8 gasoline
leaden: 4 dull, gray, grey, slow 5 bleak, drear, heavy, hefty, inert, livid 6 dismal, dreary, gloomy, taxing, torpid 7 languid, onerous, weighty 8 lifeless, listless, overcast, sluggish 9 ponderous 10 burdensome, lackluster, oppressive, spiritless
leader: 4 amir, boss, czar, dean, emir, exec, guru, head, king, lead, lion, pres., tsar, tzar 5 ameer, chair, chief, doyen, emeer, guide, nawab, pacer, pilot, ruler 6 gerent, herald, rector, top dog 7 captain, general, headman, magnate, manager, notable, officer, pioneer, skipper, viceroy 8 band boss, cynosure, director, eminence, governor, higher-up, kingfish, luminary, mistress, official, shepherd, superior 9 chieftain, commander, conductor, counselor, dignitary, downspout, executive, harbinger, key player, number one, organizer, precursor, president, principal, sovereign 10 controller, coryphaeus, counsellor, forerunner, legislator, mastermind, notability, pacesetter, politician, ringleader
combining form: 4 -agog 6 -agogue
starter: 4 band, fair, ring 5 cheer
suffix: 4 -arch
leader ___: 4 head 5 block, board, cable
___ leader: 4 bear, loss 5 civic, floor, squad 6 flight
leaderless: 8 unguided
Leader of the Band (1981 song) artist: Dan Fogelberg
Leader of the Pack (1964 song) artist: Shangri-las
leaders: 5 brass
Leaders author: 5 Nixon
leadership: 4 rule, sway 5 power, reign, skill 6 regime 7 command, conduct, control, primacy 8 capacity, guidance, hegemony, pilotage 9 authority, direction, executive, foresight, influence, supremacy 10 initiative
group: 5 cadre
position: 4 helm 5 front, reins, wheel 6 tiller
leadfooted: 5 gawky 6 clumsy, klutzy, oafish 7 awkward 8 ungainly 9 lumbering, maladroit
lead-in: 5 intro, segue 6 opener, prelim
leading: 3 big, top 4 arch, best, head, main, note, star 5 ahead, chief, first, front, grand, major, on top, prime 6 famous, master, ruling, senior, utmost 7 forward, highest, in front, initial, popular, premier, primary, stellar, supreme 8 cardinal, champion, dominant, foremost, greatest, headmost, superior 9 governing, inaugural, notorious, number one, paramount, preceding, principal, prominent, unrivaled, uppermost, well-known, worthiest 10 dominating, preeminent, unrivalled
lady: 4 star 7 actress, heroine
light: 4 rock 8 mainstay
man: 4 hero, star 5 actor
slightly: 5 one up
starter: 5 cheer
leading ___: 3 man 4 edge, lady, mark, tone, wind 5 block, light 7 article, strings
leading-edge: 6 modern 7 current 8 advanced
Leading With My Chin author: 4 Leno
Lead Me On (1979 song) artist: Maxine Nightingale
leadoff: 5 onset, start 6 advent, outset 7 opening 8 exordium 9 beginning, inception
lead-off: 5 first 7 initial
lead-pipe ___: 5 cinch
lead the ___: 3 way
lead-tin alloy: 5 terne
lead to the ___: 5 altar
leadwort: 5 shrub
leady: 4 dull 5 heavy 6 gloomy 8 listless, sluggish 10 spiritless
leaf: 2 pg. 3 pad 4 page, scan, skim 5 blade, bract, folio, frond, metal, organ, paper, petal, sheet, thumb, verso 6 browse, glance, needle, riffle 7 foliage, foliole
adjective: 5 erose
area: 6 areola, areole
calyx ~: 5 sepal
collector: 5 raker
combining form: 5 phyll- 6 phyllo-
extra ~: 6 insert
fern ~: 5 bract, frond
gatherer: 5 raker
holder: 4 limb, stem 5 shoot 6 branch 7 pedicel, pedicle 8 peduncle
in ~: 5 green
juncture: 4 axil
like an oak ~: 7 rounded
lucky ~: 6 clover 8 shamrock
opening: 4 pore 5 stoma
out: 3 bud 7 burgeon 10 burst forth
part: 3 rib 4 lobe, vein 5 pinna
plant ~: 6 earlet
point: 5 mucro
starter: 3 fly 4 shin, twin 5 broad, heart, liver, water 6 clover, copper, velvet
starting point: 3 bud 4 node 8 juncture, swelling
through: 4 read, scan, skim 5 thumb 6 browse
turn over a new ~: 6 change, reform 7 redress, shape up
walking ~: 3 bug 4 fern 6 insect
leaf ___: 3 bud, bug, fat 4 beet, lard, mold, rust, spot 5 coral, miner, scald 6 beetle, blight, blotch, insect, roller, spring 7 lettuce, mustard, warbler
___ leaf: 3 bay, end, fig 4 drop, gold, nose, palm, seed 5 scale, water 6 floral, silver 7 crinkle, vanilla, walking
___-leaf: 5 loose 6 copper, myriad 7 flannel
___ Leaf: 4 A New 5 Maple
___-leaf binder: 5 loose
___-leaf clover: 4 four
___-leaf cluster: 3 oak
leafless: 4 bare 5 naked
vine: 5 haoma
leaflet: 2 ad 4 bill 5 flier, flyer, tract 8 brochure, circular, handbill, pamphlet 10 literature
leaflike part: 5 bract
___ Leaf Rag: 5 Maple
Leafs: 3 six 4 team
home: 7 Toronto
milieu: 3 ice 4 rink
org.: 3 NHL
___-leaf table: 4 drop
___ Leaf, The: 4 Last
leafy: 5 green, shady 6 foliar, hidden, shaded, wooded 7 verdant 8 abundant 9 abounding 10 umbrageous
shelter: 5 arbor, bower 6 recess 7 pergola
league: 3 mob, soc. 4 ally, assn., band, bloc, club, crew, gang, gild, loop, pact, pool, rank, ring, tier, unit 5 bunch, class, grade, group, guild, level, order, party, union, unite 6 circle, concur, outfit, status, treaty 7 academy, circuit, combine, compact, company, conjoin, society 8 alliance, category, coadjute, congress, federate, grouping, sodality 9 anschluss, associate, coalition, cooperate 10 amalgamate, conference, consortium, federation, fellowship, join forces, membership, pigeonhole
baseball ~: 4 Amer., Natl. 8 American, National
in ~: 6 allied, joined, tied in, united 8 combined, hooked up 9 connected, in cahoots 10 affiliated, associated
in German ~: 4 bund
lowest minor ~: 6 class A
___ league: 3 big 4 bush 5 major, minor 6 marine

___ League: **3** Ivy **4** Arab, Pony **5** Human, Major **6** Delian, Junior, Little **7** Achaean, Epworth
___-league boots: **5** seven
League City: **4** town
locale: **5** Texas
League of ___ Voters: **5** Women
League of Nations
home: **6** Geneva
successor: **5** The UN
League of Their Own, A (1992 film)
cast: Geena Davis, Tom Hanks, Jon Lovitz, Madonna, Garry Marshall, Lori Petty
director: Penny Marshall
League of Youth, The author: Henrik Ibsen
___ leaguer: **3** big **4** bush **5** Texas
___-leaguer: **5** major, minor
___ Leaguer: **3** Ivy **6** Little
Leah
daughter of ~: **5** Dinah
father of ~: **5** Laban
husband of ~: **5** Jacob
son of ~: **4** Levi **5** Judah **6** Reuben, Simeon **7** Zebulun **8** Issachar
Leahy: **7** Patrick
leak: **3** run **4** blab, drip, drop, flow, hole, loss, news, ooze, seep, tell **5** chink, crack, drain, drool, exude **6** escape, expose, filter, reveal, tattle, unmask, unveil **7** come out, crevice, divulge, dribble, exhibit, fissure, lay bare, let slip, opening, release, seep out, trickle, uncover **8** aperture, decrease, disclose, exposure, give away, puncture **9** discharge, make known, percolate **10** make public, revelation
apt to ~: **5** seepy
ender: **3** age **5** proof
sound: **4** hiss
stopper: **5** O-ring **6** gasket
tanker ~: **5** spill
leakage: **6** escape
Leakey: **4** Mary **5** Louis **7** Richard
Leakey, Louis: **14** anthropologist
Leakey, Mary: **14** anthropologist
Leakey, Richard: **14** anthropologist
Leakin' ___: **4** Lena
leaking: **5** adrip
leakproof: **5** tight **6** sealed **8** airtight, hermetic
leaky: **5** holey **6** faulty, porous **7** seeping **8** dripping
device: **5** sieve **6** filter, screen **8** colander, strainer
tire sound: **4** ssss
lealty: **8** fidelity
lean: **3** fit, jut, sag, tip **4** bend, bony, cant, keel, lank, list, prop, rely, rest, slim, sway, tend, thin, tilt, trim, turn, veer, wiry **5** boney, droop, favor, gaunt, lanky, lithe, lurch, no-fat, pitch, rangy, slant, slope, spare, stoop, terse, trust, weedy **6** bank on, bear on, careen, dainty, gangly, gnomic, meager, prefer, scanty, sinewy, skinny, slight, slinky, slouch, sparse, svelte, twiggy, wasted **7** angular, gracile, haggard, incline, recline, scraggy, scrawny, slender, spidery, stringy, willowy **8** angulose, angulous, bear upon, gangling, rawboned **9** efficient, emaciated, gravitate, lithesome, sylphlike
backward: **4** arch, flex
eater: **5** Sprat
forward: **4** bend **7** bow down
make ~: **5** defat
not ~: **4** oily, rich **5** fatty, lardy **7** adipose
on: **4** abut, hurt, push **5** bully, press, trust **6** coerce, menace, rebuke **7** squeeze **8** browbeat, chastise, pressure **9** criticize, shake down **10** intimidate
(on): **4** rely, rest **5** hinge **6** depend
one: **5** scrag **8** beanpole
over: **3** bow, sag **4** bend, flex **5** droop, hunch, slump, stoop **6** hunker, slouch
to one side: **4** cant, heel, list
toward: **4** near, tend **5** favor, verge
lean ___ backward: **4** over
Lean ___: **4** on Me **7** Cuisine
lean and ___: **4** mean
Lean, David: **3** Sir **8** director
film: Blithe Spirit (1945)
Breaking the Sound Barrier (1952)
The Bridge on the River Kwai (1957, AA)
Brief Encounter (1945)
Doctor Zhivago (1965)
Great Expectations (1946)
In Which We Serve (1942)
Lawrence of Arabia (1962, AA)
Oliver Twist (1948)
A Passage to India (1984)
Ryan's Daughter (1970)
Summertime (1955)
This Happy Breed (1944)
Leander's love: **4** Hero
Leandro's love: **3** Ero
leaning: **4** bent, bias, tilt **5** alist, atilt, drift, slant, slope, taste, trend **6** aslant, liking, temper **7** mindset **8** aptitude, attitude, cup of tea, lopsided, penchant, tendency, velleity **9** appetence, inclining, incumbent, proneness, sentiment **10** partiality, preference, proclivity, propensity
Leaning ___ of Pisa: **5** Tower
leaning forward (ballet): **6** penché
Leaning on the Lamp Post (1966 song)
artist: Herman's Hermits
Leaning Tower
like the ~: **5** atilt **8** slanting
Leaning Tower, The author: Katherine Anne Porter
Leann: **6** Hunley
LeAnn: **5** Rimes
Lean on Me (1989 film)
cast: Morgan Freeman, Robert Guillaume, Beverly Todd
director: John G. Avildsen
Lean on Me (song) artist: Bill Withers, Club Nouveau
leant: **4** bent **6** canted, listed, tended, tilted **7** propped, slanted **8** inclined
lean-to: **3** hut **4** shed **5** annex, house, hovel, shack **6** shanty **7** cottage, shelter **8** addition, building
leap: **3** hop, pop **4** axel, jump, lick, Lutz, move, rise, rush, skip, soar **5** arise, bound, caper, clear, frisk, lunge, mount, start, surge, vault **6** ascend, bounce, cavort, hurdle, plunge, pounce, prance, rocket, spring **7** advance, saltate, upsurge, upswing **8** escalate, increase, jump over **9** skyrocket **10** escalation, go whole hog, hippety hop
aboard: **6** jump on
aside: **4** duck **5** avoid, dodge
at: **5** go for **6** accept, fall on, relish
ballet ~: **4** jeté **5** brisé, sauté **7** ciseaux, échappé **8** assemble, ballonné, cabriole, sissonne, soussous **9** entrechat, grand jeté, pas de chat **10** soubresaut
dressage ~: **6** curvet
ender: **4** frog
fencing ~: **4** volt
for joy: **4** crow **5** cheer, exult, glory **7** delight, triumph **9** celebrate
over: **3** hop **5** clear **6** hurdle
(over): **4** sail
skater's ~: **4** axel, lutz
leap ___: **3** day **4** year **6** second
___ leap: **7** quantum
leapfrog: **4** game, jump, skip **5** vault **6** hurtle **7** advance
leap in the ___: **4** dark
leap of ___: **5** faith
Leap of Faith (1992 film)
cast: Lolita Davidovich, Steve Martin, Liam Neeson, Debra Winger
director: Richard Pearce
Leap of Faith author: Danielle Steel
leaps and ___: **6** bounds
Lear: **4** poet **6** Edward, Evelyn, Norman
daughter: **5** Regan **7** Goneril **8** Cordelia
loyal companion: **4** Kent
Lear ___: **3** Jet
___ Lear: **4** King
Lear, Edward: **4** poet **7** British
cat: **4** Foss
elegant fowl: **3** owl
specialty: limerick
work: A Book of Nonsense
Calico Pie
The Jumblies
Laughable Lyrics
More Nonsense Songs
Nonsense Songs
The Owl and the Pussycat
The Pobble Who Has No Toes
learn: **3** con, get, see **4** cram, hear, know, read, tell **5** dig up, enrol, glean, grasp, study **6** absorb, attain, detect, enroll, master, peruse, pick up, review, soak up, take in, tumble, turn up **7** catch on, discern, drink in, find out, major in, minor in, nose out, prepare, receive, train in, uncover, unearth **8** discover, memorize, pore over, remember, smoke out **9** ascertain, brush up on, catch on to, determine, establish, figure out, get word of, lucubrate **10** apprentice, get down pat, understand
about: **6** hear of
a lesson: **3** get **5** grasp **6** digest, soak up **7** drink in **9** apprehend **10** assimilate, comprehend, understand
from: **3** use **4** gain **5** value **7** benefit, improve, realize
(from): **6** profit
how some ~: **6** by rote
in a hurry: **4** cram
one's part: **5** drill, study **6** go over **8** practice, rehearse
one way to ~: **4** rote **7** routine **10** repetition
quick to ~: **3** apt **4** able, keen **5** acute, adept, alert, canny, sharp, smart **6** astute, brainy, bright, clever, gifted, shrewd, with it **7** capable, erudite **8** well-read **9** brilliant, on the ball **10** discerning, insightful, precocious
slowly: **5** glean
something to ~: **6** lesson **7** precept, reading **8** exercise, homework, teaching **9** chalk talk **10** assignment, recitation
the ropes: **5** adapt, train **6** master
try to ~: **3** ask, dig **4** cram, heed, muse, plug, pump, quiz, read **5** probe, query, study, think, train **6** bone up, digest, go over, master, peruse, ponder, reason, review, survey, take up **7** analyze, consult, dissect, inquire, observe, reflect **8** check out, look into, meditate, mull over, polish up, pore over, practice, read up on, rehearse, research **9** grind away, pick apart, sweat over **10** crack a book, experiment
learned: **4** deep, sage **5** grave, sharp, smart, solid, sound **6** brainy, expert, posted, solemn, versed **7** bookish, erudite, sapient, skilled, studied **8** abstruse, academic, cultured, educated, esoteric, grounded, highbrow, lettered, literary, literate, pedantic, polymath, profound, skillful, studious, well-read **9** in the know, judicious, pansophic, recondite, scholarly **10** conversant, cultivated, omniscient, pedantical, scientific
about: **4** up on **6** versed
not ~: **6** innate, native **7** natural **9** intrinsic, intuitive
one: **4** guru, sage **5** guide, solon **6** critic, expert, master, mentor, Nestor, pundit, savant **7** scholar, Solomon, teacher, thinker **9** abecedary, authority, professor **10** specialist
something ~: **5** craft, skill, trade **7** know-how, mastery **9** expertise, technique
Learned: **4** Hand **7** Michael
learner: **3** cub **4** tiro, tyro **5** newie, pupil, tutee **6** intern, novice **7** interne, new hand, recruit, scholar, student, trainee **8** beginner, bookworm, disciple, initiate, neophyte **9** fledgling, greenhorn **10** apprentice, catechumen, tenderfoot
learning: **4** info, lore **5** study **6** wisdom **7** culture, letters, reading, science, tuition **8** literacy, research, training **9** education, erudition, knowledge, schooling **10** literature
basics: **3** RRR **4** ABCs **7** three Rs
branch of ~: **5** ology
place: **3** sch. **4** acad., coll., inst., univ. **6** school **7** academy, college **9** institute **10** university
learning ___: **5** curve
___ learning: **3** new **4** book **5** sleep **6** higher
Learning to Fly (1991 song) artist: Tom Petty
Learnin' the Blues (1955 song) artist: Frank Sinatra
Leary: **5** Denis **7** Timothy
Leary, Denis: **5** actor
film: The Ref (1994)
Suicide Kings (1998)
The Thomas Crown Affair (1999)
True Crime (1999)
Wag the Dog (1997)
Wide Awake (1998)
lease: **3** let **4** hire, loan, rent, take **6** engage, let out, occupy, sublet **7** charter, rent out **8** sublease **9** agreement, indenture, liability, residence
ender: **4** back, hold **6** holder
extend a ~: **5** relet, renew
holder: **6** lessee, lessor, renter, tenant **8** landlady, landlord, occupant
in law: **6** demise
___-Lease Act: **4** Lend
___ lease on life: **4** a new
leaser: **6** tenant **8** landlady, landlord
leash: **3** tie **4** bind, curb, lead, rein, rope, trio **5** chain, check, strap, tie up **6** bridle, fasten, fetter, hamper, hobble, secure, tether, triple **7** control **8** hold back, restrain, suppress **9** restraint **10** constraint
on a ~: **5** in tow **10** restrained
leash ___: **3** law
least: **3** min. **4** last **5** basal, first, nadir, third **6** atomic, barest, bottom, fewest, gutter, lowest, minute, second **7** finical, meanest, minimal, minimum, poorest, tiniest, trivial **8** atomical, feeblest, littlest, minutest, niggling, piddling, short-end, smallest **9** molecular, narrowest, slightest **10** entry-level
ender: **4** ways, wise
least ___: **5** of all, shrew **6** weasel **7** bittern, squares

least __ bound: 5 upper
least __ denominator: 6 common
least __ multiple: 6 common
__ least: 5 in the
least of __: 3 all
leather: 3 elk, kid, Mor. 4 hide, roan, skin 5 mocha, suede 6 chammy, Levant, lizard, shammy, shamoy 7 chamois, cowhide, doeskin, Morocco, pigskin, rawhide 8 cordovan, deerskin, goatskin, shagreen 9 alligator, crocodile
  armor: 6 lorica
  dressing: 6 dubbin 7 dubbing
  ender: 4 back, ette, head, neck, wear, wood, work 6 jacket, worker
  fake ~: 5 vinyl
  go hellbent for ~: 6 careen, hasten, hurtle 7 rampage 8 stampede
  item: 4 belt, rein, weft, whip 5 knout, strap, strop, thong
  split ~: 5 skive
  to-be: 4 hide, pelt
  tool: 3 awl
  treat ~ again: 5 retan
  work with ~: 3 tan 4 cure, tool
leather-__: 4 hard 6 lunged
__ leather: 3 oak, sea 4 half, ooze 5 glove, thong, white 6 chrome, patent, pebble, Russia, saddle 7 Dongola, morocco, stirrup
Leather and Lace (1981 song)
  artist: Don Henley, Stevie Nicks
leatherback: 6 animal, turtle 7 reptile
leather maker, name meaning: 7 Lederer
leatherneck: 6 gyrene, Marine
  org.: 4 USMC
Leather-Stocking Tales author: James Fenimore Cooper
leatherwood: 4 titi
leathery: 4 hard 5 rough, tough 6 rugged, strong 7 durable 8 hardened, wrinkled 10 coriaceous
Leatrice: 3 Joy
leave: 2 go, OK 3 fly, let, vac. 4 drop, exit, flee, flit, jilt, move, okay, omit, park, part, quit, sail, stop, will 5 adieu, allot, allow, be off, ditch, elope, go off, go out, let be, R and R, sally, scram, spare, split, start 6 assent, beat it, be gone, bow out, bug out, cut out, decamp, defect, depart, desert, egress, embark, escape, forget, get out, go away, go home, maroon, move on, permit, pop off, repair, resign, retire, run off, secede, set off, set out, suffer, vacate, vanish 7 abandon, abscond, back out, bail out, bequest, consent, consign, drop off, drop out, entrust, forsake, freedom, go-ahead, go forth, goodbye, head out, holiday, intrust, liberty, license, make off, migrate, move out, neglect, parting, pull out, push off, retreat, ride off, ship out, skip out, slip out, step out, take off, time off, vamoose, walk out 8 abdicate, approval, bequeath, check out, clear out, come away, emigrate, evacuate, farewell, forswear, fugitate, furlough, hand down, hightail, light out, renounce, run along, sanction, separate, set forth, shove off, skip town, slip away, step down, vacation, withdraw 9 allowance, break away, break camp, clearance, departure, disappear, foreswear, skedaddle, stand down, surrender, take a hike, throw over 10 give notice, green light, hit the road, indulgence, permission, relinquish, sabbatical, say goodbye, shuffle off, withdrawal
  alone: 5 let be 6 lay off, resist 7 neglect 10 deregulate
  behind: 4 lose, pass 5 outdo 7 abandon 8 distance, overtake, shake off, throw off 9 transcend
  compel to ~: 6 banish
  empty: 6 vacate 7 move out
  give ~: 2 OK 3 let 5 allow, grant 6 accede, free up, permit 7 approve, concede, endorse, license 8 sanction 9 authorize 10 say the word
  hanging: 4 jilt, quit 5 ditch 6 cop out, desert, maroon, reject, strand 7 abandon, forsake, let down 8 abdicate
  hastily: 3 hie, run 4 bolt, flee, skip 5 scram, split 6 bug out, decamp 7 take off, vamoose 8 shove off 9 bundle off
  in: 4 stet
  no part empty: 4 cram, pack, sate 5 crowd 6 occupy, top off 7 jampack, pervade, satiate 8 brim over, permeate
  no stone unturned: 4 seek 5 scour 6 search, strive 7 persist, ransack, rummage 9 persevere
  no trace of: 3 end 4 doom, raze, ruin, sack 5 blast, crush, level, total, wreck 6 blow up, ravage 7 butcher, despoil, destroy, flatten, pillage, scourge, scuttle, wipe out 8 bankrupt, bulldoze, clean out, decimate, demolish, lay waste 9 bring down, desecrate, devastate 10 annihilate, obliterate
  obscurity: 6 emerge
  of absence: 4 rest 5 break, leave, R and R 7 holiday, leisure, respite, time off 8 furlough, vacation 10 sabbatical
  off: 3 end 4 halt, omit, quit, stop 5 cease 6 desist, give up 7 abstain, refrain 8 give over, keep from, surcease
  on ~: 6 ashore
  one's feet: 4 jump, leap 5 bound
  one's seat: 5 arise, get up, stand 6 jump up
  open-mouthed: 3 awe, wow 4 stun 5 amaze 8 surprise
  out: 3 bar, cut 4 omit, skip, tabu 5 debar, elide, forgo 6 except, forego 7 exclude, scissor 8 overlook, pass over 9 cast aside, eliminate, gloss over
  out in the cold: 4 shun, snub 6 ignore, rebuff, reject, slight 7 high-hat, neglect 8 overlook 9 ostracize
  port: 4 sail 6 embark 7 set sail 8 go aboard, shove off
  prepare to ~: 4 pack 8 get ready
  secretly: 4 bolt, flee 5 elope 6 decamp, escape 7 abscond, run away 8 slip away, sneak off 9 steal away
  take one's ~: 2 go 4 exit 5 split 6 beat it, depart, go away, move on, retire 7 make off, pull out, push off 8 blast off, hightail, light out, set forth, shove off, slip away, withdraw
  the fold: 4 roam 6 depart, wander
  the ground: 3 fly 4 soar 5 arise, climb, vault 6 ascend, rocket 7 balloon, take off 8 levitate
  the nest: 8 take wing
  the path: 3 err 4 rove, turn, veer 5 stray 6 swerve 7 deviate, diverge
  the water: 7 surface
  town: 4 move, relo 8 relocate
  unceremoniously: 4 drop, dump, jilt 5 chuck, ditch 6 desert 7 abandon, forsake
  undone: 4 omit 5 slack 8 overlook
  wide-eyed: 3 awe, wow 4 stun 5 amaze
  without escape: 4 trap, tree 6 corner
  without paying: 5 stiff
leave __: 3 off 5 alone
leave __ dust: 5 in the
leave __ enough alone: 4 well
leave-__: 6 taking
__ leave: 4 sick 5 shore 6 family, French
Leave __ Beaver: 4 It to
Leave __ Me!: 4 It to
Leave __ that!: 4 it at
Leave __ to Heaven: 3 Her
Leave!: 4 shoo 6 begone
leaved combining form: 7 -folious
Leave Her to Heaven (1945 film)
  cast: Jeanne Crain, Gene Tierney, Cornel Wilde
  character: 5 Ellen
  director: John M. Stahl
leave in the __: 4 dust
Leave It to Beaver (CBS/ABC sitcom)
  cast: Frank Bank (Lumpy Rutherford)
    Hugh Beaumont (Ward Cleaver)
    Barbara Billingsley (June Cleaver)
    Richard Deacon (Fred Rutherford)
    Tony Dow (Wally Cleaver)
    Jerry Mathers (Beaver Cleaver)
    Ken Osmond (Eddie Haskell)
  setting: Mayfield
Leave It to Me!: 7 musical
  songwriter: 6 Porter
Leave me __!: 5 alone
Leave Me Alone (1973 song) artist: Helen Reddy
__ Leave Me Now: 5 If You
leaven: 4 barm, soda 5 yeast 7 lighten
  combining form: 3 zym- 4 zymo-
leave no __ unturned: 5 stone
Leavenworth: 4 city, Fort, town
  locale: 6 Kansas
leave of __: 7 absence
leaves: 6 fodder 7 foliage
  gather ~: 4 rake 7 clean up
  gatherer: 5 raker
  like autumn ~: 3 dry 4 sere 7 parched 9 shriveled
  like some ~: 5 lobed 6 lobate 7 lobated
  lose ~: 4 shed 9 exfoliate
  notched, as ~: 5 erose
  one who ~: 4 goer
  plant with two seed ~: 5 dicot 7 dicotyl
  tea ~: 4 lees 5 dregs 8 sediment
__ Leaves: 6 Autumn
Leaves of Grass author: Walt Whitman
leave-taking: 4 exit 5 adieu, adios, conge 6 congee 7 goodbye, parting 8 farewell
leave the __ open: 4 door
leave to one's __ devices: 3 own
leave well enough __: 5 alone
leaving: 4 exit 6 exodus 8 outgoing 10 withdrawal
  combining form: 4 lipo-
  keep from ~: 5 delay 6 detain, hold up, impede 7 set back 8 slow down 10 buttonhole
  out: 3 bar, but 5 minus 6 except 7 barring, besides, short of 8 omitting 9 apart from, aside from, excluding
__ Leaving Home: 4 She's
Leaving Las Vegas (1995 film)
  cast: Nicolas Cage, Julian Sands, Elisabeth Shue
  character: 4 Sera
  director: Mike Figgis
Leaving on a Jet Plane (1969 song)
  artist: Peter, Paul and Mary
leavings: 4 junk, orts, rest 5 ashes, chaff, dross, trash, truck, waste 6 litter, refuse 7 garbage, grounds, remains, remnant, residue, rubbish, rummage 8 detritus, leftover, oddments, remnants 9 remainder
Leawood: 4 city, font, town 8 typeface
  locale: 6 Kansas
Leb.
  neighbor: 3 Isr., Syr.
Lebanese: 4 Arab 5 Asian
Lebanon: 4 city, town 6 nation 7 country
  bovine: 6 Baladi
  capital: 6 Beirut
  city: 6 Beirut 7 Tripoli 8 Beyrouth
  group: 10 Arab League
  language: 6 Arabic
  locale: 4 Asia 7 Mideast 9 Tennessee
  money: 7 piaster, piastre
  neighbor: 5 Syria 6 Israel
  poet: 5 Accad, Adnan
  port: 4 Tyre 5 Saida, Sayda, Sidon, Sydon, Zidon 6 Beirut 8 Beyrouth
  tree: 5 cedar
  writer: 6 Gibran
LeBaron: 3 car 4 auto 8 Chrysler 10 automobile
lebbek: 4 tree
lebkuchen: 6 cookie
Leblanc: 7 Maurice, Nicolas
LeBlanc: 4 Matt
Le Bourget alternative: 4 Orly 8 de Gaulle
Lebowitz: 4 Fran
__ Lebowski, The: 3 Big
LeBrock, Kelly spouse: Steven Seagal
Le Cain: 5 Errol
Le Car: 3 car 4 auto 7 Renault 10 automobile
le Carré, John: 6 writer 7 British
  figure: 3 spy 5 agent
  work: The Honourable Schoolboy
    The Little Drummer Girl
    The Looking-Glass War
    A Perfect Spy
    Smiley's people
    The Spy Who Came in from the Cold
    Tinker, Tailor, Soldier, Spy
Lech: 5 river 6 Walesa
  city on the ~: 8 Augsburg
  locale: 5 Tirol, Tyrol 7 Austria, Bavaria, Germany
leche seller: 6 bodega
lechwe: 6 mammal 8 antelope
  relative: 3 gnu, kob 4 guib, kudu, oryx, puku, topi 5 addax, bongo, chiru, eland, goral, korin, nyala, oribi, saiga, serow 6 chammy, dik-dik, duiker, impala, koodoo, nilgai, rhebok, shammy, shamoy 7 blaubok, blesbok, chamois, defassa, gazelle, gemsbok, gerenuk, grysbok, nylghai, nylghau, sassaby 8 blesbuck, bontebok, bushbuck, gemsbuck, reedbuck, steenbok, steinbok 9 blackbuck, pronghorn, sitatunga, springbok, waterbuck 10 hartebeest, wildebeest
Le Cid author: Pierre Corneille
Le Cid composer: 8 Massenet
Le Coq d'Or: 5 opera 6 ballet
  composer: Rimsky-Korsakov
Le Création du monde composer: 7 Milhaud
lect.
  giver: 4 prof.
Lecter: 8 Hannibal
  like ~: 4 evil
lectern: 4 ambo, desk 5 ambon, stand, table 6 podium, pulpit 7 rostrum, support 8 platform
lector: 6 fellow, mentor, reader 7 academe, teacher 8 academic, educator, lecturer 9 pedagogue, preceptor, professor 10 instructor
Lectric __: 5 Shave
lecture: 3 rag, ser. 4 flay, rate, talk

5 chide, orate, pitch, scold, speak, spiel, spout, teach, tutor 6 berate, lesson, preach, punish, rank on, rebuke, recite, sermon, speech, tirade 7 address, censure, chiding, declaim, deliver, expound, monolog, oration, pep talk, prelect, reproof, reprove, soapbox, tell off 8 admonish, harangue, instruct, moralism, moralize, perorate, scolding 9 chalk talk, discourse, exprobate, going-over, hold forth, monologue, pound into, preaching, reprehend, reprimand, sermonize, talking-to 10 allocution, preachment, recitation, upbraiding, vocalizing
follower: 5 Q and A
give a ~: 4 talk 5 edify, orate, speak, spout, teach, tutor 6 advise, inform 7 address, declaim, deliver, educate, expound, instill 8 initiate, instruct 9 discourse, hold forth, inculcate, interpret, pound into, sermonize
leader: 4 prof 7 speaker 9 professor
place: 4 dais, hall 6 lyceum, podium 7 rostrum 10 auditorium
lecturer: 5 tutor 6 docent, fellow, lector, orator, reader, talker 7 academe, pedagog, speaker, teacher 8 academic, educator 9 abecedary, pedagogue, professor 10 instructor
lecturers: 5 profs 7 faculty 8 teachers 9 academics 10 professors
led
being ~: 5 in tow
easily ~: 4 meek, tame 5 mousy 6 docile 7 passive, pliable 8 amenable, obedient, yielding 9 compliant, tractable 10 submissive
in: 5 began 6 guided 7 brought 8 escorted
on: 5 lured 6 teased 7 deluded, enticed, tempted, tricked 8 beguiled, deceived 9 inveigled, misguided, toyed with 10 hoodwinked
to: 6 caused 8 preceded 9 brought on 10 eventuated, resulted in
Leda: 4 moon
daughter of ~: 5 Helen 8 Timandra
lover of ~: 4 Zeus 9 Tyndareus
parent of ~: 8 Thestius 10 Eurythemis
planet: 7 Jupiter
son of ~: 6 Castor, Pollux
Leda and the Swan author: William Butler Yeats
Le Déjeuner sur l'herbe artist: 5 Manet
Leder: 4 Mimi
Lederberg, Joshua: 8 Nobelist
Lederer: 5 Eppir 7 Francis, William
lederhosen: 5 pants 6 shorts
Lederman, Leon: 8 Nobelist 9 physicist
ledge: 3 bar, rim 4 berm, edge, reef, sill 5 bench, berme, ridge, shelf 6 mantle 7 bracket 10 projection
fireplace ~: 3 hob
rocky ~: 3 tor 4 crag 5 arête, cliff 8 pinnacle 9 precipice 10 escarpment, prominence
underwater ~: 3 bar 4 reef 5 atoll, ridge, shelf, shoal 7 sand bar
ledger: 5 books 7 account, daybook, journal 8 register
abbr.: 3 amt., YTD
check: 5 audit 10 inspection
division: 4 acct. 7 account
entry: 4 item, loss 5 asset, debit 6 credit
expert: 3 CPA 7 auditor 10 accountant, bookkeeper
put in the ~: 5 enter 7 set down
ledger ___: 4 beam, line 5 board, paper, plate, strip
___ ledger: 4 cost 5 stock 6 stores
Ledger, Heath: 5 actor
film: 10 Things I Hate About You (1999)
The Four Feathers (2002)
Monster's Ball (2001)
The Patriot (2000)
Le Docteur miracle composer: 5 Bizet
LED part: 5 diode, light 8 emitting
Le Droit locale: 6 Ottawa
Leduc: 4 city, town
locale: 6 Canada 7 Alberta
Le Duc ___: 3 Tho
Led Zeppelin
members: Plant, Page, Jones, Bonham
song: Stairway to Heaven (1970)
Whole Lotta Love (1969)
lee: 4 dreg, side 5 cover 6 refuge 7 shelter 10 protection
ender: 3 way 4 ward 5 board
opposite: 5 stoss
lee ___: 4 tide, wave 5 gauge, shore
Lee: 3 Ang, Ann, Reb 4 Anna, Fort, Joie, Sara, Stan, Yuan 5 Aaker, Alvin, Bruce, David, Elder, Grant, Peggy, Pinky, Smith, Spike, Tommy, Tracy 6 Albert, Bailey, Bowman, Brenda, Canada, Curtis, Dickey, Harper, Janzen, Johnny, Majors, Marvin, Remick, Sheryl, Tanith 7 Bernard, Brandon, Horsley, Iacocca, Krasner, Lorelei, Manfred, Michele, Robert E., Trevino 8 De Forest, Meredith, Michaels, Ritenour, Tsung-Dao, Van Cleef 9 Greenwood, Holdridge, Radziwill, Strasberg 10 Meriwether
city on the ~: 4 Cork
to Grant: 3 foe 5 enemy
Lee ___: 5 Myles
___ Lee: 4 Aura, Fort, Sara 6 Jennie 7 Annabel, Stagger
Lee, Ang: 8 director
film: Crouching Tiger, Hidden Dragon (2000)
The Ice Storm (1997)
Ride With the Devil (1999)
Sense and Sensibility (1995)
Lee Ann: 6 Womack
Lee, Bernard: 5 actor
film: From Russia With Love (1963)
Goldfinger (1964)
The Purple Plain (1954)
Whistle Down the Wind (1961)
Lee, Brenda
nickname: Little Miss Dynamite
real last name: Tarpley
song: All Alone Am I (1962)
As Usual (1963)
Break It to Me Gently (1962)
Coming On Strong (1966)
Dum Dum (1961)
Emotions (1961)
Everybody Loves Me But You (1962)
Fool #1 (1961)
Heart in Hand (1962)
I'm Sorry (1960)
Is It True (1964)
I Want to Be Wanted (1960)
Losing You (1963)
Rockin' Around the Christmas Tree (1960)
Sweet Nothin's (1960)
That's All You Gotta Do (1960)
Too Many Rivers (1965)
You Can Depend on Me (1961)
___ Lee Browne: 6 Roscoe
___ Lee Bunton: 4 Emma
leech: 3 bum 6 jackal, sponge 7 moocher, sponger 8 barnacle, deadbeat, freeload, hanger-on, parasite, scrounge 9 loan shark, scrounger, sycophant 10 freeloader
Lee, Christopher: 5 actor
film: The Creeping Flesh (1973)
The Devil's Bride (1968)
Diagnosis: Murder (1976)
The Face of Fu Manchu (1965)
The Man With the Golden Gun (1974)
Return From Witch Mountain (1978)
Scream of Fear (1961)
The Wicker Man (1973)
___ Lee Crosby: 5 Cathy
___ Lee Curtis: 5 Jamie
Lee, Curtis song: Pretty Little Angel Eyes (1961)
Lee, David: 8 Nobelist 9 physicist
Leeds: 4 city, town 6 Andrea
city near ~: 4 York
locale: 7 England 9 Yorkshire
river: 4 Aire
___ Lee Gifford: 6 Kathie
Lee, Harper work: To Kill a Mockingbird
___ Lee Hope: 5 Laura
Lee J. ___: 4 Cobb
Lee, Johnny song: Lookin' for Love (1980)
___ Lee Jones: 5 Tommy 6 Rickie
leek: 6 allium, veggie 9 vegetable
relative: 5 chive, onion
Leek: 5 Sybil
___-leekie: 5 cock-a
Leelee: 8 Sobieski
___ Lee Lewis: 5 Jerry
Lee, Lorelei creator: 4 Loos
___ Lee Masters: 5 Edgar
Lee, Michele: 7 actress
film: How to Succeed in Business Without Really Trying (1967)
The Love Bug (1969)
spouse: James Farentino
TV: Knots Landing
___ Lee, NJ: 4 Fort
___ Lee Nolin: 4 Gena
Lee, Peggy
film (voice): Lady and the Tramp
real name: Norma Jean Egstrom
song: Fever (1958)
Is That All There Is (1969)
leer: 3 eye 4 look, ogle 5 smirk, sneer, stare 6 goggle, squint 7 eyeball 10 make eyes at
___ Lee Ralph: 6 Sheryl
___ Lee Ray: 4 Dixy
leerer: 5 ogler
leeriness: 5 doubt, qualm 8 wariness 9 chariness, misgiving, suspicion 10 skepticism
Lee, Robert E.: 3 gen. 7 general
horse: 9 Traveller
nation: 3 CSA
___ Lee Roth: 5 David
Lee, Rowland V.: 8 director
film: The Count of Monte Cristo (1934)
The Ruling Voice (1931)
Son of Frankenstein (1939)
The Son of Monte Cristo (1940)
The Toast of New York (1937)
Zoo in Budapest (1933)
leery: 3 shy 4 cagy, wary 5 cagey, chary 6 unsure 7 careful, dubious, fearful, guarded, prudent 8 cautious, doubtful, doubting, overwary, skittish 9 skeptical, uncertain 10 suspicious, uneffusive
be ~: 5 doubt 7 suspect 10 disbelieve
one: 5 cynic 7 doubter, sceptic, scoffer, skeptic 8 nihilist 9 dissenter, pessimist
lees: 3 end 5 dregs 7 deposit, grounds, remnant 8 sediment 9 tea leaves
Leesburg: 4 city, town
locale: 8 Virginia
Lee, Spike: 5 actor 8 director
film: Clockers (1995)
Crooklyn (1994)
Do the Right Thing (1989)
Get on the Bus (1996)
He Got Game (1998)
Jungle Fever (1991)
Malcolm X (1992)
Mo' Better Blues (1990)
The Original Kings of Comedy (2000)
School Daze (1988)
She's Gotta Have It (1986)
Lee's Summit: 4 city, town
locale: 8 Missouri
Lee, Tommy
spouse: Pamela Anderson, Heather Locklear
Lee, Tsung-Dao: 8 Nobelist 9 physicist
___ Lee, VA: 4 Fort
Leeward Island: 4 Saba 5 Nevis 7 Antigua, Barbuda, St. Kitts 8 Anguilla, Dominica, St. Martin 10 Guadeloupe, Montserrat, Saint Kitts
leeway: 4 play, room 5 range, scope, slack, space, swing 6 extent, margin 7 freedom 8 free hand, latitude 9 elbowroom, extra time, free space, tolerance 10 room to move, wiggle room
having no ~: 4 snug 5 tight 6 narrow 7 cramped, crowded
Lee, Yuan: 7 chemist 8 Nobelist
Leeza: 7 Gibbons
Le Fanal author: Gabriel Marcel
Le Fifre artist: 5 Manet
Leflore: 3 Ron
le freak: 5 dance
Le Freak (1978 song) artist: Chic
left: 4 gone, port 5 extra, punch, split 6 extant, lonely, with us 7 gone out, liberal 8 departed, forsaken, larboard, liberals, marooned, portside, residual, sinister 9 abandoned, direction, remaining, sinistral, socialist 10 liberalism
bank: 8 bohemian
be ~: 6 remain 7 inherit, survive
behind: 7 missing 9 abandoned, forgotten
combining form: 3 lev- 4 levo- 5 laevo- 8 sinistro-
ender: 3 ist 4 most, over, ward
hang a ~: 4 turn
in heraldry: 8 sinister
in the time ~: 3 yet 4 till 5 still
not ~: 5 right
on a ship: 4 port 5 aport
one ~ holding the bag: 4 dupe, goat 5 chump 6 sucker, victim 7 cat's-paw, fall guy 9 scapegoat
out: 7 missing, omitted
to a horse: 3 haw
to the ~: 4 levo 5 aside
to the imagination: 5 tacit 6 silent, unsaid 7 implied 8 implicit, inferred, unspoken, unstated, unvoiced, wordless 10 understood
to the ~, in French: 7 à gauche
what's ~: 3 net 4 orts, rest 6 excess, profit 7 balance, overage, remains, remnant, residue, surplus 8 leavings, take-home 9 remainder
left ___: 4 face, wing 5 brain, field, stage 7 fielder
left-___: 4 hand, laid 6 handed, hander
___ left: 4 eyes, quad 5 flush, guide, hang a, stage
Left ___: 4 Bank
Left ___ of God, The: 4 Hand
___ Left: 3 New
Left Bank and Other Stories, The author: Jean Rhys
Left Banke song: Walk Away Renee (1966)
Left Bank river: 5 Seine
___ left field: 5 out in
left-handed: 6 clumsy 7 awkward,

dubious, unadept 8 inexpert 9 equivocal, maladroit 10 unexplicit
compliment: 3 cut, dig 4 slam, snub 6 insult, slight, zinger 7 affront, offense, put-down
Left Hand of God, The (1955 film)
cast: Humphrey Bogart, Lee J. Cobb, Gene Tierney
director: Edward Dmytryk
left-hand page: 5 verso
leftist: 6 Maoist 7 liberal, radical 8 ultraist 9 anarchist, communist, socialist 10 Bolshevist
Left Leg, The author: T.F. Powys
left-of-___: 6 center
leftover: 3 odd, ort 4 dreg, orts 5 crumb, extra, scrap, spare, trash 6 debris, excess, legacy, scraps, unused 7 oddment, remnant, residue, surplus, uneaten 8 leavings, oddments, remnants, residual, survivor, unwanted 9 remainder, remaining, untouched, vestigial 10 unconsumed
leftovers: 4 hash, rest 5 waste 6 others 7 remnant, residue
dish: 4 hash, stew
fix ~: 3 zap 4 heat, nuke, warm 6 reheat, rewarm
Left Right Out of Your Heart (1958 song) artist: Patti Page
Left Turn ___: 4 Only
lefty: 8 southpaw 9 portsider
Lefty: 5 Gomez, Grove 8 Frizzell
leg: 3 lap 4 limb, part, post, prop 5 brace, shank, stage, stump 6 column, member 7 portion, section, segment, stretch, support, upright 8 baluster 9 drumstick, extremity
an arm and a ~: 4 high 5 pricy, steep 6 costly, pricey 7 damages, ruinous 9 expensive 10 exorbitant
armor: 6 greave
bone: 4 shin 5 femur, tibia 6 fibula
bones: 6 femora
combining form: 4 scel- 5 scelo-
covering: 4 spat 6 gaiter, puttee 7 gambado
ender: 4 foot, horn, room, work 6 warmer
give a ~ up: 3 aid 4 help 5 boost, hoist 6 assist, succor 9 encourage
it: 3 run 4 hike, walk 7 hotfoot, vamoose
joint: 4 knee 5 ankle
muscle: 4 quad 6 soleus 10 quadriceps
muscles: 5 solei
part: 4 calf, crus, knee 5 shank, thigh
puller: 4 liar
pull one's ~: 3 guy, kid, rag, rib 4 fool, jest, joke, razz, twit 5 chaff, tease, trick 6 banter, take in 7 deceive, mislead
shake a ~: 3 fly, hie, rip, run, zip 4 dart, dash, flit, move, race, rush, stir, tear, zoom 5 hurry, scoot, speed 6 barrel, boogie, gallop, hasten, hustle, move it, rocket, scurry 7 floor it, hop to it, quicken, scamper, speed up 8 step on it 9 hotfoot it, skedaddle 10 get a move on, get hopping, hightail it
starter: 3 bow, dog 4 boot, fore, jack 5 black
up: 4 edge, hand, lift 5 boost 6 assist 9 advantage, headstart
leg ___: 3 bye, hit 4 drop 7 warmers
leg-___: 4 pull 5 break 6 puller
___ leg: 4 gate, milk, pant 5 swing 6 quiver, square 7 cluster, trumpet
legacy: 4 gift, will 6 devise, estate 7 bequest, product 8 heirloom, heritage, leftover 9 endowment, patrimony, throwback, tradition 10 birthright
recipient: 4 heir
revoke a ~: 5 adeem
sharer: 6 coheir
Legacy: 3 car 4 auto, font 6 Subaru 8 typeface 10 automobile
Legacy, The
author: Howard Fast, John Donne
legal: 3 due 4 fair, good, just 5 clean, jural, legit, licit, right, sound, valid 6 formal, kasher, kosher, lawful, proper, vested 7 allowed, decreed, granted 8 forensic, innocent, judicial, juristic, rightful, straight 9 allowable, canonical, chartered, juridical, justified, protected, statutory, warranted 10 aboveboard, admissible, authorized, legitimate, on the level, prescribed, sanctioned
action: 4 case, plea, suit 5 trial 6 appeal
adverb: 6 hereby, herein, hereof, hereon, hereto 8 hereunto, hereupon
adviser: 3 att. 4 atty. 6 jurist, lawyer 7 adviser, advisor, counsel 8 advocate, attorney 9 barrister, counselor, solicitor 10 mouthpiece
agreement: 6 escrow 8 contract
article: 6 clause 7 codicil, proviso 9 amendment
assistant: 4 para 5 clerk 10 amanuensis
bring ~ action: 3 sue 8 litigate
case statement: 5 facta
claim: 4 lien 5 droit 8 mortgage
concept: 6 intent, motive 8 volition
defense: 5 alibi
delay: 4 hold, stay, stop 5 waive 8 reprieve 9 deferment, remission 10 suspension
document: 4 deed, will, writ 5 brief, title
ender: 3 ese
force: 6 duress
joining: 6 merger 7 wedding, wedlock 8 contract, marriage, nuptials 9 matrimony
make ~: 2 OK 3 ink 4 sign 6 ratify 7 approve, certify, endorse, initial, witness 8 sanction, validate 9 authorize, establish, formalize, sign off on 10 constitute, legitimize
maturity: 8 majority
memo: 5 brief 8 abstract
not ~: 7 bootleg, illicit 8 criminal, improper, outlawed, unlawful, wrongful 9 felonious 10 contraband, prohibited, unlicensed
noun: 5 whoso
official: 2 DA 5 bench, judge 6 jurist, umpire 7 arbiter, referee 8 his Honor 9 moderator 10 arbitrator, magistrate, negotiator
phrase: 4 as to, in re 5 and/or, in rem
posting: 4 bail, bond 6 surety 7 warrant
record book: 5 liber
remove beyond ~ jurisdiction: 5 eloin
setting: 5 bench, court, venue 8 tribunal
starter: 4 para
start of a ~ conclusion: 5 I rest
substitute: 5 agent, proxy 6 deputy 7 stand-in 8 delegate 9 alternate, appointee, go-between, surrogate 10 lieutenant
tender: 3 oof 4 cash, coin, gelt, jack, kail, kale, loot, peag, pelf 5 bills, bread, bucks, dough, funds, lucre, money, moola, mopus, pesos, rhino, sewan 6 dinero, do-re-mi, mammon, mazuma, moolah, seawan, silver, specie, wampum, wealth 7 cabbage, capital, dollars, lettuce, ooftish, scratch, shekels 8 bankroll, cold cash, currency, hard cash, smackers 9 banknotes, frogskins, long green, simoleons 10 greenbacks, green stuff
under ~ age: 5 minor 8 juvenile 10 adolescent
unknown: 3 Doe, Roe
writ: 4 mise 6 elegit
see also law
legal ___: 3 age, aid, cap, fee, pad 4 list 5 eagle 6 memory, tender, weight 7 holiday, reserve
legal-___: 4 size
Legal ___ Society: 3 Aid
Legal Eagles (1986 film)
cast: Brian Dennehy, Daryl Hannah, Robert Redford, Debra Winger
director: Ivan Reitman
legality: 8 validity 10 lawfulness, legitimacy
legalize: 5 allow, enact 6 codify, decree, ordain, permit 7 approve, clean up, decrees, launder, license 8 regulate, sanction, validate 9 authorize, formulate, legislate 10 constitute, legitimate
legalized: 5 legit, licit 6 kosher, lawful 7 enacted 9 allowable 10 legitimate
Le Gallienne: 3 Eva
legally: 5 by law, right
Legally Blonde (2001 film)
cast: Selma Blair, Matthew Davis, Luke Wilson, Reese Witherspoon
director: Robert Luketic
dog: 7 Bruiser 9 Chihuahua
legan: 5 licit
Leganza: 3 car 4 auto 6 Daewoo 10 automobile
legate: 5 agent, envoy 6 consul, deputy, nuncio 7 attaché, courier 8 bequeath, delegate, diplomat, emissary, minister 9 appointee 10 ambassador
legatee: 4 heir 5 owner 6 coheir 7 grantee, heiress, heritor 9 inheritor, recipient
legation: 5 staff 6 envoys 7 embassy, mission 9 committee, delegates 10 deputation, emissaries
legato: 6 smooth 7 flowing 8 smoothly
opposite: 4 stac. 8 staccato
symbol: 4 slur
legend: 3 key 4 code, head, lore, myth, saga, tale 5 fable, motto, story, table, title 6 cipher, device, mythos, record, rubric 7 account, caption, epitaph, fiction, heading, romance 8 epigraph, folklore, folktale 9 folk story, mythology, narrative, tradition, underline 10 fairy story
___ legend: 5 urban 6 living
Legend: 3 car 4 auto 5 Acura 10 automobile
legendary: 5 famed, noted 6 fabled, famous, unreal 7 storied 8 fabulous, immortal, invented, mythical, renowned, romantic 9 imaginary, well-known 10 apocryphal, celebrated, improbable
Legend of Bagger Vance, The (2000 film)
cast: Matt Damon, Bruce McGill, Will Smith, Charlize Theron
director: Robert Redford
Legend of Hell House, The (1973 film)
cast: Pamela Franklin, Roddy McDowall, Clive Revill
director: John Hough
Legend of Sleepy Hollow, The author: Washington Irving
legends: 4 lore 5 myths, tales 6 fables 8 folklore
Legends of Our Time author: Elie Wiesel
leger ___: 4 line
Léger: 6 Aléxis 7 Fernand
Léger, Alexis: 4 poet
legerdemain: 5 magic, trick 9 dexterity
expert: 5 magus 6 wizard 8 conjurer, magician, sorcerer
Léger, Fernand: 6 artist 7 painter
homeland: 6 France
legerity: 7 agility 8 celerity, deftness 9 dexterity, quickness 10 nimbleness
___-legged: 4 duck, four 5 bandy, cross 7 feather, spindle
___-legged race: 5 three
legging: 7 gambado
leggings: 5 chaps, pants, spats 6 tights 7 gaiters, puttees 10 chaparajos
Leggo my ___!: 4 Eggo
L'eggs rival: 5 Hanes
leggy: 4 tall 5 rangy 6 gangly 7 spindly, willowy 8 gangling
leghorn: 3 hat, hen 4 bird, fowl 7 chicken
relative: 6 Bantam, Brahma, Houdan, Sussex 7 Cornish, Dorking 8 Araucana, Langshan, Shanghai 9 Dominique, Orpington, Wyandotte
Leghorn: 4 city, port, town
locale: 5 Italy
legibility: 4 ease 7 clarity 8 evenness, neatness
legible: 4 neat 5 clean, clear, lucid, plain, sharp 8 coherent, distinct, readable
legibly, write: 5 print
legion: 4 army, body, host, many, mass, rout 5 cloud, crowd, drove, flock, force, group, horde, ocean, swarm, troop 6 myriad, number, scores, sundry, throng 7 brigade, company, numbers, phalanx, various 8 division, multiple, numerous, populous 9 battalion, countless, multitude 10 numberless, voluminous
fraction: 6 cohort
___ legion: 7 foreign
___ Legion: 4 Arab 5 Black 7 British
legionary: 5 cadet 7 draftee, fighter, officer, private, recruit, soldier, trooper, veteran, warrior 8 commando 9 combatant, mercenary
Legion of ___: 5 Honor, Merit
legions: 3 sea 4 army, host, lots, many, slew, tons 5 drove, horde, hosts, ocean, scads 6 clouds, crowds, droves, flocks, hoards, masses, myriad, scores, swarms 7 myriads, numbers, throngs 8 billions, millions, quantity, very many 9 battalion, multitude, profusion, trillions 10 multitudes
legislate: 4 make, pass 5 enact, order 6 codify, decree, oblige, ordain 8 legalize, regulate 9 establish, prescribe 10 constitute
legislated: 6 lawful
législateur group: 5 senat
legislation: 3 act, law 4 bill 6 ruling 7 charter, measure, passage, statute 9 enactment, lawmaking 10 regulation
nix, as ~: 4 kill, veto 5 quash 6 reject 8 override, throw out 9 shoot down
legislative: 8 enacting 9 decreeing, lawgiving, lawmaking, ordaining, synodical 10 senatorial
appendage: 5 rider 7 proviso 9 amendment
assemblies: 5 plena
body: 5 house 6 senate 7 council 10 parliament
disciplinarian: 4 whip
excess: 4 pork
matter: 3 act 4 bill 6 debate 7 cloture 10 filibuster
meeting: 4 sess. 7 session
ordinance: 3 law 4 rule 6 assize
legislative ___: 4 veto 7 council

legislator: 6 deputy, leader, member 7 senator 8 lawgiver, lawmaker 10 politician
legislature: 4 body, diet, parl. 5 house, taxer 6 plenum, senate 7 chamber, council 8 assembly, congress, politics 9 lawmakers 10 parliament
Austria: 9 Bundesrat
Canada: 6 Senate
Croatia: 5 Sabor
Denmark: 9 Folketing
Finland: 9 Eduskunta
France: 5 Senat 6 Senate
Germany: 9 Bundesrat, Bundestag
Greek: 5 Boule
Iceland: 7 Althing
India: 6 Sansad
Ireland: 4 Dail
Israel: 7 Knesset
Italy: 6 Senate
Japan: 4 Diet
Kenya: 5 Bunge
Latvia: 6 Saeima
Lichtenstein: 4 Diet
Lithuania: 6 Seimas
Mexico: 6 Senate
Norway: 8 Storting
Poland: 4 Sejm
Russia: 4 Duma
South Korea: 6 Kukhoe
Spain: 6 Cortes
Sweden: 7 Riksdag
Ukraine: 4 Rada
legist: 6 jurist, lawyer 7 counsel 8 attorney, defender 9 barrister, counselor, solicitor 10 counsellor
legit: 2 OK 4 fair, fine, good, nice, okay, okeh, okey, real, walk 5 frank, great, jural, legal, licit, moral, noble, sound, valid 6 honest, kasher, kosher, lawful, proper, square 7 allowed, ethical, factual, genuine, logical, upright 8 accepted, all right, bona fide, credible, laudable, pleasant, pleasing, rightful, splendid, straight, superior, truthful, verified 9 admirable, agreeable, allowable, authentic, by the book, excellent, legalized, permitted, reputable, veracious, veritable, wonderful 10 aboveboard, acceptable, authorized, beneficial, creditable, forthright, on the level, reasonable, sanctioned, scrupulous
not ~: 4 fake 5 bogus, phony, shady 6 phoney, pseudo
legitimacy: 5 force, right, truth 6 weight 7 grounds 8 legality, validity 9 authority, soundness 10 lawfulness
legitimate: 4 fair, good, just, real, sure, true 5 jural, legal, licit, right, sound, typic, usual, valid 6 cogent, honest, kasher, kosher, lawful, normal, proper 7 certain, correct, genuine, logical, natural, regular, typical 8 accepted, innocent, legalize, official, orthodox, probable, received, reliable, rightful, sensible, verified 9 allowable, authentic, canonical, customary, legalized, statutory, warranted 10 admissible, authorized, consistent, on the level, reasonable, sanctioned, true to type, verifiable
legitimately: 5 right, truly 6 indeed, in fact, really 7 de facto, in truth 8 actually, for a fact, honestly 9 assuredly, certainly, genuinely, in reality, precisely 10 positively
legitimize: 5 adopt 7 certify, entitle, intitle, justify, mandate 8 sanction, validate
legitimized: 5 legal, licit, valid 6 kosher, lawful 7 enacted 8 mandated, official 9 juridical, legalized, statutory 10 authorized, legislated, legitimate
legman: 5 gofer 6 gopher 8 reporter
job: 6 errand
___ legno: 3 col
Lego: 5 block
leg-of-mutton sleeve: 5 gigot
leg-puller: 3 wag 4 card, fool 5 clown, comic, cutup 6 jester, kidder 7 buffoon, farceur, gagster, wise guy 8 comedian, funnyman, humorist, wiseacre
Legrand: 6 Michel
Le Grand Orange: 5 Staub 10 Rusty Staub
Legree: 5 Simon
LeGros, James: 5 actor
film: Drugstore Cowboy (1989)
Floundering (1994)
Guncrazy (1992)
Scotland, Pa. (2002)
leg rotation (ballet): 7 turnout
legs: 7 stamina 8 patience 9 longevity
creature with 14 ~: 6 isopod
go on hind ~: 4 ramp, rear
on its last ~: 4 weak 6 poorly 7 failing, not well 9 worsening
___ legs: 3 sea 4 crab, hind, land 5 shear
Legs: 7 Diamond
Legs (1984 song) artist: ZZ Top
Legs author: William Kennedy
leg-smoothing product: 4 Nair, Neet
___-leg table: 4 gate
legume: 3 pea, soy 4 bean, miso, soya, tofu 5 vetch 6 acacia, cowpea, frijol, lentil, manioc, mimosa, peanut 7 cassava, haricot, mesquit, red bean, snow pea, soybean, wax bean 8 bean curd, bush bean, chickpea, fava bean, garbanzo, lima bean, mesquite, mung bean, navy bean, pink bean, pole bean, snap bean, sweet pea, yard-long 9 broad bean, cover crop, green bean, pinto bean, tonka bean, vegetable, white bean 10 adzuki bean, butter bean, kidney bean, string bean
holder: 3 pod 4 hull 6 jacket 8 seed case 10 integument
tree: 3 koa 5 carob 6 cassia, cercis, locust, padauk, padouk, redbud 7 araroba, mesquit 8 mesquite, tamarind 9 poinciana
___ leg up: 4 get a 5 give a
legwear: 5 socks 7 hosiery 9 stockings
legwork: 6 search, survey 8 research
Lehár, Franz work: The Merry Widow
Le Havre: 4 city, port, town
city near ~: 4 Caen
locale: 6 France
Lehigh: 5 river 6 school
athletes: 9 Engineers
locale: 4 Penn. 9 Bethlehem
Lehigh Acres: 4 city, town
locale: 7 Florida
Lehi locale: 4 Utah
Lehman: 3 Tom 5 Engel 6 Ernest
Lehmann: 5 Lotte 7 Michael
Lehmann, Lotte: 6 singer 7 soprano
specialty: 5 opera
Lehn, Jean-Marie: 7 chemist 8 Nobelist
lehr: 4 oven
Lehr: 3 Lew
Lehrer: 3 Jim, Tom
lehua: 4 tree 5 plant 6 flower 8 hardwood
lei: 6 wreath 7 garland 9 neckpiece
land: 4 Maui, Oahu 5 Kauai 6 Hawaii
Leia: 8 princess
brother: 4 Luke
rescuer: 3 Han
Leiber: 5 Fritz, Jerry
Leibman, Ron: 5 actor
film: The Hot Rock (1972)
Norma Rae (1979)
Slaughterhouse-Five (1972)
The Super Cops (1974)
Your Three Minutes Are Up (1973)
spouse: Linda Lavin, Jessica Walter
Leibnitz, Wilhelm von: 11 philosopher
Leibovitz: 5 Annie
Leibowitz, René: 9 conductor
Leica: 6 camera
alternative: 4 Fuji 5 Canon, Kodak, Nikon 6 Konica, Pentax, Rollei 7 Minolta, Olympus, Vivitar, Yashica 8 Polaroid
Leicester: 4 city, earl, town 5 sheep 6 cheese
locale: 7 England
Leicestershire: 6 county
locale: 7 England
Leics: 6 county
locale: 7 England
Leiden: 4 city, town
locale: 7 Holland
Leie, city on the: 5 Ghent
Leif: 7 Ericson, Garrett 8 Erickson, Eriksson
father: 4 Eric
Leifer: 5 Carol
Leigh: 4 Hunt 5 Janet, Mitch 6 Vivien 7 Harline 9 McCloskey
___ Leigh Cook: 7 Rachael
Leigh, Janet: 7 actress
daughter: Jamie Lee Curtis
film: Act of Violence (1949)
Angels in the Outfield (1951)
Bye Bye Birdie (1963)
The Fog (1980)
Holiday Affair (1949)
Houdini (1953)
Living It Up (1954)
The Manchurian Candidate (1962)
My Sister Eileen (1955)
The Naked Spur (1953)
One Is a Lonely Number (1972)
Psycho (1960)
Rogue Cop (1954)
The Romance of Rosy Ridge (1947)
Scaramouche (1952)
Touch of Evil (1958)
Walking My Baby Back Home (1953)
Who Was That Lady? (1960)
spouse: Tony Curtis
Leigh, Jennifer Jason: 7 actress
film: The Anniversary Party (2001)
Crooked Hearts (1991)
Dolores Claiborne (1995)
Fast Times at Ridgemont High (1982)
Grandview, U.S.A. (1984)
The Hudsucker Proxy (1994)
Road to Perdition (2002)
Single White Female (1992)
Leigh Taylor-___: 5 Young
Leighton: 5 Laura 8 Margaret
Leighton, Margaret: 7 actress
film: The Constant Husband (1955)
Court Martial (1955)
The Winslow Boy (1948)
Leigh, Vivien: 7 actress
film: Dark Journey (1937)
Gone With the Wind (1939, AA)
The Roman Spring of Mrs. Stone (1961)
Ship of Fools (1965)
Sidewalks of London (1938)
Storm in a Teacup (1937)
A Streetcar Named Desire (1951, AA)
That Hamilton Woman (1941)
Waterloo Bridge (1940)
role: 5 O'Hara 6 Stella 8 Scarlett
spouse: Laurence Olivier
Leila: 5 Hyams
Leila author: Edward Bulwer-Lytton
___ Leilani: 5 Sweet
Leinsdorf, Erich: 9 conductor
Leinster: 6 Murray
Leipzig: 4 city, town
city near ~: 4 Gera 5 Halle 6 Dessau
locale: 7 Germany
river: 6 Parthe 7 Pleisse
see also German
Leisen, Mitchell: 8 director
film: Artists and Models Abroad (1938)
The Big Broadcast of 1938 (1938)
Captain Carey, U.S.A. (1950)
Death Takes a Holiday (1934)
Easy Living (1937)
Four Hours to Kill (1935)
Frenchman's Creek (1944)
The Girl Most Likely (1957)
Hands Across the Table (1935)
Hold Back the Dawn (1941)
Kitty (1945)
The Lady Is Willing (1942)
The Mating Season (1951)
Midnight (1939)
Remember the Night (1940)
Take a Letter, Darling (1942)
To Each His Own (1946)
leisure: 4 ease, rest, time 5 pause, quiet, range, scope 6 chance, luxury, recess, repose 7 freedom, holiday, liberty, respite, time off 8 free time, good life, vacation 9 spare time 10 recreation, relaxation, retirement, sabbatical
at ~: 4 free, idle 6 otiose
companion: 4 arts
ender: 4 wear
pursuit: 4 play 5 hobby 7 pastime
wear: 5 jeans 6 chinos, denims, slacks, T-shirt
leisure ___: 4 home, suit
Leisure: 5 David
Leisure City: 4 town
locale: 7 Florida
leisure-class: 4 rich 5 flush 6 fat-cat, loaded, uptown 7 moneyed, opulent, upscale, wealthy, well-off 8 affluent, well-to-do 10 prosperous, well-heeled
leisured: 4 free, idle 7 jobless 8 inactive, on layoff 9 at liberty, on the dole 10 unemployed
leisurely: 3 lax 4 easy, free, idly, lazy, poky, slow 5 slack 6 calmly, casual, draggy, easily, gentle, lazily, pokily, slowly 7 delayed, gradual, halting, impeded, laggard, lagging, languid, relaxed, restful, tardily, unhasty 8 bit by bit, casually, crawling, creeping, dawdling, dilatory, dragging, drawn-out, hesitant, laid-back, plodding, slothful, sluggish, toddling, torpidly 9 gradually, haltingly, laggardly, languidly, lethargic, prolonged, slackened, snaillike, unhurried 10 composedly, crawlingly, creepingly, deliberate, dilatorily, inactively, indolently, listlessly, protracted, sluggishly
leisure-suit fabric: 5 Orlon
leitmotif: 3 air 4 idea 5 theme 6 melody, notion, strain 7 subject
Le Jet d'___: 3 Eau
___ Lejeune: 4 Camp
lek: 4 coin 5 money
Lek: 5 river
locale: 7 Holland 11 Netherlands
Lela: 6 Rochon
Leland: 7 Hayward 8 Hartwell, Stanford
Lélia author: George Sand
L'Elisir d'Amore composer: 9 Donizetti
Leloir, Luis F.: 7 chemist 8 Nobelist
Lely, Peter: 6 artist 7 painter
homeland: 7 Holland
Lem: 6 Barney 9 Stanislaw
LEM: 6 lander
Apollo 11 ~: 5 Eagle
locale: 4 moon
org.: 4 NASA
part of ~: 5 Lunar 6 Module 9 Excursion
leman: 2 jo 3 pet 4 baby, dear, jill, love

5 amour, angel, chéri, cooky, cutey, cutie, deary, ducky, flame, honey, lover, lovey, novia, novio, sugar, sweet 6 bon ami, chérie, cookie, dautie, dearie, steady, sweets 7 beloved, dearest, dear one, pigsney, schatzi, squeeze, sweetie, tootsie 8 chou-chou, cutie pie, dowsabel, dulcinea, ladylove, lovebird, macushla, paramour, precious, snookums, sugar pie, sweetums, truelove 9 bonne amie, boyfriend, dreamboat, inamorata, inamorato, petit chou, valentine 10 girlfriend, heartthrob, honeybunch, mavourneen, sweetheart, sweetie pie, turtledove
LeMans: 3 car 4 auto 7 Pontiac 10 automobile
Le Mans: 4 city, race, town
  locale: 6 France
Le Mans (1971 film)
  cast: Elga Andersen, Steve McQueen
  director: Lee H. Katzin
___ Leman, Switzerland: 3 Lac
Le Marquis de Villemer author: George Sand
Lema, Tony: 6 golfer
  milieu: 5 links 6 course
  org.: 3 PGA
LeMat, Paul: 5 actor
  film: American Graffiti (1973)
    Big Bad Love (2002)
    Handle With Care (1977)
    Melvin and Howard (1980)
LeMay: 6 Curtis 7 general
  milieu: 3 SAC 8 Air Force
Le menunier d'Angibault author: George Sand
___ le mérite: 4 pour
Lemieux, Mario
  milieu: 3 ice 4 rink 5 arena
  org.: 3 NHL
Lemme ___!: 4 at 'em
lemming: 6 animal, mammal, rodent
  relative: 3 rat 4 cavy, degu, jird, paca, vole 5 coypu, gundi, mouse, xerus 6 agouti, beaver, gerbil, gopher, jerboa, marmot, murine 7 hamster, muskrat, visacha 8 chipmunk, cricetid, dormouse, squirrel, tucotuco 9 chickaree, groundhog, guinea pig, porcupine, woodchuck 10 chinchilla, prairie dog
Lemmon: 4 Jack 5 Chris
Lemmon, Jack: 5 actor
  film: Airport '77 (1977)
    The Apartment (1960)
    Avanti! (1972)
    Bell, Book and Candle (1958)
    Buddy Buddy (1981)
    The China Syndrome (1979)
    Cowboy (1958)
    Dad (1989)
    Days of Wine and Roses (1962)
    The Fortune Cookie (1966)
    The Front Page (1974)
    Glengarry Glen Ross (1992)
    Good Neighbor Sam (1964)
    The Great Race (1965)
    Grumpier Old Men (1995)
    Grumpy Old Men (1993)
    How to Murder Your Wife (1965)
    Irma la Douce (1963)
    It Should Happen to You (1954)
    JFK (1991)
    Kotch (1971)
    Luv (1967)
    Mass Appeal (1984)
    Missing (1982)
    Mister Roberts (1955, AA)
    My Fellow Americans (1996)
    My Sister Eileen (1955)
    The Odd Couple (1968)
    The Out-of-Towners (1970)
    Out to Sea (1997)
    Phffft! (1954)
    The Prisoner of Second Avenue (1975)
    Save the Tiger (1973, AA)
    Short Cuts (1993)
    Some Like It Hot (1959)
    That's Life! (1986)
    Under the Yum Yum Tree (1963)
    The Wackiest Ship in the Army (1960)
  spouse: Felicia Farr
Lemnos: 4 isle 6 island
  locale: 5 Egean 6 Aegean
Le Moko: 4 Pepe
lemon: 3 car, dog, dud 4 auto, flop, tree 5 color, fruit 6 citrus, flavor, jalopy, turkey, yellow 7 clunker, failure 8 ice cream 10 automobile, hunk of junk, rattletrap
  alternative: 5 mocha, peach 6 banana, coffee, Jamoca, toffee 7 caramel, coconut, vanilla 8 cinnamon, hazelnut 9 bubblegum, chocolate, pineapple, pistachio, raspberry, rocky road, rum raisin 10 blackberry, cheesecake, Neapolitan, peppermint, strawberry
  bit of ~: 5 twist
  candy: 4 drop
  derivative: 6 citral
  drink: 3 ade 5 juice
  ender: 3 ade 5 grass
  like ~ juice: 5 acerb 6 acidic
  partner: 4 lime
  relative: 4 buff, corn, gold, lime, rust, sand, Ugli 5 blond, brass, coral, cream, flaxy, maize, navel, ocher, ochre, peach, rusty, straw 6 blonde, canary, chammy, citron, crocus, flaxen, orange, pomelo, shammy, shamoy, tangor 7 apricot, chamois, citrine, jasmine, kumquat, mustard, nankeen, old gold, saffron, satsuma, Seville, tangelo, xanthic 8 bergamot, daffodil, mandarin, primrose, shaddock, Valencia 9 champagne, goldenrod, jessamine, tangerine 10 calamondin, grapefruit
  tree: 6 citron
lemon ___: 3 law, oil 4 balm, drop, kali, mint, sole, vine 5 grass, shark 6 squash, yellow 7 verbena
lemon-___: 4 lime
Lemon: 3 Bob 10 Meadowlark
Lemon ___: 4 Tree 5 Grove 6 Pipers
lemonade: 5 drink, juice 8 beverage
  color: 4 pink
  location: 5 stand
Lemonade Lucy: 5 Hayes
lemon balm: 4 herb
Lemon, Bob: 6 hurler, Indian 7 pitcher
LeMond: 4 Greg
___ le monde: 4 tout
Le Monde: 5 paper 6 French 9 newspaper
lemon drop: 5 candy
Lemon Drop Kid, The (1951 film)
  cast: Bob Hope, Marilyn Maxwell, Lloyd Nolan
  director: Sidney Lanfield
Lemon Grove: 4 city, town
  locale: 10 California
lemonlike fruit: 6 cedrat, citron
lemon meringue ___: 3 pie
Lemon Pipers song: Green Tambourine (1967)
Lemon Tree (1962 song) artist: Peter, Paul and Mary
lemon verbena: 4 herb
lemony: 4 acid, sour, tart 5 tangy 6 citric
Lemoore: 4 city, town
  locale: 10 California
Lempa: 5 river
  locale: 10 El Salvador
lempira: 5 money
Lemuel: 8 Gulliver
lemur: 4 maki, vari 5 indri, loris, potto 6 animal, aye-aye, colugo, macaco, monkey 7 primate
  relative: 3 ape 4 saki, titi 5 chimp, drill, jocko, magot, orang, shrew 6 baboon, Bandar, galago, gelada, gibbon, grivet, guenon, howler, langur, rhesus, uakari, vervet 7 colobus, gorilla, guereza, hoolock, macaque, sapajou, siamang, tamarin, tarsier 8 bush baby, capuchin, mandrill, mangabey, marmoset, talapoin 9 orangutan 10 Barbary ape, chimpanzee, orangutang
___ lemur: 6 flying, ruffed 7 gliding
Len: 5 Barry 6 Berman, Cariou, Dawson 7 Dykstra, Wilkens 8 Deighton
Lena: 4 Olin 5 Horne, Nyman, river 6 Stolze
  River locale: 4 Asia 6 Russia
  River people: 5 Yakut
Le Nain: 5 Louis 7 Antoine, Mathieu
___ Lenape: 4 Leni 5 Lenni
Lenard: 4 Mark
Lena the ___: 5 Hyena
Lenca: 6 Indian 7 Amerind
lend: 3 let 4 give, loan 5 allow, grant, share, stake, trust 6 afford, extend, impart, lay out, oblige, supply 7 advance, entrust, furnish, intrust, present, provide 10 contribute
  a hand: 3 aid 4 abet, help 6 assist, step in 7 bail out, pitch in, sustain 9 cooperate
  an ear: 4 heed 6 listen 7 hearken, hear out
  one's name to: 4 back, sign 5 boost 7 endorse, indorse, promote, support, warrant 8 champion, stump for, vouch for 9 get behind, guarantee, recommend, subscribe 10 go to bat for, speak up for, stand up for
lend ___: 5 a hand, an ear
lend-___: 5 lease
lender: 3 FHA, SBA 4 bank, FNMA, GNMA 5 S and L 6 banker, loaner, usurer 7 Shylock 8 creditor 9 loan shark 10 pawnbroker
  starter: 5 money
... ___ lender be: 4 nor a
lending ___: 7 library
lending, illegal: 5 usury
___ lending rate: 5 prime 7 minimum
Lendl, Ivan: 7 netster 9 tennis pro
  milieu: 5 court
  rival: 6 Becker
Lend me your ___: 4 ears
Lenexa: 4 city, town
  locale: 6 Kansas
L'Enfant: 6 Pierre
L'Enfer poet: 5 Marot
length: 4 hank, size, span, term, time, unit, year 5 limit, orbit, piece, range, reach, realm, space, stage, sweep, width 6 course, degree, extent, height, milage, period, radius, season, strand, stride 7 breadth, compass, expanse, measure, mileage, portion, purview, section, segment, stretch 8 diameter, distance, duration, interval, longness, panorama, quantity, tallness 9 dimension, expansion, linearity, loftiness, longitude, magnitude, ranginess 10 elongation, remoteness
  and width: 4 area, size 5 range, reach, scale, scope, space 6 extent, spread 7 compass 9 amplitude
  arm's ~: 5 reach
  at ~: 5 wordy 6 prolix 7 on and on 8 rambling 10 circuitous, discursive, long-winded
  ender: 4 ways, wise
  fashion ~: 4 maxi, mini
  having only ~: 4 one-d
  keep at arm's ~: 6 rebuff 7 neglect, ward off
  of office: 4 span 6 period, tenure 8 duration, interval 9 occupancy
  of time: 4 span, term 5 sweep 6 period
  speak at ~: 3 jaw, yak 4 rant 5 orate, spout 6 expand, preach, rattle 7 address, amplify, declaim, descant, enlarge, lecture, maunder 8 harangue, perorate, sound off 9 discourse, elaborate, expatiate, explicate, hold forth, sermonize, speechify 10 dissertate
  starter: 4 wave
  times width: 4 area
  unit: 2 cm., ft., in., km., mm., yd. 3 mil, rod 4 feet, foot, inch, mile, rood, span, yard 5 chain, cubit, meter 6 fathom, micron, parsec 7 furlong 8 angstrom 9 kilometer, light year 10 centimeter, millimeter
  write at ~: 6 ramble 10 dissertate
___ length: 5 cable, focal 6 cable's 7 sailing
___-length: 4 arm's, full 5 fixed, floor, waltz, whole 7 feature
lengthen: 3 hem, pad 4 draw, grow 5 add to, reach, swell 6 beef up, dilate, expand, extend, let out, spread 7 amplify, augment, broaden, burgeon, distend, drag out, draw out, enlarge, inflate, proceed, prolong, spin out, stretch 8 bourgeon, continue, elongate, increase, protract 9 string out 10 prolongate
  again: 5 rehem
lengthwise: 5 along 7 endways 8 vertical
lengthy: 4 long 5 gabby, windy, wordy 6 padded, prolix 7 diffuse, longish, tedious, unterse, verbose, voluble 8 dragging, drawn-out, elongate, extended, overlong, rambling, tiresome, very long 9 bombastic, elongated, extensive, garrulous, prolonged, talkative, wearisome 10 discursive, long-winded, loquacious, palaverous, protracted
Lengua: 6 Indian 7 Amerind
Leni ___: 6 Lenape
leniency: 4 pity 5 grace, mercy 7 charity, quarter 8 clemency, easiness, humanity, kindness, mildness, patience, softness, sympathy 9 tolerance 10 compassion, generosity, gentleness, indulgence, moderation, tenderness
lenient: 3 lax 4 easy, kind, meek, mild, soft 5 light 6 benign, decent, gentle, humane, kindly, loving, tender 7 amiable, clement, letting, liberal, sparing 8 allowing, excusing, favoring, gracious, humoring, merciful, obliging, spoiling, tolerant, unstrict, yielding 9 assuasive, benignant, compliant, condoning, easygoing, emollient, forgiving, indulgent, pampering, pardoning, soft-shell 10 altruistic, benevolent, charitable, forbearing, permissive, unhardened
  be ~: 5 spare
  become ~: 5 yield 6 relent, soften 8 unfreeze
  one: 5 softy 6 softie
Lenin: 3 Red 7 Marxist 8 Vladimir
  land: 3 Rus. 4 USSR 6 Russia
  police: 4 OGPU
  predecessor: 4 czar, tsar
Leningrad: 4 city, port, town
  locale: 6 Russia

river: 4 Neva
Leninism: 9 Communism, Socialism
Leninist: 3 Red 9 Communist
Lenin Peak: 4 peak 5 mount 8 mountain
locale: 4 Asia 10 Tajikistan
lenitive: 4 balm, soft 5 salve 6 lotion 7 anodyne, unguent 8 liniment, ointment, soothing 9 emollient
lenity: 4 pity 5 mercy 7 quarter 8 clemency, humanity, kindness, mildness, patience, softness, sympathy 10 compassion, generosity, gentleness, indulgence, moderation, toleration
Lenni ___: 6 Lenape
Lennon: 4 John, Sean 5 Janet, Kathy, Peggy 6 Dianne, Julian
Lennon, John
middle name: 3 Ono 7 Winston
song: #9 Dream (1975)
Give Peace a Chance (1969)
Imagine (1971)
Instant Karma (1970)
(Just Like) Starting Over (1980)
Mind Games (1973)
Nobody Told Me (1984)
Power to the People (1971)
Stand By Me (1975)
Watching the Wheels (1981)
Whatever Gets You Thru the Night (1974)
Woman (1980)
spouse: Yoko Ono
Lennon, Julian
song: Tool Late for Goodbyes (1985)
Valotte (1984)
stepmother: Yoko Ono
Lennon, Sean mom: 3 Ono
Lennox: 4 city, town 5 Annie, Lewis
alternative: 5 Rheem, Trane 7 Carrier, Fedders 9 Friedrich
locale: 10 California
Lennox, Annie
group: Eurythmics
song: Put a Little Love in Your Heart (1988)
Walking on Broken Glass (1992)
Lennoxville school: 7 Bishop's
Lenny: 5 Bruce, Moore, Welch 7 Dykstra, Kravitz, Wilkens
Lenny (1974 film)
cast: Dustin Hoffman, Jan Miner, Valerie Perrine
director: Bob Fosse
leno: 5 weave 6 fabric 8 material
Leno, Jay: 4 host 5 emcee
predecessor: 4 Paar 5 Allen 6 Carson
prominent feature: 4 chin
to Letterman: 5 rival
Lenore author: Edgar Allan Poe
Lenox: 4 city, town
alternative: 6 Mikasa 8 Wedgwood
locale: 4 Mass.
product: 5 china
Le Nozze di Figaro composer: 6 Mozart
lens: 4 zoom 5 glass, loupe 6 ocular 7 contact, fisheye, monocle 8 eyeglass, eyepiece, meniscus 9 magnifier, wide-angle
camera ~ scope: 5 field
cleaning aid: 6 eyecup
combining form: 4 phac-, phak- 5 phaco-, phako-
cover: 6 cornea
holder: 3 rim 5 frame
insect eye ~: 5 facet
jeweler's ~: 5 loupe
opening: 4 iris
setting: 5 f-stop
lens ___: 5 board 6 turret
___ lens: 3 eye 4 hand, hard, soft, zoom 5 crown, field, macro 6 object, taking 7 contact, fisheye, Fresnel, viewing
Lens: 4 city, town
locale: 6 France
lenses
big name in ~: 4 Lomb 6 Bausch
like some ~: 6 convex 7 bulging, concave 9 outcurved
like some contact ~: 4 soft
___-lens reflex camera: 6 single
Lent
follower: 6 Easter
observe ~: 4 fast 7 abstain
symbol: 3 ash
___ lente: 7 festina
Lenten: 6 frugal, meager 7 austere 8 rigorous
lenticular: 7 bulging, gibbose, gibbous
lentigo: 3 dot 4 spot 5 speck 7 freckle
lentil: 4 bean 6 legume, veggie 9 vegetable
combining form: 4 phac-, phak- 5 phaco-, phako-
dish: 3 dal
Lent Lily, The author: A.E. Housman
lento: 4 slow 5 tempo 6 slowly
faster than ~: 6 adagio
slower than ~: 5 largo
Lenya, Lotte: 6 singer 7 actress
film: The 3 Penny Opera (1931)
From Russia With Love (1963)
The Roman Spring of Mrs. Stone (1961)
spouse: Kurt Weill
Lenz, Kay spouse: David Cassidy
Leo: 3 cat 4 Genn, lion, pope, sign 5 Esaki, saint, Sayer 6 Fender, Gorcey, Kottke, McKern, Popkin, Rosten 7 Carroll, Delibes, McCarey, pontiff, Szilard, Tolstoy 8 Carrillo, Durocher 9 Baekeland, Buscaglia, Nomellini, Rainwater
constituent: 4 star
month: 3 Aug., Jul. 4 July 6 August
predecessor: 4 Crab 6 Cancer
singer ~: 5 Sayer
successor: 5 Virgo
see also lion
Leo ___: 5 Minor
Léo: 7 Delibes
Leo G. ___: 7 Carroll
Leominster: 4 city, town
locale: 4 Mass.
Leon: 4 Ames, Edel, Hess, Uris 5 Bakst, Errol 6 Cooper, Spinks 7 Alberti, Panetta, Redbone, Russell, Trotsky 8 Fleisher, Jaworski, Lederman
León: 4 city, town
locale: 6 Mexico 9 Nicaragua 10 Guanajuato
see also Spanish
___ León: 7 Ponce de
Léon: 5 Bakst 6 Daudet 7 Jouhaux 9 Bourgeois
see also French
Leona: 8 Helmsley, Mitchell
Leonard: 4 Buck 5 Cohen, Nimoy 6 Elmore, Maltin, Warren 7 Sheldon, Slatkin 9 Bernstein
in Russian: 6 Leonid
Leonardo: 7 da Vinci 8 DiCaprio
see also Italian
Leonard, Robert Z.: 8 director
film: Dancing Lady (1933)
The Divorcée (1930)
The Great Ziegfeld (1936)
In the Good Old Summertime (1949)
The King's Thief (1955)
Marianne (1929)
Marriage Is a Private Affair (1944)
Maytime (1937)
Peg o' My Heart (1933)
Pride and Prejudice (1940)
Strange Interlude (1932)
Weekend at the Waldorf (1945)
Ziegfeld Girl (1941)
Leonard, Sugar Ray: 5 boxer
milieu: 4 ring
___ Leonard Wood: 4 Fort
Leonato to Beatrice: 4 aunt
Leoncavallo, Ruggiero: 8 composer
work: I Pagliacci
Serafita
Zaza
leone: 5 money
Leone: 3 car 4 auto 6 Sergio, Subaru 10 automobile
___ Leone: 6 Sierra
Leone, Sergio: 8 director
film: Fistful of Dollars (1964)
For a Few Dollars More (1966)
The Good, the Bad, and the Ugly (1966)
Once Upon a Time in America (1984)
Once Upon a Time in the West (1968)
Leonhard: 5 Euler
Leonid: 8 Andreyev, Brezhnev
in English: 7 Leonard
see also Russian
leonine: 5 maned 6 feline, kingly, lordly, mighty 8 fearless 10 courageous
see also lion
Leoni, Téa: 7 actress
film: Deep Impact (1998)
The Family Man (2000)
Hollywood Ending (2002)
Jurassic Park III (2001)
spouse: David Duchovny
TV: The Naked Truth
Leonore Overture composer: 9 Beethoven
Leonowens, Anna
where ~ taught: 4 Siam
Leontief, Wassily: 8 Nobelist 9 economist
Leontyne: 5 Price
leopard: 3 cat, fur 5 felid 6 animal, big cat, feline
home: 3 zoo
relative: 4 eyra, lion, lynx, puma 5 chita, liger, ounce, tiger, tigon 6 bobcat, cheeta, chetah, cougar, jaguar, margay, ocelot, serval, tiglon 7 bay lynx, caracal, cheetah, panther 9 catamount 10 jaguarundi
snow ~: 3 cat, fur 5 ounce
sound: 5 growl, snarl
leopard ___: 4 frog, lily, moth, seal 5 shark 6 lizard
___ leopard: 4 snow 7 clouded, hunting
Leopards: 9 Lafayette
Leopard, The (1963 film)
cast: Claudia Cardinale, Alain Delon, Burt Lancaster
director: Luchino Visconti
Leopard, The composer: 4 Rota
Leopold: 4 Aldo, Auer 7 Ruzicka 8 von Ranke 9 Stokowski
colleague: 4 Loeb
Leos: 7 Janácek
leotard: 6 tights 7 costume, garment
Lepanto: 4 gulf
Le Penseur sculptor: 5 Rodin
Le Père Goriot author: Honoré de Balzac
Le Pew: 4 Pepe
lepidolite: 3 ore 7 mineral
lepidopterist gear: 3 net
Lepke (1975 film)
cast: Michael Callan, Anjanette Comer, Tony Curtis
director: Menahem Golan
Lepontine ___: 4 Alps
___ Leppard: 3 Def
leprechaun: 3 elf, fay 4 pixy 5 elfin, fairy, gnome, nisse, pixie 6 sprite 7 brownie
country: 4 Eire, Erin 7 Ireland
cousin: 3 elf 5 gnome, troll
language: 6 Gaelic
like a ~: 3 wee 5 elfin 6 little, petite 7 puckish 10 diminutive
lepton: 4 coin, muon 5 Greek, money, tauon 8 electron, particle
___ lepton: 3 tau
Lepus: 4 Hare
star in ~: 5 Arneb
Lerdo: 4 city, town
locale: 6 Mexico 7 Durango 8 Veracruz
Le Repos artist: 5 Corot
Le rève: 4 aria
Lerma: 4 city, town
locale: 6 Mexico
Lerner: 3 Max 4 Carl 7 Alan Jay, Michael
Lerner, Alan Jay: 8 lyricist
collaborator: 5 Loewe
musical: Brigadoon
Camelot
Gigi
My Fair Lady
Paint Your Wagon
song: Almost Like Being in Love
Camelot
Get Me to the Church on Time
Gigi
The Heather on the Hill
I Could Have Danced All Night
If Ever I Would Leave You
I Remember It Well
I Talk to the Trees
I've Grown Accustomed to Her Face
The Night They Invented Champagne
On the Street Where You Live
The Rain in Spain
Thank Heaven for Little Girls
They Call the Wind Maria
With a Little Bit of Luck
Wouldn't It Be Loverly
___ le roi!: 4 A bas, Vive
LeRoi: 5 Jones
Le Roi ___: 6 Soleil
Le Roi d'Ys composer: 4 Lalo
Le Roi Malgré ___: 3 Lui
Le Rossignol: 6 ballet
composer: 10 Stravinsky
lerot: 6 rodent 8 dormouse
Le Rouge ___ Noir: 4 et le
Leroux: 6 Gaston
Leroy: 3 Hal 6 Mervyn, Neiman 7 Grumman, Van Dyke 8 Anderson
___ Leroy: 4 lola
LeRoy: 4 Baby 6 Mervyn, Neiman
LeRoy, Baby: 5 actor
film: It's a Gift (1934)
The Old-Fashioned Way (1934)
Tillie and Gus (1933)
LeRoy, Mervyn: 8 director
film: Anthony Adverse (1936)
Blossoms in the Dust (1941)
Elmer the Great (1933)
Escape (1940)
The FBI Story (1959)
Five Star Final (1931)
Gold Diggers of 1933 (1933)
Gypsy (1962)
High Pressure (1932)
Home Before Dark (1958)
I Am a Fugitive From a Chain Gang (1932)
Johnny Eager (1941)
Little Caesar (1930)
Madame Curie (1943)
Million Dollar Mermaid (1952)
Mister Roberts (1955)
No Time for Sergeants (1958)
Oil for the Lamps of China (1935)
Quo Vadis? (1951)
Random Harvest (1942)
They Won't Forget (1937)
Thirty Seconds Over Tokyo (1944)
Three Men on a Horse (1936)

Three on a Match (1932)
Unholy Partners (1941)
Wake Me When It's Over (1960)
Waterloo Bridge (1940)
Without Reservations (1946)
The World Changes (1933)
Les: **4** Paul **5** Aspin, Brown, Crane **6** Baxter, Elgart **7** Nessman **8** Tremayne
Les ___: **3** Miz **5** Girls
Les ___ mousquetaires: **5** trois
Les ___-Unis: **5** États
LeSabre: **3** car **4** auto **5** Buick **10** automobile
rival: **3** LTD
Lesage, Alain: **6** French, writer
work: Gil Blas
Lesath: **4** star
___-les-Bains: **3** Aix **5** Evian
Les Bergeries author: **4** Anet
Lesbos locale: **5** Egean **6** Aegean, Greece
___ Lescaut: **5** Manon
lèse ___: **7** majesté, majesty
lèse majesty: **7** treason **8** betrayal, sedition **9** treachery
Les États-___: **4** Unis
Les Girls (1957 film)
cast: Mitzi Gaynor, Gene Kelly, Kay Kendall
composer: Cole Porter
director: George Cukor
Lesh: **4** Phil
LeShan: **3** Eda
lesion: **3** cut **4** gash, sore **5** wound **6** bruise, injury, scrape **7** scratch **8** abrasion **10** laceration
Lesley: **4** Gore **5** Stahl
Lesley Ann: **6** Warren
Lesley-Anne: **4** Down
Leslie: **4** Joan **5** Caron **6** Bethel, Howard, Uggams **7** Nielsen, Stephen **9** Charteris, Halliwell
Leslie ___ Hope: **6** Townes
Leslie, Joan: **7** actress
film: The Hard Way (1942)
The Male Animal (1942)
Repeat Performance (1947)
Rhapsody in Blue (1945)
Sergeant York (1941)
The Sky's the Limit (1943)
Thank Your Lucky Stars (1943)
This Is the Army (1943)
Yankee Doodle Dandy (1942)
Les Maîtres Mosaïstes author: George Sand
Les Maîtres Sonneurs author: George Sand
Les Misérables (1935 film)
cast: Sir Cedric Hardwicke, Charles Laughton, Fredric March
Les Misérables (1952 film)
cast: Robert Newton, Debra Paget, Michael Rennie
director: Lewis Milestone
Les Misérables (1998 film)
cast: Claire Danes, Liam Neeson, Geoffrey Rush, Uma Thurman
director: Bille August
Les Misérables author: Victor Hugo
character: **4** Jean **5** Felix **6** Azelma, Javert, Marius **7** Cosette, Fantine, Valjean **8** Gavroche **9** Pontmercy, Tholomyès **10** Thénardier
setting: **5** Paris, sewer **6** France
Les Misérables song: **5** Stars
___-les-mois: **4** tous
Les Noces: **6** ballet
composer: **10** Stravinsky
Les Nuits d'___: **3** Été
Le Soleil locale: **6** Quebec
Lesotho: **6** nation **7** country
capital: **6** Maseru
coin: **5** sente
home: **6** Africa
language: **4** Zulu
locale: **6** Africa
people: **5** Sotho **6** Basuto
river: **6** Orange
Les pêcheurs de perles composer: **5** Bizet
Le Spectre de la Rose: **6** ballet
composer: **5** Weber
Les Préludes composer: **5** Liszt
Les Rougon-Macquart author: Emile Zola
less: **5** fewer, lower, minor, minus **6** little **7** limited, reduced, shorter, smaller, wanting, without **8** inferior, slighter, take away **9** excepting, secondary, shortened **10** diminished
important: **5** lower, minor **9** auxiliary, secondary **10** derivative, incidental, peripheral
in music: **4** meno
make ~: **5** allay **6** reduce **7** lighten **8** decrease
make ~ narrow: **6** expand, spread **7** broaden, enlarge, thicken **9** spread out
make ~ wild: **5** break **6** soften **7** harness **8** tone down
more or ~: **4** near **5** quite, sorta **6** around, fairly, kind of, nearly, rather, sort of **8** slightly, somewhat, very well
than: **5** below, lower, under **7** beneath **10** inferior to, unworthy of
less ___: **4** than
___ Less Bell to Answer: **3** One
lessee: **5** liver **6** lodger, renter, roomer, tenant **7** boarder **8** occupant
payment: **4** rent
lessen: **3** cut, ebb **4** bate, clip, crop, curb, drop, ease, fade, fall, pare, sink, slow, thin, wane **5** abate, allay, break, close, drain, erode, let up, limit, lower, relax, slack, taper **6** dampen, deduct, defuse, defuze, demean, dilute, impair, minify, modify, narrow, recede, reduce, shrink, soften, temper, weaken **7** abridge, assuage, curtail, cut back, cut down, decline, degrade, depress, detract, die down, drop off, dwindle, fall off, lighten, mollify, qualify, shorten, slacken, slack up, subside, tail off, thin out, whittle **8** amputate, contract, decrease, diminish, downsize, minimize, mitigate, moderate, palliate, peter out, roll back, slow down, taper off, tone down, trail off, truncate, wind down **9** alleviate, attenuate, cut down on, extenuate, scale down, soft-pedal **10** de-escalate, smooth over
lessened: **5** lower, short **7** cut back, reduced **9** decreased, pared down **10** diminished
lessening: **3** cut, ebb **4** drop, fall **5** letup **7** cutback, decline **8** decrease **9** abatement, reduction, remission **10** diminution
lesser: **3** low **4** bush, side **5** dinky, lower, minor, small, under **6** bottom, junior, nether, second **8** inferior, slighter, small-fry **9** secondary, small-time, subjacent **10** bush-league, second-rate, subsidiary, undersized
prefix: **5** under-
lesser ___: **3** ape **5** Ionic, panda **6** weever **7** amakihi, rorqual
Lesser ___: **3** Dog **4** Bear
Lesser Antilles: **4** isls. **5** isles **7** islands
island: **6** Tobago **8** Barbados, Leewards, Trinidad **9** Windwards
native: **5** Carib
lesser of two ___: **5** evils
Lesser Sundas: **3** isl. **5** isles **7** islands
one of the ~: **4** Bali **5** Timor
Lessing: **5** Doris **8** Gotthold
Less is ___: **4** more
lesson: **4** quiz, task, test **5** class, drill, model, moral, study **6** homily, notice, period, rebuke, sermon **7** censure, chiding, lecture, message, precept, reading, reproof, warning **8** coaching, exemplar, exercise, homework, practice, scolding, teaching, tutoring **9** chalk talk, class work, deterrent, education, reprimand, schooling **10** admonition, assignment, punishment, recitation, school work
conduct a ~: **5** teach **7** lecture
first-grade ~: **8** alphabet
learn a ~: **3** get **5** grasp **6** absorb, digest, soak up **7** drink in **9** apprehend **10** assimilate, comprehend, understand
story with a ~: **4** myth **5** fable **7** parable **8** allegory, apologue
teach a ~ to: **6** punish
___ lesson: **6** object
Lesson From Aloes, A author: Athol Fugard
Lessons in Living author: Maya Angelou
___ Lesson, The: **5** Piano **7** Anatomy
Lesson, The author: Eugène Ionesco
lessor: **8** landlady, landlord
___ Less Ordinary: **5** A Life
Less Than Zero author: **5** Ellis
Les Sylphides: **6** ballet
composer: **6** Chopin
lest: **6** in case **7** perhaps **9** perchance
Lestat creator: **4** Rice
___ Lestat, The: **7** Vampire
Lester: **3** Tom **5** Flatt, Jerry, Ketty, Young **6** del Rey, Maddox **7** Pearson, Richard
Lester Pearson Award awarder: **3** NHL
Lester, Richard: **8** director
film: Cuba (1979)
The Four Musketeers (1975)
A Hard Day's Night (1964)
Help! (1965)
The Knack, and How to Get It (1965)
The Mouse on the Moon (1963)
Petulia (1968)
Robin and Marian (1976)
Royal Flash (1975)
Superman II (1980)
The Three Musketeers (1974)
Lestoil: **7** cleaner
alternative: **5** Brite, Lysol **6** Top Job **7** Mr. Clean, Pine Sol **9** Fantastik, Step Saver
Les Trois Villes author: Emile Zola
Lest we lose our ___: **5** Edens
let: **4** lend, rent **5** allow, brook, cause, grant, lease, leave, trust **6** accede, accept, do-over, enable, free up, leased, permit, suffer **7** approve, certify, charter, concede, endorse, indorse, license, rent out, warrant **8** accede to, assent to, sanction, stand for, sublease, tolerate **9** approve of, authorize, give leave, put up with **10** commission
at: **5** sic on
be: **5** leave, spare **6** lay off **10** leave alone
be known: **3** air, say **4** blab, leak, tell, warn **5** level, speak, spill, state, utter, voice **6** advise, clue in, convey, detail, fill in, impart, inform, notify, relate, report, reveal, squeal, tip off, unveil **7** apprise, breathe, confess, declare, divulge, explain, express, give out, lay bare, mention, recount, uncover, whisper **8** acquaint, announce, disclose, instruct, proclaim **9** leave word, recognize, spit it out **10** keep posted
bygones be bygones: **6** excuse, forget, pardon **7** forgive **8** overlook, play past
down: **4** fail, mock, sink **5** lower **6** dismay **7** abandon, depress **9** depressed, fall short **10** disappoint, disenchant, dissatisfy
ender: **4** down
fall: **4** drop, shed **5** spill
fall between the cracks: **4** omit **6** forget, ignore **7** neglect **9** disregard
fly: **3** lob **4** cast, fire, hurl, send, toss **5** chuck, fling, heave, pitch, shoot, sling, throw **6** launch, let off, propel **7** fire off
go: **2** ax **3** axe, can **4** axed, boot, drop, fire, free, miss, omit, oust, sack, weep **5** clear, fired, freed, loose, relax, spare, throw, untie, waive, yield **6** acquit, bounce, canned, excuse, lay off, let off, loosen, relent, sprang, spring, sprung, unhand, untied **7** abandon, cashier, dismiss, drum out, manumit, neglect, release, set free **8** cut loose, furlough, get rid of, liberate, overlook, pink-slip, released **9** discharge, disengage, dismissed, liberated, sacrifice, surrender, terminate, turn loose **10** discharged, relinquish
go of: **4** dump, shed **5** ditch, spurn **6** give up, unload **7** abandon, discard, toss out **8** renounce **9** eighty-six, repudiate, throw away **10** relinquish
happen: **6** permit **8** sanction, tolerate
in: **5** admit, alter, greet **6** accept **7** accepts, altered, embrace, include, receive, welcome **8** accepted, admitted
in on: **4** tell **5** ready **6** advise, inform, tip off **8** advise of
it all hang out: **4** bare **6** reveal **7** divulge, lay bare **8** disclose **9** make known **10** make public
it go: **6** excuse, pardon **7** forgive **8** laugh off, overlook
it happen: **6** give in, give up **7** back off **9** acquiesce **10** capitulate
it stand: **4** stet
know: **4** tell **5** cue in **6** inform, tip off
know indirectly: **4** hint **6** allude **7** suggest **8** intimate, lead up to **9** insinuate
loose: **4** free, play, yell **5** shout, unpen, unpin, untie **6** bellow, unbind, untied **8** liberate
off: **4** drop, emit, free **5** clear, spare **6** acquit, excuse, exempt, let fly, pardon, wink at **7** absolve, dismiss, excused, forgive, release, relieve **9** allow to go, discharge, exonerate
off steam: **4** rage, vent, yell **7** release
on: **3** own, say **4** avow, fool, hint, tell **5** admit, allow, grant, imply, spill **6** fess up, reveal **7** admit to, concede, confess, divulge, pretend, suggest **8** disclose, give away, indicate **9** drop a hint, make known
oneself go: **5** unlax **6** rest up, unwind **7** lay back, sit back **8** loosen up, slack off **9** hang loose **10** settle back, take it easy
one's voice be heard: **6** assert, insist **7** declare **8** sound off **10** stand up for
out: **4** blab, free, loan, vent **5** break, lease, loose, unpen, widen **6** exhale, expand, expose, loosen, reveal **7** divulge, release **8** disclose, lengthen, liberate **9** discharge, make

known, open a seam
pass: **5** allow, spend **6** ignore, wink at **7** forgive, neglect **8** overlook **9** disregard
rip: **5** begin, start **6** launch **7** kick off, lead off, take off, usher in **8** commence, get going **10** inaugurate
slide: **4** omit **6** wink at **7** neglect **8** overlook
slip: **4** blab, leak, miss, tell **5** blurt, spill **6** betray, expose, forget, reveal, unmask, unveil **7** divulge, exhibit, lay bare, uncover **8** disclose **9** make known **10** make public
the cat out of the bag: **3** air **4** bare, leak, tell **5** admit, blurt, spill **6** betray, expose, gossip, reveal, squeal, tattle **7** divulge **8** disclose, give away **9** make known
the water out: **3** tap **4** vent **6** siphon **7** draw off
to ~: **4** free, open **5** empty **6** vacant **7** for rent, untaken **8** not in use, unfilled **9** available **10** tenantless, unoccupied
up: **3** ebb **4** ease, fall, lull, quit, stop, wane **5** abate, cease, eased, pause, relax, slack **6** abated, ceased, die out, ease up, go easy, lay off, lessen, paused, relent, relief **7** back off, die down, ease off, relaxed, release, relieve, respite, slacken, stopped, subside, tail off **8** decrease, diminish, intermit, level off, mitigate, moderate, slack off, slow down, tone down **9** backed off, lose speed, mitigated, moderated **10** diminished, slacked off, slowed down
use: **4** lend, loan, pool **5** allot, cut in, split, trust **6** assign, divide, extend, oblige **7** divvy up, provide **8** go in with
let __: **3** fly, off, out **4** down, in on, it go, slip **5** alone, loose
let __ a secret: **4** in on
let __ hang out: **5** it all
...let __ put asunder: **5** no man
Let __: **4** 'Em In, It Be, Me In **5** Her In
Let __...: **5** me see
Let __ be said...: **5** it not
Let __ Cake: **5** 'em Eat
Let __ do it: **6** George
Let __, Lover: **4** Me Go
Let __ Me: **4** It Be
Let __ Praise Famous Men: **5** Us Now
Let __ the One: **4** Me Be
Let __ There: **4** Me Be
Let a __ Be...: **5** Smile
L'état, c'est __: **3** moi
letdown: **4** balk **5** baulk **7** chagrin, sadness, setback, washout **10** anticlimax, bitter pill, melancholy
let-down: **7** unhappy
__ letdown: **5** nylon
Let 'Em Eat Cake: **7** musical
song: **4** Mine
songwriter: **8** Gershwin
Let 'Em In (1976 song) artist: Paul McCartney
l'été, month of: **4** août, juin **7** juillet
Let 'er __!: **3** rip
Let George __: **4** do it
Lethal Weapon (1987 film)
cast: Gary Busey, Mel Gibson, Danny Glover
cat: **7** Burbank
director: Richard Donner
dog: **3** Sam
role: **5** Riggs **8** Murtaugh
Lethal Weapon 2 (1989 film)
cast: Mel Gibson, Danny Glover, Joe Pesci
director: Richard Donner
Lethal Weapon 3 (1992 film)
cast: Mel Gibson, Danny Glover, Joe Pesci, Rene Russo
director: Richard Donner
Lethal Weapon 4 (1998 film)
cast: Mel Gibson, Danny Glover, Joe Pesci, Rene Russo
director: Richard Donner
lethargic: **3** lax **4** blah, dopy, dozy, dull, idle, lazy, limp, logy, poky, slow **5** dopey, heavy, inert, moony, slack, tardy, weary, wimpy **6** asleep, draggy, drowsy, otiose, sleepy, snoozy, stolid, supine, torpid **7** dormant, gradual, halting, impeded, laggard, lagging, languid, nebbish, out of it, passive, wimpish **8** comatose, crawling, creeping, dawdling, dilatory, dragging, drawn-out, hesitant, inactive, indolent, laid-back, lifeless, listless, plodding, slothful, sluggish, stretchy, toddling **9** apathetic, enervated, impassive, leisurely, lymphatic, prolonged, sedentary, snaillike, somnolent, stupefied, unhurried **10** deliberate, disengaged, languorous, phlegmatic, protracted, sleepyhead, slumberous, spiritless, unreactive
feeling: **5** ennui
one: **5** snail **7** dawdler
lethargy: **4** coma **5** sleep, sloth, sopor **6** apathy, phlegm, stupor, torpor **7** boredom, inertia, languor, laxness, slumber, vacuity **8** dullness, hebetude, idleness, inaction, laziness, loginess, slowness **9** disregard, inanition, indolence, inertness, lassitude, torpidity, unconcern, weariness **10** drowsiness, inactivity, sleepiness, supineness, torpidness
Lethbridge: **4** city, town
locale: **6** Canada **7** Alberta
Lethe: **5** river
locale: **5** Hades
Let Her Cry (1995 song) artist: Hootie and the Blowfish
Let Her In (1976 song) artist: John Travolta
let it __ hang out: **3** all
Let It Be (1970 song) artist: Beatles
Let It Be Me (song)
artist: Betty Everett, Everly Brothers, Jerry Butler
Letitia: **9** Baldridge
Let Me Be the One (song) artist: Carpenters, Exposé
Let Me Be There (1973 song) artist: Olivia Newton-John
(Let Me Be Your) Teddy Bear (1957 song) artist: Elvis Presley
Let Me Call You Sweetheart: **4** song **5** novel, waltz
author: Mary Higgins Clark
Let Me Entertain You composer: **5** Styne **8** Sondheim
Let Me Go Lover (song) artist: Joan Weber, Patti Page, Teresa Brewer
Let me in!: **6** open up
Let Me Ride rapper: **5** Dr. Dre
Let Me Sing and I'm Happy (1930 song) artist: Al Jolson
composer: **6** Berlin
Let My Love Open the Door (1980 song) artist: Pete Townshend
Let No Man Write My Epitaph (1960 film)
cast: James Darren, Burl Ives, Shelley Winters
Leto: **4** city, town **5** Jared
daughter of ~: **7** Artemis
locale: **7** Florida
parent of ~: **5** Coeus **6** Phoebe
sister of ~: **7** Asteria
son of ~: **6** Apollo
L'Étoile du Nord: **4** Minn. **9** Minnesota
let one's __ down: **4** hair
L'Etranger author: Albert Camus
Let's __: **4** Do It, Ride **5** Dance **6** Groove **7** Pretend
Let's __ a Deal: **4** Make
Let's __ Again: **4** Do It **5** Twist
Let's __ an Old-Fashioned Walk: **4** Take
Let's __ Another Cup of Coffee: **4** Have
Let's __ in Love: **4** Fall
Let's __ it: **4** face
Let's __ It for the Boy: **4** Hear
Let's __ the Music and Dance: **4** Face
Let's __ the Whole Thing Off: **4** Call
Let's __ Together: **3** Get **4** Stay
Let's call __ day!: **3** it a
Let's Call the Whole Thing Off: **4** duet
composer: **8** Gershwin
Let's Dance (song) artist: Chris Montez, David Bowie
Let's do __!: **5** lunch
Let's Do It Again (1953 film)
cast: Ray Milland, Aldo Ray, Jane Wyman
director: Alexander Hall
Let's Do It Again (1975 film)
cast: Bill Cosby, Sidney Poitier, Jimmie Walker
director: Sidney Poitier
Let's Do It Again (1975 song) artist: Staple Singers
Let's Do It composer: **6** Porter
Let's Face It (1943 film): **7** musical
cast: Bob Hope, Betty Hutton, ZaSu Pitts
composer: Cole Porter
Let's Face the Music and Dance composer: **6** Berlin
Let's Fall in Love (1967 song) artist: Peaches and Herb
Let's Fall in Love composer: **5** Arlen **7** Koehler
Let's Get Away From __: **5** It All
Let's Get It On (1973 song) artist: Marvin Gaye
Let's Get Serious (1980 song) artist: Jermaine Jackson
Let's Get Together (1961 song) artist: Hayley Mills
Let's go!: **4** c'mon
Let's Go Crazy (1984 song) artist: Prince
Let's Groove (1981 song) artist: Earth, Wind & Fire
Let's Hang On (1965 song) artist: Four Seasons
Let's Have Another Cup of Coffee composer: **6** Berlin
Let's Hear It for the Boy (1984 song) artist: Deniece Williams
Let's hear more...: **6** do tell
let sleeping dogs __: **3** lie
Let's Live for Today (1967 song) artist: Grass Roots
Let's Lock the Door (1965 song) artist: Jay and the Americans
Let's Make a Deal: **8** game show
choice: **3** box **7** curtain
host: Monty Hall
prize: **4** zonk
Let's Make Love (1960 film)
cast: Marilyn Monroe, Yves Montand, Tony Randall
director: George Cukor
Let's Misbehave composer: **6** Porter
Let's Pretend: **9** radio show
Let's Ride (1998 song)
artist: Master P, Montell Jordan, Silkk the Shocker
Let's see...: **3** hmm
Let's shake on it!: **4** deal
Let's Stay Together (1971 song) artist: Al Green
Let's Take __ Around the Block: **5** a Walk
Let's Take an Old-Fashioned Walk
composer: **6** Berlin
Let's Twist Again (1961 song) artist: Chubby Checker
Let's Wait Awhile (1987 song) artist: Janet Jackson
Lett: **7** Latvian **8** European
neighbor: **4** Esth
letter: **2** ar, ef, el, em, en, ex, mu, nu, pi, xi **3** bee, cap, cee, chi, dee, ell, ess, eta, gee, jay, kay, phi, psi, rho, tau, tee, vee, wye, zee **4** beta, iota, kite, line, mail, memo, note, rune, sign, type, zeta **5** aitch, alpha, delta, gamma, kappa, omega, paper, print, prose, reply, sigma, theta **6** answer, billet, lambda, report, symbol, uncial **7** capital, double u, epistle, epsilon, initial, message, missive, omicron, receipt, upsilon, writing **8** alphabet, dispatch, junk mail, longhand **9** character, majuscule, minuscule
abbr.: **3** APO, att., FPO, RFD **4** attn.
closer: **4** seal
drop: **4** slot
ender: **3** box, man, men **4** form, head **5** press
first ~: **4** init. **7** initial
love ~ (French): **10** billet doux
starter: **4** dear, news
letter __: **3** box **4** drop **5** stock **6** ruling **7** carrier, missive
letter-__: **4** card, size **7** perfect, quality
__ letter: **3** air, day, fan, sun **4** cash, dead, dog's, drop, form, hand, moon, open **5** black, block, chain, cover, crank, night, swash, to the **6** market **7** capital, comfort, paschal, primary, pyramid
__-letter: **3** red **4** open
__ Letter, Darling: **5** Take a
__-letter day: **3** red **5** black
lettered: **7** erudite, learned, refined **8** cultured, educated, literary, literate, polished **9** scholarly **10** cultivated, well-versed
Letter for __, A: **4** Evie
__-letter fraternity: **5** Greek
Letter From an Unknown Woman (1948 film)
cast: Mady Christians, Joan Fontaine, Louis Jourdan
director: Max Ophuls
letterhead: **5** sheet **10** stationery
abbr.: **3** inc.
illustration: **4** logo
Letterman, David: **4** host **5** emcee
first item on a ~ list: **3** ten
network: **3** CBS **5** CBSTV
rival: **4** Leno
__ Letter Maria: **5** Take a
Lettermen: **4** trio
members: Butala, Pike, Enegmann
song: Come Back Silly Girl (1962)
Goin' Out of My Head-Can't Take My Eyes Off You (1968)
Hurt So Bad (1969)
Theme from 'A Summer Place' (1965)
The Way You Look Tonight (1961)
When I Fall in Love (1961)
letter of __: **6** advice, credit, intent, marque **7** comfort
__ letter office: **4** dead
letter-perfect: **5** exact **7** precise **8** accurate, faithful, verbatim
letters: **5** print **6** script **7** writing **8** booklore, learning **9** erudition, knowledge **10** literature
__ letters: **4** call **5** man of
Letters author: Plato

Letters From the Field author: Margaret Mead
__ Letters in the Sand: 4 Love
Letter (song), The artist: Box Tops, Joe Cocker
__-letter sorority: 5 Greek
Letters to Father Flye author: James Agee
Letters to Olga author: Václav Havel
Letter, The (1940 film)
cast: Bette Davis, Herbert Marshall, James Stephenson
director: William Wyler
__ Letter, The: 7 Scarlet
Letter to Three Wives, A (1949 film)
cast: Jeanne Crain, Linda Darnell, Kirk Douglas, Ann Sothern
director: Joseph L. Mankiewicz
__-letter word: 4 four
let the __ out of the bag: 3 cat
Let the Devil Wear Black (2000 film)
cast: Jacqueline Bisset, Mary-Louise Parker, Jonathan Penner, Jamey Sheridan
director: Stacy Title
Let the Good Times Roll (1973 film)
cast: Chuck Berry, Chubby Checker, Bo Diddley
director: Bob Abel, Sidney Levin
Let the Little Girl Dance (1960 song)
artist: Billy Bland
Let them eat __: 4 cake
let there be light in Latin: 7 fiat lux
Let the Sunshine In musical: 4 Hair
Letting Go author: Philip Roth
lettre de __: 6 cachet, change 7 créance
__ lettres: 6 belles
lettuce: 3 cos, oof 4 bibb, cash, gelt, jack, kail, kale, loot, peag, pelf 5 bills, bread, bucks, dough, funds, lucre, money, moola, mopus, pesos, rhino, sewan 6 dinero, do-re-mi, mammon, mazuma, moolah, seawan, silver, specie, veggie, wampum, wealth 7 cabbage, capital, dollars, ooftish, scratch, shekels 8 bankroll, cold cash, currency, hard cash, smackers 9 banknotes, frogskins, long green, simoleons, vegetable 10 greenbacks, green stuff
cousin: 4 kail, kale
layer: 3 bed
like ~: 5 crisp, leafy
sea ~: 4 ulva
unit: 4 head, leaf
__ lettuce: 3 cos, sea 4 Bibb, head, leaf, wild 5 lamb's, water 6 Boston, miner's 7 iceberg, romaine
L'Etui de nacre author: Anatole France
letup: 4 halt, lull, rest, stop 5 break, lapse, pause, truce 6 easing, recess, relief 7 anodyne, interim, respite 8 interval, reprieve 9 abatement, cessation, lessening, reduction, remission 10 mitigation, slackening, suspension
without ~: 4 a lot 5 no end, on end
Let us __: 4 pray
Let Us Now Praise Famous Men author: James Agee
let well enough __: 5 alone
Let your conscience be your __: 5 guide
Let Yourself Go composer: 6 Berlin
leu: 4 coin 5 money
leukocyte carrier: 5 lymph
Leutnant Gustl author: Arthur Schnitzler
Leutze, Emanuel: 6 artist 7 painter
lev: 5 money
Lev: 6 Landau
Levant: 5 Oscar 7 leather, Mideast
Levant __: 3 red 6 dollar, storax 7 morocco
levanter: 4 wind
Levantine: 7 Eastern, Mideast
ancient ~ city: 5 Petra
state: 5 Syria
vessel: 4 saic
weight: 4 rotl
Levant, Oscar: 7 pianist
film: An American in Paris (1951)
The Band Wagon (1953)
Humoresque (1946)
You Were Meant for Me (1948)
LeVar: 6 Burton
levee: 3 dam 4 dike, dock, pier, quay, wall 5 wharf 7 sea wall 9 reception 10 breakwater, embankment
level: 3 aim, lay, mow, par, tie 4 akin, beam, calm, cast, down, drop, even, fell, flat, like, rank, rase, raze, roll, ruin, rung, same, step, tell, tier, trim, true, turn, zone 5 alike, equal, exact, floor, flush, focus, grade, layer, pitch, plain, plane, point, press, slant, stage, story, train, waste, wreck 6 common, degree, direct, equate, even up, ground, height, in line, lay low, league, on a par, planed, rating, rolled, smooth, spread, square, stable, status, steady, topple 7 abreast, address, aligned, balance, destroy, echelon, equable, even off, even out, flatten, incline, lined up, matched, on a line, planate, plateau, precise, regular, station, stratum, surface, trimmed, unbuild, uniform 8 altitude, balanced, bulldoze, category, constant, demolish, equalize, matching, parallel, polished, position, pull down, smoothen, standard, standing, straight, take down, tear down, unbroken, zero in on 9 bring down, come clean, devastate, dismantle, elevation, gradation, identical, knock down, knock over, nivellate, prostrate, recumbent, take apart 10 comparable, consistent, continuous, dependable, equivalent, horizontal, straighten, unchanging
ender: 6 headed
not ~: 5 atilt 6 aslope
off: 3 ebb 4 ease, fall, wane 5 abate, let up 6 recede 7 decline, die down, dwindle, slacken, subside, tail off 8 decrease, moderate, taper off 10 de-escalate
on the ~: 4 fair, open, true 5 clean, frank, legal, legit, licit, no lie, solid, sound, valid 6 candid, decent, honest, infelt, lawful, proven, square, trusty 7 earnest, ethical, factual, genuine, sincere, up-front, upright 8 bona fide, credible, like it is, out-front, reliable, straight, truthful 9 authentic, blameless, confirmed, guileless, heartfelt, honorable, reputable, rock-solid, veracious 10 aboveboard, dependable, documented, forthright, legitimate, principled, scrupulous, unarguable, upstanding
top ~: 4 acme, peak, roof 6 apogee, heyday, summit 7 maximum 8 mountain, pinnacle
level __: 3 off 4 line 5 curve
level __ field: 7 playing
__ level: 3 sea, wye 4 base, foot, hand, true 5 Abney, blood, dumpy, on the, water 6 energy, ground, spirit 7 poverty, support
__-level: 3 low, mid, sub, top 4 high 5 entry, split 6 middle
levelheaded: 4 calm, cool, sane, wise 5 quiet, sober, solid, sound 6 low-key, mellow, placid, sedate, serene, steady, trusty 7 amiable, at peace, equable, pacific, prudent, relaxed, stoical, unmoved 8 all there, amicable, balanced, composed, discreet, laid-back, peaceful, rational, sensible, together, tranquil 9 collected, easy-going, impassive, judicious, practical, quiescent, realistic, temperate, unexcited, unruffled 10 cool-headed, dependable, farsighted, reasonable, unagitated, untroubled
levelheadedness: 5 sense 6 aplomb, sanity 8 presence
leveling: 6 razing 10 bulldozing, demolition
device: 4 shim 5 wedge
Leven: 4 lake, Loch
Levene: 3 Sam
Levenson: 3 Sam
__ l'Évêque: 4 Pont
lever: 3 bar, pry 4 tool 5 crank, jimmy, raise 7 crowbar 9 force open
ender: 3 age
foot ~: 5 pedal 7 treadle
November ~ puller: 5 voter
organ ~: 4 stop 5 pedal
piano ~: 5 pedal
pull the ~: 3 opt 4 vote 5 elect 6 decide
leverage: 4 drag, edge, pull, rank 5 break, clout, power, ropes 6 grease, jump on, weight 7 hostage, suction 8 purchase 9 advantage, authority, influence 10 ascendance, ascendancy, ascendence, ascendency
leveraged __: 6 buyout
Lever Brothers brand: 3 Lux
leveret: 4 hare 6 animal
coat: 5 lapin
Lever 2000: 4 soap
alternative: 3 Lux 4 Dial, Dove, Lava, Tone, Zest 5 Camay, Coast, Ivory 6 Boraxo, Caress, Shield 8 Lifebuoy 9 Palmolive, Safeguard 11 Irish Spring
Levert, Gerald
song: Casanova (1987)
Taking Everything (1999)
Thinkin' Bout It (1998)
Levertov: 6 Denise
Lévesque: 4 René
Levi: 5 Dolly, Primo, tribe 6 Eshkol, Morton, Stubbs 7 Strauss
brother of ~: 3 Dan, Gad 5 Asher, Judah 6 Joseph, Reuben, Simeon 7 Zebulun 8 Benjamin, Issachar, Naphtali
parent of ~: 4 Leah 5 Jacob
sister of ~: 5 Dinah
son of ~: 6 Kohath, Merari 7 Gershon
leviathan: 3 big 4 huge 5 giant, hippo, jumbo, rhino, titan, whale 6 beluga 7 mammoth, monster 8 behemoth, colossus, dinosaur, mastodon, Moby Dick 10 gargantuan
Leviathan author: 6 Hobbes
levigate: 3 rub 4 file, mash, mill 5 crush, grate, grind, pound 6 powder 7 break up 9 pulverize
Le Villi composer: 7 Puccini
Levi-Montalcini, Rita: 8 Nobelist
Levin: 3 Ira, Sid 4 Marc 5 Henry, Meyer
Levine, James: 9 conductor
Levin, Henry: 8 director
film: The Ambushers (1968)
Belles on Their Toes (1952)
The Guilt of Janet Ames (1947)
Jolson Sings Again (1949)
Journey to the Center of the Earth (1959)
The Lonely Man (1957)
The Man From Colorado (1948)
Mister Scoutmaster (1953)
Murderers' Row (1966)
The President's Lady (1953)
The Wonderful World of the Brothers Grimm (1962)
Levin, Ira: 6 author, writer
work: The Boys From Brazil
Critic's Choice
Deathtrap
General Seeger
A Kiss Before Dying
Rosemary's Baby
Sliver
Song of Rosemary
The Stepford Wives
This Perfect Day
Levinson, Barry: 8 director
film: Avalon (1990)
Bandits (2001)
Bugsy (1991)
Diner (1982)
Disclosure (1994)
An Everlasting Piece (2000)
Good Morning, Vietnam (1987)
Liberty Heights (1999)
The Natural (1984)
Rain Man (1988, AA)
Sleepers (1996)
Sphere (1998)
Tin Men (1987)
Wag the Dog (1997)
Le Viol artist: 5 Degas
Levi's: 5 jeans, pants 8 trousers 9 dungarees
rival: 3 Lee 6 Gitano 8 Jordache
Lévis: 4 city, town
locale: 6 Canada, Québec
Lévi-Strauss: 6 Claude
levitate: 3 fly 4 hang, rise 5 arise, float, glide, hover 6 lift up 7 elevate, lighten
Leviticus: 4 book
follower: 7 Numbers
preceder: 6 Exodus
Levitt: 7 William
Levittown: 4 city
locale: 7 New York
levity: 3 wit 5 humor, mirth 6 joking 7 gayness 8 buoyance, buoyancy, hilarity, jocosity, zaniness 9 flippancy, frivolity, funniness, giddiness, lightness, merriment, silliness 10 fickleness, jocoseness, jocularity
__ Levu: 4 Viti 5 Vanua
levulose: 5 sugar
levy: 3 fee, put, set, tax 4 call, duty, fine, toll 5 asses, draft, exact, lay on, place, put on, raise, tithe, wrest, wring 6 assess, burden, call up, charge, custom, demand, enlist, excise, extort, gather, impose, impost, muster, summon, tariff, towage 7 collect, recruit 8 exaction, shanghai, usage fee 9 conscript, gathering 10 assessment, collection, imposition
impose a new ~ on: 5 retax
union ~: 7 charges 10 assessment
Levy: 4 Marv 6 Eugene
Levy, Marv: 5 coach
sport: 8 football
Lew: 4 Hoad, Lehr 5 Ayres, Grade 6 Archer 7 Landers, Wallace 8 Burdette 10 Dockstader
lewd: 4 base, blue, fast, foul, racy 5 bawdy, dirty, gross, loose, nasty 6 coarse, erotic, impure, rakish, ribald, risqué, smutty, vulgar, wanton, X-rated 7 immoral, lustful, naughty, obscene, sensual 8 immodest, improper, indecent, off-color, shameful, unchaste, uncurbed 9 libertine, low-minded, lubricous, salacious, shameless 10 in bad taste, indelicate, lascivious, licentious, lubricious, profligate, scandalous, scurrilous, suggestive
look: 4 leer, ogle 5 smirk
Lewes: 4 city, town
locale: 8 Delaware
Lewes, George Henry: 11 philosopher
Lewis: 2 Al, C.S. 3 Ted 4 Carl, Gary, Huey 5 Allen, Bobby, Dawnn, Donna,

Jerry, Oscar, range, Shari, Stone **6** Arthur, Edward, Lennox, Ramsey, Seiler, Teague **7** Barbara, Carroll, Gilbert, Mumford, Padgett, Richard, Wyndham **8** Emmanuel, Geoffrey, Grizzard, Juliette, Sinclair **9** Charlotte, Milestone **10** Meriwether
in German: **6** Ludwig
in Italian: **8** Lodovico
in Spanish: **4** Luis
locale: **6** Canada **7** Montana
partner: **5** Clark
seat of ~ and Clark County: **6** Helena
Lewis and the News, Huey
song: Couple Days Off (1991)
Doing It All for My Baby (1987)
Do You Believe in Love (1982)
Heart and Soul (1983)
The Heart of Rock & Roll (1984)
Hip to Be Square (1986)
If This Is It (1984)
I Know What I Like (1987)
It Hit Me Like a Hammer (1991)
I Want a New Drug (1984)
Jacob's Ladder (1987)
Perfect World (1988)
The Power of Love (1985)
Stuck With You (1986)
Walking on a Thin Line (1984)
Lewis and the Playboys, Gary
song: Count Me In (1965)
Everybody Loves a Clown (1965)
Green Grass (1966)
Save Your Heart for Me (1965)
She's Just My Style (1965)
Sure Gonna Miss Her (1966)
This Diamond Ring (1965)
Lewis, Arthur: **8** Nobelist **9** economist
Lewis, Barbara
song: Baby, I'm Yours (1965)
Hello Stranger (1963)
Make Me Your Baby (1965)
Lewisburg
athletes: **5** Bison
school: **8** Bucknell
Lewis, Carl: **6** runner **8** sprinter **10** long jumper
event: **4** dash, race
Lewis, C.S.: **6** author, writer **7** British
work: The Allegory of Love
The Chronicles of Narnia
Out of the Silent Planet
The Screwtape Letters
Lewis, Edward: **8** Nobelist
Lewis grp., John L.: **3** UMW
Lewis, Jerry: **5** actor **8** comedian
film: Artists and Models (1955)
The Bellboy (1960)
Boeing Boeing (1965)
The Delicate Delinquent (1957)
The Disorderly Orderly (1964)
Don't Give Up the Ship (1959)
It'$ Only Money (1962)
The King of Comedy (1983)
The Ladies' Man (1961)
Living It Up (1954)
My Friend Irma (1949)
The Nutty Professor (1963)
Rock-a-Bye Baby (1958)
Sailor Beware (1951)
The Stooge (1953)
You're Never Too Young (1955)
song: Rock-A-Bye Your Baby with a Dixie Melody (1956)
Lewis, Jerry Lee
cousin: Jimmy Swaggart, Mickey Gilley
nickname: Killer
song: Breathless (1958)
Great Balls of Fire (1957)
High School Confidential (1958)
Whole Lot of Shakin' Going On (1957)
Lewis, Juliette: **7** actress
film: Cape Fear (1991)
Enough (2002)
The Evening Star (1996)
Husbands and Wives (1992)
Kalifornia (1993)
The Other Sister (1999)
Lewis, Lennox: **5** boxer
milieu: **4** ring
Lewis, Meriwether: **8** explorer
Lewis, Oscar: **6** writer
work: Children of Sanchez
Five Families
La Vida
Lewis, Ramsey: **7** pianist
genre: **4** jazz
song: The 'In' Crowd (1975)
Lewis, Sinclair: **6** writer **8** Nobelist
alma mater: **4** Yale
work: Ann Vickers
Arrowsmith
Babbitt
Cass Timberlane
Dodsworth
Elmer Gantry
The God-Seeker
Kingsblood Royal
Main Street
Lewiston: **4** city, town
locale: **5** Idaho, Maine
Lewisville: **4** city, town
locale: **5** Texas
__ Lewis, WA: **4** Fort
lex __: **4** loci **7** scripta
lex __ scripta: **3** non
Lex: **6** Barker, Luthor
Lex. __: **3** Ave.
lexicographer: **7** Webster **9** Partridge
creation: **3** def. **4** dict. **10** definition, dictionary
name: **4** Noah
lexicon: **3** OED **4** book, list **5** lexis, usage, vocab. **8** dict.. thes., glossary, language, wordbook, wordlist **9** thesaurus **10** cyclopedia, dictionary, vocabulary
Lexington: **2** Av. **4** city, town **6** avenue
athletes: **7** Keydets **8** Wildcats
county: **7** Fayette
locale: **8** Kentucky
school: **3** VMI
Lexington and Concord: **6** battle
lexis: **5** words **7** lexicon **8** glossary **9** thesaurus **10** dictionary, vocabulary
Lexus: **3** car **4** auto **10** automobile
ley: **6** pewter
Ley: **5** Willy
Leyden: **6** cheese
kin: **4** Edam
Leyden __: **3** jar
Leyte: **6** battle, island
neighbor: **5** Samar
LF: **3** pos.
L. Frank __: **4** Baum
LGA locale: **3** NYC
lge., smaller than: **3** med.
lgth.: **2** ft., km., yd. **4** meas.
see also length
Lhasa: **4** city, town
leader: **4** lama
locale: **4** Asia **5** Tibet **6** Thibet, Xizang **7** Sitsang
Lhasa Apso: **3** dog, pet **5** canid, pooch **6** canine
Lhotse: **4** peak **5** mount **8** mountain
locale: **4** Asia **5** Nepal, Tibet
Li: **3** Jet **4** elem., Peng **7** element, lithium
3 for ~: **4** at. no.
liability: **3** due, IOU, tab **4** bill, bite, chit, debt, drag, duty, loan, onus, risk **5** blame, debit, guilt, lease, minus, owing, peril **6** arrear, burden, chance, damage, hurdle, pledge, red ink **7** account, bad news, baggage, balance, barrier **8** breakage, contract, drawback, exposure, handicap, jeopardy, mortgage, nuisance, obstacle, openness, tendency, weakness **9** arrearage, detriment, hindrance, millstone, proneness, remainder **10** commitment, compulsion, impediment, indebtment, likelihood, misfortune, obligation, subjection
opposite: **5** asset
__ liability: **5** fixed **7** accrued, limited, product
liable: **3** apt **4** open, tied **5** bound, given, prone, wrong **6** at risk, guilty, likely **7** at fault, exposed, obliged, subject, tending, to blame **8** amenable, beatable, blamable, culpable, disposed, inclined, in danger, indebted, vincible **9** blameable, obligated, sensitive, subject to **10** answerable, assailable, attackable, chargeable, honor-bound, in the wrong, penetrable, vulnerable
be ~: **4** head, lead, mind, tend **5** do for, guard, nurse, see to, serve **6** manage **7** baby-sit, oversee, protect **8** see after, shepherd **9** look after, safeguard, supervise **10** administer, keep tabs on, minister to, ride herd on, take care of
become ~ for: **5** incur, run up **7** bring on, provoke
not ~: **4** free **5** clear **6** exempt **7** excused **8** absolved **10** off the hook, privileged
(to): **4** open **5** given
liaise: **4** link **7** contact **10** rendezvous
liaison: **2** in **3** tie **4** link **5** amour, fixer, fling **6** hookup **7** contact, romance **8** intrigue, relation **9** encounter, go-between, interface, interlude **10** connection, get a hold of, interceder
Liam: **6** Neeson **9** O'Flaherty **10** Cunningham
in English: **7** William
liana: **4** vine **5** plant
liang: **4** tael
Lianna (1983 film) director: John Sayles
Liao: **5** river
locale: **5** China
Liaodong: **4** gulf
locale: **5** China
Liaoning
city: **6** Anshan, Fushun
locale: **5** China
liar: **5** cheat, phony **6** fibber, phoney, rascal **7** deluder **8** deceiver, fabulist, palterer, perjurer **9** charlatan, con artist, falsifier, trickster **10** fabricator, tale teller
__ Liar: **5** Billy
Liar (1971 song) artist: Three Dog Night
liard: **5** money
Liard: **5** river
locale: **5** Yukon **6** Canada
Liar, liar, __ on fire!: **5** pants
Liar Liar (1997 film)
cast: Jim Carrey, Swoosie Kurtz, Maura Tierney, Jennifer Tilly
director: Tom Shadyac
liars __: **4** dice **5** poker
libate: **4** pour **5** serve **6** decant **7** pour out
libation: **4** dram **5** drink, toast **6** bracer, liquid **7** draught, potable, tribute **8** apéritif, beverage, cocktail, highball, nightcap, offering, potation **9** sacrifice, sundowner **10** intoxicant
see also beverage, drink
Libation Bearers author: Aeschylus
Libby: **5** Frank **7** Willard
Libby, Frank: **7** chemist
Libby, Willard: **7** chemist **8** Nobelist
libel: **3** dig, lie **4** barb, gibe, jeer, jibe, mock, slam, slap, slur, snub, tort **5** abuse, decry, knock, scorn, smear, spurn, taunt, wrong **6** attack, defame, deride, dump on, heckle, impugn, insult, malign, offend, rebuff, revile, slight, vilify **7** affront, asperse, blacken, calumny, catcall, degrade, disdain, mockery, obloquy, offense, put down, rank out, scandal, slander, traduce **8** backbite, badmouth, belittle, contempt, denounce, derision, derogate, ridicule, tear down, throw mud, vilipend **9** aspersion, cheap shot, contumely, denigrate, discredit, disparage, humiliate **10** calumniate, defamation, disrespect, impugnment, imputation, opprobrium, villainize
ending: **3** ous
Libeled Lady (1936 film)
cast: Jean Harlow, Myrna Loy, William Powell, Spencer Tracy
director: Jack Conway
libelous: **5** false **6** untrue **7** abusive **9** aspersive, injurious, invidious, malicious, traducing, vilifying **10** backbiting, calumnious, defamatory, derogatory, detractive, malevolent, pejorative, scandalous, scurrilous
Liberace: **3** Lee **7** pianist
brother: **6** George
liberal: **3** big **4** free, kind, left, rich **5** ample, broad, large, loose, noble, no end **6** casual, galore, giving, lavish, plenty **7** aplenty, copious, general, leftist, lenient, profuse, radical **8** abundant, advanced, catholic, flexible, generous, handsome, merciful, princely, prodigal, rational, tolerant, ultraist, unbiased, wasteful **9** bounteous, bountiful, capacious, exuberant, indulgent, plentiful, receiving, receptive, reformist, soft-touch, unbigoted, unselfish, unsparing, unthrifty **10** altruistic, avant-garde, beneficent, benevolent, bighearted, charitable, dime a dozen, free-handed, high-minded, humanistic, interested, munificent, openhanded, permissive, reasonable, ungrudging, unorthodox, unstinting
European ~: **5** Green
lead-in: **3** neo
liberal __: **4** arts
Liberal: **4** city **9** town. party
locale: **6** Kansas
liberalism: **4** left **8** left wing
liberality: **4** alms **6** bounty **7** bigness, breadth, charity, largess **8** free hand, kindness, largesse, latitude **10** generosity
liberalize: **4** ease, free, grow **5** relax, widen **6** expand, loosen, soften **7** broaden, develop, slacken
liberally: **4** much **7** largely **9** in a big way **10** handsomely
liberalness: **7** charity **8** altruism, humanity, kindness, sympathy **9** tolerance
liberals: **4** left
liberate: **3** rid, rob **4** free, lift, loot, save, take **5** let go, loose, steal, swipe, unmew, untie **6** acquit, detach, free up, let out, loosen, pilfer, ransom, redeem, rescue, unbind, unhand, unhook **7** absolve, bail out, deliver, manumit, release, set free, unchain **8** let loose **9** allow to go, discharge, extricate, unshackle **10** emancipate
liberated: **3** rid **4** free **5** loose, saved **6** untied **7** rescued, set free, unbound **8** set loose **9** unchained **10** unconfined, unfettered, unshackled
liberation: **7** freedom, liberty, release **8** delivery **9** acquittal, discharge, dismissal, salvation
liberator: **5** freer **6** savior **7** rescuer, saviour **8** redeemer

Liberia: **6** nation **7** country
capital: **8** Monrovia
flag has one: **4** star
locale: **3** Afr. **6** Africa
money: **4** cent **6** dollar
neighbor: **6** Guinea **10** Ivory Coast
people: **3** Gbe, Vei **5** Mende **6** Kpelle
Liberius: **4** pope **7** pontiff
Libertarians: **5** party
liberté, ___, fraternité: **7** égalité
___ liberties: **5** civil
libertine: **4** lewd, rake, roué, wolf **5** flirt, lover, satyr **6** amoral, bad guy, wanton **7** Don Juan, gallant, playboy, swinger, villain **8** Casanova, hedonist, lothario, prodigal, rakehell, sybarite, uncurbed **9** dissolute, epicurean **10** lascivious, licentious, profligate, voluptuary
no ~: **4** prig **5** prude **7** puritan **8** bluenose **9** nice Nelly **10** goody-goody
libertinism: **6** laxity **7** abandon, license **8** hedonism, wildness **9** looseness
liberty: **4** rest **5** leave, right, scope **6** choice, permit **7** freedom, holiday, leisure, license, release **8** autarchy, autonomy, decision, delivery, free time, furlough, immunity, latitude, sanction, suffrage, vacation **9** exemption, franchise, privilege **10** birthright, free speech, liberation, permission, relaxation
at ~: **4** free **6** untied **8** leisured **9** out of work, unengaged **10** unattached, unemployed
on ~: **6** ashore
take the ~: **4** dare **6** impose **7** presume **8** be so bold **9** go so far as
liberty ___: **3** cap **4** pole, tree
Liberty: **4** city, town **5** apple
locale: **8** Missouri
relative: **4** crab, Gala, Lodi, Rome **5** Mutsu **6** Empire, Ida Red, medlar, Pippin, russet **7** Baldwin, Bramley, costard, Freedom, Spartan, Wealthy, Winesap **8** Cortland, Jonathan, McIntosh **10** Rome Beauty
Liberty ___: **4** Bell, bond, loan, ship **5** party **6** Island **7** Heights
___ Liberty: **4** Miss **5** Ode to, Radio, Sweet
Liberty Bell, The composer: **5** Sousa
Liberty Heights (1999 film)
cast: Adrien Brody, Ben Foster, Orlando Jones, Bebe Neuwirth
director: Barry Levinson
___ liberty, or...: **6** Give me
Liberty Tree, The writer: **5** Paine
Libertyville: **4** city, town
locale: **8** Illinois
liberum ___: **4** veto
___ liberum: **4** mare
libido: **2** id **4** Eros, lust
libra: **5** money
Libra: **4** sign **6** Scales **7** air sign, Balance
month: **3** Oct. **4** Sept. **7** October **9** September
predecessor: **5** Virgo
ruler of ~ in astrology: **5** Venus
stone: **4** opal
successor: **7** Scorpio
Libra author: Don DeLillo
librairie unit: **5** livre
librarian degree: **3** BLS, MLS
library: **3** den **4** room **5** study **8** atheneum, book room **9** athenaeum
desk: **6** carrel **7** carrell
emulate a ~: **4** lend
enjoy a ~: **4** read **6** browse
feature: **5** globe **6** alcove
ID: **4** ISBN
no-no: **3** din **4** talk **5** noise **6** racket **7** chatter **9** commotion
request: **5** quiet **7** silence **9** stillness
section: **3** ref. **4** biog. **7** fiction **9** biography, reference **10** nonfiction
sorter: **5** filer
sound: **3** pst, shh **4** psst
stamp: **5** dater
transaction: **4** loan
unit: **3** vol. **4** book, tome **5** shelf, stack **6** volume
library ___: **4** card **5** paste, steps, table **7** binding, edition, science
___ library: **4** film **6** public, rental **7** lending, special
librate: **4** rock **5** pivot, swing **6** seesaw, swivel **9** alternate, oscillate
___ libre: **4** Cuba, vers
Libres: **4** city, town
locale: **6** Mexico, Puebla
librettist: **6** author, writer **9** dramatist, wordsmith **10** playwright
libretto: **4** book, text **5** story **6** script **7** writing **9** narrative
feature: **4** aria
Libreville: **4** city, town **7** capital
locale: **5** Gabon, Gabun
Libya: **6** nation **7** country
capital: **7** Tripoli
city: **4** Waha **6** Tobruk **7** Bengasi, Tripoli **8** Benghazi
desert: **6** Sahara
group: **4** OPEC **10** Arab League
gulf: **5** Sidra
it's n. of ~: **5** Medit.
money: **5** dinar **6** dirham
neighbor: **4** Chad **5** Egypt, Niger, Sudan **7** Algeria, Tunisia
people: **6** Tuareg
port: **7** Bengasi, Tripoli **8** Benghazi
Libyan: **6** desert
lice: **4** bugs **7** cooties, insects **9** parasites
Licence to Kill (1989 film)
cast: Timothy Dalton, Robert Davi, Carey Lowell, Talisa Soto
director: John Glen
license: **2** OK **3** let **4** okay, pass, room **5** allow, grant, leave, power, right, title **6** enable, excess, invest, laxity, patent, permit, ratify, suffer, ticket **7** abandon, anarchy, certify, charter, consent, empower, freedom, go-ahead, liberty, warrant **8** accredit, approval, audacity, boldness, delegate, disorder, gluttony, immunity, latitude, legalize, sanction, temerity, wildness **9** animalism, arrogance, authority, authorize, exemption, looseness, privilege, sauciness, slackness, tolerance **10** commission, debauchery, effrontery, green light, indulgence, permission, profligacy, relaxation, sensuality, sybaritism, unruliness, wantonness
charge: **3** fee
plate: **2** ID
license ___: **3** fee **5** plate
___ license: **4** hack **6** poetic **7** driver's
licensed: **6** vested **8** official **9** qualified **10** privileged
licensed practical ___: **5** nurse
license plate: **3** tag
HQ: **3** DMV
sticker: **5** decal
licentious: **3** lax **4** fast, lewd, wild **5** loose, nasty **6** amoral, animal, impure, rakish, ribald, unruly, wanton **7** corrupt, fleshly, immoral, relaxed, satyric, unmoral **8** depraved, desirous, scabrous, swinging, uncurbed **9** abandoned, corrupted, dissolute, libertine, lickerish, reprobate, salacious **10** disorderly, libidinous, lubricious, profligate
lichee: **3** nut **4** tree
lichen: **4** moss **5** plant, usnea **6** fungus
lichenology: **7** science
Licht: **6** Jeremy
Lichtenfield: **3** Ted
Lichtenstein: **3** Roy **6** artist **8** sculptor
___ Licht Idylls: **4** Auld
Licia: **8** Albanese
licit: **2** OK **4** good, okay, okeh, okey **5** jural, legal, legan, legit, right, sound, valid **6** kasher, kosher, lawful, proper **7** allowed **8** judicial, mandated, rightful **9** allowable, by the book, legalized, permitted, statutory, warranted **10** aboveboard, acceptable, admissible, authorized, legitimate, on the level, sanctioned
lick: **3** bit, dab, hit, lap, rub, tan, top **4** beat, best, burn, calm, cast, dart, dash, down, drub, flog, hint, leap, play, rout, slap, trim, wash, whip, whup **5** blaze, brush, excel, flick, gloss, graze, outdo, quiet, shoot, smack, smear, solve, spank, speck, speed, sweep, swipe, taste, throw, tinge, touch, trace, waver, whiff, worst **6** caress, defeat, fondle, glance, hurdle, ignite, kindle, master, phrase, quiver, ripple, sample, soothe, strike, stroke, thrash, tongue, wallop **7** clobber, conquer, flicker, flutter, lambast, moisten, overrun, run over, shellac, smother, surpass, tremble, trounce, vibrate **8** lambaste, move over, osculate, outstrip, overcome, pass over, play over, shellack, spoonful, surmount, vanquish **9** fluctuate, overwhelm, palpitate, vacillate **10** suggestion
and stick: **4** seal
into shape: **5** coach, groom **8** organize
not a ~: **3** nil **4** none, zero
one's chops: **5** savor **6** relish **10** anticipate
starter: **3** cow **4** boot
lick ___ promise: **4** and a
lick ___ shape: **4** into
___ lick: **3** hot **4** deer, salt
lickety-split: **3** PDQ **4** fast, soon **5** apace **6** presto **7** fleetly, hastily, quickly, rapidly, swiftly **8** in a flash, in a jiffy, in no time, pell-mell, promptly, speedily **9** forthwith, hurriedly, instantly, like a shot, posthaste
go ~: **3** hie, run **4** race **5** speed **6** hurtle
licking: **5** upset **6** defeat **7** beating, setback, tanning **8** drubbing, reversal, spanking, whipping **9** thrashing
___ licks: **4** last
lickspittle: **5** toady **6** fawner, flunky, jackal, lackey, sponge, yes man **7** flunkey, lacquey **8** adulator, hanger-on
licorice: **5** candy, plant **6** flavor
brand: **4** Nibs
flavoring: **5** anise **6** fennel
licorice ___: **5** stick
licorice root: **4** herb
lid: **3** cap, hat, tam, top **4** kepi **5** cover **6** boater, bonnet, box top, fedora, helmet, Panama, topper **7** chapeau, closure, Stetson **8** covering, headgear, sombrero **9** stovepipe **10** upper limit
flip one's ~: **4** rage, rail, rant, rave **5** freak, go ape, go mad **7** bluster, carry on, explode, flare up, go crazy **8** freak out **9** go bananas **10** hit the roof
keep a ~ on: **3** gag **4** cork, curb, lull **5** cover, limit, quash, quell **6** muffle, rein in, stifle **7** conceal, contain, control, cover up, repress **8** bottle up, hold back, restrain, restrict, suppress **9** constrain, stonewall, whitewash
remove a ~: **5** uncap
starter: **3** eye
tighten a ~: **5** screw, twist
see also hat
Liddy: **4** Dole **6** Gordon **7** G. Gordon
radio nickname: **4** G-man
Lido Shuffle (1977 song) artist: Boz Scaggs
Lidwina: **5** saint
lie: **3** con, fib, sit **4** bull, dupe, fake, hoax, laze, loll, rest, sham, snow, tale, yarn **5** bluff, couch, exist, fudge, guile, libel, phony, place, put on, rumor, story **6** deceit, delude, dupery, extend, invent, lounge, malign, palter, phoney, remain, repose, reside, sprawl, spread, take in, turn in **7** beguile, calumny, concoct, deceive, distort, evasion, falsify, falsity, fiction, go to bed, mislead, obloquy, perjure, perjury, promote, recline, slander, snow job, untruth, whapper, whopper **8** forswear, go back on, misguide, misquote, misspeak, misstate, overdraw, simulate, soft-soap **9** aspersion, deception, disinform, dissemble, falsehood, falseness, foreswear, four-flush, invention, mendacity, misinform, tall story **10** defamation, dishonesty, distortion, equivocate, exaggerate, imputation, inaccuracy, inveracity, stretch out, subterfuge
about: **4** laze **5** relax **6** lounge **7** traduce
adjacent to: **4** abut, join, meet **5** touch, verge **6** adjoin **8** border on, neighbor
against: **3** hug **6** cuddle, curl up, nestle, nuzzle **7** snuggle **8** ensconce, huddle up
along: **4** edge **5** flank, skirt, verge **6** border
around: **8** lallygag
beside: **9** juxtapose
dormant: **3** sit **6** hole up **9** hibernate
down: **4** rest **5** relax **6** repose, rest up, turn in **7** recline **9** go to sleep
down on the job: **5** slack **7** slacken **8** slack off
down on the job, in Britain: **5** sculk, skulk
fallow: **3** rot **4** idle, rust **5** decay **7** decline **8** go to seed, languish, stagnate, vegetate
give the ~ to: **4** deny **5** rebut **6** differ, impugn, negate, refute **7** confute, counter, dispute, gainsay **8** disprove **9** overthrow
in store for: **4** look, wait **5** await **10** anticipate
in the sun: **4** bake, bask, laze, loll **5** relax **6** lounge **8** sunbathe **9** luxuriate
in wait: **4** lurk **5** sculk, skulk **6** waylay
low: **4** hide, wait **5** squat **6** hole up **9** take cover
spread out: **4** flop, loll **5** slump **6** lounge, slouch, sprawl **7** stretch
to: **4** halt **7** deceive, mislead **9** misinform
under oath: **7** falsify, perjure **8** forswear
lie ___: **3** low **4** down **5** doggo
lie ___ on the job: **4** down
___ lie: **3** big **5** white **7** hanging
Lie: **6** Trygve
lie-abed: **7** dawdler
___ liebe dich: **3** Ich
Liebestraum composer: **5** Liszt
Liebfraumilch: **4** wine **5** white
origin: **7** Germany
Lieblich: **4** Amia
Liech.
neighbor of ~: **3** Aus. **4** Aust.
Liechtenstein: **6** nation **7** country

capital: 5 Vaduz
legislature: 4 Diet
locale: 3 Eur. 4 Alps 6 Europe
money: 5 franc
neighbor: 5 Switz. 7 Austria
lied: 4 hymn, song, tune 5 music
__ lied!: 3 So I
Liederkranz: 6 cheese
Lie Down in Darkness author: William Styron
lie down on the __: 3 job
__ Lied von der Erde: 3 Das
lief: 6 gladly, rather 7 readily, willing 9 willingly
liege: 5 loyal 6 steady, vassal 7 devoted, staunch, subject 8 faithful 9 steadfast
Liège: 4 city, town
locale: 7 Belgium
river: 4 Maas 5 Meuse
town near ~: 3 Spa
lie in __: 4 wait
lien: 4 mtge. 5 claim 8 mortgage 10 attachment
__ lien: 3 tax 5 first, prior 6 second
Lien: 8 Jennifer
lienee: 6 debtor
lienor: 4 bank 8 claimant, creditor 9 mortgagee
lier: 7 sleeper 8 recliner
lies: 3 gas, rot 4 blah, bosh, bull, bunk, guff, jazz, jive, tosh, wind 5 bilge, fudge, hokum, hooey, trash, tripe 6 babble, bunkum, bushwa, drivel, footle, gabble, gammon, gibber, havers, hot air, humbug, jabber, jargon, kibosh, piffle 7 baloney, bananas, blarney, blather, blether, boloney, bombast, bushwah, eyewash, garbage, hogwash, malarky, prattle, rubbish, twaddle 8 buncombe, claptrap, falderal, falderol, flimflam, flummery, folderal, folderol, malarkey, slipslop, tommyrot, trumpery 9 banana oil, moonshine, poppycock, rigmarole 10 applesauce, balderdash, bilge water, codswallop, double-talk, empty words, flapdoodle, galimatias, Jabberwock, mumbo jumbo, propaganda, rigamarole
__ Lies: 4 Here, True 6 Little
__, lies, and videotape: 3 sex
__ Lies Beneath: 4 What
Lies My Father Told Me (1975 film)
director: Jan Kadar
lie through one's __: 5 teeth
Lie, Trygve home: 4 Oslo
lieu: 5 place, stead
in ~: 8 on behalf
in ~ of: 4 than 6 rather 10 rather than
stand in ~ of: 3 sub 5 alter 6 fill in 7 replace 10 substitute
lieut.: 3 off. 4 rank
right arm: 3 sgt.
sch.: 4 USMA
Lieut. __: 3 Col. 5 Comdr.
lieutenant: 4 aide, rank 5 looey, looie, louie, proxy 6 deputy, helper, second 7 officer 8 minister 9 man Friday
future ~: 5 cadet
subordinate: 3 NCO, PFC, pvt., sgt. 7 private 8 sergeant
superior: 3 col., gen., maj. 4 capt. 5 major 7 captain, colonel, general
trainer: 3 OCS
lieutenant __: 7 colonel, general
__ lieutenant: 5 first 6 second
__ Lieutenant's Woman, The: 6 French
Liev: 9 Schreiber
lieve: 6 gladly 7 readily 9 willingly
__-lievio: 5 ring-a
Lifar, Serge: 6 dancer 7 danseur
life: 3 bio, zip 4 brio, dash, days, élan, soul, span, term, time, zest, zing 5 being, cycle, oomph, verve, vigor, world 6 bounce, breath, energy, esprit, growth, memoir, spirit 7 history, sparkle 8 activity, duration, lifetime, organism, survival, vitality, vivacity 9 animation, biography, élan vital, enjoyment, existence, happiness, longevity, sentience, viability 10 enthusiasm, excitement, exuberance, get up and go, human being, liveliness, metabolism
animal ~: 5 fauna
basis of ~: 6 carbon
big as ~: 5 plain 7 visible 8 apparent, manifest
breathe new ~ into: 6 revive 7 refresh 10 regenerate
breath of ~: 4 soul 5 anima 6 spirit 10 vital force
combining form: 3 bio-
ender: 4 boat, line, long, time, work 5 blood, guard, saver, style 6 saving
enhancer: 5 spice
family ~: 4 home 6 hearth 8 fireside
force: 3 Tao, vim 4 élan, fire, soul, will 5 sense, spark, vigor 6 energy, esprit, spirit, warmth 7 essence, passion 8 presence, vitality 9 animation, willpower
form: 5 being, human 6 animal, person 8 creature, organism
former ~: 4 past
full of ~: 4 spry 5 lusty, peppy, zingy 7 healthy, zestful, zinging 8 spirited, youthful 9 energetic, vivacious
future ~: 9 next world 10 afterworld
get extra ~ from: 5 reuse
give new ~ to: 7 refresh
give ~ to: 4 form 5 beget, breed, build, erect, forge, found, hatch, model, shape, spawn, start 6 author, create, design, devise, effect, father 7 compose, develop, dream up, fashion, imagine, produce, think up 8 conceive, engender, engineer, generate, occasion, organize 9 actualize, construct, establish, institute, originate 10 mastermind
good ~: 4 ease 6 luxury 7 comfort, leisure 9 affluence 10 bed of roses, prosperity
have ~: 2 be 4 go on, last, live 5 abide, exist 6 endure, remain 7 breathe, subsist, survive 8 continue
in French: 3 vie
in Latin: 4 esse
larger than ~: 4 epic 5 famed 6 famous, heroic 7 awesome 8 heroical, immortal, imposing, mythical, renowned, towering 9 legendary 10 celebrated, impressive
love of ~: 2 go 3 pep, zip 4 brio, élan, zest 5 gusto, oomph, punch, spice, verve 6 ginger, relish, spirit 7 passion, sparkle 8 appetite, vitality 10 enthusiasm, exuberance, heartiness
name meaning ~: 3 Eve, Zoe
not on your ~: 4 nope 5 ixnay, never, no way 6 nowise 7 I refuse, not ever 8 at no time, forget it 9 by no means, fat chance, I think not 10 count me out, not a chance
of ~: 6 biotic 8 biotical
of the party: 3 wit 5 mixer 6 joiner
partner: 4 limb
plant ~: 5 flora 10 vegetation
prime of ~: 8 fullness, majority, maturity
rudimentary ~: 4 germ, seed 5 virus 6 embryo 7 microbe 8 pathogen 9 bacterium
saver: 4 hero 7 heroine
science: 3 bio. 4 biol., zool. 7 biology, zoology
sign of ~: 5 pulse 6 breath 9 heartbeat
staff of ~: 5 bread 7 aliment
starter: 3 low, mid 4 high, wild 5 after, night
story: 3 bio 4 biog. 6 memoir 7 memoirs 9 biography
time of one's ~: 4 ball 5 blast
true to ~: 9 realistic
walk of ~: 4 turf, work 5 field, orbit, realm 6 career, métier, milieu, sphere 7 calling, pursuit, purview, station 8 business, province, vocation 9 bailiwick, situation 10 livelihood, occupation, profession
you bet your ~: 3 yep, yes, yup 4 amen, true 5 natch, roger, uh-huh 6 agreed, indeed, just so, rather 7 exactly, granted, indeedy, mais oui, quite so, right on 8 for a fact, of course 9 certainly, darn right, naturally, precisely, sure thing 10 by all means, definitely, positively, that's right
life __: 3 car, net 4 belt, buoy, form, peer, raft, span, vest 5 arrow, cycle, float, force, plant, signs 6 jacket 7 annuity, history, science
life __ party: 5 of the
life-__: 4 size 6 giving
__ life: 3 for 4 dog's, good, mean 5 big as, shelf, still 6 public 7 average, charmed, fatigue, storage
__ life!: 4 Get a
__-life: 4 half, real, true
...life __ know it: 4 as we
Life: 3 mag 5 Scout 6 cereal 8 Boy Scout, magazine
competitor: 3 Kix 4 Trix 5 Kashi, Quisp, Total 6 Kaboom, Muesli, Oreo O's, Pablum, Smacks 7 All-Bran, Crispix, Harmony, Hunny B's, Mueslix, Oat Bran, Pokemon 8 Boo Berry, Cheerios, Corn Chex, Corn Pops, Fiber One, Rice Chex, Special K, Uncle Sam, Wheaties 9 Alpha Bits, Apple Zaps, Grape Nuts, Honey Comb, Just Right, Wheat Chex 10 Apple Jacks, Bran Flakes, Cap'n Crunch, Cocoa Puffs, Froot Loops, Mini-Wheats, Nutri-Grain, Puffed Rice, Quaker Oats, Smart Start 11 Cocoa Blasts, Cookie Crisp, Golden Crisp, Lucky Charms, Puffed Wheat, Sweet Crunch, Waffle Crisp
founder: 4 Luce
rival: 4 Look
Life (1999 film)
cast: Obba Babatundé, Ned Beatty, Martin Lawrence, Eddie Murphy
director: Ted Demme
Life __ a dream: 5 is but
Life __ at Forty: 6 Begins
Life __ Beautiful: 5 Can Be
Life __ cabaret: 3 is a
Life __ Fast Lane: 5 in the
Life __ Father: 4 With
Life __ On: 4 Goes
__ Life: 3 Pop 4 A New, In My 5 All My, Big as, Still, That's 7 Country
__ Life!: 5 That's
__ Life, A: 3 New 6 Double 7 Charmed
Life Among the Modocs author: Joaquin Miller
life-and-death: 4 dire 5 acute, grave, heavy, major, vital 6 urgent 7 big-deal, crucial, pivotal, serious 8 critical, pressing 9 desperate, essential, important, paramount 10 imperative, portentous, touch-and-go
Life and Death of Colonel Blimp (1943 film)
cast: Deborah Kerr, Roger Livesey
Life and Legend of Wyatt Earp, The (ABC western)
cast: Hugh O'Brian (Wyatt Earp)
Life and Times of Judge Roy Bean, The (1972 film)
cast: Ava Gardner, Paul Newman, Victoria Principal
director: John Huston
Life as a House (2001 film)
cast: Kevin Kline, Jena Malone, Kristin Scott Thomas
director: Irwin Winkler
Life Before Man author: Margaret Atwood
Life Begins (1932 film)
cast: Glenda Farrell, Aline MacMahon, Loretta Young
Life Begins at Eight-Thirty (1942 film)
cast: Ida Lupino, Cornel Wilde, Monty Woolley
Life Begins at Forty (1935 film)
cast: Richard Cromwell, Rochelle Hudson, Will Rogers
Life Begins for Andy Hardy (1941 film)
cast: Judy Garland, Mickey Rooney, Lewis Stone
director: George B. Seitz
lifeblood: 4 core 5 basis, heart 6 marrow 7 essence 9 substance
lifeboat
lowerer: 5 crane, davit 7 derrick
Lifeboat (1944 film)
cast: Tallulah Bankhead, William Bendix, Walter Slezak
director: Alfred Hitchcock
Lifebuoy: 4 soap
alternative: 3 Lux 4 Dial, Dove, Lava, Tone, Zest 5 Camay, Coast, Ivory, Lever 6 Boraxo, Caress, Shield 9 Palmolive, Safeguard 11 Irish Spring
Life Can Be Beautiful: 9 radio show
Life Doesn't Frighten Me author: Maya Angelou
Life for the Tsar, A composer: 6 Glinka
Life Goes On (ABC drama)
cast: Christopher Burke (Corky Thatcher)
Patti LuPone (Libby Thatcher)
Kellie Martin (Becca Thatcher)
Bill Smitrovich (Drew Thatcher)
dog: 6 Arnold
lifeguard
at times: 5 saver
beat: 4 pool 5 beach
Life in London author: 4 Egan
__ life insurance: 5 group, joint, whole 6 credit
Life in the Fast Lane (1977 song)
artist: Eagles
Life is a banquet lady: 4 Mame
Life Is Beautiful (1998 film)
cast: Roberto Benigni, Nicoletta Braschi
director: Roberto Benigni
__ Life Is It Anyway?: 5 Whose
Life Is Just __ of Cherries: 5 a Bowl
Life is like __ of chocolates: 4 a box
life jacket: 7 Mae West
stuffing: 5 kapok
lifeless: 3 dry 4 arid, bare, blah, cold, drab, dull, flat, late, lazy, slow, zero 5 brute, empty, faint, inert, prosy, spent, stiff, tepid, vapid, waste 6 asleep, barren, desert, draggy, glassy, hollow, jejune, leaden, static, torpid, wooden 7 defunct, extinct, insipid, nothing, out cold, pabulum, passive, prosaic, sterile, tedious 8 listless, slothful, sluggish, stagnant 9 colorless, exanimate, inanimate, inorganic, insensate, lethargic, ponderous, prosaical 10 glassy-eyed, insensible, insentient, lackluster, lusterless, mechanical, motionless, spiritless

combining form: 4 abio-
old-style: 5 amort
lifelike: 9 realistic
lifeline: 9 salvation
locale: 4 palm
lifelong: 3 old 7 lasting 8 constant, enduring 9 perennial, permanent 10 continuing, deep-rooted, inveterate, persistent
life of __: 5 Riley
Life of Emile Zola, The (1937 film)
cast: Paul Muni, Joseph Schildkraut, Gale Sondergaard
Life of Galileo, The author: Bertolt Brecht
Life of Jimmy Dolan, The (1933 film)
cast: Douglas Fairbanks Jr., Guy Kibbee, Loretta Young
director: Archie Mayo
Life of Riley, The (NBC sitcom)
cast: William Bendix (Chester Riley) John Brown (Digger O'Dell) Marjorie Reynolds (Peg Riley)
dog: 3 Rex
life of the __: 5 party
Life of the Insects, The author: Karel Capek
__ Life of Walter Mitty, The: 6 Secret
Life or Something Like It (2002 film)
cast: Edward Burns, Angelina Jolie, Tony Shalhoub
director: Stephen Herek
lifer: 3 con 5 felon 8 internee, jailbird, prisoner
lifesaver: 4 hero 5 medic 7 release
at times: 3 net 6 airbag 9 safety net
Lifesavers: 5 candy
like ~: 5 toric
shapes: 4 tori
lifesaving
org.: 4 USCG
skill: 3 CPR
Life So Far author: Betty Friedan
Lifestyles of the Rich and Famous
host: Robin Leach
__ Life, The: 3 New 4 Good
lifetime: 3 age 4 days, span 5 years 6 career, course, period 9 endurance, existence
Lifetime alternative: 3 BET, CMT, MTV, PAX, TBS, TLC, TNN, TNT, USA 4 ESPN, HGTV 5 A and E, C-SPAN, Style 6 Noggin, Tech TV, TV Land 7 Court TV, Ovation, SoapNet
lifetimes
many ~: 3 eon 4 aeon
__ Life to Live: 3 One
Life With Father: 4 film, play
author: Clarence Day
cast: Irene Dunne, Edmund Gwenn, ZaSu Pitts, William Powell, Elizabeth Taylor
character: 4 Cora, Nora 5 Delia, Julie
director: Michael Curtiz
Life With Mikey (1993 film)
cast: Michael J. Fox, Nathan Lane, Christina Vidal
director: James Lapine
Life With Mother author: Clarence Day
lifework: 3 job 6 career 7 calling, mission, purpose, pursuit 8 business, interest, vocation 10 occupation, profession
Liffey: 5 river
city on the ~: 6 Dublin
locale: 4 Eire, Erin 7 Ireland
lift: 2 up 3 aid, cop, end, nip, rob, run 4 buoy, copy, crib, glom, hand, heft, help, hike, hook, loot, rear, ride, rise, soar, stop, take 5 annul, arise, boost, carry, cheer, climb, drive, erect, exalt, filch, goose, heave, heist, hoist, leg up, mount, pinch, put up, raise, relax, scoop, seize, steal, swipe 6 ascend, aspire, assist, buoy up, cancel, come up, draw up, haul up, hike up, jack up, jump up, move up, pick up, pilfer, pirate, pocket, recall, relief, remove, repeal, revoke, rip off, snitch, step up, succor, take up, thieve, uphold, uprear, vanish 7 advance, bring up, build up, comfort, console, dignify, elevate, enhance, improve, journey, larceny, lighten, passage, promote, purloin, ransack, rescind, reverse, secours, support, upgrade, upheave, upraise 8 abstract, disperse, elevator, heighten, liberate, pick-me-up, pump iron, simulate 9 disappear, dismantle, dissipate, terminate, transport 10 ameliorate, assistance, exhilarate, pickpocket, plagiarize
a finger: 3 aid, try 4 help 6 assist 7 help out 10 contribute
easy to ~: 3 wee 4 puny, tiny 5 light, small 6 little, slight 8 feathery, portable 10 manageable, weightless
give a ~ to: 3 aid 4 cart 5 cheer, elate 6 assist, pick up 7 enliven 8 reassure
in America: 8 elevator
kind of ~: 4 tram
off: 6 ascend
ski ~: 4 J-bar, T-bar
starter: 3 air, eye, sea 4 boat, drag, fork, shop
up: 4 heft 5 elate, exalt, hoist 7 elevate 8 levitate 10 exhilarate
up one's voice: 5 chant, croon 6 intone, warble 7 belt out, perform 8 melodize, vocalize
user: 5 skier
weights: 8 exercise, pump iron
with effort: 4 heft 5 boost, heave, hoist
lift __: 3 off 4 bolt, pump 5 truck 6 bridge, ticket
__ lift: 3 air, ski 4 auto, dead, J-bar, Poma, T-bar 5 chair 7 surface, topping
__-lift: 4 face
lift a __: 6 finger
Lift dat __: 4 bale
lifter: 4 jack 5 crane, thief, winch 6 pulley, tackle 7 derrick 8 windlass 10 dumbwaiter
mythical ~: 5 Atlas
starter: 4 shop 6 weight
wallet ~: 3 dip 10 pickpocket
lifting: 5 theft
device: 3 pry 5 crank, jimmy, lever 7 crowbar
starter: 4 face, shop 5 power 6 weight
lifting __: 4 sail
__ lifting: 5 heavy
liftoff: 6 ascent, launch 8 blastoff 9 departure
ligament: 3 tie 4 link 8 ligature, vinculum
combining form: 4 desm- 5 desmo- 7 syndesm- 8 syndesmo-
ligand: 7 hormone 8 antibody
ligate: 3 tie 4 bind 5 tie up 6 tie off
ligation: 3 tie 4 link 8 ligature
ligature: 3 tie 4 band, bond, cord, knot, link, rope, yoke 5 nexus 7 bandage, binding 8 ligament 10 connection
Ligeia author: Edgar Allan Poe
liger: 3 cat 5 felid 6 feline, hybrid
relative: 4 eyra, lion, lynx, puma 5 chita, ounce, tiger, tigon 6 bobcat, cheeta, chetah, cougar, jaguar, margay, ocelot, serval, tiglon 7 bay lynx, caracal, cheetah, leopard, panther 9 catamount 10 jaguarundi
light: 3 gay, ray, sit, sun, wee 4 airy, bulb, burn, cast, dawn, drop, easy, fair, fire, glow, high, lamp, land, mild, morn, pale, puny, rest, rich, sign, soft, spot, star, stop, thin, tiny, weak, wiry 5 agile, aglow, angle, blaze, blond, clear, dizzy, downy, faded, faint, filmy, flame, flare, flash, flood, funny, gauzy, giddy, glare, gleam, glint, lithe, lo-cal, loose, merry, minor, model, perch, perky, petty, put on, roost, sandy, sheen, sheer, shine, shiny, slant, small, spark, start, sunny, taper, teeny, torch, vivid, white, witty 6 ablaze, alight, arrive, aspect, aurora, beacon, blithe, blonde, breezy, bright, candle, casual, cheery, chirpy, dainty, facile, fickle, flimsy, fluffy, frothy, frugal, gentle, glossy, ignite, illume, kindle, little, lively, lucent, luster, meager, minute, modest, nimble, pastel, porous, scanty, settle, simple, slight, smooth, sparse, spongy, teensy, turn on, upbeat, window 7 amusing, animate, buoyant, chipper, context, crumbly, daytime, deplane, descend, detrain, enflame, example, flighty, fly down, friable, get down, glimmer, glitter, glowing, inflame, insight, lambent, lantern, morning, paragon, radiant, set down, shining, sit down, slender, sparkle, sunbeam, sunrise, trivial, unheavy 8 animated, approach, attitude, bleached, brighten, carefree, cheerful, come down, daybreak, daylight, delicate, dismount, enkindle, ethereal, exemplar, feathery, finespun, flashing, floating, get there, gossamer, graceful, humorous, illumine, lambency, luminous, lustrous, moderate, pleasing, polished, portable, radiance, radiancy, splendor, standing, step down, sunshine, switch on, trifling, untaxing 9 awareness, brilliant, burnished, cloudless, condition, disembark, diverting, easygoing, education, emanation, floatable, frivolous, gossamery, hardly any, irradiate, knowledge, lithesome, minuscule, radiation, refulgent, set fire to, spotlight, sprightly, sylphlike, touch down, towheaded, unclouded, viewpoint, whimsical 10 brightness, brilliance, brilliancy, digestible, effortless, effulgence, floodlight, fractional, illuminate, inadequate, incandesce, indistinct, low-calorie, luminosity, manageable, reflection, refulgence, restricted, settle down, shoestring, tissuelike, unexacting, unobscured, weightless
a fire under: 4 goad, spur, stir 5 rouse, spark 6 arouse, bestir, excite, fire up, incite, stir up, wake up, whip up, work up 7 animate, inflame, inspire, provoke, quicken 8 motivate 9 electrify, galvanize, stimulate
as a feather: 4 airy 6 aerial 8 gossamer
blinding ~: 5 glare 6 dazzle
bring to ~: 4 bare, find, show 5 admit, dig up 6 elicit, evince, expose, reveal, turn up, unmask, unveil 7 lay bare, uncover, unearth 8 disclose, discover 9 track down
circle of ~: 4 halo 6 corona 7 aureola, aureole
combining form: 4 luci-, phos-, phot- 5 lumin-, photo- 6 lumini-, lumino-
come to ~: 5 arise 6 arisen, emerge 7 surface
emit ~: 4 beam, glow 5 blaze, flare, flash, glare, gleam, glint, shine 6 dazzle 7 flicker, glimmer, glisten, glitter, radiate, reflect, shimmer, sparkle, twinkle 8 bedazzle, brighten, illumine 9 coruscate 10 illuminate, incandesce
ender: 4 face, foot, ship, some, wood 5 house, proof 6 headed, weight 7 hearted
film-set ~: 5 klieg
first ~: 4 dawn 5 sunup 7 genesis 8 daybreak, daylight
flash of ~: 5 blaze, gleam, spark
garish ~: 4 neon
give the green ~: 2 OK 4 okay 5 agree, allow, clear 6 accede, enable 7 endorse, indorse
green ~: 2 go, OK 3 yes 4 okay, word 5 leave 6 assent, permit, signal 7 go-ahead, license, mandate, warrant 8 approval, sanction 9 clearance 10 acceptance
guiding ~: 4 guru 6 beacon 8 cynosure, lodestar, polestar 10 apotheosis
high-tech ~: 5 laser
into: 4 flay, slam, wade 5 fight, fly at, roast, scold 6 assault, attack, hit out, oppugn 7 assault, lambast 8 lambaste 9 fustigate, haul off on, lash out at, reprimand
leading ~: 4 rock 6 pillar 8 mainstay
lower the ~: 5 bedim 6 darken
make ~ of: 3 rag 4 mock 5 scoff 6 deride, slight 7 neglect 8 minimize, overlook, palliate, play down, sneeze at 9 soft-pedal 10 understate
name meaning ~: 5 Lucia 6 Lucius
not ~: 4 dark 7 onerous
of heel: 4 fast 5 fleet, quick, rapid, swift 6 nimble, speedy, winged
on one's feet: 4 deft, spry 5 agile, fleet, lithe, quick 6 active, limber, lively, nimble, supple 7 lissome 8 graceful, spirited, vigorous 9 energetic, sprightly, vivacious
out: 3 hie, run 4 head, quit, race 5 leave 6 be gone, depart, escape 7 abscond, make off, push off, run away, take off 8 hightail 9 take a hike
pilot ~: 5 flame 6 gas jet
red ~: 4 flag 5 alert 6 signal 7 caution, warning
refractor: 5 prism 7 crystal, rainbow
regulator: 4 iris
science: 6 optics
see the ~: 5 get it 7 realize 10 understand
shaft: 3 ray 4 beam 7 sunbeam 8 moonbeam
shed ~ on: 4 show 5 solve 6 answer, unfold 7 clarify, explain, expound 8 illumine, simplify, spell out 9 bring home, elaborate, elucidate, interpret, make plain, translate 10 illuminate, illustrate
sky ~: 3 sun 4 moon, star 6 albedo, aurora
source: 4 bulb, lamp 5 torch 6 candle
starter: 3 day, fan, gas, pen, sky, sun, twi 4 back, dead, drop, fire, head, high, jack, lamp, lime, moon, rush, safe, side, spot, star, stop, tail, trap 5 earth, flash, flood 6 candle, search, street
switch: 6 dimmer
trip the ~ fantastic: 4 step 5 dance, party, rumba, tango, waltz 6 cha-cha, rhumba 7 cut a rug
unit: 3 lux 4 phot 5 lumen 10 foot-candle
up: 5 smoke 6 ignite 7 radiate, twinkle 8 brighten, illumine 9 irradiate 10 illuminate
upon: 4 find, spot 6 locate 8 discover 10 come across
vigil ~: 5 taper 6 shames 7 shammes 9 luminaria
warning ~: 5 flare 6 beacon, signal

light __: **3** air, box, pen **4** bulb, into, line, meat, pipe, show **5** as air, bread, chain, cream, curve, draft, guide, horse, meter, opera, table, valve, verse, water **6** bomber, breeze, bridge, pencil **7** colonel, cruiser, mineral, quantum
light __ feather: **3** as a
light __ under: **5** a fire
light-__: **4** duty, rail, year **5** armed **6** footed, handed, minded, struck
__ light: **3** arc, fog, hot, key, red, wax **4** beam, cold, dash, deck, dome, fill, flat, grow, hard **5** alley, angel, ashen, black, brake, bunch, carry, first, green, idiot, klieg, night, pilot, speed, spill, tidal, vault, vigil, white **6** anchor, backup, Bengal, border, bounce, hazard, Holmes, hopper, kicker, riding, strobe, yellow **7** backing, calcium, leading, running, traffic
Light: **5** Allie, Enoch **6** Judith
Light __ Failed, The: **4** That
Light-__ Harry Lee: **5** Horse
light a __ under: **4** fire
Light a Penny Candle author: Maeve Binchy
light as a __: **7** feather
Light Brigade milieu: **6** Crimea, Russia
light-complexioned: **4** fair
lighted: **6** ablaze, aflame **8** luminous
light-emitting __: **5** diode
lighten: **4** buoy, ease, free, lift, take, thin **5** allay, break, cheer, elate, empty, flash, gleam, light, relax, shift, shine **6** bleach, buoy up, change, dilute, illume, leaven, lessen, perk up, put off, reduce, remove, revive, soften, unlade, unload, whiten **7** assuage, cheer up, comfort, cut down, gladden, hearten, inspire, mollify, pour out, relieve, tail off, upraise **8** brighten, decrease, jettison, levitate, mitigate, palliate, slack off, throw out, unburden **9** alleviate, attenuate, disburden, encourage, eradicate, extenuate, irradiate **10** ameliorate, facilitate, illuminate
up: **4** slow **5** relax **6** cool it, give in, relent, soften **7** back off, ease off, give way, lay back, slacken, subside **8** go easy on, moderate **9** mellow out **10** come around
lighter: **4** boat, fuse, fuze **5** barge, flint, fusee, fuzee, match, squib **6** tender **7** lucifer **8** ignition **9** detonator
brand: **3** Bic **5** Zippo
feature: **4** fuel, wick **5** flint **6** butane
starter: **4** high, lamp
lighter __: **5** fluid
lighter-__-air: **4** than
light-fingered: **3** sly **4** deft **5** agile **6** adroit, nimble **7** crooked **8** thieving, thievish
one: **4** yegg **5** crook, ganef, thief **6** bandit, rip-off, robber **7** brigand, burglar, filcher, footpad, heister, prowler, rustler, stealer **8** cutpurse, pilferer **9** purloiner **10** bushranger, cat burglar, highwayman, pickpocket, shoplifter
light-footed: **4** spry **5** agile, light, lithe, quick **6** nimble **9** lithesome, sprightly
Lightfoot, Gordon
homeland: Canada
song: Carefree Highway (1974)
If You Could Read My Mind (1971)
Rainy Day People (1975)
Sundown (1974)
The Wreck of the Edmund Fitzgerald (1976)
light-haired: **6** blonde
lightheaded: **4** gaga, hazy **5** dizzy, empty, faint, giddy, queer, rocky, silly, tired, woozy **6** fickle, punchy, swimmy **7** flighty, foolish, reeling, shallow **8** flippant, skittish, swimming, trifling, whirling **9** delirious, frivolous **10** changeable
lighthearted: **3** gay **4** glad **5** happy, jolly, light, merry, sunny **6** blithe, breezy, bright, jocund, jovial, joyful, joyous, lively, upbeat **7** buoyant, gleeful, jocular, playful **8** carefree, cheerful, feel-good, laid-back, sanguine, spirited, volatile **9** expansive, resilient, sprightly, vivacious **10** blithesome, frolicsome, insouciant, untroubled
lightheartedness: **4** glee **5** mirth **6** gaiety, gayety, levity **7** jollity **8** pleasure
Light-Horse Harry: **3** Lee
lighthouse: **5** tower **6** Pharos, signal **10** watchtower
feature: **4** beam, lamp **5** flare **6** beacon, signal **7** lantern
lighthouse __: **4** tube **5** clock
Lighthouse at the End of the World, The author: Jules Verne
Light in August author: William Faulkner
__ lighting: **3** rim **4** cove **5** panel, track **6** bounce, direct
lighting pro: **5** wirer
Light in the __, A: **5** Attic
Light in the Forest, The (1958 film)
cast: Carol Lynley, James MacArthur, Fess Parker
Light in the Forest, The author: Conrad Richter
Light in the Piazza (1962 film)
cast: Rossano Brazzi, Olivia de Havilland, Yvette Mimieux
director: Guy Green
__ Light in the Window: **4** Put a
Light It Up (1999 film)
cast: Rosario Dawson, Usher Raymond, Marcello Robinson, Forest Whitaker
director: Craig Bolotin
lightless: **3** dim **4** dark, inky **5** black, dusky, unlit **6** gloomy, pitchy **7** shadowy, Stygian **8** jet black
lightly: **4** idly, skim **6** airily, easily, freely, gently, mildly, nimbly, simply, softly, subtly, thinly **7** agilely, faintly, quietly, timidly **8** breezily, casually, daintily, gingerly, slightly, smoothly, sparsely, tenderly **9** leniently, sparingly, tactfully, tenuously **10** carelessly, delicately, ethereally, flippantly, heedlessly, moderately, peacefully
light-minded: **5** giddy, petty, silly **7** flyaway, shallow, vacuous
Light My Fire (song) artist: Doors, Jose Feliciano
lightness: **3** joy **4** glee **5** balon, grace, mirth **6** ballon, gaiety, gayety, levity **7** agility, elation, gayness, jollity **8** airiness, bouyancy, buoyance, buoyancy, deftness, delicacy, gladness, optimism, paleness, spryness **9** flippancy, frivolity **10** volatility
lightning: **4** bolt **5** chain, flash, forky, sheet, swift **6** forked, speedy **8** fireball
by-product: **5** ozone
go like ~: **3** hie, rip, run **4** race, rush **5** hurry **6** streak
like ~: **3** PDQ **4** fast **5** apace, fleet **6** presto **7** fleetly, hastily, quickly, rapidly, swiftly **8** in a flash, in a jiffy, in no time, pell-mell, speedily **9** forthwith, hurriedly, instantly, momentary, posthaste
white ~: **5** booze, hooch **6** hootch **9** moonshine
white ~ holder: **3** jug
lightning __: **3** bug, rod **5** chess
__ lightning: **4** ball, bead, heat **5** Andes, chain, globe, pearl, sheet, white **6** ribbon **7** scarlet
Lightning: **3** six **4** team **5** novel
author: Danielle Steel, Dean Koontz
home: **5** Tampa **8** Tampa Bay
milieu: **3** ice **4** rink
org.: **3** NHL
rival: **4** Blue, King, Star, Wild **5** Bruin, Devil, Flame, Flyer, Oiler, Sabre, Shark **6** Canuck, Coyote, Ranger **7** Capital, Panther, Penguin, Red Wing, Senator **8** Canadien, Islander, Predator, Thrasher **9** Avalanche, Blackhawk, Hurricane, Maple Leaf **10** Blue Jacket, Mighty Duck
sport: **6** hockey
__ light of: **4** make
Light o' Love author: Arthur Schnitzler
__ light on: **4** shed **5** throw
lights __: **3** out
__ Lights: **4** City **5** Party **6** Harbor
__ Lights, Big City: **6** Bright
Lights, camera, __!: **6** action
Light Sleeper (1992 film)
cast: Willem Dafoe, Dana Delany, Susan Sarandon
director: Paul Schrader
lightsome: **3** gay **4** airy, glad, spry **5** agile, giddy, happy, lithe, merry, silly **6** blithe, breezy, bright, cheery, fickle, fluffy, joyous, lissom, nimble, pliant, supple **7** buoyant, chipper, flighty, foolish, gleeful, lissome, playful, smiling **8** bodiless, carefree, cheerful, debonair, ethereal, feathery, flexible, floating, gossamer, graceful, jubilant, laughing, volatile **9** debonaire **10** debonnaire, flying high
Lights Out: **9** radio show
Lights out tune: **4** Taps
__ Light Special: **3** Red **4** Blue
Light That Failed: **4** film **5** novel
author: Rudyard Kipling
cast: Ronald Colman, Walter Huston, Ida Lupino
director: William Wellman
__ Light, The: **7** Guiding
__ Light Up My Life: **3** You
lightweight: **4** thin **5** petty **6** nobody, paltry, slight **7** failing, foolish, shallow, trivial **8** feathery, portable, trifling **9** jellyfish, nonentity, worthless
ligneous: **5** woody **6** wooden
lignite: **4** coal, fuel **7** mineral
lignum vitae: **4** tree
Ligurian Sea
feeder: **4** Arno **6** Genova
locale: **5** Italy
port: **5** Genoa
lija: **4** fish
likable: **4** good, nice **5** sweet **6** genial **7** amiable, lovable, popular, winning, winsome **8** charming, engaging, friendly, loveable, pleasant, pleasing **9** agreeable, appealing, enjoyable **10** attractive, personable, preferable, relishable
Likasi: **4** city, town
locale: **5** Congo
like: **3** à la, dig **4** akin, as if, love, same, such, want **5** adore, enjoy, equal, fancy, favor, gofor, level, prize, savor **6** accept, admire, akin to, care to, choose, desire, dote on, esteem, in kind, on a par, please, prefer, relish, revere, take to **7** approve, care for, cherish, close to, cognate, equal to, feast on, idolize, kindred, related, revel in, similar, stuck on, uniform, worship **8** dote upon, hold dear, matching, parallel, selfsame, treasure **9** analogous, care about, delight in, get high on, hanker for, identical, indulge in, rejoice in, similar to **10** appreciate, comparable, compatible, conforming, consistent, equivalent, homologous, resembling, synonymous, tantamount, true to type
prefix: **3** sym-, syn-
suffix: **3** -ine, -ish, -ose **4** -eous **5** -esque
like __: **3** mad **4** it is **5** a book, a shot, as not, crazy
like __ balloon: **5** a lead
like __ from the blue: **5** a bolt
like __ in a china shop: **5** a bull
like __ in a pod: **4** peas
like __ in a trap: **4** a rat
like __, like son: **6** father
like __ not: **4** it or
like __ of bricks: **4** a ton
like __ off a log: **7** falling
like __ of potatoes: **5** a sack
like __ of sunshine: **4** a ray
like __ on a log: **5** a bump
like __ out of hell: **4** a bat
like __ out of water: **5** a fish
like __ thumb: **5** a sore
like __ to the flame: **5** a moth
like-__: **6** minded
__ like: **4** feel, make
Like __ love it!: **3** it I
Like __ not!: **4** it or
like a __: **4** book, shot
like a __ afire: **5** house
like a __ balloon: **4** lead
like a __ of bricks: **3** ton
like a __ on a log: **4** bump
like a __ out of water: **4** fish
__ like a baby: **3** cry
...like a big pizza pie, that's __: **5** amore
__ like a bird: **3** eat
likeable: **4** kind, nice, warm **6** decent, genial, kindly, mellow, polite **7** affable, amiable, cordial, helpful, winsome **8** amicable, charming, cheerful, friendly, gracious, inviting, obliging, pleasant, sociable **9** agreeable, congenial, courteous, simpatico **10** attractive, hospitable, neighborly, personable
like a bump on a __: **3** log
__ like a charm: **4** work
like a fish __ of water: **3** out
like a house __: **5** afire
like a lead __: **7** balloon
__ Like Alice: **5** A Town
__ Like a Man: **4** Walk
__ Like an Eagle: **3** Fly
Like a Prayer (1989 song) artist: Madonna
like a rat in __: **5** a trap
Like a Rock (1986 song) artist: Bob Seger
Like a Rolling Stone (1965 song) artist: Bob Dylan
like a ton of __: **6** bricks
__ like a top: **4** spin **5** sleep
Like a Virgin (1984 song) artist: Madonna
__ Like Being in Love: **6** Almost
liked: **3** big, hot **6** choice, culled, picked, trendy **7** elected, faddish, fancied, favored, in favor, in vogue, popular, selling, voguish **8** accepted, approved, embraced, endorsed, in demand, pleasing, selected **9** preferred **10** celebrated, fair-haired, handpicked, widespread
__-liked: **4** well
like falling off __: **4** a log
like father, like __: **3** son
__ like hotcakes: **4** sell
__ Like I: **5** A Girl
like it __: **5** or not
__ Like It: **5** As You

__ Like It Hot: 4 Some
__ like it is: 6 tell it
-like kin: 3 -ish, -oid
likelihood: 4 odds, prob. 5 trend 6 chance, toss-up 7 outlook, promise 8 long shot, prospect, tendency 9 direction, fair shake, liability 10 expectancy, fifty-fifty, good chance
likely: 3 apt 4 fair, true, wont 5 prone 6 adverb, doable, liable, odds-on, timely, viable 7 destine, earthly, hopeful, no doubt, seeming, subject, tending 8 apparent, assuring, credible, destined, disposed, expected, favorite, feasible, inclined, possible, probable, probably, rational, workable 9 assumably, doubtless, in favor of, inferable, plausible, potential, practical, promising, seemingly, thinkable 10 acceptable, achievable, attainable, believable, contingent, imaginable, in the cards, ostensible, presumable, presumably, prima facie, reasonable, supposable
likely story!, A: 3 hah 4 as if, I bet
__ Like Me: 4 Just 5 Black, Freak
__ Like Me Now: 4 How U
like-minded: 6 jibing, united 7 similar 8 agreeing, in accord 9 congenial, in harmony, unanimous 10 compatible, concurrent, harmonious, synchronal
like-mindedness: 5 amity, unity 6 accord, unison 7 concert, concord, harmony, oneness, rapport 8 sameness, sympathy 9 agreement, communion, consensus, unanimity 10 conformity, consonance, friendship, solidarity
liken: 6 equate 7 compare
likeness: 4 copy, form, icon, ikon 5 clone, ditto, eikon, guise, image, model, photo, study, xerox 6 carbon, double, ectype, effigy, parity, simile, sketch, statue 7 analogy, picture, profile, replica 8 affinity, equality, identity, knock-off, portrait, sameness 9 agreement, depiction, duplicate, facsimile, imitation, lineation, photocopy, semblance 10 appearance, carbon copy, comparison, conformity, dead ringer, photograph, reflection, silhouette, similarity, similitude, uniformity
  combining form: 4 icon-, ikon- 5 eicon-, icono-, ikono-, -opsis 6 eicono-
likening: 6 simile 7 analogy 9 measuring, semblance 10 comparison
Like Niobe, __ tears: 3 all
__ Like Old Times: 5 Seems
liker: 7 admirer, fancier
like the sun, name meaning: 6 Samson
__ Like the Wind: 4 Ride, She's
Like to Get to Know You (1968 song)
  artist: Spanky and Our Gang
like two peas in __: 4 a pod
__ Like Us: 5 Spies 7 Thieves
Like Water For Chocolate director: 4 Arau
__ Like We Made It: 5 Looks
likewise: 2 so 3 too, yet 4 also, more, same 5 along, ditto 6 as well, either, in kind, withal 7 besides, further 8 moreover 9 similarly 10 in addition
  not: 3 nor
__ Like You, A: 4 Girl 6 Wonder
...like you've __ ghost!: 5 seen a
liking: 4 bent, bias, love, mind, pref., will 5 fancy, taste, tooth 6 desire, loving, palate, regard, relish 7 leaning, passion, stomach, valuing 8 affinity, appetite, devotion, fondness, penchant, pleasure, soft spot, sympathy, tendency, velleity, weakness 9 affection, appetence, proneness 10 attachment, attraction, favoritism, partiality, preference, propensity
  combining form: 7 -philous
  having a ~ for: 6 fond of 9 partial to
  take a ~ (to): 6 cotton
likuta: 5 money
Lil' __: 3 Kim
Lila: 6 McCann 7 Kedrova, Wallace
Li'l Abner: 5 strip 10 comic strip
  animal: 5 Shmoo
  cartoonist: 4 Capp 6 Al Capp
lilac: 5 color, mauve, plant, shrub 6 flower, purple 7 reddish
  relative: 4 plum, puce 5 mauve, olive 6 dahlia, damson, orchid 7 heather, jasmine, petunia 8 amethyst, burgundy, eggplant, lavender, mulberry 9 forsythia, jessamine, raspberry 10 heliotrope
__ lilac: 5 Rouen 7 nodding, Persian
Lilac Bus, The author: Maeve Binchy
Lilacs author: Amy Lowell
Lil E. __: 3 Tee
Lili: 6 Damita, Taylor
Lili (1953 film)
  cast: Jean-Pierre Aumont, Leslie Caron, Mel Ferrer, Zsa Zsa Gabor
  director: Charles Walters
Lili __: 7 Marlene
__ Lili: 7 Darling
Lilia: 5 Skala
Lilienthal: 4 Otto
Lilies of the Field (1963 film)
  cast: Lisa Mann, Sidney Poitier, Lilia Skala
  character: 3 nun 5 Homer
  director: Ralph Nelson
Liliuokalani: 5 queen 8 Hawaiian
Liljekrans: 4 Olaf
Lil' Kim
  real name: Kimberly Jones
  song: It's All About the Benjamins (1997)
    No Time (1996)
    Not Tonight (1997)
Lille: 4 city, town
  locale: 6 France
Lillehammer
  city near ~: 4 Oslo
  locale: 3 Nor. 4 Norw. 6 Norway
Lilli: 6 Palmer
Lillian: 4 Gish, Roth 5 Smith 7 Hellman 8 O'Donnell
Lillie: 3 Bea 7 Langtry 8 Beatrice
Lilliputian: 3 elf, wee 4 baby, mini, puny, tiny 5 bitty, dwarf, elfin, fairy, gnome, short, small, sylph, teeny, troll 6 atomic, bantam, little, midget, minute, pee-wee, petite, shorty, sprite, teensy 7 minikin, shortie 8 atomical, atomlike, half-pint, small fry 9 itsy-bitsy, itty-bitty, miniature, pint-sized, pipsqueak 10 diminutive, homunculus, leprechaun, teeny-weeny, vest-pocket
Lilly: 3 Bob, Eli 5 Daché
Lilongwe: 4 city, town 7 capital
  locale: 6 Malawi
Lil' Red Riding Hood (1966 song)
  artist: Sam the Sham
lilt: 4 tune 5 ditty, meter, swing 6 melody, rhythm 7 cadence, cadency
lilting: 6 dulcet, poetic 7 lyrical, melodic, musical, songful 8 pleasing, rhythmic 9 melodious, rhapsodic 10 euphonious, expressive, harmonious
  syllables: 5 tra la
lily: 5 calla, plant 6 flower
  African ~: 4 aloe
  atamasco ~: 5 plant 6 flower
  calla ~: 4 arum 5 aroid
  corn ~ genus: 4 ixia
  genus: 4 aloe
  in French: 3 lis
  kin: 4 irid, leek 5 camas, chive, onion, yucca 6 camass
  maid of Astolat: 6 Elaine
  name meaning ~: 7 Susanna 8 Susannah
  part: 5 tepal
  stone ~: 6 fossil
  water ~: 3 pad 5 bloom, lotus 6 flower 7 blossom 9 perennial
lily __: 3 pad 4 iron, pond
lily __ valley: 5 of the
lily-__: 7 livered, trotter
__ lily: 3 cow, day, sea 4 arum, boat, corn, fawn, flax, frog, pond, sand, sego, snow, star, wood 5 Aztec, blood, calla, coral, fairy, peace, royal, snake, stone, sword, tiger, torch, trout, water 6 Canada, Easter, ginger, meadow, orange, rubrum, Sierra, spider, zephyr 7 African, Bermuda, glacier, leopard, Madonna, nankeen, prairie
Lily: 4 Pons 5 St. Cyr 6 Tomlin 7 Munster
  cohort: 4 Arte, Ruth
  husband: 6 Herman
lily-livered: 5 timid 6 coward, craven, yellow 7 fearful 8 cowardly, unheroic 9 spineless
lily of the __: 6 valley
lily pad
  lament: 5 croak
  locale: 4 lake, pond
  sitter: 4 frog
__ Lily, The: 3 Red 4 Lent 6 Gilded
lily-trotter: 6 jacana
lily-white: 3 wan 4 pale, pure 6 chaste, pallid 8 innocent, spotless, unsoiled, untanned, virginal
lim.: 3 max., min.
lima: 4 bean 6 legume 10 butterbean
Lima: 4 city, town 7 capital
  city near ~: 6 Callao
  locale: 4 Ohio, Peru
  river: 5 Rímac
  see also Spanish
__ Lima: 6 Rose of
limb: 3 arm, fin, gam, leg, pin 4 lobe, part, spur, stem, unit, wing 5 bough, spray, sprig, wheel 6 branch, member, pinion, spring, switch 7 process 8 offshoot 9 appendage, extension, extremity 10 projection
  combining form: 3 mel-
  feature: 4 leaf 7 foliage
  go out on a ~: 5 guess 6 hazard 7 venture
  holder: 4 bole 5 trunk
  lower ~: 3 gam, leg
  out on a ~: 5 risky, treed 9 foolhardy
  thin ~: 4 twig, wand 5 sprig, stick
__ limb: 6 out on a
limba: 4 tree
Limbaugh: 4 Rush
  medium: 5 radio
__-limbed: 5 clean, loose
limber: 4 deft, limp, spry, wiry 5 agile, lithe, loose 6 lissom, nimble, pliant, supple 7 elastic, lissome, plastic, pliable, springy, willowy 8 flexible, graceful 9 lithesome, resilient
  up: 3 jog 5 train 6 tone up 7 work out 8 exercise
limbic: 8 marginal 9 on the edge 10 borderline
limbo: 5 dance, Hades 7 nowhere, Siberia 8 oblivion 9 left field
Limbo (1999 film)
  cast: Kris Kristofferson, Vanessa Martinez, Mary Elizabeth Mastrantonio, David Strathairn
  director: John Sayles
Limbo Rock (1962 song) artist: Chubby Checker
Limburger: 6 cheese
  feature: 4 odor 5 aroma, smell
  relative: 6 Tilsit
limbus: 4 edge 6 border 8 boundary
lime: 4 tree 5 color, fruit, green, oxide 6 alkali, citrus, flavor, veggie, yellow 7 plaster 8 greenish 9 vegetable
  additive: 4 marl
  bit of ~: 5 twist
  drink: 3 ade 5 juice, sling 6 gimlet, rickey
  ender: 3 ade 4 kiln 5 light, stone, water
  relative: 4 buff, corn, gold, rust, sand, Ugli 5 blond, brass, coral, cream, flaxy, lemon, maize, navel, ocher, ochre, peach, rusty, straw 6 blonde, canary, chammy, citron, crocus, flaxen, orange, pomelo, shammy, shamoy, tangor 7 apricot, chamois, citrine, jasmine, kumquat, mustard, nankeen, old gold, saffron, satsuma, Seville, tangelo, xanthic 8 bergamot, daffodil, mandarin, primrose, shaddock, Valencia 9 champagne, goldenrod, jessamine, tangerine 10 calamondin, grapefruit
  starter: 4 bird 5 brook, quick
lime __: 4 tree, twig 5 glass, green 6 burner, rickey, sulfur 7 hydrate
__ lime: 3 Key 4 soda 5 burnt 6 slaked 7 caustic, Spanish
__-lime: 5 lemon
Lime: 5 Harry
limeade: 5 drink 8 beverage
Limeira: 4 city, town
  locale: 6 Brazil
limekiln: 4 oven
limelight: 5 light, stage 9 publicity, spotlight
  in the ~: 3 big 5 large 6 famous, public 7 eminent, popular, splashy 8 familiar, infamous 9 acclaimed, important, prominent, well-known 10 celebrated, recognized
  share the ~: 6 costar
Limelight (1952 film)
  cast: Claire Bloom, Nigel Bruce, Charles Chaplin
  director: Charles Chaplin
limelike: 4 acid, sour, tart
__ lime pie: 3 Key
limequat: 4 tree 6 hybrid
limerick: 4 poem, rime 5 rhyme, verse
  man: 4 Lear
  opener: 5 there
  writer: 4 poet 5 rimer
Limerick: 4 city, town
  county north of ~: 5 Clare
  land: 4 Eire, Erin 7 Ireland
  town near ~: 5 Adare
limes, like: 4 acid, sour, tart
limestone: 4 malm, tufa 5 chalk 7 mineral
  formation: 6 cavern, grotto
  metamorphosed ~: 6 marble
  terrain: 5 karst
limestone __: 4 fern 7 lettuce
Limey, The (1999 film)
  cast: Peter Fonda, Luis Guzman, Terence Stamp, Lesley Ann Warren
  director: Steven Soderbergh
limit: 3 bar, cap, end, fix, max, rim, set, tie, top 4 brim, cork, curb, edge, side, term, tops 5 bound, bourn, brink, check, cramp, fence, hem in, orbit, quota, stint, tie up, verge 6 apogee, border, bounds, bourne, define, degree, demark, extent, fringe, height, hinder, length, lessen, margin, modify, narrow, period, radius, ration, reduce, utmost 7 abridge, barrier, ceiling, compass, confine, control, curtail, cut back, cut down, due date, extreme, inhibit, maximum, measure, minimum, prevent, purlieu, qualify, specify

8 capacity, confines, deadline, end point, frontier, handicap, precinct, restrain, restrict, straiten, ultimate 9 constrain, constrict, demarcate, last straw, outskirts, parameter, perimeter, periphery, prescribe, restraint, terminate 10 bottom line, boundaries, keep in line
beyond the ~: 5 rabid, ultra 6 far-out 7 drastic, extreme, radical 9 excessive, fanatical 10 immoderate, outlandish
exceed the ~: 3 fly, zip 4 race, rush, tear, whiz, zoom 5 speed 6 barrel, go fast, hurtle 8 hightail, step on it 10 lose no time
go the ~: 6 plunge, strive 7 persist
outer ~: 3 rim 4 edge 5 verge 6 apogee 8 boundary
over the ~: 4 long
reach a ~: 3 max 6 max out, top out
time ~: 6 curfew
to the ~: 4 A to Z 5 fully, plumb, sheer 6 in full, in toto, wholly 7 in depth, totally, utterly 8 entirely, whole hog 9 all the way, full blast, perfectly, to the hilt 10 absolutely, completely, thoroughly
upper ~: 3 cap, lid, max, top 7 ceiling, maximum 8 pinnacle
without ~: 6 all-out 7 flat-out 8 accurate, infinite
limit ___: 5 order, point 6 switch
___ limit: 4 debt, term, time 5 Roche, speed 6 credit 7 elastic, fatigue
limitation: 3 bar, end 4 curb, snag, tabu 5 block, check, pinch, state, taboo 7 proviso 8 drawback, handicap 9 abatement, condition, hindrance, provision, restraint, stricture 10 constraint, discipline
limited: 3 set 4 less, mean, poor, slow, weak 5 bound, brief, fixed, local, scant, short, small, train 6 curbed, faulty, finite, little, meager, modest, narrow, paltry, scanty, scarce, select 7 bounded, checked, cramped, defined, insular, minimal, partial, precise, reduced, special, topical 8 confined, definite, exiguous, far apart, hampered, moderate, modified, one or two, orthodox, reserved, specific 9 confining, delimited, hardly any, parochial, qualified, sectarian, sectional 10 a handful of, compressed, contracted, controlled, diminished, inadequate, infrequent, measurable, particular, provincial, restrained, restricted, terminable
time: 4 span, term, tour 5 hitch, phase 6 period, tenure 7 stretch 8 duration, interval, semester, sentence
to: 6 at most
limited ___: 3 war 6 policy 7 company, edition, partner
limited ___ highway: 6 access
Limited: 3 car 4 auto 5 Buick 10 automobile
___ limiter: 5 noise 7 current
limiting: 6 fixing 7 binding, curbing 9 confining
limitless: 3 big 4 vast 6 cosmic, eonian, untold 7 endless, immense, no end of, no end to 8 cosmical, infinite, spacious, unending, wide-open 9 boundless, countless, excessive, no-strings, unbounded, undefined 10 bottomless, indefinite, innumerous, numberless, unnumbered
limitlessly: 5 no end
___-limit order: 4 stop
limits: 4 ends 5 range 6 bounds 8 boundary 9 perimeter, periphery
free from ~: 5 uncap
off ~: 4 tabu 5 taboo 8 outlawed 9 forbidden 10 prohibited
outer ~: 3 rim 5 ambit, ether, verge 6 aether
___ limits: 4 term
___-limits: 3 off
Limits of Interpretation, The author: Umberto Eco
___ Limits, The: 5 Outer
Limit 10 ___ or Less: 5 items
Limmat, city on the: 6 Zurich
limn: 4 draw 5 paint 6 depict, sketch 7 outline, picture, portray 8 describe 9 delineate, interpret, represent 10 illustrate
limo
see limousine
Limoges: 4 city, town 5 china 9 porcelain
locale: 6 France
river: 6 Vienne
Limoges ___: 4 ware
___ Limon, Costa Rica: 6 Puerto
limonite: 3 ore 7 mineral
Limón, José milieu: 5 dance
Limousin: 3 cow 4 bull 6 bovine, cattle
limousine: 3 car 4 auto 7 vehicle 10 automobile
capacity: 6 carful
feature: 2 TV 3 bar 5 TV set
passenger: 3 VIP
Russian ~: 3 Zil
what a ~ symbolizes: 6 status
limp: 3 lag, lax 4 halt, soft, weak 5 baggy, hitch, loose, loppy, slack, spent, tired, vapid 6 dodder, droopy, falter, feeble, flabby, flaggy, floppy, hobble, limber, pliant, sleazy, supple, totter, waddle, wilted 7 bending, flaccid, hanging, languid, plastic, pliable, relaxed, sagging, shuffle, wearied, worn out 8 dangling, drooping, flagging, flexible, lameness, listless, yielding 9 enervated, exhausted, lethargic 10 spiritless
along: 4 drag 6 schlep 7 shuffle 8 straggle
become ~: 4 wilt 5 swoon
go ~: 3 sag 5 droop, faint 6 weaken 7 crumple, pass out, shrivel 8 black out, keel over
limpet: 5 shell 7 mollusc, mollusk 8 conch kin, seashell
limpid: 4 pure, thin 5 clear, filmy, lucid, sheer 6 bright 7 obvious 8 definite, distinct, luculent, pellucid 10 see-through
limpkin: 4 bird
Limpopo: 5 river
locale: 10 Mozambique
limp-watch painter: 4 Dali
Lin: 4 Maya
Lina: 10 Wertmuller
Linares: 4 city, town
locale: 6 Mexico 9 Nuevo León
linchpin: 3 key 7 keynote 8 mainstay
locale: 4 axle 5 shaft
Lincoln: 3 Abe, car 4 auto, city, Elmo, peak, town 5 mount, sheep 7 Abraham 8 mountain, Steffens 10 automobile
athlete: 10 Cornhusker
county: 9 Lancaster
locale: 3 Neb. 4 Nebr. 6 Canada 7 Ontario, Rockies 8 Colorado, Nebraska
model: 5 Capri 6 Zephyr 7 Aviator, Town Car 8 Premiere 9 Navigator 10 Versailles 11 Continental
what a ~ symbolizes: 4 rank 5 class 6 cachet, rating, status 7 footing, station 8 eminence, position, prestige, standing 10 importance, prominence
Lincoln ___: 4 Logs 5 green
Lincoln, Abraham: 9 president
bill: 4 five
cabinet member: 5 Blair, Chase 6 Seward, Welles 7 Stanton
child: 3 Tad 6 Robert, Willie
coin: 4 cent 5 penny
feature: 5 beard
film portrayer: 5 Fonda 6 Massey
former occupation: 6 lawyer
home: 7 Indiana 8 Illinois, Kentucky
law partner: 7 Herndon
like ~: 4 tall
opponent: 4 Bell 7 Douglas 9 McClellan 12 Breckinridge
parent: 3 Tom 5 Nancy 6 Thomas
V.P.: 6 Hamlin 7 Johnson
wife: 4 Mary
Lincoln Center
attraction: 3 art, Met
___ Lincoln in Illinois: 3 Abe
Lincoln Log competitor: 4 Lego
Lincoln Memorial architect: 5 Bacon
scuptor: 6 French
Lincoln Navigator: 3 SUV
Lincoln Park: 4 city, town
locale: 8 Michigan
Lincoln Park Inn, The singer: 4 Bare
Lincoln Portrait, A composer: 7 Copland
Lincoln Red: 3 cow 4 bull 6 bovine, cattle
Lincolnshire: 6 county
locale: 7 England
Lincs: 6 county
locale: 7 England
Lind: 3 Bob 5 Jenny
Linda: 4 Dano, Gray, Hunt, Park, Purl 5 Blair, Evans, Lavin, Scott 6 Kelsey 7 Darnell, Thorson 8 Ellerbee, Hamilton, Ronstadt 9 Christian, Fratianne, Kozlowski, McCartney 10 Fiorentino
___ Linda, CA: 4 Loma 5 Yorba
Lindbergh: 4 Anne, Erik 7 Charles
Lindbergh, Charles: 7 aviator
linden: 4 teil, tree 8 basswood
Linden: 3 Hal 4 city, town 5 Kathy
locale: 9 New Jersey
Lindenhurst: 4 city, town
locale: 7 New York
Linder: 4 Kate
Lindfors: 6 Viveca
Lindgren: 6 Astrid
___ Lind Hayes: 5 Peter
Lind, Jenny: 6 singer 7 soprano, Swedish
specialty: 5 opera
Lindley: 5 Audra
Lindo, Delroy: 5 actor
film: Broken Arrow (1996)
Cider House Rules (1999)
Clockers (1995)
Crooklyn (1994)
Heist (2001)
Ransom (1996)
Romeo Must Die (2000)
Lindros: 4 Eric
Lindsay: 3 Ted 4 Mark 6 Crouse, Howard, Vachel, Wagner 8 Anderson, Margaret 9 Davenport
partner: 6 Crouse
Lindsay-Hogg: 7 Michael
Lindsay, Mark
song: Arizona (1970)
Silver Bird (1970)
Lindsay, Vachel: 4 poet
work: The Chinese Nightingale
The Congo
General William Booth Enters Into Heaven
The Ghost of the Buffaloes
In Praise of Johnny Appleseed
Rhymes to Be Traded for Bread
The Santa Fe Trail
Lindsey: 4 Mort 6 George 10 Buckingham
Lindstrom: 3 Pia
mother: 6 Ingrid 7 Bergman
Lindstrom, Phyllis
husband: 4 Lars
Lindt: 5 candy, Swiss 9 chocolate
lindy: 3 hop 5 dance
Lindy
contemporary: 6 Amelia
how ~ flew: 4 solo 5 alone
line: 3 bar, job, pad, rim, row, way 4 axis, band, cord, dash, edge, face, file, mark, note, path, pipe, rank, rope, rule, scar, seam, tack, tape, text, tick, tier, vein, wire, work, yarn 5 bound, breed, cable, craft, goods, pitch, queue, ridge, route, skill, spiel, stock, track, trade, verge, wares 6 artery, border, career, column, come-on, crease, family, figure, furrow, groove, letter, method, métier, parade, patter, policy, series, streak, string, stripe, tackle, thread 7 calling, channel, contour, descent, encrust, incrust, lanyard, message, missive, passage, product, pursuit, tracing, wrinkle 8 ancestry, boundary, business, bus route, eremitic, heredity, ideology, pedigree, postcard, province, railroad, vocation 9 commodity, reinforce, threshold, vendibles 10 employment, occupation, procession, profession, sales pitch, silhouette, succession, trajectory
at the end of the ~: 4 last 8 farthest, rearmost, remotest
be in ~ for: 4 rate 5 merit 7 deserve 10 have coming
bottom ~: 3 sum 4 cost, crux 5 limit, point, tally, total 6 outlay, payoff, profit 7 essence, meaning, reality, revenue 8 key point, receipts 9 essential, main point 10 conclusion
curved ~: 3 arc
down the ~: 4 anon, soon, then 5 later 6 in a bit, in time 7 by and by, later on, someday 8 in a while, sometime 9 afterward, hereafter, presently 10 before long, eventually
draw a ~ through: 4 X out 6 delete 8 cross off, cross out
draw the ~: 3 bar, fix 4 halt, stop 5 check, limit 6 cut off, depart, step in 8 restrict 9 determine
drop a ~: 4 fish 5 write 10 correspond
end of the ~: 5 depot 7 station 8 terminal, terminus
feeder: 4 cuer
finish ~: 3 end 4 tape, wire
first in ~: 4 next 6 eldest 7 closest, nearest
get into ~: 4 heed 6 comply, follow, submit 7 conform, observe
get out of ~: 4 defy, riot, rise 5 act up 6 mutiny, oppose, resist, revolt, rise up 7 disobey, dissent, protest 9 make waves, misbehave
get the punch ~: 4 grin, howl, roar 6 giggle, guffaw 7 chortle, chuckle, crack up, snicker, snigger
graph ~: 4 axis 5 x-axis, y-axis, z-axis
help with a ~: 3 cue 6 prompt
in ~: 4 arow 5 level, ready 6 proper 7 abreast, waiting 8 eligible, orthodox, queued up, straight
in ~ (with): 5 along
jump the ~: 5 cut in 7 intrude 9 interpose
keep in ~: 3 pin 4 curb, stem 5 check, cramp, deter, leash, limit, sit on 6 bridle, enjoin, fetter, forbid, stifle, subdue, temper, tether 7 contain, control, curtail, harness, inhibit, repress, squelch 8 hold back, moderate, prohibit, restrain, restrict, slow

down, straiten, suppress, tone down 9 constrain, crack down, hamstring 10 discourage

laying it on the ~: 4 free, open 5 bluff, blunt, frank, plain, vocal 6 abrupt, candid, direct, square 7 sincere, upfront 8 explicit, truthful 9 outspoken 10 forthright, from the hip, point-blank, unreserved

lay on the ~: 4 risk

like a straight ~: 4 one-d

map ~: 2 rd., rt. 3 hwy., riv., rte. 4 blvd., road 5 river, route 6 avenue 7 highway 9 boulevard 10 interstate

next in ~: 4 heir 7 heiress 9 inheritor

oblique ~: 3 zig 4 bias, diag. 8 diagonal

of demarcation: 4 edge 5 verge 6 border, margin 8 boundary, frontier 9 perimeter, periphery 10 outer limit

of gab: 5 pitch 6 patter

of work: 3 job 10 occupation

on the ~: 6 at risk 7 sincere 9 veracious 10 in jeopardy

out of ~: 4 flip, pert, rude 5 askew, fresh, nervy, sassy, wrong 6 awless, brazen, cheeky, snippy, unruly, untrue 7 aweless, uncivil 8 aberrant, abnormal, flippant, impolite, insolent, snippety 10 prohibited, suspicious

part: 3 seg. 7 segment

sailor's ~: 5 brail 6 hawser 7 halyard

stand in ~: 4 wait 5 await 8 lose time, mark time

starter: 3 air, bee, bow, hem, hot, rat, red, set, sky, tag, tow 4 balk, bunt, date, dead, drag, hair, hard, head, land, life, main, neck, pipe, plot, roof, side, tape, tram, trot 5 blood, coast, drive, front, guide, ridge, shore, sight, touch, waist 6 border, center, strand, stream, timber 7 clothes

time ~: 4 plan 6 agenda 8 game plan, scenario, schedule, strategy 9 blueprint, framework 10 big picture

toe the ~: 4 heed, mind, obey 5 agree, bow to, defer, yield 6 accept, adhere, behave, bend to, comply, follow, fulfil, listen, submit 7 conform, consent, fulfill, observe, respect 8 carry out 10 keep in step

top of the ~: 4 A-one, best

unscripted ~: 5 ad-lib

up: 3 get 4 book, hire 5 align, array, enrol, order, queue, range 6 engage, enroll, obtain, secure 7 acquire, arrange, marshal, procure, program 8 organize 9 string out 10 straighten

(up): 3 set

walk the ~: 4 heed 6 listen, submit

weather ~: 5 front 6 isobar, isohel

line __: 3 art, cut 4 copy, drop, gale, mark 5 dance, drive, gauge, score, space, storm 6 squall, vector 7 drawing, officer, printer, segment, trimmer, voltage

line-__: 4 haul 6 hauler 7 casting

line-__ veto: 4 item

__ line: 3 bar, bus, car, dew, end, fly, gag, hot, lag, log, net, red, tag, taw, tie, toy 4 apse, balk, base, belt, beta, blue, cell, chow, date, fall, fire, foot, foul, goal, grab, hard, jump, lash, lead, load, main, mean, neat, plot, pure, real, sash, snow, soft, spot, stag, time, toll, tree, trip, zone 5 added, agate, block, bread, chalk, check, drop a, fault, field, frame, front, grade, green, laugh, leech, leger, level, light, on the, out of, party, pitch, plumb, power, punch, range, rhumb, short, story, trawl, trunk, water, white, world 6 action, agonic, ashlar, banner, battle, border, bottom, branch, breast, broken, center, credit, dotted, feeder, finish, firing, flight, ledger, margin, number, picket, random, shroud, spring, squall, static, strand, string 7 aclinic, ballast, contour, curtain, fishing, lateral, lubber's, Maginot, meander, morning, parting, poverty, product, scratch, service, stepped, trolley, walking

__-line: 3 off, old 4 full 5 first, front

__ Line: 3 Hot 4 Main 5 Value

__ Line, A: 6 Chorus

lineage: 3 kin 4 clan, folk, race 5 birth, blood, breed, class, house, roots, stock, tribe 6 family, origin, stirps, strain 7 descent, kindred, progeny 8 ancestry, breeding, forbears, heredity, pedigree 9 forebears, genealogy, offspring, posterity 10 extraction, succession

lineal: 6 family, racial 8 familial, parental 9 ancestral 10 hereditary

not ~: 10 collateral

start: 5 matri, patri

lineament: 4 form, mark 5 shape 7 contour, feature, profile 10 silhouette

__, line and sinker: 4 hook

linear: 4 one-d 6 direct, in a row, narrow, unbent 7 unbowed 8 straight 9 arabesque 10 unswerving

extent: 4 span 5 orbit, range 6 course, length, radius 7 breadth, expanse, measure, purview, section, segment 8 diameter, distance, longness 9 longitude

lead-in: 5 recti

measure: 2 ft., km., mi., yd. 3 rod 4 foot, mile, yard 5 meter 7 furlong 9 kilometer

linear __: 5 graph, motor, space 7 algebra, measure

lineation: 5 shape 6 figure, sketch 7 profile 8 likeness, portrait 10 silhouette

lined

combining form: 8 -stichous

up: 4 arow 5 level 6 in a row

line dance: 5 conga 8 bunny hop

__ Line Fever: 5 White

__ Line Is It Anyway?: 5 Whose

line-item __: 4 veto

lineman: 2 LG, LT, RG, RT 3 end 5 wirer 6 center, tackle 9 left guard 10 footballer, left tackle, right guard

__ Lineman: 7 Wichita

__ lineman for the county: 4 I am a

linen: 5 sheet, towel 6 damask, fabric, napery, napkin, sheets, towels 7 bedding, cambric, napkins 8 bed sheet 9 bed sheets, washcloth 10 pillowcase, washcloths

ancient ~: 6 byssus

buy: 9 white sale

dirty ~: 6 exposé, gossip 7 scandal

fabric: 4 lawn 5 toile 6 canvas, damask 7 cambric 8 chambray, marcella 10 seersucker

plant: 4 flax

shade: 3 tan 4 ecru 7 neutral

tape: 5 inkle

vestment: 3 alb 5 amice

linen __: 5 panel, paper 6 closet, draper 7 pattern

__ linen: 3 bed 5 dirty, Irish, table 6 Canton 7 butcher

line of __: 4 fire, site 5 force, sight 6 battle, credit, vision 7 apsides

__ line of duty: 5 in the

__ Line of Fire: 5 In the

line one's __: 7 pockets

liner: 4 boat, QE II, ship 5 cover, craft, plane 6 makeup, vessel 7 mascara, steamer, vehicle 8 aircraft, airliner, airplane, cosmetic 9 eye pencil, eye shadow, steamship, transport 10 cruise ship, watercraft

level: 4 deck

location: 6 eyelid

ocean ~ name: 6 Cunard

place: 4 dock, mole, pier, port, quay, slip 5 berth, jetty, levee, wharf 6 harbor 7 landing 9 anchorage

starter: 3 air, eye, jet 4 head

liner __: 5 notes

__ liner: 5 cargo, ocean, party 6 helmet

__-liner: 3 day, one 4 hard 6 bottom

__ Line Railroad: 3 Soo

Liner She's a Lady, The: 4 poem

author: 7 Kipling

lines: 4 part 6 dialog, script 8 dialogue

combining form: 5 -stich

feed ~ to: 3 cue 6 prompt

forget one's ~: 4 flub, muff 5 choke, fluff 7 stumble

having ~: 4 rowy

having wavy ~: 6 gyrose

practice ~: 8 rehearse

read between the ~: 3 bet 5 glean, guess, infer, judge, wager, weigh 6 assume, call it, deduce, figure, gather, intuit, reckon, size up, take it, wonder 7 imagine, make out, presume, suppose, surmise, suspect 8 arrive at, conclude, construe 9 figure out, interpret, postulate, speculate 10 conjecture, have a hunch, understand

salesperson's ~: 4 puff, sell 5 offer, pitch, spiel 6 patter 9 promotion

Lines Composed a Few Miles Above Tintern Abbey author: William Wordsworth

line-score letters: 3 RHE

Lines on the Mermaid Tavern: 4 poem

author: 5 Keats

lineup: 3 row 4 card, list, team 5 array, order, slate 6 agenda, roster 8 schedule 9 directory

entry: 4 name

pick from a ~: 2 ID 3 tag

remove from the ~: 5 bench

vertical ~: 4 heap, mass, pile 5 mound

lin. ft.: 4 meas.

ling: 4 fish 6 burbot

kin: 3 cod

__-ling: 5 ding-a, ting-a

Lingayen __: 4 Gulf

lingcod: 4 fish

linger: 3 lag 4 bide, idle, last, laze, loaf, loll, mope, plod, poke, stay, stop, tool, wait 5 abide, amble, cling, crawl, dally, delay, drift, dwell, hover, mosey, stall, stand, stick, tarry, trail 6 dawdle, endure, falter, hang on, hobble, loiter, lumber, put off, putter, remain, slouch, stroll, totter, trapes, trifle, trudge 7 goof off, hang out, persist, saunter, shuffle, sojourn, stagger, survive, traipse 8 continue, hesitate, lollygag, lose time, straggle 9 sit around, vacillate, waste time 10 dillydally, fool around, hang around, stay a while, wait around

lingerer: 7 dawdler, laggard 8 slowpoke 9 straggler

lingerie: 3 bra, top 4 hose, robe, slip 5 pants, shift, stays, teddy 6 corset, girdle, jog bra, kimono, nighty, nylons, shimmy, undies 7 bikinis, chemise, drawers, nightie, pajamas, wrapper 8 bathrobe, bloomers, camisole, half-slip, skivvies 9 bedjacket, brassiere, hoop skirt, nightgown, pantyhose, petticoat, sleepwear, underwear 10 sleep shirt, undershirt

like some ~: 4 fine, lacy, soft 5 fancy, filmy, gauzy, sheer 6 dainty, frilly, smooth 7 elegant 8 delicate, gossamer 10 diaphanous, see-through

lingering: 8 dawdling, leftover, residual, tarrying 9 vestigial 10 continuing

__ Lingle Mungo: 3 Van

Ling-Ling: 5 panda

lingo: 4 cant, talk 5 argot, idiom, slang 6 jargon, patois, patter, speech, tongue 7 dialect 8 jive talk, language, Newspeak, parlance, pig Latin, shop talk 9 buzzwords 10 vernacular, vocabulary

lingonberry: 5 fruit

lingua: 6 tongue

lingua __: 5 geral 6 franca

__ linguae: 6 lapsus

lingual: 4 oral 6 spoken, verbal 7 sensory 9 sensorial

__-lingual: 5 audio

linguini: 5 pasta 7 noodles

alternative: 4 orzo, ziti 5 penne 6 noodle 7 lasagna, lasagne, pastina, ravioli 8 bucatini, couscous, farfalle, macaroni, rigatoni 9 agnolotti, angelhair, cavatelli, manicotti, spaghetti 10 cannelloni, fettuccini, tortellini, vermicelli

Chinese ~: 6 lo mein

topping: 5 sauce

linguist: 8 polyglot

linguistic: 8 semantic 10 semantical

comment: 5 rheme

group: 6 ethnos

root: 6 etymon

linguistic __: 4 area, form 5 atlas, stock

linguistics: 6 syntax 7 grammar 10 morphology

branch: 4 etym. 9 etymology

grp.: 3 MLA

__ Lingus: 3 Aer

liniment: 4 balm 5 cream, salve, slave 6 lotion 7 unction, unguent 8 dressing, lenitive, medicine, ointment 9 emollient 10 medication

apply, as ~: 5 rub on

target: 4 ache

lining: 6 facing, inside 7 backing 8 membrane

starter: 6 stream

stiff ~: 5 wigan

__ lining: 3 art 4 sock 5 brake, title 6 silver

link: 2 in 3 tie, wed 4 bind, bond, join, knot, lock, loop, part, ring, seam, span, unit, weld, yoke 5 annex, chain, group, hitch, joint, nexus, piece, segue, tag on, tie in, tie-up, unify, unite 6 adjoin, attach, bridge, cleave, cohere, copula, couple, fasten, hook on, hookup, joiner, liaise, member, relate, slap on, splice, tack on 7 bracket, channel, combine, conjoin, connect, contact, coupler, element, hitch on, joining, liaison, network, rapport, section 8 coupling, division, dovetail, flambeau, identify, junction, ligament, ligation, ligature, meld with, plug into, tag along, vinculum 9 associate, component, conjugate, correlate, fastening, integrate, interface, interlink, tie in with 10 attachment, connection, connective, team up with

ender: 3 age

firmly: 4 fuse, knit 5 weave 6 splice, stitch

missing ~: 6 apeman

site: 4 cuff

starter: 4 cuff, down

up: 4 dock, join, meet 5 unify, unite 6 plug in 9 get to know

with: 5 tie to

word ~: 6 hyphen
___ link: 3 lap 4 cuff, drag, snap 6 monkey, sleeve 7 missing, sausage
___-link: 5 cross, index
Link: 4 Wray 5 Lyman
linkage: 5 logic, tie up 6 hookup
linkage ___: 3 map 5 group 6 editor
linked: 6 allied, joined, united 7 related 8 hooked up
___-link fence: 5 chain
linking: 6 hookup 8 junction, juncture 10 continuity
verb: 6 copula
word: 3 and
Linklater: 7 Richard
Linkletter: 3 Art 4 host 5 emcee
links: 5 wurst 6 course 7 sausage 10 golf course
see also golf
___ links: 4 golf 7 sausage
Lin, Maya: 9 architect
Linnaeus, Carolus: 5 Swede 8 botanist
Linn-Baker: 4 Mark
linnet: 4 bird 8 songbird
Linney, Laura: 7 actress
film: Absolute Power (1997)
Primal Fear (1996)
The Truman Show (1998)
You Can Count on Me (2000)
linoleum
alternative: 3 rug 4 tile 6 carpet
measurement: 4 area
oil: 4 tung
protector: 3 wax
linseed ___: 3 oil 4 cake, meal
linseed oil source: 4 flax
linsey: 6 fabric 8 material
linsey-___: 7 woolsey
lint: 4 dust, fuzz 5 fluff
collector: 4 trap 5 drier, dryer, navel, serge
lint ___: 6 filter
lintel: 4 beam, jamb 8 crossbar 10 crosspiece
companion: 4 jamb
linty: 5 downy, fuzzy 6 fluffy, napped, woolly
Linus: 4 pope, Yale 7 Pauling, pontiff, Van Pelt
brother of ~: 7 Orpheus
father of ~: 6 Apollo
sister: 4 Lucy
son of ~: 8 Calliope
Linville: 5 Larry
liny: 5 ruled 7 striped 8 streaked
Linz: 4 city, town
locale: 7 Austria
river: 6 Danube
Linzer ___: 5 torte
Linz Symphony composer: 6 Mozart
lion: 3 cat, Leo, VIP 4 hero, Nala 5 beast, felid, mogul, Mr. Big, Simba 6 animal, big cat, big gun, bigwig, feline, leader, mammal 7 big name, big shot, magnate, wild cat 8 Clarence, luminary 9 big cheese, celebrity, dignitary
ant ~: 3 bug 6 insect
attack like a ~: 4 leap 6 pounce
beard the ~ in his den: 4 face 5 brave 8 confront
ender: 3 ess 4 fish 7 hearted
end of a ~ tail: 4 tuft
fare: 4 meat
greeting: 4 roar
home: 3 den, zoo 4 lair
like a ~: 4 wild 5 maned, tawny
MGM ~: 3 Leo 4 logo
mountain ~: 4 puma 6 cougar 7 panther
mythical ~ home: 5 Nemea
name meaning ~: 3 Leo 4 Leon
pack: 5 pride
prey: 5 zebra
pride: 4 mane
relative: 4 eyra, lynx, puma 5 chita, liger, ounce, tiger, tigon 6 bobcat, cheeta, chetah, cougar, jaguar, margay, ocelot, serval, tiglon 7 bay lynx, caracal, cheetah, leopard, panther 9 catamount 10 jaguarundi
to Tarzan: 5 simba
young: 3 cub 5 whelp
___ lion: 3 ant, sea 5 aphid, aphis 6 Nemean
Lion: 3 Leo 4 sign
month: 3 Aug., Jul. 4 July 6 August
predecessor: 4 Crab
rival: 3 Jet, Ram 4 Bear, Bill, Colt 5 Brown, Chief, Eagle, Giant, Niner, Raven, Saint, Texan, Titan 6 Bengal, Bronco, Cowboy, Falcon, Jaguar, Packer, Raider, Viking 7 Charger, Dolphin, Panther, Patriot, Redskin, Seahawk, Steeler 8 Cardinal 9 Buccaneer
successor: 6 Virgin
Lion ___, The: 4 King
Lion ___ Tonight, The: 6 Sleeps
___ Lion: 5 Paper, White 6 Little
Lion and the Mouse, The
source: 4 Esop 5 Aesop
lion-eagle in heraldry: 7 griffin
Lionel: 4 Bart 6 Atwill, Richie 7 Hampton, Johnson, Stander 8 Jeffries, Trilling 9 Barrymore
lioness: 4 Elsa
name meaning ~: 5 Leona
Lioness and the Vixen, The: 5 fable
lionet: 3 cub
Lionheart (1987 film)
cast: Gabriel Byrne, Nicola Cowper, Dexter Fletcher, Eric Stoltz
director: Franklin Schaffner
lionhearted: 4 bold, firm, game 5 brave, gutsy, manly, nervy, stout 6 awless, daring, gritty, heroic, plucky, spunky, sturdy, virile 7 aweless, defiant, doughty, gallant, leonine, staunch, valiant 8 fearless, heroical, intrepid, resolute, spirited, stalwart, unafraid, valorous 9 audacious, dauntless, dreadless, undaunted, unfearful 10 courageous
lionheartedness: 5 valor 6 daring 7 bravery, courage, heroism, prowess 8 boldness
Lion in Winter, The (1968 film)
cast: Katharine Hepburn, Jane Merrow, Peter O'Toole
director: Anthony Harvey
lionize: 4 fete, laud, tout 5 exalt, honor 6 praise 7 acclaim, adulate, glorify, idolize, worship 8 eulogize, gush over, look up to 9 celebrate 10 aggrandize
Lionizing author: Edgar Allan Poe
Lion King, The (1994 film)
director: Roger Allers, Rob Minkoff
role: 4 Nala, Scar 5 hyena, Simba, Timon 6 Mufasa
voice cast: Matthew Broderick, Whoopi Goldberg, Jeremy Irons, James Earl Jones, Moira Kelly, Nathan Lane, Cheech Marin, Jonathan Taylor Thomas
lion of God, name meaning: 5 Ariel
Lion of God, The: 3 Ali
lion's
share: 4 bulk, mass, most 7 big half, portion 8 majority
twist the ~ tail: 4 dare
lion's ___: 3 den 5 share
Lions: 4 gulf, team 6 eleven 8 Columbia
colleagues: 4 Elks 5 Moose 7 Kiwanis
home: 7 Detroit
org.: 3 NFC, NFL
sport: 8 football
Lions ___: 4 Club
___ Lions: 7 Nittany
Lions and Shadows author: Christopher Isherwood
Lion's Game, The author: Nelson Demille
Lion Sleeps Tonight (song), The artist: Tokens
artist: Robert John
___ Lions, The: 5 Young
lion-tamer: 6 catman
need: 4 hoop, whip
place: 6 circus
prop: 5 chair
lion-to-lamb time: 5 March
Liotta, Ray: 5 actor
film: Cop Land (1997)
Corrina, Corrina (1994)
Dominick and Eugene (1988)
Field of Dreams (1989)
GoodFellas (1990)
Hannibal (2001)
Heartbreakers (2001)
A Rumor of Angels (2002)
Unlawful Entry (1992)
lip: 3 rim 4 brim, edge, guff, sass, talk 5 brink, cheek, flare, mouth, reply, sauce, speak, spout, verge 6 border, flange, labium, margin 8 back talk, defiance, reaction, response, rudeness 9 freshness, impudence, insolence, sassiness, sauciness, smart talk 10 effrontery, embouchure
application: 4 balm 5 salve
balm target: 4 chap 5 crack
bite one's ~: 7 forbear, refrain, repress
button one's ~: 5 quiet 6 clam up, shut up 7 keep mum, let pass 8 play dumb 9 let it ride
combining form: 5 cheil-, chilo-, labio- 6 cheilo-
curl a ~: 4 mock, slam 5 flout, scoff, scorn, smirk, sneer 6 slight 7 grimace, put down, sniff at, snigger 8 ridicule 9 disparage 10 look down on
ender: 5 stick
give ~ to: 4 sass 8 get smart, mouth off, talk back 10 answer back
hang the ~: 4 mope, pout, sulk 5 brood
keep a stiff lower ~: 4 fume, mope, sulk 5 brood, frown 6 glower
keep a stiff upper ~: 6 bear up, hang in 8 face up to
ornament: 6 labret
service: 4 cant 7 mockery 8 pretense 9 hypocrisy, phoniness 10 pharisaism, pretension, sanctimony
shade: 3 red 4 pink, ruby 7 crimson
with a stiff upper ~: 5 stoic
lip ___: 4 balm, fern 5 gloss 6 reader 7 molding, reading, service
lip-___: 4 read, sync 5 synch
___ lip: 3 fat 6 dorsal
Lipan: 6 Indian 7 Amerind
Liparis: 4 isls. 5 isles 7 islands
one of the ~: 9 Stromboli
lip-balm target: 5 crack
lipid: 3 fat, oil, wax 7 steroid
Lipinski, Tara: 6 skater
feat: 4 axel, lutz
milieu: 3 ice 4 rink
Lipizzaner: 5 horse, steed
Lipmann, Fritz: 8 Nobelist
Lip My Reeds composer: PDQ Bach
Lipnicki: 8 Jonathan
Li Po: 4 poet 7 Chinese
lipoid: 3 wax 5 fatty 8 lecithin
lipped: 7 labiate
___-lipped: 5 close, tight
Lippi: 5 Lippo 7 Filippo
Lippizaner: 5 horse, steed 6 equine
Lippmann: 6 Walter 7 Gabriel
Lippmann, Gabriel: 8 Nobelist 9 physicist
___ Lippo Lippi: 3 Fra
lip-puckering: 4 sour, tart 5 acerb
lippy: 4 pert 5 fresh, sassy 8 impudent
one: 4 snip
lips: 5 labia, mouth 6 kisser
bloodhound's ~: 5 flews
lock ~: 3 pet 4 kiss 6 smooch 8 osculate
of the ~: 6 labial
smack one's ~: 5 eat up, enjoy, gloat, savor 6 devour, relish 7 feast on
Lipscomb, William: 7 chemist 8 Nobelist
___ Lips Houlihan: 3 Hot
lip-smacking: 4 good, rich 5 spicy, sweet, tasty, yummy 6 delish, divine, mellow, savory 8 heavenly, luscious 9 ambrosial, delicious, flavorful, succulent, toothsome 10 appetizing, delectable
lipstick: 4 tree 5 paint 6 makeup
apply ~: 4 tint 5 color, paint 6 redden
holder: 3 bag 5 purse 6 clutch 7 handbag 8 reticule 10 pocketbook
like ~: 4 oily, waxy 8 lustrous
shade: 3 red 4 puce 5 peach
target: 5 mouth
type: 5 gloss
Lipstick on Your Collar (1959 song)
artist: Connie Francis
Liptauer: 6 cheese
Lipton: 3 tea 5 Peggy
alternative: 6 Nestea, Salada, Tetley 7 Bigelow, Red Rose 8 Twinings
brand: 4 Ragu
Lipton, Peggy spouse: Quincy Jones
liq. measure: 2 pt., qt. 3 gal.
liquefied: 5 fluid 6 molten
liquefied natural ___: 3 gas
liquefy: 3 run 4 melt, thaw 8 dissolve, fluidize, unfreeze 10 deliquesce
liqueur: 4 ouzo, port 5 booze, creme, drink 6 brandy, cognac, Kahlúa, kirsch, kümmel, pastis, Pernod 7 alcohol, cordial, curaçao, ratafia, sloe gin, spirits 8 apéritif, beverage, Drambuie, Tia Maria 9 alcoholic, aqua vitae, Cointreau, inebriant 10 chartreuse, intoxicant
anise ~: 4 ouzo 6 pastis, Pernod
cherry ~: 6 kirsch
coffee ~: 6 Kahlúa 8 Tia Maria
flavoring: 4 pear 5 anise, cacao 6 cherry, coffee, orange 8 licorice
German ~: 6 kümmel
Greek ~: 4 ouzo
licorice-flavored ~: 8 absinthe
orange ~: 9 Cointreau
orange peel ~: 7 curaçao
wine ~: 7 ratafia
liquid: 3 goo, sap, tea, wet 4 aqua, damp, flow, flux, free, goop, slop, soft, thin 5 broth, drink, fluid, juice, juicy, moist, pulpy, quick, ready, runny, sappy, swill, water 6 dulcet, elixir, fluent, mellow, melted, molten, moving, nectar, serous, smooth, thawed, usable, watery 7 aqueous, extract, flowing, fluidic, fusible, hydrous, melting, running, solvent, useable, viscose, viscous, wettish 8 ichorous, libation, luscious, meltable, moisture, solution 9 dissolved, secretion, splashing, succulent 10 marketable, negotiable, realizable
brush with ~: 5 baste 7 moisten
burn with ~: 5 scald
container: 4 ewer, tube, vial 5 phial 6 beaker, bottle, flagon 7 pitcher 8 test tube
foul ~: 3 mud 4 mire, muck, ooze, scum 5 slime 6 sludge

in physics: 5 state
measure: 2 oz., pt., qt. 3 gal., tsp. 4 fl. oz., gill, pint, tbsp. 5 liter, litre, ounce, quart 6 capful, gallon 8 teaspoon 10 tablespoon
refreshment: 5 drink, juice 8 beverage
science: 10 hydraulics
sweet ~: 5 sirup, syrup
viscous ~: 4 lard 5 pitch 6 grease 9 lubricant, petroleum
liquid __: 3 air 4 fire, gold 5 asset, glass 6 oxygen, storax 7 compass, crystal, measure, protein
liquid-__ display: 7 crystal
Liquid __: 3 Sky 5 Paper, Plumr
liquidate: 3 pay 4 cash, do in, quit, sell, slay, vend 5 annul, honor, purge, repay, spend 6 cancel, cash in, divest, pay off, peddle, remove, rub out, settle, square, unload 7 abolish, cash out, convert, destroy, realize, satisfy, sell off, sell out, silence, wipe out 8 close out, dispatch, dissolve, exchange, get money, get rid of, vaporize 9 discharge, dispose of, eliminate, eradicate, finish off, polish off, reimburse, terminate 10 annihilate, auction off, do away with
liquid-crystal __: 7 display
Liquid Gold: 6 polish
alternative: 6 Behold, Endust, Pledge 10 Old English
Liquid Plumr rival: 5 Drano
liquor: 3 alc., ale, gin, rum, rye 4 beer, grog, ouzo 5 booze, broth, drink, fluid, sauce, stock, vodka 6 brandy, cognac, elixir, mescal, poison, spirit, whisky 7 alcohol, aquavit, extract, potable, solvent, spirits, tequila, whiskey 8 infusion, schnapps, vermouth 9 aqua vitae, decoction, drinkable, firewater, hard stuff, inebriant, moonshine 10 intoxicant
add ~ to: 4 lace 5 spike 7 fortify
bottle: 5 fifth, flask 6 flagon
category: 5 blend
flavoring: 4 sloe
grp. for tough ~ laws: 4 MADD
Mideast ~: 4 arak, raki 5 rakee 6 arrack
over cracked ice: 4 mist
small ~ glass: 4 pony
spot of ~: 3 nip 4 dram
strength: 5 proof
__ liquor: 3 gas, pot, red 4 corn, malt 5 black, white 6 mother 7 ammonia
liquor-free: 3 dry
Liquor is quicker poet: 4 Nash
...liquor will __ contest quicker: 4 end a
lira: 5 money 6 string, violin
origin: 6 Greece
replacement: 4 euro
lira da __: 7 braccio
lirica: 6 string, violin
origin: 10 Yugoslavia
Lisa: 4 Kirk, Loeb 5 Bonet, McRee, Rinna 6 Kudrow, Loring 7 Hartman, Presley, Simpson 8 Birnbach, Eichhorn, Whelchel 9 Eilbacher 10 Stansfield
to Bart: 3 sis 6 sister
Lisa __ Presley: 5 Marie
__ Lisa: 4 Mona 5 I'm Not
Lisa Hartman __: 5 Black
Lisa Lisa and Cult Jam
song: All Cried Out (1986)
Head to Toe (1987)
Lost in Emotion (1987)
Lisa Marie dad: 5 Elvis
Lisa Picard Is Famous (2001 film)
cast: Nat DeWolf, Griffin Dunne, Laura Kirk
director: Griffin Dunne
Lisbon: 4 city, port, town 7 capital
city near ~: 5 Evora
locale: 8 Portugal
river: 5 Tagus
Lisbon Antigua (1955 song) artist: Nelson Riddle
Lise: 7 Meitner
Lisette: 5 Reese
Lisi: 5 Virna
lisle: 6 fabric, thread
Lisle: 4 city, town
locale: 8 Illinois
lisp: 8 sibilate 9 sibilance, sigmatism 10 assibilate, sibilation
kin: 4 lall
LISP: 8 language
alternative: 3 ADA, APL, SQL 4 Alef, html, Icon, Java, Logo, Orca, Perl 5 Algol, Basic, Cecil, COBOL, Dylan, SISAL 6 Delphi, Eiffel, Erlang, Oberon, Pascal, Prolog, Sather, Scheme, Snobol 7 Fortran
lisper's challenge: 3 ess
lisse: 5 cloth 6 fabric 7 textile 8 material
lissome: 4 wiry 5 agile, lithe, loose 6 limber, nimble, pliant, rubber, supple, svelte 7 bending, elastic, pliable, springy, willowy 8 bendable, flexible, graceful, moldable, stretchy 9 adaptable, lightsome, lithesome, malleable, resilient
quality: 5 grace
list: 3 sag, tab, tip 4 bill, heel, keel, lean, menu, name, note, poll, roll, sked, tilt 5 carte, enrol, index, lurch, slant, slate, slope, table, tally 6 agenda, careen, census, detail, docket, enroll, lineup, rattle, record, report, roster, series, ticket 7 archive, catalog, incline, invoice, itemize, lexicon, outline, recline, specify, tick off 8 calendar, classify, contents, glossary, heel over, keel over, manifest, register, schedule, syllabus, tabulate 9 catalogue, checklist, directory, enumerate, inventory, keep count, thesaurus, timetable, write down 10 cyclopedia, dictionary, memorandum, prospectus, tabulation, vocabulary
A ~: 5 elite
drop from a ~: 4 x out 6 delete 8 cross off, cross out
ender: 3 etc. 4 et al. 6 et alia, et alii
heading: 4 to do
item: 3 job 4 task 5 chore, entry 6 errand
preceder: 5 colon
separator: 5 comma
starter: 4 back 5 black, check
list __: 5 price 6 server
__ list: 4 book, free, sick, to-do, want, wine, wish 5 check, dean's, legal, price, punch, short, union, watch, white 7 laundry, mailing, waiting
List: 6 Eugene
listen: 4 hark, hear, heed, mind, obey 5 admit, adopt, audit, catch, watch 6 accept, attend, comply, harken, tune in 7 conform, consent, hearken, hear out, look out, monitor, observe, pay heed, receive, welcome 8 hear tell, overhear, pick up on 9 eavesdrop, entertain, lend an ear 10 get a load of, give heed to, take advice, take notice, toe the line
a lot to ~ to: 6 earful
don't ~: 7 disobey
in: 3 pry 4 hear 5 audit 9 eavesdrop
to: 3 bug 4 hear, heed, mind 6 advert, attend, follow, fulfil, notice, regard 7 abide by, fulfill, respect
(to): 3 bow 4 bend 5 agree, defer 6 adhere 8 carry out
unwilling to ~: 4 deaf 9 unhearing
willing to ~: 4 fair 6 mellow 8 amenable, flexible, open-door, outgoing, unbiased 9 impartial, objective, receptive, welcoming 10 accessible, hospitable, responsive
listener
name meaning ~: 8 Samantha
listeners: 5 crowd 7 gallery, hearers, turnout, viewers 8 assembly, audience 9 attendees, gathering, observers, onlookers, witnesses 10 assemblage, spectators
listening: 7 all ears, hearing 9 attentive
combining form: 4 acou- 5 acouo-
device: 3 bug, ear
listening __: 4 post
__ listening: 4 easy
Listening author: Edward Albee
Listen People (1966 song) artist: Herman's Hermits
Listen to the Music (1972 song) artist: Doobie Brothers
Listen to What the Man Said (1975 song) artist: Paul McCartney
Lister: 4 peak 5 mount 6 Joseph 8 mountain
locale: 10 Antarctica
Listerine: 9 mouthwash
alternative: 3 Act 4 Plax 5 Scope 6 Signal 7 Lavoris 10 Fluorigard
target: 4 germ
use ~: 6 gargle
l'istesso __: 5 tempo
List, Eugene: 7 pianist
listing: 3 log 4 sked 5 atilt 6 agenda, roster, tilted 7 program 8 schedule 9 timetable
listless: 4 blah, down, dull, limp, logy, mopy, slow 5 bored, faint, heavy, inert, leady, moony, mopey, musty, slack, weary 6 absent, anemic, dreamy, drowsy, leaden, mopish, sleepy, stupid, supine, torpid, vacant 7 anaemic, dormant, lagging, languid, neutral, out of it, passive 8 careless, downcast, heedless, indolent, laidback, languish, lifeless, lukewarm, sluggish, stagnant 9 apathetic, easygoing, enervated, impassive, inanimate, lethargic, lymphatic 10 abstracted, energyless, insouciant, languorous, nonchalant, phlegmatic, regardless, spiritless, unreactive
become ~: 4 fade, flag, moon, mope, pine, sigh 5 brood, droop, yearn 6 grieve, repine, sicken 7 decline 8 languish, stagnate, vegetate 9 waste away
feeling: 5 ennui 6 apathy, tedium 7 boredom, languor 8 doldrums, monotony 9 lassitude, weariness 10 melancholy
listlessness: 5 blahs, ennui 6 apathy, phlegm, torpor 7 boredom, fatigue, inertia, languor 8 coolness, doldrums, dullness, laziness, lethargy 9 lassitude
showing ~: 4 mopy 5 mopey
List of Adrian Messenger, The (1963 film)
cast: Clive Brook, Tony Curtis, George C. Scott, Dana Wynter
director: John Huston
Liston, Sonny: 5 boxer
milieu: 4 ring
Liszt, Franz: 7 pianist 8 composer
piece: 5 étude
work: Dante Symphony
Faust Symphony
Hungaria
Hungarian Rhapsodies
Les Préludes
Liebestraum
Mazeppa
Mephisto Waltz
Totentanz
lit: 5 afire, aglow, shiny, tipsy 6 ablaze, aflame, agleam, bright, flashy, got off, landed 7 beaming, blazing, burning, fired up, fulgent, glowing, ignited, kindled, lambent, radiant, set down, settled, shining, torched 8 dazzling, gleaming, luminous, lustrous, turned on 9 brilliant, illumined, irrigated, set fire to, sparkling 10 came to rest, literature, touched off
on: 10 discovered
poorly ~: 3 dim 4 dark 5 murky 6 gloomy, somber 7 shadowy 9 tenebrous
softly ~: 5 aglow 7 lambent 9 refulgent
starter: 3 sun 4 back, moon, spot, star 5 flood
up: 5 aglow 6 beamed, glowed 7 beaming, glowing, grinned 8 grinning, spirited 10 brightened
lit-__: 4 crit
__ lit: 6 kiddie
__-lit: 5 wagon
__ Lit: 3 Eng. 7 English
Lita: 4 Ford, Grey
litany: 5 chant 6 prayer 7 account, catalog, recital 8 petition 9 catalogue 10 invocation, recitation, repetition
Lit.B.: 3 deg.
litchi: 3 nut 4 tree
relative: 4 akee 5 genip 6 longan, lungan 7 genipap 9 soapberry
lite: 5 lo-cal, lo-fat 6 low-cal
better than ~: 5 no-cal
make ~: 5 defat
product buyer: 6 dieter
Litel: 4 John
liter: 7 measure
about 3.8 ~s: 6 gallon
less than a ~: 5 quart
literacy: 8 learning 9 education, erudition, knowledge 10 articulacy, background, refinement
demonstrate ~: 4 read
volunteer: 5 coach, tutor
literacy __: 4 test
literal: 4 true 5 close, exact, plain, rigid 6 actual, simple, strict 7 prosaic 8 accurate, bona fide, faithful, truthful, unerring, verbatim 9 authentic, prosaical 10 unimagined
not ~: 8 symbolic 10 figurative, metaphoric
literally: 3 sic 5 truly 6 really, simply 7 exactly, plainly 8 actually, directly, strictly, verbatim 9 precisely 10 completely, faithfully, unerringly
literalness: 5 truth 7 honesty 8 accuracy, dullness, rigidity, slowness
literary: 6 formal 7 bookish, erudite, learned 8 lettered, well-read 9 classical, scholarly
adverb: 3 e'er 4 ne'er
category: 4 biog. 5 drama, genre, novel, sci-fi 6 poetry 7 romance 9 biography
composition: 4 opus 5 novel, piece 6 column, sketch 7 article, passage, romance 9 editorial
device: 5 irony, trope 6 pathos
drudge: 4 hack
form: 3 ode 5 essay, prose
medley: 5 cento
miscellany: 3 ana 5 varia
monogram: 3 LMA, PDJ, RLS, RWE, TSE
passage: 5 quote 9 quotation
pseudonym: 4 Elia, Saki
rep: 3 agt. 5 agent
sketch: 5 cameo
literary __: 4 lion

Literary Life of Tingum Bob, Esq., The author: Edgar Allan Poe
literate: 6 versed 7 erudite, learned 8 cultured, educated, lettered, schooled 9 scholarly 10 cultivated, instructed
literati: 5 elite, sages 7 pundits, savants 8 academes, scholars 9 aesthetes, highbrows, longhairs 10 illuminati, upper-crust
literatim: 7 exactly 8 verbatim 9 precisely
literature: 4 lore 5 books, drama, essay, novel, paper, poesy, prose, story, theme, tract 6 poetry, précis, report, thesis 7 article, comment, history, leaflet, letters, summary, writing 8 abstract, brochure, classics, critique, findings, learning, pamphlet, research, treatise, writings 9 biography, discourse, treatment 10 discussion, exposition, humanities
__-Lites: 3 Chi
Lith.: 3 SSR 4 once
lithe: 4 lean, slim, spry 5 agile, light 6 limber, lissom, nimble, pliant, slight, supple, svelte 7 lissome, pliable, sinuous, slender, willowy 8 flexible, graceful 9 lightsome
lithesome: 6 limber, supple 7 sinuous
Lithgow, John: 5 actor
film: 2010 (1984)
Blow Out (1981)
Cliffhanger (1993)
Footloose (1984)
Rich Kids (1979)
Terms of Endearment (1983)
The World According to Garp (1982)
film (voice): Shrek (2001)
TV: 3rd Rock from the Sun
lithic: 5 rocky, stony 6 stoney
-lithic starter: 3 neo 5 paleo
lithium: 5 metal 7 element
ore: 10 lepidolite
lithium-__ battery: 3 ion
litho-: 5 stone
lithograph: 5 plate, print 9 engraving
lithographer: 4 Ives 7 Currier
lithoid: 9 petrified, stonelike 10 adamantine
lithosphere: 5 crust, shell
Lithuania: 6 nation 7 country
capital: 5 Vilna 7 Vilnius
city: 5 Vilna 6 Kaunas 7 Vilnius
legislature: 6 Seimas
money: 5 litas
neighbor: 6 Latvia, Poland, Russia 7 Belarus
once: 3 SSR
region: 6 Baltic
Lithuanian: 4 Balt
neighbor: 4 Lett
litigant: 4 suer 5 party 6 suitor 7 accused, accuser 8 claimant, opponent 9 appellant, defendant, disputant, plaintiff 10 prosecutor
litigate: 3 sue 6 appeal 7 contest, dispute 8 file suit 9 fight over, go to court, prosecute
litigation: 4 case, feud, suit 5 cause, trial 6 action 7 dispute, lawsuit, process 10 contention
litigious: 9 bellicose, combative 10 disputable
be ~: 3 sue
litmus: 3 dye 7 pigment 8 colorant
color: 3 red 4 blue
it turns ~ blue: 3 alk. 4 base 6 alkali
it turns ~ red: 4 acid
tester: 2 pH
use ~: 4 test 7 analyze 10 experiment
litmus __: 4 test 5 paper
__-Litovsk: 5 Brest
litter: 4 cubs, hash, junk, mess, muck, rash 5 brood, dirty, offal, strew, trash, waste, young 6 debris, family, jumble, jungle, mess up, muddle, refuse, school 7 clutter, confuse, derange, garbage, kittens, piglets, progeny, puppies, rubbish, rummage, scatter, shuffle 8 detritus, disarray, disorder, leavings, mishmash, scramble 9 confusion, make a mess, stretcher, sweepings 10 collateral, disarrange, hodgepodge, scattering, untidiness
ender: 3 bag, bug 4 mate
have a ~: 5 whelp
member: 3 pup 4 runt 5 puppy
pig ~: 6 farrow
__ litter: 3 cat
__ Litter: 5 Kitty
litterbug: 3 pig 4 slob, slop 6 sloven 8 polluter
unlike a ~: 4 neat, tidy, trim 6 dainty 7 orderly 8 well-kept 10 fastidious, methodical, systematic
littered: 5 messy 6 unneat, untidy 10 topsy-turvy
litter-free: 4 neat
little: 3 bit, dab, nip, set, tad, toy, wee 4 aper, baby, base, dash, hint, less, lick, mean, mini, puny, snub, spot, tiny, whit 5 bitty, brief, cheap, dinky, elfin, hasty, light, minor, petty, pinch, scant, short, small, speck, taste, teeny, touch, trace, weeny, young 6 atomic, bantam, barely, casual, hardly, infant, junior, meager, minute, narrow, paltry, peanut, peewee, petite, pocket, rarely, scanty, seldom, skimpy, slight, sparse, stubby, teensy, trifle, vulgar, wicked 7 babyish, bigoted, cramped, limited, modicum, not many, not much, selfish, shrimpy, slender, snippet, soupçon, stunted, trivial, wizened 8 atomical, atomlike, dwarfish, fleeting, fragment, immature, not often, not quite, only just, particle, pint-size, pittance, scarcely, somewhat, trifling 9 embryonic, hardly any, hidebound, illiberal, itsy-bitsy, itty-bitty, miniature, minuscule, parochial, pint-sized, shriveled, truncated, undersize 10 diminutive, hardly ever, negligible, provincial, shoestring, short-lived, teeny-weeny, undersized, vest-pocket
a ~: 3 any 4 some 6 kind of, little, rather 8 slightly, somewhat 10 moderately
bit: 3 dab, jot 4 iota, spot 5 speck
boy: 3 imp 6 moppet 9 youngster
by little: 6 pokily 9 gradually, haltingly, languidly, leisurely, partially, piecemeal 10 crawlingly, creepingly, sluggishly
costing ~: 3 low 5 cheap 6 modest, on sale 7 cut-rate, reduced, slashed 8 for a song 9 half-price 10 economical, marked down, reasonable
darling: 3 tot 4 baby 5 angel, child 6 cherub, infant, moppet 7 neonate, newborn, toddler 8 cutie pie, dumpling, snookums 10 sweetie pie
devil: 3 imp 4 brat 5 scamp 6 urchin
do ~: 4 laze 5 slack 7 slacken
game: 4 plot, trap 5 cabal 6 racket, scheme 8 intrigue 9 coalition, collusion, treachery 10 complicity, connivance, conspiracy, disloyalty
give ~: 4 save 5 skimp 6 scrape, scrimp, slight 8 conserve, roll back, withhold 9 economize 10 cut corners
give a ~ extra: 6 slap on, tack on, toss in 8 increase
in a ~ while: 4 anon, soon 7 shortly 8 directly
in music: 4 poco
just a ~: 3 sip 4 bite, dash, dram, drop, shot 5 pinch, snort, taste 6 nibble 7 soupçon, swallow 8 spoonful
known: 3 new 4 dark 5 alien 6 exotic, hidden, humble, occult, remote, secret, unsung, untold 7 foreign, obscure, strange, unnamed, unnoted 8 nameless 9 anonymous, concealed, incognito, uncharted, unheard-of 10 mysterious, unexplored, unfamiliar, unrevealed
make ~ of: 5 gloze 6 lessen 8 discount, downplay, minimize, play down, pooh-pooh, shrug off, talk down 9 deprecate, underplay, whitewash 10 understate
more than: 4 mere
more than just a ~: 4 much 5 amply, quite 6 deeply, highly, hugely, unduly, vastly 7 greatly, largely, only too, rabidly 8 terribly 9 decidedly, extremely, seriously, unusually 10 enormously, incredibly, profoundly, remarkably, thoroughly, uncommonly
name meaning ~: 6 Vaughn 7 Vaughan
of ~ value: 4 mean, mere, poor, punk, puny 5 cheap, lousy, minor, petty, scant, small, sorry 6 crummy, feeble, humble, meager, measly, paltry, rotten, shoddy, sleazy, stingy 7 limited, pitiful, shallow, trivial 8 inferior, pathetic, picayune, piddling, trifling, wretched 9 fifth-rate, miserable, third-rate, worthless 10 fourth-rate, second-rate
one: 3 elf, kid, tot 4 babe, baby 5 minor 6 infant, sprite
people: 3 mob 4 fays, herd, imps 5 elves 6 dryads, dwarfs, gnomes, nymphs, pixies, public, rabble, sylphs, trolls 7 dwarves, fairies, midgets, sprites, squirts, workers 8 brownies, populace 9 hoi polloi
piggy: 3 toe 5 digit
prefix: 4 mini- 5 micro-
shaver: 3 boy, tot 4 tike, tyke 5 child
suffix: 3 -ino, -ule 4 -etta, -ette
think ~ of: 4 skip, snub 5 let go, scorn, spurn 6 forget, ignore, rebuff, slight 7 disdain, dismiss, let pass, neglect, tune out 8 discount, laugh off, let slide, pass over, shrug off 9 disregard, gloss over, pay no mind 10 brush aside
too ~: 3 shy 4 thin 5 short 6 meager, scanty, skimpy 7 wanting 9 deficient 10 inadequate
too ~ too late: 9 deficient, half-baked, shortfall 10 inadequate
while: 3 bit 4 jiff 5 jiffy
little __: 3 auk, Joe, man, owl, toe 4 gull, slam 5 egret, grebe, hours 6 casino, finger, office, people 7 theater, theatre
little __'ll do ya, A: 3 dab
little __ told me, A: 4 bird
little-__: 5 bitty
__ little: 4 not a
...little __ eat ivy...: 5 lambs
Little: 4 Rich 7 Cleavon
Little __: 3 Dog, Eva, Fox, Men 4 Bear, Em'ly, John, Lies, Lion, Lulu, Nemo, Star 5 Abaco, Birds, Devil, Diane, Eyolf, Giant, Honda, Horse, Rhody, Tikes, Willy, Woman, Women 6 Caesar, Cigars, Darlin', Dipper, Dorrit, Iodine, League, Odessa, Russia, Sister 7 America, Anthony, Bighorn, Jeannie, Leaguer, Murders, Richard, Russian
Little __ and Big Halsy: 5 Fauss
Little __ and the Imperials: 7 Anthony
Little __ Annie: 6 Orphan 7 Orphant
Little __ Apples: 5 Green
Little __ Blue: 4 Girl
Little __ Book: 3 Red
Little __ Boy, The: 7 Drummer
Little __ Cartwright: 3 Joe
Little __ Coupe: 5 Deuce
Little __ Echo: 3 Sir
Little __ Fauntleroy: 4 Lord
Little __ Flowers: 4 Ida's
Little __ Girl, The: 7 Drummer
Little __ Jug: 5 Brown
Little __ Lies: 5 White
Little __ Man: 3 Big, Ole
Little __ Marker: 4 Miss
Little __ Mean a Lot: 6 Things
Little __ Music, A: 5 Night
Little __ of Horrors: 4 Shop
Little __ on the Prairie: 5 House
Little __ Pretty One: 5 Bitty
Little __ Riding Hood: 3 Red
Little __ Rooney: 5 Annie
Little __ Soap, A: 5 Bit of
Little __ Tate: 3 Man
Little __ Tear, A: 5 Bitty
Little __ That Could, The: 6 Engine
Little __, The: 3 Ark 4 King 5 Foxes, Giant 6 Prince, Sister 7 Colonel, Mermaid
__ Little: 6 Stuart 7 Chicken
__ Little Acre: 4 God's
__ Little Angel Eyes: 6 Pretty
Little Annie Rooney dog: 4 Zero
Little Anthony and the Imperials
last name: Gourdine
song: Goin' Out of My Head (1964)
Hurt So Bad (1965)
Shimmy, Shimmy, Ko-Ko-Bop (1960)
Tears on My Pillow (1958)
Little Big Horn: 6 battle
Little Big Man: 4 film 5 novel
author: Thomas Berger
cast: Martin Balsam, Faye Dunaway, Dustin Hoffman
director: Arthur Penn
__ Little Billy: 5 Dirty
little bird __ me, A: 4 told
Little Birds author: Anaïs Nin
__ Little Bit Better: 5 Just a
__ Little Bit Closer: 5 Come a
Little Bit Me, A Little Bit You, A (1967 song) artist: Monkees
__ Little Bit of Luck: 5 With a
Little Bit O' Soul (1967 song) artist: Music Explosion
Little Bitty Pretty One (song) artist: Clyde McPhatter, Thurston Harris
Little Bitty Tear, A (1962 song) artist: Burl Ives
Little Boy: 5 A bomb
Little Boy __: 4 Blue, Lost
Little Boy Lost (1953 film)
cast: Bing Crosby, Claude Dauphin, Nicole Maurey
director: George Seaton
Little Brown __: 3 Jug
little by little, move: 4 edge
Little Caesar (1930 film)
cast: Douglas Fairbanks Jr., Glenda Farrell, Edward G. Robinson
director: Mervyn LeRoy
role: 4 Rico
Little Cigars (1973 film)
cast: Billy Curtis, Jerry Maren, Angel Tompkins
Little Colonel, The: 5 Reese
Little Colonel, The (1935 film)
cast: Lionel Barrymore, Bill Robinson, Shirley Temple, Evelyn Venable
dog: 5 Fritz
little cow, name meaning: 6 Vachel
Little Darlings actress: 5 O'Neal
Little Deuce __: 5 Coupe
Little Devil (1961 song) artist: Neil Sedaka

Little Diane (1962 song) artist: Dion
__ Little Dividend: 7 Father's
Little Dorrit author: Charles Dickens
character: 3 Amy, Tip 5 Casby, Doyce, Fanny, Flora 6 Arthur, Daniel, Merdle, Pancks 7 Clennam, Meagles, Sparler 8 Blandois, Finching
Little Drummer Boy syllable: 3 tum
Little Drummer Girl, The: 4 film 5 novel
author: John le Carré
cast: Sami Frey, Diane Keaton, Klaus Kinski, Yorgo Voyagis
director: George Roy Hill
Little Engine That __, The: 5 Could
Little Engine verb: 3 can
Little Eva
last name: Boyd
song: The Loco-Motion (1962)
Little Eyolf author: Henrik Ibsen
__ little faith!: 4 Ye of
__ Little Fishes: 5 Three
__ Little Fool: 4 Poor
Little Foxes, The: 4 film, play
author: Lillian Hellman
cast: Bette Davis, Herbert Marshall, Teresa Wright
character: 3 Cal, Leo 5 Addie, Oscar 6 Birdie, Horace, Regina 7 Giddens, Hubbard
director: William Wyler
__ Little Foys, The: 5 Seven
Little Giant (1946 film)
cast: Bud Abbott, Lou Costello
Little Giant, The (1933 film)
cast: Mary Astor, Edward G. Robinson, Helen Vinson
director: Roy Del Ruth
Little Gidding author: 5 Eliot
__ Little Girl: 3 Hey 6 Daddy's 7 Foolish
Little Girl Blue composer: 4 Hart 7 Rodgers
Little Green Apples (1968 song) artist: O.C. Smith
__ Little Helper: 7 Mothers
Little House on the Prairie (NBC drama)
cast: Melissa Sue Anderson (Mary Ingalls)
Richard Bull (Nels Oleson)
Melissa Gilbert (Laura Ingalls)
Karen Grassle (Caroline Ingalls)
Michael Landon (Charles Ingalls)
dog: 6 Bandit
__ Little Indians: 3 Ten
Little in Love, A (1981 song) artist: Cliff Richard
Little Iodine cartoonist: 5 Hatlo
__ Little Ironies: 5 Life's
Little Jack __: 6 Horner
Little Jeannie (1980 song) artist: Elton John
Little Joe: 10 Cartwright
brother: 4 Adam, Hoss
Little Johnny Jones composer: 5 Cohan
little-known: 3 new 4 dark, deep, rare 6 arcane, hidden, mystic, occult, orphic, secret, unsung 7 cryptic, obscure, strange, unusual 8 abstruse, esoteric, mystical, nameless, shocking, singular, uncommon 9 recondite, unheard-of 10 mysterious, unrenowned
Little League coach, usually: 3 dad
Little Lies (1987 song) artist: Fleetwood Mac
Little Lord Fauntleroy (1936 film)
cast: Freddie Bartholomew, Guy Kibbee, C. Aubrey Smith
director: John Cromwell
Little Lord Fauntleroy dog: 6 Dougal
__ Little Love in Your Heart: 4 Put a
__ Little Luck: 5 With a
Little Man Tate (1991 film)
cast: Jodie Foster, Adam Hann-Byrd, Dianne Wiest
director: Jodie Foster
Little Man, What Now? (1934 film)
cast: Alan Hale, Douglass Montgomery, Margaret Sullavan
director: Frank Borzage
Little Men author: Louisa May Alcott
Little Mermaid, The (1989 film)
character: 4 crab, Eric 5 Ariel 9 Sebastian
director: Ron Clements, John Musker
voice cast: Rene Auberjonois, Jodi Benson, Pat Carroll, Buddy Hackett, Kenneth Mars
Little Mermaid, The author: Hans Christian Andersen
Little Minister, The (1934 film)
cast: John Beal, Donald Crisp, Katharine Hepburn
Little Miss Marker (1934 film)
cast: Adolphe Menjou, Shirley Temple
director: Alexander Hall
Little Miss Muffet __ tuffet: 6 sat on a
Little More Love, A (1978 song) artist: Olivia Newton-John
Little More Time on You, A (1998 song) artist: 'Nsync
Little Murders (1971 film)
cast: Vincent Gardenia, Elliott Gould, Marcia Rodd
director: Alan Arkin
littleneck: 4 clam 6 quahog 7 quahaug
Little Nemo: 5 strip 10 comic strip
cartoonist: 5 McCay
dog: 7 Slivers
Little Night Music, A: 7 musical
songwriter: 8 Sondheim
Little Odessa (1994 film)
cast: Edward Furlong, Moira Kelly, Tim Roth
director: James Gray
__ little of: 4 make 5 think
Little Old Lady, The (1964 song) artist: Jan & Dean
Little Ole Man (1967 song) artist: Bill Cosby
Little Order, A author: Evelyn Waugh
Little Orphan Annie: 5 strip 10 comic strip
cartoonist: 4 Gray
character: 3 Asp 6 Punjab 8 Warbucks
dog: 5 Sandy
Little Orphant Annie: 4 poem
author: James Whitcomb Riley
__ little piggy...: 4 this
Little Pigs building material: 5 straw 6 bricks, sticks
Little pitchers have big __!: 4 ears
Little Poison: 5 Waner
__ Little Prayer: 5 I Say a
Little Princess, The (1939 film)
cast: Anita Louise, Shirley Temple
director: Walter Lang
Little Prince, The author: Antoine de Saint-Exupéry
Little Rascals
dog: 4 Pete 5 Petey
producer: 5 Roach
Little Red __ Hood: 6 Riding
Little Red Book author: 3 Mao
Little Red Corvette (1983 song) artist: Prince
Little Red Hen, reply to: 4 not I
Littler, Gene: 6 golfer
milieu: 5 links 6 course
org.: 3 PGA
Little, Rich: 4 aper
emulate ~: 3 ape
Little Richard
last name: Penniman
song: Good Golly, Miss Molly (1958)
Jenny, Jenny (1957)
Keep A Knockin' (1957)
Long Tall Sally (1956)
Lucille (1957)
Ooh! My Soul (1958)
Rip It Up (1956)
Slippin' and Slidin' (1956)
Tutti-Frutti (1956)
__ Little Rich Girl: 4 Poor
Little River Band
homeland: Australia
song: Cool Change (1979)
Help Is on Its Way (1977)
Lady (1979)
Lonesome Lover (1979)
Man on Your Mind (1982)
The Night Owls (1981)
The Other Guy (1982)
Reminiscing (1978)
Take It Easy on Me (1981)
Little Rock: 4 city, town 7 capital
county: 7 Pulaski
locale: 3 Ark. 8 Arkansas
river: 8 Arkansas
Little Romance, A (1979 film)
cast: Diane Lane, Laurence Olivier
director: George Roy Hill
Little Shop of Horrors (1986 film)
cast: Vincent Gardenia, Ellen Greene, Steve Martin, Rick Moranis
character: 4 Luce, Orin, Snip 6 Audrey 7 Ronette
director: Frank Oz
Little Shop of Horrors, The (1960 film)
director: Roger Corman
Little Sir __: 4 Echo
Little Sister (1961 song) artist: Elvis Presley
Little Sister, The author: Raymond Chandler
__ Little Sixteen: 5 Sweet
Little Sparrow, The: 4 Piaf
littlest: 5 least 6 lowest, merest 7 minimal, minimum, modicum, nominal, tiniest 8 smallest 9 slightest
Littlest __, The: 5 Rebel 6 Outlaw
Little Star (1958 song) artist: Elegants
Littlest Rebel, The (1935 film)
cast: John Boles, Bill Robinson, Shirley Temple
__ Little Teapot: 3 I'm a
__ Little Tenderness: 4 Try a
Little Things Mean __: 4 a Lot
__ Little Toaster, The: 5 Brave
Littleton: 4 city, town
locale: 8 Colorado
__ Little We Know: 3 How
Little White __: 4 Lies
little wolf, name meaning: 6 Lowell
Little Woman (1969 song) artist: Bobby Sherman
Little Women (1933 film)
cast: Joan Bennett, Katharine Hepburn, Paul Lukas, Edna May Oliver
director: George Cukor
Little Women (1994 film)
cast: Trini Alvarado, Gabriel Byrne, Claire Danes, Winona Ryder, Susan Sarandon
director: Gillian Armstrong
Little Women author: Louisa May Alcott
character: 2 Jo 3 Amy, Meg 4 Beth, Demi 5 Bhaer, Daisy, Kirke, March 6 Carrol, Laurie, Marmee
__ Little Words: 5 Three
littoral: 5 beach, coast, sands, shore 6 marine, strand 7 coastal, seaside 8 maritime
phenomenon: 4 tide
liturgical: 6 formal, ritual, solemn 10 ceremonial
see also church
Liturgical __: 5 Latin
liturgy: 4 form, rite 6 ritual 7 formula, service, worship 8 ceremony, services 9 formality, sacrament 10 ceremonial, observance
lituus: 4 wind 7 trumpet
origin: 4 Rome
Litvak, Anatole: 8 director
film: All This and Heaven Too (1940)
The Amazing Doctor Clitterhouse (1938)
Anastasia (1956)
Castle on the Hudson (1940)
City for Conquest (1940)
Decision Before Dawn (1952)
Goodbye Again (1961)
The Journey (1959)
Out of the Fog (1941)
The Sisters (1938)
The Snake Pit (1948)
Sorry, Wrong Number (1948)
This Above All (1942)
Tovarich (1937)
Liu: 4 Lucy
LIU locale: 3 NYC
Liu Pang dynasty: 3 Han
Liv: 5 Tyler 7 Ullmann
Broadway role for ~: 4 Mama
livable: 3 fit 4 cosy, cozy, homy, snug 5 cozey, cozie, homey 8 adequate, bearable, homelike, passable 9 endurable, habitable, tolerable 10 acceptable, worthwhile
live: 3 are, hot 4 bide, bunk, fare, feed, last, nest, real, stay 5 abide, alert, alive, crash, dwell, exist, get by, lodge, ready, roost, savor, vital, vivid 6 active, actual, belong, billet, endure, make it, occupy, remain, reside, settle, thrive 7 animate, breathe, burning, current, dynamic, organic, prevail, prosper, running, subsist, survive, topical, working 8 animated, continue, existent, flourish, get along, in person, pressing, vigorous 9 as we speak, breathing, conscious, energetic, explosive, make money, observant, operative, unsettled 10 draw breath, experience, performing, unimagined
at: 6 billet, occupy 7 inhabit
beneath one's station: 4 slum
can't ~ without: 4 need 5 crave 7 hurt for, require
ender: 4 long 5 stock
fit to ~ in: 9 habitable
high on the hog: 4 bask 5 revel 6 thrive 7 indulge, rollick 8 flourish
in: 6 occupy 7 inhabit 8 populate
it up: 4 riot 5 revel 8 roll in it 9 celebrate, luxuriate, make merry
on: 3 eat 6 endure 7 survive 8 continue
partner: 5 learn
place to ~: 4 home 5 abode 8 quarters
through: 4 bear, go on, last, stay 5 stand 6 endure, hang on, hold on, keep on, manage, suffer 7 carry on, hold out, make out, outlast, prevail, recover, ride out, survive, undergo, weather 8 overcome 9 persevere, put up with, withstand 10 keep afloat, sit through, stick it out, tough it out
up to: 5 honor 6 follow 8 practice
where most people ~: 4 Asia
wire: 4 doer, grig 6 dynamo 7 busy bee, hustler 8 fireball, go-getter 9 workhorse 10 powerhouse
with: 4 take 5 brook, stand 6 accept, suffer 8 overlook, stand for, tolerate 9 disregard
(with): 4 cope
words to ~ by: 5 adage, credo, creed, motto
live __: 3 oak 4 a lie, down, it up, load,

up to, wire, with **5** steam **6** center **7** spindle
live __ the fat of the land: 3 off
live-__: 6 action **7** forever
Live __: 3 Aid **5** or Die
Live a Little, Love a Little (1968 film)
cast: Michele Carey, Don Porter, Elvis Presley, Rudy Vallee
director: Norman Taurog
live and __: 5 learn
__ live and breathe!: 3 as I
Live and Let Die: 4 film, song **5** novel
artist: Paul McCartney
author: Ian Fleming
cast: Yaphet Kotto, Roger Moore, Jane Seymour
director: Guy Hamilton
Live at Red Rocks artist: 4 Tesh
__ Live by Night: 4 They
live by one's __: 4 wits
lived: 3 was **4** been
__-lived: 4 long **5** short
...lived happily __ after: 4 ever
lived-in: 8 occupied **9** inhabited
Live Free __: 5 or Die
Live from New York, __ Saturday Night!: 3 it's
live in __ paradise: 6 a fool's
live-in: 4 maid **6** au pair **7** servant
livelihood: 3 art, job **4** game, keep, slot, work **5** craft, grind, means, thing, trade **6** career, income, racket **7** aliment, rat race, support **8** business, vocation **9** resources **10** employment, nine-to-five, occupation, profession, sustenance, walk of life
liveliness: 3 fun, pep, vim, zip **4** brio, dash, élan, fire, glee, jazz, life, zeal, zest **5** ardor, mirth, spark, speed, spice, sport, verve, vigor **6** action, bounce, energy, esprit, fervor, gaiety, gayety, spirit, warmth **7** agility, revelry, sparkle **8** activity, airiness, alacrity, buoyance, buoyancy, vitality, vivacity **9** animation, élan vital **10** ebullience, exuberance, friskiness
livelong: 4 full **5** total, whole **6** entire
lively: 3 gay, yar **4** busy, go-go, keen, live, pert, racy, spry, yare **5** agile, alert, astir, brisk, fresh, happy, hyper, jazzy, light, merry, peart, peppy, perky, quick, salty, sassy, sharp, smart, vital, vivid, witty, zippy **6** active, at work, blithe, bouncy, breezy, bright, chirpy, dapper, feisty, festal, frisky, jaunty, jocund, madcap, nimble, snappy, speedy **7** animate, buoyant, buzzing, chipper, coltish, complex, dashing, driving, dynamic, festive, graphic, hyped-up, jumping, piquant, playful, rousing, vibrant, working, zestful **8** animated, bustling, cheerful, involved, skittish, sparking, spirited, sporting, sportive, stirring, swinging, vigorous **9** assiduous, convivial, energetic, enjoyable, exuberant, gamboling, graphical, sparkling, sprightly, vivacious, with a kick **10** blithesome, expressive, frolicsome, refreshing, rollicking
in music: 4 anim. **7** animato
name meaning ~: 6 Vivian, Vivien **8** Vivienne
__ lively!: 4 Step
__ Lively Arts: 5 Seven
liven: 4 buoy, fire, goad, prod, zest **5** cheer, elate, pep up, rouse, spark, spice, waken **6** arouse, buck up, excite, kindle, perk up, pump up, spur on, stir up, turn on, vivify **7** animate, cheer up, gladden, hearten, inspire, juice up, quicken **8** activate, charge up, energize, vitalize **9** stimulate **10** brighten up, exhilarate, invigorate
__ live nephew...: 5 A real
Livenza: 5 river
locale: 5 Italy
live off the __ of the land: 3 fat
Live or Die author: Anne Sexton
liver: 4 meat **5** gland, organ **6** lessee, lodger, native, renter, roomer, tenant **7** boarder, burgher, denizen, dweller, resider **8** occupant, resident **10** inhabitant
appetizer: 6 rumaki
combining form: 5 hepat- **6** hepato-
ender: 4 leaf, wort **5** wurst
nutrient: 4 iron
output: 4 bile
paste: 4 pâté
__ liver: 4 free, high **7** chopped
__-livered: 4 lily **5** white **6** pigeon **7** chicken
liverish: 3 wan **4** glum, pale, rude, sour **5** nasty, sulky, surly, testy **6** bitter, cranky, dismal, gloomy, grumpy, morose, sallow, sickly, sullen, touchy, yellow **7** bilious, crabbed, grouchy **8** choleric, grumpish **9** depressed, irascible, irritable, jaundiced, saturnine, spleenful **10** melancholy
Livermore: 4 city, town
locale: 10 California
__ liver oil: 3 cod
Liverpool: 4 city, port, town
locale: 7 Britain, England
river: 6 Mersey
Liverpudlian: 6 Briton
liverwort
bud: 5 gemma
cousin: 4 moss
liverwurst: 4 meat **7** sausage
livery: 4 garb, suit **5** dress, get-up, habit **6** attire, outfit **7** apparel, clothes, costume, garment, raiment, regalia, threads, uniform **8** clothing, ensemble, garments **9** trappings **10** Sunday best
livery __: 3 cab **6** colors, stable **7** company
Lives __ Bengal Lancer, The: 3 of a
__ Lives: 4 Men's **5** Three **7** Private
Livesey: 5 Roger
Lives of a Bengal Lancer, The (1935 film)
cast: Gary Cooper, Richard Cromwell, Franchot Tone
director: Henry Hathaway
__ Lives of Thomasina, The: 5 Three
livestock: 4 cows, kine, pigs **5** goats, herds, sheep, stock **6** cattle, droves, flocks, horses, steers **7** animals
meal: 3 rye **4** feed **5** spelt **6** fodder
place: 4 barn **5** ranch **6** corral
show: 4 fair
live the __ life: 4 good
Live to Tell (1986 song) artist: Madonna
__ Live With Me: 4 Come
Livia: 7 Soprano
Livia author: Lawrence Durrell
livid: 3 hot, mad, wan **4** ashy, ired, pale, sore **5** angry, ashen, cross, dusky, huffy, irate, lurid, mirky, murky, pasty, riled, upset, waxen, wroth **6** fuming, gloomy, grisly, ireful, leaden, pallid, peeved, piqued, purple, raging, raving, red-hot **7** boiling, bruised, enraged, flaming, flushed, furious, grayish, greyish, ranting **8** blanched, choleric, contused, in a pique, incensed, inflamed, maddened, offended, outraged, white-hot, wrathful **9** bloodless, colorless, indignant, irritated, resentful, seeing red, splenetic **10** discolored, freaked out, hopping mad, infuriated
be ~: 4 boil, burn, fume, rage, stew **5** froth **6** see red, seethe
Livin' for the Weekend (1976 song) artist: O'Jays
living: 3 job, way **4** born, keep, mode, salt, warm, work **5** alert, awake, brisk, in use, means, vital **6** active, actual, around, billet, career, extant, income, strong, with us **7** aliment, animate, current, dynamic, ongoing, organic, support, ticking **8** animated, existent, existing, vigorous **9** breathing, existence, lifestyle, operative **10** continuing, developing, occupation, persisting, subsisting, sustenance, unimagined
all ~ things: 5 world **6** nature **8** creation, universe
alone: 5 unwed **6** single **8** isolated, solitary **9** by oneself, on one's own, separated, unmarried **10** spouseless, unattached
combining form: 4 vivi-
daylights: 4 wits **5** sense
earn a ~: 4 fare, work **5** get by **6** make it **7** prosper, subsist, support, survive **8** get along **9** make money
high ~: 4 ease **5** style **6** luxury, wealth **7** comfort, leisure **8** elegance, hedonism, opulence, splendor **9** affluence **10** lavishness, prosperity
quarters: 4 home **5** abode, place
scratch out a ~: 3 eke **6** scrape
space: 4 area
thing: 5 being, human **6** mortal, person **8** creature, organism **10** human being, individual
living __: 3 end **4** room, unit, wage **5** large, stone, trust **6** fossil, legend **7** picture
__ living: 5 earn a
__-living: 4 free **5** clean
Living __, The: 3 End **4** Reed **5** Years **6** Desert
Living and Loving author: 5 Loren
Living Daylights, The: 4 film **5** novel
author: Ian Fleming
band: 3 A-ha
cast: Joe Don Baker, Maryam d'Abo, Timothy Dalton
director: John Glen
instrument: 5 cello
Living End, The suthor: 5 Elkin
Living Faith author: 6 Carter
Living for the City (1973 song) artist: Stevie Wonder
living fossil tree: 6 gingko, ginkgo
Living in America (1986 song) artist: James Brown
Living in Oblivion (1995 film)
cast: Steve Buscemi, Catherine Keener, Dermot Mulroney
director: Tom DiCillo
living in the __: 4 past
Living It Up (1954 film)
cast: Janet Leigh, Jerry Lewis, Dean Martin
director: Norman Taurog
Living on the Fault Line author: 5 Moore
Living Out Loud (1998 film)
cast: Danny DeVito, Martin Donovan, Holly Hunter, Queen Latifah
Living Reed, The author: Pearl S. Buck
living room
appliance of old: 5 radio
furniture: 4 sofa **6** settee **8** end table, recliner
Livingston: 3 Jay **4** city, town **5** Barry **7** Stanley
locale: 9 New Jersey
Livingstone: 4 Mark, Mary **5** David
Livingstone, David: 4 Scot **8** explorer
Livingstone, Mary spouse: Jack Benny
Livin' La Vida Loca (1999 song) artist: Ricky Martin
Livin' on a Prayer (1987 song) artist: Bon Jovi
__ Livin' to Do, A: 5 Lot of
Livonia: 4 city, town
locale: 8 Michigan
Livorno: 4 city, port, town
island south of ~: 4 Elba
locale: 5 Italy **6** Italia
livre: 4 coin **5** money
Livy: 5 Roman **6** writer **9** historian
contemporary: 4 Ovid
see also Latin
Liwung, city on the: 7 Jakarta **8** Djakarta
lixiviate: 5 leach **6** filter, strain **7** extract **8** wash away **9** percolate
lixivium: 3 lye
Liz: 5 Phair, Smith **6** Taylor **9** Claiborne
ex: 4 Dick **5** Eddie, Larry, Nicky
role for ~: 4 Cleo
Liza: 6 Snyder **8** Minnelli
half-sister: 4 Luft **5** Lorna
mother: 4 Judy
Liza (1929 song) artist: Al Jolson
composer: George Gershwin
Lizabeth: 5 Scott
__ Liza Jane: 3 Li'l
lizard: 3 eft **4** newt, uran **5** agama, anole, gecko, skink, teiid **6** agamid, animal, goanna, iguana, moloch **7** iguanid, leather, monitor, reptile, saurian **8** dinosaur **9** alligator, chameleon, crocodile
Australia: 6 goanna, moloch
color-changing ~: 5 agama, anole **9** chameleon
combining form: 4 saur- **5** -saura, sauro-
Hawaiian ~ fish: 4 ulae
like a ~: 5 scaly **8** lamellar, squamose, squamous
lounge ~: 5 idler **8** parasite
Mexico: 3 uta **6** iguana
monitor ~: 4 uran **6** goanna
__ lizard: 4 sand, worm **5** fence, giant, glass, night, spiny, tiger **6** beaded, caiman, dragon, flying, horned, Komodo, lounge **7** crested, earless, frilled, leopard
Lizard Head: 4 cape
locale: 7 England **8** Cornwall
__ lizards!: 6 Leapin'
Lizette: 5 Reese
__ lizzie: 3 tin
Lizzie Borden took __: 4 an ax **5** an axe
__ L. Jackson: 6 Samuel
Ljubljana: 4 city, town **7** capital
locale: 8 Slovenia
LL __ J: 4 Cool
L.L.: 4 Bean
llama: 6 animal, mammal
herder, once: 5 Incan
milieu: 4 Peru **5** Andes
relative: 5 camel **6** alpaca, vicuna **7** guanaco **8** Bactrian **9** dromedary
Llanelly: 4 city, port, town
locale: 5 Wales
llano: 3 lea, ley **5** plain, veldt **7** prairie **9** grassland
LL.B.: 3 deg.
holder: 3 att. **4** atty.
offerer: 4 univ.
org.: 3 ABA
LLC kin: 3 inc.
LL Cool J: 6 rapper
real name: James Todd Smith
song: Around the Way Girl (1991)
Doin It (1996)
Father (1998)
Going Back to Cali (1988)
Hey Lover (1995)
I'm That Kind of Guy (1989)
I Need Love (1987)
Loungin (1996)
Mama Said Knock You Out (1991)
This Is for the Lover in You (1996)

LL.D.: 3 deg.
Llewellyn: 7 Richard
___ L. Lewis: 4 John
Lloyd: 5 Bacon, Emily, Frank, Nolan, Price, Waner 6 Harold, Haynes 7 Bentsen, Bochner, Bridges 8 Kathleen
Lloyd, Christopher: 5 actor
film: The Addams Family (1991)
Addams Family Values (1993)
Back to the Future (1985)
Back to the Future Part II (1989)
Back to the Future Part III (1990)
The Dream Team (1989)
Eight Men Out (1988)
Goin' South (1978)
Who Framed Roger Rabbit (1988)
Lloyd, Emily: 7 actress
film: Cookie (1989)
In Country (1989)
A River Runs Through It (1992)
Wish You Were Here (1987)
Lloyd, Frank: 8 director
film: Berkeley Square (1933)
Blood on the Sun (1945)
Cavalcade (1933, AA)
The Divine Lady (1928, AA)
Forever and a Day (1943)
If I Were King (1938)
Maid of Salem (1937)
Mutiny on the Bounty (1935)
Oliver Twist (1922)
The Sea Hawk (1924)
A Tale of Two Cities (1917)
Under Two Flags (1936)
Wells Fargo (1937)
___ Lloyd Garrison: 7 William
___ Lloyd George: 5 David
Lloyd, Harold: 5 actor 8 comedian
film: For Heaven's Sake (1926)
The Freshman (1925)
Girl Shy (1924)
Grandma's Boy (1922)
Hot Water (1924)
The Kid Brother (1927)
The Milky Way (1936)
Movie Crazy (1932)
Safety Last (1923)
Speedy (1928)
Why Worry? (1923)
Lloyd's of London (1936 film)
cast: Freddie Bartholomew, Madeleine Carroll, Guy Standing
director: Henry King
Lloyd Webber, Andrew: 3 Sir 7 British 8 composer
musical: Aspects of Love
Cats
Evita
Jesus Christ Superstar
Joseph and the Amazing Technicolor Dreamcoat
The Phantom of the Opera
Starlight Express
Sunset Boulevard
___ Lloyd Wright: 5 Frank
Llullaillaco: 4 peak 5 mount 8 mountain
locale: 5 Andes, Chile
___ L. Mankiewicz: 6 Joseph
lmt.: 3 max., min.
ln.: 2 rd.
kin: 2 av., st. 3 ave. 4 blvd.
LNG vehicle: 2 RV
lo
partner: 6 behold
lo ___: 4 mein
lo-___: 3 cal, res
___ Loa: 5 Mauna
loach: 4 fish
load: 3 arm, jam, lot, tax 4 care, cram, fill, glut, haul, heap, lade, mass, onus, pack, pile, scad, stow 5 cargo, flood, goods, stack, store, stuff, swamp, trial 6 armful, bundle, burden, cumber, eyeful, hamper, heap up, infuse, lading, lumber, misery, parcel, pile on, saddle, weight 7 freight, oppress, payload, surfeit 8 contents, encumber, irritant, pile it on, pressure, quantity, shipment, truckful 9 albatross, hindrance, millstone, profusion, put aboard, weigh down 10 affliction, commission, dead weight, freightage, infliction, overburden, oversupply
carrier: 3 van 5 truck, wagon
ender: 4 star 5 stone 6 master
get a ~ of: 3 eye, see, spy 4 look, peek, peep, peer, view 5 watch 6 behold, glance, listen, look at, notice, regard 7 glimpse, observe, witness 10 sneak a look
heavy ~: 6 burden, weight
off one's mind: 6 relief
reduce a ~: 7 lighten
share the ~: 4 ease, help 6 assist, join in 7 pitch in, relieve 9 cooperate, lend a hand 10 see through
starter: 3 arm, bus, car, off, pay, van 4 boat, cart, case, down, free, ship, work 5 plane, train, truck, wagon
take a ~ off: 3 sit 5 relax 6 unload 7 lighten
up: 4 fill, heap, pile 5 amass, cache, hoard, lay by, stock, store 6 gather, supply 9 replenish, stockpile 10 accumulate
load ___: 4 fund, line 6 factor, module
___ load: 3 bed 4 base, case, dead, deck, live, work 5 rated 7 genetic
___-load: 3 off 4 back 5 carbo, front
loaded: 4 full, rich, rife 5 armed, drunk, flush, laden, tight, tipsy 6 aboard, deluxe, monied, packed, soused 7 charged, crowded, moneyed, replete, stuffed, teeming, wealthy, well-off 8 affluent, brimming, cram-full, in clover, perilous, well-to-do 9 chock-full, jam-packed, well-fixed 10 in the dough, in the money, precarious, privileged, propertied, prosperous, wall-to-wall, well-heeled
down: 10 encumbered
question: 4 bait, ruse 6 ambush, come-on, device 8 maneuver 9 booby trap, deception 10 enticement, subterfuge
loaded ___: 8 question
___ loaded: 5 bases
loaded for ___: 4 bear
loader: 9 stevedore
starter: 4 free 6 breech, muzzle
___ loader: 3 top 5 front
loading
apparatus: 5 crane, hoist, sling 7 derrick
area: 4 dock, pier, quay
loading ___: 4 coil, dock
___ loading: 4 span, wing 5 power
___-loading: 5 carbo
___ load of: 4 get a
loads: 4 a lot, lots, many, much, tons 5 horde 6 flocks, hoards, myriad, oodles, plenty, scores 7 numbers 9 multitude, quite a few
load the ___: 4 dice
loaf: 3 bun, lag, veg 4 cake, cube, idle, laze, loll, lump, rest 5 amble, block, bread, dally, dogit, dough, dream, drift, evade, mosey, relax, shirk, stall, tarry, twist 6 dawdle, linger, loiter, lounge, piddle, repose, slouch 7 hang out, saunter 8 kill time, lallygag, lollygag, malinger, pass time, slack off, slow down, straggle, vegetate 9 bum around, goldbrick, hang loose, sit around, waste time 10 dillydally, fool around, knock about, take it easy
bakery ~: 3 rye 5 white 10 whole wheat
in Britain: 5 sculk, skulk
part: 4 half, heel 5 slice
loaf ___: 3 pan 5 bread 6 around
___ loaf: 4 meat
___-loaf: 5 sugar
___ Loaf Aday: 4 Meat
loafer: 3 bum 4 lazy, shoe 5 drone, idler 6 rascal, slip-on, slouch, truant, waster 7 goof-off, laggard, lounger, shirker, slacker, sponger, wastrel 8 deadbeat, footgear, footwear, loiterer, parasite, sluggard, wanderer 9 do-nothing, goldbrick, lazybones, miscreant 10 malingerer, ne'er-do-well
___ loafer: 5 penny
loafers: 5 flats, shoes 8 footwear
wearing ~: 4 shod
loafing: 4 idle, lazy 9 loitering 10 unemployed
___ loaf is...: 5 Half a
___ Loaf Mountain: 5 Sugar
loam: 4 clay, dirt, land, soil 5 earth, loess 7 topsoil
loamy: 6 arable 7 fertile, friable
soil: 5 loess
loan: 3 mtg. 4 debt, lend, mtge. 5 allow, lease, stake, touch, trust 6 credit, let out, let use 7 advance, floater, imprest 8 mortgage 9 extension, liability
abbr.: 3 APR
arranger: 4 bank 6 banker
assist with a ~: 6 cosign
clear a ~: 5 repay 7 pay back, satisfy 8 make good, settle up, square up 9 liquidate, reimburse 10 compensate
fed. ~ agcy.: 3 FCA, FHA, SBA 4 FNMA, GNMA
fee: 3 int. 6 points 8 interest
get a ~: 3 owe 6 borrow
get a ~ on: 4 hock, pawn 6 pledge
home ~: 3 mtg. 4 mtge. 8 mortgage
home ~ org.: 3 FHA 4 FNMA, GNMA 5 S and L
shark: 5 leech 6 lender, usurer 7 Shylock
shark's crime: 5 usury
try for a ~: 5 hit up
variable-interest ~: 3 ARM
loan ___: 4 word 5 shark, value 6 office 7 officer
___ loan: 3 day 4 bank, call, time 5 swing 6 bridge, demand, policy 7 Liberty, morning, premium, takeout
loaner: 6 lender, usurer 8 creditor
loath: 4 hate 5 abhor 6 afraid, averse, remiss 7 against, counter, opposed, uneager 8 hesitant 9 reluctant, resisting, unwilling 10 indisposed, uninclined, unobliging
not ~: 3 hot 4 agog, avid, game, keen 5 eager 6 gung-ho, hungry, intent 7 burning, excited, pleased, willing 8 amenable, animated, cheerful, disposed, inclined, unforced 9 agreeable, ambitious, compliant, in the mood, psyched up 10 consenting, raring to go
to: 3 con 8 opposing 10 at odds with
loathe: 4 hate 5 abhor, spurn 6 detest, refuse, reject, revolt 7 decline, despise, dislike 8 can't take, execrate 9 abominate, can't stand, disrelish, repudiate
old-style: 5 spise
loathing: 4 hate 5 odium 6 enmity, hatred, nausea, phobia 7 disgust, dislike 8 aversion, contempt, distaste 9 antipathy, repulsion, revulsion 10 abhorrence, repugnance
look of ~: 5 frown, glare, scowl 6 glower 7 grimace
loathly: 5 skyly 6 slowly 9 haltingly 10 hesitantly
loathsome: 4 base, evil, foul, grim, poor, ugly, vile 5 awful, gross, lousy, nasty, pesky, pesty, slimy, woful 6 bitchy, creepy, crumby, crummy, dismal, filthy, horrid, odious, rancid, rotten, sleazy, uncool, woeful 7 accurst, baleful, baneful, beastly, doleful, ghastly, hateful, hideous, noisome, satanic 8 accursed, dreadful, God-awful, grievous, horrible, inferior, shameful, shocking, stinking, terrible, wretched 9 abhorrent, appalling, atrocious, defective, execrable, frightful, insidious, invidious, miserable, monstrous, obnoxious, offensive, repellant, repellent, repugnant, repulsive, revolting, satanical, unsightly 10 abominable, deplorable, despicable, detestable, disastrous, disgusting, horrendous, petrifying, unpleasant, virtueless
one: 3 cad, cur, rat 4 heel, toad, worm 5 skunk, snake, sneak, swine 6 wretch 7 stinker 9 scoundrel 10 blackguard
lob: 3 arc 4 flip, hurl, shot, toss 5 chuck, fling, pitch, sling, throw 6 let fly
ender: 4 worm 5 lolly
path: 3 arc, bow 5 curve 8 crescent, half-moon
lobbies, high-ceiling: 5 atria
lobby: 3 NRA 4 bill, drum, hall, hype, plug, push, sell, spot, sway, urge 5 alter, boost, foyer, pitch, porch, press, thump 6 affect, atrium, induce, lounge, modify, sell on, splash 7 advance, build up, doorway, faction, further, gateway, hallway, ingress, passage, promote, request, solicit 8 anteroom, arm-twist, campaign, corridor, persuade, politick, soft-sell, soft-soap 9 billboard, influence, sweet-talk, vestibule 10 passageway
ender: 3 ist
furnishing: 4 seat, sofa 5 couch, divan 6 settee 7 seating
org.: 4 assn.
lobbyist: 5 urger
lobe: 4 flap, limb 6 earlap 10 projection
adornment: 4 hoop, stud 7 earring
locale: 3 ear 4 lung 5 brain
___ lobe: 3 ear 7 frontal
lobed: 6 convex, knobby 7 rounded
combining form: 3 -fid
lobelia: 5 plant 6 flower
Lo Bianco, Tony: 5 actor
film: City of Hope (1991)
The French Connection (1971)
The Honeymoon Killers (1970)
loblolly: 4 pine, tree
lobo: 4 wolf 10 timber wolf
Lobo
song: Don't Expect Me to Be Your Friend (1973)
I'd Love You to Want Me (1972)
Me and You and a Dog Named Boo (1971)
___ Lobo: 3 Rio
___ Lobos: 3 Los
Lobo star: 5 Akins
lobscouse: 4 stew
lobster: 6 entrée 7 seafood
abdomen: 5 pleon
catcher: 3 pot 4 trap
eater's wear: 3 bib
eggs: 3 roe 5 coral
extremity: 4 claw 5 chela
feeler: 4 palp 6 palpus
feelers: 5 palpi
female ~: 3 hen
home: 5 shell
on some menus: 4 surf
pot, perhaps: 5 lagan, ligan

  sauce ingredient: 3 egg
lobster ___: 3 pot 4 bisk, roll, trap 5 shift, trick 6 bisque 7 Newburg
lobster ___ Diavolo: 3 Fra
___ lobster: 4 rock 5 Maine, spiny 7 chicken
___ Lobster: 3 Red
loc.: 3 pos.
loc. ___: 3 cit.
___ Loc: 4 Tone
loca: 5 sites 6 places
L'Oca ___ Cairo: 3 del
local: 4 home 5 civic, towny, union 6 narrow, native, parish, townee, townie 7 barroom, endemic, limited, topical 8 confined, district, indigene, regional, resident, townsman 9 endemical, home-grown, in the area, milk train, municipal, parochial, sectional, small-town 10 indigenous, inhabitant, provincial, restricted, trade union
  area: 4 hood, turf 8 environs, vicinity
  booster: 6 jaycee
  color: 8 ambiance, ambience 9 character 10 atmosphere, background
  combining form: 3 top- 4 topo-
  government unit: 2 tp. 3 twp. 8 township
  group: 5 union
  not a ~: 3 exp. 7 express
local ___: 4 time, wind 5 color, stamp 6 option 7 maximum, minimum
local ___ network: 4 area
lo-cal: 4 lite 5 light
Local Color author: Truman Capote
locale: 4 area, belt, hole, home, site, spot, turf, zone 5 haunt, place, scene, situs, stage, tract, venue 6 domain, milieu, region, sector, sphere 7 habitat, quarter, setting, theater, theatre 8 district, position, vicinity 9 bailiwick, situation, territory 10 where it's at
Local Hero (1983 film)
  cast: Burt Lancaster, Peter Riegert
  director: Bill Forsyth
localism: 4 burr 5 drawl, idiom, slang, twang 6 accent, brogue, custom, patois 7 dialect 8 practice 9 tradition 10 observance
locality: 4 area, belt, hole, home, site, spot, turf, zone 5 haunt, locus, place, scene, stage, tract, venue 6 domain, region, sector, sphere 7 quarter, section, theater, theatre 8 district, location, position, vicinity 9 bailiwick, community, situation, territory
localize: 6 finger 8 home in on, identify, pinpoint, zero in on 9 get a fix on
localized: 7 endemic 8 regional 9 parochial 10 indigenous
locally: 6 nearby 7 close-by 10 around here
Locarno ___: 4 Pact
locate: 3 fix, lay, put, set 4 base, find, hook, park, plot, read, seat, site, spot 5 dig in, dig up, dwell, get at, lodge, pitch, place, squat, stand 6 detect, orient, reside, settle, strike, turn up 7 deposit, dispose, hit upon, inhabit, pin down, situate, station, uncover, unearth 8 come upon, discover, ensconce, meet with, pick up on, pinpoint, position, smell out, smoke out, sniff out, trip over, zero in on 9 determine, establish, ferret out, get a fix on, get hold of, light upon, search out, stumble on, track down 10 come across, happen upon
  as data: 6 access
located: 3 set 5 based 6 placed, posted 8 situated 9 occupying, stationed 10 positioned
  as ~: 6 in situ
  centrally ~: 4 amid 5 among 6 amidst, mongst 7 amongst
location: 4 area, hold, part, post, seat, site, spot, turf 5 place, point, scene, space, stead, tract, venue, where 6 region 7 address, quarter, section, setting, station 8 bearings, district, position 9 situation
  starter: 4 echo
locations, add new: 6 expand
locator, position: 6 cursor
loch: 4 lake
  eerie ~: 4 Ness
Loch: 4 Ness 5 Leven 6 Lomond 7 Katrine
  locale: 8 Scotland
Loch ___ monster: 4 Ness
Lochearn: 4 city, town
  locale: 8 Maryland
loci: 4 hubs 5 areas, sites, spots 6 places, points, venues 9 positions 10 situations
lock: 3 bar, dam, fix, hug 4 bolt, bond, clog, cork, curl, grip, hair, hasp, hook, join, link, mesh, plug, seal, shut 5 block, catch, cinch, clamp, clasp, close, dam up, grasp, latch, press, tress, unite 6 button, clench, clinch, clog up, clutch, engage, fasten, plug up, seal up, secure, stop up, strand 7 close up, closure, embrace, enclose, entwine, fixture, grapple, inclose, intwine, ringlet, seal off, shutter 8 blockade, button up, deadbolt, encircle, fastener, junction, make fast, obstruct, vinculum 9 certainty, fastening 10 connection
  away: 5 store
  companion: 3 key
  ender: 3 age, jaw, nut, out, set 4 step 5 smith 6 keeper, master
  horns: 5 argue, clash 6 debate 7 compete, contend, quarrel, wrangle 8 conflict, struggle 9 have words, square off
  in: 6 ensure 7 enclose, inclose 8 imprison
  lips: 4 kiss, neck 6 smooch 8 osculate
  maker: 4 Yale
  of hair: 4 coil, curl, hair 5 tress 7 ringlet
  out: 3 bar 7 exclude, occlude, shut off 9 foreclose
  part: 4 bolt, hasp 5 catch
  place: 4 door, exit, gate 5 hatch 6 portal, window 7 postern 8 entrance, entryway
  put a ~ on: 6 ensure, secure 9 safeguard
  starter: 3 elf, gun, hem, oar, pad, row, shy, war, wed 4 anti, dead, fire, fore, grid, head, love, pick 5 flint, match, wrist 6 hammer
  stock and barrel: 6 in toto, wholly
  under ~ and key: 4 held, safe 5 bound, caged 6 in jail, jailed, secure 7 captive, guarded 8 confined 9 in custody, protected 10 imprisoned
  up: 3 tie 4 bind, cage, hold, jail 5 close, embar, tie up 6 assure, closet, detain, encage, ensure, immure, intern, secure 7 acquire, confine, interne, possess, put away 8 imprison, prohibit, restrain 10 monopolize
lock ___: 3 bay, nut, out 4 rail, seam 5 horns 6 stitch, washer
lock, ___ and barrel: 5 stock
___ lock: 3 air, man, rim 4 coin, knob, tide, time 5 scalp, shift, vapor, wheel 6 duplex, safety 7 mortise
___-lock: 5 flash 6 double
___-Locka, FL: 3 Opa
___ lock and key: 5 under
lockbox: 4 safe 5 vault 6 coffer 9 strongbox 10 repository
___-lock brakes: 4 anti
Locke: 4 John 5 Alain 6 Sondra
locked: 5 tight 6 closed, secure
  in: 3 set 5 rigid 9 immovable, obstinate, unbending 10 unyielding
  starter: 4 land
  up: 6 jailed 7 captive
Locke, John: 7 British 11 philosopher
  work: An Essay Concerning Human Understanding
    Two Treatises on Government
locker: 5 chest, trunk 6 closet 7 cabinet 8 wardrobe
  locale: 3 gym, spa 5 depot 10 health club
  photo: 5 pin-up
  starter: 4 foot
locker ___: 4 room 5 plant
___ locker: 5 chain
locker room
  supply: 4 talc 6 towels
Locke, Sondra: 7 actress
  film: Any Which Way You Can (1980)
    Bronco Billy (1980)
    Every Which Way But Loose (1978)
    The Gauntlet (1977)
    Impulse (1990)
    The Outlaw Josey Wales (1976)
    Sudden Impact (1983)
locket: 5 bijou 6 bauble 7 jewelry, pendant 8 necklace 9 lavaliere
  item: 5 cameo
  place: 4 neck
  shape: 5 heart
Lockhart: 4 Anne, Gene, June 5 Keith
Lockhart, Gene: 5 actor
  film: Abe Lincoln in Illinois (1940)
    A Christmas Carol (1938)
    Miracle on 34th Street (1947)
    Rhubarb (1951)
Lockhart, June: 7 actress
  film: T-Men (1947)
  TV: Lassie, Lost in Space, Petticoat Junction
Lockhart, Keith: 9 conductor
Lockheed ___-Star: 3 Tri
Lockheed product: 3 jet 5 plane 8 airplane
Lockhorns, The cartoonist: 5 Hoest
lock-in: 10 commitment
locking ___: 5 piece, plate 6 pliers
Locklear, Heather
  spouse: Tommy Lee, Richie Sambora
  TV: Dynasty, Melrose Place, T.J. Hooker
lockout: 8 stoppage 9 exclusion
Lockport: 4 city, town
  locale: 7 New York
Lockridge: 7 Frances, Richard
locks: 4 hair
  locale: 5 canal
  starter: 5 dread
___ Locks: 3 Soo
Locksley Hall author: Alfred Tennyson
locksmithing: 5 trade
Locksmith painter: 4 Klee
lock, stock and barrel: 3 all
___ Lock the Door: 4 Let's
lockup: 3 can, jug, pen 4 brig, coop, jail, poky, stir 5 clink, pokey 6 cooler, donjon, prison 7 dungeon, hoosgow, slammer 8 big house, hoosegow 9 calaboose 10 guardhouse, paddy wagon
Lockwood: 4 Gary 8 Margaret
Lockwood, Gary spouse: Stefanie Powers
loco: 4 amok, bats, daft 5 amuck, batty, buggy, daffy, dotty, goofy, kooky, nutty, wacky 6 cuckoo, kookie, whacky 7 bananas, bonkers 8 cockeyed, crackers 10 off the beam
  ender: 4 weed
  not ~: 4 sane
loco ___: 4 weed 6 citato
loco ___ citato: 5 primo, supra
___ loco: 3 suo 5 plumb
Loco-___, The: 6 Motion
Loco, Antonio music: 3 rap
locomotion: 6 action, motion, moving, travel 8 mobility, movement 9 traveling 10 mobileness
  organ of ~: 3 pad, paw 4 foot, hoof
loco-motion: 5 dance
Loco-Motion (song), The artist: Grand Funk, Kylie Minogue, Little Eva
locomotive: 6 barney, diesel, dinkey, engine
  part: 3 cab, cam
  slangily: 3 pig
  small ~: 5 dolly
  sound: 4 chug 5 chuff
  steam ~: 6 Big Boy
___ locomotive: 3 cog 4 rack, tank 5 steam
locoweed, like: 5 toxic
loc. primo ___: 3 cit.
locum ___: 6 tenens
locus: 4 site, spot 5 place, point 7 station 8 position 9 situation
locus in ___: 3 quo
locust: 3 bug 4 tree 6 acacia, cicada, insect 8 hardwood
  bean: 5 carob
  family: 6 legume
  group: 5 swarm
  relative: 3 koa 5 carob 6 cassia, cercis, padauk, padouk, redbud 7 araroba, mesquit 8 mesquite, tamarind 9 poinciana
locust ___: 4 bean 5 years
___ locust: 5 black, honey, swamp, water 6 desert, yellow
locution: 4 talk, word 5 idiom 6 accent 7 dialect, diction, wording 8 language, phrasing 10 expression, inflection
Lod: 4 city, town
  locale: 6 Israel
lode: 3 ore 4 mine, seam, vein 5 store 6 pocket 7 bonanza, pay dirt 8 gold mine
  ender: 4 star 5 stone
___ lode: 6 mother 8 Comstock
loden: 4 coat 5 green 6 fabric, jacket
Loder: 4 John, Kurt
lodestar: 4 sign 5 guide, model 6 beacon, signal 7 pointer, Polaris 8 cynosure
lodestone: 7 mineral
lodge: 3 den, fix, hut, inn, lay, set 4 bunk, camp, club, digs, home, lair, live, nest, park, rent, room, root, stay, stop 5 abide, abode, board, bower, cabin, catch, couch, crash, dwell, embed, haunt, hotel, house, imbed, infix, motel, perch, place, plant, put up, roost, shack, squat, stick, villa 6 belong, bestow, billet, burrow, canton, chalet, harbor, hole up, hostel, instal, locate, remain, reside, resort, settle, shanty, take in, tavern 7 auberge, coterie, cottage, domicil, engrain, harbour, hospice, implant, ingrain, install, quarter, retreat, shelter, sojourn, station 8 domicile, dwelling, entrench, hostelry, log cabin, quarters, stay over, stopover 9 dormitory, entertain, gatehouse, roadhouse 10 come to rest, guesthouse
  a complaint: 3 sue 4 cite 5 blame 6 accuse, allege, charge, impute, indict 7 arraign 8 denounce 9 prosecute
  builder: 6 beaver
  in: 5 dwell 6 occupy, reside 7 inhabit
  income: 4 dues

letters: 4 BPOE, IOOF
member: 3 Elk 4 Lion 5 Mason, Moose
Navajo ~: 5 hogan
ski ~: 6 A-frame, chalet
visitor: 5 skier
__ lodge: 5 earth, motor
__-Lodge: 5 Econo
lodgepole __: 4 pine
lodger: 5 guest, liver 6 lessee, renter, roomer, tenant 7 boarder 8 occupant, resident 10 vacationer
meals: 5 board
Lodger, The (1944 film)
cast: Laird Cregar, Merle Oberon, George Sanders
director: John Brahm
lodging: 3 inn 4 camp, dorm, flat, home, port, roof, room 5 abode, B and B, botel, cabin, cover, hotel, motel, place 6 billet, boatel, castle, harbor, hostel, palace, resort 7 address, domicil, habitat, harbour, shelter 8 chambers, domicile, dwelling, quarters 9 apartment, dormitory, residence 10 habitation, pied-à-terre, protection
military ~: 6 billet, casern 7 caserne
provide ~: 4 bunk 5 board, house, put up 6 billet, harbor 7 quarter, shelter 8 domicile
lodging __: 4 knee 5 house
lodgment: 3 inn, pad 4 digs, home, room 5 B and B, cabin, condo, hotel, house, motel, store 6 billet, hostel, tavern 7 bivouac, cottage, deposit, domicil 8 chambers, domicile, dwelling, foothold, quarters 9 apartment, beachhead, residence
Lodi: 4 city, town 5 apple
locale: 9 New Jersey 10 California
relative: 4 crab, Gala, Rome 5 Mutsu 6 Empire, Ida Red, medlar, Pippin, russet 7 Baldwin, Bramley, costard, Freedom, Liberty, Spartan, Wealthy, Winesap 8 Cortland, Jonathan, McIntosh 10 Rome Beauty
Lodovico: 7 Ariosto
in English: 5 Lewis, Louis
Lódz: 4 city, town
locale: 6 Poland
resident: 4 Pole
Loeb: 4 Lisa
__ l'oeil: 6 trompe
loess: 4 clay, loam, marl, soil 5 earth
Loesser, Frank: 8 composer
musical: Guys and Dolls
How to Succeed in Business Without Really Trying
The Most Happy Fella
Where's Charley
song: Baby It's Cold Outside
A Bushel and a Peck
Heart and Soul
I Believe in You
Luck Be a Lady
On a Slow Boat to China
Once in Love With Amy
Standing on the Corner
Two Sleepy People
Loew: 6 Marcus
Loewe, Frederick: 8 composer
collaborator: 6 Lerner
musical: Brigadoon
Camelot
Gigi
My Fair Lady
Paint Your Wagon
song: Almost Like Being in Love
Camelot
Get Me to the Church on Time
Gigi
The Heather on the Hill
I Could Have Danced All Night
If Ever I Would Leave You
I Remember It Well
I Talk to the Trees
I've Grown Accustomed to Her Face
The Night They Invented Champagne
On the Street Where You Live
The Rain in Spain
Thank Heaven for Little Girls
They Call the Wind Maria
With a Little Bit of Luck
Wouldn't It Be Loverly
Loewi, Otto: 8 Nobelist
lo-fat: 4 diet, lite
Lofgren: 4 Nils
Lofoten: 4 isls. 5 isles 7 islands
loft: 5 attic 6 dormer, garret, haymow, studio 7 atelier, storage 8 top floor 9 apartment
contents: 3 hay 4 bale, feed 5 straw 6 fodder
invite to one's ~: 5 ask up
pigeon ~: 6 aviary
singers: 5 choir 6 chorus 8 ensemble
loft __: 3 bed
__ loft: 3 fly 4 mold 5 choir
loftier than: 4 high, over 5 above 7 on top of 8 overhead, superior
loftiest: 3 top 6 apical 9 uppermost
loftiness: 5 pride 6 height, hubris, hybris, length 8 altitude, eminence, grandeur, nobility 9 arrogance, elevation, greatness 10 exaltation
lofting __: 4 iron
Lofting: 4 Hugh
lofty: 3 big 4 airy, high, tall 5 grand, great, noble, proud, royal, skyey, steep 6 aerial, Andean, august, high up, lifted, lordly, raised, snooty, superb 7 eminent, exalted, gallant, haughty, sky-high, skyward, soaring, spiring, stately, sublime, utopian 8 arrogant, cavalier, elevated, empyreal, empyrean, generous, high-rise, immodest, imposing, insolent, majestic, rarefied, renowned, striking, superior, towering, uplifted 9 ambitious, arresting, dignified, grandiose, high-flown, idealized, sovereign, visionary 10 benevolent, chivalrous, commanding, disdainful, high-minded, majestical, monumental
area: 4 peak, rise 6 atrium, height, summit 8 eminence, mountain 9 elevation, precipice 10 prominence
goal: 5 ideal 6 vision
set a ~ goal: 4 hope, wish 5 dream 6 aspire
log: 4 bole, book, cast, wood 5 chart, diary, enter, trunk 6 lumber, record, timber 7 account, daybook, Filofax, journal, listing, put down 8 register 10 journalize
a few z's: 3 nap 4 doze, rest 5 sleep 6 catnap, drowse, nod off, snooze 7 drop off, slumber 10 fall asleep
bump on a ~: 3 nub 4 knub, knur, node
cabin: 3 hut 5 abode, shack 7 retreat 8 dwelling
ender: 3 jam 4 book, roll, wood 6 normal 7 rolling
in: 6 sign on 8 register
like falling off a ~: 4 easy 6 facile, simple 7 a picnic, no sweat 8 no bother 9 no problem, no trouble 10 child's play, effortless, elementary
notation: 4 item 5 entry 6 record
off: 7 card out
on: 6 card in
splitter's aid: 3 ram 5 chock, wedge
stack: 4 rick
starter: 3 ana, dia, epi, pro 4 back, mono 5 water
transport: 5 chute, flume 6 sluice 7 channel
tread a floating ~: 4 birl
log __: 3 off, out 4 chip, line, reel, ship 5 cabin
__ log: 3 air, gas, saw 4 chip, deck, hand, well, yule 5 screw 6 ground, patent
Logan: 4 city, Ella, Josh, peak, town 5 mount 6 Joshua 8 mountain
Airport symbol: 3 BOS
athletes: 6 Aggies
info: 3 arr., ETD
locale: 4 Utah 5 Yukon 6 Canada
school: 3 USU 9 Utah State
loganberry: 5 fruit
logania: 4 bush 5 shrub
Logan, Joshua: 8 director
film: Bus Stop (1956)
Fanny (1961)
Paint Your Wagon (1969)
Picnic (1955)
Sayonara (1957)
South Pacific (1958)
Logan's Run (1976 film)
android: 3 Rem
cast: Jenny Agutter, Michael York
__ logarithm: 6 Briggs, common 7 natural
logarithm base: 4 root 5 radix
Log Cabin: 5 syrup
loge: 7 gallery 9 mezzanine
logged starter: 4 back 5 water
logger: 9 lumberman 10 lumberjack, Paul Bunyan
commodity: 4 pulp
contest: 5 roleo
ender: 4 head
leaving: 5 stump
small-scale ~: 5 gyppo
tool: 3 axe, saw
loggerhead: 4 dolt 6 animal, turtle 7 reptile
loggerheads, at: 10 quarreling
loggia: 6 arcade 7 balcony, gallery
Loggia, Robert: 5 actor
film: Big (1988)
Gaby-A True Story (1987)
Innocent Blood (1992)
Jagged Edge (1985)
The Marrying Man (1991)
Prizzi's Honor (1985)
Return to Me (2000)
Triumph of the Spirit (1989)
logging
do ~: 3 axe, hew, saw 5 saw up 7 saw down
Loggins: 4 Dave 5 Kenny
partner: 7 Messina
Loggins, Dave song: Please Come to Boston (1974)
Loggins, Kenny
song: Danger Zone (1986)
Don't Fight It (1982)
Footloose (1984)
Heart to Heart (1982)
I'm Alright (1980)
I'm Free (1984)
Meet Me Half Way (1987)
Nobody's Fool (1988)
This Is It (1979)
Whenever I Call You 'Friend' (1978)
logic: 5 sense 6 reason, sanity, thesis 7 linkage, thought 9 coherence, deduction, dialectic, good sense, induction, inference, rationale, reasoning, syllogism 10 connection, philosophy
apply ~: 3 see 4 muse 5 guess, infer, judge, study, think, weigh 6 assume, deduce, gather, ideate, ponder, reason, reckon 7 analyze, examine, presume, reflect, sort out, surmise, suspect 8 appraise, cogitate, conceive, conclude, consider, estimate, evaluate, mull over, perceive, ruminate, theorize 9 cerebrate, determine, figure out, speculate 10 conjecture, deliberate
for action: 6 excuse, motive, reason 7 big idea, grounds, purpose 9 rationale, reasoning 10 motivation
logic __: 4 gate 5 array 7 circuit
__ logic: 5 fuzzy 6 formal
logical: 4 fair, sane, wise 5 clear, legit, lucid, right, solid, sound, valid, water 6 cogent, kasher, kosher, likely, subtle 7 germane, holding, natural, obvious, telling, tenable 8 analytic, coherent, luculent, methodic, probable, rational, relevant, sensible, thinking 9 congruent, deducible, judicious, necessary, pertinent, plausible, pragmatic 10 analytical, compelling, consequent, consistent, convincing, defensible, discerning, legitimate, methodical, perceptive, persuasive, reasonable, scientific, systematic, thoughtful
not ~: 5 ditsy, ditzy
premise: 5 given, lemma
proposition: 5 axiom 6 if-then
starter: 3 eco, neo 4 ideo 5 neuro, patho, socio
logician: 7 casuist, sophist 8 reasoner
abbr.: 3 QED
transition: 4 ergo, then, thus 5 hence 9 therefore
loginess: 5 sloth 6 apathy, stupor, torpor 7 inertia, languor 8 dullness, lethargy 9 indolence
logjam: 5 tie-up 6 backup, pileup 7 impasse, traffic 8 blockage, deadlock, gridlock, obstacle 10 bottleneck, congestion, parking lot
logo: 2 TM 3 tag 4 mark, sign 5 brand, label 6 device, emblem, symbol 9 trademark
ender: 4 gram, type 5 graph
Logo: 8 language
alternative: 3 ADA, APL, SQL 4 Alef, html, Icon, Java, LISP, Orca, Perl 5 Algol, Basic, Cecil, COBOL, Dylan, SISAL 6 Delphi, Eiffel, Erlang, Oberon, Pascal, Prolog, Sather, Scheme, Snobol 7 Fortran
logophile love: 3 wds. 5 words
logophobe fear: 5 words
logrolling, engage in: 4 birl
logs
haul ~: 4 skid
saw ~: 3 nap 5 crash, sleep, snore, snort 6 nod off, retire, snooze, turn in 7 drop off, sack out, slumber, snuffle, zonk out 8 take a nap 9 cop some z's, hit the hay 10 hit the sack
sawing ~: 3 out 4 abed 6 asleep 8 snoozing 9 sacked out
__ Logs: 7 Lincoln
logwood: 4 tree
logy: 4 dull, idle, lazy 5 heavy, inert, thick 6 drowsy, sleepy, torpid 7 dormant, laggard, languid, passive 8 comatose, fainéant, inactive, indolent, listless, slothful, sluggish 9 apathetic, enervated, lethargic, stupefied 10 phlegmatic, slow-moving, unreactive
-logy cousin: 3 -ism
Lohani: 3 cow 4 bull 6 bovine, cattle
Lohengrin: 5 opera
bird: 4 swan
composer: 6 Wagner
role: 4 Elsa 5 Henry 6 Ortrud 9 Frederick, Gottfried
setting: 7 Antwerp, Belgium
loi: 3 law 6 French
it might pass une ~: 5 senat
loin: 4 meat, side 6 haunch
combining form: 4 lumb- 5 lumbo-

cut: 5 T-bone
ender: 5 cloth
leg and ~: 6 haunch
muscle: 5 psoas
muscles: 5 psoae, psoai
starter: 3 sir 6 tender
loincloth, Hindu: 5 dhoti, dhuti 6 dhooti 7 dhootie
Loire: 5 river
city on the ~: 5 Blois, Tours 6 Nantes 7 Orleans
locale: 6 France
river to the ~: 4 Cher 6 Allier
__-Loire: 5 Haute
Loir-et-__: 4 Cher
Loire Valley
city: 6 Le Mans
region: 5 Anjou
Lois: 4 Lane 6 Chiles 7 Maxwell 9 Nettleton
Lois & Clark (ABC sci-fi)
cast: Dean Cain (Clark Kent/Superman)
Teri Hatcher (Lois Lane)
John Shea (Lex Luthor)
Lane Smith (Perry White)
loiter: 3 lag 4 away, drag, flag, halt, idle, laze, loaf, loll, poke, slow, stay, wait 5 amble, dally, delay, hover, mosey, pause, stall, tarry, trail 6 dabble, dawdle, diddle, linger, lounge, put off, ramble, slough, stroll 7 fritter, hang out, saunter, shamble, shuffle, slacken, traipse 8 hang back, kill time, lollygag, lose time, pass time, straggle 9 lose speed, poke along, waste time 10 dillydally, hang around, mess around, wait around
loiterer: 5 idler 6 loafer, slouch, truant 7 dawdler, goof-off, laggard 8 slowpoke, sluggard 9 do-nothing, goldbrick, lazybones
loitering: 4 free, idle, lazy, slow 5 slack 7 loafing 8 indolent, slothful
loiteringly: 6 pokily 8 bit by bit 9 gradually, haltingly, languidly, leisurely 10 crawlingly, creepingly, sluggishly
Loki
Daughter of ~: 3 Hel
son of ~: 4 Nare 6 Fenrir
Lola: 4 Lane 6 Falana, Montez 8 Albright
Lola (1961 film)
cast: Anouk Aimée, Marc Michel
director: Jacques Demy
Lola (1970 song) artist: Kinks
Lolita: 4 Haze 10 Davidovich
Lolita (1962 film)
cast: Sue Lyon, James Mason, Peter Sellers, Shelley Winters
director: Stanley Kubrick
Lolita (1997 film)
cast: Melanie Griffith, Jeremy Irons, Frank Langella, Dominique Swain
director: Adrian Lyne
Lolita author: Vladimir Nabokov
loll: 3 lie, sag 4 bask, drop, flap, flop, idle, laze, loaf, rest 5 droop, relax, slump 6 dangle, dawdle, linger, loiter, lounge, repose, slouch, sprawl, wallow 7 goof off, recline 8 kick back, lallygag 9 hang loose 10 hang around, wait around
lollapalooza: 3 pip 4 lulu, oner 5 beaut, dandy, dilly, doozy
lolling: 6 at ease
lollipop: 5 candy, treat 9 sweetmeat
eat a ~: 4 lick
flavor: 5 grape, lemon 6 cherry, orange
__ Lollipop: 5 My Boy
Lollipop (1958 song) artist: Chordettes
Lollipop, Good Ship: 5 plane 8 airplane
Lollipops and __: 5 Roses
Lollobrigida, Gina: 7 actress
film: Beat the Devil (1954)
Buona Sera, Mrs. Campbell (1969)
Come September (1961)
Solomon and Sheba (1959)
Trapeze (1956)
lollop: 3 bob 4 leap 5 bound 6 lounge
lolly: 5 candy, sweet 6 bonbon 9 sweetmeat 10 confection
ender: 3 gag, pop
starter: 3 lob
lollygag: 3 lag 4 idle, laze, loaf 5 amble, dally, mosey, stall, tarry 6 linger, loiter, trifle 7 goof off, saunter 8 straggle 9 waste time 10 dillydally
Lolly Willowes author: Sylvia Warner
Lom: 7 Herbert
Loma __, CA: 5 Linda
Loma Bonita: 4 city, town
locale: 6 Mexico, Oaxaca
__ Loma, CA: 4 Alta, Mira
Loman, Willy
emulate ~: 4 sell
goal: 4 sale
son: 4 Biff 5 Happy
__ Loma Orchestra: 4 Casa
Lomas de Zamora: 4 city, town
locale: 9 Argentina
Lombard: 4 city, town 5 Alain 6 Carole, Karina, street
locale: 8 Illinois
Lombard, Carole: 7 actress
film: The Eagle and the Hawk (1933)
Hands Across the Table (1935)
In Name Only (1939)
Made for Each Other (1939)
Mr. and Mrs. Smith (1941)
My Man Godfrey (1936)
Nothing Sacred (1937)
The Princess Comes Across (1936)
They Knew What They Wanted (1940)
To Be or Not to Be (1942)
Twentieth Century (1934)
Vigil in the Night (1940)
We're Not Dressing (1934)
spouse: Clark Gable, William Powell
Lombardi, Vince: 5 coach
sport: 8 football
Lombardo: 3 Guy 6 Carmen
Lombardy
capital: 5 Milan
city: 5 Milan, Monza 6 Milano 7 Brescia
lake: 4 Como
locale: 5 Italy
Lombardy __: 6 poplar
Lomb partner: 6 Bausch
Lomé: 4 city, town 7 capital
locale: 4 Togo
lo-mein cooker: 3 wok
Lom, Herbert: 5 actor
film: Chase a Crooked Shadow (1958)
Flame Over India (1959)
Gambit (1966)
The Horse Without a Head (1963)
I Aim at the Stars (1960)
The Ladykillers (1955)
The Pink Panther Strikes Again (1976)
The Ringer (1952)
The Seventh Veil (1945)
State Secret (1950)
Lomita: 4 city, town
locale: 10 California
Lomme: 4 city, town
locale: 6 France
Lomond: 4 lake, Loch
locale: 8 Scotland
Lompoc: 4 city, town
locale: 10 California
Lon: 3 Nol 6 Chaney, Hinkle
__-Lon: 3 Ban
Lonborg, Jim: 6 hurler 7 pitcher
London: 3 Roy 4 city, Jack, port, town 5 Julie 6 Laurie 7 capital
art gallery: 4 Tate
botanical gardens: 3 Kew
district: 3 Kew 4 Soho 6 Barnet, Ealing
doctors' street: 6 Harley
emporium: 7 Harrod's
forecast: 3 fog 4 mist, rain
hotel: 5 Savoy
landmark: 5 tower 6 Big Ben
like ~ in 1666: 5 afire
locale: 3 Eng., Ont. 5 The UK 6 Canada 7 England, Ontario
one of a ~ pair: 5 Magog
park: 4 Hyde
river: 6 Thames
street: 5 Fleet
Tower of ~ once: 4 gaol 6 prison
see also England
London __: 3 Fog 5 broil, plane, Suite 6 Bridge, Fields, forces 7 Company
London Bridge locale: 4 Ariz. 7 Arizona
Londonderry: 4 city, port, town
college: 5 Magee
locale: 7 Ireland
Londonderry __: 3 Air
Londoner: 4 Brit 6 Briton
London Fields
author: 4 Amis
character: 5 Enola
London, Jack: 5 alias 6 author, writer
work: The Call of the Wild
The Iron Heel
John Barleycorn
Martin Eden
The Sea Wolf
Tales of Adventure
The Valley of the Moon
White Fang
London, Julie: 6 singer 7 actress
film: Man of the West (1958)
Saddle the Wind (1958)
The Third Voice (1960)
song: Cry Me a River (1955)
spouse: Bobby Troup, Jack Webb
TV: Emergency
London Suite author: Neil Simon
Londrina: 4 city, town
locale: 6 Brazil
lone: 3 odd, one 4 only, sole, solo, stag 6 single, unique 7 onliest 8 deserted, forsaken, isolated, secluded, separate, singular, solitary 9 abandoned, by oneself, separated 10 friendless, individual, one and only, unattended, unescorted, unexampled
ender: 4 some
lone __: 4 hand, wolf
Lone: 4 John
Lone __: 5 Canoe, Eagle
Lone __ State: 4 Star
Lone __, The: 6 Ranger
Lone Canoe author: David Mamet
Lone Eagle author: Danielle Steel
loneliest number, The: 3 one
loneliness: 5 gloom, grief 6 misery 7 anguish, despair, sadness 8 distress, solitude 9 bleakness, dejection, emptiness, heartache, isolation 10 depression, desolation, gloominess, heartbreak, melancholy
Loneliness of the Long Distance Runner: 4 film 5 novel
author: Alan Sillitoe
cast: Avis Bunnage, Tom Courtenay, Michael Redgrave
director: Tony Richardson
lonely: 4 down, left 5 apart, bleak, empty, quiet 6 remote, secret, single 7 forlorn, obscure, outcast, private, removed, retired 8 deserted, desolate, forsaken, homeless, isolated, rejected, secluded, solitary, unsocial 9 abandoned, by oneself, destitute, estranged, reclusive, renounced, withdrawn 10 friendless, unattended
combining form: 4 erem- 5 eremo-
Lonely __: 3 Boy 4 Days 5 Night 6 People, Street
Lonely __, The: 3 Guy, Man 4 Bull, Lady
Lonely Are the Brave (1962 film)
cast: Kirk Douglas, Walter Matthau, Gena Rowlands
Lonely Blue Boy (1960 song) artist: Conway Twitty
Lonely Boy (song) artist: Andrew Gold, Donny Osmond, Paul Anka
Lonely Bull, The (1962 song) artist: Herb Alpert and the Tijuana Brass
Lonely Days (1970 song) artist: Bee Gees
Lonely Guy, The (1984 film)
cast: Charles Grodin, Judith Ivey, Steve Martin
director: Arthur Hiller
Lonely Lady, The author: Harold Robbins
Lonely Man, The (1957 film)
cast: Elaine Aiken, Jack Palance, Anthony Perkins
director: Henry Levin
Lonely Night (1976 song) artist: Captain & Tennille
Lonely Ol' Night (1985 song) artist: John Cougar Mellencamp
Lonely People (1975 song) artist: America
Lonely Silver Rain, The author: John D. MacDonald
Lonely Street (1959 song) artist: Andy Williams
Lonely Teardrops (1958 song) artist: Jackie Wilson
loner: 3 shy 6 hermit, single 7 eremite, isolato, recluse 8 homebody, maverick, singular 9 anchorite, introvert, reclusive, singleton 10 stay-at-home, wallflower
Lone Ranger and Tonto: 3 duo 4 pair
Lone Ranger, The (TV western): 5 oater
attire: 4 mask
cast: Clayton Moore (The Lone Ranger)
Jay Silverheels (Tonto)
foe: 4 Bart 9 Black Bart
horse: 5 Scout 6 Silver
real name: John Reid
lonesome: 6 dreary, gloomy, lonely, remote 7 forlorn 8 deserted, desolate, homesick, isolated, secluded, solitary 9 cheerless 10 friendless
Lonesome __: 4 Dove, Town 5 Lover
Lonesome Dove author: Larry McMurtry
Lonesome George: 5 Gobel
lonesomeness: 8 solitude 9 isolation, seclusion 10 desolation, loneliness, withdrawal
Lonesome Town (1958 song) artist: Ricky Nelson
Lone Star Ranger, The author: Zane Grey
Lone Star State: 5 Texas
Lone Star Trail, The: 5 oater
Lonette: 5 McKee
Lone Wolf Spy Hunt, The (1939 film)
cast: Rita Hayworth, Ida Lupino, Warren William
long: 4 ache, itch, miss, pine, tall, want, wish, yowl 5 covet, crave, gabby, lanky, lathy, rangy, wordy, yearn 6 aspire, desire, gangly, hanker, hunger, prolix, thirst 7 diffuse, dream of, lengthy, spun-out, stringy, unterse, verbose, voluble 8 dragging, drawn-out, extended, gangling, languish, rambling, unending 9 bombastic, elon-

gated, extensive, garrulous, outspread, talkative **10** discursive, long-winded, loquacious, palaverous, protracted
ago: **4** once, past, yore **5** of old **6** erenow **8** formerly **9** in the past **10** previously
as ~ as: **5** since, while **6** whilst **7** because **9** providing
be ~: **3** lag **4** idle, last, plod, poke **5** dally, delay, hover, mosey, tarry **6** dawdle, linger, loiter, putter **7** goof off **8** hesitate, lose time **9** sit around, vacillate **10** dillydally, hang around, wait around
before ~: **4** anon, soon, then **5** after, later **6** in a bit, in time **7** by and by, later on, someday **8** hereupon, in a while, sometime **9** afterward, hereafter, presently, thereupon **10** eventually, in good time
combining form: **3** mec- **4** macr-, meco- **5** macro- **7** dolicho-
ender: **3** bow **4** boat, hair, hand, head, horn, neck, some, spur, time, wise **5** house, shore **6** haired, headed
ere ~: **8** hereupon **10** in good time
for: **4** love, miss, need, seek **5** covet, crave **6** desire
(for): **4** ache, burn, hope, itch, pant, pine, sigh, wish **5** spoil, yearn **6** hanker, starve, thirst
gone: **3** ago **4** late, over, past, yore **6** former **7** old-time, one-time **8** finished, obsolete **9** forgotten, out-of-date, preceding **10** historical, out of style
green: **3** oof **4** cash, gelt, jack, kail, kale, loot, peag, pelf **5** bills, bread, bucks, dough, funds, lucre, money, moola, mopus, pesos, rhino, sewan **6** dinero, do-re-mi, mammon, mazuma, moolah, seawan, silver, specie, wampum, wealth **7** cabbage, capital, dollars, lettuce, ooftish, scratch, shekels **8** bankroll, cold cash, currency, hard cash, smackers **9** banknotes, frogskins, simoleons
haul: **4** hadj, hike, trek, trip **5** fight, march, tramp **6** battle **7** journey, odyssey **8** struggle **10** expedition, pilgrimage
in for the ~ haul: **6** stable **7** abiding, durable **8** enduring **9** permanent, unabating
in Hawaiian: **3** loa
in the ~ run: **7** finally, overall **8** after all **10** eventually, ultimately
in the tooth: **3** old **4** aged **5** aging, hoary **6** ageing **7** ancient, elderly, wizened **8** grizzled **9** geriatric, getting on, senescent, up in years
jump: **5** event **7** contest
look: **4** gaze **5** stare
look too ~: **4** ogle **5** stare
not ~: **5** brief, pithy, short, terse **6** stubby **7** briefly, concise, cursory, hurried, laconic, summary **8** abridged, sawed-off, succinct **9** condensed, truncated **10** boiled down, short-lived
not ~ ago: **5** newly **6** lately **8** latterly, recently **9** yesterday
not by a ~ shot: **4** uh-uh **5** ixnay, no how **7** I refuse **8** forget it **9** fat chance, I think not **10** count me out, not a chance, thumbs down
of ~ standing: **3** old **5** early, hoary **6** age-old, senior **7** ancient, lasting, vintage **8** enduring **9** perennial, venerable **10** immemorial
row to hoe: **5** grind **6** burden
shot: **3** bet **4** risk **5** fluke, flyer, wager **6** chance, gamble, toss-up **7** venture **9** adventure, dark horse
so ~: **3** bye **4** ciao, ta-ta **5** adieu, adios, aloha, later, peace, see ya **6** bye-bye, shalom, sholom **7** cheerio, goodbye **8** au revoir, farewell, sayonara, toodle-oo
starter: **3** day, end, ere, pro **4** foot, head, hour, life, live, side, year **5** night **6** decade **7** century
suit: **5** forte
take too ~: **5** run on
the ~ and short of it: **4** core, crux, gist, pith **5** heart **6** kernel
time: **3** age, eon **4** aeon **5** years **7** century, decades
(to): **6** aspire
trip: **4** trek **7** journey, sojourn **10** pilgrimage
very ~ term: **6** eonian
very ~ time: **3** age, eon **4** aeon, ages **7** century
walk: **4** hike, trek **5** jaunt **6** ramble **7** journey **10** expedition
way: **3** far **6** far cry, far off
way around: **6** bypass, detour
wear a ~ face: **4** ache, fret, idle, moon, mope, pine, pout, sulk **5** brood, droop, gripe, scowl **6** grieve, grouse, lament **8** be silent **9** lose heart
wearing a ~ face: **3** low, sad **4** blue, dark, dour, down, glum, grim, mopy **5** moody, mopey, sulky, surly **6** crabby, dismal, gloomy, morose, sullen **8** dejected, downcast **9** bummed-out, depressed **10** despondent, dispirited, melancholy
long __: **3** ago, ess, one, run, tom, ton **4** bone, card, clam, face, game, haul, horn, iron, jump, moss, play, shot, suit, wave **5** dozen, green, horse, house, johns, meter, rifle **6** barrow, jumper, primer, splice **7** account, gallery, measure
long __ no see: **4** time
long __ of the law: **3** arm
long __ to hoe: **3** row
long __ tooth: **5** in the
long-__: **3** day, run **4** haul, term, time **5** chain, faced, lived, range **6** acting, headed, limbed, winded **7** lasting, sighted, tongued, waisted
long-__ memory: **4** term
long-__-out: **5** drawn
long-__ rose: **7** stemmed
long.
opposite: **3** lat.
__ long: **6** before
__ long...: **5** Art is
Long: **3** Nia **4** Huey, isle **6** island, Shorty **7** Richard, Shelley
successor on Cheers: **5** Alley
Long __: **5** Beach, March **6** Branch, Island
Long __ and Far Away: **3** Ago
Long __ Home, The: **4** Road, Walk **6** Voyage
Long __ Journey into Night: **4** Day's
Long __ Line, The: **4** Gray
Long __ Sally: **4** Tall
Long __ Silver: **4** John
Long __ Sound: **6** Island
Long __ Summer, The: **3** Hot
Long __, The: **3** Run **5** March **6** Riders **7** Goodbye
Long __ wave...: **5** may it
__ Longa: **4** Alba
longan: **4** tree **9** evergreen
relative: **4** akee **5** genip **6** lichee, litchi **7** genipap, leechee **9** soapberry
long and the __ of it, the: **5** short
Long and Winding Road, The (1970 song) artist: Beatles
long-answer exam: **5** essay
long-armed entity: **3** law
__ longa, vita brevis: **3** ars
Long Beach: **4** city, port, town
locale: **7** New York **10** California
Longboat __: **3** Key
longbow
ammo: **5** arrow
sound: **5** twang
user: **6** archer **9** Robin Hood
wood: **3** yew
Long Branch: **4** city, town
locale: **9** New Jersey
Long Branch, New Jersey artist: **5** Homer
long-case __: **5** clock
Long Cool Woman (1972 song) artist: Hollies
Long Day's Journey Into Night: **4** film, play
author: Eugene O'Neill
cast: Katharine Hepburn, Ralph Richardson, Jason Robards, Dean Stockwell
director: Sidney Lumet
Long Day Wanes, The author: Anthony Burgess
long-delayed: **4** slow
long-distance
cost: **4** toll
letters: **3** MCI
long-drawn-out: **4** slow **5** windy, wordy **6** boring, prolix **7** lengthy, tedious, verbose
long-eared beast: **3** ass **4** hare **5** burro **6** basset
longer: **4** more **8** expanded, extended **9** augmented **10** additional
make ~: **3** pad **5** add to **6** extend, let out **7** augment, drag out, draw out, prolong, spin out, stretch **8** continue, elongate, increase, lengthen, protract **9** string out
no ~ hungry: **5** sated **6** gorged **7** glutted, stuffed **8** satiated **9** surfeited
no ~ in use: **3** out **4** gone **5** dated, dusty, moldy, musty, passé, stale **6** old-hat **7** archaic, outworn **8** outdated, outmoded, timeworn **9** discarded, moth-eaten, out-of-date **10** antiquated, superseded
no ~ qualified: **5** stale **10** out of shape
no ~ used: **3** obs., old, out **5** dated, passé **6** bygone, old hat, square **7** archaic, outworn **8** obsolete, outdated, outmoded, timeworn **10** antiquated, out of style
of ~ standing: **5** elder, older **6** senior
__ longer: **3** any
Longer (1980 song) artist: Dan Fogelberg
Longest __, The: **3** Day **4** Time, Walk, Yard
long-established: **3** old
Longest Day, The: **4** film **5** novel
author: Cornelius Ryan
cast: Eddie Albert, Paul Anka, Richard Burton, Red Buttons, Sean Connery, Mel Ferrer, Henry Fonda, Peter Lawford, Roddy McDowall, Sal Mineo, Robert Mitchum, Robert Ryan, Rod Steiger, John Wayne
director: Ken Annakin, Andrew Marton, Bernhard Wicki
extras: **3** GIs
setting: **4** Caen, WWII **6** France
singer: **4** Anka **8** Paul Anka
Longest Time, The (1984 song) artist: Billy Joel
Longest Walk, The (1955 song) artist: Jaye P. Morgan
Longest Yard, The (1974 film)
cast: Eddie Albert, Ed Lauter, Burt Reynolds
director: Robert Aldrich
Longet: **8** Claudine
longevity: **4** legs, life, span **6** tenure **8** duration **9** endurance **10** durability
long-faced: **3** sad **4** mopy **5** mopey **7** hangdog, unhappy **8** lowering **9** woebegone
one: **5** moper
Longfellow: **5** Deeds
Longfellow, Henry Wadsworth: **4** poet
character: **5** Alden **9** Priscilla
work: Azrael
Ballads and Other Poems
The Children's Hour
The Courtship of Miles Standish
Evangeline
The Golden Legend
Hiawatha
Hyperion
O Ship of State
Paul Revere's Ride
The Song of Hiawatha
Tales of a Wayside Inn
The Village Blacksmith
Voices of the Night
The Wreck of the Hesperus
Longfellow Serenade (1974 song) artist: Neil Diamond
Long Goodbye, The author: Raymond Chandler
Long Good Friday, The (1981 film)
cast: Eddie Constantine, Bob Hoskins, Helen Mirren
Long Gray Line, The (1955 film)
cast: Robert Francis, Maureen O'Hara, Tyrone Power
director: John Ford
longhair: **3** cat **5** brain, felid, hippy **6** feline, genius, hippie **7** beatnik, bookish, egghead, erudite, esthete, scholar **8** aesthete, cerebral, highbrow **9** professor, scholarly
long-haired: **6** shaggy **7** hirsute, unshorn
longhairs: **8** academes, literati, scholars **9** aesthetes, highbrows **10** illuminati
longhand: **5** diary **6** letter, scrawl, script **7** writing **8** scribble **9** autograph, signature **10** penmanship
__ Long Has This Been Going On?: **3** How
longheaded: **4** keen, wise **6** astute, shrewd **7** prudent **8** cautious, discreet, watchful **9** astucious, farseeing
longhorn: **5** steer **6** cattle, cheese
__ longhorn: **5** Texas
long-horned __: **6** beetle
Longhorn rival: **5** Aggie
Long Hot Summer, The (1958 film)
cast: Tony Franciosa, Paul Newman, Joanne Woodward
director: Martin Ritt
Longines: **5** watch **10** wristwatch
alternative: **4** Ebel, Rado **5** Casio, Elgin, Lorus, Omega, Rolex, Seiko, Timex **6** Bulova, Fossil, Movado, Pulsar, Swatch **7** Citizen **8** Tag Heuer, Tourneau
longing: **3** yen **4** avid, hope, itch, need, urge, want, will, wish **5** eager, itchy **6** ardent, desire, hunger, hungry, pining, thirst **7** anxious, athirst, craving, wishful, wistful **8** ambition, appetite, coveting, cupidity, desirous, ravenous, yearning **9** appetence, eagerness, hankering, hungering **10** aspiration
feeling: **4** ache, pang **5** throb **6** regret **7** craving **9** hankering
one ~: **5** piner
sound: **3** sob **4** sigh
longingly, look: **4** gaze

long in the ___: 5 tooth
Longinus: 5 Greek 11 philosopher
Long Island: 3 snd. 5 sound
airport: 5 Islip 9 MacArthur
campus: 6 C.W. Post 7 Adelphi, Hofstra
newspaper: 7 Newsday
town: 5 Islip, Upton 6 Elmont 7 Merrick, Montauk, Seaford, Wantagh 8 Bellmore, Freeport 10 Massapequa
Long Island Sound
city: 3 Rye 6 Darien 8 Stamford
river to ~: 10 Housatonic
Long Island University
athletes: 10 Blackbirds
locale: 7 New York 8 Brooklyn
longitude: 6 length
line of ~: 8 meridian
unit: 6 degree, minute, second
zero ~ setting: 3 GMT, GST
longitudinal ___: 4 wave 7 framing, section
Long John Silver: 6 pirate
long jumper: 5 Lewis 6 Beamon
long-lasting: 3 old 5 solid, sound 6 aeonic, eonian, rugged, strong, sturdy 7 durable 8 lifelong, well-made 9 permanent, well-built
longleaf: 4 pine 7 conifer 9 evergreen
Long-Legged Fly author: William Butler Yeats
___ Long Legs: 5 Daddy
longlegs, daddy: 3 bug 6 insect
long-limbed: 4 tall 5 leggy, rangy 6 gangly 7 willowy 8 gangling
long-lived: 3 old 7 durable, lasting 8 enduring 10 inveterate
Long, Long ___: 3 Ago
long, long way to run, A: 3 far
Long March
leader: 3 Mao 10 Mao Tse-Tung
site: 5 China
Long March, The author: William Styron
Longmont: 4 city, town
locale: 8 Colorado
long-neck ___: 4 clam
Long, Nia: 7 actress
film: The Best Man (1999)
The Boiler Room (2000)
Boyz N the Hood (1991)
The Broken Hearts Club - A Romantic Comedy (2000)
In Too Deep (1999)
long-playing ___: 6 record
Long Riders, The (1980 film)
cast: David Carradine, Keith Carradine, Robert Carradine
director: Walter Hill
Long Road Home, The author: Danielle Steel
long row ___: 5 to hoe
___ long run: 5 in the
long-running combining form: 5 -athon
Long Run, The (1979 song) artist: Eagles
Longs ___: 4 Peak
long-serving: 7 veteran 8 seasoned 9 exercised, practiced
Long, Shelley: 7 actress
film: The Brady Bunch Movie (1995)
Caveman (1981)
Hello Again (1987)
Irreconcilable Differences (1984)
The Money Pit (1986)
Night Shift (1982)
Outrageous Fortune (1987)
Troop Beverly Hills (1989)
TV: Cheers
longshoreman: 5 lader 9 stevedore
device: 5 davit
org.: 3 ILA
longshot: 8 underdog
___ long shot: 3 by a
Longshot author: Dick Francis
longspur: 4 bird
longstanding: 6 rooted 7 chronic, lasting 9 chronical
long-stemmed ___: 4 rose
Longstocking: 5 Pippi
long-suffering: 4 meek, mild 5 stoic 7 passive, patient, stoical 8 patience, resigned, tolerant 9 forgiving
one: 3 Job 5 saint
Long Tall Glasses (1975 song) artist: Leo Sayer
Long Tall Sally (1956 song)
artist: Little Richard, Pat Boone
long-term: 6 stable 7 chronic, lasting 8 enduring 9 perennial, permanent, perpetual 10 continuing, unchanging
long-term ___: 6 memory
longtime: 7 veteran 10 deep-seated
___ long time: 5 last a
Long time ___!: 5 no see
Longtime Companion (1990 film)
cast: Stephen Caffrey, Patrick Cassidy, Brian Cousins
director: Norman René
Long Train Runnin' (1973 song) artist: Doobie Brothers
___ longue: 6 chaise
Longueuil: 4 city, town
locale: 6 Canada, Québec
Longview: 4 city, town
locale: 5 Texas 10 Washington
Long Voyage Home, The: 4 film, play
author: Eugene O'Neill
cast: Ian Hunter, Thomas Mitchell, John Wayne
director: John Ford
Long Walk Home, The (1990 film)
cast: Whoopi Goldberg, Sissy Spacek
director: Richard Pearce
___ long way: 3 go a
___ Long Way to Tipperary: 4 It's a
long-winded: 4 long 5 gabby, talky, windy, wordy 6 chatty, prolix 7 diffuse, lengthy, unterse, verbose, voluble 8 rambling 9 bombastic, garrulous, ponderous, redundant, talkative 10 bigmouthed, euphuistic, loquacious, palaverous
one: 4 bore, drag, pain, pest, pill 6 gasbag 8 nuisance
___ long, with many..., The: 6 road is
Loni: 8 Anderson
Lonigan: 5 Studs
Lonnie: 4 Mack 7 Donegan
loo: 2 WC 3 can, lav 4 bath, game, john 5 privy 6 lounge, toilet 7 latrine 8 bathroom, card game, lavatory, men's room, outhouse, rest room, toilette 10 ladies' room, powder room
looby: 3 ass, lug, oaf 4 boor, clod, dolt, fool, hick, jerk, lout, rube, yo-yo 5 booby, chump, churl, dummy, dunce, klutz, ninny, yahoo, yokel 6 duffer, lubber, lummox, nitwit 7 bumbler, bumpkin, bungler, dullard, fathead, fumbler, hayseed, jackass 8 dumbbell, lardhead, lunkhead, meathead 9 birdbrain, blockhead, blunderer, ding-a-ling, schlemiel, simpleton 10 dunderhead, stumblebum
loofah: 6 sponge
looie: 7 officer
subordinate: 3 NCO, PFC, pvt., sgt. 4 corp. 7 private 8 corporal, sergeant
superior: 3 col, gen., maj. 4 capt. 5 lt. col., major 7 captain, colonel, general
look: 3 air, eye, mug, see, spy 4 case, cast, face, gape, gawk, gaze, heed, hope, hunt, leer, mark, mien, mind, mode, note, ogle, peek, peep, peer, read, scan, seek, show, spot, tend, view 5 await, flash, focus, front, guise, scout, shape, sight, slant, sound, stare, study, trend, watch 6 admire, appear, aspect, attend, behold, beware, browse, divine, effect, expect, format, gander, glance, glower, goggle, manner, notice, regard, review, search, squint, survey, swivel, visage 7 bearing, count on, display, evil eye, exhibit, express, fashion, front on, glimpse, inspect, marking, observe, present, seeming, viewing 8 demeanor, evidence, forecast, foretell, give onto, indicate, manifest, noticing, once-over, pore over, presence, reckon on, resemble, scrutiny, seem to be, strike as 9 attention, beholding, count upon, make clear, regarding, semblance 10 anticipate, appearance, complexion, expression, get a load of, inspection, rubberneck, scrutinize
after: 3 run 4 keep, mind, tend 5 guard, nurse, see to, serve, watch 6 advert, attend, defend, tend to 7 baby-sit, care for, oversee, protect, provide, sit with 8 keep safe, maintain, shepherd 9 accompany, safeguard, supervise 10 take care of
ahead: 4 plan
alike: 5 match
amused: 10 be gracious
angry ~: 5 frown, glare, scowl, snarl, sneer
another ~: 6 review
around: 6 browse
as if: 4 seem 6 appear
askance: 6 squint
at: 3 eye, see 4 case, ogle, view 5 assay, gauge, probe, scout, try on, watch 6 advert, assess, behold, peruse, regard, size up, survey, verify 7 confirm, examine, focus on, inspect, observe, qualify 8 appraise, check out, consider, evaluate, follow up 9 flirt with 10 get a load of, scrutinize
at again: 5 resee
awestruck: 4 gape, gawk, gaze 5 stare 6 goggle, marvel
back: 4 muse 5 brood 6 ponder, recall, regret, review 7 reflect 8 dredge up, mull over, remember, ruminate 9 recollect, reminisce
brief ~: 4 peek, peep
closely: 3 eye, fix, spy 4 bore, gape, gawk, gaze, leer, ogle, peer 5 focus, rivet, stare, watch 6 appear, goggle, marvel 7 eyeball, inspect, ransack 10 get a load of, rubberneck, scrutinize
coldly upon: 4 snub
cross-eyed: 6 squint
daggers: 4 rage 5 glare, scowl, sneer 6 glower 8 threaten
dejected: 4 mope, pout
down on: 5 abhor, scorn, scout, sneer, spurn 6 jibe at 7 contemn, despise, disdain, sneer at, sniff at 9 patronize 10 depreciate, disapprove
everywhere: 4 comb, hunt, rake, seek, sift, sort 5 flush, probe, scour, sweep 6 forage, search 7 examine, inspect, ransack, rummage 9 ferret out, track down
favorably (on): 5 smile
fixed ~: 4 gaze 5 stare
for: 3 spy 4 hope, hunt, seek, shop, wait 5 await, watch 6 expect, forage, search 7 count on, prepare, require, scout up 8 scout out 9 cast about, count upon 10 anticipate
forbidding ~: 5 glare 6 glower
forward to: 4 wait 5 await 6 expect 8 envision, see ahead, watch for
good ~: 6 eyeful
good on: 3 fit 4 suit 6 become 7 flatter 10 go together
happy: 4 beam, grin 5 smile
hard: 4 gape, gawk, gaze 5 focus, glare, rivet, stare 7 eyeball
have a ~ at: 4 scan, view 5 study 6 browse, peruse, regard, survey 7 observe 8 pore over
healthy ~: 4 glow 7 sparkle 9 freshness
high and low: 4 hunt, seek 5 scour 6 search 7 ransack, rummage
impolite ~: 4 leer, ogle 5 sneer, stare
in Latin: 4 ecce
in on: 4 call 5 visit, watch
insulting ~: 4 gibe 5 smirk 7 snigger
intense ~: 3 eye 4 gaze, leer, peer 5 glare, stare
into: 3 dig 4 sift 5 audit, check, delve, probe, study 7 enquire, examine, explore, inquire, inspect, ransack 8 check out, follow up, prospect, research, see about 9 delve into 10 scrutinize
(into): 2 go 5 delve
in your eye: 3 ray 4 beam 5 gleam, glint, spark 6 glance 7 glimmer, glisten, sparkle, twinkle
knowing ~: 4 ogle 5 smirk, sneer
lewd ~: 4 ogle 5 smirk
like: 4 look, seem 5 mimic 6 appear 7 smack of 8 resemble
listlessly: 4 moon
long ~: 5 stare
lovely to ~ at: 6 comely, pretty 8 gorgeous, handsome 9 beautiful 10 attractive, enchanting
of loathing: 5 frown, glare 6 glower 7 grimace
on: 4 deem, view 5 judge, treat 6 regard 7 witness 8 consider, perceive 9 think of as
out: 3 peg, spy 4 mind, spot 5 scope 6 beware, be wary, listen, notice, size up 7 heads up, hearken, watch it 8 keep tabs, pick up on 9 be careful, be on guard, have a care
out on to: 5 front
over: 4 case, pore, read, scan 5 check 6 peruse, survey 7 examine, inspect, monitor, proctor 8 appraise, check out, evaluate, look into 10 run through, scrutinize, zip through
quick ~: 4 peek, peep 6 aperçu
right through: 3 cut 4 shun, snub 5 spurn 6 ignore, insult, rebuff, slight 7 disdain, put down, tune out 8 brush off 9 blackball, disregard, humiliate, ostracize
second ~: 6 replay, review
smug ~: 4 grin, leer 5 smirk, sneer 6 simper
sneak a ~: 3 pry, see, spy 4 peek, peep, peer 5 snoop 6 glance 7 glimpse 10 get a load of
sullen: 4 lour, pout, sulk 5 scowl
take another ~: 5 audit, check, resee, weigh 6 assess, go over, rehash, review, survey 7 analyze, examine, inspect, revisit 8 appraise, critique, evaluate, reassess 9 reexamine, think over 10 reconsider, reevaluate, run through, scrutinize
take a quick ~: 4 leaf, scan, skim 5 check 6 browse, riffle, size up, survey 7 monitor 10 glance over, run through
the joint over: 4 case
the other way: 6 ignore 7 neglect 8 overlook

to: 2 do 5 avail, trust 6 accept, assume, attend, bank on, rely on, resort 7 believe, consult, count on 8 depend on 9 count upon, make use of 10 fall back on
too long: 4 ogle 5 stare
toward: 4 face 7 eyeball 8 confront 9 front onto
unauthorized ~: 4 peep
up: 4 find, gain, mend, scan, seek 5 refer, visit 6 peruse 7 advance, confirm, go to see, hunt for, improve, seek out 8 come upon, discover, progress, research 9 come along, get better, reference, search for, track down 10 ameliorate, convalesce, recuperate
upon: 3 eye, see 4 deem, gaze, take, view 5 count, judge, opine, think, treat 6 reckon, regard, survey 8 consider 9 think of as
up to: 5 adore, defer, honor, rever 6 admire, esteem, revere 7 idolize, lionize, respect, worship 8 venerate 9 reverence
well on: 4 suit 7 enhance, flatter
look __: 3 for, out 4 in on, into, over, upon, up to 5 after, alive, sharp 7 through
look __ at: 7 daggers
look __ on: 4 down
look __ to: 7 forward
look __ you leap: 6 before
look-__: 3 see 5 alike
__ look: 3 new 5 dirty
...look __ like Christmas: 4 a lot
Look __!: 4 at me 5 alive
Look __ dancing!: 4 Ma I'm
Look __ hands!: 4 Ma no
Look __, I'm as helpless...: 4 at me
Look __, I'm Sandra Dee: 4 at Me
Look __ in Anger: 4 Back
Look __ Talking: 4 Who's
Look __ the Silver Lining: 3 for
Look __ this way...: 4 at it
Look __ ye leap: 3 Ere
look-alike: 4 copy, twin 5 clone, match 6 double, ectype, ringer 7 picture, replica, stand-in 9 duplicate, facsimile, identical 10 carbon copy, dead ringer, similarity
maybe: 4 fake, lure 5 decoy
look and __: 3 see 4 feel
Look at __ Sandra Dee: 4 Me I'm
Look at me!: 4 ta-da 5 ta-dah
Look Away (1988 song) artist: Chicago
__ Look Back: 4 Don't
Look Back in Anger: 4 film, play
author: John Osborne
cast: Claire Bloom, Richard Burton
character: 5 Cliff 6 Alison, Helena 7 Redfern
director: Tony Richardson
look before you __: 4 leap
look down one's __ at: 4 nose
looker: 3 fox 4 dish, doll, hunk 5 belle, ogler, peach 6 Apollo, beauty, eyeful, vision 7 goddess, picture, stunner, witness 8 knockout, observer, passerby 9 spectator, sightseer 10 eyewitness
looker-on: 7 witness 9 spectator 10 eyewitness
Look for the Silver Lining composer: 4 Kern 7 De Sylva
Look Homeward, Angel
author: Thomas Wolfe
character: 3 Ben 4 Gant, Luke 5 Eliza, Laura, Steve 6 Eugene, Oliver
Lookin' __ Back Door: 5 Out My
Lookin' at Me (1998 song)
artist: Mase, Puff Daddy
Lookin' for Love (1980 song) artist: Johnny Lee
looking __: 5 glass
__-looking: 4 good 5 solid 7 forward
Looking __ Goodbar: 5 for Mr.
__ looking at you, kid: 5 Here's
Looking Back (1958 song) artist: Nat King Cole
looking backward in heraldry: 9 regardant
looking combining form: 6 -scopic
Looking for a New Love (1987 song) artist: Jody Watley
Looking for Mr. Goodbar: 4 film 5 novel
author: Judith Rossner
cast: William Atherton, Richard Gere, Diane Keaton, Tuesday Weld
director: Richard Brooks
Looking Glass girl: 5 Alice
Looking Glass song: Brandy (1972)
Looking-Glass War, The author: John le Carré
Looking Through the Eyes of Love (1965 song) artist: Gene Pitney
Looking Through Your Eyes (1998 song) artist: LeAnn Rimes
Lookinland: 4 Mike
Look in My Eyes Pretty Woman (1975 song) artist: Tony Orlando & Dawn
Lookin' Out My Back Door (1970 song) artist: Creedence Clearwater Revival
...look into the __ of time...: 5 seeds
__ Look Into You Eyes: 5 When I
Look Look author: Michael Frayn
Look, Ma, no __!: 5 hands
Look Ma! toothpaste: 5 Crest
__, Look Me Over: 3 Hey
__ look now: 4 Don't
Look of Love, The (1968 song) artist: Sergio Mendes & Brasil '66
lookout: 3 spy, tip 4 case, hawk, post, view, ward 5 guard, scene, scout, tower, vigil, watch 6 anchor, beacon, cupola, patrol, picket, sentry 7 citadel, spotter, station, watcher 8 eagle eye, panorama, sentinel 9 belvedere, crow's nest, vigilance 10 gatekeeper, observance, watchtower, weather eye
be a ~: 3 aid 4 abet, help 6 assist 7 collude
on the ~: 4 wary 5 alert 7 wakeful 8 cautious, keen-eyed, vigilant, watchful 9 wide-awake
Lookout: 4 cape
locale: 4 N. Car.
Look out __!: 5 below
__ looks: 4 good
look-see: 4 peek, peep, view 5 recon 6 glance 7 glimpse 10 inspection
looks, good: 4 plus 5 class 7 glamour 8 elegance 9 advantage 10 loveliness
Looks Like We Made It (1977 song) artist: Barry Manilow
Look, up in the __!: 3 sky
Look What They've Done to My Song Ma (1970 song) artist: New Seekers
Look What You Done for Me (1972 song) artist: Al Green
Look Who's Talking (1989 film)
cast: Kirstie Alley, Olympia Dukakis, John Travolta
director: Amy Heckerling
loom: 4 hulk, near, rise 5 hover, tower 6 appear, emerge, fade in, gather, impend, impose, menace 7 overtop, portend 8 dominate, hang over, overhang, stand out, threaten 9 take shape 10 overshadow
made on a ~: 4 wove 5 woven
over: 8 dominate 10 tower above
(over): 5 tower
part: 4 slay, sley 5 dobby 6 heddle, sleigh
starter: 4 heir 5 broad
up: 5 arise 6 appear, emerge 7 surface 8 approach, threaten
use a ~: 4 knit, spin 5 weave 9 fabricate
__ loom: 3 box 5 dobby, floor, inkle 7 treadle
looming: 4 near, nigh 8 imminent, lowering, menacing, oncoming, upcoming 9 impending, in the wind
loon: 4 bird, fool, zany 5 diver 6 maniac 7 jackass 8 crackpot 9 harebrain
move like a ~: 3 fly 4 dive 5 swoop 6 plunge 7 plummet 9 sweep down
relative: 5 grebe
Looney Tunes character: 3 Taz 4 Bugs, Fudd, Pepe 5 Daffy, Elmer, Le Pew, Porky, Wile E. 6 Coyote, Tweety 8 Porky Pig 9 Bugs Bunny, Daffy Duck, Elmer Fudd, Pepe Le Pew, Sylvester 10 Road Runner
Loon Lake author: E.L. Doctorow
loop: 3 arc, bow, lap 4 arch, bend, coil, curl, flex, gird, hank, hoop, kink, knot, link, purl, ring, roll, turn, wind 5 crook, curve, noose, picot, twine, twirl, twist, whorl 6 circle, eyelet, girdle, league, spiral, wreath 7 circuit, compass, scallop, scollop, sinuate 8 encircle 9 encompass, enwreathe, sinuosity 10 wind around
anatomical ~: 4 ansa
embroidery ~: 5 picot
ender: 4 hole
keep in the ~: 4 tell, warn 5 brief 6 advise, fill in, inform, notify, tip off 7 apprise, apprize 8 forewarn 9 enlighten
knock for a ~: 3 awe, wow 4 faze, jolt, stun, wham 5 amaze, floor
needlework ~: 5 bride
rope ~: 5 bight, noose, snare
loop __: 4 back, knot 6 stitch, window
loop-__-loop: 3 the
__ loop: 3 toe 5 in the 6 closed, ground, Henle's, inside, Varley 7 outside
Loop
initials: 3 CTA
trains: 3 els
looped: 5 round 6 coiled 9 connected 10 continuous
looper: 3 bug, fly 6 insect, pop fly
loophole: 3 out 6 device, escape, outlet, way out
looping: 5 curly 6 coiled 7 winding
__ loop jump: 3 tap, toe
__ Loops: 5 Froot
loopy: 4 daft, gaga 5 dotty 7 offbeat 9 befuddled, eccentric 10 off-the-wall
not ~: 4 sane 6 normal 8 all there, balanced, rational, together
Loos: 4 city, town 5 Anita
locale: 6 France
Loos, Anita: 6 author, writer
work: But Gentlemen Marry Brunettes
Gentlemen Prefer Blondes
Gigi
A Girl Like I
Kiss Hollywood Goodby
The Talmadge Girls
This Brunette Prefers Work
The Women
loose: 3 lax 4 ease, easy, emit, fast, free, kind, limp, mild, soft, undo, wide 5 apart, baggy, let go, light, relax, roomy, slack, unbar, unfix, unpin, untie, vague 6 at ease, casual, detach, flabby, gentle, kindly, let out, limber, lissom, rakish, redeem, remiss, sloppy, unbind, unbolt, undone, unhand, unhook, unlace, unlash, unlock, unsnap, untied, unwind, wabbly, wanton, wobbly 7 asunder, at large, break up, clement, corrupt, deliver, diffuse, disjoin, ease off, escaped, flaccid, general, hanging, immoral, liberal, lissome, manumit, movable, naughty, powdery, relaxed, release, ruthful, set free, slacken, sparing, unbound, uncaged, unchain, unclasp, unhitch, unlatch, unleash, unscrew, unstick, unstrap, untwine 8 careless, detached, flexible, floating, heedless, informal, laid-back, liberate, loosened, merciful, mitigate, moveable, on the lam, placable, rambling, released, separate, slipshod, slovenly, swinging, tolerant, unbolted, unbuckle, unbutton, unchaste, uncurbed, unfasten, unfetter, unhinged, unhooked, unlocked, unpinned, unstrict, work free 9 abandoned, alleviate, assuasive, compliant, corrupted, debauched, discharge, disengage, dissolute, easygoing, extricate, forgiving, haphazard, imprecise, imprudent, indulgent, liberated, negligent, slackened, unclasped, unheedful, unlatched, unleashed, unplanned, unscrewed, unsecured, untighten, work loose 10 disconnect, disjointed, dissipated, emancipate, forbearing, ill-defined, ill-fitting, immoderate, indefinite, licentious, nonchalant, on the prowl, permissive, profligate, unattached, unbuttoned, unconfined, unexacting, unfastened, unfettered, unpackaged, unrigorous, unshackled, unspecific
at ~ ends: 6 adrift 8 dallying, drifting, wavering 9 uncertain, unsettled
break ~: 4 bail, flee 6 escape, run off 7 get away
cut ~: 4 free 5 let go, revel, untie 6 escape, unbind, untied 7 abandon, manumit, release, run wild 9 disengage
end: 6 detail, nicety 7 minutia 9 punctilio
fast and ~: 4 rash, wild 5 hasty 6 amoral, unruly, unwise 7 corrupt, immoral 8 careless, feckless, headlong, heedless, reckless 9 corrupted, foolhardy, imprudent, negligent 10 incautious, indiscreet
hang ~: 3 sag 4 flap, flop, idle, loaf, rest 5 droop, relax 6 dangle, lounge
hanging ~: 6 at ease 7 relaxed 8 carefree, composed, tranquil
in Britain: 5 lowse
knock ~: 4 bump 5 budge 8 dislodge, shake off 9 dislocate
let ~: 4 free, play, yell 5 shout, unpen, unpin, untie 6 bellow, unbind, untied 8 liberate
on the ~: 4 fled, free 5 flown 6 untied 7 at large, escaped, runaway 8 scot-free 10 unconfined
partner: 4 fast
set ~: 6 untied 9 liberated
starter: 4 foot
tie up ~ ends: 6 finish, wind up, wrap up 8 complete, finalize
loose __: 4 ends 6 cannon
loose __ goose: 3 as a
loose-__: 4 leaf 6 footed, limbed 7 fitting, jointed, tongued
__ loose: 3 cut, let 4 hang, stay, turn 5 break, on the
Loose __ sink ships: 4 lips
__ Loose: 6 Bustin'
loose as a __: 5 goose
loose-fitting: 4 wide 5 baggy 6 droopy, floppy 7 sagging 9 shapeless
loose-leaf: 6 binder
divider: 3 tab
loose-limbed: 4 spry 5 agile, lithe 6 limber, nimble, supple 7 lissome
loose-lipped: 5 gabby, talky, windy, wordy 6 blabby, chatty, mouthy, prolix 7 gossipy, verbose, voluble 8 effusive

9 expansive, garrulous, talkative 10 bigmouthed, long-winded, loquacious
loosen: 4 ease, free, thaw, undo 5 let go, ravel, relax, slack, unbar, unfix, unpeg, unpin, untie, unzip 6 detach, ease up, let out, unbind, unbolt, unfold, unhook, unlace, unlash, unlock, unsnap, unwind 7 break up, deliver, disjoin, ease off, get soft, manumit, release, set free, slacken, tear off, unchain, uncinch, unclasp, unhitch, unlatch, unleash, unravel, unscrew, unstick, unstrap 8 liberate, mitigate, separate, unbuckle, unbutton, unfasten, work free 9 alleviate, discharge, disengage, extricate, unshackle, untighten 10 disconnect, emancipate, liberalize
forcibly: 3 pry 4 tear 5 wrest 6 wrench
one's grip: 4 free 6 unhand 7 release, set free 9 disengage
one's hold: 4 free 5 untie 6 let off 7 release, set free 9 disengage
up: 5 relax 6 relent, unwind 8 calm down 10 take a break, take it easy
looseness: 4 give, vice 6 laxity 7 abandon, license, neglect 8 disorder, venality, wildness 10 corruption
combining form: 3 lyo-
loosestrife tree: 5 henna
loosey-goosey: 6 at ease
loot: 3 oof, rob 4 cash, gelt, haul, jack, kail, kale, lift, peag, pelf, raid, sack, take 5 bills, boost, booty, bread, bucks, dough, funds, goods, graft, lucre, money, moola, mopus, pesos, prize, rhino, rifle, sewan, steal, swipe 6 bounty, bundle, dinero, do-re-mi, harrow, invade, mammon, maraud, mazuma, moolah, prizes, ravage, rip off, seawan, silver, snatch, snitch, specie, spoils, thieve, wampum, wealth 7 cabbage, capital, despoil, dollars, jobbery, lettuce, ooftish, pillage, plunder, ransack, relieve, salvage, scratch, seizure, shekels, stick up 8 bankroll, cold cash, currency, embezzle, freeboot, hard cash, hot goods, liberate, pickings, smackers 9 banknotes, depredate, frogskins, long green, simoleons 10 burglarize, greenbacks, green stuff
hidden ~: 5 cache, hoard, stash 8 treasure
Loot author: 5 Orton
looter: 6 pirate, robber, vandal 7 brigand 10 freebooter, highwayman
looting: 5 theft 6 rapine 8 thievery
lop: 3 cut, top 4 chop, crop, pare, trim 5 droop, prune, sever, shear, slice 6 cut off, detach, excise, spring 7 chop off, exscind, scissor, shorten, tear off, trim off 8 hang down, shear off, slice off, truncate 9 eliminate
ender: 5 sided
lop __: 3 off
lop-__: 5 eared
Lopat: 2 Ed 5 Eddie 6 hurler 7 pitcher
lope: 3 jog, run 4 skip, trip, trot 6 canter
Lope: 6 de Vega
loper: 8 sprinter
Lopes: 5 Davey 6 Fernao
Lopes, Davey sport: 8 baseball
Lopevi: 7 volcano
locale: 4 Asia 7 Vanuatu
Lopez: 2 Al 5 Nancy, Trini 8 Jennifer
Lopez, Jennifer: 6 singer 7 actress
film: Angel Eyes (2001)
The Cell (2000)
Enough (2002)
Jack (1996)
Out of Sight (1998)
Selena (1997)
U Turn (1997)
The Wedding Planner (2001)
nickname: J. Lo
song: If You Had My Love (1999)
Waiting for Tonight (1999)
López Mateos: 4 city, town
locale: 6 Mexico
Lopez, Nancy: 6 golfer
milieu: 5 links 6 course
org.: 4 LPGA
__ Lopez opening: 3 Ruy
Lopez, Trini
homeland: Trinidad
song: If I Had a Hammer (1963)
Lopez, Vincent theme: 4 Nola
Lop Nur: 4 lake
locale: 5 China
loppy: 4 limp 6 droopy, floppy 7 sagging
lopsided: 3 wry 4 awry 5 askew, atilt 6 canted, skewed, squint, uneven, warped 7 crooked, leaning, tilting, unequal 8 cockeyed, top-heavy, unsteady 9 egg-shaped, irregular 10 ill-matched, off-balance, out of shape, unbalanced
win: 4 rout 5 upset 7 debacle, shut out 8 disaster, drubbing, walkover 9 trouncing
loquacious: 4 glib, long 5 gabby, talky, windy, wordy 6 chatty, fluent, prolix 7 diffuse, gossipy, lengthy, unterse, verbose, voluble, yacking, yakking 8 babbling, rambling 9 bombastic, expansive, garrulous, jabbering, redundant, talkative 10 bigmouthed, chattering, discursive, long-winded, motormouth, palaverous
far from ~: 4 curt 5 brief, crisp, pithy, short, terse 7 brusque, concise, laconic 8 succinct, taciturn
loquacity: 4 guff 6 babble, hot air, jabber 7 blabber, blather, blether, chatter, palaver, yakking 8 bigmouth, idle talk, verbiage 9 eloquence, garrulity, gift of gab, wordiness
loquat: 4 tree 5 fruit 9 evergreen
Lorain: 4 city, town
locale: 4 Ohio
Lora Lawton: 9 radio show
__ l'orange: 5 duck à
loran part: 3 nav. 4 long 5 range 10 navigation
Lorax, The author: Dr. Seuss
lord: 4 boss, duke, earl, male, peer 5 baron, mogul, noble, ruler, title 6 gerent, honcho, master 7 marquis 8 marquess, nobleman, viscount 9 blueblood 10 aristocrat
feudal ~: 5 liege, mesne, thane, thegn
holding: 4 land 5 manor 6 estate
In Turkish: 3 aga 4 agha
it over: 5 gloat 7 swagger 9 trample on, tyrannize
lady: 4 dame
mate: 4 dame, lady
name meaning ~: 5 Cyril
servant: 4 page, serf
starter: 3 war 4 land, slum
Lord: 3 God, Jon 4 Jack 5 Jahve, Jahwe, title, Yahve, Yahwe 6 Jahveh, Jahweh, Yahveh, Yahweh 7 Holy One, Jehovah 8 Immanuel, Marjorie, Most High
& Taylor rival: 4 Saks
Lord __: 3 Jim
Lord __ Duck: 5 Love a
Lord __ Flies: 5 of the
Lord __ Rings, The: 5 of the
Lord __ shepherd, The: 4 is my
Lord Baltimore: 4 cake
__ Lord Fauntleroy: 6 Little
Lord God Made __ All, The: 4 Them
Lord-High-Everything-__: 4 Else
Lord, is __?: 3 it I
Lord is God, name meaning: 4 Joel
Lord Jim: 4 film 5 novel
author: Joseph Conrad
cast: Curt Jurgens, James Mason, Peter O'Toole, Eli Wallach
character: 4 Dain 5 Stein, Waris 6 Marlow
director: Richard Brooks
Lord knows __ tried!: 3 I've
Lord Love a Duck (1966 film)
cast: Lola Albright, Roddy McDowall, Tuesday Weld
director: George Axelrod
lordly: 4 high, posh 5 grand, lofty, noble, proud, regal, ritzy, royal, swank 6 august, formal, lavish 7 exalted, haughty, leonine, stately 8 arrogant, baronial, cavalier, despotic, imperial, imposing, kinglike, majestic, princely, snobbish, splendid 9 arbitrary, dignified, grandiose, imperious, luxurious, masterful, sumptuous 10 commanding, despotical, high-handed, impressive, majestical, peremptory
Lord of __: 5 Hosts 7 Misrule
Lord of the __: 5 Dance
Lord of the Flies author: William Golding
Lord of the Rings, The
author: J.R.R. Tolkien
character: 3 elf, ent, orc, Sam 5 Bilbo, dwarf, Frodo, Smaug, troll 6 dragon, hobbit, Sauron, wizard 7 Baggins, Gandalf
locale: 9 Mount Doom 11 Middle Earth
Lord of the Rings - The Fellowship... (2001 film)
cast: Ian McKellen, Viggo Mortensen, Liv Tyler, Elijah Wood
director: Peter Jackson
Lord Privy __: 4 Seal
lords: 6 gentry 7 peerage, royalty 8 nobility 10 bluebloods, patricians, upper class, upper crust
Lords: 5 Traci
Lord's __: 3 day 5 table 6 Prayer, Supper
__ lords a-leaping...: 3 ten
lordship: 5 title 9 honorific
Lords of Flatbush, The (1974 film)
cast: Perry King, Sylvester Stallone, Henry Winkler
Lord's Prayer: 5 Pater
pronoun: 3 thy
Lord Weary's Castle author: Robert Lowell
Lordy!: 4 egad 5 egads
lore: 4 myth, saws 5 myths, sagas, tales 6 adages, fables, legend 7 beliefs, customs, legends, sayings 8 doctrine, learning, teaching 9 erudition, knowledge, mythology, tradition 10 fairy story, literature, refinement, traditions
starter: 4 book, folk
Lorelei: 3 Lee 5 lurer, siren
emulate ~: 5 tempt
poet: 5 Heine
river of the ~: 5 Rhine
Lorelei (1976 song) artist: Styx
Loren: 4 Dean 5 Donna 6 Sophia
Loren, Sophia: 7 actress
birthplace: 4 Rome
film: Aida (1953)
Arabesque (1966)
The Cassandra Crossing (1977)
A Countess From Hong Kong (1967)
El Cid (1961)
The Fall of the Roman Empire (1964)
Grumpier Old Men (1995)
Houseboat (1958)
Operation Crossbow (1965)
That Kind of Woman (1959)
Two Women (1961, AA)
Yesterday, Today and Tomorrow (1964)
spouse: Carlo Ponti
Lorentz, Hendrik: 8 Nobelist 9 physicist
Lorenz: 4 Hart 6 Konrad
Lorenz, Konrad: 6 writer 8 Austrian, Nobelist
work: King Solomon's Ring
On Agression
Lorenzo: 5 lamas 8 de'Medici, Ghiberti
see also Spanish
__ Lorenzo: 3 San
Lorenzo Jones: 9 radio show
Lorenzo's Oil (1992 film)
cast: Nick Nolte, Susan Sarandon, Peter Ustinov
director: George Miller
Loreto: 4 city, town
locale: 6 Mexico 9 Zacatecas
Loretta: 4 Lynn, Swit 5 Young 6 Devine
sister: 7 Crystal
lorgnette: 7 glasses 10 eyeglasses, spectacles
part: 4 lens
Lori: 5 Petty 6 Singer 8 Loughlin
lorica: 4 case 6 sheath 7 cuirass 8 corselet
lorikeet: 4 bird
Lorin: 6 Maazel 9 Hollander
Loring: 4 Lisa 6 Gloria
Loring, Gloria
song: Friends and Lovers (1986)
spouse: Alan Thicke
TV: Days of Our Lives
loris: 5 lemur 6 mammal 7 primate
relative: 3 ape 4 saki, titi 5 chimp, drill, jocko, magot, orang, potto, shrew 6 aye-aye, baboon, Bandar, galago, gelada, gibbon, grivet, guenon, howler, langur, macaco, monkey, rhesus, uakari, vervet 7 colobus, gorilla, guereza, hoolock, macaque, sapajou, siamang, tamarin, tarsier 8 bush baby, capuchin, mandrill, mangabey, marmoset, talapoin 9 orangutan 10 Barbary ape, chimpanzee, orangutang
lorn: 6 bereft 7 in a funk 8 derelict, deserted, desolate, forsaken, lovesick 9 abandoned
starter: 3 for 4 love
Lorna: 4 Luft 5 Doone
half-sister: 4 Liza
Lorna Doone: 5 cooky, novel 6 cookie
alternative: 4 Oreo 7 Droxies 9 Chips Ahoy! 10 Fig Newtons
author: 10 Blackmoore
character: 3 Fry, Tom 4 Alan, Ridd 5 Ensor 6 Carver, Faggus, Jeremy, Reuben 7 Brandir 8 Stickles 9 Huckaback
setting: 6 Exmoor 7 England
Lorne: 6 Greene, Marion 8 Michaels
Lorn port, Firth of: 4 Oban
loro: 4 fish 6 parrot 10 parrot fish
Lorraine: 4 Gary 6 Bracco 9 Hansberry
city: 5 Nancy
neighbor: 6 Alsace
__ Lorraine: 5 Sweet 6 quiche
Lorre, Peter: 5 actor
film: Black Angel (1946)
Casablanca (1942)
Casbah (1948)
The Comedy of Terrors (1964)
Crime and Punishment (1935)
The Face Behind the Mask (1941)
Lancer Spy (1937)
M (1931)
Mad Love (1935)
The Maltese Falcon (1941)
The Man Who Knew Too Much (1934)
The Mask of Dimitrios (1944)
Mr. Moto's Last Warning (1939)
My Favorite Brunette (1947)

The Raven (1963)
The Stranger on the Third Floor (1940)
Tales of Terror (1962)
Thank You, Mr. Moto (1938)
Think Fast, Mr. Moto (1937)
Three Strangers (1946)
Lorrie: 6 Morgan
lorry: 3 rig, van 4 semi 5 truck, U-Haul 6 wheels 7 vehicle 9 transport
Lorus: 5 watch 10 wristwatch
alternative: 4 Ebel, Rado 5 Casio, Elgin, Omega, Rolex, Seiko, Timex 6 Bulova, Fossil, Movado, Pulsar, Swatch 7 Citizen 8 Longines, Tag Heuer, Tourneau
lory: 4 bird 6 parrot
Los __: 5 Altos, Gatos, Lobos, Lunas 6 Alamos, Bravos, Mochis 7 Angeles, Fresnos
Los __, CA: 5 Altos, Gatos
Los __, NM: 6 Alamos
Los __ Rio: 3 Del
Los Alamos: 4 city, town
locale: 9 New Mexico
Los Altos: 4 city, town
locale: 10 California
Los Angeles: 4 city, port, town
City of ~: 5 train
college athlete: 5 Bruin 6 Trojan 10 Golden Bear
East ~: 6 barrio
forecast: 4 haze, smog
locale: 10 California
newspaper: 4 News 5 Times
pro athlete: 4 King 5 Laker 6 Dodger 7 Clipper
school: 3 USC 4 UCLA
suburb: 5 Azusa 6 Bel Air, Encino, Orange
thoroughfare: 4 Pico 6 Sunset
zone: 3 PDT, PST
Los Banos: 4 city, town
locale: 10 California
Los Cabos: 4 city, town
locale: 6 Mexico
Los Del Rio
homeland: Spain
song: Macarena (1996)
lose: 3 rid 4 bomb, bust, drop, duck, fail, flop, miss, oust, shed, slip, trip 5 avoid, dodge, drain, elude, evade, flunk, shake, spill, use up, waste, yield 6 baffle, blow it, divest, escape, expend, falter, forget, give up, go down, mislay, outrun, pass up 7 blunder, decline, default, exhaust, forfeit, founder, get beat, go under, go wrong, misstep, stumble, succumb, wash out 8 confound, displace, fall flat, flounder, get rid of, lay an egg, misplace, misspend, shake off, slip away, squander, throw off, unburden 9 disorient, dissipate, fall short, get licked, miss out on, sacrifice, strike out, surrender, take a dive, throw away 10 be defeated, capitulate, disinherit, dispossess, gamble away, get clear of, relinquish, run through
a lap: 4 rise 5 arise, get up 7 stand up
as a lead: 4 blow
balance: 4 fall, reel, slip, trip 5 lurch, slide 6 sprawl, teeter, topple, totter, tumble, wobble 7 stagger, stumble 10 go headlong
color: 4 fade, pale 5 bleed 6 blanch 8 etiolate
consciousness: 5 faint, swoon 6 go limp 7 crumple, pass out 8 black out, keel over
energy: 3 sag, tax 4 flag, fold, tire 5 droop, weary 6 weaken 7 exhaust, give out, overtax, poop out 8 collapse, enervate, overwork, wear down
faith: 7 despair 10 give up hope
focus: 5 blear, cloud, muddy
freshness: 4 wilt 5 droop, go bad, spoil 6 wither 7 shrivel
ground: 3 lag 5 slide 7 regress 8 fall back
heart: 4 mope 5 quail 6 give up 7 despair 10 give up hope
intensity: 3 ebb 4 cool, fade, flag, slow, wane 5 abate, let up 6 ease up, lessen, recede, soften, weaken 7 decline, die down, dwindle, slacken, subside, tail off 8 blow over, decrease, diminish, moderate, taper off
interest: 3 nod 4 pale, pall, tire 5 weary
it: 4 boil, flip, rage, snap 5 crack, freak, go ape, panic 6 blow up, get mad, go nuts, go wild 7 explode, flip out 8 freak out, have a fit 9 go bananas, go berserk
leaves: 9 exfoliate
luster: 4 fade, pale 7 tarnish
no time: 3 hie, run 4 race, rush 5 hurry, speed 6 hasten 10 get hopping
one's shirt: 4 fold 6 go bust
one's way: 3 err 5 drift 6 ramble 7 digress, diverge, meander 9 wander off
on purpose: 4 diet, slim 5 throw 6 reduce 8 slim down
out: 4 bomb, fail, flop, fold 6 blow it, give up, pass up 7 forfeit 8 fall flat 9 fall short 10 be defeated, capitulate
out on: 4 fail, flub, miss, muff 6 fumble, ignore, pass up 7 default, misfire 8 overlook, pass over 9 fall short
sight of: 4 miss 6 forget, ignore 7 neglect 8 overlook, pass over
speed: 3 lag 4 slow 5 brake, check, choke, delay, let up, relax, stall, unlax 6 ease up, go easy, loiter, reduce, unwind, weaken 7 bog down, lay back, sit back 8 moderate, slack off, slow down, wind down 9 soft-pedal 10 decelerate, settle back, simmer down
(to): 3 bow
traction: 4 skid, slip 5 coast, skate, slide 7 slither
value: 4 sink 5 lower 6 reduce 7 decline, deflate 8 decrease 10 depreciate
weight: 4 diet 6 reduce 8 slim down
lose __: 3 out 4 face, time 5 out on 6 ground
lose __ of: 5 track
losel: 5 rogue 6 rascal 9 reprobate, scoundrel
lose-lose situation: 5 no-win
lose one's __: 4 head 5 shirt 6 tongue
lose one's __ to: 5 heart
__, Lose or Draw: 3 Win
loser: 3 dud 4 flop, jerk, nerd, nurd, wimp 5 creep, dweeb, moron, patsy 6 lummox, misfit 7 also-ran, failure, has-been 8 deadbeat, underdog 9 nonwinner 10 ne'er-do-well
be a sore ~: 4 sulk
cry: 5 I give, uncle 6 enough
election ~: 3 out
of 1588: 6 Armada
of 1917: 4 tsar
storied ~: 4 hare
__ loser: 4 born, sore
__ Loser: 3 I'm a
__ Loses a Tail: 6 Eeyore
Losey, Joseph: 8 director
film: The Boy With the Green Hair (1948)
The Concrete Jungle (1960)
Eva (1962)
King and Country (1964)
The Romantic Englishwoman (1975)
Secret Ceremony (1968)
The Servant (1963)
Time Without Pity (1956)
Los Gatos: 4 city, town
locale: 10 California
losing: 6 behind 7 lagging 8 trailing
streak: 5 slide, slump 9 downslide
Losing __: 3 You 6 Ground, Isaiah
Losing Isaiah (1995 film)
cast: Halle Berry, Cuba Gooding Jr., Jessica Lange, David Strathairn
director: Stephen Gyllenhaal
Losing My Religion (1991 song) artist: R.E.M.
Losing You (1963 song) artist: Brenda Lee
Los Lobos song: La Bamba (1987)
Los Mochis: 4 city, town
locale: 6 Mexico 7 Sinaloa
Los Nietos: 4 city, town
locale: 10 California
Los Reyes: 4 city, town
locale: 6 Mexico 9 Michoacán
loss: 3 dud 4 bomb, bust, cost, debt, flop, harm, hurt, lack, leak, miss, ruin 5 debit, minus, trial, waste 6 damage, defeat, fiasco, injury, losing, mishap, red ink, turkey 7 bad luck, blunder, debacle, deficit, failure, misstep, setback, stumble, trouble, undoing, washout 8 accident, breakage, calamity, casualty, decrease, disaster, downfall, fatality, wreckage 9 cataclysm, depletion, detriment, privation, sacrifice, shrinkage 10 deficiency, forfeiture, impairment, misfortune, nonsuccess
at a ~: 4 asea, beat 5 at sea, blank, stuck 7 baffled, puzzled, stumped 8 confused, overcome 9 mystified, perplexed 10 bewildered, confounded, nonplussed, tongue-tied
at a ~ for words: 5 dazed 7 shocked, stunned 9 awestruck 10 bowled over, nonplussed, speechless
business ~: 4 bath 8 reversal
feel a ~: 4 miss 5 mourn
leader: 5 promo 6 come-on 7 gimmick 9 promotion
of face: 5 odium, shame 6 stigma 7 chagrin, scandal 8 disgrace, dishonor, ignominy, ridicule 9 abashment, disrepute, ill repute 10 opprobrium
take a ~: 3 eat 7 devalue 8 give up on, write off
loss __: 5 ratio 6 leader
__ loss: 3 at a 5 water 7 capital
__ loss for words: 3 at a
Loss of Breath author: Edgar Allan Poe
Loss of Roses, A author: William Inge
__-loss order: 4 stop
lost: 4 asea, gone, past, rapt 5 at sea, minus, spent, stray 6 adrift, astray, bygone, doomed, dreamy, hidden, in a fog, lapsed, missed, musing, ruined, unsure, wasted 7 bemused, extinct, faraway, mislaid, missing, misused, puzzled, strange, wayward, wrecked 8 absorbed, cast away, clueless, consumed, distrait, dreaming, finished, hopeless, misspent, obscured, off-track, perished, vanished, wiped out 9 abandoned, destroyed, engrossed, entranced, flummoxed, forfeited, forgotten, frittered, misplaced, off-course, perplexed, wandering 10 abstracted, bewildered, demolished, devastated, dissipated, distracted, eradicated, gone astray, spellbound, squandered
cause: 5 goner
face: 5 shame, stain, taint 8 disgrace, dishonor 9 disrepute
get ~: 2 go 5 scram, stray 6 beat it, begone, bug off, wander 7 push off 8 withdraw 10 go fly a kite
(in): 4 deep
in thought: 4 rapt 5 moony, taken 6 intent 7 bemused, gripped 8 absorbed, immersed, involved 9 engrossed, oblivious 10 fascinated
not ~: 6 extant
partner: 5 found
word on a ~ sign: 6 reward
lost __: 5 cause, river 6 motion, tribes
__ lost!: 3 Get
Lost __: 5 in You 6 Colony, Pleiad, Pueblo 7 Command, Horizon
Lost __, A: 4 Lady
Lost __ Harem: 3 in a
Lost __ Stars: 5 in the
Lost __, The: 3 Zoo 4 Girl 5 Angel, Chord, World 6 Moment, Patrol 7 Weekend
lost and __: 5 found
Lost Angel, The author: Mary Higgins Clark
Lost Command (1966 film)
cast: Alain Delon, Anthony Quinn, George Segal
director: Mark Robson
Lost Dutchman: 4 mine
Lost Generation coiner: 5 Stein
Lost Girl, The author: D.H. Lawrence
Lost Horizon: 4 film 5 novel
author: James Hilton
cast: Ronald Colman, Edward Everett Horton, John Howard, Sam Jaffe, Margo, Jane Wyatt
character: 4 lama
director: Frank Capra
setting: 4 Asia 5 Tibet
Lost in a Harem (1944 film)
cast: Bud Abbott, Lou Costello, Marilyn Maxwell
Lost in Alaska (1952 film)
cast: Bud Abbott, Lou Costello
Lost in America (1985 film)
cast: Albert Brooks, Julie Hagerty, Garry Marshall
director: Albert Brooks
Lost in Emotion (1987 song) artist: Lisa Lisa and Cult Jam
__ Lost in His Arms: 4 I Got
Lost in Love (1980 song) artist: Air Supply
Lost in Space (1998 film)
cast: Heather Graham, William Hurt, Matt LeBlanc, Gary Oldman, Mimi Rogers
director: Stephen Hopkins
Lost in Space (CBS sci-fi)
cast: Angela Cartwright (Penny Robinson)
Mark Goddard (Don West)
Jonathan Harris (Zachary Smith)
Marta Kristen (Judy Robinson)
June Lockhart (Maureen Robinson)
Billy Mumy (Will Robinson)
Guy Williams (John Robinson)
character: 5 robot
Lost in the Funhouse author: John Barth
Lost in the Stars: 4 film, play 7 musical
author: Maxwell Anderson
cast: Melba Moore, Brock Peters, Raymond St. Jacques
composer: 5 Weill
director: Daniel Mann
Lost in Yonkers: 4 film, play
author: Neil Simon

cast: Richard Dreyfuss, Mercedes Ruehl, David Strathairn, Irene Worth
director: Martha Coolidge
role: 3 Jay 4 Arty, Gert 5 Bella, Louie
Lost in Your Eyes (1989 song) artist: Debbie Gibson
Lost in You (song) artist: Garth Brooks, Rod Stewart
Lost Lady, A author: Willa Cather
Lost Moment, The (1947 film)
cast: Robert Cummings, Susan Hayward, Agnes Moorehead
director: Martin Gabel
Lost Patrol, The (1934 film)
cast: Wallace Ford, Boris Karloff, Victor McLaglen
director: John Ford
Lost Pueblo author: Zane Grey
Lost River: 5 range 9 mountains
__ Lost Souls: 3 Two
__ Lost, The: 5 Love I
Lost Weekend, The (1945 film)
cast: Ray Milland, Philip Terry, Jane Wyman
character: 3 Bim, Don 4 Wick 5 Helen 6 Birnam, Gloria 9 Don Birnam
director: Billy Wilder
Lost Without Your Love (1976 song) artist: Bread
Lost World of the Kalahari, The author: Laurens Van der Post
Lost World, The
author: Arthur Conan Doyle, Michael Crichton
Lost World, The - Jurassic Park (1997 film)
beast: 4 T-Rex
cast: Jeff Goldblum, Julianne Moore
director: Steven Spielberg
__ Lost You: 3 I've 5 When I
Lost Zoo, The author: Countee Cullen
lot: 3 cut, hap, mob 4 area, doom, fate, gang, heap, load, lump, mass, mess, mete, mold, much, pack, part, pile, plat, plot, raft, sort, yard 5 array, batch, block, bunch, field, group, karma, ocean, order, patch, quota, reams, share, slice, stack, stamp, store, tract, whole 6 armful, boodle, bundle, chance, kismat, kismet, number, oodles, parcel, passel, plenty, plight, ration, scores, stacks 7 acreage, destiny, fortune, grounds, numbers, portion, species, tragedy 8 frontage, homesite, movie set, property, quantity 9 abundance, aggregate, allotment, great deal, multitude, plenitude, profusion 10 assortment, collection, percentage, real estate
a ~: 3 oft, ton 4 gobs, many, much, scad, tons 5 heaps, loads, no end, often, piles, rafts, scads 6 highly, myriad, oceans, oodles, plenty, vastly 7 barrels, buckets, bunches, but good, greatly 8 beaucoup, jillions, very much, zillions 9 great deal, immensely, like crazy, many a time, quite a bit, regularly 10 ever so much
a ~ of: 4 many 6 divers, myriad, umteen, untold 7 copious, profuse, umpteen 8 abundant, manifold, numerous, umpsteen 9 bountiful, countless, quite a few
a ~ of fun: 4 howl, kick
bad ~: 7 rotters 8 stinkers, villains 10 no-goodniks, scoundrels
filler: 4 cars 5 autos
measure: 4 acre, area
not a ~: 3 few 4 some 7 handful 10 infrequent, sprinkling
starter: 4 feed, sand, wood
the ~: 3 all 5 whole 9 aggregate 10 everything
throw one's ~ in with: 3 wed 4 join 5 marry 6 go with, hook up
use a ~: 4 park
__ lot: 3 dry, job, odd 4 back, bush, not a, wood 5 round 6 broken 7 parking
Lot: 5 river
brother of ~: 5 Iscah 6 Milcah
father of ~: 5 Haran
River locale: 6 France
son of ~: 4 Moab 7 Ben-Ammi
uncle of ~: 7 Abraham
__ Lot: 6 Salem's
lothario: 4 rake, roué, wolf 5 lover, Romeo 7 Don Juan 8 Casanova, lover boy 9 ladies' man, libertine
lotion: 4 balm, Keri, wash 5 cream, Curel, Nivea, salve 6 Aveeno, bay rum 7 Eucerin, Jergens, Pacquin, soother, unguent 8 cosmetic, lenitive, liniment, medicine, ointment, sunblock 9 demulcent, emollient, Lubriderm, sunscreen 10 after-shave, medication, palliative
apply, as ~: 5 rub in, rub on, smear
ingredient: 4 aloe
__ lotion: 8 calamine
Loti, Pierre: 6 author, French, writer
work: Matelot
lots: 4 a ton, gobs, heap, many, mint, much, peck, scad, slew, tons, wads 5 acres, heaps, loads, mucho, piles, scads, slews 6 flocks, hoards, oceans, oodles, plenty, raffle, scores, stacks, worlds 7 aplenty, barrels, legions, numbers 8 good deal, mountain, numerous 9 great deal, multitude, truckload
draw ~: 4 pick 6 choose, decide, select 9 determine
of: 4 many, much 6 divers, myriad, umteen, untold 7 copious, profuse, umpteen 8 abundant, manifold, numerous, umpsteen 9 bountiful, countless, quite a few
Lots, Feast of: 5 Purim
book: 6 Esther
Lott: 5 Trent 6 Ronnie
__ Lotta Love: 5 Whole
Lotta Love singer: 6 Larson
__ Lotta Loving: 5 Whole
Lotte: 5 Lenya 7 Lehmann
lottery: 5 Lotto 6 chance, raffle 7 drawing 8 gambling 10 sweepstake
equipment: 6 hopper
org., once: 3 SSS
Lottery, The author: Shirley Jackson
Lottery Winner, The author: Mary Higgins Clark
lotto: 4 game
kin: 4 keno 5 beano, bingo
Lott, Ronnie sport: 8 football
lotus: 3 pad 5 plant 6 flower 9 water lily
lotus __: 4 land
lotus-__: 5 eater
__ lotus: 4 blue 5 white 6 Indian, sacred
Lotus-Eaters, The author: Alfred Tennyson
Lou: 4 Bega, Reed 5 Adler, Brock, Dobbs, Gramm, Grant, Groza, Holtz, Rawls 6 Gehrig, Harris, Hoover, Jacobi 7 Antonio, Breslow, Gossett 8 Boudreau, Christie, Costello, Ferrigno, Novikoff, Piniella 10 Carnesecca
Lou __ Hoover: 5 Henry
Lou __ Phillips: 7 Diamond
louche: 4 iffy 5 fishy, shady 6 shifty 7 corrupt, crooked, devious, dubious, suspect 8 doubtful, slippery 9 dishonest, unethical 10 fly-by-night, suspicious
loud: 4 deep, rude 5 aroar, boomy, brash, crass, crude, forte, gaudy, gross, noisy, pushy, rowdy, showy, vivid, vocal 6 ablare, brassy, brazen, coarse, flashy, garish, strong, tawdry, vulgar 7 blaring, blatant, booming, boorish, chintzy, hooting, intense, loutish, lowbred, raucous, ringing, roaring, uncouth 8 crashing, emphatic, piercing, powerful, resonant, sonorous, strident, turned up, vehement 9 clamorous, deafening, obnoxious, obtrusive, offensive, tasteless 10 blustering, boisterous, clangorous, flamboyant, resounding, stentorian, thundering, uproarious, vociferant, vociferous
be too ~: 6 deafen
ender: 5 mouth 7 speaker
in music: 5 forte
not ~: 3 low 4 soft, weak 5 muted, quiet 6 feeble, hushed 7 muffled 9 whispered
sound: 3 bam, din, pop, pow 4 bang, boom, slam, thud, wham, yell 5 blare, blast, crack, noise, thump, whang 6 kaboom, report
very ~ in music: 3 fff
__ loud: 3 out
loud and __: 5 clear
loud battle, name meaning: 5 Louis
louder
gradually ~ in music: 4 cres. 5 cresc. 9 crescendo
make ~: 3 amp 5 amp up
Lou Diamond __: 8 Phillips
loudly: 5 forte 8 viva voce
loudmouth: 5 raver 6 magpie 7 boaster, windbag 8 blowhard, braggart
loudmouthed: 5 noisy, rowdy 7 uncouth 9 talkative
loudness: 3 vol. 6 volume 9 amplitude, intensity, magnitude
unit: 2 db 3 bel 4 phon, sone 7 decibel
Loudon: 7 Dorothy 10 Wainwright
loudspeaker: 4 horn 8 bullhorn, intercom, PA system
loud-voiced: 10 vociferant
Louella: 7 Parsons
contemporary: 5 Hedda
successor: 3 Liz 4 Rona
Louganis, Greg: 5 diver
lough: 4 lake, mere, pond, tarn 5 basin 9 reservoir
Loughlin: 4 Lori
Lou Grant (CBS drama)
cast: Mason Adams (Charlie Hume)
Daryl Anderson (Dennis Animal Price)
Edward Asner (Lou Grant)
Linda Kelsey (Billie Newman)
Nancy Marchand (Margaret Pynchon)
Robert Walden (Joe Rossi)
dog: 6 Barney
paper: 4 Trib 7 Tribune
producer: MTM
setting: 10 California, Los Angeles
Louie: 4 duck 8 Anderson
brother: 4 Huey 5 Dewey
Donald Duck, to ~: 4 unca
Louie Louie (1963 song) artist: Kingsmen
louis __: 3 d'or
Louis: 3 Joe, Nye, roi 4 Néel 5 David, Dudek, Hémon, Horst, Malle, Mayer, Nizer, Prima, Wirth 6 Aragon, Joliet, L'Amour, Leakey, Le Nain 7 Agassiz, Bellson, Braille, Calhern, Gossett, Hayward, Ignarro, Jolliet, Jourdan, Lumière, Pasteur, Renault, Simpson, Teicher, Tiffany 8 Brandeis, Couperus, Daguerre, MacNeice, Rukeyser, Sullivan, Zukofsky 9 Armstrong, Bromfield, Chevrolet, de Broglie, Fréchette 10 Untermeyer
in German: 6 Ludwig
in Italian: 5 Luigi 8 Lodovico
in Spanish: 4 Luis
see also French
Louis __: 4 heel 5 Seize 6 Le Nain, Quinze, Treize
Louisa (1950 film)
cast: Charles Coburn, Ruth Hussey, Ronald Reagan
director: Alexander Hall
Louisa __ Alcott: 3 May
Louis B. __: 5 Mayer
louis d'or: 4 coin 5 money
Louis-Dreyfus: 5 Julia
role: 6 Elaine
Louise: 4 Labé, lake, Tina 5 Anita, Bogan, Brown, Gluck, opera, Suggs 6 Brooks, Brough, Lasser 7 Beavers, Dresser, Erdrich 8 Fletcher, Mandrell 10 Allbritton
composer: Charpentier
in French: 6 Eloise
locale: 6 Canada 7 Alberta
soprano: 4 Irma
__ & Louise: 6 Thelma
Louise, Anita: 7 actress
film: First Lady (1937)
Judge Priest (1934)
The Little Princess (1939)
The Phantom of Crestwood (1932)
The Sisters (1938)
The Story of Louis Pasteur (1936)
__-Louise Parker: 4 Mary
Louisiana: 5 state
city: 5 Houma 6 Gretna, Harvey, Kenner, Monroe, Ruston 7 Laplace, Marrero, Slidell, Sulphur 8 Metairie 9 Chalmette, Lafayette, New Iberia, Opelousas, Terrytown 10 Alexandria, Baton Rouge, New Orleans, Shreveport
cuisine: 5 Cajun 6 Creole
Indian: 5 Caddo 7 Atakapa, Washita 8 Ouachita
neighbor: 5 Texas 8 Arkansas
nickname: 10 Bayou State
once: 3 ter. 4 terr. 9 territory
parish: 6 Acadia
politician: 4 Long 8 Huey Long
port: 10 Baton Rouge, New Orleans
region: 5 bayou
school: 3 LSU, LTU 6 Tulane 9 Grambling
state beverage: 4 milk
state bird: 7 pelican
state crustacean: 8 crawfish
state flower: 8 magnolia
state freshwater fish: 10 white perch
state gemstone: 5 agate
state insect: 8 honeybee
state mammal: 9 black bear
state reptile: 9 alligator
state wildflower: 4 iris
Louisiana __: 5 heron 6 French 7 tanager
Louisiana Purchase: 7 musical
part: 3 Ark., Kan., Neb., Wyo. 4 Colo., Iowa, Minn., Miss., Mont., N. Dak., Nebr., Okla., S. Dak. 6 Kansas 7 Montana, Wyoming 8 Arkansas, Colorado, Missouri, Nebraska, Oklahoma 9 Minnesota
songwriter: 6 Berlin
Louisiana State
conference: 3 SEC
locale: 10 Baton Rouge
Louisiana Tech
athletes: 8 Bulldogs
conference: 3 WAC
locale: 6 Ruston
Louis IX: 5 saint
Louis, Joe: 5 boxer
foe: 4 Baer, Conn, Farr, Mann, Nova 5 Godoy, McCoy, Musto, Roper, Simon 6 Burman, Pastor 7 Al McCoy, Charles, Dorazio, Galento, Lou Nova, Walcott 8 Abe Simon

9 Billy Conn, Bob Pastor, Buddy Baer, Jack Roper, Mauriello, Red Burman, Schmeling, Tommy Farr, Tony Musto 10 Gus Dorazio, Nathan Mann
milieu: 4 ring
Louis Quatorze: 3 roi 5 style
see also French
___ Louis Stevenson: 6 Robert
Louisville: 4 city, town
annual event: 5 Derby
athletes: 9 Cardinals
county: 9 Jefferson
locale: 3 Ken. 8 Kentucky
river: 4 Ohio
Louis XIV: 3 roi
see also French
Louis XVI: 3 roi
wife: 5 Marie
lounge: 3 bar, bum, lag, lie, pub, sit, tap 4 bask, club, dive, idle, laze, loaf, loll, rest, sofa, spot 5 couch, divan, lobby, relax 6 bistro, dawdle, loiter, lollop, parlor, repose, saloon, slouch, sprawl, tavern 7 barroom, club car, goof off, recline, saunter, seating, taproom 8 club room, drinkery, hideaway, kill time, lallygag, lie about, pass time, rest area, restroom, taphouse 9 goldbrick, greenroom, hang loose, mezzanine, reception, waste time 10 hang around, public room, take it easy
chair: 6 chaise
cocktail ~: 3 bar 6 lounge, saloon
ender: 4 wear
entertainment: 4 band 5 combo
lizard: 5 idler 8 parasite
lounge ___: 3 car 4 suit 5 chair 6 lizard
___ lounge: 6 chaise 7 transit
lounger: 4 robe 5 drone 6 loafer 7 dawdler, laggard
loungewear: 6 caftan, kaftan 7 pajamas
Loungin (1996 song) artist: LL Cool J
lounging: 5 lying 6 at ease 7 relaxed, resting 8 reposing 9 incumbent
loup-___: 5 garou
loupe: 4 lens 6 ocular, viewer 7 monocle 8 eyeglass, eyepiece 9 magnifier
user: 7 jeweler 8 engraver, lapidary 9 craftsman 10 gemologist, horologist, watchmaker
lour: 5 frown, scowl 6 gloomy
Lourdes author: Emile Zola
Lourdes, city near: 3 Pau
___ Lou Retton: 4 Mary
louse: 3 bug, bum, cad, nit 4 heel 5 aphis, cooty, knave, scamp, sneak, swine 6 bad guy, cootie, insect, isopod 7 crumbum, screw up, spoiler, stinker 8 parasite 9 miscreant, no-goodnik
egg: 3 nit
up: 3 err, mar 4 goof, ruin 5 botch, cross, spite, wreck 6 boggle, bungle, foozle, fumble, mess up, muddle 7 butcher 9 mismanage
___ louse: 4 bark, bird, book, crab, fish, wood 5 plant 6 biting
___ Louse: 3 To a
louse-up: 5 error
lousy: 3 bad, low 4 base, foul, grim, mean, poor, punk, sick, thin, vile, weak 5 awful, cheap, dirty, nasty, woful 6 crumby, crummy, dismal, faulty, feeble, horrid, no good, odious, rotten, shoddy, skimpy, stinky, two-bit, woeful 7 accurst, baleful, baneful, beastly, doleful, ghastly, harmful, hateful, ill-done, lacking, vicious 8 accursed, disliked, dreadful, God-awful, grievous, horrible, inferior, shameful, slovenly, stinking, terrible, wretched 9 abhorrent, appalling, atrocious, defective, execrable, fifth-rate, frightful, insidious, loathsome, miserable, offensive, revolting, third-rate, unpopular, unwelcome 10 abominable, deplorable, despicable, detestable, disastrous, fourth-rate, horrendous, inadequate, lamentable, outrageous, second-rate, unpleasant
be ~: 5 stink
with: 4 gobs, lots, rife, tons 5 heaps, piles, scads 6 oodles, untold 7 no end of, profuse, teeming, umpteen 8 numerous 9 plentiful 10 numberless
(with): 7 replete 8 abundant
lout: 2 ox 3 ape, cad, lug, oaf 4 boor, bozo, clod, jerk 5 brute, chump, churl, klutz, looby, rowdy, swine, yahoo 6 duffer, galoot, lubber, lummox, wampus 7 boggler, botcher, bumbler, bumpkin, bungler, fumbler, galloot, palooka 9 blunderer, harebrain, vulgarian 10 clodhopper, stumblebum
in Britain: 3 yob
loutish: 4 loud, rude 5 crude, dense, gawky, gross, gruff, onery, rough 6 clumsy, coarse, oafish, ornery, rustic, vulgar 7 bearish, bestial, boorish, doltish, gawkish, ill-bred, raffish, swinish, uncouth 8 barbaric, bungling, churlish, cloddish, clownish, impolite 9 graceless, ungallant, unrefined 10 indecorous, uncultured, uneducated, ungracious, unmannerly, unpolished
louvar: 4 fish
louver: 4 slat, slit, vent 6 outlet 7 opening 8 aperture
l'Ouverture country: 5 Haiti
Louvre: 5 musée 6 museum
annex architect: 3 Pei 5 I.M. Pei
display: 3 art 4 Nike, oils 8 Mona Lisa
locale: 5 Paris 6 France
lovable: 5 sweet 6 cuddly, genial 7 amiable, angelic, darling, snuggly, winning, winsome 8 adorable, alluring, charming, engaging, fetching, friendly, pleasing, precious 9 agreeable, angelical, appealing, covetable, desirable, endearing, ravishing 10 attractive, bewitching, cuddlesome, delightful, enchanting, entrancing
make ~: 6 endear
name meaning ~: 7 Annabel, Erastus
lovage: 4 herb
kin: 7 parsley
lovat: 5 plaid
love: 3 hug, woo 4 beau, dear, feel, kiss, like, lust, zero 5 adore, amity, amour, ardor, court, deify, enjoy, fancy, flame, go for, honey, lover, prize, spark, swain 6 admire, caress, cosset, cuddle, dote on, esteem, fervor, fiancé, gone on, liking, prefer, regard, relish, revere, soothe, suitor, virtue 7 care for, cherish, cling to, darling, dear one, embrace, emotion, fall for, fiancée, idolize, long for, passion, rapture, regards, revel in, romance, worship 8 devotion, dote upon, fidelity, fondness, hold dear, paramour, soft spot, treasure, venerate, yearning 9 adoration, affection, betrothed, boyfriend, care about, delight in, enjoyment, hankering, inamorata, inamorato, luxuriate, sentiment, valentine 10 admiration, allegiance, attachment, bridegroom, friendship, girlfriend, high regard, honeybunch, partiality, sweetheart, sweetie pie, tenderness
and kisses: 7 devoirs 9 greetings 10 best wishes, good wishes
avenger of unrequited ~: 7 Anteros, Anterus
ender: 4 bird, lock, lorn, seat, sick
feast: 5 agape
fill with ~: 6 enamor, endear
god: 4 Amor, Eros 5 Cupid 8 amoretto
handles: 3 fat 4 flab
Hindu god of: 4 Kama
in ~: 4 gaga 5 crazy 7 amorous, far gone, hugging, smitten 8 enamored 10 dreamy-eyed
in French: 5 amour
in Italian: 5 amore
in Latin: 4 amor
in ~ old-style: 4 smit
in Spanish: 4 amor
in ~ with: 6 keen on
letter: 10 billet doux
Norse ~ goddess: 5 Freya
of life: 2 go 3 pep, zip 4 élan 5 gusto, oomph, punch, spice, verve 6 ginger, relish, spirit 7 passion, sparkle 8 appetite, vitality 10 enthusiasm, exuberance, heartiness
old-style: 5 leman
play at ~: 3 toy 4 vamp 5 flirt, tease 6 trifle 8 coquette
puppy ~: 5 ardor, crush 8 devotion, fondness 9 affection 10 admiration, attachment 11 infatuation
seat: 4 sofa 5 couch 7 seating 9 furniture
starter: 4 lady, true
story: 5 novel 7 romance
symbol: 5 heart
to cynics: 5 blind
too much: 4 dote
what ~ may mean: 4 zero
where ~ means nothing: 6 tennis
love ___: 3 bug, set 4 game, knot, nest, seat, vine 5 apple, beads, feast, match 6 arrows, potion
love-___ relationship: 4 hate
___ love: 3 for 4 calf 5 puppy, tough 7 courtly
___ love!: 4 I'm in
Love: 4 Mike 5 Davis 6 Bessie 7 Darlene 8 Courtney
Love ___: 4 Land, Me Do, Song, Zone 5 Bites, Child, Grows, Hurts, Power, Shack, Songs, Story, Touch, Train, You So 6 Affair, Stinks 7 Letters, Machine
Love ___ Andy Hardy: 5 Finds
Love ___ Around: 5 Is All
Love ___ Battlefield: 3 Is a
Love ___ Elevator: 4 in an
Love ___ Find a Way: 4 Will
Love ___ Hurtin' Thing: 3 is a
Love ___ In: 6 Walked
Love ___ in the Sand: 7 Letters
Love ___ leave it!: 4 it or
Love ___ Leave Me: 4 Me or
Love ___ Many Splendored Thing: 3 Is a
Love ___ neighbor: 3 thy
Love ___ Number Nine: 6 Potion
Love ___ of J. Alfred Prufrock, The: 4 Song
Love ___ Rocks: 5 on the
Love ___ Rooftop: 3 on a
Love ___, The: 3 Bug 4 Boat 5 I Lost 6 Parade
Love ___ the Air: 4 Is in
Love ___ the Ruins: 5 Among
Love ___ Two-Way Street: 3 on a
Love ___ you need: 5 is all
___ Love: 3 Bad, Big, Mad, Our 4 Baby, Be My, Cool, Hula, Is It, Lady, More, Real, So in, True, Your 5 April, Crazy, First, I Feel, I Need, Irish, Puppy, Sea of, Stone, Sweet, We Got, Young 6 Higher, Secret, Stoned, Tender 7 Burning, Endless, Muskrat, Tainted, Without
___ Love a Duck: 4 Lord
Love Affair (1939 film)
cast: Charles Boyer, Irene Dunne, Maria Ouspenskaya
director: Leo McCarey
Love Affair (1994 film)
cast: Warren Beatty, Annette Bening, Katharine Hepburn, Garry Shandling
director: Glenn Gordon Caron
___ Love Again: 4 I'm in
Love Among the Cannibals author: Wright Morris
Love and Affection (1990 song) artist: Nelson
Love and Basketball (2000 film)
cast: Omar Epps, Dennis Haysbert, Sanaa Lathan, Alfre Woodard
Love and Death (1975 film)
cast: Woody Allen, Harold Gould, Diane Keaton
director: Woody Allen
Love and Friendship author: Alison Lurie
Love and Marriage (1955 song)
artist: Dinah Shore, Frank Sinatra
composer: 4 Cahn 9 Van Heusen
Love and Pain (1972 film)
cast: Timothy Bottoms, Maggie Smith
director: Alan J. Pakula
love apple: 5 fruit 6 tomato
love at first ___: 5 sight
Love at First Bite (1979 film)
cast: Richard Benjamin, George Hamilton, Susan Saint James
director: Stan Dragoti
love-beads wearer: 5 hippy 6 hippie 8 longhair
___ Love Belongs..., The: 4 One I
lovebird: 3 pet 5 cooer 10 sweetheart
Love Bites (1988 song) artist: Def Leppard
Love Boat, The (ABC sitcom)
cast: Fred Grandy (Yeoman-Purser Gopher Smith)
Bernie Kopell (Dr. Adam Bricker)
Ted Lange (Bartender Isaac Washington)
Gavin MacLeod (Capt. Merrill Stubing)
Lauren Tewes (Cruise Director Julie McCoy)
locale: 5 at sea, liner 6 cruise
stop: 3 POC 10 port of call
Love Boat: The Next Wave captain: 5 Urich
Love Bug: 2 VW 3 car 6 Herbie 10 automobile, Volkswagen
Love Bug, The (1969 film)
cast: Buddy Hackett, Dean Jones, Michele Lee
director: Robert Stevenson
___ Love Call: 6 Indian
Love Came to Me (1962 song) artist: Dion
Love Can Build a Bridge singer: 4 Judd
Love Child (1968 song) artist: Supremes
love conquers ___: 3 all
Love, Courtney
band: 4 Hole
spouse: Kurt Cobain
Lovecraft, H.P.: 6 author, writer
like ~ stories: 4 eery 5 eerie
loved: 4 dear 5 sweet 7 darling 8 precious
one: 3 pet 4 dear, idol, love 7 darling 10 sweetheart
Loved him, ___ her: 5 hated
Loved Ones, The (1965 film)
cast: Anjanette Comer, Robert Morse, Jonathan Winters
director: Tony Richardson
Loved One, The author: Evelyn Waugh
___ Loved You: 3 If I

Love Finds Andy Hardy (1938 film)
cast: Judy Garland, Mickey Rooney, Lewis Stone
director: George B. Seitz
Love for Sale composer: 6 Porter
Love for Three Oranges, The composer: 9 Prokofiev
Love Grows (1970 song) artist: Edison Lighthouse
Love Hangover (1976 song) artist: Diana Ross
__ Love Has Gone: 5 Where
Love Her __: 5 Madly
__ Love Her: 4 And I
__ Love Hewitt: 8 Jennifer
Love III, Davis: 6 golfer
milieu: 5 links 6 course
org.: 3 PGA
Love I Lost, The (1973 song) artist: Harold Melvin and the Blue Notes
__ Love I'm After: 3 It's
love-in: 7 protest
Love in __: 5 Bloom
Love in a Cold Climate author: Nancy Mitford
Love in a Life author: Robert Browning
Love in an Elevator (1989 song) artist: Aerosmith
Love in the Afternoon (1957 film)
cast: Maurice Chevalier, Gary Cooper, Audrey Hepburn
director: Billy Wilder
Love in the First Degree actor: 4 Owen
Love in the Ruins author: Walker Percy
Love Is (1993 song)
artist: Brian McKnight, Vanessa Williams
Love Is a __-Splendored Thing: 4 Many
Love Is a Battlefield (1983 song) artist: Pat Benatar
Love Is a Golden Ring (1957 song) artist: Frankie Laine
Love Is a Hurtin' Thing (1966 song) artist: Lou Rawls
Love Is All Around (1968 song) artist: Troggs
Love Is a Many Splendored Thing: 4 film, song
artist: Four Aces
cast: William Holden, Jennifer Jones, Murray Matheson
director: Henry King
Love Is a Wonderful Thing (1991 song) artist: Michael Bolton
Love Is Blue (1968 song) artist: Paul Mauriat
Love Is Eternal author: Irving Stone
Love Is Forever (1986 song) artist: Billy Ocean
Love Is Here and Now You're Gone (1967 song) artist: Supremes
Love Is Here to Stay composer: 8 Gershwin
Love Is in Control (1982 song) artist: Donna Summer
Love Is Like an Itching in My Heart (1966 song) artist: Supremes
Love is not __: 4 a toy
Love Is Not All: 4 poem
author: 6 Millay
Love Is Strange (1967 song) artist: Peaches and Herb
Love Is Stronger Than Pride singer: 4 Sade
Love Is Sweeping the Country composer: 8 Gershwin
Lovejoy, Frank: 5 actor
film: Beachhead (1954)
Goodbye, My Fancy (1951)
House of Wax (1953)
In a Lonely Place (1950)
Shack Out on 101 (1955)
Try and Get Me! (1950)
Lovelace: 3 Ada 7 Richard
Lovelace, Richard: 4 poet 7 English
work: To Althea from Prison
To Lucasta, Going to the Wars
Loveland: 4 city, town
locale: 8 Colorado
loveless: 3 icy 4 cold, cool 5 hated 6 frigid 7 loathed 8 despised, detested, disliked, unwanted
Loveless: 5 Patty
love-letter letters: 4 SWAK
Love Letters (1983 film)
cast: Jamie Lee Curtis, James Keach, Amy Madigan
director: Amy Jones
Love Letters in the Sand (1957 song)
artist: Pat Boone
composer: 5 Coots
Love Letters (song) artist: Elvis Presley, Ketty Lester
love-lies-bleeding: 5 plant 6 flower
Loveliest of Trees author: A.E. Housman
loveliness: 5 charm, grace 6 allure, beauty, glamor 7 glamour 8 elegance, radiance 9 good looks
Lovell, James: 9 astronaut
portrayer: Tom Hanks
lovely: 3 def, rad 4 aces, A-one, boss, braw, cool, cute, dece, fair, fine, gear, keen, neat, nice, phat, rare, tuff 5 bonny, dandy, ducky, grand, great, marvy, neato, nobby, prime, slick, super, sweet, swell 6 bang on, bang-up, bonnie, bonzer, bosker, choice, comely, dainty, divine, dreamy, far-out, gnarly, groovy, peachy, pretty, slap-up, spot on, superb, terrif, tiptop, unreal, whizzo, wicked 7 amazing, amiable, awesome, capital, corking, darling, perfect, picture, ripping, skookum, stellar, sublime, winning, winsome 8 adorable, alluring, charming, dazzling, delicate, engaging, enticing, especial, eximious, fabulous, fetching, five-star, four-star, frabjous, glorious, gorgeous, graceful, handsome, heavenly, jim-dandy, knockout, pleasant, pleasing, slam-bang, smashing, splendid, standout, sterling, stick-out, striking, stunning, superior, terrific, top-level, topnotch, very good, wondrous 9 admirable, agreeable, beauteous, beautiful, bodacious, delicious, Endsville, enjoyable, excellent, exemplary, exquisite, first-rate, glamorous, high-grade, hunky-dory, marvelous, ravishing, sollicker, top-flight, wonderful 10 attractive, bewitching, delectable, delightful, enchanting, first-class, gratifying, hotsy-totsy, jack-a-dandy, out of sight, peachy-keen, phenomenal, remarkable, stupendous, super-duper
Lovely __, meter maid...: 4 Rita
__ lovely as a tree: 5 A poem
Lovely Day for Creve Coeur, A author: Tennessee Williams
__ Lovely Day Today: 4 It's a
Lovely to Look At composer: 4 Kern 6 Fields, McHugh
Love Machine (1975 song) artist: Miracles
__ Love Me: 5 Do You, If You
Love Me Do (1964 song) artist: Beatles
Love Me for a Reason (1974 song) artist: Osmonds
Love Me or Leave Me (1955 film)
cast: James Cagney, Doris Day, Cameron Mitchell
director: Charles Vidor
Love Me or Leave Me singer: 6 Etting
Love Me (song) artist: Elvis Presley, Mase
Love Me Tender: 4 film, song
artist: Elvis Presley
cast: Richard Egan, Debra Paget, Elvis Presley
director: Robert D. Webb
Love Me Tonight (1932 film)
cast: Maurice Chevalier, Myrna Loy, Jeanette MacDonald, Charlie Ruggles
director: Rouben Mamoulian
music: 4 Hart 7 Rodgers
tune: 4 Mimi
Love Me Tonight (1969 song) artist: Tom Jones
Love Me With All Your Heart (1964 song) artist: Ray Charles Singers
Love Nest and Other Stories, The author: Ring Lardner
__ love, not war: 4 make
Love of Four Colonels, The author: Peter Ustinov
Love of Life (CBS): 4 soap 9 soap opera
__ Love of the Game: 3 For
Love on a Dark Street author: Irwin Shaw
Love on a Rooftop (ABC sitcom)
cast: Judy Carne (Julie Willis) Peter Deuel (David Willis)
Love on the Rocks (1980 song) artist: Neil Diamond
Love or Let Me Be Lonely (1970 song) artist: Friends of Distinction
__ love or money: 3 for
Love Parade, The (1929 film)
cast: Maurice Chevalier, Jeanette MacDonald, Lillian Roth
director: Ernst Lubitsch
love-potion effect: 5 spell
Love Potion Number Nine (1964 song) artist: Searchers
Love Power (1987 song)
artist: Dionne Warwick, Jeffrey Osborne
lover: 2 jo 3 fan, pet 4 baby, beau, buff, dear, jill 5 amour, angel, chéri, cooky, cutey, cutie, deary, ducky, flame, honey, leman, novia, novio, Romeo, sugar, swain, sweet, wooer 6 bon ami, chérie, cookie, dautie, dearie, eloper, escort, fiancé, Juliet, steady, suitor, sweets 7 admirer, courter, darling, dearest, dear one, devotee, fiancée, pigsney, schatzi, squeeze, sweetie, tootsie 8 chou-chou, cutie pie, dowsabel, dulcinea, idolizer, lothario, macushla, paramour, precious, snookums, sugar pie, sweetums 9 bonne amie, boyfriend, companion, dreamboat, inamorata, inamorato, infatuate, libertine, petit chou, solicitor, suppliant, valentine 10 aficionado, enthusiast, girlfriend, heartthrob, honeybunch, mavourneen, petitioner, sweetheart, sweetie pie, turtledove
boy: 4 rake, roué 5 flirt, swain, wooer 7 Don Juan, gallant, playboy, swinger 8 Casanova, hedonist, lothario, prodigal, sybarite 9 libertine
combining form: 4 -phil 5 -phile
forsake a ~: 4 dump, jilt 5 ditch, leave 6 desert 7 abandon 8 run out on 9 cast aside, throw over
lucre ~: 7 Scrooge 8 tightwad 9 skinflint 10 cheapskate, pinchpenny
opposite: 5 hater
Lover __ Back: 4 Come
__ Lover: 3 Hey 4 Be My, Easy 5 Dream, Penny, To Be a 6 Yester
Loverboy (1984 song) artist: Billy Ocean
Lover Come Back (1961 film)
cast: Edie Adams, Doris Day, Rock Hudson, Tony Randall
director: Delbert Mann
Lovergirl (1985 song) artist: Teena Marie
Lover in Me, The (1988 song) artist: Sheena Easton
Loveroot author: Erica Jong
Lover Please (1962 song) artist: Clyde McPhatter
lovers' __: 4 knot, lane
Lovers and Idol sculptor: 4 Erté
Lovers and Other Strangers (1970 film)
cast: Bea Arthur, Bonnie Bedelia, Anne Meara, Gig Young
director: Cy Howard
Lover's Concerto, A (1965 song) artist: Toys
Lover's Question, A (1958 song) artist: Clyde McPhatter
Lovers, The (1958 film)
cast: Alain Cuny, Jeanne Moreau
director: Louis Malle
Lovers Who Wander (1962 song) artist: Dion
Lover, The author: Harold Pinter
L'Overture: 9 Toussaint
Love's __ Lost: 7 Labour's
Love's Alchemy author: John Donne
__ Loves Angela: 5 Aaron
Love's Been a Little Bit Hard on Me (1982 song) artist: Juice Newton
Love's Comedy author: Henrik Ibsen
loveseat: 6 settee
Love & Sex (2000 film)
cast: Noah Emmerich, Jon Favreau, Famke Janssen, Cheri Oteri
director: Valerie Breiman
lovesick: 4 gaga, lorn 6 doting
Love's Labour's Lost author: William Shakespeare
__ Loves Mambo: 4 Papa
__ loves me...: 3 She
Loves Me Like a Rock (1973 song) artist: Paul Simon
Loves Music, Loves to Dance author: Mary Higgins Clark
Love Sneakin' Up on You (1994 song) artist: Bonnie Raitt
__ Loves of Dobie Gillis, The: 4 Many
Loves of Harry Dancer, The author: Lawrence Sanders
Love Somebody (1984 song) artist: Rick Springfield
__ Love Song: 5 Pagan
Love Song of J. Alfred Prufrock, The: 4 poem
author: T.S. Eliot
Love Songs
author: Lawrence Sanders, Sara Teasdale
__ Love Songs: 5 Silly
Love Song (song) artist: Anne Murray, Cure, Tesla
Love So Right (1976 song) artist: Bee Gees
Loves Park: 4 city, town
locale: 8 Illinois
Love Story: 4 film 5 novel
author: Erich Segal
cast: Ali MacGraw, Ray Milland, Ryan O'Neal
composer: 3 Lai
director: Arthur Hiller
Love Story (1971 song) artist: Andy Williams
Love Story Theme (1971 song) artist: Henry Mancini
__ loves ya, baby?: 3 Who
__ Loves You: 3 She
Love Takes Time (song) artist: Orleans
artist: Mariah Carey
__ Love, The: 4 Man I, One I 5 Art of, Way of, Way to
Love the One You're With (1970 song) artist: Stephen Stills
Love the World __: 4 Away

Love thy neighbor: 5 adage, credo, motto
Love to Love You Baby (1975 song) artist: Donna Summer
Love Touch (1986 song) artist: Rod Stewart
Love Train (1973 song) artist: O'Jays
Lovett, Lyle spouse: Julia Roberts
Love Walked In composer: 8 Gershwin
Love Will Conquer All (1986 song) artist: Lionel Richie
Love Will Find a Way (1978 song) artist: Pablo Cruise
Love Will Keep Us Together (1975 song) artist: Captain & Tennille
Love Will Lead You Back (1990 song) artist: Taylor Dayne
Love Will Never Do (1990 song) artist: Janet Jackson
Love Will Save the Day (1988 song) artist: Whitney Houston
Love Will Turn You Around (1982 song) artist: Kenny Rogers
Love With the Proper Stranger (1963 film)
cast: Edie Adams, Steve McQueen, Natalie Wood
director: Robert Mulligan
Lovey Childs author: John O'Hara
lovey-dovey: 5 mushy 6 tender 7 amorous, mawkish 8 romantic
__ Love You: 3 P.S. I 5 Baby I
__ Love You in My Dreams: 3 I'll
Love You Inside Out (1979 song) artist: Bee Gees
Love You Save, The (1970 song) artist: Jackson 5
__ Love You So: 4 And I
Love Zone (1986 song) artist: Billy Ocean
loving: 3 cup 4 dear, fond, font, kind, warm 5 close, loyal, sweet 6 ardent, caring, doting, filial, kindly, liking, tender 7 adoring, amatory, amiable, amorous, anxious, bound up, cordial, devoted, earnest, fervent, kissing, lenient, valuing, zealous 8 admiring, attached, enamored, faithful, friendly, generous, intimate, parental, reverent, romantic 9 amatorial, attentive, concerned, unselfish 10 benevolent, expressive, idolatrous, infatuated, passionate, respecting, solicitous, thoughtful, worshipful
combining form: 4 phil- 5 philo- 6 -philic
touch: 3 hug, pat, pet 6 caress, cuddle, stroke 7 embrace
loving __: 3 cup
Loving: 4 soap 9 soap opera
Loving (1970 film)
cast: Sterling Hayden, Eva Marie Saint, George Segal
director: Irvin Kershner
loving cup: 5 award 6 trophy
feature: 3 ear 4 base 6 plaque
__ Loving, The: 5 Art of
Loving You: 4 film, song
artist: Elvis Presley
cast: Wendell Corey, Dolores Hart, Elvis Presley, Lizabeth Scott
director: Hal Kanter
Lovin' Spoonful
lead singer: John Sebastian
song: Darling Be Home Soon (1967)
Daydream (1966)
Did You Ever Have to Make Up Your Mind? (1966)
Do You Believe in Magic (1965)
Nashville Cats (1966)
Rain on the Roof (1966)
Six O'Clock (1967)
Summer in the City (1966)
You Didn't Have to Be So Nice (1965)
Lovin' You (1975 song) artist: Minnie Riperton
Lovitz: 3 Jon
low: 3 bad, ill, sad 4 base, bass, blue, deep, down, evil, gear, glum, mean, mopy, poor, sick, soft, ugly, vile, weak 5 bated, cheap, crass, crude, faint, fed up, gross, lousy, mangy, moody, mopey, muted, nasty, piano, quiet, scant, seamy, short, slump, squat, under, woful 6 abject, ailing, broody, coarse, common, crumby, dismal, feeble, gloomy, humble, hushed, lesser, mangey, meager, menial, modest, morose, nether, on sale, paltry, poorly, scurvy, shoddy, sickly, sleazy, sneaky, sordid, sparse, sunken, unfair, unwell, vulgar, woeful, yellow 7 bargain, beastly, beneath, bestial, crushed, cut-rate, forlorn, ignoble, ill-bred, joyless, knavish, muffled, nominal, reduced, servile, shallow, sinking, slashed, squalid, squatty, stunted, subdued, uncouth, unhappy, way down 8 baseborn, crouched, dampened, deadened, degraded, dejected, depleted, depraved, downcast, guttural, indecent, inferior, marginal, moderate, murmured, plebeian, stricken, subsided, trifling, uncostly, unworthy, wretched 9 dastardly, deficient, depressed, execrable, heartsick, in the pits, malicious, miserable, prostrate, toned down, unethical, whispered, woebegone 10 despicable, despondent, dispirited, down and out, economical, inadequate, indelicate, indisposed, lamentable, marked down, melancholy, reasonable, rock-bottom, scurrilous, spiritless, turned down, unbecoming, unelevated, virtueless
as ~ as it gets: 5 worst
below ~: 3 dry 5 empty, spent 6 devoid 8 depleted 9 exhausted
blow: 4 foul 6 insult 9 cheap shot
bring ~: 4 bust, ruin 5 abase, crush 6 defeat, demean, demote, humble, reduce, weaken 7 conquer, deflate, degrade 8 bankrupt, pull down, vanquish 9 humiliate, knock down, overpower, pauperize, subjugate 10 impoverish
combining form: 5 chame- 6 chamae-
ender: 3 boy 4 ball, born, bred, brow, down, land, life 5 lands 6 lander
go ~: 5 slump
high and ~: 7 all over 9 all around 10 everywhere
hold ~: 4 hate 5 abhor 6 detest, loathe 7 despise, dislike 8 execrate 9 abominate
in French: 3 bas
keep a ~ profile: 4 hide, lurk 6 hole up, lay low, lie low 9 take cover
keep expenses ~: 4 save 6 scrape, scrimp 8 conserve, roll back 9 economize 10 cut corners
laid ~: 3 ill 5 unfit 7 invalid 9 unhealthy
lay ~: 5 floor, level 7 flatten
lie ~: 4 hide, wait 5 squat 6 hole up 9 take cover
look high and ~: 4 hunt, seek 5 scour 6 search 7 ransack, rummage
on: 7 needing, short of
on ~: 9 simmering
one: 3 cad 5 snake
point: 5 abysm, floor, nadir 6 bottom, trough
spirits: 8 glumness
voice: 3 hum 4 alto, bass, deep 5 basso 6 breath, mumble, murmur, mutter 7 whisper
low __: 4 beam, blow, gear, road, tide, wine 5 board, brass, pitch, rider, water 6 comedy, fulham, ground, relief 7 hurdles, milling, profile
low-__: 3 cal, end, fat, key, res 4 ball, cost, down, rate, rise, tech, test 5 count, grade, level, lying, power 6 budget, income, minded, necked, priced, ticket 7 pitched, tension
low-__ district: 4 rent
low-__ mark: 5 water
__ low: 3 lay, lie 7 monsoon
Low: 4 Seth 8 Juliette
Low __: 4 Mass 5 Latin, Rider 6 Church, German, Sunday
lowball: 4 game 8 card game
lowborn: 4 mean, poor 6 humble, simple 7 obscure 8 plebeian, untitled
lowboy: 5 chest 6 bureau 9 furniture
lowbred: 4 loud 5 crass, crude 6 brassy, brazen, coarse, common, vulgar 7 boorish 8 churlish, ignorant, impolite, unseemly 9 rough-hewn 10 boisterous, indecorous, unbecoming, unladylike, unpolished
lowbrow: 5 crass, yahoo 8 barbaric 9 barbarian, barbarous 10 uneducated
love: 6 kitsch
low-cal: 4 diet, lite 5 light
Lowchen: 3 dog 5 canid 6 canine
low-class: 4 non-U
low-cost: 5 cheap 6 on sale 7 bargain, cut-rate 8 moderate 9 half-price 10 economical, reasonable
Low Countries locale: 3 Eur., Lux. 4 Belg., Neth. 6 Europe 7 Belgium, Holland 10 Luxembourg 11 Netherlands
lowdown: 4 base, dirt, dope, info, mean, news, poop 5 facts, rumor, scoop, truth 6 notice, skinny 7 account 8 the goods 9 real story
get the ~: 5 learn
give the ~: 3 cue 4 leak, talk, tell, warn 5 brief, spill, steer 6 advise, impart, let out, reveal, tip off 7 caution, confide, divulge, give out, lay bare 8 disclose
low-down: 4 mean, ugly 5 nasty 6 shabby, sordid, unjust, wicked 8 degraded, wretched 10 undeserved
Lowdown (1976 song) artist: Boz Scaggs
Lowe: 3 Jim, Rob 4 Chad, Nick 5 Chris 6 Edmund
Lowe, Chad spouse: Hilary Swank
Lowe, Edmund: 5 actor
film: Dillinger (1945)
Every Day's A Holiday (1937)
No More Women (1934)
The Squeaker (1937)
What Price Glory? (1926)
Lowell: 3 Amy 4 city, town 5 Carey 6 Robert 7 Sherman
locale: 4 Mass.
Lowell, Amy: 4 poet
work: A Dome of Many-Coloured Glass
Lilacs
Patterns
Sword Blades and Poppy Seed
What's O'Clock
Lowell, Carey spouse: Richard Gere
Lowell, James Russell: 4 poet 6 editor, writer
work: The Biglow Papers
The Vision of Sir Launfal
Lowell, Robert: 4 poet
work: Day by Day
The Dolphin
Land of Unlikeness
Lord Weary's Castle
The Mills of the Kavanaughs
The Old Glory
Lowenbrau: 4 beer
alternative: 5 Becks, Coors, Pabst 6 Amstel, Corona, Miller, Molson 7 Schlitz 8 Heineken, Michelob 10 Ballantine
low-end: 5 cheap 7 chintzy 9 downscale
lower: 3 cut, dim, dip, ebb, sag 4 clip, curb, down, drop, fall, less, mute, pare, sink, sulk 5 abase, abate, berth, couch, decry, deign, demit, droop, frown, glare, minor, prune, relax, scowl, shave, slash, stoop, under 6 bemean, debase, demean, demote, ground, humble, junior, lessen, lesser, modify, nether, reduce, second, shrink, soften, weaken 7 beneath, curtail, cut back, cut down, decline, deflate, degrade, depress, descend, detract, detrude, devalue, dwindle, fall off, let down, reduced, set down, smaller, subside, tail off 8 belittle, cast down, close out, decrease, diminish, discount, disgrace, downsize, inferior, lessened, mark down, minimize, moderate, modulate, peter out, pull down, push down, roll back, submerge, take down, tone down, write off 9 bring down, curtailed, decreased, devaluate, downgrade, humiliate, pared down, scale down, secondary, subjacent 10 bush-league, condescend, de-escalate, depreciate, diminished, underneath, undervalue
class: 4 herd, scum 5 dregs 6 masses, rabble 8 riffraff 9 commoners, hoi polloi, peasantry 10 underworld
ender: 4 case, most
get ~: 4 drop, wane 6 lessen, recede 7 decline, dwindle, retreat, subside, tail off 8 decrease, diminish, fall back, slack off
in esteem: 5 shame 6 defile, demean, vilify 7 cheapen, degrade, deprave, devalue, profane, put down, vitiate 8 disgrace, dishonor, take down 9 humiliate, shoot down, undermine 10 adulterate
keep a stiff ~ lip: 4 fume, mope, sulk 5 brood, frown 6 glower
oneself: 5 deign, kneel, stoop 6 see fit 9 patronize 10 condescend
prefix: 3 sub- 5 infra-
than: 5 neath, under 7 beneath 10 underneath
lower __: 4 deck, hold, mast 5 apsis, berth, bound, class, house, world 6 fungus, school 7 chamber
Lower __: 5 Egypt, Lakes 6 Canada, Saxony 7 Austria, Chinook
Lower __ Side: 4 East
Lower California: 4 Baja
lowercase: 5 small 9 minuscule
lower-class: 4 base 6 coarse, common, humble, vulgar 8 baseborn, plebeian 9 unrefined 10 uncultured
__ Lowered the Boom: 6 Clancy
lowering: 3 cut, dim, dip, low 4 dark, dour, drop, fall, glum, gray, grey, grim 5 angry, black, bleak, dusky, mirky, murky, surly 6 cloudy, dismal, dreary, gloomy, sullen 7 cutback, decline, descent, looming, ominous 8 brooding, darkened, darkling, frowning, menacing, minatory, overcast, scowling, sinister 9 impending, long-faced, pitch-dark, tenebrous, unsmiling 10 chapfallen, lugubrious, melancholy
Lower Klamath: 4 lake
locale: 10 California
Lower Manhattan artist: 5 Marin
lowermost: 6 bottom
Lowe, Rob: 5 actor

brother: 4 Chad
film: About Last Night ... (1986)
Austin Powers: The Spy Who Shagged Me (1999)
The Hotel New Hampshire (1984)
Masquerade (1988)
St. Elmo's Fire (1985)
Wayne's World (1992)
lowery: 4 dark 6 gloomy
lowest: 4 last 5 basal, least, nadir 6 bottom 7 minimal, minimum 8 littlest
lowest ___ denominator: 6 common
lowest ___ multiple: 6 common
lowest form of wit: 3 pun
low-fat: 4 diet, lite, skim 5 light
___ Low German: 3 Old 6 Middle
low-grade: 3 low 4 poor 6 common 8 inferior 10 second-rate
low-key: 4 calm, cool, soft 5 muted, quiet, sober, staid, stoic 6 at ease, folksy, mellow, placid, sedate, serene, subtle 7 amiable, at peace, equable, muffled, pacific, relaxed, stoical, subdued, unmoved 8 amicable, carefree, composed, fireside, laid-back, moderate, peaceful, softened, soft-sell, tranquil 9 collected, easygoing, impassive, quiescent, temperate, toned down, unexcited, unruffled 10 nonchalant, played down, restrained, unagitated, untroubled
lowland: 3 bog 4 flat, mesa, moor 5 campo, heath, marsh, plain, swale, swamp 6 meadow, morass, pampas, steppe, tundra, valley 7 plateau, prairie 8 savannah 9 champaign
South African ~: 4 vlei
lowland ___: 3 fir 7 gorilla
Low-Lands author: Thomas Pynchon
lowlands hazard: 5 flood
lowlife: 3 cad, cur 4 heel, punk, scum, toad 5 creep, knave, rogue, scamp, slime, swine, yahoo 6 bad guy 7 villain 9 miscreant, reprobate, scoundrel
hang out with ~ s: 4 slum
lowliness: 7 modesty 8 humility, meekness
lowly: 4 base, mean, meek, mild, poor 5 plain 6 common, docile, gentle, humble, menial, modest, simple 7 average, dutiful, ignoble, mundane, obscure, prosaic, servile 8 baseborn, cast down, everyday, inferior, ordinary, plebeian, retiring 9 prosaical 10 obsequious, submissive, unassuming
low-lying area: 4 dale, vale 5 swale
low-minded: 4 foul, lewd, rank 5 bawdy, crass, crude, dirty, gross, lurid 6 coarse, filthy, ribald, smutty, sordid, vulgar 7 ignoble, immoral, obscene, raunchy, uncouth 8 depraved, improper, indecent, unseemly 9 dissolute, offensive, revolting 10 disgusting
lowness: 5 depth 7 crudity
low-pH: 6 acidic
compound: 4 acid
low-pitched: 4 bass, deep 5 quiet
___-low poker: 4 high
low-power period: 6 dim-out
low-pressure: 6 breezy, casual 8 informal
low-priced: 5 cheap 7 bargain, cut-rate, good buy, nominal 8 moderate 10 economical, reasonable
___ low profile: 5 keep a
low-quality: 3 off 4 poor 5 cheap 6 cheapo 8 el cheapo, inferior
low-ranking: 4 poor 5 minor, small 6 humble, modest 7 nominal 8 marginal 9 secondary 10 bush-league, negligible
Lowry: 3 AFB 7 Malcolm
low-spirited: 3 sad 4 blue, glum 5 woful 6 gloomy, morose, somber, woeful 7 doleful, joyless, unhappy 8 dejected, downcast, troubled 9 bummed out, cheerless, heartsick, miserable, saturnine, sorrowful, woebegone 10 chapfallen, dispirited, melancholy
___ Low, Sweet Chariot: 5 Swing
low-toned: 4 bass, deep
low-water ___: 4 mark
lox: 4 fish, nova 6 salmon 9 appetizer
companion: 5 bagel
like ~: 5 salty
LOX: 4 fuel 10 propellant
user: 6 rocket
___ Loxy: 4 Foxy
loyal: 4 fast, firm, good, true 5 liege, sound, stout 6 ardent, loving, steady, trusty 7 devoted, dutiful, staunch 8 attached, constant, faithful, reliable, resolute, true-blue, yeomanly 9 allegiant, believing, dedicated, fraternal, patriotic, steadfast, unfailing 10 dependable, inviolable, unswerving, unwavering
be ~: 6 adhere, cleave 8 hold fast
be ~ to: 4 heed, mind, obey 6 follow 7 observe
ender: 3 ist
not ~: 6 fickle 9 faithless, mercurial 10 capricious, changeable, coquettish, inconstant, unfaithful, unreliable
Loyale: 3 car 4 auto 6 Subaru 10 automobile
loyalist: 4 Tory 7 diehard, patriot 8 adherent, partisan
Loyal Order of ___: 5 Moose
loyalty: 3 tie 4 bond, duty, zeal 5 ardor, faith, honor, troth, truth 6 fealty, homage 7 honesty, probity, support 8 devotion, fidelity, trueness 9 adherence, belonging, constancy, fixedness, integrity, obedience, sincerity 10 allegiance, attachment, dedication, patriotism, resolution, singleness, subjection, submission, trustiness
expect ~ from: 4 rely 5 trust 6 bank on, look to 7 count on, entrust 8 delegate, depend on, gamble on, rely upon 9 patronize
model of ~: 4 Enid
Loy, Myrna: 7 actress
costar: 4 Asta 6 Powell
film: After the Thin Man (1936)
The Animal Kingdom (1932)
Another Thin Man (1939)
The Bachelor and the Bobby-Soxer (1947)
Belles on Their Toes (1952)
The Best Years of Our Lives (1946)
Broadway Bill (1934)
Cheaper by the Dozen (1950)
A Connecticut Yankee (1931)
Double Wedding (1937)
Emma (1932)
From the Terrace (1960)
The Great Ziegfeld (1936)
I Love You Again (1940)
Libeled Lady (1936)
Love Me Tonight (1932)
Manhattan Melodrama (1934)
Mr. Blandings Builds His Dream House (1948)
Penthouse (1933)
The Prizefighter and the Lady (1933)
The Red Pony (1949)
Shadow of the Thin Man (1941)
Test Pilot (1938)
The Thin Man (1934)
The Thin Man Goes Home (1944)
Too Hot to Handle (1938)
Topaze (1933)
When Ladies Meet (1933)
Loyola: 6 school
athletes: 8 Ramblers
locale: 7 Chicago 8 Illinois
lozenge: 4 pill 6 cachou, pastil, tablet, troche 8 pastille 9 cough drop
Lozi home: 6 Africa, Zambia
LP: 4 disc, disk 5 album, vinyl 7 platter
feature: 4 hole 5 track 6 groove
holder: 5 liner 6 sleeve
make an ~: 5 press
needles: 5 styli
player: 4 hi-fi 5 phono 6 stereo
problem: 4 skip
speed: 3 rpm
spinner: 2 DJ 6 deejay 10 disk jockey
successor: 2 CD
surface: 4 side 5 A-side, B-side, side A, side B
type: 4 mono 6 stereo
L-P center: 3 MNO
LPGA
concern: 4 golf
member: 5 woman
LPN: 5 nurse
boss: 2 dr., MD
colleague: 2 RN
field: 3 med.
place: 2 ER, OR 3 ICU 4 hosp.
specialty: 3 TLC
L-Q filler: 4 MNOP
Lr
see lawrencium
___-L-Ration: 3 Ken
L. Ron: 7 Hubbard
LSAT
cousin: 3 GRE
creator: 3 ETS
L-Shaped Room, The (1963 film)
cast: Tom Bell, Leslie Caron, Brock Peters
director: Bryan Forbes
___ L. Shirer: 7 William
LST part: 4 Ship, Tank 7 Landing
___ L. Sullivan: 4 John
LSU org: 3 SEC 4 NCAA
lt.: 3 off.
employer: 3 USA, USN 4 USCG, USMC
subordinate: 3 NCO, PFC, pvt., sgt.
superior: 3 cap., col, gen., maj. 4 capt.
trainer: 3 OCS, OTS 4 ROTC, USMA
Lt. ___: 3 Col., Com., Gen., Gov. 5 Comdr.
lt. col.: 3 off.
subordinate: 3 maj., NCO, PFC, pvt., sgt. 7 cap.. capt.
superior: 3 gen.
LTD: 3 car 4 auto, Ford 10 automobile
ltd. kin: 3 inc.
LTJG
part: 2 lt. 5 grade, lieut. 6 junior
subordinate: 3 CPO, ens.
ltr.: 4 init.
addendum: 2 p.s. 3 pps
handler: 2 PO 4 USPS
lt. yr.: 4 meas.
Lu: 4 elem. 7 element 8 lutetium
71 for ~: 4 at. no.
Lualaba: 5 river
locale: 5 Congo
Luana: 6 Anders
Luanda: 4 city, town 7 capital
locale: 3 Ang. 6 Angola
tongue: 5 Bantu
Luang Prabang land: 4 Laos
Luapula: 5 river
locale: 5 Congo 6 Zambia
luau: 4 meal 5 feast 6 spread 7 banquet, blowout
entertainment: 3 uke 4 hula 7 ukulele
fare: 3 pig, poi 4 taro 6 lau lau 8 mahimahi, roast pig.
locale: 4 Maui, Oahu 5 Kauai 6 Hawaii 7 Waikiki 8 Honolulu
neckwear: 3 lei
oven: 3 imu
Luba: 8 language
home: 5 Congo 6 Africa
Lubang: 4 isls. 5 isles 7 islands
lubber: 2 ox 3 lug 4 boob, clod, dolt, dope, fool, lout, ofaf, slob 5 clown, cluck, dunce, klutz, looby, ninny 6 dimwit, galoot, lummox, nitwit 7 bumbler, dingbat, dullard, fathead, galloot, retread 8 dumbbell, meathead, peabrain 9 blockhead, ignoramus, lamebrain, numbskull, simpleton 10 clodhopper, landlubber, muttonhead, nincompoop, stumblebum
place: 6 ashore
starter: 4 land
lubberly: 4 dull 5 gawky, inept, thick 6 clumsy, klutzy, obtuse, stolid, stupid 7 awkward, gawkish 8 bungling, ungainly 9 maladroit 10 blundering
lubber's ___: 4 hole, knot, line, mark 5 point
Lubbock: 4 city, town
athletes: 10 Red Raiders
locale: 5 Texas
school: 3 TTU 9 Texas Tech
lube
see lubricate
lube ___: 3 job
___ Lube: 5 Jiffy
Lubec: 4 city, town
locale: 5 Maine
Lübeck: 4 city, port, town
locale: 7 Germany
Lubin, Arthur: 8 director
film: Buck Privates (1941)
Hold That Ghost (1941)
Impact (1949)
In the Navy (1941)
Keep 'em Flying (1941)
Phantom of the Opera (1943)
Rhubarb (1951)
Ride 'em Cowboy (1942)
Lubitsch, Ernst: 8 director
film: Broken Lullaby (1932)
Cluny Brown (1946)
Design for Living (1933)
Heaven Can Wait (1943)
The Love Parade (1929)
The Marriage Circle (1924)
The Merry Widow (1934)
Ninotchka (1939)
One Hour With You (1932)
The Shop Around the Corner (1940)
So This Is Paris (1926)
The Student Prince in Old Heidelberg (1927)
That Uncertain Feeling (1941)
To Be or Not to Be (1942)
Trouble in Paradise (1932)
Lublin: 4 city, town
locale: 6 Poland
Lubovitch: 3 Lar
lubricant: 3 oil, wax 5 salve 6 grease 7 coating 8 silicone
organic ~: 4 tear 5 sebum
textile ~: 5 olein 6 oleine
lubricate: 3 oil, wax 4 lard 5 bribe, cream, slick, smear 6 anoint, grease, smooth, tallow 9 embrocate
again: 5 reoil
lubricated: 4 oily 5 slick 6 greasy, smooth 8 slippery, unctuous
lubricious: 4 lewd, oily 6 greasy 8 slippery, uncurbed 10 capricious, licentious
lubricity: 4 lust, porn, smut, vice 7 abandon 8 impurity, lewdness, oiliness, ribaldry, salacity, waxiness 10 corruption
lubricous: 3 hot, icy 4 lewd, oily, waxy 5 crude, dirty, gross, oiled, randy,

sleek, slick, soapy **6** coarse, filthy, glassy, glossy, greasy, impure, risqué, vulgar, wanton **7** buttery, goatish, immoral **8** prurient, slippery, slithery, unchaste, unctuous
Lubriderm: 6 lotion
alternative: 4 Keri **5** Curel, Nivea **6** Aveeno **7** Eucerin, Jergens, Pacquin
Luc: 6 Besson
Luca __ Robbia: 5 Della
Lucan: 4 poet **5** Roman
Lucania: 4 peak **5** mount **8** mountain
locale: 5 Yukon **6** Canada
Lucas: 5 Jerry **6** George, Robert, Tanner
Lucas (1986 film)
cast: Kerri Green, Corey Haim, Charlie Sheen
director: David Seltzer
Lucas, George: 8 director
film: American Graffiti (1973)
Star Wars (1977)
Star Wars Episode 1: The Phantom Menace (1999)
Lucas, Jerry
milieu: 5 court
org.: 3 NBA
sport: 10 basketball
Lucas, Robert: 8 Nobelist **9** economist
Lucci, Susan role: 5 Erica
Luce: 5 Clare, Henry
colleague: 6 Hadden
publication: 4 Life, Time **7** Fortune
Luce, Clare Boothe: 6 author, writer
work: Child of the Morning
Kiss the Boys Goodbye
Margin for Error
Slam the Door Softly
Stuffed Shirts
The Women
lucent: 5 clear, light, nitid **7** beaming, radiant, shining **8** luminous, lustrous **9** brilliant
lucerne: 7 alfalfa
Lucerne: 4 lake
locale: 11 Switzerland
river: 5 Reuss
__-Luc Godard: 4 Jean
Luchino: 8 Visconti
Lucia: 4 Popp **5** saint
__ Lucia: 5 Santa
Lucia di Lammermoor: 5 opera
character: 5 Alisa **6** Arturo, Ashton, Enrico **7** Bucklaw, Edgardo **8** Normanno, Raimondo
composer: 9 Donizetti
setting: 8 Scotland
Luciano: 5 Lucky **9** Pavarotti
lucid: 4 cool, pure, sane **5** clear, gauzy, plain, right, sheer, sober, sound, vivid **6** bright, glassy, limpid, normal, simple **7** beaming, evident, graphic, lambent, legible, logical, obvious, radiant, shining **8** all there, clear-cut, coherent, distinct, explicit, gleaming, knowable, luculent, luminous, lustrous, rational, readable, sensible, together, vitreous **9** brilliant, effulgent, graphical, graspable, refulgent, unblurred, unobscure **10** articulate, diaphanous, fathomable, reasonable
prefix for ~: 3 pel
Lucida: 4 font **8** typeface
lucidity: 3 wit **4** wits **6** reason, sanity **7** clarity
Lucie: 5 Arnaz
brother or dad: 4 Desi
lucifer: 5 beast, match **6** diablo **7** evil one, lighter **9** archangel, Beelzebub
Lucifer: 3 cat **5** angel, devil, Satan, Yokum **6** diablo
forte: 4 evil
son: 5 Abner
Lucile: 6 Watson
Lucille: 4 Ball **6** Bremer **8** Fletcher
__ Lucille: 4 La-La
Lucille (song) artist: Kenny Rogers, Little Richard
Lucinda: 6 Childs
Lucite: 5 resin **9** Plexiglas
Lucius: 4 pope **7** pontiff
luck: 3 hap, win **4** fate, lady, weal **5** break, fluke, karma, smile **6** chance, hazard, health, kismat, kismet, profit, stroke, toss-up, wealth **7** destiny, fortune, godsend, portion, success, triumph, victory **8** accident, big break, blessing, fortuity, occasion, windfall **9** advantage **10** fifty-fifty, in the cards, occurrence, prosperity
as ~ would have it: 8 by chance
bad ~: 4 blow, jinx, loss, pity **6** downer, hoodoo, mishap **7** reverse, setback, tragedy, undoing **8** distress **9** adversity, mischance **10** hard knocks, ill fortune, infelicity, misfortune
bad ~ old-style: 5 unhap
bring bad ~: 3 hex **4** jinx **5** curse
down on one's ~: 4 flat, poor **5** broke, needy **6** bad off, hard up, in need, in want **7** lacking, pinched **8** dirt poor, indigent, strapped **9** dead broke, desperate, destitute, flat broke, insolvent, moneyless, penniless **10** stone-broke, straitened
hard ~: 7 setback, trouble **8** bad break, calamity **9** adversity, mischance, suffering
Irish ~: 4 cess
out: 3 win **5** score **6** make it, thrive **7** prevail, prosper, triumph **8** flourish, get ahead, go places, make good
press one's ~: 4 dare, risk **6** gamble **8** chance it
starter: 3 pot
stretch of good ~: 3 run
luck __ draw: 5 of the
luck __ Irish: 5 of the
__ luck: 5 out of, tough
__ luck!: 5 Lotsa
__ luck?: 3 Any
Luck __ Lady: 3 Be a
__ Luck: 3 Bad, Pot **4** Lady, Pure **7** Sailor's
Luck and Pluck author: Horatio Alger
__ luck charm: 4 good
__ Luck Club, The: 3 Joy
luckily: 7 happily **8** by chance
Luckinbill, Laurence spouse: Lucie Arnaz
luckless: 4 poor **5** curst, hexed, sorry, woful **6** cursed, doomed, jinxed, woeful **7** accurst, hapless, ruinous, unblest, unhappy **8** accursed, ill-fated, wretched **9** ill-omened, unblessed, unfavored **10** disastrous, ill-starred
Luckman, Sid: 2 QB
sport: 8 football
Lucknow: 4 city, town
locale: 5 India
Luck of Ginger Coffey, The (1964 film)
cast: Liam Redmond, Robert Shaw, Mary Ure
director: Irvin Kershner
Luck of Roaring Camp, The author: Bret Harte
luck of the __: 4 draw **5** Irish
Luck of the Draw singer: 5 Raitt
lucky: 3 hot **4** well **5** blest, happy **6** benign, chance, golden, timely **7** blessed, charmed, favored, hopeful, on a roll, well-off **8** enviable **9** fortunate, on a streak, opportune, promising **10** auspicious, beneficial, felicitous, fortuitous, propitious, prosperous, successful, triumphant
be ~: 3 win **8** hit it big
break: 4 boon **5** fluke **6** chance **7** godsend **8** blessing, fortuity, windfall
if you're ~: 6 at best
leaf: 6 clover **8** shamrock
number: 5 seven
strike: 5 trove
lucky __: 5 stiff
Lucky: 6 Vanous **7** Luciano
Lucky __: 3 Day, Jim **4** Star **7** Numbers
Lucky __, The: 4 Spot
Lucky Charms: 6 cereal
competitor: 3 Kix **4** Life, Trix **5** Kashi, Quisp, Total **6** Kaboom, Muesli, Oreo O's, Pablum, Smacks **7** All-Bran, Crispix, Harmony, Hunny B's, Mueslix, Oat Bran, Pokemon **8** Boo Berry, Cheerios, Corn Chex, Corn Pops, Fiber One, Rice Chex, Special K, Uncle Sam, Wheaties **9** Alpha Bits, Apple Zaps, Grape Nuts, Honey Comb, Just Right, Wheat Chex **10** Apple Jacks, Bran Flakes, Cap'n Crunch, Cocoa Puffs, Froot Loops, Mini-Wheats, Nutri-Grain, Puffed Rice, Quaker Oats, Smart Start **11** Cocoa Blasts, Cookie Crisp, Golden Crisp, Puffed Wheat, Sweet Crunch, Waffle Crisp
Lucky Day author: Mary Higgins Clark
Lucky Jim author: Kingsley Amis
Lucky Numbers (2000 film)
cast: Lisa Kudrow, Ed O'Neill, Tim Roth, John Travolta
director: Nora Ephron
Lucky Spot, The author: Beth Henley
Lucky Star (1984 song) artist: Madonna
__-Luc Picard: 4 Jean
lucrative: 4 good **5** sweet **6** paying **7** fatness, gainful **8** fruitful, well-paid **10** high-income, in the black, productive, profitable, successful, worthwhile
lucre: 3 oof **4** cash, gain, gate, gelt, jack, kail, kale, loot, peag, pelf, take **5** bills, bread, bucks, cents, dough, funds, gravy, money, moola, mopus, pesos, rhino, sewan **6** dinero, do-re-mi, income, mammon, mazuma, moolah, payola, profit, reward, riches, seawan, silver, specie, wampum, wealth **7** cabbage, capital, dollars, lettuce, ooftish, profits, revenue, scratch, shekels **8** bankroll, cold cash, currency, earnings, hard cash, proceeds, receipts, smackers **9** banknotes, frogskins, long green, resources, simoleons **10** greenbacks, green stuff
lover: 5 miser **7** Scrooge **8** tightwad **9** skinflint **10** cheapskate, pinch-penny
__ lucre: 6 filthy
Lucretia: 4 Mott
Lucretius: 4 poet **5** Roman **11** philosopher
work: On the Nature of Things
Lucrezia: 4 Bori **6** Borgia
Lucrezia Borgia composer: 9 Donizetti
Lucrezia Floriani author: George Sand
lucubrate: 3 dig **4** cram, toil **5** grind, learn, study, write **8** pore over **9** grind away
lucubration: 4 opus **5** essay, grind, paper, study, tract **6** thesis **7** writing **8** exegesis, headwork, treatise
luculent: 5 clear, lucid, sound **6** cogent, limpid **7** graphic, logical **8** manifest, rational **9** graphical, plausible **10** compelling, convincing, persuasive, reasonable
Lucy: 3 Liu **4** Ball **5** Ewing, Hayes, Stone **7** Lawless, Ricardo, Van Pelt
brother: 5 Linus
friend: 4 Fred **5** Ethel
husband: 4 Desi
role: 4 Mame **7** Ricardo
telecast: 5 rerun
to Desi: 6 costar
Lucy __ Montgomery: 4 Maud
__ Lucy: 5 Here's, I Love
Lucy author: William Wordsworth
Lucy Gayheart author: Willa Cather
Lucy Gray author: William Wordsworth
Lucy in the Sky With Diamonds (song) artist: Beatles, Elton John
Lucy Show, The (CBS sitcom)
cast: Lucille Ball (Lucy Carmichael)
Gale Gordon (Theodore Mooney)
Vivian Vance (Vivian Bagley)
Ludden, Allen spouse: Betty White
ludicrous: 3 mad, odd **4** rich, zany **5** antic, comic, crazy, droll, funny, goony, inane, silly **6** absurd, har-har, insane, stupid **7** bizarre, burlesk, comical, fatuous, foolish, jocular, risible **8** cockeyed, farcical, gelastic, humorous **9** burlesque, facetious, fantastic, grotesque, laughable, senseless **10** impossible, outlandish, ridiculous, unfeasible
ludicrousness: 5 folly **6** antics **7** foolery, inanity **8** jocosity, nonsense **9** absurdity, silliness, stupidity
Ludlum, Robert: 6 author, writer
work: The Apocalypse Watch
The Aquitaine Progression
The Bourne Identity
The Bourne Supremacy
The Bourne Ultimatum
The Cassandra Compact
The Cry of the Halidon
The Gemini Contenders
The Hades Factor
The Holcroft Covenant
The Icarus Agenda
The Janson Directive
The Matarese Circle
The Matarese Countdown
The Matlock Paper
The Osterman Weekend
The Paris Option
The Parsifal Mosaic
The Prometheus Deception
The Rhinemann Exchange
The Road to Gandolfo
The Road to Omaha
The Scarlatti Inheritance
The Scorpio Illusion
The Sigma Protocol
Trevayne
Ludovico: 7 Ariosto
Ludwig: 4 Emil **5** Tieck **6** Donath, Edward, Minkus, Quidde **8** von Drake **9** Beethoven, Bemelmans, Feuerbach
in English: 5 Lewis, Louis
Ludwig __ Beethoven: 3 van
Ludwig __ van der Rohe: 4 Mies
__ luego!: 5 Hasta
Lufkin: 4 city, town
locale: 5 Texas
Luft: 3 Sid **5** Lorna
Luftwaffe foe: 3 RAF
lug: 2 ox **3** ape, oaf, tow, tug **4** bear, cart, drag, haul, lout, pack, pull, take, tote, yank **5** bring, brute, carry, ferry, heave, looby, shlep **6** convey, galoot, lubber **7** galloot, schlepp **8** transfer **9** blockhead, drag along, transport
lug __: 3 nut, pad **4** sail **6** wrench
lug-__: 5 soled **6** rigged
__-lug: 5 chug-a
Lugano: 4 lake
locale: 5 Italy **11** Switzerland
Lugar, Richard: 3 sen. **7** senator
luge: 4 sled **5** sport
Luger: 3 gun **6** German, pistol **7** handgun
luggage: 3 bag **4** case, gear **5** stuff,

trunk **6** things, valise **7** baggage, carry-on, tote bag **8** suitcase
attachment: **5** ID tag **8** claim tag
collect, as ~: **5** claim
load ~: **4** pack
lugger: **4** boat, ship **5** toter
lug-nut protector: **6** hubcap
Lugosi, Bela: **5** actor
film: Abbott and Costello Meet Frankenstein (1948)
The Black Cat (1934)
The Body Snatcher (1945)
The Death Kiss (1933)
Dracula (1931)
Frankenstein Meets the Wolf Man (1943)
Island of Lost Souls (1933)
Mark of the Vampire (1935)
Ninotchka (1939)
The Raven (1935)
Son of Frankenstein (1939)
White Zombie (1932)
role: **4** Igor
lugubrious: **3** sad **4** dark **5** black, bleak, drear, moody **6** dismal, dreary, gloomy, morose, rueful, somber **7** doleful, elegiac, forlorn, joyless **8** dolorous, funereal, lowering, mournful **9** cheerless, depressed, elegiacal, saddening, saturnine, sorrowful, woebegone **10** depressing, lamentable, melancholy
__ lui: **4** chez
Luigi: **4** Alva **7** Capuana, Galvani **10** Pirandello
in English: **5** Louis
see also Italian
Luing: **3** cow **4** bull **6** bovine, cattle
Luis: **5** Firpo, Tiant **6** Buñuel, Puenzo, Valdez **7** Alvarez, Mandoki **8** Aparicio
in English: **5** Lewis, Louis
see also Spanish
Luisa: **10** Tetrazzini
Luisa Miller composer: **5** Verdi
__ Luis Borges: **5** Jorge
__ Luis, Brazil: **3** Sao
Luise: **6** Rainer
__ Luis Obispo, CA: **3** San
__ Luis Potosi: **3** San
Luka (1987 song) artist: Suzanne Vega
Lukas: **4** Foss, Haas, Paul
Lukas, Paul: **5** actor
film: 20,000 Leagues Under the Sea (1954)
Berlin Express (1948)
Dodsworth (1936)
Downstairs (1932)
Fun in Acapulco (1963)
Kim (1950)
The Lady Vanishes (1938)
Little Women (1933)
Watch on the Rhine (1943, AA)
Luke: **4** Duke, Keye **5** Perry, Robin, saint **6** Halpin **7** Appling **9** Skywalker
book by ~: **4** Acts
foe: **5** Darth
follower: **4** John
preceder: **4** Mark
sister: **4** Leia
town in ~ 7: **4** Nain
Luke Havergal author: Edward Arlington Robinson
lukewarm: **4** cold, cool, mild, so-so **5** tepid, unhot **6** chilly **8** hesitant, listless **9** apathetic, uncertain, undecided **10** indecisive, irresolute, nonchalant, phlegmatic, unagitated, unresolved, wishy-washy
Luleå: **4** city, port **7** seaport
locale: **6** Sweden
lull: **3** ebb, gap **4** balm, calm, cool, fall, hush, rest, stop, wane **5** abate, allay, break, cease, comma, lapse, letup, pause, quell, quiet, still, truce **6** becalm, hiatus, layoff, pacify, recess, settle, soothe, stroke, subdue, temper **7** compose, cool off, die down, dwindle, ease off, lay back, mollify, qualify, respite, silence, slacken, subside, time-out **8** abeyance, breather, calm down, calmness, chill out, decrease, diminish, downtime, interval, moderate, reprieve, slowdown **9** interlude, put a lid on, quiet down, soft-pedal, stillness, untrouble **10** quiescence, take it easy
lullaby: **4** song **5** ditty, music **8** berceuse **10** cradlesong
Irish ~ start: **5** too-ra
word: **4** hush
Lullaby of Broadway composer: **5** Dubin **6** Warren
Lully, Raymond: **11** philosopher
lulu: **3** pip **4** oner **5** beaut, dilly, doozy **6** corker, doozer **7** whapper, whopper **9** humdinger **10** ripsnorter
Lulu: **5** opera **6** singer
composer: **4** Berg
song: To Sir with Love (1967)
spouse: Maurice Gibb
__ Lulu: **6** Little
__ Lulu Bett: **4** Miss
Lulu's Back in Town composer: **5** Dubin **6** Warren
Lum and Abner: **9** radio show
setting: **5** store
lumbago: **4** ache
lumbar: **4** back **8** vertebra
lumbar __: **6** plexus
Lumbee: **6** Indian **7** Amerind
lumber: **3** log, tax **4** hulk, lade, land, load, lump, plod, roll, slog, walk, wood **5** barge, board, clump, plank, stump, weigh, woods **6** boards, burden, charge, cumber, linger, planks, saddle, timber, trudge, waddle **7** galumph, shamble, shuffle, trundle **8** encumber **10** impose upon
ender: **4** jack, yard
flaw: **4** bend, knot, warp **5** curve **6** buckle
measure: **4** bd. ft. **5** lin. ft. **9** board foot **10** linear foot
process ~: **3** cut, saw
processed, as ~: **4** sawn
source: **3** ash, oak **4** pine **5** maple
worker: **5** sawer
lumber __: **4** room **6** jacket
lumberer: **2** ox **3** ape, ass, oaf, sap **4** boob, boor, bozo, clod, dolt, fool, goon, lout **5** beast, brute, chump, clown, cluck, dummy, dunce, idiot, joker, klutz, loser, ninny, patsy, yahoo, yokel **6** big ape, dimwit, galoot, lubber, lummox, nitwit, sucker, turkey **7** bruiser, buffoon, bumpkin, dingbat, dullard, fathead, half-wit, hayseed, jackass, pinhead, saphead **8** bonehead, dumbbell, lunkhead, meathead, numskull **9** birdbrain, blockhead, blunderer, lamebrain, numbskull, simpleton **10** clodhopper, dunderhead, nincompoop
lumbering: **3** oxy **5** gawky, unapt **6** clumsy, klutzy, oafish **7** awkward, gawkish, hulking, lumpish **8** bumbling, bungling, clunking, ungainly, unwieldy **9** all thumbs, graceless, maladroit, ponderous, stumbling, unskilled, unwieldly **10** lead-footed, unskillful
lumberjack: **5** axman **6** axeman, Bunyan, logger **8** woodsman **10** Paul Bunyan
cap: **5** toque
commodity: **3** log **4** wood **6** lumber, timber
competition: **5** roleo
leaving: **5** stump
need: **3** axe, saw **4** boot
shirt pattern: **5** plaid
Lumberton: **4** city, town
locale: **4** N. Car.
lumberyard buy: **4** beam **5** joist, plank **6** girder, rafter
Lumby: **4** city, town
locale: **6** Canada
lumen-__: **4** hour
Lumet, Sidney: **8** director
film: 12 Angry Men (1957)
The Anderson Tapes (1972)
Daniel (1983)
The Deadly Affair (1967)
Deathtrap (1982)
Dog Day Afternoon (1975)
Fail-Safe (1964)
Family Business (1989)
Garbo Talks (1984)
The Group (1966)
The Hill (1965)
Long Day's Journey Into Night (1962)
Murder on the Orient Express (1974)
Network (1976)
The Pawnbroker (1965)
Prince of the City (1981)
Running on Empty (1988)
Serpico (1973)
That Kind of Woman (1959)
The Verdict (1982)
spouse: Rita Gam, Gloria Vanderbilt
__ lumière: **5** son et
Lumière: **5** Louis
Lumina: **3** car **4** auto **5** Chevy **9** Chevrolet **10** automobile
luminaria: **5** light **6** candle
luminary: **3** sun, VIP **4** hero, idol, lion, name, star **5** celeb **6** leader, worthy **7** big name, notable **8** eminence, somebody **9** celebrity, dignitary, personage, superstar
luminesce: **4** glow **5** gleam, shine **7** flicker, glimmer, glisten, glitter, radiate, shimmer
luminescence: **4** glow, tint **5** gleam, light, sheen, shine **7** insight, shimmer **8** lambency, radiance, radiancy, splendor
luminescent: **6** bright, lucent **7** glowing, lambent, radiant, shining **8** luminous **9** effulgent
luminosity: **4** glow, tint **5** gleam, light, sheen, shine **7** insight, shimmer **8** lambency, radiance, radiancy, splendor
unit: **6** candle **7** candela
luminous: **3** lit **5** aglow, clear, light, lucid, shiny, vivid **6** ablaze, bright, flashy, lucent **7** beaming, blazing, crystal, evident, fulgent, glowing, lambent, lighted, obvious, radiant, shining **8** dazzling, gleaming, knowable, lustrous **9** brilliant, effulgent, graspable, inspiring, refulgent, sparkling, unobscure **10** fathomable
luminous __: **4** flux **5** paint, range **6** energy
luminousness: **4** glow **6** luster **8** lambency, radiance **10** effulgence, refulgence
Lumley: **6** Joanna
lummox: **2** ox **3** ape, ass, oaf, sap **4** boob, boor, bozo, clod, dolt, fool, goon, gowk, lout **5** beast, brute, chump, clown, cluck, dummy, dunce, joker, klutz, looby, loser, ninny, patsy, yahoo, yokel **6** big ape, dimwit, lubber, nitwit, sucker, turkey **7** bruiser, buffoon, bumpkin, dingbat, dullard, fathead, half-wit, hayseed, jackass, pinhead, saphead **8** bonehead, dumbbell, lunkhead, meathead, numskull **9** birdbrain, blockhead, blunderer, lamebrain, numbskull, simpleton **10** clodhopper, dunderhead, nincompoop
cry: **4** oops
like a ~: **5** dense, inept **6** clumsy, gauche **7** awkward **8** bumbling, bungling, cloddish, fumbling **9** all thumbs, graceless, maladroit
lump: **3** bit, dab, gob, lot, mix, nub, pat, wad **4** ball, bear, blob, bulk, bump, cake, chip, clod, clot, glob, heap, hunk, knob, knot, knub, loaf, mass, much, node, nurl, part, peck, pile, slab, spot, take **5** abide, amass, batch, block, brook, bulge, bunch, chunk, clump, crumb, gnarl, group, knurl, piece, scrap, solid, stand, tumor, wedge **6** digest, dollop, endure, gobbet, growth, lumber, morsel, nodule, nugget, suffer **7** cluster, handful, portion, section, stomach, swallow **8** mountain, swelling, tolerate **9** aggregate, put up with, withstand **10** protrusion, tumescence
of jelly: **4** blob **6** dollop
together: **4** join **5** batch, bunch, group **6** bundle **7** bunch up, combine
lump __: **3** sum
lumper: **7** laborer **10** day laborer
lump in one's __: **6** throat
lumpish: **4** dopy, dull, slow **5** dense, dopey, heavy **6** bovine, clumsy, obtuse, stolid, stupid **7** awkward **8** backward, sluggish, ungainly **9** lumbering, ponderous **10** phlegmatic
lump of __: **5** sugar
lumps: **10** punishment
some ~: **5** sugar
__ Lumpur: **5** Kuala
lumpy: **5** bumpy, nubby **6** chunky, knobby, uneven **7** gnarled, knurled **8** unsmooth **9** irregular **10** nonuniform
not ~: **4** even **6** creamy, smooth **7** uniform, velvety
luna __: **4** moth
Luna: **4** moon **7** Barbara
Luna (1979 film)
cast: Matthew Barry, Jill Clayburgh, Veronica Lazar
director: Bernardo Bertolucci
__ Luna: **3** Eva
Luna, Barbara spouse: Doug McClure
lunacy: **5** folly, mania **6** idiocy **7** fatuity, inanity, madness **8** insanity **9** absurdity, asininity, craziness, imbalance, silliness
lunar
craft: **3** LEM **5** probe, rover **6** lander
crater: **5** Tycho
depression: **6** crater
gap between solar and ~ year: **5** epact
phase: **3** new **4** full **7** gibbous **8** crescent
phenomenon: **4** halo, tide **6** corona **7** eclipse
plain: **3** sea **4** mare
valley: **4** rill **5** rille
see also moon
lunar __: **3** day **4** year **5** cycle, month, orbit, rover **6** module **7** caustic, eclipse, landing, orbiter, rainbow
Lunar __: **7** Orbiter
lunar excursion __: **6** module
__ Lunas, NM: **3** Los
lunatic: **9** unscrewed
Lunatic Villas author: **5** Engel
lunch: **3** eat **4** bite, meal **6** spread **9** grab a bite
at ~: **3** out **5** not in
before ~: **4** morn **7** morning **8** forenoon
choice: **3** BLT, ham, sub **4** hero, Spam, to go, tuna **5** pizza, salad

6 cheese 7 bologna 8 sandwich, tuna fish 9 roast beef, submarine
ender: 3 eon 4 meat, room, time
have ~: 3 eat 4 dine, meet
out to ~: 4 gaga 7 unaware 8 confused 9 forgetful
reading: 4 menu
stop: 4 deli 5 diner 6 eatery 10 restaurant
time: 3 one 4 hour, noon 5 one p.m. 6 midday, twelve
lunch ___: 4 hour 7 counter
___ lunch: 3 box 4 free 5 Dutch, out to, power 7 potluck
luncheon: 4 meal 5 party 6 affair, social 8 function 9 blue plate, gathering
ender: 4 ette
luncheon ___: 4 meat
luncheonette: 4 café 5 diner 6 eatery 10 restaurant
Luncheon on the Grass artist: 5 Manet
Lunch Poems author: 5 O'Hara
lunchroom: 4 café 5 diner, grill 6 eatery 7 canteen 9 cafeteria 10 restaurant
lure: 5 aroma
___ Lunch, The: 5 Naked
Lund: 4 Ilsa, John
Lunda home: 5 Congo 6 Africa, Angola, Zambia
Lunden: 4 Joan
Lundgren: 5 Dolph
lundi: 4 jour 6 French, Monday
follower: 5 mardi
preceder: 8 dimanche
Lund, John: 5 actor
film: A Foreign Affair (1948)
The Mating Season (1951)
The Perils of Pauline (1947)
To Each His Own (1946)
The Wackiest Ship in the Army (1960)
Lundy: 3 isl. 4 isle 6 island
lune: 4 moon 5 leash 8 crescent, half-moon
Lunel: 4 city, town
locale: 6 France
lung: 5 organ 8 breather
combining form: 5 pneum-, pulmo- 6 pneumo-, pulmon- 7 pneumon-, pulmoni-, pulmono- 8 pneumono-
ender: 4 fish, worm, wort
fish ~: 4 gill
like a ~: 5 lobar, lobed
___-Lung: 4 Aqua
lunge: 3 cut, hit, jab 4 dart, dash, dive, jump, leap, pass, poke, push, rush, stab 5 bound, burst, drive, forge, lurch, pitch, reach, surge, swing, swipe 6 charge, hurtle, plunge, pounce, spring, strike, thrust 7 set upon 8 fall upon
(at): 3 run
___-lunged: 7 leather
lungful: 3 air
lungi: 5 scarf 6 sarong, turban 9 loincloth
lungs, use: 6 exhale, inhale 7 breathe
lunker: 4 bass
lunkhead: 2 ox 3 ape, ass, lug, nit, oaf, sap 4 boob, bozo, clod, dolt, dope, fool, gowk, lout, slob 5 clown, cluck, dummy, dunce, klutz, looby, ninny 6 dimwit, galoot, lummox, nitwit 7 bumbler, dingbat, dullard, galloot 8 dumbbell, peabrain 9 ignoramus, numbskull, simpleton 10 clodhopper, landlubber, nincompoop, stumblebum
___ lunn: 5 sally
Lunt, Alfred spouse: Lynn Fontanne
Lunts milieu: 5 stage 8 Broadway
Luo home: 5 Kenya 6 Africa
Lupe: 5 Velez
Lupin: 6 Arsene
lupine: 5 plant 6 fierce, flower, savage 7 wolfish 8 ravening, ravenous, wolflike 9 ferocious, predatory, rapacious 10 wildflower
animal: 4 wolf
Lupino, Ida: 7 actress 8 director
film: The Adventures of Sherlock Holmes (1939)
Anything Goes (1936)
The Bigamist (1953)
The Big Knife (1955)
Deep Valley (1947)
The Hard Way (1942)
High Sierra (1941)
Junior Bonner (1972)
Ladies in Retirement (1941)
Life Begins at Eight-Thirty (1942)
The Light That Failed (1939)
The Lone Wolf Spy Hunt (1939)
The Man I Love (1946)
On Dangerous Ground (1952)
Out of the Fog (1941)
Road House (1948)
The Sea Wolf (1941)
They Drive by Night (1940)
While the City Sleeps (1956)
spouse: Howard Duff
LuPone: 5 Patti
role: 5 Evita
Lupton: 4 John
Lupus: 5 Peter
lurch: 3 yaw 4 cant, duck, jerk, jump, keel, lean, list, reel, rock, roll, slip, snap, sway, tilt, toss, trip 5 dodge, heave, lunge, pitch, slide, swing, weave 6 bumble, careen, falter, plunge, seesaw, swerve, teeter, totter, wabble, wallow, wobble 7 blunder, stagger, stammer, stumble 8 flounder
forward, nautically: 5 scend
leave in the ~: 4 jilt, quit 5 ditch 6 cop out, desert, reject, strand 7 abandon, forsake, let down 8 abdicate
lure: 3 fly, jig 4 bait, coax, draw, hook, plug, pull, trap, wile 5 bribe, charm, decoy, shill, snare, spoon, tempt, trick 6 beckon, cajole, carrot, come-on, entice, entrap, induce, invite, lead on, magnet, pull in, rope in, suck in 7 attract, beguile, bewitch, capture, con game, enchant, ensnare, gimmick, insnare, mislead, spinner 8 appeal to, flypaper, interest, inveigle, persuade 9 appetence, captivate, fascinate, incentive, magnetism, mousetrap, siren song, sweetener 10 attractant, attraction, camouflage, enticement, inducement, invitation, temptation
fishing ~: 3 fly, jig 4 plug 5 spoon, troll 6 dry fly
into wrongdoing: 4 hook, trap 5 decoy, set up, snare, trick 6 entice, lead on, reel in, suck in 7 beguile, ensnare 8 entangle, inveigle
Lurene: 6 Tuttle
lurer: 5 siren 7 enticer, Lorelei 9 temptress
Luria, Salvador: 8 Nobelist
lurid: 4 gory, grim, pale, racy 5 ashen, fiery, livid, vivid 6 bloody, dismal, grisly, pallid, risqué, sultry 7 flaming, flaring, ghastly, graphic, hideous, intense, macaber, macabre, violent 8 gruesome, horrible, shocking, sinister 9 appalling, frightful, graphical, low-minded 10 horrifying, scandalous
Lurie, Alison: 6 author, writer
work: Foreign Affairs
Imaginary Friends
The Language of Clothes
Love and Friendship
Only Children
The War Between the Tates
lurk: 4 hide, slip, wait 5 creep, prowl, sculk, shirk, skulk, slide, slink, snake, sneak, snoop, steal 6 crouch, lay for, waylay 7 gumshoe, slither 9 lie in wait 10 hang around, nose around
lurker's plan: 4 trap 6 ambush
lurking: 5 snaky 6 unseen 9 potential 10 underlying, undetected
Lusaka: 4 city, town 7 capital
locale: 6 Zambia
luscious: 4 good, rich 5 juicy, sapid, sweet, tasty, yummy 6 choice, creamy, delish, liquid, mellow, savory, toothy 7 opulent 8 heavenly 9 ambrosial, delicious, exquisite, flavorful, luxuriant, luxurious, nectarous, palatable, succulent, sumptuous, toothsome 10 appetizing, delectable, flavorsome
lush: 3 sot 4 posh, rank, rich, wild, wino 5 cushy, dense, grand, green, plush, ritzy, souse, toper 6 barfly, bibber, creamy, deluxe, lavish, tender 7 fertile, guzzler, opulent, profuse, riotous, teeming, tippler, tosspot, verdant 8 abundant, heavenly, palatial, prodigal, prolific, tropical 9 exuberant, luxuriant, luxurious, overgrown, plentiful, succulent, sumptuous
lushness: 8 elegance 9 abundance, profusion
Lusitania: 4 boat, ship 5 liner
sinker: 5 U-boat
Luske, Hamilton: 8 director
film: Cinderella (1950)
Lady and the Tramp (1955)
One Hundred and One Dalmatians (1961)
Peter Pan (1953)
Pinocchio (1940)
lust: 3 sin, yen 4 ache, itch, love, need, sigh, urge, vice, want 5 covet, crave, greed, yearn 6 desire, fervor, hanker, libido, thirst 7 avidity, craving, passion 8 appetite, cupidity, salacity 9 appetence, esurience, lubricity
for: 4 want 5 covet, crave 6 desire
(for): 3 die 4 ache, itch, long, pant, pine, sigh, wish 5 yearn 6 hunger, thirst
luster: 4 glow 5 glaze, gleam, glint, gloss, light, sheen, shine 6 dazzle, finish, polish, renown 7 burnish, glitter, shimmer, sparkle, varnish 8 lambency, radiance, radiancy, splendor 9 afterglow 10 brightness, brilliance, brilliancy, effulgence, refulgence
ender: 4 ware
lose ~: 4 fade 7 tarnish
starter: 4 lack
lusterless: 3 dim, dun 4 dark, drab, dull, flat, pale 5 dingy, dirty, dusty, faded, grimy, matte, muddy 6 gritty, opaque 7 unwaxed 8 lifeless
Lust for Life: 4 film 5 novel
author: Irving Stone
cast: James Donald, Kirk Douglas, Anthony Quinn
director: Vincente Minnelli
lustful: 4 avid, lewd 5 randy 6 greedy, wanton 7 craving, goatish, hoggish, immoral, piggish, sensual, wolfish 8 covetous, desirous, prurient, ravening, unchaste, uncurbed 9 abandoned, dissolute, rapacious, salacious, voracious 10 avaricious, gluttonous, hot-blooded, insatiable, lascivious, licentious, passionate, profligate, unvirtuous
lustiness: 5 vigor 7 stamina 8 vitality
lustrous: 3 lit 4 waxy 5 aglow, glacé, light, lucid, nitid, shiny, silky, sleek, waxen 6 ablaze, bright, flashy, glassy, glazed, glossy, lucent, pearly, satiny, silver, smooth 7 beaming, blazing, fulgent, glowing, lambent, radiant, shining 8 dazzling, gleaming, glinting, glorious, luminous, nacreous, polished, splendid 9 brilliant, burnished, effulgent, refulgent, sparkling 10 glistening, iridescent, shimmering
fabric: 4 lamé, silk 5 ramee, ramie, satin
Lustrous ___ of sun: 3 orb
lusty: 4 hale, iron, wiry 5 beefy, burly, hardy, hefty, hunky, husky, stout, tough, vital 6 brawny, earthy, hearty, mighty, potent, robust, rugged, sinewy, steely, stocky, strong, sturdy, virile 7 doughty, dynamic, healthy 8 athletic, forceful, indurate, muscular, powerful, puissant, spirited, stalwart, vigorous 9 Atlantean, energetic, Herculean, strapping, strenuous, well-built 10 able-bodied, full of life, hot-blooded, red-blooded
Lusty Men, The (1952 film)
cast: Susan Hayward, Arthur Kennedy, Robert Mitchum
director: Nicholas Ray
Lut: 6 desert
locale: 4 Iran
lute: 3 oud, saz, uti 4 biwa, pipa, ruan 5 cobza 6 buzuki, string 7 bandore, kantele, mandola, pandora, samisen, tambura, theorbo 8 bousouki, bouzouki, surbahar 9 balalaika
Arab: 3 oud
cousin: 4 lyre, viol 5 rebab, rebec 6 guitar, rebeck
feature: 4 fret
Hindu: 5 sarod, sitar
lutefisk: 3 cod 8 fish dish
tenderizer: 3 lye
Lute Song author: Sidney Howard
lutetium: 7 element 9 rare earth
Luth.: 4 Prot.
school: 3 sem.
Luther: 5 Adler 6 Ingram, Martin 7 Burbank 8 Campbell, Vandross
___ Luther King: 6 Martin
Luther, Martin: 6 German 8 reformer
postings: 6 theses
work: Ninety-Five Theses
Luthor: 3 Lex
like: 4 evil
to Superman: 3 foe 5 enemy
Luton: 4 city, town
locale: 7 England
Lutuli, Albert: 8 Nobelist
Lutz: 4 leap
alternative: 4 axel
where to do a ~: 3 ice 4 rink
luv: 3 hon 4 dear 5 honey 7 darling 10 sweetheart
Luv (1967 film)
cast: Peter Falk, Jack Lemmon, Elaine May
character: 4 Milt 5 Ellen
director: Clive Donner
Luvs: 6 diaper
alternative: 7 Drypers, Huggies, Pampers
___ lux: 4 fiat
Lux: 4 soap
alternative: 4 Dial, Dove, Lava, Tone, Zest 5 Camay, Coast, Ivory, Lever 6 Boraxo, Caress, Shield 8 Lifebuoy 9 Palmolive, Safeguard 11 Irish Spring
Lux ___ Theatre: 5 Radio
luxe: 4 fine, posh, rich 5 class, plush 6 classy 7 elegant, opulent 8 elegance, fineness, opulence, opulency, poshness, richness, splendid, splendor 9 high-class, plushness, sumptuous
Luxembourg: 4 city, town 5 duchy 6 nation 7 capital, country
capital: 10 Luxembourg
locale: 3 Eur. 6 Europe

money: 5 franc
neighbor: 3 Ger. 4 Belg. 6 France 7 Belgium, Germany
Nobelist in Medicine: 6 Claude
org.: 4 NATO
Luxor: 4 city, town 6 casino
city near ~: 4 Qena 5 Aswan 6 Assuan 7 Assouan
locale: 5 Egypt, Vegas 8 Las Vegas
river: 4 Nile
luxuriance: 6 wealth 9 fecundity, fertility 10 exuberance
luxuriant: 4 lush, rank, rich, wild 5 ample, dense, fancy, plush 6 deluxe, fecund, florid, lavish, ornate 7 copious, fertile, flowery, opulent, profuse, rampant, riotous, teeming 8 abundant, fruitful, generous, luscious, palatial, prodigal, prolific, thriving 9 bountiful, elaborate, excessive, exuberant, plenteous, plentiful, profusive, sumptuous 10 flamboyant, productive
luxuriate: 4 bask, grow, love, riot, roll 5 bloom, eat up, enjoy, feast, revel 6 abound, overdo, relish, roll in, thrive, wallow, wanton 7 burgeon, delight, indulge, prosper, rollick, run riot 8 abound in, bourgeon, flourish, increase, live it up 9 delight in, feast upon 10 take it easy
in: 4 like 5 adore, enjoy, revel, savor 6 relish, wallow 7 indulge 10 appreciate
luxurious: 4 easy, lush, posh, rich 5 fancy, grand, haute, plush, ritzy, showy, silky, swank, swell 6 costly, deluxe, flashy, frilly, glitzy, lavish, lordly, ornate, plushy, swanky 7 elegant, opulent, stately, upscale 8 affluent, gorgeous, imposing, luscious, majestic, palatial, pampered, princely, prodigal, splendid 9 decorated, elaborate, epicurean, expensive, grandiose, indulgent, sumptuous, sybaritic 10 gratifying, hedonistic, immoderate, impressive, majestical, ornamented
hardly ~: 4 mean 5 dingy, mangy, ratty, seedy 6 beat-up, crummy, shabby, shoddy, sleazy, sordid 7 run-down, sagging, scruffy, squalid 8 decaying, decrepit
luxury: 4 ease, posh 5 bliss, frill, ritzy, style, treat 6 rarity, wealth 7 amenity, comfort, delight, leisure 8 delicacy, elegance, good life, grandeur, hedonism, noblesse, opulence, opulency, richness, splendor 9 affluence, enjoyment, well-being 10 high living, indulgence, lavishness, prosperity
in the lap of ~: 4 posh, rich 5 plush, ritzy, swank 6 swanky 7 upscale 8 affluent, pampered, princely 9 sumptuous, sybaritic
lap of ~: 5 means, money 6 riches, wealth 7 fortune 8 opulence 9 abundance, affluence 10 gravy train, prosperity
luxury __: 3 car, tax
__ luxury: 5 lap of
Luyendyk, Arie: 9 auto racer
milieu: 5 track
Luzinski: 4 Greg
Luzon: 3 isl. 4 isle 6 island
bay: 5 Subic
neighbor: 5 Samar
peninsula: 6 Bataan
people: 5 Bikol
port: 6 Aparri
river: 5 Pasig
volcano: 4 Taal 5 Mayon 7 Bulusan 8 Pinatubo
Lvov: 4 city, town
locale: 7 Ukraine
Lw: 4 elem. 7 element 10 lawrencium
103 for ~: 4 at. no.
Lwoff, André: 8 Nobelist
lwyr.: 3 att. 4 atty.
lycée: 6 French, school 7 academy 9 institute
kin: 5 école
lyceum: 4 hall 6 school 7 academy, gallery, theater, theatre 9 gymnasium, institute 10 auditorium
Lycia, city of ancient: 4 Myra
Lycidas author: John Milton
Lycra cousin: 5 nylon
Lydgate, John: 4 poet
Lydia: 5 Child, Lunch 7 Cornell
capital of ~: 6 Sardis
Lydia (1941 film)
cast: Alan Marshal, Merle Oberon, Edna May Oliver
Lydian __: 4 mode
Lydia poet: 4 Cato
Lydia, the Tattooed Lady composer: 5 Arlen 7 Harburg
Lydie Breeze author: John Guare
Lydon: 5 James, Jimmy
lye: 3 KOH 4 NaOH 6 alkali, potash 7 caustic 8 lixivium
Lyell, Charles: 9 geologist
Lyin' Eyes (1975 song) artist: Eagles
lying: 3 sin 4 sham 5 false, trick, wrong 6 deceit, dupery, shifty, tricky, untrue 7 crooked, fibbing, knavish, perjury 8 delusive, delusory, guileful, lounging, two-faced 9 deceitful, deception, deceptive, dishonest, incumbent, insincere, inventing, mendacity, pretended, two-timing 10 committing, dishonesty, falsifying, mendacious, misleading, misstating, perfidious, unreliable, untruthful
down: 5 level, prone 6 face up, supine 8 face down 9 prostrate, recumbent 10 horizontal
still: 4 idle 5 inert 7 dormant
stop ~: 5 sit up
__-lying: 3 low
lying down
in heraldry: 7 dormant 8 couchant
Lyle: 5 Sandy 6 Alzado, Lovett, Sparky, Talbot 7 Bettger 8 Waggoner
Lyle, Sandy: 6 golfer
Lyman: 4 Link 6 Arthur 7 Beecher, Dorothy
Lymon and the Teenagers, Frankie
song: Goody Goody (1957)
I Want You to Be My Girl (1956)
Why Do Fools Fall in Love (1956)
lymph __: 4 node 5 gland
lymphatic: 8 listless, sluggish 9 lethargic
lymph-gland location: 6 armpit
Lyn: 4 Dawn
__ Lyn Bauer: 5 Jaime
Lynch: 4 John 5 David, Kelly 8 Jennifer
Lynchburg: 4 city, town
locale: 8 Virginia
Lynch, David: 8 director
film: Blue Velvet (1986)
The Elephant Man (1980)
Eraserhead (1978)
Mulholland Dr. (2001)
The Straight Story (1999)
Lynda: 6 Carter 7 Johnson
Lynda __ George: 3 Day
Lynda Bird's sister: 4 Luci
Lynda Johnson __: 4 Robb
Lynde: 4 Paul
Lyndon: 5 Barré 7 Johnson 8 Larouche
daughter: 4 Luci 5 Lynda
__ Lyndon: 5 Barry
Lyne, Adrian: 8 director
film: Fatal Attraction (1987)
Flashdance (1983)
Indecent Proposal (1993)
Lolita (1997)
Unfaithful (2002)
Lynen, Feodor: 8 Nobelist
Lynley, Carol: 7 actress
film: Blue Denim (1959)
Hound-Dog Man (1959)
The Light in the Forest (1958)
The Poseidon Adventure (1972)
Under the Yum Yum Tree (1963)
Lynn: 4 Bari, city, Fred, town, Vera 5 Diana, Janet, Sherr, Swann 6 Carlin, Cheryl 7 Barbara, Jeffrey, Kellogg, Loretta 8 Anderson, Fontanne, Jonathan, Redgrave, Reynolds
locale: 4 Mass.
Lynn, Diana: 7 actress
film: Bedtime for Bonzo (1951)
My Friend Irma (1949)
Our Hearts Were Young and Gay (1944)
Ruthless (1948)
You're Never Too Young (1955)
Lynne: 4 Jeff 6 Shelby
__ Lynne: 4 East
Lynne, Jeff rock band: 3 ELO
__ Lynn Gorney: 5 Karen
Lynn-Holly: 7 Johnson
Lynn, Jonathan: 8 director
film: The Distinguished Gentleman (1992)
My Cousin Vinny (1992)
Sgt. Bilko (1996)
Trial and Error (1997)
The Whole Nine Yards (2000)
Lynn, Loretta: 6 singer
father: 5 miner
sister: Crystal Gayle
Lynnwood: 4 city, town
locale: 10 Washington
Lynwood: 4 city, town
locale: 10 California
lynx: 3 cat 5 felid 6 animal, bobcat, feline, mammal
relative: 4 eyra, lion, puma 5 chita, liger, ounce, tiger, tigon 6 cheeta, chetah, cougar, jaguar, margay, ocelot, serval, tiglon 7 caracal, cheetah, leopard, panther 9 catamount 10 jaguarundi
__ lynx: 3 bay 6 Canada
Lynx: 3 car 4 auto, Merc 7 Mercury 10 automobile
lynx-eyed: 4 keen 5 acute, aware, sharp 9 all-seeing, intuitive, observant 10 discerning, insightful, perceptive
Lynyrd Skynyrd
lead singer: Ronnie Van Zant
song: Free Bird (1975)
Saturday Night Special (1975)
Sweet Home Alabama (1974)
What's Your Name (1978)
Lyon: 3 Ben, Sue 4 city, town
locale: 6 France
river: 5 Rhone, Saône
see also French
lyonnaise ingredient: 5 onion
Lyons: 4 city, town 7 Douglas, Jeffrey
river: 5 Rhone, Saône
town north of ~: 5 Cluny
see also French
Lyra
neighbor: 6 Cygnus
star in ~: 4 Vega
lyre: 5 crwth, kerar 6 bagana, kissar, string 7 cithara, kithara, obukano
cousin: 4 harp
ender: 4 bird
goddess with a ~: 5 Erato
Hebrew ~: 4 asor
lyre __: 4 back 5 snake
__ lyre: 6 Aeolic 7 Aeolian
lyric: 4 song 5 verse, vocal, words 6 choral, melody, poetic 7 melodic, musical, songful, tuneful 8 poetical, songlike 9 melodious 10 coloratura
poet: 5 odist
work: 3 lai, ode 4 poem 5 epode 6 arioso
lyrical: 4 odic 6 choral, dulcet, in tune, poetic 7 chiming, lilting, melodic, musical, songful, soulful, tuneful 8 blending, operatic, pleasing, poetical, rhythmic, songlike, sonorous 9 agreeable, emotional, melodious, rhapsodic, symphonic, well-tuned 10 euphonious, expressive, harmonious, orchestral, passionate
Lyrical Ballads author: William Wordsworth
lyricism: 4 brio, fire 5 ardor 6 warmth 7 ecstasy, emotion, passion, rapture 8 rhapsody 9 intensity
lyricist: 4 poet 9 songsmith 10 songwriter
lyrics: 5 words
feature: 5 meter, rhyme 7 cadence, measure
forgo the ~: 3 hum 7 whistle
lyrist: 4 poet 7 Orpheus 8 composer, musician
Lys: 5 river
locale: 6 France 7 Belgium
Lysaght: 4 peak 5 mount 8 mountain
locale: 10 Antarctica
lysine: 9 amino acid
Lysithea: 4 moon
planet: 7 Jupiter
Lysol: 7 cleaner
alternative: 5 Brite, Tilex 6 Top Job 7 Lestoil, Mr. Clean, Pine Sol 9 Fantastik, Step Saver
target: 5 staph 6 mildew
lyssa: 6 rabies

m
to Einstein: 4 mass
m.: 4 lgth., meas.
M: 4 size 6 letter 8 thousand
followers: 3 NOP 4 NOPQ 5 NOPQR
in phonetic alphabet: 4 Mike
portrayer: 3 Lee 5 Dench
preceders: 3 JKL 4 IJKL 5 HIJKL
M (1931 film)
cast: Inge Landgut, Peter Lorre, Ellen Widmann
director: Fritz Lang
M __: 4 roof, star
M __ Mary: 4 as in
M __ the million things...: 5 is for
M-__: 3 day 4 line 5 shell 6 series
M. __ Peck: 5 Scott
M. __ Walsh: 5 Emmet
__ M?: 3 N or
'M' __ Malice: 5 Is for
ma: 6 parent
see also mother
Ma: 4 Bell, Yo-Yo 6 Barker, Rainey
Ma __: 7 Perkins
Ma __ Amie: 5 Belle
Ma! (He's Making Eyes __): 4 at Me
Má __: 5 Vlast
MA
region: 4 N. Eng.
zone: 3 EDT, EST
see also Massachusetts
M.A.: 3 deg. 6 degree
part of ~: 4 arts 6 master
pursuer's test: 3 GRE
maa: 5 bleat
sounder: 4 goat 5 nanny 6 nannie
Maalox: 7 antacid
alternative: 4 Tums 6 Pepcid, Riopan, Zantac 7 Gelusil, Lactaid, Mylanta, Rolaids 8 Gaviscon 11 Alka-Seltzer, Pepto-Bismol
__, ma'am: 3 Yes
ma'am companion: 3 sir
Ma and Pa Kettle at Home (1954 film)
cast: Percy Kilbride, Marjorie Main, Alan Mowbray
Ma and Pa operation: 5 store
__ Maarten: 4 Sint
Maas: 5 river
city on the ~: 5 Liege, Sedan 6 Verdun 9 Rotterdam
locale: 6 France 7 Belgium, Holland 11 Netherlands
Maasai home: 5 Kenya 6 Africa 8 Tanzania
Maastricht: 4 city, town
locale: 7 Holland 11 Netherlands
Maazel, Lorin: 9 conductor
Mab: 5 Queen 6 sprite
mate: 6 Oberon
__, Ma Baby: 5 Hello
Mabel: 4 King 7 Normand
__ & Mabel: 4 Mack
Ma Belle __: 4 Amie
__ Mable: 4 Dere
Mableton: 4 city, town
locale: 7 Georgia
Mabley: 4 Moms
mac: 3 bub 5 buddy 6 buster, jacket 7 slicker 8 raincoat, rainwear 10 protection
starter: 3 tar
wearer: 6 Briton
Mac: 5 Davis, Hyman 6 Bernie 8 computer 9 McAnnally
alternative: 2 PC
insert: 5 CD/ROM
producer: 5 Apple
what ~ means: 5 son of
Mac (1992 film)
cast: Michael Badalucco, Carl Capotorto, John Turturro
director: John Turturro
__ Mac: 3 Big 7 Freddie
MAC
school: 3 NIU 4 Ohio 5 Akron, Miami 6 Toledo 7 Buffalo 8 Marshall 9 Ball State, Kent State
macabre: 4 eery, gory, grim, sick 5 eerie, lurid, scary, weird 6 creepy, grisly, morbid, spooky 7 fearful, ghastly, ghostly, hideous 8 ghoulish, gruesome, horrible 9 frightful, monstrous
being: 5 ghoul
master of the ~: 3 Poe
__ Macabre: 5 Danse
macaco: 7 primate
relative: 3 ape 4 saki, titi 5 chimp, drill, jocko, lemur, loris, magot, orang, potto, shrew 6 aye-aye, baboon, Bandar, galago, gelada, gibbon, grivet, guenon, howler, langur, monkey, rhesus, uakari, vervet 7 colobus, gorilla, guereza, hoolock, sapajou, siamang, tamarin, tarsier 8 bush baby, capuchin, mandrill, mangabey, marmoset, talapoin 9 orangutan 10 Barbary ape, chimpanzee, orangutang
macadam
ingredient: 3 tar
layer: 5 paver
put down ~: 4 pave
macadamia: 3 nut 4 tree
macadamize: 4 pave
MacAfee: 4 city, town
locale: 7 Georgia
MacAllen: 4 city, town
locale: 5 Texas
Macao: 4 city, port, town
coin: 3 avo
neighbor: 5 China
macaque: 5 jocko 6 animal, rhesus 7 primate 10 Barbary ape
relative: 4 saki, titi 5 chimp, drill, lemur, loris, magot, orang, potto, shrew 6 aye-aye, baboon, Bandar, galago, gelada, gibbon, grivet, guenon, howler, langur, monkey, uakari, vervet 7 colobus, gorilla, guereza, hoolock, sapajou, siamang, tamarin, tarsier 8 bush baby, capuchin, mandrill, mangabey, marmoset, talapoin 9 orangutan 10 chimpanzee, orangutang
macarena: 5 dance
Macarena (1996 song) artist: Los Del Rio
macaroni: 3 fop 4 dude, ziti 5 pasta, penne, zitti 6 elbows, noodle 7 lasagna, lasagne, noodles, pastina, ravioli 8 bucatini, couscous, farfalle, linguine, linguini, rigatoni 9 agnolotti, angelhair, cavatelli, manicotti, spaghetti 10 cannelloni, fettuccini, jack-a-dandy, tortellini, vermicelli
salad ingredient: 4 mayo
macaroni __: 5 salad, wheat
__ macaroni: 5 elbow
macaroon: 6 cookie
MacArthur: 4 Park 5 James 7 Charles, Douglas
onetime ~ command: 5 Korea
word in a ~ quote: 5 shall 6 return
MacArthur (1977 film)
cast: Ed Flanders, Dan O'Herlihy, Gregory Peck
MacArthur, Charles spouse: Helen Hayes
MacArthur, James: 5 actor
film: The Interns (1962)
The Light in the Forest (1958)
Swiss Family Robinson (1960)
Third Man on the Mountain (1959)
The Young Stranger (1957)
mother: Helen Hayes
TV: Hawaii Five-O
MacArthur Park (song) artist: Donna Summer, Richard Harris
composer: 4 Webb
Macartney __: 4 rose
Macassar __: 3 oil 6 Strait
Macau
see Macao
Macaulay: 4 Rose 6 Culkin, Thomas
Macaulay, Rose: 4 Dame 6 writer 7 British
work: Crewe Train
The Shadow Flies
Told by an Idiot
The Towers of Trezibond
Macavity: 3 cat
macaw: 3 ara 4 bird 5 arara
Macbeth: 4 Lady, play, Scot 5 opera
composer: 5 Verdi
Macbeth (1948 film)
cast: Jeanette Nolan, Dan O'Herlihy, Orson Welles
director: Orson Welles
Macbeth (1971 film)
cast: Francesca Annis, Jon Finch, Martin Shaw
director: Roman Polanski
Macbeth (play)
author: William Shakespeare
recipe ingredient: 3 dog 4 frog, newt
role: 4 Ross 5 Angus, Witch 6 Banquo, Duncan, Hecate, Lennox, Seyton, Siward 7 Fleance, Macbeth, Macduff, Malcolm 8 Menteith 9 Caithness, Donalbain
trio: 4 hags 7 witches
MacBride, Sean: 8 Nobelist
__ Maccabaeus: 5 Judas
__ Maccabeus: 5 Judah
Macchio: 5 Ralph
MacCorkindale: 5 Simon
MacDiarmid, Alan: 7 chemist 8 Nobelist
Macdonald: 4 John, Norm, Ross 5 Carey
MacDonald: 4 Ross 8 Jeanette
__ MacDonald: 3 Old
MacDonald, Jeanette: 7 actress
film: Bitter Sweet (1940)
The Cat and the Fiddle (1934)
Love Me Tonight (1932)
The Love Parade (1929)
Maytime (1937)
The Merry Widow (1934)
One Hour With You (1932)
Rose Marie (1936)
San Francisco (1936)
partner: Nelson Eddy
MacDonald, John D.: 6 author, writer
work: Condominium
The Deep Blue Good-by
The Dreadful Lemon Sky
Free Fall in Crimson
The Green Ripper
The Lonely Silver Rain
Nightmare in Pink
Macdonald, Ross: 6 author, writer
work: The Blue Hammer
The Moving Target
Sleeping Beauty
The Underground Man
MacDowell, Andie: 7 actress
film: Four Weddings and a Funeral (1994)
Green Card (1990)
Greystoke: The Legend of Tarzan, Lord of the Apes (1984)
Groundhog Day (1993)
Just the Ticket (1999)
Michael (1996)
The Muse (1999)
The Object of Beauty (1991)
sex, lies, and videotape (1989)
Shadrach (1998)
Short Cuts (1993)
Macduff: 4 Scot
command to ~: 5 lay on
mace: 4 club 5 baton, spice, staff 6 cudgel 9 truncheon
bearer: 4 aril 6 beadle
macédoine: 5 salad 9 appetizer
Macedonia: 6 nation 7 country
ancient capital of ~: 6 Edessa
ancient ~ city: 5 Pella
bovine: 4 Busa
capital: 6 Skopje
city: 6 Bitola, Tetovo
mountain: 5 Korab
neighbor: 6 Greece 7 Albania 8 Bulgaria 10 Yugoslavia
Macedonian: 8 language
Maceió: 4 city, town
locale: 6 Brazil
macerate: 3 ret 4 mash 6 squash
macfarlane: 4 coat 6 jacket 8 overcoat
MacGibbon: 7 Harriet
MacGraw, Ali: 7 actress
film: The Getaway (1972)
Goodbye, Columbus (1969)
Love Story (1970)
spouse: Robert Evans, Steve McQueen
MacGregor: 4 clan, Mary, Scot 5 Byron
MacGregor, Mary song: Torn Between Two Lovers (1967)
MacGyver (ABC adventure) cast: Richard Dean Anderson (MacGyver)
mach __: 6 number
Mach: 5 Ernst
it travels at ~ 1: 5 sound
3 rival: 4 Atra
Machakos: 4 city, town
locale: 5 Kenya
Machala: 4 city, town
locale: 7 Ecuador
__-mâché: 5 paper 6 papier
MacHenry: 4 city, town
locale: 8 Illinois
Mach, Ernst: 8 Austrian 9 physicist
Machesney Park: 4 city, town
locale: 8 Illinois
machete: 5 knife, panga 6 guitar, string
kin: 4 bolo
origin: 8 Portugal
Machiavelli: 7 Niccolò
Machiavellian: 3 sly 6 amoral, artful, clever, crafty, shrewd 7 cunning, devious 9 deceitful, deceptive
__ Machiavelli, The: 3 New
Machida: 4 city, town
locale: 5 Japan
machinate: 4 plot 5 hatch 6 scheme, wangle 7 collude, connive, finagle 8 conspire, contrive, engineer, intrigue, maneuver 9 play games 10 manipulate
machination: 4 plan, plot, ploy, ruse, trap 5 cabal, dodge, trick 6 device, scheme 8 artifice, intrigue, maneuver 9 dirty work, stratagem
machine: 4 tool 5 gizmo, motor, robot, setup, thing, zombi 6 agency, device, engine, gadget, system, widget, zombie 7 iron man, vehicle 8 computer 9 apparatus, appliance, automaton, implement, mechanism 10 automobile, instrument
insides of a ~: 5 works 9 mechanism
part: 3 cam, cog 4 gear
pattern: 3 die
machine __: 3 gun 4 bolt, code, shop, tool, word 5 rifle, screw, steel 6 pistol, vision
machine-__: 3 gun 4 wash 6 stitch

__ machine: 3 wet 4 cash, coin, copy, ring, slot, tape, time 5 Ditto, money 6 adding, boring, flying, mowing, rowing, sewing, simple, Turing, voting 7 Atwood's, billing, carding, complex, copying, mailing, milking, milling, pinball, reaping, talking, vending, virtual, washing
__ Machine: 4 Love 5 Music 6 Flying 7 Dancing
machine-gun bunker: 4 nest
machinery: 3 rig 4 gear, tool 5 gears, means, motor, organ, plant, works 6 agency, engine, gadget, medium, system, tackle 7 vehicle 8 materiel, workings 9 apparatus, equipment, mechanism, structure 10 implements
adapt, as ~: 5 refit
lubricant: 6 ben oil
maintain the ~: 5 reoil
machine-shop
fixture: 3 jig 5 lathe 6 jigsaw
wear: 5 apron
__ Machine, The: 4 Time
macho: 4 male 5 manly, tough 6 brawny, strong, studly, virile 8 intrepid 9 assertive, masculine, two-fisted 10 aggressive, dominating
guy: 4 hunk 5 he-man
no ~ man: 4 wimp 5 sissy
not ~: 4 weak 5 timid, wimpy 6 trepid 7 fearful, wimpish
Macho Man (1978 song) artist: Village People
Machree, Mother home: 4 Eire, Erin 7 Ireland
Machu Picchu
locale: 4 Peru
resident: 4 Inca 5 Incan
MacInnes: 5 Colin, Helen
Macintosh: 5 apple
Mack: 3 Ted 5 Craig, Helen, truck 6 Connie, Jillie, Lonnie, Marion 7 Sennett
__ Mack: 5 Jimmy
MacKeesport: 4 city, town
locale: 4 Penn.
Mackenzie: 5 Astin, range, river 8 Phillips 9 Alexander
locale: 6 Canada
river to the ~: 5 Liard
MacKenzie: 6 Gisele 7 Compton
MacKenzie, Gisele: 6 singer
homeland: Canada
regular on: The Sid Caesar Show, Your Hit Parade
song: Hard to Get (1955)
Mackenzie's Hundred author: Frank Yerby
mackerel: 4 cero, fish, peto 5 wahoo
relative: 6 bonito
mackerel __: 3 sky 4 gull 5 shark
__ mackerel: 4 Atka, chub, holy, jack, king 5 horse, snake 7 frigate, Spanish
Mack, Helen: 7 actress
film: Four Hours to Kill (1935)
Mystery of the White Room (1939)
She (1935)
The Son of Kong (1933)
Mackie: 3 Bob
Mackinac __: 6 Bridge, Island
Mackinac Island locale: 5 Huron 8 Michigan
Mackinaw __: 4 boat, coat 5 trout 7 blanket
MacKinlay: 6 Kantor
MacKinney: 4 city, town
locale: 5 Texas
mackintosh: 4 coat 6 jacket 7 topcoat 8 raincoat 10 protection
Mack, Lonnie song: Memphis (1963)
Mack & Mabel
character: 4 Ella, Iris 7 Normand, Sennett
composer: Jerry Herman
Mack, Ted: 4 host 5 emcee
Mack the Knife (1959 song) artist: Bobby Darin
name: 4 Lucy 5 Lenya, Lotte, Polly
MacLachlan: 4 Kyle
MacLaine, Shirley: 7 actress
brother: Warren Beatty
film: The Apartment (1960)
Around the World in 80 Days (1956)
Around the World in Eighty Days (1956)
Ask Any Girl (1959)
Being There (1979)
The Bliss of Mrs. Blossom (1968)
Bruno (2000)
Can-Can (1960)
Career (1959)
Desperate Characters (1971)
The Evening Star (1996)
Gambit (1966)
Guarding Tess (1994)
Irma la Douce (1963)
Madame Sousatzka (1988)
The Matchmaker (1958)
Mrs. Winterbourne (1996)
The Possession of Joel Delaney (1972)
Postcards From the Edge (1990)
The Sheepman (1958)
Some Came Running (1959)
Steel Magnolias (1989)
Sweet Charity (1969)
Terms of Endearment (1983, AA)
The Trouble With Harry (1955)
The Turning Point (1977)
Two for the Seesaw (1962)
Two Mules for Sister Sara (1970)
What a Way to Go! (1964)
Woman Times Seven (1967)
The Yellow Rolls-Royce (1964)
MacLane: 6 Barton
MacLean: 4 city, town 8 Alistair
locale: 8 Virginia
MacLeish, Archibald: 4 poet 6 writer
work: Conquistador
Songs for a Summer Day
Tower of Ivory
MacLeod: 5 Gavin
Macleod, John: 8 Nobelist
MacMahon, Aline: 7 actress
film: Ah, Wilderness! (1935)
All the Way Home (1963)
Back Door to Heaven (1939)
Gold Diggers of 1933 (1933)
Guest in the House (1944)
Heroes for Sale (1933)
The Lady Is Willing (1942)
Life Begins (1932)
Once in a Lifetime (1932)
One Way Passage (1932)
The Search (1948)
The World Changes (1933)
Macmillan, Harold: 2 P.M. 7 British
predecessor: 4 Eden
successor: 11 Douglas-Home
MacMinnville: 4 city, town
locale: 6 Oregon
MacMurray, Fred: 5 actor
film: Above Suspicion (1943)
The Absent-Minded Professor (1961)
Alice Adams (1935)
The Apartment (1960)
The Caine Mutiny (1954)
Dive Bomber (1941)
Double Indemnity (1944)
The Egg and I (1947)
The Gilded Lily (1935)
Hands Across the Table (1935)
Honeymoon in Bali (1939)
The Lady Is Willing (1942)
Maid of Salem (1937)
A Millionaire for Christy (1951)
Murder, He Says (1945)
Pardon My Past (1945)
The Princess Comes Across (1936)
Remember the Night (1940)
The Shaggy Dog (1959)
Sing, You Sinners (1938)
Smoky (1946)
Son of Flubber (1963)
Take a Letter, Darling (1942)
The Texas Rangers (1936)
Too Many Husbands (1940)
The Trail of the Lonesome Pine (1936)
spouse: June Haver
TV: My Three Sons
Macnee: 7 Patrick
costar: 4 Rigg 7 Thorson
TV role: 5 Steed
MacNeice, Louis: 4 poet 5 Irish
work: Autumn Sequel
Blind Fireworks
Eighty-Five Poems
Solstices
MacNeil, Robert: 7 newsman
partner: 6 Lehrer
MacNelly, Jeff comic strip: 4 Shoe
MacNicol, Peter: 5 actor
film: Dragonslayer (1981)
Sophie's Choice (1982)
TV: Ally McBeal
Macomb: 4 city, town
locale: 8 Illinois
Macomber Affair, The (1947 film)
cast: Joan Bennett, Gregory Peck, Robert Preston
director: Zoltan Korda
Macon: 4 city, town
locale: 7 Georgia
Mâcon: 4 city, town, wine 5 white
locale: 6 France
river: 5 Saône
Mâcon's river: 5 Saône
MacPhail: 3 Lee 4 Andy 5 Larry
Macpherson: 4 Elle
MacPherson __: 5 strut
Macquarie: 5 river
locale: 9 Australia
MacRae: 6 Gordon, Sheila 8 Meredith
MacRae, Gordon spouse: Sheila MacRae
macramé: 5 craft
material: 5 twine
Macready, George: 5 actor
film: The Black Arrow (1948)
Gilda (1946)
The Missing Juror (1944)
My Name Is Julia Ross (1945)
TV: Peyton Place
macro: 10 large-scale
macrocosm: 5 world 6 nature 8 universe
macroeconomic stat: 3 GNP
macromolecular letters: 3 DNA
macrophysics: 7 science
macroscopic: 7 visible
macroscopic __: 7 anatomy
macroseism: 10 earthquake
maculate: 5 dirty, grimy, sooty, stain, sully 6 defile, filthy, fouled, grubby, grungy, impure, soiled 7 debased, defiled, dirtied, smudged, spotted, stained, sullied, tainted 8 befouled, begrimed, polluted, slovenly, vitiated 9 blackened, corrupted, tarnished 10 besmirched, unsanitary
macushla: 2 jo 3 pet 4 baby, dear, jill, love 5 amour, angel, chéri, cooky, cutey, cutie, deary, ducky, flame, honey, leman, lover, lovey, novia, novio, sugar, sweet 6 bon ami, chérie, cookie, dautie, dearie, steady, sweets 7 beloved, dearest, dear one, pigsney, schatzi, squeeze, sweetie, tootsie 8 chou-chou, cutie pie, dowsabel, dulcinea, ladylove, lovebird, paramour, precious, snookums, sugar pie, sweetums, truelove 9 bonne amie, boyfriend, dreamboat, inamorata, inamorato, petit chou, valentine 10 girlfriend, heartthrob, honeybunch, mavourneen, sweetheart, sweetie pie, turtledove
Macuspana: 4 city, town
locale: 6 Mexico 7 Tabasco
Macy: 2 R.H. 4 Bill 7 Rowland 8 William H.
Macy, Bill: 5 actor
film: The Late Show (1977)
My Favorite Year (1982)
TV: Maude
Macy's: 5 store
rival: 4 Saks 7 Gimbel's
Macy, William H.: 5 actor
film: A Civil Action (1998)
Fargo (1996)
Focus (2001)
Happy, Texas (1999)
Jurassic Park III (2001)
Mr. Holland's Opus (1995)
Panic (2000)
Pleasantville (1998)
State and Main (2000)
mad: 3 hot 4 avid, daft, ired, keen, loco, sore, wild 5 angry, batty, crazy, cross, goony, huffy, irate, kooky, livid, manic, nutty, rabid, riled, upset, vexed, wacky, wroth 6 absurd, crazed, cuckoo, fuming, insane, ireful, kookie, looney, peeved, piqued, raging, raving, red-hot, unsafe, whacky 7 bananas, berserk, boiling, enraged, excited, foolish, frantic, furious, in a snit, rampage, ranting, teed off, unsound, violent, zealous 8 agitated, choleric, crackers, frenetic, frenzied, incensed, inflamed, maniacal, outraged, provoked, unhinged, unstable, vehement, white-hot, wild-eyed, worked up, wrathful 9 fanatical, far gone on, foolhardy, illogical, imprudent, indignant, irritated, ludicrous, possessed, resentful, seeing red, senseless, splenetic, ticked off 10 distraught, freaked out, infatuated, infuriated, irrational, outrageous
about: 7 sweet on 10 enamored of, in love with
at: 9 angry with, cross with, upset with
be ~: 4 burn, fume, rage, rave, stew 6 blow up, see red, seethe
be ~ about: 4 love, rave 5 adore 6 admire
ender: 3 cap 4 wort 5 house
get ~: 3 ire, irk 4 rile 5 anger, peeve, upset 6 blow up, enrage, rear up 10 hit the roof
hopping ~: 4 sore 5 angry, cross, huffy, irate 6 ireful 7 furious 9 irritated
like ~: 6 wildly 8 fiercely 9 furiously, violently 10 vehemently, vigorously
one: 6 maniac
rush: 5 furor, hurry, panic 6 bustle, plunge, scurry 7 ferment, scamper, turmoil 8 outburst, stampede
mad __: 4 dash 5 money
mad __ hatter: 3 as a
mad __ hornet: 3 as a
mad __ March hare: 3 as a
mad __ wet hen: 3 as a
__ mad: 4 like 7 hopping
Mad: 3 mag 8 magazine
feature: 6 parody, satire
Mad __: 3 Max 4 Love
Mad __ and Glory: 3 Dog
Mad __ You: 5 About

Mad About Music (1938 film)
cast: Deanna Durbin, Herbert Marshall, Gail Patrick
director: Norman Taurog
Mad About You (NBC sitcom)
cast: Helen Hunt (Jamie Buchman) Paul Reiser (Paul Buchman)
cousin: 3 Ira
dog: 6 Murray
Mad About You (1986 song) artist: Belinda Carlisle
Madagascar: 3 isl. 4 isle 6 island, nation 7 country
beast: 4 vari 5 fossa
locale: 3 Afr. 6 Africa
money: 5 franc
primate: 5 indri, lemur 6 aye-aye
tree: 6 balata
Madalyn: 5 O'Hair
madam: 5 title, woman 6 female
mate: 3 sir
Madama Butterfly piece: 4 aria
madame: 3 gal, she 4 lady, marm 5 woman 6 female
Madame: 5 title
see also French
Madame ___: 3 Nhu 4 Rosa 5 Curie 6 Bovary 7 de Staël, LaZonga
Madame Bovary: 4 film 5 novel
author: Gustave Flaubert
cast: Van Heflin, Jennifer Jones, James Mason
character: 4 Emma, Léon 5 Binet 6 Berthe 7 Heloise
director: Vincente Minnelli
Madame Butterfly: 5 opera 6 geisha
composer: 7 Puccini
role: 4 Goro, Kate 6 Suzuki 8 Yamadori 9 Cio-Cio-San, Pinkerton, Sharpless
setting: 5 Japan 8 Nagasaki
Madame Curie (1943 film)
cast: Greer Garson, Walter Pidgeon, Henry Travers
director: Mervyn LeRoy
Madame Sousatzka (1988 film)
cast: Peggy Ashcroft, Navin Chowdhry, Shirley MacLaine
director: John Schlesinger
Madame X (1966 film)
cast: Constance Bennett, John Forsythe, Lana Turner
Madam, I'm ___: 4 Adam
Madamina: 4 aria
Madam Satan (1930 film)
cast: Reginald Denny, Kay Johnson, Roland Young
director: Cecil B. DeMille
Madam, Will You Talk? author: Mary Stewart
Mad Anthony: 5 Wayne
mad as ___ hen: 4 a wet
mad as a ___: 6 hatter, hornet
mad as a ___ hare: 5 March
madcap: 4 rash, wild, zany 5 brash, clown, crazy, goony, hasty 6 jester, lively, stupid 7 foolish 8 heedless, reckless 9 daredevil, foolhardy, frivolous, hotheaded, imprudent, impulsive, uncareful 10 ill-advised, incautious, nonserious
Mädchen: 5 Amick
MADD concern: 3 DUI, DWI
madden: 3 ire, irk, vex 4 rile 5 anger, annoy, craze, haunt, peeve, upset 6 bother, enrage, frenzy, pester 7 derange, enflame, incense, inflame, outrage, possess, provoke, shatter, steam up, unhinge 8 distract, irritate 9 infuriate, unbalance 10 drive crazy, exasperate
Madden: 4 John
maddened: 3 hot 4 ired, sore 5 angry, cross, huffy, irate, livid, riled, wroth 6 fuming, ireful, raging, raving, red-hot 7 furious, ranting, violent 8 choleric, wrathful 9 indignant, resentful, splenetic
maddening: 5 pesky, pesty
___ madder: 4 rose, wild
madder family shrub: 5 ixora 6 coffee 8 cinchona, gardenia 9 bouvardia
Mad Dog and Glory (1993 film)
cast: Robert De Niro, Bill Murray, Uma Thurman
director: John McNaughton
Maddox: 5 Garry 6 Lester
Maddox and the Rhythmasters, Johnny song: The Crazy Otto (1955)
Maddux, Greg: 3 ace 6 hurler 7 pitcher
sport: 8 baseball
made: 7 devised 8 invented 9 concocted, contrived 10 fabricated
first: 5 newer
in French: 4 fait
in heaven: 7 perfect, utopian 9 exemplary, nonpareil
just ~: 3 new 5 fresh
not ~ up: 6 actual
of (suffix): 3 -ine
starter: 3 man 4 hand, home
made ___ shade: 5 in the
___-made: 3 man 4 self, well 5 bench, judge, ready, union 6 custom, tailor
Made (2001 film)
cast: Peter Falk, Jon Favreau, Famke Janssen, Vince Vaughn
director: Jon Favreau
Made for Each Other (1939 film)
cast: Charles Coburn, Carole Lombard, James Stewart
director: John Cromwell
Made for Each Other (1971 film)
cast: Joseph Bologna, Paul Sorvino, Renee Taylor
director: Robert B. Bean
Made in ___: 3 USA
made in the ___: 3 USA 5 shade
Madeira: 4 isle, wine 5 river, white 6 island
origin: 8 Portugal
port: 7 Funchal
River locale: 6 Brazil
Madeira ___: 5 topaz
madeleine: 4 cake 6 pastry
Madeleine: 5 Stowe 6 L'Engle 7 Carroll 8 Albright 9 de Scudéry
see also French
Madeleine author: Ludwig Bemelmans
Madeleine Férat author: Emile Zola
Madeline: 4 Kahn
Madeline (1998 film)
cast: Ben Daniels, Nigel Hawthorne, Hatty Jones, Frances McDormand
director: Daisy von Scherler Mayer
___ Madelon Claudet, The: 5 Sin of
___-made man: 4 self
___ made me do it!, The: 5 devil
___ Made Me Love You: 3 You
___-made millionaire: 4 self
mademoiselle: 4 girl, lass, maid, miss 5 title, youth 6 damsel, lassie, maiden 7 colleen 8 fraülein
see also French
Mademoiselle: 3 mag 8 magazine
rival: 4 Elle 5 Vogue 7 Glamour
Mademoiselle Merquem author: George Sand
Madera: 4 city, town
locale: 6 Mexico 9 Chihuahua 10 California
Madero: 4 city, town 9 Francisco
locale: 6 Mexico 10 Tamaulipas
made-to-___: 5 order 7 measure
made-up: 5 false 6 unreal, untrue 7 assumed 8 mythical, specious 9 fictional, imaginary, unnatural 10 fabricated, fictitious
story: 7 fiction
Madge: 5 Blake, Evans 7 Bellamy 8 Sinclair
Mad Genius, The (1931 film)
cast: John Barrymore, Donald Cook, Marian Marsh
director: Michael Curtiz
madhouse: 3 zoo 5 chaos 6 bedlam, uproar 7 turmoil 8 shambles 9 mobocracy
Madhya Pradesh, capital of: 6 Bhopal
Madigan (1968 film)
cast: Henry Fonda, Harry Guardino, Richard Widmark
director: Don Siegel
___ Madigan: 6 Elvira
Madigan, Amy: 7 actress
film: Field of Dreams (1989)
Love Letters (1983)
Places in the Heart (1984)
Pollock (2000)
Uncle Buck (1989)
With Friends Like These ... (1999)
spouse: Ed Harris
Madison: 2 av. 3 ave., Guy 4 city, town 5 James, Oscar 6 avenue, Dolley
athletes: 7 Badgers
county: 4 Dane
locale: 3 Ala. 4 Wisc. 7 Alabama 9 Wisconsin
Madison Avenue
magazine: 6 Ad Week
output: 3 ads
payment: 5 ad fee
worker: 5 adman
Madison County structure: 6 bridge
Madison, Guy: 5 actor
film: 5 Against the House (1955)
Till the End of Time (1946)
TV: The Adventures of Wild Bill Hickok
Madison Heights: 4 city, town
locale: 8 Michigan
Madison, James: 9 president
alma mater: 9 Princeton
home: 8 Virginia 10 Montpelier
opponent: 7 Clinton 8 Pinckney
V.P.: 5 Gerry 7 Clinton
wife: 6 Dolley
Madison, Oscar: 4 slob
creator: Neil Simon
like ~: 5 messy
portrayer: 7 Klugman, Matthau
unlike ~: 4 neat
Madison Square Garden: 5 arena
Madlock, Bill sport: 8 baseball
Mad Love (1935 film)
cast: Colin Clive, Frances Drake, Peter Lorre
madly: 4 a lot, hard 6 keenly, rashly, wildly 7 crazily, hastily, quickly, rabidly, rapidly 8 absurdly, ardently, fiercely, insanely, speedily, stormily, urgently 9 devotedly, excitedly, extremely, fervently, foolishly, furiously, hurriedly, intensely, like crazy, viciously, violently 10 dementedly, frenziedly, recklessly
___ Madly Deeply: 5 Truly
Madlyn: 4 Rhue
___ Mad Mad Mad Mad World: 4 It's a
Madman at My Door author: Hillary Waugh
Mad Max (1979 film)
cast: Mel Gibson, Hugh Keays-Byrne, Joanne Samuel
director: George Miller
Mad Max 2 (1981 film)
cast: Mel Gibson, Bruce Spence, Vernon Wells
director: George Miller
madness: 4 rage 5 folly, mania 6 lunacy 8 nonsense
___ Madness: 5 A Fine, March
mado: 4 fish
Madonna
book: 3 Sex
documentary: Truth or Dare
film: Desperately Seeking Susan (1985)
Dick Tracy (1990)
Evita (1996)
A League of Their Own (1992)
The Next Best Thing (2000)
last name: Ciccone
role: 3 Eva 5 Evita, Perón
song: Angel (1985)
Beautiful Stranger (1999)
Borderline (1984)
Causing a Commotion (1987)
Cherish (1989)
Crazy for You (1985)
Deeper and Deeper (1992)
Don't Cry for Me Argentina (1997)
Dress You Up (1985)
Erotica (1992)
Express Yourself (1989)
Frozen (1998)
Hanky Panky (1990)
Holiday (1983)
I'll Remember (1994)
Justify My Love (1990)
Keep It Together (1990)
La Isla Bonita (1987)
Like a Prayer (1989)
Like a Virgin (1984)
Live to Tell (1986)
Lucky Star (1984)
Material Girl (1985)
Oh Father (1989)
Open Your Heart (1986)
Papa Don't Preach (1986)
The Power of Good-Bye (1998)
Rain (1993)
Ray of Light (1998)
Rescue Me (1991)
Secret (1994)
Take a Bow (1994)
This Used to Be My Playground (1992)
True Blue (1986)
Vogue (1990)
Who's That Girl (1987)
You'll See (1995)
You Must Love Me (1996)
spouse: Sean Penn, Guy Ritchie
___ Madonna: 4 Lady 7 Sistine
Madonna and ___: 5 Child
Madonna With Rosary artist: 4 Reni
Madonna With Saints artist: 5 Lippi
___ Madox Brown: 4 Ford
madras: 5 scarf 6 fabric 8 kerchief
Madras: 4 city, port, town
language: 4 Urdu
locale: 5 India
madre: 6 mother 7 Spanish
baby: 4 nene
brother: 3 tío
sister: 3 tía
___ Madre: 6 Sierra
Madre de Dios: 5 river
locale: 4 Peru 7 Bolivia
Madrid: 4 city, town 7 capital
airline to ~: 6 Iberia
city NW of ~: 4 Leon
locale: 5 Spain 6 España, Europe, Iberia
museum: 5 Prado 7 El Prado
neighbor: 5 Avila
river: 10 Manzanares
Madrid-to-Avila dir.: 3 WNW
madrigal: 4 fala, song 5 music
madrilène: 4 soup
madrone: 4 tree
relative: 5 erica, heath 6 sorrel 7 arbutus
Madsen: 7 Michael 8 Virginia
Madsen, Michael: 5 actor

film: Donnie Brasco (1997)
The Florentine (2000)
Free Willy (1993)
Reservoir Dogs (1992)
Species (1995)
Thelma & Louise (1991)
Mad Trapper, The author: Rudy Wiebe
Mad TV bit: 4 skit
Madura: 3 isl. **4** isle **6** island
locale: 4 Java **9** Indonesia
Madwoman of Chaillot, The role: **4** Irma
Mae: 4 West **5** Busch, Marsh **6** Clarke, Murray **7** Jemison, Whitman
__ Mae: 5 Daisy **6** Fannie, Ginnie, Sallie
Maebashi: 4 city, town
locale: 5 Japan
__ Mae Brown: 4 Rita
maelstrom: 4 eddy, vort **5** furor, hoo-ha, swirl **6** hoo-hah, hubbub, tumult, uproar, vortex **7** turmoil **8** sea swirl, shambles **9** whirlpool
Maelzel's Chess-Player author: Edgar Allan Poe
__ Mae Morse: 4 Ella
maenad: 8 baccanal
__ maestà: 3 con
maestro: 5 adept **6** master **9** conductor
need: 5 baton, score **9** orchestra
Maestro, Johnny: 6 singer
group: Brooklyn Bridge, Crests
Maeterlinck, Maurice: 4 poet **6** writer **8** Nobelist
Maeve: 6 Binchy
Mafia: 3 mob **9** gangsters **10** Cosa Nostra, underworld
leader: 3 don **4** capo **9** godfather
mag: 4 zine **7** fanzine, journal **10** periodical
see also magazine
mag __: 4 card, tape **5** wheel **6** wheels
mag.
edition: 3 iss., vol.
sales: 4 circ.
magazine: 3 rag **4** case, pulp **5** cache, daily, depot, ebony, issue, organ, print, shell, store **6** armory, digest, glossy, review, weekly **7** arsenal, gazette, journal, monthly **8** biweekly, circular **9** bimonthly, quarterly, warehouse **10** depository, periodical, repository, semiweekly, storehouse
Army ~: 4 Yank
business ~: 3 Inc. **6** Forbes **7** Fortune
category: 4 men's **6** women's
cheap ~: 4 pulp
computer: 4 Byte
contents: 4 ammo
current-events: 4 Time **6** US News **8** Newsweek
exec: 2 ed. **6** editor
extra: 6 insert
feature: 3 ads **4** item **5** essay **7** columns, letters **9** crossword
German ~: 5 Stern
glossy ~: 5 slick
ID: 4 ISSN
like some ~ s: 5 illus., newsy, pulpy
look: 6 format
onetime: 4 Life, Look **5** Sport
part: 2 pg. **4** page **5** cover
satire ~: 3 Mad
science ~: 4 Omni
science fiction ~: 6 Analog
section: 4 roto
space: 6 linage **7** lineage
stand: 4 rack **5** kiosk
starter: 4 news
title word: 6 Digest
women's ~: 4 Elle, Self **5** Cosmo, Vogue **6** Allure **7** Glamour
magazine __: 4 show **7** section
__ magazine: 3 fan **6** little, powder
Magaziner: 3 Ira
magazines: 5 media, press
Magda: 5 Gabor
sister: 3 Eva **6** Zsa Zsa
Magdalena: 3 bay **5** river
River locale: 8 Columbia
Magdalena __: 3 Bay
Magdalene: 4 Mary
Magdalene College student: 6 Cantab
Magdeburg: 4 city, town
locale: 7 Germany
river: 4 Elbe
mage: 6 wizard **8** sorcerer
like a ~: 4 wise
Magee, Patrick: 5 actor
film: Barry Lyndon (1975)
The Birthday Party (1968)
A Clockwork Orange (1971)
Marat/Sade (1966)
Séance on a Wet Afternoon (1964)
Telefon (1977)
Magellan: 5 probe **6** strait **10** space probe
destination: 5 Venus
org.: 4 NASA
Magellan, Ferdinand: 8 explorer **10** Portuguese
Magellania author: Jules Verne
Magellanic __: 5 cloud
Magen __: 5 David
magenta: 3 red **5** color **6** purple, purply **7** crimson **8** purplish
relative: 4 rose, ruby, rust, wine **5** brick, coral, grape, poppy, rusty, sandy **6** cerise, cherry, claret, garnet, maroon **7** carmine, crimson, fuchsia, pimento, scarlet, sultana, vermeil **8** amaranth, cardinal, dubonnet, geranium, rubicund **9** carnation, cranberry, vermilion **10** strawberry
Maggie: 3 nag **4** Kuhn **5** Smith **7** Simpson
Maggie author: Stephen Crane
Maggie May (1971 song) artist: Rod Stewart
Maggio: 6 Angelo
maggiore: 5 major **7** Italian
Maggiore: 4 Lago, lake
locale: 5 Italy **11** Switzerland
maggot: 3 bug **5** larva **6** insect **9** scoundrel
Magi: 4 trio **7** wise men
carrier: 5 camel
emulate the ~: 5 adore
guide: 4 star
member: 6 Caspar, Casper **8** Melchior **9** Balthazar
offering: 4 gift, gold **5** myrrh **12** frankincense
magic: 3 hex **4** tabu **5** charm, spell, taboo, vodun **6** hoodoo, occult, tricks, voodoo **7** charism, conjury, sorcery **8** black art, charisma, illusion, wizardry **9** bewitched, conjuring, enchanted, occultism, voodooism, witchlike **10** bewitching, divination, enchanting, entrancing, hocus-pocus, mysterious, necromancy, witchcraft
act: 5 trick **6** escape
black ~: 5 vodun **7** sorcery **9** diabolism **10** necromancy, witchcraft
charm: 4 mojo **6** fetich, fetish
do ~: 3 hex **6** invoke **7** conjure
potion: 7 arcanum
power: 4 mojo **5** spell
say ~ words: 6 incant
spirit: 5 fairy, genie
West Indies ~: 3 obi **5** obeah
white ~: 5 wicca
word: 4 poof **5** hocus, pocus, voilà **6** chango, please, presto **10** hocus-pocus **11** abracadabra
magic __: 4 wand **6** bullet, carpet, number, potion, square **7** lantern, realism
__ magic: 5 black, white
Magic: 4 five, team **7** Johnson
home: 3 Fla. **7** Florida, Orlando
org.: 3 NBA
rival: 3 Net, Sun **4** Buck, Bull, Hawk, Heat, Jazz, King, Spur **5** Knick, Laker, Pacer, Sixer **6** Celtic, Hornet, Nugget, Piston, Raptor, Rocket, Wizard **7** Clipper, Grizzly, Warrior **8** Cavalier, Maverick **10** SuperSonic, Timberwolf
sport: 10 basketball
where the ~ plays: 5 Orena
Magic __: 3 Bus, Man **4** Chef, Time, Town **6** Marker **7** Moments
Magic __, The: 3 Box **5** Flute **6** Barrel
__ Magic: 3 It's **4** Blue **5** Night
__ magica: 3 ars
magical: 3 fey **5** runic, weird **6** mystic, occult **7** uncanny **8** mystical, wizardly **9** enchanted **10** bewitching, enchanting, entrancing, miraculous, mysterious
symbol: 5 sigil
Magical Mystery Tour artist: 7 Beatles
Magic Barrel, The author: Bernard Malamud
Magic Box, The (1951 film)
cast: Robert Donat, Maria Schell
director: John Boulting
Magic Bus (1968 song) artist: Who
Magic Carpet Ride (1968 song) artist: Steppenwolf
Magic Chef alternative: 5 Amana, Norge **6** Bendix, Maytag, Tappan **7** Admiral, Jenn-Air, Kenmore **8** Hotpoint **9** Whirlpool **10** Frigidaire, Kelvinator, KitchenAid
Magic Flute, The: 5 opera
composer: 6 Mozart
role: 6 Pamina, Tamino **8** Papagena, Papageno, Sarastro **10** Monostatos
setting: 5 Egypt **7** Memphis
Magic Hour author: 6 Isaacs
magician: 3 wiz **5** magus **6** Merlin, wizard **7** charmer, diviner, warlock **8** conjurer, conjuror, sorcerer **9** enchanter
assistant: 7 famulus
need: 3 hat, saw **4** deck, wand **5** cards **6** rabbit, top hat
see also magic
__ Magic Moment: 4 This
Magic Moments (1958 song) artist: Perry Como
Magic Mountain, The author: Thomas Mann
character: 3 Leo **4** Hans **5** Albin, Berta **6** Hofrat, Naphta **7** Behrens, Castorp, Clavdia, Joachim, Marusja **8** Chauchat, Ludovico, Ziemssen **10** Peeperkorn
setting: 4 Alps **7** Germany
Magic (song) artist: Olivia Newton-John, Pilot
Magic Theater painter: 4 Klee
Magic Time author: W.P. Kinsella
Magic Town (1947 film)
cast: Kent Smith, James Stewart, Jane Wyman
director: William Wellman
__ Magic Woman: 5 Black
Maginot: 4 line **5** André
magisterial: 6 lordly **8** dogmatic **10** dogmatical
Magister Ludi author: 5 Hesse
magistrate: 5 judge, jurat **6** jurist **7** bailiff, officer **8** his Honor, official
ancient ~: 4 doge **5** edile, ephor **6** aedile, archon
attendant: 6 lictor
magistrate's __: 5 court
Maglie, Sal: 6 hurler **7** pitcher **9** the Barber
magma: 4 lava, rock **7** mineral
magna __ laude: 3 cum
Magna: 3 car **4** auto, city, town **10** automobile, Mitsubishi
locale: 4 Utah
Magna __: 5 Carta, Mater **6** Charta **7** Graecia
magnalium: 5 alloy
component: 8 aluminum **9** magnesium
Magnani, Anna Oscar: The Rose Tattoo
magnanimity: 6 lenity **7** charity **8** kindness, nobility **9** tolerance
magnanimous: 3 big **4** free, kind **5** lofty, noble **6** decent, gentle, humane, kindly, tender **7** clement, gallant, lenient, liberal, sparing **8** all heart, generous, gracious, handsome, merciful, tolerant **9** bountiful, forgiving, unselfish **10** altruistic, benevolent, bighearted, charitable
magnate: 3 VIP **4** czar, lion, tsar, tzar **5** baron, mogul, nabob, nawab **6** bigwig, leader, tycoon **7** notable **9** financier, plutocrat **10** capitalist
Magnavox: 2 TV **3** VCR **5** TV set **10** television
alternative: 3 JVC, NEC, RCA **4** Sony **6** Quasar, Zenith **7** Emerson, Hitachi, ProScan, Toshiba **8** Sylvania **9** Panasonic
magnesium: 5 metal **7** element
silicate: 4 talc
magnesium __: 5 light, oxide **7** dioxide, sulfate
magnet: 4 lure
magnet __: 6 school
__ magnet: 3 bar **5** field
Magnet and Steel (1978 song) artist: Walter Egan
magnetic: 8 alluring, charming, hypnotic, inviting **9** arresting, glamorous **10** attractive, bewitching, entrancing
alloy: 6 alnico
element: 4 iron **6** cobalt
unit: 3 ESU **5** gamma, gauss, tesla, weber **7** oersted
magnetic __: 3 dip **4** card, core, disk, drum, flux, head, lens, mine, pole, star, tape, wire **5** chart, field, force, north, storm, strip **6** bottle, bubble, course, domain, mirror, moment, needle, pickup, pulley, stripe **7** anomaly, bearing, circuit, compass, equator, pyrites
magnetic resonance __: 4 scan **7** imaging
magnetism: 4 lure, pull **5** charm, power **6** allure, appeal, glamor **7** charism, glamour **8** charisma, mystique **9** appetence, hypnotism, influence **10** attraction
__ magnetism: 6 animal
magnetite: 3 ore **7** mineral
magnetize: 4 draw **7** attract **9** captivate, electrify, hypnotize
Magnificat: 4 song
magnificence: 4 pomp **5** glory **7** majesty **8** elegance, grandeur, nobility, splendor
magnificent: 3 def, rad **4** aces, A-one, boss, braw, cool, dece, fine, gear, keen, neat, nice, phat, rich, tuff **5** dandy, ducky, grand, great, marvy, neato, nobby, noble, prime, proud, regal, royal, slick, super, swell **6** august, bang on, bang-up, bonzer, bosker, choice, divine, dreamy, far-out, gnarly, groovy, lavish, lordly, lovely, mighty, ornate, peachy, slap-up, solemn, spot on, superb, swanky, terrif, tiptop, unreal, whizzo, wicked **7** amazing, awesome, capital, corking,

exalted, opulent, perfect, radiant, ripping, skookum, stately, stellar, sublime 8 dazzling, especial, eximious, fabulous, five-star, four-star, frabjous, glorious, heavenly, imposing, jim-dandy, majestic, palatial, princely, slam-bang, smashing, splendid, standout, sterling, stickout, striking, superior, terrific, top-level, topnotch, towering, very good, wondrous 9 arresting, bodacious, brilliant, Endsville, excellent, exemplary, exquisite, first-rate, high-grade, hunky-dory, luxurious, marvelous, sollicker, sumptuous, thrilling, top-flight, wonderful 10 first-class, hotsy-totsy, jack-a-dandy, majestical, out of sight, peachy-keen, phenomenal, remarkable, stupendous, super-duper

Magnificent Ambersons, The: 4 film 5 novel
  author: Booth Tarkington
  cast: Dolores Costello, Joseph Cotten, Tim Holt
  director: Orson Welles
Magnificent Dope, The (1942 film)
  cast: Don Ameche, Lynn Bari, Henry Fonda
  director: Walter Lang
___ Magnificent Men in Their Flying Machines: 5 Those
Magnificent Obsession (1935 film)
  cast: Irene Dunne, Betty Furness, Robert Taylor
  director: John M. Stahl
Magnificent Obsession (1954 film)
  cast: Rock Hudson, Barbara Rush, Jane Wyman
  director: Douglas Sirk
Magnificent Seven, The (1960 film)
  cast: Charles Bronson, Yul Brynner, Horst Buchholz, James Coburn, Brad Dexter, Steve McQueen, Robert Vaughn, Eli Wallach
  director: John Sturges
Magnificent Yankee, The (1950 film)
  cast: Louis Calhern, Eduard Franz, Ann Harding
  director: John Sturges
magnifico: 8 nobleman, splendid
magnifier: 4 lens 5 loupe
___ Magnifique: 4 C'est
magnify: 3 pad, wax 4 grow, hike, laud 5 add to, bless, boost, color, ensky, exalt, honor, raise, run up, swell 6 blow up, deepen, dilate, expand, extend, jack up, jump up, overdo, play up, puff up, revere, step up 7 advance, amplify, augment, build up, develop, elevate, enhance, enlarge, ennoble, glorify, inflate, promote, pyramid, worship 8 escalate, eulogize, heighten, increase, multiply, overplay, overrate, redouble 9 aggravate, embellish, embroider, intensify, overstate, recommend 10 aggrandize, exaggerate, overstress
magnifying ___: 5 glass
magniloquence: 7 bombast 8 rhetoric
magniloquent: 5 tumid 7 fustian, orotund, pompous, stilted, verbose 9 bombastic, grandiose, overblown
magniloquize: 5 orate
Magnitogorsk river: 4 Ural
magnitude: 4 bulk, note, size 5 range, reach 6 amount, extent, import, length, moment, volume, weight 7 bigness, breadth, compass, expanse 8 capacity, eminence, enormity, grandeur, hugeness, loudness, strength, vastness 9 amplitude, greatness, immensity, intensity, largeness 10 dimensions, importance, proportion
magnolia: 4 tree 5 plant, shrub 6 flower
  tree: 5 yulan 7 champac 8 champaca
Magnolia (1999 film)
  cast: Tom Cruise, Julianne Moore, John C. Reilly, Jason Robards
  director: Paul Thomas Anderson
___ Magnolias: 5 Steel
Magnolia St.: 4 Miss.
___-Magnon: 3 Cro
magnum: 3 gun 6 bottle 9 container
  opus: 4 tome, work 7 classic 8 monument
magnum ___: 4 opus
Magnum: 3 car 4 auto 5 Dodge 6 Thomas 10 automobile
Magnum Force (1973 film)
  cast: Clint Eastwood, Hal Holbrook, David Soul
  director: Ted Post
Magnum, P.I. (CBS drama)
  cast: John Hillerman (Jonathan Higgins)
    Roger E. Mosley (T.C.)
    Tom Selleck (Thomas Magnum)
  dog: 4 Zeus 6 Apollo
  setting: Oahu, Hawaii
Magnus: 4 Edie 8 Albertus
Magnuson: 3 Ann
Magog
  ally: 3 Gog
  father of ~: 7 Japheth
  grandfather of ~: 4 Noah
Magoo: 5 myope 6 Quincy
  dog: 6 Bowser
  nephew: 5 Waldo
___ Magoos: 5 Blues
magot: 7 primate
  relative: 3 ape 4 saki, titi 5 chimp, drill, jocko, lemur, loris, orang, potto, shrew 6 aye-aye, baboon, Bandar, galago, gelada, gibbon, grivet, guenon, howler, langur, macaco, monkey, rhesus, uakari, vervet 7 colobus, gorilla, guereza, hoolock, macaque, sapajou, siamang, tamarin, tarsier 8 bush baby, capuchin, mandrill, mangabey, marmoset, talapoin 9 orangutan 10 Barbary ape, chimpanzee, orangutang
magpie: 3 daw 4 bird 6 yakker 7 babbler, windbag 9 loud-mouth 10 chatterbox
Magritte, René: 6 artist 7 Belgian, painter
  contemporary: 4 Dali
Magruder: 3 Jeb
maguey: 6 cactus
Maguire: 3 AFB 5 Jerry, Molly, Tobey
Maguire, Jerry: 3 rep 5 agent
Maguire, Tobey: 5 actor
  film: Cider House Rules (1999)
    Pleasantville (1998)
    Ride With the Devil (1999)
    Spider-Man (2002)
    Wonder Boys (2000)
magus: 4 sage 6 wizard 7 diviner, prophet 8 conjurer, conjuror, magician
___ Magus: 5 Simon
Magus, The: 5 novel
  author: John Fowles
  setting: 6 Greece
Magwitch: 4 Abel
Magyar tongue: 5 Ugric
mah-___: 4 jong 5 jongg
Mahabharata: 4 epic, poem
___ Mahal: 3 Taj
Mahalia: 7 Jackson
mahalo ___ loa: 3 nui
maharajah: 5 ruler, title 6 gerent, Indian
maharani: 4 lady 5 noble, ruler, title 6 gerent
  cover: 4 sari 5 saree
Maharis: 6 George
maharishi: 5 title 6 cleric
mahatma: 4 sage 6 cleric
  garment: 5 dhoti, dhuti 6 dhooti 7 dhootie
Mahatma: 5 title 6 Gandhi
Mahayana
  school: 3 Zen 4 Chan
  teacher: 4 lama
___-Mahdi: 2 Al
Maher: 4 Bill
Ma, he's making eyes ___: 4 at me
Mahfouz, Naguib: 6 writer 8 Nobelist
Mahican: 6 Indian 7 Amerind
mahimahi: 6 dorado 7 dolphin
mah-jongg: 4 game
  counter: 4 tile
  tile: 3 bam 4 soap, wind 5 crack
Mahler, Gustav: 8 Austrian, composer
  wife: 4 Alma
  work: Das Lied von der Erde
    Kindertotenlieder
    Resurrection Symphony
    Symphony of a Thousand
Mahlon, mother of: 5 Naomi
mahoe: 4 tree
mahogany: 4 tree, wood 5 brown 7 reddish 8 hardwood
  relative: 3 bay, dun, tan 4 bole, ecru, fawn, foxy, nude, seal, toon 5 amber, beige, camel, cocoa, hazel, khaki, mocha, sepia, tawny, umber 6 auburn, bister, bistre, bronze, coffee, copper, ginger, russet, sienna, sorrel, suntan, walnut 7 biscuit, caramel, dogwood 8 chestnut, cinnamon 9 butternut, chocolate
  tree: 4 neem 5 lauan 6 acajou, carapa, sapele 7 avodire 8 andiroba, crabwood
___ mahogany: 5 white 6 gaboon, sapele 7 African
mahoganylike tree: 4 agba
Mahogany Row denizen: 4 exec 9 executive
Mahogany Theme (1975 song) artist: Diana Ross
Mahoney: 4 Jock, John 5 Jerry
Mahoney, John: 5 actor
  film: Eight Men Out (1988)
    Primal Fear (1996)
    Say Anything ... (1989)
    Tin Men (1987)
  TV: Frasier
mahonia: 5 shrub
  relative: 7 agarita 8 algerita, barberry
mahout master: 5 saheb, sahib
Mahre, Phil: 5 skier
mahua: 4 tree
mahuang: 5 shrub
Mahwah: 4 city, town
  locale: 9 New Jersey
mai: 3 May 5 month 6 French
  follower: 4 juin
  preceder: 5 avril
mai ___: 3 tai
Mai: 3 May 4 mois 5 month 6 French 10 Zetterling
Maia: 4 star 6 Pleiad
  father of ~: 5 Atlas
  son of ~: 6 Hermes
maid: 4 girl, lass, miss 5 bonne, Hazel, woman 6 damsel, duster, female, lassie 7 abigail, colleen, servant 8 domestic, fraülein 9 launderer, soubrette, young lady
  at times: 6 ironer
  British ~: 4 char
  ender: 7 servant
  India: 4 ayah
  in French: 5 bonne, fille
  starter: 3 bar 4 bond, hand, milk 5 dairy, house, nurse 6 brides 7 chamber
  target: 4 dust
maid ___: 7 service
___ maid: 3 old 5 lady's, meter 6 live-in
Maid ___: 6 Marian
___ Maid: 3 Old 6 Minute
maiden: 4 girl, lass, miss 5 first, woman, youth 6 damsel, female, lassie 7 colleen, initial 8 earliest, fraülein, señorita 9 inaugural 10 demoiselle, initiatory
  lack: 3 win
  name indicator: 3 née
  starter: 4 hand
  yon ~: 3 her, she
maiden ___: 4 name, over, pink 6 speech, voyage
___ maiden: 4 fair
maidenhair: 4 fern, tree, vine 6 gingko, ginkgo
maidenly: 4 pure 6 chaste
M'aidez!: 3 SOS 4 help 5 alarm, alert
maid-in-___: 7 waiting
maid of ___: 5 honor
Maid of ___: 5 Salem 7 Orléans
Maid of Athens, ___ we part: 3 ere
maid of battle, name meaning: 5 Hilda
Maid of Orleans, The author: Friedrich von Schiller
Maid of Salem (1937 film)
  cast: Claudette Colbert, Louise Dresser, Fred MacMurray
  director: Frank Lloyd
Maid of the Mist: 4 boat
maids: 4 help
___ Maids All in a Row: 6 Pretty
___ maids a-milking...: 5 Eight
Maids, The author: Jean Genet
Maidstone county: 4 Kent
Maid to Order (1987 film)
  cast: Beverly D'Angelo, Michael Ontkean, Valerie Perrine, Ally Sheedy
  director: Amy Jones
Maidu: 5 tribe 6 Indian 7 Amerind 8 language
maigre: 4 fish
Maigret: 4 Insp. 9 Inspector
  see also French
mail: 4 post, send 5 armor, metal, remit 6 direct, letter, parcel, shield 7 arrival, express, forward, package 8 dispatch, postcard, transfer, transmit
  accompaniment: 3 SAE 4 SASE
  agcy.: 4 USPS
  Army ~ addr.: 3 APO, FPO
  beat: 3 rte. 5 route
  check one's ~ maybe: 5 log in, log on
  drop: 2 PO 3 APO, box, FPO, GPO 5 PO box
  ender: 3 bag, box, man, men 4 room
  for free: 5 frank
  holder: 3 bag, box 4 slot 5 chute, pouch
  junk ~: 3 ads 4 spam 6 letter
  motto word: 3 nor 4 rain, snow 5 sleet
  need: 5 stamp 7 zip code 8 envelope
  piece of ~: 3 ltr. 4 card 6 letter 8 postcard 10 postal card
  prepare to ~: 4 seal 5 stamp
  railroad ~ place: 3 RPO
  starter: 3 air 4 gray, grey 5 black, green
mail ___: 3 car 4 boat, call, drop, flag, room 5 order 7 carrier
___ mail: 3 air, fan 4 bulk, dead, hate, junk 5 chain, snail, voice 6 direct 7 franked, metered, surface
___ Mail: 5 Night 7 Express 8 Priority
mailed ___: 4 fist
Mailer, Norman: 6 author, writer
  work: An American Dream
    The Armies of the Night
    The Deer Park

The Executioner's Song
The Naked and the Dead
The Presidential Papers
Tough Guys Don't Dance
mailing: **8** delivery
including ~ cost: **3** ppd. **7** prepaid
mailing __: **4** list, tube **7** machine
mailing-list unit: **4** name
maillot: **5** shirt **7** costume
mail-order
benefit, perhaps: **5** no tax
charge: **3** COD **5** S and H
company: **4** K-Tel **6** L.L. Bean
Mail Order Bride actor: **5** Ebsen, Oates
mailroom
gizmo: **5** dater
stamp: **3** rcd. **8** received
work in the ~: **4** sort
maim: **4** harm, hurt, ruin **5** crush, wound **6** batter, damage, deface, impair, injure, mangle **8** lacerate **9** hamstring, indispose
maimed: **4** hurt **7** injured
Maimonides: **5** Moses **6** Jewish **7** Spanish **11** philosopher
main: **3** key, sea **4** arch, duct, head, pipe, prin., star **5** basic, briny, chief, first, grand, major, ocean, prime, sheer, trunk, utter, vital **6** ruling, staple, utmost **7** capital, central, conduit, crucial, gas line, leading, premier, primary, special, stellar, supreme **8** cardinal, critical, dominant, favorite, foremost **9** essential, governing, paramount, principal, prominent, uppermost, water line, water pipe **10** overriding, preeminent, prevailing
bounding ~: **3** sea **5** ocean
ender: **3** top **4** land, line, mast, sail, stay **5** frame, sheet **6** lander, spring, stream
event: **4** bout, duel **5** fight, match, round **7** contest, feature **8** showcase **9** headliner, highlight **10** engagement
focus: **4** gist **5** tenor, topic
give the ~ idea: **9** summarize
idea: **3** nub **4** core, crux, gist, knub, pith **5** focus, motif, point **7** essence, keynote, outline **10** bottom line
in the ~: **7** as a rule, usually **9** routinely
on the ~: **4** asea **5** at sea
part: **4** body, bulk
partner: **5** might
main __: **4** body, deck, drag, line, stem, verb, yard **5** brace, entry, shaft **6** chance, clause, course, gauche, memory **7** storage
main-__: **5** de-fer, force **7** topmast, topsail
__ main: **3** gas **5** in the, water
Main: **2** st. **5** river **6** street **8** Marjorie
city on the ~: **9** Frankfurt
River locale: **7** Germany
Main __: **4** Line **6** Street
__ Main: **7** Spanish
Maine: **4** boat, ship **5** state **8** Down East **10** battleship
animal: **5** moose **7** caribou
bay: **5** Casco **9** Penobscot
city: **4** Saco **5** Lubec, Orono **6** Auburn, Bangor, Calais **7** Augusta, Caribou, Sanford **8** Lewiston, Portland **9** Biddeford, Brunswick
Indian: **6** Abnaki **7** Abenaki **8** Malecite, Wabanaki **9** Penobscot
lake: **9** Moosehead
like a ~ woods: **5** piney
merchant: **6** L.L. Bean
motto: **6** Dirigo
mountain: **8** Katahdin
national park: **6** Acadia
neighbor: **6** Canada, Quebec
river: **4** Saco
state animal: **5** moose
state bird: **9** chickadee
state cat: **7** coon cat
state fish: **6** salmon
state gemstone: **10** tourmaline
state insect: **8** honeybee
state tree: **4** pine **9** white pine
Tom's of ~: **10** toothpaste
University of ~ locale: **5** Orono
where the ~ blew up: **4** Cuba **6** Havana
Maine Coon: **3** cat **5** felid **6** feline
Maine-et-__: **5** Loire
Maine-to-Florida route: **5** US one
Main Event, The actor: **5** O'Neal
mainframe: **3** CPU **8** computer
Main Ingredient
song: Everybody Plays the Fool (1972)
Just Don't Want to Be Lonely (1974)
mainland __: **5** China **7** Chinese
Mainline: **3** car **4** auto, Ford **10** automobile
mainly: **6** mostly **7** at large, chiefly, largely, overall, usually **8** above all, all in all **9** generally, in general, most of all, primarily **10** especially, on the whole
Main, Marjorie: **7** actress
film: The Egg and I (1947)
Friendly Persuasion (1956)
Ma and Pa Kettle at Home (1954)
Murder, He Says (1945)
The Wistful Widow of Wagon Gap (1947)
mainsail neighbor: **3** jib
mainspring: **4** root **6** motive, origin
mainstay: **4** prop, rock **5** brace **6** anchor, pillar **7** bastion, bulwark, sponsor, support **8** backbone, buttress, linchpin, lynchpin, strength, upholder **9** supporter, sustainer
mainstream: **4** mode **5** usual **6** center, middle **7** average, popular **8** mediocre, moderate
in the ~: **7** current
not ~: **5** outré
out of the ~: **5** apart
Main Street author: Sinclair Lewis
character: **3** Bea, Guy, Sam **4** Erik, Hugh, Vida **5** Carol
maintain: **3** say **4** aver, avow, bear, have, hold, keep, save, tend **5** amass, argue, cache, claim, hoard, put by, reach, state, store, swear, vouch **6** affirm, allege, assert, attest, defend, garner, insist, keep up, manage, occupy, pursue, resist, retain, save up, uphold **7** believe, care for, carry on, contend, declare, finance, nurture, persist, possess, profess, prolong, protect, protest, provide, purport, put away, reserve, stand by, support, sustain **8** conserve, continue, go on with, hang onto, hold onto, preserve, put aside **9** keep going, look after, persevere, predicate, stabilize, vindicate **10** accumulate, asseverate, perpetuate, take care of
barely ~: **6** eke out
maintainable: **7** tenable
maintenance: **4** care, keep **6** living, upkeep **7** alimony, repairs, running, service, support **10** livelihood
worker: **5** super **8** handyman
maintenance-__: **4** free
maintop: **8** platform
Mainz: **4** city, town
locale: **7** Germany
river: **5** Rhine
Mairzy __: **5** Doats
maison: **5** house **6** French
division: **5** salle
entrance: **5** porte
floor in a ~: **5** étage
__ maison: **3** à la
mais oui: **2** ay, da, ja, sí **3** aye, yea, yep, yes, yup **4** fine, okay, sure, yeah **5** good-o, natch, quite, right, roger, uh-huh **6** agreed, gladly, good-oh, indeed, just so, rather, righto, surely, you bet, yowzah **7** exactly, go ahead, indeedy, quite so, ten-four **8** all right, as you say, of course, thumbs up, very well **9** be my guest, certainly, darn right, naturally, precisely, sure thing, you betcha, you said it **10** absolutely, by all means, definitely, positively, sure enough, that's right
mai tai: **5** drink **8** beverage, cocktail
ingredient: **3** rum **7** curaçao **10** fruit juice
maître __: **6** d'hôtel
maître d' offering: **4** menu
maize: **4** corn **5** color **6** yellow
genus: **3** zea
relative: **4** buff, corn, gold, lime, rust, sand **5** blond, brass, coral, cream, flaxy, lemon, ocher, ochre, peach, rusty, straw **6** blonde, canary, chammy, citron, crocus, flaxen, shammy, shamoy **7** apricot, chamois, citrine, jasmine, mustard, nankeen, old gold, saffron, xanthic **8** daffodil, primrose **9** champagne, goldenrod, jessamine
Spanish ~ grinding stone: **4** mano
maj.: **4** rank
employer: **3** USA **4** USMC
subordinate: **3** NCO, PFC, pvt., sgt. **4** capt. **5** lieut.
superior: **3** col., gen. **5** lt. col.
Maj. __: **3** Gen.
__ Maj.: **3** Sgt.
__ Maja, The: **5** Naked
Majel: **7** Barrett
__ majesté: **4** lèse
majestic: **5** grand, large, lofty, noble, proud, regal, royal **6** august, epical, kingly, lordly, mighty, solemn, superb **7** awesome, elegant, exalted, stately, sublime **8** empyreal, empyrean, glorious, imperial, imposing, kinglike, palatial, splendid **9** luxurious, sovereign **10** impressive, monumental, statuesque
majesty: **4** king **5** glory, state **7** dignity, monarch **8** grandeur, nobility, splendor **9** sovereign **10** kingliness
lese ~: **7** treason **8** betrayal, sedition **9** treachery
__ majesty: **3** her, his **4** lese, leze, your
Majesty: **5** title
__ Majesty's Secret Service: **5** On Her
__ majeure: **5** force
majolica glaze: **3** tin
major: **3** key, top **4** arch, main, more, rank, star, ugly **5** chief, grave, vital **6** Hoople, larger, needed, senior, utmost **7** crucial, greater, leading, pivotal, primary, serious, sizable, special, weighty **8** critical, dominant, greatest, Houlihan, required, sizeable **9** big-league, governing, important, mandatory, necessary, principal, specialty, uttermost **10** overriding, preeminent
college ~: **3** art, bio, mus. **4** biol., chem., econ, educ., hist, math, phys. **5** drama, music **6** acting, anthro, cinema, French, phys. ed. **7** biology, English, geology, history, physics., poli sci **9** chemistry, economics, education
command: **6** at ease
ender: **4** ette
grad-school ~: **3** law **7** finance **8** medicine **9** dentistry, economics
in music: **3** dur **8** maggiore
not ~: **5** minor
portion: **4** bulk
major __: **3** key **4** axis, mode, suit, term **5** order, party, piece, scale, triad **6** league, planet, tenace **7** element, general, medical, penalty, premise
major-__: **4** domo **7** leaguer
__ major: **3** vis **4** drum **5** quart, quint
Major: **4** John **5** Bowes, Lance **6** Harris **7** Barbara
Major __: **3** Dad **6** League **7** Barbara, Prophet
__ Major: **4** Ursa **5** Canis **6** Syrtis
Major and the Minor, The (1942 film)
cast: Rita Johnson, Ray Milland, Ginger Rogers
director: Billy Wilder
Major Barbara: **4** film, play
author: George Bernard Shaw
cast: Rex Harrison, Wendy Hiller, Robert Morley
director: Gabriel Pascal
Majorca: **3** isl. **4** isle **6** island
neighbor: **5** Ibiza, Iviza
port: **5** Palma
see also Spanish
Major Dad (CBS sitcom)
cast: Gerald McRaney (Maj. John MacGillis)
Shanna Reed (Polly MacGillis)
major-domo: **6** butler **10** manservant
majorette
gait: **5** strut
motion: **5** twirl
twirler: **5** baton
__ majorette: **4** drum
Majorino: **4** Tina
__ Majoris: **5** Canis, Ursae
majority: **4** body, bulk, mass, most, vote **5** prime **7** manhood **8** best part, maturity **9** adulthood, plurality, womanhood **10** lion's share
attain ~: **6** mature
majority __: **4** rule **6** leader
majority __, a: **5** of one
__ majority: **6** silent, simple
Majority __, A: **5** of One
__ Majority: **5** Moral
__ Majority, The: **5** Moral
Major, John: **2** P.M. **4** Tory **7** British
predecessor: **8** Thatcher
successor: **5** Blair
major league
see baseball
major-league: **3** big **5** great
Major League: **4** Amer., Natl. **8** American, National
Major League (1989 film)
cast: Tom Berenger, Corbin Bernsen, Charlie Sheen, Margaret Whitton
director: David S. Ward
major leaguer: **3** pro
major-leaguers: **7** big boys
Majors, Lee
spouse: Farrah Fawcett
TV: The Big Valley, The Fall Guy, The Six Million Dollar Man
Majuro: **4** city, town
locale: **9** Marshalls
majuscule: **6** letter **7** capital
Makah: **6** Indian **7** Amerind
Makalu: **4** peak **5** mount **8** mountain
locale: **4** Asia **5** Nepal **9** Himalayas
Makarova: **7** Natalia
Makassar __: **6** Strait
make: **3** fix, get, net, set **4** brew, cook, earn, form, gain, mint, mold, name, sort, verb, wage **5** build, cause, clear, craft, draft, drive, elect, enact, erect, force, forge, frame, gauge, gross, hatch, impel, judge, press, put up,

reach, ready, shape, spawn **6** coerce, come to, compel, cook up, create, deduce, derive, draw up, finger, invent, kidney, lead to, oblige, ordain, parent, put out, reckon, spoils, take in, whip up **7** achieve, add up to, advance, appoint, bring in, compose, dragoon, dream up, fashion, prepare, produce, proffer, quality, realize, receive, turn out, variety **8** amount to, assemble, compound, comprise, conclude, delegate, engender, estimate, generate, knock off, nominate, pull down **9** brand name, calculate, constrain, construct, designate, establish, fabricate, formulate, legislate, originate, recognize, structure **10** bring about, bring forth, constitute, pressurize, synthesize

a break: **7** go south

a face: **3** mug **5** scowl, smirk, wince

a faux pas: **3** err **4** flub, goof, muff, slip, trip **5** botch, lapse, stray **6** booboo, bungle, foul up, fumble, mess up, slip up **7** blunder, go wrong, louse up, misstep, stumble **8** go astray

a fuss: **4** beef, carp, kick, mind, moan, rail, rant, sigh, wail, weep, yell **5** cavil, demur, gripe, groan, growl, mourn, whine **6** grouch, grouse, holler, mutter, repine, squawk, squeal, yammer **7** grumble, protest, quarrel, trouble, whimper **8** complain, sound off **9** bellyache, find fault, give a darn

a gaffe: **6** slip up **7** blunder

a getaway: **3** run **4** bolt, flee, flit, skip **5** elude, evade **6** decamp, escape **7** abscond **8** jump bail, shake off **9** cut and run, disappear, skedaddle **10** hightail it

a gift: **5** grant, offer **6** bestow, confer **8** bequeath **10** contribute

a hash of: **4** flub, goof, muff **5** botch, gum up **6** bungle, foul up, goof up, mess up **7** louse up

a hit: **7** succeed, triumph

a hole: **4** bore **5** gouge **6** burrow, dredge **8** excavate **9** hollow out

a judicial decision: **4** find **5** order **6** decide, decree, ordain **7** preside, resolve **8** sentence **9** prescribe, pronounce

a long face: **4** mope, sulk **5** brood

amends: **3** pay **5** atone, repay **6** redeem, reform, refund **7** appease, expiate, redress, requite **8** atone for **9** apologize, indemnify **10** compensate, recompense

a mess of: **4** muff **6** ball up, bungle, foul up, muddle **7** butcher, screw up **9** mishandle, mismanage

an entreaty: **3** beg **4** seek, urge **5** plead, probe, query **6** appeal **7** beseech, implore, inquire, request **8** call upon, petition

as if: **3** act **4** pose **5** feign **7** pretend **8** simulate

a stand: **4** dare, defy **5** claim, fight, query, rally **6** accost, object, take on, threat **7** contest, dispute, protest, vie with **8** confront, denounce, face down, question **9** challenge, discredit, stimulate, vindicate **10** contradict, controvert, insist upon

back: **6** regain

barely ~: **6** eke out

believe: **3** lie **4** fool, play, pose **5** dream, enact, feign **7** act as if, act like, imagine, playact, pretend **8** simulate **9** fantasize

book: **3** bet **4** punt **5** stake, wager **6** gamble **8** give odds, take bets **9** speculate

clear: **4** look, show **5** state **6** decode, define, detail, evince, refine **7** exhibit, explain **8** decipher, describe, simplify **9** bring home, emphasize, explicate, expound on, get across, put across, translate **10** illuminate, illustrate

do: **3** eke **4** cope **5** adapt, get by **6** eke out, manage **7** survive **8** get along, scrape by

do with: **3** use

ecstatic: **5** liven **6** lift up, please, thrill **7** delight, elevate, gladden, hearten, satisfy **9** enrapture **10** exhilarate

effervescent: **7** freshen **9** oxygenate, ventilate

eligible: **6** enable, permit **7** empower, qualify **8** christen **9** authorize, designate, privilege **10** legitimize

ender: **4** over **5** shift **6** weight

enemies: **5** anger **6** fire up, madden **7** incense, inflame, provoke **8** irritate **9** displease, infuriate **10** exasperate

equivalent: **5** level **7** balance

exuberant: **4** gush, rave, send **5** psych **6** excite, fire up, thrill, work up **7** impress **8** interest **9** electrify **10** bubble over, effervesce, get excited

eyes at: **3** eye **4** ogle **5** stare, tease **7** eyeball **8** coquette

fast: **3** fix, peg, tie **4** bind, lock, moor, nail **5** hitch, latch, rivet, truss

feasible: **3** let **6** permit **7** empower, license, qualify **9** authorize

feeble: **6** weaken **8** enervate **9** attenuate **10** devitalize

filthy: **4** foul, soil **5** dirty, spoil, stain, sully, taint **6** befoul, defile **7** corrupt, vitiate **9** desecrate **10** adulterate

final: **5** close **6** clinch **8** finalize **10** consummate

finer: **6** better **7** enhance, improve, sweeten **9** embellish **10** supplement

firewood: **3** cut **4** chop

firm: **3** pin, tie **4** bind, bond, gird, lock, nail, root, weld **5** brace, build, plant, rivet, shore, steel **6** anchor, cement, enroot, fasten, harden, secure, tone up **7** bolster, build up, fortify, implant, shore up, stiffen, tighten, toughen **8** buttress, entrench, nail down, rigidify, solidify **9** reinforce, stabilize **10** straighten

fit: **4** suit **5** adapt, alter, amend **6** adjust, recast, remold, revamp, revise, tailor **7** correct, reshape **8** fine-tune, renovate

flat: **4** even **8** straight

for: **7** advance, promote **8** go toward **10** facilitate, head toward

friends: **7** connect

fun of: **3** kid, rag, rib **4** bait, gibe, jape, jeer, jibe, jive, mock, razz, twit **5** fleer, mimic, taunt, tease **6** banter, deride, go like **7** lampoon, laugh at, run down, scoff at **8** ridicule

furious: **6** enrage

fuzzy: **4** blur, roil, veil **5** bedim, befog **7** obscure

gape: **3** awe **4** daze, rock, stun **5** floor **6** bemuse, boggle, dazzle, thrill **7** astound, nonplus **8** astonish, blow away, bowl over, confound, transfix **9** dumbfound, take aback **10** strike dumb

gentle: **6** mellow, soften **8** civilize

gloomy: **6** dampen, deject, sadden, shadow **7** depress, obscure **8** dispirit **9** bring down **10** demoralize, discourage, dishearten

glow: **5** shine **6** polish **7** burnish, cheer up, light up **8** illumine **10** illuminate

godlike: **5** adore, exalt, extol **7** elevate, glorify, worship **8** sanctify, venerate **10** consecrate

good: **3** pay, win **5** atone, pay up, repay **6** arrive, do well, fulfil, hack it, pan out, pay for, recoup, redeem, refund, settle, thrive **7** deliver, fulfill, luck out, pay back, prevail, prosper, realize, recover, rectify, satisfy, succeed, triumph, work out **8** atone for, flourish, get ahead, go places, hit it big, square up **9** indemnify, reimburse **10** accomplish, do all right, make amends, recompense

goo-goo eyes at: **5** flirt **8** check out

greater: **3** pad **4** feed, hike **5** add to, boost, swell, widen **6** beef up, expand, extend, jack up **7** amplify, build up, develop, enhance, enlarge, inflate, magnify, scale up **8** heighten, increase, lengthen **9** intensify **10** aggrandize, strengthen, supplement

happy: **5** cheer, elate, liven **6** lift up, please, thrill, turn on **7** beatify, content, delight, gladden, gratify, hearten, lighten, overjoy, satisfy, sweeten **8** brighten, enthrall **9** enrapture, inebriate, make happy, transport **10** exhilarate, intoxicate

harmonious: **9** reconcile

haste: **8** hightail **10** burn rubber, get hopping

hazy: **5** bedim, befog, blear, cloud, muddy, smear **7** becloud, obscure **9** adumbrate

heads or tails of: **3** see **6** fathom, follow, pick up **9** figure out **10** comprehend, understand

help to ~ up: **6** pacify, soothe **7** appease, assuage, mediate, mollify, patch up, placate, reunite, satisfy, sweeten, win over **9** arbitrate, intervene, reconcile **10** compromise, conciliate

higher: **4** hike **5** boost, raise **7** elevate **8** increase

hit the ceiling: **5** anger **6** madden, offend **7** incense **9** infuriate

hostile: **10** antagonize

ill: **5** repel, upset **6** infect, offend, revolt **7** afflict

into law: **4** pass **9** institute, legislate

it: **3** win **4** come, live **5** pop up, reach **6** arrive, attend, do well, pan out, thrive **7** luck out, prevail, prosper, qualify, succeed, triumph, weather, work out **8** flourish, get ahead, get there, go places **10** do all right

jump: **5** alarm, panic, scare, spook **7** disturb, startle **8** affright, frighten, surprise **9** galvanize, give a turn

just ~ it: **4** last **5** exist **6** endure, hang on, manage **7** ride out, survive **8** scrape by **9** stay alive **10** stick it out

keen: **5** pique, rally, rouse, strop **6** arouse, excite, kindle **7** sharpen

kind: **6** gentle, mellow, soften, temper

kiss and ~ up: **5** yield **6** accept, pardon **7** appease, let it go, let pass, patch up, placate, reunite **8** overlook, take back **9** acquiesce

knifelike: **4** file, hone, whet **5** grind, strop

known: **3** air, say **4** bare, leak, post, show, tell **5** admit, let on, speak, utter, voice **6** advise, convey, expose, herald, impart, let out, report, reveal, spread, unfold, unmask, unveil **7** declare, display, divulge, exhibit, lay bare, let slip, mention, narrate, uncover **8** advise of, announce, disclose, proclaim **9** advertise, circulate, introduce, propagate, publicize, ventilate **10** make public, promulgate

late: **4** keep **5** delay **6** hang up, hinder, hold up, impede, retard **7** bog down, set back **8** slow down **10** buttonhole

laugh: **5** cheer **6** divert, regale, tickle **7** delight **9** entertain

legal: **2** OK **3** ink **6** ratify **7** approve, certify, endorse, initial, witness **8** legalize, sanction **9** authorize, establish, formalize, sign off on **10** constitute, legitimize

less: **5** allay **6** reduce

less narrow: **6** expand, spread **7** broaden, enlarge, thicken **9** spread out

less wild: **5** break **6** soften **7** harness **8** tone down

light of: **3** rag **4** mock **5** gloze, scoff **6** deride, lessen, slight **7** neglect **8** discount, downplay, minimize, overlook, palliate, play down, pooh-pooh, shrug off, sneeze at, talk down **9** deprecate, soft-pedal, underplay, whitewash **10** understate

like: **3** ape **4** copy, echo **5** mimic **6** mirror **7** imitate

longer: **3** pad **5** add to **6** extend, let out **7** augment, drag out, draw out, prolong, spin out, stretch **8** continue, increase, protract **9** string out

merry: **4** play, romp **5** amuse, exult, laugh, party, revel **6** cavort, frolic **7** carouse, rejoice, satisfy **8** live it up **9** celebrate, entertain, have a ball

more inclusive: **6** expand, spread **7** augment, broaden, enlarge

much of: **4** tout **5** exalt **6** praise, stress **7** amplify, magnify **9** emphasize **10** compliment

naked: **4** bare **5** strip **7** disrobe, uncover, undress

neat: **4** tidy **5** clean, fix up, order **6** spruce **7** freshen, shape up **8** organize, spruce up **9** smarten up **10** straighten

nervous: **5** spook **6** rattle, unglue **7** fluster **8** unsettle **10** discompose, disconcert, intimidate

not ~ the grade: **4** bomb, flop, fold **7** lose out **8** fall flat **9** fall short

null: **6** cancel, repeal **7** rescind, reverse **8** set aside **9** supersede **10** invalidate

obligatory: **5** exact, force, order **6** charge, compel, decree, demand, enjoin **7** command, dictate, inflict **9** establish, institute, prescribe, stipulate **10** promulgate

off: **2** go **3** fly, run **4** bolt, flee, skip **5** lam it, leave, scoot, scram, split **6** beat it, be gone, cut out, decamp, depart, escape **7** abscond, bail out, go south, run away, scamper, skip out, vamoose **8** clear out, fugitate, light out, run for it, skip town, withdraw **9** cut and run, skedaddle **10** hightail it

off with: **3** rob **5** filch, steal, swipe **6** abduct, kidnap, pilfer, snatch **7** ransack

one: **3** wed **5** merge

one's flesh crawl: **5** chill, panic, scare, spook **7** horrify, petrify, terrify **8** frighten **9** terrorize

one's head swim: 5 amaze 6 dazzle 7 impress
one's own: 5 adopt 7 espouse
one's position known: 6 assert 7 declare 8 sound off 10 stand up for
orderly: 5 clean 6 neaten 8 spruce up 10 straighten
out: 2 go 3 see, win 4 cope, espy, fare, find, hint, read, spot, tell 5 get by, get on, grasp, imply, infer, sight, solve 6 deduce, descry, detect, do with, endure, fathom, follow, hack it, impute, manage, notice, reason, thrive 7 achieve, discern, observe, prevail, profess, prosper, succeed, suggest, survive, triumph 8 decipher, flourish, get ahead, get along, go places, hit it big, identify, intimate, make good, perceive, scrape by 9 insinuate, recognize 10 comprehend, do all right, understand
over: 4 redo 5 alter 6 change, reform 7 correct, remodel, reshape 8 transfer 9 transform 10 redecorate, reorganize
plain: 4 show 6 evince 7 clarify, exhibit, speak up 8 manifest, simplify, speak out 9 bring home, elucidate, explicate 10 illustrate
public: 3 air 4 bare, leak 5 break, speak 6 expose, report, reveal, spread, unmask, unveil 7 divulge, exhibit, lay bare, let slip, uncover 8 announce, disclose, proclaim 9 broadcast
quake: 5 alarm, panic 6 rattle 7 horrify, petrify, shake up, startle, terrify 8 frighten 10 intimidate
readable: 5 crack 7 decrypt 8 decipher 9 interpret, translate
ready: 3 set 4 prep 5 equip, groom, prime, train 7 arrange 8 mobilize 9 condition
ringlets: 4 coil 5 swirl, twine, twirl, twist
room for: 3 add 5 admit 6 append, insert 9 interject
sense: 4 jell 5 add up, fit in 6 cohere, figure, relate, square 7 conform, connect 8 dovetail 9 hold water 10 correspond
sure: 5 check 6 affirm, verify 7 confirm 9 ascertain, guarantee
the best of: 5 get by 6 manage 8 tolerate 9 put up with, reconcile
the cut: 6 hack it
the grade: 3 win 4 pass 5 ace it, cut it, score 6 arrive, hack it, pan out, thrive 7 luck out, prevail, prosper, qualify, satisfy, succeed, triumph, work out 8 flourish, get ahead, go places 9 measure up 10 pass muster
the rounds: 3 mix 4 walk 5 watch 6 hobnob, mingle, police 7 inspect
the scene: 4 come, show 5 enter, reach, visit 6 appear, arrive, attend, emerge, stop by 7 turn out
too much of: 8 overrate 9 overstate 10 exaggerate
tracks: 3 hie, run 4 bolt, flee, race, rush, tear 5 hurry, scoot, scram, spank 6 depart, hasten 8 fugitate 10 accelerate, get hopping
unclear: 3 dim, fog 4 blur, roil, veil 5 bedim, befog 6 darken 7 confuse, mystify, obscure 8 bewilder, confound 9 obfuscate
understandable: 7 clarify, clear up 9 elucidate, explicate, get across 10 illuminate, illustrate
unfit: 4 lame, maim, ruin 5 lay up, wreck 6 injure 8 sabotage 9 hamstring
uniform: 4 even, sand 5 level, plane
untidy: 6 jumble, mess up, ruffle, rumple, tangle, tousle 7 clutter, crumple, disturb, rummage, wrinkle 8 dishevel 10 disarrange
up: 3 fix, mix 4 coin, fill, form, meet 5 ad-lib, atone, blend, frame, hatch, ready 6 cook up, create, devise, draw up, inhere, invent, mingle, settle, soothe, whip up, wing it 7 combine, compose, concoct, fashion, imagine, prepare, redress, trump up 8 beautify, complete, compound, comprise, conceive, contrive, knock off 9 fabricate, formulate, improvise, originate, play by ear, reconcile, replenish 10 compensate, constitute, make amends, recompense, shake hands
(up): 5 dream, think
up for: 5 atone, cover, right 6 offset, recoup, redeem, refund 7 balance, expiate, rectify, redress 8 outweigh 9 apologize, do justice, reimburse 10 compensate, recompense
up-to-date: 5 fix up, refit 6 extend, resume 7 freshen, furbish, remodel, restore 8 overhaul, renovate, spruce up 9 modernize, refurbish 10 revitalize
usable: 3 fit 5 alter 6 adjust, change, modify, revise, tailor 7 remodel 8 regulate
usable again: 5 renew 9 refurbish
use of: 5 avail, exert, wield 6 employ, look to, resort 7 utilize 10 fall back on
vague: 3 fog 4 daze, mist 5 befog, blear, cloud, muddy, smear 6 smudge 7 becloud, obscure
vapid: 6 benumb, dampen, muffle, stifle 7 repress, silence 8 diminish, suppress
visible: 5 flare, flash, shine 6 ignite, illume, kindle, turn on 7 inflame, lighten 8 brighten, enkindle, illumine 9 highlight, set fire to, set on fire, spotlight 10 illuminate
waves: 4 stir 5 rebel, shake, upset 6 revolt 7 trouble 9 instigate 10 complicate, exasperate
wavy: 4 curl 5 frizz, swirl
whole: 4 cure, heal, mend 5 right, treat 6 remedy, repair 7 correct, relieve, restore 8 medicate
make ___: 3 for, hay, off, out, way 4 as if, bold, book, eyes, fast, good, like, nice, over, sail, sure, time, with 5 a face, a go of, a mint, a stab, fun of, haste, ready, up for, use of, waves 6 amends, public, tracks 7 believe, whoopee, whoopie
make ___ buck: 5 a fast
make ___ dash: 4 a mad
make ___ for: 5 a case, a play, it hot
make ___ for it: 4 a run
make ___ for oneself: 5 a name
make ___ in: 5 a dent
make ___ like a bandit: 3 out
make ___ meet: 4 ends
make ___ of: 3 a go, fun, use 4 much 5 a fool, a mess, a note, a show, light 6 little
make ___ of faith: 5 a leap
make ___ of it: 3 a go
make ___ of the tongue: 5 a slip
make ___ on: 4 book 5 a move
make ___ with: 3 off 4 a hit, away 6 points 7 friends
make-___: 4 work 5 ahead, peace, ready 7 believe
Make ___!: 4 it so
Make ___ double!: 3 it a
Make ___ for Daddy: 4 Room
Make ___ Happy: 7 Someone
Make ___ Music: 4 Mine
Make-___ Foundation: 5 a-Wish
make a ___: 4 face, go of 5 stink
make a ___ breast of: 5 clean
make a ___ for: 4 case, play
make a ___ for oneself: 4 name
make a ___ it: 4 go of
make a ___ of: 4 show 5 point
make a ___ on: 4 move
make a ___ out of: 6 monkey
make a day ___: 4 of it
___ Make a Deal: 4 Let's
make a go ___: 4 of it
Make a Move on Me (1982 song) artist: Olivia Newton-John
make-and-___: 5 break
Make and Break author: Michael Frayn
make a run ___: 5 for it
Makeba, Miriam
homeland: South Africa
song: Pata Pata (1967)
make-believe: 4 fake, mock, sham 5 bogus, false, phony, put-on 6 ersatz, fakery, forged, phoney, pseudo, unreal 7 assumed, charade, fantasy, feigned, pretend 8 imagined, pretense, spurious 9 fairy-tale, fictional, imaginary, imitation, pretended, simulated, synthetic, unnatural, unreality 10 artificial, fabricated, fictitious, fraudulent
___ Make Believe: 4 Only
Make Believe (1969 song) artist: Tony Orlando & Dawn
Make Believe composer: 4 Kern 11 Hammerstein
make both ends ___: 4 meet
make-do: 9 makeshift, temporary 10 pro tempore
make it ___: 6 snappy
Make it ___ for my baby...: 3 one
Make It Happen (1992 song) artist: Mariah Carey
Make It Hot (1998 song)
artist: Missy Elliott, Nicole
Make it snappy!: 4 ASAP, stat
Make It With You (1970 song) artist: Bread
Make like ___ and leave: 5 a tree
Make Me Lose Control (1988 song)
artist: Eric Carmen
___ Make Me Over: 4 Don't
Make Me Smile (1970 song) artist: Chicago
Make my day!: 4 dare
make no ___ about: 5 bones
make one's ___: 3 way 4 case, mark
make one's ___ water: 5 mouth
make oneself ___: 6 scarce
make-or-___: 5 break
make out ___ bandit: 5 like a
___ Makepeace Thackeray: 7 William
maker: 5 cause 6 framer, wright 7 creator 8 designer, inventer, inventor, producer 9 architect, artificer, craftsman 10 fabricator
combining form: 3 -fex
starter: 3 car, hay, ice, law, map 4 auto, book, chip, deal, film, home, king, myth, news, odds, pace, play, rain, shoe, tool, wine 5 dress, glass, match, merry, money, movie, noise, paper, peace, print, taste, watch 6 boiler, coffee, phrase, policy, speech, violin 7 cabinet, holiday, pattern, trouble
suffix: 3 -ist
___ maker: 3 tea 6 coffee, market
Maker: 3 God 7 Creator 8 Almighty
makeshift: 4 rude, temp 5 crude, rough 6 coarse, refuge, shoddy 7 interim, stopgap 8 homemade, slapdash 9 expedient, hit-or-miss, inelegant, patchwork, primitive, temporary, unrefined 10 amateurish, improvised, jury-rigged, last resort, pro tempore, substitute, unpolished, unreliable
make short ___ of: 4 work
...makes Jack ___ boy: 5 a dull
Make Someone Happy composer: 5 Green, Styne 6 Comden
___ Makes Sammy Run?: 4 What
___ makes two of us!: 4 That
make the ___: 5 grade, scene 6 rounds
make the ___ fly: 3 fur 4 dust
make the ___ of: 4 most
Make thee ___ of greatness: 5 a name
make the fur ___: 3 fly
make the most ___: 4 of it
Make the World Go Away (1965 song) artist: Eddy Arnold
makeup: 4 Avon, body, mold 5 Almay, blush, gloss, humor, liner, paint, rouge, stamp 6 design, format, nature, powder, Revlon, shadow, stripe, temper 7 anatomy, Lancome, Mary Kay, mascara, pancake, texture 8 Clinique, cosmetic, eyeliner, lipstick 9 character, cosmetics, Cover Girl, eye shadow, formation, Max Factor, mentality, structure 10 complexion, foundation, maquillage, Maybelline 11 Estée Lauder, Merle Norman
apply ~: 3 dab
eye ~: 4 kohl 5 liner
fuss with ~: 5 primp
take a ~ exam: 5 resit
makeup ___: 4 exam
___ makeup: 4 cake 7 Pan-Cake
make up one's ___: 4 mind
___ Make Waves: 4 Don't
Make Way for Tomorrow (1937 film)
cast: Fay Bainter, Beulah Bondi, Victor Moore
director: Leo McCarey
Make yourself ___: 6 at home
Make Yourself Comfortable (1954 song) artist: Sarah Vaughan
maki: 5 lemur
Makin' ___: 7 Whoopie
making: 8 creation
combining form: 7 -facient, -poiesis
not ~ it: 7 failing
starter: 3 law, map 4 book, film, home, king, myth, play, rain, rate, shoe, snow, wine 5 glass, match, merry, money, movie, paper, peace, print 6 phrase, policy, speech, violin 7 cabinet, pattern
___ making eyes at me: 5 Ma he's
Making Love out of Nothing at All (1983 song) artist: Air Supply
Making Mr. Right (1987 film)
cast: Glenne Headly, Ann Magnuson, John Malkovich
director: Susan Seidelman
Making of an American, The author: Jacob Riis
Making of the President, The author: Theodore H. White
makings: 8 capacity 9 potential
Making Tracks author: Alan Ayckbourn
Makin' Whoopee composer: 4 Kahn 9 Donaldson
mako: 4 fish 5 shark
Makonde home: 6 Africa 8 Tanzania 10 Mozambique
Maksim: 5 Gorki, Gorky
Makua home: 6 Africa 8 Tanzania 10 Mozambique
mal ___: 5 de mer
mal-: 3 bad, ill
mala ___: 4 fide
Mala: 6 Powers
Malabar Coast district: 3 Goa
Malabo: 4 city, town 7 capital

Malacca: **3** str. **4** cane **6** strait
Malachi: **6** Throne
preceder: **9** Zechariah
malachite: **3** ore **7** mineral
maladroit: **5** gawky, inapt, inept, unapt **6** clumsy, gauche, klutzy, oafish, wooden **7** awkward, gawkish, halting, labored, unadept, unhandy **8** bumbling, bungling, cloddish, fumbling, inexpert, lubberly, tactless, ungainly **9** all thumbs, graceless, impolitic, lumbering, stumbling, unskilled, untactful **10** blundering, leadfooted, left-handed, unbecoming, ungraceful, unskillful
malady: **3** bug, ill **7** ailment, disease, illness, trouble **8** disorder, sickness, syndrome **9** complaint, condition, infirmity **10** affliction, unwellness
childhood ~: **5** colic, croup, mumps **7** measles **10** chicken pox
suffix: **4** -itis
mala fide: **8** bad faith
Malaga: **4** wine
origin: **5** Spain
Málaga: **4** city, port, town
locale: **5** Spain
malagueña: **5** dance
malaise: **4** pain **5** angst, gloom **6** unease **7** anxiety, despair, fidgets, illness **8** debility, disquiet, distress, doldrums, sickness, weakness **9** infirmity, lassitude **10** depression, discomfort, enervation, feebleness, infirmness, inquietude, melancholy, sickliness, uneasiness, unwellness, woefulness
Malamud, Bernard: **6** author, writer
work: The Assistant
The Fixer
Idiots First
The Magic Barrel
The Natural
The Tenants
malamute: **3** dog, pet **5** pooch **6** canine
burden: **4** sled
command to a ~: **4** mush
__ malamute: **7** Alaskan
Malang: **4** city, town
locale: **9** Indonesia
__ Malaprop: **3** Mrs.
malapropism: **6** misuse **8** wordplay
malapropos: **5** badly, inapt, unapt, wrong **8** improper, unseemly, untimely
malar: **4** bone **9** cheekbone
malaria symptom: **4** ague
malarkey: **3** rot **4** bosh, bull, bunk, guff, jazz, jive **5** bilge, hokum, stuff, trash **6** bunkum, bushwa, dupery, hot air **7** baloney, blather, blether, boloney, bushwah, garbage, hogwash, rubbish, twaddle **8** buncombe, claptrap, fast talk, flummery, nonsense, tommyrot **9** deception, poppycock **10** applesauce, balderdash, empty words
Malawi: **4** lake **6** nation **7** country
city: **5** Zomba **8** Lilongwe
Lake locale: **8** Tanzania **10** Mozambique
money: **6** kwacha **7** tambala
neighbor: **6** Zambia **8** Tanzania **10** Mozambique
people: **3** Yao **4** Cewa **5** Bemba, Chewa, Makua, Ngoni, Nguni **6** Nyanja
Malay: **8** language **10** Indonesian
address: **4** tuan
boat: **4** prao, prau, proa **5** prahu
bovine: **4** gaur **5** gayal **6** mithan **7** banteng, banting
cuckoo: **4** koel
dagger: **4** kris **6** crease, creese
gecko: **5** tokay
island: **5** Timor
isthmus: **3** Kra
mammal: **5** tapir
native: **4** Moro
primate: **3** lar **7** siamang
prince: **4** raja
region: **6** Indies
reptile: **5** krait
sea: **7** Andaman
sultanate: **6** Brunei
tree: **5** areca, mahua, mahwa, mohwa, mowra **6** mowrah **8** jelutong
__-Malayan: **4** Indo
Malay Archipelago: **4** isls. **5** isles **7** islands
island: **4** Java **5** Luzon **6** Borneo, Sundas **7** Celebes, Sumatra **8** Mindanao, Sulawesi **9** Indonesia, New Guinea **10** East Indies
Malaysia: **6** nation **7** country
bay: **6** Brunei
capital: **11** Kuala Lumpur
city: **4** Ipoh **6** Penang
export: **3** tin **5** copra **8** copperah
money: **3** sen
neighbor: **6** Brunei **8** Thailand **9** Indonesia
port: **6** Penang **10** George Town
river: **5** Perak
sarong: **4** kain
state: **5** Johor, Kedah, Perak, Sabah **6** Melaka, Pahang, Penang, Perlis **7** Sarawak **8** Kelantan, Selangor
Malcolm: **4** Gets **5** Lowry, Young **6** Forbes **7** McLaren, Sargent **8** Bradbury, McDowell **9** Baldridge **10** Muggeridge
Malcolm __ Middle: **5** in the
Malcolm author: James Purdy
Malcolm-Jamal: **6** Warner
Malcolm X (1992 film)
cast: Angela Bassett, Albert Hall, Denzel Washington
director: Spike Lee
malcontent: **4** crab **5** grump, rebel **6** griper, grouch, moaner **7** crybaby, heretic **8** agitator, maverick, renegade **9** anarchist, dissenter, insurgent, protester **10** iconoclast
Malcontent, The author: John Marston
mal de __: **3** mer **4** tête **5** dents
mal de mer: **6** nausea
Malden: **4** city, Karl, town
locale: **4** Mass.
Malden, Karl: **5** actor
film: All Fall Down (1962)
Baby Doll (1956)
Billion Dollar Brain (1967)
Birdman of Alcatraz (1962)
Cheyenne Autumn (1964)
The Cincinnati Kid (1965)
Fear Strikes Out (1957)
The Great Impostor (1961)
Gypsy (1962)
The Hanging Tree (1959)
Murderers' Row (1966)
Nevada Smith (1966)
Nuts (1987)
One-Eyed Jacks (1961)
On the Waterfront (1954)
Patton (1970)
A Streetcar Named Desire (1951, AA)
Take the High Ground (1953)
Time Limit (1957)
Wild Rovers (1971)
TV: Skag, The Streets of San Francisco
Maldives: **4** isls. **5** isles **6** nation **7** country, islands
capital: **4** Male
coin: **4** lari **5** laree
mal du __: **4** pays
male: **2** he, Mr., pa **3** boy, cob, dad, guy, him, man, pop, ram, sir, son **4** bass, boar, buck, bull, chap, colt, czar, gent, hero, hunk, papa, sire, stag, stud, tsar, tzar **5** bloke, calif, capon, daddy, drake, drone, groom, kalif, macho, manly, pappy, Romeo, steer, swain, tenor, uncle, youth **6** butler, caliph, father, feller, fellow, gender, kaliph, khalif, laddie, mister, nephew, potent, spouse, tomcat, virile **7** brother, danseur, husband, rooster **8** bachelor, baritone, barytone, cardinal, paternal, stallion **9** boyfriend, chevalier, gentleman, masculine
combining form: **4** andr- **5** andro-, -andry **7** -androus
vain ~: **4** dude **5** dandy **9** pretty boy
male __: **4** fern **7** bonding
__ male: **5** alpha
Malé: **4** city, town **7** capital
locale: **8** Maldives
Male and Female author: **4** Mead
Male Animal, The (1942 film)
cast: Olivia de Havilland, Henry Fonda, Joan Leslie
director: Elliott Nugent
Male Animal, The author: James Thurber
Malebranche, Nicolas de: **6** French **11** philosopher
Malecite: **6** Indian **7** Amerind
malediction: **4** jinx, oath **5** curse **6** tirade, whammy **8** anathema **9** damnation, profanity
malefaction: **3** sin **4** evil, harm, vice **5** guilt **7** misdeed
malefactor: **5** felon, scamp **6** bad guy **7** villain **9** miscreant **10** delinquent, holy terror
malefic: **4** evil **6** malign **7** baneful, harmful, ominous, satanic **8** sinister **9** satanical
maleficent: **4** base, evil, foul **6** malign, wicked **7** harmful, hurtful **8** diabolic, fiendish **9** injurious **10** diabolical, villainous
males and females, for: **4** coed **6** unisex
malevolence: **4** evil **5** spite, venom, wrong **6** animus, malice, rancor **8** acrimony
malevolent: **3** ill **4** cold, evil, mean, ugly **5** catty, cruel, nasty, onery, surly **6** chilly, malign, ornery, wanton, wicked **7** baleful, hateful, hellish, hostile, satanic, vicious, waspish **8** infernal, inimical, libelous, sinister, spiteful, vengeful, venomous, virulent **9** bellicose, malicious, poisonous, rancorous, satanical **10** derogatory, evil-minded, ill-natured, pugnacious, virtueless
one: **5** hater
__ Male War Bride: **5** I Was a
malfeasance: **5** abuse, fault, guilt **7** offense **9** improbity
malformed: **6** skewed, warped **7** crooked, twisted **8** abnormal **9** contorted, distorted, grotesque, irregular, misshapen, shapeless
malfunction: **3** bug **4** fail, flaw, slip **5** act up, crash, fault **6** defect, glitch **7** failure, gremlin, trouble **9** breakdown
malfunctioning: **6** faulty
__ malgre lui: **5** Le roi
Malherbe, François de: **4** poet **6** French
Mali: **6** nation **7** country
capital: **6** Bamako
city: **3** Gao **5** Mopti, Ségou **6** Bamako **7** Sikasso
desert: **6** Sahara
locale: **3** Afr. **6** Africa
money: **5** franc
neighbor: **5** Niger **6** Guinea **7** Algeria, Senegal **10** Ivory Coast, Mauritania
people: **4** Fula **5** Dogon **6** Fulani, Senufo, Tuareg **7** Bambara, Malinka, Malinke, Songhai **8** Mandingo, Mandinka
river: **5** Niger
Malibu: **3** car **4** auto **5** beach, Chevy **9** Chevrolet **10** automobile
athletes: **5** Waves
locale: **10** California
school: **10** Pepperdine
sight: **4** surf
malic: **4** acid
malice: **3** ill **4** bile, evil, hate **5** odium, spite, venom **6** animus, enmity, grudge, hatred, rancor, spleen **7** cruelty, ill will, umbrage **8** acrimony, bad blood, contempt, meanness **9** animosity, antipathy, hostility, mordacity, nastiness **10** abhorrence, backbiting, bitterness, resentment, unkindness
bear ~ toward: **4** hate **7** dislike
Malice (1993 film)
cast: Alec Baldwin, Nicole Kidman, Bebe Neuwirth, Bill Pullman
director: Harold Becker
Malice author: Danielle Steel
malicious: **3** ill, low **4** evil, mean **5** catty, nasty, onery, petty, snide, surly **6** bitter, cussed, ornery, sneaky, uncool, unkind, wanton, wicked **7** baleful, beastly, cutting, envious, harmful, hateful, hostile, hurtful, jealous, vicious **8** fiendish, inimical, libelous, spiteful, vengeful, venomous, virulent **9** bellicose, green-eyed, injurious, poisonous, rancorous, resentful, splenetic **10** bad-natured, derogatory, evil-minded, ill-natured, malevolent, pernicious, pugnacious, unfriendly, vindictive, virtueless
intent: **6** enmity, hatred, malice, rancor **7** cruelty, ill will **8** acrimony **9** animosity, hostility, vengeance
one: **5** viper, vixen
tale: **6** canard
Malick: **6** Wendie **8** Terrence
malign: **3** dis, hit, lie, rap **4** evil, gibe, harm, jeer, jibe, mock, slam, slur, snub, soil **5** abuse, curse, decry, libel, roast, scorn, smear, spurn, stain, sully, taint, taunt, toxic, wrong **6** accuse, assail, befoul, defame, defile, deride, dump on, heckle, impugn, injure, insult, nocent, offend, rebuff, revile, slight, vilify, wicked **7** adverse, affront, asperse, baleful, baneful, blacken, degrade, detract, disdain, harmful, hateful, hostile, hurtful, inhuman, malefic, put down, rank out, rip into, ruinous, run down, slander, tarnish, traduce, vicious **8** backbite, badmouth, belittle, besmirch, damaging, denounce, derogate, inhumane, inimical, mudsling, negative, ridicule, sinister, spiteful, tear down, throw mud, vilipend, virulent **9** bespatter, dangerous, denigrate, deprecate, discredit, disparage, humiliate, injurious, rancorous **10** blackguard, calamitous, calumniate, disastrous, disrespect, maleficent, malevolent, pernicious, speak ill of, villainize, vituperate
maligner: **6** critic **8** vilifier **9** detractor
maligning: **5** abuse **9** invidious **10** defamatory, derogatory, detraction, muckraking
malignity: **4** evil **6** animus, rancor **9** animosity
malinger: **4** idle, loaf **5** shirk, slack **7** goof off, pretend **8** slack off **9** goldbrick
in Britain: **5** sculk, skulk

malingerer: **5** shirk **6** loafer, truant **7** shirker, slacker **10** ne'er-do-well
Malinka home: **4** Mali **6** Africa, Guinea **10** Ivory Coast
Malinke: **8** language
Malinowski, Bronislaw: **6** Polish **14** anthropologist
malkin: **3** cat, mop **4** hare
Malkovich, John: **5** actor
film: Being John Malkovich (1999)
Con Air (1997)
Dangerous Liaisons (1988)
Eleni (1985)
Empire of the Sun (1987)
The Glass Menagerie (1987)
In the Line of Fire (1993)
The Killing Fields (1984)
Making Mr. Right (1987)
Man in the Iron Mask (1998)
The Object of Beauty (1991)
Of Mice and Men (1992)
Places in the Heart (1984)
Shadow of the Vampire (2000)
spouse: Glenne Headly
mall: **4** mart, walk **5** plaza **6** arcade, market **9** boulevard, esplanade, promenade
binge: **5** spree
feature: **3** map **4** sale, shop **5** kiosk, store **6** arcade, atrium, cinema **8** boutique **9** food court
forerunner: **5** agora
frequenter: **4** teen **7** shopper
hit the ~: **4** shop **5** spend
shopping ~: **4** mart **5** plaza **6** market
__ mall: **5** strip
__ Mall: **4** Pall
mallard: **4** bird, duck, fowl
flock: **4** sute
relative: **4** smew, teal **5** eider, koloa, Pekin, Rouen, scaup **6** Cayuga, scoter, wigeon **7** gadwall, pintail, pochard, redhead, sea duck, widgeon **8** garganey, gray duck, mandarin, musk duck, oldsquaw, shoveler, surf duck, wood duck **9** black duck, broadbill, goldeneye, goosander, greenhead, merganser, ruddy duck, sprigtail **10** bufflehead, canvasback, surf scoter, tufted duck
Mallarmé, Stéphane: **4** poet **6** French
malleable: **4** soft **5** fluid **6** clayey, lissom, pliant, supple **7** clayish, ductile, lissome, plastic, pliable **8** flexible, formable, moldable, obedient, tractile, workable, yielding **9** adaptable, compliant, formative, tractable **10** governable, manageable, submissive
Malle, Louis: **8** director
film: Atlantic City (1981)
Au Revoir, Les Enfants (1987)
God's Country (1985)
Lacombe, Lucien (1974)
The Lovers (1958)
Pretty Baby (1978)
The Silent World (1956)
The Thief of Paris (1967)
Vanya on 42nd Street (1994)
spouse: Candice Bergen
mallemuck: **4** bird
mallet: **4** club, tool **5** gavel **6** hammer
game: **4** polo **5** roque **7** croquet
target: **4** gong
malleus: **4** bone
locale: **3** ear
Mallon: **3** Meg **4** Mary
Mallon, Meg: **6** golfer
milieu: **5** links **6** course
org.: **4** LPGA
Mallorca: **3** isl. **4** isla, isle **6** island
see also Majorca, Spanish
Mallory: **6** George
mallow: **5** plant **6** flower
family shrub: **4** ocra, okra, okro **5** urena **8** abutilon
genus: **5** malva
starter: **5** marsh
tree: **8** hibiscus
mallow __: **4** rose
__ mallow: **4** musk, rose **5** dwarf, marsh, swamp **6** common, Indian
Malmö: **4** city, port, town
city near ~: **4** Lund
locale: **6** Sweden
malmsey: **4** wine
origin: **6** Greece **8** Portugal
malnourished: **6** skinny **7** starved **8** starving
malodor: **4** reek **5** smell, stink **6** stench **9** fetidness
malodorous: **3** bad, off **4** foul, gamy, high, olid, rank, vile **5** fetid, fusty, gamey, musty, nasty, stale **6** foetid, frowsy, frowzy, rancid, rotten, smelly, stinky, strong **7** decayed, noisome, noxious, reeking, tainted **8** mephitic, overripe, stinking **9** offensive
Malone: **3** Sam **4** Jena, Karl **5** Moses **7** Dorothy
Malone Dies author: Samuel Beckett
Malone, Dorothy: **7** actress
film: Beach Party (1963)
The Last Sunset (1961)
The Last Voyage (1960)
Man of a Thousand Faces (1957)
The Tarnished Angels (1958)
Tip on a Dead Jockey (1957)
Written on the Wind (1957, AA)
TV: Peyton Place
Malone, Karl
milieu: **5** court
org.: **3** NBA
sport: **10** basketball
Malone, Moses
milieu: **5** court
org.: **3** NBA
sport: **10** basketball
Malory: **6** Thomas
malpractice: **5** abuse **7** misdeed, offense **9** improbity, violation
Malraux: **5** André
malt
beverage: **3** ale **4** beer, suds **5** lager, stout **6** porter
dryer: **4** oast
ender: **3** ase, ose
fermenting ~ infusion: **4** wort
liquor yeast: **4** barm
vinegar: **6** alegar
malt __: **4** shop **5** sugar **6** liquor, whisky **7** extract
Malta: **3** isl. **4** isle **6** island, nation **7** country
capital: **8** Valletta
locale: **3** Eur. **5** Medit. **6** Europe
money: **4** cent, lira, lire, tari **6** sequin
Maltbie: **5** Roger
Maltby: **7** Richard
malted: **8** beverage
malted __: **4** milk
Maltese: **3** cat, dog **5** canid, felid **6** canine, feline
remark: **3** mew **4** meow **5** miaou, miaow, miaul
Maltese __: **3** cat, dog **5** cross
Maltese __, The: **5** Bippy **6** Falcon
Maltese Falcon, The: **4** film **5** novel
author: Dashiell Hammett
cast: Mary Astor, Humphrey Bogart, Ward Bond, Elisha Cook Jr., Sydney Greenstreet, Peter Lorre
character: **3** Iva, Sam **4** Cook, Joel, Rhea **5** Cairo, Effie, Floyd, Miles, Spade **6** Archer, Brigid, Casper, Gutman, Jacobi, Perine, Wilmer **7** Kemidov, Thursby **8** Sam Spade **9** Iva Archer, Joel Cairo **10** Rhea Gutman, Wilmer Cook
director: John Huston
Malthus, Thomas: **7** British **9** economist
Maltin: **7** Leonard
maltose: **5** sugar
Maltrata: **4** city, town
locale: **6** Mexico **8** Veracruz
maltreat: **4** beat, harm, hurt, mall, maul **5** abuse, wrong **6** ill-use, injure, misuse **7** corrupt, oppress, outrage, rough up **8** aggrieve, keep down **9** manhandle, persecute **10** excruciate, kick around
maltreatment: **5** abuse **6** misuse **8** inequity
malt-shop
freebie: **5** straw
order: **4** soda **5** float
malvasia: **5** grape
relative: **5** Gamay, pinot, Tokay **6** Merlot **7** Catawba, Concord, Niagara **8** Cabernet, muscatel **9** muscadine, Sauvignon, zinfandel **10** Chardonnay
Malvi: **3** cow **4** bull **6** bovine, cattle
__ Malvinas: **5** Islas
mama: **3** dam **4** mate **6** mother, parent **8** baby talk
Mama: **4** Cass **8** Michelle
warning: **4** don't, no-no
Mama (CBS sitcom)
cast: Judson Laire (Lars Hansen)
Rosemary Rice (Katrin Hansen)
Dick Van Patten (Nels Hansen)
Peggy Wood (Marta Hansen)
dog: **6** Willie
Mama (1960 song) artist: Connie Francis
mama and __: **4** papa
Mama Can't Buy You Love (1979 song) artist: Elton John
__ Mama Don't Dance: **4** Your
Mama from the Train (1956 song) artist: Patti Page
Mama Said (1961 song) artist: Shirelles
Mama Said Knock You Out (1991 song) artist: LL Cool J
mama's boy: **4** wimp **5** sissy **7** milksop **8** weakling **10** namby-pamby
Mama's Family (NBC sitcom)
cast: Ken Berry (Vinton Harper)
Vicki Lawrence (Mama Harper)
Dorothy Lyman (Naomi Harper)
Mama's Pearl (1971 song) artist: Jackson 5
Mamas & the Papas
members: **6** Elliot **7** Doherty, Elliott **8** Phillips
song: California Dreamin' (1966)
Creeque Alley (1967)
Dedicated to the One I Love (1967)
I Saw Her Again (1966)
Monday, Monday (1966)
Twelve Thirty (1967)
Words of Love (1966)
Mama Told Me (1970 song) artist: Three Dog Night
mamba: **5** snake **6** animal **7** reptile
relative: **3** asp, boa **5** aboma, adder, cobra, krait, racer, viper **6** dhaman, python, taipan **7** markhor, rattler **8** anaconda, moccasin, ringhals **9** boomslang, coachwhip **10** bushmaster, copperhead, sidewinder
mambo: **5** dance
relative: **5** rumba **6** cha-cha, rhumba
Mambo Italiano (1954 song) artist: Rosemary Clooney
Mame: **7** musical
songwriter: **6** Herman
to Patrick: **4** aunt
__ Mame: **6** Auntie
Mame (1966 song) artist: Herb Alpert and the Tijuana Brass
Ma mère, je la vois: **4** duet
Mamet, David: **6** author **8** director **9** dramatist **10** playwright
film: Heist (2001)
House of Games (1987)
The Spanish Prisoner (1998)
State and Main (2000)
The Winslow Boy (1999)
spouse: Lindsay Crouse
work: American Buffalo
Glengarry Glen Ross
Lone Canoe
mamey: **5** fruit
Mamie: **8** Van Doren **10** Eisenhower
predecessor: **4** Bess
spouse: **3** Ike
successor: **6** Jackie **10** Jacqueline
Mamie Eisenhower, __ Doud: **3** née
Mamma __!: **3** Mia
mammal: **2** ai **3** ape, bat, cat, cow, dog, elk, fox, gnu, kob, man, pig, yak **4** anoa, bear, boar, cavy, deer, goat, guib, hare, ibex, kudu, lion, lynx, mink, mole, mule, orca, oryx, paca, peba, pika, puku, puma, saki, seal, titi, topi, unau, vole, wolf, zebu **5** addax, apara, bison, bongo, camel, chimp, chiru, civet, coati, dhole, drill, eland, genet, goral, hippo, horse, human, hyena, hyrax, jocko, koala, korin, lemur, llama, loris, magot, moose, mouse, nyala, okapi, orang, oribi, otary, otter, panda, potto, ratel, rhino, sable, saiga, serow, sheep, shrew, skunk, sloth, stoat, tapir, tiger, whale, zebra **6** agouti, alpaca, aye-aye, baboon, badger, Bandar, beaver, bobcat, canine, chammy, cougar, coyote, dassie, desman, dik-dik, dugong, duiker, ermine, feline, ferret, galago, gelada, gerbil, gibbon, gopher, grivet, guenon, howler, hyaena, impala, jackal, jaguar, jerboa, koodoo, langur, lechwe, macaco, marmot, marten, monkey, nilgai, ocelot, peludo, possum, rabbit, racoon, rhebok, rhesus, shammy, shamoy, tanrec, tenrec, uakari, vervet, vicuna, walrus, wapiti, weasel **7** blaubok, blesbok, buffalo, chamois, cheetah, colobus, defassa, dolphin, echidna, gazelle, gemsbok, gerenuk, giraffe, gorilla, grysbok, guanaco, guereza, hamster, hoolock, lemming, leopard, macaque, manatee, meerkat, muskrat, narwhal, nylghai, nylghau, opossum, panther, peccary, polecat, primate, raccoon, rorqual, sapajou, sassaby, sea lion, siamang, tamarin, tarsier, tatuasu, wallaby, warthog **8** aardvark, aardwolf, anteater, antelope, blesbuck, bontebok, bush baby, bushbuck, capuchin, capybara, chipmunk, dormouse, elephant, gemsbuck, hedgehog, kangaroo, kinkajou, mandrill, mangabey, marmoset, mongoose, pangolin, platypus, porpoise, reedbuck, reindeer, ruminant, squirrel, steenbok, steinbok, talapoin, wallaroo **9** armadillo, bandicoot, blackbuck, dromedary, guinea pig, marsupial, orangutan, porcupine, pronghorn, razorback, sitatunga, springbok, waterbuck, wolverine **10** Barbary ape, chimpanzee, coatimundi, hartebeest, orangutang, prairie dog, rhinoceros, wildebeest
aquatic ~: **4** seal **5** hippo, otary, otter **6** desman, dugong
arboreal ~: **5** koala, lemur, sloth
characteristic: **4** hair
largest ~: **5** whale
Mamma Mia (1976 song) artist: ABBA
mammee: **4** tree

mammon: 3 oof 4 cash, gelt, jack, kail, kale, loot, peag, pelf 5 bills, bread, bucks, dough, funds, lucre, money, moola, mopus, pesos, rhino, sewan 6 dinero, do-re-mi, mazuma, moolah, riches, seawan, silver, specie, wampum, wealth 7 cabbage, capital, dollars, lettuce, ooftish, scratch, shekels 8 bankroll, cold cash, currency, hard cash, smackers 9 banknotes, frogskins, long green, simoleons 10 greenbacks, green stuff

mammoth: 3 big 4 huge, vast 5 bulky, giant, great, jumbo, large 6 animal 7 hulking, immense, massive, monster, sizable, titanic 8 colossal, colossus, elephant, enormous, gigantic, king-size, oversize, sizeable, towering, whapping, whopping 9 Herculean, humongous, leviathan, monstrous, overlarge 10 behemothic, formidable, gargantuan, monumental, prodigious, stupendous, tremendous

feature: 4 tusk 5 trunk

period: 6 ice age

___ mammoth: 6 woolly

Mammoth Cave: 4 Park

locale: 3 Ken. 8 Kentucky

Mammoth Hunters, The author: Jean Auel

character: 4 Ayla

period: 6 Ice Age

Mamoré: 5 river

locale: 6 Brazil 7 Bolivia

Mamoulian, Rouben: 8 director

film: Applause (1929)
Blood and Sand (1941)
City Streets (1931)
Dr. Jekyll and Mr. Hyde (1932)
Love Me Tonight (1932)
The Mark of Zorro (1940)
Queen Christina (1933)
Silk Stockings (1957)

man: 2 he 3 dad, guy, him, wow 4 chap, male, stag 5 adult, fella, human, señor, staff 6 animal, butler, feller, fellow, mensch, mister, mortal, person, senhor, spouse, suitor 7 checker, fortify, grown-up, operate 8 monsieur, naked ape 9 earthling, game piece, human race 10 chess piece, human being, individual

combining form: 5 homin- 6 homini-

ender: 3 age 4 hole, hunt, kind, made, rope, trap, ward, wise 5 drake, drill, power, wards 6 handle 7 servant

Friday: 4 aide, asst. 9 assistant

Lady's ~: 4 earl, lord, peer

name meaning ~: 7 Charles

starter: 3 air, bag, bar, bat, bow, bus, cab, cow, foe, gag, gun, ice, law, lay, mad, pen, pit, rag, rod, sea, tax 4 alms, base, bats, bell, bird, boat, bogy, bond, cave, club, desk, door, dray, fire, flag, foot, fore, free, frog, glee, good, head, jazz, line, mail, Manx, milk, news, oars, pack, plow, post, reed, sand, ship, show, side, snow, swag, wing, wire, wood, work, yard 5 alder, bails, bands, barge, blues, bogey, bonds, brake, chain, chair, chess, clans, coach, corps, dairy, Dutch, earth, freed, fresh, fugle, funny, games, gowns, handy, helms, herds, horse, house, hunts, Irish, lands, leads, liege, lines, marks, money, motor, noble, Norse, North, pitch, place, press, radio, ranch, rifle, sales, Scots, sound, spear, stock, stunt, swing, towns, track, train, watch, water, wheel, woods 6 anchor, boogie, bushel, camera, cattle, church, clergy, crafts, drafts, fellow, fields, fisher, French, gentle, grooms, guards, guilds, letter, livery, middle, minute, muscle, oyster, patrol, plains, police, repair, rounds, safety, school, select, spokes, sports, states, steers, strong, switch, swords, trades, tribes, vestry, wheels, yachts 7 advance, cavalry, Cornish, council, counter, country, defense, English, harvest, highway, husband, journey, midship, militia, service, trigger, working 8 assembly, business, crossbow, infantry, merchant, outdoors, trencher 9 artillery, committee, longshore, newspaper

traveling ~: 5 nomad

man ___: 4 lock 5 of God, power 6 Friday

man ___ cloth: 5 of the

man ___ hour: 5 of the

man ___ house: 5 of the

man ___ moon: 5 in the

man ___ mouse: 3 or a

man ___ street: 5 in the, on the

man ___ town: 5 about

man ___ world: 5 of the

man ___ year: 5 of the

man-___: 3 day 4 hour, made, trap, year 5 child, of-war, sized 6 at-arms, minute

man-___ bird: 4 o'-war

___ man: 3 bad, con, day, end, old, rim, to a, yes 4 beat, best, cave, idea, iron, Java, mass, ring, slot, Solo, wild 5 Arago, as one, inner, lady's, party, point, sixth, sound, straw, stunt, third, trail, young 6 Boskop, button, cutoff, detail, family, finger, Folsom, holdup, ladies', little, Marmes, Peking, safety, single 7 advance, company, conjure, hatchet, leading, miracle, stickup, Tollund, trouble, utility

___-man: 3 ape, God, yes 4 byre 7 gombeen

Man: 3 isl., Ray 4 isle 6 island

locale: 7 England

Man ___ All Seasons, A: 3 for

Man ___ Dog: 5 Bites

Man ___ Gray Flannel Suit, The: 5 in the

Man ___ Iron Mask, The: 5 in the

Man ___ Knew Too Much, The: 3 Who

Man ___ Mancha: 4 of La

Man ___ social animal: 3 is a

Man ___, The: 5 I Love

Man ___ Thousand Faces: 3 of a

Man ___ Would Be King, The: 3 Who

Man-___: 4 o'War

Man.: 4 prov.

neighbor: 3 Ont. 4 N. Dak., Sask.

see also Manitoba

___ Man: 3 Ape, Big, I'm a, Tin 4 Dead, Rain, Repo, Soul 5 Gypsy, Handy, Macho, Magic, No One, Piano, Son of 6 Better, Encino, Family, Lawyer, Method, Poetry, Rocket, Whatta, Wonder 7 Nowhere, Raggedy, Ramblin, Trouble

___-Man: 3 Pac 6 Spider

man, a ___, a canal..., A: 4 plan

Mana: 4 peak 5 mount 8 mountain

locale: 4 Asia 5 India 9 Himalayas

man about ___: 4 town

manacle: 4 bind, bond, cuff, iron 5 chain 6 fetter, pinion 7 enchain 8 bracelet, handcuff, restrain

place for a ~: 5 wrist

manacled: 7 in irons

manacles: 5 irons 6 chains 8 shackles, trammels 9 bracelets, handcuffs

manacode: 4 bird

Manadalay river: 9 Irrawaddy

Manado: 4 city, town

locale: 9 Indonesia

Man Against the Sky, The author: E.A. Robinson

manage: 3 con, ply, run, use 4 boss, cope, fare, head, keep, lead, rule, tend 5 get by, guide, pilot, shift, steer, swing 6 afford, bear up, direct, eke out, endure, govern, hack it, handle, make do, wangle 7 achieve, captain, care for, carry on, command, conduct, control, make out, operate, oversee, preside, pull off, subsist, succeed, survive 8 bring off, carry out, contrive, deal with, dispense, dominate, engineer, get along, hold down, maintain, minister, regulate, scrape by, take over, transact 9 influence, negotiate, officiate, play games, supervise, watch over 10 accomplish, administer, manipulate, mastermind, run the show

just ~: 5 get by

without: 5 spare

___-manage: 5 floor, stage

manageable: 4 easy, meek, ruly, soft, tame 5 light 6 broken, docile, pliant, simple 7 subdued, trained 8 lamblike, obedient, portable, untaxing 9 compliant, malleable, tractable 10 governable, submissive

managed-care option: 3 HMO

management: 4 care, head 5 board, brass, execs, power, suits, usage 6 bosses, charge, policy, regime 7 command, conduct, control, running 8 guidance, handling, top brass, upstairs 9 authority, direction, directors, employers, executive, operation, overseers, oversight, treatment 10 executives, government

combining form: 4 -nomy

group: 5 board

level: 4 tier

opposite: 5 labor

prefix for ~: 5 micro

___ management: 4 risk 5 yield 6 crisis, middle

manager: 4 boss, exec, head, host, suit 5 chief, coach, hirer 6 gerent, leader, top dog, warden 7 curator, foreman, headman, officer 8 brass hat, director, employer, governor, higher-up, official, overseer, superior, watchdog 9 custodian, executive, organizer, straw boss 10 mastermind, proprietor, supervisor

spot: 6 dugout, office

___ manager: 4 city, town 5 floor, house, stage 6 credit, middle 7 traffic 8 district

managing ___: 6 editor 8 director

Managua: 4 city, lake, town 7 capital

locale: 9 Nicaragua

see also Spanish

___ man a horse he can ride: 5 Give a

manakin: 4 bird

Manam: 7 volcano

locale: 4 Asia

Manama: 4 city, town 7 capital

locale: 7 Bahrain, Bahrein

mañana: 5 later 7 Spanish

marking: 5 tilde

opposite: 4 ayer

___ mañana!: 5 Hasta

Man and a Woman, A (1966 film)

cast: Anouk Aimée, Pierre Barouh, Jean-Louis Trintignant

composer: 3 Lai

director: Claude Lelouch

___ Man and Little Boy: 3 Fat

Man and Superman author: Shaw

character: 3 Ana, Ann 5 Rhoda 6 Hector

___ Man and the Sea, The: 3 Old

Manannan's father: 3 Ler, Lir

___ Man Answers: 3 If a

Manaslu: 4 peak 5 mount 8 mountain

locale: 4 Asia

Manassas: 4 city, town 6 battle

locale: 8 Virginia

man-at-___: 4 arms

manatee: 5 siren 6 animal, mammal

kin: 6 dugong

Manaus: 4 city, port, town

locale: 6 Brazil

___-man band: 3 one

Man Called Peter, A (1955 film)

cast: Jean Peters, Marjorie Rambeau, Richard Todd

director: Henry Koster

Manche capital: 4 St. Lô

Manchester: 4 city, town 7 Melissa, William

city near ~: 5 Leeds

locale: 7 England

Manchester, Melissa

song: Don't Cry Out Loud (1979)
Midnight Blue (1975)
You Should Hear How She Talks About You (1982)

Manchild in the Promised Land

author: Claude Brown

Manchu: 8 language

Manchurian Candidate, The (1962 film)

cast: Laurence Harvey, Angela Lansbury, Janet Leigh, Frank Sinatra

director: John Frankenheimer

Manchuria river: 4 Amur, Liao, Yalu

Mancini: 3 Ray 5 Henry

Mancini, Henry: 8 composer 9 conductor

film score: Breakfast at Tiffany's
Charade
Days of Wine and Roses
The Great Race
Hatari!
The Pink Panther
Victor/Victoria
Wait Until Dark

song: Charade (1964)
Days of Wine and Roses (1963)
Love Theme from Romeo & Juliet (1969)
Moon River (1961)
Mr. Lucky (1960)
The Pink Panther Theme (1964)
Theme From Love Story (1971)

Man Crazy author: Joyce Carol Oates

mandala: 4 icon, ikon 5 eikon

Mandala author: Pearl S. Buck

Mandalay: 4 city, poem, town

author: Rudyard Kipling

locale: 5 Burma 7 Myanmar

Mandan: 6 Indian, Robert 7 Amerind

mandarin: 4 fowl, tree 5 fruit 6 citrus 7 scholar

relative: 4 lime, smew, teal, Ugli 5 eider, lemon, navel, Pekin, Rouen, scaup 6 Cayuga, orange, pomelo, scoter, tangor 7 gadwall, kumquat, mallard, pintail, pochard, redhead, satsuma, sea duck, Seville, tangelo, widgeon 8 bergamot, garganey, gray duck, musk duck, oldsquaw, shaddock, shoveler, surf duck, Valencia, wood duck 9 black duck, broadbill, goldeneye, goosander, greenhead, merganser, ruddy duck, sprigtail, tangerine 10 bufflehead, calamondin, canvasback, grapefruit, surf scoter, tufted duck

mandarin ___: 4 duck 6 collar, orange

Mandarin: 5 Kuoyu 8 language

Mandarins, The author: Simone de Beauvoir

mandate: **2** OK **3** law **4** fiat, must, okay, word, writ **5** bylaw, edict, order **6** behest, charge, decree, dictum, firman **7** bidding, command, dictate, go-ahead, precept, warrant **8** sanction **9** directive, ordinance, territory **10** blank check, commission, green light, imperative, injunction, legitimize
mandated: **5** licit **6** lawful
mandatory: **5** major, vital **6** forced, needed **7** binding, crucial, needful, pivotal, primary **8** required **9** de rigueur, essential, important, necessary, requisite **10** compelling, compulsory, imperative, obligatory, peremptory
Mandel: **5** Howie **6** Johnny
Mandela: **6** Nelson, Winnie
Mandela, Nelson: **8** Nobelist
land: **3** RSA **11** South Africa
Mandeville, Bernard: **7** British **8** satirist
Mandeville, John: **3** Sir
mandible: **3** jaw **4** bone, jowl **7** jawbone
mandilion: **5** cloak
Mandingo home: **4** Mali **6** Africa, Gambia, Guinea **10** Ivory Coast
Mandlikova, Hana: **7** netster **9** tennis pro
milieu: **5** court
Mandoki, Luis: **8** director
film: Angel Eyes (2001)
Gaby-A True Story (1987)
Message in a Bottle (1999)
When a Man Loves a Woman (1994)
White Palace (1990)
mandola: **4** lute **6** string
origin: **5** Italy
mandolin: **6** string
ancestor: **4** lute
part: **3** peg
play a ~: **5** strum
mandrake: **5** plant **7** anodyne
Mandrell: **6** Irlene, Louise **7** Barbara
Mandrells: **4** trio
mandrill: **5** jocko **6** animal **7** primate
kin: **6** baboon
relative: **3** ape **4** saki, titi **5** chimp, drill, jocko, lemur, loris, magot, orang, potto, shrew **6** aye-aye, baboon, Bandar, galago, gelada, gibbon, grivet, guenon, howler, langur, macaco, monkey, rhesus, uakari, vervet **7** colobus, gorilla, guereza, hoolock, macaque, sapajou, siamang, tamarin, tarsier **8** bush baby, capuchin, mangabey, marmoset, talapoin **9** orangutan **10** Barbary ape, chimpanzee, orangutang
Mandy: **8** Patinkin
Mandy (1974 song) artist: Barry Manilow
mandyas: **5** cloak
Mandy composer: **6** Berlin
mane: **3** mop **4** hair, ruff
clip a horse's ~: **5** roach
like some ~ s: **5** tawny
owner: **4** lion, mare **5** horse **6** equine
site: **4** nape
Maneater (1982 song) artist: Hall and Oates
Manet, Édouard: **6** artist, French **7** painter
medium: **3** oil
maneuver: **3** act, fix, ply, rig **4** move, plan, play, plot, ploy, ruse, scam, step, trap, urge, wile, work **5** angle, dodge, drill, pilot, shift, steer, trick **6** action, design, device, gambit, handle, jockey, scheme, tactic, wangle **7** finagle, finesse, gimmick, operate, sleight **8** artifice, conspire, contrive, engineer, intrigue, inveigle, movement, navigate **9** imposture, machinate, negotiate, operation, play games, stratagem **10** manipulate, reposition, subterfuge
in basketball: **4** pass **5** block, press, steal **7** dribble, rebound
in boxing: **3** bob **5** feint **6** clinch
in fencing: **5** feint, lunge, parry **6** remise, thrust **7** riposte
in football: **4** rush, snap **5** blitz, block, sneak **6** end run **7** hand-off, reverse **8** drop kick, pitch-out
maneuverable: **3** yar **4** yare
maneuvering: **7** tactics **9** diplomacy
maneuvers: **5** drill **8** war games **9** exercises **10** inspection
__ Man Flint: **3** Our
Man for All Seasons, A (1966 film)
cast: Wendy Hiller, Leo McKern, Paul Scofield, Robert Shaw, Orson Welles, Susannah York
director: Fred Zinnemann
man for all seasons, The: **4** More
__ man for himself!: **5** Every
Man For Himself author: Erich Fromm
Manfred: **3** Lee **4** Mann, poem **5** Eigen
manfreda: **5** amole
Manfred author: Byron
Manfred Overture composer: **8** Schumann
Manfred Symphony composer: **11** Tchaikovsky
Man From Colorado, The (1948 film)
cast: Ellen Drew, Glenn Ford, William Holden
director: Henry Levin
Man From Laramie, The (1955 film)
cast: Donald Crisp, Arthur Kennedy, James Stewart
director: Anthony Mann
Man From Snowy River, The (1982 film)
cast: Tom Burlinson, Kirk Douglas, Sigrid Thornton
director: George Miller
Man From the Alamo, The (1953 film)
cast: Julie Adams, Glenn Ford, Victor Jory
director: Budd Boetticher
Man From U.N.C.L.E., The (NBC adventure)
cast: Leo G. Carroll (Alexander Waverly)
David McCallum (Illya Kuryakin)
Robert Vaughn (Napoleon Solo)
foe: THRUSH
Man From Yesterday, The (1932 film)
cast: Charles Boyer, Clive Brook, Claudette Colbert
mangabey: **7** primate
relative: **3** ape **4** saki, titi **5** chimp, drill, jocko, lemur, loris, magot, orang, potto, shrew **6** aye-aye, baboon, Bandar, galago, gelada, gibbon, grivet, guenon, howler, langur, macaco, monkey, rhesus, uakari, vervet **7** colobus, gorilla, guereza, hoolock, macaque, sapajou, siamang, tamarin, tarsier **8** bush baby, capuchin, mandrill, marmoset, talapoin **9** orangutan **10** Barbary ape, chimpanzee, orangutang
manganese: **5** metal **7** element
alloy: **5** Monel **7** Everdur **8** bismanol, Manganin
Manganin: **5** alloy
component: **6** copper, nickel **9** manganese
Mangano: **7** Silvana
mangel-wurzel: **4** beet
manger: **3** bin **4** crib **6** trough
locale: **4** barn
scene: **6** crèche
visitors: **4** Magi
Mangia!: **3** eat **5** dig in
Mangione, Chuck: **9** trumpeter
genre: **4** jazz
instrument: flugelhorn
song: Feels So Good (1978)
mangle: **3** cut, mar **4** claw, hack, iron, maim, mall, maul, rend, ruin, tear **5** crush, press, slash, spoil, wound, wreck **6** damage, deface, deform, hackle, heckle, impair, injure **7** contort, destroy, distort **8** lacerate, mutilate
use a ~: **4** iron
mango: **4** tree **5** fruit
relative: **5** sumac **6** cashew, fustet, mastic, sumach **9** pistachio
Mangoky: **5** river
locale: **3** Afr. **6** Africa **10** Madagascar
Mangos (1957 song) artist: Rosemary Clooney
mangosteen: **4** tree **5** fruit
mangrove: **4** tree **5** shrub
__-Manguean: **3** Oto
mangy: **3** low **4** mean **5** dirty, seedy **6** filthy, ragtag, shabby, shoddy, sleazy, sordid **7** rundown, scruffy, squalid **8** decrepit, tattered **9** moth-eaten, ungroomed
manhandle: **3** paw **4** mawl **5** abuse, knock, paw at **6** bang up **7** rough up **8** ill-treat, maltreat, mistreat **10** kick around, knock about
manhandling: **5** abuse
Manhattan: **3** isl. **4** city, isle, NY NY, town **5** drink **6** island **8** beverage, cocktail
athletes: **8** Wildcats
district: **4** Soho **6** Harlem **7** Tribeca
eatery: **6** Lutèce, Sardi's **7** Elaine's
ender: **3** -ite
ingredient: **3** rye **7** bitters, whiskey **8** vermouth
island off ~: **5** Ellis
locale: **3** Kan., NYC **4** Kans. **6** Kansas **7** New York
school: **3** KSU, NYU **6** Hunter
subway: **3** BMT, IRT
Manhattan (1979 film)
cast: Woody Allen, Mariel Hemingway, Diane Keaton, Michael Murphy, Meryl Streep
director: Woody Allen
dog: **7** Waffles
Manhattan __: **5** Beach **6** Island **7** Project
Manhattan __ chowder: **4** clam
Manhattan Beach: **4** city, town **5** march
composer: **5** Sousa
locale: **10** California
Manhattan Mary artist: **4** Erté
Manhattan Melodrama (1934 film)
cast: Clark Gable, Myrna Loy, William Powell
director: W.S. Van Dyke
Manhattan Murder Mystery (1993 film)
cast: Alan Alda, Woody Allen, Anjelica Huston, Diane Keaton
director: Woody Allen
Manhattan Project
event: **5** A test
participant: **4** Urey
result: **5** A bomb
Manhattan (song) composer: **4** Hart **7** Rodgers
Manhattan Transfer: **5** novel **7** singers
author: Dos Passos
character: **3** Gus **4** Herf, Stan **5** Ellen, Emery, Emile, Susie **6** Cecily
song: Boy from New York City (1981)
Operator (1975)
Twilight Zone (1980)
Manheim: **6** Camryn
manhood: **8** majority, maturity
manhunt: **3** APB **7** dragnet
Man Hunt (1941 film)
cast: Joan Bennett, Walter Pidgeon, George Sanders
director: Fritz Lang
Manhunter (1986 film)
cast: Joan Allen, Kim Greist, William L. Petersen
director: Michael Mann
mania: **3** bug, fad **4** rage, to-do, zeal **5** craze, thing **6** fetich, fetish, frenzy, hang-up, lunacy, uproar **7** craving, madness, passion **8** delirium, disorder, fixation, idée fixe, insanity **9** commotion, craziness, obsession **10** aberration, compulsion, enthusiasm, hullabaloo, partiality
maniac: **3** fan, nut **4** kook **5** crank, fiend, flake **7** fanatic **8** crackpot **9** screwball **10** enthusiast
Maniac (1983 song) artist: Michael Sembello
maniacal: **3** mad **4** wild **5** crazy, nutty, rabid **6** crazed, freaky, raving **7** berserk, demonic, excited, frantic, hog-wild, violent **8** daemonic, frenetic, frenzied, wild-eyed **9** demonical **10** flipped out, freaked out
manic: **3** mad **4** wild **5** crazy, hyper, nutty, rabid, wired **6** crazed, freaky, raving **7** berserk, demonic, excited, frantic, hog-wild **8** agitated, daemonic, frenzied, in a tizzy, wild-eyed **9** demonical, fanatical, wrought-up **10** flipped out, freaked out, off-the-wall
manicotti: **5** pasta **7** noodles
alternative: **4** orzo, ziti **5** penne **6** noodle **7** lasagna, lasagne, pastina, ravioli **8** bucatini, couscous, farfalle, linguine, linguini, macaroni, rigatoni **9** agnolotti, angelhair, cavatelli, spaghetti **10** cannelloni, fettuccini, tortellini, vermicelli
manicurist: **5** filer
concern: **4** nail
item: **4** file **5** emery **6** enamel
manifest: **4** bold, easy, give, list, look, open, show **5** clear, gross, known, occur, overt, plain, prove, shown, vivid **6** attest, cogent, embody, evince, imbody, in view, marked, patent, public, reveal, unfold **7** declare, display, evident, exhibit, exposed, express, for sure, glaring, obvious, reflect, signify, visible **8** apparent, clear-cut, distinct, evidence, explicit, indicate, knowable, luculent, palpable, proclaim, register, revealed, tangible, unhidden, unveiled **9** axiomatic, barefaced, big as life, bring home, disclosed, graspable, make plain, personify, touchable, unobscure **10** illustrate, noticeable, observable, ostensible, spelled out, undeniable, unshrouded
be ~: **6** appear
Manifest __: **7** Destiny
manifestation: **4** form, mark, show, sign **5** token **7** display, symptom **8** epiphany, instance, presence **9** testimony
manifestly: **6** surely **7** plainly **8** markedly **9** evidently, expressly **10** apparently
manifestness: **7** clarity
manifesto: **5** edict **6** firman **8** platform **9** statement
manifold: **4** many **6** a lot of, divers, gobs of, lots of, myriad, sundry, umteen, untold, varied **7** a host of, a slew of, complex, copious, diverse, heaps of, no end of, piles of, profuse, scads of, umpteen, various **8** a bunch of, abundant, an army of, assorted,

frequent, iterated, multiple, multiply, numerous, oodles of, scores of, umpsteen 9 a passel of, bountiful, countless, different, multifold, multiform, quite a few 10 unnumbered, zillions of
___ manifold: 6 intake, linear 7 exhaust
manikin: 5 model 6 puppet 10 homunculus
manila: 5 paper
Manila: 3 bay 4 city, port, town 7 capital
  hemp: 5 abaca
  locale: 5 Luzon 11 Philippines
  river: 5 Pasig
Manila ___: 3 Bay 4 hemp, rope 5 paper
Manila Bay: 6 battle
  city: 6 Cavite
Man I Love, The (1946 film)
  cast: Robert Alda, Bruce Bennett, Ida Lupino
  director: Raoul Walsh
Man I Love, The composer: 8 Gershwin
Manilow, Barry
  instrument: 5 piano
  song: Can't Smile Without You (1978)
    Copacabana (1978)
    Could It Be Magic (1975)
    Even Now (1978)
    I Made It Through the Rain (1980)
    It's a Miracle (1975)
    I Write the Songs (1975)
    Looks Like We Made It (1977)
    Mandy (1974)
    The Old Songs (1981)
    Read 'Em and Weep (1983)
    Ready to Take a Chance Again (1978)
    Ships (1979)
    Somewhere in the Night (1979)
    This One's for You (1976)
    Tryin' to Get the Feeling Again (1976)
    Weekend in New England (1976)
    When I Wanted You (1980)
Man I Married, The (1940 film)
  cast: Joan Bennett, Francis Lederer, Lloyd Nolan
Man in a Slouch Hat painter: 4 Hals
Man in Black, The: 4 Cash
Man in Full, A author: Tom Wolfe
___ Man in Havana: 3 Our
___ Man in His Humour: 5 Every
Man in Lower Ten, The author: Mary Roberts Rinehart
man in the ___: 4 moon 6 street
Man in the Gray Flannel Suit, The: 4 film 5 novel
  author: Sloan Wilson
  cast: Jennifer Jones, Fredric March, Gregory Peck
  character: 4 Rath, Saul 5 Ogden
  director: Nunnally Johnson
Man in the Iron Mask (1998 film)
  cast: Gérard Depardieu, Leonardo DiCaprio, Jeremy Irons, John Malkovich
  director: Randall Wallace
Man in the Iron Mask, The (1939 film)
  cast: Joan Bennett, Louis Hayward, Warren William
  director: James Whale
Man in the Iron Mask, The author: 5 Dumas
Man in the Mirror (1988 song) artist: Michael Jackson
Man in the Moon, The (1991 film)
  cast: Tess Harper, Gail Strickland, Sam Waterston
  director: Robert Mulligan
Man in the White Suit, The (1951 film)
  cast: Joan Greenwood, Alec Guinness, Cecil Parker
Man in the Wilderness (1971 film)
  cast: John Bindon, Richard Harris, John Huston
  director: Richard C. Sarafian
manioc: 6 legume
maniple: 5 fanon, orale 10 canonicals
manipulate: 3 fix, ply, rig, use 4 feel, hoke, play, work 5 knead, shape, steer, touch, wield 6 direct, employ, finger, handle, jigger, jockey, juggle, manage, tamper 7 control, exploit, finagle, finesse, massage, operate 8 contrive, engineer, maneuver 9 influence, machinate, play games
manipulated one: 4 pawn 5 patsy
manipulation: 8 intrigue 9 treatment
manipulative one: 4 user 5 toyer
Manipur, capital of: 6 Imphal
___ Man is Hard to Find: 5 A Good
Manitoba: 4 lake 8 province
  city: 6 Birtle, The Pas 7 Brandon 8 Flin Flon, Winnipeg
  Indian: 4 Cree 9 Saulteaux
  lake: 8 Winnipeg
  locale: 6 Canada
  school: 7 Brandon
Manitoulin Islands lake: 5 Huron
Manitowoc: 4 city, town
  locale: 9 Wisconsin
___ man jack: 5 every
Mankato: 4 city, town
  locale: 9 Minnesota
Mankiewicz, Joseph L.: 8 director
  film: 5 Fingers (1952)
    All About Eve (1950, AA)
    The Barefoot Contessa (1954)
    Cleopatra (1963)
    Escape (1948)
    The Ghost and Mrs. Muir (1947)
    Guys and Dolls (1955)
    House of Strangers (1949)
    Julius Caesar (1953)
    The Late George Apley (1947)
    A Letter to Three Wives (1949, AA)
    No Way Out (1950)
    People Will Talk (1951)
    Sleuth (1972)
    Suddenly, Last Summer (1959)
    There Was a Crooked Man ... (1970)
mankind: 5 Earth, world 6 people 9 human race
Mankind in the Making author: H.G. Wells
Man Lay Dead, A author: Ngaio Marsh
___ Manley Hopkins: 6 Gerard
___ Man Loves a Woman: 5 When a
manly: 4 bold, male 5 brave, macho 6 virile 9 masculine 10 courageous
  name meaning ~: 6 Andrew
  not ~: 5 sissy
man-made: 9 synthetic 10 artificial
Mann: 3 Ron 5 Aimee, Barry, Carol 6 Daniel, Herbie, Horace, Thomas 7 Anthony, Delbert, Manfred, Michael 8 Heinrich
manna: 7 aliment 8 blessing, windfall
  book: 6 Exodus
  from heaven: 4 boon 7 godsend 8 windfall
  Mormon ~: 4 sego
Mann, Anthony: 8 director
  film: Bend of the River (1952)
    Border Incident (1949)
    The Devil's Doorway (1950)
    El Cid (1961)
    The Fall of the Roman Empire (1964)
    The Far Country (1955)
    The Glenn Miller Story (1954)
    God's Little Acre (1958)
    The Man From Laramie (1955)
    Man of the West (1958)
    The Naked Spur (1953)
    Railroaded! (1947)
    Raw Deal (1948)
    Reign of Terror (1949)
    Side Street (1949)
    Strange Impersonation (1946)
    The Tall Target (1951)
    Thunder Bay (1953)
    The Tin Star (1957)
    T-Men (1947)
    Winchester '73 (1950)
Mannar: 3 isl. 4 gulf, isle 6 island
  locale: 8 Sri Lanka
Mann, Carol: 6 golfer
  milieu: 5 links 6 course
  org.: 4 LPGA
Mann, Daniel: 8 director
  film: About Mrs. Leslie (1954)
    Ada (1961)
    Butterfield 8 (1960)
    Come Back, Little Sheba (1952)
    A Dream of Kings (1969)
    I'll Cry Tomorrow (1955)
    The Last Angry Man (1959)
    Lost in the Stars (1974)
    The Rose Tattoo (1955)
    The Teahouse of the August Moon (1956)
Mann, Delbert: 8 director
  film: The Bachelor Party (1957)
    Birch Interval (1977)
    Brontë (1983)
    The Dark at the Top of the Stairs (1960)
    Dear Heart (1964)
    A Gathering of Eagles (1963)
    Lover Come Back (1961)
    Marty (1955, AA)
    The Outsider (1961)
    Separate Tables (1958)
mannequin: 5 dummy, model
  part: 3 arm, leg 4 head
  topper: 3 wig
manner: 3 air, way 4 cast, form, kind, look, mien, mode, sort, tone, type, vein, wise, wont 5 brand, breed, class, means, style, usage 6 aspect, custom, method, system 7 bearing, conduct, fashion, process, variety 8 approach, attitude, behavior, category, demeanor, practice, presence 9 procedure, technique 10 appearance, deportment
  affected ~: 4 airs
  all ~ of: 4 many 6 sundry 7 various
  assume the ~ of: 2 do 3 ape 7 emulate, imitate
  dignity of ~: 5 poise
  in a ~: 4 as if 8 as it were 9 so to speak
  in the ~ of: 3 à la 4 like
  in the same ~: 8 likewise
  in this ~: 2 so 6 like so
  in what ~: 3 how
  of a ~: 5 modal
  of walking: 4 pace, step
  to the ~ born: 5 noble 7 genteel 9 patrician
___ manner: 7 bedside
___ manner born: 5 to the
mannered: 5 artsy, campy, posed, put-on, stiff 6 chichi, la-de-da, la-di-da, poised 7 stilted 8 affected, lah-di-dah 9 unnatural 10 artificial, theatrical
___-mannered: 3 ill 4 mild, well
Mannerhouse author: Thomas Wolfe
mannerism: 3 air, tic, way 4 mien, pose 5 habit, quirk, trait 6 foible, manner 7 oddness 10 pretension
mannerless: 8 impolite
  one: 3 cad, oaf 4 boor
mannerly: 4 good 5 civil 6 decent, polite, proper, social, urbane 7 genteel, refined 8 charming, decorous, gracious, polished, well-bred 9 civilized, courteous 10 respectful
___ manner of speaking: 3 in a
manners: 5 couth, mores 6 polish 7 conduct, culture, decorum, p's and q's 8 behavior, breeding, civility, courtesy, folkways, protocol, urbanity 9 etiquette, politesse, propriety 10 civilities, deportment, politeness, refinement
  mind one's ~: 6 behave
___ manners: 3 bad 5 table
Manners: 5 David
Manners, Miss subject: 4 tact
Mannheim: 4 city, town
  locale: 7 Germany
Mann, Herbie: 7 flutist 8 flautist, musician
  genre: 4 jazz
  song: Hijack (1975)
    Superman (1979)
Manning: 6 Archie 8 Adelaide, Frederic
Manning, Frederic: 6 writer 10 Australian
mannish: 9 masculine
Mannix (CBS drama)
  cast: Joseph Campanella (Lou Wickersham)
    Mike Connors (Joe Mannix)
    Gail Fisher (Peggy Fair)
Mann, Manfred
  homeland: South Africa
  real name: Michael Lubowitz
  song: Blinded by the Light (1976)
    Do Wah Diddy Diddy (1964)
    Mighty Quinn (1968)
    Sha La La (1964)
Mann, Michael: 8 director
  film: Ali (2001)
    Heat (1995)
    The Insider (1999)
    The Last of the Mohicans (1992)
    Manhunter (1986)
    Thief (1981)
Mann, Thomas: 6 German, writer 8 essayist, Nobelist
  work: Buddenbrooks
    Confessions of Felix Krull
    Death in Venice
    Joseph and His Brothers
    The Magic Mountain
    Tonio Kroger
Mannucci: 4 Aldo
Manny: 4 Mota 6 Trillo 7 Ramirez
man-o'-___ bird: 3 war
Manoah, son of: 6 Samson
man of ___: 3 God 5 straw 7 letters
man-of-___: 3 war
Man of ___: 4 Aran, Iron 5 Steel 7 Destiny, Galilee, Sorrows
Man of Aran (1934 film)
  cast: Maggie Dillane, Tiger King
  director: Robert Flaherty
Man of a Thousand Faces (1957 film)
  cast: James Cagney, Jane Greer, Dorothy Malone
  director: Joseph Pevney
Man of a Thousand Faces, The: 3 Lon 6 Chaney
Man of Destiny, The author: George Bernard Shaw
Manoff: 5 Dinah
Man of God, A author: Gabriel Marcel
Man of Iron (1980 film) director: Andrzej Wajda
Man of La Mancha star: 5 Kiley
Man of Marble (1977 film) director: Andrzej Wajda
___ man of means...: 3 I'm a
Man of Steel monogram: 3 ess
  see also Superman
man of the ___: 4 hour, year 5 cloth, house, world
Man of the Crowd, A author: Edgar Allan Poe
Man of the Forest, The author: Zane Grey

Man of the West (1958 film)
cast: Lee J. Cobb, Gary Cooper, Julie London
director: Anthony Mann
Man of the Year magazine: 4 Time
man-of-war: 4 boat 7 flattop, frigate, gunboat 9 destroyer 10 battleship
___, ma! No hands!: 4 Look
Manolete: 6 torero 7 matador 11 bullfighter
foe: 4 bull, toro
see also Spanish
Manon: 5 opera
composer: 8 Massenet
piece: 4 aria
role: 7 Lescaut 9 des Grieux
setting: 5 Paris 6 Amiens, France 7 Le Havre
Man on a String (1960 film)
cast: Ernest Borgnine, Colleen Dewhurst, Kerwin Mathews
director: Andre de Toth
Manon Lescaut: 5 opera
composer: 7 Puccini
Manon Lescaut author: Abbé Prévost
man on the ___: 6 street
Man on the Eiffel Tower, The (1949 film)
cast: Charles Laughton, Burgess Meredith, Franchot Tone
director: Burgess Meredith
Man on the Flying Trapeze, The (1935 film)
cast: Mary Brian, W.C. Fields
Man on the Moon (1999 film)
cast: Jim Carrey, Danny DeVito, Courtney Love
director: Milos Forman
Man on the Moon (1993 song) artist: R.E.M.
man-on-the-moon org.: 4 NASA
manor: 4 home, land 5 abode 6 castle, estate, palace 7 mansion 9 residence 10 plantation
house: 7 chateau
master: 3 esq. 4 lord 7 esquire
worker: 4 serf
manorial court: 4 leet
___ man out: 3 odd
man-o'-war: 4 bird
Man O'War: 5 horse 9 racehorse
only horse to beat ~: 5 Upset
___ Man, Poor Man: 4 Rich
manpower: 9 personnel
Manpower (1941 film)
cast: Marlene Dietrich, George Raft, Edward G. Robinson
director: Raoul Walsh
...___ man put asunder: 5 let no
manqué: 6 failed
Man Ray: 6 artist 7 painter
art: 4 Dada
Manrique, Jorge: 4 poet 7 Spanish
man's
best friend: 3 dog
no ~ land: 3 DMZ
that ~: 3 his
man's ___ friend: 4 best
mansard: 4 roof 5 attic 6 garret
part: 4 eave
Man's Castle (1933 film)
cast: Marjorie Rambeau, Spencer Tracy, Loretta Young
director: Frank Borzage
___ Man's Curve: 4 Dead
manse: 7 rectory 8 vicarage 9 parsonage
manservant: 5 valet 6 butler 7 steward 9 major-domo
___ Manse, The: 3 Old
___ Man's Family: 3 One
Mansfield: 4 city, town 5 Jayne 9 Katherine
locale: 4 Ohio 5 Texas
Mansfield, Jayne film: Will Success Spoil Rock Hunter? (1957)
Mansfield, Katherine: 6 author, writer
work: Bliss
A Dill Pickle
The Dove's Nest
The Garden Party
Mansfield Park author: Jane Austen
Mansfield, Peter book: 8 The Arabs
man's home is ___ castle, A: 3 His
___-man show: 3 one
mansion: 4 hall, home, seat 5 abode, house, manor, villa 6 castle, estate, palace 7 chateau, domicil, housing 8 building, domicile, dwelling, hacienda 9 residence 10 habitation
and grounds: 6 estate
like a ~: 5 roomy
opposite: 3 hut 5 hovel
___ Mansion: 6 Gracie
___ Mansions: 5 Green
man-size: 3 big
Manson: 7 Marilyn, Shirley
manta: 3 ray 4 fish 5 cloak, shawl 8 devil ray 9 devilfish
kin: 5 skate
Manta: 3 bay, car 4 auto, city, Opel, town
locale: 7 Ecuador
Mantaro: 5 river
locale: 4 Peru
___ Man Tate: 6 Little
manteau: 4 cape 5 cloak
Manteca: 4 city, town
locale: 10 California
Mantegna: 3 Joe 6 Andrea
Mantegna, Joe: 5 actor
film: Celebrity (1998)
Forget Paris (1995)
The Godfather Part III (1990)
Hoods (1999)
House of Games (1987)
Lakeboat (2001)
Searching for Bobby Fischer (1993)
The Wonderful Ice Cream Suit (1999)
mantel: 5 shelf
ender: 4 tree 5 piece, shelf
Man That Got Away, The composer: 5 Arlen 8 Gershwin
Man That Was Used Up, The author: Edgar Allan Poe
Man, The: 4 Stan 6 Musial
___ Man, The: 4 Best, Next, Thin, Wolf 5 Candy, Great, Green, Minus, Music, Omega, Quiet, Squaw, Stunt, Tenth, Third, Wrong 6 Double, Family, Ladies', Lonely, Murder, Strong, Wicker 7 Outside, Raggedy, Running, Working
mantic: 9 prophetic
mantilla: 4 cape, veil 5 scarf, shawl, throw 8 covering, kerchief 9 headcloth
mantis: 3 bug 6 insect, prayer
___ mantis: 7 praying
Mantis actor: 4 Rees
Mantissa author: John Fowles
mantle: 4 cape, pall, rock, veil, wrap 5 capot, cloak, cover, ledge, shelf 6 capote, dolman, redden, screen 7 chlamys 8 covering
layer between Earth's crust and ~: 4 moho
Mantle: 5 Burns 6 Mickey
Mantle, Mickey: 4 Yank 6 Yankee 7 slugger 10 outfielder
number: 5 seven
mantlet: 4 cape 5 cloak
man-to-man ___: 4 talk 7 defense
Mantooth: 8 Randolph
Mantovani and His Orchestra
song: Around the World (1957)
Cara Mia (1954)
Main Theme from Exodus (1961)
Mantovani, Annunzio: 9 conductor
mantra: 2 om 3 aum 5 chant
beads: 4 mala
___ Man Triathlon: 4 Iron
mantua: 4 robe
Manua: 4 isls. 5 isles 7 islands
locale: 5 Samoa
manual: 4 book, text 5 bible, guide, how-to 6 primer 8 cookbook, handbook, physical, textbook, workbook 9 guidebook 10 compendium
arts workroom: 4 shop
skill: 5 craft
training system: 5 sloid, slojd, sloyd
worker: 5 prole 7 laborer
manually: 6 by hand
Manuel: 5 Rojas 6 Gálvez 7 de Falla, Noriega, Padilla 8 Bandeira
see also Spanish
manufacture: 4 form, make, mill, mold, tool, work 5 build, forge, frame, hatch 6 cook up, create, devise, invent, output, prefab, put out 7 concoct, fashion, produce, think up, trump up, turn out 8 assemble, assembly, contrive 9 construct, fabricate
manufactured: 5 false 9 synthetic
manufactured ___: 4 home 7 housing
manufacturer: 5 maker
claim: 3 new 8 improved
come-on: 6 coupon, rebate
tag: 5 label
manufacturing: 6 making, output 7 casting, tooling 8 assembly 9 producing 10 production
plant: 4 mill
manufacturing ___: 5 plant
Manukau: 4 city, town
locale: 10 New Zealand
manumission: 7 freedom, release
manumit: 4 free 5 let go, loose 6 loosen, redeem 7 release, set free 8 liberate, set loose, unfetter 9 discharge, turn loose, unshackle 10 emancipate
manuscript: 5 draft 6 record, script 7 galleys, writing
ancient ~: 5 codex
correct a ~: 4 edit 5 emend
enclosure: 3 SAE 4 SASE
marking: 6 obelus
markings: 5 obeli
notation: 4 stet
page: 5 folio
polisher: 6 editor
manuscripts, unsolicited: 5 slush
Manush: 6 Heinie
Manute: 3 Bol
Manutius: 5 Aldus
___ Man Walking: 4 Dead
Man Who Came to Dinner, The: 4 film, play
author: George S. Kaufman, Moss Hart
cast: Bette Davis, Ann Sheridan, Monty Woolley
director: William Keighley
Man Who Cried I AM, The author: John Williams
Man Who Died Twice, The author: E.A. Robinson
Man Who Fell to Earth, The (1976 film)
cast: David Bowie, Candy Clark, Rip Torn
director: Nicolas Roeg
Man Who Had Three Arms, The author: Edward Albee
Man Who Knew Too Much, The (1934 film)
cast: Leslie Banks, Edna Best, Peter Lorre
director: Alfred Hitchcock
Man Who Knew Too Much, The (1956 film)
cast: Doris Day, James Stewart
composer: 8 Herrmann
director: Alfred Hitchcock
Man Who Loved Cat Dancing, The (1973 film): 5 oater
cast: George Hamilton, Sarah Miles, Burt Reynolds
director: Richard C. Sarafian
Man Who Loved Children, The author: Christina Stead
Man Who Mistook His Wife For ___, The: 4 a Hat
Man Who Owned Broadway, The: 5 Cohan
Man Who Reclaimed His Head, The (1934 film)
cast: Lionel Atwill, Joan Bennett, Claude Rains
Man Who Shot Liberty Valance, The (1962 film): 5 oater
cast: Lee Marvin, Vera Miles, Jeanette Nolan, James Stewart, John Wayne
director: John Ford
Man Who Shot Liberty Valance, The (1962 song) artist: Gene Pitney
Man Who Wasn't There, The (2001 film)
cast: James Gandolfini, Frances McDormand, Billy Bob Thornton
director: Joel Coen
Man Who Would Be King, The: 4 film 10 short story
author: Rudyard Kipling
cast: Michael Caine, Sean Connery, Christopher Plummer
director: John Huston
Man With a Cloak, The (1951 film)
cast: Louis Calhern, Joseph Cotten, Barbara Stanwyck
director: Fletcher Markle
___ Man With a Horn: 5 Young
Man With One Red Shoe, The (1985 film)
cast: Dabney Coleman, Charles Durning, Tom Hanks, Lori Singer
director: Stan Dragoti
Man Without a Country, The
author: 4 Hale
character: 5 Nolan
Man Without a Face, The (1993 film)
cast: Mel Gibson, Nick Stahl, Margaret Whitton
director: Mel Gibson
Man Without a Star, The (1955 film)
cast: Jeanne Crain, Kirk Douglas, Claire Trevor
director: King Vidor
___ man with seven...: 5 I met a
Man with the Blue Guitar, The author: Wallace Stevens
Man With the Golden Arm, The: 4 film 5 novel
author: Nelson Algren
cast: Kim Novak, Eleanor Parker, Frank Sinatra
director: Otto Preminger
Man With the Golden Gun, The: 4 film 5 novel
author: Ian Fleming
cast: Maud Adams, Britt Ekland, Christopher Lee, Roger Moore
director: Guy Hamilton
Man With the Hoe, The: 4 poem
author: 7 Markham
Man With Two Brains, The (1983 film)
cast: Steve Martin, Kathleen Turner, David Warner
cat: 6 Jarvis
director: Carl Reiner
Man, Woman and Chil
cast: Blythe Danner,
Manx: 3 cat 5 felid 6 fel
cat's lack: 4 tail

language: **4** Erse **6** Gaelic
many: **4** a lot, gobs, lots, much, rife, tons **5** heaps, horde, loads, piles, scads **6** a lot of, divers, dozens, legion, lots of, myriad, oodles, plenty, scores, sundry, throng, umteen, untold, varied **7** copious, jillion, legions, no end of, numbers, profuse, several, teeming, umpteen, various **8** abundant, frequent, jillions, manifold, millions, multiple, numerous, umpsteen, zillions **9** abundance, bountiful, countless, legions of, multitude, plentiful, quite a few, thousands, uncounted **10** bezillions, innumerous, numberless
a good ~: **8** numerous
a time: **3** oft **4** a lot, much **5** often **9** quite a bit, regularly, routinely **10** frequently, habitually, repeatedly
combining form: **4** mult-, poly- **5** multi-, pluri-
ender: **4** fold
eras: **3** age **4** ages **6** period **8** long time
find how ~: **5** count
in Greek: **6** polloi
in Spanish: **5** mucha, mucho
not ~: **3** few **4** a few **5** light **6** little
too ~: **9** excessive
with ~ irons in the fire: **6** hectic
many ___: **5** a time **6** thanks
many ___ ago: **5** moons, years
many ___ returns: **5** happy
Many ___ Day: **4** a New
Many ___ has to fall...: **5** a tear
Many ___ of Dobie Gillis, The: **5** Loves
many a ___: **4** time
Many a New Day composer: **7** Rodgers **11** Hammerstein
___ many cooks...: **3** Too
___ Many Girls: **3** Too
many happy ___: **7** returns
___ Many Husbands: **3** Too
___ many irons in the fire: **3** too
Many Loves of Dobie Gillis, The (CBS sitcom)
cast: Warren Beatty (Milton Armitage) Bob Denver (Maynard G. Krebs) Dwayne Hickman (Dobie Gillis) Sheila James (Zelda Gilroy) Tuesday Weld (Thalia Menninger)
many moons ___: **3** ago
many-sided: **9** versatile
many splendored thing, A: **4** love
Many Tears Ago (1960 song) artist: Connie Francis
___ many words: **4** in so
Manzanares, city on the: **6** Madrid
Manzanillo: **4** city, town
locale: **6** Colima, Mexico
manzanita: **5** fruit
Manzarek: **3** Ray
Manzini: **4** city, town
locale: **9** Swaziland
Manzoni, Alessandro: **6** writer **7** Italian
mao-___: **3** tai
Mao: **6** Zedong **7** Tse-tung
colleague: **4** Chou, Deng, Zhou
opponent: **6** Chiang
Mao ___: **4** suit **6** jacket
Mao II author: Don DeLillo
Maoist: **3** Red **7** leftist **9** Communist
Maori: **8** language **10** Polynesian
bird the ~ once hunted: **3** moa
greeting: **5** hongi
war dance: **4** haka
map: **4** plan, plat, plot **5** atlas, chart, draft, frame, globe, graph, trace **6** design, layout, sketch, survey **7** diagram, drawing, outline, picture **9** formulate, visual aid **10** projection
.: **2** av., st. **3** alt., Atl., ave., hwy., isl., lat., mtn., mts., Pac., str., ter. **4** elev., N. Lat., terr.
be all over the ~: **5** stray **6** ramble **7** meander
blue spot on a ~: **4** lake
city ~: **4** plat
direction: **3** ENE, ESE, NNE, NNW, SSE, SSW, WNW, WSW **4** east, west **5** north, south **9** northeast, northwest, southeast, southwest
dot: **4** town **5** islet **6** island
ender: **5** maker **6** making
feature: **4** grid **5** inset, scale **6** legend
former ~ abbr.: **4** USSR
line: **2** rt. **3** riv., rte. **4** road **5** river, route **6** avenue, border, street
on the ~: **5** known
out: **4** plan, plot **5** frame **6** depict, devise, sketch **7** pioneer, program, project **9** formulate
put on the ~: **9** publicize
science: **9** geography **10** topography
starter: **4** road **5** photo
wipe off the ~: **4** rase, raze, ruin, sack, undo **5** blast, crush, level, smash, total, trash, waste, wreck **6** defeat, ravage, uproot **7** despoil, destroy, flatten, shatter, torpedo **8** bulldoze, decimate, demolish, desolate, spoliate **9** depredate, devastate, eradicate, extirpate, overwhelm, pulverize, take apart **10** annihilate, obliterate
map ___: **3** out **6** turtle
___ map: **3** air, bit **4** base, road, star **5** strip **6** mosaic, relief, sketch **7** contour, genetic, linkage, weather
Ma Perkins: **9** radio show
___ Mapes Dodge: **4** Mary
maple: **4** tree, wood **8** hardwood **10** bowling pin
extract: **3** sap
genus: **4** acer
like a ~ leaf: **5** erose
like ~ seeds: **4** alar **5** alary
of ~ trees: **6** aceric
maple ___: **5** honey, sugar, syrup
___ maple: **3** red **4** hard, rock, vine **5** black, sugar, swamp **6** Norway, Oregon, silver **7** ash-leaf, bigleaf, striped
Maple Grove: **4** city, town
locale: **9** Minnesota
Maple Heights: **4** city, town
locale: **4** Ohio
Maple Leaf: **4** coin
rival: **4** Blue, King, Star, Wild **5** Bruin, Devil, Flame, Flyer, Oiler, Sabre, Shark **6** Canuck, Coyote, Ranger **7** Capital, Panther, Penguin, Red Wing, Senator **8** Canadien, Islander, Predator, Thrasher **9** Avalanche, Blackhawk, Hurricane, Lightning **10** Blue Jacket, Mighty Duck
Maple Leaf ___: **3** Rag
Maple Leafs: **3** six **4** team
home: **7** Toronto
milieu: **3** ice **4** rink
org.: **3** NHL
sport: **6** hockey
target: **3** net
Maple Ridge: **4** city, town
locale: **6** Canada
Maples, Marla spouse: Donald Trump
maple walnut: **8** ice cream
alternative: **5** lemon, mocha, peach **6** banana, coffee, Jamoca, toffee **7** caramel, coconut, vanilla **8** cinnamon, hazelnut **9** bubblegum, chocolate, pineapple, pistachio, raspberry, rocky road, rum raisin **10** blackberry, cheesecake, Neapolitan, peppermint, strawberry
Maplewood: **4** city, town
locale: **9** Minnesota, New Jersey
mapo: **4** fish
Mapocho, city on the: **8** Santiago
Map of the World, A (1999 film)
cast: Julianne Moore, David Strathairn, Sigourney Weaver
___ mapping: **4** gene
Maputo: **4** city, port, town **7** capital
locale: **10** Mozambique
Map, Walter: **5** Welsh **6** writer
maqui: **5** fruit, shrub
maquillage: **4** kohl **6** makeup
mar: **4** bend, blot, dent, ding, harm, hurt, nick, ruin, scar, soil, warp **5** abuse, botch, break, score, scuff, spoil, stain, sully, taint, wreck **6** bang up, befoul, blight, bruise, damage, deface, foul up, impair, injure, mangle, mess up **7** blemish, despoil, detract, louse up, scratch, tarnish, vitiate **8** discolor **9** vandalize **10** adulterate
Mar ___ Plata: **3** del
Mar.: **2** mo.
follower: **3** Apr.
honoree: **5** St. Pat
it starts in ~: **3** spr.
preceder: **3** Feb.
see also March
Mara: **3** Tim **5** Adele **6** Corday, Wilson **10** Wellington
marabou: **4** bird **5** stork
Maracaibo: **4** city, gulf, Lago, lake, port, town
locale: **9** Venezuela
maracas: **10** percussion
Maracot Deep, The author: Arthur Conan Doyle
Maradi: **4** city, town
locale: **5** Niger
Maranello: **3** car **4** auto **7** Ferrari **10** automobile
Marañón: **5** river
locale: **4** Peru
Maranville: **6** Rabbit
marasca: **5** fruit **6** cherry
relative: **4** Bing **7** morello, oxheart
maraschino cherry: **7** marasca
Marat: **8** Jean Paul
see also French
marathon: **4** race **5** event **10** protracted
award: **6** anadem, laurel
city: **6** Boston
contender: **5** racer **6** runner
handout: **5** water
terminus: **4** tape
unit: **4** mile
Marathon: **3** car **4** auto **6** battle **7** Checker **10** automobile
marathoner: **6** Benoit, Bikila **7** athlete, Shorter
bane: **5** cramp
breaking point: **4** wall
load-up: **4** carb
ordeal: **4** hill
Marathon Man (1976 film)
cast: William Devane, Dustin Hoffman, Laurence Olivier, Roy Scheider
director: John Schlesinger
Marat/Sade: **4** film, play
author: Peter Weiss
cast: Glenda Jackson, Patrick Magee, Ian Richardson, Clifford Rose
director: Peter Brook
maraud: **4** loot, raid, sack **5** foray, harry **6** harass, invade, ravage **7** despoil, pillage, plunder, ransack **8** freeboot, spoliate **9** depredate **10** encroach on
marauder: **3** Hun **5** thief **6** bandit, outlaw, pirate, robber **7** brigand, corsair, rustler **8** rapparee **9** buccaneer **10** freebooter, highwayman
Marauder: **3** car **4** auto **7** Mercury **10** automobile
marauding: **9** predatory, rapacious
Maravatío: **4** city, town
locale: **6** Mexico **9** Michoacán
maravedi: **5** money
Maravich, Pete
milieu: **5** court
org.: **3** NBA
sport: **10** basketball
marble: **4** cake, rock **5** agate **6** camlet, sphere, statue, streak **7** mineral
Belgian ~: **5** rance
big blue ~: **5** Earth
block: **4** slab
Greek ~ island: **5** Paros
Italian ~ city: **5** Massa
marking: **4** vein
playing ~: **3** mib, mig, taw **4** migg **5** aggie, immie
marble ___: **4** cake **7** orchard
___ marble: **4** onyx **7** Carrara, cat's-eye
Marble, Alice: **7** netster **9** tennis pro
milieu: **5** court
marbled: **7** mottled **8** brindled
Marble Faun, The
author: Nathaniel Hawthorne, William Faulkner
Marblehead: **4** city, town
locale: **4** Mass.
marbles: **3** wit **4** game, mind, wits **6** reason
having all one's ~: **4** sane **5** lucid **8** sensible
___ Marbles: **5** Elgin
marc: **5** drink **6** brandy **8** beverage
Marc: **5** Levin, Price **6** Antony, Singer **7** Anthony, Chagall, McClure, Summers **8** Allegret, Connelly **10** Blitzstein
beloved: **4** Cleo
Marcal alternative: **5** Scott **7** Charmin **8** Northern, Soft Weve **10** Cottonelle, White Cloud
marcando: **8** accented
Marceau: **6** Marcel, Sophie
marcel: **4** coif **6** hairdo **8** coiffure
Marcel: **4** Aymé **5** Carné **6** Dionne, Ophuls, Pagnol, Proust **7** Duchamp, Gabriel, Marceau
see also French
Marcel, Gabriel: **6** French, writer
work: Being and Having
La Grâce
Le Fanal
A Man of God
The Mystery of Being
marcella: **6** fabric **8** material
Marcellinus: **4** pope **7** pontiff
Marcello: **8** Malpighi **11** Mastroianni
Marcellus: **4** pope **7** pontiff
Marcels
song: Blue Moon (1961)
Heartaches (1961)
march: **4** gait, hike, move, pace, slog, trek, walk **5** drill, jaunt, music, stalk, strut, tramp, tread, troop **6** course, file by, foot it, parade, stride, trudge **7** advance, journey, proceed, protest, step out **8** long haul, neighbor, progress **9** go forward, promenade **10** forge ahead, procession
against: **3** war **5** fight **6** battle
day's ~: **5** étape
ender: **4** halt, land, pane
line of ~: **9** direction
off: **6** decamp
on the ~: **6** moving **9** advancing
starter: **7** counter
steal a ~ on: **5** one-up
___ march: **5** grand, on the, quick, route **6** forced, rogue's **7** freedom, wedding
March: **2** Jo **3** Amy, Hal, Meg **4** Alex, Beth, Jane **5** month **7** Fredric
birthstone: **10** aquamarine
date: **4** ides **5** nones
follower: **3** Apr. **5** April

honoree: 5 St. Pat
like a ~ day: 5 gusty
like a ~ hare: 3 mad 4 daft
one of the ~ sisters: 2 Jo 3 Amy, Meg 4 Beth
preceder: 3 Feb. 8 February
17th color: 5 green
sign: 3 Ram 4 Fish 5 Aries 6 Pisces
March __ said: 4 on he
__ March: 4 Long
Marchand: 5 Nancy
march-command word: 3 hep, hup
__ marché: 3 bon, pas
Marche __: 5 Slave 7 Funèbre
Marche Funèbre composer: 5 Bizet
marché, pas: 4 step
marchers, univ.: 4 ROTC
marchesa: 4 rank 5 title
marchese: 4 rank 5 title
Marche Slave composer: 11 Tchaikovsky
Marchetti, Gino sport: 8 football
March, Fredric: 5 actor
film: An Act of Murder (1948)
The Adventures of Mark Twain (1944)
Affairs of Cellini (1934)
Alexander the Great (1956)
Anna Karenina (1935)
Another Part of the Forest (1948)
Anthony Adverse (1936)
The Barretts of Wimpole Street (1934)
Bedtime Story (1941)
The Best Years of Our Lives (1946, AA)
The Bridges at Toko-Ri (1955)
The Buccaneer (1938)
Christopher Columbus (1949)
Death of a Salesman (1951)
Death Takes a Holiday (1934)
Design for Living (1933)
The Desperate Hours (1955)
Dr. Jekyll and Mr. Hyde (1932, AA)
The Eagle and the Hawk (1933)
Hombre (1967)
The Iceman Cometh (1973)
I Married a Witch (1942)
Inherit the Wind (1960)
Les Miserables (1935)
The Man in the Gray Flannel Suit (1956)
Mary of Scotland (1936)
Nothing Sacred (1937)
One Foot in Heaven (1941)
The Road to Glory (1936)
The Royal Family of Broadway (1930)
Seven Days in May (1964)
Smilin' Through (1932)
So Ends Our Night (1941)
A Star Is Born (1937)
There Goes My Heart (1938)
Tomorrow the World (1944)
Trade Winds (1938)
Victory (1940)
The Young Doctors (1961)
marching: 5 drill
give ~ orders: 4 sack
order: 3 hup, hut 4 halt
syllable: 3 hut
marching __: 6 orders
Marching __ war: 4 as to
Marching Along author: 5 Sousa
marching band
hat: 5 shako
instrument: 4 drum, fife, tuba 5 flute 8 clarinet
Marching Man author: Sherwood Anderson
marchioness: 4 lady, peer, rank 5 noble, title
March King, The: 5 Sousa
March, Little Peggy song: I Will Follow Him (1963)
March Madness org.: 4 NCAA
March of __: 5 Dimes
March of Time, The: 9 radio show
marchpane: 5 candy
march-past: 9 cavalcade
March 7: 5 nones
March to Quebec author: Kenneth Roberts
__ marcia: 4 alla
Marcia: 4 Rodd 5 Cross 7 Wallace 9 Strassman
Marcia __ Harden: 3 Gay
Marciano, Rocky: 5 boxer
milieu: 4 ring
Marco: 4 Polo
see also Italian
Marconi __: 3 rig 4 mast
Marconi, Guglielmo: 8 Nobelist 9 physicist, scientist
invention: 5 radio
Marco Polo Sings a Solo author: John Guare
Marcos: 6 Imelda 9 Ferdinand
__ Marcos, TX: 3 San
Marcovicci: 6 Andrea
Marcus: 4 Loew, pope 5 Allen, Welby 6 Garvey 7 pontiff, Rudolph 8 Aurelius
__ Marcus: 6 Neiman
Marcus Aurelius: 5 Roman, Stoic 6 Caesar 11 philosopher
physician of ~: 5 Galen
see also Latin
Marcuse, Herbert: 6 writer 11 philosopher, sociologist
work: Eros and Civilization
One-Dimensional Man
Marcus, Rudolph: 7 chemist 8 Nobelist
Marcus Welby M.D. (ABC drama)
cast: James Brolin (Dr. Steven Kiley)
Elena Verdugo (Consuelo Lopez)
Robert Young (Dr. Marcus Welby)
Marcy: 4 peak 5 mount 6 Carsey, Walker 7 William 8 mountain
locale: 7 New York 11 Adirondacks
Mar del Plata: 4 city, town
locale: 9 Argentina
mardi: 6 French 7 Tuesday
follower: 8 mercredi
preceder: 5 lundi
Mardi Gras: 3 Tue. 4 gala, Tues. 7 Tuesday 8 carnival 10 masquerade
city: 3 Rio 4 Nice
event: 6 parade
follower: 4 Lent
organizers: 5 krewe
VIP: 3 Rex
wear: 6 domino 7 costume
mare: 3 dam, she 5 filly, horse, mount, steed 6 animal, equine
go by shanks' ~: 4 slog, walk 5 leg it, march 6 foot it, hoof it, trudge
offspring: 4 colt, foal 5 filly
sound: 5 neigh 6 whinny
starter: 5 night
mare __: 7 clausum, liberum, nostrum
__ mare: 6 shanks'
Mare: 10 Winningham
Mare __: 6 Boreum, Island, Nubium 7 Crisium, Humorum, Imbrium, Sirenum, Undarum, Vaporum
Maren: 5 Jerry
Marengo: 5 horse, steed 6 battle
Maresca: 5 Ernie
Mares eat __: 4 oats
mare's-nest: 3 zoo 4 fake, hoax, mess, sham 5 fraud, snafu 6 dupery, foul-up, jumble, muddle 8 delusion 9 deception
mare's-tail: 5 cloud 6 cirrus
Marfil: 4 city, town
locale: 6 Mexico 10 Guanajuato
Margaret: 3 Cho, Rey 4 Ladd, Mead 5 Colin, Court, saint, Smith 6 Atwood, Avison, Dumont, Farrar, Fuller, Hillis, O'Brien, Sanger, Truman, Walker 7 Drabble, Lindsay, Whiting 8 Hamilton, Leighton, Lockwood, Mitchell, Sullavan, Thatcher 10 Rutherford
dad's monogram: 3 HST
in French: 7 Margaux
in German: 8 Gretchen
mother: 4 Bess
nickname: 3 Meg, Peg 5 Marge, Peggy
Margaret __ Smith: 5 Chase
Margaret __ Thatcher: 5 Hilda
Margaret Bourke-__: 5 White
Margaret of __: 5 Anjou 6 France, Valois 7 Navarre 9 Clitherow
Margaret of Clitherow: 5 saint
Margaret of Navarre: 5 queen 6 French, writer
margarine: 4 oleo 6 Parkay, Shedd's, spread 7 Promise 8 Imperial
fat: 5 olein 6 oleine
serving: 3 pat
margarita: 5 drink 8 beverage, cocktail
ingredient: 4 salt 7 tequila 9 lime juice 10 lemon juice
Margaritaville (1977 song) artist: Jimmy Buffett
margate: 4 fish
Margate: 4 city, town
locale: 4 Kent 7 England, Florida
Margaux: 9 Hemingway
grandfather: 6 Ernest
in English: 8 Margaret
sister: 6 Mariel
margay: 3 cat 5 felid 6 feline
relative: 4 eyra, lion, lynx, puma 5 chita, liger, ounce, tiger, tigon 6 bobcat, cheeta, chetah, cougar, jaguar, ocelot, serval, tiglon 7 bay lynx, caracal, cheetah, leopard, panther 9 catamount 10 jaguarundi
Marge: 7 Simpson 8 Champion
Margie (1946 film)
cast: Lynn Bari, Jeanne Crain
director: Henry King
margin: 3 hem, lip, rim 4 brim, edge, lead, play, room, side 5 bound, brink, extra, limit, scope, shore, skirt, space, verge 6 border, fringe, leeway 7 selvage, surplus 8 boundary, latitude, selvedge 9 allowance, extremity, perimeter, periphery
for error: 4 room 5 range, slack, space 6 leeway 8 latitude 9 elbowroom 10 room to move
make a larger ~: 6 indent
narrow ~: 4 hair, inch, neck, nose
not on the ~: 5 set in
margin __: 4 call, line 5 plank 7 account
margin __ error: 3 for
__ margin: 4 head 6 profit
marginal: 3 low 4 side 5 minor, small 6 limbic, slight 7 minimal, outside 9 on the edge 10 borderline, low-ranking, negligible, peripheral
notation: 4 dele, stet
marginal __: 3 man, sea 4 cost 7 utility
marginalia: 5 notes 7 doodles
marginally: 8 slightly
margin for __: 5 error
Margin for Error author: Clare Boothe Luce
margin of __: 6 safety
Margo: 7 actress 8 Channing
spouse: Eddie Albert
Margolin: 5 Janet 6 Stuart
Margolin, Janet: 7 actress
film: David and Lisa (1962)
Last Embrace (1979)
Take the Money and Run (1969)
Your Three Minutes Are Up (1973)
Margot: 6 Kidder 7 Fonteyn
role for ~: 4 Lois
margrave: 5 title
__-Margret: 3 Ann
Margrethe II: 4 Dane 5 queen
marguerite: 5 daisy, plant 6 flower
Marguerite: 5 Duras 9 Yourcenar
see also French
Maria: 5 Bueno, McKee 6 Agnesi, Bombal, Callas, Montez, Schell 7 Jeritza, Muldaur, Pitillo, Shriver 8 von Trapp 9 Edgeworth, Tallchief 10 Montessori
husband: 6 Arnold
in the song: 4 wind
to Ted: 5 niece
see also Spanish
Maria __: 5 Elena 7 Theresa
Maria __ Alonso: 8 Conchita
Maria __ Trapp: 3 Von
__ Maria: 3 Ave, Tia 5 Black, Santa
__ Maria Alberghetti: 4 Anna
Maria author: 6 Isaacs
__ Maria Brandauer: 5 Klaus
mariachi
gig: 6 fiesta
wear: 6 sarape, serape
Maria Conchita __: 6 Alonso
Mariah: 5 Carey
__ Maria Horsford: 4 Anna
Marian: 5 Engel, Marsh 6 Jordan, Mercer 8 Anderson 10 McPartland
the Librarian's last name: 5 Paroo
__ Marian: 4 Maid
Mariana __: 6 Trench 7 Islands
Mariana author: Alfred Tennyson
Marianas: 4 isls. 5 isles 7 islands
island: 4 Guam, Rota 5 Pagan 6 Guguan, Saipan, Tinian 7 Agrihan, Aguijan
port: 4 Apra
Mariana Trench, like the: 4 deep
Marianne: 5 Moore 9 Faithfull 10 Sägebrecht
Marianne (1929 film)
cast: George Baxter, Marion Davies, Lawrence Gray
Marianne (1957 song)
artist: Hilltoppers, Terry Gilkyson and the Easy Riders
__ Marianne: 4 C'mon
Marianne author: George Sand
__ Maria Olazabal: 4 Jose
__ Maria Remarque: 5 Erich
__ Maria Rilke: 6 Rainer
Marías, Julián: 6 writer 7 Spanish 11 philosopher
Maribor: 4 city, town
locale: 8 Slovenia
Marichal, Juan: 5 Giant 7 pitcher
Maricopa: 6 Indian 7 Amerind
__-marie: 4 bain
Marie: 3 Ste. 4 Rose 5 Curie, Teena 6 Dionne, Osmond, sainte, Wilson 7 Corelli, Tempest 8 Dressler 9 de Médicis 10 Antoinette, LaChapelle
brother: 5 Donny
in English: 4 Mary
see also French
Marie (1985 film)
cast: Jeff Daniels, Sissy Spacek
director: Roger Donaldson
Marie __: 6 Claire
Marie __ Land: 4 Byrd
__ Marie: 4 Rose, Tina 5 Teena
Marie Antoinette: 5 queen, reine 6 French
Marie Byrd Land, toward: 5 south
Marie de France: 4 poet 6 French
Mariel: 4 city, port, town 9 Hemingway
grandpa: 6 Ernest
locale: 4 Cuba
Marienbad: 3 spa 4 city, town
locale: Czech Republic
__ Marie Presley: 4 Lisa

__ Marie Saint: 3 Eva
Marietta: 4 city, town
locale: 7 Georgia
Mariette: 7 Hartley
marigold: 5 plant 6 annual, flower
__ marigold: 3 bur, fig, pot 4 Cape, corn 5 Aztec, marsh 6 French 7 African
Marilu: 6 Henner
Marilyn: 5 Horne, McCoo 6 French, Manson, Martin, Miller, Monroe 7 Bergman, Maxwell, Munster
real first name: 5 Norma
Marilyn __ Savant: 3 Vos
marimba: 7 kalimba 10 percussion
Marin: 4 John 6 Cheech
marina: 4 dock 5 wharf 6 harbor 7 harbour
hoist: 5 davit
place: 4 cove 5 inlet
sight: 4 mast, spar 5 yacht 8 boat. slip
Marina: 4 city, town 6 Sirtis
locale: 10 California
see also Russian
marinade: 5 steep 6 pickle
Marina del __, CA: 3 Rey
marinara: 5 sauce
alternative: 5 pesto
ingredient: 6 garlic, tomato
Marinaro: 2 Ed
marinate: 4 soak 5 souse, steep
Marin, Cheech: 5 actor 8 comedian
film: Paulie (1998)
Tin Cup (1996)
Up in Smoke (1978)
Yellowbeard (1983)
partner: Tommy Chong
TV: Nash Bridges
marine: 4 naut. 5 naval 7 aquatic, coastal, deep-sea, oceanic, pelagic, soldier 8 littoral, maritime, natatory, nautical 9 salt-water, seafaring 10 oceangoing
life: 4 alga, fish 5 algae 7 seaweed
starter: 3 sub 4 aqua 5 ultra
see also ocean, sea
marine __: 3 ivy 4 alga, belt, glue 6 league 7 biology, geology, railway
__ marine: 5 horse 7 trumpet
Marine: 6 gyrene
officer: 3 col., gen., maj. 4 capt. 5 lieut., lt. col., major 7 captain, colonel, general 10 lieutenant
poster words: 4 a few
response: 5 no sir 6 yes sir
Marine __: 5 Corps
mariner: 3 gob, tar 4 mate, salt, swab, swob 6 sailor, sea dog, seaman 7 captain, jack tar, yachtie 8 deckhand, helmsman, seafarer, shipmate 9 navigator 10 bluejacket
aid: 4 buoy 6 beacon 10 lighthouse
ancient ~: 4 Eric, Leif, Noah 7 Ericson 8 Columbus
danger: 4 reef 5 rocks
heading: 3 ENE, ESE, NNE, NNW, SSE, SSW, WNW, WSW
see also sailor
Mariner rival: 3 Cub, Met, Red 4 Expo, Twin 5 Angel, Astro, Brave, Giant, Padre, Rocky, Royal, Tiger 6 Brewer, Dodger, Indian, Marlin, Oriole, Philly, Pirate, Ranger, Red Sox, Yankee 7 Blue Jay 8 Athletic, Cardinal, Devil Ray, White Sox
Mariners: 3 ten 4 team
home: 7 Seattle
org.: 3 ALW, MLB
sport: 8 baseball
Marines: 5 Corps 8 military
join the ~: 6 enlist
stay in the ~: 4 reup

Maringá: 4 city, town
locale: 6 Brazil
__ Marino: 3 San
Marino, Dan: 2 QB 11 quarterback
sport: 8 football
Marino, Giambattista: 4 poet 7 Italian
Marinus: 4 pope 7 pontiff
Mario: 3 Pei 4 Puzo 5 Cuomo, Lanza, Zampi 6 Molina 7 Andrade, Lemieux, Soldati 8 Andretti 9 Benedetti, Monicelli 10 Van Peebles
see also Italian
Mario __ Llosa: 6 Vargas
Mario __ Peebles: 3 Van
Marion: 4 city, Mack, Ross, town 5 Barry, Lorne, Marty 6 Davies, Motley 7 Donovan, Francis 10 Van Peebles
locale: 4 Iowa, Ohio 7 Indiana
marionette: 4 doll 6 puppet
Mario Vargas __: 5 Llosa
mariposa __: 4 lily 5 tulip
Maris: 3 Ada 5 Roger
__ Maris: 6 Stella
Marisa: 5 Pavan, Tomei 8 Berenson
Mariska: 8 Hargitay
mother: 5 Jayne
Maris, Roger sport: 8 baseball
Maritain, Jacques: 6 French, writer 11 philosopher
marital: 6 bridal, wedded 7 nuptial, spousal 8 conjugal 9 connubial
rites: 7 wedding 9 matrimony
maritime: 3 nav. 4 naut. 5 naval 6 marine 7 aquatic, coastal, deep-sea, oceanic, pelagic 8 littoral, maritime, nautical, seagoing 9 salt-water, seafaring 10 oceangoing
clandestine ~ org.: 3 ONI
convoy: 6 armada
outpost: 3 NAS
pal: 5 matey
rescue org.: 4 USCG
saint: 4 Elmo
see also navy, ocean, sea
maritime __: 3 law 4 belt
Maritime __: 4 Alps
__ Maritime: 5 Seine
Maritime Provinces locale: 6 Canada
__-Maritimes: 5 Alpes
Maritsa: 5 river
locale: 6 Greece, Turkey 8 Bulgaria
Marius the Epicurean author: 5 Pater
Marjoe: 7 Gortner
marjoram: 4 herb
__ marjoram: 3 pot 4 wild 5 sweet
Marjorie: 4 Lord, Main 8 Reynolds
Marjorie __ Rawlings: 6 Kinnan
Marjorie Merriweather __: 4 Post
Marjorie Morningstar: 4 film 5 novel
author: Herman Wouk
cast: Gene Kelly, Claire Trevor, Natalie Wood, Ed Wynn
character: 3 Guy 4 Eden, Noel
composer: 7 Steiner
director: Irving Rapper
mark: 2 ID 3 add, aim, bar, bit, con, cue, cut, dab, dot, eye, IOU, jot, log, mar, nip, opt, peg, pit, rub, rut, sap, say, see, tab, tag, tip 4 atom, aura, band, blob, blot, blur, boob, butt, call, cash, chip, cite, claw, clew, clue, coin, dash, data, daub, dent, draw, dupe, edit, etch, fame, feel, file, find, flaw, fool, form, foul, gain, gash, goal, goat, gull, heed, hint, hurt, iota, kind, lamb, lead, line, list, logo, look, make, mean, mind, mint, mite, name, nick, note, omen, pawn, pick, pink, plan, plot, prey, rank, rate, scab, scan, scar, seal, seam, show, sign, slit, soil, sort, spot, stub, tack, take, tear, tend, tick, tier, tint, tool, view, vote, welt, whit, wisp 5 affix, augur, badge, blaze, brand, carve, catch, chart, cheat, check, chump, claim, class, count, crest, cross, dirty, dough, draft, éclat, elect, enter, fleck, gauge, gouge, grade, grain, graph, graze, guard, guide, honor, image, imply, index, judge, label, money, notch, odium, patsy, point, prick, print, proof, quirk, refer, ridge, savor, score, scout, sense, shade, shame, shape, slash, smear, speck, stain, stamp, sully, taint, tally, tilde, tinge, token, total, touch, trace, track, trail, trait, value, vouch, watch, weigh, worth, wound, write 6 accent, advert, affect, append, aspect, assess, assign, assort, attend, attest, augury, bang up, batter, beacon, bedaub, behold, blotch, boo-boo, bruise, cachet, center, change, choose, course, crater, crease, credit, crud up, damage, dapple, darken, debase, decide, deface, defect, defile, define, denote, depict, descry, design, detail, detect, dimple, emblem, evince, figure, finger, flavor, flunky, follow, groove, herald, hunted, incise, injure, intend, intent, lackey, lay out, lesion, listen, locate, martyr, mottle, nature, notice, oddity, opt for, pepper, pigeon, pimple, play up, pledge, puppet, rating, record, regard, schook, scrape, scrawl, screen, select, signal, size up, sketch, smirch, smudge, status, stigma, stooge, streak, stress, stripe, stroke, sucker, survey, symbol, take in, target, ticket, tip-off, victim, wretch 7 abide by, acclaim, archive, auspice, begrime, besmear, betoken, blacken, blemish, catalog, certify, chalk up, comment, confirm, connote, contour, discern, doormat, earmark, earnest, endorse, engrave, exhibit, explain, express, extract, eyeball, fall guy, feature, freckle, glimpse, hearken, implant, impress, imprint, ingrain, initial, inkling, insigne, instill, itemize, jot down, jotting, license, look out, make out, meaning, measure, mention, monitor, nebbish, observe, outline, pick out, pin down, pointer, point to, point up, portend, portent, presage, put down, quality, recount, refer to, reflect, reserve, scratch, set down, signify, smidgen, snippet, sort out, spatter, specify, speckle, splotch, stipple, suggest, symptom, tarnish, tracing, unknown, vestige, witness 8 abrasion, adhere to, allocate, allude to, annotate, appraise, attest to, besmirch, black eye, boundary, bull's-eye, check off, check out, classify, colophon, currency, delegate, describe, diagnose, discolor, disgrace, dishonor, document, eminence, estimate, evaluate, evidence, flyspeck, home in on, identify, ideogram, impurity, indicate, inscribe, insignia, intimate, lacerate, maculate, milepost, particle, perceive, pinpoint, point out, position, pushover, register, reminder, scribble, see after, set aside, squiggle, stake out, stand for, standing, sure sign, swelling, take down, take heed, tincture, zero in on 9 adumbrate, appraisal, apprehend, assertion, attribute, authorize, bespatter, bespeckle, born loser, brand name, calibrate, catalogue, celebrate, character, chronicle, condition, contusion, criterion, delineate, designate, determine, disfigure, disrepute, emphasize, engraving, enumerate, footprint, greatness, harbinger, highlight, indicator, influence, insinuate, intention, interpret, italicize, keep score, lend an ear, lineament, look after, objective, parameter, pay heed to, precursor, punctuate, recognize, reinforce, represent, scapegoat, schlemiel, scintilla, semicolon, signifier, single out, soft touch, solemnize, symbolize, touch upon, underline, valuation, write down, yardstick 10 accentuate, annotation, apostrophe, assessment, beauty spot, blame-taker, categorize, coat of arms, denotation, depression, evaluation, foreshadow, get a load of, illustrate, impression, imputation, indication, intimation, keep tabs on, laceration, predispose, prognostic, reputation, stigmatize, take care of, traumatize, underscore
black ~: 4 slur, smut 5 stain 6 stigma
black-and-blue ~: 4 hurt 6 boo-boo, bruise
diacritical ~: 4 shwa 5 breve, hacek, schwa, tilde 6 macron, obelus, umlaut
down: 3 cut 4 note 5 enter, lower, price, retag, slash, tally, write 6 notate, record, reduce 7 devalue 8 close out, decrease, discount 9 devaluate, keep score
easy ~: 3 sap 4 butt, dupe, goat, lamb, simp, tool 5 chump, patsy, setup 6 pigeon, sucker, victim 8 pushover
high-water ~: 4 acme, apex, peak 5 crest 6 apogee, summit, zenith 8 pinnacle
hunter ~: 4 game 6 quarry
leave a ~: 4 scar
make one's ~: 7 prosper
miss the ~: 3 err 4 fail
off: 4 drop 8 cross out, graduate 10 measure out
off the ~: 4 awry 5 amiss, wrong 6 afield, astray, errant, faulty 7 inexact 8 mistaken 9 erroneous, imprecise 10 inaccurate
on the ~: 3 apt 4 true 5 right 7 correct 8 accurate
out: 4 pace, plan 6 define
punctuation ~: 4 dash 5 colon, comma, paren. 6 hyphen
replacement: 4 euro
starter: 3 ear, pug, sea 4 book, foot, hall, land, mint, post, tide 5 bench, birth, metal, press, trade, water 7 chatter
time: 4 drag, idle, tick, wait
up: 4 edit, hike 5 boost, price, raise 8 increase
see also grade
mark __: 3 off 4 down, time
__ mark: 3 hex, pin 4 chop, hash, line, view 5 bench, black, caste, check, class, ditto, draft, house, King's, plate, quote, shelf, space 6 accent, beauty, finger, maker's, ripple, stress, thread, witch's 7 chatter, leading, lubber's, product, section, service
Mark: 4 Lane, Roth 5 Clark, Damon, Grace, saint, Shera, Spitz, Twain, Wills 6 Antony, Hamill, Harmon, Lenard, McEwen, O'Meara, Robson, Rothko, Rydell, Strand 7 Dinning, Fidrych, Goddard, Goodson, Lindsay, McGwire, Messier, Russell, Stevens 8 Hatfield, Morrison, Sandrich, Van Doren, Wahlberg 9 Linn-Baker
follower: 4 Luke
preceder: 7 Matthew
to Tristan: 5 uncle
Mark __-Baker: 4 Linn
Markab: 4 star
Markandaya, Kamala: 6 Indian, writer
work: Nectar in a Sieve
markdown: 4 sale 7 bargain 8 discount

9 abatement, reduction
marked: 3 x'ed 5 clear, sharp 6 patent, signal, strong 7 decided, evident, intense, notable, salient, special, telling, visible 8 apparent, definite, distinct, manifest, striking 9 arresting, prominent 10 noticeable, pronounced
be ~ at: 4 cost
down: 3 low 5 cheap 6 on sale 7 reduced 8 a good buy, uncostly 9 half-price 10 economical
markedly: 5 extra 6 vastly 7 clearly, greatly, notably 8 patently, severely, signally, terribly 9 decidedly, evidently, extremely, obviously 10 distinctly, especially, incredibly, manifestly, noticeably, remarkably, strikingly
Marked Woman (1937 film)
cast: Humphrey Bogart, Bette Davis, Lola Lane
director: Lloyd Bacon
marker: 3 IOU, pen, tab, tag 4 buoy, chit, cone, debt 5 arrow, chalk, pylon, stela, stele 6 ticket 7 felt-tip, waypost 8 landmark, monument
marker __: 3 pen 4 gene 5 crude
__ marker: 4 felt 6 phrase 7 genetic
__ Marker: 5 Magic
markers
having ~ out: 6 in debt
one with ~: 4 ower
market: 4 co-op, deli, fair, hawk, mall, mart, sell, shop, souk, vend 5 bazar, booth, stall, store, trade 6 bazaar, bourse, outlet, peddle, retail 7 grocery 8 business, emporium, exchange 9 advertise, dime store, drugstore, move goods, wholesale 10 chain store, Wall Street
abroad: 6 export
aid: 4 cart
collapse: 5 crash
corner the ~: 5 buy up, sew up 7 possess
downturn: 5 slide
employee: 3 arb 5 clerk 6 bagger, broker 7 cashier
ender: 5 place
flood the ~: 4 glut
free ~: 10 capitalism
in the ~: 7 looking, seeking, wanting
just on the ~: 3 new
letters: 3 IPO, OTC 4 AMEX, NYSE 6 NASDAQ
Mideast ~: 3 suk, suq 4 souk 5 bazar 6 bazaar
offering: 5 stock
off the ~: 4 sold
on the ~: 7 for sale 9 available, up for sale
order: 3 buy 4 sell
play the ~: 5 trade 6 invest 7 venture 9 speculate
price: 4 cost 5 quote, value 9 quotation
put on the ~: 5 offer
segment: 5 niche
starter: 4 down 5 green
upturn: 5 rally 6 uptick 8 recovery 10 turnaround
visit the ~: 4 shop 6 browse
market __: 4 boat, crab, town 5 maker, order, price, share, value 6 basket, garden, letter
__ market: 3 job 4 bear, bull, call, curb, flea, gray, grey, open, spot 5 black, labor, money, on the, stock, white 6 buyer's 7 farmers', futures, seller's
__-market: 4 down, mass, test 5 after
__ Market: 6 Boston, Common
marketability: 5 value
marketable: 3 hot 6 liquid 7 popular, salable 8 bankable, in demand, saleable, sellable, vendible 10 commercial
marketable __: 5 title
marketer: 6 dealer, seller
__-market fund: 5 money
marketing
budget item: 2 ad
device: 5 tie in
online ~: 5 e-tail
starter: 4 tele
target: 5 buyer
__ marketing: 4 mass 5 viral 6 direct
__-market paperback: 4 mass
marketplace: 5 bazar, plaza 6 bazaar
ancient ~: 5 agora, Forum
__-market price: 4 fair
Markevich, Igor: 7 Russian 9 conductor
Markey: 4 Enid, Gene
Markham: 4 city, peak, town 5 Beryl, Edwin, Monte, mount 7 Pigmeat 8 mountain
locale: 6 Canada 7 Ontario 10 Antarctica
Markham, Beryl: 5 pilot
Markham, Edwin: 4 poet
subject: 4 hoer
Markham, Pigmeat song: Here Comes the Judge (1968)
markhor: 4 goat 5 snake 6 animal 7 reptile
relative: 3 asp, boa 4 geep, ibex, tahr, thar 5 aboma, adder, cobra, krait, mamba, racer, viper 6 Angora, dhaman, python, taipan 7 rattler 8 anaconda, moccasin, ringhals 9 boomslang, coachwhip 10 bushmaster, copperhead, sidewinder
Markie: 4 Post
__ Markie: 3 Biz
marking: 4 look 5 brand 7 pattern
marking __: 3 pen 4 gage
markka: 5 money
Mark Mc__: 4 Ewen
Mark of the Vampire (1935 film)
cast: Elizabeth Allan, Lionel Barrymore, Bela Lugosi
director: Tod Browning
Mark of Zorro, The (1940 film)
cast: Linda Darnell, Tyrone Power, Basil Rathbone
director: Rouben Mamoulian
Markova, Alicia: 6 dancer 7 British 8 danseuse 9 ballerina
Markowitz, Harry: 8 Nobelist 9 economist
Marks and Spencer: 4 shop 5 store
marksman: 4 shot 7 deadeye
order: 3 aim 4 fire 5 ready
Mark Trail dog: 4 Andy
Mark Twain National Forest, site of: 6 Ozarks
Mark Twain Suite composer: 5 Grofé
markup: 6 profit
basis: 4 cost
sans ~: 6 at cost
Mark Van __: 5 Doren
Marky Mark and the Funky Bunch song: Good Vibrations (1991) Wildside (1991)
marl: 4 clay 5 earth, loess
Marla: 5 Gibbs 6 Maples
Marlborough: 4 city, town
locale: 4 Conn.
Marlee: 6 Matlin
Marlene: 8 Dietrich
__ Marlene: 4 Lili
Marley: 3 Bob 5 Jacob, Ziggy
marlin: 4 fish
__ marlin: 4 blue 5 white 7 striped
Marlin: 3 AMC, car 4 auto 7 Perkins, Rambler 9 Fitzwater 10 automobile
rival: 3 Cub, Met, Red 4 Expo, Twin 5 Angel, Astro, Brave, Giant, Padre, Rocky, Royal, Tiger 6 Brewer, Dodger, Indian, Oriole, Philly, Pirate, Ranger, Red Sox, Yankee 7 Blue Jay, Mariner 8 Athletic, Cardinal, Devil Ray, White Sox
marline: 5 twine
Marlins: 4 nine, team
home: 3 Fla. 5 Miami 7 Florida
org.: 3 MLB, NLE
sport: 8 baseball
Marlo: 6 Thomas
hubby: 4 Phil
Marlon: 6 Brando 7 Jackson
Marlow Chronicles, The author: Lawrence Sanders
Marlowe: 4 Hugh 6 Philip
contemporary: 3 Kid, Kyd
Marlowe (1969 film)
cast: James Garner, Gayle Hunnicutt, Carroll O'Connor
director: Paul Bogart
Marlowe, Christopher: 4 poet 7 British 10 playwright
work: Come live with me...
Hero and Leander
The Jew of Malta
Tamburlaine the Great
The Tragical History of Dr. Faustus
see also poet
Marlowe, Hugh: 5 actor
film: Come to the Stable (1949)
The Day the Earth Stood Still (1951)
Earth vs. the Flying Saucers (1956)
Twelve O'Clock High (1949)
Wait 'Til the Sun Shines, Nellie (1952)
marm: 6 madame
Marmaduke: 3 dog, pet
marmalade: 3 cat 6 spread 9 conserves, preserves
ingredient: 4 peel, rind 6 orange
kin: 5 jelly
marmalade __: 3 box 4 bush, plum, tree
__ Marmalade: 4 Lady
Marmara: 3 sea
locale: 6 Turkey
Sea of ~ port: 5 Izmit
Marmion author: Walter Scott
Marmolejo: 4 peak 5 mount 8 mountain
locale: 5 Andes, Chile 9 Argentina
marmoset: 5 jocko 6 animal 7 primate, tamarin
fare: 6 insect
relative: 3 ape 4 saki, titi 5 chimp, drill, jocko, lemur, loris, magot, orang, potto, shrew 6 aye-aye, baboon, Bandar, galago, gelada, gibbon, grivet, guenon, howler, langur, macaco, monkey, rhesus, uakari, vervet 7 colobus, gorilla, guereza, hoolock, macaque, sapajou, siamang, tamarin, tarsier 8 bush baby, capuchin, mandrill, mangabey, talapoin 9 orangutan 10 Barbary ape, chimpanzee, orangutang
marmot: 6 animal, mammal, rodent
relative: 3 rat 4 cavy, degu, jird, paca, vole 5 coypu, gundi, mouse, xerus 6 agouti, beaver, gerbil, gopher, jerboa, murine 7 hamster, lemming, muskrat, visacha 8 chipmunk, cricetid, dormouse, squirrel, tuco-tuco 9 chickaree, groundhog, guinea pig, porcupine, woodchuck 10 chinchilla, prairie dog
Marne: 5 river 6 battle
locale: 6 France
__-Marne: 5 Haute
Marner: 5 Silas
Marnie (1964 film)
cast: Diane Baker, Sean Connery, Tippi Hedren
composer: 8 Herrmann
director: Alfred Hitchcock
__ Marnier: 5 Grand
marocain: 5 crepe 6 fabric 8 material
maroon: 3 red 5 beach, color, leave 6 desert, enisle, strand 7 abandon, crimson, forsake, isolate 8 forswear 9 foreswear 10 cast ashore
relative: 4 rose, ruby, rust, wine 5 brick, coral, grape, poppy, rusty, sandy 6 cerise, cherry, claret, garnet 7 carmine, crimson, fuchsia, magenta, pimento, scarlet, sultana, vermeil 8 amaranth, cardinal, dubonnet, geranium, rubicund 9 carnation, cranberry, vermilion 10 strawberry
marooned: 4 left 5 alone 7 aground 8 castaway, forsaken, stranded 9 foundered 10 high and dry
Marot, Clément: 4 poet 6 French
Maroua: 4 city, town
locale: 8 Cameroon
Marouf, baritone in: 3 Ali
Marple, Miss: 4 Jane
Marquand: 2 J.P. 7 Richard
Marquand, J.P.: 6 author, writer
sleuth: Mr. Moto
work: The Late George Apley
Wickford Point
Marquard, Rube: 6 hurler 7 pitcher
__ marqué: 3 sou
marquee: 6 awning, canopy
light: 4 neon
share the ~: 6 costar
word: 4 nite
Marquesas: 4 isls. 5 isles 7 islands
island: 4 Eïao, Ua Pu 6 Hatutu, Hiva Oa, Ua Huka 7 Tahuata 8 Fatu Hiva, Nuku Hiva
marquess: 4 peer 5 noble, title
Marquette: 4 city, Père, town
locale: 8 Michigan 9 Milwaukee, Wisconsin
Márquez, Gabriel García: 6 author, writer 8 Nobelist 9 Colombian
work: One Hundred Years of Solitude
Marquina, Eduardo: 6 writer 7 Spanish
marquis: 4 lord, male, peer, rank 5 noble, title 8 nobleman
rank above ~: 4 duke
rank below ~: 4 earl
Marquis: 3 car, Don 4 auto 6 Childs 7 Mercury 10 automobile
Marquis de __: 4 Sade 9 Condorcet, Lafayette
Marquis, Don: 6 author, writer
work: Archy and Mehitabel
The Lantern
The Sun Dial
marquise: 3 gem
marquise __: 3 cut 5 chair
marquisette: 5 gauze 6 fabric
Marquis of Queensberry __: 5 rules
Marrakesh: 4 city, town
locale: 7 Morocco
section: 6 casbah
Marrakesh Express (1969 song) artist: Crosby, Stills & Nash
marred: 4 hurt 6 broken, faulty, flawed 7 injured, unsound 8 fallible 9 defective, imperfect
Marrero: 4 city, town
locale: 9 Louisiana
marriage: 4 bond, rite 5 match, union 6 mating, merger 7 wedding, wedlock 8 alliance, contract, espousal, monogamy, nuptials, polygamy 9 matrimony, sacrament
absence of ~ laws: 5 agamy
before ~: 3 née
combining form: 4 -gamy 6 -gamous
document: 3 lic. 7 license
it's given in ~: 4 hand

notice: 4 bans 5 banns
of ~: 7 marital
offer ~: 7 propose
perform a ~: 5 unite
place: 5 altar 6 chapel
relative by ~: 5 in-law 6 affine
seek in ~: 3 woo
symbol: 4 ring
vows: 5 troth
vow word: 5 worse 6 better, poorer, richer
marriage __: 6 broker 7 portion
__ marriage: 5 civil, proxy, royal 6 Boston
marriageable one: 4 miss
Marriage at __: 4 Cana
Marriage Circle, The (1924 film)
cast: Monte Blue, Florence Vidor
director: Ernst Lubitsch
Marriage Is a Private Affair (1944 film)
cast: James Craig, John Hodiak, Lana Turner
director: Robert Z. Leonard
Marriage Italian Style actress: 5 Loren
Marriage of Figaro, The: 5 opera
composer: 6 Mozart
role: 6 Curzio 7 Antonio, Bartolo, Basilio, Susanna 8 Almaviva 9 Don Curzio 10 Don Basilio, Marcellina
setting: 5 Spain 7 Seville
Marriage Play author: Edward Albee
married
get ~: 3 wed
name meaning ~: 6 Beulah
not ~: 5 unwed 6 single
one: 4 wife 5 bride, groom 6 spouse 7 husband
Married to the Mob (1988 film)
cast: Alec Baldwin, Joan Cusack, Matthew Modine, Michelle Pfeiffer, Mercedes Ruehl, Dean Stockwell
director: Jonathan Demme
dog: 5 Lucky
Married...With Children (Fox sitcom)
cast: Christina Applegate (Kelly Bundy)
David Faustino (Bud Bundy)
Ed O'Neill (Al Bundy)
Katey Sagal (Peg Bundy)
dog: Buck
Marriner, Neville: 7 British 9 conductor
marring: 6 defect 8 graffiti
Marriott: 5 hotel
alternative: 4 Omni 5 Hyatt 6 Hilton, Westin 7 Wyndham 8 Radisson, Sheraton 10 DoubleTree 11 Crowne Plaza, Four Seasons
marrons glacés: 7 dessert 9 chestnuts
marrow: 4 core, gist, meat, pith, root, soul 5 cream, heart, point, quick 6 kernel, middle 7 essence, keynote 8 interior, key point 9 innermost, lifeblood, substance
combining form: 4 myel- 5 myelo-
__ marrow: 4 bone
marry: 3 tie, wed 4 bond, join, mate, take, wive, yoke 5 blend, catch, merge, unify, unite 6 splice 7 combine, espouse 10 get hitched, settle down, tie the knot
again: 5 rewed
on the run: 5 elope
persuade to ~: 3 win
promise to ~: 5 troth
__ Marry a Millionaire: 5 How to
Marryat, Frederick: 6 writer 7 British
work: Frank Mildmay, or the Naval Officer
Masterman Ready
Mr. Midshipman Easy
Peter Simple
Marryin' __: 3 Sam
Marrying Kind, The (1952 film)
cast: Judy Holliday, Madge Kennedy, Aldo Ray
director: George Cukor
marrying man: 2 JP 6 parson, priest
Marrying Man, The (1991 film)
cast: Alec Baldwin, Kim Basinger, Robert Loggia, Elisabeth Shue
director: Jerry Rees
Mars: 3 bar, deo, god, orb 4 Ares, Mick, mois 5 candy, March, month 6 French, planet 7 Kenneth 9 chocolate 10 candy maker
alternative: 4 Twix 5 Clark, Heath 6 Kit Kat, Mounds, PayDay, Reese's, Zagnut 7 Krackel, Oh Henry 8 Baby Ruth, Hershey's, Milky Way, Snickers 9 Almond Joy, Mr. Goodbar 10 NutRageous
combining form: 4 areo-
equivalent: 4 Ares
explorer: 5 probe
Explorer: 5 robot
feature: 5 canal 6 crater, icecap
follower: 5 Avril
from ~: 5 alien
moon of ~: 6 Deimos, Phobos
neighbor: 5 Earth 7 Jupiter
opposite: 3 Pax
parent of ~: 4 Juno 7 Jupiter
Pathfinder org.: 4 NASA
preceder: 7 Février
sister of ~: 7 Bellona
son of ~: 5 Remus 7 Romulus
Mars __: 3 red 5 brown 6 violet, yellow
__ marsala: 4 veal 7 chicken
Marsala: 4 port, wine
origin: 5 Italy 6 Sicily
Marsalis: 5 Ellis 6 Wynton 8 Branford
Marsalis, Branford: 11 saxophonist
genre: 4 jazz
Marsalis, Ellis: 7 pianist
genre: 4 jazz
Marsalis, Wynton: 9 trumpeter
genre: 4 jazz
Mars Attacks! (1996 film)
cast: Annette Bening, Pierce Brosnan, Glenn Close, Jack Nicholson
director: Tim Burton
dog: 5 Rusty
Marsden: 5 Gerry
Marseille: 4 city, port, town
city near ~: 4 Lyon 5 Lyons
locale: 6 France
marseilles: 6 fabric 8 material
Marseilles: 4 city, port, town
city near ~: 3 Aix 5 Nîmes
locale: 6 France
marsh: 3 bog, fen 4 mire, sink 5 bayou, swale, swamp 6 lagoon, morass, slough 7 estuary, lowland, wetland 8 quagmire 9 backwater, everglade, swampland 10 everglades
bird: 4 rail, sora 5 crake, egret, heron, snipe 8 water hen
combining form: 4 helo- 6 paludi-
dweller: 4 frog
elder: 3 iva
ender: 4 land 5 lands 6 mallow
like a ~: 5 boggy, fenny, rushy, sedgy 6 swampy
plant: 4 reed, rush 5 ament, calla, sedge 6 catkin 8 arum lily
marsh __: 3 gas, hen 4 deer, fern, hawk, pink, wren 5 buggy, cress, elder, grass 6 mallow 7 trefoil
__ marsh: 4 salt
Marsh: 3 Mae 4 Jean 5 Ngaio 6 Marian
__ Marsh: 4 Pink 6 Romney
Marsha: 4 Hunt 5 Mason 6 Norman 8 Warfield
marshal: 5 align, aline, array, group, order, rally, usher 6 deploy, draw up, gather, lawman, line up, muster 7 arrange, bailiff, collect, compile, convoke, dispose, officer, round up, sheriff 8 assemble, mobilize, muster up, official, organize 9 fire chief
force: 5 posse
__ marshal: 3 air, sky 4 fire 5 field, grand 7 provost
Marshal __: 4 Tito
Marshall: 2 E.G. 4 city, John, town 5 Field, Frank, Garry, Penny, Peter 6 Brenda, George 7 Herbert, McLuhan 8 Thurgood 9 Nirenberg
locale: 5 Texas
Marshall __: 4 Plan 7 Islands
__ Marshall, Counselor at Law: 4 Owen
Marshall, E.G.: 5 actor
film: 12 Angry Men (1957)
The Bachelor Party (1957)
Interiors (1978)
Nixon (1995)
Town Without Pity (1961)
TV: The Defenders
Marshall, Garry: 8 director
film: Beaches (1988)
The Flamingo Kid (1984)
Frankie and Johnnie (1991)
Frankie and Johnny (1991)
A League of Their Own (1992)
Lost in America (1985)
Nothing in Common (1986)
The Other Sister (1999)
Overboard (1987)
Pretty Woman (1990)
The Princess Diaries (2001)
Runaway Bride (1999)
Marshall, George: 8 director
film: The Blue Dahlia (1946)
Destry Rides Again (1939)
Fancy Pants (1950)
The Gazebo (1959)
The Ghost Breakers (1940)
The Guns of Fort Petticoat (1957)
Hold That Co-ed (1938)
Houdini (1953)
How the West Was Won (1962)
Incendiary Blonde (1945)
Life Begins at Forty (1935)
The Mating Game (1959)
A Message to Garcia (1936)
A Millionaire for Christy (1951)
Monsieur Beaucaire (1946)
Murder, He Says (1945)
My Friend Irma (1949)
The Perils of Pauline (1947)
The Sheepman (1958)
Show Them No Mercy! (1935)
Star Spangled Rhythm (1942)
Texas (1941)
True to Life (1943)
Valley of the Sun (1942)
When the Daltons Rode (1940)
You Can't Cheat an Honest Man (1939)
Marshall, George C.: 7 general 8 Nobelist
Marshall, Herbert: 5 actor
film: Blonde Venus (1932)
Foreign Correspondent (1940)
The Good Fairy (1935)
High Wall (1947)
If You Could Only Cook (1935)
The Letter (1940)
The Little Foxes (1941)
Mad About Music (1938)
The Moon and Sixpence (1942)
Riptide (1934)
The Secret Garden (1949)
Trouble in Paradise (1932)
The Underworld Story (1950)
A Woman Rebels (1936)
Marshall Islands
capital: 6 Majuro
island: 6 Bikini 8 Eniwetok
Marshall, Penny: 7 actress 8 director
film: Awakenings (1990)
Big (1988)
A League of Their Own (1992)
The Preacher's Wife (1996)
Renaissance Man (1994)
spouse: Rob Reiner
TV: Laverne and Shirley, The Odd Couple
Marshall Plan agcy.: 3 ECA
Marshalls: 4 isls. 5 isles 7 islands
Marshalltown: 4 city
locale: 4 Iowa
Marshall University locale: 10 Huntington
Marshes of Glynn, The: 4 poem
author: Sidney Lanier
marshland: 4 mire, quag 5 swamp, waste 8 quagmire
marshmallow: 5 plant, snack
chocolate ~ snack: 5 Smore
holder: 4 twig
like a ~: 4 soft
Marsh, Marian: 7 actress
film: The Black Room (1935)
Crime and Punishment (1935)
Five Star Final (1931)
The Mad Genius (1931)
Svengali (1931)
Marsh, Ngaio: 6 author, writer
sleuth: Roderick Alleyn
work: Artists in Crime
Black as He's Painted
Hand in Glove
A Man Lay Dead
Night at the Vulcan
Photo Finish
marshy: 5 boggy, fenny, muddy 6 swampy, watery
Marsilius of Padua: 11 philosopher
Mars, Kenneth: 5 actor
film: Desperate Characters (1971)
The Producers (1968)
What's Up, Doc? (1972)
Young Frankenstein (1974)
Marston __: 4 Moor
Marston, John: 6 writer 7 British
work: The Dutch Courtezan
The Malcontent
marsupial: 3 'roo 4 euro, tait 5 bilbi, bilby, koala 6 animal, numbat, wombat 7 bettong, dasyure, opossum, wallaby 8 kangaroo, wallaroo 9 bandicoot, phalanger
place for a young ~: 5 pouch
marsupial __: 3 rat 4 mole 5 mouse
marsupium: 3 sac 5 pouch
mart: 4 co-op, deli, fair, mall, shop, souk 5 bazar, booth, stall, store 6 bazaar, market, outlet 8 boutique, business, emporium, exchange, showroom 9 dime store, drugstore 10 chain store
__-Mart: 3 Wal
Marta: 7 Kristen
in English: 6 Martha
Martaban: 4 gulf
locale: 5 Burma 7 Myanmar
Martel: 7 Charles
marten: 3 fur 5 pekan, tayra 6 animal, fisher, weasel
relative: 4 mink 5 fitch, otter, ratel, sable, skunk, stoat, tayra 6 badger, ermine, ferret 7 foumart, polecat 8 carcajou, foulmart, kolinsky, muishond 9 wolverine
__ marten: 4 baum, pine 5 beech, stone, sweet
martes: 3 día 7 Spanish, Tuesday
follower: 9 miércoles
preceder: 5 lunes
Martha: 4 Hyer, Raye 5 opera, saint, Scott 6 Graham, Grimes, Reeves 7 Stewart, Vickers 8 Coolidge, Plimpton 9 Jefferson 10 Washington

in Italian: 5 Marta
in Spanish: 5 Marta
to George: 4 wife
Martha's Vineyard: 3 isl. **4** isle **6** island
Martha & the Vandellas
last name: Reeves
song: Dancing in the Street (1964)
Heat Wave (1963)
Honey Chile (1967)
I'm Ready for Love (1966)
Jimmy Mack (1967)
Nowhere to Run (1965)
Quicksand (1963)
Martha Washington __: 5 chair, table **6** mirror
Marthe: 6 Keller
Martí: 4 José
martial: 7 hawkish, hostile, warlike **8** fighting, military, ructious **9** bellicose, combative, soldierly **10** aggressive, pugnacious
court ~: 5 trial
god: 4 Ares, Mars
martial __: 3 law **4** arts
__-martial: 5 court
Martial: 4 poet **5** Roman **6** writer
martial art: 4 judo **5** kendo, taebo, wushu **6** aikido, karate, kung fu, t'ai chi **7** jujitsu **9** tae kwon do
attire: 2 gi **4** belt **9** black belt
blow: 4 chop
exercise: 4 kata
expert: 5 ninja **6** judoka, sansei
legend: 3 Lee **8** Bruce Lee
school: 4 dojo
Martian: 2 ET **5** alien
craft, maybe: 3 UFO
invasion report: 4 hoax
Martian Chronicles, The author: Ray Bradbury
Martí, José: 4 poet **5** Cuban **6** writer
martin: 4 bird **8** boundary
__ martin: 3 bee **4** sand **5** house **6** purple, vernis
Martin: 3 Don **4** Amis, Beck, Dean, Dick, Eden, Kiel, Mary, Moon, Mull, Nexo, Perl, pope, Ritt, Ross, Ryle, Tony **5** Billy, Brest, Buber, Denny, Gabel, Ricky, Sheen, Short, Steve **6** Archer, Balsam, Behaim, Kellie, Landau, Luther, Milner, Pepper, Walser **7** Darnell, Gregory, Marilyn, Melcher, pontiff, Rodbell **8** Agronsky, de Porres, Lawrence, Scorsese, Strother, Van Buren **9** Frobisher, Heidegger
partner: 5 Aston, Rowan
Martin __ King: 6 Luther
Martin __ Smith: 4 Cruz
__ Martin: 4 Remy **5** Aston
__ Martín: 3 San
Martin (1978 film) director: George A. Romero
Martina: 6 Hingis **7** McBride
Chris, to ~: 5 rival
__, Martin and John: 7 Abraham
Martin, Archer: 7 chemist **8** Nobelist
Martin Chuzzlewit author: Charles Dickens
Martindale, Wink: 2 MC **5** emcee
song: Deck of Cards (1959)
TV: Gambit, Tic Tac Dough
Martin, Dean: 5 actor **6** singer
film: 4 for Texas (1963)
Ada (1961)
Airport (1970)
The Ambushers (1968)
Artists and Models (1955)
Bandolero! (1968)
Bells Are Ringing (1960)
Career (1959)
Kiss Me, Stupid (1964)
Living It Up (1954)
Murderers' Row (1966)
My Friend Irma (1949)
Ocean's Eleven (1960)
Rio Bravo (1959)
Robin and the Seven Hoods (1964)
Sailor Beware (1951)
The Silencers (1966)
Some Came Running (1959)
The Sons of Katie Elder (1965)
The Stooge (1953)
Texas Across the River (1966)
Who Was That Lady? (1960)
The Wrecking Crew (1969)
The Young Lions (1958)
You're Never Too Young (1955)
film role: Matt Helm
movie partner: Jerry Lewis
real name: Dino Crocetti
song: The Door Is Still Open to My Heart (1964)
Everybody Loves Somebody (1964)
In the Chapel in the Moonlight (1967)
I Will (1965)
Memories Are Made of This (1955)
Return to Me (1958)
Send Me the Pillow You Dream On (1965)
That's Amore (1953)
Volare (1958)
You're Nobody Till Somebody Loves You (1965)
specialty: 5 roast
Martin de Porres: 5 saint
Martin du Gard, Roger: 6 French, writer
work: The Postman
Martin Eden author: Jack London
Martinelli: 4 Elsa
martinet: 4 ogre **6** ramrod, tyrant **8** stickler **10** taskmaster
Martinez: 4 city, town **5** Edgar
locale: 7 Georgia **10** California
Martínez: 4 city, town
locale: 6 Mexico **8** Veracruz
Martinez, Edgar sport: 8 baseball
Martínez Ruiz, José: 6 writer **7** Spanish
Martínez Sierra, Gregorio: 6 writer **7** Spanish
work: Cradle Song
martini: 5 drink **8** beverage, cocktail
impact: 4 kick
ingredient: 3 gin **5** olive, vodka **8** vermouth
maker: 6 barman **9** bartender
preference: 3 dry
with an onion: 6 Gibson
Martini and __: 5 Rossi
martinico: 4 fish
Martinique: 3 île, isl. **4** isle **6** banana, island
money: 4 euro **5** franc
poet: 7 Césaire
volcano: 5 Pelee
writer: 8 Glissant
see also French
Martin Luther __: 4 King
Martino, Al
real name: Alfred Cini
song: I Love You Because (1963)
I Love You More and More Every Day (1964)
Spanish Eyes (1965)
Tears and Roses (1964)
Martin of Tours: 5 saint
Martin, Ricky
song: Livin' La Vida Loca (1999)
She's All I Ever Had (1999)
TV: General Hospital
Martinson, Harry: 6 writer **8** Nobelist
Martins, Peter: 6 dancer **7** danseur
specialty: 6 ballet
Martin, Steve: 5 actor **8** comedian
birthplace: 4 Waco **5** Texas
film: All of Me (1984)
Bowfinger (1999)
Dead Men Don't Wear Plaid (1982)
Dirty Rotten Scoundrels (1988)
Father of the Bride (1991)
Grand Canyon (1991)
The Jerk (1979)
L.A. Story (1991)
Leap of Faith (1992)
Little Shop of Horrors (1986)
The Lonely Guy (1984)
The Man With Two Brains (1983)
My Blue Heaven (1990)
Novocaine (2001)
The Out-of-Towners (1999)
Parenthood (1989)
Pennies From Heaven (1981)
Planes, Trains & Automobiles (1987)
Roxanne (1987)
Sgt. Bilko (1996)
A Simple Twist of Faith (1994)
The Spanish Prisoner (1998)
Three Amigos! (1986)
song: King Tut (1978)
spouse: Victoria Tennant
Martin, Strother: 5 actor
film: Cool Hand Luke (1967)
Hard Times (1975)
Pocket Money (1972)
Rooster Cogburn (1975)
SSSSSSS (1973)
Martin, Tony
real name: Alvin Morris
song: Walk Hand in Hand (1956)
spouse: Cyd Charisse, Alice Faye
Marton: 3 Eva **6** Andrew
Marton, Andrew: 8 director
film: Clarence, the Cross-Eyed Lion (1965)
King Solomon's Mines (1950)
The Longest Day (1962)
Men of the Fighting Lady (1954)
Marty: 5 Balin **6** Ingels, Marion **7** Feldman, Melcher, Riessen, Robbins
Marty (1955 film)
cast: Betsy Blair, Ernest Borgnine, Joe Mantell
director: Delbert Mann
Marty author: Paddy Chayefsky
Marv: 4 Levy **6** Albert **7** Johnson **11** Throneberry
marvel: 3 awe **4** gape, whiz **5** stare **6** genius, goggle, puzzle, wonder **7** miracle, portent, prodigy, stunner **8** surprise **9** amazement, curiosity, sensation, spectacle **10** phenomenon
Marvelettes
song: Beechwood 4-5789 (1962)
Don's Mess with Bill (1966)
The Hunter Gets Captured by the Game (1967)
Playboy (1962)
Please Mr. Postman (1961)
Marvell, Andrew: 4 poet **7** British
work: To His Coy Mistress
marvelous: 3 ace, def, fab, rad **4** aces, A-one, boss, braw, cool, dece, fine, gear, good, keen, neat, nice, phat, tuff **5** dandy, ducky, grand, great, neato, nifty, nobby, prime, slick, super, swell **6** bang on, bang-up, bonzer, bosker, choice, divine, dreamy, far-out, gnarly, groovy, lovely, peachy, slap-up, spot on, superb, terrif, tiptop, unreal, whizzo, wicked **7** amazing, awesome, capital, corking, perfect, ripping, skookum, stellar, strange, sublime, supreme, unusual **8** colossal, dazzling, especial, eximious, fabulous, five-star, four-star, frabjous, glorious, greatest, heavenly, jim-dandy, singular, slam-bang, smashing, splendid, standout, sterling, stickout, striking, stunning, superior, terrific, top-level, topnotch, very good, wondrous **9** beautiful, bodacious, Endsville, enjoyable, excellent, exemplary, exquisite, fantastic, first-rate, high-grade, hunky-dory, solid gold, sollicker, top-flight, unrivaled, wonderful, wunderbar **10** astounding, first-class, hotsy-totsy, incredible, jack-a-dandy, miraculous, out of sight, peachy-keen, phenomenal, prodigious, remarkable, staggering, stupendous, super-duper, surprising, tremendous, unrivalled, world-class
Marvelous!: 3 ooh
__ Marvelous for Words: 3 Too
Marvin: 3 Lee **4** Gaye, Kalb **6** Hagler, Miller **8** Hamlisch **9** Rainwater
Marvin dog: 5 Bitsy
Marvin, Lee: 5 actor
film: Attack! (1956)
The Big Red One (1980)
Cat Ballou (1965, AA)
The Comancheros (1961)
The Dirty Dozen (1967)
Donovan's Reef (1963)
Emperor of the North (1973)
Gorky Park (1983)
Hell in the Pacific (1968)
The Iceman Cometh (1973)
The Man Who Shot Liberty Valance (1962)
Monte Walsh (1970)
Paint Your Wagon (1969)
Pocket Money (1972)
Point Blank (1967)
Prime Cut (1972)
The Professionals (1966)
Seven Men From Now (1956)
Shack Out on 101 (1955)
marvy: 3 fab **5** great, neato, nifty, super, swell **6** dreamy, groovy **8** splendid, terrific **9** wonderful **10** tremendous
Marx: 3 red **4** Karl **5** Chico, Gummo, Harpo, Zeppo **7** Groucho, Richard
ender: 3 ism, ist
instrument: 4 harp **5** piano
Marx __: 8 Brothers
Marx, Arthur: 5 Harpo
Marx, Groucho: 3 wit **4** host **5** emcee
brother: 5 Chico, Gummo, Harpo, Zeppo
cap: 5 beret
glance from ~: 4 leer
specialty: 5 ad-lib
Marxism: 9 Communism, Socialism
Marxist: 9 Communist, Socialist
Marx, Karl: 6 German, writer **9** socialist **11** philosopher
collaborator: 6 Engels
exhortation: 5 unite
work: Das Kapital
Marx, Richard
song: Angelia (1989)
Children of the Night (1990)
Don't Mean Nothing (1987)
Endless Summers Nights (1988)
Hazard (1992)
Hold On to the Nights (1988)
Keep Coming Back (1991)
Now and Forever (1994)
Right Here Waiting (1989)
Satisfied (1989)
Should've Known Better (1987)
Take This Heart (1992)
Too Late to Say Goodbye (1990)
Mary: 3 Ure **4** Hart **5** Astor, Brian, Frann, Gross, O'Hara, Quant, saint, Tudor, Wells **6** Boland, Crosby, Decker, Garden, Hopkin, Leakey, Mallon, Martin, Norton, Stuart, Wilson **7** Cassatt, Lincoln, Matalin, McGrory, Poppins, Renault, Shelley, Stewart, Travers, Woronov **8** McCarthy,

McFadden, Pickford **9** MacGregor, Magdalene, McCormack, McDonnell, McDonough
boss at WJM: 3 Lou
follower: 4 lamb
friend: 5 Rhoda
in French: 5 Marie
in Irish: 5 Moira
in Scottish: 5 Moira
to Abe: 4 wife
Mary __: 3 Kay **5** Janes
Mary __ a little lamb: 3 had
Mary __ Ash: 3 Kay
Mary __, Backstage Wife: 5 Noble
Mary __ Carpenter: 6 Chapin
Mary __ Clark: 7 Higgins
Mary __ Dodge: 5 Mapes
Mary __ Eddy: 5 Baker
Mary __ Hurt: 4 Beth
Mary __ Lincoln: 4 Todd
Mary __ Masterson: 6 Stuart
Mary __ Mobley: 3 Ann
Mary __ Moore: 5 Tyler
Mary __ Place: 3 Kay
Mary __ Retton: 3 Lou
Mary __ Rinehart: 7 Roberts
Mary, __ of Scots: 5 Queen
Mary-__ Olsen: 4 Kate
Mary-__ Parker: 6 Louise
__ Mary: 4 Hail **5** Proud, Sweet **6** Bloody, Virgin **7** Typhoid
Maryam: 4 d'Abo
Mary Ann: 6 Mobley
Mary author: Sholem Asch
Mary Baker __: 4 Eddy
Mary Beth: 4 Hurt
Mary Burns, Fugitive (1935 film)
cast: Melvyn Douglas, Pert Kelton, Sylvia Sidney
Mary Chapin __: 9 Carpenter
Mary Had a Little Lamb author: 4 Hale
Mary Hartman, Mary Hartman (TV sitcom)
cast: Dody Goodman (Martha Shumway)
Louise Lasser (Mary Hartman)
Greg Mullavey (Tom Hartman)
Mary Kay Place (Loretta Haggers)
setting: Fernwood, Ohio
Mary Higgins __: 5 Clark
Mary J. __: 5 Blige, Latis
Mary Janes: 5 shoes **8** footwear
Mary Jane's Last Dance (1994 song)
artist: Tom Petty
Mary-Kate: 5 Olsen
sister: 6 Ashley
Mary Kay: 3 Ash **5** Place **6** makeup
alternative: 4 Avon **5** Almay **6** Revlon **7** Lancome **8** Clinique **9** Cover Girl, Max Factor **10** Maybelline **11** Estée Lauder, Merle Norman
Maryland: 5 state
athlete: 4 Terp **8** Terrapin
bay: 10 Chesapeake
capital: 9 Annapolis
city: 5 Bowie, Essex, Olney **6** Arnold, Bel Air, Carney, Elkton, Laurel, Severn, Towson **7** Arbutus, Chillum, Clinton, Crofton, Dundalk, Odenton, Potomac, Waldorf, Wheaton **8** Aberdeen, Bethesda, Columbia, Edgewood, Elkridge, Fairland, Glenmont, Landover, Lochearn, Oxon Hill, Suitland, White Oak, Woodlawn **9** Annapolis, Aspen Hill, Baltimore, Fort Meade, Frederick, Greenbelt, Parkville, Perry Hall, Rockville, Salisbury, South Gate, St. Charles **10** Chevy Chase, Colesville, Cumberland, Eldersburg, Germantown, Glassmanor, Glen Burnie, Hagerstown, Montgomery, Pikesville, Silver Hill
conference: 3 ACC
fort: 5 Meade
Indian: 9 Nanticoke
mountains: 8 Catoctin
neighbor: 8 Delaware, Virginia
once: 6 colony
port: 9 Baltimore
school: 4 Navy, USNA
state beverage: 4 milk
state bird: 6 oriole
state boat: 8 skipjack
state crustacean: 8 blue crab
state fish: 8 rockfish
state sport: 8 jousting
state tree: 3 oak **8** white oak
zone: 3 EDT, EST
Maryland Heights: 4 city, town
locale: 8 Missouri
Mary Lincoln, __ Todd: 3 née
Mary Lou: 6 Retton
__ Mary Lou: 5 Hello
Mary-Louise: 6 Parker
Mary Magdalene: 5 saint
Mary Mapes __: 5 Dodge
Mary McLeod __: 7 Bethune
Mary Montagu: 4 Lady
Mary Noble, Backstage Wife: 9 radio show
Mary of __: 4 Teck
Mary of Scotland (1936 film)
cast: Florence Eldridge, Katharine Hepburn, Fredric March
director: John Ford
Mary of Scotland author: Maxwell Anderson
__ Mary pass: 4 Hail
Mary Poppins: 4 film **5** novel
author: P.L. Travers
cast: Julie Andrews, Glynis Johns, David Tomlinson, Dick Van Dyke
director: Robert Stevenson
song: Chim Chim Cheree
Mary, Queen of Scots (1971 film)
cast: Glenda Jackson, Patrick McGoohan, Vanessa Redgrave
director: Charles Jarrott
Mary Queen of Scots' son: 5 James
Mary Roberts __: 8 Rinehart
Mary's a Grand Old Name composer: 5 Cohan
Mary Stuart __: 9 Masterson
Marysville: 4 city, town
locale: 10 Washington
Mary Todd __: 7 Lincoln
Mary Tyler Moore Show, The (CBS sitcom)
cast: Edward Asner (Lou Grant)
Georgia Engel (Georgette Baxter)
Valerie Harper (Rhoda Morgenstern)
Ted Knight (Ted Baxter)
Cloris Leachman (Phyllis Lindstrom)
Gavin MacLeod (Murray Slaughter)
Mary Tyler Moore (Mary Richards)
Betty White (Sue Ann Nivens)
Lou Grant ex: Edie
setting: 9 Minnesota **11** Minneapolis
spinoff: Rhoda, Phyllis
station: WJM
Maryville: 4 city, town
locale: 9 Tennessee
marzipan: 5 candy
base: 6 almond
masa: 5 grain
Masai: 8 language
home: 5 Kenya **6** Africa **8** Tanzania
Masaka: 4 city, town
locale: 6 Uganda
Masaoka Shiki: 4 poet **8** Japanese
specialty: haiku
Masaya: 4 city, town **7** volcano
locale: 9 Nicaragua
masc.: 6 gender
not ~: 3 fem. **4** neut.
Mascagni, Pietro: 7 Italian **8** composer
work: Amica
Cavalleria Rusticana
Iris
Isabeau
Nero
Parisina
Pinotta
Silvano
Zanetto
mascara: 4 kohl **5** liner **6** makeup
applicator: 4 wand
apply ~: 6 darken
site: 4 brow, lash **7** eyebrow, eyelash
mascarpone: 6 cheese
Mascouche: 4 city, town
locale: 6 Canada, Québec
masculine: 4 male **5** macho, manly **6** gender, virile **7** mannish
principle: 4 yang **6** animus
masculinity: 8 machismo, maleness, virility **9** manliness
Masefield, John: 4 poet **7** British
work: Dauber
The Everlasting Mercy
Reynard the Fox
Salt-Water Ballads
The Tragedy of Nan
Masekela, Hugh: 9 trumpeter
homeland: South Africa
song: Grazing in the Grass (1968)
Maserati: 7 Ernesto
Maseru: 4 city, town **7** capital
locale: 7 Lesotho
mash: 3 pap **4** beat, pulp, wort **5** cream, crush, grind, pound, press, purée, smash, sqush **6** bruise, pestle, soften, squash, squish, squush **7** scrunch, squeeze, squoosh **8** levigate, macerate **9** pulverize
preceder: 4 mish
__ mash: 4 sour
__ Mash: 7 Monster
MASH (1970 film)
cast: Robert Duvall, Elliott Gould, Sally Kellerman, Tom Skerritt, Donald Sutherland
director: Robert Altman
MASH (CBS sitcom)
cast: Alan Alda (Capt. Hawkeye Pierce)
Gary Burghoff (Cpl. Walter Radar O'Reilly)
Mike Farrell (Capt. B.J. Hunnicutt)
Jamie Farr (Cpl. Maxwell Klinger)
Larry Linville (Maj. Frank Burns)
Harry Morgan (Col. Sherman Potter)
Wayne Rogers (Capt. Trapper John McIntyre)
McLean Stevenson (Lt. Col. Henry Blake)
David Ogden Stiers (Maj. Charles Winchester)
Loretta Swit (Maj. Margaret Hot Lips Houlihan)
cook: 4 Igor
drink: 4 Ne-Hi **7** martini
extra: 2 GI, MP **5** medic, nurse
hangout: Rosie's
Hawkeye's home: Maine
meal: 4 mess, Spam
nurse: 4 Able
protocol: 6 triage
Radar's drink: Nehi
Radar's home: Iowa
remove to a ~ maybe: 4 evac
setting: Korea
shelter: 4 tent
soldier: 3 ROK
vehicle: 4 jeep
mashed potato: 5 dance
Mashed Potato Time (1962 song)
artist: Dee Dee Sharp
masher: 4 roué **5** flirt, ogler **6** pestle
comeuppance: 4 slap
expression: 4 leer
Masherbrum: 4 peak **5** mount **8** mountain
locale: 4 Asia **5** India **9** Himalayas
Mashhad: 4 city, town
locale: 4 Iran
mashie: 4 club, iron **8** golf club
Mashona: 3 cow **4** bull **6** bovine, cattle
home: 6 Africa **8** Zimbabwe **10** Mozambique
mask: 3 air **4** hide, hood, loup, pose, veil, wrap **5** beard, blind, cache, cloak, couch, cover, front, guise, shade, visor, vizor **6** aspect, domino, facade, screen, veneer **7** conceal, cover up, obscure, posture, pretext, secrete, shut off, shut out **8** disguise, pretense **9** dissemble, false face, semblance **10** appearance, camouflage, false front
part: 4 slit **7** eyehole
starter: 4 face
the smell of: 6 purify **7** freshen, sweeten **8** sanitize **9** deodorize
wearer: 5 Robin, Zorro **6** Batman **10** Lone Ranger
__ mask: 3 gas, ski **4** face, swim **6** oxygen, shadow
Mask (1985 film)
cast: Cher, Sam Elliott, Eric Stoltz
director: Peter Bogdanovich
masked: 6 covert, hidden, larval, secret, unseen **7** furtive, larvate, private **8** hush-hush **9** incognito, unexposed **10** undercover, under wraps
critter: 4 coon **7** raccoon
man: 6 bandit
masked __: 4 ball
Masked Ball, A aria: 5 Eri tu
Masked Man companion: 5 Tonto
masking __: 4 tape **5** frame, piece
Mask of Dimitrios, The: 4 film **5** novel
author: Eric Ambler
cast: Sydney Greenstreet, Peter Lorre, Zachary Scott
director: Jean Negulesco
Mask of Zorro, The (1998 film)
cast: Antonio Banderas, Anthony Hopkins, Stuart Wilson, Catherine Zeta-Jones
director: Martin Campbell
role: 5 Elena
Mask, The (1994 film)
cast: Jim Carrey, Cameron Diaz, Peter Greene, Peter Riegert
director: Charles Russell
Mask, The author: Dean Koontz
mason: 7 builder **10** bricklayer
device: 3 hod **4** shim **6** trowel
helper: 6 hodman
name meaning ~: 5 Dyker
starter: 4 free **5** stone
mason __: 3 bee, jar **4** wasp
Mason: 3 A.E.W. **4** city, Dave, town **5** Adams, James, Perry, Reese, Weems **6** Daniel, Jackie, Marsha, Pamela **7** Barbara **8** Williams
locale: 4 Ohio
partner: 4 Legg
Mason __: 3 jar
Mason-__ line: 5 Dixon
Mason, A.E.W.: 6 writer **7** British
work: The Four Feathers
Mason, Barbara song: Yes, I'm Ready (1965)
Mason City: 4 town
locale: 4 Iowa
Mason-Dixon
below the ~ line: 5 south
Masonic doorkeeper: 5 tiler
Mason, James: 5 actor

film: 11 Harrowhouse (1974)
20,000 Leagues Under the Sea (1954)
5 Fingers (1952)
Bigger Than Life (1956)
Caught (1949)
Cross of Iron (1977)
Cry Terror (1958)
The Deadly Affair (1967)
The Desert Fox (1951)
The Desert Rats (1953)
The Destructors (1974)
The Fall of the Roman Empire (1964)
ffolkes (1980)
Georgy Girl (1966)
Journey to the Center of the Earth (1959)
Julius Caesar (1953)
The Last of Sheila (1973)
Lolita (1962)
Lord Jim (1965)
Madame Bovary (1949)
North by Northwest (1959)
Odd Man Out (1947)
The Pumpkin Eater (1964)
The Reckless Moment (1949)
The Seventh Veil (1945)
The Shooting Party (1984)
Spring and Port Wine (1970)
A Star Is Born (1954)
A Touch of Larceny (1959)
The Upturned Glass (1947)
The Verdict (1982)
role: 4 Nemo 5 Maine
Mason jar topper: 3 lid
Mason, Marsha: 7 actress
film: Cinderella Liberty (1973)
The Goodbye Girl (1977)
Heartbreak Ridge (1986)
Max Dugan Returns (1983)
Only When I Laugh (1981)
spouse: Neil Simon
Mason, Perry: 3 att. 4 atty. 6 lawyer 8 attorney
assistant: 4 Paul 5 Della, Drake 6 Street 9 Paul Drake
creator: Erle Stanley Gardner
job for ~: 4 case
opponent: 6 Berger
profession: 3 law
masonry: 5 trade
face with ~: 5 revet
starter: 4 free 5 stone
stone: 6 ashlar, ashler
___ masqué: 3 bal
Masque of Alfred, The composer: 4 Arne
Masque of the Red Death, The (1964 film)
author: Edgar Allan Poe
cast: Jane Asher, Hazel Court, Vincent Price
director: Roger Corman
masquerade: 3 act 4 pose 5 cloak, front, guise, put on, revel 6 domino, dupery, facade, fake it 7 costume, cover-up, mummery, posture, pretend, pretext 8 carnival, disguise, pretense 9 deception, dissemble, festivity, imposture, Mardi Gras 10 camouflage, impression
wear: 3 wig 6 domino
Masquerade (1988 film)
cast: Kim Cattrall, Rob Lowe, Meg Tilly
director: Bob Swaim
___ Masquerade: 4 This
masquerader: 8 baccanal, imposter, impostor
mass: 3 gob, lot, mob, wad 4 blob, body, bulk, cake, clot, glob, heap, heft, herd, host, hunk, knot, load, lump, pile, rite, ruck, size 5 batch, block, bunch, chunk, clump, crowd, flock, group, hoard, horde, mound, press, shock, stack, swarm, total, troop 6 gather, gobbet, huddle, jungle, legion, matter, number, rabble, throng, volume, weight 7 cluster, collect, pyramid 8 assemble, majority, mountain, quantity 9 aggregate, amplitude, bulkiness, congeries, gathering, great deal, heaviness, immensity, largeness, multitude, plurality, profusion, stockpile, wholesale 10 accumulate, collection, concretion, cumulation, large-scale, lion's share
combining form: 5 cumul- 6 cumuli-, cumulo-
unit: 3 mol 4 gram, kilo 8 kilogram
mass ___: 3 man 4 noun 5 media 6 defect, number 7 meeting, society, transit, wasting
mass-___: 6 market 7 produce
mass-___ paperback: 6 market
___ mass: 3 air 4 blue, folk, hard, high, land, rest 5 solar 6 active, atomic 7 missing, nuptial, reduced
Mass
composer: 4 Bach 9 Bernstein
exclamation ~: 4 amen 7 hosanna 10 hallelujah
like ~ music: 6 choral
part of the ~: 5 canon
place: 5 abbey, altar 6 chapel, church 9 cathedral
plate: 5 paten
seating: 3 pew
vestment: 3 alb 5 orale
see also Latin
Mass ___: 4 book, card 6 Appeal
Mass.
neighbor: 3 Atl. 4 Conn.
see also Massachusetts
___ Mass: 3 Low, Red 4 High, sung 6 Solemn, votive 7 Requiem
Massachusetts: 5 state
bay: 8 Buzzard's
cape: 3 Ann, Cod
capital: 6 Boston
city: 4 Lynn 5 Lenox, Salem, Truro 6 Agawam, Boston, Dedham, Lowell, Malden, Milton, Newton, Quincy, Revere, Saugus, Woburn 7 Amherst, Belmont, Beverly, Chelsea, Danvers, Everett, Gardner, Holyoke, Ipswich, Medford, Melrose, Methuen, Milford, Needham, Norwood, Peabody, Reading, Taunton, Waltham 8 Brockton, Chicopee, Franklin, Lawrence, Randolph, Stoneham, Weymouth 9 Arlington, Attleboro, Braintree, Brookline, Cambridge, Fall River, Fitchburg, Haverhill, Lexington, Wakefield, Watertown, Wellesley, Westfield, Worcester 10 Barnstable, Burlington, Framingham, Gloucester, Leominster, Marblehead, New Bedford, Pittsfield, Somerville, Wilmington, Winchester
Indian: 7 Nipmuck 9 Wampanoag
neighbor: 7 New York, Vermont
nickname: 8 Bay State
port: 9 Nantucket 10 New Bedford
school: 3 MIT 5 Regis, Tufts 6 Babson 7 Amherst, Harvard 9 Holy Cross, Radcliffe
start of ~ motto: 4 Ense
state bean: 8 navy bean
state bird: 9 chickadee
state building rock: 7 granite
state cat: 5 tabby
state fish: 3 cod
state flower: 9 mayflower
state game bird: 10 wild turkey
state gem: 9 rhodonite
state horse: 6 Morgan
state insect: 7 ladybug
state marine mammal: 10 right whale
state muffin: 10 corn muffin
state shell: 7 Neptune
state tree: 3 elm
Massachusetts ___: 3 Bay 6 ballot
Massachusetts ___ Company: 3 Bay
___ Massacre: 6 Boston
massage: 3 rub 4 edit 5 knead, touch 7 back rub, rolfing, rubbing, rub down 9 stimulate 10 manipulate
milieu: 3 spa 6 day spa 9 health spa
need: 3 oil 5 towel 6 hot oil
needing a ~: 4 achy 5 tense
target: 4 ache, kink
___ massage: 7 Swedish
Massapequa: 4 city, town
locale: 7 New York
Mass Appeal (1984 film)
cast: Charles Durning, Jack Lemmon
massé: 4 shot
masse, en: 6 bodily, wholly 8 in unison, mutually, together 10 altogether, completely
Massen: 3 Osa
Massena: 4 city, town
locale: 7 New York
Massenet, Jules: 6 French 8 composer
genre: 5 opera
work: Eve
Le Cid
Manon
Narcisse
Phèdre
Thaïs
Werther
masses: 3 mob 4 raff 5 crowd, reams 6 cattle, people, plenty, public, rabble, scores 7 legions 8 populace, riffraff 9 hoi polloi, multitude 10 lower class
one of the ~: 4 pleb 8 plebeian
masseur
see massage
masseuse employer: 6 day spa
Massey: 5 Ilona 7 Raymond
Massey, Raymond: 5 actor
film: Abe Lincoln in Illinois (1940)
Action in the North Atlantic (1943)
Arsenic and Old Lace (1944)
Desperate Journey (1942)
Drums (1938)
East of Eden (1955)
The Great Impostor (1961)
The Naked and the Dead (1958)
Possessed (1947)
The Scarlet Pimpernel (1935)
Seven Angry Men (1955)
Stairway to Heaven (1946)
Things to Come (1936)
TV: Dr. Kildare
___ Massif: 6 Vinson
Massillon: 4 city, town
locale: 4 Ohio
Mass in B Minor composer: 4 Bach
Massine, Léonide: 6 dancer 7 danseur
specialty: 6 ballet
Massinger, Philip: 7 British 10 playwright
work: A New Way to Pay Old Debts
massive: 3 big 4 huge, vast 5 beefy, bulky, giant, grand, great, gross, heavy, hefty, jumbo, large, thick 6 mighty 7 hulking, immense, mammoth, sizable, stately, titanic, weighty 8 colossal, enormous, gigantic, imposing, king-size, oversize, sizeable, towering, unwieldy, whapping, whopping 9 extensive, fantastic, Herculean, humongous, monstrous, overlarge, ponderous, unwieldly, walloping, whalelike 10 cumbersome, gargantuan, impressive, monumental, overweight, prodigious, stupendous, tremendous, voluminous
massiveness: 4 bulk 8 enormity 9 immensity
Masson, Paul: 7 vintner 9 winemaker
mass transit: 3 bus 5 train 6 subway
problem: 5 delay
Massy: 4 city, town
locale: 6 France
mast: 4 boom, pole, post, spar 5 mizen, stick, tower 6 mizzen, timber 7 spanker 8 flagpole
attachment: 4 gaff
bracket: 4 bibb
ender: 4 head
rope: 3 tye
starter: 3 top 4 main 5 mizen, royal 6 mizzen 7 foretop
support: 4 stay
mast ___: 3 bed 4 ball, band, cell, hasp 5 clamp, cloth, cover, house
___ mast: 4 pole 5 after, beech, block, lower, royal 7 built-up, Marconi, mooring, trysail
___-mast: 4 half
master: 3 ace, win 4 cram, guru, head, lick, lord, sage, whiz 5 adept, chief, grasp, learn, maven, mavin, owner, prime, ruler, study, swami, swamy, tutor 6 artist, bone up, defeat, expert, genius, old pro, pick up, pundit, reduce, savant, top dog, victor, wizard 7 artisan, artiste, captain, conquer, excel in, leading, maestro, major in, old hand, pedagog, skipper, supreme, teacher 8 champion, director, employer, foremost, governor, graduate, kingfish, original, overcome, overlord, overseer, virtuoso 9 abecedary, authority, chieftain, commander, conqueror, pedagogue, preceptor, principal, sovereign 10 commandant, comprehend, controller, instructor, journeyman, past master, subjugator, supervisor, taskmaster, understand
ender: 3 dom, ful 4 mind, ship, work 5 piece 6 singer
in Arabic: 5 saheb, sahib
of ceremonies: 4 host 5 emcee
starter: 3 pay, spy 4 band, brew, bush, head, jump, load, lock, over, post, ring, ship, task, yard 5 choir, drill, grand, house, scout, toast, whore 6 harbor, school 7 concert, harbour, quarter, station
master ___: 3 key 4 bath, file, hand, plan 5 alloy, class, mason, point 6 policy, stroke 7 bedroom, builder, mariner, workman
___ master: 3 old 4 past, task 5 scene, wagon 6 ballet, harbor, riding 7 harbour
Master ___ Game: 5 of the
master-at-___: 4 arms
Master Blaster (1980 song) artist: Stevie Wonder
Master Blaster, The: Joe Weider
Master Builder, The author: Henrik Ibsen
character: 4 Kaia, Knut 5 Aline, Fosli, Hilda 6 Brovik, Wangel 7 Halvard, Solness
MasterCard, use: 3 owe 6 charge
Master Class subject: 6 Callas
mastered, easily: 6 facile
masterful: 3 ace 4 able, deft, fine 5 adept, slick 6 adroit, au fait, clever, expert, habile, lordly, nimble, virile 7 capable, cunning, dynamic, skilled, trained 8 dextrous, forceful, graceful, resolute, seasoned, skillful, talented 9 competent, dexterous, efficient,

excellent, exquisite, first-rate, practiced, virtuosic **10** aggressive, consummate, proficient
Masterman Ready author: Frederick Marryat
Master Melvin: 3 Ott
mastermind: 3 ace **4** lead, plan, whiz **5** brain **6** brains, create, design, devise, direct, genius, invent, leader, manage **7** builder, creator, develop, dream up, egghead, execute, manager, planner, prodigy, thinker, think up **8** conceive, designer, director, Einstein, engineer, highbrow, kingfish, virtuoso **9** architect, commander, fashioner, organizer, originate, tactician **10** originator, strategist
Mastermind (1976 film)
cast: Bradford Dillman, Zero Mostel
Master Mosaic Workers, The author: George Sand
Master of __: 4 Arts **7** Science
Master of Ballantrae, The author: Robert Louis Stevenson
Master of the Game author: Sidney Sheldon
Master of the World (1961 film)
cast: Charles Bronson, Vincent Price
Master of the World, The author: Jules Verne
masterpiece: 3 gem **4** work **5** jewel **7** classic **8** treasure **9** specialty, work of art
Masterpiece (song) artist: Atlantic Starr, Temptations
Masterpiece Theatre network: 3 PBS
Master Pipers, The author: George Sand
master's: 6 degree
paper: 6 thesis
Masters, Edgar Lee: 4 poet **6** writer
work: Spoon River Anthology
Masters golf champs:
2004 - Phil Mickelson
2003 - Mike Weir
2002 - Tiger Woods
2001 - Tiger Woods
2000 - Vijay Singh
1999 - Jose Maria Olazabal
1998 - Mark O'Meara
1997 - Tiger Woods
1996 - Nick Faldo
1995 - Ben Crenshaw
1994 - Jose Maria Olazabal
1993 - Bernhard Langer
1992 - Fred Couples
1991 - Ian Woosnam
1990 - Nick Faldo
1989 - Nick Faldo
1988 - Sandy Lyle
1987 - Larry Mize
1986 - Jack Nicklaus
1985 - Bernhard Langer
1984 - Ben Crenshaw
1983 - Seve Ballesteros
1982 - Craig Stadler
1981 - Tom Watson
1980 - Seve Ballesteros
1979 - Fuzzy Zoeller
1978 - Gary Player
1977 - Tom Watson
1976 - Ray Floyd
1975 - Jack Nicklaus
1974 - Gary Player
1973 - Tommy Aaron
1972 - Jack Nicklaus
1971 - Charles Coody
1970 - Billy Casper
1969 - George Archer
1968 - Bob Goalby
1967 - Gay Brewer
1966 - Jack Nicklaus
1965 - Jack Nicklaus
1964 - Arnold Palmer
1963 - Jack Nicklaus
1962 - Arnold Palmer
1961 - Gary Player
1960 - Arnold Palmer
1959 - Art Wall
1958 - Arnold Palmer
1957 - Doug Ford
1956 - Jack Burke
1955 - Cary Middlecoff
1954 - Sam Snead
1953 - Ben Hogan
1952 - Sam Snead
1951 - Ben Hogan
1950 - Jimmy Demaret
1949 - Sam Snead
1948 - Claude Harmon
1947 - Jimmy Demaret
1946 - Herman Keiser
1943–1945 - NOT PLAYED
1942 - Byron Nelson
1941 - Craig Wood
1940 - Jimmy Demaret
1939 - Ralph Guldahl
1938 - Henry Picard
1937 - Byron Nelson
1936 - Horton Smith
1935 - Gene Sarazen
1934 - Horton Smith
Masterson: 3 Bat, Sky **5** Peter
colleague: 4 Earp
prop: 4 cane
Masterson, Mary Stuart: 7 actress
film: Benny & Joon (1993)
The Book of Stars (2000)
Chances Are (1989)
The Florentine (2000)
Fried Green Tomatoes (1991)
Gardens of Stone (1987)
Immediate Family (1989)
My Little Girl (1986)
Some Kind of Wonderful (1987)
Masterson, Mrs. Sky: 5 Sarah
Masters org.: 3 PGA
masterstroke: 4 coup
__ Master's Voice: 3 His
mastery: 3 art **4** grip **5** grasp, knack, power, reach, skill, touch **7** ability, command, control, finesse, know-how, prowess **8** artistry, deftness, hang of it **9** adeptness, dexterity, dominance, expertise **10** adroitness, ascendance, ascendancy, ascendence, ascendency, attainment, expertness, virtuosity
masthead listing: 3 eds. **5** staff **6** editor
mastic: 4 tree **5** resin
relative: 5 mango, sumac **6** cashew, fustet, sumach **9** pistachio
masticate: 3 eat **4** bite, chaw, chew, gnaw **5** graze, munch **6** chew on, crunch, gnaw on, nibble **7** munch on **8** crunch on, nibble on
mastiff: 3 dog **5** canid, pooch **6** canine
__ mastiff: 4 bull
mastodon: 6 animal **9** leviathan
mastoid __: 4 bone **7** process
Mastrantonio, Mary Elizabeth: 7 actress
film: The Abyss (1989)
Class Action (1991)
The Color of Money (1986)
Limbo (1999)
Robin Hood: Prince of Thieves (1991)
Scarface (1983)
White Sands (1992)
Mastroianni, Marcello: 8 director
costar: 5 Loren
film: 8 1/2 (1963)
Big Deal on Madonna Street (1958)
Dark Eyes (1987)
Divorce-Italian Style (1962)
La Dolce Vita (1960)
Yesterday, Today and Tomorrow (1964)
masts, change: 5 rerig
masu: 4 fish
Masur, Kurt: 9 conductor
mat: 3 pad **4** yapa **6** darken, tangle, tatami **7** cushion, zabuton **9** interlace
Buddhist sitting ~: 7 zabuton
go to the ~ for: 4 back **5** stake, vouch **7** endorse, promote, sponsor, support, warrant **8** champion **9** get behind **10** underwrite
Japanese: 6 tatami
place ~: 5 doily **6** doyley
South American ~: 4 yapa
starter: 4 bath, door
victory: 3 pin
__ mat: 6 mahala **7** welcome
Mata __: 4 Hari
Matabele: 5 Bantu
home: 6 Africa **8** Zimbabwe
Matadi: 4 city, port, town
locale: 3 Afr. **5** Congo **6** Africa
matador: 6 torero **8** toreador
cape color: 4 rojo
foe: 4 bull, toro **6** el toro
maneuver: 4 pase **5** faena
wear: 4 capa **6** bolero
Matador: 3 car **4** auto **5** Dodge **10** automobile
Mata Hari: 3 spy
Mata Hari (1932 film)
cast: Lionel Barrymore, Greta Garbo, Ramon Novarro
Matalin, Mary spouse: James Carville
Matamoros: 4 city, port, town
locale: 6 Mexico **8** Coahuila **10** Tamaulipas
Matanzas: 4 city, town
locale: 4 Cuba
Matapan: 4 cape
locale: 6 Greece
Mataram: 4 city, town
locale: 9 Indonesia
Matarese Circle, The author: Robert Ludlum
Matarese Countdown, The author: Robert Ludlum
match: 2 go **3** fit, pit, tie, vie **4** boot, bout, duel, even, game, gybe, jibe, mate, meet, pair, peer, race, sort, suit, twin **5** agree, equal, event, fight, fusee, fuzee, rival, tie up, union, vesta **6** beseem, couple, double, equate, mating, ringer, square, take on **7** compeer, conform, contest, lighter, lucifer, pairing, reflect, replica, rivalry **8** arsonist, coincide, dovetail, equalize, espousal, marriage, opponent, parallel, rank with, resemble **9** companion, correlate, duplicate, harmonize, look alike, matrimony **10** competitor, complement, coordinate, correspond, dead ringer, engagement, go together, keep up with, tournament
be a ~ for: 5 equal, rival
division: 3 set
don't ~: 5 clash **6** differ **8** disagree
end: 2 KO **3** TKO **4** kayo
ender: 3 box **4** book, lock, wood **5** board, maker, stick **6** making
make a ~: 3 wed
partner: 3 mix
prepare for a ~: 4 spar
put another ~ to: 5 relit
put a ~ to: 5 light **6** ignite, kindle, set off **8** enkindle
start a ~: 5 serve
up: 4 pair, test **5** unite
wrestling ~: 5 fight, round **6** tussle **7** contest **9** encounter
match __: 4 play **5** plate, point
__ match: 4 book, love, slow, test **5** paper **6** rubber, safety **7** kitchen, lucifer
__-match: 5 cross
matched: 5 equal, level **6** in sync **7** coequal
group: 3 set **4** pair, suit, team **5** suite
Match Game, The: 8 game show
host: Gene Rayburn
matching: 4 even, like, same, twin **5** level **6** on a par, paired **7** similar **8** parallel **9** analogous, duplicate, identical **10** comparable, equivalent, reciprocal
not ~: 3 odd
piece: 4 mate
matchless: 3 ace **4** best, only, rare, sole **5** alone, prime **6** superb, unique **7** optimum, perfect, supreme **8** peerless, splendid, superior **9** excellent, exquisite, nonpareil, topflight, unequaled, unmatched, unrivaled, virtuosic **10** consummate, inimitable, preeminent, unequalled, unexampled, unrivalled
matchmaker: 4 Amor, Eros **5** Cupid **9** go-between
Matchmaker, The: 4 film, play
author: Thornton Wilder
cast: Shirley Booth, Shirley MacLaine, Anthony Perkins
director: Joseph Anthony
matchsticks game: 3 nim
mate: 3 bro, pal, wed **4** ally, chum, join, papa, peer, twin, wife **5** bride, buddy, crony, groom, hubby, marry, match **6** cohort, defeat, double, frater, friend, helper, missis, missus, mister, splice, spouse **7** coequal, comrade, consort, mariner, partner **8** alter ego, confrere, coworker, deckhand, familiar, helpmate, intimate, playmate, roommate, sidekick **9** assistant, associate, classmate, colleague, companion, duplicate **10** bridegroom, complement, coordinate, schoolmate, tie the knot
starter: 3 bed **4** bunk, case, cell, crew, help, mess, play, room, seat, ship, team **5** check, class, house, stale, table **6** litter, school
__ mate: 4 soul **5** chief, first, third **6** second **7** running
maté: 8 beverage
__ maté: 5 yerba
__ Mate: 5 Paper
Matehuala: 4 city, town
locale: 6 Mexico
matelassé: 6 fabric **8** material
mateless: 3 odd **8** unpaired **10** unattached
matelot: 3 gob, tar **4** salt **6** sailor **7** jack tar
Matelot author: Pierre Loti
matelote: 4 stew **8** fish stew
__ Mateo, CA: 3 San
Mateo in English: 7 Matthew
mater: 5 mumsy
mate: 5 pater
__ mater: 3 pia **4** alma, dura **5** terra
__ Mater: 5 Magna, Terra **6** Stabat
materia __: 6 medica
material: 3 key **4** bolt, data, felt, fuel, gear, real, text **5** ad rem, cloth, facts, frisé, goods, lisse, notes, solid, stock, stuff, thing, wares **6** actual, fabric, matter, ratiné, supply **7** apropos, earthly, element, fleshly, germane, telling, textile, worldly, worsted **8** apposite, concrete, jacquard, physical, relevant, tangible, temporal **9** commodity, component, corporeal, essential, grosgrain, important, momentous, pertinent, substance, touchable **10** applicable, ingredient, phenomenal, unimagined
building ~: 4 wood **5** adobe, brick, steel **6** cement, stucco
foil ~: 8 aluminum

foundation ~: 8 concrete
golf-course ~: 4 lawn, turf 5 grass, sward
goods: 9 resources
introductory ~: 6 basics
jacket ~: 7 leather
organic ~: 5 mulch 7 compost 10 fertilizer
outfield ~: 4 turf 5 grass
raw ~: 3 ore
sample: 4 snip 6 swatch
suffix: 3 -ine
see also fabric
material __: 5 cause 7 culture
__ material: 3 raw 6 source
Material Girl (1985 song) artist: Madonna
materialistic: 6 greedy 7 mundane, profane, secular, worldly 8 banausic, temporal
materiality: 7 reality
materialization: 8 fruition
materialize: 3 pop 4 come, form, show 5 bob up, occur, reify 6 appear, embody, emerge, evolve, happen, imbody, turn up, unfold 7 develop, realize, surface 8 coalesce, manifest, take form 9 actualize, come about, take place, take shape
materials: 5 goods, order 8 supplies
__ materials: 3 raw
matériel: 4 ammo, arms, guns 6 outfit, tackle 7 cannons, weapons 8 ordnance, weaponry 9 armaments, artillery, firepower, machinery, munitions 10 ammunition
issue ~: 3 arm
maternal: 4 kind, warm 6 caring, gentle, tender 7 devoted 8 motherly, parental 10 protective
kin: 5 enate
__ maternelle: 5 école
maternity: 10 motherhood, parenthood
ward stat: 2 wt. 3 hgt. 4 lgth. 6 height, length, weight
maternity __: 4 ward 5 leave
Maté, Rudolph: 8 director
film: The Dark Past (1948)
D.O.A. (1950)
No Sad Songs for Me (1950)
When Worlds Collide (1951)
mates: 4 pair
former ~: 4 exes
Matewan (1987 film)
cast: Chris Cooper, Mary McDonnell, Will Oldham
director: John Sayles
matey: 3 pal 4 Brit
matgrass: 4 nard
__ math: 3 new 5 fuzzy
mathematical: 9 algebraic, numerical
relation: 8 equation, fraction
mathematical __: 5 logic
mathematician: 4 Omar, Venn 5 Euler, Gauss 6 Kepler, Napier, Newton, Pascal 7 Doppler, Laplace, Ptolemy 8 Lagrange 9 Whitehead 10 Archimedes, Pythagoras
Austrian ~: 7 Doppler
British ~: 6 Newton 7 Russell 9 Whitehead
Egyptian ~: 7 Ptolemy
French ~: 6 Pascal 7 Laplace 8 Lagrange
German ~: 5 Gauss 6 Kepler
Greek ~: 10 Pythagoras
letters: 3 QED
Persian ~: 4 Omar
Scottish ~: 6 Napier
starter: 4 meta
Swiss ~: 5 Euler
mathematics: 3 alg. 4 calc., geom., trig 5 arith. 7 algebra, geodesy 8 calculus, geometry 10 arithmetic
abbr.: 3 div., exp., GCD, iff, LCD, lim., pct., QED 5 recip.
concept: 2 pi 3 set 5 limit, ratio 10 reciprocal
do ~: 3 add 5 graph 6 divide 8 multiply, subtract 9 calculate
expression: 4 is to
rule: 3 law 5 axiom 9 postulate
work: 4 area 5 proof
__ mathematics: 6 higher
Mather: 6 Cotton 8 Increase
Mathers: 5 Jerry
Matheson: 3 Tim 7 Richard
Mathew: 5 Brady
Mathews: 5 Eddie, Larry 6 Kerwin
Mathews, Eddie: 5 Brave
Mathews, Kerwin: 5 actor
film: The 3 Worlds of Gulliver (1960)
The 7th Voyage of Sinbad (1958)
Jack the Giant Killer (1962)
Man on a String (1960)
Mathewson, Christy: 5 Giant 6 hurler 7 pitcher
Mathias, Bob: 10 decathlete
Mathilde: 8 asteroid
Mathis: 6 Johnny 8 Samantha
Mathis, Johnny
song: Call Me (1958)
A Certain Smile (1958)
Chances Are (1957)
Come to Me (1958)
Gina (1962)
It's Not for Me to Say (1957)
Misty (1959)
Too Much, Too Little, Too Late (1978)
The Twelfth of Never (1957)
What Will Mary Say (1963)
Wonderful! Wonderful! (1957)
Mathison, Melissa spouse: Harrison Ford
Matías Romero: 4 city, town
locale: 6 Mexico, Oaxaca
matin: 6 French 7 morning
opposite: 4 soir
matinal period: 4 morn 7 morning
Matineau, Harriet: 6 writer 7 British
matinée: 4 show 9 reception
time: 3 aft. 9 afternoon
matinée __: 4 idol
Matinee (1993 film)
cast: Simon Fenton, John Goodman, Cathy Moriarty
director: Joe Dante
mating: 5 match 8 marriage
game: 5 chess
Mating Game, The (1959 film)
cast: Paul Douglas, Tony Randall, Debbie Reynolds
director: George Marshall
Mating Season, The (1951 film)
cast: Miriam Hopkins, John Lund, Gene Tierney
director: Mitchell Leisen
matins: 4 hour 7 worship
Matinson, Harry: 6 writer 7 Swedish
work: Cape Farewell
The Road
Matisse: 4 font 5 Henri 8 typeface
Matisse, Henri: 6 artist 7 painter
homeland: 6 France
medium for ~: 3 oil
piece: 3 art 8 painting
matjes __: 7 herring
matka: 4 seal
Matlin, Marlee Oscar: Children of a Lesser God
Matlock: 3 Ben
job: 3 att. 4 atty. 6 lawyer 8 attorney
matter: 4 case
org.: 3 ABA
Matlock (NBC/ABC drama)
cast: Andy Griffith (Ben Matlock)
setting: Atlanta, Georgia
Matlock Paper, The author: Robert Ludlum
Mato __: 6 Grosso
matriarch: 5 elder 6 female, granny, senior 7 grannie 10 forebearer
matriarchal: 6 lineal
kin: 5 enate
matriculate: 4 join 5 begin, enrol, enter, learn 6 enroll, record, sign up 8 register
matrimonial: 6 bridal, wedded 7 marital, nuptial, spousal 8 conjugal 9 connubial
hopeful: 5 swain, wooer
matrimony: 5 match, union 7 wedding, wedlock 8 alliance, marriage, nuptials 9 sacrament
commit ~: 3 wed 5 marry
__ Matrimony: 4 Holy
matrix: 4 cast, grid, mold 5 array 6 origin, source
Matrix: 3 car 4 auto 6 Toyota 10 automobile
__-matrix printer: 3 dot
Matrix, The (1999 film)
cast: Laurence Fishburne, Carrie-Anne Moss, Keanu Reeves
character: 3 Neo
matron: 3 Mrs. 4 dame, lady, wife 5 woman 6 female 10 noblewoman
matron of __: 5 honor
Mats: 8 Wilander
Matson: 5 Ollie
Matsudo: 4 city, town
locale: 5 Japan
Matsue: 4 city, town
locale: 5 Japan
matsu-take: 6 fungus 8 Japanese
Matt: 4 Helm 5 Damon, Lauer, Stone 6 Biondi, Dillon, Drudge, Frewer 7 Houston, Keeslar, LeBlanc 8 Groening, Lattanzi
matte: 4 dull, flat 10 lusterless
matte __: 4 shot
Mattea: 5 Kathy
matted: 5 kinky 7 knotted, rumpled, snarled, tangled, tousled, twisted 8 uncombed
Matteo in English: 7 Matthew
matter: 3 job 4 body, mass, text, to-do 5 being, count, issue, sense, stuff, thing, topic, weigh, worry 6 affair, affect, cut ice, entity, regard 7 content, episode, problem, project, purport, reality, trouble 8 argument, business, elements, incident, interest, material, question, sediment 9 grievance, situation, substance 10 difficulty, phenomenon, protoplasm
as a ~ of fact: 5 truly 6 really 7 in truth 8 actually 9 in reality
at hand: 3 job 5 theme, topic 7 subject
bit of ~: 4 atom
combining form: 3 hyl- 4 hylo-
foreign ~: 5 taint
gray ~: 4 head, mind 5 brain 9 mentality
heart of the ~: 3 nub 4 crux, gist, knub 5 nexus, point
in the ~ of: 4 as to 5 about, as for
laughing ~: 3 fun, wit 4 gags 5 farce, jests, jokes 6 comedy, gaiety, levity 8 drollery, raillery 10 wisecracks
no ~: 6 drop it 8 forget it 9 never mind
no laughing ~: 3 bad, big 4 grim, ugly 5 grave, heavy, major, tough 6 urgent 7 weighty 8 grievous, sobering, terrible 9 dangerous, important 10 formidable
no ~ what: 5 still 6 anyhow, anyway 9 at any rate 10 in any event, regardless
science of ~: 7 physics
starter: 4 anti
state of ~: 3 gas 5 solid 6 liquid
to, old-style: 4 reck
use the gray ~: 5 think 6 ideate, reason
worthless ~: 5 dregs 6 debris, refuse 7 rubbish
matter __: 4 wave 5 of law
__ matter: 3 end 4 back, dark, dead, foul, gray, grey 5 front, white 7 print-ed, subject
Matterhorn: 3 alp, mtn. 4 peak 5 mount 8 mountain
echo: 5 yodel, yodle
locale: 4 Alps 6 Europe 11 Switzerland
matter of __: 3 law 4 fact 6 course, record
matter-of-course: 5 usual
matter-of-fact: 4 calm, cool 5 blunt, brusk, frank, plain, stoic 6 abrupt, candid, direct, honest, stolid 7 brusque, factual, prosaic, stoical 8 accurate, impolite, sensible, tactless 9 objective, outspoken, practical, pragmatic, prosaical, realistic 10 indelicate
__ matter of fact: 3 as a
Matter of Fact columnist: 5 Alsop
matter-of-factly: 6 simply
Matter of Trust, A (1986 song) artist: Billy Joel
matters: 6 doings 7 affairs 8 dealings
Matthau, Walter: 5 actor
film: The Bad News Bears (1976)
Buddy Buddy (1981)
Cactus Flower (1969)
California Suite (1978)
Charade (1963)
Charley Varrick (1973)
A Face in the Crowd (1957)
Fail-Safe (1964)
The Fortune Cookie (1966, AA)
The Front Page (1974)
The Grass Harp (1996)
Grumpier Old Men (1995)
Grumpy Old Men (1993)
A Guide for the Married Man (1967)
Hanging Up (2000)
Hello, Dolly! (1969)
Hopscotch (1980)
House Calls (1978)
The Indian Fighter (1955)
I.Q. (1994)
JFK (1991)
Kotch (1971)
Lonely Are the Brave (1962)
Mirage (1965)
A New Leaf (1971)
The Odd Couple (1968)
Out to Sea (1997)
Plaza Suite (1971)
The Sunshine Boys (1975)
The Taking of Pelham One Two Three (1974)
Matthew: 3 Fox 5 Perry, saint 6 Arnold, Garber, Modine, Wilder 8 Flinders 9 Broderick
follower: 4 Mark
in Italian: 6 Matteo
in Spanish: 5 Mateo
original name: 4 Levi
Matthews: 4 city, Dave, town
locale: 4 N. Car.
Matthews Band, Dave song: Crash Into Me (1997)
Matthiessen, Peter: 6 author, writer
work: At Play in the Fields of the Lord
Blue Meridian
The Cloud Forest
Far Tortuga
Men's Lives
Sand Rivers

The Snow Leopard
Under the Mountain Wall
Matt Houston (ABC adventure)
cast: Pamela Hensley (C.J. Parsons)
Lee Horsley (Matt Houston)
Mattingly: 3 Don
Matto __: 6 Grosso
mattock: 4 tool
use a ~: 3 dig
mattress: 3 bed, pad 5 futon
brand: 5 Sealy, Serta 7 Simmons
category: 4 firm, hard 9 extra-firm, super-firm
covering: 3 pad 5 sheet
filling: 3 air 5 kapok
in England: 4 lilo
on the ~: 4 abed 8 sleeping
part: 4 coil 6 spring 7 ticking
problem: 4 lump
support: 4 slat 9 box spring
__ mattress: 3 air
Matty: 4 Alou
brother: 5 Jesus 6 Felipe
maturate: 4 grow 5 ripen 7 develop
maturation: 6 growth 9 evolution, expansion, gestation
mature: 3 age, big, old 4 aged, form, grow, ripe 5 adult, bloom, grown, of age, owing, ready, ripen 6 arrive, evolve, flower, grow up, mellow, season, trusty, unfold, unpaid 7 advance, blossom, come due, develop, fill out, grown-up, payable, perfect, ripened, settled, shoot up, vintage 8 complete, cultured, full-size, incubate, mellowed, mushroom, progress, seasoned 9 come of age, culminate, developed, full-blown, full-grown 10 fully grown, precocious, settle down
into: 6 become
not ~: 5 green, young
Mature, Victor: 5 actor
film: Easy Living (1949)
Footlight Serenade (1942)
I Wake Up Screaming (1941)
Kiss of Death (1947)
Million Dollar Mermaid (1952)
My Darling Clementine (1946)
My Gal Sal (1942)
Samson and Delilah (1949)
Song of the Islands (1942)
Violent Saturday (1955)
Wabash Avenue (1950)
Maturin, Charles Robert: 5 Irish 6 writer
work: Melmoth the Wanderer
maturing agent: 4 ager
maturity: 5 prime 6 wisdom 7 manhood 8 fruition, fullness, majority, ripeness 9 adulthood, readiness, stability, womanhood 10 completion, experience, perfection
Matute, Ana María: 6 writer 7 Spanish
matzo __: 4 ball, brei, meal 6 farfel
matzo ball __: 4 soup
matzoh: 5 bread
lack: 5 yeast 9 leavening
meal with ~: 5 seder
Mauá: 4 city, town
locale: 6 Brazil
Mauch: 4 Gene 5 Billy, Bobby
Maud: 5 Adams
Maud __: 6 Martha, Muller
Maud author: Alfred Tennyson
Maude (CBS sitcom)
cast: Bea Arthur (Maude Findlay)
Conrad Bain (Arthur Harman)
Adrienne Barbeau (Carol Findlay)
Bill Macy (Walter Findlay)
Rue McClanahan (Vivian Harman)
producer: Norman Lear
__ + Maude: 5 Micki
__ Maud Land: 5 Queen
maudlin: 4 weak 5 gooey, gushy, mushy, sappy, soppy, teary, weepy 6 sirupy, slushy, syrupy 7 cloying, insipid, mawkish, tearful 8 bathetic, cornball, romantic, schmalzy, shmaltzy 9 schmaltzy, sniveling 10 lachrymose
Maud Martha author: Gwendolyn Brooks
__ Maud Montgomery: 4 Lucy
Maud Muller author: John Greenleaf Whittier
Maugham, W. Somerset: 6 author, writer 7 British
work: Cakes and Ale
The Circle
The Constant Wife
Hero, The
Miss Thompson
The Moon and Sixpence
Of Human Bondage
Our Betters
Rain
The Razor's Edge
Maui: 3 isl. 4 isle 6 island
locale: 6 Hawaii
neighbor: 5 Lanai
maul: 3 hit, paw 4 bash, beat, claw, drub, hurt, maim 5 abuse, paste, pound 6 bang up, batter, beat up, bruise, injure, mangle, misuse, pummel, savage, thrash 7 rough up, trample, trounce 8 bludgeon, ill-treat, lacerate, maltreat, mistreat, work over 9 mishandle 10 knock about, take care of
ender: 5 stick
Mauldin: 4 Bill
mauling: 5 abuse
Maumee: 5 river
locale: 4 Ohio 7 Indiana
Mauna __: 3 Kea, Loa
Mauna Loa: 7 volcano
locale: 4 Hilo 6 Hawaii
maunder: 3 yak 4 roam, rove 5 run on, stray 6 babble, mumble, ramble, wander 7 chatter 8 ramble on
maundering: 10 incoherent
maundy money: 4 alms
Maupassant, Guy de: 6 author, French, writer
work: The Necklace
The Umbrella
Maupin: 9 Armistead
Mauprat author: George Sand
Maura: 7 Tierney 8 Jacobson
Maure: 3 cow 4 bull 6 bovine, cattle
Maureen: 5 O'Hara 8 Connolly, McGovern 9 McCormick, O'Sullivan, Stapleton
daughter: 3 Mia
Mauriac, François: 6 French, writer 8 Nobelist
work: Asmodée
The Desert of Love
Genitrix
God and Mammon
Vipers' Tangle
A Woman of the Pharisees
Mauriat and His Orchestra, Paul
homeland: France
song: Love Is Blue (1968)
Maurice: 4 Gibb 5 Evans, Jarre, Ravel, saint, Scève 6 Allais, Barrès, Béjart, Sendak 7 Leblanc, Richard, Utrillo, Wilkins 8 Williams 9 Chevalier
see also French
Mauritania: 6 nation 7 country
bovine: 5 Maure
capital: 10 Nouakchott
desert: 6 Sahara
group: 10 Arab League
neighbor: 4 Mali 7 Algeria, Senegal
people: 4 Fula 6 Fulani
Mauritanian: 4 Arab
Mauritius: 4 isle 6 island, nation 7 country
bird, once: 4 dodo
capital: 9 Port Louis
money: 4 cent 5 rupee
Maurois, André: 6 French, writer 10 biographer
work: Ariel
Disraeli
The Family Circle
Prometheus
The Silence of Colonel Bramble
The Titans
Maury: 5 Wills 6 Povich
mauve: 4 plum 5 color, lilac 6 bluish, purple, violet 7 blueish 8 lavender
relative: 4 plum, puce 5 lilac 6 dahlia, damson, orchid 7 heather, petunia 8 amethyst, burgundy, eggplant, lavender, mulberry 9 raspberry 10 heliotrope
mauve __: 6 decade
Mauve Gloves & Madmen, Clutter & Vine author: Tom Wolfe
Mav
see Maverick
maven: 3 pro 4 buff, guru, whiz 6 expert, master 8 virtuoso 9 authority, know-it-all 10 specialist
maverick: 4 calf 5 leppy, loner, rebel, stray 7 heretic, oddball, radical 8 newcomer, renegade, ultraist 9 dissenter, protester 10 iconoclast, malcontent
Maverick: 3 car 4 auto, Bart, Bret, Ford 10 automobile
rival: 3 Net, Sun 4 Buck, Bull, Hawk, Heat, Jazz, King, Spur 5 Knick, Laker, Magic, Pacer, Sixer 6 Celtic, Hornet, Nugget, Piston, Raptor, Rocket, Wizard 7 Clipper, Grizzly, Warrior 8 Cavalier 10 SuperSonic, Timberwolf
Maverick (1994 film)
cast: Jodie Foster, James Garner, Mel Gibson
director: Richard Donner
Maverick (ABC western)
cast: James Garner (Bret Maverick)
Jack Kelly (Bart Maverick)
Maverick Queen, The author: Zane Grey
Mavericks: 4 five, team
home: 5 Texas 6 Dallas
org.: 3 NBA
sport: 10 basketball
mavin
see maven
mavis: 4 bird 6 thrush 8 songbird
Mavis: 7 Gallant
Má Vlast composer: 7 Smetana
mavourneen: 2 jo 3 pet 4 baby, dear, jill, love 5 amour, angel, chéri, cooky, cutey, cutie, deary, ducky, flame, honey, leman, lover, lovey, novia, novio, sugar, sweet 6 bon ami, chérie, cookie, dautie, dearie, steady, sweets 7 beloved, dearest, dear one, pigsney, schatzi, squeeze, sweetie, tootsie 8 chou-chou, cutie pie, dowsabel, dulcinea, ladylove, lovebird, macushla, paramour, precious, snookums, sugar pie, sweetums, truelove 9 bonne amie, boyfriend, dreamboat, inamorata, inamorato, petit chou, valentine 10 girlfriend, heartthrob, honeybunch, sweetheart, sweetie pie, turtledove
home: 4 Eire, Erin 7 Ireland
maw: 4 craw, crop, hole 5 chops, mouth 6 gullet, throat 7 gizzard, stomach
partner: 3 paw
mawkish: 5 corny, gooey, gushy, hokey, mushy, sappy, soppy, teary 6 drippy, feeble, sickly, sirupy, sloppy, syrupy 7 cloying, gushing, maudlin 8 bathetic, schmalzy, shmaltzy 9 emotional, schmaltzy 10 lovey-dovey, saccharine
mawkishness: 4 corn, glop, mush 5 slush 6 bathos
mawl: 9 manhandle
__ Mawr: 4 Bryn
Mawson, Douglas: 8 explorer 10 Australian
max: 4 most 5 limit 8 ultimate 10 upper limit
out: 4 peak
to the ~: 6 all-out
max __: 3 out
max.: 3 lim., lmt.
factor: 3 GCD
opposite: 3 min.
__ max: 5 to the
Max: 3 Aub 4 Baer, Born, Euwe, Gail 5 Brand, Bruch, Ernst, Jacob, Peter, Roach, Weber 6 Factor, Frisch, Lerner, Morath, Ophuls, Perutz, Planck, Rudolf 7 Eastman, Klinger, Shulman, Steiner, Theiler, von Laue 8 Beckmann, Beerbohm, Delbrück, Pomeranc, Schuster, von Sydow 9 Fleischer, Schmeling 10 Bialystock, Liebermann
Max __ Returns: 5 Dugan
__ Max: 3 Mad
Max and the White Phagocytes author: Henry Miller
Max author: Howard Fast
Maxcanú: 4 city, town
locale: 6 Mexico 7 Yucatán
Max Dugan Returns (1983 film)
cast: Marsha Mason, Jason Robards, Donald Sutherland
director: Herbert Ross
Maxene: 7 Andrews
sister: 5 Patty 7 LaVerne
Max Factor: 6 makeup
alternative: 4 Avon 5 Almay 6 Revlon 7 Lancome, Mary Kay 8 Clinique 9 Cover Girl 10 Maybelline 11 Estée Lauder, Merle Norman
maxi: 4 coat 5 skirt 9 extra-long
make a ~: 5 rehem
terminus: 5 ankle
Maxie: 10 Rosenbloom
Maxie (1985 film)
cast: Glenn Close, Ruth Gordon, Barnard Hughes, Mandy Patinkin
director: Paul Aaron
maxilla: 3 jaw 4 bone 7 jawbone
maxim: 3 law, saw 4 rule 5 adage, axiom, moral, motto, truth 6 belief, byword, dictum, phrase, saying, truism 7 precept, proverb 8 aphorism, laconism 9 catchword, platitude, principle
like a ~: 5 pithy
Maxim: 5 Gorki, Gorky
Maxim __: 3 gun
Maxima: 3 car 4 auto, font 6 Nissan 8 typeface 10 automobile
maximal: 6 utmost 7 maximum, topmost
maximally: 6 at best, at most
Maximilian: 6 Schell
maximum: 3 cap, nth, top, ult. 4 apex, full, most, peak 5 crest, limit 6 all-out, apogee, climax, height, record, summit, utmost, zenith 7 biggest, ceiling, highest, largest, optimum, outside, supreme, topmost 8 greatest, pinnacle, ultimate 9 uttermost 10 upper limit
number: 5 quota
reach a ~: 4 peak
Maximus, Circus: 5 arena
Maximus Poems, The author: Charles Olson
Maxine: 5 Kumin
Maxwell: 3 AFB, car 4 auto, Elsa, Lois

5 Gavin, Shane, Smart 7 Marilyn 8 Anderson 9 Bodenheim, Caulfield
contemporary: 3 Reo
Don Adams' ~: 5 Smart
nanny: 4 Fran
Maxwell House: 6 coffee
alternative: 5 Sanka, Yuban 7 Folgers, Melitta, Nescafe, Savarin 9 Hills Bros.
Maxwell, James Clerk: 8 Scottish 9 physicist
Maxwell, Marilyn: 7 actress
film: Champion (1949)
The Lemon Drop Kid (1951)
Lost in a Harem (1944)
Rock-a-Bye Baby (1958)
may: 5 might
be that as it ~: 6 anyhow, anyway, even so 7 however
come what ~: 6 surely 7 somehow 10 in any event
ender: 3 day, fly, hap, pop 4 pole, weed 6 flower
may ___: 4 tree 5 apple
May: 3 Joe 4 cape, Phil 5 Brian, Britt, month 6 Elaine, McAvoy, Robson, Sarton, Whitty 7 Swenson
birthstone: 5 agate 7 emerald
ender: 4 pole
event, familiarly: 4 Indy
follower: 3 Jun. 4 June
honoree: 3 mom 6 mother
in French: 3 Mai
in Spanish: 4 mayo
preceder: 3 Apr. 5 April
sign: 4 Bull 5 Twins 6 Gemini, Taurus
May ___: 3 Day 4 wine 5 apple, queen 6 beetle
May ___ to You: 5 I Sing
May ___ you?: 5 I help
___ May: 3 If I 4 Cape 6 Maggie
Maya: 3 Lin 6 Indian 7 Amerind, Angelou, Yucatec
ancient ~ city: 5 Tikal, Uxmal
archeological site: 5 Copan
farmland: 5 milpa
food staple: 5 maize
predecessor: 5 Olmec
sacrificial pool: 6 cenote
tree: 6 balche
Mayakovsky, Vladimir: 4 poet 7 Russian
___ May Alcott: 6 Louisa
Mayall: 4 John
Mayan: 3 Mam 8 language
maybe: 6 I'll see 7 perhaps, we'll see 8 possibly 9 perchance 10 God willing, imaginably
Maybe ___ ragged and funny...: 4 we're
Maybe author: Lillian Hellman
Maybe composer: 8 Gershwin
Maybe I'm Amazed (1977 song) artist: Paul McCartney
Maybe It Was Memphis singer: 6 Tillis
Maybelle: 6 Carter
Maybellene (song) artist: Chuck Berry, Johnny Rivers
Maybelline: 6 makeup
alternative: 4 Avon 5 Almay 6 Revlon 7 Lancome, Mary Kay 8 Clinique 9 Cover Girl, Max Factor 11 Estée Lauder, Merle Norman
___ May Be Right: 3 You
Mayberry
see Andy Griffith Show
maybes: 3 ifs
___-may-care: 5 devil
___ May Clampett: 4 Elly
Mayday: 3 SOS 4 help 5 alarm, alert 6 signal 7 warning
Mayday author: Nelson Demille
May-Day author: Ralph Waldo Emerson
May Day dance: 6 morris
May 8, 1945: 5 V-E Day
May, Elaine: 7 actress 8 director
film: California Suite (1978)
The Heartbreak Kid (1972)
Ishtar (1987)
Luv (1967)
A New Leaf (1971)
Small Time Crooks (2000)
partner: Mike Nichols
___ Mayer: 5 Oscar
Mayfield, Curtis
leader of: The Impressions
song: Freddie's Dead (1972)
Superfly (1972)
___ mayflower: 6 Canada
Mayflower: 4 ship 5 mover
competitor: 6 Allied, Global
passenger: 5 Alden 8 Standish, Winthrop
mayfly: 3 bug, dun 6 insect
larva: 5 nymph
mayhem: 4 mess 5 chaos, havoc 6 bedlam, fracas, tumult, unrest, uproar 7 anarchy, battery, ferment, rioting, trouble, turmoil 8 disarray, disorder, upheaval, violence 9 commotion, confusion, mobocracy
May I help you?: 3 yes
May I interrupt?: 4 ahem
Mayim: 6 Bialik
May, Joe: 8 director
film: Confession (1937)
The House of Seven Gables (1940)
The Invisible Man Returns (1940)
Music in the Air (1934)
___ May Lester: 5 Ellie
___ may look at a king: 4 A cat
Maynard: 3 Don, Ken 7 Jackson 8 Ferguson
Maynard G. ___: 5 Krebs
Maynard, Ken film: 5 oater
___ Maynard Keynes: 4 John
___ May, NJ: 4 Cape
mayo: 3 mes 5 month 7 Spanish
follower: 5 junio
preceder: 5 abril
see also mayonnaise
Mayo: 4 city, town 6 Archie, county 7 Charles, Whitman, William 8 Virginia
locale: 6 Canada 7 Ireland
neighbor: 5 Sligo
Mayo, Archie: 8 director
film: Angel on My Shoulder (1946)
Black Legion (1936)
Bordertown (1935)
It's Love I'm After (1937)
The Life of Jimmy Dolan (1933)
The Mayor of Hell (1933)
A Night in Casablanca (1946)
The Petrified Forest (1936)
Svengali (1931)
They Shall Have Music (1939)
___ May Oliver: 4 Edna
Mayon: 7 volcano
locale: 4 Asia 5 Luzon
mayonnaise: 8 dressing
cover: 3 lid
garlic-flavored ~: 5 aioli
holder: 3 jar
serving: 4 glob
mayor: 8 Hizzoner, official
bailiwick: 4 city
name meaning ~: 7 Schultz
___ mayor: 4 lord
Mayor author: 4 Koch
Mayor of Casterbridge, The author: Thomas Hardy
Mayor of Hell, The (1933 film)
cast: James Cagney, Madge Evans, Allen Jenkins
director: Archie Mayo
Mayo, Virginia: 7 actress
film: The Best Years of Our Lives (1946)
Captain Horatio Hornblower (1951)
Colorado Territory (1949)
The Flame and the Arrow (1950)
French Quarter (1978)
The Kid From Brooklyn (1946)
The Princess and the Pirate (1944)
The Secret Life of Walter Mitty (1947)
White Heat (1949)
Wonder Man (1945)
Ma, Yo-Yo: 7 cellist, Chinese
birthplace: 5 Paris
maypop: 5 fruit, plant 6 flower
Mayron, Melanie: 7 actress
film: Girlfriends (1978)
Harry and Tonto (1974)
Missing (1982)
TV: thirtysomething
May 7: 5 nones
Mays, Willie: 5 Giant 10 outfielder
Maytag alternative: 5 Amana, Norge 6 Bendix, Tappan 7 Admiral, Jenn-Air, Kenmore 8 Hotpoint 9 Magic Chef, Whirlpool 10 Frigidaire, Kelvinator, KitchenAid
Maytag dog: 6 Newton
mayten: 4 tree
May the ___ be with you: 5 Force
Maytime (1937 film)
cast: John Barrymore, Nelson Eddy, Jeanette MacDonald
director: Robert Z. Leonard
mayweed: 5 plant 6 flower
___ May Wong: 4 Anna
Maywood: 4 city, town
locale: 8 Illinois 10 California
May You Always (1959 song) artist: McGuire Sisters
Mazama lake, Mount: 6 Crater
Mazar: 4 Debi
Mazar-i-Sharif: 4 city, town
locale: 11 Afghanistan
Mazatec: 6 Indian 7 Amerind
Mazatlán: 4 city, port, town
locale: 6 Mexico 7 Sinaloa
see also Spanish
Mazda: 3 car 4 auto 10 automobile
competitor: 5 Isuzu
model: 3 MPV 5 Miata 7 Protege, Tribute 8 Millenia
maze: 3 web 5 snarl 6 jungle, morass, riddle, tangle 7 complex, network, red tape 9 catacombs, confusion, imbroglio, labyrinth 10 perplexity
part: 4 wall
runner: 6 lab rat
word: 5 Enter, Start
Mazel ___!: 3 tov
Mazeppa composer: 5 Liszt
mazer: 6 goblet
Mazeroski, Bill: 6 Pirate
Mazes and Monsters author: 5 Jaffe
Mazo ___ Roche: 4 de la
Mazola: 3 oil 10 cooking oil
alternative: 6 Crisco, Wesson 7 Puritan
mazuma: 3 oof 4 cash, gelt, jack, kail, kale, loot, peag, pelf 5 bills, bread, bucks, dough, funds, lucre, money, moola, mopus, pesos, rhino, sewan 6 dinero, do-re-mi, mammon, moolah, seawan, silver, specie, wampum, wealth 7 cabbage, capital, dollars, lettuce, ooftish, scratch, shekels 8 bankroll, cold cash, currency, hard cash, smackers 9 banknotes, frogskins, long green, simoleons 10 greenbacks, green stuff
mazurka: 5 dance, music
Mazursky, Paul: 8 director
film: Blume in Love (1973)
Bob & Carol & Ted & Alice (1969)
Down and Out in Beverly Hills (1986)
Enemies, A Love Story (1989)
Harry and Tonto (1974)
Moon Over Parador (1988)
Moscow on the Hudson (1984)
Next Stop, Greenwich Village (1976)
An Unmarried Woman (1978)
Willie and Phil (1980)
mazy: 6 knotty 7 winding 8 tortuous
MBA: 3 deg. 6 degree
course: 4 econ. 9 economics
Mbabane: 4 city, town 7 capital
locale: 9 Swaziland
Mbale: 4 city, town
locale: 6 Uganda
___ M. Barrie: 5 James
Mbeki org.: 3 ANC
Mbeya: 4 city, town
locale: 8 Tanzania
mbira: 10 percussion
origin: 6 Africa
Mbundu: 8 language
home: 6 Africa, Angola
M. Butterfly star: 4 Wong
M.C.: 4 host 6 Hammer
need: 4 mike 10 microphone
McAdoo, Bob
milieu: 5 court
org.: 3 NBA
sport: 10 basketball
___ M. Cain: 5 James
McAnuff, Des: 8 director
film: The Adventures of Rocky and Bullwinkle (2000)
Cousin Bette (1998)
McArdle, Andrea role: 5 Annie
McAuliffe: 7 Christa
McAvoy: 3 May
McBain: 2 Ed 5 Diane
McBeal: 4 Ally
McCabe & Mrs. Miller (1971 film)
cast: Rene Auberjonois, Warren Beatty, Julie Christie
director: Robert Altman
McCall: 2 C.W. 5 Mitzi
McCall, C.W. song: Convoy (1975)
McCallum, David: 5 actor
film: The Great Escape (1963)
A Night to Remember (1958)
spouse: Jill Ireland
TV: The Man From U.N.C.L.E.
McCambridge, Mercedes Oscar: All the King's Men
McCann: 4 Lila 5 Chuck, Peter
McCarey, Leo: 8 director
film: The Awful Truth (1937, AA)
Belle of the Nineties (1934)
The Bells of St. Mary's (1945)
Duck Soup (1933)
Going My Way (1944, AA)
The Kid From Spain (1932)
Love Affair (1939)
Make Way for Tomorrow (1937)
The Milky Way (1936)
Ruggles of Red Gap (1935)
Six of a Kind (1934)
McCarthy: 3 Joe 4 Mary 5 Jenny, Kevin, Peter 6 Andrew, Eugene
partner: 6 Bergen
trunkmate: 5 Snerd 7 Klinker
McCarthy, Andrew: 5 actor
film: Heaven Help Us (1985)
I'm Losing You (1999)
Pretty in Pink (1987)
St. Elmo's Fire (1985)
McCarthy, Kevin: 5 actor
film: Death of a Salesman (1951)
Innerspace (1987)
Invasion of the Body Snatchers (1956)
Piranha (1978)
McCarthy, Mary: 6 author, writer
work: Cannibals and Missionaries
A Charmed Life

The Company She Keeps
The Group
The Groves of Academe
Memories of a Catholic Girlhood
The Oasis
McCartney: **4** Paul **5** Linda
McCartney, Paul: **3** Sir
album: **3** Ram
colleague: **5** Starr **6** Lennon **8** Harrison
instrument: bass guitar
real first name: James
song: Another Day (1971)
Band on the Run (1974)
Coming Up (1980)
Ebony and Ivory (1982)
Getting Closer (1979)
The Girl Is Mine (1982)
Goodnight Tonight (1979)
Helen Wheels (1973)
Hi, Hi, Hi (1972)
Jet (1974)
Junior's Farm (1974)
Let 'Em In (1976)
Listen to What the Man Said (1975)
Live and Let Die (1973)
Maybe I'm Amazed (1977)
My Love (1973)
No More Lonely Nights (1984)
Sally G (1974)
Say Say Say (1983)
Silly Love Songs (1976)
So Bad (1984)
Spies Like Us (1985)
Take It Away (1982)
Uncle Albert/Admiral Halsey (1971)
With a Little Luck (1978)
spouse: Linda Eastman, Heather Mills
McCarver: **3** Tim
McCay: **6** Winsor
McClain: **6** Charly
McClanahan: **3** Rue
McClellan: **6** George
adversary: **3** Lee
colleague: **5** Meade
McClintock, Barbara: **8** Nobelist
McCloskey: **5** Leigh
McCloud (NBC drama)
cast: J.D. Cannon (Peter Clifford)
Terry Carter (Joe Broadhurst)
Dennis Weaver (Sam McCloud)
hometown: **4** Taos
McClure: **2** S.S. **4** Doug, Marc
McClure, Doug: **5** actor
film: Humanoids From the Deep (1980)
Shenandoah (1965)
spouse: Barbara Luna
TV: The Virginian
McClurg: **4** Edie
McConaughey, Matthew: **5** actor
film: Amistad (1997)
Boys on the Side (1995)
Contact (1997)
Ed TV (1999)
Thirteen Conversations About One Thing (2001)
A Time to Kill (1996)
U-571 (2000)
The Wedding Planner (2001)
McConnell Story, The (1955 film)
cast: June Allyson, Alan Ladd, James Whitmore
director: Gordon Douglas
McCoo, Marilyn spouse: Billy Davis Jr.
McCord: **4** Kent
McCormack: **4** Eric, Mary
McCormack, John: **5** tenor
McCormick: **5** Cyrus, Myron **7** Maureen
McCourt, Frank: **6** author, writer
work: Angela's Ashes, Brotherhood, 'Tis

McCovey, Willie: **5** Giant **7** slugger
McCowen: **4** Alec
McCoy: **3** Van **4** Amos, Neal **6** Elijah **7** Charlie
Hatfield, to a ~: **3** foe **5** enemy
the real ~: **5** legit
__ McCoy: **4** real
McCoys: **4** clan
song: Fever (1965)
Hang on Sloopy (1965)
McCoy, Van song: The Hustle (1975)
__ McCoy, WI: **4** Fort
McCrae: **4** Gwen, John **6** George
McCrae, John: **4** poet
McCrary, Tex spouse: Jinx Falkenburg
McCready: **5** Mindy
McCrea, Joel: **5** actor
film: Banjo on My Knee (1936)
Barbary Coast (1935)
Bed of Roses (1933)
Colorado Territory (1949)
Come and Get It (1936)
Dead End (1937)
Foreign Correspondent (1940)
Girls About Town (1931)
The More the Merrier (1943)
The Most Dangerous Game (1932)
Mustang Country (1976)
The Palm Beach Story (1942)
The Richest Girl in the World (1934)
Ride the High Country (1962)
Stars in My Crown (1950)
Sullivan's Travels (1941)
These Three (1936)
They Shall Have Music (1939)
Union Pacific (1939)
Wells Fargo (1937)
McCullers, Carson: **6** author, writer
work: The Ballad of the Sad Cafe
Clock without Hands
The Heart is a Lonely Hunter
The Member of the Wedding
Reflections in a Golden Eye
The Square Root of Wonderful
McCullough: **5** David **7** Colleen
McCullough, Colleen: **6** writer **10** Australian
MCCX halved: **3** DCV
work: An Indecent Obsession
The Thorn Birds
McDaniel: **3** Mel **6** Hattie, Xavier
McDaniel, Hattie Oscar: Gone With the Wind
McDaniels, Gene
song: Chip Chip (1962)
A Hundred Pounds of Clay (1961)
Tower of Strength (1961)
McDermott: **5** Dylan
McDonald's
alternative: **3** KFC **6** Wendy's **8** Pizza Hut **10** Burger King
freebie: **5** straw **6** catsup, napkin **7** ketchup
McDonnell, Mary: **7** actress
film: Dances With Wolves (1990)
Grand Canyon (1991)
Independence Day (1996)
Matewan (1987)
Passion Fish (1992)
Sneakers (1992)
McDonough: **4** Mary
McDormand, Frances: **7** actress
film: Almost Famous (2000)
Blood Simple (1984)
Darkman (1990)
Fargo (1996, AA)
Laurel Canyon (2002)
Madeline (1998)
The Man Who Wasn't There (2001)
Mississippi Burning (1988)
Talk of Angels (1998)
Wonder Boys (2000)

McDowall, Roddy: **5** actor
film: The Adventures of Bullwhip Griffin (1967)
Dead of Winter (1987)
Escape From the Planet of the Apes (1971)
Holiday in Mexico (1946)
How Green Was My Valley (1941)
Inside Daisy Clover (1965)
Lassie Come Home (1943)
The Legend of Hell House (1973)
The Longest Day (1962)
Lord Love a Duck (1966)
Molly and Me (1945)
My Friend Flicka (1943)
The Pied Piper (1942)
Planet of the Apes (1968)
The Poseidon Adventure (1972)
McDowell: **6** Ronnie **7** Malcolm
McDowell, Malcolm: **5** actor
film: Aces High (1977)
Bopha! (1993)
A Clockwork Orange (1971)
Cross Creek (1983)
Get Crazy (1983)
if ... (1968)
O Lucky Man! (1973)
Royal Flash (1975)
Star Trek Generations (1994)
Sunset (1988)
Time After Time (1979)
spouse: Mary Steenburgen
McElhone: **8** Natascha
McElligot's Pool author: Dr. Seuss
McEnroe, John: **7** netster **9** tennis pro
doubles partner: **5** Stich
milieu: **5** court
rival: **4** Borg **5** Lendl
spouse: Tatum O'Neal
McEntire: **4** Reba
McEveety: **7** Vincent
McEwan: **3** Ian
McEwen: **4** Mark
McFadden: **4** Mary **5** Gates **6** Daniel
McFadden, Daniel: **8** Nobelist **9** economist
McFarland: **6** Spanky
McFerrin, Bobby
sing like ~: **4** scat
song: Don't Worry Be Happy (1988)
McGavin: **6** Darren
McGee: **5** Molly **6** Fibber, Willie
McGee, Fibber
medium: **5** radio
mess: **6** closet
McGillis, Kelly: **7** actress
film: The Accused (1988)
At First Sight (1998)
The Babe (1992)
Reuben, Reuben (1983)
Top Gun (1986)
Witness (1985)
McGill University
location: **6** Canada, Quebec **8** Montreal
McGinley: **3** Ted **7** Phyllis
McGinnis: **6** George
McGinnity: **3** Joe
McGoohan, Patrick: **5** actor
film: Braveheart (1995)
Escape From Alcatraz (1979)
Ice Station Zebra (1968)
Mary, Queen of Scots (1971)
The Quare Fellow (1962)
The Three Lives of Thomasina (1964)
Walk in the Shadow (1966)
TV: The Prisoner
Secret Agent
McGovern: **6** George **7** Maureen **9** Elizabeth
McGovern, Elizabeth: **7** actress
film: Bedroom Window (1987)
Once Upon a Time in America (1984)

Racing With the Moon (1984)
Ragtime (1981)
She's Having a Baby (1988)
McGovern, George home: **4** S. Dak.
McGovern, Maureen song: The Morning After (1973)
McGraw: **3** Tim, Tug **4** John **5** James **7** Charles
McGraw-__: **4** Hill
McGraw, Tim
father: Tug
song: Indian Outlaw (1994)
It's Your Love (1997)
Please Remember Me (1999)
spouse: Faith Hill
McGregor: **4** Ewan
McGrew: **3** Dan
lady: **3** Lou
McGriff, Fred sport: **8** baseball
McGuire: **2** Al **3** Don **5** Barry **7** Dorothy, Phyllis **9** Christine
McGuire, Barry
member: New Christy Minstrels
song: Eve of Destruction (1965)
McGuire, Dorothy: **7** actress
film: Claudia (1943)
Claudia and David (1946)
The Dark at the Top of the Stairs (1960)
Friendly Persuasion (1956)
Gentleman's Agreement (1947)
I Want You (1951)
Mister 880 (1950)
Old Yeller (1957)
The Spiral Staircase (1946)
A Summer Place (1959)
Swiss Family Robinson (1960)
Three Coins in the Fountain (1954)
Till the End of Time (1946)
A Tree Grows in Brooklyn (1945)
Trial (1955)
McGuire Sisters: **4** trio
members: Phyllis, Christine, Dorothy
song: Delilah Jones (1956)
Doesn't Anybody Love Me? (1955)
He (1955)
It May Sound Silly (1955)
May You Always (1959)
Picnic (1956)
Rhythm 'N' Blues (1955)
Sincerely (1955)
Something's Gotta Give (1955)
Sugartime (1958)
McGwire, Mark: **7** slugger
rival: **4** Sosa **9** Sammy Sosa
sport: **8** baseball
stat for ~: **3** RBI **5** homer
McHale's Navy (ABC sitcom)
cast: Ernest Borgnine (Lt. Cmdr. Quinton McHale)
Tim Conway (Ens. Charles Parker)
Joe Flynn (Capt. Wallace Binghamton)
catchphrase: **5** why me
M.C. Hammer: **6** rapper
real name: Stanley Burrell
song: 2 Legit 2 Quit (1991)
Addams Groove (1991)
Have You Seen Her (1990)
Pray (1990)
U Can't Touch This (1990)
McHenry: **4** Fort
McHugh: **5** Frank, Jimmy
McHugh, Frank: **5** actor
film: Elmer the Great (1933)
High Pressure (1932)
I Love You Again (1940)
It Happens Every Thursday (1953)
Three Men on a Horse (1936)
McInerney: **3** Jay
McIntire: **3** Tim **4** John
McIntire, John: **5** actor
film: Honkytonk Man (1982)
The Phenix City Story (1955)
The President's Lady (1953)

The World in His Arms (1952)
McIntire, Tim: 5 actor
film: American Hot Wax (1978)
The Gumball Rally (1976)
The Sterile Cuckoo (1969)
McIntosh: 5 apple
relative: 4 crab, Gala, Lodi, Rome **5** Mutsu **6** Empire, Ida Red, medlar, Pippin, russet **7** Baldwin, Bramley, costard, Freedom, Liberty, Spartan, Wealthy, Winesap **8** Cortland, Jonathan **10** Rome Beauty
McIntyre: 3 Hal, Joe **4** Joey
McKay: 3 Jim **4** John **6** Claude **7** Gardner
McKean, Michael: 5 actor
film: Best in Show (2000)
The Brady Bunch Movie (1995)
Planes, Trains & Automobiles (1987)
This Is Spinal Tap (1984)
TV: Laverne & Shirley
McKechnie: 4 Bill
McKee: 5 Maria **7** Lonette
McKellen, Ian: 3 Sir **5** actor
film: The Ballad of Little Jo (1993)
Gods and Monsters (1998)
The Lord of the Rings: The Fellowship of The Ring (2001)
Priest of Love (1981)
Richard III (1995)
Six Degrees of Separation (1993)
Thank You All Very Much (1969)
X-Men (2000)
McKenna: 7 Siobhan **8** Virginia
McKenna, Virginia: 7 actress
film: Born Free (1966)
Carve Her Name With Pride (1958)
Ring of Bright Water (1969)
Simba (1955)
The Smallest Show on Earth (1957)
McKennitt, Loreena instrument: harp
McKenzie Break, The (1970 film)
cast: Helmut Griem, Ian Hendry, Brian Keith
director: Lamont Johnson
McKenzie, Scott song: San Francisco (1967)
McKeon: 4 Doug **5** Nancy **6** Philip
McKern, Leo: 5 actor
film: The Blue Lagoon (1980)
The Day the Earth Caught Fire (1962)
The French Lieutenant's Woman (1981)
The Horse Without a Head (1963)
King and Country (1964)
Ladyhawke (1985)
A Man for All Seasons (1966)
Ryan's Daughter (1970)
McKim: 7 Charles
McKinley: 2 mt. **3** Ida, mtn. **4** peak **5** mount **7** William **8** mountain
birthplace: 4 Ohio
locale: 6 Alaska
McKinley, William: 9 president
assassin: 8 Czolgosz
birthplace: 4 Ohio **5** Niles
former occupation: 6 lawyer
opponent: 5 Bryan
V.P.: 6 Hobart **9** Roosevelt
wife: 3 Ida
McKinney, Ruth work: My Sister Eileen
McKinney, Tamara: 5 skier
McKuen: 3 Rod
McLachlan, Sarah
homeland: Canada
song: Adia (1998)
Angel (1998)
Building a Mystery (1997)
I Will Remember You (1999)
Sweet Surrender (1998)
McLaglen, Andrew V.: 8 director
film: Bandolero! (1968)
ffolkes (1980)
McLintock! (1963)
The Sea Wolves (1980)
Shenandoah (1965)
McLaglen, Victor: 5 actor
film: Captain Fury (1939)
Gunga Din (1939)
The Informer (1935, AA)
Klondike Annie (1936)
The Lost Patrol (1934)
No More Women (1934)
The Quiet Man (1952)
This Is My Affair (1937)
Under Two Flags (1936)
Wee Willie Winkie (1937)
What Price Glory? (1926)
McLain: 5 Denny
McLean: 3 Don **9** Stevenson
McLean, Don
song: American Pie (1971)
Castles in the Air (1972)
Crying (1981)
Vincent (1972)
McLean, Va. org.: 3 CIA
__ McLeod Bethune: 4 Mary
McLeod, Norman Z.: 8 director
film: Alias Jesse James (1952)
Casanova's Big Night (1954)
Horse Feathers (1932)
It's a Gift (1934)
The Kid From Brooklyn (1946)
Lady Be Cool (1941)
Merrily We Live (1938)
Monkey Business (1931)
My Favorite Spy (1951)
The Paleface (1948)
Road to Rio (1947)
The Secret Life of Walter Mitty (1947)
There Goes My Heart (1938)
Topper (1937)
Topper Takes a Trip (1939)
McLintock! (1963 film)
cast: Maureen O'Hara, John Wayne, Patrick Wayne
director: Andrew V. McLaglen
McLuhan, Marshall: 6 author, critic, writer **8** Canadian
work: The Gutenberg Galaxy
The Mechanical Bride
The Medium is the Massage
Understanding Media
McMahon: 2 Ed **3** Jim **6** Horace
word: 5 Here's **6** Johnny
McManus: 6 George
McMartin: 4 John
McMaster University
location: 6 Canada **7** Ontario **8** Hamilton
McMillan: 5 Edwin, Terry **6** Donald
McMillan and Wife (NBC drama)
cast: Rock Hudson (Stewart McMillan)
Susan Saint James (Sally McMillan)
Nancy Walker (Mildred)
McMillan, Edwin: 7 chemist **8** Nobelist
McMurdo: 5 Sound
locale: 10 Antarctica
McMurtry, Larry: 6 author, writer
work: All My Friends Are Going to Be Strangers
Anything for Billy
Boone's Lick
Buffalo Girls
Cadillac Jack
Dead Man's Walk
Duane's Depressed
The Evening Star
Horseman Pass By
The Last Picture Show
The Late Child
Lonesome Dove
Panhandle Cowboy
Paradise
Rodeo
Sin Killer
Somebody's Darling
Some Can Whistle
Streets of Laredo
Terms of Endearment
Texasville
Whatever Happened to Jacy Farrow?
McNair: 4 Fort **7** Barbara
McNally: 4 Dave **7** Stephen **8** Terrence
partner: 4 Rand
McNally's Alibi author: 7 Sanders
McNally's Caper author: 7 Sanders
McNally's Chance author: 7 Sanders
McNally's Dilemma author: 7 Sanders
McNally's Folly author: 7 Sanders
McNally's Gamble author: 7 Sanders
McNally's Luck author: 7 Sanders
McNally's Puzzle author: 7 Sanders
McNally's Risk author: 7 Sanders
McNally's Secret author: 7 Sanders
McNally, Stephen: 5 actor
film: Diplomatic Courier (1952)
The Lady Gambles (1949)
No Way Out (1950)
Tribute to a Bad Man (1956)
Violent Saturday (1955)
McNally's Trial author: 7 Sanders
McNamara: 5 Robin **6** Robert
McNaughton: 3 Ian
__ McNeill Whistler: 5 James
McNichol: 5 Jimmy **6** Kristy
McNichol, Kristy: 7 actress
film: Just the Way You Are (1984)
Only When I Laugh (1981)
TV: Empty Nest, Family
__ McNutt: 4 Boob
__ M. Cohan: 6 George
McPartland, Marian: 7 pianist
genre: 4 jazz
McPhatter, Clyde
member: The Dominoes, The Drifters
song: Little Bitty Pretty One (1962)
Lover Please (1962)
A Lover's Question (1958)
Treasure of Love (1956)
McPherson: 5 Aimee
__ McPherson, GA: 4 Fort
McQ (1974 film)
cast: Eddie Albert, Colleen Dewhurst, Diana Muldaur, John Wayne
director: John Sturges
McQueen: 5 Steve **9** Butterfly
McQueen, Steve: 5 actor
film: Baby The Rain Must Fall (1965)
Bullitt (1968)
The Cincinnati Kid (1965)
The Getaway (1972)
The Great Escape (1963)
Hell Is for Heroes (1962)
Junior Bonner (1972)
Le Mans (1971)
Love With the Proper Stranger (1963)
The Magnificent Seven (1960)
Nevada Smith (1966)
On Any Sunday (1971)
Papillon (1973)
The Reivers (1969)
The Sand Pebbles (1966)
Soldier in the Rain (1963)
The Thomas Crown Affair (1968)
The Towering Inferno (1974)
spouse: Ali MacGraw
TV: Wanted: Dead or Alive
McRae: 6 Carmen
McRaney, Gerald spouse: Delta Burke
McRee: 4 Lisa
McShane: 3 Ian
McSorley's Bar artist: 5 Sloan
McTeague author: Frank Norris
McTiernan, John: 8 director
film: The 13th Warrior (1999)
Die Hard (1988)
Die Hard With a Vengeance (1995)
The Hunt for Red October (1990)
Last Action Hero (1993)
Medicine Man (1992)
Predator (1987)
The Thomas Crown Affair (1999)
McVie: 4 John **9** Christine
McVie, Christine
homeland: England
member: Fleetwood Mac
song: Got a Hold of Me (1984)
McWhirter: 4 Ross **6** Norris
Md: 4 elem. **7** element **11** mendelevium
101 for ~: 4 at. no.
M.D.: 2 dr., GP **3** deg., doc **6** degree, doctor **9** physician
assistant: 2 RN
employer: 3 HMO
needle: 4 hypo
order: 2 Rx **4** stat
org.: 3 ACP, AMA
place: 2 ER, OR **4** hosp.
publication: 4 JAMA
reference: 3 PDR
request: 3 ECG, EEG, EKG, MRI, NMR **4** X-ray
specialty: 3 ENT
see also doctor, physician
Md. neighbor: 3 Del., W.Va. **4** Virg.
see also Maryland
mdse.: 3 gds., stk.
bars: 3 UPC
bill: 3 inv.
outlet: 3 mkt.
second-quality ~: 4 impf. **5** irreg.
MDT part: 3 Mtn., Std. **4** Time **8** Mountain, Standard
MDX: 3 SUV **5** Acura
me: 4 pron., self **7** pronoun
ah ~: 4 alas, sigh
belonging to ~: 4 mine
between you and ~: 7 sub rosa **8** in secret, secretly **9** entre nous, privately
count ~ out: 4 uh-uh **10** not a chance
dear ~: 7 my stars **10** I do declare, my goodness
excuse ~: 4 ahem, oops **5** sorry **6** whoops
in French: 3 moi
in German: 3 mir
it wasn't ~: 4 not I
not ~: 3 you
suits ~: 2 OK **3** yes **4** fine, okay **5** swell **8** very well
too: 5 ditto
me __: 6 decade
me-__: 3 too **5** tooer
__ me!: 5 Woe is **6** Search
__ me?: 3 Why
__, me?: 3 Who
Me __ Shadow: 5 and My
Me __, The: 6 decade
Me, __ I call myself: 5 a name
Me, __ & Irene: 6 Myself
Me.
neighbor: 3 Que.
region: 4 N. Eng.
see also Maine
__ Me: 3 Ask, Sue, Use **4** Call, Dang, Dare, Help, Hold, Kiss, Love, Play, Rock, Tell **5** All of, Bad to, Cover, Freak, Pinch, Rock'n, Touch **6** Choose, Groove, Jammin', Rescue, Tickle **7** Release
M.E.: 3 deg.
awarder: 3 MIT
part of ~: 3 Eng. **4** Engr., Mech. **8** Engineer **10** Mechanical
__, M.E.: 6 Quincy
mea culpa: 5 sorry **7** apology, I'm sorry, my fault

mead: 5 drink 6 meadow 8 beverage
ingredient: 5 honey
Mead: 4 lake 8 Margaret
locale: 5 Samoa
Meade: 5 James 6 George
__ Meade: 4 Fort
Meade, James: 8 Nobelist 9 economist
Mead Johnson cereal: 6 Pablum
Mead, Margaret: 6 author, writer 14 anthropologist
work: Blackberry Winter
Coming of Age in Samoa
Growing Up in New Guinea
Letters From the Field
Male and Female
meadow: 3 fld., lea, ley, sod 4 mead, park 5 field, grass, heath, plain, range, sward, veldt 6 steppe, swarth 7 bottoms, lowland, pasture, prairie, verdure 9 grassland
ender: 4 land, lark 5 lands, sweet
grazer: 3 cow, ewe 5 sheep
munch in the ~: 5 graze
remark: 3 baa, maa, moo 5 bleat
rolling ~: 4 down
meadow __: 3 rue 4 bird, fern, lily, vole 5 grass, mouse 6 beauty, fescue 7 parsnip, saffron, salsify
Meadowlands Arena team: 4 Nets
Meadowlark: 5 Lemon
meadowlark cousin: 4 wren
Meadows: 3 Tim 5 Jayne 6 Audrey
Meadows, Jayne spouse: Steve Allen
meager: 3 low 4 bare, bony, lank, lean, poor, puny, slim, thin 5 boney, gaunt, lanky, light, scant, short, small, spare 6 flimsy, gangly, humble, Lenten, little, measly, paltry, scanty, scrimp, shabby, skimpy, skinny, slight, sparse, stingy 7 angular, lacking, limited, scraggy, scrawny, scrimpy, slender, stinted, trivial, wanting 8 angulose, angulous, beggarly, exiguous, gangling, pathetic, rawboned, underfed 9 deficient, emaciated, miserable 10 inadequate, infrequent, lamentable, pathetical, unfruitful
not ~: 8 generous 9 plentiful
meagerness: 4 lack, want 6 dearth 7 paucity, poverty 8 exiguity, scarcity, sparsity 10 deficiency, inadequacy
meal: 3 tea 4 chow, dish, eats, fare, feed, food, grub, luau, mess 5 board, feast, flour, lunch, plate, snack, table 6 brunch, buffet, din-din, dinner, entrée, farina, picnic, powder, repast, spread, supper 7 aliment, banquet, cookout, dessert, fish fry, high tea, potluck, special 8 barbecue, carryout, clambake, luncheon, munchies, prix fixe, TV dinner, victuals 9 blue plate, breakfast, collation, refection
afternoon ~: 5 lunch
Army ~: 4 chow, hash, mess 7 K-ration
baby's ~: 6 din-din
ender: 4 time, worm
enjoy your ~ in French: 10 bon appétit
evening ~: 6 dinner, repast, supper 9 collation
fix a ~: 4 cook 6 whip up
for the humbled: 4 crow
gluttonous ~: 5 gorge
ground ~: 5 flour
have a ~: 3 eat, sup 4 dine 5 feast
horse ~: 4 feed 6 fodder
ingredient: 3 oat 4 corn
in need of a ~: 5 unfed 6 hungry
light ~: 4 bite 5 salad, snack 9 collation
Mexican ~: 6 flauta
morning ~: 9 breakfast
oater ~: 4 chow, grub 7 vittles
outdoor ~: 6 picnic 8 barbecue
part: 5 drink 6 entrée 7 dessert 9 appetizer
prayer: 5 grace
starter: 3 oat 4 corn, fish, inch 5 piece, salad
sumptuous ~: 5 feast 7 banquet
unappetizing ~: 4 slop 5 gruel
meal __: 6 ticket
__ meal: 3 oil 4 bone, corn, fish 5 blood, matzo 6 almond, Indian, matzah, matzoh, square 7 glacial, linseed
__ Me Along: 4 Take
meals: 4 fare 5 board
meals on __: 6 wheels
mealy: 3 dry 4 oaty, pale, soft 6 floury, sallow 7 crumbly, powdery 8 granular
ender: 3 bug
mealy-__: 7 mouthed
mealybug: 6 insect
mean: 2 av. 3 aim, avg., bad, low, par 4 base, cold, cool, evil, hard, norm, plan, poor, rude, sour, ugly, vile 5 augur, catty, cheap, close, dirty, harsh, imply, lousy, lowly, mangy, nasty, onery, petty, rough, seedy, snide, spell, surly, testy, tight, tough 6 animal, aspire, attest, brutal, chilly, convey, denote, entail, fierce, herald, hint at, humble, intend, little, mangey, measly, medial, median, mesial, middle, modest, narrow, odious, ogrish, ornery, paltry, ragged, remote, rotten, savage, shabby, sleazy, sneaky, sordid, stingy, tawdry, unfair, unkind, wanton, wicked 7 add up to, average, balance, beastly, bestial, betoken, callous, connote, crabbed, drive at, halfway, hateful, hostile, hurtful, ignoble, inhuman, knavish, limited, lowborn, lowdown, miserly, peevish, pitiful, point to, portend, presage, propose, purport, run-down, scruffy, selfish, servile, signify, squalid, suggest, thrifty, trivial, vicious, waspish 8 allude to, barbaric, beggarly, churlish, contrary, degraded, fiendish, foreshow, foretell, indicate, inferior, inhumane, inimical, intimate, midpoint, moderate, ordinary, pitiless, plebeian, ruthless, sadistic, spell out, spiteful, standard, stand for, ungiving, vengeful, venomous, wretched 9 adumbrate, bellicose, cutthroat, dangerous, dastardly, determine, ferocious, fractious, hardnosed, malicious, merciless, miserable, monstrous, obnoxious, penurious, represent, sarcastic, shameless, symbolize, truculent, unpitying, vexatious, withdrawn 10 anticipate, catchpenny, despicable, diabolical, evilminded, foreshadow, have in mind, illnatured, lamentable, malevolent, oppressive, pugnacious, scurrilous, ungenerous, vindictive
ender: 4 time 5 while
kid: 3 imp 4 brat
lean and ~: 4 wiry
look: 5 scowl, sneer
not ~: 4 nice
one: 3 cur 4 ogre 5 brute, fiend 6 despot
partner: 4 lean
something: 6 matter
take to ~: 4 draw, make 5 glean, guess, infer, think 6 assume, decode, deduce, derive, gather 7 imagine, surmise 8 conclude, construe 10 understand
(to): 3 aim 4 hope
words: 5 venom
mean __: 3 sun 4 life, line, noon, well 5 value 6 planet 7 anomaly
__ mean: 6 golden
Mean __ Greene: 3 Joe
Me and Bobby McGee (1971 song) artist: Janis Joplin
meander: 3 gad 4 coil, roam, rove, turn, walk, wind 5 amble, drift, range, slink, snake, stray, twine, twist, weave 6 browse, change, cruise, ramble, stroll, trapes, wander, zigzag 7 saunter, sinuate, slither, traipse 8 straggle 9 bat around, gallivant
meanderer: 5 rover 8 wanderer, wayfarer
meandering: 5 snaky, twiny, windy 6 errant, zigzag 7 crooked, erratic, sinuous, winding 8 indirect, tortuous 9 difficult, irregular 10 circuitous, convoluted, serpentine
Me and Juliet: 7 musical
songwriter: 7 Rodgers 11 Hammerstein
Me and Julio... (1972 song) artist: Paul Simon
Me and Mrs. Jones (1972 song) artist: Billy Paul
Me and My __: 6 Shadow
Me and My Gal (1932 film)
cast: Joan Bennett, Marion Burns, Spencer Tracy
director: Raoul Walsh
__ Me and My Gal: 3 For
Me and My Shadow composer: 4 Rose
meandrous: 5 snaky 7 sinuous
Me and You and a Dog Named Boo (1971 song) artist: Lobo
Meanest Man in the World, The (1943 film)
cast: Eddie Anderson, Jack Benny, Priscilla Lane
director: Sidney Lanfield
Meaney, Colm: 5 actor
film: The Snapper (1993)
TV: Star Trek: Deep Space Nine, Star Trek: The Next Generation
Mean Green: 10 North Texas
meanie: 4 ogre 5 fiend
meaning: 3 aim, use 4 gist, goal, pith 5 drift, heart, point, sense, tenor, value, worth 6 effect, import, intent, nuance, object, spirit, thrust, upshot 7 bearing, content, context, essence, message, purport, purpose 8 overtone 9 intention, substance 10 bottom line, definition, denotation
business: 7 serious 8 resolute 9 tenacious
different ~: 5 twist
fraught with ~: 4 deep 8 profound
give the ~ of: 6 define 7 explain 8 spell out 9 interpret
having a secret ~: 5 runic
__-meaning: 4 well
meaningful: 3 big 4 deep, rich 5 meaty, pithy, valid, vital 6 cogent 7 earnest, pointed, serious, weighty 8 eloquent, pregnant, telltale 9 important, momentous 10 expressive, portentous, suggestive, worthwhile
meaningless: 4 idle, vain, void 5 empty, inane, silly, vague, vapid 6 absurd, futile, hollow 7 aimless, shallow, trivial, useless 8 nugatory, trifling 9 pointless, senseless, valueless, worthless
Mean Joe: 6 Greene
meanness: 4 evil 5 spite 6 malice 8 asperity 9 hostility
means: 3 job, way 4 mode, path, road, step, tool 5 agent, dough, funds, kitty, money, organ, power, purse, route, stake, thing 6 agency, assets, avenue, budget, bundle, engine, estate, income, living, manner, medium, method, riches, system, tactic, wealth 7 backing, capital, channel, fortune, ingress, measure, nest egg, process, revenue, savings, support, tactics, vehicle 8 approach, bankroll, finances, holdings, property, reserves 9 affluence, apparatus, equipment, expedient, implement, machinery, mechanism, resources, substance, technique 10 capability, expediency, instrument, livelihood, pocketbook, securities
by all ~: 2 ay, da, ja, OK, sí 3 aye, oui, yea, yep, yes, yup 4 fine, okay, okeh, okey, sure, yeah 5 good-o, natch, quite, right, roger, uh-huh 6 agreed, gladly, good-oh, indeed, just so, rather, righto, surely, you bet, yowzah 7 exactly, for sure, go ahead, indeedy, mais oui, quite so, ten-four 8 all right, as you say, for a fact, of course, thumbs up, very well 9 be my guest, certainly, darn right, decidedly, naturally, precisely, sure thing, you betcha, you said it 10 absolutely, definitely, far and away, positively, sure enough, that's right
by any ~: 5 at all
by no ~: 3 nah, naw, nay, nix, non 4 nein, nope, nyet, uh-uh 5 I won't, ixnay, never, no way 6 hardly, noways, nowise 7 I refuse 8 forget it, I will not, negative, negatory 9 fat chance, I think not 10 count me out, not a chance, thumbs down
by ~ of: 3 via 5 using 6 hereby 7 through
by what ~: 3 how
have the ~ for: 6 afford
having the ~: 4 able 6 able to
justifiers: 4 ends
man of ~: 5 nabob 6 fat cat 9 moneybags, plutocrat
of getting there: 4 belt, lane, path, pike, road, ship 5 guide, route, trail 6 access, artery, avenue, detour, street 7 channel, freeway, highway, parkway, passage, roadway, thruway, viaduct 8 short cut, turnpike 9 boulevard, itinerary 10 expressway, throughway
of independent ~: 4 rich 5 flush 6 loaded 7 moneyed, opulent, upscale, wealthy, well-off 8 affluent, thriving, well-to-do 10 in the money, privileged, prosperous, successful, well-heeled
partner: 4 ways
ways and ~: 7 capital, revenue
means __: 4 test
means __ end: 4 to an
__ means: 4 by no 5 by all, by any
meanspirited: 5 harsh, nasty, petty 10 ungenerous
Mean Streets (1973 film)
cast: Robert De Niro, Harvey Keitel, Amy Robinson
director: Martin Scorsese
__ means war!: 4 This
meant: 6 wilful 7 planned, sincere, willful 8 destined, intended 9 voluntary 10 deliberate, preplanned, purposeful, volitional
mean-tempered: 4 evil, sour, ugly 5 catty, cruel, nasty, onery, surly 6 chilly, malign, ornery, wanton, wicked 7 baleful, hateful, hostile, satanic, vicious, waspish 8 inimical, spiteful, vengeful, venomous 9 bellicose, malicious, rancorous 10 derogatory, ill-natured, pugnacious
meantime: 5 while 7 interim
in the ~: 4 till 5 until 6 for now
meanwhile: 4 till 5 until 6 for now
Meanwhile, back at the __: 5 ranch

Mean Woman Blues (1963 song)
artist: Roy Orbison
Meany: 6 George
Meara, Anne spouse: Jerry Stiller
son: Ben Stiller
__ Me a River: 3 Cry
Mears, Rick: 9 auto racer
milieu: 5 track
meas.: 2 cc., cm., ft., in., kg., km., lb., mg., mi., mm., oz., pt., qt., yd. 3 deg., fth., gal., qty., tsp. 4 cu. ft., cu. in., fath., fl. oz., sq. ft., sq. yd., tbsp. 6 cu. yd. oz.
area ~: 4 sq. ft., sq. mi., sq. yd.
heat ~: 3 deg.
length ~: 2 cm., ft., km., mi., mm., yd. 3 fth. 4 fath.
liquid ~: 2 oz., pt., qt. 3 gal., tsp. 4 fl. oz., tbsp.
volume ~: 2 cc. 4 cu. ft., cu. in., cu. yd.
weight: 2 kg., lb., mg., oz.
see also measure
__ measles: 6 German
measles, like: 5 viral
measly: 4 mean, mere, poor, puny 5 petty 6 humble, meager, paltry, scanty, skimpy, stingy 7 miserly, pitiful 8 beggarly, niggling, pathetic, picayune, piddling, trifling 9 miserable 10 pathetical
measurable: 6 finite 7 bounded, limited 9 weighable 10 calculable, terminable
measure: 3 act, bar, eye, fit, law, peg 4 beat, bill, dose, mark, mete, move, norm, pace, rank, rate, read, rime, rule, span, step, time 5 bylaw, check, gauge, grade, judge, limit, means, meter, plumb, quota, ratio, reach, rhyme, scale, scope, share, sound, swing, tempo, weigh, width 6 action, amount, assess, bounds, course, degree, effort, extent, figure, length, method, ration, reckon, resort, rhythm, size up, strain, stress, survey, tailor 7 cadence, cadency, compute, dope out, pace off, portion, process, statute, stopgap 8 appraise, estimate, evaluate, keep tabs, proposal, quantify, quantity, regulate, resource, standard 9 allotment, benchmark, calculate, calibrate, criterion, determine, dimension, enactment, expedient, immensity, procedure, restraint, stratagem, yardstick 10 proceeding, proportion, resolution, touchstone
area ~: 4 acre, sq. ft., sq. mi., sq. yd. 7 hectare 10 square foot, square mile, square yard
combining form: 5 -meter, metro-
heat ~: 3 deg. 6 degree
in music: 3 bar
lateral ~: 4 span 5 girth 6 spread 7 breadth 9 broadness
length ~: 2 cm., ft., km., mi., mm., yd. 3 fth., rod 4 fath., foot, inch, mile, yard 5 meter 6 fathom 8 kilogram 9 kilometer 10 centimeter, millimeter
liquid ~: 2 oz., pt., qt. 3 gal., tsp. 4 fl. oz., pint, tbsp. 5 ounce, quart 8 teaspoon 10 fluid ounce, tablespoon
starter: 7 counter
volume ~: 2 cc. 4 cu. ft., cu. in., cu. yd. 9 cubic foot, cubic inch, cubic yard
weight ~: 2 kg., lb., mg., oz. 3 ton 5 ounce, pound 8 kilogram 9 milligram
__ measure: 3 dry 4 coal, land, long, tape 5 board, chain, cubic, duple 6 beyond, common, linear, liquid, simple, square, struck, triple 7 angular
measured: 5 paced 7 regular, stately 8 moderate
amount: 4 dose 6 dosage
combining form: 6 -metric
Measure for Measure: 4 play
author: William Shakespeare
character: 5 Lucio 6 Angelo 7 Escalus, Mariana 8 Isabella
measureless: 3 big 4 vast 6 cosmic, untold 7 endless 8 cosmical, infinite 9 limitless, unlimited
measurement: 4 area, mass, size 5 depth, width 6 amount, degree, extent, height, length, survey, volume, weight 7 density 8 altitude, analysis, capacity, distance, quantity 9 amplitude, appraisal, dimension, frequency, magnitude, thickness, valuation
combining form: 5 -metry
see also measure
measurements: 4 data 7 figures 10 statistics
measurers' org.: 4 ANSI
measures: 6 action
take ~: 3 act
Measure twice, cut __: 4 once
measuring: 8 checking, likening 9 analyzing, balancing 10 comparison, estimation
device: 4 dial, rule 5 gauge, ruler, sizer, spoon
science: 7 metrics
measuring __: 3 cup 5 spoon
meat: 3 ham, nub, nut 4 beef, chop, chow, core, crux, duck, fare, fish, food, fowl, gist, goat, grub, knub, lamb, loin, pâté, pith, pork, ribs, Spam, veal 5 bacon, brawn, chops, flank, frank, goose, heart, jerky, liver, point, roast, sense, shank, sheep, steak, T-bone, Treet, tripe, wings, wurst 6 banger, burger, collop, cutlet, entrée, fillet, hot dog, kernel, marrow, muscle, mutton, ragout, rib eye, saddle, salami, thrust, turkey, upshot, vittle, wiener 7 aliment, biltong, bologna, brisket, charqui, chicken, chorizo, cold cut, edibles, essence, giblets, nucleus, pemican, poultry, purport, rissole, roulade, sausage, sirloin, terrine, venison, victual 8 baked ham, barbecue, braciola, chili dog, cold cuts, foie gras, key point, kielbasa, lamb chop, linguiça, noisette, pastrami, pemmican, pork chop, pot-au-feu, pot roast, quenelle, rib roast, rib steak, salt pork, scrapple, shoulder, teriyaki, top round 9 andouille, beefsteak, bratwurst, carbonado, club steak, croquette, cube steak, drumstick, foodstuff, forcemeat, fricassee, galantine, hamburger, liver pâté, lunchmeat, medallion, nutriment, pork roast, provender, roast duck, rump steak, short ribs, spareribs, substance 10 beefburger, blade steak, boudin noir, comestible, corned beef, Cornish hen, cracklings, deviled ham, flank steak, headcheese, knockwurst, liverwurst, main course, mortadilla, prosciutto, provisions, roast goose, round steak, scaloppine, scaloppini, shank steak, shell steak, shish kebab, skirt steak, sustenance, tenderloin
accompaniment: 6 potato 9 vegetable
alternative: 4 tofu 8 bean curd
avoider: 5 vegan 10 vegetarian
breakfast ~: 3 ham 5 bacon
canned ~: 4 Spam
cured ~: 5 jerky
cut: 4 chop, loin 5 flank, shank, T-bone 6 fillet
dark ~: 3 leg 5 thigh 9 drumstick
deli ~: 3 ham 6 salami 7 bologna 8 pastrami 10 corned beef
dish: 4 stew
dried ~: 5 jerky
ender: 4 ball, head, loaf 6 packer 7 packing
exotic ~: 3 emu 4 emeu
GI ~: 4 Spam
grade: 5 prime 6 choice
in Spanish: 5 carne
jelly: 5 aspic
juices: 5 gravy
made without milk or ~: 5 parve 6 pareve
moisten ~: 5 baste
on a stick: 5 cabob, kabab, kabob, kebab, kebob
pie: 5 pasty
red ~: 4 beef 5 steak
seller: 7 butcher
site: 6 locker
slice of ~: 6 collop
starter: 3 nut 4 crab 5 force, lunch, mince, sweet
strong, as ~: 4 gamy 5 gamey
treat ~: 4 corn, cure 5 smoke
trim ~: 5 defat
meat __: 3 tea 4 hook, loaf 5 house 7 grinder, packing
__ meat: 3 fat, red 4 dark, side 5 baked, light, white 7 variety
Meat __ Aday: 4 Loaf
meat-and-potatoes: 5 vital 7 radical
concoction: 4 hash
__ meatball: 7 Swedish
Meatballs (1979 film)
cast: Harvey Atkin, Kate Lynch, Bill Murray
director: Ivan Reitman
setting: 4 camp
meathead: 3 ass, nit, oaf, sap 4 boob, clod, dolt, fool 5 chump, clown, cluck, dummy, dunce, joker, looby, ninny, patsy 6 dimwit, lubber, lummox, nitwit, sucker, turkey 7 buffoon, dingbat, dullard, half-wit, jackass 8 dumbbell, numskull 9 birdbrain, lamebrain, numbskull, simpleton 10 nincompoop
Meathead: 4 Mike 6 Stivic
father-in-law: 6 Archie
mother-in-law: 5 Edith
wife: 6 Gloria
Meat Loaf
real name: Marvin Lee Aday
song: I'd Do Anything for Your Love (1993)
I'd Lie for You (1995)
Paradise by the Dashboard Light (1978)
Rock and Roll Dreams Come Through (1994)
Two Out of Three Ain't Bad (1978)
meatus site: 3 ear
meaty: 4 rich 5 beefy, pithy 7 weighty 8 profound 10 meaningful
__ Me Back to Old Virginny: 5 Carry
__ Me Badd: 5 Color
__ Me Be the One: 3 Let
__ Me Be There: 3 Let
Mebsuta: 4 star
__ Me By: 4 Pass
__ Me Call You Sweetheart: 3 Let
Mecca: 3 hub 4 city, town 10 attraction
locale: 5 Hejaz, Hijaz 6 Hedjaz 11 Saudi Arabia
pilgrim: 5 hadji
pilgrimage to ~: 3 haj 4 hadj, hajj
port: 5 Jedda, Jidda
resident: 5 Saudi
shrine: 4 Kaba 5 Kaaba, Kabah 6 Kaabah
Mecca (1963 song) artist: Gene Pitney
Mecham: 4 Evan
mechanic: 8 repairer 10 technician
concern: 6 engine
device: 5 dolly, U-bolt
job: 4 lube 6 tuneup
specialty ~: 3 car 4 auto 10 automobile
__ mechanic: 6 master
mechanical: 4 cold 5 fixed, stiff 6 useful 7 cursory, regular, routine 8 habitual, knee-jerk, lifeless 9 automated, automatic, technical, unfeeling 10 industrial
man: 5 droid, robot 7 android
person: 5 droid
procedure: 4 rote
mechanical __: 3 man 4 bank, pulp, twin 6 pencil 7 drawing
Mechanical Bride, The author: Marshall McLuhan
mechanics: 7 science
study: 6 forces, motion
mechanic's __: 4 lien
__ mechanics: 4 body, soil, wave 5 fluid 6 matrix 7 quantum
__ Mechanics: 7 Popular
Mechanicsville: 4 city, town
locale: 8 Virginia
mechanism: 4 mode, tool 5 gears, means, motor, thing, works 6 agency, device, engine, gadget, medium, method, system 7 gimmick, innards, machine, process, vehicle 8 black box, workings 9 apparatus, appliance, doohickey, machinery, operation, procedure 10 components, instrument
__ mechanism: 6 coping, escape 7 defense, trigger
mechanized: 9 automated, automatic 10 electrical, industrial
mecum, vade: 5 bible, guide 8 handbook
med __: 6 school
med.
bigger than ~: 2 XL 3 lge.
conglomerate: 3 HMO
degree: 2 MD 3 DMD 4 M.Sc.D.
facility: 4 hosp.
staffer: 2 RN 3 LPN
test: 3 ECG, EEG, EKG, MRI
__ Med: 4 Club
medaka: 4 fish
medal: 3 DCM, DFC, DSM, DSO 4 gold 5 award, badge, honor, prize, title 6 bronze, reward, ribbon, trophy 9 Navy Cross 10 Bronze Star, decoration, Silver Star
attachment: 5 clasp
British ~: 3 DCM, DSO
bronze ~: 3 DSC
give a ~ to: 4 cite 5 honor 8 decorate
grounds for a ~: 5 valor
material: 4 gold 6 bronze, silver
shape: 4 star
winner: 4 best, hero
medal __: 4 play
__ medal: 4 gold 6 bronze, silver 7 service
Medal for Benny, A (1945 film)
cast: Arturo de Cordova, Dorothy Lamour, J. Carrol Naish
director: Irving Pichel
medalist: 6 victor, winner 8 champion
gold ~: 4 hero 5 first 6 winner 8 champion
Medalist: 3 car 4 auto 7 Mercury 10 automobile
medallion: 4 meat, seal 5 badge, prize
Medallion: 3 car 4 auto 5 Dodge 10 automobile
Medal of __: 5 Honor 7 Freedom
Medan: 4 city, town
locale: 9 Indonesia
Medard: 5 saint
Medawar, Peter: 7 British 8 Nobelist 9 zoologist
meddle: 3 pry, spy 4 nose, poke 5 mix in, snoop 6 butt in, horn in, impose,

kibitz, tamper, worm in 7 barge in, break in, chime in, enquire, inquire, intrude, obtrude 8 encroach, infringe, trespass 9 interfere, interpose, intervene
don't ~: 5 let be 10 deregulate
ender: 4 some
meddler: 5 snoop, yenta 6 gossip 8 busybody, intruder, quidnunc
meddlesome: 4 busy, nosy 5 nosey, pushy 6 prying, snoopy 7 curious 8 busybody, snooping 9 intrusive, kibitzing, obtrusive, officious
in Britain: 5 nebby
meddling: 4 nosy 5 nosey 7 curious 9 intrusive, obtrusive, officious 10 snoopiness
Medea
brother of ~: 8 Apsyrtus
daughter of ~: 7 Eriopis
father of ~: 6 Aeetes, Hecate, Hekate
husband of ~: 5 Jason 6 Aegeus
sailed on it: 4 Argo
sister of ~: 5 Aeaea, Circe, Kirke 9 Chalciope
son of ~: 5 Argus, Medus 6 Medeus, Pheres 8 Mermerus, Tisander 9 Alcimedes, Alcimenes, Thessalus, Tisandrus
Medea author: Euripides
character: 5 Creon, Jason 6 Aegeus, Glauce
__ Me Deadly: 4 Kiss
Médée author: Pierre Corneille
Medeiros: 5 Glenn
Medellín: 4 city, town
locale: 8 Colombia
Medford: 3 Don 4 city, town
locale: 4 Mass. 6 Oregon 7 New York
school: 5 Tufts
Medgar: 5 Evers
media: 4 news, oils 5 cable, press, radio 7 dailies 9 magazines 10 newspapers, publishing, television
barrage: 4 hype 5 blitz
center: 7 library
initials: 3 ABC, CBS, NBC
messages: 3 ads
monitor: 3 FCC
one of the news ~: 2 TV 5 print, radio 10 television
prefix: 5 multi
room: 3 den
star: 5 celeb 9 celebrity
workers' union: 5 AFTRA
media __: 5 blitz, event, hound, mogul 6 center
__ media: 3 new, via 4 mass, news 5 mixed
Media
today: 4 Iran
medial: 4 mean 6 center
median: 3 avg., par 4 mean, norm 6 middle 7 average, central, halfway 8 midpoint, standard
median __: 5 plane, point, strip
mediate: 5 judge 6 settle, step in, umpire 7 referee, resolve 8 moderate, trade off 9 arbitrate, intercede, interpose, intervene, make a deal, make peace, negotiate, reconcile, take a hand 10 adjudicate, conciliate, propitiate
Mediate, Rocco: 6 golfer
milieu: 5 links 6 course
org.: 3 PGA
mediation: 9 agreement
agcy.: 4 NLRB
mediator: 5 fixer 6 broker, umpire 7 arbiter, referee 9 appointee, go-between, moderator 10 arbitrator, interceder, negotiator, peacemaker
goal: 5 peace 6 accord 8 contract 9 agreement 10 settlement
medic: 3 doc, EMT 6 aidman, doctor, healer, intern 7 interne 8 corpsman 9 lifesaver, physician
starter: 4 para
medical: 6 iatric 8 curative, iatrical
British ~ journal: 6 Lancet
British ~ org.: 3 NHS
center: 4 hosp. 6 clinic 8 hospital 9 infirmary 10 dispensary
charge: 3 fee
deg.: 2 MD 3 DDS, DMD
discovery: 4 cure 9 treatment
meas.: 2 cc.
org.: 3 AMA
prefix: 4 neur- 5 iatro-, neuro-
research agcy.: 3 CDC, NIH
school subject: 4 anat. 7 anatomy
specialty: 3 ENT
suffix: 4 -itis, -osis 5 -iatry
test: 3 ECG, EEG, EKG, MRI, NMR 4 X-ray
tool: 5 laser 6 lancet
worker: 2 dr., MD, RN 3 LPN 5 nurse 6 doctor, extern, intern 7 interne 8 resident 9 physician
medical __: 3 law 6 doctor
__ medical: 5 major
Medical Center (CBS drama)
cast: James Daly (Dr. Paul Lochner) Chad Everett (Dr. Joe Gannon)
Medicare org.: 3 SSA
medicaster: 5 quack
medicate: 4 drug 5 treat 6 doctor
medicated: 10 antiseptic
medication: 4 balm, cure, dose, drug, pill 5 salve, serum, tonic 6 elixir, lotion, physic, potion, remedy, tablet 7 capsule, vaccine 8 antidote, liniment, ointment, sedative, tincture 9 antitoxin, injection, treatment 10 antibiotic
amount: 4 dose 6 dosage
Medici in-law: 4 Este
medicinal: 4 herb 6 iatric 8 curative, iatrical, remedial, sanative
application: 5 salve
in taste: 6 bitter
medium: 4 pill 5 serum 6 caplet 7 vaccine
paper: 6 charta
plant: 3 rue 4 aloe, sage 5 jalap, senna, sumac, urena 6 arnica, cassia, croton, ipecac, sumach
plant derivative: 5 aloin
tea: 5 tansy
medicine: 4 balm, cure, dose, drug, pill 5 salve, serum, tonic 6 elixir, lotion, physic, potion, remedy, tablet 7 capsule, science, therapy, vaccine 8 antidote, liniment, ointment, sedative, tincture 9 antitoxin, injection, treatment 10 antibiotic, profession
agency: 3 FDA
chest item: 4 Q-Tip 5 floss, gauze 6 iodine 9 boric acid, mouthwash 10 toothpaste
combining form: 5 iatro-, -iatry 7 -iatrics
dispenser: 5 doser
folk ~: 4 lore
give ~ to: 4 dose
holder: 4 vial 5 ampul, phial 6 ampule 7 ampoule
like some ~: 3 OTC
man: 6 healer, shaman
measure: 6 capful
open, as a ~ bottle: 5 uncap
patent ~: 6 elixir 7 panacea
sugarcoated ~: 6 dragée
medicine __: 3 man 4 ball, show 5 dance, lodge
__ medicine: 4 folk 5 cough, group, legal, space, state 6 family, patent, sports 7 nuclear
Medicine Hat: 4 city, town
locale: 6 Canada 7 Alberta
Medicine Man (1992 film)
cast: Lorraine Bracco, Sean Connery
director: John McTiernan
medico: 3 doc 6 doctor, healer 9 physician
medieval: 6 feudal, Gothic 7 buisine 10 antiquated
entertainer: 4 poet 8 minstrel
laborer: 5 helot 6 vassal 7 bondman, chattel, villein
trade union: 4 club
Medina: 4 city, town
locale: 4 Ohio 5 Hejaz, Hijaz 6 Hedjaz 11 Saudi Arabia
resident: 4 Arab 5 Saudi
mediocre: 4 blah, dull, fair, poor, so-so 5 cheap 6 decent 7 average, humdrum, vanilla 8 inferior, middling, moderate, ordinary, passable, standard 9 colorless, tolerable, unnotable 10 fairly good, mainstream, pedestrian, second-rate, uninspired
meditate: 4 mull, muse, pore 5 study, think, weigh 6 ponder 7 reflect 8 cogitate, consider, mull over, ruminate, turn over 9 think over 10 deliberate, introspect, puzzle over
meditation: 6 revery 7 reverie, thought 9 deduction 10 cogitation
aid: 5 chant
breakthrough in ~: 6 satori
exercise: 4 yoga
room: 5 zendo
sound: 2 om
meditative: 6 broody 7 pensive, wistful 8 studious
one: 5 muser
sect: 3 Zen
Mediterranean: 3 sea
arm of the ~: 5 Egean 6 Aegean, Ionian
country: 3 Alg., Isr., Leb., Mor., Syr. 5 Egypt, Italy, Libya, Spain, Syria 6 France, Greece, Israel, Turkey 7 Algeria, Lebanon, Morocco, Tunisia
eastern ~: 6 Levant
fish: 5 porgy 6 nonnat 7 anchovy 8 gilthead
gulf: 5 Gabès, Lions, Sidra
island: 3 Sar. 4 Elba 5 Capri, Corfu, Crete, Egadi, Ibiza, Iviza, Malta 6 Candia, Cyprus, Sicily 7 Corsica 8 Sardinia
locale: 3 Afr., Eur. 4 Asia 6 Africa, Europe
port: 4 Gaza, Oran, Yafo 5 Haifa, Jaffa, Tunis 6 Beirut, Naples 8 Beyrouth 10 Marseilles
resort: 4 Nice 7 Antibes
river to the ~: 4 Ebro, Nile 5 Rhone, Tiber 6 Seyhan 7 Orontes
ship: 5 xebec, zebec 6 caique, zebeck 7 chebeck
shrub: 5 caper 8 rosemary
staple: 5 olive
tree: 4 cork 5 carob 6 mastic
wind: 6 solano 7 sirocco 8 levanter
Mediterranean __: 3 Sea 7 climate
__ Méditerranée: 3 Mer
medium: 3 art, par 4 fair, form, mode, norm, seer, size, so-so, tool 5 agent, dance, drama, means, music, organ, sibyl 6 agency, avenue, factor, median, milieu, normal, speech 7 average, channel, habitat, neutral, prophet, psychic, setting, vehicle, writing 8 ambience, middling, moderate, ordinary, painting, passable, standard 9 machinery, mechanism, sculpture, temperate, tolerable, unextreme 10 instrument
device: 5 Ouija, tarot 7 crystal 10 Ouija board
in music: 5 mezzo
skill: 3 ESP
medium __: 4 shot 5 strip 6 bomber, octavo, quarto
__ medium: 4 mass 7 culture
medium-dry: 3 sec
Medium is the Massage, The author: Marshall McLuhan
medlar: 4 tree 5 apple
family: 4 rose
relative: 4 crab, Gala, Lodi, pear, plum, Rome 5 apple, Mutsu, peach 6 almond, cherry, Empire, Ida Red, Pippin, quince, russet 7 apricot, Baldwin, Bramley, costard, Freedom, Liberty, Spartan, Wealthy, Winesap 8 Cortland, hawthorn, Jonathan, McIntosh, oiticica 10 blackthorn, Rome Beauty
medley: 3 mix 4 brew, hash, olio, stew 5 combo 6 jumble 7 farrago, mélange, mixture, variety 8 mishmash, mixed bag, pastiche 9 composite, diversity, patchwork, potpourri 10 assortment, collection, cumulation, hodgepodge, miscellany, salmagundi
play a ~: 5 segue
medley __: 5 relay
Medley: 4 Bill
__ Me Do: 4 Love
Médoc: 3 red, vin 4 wine 6 claret 7 red wine
origin: 6 France
__-me-down: 4 hand 5 reach
medregal: 4 fish
__-med student: 3 pre
Medusa
bearer: 4 egis 5 aegis
home: 3 sea 5 ocean
parent of ~: 4 Ceto 7 Phorcys
sister of ~: 6 Stheno 7 Euryale
slayer of ~: 7 Perseus
son of ~: 7 Pegasus 8 Chrysaor
tress: 5 snake
Medwick, Joe: 8 Cardinal 10 outfielder
meed: 6 ration, reward
meek: 3 shy 4 mild, soft, tame, weak, zero 5 lowly, mousy, quiet, timid 6 demure, docile, gentle, humble, modest, mousey, serene 7 lenient, passive, patient, servile, slavish, subdued 8 lamblike, obedient, peaceful, resigned, retiring, tolerant, yielding 9 compliant, diffident, flinching, spineless, tractable 10 forbearing, manageable, obsequious, spiritless, submissive, unassuming
inheritance: 5 Earth
one: 4 lamb 5 sheep
meek as __: 5 a lamb
Meek comic-strip partner: 3 Eek
Meeker: 5 Howie, Ralph
Meeker, Ralph: 5 actor
film: The Detective (1968)
Kiss Me Deadly (1955)
The Naked Spur (1953)
Paths of Glory (1957)
meekness: 7 modesty 8 humility 9 lowliness, timidness 10 diffidence, submission
__ Me Entertain You: 3 Let
meeny preceder: 4 eeny
meerkat: 8 mongoose
milieu: 3 Afr. 6 Africa, desert
meerschaum: 4 pipe 7 mineral
Meese: 2 Ed 5 Edwin
meet: 3 apt, fit, see, sit, tie 4 abut, face, find, good, join, just, race, tilt 5 event, flock, focus, front, greet, match, merge, moral, rally, reach, right, rival, touch, unite 6 accost, adjoin, answer, border, caucus, comply, confab,

engage, fulfil, gather, handle, huddle, link up, make up, muster, powwow, proper, redeem, timely **7** collide, condign, conform, connect, contact, contest, convene, do lunch, fitting, fulfill, qualify, receive, run into, satisfy, session, tourney, welcome **8** adhere to, apposite, approach, assemble, bump into, carry out, chance on, coincide, come up to, confront, converge, cope with, deal with, deserved, face up to, happen on, keep pace, suitable **9** discharge, encounter, expedient, forgather, get to know, intersect, juxtapose, measure up, opportune, road rally, run across, stand up to **10** applicable, chance upon, come across, comply with, congregate, convention, engagement, experience, get a hold of, hook up with, keep up with, rendezvous, tournament
again: **5** resee, resit
a raise: **3** see **4** call
halfway: **7** mediate **9** arbitrate, negotiate, reconcile **10** compromise, conciliate
head on: **8** confront, cope with, deal with
make ends ~: **3** eke **4** live, save **5** skimp, stint **6** eke out **7** subsist
one's enemy: **4** face **6** attack, line up, take on **7** assault **9** fight with
participant: **5** racer **6** runner **8** sprinter
requirements: **2** do **4** pass, suit **5** serve **7** fulfill, qualify, satisfy
segment: **3** run **4** race **5** event **6** sprint
starter: **4** help
with: **3** see **4** spot **5** taste **6** endure, fall on, locate, suffer **7** receive, run into, undergo **8** come upon, fall upon **9** encounter **10** experience
meet __: **7** halfway
__ meet: **4** swap **5** track
...meet __ coming...: **5** a body
Meet __ Black: **3** Joe
Meet __ Doe: **4** John
Meet __ St. Louis: **4** Me in
Meet Boston Blackie (1941 film)
cast: Rochelle Hudson, Richard Lane, Chester Morris
director: Robert Florey
Meet Corliss Archer: **9** radio show
meeting: **4** conf., conv., date, sess., talk **5** forum, Q and A, rally, tryst **6** caucus, confab, huddle, parley, powwow **7** contact, hearing, joining, reunion, session, turnout **8** assembly, audience, conclave, congress, crossing, junction, juncture, showdown **9** concourse, confluent, encounter, gathering, reception, symposium **10** cattle call, conference, confluence, contiguity, convention, convergent, discussion, engagement, rendezvous
attend a ~: **3** sit
call a ~: **6** gather, muster, summon **7** convene, convoke, marshal **8** assemble
ender: **5** house
have another ~ with: **5** resee
hold a ~: **3** sit **4** call **5** rally **6** confer, gather, muster, summon **7** conduct, convene, convoke **8** assemble **10** congregate
in a ~: **4** busy
nautical ~: **3** gam
never ~: **8** parallel
of the minds: **6** accord **7** concord, harmony **9** agreement, consensus
outline: **6** agenda
place: **3** hub **5** forum, haunt
plan: **6** agenda
run the ~: **5** chair **7** preside
secret ~: **5** tryst **10** rendezvous
the quota: **8** adequate **10** acceptable, sufficient
unpleasant ~: **5** run-in
meeting __: **4** post, rail **5** house
__ meeting: **4** camp, mass, tent, town **5** watch **6** prayer, Quaker, summit **7** monthly
__-meeting: **4** go-to
meeting of the __: **5** minds
Meet Joe Black (1998 film)
cast: Claire Forlani, Anthony Hopkins, Brad Pitt
director: Martin Brest
Meet John Doe (1941 film)
cast: Edward Arnold, Gary Cooper, Barbara Stanwyck
composer: **7** Tiomkin
director: Frank Capra
Meet Me Half Way (1987 song) artist: Kenny Loggins
Meet Me in St. Louis (1944 film)
cast: Mary Astor, Lucille Bremer, Judy Garland, Margaret O'Brien
director: Vincente Minnelli
meetness: **8** justness **9** propriety
meet one's __: **5** match
__ Meets Girl: **3** Boy
Meet the Parents (2000 film)
cast: Blythe Danner, Robert De Niro, Teri Polo, Ben Stiller
cat: **6** Mr. Jinx
director: Jay Roach
Meet the Press (NBC news)
host: Ned Brooks, Marvin Kalb, Bill Monroe, Roger Mudd, Martha Rountree, Tim Russert, Lawrence Spivak, Garrick Utley, Chris Wallace
Mefistofele: **5** opera
composer: **5** Boito
role: **5** Elena, Faust, Marta **6** Wagner **10** Margherita
setting: **6** Greece, Heaven **7** Germany
Meg: **4** Ryan **5** Tilly **6** Foster, Mallon **8** Wolitzer
daughter: **4** Demi
sister: **2** Jo **3** Amy **4** Beth
mega: **4** huge, much
megacorporation: **5** giant, trust **9** syndicate
megalomaniac's craving: **5** power
megalopolis: **4** city
Megan: **7** Follows
Megane: **3** car **4** auto **7** Renault **10** automobile
megaphone
inventor: **6** Edison
like a ~: **5** conic **7** conical
megapode: **4** bird
megastar: **4** idol
megatherian: **3** big
__ Me Gently: **4** Rock
megilla: **4** tale
Meg Merrilies author: John Keats
Megna: **4** John
__ Me Go, Lover: **3** Let
Megrez: **4** star
megrim: **8** headache
__ Me Half Way: **4** Meet
mehitabel: **3** cat
friend: **5** Archy, roach **9** cockroach
Mehlville: **4** city, town
locale: **8** Missouri
Mehta: **3** Ved **5** Zubin
successor: **5** Masur
Mehta, Ved: **6** Indian, writer
Mehta, Zubin: **6** Indian **9** conductor
__ Meigs: **4** Fort
__ mein: **4** chow
__ me in!: **3** Let **4** Deal **5** Count
Mein Gott!: **3** ach
Mein Herr Marquis: **4** aria
Meins: **3** Gus
__ Me in St. Louis: **4** Meet
__ Me in the Morning: **5** Touch
Meir, Golda: **2** P.M. **7** Israeli
predecessor: **6** Eshkol
successor: **5** Rabin
__ Me Irresponsible: **4** Call
Meishan: **3** pig **5** swine
Meisner: **5** Randy
Meissa: **4** star
__ Meistersinger: **3** Die
Meitner, Lise: **9** physicist, scientist
Mejicanos: **4** city, town
locale: **10** El Salvador
__ Me Kangaroo Down, Sport: **3** Tie
__ Me Kate: **4** Kiss
Mekbuda: **4** star
Mekka: **5** Eddie
Mekong: **5** Delta, river
locale: **4** Laos **5** China **7** Myanmar, Vietnam **8** Thailand
Mel: **3** Ott **4** Hein **5** Allen, Blanc, Torme **6** Brooks, Carter, Ferrer, Gibson, Harris, Renfro, Stuart, Tillis **8** McDaniel
Melancholia engraver: **5** Durer
melancholy: **3** low, sad, woe **4** blue, dark, down, funk, glum, mood, mopy, pall **5** blahs, bleak, blues, dolor, ennui, funky, gloom, grief, heavy, moody, moony, mopey, sorry, woful **6** broody, dismal, dreary, droopy, gloomy, misery, moping, morbid, morose, somber, sorrow, tedium, woeful **7** anguish, boredom, despair, dim view, dismals, doleful, elegiac, emotion, hangdog, in a funk, joyless, letdown, malaise, pensive, sadness, unhappy, wistful **8** blue funk, dejected, desolate, dolorous, downcast, glumness, liverish, lowering, mournful, saddened, the blues, troubled, wretched **9** bummed out, cheerless, dejection, depressed, heartache, heartsick, mirthless, miserable, pessimism, plaintive, saddening, saturnine, sorrowful, woebegone **10** chapfallen, deplorable, depressing, depression, desolation, despairing, despondent, dispirited, heavy heart, in the dumps, lamentable, loneliness, lugubrious, out of sorts, woefulness
in music: **5** mesto
mood: **4** funk
with ~: **5** sadly
__ Melancholy: **5** Ode on
Melanesian: **6** Fijian
mélange: **3** mix **4** hash, olio, stew **5** combo **6** jumble, medley **7** farrago, goulash, mixture, variety **8** mishmash, mixed bag, pastiche **9** admixture, pasticcio, patchwork, potpourri **10** assortment, hodgepodge, miscellany, salmagundi
Melanie: **6** Mayron **8** Griffith
last name: Safka
song: Brand New Key (1971)
Lay Down (1970)
to Pittypat: **5** niece
Melba: **5** Moore **6** Nellie
Melba __: **5** sauce, toast
__ Melba: **5** peach, pêche
Melba, Nellie: **4** Dame, diva **6** singer **7** soprano **10** Australian
specialty: **5** opera
melba toast: **5** bread
Melbourne: **4** city, port, town
locale: **7** Florida **9** Australia
river: **5** Yarra
Melcher: **5** Marty **6** Martin
Melchiades: **4** pope **7** pontiff
Melchior: **5** magus **7** Lauritz
and others: **4** Magi
colleague: **6** Caspar **9** Balthazar
like ~: **4** wise
Melchior, Lauritz: **5** tenor **6** singer
specialty: **5** opera
Melchor Ocampo: **4** city, town
locale: **6** Mexico
meld: **3** mix **4** fuse, link **5** blend, immix, merge, unify **6** mingle **7** connect **8** conflate **9** commingle, integrate **10** amalgamate
melded: **4** mixt **5** fused, mixed **6** merged **7** blended **9** composite
melding: **5** union
melee: **3** ado, row **4** fray, to-do **5** brawl, broil, brush, clash, fight, set-to, storm **6** affray, barney, fracas, ruckus, rumpus, tussle, uproar **7** ruction, scuffle **8** brouhaha, rowdydow, scramble, skirmish **9** brannigan, scrimmage **10** donnybrook, free-for-all, hullabaloo
Melendez: **4** Bill
Melfort: **4** city, town
locale: **6** Canada
meliad: **5** nymph
__ Me Like a Rock: **5** Loves
Melina: **8** Mercouri
Melinda: **6** Dillon
Melior: **4** font **8** typeface
meliorate: **5** fix up **6** better, enrich, polish, reform **7** enhance, improve, shape up, sharpen, upgrade **8** spruce up
Melisande artist: **4** Erté
Melissa: **6** Hayden **7** Gilbert **8** Mathison **9** Etheridge **10** Manchester
Melissa __ Anderson: **3** Sue
Melissa Joan __: **4** Hart
Melitta: **6** coffee
alternative: **5** Sanka, Yuban **7** Folgers, Nescafe, Savarin **9** Hills Bros.
__-mell: **4** pell
Mell: **7** Lazarus
Mellencamp, John Cougar
song: Authority Song (1984)
Check It Out (1988)
Cherry Bomb (1987)
Crumblin' Down (1983)
Get a Leg Up (1991)
Hand to Hold on to (1982)
Hurts So Good (1982)
Jack and Diane (1982)
Key West Intermezzo (1996)
Lonely Ol' Night (1985)
Paper in Fire (1987)
Pink Houses (1983)
Pop Singer (1989)
R.O.C.K. in the U.S.A. (1986)
Small Town (1985)
Wild Night (1994)
mellifluous: **4** rich, soft **5** lyric, round, sweet **6** dulcet, honied, liquid, smooth **7** flowing, melodic, tuneful **8** euphonic **9** melodious **10** euphonical
Mello __: **5** Yello
Mellon: **6** Andrew
Mellonta Tauta author: Edgar Allan Poe
mellow: **3** age **4** aged, calm, cool, mild, open, rich, ripe, soft **5** juicy, quiet, relax, ripen, staid, stoic, sweet, tasty, tipsy **6** at ease, casual, docile, gentle, go soft, liquid, low-key, mature, placid, relent, season, sedate, serene, smooth, soften, subdue, toothy **7** amiable, at peace, cordial, develop, equable, mollify, musical, offhand, pacific, relaxed, ripened, stoical, subdued, unmoved **8** amicable, carefree, composed, humanize, informal, laidback, likeable, luscious, peaceful, resonant, seasoned, tranquil **9** collected, congenial, easy-going, impassive, melodious, quiescent, succulent, tem-

perate, unexcited, unruffled **10** come around, full-bodied, nonchalant, settle down, unagitated, unhardened, untroubled
out: 9 lighten up
mellow __: 3 out
mellowed: 6 mature
Mellow Yellow (1966 song) artist: Donovan
Mello Yello: 9 soft drink
alternative: 3 TAB **4** Nehi **5** Fanta **6** Fresca, Sprite **8** Diet Rite, Dr Pepper **9** Canada Dry **10** Royal Crown **11** Mountain Dew
Melmac native: 3 Alf
Melmoth the Wanderer author: Charles Robert Maturin
melodeon: 8 keyboard **10** instrument
part: 4 reed
melodic: 4 soft **5** clear, lyric, sweet, tonal **6** ariose, arioso, dulcet, in tune, mellow, poetic **7** lilting, lyrical, musical, silvery, tuneful **8** poetical, resonant, sonorous **9** agreeable, well-tuned **10** euphonious, harmonious
not ~: 6 atonal
phrase: 4 riff
subject: 4 tema
Melodie d'Amour (1957 song) artist: Ames Brothers
__ Melodies: 6 Merrie
melodious: 4 soft **5** clear, in key, lyric, on key, sweet, tonal **6** ariose, arioso, dulcet, in tune, mellow, poetic **7** lilting, lyrical, musical, silvery, tuneful **8** poetical, resonant, sonorous **9** agreeable, well-tuned **10** euphonious, harmonious
melodiousness: 7 harmony **8** lyricism
melodist: 6 singer
melodize: 4 sing
melodrama: 4 play **5** genre **7** romance **10** excitement, production
role: 4 hero **6** damsel **7** villain
melodramatic: 5 hammy, hokey, lurid, soapy, stagy, sudsy, teary **6** stagey **8** affected **10** theatrical
cry: 3 oho **4** alas **5** never
get ~: 3 act **5** emote **7** carry on, overact
one: 3 ham
melodramatize: 5 emote
melody: 3 air, lay **4** aria, lilt, pean, raga, riff, song, tema, tune **5** canto, chant, dirge, ditty, lyric, music, paean, sound, theme **6** chorus, strain **7** descant, discant, euphony, harmony, refrain **8** diapason **9** leitmotif
partner: 5 lyric **6** lyrics
recurring ~: 5 motif, thema
Melody: 8 Anderson **9** Patterson
Melody of Love (1955 song)
artist: Billy Vaughan, David Carroll, Four Aces
Melody Ranch: 9 radio show
host: Gene Autry
melon: 4 pepo, pink **5** color, fruit, gourd **6** casaba **7** cassaba, Persian **8** Crenshaw, honeydew, windfall **9** cantaloup **10** cantaloupe
like a ~: 5 juicy
relative: 4 nude **6** damask, salmon **7** apricot **8** flamingo **9** carnation
starter: 4 musk **5** water
throwaway: 4 rind
__ melon: 6 casaba, citron, netted, nutmeg, winter **7** cassaba, Persian
melonlike fruit: 5 papaw
__ Me Loose: 4 Turn
Melos: 3 isl. **4** isle **6** island
Melpomene: 4 Muse
colleague: 4 Clio **5** Erato **6** Thalia, Urania **7** Euterpe **8** Calliope **10** Polyhymnia **11** Terpsichore
parent of ~: 4 Zeus **9** Mnemosyne
Melrose: 4 city, town
locale: 4 Mass.
Melrose Park: 4 city, town
locale: 8 Illinois
Melrose Place (Fox drama)
cast: Thomas Calabro (Michael Mancini)
Rob Estes (Kyle McBride)
Heather Locklear (Amanda Woodward)
Grant Show (Jake Hanson)
Andrew Shue (Billy Campbell)
Courtney Thorne-Smith (Alison Parker)
Jack Wagner (Peter Burns)
Mel's Diner waitress: 3 Flo **4** Vera **5** Alice
melt: 3 run **4** fade, fuse, join, thaw, warm **5** deice, touch, yield **6** ablate, disarm, give in, relent, render, scorch, soften, vanish, warm up **7** diffuse, liquefy, liquify **8** disperse, dissolve, evanesce, fluidize, unfreeze **9** blend into, disappear **10** deliquesce
away: 3 die **4** fade, thaw **9** dissipate
down: 4 heat **6** render
ender: 3 age **4** down
into: 5 merge
starter: 4 snow
together: 4 weld **5** blend
__ melt: 4 tuna **5** patty
meltdown: 9 emergency
site: 4 core **7** reactor
melted: 6 fusile, liquid, molten
melting __: 3 pot **5** point
Melton: 3 Sid
Melun: 4 city, town
locale: 6 France
Melvil: 5 Dewey
Melville: 6 Cooper, Herman **9** Shavelson
Melville, Herman: 6 author, writer
captain: 4 Ahab
setting: 3 sea **5** ocean
work: Benito Cereno
Billy Budd
Moby-Dick
Omoo
Typée
Melvin: 5 Belli, Frank, Laird **6** Calvin, Harold **8** Schwartz
Melvin and Howard (1980 film)
cast: Paul LeMat, Jason Robards, Mary Steenburgen
director: Jonathan Demme
Melvin and the Blue Notes, Harold
song: Bad Luck (1975)
If You Don't Know Me by Now (1972)
The Love I Lost (1973)
Wake Up Everybody (1975)
Melvyn: 7 Douglas
mem: 6 Hebrew, letter
predecessor: 5 lamed **6** lamedh
successor: 3 nun
__ Me Madam: 4 Call
member: 3 arm, leg, toe **4** beam, foot, hand, limb, link, part, unit, wing **5** bough, digit, organ, shoot **6** branch, finger, joiner **7** chapter, element, segment **8** division **9** affiliate, appendage, associate, component, extremity, layperson **10** legislator
member __: 4 firm
__ member: 3 end, web **7** charter
Member of the Wedding, The: 4 film, play
author: Carson McCullers
cast: Brandon de Wilde, Julie Harris, Ethel Waters
director: Fred Zinnemann
Members __: 4 Only
membership: 4 body, club, roll **6** league, roster **7** company, fellows, society **9** personnel
fee: 4 dues
have a ~ card: 6 belong
membrane: 3 web **4** film, skin, wall **5** sheet **6** intima, lamina, lining, septum, sheath, tissue **10** integument
combining form: 5 chori- **6** chorio-, hymeno-
__ membrane: 4 cell **6** plasma, serous **7** basilar, choroid, hyaloid, nuclear
Memel: 5 river
locale: 6 Russia
memento: 5 favor, relic, token **6** trophy **7** vestige **8** keepsake, reminder, souvenir
Memento Mori author: Muriel Spark
M. Emmet __: 5 Walsh
Memnoch the Devil author: Anne Rice
memo: 4 list, note **5** aviso **6** advice, letter, notice, record, report **7** jotting, message, missive, tickler **8** dispatch, notation, register, reminder **9** directive
abbr.: 3 FYI **4** ASAP, attn.
high-tech ~: 3 fax **5** e-mail
legal ~: 5 brief **8** abstract
starter: 4 in re
__ memo: 6 credit
memoir: 3 bio **4** life **5** diary, story **6** record **7** account, journal **9** biography, chronicle, life story, narrative, recountal
__-mémoire: 4 aide
Memoires author: François de La Rouchefoucauld
memoirs: 3 bio **9** life story
Memoirs of a Fox-Hunting Man
author: Siegfried Sassoon
memorabilia: 3 ana **6** trivia **9** souvenirs
memorable: 5 great, noted, vivid **6** famous, signal **7** crucial, lasting, notable, special, unusual **8** critical, decisive, enduring, eventful, glorious, haunting, historic, striking **9** bodacious, deathless, important, indelible, momentous, red-letter, top-drawer **10** celebrated, monumental, noteworthy, remarkable
memorandum: 4 list, note **5** aviso **6** advice, letter, notice, record, report **7** jotting, message, missive, tickler **8** dispatch, notation, register, reminder **9** directive
maker: 5 noter
__ Memorandum, The: 7 Quiller
Memorandum, The author: Václav Havel
__ memoria: 3 pro
memorial: 4 carn **5** cairn, stela, stele **6** column, pillar, plaque, record, statue, tablet **7** obelisk, tribute **8** landmark, monolith, monument **10** dedicatory
__ Memorial: 7 Lincoln **9** Jefferson
Memorial Day race: 4 Indy
Memorial University
location: 6 Canada **7** St. John's
memories
awaken ~: 6 remind
Memories Are Made of This (1955 song)
artist: Dean Martin, Gale Storm
Memories of __: 3 Eld
Memories of a Catholic Girlhood
author: Mary McCarthy
Memories of Another Day author: Harold Robbins
Memories of Me (1988 film)
cast: Billy Crystal, Alan King, JoBeth Williams
director: Henry Winkler
Memories of Midnight author: Sidney Sheldon
Memories of You composer: 5 Blake, Razaf
memorization process: 4 rote
memorize: 4 know **5** learn **6** retain **8** remember
memorized, have: 4 know
memory: 4 game **6** recall **8** card game, mind's eye **9** anamnesis, awareness, flashback, retention **10** cognizance, impression, retrospect
book: 5 album
combining form: 4 mnem- **5** mnemo-
commit to ~: 4 etch **5** learn
computer ~: 3 ram **4** core **5** EPROM
fetch from ~: 6 call up, recall
flub: 5 lapse
from ~: 6 by rote
jogger: 4 list, note **8** reminder
jog the ~: 4 prod **5** tweak **6** remind
Muse: 5 Mneme
refresh one's ~ in Britain: 5 rub up
site: 6 cortex
trace: 6 engram
unit: 3 bit **4** byte
memory __: 4 bank, cell, lane **5** trace, verse **6** engram
__ memory: 4 core, drum, main, real **5** cache, flash, legal **6** bubble, screen **7** primary, virtual
Memory musical: 4 Cats
memory of God, name meaning: 7 Zachary
Memory of Trees, The singer: 4 Enya
Memphis: 4 city, font, town **8** typeface
athletes: 6 Tigers
county: 6 Shelby
locale: 4 Tenn. **5** Egypt **9** Tennessee
pro team: 9 Grizzlies
river: 4 Nile **11** Mississippi
street: 5 Beale
Memphis (song) artist: Johnny Rivers, Lonnie Mack
Me, Myself, __: 4 and I
Me, Myself & Irene (2000 film)
cast: Jim Carrey, Robert Forster, Renée Zellweger
director: Bobby Farrelly, Peter Farrelly
men: 3 he's **6** messr.'s
and women: 4 folk **6** masses, people, public, voters **7** society **8** citizens **9** hoi polloi, personnel
for ~ and women: 4 coed **6** unisex
for ~ only: 4 stag
in blue: 6 police
of ~: 4 masc. **9** masculine
org. for a few good ~: 4 USMC
Men __ From Mars...: 3 Are
Men __ Leave: 4 Don't
__ Men: 3 Tin, Two **4** Mojo, Safe **5** I Hate, King's, Metal **6** Little, Public, Simple **7** Diamond, Mystery
Mena: 6 Suvari
menace: 4 loom, risk, thug **5** bully, daunt, peril, scare **6** danger, hazard, impend, lean on, threat **7** imperil, portend, terrify, torment **8** browbeat, domineer, endanger, frighten, jeopardy, threaten **9** strong-arm, terrorize **10** intimidate, jeopardize, scare stiff
Menace II Society (1993 film)
cast: Jada Pinkett, Larenz Tate, Tyrin Turner
director: Albert Hughes, Allen Hughes
Menachem: 5 Begin
menacing: 4 ugly **5** scary **6** fierce, stormy **7** baleful, harmful, looming, ominous, parlous, serious **8** alarming, coercion, lowering, minatory, perilous, sinister **9** dangerous, frightful, impending **10** forbidding, formidable, pugnacious
be vaguely ~: 4 loom

look: 5 scowl
sound: 3 grr
menad: 9 bacchante
ménage: 9 household
menagerie: 3 zoo
member: 5 beast 6 animal
__ Menagerie, The: 5 Glass
Menahem: 5 Golan
Menai __: 6 Strait
Mena, Juan de: 4 poet 7 Spanish
__ Men and a Baby: 5 Three
Menander: 5 Greek 10 playwright
Men at Arms author: Evelyn Waugh
__ Men Can't Jump: 5 White
Mencius: 7 Chinese 11 philosopher
Mencken, H.L.: 6 author, writer
work: A Book of Burlesques
Damn: A Book of Calumny
In Defense of Women
Newspaper Days
Prejudices
mend: 3 fix, sew 4 cure, darn, gain, heal, knit, vamp 5 fix up, patch, piece, renew, resew, right 6 doctor, reform, repair, revamp, revise, stitch, tape up 7 correct, get well, improve, patch up, rebound, recover, rectify, redress, restore, retouch, service 8 overhaul, renovate 9 get better, refurbish 10 convalesce, recuperate
on the ~: 6 better 7 healing 9 improving 10 recovering
mend __: 6 fences
__ mend: 5 on the
mendacious: 5 false, lying, wrong 6 shifty, tricky, untrue 7 crooked, devious, fibbing 8 delusive, guileful, perjured, spurious 9 deceitful, deceptive, dishonest, erroneous, insincere, paltering 10 ungrounded, untruthful
mendacity: 3 fib, lie 4 tale 5 lying 6 dupery 7 falsity, untruth, whapper, whopper 9 deception, falsehood 10 dishonesty
Mende home: 6 Africa 7 Liberia
Mendeleev, Dmitri: 7 chemist, Russian
mendelevium: 7 element
Mendel, Gregor: 8 botanist 9 biologist, scientist
Mendelssohn: 5 Felix, Moses
Mendelssohn, Felix: 6 German 8 composer
work: Hebrides Overture
Italian Symphony
A Midsummer Night's Dream
Ruy Blas Overture
Scottish Symphony
Songs Without Words
St. Paul
Trumpet Overture
Mendelssohn, Moses: 11 philosopher
mender: 6 healer
target: 4 hole
Menderes: 5 river
locale: 6 Turkey 9 Asia Minor
Mendes: 3 Sam 6 Sergio
Mendes & Brasil '66, Sergio
song: The Fool on the Hill (1968)
The Look of Love (1968)
Never Gonna Let You Go (1983)
Scarborough Fair (1968)
Mendes, Sam Oscar: American Beauty
mendicant: 5 faker, fakir, faqir, friar 6 beggar, faquir, pauper 7 have-not
desire: 4 alms
home: 6 friary
mendicate: 3 beg 9 impetrate
__-mending: 5 fence
Mending Wall: 4 poem
author: Robert Frost
Mendocino: 4 cape
locale: 10 California
Men Don't Leave (1990 film)
cast: Joan Cusack, Arliss Howard, Jessica Lange
director: Paul Brickman
__ Men Don't Wear Plaid: 4 Dead
Mendoza: 4 city, town
locale: 6 Mexico 8 Veracruz
Me neither!: 4 Nor I
Menelaus
brother of ~: 9 Agamemnon
daughter of ~: 8 Hermione
parent of ~: 6 Aerope, Atreus
wife of ~: 5 Helen
mene, mene, __, upharsin: 5 tekel
Menen, Aubrey: 6 writer 7 British
menhaden: 4 fish, pogy
cousin: 4 shad
menial: 3 low 4 base 5 lowly, slave 6 abject, drudge, flunky, humble, lackey, nobody 7 fawning, flunkey, ignoble, lacquey, servant, servile, slavish 9 degrading, demeaning, groveling, low-status, nonentity 10 obsequious
worker: 4 peon, serf 6 drudge
__ Me Nice: 5 Treat
__ men in a tub: 5 three
Men in Black (1997 film)
cast: Linda Fiorentino, Tommy Lee Jones, Will Smith, Rip Torn
cat: 5 Orion
director: Barry Sonnenfeld
menace: 2 ET 5 alien
Men in Black (1997 song) artist: Will Smith
Men in Black II (2002 film)
cast: Lara Flynn Boyle, Rosario Dawson, Tommy Lee Jones, Will Smith
director: Barry Sonnenfeld
Men in My Little Girl's Life, The (1966 song) artist: Mike Douglas
meniscus: 4 lens 8 crescent
Menjou, Adolphe: 5 actor
film: A Farewell to Arms (1932)
The Front Page (1931)
Gold Diggers of 1935 (1935)
Little Miss Marker (1934)
The Mighty Barnum (1934)
The Milky Way (1936)
Morning Glory (1933)
Morocco (1930)
One Hundred Men and a Girl (1937)
One in a Million (1936)
Paths of Glory (1957)
The Sheik (1921)
Sing, Baby, Sing (1936)
The Sniper (1952)
Stage Door (1937)
A Star Is Born (1937)
Step Lively (1944)
The Tall Target (1951)
A Woman of Paris (1923)
You Were Never Lovelier (1942)
Menkar: 4 star
Menkent: 4 star
Menkib: 4 star
Men Like Gods author: H.G. Wells
Menlo Park: 4 city, town
initials: 3 TAE
locale: 9 New Jersey 10 California
name: 4 Alva 6 Edison, Thomas
Mennen rival: 5 Arrid
Menninger: 4 Karl
Mennonites: 4 sect 5 Amish
meno: 4 less
meno __: 5 mosso
Men of Honor (2000 film)
cast: Robert De Niro, Cuba Gooding Jr., Charlize Theron
director: George Tillman Jr.
__ Me No Flowers: 4 Send
Men of the Fighting Lady (1954 film)
cast: Louis Calhern, Van Johnson, Walter Pidgeon
Menominee: 6 Indian 7 Amerind
Menomonee, city on the: 9 Milwaukee
Menomonee Falls: 4 city, town
locale: 9 Wisconsin
__ Men on a Horse: 5 Three
__ me no questions...: 3 Ask
__-me-not: 5 touch 6 forget
Menotti, Gian Carlo work: Amahl and the Night Visitors
__ Men Out: 5 Eight
mens __: 3 rea
mens __ in corpore sano: 4 sana
men's __: 4 wear
Mensa: 4 club
like a ~ member: 5 smart
member: 5 brain 6 genius
qualifier: 6 IQ test
mensch: 3 man 7 good egg
mense: 8 civility 9 propriety 10 discretion
Men's Lives author: Peter Matthiessen
men's org.: 4 YMCA, YMHA
mens sana in corpore __: 4 sano
...__ men's souls: 3 try
Mentadent: 10 toothpaste
alternative: 3 Aim 5 Crest, Gleem, Topol 7 Close-Up, Colgate, Viadent 9 Aquafresh, Pepsodent, Rembrandt, Sensodyne 10 Pearl Drops, Ultra Brite
mental: 7 psychic 8 cerebral, rational, thinking 9 reasoning 10 subjective, subliminal, telepathic
ability: 3 ken 4 wits 6 brains, reason 9 knowledge
discipline: 4 will, yoga
faculties: 4 mind 5 sense 6 brains, reason, wisdom 8 judgment, lucidity, sagacity, sapience 9 intellect 10 perception
giant: 3 ace 4 whiz 5 brain 6 genius 7 egghead, prodigy, thinker 8 Einstein, highbrow, virtuoso 10 mastermind
health: 6 sanity
impression: 5 image 6 memory, vision
invention: 7 figment
picture: 4 idea 5 image 6 memory, vision 7 concept
state: 4 mood 6 esprit, fettle 7 emotion 8 attitude
mental __: 3 age 5 image 6 health
mentalist asset: 3 ESP
mentality: 2 IQ 3 wit 4 head, mind, wits 5 brain 6 acumen, brains, makeup, reason, smarts 7 mindset, outlook 8 attitude 9 character, intellect 10 brainpower, gray matter
__ mentality: 4 herd 5 siege
mentally: 8 inwardly
Men, The (1950 film)
cast: Marlon Brando, Everett Sloane, Teresa Wright
director: Fred Zinnemann
__ Men, The: 3 New 4 Tall 5 Lusty 6 Hollow
menthol, with: 5 minty
mention: 3 say 4 cite, name, note, plug, tell 5 infer, quote, refer, state, touch, voice 6 adduce, advert, broach, hint at, impart, notice, recite, remark, report, reveal 7 bring up, comment, discuss, divulge, itemize, observe, recount, refer to, speak of, specify, suggest, touch on, tribute 8 acquaint, allude to, allusion, citation, disclose, footnote, intimate, point out, throw out 9 enumerate, make known, recognize, reference, statement, touch upon 10 speak about
again: 5 resay
favorable ~: 4 plug, puff
not to ~: 3 and 4 also, plus 7 besides 8 as well as
__ mention: 5 not to
mentioned: 6 spoken
heretofore ~: 5 above
starter: 5 afore
those not ~: 6 others
mentioning: 9 reference
keep ~: 5 rub in
not worth ~: 5 minor, petty 7 trivial 8 trifling 9 small-time 10 incidental
mentis, compos: 4 sane 5 lucid, right, sound
mentor: 4 guru, sage 5 coach, guide, tutor 6 lector, pundit 7 adviser, advisor, teacher, trainer 8 educator 9 abecedary, counselor 10 connection, instructor
charge: 7 student, trainee
Mentor: 4 city, town
father of ~: 8 Heracles
locale: 4 Ohio
Mentos alternative: 5 Certs 6 Binaca, Tic Tac 7 Altoids, Clorets, Dentyne
menu: 4 diet, fare, list 5 carte, table 6 dishes 7 cuisine 10 bill of fare, gastronomy
kind of ~: 5 pop up
lighten one's ~: 4 diet
phrase: 3 a la 5 au jus 6 du jour
selection: 4 soup 5 order, salad 6 course, entrée 7 dessert
symbol: 4 icon
menu-__ software: 6 driven
menudo: 4 soup
ingredient: 5 tripe
Menuhin, Yehudi: 9 violinist
contemporary: 5 Stern
Men With Guns (1998 film) director: John Sayles
Menzies: 7 Heather
__ Me On: 4 Lead
Meoqui: 4 city, town
locale: 6 Mexico 9 Chihuahua
__ Me or Leave Me: 4 Love
__ me out!: 4 Hear
__ Me Out to the Ball Game: 4 Take
meow: 9 caterwaul
__ meow: 4 cat's
Meow __: 3 Mix
Mephistopheles: 5 Devil, Satan 7 Lucifer
forte: 4 evil
Mephistophelian: 3 bad 4 evil 5 cruel 6 wicked 7 demonic, hellish, satanic 8 daemonic, demoniac, devilish, diabolic, fiendish, infernal 9 demonical, nefarious, satanical 10 diabolical, maleficent, unhallowed
Mephisto Waltz composer: 5 Liszt
Mephisto Waltz, The (1971 film)
cast: Alan Alda, Jacqueline Bisset, Barbara Parkins
director: Paul Wendkos
mephitic: 4 foul, rank 5 fetid, reeky 6 foetid, smelly, stinky 7 noisome, noxious, odorous, reeking 8 stinking 10 malodorous
mephitis: 3 gas 6 stench
Mequon: 4 city, town
locale: 9 Wisconsin
__ mer: 5 mal de
Merak: 4 star
Merapi: 7 volcano
locale: 4 Asia, Java 9 Indonesia
mercantile: 8 economic 10 commercial
mercantilism: 5 trade
Mercator: 8 Gerardus 9 Gerhardus
Mercator, Gerhardus: 7 Flemish 12 cartographer
creation: 3 map 5 atlas
Merce: 10 Cunningham
Merced: 4 city, town
locale: 10 California
Mercedario: 4 peak 5 mount 8 mountain
locale: 9 Argentina

Mercedes: 5 Ruehl 11 McCambridge
Mercedes-Benz: 3 car 4 auto 6 German 10 automobile
category: 6 A class, E class
competitor: 3 BMW 4 Audi 5 Lexus 8 Infiniti
mercenary: 5 ninja, venal 6 grabby, greedy, rotten, sordid, stingy 7 corrupt, fighter, selfish, soldier, warrior 8 bribable, covetous, grasping, hireling, ungiving 9 legionary, unethical, warmonger 10 adventurer, avaricious, commercial
job: 6 combat
Mercer: 6 Johnny, Marian 9 Ellington
Mercer Island: 4 city, town
locale: 10 Washington
Mercer University's home: 5 Macon
Mercerville: 4 city, town
locale: 9 New Jersey
merchandise: 4 line, sell, vend 5 goods, stock, trade, wares 6 deal in, job lot, lading, market, retail 7 freight, produce, product, promote, seconds, staples 9 advertise, publicize, traffic in, wholesale
group: 3 lot
ID: 3 SKU, UPC
outlet: 3 mkt. 4 shop 5 store 6 market 8 boutique
piece of ~: 4 ware
shrinkage: 5 theft
warning: 4 as is
Merchandise ___: 4 Mart
merchandiser: 6 broker, dealer, jobber, seller, trader, vender, vendor 8 marketer, retailer 10 wholesaler
___ merchandiser: 4 mass
merchant: 6 broker, dealer, grocer, jobber, seller, trader, vender, vendor 7 shipper 8 exporter, operator, retailer 9 consigner 10 franchisee, shopkeeper, trafficker, wholesaler
guild: 5 hansa, hanse
help the ~: 3 buy
name meaning ~: 7 Kaufman
ship: 6 argosy, carack, trader 7 carrack, clipper, galleon 8 schooner 9 freighter 10 brigantine, tea clipper
wholesale ~: 6 jobber
merchant ___: 4 bank, flag, ship 5 guild 6 marine, prince, seaman, vessel
___ merchant: 3 law 5 dream 7 feather
Merchant: 6 Ismail, Vivien 7 Natalie
Merchant, Natalie
song: Carnival (1995)
Jealousy (1996)
Kind & Generous (1998)
Wonder (1996)
Merchant of Venice, The: 4 play
author: William Shakespeare
character: 5 Gobbo, Tubal 6 Portia 7 Antonio, Jessica, Lorenzo, Nerissa, Shylock 8 Bassanio, Gratiano
merchantry: 5 trade
___ Merchants, The: 5 Dream
merci: 6 French, thanks 7 gracias, spasibo 8 thank you
___ Mercies: 6 Tender
merciful: 3 lax 4 easy, good, kind, mild, soft 5 loose 6 benign, decent, gentle, humane, kindly, tender 7 clement, lenient, liberal, pitying, ruthful, sparing 8 all heart, empathic, flexible, generous, gracious, laid-back, placable, tolerant 9 assuasive, compliant, easygoing, forgiving, indulgent, pardoning 10 altruistic, beneficent, benevolent, charitable, forbearing, permissive, unexacting
be ~: 5 spare 6 relent 10 have a heart
name meaning ~: 5 Miles
mercifulness: 4 pity 5 grace 6 lenity, pardon 7 charity, quarter, release 8 clemency, kindness, lenience, leniency 9 tolerance 10 compassion, gentleness
merciless: 4 grim, hard, iron, mean 5 cruel, harsh, nasty, stony, tough 6 animal, brutal, fierce, savage, severe, stoney, unkind, wanton 7 beastly, callous, hurtful, onerous, vicious 8 barbaric, fiendish, inhumane, pitiless, ruthless, sadistic, vengeful 9 barbarian, barbarous, cutthroat, dog-eat-dog, ferocious, heartless, inclement, monstrous, truculent, unfeeling, unpitying, unsparing 10 implacable, inexorable, ironfisted, relentless, unmerciful, unyielding, vindictive
mercilessly: 4 hard
mercilessness: 7 cruelty 8 hardness
Merck competitor: 5 Glaxo, Lilly 6 Pfizer
Merckx: 4 Eddy
Mercouri: 6 Melina
Mercredi: 6 French 9 Wednesday
follower: 5 Jeudi
preceder: 5 Mardi
Merc rival: 5 Chevy, COMEX
Mercure composer: 5 Satie
mercurial: 4 yo-yo 5 fluid, moody, quick 6 fickle, mobile, uneven 7 erratic, flighty, mutable, protean 8 shifting, ticklish, unstable, unsteady, variable, volatile, wavering 9 excitable, impulsive, uncertain, up-and-down, vagarious 10 capricious, changeable, inconstant
mercury: 5 azoth, metal 6 liquid 7 element
alloy: 7 amalgam
ore: 8 cinnabar
mercury ___: 3 arc 6 switch 7 sulfide
mercury-___ lamp: 5 vapor
Mercury: 3 car, deo, god, orb 4 auto, Ford 7 Freddie 10 automobile
astronaut: 5 Glenn 6 Cooper 7 Grissom, Schirra, Shepard, Slayton 9 Carpenter, John Glenn 10 Gus Grissom
equivalent: 6 Hermes
father of ~: 7 Jupiter
follower: 6 Gemini
model: 4 Lynx 5 Capri, Comet, sable, Topaz 6 Bobcat, Cougar, Meteor, Tracer, Zephyr 7 Cougars, Marquis, Monarch, Montego, Voyager 8 Marauder, Medalist, Monterey, Mystique, Park Lane, Villager 9 Montclair 10 Colony Park 11 Mountaineer
neighbor: 5 Venus
org.: 4 NASA
Mercury ___: 4 dime 6 Rising
Mercury News: 5 paper 9 newspaper
locale: 7 San Jose
Mercury Rising (1998 film)
cast: Alec Baldwin, Miko Hughes, Chi McBride, Bruce Willis
director: Harold Becker
Mercury Theatre name: 5 Orson
Mercutio friend: 5 Romeo
mercy: 4 pity 5 grace 6 lenity, pardon 7 charity, quarter 8 blessing, clemency, humanity, kindness, lenience, leniency, mildness, sympathy 9 tolerance 10 compassion, generosity, gentleness, kindliness, tenderness
show ~: 4 pity 5 spare 6 relent 10 sympathize
Mercy!: 4 oh my 5 lordy
Mercy, Mercy, Mercy (1967 song)
artist: Buckinghams
Mercy Mercy Me (song) artist: Marvin Gaye
artist: Robert Palmer
...mercy on such ___: 4 as we
mere: 4 just, lake, pond, pool, pure, very 5 lough, scant, sheer, small, utter 6 measly, paltry, simple, simply, slight 8 trifling 9 unadorned 10 negligible
combining form: 4 psil- 5 psilo-
mère: 6 French, mother
brother: 5 oncle
partner: 4 père
Meredith: 3 Don, Lee 6 Baxter, George, MacRae, Vieira 7 Burgess, Willson
Meredith ___-Birney: 6 Baxter
Meredith, Burgess: 5 actor
film: The Day of the Locust (1975)
Foul Play (1978)
Grumpier Old Men (1995)
Grumpy Old Men (1993)
The Man on the Eiffel Tower (1949)
Of Mice and Men (1939)
Rocky (1976)
Rocky II (1979)
Stay Away, Joe (1968)
The Story of G.I. Joe (1945)
That Uncertain Feeling (1941)
spouse: Paulette Goddard
TV: Batman
Meredith, George: 6 writer 7 British
work: The Egoist
The Ordeal of Richard Feverel
Rhoda Fleming
merely: 3 but 4 just, only 6 purely, simply, solely 10 nothing but
merengue: 5 dance 7 Haitian 9 Dominican
merest: 7 minimum 8 littlest 9 narrowest
bit: 4 wisp
meretricious: 4 sham 5 bogus, gaudy, phony, showy, tacky 6 flashy, garish, phoney, tawdry, tinsel, trashy, untrue 7 chintzy, glaring 8 spurious 9 insincere
merganser: 4 bird, duck, fowl, smew
relative: 4 teal 5 eider, Pekin, Rouen, scaup 6 Cayuga, scoter 7 gadwall, mallard, pintail, pochard, redhead, sea duck, widgeon 8 garganey, gray duck, mandarin, musk duck, oldsquaw, shoveler, surf duck, wood duck 9 black duck, broadbill, goldeneye, goosander, greenhead, ruddy duck, sprigtail 10 bufflehead, canvasback, surf scoter, tufted duck
merge: 3 mix, wed 4 band, fuse, join, meet, meld, pool, sign 5 blend, focus, immix, marry, tie in, unify, unite 6 cement, cohere, commix, embody, gather, imbody, mingle, team up 7 combine, network 8 assemble, coalesce, converge, cumulate, federate, intermix, road sign 9 commingle, integrate, syndicate 10 amalgamate, centralize, join forces, synthesize
(into): 4 melt
merger: 3 LBO 4 deal 5 union 6 buyout 8 marriage, takeover
Merger ___: 5 Mania
merging: 7 joining 8 blending 10 convergent
___ Me, Rhonda: 4 Help
Mérida: 4 city, town
locale: 6 Mexico 7 Yucatán
Meriden: 4 city, town
locale: 4 Conn.
meridian: 4 acme, apex, noon, peak 5 crest 6 apogee, summit, zenith 8 high noon, pinnacle
___ meridian: 5 prime
Meridian: 4 city, town
locale: 4 Miss. 5 Idaho 10 Washington
Meridian author: Alice Walker
___ meridiem: 4 ante, post
meridiem, ante: 7 morning
Meridien: 4 font 8 typeface
Mérimée, Prosper: 6 French, writer
work: Carmen
meringue: 6 pastry 7 dessert
ingredient: 3 egg 8 egg white
it's not in ~: 4 yolk 7 egg yolk
like ~: 4 eggy 6 beaten
make ~: 4 whip
___ meringue pie: 5 lemon
merino: 5 sheep 6 fabric
relative: 4 geep 5 argal, shapu, urial 6 aoudad, argali, bharal 7 bighorn, burrhel, mouflon 8 cimarron, moufflon
merit: 4 earn, rate 5 honor, title, value, worth 6 beauty, credit, reward, status, virtue 7 benefit, deserve, dignity, justify, quality, stature, warrant 8 goodness 9 advantage 10 excellence, have coming, worthiness
artistic ~: 5 vertu, virtu
award: 5 badge, bonus
merit ___: 3 pay 5 badge, raise 6 system
merit badge
holder: 4 sash
org.: 3 BSA
merited: 3 due 4 just 5 right 8 deserved, rightful
meritorious: 5 moral, noble 6 worthy 8 laudable, virtuous 9 admirable, deserving, estimable, excellent, exemplary, righteous
meritoriously: 4 well
Meriwether: 3 Lee 5 Lewis
Merkel, Una: 7 actress
film: The Bank Dick (1940)
The Merry Widow (1934)
A Millionaire for Christy (1951)
On Borrowed Time (1939)
Private Lives (1931)
Red-Headed Woman (1932)
Road to Zanzibar (1941)
Summer and Smoke (1961)
merl: 4 bird 9 blackbird
Merl: 6 Reagle
merle: 4 bird, gray, grey 6 bluish 7 blueish 9 blackbird
relative: 3 ash 4 dove, drab 5 beige, dusty, pearl, putty, slate, taupe 6 silver 7 grizzly 8 charcoal, gunmetal, platinum
Merle: 6 Miller, Oberon 7 Haggard
Merle Norman: 6 makeup
alternative: 4 Avon 5 Almay 6 Revlon 7 Lancome, Mary Kay 8 Clinique 9 Cover Girl, Max Factor 10 Maybelline 11 Estée Lauder
merlin: 4 bird
Merlin: 5 Olsen 6 wizard 8 conjurer, conjuror
Merlot: 5 grape
relative: 5 Gamay, pinot, Tokay 7 Catawba, Concord, Niagara 8 Cabernet, malvasia, muscatel 9 muscadine, Sauvignon, zinfandel 10 Chardonnay
mermaid: 6 biform
feature: 4 tail
habitat: 3 sea 5 ocean
Mermaids (1990 film)
cast: Cher, Bob Hoskins, Winona Ryder
director: Richard Benjamin
___ Mermaid, The: 6 Little
Merman, Ethel: 6 singer
role: 4 Reno 5 Annie, Mesta, Perle 10 Perle Mesta
spouse: Ernest Borgnine
mero: 4 fish 7 grouper
Merope: 4 star 6 Pleiad
father of ~: 5 Atlas
husband of ~: 8 Sisyphus
Merops: 4 seer

Merriam: 3 Eve
Merrick: 4 city, town 5 David
locale: 7 New York
Merrick author: Anne Rice
merrie ___ England: 4 olde
Merrie Melodies name: 4 Bugs, Fudd, Pepe 5 Daffy, Elmer, Porky 6 Tweety 9 Sylvester
Merrifield, Robert: 7 chemist 8 Nobelist
Merrill: 4 Dina, Gary 5 James, Stump 6 Robert 7 Charles
partner: 5 Beane, Lynch, Smith 6 Fenner, Pierce
Merrill, Dina: 7 actress
film: Don't Give Up the Ship (1959)
Operation Petticoat (1959)
Running Wild (1973)
The Young Savages (1961)
spouse: Cliff Robertson
Merrillee: 4 Rush
Merrill, Gary: 5 actor
film: Decision Before Dawn (1952)
The Frogmen (1951)
Phone Call From a Stranger (1952)
Twelve O'Clock High (1949)
Where the Sidewalk Ends (1950)
Witness to Murder (1954)
Merrill, James: 6 author, writer
work: Divine Comedies
Merrill, Robert: 6 singer 8 baritone, barytone
specialty: 5 opera
Merrillville: 4 city, town
locale: 7 Indiana
merrily: 5 gaily, gayly
Merrily we ___ along: 4 roll
Merrily We Live (1938 film)
cast: Brian Aherne, Constance Bennett, Alan Mowbray
director: Norman Z. McLeod
Merrimac: 4 boat, ship 8 ironclad
Merrimack: 4 city, town 5 river
city on the ~: 7 Concord
Merriman, Nan: 5 mezzo 6 singer
specialty: 5 opera
merriment: 3 fun, joy 4 glee 5 cheer, laugh, mirth, sport 6 frolic, gaiety, gayety, laughs, levity 7 gayness, jollity, revelry, triumph 8 felicity, hilarity, jocosity, laughter, pleasure 9 amusement, enjoyment, festivity, happiness, jocundity, joviality 10 buffoonery, exultation, jocularity, risibility
Merritt Island: 4 city, town
locale: 7 Florida
Merrivale, Henry: 3 Sir
___ Merriweather Post: 8 Marjorie
merry: 3 fun, gay 4 glad 5 happy, jolly, light, sunny, tipsy 6 blithe, bright, cheery, festal, genial, jocose, jocund, jovial, joyful, joyous, lively, upbeat 7 amusing, chipper, festive, gleeful, jesting, jocular, playful, pleased, rocking, romping, tickled 8 blissful, carefree, cheerful, ecstatic, euphoric, exultant, giggling, grooving, humorous, jubilant, laughing, mirthful, sporting, sportive, thrilled 9 convivial, delighted, enjoyable, fun-loving, hilarious, lightsome, overjoyed, rejoicing, vivacious 10 flying high, frolicsome, optimistic, rollicking, skylarking, uproarious
ender: 5 maker 6 making 7 thought
in music: 7 festoso
make ~: 4 play, romp 5 amuse, exult, laugh, party, revel 6 cavort, frolic 7 carouse, rejoice, satisfy 8 live it up 9 celebrate, entertain, have a ball
merry-___: 5 bells 6 andrew
Merry ___, The: 5 Widow
merry-andrew: 5 clown 7 buffoon 9 harlequin
Merry Christmas preceder: 6 ho ho ho
Merry Company artist: 5 Steen
merry-go-round: 4 ride 5 spree
Merry Madcap: 4 Baer 7 Max Baer
merrymaker: 9 wassailer
merrymaking: 3 fun, joy 4 glee, play 5 cheer, mirth, revel, sport 6 fiesta, frolic, gaiety, gayety, laughs, levity 7 jollity, revelry 8 festival, hilarity, laughter 9 amusement, enjoyment, festivity, happiness, joviality
___ Merry Oldsmobile: 4 In My
Merry Widow, The: 8 operetta
composer: Franz Lehár
role: 4 Zeta 5 Hanna, Vilja 6 Danilo 7 Glawari
Merry Widow, The (1934 film)
cast: Maurice Chevalier, Jeanette MacDonald, Una Merkel
director: Ernst Lubitsch
Merry Widow, The (1952 film)
cast: Fernando Lamas, Una Merkel, Lana Turner
Merry Wives of Windsor, The: 4 play 6 comedy
author: William Shakespeare
role: 3 Nym 4 Ford, Hugh, Page 5 Caius, Evans, Robin 6 Fenton, Pistol, Simple 7 Quickly, Shallow, Slender 8 Anne Page, Bardolph, Falstaff 9 Hugh Evans
Mersey: 5 river
city on the ~: 9 Liverpool
locale: 7 England
Merton: 6 Miller, Robert, Thomas
Merton, Robert: 8 Nobelist 9 economist
Merton, Thomas: 6 author, writer
work: Mystics and Zen Masters
The Seven Storey Mountain
Mertz: 4 Fred 5 Ethel
Meru: 4 city, peak, town 5 mount 8 mountain
locale: 5 Kenya 6 Africa 8 Tanzania
Merv: 7 Griffin
Mervyn: 5 LeRoy
Merwin, W.S.: 4 poet
Meryl: 6 Streep
mes: 4 mayo 5 abril, enero, julio, junio, marzo, month 6 agosto 7 febrero, octubre, Spanish 9 diciembre, noviembre 10 septiembre
mesa: 4 hill 5 table 7 flattop, lowland, plateau 9 tableland 10 prominence
dweller: 4 Hopi
Mesa: 4 city, town
county: 8 Maricopa
locale: 7 Arizona
Mesa ___: 5 Falls, Verde
Mesabi: 5 Range
product: 3 ore 4 iron
workplace: 4 mine
___ Mesa, CA: 5 Costa
Mesa Verde: 4 park
locale: 8 Colorado
sight: 4 ruin
mescal: 4 bean 5 drink 6 cactus 8 beverage
source: 5 agave
Mescalero: 5 tribe 6 Indian 7 Amerind
mesh: 2 go 3 net, web 4 gybe, jibe, lace, lock, rete 5 agree, catch, gauze, snarl, toils 6 belong, cobweb, engage, fabric, screen, splice, tangle 7 combine, conjoin, connect, ensnare, insnare, lattice, netting, network, weaving 8 coincide, dovetail, entangle 9 harmonize, integrate, interlink, interlock, labyrinth, screening 10 coordinate, interspace, intertwine, interweave
ender: 4 work
fabric: 3 net 4 leno 7 fishnet, netting, tiffany 8 tarlatan
___ Me, Shape Me: 4 Bend
Meshed: 4 city, town
locale: 4 Iran
meshlike: 4 lacy 5 netty
fabric: 5 gauze, tulle
meshy: 7 netlike
___ Me Sing and I'm Happy: 3 Let
mesmeric: 8 hypnotic
Mesmeric Revelation author: Edgar Allan Poe
mesmerism: 5 spell 8 hypnosis
mesmerize: 4 grip 5 charm 7 catch up, control, enchant, enthral, inthral 8 enthrall, entrance, inthrall, transfix 9 captivate, fascinate, hypnotize, spellbind
mesmerized: 4 rapt 5 under 6 enrapt 9 bewitched 10 fascinated
mesmerizing: 8 magnetic 9 soporific 10 magnetical
mesne: 4 lord
___ Me Softly: 7 Killing
meson: 4 kaon, pion 5 boson 8 particle
place: 4 atom
mesophyte: 5 plant
Mesopotamia
ancient city of ~: 4 Kish 6 Edessa
kingdom: 4 Elam
neighbor: 6 Arabia
region: 5 Sumer
today: 4 Irak, Iraq
Mesozoic: 3 Era
mesquite: 4 tree 5 shrub 6 legume
family: 6 legume
relative: 3 koa 5 carob 6 cassia, cercis, locust, padauk, padouk, redbud 7 araroba 8 tamarind 9 poinciana
treat with ~: 5 smoke
___ mesquite: 5 honey
Mesquite: 4 city, town
locale: 5 Texas
mess: 3 fix, jam, lot 4 food, hash, meal, much, muck, muff, soil, spot 5 botch, chaos, mix-up, sapfu, sight, snafu, snarl, wreck 6 bedlam, fiasco, fright, huddle, jumble, litter, mayhem, muddle, pickle, pigpen, pigsty, plight, scrape, strait, tangle, tinker, tumult, unrest, uproar 7 anarchy, clutter, dilemma, eyesore, farrago, ferment, piggery, problem, screwup, trouble, turmoil 8 bad scene, disarray, dishevel, disorder, mishmash, shambles, upheaval 9 confusion, deep water, dirtiness, mare's nest, mobocracy, profusion 10 difficulty, dining hall, dining room, hodgepodge, miscellany, untidiness
around: 3 toy 4 play 5 dally 6 dabble, dawdle, doodle, fiddle, loiter, potter, putter, tinker, trifle 7 goof off 8 fool with
ender: 3 age 4 mate
gooey ~: 4 glop
in a ~: 7 trapped 10 on the ropes
make a ~: 4 slop 6 litter
make a ~ of: 4 muff 6 ball up, bungle, foul up, muddle 7 butcher 9 mishandle, mismanage
sergeant: 4 cook
unholy ~: 5 havoc 7 debacle 8 collapse, disaster
up: 3 err, mar 4 blow, flub, goof, harm, hurt, muff, muss, ruin, soil 5 botch, dirty, misdo, smear, snarl, spoil, upset 6 blight, bobble, boggle, bollix, bungle, damage, foozle, fumble, jumble, litter, misuse, ruffle 7 clutter, disrupt, disturb 8 dishevel, disorder, mistreat, mutilate 9 mishandle, mismanage 10 complicate, disarrange, disconcert
(up): 3 gum, mix 4 foul, goof 5 louse 6 bollix
with: 6 pester 7 disturb
(with): 6 fiddle, monkey, tamper, tinker
working in a ~: 4 on KP
mess ___: 3 kit 4 call, gear, hall 6 around, jacket
message: 3 fax 4 info, line, mail, memo, news, note, wire, word 5 moral, point, sense, telex, theme 6 earful, import, lesson, letter, notice, report 7 epistle, meaning, missive, purport, tidings 8 bulletin, dispatch, telegram 9 directive, radiogram 10 communiqué, memorandum
bearer: 4 aide, page 5 e-mail
combining form: 4 -gram
conceal a ~: 6 encode
concealed: 4 code 6 cipher 10 cryptogram
get the ~: 3 see 4 hear 8 perceive
holder: 5 in-box, pager 6 bottle, letter 8 postcard 9 enveloper
mangle a ~: 6 garble
return a ~: 5 reply
send a ~ to: 4 wire
message ___: 4 unit 6 center
___ message: 4 veto 5 send a
Message from Nam author: Danielle Steel
Message in a Bottle (1999 film)
cast: Kevin Costner, Paul Newman, John Savage, Robin Wright
director: Luis Mandoki
Message in the Bottle, The author: Walker Percy
Message received: 5 Roger
Message, The author: John Donne
Message to Garcia, A (1936 film)
cast: Wallace Beery, John Boles, Barbara Stanwyck
director: George Marshall
Message to Michael (1966 song)
artist: Dionne Warwick
messed up: 7 tousled 8 slovenly
messenger: 5 agent, envoy, gofer 6 bearer, gopher, herald, runner 7 carrier, courier, prophet 8 delegate, emissary 9 errand boy, go-between, harbinger, precursor, town crier 10 ambassador, connection, dispatcher, forerunner, missionary
divine ~: 5 angel
Greek ~ of the gods: 4 Iris
name meaning ~: 6 Angela, Angelo
vehicle: 4 bike
messenger ___: 3 RNA
Messerschmitt: 5 Willy
mess hall: 10 dining room
amenity: 4 tray
meal: 4 chow, hash
staff: 2 KP
messiah: 5 Mahdi 6 savior 7 saviour 8 redeemer 9 deliverer
Messiah: 8 oratorio
composer: 6 Handel
piece: 4 aria
Messick: 3 Don 4 Dale
Messier: 4 Mark
Messina: 3 Jim 4 city, port, town
locale: 5 Italy
partner: 7 Loggins
Messing, Debra: 7 actress
film: Hollywood Ending (2002)
TV: Ned and Stacey, Will & Grace
___ Mess with Bill: 4 Don't
messy: 4 ugly, wild 5 dirty, dowdy, grimy, tacky, upset 6 blowsy, blowzy, grubby, grungy, sloppy, unneat, untidy 7 awkward, blotchy, blowsed, blowzed, chaotic, jumbled, muddled, rumpled, scruffy, tousled, unclean, unkempt, unswept 8 careless, confused, littered, slapdash, slipshod, slovenly 9 cluttered, difficult, inside-out, ungroomed 10 bothersome, disheveled, disordered, disorderly,

disturbing, in disarray, topsy-turvy
one: 4 slob
place: 3 sty 6 pigsty
Mesta: 5 Perle
__ Me, Stupid: 4 Kiss
met: 6 solved 7 reached
hail-fellow well ~: 7 mingler 9 extrovert 10 socializer
not ~: 3 due
seldom ~ with: 6 scarce
Met: 4 NLer 10 opera house
Hall of Famer: 6 Seaver
performance: 4 aria, solo 5 opera
rival: 3 Cub, Met, Red 4 Expo, Twin 5 Angel, Astro, Brave, Giant, Padre, Rocky, Royal, Tiger 6 Brewer, Dodger, Indian, Marlin, Oriole, Philly, Pirate, Ranger, Red Sox, Yankee 7 Blue Jay, Mariner 8 Athletic, Cardinal, Devil Ray, White Sox
singer: 4 alto, bass, diva 5 basso, mezzo, tenor
metabolism chemical: 3 ADP, ATP
metacarpus: 4 bone
locale: 5 wrist
Metairie: 4 city, town
locale: 9 Louisiana
metal: 3 ore, tin 4 foil, gold, iron, lead, leaf, mail, vein, zinc 5 alloy, brass, ingot, plate, steel 6 cerium, cesium, cobalt, copper, curium, indium, nickel, ormolu, osmium, radium, silver, sodium, solder 7 caesium, casting, fermium, gallium, hafnium, iridium, lithium, mercury, mineral, niobium, rhenium, rhodium, terbium, thorium, uranium, wolfram, yttrium 8 chromium, electrum, francium, hardware, platinum, polonium, rubidium, samarium, scandium, tantalum, thallium, titanium, tungsten, vanadium 9 conductor, lanthanum, magnesium, manganese, neptunium, palladium, plutonium, potassium, rare earth, ruthenium, strontium, tellurium, zirconium 10 gadolinium, molybdenum
bar: 5 ingot
blend: 5 alloy
cloth: 4 lamé
coat with ~: 5 plate
cylinder: 6 gabion
deposit: 3 ore 4 lode, mine
ender: 4 mark, work 6 worker
fastener: 4 bolt, brad, nail 5 rivet, screw, U-bolt
filings: 5 swarf
framework: 5 grate
fuse ~: 4 weld 6 solder
heavy ~: 4 iron, lead 5 armor, brass, music
in heraldry: 8 tincture
mold: 3 pig
mold opening: 5 sprue
precious ~: 4 gold 6 silver 8 platinum
problem: 4 rust 9 corrosion
rare earth ~: 6 cerium, cesium, erbium 7 caesium, holmium, terbium, thulium, yttrium 8 europium, lutetium, samarium, scandium 9 neodymium, ytterbium 10 dysprosium, gadolinium, promethium 12 praseodymium
receptacle: 3 can, pan, pot, tin
refine ~: 5 smelt
refuse: 4 slag 5 dross
shaper: 5 swage
sound: 4 ding, ping, tick 5 clack, clang, clank, click, clink
starter: 3 gun
thin ~: 4 foil 7 coating
treat ~: 6 anneal
worker: 5 smith 7 smelter 8 tinsmith 9 goldsmith
write on ~: 4 etch
yarn: 5 lurex
__ metal: 3 Dow, hot, ply, pot 4 base, bell, dead, foam, road, shot, type 5 heavy, misch, Monel, Muntz, noble, sheet, speed, terne, white, Wood's 6 alkali, cerium, foamed, virgin 7 Babbitt, brazing, fusible, primary, terbium, yttrium
Metalious, Grace: 6 author, writer
work: Peyton Place
__ Metal Jacket: 4 Full
metallic __: 4 bond, soap 5 glass 6 luster
metallurgy: 7 science
study: 4 ores 6 alloys, metals
metalware: 4 tole
metalworker's
joint: 4 bond 6 solder 8 juncture
metamorphic rock: 5 slate 6 gneiss, schist 9 quartzite
metamorphose: 4 turn 5 alter 6 change, evolve, mutate 7 convert 8 innovate 9 transform, transmute
Metamorphoses author: Ovid
metamorphosis: 6 change 8 mutation
stage: 4 pupa 5 larva
Metamorphosis, The author: Franz Kafka
__ me tangere: 4 noli
metaphor: 5 image, trope 6 symbol 7 analogy 8 allegory 10 comparison, similitude
__ metaphor: 5 mixed
metaphysical: 4 deep 6 mystic 7 psychic 8 abstract, abstruse, esoteric, mystical, numinous, profound 9 recondite, spiritual
beings: 5 entia
metaphysics: 10 philosophy
unit: 5 monad
Metaphysics of Morals author: 4 Kant
Me Tarzan, you __!: 4 Jane
metatarsal __: 4 arch
metatarsus: 4 bone
locale: 5 ankle
metate, use a: 5 grind
Metcalf: 6 Laurie
Metchnikoff, Elie: 7 Russian 8 Nobelist 9 zoologist
mete: 3 lot 4 deal, dole, give 5 allot, allow, share 6 assign, divide, parcel, ration 7 give out, hand out, measure, portion 8 allocate, boundary, disburse, dispense 9 apportion 10 distribute
out: 5 allot, divvy, issue, share, split 6 assign, ration 7 divvy up, inflict, portion 8 allocate, disburse, dispense, sentence 9 apportion 10 administer, distribute
(out): 4 deal, dish, dole 6 parcel, ration
mete __: 3 out
__ Me Tender: 4 Love
meteor: 6 bolide
impact site: 6 crater
path: 3 arc
shower: 6 Lyrids 7 Cygnids, Leonids 8 Perseids
suffix: 3 -ite
meteor __: 5 swarm 6 shower
Meteor: 3 car 4 auto 7 Mercury 10 automobile
Meteor __: 6 Crater
Meteor author: Karel Capek
meteoric: 5 brief, fleet, rapid, swift 6 speedy, sudden 8 dazzling, flashing, fleeting 9 ephemeral, momentary, overnight, transient
meteorology: 7 climate, science, weather
event: 4 tide 5 storm 6 aurora, shower 7 cyclone, tornado, typhoon 8 blizzard 9 hurricane
govt. ~ agcy.: 3 NWS
info: 4 temp 8 forecast
line: 6 isobar, isohel
prefix: 3 aer- 4 aero-, atmo-
region: 5 front, ridge 9 cold front, warm front
unit: 6 degree 9 degree day
zone: 5 clime
Metepec: 4 city, town
locale: 6 Mexico
meter: 4 beat, feet, lilt, rime 5 gauge, rhyme, swing, tempo 6 rhythm 7 cadence, cadency, measure 9 indicator
cubic ~: 5 stere
fraction ~: 6 micron
gas ~: 9 indicator
marker: 6 needle
reader: 5 cabby 6 cabbie, gasman
reading: 4 fare
relative: 4 yard
starter: 3 odo, ohm 4 alti, kilo, nano, taxi, volt, watt 5 audio, centi, milli, penta, radio, tacho 6 alkali 7 alcohol
two-foot ~: 6 dipody
user: 4 poet
Welsh ~: 6 cywydd
meter __: 4 maid
__ meter: 3 air, gas, TTL 4 long, spot 5 drift, light, water 6 common, heroic, square 7 gravity, parking, postage
meter-candle: 3 lux
metered __: 4 mail
metered vehicle: 3 cab
meter maid, Beatles': 4 Rita
meters
100 square ~: 7 hectare
1000 ~: 4 one K
1000 square ~: 6 decare
10,000 ~: 4 ten K
meth.: 3 sys. 4 syst.
Meth.: 4 Prot.
methane: 6 alkane
liquid ~: 3 LNG
Metheny: 3 Pat
__ Me the Pillow You Dream On: 4 Send
__ Me the Simple Life: 4 Give
__ Me the Way: 4 Show
method: 3 sys., way 4 form, line, mode, plan, syst., tack, wise 5 means, style, trick, usage 6 course, custom, manner, recipe, schema, scheme, system 7 fashion, formula, measure, process, program, purpose, routine, science, tactics, wrinkle 8 approach, hang of it, practice, strategy 9 expedient, mechanism, procedure, technique, treatment 10 expediency
by what ~: 3 how
__ method: 4 case 5 Gram's, Milne 6 access, Bessel, direct, Lamaze, powder 7 Graeffe, Horner's, Newton's, raw-pack, simplex
methodical: 4 neat, nice, tidy 5 exact, fixed, sound 6 cogent, formal 7 careful, logical, ordered, orderly, planned, precise, regular, tenable 8 accurate, analytic, coherent, habitual, rational, sensible 9 by the book, efficient, organized, pragmatic 10 analytical, consistent, deliberate, economical, meticulous, scrupulous, structured, systematic
Methodius: 5 saint
methodize: 5 array, order 7 arrange 8 regulate
Method of Modern Love (1985 song) artist: Hall and Oates
methodology: 4 mode 6 system
Methuen: 4 city, town
locale: 4 Mass.
Methuselah: 7 measure, oldster
father of ~: 8 Mehujael
fraction: 5 quart 6 magnum 8 jereboam
grandfather of ~: 5 Jared
grandson of ~: 4 Noah
like ~: 3 old 4 aged
son of ~: 6 Lamech
__ Methuselah: 5 old as
methyl __: 3 red 6 oleate, orange, phenol 7 acetate, alcohol, bromide, formate, lactate, sulfate
meticulous: 4 nice 5 exact, fussy 6 minute, strict 7 careful, correct, finicky, heedful, precise, prudent 8 accurate, cautious, detailed, exacting, finiking, finnicky, methodic, rigorous, thorough, whole-hog 9 assiduous, attentive, exquisite, judicious, observant 10 deliberate, fastidious, particular, scrupulous, soup-to-nuts
meticulously: 8 in detail
meticulousness: 4 care 5 rigor 8 accuracy 9 precision
métier: 3 job 4 area, line, work 5 field, forte, place, trade 6 career 7 calling 8 business, vocation 9 specialty 10 occupation, profession, walk of life
__ me timbers: 6 shiver
Metis: 4 moon
planet: 7 Jupiter
__ Me Tonight: 4 Love, Rock 5 Teach
metonymy: 5 trope
Me too!: 5 ditto, so am I, so do I
__ Me to the Church on Time: 3 Get
__ Me to the Moon: 3 Fly
metric
area measure: 3 are 5 stere 6 decare 7 hectare
prefix: 3 exa- 4 atto-, deci-, deka-, giga-, kilo-, mega-, nano-, peta-, pico-, tera- 5 centi-, femto-, hecto-, micro-, milli-, yocto-, yotta-, zepto-, zetta-
volume measure: 2 cL., dL., hL., kL. 3 daL. 5 liter 9 dekaliter, kiloliter 10 centiliter, hectoliter, milliliter
weight: 2 cg., dg., hg., kg. 3 dag., mcg., ton 4 gram, kilo 5 tonne 8 decigram, dekagram, kilogram 9 centigram, hectogram, microgram, milligram
metric __: 3 ton 5 space 6 system 7 centner
metrical: 6 poetic 8 poetical
foot: 4 iamb 6 dactyl 7 anapest, spondee, trochee
unit: 4 mora
writing: 4 poem 5 poesy, verse
metro: 4 city 6 subway 8 railroad
alternative: 3 bus, cab
area: 3 urb 4 city
ending: 4 plex 5 polis
part of the ~: 5 exurb
Metro: 3 car, Geo 4 auto 10 automobile
Metroliner company: 6 Amtrak
metronome setting: 5 tempo
__ Metropole: 4 Café
metropolis: 4 burg, city, town 7 capital
Metropolis (1926 film) director: Fritz Lang
metropolitan: 4 city 5 civic, urban 6 bishop, public 9 municipal
Metropolitan: 3 car 4 auto, Nash 10 automobile
Metropolitan __: 4 Life 5 Opera
Mets: 4 nine, team
home: 4 Shea 6 Queens 7 New York
org.: 3 MLB, NLE
sport: 8 baseball
mettle: 4 grit, guts 5 heart, moxie, nerve, pluck, spine, spunk, valor 6 morale, spirit, starch 7 bravery, courage, prowess, resolve, stamina 8 audacity, backbone, boldness,

gameness **9** character, endurance, fortitude, gallantry **10** confidence, feistiness, resolution
man of ~: 4 hero
mettlesome: 4 bold, game **5** brave, gutsy **6** gritty, heroic, plucky, spunky **7** valiant **8** fearless, heroical, intrepid, spirited **9** dauntless, undaunted, unfearing **10** courageous, undismayed
Metuchen: 4 city, town
locale: 9 New Jersey
Metz: 4 city, town
city near ~: 5 Nancy
locale: 6 France
river: 5 Mosel **7** Moselle
Metzengerstein author: Edgar Allan Poe
Meudon: 4 city, town
locale: 6 France
meum et ___: 4 tuum
___-me-up: 4 pick
___ me up, Scotty!: 4 Beam
Meursault: 4 wine **5** white
origin: 6 France
Meurthe, city on the: 5 Nancy
Meuse: 4 Maas **5** river
city on the ~: 5 Liege, Namur, Ornes, Sedan **6** Verdun **9** Rotterdam
locale: 6 France **7** Belgium
river to the ~: 3 Lek **4** Waal **6** Sambre
mew: 3 cry **4** bird, gull **7** seabird, seagull **8** hideaway
Mewati: 3 cow **4** bull **6** bovine, cattle
___ Me Why: 4 Tell
___ me with a spoon!: 3 Gag
mewl: 3 cry, sob **4** bawl, pule, wail, weep, yowl **5** whine **6** boohoo, snivel **7** blubber, whimper **9** shed tears
mews: 5 alley
Mex.
locale: 5 N. Amer.
neighbor: 3 Cal, Tex. **4** Ariz.
org.: 3 OAS **4** NATO
see also Mexico
___-Mex: 3 Tex
Mexicali: 4 city, town
locale: 4 Baja **6** Mexico
see also Spanish
Mexicali Rose: 5 oater **7** western
Mexican ___: 3 ivy, tea, War **4** jade, onyx, star **5** apple, poppy **6** bamboo, orange **7** Hayride, Spanish
Mexican ___ bean: 7 jumping
Mexican ___ dance: 3 hat
Mexican Hayride: 7 musical
songwriter: 6 Porter
Mexican Hayride (1948 film)
cast: Bud Abbott, Lou Costello, Virginia Grey
director: Charles Barton
Mexican Spitfire (1939 film)
cast: Leon Errol, Lupe Velez
Mexico: 4 gulf **6** nation **7** country
agreement with ~: 5 NAFTA
appetizer: 5 nacho **6** fajita
basket grass: 5 otate
bay: 9 Magdalena
bean: 6 frijol **7** frijole
beer: 6 Corona **8** Dos Equis
bird: 5 potoo
blanket: 6 sarape, serape
city: 4 Apan, Ario, Isla, Kino, León, Muná, Nava, Peto, Ruiz, Tala, Tula, Umán, Xico **5** Acala, Acuña, Ahome, Alamo, Ameca, Canoa, Clara, Ébano, Jalpa, Jamay, Jérez, La Paz, Lerdo, Lerma, Mitla, Motul, Oluta, Palau, Silao, Taxco, Teapa, Tekax, Tepic, Tetla, Ticul, Tlapa, Yaquí **6** Acatic, Ajijic, Aldama, Amozoc, Apaxco, Atempa, Atenco, Atoyac, Autlán, Bochil, Cabada, Cancún, Carmen, Celaya, Chalco, Chemax, Cherán, Chiapa, Chilac, Cocula, Colima, Contla, Cotija, Coyuca, Fortín, García, Guzmán, Iguala, Ixtapa, Izamal, Izúcar, Jacona, Jalapa, Juárez, La Doce, La Joya, La Mira, La Poza, Libres, Loreto, Madera, Madero, Marfil, Meoqui, Mérida, México, Oaxaca, Ozumba, Pánuco, Perote, Poanas, Puebla, Romita, Sayula, Serdán, Tamuín, Tecate, Tecpan, Tepeji, Tixtla, Tlaxco, Toluca, Tonalá, Tuxpam, Tuxpan, Tuxtla, Vindho, Zacapú, Zamora **7** Abasolo, Acajete, Acatlán, Actopan, Ajalpán, Allende, Anáhuac, Apizaco, Apodaca, Arandas, Arcelia, Armería, Arriaga, Atlixco, Autopan, Ayotlán, Caborca, Calkiní, Camargo, Cananea, Chapala, Charcas, Chilapa, Cholula, Comitan, Córdoba, Cozumel, Cuautla, Durango, El Mante, El Salto, El Tejar, Empalme, Guasave, Guaymas, Hidalgo, Huetamo, Huixtla, Hunucmá, Ixtapan, Ixtepec, Jiménez, Jojutla, Kanasín, La Barca, Linares, Maxcanú, Mendoza, Metepec, Miramar, Morelia, Múzquiz, Navajoa, Nogales, Obregón, Ocotlán, Octopan, Ojinaga, Orizaba, Oteapan, Pachuca, Pacueco, Palmira, Panotla, Paracho, Paraíso, Pénjamo, Peribán, Quiroga, Reforma, Reynosa, Sabinas, Sahagún, Sahuayo, Soledad, Tampico, Tecámac, Tecomán, Tecuala, Temixco, Tempoal, Tepeaca, Tequila, Texcoco, Tijuana, Tizimín, Torreón, Uruapan, Yajalón, Yuriria, Zapopan, Zimapán **8** Acámbaro, Acapulco, Acayucan, Acuautla, Alborada, Altamira, Altepexi, Alvarado, Apatlaco, Atlautla, Balancán, Calvillo, Campeche, Canatlán, Cárdenas, Carrillo, Castaños, Catemaco, Cerritos, Chetumal, Chiautla, Coacalco, Coahuila, Coatepec, Colotlán, Cortazar, Culiacán, Delicias, Ecatepec, El Colomo, El Grullo, Ensenada, Etzatlán, Frontera, Huatusco, Huejutla, Huilango, Huitzuco, Irapuato, Jáltipan, Jardines, Jauregui, Jiutepec, Juchitán, La Piedad, Las Varas, Los Cabos, Los Reyes, Maltrata, Martínez, Mazatlán, Mexicali, Misantla, Monclova, Moroleón, Nacozari, Naranjos, Navolato, Ocosingo, Ometepec, Palenque, Papantla, Parrilla, Petatlán, Pochutla, Poza Rica, Progreso, Purépero, Río Bravo, Ríoverde, Rosarito, Saltillo, San Pedro, Santiago, Saucillo, Tarimoro, Tehuacán, Tesistán, Tia Juana, Tizayuca, Tlaxcala, Tlaxiaco, Tototlán, Trancoso, Tultepec, Tuxtepec, Veracruz, Victoria, Xaloztoc, Yautepec, Zaachila, Zacatlán, Zacoalco, Zaragoza, Zumpango **9** Acatzingo, Agua Dulce, Amecameca, Azcatepec, Cadereyta, Cerro Azul, Champotón, Chihuahua, Cintalapa, Comonfort, El Rosario, Escárcega, Escuinapa, Esperanza, Fernández, Fresnillo, Guadalupe, Guamúchil, Huajuapan, Huamantla, Jiquilpan, Las Pintas, Los Mochis, Macuspana, Maravatío, Matamoros, Matehuala, Monterrey, Nanchital, Naucalpan, Ocoyoacac, Ojo de Agua, Pátzcuaro, Querétaro, Río Grande, Salamanca, Sanctórum, San Felipe, Tacámbaro, Tantoyuca, Tapachula, Tejupilco, Tenosique, Teziutlán, Tultitlán, Uriangato, Villagrán, Xalatlaco, Xicotepec, Yurécuaro, Zacatecas, Zacatelco, Zacatepec, Zitácuaro **10** Agua Prieta, Altamirano, Alto Lucero, Apatzingán, Buenavista, Coatzintla, Comalcalco, Cuauhtémoc, Cuautitlán, Cuernavaca, El Pueblito, Guanajuato, Hermosillo, Huatabampo, Ixtapaluca, Juan Aldama, Las Choapas, Loma Bonita, Manzanillo, Minatitlán, Moyotzingo, Puruándiro, Salina Cruz, San Agustín, Teloloapan, Tenancingo, Teoloyucan, Tepatitlán, Texmelucan, Teyahualco, Tezontepec, Tlapacoyan, Tulancingo, Valladolid, Xoxocotlan, Zapotiltic **11** Encarnación, Garza García, López Mateos, Nuevo México, Teotihuacán, Tepotzotlán
condiment: 5 salsa
corn flour: 4 masa
cowboy: 6 charro
critic: 3 Paz
dance: 5 raspa
desert: 7 Sonoran **10** Chihuahuan
essayist: 5 Reyes
explorer: 6 Cortés
export: 4 opal
feline: 6 ocelot
figurine mineral: 4 onyx
fish: 7 garlopa **8** anableps
fruit: 7 chayote **8** eggfruit **9** sapodilla, tomatillo
gulf: 8 Campeche
Gulf of ~ port: 6 Biloxi
hut: 5 jacal
Indian: 3 Mam **4** Maya, Pima, Seri **5** Aztec, Mayan, Nahua, Olmec, Otomi, Yaqui **6** Papago, Toltec **7** Huastec, Mazatec, Yucatec, Zapotec **8** Tarascan **10** Tarahumara
land unit: 6 fanega
language: 4 Maya **5** Aztec, Mayan, Yaqui **6** Papago **7** Nahuatl, Spanish **10** Tarahumara
legislature: 6 Senate
meal: 6 flauta
money: 4 peso, tlac **5** tlaco **7** centavo
neighbor: 3 USA **6** Belize **9** Guatemala
Nobelist in Chemistry: 6 Molina
Nobelist in Literature: 3 Paz
Nobelist in Peace: 6 Robles
org.: 3 OAS
painter: 5 Kahlo **6** Rivera **10** Frida Kahlo
pastry: 6 churro
poet: 3 Paz **4** Cruz **5** Nervo, Reyes
political party: 3 PRI
port: 7 Guaymas, Tampico **8** Acapulco, Vera Cruz
prepare ~ beans: 5 refry
promenade: 5 paseo
raccoon: 5 coati
region: 4 Baja
reptile: 3 uta **6** iguana **9** coachwhip
resort: 6 Cancún **7** Cozumel **8** Acapulco
river: 5 Yaqui **6** Pánuco **7** Conchos **8** Rio Bravo
rodent: 7 rice rat
sauce: 4 mole
shrub: 6 jojoba **7** goldcup, guayule **8** ocotillo
state of ~: 6 Colima, Oaxaca, Puebla, Sonora **7** Chiapas, Durango, Hidalgo, Jalisco, Morelos, Nayarit, Sinaloa, Tabasco, Yucatán **8** Campeche, Coahuila, Guerrero, Tlaxcala, Veracruz **9** Chihuahua, Michoacán, Nuevo León, Querétaro, Zacatecas
tree: 5 cirio **6** boojum, sapota
volcano: 4 Popo **6** Colima, Toluca **7** Orizaba
weasel: 5 tayra
writer: 5 Rulfo, Yañez **6** Azuela, Guzmán **7** Fuentes
see also Spanish
Mexico City: 4 town **7** capital
newspaper: 5 El Sol
town near ~: 5 Taxco
Meyer: 3 Ray **4** Dina, Russ **5** Levin **6** Debbie, Lansky **8** Nicholas
Meyerbeer, Giacomo: 6 German **8** composer
Meyer, Conrad Ferdinand: 5 Swiss **6** writer
Meyerhof, Otto: 8 Nobelist
Meyer, Nicholas: 8 director
film: Star Trek II: The Wrath of Khan (1982)
Star Trek VI: The Undiscovered Country (1991)
Time After Time (1979)
Volunteers (1985)
Meyers: 3 Ann, Ari
Meyers, Ann
milieu: 5 court
org.: 3 NBA
sport: 10 basketball
Meynell, Alice Thompson: 6 writer **7** British
...___ me your ears: 4 lend
mezereum: 5 shrub
mezza ___: 4 voce
mezz. alternative: 4 orch.
mezza-mezza: 4 so-so
mezzanine: 4 loge, tier **5** floor **6** lounge **7** gallery
mezzo: 4 half **6** medium, middle
mezzo ___: 5 forte, piano
mezzo-___: 7 relievo, soprano
mezzo-soprano: 5 Horne, Stade, voice **6** singer **7** Stevens **8** Merriman, Troyanos
mezzotint: 7 engrave, etching **9** engraving
MFA: 3 deg.
___ M for Murder: 4 Dial
mfr.: 4 bldr.
bill: 3 inv.
mg.: 2 wt. **4** meas.
Mg: 4 elem. **7** element **9** magnesium
12 for ~: 4 at. no.
MGM: 6 studio
competitor: 3 Fox **6** Disney **7** Miramax, New Line **8** Columbia **9** Paramount, Universal **10** Dreamworks, Warner Bros.
creation: 4 film **5** movie **7** musical
former ~ head: 5 Mayer
former rival: 3 RKO
mascot: 3 Leo **4** lion
motto word: 3 Ars **5** Artis **6** Gratia
offering: 5 movie
part: 5 Mayer, Metro **7** Goldwyn
sound effect: 4 roar
workplace: 3 lot **10** soundstage
MGM ___ Hotel: 5 Grand
MGM Grand locale: 5 Vegas **8** Las Vegas
mgmt.: 5 admin.
VIP: 3 CEO, CFO, COO **4** pres.
mgr.: 3 ldr. **4** exec., supt. **5** admin., supvr.
mi: 4 note
follower: 2 fa
preceder: 2 re

mi.: 4 meas.
about .62 ~: 2 km. 3 kil.
about 6 billion ~: 4 lt. yr.
Mi __ es su...: 4 casa
__ Mi: 4 Do Re
MI
see Michigan
Mia: 4 Hamm, Sara 6 Farrow 9 Kirschner
sister: 4 Tisa
__ Mia: 4 Cara 5 Mamma
Miami: 4 city, port, town 5 river 6 Indian 7 Amerind
athlete: 4 Cane 7 RedHawk 9 Hurricane
city on the ~: 6 Dayton
conference: 3 MAC 7 Big East
county: 4 Dade 9 Miami-Dade
golf tournament: 5 Doral
locale: 4 Ohio 7 Florida
newspaper: 6 Herald
pro team: 4 Heat 7 Marlins 8 Dolphins
River locale: 4 Ohio
zone: 3 EDT, EST
Miami __: 4 Vice 5 Beach
Miami-__ County: 4 Dade
Miami author: Joan Didion
Miami Beach: 4 city, town
locale: 7 Florida
Miami of __: 4 Ohio
Miami University
athletes: 8 RedHawks
locale: 4 Ohio 6 Oxford
Miami Vice (NBC drama)
cast: Don Johnson (Det. Sonny Crockett)
Philip Michael Thomas (Det. Ricardo Tubbs)
theme artist: Jan Hammer
miaow sayer: 3 cat 5 tabby
miasma: 5 vapor 9 effluvium
miasmic: 4 fumy 5 gassy 7 odorous 10 pernicious
Miata: 3 car 4 auto 5 Mazda 10 automobile
mib: 5 aggie 6 marble
relative: 5 immie
mica: 4 rock 7 biotite, mineral 9 isinglass, muscovite
Micah
follower: 5 Nahum
preceder: 5 Jonah
son of ~: 4 Ahaz
Micah Clarke author: Arthur Conan Doyle
Micawber: 7 Wilkins
mice to cats: 4 prey
Mich.
co.: 2 GM
neighbor: 3 Ind., Ont. 4 Ohio, Wisc.
see also Michigan
Michael: 4 Cole, Dorn, Dunn, Gore, Kidd, Mann, Paré, York 5 angel, Apted, Arlen, Biehn, Brown, Caine, Chang, Frayn, Gross, Innes, Jeter, Korda, Moore, Nouri, O'Shea, Ovitz, Palin, Parks, saint, Sarne, Smith, Stipe 6 Ansara, Bishop, Bolton, Callan, Cimino, Conrad, Curtiz, Damian, Eisner, George, Gordon, Jordan, Keaton, Landon, Lerner, Madsen, McKean, Murphy, Powell, Rennie, Rooker, Spence, Spinks, Tucker, Warren, Winner 7 Collins, De Bakey, Douglas, Drayton, Dukakis, Faraday, Jackson, Learned, Lehmann, Murphey, Ontkean, Radford, Ritchie, Wilding 8 Anderson, Corleone, Crawford, Crichton, Dudikoff, McDonald, Moriarty, Redgrave, Richards, Sarrazin, Schenker, Sembello 9 Feinstein, Hutchence, Montaigne, Rosenbaum 10 Caton-Jones, Harrington
in French: 6 Michel
in Italian: 7 Michele
in Russian: 7 Mikhail
in Spanish: 6 Miguel
sister: 5 Janet 6 La Toya
Michael (1996 film)
cast: William Hurt, Andie MacDowell, John Travolta
director: Nora Ephron
dog: 6 Sparky
Michael __-Hogg: 7 Lindsay
Michael __-Jones: 5 Caton
Michael __ Thomas: 6 Tilson
Michael (1961 song) artist: Highwaymen
Michael author: William Wordsworth
Michael Clarke __: 6 Duncan
Michael Collins (1996 film)
cast: Liam Neeson, Aidan Quinn, Stephen Rea, Julia Roberts
director: Neil Jordan
Michael Collins actor: 3 Rea
Michael, George
homeland: England
member of: Wham!
song: Careless Whisper (1984)
A Different Corner (1986)
Don't Let the Sun Go Down on Me (1991)
The Edge of Heaven (1987)
Everything She Wants (1985)
Faith (1987)
Fastlove (1996)
Father Figure (1988)
Freedom (1985)
Heaven Help Me (1989)
I Knew You Were Waiting (1987)
I'm Your Man (1985)
Jesus to a Child (1996)
Kissing a Fool (1988)
Monkey (1988)
One More Try (1988)
Praying for Time (1990)
Too Funky (1992)
Wake Me Up Before You Go-Go (1984)
__ Michael Glaser: 4 Paul
__ Michael Hall: 7 Anthony
Michael J. __: 3 Fox 7 Pollard
Michaelmas __: 3 Day 5 daisy
Michaelmas daisy: 5 aster, plant 6 flower
Michael, Row Your Boat __: 6 Ashore
Michaels: 2 Al 3 Lee 4 Bret 5 Lorne 7 Barbara
Michael Strogoff author: Jules Verne
Michael Tilson __: 6 Thomas
__-Michael Vincent: 3 Jan
Michaux, Henri: 4 poet 6 French
Michel: 5 Butor 6 Fokine 7 Hartmut, Legrand, Piccoli
in English: 7 Michael
Michelangelo: 6 artist 7 Italian, painter 8 sculptor
sculpture: 5 Pietà
work: 4 arte
see also Italian
Michele: 3 Lee 6 Greene
Michel, Hartmut: 7 chemist 8 Nobelist
Michelin: 4 tire
rival: 6 Dunlop 7 General, Pirelli 8 Goodrich, Goodyear 9 Firestone 11 Bridgestone
Michelle: 4 Kwan, Mama, Yeoh 7 Johnson 8 Pfeiffer, Phillips, Williams
__ Michelle Gellar: 5 Sarah
Michelob: 4 beer
alternative: 5 Becks, Coors, Pabst 6 Amstel, Corona, Miller, Molson, Stroh's 7 Schlitz 8 Heineken 9 Lowenbrau 10 Ballantine
Michelson, Albert: 8 Nobelist 9 physicist, scientist
Michener, James A.: 6 author, writer
work: Alaska
Centennial
Chesapeake
The Covenant
Hawaii
Iberia
Poland
The Source
Space
Tales of the South Pacific
Texas
Mi chiamano Mimi: 4 aria
Michigan: 4 game, lake 5 rummy, state 6 avenue 8 card game
bay: 7 Saginaw
canals: 3 Soo
capital: 7 Lansing
city: 4 Novi, Troy 5 Flint, Niles 6 Adrian, Burton, Canton, Monroe, Okemos, Paw Paw, Taylor, Walker, Warren 7 Bay City, Clinton, Detroit, Holland, Inkster, Jackson, Lansing, Livonia, Midland, Oak Park, Pontiac, Portage, Redford, Romulus, Saginaw, Trenton, Wyoming 8 Ann Arbor, Dearborn, Ferndale, Harrison, Kentwood, Muskegon, Royal Oak, Westland 9 Allen Park, Hazel Park, Kalamazoo, Marquette, Port Huron, Roseville, Southgate, Waterford, Wyandotte, Ypsilanti 10 Bloomfield, Eastpointe, Garden City, Southfield
college: 4 Alma
conference: 6 Big Ten
Indian: 5 Miami 10 Potawatomi
lake: 4 Erie 5 Black, Huron 6 Beaver, Turtle 8 Houghton, Superior
national park: 10 Isle Royale
neighbor: 3 Ind., Ont., Wis. 4 Minn., Ohio, Wisc. 6 Canada 7 Indiana, Ontario 9 Minnesota, Wisconsin
port: 7 Detroit, Saginaw 8 Green Bay
state bird: 5 robin
state fish: 10 brook trout
state tree: 9 white pine
Michigan __: 4 roll 5 rummy
__ Michigan: 5 Lower, Upper
Michigan City: 4 town
locale: 7 Indiana
Michigan rummy: 4 game 8 card game
Michigan State
athletes: 8 Spartans
conference: 6 Big Ten
Michoacán: 5 state 7 Mexican
city: 4 Ario 6 Cherán, Cotija, Jacona, La Mira, Zacapú, Zamora 7 Hidalgo, Huetamo, Morelia, Paracho, Peribán, Quiroga, Sahuayo, Uruapan 8 La Piedad, Los Reyes, Purépero 9 Jiquilpan, Maravatío, Pátzcuaro, Tacámbaro, Yurécuaro, Zitácuaro 10 Apatzingán, Puruándiro
Mick: 4 Mars 6 Jagger 9 Fleetwood
Mickelson, Phil: 6 golfer
milieu: 5 links 6 course
org.: 3 PGA
Mickey: 4 Owen 5 drink, mouse 6 Dolenz, Gilley, Mantle, Rivers, Rooney, Rourke, Wright 8 beverage, Cochrane, Hargitay, Spillane
Mickey __: 4 Finn 5 Mouse
Mickey Finn: 5 drink 8 beverage
Mickey Mouse Club, The
leader: 4 Dodd
member: 5 Cubby, Karen 6 Cheryl, Doreen 7 Annette, Darlene
Mickey Mouse nephew: 5 Morty 6 Ferdie
Mickey's Magix: 6 cereal
competitor: 3 Kix 4 Life, Trix 5 Kashi, Quisp, Total 6 Kaboom, Muesli, Oreo O's, Pablum, Smacks 7 All-Bran, Crispix, Harmony, Hunny B's, Mueslix, Oat Bran, Pokemon 8 Boo Berry, Cheerios, Corn Chex, Corn Pops, Fiber One, Rice Chex, Special K, Uncle Sam, Wheaties 9 Alpha Bits, Apple Zaps, Grape Nuts, Honey Comb, Just Right, Wheat Chex 10 Apple Jacks, Bran Flakes, Cap'n Crunch, Cocoa Puffs, Froot Loops, Mini-Wheats, Nutri-Grain, Puffed Rice, Quaker Oats, Smart Start 11 Cocoa Blasts, Cookie Crisp, Golden Crisp, Lucky Charms, Puffed Wheat, Sweet Crunch, Waffle Crisp
Mickey's Monkey (1963 song) artist: Miracles
Mickiewicz, Adam: 4 poet 6 Polish
Micki + Maude (1984 film)
cast: Amy Irving, Dudley Moore, Ann Reinking
director: Blake Edwards
__ Micklin Silver: 4 Joan
Micky: 6 Dolenz
Micmac: 5 tribe 6 Indian 7 Amerind
micraner: 3 ant
micro: 2 PC 8 computer
microbe: 3 bug 4 germ 5 virus 6 amoeba 8 bacillus, pathogen 9 bacterium
microbes: 8 bacteria
microbiology: 7 science
microbrewery product: 3 ale 4 beer
microchip giant: 5 Intel
microfilm: 5 fiche
micromanager concern: 6 detail
Micronesia: 4 isls. 5 isles 7 islands
island: 3 Yap 4 Guam, Truk 5 Nauru, Palau 6 Tuvalu 8 Gilberts, Kiribati, Marianas 9 Carolines, Marshalls
micronutrient: 4 iron, zinc 9 magnesium
microorganism: 3 bug 4 germ 6 aerobe, amoeba 7 microbe
microorganisms: 8 bacteria
__ microphone: 3 lap 6 ribbon, throat 7 shotgun
microphone, hidden: 3 bug
microphysics: 7 science
microprocessor
maker: 5 Intel
speed unit: 3 MHz 9 megahertz
microscope
accessory: 5 slide
adjust a ~: 5 focus
part: 4 lens
__ microscope: 3 ion 5 light, phase 6 simple
microscopic: 3 wee 4 baby, puny, tiny 5 bitty, least, small, teeny 6 atomic, bantam, little, minute, peewee, petite, teensy 7 trivial 8 atomical, atomlike 9 invisible, itsy-bitsy, itty-bitty, miniature, minuscule, pint-sized 10 diminutive, teeny-weeny, vest-pocket
amount: 5 trace
Microsoft
founder: 5 Allen, Gates 9 Bill Gates, Paul Allen
product: 3 DOS 4 Word, Xbox 5 Excel 6 Access 7 Windows
rival: 3 IBM 5 Apple
__ Microsystems: 3 Sun
microwave: 3 fix 4 cook, oven, warm
brand: 5 Amana
device: 5 maser, timer
no-no: 4 foil
one way to ~: 5 on low
use a ~: 3 zap 4 bake, cook, warm
mid: 5 among, cadet 6 center, mongst 7 amongst, central, halfway
mid-__: 3 cap 4 rise, size, teen 5 level 6 mashie
mid-__ car: 4 size

mid.: 3 ctr.
'mid: 5 'twixt
Mid-___ Sunday: 4 Lent
midafternoon: 5 three 7 three p.m.
midair, float in: 9 hover. hang
Mid-American Conference
  school: 3 NIU 4 Ohio 5 Akron, Miami 6 Toledo 7 Buffalo 8 Marshall 9 Ball State, Kent State
Midas: 4 king 8 Phrygian
  father of ~: 7 Gordius
  mother of ~: 6 Cybebe, Cybele
  son of ~: 8 Anchurus 9 Lityerses
Midas ___: 5 touch
midday: 4 noon 6 twelve 10 eight bells
middie: 7 student
  counterpart: 5 cadet
  sch.: 4 USNA
middle: 3 hub, tum 4 core, mean 5 heart, inner, mezzo, thick, tummy, waist 6 center, inside, marrow, median 7 abdomen, average, between, central, halfway 10 mainstream
  combining form: 3 mes- 4 meso- 5 centr- 6 centri-, centro-
  ender: 3 man, men 4 brow, most 6 weight
  in the ~: 5 'tween 6 inside 9 undecided
  in the ~ of: 4 amid 5 among 6 atween, during, mongst 7 amongst, between
  of nowhere: 5 limbo, wilds
  person: 5 agent 6 broker, jobber 8 mediator 9 go-between
middle ___: 3 age, ear 4 game, name, term 5 class, guard, plane, stump, watch 6 finger, ground, school 7 lamella, manager, passage
middle-___: 4 aged, born 5 level, sized 6 income
middle-___-road: 5 of-the
Middle ___: 4 Ages, East, Path, West 5 Congo, Dutch, Greek, Irish, Latin 6 Comedy, French, States, Temple 7 America, Chinese, Eastern, English, Flemish, Kingdom, Persian, Western
Middle-Aged Man on the Flying Trapeze, The author: James Thurber
Middle Ages
  of the ~: 8 medieval 9 mediaeval
Middlecoff, Cary: 6 golfer
  milieu: 5 links 6 course
  org.: 3 PGA
Middle Earth
  inhabitant: 3 Ent, orc 6 hobbit
Middle East
  see Mideast
middleman: 3 rep 5 agent 6 broker, jobber 9 appointee, go-between, negotiant 10 interceder
Middlemarch author: George Eliot
  character: 3 Ben, Ned 4 Dodo, Fred, Rigg, Tyke 5 Caleb, Celia, Garth, Letty, Vincy 6 Cranch, Selina
Middle of the Night author: Paddy Chayefsky
middle-of-the-road: 7 neutral 8 centrist, moderate
Middle of the Road (1984 song) artist: Pretenders
Middle River: 4 city, town
  locale: 8 Maryland
middle-school grade: 5 ninth 6 eighth 7 seventh
Middlesex: 6 county
  locale: 7 England
Middleton, Thomas: 7 British 10 playwright
  work: The Changeling
    The Roaring Girl
    A Trick to Catch the Old One
Middletown: 4 city
  locale: 4 Ohio 7 New York
Middletown author: 4 Lynd
middling: 2 OK 4 fair, okay, okeh, okey, so-so 6 decent, medium, modest 7 average 8 adequate, all right, inferior, mediocre, moderate, ordinary, passable 9 tolerable, unnotable 10 fairly good
  fair to ~: 4 so-so 8 mediocre, moderate 9 tolerable
  grade: 3 cee 5 C plus
Middx: 6 county
  locale: 7 England
middy: 5 shirt 6 blouse, sailor 7 jack tar
  opponent: 5 cadet
middy ___: 6 blouse
Mideast: 6 Levant
  airline: 4 El Al
  airport: 3 Lod
  ancient ~ nomads: 5 Alani
  ancient ~ region: 4 Moab 5 Sumer
  bay: 6 Abukir
  bovine: 6 Baladi, Jaulan
  bread: 4 pita
  capital: 4 Aden, Doha, Sana 5 Amman, Cairo, Sanaa 6 Bagdad, Beirut, Manama, Muscat, Riyadh, Tehran 7 Baghdad, Teheran 8 Abu Dhabi, Beyrouth, Damascus 9 Jerusalem 10 Kuwait City
  coffee cup: 6 finjan
  cup holder: 4 zarf, zurf
  dam: 5 Aswan
  desert: 5 Negeb, Negev, Sinai
  dish: 5 pilaf, pilau, pilaw 6 pilaff
  dough: 4 filo
  emirate: 5 Dibai, Dubai, Katar, Qatar 6 Kuwait
  export: 3 oil
  federation: 3 UAE
  fiddle: 5 rebab
  former ~ alliance: 3 UAR
  garment: 3 aba 4 abba
  grp.: 3 PLO
  gulf: 4 Aden, Oman, Suez 5 Akaba, Aqaba, Sidra 7 Arabian, Persian
  headgear: 3 fez
  head of state: 4 amir, emir 5 ameer, emeer
  inn: 5 serai
  instrument: 3 oud
  language: 5 Farsi 6 Arabic, Hebrew 7 Aramaic, Kurdish, Semitic
  liquor: 4 arak, raki 5 rakee 6 arrack
  market: 3 suk, suq 4 souk 5 bazar 6 bazaar
  messiah: 5 Mahdi
  missile: 4 Scud
  money: 4 rial 5 dinar 6 shekel, talent
  name: 3 Ali
  nation: 3 Isr., Leb., Syr. 4 Irak, Iran, Iraq, Oman 5 Egypt, Katar, Qatar, Yemen 6 Israel, Jordan, Kuwait 7 Lebanon
  native: 4 Arab, Kurd 5 Adeni, Iraki, Irani, Iraqi, Omani, sabra, Saudi 6 Qatari 7 Israeli, Kuwaiti 8 Lebanese 9 Jordanian
  palace area: 5 haram, harem, harim 6 hareem
  pilgrimage: 3 haj 4 hadj, hajj
  port: 4 Aden
  porter: 5 hamal 6 hammal
  region: 4 Gaza 5 Sinai 6 Arabia
  religion: 5 Baha'I, Islam 7 Judaism
  ruler: 3 aga 4 agha, amir, emir 5 ameer, emeer
  shrub: 5 retem
  title: 3 aga 4 agha, imam 5 imaum, rebbe
  weapon: 3 Uzi
  weight: 4 rotl
midevening: 5 eight, seven 7 eight p.m., seven p.m.
midge: 3 bug 4 gnat, pest 6 insect
midget: 4 baby, runt, tiny 5 gnome, small, teeny, weeny 6 bantam, pocket, teensy 8 knee-high 9 miniature, undersize 10 diminutive, homunculus
midget ___: 4 golf
midi: 5 skirt 10 calf-length
___-midi: 5 après
Midianite king: 4 Reba
midiron: 4 club
Midkiff: 4 Dale
Midland: 4 city, town
  locale: 5 Texas 8 Michigan
Midler, Bette: 6 singer 7 actress
  film: Beaches (1988)
    Big Business (1988)
    Down and Out in Beverly Hills (1986)
    Drowning Mona (2000)
    The First Wives Club (1996)
    For the Boys (1991)
    Outrageous Fortune (1987)
    The Rose (1979)
    Ruthless People (1986)
  nickname: 5 Miss M
  song: Boogie Woogie Bugle Boy (1973)
    Do You Want to Dance? (1973)
    From a Distance (1990)
    The Rose (1980)
    Wind Beneath My Wings (1989)
midmonth day: 4 ides
midmorning: 3 ten 4 nine 5 ten a.m. 6 nine a.m.
midnight: 3 jet 5 night
  after ~: 4 late 7 morning
  approach ~: 5 laten
  burn the ~ oil: 4 cram 5 study
  follower: 3 one 5 one a.m.
  on some clocks: 3 XII
  opposite: 4 noon
midnight ___: 3 sun 5 snack
Midnight (1939 film)
  cast: Don Ameche, John Barrymore, Claudette Colbert
  director: Mitchell Leisen
Midnight ___: 3 Run 4 Blue, Lace, Mary 5 Rider 6 Cowboy 7 Express, Special
Midnight ___ to Georgia: 5 Train
___ Midnight: 5 After, Round
Midnight at the Oasis (1974 song)
  artist: Maria Muldaur
Midnight author: Dean Koontz
Midnight Blue (song) artist: Lou Gramm, Melissa Manchester
Midnight Choo Choo destination: 6 Alabam'
Midnight Clear, A (1992 film)
  cast: Peter Berg, Kevin Dillon, Arye Gross, Ethan Hawke
Midnight Confessions (1968 song)
  artist: Grass Roots
Midnight Cowboy (1969 film)
  cast: Dustin Hoffman, Sylvia Miles, Jon Voight
  director: John Schlesinger
  like: 6 X-rated
  role: 3 Joe 4 Buck 5 Ratso, Rizzo 7 Joe Buck 10 Ratso Rizzo
Midnight Express (1978 film)
  cast: Brad Davis, Bo Hopkins
  director: Alan Parker
Midnight in the Garden of Good and Evil (1997 film)
  cast: John Cusack, Kevin Spacey, Jack Thompson
  director: Clint Eastwood
Midnight Lace (1960 film)
  cast: Doris Day, John Gavin, Rex Harrison
Midnight Mary (1933 film)
  cast: Ricardo Cortez, Franchot Tone, Loretta Young
  director: William Wellman
Midnight Rider (1975 song) artist: Allman Brothers Band
Midnight Run (1988 film)
  cast: Robert De Niro, Charles Grodin, Yaphet Kotto
  director: Martin Brest
Midnight's Children author: Salman Rushdie
Midnight Special (1965 song) artist: Johnny Rivers
Midnight Sun dweller: 4 Lapp
Midnight Train to Georgia (1973 song) artist: Gladys Knight and the Pips
midocean
  in ~: 4 asea 5 at sea
Midori: 3 Ito 8 Japanese, musician 9 violinist
midpoint: 2 av. 3 avg. 4 mean 5 midst 6 center, median, middle 7 average
midpt.: 3 ctr.
___ Midrash: 4 Beth
midsection: 3 gut, tum 4 core 5 belly, tummy, waist 6 center 7 abdomen
midshipman: 6 sailor 7 jack tar
  counterpart: 5 cadet
Midshipmen: 4 Navy, USNA
midshipwoman: 6 sailor
mid-size ___: 3 car
midst: 3 hub 4 core 5 heart, thick 6 center, depths, middle 7 halfway, nucleus 8 interior, presence
  in the ~ of: 5 among, 'twixt 6 during, mongst 7 amongst, between
  in the ~ of (prefix): 5 inter-
midsummer: 4 July
Midsummer ___: 3 Day, Eve 5 Night
Midsummer Night's Dream, A: 4 play 6 comedy
  author: William Shakespeare
  character: 4 Nick, Puck, Snug 5 Egeus, Flute, Peter, Snout 6 Bottom, Helena, Hermia, Oberon, Quince 7 Theseus, Titania 8 Lysander 9 Demetrius, Hippolyta 10 Nick Bottom, Starveling
Midsummer Night's Dream, A (1935 film)
  cast: Joe E. Brown, James Cagney, Olivia de Havilland, Dick Powell, Mickey Rooney
Midsummer Night's Dream, A (1999 film)
  cast: Rupert Everett, Kevin Kline, Michelle Pfeiffer, Stanley Tucci
  director: Michael Hoffman
Midsummer Night's Sex Comedy, A (1982 film)
  cast: Woody Allen, Mia Farrow, José Ferrer, Julie Hagerty, Tony Roberts, Mary Steenburgen
  director: Woody Allen
midterm: 4 exam, test
Midvale: 4 city, town
  locale: 4 Utah
midway: 7 between, en route 8 moderate
  attraction: 4 ride
  prize: 4 doll 6 kewpie 8 goldfish 10 kewpie doll
Midway: 3 isl. 4 isle 6 battle, island 7 airport
  alternative: 5 O'Hare
  like the Battle of ~: 5 naval
  loc.: 3 Chi. 7 Chicago
Midwest
  city: 5 Omaha 7 Chicago, St. Louis, Wichita 9 Des Moines
  crop: 4 corn 5 grain, wheat
  Indian: 3 Ute 5 Osage
  sight: 4 silo
  state: 3 Ill., Ind., Kan., Neb. 4 Iowa, N. Dak., Nebr., S. Dak. 6 Kansas 7 Indiana 8 Illinois, Missouri, Nebraska
  zone: 3 CDT, CST

Midwest City: 4 town
locale: 8 Oklahoma
Midwinter's Tale, A author: Andrew Greeley
midyear: 4 exam, test
Mielziner: 2 Jo
mien: 3 air, set 4 aura, cast, look, pose 5 front, guise 6 aspect, manner 7 bearing, conduct, posture 8 attitude, carriage, demeanor, features, presence 9 mannerism 10 appearance, deportment, expression
Mies van der Rohe, Ludwig: 9 architect
miff: 3 irk, vex 4 hurt, roil, tiff 5 anger, annoy, peeve, pique, upset 6 bother, nettle, offend, put out, tee off 7 perturb, provoke, tick off 8 aggrieve, irritate 9 displease
miffed: 4 hurt, sore 5 angry 9 indignant, resentful
easily ~: 5 pouty 6 touchy
more than ~: 3 mad 5 het up, livid 7 furious
Mifune, Toshiro: 5 actor
film: Hell in the Pacific (1968)
Rashomon (1950)
The Seven Samurai (1954)
Stray Dog (1949)
Throne of Blood (1957)
Yojimbo (1961)
MiG: 3 jet
weapon: 3 AAM
might: 3 may, vim 4 beef, dint, sway, thew 5 brawn, clout, could, force, power, steam, thews, vigor 6 energy, muscle 7 ability, command, control, fitness, muscles, potence, potency, prowess, stamina 8 capacity, strength, violence, vitality 9 authority, beefiness, endurance, fortitude, hardiness, huskiness, intensity, puissance, stoutness, strong arm, toughness 10 brawniness, brute force, capability, competence, robustness, ruggedness, sturdiness
partner: 4 main
symbol of ~: 4 fist
with all one's ~: 4 hard 5 amain
__ Might Be Giants: 4 They
Might I interrupt?: 4 ahem
mightily: 7 greatly 8 forcibly, strongly 9 arduously, intensely 10 forcefully, incredibly, powerfully, vigorously
mighty: 3 big 4 hale, huge, iron, vast, wiry 5 beefy, burly, hardy, hefty, hunky, husky, jumbo, large, lusty, nervy, stout, tough 6 brawny, hearty, heroic, potent, robust, rugged, sinewy, steely, stocky, strong, sturdy, virile 7 doughty, immense, leonine, massive, titanic, violent 8 athletic, colossal, enormous, forceful, gigantic, heroical, imposing, indurate, majestic, muscular, powerful, puissant, renowned, stalwart, towering, vigorous, whapping, whopping 9 Atlantean, herculean, strapping, unusually, well-built 10 able-bodied, formidable, impressive, majestical, monumental, omnipotent, prodigious, red-blooded, stupendous, tremendous
combining form: 3 din- 4 dein-, dino- 5 deino-
high and ~: 5 lofty 7 haughty, pompous 8 arrogant, dogmatic, snobbish 10 dogmatical
partner: 4 high
mighty __ oak: 4 as an
Mighty __: 5 Mouse, Quinn
Mighty __ a Rose: 3 Lak'
Mighty __, The: 5 Ducks 6 Barnum 7 Orinoco
Mighty __ Young: 3 Joe
Mighty Aphrodite (1995 film)
cast: F. Murray Abraham, Woody Allen, Claire Bloom, Helena Bonham Carter, Olympia Dukakis, Mira Sorvino
director: Woody Allen
Mighty Barnum, The (1934 film)
cast: Wallace Beery, Virginia Bruce, Adolphe Menjou
director: Walter Lang
Mighty Dog rival: 4 Alpo, Iams 6 Purina 10 Ken-L-Ration
Mighty Duck rival: 4 Blue, King, Star, Wild 5 Bruin, Devil, Flame, Flyer, Oiler, Sabre, Shark 6 Canuck, Coyote, Ranger 7 Capital, Panther, Penguin, Red Wing, Senator 8 Canadien, Islander, Predator, Thrasher 9 Avalanche, Blackhawk, Hurricane, Lightning, Maple Leaf 10 Blue Jacket
Mighty Ducks: 3 six 4 team
home: 7 Anaheim
milieu: 3 ice 4 rink
org.: 3 NHL
sport: 6 hockey
Mighty Ducks, The (1992 film)
cast: Joss Ackland, Emilio Estevez, Lane Smith
director: Stephen Herek
Mighty Joe Young: 3 ape 7 gorilla
Mighty Joe Young (1949 film)
cast: Robert Armstrong, Ben Johnson, Terry Moore
Mighty Joe Young (1998 film)
cast: Regina King, Bill Paxton, David Paymer, Charlize Theron
director: Ron Underwood
Mighty Lak' a Rose composer: 5 Nevin
Mighty Morphin Power Rangers: The Movie villain: 4 Ooze
Mighty Mouse: 4 hero, toon
garb: 4 cape
Mighty Orinoco, The author: Jules Verne
Mighty Quinn (1968 song) artist: Manfred Mann
composer: Bob Dylan
Mighty, The (1998 film)
cast: Kieran Culkin, Gena Rowlands, Sharon Stone
__ mignon: 5 filet
mignonette: 5 plant 6 flower
migraine: 4 ache 8 headache
so to speak: 4 vise
migrant: 4 hobo 5 gypsy, mover, nomad, tramp 6 jobber, mobile, moving, roving 7 drifter, nomadic, ranging 8 changing, drifting, stranger, traveler, vagabond 9 itinerant, on the move, temporary, transient, unsettled, wandering
worker: 7 laborer
worker's org.: 3 UFW
migrate: 2 go 4 move, roam, rove, trek 5 drift, leave, range 6 depart, travel, wander 7 journey, scatter 8 emigrate, relocate
migration: 4 trek 6 hejira 7 journey 8 movement 9 departure
plant ~: 6 ecesis
migratory: 5 gypsy 6 mobile, moving, roving 7 nomadic, ranging 8 drifting, seasonal 9 itinerant, on the move, peregrine, temporary, transient, traveling, unsettled, wandering
animal: 4 loon, tern 5 goose, vireo, whale 6 locust
mammal: 5 whale
Miguel: 6 Barnet, Ferrer, Mihura 7 Unamuno 8 Asturias 9 Cervantes
in English: 7 Michael
Miguel Alemán: 4 city, town
locale: 6 Mexico 10 Tamaulipas
__ Miguel, Azores: 3 Sao
Mihura, Miguel: 7 Spanish 10 playwright
mikado: 5 ruler 6 gerent 8 Japanese
Mikado, The: 8 operetta
character: 4 Ko-Ko 6 Mikado, Peep-Bo, Yum-Yum 7 Katisha, Pooh-Bah 8 Nanki-Poo, Pish-Tush 9 Pitti-Sing
composer: 7 Gilbert 8 Sullivan
sash: 3 obi
trio: 5 maids
Mikan, George
milieu: 5 court
org.: 3 NBA
sport: 10 basketball
Mikasa competitor: 5 Lenox
Mikasuki: 6 Indian 7 Amerind
mike: 3 bug
adjunct: 3 amp
place for a ~: 5 lapel
problem: 4 echo
user: 2 DJ, MC 5 emcee 6 deejay
mike __: 6 fright
__ mike: 4 body 5 lapel
Mike: 4 Fink, Love, Post, Reno, Todd, Weir 5 Aulby, Bossy, Ditka, Judge, Myers, Royko, Tyson 6 Brewer, Figgis, Hodges, Newell, Piazza 7 Connors, Douglas, Farrell, Nesmith, Nichols, Schmidt, Stoller, Wallace 8 Oldfield 10 Lookinland
in Russian: 5 Misha
Mike and __: 3 Ike
__ Mike Tyson: 4 Iron
Mikhail: 3 Tal 4 tsar 6 Glinka 7 Bakunin, Kutuzov, Romanov 8 Bulgakov, Saltykov 9 Botvinnik, Gorbachev, Sholokhov 10 Zoshchenko
in English: 7 Michael
spouse: 5 Raisa
successor: 5 Boris
see also Russian
Mikita, Stan
milieu: 3 ice 4 rink 5 arena
org.: 3 NHL
Mikrokosmos composer: 6 Bartók
mil: 5 money
1/1000 of a ~: 5 grand
mil.: 3 GIs
address: 3 APO, FPO
aide: 3 GSO
award: 3 DFC, DSC, DSM
boat: 3 LST
branch: 3 USN, WAC 4 RCAF, USAF, USMC
British ~ branch: 3 RNR
college: 3 VMI
concern: 3 def.
former ~ auxiliary: 3 WAF
group: 2 tp. 3 div., reg., trp.
offender: 4 AWOL
plane: 4 STOL, VTOL
post: 2 HQ 3 AFB, NAS
rank: 2 BG 3 cdr., CNO, Col., cpl., CPO, ens., gen., maj., NCO, PFC, pvt., SFC, sgt. 4 capt., cmdr., genl., m.sgt., serg., SSgt. 5 lieut., lt. col., lt. gen.
sign up for ~ service: 3 enl.
spy org.: 3 ONI
staff officer: 4 adjt.
training place: 3 OCS, OTC, OTS 4 ROTC
see also military
Mila 18 author: Leon Uris
Milagro: 4 city, town
locale: 7 Ecuador
Milagro Beanfield War, The (1988 film)
cast: Ruben Blades, Richard Bradford, Sonia Braga
director: Robert Redford
Milan: 4 city, town 7 Kundera
city near ~: 4 Lodi 5 Parma
ender: 3 ese
locale: 5 Italy
Milanese: 6 fabric 8 material
Milano: 3 car 4 auto, city, town 6 Alyssa 9 Alfa Romeo 10 automobile
locale: 5 Italy 6 Italia
Milburn: 5 Stone
mild: 3 lax 4 blah, calm, cool, dull, easy, fair, fine, flat, kind, meek, soft, tame, warm, weak 5 balmy, bland, clear, ho-hum, light, loose, lowly, quiet, sunny, sweet, tepid, vapid, wimpy 6 benign, breezy, docile, genial, gentle, humane, irenic, kindly, mellow, placid, polite, serene, simple, smooth, tender 7 amiable, clement, equable, insipid, lenient, patient, ruthful, sparing, subdued, vanilla, warmish, wimpish 8 flexible, irenical, laid-back, lamblike, lukewarm, merciful, moderate, not so hot, obliging, peaceful, placable, pleasant, reserved, soothing, tolerant, tranquil 9 assuasive, compliant, easygoing, forgiving, indulgent, innocuous, peaceable, tasteless, temperate, unextreme 10 forbearing, permissive, restrained, springlike, submissive, unagitated, unassuming, unexacting, unhardened
mildew: 4 mold 5 ergot, mould, plant, spoil 6 blight, fungus, go sour
mildew-fighting product: 5 Tilex
mildewy: 4 damp, dank 5 fusty, musty, trite
mild-mannered: 4 meek, mild, tame 8 ladylike, pleasant
mildness: 5 mercy 6 lenity 8 lenience 9 balminess 10 moderation
Mildred: 6 Bailey, Pierce 7 Natwick
Mildred Pierce: 4 film 5 novel
author: James M. Cain
cast: Eve Arden, Ann Blyth, Jack Carson, Joan Crawford, Zachary Scott
composer: 7 Steiner
director: Michael Curtiz
mile
a ~ a minute: 5 sixty
ender: 3 age 4 post 5 stone
equivalent: 4 miss 5 a miss
off by a ~: 5 wrong
__ mile: 3 air, sea 4 land 5 Roman 6 square 7 country, miracle, statute 8 nautical
__-mile: 3 ton 4 half
mileage: 3 use 4 wear 6 length
get extra ~ from: 5 reuse 7 recycle
get ~ out of: 3 use 7 exploit
Mile High __: 6 Center 7 Stadium
Mile High Center architect: 3 Pei
mile-high city: 5 Kabul 6 Denver
__ Mile in My Shoes: 5 Walk a
__ Mile Island: 5 Three
__-mile limit: 5 three 6 twelve
milepost: 8 landmark, occasion
miler: 3 Coe 4 Ryun 5 Ovett, racer 6 runner 7 Jim Ryun 9 Bannister 10 Steve Ovett
concern: 4 pace
miles: 3 far
about three ~: 6 league
away: 4 afar
per hour: 4 rate
Miles: 4 Vera 5 Buddy, Davis, Sarah 6 Sylvia 8 Franklin, Standish 9 Josephine
Miles, Josephine: 4 poet
__ Miles Minter: 4 Mary
__ Miles of Bad Road: 5 Forty
Miles, Sarah: 7 actress
film: Blowup (1966)
Hope and Glory (1987)
The Man Who Loved Cat Dancing (1973)

Ryan's Daughter (1970)
The Servant (1963)
Those Magnificent Men in Their Flying Machines (1965)
Time Lost and Time Remembered (1966)
White Mischief (1988)
milestone: 5 event 7 waypost 8 landmark, occasion 9 happening
Milestone, Lewis: 8 director
film: All Quiet on the Western Front (1930, AA)
Anything Goes (1936)
Arch of Triumph (1948)
Edge of Darkness (1943)
The Front Page (1931)
The General Died at Dawn (1936)
Hallelujah, I'm a Bum (1933)
Les Miserables (1952)
Ocean's Eleven (1960)
Of Mice and Men (1939)
Pork Chop Hill (1959)
The Purple Heart (1944)
The Red Pony (1949)
The Strange Loves of Martha Ivers (1946)
Two Arabian Knights (1927, AA)
A Walk in the Sun (1945)
Miles, Vera: 7 actress
film: 23 Paces to Baker Street (1956)
Beau James (1957)
The FBI Story (1959)
Gentle Giant (1967)
The Man Who Shot Liberty Valance (1962)
Psycho (1960)
The Searchers (1956)
Those Calloways (1965)
The Wrong Man (1957)
___ Mile, The: 4 Last 5 Green
Milford: 4 city, town
locale: 4 Conn.
Milford Mill: 4 city, town
locale: 8 Maryland
Milhaud, Darius: 6 French 8 composer
work: The Creation of the World
milieu: 3 job 4 area, nabe 5 place, scene, world 6 locale, medium, sphere 7 climate, element, purlieu, setting 8 ambience 10 atmosphere, background, walk of life
Mililani: 4 city, town
locale: 6 Hawaii
___ militaire: 5 école
militancy: 5 fight 6 hatred
militant: 5 pushy 7 fanatic, hawkish, hostile, radical, scrappy, warlike 8 activist, fighting, partisan, ructious, up in arms 9 assertive, bellicose, combative, embattled, protester, truculent 10 aggressive, jingoistic, pugnacious
god: 4 Ares, Mars
militaristic: 7 warlike 8 fighting
militarize: 3 arm 8 embattle
military: 4 army, navy 6 troops 7 Marines, martial, service, warlike 8 air force 9 combative, soldierly 10 aggressive
acronym: 5 NORAD 6 DEFCON
action: 3 war 7 warfare
address: 3 APO, FPO, sir
advisory grp.: 3 NSC
aircraft: 5 AWACS 6 Apache
alliance: 3 OAS 4 NATO
ammo: 4 ordn. 8 ordnance
assignment: 6 KP duty, patrol
assistant: 3 ADC 6 yeoman 8 adjutant
backup org.: 4 USAR, USNR
base: 4 post 8 garrison
bed: 3 cot
careerist: 5 lifer
cash: 5 scrip
coat: 5 tunic 9 pea jacket 10 flak jacket
command: 4 fire, halt 5 march 6 at ease
commando: 4 SEAL
council: 5 junta
decoration: 5 medal
defense: 5 stand
education facility: 3 OCS, OTC, OTS 4 acad., ROTC 7 academy
elite ~ group: 5 A-team
encampment: 5 étape
encounter: 6 action, battle 8 skirmish
flag: 6 colors, ensign
formation: 5 wedge
former ~ grp.: 3 WAF
fortification: 5 redan
group: 2 tp. 3 rgt., trp. 4 regt., unit 5 cadre, force, squad, troop 6 legion, patrol 7 brigade 8 regiment 9 battalion
hat: 5 beret, busby, shako
installation: 4 silo
instrument: 4 drum 5 bugle
join the ~: 6 enlist, sign up 9 volunteer
make a ~ stopover: 6 encamp
mission, in Britain: 5 recce, recco
mix-up: 5 snafu
musician: 6 bugler
neckwear: 6 dogtag
no-show: 8 deserter
not ~: 5 civvy 8 civilian
offender: 4 AWOL
org.: 3 SAC, USN 4 USAF
person: 7 soldier
physician: 5 medic
prison: 4 brig
quarters: 4 base, tent 6 armory, billet 7 bivouac 8 barracks
rank: 2 BG 3 cdr., CNO, col., cpl., CPO, ens., gen., maj., NCO, PFC, pvt., SFC, sgt. 4 capt., cmdr., genl., m.sgt., serg., SSgt. 5 lieut., lt. col., lt. gen., major 6 airman, ensign, seaman 7 captain, colonel, general, private 8 corporal, sergeant 10 lieutenant
response: 5 no sir 6 yes sir
rookie: 3 rct. 7 recruit
salute: 5 salvo
stay in the ~: 4 reup
stint: 4 tour 5 hitch
store: 2 PX
student: 4 pleb 5 cadet, middy, plebe 6 middie
tactic: 5 recon, siege 6 attack
takeover: 4 coup
tune: 4 Taps 5 march
uniform: 3 ODs 4 camo 6 khakis
vacation: 5 leave 8 furlough
vehicle: 3 LCT, LST 4 jeep, tank 6 amtrac, camion 7 amtrack
VIPs: 5 brass
woman: 3 WAC 4 WAAC, Wave
see also army, navy
military ___: 3 law 4 pace 5 brush, march 6 police, school 7 academy, attaché, science
military-industrial ___: 7 complex
Military Symphony composer: 5 Haydn
militate: 4 tell 5 weigh
Milius: 4 John
milk: 3 tap, use 4 pump, skim 5 bleed, cream, dairy, drain, press, white, wring 6 elicit, extort, fleece 7 defraud, deplete, draw off, draw out, exhaust, exploit, extract, formula, squeeze 8 beverage, moo juice 9 siphon off 10 buttermilk, one-percent, two-percent
acid in ~: 5 color, oleic, white 6 lactic
alternative: 3 tea 5 cream 6 coffee
amount: 2 pt., qt. 3 gal. 4 pint 5 quart 6 gallon
buying ~: 6 errand
combining form: 4 lact- 5 lacti-, lacto- 6 galact- 7 galacto-
component: 3 fat 4 whey 6 casein
cry over spilled ~: 5 whine 6 regret
drinker: 3 boy, cat 4 girl 9 youngster
ender: 3 man, men, sop 4 fish, maid, weed
fermented ~ drink: 5 kefir 6 kumiss
go bad, as ~: 4 sour 6 curdle
grader: 4 USDA
holder: 4 pail 5 udder 6 bottle, bucket, carton
in French: 4 lait
in Italian: 5 latte
in prescriptions: 3 lac
in Spanish: 5 leche
land of ~ and honey: 6 utopia 7 Arcadia, Erehwon 8 paradise 9 Shangri-la
like a ~ shake: 5 foamy
like some ~: 5 spilt 6 low-fat
like supermarket ~: 5 dated
made without ~ or meat: 5 parve 6 pareve
of ~: 6 lactic
produce skim ~: 5 defat
product: 4 curd 6 yogurt 7 yoghurt 8 ice cream, yoghourt
rating: 6 grade A
relative: 4 bone, snow 5 cream, ivory 6 argent, oyster, silver 8 eggshell
sans ~: 5 black
source: 3 cow, ewe 4 goat 5 dairy, udder 6 Jersey
starter: 6 butter
milk ___: 3 bar, cow, leg, run 5 adder, bench, float, glass, gravy, punch, shake, snake, sugar, toast, tooth, train, vetch 6 powder 7 thistle
___ milk: 3 dry, ice 4 rock, skim, soya 5 dried, thick, whole 6 almond, filled, malted, pigeon 7 coconut, glacial, skimmed, soybean 8 cocoanut
Milk-___: 4 Bone
___ Milk?: 3 Got
Milk and Honey author: Faye Kellerman
milk-cap collectible: 3 pog
Milk Duds: 5 candy
milking: 5 chore
need: 5 stool
time: 4 dawn 5 sunup 8 daybreak
milking ___: 5 stool 6 parlor 7 machine
milk shake: 7 dessert 8 beverage
alternative: 5 bombe 6 frappe 10 peach Melba
ingredient: 8 ice cream
milksop: 4 wimp 6 coward 8 mama's boy, recreant
lack: 5 nerve, spine
unlike a ~: 5 brave, macho, manly
Milk Train Doesn't Stop Here Anymore, The author: Tennessee Williams
milkwood: 4 tree
___ Milk Wood: 5 Under
milkwort: 5 shrub
milky: 5 white 6 chalky, opaque, pearly 7 clouded, lacteal, opaline, whitish 9 alabaster, albescent 10 opalescent
relative: 4 bone, snow 5 cream, ivory 6 argent, oyster, silver 8 eggshell
Milky Way: 3 bar 5 candy 6 galaxy 9 chocolate, Via Lactea
alternative: 4 Mars, Twix 5 Clark, Heath 6 Kit Kat, Mounds, PayDay, Reese's, Zagnut 7 Krackel, Oh Henry 8 Baby Ruth, Hershey's, Snickers 9 Almond Joy, Mr. Goodbar 10 NutRageous
unit: 4 star
Milky Way, The (1936 film)
cast: Harold Lloyd, Adolphe Menjou, Verree Teasdale
director: Leo McCarey
mill: 4 shop 5 churn, crush, flour, grind, money, plant, pound, press, works 7 factory, foundry 8 levigate 9 granulate, pulverize, sweatshop
around: 6 dither 9 circulate
(around): 4 move
ender: 3 age, dam, run 4 pond, race, work 5 board, stone 6 stream, wright
gin ~: 3 pub 6 tavern 7 barroom 8 taphouse
input: 4 iron
lumber ~ worker: 5 sawer
output: 5 steel
paper ~ commodity: 4 pulp
primitive ~: 5 quern
starter: 3 saw 4 wind 5 grist, tread
to a cent: 5 tenth
use a ~: 5 grind
mill ___: 3 end 4 hole, work 5 scale, wheel 6 chisel
___ mill: 3 end, gig, gin, per, pug, rod 4 ball, band, beam, food, tide 5 draft, flour, grist, paper, rumor, smock, stamp, steel, water 6 boring, coffee, cotton, degree, hammer, pepper, powder, roller, timber 7 diploma, fanning, flutter, gastric, looping, rolling, stretch
Mill ___ Floss, The: 5 on the
___ Mill: 7 Sutter's
Milla: 8 Jovovich
Milland, Ray: 5 actor
film: Alias Nick Beal (1943)
Beau Geste (1939)
The Big Clock (1948)
Close to My Heart (1951)
Dial M for Murder (1954)
The Doctor Takes a Wife (1940)
Easy Living (1937)
Escape to Witch Mountain (1975)
The Gilded Lily (1935)
It Happens Every Spring (1949)
The Jungle Princess (1936)
Kitty (1945)
Let's Do It Again (1953)
The Lost Weekend (1945, AA)
Love Story (1970)
The Major and the Minor (1942)
Ministry of Fear (1944)
Next Time We Love (1936)
Night Into Morning (1951)
Reap the Wild Wind (1942)
Rhubarb (1951)
The River's Edge (1957)
Skylark (1941)
So Evil My Love (1948)
Star Spangled Rhythm (1942)
The Uninvited (1944)
A Woman of Distinction (1950)
Millard: 8 Fillmore
Millau: 4 city, town
locale: 6 France
Millay, Edna St. Vincent: 4 poet
work: The Buck in the Snow
A Few Figs From Thistles
The Harp Weaver and Other Poems
Renascence and Other Poems
Millbrae: 4 city, town
locale: 10 California
Millburn: 4 city, town
locale: 9 New Jersey
Millcreek: 4 city, town
locale: 4 Utah
milled: 7 powdery
mille-feuilles: 6 pastry 7 dessert
Millenia: 3 car 4 auto 5 Mazda 10 automobile
millennia: 4 ages
many ~: 3 eon 4 aeon

millennium
part: 2 yr. 3 cen. 4 year 6 decade 7 century
Millennium Falcon: 4 ship 10 spacecraft
pilot: 3 Han 4 Solo 7 Han Solo
Miller: 3 Ann, Ned 4 beer 5 David, Glenn, Henry, Jason, Merle, Mitch, Roger, Steve 6 Arthur, Barney, Cheryl, Dennis, George, Jeremy, Johnny, Marvin, Merton 7 Christa, Huggins, Joaquin, Marilyn, Shannon 9 Stephanie
alternative: 5 Becks, Coors, Pabst 6 Amstel, Corona, Molson 7 Schlitz 8 Heineken, Michelob 9 Lowenbrau 10 Ballantine
__ Miller: 3 Joe 5 Daisy, Luisa, Molly
Miller, Ann: 6 dancer 7 actress
film: Kiss Me Kate (1953)
Mulholland Dr. (2001)
On the Town (1949)
Room Service (1938)
Miller, Arthur: 10 playwright
spouse: Marilyn Monroe
work: After the Fall
All My Sons
The Crucible
Death of a Salesman
Incident at Vichy
The Misfits
A View from the Bridge
Miller Band, Steve
song: Abracadabra (1982)
Fly Like an Eagle (1977)
Jet Airliner (1977)
The Joker (1973)
Rock'n Me (1976)
Swingtown (1977)
Take the Money and Run (1976)
Miller, David: 8 director
film: Captain Newman, M.D. (1963)
Flying Tigers (1942)
Lonely Are the Brave (1962)
Midnight Lace (1960)
The Opposite Sex (1956)
Sudden Fear (1952)
Miller, George: 8 director
film: André (1994)
Lorenzo's Oil (1992)
Mad Max (1979)
Mad Max 2 (1981)
The Man From Snowy River (1982)
The Witches of Eastwick (1987)
Miller, Glenn: 10 trombonist
Miller, Henry: 6 author, writer
work: The Air-Conditioned Nightmare
The Colossus of Maroussi
The Cosmological Eye
Max and the White Phagocytes
Tropic of Cancer
Tropic of Capricorn
millerite: 3 ore 7 mineral
Miller, Joaquin: 4 poet 6 writer
work: Columbus
Kit Carson's Ride
Life among the Modocs
Songs of the Sierras
Miller, Joe material: 4 corn, joke
Miller, Johnny: 6 golfer
milieu: 5 links 6 course
org.: 3 PGA
Miller, Merton: 8 Nobelist 9 economist
Miller, Mitch
song: The Children's Marching Song (1959)
The Yellow Rose of Texas (1955)
Miller of Angibault, The author: George Sand
Miller, Penelope Ann: 7 actress
film: Big Top Pee-wee (1988)
Carlito's Way (1993)
The Freshman (1990)
Kindergarten Cop (1990)
Other People's Money (1991)
The Shadow (1994)
Miller, Roger
song: Chug-A-Lug (1964)
Dang Me (1964)
Do-Wacka-Do (1965)
Engine Engine #9 (1965)
England Swings (1965)
King of the Road (1965)
millet: 5 grain 6 cereal
Indian ~: 5 doura, durra 6 dourah
__ millet: 5 pearl, spray 6 Indian 7 African, foxtail
Millett: 4 Kate
Milli __: 7 Vanilli
Millie: 3 dog, pet 4 aunt 5 Small 7 Jackson, Perkins, spaniel
millieme: 5 money
Millie's Book author: 4 Bush
Milligan: 5 Spike
Millikan, Robert: 8 Nobelist 9 physicist
milliliters, 237: 3 cup
milliner: 6 hatter
millinery item: 3 hat 5 toque, tuque 6 cloche, hatpin
Millinery Shop, The artist: 5 Degas
million
combining form: 3 meg- 4 mega-
ender: 4 aire
one in a ~: 4 rare
prefix: 4 mega-
worth a ~: 4 rich
million __, a: 5 to one
__ million: 6 one in a
millionaire: 9 moneybags, plutocrat
home: 5 manor 6 estate
maker: 5 lotto
prefix for ~: 5 multi
toy: 5 yacht
Millionaire for Christy, A (1951 film)
cast: Richard Carlson, Fred MacMurray, Una Merkel, Eleanor Parker
director: George Marshall
Millionairess, The: 4 film, play
author: George Bernard Shaw
cast: Sophia Loren, Peter Sellers, Alastair Sim
director: Anthony Asquith
Millionaire, The (CBS drama)
boss: Tipton
cast: Marvin Miller (Michael Anthony)
Million Dollar Legs (1932 film)
cast: W.C. Fields, Susan Fleming, Jack Oakie
director: Edward Cline
__ Million Dollar Man, The: 3 Six
Million Dollar Mermaid (1952 film)
cast: Victor Mature, Walter Pidgeon, Esther Williams
director: Mervyn LeRoy
__ Million Frenchmen: 5 Fifty
millions: 4 many, mint 6 flocks, hoards, scores 7 legions
__ Millions: 3 Kid 5 Marco
million-selling: 4 gold
Million to One (song), A artist: Donny Osmond, Jimmy Charles
__ Million Years B.C.: 3 One
Milli Vanilli
members: Pilatus, Morvan
song: All or Nothing (1990)
Baby Don't Forget My Number (1989)
Blame It on the Rain (1989)
Girl I'm Gonna Miss You (1989)
Girl You Know It's True (1989)
Mill, James: 8 Scottish 11 philosopher
Mill, John Stuart: 7 British 11 philosopher
Mill on the Floss, The author: George Eliot
character: 4 Kenn 5 Deane, Glegg, Jakin, Moggs, Sophy, Wakem
dog: 3 Yap
millpond: 4 lake, pond, pool
Mills: 4 Enos, Erie, John 5 Alley, Donna, Frank 6 Hayley, Juliet, Robert 9 Stephanie
__ Mills: 7 General
Mills, Erie: 6 singer 7 soprano
specialty: 5 opera
Mills, Hayley: 7 actress
father: 4 John
film: The Chalk Garden (1964)
Deadly Strangers (1974)
Endless Night (1971)
The Family Way (1966)
The Parent Trap (1961)
Pollyanna (1960)
That Darn Cat! (1965)
Tiger Bay (1959)
The Truth About Spring (1965)
Whistle Down the Wind (1961)
song: Let's Get Together (1961)
Mills, John: 3 Sir 5 actor
film: The Chalk Garden (1964)
The Colditz Story (1957)
Desert Attack (1960)
The Family Way (1966)
Great Expectations (1946)
In Which We Serve (1942)
Oklahoma Crude (1973)
The Rocking Horse Winner (1949)
Ryan's Daughter (1970, AA)
So Well Remembered (1947)
Swiss Family Robinson (1960)
This Happy Breed (1944)
Tiger Bay (1959)
Times of Glory (1960)
The Truth About Spring (1965)
Waterloo Road (1944)
The Way to the Stars (1945)
The Wrong Box (1966)
__ Mills, MD: 6 Owings
Mills of the Kavanaughs, The author: Robert Lowell
mills, ten: 4 cent
millstone: 4 buhr, load, onus, task 6 burden, weight 9 albatross, hindrance, liability 10 difficulty, impediment
bar: 4 rynd
product: 5 grist
Millville: 4 city, town
locale: 9 New Jersey
Milne, A.A.: 6 author, writer 7 British
character: 3 Owl, Roo 4 Pooh 5 Kanga 6 Eeyore
first name: 4 Alan
work: Eeyore Has a Birthday
Eeyore Loses a Tail
Hello, Eeyore!
The House at Pooh Corner
Now We Are Six
Pooh Goes Visiting
Santa Roo and Pooh Box
Tigger Comes to the Forest
When We Were Very Young
Winnie the Pooh
Milner, Martin: 5 actor
film: Sweet Smell of Success (1957)
TV: Adam 12, Route 66
Milnes, Sherrill: 6 singer 8 baritone, barytone
specialty: 5 opera
milo: 5 grain 7 sorghum
Milo: 5 O'Shea
Milos: 6 Forman
Milosz, Czeslaw: 6 Polish, writer 8 Nobelist
Milpitas: 4 city, town
locale: 10 California
Milquetoast: 4 meek, wimp 5 sissy, timid, vapid 6 Caspar 8 mama's boy, recreant, weakling 9 jellyfish
like a ~: 4 meek 5 timid
unlike a ~: 5 bossy, manly
milreis: 5 money
Milsap, Ronnie song: (There's) No Gettin' Over Me (1981)
Milstein: 5 César 6 Nathan
Milstein, César: 8 Nobelist
Milstein, Nathan: 7 Russian 9 violinist
teacher: 4 Auer
Milt: 5 Gross 6 Caniff, Pappas 7 Jackson
Miltie, Uncle: 5 Berle
contemporary: 3 Sid
Milton: 4 Ager, city, John, town 5 Berle 6 Caniff, Delugg 7 Hershey 8 Friedman 10 Eisenhower
locale: 6 Canada 7 Ontario
Milton, John: 4 poet 6 writer 7 British
nutbrown brew: 3 ale
work: Areopagitica
Comus
Il Penseroso
Lycidas
On His Blindness
Paradise Lost
Paradise Regained
Samson Agonistes
Milwaukee: 4 city, town
beverage: 4 beer
locale: 3 Wis. 4 Wisc. 9 Wisconsin
pro team: 5 Bucks 7 Brewers
river: 9 Menomonee
school: 9 Marquette
Milwaukie: 4 city, town
locale: 6 Oregon
Mimas: 4 moon
planet: 6 Saturn
mime: 3 ape 4 aper, mock 5 clown, farce 6 acting, jester, parrot, player 7 copycat, gesture, pierrot 9 performer
like a ~: 3 mum 6 silent
prefix with ~: 5 panto
mimeo: 4 copy, dupe 6 ectype, run off 9 duplicate, facsimile, reproduce
mimeograph: 4 copy 6 ectype, run off 7 replica 9 reproduce
inventor: 6 Edison
mimer: 3 ape 4 aper 6 jester 7 copycat
mimetic: 9 imitative
Mimi: 5 Leder 6 Rogers 7 Benzell, Kennedy
see also French
mimic: 3 ape 4 aper, copy, echo, mock 5 actor, ditto, mynah 6 assume, echoer, follow, mirror, mummer, parody, parrot, player 7 act like, burlesk, copycat, emulate, imitate, portray, pretend, take off 8 comedian, imitator, imposter, impostor, look like, make like, resemble, ridicule, simulate, thespian 9 burlesque, make fun of, pantomime 10 caricature
natural ~: 4 mina, myna 5 minah, mynah
mimicking: 9 emulative
Mimi composer: 4 Hart 7 Rodgers
mimicry: 5 apery 6 acting 7 mockery 9 imitation
Mimieux, Yvette: 7 actress
film: Dark of the Sun (1968)
Light in the Piazza (1962)
The Time Machine (1960)
mimosa: 4 tree 5 drink, plant, shrub 6 flower, legume 8 beverage, cocktail
family shrub: 6 acacia
ingredient: 2 OJ 9 champagne
relative: 6 acacia
Mimosa: 4 star
__ Mims: 4 Fort
min.: 3 lim., lmt. 4 inst. 5 least
division: 3 sec. 4 msec., nsec.
many ~: 3 hrs.
Min: 4 Gump
mina: 4 bird 5 money

Min and Bill (1930 film)
cast: Wallace Beery, Marie Dressler
minaret: **5** tower
call from a ~: **4** azan
Minatitlán: **4** city, town
locale: **6** Mexico **8** Veracruz
minatory: **7** ominous **8** lowering, menacing
mince: **3** cut, pie **4** chop, cube, dice, hack, hash, pose **5** grate, grind, shred, spare, strut **6** prance, sashay, soften, weaken **7** crumble, posture **8** mitigate, palliate, tone down **9** euphemize, gloss over, pulverize, put on airs, whitewash
ender: **4** meat
words: **10** equivocate
mince ___: **3** pie
minced oath: **4** darn, drat, rats
mincemeat: **3** pie **7** dessert
make ~ of: **5** smash **7** trounce
mincing: **4** nice **5** fussy, sissy **6** dainty, la-de-da, la-di-da, too-too **7** finicky, prudish **8** affected, delicate, finiking, finnicky, lah-di-dah, precious **9** insincere, squeamish, unnatural **10** artificial, effeminate, fastidious
not ~ words: **5** blunt, frank **6** candid **10** forthright, from the hip, unreserved
mind: **3** wit **4** care, head, heed, keep, look, mark, nous, obey, soul, tend, view, wits **5** bow to, brain, guard, sense, watch **6** accept, advert, animus, attend, behave, bend to, beware, be wary, brains, comply, ensure, follow, fulfil, genius, liking, listen, noggin, noodle, object, psyche, reason, recall, regard, remark, resent, tend to, wisdom **7** abide by, agree to, baby-sit, care for, defer to, fulfill, look out, marbles, observe, opinion, oversee, respect **8** adhere to, attend to, carry out, cerebrum, complain, listen to, object to, remember, take heed, thoughts, watch out **9** attention, conform to, consent to, frown upon, give a damn, give a darn, give a hoot, intellect, look after, make a fuss, mentality, pay heed to, recollect, supervise, watch over **10** brainpower, disapprove, gray matter, ride herd on, toe the line
bear in ~: **4** heed **6** recall **7** bethink **8** remember **9** entertain, recognize, recollect **10** reckon with
be of one ~: **5** agree
blow one's ~: **3** awe **5** amaze
bring to ~: **5** evoke, think **6** recall, review **7** suggest **8** remember **9** recollect, visualize
change of ~: **5** U-turn
change one's ~: **4** bend **6** relent **7** retract **9** vacillate
combining form: **3** noo- **5** menti-, phren-, psych- **6** phreni-, phreno-, psycho-
come back to ~: **5** recur
come to ~: **4** dawn **5** arise, occur **6** strike
dismiss from one's ~: **6** forget
don't ~: **7** disobey
ender: **5** scape
fix in one's ~: **3** con **4** etch **5** learn
frame of ~: **4** mood, vein **5** frame, humor, state **6** spirit, temper **7** feeling, outlook, posture **8** attitude **9** mentality
give a piece of one's ~: **7** lecture, tell off **8** admonish
have in ~: **4** know, mean, plan **5** think **6** intend **7** propose
healthy ~: **6** sanity
improve a ~: **5** learn, teach
in philosophy: **4** nous
load off one's ~: **6** relief
make up one's ~: **5** elect **6** choose, decide **7** resolve **9** determine
name meaning ~: **4** Hugh
never ~: **8** forget it, no matter **10** don't bother
of a ~ (to): **3** apt **5** prone **8** disposed, prepared
of one ~: **6** united **9** unanimous **10** harmonious, like-minded
of sound ~: **4** able, sane **5** lucid **8** rational, sensible **10** reasonable
of the ~: **5** inner **6** mental
one's manners: **6** behave
one's p's and q's: **10** toe the line
one-track ~: **5** mania **6** hang-up **8** fixation, idée fixe **9** monomania, obsession
pay no ~ to: **6** ignore **7** neglect, tune out **8** file away, lay aside, overlook **9** disregard
peace of ~: **4** ease **8** security, serenity
picture: **5** image
presence of ~: **5** poise **6** aplomb **8** calmness **9** composure, sangfroid, stability
prey on one's ~: **6** plague
put one's ~ to rest: **4** buoy **5** cheer **7** cheer up, comfort, console, hearten, satisfy **8** inspirit, reassure
rational ~: **3** ego
science of ~: **10** psychology
sound ~: **6** reason
strength of ~: **4** will **5** spine **7** resolve **8** backbone, decision, firmness **9** fortitude, will power **10** resolution
trip: **6** revery **7** reverie **8** daydream
mind ___: **4** game **6** bender, reader **7** reading
mind-___: **3** set **7** blowing
___ mind: **5** of one
___ mind!: **5** Never
___ mind?: **5** Do you
Mindanao: **3** isl., sea **4** isle **6** island
city: **6** Butuan
gulf: **5** Davao
native: **4** Aeta, Moro
neighbor: **5** Leyte
volcano: **3** Apo
Mind at the End of Its Tether author: H.G. Wells
Mindbend author: Robin Cook
mind-bender: **5** poser **6** enigma, puzzle **7** mystery, problem, stumper
mind-blowing: **6** moving **7** awesome **8** fabulous, imposing **9** memorable, thrilling
mind-changing mark: **4** stet
___-minded: **3** air, ear, eye, low **4** even, evil, fair, high, like, open, weak **5** broad, civic, close, large, light, motor, noble, right, small, sober, tough **6** absent, bloody, closed, double, feeble, fickle, narrow, single, social, strong, tender **7** literal, serious, worldly
Minderbinder: **4** Milo
mindful: **3** hep, hip **4** cagy, kind, wary, wise **5** alert, aware, cagey, chary, savvy **6** kindly, polite, versed, wise to, with it **7** alive to, careful, gallant, heedful, knowing, tactful, tuned in **8** apprised, cautious, gracious, informed, obliging, on the job, sensible, vigilant, watchful **9** attentive, cognizant, conscious, in the know, observant, on the ball, plugged in, regardful, sensitive, unselfish **10** on one's toes, solicitous, thoughtful
be ~: **7** observe
of: **4** onto
mindfulness: **9** chariness **10** discretion, weather eye
Mind Games (1973 song) artist: John Lennon
___ Minding the Mint?: **4** Who's
mindless: **4** dopy, rash **5** blind, dense, dopey, inane, moony, silly **6** obtuse, simple, wanton **7** asinine, doltish, fatuous, foolish, out of it, unaware, witless **8** careless, headless, heedless, knee-jerk, reckless **9** automatic, dim-witted, forgetful, negligent, nitwitted, oblivious, senseless, spaced-out, unheedful **10** gratuitous, irrational, neglectful, regardless, unthinking
Mind Murders, The author: Janwillem van de Wetering
Mind of Mr. Soames, The (1970 film)
cast: Nigel Davenport, Terence Stamp, Robert Vaughn
director: Alan Cooke
mind one's ___ Q's: **5** P's and
Mindoro: **3** isl. **4** isle **6** island
neighbor: **5** Panay
mind reader: **4** seer **9** mentalist
gift: **3** ESP
mind-reading: **9** telepathy
minds
meeting of ~: **6** accord **7** concord, harmony **9** agreement, consensus
of two ~: **4** torn **8** wavering **9** undecided **10** ambivalent, indecisive, on the fence
mind's
heat: **4** zeal **6** fervor **7** avidity, passion
mind's ___: **3** eye
mind-set: **4** mood **6** belief **7** leaning, outlook **8** attitude, tendency **9** mentality, prejudice **10** standpoint
mind's eye: **5** image **6** memory
view: **7** concept **10** appearance, envisaging, impression, perception, projection
Mindspring: **3** ISP
Mindy: **4** Cohn **8** McCready
friend: **4** Mork
portrayer: **3** Pam
mine: **3** dig, pan, pit **4** bomb, bore, fund, lode, vein **5** cache, delve, dig up, fount, hoard, shaft, stock, store **6** burrow, dig for, quarry, source, supply, tunnel, wealth **7** bonanza, deposit, extract, pronoun, reserve **8** excavate, fountain, treasury **9** abundance, booby trap, explosive **10** excavation, mother lode, wellspring
car: **4** tram
detector: **5** sonar
ender: **5** field, layer, shaft **6** worker **7** sweeper
entrance: **4** adit
excavation: **5** stope
find: **3** ore **4** coal, gold, lode, seam, vein **6** silver **7** diamond
gold ~: **4** lode **5** cache, stock, store **6** source, supply, wealth **7** bonanza, cash cow, deposit, fortune, reserve **8** windfall **10** mother lode
in French: **4** à moi
in part: **4** ours
like ~: **4** poss. **10** possessive
machine: **6** dredge
mishap: **6** cave-in
nail: **4** spad
not ~: **3** his **4** hers, your **5** thine, yours
passage: **3** pit **5** shaft, winze **6** airway
timber: **5** brace, sprag, stull
vapor: **4** damp
work a ~: **3** dig **8** prospect
yours and ~: **3** our **4** ours
___ mine: **4** coal, gold, salt **5** drift, sonic **6** aerial **7** contact
___-mine: **5** strip
Mine ___ dog, though he had bit me...: **6** enemy's
___ Mine: **3** He's, I Me, Not **4** She's **5** Enemy
___, Mine and Ours: **5** Yours
mine and yours in Latin: **10** meum et tuum
Mine composer: **8** Gershwin
Mine eyes have ___...: **4** seen
minelayer: **4** boat
Mineo, Sal: **5** actor
film: Cheyenne Autumn (1964) Exodus (1960) The Longest Day (1962) Rebel Without a Cause (1955)
song: Start Movin' (1957)
miner: **9** excavator, sourdough **10** forty-niner, prospector
name meaning ~: **6** Pitman **7** Collier
need: **5** claim **7** lantern
org.: **3** UMW
tool: **3** gad **4** pick
___ miner: **4** coal, leaf
Miner: **3** Jan **5** Steve
mineral: **3** oil, ore **4** coal, jade, lava, mica, opal, rock, ruby, talc, trap, tuff **5** agate, beryl, chalk, chert, emery, flint, geode, lapis, magma, metal, niter, ocher, ochre, shale, slate, stone, topaz, trass, wacke **6** basalt, gabbro, galena, garnet, gneiss, gypsum, halite, iolite, marble, natron, oolite, ophite, pyrite, quartz, rutile, schist, scoria, silica, spinel, zircon **7** azurite, bauxite, biotite, breccia, citrine, diamond, emerald, granite, hyalite, kernite, lignite, olivine, realgar, sylvite, thorite, zincite, zoisite **8** asbestos, cinnabar, corundum, cryolite, dolerite, dolomite, feldspar, fluorite, graphite, hematite, ilmenite, limonite, mudstone, obsidian, plumbago, porphyry, resource, rhyolite, rock salt, sapphire, siderite, smaltite, stannite, stibnite, taconite **9** alabaster, amazonite, argentite, celestite, columbite, graywacke, insensate, limestone, lodestone, magnetite, malachite, millerite, niccolite, pipestone, quartzite, sandstone, scheelite, soapstone, sylvanite, turquoise, uraninite, willemite, wulfenite **10** chalcedony, chrysolite, hornblende, insentient, iron pyrite, lepidolite, meerschaum, polybasite, rose quartz, serpentine, sphalerite, tourmaline, travertine, vanadinite
abrasive ~: **6** garnet **8** corundum
blue ~: **5** lapis **6** iolite **8** fluorite, sapphire **9** turquoise **10** tourmaline
clear ~: **6** zircon **10** tourmaline
combining form: **4** -lite, -lyte **5** oryct- **6** orycto-
commonest ~: **6** quartz
deposit: **4** lode, seam, vein **5** scale
green ~: **4** jade **5** prase **7** olivine **8** fluorite **9** malachite **10** hornblende, serpentine, tourmaline
igneous ~: **6** basalt, gabbro **7** granite, olivine **8** dolerite, feldspar, rhyolite **10** hornblende
metamorphic ~: **5** slate **6** gneiss, schist **9** soapstone
nutrient: **4** iron, zinc **9** magnesium
ornamental stonework ~: **7** zoisite
partner: **3** vit. **7** vitamin
red ~: **4** ruby, sard **6** garnet, rutile, spinel **7** sardine, sardius **8** cinnabar, porphyry **10** rose quartz
residue: **4** calx
Roman ~: **5** murra **6** murrha
sedimentary ~: **5** shale **8** dolomite, mudstone **9** limestone, sandstone
silica ~: **4** mica **6** quartz
soft ~: **4** talc **8** graphite **9** soapstone
suffix: **3** -ite **4** -lite

translucent ~: 4 mica, opal 9 alabaster
volcanic ~: 4 lava, tuff 6 basalt, scoria 8 porphyry
white ~: 5 chalk 6 gypsum 9 alabaster 10 meerschaum
worthless ~: 6 gangue
yellow ~: 5 topaz 8 fluorite
mineral __: 3 oil, tar, wax 4 wool 5 jelly, pitch, water 6 spring 7 kingdom, spirits
__ mineral: 3 gel 4 clay, dark 5 light 6 agaric
__ minérale: 3 eau
mineralize: 7 petrify
mineralogy: 7 science
miner's __: 4 dial, inch 7 lettuce
Miners: 4 UTEP
__ Miner's Daughter: 4 Coal
Miner, Steve: 8 director
film: Forever Young (1992)
Halloween H20: 20 Years Later (1998)
My Father, The Hero (1994)
Wild Hearts Can't Be Broken (1991)
Minerva: 3 dea 5 Roman 7 goddess
equivalent: 6 Athena, Athene
father of ~: 7 Jupiter
symbol: 3 owl
mines
look for ~: 5 sweep
salt ~: 4 work 6 office
minestrone: 4 soup
follower, maybe: 5 pasta
minesweeper: 4 boat
fictional ~: 5 Caine
__ Mine, The: 5 Boy Is
miney
follower: 3 moe
preceder: 5 meeny
Ming __: 4 vase 7 Dynasty
Minghella, Anthony Oscar: The English Patient
mingle: 3 mix 4 fuse, join, meld, pool 5 admix, alloy, blend, cross, immix, merge, tie in, unite 6 hobnob, make up 7 combine, consort, hang out, network 8 intermix 9 associate, circulate, interlace, socialize 10 assimilate, fraternize, interbreed, interweave
unlikely to ~: 3 shy
mingling with: 4 amid 5 among 6 amidst, mongst 7 amongst
Mingo: 6 Norman
portrayer: 4 Ames 6 Ed Ames
__ Ming Pei: 4 Ieoh
Ming the Merciless' daughter: 4 Aura
Mingus, Charles: 7 bassist
genre: 4 jazz
__ Minh: 4 Viet 5 Ho Chi
Minho: 5 river
locale: 5 Spain 8 Portugal
mini: 2 PC 4 tiny 5 skirt, small, teeny 6 little, teensy 8 computer
change a ~: 5 rehem
opposite: 4 maxi
smaller than ~: 5 micro
mini-: 4 tiny 5 teeny 6 teensy
Mini-__: 3 Vac
mini-album: 2 EP
miniature: 3 toy, wee 4 baby, puny, tiny 5 bitty, dwarf, eensy, model, pigmy, pygmy, small, teeny, weeny 6 atomic, bantam, little, midget, minute, peewee, petite, pocket, teensy 7 replica 8 atomical, atomlike, nicknack 9 facsimile, itsy-bitsy, itty-bitty, minuscule, pint-sized, undersize 10 diminutive, homunculus, knickknack, scaled-down, teeny-weeny, vest-pocket
suffix: 3 -ino, -ita, -ito, -ock 4 -ella, -ette
miniature __: 4 golf 6 camera
miniature-golf shot: 4 putt
minibike kin: 5 moped
minibus: 6 jitney
minicomputer, '70s: 3 Vax
Miniconjou: 6 Indian 7 Amerind
Minicoy: 3 isl. 4 isle 6 island
locale: 5 India
minify: 6 lessen
minikin: 3 wee 4 tiny 5 small, teeny 6 little, teensy
minim: 4 note 7 modicum 8 half note, molecule, particle
minimal: 5 basic, least, scant, token 6 barest, lowest, minute, scanty 7 limited, nominal 8 littlest, marginal, smallest 9 essential, narrowest, slightest
amount: 3 bit, tad 4 hoot, iota
exert ~ effort: 5 glide, slide 6 cruise
minimize: 3 pan 4 pare 5 dwarf, gloze, knock, lower, prune 6 lessen, reduce, shrink, weaken 7 cheapen, curtail, detract, put down, run down, shorten 8 belittle, decrease, derogate, diminish, discount, downplay, palliate, play down, pooh-pooh, shrug off, talk down 9 attenuate, deprecate, disparage, extenuate, knock down, poor-mouth, soft-pedal, underplay, underrate, whitewash 10 abbreviate, understate
minimizing: 8 critical, scornful, spiteful 9 slighting 10 belittling, derogatory, detracting, disdainful, pejorative
minimum: 3 dab, jot 4 hair, iota, tiny, whit 5 basal, grain, least, limit, point, spark, speck, teeny 6 barest, bottom, lowest, merest, shadow, teensy 7 modicum, smidgen, smidgin, soupçon, tiniest 8 littlest, pittance, smallest, smidgeon 9 narrowest, scintilla, slightest
number: 5 quota
minimum __: 4 wage 7 tillage
__ minimum: 4 bare 5 local
__ mining: 4 coal 5 strip 6 placer
minion: 4 pawn, tool 5 toady 6 flunky, jackal, lackey, yes man 7 flunkey, lacquey, servant 8 follower, kowtower, truckler 9 sycophant, underling 10 handshaker
Minion: 4 font 8 typeface
miniseries
landmark ~: 5 Roots
maybe: 4 epic
minister: 3 rev. 4 abbé, aide, dean, give, heal, help, tend 5 abbot, agent, do for, envoy, nurse, padre, rabbi, rebbe, serve, treat, vicar 6 bishop, clergy, cleric, consul, curate, deacon, deputy, doctor, father, foster, legate, manage, parson, pastor, priest, rector, succor, supply, wait on 7 prelate, premier, sit with 8 chaplain, delegate, diplomat, official, preacher, reverend, shepherd, wait upon 9 assistant, confesser, confessor, secretary 10 ambassador, archbishop, evangelist, lieutenant, missionary, take care of
assistant: 6 deacon
home: 5 manse
school: 3 sem. 8 seminary
to: 4 keep, tend 5 nurse, serve, treat 6 attend, wait on 8 wait upon
(to): 5 cater
minister __ portfolio: 7 without
__ minister: 5 prime 7 cabinet, foreign
Minister: 4 font 8 typeface
ministerial: 8 clerical 9 religious
Minister's Wooing, The author: Harriet Beecher Stowe
ministration: 3 aid 4 care, help 6 relief, solace, succor 7 service
ministry: 5 abbey 6 clergy 9 rabbinate
former TV ~: 3 PTL
Ministry of Fear (1944 film)
cast: Ray Milland, Marjorie Reynolds
director: Fritz Lang
miniver: 3 fur 4 vair
Miniver: 3 Kay
Mr. ~: 4 Clem
__ Miniver: 3 Mrs.
Miniver Cheevy author: E.A. Robinson
Mini-Wheats: 6 cereal
competitor: 3 Kix 4 Life, Trix 5 Kashi, Quisp, Total 6 Kaboom, Muesli, Oreo O's, Pablum, Smacks 7 All-Bran, Crispix, Harmony, Hunny B's, Mueslix, Oat Bran, Pokemon 8 Boo Berry, Cheerios, Corn Chex, Corn Pops, Fiber One, Rice Chex, Special K, Uncle Sam, Wheaties 9 Alpha Bits, Apple Zaps, Grape Nuts, Honey Comb, Just Right, Wheat Chex 10 Apple Jacks, Bran Flakes, Cap'n Crunch, Cocoa Puffs, Froot Loops, Nutri-Grain, Puffed Rice, Quaker Oats, Smart Start 11 Cocoa Blasts, Cookie Crisp, Golden Crisp, Lucky Charms, Puffed Wheat, Sweet Crunch, Waffle Crisp
mink: 3 fur 4 wrap 6 animal, mammal, weasel 8 kolinsky
home: 5 ranch
relative: 5 fitch, otter, ratel, sable, skunk, stoat, tayra 6 badger, ermine, ferret, marten 7 foumart, polecat 8 carcajou, foulmart, muishond 9 wolverine
Minn.
neighbor: 2 N.D. 3 Man., Ont., Wis. 4 N. Dak., S. Dak., Wisc.
see also Minnesota
Minneapolis: 4 city, town
county: 8 Hennepin
exurb: 5 Edina
locale: 9 Minnesota
river: 11 Mississippi
suburb: 5 Anoka, Eagan, Edina, Osseo
town near ~: 5 Osseo
Minneapolis-to-Fargo highway: 5 US ten
Minnelli: 4 Liza 8 Vincente
Minnelli, Liza: 6 singer 7 actress
film: Arthur (1981)
Cabaret (1972, AA)
New York, New York (1977)
The Sterile Cuckoo (1969)
Tell Me That You Love Me, Junie Moon (1970)
mother: Judy Garland
sister: Lorna Luft
spouse: Peter Allen, Jack Haley Jr.
Minnelli, Vincente: 8 director
film: An American in Paris (1951)
The Bad and the Beautiful (1952)
The Band Wagon (1953)
Bells Are Ringing (1960)
Brigadoon (1954)
Cabin in the Sky (1943)
The Clock (1945)
The Courtship of Eddie's Father (1963)
Designing Woman (1957)
Father of the Bride (1950)
Father's Little Dividend (1951)
Gigi (1958, AA)
Home From the Hill (1960)
Lust for Life (1956)
Madame Bovary (1949)
Meet Me in St. Louis (1944)
On a Clear Day You Can See Forever (1970)
The Pirate (1948)
The Sandpiper (1965)
Some Came Running (1959)
The Story of Three Loves (1953)
Tea and Sympathy (1956)
Two Weeks in Another Town (1962)
Ziegfeld Follies (1946)
spouse: Judy Garland
Minnesota: 5 river, state
capital: 6 St. Paul
city: 5 Eagan, Edina, Osseo 6 Austin, Blaine, Duluth, Savage, St. Paul, Winona 7 Andover, Crystal, Fridley, Hibbing, Mankato, New Hope, Oakdale, St. Cloud, Wabasha 8 Champlin, Moorhead, Owatonna, Plymouth, Shakopee, Woodbury 9 Albert Lea, Faribault, Lakeville, Maplewood, Richfield, Rochester, Roseville, Shoreview 10 Burnsville, Chanhassen, Coon Rapids, Maple Grove, Minnetonka, Sauk Centre
clinic: 4 Mayo
conference: 6 Big Ten
county: 5 Anoka 6 Dakota, Isanti, Itasca, McLeod, Meeker, Sibley, Wadena, Waseca, Winona 7 Le Sueur, Olmsted, Red Lake 8 Chippewa, Hennepin, Nicollet 9 Otter Tail
lake: 5 Rainy 6 Itasca
national park: 9 Voyageurs
neighbor: 4 Iowa 6 Canada 7 Ontario 8 Manitoba, Michigan 9 Wisconsin
port: 6 Duluth
pro team: 5 Twins 7 Vikings 12 Timberwolves
state beverage: 4 milk
state bird: 4 loon
state fish: 7 walleye
state gemstone: 5 agate
state grain: 8 wild rice
state mineral: 6 galena
state muffin: 9 blueberry
state mushroom: 5 morel
state tree: 10 Norway pine
University of ~ athlete: 6 Gopher
Minnesota Fats
game: 4 pool
need: 3 cue
shot: 5 carom, massé 6 carrom
Minnetonka: 4 city, town
locale: 9 Minnesota
Minnie: 4 Marx 5 mouse, Pearl 6 Driver 8 Riperton
Minnie and Moskowitz (1971 film)
cast: Val Avery, Seymour Cassel, Gena Rowlands
director: John Cassavetes
Minnie Mouse dog: 4 Fifi
Minnie the Moocher artist: Cab Calloway
minnow: 4 bait, dace, fish 5 danio
alternative: 4 worm
eater: 4 tern
kin: 4 carp, chub 5 bream
Miño: 5 river
locale: 5 Spain 8 Portugal
Minoan
capital: 7 Cnossus, Gnossus, Knossos
island: 5 Crete 6 Candia
Minogue, Kylie song: The Loco-Motion (1988)
Minolta: 6 camera
alternative: 4 Fuji 5 Canon, Kodak, Leica, Nikon, Ricoh 6 Konica, Pentax, Rollei 7 Olympus, Vivitar, Yashica 8 Polaroid
Minoo: 4 city, town
locale: 5 Japan
minor: 3 boy, kid, lad 4 baby, girl, less, side, teen, ward 5 child, dinky, light, lower, petty, small, youth 6 infant, junior, lesser, little, paltry, slight, two-bit 7 smaller, trivial, younger 8 inferior, juvenile, marginal, picayune, piddling, small-fry, teenager, trifling, underage

9 accessory, ancillary, dependent, little one, schoolboy, secondary, small-time, stripling, youngster 10 adolescent, bush-league, incidental, low-ranking, negligible, peripheral, schoolgirl, second-rate, subsidiary
falling-out: 4 spat 5 scrap 8 squabble
flaw: 4 nick
in law: 5 petit
in music: 4 moll
no longer a ~: 5 adult
not ~: 5 major 7 crucial, serious
weakness: 6 foible
minor __: 3 key 4 axis, coin, mode, suit, term 5 canon, order, party, piece, scale, triad 6 league, planet, tenace 7 element, penalty, premise
minor-__: 7 leaguer
Minor __: 7 Prophet
__ Minor: 3 Leo 4 Asia, Ursa 5 Canis, Friar
Minorca: 3 isl. 4 isle 6 island
port: 5 Mahon
__ Minoris: 5 Canis, Ursae
minority: 5 youth 9 childhood
minority __: 5 group 6 leader
Minority Report (2002 film)
cast: Tom Cruise, Steve Harris, Neal McDonough, Max von Sydow
director: Steven Spielberg
minor-league: 4 bush 5 dinky, small 6 lesser 9 secondary
club: 8 farm team
roundball org.: 3 CBA
Minor Prophet: 4 Amos, Joel 5 Hosea, Micah, Nahum 6 Haggai 7 Malachi, Obadiah 8 Habakkuk 9 Zechariah, Zephaniah
Minos
daughter of ~: 7 Ariadne, Euryale, Phaedra 8 Xenodice 9 Acacallis
home: 5 Crete 6 Candia
parent of ~: 4 Zeus 6 Europa
son of ~: 5 Molus 7 Catreus, Chryses, Glaucus 9 Androgeus, Deucalion, Eurymedon, Nephalion, Philolaus
wife of ~: 8 Pasiphae
Minot: 4 city, town 6 George
locale: 4 N. Dak.
Minotaur
home: 4 maze 5 Crete 6 Candia
slayer of ~: 7 Theseus
Minot, George: 8 Nobelist
Minsk: 4 city, town 7 capital
locale: 7 Belarus
minstrel: 4 bard, scop 6 singer 10 troubadour
instrument: 4 lute
name meaning ~: 6 Harper
poem: 3 lay
minstrel show: 5 revue 6 review
figure: 6 endman
instrument: 5 banjo
mint: 3 new, pot, wad 4 coin, heap, herb, lots, make, pile 5 candy, forge, fresh, issue, shape, stamp, whole 6 boodle, bundle, intact, invent, myriad, packet, unused, virgin 7 fortune, like new 8 billions, brand-new, millions, original, unmarred 9 high grade, undamaged
ender: 3 age 4 mark
family plant: 4 chia, sage 5 thyme 6 betony, catnip, henbit, hyssop 8 lavender, rosemary
jelly: 5 aspic
jelly accompaniment: 4 lamb
not ~: 4 used
output: 4 cent, coin, dime 5 money 6 nickel 7 quarter 10 half-dollar
starter: 3 cat 5 horse, spear 6 pepper
mint __: 5 julep
__ mint: 5 field, lemon, stone 6 brandy
Mintaka: 4 star
constellation: 5 Orion
mint chocolate: 8 ice cream
alternative: 5 lemon, mocha, peach 6 banana, coffee, Jamoca, toffee 7 caramel, coconut, vanilla 8 cinnamon, hazelnut 9 bubblegum, pineapple, pistachio, raspberry, rocky road, rum raisin 10 blackberry, cheesecake, Neapolitan, peppermint, strawberry
Mint Condition song: Breakin' My Heart (1992)
mint julep: 5 drink 8 beverage
Minto: 4 peak 5 mount 8 mountain
locale: 10 Antarctica
minty: 5 tangy 7 piquant
minuet: 5 dance, music, piece
movement: 4 trio
Minuet __: 3 in G
minus: 4 lack, less, loss, lost, sans 6 absent, except, hurdle 7 barrier, deficit, lacking, missing, needing, wanting, without 8 drawback, handicap, negative, obstacle, take away, weakness, weak spot 9 detriment, hindrance, liability 10 deficiency, impediment, leaving out
entry: 5 debit
toppings: 5 plain
minus __: 4 sign, tick 5 sight
minuscule: 3 wee 4 itsy, puny, tiny 5 bitty, light, small, teeny, weeny 6 atomic, bantam, letter, little, paltry, peewee, petite, teensy 7 trivial 8 atomical, atomlike, picayune, piddling, trifling 9 itsy-bitsy, itty-bitty, pint-sized 10 teeny-weeny, vest-pocket
Minus Man, The (1999 film)
cast: Brian Cox, Sheryl Crow, Janeane Garofalo, Owen Wilson
director: Hampton Fancher
minute: 3 sec, wee 4 baby, full, jiff, nice, puny, tick, tiny, wink 5 bitty, close, flash, jiffy, least, light, shake, small, teeny, weeny 6 atomic, bantam, breath, little, moment, paltry, peewee, petite, pocket, second, slight, teensy 7 careful, instant, precise, slender, trivial 8 atomical, atomlike, critical, detailed, exiguous, picayune, piddling, thorough, trifling 9 invisible, itsy-bitsy, itty-bitty, pint-sized, twinkling, undersize, very small 10 diminutive, exhaustive, meticulous, negligible, scrupulous, teeny-weeny, unviewable, vest-pocket
a mile a ~: 5 sixty
any ~ now: 4 anon, soon 7 shortly
fraction: 3 sec. 6 second
hands, essentially: 5 radii
in a ~: 4 soon 9 presently
in a New York ~: 9 instantly, posthaste, right away
New York ~: 5 trice
quantity: 4 drib
this ~: 3 now 4 stat 5 today 6 at once 8 promptly, right now, right off 9 at present, forthwith, instantly, presently, right away 10 here and now
minute __: 3 gun 4 hand 5 steak
__ minute: 3 any, in a 4 last 5 mile a, wait a
__-minute: 3 man
Minute __: 4 Maid, Rice 5 Waltz
Minute Maid product: 2 OJ
Minuteman: 4 ICBM 7 missile
Minutemen: 5 U Mass
Redcoats, to ~: 5 enemy
Minute Rice alternative: 7 Success 8 Carolina 9 Uncle Ben's
minutes: 3 log 6 record
boxer's three ~: 5 round
every 60 ~: 5 horal
fifty ~ past: 5 ten of, ten to
in a few ~: 4 anon, soon 5 later 7 erelong, shortly 8 directly 9 presently 10 before long
keep ~: 4 note 6 record
keeper: 5 noter 9 secretary
one who keeps ~: 5 noter
sixty ~: 4 hour
__ Minutes More: 4 Five
minutest: 5 least
__ Minutes With Andy Rooney, A: 3 Few
Minute Waltz composer: 6 Chopin
__-minute warning: 3 two
minutiae: 6 trivia 7 details, trifles 8 niceties
expert: 4 wonk
minx: 4 miss, snip, vamp 5 flirt, hussy 8 coquette
like a ~: 4 pert 5 saucy
Minya Konka: 4 peak 5 mount 8 mountain
locale: 4 Asia 5 China
Minzhu: 3 pig 5 swine
__ Mio: 4 O Dio 5 O Sole
Miocene: 5 Epoch
Mir
milieu: 5 space
Mira: 4 star 6 pulsar 7 Sorvino 8 red giant
Mirabel: 4 city, town
locale: 6 Canada, Québec
Mirabella: 5 Grace
mirabile __: 5 dictu
__ mirabiles: 4 anni
__ mirabilis: 5 annus
Mirach: 4 star
miracle: 6 marvel, rarity, wonder 7 prodigy, stunner 8 surprise 9 sensation 10 phenomenon
combining form: 8 thaumato-
food: 5 manna
Islam ~: 5 miraj
subject of a Biblical ~: 6 loaves
miracle __: 3 man 4 drug, mile, play 5 berry, fruit
Miracle __: 4 Mile, Whip
Miracle __, The: 5 Woman 6 Worker
Miracle-__: 3 Gro
__ Miracle: 4 It's a
Miracle (1991 song) artist: Whitney Houston
Miracle at Indian River author: Alden Nowlan
Miracle Mile star: 4 Agar
Miracle of Morgan's Creek, The (1944 film)
cast: Eddie Bracken, William Demarest, Betty Hutton
director: Preston Sturges
Miracle of the Rose author: Jean Genet
Miracle on 34th Street (1947 film)
boss: 4 Macy
cast: Edmund Gwenn, Gene Lockhart, Maureen O'Hara, John Payne, Natalie Wood
director: George Seaton
Miracles
lead singer: Smokey Robinson
song: Baby, Baby Don't Cry (1969)
Do It Baby (1974)
Going to a Go-Go (1966)
If You Can Want (1968)
I Second That Emotion (1967)
Love Machine (1975)
Mickey's Monkey (1963)
My Girl Has Gone (1965)
Ooo Baby Baby (1965)
Shop Around (1960)
The Tears of a Clown (1970)
The Tracks of My Tears (1965)
Yester Lover (1968)
You've Really Got A Hold on Me (1963)
Miracles (1975 song) artist: Jefferson Starship
Miracle Whip maker: 5 Kraft
Miracle Woman, The (1931 film)
cast: Sam Hardy, David Manners, Barbara Stanwyck
director: Frank Capra
Miracle Worker, The (1962 film)
cast: Anne Bancroft, Patty Duke, Victor Jory
director: Arthur Penn
role: 5 Annie, Helen 6 Keller 8 Sullivan
miraculous: 7 amazing, awesome, magical, strange, uncanny 8 fabulous, numinous, wondrous 9 marvelous, thrilling, wonderful
Miraculous Mandarin, The: 6 ballet
composer: 6 Bartók
Mirada: 3 car 4 auto 5 Dodge 10 automobile
mirage: 6 fantom, vision 7 fantasm, fantasy, phantom 8 delusion, illusion, phantasm
perhaps: 5 oasis
site: 6 desert
Mirage: 3 car 4 auto 10 automobile, Mitsubishi
locale: 5 Vegas
Mirage (1965 film)
cast: Diane Baker, Walter Matthau, Gregory Peck
director: Edward Dmytryk
Mirage (1967 song) artist: Tommy James and the Shondells
__ Mirage, CA: 6 Rancho
Miramar: 4 city, town
locale: 6 Mexico 7 Florida 10 Tamaulipas
Miramax: 6 studio
competitor: 3 Fox, MGM 6 Disney 7 New Line 8 Columbia 9 Paramount, Universal 10 Dreamworks, Warner Bros.
creation: 4 film 5 movie
Miramichi: 4 city, town
locale: 6 Canada
Miranda: 3 Isa 4 moon 6 Carmen 10 Richardson
planet: 6 Uranus
Miranda, Carmen: 7 actress
film: Down Argentine Way (1940)
Springtime in the Rockies (1942)
Week-end in Havana (1941)
__ Mir Bist du Schön: 3 Bei
mire: 3 bog, fen, mud 4 dirt, muck, ooze, quag, sink 5 delay, marsh, slime, slush, snare, swamp 6 detain, enmesh, entrap, immesh, inmesh, morass 7 bog down, embroil, ensnare, insnare, involve, set back 8 entangle 9 catch up in, implicate, marshland, quicksand, swampland
down: 5 embog
drag through the ~: 5 sully
in a ~: 5 stuck
move in ~: 5 slosh
starter: 4 quag
Mirfak: 4 star
Miriam: 6 Makeba 7 Hopkins
brother of ~: 5 Aaron, Moses
father of ~: 5 Amram
Mirisch: 6 Walter
mirliton: 5 fruit
Miró, Joan: 6 artist 7 painter, Spanish
contemporary: 4 Sert
Mirren, Helen: 7 actress
film: 2010 (1984)
Cal (1984)
Excalibur (1981)
Greenfingers (2001)
The Long Good Friday (1981)
The Mosquito Coast (1986)

Mirrlees, James: **8** Nobelist **9** economist
mirror: **3** ape **4** copy, echo, mock, show **5** glass, image, mimic, shine **6** follow, typify **7** act like, emulate, imitate, reflect **8** make like, resemble, simulate **9** personify, reflector, represent, symbolize **10** illustrate
backing: **4** foil, tain
element: **6** indium **7** silicon
fogger: **5** steam
image: **4** refl. **10** reflection
like a ~: **6** glassy, smooth
stand before a ~: **5** preen, prink
mirror __: **5** image, plant
Mirror Crack'd, The (1980 film)
cast: Rock Hudson, Angela Lansbury, Kim Novak, Elizabeth Taylor
director: Guy Hamilton
Mirror Has Two Faces, The (1996 film)
cast: Lauren Bacall, Jeff Bridges, Mimi Rogers, Barbra Streisand
director: Barbra Streisand
Mirror Image author: Danielle Steel
Mirror, Mirror (1982 song) artist: Diana Ross
mirrors, smoke and: **6** deceit
mirth: **3** fun, joy **4** glee **5** cheer, kicks, laugh, sport **6** frolic, gaiety, gayety, laughs, levity **7** gayness, jollity, revelry **8** felicity, gladness, hilarity, laughter, pleasure **9** amusement, festivity, frivolity, happiness, jocundity, joviality, lightness, merriment, rejoicing **10** jocularity, joyousness, liveliness, recreation, regalement, risibility
mirthful: **3** gay **4** glad **5** funny, happy, jolly, merry, riant, sunny **6** blithe, cheery, jovial, joyous, upbeat **7** buoyant, chipper, festive, gleeful, playful, pleased, tickled **8** ecstatic, euphoric, exultant, giggling, grooving, jubilant, laughing, thrilled **9** convivial, delighted, laughable, overjoyed, rejoicing
sound: **4** ha-ha
mirthless: **6** gloomy **7** unhappy **10** melancholy
MIRV: **4** ICBM **7** missile
miry: **5** boggy, mucky, muddy, slimy **6** swampy
not ~: **5** solid
terrain: **3** bog, fen **4** quag **5** swamp
Mirzam: **4** star
mis-: **3** bad, ill **4** lack
misadd: **3** err
misadventure: **3** woe **4** loss, slip **5** folly **6** mishap **7** bad luck, blunder, debacle, failure, reverse, setback, tragedy **8** accident, bad break, calamity, casualty, disaster **9** adversity, cataclysm, mischance
misanthrope: **5** cynic, hater, loner **6** hermit **7** doubter, recluse, sceptic, skeptic **9** pessimist
Misanthrope, The author: Molière
misanthropic: **6** crabby, hating **7** cynical, recluse **8** eremitic, reserved, solitary **9** reclusive, sarcastic
Misantla: **4** city, town
locale: **6** Mexico **8** Veracruz
misapplication: **5** abuse **6** misuse **7** mistake
misapply: **5** abuse, waste **6** misuse
misapprehend: **3** err **4** miss **7** blunder, confuse, misread, mistake **8** misjudge
misapprehension: **7** fallacy, mistake **8** delusion, illusion
misappropriate: **3** rob **4** crib, grab **5** abuse, filch, steal, usurp **6** misuse, pocket, thieve **7** plunder, swindle **8** embezzle, misapply, misspend, peculate **9** defalcate
misappropriation: **5** abuse, theft **7** larceny
misarrange: **6** muddle
Misato: **4** city, town
locale: **5** Japan
misbegotten: **5** inept **7** illegal, illicit, natural **8** baseborn, spurious, unlawful
misbehave: **3** err, sin **5** act up, be bad, cut up **6** offend **7** carry on, deviate, do wrong, go wrong **8** go astray, trespass **10** fool around, misconduct, roughhouse, transgress
__ Misbehave: **4** Let's
misbehaver: **3** imp
__ Misbehaves: **5** Julia
__ Misbehavin': **4** Ain't
misbehaving: **3** bad **4** wild **6** errant
child: **3** imp **4** brat, tike, tyke
misbehavior: **5** guilt **7** misdeed **8** acting up, mischief, misdoing, rudeness
misbelief: **5** error **8** delusion, illusion
misbeliever: **7** sceptic, skeptic
misc.: **3** var.
miscalculate: **3** err **4** goof, slip, trip **5** mix up **6** mess up, slip up **7** blunder, misread, mistake, stumble **8** get wrong, miscount, misjudge, overlook, overrate **9** overvalue, underrate
miscalculated: **5** wrong
miscalculation: **5** boner, error **7** mistake **8** surprise
miscellaneous: **3** NOC, odd **4** many, mixt **5** mixed **6** divers, motley, sundry, varied **7** diverse, jumbled, mingled, oddball, various **8** assorted, multiple, unsorted **9** different, disparate, divergent, unmatched
miscellany: **3** mix **4** hash, mess, olio, stew **5** combo **6** jumble, medley **7** farrago, mélange, mixture, variety **8** mishmash, mixed bag, pastiche **9** anthology, diversity, patchwork, potpourri **10** assortment, collection, cumulation, hodgepodge, salmagundi
literary ~: **3** ana **5** varia
Mischa: **4** Auer **5** Elman
mischance: **4** pity **5** fluke **6** mishap **7** bad luck, reverse, tragedy, undoing **8** hard luck **9** adversity **10** hard knocks, misfortune
mischief: **3** gag **4** evil, harm, hurt **5** antic, caper, prank **6** damage, injury **7** devilry, hot foot, knavery, outrage, roguery, trouble **8** deviltry, sabotage **9** devilment, high jinks, rascality, vandalism **10** dirty trick, friskiness, impishness, misconduct, tomfoolery, wrongdoing
fond of ~: **3** sly
get into ~: **5** act up, cut up **8** go astray **9** misbehave **10** fool around, roughhouse
maker: **3** imp **4** pixy, punk **5** demon, pixie **6** daemon, daimon **7** hellion
mischief __: **5** night
mischief-maker: **3** elf **5** rogue, scamp **6** rascal, vandal **7** gremlin **9** scoundrel
mischieviously: **5** in fun
mischievous: **3** bad, sly **4** arch, evil, foxy **5** apish, elfin, rowdy **6** artful, elfish, elvish, impish, tricky, vexing, wicked **7** coltish, harmful, hurtful, irksome, jocular, knavish, naughty, nocuous, playful, puckish, teasing, vicious, wayward **8** damaging, devilish, prankish, rascally, sinister, spiteful, sporting, sportive **9** injurious, insidious, malicious, vexatious
be ~: **5** act up **9** misbehave
child: **3** imp **4** tike, tyke **6** gamine, urchin
one: **3** elf **5** rogue, scamp
mischievousness: **7** devilry **8** deviltry
misch metal: **5** alloy
component: **6** cerium **9** lanthanum
misconceive: **7** mistake **8** misjudge
misconception: **5** error, fault **7** fallacy, mistake **8** delusion, illusion
misconduct: **3** sin **4** evil **5** fault, guilt **7** misdeed, offense **8** mischief, misdoing, rudeness **9** improbity, misbehave, vandalism, veniality
misconstrue: **4** skew **7** distort, misread, mistake **8** get wrong, misjudge
misconstrued: **5** wrong **8** mistaken
miscount: **5** error
miscreancy: **8** iniquity
miscreant: **3** cad, cur, rat **4** evil, fink, heel, scum, worm **5** bully, churl, felon, hater, knave, louse, rogue, rowdy, scamp, sneak **6** loafer, outlaw, rascal, wicked, wretch **7** caitiff, convict, corrupt, culprit, hoodlum, immoral, lowlife, outcast, ruffian, vicious, villain **8** criminal, depraved, evildoer, infamous, jailbird, perverse, picaroon, rakehell, rascally, scalawag **9** heretical, nefarious, racketeer, reprobate, scallawag, scallywag, scoundrel, vulgarian, wrongdoer **10** blackguard, black sheep, bootlegger, degenerate, delinquent, holy terror, iniquitous, malefactor, pickpocket, villainous
miscue: **3** err **5** boner, error, fault, fluff, lapse **6** fumble, slip-up **7** misstep **9** oversight
remover: **6** eraser
misdeal: **3** err
misdeed: **3** sin **4** no-no, slip **5** crime, error, fault, wrong **6** slip-up **7** offense **8** trespass, villainy **9** dirty pool, veniality, violation **10** illegality, misconduct, peccadillo, wrongdoing
misdemeanor: **3** sin **5** crime, fault, wrong **6** delict, miscue, slip-up **7** offense **8** trespass, villainy **9** dirty deed, dirty pool, violation
misdirect: **8** throw off **9** misinform **10** lead astray
misdirected: **5** led on **6** astray
misdo: **3** err **4** muff **5** botch **6** blow it, bungle, foul up, mess up **7** go wrong
misdoing: **5** wrong **7** outrage **10** misconduct
mise: **4** writ **9** agreement **10** settlement
mise en __: **5** scène
misemploy: **5** abuse, waste **6** misuse
misemployment: **5** abuse
miser: **5** churl **6** cheapo **7** hoarder, Scrooge **8** el cheapo, muckworm, tightwad **9** skinflint **10** cheapskate, pinchpenny
like a ~: **6** stingy **7** chintzy
motivation: **5** greed
no ~: **5** donor, giver
stash: **5** hoard
miserable: **3** bad, ill, low, sad **4** blue, down, foul, glum, grim, hurt, mean, poor, sick, vile **5** awful, lousy, moody, needy, sorry, woful **6** abject, ailing, broody, crumby, crummy, dismal, gloomy, horrid, humble, in pain, meager, measly, morose, odious, pained, paltry, racked, rotten, rueful, scanty, scurvy, shabby, sickly, somber, sordid, tragic, woeful **7** accurst, baleful, baneful, beastly, doleful, forlorn, ghastly, hapless, hurting, ill-done, in a funk, injured, joyless, piteous, pitiful, ruthful, squalid, unhappy, wounded **8** accursed, beggarly, dejected, desolate, dolorous, downcast, dreadful, God-awful, grievous, hopeless, horrible, indigent, inferior, mournful, pathetic, pitiable, shameful, stinking, strained, terrible, tortured, tragical, troubled, wretched **9** abhorrent, afflicted, appalling, atrocious, bummed out, cheerless, defective, depressed, destitute, destroyed, execrable, frightful, heartsick, insidious, loathsome, offensive, penniless, revolting, sorrowful, suffering, thankless, third-rate, tormented, woebegone, worthless **10** abominable, chapfallen, deplorable, despairing, despicable, despondent, detestable, disastrous, dispirited, distressed, horrendous, lamentable, melancholy, pathetical
feeling: **5** agony
__ Misérables: **3** Les
Miserere: **5** psalm
miserliness: **7** avarice
miserly: **4** mean **5** cheap, close, tight **6** greedy, measly, shabby, skimpy, stingy **7** ignoble, selfish **8** churlish, covetous, grasping, ungiving **9** illiberal, penurious, skinflint **10** avaricious, cheapskate, inadequate, skinflinty, ungenerous
misery: **3** ill, woe **4** ache, bane, hell, load, need, pain, pang, want **5** agony, blues, curse, dolor, gloom, grief, throe, trial, worry **6** burden, ordeal, penury, sorrow, stitch, twinge **7** anguish, anxiety, bad news, despair, hurting, passion, poverty, problem, sadness, squalor, torment, torture, travail, trouble **8** calamity, disaster, distress, hardship, headache, the blues **9** adversity, dejection, heartache, indigence, privation, suffering **10** affliction, bitter pill, depression, desolation, difficulty, discomfort, heartbreak, heavy heart, infelicity, loneliness, melancholy, misfortune, oppression, sordidness, woefulness
cause of ~: **4** bane
misery __: **5** index
Misery: **4** film **5** novel
author: Stephen King
cast: Kathy Bates, James Caan, Richard Farnsworth, Frances Sternhagen
director: Rob Reiner
misfeasance: **5** abuse
misfield: **6** fumble
misfigured: **5** wrong
misfire: **4** miss **6** fizzle, glitch **7** lose out **8** fall flat
misfit: **4** geek, nerd, nurd **5** dweeb, loser **6** wretch **7** oddball
high-school ~: **4** nerd **7** egghead
Misfits, The (1961 film)
author: Arthur Miller
cast: Montgomery Clift, Clark Gable, Marilyn Monroe, Thelma Ritter, Eli Wallach
director: John Huston
dog: **9** Tom Dooley
'M' Is for Malice author: Sue Grafton
misfortunate: **7** unhappy
misfortune: **3** ill, woe **4** blow, harm, loss, pity **5** cross, trial **6** crunch, misery, sorrow **7** bad luck, bad news, debacle, failure, reverse, setback, tragedy, trouble, undoing **8** accident, bad break, calamity, casualty, disaster, distress, hard luck, hardship **9** adversity, cataclysm, liability, mischance, suffering, tough luck **10** affliction, difficulty, hard knocks
cause of ~: **3** hex **4** jinx **5** curse **6** hoodoo
misgiving: **8** bad vibes **9** nonbelief
misgivings: **4** care, fear, pang **5** doubt, qualm, worry **6** regret, unease **7** anxiety, scruple **8** distrust, mistrust, question, wariness **9** leeriness, suspicion **10** foreboding, hesitation, insecurity, skepticism
have ~ about: **3** rue
more than ~: **5** dread
misguess: **3** err

misguide: 3 lie 6 delude 7 mislead 9 disinform, misinform
misguided: 5 led on, wrong 6 misled, unwise 7 deluded, foolish 8 confused, deceived, faked-out, mistaken 9 erroneous, impolitic, imprudent, misplaced 10 ill-advised, indiscreet
act: 5 folly
Misha: 7 Dichter
in English: 4 Mike
mishandle: 3 err 4 blow, flub, goof, harm, mall, maul, muff 5 abuse, botch, gum up 6 blow it, bungle, foozle, foul up, fumble, goof up, mess up, misuse 7 blunder 8 aggrieve, mistreat, overlook
mishandled: 5 wrong
mishandling: 5 abuse
mishap: 3 dud 4 blow, bomb, bust, flop, harm, loss, pity 5 event, hitch, snafu 6 defeat, fiasco, glitch, turkey 7 blunder, debacle, misstep, reverse, setback, stumble, tragedy, trouble, washout 8 accident, bad break, calamity, casualty, disaster, downfall, hard luck, hardship 9 adversity, breakdown, cataclysm, mischance, tough luck 10 visitation
razor ~: 3 cut
Mishawaka: 4 city, town
locale: 7 Indiana
mishearing: 6 otosis
Mishima: 4 city, town 5 Yukio
locale: 5 Japan
Mishima, Yukio: 6 author, writer 8 Japanese
work: The Sailor Who Fell From Grace With the Sea
The Sound of Waves
The Temple of the Golden Pavilion
mishmash: 3 mix 4 hash, mess, muss, olio, stew 5 mix-up, snarl 6 jumble, litter, medley 7 farrago, goulash, mélange, mixture, variety 8 pastiche, scramble 9 pasticcio, patchwork, potpourri 10 assortment, hodgepodge, miscellany, salmagundi
Mishnah: 4 laws 6 Jewish
authority: 5 rabbi, rebbe
misimpression: 8 illusion
misinform: 3 lie 5 lie to 7 cover up, deceive, mislead 8 misguide, misstate 9 misdirect, mousetrap 10 lead astray, put on an act, steer wrong
misinformed: 6 lied to 8 mistaken 9 misguided
misinstruct: 3 lie
misinterpret: 4 skew 6 garble 7 distort, mistake
misinterpretation: 5 error
misjudge: 3 err 4 slip 7 mistake, presume 8 be misled, overrate, prejudge 9 dogmatize, underrate 10 presuppose
misjudgment: 5 error 7 mistake
Miskito: 6 Indian 7 Amerind
Miskolc: 4 city, town
locale: 7 Hungary
mislaid: 4 lost 7 missing
mislay: 4 lose, miss 8 misplace
mislead: 3 con, lie 4 bait, bilk, dupe, fool, gull, hoax, hose, jive, lure, nick, rook, scam, sell, sham, snow 5 bluff, cheat, cozen, lie to, put on, shaft, tempt, trick 6 betray, delude, entice, outwit, rip off, rope in, suck in, take in 7 beguile, confuse, deceive, defraud, ensnare, insnare, pretend, sell out, two-time 8 confound, hoodwink, inveigle, misguide, outsmart, throw off 9 disinform, four-flush, misinform, victimize
misleading: 4 sham 5 false, lying, wrong 6 tricky, unreal, untrue 7 devious, evasive 8 deluding, delusive, delusory, puzzling, specious, spurious 9 ambiguous, beguiling, confusing, deceitful, deceiving, deception, deceptive, dishonest, equivocal 10 fallacious, fictitious, inexplicit, unexplicit, ungrounded
move: 4 ruse
one: 4 liar
Misled (1985 song) artist: Kool and the Gang
mismanage: 3 err 4 flub, goof, harm, muff 5 abuse, botch, gum up 6 blow it, bungle, foozle, foul up, fumble, goof up, mess up, misuse 7 blunder, louse up 8 overlook
mismatch: 6 differ 8 contrast 9 disparity
mismatched: 6 unlike 7 unalike, unequal 9 different 10 dissimilar
miso: 4 soup 6 legume
ingredient: 3 soy
misogynist: 5 hater
mispickel: 3 ore
misplace: 4 lose, miss 6 mislay 7 misfile
misplaced: 4 lost 7 missing 9 misguided
combining form: 7 chorist- 8 choristo-
misplay: 3 err 4 muff 5 error
misprint: 4 typo 5 error 7 erratum, mistake
misprints: 6 errata
misquote: 3 lie 4 skew, warp 5 slant, twist 6 garble 7 distort, falsify, stretch, trump up 8 miscolor 9 embellish, embroider, overstate 10 equivocate, exaggerate
Misreadings author: Umberto Eco
misreckon: 3 err
misrender: 4 skew 5 color
misreport: 4 skew 10 exaggerate
misrepresent: 3 con, lie 4 hoke, skew, snow, warp 5 belie, color, fudge, slant, twist, wrong 6 garble, palter 7 cover up, distort, falsify, mislead, stretch, trump up 8 disguise, miscolor, simulate 9 embellish, embroider, overstate
misrepresentation: 3 fib, lie 4 hoax, ruse, sham 5 feint, fraud 6 deceit, humbug 7 falsity, slander, snow job, swindle 8 artifice, pretense 9 imposture 10 subterfuge
Misr, natives call it: 5 Egypt
miss: 3 deb, err 4 fail, flub, girl, jump, lack, lass, long, lose, loss, maid, minx, muff, need, omit, skip, slip, trip, verb, want, wish 5 botch, crave, error, fault, fluff, forgo, let go, mourn, title, woman, yearn 6 blow it, damsel, desire, falter, female, forego, forget, fumble, gamine, ignore, lassie, maiden, mislay, pass up, regret, tomboy 7 blunder, colleen, default, failure, let slip, long for, misfire, misstep, mistake, neglect, pine for, require 8 fraülein, misjudge, misplace, omission, overlook, pass over 9 debutante, disregard, fall short, go without, lose out on, overshoot, oversight 10 bobbysoxer, schoolgirl, undershoot
any ~: 3 her, she
hit or ~: 6 random 10 undesigned
in French: 4 mlle.
in Japanese: 3 san
in Spanish: 4 srta. 8 señorita
partner: 3 hit
the boat: 4 fail 7 lose out
miss __: 4 a cue 5 out on
miss __ good..., A: 4 is as
miss __ mile: 3 by a
miss __ on: 3 out
__ miss: 4 near 5 hit or 6 junior
Miss __: 3 USA,You 5 Julie, Peach, Piggy 6 Saigon 7 America, Liberty, Manners 8 Universe
Miss __ at the Cirque Fernando: 4 Lola
Miss __ Bett: 4 Lulu
Miss __ Disposes: 3 Pym
Miss __ Like Crazy: 3 You
Miss __ Regrets: 4 Otis
Miss __ Thompson: 5 Sadie
Miss __ USA: 4 Teen
Miss.
city on the ~: 3 St. L.
neighbor: 3 Ala., Ark., Tex. 4 Tenn.
see also Mississippi
__ Miss: 3 Old, Ole
missa __: 7 cantata
miss a __: 3 cue
Missa Hilarious composer: PDQ Bach
Miss America
former ~ host: 3 Ely 5 Parks 6 Ron Ely 9 Bert Parks
wear: 4 sash 5 tiara 8 swimsuit
Miss America author: 5 Stern
Missa Solemnis composer: 9 Beethoven
__ Miss Brooks: 3 Our
miss by __: 5 a mile
Miss Congeniality (2000 film)
cast: Benjamin Bratt, Sandra Bullock, Michael Caine, William Shatner
director: Donald Petrie
__ Miss Daisy: 7 Driving
missed: 4 lost 5 unhit
Miss Firecracker (1989 film)
cast: Holly Hunter, Tim Robbins, Mary Steenburgen
Miss Firecracker Contest, The author: Beth Henley
misshape: 4 warp 6 deform 7 contort
misshapen: 9 grotesque, malformed
missile: 2 MX 3 bat, SAM 4 ammo, bolt, bomb, dart, ICBM, MIRV, Nike, nuke, Scud, shot, Thor 5 arrow, lance, spear, Titan 6 bullet, pellet, rocket, weapon 9 cartridge, explosive 10 ammunition, projectile, trajectile
housing: 4 silo
of yore: 5 arrow, spear, stone
part: 4 cone
path: 3 arc 4 traj. 10 trajectory
treaty acronym: 4 SALT 5 START
warning grp.: 5 NORAD
missile __: 3 gap
__ missile: 6 cruise, guided
__-missile: 4 anti
__ Missile Crisis: 5 Cuban
missing: 4 away, AWOL, gone, lost 5 minus, out of, short 6 absent, astray, bereft 7 at large, lacking, left out, mislaid, needing, omitted, removed, wanting 8 vanished 9 elsewhere, misplaced 10 left behind
link: 6 apeman
not ~ a trick: 8 watchful 9 observant
nothing: 4 full 6 entire 8 complete, thorough 10 exhaustive, unabridged
part: 4 hole 6 lacuna
something ~: 4 lack
missing __: 4 link, mass
Missing (1982 film)
cast: Jack Lemmon, Melanie Mayron, John Shea, Sissy Spacek
director: Costa-Gavras
setting: 5 Chile
Missing You (song) artist: Diana Ross, John Waite, Ray Peterson
mission: 3 aim, end, job 4 duty, goal, task, work 5 quest, trust 6 affair, charge, church, errand, object, sortie 7 calling, embassy, purpose, pursuit 8 business, function, legation, lifework, vocation 9 objective, operation 10 assignment, commission, profession
military ~: 5 recon
military ~ in Britain: 5 recce, recco
scrap a ~: 5 abort
starter: 5 trans
mission __: 7 control
__ mission: 4 home 5 inner 6 rescue 7 foreign, support
Mission: 4 city, town
locale: 5 Texas 6 Canada, Kansas
Mission __, CA: 5 Viejo
missionary: 6 clergy, herald, jesuit, pastor 7 apostle, teacher 8 minister, preacher, promoter 9 converter, messenger
book: 5 Bible
Missionary __: 5 Ridge
Mission Bend: 4 city, town
locale: 5 Texas
Mission Control concern: 6 G force
Mission Impossible (1996 film)
cast: Emmanuelle Béart, Tom Cruise, Emilio Estevez, Vanessa Redgrave, Ving Rhames, Jon Voight
director: Brian De Palma
Mission Impossible (CBS drama)
cast: Barbara Bain (Cinnamon Carter)
Lynda Day George (Lisa Casey)
Peter Graves (Jim Phelps)
Steven Hill (Dan Briggs)
Martin Landau (Rollin Hand)
Peter Lupus (Willy Armitage)
Greg Morris (Barney Collier)
Leonard Nimoy (Paris)
Mission Impossible II (2000 film)
cast: Tom Cruise, Thandie Newton, Ving Rhames, Dougray Scott
director: John Woo
Mission: Impossible org.: 3 IMF
Mission to __: 4 Mars
Mission to Moscow (1943 film)
cast: Ann Harding, Oscar Homolka, Walter Huston
director: Michael Curtiz
Mission Viejo: 4 city, town
locale: 10 California
town near ~: 6 El Toro
missis: 4 mate, wife 5 bride, woman 6 female, spouse 9 other half
miss is as good as __, A: 5 a mile
Mississauga: 4 city, town
locale: 6 Canada 7 Ontario
Mississippi: 3 riv. 5 river, state
capital: 7 Jackson
city: 5 Pearl 6 Biloxi, Tupelo 7 Clinton, Jackson, Natchez 8 Columbus, Gulfport, Meridian 9 Southaven, Vicksburg 10 Clarksdale, Greenville, Pascagoula, Southhaven, Starkville
conference: 3 SEC
neighbor: 3 Ala., Ark. 4 Tenn. 7 Alabama 8 Arkansas 9 Louisiana, Tennessee
river: 5 Yazoo
state beverage: 4 milk
state flower: 8 magnolia
state game bird: 8 wood duck
state insect: 8 honeybee
state shell: 6 oyster
state tree: 8 magnolia
Mississippi (1935 film)
cast: Joan Bennett, Bing Crosby, W.C. Fields
director: A. Edward Sutherland
Mississippi __: 3 Mud 5 Blues, Delta, Suite 6 Masala, Valley 7 Burning
Mississippi Burning (1988 film)
cast: Willem Dafoe, Gene Hackman, Frances McDormand
director: Alan Parker
Mississippi River
city on the ~: 6 Keokuk, St. Paul 7 Memphis, St. Louis 10 Baton Rouge

explorer: 6 Joliet 7 Jolliet, La Salle
feature: 4 silt 5 bayou, delta
flatboat: 3 ark
river to the ~: 3 Red 4 Iowa, Ohio 5 White, Yazoo 7 St. Croix 8 Arkansas, Big Muddy, Illinois 9 Minnesota, Wisconsin
source: 6 Itasca
state: 3 Ill, Ken., Wis. 4 Iowa, Minn., Tenn., Wisc. 8 Illinois, Kentucky, Missouri 9 Louisiana, Minnesota, Tennessee, Wisconsin
vessel: 3 ark, str. 7 steamer 8 flatboat
Mississippi State
athletes: 8 Bulldogs
conference: 3 SEC
locale: 10 Starkville
Mississippi Suite composer: 5 Grofé
missive: 3 ltr. 4 line, memo, note, word 6 letter, report 7 epistle, message 8 dispatch 10 memorandum
Miss Julie author: August Strindberg
Miss Julie composer: Ned Rorem
Miss Kitty's friend: 4 Matt 6 Dillon
Miss Liberty: 7 musical
songwriter: 6 Berlin
Miss Lonelyhearts author: Nathanael West
Miss Lulu Bett author: Zona Gale
Miss Mama __: 5 Aimee
__ Miss Marker: 6 Little
Miss Me Blind (1984 song) artist: Culture Club
Miss Otis Regrets composer: 6 Porter
Missoula: 4 city, town
athletes: 9 Grizzlies
locale: 4 Mont. 7 Montana
Missouri: 3 riv 5 river, state 6 Indian 7 Amerind 10 battleship
capital: Jefferson City
city: 3 St. L. 5 Lamar, Rolla, St. Joe 6 Affton, Arnold, Belton, Joplin 7 Ballwin, Branson, Liberty, O'Fallon, Raytown, Sedalia, St. Louis 8 Columbia, Ferguson, Kirkwood, Oakville, St. Joseph, St. Peters, Wildwood 9 Gladstone, Grandview, Hazelwood, Mehlville, St. Charles 10 Florissant, Kansas City, Lee's Summit
conference: 9 Big Twelve
motto word: 4 esto
mountain range: 6 Ozarks
neighbor: 3 Ark., Ill., Kan., Ken., Neb. 4 Iowa, Nebr., Okla., Tenn. 6 Kansas 8 Arkansas, Illinois, Kentucky, Nebraska, Oklahoma 9 Tennessee
plateau: 5 Ozark
port: 7 St. Louis
state animal: 4 mule
state aquatic animal: 10 paddlefish
state bird: 8 bluebird
state fish: 7 catfish
state fossil: 7 crinoid
state insect: 8 honeybee
state mineral: 6 galena
state musical instrument: 6 fiddle
state rock: 9 mozarkite
state tree: 7 dogwood
__ Missouri: 3 USS
Missouri City: 4 town
locale: 5 Texas
Missouri River
city: 5 Omaha 6 Pierre 8 Bismarck, St. Joseph 9 Sioux City 10 Great Falls
city on the ~: 5 Omaha 6 Pierre 8 Bismarck 10 Kansas City
river to the ~: 5 Osage 6 Kansas 8 Cheyenne, Niobrara
tribe: 3 Oto 4 Otoe

Miss Peach: 5 comic 10 comic strip
artist: Mell Lazarus
character: 3 Ira
misspeak: 3 err, lie
misspell: 3 err
misspend: 4 lose 5 waste 8 squander 9 dissipate
misspent: 4 idle, lost 5 blown 6 wasted 8 prodigal 10 dissipated, misapplied, profitless, squandered, thrown away
Miss Piggy: 3 sow 6 Muppet
friend: 6 Kermit
pronoun: 3 moi
Miss Pym Disposes author: Josephine Tey
Miss Sadie Thompson (1953 film)
cast: José Ferrer, Rita Hayworth, Aldo Ray
Miss Saigon setting: 3 Nam 7 Vietnam
misstate: 3 lie 4 skew 5 twist 6 invent 7 falsify 9 misinform
misstatement: 3 lie 5 error, gaffe 7 blooper, mistake 8 pretense
misstep: 3 dud, err 4 bomb, bust, flop, lose, loss, slip, trip 5 boner, error, fluff, flunk, gaffe, guilt, lapse 6 blow it, boo-boo, bungle, defeat, falter, fiasco, miscue, slip-up, turkey 7 blunder, debacle, failure, faux pas, founder, go under, go wrong, mistake, stumble, washout 8 downfall, fall flat, flounder, lay an egg 9 indecorum, strike out
miss the __: 4 boat
Miss Thompson author: W. Somerset Maugham
Miss Universe wear: 5 tiara
missus: 4 mate, wife 5 woman 6 female, spouse 9 other half
missy: 4 girl, lass 5 woman
Missy: 4 Gold 7 Elliott, Francis
Miss You (1978 song) artist: Rolling Stones
Miss You Like Crazy (1989 song)
artist: Natalie Cole
Miss You Much (1989 song) artist: Janet Jackson
mist: 3 dew, dim, fog 4 blur, film, haze, mirk, murk, rain, smog, soup 5 befog, blear, brume, cloud, spray, steam, vapor 6 mizzle, shower 7 drizzle, moisten, obscure, steam up 8 moisture, sprinkle 9 overcloud
__ mist: 3 sea 6 Scotch
__ Mist: 5 Irish
mistake: 3 err 4 fail, flub, goof, miss, omit, slip, trip, typo 5 boner, botch, error, fault, fluff, gaffe, lapse, mix-up, snafu, snarl 6 barney, bobble, boo-boo, bungle, goof-up, gotcha, howler, jumble, lapsus, muddle, slip-up, tangle 7 blooper, blunder, confuse, erratum, faux pas, misread, misstep, neglect 8 confound, delusion, get wrong, illusion, miscount, misjudge, misprint, omission, overlook, solecism 9 confusion, false move, false step, oversight 10 aberration, inaccuracy
by ~: 7 in error 8 unawares
exclamation: 4 oh-oh, oops, uh-oh 6 whoops
indicated a ~: 3 x'ed
make a ~: 3 err 4 goof, miss, slip
no ~: 5 truly 6 surely 7 flat out 8 in spades 9 certainly, decidedly, downright 10 absolutely, definitely, distinctly, positively
remover: 6 eraser
mistaken: 5 duped, false, wrong 6 all wet, erring, faulty, fooled, misled, unreal, untrue, way off 7 at fault, deluded, off-base, tricked, unsound 8 confused, deceived 9 erroneous, illogical, incorrect, misguided, unadvised, unfounded 10 confounded, fallacious, ill-advised, inaccurate, misjudging, ungrounded, unreliable
__ mistaken: 5 sadly
mistakenly: 5 amiss, wrong 9 foolishly
mistakes: 6 errata
mister: 2 he 3 guy, man, sir 4 chap, gent, male, mate 5 bloke, hubby 6 feller, fellow, spouse 7 grown-up, husband
in French: 8 monsieur
in German: 4 herr
in India: 3 sri 4 shri 5 saheb, sahib
in Spanish: 5 señor
Mister __: 7 Roberts, Sandman
Mister 880 (1950 film)
cast: Edmund Gwenn, Burt Lancaster, Dorothy McGuire
Mister Ed (CBS sitcom)
cast: Connie Hines (Carol Post) Alan Young (Wilbur Post)
title character: 5 horse
Mister Roberts (1955 film)
cast: James Cagney, Henry Fonda, Jack Lemmon, William Powell
director: John Ford, Mervyn LeRoy
Mister Sandman (1954 song) artist: Four Aces
Mister Scoutmaster (1953 film)
cast: Edmund Gwenn, Clifton Webb
director: Henry Levin
mistimed: 3 off 5 wrong
mistletoe: 5 plant, shrub
month: 3 Dec. 8 December
ritual: 4 kiss
unit: 5 sprig
mistletoe __: 6 cactus
__ misto: 6 fritto
mistral: 4 wind
Mistral: 8 Frédéric, Gabriela
Mistral, Frédéric: 4 poet 6 French, writer 8 Nobelist
Mistral, Gabriela: 4 poet 6 writer 7 Chilean 8 Nobelist
Mistral's Daughter author: Judith Krantz
mistranscription: 4 typo
mistreat: 3 rip 4 bash, harm, mall, maul 5 abuse, trash, wound, wrong 6 dump on, ill-use, injure, mess up, misuse 7 corrupt, outrage, rough up, shake up, torment, torture 8 aggrieve, backbite, maltreat 9 brutalize, manhandle, mishandle 10 excruciate, kick around, push around, roughhouse
mistreatment: 5 abuse 6 misuse 8 inequity
__, Mistress of the Dark: 6 Elvira
mistrust: 4 fear 5 doubt, query 6 beware, wonder 7 dispute, suspect 8 bad vibes, discount, disfavor, distrust, question, wariness 9 challenge, chariness, disbelief, discredit, misgiving, nonbelief, smell a rat, suspicion 10 disbelieve, foreboding, skepticism
mistrustful: 4 wary 5 chary 6 unsure 7 dubious, guarded 8 cautious, doubting, hesitant 9 skeptical, uncertain 10 suspicious
misty: 3 dim, wet 4 damp, dark, dewy, hazy 5 foggy, fuzzy, mirky, moist, murky, soupy, undry, vague 6 bleary, cloudy, opaque, steamy 7 blurred, clouded, obscure, unclear, wettish 8 closed in, nebulous, overcast, shrouded, socked in, vaporous 9 drizzling 10 indistinct
become ~: 5 fog up
get ~: 3 sob 4 weep 7 blubber 9 shed tears
Misty (1959 song) artist: Johnny Mathis
misty-eyed: 5 teary
__ Misty for Me: 4 Play
misunderstand: 4 miss 7 confuse, misread, mistake 8 confound, get wrong, misapply, misjudge 9 take amiss
misunderstanding: 3 row 4 feud, fuss, rift, spat, tiff 5 break, clash, error, fight, mix-up, run-in, set-to, words 6 blowup, breach 7 discord, mistake, quarrel, rupture 8 argument, bad vibes, conflict, delusion, mistaken, sour note, squabble, variance 9 confusion
misuse: 4 harm, mall, maul 5 abuse, spend, waste 6 injury, mess up, play on, punish, trifle 7 corrupt, exploit, outrage, profane 8 aggrieve, ill-treat, maltreat, misapply, mistreat, play upon, solecism, squander 9 brutalize, desecrate, go through, misemploy, mishandle, mismanage, pollution 10 gamble away, run through
misused: 4 lost 7 injured
mit: 4 with 6 German
in French: 4 avec
in Spanish: 3 con
MIT: 3 sch. 4 coll. 6 school 7 college
degree: 2 EE, IE, ME 3 BME
grad: 3 eng. 4 engr.
part: 4 inst., Mass., Tech.
stat: 3 GPA
Mitaka: 4 city, town
locale: 5 Japan
Mitch: 5 Leigh, Ryder 6 Miller 7 Gaylord, Pileggi
Mitchell: 3 Don, Guy 4 diva, Eric, Joni, peak 5 Ayres, Bobby, Brian, Kevin, Leona, mount, Peter, Sasha 6 Andrea, Arthur, Leisen, Thomas, Yvonne 7 Cameron 8 Margaret, mountain
locale: 4 N. Car.
Mitchell, Andrea spouse: Alan Greenspan
Mitchell, Arthur: 6 dancer 7 danseur
specialty: 6 ballet
Mitchell, Cameron: 5 actor
film: Carousel (1956)
Death of a Salesman (1951)
Face of Fire (1959)
Gorilla at Large (1954)
Haunts (1977)
Love Me or Leave Me (1955)
Mitchell, Guy
song: Heartaches by the Numbers (1959)
Rock-A-Billy (1957)
Singing the Blues (1956)
Mitchell, John Leslie: 6 writer 8 Scottish
Mitchell, Joni
homeland: Canada
song: Big Yellow Taxi (1975)
Help Me (1974)
Mitchell, Margaret: 6 author, writer
heroine: 5 O'Hara
mansion: 4 Tara
work: Gone With the Wind
Mitchell, Peter: 7 chemist 8 Nobelist
Mitchell, Thomas: 5 actor
film: Angels Over Broadway (1940)
The Dark Mirror (1946)
Flight From Destiny (1941)
Gone With the Wind (1939)
High Noon (1952)
The Hunchback of Notre Dame (1939)
It's a Wonderful Life (1946)
Joan of Paris (1942)
The Keys of the Kingdom (1944)
The Long Voyage Home (1940)
Out of the Fog (1941)
The Romance of Rosy Ridge (1947)
Stagecoach (1939, AA)
The Sullivans (1944)
Swiss Family Robinson (1940)
Theodora Goes Wild (1936)

This Above All (1942)
Wilson (1944)
Mitchell, Yvonne: 7 actress
film: Conspiracy of Hearts (1960)
Demons of the Mind (1971)
The Divided Heart (1954)
The Trials of Oscar Wilde (1960)
Woman in a Dressing Gown (1957)
Mitchison, Naomi: 6 writer 7 British
Mitchum: 6 Robert 9 deodorant
alternative: 3 Ban 4 Sure 5 Arrid, Tussy 6 Degree, Secret 7 Dry Idea 10 Right Guard, Soft and Dri, Speed Stick
Mitchum, Robert: 5 actor
film: The Ambassador (1984)
Bandido (1956)
Big Steal (1949)
Blood on the Moon (1948)
Cape Fear (1962)
Crossfire (1947)
El Dorado (1967)
The Enemy Below (1957)
The Friends of Eddie Coyle (1973)
Going Home (1971)
The Grass Is Greener (1960)
Heaven Knows, Mr. Allison (1957)
His Kind of Woman (1951)
Holiday Affair (1949)
Home From the Hill (1960)
The Last Tycoon (1976)
The Longest Day (1962)
The Lusty Men (1952)
The Night of the Hunter (1955)
Not as a Stranger (1955)
Out of the Past (1947)
Pursued (1947)
Rachel and the Stranger (1948)
The Racket (1951)
The Red Pony (1949)
Ryan's Daughter (1970)
Secret Ceremony (1968)
The Story of G.I. Joe (1945)
The Sundowners (1960)
Thunder Road (1958)
Till the End of Time (1946)
Two for the Seesaw (1962)
What a Way to Go! (1964)
When Strangers Marry (1944)
The Yakuza (1975)
mite: 3 bit, bug, dot, jot, tad 4 atom, iota, pest, snip, tick, whit 5 child, crumb, grain, pinch, scrap, speck 6 acarid, acarus, insect, tittle 7 granule, modicum, smidgen, smidgin 8 arachnid, molecule, particle, pittance, smidgeon 9 scintilla
a ~: 8 slightly, somewhat
combining form: 4 acar- 5 acari-, acaro-
___ mite: 4 gall, rust 5 straw 6 purple, spider, widow's 7 harvest
miter: 3 cut, hat 5 bevel 6 joiner
wearer: 4 Pope 6 bishop
miter ___: 3 box, jib, saw 4 gear, post 5 joint 6 square
Mitford: 5 Nancy 7 Jessica
Mitford, Jessica: 6 author, writer
work: The American Way of Death
Daughters and Rebels
A Fine Old Conflict
Mitford, Nancy: 6 author, writer 7 British
concept: 4 non-U
work: The Blessing
Love in a Cold Climate
The Pursuit of Love
mithan: 5 bovid 6 bovine
relative: 3 yak 4 anoa, arna, gaur, urus, zebu 5 bison, takin 6 muskox 7 aurochs, banteng, banting, beefalo, buffalo, carabao, cattalo, kouprey, tamarao, tamarau, timarau
mitigate: 4 calm, cool, dull, ease, help 5 abate, allay, blunt, check, let up, loose, mince, quell, quiet, relax, remit 6 lessen, loosen, modify, pacify, quench, reduce, remedy, smooth, soften, solace, soothe, subdue, temper, weaken 7 appease, assuage, comfort, commute, lighten, mollify, placate, qualify, relieve 8 diminish, moderate, palliate, tone down 9 alleviate, attenuate, extenuate, reconcile 10 ameliorate
mitigation: 4 balm, ease 5 letup 6 easing, relief 7 anodyne 8 easement 9 abatement
Mitla Pass author: Leon Uris
Mito: 4 city, town
locale: 5 Japan
mitosis, undergo: 6 divide
mitral ___: 5 valve
Mitropoulos, Dimitri: 5 Greek 9 conductor
Mitsou author: Colette
Mitsubishi: 3 car 4 auto 10 automobile
model: 3 FTO 4 Colt, Expo 5 Magna, Sigma 6 Cordia, Galant, Lancer, Mirage, Precis, Tredia 7 Eclipse, Montero, Starion 8 Diamante 9 Evolution
mitt: 3 paw 4 hand 5 glove 6 holder
___ mitt: 4 oven 8 catcher's
mitten
lack: 7 fingers
part: 4 palm 5 thumb
Mitterrand, François: 6 French 9 president
mitts on, get one's: 5 seize
Mitty: 6 Walter
Mitty, Mrs.: 3 nag
Mitumba: 3 mts. 4 mtns. 5 range 9 mountains
locale: 5 Congo 6 Africa
Mitzi: 6 Gaynor, McCall 7 Kapture
___ mitzvah: 3 bar, bas, bat 4 bath
Miuazaki: 4 city, town
locale: 5 Japan
Miwok: 6 Indian 7 Amerind
mix: 4 beat, fuse, join, lace, lump, meld, soup, stew, stir, whip 5 alloy, blend, combo, cross, dough, knead, merge, union, unite 6 batter, commix, hobnob, hybrid, infuse, jumble, make up, medley, mingle, mosaic, muddle, tangle, work in 7 amalgam, combine, conjoin, consort, goulash, grab bag, hang out, mélange, shake up, suffuse, variety 8 coalesce, compound, get along, mishmash, solution, table-hop 9 admixture, aggregate, associate, commingle, composite, diversify, hybridize, integrate, interlace, potpourri, socialize 10 adulterate, amalgamate, assortment, concoction, confection, fraternize, hodgepodge, homogenize, infiltrate, interbreed, interweave, miscellany, salmagundi
ending: 5 ology
in: 6 meddle 8 dissolve 9 intercede, interfere, interlard, intervene
it up: 4 spat 5 argue, clash, fight 6 battle, go at it, tussle 7 quarrel, scuffle
up: 4 goof, mess 5 addle, botch, churn, dizzy, throw, upset 6 garble, hassle, jumble, muddle, puzzle, tangle 7 confuse, disrupt, disturb, fluster, mistake, perplex, shuffle, trouble 8 befuddle, bewilder, confound, disorder, distract, entangle, scramble 9 confusion, dislocate 10 complicate, disarrange, disconcert, disorderly
mix ___: 4 it up
mix-___: 3 ups
___ mix: 4 cake 5 trail
___-mix: 5 ready
Mix: 3 Ron, Tom
___ Mix: 4 Meow
___ Mix-a-Lot: 3 Sir
mix-and-___: 5 match
Mixco: 4 city, town
locale: 9 Guatemala
mixed: 5 fused, joint 6 melded, merged, motley, united, varied 7 alloyed, blended, diverse, infused, kneaded, mingled, unalike, various 8 assorted, combined, multiple 9 aggregate, composite, crossbred, different, interbred 10 compounded, hybridized, transfused
bag: 4 misc., olio, stew 6 medley 7 mélange, variety 9 diversity, potpourri 10 assortment, hodgepodge, miscellany, salmagundi
breed: 3 mut 4 mule, mutt 7 mongrel
up: 6 addled 7 tangled 8 pell-mell 10 disorderly, topsy-turvy, upside-down
mixed ___: 3 bag, bud 4 acid, nuts 5 drink, grill, layer, media, nerve 6 number 7 company, doubles, economy
Mixed Blessings author: Danielle Steel
Mixed Company author: Irwin Shaw
Mixed Emotions (1989 song) artist: Rolling Stones
mixer: 2 do 4 cola, soda 5 dance, whisk 6 beater, joiner, social 7 blender, mingler, seltzer 8 club soda 9 eggbeater, extrovert, ginger ale 10 socializer, tonic water
alternative: 5 whisk
bar ~: 4 cola, soda 5 tonic, water 7 bitters, seltzer 8 club soda 9 ginger ale 10 tonic water
maker: 5 Oster
without a ~: 4 neat 8 straight
___ mixer: 6 cement
mixing ___: 4 bowl 5 ratio, valve 6 faucet
mixing bowl: 6 krater
mixologist: 6 barman 9 bartender
cube: 4 rock
measure: 4 shot
Mixtec: 8 language
Mix, Tom
film: 5 oater 7 western
horse: 4 Tony
mixture: 4 hash, olio, soup, stew 5 alloy, batch, blend, combo, cross, dough, union 6 batter, fusion, hybrid, jumble, medley, mosaic, potion 7 amalgam, collage, combine, farrago, goulash, grab bag, mélange, mongrel, variety 8 compound, mishmash, pastiche, solution 9 composite, potpourri 10 assortment, concoction, confection, hodgepodge, miscellany, salmagundi, sprinkling
flour ~: 6 batter
mix-up: 3 row 4 fray, mess, riot 5 brawl, chaos, fight, snafu, twist 6 battle, fracas, jumble, muddle, rumpus, tangle, tussle, uproar 7 mistake, problem, turmoil 8 disorder, mishmash, shambles, skirmish 9 commotion, confusion, imbroglio, scrimmage 10 donnybrook, free-for-all
Miyoshi: 5 Umeki
___ Miz: 3 Les
Mizar: 4 star
Mize: 5 Larry 6 Johnny
Mize, Larry: 6 golfer
milieu: 5 links 6 course
org.: 3 PGA
Mizner: 6 Wilson
mizzen: 4 mast, sail
mizzen-royal: 4 mast
mizzle: 4 mist
___ M. Kennedy: 6 Edward
mkt.: 3 OTC 4 AMEX, NYSE 6 NASDAQ
MLB
award: 3 MVP
league: 4 Amer., Natl.
part: 5 Major 6 League 8 Baseball
stat: 3 ABs, avg., ERA, HRs 4 RBIs
team: 4 Cubs, Mets, Reds 5 Expos, Twins 6 Angels, Astros, Braves, Giants, Padres, Red Sox, Royals, Tigers 7 Brewers, Dodgers, Indians, Marlins, Orioles, Pirates, Rangers, Rockies, Yankees 8 Blue Jays, Mariners, Phillies, White Sox 9 Athletics, Cardinals, Devil Rays
see also baseball
M'Liss author: 5 Harte
MLK title: 3 Rev.
mlle.: 2 Ms.
Mlle.
canonized ~: 3 Ste.
in Spanish: 4 Srta.
married ~: 3 Mme.
mm.: 4 meas.
Mme.
daughter: 4 mlle.
in Spanish: 3 Sra.
in the US: 3 Mrs.
Mme. Tussaud's ___ Museum: 3 Wax
MMMBop (1997 song) artist: Hanson
M&M's: 5 candy, snack 9 chocolate
Mn: 4 elem. 7 element 9 manganese
25 for ~: 4 at. no.
MN
see Minnesota
MNA holder: 5 nurse
mnemonic: 3 cue, tip 4 hint, prod, sign 6 prompt, signal 8 reminder 10 indication
mnemonic ___: 6 device
Mnemosyne: 5 giant, Titan
daughter of ~: 4 Clio 5 Erato 6 Thalia, Urania 7 Euterpe 8 Calliope 9 Melpomene 10 Polyhymnia 11 Terpsichore
lover of ~: 4 Zeus
parent of ~: 4 Gaea 6 Uranus
mngr.: 4 exec.
MNO on a phone: 3 six
mo
half a ~: 4 jiff 5 jiffy
mo.: 3 Apr., Aug., Dec., Feb., Jan., Jul., Jun., Mar., Nov., Oct. 4 Sept.
autumn ~: 3 Dec., Nov., Oct. 4 Sept.
equinox ~: 3 Mar., Sep.
first ~: 3 Jan.
fraction: 2 wk.
last ~: 3 Dec., ult.
spring ~: 3 Apr., Jun., Mar.
summer ~: 3 Aug., Jul., Jun. 4 Sept.
30-day ~: 3 Apr., Jun., Nov., Sep.
valentine ~: 3 Feb.
winter ~: 3 Dec., Feb., Jan., Mar.
see also month
___-mo: 3 slo
Mo: 4 elem. 7 element 10 molybdenum
42 for ~: 4 at. no.
Mo' ___: 5 Money
Mo' ___ Blues: 6 Better
Mo.
city: 3 St. L. 5 St. Joe
neighbor: 3 Ark., Ill., Kan., Ken., Neb. 4 Iowa, Tenn.
president from ~: 3 HST
see also Missouri
___ Mo: 4 Ko Ko
M.O.
part: 5 modus 8 operandi
M-1 inventor: 6 Garand
moa: 4 bird
relative: 4 kiwi
Moab: 4 city, town 7 kingdom
father of ~: 3 Lot
locale: 4 Utah
today: 6 Jordan

moan: 3 cry, sob 4 beef, carp, howl, keen, sigh, wail, weep 5 gripe, groan, growl, mourn, sound, whine 6 bewail, grieve, grouch, grouse, lament, murmur, mutter, plaint, regret, repine, sorrow, yammer 7 deplore, grumble, whimper 8 complain, vocalize 9 bellyache, complaint, make a fuss 10 take it hard
about: 6 bewail
moan and __: 5 groan
moaner: 4 wimp 5 sissy 6 critic, griper, grouch, whiner 7 crybaby 8 grumbler 10 bellyacher, complainer, malcontent
moat: 4 foss 5 ditch, fosse 6 trench, trough 7 barrier
place: 6 castle
mob: 3 jam, lot, set 4 army, body, clan, crew, fill, gang, herd, host, mass, pack, ring, riot 5 cabal, crowd, crush, drove, flock, horde, Mafia, posse, press, swarm, troop 6 attack, cattle, circle, clique, hustle, jostle, justle, league, masses, people, public, rabble, throng 7 company, coterie, overrun, set upon 8 canaille, populace, riffraff, surround 9 gangsters, gathering, multitude, syndicate 10 assemblage, converge on, Cosa Nostra, underworld
boss: 3 don 4 capo 9 godfather
ender: 3 cap 4 ster
member: 4 thug 7 hoodlum
rule: 7 anarchy 8 disorder, nihilism
scene: 4 riot
mob __: 4 rule 5 scene
Moberg, Vilhelm: 6 writer 7 Swedish
Mo' Better Blues (1990 film)
cast: Spike Lee, Wesley Snipes, Denzel Washington
director: Spike Lee
Mobil: 3 oil 8 gasoline
partner: 5 Exxon
rival: 4 Arco, Gulf, Hess 5 Amoco, Getty, Shell 7 Chevron
mobile: 3 art 5 fluid 6 motile, moving 7 migrant, movable, mutable, nomadic, ranging 8 moveable, portable, restless, unstable 9 adaptable, itinerant, mercurial, migratory, motorized, sculpture, traveling, unsettled, versatile 10 changeable
home: 4 tent, tipi 5 tepee 6 camper, teepee
sculptor: 6 Calder
starter: 3 air, art, Bat, ski 4 auto, book, snow 5 blood
mobile __: 4 home, unit 5 phone
Mobile: 3 bay 4 city, town 5 river
locale: 3 Ala. 7 Alabama
newspaper: 8 Register
Mobile Bay: 6 battle
mobileness: 10 locomotion
__ Mobilier: 6 Crédit
mobility: 6 motion 8 movement 10 locomotion
__ mobility: 6 social, upward
mobilize: 5 impel, raise, rally, ready 6 call up, enlist, gather, gear up, get set, muster, propel, summon 7 actuate, harness, marshal, prepare, recruit 8 activate, assemble, embattle, get ready, organize 9 make ready 10 call to arms, coordinate
again: 5 rearm
Möbius __: 4 band 5 strip
Möbius strips have one: 4 side
Mobley, Mary Ann spouse: Gary Collins
mobocracy: 4 mess, riot 5 chaos, havoc, snarl 6 bedlam, jungle, mayhem, muddle, uproar 7 anarchy, discord, entropy, turmoil 8 disarray, disorder, madhouse, shambles 9 confusion 10 unruliness
mobs, like some: 4 ugly
mobster: 4 hood 6 gunsel, outlaw 7 hoodlum 8 criminal, gangster, hooligan 9 racketeer
lady: 4 moll 7 gun moll
weapon: 3 gat
Mobuto: 4 lake
locale: 5 Zaire 6 Uganda
Mobutu __ Seko: 4 Sese
Moby-Dick: 4 film 5 novel, whale 9 leviathan
author: Herman Melville
cast: Richard Basehart, Friedrich Ledebur, Gregory Peck
character: 3 Pip 4 Ahab 5 Flask, Peleg, Perth, Stubb 6 Bildad, Daggoo, Elijah, Fleece, Mapple 7 Ishmael 8 Dough-Boy, Fedallah, Queequeg, Starbuck, Tashtego 10 Bulkington
Crossed Harpoons, in ~: 3 inn
director: John Huston
setting: 3 sea 5 ocean
ship: 6 Pequod
moccasin: 3 pac 4 shoe 5 snake 6 animal 7 reptile 8 footgear, footwear
defense: 4 fang 5 venom
relative: 3 asp, boa 5 aboma, adder, cobra, krait, mamba, racer, viper 6 dhaman, python, taipan 7 markhor, rattler 8 anaconda, ringhals 9 boomslang, coachwhip 10 bushmaster, copperhead, sidewinder
water ~: 7 serpent
__ moccasin: 5 water
Mocedades song: Eres Tu (1974)
mocha: 3 joe, mud 4 brew, java 5 brown, color, drink 6 coffee 7 leather 8 beverage, goatskin, ice cream
alternative: 5 lemon, peach 6 banana, coffee, Jamoca, toffee 7 caramel, coconut, vanilla 8 cinnamon, hazelnut 9 bubblegum, chocolate, pineapple, pistachio, raspberry, rocky road, rum raisin 10 blackberry, cheesecake, Neapolitan, peppermint, strawberry
relative: 3 bay, dun, tan 4 bole, ecru, fawn, foxy, nude, seal 5 amber, beige, camel, cocoa, hazel, khaki, sepia, tawny, umber 6 auburn, bister, bistre, bronze, coffee, copper, ginger, russet, sienna, sorrel, suntan, walnut 7 biscuit, caramel, dogwood 8 chestnut, cinnamon, mahogany 9 butternut, chocolate
mocha __: 4 java
Mocha: 4 city, port, town 7 seaport
land: 5 Yemen
Mochrie: 5 Colin
mock: 3 ape, kid, rag, rib 4 bait, copy, defy, dupe, fake, faux, gibe, hoke, hoot, jape, jeer, jibe, jive, mime, sham, slam, slur, snub, twit 5 abuse, belie, bogus, chaff, decry, ditto, dummy, faked, false, feign, fleer, flout, hokey, libel, mimic, phony, put on, quasi, rally, roast, scoff, scorn, sneer, spoof, sport, spurn, taunt, tease 6 banter, defame, deride, dump on, ersatz, forged, heckle, hoot at, impugn, insult, jeer at, jibe at, malign, mirror, needle, offend, parody, phoney, pseudo, rebuff, send up, slight, thwart, unreal, vilify 7 affront, asperse, degrade, disdain, feigned, imitate, lampoon, laugh at, let down, profane, put down, rank out, slander, traduce 8 belittle, denounce, ridicule, satirize, simulate, sneeze at, so-called, spurious, travesty, vilipend 9 challenge, denigrate, discredit, disparage, frustrate, humiliate, imitation, make fun of, poke fun at, pretended, simulated, synthetic 10 artificial, calumniate, caricature, disappoint, disrespect, factitious, fraudulent, substitute
mock __: 3 sun 4 epic, mold, moon 6 orange 7 chicken
mock __ soup: 6 turtle
mock-__: 3 ups 6 heroic
mockado: 6 fabric 8 material
Mocker Mocked, The artist: 4 Klee
mockery: 3 dig 4 barb, gibe, jeer, jest, jibe, joke, quip, sham, slam, slap, slur, snub 5 abuse, farce, libel, put-on, scorn, spoof, sport, taunt 6 insult, parody, rebuff, satire, send-up, slight 7 affront, burlesk, calumny, catcall, disdain, fooling, lampoon, mimicry, obloquy, offense, put-down, sarcasm, slander, takeoff 8 contempt, derision, pretense, ridicule, scoffing, travesty 9 aspersion, burlesque, cheap shot, contumely, hypocrisy, imitation, sacrilege 10 caricature, defamation, disrespect, lip service, opprobrium
mocking: 3 wry 6 japery 7 cynical, jeering, satiric 8 derisive, sardonic 9 laughable, quizzical, sarcastic, satirical, vitriolic 10 irreverent
ender: 4 bird
mockingbird: 4 aper 5 mimic
relative: 8 thrasher
Mockingbird (song)
artist: Carly Simon, James Taylor 8 Inez Foxx
mock turtle: 4 soup
mock-up: 5 model 9 prototype
mod: 2 in 3 hip, neo 4 chic, tony 5 faddy, toney, vogue 6 chi-chi, trendy 7 current, in style, popular, stylish, voguish 8 last word 9 in fashion 10 all the rage
ender: 3 ule 4 ular
Mod __, The: 5 Squad
mode: 3 fad, way 4 chic, form, look, rage, rule, vein, wise 5 craze, decor, means, state, style, trend, usage, vogue 6 course, custom, living, manner, medium, method, status, system 7 fashion, process 8 approach, channels, last word, practice 9 mechanism, procedure, situation, technique 10 convention, dernier cri, mainstream
à la ~: 4 chic, tony 5 faddy, toney 6 chi-chi, modish, trendy 7 current, in style, popular, stylish, voguish 8 up-to-date 9 in fashion 10 all the rage
in the ~ of: 3 à la
__ mode: 3 à la 5 major, minor 6 Aeolic, church, Dorian, Ionian, Lydian 7 Aeolian
__ Mode: 7 Depeche
model: 3 kit, sit 4 base, cast, form, hero, Iman, kind, lead, mold, norm, nude, pose, rule, type, wear 5 carve, clone, dummy, frame, gauge, ideal, image, light, poser, saint, shape, sport, style, Tiegs, typic 6 create, design, effigy, lesson, mock-up, parade, relief, sample, sculpt, sitter, statue, symbol, Twiggy 7 classic, display, epitome, example, fashion, manikin, nonsuch, paragon, paste-up, pattern, perfect, portray, replica, show off, subject, typical, version, whittle 8 assemble, exemplar, figurine, flawless, game plan, likeness, lodestar, mannikin, nonesuch, original, paradigm, specimen, standard 9 archetype, beau ideal, blueprint, classical, cover girl, criterion, duplicate, exemplary, facsimile, faultless, mannequin, miniature, nonpareil, precedent, prototype, sculpture, statuette, Tyra Banks 10 archetypal, embodiment, touchstone
asset: 5 poise, smile 6 allure
binder: 4 glue
combining form: 3 typ- 4 typo-
display ~: 4 demo
earth ~: 3 map, orb 6 sphere
male ~: 4 hunk 5 he-man
material: 4 clay, wood 5 balsa
need: 3 rep 5 agent 6 agency
oneself on: 6 follow 7 imitate
role ~: 4 hero, idol 5 ideal, model
very thin ~: 4 waif
__ model: 4 role 5 floor, quark, scale
Model __: 5 A Ford, B Ford, T Ford
Model A: 3 car 4 auto, Ford 10 automobile
Model and the Marriage Broker, The (1951 film)
cast: Scott Brady, Jeanne Crain, Thelma Ritter
director: George Cukor
Model B: 3 car 4 auto, Ford 10 automobile
Model T: 3 car 4 auto, Ford 10 automobile
contemporary: 3 Reo
model-train brand: 4 Tyco 6 Lionel
modem
high-speed ~ connection: 3 DSL
message: 3 fax 5 E-mail
name: 5 Hayes
speed unit: 3 bps 4 baud
use a ~: 6 dial in
__ modem: 3 fax
Modena: 3 car 4 auto, city, town 7 Ferrari 10 automobile
locale: 5 Italy
mode of life combining form: 6 -biosis
moderate: 3 ebb, low 4 bate, calm, cool, curb, ease, even, fair, fall, lull, mean, mild, mute, sane, slow, soft, so-so, wane, warm 5 abate, allay, break, chair, cheap, check, judge, let up, light, lower, quell, quiet, relax, sober, tepid 6 dampen, defuse, defuze, gentle, lessen, low-key, medium, midway, modest, modify, obtund, pacify, reduce, relent, soften, subdue, temper, umpire, weaken 7 appease, assuage, average, bargain, control, cut-rate, decline, die down, ease off, equable, limited, low-cost, mediate, mollify, neutral, pacific, preside, qualify, referee, relieve, slacken, subside, tail off, warmish 8 balanced, bearable, cautious, decrease, diminish, level off, measured, mediocre, middling, mitigate, modulate, ordinary, palliate, passable, play down, pleasant, regulate, reserved, restrain, restrict, tolerant, tone down 9 abstinent, alleviate, constrain, extenuate, impartial, judicious, lighten up, low-priced, make peace, negotiate, peaceable, retrocede, soft-pedal, temperate, tolerable, unextreme, unslanted 10 abstemious, considered, controlled, deliberate, economical, keep in line, mainstream, reasonable, restrained, smooth over, unagitated, unhardened, well-chosen
moderately: 4 some, so-so 5 quite 6 enough, fairly, gently, kind of, pretty, rather, sort of 7 a little, lightly 8 passably, slightly, somewhat 9 gradually, quite a bit, to a degree, tolerably
moderating: 10 abstemious
moderation: 5 poise 6 lenity, reason 7 balance 8 calmness, coolness, eschewal, fairness, justness, lenience, mildness, patience, sobriety 9 abate-

ment, composure, frugality, restraint **10** abstinence, temperance
without ~: **6** arrant
moderato: **5** tempo
faster than ~: **7** allegro
slower than ~: **7** andante
moderator: **4** host **5** fixer, judge **6** umpire **8** mediator **10** negotiator
milieu: **5** forum
modern: **3** new, now **4** late **5** fresh, in use, novel, today, young **6** extant, hi-tech, latest, latter, recent, timely, with-it **7** current, new-wave, present, stylish, topical, updated **8** contempo, last word, neoteric, up-to-date **9** latter-day **10** avant-garde, newfangled, present-day
not ~: **3** old **5** olden
prefix: **3** neo-
starter: **5** ultra
modern __: **3** art, cut **4** jazz **5** dance
__-modern: **4** post
Modern: **4** font **8** typeface
Modern __: **5** Greek, Times, Woman **6** Fables, French, Hebrew **7** English, Persian
__ Modern: **6** Danish, France
Modern American Poetry author: Louis Untermeyer
moderne, not: **6** ancien
Modern Fables author: George Ade
modernism: **10** innovation
modernist: **3** neo
modernistic: **3** new **5** novel **6** recent **8** up-to-date
modernize: **4** redo **5** renew **6** remake, revamp, revive, update **7** improve, refresh, remodel, restore, restyle **8** innovate, overhaul, renovate **9** refurbish **10** regenerate, rejuvenate, streamline
Modern Maturity publisher: **4** AARP
Modern Painters author: John Ruskin
Modern Problems (1981 film)
cast: Nell Carter, Chevy Chase, Patti D'Arbanville, Mary Kay Place
Modern Times (1936 film)
cast: Henry Bergman, Charles Chaplin, Paulette Goddard
director: Charles Chaplin
tune: **5** Smile
Modern Utopia, A author: H.G. Wells
Modern Woman (1986 song) artist: Billy Joel
modest: **3** coy, low, shy **4** bare, fair, mean, meek, nice, poor, pure, so-so **5** cheap, light, lowly, moral, plain, quiet, small, spare, timid **6** chaste, demure, folksy, humble, proper, seemly, simple, slight **7** average, bashful, ignoble, limited **8** blushing, discreet, middling, ordinary, reserved, reticent, retiring, spotless, uncostly, virginal **9** diffident, temperate, unadorned, unextreme **10** economical, low-ranking, reasonable, unaffected, unassuming, uneffusive
not ~: **6** brassy
overly ~ one: **5** prude
Modest: **10** Mussorgsky
Modesto: **4** city, town
locale: **10** California
winery: **5** Gallo
Modest Proposal, A author: Jonathan Swift
modesty: **5** shame **6** purity, virtue **7** coyness, decency, prudery, reserve, shyness **8** chastity, delicacy, humility, meekness, timidity **9** lowliness, propriety, reticence, timidness **10** demureness, diffidence, humbleness, simplicity
modesty __: **5** panel
modicum: **3** bit, jot **4** atom, dash, drop, inch, iota, mite, mote, whit **5** crumb, grain, minim, ounce, pinch, scrap, shred, speck, tinge, touch **6** little, smidge, trifle **7** minimum **8** fraction, fragment, littlest, molecule, particle, pittance **9** scintilla
modicum of __: **5** sense
modifiable: **9** adaptable
modification: **5** shift **6** change **7** variant **8** revision **9** variation
make ~ to: **4** edit **5** adapt, alter, amend, emend
without ~: **4** as is
modified: **7** limited, variant **9** qualified
combining form: **2** ne- **3** neo-
it's often ~: **4** noun
modified American __: **4** plan
modifier: **3** adj., adv. **6** adverb **9** adjective
modify: **3** fit **4** curb, redo, suit, turn, vary **5** abate, act on, adapt, alter, amend, limit, lobby, lower, relax, remit, reset, shape, tweak **6** adjust, affect, become, change, divert, doctor, lessen, mutate, recast, reduce, reform, repair, revise, rework, soften, tailor, temper **7** act upon, convert, correct, mollify, permute, qualify, remodel, reshape, restyle, slacken, touch up **8** decrease, mitigate, moderate, modulate, readjust, restrict, tone down **9** condition, customize, diversify, refashion, transform, transmute **10** reorganize, shift gears, switch over
Modigliani, Amedeo: **6** artist **7** Italian, painter
Modigliani, Franco: **8** Nobelist **9** economist
Modine, Matthew: **5** actor
film: Birdy (1984)
Bye Bye, Love (1995)
Cutthroat Island (1995)
Fluke (1995)
Full Metal Jacket (1987)
Gross Anatomy (1989)
Married to the Mob (1988)
Pacific Heights (1990)
The Real Blonde (1998)
Streamers (1983)
modish: **2** in **3** hip, new, now **4** chic, posh, tony **5** faddy, fresh, funky, smart, swank, swell, toney, vogue **6** chi-chi, classy, latest, snappy, trendy, with-it **7** current, dashing, elegant, in style, in-thing, in vogue, popular, stylish, voguish **8** last word, up-to-date **9** exclusive, happening, in fashion **10** all the rage
modishness: **4** chic **5** style, vogue
modiste: **10** dressmaker
Modoc: **5** tribe **6** Indian **7** Amerind
Mod Squad, The (1999 film)
cast: Claire Danes, Omar Epps, Dennis Farina, Giovanni Ribisi
director: Scott Silver
Mod Squad, The (ABC drama)
cast: Tige Andrews (Capt. Adam Greer)
Michael Cole (Pete Cochran)
Peggy Lipton (Julie Barnes)
Clarence Williams III (Linc Hayes)
Modugno, Domenico song: Volaré (1958)
modulate: **4** pace, tune, vary **5** lower, relax, speak **6** adjust, change, modify, reduce, soften, switch, temper **7** balance, inflect, qualify **8** fine-tune, moderate, regulate, tone down **9** harmonize
modulation: **4** tone **5** pitch, sound **6** accent, change **7** cadence, cadency **8** delivery **10** inflection
modulator, prefix with: **5** neuro-
module: **4** unit
__ module: **4** load **5** lunar **7** command, service
modus __: **7** vivendi
modus operandi: **3** way **4** line **5** means **6** method, recipe **7** process **9** procedure, technique
Moe: **4** Berg **5** Bandy, Tommy **6** Howard, Stooge
brother of ~: **5** Curly, Shemp
partner: **3** Joe **5** Larry **8** Curly Joe
__ Moe Dee: **4** Kool
Moesha (UPN sitcom) cast: Brandy (Moesha Mitchell)
Moet: **4** wine **6** French
Moe, Tommy: **5** skier
Moffat: **6** Donald
Moffo, Anna: **6** singer **7** soprano
specialty: **4** aria **5** opera
Mogadishu: **4** city, town **7** capital
locale: **7** Somalia
model from ~: **4** Iman
Mogador: **6** fabric **8** material
Mogambo (1953 film)
cast: Clark Gable, Ava Gardner, Grace Kelly
director: John Ford
Mogen __: **5** David
Mogg: **4** Phil
moggy: **3** cat
Mogollon: **5** range **7** plateau **9** mountains
locale: **9** New Mexico
mogul: **3** VIP **4** bump, czar, king, lord, tsar, tzar **5** baron, nabob, nawab, ruler, titan, wheel **6** bigwig, fat cat, gerent, prince, tycoon **7** bigshot, magnate, notable **8** big wheel, top brass **9** big cheese, executive, potentate
home: **6** estate
lover: **5** skier
Mogul: **3** Era
capital of India: **4** Agra **5** Delhi
ruler: **5** nawab
mohair: **6** fabric **7** grogram **8** material, sanglier
source: **4** goat **6** angora
Mohammed
birthplace of ~: **5** Mecca
religion: **5** Islam
son-in-law: **3** Ali
wife of ~: **6** Ayesha
Mohammed __ Pahlevi: **4** Reza
Mohandas: **6** Gandhi
Mohave: **5** tribe **6** desert, Indian **7** Amerind
Mohawk: **4** coif **5** river, tribe **6** hairdo, Indian **7** Amerind, haircut **8** coiffure, language **9** hairstyle
ally: **6** Cayuga, Oneida, Seneca **8** Onondaga **9** Tuscarora
city on the ~: **5** Utica
craft: **5** canoe
River locale: **7** New York
sporter: **3** Mr. T
sporting a ~: **5** shorn
Valley city: **6** Elmira
Valley tribe: **6** Oneida
Mohegan: **6** Indian **7** Amerind **8** language
Mohican: **5** tribe **6** Indian **7** Amerind
Mohl: **4** peak **5** mount **8** mountain
locale: **10** Antarctica
moho: **5** layer
Mohs scale minerals:
1 - Talc
2 - Gypsum
3 - Calcite
4 - Fluorite
5 - Apatite
6 - Orthoclase
7 - Quartz
8 - Topaz
9 - Corundum
10 - Diamond
mohur: **4** coin **5** money
__ moi: **4** chez
__-moi: **7** excusez
moidore: **4** coin **5** money
moiety: **4** half, part **7** portion, section, segment
moil: **4** plod, toil, work **5** churn, labor, slave, sweat **6** drudge, strain, strive **8** drudgery, hard work, work hard **9** grunt work, plug along, pound away
__ moi, le déluge: **5** Après
moiling: **9** turbulent
__ Moines, IA: **3** Des
Moira: **5** Kelly **7** Shearer
in English: **4** Mary
moiré: **6** fabric **8** material
mois: **3** mai **4** août, juin, mars **5** avril, month **6** French **7** février, janvier, juillet, octobre **8** décembre, novembre **9** septembre
douze ~: **5** année
Moises: **4** Alou
uncle of ~: **5** Jesus, Matty
Moissan, Henri: **7** chemist **8** Nobelist
moist: **3** wet **4** damp, dank, dewy **5** humid, juicy, misty, muggy, rainy, soggy, teary, undry **6** basted, clammy, drippy, hygric, liquid, oozing, steamy, sweaty, watery **7** bedewed, drizzly, tearful, wettish **8** dampened, dripping **9** drizzling, succulent
adapted to a ~ habitat: **5** mesic
combining form: **5** hygro-
ender: **3** ure
moisten: **3** dip, sog, sop, wet **4** damp, lick, mist, soak, wash **5** baste, bathe, bedew, rinse, spray, steam, steep, water **6** dampen, drench, humify, quench, rain on, shower, soften, splash, squirt **8** humidify, irrigate, saturate, splatter, sprinkle, waterlog **10** moisturize
again: **5** rewet
with water: **4** soak **5** bathe, douse, flush **6** drench, shower **7** immerse
moist-eyed: **5** teary
moisture: **3** dew, fog, wet **4** damp, mist, rain, tear **5** sweat, tears, vapor, water **6** liquid **7** drizzle, wetness **8** dampness, dankness, humidity, teardrop **9** mugginess, sogginess
exude ~: **5** sweat
lacking ~: **3** dry **4** arid, sere **7** parched **8** droughty **10** dehydrated
lose ~: **4** seep **6** dry out
remove ~: **3** dry **5** defog
remover: **5** drier, dryer
requiring little ~: **5** xeric
moisturize: **8** humidify
moisturizer: **4** balm **5** cream, salve **6** lotion **7** unguent **8** cosmetic, ointment **9** emollient
skin ~: **4** aloe **6** lotion
mojarra: **4** fish
Mojave: **5** tribe **6** desert, Indian **7** Amerind
like the ~: **3** dry **4** arid
plant: **5** agave **6** cactus, cholla
Moji das Cruzes: **4** city, town
locale: **6** Brazil
mojo: **4** doll, juju **5** charm, spell **6** amulet **8** talisman
moke: **3** ass **5** horse **6** equine **7** jackass
mokugyo: **6** blocks **10** percussion
origin: **5** Japan, Korea
mol: **6** weight
Mol: **8** Gretchen
mola: **4** fish
molar: **5** tooth **7** grinder
hole: **6** cavity
malady: **4** ache
material: **4** pulp **6** enamel

molars
use the ~: 4 chew 5 grind
molasses
like ~: 4 poky, slow
move like ~: 3 lag 4 ooze
product: 3 rum 5 taffy, toffy 6 toffee
___ molasses: 6 slow as
mold: 3 die, lot, pat, pig, rot 4 bend, cast, form, kind, last, make, must, plan, plot, rust, sort, turn, type 5 build, class, ergot, forge, frame, image, knead, model, plant, shape, stamp, train 6 beetle, cavity, design, devise, dry rot, fungus, kidney, makeup, matrix, mildew, nature, sculpt 7 fashion, ferment, pattern, whittle 8 assemble, jaundice 9 character, construct, container, influence, sculpture 10 depression, impression
filler: 5 Jell-O 7 gelatin
like ~: 6 fungal
mold ___: 4 loft, wash 5 spore
___ mold: 4 blow, blue, gray, grey, iron, leaf, mock, snow 5 black, bread, green, paste, slime, sooty, water 7 picture
moldable: 4 soft 6 lissom 7 lissome, plastic 8 flexible 9 formative, malleable
Moldau: 5 river
city on the ~: 6 Prague
Moldavia once: 3 SSR
molder: 3 rot 4 turn 5 decay, spoil 7 crumble 9 decompose
moldering: 6 rotten
molding: 4 cyma, edge, ogee, trim 5 ledge, ogive, ovolo
combining form: 6 -plasty
profile: 3 ess
molding ___: 5 board, plane
___ molding: 3 bed, lip 4 back, bead, blow, edge, hood, wall 5 brace, cable, churn, pearl 6 spring, sprung
moldings: 4 tori 5 ovoli
Moldova: 6 nation 7 country
capital: 8 Chisinau
neighbor: 7 Romania, Ukraine
moldy: 3 bad 4 rank 5 fusty, musty 6 frowsy, frowzy, rancid, rotten 7 odorous 8 inedible, obsolete, outmoded 9 hackneyed 10 antiquated
get ~: 3 rot
mole: 3 spy 4 pier 5 agent, plant 6 animal, mammal, naevus, rodent 8 burrower, hot sauce 9 birthmark 10 breakwater
combining form: 5 talpi-
cousin: 5 shrew
ender: 4 hill, skin
mole ___: 3 rat 4 crab, plow 6 volume 7 cricket
molecular
component: 4 atom
variation: 6 isomer
molecular ___: 3 ray 4 beam, film 5 clock, sieve 6 weight 7 biology, formula, orbital
molecular biologist, Japanese: 6 Susumu
molecular biology: 7 science
study: 3 DNA, RNA 4 gene 8 genetics
molecule: 3 bit, jot 4 iota, mite, mote, spot, unit 5 grain, minim, ounce, speck 7 modicum 8 fragment, particle
part: 4 atom
___ molecule: 4 gram 5 polar
molehill: 5 mound
make a mountain of a ~: 7 magnify 10 exaggerate
Mole People, The star: 4 Agar
moles: 4 nevi 5 naevi
moleskin: 6 fabric 8 material
color: 5 taupe
moleskins: 5 pants 8 trousers
molest: 3 paw 4 harm 5 abuse, harry 6 bother 7 disturb
molestation: 5 abuse
Molière: 6 French 10 playwright
character: 5 Elise
work: The Misanthrope
The School for Wives
Molina: 5 Mario 6 Alfred
Molina, Alfred: 5 actor
film: Dudley Do-Right (1999)
Frida (2002)
The Imposters (1998)
Not Without My Daughter (1991)
Prick Up Your Ears (1987)
Molina, Mario: 7 chemist 8 Nobelist
Molinaro: 2 Al
Moline: 4 city, town
locale: 8 Illinois
manufacturer: 5 Deere
Molitor, Paul sport: 8 baseball
moll: 5 minor
man: 6 gunsel 7 hoodlum
___ moll: 3 gun
Moll: 7 Richard
Moll Flanders author: Daniel Defoe
mollification: 7 anodyne 9 abatement
mollifier: 5 salve
mollify: 4 calm, cool, ease, lull 5 abate, allay, blunt, fix up, humor, quell, quiet, salve, slake 6 defuse, defuze, lessen, mellow, modify, pacify, reduce, smooth, soften, soothe, temper 7 appease, assuage, compose, cushion, lighten, placate, relieve, satisfy, sweeten 8 decrease, diminish, mitigate, moderate, palliate 9 alleviate, untrouble 10 ameliorate, conciliate, propitiate, smooth over
mollifying: 6 irenic 8 irenical 9 demulcent
Molloy author: Samuel Beckett
mollusk: 4 clam, slug 5 conch, snail, squid, whelk 6 chiton, limpet, oyster, quahog 7 bivalve, geoduck, octopus, quahaug, scallop 8 escargot, nautilus 9 gastropod 10 cuttlefish
part: 5 valve
ridge on a ~ shell: 5 varix
shell lining: 5 nacre
tongue: 6 radula
molly: 3 pet
ender: 6 coddle
Molly: 4 Berg, Yard 5 Ivins, Picon 6 Malone 7 Pitcher 8 Ringwald
Molly ___: 5 and Me 6 Miller 7 Maguire
Molly and Me (1945 film)
cast: Gracie Fields, Roddy McDowall, Monty Woolley
director: Lewis Seiler
mollycoddle: 4 baby 5 nurse, spoil 6 dote on, pamper 7 cater to, indulge 8 dote upon 9 spoon-feed
mollycoddling: 4 easy 7 lenient
Molly Maguire: 5 miner
mollymawk: 4 bird
mollymoke: 4 bird
Molnár, Ferenc: 6 writer 9 Hungarian 10 playwright
work: The Devil
Liliom
The Red Mill
The Swan
moloch: 6 animal 7 reptile
Molokai neighbor: 4 Maui, Oahu
see also Hawaii
Molonglo, city on the: 8 Canberra
Molopo: 5 river
locale: 3 Afr. 6 Africa 8 Botswana
Molotov cocktail: 4 bomb
Molson: 4 beer
alternative: 5 Becks, Coors, Pabst 6 Amstel, Corona, Miller 7 Schlitz 8 Heineken, Michelob 9 Lowenbrau 10 Ballantine
molt: 4 peel, shed 6 slough 7 cast off, peel off 8 exuviate 9 exfoliate 10 desquamate
molten: 5 fluid 6 fusile, liquid, melted 9 liquefied
material: 4 lava 5 magma
metal channel: 6 ingate
work ~ glass: 4 blow
molting: 7 ecdysis
molto: 4 much, very 9 extremely
opposite of ~: 4 poco
Moluccas: 4 isls. 5 isles 7 islands
island: 3 Aru 4 Aroe, Arru, Buru, Leti 5 Ambon, Babar, Banda, Ceram, Wetar 6 Serang, Tidore 7 Morotai, Ternate 8 Tanimbar 9 Halmahera
___ moly: 4 holy
molybdenite: 3 ore 7 mineral
molybdenum: 5 metal 7 element
alloy: 9 Vitallium
ore: 9 wulfenite
mom: 6 mother, parent 8 relative
admonition: 6 be good, be nice
brother of ~: 3 unc, unk 5 uncle
expectant ~ visitor: 5 stork
like a ~ at a wedding: 5 weepy
mom's ~: 4 gran, nana 6 granny 7 grannie
month: 3 May
on ~ 's side: 5 enate
partner: 3 dad, pop 5 daddy 6 father
sister of ~: 4 aunt 5 aunty 6 auntie
___ mom: 6 soccer
___ Mom: 6 Serial
MOMA
artist: 4 Dali, Klee
exhibit: 4 Dada 5 op art
locale: 3 NYC 4 NY NY 9 Manhattan
part of ~: 3 Art 6 Modern, Museum
mom and ___ store: 3 pop
Mombasa: 4 city, isle, port, town 6 island
locale: 5 Kenya
moment: 3 bit, sec, use 4 hour, jiff, note, pith, tick, time, wink 5 flash, jiffy, point, stage, trice, value, while, worth 6 import, minute, second, weight 7 concern, eyewink, gravity, instant 8 juncture, occasion 9 magnitude, substance, twinkling 10 importance, time period
a ~ ago: 4 just 10 just before
at that ~: 4 then
at this ~: 3 now 5 as yet, today 8 promptly, right now, right off 9 forthwith, presently, right away 10 here and now, this minute
ending: 3 ous
for the ~: 8 meantime 9 meanwhile
in a ~: 4 anon, soon 8 directly 9 presently
of truth: 4 D-day, test 8 showdown, zero hour
on the spur of the ~: 5 ad-lib 6 rashly 7 brashly, hastily 8 abruptly, headlong, pell-mell, suddenly 9 headfirst
spare: 7 leisure
vital ~: 4 D-day 6 crisis 8 juncture 9 crossroad, emergency
___ moment: 3 in a 6 dipole, senior 7 bending, central
momentarily: 3 now 4 anon, nigh, soon 6 awhile, in a sec 7 briefly 8 right now 9 instantly
momentary: 5 brief, hasty, quick, short 6 flying 7 cursory, passing, regular, summary, trivial 8 flashing, fleeting, flitting, fugitive, meteoric, shifting, temporal, volatile 9 dreamlike, ephemeral, impulsive, spasmodic, temporary, transient, vanishing 10 evanescent, short-lived, transitory, unenduring
Momentary ___ of Reason, A: 5 Lapse
___ Moment in Time: 3 One
___ momento!: 3 Uno
moment of ___: 4 sail 5 truth 7 inertia
momentous: 3 big 5 grave, heavy, vital 6 signal, solemn, urgent 7 crucial, epochal, fateful, notable, pivotal, serious, special, weighty 8 critical, decisive, eventful, historic, material, pregnant 9 front-page, high-level, important, memorable 10 impressive, meaningful, portentous
momentousness: 6 import, weight 9 magnitude
___ Moments: 5 Magic
___ moment's notice: 3 at a, on a
Moments to Remember (1955 song)
artist: Four Lads
___ moment too soon!: 4 Not a
momentum: 4 pace, push 5 drive, force, power, speed, tempo 6 energy, thrust 7 impetus, impulse 8 progress, strength 10 propulsion
component: 5 speed 8 velocity
forward ~: 4 birr
gather ~: 5 speed 10 accelerate
___ momentum: 6 linear 7 angular
___ Momma From the Train: 5 Throw
momma's partner: 5 poppa
Mommie Dearest: 4 book, film
author: Christina Crawford
cast: Howard da Silva, Faye Dunaway, Steve Forrest, Diana Scarwid
director: Frank Perry
Mommsen, Theodor: 6 writer 8 Nobelist
mommy: 6 mother, parent 8 relative
see also mom
mommy ___: 5 track
___ Mommy Kissing...: 4 I Saw
Momo author: 4 Ende
Mo Money Mo Problems (1997 song)
artist: Mase, Notorious B.I.G., Puff Daddy
Momotombo: 7 volcano
locale: 9 Nicaragua
Moms: 6 Mabley
momus: 3 nag 5 shrew
Momus, mother of: 3 Nyx
mon ___: 3 ami 4 cher
mon-: 3 one, uni-
Mon ___: 5 Oncle
Mon ___!: 4 Dieu
Mon.: 3 day
follower: 3 Tue. 4 Tues.
preceder: 3 Sun.
to Tues.: 4 yest.
Mona: 6 Barrie 7 Freeman, Simpson, Van Duyn 10 Washbourne
Mona ___: 4 Lisa 7 Passage
Monaca: 4 font 8 typeface
monacillo: 5 shrub
Monaco: 3 car 4 auto, city, town 5 Dodge 6 nation 7 country 10 automobile
capital: 11 Monaco-Ville
city: 10 Monte Carlo
city near ~: 4 Nice
locale: 3 Eur. 6 Europe
money: 5 franc
neighbor: 6 France
monad: 3 one 4 unit 6 amoeba, single 9 protozoan
Mona Lisa: 8 painting
attribute: 5 smile
home: 5 Paris 6 France, Louvre
painter: 7 da Vinci
Mona Lisa (1950 song) artist: Nat King Cole
composer: 5 Evans 10 Livingston
monarch: 4 amir, czar, emir, king, raja, shah, tsar, tzar 5 ameer, crown,

emeer, queen, rajah, royal, ruler **6** despot, gerent, prince, sultan **7** emperor, empress, majesty, viceroy **8** autocrat, princess **9** butterfly, potentate, sovereign
  become a ~: 6 accede
  future ~: 5 larva **6** prince **8** princess
  hazard: 4 nets
  in French: 3 roi **5** reine
  in Latin: 3 rex
  in Spanish: 3 rey **5** reina
  letters: 3 HRH
Monarch: 3 car **4** auto **7** Mercury **10** automobile
monarchal: 8 imperial **9** sovereign
monarchical: 5 royal
...monarch of ___ survey: 4 all I
monarchy: 5 realm, reign **6** nation **7** kingdom **8** kingship
monarque: 3 roi
monastery: 5 abbey, house **6** friary, priory, temple **7** convent **8** cloister, lamasery
  chamber: 4 cell
  figure: 4 abbé, monk **5** abbot, friar, prior
  office: 6 abbacy
  Tibetan ~: 5 gompa
  title: 3 dom, fra
Monastery of ___: 4 Iona
monastic: 4 abbé, monk **5** friar **6** Essene **7** recluse **8** clerical **9** reclusive, religious
monaural, not: 6 stereo
monazite: 3 ore
Monclova: 4 city, town
  locale: 6 Mexico **8** Coahuila
Moncton: 4 city, town
  locale: 6 Canada
Mondale: 5 Fritz **6** Walter **7** Eleanor
Monday ___ quarterback: 7 morning
___ Monday: 4 blue **5** Manic **6** Easter, Shrove, Stormy
Monday feeling: 5 blahs
Monday, Monday (1966 song) artist: Mamas & the Papas
Monday Night Football
  network: 3 ABC **5** ABC-TV
monde: 5 world **6** French
  haute ~: 6 gentry, jet set **7** society, who's who **10** upper class, upper crust
  starter: 4 demi
___ monde: 4 beau, haut
___ mondes: 5 beaux
___-mondi: 5 coati
Mondial: 3 car **4** auto **7** Ferrari **10** automobile
Mon dieu!: 4 oh no
mondo: 3 big **4** huge **5** great
Mondo Cane theme: 4 More
Mondrian, Piet: 6 artist **7** painter
  homeland: 7 Holland **11** Netherlands
Monel: 5 alloy
  component: 4 iron **6** copper, nickel **9** manganese
Moneta, Ernesto: 7 Italian **8** Nobelist
monetary: 4 cash **6** fiscal **7** capital **8** economic **9** budgetary, financial, pecuniary **10** commercial
  award: 5 prize, purse
  gain: 5 lucre
  punishment: 4 fine
  value: 5 worth
monetary ___: 4 gain, unit
Monet:, Claude: 6 artist, French **7** painter
  contemporary: 5 Degas
  setting: 5 Rouen
money: 2 as, at, xu **3** ban, bit, bob, cob, ecu, fen, kip, lat, lek, leu, lev, ley, mil, oof, ore, pay, pie, pul, pya, sen, sol, sou, tip, wad, won, yen **4** anna, baht, bill, birr, buck, cash, cedi, cent, chon, coin, dime, doit, dong, duit, euro, fils, fund, gelt, gold, inti, jack, jeon, joey, kail, kale, kobo, kran, kyat, lira, loot, mark, merk, mill, mina, obol, para, peag, pelf, peso, pice, pile, pony, pula, quid, rand, real, rial, riel, roll, tael, taka, tala, wage, yuan **5** agora, angel, asper, belga, bills, bread, broad, bucks, butut, check, chips, coins, colon, conto, crown, daric, dimes, dinar, dough, ducat, eagle, eyrir, franc, funds, girsh, gravy, groat, grosz, gursh, kopec, kopek, krona, krone, kroon, kurus, leone, liard, libra, litas, livre, louis, lucre, means, mohur, mongo, moola, naira, ngwee, noble, paisa, pengo, penni, penny, pesos, plack, pound, purse, qirsh, qursh, riyal, ruble, rupee, sceat, scudi, scudo, semis, sewan, soldo, sucre, sycee, taler, thebe, tical, uncia, unite, zaire, zloty **6** assets, aureus, balboa, bawbee, bezant, boodle, bundle, change, condor, copeck, dalasi, decime, dinero, dirham, doblon, dollar, do-re-mi, drachm, escudo, filler, florin, forint, ghirsh, gilder, gourde, guinea, gulden, heller, income, kopeck, korona, koruna, kwacha, lepton, likuta, makuta, mammon, markka, mazuma, monkey, moolah, nickel, peseta, pesewa, poisha, qindar, qintar, quezal, qurush, riches, rouble, salary, seawan, sequin, shekel, silver, specie, stater, stiver, talent, tanner, tester, teston, thaler, tipoff, tugrik, wampum, wealth **7** afghani, austral, bolivar, cabbage, capital, carolus, centavo, centime, centimo, coinage, cordoba, cruzado, denarii, dollars, drachma, guarani, guilder, halalas, jacobus, lempira, lettuce, milreis, moidore, nickels, payment, pennies, pfennig, piaster, piastre, pistole, quarter, quetzal, revenue, rughrik, sceatta, scratch, sextans, shekels, support, tambala, testoon, tukhrik, unicorn **8** banknote, bankroll, big bucks, cold cash, cruzeiro, currency, denarius, doubloon, ducatoon, farthing, finances, florence, groschen, hard cash, johannes, kreutzer, louis d'or, maravedi, millieme, napoleon, new pence, new penny, picayune, property, quarters, receipts, services, sesterce, shilling, sixpence, stotinka, treasure, tuppence, twopence **9** affluence, banknotes, boliviano, centesimo, didrachma, dupondius, greenback, half-crown, halfpenny, long green, pistareen, principal, resources, rix-dollar, rose-noble, schilling, sestertia, sestertii, simoleons, sovereign **10** gold stater, greenbacks, half dollar, half-guinea, sestertium, threepence, tripondius
  back: 6 rebate, refund
  broker: 6 banker, lender
  color of ~: 5 green
  dirty ~: 4 pelf **5** lucre
  earn ~: 4 live, work
  emergency ~: 5 scrip
  ender: 3 bag, man, men **4** wort **5** maker **6** lender, making **7** changer, grubber
  finish in the ~: 3 win **4** show **5** place
  front ~: 4 loan **7** advance
  funny ~: 4 slug
  get ~: 6 redeem **9** liquidate
  get ~ for: 4 sell **6** cash in, redeem
  give ~: 4 lend, loan **6** donate **7** advance
  give ~ for: 3 buy, pay **6** lay out
  hunger: 5 greed
  hush ~: 5 bribe, graft **6** payoff **7** jobbery **8** kickback **9** blackmail
  in the ~: 4 rich **5** flush **6** loaded, monied **7** wealthy, well-off **8** affluent, well-to-do **9** well-fixed **10** privileged, propertied, prosperous, well-heeled
  in the bank: 4 acct. **5** asset **7** deposit, savings
  like funny ~: 5 bogus **11** counterfeit
  lot of ~: 3 wad **4** mint, pile **5** stack **8** bankroll
  make ~: 3 pay **4** coin, earn, live, mint **6** profit **7** prosper
  make ~ the old- fashioned way: 6 earn it
  management: 7 finance
  manager: 6 banker, broker
  medium: 4 coin **5** paper
  minimal ~: 4 cent, song
  of ~: 6 fiscal **8** monetary
  old ~: 4 rich **5** elite
  on the ~: 5 exact, right **7** correct, exactly, perfect, precise **8** accurate, very well **10** absolutely
  owed: 4 debt **6** arrear **7** arrears
  paper ~: 4 bill, note **8** currency **9** greenback
  place: 3 ATM **4** bank, belt, safe, till **5** chest, purse, S and L **6** coffer, wallet **8** register, treasury **9** piggy bank **10** pocketbook
  pocket ~: 4 cash, ones, tens **5** bills, coins, dimes, fives **6** change **7** coinage, nickels, pennies, singles **8** quarters, twenties
  pool: 4 fund **5** kitty
  press for ~: 3 dun
  provide ~ at interest: 4 loan
  put (down) ~: 5 plunk
  put ~ (on): 4 bank, rely **6** depend
  put up ~: 3 bet **4** ante, back, fund **5** wager **6** invest **7** finance, sponsor **9** speculate
  rainy-day ~: 4 fund
  recipient: 5 payee
  save ~: 6 scrimp **9** economize
  send ~: 3 pay **5** remit
  set aside: 6 escrow
  slangily: 3 oof, wad **4** cash, gelt, jack, kail, kale, loot, peag, pelf **5** bills, bread, bucks, dough, green, lucre, moola, mopus, pesos, rhino **6** dinero, do-re-mi, mazuma, moolah, wampum, wealth **7** cabbage, lettuce, ooftish, scratch, shekels **8** smackers **9** banknotes, frogskins, long green, simoleons **10** green stuff
  solicit ~: 5 hit up **7** squeeze
  source: 4 loan
  waste ~: 6 lavish **8** squander
  without ~: 4 poor **5** broke, needy, short **6** bad off, hard up, ill off, in need, in want **7** pinched **8** badly off, bankrupt, beggarly, deprived, indigent, strapped **9** destitute, insolvent, penniless, penurious **10** down and out, pauperized, straitened
  see also coin
money ___: 3 box **4** belt, fund, tree **5** order, plant, shell **6** cowrie, market, player, supply **7** machine
money-___ fund: 6 market
___ money: 3 big, hot, key, mad, old, pin, tea **4** bank, call, cash, door, easy, even, fiat, head, hush, near, play, seed, ship, side, soft, till, time **5** black, blood, found, front, funny, in the, on the, paper, prize, ready, smart **6** maundy, pocket, street **7** deposit, earnest, folding
Money ___ everything!: 4 isn't
Money ___ Nothing: 3 for
Money ___ object!: 4 is no
___ Money: 3 Hot **4** Blue **5** Blood **6** Pocket
Money (1973 song) artist: Pink Floyd
Money author: Emile Zola, Martin Amis
moneybag: 5 purse
moneybags: 5 nabob **6** fat cat **9** financier, plutocrat **10** capitalist, man of means
moneychanger, name meaning: 8 Wechsler
moneyed: 4 rich **5** flush **6** fat-cat, loaded, uptown **7** opulent, upscale, wealthy, well-off **8** affluent, in clover, well-to-do **9** well-fixed **10** in the dough, privileged, propertied, prosperous, upper-class, well-heeled
  class: 6 jet set
Money, Eddie
  song: Baby Hold On (1978)
    Endless Nights (1987)
    I'll Get By (1992)
    I Wanna Go Back (1987)
    Peace in Our Time (1989)
    Take Me Home Tonight (1986)
    Think I'm in Love (1982)
    Two Tickets to Paradise (1978)
    Walk on Water (1988)
Money for Nothing (1985 song) artist: Dire Straits
moneygrubber: 5 miser, piker **10** cheapskate
moneygrubbing: 5 cheap, crass **6** greedy, stingy **7** sparing **9** mercenary
Money Honey (1976 song) artist: Bay City Rollers
Money isn't everything: 5 adage
...money is the ___ of...: 4 root
moneylender: 4 bank **6** banker, factor, loaner, usurer **7** Shylock **8** creditor
moneyless: 4 poor **5** broke, needy **6** bad off, hard up, ill off, in need, in want **7** pinched **8** badly off, bankrupt, beggarly, deprived, indigent, strapped **9** destitute, insolvent, penniless, penurious **10** down and out, pauperized, straitened
  in Britain: 5 skint
Moneyline network: 3 CNN
moneymaking: 4 good **5** going **6** paying **7** gainful **8** economic, thriving **9** lucrative **10** profitable, worthwhile
money-market ___: 4 fund
Money, Money, Money artist: 4 ABBA
___ money on: 3 put
money order: 5 draft
  recipient: 5 payee
  sender: 6 drawee
Money Pit, The (1986 film)
  cast: Alexander Godunov, Tom Hanks, Shelley Long, Maureen Stapleton
  director: Richard Benjamin
Moneytalks artist: 4 AC/DC
___ Money, The: 3 Big
Mong Cai: 3 pig **5** swine
monger: 6 seller **7** peddler **8** merchant
  starter: 3 war **4** fish, iron, news, word **5** rumor, scare **6** gossip, phrase **7** fashion, scandal
Mongibello: 4 Etna **5** Aetna **7** volcano
Mongkut, King
  domain: 4 Siam
  nanny: 4 Anna
  portrayer: 3 Yul **7** Brynner
mongo: 5 money
Mongo: 4 Beti
  home: 5 Congo **6** Africa
Mongol: 3 Hun **5** Asian, Tatar **6** empire
  dynasty: 4 Yuan
  locale: 4 Asia
  monk: 4 lama
  ruler: 4 khan

tent: 4 yurt
tribe: 5 horde
Mongolia: 6 nation 7 country
bovine: 5 Sanhe
city: 6 Hohhot 9 Ulan Bator
equine: 5 kiang 8 chigetai 9 dziggetai
language family: 6 Altaic
like ~: 3 dry 4 arid
locale: 4 Asia
money: 5 mongo 6 tugrik 7 rughrik, tukhrik
much of ~: 4 Gobi 6 desert
neighbor: 5 China 6 Russia
people: 3 Lai
range: 5 Altai
sheep: 5 argal 6 argali
__ Mongolia: 5 Inner, Outer
Mongolian: 8 language
Mongolian __ pot: 3 hot
mongoose: 6 animal, mammal
foe: 5 cobra
Mongoose, The: Archie Moore
mongrel: 3 cur, dog, mut 4 mutt 5 cross, feist, hound, scrub, stray 6 hybrid 7 mixture 10 crossbreed, mixed breed
Monica: 5 saint, Seles 6 Potter
brother on Friends: 4 Ross
in French: 7 Monique
__ Monica, CA: 5 Santa
monied class: 5 haves
monies
see money
moniker: 4 name 5 alias, title 6 handle 8 nickname 9 sobriquet
Monique
in English: 6 Monica
see also French
monitor: 2 TV 3 VDT 4 scan 5 audit, check, guide, see to, track, TV set 6 censor, follow, listen, lizard, record, survey 7 auditor, control, observe, oversee, proctor, scanner 8 look over, overseer, regulate, terminal, watchdog 9 check up on, eavesdrop, informant, inspector, supervise 10 gatekeeper, supervisor
lizard: 4 uran 6 goanna
Monitor: 4 ship 6 vessel 8 ironclad
feature: 6 turret
Moniz, Antonio: 8 Nobelist 10 Portuguese
monja: 3 nun
monk: 3 Fra 4 abbé, lama 5 abbot, friar, prior 6 hermit, priest, sensei 7 ascetic, bhikshu, brother, eremite, recluse 8 cenobite, monastic, rinpoche, solitary, Trappist 9 anchorite, religious 10 monastical
Asian ~: 4 lama 5 bonze, sadhu 7 bhikshu 9 bhikshuni
French ~: 5 frère
garb: 4 cowl, hood 5 frock, habit 7 mandyas
group: 5 skete
habitat: 4 cell 5 abbey 6 friary
like a ~: 6 hooded
monotone: 5 chant
of yore: 6 Essene
superior: 5 abbot
title: 3 dom, fra
Monk: 10 Thelonious
Monkees
film: Head (1968)
song: Daydream Believer (1967)
I'm a Believer (1966)
Last Train to Clarksville (1966)
A Little Bit Me, A Little Bit You (1967)
Pleasant Valley Sunday (1967)
She (1967)
Steppin' Stone (1966)
That Was Then, This Is Now (1986)
Valleri (1968)
Words (1967)
Monkees, The (NBC sitcom)
cast: Micky Dolenz
Davy Jones
Mike Nesmith
Peter Tork
monkey: 4 saki, titi 5 dance, jocko, lemur, money, scamp 6 animal, baboon, Bandar, fiddle, gelada, grivet, guenon, howler, langur, rascal, rhesus, simian, tamper, tinker, trifle, uakari, vervet 7 colobus, guereza, hoolock, macaque, primate, sapajou, tamarin 8 capuchin, imitator, mandrill, mangabey, marmoset, mess with, talapoin 9 obsession 10 anthropoid, fool around, jackanapes
African ~: 6 grivet, guenon
around: 6 cavort 7 fribble, goof off
Asian ~: 6 Bandar, langur, rhesus
business: 6 deceit 7 foolery 8 falderal, falderol, mischief
Capuchin ~: 3 sai
combining form: 6 pithec- 7 pitheco-
ender: 5 shine 6 shines
food: 6 banana
home: 3 zoo
make a ~ of: 6 outwit 8 outsmart 9 embarrass, humiliate
pot: 4 tree
puzzle: 4 tree
relative: 3 ape 5 chimp, drill, loris, magot, orang, potto, shrew 6 aye-aye, galago, gibbon, macaco 7 gorilla, siamang, tarsier 8 bush baby 9 orangutan 10 Barbary ape, chimpanzee, orangutang
South American ~: 3 sai 4 titi 6 howler
suit: 3 tux 4 tuck 5 tails 6 tuxedo
throw a ~ wrench into: 5 block 6 hamper, hinder 7 disrupt 8 obstruct, sabotage 9 frustrate, undermine
(with): 4 fool 6 fiddle, tamper, trifle
wrench: 4 snag 5 block, crimp, hitch, snarl 7 barrier, problem, setback 8 handicap, obstacle 10 impediment
monkey __: 3 dog, nut, paw, pot 4 bars, link, suit, tail 5 block, bread, flush 6 bridge, flower, island, jacket, puzzle, wrench
__ monkey: 3 owl 5 green, night 6 bonnet, grease, howler, powder, rhesus, spider, woolly 7 colobus, savanna
Monkey __: 5 Trial 7 Trouble
Monkey __, monkey do: 3 see
Monkey (1988 song) artist: George Michael
monkey bread: 5 fruit
tree: 6 baobab
Monkey Business (1931 film)
cast: Chico Marx, Groucho Marx, Harpo Marx, Zeppo Marx, Thelma Todd
director: Norman Z. McLeod
Monkey Business (1952 film)
cast: Charles Coburn, Cary Grant, Marilyn Monroe, Ginger Rogers
director: Howard Hawks
__ monkey out of: 5 make a
Monkey's __, The: 3 Paw
__ Monkeys: 6 Twelve
monkeyshine: 3 gag 4 dido, jape, joke 5 antic, caper, prank, trick 6 frolic 7 foolery 8 escapade, jocosity 10 hanky-panky, tomfoolery
Monkey, the: 5 dance
__ Monkey, The: 5 Fifth
Monkey Trial
defendant: 6 Scopes
lawyer: 5 Bryan 6 Darrow
locale: 6 Dayton 9 Tennessee
Monkey Trouble (1994 film)
cast: Thora Birch, Harvey Keitel, Mimi Rogers
director: Franco Amurri
monkfish: 5 lotte
monkish: 8 clerical
monklike: 5 pious
monkshood: 5 plant 6 flower
Monk, Thelonious: 7 pianist
genre: 3 bop 4 jazz
__ Monmouth, NJ: 4 Fort
mono
not ~: 6 stereo
monocle: 4 lens 5 glass, loupe
mono- cousin: 3 uni
monocratic: 8 absolute 9 arbitrary
Monod, Jacques: 6 French 7 chemist 8 Nobelist
monody: 5 dirge
monogamist: 4 wife 6 spouse 7 husband
monogamy: 8 marriage 9 matrimony
monogrammed item: 5 shirt, towel
monogram unit: 4 init. 6 letter 7 initial
monograph: 5 paper 6 thesis 8 treatise 9 discourse 10 exposition
monolith: 5 pylon, tower 6 column 8 memorial, monument
monolithic: 7 uniform
monologist: 5 comic 6 diseur 8 comedian
seating: 5 stool
monologue: 4 talk 6 sermon, speech 7 address, descant, discant, lecture, stand-up 8 harangue 9 discourse, soliloquy 10 recitation, vocalizing
material: 3 gag 4 joke, news, quip 8 one-liner
Monologue author: Harold Pinter
monomania: 4 zeal 6 fervor 8 fixation 9 obsession 10 fanaticism
Mon Oncle (1958 film)
cast: Jacques Tati
director: Jacques Tati
Monongahela: 5 river
city on the ~: 10 Pittsburgh
monopolist's trait: 5 greed
monopolize: 3 hog, own 4 have, hold 5 buy up, sew up, sit on 6 absorb, corner, devour, engage, lock up, occupy, patent, take up 7 acquire, consume, control, engross, exclude, possess 8 dominate, take over 9 copyright, syndicate
monopoly: 4 pool 5 trust 6 cartel, corner, patent 7 holding 8 business 9 copyright, oligopoly, ownership, syndicate 10 consortium
get a ~ on: 5 sew up 6 corner
Monopoly: 4 game 9 board game
collection: 4 rent
company: 6 Hasbro
need: 4 dice 5 board, deeds, money 6 hotels, houses
player: 6 banker
Monopoly pieces:
battleship
cannon
dog
iron
race car
shoe
thimble
top hat
Monopoly railroads:
B and O
Pennsylvania
Reading
Short Line
Monopoly squares (misc.):
Chance
Community Chest
Free Parking
Go to Jail
Income Tax
Jail
Luxury Tax
Monopoly streets:
Atlantic Avenue
Baltic Avenue
Boardwalk
Connecticut Avenue
Illinois Avenue
Indiana Avenue
Kentucky Avenue
Marvin Gardens
Mediterranean Avenue
New York Avenue
North Carolina Avenue
Oriental Avenue
Pacific Avenue
Park Place
Pennsylvania Avenue
States Avenue
St. Charles Place
St. James Place
Tennessee Avenue
Ventnor Avenue
Vermont Avenue
Virginia Avenue
Monopoly utilities:
Electric Company
Water Works
monosaccharide: 5 sugar 6 aldose
suffix: 3 ose
monotone: 5 drone
in a ~: 6 evenly
Monotones song: Book of Love (1958)
monotonous: 3 dry 4 blah, dull, flat, tame 5 bland, ho-hum, plain, unfun 6 boring, dreary, smooth, stodgy 7 droning, humdrum, prosaic, tedious, uniform 8 banausic, constant, dragging, plodding, sing-song, tiresome, toneless, unlively, unvaried, wearying 9 colorless, incessant, ponderous, prosaical, recurrent, soporific, treadmill, unchanged, unvarying, wearisome 10 enervating, invariable
monotony: 3 rut 5 ennui 6 tedium 7 boredom, dryness, humdrum, routine 8 drabness, dullness, evenness, flatness, sameness 9 levelness 10 continuity, dreariness, equability, insipidity, uniformity
__ monoxide: 4 iron, lead 6 barium, carbon, sodium
Monroe: 4 Bill, city, Earl, fort, town 5 James 6 Vaughn 7 Harriet, Marilyn
coll.: 3 NLU
locale: 8 Michigan 9 Louisiana
Monroe, Earl
milieu: 5 court
org.: 3 NBA
sport: 10 basketball
Monroe, Harriet: 4 poet
Monroe, James: 9 president
home: 7 Oak Hill 8 Virginia
opponent: 4 King
predecessor: 7 Madison
successor: 5 Adams
V.P.: 8 Tompkins
wife: 9 Elizabeth
Monroe, Marilyn: 7 actress
contemporary: 6 Bardot 9 Mansfield
film: The Asphalt Jungle (1950)
Bus Stop (1956)
Clash by Night (1952)
Gentlemen Prefer Blondes (1953)
How to Marry a Millionaire (1953)
Let's Make Love (1960)
The Misfits (1961)
Monkey Business (1952)
Niagara (1953)
The Seven Year Itch (1955)
Some Like It Hot (1959)
spouse: Joe DiMaggio, Arthur Miller
__ Monroe, VA: 4 Fort

Monroeville: **4** city, town
locale: **4** Penn. **5** Penna.
Monro, Harold: **4** poet **6** editor **7** British
Monrovia: **4** city, town **7** capital
locale: **7** Liberia **10** California
Mons: **4** city, town
locale: **7** Belgium
monsieur: **3** man **5** title **6** French
in German: **4** herr
in Italian: **6** signor
in Spanish: **5** señor
Monsieur Beaucaire (1946 film)
cast: Joan Caulfield, Bob Hope, Patric Knowles
director: George Marshall
Monsieur Verdoux (1947 film)
cast: Charles Chaplin, Martha Raye
director: Charles Chaplin
monsignor: **5** title **6** cleric, priest
monsoon: **4** rain, wind **5** storm **8** downpour **9** hurricane **10** inundation
monsoon __: **3** low **6** season
monster: **3** big **4** huge, ogre **5** beast, brute, demon, devil, fiend, freak, ghoul, giant, whale **6** bad guy, daemon, daimon, dragon, horror, mutant, savage **7** chimera, hellion, mammoth, villain, werwolf **8** behemoth, bogeyman, chimaera, colossus, gargoyle, gigantic, werewolf **9** archfiend, barbarian, hellhound, leviathan
combining form: **5** terat- **6** terato-
green-eyed ~: **4** envy
home: **4** loch **8** Loch Ness
of myth: **5** harpy, hydra, lamia **6** dragon, gorgon, Medusa
__ monster: **4** Gila **6** sacred **7** hopeful **8** Loch Ness
Monster __ Closet: **5** in the
__ Monster: **6** Cookie
Monster artist: **3** R.E.M.
Monster author: Jonathan Kellerman
Monster Mash (1962 song) artist: Bobby Pickett
Monster's Ball (2001 film)
cast: Halle Berry, Peter Boyle, Heath Ledger, Billy Bob Thornton
director: Marc Forster
Monsters, Inc. (2001 film)
voice cast: Steve Buscemi, Billy Crystal, John Goodman
monstrosity: **4** ogre **5** sight **6** fright
monstrous: **4** evil, foul, huge, mean, ugly, vast, vile **5** awful, cruel, enorm, giant, great, gross, harsh, nasty **6** animal, brutal, fierce, morbid, odious, savage, unkind, wanton **7** beastly, callous, fearful, heinous, hellish, hideous, hurtful, immense, inhuman, macaber, macabre, mammoth, massive, obscene, ominous, satanic, titanic, ungodly, vicious **8** aberrant, barbaric, colossal, diabolic, dreadful, enormous, fiendish, flagrant, freakish, gigantic, grievous, gruesome, horrible, infamous, infernal, inhumane, pitiless, ruthless, sadistic, shocking, teratoid, terrible, terrific, towering, vengeful, whapping, whopping, wretched **9** appalling, atrocious, barbarous, cutthroat, desperate, egregious, execrable, fantastic, ferocious, frightful, grandiose, grotesque, loathsome, merciless, nefarious, offensive, repellant, revolting, satanical, truculent, unnatural, unpitying, unsightly **10** detestable, diabolical, disgusting, gargantuan, horrendous, horrifying, impressive, monumental, outrageous, petrifying, prodigious, scandalous, stupendous, tremendous, unmerciful, unpleasant, villainous, vindictive, virtueless
Mont: **4** alpe **5** Blanc **6** Cervin
Mont-__-Michel: **5** Saint
Mont.
neighbor: **3** Alb., Ida., Wyo. **4** Alta., N. Dak., Sask., S. Dak.
see also Montana
Montadale: **5** sheep
montagne: **6** French **8** mountain
opposite: **3** val
Montagu: **4** John **6** Ashley
Montague: **5** Romeo
Montagu, Mary Wortley: **6** author, writer **7** British
work: Turkish Letters
Montaigne, Michel de: **6** French, writer **8** essayist
Montalban, Ricardo: **5** actor
film: Battleground (1949)
Border Incident (1949)
Joe Panther (1976)
The Naked Gun: From the Files of Police Squad! (1988)
On an Island With You (1948)
Sayonara (1957)
Star Trek II: The Wrath of Khan (1982)
Sweet Charity (1969)
TV: Fantasy Island
Montale, Eugenio: **4** poet **6** writer **7** Italian **8** Nobelist
Montalvo, Juan: **6** writer **8** essayist **10** Ecuadorian
Montana: **3** Bob, Joe, van **5** state **6** Big Sky **7** Pontiac
capital: **6** Helena
city: **5** Butte **6** Helena **7** Bozeman **8** Billings, Missoula **9** Kalispell, Silver Bow **10** Great Falls
Indian: **4** Cree, Crow **7** Kutenai **8** Cheyenne **10** Assiniboin
motto word: **3** oro **5** plata
mountain: **5** Lewis **7** Granite, Purcell
national park: **7** Glacier
neighbor: **5** Idaho **6** Canada **7** Alberta, Wyoming
state bird: **10** meadowlark
state flower: **10** bitterroot
Montana, Joe: **2** QB **11** quarterback
sport: **8** football
Montand, Yves: **5** actor **6** French
film: The Crucible (1957)
Goodbye Again (1961)
La Guerre Est Finie (1966)
Let's Make Love (1960)
On a Clear Day You Can See Forever (1970)
Vincent, François, Paul and the Others (1974)
Z (1969)
spouse: Simone Signoret
Montauk: **4** city, town **5** tribe **6** Indian **8** language
locale: **7** New York
Montauk __, NY: **5** Point
Mont Blanc: **3** alp **4** alpe, peak **5** mount **8** mountain
covering: **4** snow **5** neige
locale: **4** Alps **5** Italy **6** Europe, France
neighbor: **5** Aosta
Montclair: **3** car **4** auto, city, town **7** Mercury **10** automobile
locale: **9** New Jersey **10** California
monte: **4** game, scam **8** card game
Monte: **5** Irvin **7** Hellman, Markham
Monte __: **4** Rosa **5** Albán, Carlo, Corno, Walsh **6** Cristo **7** Cassino
Monte __ sandwich: **6** Cristo
__ Monte: **3** Del
Montebello: **4** city, town
locale: **10** California
Monte Carlo: **3** car **4** auto, city, town **5** Chevy **9** Chevrolet **10** automobile
action: **3** bet
game: **6** écarté **8** baccarat, roulette **9** blackjack
locale: **6** Monaco
Monte Corno: **4** peak **5** mount **8** mountain
locale: **5** Italy **6** Europe **8** Apenines
__ Monte Cristo, The: **5** Son of
Montego: **3** car **4** auto **7** Mercury **10** automobile
Montego Bay: **4** city, port, town
locale: **7** Jamaica
Montego Bay (1970 song) artist: Bobby Bloom
Montel: **8** Williams
colleague: **5** Oprah
Montemezzi: **5** Italo
Montemorelos: **4** city, town
locale: **6** Mexico **9** Nuevo León
Montenegro, Hugo song: The Good, the Bad, and the Ugly (1968)
Monterey: **3** bay, car **4** auto, city, town **7** Mercury **10** automobile
locale: **10** California
Monterey __: **3** Bay, Pop **4** Jack, pine **7** cypress
Monterey Jack: **6** cheese
Monterey Park: **4** city, town
locale: **10** California
Montería: **4** city, town
locale: **8** Colombia
montero: **3** cap, hat **8** headgear
feature: **6** earlap
Montero: **3** SUV **10** Mitsubishi
Monte Rosa: **3** alp **4** peak **5** mount **8** mountain
locale: **4** Alps **6** Europe **11** Switzerland
Monterrey: **4** city, town
locale: **6** Mexico **9** Nuevo León
see also Spanish
Montesquieu: **6** French, writer **11** philosopher
Montessori __: **6** method, system
Montessori, Maria: **7** Italian, teacher **8** educator
Monteux, Pierre: **6** French **9** conductor
Monteverdi, Claudio: **7** Italian **8** composer
Montevideo: **4** city, port, town **7** capital
estuary: **5** Plata
locale: **3** Uru. **7** Uruguay
see also Spanish
Monte Walsh (1970 film)
cast: Lee Marvin, Jeanne Moreau, Jack Palance
Montez: **4** Lola **5** Chris, Maria
Montgomery: **3** Wes **4** city, town, Ward **5** Clift **6** George, Robert **7** Anthony, Bernard **8** Douglass **9** Elizabeth
locale: **3** Ala. **7** Alabama **8** Maryland
milieu: **3** ETO
river: **7** Alabama
sch.: **3** ASU
Montgomery __: **4** Ward
Montgomery, Elizabeth spouse: Gig Young
__ Montgomery Flagg: **5** James
Montgomery, George: **5** actor
film: Coney Island (1943)
Ten Gentlemen From West Point (1942)
Three Little Girls in Blue (1946)
spouse: Dinah Shore
Montgomery, Lucy Maud: **6** author, writer **8** Canadian
work: Anne of Green Gables
Montgomery, Robert: **5** actor
film: Another Language (1933)
The Big House (1930)
The Gallant Hours (1960)
Here Comes Mr. Jordan (1941)
June Bride (1948)
The Last of Mrs. Cheyney (1937)
Mr. and Mrs. Smith (1941)
The Mystery of Mr. X (1934)
Night Must Fall (1937)
Private Lives (1931)
Ride the Pink Horse (1947)
Riptide (1934)
The Saxon Charm (1948)
They Were Expendable (1945)
Trouble for Two (1936)
When Ladies Meet (1933)
Montgomery, Wes: **9** guitarist
genre: **4** jazz
month: **3** Apr., Aug., Dec., Feb., Jan., Jul., Jun., Mar., May, Nov., Oct., Sep. **4** July, June, moon, Sept., time **5** April, March **6** August **7** January, October, Ramadan **8** December, February, November **9** September
autumn ~: **3** Dec., Nov., Oct., Sep. **4** Sept. **7** October **8** December, November **9** September
combining form: **3** men- **4** meno-
fraction: **2** wk. **4** week
French ~: **3** mai **4** août, juin, mars **5** avril **7** février, janvier, juillet, octobre **8** décembre, novembre **9** septembre
German ~: **3** Mai **4** Juli, Juni, März **5** April **6** August, Januar **7** Februar, Oktober **8** Dezember, November **9** September
Hebrew ~: **2** Av **4** Adar, Elul, Iyar **5** Iyyar, Nisan, Sivan, Tevet **6** Kislev, Nissan, Shevat, Tammuz, Tishri **7** Heshvan
Islamic ~: **4** Magh, Rabi **5** Rajab, Safar **6** Jumada, Sha'ban **7** Ramadan, Shawwal **8** Muharram
Italian ~: **5** marzo **6** agosto, aprile, giugno, lùglio, màggio **7** gennaio, ottobre **8** dicèmbre, febbraio, novèmbre **9** settèmbre
last ~: **3** ult. **6** ultimo
Spanish ~: **4** mayo **5** abril, enero, julio, junio, marzo **6** agosto **7** febrero, octubre **9** diciembre, noviembre **10** septiembre
spring ~: **3** Apr., Mar., May **4** June **5** April **8** March. Jun.
summer ~: **3** Aug., Jul., Jun., Sep. **4** July, June, Sept. **6** August **9** September
winter ~: **3** Dec., Feb., Jan., Mar. **5** March **7** January **8** December, February
__ month: **5** lunar, solar **7** nodical, synodic
Month in the Country, A author: Ivan Turgenev
monthly: **5** paper **8** magazine, periodic **10** periodical
in Latin: **9** per mensum
month of __: **7** Sundays
months
every twelve ~: **6** yearly
twelve ~: **4** year
Monticello: **6** estate
locale: **8** Virginia
owner: **9** Jefferson
Montilla: **4** wine **7** Spanish
Montmartre locale: **5** Paris **6** France
Montoya, Carlos: **7** Spanish **9** guitarist
Montpelier: **4** city, town
county: **10** Washington
locale: **7** Vermont
river: **8** Winooski
Montpellier: **4** city, town
locale: **6** France
neighbor of ~: **5** Nîmes
Montrachet: **4** wine **5** white **6** French
Montréal: **4** city, port, town
locale: **3** Que. **6** Canada, Québec
newspaper: **7** Gazette, Journal **8** La Presse
pro team: **5** Expos **9** Canadiens
river: **10** St. Lawrence

school: 6 McGill 9 Concordia
suburb: 5 Laval
subway: 5 Metro
see also French
Montrose: 4 Scot 6 Ronnie
Mont-Saint-__: 6 Michel
Montserrat: 3 isl. 4 isle 6 island
Monty: 4 Hall 7 Woolley
colleague: 3 Ike 4 Omar
Monty Python's The Meaning of Life (1983 film)
cast: Graham Chapman, John Cleese, Terry Gilliam, Eric Idle, Terry Jones, Michael Palin
director: Terry Jones
__ Monty's Double: 4 I Was
monument: 4 carn, slab, tomb, tope 5 cairn, henge, pylon, relic, stela, stele, stone, tower 6 column, ledger, marker, pillar, record, shrine, statue, tablet 7 obelisk, tribute 8 cenotaph, landmark, memorial, monolith 10 magnum opus
monumental: 3 big 4 epic, huge, vast 5 giant, grand, great, jumbo, large, lofty 6 mighty, mortal 7 awesome, classic, Homeric, hulking, immense, lasting, mammoth, massive, sizable, stately, titanic 8 colossal, enduring, enormous, gigantic, historic, immortal, imposing, king-size, majestic, oversize, sizeable, towering, whapping, whopping 9 fantastic, grandiose, Herculean, humongous, important, memorable, monstrous, overlarge 10 gargantuan, impressive, majestical, prodigious, stupendous, tremendous
Mony Mony (song) artist: Billy Idol, Tommy James and the Shondells
Monza: 3 car 4 auto, city, town 5 Chevy 9 Chevrolet 10 automobile
locale: 5 Italy
moo: 5 bleat
juice: 4 milk
relative: 3 baa, maa 4 oink
moo __: 5 juice
moo __ gai pan: 3 goo
moo __ pork: 3 shu
mooch: 3 beg, bum 5 cadge, sneak 6 borrow, sponge 7 solicit, sponger 8 freeload, scrounge 9 impetrate, panhandle
from: 5 hit up 7 squeeze
moocher: 5 leech 6 sponge 7 sponger 8 deadbeat, parasite 9 do-nothing
mood: 3 air 4 aura, feel, huff, stew, tone, vein 5 humor, pique, state, tenor 6 desire, esprit, nature, spirit, temper 7 climate, feeling, mind-set 8 ambiance, ambience, attitude 9 character, semblance 10 atmosphere
bad ~: 3 pet 4 funk, huff, rage, snit, sulk, tiff 6 temper 9 surliness 10 grumpiness
dejected ~: 4 funk 5 blues, dumps 8 doldrums 10 depression, melancholy
in a bad ~: 3 mad 4 sore, sour 5 cross, huffy, irate, riled, upset 6 crabby, grumpy, morose 8 grumpish
in a good ~: 4 glad 5 happy, merry 6 cheery, elated
in the ~: 7 willing
not in the ~: 9 unwilling
rings: 3 fad 5 craze
mood __: 4 ring 5 music
Mood __: 6 Indigo
__ Mood: 5 In the
Moodie, Susanna: 6 author, writer 8 Canadian
work: Roughing It in the Bush
moodiness: 8 glumness
moody: 3 low, sad 4 blue, dour, down, glum, mopy 5 angry, cross, huffy, mopey, sulky, testy 6 crabby, cranky, crusty, dismal, fickle, fitful, gloomy, grumpy, moping, mopish, morbid, morose, piqued, sullen, touchy 7 crabbed, doleful, erratic, flighty, grouchy, in a huff, peevish, pensive 8 brooding, downcast, grumpish, offended, petulant, snappish 9 crotchety, depressed, impulsive, irascible, irritable, mercurial, miserable, saturnine, splenetic 10 capricious, changeable, ill-humored, lugubrious, melancholy, out of sorts
be ~: 4 mope, pout, sulk 5 brood
Moody: 3 Ron 6 Dwight
Moody __: 5 Blues, River
Moody Blues
song: Gemini Dream (1981)
Go Now! (1965)
I'm Just a Singer (1973)
Nights in White Satin (1972)
The Voice (1981)
Your Wildest Dreams (1986)
Moody, Helen Wills: 7 netster 9 tennis pro
milieu: 5 court
Moody River (1961 song) artist: Pat Boone
Moody, Ron: 5 actor
film: Dogpound Shuffle (1975)
The Mouse on the Moon (1963)
Murder Most Foul (1965)
Oliver! (1968)
The Twelve Chairs (1970)
Moody's: 5 rater
alternative: 5 S and P
best rating: 3 AAA
Moog: 6 Robert 8 keyboard 10 instrument
familiarly: 5 synth
moo goo __ pan: 3 gai
Mookie: 6 Wilson
moolah: 3 oof, wad 4 cash, gelt, jack, kail, kale, loot, peag, pelf 5 bills, bread, bucks, dough, funds, green, lucre, money, mopus, pesos, rhino, sewan 6 dinero, do-re-mi, mammon, mazuma, seawan, silver, specie, wampum, wealth 7 cabbage, capital, dollars, lettuce, ooftish, scratch, shekels 8 bankroll, cold cash, currency, hard cash, smackers 9 banknotes, frogskins, long green, simoleons 10 greenbacks, green stuff
moon: 2 Io 3 orb, Pan 4 idle, Leda, Luna, mope, pine, Puck, Rhea, sulk 5 Ariel, Atlas, Carme, Dione, dream, Elara, Janus, Metis, Mimas, month, Naiad, Thebe, Titan, yearn 6 Ananke, Bianca, Charon, Deimos, Europa, Helene, Juliet, Nereid, Oberon, Phobos, Phoebe, Portia, Sinope, Tethys, Triton 7 Belinda, Caliban, Calypso, Despina, Galatea, Himalia, Iapetus, Larissa, Miranda, Ophelia, Pandora, Proteus, Sycorax, Telesto, Titania, Umbriel 8 Adrastea, Amalthea, Callisto, Cordelia, crescent, Cressida, daydream, Ganymede, Hyperion, languish, Lysithea, Pasiphae, Rosalind, Thalassa 9 Desdemona, Enceladus, fantasize, satellite, waste time 10 Epimetheus, Prometheus, woolgather
combining form: 4 luni- 5 selen- 6 seleni-, seleno-
crater: 5 Tycho
ender: 3 eye, lit, set 4 beam, calf, eyed, fish, rise, seed, walk, wort 5 blind, child, light, quake, scape, shine, stone 6 flower, shiner, struck 8 children, lighting, stricken
feature: 3 sea 4 mare 5 rille 6 crater
goddess: 4 Luna 5 Diana
greet the ~: 3 bay 4 howl 7 ululate
hider: 5 cloud
in Italian: 4 luna
in Latin: 4 luna
Jupiter ~: 2 Io 4 Leda 5 Carme, Elara, Metis, Thebe 6 Ananke, Europa, Sinope 7 Himalia 8 Adrastea, Amalthea, Callisto, Ganymede, Lysithea, Pasiphae
man on the ~: 4 Bean, Duke 5 Irwin, Scott, Young 6 Aldrin, Cernan, Conrad 7 Schmitt, Shepard 8 Alan Bean, Mitchell 9 Armstrong, John Young 10 Buzz Aldrin, David Scott, James Irwin
Mars ~: 6 Deimos, Phobos
Neptune ~: 5 Naiad 6 Nereid, Triton 7 Despina, Galatea, Larissa, Proteus 8 Thalassa
of the ~: 5 lunar
once in a blue ~: 6 rarely, seldom
over the ~: 6 elated
phase: 3 new 4 full 7 gibbous 8 crescent
Pluto ~: 6 Charon
project: 6 Apollo
pull: 4 tide
ring: 4 halo
Saturn ~: 3 Pan 4 Rhea 5 Atlas, Dione, Janus, Mimas, Titan 6 Helene, Phoebe, Tethys 7 Calypso, Iapetus, Pandora, Telesto 8 Hyperion 9 Enceladus 10 Epimetheus, Prometheus
shoot for the ~: 6 aspire, gamble
starter: 5 honey
track: 5 orbit
Uranus ~: 4 Puck 5 Ariel 6 Bianca, Juliet, Oberon, Portia 7 Belinda, Caliban, Miranda, Ophelia, Sycorax, Titania, Umbriel 8 Cordelia, Cressida, Rosalind 9 Desdemona
USSR ~ probe: 5 Lunik
vehicle: 3 LEM 5 Rover 6 lander
moon __: 3 dog 4 gate, shot 5 knife, shell 6 letter, pillar
moon-__: 4 eyed 5 faced
__ moon: 3 new, old 4 blue, full, mock 6 waning, waxing 7 harvest, hunter's
__-moon: 4 half
Moon: 5 Keith 6 Martin, Warren 7 Mullins
Moon __: 4 Lady 5 Music, Pilot, River 6 Shadow
Moon __ Miami: 4 Over
Moon __ Parador: 4 Over
Moon __ Sixpence, The: 3 and
Moon __ Zappa: 4 Unit
__ Moon: 4 Blue, Dark, June 5 Crazy, Paper, Sugar 6 Desert, Winter
__ Moon and Empty Arms: 4 Full
Moon and Sixpence, The: 4 film 5 novel
author: W. Somerset Maugham
cast: Doris Dudley, Herbert Marshall, George Sanders
character: 3 Amy, Ata 4 Dirk 7 Blanche
director: Albert Lewin
moonbeam: 3 ray
mooneye: 4 fish
moonfish: 4 opah
Moon for the Misbegotten, A: 4 play 5 drama
author: Eugene O'Neill
character: 4 Mike, Phil 5 Josie 6 Harder, Tyrone
__ Moon Frye: 6 Soleil
Moon Is __, The: 4 Blue
Moon Is Down, The (1943 film)
cast: Lee J. Cobb, Cedric Hardwicke, Henry Travers
director: Irving Pichel
Moon, Keith: 5 Stone 7 drummer
Moon Lady author: Amy Tan
moonless: 4 dark
planet: 5 Venus
moonlight: 4 work 5 labor 10 occupation
Moonlight __: 3 Bay 6 Sonata 7 Gambler
Moonlight and Valentino (1995 film)
cast: Whoopi Goldberg, Elizabeth Perkins, Kathleen Turner
director: David Anspaugh
Moonlight Becomes You: 4 song 5 novel
author: Mary Higgins Clark
composer: 5 Burke 9 Van Heusen
Moonlight Feels Right (1976 song)
artist: Starbuck
Moonlight Gambler (1956 song) artist: Frankie Laine
Moonlighting (ABC sitcom)
cast: Allyce Beasley (Agnes Dipesto) Cybill Shepherd (Maddie Hayes) Bruce Willis (David Addison)
Moonlight Sonata composer: 9 Beethoven
moonlit: 6 bright
Moon Mullins: 5 strip 10 comic strip
artist: Frank Willard
character: 4 Kayo 5 Mamie 6 Willie
Moon Music author: Faye Kellerman
Moon Over Miami (1941 film)
cast: Don Ameche, Robert Cummings, Betty Grable
director: Walter Lang
Moon Over Parador (1988 film)
cast: Sonia Braga, Richard Dreyfuss, Raul Julia, Jonathan Winters
director: Paul Mazursky
Moon Pilot (1962 film)
cast: Brian Keith, Edmond O'Brien, Tom Tryon
Moonraker: 4 film 5 novel
author: Ian Fleming
cast: Lois Chiles, Richard Kiel, Michael Lonsdale, Roger Moore
director: Lewis Gilbert
villain: 4 Jaws
__ Moon Rising: 3 Bad
Moon River: 4 song 5 waltz
composer: 6 Mercer 7 Mancini
Moon's a Balloon, The author: 5 Niven
__ moons ago: 4 many
Moon Shadow (1971 song) artist: Cat Stevens
moonshine: 3 gas, rot 4 blah, bosh, bull, bunk, guff, jazz, jive, pooh, tale, tosh 5 bilge, booze, drink, fudge, hokum, hooch, hooey, prate, stuff, trash, tripe 6 bunkum, bushwa, drivel, footle, gabble, gammon, gibber, havers, hootch, hot air, humbug, jabber, jargon, kibosh, liquor, piffle, whisky 7 alcohol, baloney, blarney, blather, blether, boloney, bushwah, eyewash, flannel, flubdub, fustian, garbage, hogwash, inanity, rubbish, spirits, twaddle, whiskey 8 beverage, buncombe, claptrap, falderal, falderol, flimflam, flummery, folderal, folderol, nonsense, slipslop, tommyrot, trumpery 9 banana oil, gibberish, goofiness, inebriant, kidstakes, poppycock, rigmarole 10 applesauce, balderdash, bilge water, codswallop, contraband, double-talk, empty words, flapdoodle, galimatias, Jabberwock, mumbo jumbo, rigamarole, taradiddle
container: 3 jug
ingredient: 4 corn, mash
machine: 5 still

quantity: 6 jugful
moonstone: 3 gem
Moonstone, The author: Wilkie Collins
__ Moon Street: 4 Half
moonstruck: 4 rapt 7 bananas 8 ravished
Moonstruck (1987 film)
cast: Danny Aiello, Nicolas Cage, Cher, Olympia Dukakis, Vincent Gardenia
director: Norman Jewison
Moon Unit: 5 Zappa
to Dweezil: 3 sis
moonwalk: 5 dance
moonwalker: 9 astronaut
Moon, Warren: 2 QB 11 quarterback
sport: 8 football
moonwort: 4 fern
moony: 6 dreamy 7 languid, passive 8 listless, mindless 9 lethargic
moor: 3 fix, tie 4 dock, down, fell, lash, wold 5 berth, chain, heath, hitch, plain, swamp, tie up, waste 6 anchor, fasten, secure, steppe, tether, tundra 7 lowland, peat bog, savanna 8 make fast, savannah 9 wasteland
ender: 3 age, hen 4 fowl, land
plant: 4 nard 5 gorse
Moor: 5 Azeem 6 Berber 7 Othello
betrayer: 4 Iago
see also Moorish
__ Moor: 7 Marston
Moore: 2 G.E. 3 Bob 4 Alvy, Demi, diva, poet 5 Brian, Dinty, Garry, Grace, Henry, Lenny, Melba, Robin, Roger, Terry 6 Archie, Chanté, Dudley, George, Hannah, Kieron, Robert, Thomas, Victor 7 Clayton, Clement, Colleen, Dorothy, Douglas, Michael 8 Julianne, Marianne, Stanford 9 Constance
Moore, Archie: 5 boxer
milieu: 4 ring
Moore, Brian: 6 writer 8 Canadian
Moore, Clement: 4 poet
character: 5 Santa
first word: 4 'Twas
moored: 10 stationary
not ~: 6 adrift
Moore, Demi: 7 actress
film: About Last Night ... (1986)
Blame It on Rio (1984)
Disclosure (1994)
A Few Good Men (1992)
Ghost (1990)
G.I. Jane (1997)
Indecent Proposal (1993)
The Juror (1996)
St. Elmo's Fire (1985)
spouse: Bruce Willis
Moore, Dudley: 5 actor
film: 10 (1979)
Arthur (1981)
Bedazzled (1967)
Foul Play (1978)
Micki + Maude (1984)
spouse: Tuesday Weld
Moore, George: 5 Irish 6 author, writer
work: Aphrodite in Aulis
Héloise and Abélard
Moore, Grace: 6 singer 7 soprano
specialty: 5 opera
Moore, Hannah: 6 writer 7 British
work: Percy
Moorehead: 4 Alan 5 Agnes
Moorehead, Agnes: 7 actress
film: Caged (1950)
Citizen Kane (1941)
Hush ... Hush, Sweet Charlotte (1965)
Johnny Belinda (1948)
The Lost Moment (1947)
Tomorrow the World (1944)
Untamed (1955)
TV: Bewitched

Moorehead, Alan: 6 author, writer 10 Australian
work: Gallipoli
No Room in the Ark
Moore, Henry: 6 artist 7 British 8 sculptor
Moore, Julianne: 7 actress
film: Assassins (1995)
The Big Lebowski (1998)
Boogie Nights (1997)
Cookie's Fortune (1999)
Far From Heaven (2002)
Hannibal (2001)
The Hours (2002)
The Lost World: Jurassic Park (1997)
Magnolia (1999)
A Map of the World (1999)
Nine Months (1995)
The Shipping News (2001)
Short Cuts (1993)
Vanya on 42nd Street (1994)
Moore, Marianne: 4 poet
Moore, Mary Tyler: 7 actress
film: Change of Habit (1969)
Ordinary People (1980)
Thoroughly Modern Millie (1967)
spouse: Grant Tinker
TV: The Dick Van Dyke Show, The Mary Tyler Moore Show
Moore, Michael: 8 director
film: Bowling for Columbine (2002)
Canadian Bacon (1995)
Roger and Me (1989)
Moore, Roger: 5 actor
film: The Cannonball Run (1981)
ffolkes (1980)
For Your Eyes Only (1981)
Interrupted Melody (1955)
Live and Let Die (1973)
The Man With the Golden Gun (1974)
Moonraker (1979)
Octopussy (1983)
The Sea Wolves (1980)
The Spy Who Loved Me (1977)
A View to a Kill (1985)
TV: The Saint
Moore, Stanford: 7 chemist 8 Nobelist
Moore, Terry: 7 actress
film: Beneath the 12 Mile Reef (1953)
Come Back, Little Sheba (1952)
Mighty Joe Young (1949)
Shack Out on 101 (1955)
spouse: Howard Hughes
Moore, Thomas: 4 poet 5 Irish
work: Lalla Rookh
Moore, Victor: 5 actor
film: Make Way for Tomorrow (1937)
Swing Time (1936)
We're Not Married (1952)
moorfowl: 4 bird
relative: 5 poult, quail, snipe 6 chukar, grouse, peahen, turkey 7 peacock 8 curassow, pheasant, woodcock 9 partridge 10 wild turkey
Moorhead: 4 city, town
locale: 9 Minnesota
mooring: 6 harbor 7 harbour, landing 9 anchorage
line: 6 hawser
place: 4 cove, dock, pier 5 berth, inlet, layby, wharf
post: 4 bitt 7 bollard
mooring __: 4 buoy, mast, rack 5 screw, tower
Moorish: 5 style
drum: 6 atabal
faith: 5 Islam
money: 8 maravedi
Moorish __: 4 arch, idol
Moorpark: 4 city, town
locale: 10 California
moose: 6 animal, cervid, mammal 10 Bullwinkle

ender: 4 bird, wood
feature: 6 antler
female: 3 cow
genus: 5 alces
male: 4 bull
relative: 3 elk, roe 4 axis, deer, pudu, shou, sika 6 chital, guemal, hangul, huemul, sambar, sambur, thamin, wapiti 7 brocket, caribou, muntjac, muntjak, sambhar, sambhur 8 reindeer 9 barasingh
young: 4 calf
Moosehead: 4 lake
locale: 5 Maine
Moose Jaw: 4 city, town
locale: 4 Sask. 6 Canada
moosemilk: 5 drink 8 beverage, cocktail
ingredient: 3 rum 4 milk 7 whiskey
__ Moose Party: 4 Bull
moot: 4 open 7 at issue, dubious, suspect 8 academic, arguable, doubtful, forensic 9 debatable, uncertain, undecided, unsettled 10 disputable, irrelevant, unresolved
moot __: 4 hall 5 court, point
__ moo, there...: 5 Here a
mop: 3 rub 4 dust, hair, mane, swab, swob, wash, wipe 5 clean, scrub, shock, sweep 6 duster, soak up, sponge, tangle, thatch 7 tresses
like a ~: 6 shaggy, unruly
starter: 4 roll
the floor with: 4 rout 6 defeat
up: 4 swab, swob, whip 5 clean 6 absorb, finish 9 finish off
__ mop: 3 dry, wet 4 dust
__-mop: 4 damp
__ Mop: 3 Rag
mope: 4 ache, fret, idle, moon, pine, pout, stew, sulk 5 bleed, brood, chafe, droop, grump, piner, sweat, yearn 6 grieve, lament, linger, pouter, regret, repine, sulker 7 brooder, despair, grumble 8 languish, sourpuss 9 gloomy Gus, lose heart, waste time 10 take it hard
moped: 4 bike 9 motorbike
kin: 5 cycle 10 motorcycle
user: 5 rider
mopes: 5 gloom 7 sadness 8 glumness
mopey: 3 low, sad 4 blue, down, glum 5 moody, sulky 6 broody, sullen 7 forlorn, hangdog, joyless 8 dejected, downcast, listless 9 cheerless, depressed, long-faced, woebegone 10 despondent, dispirited, melancholy, out of sorts
Mop & Glo: 7 cleaner
alternative: 5 Brite, Lysol 6 Top Job 7 Lestoil, Mr. Clean, Pine Sol 9 Fantastik, Step Saver
mopish: 5 moody 6 broody, gloomy 8 dejected, listless
__ M-O-P-P...: 4 R-A-G-G
moppet: 3 kid, tot 4 tike, tyke 5 child, kiddy, youth 6 cherub 9 youngster
mopping: 5 chore 9 housework
Mopsus: 4 seer 8 Argonaut
father of ~: 6 Apollo
mop the __ with: 5 floor
Mopti: 4 city, town
locale: 3 Afr. 4 Mali 6 Africa
mopus: 3 oof 4 cash, gelt, jack, kail, kale, loot, peag, pelf 5 bills, bread, bucks, dough, funds, lucre, moola, pesos, rhino, sewan 6 dinero, do-re-mi, mammon, mazuma, moolah, seawan, silver, specie, wampum, wealth 7 cabbage, capital, dollars, lettuce, ooftish, scratch, shekels 8 bankroll, cold cash, currency, hard cash, smackers 9 banknotes, frogskins, long green, simoleons 10 greenbacks, green stuff

moquette: 6 fabric 8 material
Moraes, Dom: 4 poet 6 Indian 10 journalist
moraine: 5 ridge
__ moraine: 6 medial 7 lateral
moral: 3 saw 4 fine, good, just, meet, nice, okay, pure, rule 5 adage, axiom, clean, gnome, great, legit, maxim, motto, noble, point, right 6 chaste, decent, dictum, honest, kasher, kindly, kosher, lesson, modest, proper, saying, seemly, square, truism, worthy 7 correct, dutiful, epigram, ethical, message, precept, proverb, saintly, upright 8 all right, aphorism, decorous, elevated, laudable, pleasant, pleasing, splendid, straight, superior, true-blue, truthful, virtuous 9 admirable, agreeable, blameless, courteous, excellent, exemplary, high-toned, honorable, religious, reputable, righteous, wholesome, wonderful 10 aboveboard, acceptable, apophthegm, beneficial, creditable, folk wisdom, goody-goody, high-minded, inculcable, principled, scrupulous, upstanding
error: 3 sin 5 lapse
fiber: 4 grit, guts, will 5 pluck, spine, spunk, valor 6 mettle, spirit 7 bravery, courage 8 backbone, firmness, tenacity 9 fortitude, toughness 10 resolution
principle: 5 ethic, honor 6 ethics
sense: 8 superego 10 conscience, small voice
tale with a ~: 5 fable 7 apology 8 apologue
moral __: 5 sense 6 hazard 7 support
morale: 5 heart 6 esprit, mettle, spirit 7 outlook, resolve 8 attitude, optimism 9 character 10 confidence
Morales, Esai: 5 actor
film: Bad Boys (1983)
La Bamba (1987)
My Family/Mi Familia (1995)
The Wonderful Ice Cream Suit (1999)
TV: N.Y.P.D. Blue
Moralia author: Plutarch
moralist: 4 Cato, Esop 5 Aesop
moralistic: 8 virtuous
morality: 4 good 5 honor, mores, right 6 ethics, ideals, purity, virtue 7 conduct, decency, honesty, justice, probity 8 chastity, goodness 9 integrity, principle, rectitude, rightness, standards 10 gentleness, good habits, honestness, principles, worthiness
morality __: 4 play
moralization: 6 homily
moralize: 6 preach 7 lecture 9 exprobate
morally: 9 honorably 10 virtuously
morals: 5 ethic, mores 6 ideals, values 7 customs 8 behavior, policies, scruples, standard 9 standards 10 principles
Moran: 4 Bugs, Erin 5 Julie
contemporary: 6 Capone
Moranis, Rick: 5 actor
film: Honey, I Blew Up the Kid (1992)
Honey, I Shrunk the Kids (1989)
Little Shop of Horrors (1986)
My Blue Heaven (1990)
Parenthood (1989)
Spaceballs (1987)
Streets of Fire (1984)
__ Morant: 7 Breaker
Morante, Elsa: 4 poet 6 writer 7 Italian
morass: 3 bog, fen, web 4 maze, mire 5 marsh, snarl, swamp 6 tangle 7 lowland 8 quagmire 9 labyrinth

Morath: 3 Max **4** Inge
Morath, Max: 7 pianist
moratorium: 5 pause, truce **7** respite **9** white flag
Morava: 5 river
  locale: 10 Yugoslavia
Moravia: 6 Albert
  old capital of ~: 4 Brno
Moravia, Albert: 6 writer **7** Italian
  pen name of: Alberto Pincherle
  work: The Fancy Dress Party
    Two Women
Moravian: 4 Slav **5** Czech
moray: 3 eel **4** fish
  catcher: 5 eeler **6** eelpot
  home: 3 sea **5** ocean **6** eelery
  kin: 6 conger
  like a ~: 4 eely
  young ~: 5 elver
Moray Firth locale: 8 North Sea, Scotland
morbid: 4 dark, grim, sick **5** moody **6** gloomy, grisly, horrid, sickly, somber **7** ghastly, hideous, macaber, macabre, unsound **8** aberrant, abnormal, brooding, ghoulish, gruesome **9** depressed, frightful, monstrous, saturnine, unhealthy, unnatural **10** despondent, melancholy
mordancy: 6 malice, rancor **8** acerbity, acrimony **10** bitterness
mordant: 4 acid **5** acerb **6** biting, ireful, severe **7** caustic, cutting, pungent, satiric **8** derisive, incisive, sardonic, scornful **9** sarcastic, satirical, trenchant
Mordecai: 7 Richler **10** Anielewicz
  cousin of ~: 6 Esther
mordent relative: 5 trill
more: 3 and, new, too, yet **4** also, else, over **5** extra, fresh, major, other, spare, wider **6** as well, better, beyond, encore, higher, larger, longer **7** another, besides, farther, further, greater, heavier **8** enhanced, expanded, extended, likewise **9** along with, augmented, exceeding, increased **10** additional, in addition
  combining form: 4 pleo-, plio **5** pleio-
  ender: 4 over
  excellent: 5 finer **6** enrich, fitter **7** enhance, greater, surpass, upgrade **8** improved, souped up, stronger, superior, worthier **9** healthier, sharpened **10** preferable
  in music: 3 piu
  in Spanish: 3 más
  make ~ inclusive: 6 expand, spread **7** augment, broaden, enlarge
  no ~: 4 once, stop **5** kaput **6** lapsed
  no ~ than: 4 just, mere, only **6** at most, merely
  nothing ~ than: 4 just **6** merely, simply, solely, wholly **7** totally, utterly **8** entirely
  often than not: 6 simply **7** as a rule, usually **8** commonly, normally **9** naturally **10** ordinarily
  once ~: 4 anew, over **5** again **6** afresh, de novo, encore
  one or ~: 3 any
  or less: 4 near **5** quite, sorta **6** approx., around, fairly, kind of, nearly, rather, sort of **8** slightly, somewhat
  prefix: 5 super-
  provide ~: 6 refill **9** replenish
  recent: 6 latter **9** following
  starter: 3 any **4** ever **5** never **7** further
  than: 4 over **5** above **6** beyond **7** besides **9** upwards of
  than a few: 4 gobs, lots, much, tons **5** heaps, piles, scads **6** oodles, plenty, scores **7** copious, umpteen **8** abundant, numerous **9** bountiful, multitude, thousands
  than a little: 4 much **5** amply, quite **6** deeply, highly, hugely, unduly, vastly **7** greatly, largely, only too, rabidly **8** terribly **9** decidedly, extremely, seriously, unusually **10** enormously, incredibly, profoundly, remarkably, thoroughly, uncommonly
  than enough: 5 ample, spare, undue **6** excess, galore, oodles
  than one: 3 plu. **4** plur., some **5** group **6** plural
  to minimalists: 4 less
  what's ~: 3 and **4** also, plus **7** besides
more ___ meets the eye: 4 than
___ more: 6 less is
More: 6 Thomas **7** Kenneth
More ___ Feeling: 5 Than a
More ___ You Know: 4 Than
More ___ You, The: 4 I See
More!: 6 encore
Moreau, Jeanne: 7 actress
  film: The Bride Wore Black (1968)
    Chimes at Midnight (1967)
    Diary of a Chambermaid (1964)
    Eva (1962)
    Jules and Jim (1961)
    The Last Tycoon (1976)
    The Lovers (1958)
    Monte Walsh (1970)
    The Summer House (1993)
    The Train (1965)
  spouse: William Friedkin
More deadly than ___ dog's tooth: 4 a mad
More Die of Heartbreak author: Saul Bellow
moreen: 6 fabric **8** material
More I See You, The composer: 6 Gordon, Warren
morel: 6 fungus **8** mushroom
Morelia: 4 city, town
  locale: 6 Mexico **9** Michoacán
Morel, Jean: 6 French **9** conductor
Morella author: Edgar Allan Poe
morello: 4 tree **6** cherry
  relative: 4 Bing **7** marasca, oxheart
Morelos: 5 state **7** Mexican
  city: 7 Cuautla, Jojutla, Temixco **8** Apatlaco, Jiutepec, Yautepec **9** Zacatepec **10** Cuernavaca
More Love (1980 song) artist: Kim Carnes
___ More Night: 3 One
More Nonsense Songs author: Edward Lear
Moreno, Rita: 7 actress
  film: The Boss's Son (1978)
    Carnal Knowledge (1971)
    The Four Seasons (1981)
    The King and I (1956)
    Popi (1969)
    The Ring (1952)
    West Side Story (1961, AA)
Moreno Valley: 4 city, town
  locale: 10 California
Morenz: 5 Howie
more or ___: 4 less
moreover: 3 and, too, yet **4** also **5** again **6** as well, to boot **7** besides, further **8** likewise **10** in addition
More powerful ___ locomotive: 5 than a
mores: 5 ethos **6** ethics, morals, values **7** culture, customs, manners **8** folkways, morality, niceties **9** ethnology, propriety, tradition
More (song) artist: Kai Winding, Perry Como
more than ___ the eye: 5 meets
More Than a Feeling (1976 song) artist: Boston
More Than Ever (1991 song) artist: Nelson
More Than I Can Say (1980 song) artist: Leo Sayer
more than one way to skin ___: 4 a cat
More Than That (2001 song) artist: Backstreet Boys
More Than Words Can Say (1990 song) artist: Alias
More the Merrier, The (1943 film)
  cast: Jean Arthur, Charles Coburn, Joel McCrea
  director: George Stevens
More, Thomas: 3 Sir **5** saint **6** writer **7** British **8** essayist, humanist **9** statesman
  work: Utopia
___ more time!: 3 One
Morey: 9 Amsterdam
Morgan: 2 J.P. **3** Gil, Joe, Rex **4** Earp, Jane, Russ **5** Debbi, Frank, Harry, Helen, Henry, horse **6** Dennis, Lorrie, Thomas **7** Charles, Freeman **8** Brittany **9** Fairchild
  brother of ~: 5 Wyatt **6** Virgil
  marking: 4 star
Morgan ___: 7 Stanley
Morgan! (1966 film)
  cast: Vanessa Redgrave, Robert Stevens, David Warner
  director: Karel Reisz
Morgana: 4 King
___ Morgana: 4 Fata
Morgan, Charles: 6 writer **7** British **10** playwright
Morgan, Dennis: 5 actor
  film: Bad Men of Missouri (1941)
    Captains of the Clouds (1942)
    Christmas in Connecticut (1945)
    The Hard Way (1942)
    Kitty Foyle (1940)
    Thank Your Lucky Stars (1943)
Morgan, Frank: 5 actor
  film: Bombshell (1933)
    The Cat and the Fiddle (1934)
    The Good Fairy (1935)
    Hallelujah, I'm a Bum (1933)
    The Human Comedy (1943)
    Lady Luck (1946)
    Reunion in Vienna (1933)
    The Shop Around the Corner (1940)
    The Stratton Story (1949)
    Success at Any Price (1934)
    Trouble for Two (1936)
    The Vanishing Virginian (1942)
    The Wizard of Oz (1939)
Morgan, Gil: 6 golfer
  milieu: 5 links **6** course
  org.: 3 PGA
Morgan, Harry: 5 actor
  film: Dragnet (1987)
    Frankie and Johnny (1966)
    The Well (1951)
  TV: Dragnet, MASH
Morgan Hill: 4 city, town
  locale: 10 California
morganite: 3 gem **8** gemstone
Morgan, Jane song: Fascination (1957)
Morgan, Jaye P.
  song: Chee Chee-oo Chee (1955)
    If You Don't Want My Love (1955)
    The Longest Walk (1955)
    Pepper-Hot Baby (1955)
    That's All I Want from You (1954)
    Two Lost Souls (1955)
  TV: The Gong Show
Morgan's Passing author: Anne Tyler
Morgan, Thomas: 8 Nobelist
Morgantown: 4 city
  locale: 3 W. Va.
  school: 3 WVU
Morgenstern: 3 Ida **5** Rhoda
Morgenthau: 5 Henry
Moriarty: 5 Cathy **7** Michael
Moriarty, Cathy: 7 actress
  film: Crazy in Alabama (1999)
    Matinee (1993)
    Neighbors (1981)
    Raging Bull (1980)
    Soapdish (1991)
    White of the Eye (1987)
Moriarty, Michael: 5 actor
  film: Bang the Drum Slowly (1973)
    Pale Rider (1985)
    Q (1982)
    Who'll Stop the Rain (1978)
moribund: 8 stagnant
Mörike, Eduard: 4 poet **6** German
Morini, Erika: 8 Austrian **9** violinist
Mori Ōgai: 6 writer **8** Japanese
  work: The Abe Family
    The Wild Geese
Morioka: 4 city, town
  locale: 5 Japan
Morissette, Alanis
  homeland: Canada
  song: Hand in My Pocket (1995)
    Head over Feet (1997)
    Ironic (1996)
    Thank U (1998)
    Uninvited (1998)
    You Learn (1996)
    You Oughta Know (1995)
Morita: 3 Pat **4** Akio
Moritat (1956 song) artist: Dick Hyman
___ Moritz: 5 Saint
Mork: 2 ET **5** alien
  spaceship: 3 egg
Mork & Mindy (ABC sitcom)
  cast: Pam Dawber (Mindy McConnell)
    Ralph James (Orson)
    Conrad Janis (Frederick McConnell)
    Tom Poston (Mr. Bickley)
    Robin Williams (Mork)
    Jonathan Winters (Mearth)
  Mork's home: Ork
  Mork's word: nanu
  setting: Boulder, Colorado
Morley: 5 Karen, Safer **6** Robert **9** Callaghan
Morley, Christopher: 6 author, writer
  founder of: Saturday Review
  work: Kitty Foyle
    Parnassus on Wheels
Morley, Robert: 5 actor
  film: The African Queen (1951)
    Around the World in 80 Days (1956)
    The Battle of the Sexes (1960)
    The Boys (1961)
    Major Barbara (1941)
    Murder at the Gallop (1963)
    Topkapi (1964)
    Who Is Killing the Great Chefs of Europe? (1978)
Morlocks' prey: 4 Eloi
Mormon ___: 6 Church **7** cricket
Mormons: 3 LDS
  manna: 4 sego
  official: 5 elder
  predecessor: 3 Ute
  state: 4 Utah
morn
  opposite: 3 eve
  see also morning
Mornay: 5 sauce
Mornay, Rebecca De: 7 actress
  film: Backdraft (1991)
    The Hand That Rocks the Cradle (1992)
    Risky Business (1983)
    Runaway Train (1985)
___ Morne National Park: 4 Gros
Mornin' Beautiful (1975 song) artist: Tony Orlando & Dawn

morning: **2** a.m. **4** dawn **5** early, light, prime, sunup **6** aurora, morrow **7** sunrise **8** cockcrow, daybreak, daylight, forenoon **9** dayspring **10** break of day, first blush
activity: **5** shave
and afternoon: **6** all day
beverage: **3** tea **5** latte **6** coffee
draw toward ~: **5** laten
early ~: **3** one, two **4** dawn, five, four **5** one a.m., sunup, three, two a.m. **6** five a.m., four a.m. **7** sunrise, three a.m. **8** wee hours
every ~: **5** daily **7** diurnal, regular, routine **9** quotidian
follower: **3** aft. **4** noon **9** afternoon
good ~ in French: **7** bon jour
good ~ in German: **8** guten tag
good ~ in Japanese: **5** ohayo
good ~ in Spanish: **10** buenos días
greet the ~: **4** rise, wake **5** arise, awake, get up, waken **6** awaken
hour: **3** six, ten **4** nine **5** eight, seven, six a.m., ten a.m. **6** eleven, nine a.m. **7** eight a.m., seven a.m. **8** eleven a.m.
like ~ air: **5** brisk
like grass in the ~: **3** wet **4** damp, dewy **5** moist
meal: **6** brunch **9** breakfast
mist: **3** fog **4** haze
moisture: **3** dew
poem: **6** aubade
prayer: **5** matin
prefix for ~: **3** mid
service: **5** terce
sound: **5** alarm
morning ___: **3** gun **4** coat, line, loan, star **5** dress, glory, watch
___ morning: **4** good
Morning ___: **5** Glory, Train **6** Prayer
Morning ___, The: **5** After, Watch
___ Morning: **5** April, Every **6** Sunday **7** Chelsea
Morning After, The (1973 song) artist: Maureen McGovern
___ Morning, America: **4** Good
Morning Edition network: **3** NPR
morning glory: **5** plant **6** flower
dried ~ root: **5** jalap
Morning Glory (1933 film)
cast: Douglas Fairbanks Jr., Katharine Hepburn, Adolphe Menjou
flower: **5** calla
Morning Has Broken (1972 song)
artist: Cat Stevens
Morning News: **5** paper **9** newspaper
locale: **6** Dallas
Morning Noon and Night author: Sidney Sheldon
___ morning quarterback: **6** Monday
___ Morning Rain: **5** Early
Morning Side of the Mountain (1974 song) artist: Donny and Marie Osmond
Mornings in Mexico author: D.H. Lawrence
___ Morning Starshine: **4** Good
Morning Train (1981 song) artist: Sheena Easton
___ Morning, Vietnam: **4** Good
Morning Watch, The author: James Agee
Moro: **4** Aldo **5** César **7** Malayan **8** Filipino
morocco ___: **7** leather
___ morocco: **6** Levant
Morocco: **6** nation **7** country
capital: **5** Rabat
city: **3** Fez **4** Ujda **5** Oujda, Rabat **6** Agadir, Meknes, Oudjda **7** Tangier **8** Tangiers **9** Marrakesh **10** Casablanca
desert: **6** Sahara
group: **10** Arab League
money: **6** dirham
mount: **5** camel
mountain: **5** Atlas **7** Toubkal
neighbor: **5** Spain **7** Algeria **14** Gibraltar. Medit.
people: **4** Riff **5** Shilh
port: **4** Safi **5** Rabat, Saffi **6** Agadir **7** Tangier **8** Tangiers **10** Casablanca
region: **3** Rif **4** Ifni
writer: **10** Ben Jelloun
Morocco (1930 film)
cast: Gary Cooper, Marlene Dietrich, Adolphe Menjou
director: Josef von Sternberg
Moro, César: **4** poet **8** Peruvian
Moroder: **7** Giorgio
Morogoro: **4** city, town
locale: **8** Tanzania
Moroleón: **4** city, town
locale: **6** Mexico **10** Guanajuato
Moron: **4** city, town
locale: **9** Argentina
Moroni: **4** city, town **5** angel **7** capital
locale: **7** Comoros
morose: **3** low, sad **4** blue, dark, dour, down, glum, grim, sick, sour, ugly **5** brusk, cross, gruff, harsh, moody, sulky, surly, testy, woful **6** broody, crabby, cranky, gloomy, moping, sickly, somber, sullen, woeful **7** brusque, crabbed, doleful, grouchy, joyless, peevish, unhappy **8** choleric, churlish, dejected, downcast, frowning, liverish, mournful, perverse, snappish, taciturn, troubled **9** bummed out, cheerless, depressed, heartsick, irritable, miserable, saturnine, sorrowful, splenetic, woebegone **10** chapfallen, despondent, dispirited, ill-humored, lugubrious, melancholy
be ~: **4** sulk
Moross: **6** Jerome
morph: **6** change
into: **6** become
starter: **4** ecto, endo, meso
morpheme: **4** word
Morpheus, father of: **6** Hypnos
morphology: **7** grammar, science **9** structure
Morphy, Paul game: **5** chess
Morricone, Ennio: **7** Italian **8** composer
morris: **5** dance
Morris: **3** cat, Jan, pet **4** Greg, Phil, West **5** Anita, Cohen, Errol, Wayne **6** Albert, Howard, Willie, Wright **7** Chester, Garrett, Stoloff, William **9** Carnovsky
Morris ___: **5** chair
Morris, Chester: **5** actor
film: The Big House (1930)
Blind Spot (1947)
Boston Blackie Goes Hollywood (1942)
Confessions of Boston Blackie (1941)
The Divorcée (1930)
Five Came Back (1939)
Flight From Glory (1937)
Meet Boston Blackie (1941)
One Mysterious Night (1944)
Red-Headed Woman (1932)
Secret Command (1944)
Three Godfathers (1936)
Morris, Jack: **6** hurler **7** pitcher
Morris, Jan: **6** writer **7** British **10** journalist
Morris Jesup: **4** cape
locale: **9** Greenland
Morrison: **3** Jim, Van **4** Jane, Mark, Toni **5** Waite
Morrison, Jim: **4** Door
Morrison, Toni: **6** author, writer **8** Nobelist
work: Beloved
The Bluest Eye
Jazz
Paradise
Song of Solomon
Sula
Tar Baby
Morrison, Van
homeland: Ireland
song: Blue Money (1971)
Brown Eyed Girl (1967)
Come Running (1970)
Domino (1970)
Wild Night (1971)
Morristown: **4** city
locale: **9** New Jersey, Tennessee
Morris, William: **4** poet **6** agency, artist **7** British, printer **8** designer **9** architect
employee: **3** rep **5** agent
Morris, Wright: **6** author, writer
work: Love Among the Cannibals
The Works of Love
Morro Bay: **4** city, town
locale: **10** California
Morro Castle site: **4** Cuba **6** Havana
morrow: **4** morn **7** morning
Morrow: **3** Rob, Vic
Morrow, Vic: **5** actor
film: The Bad News Bears (1976)
Blackboard Jungle (1955)
Humanoids From the Deep (1980)
TV: Combat
Morse: **5** Barry, David, Wayne **6** Robert, Samuel
invention: **4** code **9** telegraph
Morse ___: **4** code, lamp
Morse code
code unit: **3** dah, dit, dot **4** dash
e, in ~: **3** dit, dot
message: **3** SOS
send ~: **3** tap
sound: **5** click
t, in ~: **3** dah **4** dash
Morse, David: **5** actor
film: Crazy in Alabama (1999)
The Green Mile (1999)
The Indian Runner (1991)
The Negotiator (1998)
Personal Foul (1987)
Proof of Life (2000)
morsel: **3** bit, ort **4** atom, bite, drop, hunk, iota, lump, nosh, part, snip **5** chunk, crumb, grain, piece, scrap, slice, snack, taste, treat **6** nibble, sample, tidbit **7** portion, soupçon **8** delicacy, fraction, fragment, mouthful, particle, spoonful
Morse, Robert: **5** actor
film: A Guide for the Married Man (1967)
How to Succeed in Business Without Really Trying (1967)
The Loved Ones (1965)
Mort: **4** Sahl **6** Walker **7** Drucker, Lindsey
mortadella: **4** meat **7** Italian, sausage
mortal: **3** man **4** body, soul **5** alive, being, great, human, woman **6** finite, person **7** animate, earthly, passing **8** creature, temporal **9** earthborn, earthling, ephemeral, transient **10** evanescent, individual, inexpiable
mortal ___: **3** sin
Mortal Fear author: Greg Iles, Robin Cook
Mortal Storm, The (1940 film)
cast: James Stewart, Margaret Sullavan, Robert Young
director: Frank Borzage
mortar: **3** gun **5** grout **6** cannon, cement
mixer: **3** rab
support: **5** bipod
trough: **3** hod
mortarboard: **3** cap
Morte d'Arthur: **4** poem
author: **8** Tennyson
Mortensen, Viggo: **5** actor
film: 28 Days (2000)
G.I. Jane (1997)
The Indian Runner (1991)
The Lord of the Rings: The Fellowship of The Ring (2001)
A Perfect Murder (1998)
A Walk on the Moon (1999)
mortgage: **3** IOU **4** debt, lien, loan **6** credit, red ink **9** liability
bearer: **4** ower **6** lienee
datum: **3** APR **4** rate **7** payment
get a ~: **3** owe **6** borrow
grant a ~: **4** lend, loan
issuer: **3** FHA **4** bank, FNMA, GNMA **5** S and L **6** lienor
second ~ to brokers: **4** refi
___ mortgage: **5** first **6** second **7** balloon, chattel, reverse, takeout
mortgaged: **6** in debt **8** indebted
Morticia: **6** Addams
cousin: **3** Itt
husband: **5** Gomez
to Fester: **5** niece
mortification: **8** distress **9** abashment
mortified: **5** stern **6** aghast **7** abashed **8** sheepish
mortify: **4** deny **5** abash, appal, shame **6** appall, humble, rankle **7** chagrin, chasten, deflate **8** belittle, confound, disgrace, ridicule, take down **9** discomfit, embarrass, humiliate **10** disgruntle, put to shame
mortifying: **8** shameful
Mortimer: **5** Adler, Snerd **8** Penelope
voice of ~: **5** Edgar
Mortimer, Penelope: **6** writer **7** British
work: The Pumpkin Eater
mortise: **6** fasten **8** junction, juncture
partner: **5** tenon
mortise ___: **4** lock **5** block, joint **6** chisel
Morton: **3** Joe **4** Levi, salt **5** Gould **6** Downey **7** Da Costa, Feldman, Janklow, William
Morton Grove: **4** city, town
locale: **8** Illinois
Morton, Jelly Roll: **7** pianist
genre: **4** jazz
Morton, Joe: **5** actor
film: Blues Brothers 2000 (1998)
Bounce (2000)
The Brother From Another Planet (1984)
City of Hope (1991)
Dragonfly (2002)
___ Morton Stanley: **5** Henry
mos.
every 12 ~: **4** yrly.
3 ~: **3** qtr.
mosaic: **3** mix **4** tile **5** inlay **6** inlaid **7** mixture **8** speckled
detail: **5** inset
mosaic ___: **3** map **4** gold **5** glass **6** vision
Mosaic ___: **3** Law
mosaic gold: **5** alloy
component: **4** zinc **6** copper
Mosconi, Willie
game: **4** pool
prop: **3** cue **4** rack **5** chalk **6** bridge
Moscow: **4** city, town **7** capital
athletes: **7** Vandals
city near ~: **4** Orel **5** Gorki, Kirov
department store: **3** GUM
locale: **5** Idaho **6** Russia
school: **3** Ida. **5** Idaho
Moscow ___ Theater: **3** Art
Moscow mule: **5** drink **8** beverage, cocktail
ingredient: **5** vodka **9** lime juice **10** ginger beer

Moscow on the Hudson (1984 film)
cast: Maria Conchita Alonso, Alejandro Rey, Robin Williams
director: Paul Mazursky
Mose: 7 Allison
Mosè composer: 7 Rossini
Mosel: 3 Tad 5 river
city on the ~: 7 Coblenz, Koblenz
locale: 7 Germany
Moselle: 4 wine 5 river, white
city on the ~: 4 Metz 5 Trier 6 Épinal, Treves
locale: 6 France
river to the ~: 4 Saar
Moses: 4 Gunn 5 Edwin 6 Malone
attire: 4 robe
book of ~: 3 Lev. 4 Deut., Exod. 6 Exodus 7 Genesis, Numbers. 9 Leviticus
books of ~: 4 Tora 5 Torah
brother of ~: 5 Aaron
father-in-law of ~: 6 Jethro
grandson of ~: 8 Jonathan, Rehabiah
mountain: 5 Sinai
parent of ~: 5 Amram 8 Jochebed
sister of ~: 6 Miriam
son of ~: 7 Eliezer, Gershom
uncle of ~: 6 Hebron
where baby ~ was found: 6 rushes
wife of ~: 8 Zipporah
__ Moses: 4 Amos, holy 5 Law of 7 Grandma
Moses author: Sholem Asch
Moses, Grandma: 4 Anna 6 artist 7 painter
Moses und __: 4 Aron
mosey: 2 go 3 lag 4 idle, laze, loaf, move, poke 5 amble, dally, drift, stall, tarry 6 dawdle, linger, loiter, sashay, stroll 7 saunter 8 lollygag, straggle 9 waste time 10 dillydally
mosh: 9 slam-dance
mosh __: 3 pit
Moshe: 5 Dayan 7 Sharett
Moshi: 4 city, town
locale: 8 Tanzania
Moslem
Almighty: 5 Allah
ascetic: 4 Sufi 5 faker, fakir, faqir 6 faquir
bridge to paradise: 5 sirat
call from a ~: 4 azan
cap: 3 taj
edict: 5 irade
festival: 6 Bairam
garment: 4 izar 5 burga, burka, ihram, jibba 6 burkha, chadar, chador, jubbah 7 bourkha, chaddar, chuddar
high-ranking ~ woman: 5 begum
holy book: 5 Koran, Quran
holy man: 4 imam 5 imaum, mulla 6 mullah
holy place: 5 Mecca 6 Medina
household: 5 haram, harem, harim 6 hareem
judge: 4 cadi, kadi, qadi, qaid 5 mufti
law: 5 sunna
messiah: 5 Mahdi
miracle: 5 miraj
month: 4 Rabi 5 Rajab, Safar 6 Jumada, Shaban 7 Ramadan, Shawwal 8 Muharram 9 Dhu al-Qa'da 10 Dhu al-Hijja
nymph: 5 houri
of a ~ sect: 5 Sufic
people: 5 Kazak 6 Kazakh
physician: 5 hakim
pilgrimage: 3 haj 4 hadj, hajj
pilgrimage center: 4 Kufa
ritual: 4 raka
ruler: 3 aga 4 agha, amir, emir 5 ameer, calif, emeer, kalif, mogul 6 caliph, kaliph, khalif
saint: 3 pir
scholar: 4 imam 5 imaum
scholars: 5 ulama, ulema
sect: 4 Shi'i 5 Sunni
shrine: 4 Kaba 5 Kaaba, Kabah 6 Kaabah
soldier: 5 ghazi
student: 5 softa
temple: 6 mosque
title: 5 sayid
weight: 4 rotl
world: 5 Islam
Mosque of __: 4 Omar
mosquito: 3 bug 4 fern, pest 5 biter, culex 6 insect
barrier: 3 net
combining form: 5 culic- 6 culici-
genus: 5 aedes
like a ~ bite: 5 itchy
sound: 4 buzz 5 whine
young: 5 nymph
mosquito __: 3 net 4 bite, boat, fern, hawk 5 fleet 7 netting
__ mosquito: 5 tiger
Mosquito Coast, The: 4 film 5 novel
author: Paul Theroux
cast: Harrison Ford, Helen Mirren, River Phoenix
character: 5 Allie
director: Peter Weir
mosquito-like insect: 5 midge
moss: 5 color, plant, pyxie 6 lichen 8 sphagnum 9 bryophyte
combining form: 3 bry- 4 bryo-, musc- 5 musci-, -musco
ender: 4 back 5 grown 6 bunker
science: 8 bryology
source: 4 peat
undersea: 6 obelia
moss __: 4 rose 5 agate, green 6 animal 7 campion
__ moss: 3 bog, sea, sun 4 club, long, peat, rose 5 beard, dyer's, house, Irish, scale, spike 6 Ceylon 7 Florida, Iceland, Spanish
Moss: 4 Hart, Kate 6 Arnold 8 Stirling 10 Carrie-Anne
mossback: 4 fogy 5 fogey 7 diehard
Mössbauer, Rudolf: 6 German 8 Nobelist 9 physicist
Mosses From an Old __: 5 Manse
moss-grown: 8 out of use
Mossi home: 6 Africa
mosslike: 5 peaty
plant: 5 sedum, usnea
mosso: 6 motion
__ mosso: 4 meno
mosspink: 5 plant 6 flower
mossy: 9 overgrown 10 antiquated
most: 3 max, too 4 best, bulk, much, nigh, very 6 all but, almost, nearly, utmost 7 biggest, greatly, highest, largest, maximum 8 about all, greatest, majority, ultimate, well-nigh 9 extremely, nearly all, plurality 10 lion's share
in Spanish: 3 más
opposite: 5 least
starter: 3 aft, end, top 4 head, hind, left 5 after, inner, lower, outer, right, stern, upper, utter 6 bottom, hinder, hither, middle 7 eastern, farther, further, western
most __ list: 6 wanted
most-__-nation: 7 favored
Most: 5 Donny
Most __ Fella, The: 5 Happy
mostaccioli: 5 pasta
alternative: 4 orzo, ziti 5 penne 6 noodle 7 lasagna, lasagne, pastina, ravioli 8 bucatini, couscous, farfalle, linguine, linguini, macaroni, rigatoni 9 agnolotti, angelhair, cavatelli, manicotti, spaghetti 10 cannelloni, fettuccini, tortellini, vermicelli
Mostar: 4 city, town
locale: 6 Bosnia
Most Beautiful Girl in the World, The (1994 song) artist: Prince
Most Beautiful Girl in the World, The composer: 4 Hart 7 Rodgers
Most Beautiful Girl, The (1973 song) artist: Charlie Rich
Most Dangerous Game, The (1932 film)
cast: Leslie Banks, Joel McCrea, Fay Wray
Mostel: 4 Josh, Zero
Mostel, Zero: 5 actor
film: The Angel Levine (1970) The Enforcer (1951) The Front (1976) Mastermind (1976) The Producers (1968)
most-favored-__: 6 nation
__ Most Foul: 6 Murder
Most Happy Fella, The: 7 musical
songwriter: 7 Loesser
__ Most Likely, The: 4 Girl
mostly: 5 often 6 mainly 7 as a rule, chiefly, largely, overall, usually 8 above all 9 generally, primarily, regularly 10 frequently, on the whole
Most of It, The author: Robert Frost
__ Most Unusual Day: 4 It's a
Most Valuable Player: 5 award
most wanted __: 4 list
Most Wanted
agcy.: 3 FBI
subject: 5 felon
Mosul: 4 city, town
locale: 4 Irak, Iraq
mot: 4 word 6 French
bon ~: 3 pun 4 jest, joke, quip 6 remark, zinger 7 epigram 8 laconism, repartee, wordplay 9 wisecrack, witticism 10 pleasantry
polite ~: 5 merci
mot __: 5 juste
__ mot: 3 bon
Motagua: 5 river
locale: 9 Guatemala
Mota, Manny sport: 8 baseball
mote: 3 bit, dot, jot 4 atom, iota, whit 5 crumb, fleck, grain 7 modicum 8 flyspeck, molecule, particle 9 scintilla
motel: 3 inn 5 court, lodge 7 Days Inn, lodging 8 lodgment, rest stop, stopover 9 Ramada Inn 10 Comfort Inn, Econo Lodge, Hampton Inn, Holiday Inn, motor court, motor lodge, Quality Inn, Red Roof Inn, Travelodge 11 Best Western
amenity: 2 AC 4 pool 5 Bible, sauna
approver: 3 AAA
freebie: 3 ice 4 soap 7 shampoo 9 sewing kit
offering: 2 rm. 4 room
on wheels: 2 RV
sign: 6 no pets 7 vacancy
__ Motel: 5 Roach
Motel 6 alternative: 7 Days Inn 9 Ramada Inn 10 Comfort Inn, Econo Lodge, Hampton Inn, Holiday Inn, Quality Inn, Red Roof Inn, Travelodge 11 Best Western
motes: 4 dust
motet: 5 music
moth: 2 lo 3 bug 5 egger 6 bogong, insect 8 bombycid
detractor: 5 cedar
ender: 4 ball 5 proof
lure: 5 flame
stage: 4 pupa 5 pupae
__ moth: 3 bee, wax 4 buck, hawk, luna 5 ghost, gypsy, owlet, peach, regal, swift, tiger, witch, yucca 6 cactus, carpet, potato, sphinx 7 cabbage, clothes, codling, emperor, leopard, tussock
mothball: 5 store 6 shelve 8 preserve
mothballed: 4 idle
moth-eaten: 3 old 4 worn 5 holey, mangy, musty, ratty, tatty, trite 6 mangey, ragged, shabby 8 obsolete, outdated, outmoded 9 hackneyed, out-of-date 10 threadbare
mother: 3 mom, nun, she 4 mama 5 mamma, mommy, woman 6 female, mommie, origin, parent, source 7 creator, kinsman 8 ancestor, forebear, relative 9 kinswoman, religious 10 progenitor
combining form: 4 matr- 5 matri-, matro-
directive: 3 eat 4 don't
ender: 4 land, wort 5 board
in French: 4 mère
in Italian: 7 madonna
in Spanish: 5 madre
kin: 5 enate
person without a ~: 3 Eve 4 Adam
sibling: 4 aunt 5 uncle
starter: 3 god 4 step 5 birth, grand, house
Whistler's ~ wear: 5 shawl
mother __: 3 hen, wit, yaw 4 lode, ship 5 earth, house 6 church, figure, liquor, tongue 7 country
mother __ bride: 5 of the
mother-__: 5 in-law
__ mother: 3 den 4 room 5 birth, earth, queen 6 foster
Mother __; 5 Goose, of God, o' Mine 6 Teresa 7 Goddess, Hubbard
Mother __ All, The: 4 of Us
Mother __ Tights: 4 Wore
Mother, __ I?: 3 may
__ Mother: 4 Holy, To My 6 Divine 7 Sylvia's
Mother and Child Reunion (1972 song) artist: Paul Simon
Mother Courage and Her Children author: Bertolt Brecht
Mother Goose dwelling: 4 shoe
Mother Goose Suite composer: 5 Ravel
motherhood: 9 maternity
motherhouse: 6 temple
mother-in-__: 3 law
Mother, Jugs & Speed (1976 film)
cast: Bill Cosby, Harvey Keitel, Raquel Welch
director: Peter Yates
motherly: 4 kind 8 maternal, parental 10 protective
mother-of-__: 5 pearl, thyme
mother of all living, The: 3 Eve
Mother of Cities, The: 4 Kiev
mother-of-pearl: 5 nacre
mother of the __: 5 bride
Mother of Us All, The composer: 7 Thomson
mother's __: 6 helper
Mother's __: 3 Day
Mothers and Sons author: Isabel Allende
__ Mother Should Know: 4 Your
Mother's Little Helper (1966 song) artist: Rolling Stones
mothers' org.: 4 MADD
__ Mothers' Son: 5 Every
mother superior: 6 cleric
counterpart: 5 abbot
Mother Teresa: 3 nun 8 Albanian, Nobelist
__ Mother, The: 4 Good
Mother Wore Tights (1947 film)
cast: Dan Dailey, Mona Freeman, Betty Grable

director: Walter Lang
motherwort: **5** plant **6** flower
__ Moths, The: **5** Gypsy
Moth, The author: James M. Cain
motif: **5** theme, topic **6** design, symbol **7** pattern, subject **9** arabesque
music ~: **4** riff, tema
motile: **6** mobile, moving
motility: **6** motion **8** movement
motion: **3** nod **4** flow, flux, move, sign, step, wave **5** drift **6** action, beckon, change, signal, stream, travel **7** advance, gesture, passage, transit **8** activity, dynamics, high sign, kinetics, mobility, motility, movement, progress, proposal, question, stirring **9** agitation, full swing **10** resolution, suggestion
be in ~: **4** move
circular ~: **4** gyre, spin **5** twist **8** gyration
combining form: **3** cin-, kin- **4** cino-, kine-, kino- **6** kinesi- **7** -cinesia, -kinesia, kinesio-
in ~: **5** about, afoot, astir **6** moving **7** kinetic **8** on the fly, stirring, underway **9** on the move
make a ~: **5** offer **7** propose
not in ~: **5** inert **6** at rest
picture: **3** pic **4** cine, film, show **5** flick, movie **6** talkie
pictures: **6** cinema
put in ~: **3** set **4** open, spur **5** begin, impel, shake, spark, start **6** arouse, launch **7** trigger **8** activate, mobilize, touch off **9** originate **10** lead the way
rate of ~: **5** speed **8** velocity
rotary ~: **5** twirl
science: **7** physics **8** kinetics **9** mechanics
sudden ~: **4** dart **5** slash, start
motion __: **4** work **5** study **7** picture
__ motion: **4** fast, lost, slow, stop **5** law of, rigid, set in **6** proper, radial **7** apsidal, diurnal, oblique
Motion, Andrew: **4** poet
__-motion cinematography: **4** stop
motionless: **3** put **4** calm, dead, firm, idle, numb **5** at bay, fixed, inert, quiet, still **6** at rest, frozen, halted, rooted, stable, static, torpid **7** stalled, unmoved **8** becalmed, immobile, inactive, lifeless, stagnant, unmoving **9** immovable, inanimate, paralyzed, petrified, quiescent, sedentary, unmovable **10** stock-still, unreactive
become ~: **6** freeze
not ~: **5** astir **6** moving
motion picture prefix: **4** cine-
__-Motion, The: **4** Loco
motivate: **4** draw, fire, goad, lead, move, prod, push, spur, stir, sway, urge, whet **5** bring, cause, drive, egg on, goose, hop up, impel, prime, rouse, spark, tempt **6** arouse, bestir, buck up, excite, incite, induce, prompt, propel, stir up **7** actuate, dispose, hearten, incline, inspire, provoke, quicken, suggest, trigger **8** embolden, energize, enspirit, imbolden, inspirit, persuade, psyche up, set astir, touch off **9** enhearten, galvanize, impassion, instigate, stimulate **10** predispose
hard to ~: **4** lazy
motivated: **5** can-do **8** sedulous, studious **9** assiduous
motivation: **4** goad, spur, urge **5** angle, cause, drive **6** reason, spirit **7** gimmick, impetus, impulse, purpose **8** catalyst, interest, occasion **9** impulsion, incentive, rationale **10** excitement
lack of ~: **5** ennui
motive: **3** aim, end **4** idea, root, sake, spur **5** basis, cause, drive, point **6** intent, object, origin, reason, spring **7** grounds, impulse, inspire, purpose **8** occasion, thinking **9** incentive, intention, rationale **10** incitement, inducement, mainspring
a question of ~: **3** why
having a ~: **6** causal
questioner: **5** cynic **7** doubter, skeptic
secret ~: **5** angle
__ motive: **6** profit **8** ulterior
motiveless: **6** wanton
mot juste, like a: **3** apt **7** apropos
motley: **4** mixt, pied **5** mixed **6** unlike, varied **7** dappled, mottled, rainbow, various **8** assorted, speckled **9** disparate, harlequin, multihued **10** dissimilar, multicolor, variegated
Motley: **6** Marion **7** Willard
Mötley __: **4** Crüe
Motley, Willard: **6** writer
motmot: **4** bird
__ moto: **3** con
__ motocross: **7** bicycle
Moto, Mr. portrayer: **5** Lorre
motor: **4** ride, V-six **5** drive, V-four **6** engine, travel, V-eight **7** machine, turbine **8** outboard **9** machinery, mechanism, take a ride, take a trip, tool along **10** go for a ride
along: **5** scoot
court: **5** motel **8** rest stop
ender: **3** bus, car, man, men, way **4** bike, boat **5** cycle
gun a ~: **3** rev
home: **2** RV
part: **3** cam
sound: **3** hum **4** ping, whir **5** vroom, whirr **6** varoom
trip: **4** spin
motor __: **3** inn, oil, van **4** home, pool, root, unit **5** coach, court, drive, lodge, lorry, mouth, truck **6** cortex, neuron, sailer **7** scooter, vehicle
motor __ law: **5** voter
motor-__: **5** mouth **6** minded
__ motor: **3** jet **5** water **6** linear, rocket
Motor __: **5** Trend
motorbike: **5** moped
motorboat trail: **4** wake
motorcade: **7** pageant **10** procession
Motor City: **7** Detroit
motorcycle: **3** hog **4** bike **7** vehicle
hero: **4** Evel **7** Knievel
maker: **5** Honda **6** Harley, Suzuki, Yamaha **8** Kawasaki
race: **6** enduro
sound: **5** vroom **6** varoom
motoring: **7** en route
motorist: **6** driver, honker
choice: **3** rte. **5** route
crime: **3** DUI, DWI **8** speeding
diversion: **6** detour
invitation: **5** hop in
maneuver: **5** U-turn
org.: **3** AAA
motorized: **5** power **6** mobile **8** electric **9** automated, automatic **10** electrical
motorless craft: **6** glider
motormouth: **6** gabber **10** chatterbox
motor-oil measurement: **5** quart
Motorola: **5** pager, phone **9** cell phone
alternative: **5** Nokia **6** Nextel **8** Ericsson
__ Motors: **7** General
Motown: **5** label
founder: Berry Gordy
group: **4** Pips **8** Four Tops, Jacksons, Miracles, Supremes **9** Vandellas **11** Temptations
megastar: **4** Gaye, Ross **9** Diana Ross **10** Marvin Gaye
music: **4** soul
purchaser: **3** MCA
see also Detroit
Motown __: **5** sound
Motownphilly (1991 song) artist: Boyz II Men
Motown Song, The (1991 song) artist: Rod Stewart, Temptations
Motrin alternative: **3** APF **4** Cope **5** Advil, Aleve, Bayer **6** Anacin, Datril **7** Ecotrin, Tylenol **8** Bufferin, Excedrin, St. Joseph, Vanquish **9** Ascriptin
__ mots: **5** jeu de
Mott: **4** John **6** Nevill **8** Lucretia
Mottelson, Ben: **8** Nobelist **9** physicist
Mott, John: **8** Nobelist
mottle: **5** fleck, stain **6** dapple **7** spatter
mottled: **6** motley **7** blotchy, dappled, flecked, marbled, spotted **8** brindled, freckled, speckled, splotchy, streaked
garment: **4** camo
mottling: **6** blotch
Mott, Nevill: **8** Nobelist **9** physicist
motto: **3** cry, saw **5** adage, axiom, maxim, moral **6** byword, dictum, legend, phrase, saying, slogan, truism, war cry **7** epigram, precept, proverb **8** aphorism, apothegm, epigraph, laconism **9** battle cry, catchword, platitude, watchword **10** apophthegm, shibboleth
Motul: **4** city, town
locale: **6** Mexico **7** Yucatán
moue: **3** mug **4** pout **7** grimace
moufflon: **5** sheep
relative: **4** geep **5** argal, shapu, urial **6** aoudad, argali, bharal, merino **7** bighorn, burrhel **8** cimarron
Moulin Rouge (1952 film)
cast: José Ferrer, Suzanne Flon, Zsa Zsa Gabor
director: John Huston
Moulin Rouge (2001 film)
cast: Jim Broadbent, Nicole Kidman, John Leguizamo, Ewan McGregor
director: Baz Luhrmann
__ Moultrie: **4** Fort
mound: **4** bank, dune, heap, hill, hump, mass, pile, rise **5** drift, knoll, ridge, shock, stack **6** barrow **7** anthill, hayrick, hillock, hummock, rampart, tumulus **8** haystack, molehill, mountain **10** embankment, prominence
of earth: **4** berm **5** berme
see also pitcher
Mound Builders: **5** tribe
Moundou: **4** city, town
locale: **3** Afr. **4** Chad **6** Africa
Mounds: **5** candy **9** chocolate
alternative: **4** Mars, Twix **5** Clark, Heath **6** Kit Kat, PayDay, Reese's, Zagnut **7** Krackel, Oh Henry **8** Baby Ruth, Hershey's, Milky Way, Snickers **9** Almond Joy, Mr. Goodbar **10** NutRageous
mount: **3** fit, set, wax **4** go up, grow, hoss, leap, lift, mare, peak, pony, rise, show, zoom **5** bronc, build, camel, climb, frame, get on, hop on, horse, pacer, raise, scale, set up, stage, stand, steed, surge, swell, tower, vault **6** ascend, bronco, cayuse, deepen, dobbin, equine, instal, pile up, shinny **7** augment, broncho, charger, clamber, cow pony, enlarge, get up on, install, mustang, palfrey, produce, shinney **8** bangtail, elephant, escalate, heighten, increase, multiply, position, stallion, straddle **9** clamber up, intensify, skyrocket **10** accumulate, strengthen
up: **4** grow, ride, rise **5** total **6** accrue **7** balloon **8** increase
up to: **5** total
Mount __ Observatory: **6** Wilson
mountain: **3** alp, Api, ton, tor **4** Anne, Batu, Bear, Bona, Cook, crag, dome, glob, Guna, heap, Hood, hump, Jaja, King, lots, lump, Mana, mass, Meru, Mohl, much, Muir, peak, pile, Rysy, Sill, Solo, Toro, Wade, Yale, Zupo **5** Adams, Aneto, Astor, bluff, Borah, Bross, Cachi, Chani, cliff, Coman, Cusco, Cuzco, Eiger, Elgon, Eolus, Evans, Falla, Galan, Gughe, Horeb, Kabru, Kamet, Kekes, Korab, Laudo, Logan, Marcy, Minto, Negro, Press, Pular, Quela, range, ridge, Shear, Shinn, Sinai, stack, Teide, Tyree, Walsh **6** Alaska, Ampato, Antero, Ararat, Bonete, Castor, Cho Oyu, Denali, Ecrins, Elbert, Elbrus, Elbruz, Erebus, Estats, Gilead, Harney, height, Hermon, Hunter, Juncal, Kangto, Kaplan, Katmai, Kungur, Lassen, Lhotse, Lister, Makalu, Musala, myriad, Nunkun, Nuptse, Oxford, Pisgah, Pissis, Posets, Robson, Rogers, Sabine, Sajama, Shasta, Sidley, sierra, Snezka, Steele, Trisul, Wexler, Wilson **7** Aragats, Augusta, Belford, Bernina, Cameron, Epperly, Everest, Foraker, Gardner, Granite, Harvard, Huandoy, Hubbard, Illampu, Langley, Lincoln, Lucania, Lysaght, Manaslu, Markham, Odishaw, Olympus, Ostenso, Palermo, Palomar, Pyramid, Rainier, Russell, Sanford, San Juan, Sellery, Shavano, Sherman, St. Elias, Toubkal, Triglov, Trikora, Trisuli, Tyndall, volcano, Wheeler, Whitney **8** Anapurna, Ancohuma, Baruntse, Ben Nevis, Caubvick, Chamlang, Changtzu, Columbia, Coropuna, Democrat, Dunagiri, El Condor, El Muerto, eminence, Famatina, Illimani, Jungfrau, Katahdin, landmark, McKinley, Mitchell, obstacle, Pauhunri, Polleras, Sneffels, Solimana, St. Helens, Tent Peak, Tortolas, Wrangell, Yerupaja **9** abundance, Aconcagua, Ama Dablam, Annapurna, Antofalla, Badrinath, Bierstadt, Blackburn, Broad Peak, Churchill, Condoriri, El Capitan, elevation, Huascarán, Incahuasi, Istoro Nal, Kanjut Sar, Kings Peak, Kosciusko, Lenin Peak, Marmolejo, Mont Blanc, Monte Rosa, Nanda Devi, Nepal Peak, Pikes Peak, precipice, Princeton, profusion, Pumasillo, Rakaposhi, Ras Dashan, Salcantay, Sia Kangri, Tirich Mir, Tupungato, Vancouver **10** Alverstone, Amne Machin, Chimborazo, Chomo Lhari, Dhaulagiri, Gasherbrum, high ground, Himalchuli, Kula Kangri, Masherbrum, Matterhorn, Mercedario, Minya Konka, Monte Corno, Muztagh Ata, Nacimiento, Parinacota, prominence, Tres Cruces, Williamson
basin: **3** cwm **6** cirque
Biblical ~: **4** Nebo **5** Horeb **6** Ararat, Carmel, Pisgah
chain: **5** range, ridge
combining form: **3** ore-, oro- **4** oreo-
crest: **5** arete, ridge
curve: **3** ess
debris: **5** scree
deity: **5** nymph, oread
ending: **3** eer, ous, top **4** side
feature: **4** crag **5** ridge
home: **4** aery, eyry **5** aerie, cabin, eyrie **6** chalet
in Greek: **4** oros

lake: 4 pool, tarn 9 reservoir
like ~ roads: 5 curvy 6 curvey
make a ~ of a molehill: 7 magnify
range: 4 ghat 5 chain, ghaut
road abbr.: 3 alt. 4 elev.
round ~ peak: 4 dome
route: 3 col, gap 4 ghat, pass 5 ghaut, notch 6 defile
sacred to Buddhism: 4 Omei
science: 7 orology
song: 5 yodel, yodle
sound: 4 echo
top: 4 acme, apex 5 crest 6 summit
transport: 4 mule 5 burro
wind: 5 foehn 9 katabatic

mountain ___: 3 ash, cat, dew, man 4 bike, goat, lion, mint, wave, wind 5 avens, bluet, chain, daisy, ebony, maple, range, sheep 6 beaver, laurel, system 7 currant, dogwood, gorilla, rosebay

___-mountain: 4 cat-o'

___ Mountain Boys: 5 Green

Mountain Brook: 4 city, town
locale: 7 Alabama

mountain climber
see mountaineer

___ Mountain Daisy: 3 To a

mountain dew: 5 drink, hooch 6 hootch, whisky 7 whiskey 8 beverage 9 moonshine
maker: 5 still

Mountain Dew: 4 soda 9 soft drink
alternative: 3 TAB 4 Nehi 5 Fanta 6 Fresca, Sprite 8 Diet Rite, Dr Pepper 9 Canada Dry 10 Mello Yello, Royal Crown

mountaineer
activity: 5 climb 6 ascent
foothold: 4 crag
gear: 5 belay, ice ax, piton
goal: 4 acme 6 summit
wear: 5 parka

Mountaineer: 3 SUV 7 Mercury

Mountain Greenery composer: 4 Hart 7 Rodgers

Mountain Hawks: 6 Lehigh

___ Mountain High: 5 Rocky

___ Mountain Landis: 7 Kenesaw

mountain lion: 3 cat 5 felid 6 feline
relative: 4 eyra, lynx, puma 5 chita, liger, ounce, tiger, tigon 6 bobcat, cheeta, chetah, cougar, jaguar, margay, ocelot, serval, tiglon 7 bay lynx, caracal, cheetah, leopard, panther 9 catamount 10 jaguarundi

Mountain of Love (1964 song) artist:
Johnny Rivers

mountainous: 3 big 4 huge 5 hilly, large, rocky, steep 6 alpine, craggy, rugged 7 cragged, mammoth, massive 8 whopping, surpassing

mountain ranges (Africa):
Atlas (Morocco/Algeria/Tunisia)
Mitumba (Congo)

mountain ranges (Antarctica):
Admiralty Range
Edsel Ford Range
Queen Maud Range

mountain ranges (Asia):
Ala Dagh (Turkey)
Alai (Kirghyzstan)
Altai (Russia)
Anadir (Russia/Siberia)
Cardamom (India)
Elburz (Iran)
Ghats (India)
Himalayas (India/Tibet)
Hindu Kush (Afghanistan)
Karakoram/Mustagh (Kashmir)
Kolyma (Russia/Siberia)
Kunlun (China)
Nan Ling (China)
Owen Stanley (New Guinea)
Pontic (Turkey)
Sayan (Russia)
Stanovoi (Asia)
Taurus (Turkey)
Tien Shan/Tian Shan (China/Kyrgyzstan)
Trans Alai (Kyrgyzstan/Tajikistan)
Urals (Russia)
Zagros (Iran/Turkey/Iraq)

mountain ranges (Australia/New Zealand):
Alps (Australia)
Darling Range (Australia)
Flinders (Australia)
James Range (Australia)
Southern Alps (New Zealand)

mountain ranges (Europe):
Alps
Apennines (Italy)
Athos (Greece)
Balkan
Bernese Alps (Switzerland)
Cadore (Italy)
Carnic Alps (Austria/Italy)
Carpathian
Caucasus (Russia/Georgia/Azerbaijan)
Cevennes (France)
Cottian Alps (France/Italy)
Dolomites (Italy)
Erz (Germany/Czech Republic)
Harz (Germany)
Jura (France/Switzerland)
Kjölen (Norway/Sweden)
Pennine Alps (Switzerland/Italy)
Pindus (Greece)
Pyrenees (Spain/France)
Rhodope (Bulgaria)
Rhon (Germany)
Savoy Alps (France)
St. Gotthard (Switzerland)
Sudeten (Czech Republic)
Tatra (Slovakia/Poland)
Transylvanian Alps (Romania)
Urals (Russia)

mountain ranges (North America):
Adirondacks (New York)
Aleutians (Alaska)
Alleghenies (U.S.)
Appalachians (U.S./Canada)
Baird (Alaska)
Bighorn (Wyoming)
Black (North Carolina)
Blue Ridge (U.S.)
Brooks (Alaska)
Cariboo (Canada)
Cascades (U.S./Canada)
Catoctin (Virginia/Maryland)
Green (Vermont)
Laramie (Colorado/Wyoming)
Lasal (Utah)
Laurentians (Canada)
Lewis (Montana/Canada)
Mackenzie (Canada)
Mogollon (New Mexico)
Ozarks (Missouri/Arkansas/Oklahoma)
Panamint (California)
Poconos (Pennsylvania)
Purcell (Montana/Canada)
Rockies (U.S./Canada)
San Bernardino (California)
Sangre de Cristo (Colorado/New Mexico)
San Juan (Colorado/New Mexico)
Sawatch (Colorado)
Selkirk (Canada)
Sierra Madres (Wyoming/Colorado)
Sierra Nevadas (California)
St. Elias (Canada)
Tetons (Wyoming/Idaho)
Torngat (Canada)
Uinta (Utah)
Wasatch (Utah/Idaho)
White (New Hampshire)

mountain ranges (South America):
Andes
Serra do Mar (Brazil)

mountains: 4 lots 5 loads, scads 6 plenty 8 outdoors 9 highlands

mountains (Africa):
Batu (Ethiopia)
Elgon (Kenya/Uganda)
Gughe (Ethiopia)
Guna (Ethiopia)
Kilimanjaro (Tanzania)
Meru (Tanzania)
Ras Dashan (Ethiopia)
Toubkal (Morocco)

mountains (Antarctica):
Anne
Astor
Coman
Epperly
Erebus
Falla
Gardner
Kaplan
Lister
Lysaght
Markham
Minto
Mohl
Odishaw
Ostenso
Press
Sabine
Sellery
Shear
Shinn
Sidley
Tyree
Vinson Massif
Wade
Wexler

mountains (Asia):
Ama Dablam (Nepal, Himalayas)
Amne Machin (China)
Annapurna (Nepal, Himalayas)
Api (Nepal (Himalayas)
Ararat (Turkey)
Asia Alung Gangri (Tibet, Himalayas)
Badrinath (India, Himalayas)
Baltoro Kangri (Kashmir, Himalayas)
Baruntse (Nepal, Himalayas)
Broad Peak (Pakistan/China)
Chamlang (Nepal, Himalayas)
Changtzu (Tibet, Himalayas)
Chomo Lhari (Tibet/Bhutan, Himalayas)
Cho Oyu (Nepal/Tibet, Himalayas)
Dhaulagiri (Nepal, Himalayas)
Disteghil Sar (Pakistan)
Dunagiri (India, Himalayas)
Everest (Nepal/Tibet, Himalayas)
Fuji (Japan)
Gasherbrum (Pakistan/China)
Gauri Sankar (Nepal/Tibet, Himalayas)
Gilead (Jordan)
Gurla Mandhata (Tibet, Himalayas)
Gyachung Kang (Nepal, Himalayas)
Haramosh Peak (Pakistan)
Hermon (Syria)
Himalchuli (Nepal, Himalayas)
Ismail Samani Peak (Tajikistan)
Istoro Nal (Pakistan)
Jaja (New Guinea)
Jongsong Peak (Nepal, Himalayas)
K2/Godwin Austen (Pakistan/China)
Kabru (Nepal, Himalayas)
Kamet (India/Tibet, Himalayas)
Kanchenjunga (India/Nepal, Himalayas)
Kangto (Tibet, Himalayas)
Kanjut Sar (Pakistan)
Kula Kangri (Bhutan, Himalayas)
Kungur (China)
Lenin Peak (Tajikistan)
Lhotse (Nepal/Tibet, Himalayas)
Makalu (Nepal/Tibet, Himalayas)
Mana (India, Himalayas)
Manaslu (Nepal, Himalayas)
Masherbrum (Kashmir)
Minya Konka (China)
Muztagh Ata (China)
Namcha Barwa (Tibet, Himalayas)
Nanda Devi (India, Himalayas)
Nanga Parbat (Pakistan, Himalayas)
Nebo (Jordan)
Nepal Peak (Nepal, Himalayas)
Nunkun (Kashmir, Himalayas)
Nuptse (Nepal, Himalayas)
Oyama (Japan)
Pauhunri (India/Tibet, Himalayas)
Pisgah (Jordan)
Pyramid (Nepal, Himalayas)
Rakaposhi (Pakistan)
Sia Kangri (Kashmir, Himalayas)
Skyang Kangri (Kashmir, Himalayas)
Tabor (Israel)
Tent Peak (Nepal, Himalayas)
Tirich Mir (Pakistan)
Trikora (New Guinea)
Trisuli (India, Himalayas)
Trisul (India, Himalayas)
Ulugh Muztagh (Tibet)

mountains (Australia/New Zealand):
Cook (New Zealand)
Kosciusko (Australia)
Ossa (Tasmania)

mountains (Europe):
Aneto (Spain, Pyrenees)
Aragats (Armenia)
Ben Nevis (Scotland)
Bernina (Italy/Switzerland, Alps)
Castor (Switzerland, Alps)
Ecrins (France, Alps)
Eiger (Switzerland, Alps)
Elbrus (Russia, Caucasus)
Estats (Spain, Pyrenees)
Etna/Aetna (Sicily)
Ida (Crete)
Jungfrau (Switzerland, Alps)
Kekes (Hungary)
Korab (Macedonia/Albania)
Matterhorn (Switzerland, Alps)
Mont Blanc (France/Italy, Alps)
Monte Corno (Italy, Apenines)
Monte Rosa (Switzerland, Alps)
Musala (Bulgaria)
Narodnaya (Russia, Urals)
Oeta (Greece)
Olympus (Greece)
Ossa (Greece)
Posets (Spain, Pyrenees)
Rysy (Poland)
Snezka (Czech Republic)
Teide (Spain)
Triglov (Croatia)
Zupo (Switzerland, Alps)

mountains (North America):
Adams (Washington, Cascades)
Alverstone (Alaska)
Antero (Colorado, Sawatch/Rockies)
Augusta (Alaska)
Bear (Alaska)
Belford (Colorado, Rockies)
Bierstadt (Colorado, Rockies)
Blackburn (Alaska)
Bona (Alaska)
Borah (Idaho)
Bross (Colorado, Rockies)
Cameron (Colorado, Rockies)
Caubvick (Newfoundland and Labrador)
Churchill (Alaska)
Columbia (Alberta)
Columbia (Colorado, Rockies)
Democrat (Colorado, Rockies)
Elbert (Colorado, Rockies)
El Capitan (California, Sierra

Nevadas)
Eolus (Colorado, Rockies)
Evans (Colorado, Rockies)
Fairweather (Alaska)
Foraker (Alaska)
Granite (California, Sierra Nevadas)
Granite (Montana)
Harney (South Dakota, Black Hills)
Harvard (Colorado, Sawatch/Rockies)
Hood (Oregon, Cascades)
Hubbard (Alaska)
Hunter (Alaska)
Katahdin (Maine, Appalachians)
Katmai (Alaska)
Kings Peak (Utah, Uintas)
King (Yukon)
Langley (California, Sierra Nevadas)
Lassen (California, Cascades)
Lincoln (Colorado, Rockies)
Logan (Yukon)
Lucania (Yukon)
Marcy (New York, Adirondacks)
Mauna Kea (Hawaii)
Mauna Loa (Hawaii)
McKinley/Denali (Alaska)
Mitchell (North Carolina, Appalachians)
Muir (California, Sierra Nevadas)
Oxford (Colorado, Rockies)
Palomar (California)
Pikes Peak (Colorado, Rockies)
Princeton (Colorado, Sawatch/Rockies)
Rainier (Washington, Cascades)
Robson (British Columbia, Rockies)
Rogers (Virginia, Appalachians)
Rushmore (South Dakota, Black Hills)
Russell (California, Sierra Nevadas)
Sanford (Alaska)
Shasta (California, Cascades)
Shavano (Colorado, Sawatch/Rockies)
Sherman (Colorado, Rockies)
Sill (California, Sierra Nevadas)
Sneffels (Colorado, Rockies)
Steele (Yukon)
St. Elias (Alaska, Canada)
St. Helens (Washington, Cascades)
Tyndall (California, Sierra Nevadas)
Vancouver (Alaska)
Walsh (Yukon)
Wheeler (New Mexico)
Whitney (California, Sierra Nevadas)
Williamson (California, Sierra Nevadas)
Wilson (California)
Wilson (Colorado, Rockies)
Wrangell (Alaska)
Yale (Colorado, Sawatch/Rockies)

mountains (South America):
Aconcagua (Argentina, Andes)
Ampato (Peru, Andes)
Ancohuma (Bolivia, Andes)
Antofalla (Argentina, Andes)
Bonete (Argentina/Chile, Andes)
Cachi (Argentina, Andes)
Chañi (Argentina, Andes)
Chimborazo (Ecuador, Andes)
Condoriri (Bolivia, Andes)
Coropuna (Peru, Andes)
Cuzco (Peru, Andes)
El Condor (Argentina, Andes)
El Libertador (Argentina, Andes)
El Muerto (Argentina/Chile, Andes)
Famatina (Argentina, Andes)
Galan (Argentina, Andes)
Huandoy (Peru, Andes)
Huascarán (Peru, Andes)
Illampu (Bolivia, Andes)
Illimani (Bolivia, Andes)
Incahuasi (Argentina/Chile, Andes)
Juncal (Argentina/Chile, Andes)
Laudo (Argentina, Andes)
Llullaillaco (Argentina/Chile, Andes)
Marmolejo (Argentina/Chile, Andes)
Mercedario (Argentina/Chile, Andes)
Nacimiento (Argentina, Andes)
Negro (Argentina, Andes)
Ojos del Salado (Argentina/Chile, Andes)
Palermo (Argentina, Andes)
Parinacota (Bolivia/Chile, Andes)
Pissis (Argentina, Andes)
Polleras (Argentina, Andes)
Pular (Chile, Andes)
Pumasillo (Peru, Andes)
Quela (Argentina, Andes)
Sajama (Bolivia, Andes)
Salcantay (Peru, Andes)
San Juan (Argentina/Chile, Andes)
Solimana (Peru, Andes)
Solo (Argentina, Andes)
Toro (Argentina/Chile, Andes)
Tortolas (Argentina/Chile, Andes)
Tres Cruces (Argentina/Chile, Andes)
Tupungato (Argentina/Chile, Andes)
Yerupaja (Peru, Andes)

___ Mountain, The: 5 Magic
Mountain Time state: 3 Ida., Neb., Tex., Wyo. **4** Ariz., Colo., Mont., N. Dak., Nebr., N. Mex, S. Dak., Utah **5** Idaho, Texas **7** Arizona, Montana, Wyoming **8** Colorado, Nebraska **9** New Mexico
mountaintop: 4 acme, apex, peak **6** summit
Mountain View: 4 city, town
  locale: 10 California
Mountbatten: 5 Louis
Mount Dora: 4 city, town
  locale: 7 Florida
mountebank: 4 fake, sham **5** faker, fraud, knave, phony, quack, rogue **6** bad guy, phoney **8** huckster, imposter, impostor, swindler **9** charlatan, scoundrel
Mount Everest pioneer: 6 Norgay **7** Hillary
Mount Hamilton observatory: 4 Lick
Mount Helix: 4 city, town
  locale: 10 California
Mount Holyoke grad: 5 woman **6** alumna
Mounties: 4 RCMP
mounting: 4 rise **5** frame **7** setting
Mountlake Terrace: 4 city, town
  locale: 10 Washington
Mount Lorne: 4 city, town
  locale: 6 Canada
Mountolive author: Lawrence Durrell
Mount Pearl: 4 city, town
  locale: 6 Canada
Mount Pleasant: 4 city, town
  athletes: 9 Chippewas
  locale: 8 Michigan **9** Wisconsin
  school: 3 CMU
Mount Prospect: 4 city, town
  locale: 8 Illinois
Mount Saint Helens
  emulate ~: 4 spew, spue **5** erupt
  output: 3 ash **4** lava
Mount St. ___: 5 Elias **6** Helens
Mount Vernon: 4 city, town **6** estate
  locale: 7 New York **8** Virginia **10** Washington
mourn: 3 cry, rue, sob **4** ache, fret, keen, miss, moan, pine, sigh, wail, weep **5** bleed **6** bemoan, bewail, cry for, grieve, lament, regret, sorrow **7** agonize, carry on, deplore **10** take it hard
Mourners Below author: James Purdy
mournful: 3 sad **5** bleak, funky, sorry, woful **6** dreary, morose, somber, tragic, woeful **7** doleful, elegiac, joyless, pitiful, tearful, unhappy, wistful **8** dolorous, grievous, tragical **9** heartsick, miserable, plaintive, regretful, saddening, sniveling, sorrowful, woebegone **10** deplorable, depressing, lamentable, lachrymose, lugubrious, melancholy
  poem: 5 dirge, elegy
  sound: 4 sigh, wail, yowl **5** dirge, groan, knell
mournfulness: 5 blues, grief **7** sadness
mourning: 3 woe **5** crape, grief **6** lament, sorrow **7** keening, sadness, wailing, weeping **8** grieving
  cloak: 3 bug **6** insect
mourning ___: 4 dove, iris **5** cloak **7** warbler
Mourning, Alonzo
  milieu: 5 court
  org.: 3 NBA
  sport: 10 basketball
Mourning Becomes Electra
  author: Eugene O'Neill
  character: 3 Ira **4** Adam, Ames, Amos, Emma, Ezra, Orin, Seth **5** Abner, Brant, Hazel, Niles, Silva **6** Louisa, Mannon, Minnie
mouse: 4 pest, welt **5** dance, Dixie, Jerry, murid, Pixie **6** animal, coward, Ignatz, mammal, Mickey, Minnie, murine, rodent, shiner, vermin **7** quitter **8** black eye, squeaker
  appendage: 4 tail
  catcher: 3 cat **4** trap **6** feline
  cat with a ~ perhaps: 5 toyer
  clicker: 6 button
  combining form: 3 -mys
  ender: 4 trap
  female: 3 doe
  field ~: 4 vole
  like a ~: 5 timid
  male: 4 buck
  move like a ~: 4 dart **5** scoot
  relative: 3 rat **4** cavy, degu, jird, paca, vole **5** coypu, gundi, xerus **6** agouti, beaver, gerbil, gopher, jerboa, marmot, murine **7** hamster, lemming, muskrat, visacha **8** chipmunk, cricetid, squirrel, tuco-tuco **9** chickaree, groundhog, guinea pig, porcupine, woodchuck **10** chinchilla, prairie dog
  spotter reaction: 3 eek
  target: 4 icon
  to an owl: 4 prey **6** quarry
  use a ~: 4 drag **5** click
  young: 3 pup **6** kitten
mouse ___ the clock, The: 5 ran up
___ mouse: 3 sea **4** deer, dust, nude, pine, wood **5** field, house **6** flying, meadow, pocket, vesper **7** harvest, jumping
___ Mouse: 3 To a **6** Ignatz, Mickey, Mighty, Minnie
mouse!, A: 3 eek
___ Mouse Detective, The: 5 Great
Mouse Hunt (1997 film)
  cast: Lee Evans, Nathan Lane, Vicki Lewis
  cat: 8 Catzilla
mouselike animal: 4 vole **5** shrew **6** jerboa **7** lemming
Mouse of hockey: 6 Mikita
Mouse on the Moon, The (1963 film)
  cast: Ron Moody, Margaret Rutherford
  director: Richard Lester
mouser: 3 cat **4** puss **5** felid **6** feline
mouse ran up the ___, The: 5 clock
mouse-tail: 5 plant
Mouse That Roared, The (1959 film)
  cast: David Kossoff, Jean Seberg, Peter Sellers
  director: Jack Arnold
mousetrap: 4 lure **5** tempt **7** pitfall **9** misinform **10** enticement
  bait: 6 cheese
Mousetrap, The: 4 play **5** drama
  author: Agatha Christie
  character: 4 Wren **5** Giles **6** Mollie
mousiness: 9 timidness **10** diffidence
Mouskouri: 4 Nana
mousquetaires, number of: 5 trois
moussaka: 5 Greek **6** entrée
  drink with ~: 4 ouzo
  ingredient: 4 lamb **5** onion **6** cheese, tomato **8** cinnamon, eggplant
mousse: 5 aspic **7** dessert, pudding **8** hair foam
  alternative: 3 gel
mousseline de ___: 4 soie **5** laine
mousy: 3 shy **4** drab, dull, gray, grey, meek **5** plain, timid **6** docile **7** bashful, fearful **8** obedient, timorous **9** colorless, compliant, easily led **10** lackluster, unassuming, uneffusive
mouth: 3 gas, jaw, lip, maw, mug, rim, yap **4** beak, guff, jaws, lips, puss, sass, trap **5** bazoo, cheek, chops, delta, firth, frith, inlet, sauce, speak, utter **6** cavity, crater, hot air, intone, kisser, parrot, recess **7** estuary, opening, orifice **8** aperture, back talk, entrance, rudeness **9** impudence, insolence, sauciness **10** embouchure
  away from the ~: 6 aboral
  be down in the ~: 4 mope, sulk
  big ~: 7 tattler **10** taleteller, tattletale
  combining form: 3 ori-, oro- **5** bucco-, -stoma, -stome **6** stomat- **7** stomato-
  down in the ~: 3 low, sad **4** blue, glum, mopy **5** moody, mopey **6** abject, morose **7** daunted, joyless, unhappy **8** dejected **9** depressed, miserable **10** dispirited
  ender: 4 part, wash **5** piece **7** breeder **8** watering
  foam at the ~: 4 rage **6** seethe
  foaming at the ~: 4 wild **5** manic, rabid, upset **6** raging **7** frantic, unglued **8** agitated, frenzied, maniacal, unstrung, vehement **9** bummed-out, fanatical **10** freaked out, hysterical
  from the horse's ~: 6 direct
  gaping ~: 3 maw
  have a big ~: 6 tattle
  horse's ~: 6 expert, origin, source **9** authority **10** originator
  hush one's ~: 6 shut up
  it's down in the ~: 5 uvula
  locale: 4 head **5** river
  make one's ~ water: 5 tempt **9** tantalize
  off: 3 dis, yap **4** sass **7** observe **8** get fresh, get smart, talk back **9** give lip to
  of the ~: 4 oral
  open one's ~: 4 talk **5** speak
  part: 3 jaw, lip **4** roof
  run off at the ~: 3 yak **4** blab **6** babble, jabber **7** blather, blether
  shoot off one's ~: 4 brag **5** spout **7** bluster
  starter: 3 bad, big **4** frog, loud, poor **5** snake **6** cotton **7** blabber
  toward the ~: 4 orad
  with ~ shut: 3 mum
  word of ~: 5 parol **7** hearsay
mouth ___: 3 off **4** harp **5** organ
___ mouth: 4 poor **5** bird's, motor **7** dragon's
___-mouth: 3 bad **5** motor **6** adder's
___-mouthed: 4 foul, full, open **5** close, mealy, tight
mouthed combining form: 7 -stomous
mouthful: 3 gob **4** bite, gulp, swig **5** scrap, taste **6** morsel, tidbit **8** spoonful

mouthlike opening: 5 stoma
mouthpiece: 3 att., rep 4 atty., reed 5 agent 6 fipple, lawyer, puppet 7 counsel 8 attorney 9 counselor 10 figurehead
mouths in Latin: 3 ora
mouth-to-mouth: 4 oral
mouthwash: 3 Act 4 Plax 5 Scope 6 Signal 7 Lavoris 9 Listerine 10 Fluorigard
approving org.: 3 ADA
like some ~: 5 minty
use ~: 5 rinse 6 gargle
mouth-watering: 5 sapid, tasty, yummy 6 savory 8 inviting, luscious, tempting 9 palatable, succulent
mouthy: 8 impudent 9 talkative 10 rhetorical
movable: 5 loose 6 mobile 8 floating, haulable, on wheels, portable 10 adjustable, detachable, unattached
movable ___: 4 type 5 feast
Movado: 5 watch 10 wristwatch
alternative: 4 Ebel, Rado 5 Casio, Elgin, Lorus, Omega, Rolex, Seiko, Timex 6 Bulova, Fossil, Pulsar, Swatch 7 Citizen 8 Longines, Tag Heuer, Tourneau
move: 2 go 3 act, fly, run 4 cart, deed, drag, flow, haul, jump, leap, ploy, push, send, ship, slip, step, stir, sway, trot, turn, urge, walk 5 budge, carry, cause, climb, crawl, drift, drive, glide, hurry, impel, leave, march, offer, prime, reach, rouse, scram, shake, shift, shove, touch 6 action, affect, bestir, betake, bustle, change, convey, depart, excite, incite, induce, jockey, motion, prompt, propel, reason, thrill, travel, uproot, work up 7 actuate, advance, agitate, cart off, disturb, get busy, give way, head out, hop to it, impress, inspire, measure, migrate, proceed, propose, provoke, pull out, quicken, skip out, suggest, take off 8 cart away, displace, get going, interest, maneuver, motivate, persuade, position, relocate, resettle, run along, transfer, traverse, withdraw 9 galvanize, influence, recommend, shake a leg, stratagem, transport, transpose 10 get hopping, get started, put forward, reposition, shuffle off, take action, transplant
along: 2 go 4 ride 5 scoot, slide
around: 3 gad 4 mill, ring, roam, rove, stir 5 drift, shift 6 mingle, wander 9 circulate 10 reposition
awkwardly: 6 gangle
back: 6 return
bad ~: 4 trip 5 boner, error, folly 7 misstep, mistake 9 indecorum
be reluctant to ~: 8 hang back
blithely: 4 skip
clever ~: 4 coup, ruse 6 device
close: 6 cuddle, nestle 7 snuggle
deceptive ~: 4 deke 5 feint
don't ~: 4 stay 5 stall 6 freeze
down: 4 drop, fall, sink 5 slide 7 descend
erratically: 3 zag, zig 4 dart, flit
forward: 4 gain 8 progress
get a ~ on: 2 go 3 fly, hie, rip, run, zip 4 dart, dash, flit, race, rush, stir, tear, zoom 5 hurry, scoot, spank, speed 6 barrel, gallop, hasten, hustle, rocket, scurry 7 floor it, hop to it, quicken, scamper, speed up 8 step on it 9 hotfoot it, shake a leg, skedaddle 10 hightail it
get ready to ~: 4 pack
goods: 4 hawk, push, sell, vend 5 pitch, trade 6 barter, handle, hustle, market, peddle, retail, unload 7 auction, promote, traffic 9 wholesale
hard to ~: 6 leaden
hither and thither: 3 gad 4 roam 6 ramble, wander 7 meander, traipse 8 ambulate, nomadize 9 bum around, gallivant, globe-trot
in: 5 enter
in on: 5 usurp
into: 10 infiltrate
laterally: 3 zag 4 edge, skew 5 sidle
lazily: 5 amble, mosey 7 shuffle
make a ~: 3 act
make a wrong ~: 3 err
nautically: 5 heave
not inclined to ~: 4 lazy
on: 4 pass 5 leave 6 depart 7 advance, proceed 8 progress 9 go forward
one on the ~: 4 goer 5 nomad
on one's hands and knees: 4 inch 5 crawl, creep, slink, sneak, steal 7 clamber, slither, wriggle
on the ~: 4 at it, busy 5 afoot, astir 6 active, at work 7 engaged, migrant, working 8 employed, in motion, occupied, underway 9 advancing, migratory, traveling, wayfaring 10 proceeding
out: 2 go 4 exit 5 leave 6 set off, vacate 7 ride off 8 set forth
over: 4 lick 5 shift, slide
room to ~: 4 give, play 6 leeway 8 latitude
rudely: 4 push 5 elbow, shove 6 jostle
secretly: 4 lurk 5 prowl, sculk, sidle, skulk, slink, sneak, steal
slightly: 4 stir 5 budge
slowly: 3 lag 4 drag, ease, inch, nose, poke 5 crawl, creep, mosey 9 limp along
smoothly: 4 flow, sail 5 coast, glide, slide
softly: 3 pad 6 tiptoe
suddenly: 4 dart, jerk, jump, leap 5 lunge, lurch, shoot, swoop
(to): 3 try 7 attempt
to action: 6 arouse
to and fro: 3 wag 4 rock, sway, wave 5 swing 9 oscillate
to tears: 3 get 4 move 6 affect
toward: 4 near, tend 6 go up to 7 head for 8 approach 9 gravitate
(toward): 4 come, head, tend
unsteadily: 3 yaw 4 reel 6 teeter, totter
up: 4 bump, lift, rise, soar 5 arise, climb, raise, surge 6 ascend 7 advance, elevate, promote, surface, upgrade 8 escalate
up and down: 3 bob
up in the world: 6 make it 7 prosper, succeed 8 get ahead
wildly: 6 careen, career
wrong ~: 4 slip 5 boner, error, fluff, gaffe, lapse 6 bungle, miscue, slipup 7 blunder, faux pas, misdeed, misstep, mistake
move ___: 3 out 4 away, in on
move ___ and earth: 6 heaven
___ move: 5 false, on the 6 career
Move!: 4 C'mon
Moveable Feast, A author: Ernest Hemingway
moved: 4 gone
be ~: 3 cry, sob 5 react
move heaven and ___: 5 earth
movement: 4 flow, flux, play, tide 5 cause, shift, steps, trend 6 action, change, course, flight, motion, signal, stroke, travel, unrest 7 advance, crusade, gesture, journey, process, transit 8 activity, campaign, exercise, kinetics, maneuver, mobility, motility, progress, stirring, transfer, velocity 9 agitation, animation, migration 10 locomotion, procession, regression, transferal, transition
combining form: 6 kinesi- 7 -cinesia, -kinesia, kinesio-, -kinesis
freedom of ~: 4 room 5 range, scope 6 leeway 8 latitude 9 elbowroom
in music: 4 moto
lack of ~: 6 stasis
last ~: 6 finale
of ~: 6 gestic 8 gestical
unexpected ~: 3 jab 4 dash, dive, jump, leap, poke 5 bound, burst, lurch, pitch, surge, swing, swipe 6 charge, plunge, pounce, spring, strike, thrust
upward ~: 4 rise
see also move
___ movement: 4 mass 5 labor 6 Oxford, pincer, quartz
___ move on: 4 get a 5 make a
mover: 3 VIP 5 lader 6 Allied, dynamo, Global 7 migrant, van line 8 go-getter 9 Mayflower
and shaker: 4 doer 5 mogul
burden: 3 box 5 piano 9 furniture
device: 5 dolly 6 bungee, caster
earth ~: 3 hoe 6 dredge
prime ~: 5 cause 9 architect
starter: 5 earth
vehicle: 3 van 5 truck, U-Haul
___ mover: 5 prime 6 people
mover and ___: 6 shaker
___ Moves: 5 Night
___ Moves South: 5 Grant
movie: 3 pic 4 cine, film, show 5 flick 6 cinema, silent, talkie 7 feature, picture, theater, theatre 9 photoplay, spectacle, videotape 10 production, screenplay
ad photo: 5 still
be in a ~: 3 act
board member: 5 rater
combining form: 4 cine-
ender: 3 dom 4 goer 5 going, maker 6 making
lot locale: 3 set 6 studio 10 soundstage
promo: 4 clip 7 trailer
rating org.: 4 MPAA
studio: 3 Fox, MGM 6 Disney 7 Miramax, New Line 8 Columbia 9 Paramount, Universal 10 Dreamworks, Warner Bros.
theater suffix: 4 plex
union: 3 SAG
movie ___: 5 house 7 theater, theatre
___ movie: 4 home 7 drive-in
___ Movie: 5 Scary 6 Silent
moviegoer: 6 viewer 9 spectator
moviegoers: 5 crowd 8 audience
Moviegoer, The author: Walker Percy
Movie Movie (1978 film)
cast: George C. Scott, Trish Van Devere, Eli Wallach
director: Stanley Donen
movies: 3 pix 6 cinema
like some ~: 4 gory 6 G-rated, R-rated 8 animated
like vampire ~: 5 lurid 6 bloody
sound at the ~: 3 shh
Movin' ___: 3 Out 4 on Up
moving: 5 about, astir 6 active, liquid, mobile, motile, onward, tender 7 dynamic, migrant, onwards, piteous, pitiful, sensual, soulful 8 dramatic, eloquent, exciting, gripping, in motion, pathetic, poignant, touching, underway 9 emotional, impelling, inspiring, migratory 10 convincing, emigration, expressive, impressive, locomotion, on the march, pathetical, persuasive
combining form: 4 plan- 5 -grade, plano- 6 kineto- 7 -kinetic
get ~: 3 hie, run 4 roll, stir 5 speed 6 bestir 7 speed up 8 hightail, run along
not ~: 5 inert, still 6 at rest
picture: 4 film 5 flick
vehicle: 5 truck, U-Haul
see also mover
moving ___: 3 van 6 target 7 average, picture
___-moving: 4 fast, slow
Moving right ___...: 5 along
Moving Target, The author: Ross Macdonald
Moving the Mountain (1994 film) director: Michael Apted
Movin' Out (1978 song) artist: Billy Joel
mow: 3 cut 4 clip, crop, reap, trim 5 level, prune, shave, shear 6 scythe 7 hayloft
again: 5 recut
down: 4 rase, raze 6 defeat 9 eradicate
starter: 3 hay
mow ___: 4 down
Mowat, Farley: 6 writer 8 Canadian
work: The Desperate People
People of the Deer
The Snow Walker
Mowbray, Alan: 5 actor
film: Ma and Pa Kettle at Home (1954)
Merrily We Live (1938)
That Hamilton Woman (1941)
mowed area: 5 swath 6 swathe
mower: 4 tool
place: 4 shed 6 garage
starter: 4 lawn
___ mower: 4 hand, lawn 5 power
Mowgli
friend: 5 Akela, Baloo
rearer: 4 wolf
mowing: 5 chore
place: 4 lawn 5 grass
the lawn: 4 task
Mowing author: Robert Frost
___-mown: 3 new
moxie: 3 pep 4 grit, guts, will, zest 5 brass, drive, heart, nerve, pluck, skill, spine, spunk, valor, verve, vigor 6 daring, energy, mettle, spirit 7 courage, know-how, stamina 8 audacity, chutzpah, gumption, tenacity 9 endurance, fortitude, gutsiness 10 durability, feistiness, get-up-and-go, initiative
having ~: 4 game 5 brash, gutsy, nervy 6 brassy, daring, gritty, plucky, spunky 9 audacious 10 courageous
Moyers: 4 Bill
Moyet: 6 Alison
Moynihan: 3 Pat
Moyotzingo: 4 city, town
locale: 6 Mexico, Puebla
Mozambique: 6 nation 7 country
bay: 7 Delagoa
bovine: 5 Nguni 7 Mashona
capital: 6 Maputo
city: 4 Sena 5 Beira 6 Maputo
lake: 5 Nyasa 6 Malawi
nation off ~: 7 Comoros
neighbor: 6 Malawi, Zambia 8 Tanzania, Zimbabwe 9 Swaziland
people: 3 Yao 4 Cewa 5 Chewa, Makua, Shona 6 Nyanja 7 Makonde, Mashona
Mozambique ___: 7 Channel, Current
___ Mozart: 6 Mostly
Mozart, Wolfgang Amadeus: 8 Austrian, composer
contemporary: 5 Haydn

father: 7 Leopold
genre: 5 opera 6 sonata 8 concerto, symphony
work: Così fan tutte
Don Giovanni
Eine Kleine Nachtmusik
Haffner Symphony
Idomeneo
Jupiter Symphony
La Clemenza di Tito
Linz Symphony
The Magic Flute
The Marriage of Figaro
Paris Symphony
Prague Symphony
mozetta: 4 cape
mozo: 6 waiter
mozzarella: 6 cheese 7 Italian
mozzetta: 4 cape
MP
part: 3 Mil., Pol. 6 Police 8 Military
quest: 4 AWOL
task: 6 arrest
MPAA employee: 5 rater
MPG
monitor: 3 EPA
part of ~: 3 gal., per 5 miles 6 gallon
MPH part: 3 per 4 hour 5 miles
MPV: 3 van 5 Mazda
Mr.: 3 man 4 male 5 title
Mr. __: 3 Big, Lee, Mom 4 Blue, Cool, Jaws, Moto 5 Bones, Clean, Fixit, Jones, Lucky, Right, Tambo, Wrong 6 Burden, Custer, Lonely, Mister, Murder, Roboto, Wendal 7 America, Palomar, Peepers, Sandman
Mr. __ Goes to Town: 5 Deeds
Mr. __ Goes to Washington: 5 Smith
Mr. __ Guy: 4 Nice
Mr. __ Jeans: 5 Green
Mr. __ Neighborhood: 6 Rogers'
Mr. __ Passes By: 3 Pim
Mr. __ Stuff: 3 Big
Mr. __, Tracer of Lost Persons: 4 Keen
MR __: 4 scan 6 imager 7 scanner
Mr. and __: 3 Mrs.
Mr. and Mrs. Smith (1941 film)
cast: Carole Lombard, Robert Montgomery, Gene Raymond
director: Alfred Hitchcock
Mr. Beluncle author: V.S. Pritchett
Mr. Belvedere (ABC sitcom)
cast: Ilene Graff (Marsha Owens)
Christopher Hewitt (Lynn Belvedere)
George Owens (Bob Uecker)
Mr. Big: 3 VIP 4 lion 5 mogul
Mr. Big Stuff (1971 song) artist: Jean Knight
Mr. Blandings Builds His Dream House (1948 film)
cast: Melvyn Douglas, Cary Grant, Myrna Loy
director: H.C. Potter
Mr. Blue (1959 song) artist: Fleetwoods
Mr. Bojangles (1971 song) artist: Nitty Gritty Dirt Band
Mr. Burden author: Hilaire Belloc
__, Mr. Chips: 7 Goodbye
Mr. Clean alternative: 5 Brite, Lysol 6 Top Job 7 Lestoil, Pine Sol 9 Fantastik, Step Saver
Mr. Deeds Goes to Town (1936 film)
cast: Jean Arthur, George Bancroft, Gary Cooper
director: Frank Capra
MRE consumer: 2 GI 7 soldier
Mr. Flood's Party: 4 poem
author: E.A. Robinson
Mr. Goodbar: 5 candy 9 chocolate
alternative: 4 Mars, Twix 5 Clark, Heath 6 Kit Kat, Mounds, PayDay, Reese's, Zagnut 7 Krackel, Oh Henry 8 Baby Ruth, Hershey's, Milky Way, Snickers 9 Almond Joy 10 NutRageous
Mr. Guitar: 6 Atkins
Mr. Holland's Opus (1995 film)
cast: Richard Dreyfuss, Olympia Dukakis, Glenne Headly, William H. Macy, Jay Thomas, Alicia Witt
director: Stephen Herek
Mr. Hulot's Holiday star: 4 Tati
MRI: 6 imager 7 scanner
Mr. Jealousy (1998 film)
cast: Annabella Sciorra, Eric Stoltz
Mr. Keen, Tracer of Lost Persons: 9 radio show
Mr. Lee (1957 song) artist: Bobbettes
__ Mr. Lincoln: 5 Young
Mr. Lincoln's Army author: Bruce Catton
Mr. Lonely (1964 song) artist: Bobby Vinton
Mr. Lucky (1943 film)
cast: Charles Bickford, Laraine Day, Cary Grant
director: H.C. Potter
Mr. Lucky (1960 song) artist: Henry Mancini
Mr. Midshipman Easy author: Frederick Marryat
Mr. Mom (1983 film)
cast: Teri Garr, Ann Jillian, Michael Keaton, Martin Mull
director: Stan Dragoti
Mr. Moto's Last Warning (1939 film)
cast: Ricardo Cortez, Virginia Field, Peter Lorre
director: Norman Foster
Mr. & Mrs. Bridge (1990 film)
cast: Blythe Danner, Paul Newman, Joanne Woodward
director: James Ivory
Mr. Murder author: Dean Koontz
Mr. Nice __: 3 Guy
Mr. Norris Changes Trains author: Christopher Isherwood
Mrozek, Slawomir: 6 Polish, writer
Mr. Palomar author: Italo Calvino
Mr. Peepers (NBC sitcom) cast: Wally Cox (Robinson Peepers)
Mr. Perrin and Mr. Traill author: Hugh Walpole
__ Mr. Postman: 6 Please
Mr. President: 7 musical
songwriter: 6 Berlin
Mr. Republican: 4 Taft
__ Mr. Right: 6 Making
Mr. Robinson Crusoe (1932 film)
cast: Douglas Fairbanks Sr., William Farnum
director: Edward Sutherland
dog: 6 Rooney
Mr. Roboto (1983 song) artist: Styx
Mrs.: 4 wife 5 title, woman 6 female
in French: 3 Mme.
in Japanese: 3 san
in Spanish: 3 Sra.
new ~: 5 bride
Mrs. __: 6 Grundy 7 Miniver
Mrs. __ Goes to Paris: 5 'Arris
__ Mrs.: 5 Mr. and
Mr. Sammler's Planet author: Saul Bellow
Mr. Sandman (1954 song) artist: Chordettes
Mr. Saturday Night (1992 film)
cast: Billy Crystal, Helen Hunt, David Paymer, Julie Warner
director: Billy Crystal
Mrs. Battle's Opinions of Whist
author: Charles Lamb (Elia)
Mrs. Brown You've Got a Lovely Daughter (1965 song) artist: Herman's Hermits
Mrs. Butterworth's: 5 syrup
alternative: 8 Log Cabin
__ Mrs. Carrolls, The: 3 Two
Mrs. Dalloway: 5 novel
author: Virginia Woolf
character: 5 Doris, Rezia, Walsh 8 Clarissa
Mrs. Doubtfire (1993 film)
cast: Pierce Brosnan, Sally Field, Robin Williams
director: Chris Columbus
Mrs. Fields alternative: 7 Archway, Keebler, Nabisco 8 Sunshine 10 Famous Amos, Peak Freans
__ Mrs. Jones: 5 Me and
Mr. Skeffington (1944 film)
cast: Walter Abel, Bette Davis, Claude Rains
__ Mrs. Leslie: 5 About
__ & Mrs. Miller: 6 McCabe
Mrs. Miniver (1942 film)
cast: Greer Garson, Reginald Owen, Walter Pidgeon, May Whitty, Teresa Wright
character: 3 Kay 4 Clem
director: William Wyler
studio: 3 MGM
Mr. Smith Goes to Washington (1939 film)
cast: Jean Arthur, Claude Rains, James Stewart
composer: 7 Tiomkin
director: Frank Capra
Mrs. Parkington (1944 film)
cast: Edward Arnold, Greer Garson, Walter Pidgeon
director: Tay Garnett
Mrs. Robinson (1968 song) artist: Simon and Garfunkel
Mrs. Warren's Profession author: Shaw
Mrs. Wiggs of the Cabbage Patch (1934 film)
cast: W.C. Fields, Pauline Lord, ZaSu Pitts
director: Norman Taurog
Mrs. Winterbourne (1996 film)
cast: Brendan Fraser, Ricki Lake, Shirley MacLaine
director: Richard Benjamin
Mr. Tambourine Man (1965 song)
artist: Byrds
Mr. Television: 5 Berle
Mr. T group: 5 A-Team
Mr Weston's Good Wine author: T.F. Powys
__ Mr. Wizard: 5 Watch
Mr. Wonderful (1956 song) artist: Sarah Vaughan
Mr. Wrong (1996 film)
cast: Joan Cusack, Ellen DeGeneres, Bill Pullman, Dean Stockwell
director: Nick Castle
ms.
enclosure: 3 SAE
reader: 2 ed.
Ms.: 5 title, woman 6 female
MS
see Mississippi
MS-__: 3 DOS
M.Sc.D.: 3 deg.
M. Scott: 4 Peck
MS-DOS popularizer: 3 IBM
MS. Found in a Bottle author: Edgar Allan Poe
MSG part: 4 mono 6 sodium 9 glutamate
Msgr.'s faith: 4 Cath.
M.Sgt.: 3 NCO
subordinate: 3 SFC
MSNBC: 7 channel
rival: 3 CNN 4 CNBC
MSN holder: 5 nurse
M.S., part of: 3 sci. 6 master 7 science
Ms. rival: 4 Elle
MST part: 3 Mtn., Std. 4 Time 8 Mountain, Standard
MSU
conference: 6 Big Ten
locale: 7 Bozeman
mt.: 3 hgt. 15 See also mountain
MT
see Montana
M.T.A. (1959 song) artist: Kingston Trio
mtg.: 4 appt., sess.
mtge.
lender: 3 FHA 4 FNMA, GNMA 5 S and L
obligation: 3 pmt 4 payt.
see also mortgage
Mt. St. __: 6 Helens
MTV: 7 channel
alternative: 3 BET, CMT, PAX, TBS, TLC, TNN, TNT, USA 4 ESPN, HGTV 5 A and E, C-SPAN, Style, VH one 6 Noggin, Tech TV, TV Land 7 Court TV, Ovation, SoapNet 8 Lifetime
employee: 2 VJ 6 veejay
music: 3 rap
offering: 4 trax 5 video
part of ~: 4 tele 5 music 6 vision
prize: 3 Ava
viewer: 4 teen
Mtwara: 4 city, town
locale: 8 Tanzania
mu: 5 Greek 6 letter
follower: 2 nu
preceder: 6 lambda
Mubarak: 4 Arab 5 Hosni 8 Egyptian 9 president
capital: 5 Cairo
predecessor: 5 Sadat
much: 3 far, lot, oft 4 a lot, gobs, lots, lump, many, mega, mess, most, peck, pile, tons, very 5 ample, heaps, loads, lotsa, no end, often, scads 6 barrel, excess, galore, highly, hugely, lavish, lots of, nearly, oodles, plenty, vastly, volume 7 aplenty, awfully, copious, endless, greatly, notably, profuse, sizable 8 abundant, beaucoup, generous, mountain, plethora, sizeable, terribly, very many 9 abundance, copiously, extremely, immensely, in a big way, liberally, many a time, plenteous, plentiful, profusely, quite a bit, regularly, thousands 10 abundantly, a great deal, all kinds of, enormously, frequently, oversupply, repeatedly, voluminous
a bit ~: 10 untempered
as: 5 while 6 though
as ~ as: 4 up to
be too ~: 4 cloy
combining form: 4 poly-
ever so ~: 4 many 6 highly 7 greatly
give too ~: 4 cloy, glut 5 gorge 7 surfeit
in music: 5 molto
make ~ of: 4 tout 5 exalt 6 praise, stress 7 amplify, magnify 9 emphasize 10 compliment
make too ~ of: 8 overrate 9 overstate 10 exaggerate
not ~: 4 a bit, a dab 5 light 6 hardly, little 8 somewhat
obliged: 5 danke, merci 6 grazie, thanks 7 gracias, spasibo 8 beholden, grateful, indebted, thank you
prefix: 4 poly-
so ~ in music: 5 tanto
the same: 4 like 5 alike 7 similar
too ~: 5 ultra, undue 6 de trop, excess, overly 8 annoying, tiresome, to a fault 9 excessive, overblown 10 inordinate, outra-

geous, stupendous, unbearable, untempered
too ~ in French: 6 de trop
too ~ of a good thing: 4 glut 5 flood 7 surfeit, surplus 8 overload 10 indulgence, oversupply
used: 4 flat 5 banal, corny, stale, stock, tired 6 common, jejune 7 clichéd, insipid, worn-out 8 bathetic, bromidic, cornball, ordinary, shopworn, timeworn, well-worn 9 hackneyed, moth-eaten, played out 10 pedestrian, uninspired, unoriginal, warmed-over
very ~: 3 far 4 a lot, well 5 badly, by far, no end 6 highly, indeed 7 greatly 10 incredibly
__ much: 4 very 6 pretty
__ Much!: 5 No Not
__, muchachos: 5 Adios
Much Ado About Nothing: 4 film, play
author: William Shakespeare
cast: Kenneth Branagh, Michael Keaton, Robert Sean Leonard, Keanu Reeves, Emma Thompson, Denzel Washington
director: Kenneth Branagh
role: 4 Hero 6 Ursula, Verges 7 Claudio, Conrade, Leonato 8 Beatrice, Don Pedro
much-heard: 5 banal
__ Much Heaven: 3 Too
mucho: 4 lots, very 5 lotsa 6 highly 7 but good, Spanish
__ Mucho: 6 Bésame
__ much of: 4 make 5 think
much-wanted: 3 hot 7 popular 8 in demand
mucilage: 3 gum 4 glue 5 paste 6 cement 8 adhesive, fixative
mucilaginous: 5 gooey, gummy 7 viscose, viscous 8 adhesive
muck: 3 goo, mud 4 crud, dirt, glop, gunk, mess, mire, ooze, soil 5 filth, grime, slime, snarl 6 litter, muddle, refuse
about: 6 tamper, tinker
ender: 4 rake, worm 5 raker 6 raking
move in ~: 5 slosh
up: 4 harm, soil 5 botch, spoil 7 disrupt, screw up 10 complicate
muck __: 3 bar 5 about 6 around
muck-a-muck: 3 VIP 7 big shot
__-muck-a-muck: 4 high
muckraker: 6 critic 8 vilifier
muckraking: 7 slander 9 aspersion, disesteem, maligning, traducing 10 backbiting, defamation, derogation, detraction, revilement, scurrility
muckworm: 3 bug 5 churl, miser 6 cheapo, insect 7 hoarder, Scrooge 8 el cheapo, tightwad 9 skinflint 10 cheapskate, pinchpenny
mucky: 4 miry, oozy 5 grimy, muddy, muggy, slimy, soggy 6 sticky
make ~: 5 sully
mud: 4 dirt, mire, muck, ooze, slop, soil 5 earth, mocha, slime, swamp 6 coffee, gossip, jamoke 7 earthen, scandal, slander
clear as ~: 5 mirky, murky, vague 9 equivocal 10 unexplicit
combining form: 3 pel- 4 pelo-
dauber: 4 wasp
ender: 3 bug 4 fish, flow, sill 5 guard, puppy, slide, stone 7 skipper, slinger 8 slinging
like ~: 4 oozy 5 slimy
lover: 3 hog, pig 5 swine
move through ~: 4 slog 5 slosh
product: 3 pie 4 pack
propel ~: 5 sling
sink in ~: 4 mire
throw ~ at: 4 slam, slur 5 knock, libel, smear, sully, taint, wrong 6 defame, malign, vilify 7 asperse, blacken, run down, slander, tarnish, traduce 8 backbite, badmouth, besmirch, dishonor 9 denigrate, discredit, disparage 10 calumniate, stigmatize, vituperate
mud __: 3 bug, cat, eel, hen, pie, pot 4 bath, flap, flat, room, wasp 5 berth, crack, puppy, slide, snake 6 dauber, puddle, stream, turtle 7 volcano
Mud & Bugs: 6 cereal
competitor: 3 Kix 4 Life, Trix 5 Kashi, Quisp, Total 6 Kaboom, Muesli, Oreo O's, Pablum, Smacks 7 All-Bran, Crispix, Harmony, Hunny B's, Mueslix, Oat Bran, Pokemon 8 Boo Berry, Cheerios, Corn Chex, Corn Pops, Fiber One, Rice Chex, Special K, Uncle Sam, Wheaties 9 Alpha Bits, Apple Zaps, Grape Nuts, Honey Comb, Just Right, Wheat Chex 10 Apple Jacks, Bran Flakes, Cap'n Crunch, Cocoa Puffs, Froot Loops, Mini-Wheats, Nutri-Grain, Puffed Rice, Quaker Oats, Smart Start 11 Cocoa Blasts, Cookie Crisp, Golden Crisp, Lucky Charms, Puffed Wheat, Sweet Crunch, Waffle Crisp
Mudd: 5 Roger
mudder: 5 horse 9 racehorse
muddied: 5 dirty, grimy 6 opaque, turbid 10 bedraggled
muddle: 3 fog, mix 4 daze, hash, haze, mess, muck, muss, stir 5 addle, befog, boner, botch, chaos, cloud, mix up, snafu, snarl, upset 6 baffle, bumble, bungle, foul up, fuddle, jumble, litter, plight, rattle, tangle 7 bedevil, blunder, clutter, confuse, dilemma, disrupt, disturb, fluster, louse up, mistake, nonplus, perplex, screwup, shuffle, snarl up, stupefy 8 befuddle, bewilder, confound, disarray, disorder, entangle, flounder, quagmire, quandary, scramble, shambles 9 adumbrate, confusion, disorient, inebriate, mare's nest, mobocracy, patchwork 10 complexity, complicate, intoxicate, misarrange
through: 4 cope 5 get by 6 manage 7 make out, press on
muddle __: 7 through
muddled: 4 asea, hazy 5 at sea, dizzy, messy, mussy, upset, wooly, woozy 6 turbid, woolly 7 out of it 8 pell-mell 9 equivocal, inside-out 10 disjointed, disorderly, incohesive, topsy-turvy, unexplicit
muddleheaded: 4 asea, daft, loco 5 at sea, balmy, dense, dotty, flaky, inane, kooky, wacky 6 absurd 7 asinine, bonkers, doltish, foolish, witless 9 brainless, half-baked
muddy: 3 dim, fog 4 blur, damp, dull, hazy, miry, oozy, roil, soil 5 boggy, caked, dirty, fuzzy, grimy, gummy, gunky, mirky, mucky, murky, roily, silty, slimy, soggy, taint, thick, undry, vague 6 bemire, cloudy, crud up, filthy, grubby, marshy, opaque, sloppy, slushy, sodden, soiled, swampy, turbid 7 bemired, confuse, obscure, unclean, unclear, wettish 8 abstruse, besmirch, confused, darkened, roiled up, unwashed 9 obfuscate, uncertain, unfocused 10 lusterless
not ~: 5 clear
spot: 3 sty 6 pigpen, pigsty
Muddy: 6 Waters
__ Muddy: 3 Big
Muddy Water (1966 song) artist: Johnny Rivers
mudguard: 6 fender
Mud Hens home: 6 Toledo
__ mud in your eye!: 5 Here's
mudlark: 4 bird
Mudlark, The (1950 film)
cast: Finlay Currie, Irene Dunne, Alec Guinness, Anthony Steel
director: Jean Negulesco
mudminnow: 4 fish
mudpack: 6 facial
mudpuppy: 9 amphibian 10 salamander
mudslide: 9 earthfall
mudsling: 5 smear 6 malign, vilify 7 slander 9 denigrate 10 villainize
mudstone: 7 mineral
Mueller-Stahl, Armin: 5 actor
film: Avalon (1990)
The Last Good Time (1994)
Music Box (1989)
Shine (1996)
The Third Miracle (1999)
muenster: 6 cheese
Mueslix: 6 cereal
competitor: 3 Kix 4 Life, Trix 5 Kashi, Quisp, Total 6 Kaboom, Muesli, Oreo O's, Pablum, Smacks 7 All-Bran, Crispix, Harmony, Hunny B's, Oat Bran, Pokemon 8 Boo Berry, Cheerios, Corn Chex, Corn Pops, Fiber One, Rice Chex, Special K, Uncle Sam, Wheaties 9 Alpha Bits, Apple Zaps, Grape Nuts, Honey Comb, Just Right, Wheat Chex 10 Apple Jacks, Bran Flakes, Cap'n Crunch, Cocoa Puffs, Froot Loops, Mini-Wheats, Nutri-Grain, Puffed Rice, Quaker Oats, Smart Start 11 Cocoa Blasts, Cookie Crisp, Golden Crisp, Lucky Charms, Puffed Wheat, Sweet Crunch, Waffle Crisp
muezzin's call: 4 azan
Mufasa: 4 lion
muff: 3 err 4 blow, boot, fail, flub, mess, miss, slip, wrap 5 boner, botch, fluff, misdo, snafu 6 bobble, boggle, bumble, bungle, foozle, foul up, fumble, mess up, slip up 7 blunder, failure, lose out, misplay, screw up, stumble 9 gaucherie, mishandle, mismanage
starter: 3 ear
muffed grounder: 5 error
Muffet, emulate: 3 eat, sit
muffin: 3 gem 5 bread
starter: 4 raga
muffin __: 3 pan 5 stand
__ muffin: 4 bran, corn 7 English
Muffin Man's lane: 5 Drury
muffins, make: 4 bake
muffle: 3 gag 4 dull, hush, mute, wrap 5 drown, quiet, still 6 dampen, deaden, muzzle, obtund, soften, stifle, subdue 7 cushion, envelop, quieten, repress, silence, smother, squelch 8 bundle up, decrease, suppress, tone down
up: 4 wrap 6 swathe 7 envelop, swaddle
muffled: 3 low 4 dull, mute, weak 5 faint, muted, piano, quiet 6 hollow, low-key 8 deadened, hushed up
muffler: 4 mute 5 scarf, throw 8 kerchief
car ~ in Britain: 8 silencer
support: 4 nape 5 U-bolt
mufti: 6 civies 7 civvies, clothes
mug: 3 cup, rob 4 face, gull, look, moue, phiz, pose, puss, toby 5 mouth, stein 6 ambush, attack, beat up, kisser, prey on, visage 7 assault, grimace, tankard 8 features, overplay, schooner 9 coffee cup, make a face, steal from, strong-arm 10 expression
filler: 3 ale 4 beer, java, suds 6 coffee
shot subject: 4 perp 7 suspect
mug __: 4 shot
Mugabe: 6 Robert
mugger: 4 thug 5 rowdy, thief 6 outlaw, robber 7 brigand 8 attacker 9 assailant
deterrent: 4 mace
__-mugger: 6 hugger
Muggeridge, Malcolm: 6 writer 7 British
mugginess: 8 humidity, moisture
mugging: 5 theft 6 attack, holdup 7 offense, robbery 8 thievery
Muggs, J. Fred: 5 chimp 10 chimpanzee
show: 5 Today
muggy: 3 wet 4 damp, dank 5 close, humid, moist, mucky, soggy, undry 6 clammy, steamy, sticky, stuffy, sultry 7 wettish 10 oppressive
mugho: 4 pine, tree 8 pine tree
mugo: 4 pine, tree 8 pine tree
Muhammad: 3 Ali 5 Iqbal 6 Elijah
birthplace: 5 Mecca
book: 5 Koran, Quran
cat: 6 Muezza
daughter of ~: 5 Laila 6 Fatima
faith: 5 Islam
horse: 7 Alborak
wife of ~: 5 Aisha
Muir: 4 John, peak 5 Edwin, Gavin, mount 7 glacier 8 mountain
locale: 10 California
Muir __ National Monument: 5 Woods
Muir, Edwin: 4 poet 8 Scottish
work: The Labyrinth
Muir, John: 6 writer 10 naturalist
muishond: 6 weasel
relative: 4 mink 5 fitch, otter, ratel, sable, skunk, stoat, tayra 6 badger, ermine, ferret, marten 7 foumart, polecat 8 carcajou, foulmart, kolinsky 9 wolverine
mujer: 5 woman 7 Spanish
husband: 6 hombre
__ Mujeres, Mexico: 4 Isla
mukluk: 4 boot 5 kamik
wearer: 3 Esk. 5 Inuit 6 Eskimo, Innuit, Inupik
Mukota: 3 pig 5 swine
Mulan (1998 film)
director: Tony Bancroft, Barry Cook
voice cast: Eddie Murphy, Lea Salonga, B.D. Wong
mulberry: 4 tree 5 color, fruit 6 banian, banyan, fustic, purple 7 grayish
bark: 4 tapa
relative: 4 plum, puce 5 lilac, mauve 6 dahlia, damson, orchid 7 heather, petunia 8 amethyst, burgundy, eggplant, lavender 9 raspberry 10 heliotrope
tree: 3 fig 4 upas 5 ficus, ramon 6 antiar, fustic 10 breadfruit
__ mulberry: 3 red 5 black, paper, white 6 French, Indian
Mulberry Bush, The author: Angus Wilson
mulch: 4 till 5 humus 7 compost 9 fertilize
mulct: 4 fine, gull 5 cheat 6 amerce, extort, fleece, punish 7 defraud, swindle 8 penalize 10 amercement, forfeiture
Muldaur: 5 Diana, Maria
Muldaur, Maria
song: I'm a Woman (1975)
Midnight at the Oasis (1974)
Mulder: 3 Fox 5 agent
org.: 3 FBI
Muldoon: 3 cop 7 Francis
partner: 5 Toody
Muldowney, Shirley: 6 Cha Cha 9 auto racer
milieu: 5 track
mule: 3 Sal 4 sail, shoe 5 scuff 6 ani-

mal, brayer, equine, hybrid, mammal **7** Francis, holdout **8** footgear, footwear **10** crossbreed, mixed breed
blanket: 5 manta
burden: 4 plow
command to a ~: 3 gee, haw
cousin: 5 burro
emulate a ~: 4 balk, bray **5** baulk
father: 3 ass **6** donkey
foot: 4 hoof
its mascot is a ~: 4 Army
mother: 4 mare
of song: 3 Sal
mule __: 4 deer **5** chest, train **7** skinner
__ mule: 4 pack **5** white **6** Moscow
Mule __ Blues: 7 Skinner
Mule Bone author: Langston Hughes, Zora Neale Hurston
__ Mules for Sister Sara: 3 Two
muleta: 4 cape
color: 3 red
Mule Train artist: Frankie Laine
mulga: 4 tree **5** shrub
Mulgrew: 4 Kate
Mulhare: 6 Edward
Mulholland Dr. (2001 film)
cast: Laura Elena Harring, Ann Miller, Justin Theroux, Naomi Watts
director: David Lynch
Mulholland Falls actor: 5 Nolte
muliebral: 6 female **8** feminine
mulish: 5 balky, onery, rigid **6** ornery, wilful **7** decided, hard-set, piggish, wayward, willful **8** contrary, indocile, obdurate, perverse, stubborn **9** hard-nosed, impliable, iron-jawed, obstinate, pigheaded, tenacious, unbending **10** hard-bitten, headstrong, inflexible, refractory, unyielding
Mulk __ Anand: 3 Raj
mull: 4 muse **5** study, weigh **6** figure, ponder, review **7** revolve, sweeten **8** chaw over, chew over, cogitate, consider, headland, meditate, pore over, question, ruminate, turn over **9** brood over, reflect on, sweat over, think over **10** deliberate, meditate on
over: 4 muse, roll **5** study, think, weigh **6** ponder, puzzle **7** focus on, reflect, revolve, sleep on **8** cogitate, consider, look back, meditate, ruminate, turn over **9** reflect on **10** cogitate on, deliberate, reconsider, think about
Mull: 6 Martin
mullah
text: 5 Koran, Quran
tongue: 6 Arabic
Mullavey: 4 Greg
mullein: 5 plant **6** flower
__ Muller: 4 Maud
Müller: 4 Paul **7** Hermann **9** Alexander
Müller, Alexander: 8 Nobelist **9** physicist
Müller, Hermann: 8 Nobelist
Müller, Paul: 7 chemist **8** Nobelist
mullet: 4 fish
mulliatelle: 4 meat
mulligan: 4 soup, stew
Mulligan: 5 Gerry **6** Robert **7** Richard
Mulligan, Gerry: 11 saxophonist
genre: 4 jazz
Mulligan, Richard: 5 actor
film: One Potato, Two Potato (1964)
TV: Empty Nest, Soap
Mulligan, Robert: 8 director
film: Baby The Rain Must Fall (1965)
Come September (1961)
Fear Strikes Out (1957)
The Great Impostor (1961)
Inside Daisy Clover (1965)
Love With the Proper Stranger (1963)
The Man in the Moon (1991)
The Other (1972)
The Pursuit of Happiness (1971)
The Rat Race (1960)
Same Time, Next Year (1978)
Summer of '42 (1971)
To Kill a Mockingbird (1962)
Up the Down Staircase (1967)
mulligatawny: 4 soup
ingredient: 5 curry
Mulliken, Robert: 7 chemist **8** Nobelist
Mullins: 4 Moon **5** Shawn **9** Priscilla
Mullis, Kary: 7 chemist **8** Nobelist
mulloway: 4 fish
Mulroney: 5 Brian **6** Dermot
Mulroney, Brian: 2 P.M. **8** Canadian
predecessor: 6 Turner
successor: 8 Campbell
Mulroney, Dermot: 5 actor
film: Copycat (1995)
Living in Oblivion (1995)
My Best Friend's Wedding (1997)
There Goes My Baby (1994)
Mulsanne: 3 car **4** auto **7** Bentley **10** automobile
Multi-Bran Chex: 6 cereal
competitor: 3 Kix **4** Life, Trix **5** Kashi, Quisp, Total **6** Kaboom, Muesli, Oreo O's, Pablum, Smacks **7** All-Bran, Crispix, Harmony, Hunny B's, Mueslix, Oat Bran, Pokemon **8** Boo Berry, Cheerios, Corn Chex, Corn Pops, Fiber One, Rice Chex, Special K, Uncle Sam, Wheaties **9** Alpha Bits, Apple Zaps, Grape Nuts, Honey Comb, Just Right, Wheat Chex **10** Apple Jacks, Bran Flakes, Cap'n Crunch, Cocoa Puffs, Froot Loops, Mini-Wheats, Nutri-Grain, Puffed Rice, Quaker Oats, Smart Start **11** Cocoa Blasts, Cookie Crisp, Golden Crisp, Lucky Charms, Puffed Wheat, Sweet Crunch, Waffle Crisp
multicolor: 6 motley **7** dappled
multicolored: 4 pied **5** plaid **6** motley, veined **7** dappled, flecked, marbled, mottled, piebald, rainbow, spotted, striped **8** speckled, streaked **9** checkered, harlequin, prismatic
multiculturalism: 9 diversity
multifaceted: 9 versatile
multifarious: 4 many, mixt **5** mixed **6** legion, motley, sundry, varied **7** diverse, various **8** assorted, manifold, numerous, populous **9** different
multiflora: 4 rose
multiform: 7 unalike **8** manifold **9** different
multihued: 6 motley **7** dappled
multi- kin: 4 poly-
multilingual: 8 polyglot
multiloquent: 9 talkative **10** loquacious
multimedia format: 5 CD/ROM
multinational: 9 universal, worldwide
multiple: 4 many, mixt **5** mixed **6** legion, sundry, varied **7** diverse, various **8** assorted, manifold, numerous **9** different
multiple __: 4 shop, star **5** drill, store **6** allele, voting **7** factors, fission
multiple-__: 6 choice, valued
Multiple __ Service: 7 Listing
multiple-choice
not ~: 5 essay
option: 4 true **5** false, guess
word: 3 any
multiplex: 5 movie **6** cinema **7** theater, theatre
multiplication: 6 growth
symbol: 3 dot
multiplication __: 4 sign **5** table
multiplicity: 3 lot, ton **4** heap, host, pile, slew **5** bunch, ocean, stack **7** variety **9** abundance, great deal
multiply: 3 add **4** cube, grow, rise **5** boost, breed, build, mount, raise, spawn **6** double, expand, extend, repeat, spread, square **7** augment, build up, burgeon, compute, enlarge, magnify, produce, prosper **8** bourgeon, compound, generate, heighten, increase, manifold **9** calculate, propagate, reinforce, reproduce **10** accumulate, aggrandize, strengthen
multitude: 3 jam, lot, mob, sea **4** army, heap, herd, host, lots, many, mass, raff, slew **5** bunch, crowd, crush, drove, flock, horde, loads, ocean, press, stack, swarm, troop **6** legion, masses, myriad, number, oodles, people, public, rabble, scores, throng **7** legions, numbers, turnout **8** assembly, infinity, populace, quantity **9** battalion, concourse, profusion **10** confluence
multitudes: 4 lots **6** scores **7** legions
multitudinous: 4 many, rife **5** heaps **6** a lot of, divers, gobs of, legion, lots of, myriad, umteen, untold **7** a host of, a slew of, copious, heaps of, no end of, piles of, profuse, scads of, teeming, umpteen, various **8** a bunch of, abundant, an army of, infinite, manifold, numerous, oodles of, scores of, umpsteen **9** abounding, a passel of, bountiful, countless, quite a few, uncounted **10** zillions of
mum: 4 beer, mute **5** plant, quiet **6** flower, silent **7** aphonic **8** hushed up, nonvocal, taciturn, wordless **9** clammed up, secretive, soundless, voiceless **10** pantomimic, speechless, tongue-tied, unspeaking
half of a ~: 3 pom
maybe: 4 word
move a ~: 5 repot
not ~: 7 talking
one: 4 mime **5** mimer
Mumbai: 4 city, town **6** Bombay
locale: 5 India
mumble: 3 hum **4** slur, talk **5** speak, utter, voice **6** babble, murmur, mutter, ramble, rumble **7** grumble, maunder, stammer, stutter, whisper **8** vocalize **9** undertone, verbalize
mumbletypeg: 4 game
need: 5 knife
mumbo jumbo: 3 gas, rot **4** blah, bosh, bull, bunk, guff, jazz, jive, pooh, tosh **5** bilge, fudge, hokum, hooey, prate, stuff, trash, tripe **6** bunkum, bushwa, drivel, footle, gabble, gammon, gibber, havers, hot air, humbug, jabber, jargon, kibosh, piffle **7** baloney, blarney, blather, blether, boloney, bushwah, eyewash, flannel, flubdub, fustian, garbage, hogwash, inanity, rubbish, twaddle **8** buncombe, claptrap, falderal, falderol, flimflam, flummery, folderal, folderol, nonsense, slipslop, tommyrot, trumpery **9** banana oil, gibberish, goofiness, kidstakes, moonshine, poppycock, rigmarole **10** applesauce, balderdash, bilge water, codswallop, double-talk, empty words, flapdoodle, galimatias, hocus-pocus, invocation, Jabberwock, rigamarole, taradiddle
Mumetal: 5 alloy
component: 4 iron **6** copper, nickel
Mumford (1999 film)
cast: Hope Davis, Loren Dean, Jason Lee, Alfre Woodard
director: Lawrence Kasdan
Mumford, Lewis: 6 author, writer
work: The Culture of Cities
Myth and Machine
The Urban Prospect
mummer: 5 actor, clown, mimic **6** player **7** pierrot
mummery: 10 masquerade
mummy: 3 Tut **7** King Tut
Mummy's Hand, The (1940 film)
cast: Dick Foran, Wallace Ford, Peggy Moran
Mummy, The (1999 film)
cast: Brendan Fraser, John Hannah, Rachel Weisz
Mummy, The (1932 film) cast: Boris Karloff
Mummy, The author: Anne Rice
mumps: 9 parotitis
Mum's __ word!: 3 the
mumsy: 5 mater
Mumy: 5 Billy
Muná: 4 city, town
locale: 6 Mexico **7** Yucatán
munch: 3 eat **4** bite, chew, gnaw, nosh **5** champ, chomp, crush, grind, snack **6** crunch, nibble **7** scrunch **9** masticate
on: 9 grab a bite
Munchausen: 4 liar **5** baron
like ~ 's tales: 4 tall
Münch, Charles: 6 French **9** conductor
Munch, Edvard: 6 artist **7** painter **9** Norwegian
home: 4 Oslo
München: 4 city, town **5** stadt **6** Munich
locale: 7 Germany
munchies: 4 nosh **5** snack **6** hunger **7** craving
Munchkin
kin: 3 elf
official: 5 mayor
Muncie: 4 city, town
athletes: 9 Cardinals
locale: 3 Ind. **7** Indiana
school: 3 BSU **9** Ball State
mundane: 5 banal, ho-hum, lowly, vapid **6** normal **7** earthly, humdrum, insipid, profane, prosaic, routine, workday, worldly **8** day-to-day, everyday, ordinary, temporal, workaday **9** prosaical **10** pedestrian
Mundelein: 4 city, town
locale: 8 Illinois
Mundell, Robert: 8 Nobelist **9** economist
__ mundi: 4 anno
__-mundi: 5 coati
mung: 3 urd **4** bean **6** legume
bean relative: 4 urad
mung bean: 6 legume
Mungo: 4 Park
Mungojerrie: 3 cat
Mungo Jerry song: In the Summertime (1970)
muni: 4 bond
Munich: 4 city, town
locale: 7 Germany
river: 4 Isar
municipal: 4 city, town **5** civic, civil, local, urban **6** public **9** community
see also city
municipal __: 4 bond **5** court
municipality: 4 city, town **6** hamlet **7** borough, village **8** township **10** metropolis
munificent: 3 big **4** free **5** ample **6** giving, lavish **7** liberal, profuse **8** generous, handsome, prodigal **9** bounteous, bountiful, unsparing **10** altruistic, free-handed, open-handed, ungrudging
Muni, Paul: 5 actor
film: Angel on My Shoulder (1946)
Black Fury (1935)
Bordertown (1935)
Dr. Socrates (1935)
The Good Earth (1937)
I Am a Fugitive From a Chain Gang (1932)

Juarez (1939)
The Last Angry Man (1959)
The Life of Emile Zola (1937)
Scarface (1932)
The Story of Louis Pasteur (1936, AA)
The World Changes (1933)
munition: 3 arm 8 accouter
munitions: 4 ammo, arms, guns 5 bombs 7 cannons, weapons 8 equipage, grenades, materiel, ordnance, weaponry 9 armaments, artillery, firepower, torpedoes 10 explosives
place: 4 dump 6 armory 8 magazine
Munonye, John: 6 writer 8 Nigerian
Munro: 2 H.H. 5 Alice, Janet
Munro, Alice: 6 writer 8 Canadian
Munro, H.H.: 4 Saki 6 author, writer 8 Scottish
Munsee: 6 Indian 7 Amerind
Munshin: 5 Jules
Munson: 3 Ona 7 Thurman
Munster: 4 city, Lily, town 5 Eddie 6 Herman 7 Marilyn
county: 5 Clare
locale: 7 Indiana
Münster: 4 city, port, town
locale: 7 Germany
Munsters, The (CBS sitcom)
cast: Yvonne DeCarlo (Lily Munster)
Fred Gwynne (Herman Munster)
Al Lewis (Grandpa)
Butch Patrick (Eddie Munster)
Pat Priest (Marilyn Munster)
pet: Spot, Igor
muntjac: 4 deer 6 animal
relative: 3 elk, roe 4 axis, pudu, shou, sika 5 moose 6 chital, guemal, hangul, huemul, sambar, sambur, thamin, wapiti 7 brocket, caribou, sambhar, sambhur 8 reindeer 9 barasingh
muon: 6 lepton 8 particle
Muphrid: 4 star
Muppet: 3 Sam 4 Bert, Elmo 5 Ernie, Gonzo, Oscar, Piggy, Rizzo, Rowlf 6 Animal, Fozzie, Kermit 7 Statler, Waldorf 9 Miss Piggy
Muppet Christmas Carol, The (1992 film)
cast: Michael Caine, Fozzie Bear, Kermit the Frog, Miss Piggy
director: Brian Henson
Muppet Movie, The (1979 film)
cast: Fozzie Bear, Kermit the Frog, Miss Piggy
director: James Frawley
Muppets From Space (1999 film)
cast: Gonzo, Kermit the Frog, Miss Piggy, Jeffrey Tambor
director: Tim Hill
Muppets Take Manhattan, The (1984 film)
cast: Fozzie Bear, Gonzo, Kermit the Frog, Miss Piggy
director: Frank Oz
Murad, Ferid: 8 Nobelist
mural: 3 art 5 décor, secco 6 fresco 8 painting 9 landscape
place: 4 wall
starter: 5 inter, intra
Murano: 3 SUV 6 Nissan
Murasaki Shikibu: 6 writer 8 Japanese
work: The Tale of Genji
Murat: 5 river
locale: 6 Turkey
Murcia: 4 city, town
locale: 5 Spain
Murcielago: 3 car 4 auto 10 automobile 11 Lamborghini
Murder, __ Wrote: 3 She
Murder at 1600 (1997 film)
cast: Alan Alda, Diane Lane, Wesley Snipes
Murder at the Gallop (1963 film)
cast: Robert Morley, Margaret Rutherford
Murder by Death (1976 film)
cast: Eileen Brennan, James Coco, Peter Falk, Alec Guinness, Elsa Lanchester, David Niven, Peter Sellers, Maggie Smith
director: Robert Moore
dog: 5 Myron
Murder by Numbers (2002 film)
cast: Sandra Bullock, Ben Chaplin, Ryan Gosling
director: Barbet Schroeder
Murderers' Row (1966 film)
cast: Ann-Margret, Karl Malden, Dean Martin
director: Henry Levin
Murder, He Says (1945 film)
cast: Fred MacMurray, Marjorie Main, Helen Walker
director: George Marshall
Murder, Inc. (1960 film)
cast: May Britt, Henry Morgan, Stuart Whitman
director: Burt Balaban, Stuart Rosenberg
Murder in the Cathedral author: T.S. Eliot
Murder Man, The (1935 film)
cast: Lionel Atwill, Virginia Bruce, Spencer Tracy
director: Tim Whelan
Murder Most __: 4 Foul
Murder Must Advertise author: 6 Sayers
Murder, My Sweet (1944 film)
cast: Dick Powell, Anne Shirley, Claire Trevor
director: Edward Dmytryk
Murder of Roger Ackroyd, The
author: Agatha Christie
Murder on the Orient Express: 4 film 5 novel
author: Agatha Christie
cast: Lauren Bacall, Martin Balsam, Ingrid Bergman, Jacqueline Bisset, Sean Connery, Albert Finney, John Gielgud, Wendy Hiller, Anthony Perkins, Vanessa Redgrave, Rachel Roberts, Richard Widmark, Michael York
director: Sidney Lumet
murderous: 4 fell 5 cruel 6 brutal, savage 7 arduous, hellish, ruinous, vicious, violent 8 criminal, ruthless 9 dangerous, difficult, ferocious, harrowing, rapacious, strenuous 10 exhausting, malevolent
Murder, She Wrote (CBS drama)
cast: Tom Bosley (Amos Tupper)
Angela Lansbury (Jessica Fletcher)
William Windom (Dr. Seth Hazlitt)
setting: Cabot Cove, Maine
Murders in the Rue Morgue, The
author: Edgar Allan Poe
beast: 3 ape
Murders in the Zoo (1933 film)
cast: Lionel Atwill, Charles Ruggles, Randolph Scott
director: A. Edward Sutherland
Murdoch: 4 Iris 6 Rupert
Murdoch, Iris: 5 Irish 6 writer
work: An Accidental Man
The Bell
Henry and Cato
The Sandcastle
The Sea, the Sea
A Severed Head
Under the Net
The Unicorn
An Unofficial Rose
Murdoch University home: 5 Perth
Mures: 5 river
city on the ~: 4 Arad
locale: 7 Hungary, Romania, Rumania 8 Roumania
Muret: 4 city, town
locale: 6 France
murex: 5 shell 8 seashell 9 gastropod
Murfreesboro: 4 city, town
athletes: 11 Blue Raiders
locale: 9 Tennessee
school: 4 MTSU
muriatic __: 4 acid
murid: 5 mouse
Muriel: 5 Spark 8 Humphrey, Rukeyser
Muriel's Wedding (1994 film)
cast: Toni Collette, Rachel Griffiths, Bill Hunter
director: P.J. Hogan
murine: 5 mouse 6 animal, mammal, rodent
relative: 3 rat 4 cavy, degu, jird, paca, vole 5 coypu, gundi, mouse, xerus 6 agouti, beaver, gerbil, gopher, jerboa, marmot 7 hamster, lemming, muskrat, visacha 8 chipmunk, cricetid, dormouse, squirrel, tuco-tuco 9 chickaree, groundhog, guinea pig, porcupine, woodchuck 10 chinchilla, prairie dog
murk: 3 fog 4 dark, haze, mist 5 gloom 8 darkness
murky: 3 dim 4 dark, drab, dull, gray, grey, grim, hazy 5 black, dingy, dusky, faded, foggy, fuzzy, livid, misty, muddy, muted, smoky, thick, vague 6 cloudy, dismal, dreary, gloomy, ill-lit, opaque, somber, turbid 7 cryptic, obscure, shadowy, unclear 8 darkened, lowering, nebulous, overcast, puzzling, roiled up 9 ambiguous, cheerless, cryptical, enigmatic, tenebrous, unlighted 10 caliginous, clear as mud, depressing, indistinct, perplexing, tenebrific
make ~: 5 cloud
Murmansk: 4 city, port, town
locale: 6 Russia
murmur: 3 coo, hum, pur 4 buzz, moan, purl, purr, sigh, wash 5 drone, sough, sound, speak, voice, whine 6 babble, breath, burble, gurgle, intone, mumble, mutter, ripple, rumble, rustle, tinkle 7 buzzing, grumble, humming, lapping, trickle, whisper 8 susurrus, vocalize 9 undertone, verbalize
murmured: 3 low 4 soft 5 bated, faint, muted, piano, quiet 6 hushed 7 muffled, subdued 8 dampened, deadened 9 toned down 10 turned down
__ muros: 5 intra
Murphey, Michael
song: What's Forever For (1982)
Wildfire (1975)
Murphy: 3 bed, Ben 4 Dale 5 Audie, Brown, Eddie 6 Calvin, George, Walter 7 Michael, William 8 Brittany
bed's place: 6 closet
Murphy __: 3 bed 5 Brown
__ Murphy: 6 Father
Murphy, Audie: 5 actor
film: The Guns of Fort Petticoat (1957)
Night Passage (1957)
No Name on the Bullet (1959)
The Red Badge of Courage (1951)
To Hell and Back (1955)
The Unforgiven (1960)
Walk the Proud Land (1956)
Murphy author: Samuel Beckett
Murphy Brown (CBS sitcom)
cast: Candice Bergen (Murphy Brown)
Faith Ford (Corky Sherwood)
Charles Kimbrough (Jim Dial)
Joe Regalbuto (Frank Fontana)
housekeeper: 5 Eldin
program: F.Y.I.
setting: 10 Washington
son: Avery
tavern owner: 4 Phil
Murphy, Eddie: 5 actor 8 comedian
film: 48HRS. (1982)
Beverly Hills Cop (1984)
Bowfinger (1999)
Coming to America (1988)
The Distinguished Gentleman (1992)
Doctor Dolittle (1998)
Dr. Doolittle 2 (2001)
Life (1999)
The Nutty Professor (1996)
Showtime (2002)
Trading Places (1983)
film (voice): Mulan (1998)
Shrek (2001)
TV: Saturday Night Live
Murphy, George: 5 actor
film: Bataan (1943)
Border Incident (1949)
Broadway Melody of 1940 (1940)
For Me and My Gal (1942)
Hold That Co-ed (1938)
Step Lively (1944)
This Is the Army (1943)
Tom, Dick and Harry (1941)
Murphy, Michael: 5 actor
film: Cloak & Dagger (1984)
Manhattan (1979)
An Unmarried Woman (1978)
Murphy, Rose Mary hubby: 4 Abie
Murphy's __: 3 Law, War 7 Romance
Murphy's Law word: 5 wrong
Murphy's Romance (1985 film)
cast: Sally Field, James Garner, Brian Kerwin
director: Martin Ritt
Murphy's War (1971 film)
cast: Horst Janson, Philippe Noiret, Peter O'Toole, Sian Phillips
director: Peter Yates
Murphy, Walter song: A Fifth of Beethoven (1976)
Murphy, William: 8 Nobelist
Murray: 3 Don, Jan, Ken, Mae 4 Anne, Bill, city, Head, town 5 river 6 Arthur, Butler, Joseph 7 Kempton 8 Gell-Mann, Hamilton, Leinster
locale: 4 Utah
River locale: 9 Australia
Murray __: 4 the K
Murray, Anne
homeland: Canada
song: Broken Hearted Me (1979)
Danny's Song (1973)
Daydream Believer (1980)
I Just Fall in Love Again (1979)
Love Song (1974)
Snowbird (1970)
You Needed Me (1978)
You Won't See Me (1974)
Murray, Arthur
lesson: 4 step 5 tango
Murray, Bill: 5 actor 8 comedian
film: Caddyshack (1980)
Charlie's Angels (2000)
Ed Wood (1994)
Ghostbusters (1984)
Ghostbusters II (1989)
Groundhog Day (1993)
Kingpin (1996)
Mad Dog and Glory (1993)
Meatballs (1979)
Quick Change (1990)
Rushmore (1998)
Scrooged (1988)
Stripes (1981)
Tootsie (1982)

What About Bob? (1991)
TV: 17 Saturday Night Live
Murray, Don: 5 actor
film: Advise & Consent (1962)
The Bachelor Party (1957)
Bus Stop (1956)
A Hatful of Rain (1957)
The Hoodlum Priest (1961)
One Man's Way (1964)
Shake Hands With the Devil (1959)
These Thousand Hills (1959)
Murray Grey: 3 cow **4** bull **6** bovine, cattle
Murray, J.A.H. lexicon: 3 OED
Murray, Joseph: 8 Nobelist
murre: 4 bird **9** guillemot
emulate a ~: 4 dive
genus: 4 uria
murrelet: 4 bird
murrey: 3 red **5** color
Murrieta: 4 city, town
locale: 10 California
Murrow, Edward R.
milieu: 4 news
network: 3 CBS **5** CBS-TV
Murry, John Middleton: 6 critic, editor, writer **7** British
murumbu: 4 drum
mus.
adaptation: 3 arr.
detached, in ~: 4 stac.
ensemble: 4 orch.
slower, in ~: 3 rit. **4** rall.
strongly accented, in ~: 3 sfz.
see also music
Musala: 4 peak **5** mount **8** mountain
locale: 6 Europe **8** Bulgaria
Musante: 4 Tony
Musberger: 5 Brent
Muscadet: 4 wine **5** white
origin: 6 France
muscadine: 5 fruit, grape
relative: 5 Gamay, pinot, Tokay **6** Merlot **7** Catawba, Concord, Niagara **8** Cabernet, malvasia, muscatel **9** Sauvignon, zinfandel **10** Chardonnay
muscat: 4 wine
Muscat: 4 city, town **5** grape **7** capital
locale: 4 Oman
native: 4 Arab
muscatel: 3 red **4** wine **5** grape
relative: 5 Gamay, pinot, Tokay **6** Merlot **7** Catawba, Concord, Niagara **8** Cabernet, malvasia **9** muscadine, Sauvignon, zinfandel **10** Chardonnay
Muscatine: 4 city, town
locale: 4 Iowa
Muscida: 4 star
muscle: 3 vim **4** beef, dint, meat, push, thew, work **5** brawn, clout, flesh, force, might, power, sinew, steam, thews, vigor **6** energy, flexor, tendon, tissue **7** fitness, potence, potency, stamina **8** strength, vitality **9** beefiness, endurance, fortitude, hardiness, huskiness, influence, puissance, stoutness, toughness **10** brawniness, brute force, horsepower, mightiness, robustness, ruggedness, sturdiness
arm ~: 6 biceps
back ~: 3 lat
belly ~: 2 ab **6** rectus
cell: 5 fiber, stria
chest ~: 3 pec
combining form: 2 my- **3** myo-
contract a ~: 4 flex
contraction chemical: 3 ATP
ender: 3 man, men **5** bound
hip ~: 5 psoas
hired ~: 4 goon **7** torpedo
in: 5 usurp **8** trespass **9** insinuate, interpose, intervene
(in): 5 barge
injury: 4 pull, tear
in on: 6 invade
lacking ~: 4 puny, weak **6** flabby
leg ~: 4 quad **6** rectus, soleus, vastus **9** hamstring
loss of ~ coordination: 5 ataxy **6** ataxia
move a ~: 4 stir
pain: 4 ache, kink, knot, pang **5** cramp, crick, spasm **6** twinge
protein: 5 actin
quality: 4 tone **5** tonus
science: 7 myology
shoulder ~: 4 delt
show some ~: 5 exert
soother: 3 spa **6** hot tub **7** Jacuzzi
straight ~: 6 rectus
treat a ~ pull: 5 chill
weakness: 5 atony **6** atonia
muscle __: 3 car **5** beach, fiber, sense, shirt **7** spindle
Muscle __, AL: 6 Shoals
Muscle Beach Party (1964 film)
cast: Frankie Avalon, Annette Funicello, Buddy Hackett
director: William Asher
muscleman, mythical: 5 Atlas
Muscles (1982 song) artist: Diana Ross
muscovado: 5 sugar
muscovite: 4 mica
Muscovy duck: 4 fowl
relative: 4 smew, teal **5** eider, Pekin, Rouen, scaup **6** Cayuga, scoter **7** gadwall, mallard, pintail, pochard, redhead, widgeon **8** garganey, mandarin, oldsquaw, shoveler **9** broadbill, goldeneye, goosander, greenhead, merganser, sprigtail **10** bufflehead, canvasback, surf scoter
muscular: 3 fit **4** buff, hale, iron, wiry **5** beefy, burly, hardy, hefty, hunky, husky, lusty, nervy, stout, thewy, tough **6** brawny, hearty, mighty, potent, robust, rugged, sinewy, steely, stocky, strong, sturdy, virile **7** doughty, healthy, hulking **8** athletic, forceful, indurate, powerful, puissant, pumped up, stalwart, vigorous **9** Atlantean, herculean, strapping, well-built **10** able-bodied, red-blooded
not ~: 4 puny, weak **6** flabby
one: 5 he-man
muscularity: 5 power, thews
musculature: 8 physique
muse: 4 mull **5** dream, study, think, weigh **6** ponder, puzzle, trance **7** reflect, revolve **8** chew over, cogitate, consider, look back, meditate, mull over, ruminate, turn over **9** cerebrate, percolate, speculate, think over **10** brown study, deliberate, introspect, puzzle over
Muse
complement: 4 nine
domain: 4 arts
gift from a ~: 4 idea
instrument: 4 lyre
musée: 6 Louvre
Musée des Beaux Arts author: W.H. Auden
Museo del __: 5 Prado
muser: 8 ponderer, theorist **9** meditator
Muses:
Calliope (epic poetry)
Clio (history)
Erato (lyric poetry)
Euterpe (music)
Melpomene (tragedy)
Polyhymnia (sacred music)
Terpsichore (dance)
Thalia (comedy)
Urania (astronomy)
parent: 4 Zeus **9** Mnemosyne
Muses are Heard, The author: Truman Capote
Muse, The (1999 film)
cast: Jeff Bridges, Albert Brooks, Andie MacDowell, Sharon Stone
director: Albert Brooks
musette: 4 wind **7** bagpipe **10** instrument
origin: 6 France
museum: 4 hall **7** archive, gallery **8** building, landmark, treasury **10** exhibition, foundation, repository, storehouse
add-on: 4 wing
employee: 5 guard **7** curator **8** restorer
funder: 3 NEA
guide: 6 docent
piece: 3 art, urn **4** bust **5** relic, torso **6** fossil
regular: 4 goer
room: 6 atrium
vessel: 7 samovar
worker's deg.: 3 MFA
museum __: 5 piece
__ museum: 3 wax
__ Museum: 7 British
mush: 4 glop, pulp, samp **5** slush **6** batter **8** porridge
ender: 4 room
musher conveyance: 4 sled
mushroom: 3 cep **4** boom, cepe **5** burst, enoki, morel, plant, swell **6** agaric, blewit, blow up, button, expand, fungus, mature, spread, spring, sprout, thrive **7** blewitt, blueleg, bluette, burgeon, explode, shoot up, truffle **8** bourgeon, flourish, increase, shiitake, spring up **9** shaggy cap **10** champignon, shaggymane
cloud maker: 5 A bomb, A test, H bomb, N test
combining form: 3 myc- **4** myco- **6** -mycete
like some ~ s: 6 edible
part: 5 stipe, theca **6** pileus
source: 5 spore
mushroom __: 5 cloud **6** anchor
__ mushroom: 4 milk **5** field, honey, horse, straw **6** meadow, oyster, sponge **7** chicken, parasol
mushy: 4 soft **5** corny, pulpy, sappy, soggy, soppy, sweet, weepy **6** sirupy, sloppy, slushy, spongy, sugary, syrupy, tender **7** maudlin, mawkish, squashy, squishy **8** bathetic, effusive, romantic, schmalzy, shmaltzy, yielding **9** emotional, pastelike, schmaltzy, semisolid **10** lovey-dovey, saccharine, semiliquid
Musial, Stan: 8 Cardinal **10** outfielder
music: 3 air, art, bop, jig, lay, pop, rag, rap, ska **4** aria, duet, folk, hymn, jazz, lied, opus, raga, reel, rock, scat, song, soul, trio, tune **5** bebop, blues, C and W, canon, carol, chant, dirge, ditty, etude, fugue, galop, gavot, gigue, largo, march, motet, octet, opera, pavan, pavin, piece, polka, R and B, rondo, rumba, salsa, samba, score, sound, suite, swing, tango, waltz **6** adagio, anthem, ballad, bolero, chorus, doo-wop, gospel, medium, melody, minuet, pavane, reggae, rhumba, sonata, strain **7** andante, arietta, ariette, big band, calypso, cantata, caprice, chamber, chanson, chorale, country, euphony, foxtrot, gavotte, harmony, klezmer, lullaby, mazurka, octette, prelude, ragtime, refrain, scherzo, singing, skiffle, toccata, two-step **8** acid rock, acoustic, canticle, canzonet, cavatina, concerto, fantasia, folk rock, hard rock, hornpipe, mazourka, nocturne, operetta, oratorio, overture, punk rock, rhapsody, serenade, serenata, soft rock, symphony **9** a cappella, bluegrass, bossa nova, capriccio, classical, Dixieland, honky-tonk, pastorale, plainsong, polonaise **10** acoustical, heavy metal, trumpeting
copyright org.: 3 BMI **5** ASCAP
enhancer: 3 amp
holder: 5 stand
knack for ~: 3 ear
like modern ~: 6 atonal
media: 3 CDs
sheet ~ abbr.: 3 arr.
music __: 3 box **4** hall, roll **5** drama, stand, video
music __ spheres: 5 of the
__ music: 3 rap **4** chin, folk, mood, part, soul, surf **5** house, salon, sheet, swing **6** chance, choral, gospel **7** chamber, country, klezmer, program, surfing
Music __ charms...: 4 hath
Music __ Revue: 3 Box
Music __, The: 3 Man
__ Music: 4 Moon **5** I Hear, I Love, Night, Water
musica __: 5 falsa, ficta
musical: 4 play, show **5** in key, lyric, revue, sweet, tonal **6** ariose, choral, dulcet, mellow, poetic, review **7** lilting, lyrical, melodic, recital, silvery, songful, tuneful **8** pleasing, poetical, rhythmic **9** agreeable, melodious **10** euphonious, harmonious, production
accompaniment: 6 backup
beginning: 4 vamp **5** intro **8** overture
Broadway: 3 Big **4** Cats, Coco, Hair, Mame, Nine, Rent **5** Annie, Dolly!, Evita, Gypsy, Hello, Zorba **6** Barnum, Can-Can, Grease, I Do! I Do!, Kismet, Les Miz, Oliver!, Pippin, Purlie, The Wiz **7** Allegro, Cabaret, Camelot, Chicago, Company, Follies, Pal Joey, Passion, Ragtime, Titanic, Whoopee **8** Applause, Big River, Carousel, Fiorello!, Godspell, Oklahoma!, Peter Pan, Show Boat, Two by Two **9** Brigadoon, Funny Girl, Girl Crazy, No Strings, On the Town, Pipe Dream **10** Dreamgirls, Kiss Me Kate, Lady Be Good!, Miss Saigon, My Fair Lady, Shenandoah **11** A Chorus Line, Crazy For You, Damn Yankees, Leave It to Me, Me and Juliet, No No Nanette, Of Thee I Sing, Sweeney Todd, The King and I, The Lion King, The Music Man
direction: 3 rit., sfz. **4** a due, anim., stac. **5** assai, dolce, forte, grave, largo, lento, piano, secco, tutti **6** adagio, al fine, arioso, da capo, legato, presto, rubato, subito, vivace **7** agitato, allegro, amoroso, andante, animato, con brio, con moto, marcato, tremolo, vibrato, volante **8** con amore, con anima, grazioso, maestoso, moderato, parlando, semplice, spiccato **9** alla breve, andantino, cantabile, crescendo, glissando, larghetto, non troppo, pizzicato, sforzando, sostenuto **10** allegretto, fortissimo, pianissimo, ritardando, scherzando
epilogue: 4 coda
Greek ~ note: 4 nete
group: 4 band, trio **5** combo, nonet, octet **6** sestet, sextet **7** nonette, octette, quartet, quintet **8** sextette
hall: 5 odeon, odeum

halls: 4 odea
instrument: 3 sax, uke 4 fife, gong, harp, horn, lute, lyre, Moog, oboe, tuba, viol 5 banjo, bongo, bugle, cello, flute, kazoo, organ, piano, viola 6 chimes, cornet, fiddle, guitar, tam-tam, tom-tom, violin, zither 7 alto sax, bagpipe, bassoon, celesta, cymbals, helicon, maracas, marimba, musette, ocarina, panpipe, piccolo, saxhorn, trumpet, ukulele 8 altohorn, autoharp, bass drum, bass viol, calliope, castanet, clarinet, dulcimer, mandolin, melodeon, recorder, theremin, triangle, trombone 9 accordion, alpenhorn, balalaika, euphonium, harmonica, harmonium, saxophone, vibraharp 10 clavichord, concertina, contrabass, flugelhorn, hurdy-gurdy, kettledrum, sousaphone, squeezebox, tambourine, vibraphone 11 harpsichord
interval: 4 step 5 fifth, ninth, sixth, third 6 fourth, octave 7 seventh 8 half-step
key: 4 A maj., B maj., C maj., D maj., E maj., F maj., G maj. 5 A flat, B flat, E flat 6 A major, A minor, B major, B minor, C major, C minor, D major, D minor, E major, E minor, F major, F minor, G major, G minor 8 A flat maj., B flat maj., E flat maj. 10 A flat major, B flat major, B flat minor, E flat major 11 C sharp minor
liability: 5 no ear 6 tin ear
measure: 3 bar
motif: 4 riff
notation: 3 tie 4 clef, flat, neum, rest, slur 5 C clef, F clef, G clef, neume, sharp 6 accent 7 mordent, natural 8 alto clef, bass clef 9 signature
note: 2 do, fa, la, mi, re, so, ti 3 sol
notes: 5 chord, triad
phrase: 5 tra la
sample: 4 demo
sound: 4 note, tone 5 trill
staff letters: 4 FACE 5 EGBDF
style: 5 sound
syllables: 5 solfa
tempo: 4 time
theme: 4 tema
toy: 5 gazoo, kazoo 8 mirliton
transition: 5 segue 6 bridge
musical ___: 3 saw 6 chairs, comedy 7 glasses
musical chairs: 4 game
quest: 4 seat
musicale: 3 gig 4 show 6 accord, unison 7 concert, harmony, recital 9 agreement, festivity 10 jam session
Music Box (1989 film)
cast: Frederic Forrest, Jessica Lange, Donald Moffat, Armin Mueller-Stahl
director: Costa-Gavras
Music Box Dancer (1979 song) artist: Frank Mills
Music Box Revue composer: 6 Berlin
Music for Airports composer: 3 Eno
Music for Chameleons author: Truman Capote
Music for the Millions author: 4 Ewen
musician: 4 diva 5 fifer, piper 6 artist, bugler, harper, lutist, lyrist, oboist, player, singer 7 artiste, bassist, cellist, drummer, flutist, harpist, pianist, soloist, violist 8 banjoist, composer, flautist, lyricist, organist, virtuoso, vocalist 9 conductor, cornetist, guitarist, performer, violinist 10 trombonist
job: 3 gig
street ~: 6 busker
musicians: 4 band, orch. 8 ensemble 9 orchestra
Music in the Air (1934 film)
cast: John Boles, Douglass Montgomery, Gloria Swanson
director: Joe May
Music in the Air composer: 4 Kern 11 Hammerstein
Music Man, The (1962 film)
cast: Paul Ford, Hermione Gingold, Buddy Hackett, Ron Howard, Shirley Jones, Pert Kelton, Robert Preston
character: 3 Hix 4 Alma, Hill, Maud 5 Ewart, Jacey, Paroo, Shinn 6 Dunlop, Harold, Marian, Oliver 7 Alma Hix, Eulalie, Squires 9 Oliver Hix 10 Harold Hill, Maud Dunlop
composer: Meredith Willson
director: Morton Da Costa
setting: 4 Iowa 9 River City
Music of My Heart (1999 song) artist: Gloria Estefan, 'Nsync
music of the ___: 7 spheres
Music of the Heart (1999 film)
cast: Angela Bassett, Gloria Estefan, Aidan Quinn, Meryl Streep
director: Wes Craven
Music of the Night, The: 4 aria
Musigny: 3 red 4 wine
origin: 6 France
Musil, Robert: 6 writer 8 Austrian
musing: 4 lost 6 revery 7 pensive, reverie, thought, wistful 10 reflection, thoughtful
musk: 4 odor
ender: 3 rat 4 oxen, root 5 melon
source: 5 civet
musk ___: 3 hog 4 deer, duck, oxen, rose 5 plant 6 flower, mallow, turtle 7 thistle
musk duck: 4 fowl
relative: 4 smew, teal 5 eider, Pekin, Rouen, scaup 6 Cayuga, scoter 7 gadwall, mallard, pintail, pochard, redhead, widgeon 8 garganey, mandarin, oldsquaw, shoveler 9 broadbill, goldeneye, goosander, greenhead, merganser, sprigtail 10 bufflehead, canvasback, surf scoter
muskeg: 3 fen 5 swamp
Muskego: 4 city, town
locale: 9 Wisconsin
Muskegon: 4 city, town
locale: 8 Michigan
muskellunge: 4 fish, pike
Musker, John: 8 director
film: Aladdin (1992)
The Great Mouse Detective (1986)
The Little Mermaid (1989)
musket: 3 arm, gun 5 fusil, rifle 6 jingal, weapon 7 firearm 9 flintlock
ball: 4 slug
ender: 3 eer
musketeer: 7 soldier
Musketeers: 6 Xavier
motto word: 3 all, one
one of the ~: 5 Athos 6 Aramis 7 Porthos 9 d'Artagnan
___ Musketeers, The: 4 Four 5 Three
Muskie, Edmund: 3 sen. 7 senator
state: 5 Maine
muskmelon: 4 pepo 5 fruit 6 casaba 7 cassaba
Muskogee: 4 city, town 6 Indian 7 Amerind
locale: 8 Oklahoma
muskox: 5 bovid 6 bovine
relative: 3 yak 4 anoa, arna, gaur, urus, zebu 5 bison, gayal, takin 6 mithan 7 aurochs, banteng, banting, beefalo, buffalo, carabao, cattalo, kouprey, tamarao, tamarau, timarau
muskrat: 6 animal, mammal, rodent
relative: 4 cavy, degu, jird, paca, vole 5 coypu, gundi, mouse, xerus 6 agouti, beaver, gerbil, gopher, jerboa, marmot, murine 7 hamster, lemming, visacha 8 chipmunk, cricetid, dormouse, squirrel, tuco-tuco 9 chickaree, groundhog, guinea pig, porcupine, woodchuck 10 chinchilla, prairie dog
Muskrat Love (1976 song) artist: Captain & Tennille
Muskrat Ramble composer: 3 Ory
Muslim: 3 Era
see also Moslem
___ Muslim: 5 Black
muslin: 4 mull 6 fabric 8 material
___ muslin: 5 Swiss 6 butter
Musoma: 4 city, town
locale: 8 Tanzania
musophobe fear: 4 mice
muss: 4 hash, mess 6 jumble, mess up, muddle, ruck up, ruffle, rumple, tangle, tousle, touzle 7 clutter, crumple, disturb, rummage, wrinkle 8 disarray, dishevel, mishmash 9 bedraggle 10 disarrange, untidiness
up: 4 soil 6 ruffle, rumple, tousle, touzle 7 derange 8 disarray, dishevel, scramble
mussed: 7 tousled, unkempt
mussel: 4 unio 5 naiad, shell 6 cockle 8 seashell
cousin: 4 clam 6 oyster
prepare ~ s: 5 steam
mussel ___: 4 crab 6 shrimp
___ mussel: 4 date 5 zebra
Musset, Alfred de: 4 poet 6 French 10 playwright
Mussolini: 6 Benito
son-in-law: 5 Ciano
Mussorgsky, Modest: 7 Russian 8 composer
work: Boris Godunov
Edipo
A Night on Bald Mountain
Pictures at an Exhibition
mussy: 6 sloppy, unneat, untidy 7 chaotic, jumbled, muddled, rumpled, tousled, unkempt 8 slovenly 9 cluttered 10 disheveled, disordered, disorderly, in disarray, out of order, out of place, topsy-turvy
not ~: 4 neat, tidy
must: 4 duty, need 5 has to, ought, vital 6 devoir, have to, need to, should 9 condition, essential, moldiness, necessary, necessity, obsession, requisite 10 commitment, imperative, obligation, sine qua non
must-___: 3 see 4 have, read
mustache
application: 3 wax
get rid of a ~: 5 shave
site: 3 lip
teen ~: 4 wisp
mustache ___: 3 cup, wax
___ mustache: 6 walrus, Zapata 9 handlebar
Mustagh: 5 range
locale: 4 Asia 7 Kashmir 8 Cashmere
mustang: 4 pony 5 horse, mount 6 animal, equine
Mustang: 3 car 4 auto, Ford 10 automobile
competitor: 6 Camaro
Mustang Country (1976 film)
cast: Robert Fuller, Joel McCrea, Patrick Wayne
Mustangs: 3 SMU
Mustang Sally (1966 song) artist: Wilson Pickett
mustard: 4 herb, seed 5 color, Dijon, spice 6 yellow 7 French's, Gulden's 9 condiment 10 Grey Poupon
alternative: 4 mayo 6 catsup
cut the ~: 6 hack it 7 succeed
family plant: 4 cole, kail, kale 5 cress
like some ~: 4 mild
relative: 4 buff, corn, gold, lime, rust, sand 5 blond, brass, coral, cream, flaxy, lemon, maize, ocher, ochre, peach, rusty, straw 6 blonde, canary, chammy, citron, crocus, flaxen, shammy, shamoy 7 apricot, chamois, citrine, jasmine, nankeen, old gold, saffron, xanthic 8 daffodil, primrose 9 champagne, goldenrod, jessamine
mustard ___: 3 oil 7 plaster
___ mustard: 4 leaf, wild 5 black, brown, Dijon, white 6 garlic, Indian 7 Chinese
Mustard, Colonel game: 4 Clue
___-mustard dressing: 5 honey
Mustard, Mr., like: 4 mean
___ Must Be Crazy, The: 4 Gods
musteline mammal: 4 mink
muster: 4 bevy, bloc, crew, gang, levy, meet, roll 5 array, bunch, crowd, draft, enrol, enter, group, raise, rally, troop 6 call up, enlist, enroll, gather, roster, sign up, summon, throng, troupe 7 collect, compile, convene, convoke, marshal, pluck up, produce, recruit, roundup, send for 8 assemble, assembly, mobilize, roll call 9 coalition, forgather, gathering 10 congregate
out: 9 allow to go, discharge
pass ~: 4 suit 6 hack it 7 qualify, satisfy
up: 6 gather, summon 7 collect, marshal
muster ___: 3 out 4 roll
___ muster: 4 pass
___ Must Fall: 5 Night
___ must go on, The: 4 show
Must to Avoid, A (1966 song) artist: Herman's Hermits
Must've been something ___: 4 I ate
musty: 3 old 4 dank, dull, rank, sour 5 banal, fusty, hoary, moldy, passé, stale, tired, trite 6 frowsy, frowzy, old hat, rancid, smelly, spoilt, stuffy 7 airless, clichéd, decayed, mildewy, noisome, odorous, spoiled 8 decrepit, listless, mildewed, obsolete, outdated, outmoded, overripe 9 apathetic, crumbling, hackneyed, moth-eaten, old-school, out-of-date 10 antiquated, malodorous, threadbare
make less ~: 6 air out 9 ventilate
mut
see mutt
mutability: 4 flux
mutable: 5 fluid 6 fickle, labile, mobile, uneven 7 erratic, protean, varying 8 changing, shifting, unstable, unsteady, variable, wavering 9 mercurial, uncertain, unsettled 10 capricious, changeable, inconstant
mutant: 5 freak 7 monster
Mutare: 4 city, town
locale: 8 Zimbabwe
mutate: 4 turn, vary 5 alter, morph 6 change, evolve, modify 9 transform
mutation: 5 freak 6 change, mutant 7 anomaly 9 deviation, variation 10 alteration
gene ~: 6 allele
starter: 5 trans
subject: 4 gene
___ mutation: 3 bud 4 back 5 point 7 reverse
Mutation author: Robin Cook
mute: 3 mum 4 hush 5 lower, quiet, tacit 6 dampen, damper, deaden, muffle,

reduce, silent, soften, subdue 7 muffled, silence 8 moderate, nonvocal, reticent, silenced, taciturn, tone down, turn down, unvoiced, wordless 9 noiseless, soft-pedal, unsounded, voiceless 10 speechless, tongue-tied, unspeaking
effect: 4 wawa
in music: 7 sordino 8 sourdine
performer: 4 mime 5 mimer

mute ___: 4 swan

muted: 3 dim, low 4 dark, soft 5 dusky, faded, faint, fuzzy, mirky, murky, piano, quiet 6 bleary, blurry, gentle, hollow, low-key, pastel, silent 7 muffled, shadowy, subdued 8 murmured, nonvocal 9 noiseless, whispered 10 indistinct, lackluster, restrained, unspeaking

muteness: 7 secrecy, silence

Muti: 8 Riccardo

mutineer: 5 rebel 7 traitor 8 renegade 9 insurgent

mutinous: 6 unruly 7 defiant, lawless, radical 8 factious, renegade 9 insurgent 10 rebellious, unpeaceful

mutiny: 4 riot, rise 5 rebel 6 resist, revolt, rise up 7 disobey, treason 8 defiance, outbreak, uprising 9 overthrow 10 resistance, revolution

___ Mutiny: 5 Sepoy 6 Indian

Mutiny on the Bounty: 4 book
author: 4 Hall 8 Nordhoff
character: 4 Byam 5 Bligh, Peggy, Roger 6 Tehani 7 Maimiti 8 Fletcher, Hitihiti 9 Christian, Roger Byam

Mutiny on the Bounty (1935 film)
cast: Clark Gable, Charles Laughton, Franchot Tone
director: Frank Lloyd

Mutiny on the Bounty (1962 film)
cast: Marlon Brando, Richard Harris, Trevor Howard
director: Lewis Milestone
music: Bronislau Kaper

___ Mutiny, The: 5 Caine

Muti, Riccardo: 7 Italian 9 conductor

Mutsu: 5 apple
relative: 4 crab, Gala, Lodi, Rome 6 Empire, Ida Red, medlar, Pippin, russet 7 Baldwin, Bramley, costard, Freedom, Liberty, Spartan, Wealthy, Winesap 8 Cortland, Jonathan, McIntosh 10 Rome Beauty

mutt: 3 cur, dog 5 canid, feist, hound, pooch, scrub 6 canine 7 jackass, mongrel 10 mixed breed
see also canine, dog

Mutt and Jeff: 3 duo 4 pair

mutter: 4 bark, moan 5 croak, gripe, groan, growl, grunt, snarl, speak, utter, voice 6 grouch, grouse, jabber, mumble, murmur, rumble 7 grumble, sputter, whisper 8 complain 9 make a fuss, undertone

Mutter, Anne-Sophie: 6 German 9 violinist

mutton: 4 lamb, meat
dish: 6 hot pot
ender: 4 fish, head 5 chops 6 headed

mutton ___: 4 bird, corn 7 snapper

___-mutton: 4 leg-o' 5 leg-of

muttonbird: 3 oii

muttonfish: 4 sama

muttonhead: 3 ass, oaf, sap 4 boob, clod, dolt, fool 5 chump, clown, cluck, dummy, dunce, joker, ninny, patsy 6 dimwit, lubber, lummox, nitwit, sucker, turkey 7 buffoon, dingbat, dullard, half-wit, jackass 8 dumbbell, numskull 9 birdbrain, harebrain, lamebrain, numbskull, simpleton 10 nincompoop

muttonheaded: 4 daft, dopy, loco, rash 5 balmy, dense, dopey, dotty, flaky, inane, kooky, moony, silly, wacky 6 absurd, obtuse, simple, wanton 7 asinine, bonkers, doltish, fatuous, foolish, out of it, witless 8 careless, headless, heedless, mindless, reckless 9 brainless, dim-witted, half-baked, nitwitted, senseless, spaced-out

Mutts: 5 comic 10 comic strip
cat: 5 Mooch
dog: 4 Earl 6 Woofie

mutual: 5 joint 6 common, shared 7 grouped, related 8 communal, conjoint, requited, returned 9 bilateral, concerted, dependant, dependent 10 agreed upon, associated, collective, reciprocal
prefix: 5 inter-

___ Mutual Friend: 3 Our

mutual fund
acct.: 3 IRA 5 Keogh 7 Roth IRA 8 Roth plan
charge: 4 load
fund price: 3 NAV
type: 4 bond, muni, REIT 5 stock 6 growth, income

mutuality: 10 dependence

mutually: 7 en masse, jointly 8 as a group, together 9 in concert 10 conjointly

Mutual of ___: 5 Omaha

___-mutuel: 4 pari

muumuu: 5 dress 8 Hawaiian
accessory: 3 lei

Muy ___!: 4 bien

Muzhik: 7 peasant, Russian

Múzquiz: 4 city, town
locale: 6 Mexico 8 Coahuila

Muztagh Ata: 4 peak 5 mount 8 mountain
locale: 4 Asia

muzzle: 3 gag, jaw 4 curb, hush, jowl, stop 5 check, quiet, snout, still 6 bridle, censor, muffle, rein in, shut up, stifle 7 prevent, repress, silence 8 restrain, suppress, throttle 9 keep still

muzzled: 4 tame 10 unspeaking

muzzleloader: 3 gun 5 rifle 6 weapon 7 firearm

muzzy: 4 dull, hazy 7 blurred 8 confused 9 equivocal 10 unexplicit

MVP part: 4 Most 6 Player 8 Valuable

Mwanza: 4 city, town
locale: 8 Tanzania

Mweru: 4 lake
locale: 5 Zaire 6 Zambia

MX: 4 ICBM 7 missile

my
in Italian: 3 mia, mio
oh ~: 6 dear me, oh dear 7 heavens 8 goodness, well well

My ___: 3 All, Boy, Dad, Guy, Lai, Man, Sin, Way 4 Body, Days, Girl, Life, Love, Turn 5 Giant, Ideal, Lovin', Mammy, Maria, Shawl 6 Prayer 7 Antonia, Sharona

My ___!: 3 eye 4 hero 5 stars 7 heavens

My ___ Adored You: 4 Eyes

My ___ Amour: 6 Cherie

My ___ and Only: 3 One

My ___ and Welcome to It: 5 World

My ___ Angel: 7 Special

My ___ are sealed!: 4 lips

My ___ Belongs to Daddy: 5 Heart

My ___ Chickadee: 6 Little

My ___ Clementine: 7 Darling

My ___ Dads: 3 Two

My ___ Duchess: 4 Last

My ___ Eileen: 6 Sister

My ___ Fat Greek Wedding: 3 Big

My ___ Flame: 3 Old

My ___ Flicka: 6 Friend

My ___ Foot: 4 Left

My ___ Friend's Wedding: 4 Best

My ___ Godfrey: 3 Man

My ___ Heaven: 4 Blue

My ___ in the Highlands: 6 Heart's

My ___ Irish Rose: 4 Wild

My ___ Irma: 6 Friend

My ___ Is Aram: 4 Name

My ___ is as a lusty winter...: 3 age

My ___ Is Asher Lev: 4 Name

My ___ Lady: 4 Fair

My ___ Leaps Up: 5 Heart

My ___ Lollipop: 3 Boy

My ___ Lord: 5 Sweet

My ___ Margie: 6 Little

My ___ of Town: 4 Kind

My ___ perfume: 3 Sin

My ___ Private Idaho: 3 Own

My ___ Runneth Over: 3 Cup

My ___ Sal: 3 Gal

My ___ Sons: 5 Three

My ___ Star: 5 Lucky

My ___ Stood Still: 5 Heart

My ___ Story: 3 Own 4 True

My ___ Town: 4 Home 6 Little

My ___ Trigger: 3 Pal

My ___ True: 5 Aim Is

My ___ Valentine: 5 Funny

My ___, Vietnam: 3 Lai

My ___ Vinny: 6 Cousin

My ___ Will Go On: 5 Heart

My ___ Years in a Quandary: 3 Ten

My-___: 5 T-Fine

My All (1998 song) artist: Mariah Carey

Myanmar: 5 Burma 6 nation 7 country
bay: 6 Bengal
bovine: 5 takin
capital: 6 Yangon 7 Rangoon
city: 6 Yangon 7 Rangoon 8 Mandalay
export: 4 teak
garment of ~: 5 lungi 6 lungee, lungyi
gulf: 8 Martaban
locale: 4 Asia
money: 3 pya 4 kyat
native: 4 Nosu, Shan 6 Burman
neighbor: 4 Laos 5 China, India 8 Thailand 10 Bangladesh
Nobelist in Peace: 6 Suu Kyi
robber: 6 dacoit, dakoit

___ my Annabel Lee: 4 I and

My Antonia: 5 novel
author: Willa Cather
character: 3 Jan, Leo 4 Anna, Lena, Nina, Otto 5 Cuzak, Lucie, Marek, Pavel, Yulka

___ My Baby Back Home: 7 Walking

___ my backyard!: 5 Not in

My Beautiful Laundrette (1985 film)
cast: Daniel Day Lewis, Saeed Jaffrey, Roshan Seth
director: Stephen Frears

My Best Friend's Wedding (1997 film)
cast: Cameron Diaz, Rupert Everett, Dermot Mulroney, Julia Roberts
director: P.J. Hogan

My Big Fat Greek Wedding (2002 film)
cast: Michael Constantine, John Corbett, Lainie Kazan, Nia Vardalos
director: Joel Zwick

___ my big mouth!: 5 Me and

My Blue Heaven (1990 film)
cast: Joan Cusack, Steve Martin, Rick Moranis
director: Herbert Ross

My bologna ___ first name...: 4 has a

My Bonnie ___ over...: 4 lies

My Bonnie Lassie (1955 song) artist: Ames Brothers

My Boy (1975 song) artist: Elvis Presley

My Boyfriend's Back (1963 song) artist: Angels

My Boy Lollipop (1964 song) artist: Millie Small

My Brilliant Career (1979 film)
cast: Judy Davis, Sam Neill
director: Gillian Armstrong

...___ my brother: 3 he's

___ my brother's keeper?: 3 Am I

My Bucket's Got a Hole in It (1958 song) artist: Ricky Nelson

My Buddy composer: 4 Kahn 9 Donaldson

___ my case: 5 I rest

Mycenaean: 3 Era 5 Greek

My Cherie Amour (1969 song) artist: Stevie Wonder

___ My Children: 3 All

mycology: 7 science
study: 6 fungus

___ My Co-Pilot: 5 God Is

My country ___ of thee...: 3 'tis

My Country author: 4 Eban

My Cousin in Milwaukee composer: 8 Gershwin

My Cousin Rachel (1952 film)
cast: Richard Burton, Audrey Dalton, Olivia de Havilland
director: Henry Koster

My Cousin Vinny (1992 film)
cast: Fred Gwynne, Ralph Macchio, Joe Pesci, Marisa Tomei
director: Jonathan Lynn

___ my cup of tea: 3 not

My Cup Runneth Over (1967 song)
artist: Ed Ames
musical: 6 I Do! I Do!

My Dad (1962 song) artist: Paul Petersen

...my dainty ___! I shall miss thee: 5 Ariel

My dame has lost her ___: 4 shoe

My Darling Clementine (1946 film)
cast: Walter Brennan, Linda Darnell, Henry Fonda, Victor Mature
director: John Ford

My Days author: Eleanor Roosevelt

My Ding-a-Ling (1972 song) artist: Chuck Berry

My Dinner With ___: 5 André

My dog has ___: 5 fleas

My Dog Skip (2000 film)
cast: Kevin Bacon, Diane Lane, Frankie Muniz, Luke Wilson

___ my drift?: 3 Get

___ my dust!: 3 Eat

My Empty Arms (1961 song) artist: Jackie Wilson

___ Myer: 4 Fort

Myers: 3 Ned 4 Mike 7 Russell

___-Myers: 7 Bristol

Myers, Mike: 5 actor 8 comedian
film: Austin Powers in Goldmember (2002)
Austin Powers: International Man of Mystery (1997)
Austin Powers: The Spy Who Shagged Me (1999)
Wayne's World (1992)
film (voice): Shrek (2001)

Myerson: 4 Alan, Bess

___ My Ex's Live in Texas: 3 All

My eye!: 5 no way 8 forget it

___ My Eye: 7 Earache

My Eyes Adored You (1975 song) artist: Frankie Valli

My Fair Lady (1964 film): 7 musical
cast: Jeremy Brett, Gladys Cooper, Rex Harrison, Audrey Hepburn, Stanley Holloway, Wilfrid Hyde-White
director: George Cukor
role: 5 Eliza, Henry 6 Alfred, Zoltan 7 Higgins 8 Karpathy 9 Doolittle, Pickering

setting: 5 Ascot 6 London 7 England
songwriter: 5 Loewe 6 Lerner
My Family (1995 film)
cast: Esai Morales, Edward James Olmos, Jimmy Smits
director: Gregory Nava
My father moved through dooms of love: 4 poem
author: e.e. cummings
My Father, The Hero (1994 film)
cast: Gérard Depardieu, Katherine Heigl, Dalton James
director: Steve Miner
__ My Father Told Me: 4 Lies
My fault!: 5 sorry 7 so sorry 8 mea culpa 9 forgive me
My Favorite __: 3 Spy 4 Wife, Year 6 Blonde 7 Martian
My Favorite Blonde (1942 film)
cast: Madeleine Carroll, Bob Hope, Gale Sondergaard
director: Sidney Lanfield
My Favorite Brunette (1947 film)
cast: Bob Hope, Dorothy Lamour, Peter Lorre
director: Elliott Nugent
My Favorite Martian (CBS sitcom)
cast: Bill Bixby (Tim O'Hara) Ray Walston (Martin)
My Favorite Spy (1951 film)
cast: Bob Hope, Hedy Lamarr, Francis L. Sullivan
director: Norman Z. McLeod
My Favorite Things composer: 7 Rodgers 11 Hammerstein
My Favorite Wife (1940 film)
cast: Irene Dunne, Cary Grant, Gail Patrick
director: Garson Kanin
My Favorite Year (1982 film)
cast: Joseph Bologna, Selma Diamond, Jessica Harper, Lainie Kazan, Mark Linn-Baker, Bill Macy, Peter O'Toole
director: Richard Benjamin
My Fellow Americans (1996 film)
cast: Dan Aykroyd, Lauren Bacall, James Garner, Jack Lemmon
director: Peter Segal
__ My Fire: 5 Light
My First Mister (2001 film)
cast: Albert Brooks, Carol Kane, Leelee Sobieski
director: Christine Lahti
My Foolish Heart (1949 film)
cast: Dana Andrews, Susan Hayward, Kent Smith
director: Mark Robson
My Friend __: 4 Irma 6 Flicka
My Friend Flicka: 4 film 5 novel
author: Mary O'Hara
cast: Preston Foster, Rita Johnson, Roddy McDowall
director: Harold Schuster
My Friend Irma (1949 film)
cast: Jerry Lewis, Diana Lynn, Dean Martin, Marie Wilson
director: George Marshall
My Funny Valentine composer: 4 Hart 7 Rodgers
__ My Gal: 5 Me and
My Gal Sal (1942 film)
cast: Rita Hayworth, Victor Mature, John Sutton
My Gal Sunday author: Mary Higgins Clark
My Game author: 3 Orr
My Giant (1998 film)
cast: Billy Crystal, Gheorghe Muresan, Joanna Pacula, Kathleen Quinlan
director: Michael Lehman
My Girl (1991 film)
cast: Dan Aykroyd, Anna Chlumsky, Macaulay Culkin, Jamie Lee Curtis
director: Howard Zieff
My Girl (1965 song) artist: Temptations
My Girl Has Gone (1965 song) artist: Miracles
__, My God, to Thee: 6 Nearer
My goodness!: 3 gee, wow 4 egad, gosh 5 egads
My Guy (1974 song) artist: Mary Wells
My Happiness (1958 song) artist: Connie Francis
__ My Heart: 4 Peg o' 7 Un-Break, Unchain
My Heart and I author: Elizabeth Barrett Browning
My Heart Belongs to Daddy composer: 6 Porter
My Heart Belongs to Me (1977 song) artist: Barbra Streisand
My Heart Belongs to Only You (1964 song) artist: Bobby Vinton
My Heart Can't Tell You No (1989 song) artist: Rod Stewart
My Heart Has a Mind of Its Own (1960 song) artist: Connie Francis
__ My Heart in San Francisco: 5 I Left
My Heart Leaps Up: 4 poem
author: Wordsworth
My Heart Reminds Me (1957 song) artist: Kay Starr
My Heart's in the Highlands: 4 poem 5 novel
author: William Saroyan
poet: Robert Burns
My heart skipped __: 5 a beat
My Heart Stood Still composer: 4 Hart 7 Rodgers
My Heart Will Go On (1998 song) artist: Celine Dion
My Home Town (1960 song) artist: Paul Anka
My Hometown (1985 song) artist: Bruce Springsteen
My Kind of Town composer: 4 Cahn 9 Van Heusen
My kingdom for a __!: 5 horse
Mykonos: 3 isl. 4 isle 6 island
locale: 6 Aegean, Greece
neighbor: 5 Delos
__ my lamp beside...: 5 I lift
Mylanta: 7 antacid
alternative: 4 Tums 6 Maalox, Pepcid, Riopan, Zantac 7 Gelusil, Lactaid, Rolaids 8 Gaviscon 11 Alka-Seltzer, Pepto-Bismol
My Last Duchess: 4 poem
author: Robert Browning
My Left Foot (1989 film)
cast: Daniel Day Lewis, Brenda Fricker, Ray McAnally
director: Jim Sheridan
Myles: 7 Alannah 8 Standish
My life __ open book!: 4 is an
My Life (1978 song) artist: Billy Joel
My Life as __: 4 a Dog
My Life as a Man author: Philip Roth
My Life autobiographer: 4 Meir
My Life in Court author: 5 Nizer
My Life on Trial author: 5 Belli
__ My Line?: 5 What's
__ my lips...: 4 Read
My lips are __: 6 sealed
My Little Chickadee (1940 film)
cast: W.C. Fields, Mae West
director: Edward Cline
My Little Girl (1986 film)
cast: James Earl Jones, Mary Stuart Masterson, Anne Meara, Geraldine Page
My Little Margie (CBS/NBC sitcom)
cast: Charles Farrell (Vern Albright) Gale Storm (Margie Albright)
My Little Town (1975 song) artist: Simon and Garfunkel
My Lost Youth: 4 poem
author: Longfellow
__ My Love: 5 Never, Sleep 7 Justify
__, My Love: 6 Angelo
My Love Is a Fire (1990 song) artist: Donny Osmond
My Love Is Like a Red, Red Rose: 4 poem
author: Robert Burns
My Love Is Your Love (1999 song) artist: Whitney Houston
My Love (song) artist: Lionel Richie, Paul McCartney, Petula Clark
My Lovin' (1992 song) artist: En Vogue
My mama done __ me: 3 tol'
My Mammy (1928 song) artist: Al Jolson
My man!: 3 bro
My Man Godfrey (1936 film)
cast: Mischa Auer, Gail Patrick, William Powell 6 Carole 7 Lombard`$
director: Gregory La Cava
__ my Maypo!: 5 I Want
My Melody of Love (1974 song) artist: Bobby Vinton
My Mortal Enemy author: Willa Cather
My Mother the Car (NBC sitcom)
car: Porter
cast: Ann Sothern (The Car) Jerry Van Dyke (Dave Crabtree)
__ my MTV!: 5 I Want
My, my!: 3 tsk 6 do tell, tsk tsk
mynah: 3 pet 4 bird 5 mimic 6 talker
My Name Is Aram author: William Saroyan
My Name Is Asher Lev author: Chaim Potok
My Name Is Julia Ross (1945 film)
cast: Nina Foch, George Macready, May Whitty
Mynheer: 3 sir 5 Dutch, title 6 mister
MYOB, part of: 3 own 4 mind, your 8 business
My Old __: 5 Flame
My Old Kentucky Home composer: 6 Foster
myology: 7 science
study: 7 muscles
My One and Only composer: 8 Gershwin
myopic: 6 biased 11 nearsighted
mammal: 5 rhino
myoporum: 5 shrub
My Own Private Idaho (1991 film)
cast: River Phoenix, Keanu Reeves, James Russo
director: Gus Van Sant
My Pal Trigger: 5 oater
__ My Party: 3 It's
My People author: 4 Eban
My pleasure!: 6 glad to
My Prayer (1956 song) artist: Platters
My Prerogative (1988 song) artist: Bobby Brown
Myra: 4 Hess
Myra Breckinridge (1970 film)
author: Gore Vidal
cast: John Huston, Rex Reed, Raquel Welch, Mae West
director: Michael Sarne
Myrdal: 4 Alva 6 Gunnar
Myrdal, Alva: 7 Swedish 8 diplomat, Nobelist
Myrdal, Gunnar: 6 writer 7 Swedish 8 Nobelist 9 economist
__ My Regards to Broadway: 4 Give
My Reputation (1946 film)
cast: George Brent, Barbara Stanwyck
myriad: 4 a lot, army, gobs, heap, host, many, mint, slew 5 flood, horde, loads, swarm 6 a lot of, divers, gobs of, legion, lots of, oodles, scores, stacks, umteen, untold 7 a host of, a slew of, copious, endless, heaping, heaps of, legions, no end of, numbers, piles of, profuse, scads of, umpteen 8 a bunch of, abundant, an army of, infinite, manifold, mountain, numerous, oodles of, prodigal, scores of, umpsteen, variable 9 abundance, a passel of, bountiful, countless, multitude, quite a few, thousands, uncounted 10 innumerous, numberless, unnumbered, zillions of
Myriad: 4 font 8 typeface
myrmecology: 7 science
study: 4 ants
Myrna: 3 Loy
role for ~: 4 Nora
myrobalan: 4 plum
relative: 4 sloe 6 cherry, damson 9 greengage
Myron: 5 Cohen 7 Scholes 9 McCormick
Myrt and Marge: 9 radio show
myrtle: 5 green, plant, shrub 6 bluish, flower 7 blueish
family shrub: 6 feijoa
relative: 3 pea 4 cyan, jade, sage 5 beryl, breen, guava, olive, virid 6 reseda 7 avocado, celadon, emerald, verdant 9 pistachio, turquoise 10 aquamarine, chartreuse
tree: 5 guava 7 cajeput 10 eucalyptus
__ myrtle: 3 bog, gum, wax 4 blue, moor, sand 5 crape, crepe 6 Oregon 7 running
Myrtle Beach: 4 city, town
locale: 4 S. Car.
My Saber Is Bent author: 4 Paar
__ My Sarong: 6 Pardon
__ Myself: 5 All by
My Several Worlds author: Pearl S. Buck
__ My Shadow: 5 Me and
My Sharona (1979 song) artist: Knack
Myshkin, Prince: 5 Idiot
My Sin: 7 perfume
My Sister __: 3 Sam 6 Eileen
My Sister Eileen: 4 book, film
author: Ruth McKinney
cast: Betty Garrett, Janet Leigh, Jack Lemmon
director: Richard Quine
__ My Sons: 3 All
mysophobe fear: 4 dirt
mysost: 6 cheese
__ my soul!: 5 Bless
__ My Souvenirs: 5 Among
My Special Angel (song) artist: Bobby Helms, Vogues
My Stepmother Is an Alien (1988 film)
cast: Dan Aykroyd, Kim Basinger, Jon Lovitz
director: Richard Benjamin
dog: 4 Dave
mysteries: 6 arcana
Mysteries of Marseilles author: Emile Zola
Mysteries of Paris, The author: Eugène Sue
Mysteries of Udolpho, The author: Ann Radcliffe
Mysteries of Winterthurn author: Joyce Carol Oates
mysterious: 4 dark, deep, eery 5 eerie, magic, queer, weird 6 arcane, hidden, occult, secret, spooky, veiled 7 cryptic, curious, elusive, elusory, magical, obscure, strange, uncanny, unknown 8 abstruse, baffling, esoteric, mystical, oracular, profound, puzzling, romantic 9 cryptical, difficult, enigmatic, insolu-

ble, recondite, secretive, spiritual **10** unknowable
Mysterious Affair at Styles, The author: Agatha Christie
Mysterious Island, The author: Verne
character: 3 Neb **4** Jack **5** Brown **6** Ayrton, Gideon **7** Harding, Herbert, Spilett **8** Pencroft **9** Nemo. Cyrus
Mysterious Rider, The author: Zane Grey
mystery: 5 genre, novel, story, vexer **6** enigma, puzzle, riddle, secret **7** arcanum, chiller, grabber, problem, romance, secrecy **8** question, subtlety, thriller, whodunit **9** conundrum **10** closed book, puzzlement
element: 4 clew, clue
man: 3 Mr X
not a ~: 5 known
writers' award: 5 Edgar
mystery __: 4 play
Mystery __ X, The: 4 of Mr.
Mystery!
host: 4 Rigg
Mystery Men (1999 film)
cast: Hank Azaria, Claire Forlani, Janeane Garofalo, Greg Kinnear
director: Kinka Usher
Mystery of Being, The author: Gabriel Marcel
Mystery of Cloomber, The author: Arthur Conan Doyle
Mystery of Edwin Drood, The author: Charles Dickens
character: 3 Bud **4** Rosa **6** Helena, Jasper **7** Durdles, Neville, Rosa Bud **8** Datchery, Landless **9** Grewgious **10** Crisparkle
Mystery of Marie Roget, The author: Poe
mystic: 4 seer, yogi **5** faker, fakir, faqir, swami, swamy, yogin **6** arcane, faquir, hidden, occult, secret **7** magical, psychic **8** abstruse, anagogic, esoteric, numinous **9** enigmatic, recondite, spiritual, visionary **10** anagogical, enshrouded, paranormal, unknowable
Hindu ~: 4 yogi **5** faker, fakir, faqir, swami, swamy, yogin **6** faquir
Mystic: 4 city, town
locale: 4 Conn.
mystical: 5 runic **6** arcane, hidden, occult, secret **7** magical **8** abstruse, anagogic, esoteric, numinous, oracular, profound **9** recondite, spiritual, visionary **10** anagogical, mysterious, paranormal, unknowable
emanation: 4 aura
force: 5 karma **6** kismet
knowledge: 6 gnosis
society: 4 cult
mysticism: 6 cabala, kabala **7** cabbala, kabbala **8** dzogchen
Mystic Pizza (1988 film)
cast: Vincent D'Onofrio, Annabeth Gish, Julia Roberts, Lili Taylor
director: Donald Petrie
Mystics and Zen Masters author: Thomas Merton
Mystification author: Edgar Allan Poe
mystified: 5 at sea **7** at a loss, bemused, puzzled, stumped **8** clueless, confused **9** buffaloed, flummoxed, in the dark, perplexed **10** bewildered
mystify: 4 beat **5** befog, elude, floor, stump, throw **6** baffle, bemuse, boggle, escape, puzzle **7** becloud, buffalo, confuse, nonplus, perplex **8** bewilder, confound **9** bamboozle
mystifying: 4 dark **6** knotty **7** strange, uncanny **8** puzzling **9** difficult, insoluble
mystique: 4 aura **6** glamor **7** charism, glamour **8** charisma **9** character, magnetism
Mystique: 3 car **4** auto **7** Mercury **10** automobile
My Sweet Lord (1970 song) artist: George Harrison
My-T-__: 4 Fine
My Ten Years in a Quandary author: Robert Benchley
myth: 4 lore, tale **5** fable, story **6** legend, mythos **7** fantasy, fiction **8** allegory, delusion, folktale, illusion, nonsense, religion **9** falsehood, half-truth, invention **10** fairy story
__ myth: 5 urban
Myth and Machine author: Lewis Mumford
My Theodosia author: Anya Seton
mythical: 5 false **6** fabled, made-up, unreal **7** storied **8** fabulous, invented **9** fairy-tale, imaginary, legendary, visionary **10** fabricated, fictitious
Myth of Sisyphus, The author: Albert Camus
mythology: 4 lore **5** myths **6** legend **8** religion **9** tradition
branch of ~: 5 Greek, Norse, Roman
mythomaniac: 4 liar
mythos: 6 legend **9** tradition
My Three Sons (ABC/CBS sitcom)
cast: Tina Cole (Katie Douglas)
Tim Considine (Mike Douglas)
William Demarest (Charlie O'Casey)
William Frawley (Michael Bub O'Casey)
Beverly Garland (Barbara Douglas)
Don Grady (Robbie Douglas)
Barry Livingston (Ernie Douglas)
Stanley Livingston (Chip Douglas)
Fred MacMurray (Steve Douglas)
dog: Tramp
myths: 4 lore **7** legends
__-my-thumb: 4 hop-o'
__ My Time: 5 Bidin'
__ My Turn: 3 It's
My Two Dads (NBC sitcom)
cast: Greg Evigan (Joey Harris)
Paul Reiser (Michael Taylor)
__ my type: 3 not
__ Myung Moon: 3 Sun
__ My Way: 4 I'm on **5** Going, Swing
My Way (1969 song) artist: Frank Sinatra
My Wide World author: 5 McKay
My Wild Irish __: 4 Rose
My Wish Came True (1959 song)
artist: Elvis Presley
__ my wits' end!: 4 I'm at
__ my word!: 4 Upon
My word!: 4 egad, I say **5** egads
__ my words!: 4 Mark
My World Is Empty Without You (1966 song) artist: Supremes

N

9
figure above ~: 5 paren.
to 5: 5 shift
9 A.M. service: 5 terce
#9 Dream (1975 song) artist: John Lennon
9 Lives: 7 cat food
alternative: 5 Amore 6 Figaro, Purina 7 Whiskas 8 Friskies 10 Chef's Blend, Fancy Feast
___ 9 'til 5: 4 open
9 to 5 (1980 song) artist: Dolly Parton
19th ___: 4 hole
19th Amendment beneficiary: 5 woman
19th Nervous Breakdown (1966 song) artist: Rolling Stones
92 in the Shade (1975 film)
cast: Peter Fonda, Margot Kidder, Warren Oates
director: Thomas McGuane
94th ___ Squadron: 4 Aero
96 Tears (1966 song) artist: Question Mark and the Mysterians
98°
song: Because of You (1998)
The Hardest Thing (1999)
I Do (Cherish You) (1999)
Invisible Man (1997)
98.6 (1967 song) artist: Keith
99: 5 agent
99 and 44/100% ___: 4 pure
99 beautiful names, one with: 5 Allah
99 Luftballons (1984 song) artist: Nena
99 River Street (1953 film)
cast: Brad Dexter, Evelyn Keyes, John Payne
director: Phil Karlson
911
like a ~ call: 4 emer.
___ 911: 6 Rescue
1910 Fruitgum Co.
song: 1, 2, 3, Red Light (1968)
Indian Giver (1969)
Simon Says (1968)
1914-1918 conflict: 3 WWI
1917
leader until ~: 4 czar, tsar, tzar
1929 event: 5 crash
1930s
agcy.: 3 WPA
migrant worker: 4 Okie
org.: 3 CCC
1940s conflict: 4 WWII
1941 (1979 film)
cast: Dan Aykroyd, Ned Beatty, John Belushi, Treat Williams
director: Steven Spielberg
1979 (1996 song) artist: Smashing Pumpkins
1984: 5 novel
author: George Orwell
character: 5 Julia, Smith 6 O'Brien 7 Winston
1984 (1956 film)
cast: Edmond O'Brien, Michael Redgrave, Jan Sterling
director: Michael Anderson
****1999** (1983 song) artist:** Prince
9000 automaker: 4 Saab
90125 band: 3 Yes
N: 2 nu 3 dir. 4 elem. 5 point 6 letter 7 element 8 nitrogen 9 direction
followers: 3 OPQ 4 OPQR 5 OPQRS
in phonetic alphabet: 8 November
not quite ~: 3 NNW
preceders: 3 KLM 4 JKLM 5 IJKLM
7 for ~: 4 at. no.
star: 3 sun
N ___?: 3 or M
N ___ Nancy: 4 as in
N-___: 4 bomb 5 shell
N. ___: 3 Eng., Heb., Lat. 4 Zeal.
'N'___ Noose: 5 Is for
Na: 4 elem. 6 sodium 7 element
11 for ~: 4 at. no.
N.A.: 4 cont.
nation: 3 Can., Mex., USA
part of ~: 4 Amer.
NAACP
concern: 6 rights
part: 4 Assn., Natl. 5 Assoc. 6 People 7 Colored
NAA member: 5 flyer, pilot 7 aviator
nab: 3 bag, cop, get, net 4 bust, grab, jail, nail, snag, take, trap 5 catch, pinch, run in, seize, snare, swipe 6 arrest, collar, corner, detain, kidnap, obtain, pick up, pull in, rip off, snap up, snatch 7 capture, ensnare, insnare 8 grab away, surprise 9 apprehend, lay hold of 10 bring to bay
Nabisco: 6 cookie
alternative: 7 Archway, Keebler 8 Sunshine 9 Mrs. Fields 10 Famous Amos, Peak Freans
brand: 4 Oreo, Ritz 5 Nilla 6 Newton
___ Nabisco: 3 RJR
nabob: 3 VIP 4 czar, king 5 mogul 6 bigwig, fat cat, tycoon 7 big shot, magnate 8 big wheel, somebody 9 big cheese, dignitary, moneybags, plutocrat 10 man of means
residence: 6 estate 7 mansion
Nabokov, Vladimir: 6 author, writer 7 Russian
work: Ada
Lolita
Pnin
Nabors: 3 Jim
role: 4 Pyle 5 Gomer
Nabucco composer: 5 Verdi
nachos: 5 chips, snack 9 appetizer
dip: 5 salsa
like ~: 5 crisp, spicy 6 spicey
make ~: 5 broil
___ Nacht: 4 Gute 6 Stille
___ Nacht in Venedig: 4 Eine
Nacimiento: 4 peak 5 mount 8 mountain
Nacio ___ Brown: 4 Herb
nación: 6 España, Méjico
NaCl: 4 salt 9 table salt
remove ~: 6 desalt 10 desalinate, desalinize
Nacogdoches: 4 city, town
locale: 5 Texas
Nacozari: 4 city, town
locale: 6 Mexico, Sonora
nacreous: 6 pearly 8 lustrous 10 iridescent
nacre source: 5 conch 6 oyster
nada: 3 nil, nix, zip 4 none, zero 5 squat, zilch, zippo 6 bubkes, bupkis, naught, nought 7 nothing 8 goose egg
in French: 4 rien
Nadab, father of: 5 Aaron
Nada the Lily author: H. Rider Haggard
Nadelman: 4 Elie
Nader: 5 Ralph
Nader's ___: 7 Raiders
Nadia: 8 Comaneci 9 Boulanger
predecessor: 4 Olga
Nadia's Theme (1976 song) artist: DeVorzon, Botkin
Nadine: 8 Gordimer
Nadine (1987 film)
cast: Kim Basinger, Jeff Bridges, Rip Torn
director: Robert Benton
nadir: 4 foot, zero 5 depth, floor, least, worst 6 bathos, bottom, depths, low ebb 7 the pits 8 low point 10 rock bottom
Nadja (1994 film)
cast: Suzy Amis, Peter Fonda
nae: 2 no 8 Scottish
naevus: 4 mole
N. Afr. country: 3 Alg., Mor., Tun. 4 Egyp.
NAFTA
forerunner: 4 GATT
opponent: 5 Perot
part: 4 Amer., Free 5 North, Trade 8 American 9 Agreement
signatory: 3 USA 6 Canada, Mexico
topic: 6 tariff
nag: 3 bug, dog, dun, vex 4 bait, carp, coax, fret, fuss, goad, harp, pest, plug, prod, ride 5 annoy, cavil, chide, gripe, groan, harry, horse, hound, momus, nudge, press, scold, shrew, worry 6 badger, berate, bother, carp at, carper, chivvy, critic, equine, harass, harper, harp on, hassle, heckle, hector, Maggie, needle, noodge, peck at, pester, pick at, plague, virago, work on 7 annoyer, henpeck, needler, nitpick, provoke, torment, upbraid 8 browbeat, harangue, harridan, irritate 9 aggravate, find fault, henpecker, importune, keep after, Xanthippe 10 complainer, complain to, tongue-lash
Nagai Kafu: 6 writer 8 Japanese
Nagaland, capital of: 6 Kohima
Naga locale: 4 Cebu
nagami ___: 7 kumquat
Nagano: 4 city, town
locale: 5 Japan
volcano near ~: 5 Asama
Nagano Olympics
network: 3 CBS 5 CBS-TV
Nagaoka: 4 city, town
locale: 5 Japan
Nagasaki: 4 city, port, town
locale: 5 Japan 6 Kiushu, Kyushu
Nagel: 6 Conrad
nagging: 5 pesky, pesty 7 carping 8 captious, critical, haunting 9 annoyance, demanding, vexatious
feeling: 6 déjà vu
naggy: 8 shrewish
___ Nagila: 4 Hava
Nagori: 3 cow 4 bull 6 bovine, cattle
Nagoya: 4 city, town
locale: 5 Japan
Naguib: 7 Mahfous, Mahfouz
Nagurski, Bronko sport: 8 football
Nagy: 4 Imre
nah: 2 no 3 naw, nay, nix, non 4 nein, nope, nyet, uh-uh 5 I won't, ixnay, never, no how, no way 6 no deal, noways, nowise, unh-unh 7 I refuse 8 forget it, I will not, negative, negatory 9 by no means, fat chance, I think not 10 count me out, not a chance, thumbs down
Naha: 4 city, port, town
locale: 5 Japan
Nahath, grandfather of: 4 Esau
NaHCO3: 6 bicarb
Nahua: 5 Aztec 6 Toltec
Nahuatl: 8 language
language: 5 Aztec
Nahum: 4 Tate
follower: 8 Habakkuk
preceder: 5 Micah
naiad: 5 nymph 10 water nymph
Naiad: 4 moon
planet: 7 Neptune
Naidu, Sarojini: 4 poet
naif: 4 babe, tiro, tyro 7 ingenue, new hand 8 innocent 9 credulous, greenhorn 10 unaffected
___-naïf: 4 faux
nail: 3 bag, fix, get, nab, pin 4 brad, claw, grab, join, snag, sock, spad, tack, take, trap 5 catch, pinch, place, pound, seize, spike, whack 6 arrest, attach, clinch, collar, detain, expose, fasten, hammer, pull in, secure, snatch, tackle, unguis 7 capture, pin down 8 fastener, transfix 9 apprehend, recognize 10 tenterhook
biting: 4 vice
combining form: 4 helo- 5 onych-, ungui- 6 onycho-
container: 3 box, keg
down: 3 fix 5 sew up 6 assure, batten, clinch, define, ensure, firm up, recall, settle 7 resolve 8 finalize 9 determine, formalize
drive a ~ aslant: 3 toe
ender: 5 brush
groomer: 4 file 5 emery 8 scissors
like some ~ polish: 5 clear
locale: 3 toe 6 finger
polish: 5 Cutex, paint 6 enamel
relative: 4 tack 5 screw, spike
starter: 3 hob, toe 4 door, hang, tree 5 thumb 6 finger
tooth and ~: 5 madly 6 wildly 8 fiercely, savagely 9 violently
nail ___: 3 set 4 down, file 6 enamel, polish, violin 7 varnish
___ nail: 3 box, cut, dog 4 boat, fine, form, stub 5 clout, screw, spoon 6 casing, common, dating, wiggle 7 roofing
nailed: 4 firm 5 exact, tight 6 secure, stable 8 immobile 10 definitive
nail-polish color: 3 red 4 pink
nails
bite one's ~: 5 worry 7 agonize
hard as ~: 5 rigid, tough 6 steely, strong 9 unbending
___ nails: 5 bed of 6 hard as
Naina predecessor: 5 Raisa
nainsook: 6 fabric 8 material
Naipaul, V.S.: 6 writer 8 essayist, Nobelist 10 West Indian
Nair: 10 depilatory
alternative: 4 Neet 5 razor
naira: 5 money
Nairn: 6 county
locale: 8 Scotland
Nairobi: 4 city, town 7 capital
locale: 5 Kenya
Nairobi ___, The: 4 Trio
nais: 5 nymph
Naismith: 5 James
naître, form of: 3 née
naive: 4 easy, open 5 fresh, green, plain 6 callow, candid, honest, jejune, simple, stupid, trusty, unwary, unwise 7 artless, genuine, natural, sincere, unjaded 8 foolable, gullable, gullible, ignorant, innocent, lamblike, trustful, trusting, unartful, untaught, unversed, wide-eyed 9 backwater, childlike, confiding, credulous, deludable, guileless, ingenuous, unfledged, unguarded, unknowing, unworldly 10 deceivable, falling for, sophomoric, unaffected, uninformed, unschooled, unseasoned
be ~: 6 accept 7 believe, fall for, swallow
not ~: 4 foxy, wily 5 cagey, canny, slick, smart 6 artful, astute, crafty, shrewd 7 cunning, furtive 8 guileful
one: 4 babe, lamb 8 innocent
naiveté: 6 candor 8 openness 9 credulity, frankness, greenness, ignorance, innocence 10 simplicity
Najimy: 5 Kathy
naked: 3 raw 4 bald, bare, nude, open, pure 5 frank, overt, plain, sheer, stark 6 patent, peeled, simple, unclad 7 blatant, denuded, evident, exposed, obvi-

ous **8** disrobed, divested, glabrous, helpless, in the raw, knowable, leafless, palpable, revealed, starkers, stripped, undraped, unveiled, wide-open **9** au naturel, in the buff, unadorned, unattired, unclothed, uncovered, undressed, unobscure **10** unshielded, vulnerable
ape: **3** man **5** being, human **6** mortal
combining form: **4** gymn-, nudi- **5** gymno-
make ~: **4** bare **5** strip **6** denude **7** disrobe, uncover, undress
naked __: **3** eye **5** truth
naked __ jaybird: **3** as a
__-naked: **4** buck **5** stark
Naked __: **4** City, Eyes **5** Lunch
Naked __, The: **3** Ape, God, Gun, Sun **4** City, Face, Kiss, Maja, Prey, Spur **5** Truth **6** Jungle
Naked and the Dead, The (1958 film)
cast: Raymond Massey, Aldo Ray, Cliff Robertson
director: Raoul Walsh
Naked and the Dead, The author: Norman Mailer
Naked Ape, The author: Desmond Morris
Naked City (ABC drama) cast: Horace McMahon (Lt. Mike Parker)
Naked City, The (1948 film)
cast: Howard Duff, Barry Fitzgerald
Naked Face, The author: Sidney Sheldon
Naked God, The author: Howard Fast
Naked Gun 2 1/2 (1991 film)
cast: George Kennedy, Leslie Nielsen, Priscilla Presley
director: David Zucker
Naked Gun 33 1/3 (1994 film)
cast: George Kennedy, Leslie Nielsen, Priscilla Presley
Naked Gun, The (1988 film)
cast: George Kennedy, Ricardo Montalban, Leslie Nielsen, Priscilla Presley
director: David Zucker
Naked Jungle, The (1954 film)
cast: Charlton Heston, Eleanor Parker
menace: **4** ants
Naked Lunch author: William S. Burroughs
Naked Maja artist: **4** Goya
Naked Spur, The (1953 film)
cast: Janet Leigh, James Stewart
director: Anthony Mann
Naked Sun, The author: Isaac Asimov
Naked Truth, The (ABC/NBC sitcom)
cast: Téa Leoni (Nora Wilde)
nakers: **4** drum
origin: **6** Europe
Nakuru: **4** city, town
locale: **5** Kenya
nal: **4** reed
Nala: **4** lion
Naldi: **4** Nita
__ Nam: **4** Viet
Nama home: **6** Africa **7** Namibia
Namath: **3** Joe **9** Joe Willie
alma mater: **4** Bama **7** Alabama
once: **3** Jet, Ram
namaycush: **4** fish **5** trout
namby-pamby: **4** soft, weak **5** sissy, timid **8** mama's boy **9** spineless
Namcha Barwa: **4** peak **5** mount **8** mountain
locale: **5** China, Tibet **9** Himalayas
name: **3** dub, peg, rep, set, tab, tag, tap **4** call, cite, fame, flag, list, make, pick, sign, star, term, word **5** alias, brand, celeb, elect, honor, label, nomen, place, style, title **6** anoint, assign, choose, credit, define, denote, eponym, finger, handle, indict, renown, report, repute, select **7** agnomen, appoint, baptize, big star, declare, entitle, epithet, heading, imprint, intitle, mention, moniker, pin down, point to, propose, qualify, refer to, speak of, specify **8** christen, classify, cognomen, delegate, deputize, eminence, identify, luminary, monicker, nominate, prenomen, snitch on, somebody, subtitle **9** autograph, celebrity, designate, enumerate, headliner, personage, pseudonym, recognize, signature, single out, sobriquet, stipulate, superstar **10** commission, denominate, nom de plume, prominence, reputation, settle upon
combining form: **4** -onym **7** onomato-
ender: **3** tag **4** sake, tape **5** plate
fake ~: **5** alias **6** anonym **10** nom de plume
in French: **3** nom
in Spanish: **6** nombre
names: **3** rat **4** bare, blab, leak
starter: **3** pen **4** nick
name __: **3** day **4** tape **5** brand, names **7** dropper
name __ game: **5** of the
name-__: **4** drop **6** caller **7** calling, dropper
__ name: **3** big, day, pen, pet **4** code, font, last **5** birth, brand, first, given, trade **6** common, domain, family, maiden, middle, proper, street
Name __ Rose, The: **5** of the
Name __, The: **4** Game
Name __ Tune: **4** That
__ Name: **5** I Got a, Say My
Name (1995 song) artist: Goo Goo Dolls
Name Above the Title, The author: **5** Capra
named: **6** cleped, yclept **7** nominal, ycleped **9** preferred
commonly ~: **8** so-called
derived from a person: **6** eponym
originally ~: **3** née
__ Named Charlie Brown: **4** A Boy
name-dropper: **4** snob **5** snoot **7** elitist **8** braggart
__ Named Sue: **4** A Boy
__ name for oneself: **5** make a
Name Game, The (1965 song) artist: Shirley Ellis
nameless: **6** unsung **7** obscure, unfamed, unknown **8** untitled **9** anonymous, incognito, unheard-of **10** unrenowned
namely: **3** viz. **4** scil. **5** id est, to wit **6** such as **8** scilicet **9** expressly, videlicet **10** especially
__ name of: **5** in the
name of God, name meaning: **6** Samuel
name of the __: **4** game
__ Name of the Father: **5** In the
Name of the Game, The (NBC drama)
cast: Gene Barry (Glenn Howard)
Tony Franciosa (Jeff Dillon)
Susan Saint James (Peggy Maxwell)
Robert Stack (Dan Farrell)
Name of the Rose, The: **4** film **5** novel
author: Umberto Eco
cast: F. Murray Abraham, Sean Connery, Christian Slater
setting: Italy
nameplates, make: **6** emboss
namer: **3** rat **4** fink **6** parent **7** tattler **8** informer **9** informant **10** tattletale
names
inability to recognize ~: **6** anomia
name ~: **3** rat **4** bare, blab, leak
__ names: **4** call, name
namesake: **6** eponym, junior
names - English/French:
Alan - Alain
Henry - Henri
John - Jean
Mary - Marie
names - English/German:
Frank - Franz
John - Hans
names - English/Irish:
Jane - Shana
John - Sean
Mary - Moira
Shane - John
names - English/Italian:
Donald - Aldo
Ellen - Elena
Guy - Guido
Helen - Elena
Hugh - Ugo
Louis - Luigi
Paul - Paolo
names - English/Russian:
Ann - Nina
Elijah - Ilya
George - Yuri
Irene - Irina
Jacob - Yakov
John - Ivan
Mike - Misha
Paul - Pavel
Peter - Pyotr
names - English/Scottish:
Jane - Sheena
Jane - Shona
John - Iain
John - Ian
Mary - Moira
names - English/Spanish:
Ellen - Elena
Helen - Elena
James - Diego
James - Iago
James - Jaime
John - Juan
Joseph - José
Lewis - Luis
Louis - Luis
Paul - Pablo
Peter - Pedro
Thomas - Tomás
names - French/English:
Alain - Alan
André - Andrew
Henri - Henry
Jean - John
Marie - Mary
names - German/English:
Franz - Frank
Hans - John
names - Irish/English:
Moira - Mary
Sean - John
Shana - Jane
Shane - John
names - Italian/English:
Aldo - Donald
Guido - Guy
Luigi - Louis
Paolo - Paul
Ugo - Hugh
names, meaning of:
Ada - noble
Adele - noble
Adler - eagle
Agatha - good
Alice - noble
Alissa - joy
Alma - kind
Amos - burden
Amy - beloved
Anne - grace
Ava - water
Barry - spear
Basil - royal
Baum - tree
Beck - baker
Bjorn - bear
Bonnie - good
Bruno - brown
Caleb - dog
Calvin - bald
Carmen - song
Casey - brave
Cecil - blind
Charles - man
Claude - lame
Cora - girl
Cosmo - order
Craig - rock
Cyril - lord, ruler
Daniel - the Lord is my judge
Dean - valley
Deborah - bee
Dora - gift
Drew - trusty
Dyker - mason
Earl - noble
Edna - birth
Eli - height
Ella - all
Elmo - helmet
Elroy - king
Eric - ruler
Erna - eagle
Ethel - noble
Eve - life
Ezra - help
Felix - happy
Gail - joy
Grant - great, large
Guy - woods
Haas - hare
Helga - holy
Hiram - noble
Horst - wood
Hoyt - glee
Hugh - heart, mind
Ida - happy
Jemima - dove
Jonah - dove
Jonas - dove
Jonathan - God gave
Kay - rejoice
Klein - small
Leah - weary
Leila - night
Leon - lion
Leroy - king
Linus - flax
Lloyd - gray
Lucia - light
Martha - lady
Nadia - hope
Nathan - gift
Noah - rest
Nora - honor
Olga - holy
Paul - small
Peter - rock
Rachel - lamb
Roth - red
Roy - red
Russell - red
Samuel - name of God
Stanley - stone field
Stella - star
Tara - hill
Thomas - twin
Tristan - sad
Ursula - bear
Vera - faith, truth
Vogel - bird
Weiss - white
Yves - yew
Zoe - life

names - Russian/English:
Ilya - Elijah
Irina - Irene
Ivan - John
Misha - Mike
Nina - Ann
Pavel - Paul
Pyotr - Peter
Yakov - Jacob
Yuri - George
names - Scottish/English:
Iain - John
Ian - John
Moira - Mary
Sheena - Jane
Shona - Jane
names - Spanish/English:
Diego - James
Iago - James
Jaime - James
José - Joseph
Juan - John
Pablo - Paul
Pedro - Peter
Tomás - Thomas
Names, The author: Don DeLillo
nametag site: 5 lapel 6 pocket
nametags, like some: 6 clip-on
Name That Tune: game show
clue: note
Namib: 6 desert
locale: 6 Africa
Namibia: 6 nation 7 country
bay: 6 Walvis 7 Walfish
bovine: 6 Ovambo
capital: 8 Windhoek
desert: 8 Kalahari
money: 4 cent
native: 4 Nama 5 Bantu 6 Herero
neighbor: 3 Ang., Bot., RSA, Zam. 6 Angola, Zambia 8 Botswana
once: 3 SWA
Namouna composer: 4 Lalo
Nampa: 4 city, town
locale: 5 Idaho
Nampo: 4 city, town
locale: 10 North Korea
nan: 5 bread
Nan: 4 Grey 7 Bobbsey 8 Merriman
sibling: 4 Bert 7 Flossie, Freddie
nana: 4 gran 6 granny 7 grandma, grannie 8 babushka 9 governess, nursemaid
husband: 5 gramp 6 grampa
son: 5 uncle
Nana: 7 Visitor 9 Mouskouri
portrayer: 4 Anna, Sten
__ Na Na: 3 Sha
Nana author: Émile Zola
Na Na Hey Hey... band: 5 Steam
Nanaimo: 4 city, town
locale: 6 Canada
__ Nance Garner: 4 John
Nancy: 4 Ames, city, Drew, Kulp, Kwan, town 5 Allen, Astor, comic, Davis, Kelly, Lopez, Olson, strip 6 McKeon, Savoca, Travis, Walker, Wilson 7 Mitford, Sinatra 8 Dussault, Kerrigan, Marchand, Schuster 10 Cartwright, comic strip
character: 4 Irma, Ritz 5 Rollo 6 Fritzi, Sluggo
dog: 7 Poochie
locale: 6 France
river: 7 Meurthe
Nancy __ Kassebaum: 6 Landon
NAND __: 4 gate 7 circuit
Nanda Devi: 4 peak 5 mount 8 mountain
locale: 4 Asia
Nandi home: 5 Kenya 6 Africa
nandina: 5 shrub
__ 'n' Andy: 4 Amos

Nanette: 6 Fabray, Newman
__, Nanette: 4 No No
Nanga Parbat: 4 peak 5 mount 8 mountain
locale: 4 Asia 7 Kashmir
Nanjing: 4 city, town
locale: 5 China
nankeen: 4 lily 6 fabric, yellow 8 brownish
relative: 4 buff, corn, gold, lime, rust, sand 5 blond, brass, coral, cream, flaxy, lemon, maize, ocher, ochre, peach, rusty, straw 6 blonde, canary, chammy, citron, crocus, flaxen, shammy, shamoy 7 apricot, chamois, citrine, jasmine, mustard, old gold, saffron, xanthic 8 daffodil, primrose 9 champagne, goldenrod, jessamine
Nanking
Treaty of ~ port: 4 Amoy
see also Nanjing
Nanking __: 4 ware 5 china
Nanki-Poo's beloved: 6 Yum Yum
Nan Ling: 5 range
locale: 4 Asia 5 China
nanna: 6 granny 7 grannie
nanny: 4 goat 6 au pair 7 watcher 9 governess, nursemaid
a ~ pushes it: 4 pram
Asian ~: 3 ama 4 amah, ayah
concern: 3 tot 5 child
cry: 3 maa
ender: 5 berry
mate: 5 billy
offspring: 3 kid
nanny __: 3 tax 4 goat, plum
nannygai: 4 fish
Nanny, The (CBS sitcom)
cast: Fran Drescher (Fran Fine) Maxwell Shaughnessy (Maxwell Sheffield) Renée Taylor (Sylvia Fine)
dog: Chester
nano-: 4 tiny 5 teeny 6 teensy
Nanon author: George Sand
Nanook
home: 4 iglu 5 igloo
vehicle: 4 sled 5 kayak
Nanook of the North (1922 film) director: Robert Flaherty
Nanook of the North sequel: 5 Moana
Nansen: 8 Fridtjof
Nansen __: 6 bottle
Nansen, Fridtjof: 8 explorer, Nobelist
Nantes: 4 city, port, town
locale: 6 France
river: 5 Loire
Nanticoke: 4 city, town 6 Indian 7 Amerind
locale: 6 Canada 7 Ontario
Nantucket: 4 isle, port 6 island
locale: 3 Atl. 8 Atlantic
TV sitcom set on ~: 5 Wings
NaOH: 3 lye 4 base 6 alkali
Naomi: 4 Judd 8 Campbell 9 Mitchison
colleague of ~: 4 Elle
daughter: 6 Ashley 7 Wynonna
daughter-in-law of ~: 4 Ruth 5 Orpah
husband of ~: 9 Elimelech
son of ~: 6 Mahlon 7 Chilion
naos: 5 cella 6 temple
Naos: 4 star
nap: 3 nod 4 down, doze, fuzz, game, pile, rest, shag, woof, yawn 5 fiber, fluff, relax, sleep 6 drowse, nod off, siesta, snooze, turn in 7 doze off, drop off, respite, shuteye, slumber, surface, texture, time-out 8 card game, dog ender, down time 9 go to sleep 10 fall asleep, forty winks
end a ~: 4 rise, stir, wake 5 arise, awake, get up, waken 6 awaken, bestir, wake up
ender: 4 time
inducer: 4 bore
sound: 3 zzz 5 snore
starter: 3 cat, dog, kid
unit: 4 wink
Nap: 6 Lajoie
Napa: 4 city, town 6 valley
locale: 10 California
product: 4 wine 5 pinot
winery: 5 Gallo
Napaeus: 5 satyr
N/A, part of: 3 not 4 appl. 10 applicable
nape: 4 neck 5 nucha, scrag 6 scruff
coverer: 6 collar
knot: 3 bun
Naperville: 4 city, town
locale: 8 Illinois
napery: 5 linen
Naphtali
parent of ~: 5 Jacob 6 Bilhah
sibling of ~: 3 Dan, Gad 4 Levi 5 Asher, Dinah, Judah 6 Joseph, Reuben, Simeon 7 Zebulun 8 Benjamin, Issachar
napier: 5 grass
Napier: 4 Alan, John 7 Charles
Napier's __: 4 rods 5 bones
napkin: 3 bib 5 doily, linen 6 doyley
in Britain: 9 serviette
material: 6 damask
place: 3 lap 5 table
napkin __: 4 ring
Naples: 3 bay 4 city, port, town
city near ~: 5 Gaeta 6 Amalfi
island near ~: 5 Capri 6 Ischia
lake near ~: 6 Averno
locale: 5 Italy 7 Florida
Napo: 5 river
locale: 4 Peru 7 Ecuador
napoleon: 4 coin, game 5 money 6 pastry 7 dessert 8 card game
cousin: 6 éclair
locale: 6 bakery
Napoleon: 4 Solo 5 exile 6 Lajoie 9 Bonaparte
emblem: 5 eagle
horse: 7 Marengo
island: 4 Elba 7 Corsica 8 St. Helena
river ~ navigated: 4 Nile
victory site: 4 Lodi, Yafo 5 Jaffa
word in a ~ palindrome: 3 ere, saw, was 4 able, Elba
see also French
__ Napoléon: 4 Code
Napoleon (1927 film) director: Abel Gance
__ Napoleon Duarte: 4 José
Napoleonic __: 3 Era 4 Code, Wars
__ Napoleon, The: 5 Age of
Napoli: 4 city, town
locale: 5 Italy 6 Italia
napped: 5 downy, fuzzy 6 fluffy
fabric: 5 baize 7 flannel
napping: 5 adoze 6 asleep, at rest 7 dormant 9 sacked out, somnolent, unmindful
caught ~: 6 dozing, spacey 7 in a daze, out of it, unaware 8 heedless 9 negligent, unmindful, unwitting 10 out to lunch
place: 4 sofa 8 recliner
quit ~: 4 rise, wake 5 arise, awake, get up, waken 6 awaken
nappy: 4 soft 5 curly, downy, furry, fuzzy, plush 6 diaper, fleecy, fluffy, shaggy 7 squishy, velvety 8 cushiony
Napster opponent: 4 RIAA
naqara: 4 drum
origin: 7 Mideast
Nara: 4 city, town
locale: 5 Hondo, Japan 6 Honshu
Naranjos: 4 city, town
locale: 6 Mexico 8 Veracruz

NARAS award: 6 Grammy
part of: 3 Nat. 4 Acad., Arts, Natl., Scis. 7 Academy 8 National, Sciences 9 Recording
Narayan, R.K.: 6 author, Indian, writer
Narbada: 5 river
locale: 5 India
narc: 3 cop 4 G-man 6 buster, shamus 9 detective, policeman
activity: 4 bust, raid 5 pinch 6 arrest, collar 7 seizure
find: 4 kilo, perp 5 drugs
org.: 3 DEA
Narcisse author: George Sand
Narcisse composer: 8 Massenet
narcissism: 3 ego 5 pride 6 egoism, vanity 7 conceit, egotism, hauteur 8 self-love, snobbery 9 immodesty, vainglory 10 pretension
narcissist: 4 snob 6 egoist 9 introvert 10 self-seeker, self-server
narcissistic: 4 smug, vain 5 cocky, proud 6 snobby, stuffy 7 fustian, haughty, pompous, selfish, stuck-up 8 arrogant, boastful, snobbish 9 bigheaded, conceited, egotistic
narcissus: 5 plant 6 flower
Narcissus
like ~: 4 vain
love: 3 ego 4 Echo, self 5 image
parent of ~: 6 Selene 7 Liriope 8 Endymion 9 Cephissus
play ~: 5 preen
__ Narcissus: 5 Black
nard: 5 grass 8 matgrass
nardin: 5 shrub
nares: 8 nostrils
Narew: 5 river
locale: 6 Poland
naris: 7 nostril
nark: 3 rat 4 fink 6 canary, snitch, weasel 7 stoolie, tattler, traitor 8 informer, squealer, turncoat 10 tattletale
Narnia creator: 5 Lewis
Narragansett: 3 bay
narrate: 4 tell, yarn 5 state 6 depict, detail, recite, relate, repeat, report, unfold 7 portray, recount 8 describe, rehearse, set forth 9 chronicle, hold forth, make known
narrated: 4 oral 5 vocal 6 spoken, verbal 9 unwritten, vocalized
narration: 4 news, tale, yarn 5 story 6 report 7 account, reading, recital 8 anecdote 9 chronicle, recountal, voice-over 10 commentary, confession, expression, recitation, recounting
narrative: 4 acct., book, epic, plot, saga, tale, yarn 5 novel, story 6 legend, memoir, report 7 account, article, fiction, history, recital, romance, version 8 anecdote, libretto, thriller, whodunit 9 chronicle, potboiler, recountal, statement 10 recounting, short story
French ~ poem: 3 lai
poem: 4 idyl 5 idyll
song: 6 ballad
Narrative of A. Gordon Pym author: Edgar Allan Poe
narrow: 3 set 4 fine, mean, slim, thin 5 close, fixed, limit, local, scant, small, taper, tight 6 biased, lessen, linear, little, recede, reduce, shrink 7 abridge, bigoted, compact, cramped, curtail, insular, limited, partial, pinched, shallow, shorten, slender, thin out, tighten 8 compress, condense, contract, decrease, dogmatic, hemmed in, isolated, obdurate, orthodox, restrict, shrunken, tapering, taper off 9 confining, exclusive, hidebound, illiberal, parochial, sectarian 10 abbreviate, attenuated, compressed, contracted,

dogmatical, inflexible, intolerant, prejudiced, provincial, restricted, threadlike
band: 4 rein 5 leash, strap
board: 4 lath
boat: 5 canoe, kayak, skiff 9 outrigger
combining form: 4 sten- 5 steno- 7 augusti-, dolicho-
conduit: 4 tube
connector: 4 neck
ender: 4 back, cast 7 casting
get ~: 5 taper
land: 4 spit
make less ~: 5 widen 6 expand, spread 7 broaden, enlarge, thicken 9 spread out
margin: 4 hair, neck, nose
not ~: 4 wide 5 broad, roomy 8 spacious 9 capacious, expansive, extensive 10 commodious
off the straight and ~: 4 awry, lost 5 amiss 6 adrift, afield, astray 7 missing, roaming 9 wandering
opening: 4 slit, slot 5 chink 6 cranny
passage: 4 lane 5 alley, fiord, fjord, inlet
route: 4 pass 6 strait
shelf: 5 ledge
shoe: 3 AAA 4 AAAA, ten A
the gap: 4 near 5 close 6 gain on 7 catch up, close in 8 approach, overtake 9 close in on
valley: 5 combe, coomb 6 coombe
waterway: 5 sound 7 channel
window opening: 6 louver, louvre
narrow ___: 5 gauge 6 escape, margin
narrow-___: 6 fisted, minded
Narrow Corner, The (1933 film)
cast: Ralph Bellamy, Douglas Fairbanks Jr.
narrowest: 5 least 6 lowest, merest 7 minimal, minimum, tiniest 8 smallest 9 slightest
narrow horizontal
in heraldry: 5 label 6 fillet
narrowly: 4 just 6 almost, barely, nearly 7 by a hair, by a nose, closely 8 only just, scarcely 10 by a whisker
narrow-minded: 5 petty, rabid, rigid, small 6 biased, little, narrow, stuffy 7 bigoted, insular, prudish, selfish, shallow 8 dogmatic 9 hidebound, illiberal, parochial, sectarian 10 dogmatical
one: 5 bigot
narrowness: 4 bias 8 jingoism 9 prejudice 10 chauvinism, fanaticism
Narrow Rooms author: James Purdy
narrows: 4 neck 6 strait 7 channel
narrow-waisted stinger: 4 wasp
narthex: 8 anteroom
neighbor: 4 apse, nave
Narvik: 4 city, port, town
locale: 6 Norway
narwhal: 6 animal 8 cetacean
feature: 4 tusk
nosh: 5 krill
relative: 3 orc, sei 5 whale 6 beluga 7 cowfish, dolphin, finback, grampus, rorqual 8 porpoise
nary: 3 not 4 none, zero 5 never 6 not any
a soul: 4 none 5 no one
nary ___: 4 a one 5 a soul
NASA
acronym: 3 ELV, EVA, LEM
affirmative: 3 A-OK 5 A-okay
chimp: 4 Enos
concern: 7 shuttle
countdown word: 3 one, six, ten, two 4 five, four, nine 5 eight, minus, seven, three 7 liftoff 8 ignition
counterpart: 3 ESA
creation: 5 robot
decision: 4 no-go
destination: 3 Mir 4 Mars, moon 5 orbit
event: 6 launch
gasket: 5 O-ring
1960 ~ launch: 5 Tiros
name: 3 Gus 4 Alan, Buzz, Deke, Neil, Ride 5 Glenn 6 Aldrin 7 Grissom, Shepard, Slayton 9 Armstrong
normal gravity, to ~: 4 one G
number: 5 niner
outfit: 5 G-suit
part: 3 Nat. 4 Natl. 5 Admin., Space 8 National
project: 6 Apollo, Aurora, Gemini 7 Mercury
spacewalk: 3 EVA
vehicle: 3 LEM 5 Agena, Atlas 6 Skylab 7 orbiter
nasal: 6 rhinal, twangy 9 adenoidal
bone: 5 vomer
input: 4 odor 5 aroma, scent, smell, whiff 9 fragrance
of the ~ cavity: 5 naric
opening: 5 naris 7 nostril
openings: 5 nares
passage: 5 sinus
sound: 5 snore, snort, twang, whine
nasal ___: 5 index, spray 6 concha
nasally offensive: 4 olid, rank 6 stinky
NASCAR
broadcaster: 4 ESPN
event: 4 race
part: 3 Car 4 Assn., Auto 5 Assoc., Stock 6 Racing
sponsor: 3 STP
nascence: 5 birth 7 genesis, infancy 9 childhood
nascent: 5 early 6 infant 7 initial 9 beginning, inceptive
Nascimento, Edson Arantes do: 4 Pelé
NASDAQ: 3 mkt.
how ~ stocks trade: 3 OTC
offering: 3 IPO, stk. 4 shrs. 5 stock
orgs.: 3 cos.
rival: 4 AMEX, NYSE
transaction: 5 trade
Nash: 3 car 4 auto, John, poet 5 Ogden 6 Graham, Johnny 7 Bridges, Charles 8 Clarence 10 automobile
colleague: 5 Young 6 Crosby, Stills
competitor: 6 De Soto
model: 7 Rambler 9 Lafayette, Statesman 10 Ambassador
Nash Bridges (CBS drama)
cast: Don Johnson (Insp. Nash Bridges)
Cheech Marin (Insp. Joe Dominguez)
employer: SFPD
Nashe, Thomas: 7 English 8 satirist 10 playwright
Nashira: 4 star
Nash, John: 8 Nobelist 9 economist
Nash, Johnny
song: Hold Me Tight (1968)
I Can See Clearly Now (1972)
Stir It Up (1973)
Nash, Ogden: 4 poet 6 writer
one-L priest: 4 lama
two-L beast: 5 llama
work: Bed Riddance
Everyone But Thee and Me
Nashua: 4 city, town 5 horse 9 racehorse
locale: New Hampshire
Nashville: 4 city, town
athletes: 9 Predators 10 Commodores
county: 8 Davidson
locale: 9 Tennessee
music hall: 4 Opry
river: 10 Cumberland
school: 3 TSU 4 Fisk 10 Vanderbilt
Nashville (1975 film)
cast: Karen Black, Ronee Blakley, Keith Carradine, Geraldine Chaplin, Henry Gibson, Lily Tomlin
director: Robert Altman
song: 6 I'm Easy
Nashville ___: 4 Cats 7 warbler
Nashville Cats (1966 song) artist: Lovin' Spoonful
Nashville-to-Chicago dir.: 3 NNW
Naskapi: 6 Indian 7 Amerind
nasolacrimal ___: 4 duct
NAS org.: 3 USN
Nassau: 4 city, port, town 7 capital
locale: 7 Bahamas
Nasser: 4 lake 5 Gamal
locale: 5 Egypt
org.: 3 UAR
successor: 5 Sadat
Nast: 5 Condé 6 Thomas
symbol: 6 donkey 8 elephant
target: 5 Tweed
Nastase, Ilie: 7 netster 9 tennis pro
milieu: 5 court
Nastassja: 6 Kinski
nastiness: 5 spite, venom 6 enmity, malice, rancor 7 cruelty, ill will 8 acrimony, bad blood 9 animosity, hostility 10 resentment
Nast, Thomas: 10 cartoonist
nasturtium: 5 bloom, plant 6 flower 7 blossom
nasty: 3 bad, low 4 acid, cold, cool, evil, foul, icky, lewd, mean, rank, ugly, vile 5 awful, catty, cruel, dance, dirty, gross, harsh, lousy, onery, rough, snide, surly, yucky 6 animal, bad guy, bitter, bratty, brutal, chilly, coarse, crabby, fierce, filthy, grubby, horrid, odious, ornery, putrid, rancid, remote, ribald, rotten, savage, severe, smutty, snappy, sneaky, sordid, sticky, unkind, vulgar, wanton, wicked 7 abusive, beastly, brutish, callous, cutting, glacial, hateful, heinous, hellish, hostile, hurtful, immoral, knavish, lowdown, noisome, noxious, obscene, painful, profane, raunchy, squalid, unclean, vicious 8 abrasive, annoying, barbaric, contrary, critical, diabolic, fiendish, horrible, immodest, improper, indecent, inhumane, inimical, liverish, pitiless, polluted, ruthless, sadistic, shameful, sinister, spiteful, stinking, unsavory, unseemly, vengeful 9 abhorrent, bellicose, cutthroat, dangerous, ferocious, inclement, loathsome, malicious, merciless, monstrous, obnoxious, offensive, poisonous, repellent, repugnant, repulsive, revolting, sarcastic, truculent, withdrawn 10 despicable, diabolical, disgusting, ill-humored, ill-natured, indecorous, indelicate, iniquitous, malevolent, malodorous, pugnacious, scurrilous, unfriendly, unpleasant, villainous, vindictive
comment: 3 heh, mud 7 put-down
habit: 4 vice
look: 4 leer 5 sneer
mood: 4 snit 5 pique
one: 3 cur 4 ogre 5 meany 6 meanie
Nasty (1986 song) artist: Janet Jackson
Nasty on the courts: 4 Ilie
Nasu: 7 volcano
locale: 4 Asia 5 Japan
nasus: 4 nose
part of a ~: 5 nares, naris
Nat: 4 Cole 5 Hiken 6 Holman, Turner 7 Currier, Hentoff 9 Fleischer
Nat ___ Cole: 4 King
Natal: 4 city, town
locale: 6 Brazil
native: 4 Zulu
seaport: 6 Durban
Natal ___: 4 plum 6 orange
Natalia: 8 Ginzburg, Makarova
see also Italian
Natalie: 4 Cole, Wood 6 Maines 7 Portman, Schafer 8 Merchant 9 Imbruglia
father: 3 Nat
in Russian: 7 Natasha
played her: 5 Maria
natality: 5 birth
natal starter: 3 neo
Natascha: 8 McElhone
Natasha: 6 Lyonne 10 Henstridge, Richardson
aunt: 4 Lynn
husband: 4 Liam
in English: 7 Natalie
mother: 7 Vanessa
see also Russian
Natasha ___ Wagner: 7 Gregson
natatorium: 4 pool
natatory: 6 marine 7 aquatic, oceanic
natch: 2 ay, da, ja, sí 3 aye, oui, yea, yep, yup 4 fine, okay, sure, yeah 5 good-o, quite, right, roger, uh-huh 6 agreed, gladly, good-oh, indeed, just so, rather, righto, surely, you bet, yowzah 7 exactly, for sure, go ahead, indeedy, mais oui, quite so, ten-four 8 all right, as you say, of course, thumbs up, very well 9 be my guest, certainly, darn right, precisely, sure thing, you betcha, you said it 10 absolutely, by all means, definitely, positively, sure enough, that's right
Natchez: 4 city, town
locale: 4 Miss.
Natchez ___: 5 Trace
Nate: 4 Dogg 8 Thurmond 9 Archibald
Nathalie: 8 Sarraute
Nathan: 4 Hale, Lane 5 Juran 8 Alterman, Milstein 9 Söderblom
Nathanael: 4 West 5 saint
Nathaniel: 7 Currier 9 Hawthorne
Nathans, Daniel: 8 Nobelist
nation: 4 land, race 5 realm, state, tribe, union 6 domain, empire, people, public 7 country, kingdom, society 8 dominion, monarchy, republic 9 democracy, territory
ender: 4 wide
nation-___: 5 state
Nation: 5 Carry
___ Nation: 5 Alien 6 Rhythm
national: 6 ethnic, public, racial 7 citizen, federal 8 domestic, interior, internal, societal 10 interstate
song: 6 anthem
spirit: 5 ethos
starter: 5 inter, multi
symbol: 4 flag 8 standard
national ___: 4 bank, debt, park 6 church, forest, income 7 holiday, library
National: 9 car rental 10 auto rental
alternative: 4 Avis 5 Alamo, Hertz 6 Budget, Dollar 7 Thrifty 10 Enterprise
National ___: 5 Guard 6 League, Velvet 7 Charter
National ___ Award: 4 Book
National ___ Foundation: 7 Science
National ___ of Sciences: 7 Academy
National ___ of Standards: 6 Bureau
National ___ Radio: 6 Public
National ___ Relations Act: 5 Labor
National ___ Scholarship: 5 Merit
National ___ Service: 4 Park 7 Weather
National Assembly locale: 6 France
National Enquirer rival: 4 Star

National Forest: **4** Gila, Inyo, Pike **5** Boise, Delta, Dixie, Huron, Modoc, Ocala, Ozark, Routt, Tahoe, Teton, Tonto, Twain, Uinta, Wayne **6** Apache, Ashley, Carson, Cibola, Custer, De Soto, Helena, Kaibab, Lassen, Marion, Ochoco, Oconee, Oglala, Ottawa, Pawnee, Pisgah, Plumas, Sabine, Salmon, Shasta, Sierra, Sumter, Umpqua, Winema **7** Angeles, Arapaho, Bighorn, Bridger, Caribou, Challis, Chugach, Conecuh, Fremont, Hoosier, Houston, Klamath, Lincoln, Malheur, Nicolet, Olympic, Osceola, Payette, Pinchot, San Juan, Santa Fe, Sequoia, Shawnee, Siuslaw, Targhee, Tongass, Trinity, Wasatch **8** Angelina, Bankhead, Cherokee, Chippewa, Coconino, Colville, Croatoan, Crockett, Eldorado, Fishlake, Flathead, Gallatin, Hiawatha, Humboldt, Kootenai, Manistee, Nez Perce, Okanogan, Ouachita, Prescott, Sawtooth, Shoshone, Superior, Tombigee, Tuskegee, Uwharrie **9** Allegheny, Bienville, Deschutes, Kisatchie, Roosevelt, Talladega, Wenatchee
National Gallery ___: **5** of Art
National Geographic insert: **3** map
___ National Guard: **3** Air
National Guard building: **6** armory
nationalism: **8** jingoism **10** chauvinism, flag-waving, patriotism
nationalist: **5** jingo **7** patriot **8** jingoist **9** flag-waver
  org.: **3** IRA
Nationalist ___: **5** China
nationality: **4** race **6** origin, people **7** country, society
  indicator: **6** ensign
  suffix: **3** -ese, -ish
___ nationality: **4** dual
National Labor Relations ___: **3** Act
National Lampoon's Animal House (1978 film)
  attire: toga
  cast: Kevin Bacon, John Belushi, Stephen Furst, Tom Hulce, Tim Matheson, Peter Riegert, Donald Sutherland, John Vernon
  director: John Landis
  role: **4** D-Day, Doug, Greg, Katy **5** Bluto, Mandy, Otter, Pinto **6** Wormer **8** Flounder
National Lampoon's Christmas Vacation (1989 film)
  cast: Chevy Chase, Beverly D'Angelo, Randy Quaid
National Lampoon's Vacation (1983 film)
  cast: Chevy Chase, Beverly D'Angelo, Anthony Michael Hall
  director: Harold Ramis
National League
  city: **3** Atl., Chi., NYC, St. L. **4** Milw. **5** Miami, Phila. **6** Denver **7** Atlanta, Chicago, Houston, New York, Phoenix, St. Louis **8** Montreal, San Diego **9** Milwaukee **10** Cincinnati, Los Angeles, Pittsburgh **12** Philadelphia, San Francisco
  division: **4** East, West
  player: **3** Cub, Met, Red **4** Card, Expo **5** Astro, Brave, Giant, NY Met, Padre, Rocky **6** Brewer, Dodger, Marlin, Pirate **7** Phillie **8** Cardinal **11** Diamondback
  stadium: **4** Shea
National Park: **4** Zion **5** Banff **6** Acadia, Arches, Denali, Katmai **7** Big Bend, Glacier, Olympic, Redwood, Saguaro, Sequoia **8** Badlands, Biscayne, Wind Cave, Yosemite **9** Haleakala, Lake Clark, Mesa Verde, Voyageurs **10** Crater Lake, Everglades, Glacier Bay, Grand Teton, Great Basin, Hot Springs, Isle Royale, Joshua Tree **11** Yellowstone
National Park ___: **7** Service
___ national product: **3** net **5** gross
National Public ___: **5** Radio
Nationalrat locale: **7** Austria
National Security ___: **6** Agency **7** Council
National Velvet (1944 film)
  cast: Donald Crisp, Angela Lansbury, Anne Revere, Mickey Rooney, Elizabeth Taylor
  highlight: race
National Weather Service agency: **4** NOAA
Nation, Carry: **3** dry
  like ~: **5** sober
  weapon: **3** axe
___ nation indivisible...: **3** one
___ Nations: **3** Six **4** Five **6** United
nations, allied: **4** bloc
___ Nations Day: **6** United
native: **4** real, wild **5** liver, local, voter **6** ethnic, inborn, inbred, innate, vulgar **7** ancient, built-in, citizen, denizen, endemic, natural, radical, resider **8** domestic, indigene, inherent, original, primeval, regional, resident **9** aborigine, belonging, endemical, homegrown, indweller, inherited, intrinsic, primaeval, primitive **10** aboriginal, autochthon, indigenous, inhabitant, unacquired
  (suffix): **3** ese, ite, ote
native ___: **3** cat, son
native-___: **4** born
Native ___: **3** Son **6** States
Native American: **3** Fox, Han, Kaw, Oto, Sac, Ute **4** ALer, Cree, Crow, Cuna, Erie, Eyak, Hopi, Inca, Iowa, Maya, Otoe, Pima, Pomo, Sauk, Seri, Tama, Taos, Tewa, Tiwa, Tupi, Yana, Yuma, Zuni **5** Ahtna, Asian, brave, Brulé, Caddo, Carib, Creek, Haida, Huron, Kansa, Kaska, Kiowa, Lenca, Lipan, Maidu, Makah, Miami, Miwok, Modoc, Omaha, Osage, Otomi, Piute, Ponca, Sioux, Taino, Teton, Unami, Washo, Wintu, Yaqui **6** Abnaki, Ahtena, Apache, Arawak, Aymara, Cayuga, Cayuse, Dakota, Feller, Galibi, Indian, Jivaro, Kechua, Laguna, Lakota, Lengua, Lumbee, Mandan, Micmac, Mohave, Mohawk, Mojave, Munsee, Navaho, Navajo, Nootka, Oglala, Ojibwa, Oneida, Ottawa, Paiute, Papago, Patwin, Pawnee, Pequot, Plains, Pueblo, Quapaw, Salish, Santee, Seneca, Tanana, Toltec, Wintun, Yahgan, Yakima, Yokuts **7** Abenaki, Arapaho, Arikara, Atakapa, Bannock, Chibcha, Chilcat, Chilkat, Chinook, Choctaw, Chumash, Guarani, Huastec, Kechuan, Klamath, Koyukon, Kutchin, Kutenai, Lakhota, Mahican, Mazatec, Miskito, Mohegan, Mohican, Naskapi, Nipmuck, Ojibway, Quechua, Quichua, San Blas, Shawnee, Takelma, Tanaina, Tlingit, Washita, Wichita, Wyandot, Yankton, Yavapai, Yucatec, Zapotec **8** Arapahoe, Cahuilla, Caingang, Cherokee, Cheyenne, Chippewa, Comanche, Delaware, Hunkpapa, Illinois, Iroquois, Kickapoo, Kwakiutl, Malecite, Maricopa, Mikasuki, Missouri, Muskogee, Nez Percé, Onondaga, Ouachita, Puyallup, Quechuan, Sahaptin, Seminole, Squamish, Tarascan, Wabanaki, Wahpeton **9** Blackfoot, Chickasaw, Havasupai, Jicarilla, Karankawa, Menominee, Mescalero, Nanticoke, Penobscot, Saulteaux, Suquamish, Tehuelche, Tiger Lily, Tsimshian, Tuscarora, Wahpekute, Wampanoag, Winnebago, Wyandotte **10** Adirondack, Araucanian, Assiniboin, Athabaskan, Bellabella, Bellacoola, Chiricahua, Miniconjou, Potawatomi, Tarahumara
  corn: **5** maize
  group: **5** tribe
  see also Indian
natives: **10** population
Native Son: **5** novel
  author: Richard Wright
  character: **6** Bigger, Thomas
nativity: **5** birth **6** origin
  figures: **4** Magi
  scene: **6** crèche
Nat King ___: **4** Cole
natl.: **3** fed. **9** govt.-owned
NATO: **4** pact **8** alliance
  cousin: **3** OAS
  former ~ commander: **3** DDE **4** Haig
  member: **3** Can., Eng., Ger., Lux., Mex., Nor., USA **4** Belg., Holl., Icel., Neth., Norw., Port. **5** Italy, Spain **6** Canada, France, Greece, Norway, Poland, Turkey **7** Belgium, Denmark, Germany, Hungary, Iceland **8** Portugal **10** Luxembourg
  part: **3** Atl., Org. **5** North **6** Treaty **8** Atlantic
natron: **7** mineral
Natta, Giulio: **7** chemist **8** Nobelist
natter: **3** gab, yak **4** chat **7** chatter, grumble
nattering nabobs coiner: **5** Agnew
natterjack: **4** toad **9** amphibian
nattiness: **4** chic **5** style, swank, vogue
natty: **4** chic, neat **5** dandy, sharp, sleek, smart, swank **6** dapper, dressy, jaunty, rakish, snazzy, spiffy, sporty, spruce, swanky **7** duded up, groomed, stylish, voguish **9** decked out, gussied up
Natty's dog: **6** Hector
___ naturae: **3** jus **5** ferae **7** domitae
natural: **3** raw, tan **4** Afro, easy, homy, naif, open, pure, real, true, wild **5** crude, frank, homey, naive, plain, typic, usual **6** candid, direct, earthy, folksy, inborn, innate, native, normal, simple **7** artless, genuine, logical, organic, outdoor, radical, regular, sincere, typical, up-front **8** everyday, familiar, habitual, inherent, laid-back, ordinary, physical, unartful, unforced **9** childlike, customary, guileless, hairstyle, ingenuous, intrinsic, intuitive, primitive, realistic, unfeigned, universal, unlabored, unrefined, unstudied **10** forthright, indigenous, legitimate, reasonable, unacquired, unaffected, unbleached
  ability: **4** gift **5** flair, knack **6** genius **8** instinct **9** endowment
  casino ~: **5** seven **6** eleven
  combining form: **7** physico-
  fiber: **4** jute, wool
  history museum display: **4** T-rex
  mimic: **4** mina, myna **5** minah, mynah
  resource: **3** gas, oil, ore **5** water
  toxin: **5** venin **6** venene, venine
  undergo ~ selection: **6** evolve
  world: **8** creation, universe
natural ___: **3** gas, law **4** aids, food **5** levee, right **6** gender, number, person, rubber, virtue **7** history, realism, science, varnish
natural-___: **4** born
Natural ___: **4** High **5** Woman **6** Bridge **7** History
Natural ___, A: **3** Man **5** Woman
Natural Blonde author: **8** Liz Smith
___ naturale: **3** jus
natural food additive: **4** herb
natural gas
  constituent: **6** ethane **8** dimethyl
Natural High (1973 song) artist: Bloodstone
natural historian: **3** Ray **4** Baer **6** Buffon, Cuvier, Darwin, Gesner **7** Agassiz, Lamarck, Wallace
  British ~: **3** Ray **6** Darwin **7** Wallace
  French ~: **6** Buffon, Cuvier **7** Lamarck
  German ~: **4** Baer
  Swiss ~: **6** Gesner
natural history: **7** science
  study: **6** nature **9** organisms
Natural History author: **5** Pliny
naturalist study: **5** flora
naturally: **2** ay, da, ja, sí **3** aye, oui, yea, yep, yes, yup **4** fine, okay, sure, yeah **5** good-o, quite, right, roger, uh-huh **6** agreed, easily, freely, gladly, good-oh, indeed, just so, openly, rather, righto, simply, surely, you bet, yowzah **7** by birth, exactly, go ahead, indeedy, mais oui, quite so, readily, ten-four **8** all right, as you say, by nature, candidly, casually, commonly, normally, of course, thumbs up, very well **9** artlessly, be my guest, certainly, darn right, genuinely, precisely, sure thing, typically, you betcha, you said it **10** absolutely, by all means, definitely, habitually, informally, innocently, ordinarily, positively, sure enough, that's right
  exist ~: **6** inhere
___ Naturally: **3** Act
Natural Man, A (1971 song) artist: Lou Rawls
naturalness: **4** ease **7** naiveté
Natural, The: **4** film **5** novel
  author: Bernard Malamud
  cast: Kim Basinger, Glenn Close, Robert Duvall, Robert Redford
  director: Barry Levinson
  role: **3** Roy **5** Hobbs **8** Roy Hobbs
Natural Woman, A (1967 song) artist: Aretha Franklin
nature: **3** ilk, way **4** cast, kind, mold, mood, self, sort, type, vein **5** being, color, earth, fiber, heart, humor, order, state, style, world **6** aspect, cosmos, entity, forest, makeup, stripe, temper, traits **7** essence, meaning, outlook, quality, scenery, species **8** creation, features, outdoors, seascape, universe **9** character, framework, landscape, macrocosm, structure **10** attributes, complexion
  building block of ~: **4** atom
  by ~: **5** per se **8** normally **10** inherently
  combining form: **3** eco- **5** physi- **6** physio-
  good ~: **6** gaiety, warmth **9** geniality, joviality, pleasance, sunniness **10** affability, amiability, cheeriness, cordiality, kindliness
  imitator: **3** art
  of the ~ of (suffix): **3** -ine
  prefix: **3** eco-
  preserve: **4** park **9** sanctuary
  second ~: **5** habit
  spirit of Africa: **4** ngai
  walk: **4** hike **5** trail
nature ___: **4** walk **5** study, trail **7** worship
___ nature: **3** ill **4** good **5** human **6** second
Nature ___: **3** Boy
Nature author: Ralph Waldo Emerson

nature concentrated: 3 art
__-natured: 3 ill 4 good
naturel, au: 3 raw 4 bare, nude 5 naked 9 in the buff, unattired
nature-loving: 6 rustic 7 outdoor
Nature network: 3 PBS
__ Nature of Things: 5 On the
...nature's copy's not __: 6 eterne
nature-walk snack: 7 berries
Natwick: 7 Mildred
Naucalpan: 4 city, town
locale: 6 Mexico
Naugahyde: 6 fabric
coating: 5 vinyl
Naugatuck: 4 city, town
locale: 4 Conn.
naught: 3 nil, zip 4 nada, none, zero 5 squat, zilch 6 bubkes, bupkes, cipher 7 nothing 8 goose egg
bring to ~: 4 undo 5 annul 6 cancel, negate 7 abolish, destroy, nullify, reverse 8 abrogate, demolish 10 invalidate, neutralize
come to ~: 4 bomb, bust, fail, flop, sink 6 fizzle 7 founder 8 backfire, fall flat, flounder 10 run aground
for ~: 4 idle, vain 6 futile, otiose 7 inutile, useless 8 bootless, hopeless 9 fruitless, pointless, worthless 10 unavailing
naughtiness: 5 prank 7 knavery, roguery, trouble 8 deviltry, mischief 9 high jinks, rascality, vandalism 10 misconduct, wrongdoing
Naughton: 4 Greg 5 David, James, Keira 6 Amanda
naughts-and-crosses: 9 tic-tac-toe
nonwinner: 3 OOX, OXO, OXX, XOO, XOX, XXO
winner: 3 OOO, XXX
naughty: 3 bad 4 blue, lewd, racy 5 bawdy, dirty, loose, onery, rough, rowdy, wrong 6 erotic, errant, feisty, impish, ornery, ribald, risqué, steamy, unruly, vulgar, wanton, wicked, wilful 7 defiant, knavish, obscene, playful, raunchy, teasing, wayward, willful 8 annoying, contrary, improper, off-color, perverse, rascally, stubborn 9 fractious 10 headstrong, indecorous, rebellious, refractory
one: 3 cad, cur, imp 4 brat 5 churl, knave, louse, rogue, scamp 6 rascal 7 bounder, stinker 8 blighter, picaroon, scalawag, spalpeen 9 miscreant, prankster, reprobate, scoundrel 10 blackguard, holy terror, ne'er-do-well
Naughty __ of Shady Lane, The: 4 Lady
Naughty by Nature
song: Feel Me Flow (1995)
Hip Hop Hooray (1993)
Jamboree (1999)
O.P.P. (1991)
Naughty Lady of Shady Lane, The (1954 song) artist: Ames Brothers
Naughty, naughty!: 3 tsk, tut 6 tsk tsk, tut-tut
Naughty Nineties, The (1945 film)
cast: Bud Abbott, Lou Costello
Nauru money: 4 cent 6 dollar
Nausea author: Jean-Paul Sartre
__ Nautica: 5 Pyxis
nautical: 5 naval 6 marine 7 aquatic, deep-sea, oceanic, pelagic 8 maritime, sailorly, seagoing, yachting 9 seafaring, thalassic 10 oceangoing
adjective: 3 yar 4 yare
adverb: 3 aft 4 alee, alow 6 astern
AFB's ~ counterpart: 3 NAS
art: 5 navig. 10 navigation
assent: 3 aye
boom: 5 sprit
chain: 3 tye
CIA's ~ cousin: 3 ONI
diary: 3 log
direction: 3 aft, EbN, EbS, ENE, ESE, NbE, NbW, NNE, NNW, SbE, SbW, SSE, SSW, WbN, WbS, WNW, WSW 4 alee, fore 5 abeam, aport 6 astern
distance: 6 league
exclamation: 4 ahoy 5 avast, heave 7 heave ho
gear: 3 rig
greeting: 4 ahoy
group: 4 crew 5 hands 7 sailors
law enforcers: 4 USCG
line: 6 inhaul
measure: 2 kn., kt. 4 knot 6 fathom, league
nose: 4 prow
pole: 4 spar 5 sprit
quarters: 5 berth, cabin
rope: 3 tye 4 vang 6 cablet, earing, hawser
signal: 4 bell
starter: 4 aero 5 astro
see also naval, Navy
nautical __: 3 day 4 mile
nautilus: 5 shell 8 seashell
__ nautilus: 5 paper 6 pearly
Nautilus
branch: 3 USN 4 Navy
captain: 4 Nemo
locale: 3 gym, spa
use a ~: 4 lift, tone 5 train 6 tone up 7 work out 8 exercise
user's muscle: 2 ab 3 pec 4 delt, quad 9 hamstring
Nava: 4 city, town
locale: 6 Mexico 8 Coahuila
Navajo: 5 tribe 6 Indian 7 Amerind 8 language
hello: 6 yateeh
kin: 6 Apache
lodge: 5 hogan
silver: 6 concha
Navajoa: 4 city, town
locale: 6 Mexico, Sonora
naval: 6 marine 7 aquatic, deep-sea, oceanic, pelagic 8 maritime, nautical, sailorly, seagoing, yachting 9 seafaring, thalassic 10 oceangoing
alert: 3 SOS
arena: 3 sea 5 ocean
barrage: 5 salvo 6 volley 7 barrage 9 broadside, cannonade, fusillade
cadet: 3 mid 5 middy 6 middie
call: 4 ahoy 5 avast
force: 5 fleet 6 argosy, armada 8 flotilla
German WWII ~ base: 5 Emden
guide: 6 beacon 10 lighthouse, watchtower
inits.: 3 HMS, USN, USS
officer: 6 gunner
on ~ maneuvers: 4 asea 5 at sea
rank: 2 lt. 3 cdr., com., CPO, ens., yeo. 4 cmdr., lt. jg., RAdm., VAdm. 5 lieut. 6 ensign, yeoman 7 admiral, captain 9 commander
response: 3 aye 6 aye aye 9 aye aye sir
second-in-command: 4 exec
tracking system: 5 loran
US ~ base, familiarly: 5 Gitmo
vessel: 4 boat 6 PT boat 10 battleship
see also nautical, Navy
naval __: 5 brass 6 stores 7 academy
Naval Academy
freshman: 4 pleb 5 plebe
Navarre
see Spanish
Navarro: 4 Dave, Fats
nave: 3 hub
bisector: 5 aisle
neighbor: 4 apse
seat: 3 pew
navel: 5 innie, outie 8 omphalos 9 umbilicus 11 belly button
combining form: 6 omphal- 7 omphalo-
ender: 4 wort
filler: 4 lint
navel orange: 5 fruit 6 citrus
relative: 4 lime, Ugli 5 lemon 6 pomelo, tangor 7 kumquat, satsuma, Seville, tangelo 8 bergamot, mandarin, shaddock, Valencia 9 tangerine 10 calamondin, grapefruit
__ Navidad!: 5 Feliz
navigable: 4 open 5 clear 8 passable 9 unblocked
navigate: 4 plot, sail 5 cross, guide, pilot, steer 6 aviate, cruise, direct, jockey, paddle, voyage 7 captain, journey, operate, ride out 8 maneuver
on snow: 3 ski 4 skee
tricky to ~: 5 reefy
navigation: 6 flying, travel 7 boating, sailing 8 cruising, piloting, shipping, steering, voyaging, yachting 9 seafaring, traveling
aid: 3 map, oar 5 chart, racon
device: 4 gyro 5 loran, radar, sonar
hazard: 3 fog 4 berb, reef 5 shoal
navigational: 5 naval 8 maritime, nautical
navigator: 5 flyer, pilot 7 mariner 8 helmsman, traveler
concern: 5 route 6 course 7 heading
heading: 3 EbS, ENE, ESE, NbE, NbW, NNE, NNW, SbE, SbW, SSE, SSW, WbN, WbS, WNW, WSW 9 SbE EbN EbN
Navigator: 3 SUV 4 Linc 7 Lincoln
Navigator Islands: 5 Samoa
Navolato: 4 city, town
locale: 6 Mexico 7 Sinaloa
Navratilova, Martina: 5 Czech 7 netster 9 tennis pro
milieu: 5 court
rival: 4 Graf 5 Evert
navy: 4 bean, blue 5 color, fleet 6 armada 8 dark blue, flotilla, military
relative: 4 anil, cyan, Nile, teal 5 Alice, azure, slate 6 cobalt, indigo, raisin, violet 7 peacock 8 cerulean, sapphire 9 turquoise 10 aquamarine, periwinkle
navy __: 4 bean, blue, gray, grey, yard
Navy: 4 USNA
athletes: 10 Midshipmen
CIA: 3 ONI
diver: 4 Seal
join the ~: 6 enlist, sign on
lawyer TV show: 3 JAG
locale: 8 Maryland 9 Annapolis
man: 3 gob
policemen: 2 SP
position: 4 rank
rank: 2 lt. 3 cdr., com., CPO, ens., yeo. 4 cmdr., lt. jg., RAdm., VAdm. 5 lieut., lt. com. 6 ensign, yeoman 7 admiral, captain 9 commander
reply: 3 aye 5 no sir 6 aye aye
rival: 4 Army
signal pennant: 6 cornet
stay in the ~: 4 reup
VIP: 3 Adm., CNO 4 RAdm., VAdm.
see also nautical, naval
Navy __: 4 Blue 5 Blues, Cross, Seals
__ Navy: 3 Old 5 In the 7 McHale's
navy bean: 6 legume
Navy Blues (1941 film)
cast: Jack Oakie, Martha Raye, Ann Sheridan
Navy Cross: 5 medal
__-navy store: 4 army
naw: 2 no 3 nah, nay, nix, non 4 nein, nope, nyet, uh-uh 5 I won't, ixnay, never, no how, no way 6 no deal, noways, nowise 7 I refuse 8 forget it, I will not, negative, negatory 9 by no means, fat chance, I think not 10 count me out, not a chance, thumbs down
nawab: 3 VIP 4 czar, king 5 baron, chief, mogul, ruler 6 bigwig, fat cat, leader, tycoon 7 big shot, magnate 8 big wheel, somebody 9 big cheese, dignitary, moneybags, plutocrat 10 man of means
Naxos: 4 isle 6 island
locale: 6 Greece
nay: 2 no 3 nah, naw, nix, non 4 nein, nope, nyet, uh-uh, veto, vote 5 I won't, ixnay, never, no how, noway 6 indeed, no deal, noways, nowise 7 I refuse 8 forget it, I will not, negative, negatory, to be sure 9 by no means, fat chance, I think not 10 count me out, not a chance, thumbs down
ender: 3 say 4 said 5 sayer 6 saying
not ~: 2 ay 3 aye, yea
sayer: 4 anti
Naya: 5 water
alternative: 5 Evian 7 Perrier 8 Aquafina 9 Arrowhead
Nayarit: 5 state 7 Mexican
city: 4 Ruiz 5 Tepic 6 Tuxpan 7 Tecuala 8 Las Varas
naysay: 6 negate, refute 7 confute, dispute 8 disagree, disprove 9 disaffirm, discredit 10 contradict, contravene
naysayer: 4 anti 5 cynic 6 censor, denier
perhaps: 5 voter
naysaying: 8 negative
Nazarenes: 4 sect
Nazarene, The author: Sholem Asch
Nazareth: 4 band, city, town
locale: 6 Israel
mountain near ~: 5 Tabor
song: Love Hurts (1976)
Nazimova: 4 Alla
Nb: 4 elem. 7 element, niobium
41 for ~: 4 at. no.
N.B.: 4 prov.
part of ~: 4 bene, nota
see also New Brunswick
NBA: 6 cagers, league.
arena: 5 court 6 Garden
broadcaster: 4 ESPN
former ~ venue: 4 Omni
like most ~ players: 4 tall
locale: 3 Atl., Chi. 4 Milw., Utah 5 Miami, Phila. 6 Boston, Dallas, Denver 7 Atlanta, Chicago, Detroit, Houston, Memphis, New York, Oakland, Orlando, Phoenix, Seattle, Toronto 8 Portland 9 Cleveland, Milwaukee 10 Los Angeles, New Orleans, Sacramento, San Antonio, Washington 11 Minneapolis 12 Indianapolis, Philadelphia 14 Salt Lake locale
official: 3 ref 7 referee
part: 3 Nat. 4 Assn., Natl. 5 Assoc. 10 Basketball
period: 3 qtr. 7 quarter
position: 3 fwd. 5 guard 6 center 7 forward
score: 2 pt. 5 point 9 field goal, free throw
shot: 5 lay-up
statistic: 6 assist
team: 4 Heat, Jazz, Nets, Suns 5 Bucks, Bulls, Celts, Hawks, Kings, Magic, Spurs 6 Knicks, Lakers, Pacers, Sixers, Sonics 7 Celtics, Hornets, Nuggets,

Pistons, Raptors, Rockets, Wizards 8 Clippers, Warriors 9 Cavaliers, Grizzlies, Mavericks 11 SuperSonics 12 Timberwolves, Trail Blazers
tiebreaker: 2 OT
NBAer: 3 pro 5 cager
__ 'N Bake: 5 Shake
NBC: 7 network
former ~ owner: 3 RCA
HQ: 3 NYC
overseer: 3 FCC
part of ~: 3 Nat 4 Natl.
peacock: 4 logo
rival: 3 ABC, CBS, Fox, UPN 5 ABCTV, CBSTV
show: 3 SNL 5 Today
__ 'n Boots: 4 Puss
N.C.
city: 3 Ral.
neighbor: 4 S. Car., Tenn.
water off ~: 3 Atl.
zone: 3 EDT, EST
see also North Carolina
NCAA
division: 3 ACC
part of ~: 4 assn.
regional: 4 East, West
rival: 3 NIT
tiebreaker: 2 OT
NCO: 2 DI, G.I. 3 cpl., CPO, SFC, sgt. 4 MSgt., serg., SSgt., TSgt. 5 sarge 6 noncom, sgt. maj. 8 corporal
part of ~: 3 com., non, off.
store: 2 PX
subordinate: 3 PFC
superior: 2 lt.
NCR
product: 3 ATM 4 till
NC-17: 6 rating
issuer: 4 MPAA
Nd: 4 elem. 7 element 9 neodymium
60 for ~: 4 at. no.
ND
neighbor: 3 Man. 4 Minn.
see also North Dakota
N'dama: 3 cow 4 bull 6 bovine, cattle
Ndebele: 8 language
home: 6 Africa 8 Zimbabwe
Ndegeocello: 7 Meshell
__ 'n dip: 4 chip
N'Djamena: 4 city, town 7 capital
locale: 4 Chad
Ndola: 4 city, town
locale: 6 Zambia
__ 'n Dri: 4 Wash
NDU conference: 7 Big East
Ne: 4 elem., neon 7 element
10 for ~: 4 at. no.
NE: 3 dir.
see also Nebraska
NEA: 5 union
be eligible for the ~: 5 teach
beneficiary: 3 PBS
chapter: 3 lcl. 5 local
concern: 7 three R's
member: 4 tchr. 7 teacher
part of ~: 3 Nat. 4 Arts, Assn., Educ., Natl. 8 National 9 Endowment
rival: 3 AFT, UFT
Neagle: 4 Anna
Neal: 5 Conan, Curly, Elise, Hefti, McCoy 6 Gabler 7 Jiminez 8 Patricia
Neale: 6 Fraser, Greasy
Neale, Greasy: 5 coach
sport: 8 football
__ Neale Hurston: 4 Zora
Neal, Patricia: 7 actress
film: Baxter (1973)
Breakfast at Tiffany's (1961)
The Breaking Point (1950)
The Day the Earth Stood Still (1951)
Diplomatic Courier (1952)
A Face in the Crowd (1957)
Hud (1963, AA)
Operation Pacific (1951)
The Subject Was Roses (1968)
Three Secrets (1950)
spouse: Roald Dahl
Neame, Ronald: 8 director
film: The Chalk Garden (1964)
Gambit (1966)
Hopscotch (1980)
The Horse's Mouth (1958)
The Odessa File (1974)
The Poseidon Adventure (1972)
The Prime of Miss Jean Brodie (1969)
The Promoter (1952)
Scrooge (1970)
Times of Glory (1960)
Windom's Way (1957)
Neanderthal: 3 man 7 caveman
neap: 4 tide
neaped: 8 grounded
Neapolitan: 5 pizza 7 Italian 8 ice cream
alternative: 5 lemon, mocha, peach 6 banana, coffee, Jamoca, toffee 7 caramel, coconut, vanilla 8 cinnamon, hazelnut 9 bubblegum, chocolate, pineapple, pistachio, raspberry, rocky road, rum raisin 10 blackberry, cheesecake, peppermint, strawberry
flavor: 7 vanilla 9 chocolate 10 strawberry
near: 4 akin, dear, loom, nigh 5 aside, cheap, close, handy, quasi, ready, tight 6 almost, around, at hand, beside, hard by, impend, stingy 7 abreast, advance, close by, close to, handy to, looming, up close, verge on 8 abutting, adjacent, approach, imminent, intimate, next door, proximal, relative, touching 9 adjoining, affecting, alongside, belly up to, bordering, close in on, hereabout, immediate, impending, in the area, in the wind, penurious, proximate, sneak up on 10 accessible, adjacent to, contiguous, convenient, converge on, get close to, in the cards, juxtaposed, near-at-hand, side-by-side, skinflinty, ungenerous
combining form: 4 peri-, pros- 5 juxta-, plesi- 6 plesio-
ender: 7 sighted
in German: 4 nahe
prefix: 3 epi- 4 para-
suffix: 3 -ish
near __: 4 beer, miss 5 money, rhyme 6 at hand
near-__: 4 term 5 point
Near: 5 Holly
Near __: 3 You 4 East 7 Eastern, Islands
near and __: 3 far
nearby: 4 nigh 5 about, aside, close, handy, ready 6 around, at hand, at heel 7 locally, present 8 adjacent, imminent, next-door 9 adjoining, bordering, immediate, impending, proximate 10 contiguous, convenient, timesaving
objects ~: 5 these
place ~: 6 appose
resident: 8 neighbor
wait ~: 5 hover 6 linger, loiter, remain
Near East
see Mideast
nearer
get ~: 6 gain on
prefix: 3 cis-
Nearer, My __, to Thee: 3 God
nearest: 4 next 6 direct 9 proximate
one: 4 this
Nearest the Pole author: 5 Peary
nearing: 7 close to 8 imminent, oncoming, upcoming 9 impending, in the wind 10 in the cards
the hour: 5 ten of, ten to
Near Island: 4 Attu 6 Agattu 7 Semichi
nearly: 4 most, much, nigh 5 about, circa, round 6 all but, almost, toward 7 halfway, roughly, towards 8 as good as, in effect, narrowly, not quite 9 in essence, just about, upwards of, virtually 10 more or less
near miss: 6 escape 9 close call
exclamation: 4 whew
nearness: 8 presence, vicinity 9 adjacency, immediacy, proximity
Nearness __, The: 5 of You
nearsighted: 4 owly 6 myopic
one: 5 myope
__ near!, The: 5 end is
Near You (1958 song) artist: Roger Williams
Near You was his theme: 5 Berle
__ 'n' Easy: 4 Nice
neat: 3 def, rad 4 aces, A-one, boss, braw, cool, dece, deft, fine, gear, good, keen, nice, phat, pure, tidy, trim, tuff 5 clean, dandy, ducky, grand, great, kempt, marvy, natty, nifty, nobby, noice, prime, sleek, slick, smart, super, swell, swept 6 adroit, bang on, bang-up, bonzer, bosker, choice, clever, dainty, dapper, deftly, divine, dreamy, far out, gnarly, groovy, lovely, peachy, pretty, shrewd, slap-up, spot on, spruce, superb, terrif, tiptop, unmixt, unreal, whizzo, wicked 7 adeptly, amazing, awesome, capital, corking, finicky, groomed, handily, iceless, in place, legible, nattily, ordered, orderly, perfect, precise, ripping, shapely, skookum, slickly, smartly, stellar, stylish, sublime, unmixed 8 adroitly, clean-cut, cleverly, dazzling, dextrous, especial, eximious, expertly, fabulous, finiking, finnicky, five-star, four-star, frabjous, glorious, graceful, heavenly, jim-dandy, methodic, skillful, slambang, smashing, splendid, spotless, standout, sterling, stickout, straight, superior, terrific, top-level, topnotch, very good, well-kept, wondrous 9 admirable, bodacious, dexterous, effective, efficient, Endsville, excellent, exemplary, exquisite, first-rate, high-grade, hunky-dory, marvelous, organized, practiced, shipshape, sollicker, spruced up, top-flight, unblended, wonderful, wunderbar 10 fastidious, first-class, hotsy-totsy, immaculate, jack-a-dandy, methodical, nicely done, out of sight, peachy keen, phenomenal, remarkable, skillfully, straight up, stupendous, super-duper, systematic
ender: 3 nik 4 ness
in England: 4 trig
make ~: 4 tidy 5 clean, fix up, order 6 spruce, tidy up 7 freshen, shape up 8 organize, spruce up 9 smarten up 10 straighten
stiffly ~: 4 prim 7 stilted 8 starched
neat __ pin: 3 as a
neaten: 4 tidy, trim, wash 5 brush, clean, fix up, groom, order 6 spruce, tidy up 7 clean up 8 spruce up 9 smarten up 10 straighten
neath: 5 below, under
opposite of ~: 3 o'er
Neath: 4 city, town
locale: 5 Wales
neatness: 4 trim 5 order 8 symmetry 10 legibility
neatnik bane: 4 dirt, dust, slob
neato: 3 rad 4 cool, keen, phat 5 marvy, nifty, super, swell 6 far out, groovy, peachy
neat's-__ oil: 4 foot
neb: 4 beak, bill 5 point 8 penpoint
nebbish: 4 drip, nerd, nurd, wimp 5 dweeb, patsy, twerp, twirp 7 languid 9 jellyfish, lethargic
Nebraska: 5 state
airport code: 3 OMA
capital: 7 Lincoln
city: 4 Elko 5 Omaha, Wahoo 7 Fremont, Kearney, Lincoln, Norfolk 8 Bellevue, Columbus, Hastings
conference: 9 Big Twelve
county: 4 Otoe 5 Sioux 6 Pawnee, Platte
Indian: 5 Omaha, Ponca 9 Winnebago 10 Miniconjou
institution: 8 Boys Town
like ~: 6 inland
mil. group headquartered in ~: 3 SAC
neighbor: 3 Kan., Wyo. 4 Colo., Iowa, Kans., S. Dak. 6 Kansas 7 Wyoming 8 Colorado, Missouri
river: 4 Loup 6 Platte
school: 9 Creighton
state beverage: 4 milk
state bird: 10 meadowlark
state fish: 7 catfish
state flower: 9 goldenrod
state fossil: 7 mammoth
state insect: 8 honeybee
state river: 6 Platte
state rock: 5 agate
state soft drink: 7 Kool-Aid
state tree: 10 cottonwood
student: 6 Husker 10 Cornhusker
__-Nebraska Act: 6 Kansas
__ nebula: 4 dark 6 spiral 7 diffuse
__ Nebula: 4 Crab, Ring 5 Orion
nebulous: 3 dim 4 dark, hazy 5 foggy, mirky, misty, murky, vague 6 arcane, cloudy 7 cryptic, obscure, shadowy, tenuous, unclear 8 abstruse, confused, puzzling, unformed 9 ambiguous, amorphous, confusing, cryptical, enigmatic, imprecise, shapeless, uncertain 10 indefinite, indistinct, perplexing, unspecific
NEC: 2 TV 5 TV set 10 television
alternative: 3 JVC, RCA 4 Sony 6 Quasar, Zenith 7 Emerson, Hitachi, ProScan, Toshiba 8 Magnavox, Sylvania 9 Panasonic
necessaries: 4 food 6 viands 7 aliment, rations 8 victuals 9 nutriment, provender 10 provisions, sustenance
necessarily: 8 perforce
necessary: 3 req. 4 must, reqd. 5 basic, fated, major, vital 6 needed, staple, urgent 7 binding, crucial, logical, needful, pivotal, primary 8 decisive, integral, pressing, required 9 de rigueur, essential, expedient, important, mandatory, paramount, requisite, specified, strategic 10 compelling, compulsory, imperative, inevitable, inexorable, obligatory, undeniable, underlying
amount: 5 quota 7 minimum
find ~: 4 need 6 have to
part: 3 cog
necessitate: 3 ask 4 make, need, take 5 force, impel 6 compel, demand, entail, oblige 7 behoove, call for, involve, require 9 constrain
__ necessities: 4 bare
necessitude: 4 need 7 urgency 8 exigency 9 privation
necessity: 4 call, lack, must, need

5 cause, pinch 6 demand, duress 7 essence, poverty, urgency 8 exigence, exigency, pressure 9 condition, emergency, essential, requisite, vital part 10 compulsion, constraint, imperative, obligation, sine qua non
neck: 4 kiss, nape 5 scrag, spoon 6 giblet, scruff, smooch, strait, throat 7 channel, isthmus, narrows, snuggle 8 osculate, pitch woo 10 bill and coo
and neck: 4 even, tied 5 close, tight 10 nose to nose
annoyance: 4 kink, pain 5 crick, spasm 6 twinge 9 stiffness
back of the ~: 4 nape 5 nucha, nuque
break one's ~: 4 toil 5 slave, sweat 6 hustle, strain, strive 8 bear down, struggle
combining form: 3 der- 4 dero- 7 trachei- 8 tracheio-
cover: 3 boa 5 dicky, scarf 6 collar, dickey, dickie 7 muffler
crew ~: 7 sweater
ender: 3 tie 4 band, lace, line, wear 5 piece
feather: 6 hackle, heckle 7 hatchel
feature: 6 dewlap 10 Adam's apple
front of the ~: 4 gula
hair: 7 hackles
jewelry: 5 chain 6 choker, pearls, shells
of land: 4 isth. 7 isthmus
of the ~: 5 napal
of the woods: 4 area 6 locale, region, sphere 7 quarter 8 locality, location, purlieus, vicinity 9 territory
pain in the ~: 4 ache, kink, pest, pill 5 crick, trial 6 bother, hassle, noodge, nudnik, odious 8 headache, irritant 9 annoyance
save one's ~: 4 free, save 5 spare 6 let off, pardon, rescue 7 bail out, manumit, release, set free, unchain 8 liberate 9 extricate, unshackle
starter: 3 wry 4 long 5 break, crook, goose, rough 6 bottle, little, rubber, turtle 7 leather
stick one's ~ out: 4 gawk, risk 5 crane 6 gamble 7 venture 9 speculate
neck __ woods: 5 of the
__ neck: 4 boat, crew 5 bevel, scoop, swan's 6 bateau, horse's
__-neck: 3 ewe
Neckar: 5 river
city on the ~: 9 Stuttgart 10 Heidelberg
River locale: 7 Germany
__-necked: 3 low 4 bull, high, ring 5 stiff
neckerchief: 5 scarf 8 bandanna
necklace: 5 beads 6 choker 7 jewelry 8 ornament
flowery ~: 3 lei
Hawaiian ~ shell: 4 puka
make a ~: 4 link
part: 4 bead 5 charm, clasp 6 amulet, locket
place for a ~ clasp: 4 nape
Necklace, The author: Guy de Maupassant
__ neckline: 4 boat 5 scoop 6 bateau
neckline shape: 3 vee
neckpiece: 3 boa, lei 5 scarf
neckwear: 3 boa, lei, tie 4 bola, bolo 5 ascot 6 bowtie, clip-on, cravat, dogtag 7 bandana, bola tie, bolo tie, foulard, paisley 8 bandanna, kerchief 10 four-in-hand
like some ~: 4 loud 6 clip-on
necromancer: 4 mage 5 magus, witch 6 wizard 7 warlock 8 conjurer, magician, sorcerer
necromancy: 5 magic 7 conjury, sorcery 8 black art, wizardry 9 occultism 10 black magic, divination, witchcraft
nectar: 3 sap 5 drink, fluid, juice 6 elixir, liquid 7 extract 8 beverage
amber ~: 4 beer, brew, suds 5 lager 7 brewski
collector: 3 bee 4 hive
ender: 3 ine
finally: 5 honey
Hindu ~: 6 amrita 7 amreeta
source: 4 pear 5 apple, bloom, peach 6 flower 7 blossom
nectared: 5 sweet 7 honeyed
Nectar in a Sieve author: Kamala Markandaya
nectarine: 4 tree 5 fruit
relative: 5 peach
__ Nectaris: 4 Mare
nectarous: 5 sapid, sweet, tasty, yummy 6 divine, savory 8 heavenly, luscious 9 ambrosial, delicious, flavorful, palatable, succulent, toothsome 10 appetizing, delectable, delightful
Ned: 4 Land 5 Rorem, Uncle 6 Beatty, Miller, Romero, Sparks 8 Buntline, Flanders 10 Washington
Ned and Stacey (Fox sitcom)
cast: Thomas Haden Church (Ned Dorsey)
Debra Messing (Stacey Colbert)
neddy: 5 horse 6 donkey 7 jackass
Ned's __ Dustbin: 6 Atomic
née: 4 born 8 formerly 10 christened, heretofore, previously
need: 3 use, yen 4 call, duty, food, itch, lack, lust, miss, must, take, want 5 covet, crave, ought 6 dearth, demand, desire, devoir, hanker, hunger, misery, penury, thirst 7 absence, beggary, call for, craving, hope for, hurt for, long for, longing, paucity, pine for, poverty, require, urgency, wish for 8 distress, exigence, exigency, go hungry, must have, occasion, poorness, shortage, sparsity, weakness, yearn for 9 appetence, be without, cry out for, do without, emergency, emptiness, essential, extremity, indigence, necessity, privation, requisite, shortfall 10 compulsion, deficiency, difficulty, have use for, inadequacy, obligation
needed: 5 major, vital 7 crucial, lacking, pivotal, primary 8 required 9 essential, important, mandatory, necessary
as ~ on prescriptions: 3 p.r.n.
something ~: 4 lack 9 necessity
__ needed: 6 sorely
__ Needed Me: 3 You
needful: 8 required 9 essential, mandatory, necessary, requisite
needfulness: 8 exigency 9 necessity
Needful Things author: Stephen King
Needham: 3 Hal 4 city, town
locale: 4 Mass.
Needham, Hal: 8 director
film: The Cannonball Run (1981)
Hooper (1978)
Smokey and the Bandit (1977)
neediness: 4 want 6 penury 7 beggary
needing: 3 shy 4 sans 5 low on, minus, short 7 lacking, missing, without 8 bereft of 10 deprived of
immediate attention: 4 dire 5 acute 7 crucial, exigent, serious 8 critical, pressing 9 desperate, important 10 compelling, imperative
__ Need Is a Miracle: 4 All I
__ Need Is the Girl: 4 All I
needle: 3 bug, egg, irk, nag, rib, vex 4 bait, barb, goad, hypo, leaf, mock, prod, ride, rile, spur, twit 5 annoy, peeve, pique, prick, spite, sting, taunt, tease, worry 6 badger, bother, darner, harass, heckle, hector, nettle, noodge, pester, pick on, plague, ruffle, stylus 7 bedevil, disturb, henpeck, perturb, pointer, provoke, unnerve 8 distress, irritate, pinnacle, question, ridicule, splinter 9 aggravate, injection, instigate, poke fun at
bug: 4 nepa
case: 4 etui 5 etwee
combining form: 3 acu-
ender: 4 fish, work 5 craft, point
feature: 3 eye 4 hole 5 point
locale: 6 groove
phonograph: 6 stylus
ply a ~: 3 sew 4 darn 5 baste 6 stitch 9 embroider
point: 3 ENE, ESE, NNE, NNW, SSE, SSW, WNW, WSW 4 east, west 5 north, south
producer: 4 pine
whelk: 5 shell 8 seashell
worker: 6 tailor 8 clothier 9 couturier 10 dressmaker
needle __: 5 grass, shell, valve 6 trades
__ needle: 3 dip 4 pine 5 latch 6 sewing 7 crochet, darning
needle and __: 6 thread
needlefish: 3 gar 7 garpike
needlelike: 4 thin 5 sharp 7 pointed
needlepoint: 5 craft
need: 4 mesh 6 thread
needler: 3 nag 5 scold, shrew 6 kvetch, virago 8 fishwife 9 termagant
__ needles: 3 ice 7 Spanish
Needles and Pins (1964 song) artist: Searchers
needles, on pins and: 4 edgy 5 antsy, itchy, jumpy, tense 6 sweaty, uneasy 7 anxious, jittery, keyed up, nervous, restive, uptight, worried 8 agitated, restless, skittish, troubled 9 concerned, excitable, ill at ease 10 highstrung
needless: 5 extra, minor, undue 6 wanton 7 trivial, useless 8 optional, overmuch, picayune, trifling, unwanted, wasteful 9 causeless, excessive, pointless, redundant, undesired 10 expendable, gratuitous, groundless, inordinate, undeserved, unrequired
to say: 7 clearly 8 of course 9 naturally, obviously
needlework: 6 crewel 10 embroidery
do ~: 3 sew 4 knit, purl 6 stitch
needs: 5 hasn't
like some ~: 5 unmet
__ need-to-know basis: 3 on a
needy: 4 flat, poor 5 broke, short, sorry 6 bad off, hard up, ill off, in want 7 pinched 8 badly off, bankrupt, beggarly, deprived, dirt poor, indigent, strapped 9 dead broke, dependant, dependent, destitute, insolvent, miserable, moneyless, on welfare, penniless, penurious 10 down and out, down at heel, pauperized, straitened
help for the ~: 7 charity
__ Need You: 5 I Don't, When I
Need You Tonight (1987 song) artist: INXS
Neel, Alice: 6 artist 7 painter
Néel, Louis: 8 Nobelist 9 physicist
neem: 4 tree
family: 8 mahogany
relative: 6 acajou, carapa, sapele 7 avodire 8 andiroba, crabwood
Neenah: 4 city, town
locale: 9 Wisconsin
ne'er-do-well: 3 bum, cad, cur 5 drone, idler, knave, loser, rogue, scamp 6 bad hat, loafer, rascal 7 goof-off, shirker, wastrel 8 derelict, fainéant, layabout, picaroon, scalawag, sluggard 9 do-nothing, goldbrick, no-account, reprobate, scallawag, scallywag, scoundrel 10 blackguard, malingerer, scapegrace
Neeson, Liam: 5 actor
film: Before and After (1996)
Darkman (1990)
The Dead Pool (1988)
The Good Mother (1988)
Gun Shy (2000)
Husbands and Wives (1992)
Leap of Faith (1992)
Les Misérables (1998)
Michael Collins (1996)
Nell (1994)
Rob Roy (1995)
Schindler's List (1993)
Shining Through (1992)
Star Wars Episode 1 - The Phantom Menace (1999)
Suspect (1987)
spouse: Natasha Richardson
Neet alternative: 4 Nair 5 razor
nefarious: 3 bad 4 base, evil, foul, rank, vile 5 gross 6 odious, rotten, wicked 7 corrupt, crooked, glaring, heinous, hellish, immoral, satanic, vicious 8 criminal, depraved, devilish, diabolic, dreadful, fiendish, flagrant, horrible, infamous, infernal, perverse, shameful, unlawful 9 atrocious, egregious, execrable, miscreant, monstrous, satanical, unhealthy 10 abominable, degenerate, detestable, diabolical, flagitious, iniquitous, outrageous, pernicious, villainous, virtueless
Nefertiti
god: 4 Aten, Aton
river: 4 Nile
to Tut: 4 aunt
Neff: 10 Hildegarde
Nefud: 6 desert
locale: 6 Arabia 7 Mideast
neg.: 3 chg.
maker: 3 SLR
not ~: 3 aff., pos.
see also negative
negate: 3 nix 4 deny, undo, veto, void 5 annul, belie, erase, quash, rebut 6 cancel, impugn, naysay, offset, oppose, refute, repeal, revoke 7 abolish, confute, dispute, gainsay, nullify, put down, redress, rescind, retract, reverse, vitiate 8 abrogate, disagree, disallow, disprove 9 cancel out, disaffirm, discredit, frustrate 10 annihilate, contradict, contravene, controvert, counteract, disconfirm, invalidate, neutralize, prove wrong
negation: 4 veto 6 denial 7 inverse, refusal, reverse 9 disavowal, rejection 10 antithesis, disclaimer, gainsaying, opposition
negative: 3 nah, naw, nay, nix, non, not 4 anti, nein, nope, nyet, uh-uh 5 balky, I won't, ixnay, minus, never, no how, no way, toxic 6 gloomy, malign, no deal, noways, nowise 7 adverse, baleful, baneful, cynical, denying, I refuse, redress, ruinous 8 contrary, damaging, downbeat, forget it, I will not, negatory, nugatory, opposing 9 by no means, dangerous, fat chance, impugning, injurious, I think not, jaundiced, naysaying, rejecting, resistive, unhealthy, unhopeful, unwilling 10 calamitous, count me out, disastrous, dissenting, gainsaying, not a chance, pejorative, photograph, thumbs down
contraction: 4 ain't, can't, don't, isn't, won't 5 aren't, didn't, shan't 6 mustn't 7 couldn't, wouldn't 8 shouldn't
emotion: 4 hate, rage 5 anger,

odium, pique, scorn, spite, wrath 6 animus, enmity, malice, rancor 7 disgust, ill will, offense, outrage, umbrage 8 acrimony, loathing, vexation 9 animosity, antipathy, petulance, revulsion 10 abhorrence, repugnance
in French: 3 non
in German: 4 nein
in Scottish: 3 nae
make a positive from a ~: 5 print
nonstandard ~: 4 ain't 5 t'isn't
polite ~: 5 no sir
prefix: 3 dis-, non-
slangy ~: 3 nah, naw 4 nope 5 ixnay, no how, no way
suffix: 4 -less
toward: 6 down on 8 averse to 9 hostile to
vote: 2 no 3 nay
negative ___: 3 ion 4 flag, glow, lens 6 option
negative ___ tax: 6 income
___ negative: 4 copy 6 double
___-negative: 4 Gram 5 false
negatively charged atom: 5 anion
negatory: 3 nah, naw, nay, nix, non 4 nein, nope, nyet, uh-uh 5 I won't, ixnay, never, no how, no way 6 no deal, noways, nowise 7 I refuse 8 forget it, I will not, negative 9 by no means, fat chance, I think not 10 count me out, not a chance, thumbs down
Negev: 6 desert
like the ~: 3 dry 4 arid 7 parched 8 rainless 9 waterless
locale: 6 Israel
neglect: 4 fail, miss, omit, shun, skip, snub 5 defer, delay, evade, lapse, leave, let go, scorn, shirk, slack, spurn 6 bypass, disuse, forget, ignore, laxity, pass by, rebuff, slight 7 default, disdain, dismiss, laxness, let pass, mistake, slacken, suspend, tune out 8 brush off, coolness, discount, laugh off, let slide, omission, overleap, overlook, pass over, postpone, shrug off 9 disregard, gloss over, looseness, oversight, pay no mind, slackness, unconcern 10 brush aside, disrespect, leave alone, negligence, remissness
sign of ~: 3 rot 4 dust 6 cobweb
state of ~: 5 limbo
neglected: 4 wild 5 rusty, seedy 6 shabby 7 run-down, unkempt 8 derelict, deserted, slipshod, untended 9 abandoned, unnoticed
as a garden: 5 weedy
be ~: 8 languish, stagnate, vegetate
neglectful: 3 lax 4 lazy 5 slack 6 otiose, remiss 8 careless, dallying, derelict, heedless, indolent, mindless, slothful, uncaring 9 apathetic, forgetful, negligent, shiftless, unheedful, unmindful 10 delinquent, incautious, regardless
negligee: 7 nightie 9 nightgown
like a ~: 4 lacy 10 diaphanous
negligence: 5 fault, lapse 6 laxity 8 laziness 9 disregard, injustice
in law: 6 laches
negligent: 3 lax 4 slow 5 hasty, loose, slack 6 otiose, remiss, sloppy 7 cursory, offhand, unaware 8 careless, dallying, derelict, heedless, indolent, mindless, off-guard, reckless, slapdash, slipshod, slothful, slovenly 9 apathetic, forgetful, imprudent, shiftless, unheedful, unmindful 10 behindhand, delinquent, incautious, neglectful, nonchalant, regardless, unthinking, unthorough
negligently: 5 laxly 7 hastily 8 absently, sloppily 10 carelessly
negligible: 4 mere, poor, slim, tiny 5 minor, petty, small, teeny 6 little, minute, remote, slight, teensy 7 outside, slender, trivial 8 exiguous, marginal, trifling
amount: 4 crop, drab, drib 7 smidgen
negotiable: 4 open 6 liquid 8 flexible
negotiant: 5 agent 6 broker 8 emissary 9 go-between, middleman
negotiate: 4 deal, swap, swop, talk 5 agree, clear, swing, vault 6 adjust, confer, debate, dicker, haggle, handle, jockey, manage, parley, settle, step in 7 achieve, arrange, bargain, consult, discuss, get over, get past, mediate, network, referee, work out 8 contract, cut a deal, engineer, maneuver, moderate, surmount, transact, traverse 9 arbitrate, get around, hammer out, intercede, intervene, make a deal, make peace 10 adjudicate, compromise, horse trade
unwilling to ~: 4 firm, iron 5 rigid 6 flinty, intent, steely 7 adamant, diehard 8 hardened, hard-line, hellbent, obdurate, resolute, stubborn 9 immovable, immutable, obstinate, steadfast 10 inflexible
negotiation: 6 debate, treaty 7 bargain, meeting 9 agreement, diplomacy, mediation 10 bargaining, discussion
conclude a ~: 5 agree 6 settle
point of ~: 6 demand
stage: 4 snag 5 offer 10 settlement
negotiator: 3 rep 5 agent, fixer, judge 6 broker, umpire 8 delegate, diplomat, mediator 9 go-between, moderator 10 interceder
asset: 4 tact 8 delicacy 9 diplomacy
Negotiator, The (1998 film)
cast: Samuel L. Jackson, Kevin Spacey
Negri: 4 Pola
Negro: 4 peak 5 mount, river 8 mountain
locale: 5 Andes 6 Brazil 8 Colombia 9 Argentina
___ Negro: 3 Rio
negroni: 5 drink 8 beverage, cocktail
ingredient: 3 gin 7 bitters 8 vermouth
Negulesco, Jean: 8 director
film: The Best of Everything (1959)
Daddy Long Legs (1955)
Deep Valley (1947)
How to Marry a Millionaire (1953)
Humoresque (1946)
Johnny Belinda (1948)
The Mask of Dimitrios (1944)
The Mudlark (1950)
Nobody Lives Forever (1946)
Phone Call From a Stranger (1952)
Road House (1948)
Three Came Home (1950)
Three Coins in the Fountain (1954)
Three Strangers (1946)
Titanic (1953)
Woman's World (1954)
negus: 5 drink 8 beverage
ingredient: 4 wine
Nehemiah: 7 Persoff
follower: 6 Esther
preceder: 4 Ezra
Neher, Erwin: 8 Nobelist
Nehi: 5 drink 9 soft drink
alternative: 3 TAB 5 Fanta 6 Fresca, Sprite 8 Diet Rite, Dr Pepper 9 Canada Dry 10 Mello Yello, Royal Crown 11 Mountain Dew
drinker: 5 Radar
flavor: 5 grape, peach 6 cherry, orange
Nehru: 10 Jawaharlal
daughter: 6 Indira
see also India
neigh
cousin: 4 bray 6 whinny
homophone: 3 nay, née
sayer: 4 mare 5 filly, horse 6 equine
neighbor: 4 abut, join 5 march, touch, verge 6 adjoin, border, friend 7 connect 8 surround
...___ neighbor and weigh: 4 as in
neighborhood: 3 vic. 4 area, slum, turf, ward, zone 5 block, local, place, range, tract 6 ghetto, locale, milieu, parish, region, street, suburb 7 quarter, section 8 confines, district, environs, locality, location, precinct, presence, purlieus, vicinity 9 community, territory
hangout: 5 stoop 8 malt shop
Hispanic ~: 6 barrio
in the ~: 4 near 5 close, local 6 around, nearby, nearly 7 close by, locally
in the ~ of: 4 near 5 about, anear 6 almost, around 7 close to
rundown ~: 4 slum 5 slurb
sign: 4 lost 7 lost dog 8 yard sale
upscale ~: 5 exurb
neighborhood ___: 5 watch
neighboring: 4 near, next, nigh 5 close 6 at hand, beside, nearby 8 adjacent, imminent 9 impending, proximate 10 convenient
neighborliness: 5 amity 6 comity 8 goodwill 10 cordiality, friendship
neighborly: 4 kind 5 civil, close 6 chummy, clubby, genial, kindly, polite, social 7 affable, amiable, cordial, helpful 8 amicable, friendly, gracious, intimate, obliging, outgoing, sociable 9 brotherly, convivial 10 benevolent, buddy-buddy, hospitable, solicitous
___ Neighbor Policy: 4 Good
Neighbors (1981 film)
cast: Dan Aykroyd, John Belushi, Cathy Moriarty
director: John G. Avildsen
___ Neighbor Sam: 4 Good
Neighbors author: Thomas Berger
neighbors, friends and: 4 kith
___ Neighbor's Wife: 3 Thy
Neil: 5 Simon, Vince, Young 6 Harris, Jordan, Sedaka 7 Diamond, Sheehan 8 Hamilton 9 Armstrong
Neil ___ Harris: 7 Patrick
Neill: 3 Sam 4 Noel
Neill, Sam: 5 actor
film: Bicentennial Man (1999)
Country Life (1995)
A Cry in the Dark (1988)
Dead Calm (1989)
The Horse Whisperer (1998)
Jurassic Park (1993)
Jurassic Park III (2001)
My Brilliant Career (1979)
The Piano (1993)
Restoration (1995)
Neilson: 5 James
Neiman: 5 Leroy
Neiman ___: 6 Marcus
nein: 2 no 3 nah, naw, nay, nix, non 4 nope, nyet, uh-uh 5 I won't, ixnay, never, no how, noway 6 no deal, noways, nowise 7 I refuse 8 forget it, I will not, negative, negatory 9 by no means, fat chance, I think not 10 count me out, not a chance, thumbs down
in French: 3 non
in Latin: 3 non
in Russian: 4 nyet
in Scottish: 3 nae
opposite: 2 ja
Neisse: 5 river
locale: 6 Poland 7 Germany
___-Neisse Line: 4 Oder
neither ___ nor fowl: 4 fish
neither ___ nor there: 4 here
Neither ___ of Us: 3 One
Neither One of Us (1973 song) artist: Gladys Knight and the Pips
neither partner: 3 nor
Neither snow, ___ rain,...: 3 nor
Neiva: 4 city, town
locale: 8 Colombia
Nejd
native: 5 Saudi
where ~ is: 6 Arabia
Nekkar: 4 star
Nekrasov: 6 Viktor 7 Nikolay
Nekrasov, Nikolay: 4 poet 7 Russian
Nekrasov, Viktor: 6 writer 7 Russian
Nel ___ dipinto...: 3 blu
Nel Blu Dipinto Di Blu (Volaré) (1958 song) artist: Domenico Modugno
Nell: 4 Gwyn 6 Carter 8 Campbell
Nell (1994 film)
cast: Jodie Foster, Liam Neeson, Natasha Richardson
director: Michael Apted
___ Nell: 3 Our
Nellie: 3 Bly, Fox 4 Ross 5 Melba 7 Forbush
man: 5 Emile
nosy ~: 5 prier, pryer
Nellie ___ Ross: 6 Tayloe
___ Nellie: 7 nervous
___, Nellie!: 4 Whoa
Nelligan, Kate: 7 actress
film: Bethune (1977)
Eleni (1985)
Eye of the Needle (1981)
U.S. Marshals (1998)
Nellis: 3 AFB
Nelly: 5 Sachs
nice ~: 4 prig 5 prude 7 puritan 8 bluenose 10 goody-goody
Nelore: 3 cow 4 bull 6 bovine, cattle
nelson: 4 hold
___ nelson: 4 full, half 7 quarter
Nelson: 2 Ed 3 duo, Fox 4 Eddy, Gene, Judd, Kris 5 Barry, Byron, David, Ozzie, Ralph, Ricky, river, Sandy 6 Algren, Burton, Craig T., Riddle, Willie 7 Demille, Harriet, Horatio, Mandela 9 Doubleday
River locale: 6 Canada 8 Manitoba
song: After the Rain (1990)
Love and Affection (1990)
More Than Ever (1991)
Nelson, Byron: 6 golfer
milieu: 5 links 6 course
org.: 3 PGA
Nelson, Craig T.: 5 actor
film: All the Right Moves (1983)
Ghosts of Mississippi (1996)
Poltergeist (1982)
Troop Beverly Hills (1989)
Turner & Hooch (1989)
TV: Coach
Nelson, Harriet spouse: Ozzie Nelson
Nelson, Judd: 5 actor
film: The Breakfast Club (1985)
St. Elmo's Fire (1985)
TV: Suddenly Susan
Nelson, Ozzie spouse: Harriet Nelson
Nelson, Ralph: 8 director
film: Charly (1968)
Duel at Diablo (1966)
Father Goose (1964)
Lilies of the Field (1963)
Requiem for a Heavyweight (1962)
Soldier in the Rain (1963)
The Wilby Conspiracy (1975)
___ Nelson Reilly: 7 Charles
Nelson, Ricky
brother: 5 David
film: Rio Bravo (1959)
The Wackiest Ship in the Army (1960)

parent: 5 Ozzie 7 Harriet
song: Be-Bop Baby (1957)
Believe What You Say (1958)
Everlovin' (1961)
Fools Rush In (1963)
For You (1964)
Garden Party (1972)
Hello Mary Lou (1961)
I Got a Feeling (1958)
I'm Walking (1957)
It's Late (1959)
It's Up to You (1962)
Just a Little Too Much (1959)
Lonesome Town (1958)
My Bucket's Got a Hole in It (1958)
Never Be Anyone Else But You (1959)
Poor Little Fool (1958)
Stood Up (1957)
String Along (1963)
Sweeter Than You (1959)
Teen Age Idol (1962)
A Teenager's Romance (1957)
Travelin' Man (1961)
A Wonder Like You (1961)
Young Emotions (1959)
Young World (1962)
TV: The Adventures of Ozzie and Harriet
Nelson, Tony servant: 5 genie 7 Jeannie
Nelson, Willie
cause: 7 Farm Aid
film: Barbarosa (1982)
The Electric Horseman (1979)
Honeysuckle Rose (1980)
Thief (1981)
song: Always on My Mind (1982)
Blue Eyes Crying in the Rain (1975)
Good Hearted Woman (1976)
On the Road Again (1980)
To All the Girls I've Loved Before (1984)
Nels to Marta: 3 son
nema: 4 worm 7 eelworm 9 roundworm
Neman: 5 river
locale: 7 Belarus 9 Lithuania
Nemean __: 4 lion 5 Games
Nemec: 5 Corin, Corky
Nemerov, Howard: 4 poet
work: Inside the Onion
nemesis: 3 foe 4 bane, ruin 5 enemy, rival 8 opponent 9 ill-wisher 10 infliction
Nemesis: 8 asteroid
lover of ~: 4 Zeus
parent of ~: 6 Erebus
play ~: 6 avenge
Nen: 4 Robb
nene: 4 bird, fowl 5 goose
home: 6 Hawaii
relative: 5 brant 7 graylag 9 snow goose
Neneh: 6 Cherry
Nennius: 5 Welsh 6 writer 9 historian
Nen, Robb sport: 8 baseball
neo: 3 mod 8 newcomer 9 modernist 10 revivalist
neo-: 3 new 4 late
opposite: 5 paleo-
neoclassical: 5 style
architect: 4 Adam
neodymium: 7 element
Neolithic: 7 ancient
chisel: 4 celt
monument: 5 henge
neologism: 5 slang 7 coinage, new word 8 buzzword
neon: 3 gas 4 bulb 7 element 8 inert gas, noble gas
tetra: 3 pet 4 fish
neon __: 4 lamp 5 tetra
Neon: 3 car 4 auto 5 Dodge 8 Plymouth
neonate: 4 babe, baby 5 child 6 infant 7 newborn
garment: 6 bootee, bootie
neon tetra: 4 fish
Neon Wilderness, The author: Nelson Algren
neophyte: 4 tiro, tyro 5 newie, pupil 6 greeny, newbie, novice, rookie 7 convert, entrant, learner, new hand, recruit, trainee 8 beginner, newcomer 9 fledgling, greenhorn, layperson 10 apprentice, catechumen, tenderfoot
Neopolitan poet: 10 Sannazzaro
neoteric: 5 fresh, novel 6 modern, recent 8 up-to-date
nep: 4 knot
Nepal: 6 nation 7 country
capital: 8 Katmandu 9 Kathmandu
ender: 3 ese
knife: 5 kukri
locale: 4 Asia
money: 4 pice 5 paisa, rupee
mountain: 3 Api 5 Kabru 6 Cho Oyu, Lhotse, Makalu, Nuptse 7 Everest, Manaslu, Pyramid 8 Anapurna, Baruntse, Chamlang, Tent Peak 9 Ama Dablam, Annapurna, Nepal Peak 10 Dhaulagiri, Himalchuli
neighbor: 5 China, India
people: 6 Lepcha
soldier: 6 Gurkha
Nepali: 8 language
Nepal Peak: 5 mount 8 mountain
locale: 4 Asia 9 Himalayas
Nepean: 4 city, town
locale: 6 Canada 7 Ontario
nepenthe: 7 anodyne 8 narcotic 9 analgesic 10 palliative
Nephalion, father of: 5 Minos
nephew: 4 male 7 kinsman 8 relative
sister: 5 niece
starter: 5 grand
__-nephew: 5 great
Nephew, The author: James Purdy
nephric: 5 renal
nephrite: 3 gem 4 jade 8 gemstone
Nephthys, sister of: 4 Isis
ne plus ultra: 3 top 4 acme, A-one, apex, best, peak, tops 5 crest, crown, elite, first, ideal, model, prime 6 apogee, choice, far-out, finest, select, superb, unique, zenith 7 highest, maximum, optimal, optimum, paragon, perfect, stellar, sublime, supreme 8 choicest, exemplar, five-star, foremost, four-star, greatest, high spot, lodestar, nonesuch, paradigm, peerless, pinnacle, superior, topnotch, ultimate, very good 9 beau ideal, Endsville, excellent, exemplary, first-rate, high point, matchless, nonpareil, top-flight, unequaled, unrivaled 10 consummate, first-class, inimitable, out of sight, phenomenal, preeminent, touchstone, unrivalled
nepotism: 8 inequity 9 injustice 10 corruption, favoritism, partiality, unfairness
Neptune: 3 deo, god, orb 6 planet
brother of ~: 5 Pluto 7 Jupiter
Celtic ~: 3 Ler, Lir
daughter of ~: 7 Minerva
domain: 3 sea 5 ocean
equivalent: 8 Poseidon
moon: 5 Naiad 6 Nereid, Triton 7 Despina, Galatea, Larissa, Proteus 8 Thalassa
neighbor: 5 Pluto 6 Uranus
parent: 3 Ops 6 Saturn
sister of ~: 4 Juno 5 Ceres, Vesta
wife of ~: 7 Salacia
Neptune's Daughter (1949 film)
cast: Red Skelton, Esther Williams, Keenan Wynn
neptunium: 5 metal 7 element
Ner
grandson of ~: 4 Saul
son of ~: 5 Abner
Nerbudda: 5 river
locale: 5 India
nerd: 3 sap 4 clod, dork, drip, geek, jerk, wimp, wonk, wuss 5 dufus, dweeb, loser, schmo, sissy, twerp, twirp, weeny 6 doofus, schmoe, square, techie, tekkie 7 egghead, nebbish, oddball 8 bookworm, goofball
like a ~: 5 unhip 6 square
no ~: 4 BMOC, jock 7 hipster
Nerd, The author: Larry Shue
nerdy: 5 sissy, unhip 6 square, uncool 8 dweebish 9 unpopular
Nereid: 4 Ione, moon 5 nymph 6 Thetis 7 Cydippe, Galatea 8 Arethusa, Psamathe, sea nymph 10 Amphitrite
planet: 7 Neptune
Nereus: 8 asteroid
daughter of ~: 7 Galatea
mother of ~: 4 Gaea
Nerf: 3 orb 4 ball
like a ~: 4 soft 6 spongy 7 squishy
Neri, Philip: 5 saint
Nernst, Walther: 7 chemist 8 Nobelist 9 physicist
Nero: 5 Peter, Roman, Wolfe 6 Caesar, Franco
city: 4 Rome
friend of ~: 4 Otho
instrument: 5 piano
mother: 9 Agrippina
outfit for ~: 4 toga
see also Latin
Nero composer: 8 Mascagni
neroli: 3 oil
Nero, Peter: 7 pianist
instrument: piano
song: Summer of '42 (1971)
nerts: 4 dang, darn, drat, oath, phoo 6 darn it, phooey
Neruda: 3 Jan 5 Pablo
Neruda, Jan: 4 poet 5 Czech
Neruda, Pablo: 4 poet 6 writer 7 Chilean 8 Nobelist
nerve: 4 face, gall, grit, guts, will 5 brass, cheek, crust, heart, moxie, pluck, sauce, spunk, steel, valor 6 daring, hubris, hutzpa, hybris, mettle, spirit, starch 7 bravery, chutzpa, courage, hauteur, hutzpah, prowess, sciatic 8 audacity, backbone, boldness, chutzpah, coolness, firmness, gameness, gumption, rudeness, strength, temerity, tenacity 9 arrogance, assurance, brashness, fortitude, gallantry, impudence, insolence 10 brazenness, confidence, effrontery, resolution
cell: 5 fiber
cells: 4 glia
center: 3 hub 4 seat 5 focus
combining form: 4 neur- 5 neuro-
deprive of one's ~: 5 unman
have the ~: 4 dare, defy 7 venture 9 challenge, speculate
like some ~ cells: 6 apolar
lose one's ~: 5 blink, choke 6 freeze 7 back out 10 chicken out
part of a ~ cell: 4 axon 5 axone
nerve __: 3 net 4 cell, cord, root 5 block, fiber, trunk 6 center 7 impulse
__ nerve: 4 hit a 5 mixed, optic, ulnar, vagus 6 facial, sacral, spinal 7 cranial, sciatic
__ nerve!: 4 Some, What
Nerve author: Dick Francis
nerveless: 4 calm, cool, weak 5 timid 6 afraid, feeble 7 fearful 8 composed, cowardly, intrepid, tranquil 9 collected, enervated, impassive, petrified, spineless 10 controlled, unagitated
nerve-racking: 5 hairy, jumpy, tense 7 anxious 9 stressful
nerves: 4 glia 6 strain, stress 7 anxiety, fidgets, ganglia, jitters, tension 8 hysteria 9 imbalance, tenseness, tightness 10 irritation, uneasiness
bundle of ~: 4 edgy 5 antsy, itchy, jumpy, tense 6 on edge, uneasy 7 anxious, jittery, keyed up, nervous, restive, uptight 8 agitated, restless, skittish, troubled 9 concerned, excitable, ill at ease 10 high-strung
cranial ~: 4 vagi
get on one's ~: 3 bug, get, ire, irk, jar, vex 4 fret, goad, miff, rile, weed 5 anger, annoy, chafe, grate, peeve, pique, shrub, spite, upset 6 bother, burn up, harass, needle, noodge, offend, pester, pother, put out, rankle, ruffle 7 bramble, disturb, incense, prickle, provoke 8 irritate 9 aggravate, displease 10 discompose, exasperate
__ nerves: 5 war of
nerves of __: 5 steel
Nervo, Amado Ruiz de: 4 poet 7 Mexican
nervous: 3 shy 4 edgy, taut, weak 5 antsy, fazed, fussy, itchy, jumpy, shaky, tense, timid, upset, wired 6 afraid, gun-shy, jangly, on edge, pacing, queasy, queazy, scared, sweaty, trepid, uneasy 7 abashed, alarmed, anxious, chicken, daunted, dithery, excited, fearful, fidgety, jittery, keyed up, panicky, restive, ruffled, spooked, twitchy, uptight, worried 8 agitated, cowardly, fearsome, fluttery, hesitant, restless, skittish, snappish, timorous, troubled, unstrung, volatile 9 concerned, disturbed, emotional, excitable, flustered, ill at ease, irritable, petrified, querulous, sensitive, shrinking, terrified, tremulous 10 distressed, frightened, high-strung, hysterical, solicitous
make ~: 5 spook 6 rattle, unglue 7 fluster 8 psych out, unsettle 10 discompose, disconcert, intimidate
nervous __: 5 Nelly 6 Nellie, system
nervously, react: 4 jump 5 start, wince
nervousness: 5 alarm, qualm, tizzy, worry 6 creeps, shakes, stress 7 anxiety, dithers, fidgets, jimjams, jitters, quivers, tension, willies 8 disquiet, timidity 9 agitation, cold sweat, jumpiness
__ nervous system: 7 central
nervy: 4 bold, flip, game, pert, rude, wise 5 brash, brave, cocky, crass, crude, fresh, gutsy, pushy, sassy, saucy, smart, stout 6 awless, brassy, brawny, brazen, cheeky, daring, gritty, heroic, mighty, on edge, plucky, sinewy, snippy, spunky, strong 7 anxious, aweless, boorish, defiant, doughty, forward, gallant, impavid, jittery, selfish, staunch, uncivil, valiant 8 cocksure, familiar, fearless, flippant, forceful, heedless, heroical, impolite, impudent, insolent, intrepid, muscular, powerful, resolute, restless, skittish, snippety, spirited, stalwart, tactless, unafraid, valorous, vigorous 9 audacious, bumptious, dauntless, dreadless, excitable, out of line, tenacious, undaunted, unfearful 10 courageous, undismayed, ungracious, unthinking
Nesbitt: 8 Cathleen
Nescafé: 6 coffee

alternative: 5 Sanka, Yuban 7 Folgers, Melitta, Savarin 9 Hills Bros.
nescient: 7 unaware 8 ignorant, innocent
Nesmith: 4 Mike 6 Monkee
colleague: 4 Tork 5 Jones 6 Dolenz
ness: 6 suffix 8 headland 10 promontory
Ness: 3 Fed 4 lake, Loch, T-man 5 Eliot
locale: 8 Scotland
to Capone: 3 foe 5 enemy
Nessen: 3 Ron
Nessie's home: 4 loch
Nessman: 3 Les 7 newsman
employer: 4 WKRP
Nessun dorma: 4 aria
Nessus: 7 centaur
nest: 3 den 4 aery, coop, eyry, hive, home, lair, live, stay 5 aerie, covey, dwell, embed, eyrie, haunt, haven, imbed, lodge, nidus, perch, roost 6 asylum, colony, hotbed, refuge, reside 7 anthill, beehive, cluster, habitat, hangout, hideout, retreat, shelter, sojourn 8 cloister, hideaway, settle in, snuggery, vespiary 9 formicary
bird with a cup-shaped ~: 5 vireo
crow's ~: 7 lookout, station
eagle's ~: 4 aery, eyry 5 aerie, eyrie
egg: 3 IRA 5 cache, funds, means, store 7 reserve, savings 9 resources
feather one's ~: 4 save 6 make it, thrive 7 advance, develop, make out, prosper, succeed 8 flourish, go places, grow rich, hit it big, make good, progress
hornet's ~: 3 ado, fix 4 hive, mess, stir 5 furor 6 clamor, pickle, plight, rumpus, scrape, tumult, uproar 7 travail, trouble, turmoil 8 quagmire, quandary
insect ~: 5 nidus
leave the ~: 3 fly 8 take wing
like a ~: 4 cozy, snug 5 comfy, homey
locale: 4 limb, tree 5 hedge
mare's ~: 3 zoo 4 fake, hoax, mess, sham 5 fraud, snafu 6 foul-up, jumble, muddle 8 delusion 9 deception
noise: 5 cheep, tweet
of an insect ~: 5 nidal
paper ~ builder: 4 wasp
rob a ~: 5 poach
sound: 3 coo 4 peep 5 cheep, chirp, tweet
(within): 3 sit
nest __: 3 egg
__ nest: 4 love, rat's 5 bird's 7 hornet's
__-nest: 5 crow's, mare's
__ Nest: 4 Love 5 Empty
n'est-ce pas?: 3 yes 4 okay 5 right
Nestea: 9 soft drink
alternative: 6 Lipton, Salada, Tetley 7 Bigelow, Red Rose 8 Twinings
__ nester: 5 empty
nesting __: 5 table
nestle: 3 hug 4 seat, snug 6 burrow, cradle, cuddle, curl up, huddle, nuzzle 7 snuggle 8 ensconce, huddle up, settle in 9 keep close 10 settle down
Nestlé: 5 candy 9 chocolate
product: 4 Alpo, Baci, Quik 5 Wonka 6 Chunky, Crunch 7 Buitoni, Goobers, Oh Henry, Sno-Caps 8 Baby Ruth, Friskies, Perugina, PowerBar 9 Bit-O-Honey, Carnation, Mighty Dog, Raisinets, Stouffer's 10 Coffee-Mate, Fancy Feast, Juicy Juice
nestled: 4 cosy, cozy 5 cozey, cozie 8 tucked in
nestling: 4 baby, bird 5 owlet 6 eaglet 9 fledgling
call: 5 chirp, tweet
nestlings: 5 brood
nest of __: 7 drawers
nest of robins..., A poem: 5 Trees
Nest of Simple Folk, A author: Sean O'Faolain
Nestor: 4 sage
daughter of ~: 8 Pisidice 9 Polycaste
like ~: 4 sage, wise 9 sagacious
parent of ~: 6 Neleus 7 Chloris
son of ~: 6 Aretus 7 Perseus 10 Antilochus, Stratichus
wife of ~: 8 Anaxibia, Eurydice
__-nest soup: 5 bird's
__ nest syndrome: 5 empty
net: 3 bag, get, nab, web 4 earn, hook, lace, make, mesh, trap, veil 5 catch, clear, cloth, crisp, final, snare, snood, yield 6 collar, enmesh, entrap, fabric, garner, immesh, inmesh, profit, return, screen 7 bring in, capture, ensnare, insnare, lattice, realize, revenue 8 entangle, lacework, openwork, pull down, receipts, residual, take home 9 bring home, end up with, profiting, remaining 10 after taxes, bottom line, conclusive
alternative: 4 gaff
combining form: 5 dicty- 6 dictyo-
ender: 4 back, ball, work 6 keeper
fabric: 4 lace 5 tulle
feat: 5 spike
fish ~: 5 seine, trawl
game: 6 hockey, tennis 8 Ping Pong 9 badminton 10 volleyball
holder: 3 rim
org.: 4 USTA
plus expenses: 5 gross
starter: 4 drag, fish, gill
work without a ~: 4 dare, defy, risk 6 hazard 9 take a risk
worth: 6 estate
see also basketball
net __: 3 pay, ton 4 gain, line, loss, silk 5 worth 6 assets, income, profit 7 tonnage
net __ value: 5 asset
net-__: 6 veined, winged
__ net: 3 bow, fly 4 gill, hair, life 5 drift, nerve, pound, trawl 6 neural, safety 7 landing, trammel 9 butterfly
Net: 3 Web
access the ~: 5 log on 6 dial up
address: 3 URL, www
connector: 5 modem
giant: 3 AOL
rival: 3 Sun 4 Buck, Bull, Celt, Hawk, Heat, Jazz, King, Spur 5 Knick, Laker, Magic, Pacer, Sixer, Sonic 6 Celtic, Hornet, Nugget, Piston, Raptor, Rocket, Wizard 7 Clipper, Grizzly, Warrior 8 Cavalier, Maverick 10 SuperSonic, Timberwolf
surfer: 4 user
Netanya: 4 city, town
locale: 6 Israel
Netanyahu, Benjamin: 4 Bibi 7 Israeli
predecessor: 5 Peres
successor: 5 Barak
Neth.
locale: 3 Eur.
neighbor: 3 Ger. 4 Belg.
org.: 4 NATO
see also Netherlands
nether: 3 low 5 lower, under 6 lesser 7 Stygian 8 infernal 10 underneath
ender: 5 world
region: 4 hell 5 Hades, Sheol 7 inferno 10 underworld
nether __: 5 world
__ Netherland: 3 New
Netherlands: 6 nation 7 country
airline: 3 KLM
astronomer: 6 Sitter 7 Huygens
beer: 6 Amstel
botanist: 5 Vries
bovine: 8 Holstein
capital: 7 Den Haag 8 The Hague 9 Amsterdam
cheese: 4 Brie, Edam 5 Gouda 6 Leyden
city: 3 Ede 4 Edam 5 Breda, Delft, Emmen, Gouda, Venlo, Zeist 6 Arnhem, Beilen, Leiden, Leyden, Venloo 7 Den Haag, Haarlem, Tilburg, Utrecht 8 The Hague 9 Amsterdam, Rotterdam 10 Maastricht
colonist: 4 Boer
conductor: 7 De Waart
explorer: 6 Tasman 7 Barents
export: 4 bulb, Edam 5 Gouda, tulip 6 cheese
farmer: 4 Boer
fishing boat: 6 dogger
former colony: 5 Timor
lake: 9 Zuider Zee 10 Ijsselmeer
language: 5 Dutch
Meuse in ~: 4 Maas
money: 4 cent, doit, duit, euro 6 florin, gilder, gulden, stiver 7 guilder 8 ducatoon 9 rix-dollar
neighbor: 7 Belgium, Germany
Nobelist in Chemistry: 5 Debye 7 Crutzen 8 van't Hoff
Nobelist in Economics: 8 Koopmans 9 Tinbergen
Nobelist in Medicine: 7 Eijkman 9 Einthoven
Nobelist in Peace: 5 Asser
Nobelist in Physics: 5 Hooft 6 Zeeman 7 Lorentz, Veltman, Zernike 10 van der Meer 11 van der Waals
org.: 4 NATO
painter: 4 Hals, Lely 5 Steen 7 van Gogh, Vermeer 8 Mondrian, Ter Borch 9 de Kooning, Rembrandt
philosopher: 7 Spinoza
physicist: 7 Huygens 11 van der Waals
port: 5 Delft 8 Flushing 9 Amsterdam, Rotterdam 10 Vlissingen
river: 3 Lek 4 Maas, Rijn, Waal 5 Issel, Yssel 6 Ijssel
royal house: 6 Orange
scientist: 5 Vries 6 Sitter 7 Huygens 11 van der Waals
shoe: 5 sabot
South African: 4 Boer
waterway: 3 zee
writer: 7 Erasmus, Spinoza 8 Couperus
see also Dutch, Holland
Netherlands Antilles
money: 4 cent 6 gilder, gulden 7 guilder
one of the ~: 4 Saba 7 Bonaire, Curaçao
nethermost point: 5 nadir 6 bottom
netherworld: 4 hell 5 Hades, Sheol 7 inferno
net judge call: 3 let
netkeeper: 6 goalie
netlike: 4 fine, lacy 5 meshy 6 dainty, frilly 8 delicate, gossamer
cap: 5 snood
fabric: 4 lace
Nets: 4 five, team
home: 9 New Jersey
org.: 3 NBA
sport: 10 basketball
Netscape purchaser: 3 AOL
netster: 4 Ashe, Borg, Hoad, King, Wade 5 Budge, Bueno, Chang, Court, Evert, Kodes, Laver, Lendl, Moody, Riggs, Seles, Smith, Vilas 6 Agassi, Austin, Casals, Fraser, Gibson, Hingis, Kramer, Marble, Rafter, Segura, Stolle, Tilden 7 Connors, Emerson, Lacoste, Lew Hoad, McEnroe, Nastase, Ralston, Roddick, Sampras, Trabert 8 Capriati, Connolly, Don Budge, Gonzales, Newcombe, Rod Laver, Rosewall, Williams 9 Bjorn Borg, Davenport, Goolagong, Ivan Lendl, Stan Smith, tennis pro 10 Arthur Ashe, Bill Tilden, Bobby Riggs, Chris Evert, Fred Stolle, Jack Kramer, Kournikova, Mandlikova, Maria Bueno 11 Navratilova
Nets to Catch the Wind author: Elinor Wylie
netsuke container: 4 inro
__-netter: 4 gill
Net, The (1995 film)
cast: Diane Baker, Sandra Bullock, Dennis Miller, Jeremy Northam
director: Irwin Winkler
netting: 3 web 4 lace, mesh 6 fabric
like ~: 5 meshy
nettle: 3 bug, get, ire, irk, jar, vex 4 fret, goad, miff, rile, weed 5 anger, annoy, chafe, grate, peeve, pique, shrub, spite, tease, upset, worry 6 bother, burn up, harass, needle, noodge, offend, pester, pother, put out, rankle, ruffle 7 bramble, disturb, incense, prickle, provoke 8 irritate 9 aggravate, displease 10 discompose, exasperate
family shrub: 5 pilea, ramee, ramie
__ nettle: 3 sea 4 hemp 5 hedge, horse
nettled: 5 huffy, irate, upset 9 irritated
Nettles, Graig sport: 8 baseball
nettlesome: 5 pesky, pesty 6 thorny 7 prickly 8 annoying, worrying 10 in one's hair
Nettleton: 4 Lois
network: 3 net, sys., tie, web 4 bond, grid, link, maze, mesh, syst., talk 5 merge, nexus 6 hookup, medium, mingle, plexus, scheme, system 7 complex, lattice, society 8 interact 9 broadcast, circuitry, labyrinth, negotiate, structure
electrical ~: 4 grid
English ~: 3 BBC
link: 5 modem
transmission: 4 feed
TV ~: 3 ABC, CBS, Fox, UPN
__ network: 4 star 6 neural, old-boy 7 old-girl
Network (1976 film)
cast: Faye Dunaway, Robert Duvall, Peter Finch, William Holden, Beatrice Straight
director: Sidney Lumet
network: 3 UBS
networks, TV: 5 media
net worth component: 5 asset
Neuchâtel: 4 lake
locale: Switzerland
Neufchâtel: 6 cheese
Neuharth: 2 Al
Neuilly-__-Seine: 3 sur
Neuman, Alfred E. mag: 3 Mad
Neumann: 4 Kurt
neural: 7 sensory 9 sensorial
network: 4 rete
tissue: 4 glia
transmitter: 4 axon 5 axone
neural __: 3 net 4 tube 5 crest 7 network
neurological: 7 sensory 9 sensorial
exam.: 3 EEG
__ neuron: 5 motor 7 sensory
neuron appendage: 4 axon 5 axone
neurotransmitter: 4 dopa
Neuss: 4 city, town
locale: 7 Germany

neuter: 4 geld, spay 5 alter 6 gender
not ~: 3 fem. 4 masc. 8 feminine 9 masculine
neutral: 3 tan 4 cool, drab, ecru, gray, grey, just 5 aloof, beige, cream, ivory, white 6 medium 7 subdued 8 clinical, detached, listless, moderate, peaceful, unbiased 9 impartial, objective, unaligned, undecided, unslanted 10 achromatic, disengaged, even-handed, fair-minded, impersonal, nonaligned, nonchalant, on the fence, pacifistic, poker-faced, unagitated, uninvolved
color: 3 tan 4 ecru, gray, grey 5 beige, flesh, taupe
ethically ~: 6 amoral
run in ~: 3 rev 4 idle 5 coast
zone: 3 DMZ 6 buffer
neutral __: 4 axis, zone 6 corner, ground 7 spirits
__-neutral: 3 day 6 gender
neutrality: 8 coolness 9 aloofness, unconcern 10 detachment, equanimity
neutralize: 4 undo 5 annul, unarm 6 cancel, defeat, negate, offset, oppose, scotch 7 balance, nullify, redress 8 abrogate, overcome 9 frustrate 10 antagonize, compensate, counteract, invalidate
neutrino: 8 particle
neutron: 8 particle
neutron __: 4 star 5 dance 6 number
__ neutron: 4 slow 7 thermal
Neutron Dance (1984 song) artist: Pointer Sisters
Neuwirth, Bebe: 7 actress
film: Green Card (1990) Liberty Heights (1999) Malice (1993)
TV: Cheers
Neva: 5 river
locale: 6 Russia
Nevada: 5 state
capital: 10 Carson City
casino: 5 Luxor, Sands 6 Sahara 7 Harrah's 8 MGM Grand
city: 3 Ely 4 Elko, Reno 5 Vegas 6 Sparks 7 Pahrump 8 Las Vegas, Paradise 9 Henderson, Sun Valley 10 Carson City, Winchester
conference: 3 WAC
county: 3 Nye 4 Elko 6 Washoe
desert: 11 Death Valley
Indian: 5 Piute, Washo 6 Paiute
lake: 4 Mead 5 Tahoe 8 Lahontan
national park: 10 Great Basin
neighbor: 4 Utah 5 Idaho 6 Oregon 7 Arizona 10 California
peak: 3 Ely 5 Mt. Ely
state bird: 8 bluebird
state flower: 9 sagebrush
state metal: 6 silver
state precious gemstone: 8 fire opal
state rock: 9 sandstone
state semi-precious gemstone: 9 turquoise
University of ~ site: 4 Reno
waterfall: 6 Ribbon
Nevada __: 5 Smith
__ Nevada: 5 Wanda 6 Sierra
Nevada author: Zane Grey
Nevada Smith (1966 film)
cast: Brian Keith, Karl Malden, Steve McQueen
director: Henry Hathaway
__ ne va plus: 4 rien
névé: 4 firn, snow
Neve: 8 Campbell
never: 2 no 3 nah, naw, nay, nix, non 4 nary, ne'er, nein, nope, nyet, uh-uh 5 I won't, ixnay, no how, no way 6 no deal, noways, nowise 7 I refuse, not ever 8 at no time, forget it, I will not, negative, negatory, not at all 9 by no means, fat chance, I think not, nevermore 10 count me out, impossible, not a chance, thumbs down
almost ~: 6 rarely, seldom 8 not often 10 hardly ever, now and then
before seen: 3 new 6 all-new
ender: 4 more
meeting: 8 parallel
mind: 6 skip it 8 forget it, no matter 10 don't bother
still: 5 antsy, hyper, jumpy 6 on edge 7 fidgety, jittery 8 restless
used, in coin-collecting: 3 unc.
never __ die: 3 say
never-__: 6 ending
__ never: 5 now or
Never __: 3 Lie 4 Ever 5 Again 6 Enough
Never __ Diet: 3 Say
Never __ moment!: 5 a dull
Never __ Never Again: 3 Say
Never __ Say Goodbye: 3 Can
Never (1985 song) artist: Heart
Never Again author: Flora Nwapa
Never Be Anyone Else But You (1959 song) artist: Ricky Nelson
Never Been Kissed (1999 film)
cast: David Arquette, Drew Barrymore, Molly Shannon
__ Never Been to Me: 3 I've
Never Been to Spain (1972 song) artist: Three Dog Night
__ never believe me...: 5 They'd
Never Bet the Devil Your Head author: Edgar Allan Poe
Never Call Retreat author: Bruce Catton
Never Can Say Goodbye (song) artist: Gloria Gaynor, Jackson 5
__ Never Can Tell: 3 You
Never Come Morning author: Nelson Algren
Never Cry Wolf (1983 film)
cast: Brian Dennehy, Charles Martin Smith
never-ending: 4 vast 6 eonian, eterne, steady 7 abiding, chronic, eternal, nonstop, undying 8 constant, enduring, immortal, infinite, timeless, unbroken 9 boundless, ceaseless, chronical, continual, countless, deathless, incessant, limitless, perennial, permanent, perpetual, unceasing, unlimited
NeverEnding Story, The author: 4 Ende
Never Enough author: Harold Robbins
never-failing: 4 sure 6 steady 9 steadfast, unfailing
__ Never Get Rich: 5 You'll
Never Give a Sucker an Even Break (1941 film)
cast: Leon Errol, W.C. Fields
Never Gonna Give You Up (1988 song) artist: Rick Astley
Never Gonna Let You Go (1983 song) artist: Sergio Mendes & Brasil '66
__ never heard them at all...: 3 No I
Never Knew Lonely artist: Vince Gill
Never Knew Love Like This Before (1980 song) artist: Stephanie Mills
__ Never Know: 5 You'll
Never Leave Me author: Harold Robbins
Never Love a Stranger author: Harold Robbins
...never met __ I didn't like: 4 a man
never missing __: 5 a beat
Nevermore! bird: 5 raven
Never My Love (song) artist: Association, Blue Swede
Never, Never Gonna Give Ya Up (1973 song) artist: Barry White
never-never land: 6 heaven, utopia 8 paradise 9 fairyland, Shangri-la
Never on Sunday (1960 film)
cast: Jules Dassin, Melina Mercouri
director: Jules Dassin
setting: 6 Greece
Nevers: 4 city, town 5 Ernie
locale: 6 France
Never Say __: 3 Die 4 Diet
Never Say Die (1939 film)
cast: Andy Devine, Bob Hope, Martha Raye
Never Say Never Again (1983 film)
cast: Kim Basinger, Klaus Maria Brandauer, Barbara Carrera, Sean Connery, Max von Sydow
director: Irvin Kershner
__ Never Seen Those Eyes: 5 Mama's
Nevers, Ernie sport: 8 football
__ Never Smile Again: 3 I'll
Never Tear Us Apart (1988 song) artist: INXS
nevertheless: 3 but, tho, yet 5 altho, still 6 anyway, even so, though 7 howbeit, however 8 after all, although
__ never too late...: 3 it's
__ Never Walk Alone: 5 You'll
__ never work!: 4 It'll
nevi: 5 moles 10 birthmarks
Nevil: 5 Shute 6 Robbie
Nevill: 4 Mott
Neville: 3 Art 5 Aaron, Brand, Cyril 7 Charles 8 Marriner 11 Chamberlain
Neville, Aaron
song: Don't Know Much (1989) Everybody Plays the Fool (1991) Tell It Like It Is (1966)
Nevin: 9 Ethelbert
Nevins, Allan: 6 writer 9 historian
Nev. neighbor: 3 Cal., Ida., Ore. 4 Ariz., Oreg. 5 Calif.
see also Nevada
Nevsky: 9 Alexander
Nevsky Cathedral
locale: 5 Sofia 6 Sofiya 8 Bulgaria
nevus: 4 mole 9 birthmark
new: 3 mod, now, raw 4 dewy, late, mint, more 5 added, faddy, fresh, green, novel, other, sweet, young 6 afresh, clever, just in, latest, modern, modish, of late, recent, red-hot, unique, unlike, unused, virgin 7 altered, current, just out, revived, strange, topical, unknown, untried, unusual, updated 8 advanced, creative, directly, improved, inspired, original, restored, singular, spanking, untapped, up-to-date, virginal, youthful 9 au courant, different, increased, ingenious, inventive, unhandled, unheard-of, unskilled, unspoiled, untouched, untrained, untrodden 10 additional, dissimilar, innovative, redesigned, refreshing, starting up, unfamiliar, unseasoned
breathe ~ life into: 6 revive 7 refresh 10 regenerate
combining form: 2 ne- 3 neo-, nov- 4 ceno-, novo-
ender: 4 born 5 comer, found, speak 6 sprint
face a ~ day: 4 rise, wake 5 awake, waken 6 awaken
growth: 4 twig, wand 5 shoot
hand: 4 babe, lamb, naif, tiro, tyro 6 intern, novice 7 learner, recruit 8 beginner, freshman, neophyte 9 fledgling 10 tenderfoot
homophone of ~: 3 gnu 4 knew
in French: 7 nouveau 8 nouvelle
in German: 3 neu 4 neue
in Spanish: 5 nueva, nuevo
like ~: 4 mint 5 fresh 9 unspoiled
like a ~ coin: 5 shiny 6 agleam, bright 8 gleaming
like ~ to a coin collector: 3 unc.
make ~: 3 fix 4 heal 6 repair 7 refresh, restore
open to ~ ideas: 7 pliable 8 amenable, tolerant 9 acceptive, sensitive 10 hospitable, responsive
person: 4 baby, tiro, tyro 5 hiree 7 recruit 8 beginner 9 greenhorn
phrase: 7 coinage 9 neologism
turn over a ~ leaf: 6 change, reform 7 redress, shape up
version: 6 change, update 7 redraft, rewrite 8 overhaul, revision 9 amendment, redaction 10 adjustment, alteration, correction, emendation
wave: 5 novel 6 exotic, modern 7 radical 8 vanguard 9 inventive 10 avant-garde, innovative, pioneering
wrinkle: 6 change 7 novelty 9 departure 10 innovation
new __: 4 look, math, moon, town, wave, year 5 blood, media, order, penny, thing 7 biology, cuisine
new __ in old bottles: 4 wine
new __ order: 5 world
new-__: 4 mint, mown, rich 6 sprung
__ new?: 5 What's
__-new: 4 span 5 brand
New __: 3 Age 4 Ager, Deal, Left, Look, Test., York 5 Delhi, Greek, Haven, Latin, Norse, Right, Spain, Style, World 6 Albany, Comedy, Dealer, Forest, France, Guinea, Hebrew, Iberia, Jersey, London, Mexico, Sweden, Yorker 7 Balance, Edition, England, English, Granada, Kingdom, Orleans, Realism, Seekers, Thought 9 Amsterdam, Caledonia, Hampshire
New __, A: 4 Leaf, Life
New __ City: 4 York
New __ clam chowder: 7 England
New __, CT: 5 Haven 6 Canaan
New __ Day: 5 Year's
New __ Eve: 5 Year's
New __, India: 5 Delhi
New __ in Town: 3 Kid
New __, LA: 6 Iberia
New __ Mets: 4 York
New __ minute: 4 York
New __ on the Block: 4 Kids
New __ Pay Old Debts, A: 5 Way to
New __ steak: 4 York
New __ Stock Exchange: 4 York
New __ Symphony: 5 World
New __, The: 3 Men 6 Tenant 7 Yorkers
New __ theology: 5 Haven 7 England
New __ Wales: 5 South
New Age
glow: 4 aura
philosophy: 6 holism
pianist: 4 Tesh
syllable: 2 om
New Albany: 4 city, town
locale: 7 Indiana
Newark: 3 bay 4 city, port, town
athletes: 8 Blue Hens
county: 5 Essex
locale: 3 Cal., Del. 4 Ohio 5 Calif. 8 Delaware 9 New Jersey 10 California
newspaper: 10 Star-Ledger
New Attitude (1985 song) artist: Patti LaBelle
New Balance competitor: 4 Avia, Keds 6 Adidas, Reebok 8 Converse
__ new ball game: 5 whole
New Baskerville: 4 font 8 typeface
New Bedford: 4 city, port, town
locale: 4 Mass.
New Berlin: 4 city, town
locale: 9 Wisconsin

New Bern: 4 city, town
locale: 4 N. Car.
Newbery: 4 John 5 Award, medal
Newbery, John: 7 English 9 publisher
newbie: 4 tiro, tyro 6 novice 8 neophyte
newborn: 4 babe, baby 5 child, young 6 infant, recent 7 neonate
bed: 4 crib 6 cradle
New Brighton: 4 city, town
locale: 9 Minnesota
New Britain: 4 city, town
locale: 4 Conn.
New Brunswick: 4 city, town 8 province
city: 6 St. John 7 Cap-Pelé, Moncton 9 Miramichi, Port Elgin
Indian: 8 Malecite
locale: 6 Canada 9 New Jersey
neighbor: 5 Maine
school: 7 Rutgers
Newburg: 4 city, town
locale: 8 Kentucky
__ Newburg: 7 lobster
Newburgh: 4 city, town
locale: 7 New York
New Caledonia: 3 isl. 4 isle 6 island
bird: 4 kagu
capital: 6 Nouméa
Newcastle: 4 city, port, town
locale: 7 England 9 Australia
product: 4 coal
New Castle: 4 city, town
locale: 7 Indiana 8 Delaware
Newcastle-under-__: 4 Lyme
Newcastle-upon-__: 4 Tyne
New Centurions, The (1972 film)
cast: Jane Alexander, Stacy Keach, George C. Scott
New Colossus, The author: Emma Lazarus
Newcombe: 3 Don 4 John
Newcombe, Don: 6 Dodger, hurler 7 pitcher
Newcombe, John: 7 netster 9 tennis pro
milieu: 5 court
rival: 4 Ashe
newcomer: 3 neo 4 colt, tiro, tyro 5 alien 6 blow-in, novice, rookie 7 entrant, recruit, settler 8 beginner, maverick, neophyte, outsider, stranger 9 foreigner, greenhorn, immigrant, latecomer 10 apprentice, tenderfoot
academy ~: 4 pleb 5 frosh, plebe
__ New Day: 5 Many a
New Day Has Come, A (2002 song)
artist: Celine Dion
New Deal agcy.: 3 AAA, CCC, FHA, FSA, NRA, NYA, PWA, REA, RFC, SSA, TVA, WPA 4 FDIC, NLRB
New Deal for Christmas, A show: 5 Annie
New Delhi: 4 city, town 7 capital
locale: 5 India
New Diplomacy, The author: 4 Eban
New Edition
song: Cool It Now (1984)
Hit Me Off (1996)
If It Isn't Love (1988)
I'm Still in Love with You (1996)
Mr. Telephone Man (1985)
newel: 4 post 9 stairpost
Newell, Mike: 8 director
film: Dance With a Stranger (1985)
Donnie Brasco (1997)
Enchanted April (1991)
Four Weddings and a Funeral (1994)
Pushing Tin (1999)
new-employee offering (abbr.): 3 OJT
New England
campus: 3 MIT, UNH, URI 4 Yale 5 Brown, Tufts, U Mass 7 Amherst, Harvard 9 Dartmouth
cape: 3 Ann, Cod
fish: 5 scrod 6 schrod
native: 4 Yank 6 Mainer 9 Bay Stater, Nutmegger, Vermonter
port: 6 Boston 10 New Bedford
pro team: 6 Bruins, Red Sox 7 Celtics 8 Patriots
soda fountain: 3 spa
state: 4 Conn., Mass. 5 Maine 7 Vermont
New England Suite composer: 5 Grofé
New English __: 5 Bible
newest: 4 last 6 latest 8 up-to-date
wrinkle: 3 fad 4 rage 5 style, trend, vogue 7 fashion 10 dernier cri
Newf.: 3 isl. 4 prov.
newfangled: 5 fresh, novel 6 modern, recent 7 in vogue, popular, strange 8 gimmicky, up-to-date 10 innovative
Newfoundland: 3 dog, isl. 4 isle, prov. 5 canid 6 canine, island 8 province
airport: 6 Gander
city: 6 Brigus 7 Botwood, St. John's 10 Mount Pearl
explorer: 7 Gilbert
fisherman: 6 banker
hrs.: 3 AST
mountain: 8 Caubvick
school: 8 Memorial
New Glasgow: 4 city, town
locale: 6 Canada 10 Nova Scotia
__ new ground: 5 break
New Guinea: 3 isl. 4 isle 6 island
bay: 6 Sarera
bird: 7 mudlark 8 manacode 9 bower-bird, cassowary
city: 3 Lae
gulf: 5 Papua
island off ~: 4 Biak
islands near ~: 3 Aru 4 Aroe, Arru
mountain: 4 Jaja 7 Trikora
reptile: 6 taipan
sea: 5 Coral 7 Arafura 8 Bismarck
snake: 6 taipan
strait off ~: 6 Torres
territory: 5 Papua
to Indonesians: 5 Irian
__ New Guinea: 5 Dutch
New Hampshire: 3 hen 4 fowl 5 state 7 chicken, poultry
capital: 7 Concord
city: 5 Derry, Dover, Keene, Salem 6 Exeter, Hudson, Nashua 7 Concord, Laconia 9 Merrimack, Rochester 10 Manchester, Portsmouth
mountain: 5 White
neighbor: 5 Maine 6 Canada, Quebec 7 Vermont
relative: 6 Bantam, Brahma, Houdan, Sussex 7 Cornish, Dorking, Leghorn 8 Araucana, Langshan, Shanghai 9 Dominique, Orpington, Wyandotte
school: 9 Dartmouth
state amphibian: 4 newt
state bird: 5 finch
state flower: 5 lilac
state game fish: 10 brook trout
state insect: 7 ladybug
state mineral: 5 beryl
state rock: 7 granite
state sport: 6 skiing
state tree: 10 white birch
__ New Hampshire, The: 5 Hotel
New Harmony founder: 4 Owen
Newhart (CBS sitcom)
cast: Julia Duffy (Stephanie Vanderkellen)
Mary Frann (Joanna Loudon)
Bob Newhart (Dick Loudon)
Tom Poston (George Utley)
producer: MTM
setting: 3 inn 7 Vermont 9 Stratford
Newhart, Bob: 5 actor 8 comedian
film: Catch-22 (1970)
Cold Turkey (1971)
On a Clear Day You Can See Forever (1970)
TV: Newhart, The Bob Newhart Show
Newhaven: 4 port
locale: 6 Sussex 7 England
New Haven: 4 city, town
locale: 4 Conn.
neighbor: 6 Hamden
school: 4 Yale 5 Yale U
student: 3 Eli 5 Yalie 7 Bulldog
tree: 3 elm
New Haven __: 4 stem 6 Colony
New Hebrides: 5 isles 7 islands
see also Vanuatu
New High __: 6 German
New Hope: 4 city, town
locale: 4 Penn. 9 Minnesota
Newhouse: 2 S.I.
Newhouser, Hal: 5 Tiger 6 hurler 7 pitcher
New Iberia: 4 city, town
locale: 9 Louisiana
newie: 4 tiro, tyro 5 plebe 6 novice, rookie 7 learner, recruit, trainee 8 beginner, initiate, neophyte 9 fledgling, greenhorn 10 apprentice, tenderfoot
Newington: 4 city, town
locale: 8 Virginia
New Jack City actor: 4 Ice-T
New Jersey: 5 state
bay: 6 Newark 8 Delaware
cape: 3 May
capital: 7 Trenton
city: 4 Lodi 5 Brick, Ewing, Union, Wayne 6 Camden, Edison, Iselin, Kearny, Leonia, Linden, Mahwah, Newark, Nutley, Orange, Rahway, Summit 7 Bayonne, Cape May, Clifton, Fort Dix, Fort Lee, Hoboken, Paramus, Passaic, Roselle, Teaneck, Tenafly, Trenton 8 Carteret, Cranbury, Cranford, Fair Lawn, Freehold, Garfield, Hamilton, Hillside, Lakewood, Metuchen, Millburn, Paterson, Somerset, Vineland 9 Bridgeton, Elizabeth, Englewood, Irvington, Maplewood, Millville, Montclair, Old Bridge, Princeton, Ridgewood, Toms River, Union City, Westfield 10 Belleville, Bloomfield, Cherry Hill, East Orange, Hackensack, Jersey City, Livingston, Long Branch, Parsippany, Pennsauken, Perth Amboy, Plainfield, Sayreville, West Orange
ender: 3 ite
fort: 3 Dix
neighbor: 4 Penn. 5 Penna. 7 New York 8 Delaware
pro team: 4 Nets 6 Devils
school: 4 Drew 7 Rutgers 9 Princeton, Seton Hall
state bird: 9 goldfinch
state fish: 10 brook trout
state flower: 6 violet
state insect: 8 honeybee
state mammal: 5 horse
state shell: 5 whelk
state tree: 6 red oak
New Jersey __: 3 tea 4 plan
New Kid in Town (1976 song) artist: Eagles
New Kids on the Block
hometown: Boston
members: McIntyre, Wahlberg, Wood, Knight
song: Cover Girl (1989)
Didn't I (Blow Your Mind) (1989)
Hangin' Tough (1989)
I'll Be Loving You (1989)
Please Don't Go Girl (1988)
Step by Step (1990)
This One's for the Children (1989)
Tonight (1990)
You Got It (1980)
New Leaf, A (1971 film)
cast: Walter Matthau, Elaine May, Jack Weston
director: Elaine May
__ new lease on life: 4 get a
New Left org.: 3 SDS
Newley, Anthony spouse: Joan Collins
New Life, A (1988 film)
cast: Alan Alda, Ann-Margret, Veronica Hamel, Hal Linden
director: Alan Alda
New Life, The author: Dante
New Line: 6 studio
competitor: 3 Fox, MGM 6 Disney 7 Miramax 8 Columbia 9 Paramount, Universal 10 Dreamworks, Warner Bros.
creation: 4 film 5 movie
New London: 4 city, town
locale: 4 Conn.
river: 6 Thames
sch.: 5 USCGA
New Look designer: 4 Dior
Newlove, John: 4 poet 8 Canadian
newly: 4 anew, just 6 afresh, lately, of late 7 freshly 8 recently
arrived: 6 just in
ender: 3 wed
produced: 5 fresh 6 recent 7 just out 8 just made
newlywed: 5 bride, groom 10 bridegroom
promise: 3 I do
Newlywed Game, The: 8 game show
host: Bob Eubanks
newlyweds: 6 couple 7 twosome
New Machiavelli, The author: H.G. Wells
Newman: 4 Paul 5 Barry, Edwin, Randy 6 Alfred, Thomas 7 Laraine, Nanette
__ Newman, M.D.: 7 Captain
Newman, Paul: 5 actor
film: Absence of Malice (1981)
Blaze (1989)
Butch Cassidy and the Sundance Kid (1969)
Cat on a Hot Tin Roof (1958)
The Color of Money (1986, AA)
Cool Hand Luke (1967)
Exodus (1960)
Fat Man and Little Boy (1989)
Fort Apache, The Bronx (1981)
From the Terrace (1960)
The Glass Menagerie (1987)
Harper (1966)
Hombre (1967)
Hud (1963)
The Hudsucker Proxy (1994)
The Hustler (1961)
The Life and Times of Judge Roy Bean (1972)
The Long Hot Summer (1958)
Message in a Bottle (1999)
Mr. & Mrs. Bridge (1990)
Nobody's Fool (1994)
Paris Blues (1961)
Pocket Money (1972)
The Prize (1963)
Rachel, Rachel (1968)
The Rack (1956)
Road to Perdition (2002)
Slap Shot (1977)
Somebody Up There Likes Me (1956)
The Sting (1973)
Sweet Bird of Youth (1962)
Torn Curtain (1966)
The Towering Inferno (1974)
Twilight (1998)

The Verdict (1982)
What a Way to Go! (1964)
Winning (1969)
WUSA (1970)
The Young Philadelphians (1959)
spouse: Joanne Woodward
Newman, Randy song: Short People (1977)
Newman's Own: 10 pasta sauce
alternative: 4 Ragu **5** Prego **6** Prince **8** Classico
Newmar: 5 Julie
Newmarket: 4 city, town
locale: 6 Canada **7** Ontario
New Men, The author: C.P. Snow
New Mexico: 5 state
capital: 7 Santa Fe
city: 4 Taos **5** Hobbs **6** Clovis, Gallup **7** Roswell, Santa Fe **8** Carlsbad **9** Las Cruces, Los Alamos, Rio Rancho **10** Alamogordo, Farmington
county: 3 Lea **4** Eddy, Luna, Mora, Quay, Taos **5** Otero **6** Cibola
desert: 10 Chihuahuan
Indian: 3 Sia, Ute **4** Piro, Tano, Taos, Tewa, Tiwa, Zuni **6** Laguna, Navaho, Navajo, Pueblo **9** Jicarilla, Mescalero **10** Chiricahua
lake: 3 Ute
mountain: 7 San Juan, Wheeler **8** Mogollon
neighbor: 4 Utah **5** Texas **6** Mexico **7** Arizona **8** Colorado, Oklahoma
pueblo: 5 Acoma
state bird: 10 roadrunner
state flower: 5 yucca
state gem: 9 turquoise
state mammal: 9 black bear
state tree: 5 piñon
New Mexico State
athletes: 6 Aggies
locale: 9 Las Cruces
New Minas: 4 city, town
locale: 6 Canada **10** Nova Scotia
Newnan: 4 city, town
locale: 7 Georgia
newness: 7 novelty **10** innovation
New Orleans: 3 spt. **4** city, port, town **6** battle **7** seaport
athletes: 9 Green Wave
city near ~: 5 Houma **6** Kenner
City of ~: 5 train
cuisine: 6 creole
locale: 9 Louisiana
music: 4 jazz
pro team: 6 Saints
sandwich: 5 po boy
school: 6 Loyola, Tulane
New Orleans __: 5 style **6** lugger, Saints
New Orleans (1960 song) artist: Gary U.S. Bonds
Newport: 3 car **4** auto, city, town **8** Chrysler **10** automobile
locale: 5 Wales
New Port __, FL: 6 Richey
Newport Beach: 4 city, town
locale: 10 California
Newport News: 4 city, town
locale: 8 Virginia
__ New, Pussycat?: 5 What's
New Republic: 3 mag **8** magazine
founder: 5 Croly
piece: 5 essay
New Rochelle: 4 city, town
athletes: 5 Gaels
locale: 7 New York
school: 4 Iona
news: 3 tip **4** copy, data, dope, info, leak, word **5** cable, media, paper, rumor, scoop, story, telex **6** expose, latest, report, tip-off **7** account, hearsay, lowdown, message, release, scandal, tidings **8** bulletin, dispatch, telecast, telegram **9** broadcast, discovery, eyeopener, headlines, narration, statement **10** communiqué, disclosure, journalism, revelation
bad ~: 4 blow **5** rogue, worry **6** downer, misery, sorrow **7** problem, trouble **9** liability, reckoning, scoundrel **10** misfortune, unpleasant
break the ~: 3 air **4** leak, tell **6** advise, clue in, inform, report, reveal, tip off **7** let slip **8** announce, disclose **9** make known **10** make public
center: 6 agency, bureau
clip: 5 video
ender: 3 boy, man, men **4** cast, girl, reel, room **5** break, maker, paper, print, stand, woman, women **6** caster, letter, monger, people, person, weekly, worthy **8** magazine **9** gathering
exclusive: 5 scoop
flash: 6 notice **8** bulletin, dispatch **10** communiqué, revelation
fresh ~: 4 poop **6** latest
govt. ~ source: 4 USIA
hour: 3 six **4** five, noon **5** seven, six p.m. **6** eleven, five p.m. **7** seven p.m.
in the ~: 3 now **5** fresh **6** recent, trendy **7** current, ongoing, popular, topical **9** happening, immediate **10** in progress, widespread
Italian ~ agency: 4 ANSA
item: 4 clip, obit **5** event, flash, squib, story **9** sound bite **10** communiqué
like a ~ bulletin: 6 just in
like bad ~: 4 glum, grim **5** bleak **6** gloomy **7** ghastly, serious, unhappy **9** cheerless **10** lamentable
like the evening ~: 4 on TV
magazine: 4 Time
maker: 4 star **5** celeb **9** celebrity
medium: 5 daily, press, print, radio
noncommercial ~ source: 3 NPR, PBS
org.: 3 UPI **4** USIA **7** Reuters
perspective: 5 slant
reaction to bad ~: 4 oh no
receive, as ~: 4 hear **5** catch, learn **6** pick up **7** find out **8** discover **9** get wind of
reporter of yore: 5 crier
Russian ~ agency: 4 Tass **8** ITAR-Tass
source: 3 CNN **4** leak **5** MSNBC, paper, radio **6** herald
summary: 5 recap **6** review **8** synopsis
top ~ story: 4 lead **6** leader **8** headline
news __: 3 peg **4** case, clip **5** flash, media, story **6** agency **7** analyst, release, service
__ news: 3 bad **4** good, hard, soft, spot
News: 5 paper
locale: 7 Buffalo, Detroit, Halifax, New York **9** Anchorage **10** Los Angeles
__ News: 4 Good, Nick
__ News Bears, The: 3 Bad
newsboy cry: 5 extra
newscaster: 6 anchor **8** reporter **9** announcer
colonial ~: 5 crier
newscast segment: 5 recap **6** sports
news conference
attendees: 5 media, press
Newsday: 5 paper **9** newspaper
locale: 7 New York **10** Long Island
New Seekers
song: I'd Like to Teach the World to Sing (1971)
Look What They've Done to My Song, Ma (1970)
New Sensation (1988 song) artist: INXS
newsgroup
problem: 4 spam
protocol: 4 nntp
newshawk: 8 reporter
goal: 5 scoop
novice ~: 3 cub
pursuit: 5 story
query: 3 how, who, why **4** what, when **5** where
newsmen: 5 press **7** editors, scribes
News-Miner: 5 paper **9** newspaper
locale: 9 Fairbanks
Newsom, Bobo sport: 8 baseball
Newsome: 5 Ozzie
New South Wales: 5 state **10** Australian
capital: 6 Sydney
city: 6 Sydney **9** Newcastle **10** Wollongong
newspaper: 3 rag **5** daily, extra, organ, press, print, sheet, trade **6** medium, review, weekly **7** gazette, journal, tabloid **8** biweekly **10** periodical
bygone New York ~: 3 Sun **5** World **6** Herald **7** Journal, Tribune **8** American, Telegram
edition: 5 final
employee: 2 ed. **6** critic, editor, writer **8** pressman, reporter
ender: 3 man **5** woman
feature: 3 ads, col. **4** item, obit, Op-Ed, roto **5** piece **6** byline, column, comics **7** funnies, section
filler: 5 squib
holder: 5 twine
Italian ~: 6 Avanti
old ~ machine: 3 TTY **8** teletype
post: 4 beat, desk
section: 4 desk **5** metro **6** insert, sports
space: 6 linage **7** lineage
special edition: 5 extra
stand: 5 kiosk
third-rate ~: 3 rag
typography: 5 agate, print
Newspaper Days author: H.L. Mencken
newspaperman: 6 editor, scribe **8** reporter **10** ink slinger, journalist
newspapers: 5 media, press
newspapers (Canada):
Calgary - Herald, Sun
Edmonton - Journal, Sun
Halifax - News, Herald
Montreal - Gazette, Journal, La Presse
Ottawa - Citizen, Le Droit, Sun
Quebec - Le Soleil
Toronto - Globe and Mail, Star, Sun
Vancouver - Province, Sun
Winnipeg - Free Press
newspapers (U.S.):
Albuquerque - Journal, Tribune
Anchorage - News
Atlanta - Journal-Constitution
Baltimore - Sun
Boise - Idaho Statesman
Boston - Globe, Herald
Buffalo - News
Charlotte - Observer
Chicago - Sun-Times, Tribune
Cincinnati - Enquirer, Post
Cleveland - Plain Dealer
Columbus - Dispatch
Dallas - Morning News
Denver - Post, Rocky Mountain News
Des Moines - Register
Detroit - Free Press, News
Fairbanks - News-Miner
Fresno - Bee
Ft. Lauderdale - Sun-Sentinel
Ft. Worth - Star-Telegram
Hartford - Courant
Honolulu - Advertiser, Star-Bulletin
Houston - Chronicle
Indianapolis - Star
Jacksonville - Florida Times-Union
Kansas City - Star
Las Vegas - Review-Journal, Sun
Little Rock - Democrat-Gazette
Long Island - Newsday
Los Angeles - News, Times
Louisville - Courier Journal
Memphis - Commercial Appeal
Miami - Herald
Milwaukee - Journal Sentinel
Minneapolis/St. Paul - Pioneer Press, Star Tribune
Mobile - Register
Nashville - Tennesseean
Newark - Star-Ledger
New Orleans - Times-Picayune
New York - News, Post, Times
Norfolk - Virginian-Pilot
Oakland - Tribune
Omaha- World-Herald
Orlando - Sentinel
Philadelphia - Inquirer, News
Phoenix - Arizona Republic
Pittsburgh - Post-Gazette, Tribune-Review
Portland - Oregonian
Providence - Journal-Bulletin
Richmond - Times-Dispatch
Sacramento - Bee
Salt Lake City - Deseret News, Tribune
San Diego - Union-Tribune
San Francisco - Chronicle
San Jose - Mercury News
Santa Ana - Orange County Register
Seattle - Post-Intelligencer, Times
St. Louis - Post-Dispatch
St. Petersburg - Times
Tampa - Tribune
Toledo - Blade
Tombstone - Epitaph
Tulsa - World
Washington, D.C. - Post, Times
Newspeak: 5 lingo **10** propaganda
newsprint material: 4 pulp
newsreel: 7 feature
name: 5 Pathé
newsstand: 5 kiosk
Newsweek: 3 mag **8** magazine
items: 3 ads
rival: 4 Time
newsy: 7 gossipy, topical **9** au courant
newt: 3 eft **6** triton **7** axolotl **9** amphibian **10** salamander
__ newt: 5 eye of
Newt: 8 Gingrich
New Tenant, The author: Eugène Ionesco
New Testament
book: 3 Col., Eph., Gal., Heb., Rev., Rom., Tim. **4** Acts, Hebr., John, Jude, Luke, Mark, Matt., Thes. **5** James, Peter, Thess., Titus **6** Romans **7** Hebrews, Matthew, Timothy **8** Philemon **9** Ephesians, Galatians **10** Colossians, Revelation **11** Corinthians, Philippians **13** Thessalonians
sages: 4 Magi
villain: 5 Herod
see also Bible
Newton: 4 city, Huey, town **5** Isaac, Juice, Minow, Wayne **6** Robert **7** Thandie
contemporary: 6 Halley
__ Newton: 3 Fig
newton cousin: 3 erg **4** dyne **5** joule
Newton, Isaac: 3 Sir **9** physicist, scientist

Newton-John, Olivia
grandfather: Max Born
song: Have You Never Been Mellow (1975)
Heart Attack (1982)
Hopelessly Devoted to You (1978)
I Can't Help It (1980)
If Not for You (1971)
If You Love Me (1974)
I Honestly Love You (1974)
Let Me Be There (1973)
A Little More Love (1978)
Magic (1980)
Make a Move on Me (1982)
Physical (1981)
Please Mr. Please (1975)
Suddenly (1980)
Summer Nights (1978)
Twist of Fate (1983)
Xanadu (1980)
You're the One That I Want (1978)
Newton, Juice
song: Angel of the Morning (1981)
Break It to Me Gently (1982)
Love's Been a Little Bit Hard on Me (1982)
Queen of Hearts (1981)
The Sweetest Thing (1981)
Newton, Robert: 5 actor
film: The Beachcomber (1955)
The Desert Rats (1953)
Henry V (1945)
Les Miserables (1952)
Odd Man Out (1947)
Oliver Twist (1948)
This Happy Breed (1944)
Tom Brown's Schooldays (1951)
Treasure Island (1950)
Newton's ___: 5 rings 6 method
Newton's ___ of motion: 3 law
Newton, Thandie: 7 actress
film: Jefferson in Paris (1995)
The Journey of August King (1995)
Mission: Impossible II (2000)
Newton, Wayne
song: Daddy Don't You Walk So Fast (1972)
Danke Schoen (1963)
New Vaudeville Band song: Winchester Cathedral (1966)
new-wave prefix: 3 neo
New Wave rock group: 4 Devo
New Way to Pay Old Debts, A author: Philip Massinger
___ New Window: 5 Open a
new wine in ___ bottles: 3 old
New Woman rival: 4 Self
new world ___: 5 order
New World: 4 Amer. 7 America
___ New World: 5 Brave
___ New World, A: 5 Whole
New World Symphony composer: 6 Dvorák
New Year
lunar ~: 3 Tet
noise: 4 toot
resolution: 4 diet
word: 4 auld, lang, syne
New Year's ___: 3 Day, Eve
New Year's game: 4 Bowl
New York: 4 city, port, town 5 state
canal: 4 Erie
capital: 6 Albany
city: 3 Rye 4 Rome, Troy 5 Coram, Depew, Islip, Nyack, Olean, Owego, Utica 6 Albany, Armonk, Attica, Auburn, Cohoes, Elmira, Elmont, Ithaca, Selden 7 Baldwin, Buffalo, Commack, Massena, Medford, Merrick, Montauk, New City, New York, Oneonta, Penn Yan, Shirley, Yonkers 8 Bay Shore, Brighton, Copiague, Deer Park, Dix Hills, Freeport, Glen Cove, Harrison, Holbrook, Kingston, Lockport, Newburgh, Ossining, Syracuse 9 Amsterdam, Brentwood, Great Neck, Hauppauge, Hempstead, Jamestown, Levittown, Long Beach, Oceanside, Peekskill, Plainview, Rochester, Rotterdam, Sag Harbor, Smithtown, Tonawanda, Uniondale, Watertown, West Islip 10 Binghamton, Centereach, East Meadow, Garden City, Hicksville, Huntington, Lackawanna, Massapequa, Middletown, Ronkonkoma, West Seneca
college: 4 Iona, Pace 5 Mercy, Siena, Touro 6 C.W. Post, Hunter, Marist, Vassar 7 Adelphi, Colgate, Cornell, Fordham, Hofstra, St. John's 8 Columbia 9 West Point 10 Saint John's
county: 4 Erie 5 Bronx, Tioga, Yates 6 Albany, Cayuga, Nassau, Oneida, Otsego, Seneca, Ulster 7 Genesee, Ontario, Steuben, Suffolk 8 Saratoga
in a ~ minute: 4 fast 6 at once 9 instantly, posthaste, right away
Indian: 4 Erie 6 Cayuga, Mohawk, Oneida, Seneca 7 Mahican, Mohican 8 Onondaga 9 Tuscarora
island: 4 Fire 5 Coney, Ellis 6 Rikers
lake: 5 Keuka 6 Cayuga, Oneida, Seneca 9 Champlain 10 Chautauqua, Lake Placid
minute: 5 trice
mountain: 5 Marcy
neighbor: 6 Canada, Quebec 7 Ontario, Vermont 9 New Jersey
pro team: 4 Jets, Mets 5 Bills 6 Giants, Knicks 7 Rangers, Yankees 9 Islanders
river: 4 East 5 Tioga 6 Harlem, Hudson, Mohawk
state beverage: 4 milk
state bird: 8 bluebird
state fish: 10 brook trout
state flower: 4 rose
state fruit: 5 apple
state gem: 6 garnet
state insect: 7 ladybug
state mammal: 6 beaver
state motto: 9 Excelsior
state muffin: 5 apple
state shell: 7 scallop
state tree: 10 sugar maple
waterfall: 7 Niagara
New York ___: 3 Bay, cut 4 City, fern, Post 5 steak, strip, Times 6 minute, school
New York ___ Exchange: 5 Stock
New York ___ of Mind: 5 State
___ New York: 3 Old 7 Greater
New York Bay
island: 4 Long 5 Ellis 6 Staten 7 Liberty 9 Manhattan
river to ~: 6 Hudson
New York City: 3 spt. 4 port 6 Gotham 7 seaport 8 Big Apple
area: 4 Soho 6 Bowery, Harlem 7 Chelsea, Tribeca
avenue: 4 Park 5 Fifth 7 Madison 9 Lexington
ballpark: 4 Shea
baseballer: 3 Met 4 Yank 6 Yankee
borough: 5 Bronx 6 Queens 8 Brooklyn 9 Manhattan
cager: 5 Knick
county: 5 Bronx, Kings 6 Queens 7 New York 8 Richmond
footballer: 3 Jet 5 Giant
hotel: 5 Plaza
newspaper: 4 News, Post 5 Times
restaurant: 6 Sardi's 7 Elaine's
river: 4 East 6 Harlem, Hudson
store: 4 Saks 5 Macy's
street: 4 Wall 8 Broadway
suburb: 3 Rye 5 Nyack
New York Cosmos star: 4 Pelé
New York cut: 5 steak
New York Enquirer boss: 4 Kane
New Yorker: 3 car 4 auto 8 Chrysler
New Yorkers, The: 7 musical
songwriter: 6 Porter
New Yorker, The: 3 mag
cartoonist: 3 Rea 4 Arno 5 Chast, Steig 6 Addams 7 Thurber
editor: 5 Brown, Shawn
founder: 4 Ross
mascot: 6 Tilley 7 Eustace
___ New York in June...: 5 I like
New York Liberty org.: 4 WNBA
New York Life competitor: 5 Aetna 6 Kemper 8 Hartford 9 Traveler's
___ New York minute: 3 in a
New York, New York (1977 film)
cast: Robert De Niro, Liza Minnelli, Lionel Stander
director: Martin Scorsese
New York's ___: 6 Finest
New York Times
onetime ~ publisher: 4 Ochs
New York World journalist: 3 Bly
New Zealand: 4 isls. 5 isles 6 nation 7 country, islands
aborigine: 5 Maori
bird: 3 kea, moa, oii, tui 4 huia, kaka, kiwi, weka 6 kakapo, takahe 8 notornis
capital: 10 Wellington
city: 6 Nelson 7 Dunedin, Manukau 8 Auckland, Hamilton 10 Wellington
evergreen: 5 kauri
explorer: 6 Tasman
export: 4 lamb, wool
fish: 3 ihi 4 hiku 6 hapuku, inanga 7 whapuku 8 hiwi hiwi
island: 4 Niue 5 North, South 9 Antipodes
lake: 5 Taupo
language: 5 Maori
money: 4 cent 6 dollar
mountain: 4 Cook
nation north of ~: 4 Fiji
native: 4 kiwi 5 Maori
parrot: 3 kea 4 kaka 6 kakapo
playwright: 8 Sargeson
poet: 6 Adcock, Baxter, Curnow
river: 6 Clutha
sea: 4 Ross 6 Tasman
sheep: 10 Corriedale
shrub: 4 hebe, karo 7 geebung 8 myoporum
soldier: 5 Anzac
soprano: 4 Alda 8 te Kanawa
tree: 4 hebe, karo, rimu 5 kauri, mapau 6 kapuka, kowhai, tarata
volcano: 7 Ruapehu
waterfall: 6 Helena
writer: 5 Frame, Marsh 8 Ihimaera, Sargeson 9 Mansfield
New Zealand ___: 4 flax 7 spinach
Nexö, Martin Andersen: 6 Danish, writer
work: Pelle the Conqueror
next: 4 then 5 close, later 6 behind, beside, hard by, on deck, second 7 closest, ensuing, nearest 8 abutting, adjacent, coming up, touching 9 adjoining, after that, afterward, alongside, following, proximate, thereupon 10 back-to-back, consequent, sequential, subsequent, succeeding, successive, thereafter
be ~ to: 4 abut 6 adjoin, appose 8 neighbor
come ~: 5 ensue 6 follow 7 succeed
coming ~: 3 fol. 5 after 9 following
door: 4 near 5 close 6 at hand, nearby 8 abutting, adjacent, touching 9 adjoining, bordering, immediate, in contact 10 contiguous, convenient, juxtaposed
get ~ to: 3 woo 7 flatter, promote 8 butter up 9 cultivate, shine up to 10 curry favor
go ~: 7 succeed 9 come after
in baseball: 6 on deck
in line: 4 heir 5 first 7 heiress, legatee 9 inheritor
to: 4 with 6 at hand, beside 8 abutting, adjacent 9 alongside
to nothing: 5 least, scant 6 meager
world: 6 heaven 7 Elysium 8 paradise 9 hereafter
next-___ neighbor: 4 door
___ next?: 4 Who's
Next
song: I Still Love You (1998)
Too Close (1998)
Next Best Thing, The (2000 film)
cast: Benjamin Bratt, Rupert Everett, Madonna
director: John Schlesinger
___ next door: 3 boy 4 girl
Next Door to an Angel (1962 song)
artist: Neil Sedaka
Nextel alternative: 5 Nokia 7 T-Mobile 8 Ericsson, Motorola
next in ___: 4 line
next of ___: 3 kin
Next Stop, Greenwich Village (1976 film)
cast: Ellen Greene, Shelley Winters
director: Paul Mazursky
Next Time I Fall, The (1986 song)
artist: Amy Grant, Peter Cetera
___ Next Time, The: 4 Fire
Next Time We Love (1936 film)
cast: Ray Milland, James Stewart, Margaret Sullavan
nexus: 3 tie 4 link, yoke 5 focus, joint 6 center 7 network 8 ligature, vinculum 10 connection
Neyagawa: 4 city, town
locale: 5 Japan
Neyman: 5 Jerzy
___-nez: 5 pince
___-Nez: 4 Gris
Nezahualcóyotl: 4 city, town
locale: 6 Mexico
Nez Percé: 5 tribe 6 Indian 7 Amerind 8 language
NFC
division: 4 East, West
team: 4 Bucs, Rams 5 Bears, Lions, Skins, Vikes 6 Eagles, Giants, Niners, Saints 7 Cowboys, Falcons, Packers, Vikings 8 Panthers, Redskins, Seahawks 9 Cardinals 10 Buccaneers
NFL
broadcaster: 4 ESPN
city: 5 Miami, Tampa 6 Dallas, Denver 7 Atlanta, Buffalo, Chicago, Detroit, New York, Oakland, Seattle, St. Louis 8 Green Bay, San Diego 9 Baltimore, Cleveland 10 Cincinnati, Kansas City, New Orleans, Pittsburgh, Washington 12 Indianapolis, Jacksonville, Philadelphia, San Francisco
conference: 4 East, West
div.: 3 AFC, NFC
exec: 2 GM
honor: 6 All-Pro
official: 3 ref 5 zebra 7 referee
part: 4 Natl. 6 League 8 Football, National
period: 2 OT 3 qtr. 7 quarter 8 overtime

player: **2** FB, LG, LH, LT, QB, RB, RG, RT **3** end, pro, RFB, RHB **4** back **5** guard **6** center, tackle **8** fullback, halfback
score: **2** FG, pt., TD **5** point **9** field goal, touchdown
squad: **3** def., off. **7** defense, offense
team: **4** Jets, Rams **5** Bears, Bills, Colts, Lions **6** Browns, Chiefs, Eagles, eleven, Giants, Niners, Ravens, Saints, Sharks, Texans, Titans **7** Bengals, Broncos, Cowboys, Falcons, Jaguars, Packers, Raiders, Vikings **8** Chargers, Dolphins, Panthers, Patriots, Redskins, Seahawks, Steelers **9** Cardinals **10** Buccaneers
see also football
Nfld.: **3** isl. **4** prov.
see also Newfoundland
Ngaio: **5** Marsh
Ngami: **4** lake
locale: **8** Botswana
Ngo __ Diem: **4** Dinh
ngoma: **4** drum
Ngoni home: **6** Africa, Malawi, Zambia **8** Tanzania
Ngor, Haing S. Oscar: The Killing Fields
Nguni: **3** cow **4** bull **6** bovine, cattle
home: **6** Africa, Malawi, Zambia **8** Tanzania
nguru: **5** flute **6** string
origin: **5** Maori
Nguyen Van __: **5** Thieu
ngwee: **5** money
NH
neighbor: **3** Que. **4** Mass.
region: **4** N. Eng.
see also New Hampshire
Nha Trang: **4** city, town
locale: **7** Vietnam
NHL
city: **5** Tampa **6** Boston, Dallas, Ottawa **7** Buffalo, Calgary, Chicago, Detroit, New York, Phoenix, San Jose, St. Louis, Toronto **8** Columbus, Edmonton, Montreal **9** Nashville, Vancouver **10** Los Angeles, Pittsburgh, Washington **12** Philadelphia
fake-out: **4** deke
Hall-of-Famer: **3** Orr **4** Howe, Hull, Park **5** Bossy **6** Dionne, Mikita, Parent, Plante, Potvin **7** Federko, Gilbert, Gillies, Gretzky, Lafleur, Langway, Lemieux, Richard, Sawchuk, Worsley **8** Bathgate, Bobby Orr, Brad Park, Esposito, Trottier **9** Bobby Hull, Geoffrion, Mike Bossy **10** Gordie Howe, Guy Lafleur, Rod Gilbert, Stan Mikita
player: **2** LW, RW **3** pro **6** center, goalie, iceman, skater **8** left wing **9** right wing
player at times: **4** icer
stat: **3** pts. **5** goals **6** points **7** assists.
team: **3** six **4** Caps, Habs, Wild **5** Blues, Isles, Kings, Leafs, Stars **6** Bruins, Devils, Flames, Flyers, Oilers, Sabres, Sharks **7** Canucks, Coyotes, Rangers **8** Capitals, Panthers, Penguins, Red Wings, Senators **9** Avalanche, Canadiens, Islanders, Lightning, Predators, Thrashers **10** Blackhawks, Hurricanes, Maple Leafs
tiebreaker: **2** OT **8** overtime
venue: **3** ice **4** rink
see also hockey
NH2, compound with: **5** amide
NH3, derived from: **6** ammono
Ni: **4** elem. **6** nickel **7** element
28 for ~: **4** at. no.
Nia: **4** Long **7** Peeples **8** Vardalos
niacin: **4** acid **7** vitamin **8** B vitamin
niagara: **7** cascade, torrent **9** waterfall
Niagara: **5** falls, grape, green, river **9** waterfall
fort: **4** Erie
relative: **5** Gamay, pinot, Tokay **6** Merlot **7** Catawba, Concord **8** Cabernet, malvasia, muscatel **9** muscadine, Sauvignon, zinfandel **10** Chardonnay
Niagara (1953 film)
cast: Joseph Cotten, Marilyn Monroe, Jean Peters
director: Henry Hathaway
Niagara Falls: **4** city, town
craft: **6** barrel
like ~: **3** wet **5** aroar, misty
locale: **6** Canada **7** New York, Ontario
Niamey: **4** city, town **7** capital
locale: **5** Niger
nib: **3** pen, tip **4** beak, bill **5** point, tinge **8** penpoint
nibble: **3** eat, nip **4** bite, chew, crop, gnaw, nosh, peck **5** crumb, eat at, graze, munch, snack, taste **6** morsel, nosh on, pick at, tidbit **7** consume, soupçon **8** spoonful **9** grab a bite, masticate
nibbler: **4** fish
__ Nibelungen: **3** Die
Nibelungenlied: **4** epic, saga
Nibelung hoard: **4** gold
niblick: **4** club, iron **8** golf club
__ niblick: **6** mashie
Niblo: **4** Fred
__ nibs: **3** her, his
nibs, his: **4** king
nicad __: **7** battery
Nicaragua: **6** nation **7** country
capital: **7** Managua
city: **4** León **6** Estelí, Masaya **7** Managua
from ~: **6** Latino
Indian: **7** Miskito
money: **7** cordoba
neighbor: **8** Honduras **9** Costa Rica
org.: **3** OAS
poet: **5** Darío **8** Cardinal
rebel: **6** Contra
volcano: **6** Masaya **9** Momotombo
see also Spanish
niccolite: **3** ore **7** mineral
Niccolò: **8** Paganini
NiCd __: **7** battery
nice: **2** OK **3** def, rad **4** aces, A-one, boss, braw, cool, cosy, cozy, dece, fair, fine, gear, good, homy, keen, kind, neat, okay, okeh, okey, phat, prim, tidy, trim, tuff, warm **5** cozey, cozie, dandy, ducky, exact, fussy, grand, great, homey, legit, marvy, moral, neato, nifty, nobby, noble, picky, prime, right, slick, super, sweet, swell, tasty **6** bang on, bang-up, bonzer, bosker, choice, dainty, dead-on, decent, deluxe, divine, dreamy, far-out, genial, gentle, gnarly, groovy, kindly, lovely, minute, modest, peachy, polite, pretty, proper, savory, seemly, slap-up, smooth, social, spot on, subtle, superb, terrif, tiptop, toothy, unreal, whizzo, wicked **7** affable, amazing, amiable, amusing, awesome, capital, careful, cordial, corking, correct, elegant, ethical, genteel, helpful, likable, mincing, perfect, precise, refined, ripping, skookum, stellar, sublime, upscale, welcome, winning, winsome **8** all right, becoming, charming, cheerful, clean-cut, cultured, dazzling, decorous, delicate, especial, esthetic, eximious, fabulous, faithful, five-star, flawless, four-star, frabjous, friendly, generous, glorious, graceful, gracious, heavenly, humorous, inviting, jim-dandy, ladylike, laudable, likeable, obliging, pleasant, pleasing, polished, slam-bang, smashing, splendid, standout, sterling, stickout, superior, tasteful, terrific, ticklish, top-level, topnotch, very good, virtuous, well-bred, wondrous **9** admirable, agreeable, befitting, bodacious, civilized, courteous, delicious, Endsville, excellent, exemplary, exquisite, faultless, favorable, first-rate, high-grade, hunky-dory, marvelous, reputable, simpatico, sollicker, succulent, top-flight, wonderful **10** acceptable, attractive, beneficial, charitable, creditable, cultivated, delightful, fastidious, first-class, hotsy-totsy, jack-a-dandy, methodical, meticulous, out of sight, particular, peachy-keen, personable, phenomenal, remarkable, satisfying, scrupulous, stupendous, super-duper
insincerely ~: **4** oily **6** greasy, smarmy **7** servile **8** unctuous **10** obsequious
make ~: **3** pat **6** caress, soothe **7** appease
Nelly: **4** prig **7** puritan **8** bluenose **10** goody-goody
no ~ guy: **4** ogre **5** meany **6** meanie
nice __: **5** as pie, nelly
__ nice: **4** make
Nice: **4** city, town
locale: **6** France
port near ~: **7** Antibes
Nice __: **5** 'n' Easy
Nice __!: **5** catch, going
Nice __ With You: **4** to Be
__ Nice Clambake: **5** A Real
__ nice day!: **5** Have a
Nice Girl? (1941 film)
cast: Walter Brennan, Deanna Durbin, Franchot Tone
Nice guys finish __: **4** last
nicely: **8** worthily
Nice 'N' __: **4** Easy
Nicene __: **5** Creed **7** Council
Nicene Council concern: **6** heresy
__ nice place to visit...: **4** It's a
Nice & Slow (1998 song) artist: Usher
niceties: **5** mores **7** decency, decorum, details, nuances **8** courtesy, minutiae, protocol **9** etiquette, fine print, gentility, politesse, propriety, punctilio **10** convention, politeness, refinement, seemliness
Nice to Be With You (1972 song)
artist: Gallery
__ Nice to Have a Man...: **5** It's So
nicety: **5** point **6** detail, nuance **8** ceremony, quiddity, subtlety **9** fine point, punctilio **10** refinement
Nice Work if You Can Get It composer: **8** Gershwin
niche: **3** bay, job **4** hole, nest, nook, room, slot **5** cubby, place **6** alcove, corner, cranny, hollow, recess **7** calling, opening **8** position, vocation **9** cubbyhole, specialty **10** pigeonhole
Nichelle: **7** Nichols
Nicholas: **3** Ray **4** Gage, Paul, pope, Rowe, tsar **5** Brady, Meyer, saint **6** Biddle, Denise, Fayard, Harold **7** Boileau, Brendon, Pileggi, pontiff, Webster **9** Colasanto
in German: **5** Klaus
in Italian: **6** Nicola
Nicholas, Denise: **7** actress
film: Blacula (1972)
A Piece of the Action (1977)
TV: In the Heat of the Night, Room 222
Nicholas Nickleby
author: Charles Dickens
character: **3** Peg **4** Bray, Kate, Knag, Pyke **5** Celia, Edwin, Fanny, Gride, Noggs, Ralph, Smike **7** Matilda, Squeers
Nicholas Nickleby actor: **4** Rees
Nichols: **3** Kid, Red **4** Anne, Mike **5** Peter **8** Nichelle
Nichols, Anne hero: **4** Abie
Nichols, Mike: **8** director
collaborator: Elaine May
film: Biloxi Blues (1988)
the birdcage (1995)
Carnal Knowledge (1971)
Catch-22 (1970)
The Graduate (1967, AA)
Heartburn (1986)
Postcards From the Edge (1990)
Primary Colors (1998)
Regarding Henry (1991)
Silkwood (1983)
What Planet Are You From? (2000)
Who's Afraid of Virginia Woolf? (1966)
Wolf (1994)
Working Girl (1988)
spouse: Diane Sawyer
Nicholson, Jack: **5** actor
film: As Good as It Gets (1997, AA)
Batman (1989)
The Border (1982)
Carnal Knowledge (1971)
Chinatown (1974)
Easy Rider (1969)
A Few Good Men (1992)
Five Easy Pieces (1970)
Goin' South (1978)
Heartburn (1986)
Hoffa (1992)
Ironweed (1987)
The King of Marvin Gardens (1972)
The Last Detail (1973)
Mars Attacks! (1996)
One Flew Over the Cuckoo's Nest (1975, AA)
The Pledge (2001)
Prizzi's Honor (1985)
Reds (1981)
The Shining (1980)
The Shooting (1967)
Terms of Endearment (1983, AA)
The Two Jakes (1990)
The Witches of Eastwick (1987)
Wolf (1994)
Nichols, Peter: **7** English **10** playwright
Nichols, Red: **9** trumpeter
genre: **4** jazz
Nichrome: **5** alloy
component: **4** iron **6** nickel **8** chromium
nicht __: **4** wahr
nick: **3** con, cut, jag, mar **4** bilk, chip, dent, ding, dupe, gaol, hurt, jail, mark, rook, scar, slit, snip **5** cheat, gouge, knock, notch, score, swipe, trick, wound **6** damage, delude, fleece, incise, injury, take in **7** defraud, mislead, scratch, swindle, two-time **8** flimflam, hoodwink, puncture, sucker in **9** bamboozle, victimize
cause: **5** razor
ender: **4** name
in the ~ of time: **6** barely **9** opportune **10** felicitous
Nick: **4** Lowe **5** Adams, Faldo, Nolte, Price, Stahl **6** Gilder, Lachey, Searcy **7** Ashford, Charles, Clooney **10** Buoniconti, Cassavetes
dog: **4** Asta
wife: **4** Nora
Nick __ Forte: **6** Apollo
__ Nick: **3** Old **5** Saint

Nick at Nite staple: 5 rerun
nickel: 4 cash, coin **5** bread, dough, metal, money **6** change **7** element
  alloy: 5 Invar, Monel **6** alnico **7** Elinvar, Inconel, Mumetal, nitinol **8** electrum, kamacite, Manganin, Nichrome **9** barberite, Platinite, platinoid, white gold **10** constantan, superalloy
  bad ~: 4 slug
  ender: 5 odeon
  like a new ~: 5 shiny **6** bright
  ore: 9 millerite, niccolite
  word on a ~: 3 God **4** five, unum **5** cents, trust **7** liberty **8** pluribus
nickel ___: 5 oxide, plate, steel **6** silver **7** acetate
nickel-___ battery: 7 cadmium
___ nickel: 4 plug **7** plugged
___-nickel: 6 double
nickel-and-___: 4 dime
nickelodeon
  heroine: 6 damsel
  opening: 4 slot
Nickelodeon (1976 film)
  cast: Ryan O'Neal, Tatum O'Neal, Burt Reynolds
  director: Peter Bogdanovich
Nicklaus, Jack: 6 golfer **10** Golden Bear
  alma mater: 3 OSU
  milieu: 5 links **6** course
  org.: 3 PGA
  rival: 6 Palmer, Player
Nickleby portrayer: 4 Rees
nickname: 3 dub, tag **5** alias, label **6** handle **7** entitle, epithet, intitle, moniker **8** cognomen, monicker **9** sobriquet **10** diminutive
  in Spanish: 4 mote
Nick News (Nickelodeon) host: Linda Ellerbee
nick of ___: 4 time
Nick of Time singer: 5 Raitt
Nickolas: 7 Ashford
Nicks, Stevie
  member: Fleetwood Mac
  song: Edge of Seventeen (1982)
    I Can't Wait (1986)
    If Anyone Falls (1983)
    Leather and Lace (1981)
    Rooms on Fire (1989)
    Stand Back (1983)
    Stop Draggin' My Heart Around (1981)
    Talk to Me (1985)
Nicobar: 4 isls. **5** isles **7** islands
  locale: 5 India
Nicol: 10 Williamson
Nicolai: 4 Otto
Nicolaou: 3 Ted
Nicolas: 4 Cage, Roeg **6** Appert **7** Leblanc, Poussin
  aunt: 5 Talia
  see also French
Nicolás: 7 Guillén
Nicolaus: 10 Copernicus
Nicolay: 5 Basov
Nicole: 6 Eggert, Kidman
___ Nicole Carson: 4 Lisa
Nicolet: 4 Jean
Nicolette: 6 Larson **8** Sheridan
Nicolle, Charles: 6 French **8** Nobelist
Nicollette: 8 Sheridan
Nicolo: 5 Amati
Nicolson: 5 Adela
Nicosia: 4 city, town **7** capital
  locale: 6 Cyprus
nicotinic ___: 4 acid
nictate: 4 wink **5** blink
nictitate: 4 wink **5** blink
___ Nidal: 3 Abu
Nidetch: 4 Jean
nidge: 6 quiver
___ Nidre: 3 Kol
nidus: 4 nest **6** hotbed
  builder: 4 wasp **6** insect, spider
Niebuhr: 8 Reinhold
niece: 3 kin **5** woman **7** kinsman **8** relative **9** kinswoman
  maybe: 4 heir **9** inheritor
  starter: 5 grand
___-niece: 5 great
Niekro: 3 Joe **4** Phil
Niekro, Phil: 6 hurler **7** pitcher
Niels: 4 Bohr **5** Jerne **6** Finsen
Nielsen: 4 Rick **5** rater **6** Arthur, Leslie **8** Brigitte
  family need: 2 TV **5** TV set **10** television
  letters: 3 ABC, CBS, Fox, NBC, UPN
Nielsen ___: 6 rating
Nielsen, Brigitte spouse: Sylvester Stallone
Nielsen, Leslie: 5 actor
  film: Airplane! (1980)
    Dark Intruder (1965)
    Forbidden Planet (1956)
    The Naked Gun (1988)
    The Naked Gun 2 1/2 (1991)
    Naked Gun 33 1/3 (1994)
    The Poseidon Adventure (1972)
    Prom Night (1980)
    The Sheepman (1958)
    Spy Hard (1996)
    Tammy and the Bachelor (1957)
Niemen: 5 river
  locale: 6 Russia
Nietzsche, Friedrich: 4 poet **6** German **11** philosopher
  concept: 10 Ubermensch
  work: Beyond Good and Evil
    Thus Spake Zarathustra
nifty: 4 chic, cool, good, keen, neat, nice **5** dandy, great, marvy, neato, quick, sharp, smart, super, swell **6** adroit, clever, dapper, far-out, groovy, peachy, spruce **7** corking, stylish, voguish **8** pleasing, terrific **9** agreeable, enjoyable, excellent, ingenious, marvelous **10** out of sight, peachy-keen
Nigel: 5 Bruce, Green **6** Havers **7** Patrick **9** Davenport, Hawthorne
Niger: 5 river **6** nation **7** country
  bovine: 4 Kuri
  capital: 6 Niamey
  city: 6 Agadez, Maradi, Niamey, Tahoua, Zinder
  city on the ~: 8 Timbuktu
  delta resident: 3 Ijo
  lake: 4 Chad
  language of ~: 5 Hausa
  money: 5 franc
  neighbor: 4 Chad, Mali **5** Benin, Libya **7** Algeria, Nigeria
  people: 3 Ebo, Ibo **4** Eboe, Igbo **5** Hausa **6** Haussa, Kanuri, Tuareg **7** Songhai
  River locale: 4 Mali **6** Guinea **7** Nigeria
  river to the ~: 5 Benue
Nigeria: 6 nation **7** country
  bovine: 4 Kuri
  capital: 5 Abuja
  city: 3 Aba, Ede, Ife, Ila, Oyo **4** Kano **5** Abuja, Lagos, Zaria **6** Ibadan, Ilesha, Ilorin, Kaduna **9** Benin City
  district: 5 Benin
  former ~ region: 6 Biafra
  lake: 4 Chad
  language: 3 Ebo, Gbe, Ibo **4** Eboe, Igbo **6** Ibibio
  locale: 6 Africa
  money: 4 kobo **5** naira
  neighbor: 4 Chad **5** Benin, Niger **8** Cameroon
  Nobelist in Literature: 7 Soyinka
  org.: 4 OPEC
  people: 3 Ebo, Edo, Ibo, Ijo, Tiv **4** Bini, Eboe, Efik, Ekoi, Fula, Igbo, Ijaw, Yedo **5** Gbari, Gwari, Hausa, Yeddo **6** Fulani, Haussa, Ibibio, Kanuri, Yoruba
  singer: 4 Sade
  writer: 5 Aluko, Amadi, Nwapa, Okara **6** Achebe **7** Ekwensi, Equiano, Munonye, Soyinka
niggle: 4 carp **5** argue, cavil, gripe **6** bicker, dabble, tinker **7** nitpick, quibble **8** pettifog, squabble **9** criticize **10** play around, split hairs
niggling: 4 puny **5** least, petty **6** measly **7** trivial **8** piddling, trifling
nigh: 4 most, near, soon **5** anear, close **6** almost, at hand, hard by, nearby, nearly **7** close by, looming **8** adjacent, imminent **9** bordering, impending, in the wind, presently, proximate, virtually **10** convenient
___-nigh: 4 well
night: 4 dark **5** gloom **6** sunset **7** bedtime, evening, sundown **8** darkness, eventide, twilight, wee hours **9** after dark, nocturnal, pitch dark **10** after hours
  and day: 7 nonstop **9** endlessly **10** unendingly
  attire: 3 PJs **4** gown, robe **6** kimono **7** jammies, pajamas **8** lingerie, negligee
  before: 3 eve
  biter: 6 bedbug
  combining form: 4 noct-, nyct- **5** nocti-, nycti-, nycto-
  dance all ~: 5 party, revel **9** celebrate, make merry
  display: 6 aurora
  duty: 5 vigil
  ender: 3 cap, jar **4** club, fall, glow, gown, hawk, life, long, mare, spot, time, wear **5** dress, rider, scape, shade, shift, shirt, stand, stick **7** clothes
  end of the ~: 4 dawn **5** sunup **7** sunrise
  flyer: 3 bat, owl **4** moth
  hunter: 5 civet
  in French: 4 nuit
  in German: 5 nacht
  in Spanish: 5 noche
  light: 4 neon, star
  name meaning ~: 5 Leila
  opening ~: 5 debut **8** premiere
  place to spend the ~: 3 bed, inn, pad **4** room **5** B and B, hotel, motel **6** hostel **8** motor inn **10** motor lodge
  preceder: 4 dusk **6** sunset **7** sundown **8** twilight
  prepare to spend the ~: 6 encamp
  Roman goddess of ~: 3 Nox
  shade: 4 ebon **5** sable
  sound: 3 ZZZ **5** snore
  spot: 3 bar, bed **4** bunk, café, dive, spot **5** boîte, disco, joint, venue **6** bistro, casino, tavern **7** cabaret **8** hideaway **9** honky-tonk, roadhouse, speakeasy **10** restaurant, supper club
  starter: 3 mid, twi **4** fort, over, week
  they're counted at ~: 5 sheep
  three-dog ~: 3 raw **6** chilly, frigid, wintry **7** wintery **8** freezing
  to poets: 3 e'en
  watchman: 5 guard **6** sentry **7** lookout
night ___: 3 key, owl **4** bolt, robe, soil **5** coach, court, heron, latch, light, raven, shift, snake, stick, table, watch **6** editor, letter, lizard, monkey, office, person, school **7** crawler, jasmine
___ night: 4 bank, dish, good **5** first, watch **6** school **7** amateur, opening
___-night: 3 all **4** late **5** fly-by **6** nighty
Night ___: 4 Mail **5** Court, Fever, Magic, Moves, Music, Nurse, Shift, Train, World **6** and Day, Chills, Flight, People, Ranger **7** Gallery, Journey, Passage
Night ___ a Thousand Eyes, The: 3 Has
Night ___ Lane: 5 Train
Night ___, The: 4 Owls **5** Flier **6** Walker **7** Awakens
___ Night: 3 One **4** Last, Prom, Wild **5** Such a **6** Fright, Ladies, Lonely, Silent, Starry **7** Another, Endless, Opening, Twelfth
Night (1960 song) artist: Jackie Wilson
Night and Day (1946 film): 7 musical
  cast: Cary Grant, Alexis Smith
  director: Michael Curtiz
Night and Day composer: 6 Porter
Night at the Opera, A (1935 film)
  cast: Kitty Carlisle, Margaret Dumont, Allan Jones, Chico Marx, Groucho Marx, Harpo Marx
  director: Sam Wood
  role: 4 Otis, Rosa **6** Baroni **7** Tomasso **8** Claypool, Fiorello **9** Driftwood
  song: 5 Alone **8** Cosi Cosa
Night at the Vulcan author: Ngaio Marsh
Night author: Elie Wiesel
Night Awakens, The author: Mary Higgins Clark
nightcap: 4 game **5** drink **8** libation
Night Chicago Died, The (1974 song) artist: Paper Lace
Night Chills author: Dean Koontz
nightclothes: 3 PJs **4** gown, robe **6** kimono **7** jammies, pajamas **8** lingerie, negligee
nightclub: 3 bar **4** café, dive, spot **5** boîte, disco, joint, venue **6** bistro, casino **7** cabaret **8** hideaway **9** honky-tonk, roadhouse, speakeasy **10** restaurant
  charge: 5 cover
  New York ~: 4 Copa
  number: 4 song **6** ballad
  production: 3 act **5** revue **6** review
  worker: 2 MC **5** B-girl, comic, emcee **6** singer, waiter **8** comedian, waitress **9** bartender
Night Court (NBC sitcom)
  cast: Harry Anderson (Judge Harry Stone)
    Selma Diamond (Selma Hacker)
    John Larroquette (Dan Fielding)
    Richard Moll (Bailiff Bull Shannon)
    Markie Post (Christine Sullivan)
    Marsha Warfield (Bailiff Roz Russell)
nightcrawler: 4 bait, worm
___-night doubleheader: 3 twi
___-nighter: 3 all
___ Nighter: 5 First
nightfall: 4 dark, dusk **6** curfew, sunset **7** day's end, evening, sundown **8** darkness, eventide, gloaming, moonrise, twilight **10** crepuscule
Nightfall (1956 film)
  cast: Anne Bancroft, Brian Keith, Aldo Ray
Night Fever (1978 song) artist: Bee Gees
Night Flight author: Antoine de Saint-Exupéry
Night Gallery (NBC sci-fi) host: Rod Serling
nightgown: 8 lingerie **10** sleep shirt
Night Has a Thousand Eyes, The (1962 song) artist: Bobby Vee
nighthawk: 4 bird

Nighthawks (1981 film)
cast: Sylvester Stallone, Lindsay Wagner, Billy Dee Williams
nightie: **8** lingerie
Night in Casablanca, A (1946 film)
cast: Chico Marx, Groucho Marx, Harpo Marx
nightingale: **4** bird **6** bulbul, singer
Nightingale: **5** nurse **6** Maxine **8** Florence
prop: **4** lamp
Nightingale (1975 song) artist: Carole King
Nightingale, Maxine
song: Lead Me On (1979)
Right Back Where We Started From (1976)
__ Night in the Tropics: **3** One
Night Into Morning (1951 film)
cast: Nancy Davis, John Hodiak, Ray Milland
__ Night, Irene: **4** Good
nightjar: **4** bird **10** goatsucker
__ Night, Ladies: **4** Good
Nightline
name: **3** Ted **6** Koppel
network: **3** ABC **5** ABC-TV
__ Night Long: **3** All
nightly: **9** after dark, nocturnal
Night Magic author: Thomas Tryon
Night Mail author: W.H. Auden
nightmare: **4** bane, hell **5** dream, trial **6** blight, ordeal, plague, vision **7** bugbear, incubus **8** bad dream, calamity, disaster, illusion **9** detriment, ruination
Nightmare __: **5** Abbey, Alley **7** Journey
Nightmare Abbey author: Thomas Peacock
Nightmare Alley (1947 film)
cast: Joan Blondell, Tyrone Power
Nightmare in Pink author: John D. MacDonald
Nightmare Journey author: Dean Koontz
Nightmare on Elm Street, A (1984 film)
cast: Ronee Blakley, Heather Langenkamp, John Saxon
director: Wes Craven
nightmarish: **4** dire **5** awful, scary, weird **6** creepy, horrid **7** ghastly, surreal **8** alarming, dreadful, horrible **9** frightful, harrowing, unearthly **10** terrifying
'Night, Mother: **4** film, play
author: Marsha Norman
cast: Anne Bancroft, Sissy Spacek
Night Moves (1975 film)
cast: Susan Clark, Gene Hackman, Jennifer Warren
director: Arthur Penn
Night Moves (1977 song) artist: Bob Seger
__ Night Music, A: **6** Little
Night Music author: Clifford Odets
Night Must Fall (1937 film)
cast: Robert Montgomery, Rosalind Russell, May Whitty
Night Nurse (1931 film)
cast: Joan Blondell, Ben Lyon, Barbara Stanwyck
director: William Wellman
Night of Camp David author: Fletcher Knebel
Night of the Grizzly, The actor: **3** Ely **4** Elam, Hyer
Night of the Hunter, The (1955 film)
cast: Lillian Gish, Robert Mitchum, Shelley Winters
director: Charles Laughton
screenwriter: **4** Agee
Night of the Iguana, The: **4** film, play
author: Tennessee Williams
cast: Richard Burton, Ava Gardner, Deborah Kerr
director: John Huston
Night of the Living Dead (1968 film)
director: George A. Romero
Night of the Moonbow author: Thomas Tryon
Night on Bald Mountain, A composer: **10** Mussorgsky
Night on Earth (1991 film)
cast: Giancarlo Esposito, Gena Rowlands, Winona Ryder
director: Jim Jarmusch
Night Over Taos author: Maxwell Anderson
Night Passage (1957 film)
cast: Dan Duryea, Audie Murphy, James Stewart
Night People (1954 film)
cast: Broderick Crawford, Gregory Peck
director: Nunnally Johnson
__ Nights: **6** Boogie, Summer **7** Endless
Nights Are Forever Without You (1976 song) artist: England Dan and John Ford Coley
nightshade: **4** weed **5** plant **6** datura
__ nightshade: **5** black, woody **6** deadly
Night Shift (1982 film)
cast: Michael Keaton, Shelley Long, Henry Winkler
director: Ron Howard
Nightshift (1985 song) artist: Commodores
Night Shift author: Stephen King
nightshirt, British: **4** sark
Nights in White Satin (1972 song)
artist: Moody Blues
Nights on Broadway (1975 song)
artist: Bee Gees
nightspot: **3** bar **4** café, dive, spot **5** boîte, disco, joint, venue **6** bistro, casino **7** cabaret **8** hideaway, taphouse **9** honky-tonk, roadhouse, speakeasy **10** restaurant, supper club
nightstick: **4** club **5** baton **6** cudgel **8** bludgeon **9** billy club, truncheon
__ Night, Sweetheart: **4** Good
Night the Lights Went Out in Georgia, The (1973 song) artist: Vicki Lawrence
Night They Drove Old Dixie Down, The (1971 song) artist: Joan Baez
Night They Invented Champagne, The
composer: **5** Loewe **6** Lerner
musical: **4** Gigi
Night They Raided Minsky's, The (1968 film)
cast: Britt Ekland, Jason Robards, Norman Wisdom
director: William Friedkin
nighttime: **3** eve **7** evening **8** eventide, twilight, wee hours **9** after dark **10** after hours
to a poet: **3** e'en
Night to Remember, A (1943 film)
cast: Brian Aherne, Jeff Donnell, Loretta Young
director: Richard Wallace
Night Train: **4** Lane
Night Walker, The (1964 film)
cast: Lloyd Bochner, Barbara Stanwyck, Robert Taylor
Nightwatch (1998 film)
cast: Patricia Arquette, Josh Brolin, Ewan McGregor, Nick Nolte
nightwear: **3** PJs **7** jammies, pajamas
Nightwood author: **6** Barnes
Night World (1932 film)
cast: Lew Ayres, Mae Clarke, Boris Karloff
NIH
department: **3** HHS
part: **3** Nat. **4** Inst., Natl. **6** Health **8** National **10** Institutes
Nihal: **4** star
nihilism: **6** denial **7** anarchy, atheism, mob rule **8** disorder **9** disbelief, nonbelief, rejection, terrorism **10** skepticism
nihilist: **5** rebel **7** radical, sceptic, skeptic **8** ultraist
nihilistic: **7** lawless, radical
nihility: **4** hole, void, zero **5** abyss **6** vacuum **7** vacuity
Niigata: **4** city, port, town
locale: **5** Japan
Niiza: **4** city, town
locale: **5** Japan
Nijinsky, Vaslav: **6** dancer **7** danseur
specialty: **5** dance **6** ballet
Nik: **7** Kershaw
Nike: **6** sneaks **7** missile **8** sneakers
endorser: **5** Tiger, Woods **7** athlete
parent of ~: **4** Ares, Styx **6** Pallas
rival: **4** Avia, Keds **6** Adidas, Etonic, Reebok
swoosh: **4** logo
Niki: **5** Lauda
Nikita: **10** Khrushchev
see also Russian
Nikita (1986 song) artist: Elton John
Nikki: **3** Cox **8** Giovanni
Nikola: **5** Tesla
Nikolaas: **9** Tinbergen
Nikolai: **5** Gogol **8** Berdyaev
see also Russian
Nikolai __-Korsakov: **6** Rimsky
Nikolaidi: **5** Elena
Nikolaus: **4** Otto
Nikolay: **7** Semenov **8** Karamzin, Nekrasov **10** Zabolotsky
Nikon: **3** SLR **6** camera
rival: **4** Fuji **5** Canon, Kodak, Leica **6** Konica, Pentax, Rollei **7** Minolta, Olympus, Vivitar, Yashica **8** Polaroid
nil: **3** nix, zip **4** nada, none, zero **5** aught, ought, zilch, zippo **6** bubkes, bupkis, cipher, naught, nought **7** nothing **8** goose egg **9** valueless
in Spanish: **4** nada
nil __ bonum: **4** nisi
nil __ numine: **4** sine
Nile: **4** blue **5** green, river **6** battle **8** greenish
ancient ~ city: **4** Sais **5** Meroe, Tanis **6** Thebes
ancient ~ kingdom: **5** Nubia
annual ~ event: **5** flood
city on the ~: **4** Giza **5** Aswan, Asyut, Cairo, Luxor, Tanta **6** Assiut, Assuan **7** Assouan **10** Alexandria
dam: **5** Aswan
denizen: **4** croc, ibis
desert bordering the ~: **6** Sahara
feature: **4** bank **5** delta
feeder: **6** Atbara
gift: **4** silt
island: **6** Philae
locale: **5** Egypt, Sudan **6** Africa
obstruction: **4** sudd
people: **5** Dinka
queen: **4** Cleo
relative: **4** anil, cyan, navy, teal **5** Alice, azure, slate **6** cobalt, indigo, raisin, violet **7** peacock **8** cerulean, sapphire **9** turquoise **10** aquamarine, periwinkle
reptile: **3** asp
symbol of life: **4** ankh
Nile __: **4** blue **5** green
__ Nile: **4** Blue **5** White
Niles: **4** city, town
locale: **4** Ohio **8** Illinois
Niles Crane wife: **5** Maris
nilgai: **8** antelope
relative: **3** gnu, kob **4** guib, kudu, oryx, puku, topi **5** addax, bongo, chiru, eland, goral, korin, nyala, oribi, saiga, serow **6** chammy, dikdik, duiker, impala, koodoo, lechwe, rhebok, shammy, shamoy **7** blaubok, blesbok, chamois, defassa, gazelle, gemsbok, gerenuk, grysbok, sassaby **8** blesbuck, bontebok, bushbuck, gemsbuck, reedbuck, steenbok, steinbok **9** blackbuck, pronghorn, sitatunga, springbok, waterbuck **10** hartebeest, wildebeest
__-nilly: **5** willy
Nils: **5** Dalén **6** Asther **7** Lofgren
Nilsson: **3** Ulf **5** Harry **6** Birgit
song: Coconut (1972)
Everybody's Talkin' (1969)
Without You (1972)
Nilsson, Birgit: **6** singer **7** soprano, Swedish
specialty: **5** opera
nim: **4** game
__ 'n' image: **4** spit
Nimari: **3** cow **4** bull **6** bovine, cattle
nimbi: **5** auras, halos **6** clouds, haloes
nimble: **4** deft, pert, spry **5** adept, agile, alert, brisk, canny, fleet, handy, light, lithe, quick, sharp, slick, smart, swift **6** active, adroit, au fait, clever, dapper, expert, limber, lissom, lively, speedy **7** capable, lissome, skilled, trained **8** dextrous, graceful, masterly, seasoned, skillful **9** competent, dexterous, efficient, lightsome, lithesome, masterful, sprightly **10** proficient
nimbleness: **4** ease **5** skill **7** agility **8** deftness, legerity **9** adeptness, dexterity, handiness, quickness **10** adroitness
nimbostratus: **5** cloud
nimbus: **4** aura, halo **5** cloud **7** aureola, aureole **8** gloriole
product: **4** rain, snow
NIMBY
part of ~: **3** not **4** back, yard
Nîmes: **4** city, town
locale: **6** France
neighbor: **4** Alès
nimiety: **4** glut **6** excess **7** surfeit, surplus **8** plethora **9** profusion **10** oversupply
niminy-__: **6** piminy
Nimitz: **7** Chester
org.: **3** USN
__ Nimitz: **3** USS
Nimoy, Leonard: **5** actor **8** director
film: 3 Men and a Baby (1987)
The Good Mother (1988)
Invasion of the Body Snatchers (1978)
Star Trek III: The Search for Spock (1984)
Star Trek II: The Wrath of Khan (1982)
Star Trek IV: The Voyage Home (1986)
Star Trek-The Motion Picture (1979)
Star Trek VI: The Undiscovered Country (1991)
role: **5** Paris, Spock
TV: Mission: Impossible, Star Trek
Nimrod: **6** hunter
father of ~: **4** Cush
grandfather of ~: **4** Noah
Nims, John Frederick: **4** poet
Nimzowitsch: **4** Aron
Nina: **4** Foch **5** Ricci **6** Simone **7** Persson
in English: **3** Ann
Niña: **4** boat, ship
companion: **5** Pinta **10** Santa Maria

Nin, Anaïs: 6 author, French, writer
work: Cities of the Interior
Collages
The Delta of Venus
The Diary of Anaïs Nin
Glass Bell
Ladders to Fire
Little Birds
Solar Barque
A Spy in the House of Love
Under a Glass Bell
Winter of Artifice
niña's parent: 5 madre, padre
nincompoop: 3 ass, nit, oaf 4 bozo, dodo, dolt, dope, fool, gowk, jerk, simp, twit, yo-yo 5 dummy, dunce, goose, ninny, schmo 6 dimwit, lubber, lummox, nitwit, schmoe 7 dingbat, dullard, jackass, pinhead 8 bonehead, dumbbell, lunkhead, meathead 9 birdbrain, blockhead, ding-a-ling, harebrain, simpleton 10 dunderhead
nine: 5 digit 6 ennead, number
cloud ~: 6 heaven 7 rapture 8 paradise
combining form: 3 non- 4 nona- 5 ennea-
ender: 3 pin 4 bark, teen
group of ~: 5 nonet 6 ennead
inches: 4 span
in French: 4 neuf
in German: 4 neun
in Italian: 4 nove
in Japanese: 3 kyu
in Portuguese: 4 nove
in Spanish: 5 nueve
on cloud ~: 4 glad, high 5 happy, merry 6 blithe, cheery, elated, jovial, joyful, joyous, upbeat 7 gleeful, pleased, tickled 8 blissful, cheerful, ecstatic, euphoric, exultant, jubilant, mirthful, thrilled 9 delighted, overjoyed, rapturous, rejoicing, rhapsodic
one of ~: 4 Clio, Muse 5 Erato 6 inning, Thalia, Urania 7 Euterpe 8 Calliope 9 Melpomene 10 Polyhymnia 11 Terpsichore
put on cloud ~: 5 cheer, elate, exult 6 buck up, perk up, uplift 7 cheer up, delight, gladden, hearten 8 inspirit 10 exhilarate
to Mohs: 8 corundum
whole ~ yards: 3 all 4 a to z 5 whole 8 entirety 10 everything
nine __: 4 ball, iron
nine __ wonder: 4 days'
__ nine: 4 back 5 cloud, front
Nine, __ big fat hen: 4 ten a
__ Nine: 5 Cloud 6 Sacred
ninebark: 5 shrub
relative: 4 rose, sloe 6 kerria, spirea 7 bramble, jetbead, spiraea 8 hardhack, photinia 9 firethorn, raspberry
nine-digit number: 3 SSN, Zip
nine-headed monster: 5 hydra
Nine Inch Nails
member: Trent Reznor
song: The Day the World Went Away (1999)
nine-iron, use a: 4 loft
Nine Lives cat: 6 Morris
Nine Months (1995 film)
cast: Tom Arnold, Joan Cusack, Jeff Goldblum, Hugh Grant, Julianne Moore
director: Chris Columbus
ninepins: 4 game 5 sport 7 bowling
__-niner: 5 forty
__ nines: 5 to the
Nine Tailors, The author: Dorothy Sayers
__-nine-tails: 4 cat-o'
Nineteen Eighty-Four (1984 film)
cast: Richard Burton, Suzanna Hamilton, John Hurt
nineteenth __: 4 hole
__ Nineties, The: 3 Gay 7 Naughty
nine-to-five: 3 job 4 toil, work 5 grind 8 position, vocation 10 livelihood
Nine to Five (1980 film)
cast: Dabney Coleman, Jane Fonda, Dolly Parton, Lily Tomlin
nine-to-fiver: 6 worker 8 employee 10 blue collar, wage earner
cry: 4 TGIF
Ninette: 8 De Valois
ninety-__ wonder: 3 day
Ninety-Eight: 3 car 4 auto, Olds 10 automobile, Oldsmobile
Ninety-Five Theses author: Martin Luther
Nineveh: 4 city
locale: 4 Irak, Iraq 7 Assyria
river: 6 Tigris
Nine Women author: Shirley Ann Grau
__ Nine Yards, The: 5 Whole
Ninja Turtles: 7 quartet
home: 5 sewer
meal: 5 pizza
ninny: 3 ass, nit, oaf, sap 4 boob, clod, ditz, dolt, fool, gowk, jerk, simp 5 chump, clown, cluck, dummy, dunce, goose, joker, patsy, stupe 6 dimwit, lubber, lummox, nitwit, sucker, turkey 7 buffoon, dingbat, dullard, fathead, halfwit, jackass, pinhead, saphead 8 bonehead, dumbbell, meathead, numskull 9 birdbrain, blockhead, harebrain, lamebrain, numbskull, simpleton 10 dunderhead, nincompoop
in French: 3 ane
niño: 3 boy, lad, tot 7 Spanish
Nino: 4 Rota 5 Tempo 9 Benvenuti
ninon: 5 voile 6 fabric 7 chiffon
Ninotchka (1939 film)
cast: Ina Claire, Melvyn Douglas, Greta Garbo, Bela Lugosi
director: Ernst Lubitsch
Nintendo: 4 game 9 video game
competitor: 4 Sega
fanatic: 5 gamer
hero: 5 Mario
predecessor: 5 Atari
Ninth Configuration, The (1980 film)
cast: Stacy Keach, Jason Miller, Scott Wilson
director: William Peter Blatty
Niobe
brother of ~: 6 Pelops 7 Broteas
father of ~: 8 Tantalus
husband of ~: 7 Amphion
like ~: 5 teary, weepy 10 lachrymose
lover of ~: 4 Zeus
son of ~: 5 Argus 7 Amyclas
niobium: 5 metal 7 element
ore: 9 columbite
Niobrara: 5 river
locale: 7 Wyoming 8 Nebraska
Niort: 4 city, town
locale: 6 France
nip: 3 sip, tip 4 bite, clip, dash, dram, drop, lift, shot, slug, snap, snip, spot, stop, tang 5 catch, check, chill, nab at, pinch, snort, taste, tweak 6 arrest, nibble, thieve, thwart, tip-off 7 soupçon, squeeze, swallow 8 compress, cut short, piquancy, pungency, spoonful 9 briskness, crispness, frustrate, jiggerful, sharpness 10 frostiness
and tuck: 5 close, tight
in sports: 4 edge 6 defeat 7 nose out
in the air: 4 bite, cold 5 chill
in the bud: 4 foil, halt, stem, stop 5 avert, quash 6 arrest, put out, scotch 7 obviate, prevent, put down, squelch 8 preclude, stamp out 9 forestall 10 extinguish, put an end to
more than a ~: 4 swig
partner: 4 tuck
starter: 3 cat
nipa: 4 palm 6 thatch
palm: 4 atap
Nipawin: 4 city, town
locale: 6 Canada
Nipigon: 4 lake
locale: 6 Canada 7 Ontario
Nipmuck: 6 Indian 7 Amerind
nipper: 3 dog 4 baby 5 child, kiddy
nose: 9 Jack Frost
Nipper company: 3 RCA
Nippon: 5 Japan
nippy: 3 icy 4 cold, cool 5 brisk, chill, crisp, polar 6 arctic, biting, chilly, frigid, frosty, frozen, wintry 7 glacial, numbing, shivery, wintery 8 freezing
__ Nips: 6 Cheese
Nipsey: 7 Russell
Nirenberg, Marshall: 8 Nobelist
Nirvana: 4 Eden 5 bliss 6 heaven 7 Elysium, rapture
attainer: 5 arhat
members: Cobain, Novoselic, Grohl
seeker: 5 Hindu 6 Hindoo
song: About a Girl (1994)
Come As You Are (1992)
Smells Like Teen Spirit (1991)
Nis: 4 city, town
locale: 10 Yugoslavia
Nisan: 5 month 6 Hebrew
follower: 4 Iyar 5 Iyyar
preceder: 4 Adar
Nisei's parent: 5 Issei
'N' Is for Noose author: Sue Grafton
__ nisi bonum: 3 nil
Nissan: 3 car 4 auto 10 automobile
competitor: 5 Mazda
formerly: 6 Datsun
model: 5 Quest 6 Altima, Axxess, Maxima, Murano, Pulsar, Sentra, Stanza, Xterra 8 Frontier 10 Pathfinder
nisse: 3 elf 5 pixie 6 sprite 7 brownie 10 leprechaun
Nissen __: 3 hut
nit: 3 bug, oaf 4 boob, dodo, dolt, fool, jerk 5 cluck, dunce, louse, ninny 6 dimwit, insect 7 airhead, buffoon, dullard, halfwit, jackass, pinhead 8 bonehead, dumbbell, lunkhead, meathead 9 birdbrain, blockhead, ignoramus, lamebrain, numbskull, simpleton 10 dunderhead, nincompoop
ender: 3 wit 4 pick, rite 6 picker
Nita: 5 Naldi 6 Talbot
Nite and Day (1988 song) artist: Al B. Sure
niter: 7 mineral
Niterói: 4 city, town
locale: 6 Brazil
nitid: 5 shiny 6 bright, glossy, lucent 7 lambent, radiant, shining 8 lustrous 9 effulgent, refulgent
nitinol: 5 alloy
component: 6 nickel 8 titanium
nitpick: 3 nag 4 carp 5 cavil, whine 6 jibe at, niggle 7 quibble 8 pettifog 9 criticize, find fault 10 split hairs
nitpicker: 3 nag 4 prig 6 critic 8 stickler 10 fussbudget
nit-picking: 4 prim 5 fussy, petty 7 finicky 8 captious, critical, exacting, finiking, pedantic 9 criticism 10 pedantical
nitrate: 4 film, salt 5 ester
potassium ~: 5 niter
__ nitrate: 5 ethyl 6 silver, sodium 7 calcium 9 potassium
nitric __: 4 acid 5 oxide
nitrite: 4 salt 5 ester
__ nitrite: 4 amyl 5 butyl, ethyl 6 sodium 7 isoamyl
NIT rival: 4 NCAA
tiebreaker: 2 OT 8 overtime
nitro: 4 soup 9 explosive
nitrogen: 3 gas 5 azote 7 element
based dye: 3 azo
combining form: 3 azo-
compound: 5 amide, amine, azide, azole
it's mostly ~: 3 air
liquid ~ container: 5 Dewar
nitrogen __: 5 cycle, fixer 7 balance, dioxide
__ nitrogen: 5 heavy
__-nitrogen cycle: 6 carbon
nitrous __: 4 acid 5 ether, oxide
Nitschke, Ray sport: 8 football
Nittany Lions school: 3 PSU 9 Penn State
Nitti nabber: 4 Ness, T-man
nitty-gritty: 3 nub 4 core, crux, gist, knub, pith 5 heart, point, sense, truth 6 detail 7 essence, meaning
Nitty Gritty Dirt Band
song: An American Dream (1980)
Mr. Bojangles (1971)
Nitty Gritty, The (1963 song) artist: Shirley Ellis
nitwit: 3 ass, oaf, sap 4 boob, clod, dolt, dope, fool, gowk, yo-yo 5 chump, clown, cluck, dummy, dunce, joker, ninny, patsy 6 lubber, lummox, sucker, turkey 7 buffoon, dingbat, dullard, fathead, jackass, pinhead, saphead 8 bonehead, dumbbell, lunkhead, meathead, numskull 9 birdbrain, blockhead, ding-a-ling, harebrain, lamebrain, numbskull, simpleton 10 dunderhead, nincompoop
Nitwits, The (1935 film)
cast: Betty Grable, Bert Wheeler, Robert Woolsey
director: George Stevens
nitwitted: 5 silly 6 simple 8 mindless
NIU conference: 3 MAC
Niva: 3 car 4 auto, Lada 7 Russian 10 automobile
Nivea: 6 lotion
rival: 4 Keri 5 Curel 6 Aveeno 7 Eucerin, Jergens, Pacquin 9 Lubriderm
nivellate: 5 level
Niven: 3 Kip 5 Busch, David, Larry
Niven, David: 5 actor
film: 55 Days at Peking (1963)
Around the World in Eighty Days (1956)
Ask Any Girl (1959)
Bachelor Mother (1939)
The Best of Enemies (1961)
The Bishop's Wife (1947)
Bonjour Tristesse (1958)
Casino Royale (1967)
Court Martial (1955)
The Dawn Patrol (1938)
Dodsworth (1936)
Enchantment (1948)
The Guns of Navarone (1961)
The King's Thief (1955)
Murder by Death (1976)
The Pink Panther (1964)
Please Don't Eat the Daisies (1960)
The Real Glory (1939)
The Sea Wolves (1980)
Separate Tables (1958, AA)
Soldiers Three (1951)
Spitfire (1942)
Stairway to Heaven (1946)
Tonight's the Night (1954)
The Way Ahead (1944)
Where the Spies Are (1965)
Wuthering Heights (1939)

niveous: 5 snowy, white 9 alabaster
nix: 2 no 3 ban, bar, nah, naw, nay, nil, non 4 deny, kill, nada, nein, nope, nyet, stop, uh-uh, veto, void, zero 5 annul, debar, I won't, never, no how, no way, quash, spurn, zilch 6 abjure, cancel, cool it, diddly, forbid, negate, no deal, noways, nowise, rebuff, refuse, reject, repeal, sprite 7 abolish, decline, I refuse, nothing, nullify, refusal, rule out, silence, squelch 8 abrogate, disallow, forget it, I will not, negative, negatory, overrule, prohibit, suppress, turn down 9 by no means, eighty-six, fat chance, I think not, proscribe, rejection, strike out 10 count me out, invalidate, not a chance, put an end to, thumbs down
nixie: 3 elf 6 goblin, sprite
Nixon (1995 film)
cast: Joan Allen, Powers Boothe, Ed Harris, Anthony Hopkins, Bob Hoskins, E.G. Marshall, David Paymer, David Hyde Pierce, Paul Sorvino, Mary Steenburgen, James Woods
director: Oliver Stone
Nixon in China: 5 opera
composer: John Adams
role: 3 Mao
Nixon, Richard: 9 president
alma mater: 4 Duke 8 Whittier
birthplace: 10 California, Yorba Linda
book: 7 Leaders 9 Real Peace, Six Crises 10 In the Arena, The Real War
cabinet member: 4 Butz, Dent, Lynn 5 Finch, Laird, Saxbe, Simon, Stans, Volpe 6 Blount, Hickel, Morton, Rogers, Romney, Shultz 8 Connally 9 Kissinger
child: 5 Julie 6 Tricia
former occupation: 6 lawyer
middle name: 7 Milhous
opponent: 3 JFK 7 Kennedy, Wallace 8 Humphrey, McGovern
parent: 5 Frank 6 Hannah
V.P.: 4 Ford 5 Agnew
wife: 3 Pat 6 Thelma
Nizer, Louis: 3 att. 4 atty. 6 lawyer 8 attorney
N.J.
neighbor: 3 Del. 4 Penn. 5 Penna.
ocean: 3 Atl.
see also New Jersey
NJ base: 5 Ft. Dix
Nkrumah: 5 Kwame
NL
award: 3 MVP
city: 3 Atl., Chi., NYC, St. L. 4 Milw. 5 Miami, Phila. 6 Denver 7 Atlanta, Chicago, Houston, New York, Phoenix, St. Louis 8 Montreal, San Diego 9 Milwaukee 10 Cincinnati, Los Angeles, Pittsburgh 12 Philadelphia, San Francisco
division: 4 East, West
part of ~: 3 Nat. 4 Natl. 6 League 8 National
player: 3 Buc, Cub, Met, Red 4 Card, Expo 5 Astro, Brave, D-back, Giant, NY Met, Padre, Rocky 6 Brewer, Dodger, Marlin, Pirate 7 Phillie 8 Cardinal 11 Diamondback
stat: 3 HRs 4 RBIs
see also baseball, National League
NLC team: 4 Cubs, Reds 6 Astros 7 Brewers, Pirates 9 Cardinals
NLE team: 4 Mets 5 Expos 6 Braves 7 Marlins 8 Phillies
NLRB
part of ~: 3 Lab., Nat, Rel. 4 Natl. 5 Board, Labor 8 National 9 Relations
NLU locale: 6 Monroe
NLW team: 6 Giants, Padres 7 Dodgers 13 Rockies. D-backs
NM
see New Mexico
N. Mex.
see New Mexico
NMR __: 4 scan 7 scanner
NNE: 3 dir.
opposite: 3 SSW
NNP, part of: 3 Nat., Net 4 Natl., Prod. 7 Product 8 National
NNW: 3 dir.
opposite: 3 SSE
no: 3 nah, naw, nay, nix 4 nein, nope, nyet, uh-uh, veto, vote 5 I won't, ixnay, never 6 denial, rebuff 7 denials, dissent, I refuse, refusal 8 forget it, turndown 9 rejection 10 count me out, refutation, thumbs down
big thing: 3 pip 4 blip 6 trifle 7 trivial 10 immaterial
contest: 4 plea 9 hands down
don't take ~ for an answer: 6 insist 7 persist, protest 8 speak out 9 stand firm
doubt: 5 truly 6 likely 8 of course, probably 9 certainly
end: 4 a lot, much 6 vastly 7 liberal 8 very many, very much 9 eternally, extremely, immensely, in a big way 10 a great deal
ender: 5 siree
end of: 4 many 6 divers, myriad, umteen, untold 7 copious, profuse, umpteen 8 abundant, manifold, numerous, umpsteen 9 bountiful, countless, limitless, quite a few, unlimited
fooling: 5 truly 6 honest, really, solemn 7 serious, sincere 8 honestly 9 precisely, sincerely
get ~ place fast: 4 flag, idle, limp, plod, poke 5 delay, tarry 6 dabble, dawdle, diddle 7 fall off, fritter, slacken 8 hang back 9 inch along, poke along, waste time 10 dillydally, lose ground, mess around, wait around
give ~ ground: 5 force, order, press 6 demand 8 pressure 9 stand firm
good: 4 evil, junk 5 lousy 7 of no use, useless 10 virtueless
great shakes: 4 so-so 8 mediocre, ordinary
holds barred: 8 absolute, straight 9 limitless
ifs ands or buts: 7 exactly 10 absolutely, definitely, positively
in French: 3 non
in German: 4 nein
in Latin: 3 non
in music: 3 non
in Portuguese: 3 nao
in Russian: 4 nyet
in Scottish: 3 nae
in ~ time: 3 PDQ 4 anon, fast, soon 5 apace 6 presto 7 fleetly, hastily, quickly, rapidly, readily, swiftly 8 pell-mell, speedily 9 forthwith, hurriedly, instantly, like a shot, posthaste
it waits for ~ man: 4 tide, time
joke: 4 ugly 5 heavy, tough 6 severe, urgent 7 arduous, crucial, weighty 8 menacing, sobering, terrible 9 dangerous, difficult, laborious, momentous, strenuous 10 formidable
leave ~ stone unturned: 4 seek 5 scour 6 search, strive 7 persist, ransack, rummage 9 persevere
leave ~ vestige of: 3 mar 4 doom, raze, sack 5 crush, level, total, wreck 6 blow up, ravage 7 butcher, destroy, flatten, pillage, wipe out 8 bankrupt, bulldoze, clean out, decimate, demolish 9 bring down, desecrate, devastate 10 annihilate, obliterate
longer used: 3 obs., old, out 4 gone 5 dated, dusty, moldy, musty, passé, stale 6 bygone, old hat, square 7 archaic, outworn 8 obsolete, outdated, outmoded, timeworn 9 discarded, moth-eaten, out-of-date 10 antiquated, out of style, superseded
matter: 6 drop it 8 forget it 9 never mind
matter what: 5 still 6 anyhow, anyway 9 at any rate 10 in any event, regardless
mistake: 5 truly 6 surely 7 flat out 8 in spades 9 certainly, decidedly, downright 10 absolutely, definitely, distinctly, positively
more: 4 once, stop 5 kaput 6 lapsed
more than: 4 just, mere, only 6 at most
of ~ importance: 4 moot 7 trivial, useless 9 worthless
of ~ use: 4 vain 6 futile, hollow 7 inutile, worn-out 8 bootless, hopeless, pathetic 9 pointless, worthless 10 not working, profitless, unavailing, unworkable
one: 4 none 6 nobody 7 pronoun 9 nary a soul
on ~ occasion: 7 not ever 8 not at all 9 nevermore
pay ~ attention to: 6 forget, ignore 7 disobey, neglect, tune out 8 file away, lay aside, overlook, sneeze at 9 disregard
picnic: 4 hard 5 bumpy, harsh, rough, tough 6 brutal, rugged, severe, taxing, thorny, trying, woolly 7 arduous, painful, serious 8 terrible 9 strenuous 10 formidable, unpleasant
problem: 4 easy, snap 5 cinch 6 simple 8 workable 10 attainable, effortless, obtainable
say ~ to: 3 nix 4 deny, shun, veto 5 spurn 6 bounce, forbid, pass on, rebuff, refuse, reject, resist 7 decline, disdain, dismiss, exclude, protest 8 disallow, override, overrule, turn down 9 blackball, cast aside, repudiate
show: 4 AWOL 8 absentee
strings: 8 optional 9 boundless, limitless, unlimited
sweat: 4 easy, snap 6 simple 8 duck soup 9 easy as pie 10 child's play, effortless
take ~ note of: 6 ignore 7 neglect 8 brush off, skip over 9 disregard
to ~ avail: 4 vain 6 futile, in vain, otiose, vainly 8 bootless, hopeless 9 fruitless, pointless, uselessly 10 for nothing
unable to say ~: 4 meek 5 timid 6 docile 7 lenient, servile, slavish 8 lamblike, yielding 9 spineless 10 obsequious, submissive
vote ~: 6 oppose
voter: 4 anti 8 opponent
no __: 3 end, one, use, way 4 ball, bill, dice, fair, sale, soap 5 doubt, sweat 6 longer, matter 7 contest
no __ attached: 7 strings
no __ at the inn: 4 room
no __ barred: 5 holds
no __ feat: 4 mean
no __ intended: 3 pun
no __ land: 4 man's
no __ lost: 4 love
no __, no return: 7 deposit
no __ roses: 5 bed of
no __ shakes: 5 great
no __ sight: 5 end in
no __ than: 6 sooner
no __ to: 6 thanks
no __ ways about it: 3 two
no-__: 3 cal, hit, win 4 good, host, iron, load, lose, name, show 5 hoper, knock, see-um, stick, trump 6 frills, growth, hitter, strike 7 account, brainer, goodnik, tillage
no-__ clause: 5 trade
no-__ contract: 3 cut
no-__ fund: 4 load
no-__ insurance: 5 fault
no-__ stock: 3 par
no-__-um: 3 see
no-__ zone: 3 fly
no.: 3 amt., fig., qty.
kind of ~: 3 neg., pos.
see also number
No: 2 Dr. 4 elem., lake 5 drama 6 doctor 7 element 8 nobelium
lake locale: 5 Sudan 6 Africa
102 for ~: 4 at. no.
No __: 3 más, MSG 4 Exit, More, Time 5 Doubt, Mercy, U-Turn 6 Scrubs 7 Diggity, Highway, Strings
No __!: 3 way 4 dice, joke, prob 5 can do, siree, sweat 6 foolin' 7 fooling, kidding, problem
No __, ands, or buts!: 3 ifs
No __ an island: 5 man is
No __ Bob!: 5 siree
No __ for Sergeants: 4 Time
No __ for the weary: 4 rest
No __ Land: 4 Man's
No __ Love: 5 Other 7 Greater
No __ luck!: 4 such
No __, no gain: 4 pain
No __, no glory!: 4 guts
No __ on Red: 4 Turn
No __ Out: 3 Way
No __ talk to...: 5 one to
No __ Tears: 4 More
No __ Traffic: 4 Thru
No, __ Much!: 3 Not
No-__: 3 Doz
NOAA
department: 8 Commerce
part: 3 Nat. 4 Natl. 5 Admin. 7 Oceanic 8 National
no-account: 5 idler 8 unusable, unworthy 9 worthless 10 ne'er-do-well
Noachian: 3 old 7 ancient
Noah: 4 Wyle 5 Beery 7 Webster, Yannick 8 Emmerich
count: 3 two
craft: 3 ark
father of ~: 6 Lamech
grandson of ~: 3 Lud, Put 4 Aram, Cush, Elam 5 Egypt, Gomer, Madai, Magog, Tiras, Tubal 6 Asshur, Canaan, Nimrod 10 Arpachshad
landing place: 6 Ararat
passengers: 5 pairs 6 beasts 7 animals
son of ~: 3 Ham 4 Shem 7 Japheth
Noam: 7 Chomsky
__ No Angels: 4 We're
nob: 4 bean, gent 6 aristo, noodle
starter: 3 hob
Nob __: 4 Hill
nobby: 3 def, rad 4 aces, A-one, boss, braw, cool, dece, fine, gear, keen, neat, nice, phat, tuff 5 dandy, ducky, grand, great, marvy, neato, prime, slick, super, swell 6 bang on, bang-up, bonzer, bosker, choice, divine, dreamy, far-out, gnarly, groovy, lovely, peachy, slap-up, spot on, superb,

terrif, tiptop, unreal, whizzo, wicked **7** amazing, awesome, capital, corking, perfect, ripping, skookum, stellar, sublime **8** dazzling, especial, eximious, fabulous, five-star, four-star, frabjous, glorious, heavenly, jim-dandy, slam-bang, smashing, splendid, standout, sterling, stickout, superior, terrific, top-level, topnotch, very good, wondrous **9** bodacious, Endsville, excellent, exemplary, exquisite, first-rate, high-grade, hunky-dory, marvelous, sollicker, top-flight, wonderful **10** first-class, hotsy-totsy, jack-a-dandy, out of sight, peachy-keen, phenomenal, remarkable, stupendous, super-duper

Nobel, Alfred: 7 chemist, Swedish
invention: 3 TNT

nobelium: 7 element

Nobel Prize: 5 award
city: 4 Oslo **9** Stockholm

Nobel Prizes - Chemistry:
2003 - Peter Agre, Roderick MacKinnon
2002 - John Fenn, Koichi Tanaka, Kurt Wüthrich
2001 - William S. Knowles, Ryoji Noyori, Barry Sharpless
2000 - Alan Heeger, Alan MacDiarmid, Hideki Shirakawa
1999 - Ahmed Zewail
1998 - Walter Kohn, John Pople
1997 - Paul Boyer, John Walker, Jens Skou
1996 - Robert Curl, Harold Kroto, Richard Smalley
1995 - Paul Crutzen, Mario Molina, Sherwood Rowland
1994 - George Olah
1993 - Kary Mullis, Michael Smith
1992 - Rudolph Marcus
1991 - Richard Ernst
1990 - Elias Corey
1989 - Sidney Altman, Thomas Cech
1988 - Johann Deisenhofer, Robert Huber, Hartmut Michel
1987 - Donald Cram, Jean-Marie Lehn, Charles Pedersen
1986 - Dudley Herschbach, Yuan Lee, John Polanyi
1985 - Herbert Hauptman, Jerome Karle
1984 - Robert Merrifield
1983 - Henry Taube
1982 - Aaron Klug
1981 - Kenichi Fukui, Roald Hoffmann
1980 - Paul Berg, Walter Gilbert, Frederick Sanger
1979 - Herbert Brown, Georg Wittig
1978 - Peter Mitchell
1977 - Ilya Prigogine
1976 - William Lipscomb
1975 - John Cornforth, Vladimir Prelog
1974 - Paul Flory
1973 - Ernst Fischer, Geoffrey Wilkinson
1972 - Christian Anfinsen, Stanford Moore, William Stein
1971 - Gerhard Herzberg
1970 - Luis F. Leloir
1969 - Derek Barton, Odd Hassel
1968 - Lars Onsager
1967 - Manfred Eigen, Ronald Norrish, George Porter
1966 - Robert Mulliken
1965 - Robert Woodward
1964 - Dorothy Hodgkin
1963 - Karl Ziegler, Giulio Natta
1962 - Max Perutz, John Kendrew
1961 - Melvin Calvin
1960 - Willard Libby
1959 - Jaroslav Heyrovsky
1958 - Frederick Sanger
1957 - Alexander Todd
1956 - Cyril Hinshelwood, Nikolay Semenov
1955 - Vincent du Vigneaud
1954 - Linus Pauling
1953 - Hermann Staudinger
1952 - Archer Martin, Richard Synge
1951 - Edwin McMillan, Glenn Seaborg
1950 - Otto Diels, Kurt Alder
1949 - William Giauque
1948 - Arne Tiselius
1947 - Robert Robinson
1946 - James Sumner, John Northrop, Wendell Stanley
1945 - Artturi Virtanen
1944 - Otto Hahn
1943 - George de Hevesy
1942 - NO AWARD
1941 - NO AWARD
1940 - NO AWARD
1939 - Adolf Butenandt, Leopold Ruzicka
1938 - Richard Kuhn
1937 - Walter Haworth, Paul Karrer
1936 - Peter Debye
1935 - Frédéric Joliot-Curie, Irène Joliot-Curie
1934 - Harold Urey
1933 - NO AWARD
1932 - Irving Langmuir
1931 - Carl Bosch, Friedrich Bergius
1930 - Hans Fischer
1929 - Arthur Harden, Hans von Euler-Chelpin
1928 - Adolf Windaus
1927 - Heinrich Wieland
1926 - Theodor Svedberg
1925 - Richard Zsigmondy
1924 - NO AWARD
1923 - Fritz Pregl
1922 - Francis Aston
1921 - Frederick Soddy
1920 - Walther Nernst
1919 - NO AWARD
1918 - Fritz Haber
1917 - NO AWARD
1916 - NO AWARD
1915 - Richard Willstötter
1914 - Theodore Richards
1913 - Alfred Werner
1912 - Victor Grignard, Paul Sabatier
1911 - Marie Curie
1910 - Otto Wallach
1909 - Wilhelm Ostwald
1908 - Ernest Rutherford
1907 - Eduard Buchner
1906 - Henri Moissan
1905 - Adolf von Baeyer
1904 - William Ramsay
1903 - Svante Arrhenius
1902 - Hermann Fischer
1901 - Jacobus van't Hoff

Nobel Prizes - Economics:
2003 - Robert Engle, Clive Granger
2002 - Daniel Kahneman, Vernon Smith
2001 - George Akerlof, Michael Spence, Joseph Stiglitz
2000 - James Heckman, Daniel McFadden
1999 - Robert Mundell
1998 - Amartya Sen
1997 - Robert Merton, Myron Scholes
1996 - James Mirrlees, William Vickrey
1995 - Robert Lucas
1994 - John Harsanyi, John Nash, Reinhard Selten
1993 - Robert Fogel, Douglass North
1992 - Gary Becker
1991 - Ronald Coase
1990 - Harry Markowitz, Merton Miller, William Sharpe
1989 - Trygve Haavelmo
1988 - Maurice Allais
1987 - Robert Solow
1986 - James Buchanan
1985 - Franco Modigliani
1984 - Richard Stone
1983 - Gerard Debreu
1982 - George Stigler
1981 - James Tobin
1980 - Lawrence Klein
1979 - Theodore Schultz, Arthur Lewis
1978 - Herbert Simon
1977 - Bertil Ohlin, James Meade
1976 - Milton Friedman
1975 - Leonid Kantorovich, Tjalling Koopmans
1974 - Gunnar Myrdal, Friedrich von Hayek
1973 - Wassily Leontief
1972 - John Hicks, Kenneth Arrow
1971 - Simon Kuznets
1970 - Paul Samuelson
1969 - Ragnar Frisch, Jan Tinbergen

Nobel Prizes - Literature:
2003 - J.M. Coetzee
2002 - Imre Kertész
2001 - V.S. Naipaul
2000 - Gao Xingjian
1999 - Günter Grass
1998 - José Saramago
1997 - Dario Fo
1996 - Wislawa Szymborska
1995 - Seamus Heaney
1994 - Kenzaburo Oe
1993 - Toni Morrison
1992 - Derek Walcott
1991 - Nadine Gordimer
1990 - Octavio Paz
1989 - Camilo Cela
1988 - Naguib Mahfouz
1987 - Joseph Brodsky
1986 - Wole Soyinka
1985 - Claude Simon
1984 - Jaroslav Seifert
1983 - William Golding
1982 - Gabriel García Márquez
1981 - Elias Canetti
1980 - Czeslaw Milosz
1979 - Odysseus Elytis
1978 - Isaac Bashevis Singer
1977 - Vicente Aleixandre
1976 - Saul Bellow
1975 - Eugenio Montale
1974 - Eyvind Johnson, Harry Martinson
1973 - Patrick White
1972 - Heinrich Böll
1971 - Pablo Neruda
1970 - Aleksandr Solzhenitsyn
1969 - Samuel Beckett
1968 - Yasunari Kawabata
1967 - Miguel Asturias
1966 - Shmuel Agnon, Nelly Sachs
1965 - Mikhail Sholokhov
1964 - Jean-Paul Sartre
1963 - Giorgos Seferis
1962 - John Steinbeck
1961 - Ivo Andric
1960 - St.-John Perse
1959 - Salvatore Quasimodo
1958 - Boris Pasternak
1957 - Albert Camus
1956 - Juan Ramón Jiménez
1955 - Halldór Laxness
1954 - Ernest Hemingway
1953 - Winston Churchill
1952 - François Mauriac
1951 - Pär Lagerkvist
1950 - Bertrand Russell
1949 - William Faulkner
1948 - T.S. Eliot
1947 - André Gide
1946 - Hermann Hesse
1945 - Gabriela Mistral
1944 - Johannes Jensen
1943 - NO AWARD
1942 - NO AWARD
1941 - NO AWARD
1940 - NO AWARD
1939 - Frans Sillanpöö
1938 - Pearl S. Buck
1937 - Roger du Gard
1936 - Eugene O'Neill
1935 - NO AWARD
1934 - Luigi Pirandello
1933 - Ivan Bunin
1932 - John Galsworthy
1931 - Erik Karlfeldt
1930 - Sinclair Lewis
1929 - Thomas Mann
1928 - Sigrid Undset
1927 - Henri Bergson
1926 - Grazia Deledda
1925 - George Bernard Shaw
1924 - Wladyslaw Reymont
1923 - William Butler Yeats
1922 - Jacinto Benavente
1921 - Anatole France
1920 - Knut Hamsun
1919 - Carl Spitteler
1918 - NO AWARD
1917 - Karl Gjellerup, Henrik Pontoppidan
1916 - Verner von Heidenstam
1915 - Romain Rolland
1914 - NO AWARD
1913 - Rabindranath Tagore
1912 - Gerhart Hauptmann
1911 - Maurice Maeterlinck
1910 - Paul Heyse
1909 - Selma Lagerlöf
1908 - Rudolf Eucken
1907 - Rudyard Kipling
1906 - Giosuè Carducci
1905 - Henryk Sienkiewicz
1904 - Frédéric Mistral, José Echegaray
1903 - Bjornstjerne Bjornson
1902 - Theodor Mommsen
1901 - Sully Prudhomme

Nobel Prizes - Medicine:
2003 - Paul Lauterbur, Peter Mansfield
2002 - Sydney Brenner, Robert Horvitz, John Sulston
2001 - Leland Hartwell, Tim Hunt, Paul Nurse
2000 - Arvid Carlsson, Paul Greengard, Eric Kandel
1999 - Günter Blobel
1998 - Robert Furchgott, Louis Ignarro, Ferid Murad
1997 - Stanley B. Prusiner
1996 - Peter Doherty, Rolf Zinkernagel
1995 - Edward Lewis, Christiane Nüsslein-Volhard, Eric Wieschaus
1994 - Alfred Gilman, Martin Rodbell
1993 - Richard Roberts, Phillip Sharp
1992 - Edmond Fischer, Edwin Krebs
1991 - Erwin Neher, Bert Sakmann
1990 - Joseph Murray, Donnall Thomas
1989 - Michael Bishop, Harold Varmus
1988 - James Black, Gertrude Elion, George Hitchings
1987 - Susumu Tonegawa
1986 - Stanley Cohen, Rita Levi-Montalcini
1985 - Michael Brown, Joseph Goldstein
1984 - Niels Jerne, Georges Köhler, César Milstein
1983 - Barbara McClintock
1982 - Sune Bergström, Bengt Samuelsson, John Vane

1981 - Roger Sperry, David Hubel, Torsten Wiesel
1980 - Baruj Benacerraf, Jean Dausset, George Snell
1979 - Allan Cormack, Godfrey Hounsfield
1978 - Werner Arber, Daniel Nathans, Hamilton Smith
1977 - Roger Guillemin, Andrew Schally, Rosalyn Yalow
1976 - Baruch Blumberg, Carleton Gajdusek
1975 - David Baltimore, Renato Dulbecco, Howard Temin
1974 - Albert Claude, Christian de Duve, George Palade
1973 - Karl von Frisch, Konrad Lorenz, Nikolaas Tinbergen
1972 - Gerald Edelman, Rodney Porter
1971 - Earl Sutherland
1970 - Bernard Katz, Ulf von Euler, Julius Axelrod
1969 - Max Delbrück, Alfred Hershey, Salvador Luria
1968 - Robert Holley, Gobind Khorana, Marshall Nirenberg
1967 - Ragnar Granit, Haldan Hartline, George Wald
1966 - Peyton Rous, Charles Huggins
1965 - François Jacob, André Lwoff, Jacques Monod
1964 - Konrad Bloch, Feodor Lynen
1963 - John Eccles, Alan Hodgkin, Andrew Huxley
1962 - Francis Crick, James Watson, Maurice Wilkins
1961 - Georg von Békésy
1960 - Frank Burnet, Peter Medawar
1959 - Severo Ochoa, Arthur Kornberg
1958 - George Beadle, Edward Tatum, Joshua Lederberg
1957 - Daniel Bovet
1956 - André Cournand, Werner Forssmann, Dickinson Richards
1955 - Axel Theorell
1954 - John Enders, Thomas Weller, Frederick Robbins
1953 - Hans Krebs, Fritz Lipmann
1952 - Selman Waksman
1951 - Max Theiler
1950 - Edward Kendall, Tadeus Reichstein, Philip Hench
1949 - Walter Hess, Antonio Moniz
1948 - Paul Müller
1947 - Carl Cori, Gerty Cori, Bernardo Houssay
1946 - Hermann Muller
1945 - Alexander Fleming, Ernst Chain, Howard Florey
1944 - Joseph Erlanger, Herbert Gasser
1943 - Henrik Dam, Edward Doisy
1942 - NO AWARD
1941 - NO AWARD
1940 - NO AWARD
1939 - Gerhard Domagk
1938 - Corneille Heymans
1937 - Albert von Szent-Györgyi
1936 - Henry Dale, Otto Loewi
1935 - Hans Spemann
1934 - George Whipple, George Minot, William Murphy
1933 - Thomas Morgan
1932 - Charles Sherrington, Edgar Adrian
1931 - Otto Warburg
1930 - Karl Landsteiner
1929 - Christiaan Eijkman, Frederick Hopkins
1928 - Charles Nicolle
1927 - Julius Wagner-Jauregg
1926 - Johannes Fibiger
1925 - NO AWARD
1924 - Willem Einthoven
1923 - Frederick Banting, John Macleod
1922 - Archibald Hill, Otto Meyerhof
1921 - NO AWARD
1920 - Schack Krogh
1919 - Jules Bordet
1918 - NO AWARD
1917 - NO AWARD
1916 - NO AWARD
1915 - NO AWARD
1914 - Robert Bárány
1913 - Charles Richet
1912 - Alexis Carrel
1911 - Allvar Gullstrand
1910 - Albrecht Kossel
1909 - Emil Kocher
1908 - Elie Metchnikoff, Paul Ehrlich
1907 - Charles Laveran
1906 - Camillo Golgi, Santiago Ramón y Cajal
1905 - Robert Koch
1904 - Ivan Pavlov
1903 - Niels Finsen
1902 - Ronald Ross
1901 - Emil von Behring

Nobel Prizes - Peace:

2003 - Shirin Ebadi
2002 - Jimmy Carter
2001 - United Nations, Kofi Annan
2000 - Kim Dae Jung
1999 - Doctors Without Borders
1998 - John Hume, David Trimble
1997 - International Campaign to Ban Landmines (ICBL), Jody Williams
1996 - Carlos Belo, José Ramos-Horta
1995 - Joseph Rotblat, Pugwash Conferences on Science and World Affairs
1994 - Yasser Arafat, Shimon Peres, Yitzhak Rabin
1993 - Nelson Mandela, F.W. de Klerk
1992 - Rigoberta Tum
1991 - Aung San Suu Kyi
1990 - Mikhail Gorbachev
1989 - Dalai Lama
1988 - United Nations Peacekeeping Forces
1987 - Oscar Arias Sanchez
1986 - Elie Wiesel
1985 - International Physicians for the Prevention of Nuclear War Inc.
1984 - Desmond Tutu
1983 - Lech Walesa
1982 - Alva Myrdal, Alfonso García Robles
1981 - Office of the United Nations High Commissioner for Refugees
1980 - Adolfo Pérez Esquivel
1979 - Mother Teresa
1978 - Anwar Sadat, Menachem Begin
1977 - Amnesty International
1976 - Betty Williams, Mairead Corrigan
1975 - Andrei Sakharov
1974 - Sean MacBride, Eisaku Sato
1973 - Henry Kissinger, Le Duc Tho
1972 - NO AWARD
1971 - Willy Brandt
1970 - Norman Borlaug
1969 - International Labor Organization (ILO)
1968 - René Cassin
1967 - NO AWARD
1966 - NO AWARD
1965 - UNICEF
1964 - Martin Luther King
1963 - International Committee of the Red Cross, League of Red Cross Societies
1962 - Linus Pauling
1961 - Dag Hammarskjöld
1960 - Albert Lutuli
1959 - Philip Noel-Baker
1958 - Georges Pire
1957 - Lester Pearson
1956 - NO AWARD
1955 - NO AWARD
1954 - Office of the United Nations High Commissioner for Refugees
1953 - George Marshall
1952 - Albert Schweitzer
1951 - Léon Jouhaux
1950 - Ralph Bunche
1949 - John Boyd Orr
1948 - NO AWARD
1947 - Friends Service Council, American Friends Service Committee
1946 - Emily Balch, John Mott
1945 - Cordell Hull
1944 - International Committee of the Red Cross
1943 - NO AWARD
1942 - NO AWARD
1941 - NO AWARD
1940 - NO AWARD
1939 - NO AWARD
1938 - Nansen International Office for Refugees
1937 - Edgar Cecil
1936 - Carlos Lamas
1935 - Carl von Ossietzky
1934 - Arthur Henderson
1933 - Norman Angell
1932 - NO AWARD
1931 - Jane Addams, Murray Butler
1930 - Nathan Söderblom
1929 - Frank Kellogg
1928 - NO AWARD
1927 - Ferdinand Buisson, Ludwig Quidde
1926 - Aristide Briand, Gustav Stresemann
1925 - Austen Chamberlain, Charles Dawes
1924 - NO AWARD
1923 - NO AWARD
1922 - Fridtjof Nansen
1921 - Karl Branting, Christian Lange
1920 - Léon Bourgeois
1919 - Woodrow Wilson
1918 - NO AWARD
1917 - International Committee of the Red Cross
1916 - NO AWARD
1915 - NO AWARD
1914 - NO AWARD
1913 - Henri La Fontaine
1912 - Elihu Root
1911 - Tobias Asser, Alfred Fried
1910 - Permanent International Peace Bureau
1909 - Auguste Beernaert, Paul Balluet, Paul d'Estournelles de Constant
1908 - Klas Arnoldson, Fredrik Bajer
1907 - Ernesto Moneta, Louis Renault
1906 - Theodore Roosevelt
1905 - Bertha von Suttner
1904 - Institute of International Law
1903 - William Cremer
1902 - Élie Ducommun, Charles Gobat
1901 - Jean Dunant, Frédéric Passy

Nobel Prizes - Physics:

2003 - Alexei Abrikosov, Vitaly Ginzburg, Anthony Leggett
2002 - Raymond Davis, Masatoshi Koshiba, Riccardo Giacconi
2001 - Eric Cornell, Wolfgang Ketterle, Carl Wieman
2000 - Zhores Alferov, Herbert Kroemer, Jack Kilby
1999 - Gerardus 't Hooft, Martinus Veltman
1998 - Robert Laughlin, Horst Störmer, Daniel Tsui
1997 - Steven Chu, Claude Cohen-Tannoudji, William Phillips
1996 - David Lee, Douglas Osheroff, Robert Richardson
1995 - Martin Perl, Frederick Reines
1994 - Bertram Brockhouse, Clifford Shull
1993 - Russell Hulse, Joseph Taylor
1992 - Georges Charpak
1991 - Pierre-Gilles de Gennes
1990 - Jerome Friedman, Henry Kendall, Richard Taylor
1989 - Norman Ramsey, Hans Dehmelt, Wolfgang Paul
1988 - Leon Lederman, Melvin Schwartz, Jack Steinberger
1987 - Georg Bednorz, Alexander Müller
1986 - Ernst Ruska, Gerd Binnig, Heinrich Rohrer
1985 - Klaus von Klitzing
1984 - Carlo Rubbia, Simon van der Meer
1983 - Subramanyan Chandrasekhar, William Fowler
1982 - Kenneth Wilson
1981 - Nicolaas Bloembergen, Arthur Schawlow, Kai Siegbahn
1980 - James Cronin, Val Fitch
1979 - Sheldon Glashow, Abdus Salam, Steven Weinberg
1978 - Pyotr Kapitsa, Arno Penzias, Robert Wilson
1977 - Philip Anderson, Nevill Mott, John van Vleck
1976 - Burton Richter, Samuel Ting
1975 - Aage Bohr, Ben Mottelson, Leo Rainwater
1974 - Martin Ryle, Antony Hewish
1973 - Leo Esaki, Ivar Giaever, Brian Josephson
1972 - John Bardeen, Leon Cooper, John Schrieffer
1971 - Dennis Gabor
1970 - Hannes Alfvén, Louis Néel
1969 - Murray Gell-Mann
1968 - Luis Alvarez
1967 - Hans Bethe
1966 - Alfred Kastler
1965 - Sin-Itiro Tomonaga, Julian Schwinger, Richard Feynman
1964 - Charles Townes, Nicolay Basov, Aleksandr Prokhorov
1963 - Eugene Wigner, Maria Goeppert-Mayer, J. Hans Jensen
1962 - Lev Landau
1961 - Robert Hofstadter, Rudolf Mössbauer
1960 - Donald Glaser
1959 - Emilio Segrè, Owen Chamberlain
1958 - Pavel Cherenkov, Ilja Frank, Igor Tamm
1957 - Chen Ning Yang, Tsung-Dao Lee
1956 - William Shockley, John Bardeen, Walter Brattain
1955 - Willis Lamb, Polykarp Kusch
1954 - Max Born, Walther Bothe
1953 - Frits Zernike
1952 - Felix Bloch, Edward Purcell
1951 - John Cockcroft, Ernest Walton
1950 - Cecil Powell
1949 - Hideki Yukawa
1948 - Patrick Blackett
1947 - Edward Appleton
1946 - Percy Bridgman
1945 - Wolfgang Pauli
1944 - Isidor Rabi
1943 - Otto Stern
1942 - NO AWARD

1941 - NO AWARD
1940 - NO AWARD
1939 - Ernest Lawrence
1938 - Enrico Fermi
1937 - Clinton Davisson, George Thomson
1936 - Victor Hess, Carl Anderson
1935 - James Chadwick
1934 - NO AWARD
1933 - Erwin Schrödinger, Paul Dirac
1932 - Werner Heisenberg
1931 - NO AWARD
1930 - Chandrasekhara Raman
1929 - Louis de Broglie
1928 - Owen Richardson
1927 - Arthur Compton, Charles Wilson
1926 - Jean Perrin
1925 - James Franck, Gustav Hertz
1924 - Karl Siegbahn
1923 - Robert Millikan
1922 - Niels Bohr
1921 - Albert Einstein
1920 - Charles Guillaume
1919 - Johannes Stark
1918 - Max Planck
1917 - Charles Barkla
1916 - NO AWARD
1915 - William Bragg
1914 - Max von Laue
1913 - Heike Kamerlingh-Onnes
1912 - Nils Dalén
1911 - Wilhelm Wien
1910 - Johannes van der Waals
1909 - Guglielmo Marconi, Carl Braun
1908 - Gabriel Lippmann
1907 - Albert Michelson
1906 - Joseph Thomson
1905 - Philipp von Lenard
1904 - John Strutt
1903 - Antoine Becquerel, Pierre Curie, Marie Curie
1902 - Hendrik Lorentz, Pieter Zeeman
1901 - Wilhelm Röntgen

Nobeoka: 4 city, town
locale: 5 Japan
No bid: 4 pass 5 I pass
Nobile, Umberto: 7 Italian 8 explorer
nobility: 4 rank, soul 5 elite, glory, honor, lords 6 gentry, virtue 7 culture, dignity, majesty, peerage, royalty 8 elegance, eminence, grandeur 9 elevation, gallantry, greatness, integrity, loftiness, sublimity 10 bluebloods, excellence, generosity, knighthood, patricians, upper class, upper crust
name meaning ~: 8 Adelaide
__ nobis pacem: 4 dona
noble: 3 big 4 dame, duke, earl, fine, high, king, lady, lord, nice, okay, peer, raja, rani 5 baron, count, elite, grand, great, legit, lofty, money, moral, proud, queen, rajah, regal, royal 6 august, benign, gentle, heroic, humane, kingly, knight, lordly, prince, proper, superb, titled, worthy 7 baronet, courtly, czarina, duchess, eminent, emperor, empress, ethical, exalted, gallant, genteel, liberal, marquis, peeress, queenly, refined, royalty, stately, sublime, supreme, tsarina, tzarina, upright, valiant 8 all right, archduke, baroness, baronial, countess, elevated, empyreal, empyrean, generous, glorious, gracious, heroical, highborn, highbred, imperial, imposing, kinglike, knightly, laudable, maharaja, maharani, majestic, marquess, pleasant, pleasing, princely, princess, splendid, superior, tolerant, virtuous, viscount, wellborn, well-bred 9 admirable, agreeable, blue blood, bounteous, brilliant, chevalier, dignified, excellent, gentleman, grandiose, honorable, maharajah, patrician, reputable, unselfish, venerable, wonderful 10 acceptable, aristocrat, beneficent, beneficial, benevolent, bighearted, charitable, creditable, cultivated, highminded, impressive, majestical, preeminent, remarkable, upper-class
action: 4 deed, feat 5 geste 6 lesson
domain: 6 barony 7 dukedom, earldom
gas: 4 neon 5 argon, radon, xenon 6 helium 7 krypton
like a ~: 5 ducal, regal, royal 8 baronial, knightly
name meaning ~: 3 Ada 4 Earl 5 Adela, Adele, Alice, Ethel, Hiram 7 Patrick 8 Patricia
noble __: 3 fir, gas 4 opal 5 metal
__ noble: 4 rose 7 danseur
Noble: 5 James 7 Chelsea 10 Willingham
__ Noble, Backstage Wife: 4 Mary
Noble House author: James Clavell
nobles: 5 class 6 estate
noblesse: 6 luxury 7 culture, hauteur 8 breeding, elegance 9 gentility 10 refinement
noblesse __: 6 oblige
noblest __ of them all, The: 5 Roman
Noblesville: 4 city, town
locale: 7 Indiana
__ Noble Truths: 4 Four
noblewoman: 4 dame, lady 6 matron 7 dowager, peeress 8 baroness 9 blueblood 10 aristocrat
nobody: 4 none, wimp, zero 6 menial, squirt 7 parvenu, upstart 8 not a soul 9 nonentity
in Latin: 4 nemo
nobody __ business: 5 else's
Nobody __: 5 but Me, I Know, Knows
Nobody but You composer: 8 Gershwin
Nobody Does It Better (song) artist: Carly Simon, Nate Dogg
Nobody doesn't like __ Lee: 4 Sara
Nobody I Know (1964 song) artist: Peter and Gordon
Nobody Knows My Name author: James Baldwin
Nobody Knows the Trouble __: 5 I Seen
Nobody Lives Forever (1946 film)
cast: Walter Brennan, Geraldine Fitzgerald, John Garfield
director: Jean Negulesco
nobody's fool: 4 keen 5 sharp 8 lynx-eyed 10 discerning
Nobody's Fool (1994 film)
cast: Melanie Griffith, Paul Newman, Jessica Tandy, Bruce Willis
director: Robert Benton
Nobody's Fool (1988 song) artist: Kenny Loggins
Nobody Told Me (1984 song) artist: John Lennon
__ no bones about: 4 make
__ No Business...: 6 There's
no-cal: 4 diet 8 dietetic
nocent: 6 malign 7 baleful, baneful, harmful, hurtful 8 damaging 9 dangerous, injurious, unhealthy 10 pernicious
No chance!: 5 never 8 forget it
__ noches: 6 buenas
__ no circumstances: 5 under
No Clouds of Glory author: Marian Engel
__ No Crime: 3 It's 4 Ain't
nocturnal: 4 late 5 night 7 nightly 9 after dark
animal: 3 bat, owl 4 paca, vari 5 cimex, gecko, krait, lemur 6 aye-aye
sound: 3 ZZZ 4 hoot 5 snore
nocturne: 5 music, piece
nocuous: 5 toxic 7 baneful, harmful, hurtful, noisome 9 injurious, poisonous
nod: 3 bow, dip, nap, wag 4 beck, bend, doze, duck, rest, sign 5 agree, droop, greet, sleep, slump 6 assent, beckon, concur, curtsy, drowse, motion, salute, signal 7 approve, consent, doze off, drop off, gesture, go-ahead, respond 8 drift off, greeting, indicate, sanction 9 acquiesce, recognize 10 acceptance, fall asleep, permission
ender: 3 ule 4 ular
give the ~: 2 OK 3 cue 4 okay 5 admit, adopt, allow, go for 6 accept, assent, comply, concur 7 consent, endorse, include, indorse, sign off, welcome 8 sanction, stand for 9 recognize
off: 3 nap 4 doze 5 sleep 6 drowse, snooze
to: 5 greet 7 welcome
Nod: 9 dreamland
in the land of ~: 3 out 6 asleep, dozing 7 napping 8 dreaming, snoozing 9 somnolent 10 slumbering
land west of ~: 4 Eden
partner: 6 Wynken 7 Blynken
visit ~: 3 nap 4 doze, rest 6 catnap, drowse, repose, retire, snooze, turn in 7 drop off, shuteye, slumber 8 take a nap 9 hibernate, hit the hay 10 hit the sack
Noda: 4 city, town
locale: 5 Japan
nodal: 6 knobby, knotty 8 knotlike
nodding: 6 asleep, sleepy 9 soporific
noddy: 4 bird, tern
node: 3 bud 4 bump, burl, knar, knob, knot, lump, nurl 5 bulge, joint, knurl, stage 6 growth, vertex 8 junction, juncture, swelling 10 connection, focal point
__ node: 5 lymph, north, sinus, south
no deposit, no __: 6 return
No Diggity (1996 song)
artist: Blackstreet, Dr. Dre
No doubt in my mind!: 6 I'm sure
No Down Payment (1957 film)
cast: Jeffrey Hunter, Sheree North, Joanne Woodward
director: Martin Ritt
nodular: 5 bumpy 6 knobby, knotty
nodule: 3 bud 4 bump, burl, knar, knob, knot, lump 5 bulge 6 growth 8 swelling
nodus: 4 knot
Noel: 4 song, Xmas, yule 5 Black, carol, Neill 7 Buckner 8 Harrison, Yuletide 9 Christmas, Gallagher
see also Christmas
Noël: 4 Père 6 Coward
Noel-Baker, Philip: 7 British 8 Nobelist
__ no evil: 3 see 4 hear 5 speak
No Excuses rival: 6 Gitano
No Exit author: Jean-Paul Sartre
__ No. 5: 5 Mambo 6 Chanel
no-fat: 4 lean
no-fly __: 4 zone
NO follower: 3 PQR 4 PQRS 5 PQRST
__ no fool like...: 6 There's
Nofret: 4 font 8 typeface
no-frills: 5 plain 7 vanilla
nog: 5 drink, quaff 8 beverage, cocktail
ingredient: 3 egg, rum 4 milk 6 brandy
Nogales: 4 city, town
locale: 6 Mexico, Sonora 7 Arizona 8 Veracruz
see also Spanish
noggin: 4 bean, dome, head, mind, pate 5 gourd 6 noodle, sconce 7 cranium 9 braincase
hit on the ~: 3 bop 4 bonk, conk
Noggin alternative: 3 BET, CMT, MTV, PAX, TBS, TLC, TNN, TNT, USA 4 ESPN, HGTV 5 A and E, C-SPAN, Style 6 Tech TV, TV Land 7 Court TV, Ovation, SoapNet 8 Lifetime
no-good: 5 awful 6 crumby 8 unusable, unworthy 9 worthless 10 despicable
__ no good: 4 up to
__ No Good: 5 You're
no-goodnik: 3 bum, cad, rat 5 baddy, crook, louse, rogue, scamp, viper 6 baddie, bad egg 10 ne'er-do-well
no-goodniks: 6 bad lot
no great __: 6 shakes
No Greater Love author: Danielle Steel
Noguchi: 5 Isamu 6 Thomas
Noguchi, Isamu: 6 artist 8 sculptor
No guts, no __!: 5 glory
Noh: 5 drama 8 Japanese
prop: 3 fan
__, no hands!: 6 Look ma
Nohant author: George Sand
no-hat: 10 bareheaded
No Highway author: Nevil Shute
No Highway in the Sky (1951 film)
cast: Marlene Dietrich, Glynis Johns, James Stewart
director: Henry Koster
no-hitter line score, maybe: 3 OOO
no-holds-barred: 6 all-out
__ No Hooks: 3 Use
__ no ice: 3 cut
__ no idea!: 4 I had
no ifs, __, or buts: 4 ands
noil: 5 fiber
noir: 3 bet 5 black 6 French
opposite: 5 blanc
__ noir: 4 café, film 6 beurre, boudin
noise: 3 din, row, yak 4 bang, boom, buzz, fuss, peal, ring, roar, shot, talk, thud 5 blare, blast, clang, crack, crash, drone, hoo-ha, sound 6 babble, bedlam, bellow, clamor, fracas, hubbub, jabber, jangle, outcry, racket, rumors, squawk, tumult, uproar 7 buzzing, chatter, clangor, clatter, discord, fanfare, hearsay, yelling 8 babbling, disquiet, drumming, eruption, shouting 9 cacophony, commotion, explosion, fireworks, stridency 10 clattering, detonation, dissonance, hullabaloo, turbulence
about: 5 bruit, rumor 6 gossip
dull ~: 4 thud 5 clonk, clunk, thunk
ender: 5 maker
grating ~: 6 squeak, squeal
loud ~: 3 bam, din, pop, pow 4 bang, thud, wham, yell 5 alarm, blare, siren, whang 6 kaboom, report, scream
overwhelm with ~: 6 deafen 8 drown out
urban ~: 4 beep, toot 5 blare, blast
noise __: 6 factor, figure 7 limiter
__ noise: 4 pink, shot 5 white 6 cosmic 7 ambient, surface, thermal
noiseless: 4 mute 5 muted, quiet, still 6 hushed, silent 8 stealthy, wordless 9 inaudible, soundless, voiceless 10 speechless
noiselessness: 4 calm 5 peace, quiet, still 7 silence
Noiseless Patient Spider, A: 4 poem
author: Walt Whitman
Noises Off: 4 film, play 5 farce
author: Michael Frayn
cast: Carol Burnett, Michael Caine, Denholm Elliott, Julie Hagerty, Marilu Henner, Christopher Reeve, John Ritter, Nicollette Sheridan
director: Peter Bogdanovich

noisette: 4 loin, meat, rose 6 fillet
noisome: 3 bad 4 foul, rank, ugly, vile 5 fetid, funky, musty, nasty 6 deadly, foetid, frowsy, frowzy, horrid, rancid, rotten, smelly, stinky, strong 7 baneful, harmful, hurtful, nocuous, noxious, odorous, reeking 8 mephitic, stinking 9 dangerous, injurious, loathsome, offensive, poisonous, repugnant, repulsive, revolting, unhealthy 10 disgusting, insalutary, malodorous
noisy: 4 loud, wild 5 aroar, forte, harsh, rowdy, vocal 7 bawling, blaring, booming, gabbing, grating, hooting, jarring, jumping, pealing, rackety, raucous, reboant, riotous, roaring, wailing, yelling 8 babbling, blasting, clanging, crashing, piercing, plangent, rumbling, shouting, sonorous, strident, turned up, whooping 9 bellowing, bigvoiced, clamorous, deafening, dissonant, hollering, jabbering, loudmouth, screaming, shrieking, turbulent 10 boisterous, chattering, clangorous, clattering, discordant, disorderly, earpopping, resounding, rip-roaring, screeching, stentorian, strepitous, stridulous, thundering, tumultuous, uproarious, vociferant, vociferous
bird: 3 pie 5 goose, macaw
disturbance: 5 brawl, melee 6 fracas
not ~: 4 calm, mute 5 quiet, still 6 at rest, hushed, placid, serene, silent 8 peaceful 9 soundless
Nokia: 5 phone 9 cell phone
alternative: 6 Nextel 8 Ericsson, Motorola
__ no kick...: 4 I get
No kidding!: 3 gee, wow 4 gosh 6 do tell, honest, really
nol-__: 4 pros
Nolan: 4 Ryan 5 Kathy, Kenny, Lloyd 6 Philip 8 Jeanette, Kathleen
Nolan, Kenny song: I Like Dreamin' (1976)
Nolan, Lloyd: 5 actor
film: Guadalcanal Diary (1943)
Hannah and Her Sisters (1986)
The House on 92nd St. (1945)
The Lemon Drop Kid (1951)
The Man I Married (1940)
Peyton Place (1957)
St. Louis Blues (1939)
The Street With No Name (1948)
TV: Julia
Nolan, Philip fate: 5 exile
no-lead: 3 gas 6 petrol 7 premium, regular 8 gasoline
nolens volens: 10 willy-nilly
noli me tangere: 10 touch me not
Nolin: 7 Gena Lee
Noll, Chuck: 5 coach
sport: 8 football
no-load __: 4 fund
nolo contendere: 4 plea
no love __: 4 lost
Nolte, Nick: 5 actor
film: 48HRS. (1982)
Affliction (1998)
Cannery Row (1982)
Cape Fear (1991)
The Deep (1977)
Down and Out in Beverly Hills (1986)
The Golden Bowl (2001)
Jefferson in Paris (1995)
Lorenzo's Oil (1992)
Nightwatch (1998)
North Dallas Forty (1979)
The Prince of Tides (1991)
Teachers (1984)
Under Fire (1983)
U Turn (1997)
Who'll Stop the Rain (1978)
nomad: 3 vag 4 hobo, Lapp 5 gypsy, rover 6 Berber, roamer 7 Bedouin, drifter, migrant, pilgrim, rambler 8 gadabout, traveler, vagabond, wanderer, wayfarer 9 itinerant
be a ~: 3 gad 4 roam, rove 6 ramble, wander 7 migrate 9 itinerate
home: 4 tent
Nomad: 3 car 4 auto 5 Chevy 9 Chevrolet 10 automobile
nomadic: 5 gypsy 6 mobile, roving 7 migrant, roaming, vagrant 8 drifting, pastoral, vagabond 9 itinerant, migratory, traveling, wandering, wayfaring
No man __ island: 4 is an
No Man __ Own: 5 of Her
...no man has __ before: 4 gone
No man is __ to his valet: 5 a hero
No man is an island author: 5 Donne
no man's __: 4 land
No Man's Land author: Harold Pinter
No más boxer: 5 Duran
nom de __: 5 plume 6 guerre
nom de plume: 4 name 5 alias, title 6 anonym 7 pen name 8 cognomen 9 false name, pseudonym
__ nome: 4 Caro
Nome: 4 city, port, town
home: 4 iglu 5 igloo 6 Alaska
native: 5 Inuit 6 Eskimo
no mean __: 4 feat
Nomellini: 3 Leo
nomen: 4 name 5 title
nomenclature: 4 name, term 8 glossary, taxonomy
No Mercy
song: Please Don't Go (1997)
Where Do You Go (1996)
nominal: 3 low 5 cheap, given, named, quasi, small, token 6 formal, puppet, stated 7 alleged, minimal, seeming, titular, trivial 8 apparent, honorary, so-called, supposed, symbolic, trifling 9 low-priced, pretended, professed, purported, suggested 10 in name only, ostensible, self-styled
lacking ~ value: 5 no par
nominal __: 3 par 5 value, wages 7 damages
nominate: 3 tab, tap 4 call, make, name, pick, term 5 draft, elect, put up, slate 6 assign, choose, decide, select, submit, tender 7 appoint, elevate, empower, present, propose, purpose, specify, suggest 8 delegate, handpick, settle on 9 designate, recommend 10 commission, settle upon
nomination: 6 choice, naming 8 election, proposal 9 selection 10 assignment, delegation
nominee: 6 runner 7 hopeful 8 prospect 9 appointee, candidate, contender 10 contestant
nominees: 5 field, slate
Nomo, Hideo sport: 8 baseball
nomologist forte: 3 law
No more!: 4 stop 5 uncle 6 cool it, enough, quit it, stop it
No More Lonely Nights (1984 song)
artist: Paul McCartney
No more Mr. __ Guy!: 4 Nice
__ No More, My Lady: 4 Weep
No More Tears (1979 song)
artist: Barbra Streisand, Donna Summer
No More Vietnams author: 5 Nixon
__ No Mountain High Enough: 4 Ain't
non: 3 nah, naw, nay, nix, not 4 nein, nope, nyet, uh-uh 5 I won't, ixnay, never, no how, noway 6 no deal, noways, nowise 7 I refuse 8 forget it, I will not, negative, negatory 9 by no means, fat chance, I think not 10 count me out, not a chance, thumbs down
in German: 4 nein
in Russian: 4 nyet
in Scottish: 3 nae
persona ~ grata: 3 bum 5 tramp 6 pariah 7 outcast 8 derelict 9 miscreant, reprobate
sine qua ~: 4 must, need 9 condition, essential, necessity, requisite
non __: 3 est 5 grata, licet 6 liquet, placet, troppo
non __ mentis: 6 compos
non-__: 4 pros 7 smoking
non-__ employee: 6 exempt
Nona: 4 Gaye 7 Hendryx
nonabrasive: 4 mild 6 benign, genial, gentle, mellow, placid, serene 7 tactful 8 harmless, laid back, pleasant, tranquil 9 easygoing
nonacceptance: 4 veto 6 denial, rebuff 7 refusal 8 turndown 9 disavowal, rejection 10 gainsaying, refutation
nonage: 5 youth 8 minority 10 immaturity
nonalcoholic beer brand: 6 O'Doul's
nonaligned: 7 neutral
nonattendance: 7 absence
nonbelief: 5 doubt, qualm 7 atheism 8 cynicism, distrust, mistrust, nihilism, wariness 9 chariness, misgiving, suspicion 10 skepticism
nonbeliever: 5 cynic, pagan 7 atheist, heathen, infidel
nonbelieving: 7 cynical, godless, mocking 8 doubtful 9 skeptical 10 suspicious
nonbelligerent: 6 irenic, placid, serene 7 neutral, pacific 8 amicable, friendly, peaceful, tranquil 9 peaceable 10 harmonious, pacifistic
noncarbonated: 4 flat 5 still
drink: 7 iced tea
nonce: 7 present 9 time being
nonce __: 4 word
nonchalance: 4 ease 5 poise, skill 6 aplomb, laxity 7 fluency 8 calmness, facility 9 composure, dexterity 10 adroitness, facileness, nimbleness
nonchalant: 3 lax 4 airy, calm, cool 5 aloof, blasé, happy, hasty, loose, staid, stoic 6 at ease, casual, low-key, mellow, placid, remiss, sedate, serene, sloppy, smooth 7 at peace, neutral, offhand, relaxed, stoical 8 carefree, careless, composed, detached, laid back, listless, lukewarm, slipshod, tranquil, uncaring 9 apathetic, collected, easygoing, impassive, imprudent, incurious, negligent, temperate, unexcited, unfeeling, unheedful, unmindful, unruffled, unworried 10 incautious, insouciant, unagitated, unthinking, untroubled
nonchooser: 6 beggar
noncitizen: 5 alien
non-civilian: 4 navy 7 soldier 8 military
nonclergy: 5 laity
nonclerical: 3 lay 4 laic 6 laical
noncom: 3 cpl., CPO, CWO, NCO, SFC, sgt. 4 MSgt., serg., SSgt., TSgt. 5 sarge
sch. for a ~: 3 OCS, OTS
superior: 5 looey, looie, louie
noncombatant: 7 neutral
noncommercial news source: 3 NPR, PBS
noncommissioned __: 7 officer
noncommittal: 3 coy, mum 4 mute, wary 5 blank, vague 7 careful, evasive, guarded, neutral, politic, prudent, tactful 8 cautious, discreet, reserved 9 ambiguous, equivocal, judicious, tentative 10 wishy-washy
be ~: 4 duck 5 evade, fudge, hedge, stall 6 waffle 7 shuffle 8 flip-flop, hesitate 9 hem and haw, pussyfoot, stonewall, vacillate 10 equivocate
response: 4 I see 5 maybe 7 perhaps 8 possibly, probably 9 it could be, it might be
noncompetitive __: 3 bid 7 bidding
noncompliance: 5 break, lapse 6 breach, schism 7 discord, refusal 9 violation 10 infraction
noncompliant: 5 rowdy 6 unruly 7 chaotic, lawless 8 anarchic, mutinous, refusing 9 divergent, irregular, objecting, truculent 10 anarchical, disorderly, dissenting, rebellious
non compos __: 6 mentis
noncompulsory: 8 optional
nonconcrete: 8 abstract 9 imaginary 10 intangible
nonconforming: 6 atypic 8 atypical, contrary 10 unorthodox
nonconformism: 6 heresy, revolt, schism, strife 7 discord, dissent, protest 8 conflict, disunity 9 rebellion 10 heterodoxy, resistance
nonconformist: 5 flake, hippy, rebel 6 defier, hippie, weirdo 7 beatnik, dropout, heretic, lawless, liberal, oddball, offbeat, radical, swinger 8 bohemian, maverick, original 9 dissenter, dissident, eccentric, heretical, heterodox, protester 10 unorthodox
nonconformity: 6 breach, denial, heresy 7 dissent 8 negation 9 exception, objection, rebellion, rejection, violation
nonconsent: 4 veto 6 rebuff 7 refusal 8 turndown 9 rejection
nondescript: 4 blah, dull 5 mousy, plain 6 common, mousey 7 insipid, prosaic 8 mediocre, ordinary, uncommon 9 colorless, prosaical
nondiscriminatory: 4 fair, just, open 8 unbiased
nondrinker: 3 dry 10 teetotaler
nondurable: 5 shaky 6 flimsy 7 brittle, crumbly, fragile 9 frangible
none: 3 nil, zip 4 nada, nary, zero 5 aught, ought, zilch 6 naught, nobody, not any, not one, nought 7 not a bit, nothing, pronoun 8 goose egg, not a soul 9 nary a soul, not a thing
bar ~: 3 all 8 everyone
combining form: 5 nulli-
ender: 4 such
in French: 4 rien
in law: 3 nul
in Scottish: 4 naen
in Spanish: 4 nada
of the above: 5 other
omitting ~: 4 full 5 fully 6 entire, wholly 7 totally 8 complete, entirely, everyone 9 everybody 10 completely, everything
second to ~: 4 A-one, best, tops 5 first, prime 8 peerless 9 unequaled 10 preeminent
none __ above: 5 of the
__ none: 3 bar
__-none: 5 all-or
non-earthling: 2 ET 5 alien
None But the Lonely Heart: 4 film, play
author: Clifford Odets
cast: Ethel Barrymore, Cary Grant
director: Clifford Odets
role: 3 Ada
nonecclesiastic: 4 laic 6 laical
nonemployment: 6 disuse
nonentity: 4 wimp, zero 6 cipher, menial, nobody, squirt 7 parvenu, upstart 10 figurehead
none of __ business: 4 your
none of the above: 5 other

nones: 4 date, hour
plus eight: 4 ides
None Shall Escape (1944 film)
cast: Marsha Hunt, Alexander Knox, Henry Travers
director: Andre de Toth
nonessential: 4 side 5 extra, petty, spare, undue 6 luxury 7 trivial 8 deadwood, needless 9 excessive
nonesuch: 5 ideal, model 7 paragon
nonet: 4 nine 5 choir, Muses 6 ennead 8 ensemble, ninesome
none the __: 5 wiser
none the __ for wear: 5 worse
nonetheless: 3 tho, yet 6 anyway, even so, though 7 however
non-ethical: 6 amoral
No news is __ news!: 4 good
non-exchange mkt.: 3 OTC
nonexclusive: 4 open 7 generic 8 exoteric 9 generical
nonexistent: 3 nil 4 dead, gone, lost, null, void 5 blank, empty, false, vague 6 absent, dreamy, fantom, unreal 7 defunct, extinct, fancied, missing, phantom, shadowy, tenuous 8 baseless, departed, ethereal, fanciful, illusive, illusory, imagined, mythical, vaporous 9 dreamlike, fictional, imaginary, legendary
nonexpert: 6 layman
nonfeasance: 6 laxity 8 leniency
nonfiction: 4 real 5 prose, story
category: 4 biog. 7 history 9 biography
nonfiction __: 5 novel
nonflowering plant: 4 fern, moss
nonforfeiture __: 5 value 7 benefit
nonforthcoming: 3 coy 6 demure 7 evasive 9 diffident 10 coquettish
nonfunctional: 6 barren, no good, otiose 7 useless 9 valueless, worthless
nongamblers play for it: 3 fun 5 kicks, sport 9 enjoyment
nongermane: 5 inapt, unapt, unfit 9 ill-suited 10 inapposite, irrelevant, out of order, out of place
Nongogo author: Athol Fugard
__ non grata: 7 persona
nongregarious: 3 coy, shy 4 meek 5 timid 6 demure 7 bashful, private 8 detached, reserved, reticent, retiring, sheepish, solitary 9 reclusive, secretive, shrinking, withdrawn 10 antisocial, unsociable
nonharmonious sound: 4 bang 5 blare, crash, noise 6 jangle, squawk 7 clangor 9 cacophony, commotion, explosion, stridency 10 clattering, dissonance
noninclusion: 4 skip 5 lapse 8 omission
nonindulgent: 5 sober, staid, stoic 7 ascetic, austere, stoical 8 reserved, sensible 9 abstinent, temperate 10 abstaining, abstemious, controlled, restrained
nonirritating: 4 mild, safe, soft 6 benign, gentle 8 harmless
nonitalicized: 5 Roman
nonliable: 4 free 6 exempt 8 excluded
nonmaterial: 9 spiritual
nonmetal: 4 neon 5 argon, boron, xenon 6 carbon, helium, iodine, oxygen, sulfur 7 bromine, krypton, silicon, sulphur 8 chlorine, fluorine, hydrogen, nitrogen 10 phosphorus
nonmilitary: 8 civilian
nonministerial: 3 lay 4 laic 6 laical
non-motorized vehicle: 4 bike, luge, sled 5 trike, wagon
non-Muslim: 6 giaour
nonnat: 4 fish
nonnative: 5 alien 7 foreign
nonnegotiable, it's: 4 must
non-nocturnal: 7 diurnal
no-no: 4 don't, rule, tabu 5 taboo 7 misdeed 9 profanity
nonobligatory: 8 elective, optional 9 voluntary
nonobservance: 4 foul 5 wrong 6 breach, laxity 7 neglect, offense 9 disregard, violation 10 infraction, remissness
No, No, Nanette composer: 6 Caesar 7 Harbach, Youmans
No, No, No (1997 song)
artist: Destiny's Child, Wyclef Jean
No-No Nonette composer: PDQ Bach
no-nonsense: 4 firm, hard 5 bossy, cruel, picky, rigid, sober, staid, stern, tough 6 severe, solemn, somber, strict 7 austere, deadpan, earnest, serious, sincere, Spartan 8 despotic, exacting, hard-line, rigorous 9 demanding, draconian, humorless, stringent, unamusing, unbending, unsparing 10 despotical, inflexible, iron-fisted, oppressive, point-blank, tyrannical, unhumorous
nonordained: 3 lay 4 laic 6 laical
No No Song (1975 song) artist: Ringo Starr
No, Not Much! (1956 song) artist: Four Lads
non-oyster months, like: 5 r-less
nonpareil: 3 gem 4 A-one, best, oner, sole 5 candy, ideal, model, prime 6 unique 7 in front, paragon, supreme 8 champion, peerless, treasure 9 just right, matchless, unequaled, unmatched, unrivaled, worthiest 10 inimitable, phenomenon, unbeatable, unequalled, unexampled, unrivalled
nonpartisan: 4 even, fair, just 5 equal 7 neutral 8 detached, moderate, unbiased 9 equitable, impartial, objective, on one's own, unbigoted, uncolored 10 evenhanded, on the fence
nonpastoral: 3 lay 4 laic 6 laical 7 secular 8 temporal
nonpayment: 5 lapse 7 default, failure 10 bankruptcy, insolvency
result: 4 repo
nonperformer: 3 dud 5 lemon 7 failure
nonphysical: 8 ethereal 9 ineffable, spiritual, unearthly 10 intangible
Non più andrai: 4 aria
nonplus: 3 get 4 balk, daze, faze, stun 5 addle, baulk, floor, stimy, stump, stymy, throw 6 baffle, bemuse, boggle, dismay, flurry, fuddle, muddle, puzzle, rattle, stymie, thwart, unglue 7 astound, buffalo, confuse, fluster, mystify, perplex, stagger 8 astonish, bewilder, confound, paralyse, paralyze, surprise 9 discomfit, dumbfound, embarrass, frustrate, take aback 10 demoralize, disconcert
nonplussed: 4 asea 5 at sea, blank 7 at a loss, puzzled 10 distraught
nonpoisonous: 4 safe 6 edible 8 harmless 9 innocuous
non-Polynesian: 5 haole
nonporous: 4 firm 5 solid, tight 6 sealed 8 hermetic 10 impervious
nonprescription: 3 OTC
nonproductive: 4 arid, drab, idle 5 dusty 6 barren, fallow 7 dormant, humdrum, sterile 8 inactive 10 lackluster, unanimated
nonprofessional: 3 lay 6 layman 7 amateur, dabbler 9 layperson
nonproliferation treaty: 4 SALT 6 SALT II
non-pro sports org.: 3 AAU 4 NCAA
nonpublic: 5 inner 6 covert, hidden, secret 7 private 8 hush-hush, isolated, personal 9 concealed, reclusive, secretive 10 restricted, tucked away, undercover, under wraps
nonreactive: 5 inert 9 impassive, insensate
non-realist: 7 dreamer, ostrich 8 escapist, idealist 9 fantasist 10 daydreamer
nonreligious: 3 lay 4 laic 6 laical 7 secular, worldly
nonresident __: 5 alien
nonresident professional: 6 extern
nonresistant: 7 passive 8 resigned, yielding
non-returnable: 9 throwaway 10 disposable
non-rural: 4 city 5 civic, urban 9 municipal
nonsense: 3 fun, gas, pap, rot 4 blah, bosh, bull, bunk, guff, jazz, jest, jive, joke, myth, pooh, talk, tosh, wind 5 bilge, farce, folly, fudge, hokum, hooey, prate, stuff, trash, tripe 6 babble, bunkum, bushwa, drivel, footle, gabble, gammon, gibber, havers, hot air, humbug, jabber, jargon, kibosh, piffle 7 baloney, bananas, blarney, blather, blether, boloney, bombast, bushwah, eyewash, fatuity, flannel, flubdub, fooling, fustian, garbage, hogwash, inanity, madness, malarky, palaver, prattle, rubbish, twaddle 8 babbling, buncombe, claptrap, falderal, falderol, flimflam, flummery, folderal, folderol, malarkey, slipslop, soft soap, tommyrot, trumpery 9 absurdity, banana oil, craziness, frivolity, gibberish, giddiness, goofiness, kidstakes, moonshine, poppycock, rigmarole, silliness, stupidity 10 applesauce, balderdash, bilge water, codswallop, double-talk, empty words, flapdoodle, galimatias, Jabberwock, mumbo jumbo, rigamarole, taradiddle
partner: 5 stuff
talk ~: 4 jive 5 prate 6 babble, footle, gabble, ramble, wander 7 blather, blether
Nonsense!: 3 bah, rot, tut 4 pooh 5 pshaw 6 phooey 7 baloney
Nonsense Songs author: Edward Lear
nonsensical: 3 mad 4 idle, wild 5 crazy, daffy, flaky, goofy, inane, kooky, nutty, silly, wacky 6 absurd, flakey, kookie, screwy, whacky 7 asinine, fatuous, foolish 8 cockeyed 9 laughable, ludicrous, pointless
nonserious: 4 flip 5 giddy, inane, silly 6 madcap 7 puerile, shallow, trivial 8 childish, juvenile 9 facetious, frivolous, whimsical
nonsocial one: 4 geek, nerd, nurd 5 dweeb, loner
nonspecialist: 6 layman 10 generalist
nonspecific adjective: 3 any, few 4 some 9 whichever
nonspiritual: 7 earthly, fleshly, mundane, secular, worldly 8 material, physical, tangible, temporal 9 corporeal
nonspoken tongue: 3 ASL
non-staff: 9 freelance
nonstandard: 3 var. 7 variant 8 aberrant
nonstop: 6 direct, steady 7 endless, express, through 8 constant, enduring, straight, unbroken, unending 9 ceaseless, incessant, perennial, perpetual 10 continuous, relentless
non-studio film: 5 indie
nonsuccess: 3 dud 4 bomb, bust, flop, loss 6 defeat, fiasco, turkey 7 failure, washout 8 collapse, disaster
nonsupporter: 3 foe 4 anti 8 opponent
non-surfing surfer: 5 ho-dad
non-swimmer: 5 wader
nonsymmetrical: 6 uneven 7 unequal 8 lopsided 10 unbalanced
nontoxic: 4 safe 6 edible, gentle 8 harmless 9 innoxious
nontransparent: 6 opaque, turbid
non-U: 5 inapt 7 uncouth 8 low-class 9 bourgeois 10 uncultured
nonuniform: 5 bumpy, jerky, lumpy, rough 6 jagged, patchy, random, wobbly, zigzag 7 crooked, erratic 8 aberrant, shifting, sporadic, unsteady 9 divergent, haphazard, hit-or-miss, irregular 10 inconstant
nonunion __: 4 shop
nonuse result: 4 dust, rust
nonvarsity player: 5 scrub
nonverbal feedback: 3 nod 5 vibes
nonviolent: 5 quiet 6 irenic 7 orderly, passive 8 irenical, pacifist, peaceful 9 peaceable
demonstration: 5 lie in, sit-in
nonvocal: 3 mum 4 mute 5 muted, quiet 6 silent 7 aphonic 8 wordless 9 soundless 10 speechless, tongue-tied
nonvoter: 3 tot 4 baby 5 child, minor 6 infant 8 juvenile
before 1920: 5 woman
nonwinner: 4 flop 5 loser 7 also-ran
nonwoven fabric: 4 felt
noodge: 3 bug, irk, nag, rag, vex 4 goad, pest 5 annoy, beset, harry, hound, shrew, taunt 6 badger, bother, critic, harass, hassle, heckle, hector, needle, nettle, pester, plague, rattle, ruffle, virago 7 bedevil, disturb, henpeck, torment 8 irritate 9 beleaguer, Xanthippe 10 complainer
noodle: 3 nob, nut 4 bean, head, mind 5 pasta, skull 6 noggin, sconce 7 cranium 9 braincase
around: 4 muse 5 think 6 ponder, reason 7 reflect 8 cogitate, conceive, mull over, ruminate 9 cerebrate, speculate 10 brainstorm
like a wet ~: 4 limp 5 saggy 6 droopy, flabby 7 flaccid
use one's ~: 5 think 6 deduce, ideate, reason 7 analyze 8 cogitate 9 cerebrate, figure out
noodlehead: 3 ass, oaf, sap 4 bozo, dodo, dolt, dope, fool, jerk, simp, twit, yo-yo 5 dummy, dunce, goose, ninny, schmo 6 dimwit, lubber, lummox, nitwit, schmoe 7 dingbat, dullard, jackass 8 dumbbell 9 birdbrain, ding-a-ling, ignoramus, simpleton
noodleheaded: 3 mad 4 bats, daft, loco, zany 5 balmy, daffy, dotty, flaky, goofy, inane, manic, nutty, silly, wacky 6 absurd, flakey, whacky 7 asinine, bonkers, doltish, foolish, witless 8 maniacal 9 brainless, eccentric, half-baked, illogical, laughable, pointless, screwball, senseless 10 off-the-wall, ridiculous
noodles: 4 ziti 5 pasta 6 ditali, elbows, lo mein, rigati, shells 7 fusilli, gnocchi, lasagna, ravioli, rotelle 8 farfalle, linguini, macaroni, rigatoni 9 manicotti, spaghetti 10 cannelloni, fettuccini, tagliarini, tortellini, vermicelli
Japanese ~: 5 ramen 6 larmen
__ noodles: 3 egg
nook: 3 bay, den 4 hole 5 coign, cubby, niche, place, quoin 6 alcove, cavity, coigne, corner, cranny, recess 7 crevice, cubicle, dinette, hideout, opening, retreat 8 hideaway 9 cubbyhole, inglenook 10 pigeonhole
shady ~: 5 bower
starter: 5 ingle

nook and ___: 6 cranny
noon: 4 apex 6 midday, twelve, zenith 8 meridian
before ~: 7 morning
ender: 3 day 4 tide, time
in French: 4 midi
meal: 5 lunch
on some clocks: 3 XII
starter: 4 fore 5 after
___ Noon: 4 High
Noonan: 3 Tom 4 Fred 5 Chris
Noone: 5 Peter 6 Jimmie 8 Kathleen
Noon Wine author: Katherine Anne Porter
___-noor Diamond: 4 Koh-i
No Ordinary Love singer: 4 Sade
noose: 4 loop, trap 5 snare 8 slipknot
Noose Hangs High, The (1948 film)
cast: Bud Abbott, Lou Costello
Nootka: 3 fir 6 Indian 7 Amerind
___ no pain: 4 feel 7 feeling
No pain, no ___: 4 gain
nopal: 5 fruit 6 cactus
no-par ___: 5 stock
No Particular Place to Go (1964 song)
artist: Chuck Berry
nope: 3 nah, naw, nay, nix, non 4 nein, nyet, uh-uh 5 I won't, ixnay, never, no how, no way 6 no deal, noways, nowise 7 I refuse 8 forget it, I will not, negative, negatory 9 by no means, fat chance, I think not 10 count me out, not a chance, thumbs down
opposite: 3 yep, yup
___ no place like home: 6 There's
___-no-prisoners: 4 take
No problem!: 4 easy, sure, yeah 5 a snap, can do, it's OK 6 glad to, OK by me 7 happy to 8 of course
___ no questions...: 5 Ask me
nor: 9 connector 10 connective
partner: 7 neither
Nor.
neighbor: 3 Den, Fin., Swe. 4 Swed.
see also Norway
NOR ___: 4 gate 7 circuit
...nor a ___ be: 6 lender
Nora: 4 Dunn 5 Bayes 6 Ephron 7 Charles
dog: 4 Asta
partner: 4 Nick
portrayer: 5 Myrna
NORAD resident: 4 ICBM
Noranda: 4 city, town
locale: 6 Canada, Québec
Norbert: 10 Burgmüller
Norco: 4 city, town
locale: 10 California
Norcross: 4 city, town
locale: 7 Georgia
Nord
capital of ~: 5 Lille
Norden: 5 Tommy
Nordenskjöld: 4 Nils 5 Adolf
Nordheim: 4 Arne
Nordhoff, Charles: 6 author, writer
partner: 4 Hall
work: Mutiny on the Bounty
Nordic: 5 Arian, Aryan
alternative: 6 Alpine
enthusiast: 5 skier
name: 4 Erik, Leif
Nordkyn: 4 cape
nord, opposite of: 3 sud
Nordstrom: 5 Elmer
competitor: 4 Saks 5 Macy's
nor'easter: 4 wind
Noreen: 8 Corcoran
Norelco: 5 razor
alternative: 5 Braun 9 Remington
Norfolk: 3 isl. 4 city, isle, port, town 6 county, island
locale: 7 England 8 Nebraska, Virginia
sch.: 3 ODU
Norfolk ___: 4 coat, pine 6 jacket 7 terrier
Norfolk Terrier: 3 dog 5 canid 6 canine
Norgay, Tenzing: 6 Nepali 7 climber
Norge: 9 appliance
alternative: 5 Amana 6 Bendix, Maytag, Tappan 7 Admiral, Jenn-Air, Kenmore 8 Hotpoint 9 Magic Chef, Whirlpool 10 Frigidaire, Kelvinator, KitchenAid
___ nor hair: 4 hide
noria: 5 wheel 10 water wheel
Noriega: 6 Manuel
No Right ___: 5 on Red
Nor iron bars ___: 5 a cage
Noritake competitor: 5 Lenox 6 Mikasa 8 Wedgwood
Norland: 4 city, town
locale: 7 Florida
norm: 3 avg., par, std. 4 mean, rule, type 5 gauge, model, scale, usual 6 median, medium 7 average, measure, pattern 8 standard 9 barometer, benchmark, criterion, prototype, yardstick 10 touchstone
departure from the ~: 8 variance 9 deviation, disparity, variation 10 aberration, divergence
Norm: 4 Cash 6 Crosby, Ullman 9 Macdonald
occupation on Cheers: 3 CPA
wife on Cheers: 4 Vera
Norm ___ Brocklin: 3 Van
Norma: 4 font 5 Klein, opera 6 Kamali 7 Desmond, Shearer 8 Talmadge, typeface
composer: 7 Bellini
neighbor: 5 Lupus
piece: 4 aria
Norma ___: 3 Rae 4 Ashe
normal: 3 par, reg., std. 4 sane 5 lucid, right, stock, typic, usual 6 common, medium, wonted 7 average, general, mundane, natural, regular, routine, typical 8 accepted, everyday, habitual, ordinary, orthodox, rational, standard 9 customary, prevalent 10 accustomed, legitimate, prevailing, uneventful
back to ~: 4 fine 5 cured 6 aright, healed, itself, mended 8 all right
not ~: 3 odd 5 flaky, outré, weird 6 way-out 7 bizarre, deviant, strange, unusual 8 aberrant, atypical, peculiar, uncommon 9 anomalous, eccentric, grotesque, irregular
starter: 3 log
normal ___: 5 curve, fault, pitch 6 school, series 7 divisor, pentane
Normal: 4 city, town
campus: 3 ISU
locale: 8 Illinois
normalize: 8 regulate 10 stereotype
normally: 7 as a rule, as usual, usually 8 by nature 9 in general, most often 10 by and large
Norman: 4 city, diva, Fell, Greg, Lear, René, town 5 Merle, Mingo, Stone, Tokar 6 Angell, Foster, Jessye, Krasna, Mailer, Marsha, McLeod, Norell, Panama, Ramsey, Taurog, Thomas, Wisdom 7 Borlaug, Cousins, Douglas, Jewison 8 Rockwell 9 Bel Geddes, Dello Joio, Greenbaum, Podhoretz
athletes: 7 Sooners
city: 4 Caen
crown tax: 4 geld
enemy: 5 Saxon
locale: 4 Okla. 8 Oklahoma
neighbor: 6 Breton
poet: 4 Wace
Norman ___: 6 French 7 dynasty
Norman ___ Geddes: 3 Bel
Norman ___ Joio: 5 Dello
Norman ___ Peale: 7 Vincent
Norman Conquest tapestry: 6 Bayeux
Normand: 5 Mabel
___ Normandes: 4 Iles
Normandy
beach: 4 Gold, Juno, Utah 5 Omaha, Sword
event: 4 D-Day
river: 4 Orne
town: 4 Caen, St. Lô 5 Rouen
see also French
Norman, Greg: 5 Shark 6 golfer
milieu: 5 links 6 course
org.: 3 PGA
Norman, Jessye: 4 diva 6 singer 7 soprano
specialty: 4 aria 5 opera
Norman Vincent: 5 Peale
Norma Rae (1979 film)
cast: Beau Bridges, Sally Field, Ron Leibman
director: Martin Ritt
focus: 5 union
setting: 3 Ala. 7 Alabama, factory
norms
lack of ~: 5 anomy 6 anomie
Norm Van ___: 8 Brocklin
No Room in the Ark author: Alan Moorehead
___ nor reason: 5 rhyme
Norris: 5 Chuck, Frank 6 Church 8 Kathleen 9 McWhirter
Norris Division org.: 3 NHL
Norris, Frank: 6 author, writer
work: McTeague
The Octopus
The Pit
Norrish, Ronald: 7 chemist 8 Nobelist
Norristown: 4 city
locale: 4 Penn.
Norse: 7 Vikings 8 language
ender: 3 man, men
epic: 4 edda, saga
giant: 4 Ymer, Ymir 5 Jotun
god: 4 Frey, Loki, Odin, Thor 5 Aegir, Njord, Othin 6 Balder 7 Forseti
goddess: 3 Hel, Urd, Vor 4 Norn 5 Freya, Frigg
gods: 5 Aesir, Vanir
mariner: 4 Eric
mythical king: 4 Atli
of old ~ poetry: 5 eddic
Olympus: 6 Asgard
royal name: 4 Olaf, Olav
symbol: 4 rune
toast: 5 skoal
north: 2 pt. 5 point 6 Arctic, boreal 9 direction
combining form: 4 arct- 5 arcto-
ender: 3 ern 4 ward, west 5 bound, wards 6 lander, wester 7 eastern, western 8 easterly, eastward, westerly, westward
of: 4 over 5 above 6 beyond 8 more than
___ north: 4 true 7 compass
North: 3 Jay, sea 5 Ollie, Union 6 Oliver, Sheree 8 Douglass 9 Frederick
ender: 3 man, men 4 east, land 5 ridge
North ___: 3 Sea 4 Cape, Pole, Side, Star 5 Slope 6 Africa, Island 7 America, Channel, Country, Vietnam
North ___ Forty: 6 Dallas
North ___ Islands: 7 Frisian, Mariana
North ___, NE: 6 Platte
North ___-Westphalia: 5 Rhine
North ___ Zone: 6 Frigid
North Africa
antelope: 5 addax
fortress: 6 Casbah, Kasbah
language: 6 Berber
mountains: 5 Atlas
official: 3 dey 5 pacha, pasha
port: 4 Oran
saint: 7 Cyprian 9 Augustine
stew: 8 couscous
wind: 6 ghibli
North African: 6 Berber
North America
canine: 6 coyote
capital: 6 Ottawa 10 Mexico City, Washington
cat: 4 lynx, puma 6 cougar 7 panther 9 catamount
deer: 3 elk 6 wapiti 7 caribou
desert: 6 Mohave 7 Sonoran 10 Chihuahuan 11 Death Valley
explorer: 5 Cabot 6 Balboa, Hudson 8 Columbus, Vespucci
feline: 4 lynx, puma 6 cougar 7 panther 9 catamount
horse: 5 bronc 6 bronco 7 mustang
weasel: 4 mink 5 skunk 6 badger, marten 7 polecat 8 carcajou 9 wolverine
Northampton: 4 city, town
locale: 4 Mass.
Northamptonshire: 6 county
locale: 7 England
river: 4 Ouse
North and South author: 5 Jakes
Northanger Abbey author: Jane Austen
Northants: 6 county
locale: 7 England
North Atlantic
fish: 3 cod
island: 6 Azores 7 Faeroes, Iceland, Ireland 9 Greenland 10 West Indies
sighting: 4 berg, floe
North Atlantic ___: 5 Drift, Ocean 6 Treaty 7 Current
North Bay: 4 city, town
locale: 6 Canada 7 Ontario
North Bergen: 4 town
locale: 9 New Jersey
Northbrook: 4 city, town
locale: 8 Illinois
North Brunswick: 4 town
locale: 9 New Jersey
north by ___: 4 east, west
North by Northwest (1959 film)
cast: Leo G. Carroll, Cary Grant, Martin Landau, James Mason, Eva Marie Saint
composer: 8 Herrmann
director: Alfred Hitchcock
North Carolina: 5 state
capital: 7 Raleigh
city: 4 Apex, Cary 6 Durham, Monroe, Shelby, Wilson 7 Concord, Hickory, Kinston, New Bern, Raleigh, Sanford 8 Asheboro, Gastonia, Havelock, Matthews 9 Asheville, Charlotte, Fort Bragg, Goldsboro, High Point, Lexington, Lumberton, Salisbury 10 Burlington, Chapel Hill, Greensboro, Greenville, Kannapolis, Rocky Mount, Wilmington
conference: 3 ACC
county: 3 Lee 4 Ashe, Eden, Hoke 5 Avery, Selma, Surry 6 Bertie, Yancey 7 Pamlico
fort: 5 Bragg
Indian: 6 Lumbee 8 Cherokee
island off ~: 7 Roanoke
mountain: 5 Black 8 Mitchell
neighbor: 7 Georgia 8 Virginia 9 Tennessee
school: 4 Duke, Elon 10 Wake Forest
start of ~ motto: 4 esse

state beverage: 4 milk
state bird: 8 cardinal
state dog: 10 Plott hound
state flower: 7 dogwood
state insect: 8 honeybee
state mammal: 8 squirrel
state precious stone: 7 emerald
state reptile: 9 box turtle
state rock: 7 granite
state tree: 4 pine
North Carolina State
athletes: 8 Wolfpack
conference: 3 ACC
locale: 7 Raleigh
North Cascades: 4 park
locale: 10 Washington
North Dakota: 5 state
capital: 8 Bismarck
city: 5 Fargo, Minot, Rolla, Rugby 8 Bismarck 10 Grand Forks
Indian: 6 Mandan
neighbor: 6 Canada 7 Montana 8 Manitoba 9 Minnesota
state beverage: 4 milk
state bird: 10 meadowlark
state fish: 4 pike
state tree: 3 elm
Northdale: 4 city, town
locale: 7 Florida
North Dallas Forty (1979 film)
cast: Mac Davis, Charles Durning, Nick Nolte
North, Douglass: 8 Nobelist **9** economist
Northeast __: 7 Passage
northeaster: 4 wind
Northeastern: 6 school
athletes: 7 Huskies
locale: 6 Boston
neighbor: 3 MIT
Northeasterner: 4 Yank **6** Yankee
Northeast Sudan once: 5 Nubia
norther: 4 wind
northerly: 4 wind
more ~: 5 upper
northern: 6 boreal
northern __: 4 pike **5** canoe **6** lights, oriole, sennet **7** harrier, whiting
Northern: 10 paper towel
alternative: 5 Scott 6 Marcal 7 Charmin 8 Soft Weve 10 Cottonelle, White Cloud
constellation: 4 Lyra
lights: 6 aurora
Northern __: 3 Spy **4** blot **5** Cross, Crown, Piute **6** Lights, Paiute
Northerner: 4 Yank **6** Yankee
Northern Exposure (CBS drama)
animal: 4 bear 5 moose
cast: Rob Morrow (Dr. Joel Fleischman)
Janine Turner (Maggie O'Connell)
radio station: 4 KBHR
setting: 6 Alaska, Cicely
Northern Illinois: 6 school
athletes: 7 Huskies
conference: 3 MAC
locale: 6 De Kalb
Northern Ireland
capital: 7 Belfast
city: 5 Larne, Newry 6 Antrim, Lurgan 7 Belfast, Lisburn
Northern Spy: 5 apple
relative: 4 crab, Gala, Lodi, Rome 5 Mutsu 6 Empire, Ida Red, medlar, Pippin, russet 7 Baldwin, Bramley, costard, Freedom, Liberty, Spartan, Wealthy, Winesap 8 Cortland, Jonathan, McIntosh 10 Rome Beauty
Northern Territory city: 6 Darwin
north forty unit: 4 acre
__ North Frederick: 3 Ten
North Frigid __: 4 Zone
Northglenn: 4 city, town
locale: 8 Colorado
North Haven: 4 city, town
locale: 4 Conn.
North Korea: 6 nation **7** country
capital: 9 Pyongyang
city: 5 Nampo 7 Hamhung 8 Chongjin 9 Pyongyang
money: 3 won 4 chon
neighbor: 5 China 6 Russia
North Lauderdale: 4 city, town
locale: 7 Florida
north-of-the-border
see Canada
North, Oliver rank: 3 Col.
North Olmsted: 4 city, town
locale: 4 Ohio
North Pacific __: 5 Ocean **7** Current
North Platte: 4 city, town **5** river
city on the ~: 6 Casper
locale: 8 Nebraska
North Pole
denizen: 3 elf 5 Santa
explorer: 5 Peary 6 Nansen, Nobile
near the ~: 6 Arctic
Northrop, John: 7 chemist **8** Nobelist
North Royalton: 4 city, town
locale: 4 Ohio
North Sea
hazard: 4 berg, floe 7 iceberg, ice floe
inlet: 5 fiord, fjord
island: 7 Frisian, Orkneys
port: 5 Emden
river to the ~: 3 Dee, Ems 4 Elbe, Maas, Oder, Odra, Tees, Tyne, Yser 5 Meuse, Rhine, Tweed, Weser 6 Thames 7 Schelde, Scheldt
__ Northside 777: 4 Call
North Slope
garment: 5 parka
quest: 3 oil
state: 6 Alaska
North Temperate __: 4 Zone
North Texas
athletes: 9 Mean Green
locale: 6 Denton
North to Alaska: 4 film, song
artist: Johnny Horton
cast: Stewart Granger, Ernie Kovacs, John Wayne
director: Henry Hathaway
North to the Future state: 6 Alaska
Northumberland: 6 county
city: 5 Blyth 7 Berwick
locale: 7 England
neighbor: 4 Scot
river: 4 Tyne
Northwest: 7 airline
former rival: 3 TWA 5 Pan Am 7 Braniff, Eastern
rival: 5 Delta 6 United 8 American 11 Continental
northwester: 4 wind
Northwestern: 10 university
athletes: 8 Wildcats
capital: 5 Boise, Salem 6 Helena 7 Olympia
conference: 6 Big Ten
locale: 8 Evanston, Illinois
sound: 5 Puget
state: 5 Idaho 6 Oregon 7 Montana 10 Washington
Northwest Passage
author: Kenneth Roberts
explorer: 5 Parry 6 Baffin 7 Gilbert 8 Franklin 9 Frobisher
locale: 6 Canada
Northwest Passage (1940 film)
cast: Walter Brennan, Ruth Hussey, Spencer Tracy, Robert Young
director: King Vidor
Northwest Territories
city: 6 Inuvik 8 Hay River
__ North Whitehead: 6 Alfred
North Woods state: 4 Minn. **9** Minnesota
Norton: 2 Ed **3** Ken **4** Mary **5** André, Simon, sound **6** Edward, Trixie **7** Charles
Norton, Charles: 6 writer
Norton, Ed: 3 Art **6** Carney
to Kramden: 3 pal
wear: 3 hat 4 vest
wife: 6 Trixie
workplace: 5 sewer
Norton, Edward: 5 actor
film: American History X (1998)
Death to Smoochy (2002)
Keeping the Faith (2000)
Primal Fear (1996)
Red Dragon (2002)
Rounders (1998)
The Score (2001)
Norton, Ken: 5 boxer
foe: 3 Ali
milieu: 4 ring
Norton Shores: 4 city, town
locale: 8 Michigan
Norton-Taylor: 4 Judy
Norval the Great author: Dr. Seuss
Norville: 7 Deborah
Norvo: 3 Red
Norwalk: 4 city, town
locale: 4 Conn. 10 California
Norway: 6 nation **7** country
bay: 5 fiord, fjord
capital: 4 Oslo
cheese: 9 Jarlsberg
city: 4 Oslo, Voss 6 Bergen, Narvik, Tromsö 9 Stavanger, Trondheim 10 Hammerfest
explorer: 6 Nansen 7 Ericson 8 Amundsen 9 Heyerdahl
figure skater: 5 Henie
in Norway: 5 Norge
legislature: 8 Storting
locale: 3 Eur. 5 Scand. 6 Europe
money: 3 öre 5 krone
mountain: 6 Kjölen
native: 4 Lapp
neighbor: 6 Russia, Sweden 7 Finland
Nobelist in Chemistry: 6 Hassel
Nobelist in Economics: 6 Frisch 8 Haavelmo
Nobelist in Literature: 6 Hamsun, Undset 8 Bjornson
Nobelist in Peace: 5 Lange 6 Nansen
org.: 4 NATO
painter: 5 Munch
patron saint: 4 Olaf, Olav
playwright: 5 Ibsen
rug: 3 rya
sea monster: 7 krakens
sea near ~: 7 Barents
soprano: 8 Flagstad
toast: 5 skoal
violinist: 4 Bull 7 Ole Bull
writer: 4 Duun 5 Bojer 6 Hamsun, Sandel 10 Falkberget
Norway __: 3 rat **4** pine **5** maple **6** spruce
Norwegian: 3 sea **8** language
to Norwegians: 5 Norsk
Norwegian __: 3 Sea **7** Current
Norwegian elkhound: 3 dog **5** canid **6** canine
Norwegian Forest: 3 cat **5** felid **6** feline
Norwegian Wood group: 7 Beatles
instrument: 5 sitar
nor'wester: 4 wind
Norwich: 4 city, town **7** terrier
locale: 7 England, Norfolk
Norwich terrier: 3 dog **5** canid **6** canine
Norwood: 4 city, town **6** Brandy
locale: 4 Ohio
nos.: 4 data **6** digits **7** figures **10** statistics
No Sad Songs for Me director: 4 Maté
No Scrubs (1999 song) artist: TLC
nose: 3 pry **4** beak, gift, odor, root, seek **5** aroma, flair, knack, organ, scent, snoot, snout **6** butt in, meddle, schnoz, talent **7** bouquet, edge out, intrude, schnozz, smeller **8** instinct **9** fragrance, interfere, proboscis, schnozzle **10** schnozzola
around: 4 lurk 5 prowl, skulk, slink, sneak 7 slither
bone: 5 vomer
by a ~: 4 just 6 barely 8 narrowly
combining form: 3 nas- 4 nasi-, naso-, rhin- 5 rhino-
ender: 3 bag, gay 4 band, dive 5 bleed, piece
follow one's ~: 3 gad 4 roam, rove 6 ramble, wander 7 meander, traipse 9 gallivant, itinerate
get one's ~ out of joint: 6 resent
hurt a ~: 5 tweak
in French: 3 nez
in Latin: 5 nasus
keep one's ~ clean: 6 behave 10 toe the line
keep one's ~ to the grindstone: 4 moil, plod, toil, work 5 labor, sweat 6 drudge, strain, strive 8 work hard 9 plug along, pound away
long ~: 5 trunk
nautical ~: 4 prow
noise: 5 achoo, snore, snort 6 ahchoo, hachoo 7 kerchoo
nose to ~: 4 even 5 equal, level
offend the ~: 4 reek 5 smell, stink
of the ~: 5 nasal
on the ~: 4 to a T 5 exact, right, sharp 6 just so, prompt, to a tee 7 correct, exactly 8 accurate, for a fact, promptly, very well 9 befitting, just right, perfectly, precisely 10 absolutely, applicable, positively
opening: 6 meatus
out: 4 beat, edge 5 learn, trail 6 defeat 8 discover, squeak by
part of the ~: 5 naris 6 septum 7 nostril
parts of the ~: 5 nares, septa
perceive with the ~: 5 smell, sniff, whiff
poke one's ~ in: 3 pry 5 snoop 6 meddle 7 intrude 9 eavesdrop, interfere
snowman's ~: 6 carrot
starter: 4 blue, cone, hook, tube 6 shovel 7 bladder
stick one's ~ in: 3 pry 5 snoop 6 meddle 7 obtrude 9 interfere
stimulus: 4 odor 5 aroma, scent, smell, whiff 7 perfume 9 fragrance
thumb one's ~ at: 4 defy, mock 5 flout
turn up one's ~: 5 sneer, spurn 7 disdain 10 look down on
under one's ~: 4 near 5 close 6 nearby, openly 7 visible
nose __: 3 bag, job, out **4** clip, cone, dive, leaf, ring **5** about, drops, ender, guard **6** around **7** glasses
__ nose: 3 by a, pug, war **5** on the, pope's, Roman **7** parson's
No seats available: 3 SRO
nosebag
don the ~: 3 eat, sup 4 dine
fill: 4 feed, oats 6 fodder
__-nosed: 3 pug **4** hard, snub, tube **5** sharp **6** shovel, toffee
__-nosed dolphin: 6 bottle
nosedive: 3 dip **4** drop, fall **5** slump,

swoop 6 plunge 7 decline, descend, descent, plummet 8 tailspin 9 worsening
no-see-um: 3 bug 4 gnat, pest 6 insect
nosegay: 4 posy 7 bouquet
holder: 4 vase
nose-in-air type: 4 snob 5 snoot
nosepiece: 5 armor
noser: 4 gale, wind 5 snoop 6 squall
noses
count ~: 4 poll 6 reckon 9 enumerate
like some ~: 5 Roman, runny, shiny
nosey
see nosy
Nosey Parker
see Nosy Parker
Nosferatu garb: 4 cape
Nosferatu the Vampyre (1979 film)
cast: Isabelle Adjani, Klaus Kinski
nosh: 3 eat 4 bite, grub 5 munch, snack 6 ingest, morsel, munchy, nibble 7 consume, munchie 8 junk food 9 collation, grab a bite
party ~: 3 dip, nut 4 chip 6 canapé
noshable: 5 tasty, yummy 6 savory 9 delicious
no-show: 6 absent 8 absentee
military ~: 4 AWOL 8 deserter
no sooner ___: 4 than
nosophobe fear: 7 disease
nostalgic: 6 quaint 7 wistful 8 haunting, romantic 9 regretful
clothes style: 5 retro
feel ~ for: 4 miss
one: 5 piner
record label: 5 Rhino
song: 4 oldy 5 oldie
sound: 4 sigh
time: 4 yore 10 yesteryear
nostoc: 4 alga
___ no stone unturned: 5 leave
___ Nostra: 4 Cosa
Nostradamus: 4 seer 7 diviner, prophet
nostril: 5 naris
parrot's ~: 4 cere
nostrils: 5 nares
assault the ~: 4 reek 5 smell, stink
No Strings: 7 musical
songwriter: 7 Rodgers
No Strings Attached artist: 5 'N Sync
Nostromo author: Joseph Conrad
nostrum: 4 cure 6 elixir, potion 7 arcanum, cure-all, panacea
peddler: 5 quack 9 charlatan
___ nostrum: 4 mare
___ No Sunshine: 4 Ain't
No sweat!: 4 easy 6 simple
nosy: 4 busy 6 prying, snoopy 7 curious, peering 8 meddling, snooping 9 butting in, inquiring, intrusive, obtrusive 10 meddlesome
be ~: 3 ask, pry 5 snoop 6 butt in
one: 5 prier, pryer, yenta
Nosy Parker: 5 prier, pryer, snoop, yenta 7 meddler 8 busybody, quidnunc
be a ~: 3 pry 5 snoop 6 butt in, meddle 7 intrude, obtrude
not: 4 nary 6 untrue 8 negative
in French: 3 pas
in music: 3 non
in Scottish: 3 nae
(prefix): 3 dis-, non-
not ___: 3 bad 4 a lot, a one 5 so bad
not ___ a finger: 4 lift
not ___ a hair: 4 turn
not ___ a sou: 5 worth
not ___ a trick: 4 miss
not ___ bad: 3 too 4 half
not ___ eye in the house: 4 a dry
not ___ from Adam: 4 know
not ___ heads or tails of: 4 make
not ___ in the world: 5 a care
not ___ least: 5 in the
not ___ long shot: 3 by a
not ___ of tea: 5 my cup
not ___ red cent: 3 one
not ___ trick: 5 miss a
not-___-profit: 3 for
___-not: 4 have, what
...not ___ a mouse: 4 even
...not ___ do: 3 as I
Not ___!: 5 again, at all 6 on a bet
Not ___ can help it!: 3 if I
Not ___ many words: 4 in so
Not ___ million years!: 3 in a
Not ___ Stranger: 3 as a
NOT ___: 4 gate 7 circuit
nota ___: 4 bene
not a ___: 3 lot, one 6 little
not a ___ in the sky: 5 cloud
not a ___ in the world: 4 care
not a ___ too soon: 6 moment
nota bene: 10 take notice
notability: 4 fame 6 leader 8 eminence, luminary 9 celebrity 10 importance
notable: 3 VIP 4 idol, star 5 celeb, famed, great, mogul 6 big gun, bigwig, famous, figure, leader, marked, signal 7 big name, big shot, eminent, magnate, salient 8 big wheel, historic, luminary, renowned, somebody, uncommon 9 big cheese, celebrity, dignitary, honorable, important, memorable, momentous, personage, prominent, well-known 10 celebrated, impressive, pronounced, remarkable, successful
notably: 4 much 6 rarely, vastly 7 greatly 8 markedly 9 extremely 10 especially, thoroughly
Not a chance!: 4 nope 8 forget it
...not always what they ___: 4 seem
___ not amused: 5 We are
notarize: 2 OK 4 okay, sign 6 enseal 7 approve, endorse, indorse
notary ___: 6 public
notary need: 4 seal 5 stamp
Not as a Stranger (1955 film)
cast: Olivia de Havilland, Robert Mitchum, Frank Sinatra
director: Stanley Kramer
notate: 5 tally 6 record 8 mark down
notation: 5 entry 6 record 7 jotting 10 memorandum
not by ___ shot: 5 a long
not care ___: 4 a fig, a rap
notch: 3 cut 4 chip, dent, kerf, mark, nick, pink, slot, step 5 gouge, score, stage 6 degree, groove, hollow, incise, indent, ravine, valley 7 chalk up, cut into
arrow ~: 4 nock
ender: 4 back
parapet ~: 6 crenel 8 crenelle
starter: 3 top
notch ___: 4 baby
notched: 5 jaggy 6 jagged, ragged, uneven 7 incised 8 serrated
as leaves: 5 erose
bar: 5 ratch 7 ratchet
notched ___: 5 lapel 6 collar
___ Not Dressing: 4 We're
note: 2 do, fa, la, mi, re, so, ti 3 IOU, key, see, sol, tag 4 cite, fame, line, list, look, mark, memo, sign, tone, vein 5 A flat, B flat, breve, D flat, E flat, G flat, gloss, high C, input, minim, sound, token, watch, worth 6 A sharp, C sharp, detect, D sharp, F sharp, G sharp, letter, moment, quaver, record, regard, remark, report, symbol, take in, ticket 7 comment, crochet, discern, jot down, jotting, leading, mention, message, middle C, missive, observe, refer to, set down, witness 8 annotate, eminence, interest, mark down, perceive, point out, register, remark on, reminder, take down 9 greatness, magnitude, recognize, reference, semibreve, touch upon, write down 10 annotation, importance, memorandum, prominence, remark upon, semiquaver, understand
bad ~: 4 clam
bank ~: 4 bill
double whole ~: 5 breve
drop a ~: 5 write 10 correspond, epistolize
eighth ~ in music: 6 quaver
ender: 3 pad 4 book 5 paper 6 worthy
explanatory ~: 5 gloss 7 comment
extended ~ in music: 5 longa
federal promissory ~ for short: 5 T-bill, T-bond
from the boss: 5 see me
Greek musical ~: 4 nete
Guido's ~: 3 é la
half ~: 5 minim
high ~: 3 alt, cee, é la
hit a sour ~: 5 clash 6 jangle, rattle
hitting the right ~: 5 on key
holder: 5 payee 8 creditor
journal ~: 4 item 5 entry 6 record
key ~: 5 tonic
make a ~ of: 3 jot 5 write 7 jot down 8 take down 9 write down
notation: 4 flat 5 sharp 7 natural
of ~: 8 laudable, renowned 9 important
office ~: 7 message, missive, tickler 8 reminder 9 directive
online ~: 5 e-mail
person of ~: 3 VIP 4 name, star 7 notable 8 luminary, somebody 9 celebrity, dignitary
piano ~: 5 A flat, B flat, D flat, E flat, G flat 6 A sharp, C sharp, D sharp, F sharp, G sharp
promissory ~: 3 IOU 4 chit
quarter ~: 8 crotchet
scale ~: 2 do, fa, la, mi, re, so, ti, ut 3 sol
signer: 4 ower 6 debtor
soprano's ~: 5 high C
sour ~: 5 clash 6 jangle, off-key 7 discord 9 cacophony 10 disharmony
starter: 3 end, key 4 foot, wood
strike a ~: 6 recall 8 remember, summon up 10 call to mind
take no ~ of: 4 snub 6 ignore 7 neglect 8 brush off, skip over 9 disregard
take ~ of: 3 see 4 heed 6 advert 9 recognize 10 reckon with
whole ~: 9 semibreve
note ___: 3 row 6 broker 7 verbale
___ note: 4 bank, blue, gold, half, time, wolf 5 grace, pedal, shape 6 demand, prompt 7 passing, project, quarter
___-note: 4 half 5 whole 6 eighth 7 quarter
___ Note: 6 Post-It, Sticky
notebook: 2 PC 3 pad 6 binder, laptop, tablet 8 computer 10 scratch pad
contents: 4 leaf 5 paper
noted: 5 famed, grand, great, known 6 fabled, famous 7 big-name, big-time, eminent, exalted, honored 8 esteemed, glorious, laureate, renowned 9 acclaimed, legendary, memorable, prominent, respected, well-known 10 celebrated, preeminent
___ Not Enough: 6 Once Is
notepad: 4 book 5 paper 6 tablet
notes: 8 material 10 marginalia
compare ~: 4 meet, talk 6 confer, huddle, parley, powwow 7 consult, discuss 8 converse 9 interface, touch base 10 brainstorm, chew the fat, deliberate
place for ~: 3 pad 5 staff
played together: 5 chord
___ notes: 5 liner 7 compare
Notes ___ the Underground: 4 From
___ Notes: 6 Cliffs
___ Note Samba: 3 One
Notes From a Sea Diary author: Nelson Algren
Notes From the Underground author: Fyodor Dostoyevsky
Notes of a Native Son author: James Baldwin
Notes on a Cowardly Lion subject: 4 Lahr
___ note to follow sew: 3 La a
noteworthy: 5 great 6 famous, signal 7 unusual 8 singular, striking, superior, uncommon 9 arresting, important, memorable
not-for-___: 6 profit
___ Not for Burning, The: 5 Lady's
___ Not for Me: 3 But
___ Not for Me to Say: 3 It's
Not from where ___!: 4 I sit
Not Gon' Cry (1996 song) artist: Mary J. Blige
not guilty: 4 plea
not half ___: 3 bad
nothing: 3 nil, nix, zip 4 nada, none, zero 5 aught, ought, squat, zilch, zippo 6 bubkes, bupkes, bupkis, cipher, naught, nought 7 trinket 8 goose egg, lifeless 10 lackluster
better than ~: 4 fair, so-so 6 decent 8 adequate, bearable, mediocre, passable 9 tolerable 10 acceptable
but: 3 all 4 just, mere, only 6 merely, purely, simply, solely
come to ~: 4 fail, flop, wane 6 fizzle, lessen, run dry, run out 7 dwindle, founder, misfire, run down, subside, tail off, thin out 8 collapse, peter out, taper off 9 evaporate
containing ~: 4 bare, void 5 empty 6 barren, hollow, vacant 7 vacated 9 evacuated
do ~: 3 veg 4 idle, laze, loll 5 sit by, slack 6 rest up 7 slacken
do ~ about: 5 sit on 6 stifle 7 squelch 8 suppress, withhold
doing: 2 no 3 nah, naw, nay, nix, non 4 nein, nope, nyet, uh-uh 5 I won't, ixnay, never, no how, no way 6 no deal, noways, nowise, rebuff 7 I refuse 8 forget it, I will not, negative, negatory 9 by no means, fat chance, I think not, rejection 10 count me out, not a chance, thumbs down
doing ~: 4 idle, lazy 5 inert 6 otiose, torpid 7 dormant, jobless, loafing, out of it, resting 8 inactive, indolent, slothful, sluggish, stagnant 9 lethargic, loitering, out of work, sedentary, shiftless 10 motionless, on the shelf, stationary
flat: 6 minute, moment, second
for ~: 4 free, vain 6 futile, gratis, vainly 7 as a gift, useless 8 futilely 9 on the cuff, to no avail, uselessly 10 gratuitous, on the house
good for ~: 3 bad 5 sorry 6 abject, dismal, rotten 7 pitiful 8 wretched 9 miserable, worthless 10 deplorable, despicable, detestable
gripe about ~: 3 nag 4 carp 5 whine 6 bicker, grouse 7 nitpick, quibble 8 pettifog 9 find fault, make a fuss
have ~ to do with: 4 shun 5 avoid 6 eschew
hiding ~: 4 bare, open 5 frank, overt, plain 7 exposed, obvious 8 wide-open
if ~ changes: 6 as it is

in ~ flat: 3 PDQ 4 anon, fast 5 apace 6 presto 7 fleetly, hastily, quickly, rapidly, swiftly 8 pell-mell, promptly, speedily 9 forthwith, hurriedly, instantly, like a shot, posthaste
in French: 4 rien
in Spanish: 4 nada
in tennis: 4 love
keep ~ back: 5 level
missing ~: 4 full 6 entire 8 complete, thorough 10 exhaustive, unabridged
more than: 4 just, mere 6 merely, simply, solely, wholly 7 totally, utterly 8 entirely
much: 4 mild, so-so
one with ~ to say: 4 mime 5 mimer
opposite: 3 all 10 everything
plenty of ~: 3 OOO 4 OOOO 5 OOOOO
saying ~: 3 mum 4 mute 5 quiet 6 silent 7 aphonic 8 nonvocal, taciturn, wordless 9 secretive, soundless, voiceless 10 pantomimic, speechless, tongue-tied
special: 5 plain, usual 7 average, routine, typical 8 ordinary, standard
to it: 4 easy 6 simple 7 a picnic 9 a pushover 10 child's play
to write home about: 4 fair 7 average 8 mediocre, middling, ordinary, passable 9 tolerable
where love means ~: 6 tennis
with ~ on: 3 raw 4 bare, nude 5 naked 6 unclad 7 unrobed 8 disrobed, in the raw, starkers, stripped, undraped 9 au naturel, in the buff, unadorned, unattired, unclothed, uncovered, undressed
nothing ___: 4 much 5 at all
___-nothing: 4 know 5 all-or
Nothing ___!: 4 to it 5 doing
Nothing ___?: 4 else
___ Nothing: 4 Fear 5 All or, I Have
___ Nothing at All: 5 All or
Nothing but blue skies do ___: 4 I see
Nothing But Heartaches (1965 song)
artist: Supremes
Nothing but net: 5 swish
Nothing but the ___: 4 best
Nothing but the Truth (1941 film)
cast: Edward Arnold, Paulette Goddard, Bob Hope
Nothing can stop ___!: 5 me now
Nothing Compares 2 U (1990 song)
artist: Sinéad O'Connor
Nothing doing!: 2 no 3 nah, naw, nay, nix, non 4 nein, nope, nyet, uh-uh 5 I won't, ixnay, never, no how, no way 6 no deal, noways, nowise, rebuff 7 I refuse 8 forget it, I will not, negative, negatory 9 by no means, fat chance, I think not, rejection 10 count me out, not a chance, thumbs down
Nothing From Nothing (1964 song)
artist: Billy Preston
Nothing Gold Can Stay: 4 poem
author: Robert Frost
Nothing in Common (1986 film)
cast: Jackie Gleason, Tom Hanks, Eva Marie Saint, Sela Ward
director: Garry Marshall
Nothing Lasts Forever author: Sidney Sheldon
nothingness: 4 void 5 limbo 6 vacuum
___ nothing of: 5 think, to say
Nothing runs like a ___: 5 Deere
___ nothings: 5 sweet
___-Nothings: 4 Know
Nothing Sacred (1937 film)
cast: Carole Lombard, Fredric March
director: William Wellman
Nothing's Gonna Stop Us Now (1987 song) artist: Starship
nothing to ___ at: 6 sneeze
Nothin' Yet (1967 song) artist: Blues Magoos
notice: 3 att., eye, see, spy 4 attn., call, data, dope, espy, find, heed, info, look, mark, memo, poop, sign, spot, view, wind, word 5 sense, watch 6 advert, attend, behold, caveat, credit, descry, detect, espial, lesson, regard, remark, report, take in, ticket, tipoff 7 account, caution, discern, handout, look out, lowdown, make out, mention, message, observe, pay heed, receipt, release, warning 8 advisory, bulletin, discover, interest, keep tabs, listen to, perceive, reminder 9 attention, give ear to, news flash, recognize 10 admonition, communiqué, get a load of, memorandum
at short ~: 7 quickly 9 summarily
don't ~: 4 miss 6 forget, ignore, pass up 7 tune out 8 overlook, pass over
favorable ~: 4 rave
give ~: 4 quit, warn 5 leave 6 be gone, resign
in French: 4 avis
put on ~: 4 warn 5 alert 6 inform, remind, signal, tip off 7 caution 8 admonish, forewarn, threaten
put up a ~: 4 post
take ~: 5 sit up, watch 6 listen
take ~ of: 3 see 4 heed, mark 6 regard
___ notice: 4 give, take 5 put on, short 7 advance, reading
noticeable: 5 plain 6 marked, signal 7 evident, glaring, obvious, outward, salient, visible 8 apparent, distinct, flagrant, manifest, palpable, striking 9 arresting, obtrusive, prominent
noticeably: 4 very 5 extra, plain, quite 6 rather 8 markedly
___ notice of: 4 take
notices, old-style: 5 seest
Not if ___ help it!: 4 I can
notification: 4 info 5 alert 6 report, signal 7 heads-up, message, warning
notify: 4 call, post, tell, warn 5 alert, phone, prime, write 6 advise, fill in, inform, report, tip off 7 apprise, apprize, caution 8 advise of, instruct 9 telephone, touch base 10 send word to
No Time (1996 song)
artist: Lil' Kim, Puff Daddy
No Time (1970 song) artist: Guess Who
No Time for Sergeants (1958 film)
cast: Nick Adams, Andy Griffith, Don Knotts
director: Mervyn LeRoy
dog: 7 Old Blue
Not interested!: 3 nah 4 nope
not in the ___: 5 least
notion: 4 idea, view, whim 5 guess, hunch, image, stand, thing 6 belief, intent, reason, vagary 7 caprice, concept, feeling, inkling, opinion, surmise, thought 8 nicknack 9 intention, leitmotif, suspicion 10 conception, impression, knickknack, suggestion
case: 4 etui 5 etwee
combining form: 4 ideo-
false ~: 4 myth 7 fantasy 8 delusion, illusion
form a ~: 5 think 6 ideate
in French: 4 idée
odd ~: 4 whim 5 fancy 6 vagary 7 caprice 8 crotchet
preconceived ~: 4 bias, tilt 5 slant 7 bigotry, leaning 9 prejudice 10 partiality
notional: 6 unreal 8 academic 9 imaginary 10 capricious
not know from ___: 4 Adam
not lift a ___: 6 finger
not make ___ or tails of: 5 heads
not miss ___: 5 a beat 6 a trick
not my ___: 4 type
not my ___ of tea: 3 cup
not on ___ life: 4 your
Not on a bet!: 4 uh-uh 8 forget it
not one ___ cent: 3 red
...not one ___ for tribute: 4 cent
Not One Minute More (1959 song)
artist: Della Reese
Not on your life!: 3 nay 4 as if, nope 5 never, no sir 8 forget it
notoriety: 4 fame 6 infamy, renown 7 obloquy 8 dishonor 9 celebrity, disrepute, ill repute, publicity, spotlight 10 reputation
notorious: 3 bad 4 evil, foul 5 shady 6 arrant, famous 7 leading 8 infamous, shameful 9 egregious, well-known 10 outrageous, villainous
Notorious (1946 film)
cast: Ingrid Bergman, Cary Grant, Claude Rains
director: Alfred Hitchcock
setting: 3 Rio 6 Brazil
Notorious (1986 song) artist: Duran Duran
Notorious B.I.G.
song: Been Around the World (1998)
Big Poppa (1995)
Can't You See (1995)
Hypnotize (1997)
It's All About the Benjamins (1997)
Juicy (1994)
Mo Money Mo Problems (1997)
One More Chance (1995)
Victory (1998)
notornis: 4 bird
no-trade ___: 6 clause
Notre Dame: 6 school 9 cathedral
abbr.: 3 UND
conference: 7 Big East
former ~ name: 3 Ara 5 Knute
locale: 5 Paris 6 France 7 Indiana
river: 5 Seine
service: 5 messe
sight: 3 île
team: 5 Irish
see also French
not so ___: 3 bad, far, hot 4 fast
not so bad: 2 OK 4 fair, okay, so-so 8 adequate, passable
Not so fast!: 4 stop 6 hold it
Not So Stories author: 4 Saki
___ Not Spock: 3 I Am
___ Not Taken, The: 4 Road
___ notte: 5 buona
not the ___ of it: 4 half
___ Not the Cat: 5 Touch
___ Not There: 4 She's
Nottingham: 4 city, town
locale: 7 England
river: 5 Trent
Nottinghamshire: 6 county
locale: 7 England
Notting Hill (1999 film)
cast: Hugh Grant, Julia Roberts
not to ___: 5 worry 7 mention
Not to Keep author: Robert Frost
Not Tonight (1997 song)
artist: Da Brat, Lil' Kim, Missy Elliott
not too ___: 3 bad 6 shabby
___ not to reason why...: 4 ours 6 theirs
Not to worry!: 5 it's OK
Notts: 6 county
locale: 7 England
not turn ___: 5 a hair
___ Not Unusual: 3 It's
No Turn ___: 5 on Red
Notus, mother of: 3 Eos
___ not what your country...: 3 Ask
Not with ___ but...: 5 a bang
Not With My Wife You Don't! (1966 film)
cast: Tony Curtis, Virna Lisi, Carroll O'Connor, George C. Scott
director: Norman Panama
Not Without My Daughter (1991 film)
cast: Sally Field, Alfred Molina
notwithstanding: 3 but, tho, yet 5 altho, aside, still 6 albeit, anyhow, anyway, though 7 despite, however 8 after all, although 9 at any rate, in any case, in spite of 10 in any event, regardless
no two ___ about it: 4 ways
not worth ___: 4 a fig, a sou 5 a cent
not worth ___ cent: 4 a red
not worth ___ of beans: 5 a hill
not worth his ___: 4 salt
no two ways ___ it: 5 about
Not Yet the Dodo author: Noël Coward
Not you ___!: 5 again
NO U-___: 4 TURN
Nouakchott: 4 city, port, town 7 capital
locale: 10 Mauritania
nougat: 5 candy 6 bonbon 9 sweetmeat
nought: 3 nil, zip 4 nada, zero 5 squat, zilch 6 bubkes, bupkes, bupkis, cipher 7 nothing 8 goose egg
bring to ~: 4 do in, raze, ruin, undo 5 total 7 destroy, wipe out 8 bulldoze, demolish 9 devastate 10 annihilate, obliterate
starter: 5 dread
noughts-and-crosses: 9 tic-tac-toe
nonwinner: 3 OOX, OXO, OXX, XOO, XOX, XXO
winner: 3 OOO, XXX
noun: 4 word 6 object 7 subject
in French: 3 nom
starter: 3 pro
suffix: 3 -acy, -ade, -age, -ana, -ant, -ard, -ary, -ase, -ate, -cle, -dom, -een, -eer, -ent, -eon, -ery, -ese, -ess, -eum, -eur, -ian, -ice, -ics, -ier, -ile, -ine, -ion, -ism, -ist, -ite, -ity, -ium, -kin, -let, -mas, -nik, -oid, -ola, -oon, -ory, -ose, -ton, -tor, -ude, -ure 4 -aire, -ance, -ancy, -ator, -cade, -ella, -elle, ence, -ency, -enne, -eroo, -ette, -etum, -euse, -goer, -hood, -iana, -itis, -kins, -ling, -ment, -mony, -ness, -osis, -plex, -ship, -some, -ster, -tain, -tion, -tory, -trix, -tude 5 -acity, -arian, -arium, -aster, -athon, -ation, -ician, -ition, -maker, -ology, -orial, -scape, -shire 6 -making, -mobile 7 -ability, -escence, -faction, -fulness, -ibility, -ization, -manship, -meister 8 -fication
noun ___: 6 clause, phrase 7 adjunct
___ noun: 4 mass 5 agent, count 6 bloody, common, proper, verbal 7 passive
nouns, like some foreign: 3 fem. 4 masc., neut. 6 neuter 8 feminine 9 masculine
Nouri: 7 Michael
nourish: 4 feed, fuel, keep, rear 5 breed, raise 6 foster 7 bring up, care for, nurture, support, sustain 9 cultivate 10 strengthen
nourished: 3 fed
was ~: 3 ate
was ~ by: 5 fed on
nourishing: 4 rich 6 alible, edible 7 healthy 9 wholesome 10 alimentary
nourishing, name meaning: 4 Alma
nourishment: 4 chow, diet, eats, food, fuel, grub, meat 5 bread 6 intake, viands 7 aliment, vittles 8 victuals 9 provender 10 provisions
combining form: 5 troph- 6 tropho-
divine ~: 5 manna
needing ~: 5 unfed 6 hungry 9 famishedd

take ~: **3** eat, sup **4** dine, nosh **5** feast, graze **6** ingest **7** consume, partake **9** have a bite **10** gormandize
nous: 5 brain **6** reason **9** intellect, mentality, reasoning
entre ~: 7 sub rosa **8** in secret, secretly **9** between us, privately
__ no use!: 3 It's
__ no use for: 4 have
nouveau __: 5 riche **6** pauvre
__ Nouveau: 3 Art **4** Club
nouveau riche: 7 parvenu, upstart **9** arriviste
nouvelle __: 5 vague **7** cuisine
Nov.: 2 mo.
event: 4 elec.
follower: 3 Dec.
predecessor: 3 Oct.
see also November
nova: 3 lox **6** salmon
bossa ~: 5 dance, music
Nova: 3 car **4** auto **5** Chevy **9** Chevrolet
Nova __: 6 Scotia **7** Express
__ Nova: 3 Ars
Nova Express author: William S. Burroughs
Novak: 3 Eva, Kim **6** Robert
colleague: 5 Evans
Novak, Kim: 7 actress
film: 5 Against the House (1955)
Bell, Book and Candle (1958)
Boys' Night Out (1962)
Kiss Me, Stupid (1964)
The Man With the Golden Arm (1955)
The Mirror Crack'd (1980)
Pal Joey (1957)
Picnic (1955)
Vertigo (1958)
Novalis: 6 German, writer
Nova network: 3 PBS
subject: 3 sci. **7** science
Novarese: 4 font **8** typeface
Novarro, Ramon: 5 actor
film: Ben-Hur (1926)
The Cat and the Fiddle (1934)
Mata Hari (1932)
The Student Prince in Old Heidelberg (1927)
Nova Scotia
bay: 5 Fundy
cape: 5 Canso
capital: 7 Halifax
city: 5 Truro **6** Argyle, Pictou **7** Baddeck, Halifax **8** New Minas **9** Dartmouth, Sackville **10** Cape Breton, New Glasgow
hrs.: 3 AST
Indian: 6 Micmac
locale: 6 Canada
once: 6 Acadia
school: 6 Acadia **9** Dalhousie
Nova Scotia __: 3 lox **6** salmon
Novatian: 4 pope **7** pontiff
Novato: 4 city, town
locale: 10 California
nove: 4 nine **7** Italian
follower: 5 dieci
preceder: 4 otto
novel: 3 new **4** book, saga, tale **5** fresh, genre, prose, story **6** clever, modern, recent, unique **7** fiction, mystery, new wave, offbeat, romance, strange, unusual, Western, writing **8** brand-new, creative, inspired, neoteric, original, thriller, uncommon, whodunit **9** adventure, different, ingenious, inventive, love story, narrative, paperback, potboiler, unheard-of **10** avant-garde, bestseller, futuristic, innovative, literature, newfangled, pocket book, refreshing, roman à clef, unexplored, unfamiliar
ender: 3 ist **4** ette
__ novel: 4 dime, saga **6** Gothic **7** graphic
novelist: 6 author, writer **9** wordsmith
concern: 4 plot **9** story line
Novell, home of: 4 Orem, Utah
Novello: 3 Don
novelty: 3 fad **5** curio, gismo, gizmo **6** change, dingus, doodad, gadget, trifle **7** newness, trinket **8** nicknack, original **9** departure, doohickey, freshness, invention **10** innovation, knickknack, new wrinkle, uniqueness
novelty __: 3 act **6** siding
November: 5 month
birthstone: 5 topaz
form: 6 ballot
honoree: 3 vet **7** veteran
lever puller: 5 voter
lineup: 5 slate
sign: 6 Archer **7** Scorpio **8** Scorpion
victors: 3 ins
November 5: 5 nones
November Rain (1992 song) artist: Guns N' Roses
November Woods composer: 3 Bax
Novembre: 4 mois **5** month **6** French
Novgorod: 4 city
locale: 6 Russia
Novi: 4 city, town
locale: 8 Michigan
Novi __: 3 Sad
novia: 2 jo **3** pet **4** baby, dear, jill, love **5** amour, angel, cooky, cutey, cutie, deary, ducky, flame, honey, leman, lover, lovey, sugar, sweet **6** chérie, cookie, dautie, dearie, steady, sweets **7** beloved, dearest, dear one, pigsney, schatzi, squeeze, sweetie, tootsie **8** chou-chou, cutie pie, dowsabel, dulcinea, ladylove, lovebird, macushla, paramour, precious, snookums, sugar pie, sweetums, truelove **9** bonne amie, dreamboat, inamorata, petit chou, valentine **10** girlfriend, heartthrob, honeybunch, mavourneen, sweetheart, sweetie pie, turtledove
novice: 3 cub **4** tiro, tyro **5** newie, pupil **6** greeny, intern, newbie, rookie **7** amateur, convert, dabbler, entrant, interne, learner, new hand, recruit, student, trainee **8** beginner, freshman, green one, neophyte, newcomer, putterer **9** fledgling, greenhorn, layperson, religious **10** apprentice, catechumen, dilettante, tenderfoot
academy ~: 4 pleb **5** frosh, plebe
Novikoff: 3 Lou
novio: 5 chéri **6** bon ami **9** boyfriend, inamorato
see also novia
Novi Sad: 4 city, town
locale: 6 Serbia
novitiate: 4 tiro, tyro **7** convert, recruit **8** beginner **10** apprentice, catechumen
novo
de ~: 4 anew **5** again **6** afresh **10** from the top
novocaine
give ~: 4 numb **6** benumb, deaden, inject
target: 5 nerve
Novocaine (2001 film)
cast: Helena Bonham Carter, Laura Dern, Steve Martin
Novotna: 4 Jana
__ novus seclorum: 4 ordo
now: 2 in **3** new, PDQ, yet **4** anon, ASAP, chic, stat **5** as yet, faddy, today, vogue **6** at once, modern, modish, pronto, timely, trendy, with it **7** current, in vogue, popular, present, stylish **8** promptly, right off, up-to-date **9** at present, currently, forthwith, on the spot, presently, right away **10** at this time, the present, this minute
and forever: 7 eternal **8** immortal, timeless, unending **9** perpetual
and then: 6 rarely, seldom **7** at times **9** sometimes **10** on occasion
any minute ~: 4 anon, soon **7** shortly
before ~: 3 ago **7** already **8** hitherto
between then and ~: 5 since, so far
by ~: 3 yet **5** so far **7** already **10** beforehand, heretofore, previously
for ~: 8 meantime **9** meanwhile
from Jan. 1 to ~: 3 YTD **5** so far
from ~ on: 5 hence **8** evermore **9** hereafter **10** henceforth
happening ~: 4 live **7** current, running
here and ~: 5 today **6** at once **7** quickly **8** promptly, right off **9** at present, forthwith, presently, right away **10** at this time, this minute
hours from ~: 5 after **6** in time **7** by and by **8** in a while **9** afterward **10** thereafter
how ~: 4 ciao **5** aloha, hello **6** shalom **7** bon jour **8** greeting
not ~: 4 anon, then **5** after, later **6** in a bit, in time **7** by and by **8** in a while **9** afterward **10** eventually, thereafter
only ~: 4 just **6** lately **8** latterly, recently
partner: 4 here, then
right ~: 3 PDQ **4** anon, ASAP, stat **5** as yet, today **6** at once, pronto **7** quickly, swiftly **8** promptly **9** at present, forthwith, instantly, on the spot, presently **10** at this time, the present, this minute
starter: 3 ere
until ~: 3 ago, yet **4** once, till **5** as yet, so far, still **6** before, hereto, of late, to date **7** earlier, prior to, thus far **8** formerly, hereunto, hitherto **9** preceding, to this day **10** before this, heretofore, previously, to this time
__ now: 4 as of, just, up to **5** until
__ now!: 3 Act
Now __ here!: 3 see
Now __ me...: 4 I lay
Now __ seen everything!: 3 I've
Now __ theater near you!: 3 at a
Now __ this!: 4 hear
Now __ time for all...: 5 is the
Now __ you!: 4 I ask
__ Now: 3 'Til **4** Even **5** See It
NOW
cause: 3 ERA
part of ~: 3 Org. **4** Natl. **5** Women
NOW __: 7 account
nowadays: 6 lately **9** presently
Nowadays musical: 7 Chicago
now and __: 4 then **5** again
Now and Forever (1994 song) artist: Richard Marx
__ now and then: 5 every
No way!: 3 nah **4** as if, uh-uh **5** never **6** can't be
No way, __!: 4 José
__ No Way: 4 Ain't
No Way Out (1950 film)
cast: Linda Darnell, Stephen McNally, Richard Widmark
director: Joseph L. Mankiewicz
No Way Out (1987 film)
cast: Kevin Costner, Gene Hackman, Sean Young
No Way to Treat a Lady (1968 film)
cast: Lee Remick, George Segal, Rod Steiger
__ No Way to Treat a Lady: 4 Ain't
__ now, brown cow: 3 How
Now hear __!: 4 this
nowhere: 4 dull **5** ho-hum, limbo **6** boring, uncool **7** humdrum **8** tiresome **10** dullsville
come out of ~: 5 bob up, pop up
going ~: 6 adrift, in a rut **9** pointless
middle of ~: 5 limbo, wilds **6** remote
near: 4 afar **6** remote
to be found: 4 away, AWOL, gone, lost **6** absent **7** far away, missing **8** vanished
__ nowhere: 3 get **5** out of
Nowhere __: 3 Man **5** to Run
Nowhere author: Thomas Berger
Nowhere Man (1966 song) artist: Beatles
Nowhere to Run (1965 song) artist: Martha & the Vandellas
Now I __ me...: 3 lay
Now I get it!: 3 aha, oho
no-win: 4 grim, vain **5** bleak **6** futile **7** useless **8** hopeless **9** desperate, fruitless, pointless, senseless **10** impossible, irremedial
situation: 3 tie **4** bind **7** dilemma **8** dead heat, deadlock, quandary, standoff **9** stalemate
nowise: 3 nah, naw, nay, nix, non **4** nein, nope, nyet, uh-uh **5** I won't, ixnay, never **7** I refuse **8** forget it, I will not, negative, negatory **9** fat chance, I think not **10** count me out, not a chance, thumbs down
Now It Can Be __: 4 Told
Now I understand!: 3 Aha
Now I've __ everything!: 4 seen
Nowlan: 4 Phil **5** Alden
Nowlan, Alden: 6 writer **8** Canadian
work: Between Tears and Laughter
Bread, Wine and Salt
I'm a Stranger Here Myself
Miracle at Indian River
now more __ ever: 4 than
__ Now My Love?: 4 What
__ no wonder!: 3 It's
now or __: 5 never
__ Now or Never: 3 It's
__ Now Praise Famous Men: 5 Let Us
Now see __!: 4 here
Now that __ there: 6 April's
Now, Voyager (1942 film)
cast: Bette Davis, Paul Henreid, Claude Rains
composer: 7 Steiner
director: Irving Rapper
Now We Are Six author: A.A. Milne
Now you __...: 5 see it
Now You Know author: Michael Frayn
noxious: 4 foul, rank, vile **5** fetid, nasty, toxic **6** foetid, lethal, rancid, rotten, sickly, smelly, stinky **7** baneful, harmful, hurtful, noisome, odorous, reeking **8** inimical, mephitic, stinking **9** injurious, pestilent, poisonous, unhealthy **10** insanitary, malodorous, pernicious
plant: 4 weed **9** stinkweed
vapor: 4 fume
Noyce: 6 Robert **7** Phillip
Noyce, Phillip: 8 director
film: Backroads (1977)
The Bone Collector (1999)
Clear and Present Danger (1994)
Dead Calm (1989)
Patriot Games (1992)
The Saint (1997)
Noyes, Alfred: 4 poet **6** writer **7** British
work: The Barrel-Organ
Drake
The Highwayman
The Torch-Bearers
Noyori, Ryoji: 7 chemist **8** Nobelist
nozzle: 3 tap **5** spout **6** outlet
output: 4 mist **5** spray, water

Np: 4 elem. 7 element 9 neptunium
  93 for ~: 4 at. no.
___-n-Pepa: 4 Salt
NPR part: 3 Nat. 4 Natl. 5 Radio 6 Public 8 National
NPS
  department: 8 Interior
  part: 3 Nat. 4 Natl., Park 7 Service 8 National
NRA: 5 lobby
  part: 3 Nat. 4 Assn., Natl. 5 Admin., Assoc., Rifle 8 National, Recovery
  program: 3 CCC
  symbol: 5 eagle
NRC
  part: 3 Reg. 4 Comm. 7 Nuclear 10 Regulatory
  predecessor: 3 AEC
N-R connection: 3 OPQ
___-'n'-roll: 4 rock
NSA: 3 org.
  part: 3 Nat., Sec. 4 Agcy., Natl. 6 Agency 8 National, Security
  worker: 3 spy
NSC
  org. that advises the ~: 3 CIA
  part: 3 Nat., Sec. 4 Natl. 7 Council 8 National, Security
N-S connection: 4 OPQR
NSF part: 3 Nat., not, Sci. 4 Natl. 5 funds 7 Science 8 National 10 Foundation, sufficient
NSX: 3 car 4 auto 5 Acura 10 automobile
  automaker: 5 Acura
'N Sync
  hometown: Orlando
  members: Kirkpatrick, Chasez, Fatone, Timberlake, Bass
  song: I Want You Back (1998) A Little More Time on You (1998) Music of My Heart (1999)
N.T.
  book: 3 Col., Eph., Gal., Heb., Rev., Rom., Tim. 4 Hebr., Matt., Thes. 5 Thess.
  letter: 5 Epist.
  passage: 3 ver.
  see also Bible, New Testament
N-T connection: 5 OPQRS
ntenga: 4 drum
  origin: 6 Uganda
nth: 3 ult. 6 utmost 7 extreme, highest, maximum 8 ultimate
  degree: 3 max 7 extreme 8 ultimate
  to the ~ degree: 6 in full, in toto, wholly 7 utterly 9 all the way, extremely, to the hilt 10 altogether, thoroughly
nth ___: 5 power 6 degree
___ N the Hood: 4 Boyz
NTSB
  part of ~: 3 Nat. 4 Natl. 5 Board, Trans. 6 Safety
___-'n'-turf: 4 surf
nu: 5 Greek 6 letter
  follower: 2 xi
  preceder: 2 mu
nuance: 5 sense, shade, tinge, trace 6 nicety 7 meaning, shading 8 delicacy, overtone, quiddity, subtlety 9 fine point, punctilio 10 refinement
nub: 4 core, crux, gist, knob, lump, meat, root 5 focus, heart, piece, point, stump 6 center, kernel 7 essence, keynote, nucleus, purport 8 key point 9 main point, substance 10 protrusion
nubbin: 5 stump
nubby: 5 bumpy, rough 6 coarse 7 bristly, grating, scruffy, stubbly 8 abrasive
nubia: 5 scarf
Nubia
  ancient city: 5 Meroe
  ancient kingdom: 4 Cush
Nubian: 6 desert
  locale: 5 Sudan 6 Africa
Nubian ___: 4 goat 6 Desert
Nubira: 3 car 4 auto 6 Daewoo 10 automobile
___ Nubium: 4 Mare
nucha: 4 nape 6 scruff
  site: 4 neck
nuclear: 6 atomic 7 central 8 atomical
  element used in ~ reactors: 5 boron
  energy source: 4 atom
  energy watchdog: 3 AEC, NRC
  experiment: 5 A test, H test, N test
  1979 ~ accident site: 3 TMI
  reaction: 6 fusion 7 fission
  reactor part: 4 core, pile
  tryout: 5 A test
  weapon: 4 ICBM, MIRV 5 A bomb, H bomb, N bomb
nuclear ___: 3 age 4 fuel 5 power 6 energy, family, fusion, isomer, weapon 7 fission, physics, reactor
Nuclear ___-Ban Treaty: 4 Test
nuclear physics: 7 science
  study: 5 atoms
nucleic: 4 acid
  compound: 3 DNA, RNA
  starter: 4 ribo
nucleotide, DNA: 3 ATP
nucleus: 3 hub, nub 4 core, germ, knub, meat, pith, seed 5 basis, cadre, heart, midst, spark 6 center, embryo, kernel, origin 7 essence
  combining form: 5 caryo-, karyo-
nuclide: 6 isomer
nude: 3 raw 4 bare, pink 5 brown, model, naked 6 unclad 7 exposed, grayish 8 brownish, disrobed, in the raw, starkers, undraped 9 au naturel, in the buff, unattired, unclothed, uncovered, undressed, yellowish 10 unshielded
  relative: 3 bay, dun, tan 4 bole, ecru, fawn, foxy, seal 5 amber, beige, camel, cocoa, hazel, khaki, melon, mocha, sepia, tawny, umber 6 auburn, bister, bistre, bronze, coffee, copper, damask, ginger, russet, salmon, sienna, sorrel, suntan, walnut 7 apricot, biscuit, caramel, dogwood 8 chestnut, cinnamon, flamingo, mahogany 9 butternut, carnation, chocolate
nudge: 3 jab, jog 4 bump, poke, prod, push, wake 5 brush, elbow, punch, shove, tease, touch, waken 6 badger, bother, jiggle, jostle, justle, pester, prompt, thrust 8 shoulder
nudnik: 4 pest, pill, twit 5 twerp, twirp
Nueces: 5 river
  locale: 5 Texas
Nuer home: 5 Sudan 6 Africa
Nueva Rosita: 4 city, town
  locale: 6 Mexico 8 Coahuila
nueve: 4 nine 7 Spanish
  follower: 4 diez
  preceder: 4 ocho
___ nuevo: 3 año
Nuevo Laredo: 4 city, town
  locale: 6 Mexico 10 Tamaulipas
Nuevo León: 5 state 7 Mexican
  city: 6 García 7 Allende, Anáhuac, Apodaca, Linares 8 Coahuila, Jardines, Santiago 9 Cadereyta, Guadalupe, Monterrey
Nuevo México: 4 city, town
  locale: 6 Mexico 7 Jalisco
___ nuff!: 3 Sho'
nugatory: 4 vain 6 futile 7 invalid, trivial 8 negative, trifling
Nugent: 3 Ted 7 Elliott
nugget: 4 hunk, lump, plum 5 chunk, clump 8 valuable
  material: 4 gold 6 silver
Nugget: 5 cager
  rival: 3 Cav, Mav, Net, Sun 4 Buck, Bull, Hawk, Heat, Jazz, King, Spur 5 Knick, Laker, Magic, Pacer, Sixer, Sonic 6 Celtic, Hornet, Piston, Raptor, Rocket, Wizard 7 Clipper, Grizzly, Warrior 8 Cavalier, Maverick 10 SuperSonic, Timberwolf
Nuggets: 4 five, team
  home: 6 Denver
  org.: 3 NBA
  sport: 10 basketball
___ Nui: 4 Rapa
nuisance: 4 bane, bore, drag, pain, pest, pill 5 trial 6 bother, gadfly, hassle, plague 7 trouble 8 headache, irritant, vexation 9 annoyance, liability
  winged ~: 3 fly 4 gnat 5 midge
nuisance ___: 3 tax 6 ground
___ nuit!: 5 Bonne
___ Nuits: 3 Les
nuke: 3 fix, zap 4 cook 5 blast
Nukualofa: 4 city, town 7 capital
  locale: 5 Tonga
null: 4 vain, void, zero 5 blank, empty 6 futile 7 inutile, invalid, useless, vacuous 8 goose egg 9 senseless, valueless, worthless 10 groundless, unavailing
  make ~: 5 quash 6 cancel, repeal, revoke 7 rescind, reverse 8 override, overrule, set aside 9 repudiate, supersede 10 invalidate
null ___: 3 set
___-null: 5 aleph
null and ___: 4 void
nullification: 6 recall 8 negation
nullify: 3 nix 4 kill, undo, void 5 erase, quash 6 cancel, defeat, negate, offset, recall, recant, repeal, revoke, scotch, vacate 7 abolish, balance, destroy, rescind, reverse 8 abrogate, override, overrule, overturn 9 frustrate, repudiate 10 invalidate, neutralize
nullity: 4 zero 10 invalidity
nullius ___: 5 juris 6 filius
num.: 3 amt., qty.
Numan: 4 Gary
Numa, wife of: 6 Egeria
Numazu: 4 city, town
  locale: 5 Japan
numb: 4 stun 5 dazed, inert, shock, stiff 6 asleep, deaden, freeze, frozen, tingly, torpid 7 petrify, sedated, stupefy 8 deadened, hardened, paralyse, paralyze, tuned out 9 apathetic, insensate, senseless, unfeeling 10 anesthetic, impervious, insentient, motionless
  ender: 4 fish 5 skull
  perhaps: 3 ice
numbat: 9 marsupial
  relative: 4 euro 5 bilbi, bilby, koala 6 wombat 7 bettong, dasyure, opossum, wallaby 8 kangaroo, wallaroo 9 bandicoot, phalanger
  tidbit: 3 ant
number: 3 add, amt., lot, one, qty., six, sum, ten, two 4 five, four, mass, nine, page, poll, song, sort, tell, tune, zero 5 count, digit, ditty, eight, gauge, seven, tally, three, total, tot up, troop 6 amount, cipher, figure, legion, reckon, volume 7 add up to, compute, include, itemize, species, tick off 8 amount to, classify, quantity 9 aggregate, calculate, character, enumerate, multitude, specialty
  additional ~: 6 encore
  a ~ of: 4 some 7 several
  a ~ of times: 5 often 9 regularly 10 frequently, repeatedly
  back ~: 7 vintage 8 obsolete, outdated, outmoded 9 out-of-date 10 antiquated
  base of a ~ system: 5 radix
  combining form: 7 arithmo-
  countdown ~: 3 one, six, ten, two 4 five, four, nine, zero 5 eight, seven, three
  cruncher: 3 CPA 4 acct. 7 analyst
  do a ~: 4 sing 5 croon 6 warble 7 perform 8 vocalize
  do a ~ on: 3 con 4 bilk, dupe, gull, rook 5 cheat, shaft 6 defame, delude, take in 7 deceive, defraud, swindle 8 flimflam
  five-digit ~: 3 Zip
  French ~: 2 un 3 dix, six 4 cent, cinq, deux, huit, neuf, onze, sept, zero 5 douze, mille, seize, trois, vingt 6 quatre, quinze, treize, trente 8 quarante, quatorze, soixante 9 cinquante
  German ~: 3 elf 4 acht, drei, eins, fünf, neun, null, vier, zehn, zwei 5 sechs, zwölf 6 sieben 7 achtzig, fünfzig, hundert, neunzig, sechzig, siebzig, tausend, vierzig, zwanzig
  goodly ~: 4 gobs, lots, tons 5 heaps, horde, piles, scads 6 divers, legion, myriad, oodles, plenty, scores, throng, untold 7 jillion, no end of, umpteen 8 numerous 9 abundance, countless, multitude, thousands, uncounted 10 numberless
  indefinite ~: 3 any, few 4 many, some
  irrational ~: 4 surd
  Italian ~: 3 due, sei, tre, uno 4 nove, otto, zero 5 cento, dieci, mille, sette, venti 6 cinque, dodici, sedici, trenta, undici 7 novanta, ottanta, quattro, tredici 8 diciotto, quaranta, quindici, sessanta 9 cinquanta
  large ~: 3 lot, ton 4 host, load, lots, many, raft, scad, slew, tons 5 crowd, loads, scads, spate 6 googol, scores 9 multitude
  lucky ~: 5 seven
  next to a plus sign: 6 addend
  nightclub ~: 4 song 6 ballad
  nine-digit ~: 3 Zip
  one: 3 ace, top 4 best, tops 5 champ, chief, first, great, prime 6 leader, select, top dog, winner 7 leading, primary 8 champion, favorite, foremost, stunning 9 governing 10 celebrated, overriding, preeminent
  out for ~ one: 6 greedy 7 hoggish, selfish 8 egoistic 9 egotistic 10 egocentric, egoistical
  small ~: 3 few 7 handful, not many 10 scattering, smattering
  Spanish ~: 3 dos, mil, uno 4 cero, cien, diez, doce, ocho, once, seis, tres 5 cinco, nueve, siete, trece 6 quarto, quince, veinte 7 catorce, noventa, ochenta, sesenta, setenta, treinta 8 cuarenta 9 cincuenta
  system: 5 octal 6 binary
  target: 5 quota
  two: 4 veep, vice 6 veepee
number ___: 3 one 4 line, sign 5 opera 6 please, theory
___ number: 4 Abbe, acid, back, call, mach, mass, real, stop, wave, Wolf 5 index, lucky, magic, mixed, prime, whole, wrong 6 atomic, baryon, beyond, binary, cetane, Cutter, Köchel, lepton, octane, proton, random, serial, signed, square 7 Brinell, complex, Messier, natural, neutron, ordinal, perfect, Prandtl, quantum, sunspot, transit, Vickers, winding, without

___ number can play: 3 any
numbered ___: 7 account
numbered composition: 4 opus
numbering: 5 count, tally 9 reckoning
 computer ~ system: 5 octal 6 binary
numberless: 4 many 6 legion, myriad, untold 8 prodigal 9 countless, limitless, unlimited
___ number on: 3 do a
___ number one!: 4 We're
Number One Son
 father: Charlie Chan
 portrayer: Keye Luke
Number One Son portrayer: Keye Luke
numbers: 3 lot, mob, sea 4 heap, herd, host, lots, many, mass, math, slew 5 bunch, crowd, crush, drove, horde, loads, ocean, swarm, troop 6 legion, myriad, oodles, scores, throng 8 quantity 9 multitude, profusion 10 regulation
 by the ~: 5 exact 6 proper 7 exactly 8 methodic, properly 9 stringent
 change the ~: 5 fudge
 combine ~: 3 add, sum, tot 5 count, sum up, tally, total, tot up 6 figure 7 compute, count up 9 calculate
 exist in great ~: 4 teem 5 swarm 6 abound, thrive 8 flourish, overflow
 game: 4 keno 5 beano, bingo, lotto 7 lottery
 in great ~: 6 galore 9 profusely
 like our ~: 6 Arabic
numbers ___: 4 game 6 racket
___ numbers: 5 by the
Numbers
 follower: 4 Deut. 11 Deuteronomy
 preceder: 3 Lev. 5 Levit. 9 Leviticus
Number Two Son portrayer: Victor Sen Yung
numbing: 3 icy, raw 4 cold 5 chill, nippy, polar 6 arctic, biting, chilly, frigid, frosty, frozen, wintry 7 shivery, wintery 8 freezing, narcotic, piercing 9 soporific 10 anesthetic
numbskull
 see numskull
numbskulled: 4 dull, slow 5 dopey 6 obtuse 9 dim-witted 10 dull-witted, half-witted, slow-witted
numen: 5 deity
numeral: 5 digit 6 figure, symbol 9 character
 clock ~: 3 III, VII, XII 4 IIII, VIII
___ numeral: 5 Roman 6 Arabic 7 ordinal
numerals, like our: 6 Arabic
Numerals, The painter: 4 Erté
numerate: 4 tell 5 count, tally 9 keep score
numeric ___: 6 keypad
numerical
 base: 5 radix
 correspondence: 5 ratio
 fact: 4 stat 5 datum 9 statistic
 goal: 5 quota
 prefix: 3 ter-, tri-, uni- 4 hexa-, mono-, octa-, octo- 5 hepta-, penta-, septi-, tetra- 6 quadri-
 suffix: 3 -eth 4 -teen
numerical ___: 5 value 7 control
numeric starter: 5 alpha
numero uno: 4 boss 5 first 8 champion 10 celebrated
 place: 5 on top
numerous: 4 lots, many, rife 5 lotsa, thick 6 a lot of, divers, gobs of, legion, lots of, myriad, umteen, untold 7 a host of, a slew of, copious, heaps of, no end of, piles of, profuse, scads of, several, teeming, umpteen, various 8 a bunch of, abundant, an army of, frequent, iterated, manifold, multiple, oodles of, prodigal, scores of, umpsteen 9 a good many, a passel of, bountiful, countless, prevalent, quite a few 10 zillions of
 be ~: 4 teem 5 swarm 6 abound
 combining form: 4 myri- 5 myrio-
numinous: 4 holy 6 mystic, sacred 8 mystical 10 miraculous
numismatic grade: 3 unc. 4 fine
nummulite: 6 fossil
numskull: 3 ass, oaf, sap 4 boob, bozo, clod, dodo, dolt, dope, fool, simp 5 chump, clown, cluck, dummy, dunce, joker, ninny, patsy 6 dimwit, lubber, lummox, nitwit, sucker, turkey 7 buffoon, dingbat, dullard, fathead, half-wit, jackass, pinhead, saphead 8 bonehead, dumbbell, meathead 9 birdbrain, blockhead, harebrain, lamebrain, simpleton 10 dunderhead
nun: 6 abbess, Hebrew, letter, mother, sister 7 recluse 8 prioress 9 anchoress, Carmelite, Poor Clare, postulant, religious 10 conventual
 Albanian-born ~: 6 Teresa
 group: 6 clergy
 home: 4 cell 5 abbey 7 convent
 predecessor: 3 mem
 Spanish ~: 5 monja
 successor: 6 samech, samekh
 wear: 4 coif, veil 5 habit 6 wimple
nun ___: 4 buoy
Nunavut city: 7 Iqaluit
nuncio: 5 envoy 6 legate 8 delegate, emissary
___ Núñez de Balboa: 5 Vasco
Nunki: 4 star
Nunkun: 4 peak 5 mount 8 mountain
 locale: 4 Asia 7 Kashmir 8 Cashmere 9 Himalayas
Nunn: 3 Sam 6 Trevor
Nunnally: 7 Johnson
nunnery: 5 abbey 7 convent 8 cloister
nun's ___: 6 fiddle 7 veiling
Nun's Story, The (1959 film)
 cast: Dame Edith Evans, Peter Finch, Audrey Hepburn
 director: Fred Zinnemann
___ Nun, The: 6 Flying
nuptial: 6 bridal, wedded 7 marital, spousal 9 connubial
 party member: 5 bride, groom, usher 7 best man 8 newlywed 10 ring bearer
 phrase: 3 I do
 starter: 3 pre
nuptial ___: 4 mass 7 plumage
nuptials: 7 wedding 8 espousal, marriage 9 matrimony
 site: 5 altar
Nuremberg: 4 city, town
 city near ~: 5 Furth 6 Coburg
 locale: 7 Germany
Nureyev, Rudolf: 6 dancer 7 danseur
 specialty: 6 ballet
Nurmi, Paavo: 6 runner 7 Finnish 10 Flying Finn
Nürnberg: 4 city, town 5 stadt
 locale: 7 Germany
nurse: 2 RN 3 LPN 4 baby, heal, tend 5 carer, serve, shark, train, treat 6 attend, Barton, coddle, foster, pamper, tend to, wait on 7 bring up, care for, nurture, sit with, support, sustain 8 attend to, Houlihan, minister, wait upon 9 governess, look after 10 minister to, take care of
 a drink: 3 sip 5 sip at
 Asian ~: 3 aia, ama 4 amah, ayah
 deg.: 3 BSN, MNA, MSN
 ender: 4 maid
 helper: 4 aide
 name: 5 Clara
 org.: 3 ANA
 portion: 3 CCs 4 dose 5 ampul 6 ampule 7 ampoule
 specialty: 3 TLC
 subject: 4 anat. 7 anatomy
nurse ___: 4 crop 5 shark
___ nurse: 5 scrub 6 flight 7 student, trained
Nurse Betty (2000 film)
 cast: Morgan Freeman, Greg Kinnear, Chris Rock, Renée Zellweger
Nurse Edith Cavell (1939 film)
 cast: Anna Neagle, Edna May Oliver, George Sanders
nursemaid: 4 nana 5 nanny 6 au pair, nannie 9 governess
 Asian ~: 3 aia, ama 4 amah, ayah
Nurse, Paul: 8 Nobelist
nursery: 4 room 6 hotbed
 color: 4 blue, pink
 complaint: 5 colic
 cry: 3 mom 4 dada, mama 5 mamma
 do a ~ chore: 5 repot
 item: 4 crib, wipe 6 cradle, diaper 8 bassinet
 noise: 3 wah 6 gurgle
 playmate: 3 tot 4 baby 6 infant, sister 7 brother 9 youngster
 purchase: 4 peat, seed, soil 5 plant
 worker: 5 nanny 6 nannie
nursery ___: 5 rhyme 6 school
___ nursery: 3 day
nursery rhyme
 crooked gate of ~: 5 stile
 flower: 4 posy
 food: 4 whey 5 curds, pease
 home of ~: 4 shoe
 merry king of ~: 4 Cole
 start: 6 baa baa
 trio: 4 mice
nursery school: 4 pre-K
 attendee: 3 tot
 item: 4 clay
 ritual: 3 nap
nurse's ___: 4 aide
nurture: 4 back, feed, keep, rear, tend 5 boost, breed, groom, nurse, raise, teach, train 6 cradle, foster, regale, school, uplift 7 advance, aliment, bring up, care for, develop, educate, forward, further, nourish, promote, support, sustain 8 advocate, incubate, instruct, maintain 9 cultivate, encourage, stimulate 10 strengthen, take care of
Nusakan: 4 star
nut: 3 fan 4 bean, buff, cola, kola, kook, meat, seed, zany 5 acorn, betel, crank, fiend, freak, fruit, funds, pecan, piñon 6 addict, almond, budget, cashew, cobnut, kernel, lichee, litchi, maniac, noodle, peanut, pignut, pinyon, quinoa, souari, walnut, zealot 7 admirer, booster, buckeye, caltrop, coconut, devotee, fanatic, filbert, groupie, hickory, leechee, pignoli 8 adherent, beechnut, betelnut, chestnut, fastener, follower, hazelnut, pignolia, shagbark 9 butternut, candlenut, ding-a-ling, macadamia, pistachio 10 aficionado, chinquapin, enthusiast
 astringent ~: 8 betelnut
 bitter ~: 6 pignut
 brittle-shelled ~: 6 lichee, litchi
 cake: 5 torte
 candy: 6 comfit, confit
 candy ~: 6 almond
 case: 3 bur 4 hull, kook 5 crank, shell
 Chinese ~: 6 lichee, litchi 7 leechee
 combining form: 4 nuci- 5 caryo-, karyo-
 ender: 4 gall, meat, pick 5 hatch, shell 7 cracker
 greenish ~: 9 pistachio
 hard-shelled ~: 7 coconut, hickory 8 shagbark 9 macadamia
 holder: 4 bolt
 oily ~: 6 souari 9 butternut, candlenut
 part: 4 meat 6 kernel
 piñon ~: 7 pignoli 8 pignolia
 prickly ~: 8 chestnut 10 chinquapin
 source: 4 tree
 starter: 3 cob, pea, pig 4 gall, lock 5 beech, betel, bread, chest, cocoa, dough, earth, hazel, thumb 6 bitter, butter, candle, ground 7 bladder
 sugarcoated ~: 6 dragée
 tough ~ to crack: 5 poser 6 enigma 7 mystery, stumper, toughie
 tree: 4 kola, pili 5 beech, hazel, pecan 6 acajou, almond, cashew, lichee, litchi 7 buckeye, filbert, leechee 9 macadamia, pistachio
nut ___: 4 coal, dash, pine, quad 5 grass, sedge 6 weevil
___ nut: 3 hex, jam, lug 4 cola, kola, lock, pine, shea, wing 5 areca, betel, ivory, piñon, screw 6 Brazil, cashew, castle, lichee, litchi, monkey, rating, souari 7 leechee, packing
Nut
 daughter of ~: 4 Isis
 son of ~: 6 Osiris
___-Nut: 5 Beech
nutbrown: 5 hazel
___ Nut Cheerios: 5 Honey
nutcracker: 4 bird
 suite: 4 nest
Nutcracker ___: 5 Suite
Nutcracker, The: 6 ballet
 composer: 11 Tchaikovsky
 role: 5 Clara, fairy
nuthatch: 4 bird
 home: 4 nest
Nuthin' But a 'G' Thang (1993 song)
 artist: Dr. Dre, Snoop Doggy Dogg
Nutley: 4 city, town
 locale: 9 New Jersey
nutmeat: 6 kernel
nutmeg: 4 tree 5 spice 9 seasoning
 cousin: 4 mace
 cover: 4 aril
 drink topped with ~: 4 flip
NutRageous: 5 candy 8 candy bar 9 chocolate
 alternative: 4 Mars, Twix 5 Clark, Heath 6 Kit Kat, Mounds, PayDay, Reese's, Zagnut 7 Krackel, Oh Henry 8 Baby Ruth, Hershey's, Milky Way, Snickers 9 Almond Joy, Mr. Goodbar
Nutri-___: 5 Grain
nutria: 3 fur 5 coypu 6 rodent
nutrient
 add a ~ to: 6 enrich
 combining form: 5 troph- 6 tropho-
 mineral ~: 4 iron, zinc
nutrient-___: 5 dense
Nutri-Grain: 6 cereal
 competitor: 3 Kix 4 Life, Trix 5 Kashi, Quisp, Total 6 Kaboom, Muesli, Oreo O's, Pablum, Smacks 7 All-Bran, Crispix, Harmony, Hunny B's, Mueslix, Oat Bran, Pokemon 8 Boo Berry, Cheerios, Corn Chex, Corn Pops, Fiber One, Rice Chex, Special K, Uncle Sam, Wheaties 9 Alpha Bits, Apple Zaps, Grape Nuts, Honey Comb, Just Right, Wheat Chex 10 Apple Jacks, Bran Flakes, Cap'n Crunch, Cocoa Puffs, Froot Loops, Mini-Wheats, Puffed Rice, Quaker Oats, Smart Start 11 Cocoa Blasts, Cookie Crisp, Golden Crisp, Lucky Charms, Puffed Wheat, Sweet Crunch, Waffle Crisp

nutriment: **4** diet, food, meat **6** viands **7** aliment, victual **8** victuals
nutrition: **4** diet, food **10** sustenance
  stat: **3** RDA
  supplement: **5** yeast
  watchdog: **3** FDA
nutritional: **10** alimentary
nutritious: **4** rich **7** healthy **9** healthful, wholesome **10** alimentary
  snack: **4** gorp **8** trail mix
nutritive: **6** edible **7** dietary **9** palatable, wholesome **10** alimentary, comestible
  acid: **5** folic
  mineral: **4** iron, zinc
Nutro: **7** dog food
  alternative: **4** Alpo, Iams **6** Purina **8** Eukanuba **10** Ken-L Ration
nuts
  and bolts: **3** nub **4** knub, pith **6** detail **7** reality
  open ~: **5** crack
  sans ~: **5** plain
  soup to ~: **4** A to Z **6** all-out **7** in-depth **8** complete, sweeping, thorough **9** extensive **10** exhaustive, meticulous
__ nuts: **6** tavern
Nuts (1987 film)
  cast: Richard Dreyfuss, Karl Malden, Maureen Stapleton, Barbra Streisand, Eli Wallach
  director: Martin Ritt
Nuts!: **4** darn, rats **6** darn it, phooey
__ Nuts: **4** Beer **5** Grape
nuts-and-bolts: **9** practical
nuts-and-honey confection: **5** halva **6** halvah **7** halavah
nutshell
  contents: **4** meat
  in a ~: **5** short, terse **8** succinct
  put in a ~: **4** trim **5** sum up **6** digest **7** abridge, shorten **8** simplify **9** summarize
Nuttin' for Christmas (1955 song)
  artist: Art Mooney, Barry Gordon, Ricky Zahnd and the Blue Jeaners
__ nut to crack: **4** hard **5** tough
Nutty Professor, The (1963 film)
  cast: Jerry Lewis, Stella Stevens
  director: Jerry Lewis
Nutty Professor, The (1996 film)
  cast: James Coburn, Eddie Murphy, Jada Pinkett
  director: Tom Shadyac
Nuyen: **6** France
nuzzle: **6** cuddle, nestle **7** embrace, snuggle
NV
  see Nevada
NW: **3** dir.
  state: **3** Ida., Ore. **4** Oreg., Wash.
Nwapa, Flora: **6** writer **8** Nigerian
  work: Efuru
    Idu
    Never Again
    One Is Enough
__ 'N Wash: **5** Spray
NWT
  locale: **3** Can.
  native: **3** Esk.
  part of ~: **3** Ter. **4** Terr., West **5** North
NY
  college: **3** LIU, RIT, RPI, SBU
  neighbor: **3** Ont., Que. **4** Conn., Mass., Penn. **5** Penna.
  setting: **3** EDT, EST
  see also New York
Nyack: **4** city, town
  locale: **7** New York
nyala: **8** antelope
  relative: **3** gnu, kob **4** guib, kudu, oryx, puku, topi **5** addax, bongo, chiru, eland, goral, korin, oribi, saiga, serow **6** chammy, dik-dik, duiker, impala, koodoo, lechwe, nilgai, rhebok, shammy, shamoy **7** blaubok, blesbok, chamois, defassa, gazelle, gemsbok, gerenuk, grysbok, nylghai, nylghau, sassaby **8** blesbuck, bontebok, bushbuck, gemsbuck, reedbuck, steenbok, steinbok **9** blackbuck, pronghorn, sitatunga, springbok, waterbuck **10** hartebeest, wildebeest
Nyamwezi home: **6** Africa **8** Tanzania
Nyanja home: **6** Africa, Malawi **10** Mozambique
Nyasa: **4** lake
  locale: **8** Tanzania **10** Mozambique
Nyby: **9** Christian
NYC: **3** spt. **8** Big Apple
  airport: **3** EWR, JFK, LGA
  art center: **4** MOMA
  borough: **3** Man., Qns. **4** Manh. **5** Bklyn.
  clock setting: **3** EDT, EST
  commuter line: **4** LIRR
  dance co.: **3** ABT
  division: **3** bor.
  dwelling: **3** apt.
  HQ: **5** The UN
  like some ~ plays: **3** OOB
  opera house: **3** Met
  part: **3** bor., Man., New, Qns. **4** City, Manh., York **5** Bklyn.
  PBS affiliate: **4** WNET
  race track: **4** Big A
  radio station: **3** WOR
  sports venue: **3** MSG
  subway: **3** BMT, IND, IRT **6** A Train
  transit org.: **3** MTA
  see also New York City
NY Central: **2** RR
nyctophobe fear: **8** darkness
Nye: **4** Bill **5** Louis **6** Carrie
Nye, Bill subject: **3** sci. **7** science
Nye, Carrie spouse: Dick Cavett
NYer: **9** Gothamite
Nyeri: **4** city, town
  locale: **5** Kenya
nyet: **2** no **3** nah, naw, nay, nix, non **4** nein, nope, uh-uh, veto **5** I won't, ixnay, never, no how, no way **6** no deal, noways, nowise **7** I refuse **8** forget it, I will not, negative, negatory **9** by no means, fat chance, I think not **10** count me out, not a chance, thumbs down
  in French: **3** non
  in Latin: **3** non
  in Scottish: **3** nae
Nyiragongo: **7** volcano
  locale: **5** Congo **6** Africa
nylghai: **8** antelope
  relative: **3** gnu, kob **4** guib, kudu, oryx, puku, topi **5** addax, bongo, chiru, eland, goral, korin, nyala, oribi, saiga, serow **6** chammy, dik-dik, duiker, impala, koodoo, lechwe, rhebok, shammy, shamoy **7** blaubok, blesbok, chamois, defassa, gazelle, gemsbok, gerenuk, grysbok, sassaby **8** blesbuck, bontebok, bushbuck, gemsbuck, reedbuck, steenbok, steinbok **9** blackbuck, pronghorn, sitatunga, springbok, waterbuck **10** hartebeest, wildebeest
nylon: **4** hose **5** fiber **6** fabric **7** hosiery **8** stocking
  fabric: **5** satin, tulle **6** gloria, jersey, tricot, velvet **7** chiffon, organza, taffeta **8** Milanese **9** grenadine, sailcloth
  fiber: **6** Antron
  like ~: **5** sheer
  ruin a ~: **3** jag **4** snag
  shade: **4** nude **5** flesh, taupe
Nyman: **4** Lena **7** Michael
nymph: **3** Soe **4** Arne, Ceto, Echo, Hora, Ione, Lara, Loxo, Neda, Nyse, Opis, Sose, Urea **5** Aegle, Aetna, Batia, Clite, Cyane, dryad, Gorge, Hagno, Harpe, Hyale, Iaera, Iasis, Idaea, larva, Lotis, Lygea, Melie, Methe, Moria, Myrto, naiad, Nomia, Oenoe, oread, Paria, Phaeo, Phlio, Phyto, Pitys, Rhene, Rhode, Sinoe, Siren **6** Acrete, Aglaia, Argyra, Bromie, Bryusa, Byblis, Calybe, Chorea, Chryse, Cleeia, Clonia, Codone, Cranae, Creusa, Cyrene, Danais, Daulis, Dryope, Egeria, Eriphe, Eudore, Euryte, Glauce, helead, Helice, Ithome, Macris, Marica, Medeia, meliad, Melite, nereid, Nicaea, Ocynoe, Oenone, Orphne, Orseis, Othris, Pedile, Pegaea, Phiale, Phoebe, Phrixa, Pirene, Polyxo, Pomona, Pronoe, Psecas, Rhanis, Silene, sprite, Syllis, Syrinx, Theope, Thisbe, Thoosa, Thyone, Trygie **7** Alcinoe, Argiope, Astacia, Calypso, Chloris, Cisseis, Clymene, Cnossia, Coronis, Corycia, Crocale, Cyllene, Daphnis, Deiopea, Drosera, Ereutho, Erythia, Ethemea, Gigarto, Himalia, hydriad, Ismenis, Limnaee, Liriope, Lycaste, Nephele, oceanid, Pegasis, Prothoe, Sterope, Theisoa, Venilia **8** Adrastia, Amalthea, Anchiale, Anchiroe, Anthedon, Arethusa, Asterope, Atlantia, Caliadne, Carthago, Cassotis, Cercetis, Chariclo, Cleodora, Cymodore, Cynosura, Diopatra, Echenais, Eidothea, Erytheis, Eupetale, Eurypyle, Harmonia, Hecaerge, Hesperia, Menodice, Oinanthe, Orithyia, Periboea, Phaesyla, Phigalia, Salmacis, Salmonis, Sebethis, Staphyle, Teledice, Telphusa, Thelpusa, Tithorea **9** Abarbarea, Anthracia, Asterodia, Carmentis, Charopeia, epimeliad, hamadryad, Hegetoria, Melanippe, Myrtoessa, Phasyleia, Praxithea, Sagaritis **10** Chalcomede, Cleocharia, Melictaina, Stesichore, Synallasis
  aquatic ~: **4** nais **5** naiad
  chaser: **5** satyr
  mountain ~: **5** oread
  Muslim ~: **5** houri
  sea ~: **4** Ione **5** siren **6** nereid
  tree ~: **5** dryad
__ nymph: **3** sea **4** wood **5** water
Nymphéas artist: **5** Monet
NYPD
  call: **3** APB
  part of ~: **4** Dept.
  rank: **4** insp.
NYPD Blue (ABC drama)
  cast: Amy Brenneman (Off. Janice Licalsi)
    David Caruso (Det. John Kelly)
    Kim Delaney (Det. Diane Russell)
    Dennis Franz (Det. Andy Sipowicz)
    Sharon Lawrence (Sylvia Costas)
    Esai Morales (Lt. Tony Rodriguez)
    Rick Schroder (Det. Danny Sorenson)
    Jimmy Smits (Det. Bobby Simone)
Nyquil
  alternative: **5** Afrin **6** Contac, Tavist **7** Actifed, Comtrex, Dayquil, Dristan, Sinutab, Sudafed **8** Benadryl, Dimetapp, Drixoral, TheraFlu **9** Coricidin, Triaminic **10** Robitussin
  maker: **5** Vicks
Nyro, Laura: **6** singer **8** composer
  song: And When I Die
    Blowing Away
    Eli's Coming
    Stoned Soul Picnic
    Stoney End
    Sweet Blindness
    Wedding Bell Blues
NYSE: **3** mkt.
  abbr.: **3** IPO, pfd., rts., shr. **4** util.
  alternative: **3** OTC **4** AMEX **6** NASDAQ
  buy: **3** stk. **5** stock
  listing: **2** co. **3** GTE, ITT **4** corp.
  membership: **4** seat
  number: **5** quote
  regulator: **3** SEC
  street: **4** Wall
  worker: **3** arb **6** trader
Nytol: **8** sleep aid
  alternative: **6** Compoz, Unisom **7** Sominex
NYU: **3** sch. **4** coll.
  locale: **9** Manhattan
  part of ~: **4** Univ.
Nyx
  brother of ~: **6** Erebus
  daughter of ~: **4** Eris **6** Hemera **7** Hespera, Nemesis
  father of ~: **5** Chaos
  husband of ~: **5** Chaos
  son of ~: **4** Eros **5** Momus **6** Erebus, Hypnos, Somnus
N.Z.
  see New Zealand

1
prior to yr. ~: 3 BCE
scale where talc = ~: 4 Mohs
1%: 4 milk
1,2,3,4 (1996 song) artist: Coolio
1-2-3 software company: 5 Lotus
1-2-3 (song) artist: Gloria Estefan, Len Barry
1/1
since: 3 YTD
100%: 6 all-out
100-__ dash: 4 yard 5 meter
$100
bill: 5 C-note, C-spot
100-lb. unit: 3 cwt
100% Pure Love (1994 song) artist: Crystal Waters
101 Dalmatians (1996 film)
cast: Glenn Close, Jeff Daniels, Joan Plowright, Joely Richardson
director: Stephen Herek
dog: 5 Pongo 7 Perdita
101-digit number: 6 googol
__ 110th Street: 6 Across
112
hometown: Atlanta
song: All Cried Out (1997)
Anywhere (1999)
Cupid (1997)
I'll Be Missing You (1997)
Love Me (1998)
Only You (1996)
144 objects: 3 gro. 5 gross
180
do a ~: 7 retreat 9 back-pedal
180-degree
maneuver: 5 U-turn
turn: 3 uey
1000: 1 M 4 thou
kilocalories: 5 therm 6 therme
kilograms: 5 tonne
meters: 4 one K
pounds: 3 kip
square meters: 6 decare
yards: 4 one K
1,001 __: 4 uses
1024 bytes: 4 one K
10001: 3 NYC 4 NY NY
100,000
BTUs: 5 therm 6 therme
rupees: 4 lakh
O: 4 elem., type 5 vowel 6 letter, oxygen 7 element 9 blood type
code word for ~: 4 oboe 5 Oscar
8 for ~: 4 at. no.
followers: 3 PQR 4 PQRS 5 PQRST
in phonetic alphabet: 5 Oscar
meaning of ~ in XOXOX: 3 hug
one ~, maybe: 3 tac, tic, toe
preceders: 3 ens, LMN 4 KLMN 5 JLKMN
star: 7 blue sun
O (2001 film)
cast: Josh Hartnett, Martin Sheen, Julia Stiles
O __: 4 star 5 gauge, Henry, level 6 Canada 7 horizon
O __ All Ye Faithful: 4 Come
O __ babbino caro: 3 mio
O __ can you see...: 3 say
O __ Mio: 3 Dio 4 Sole
O __ odd: 4 as in
O __ of State: 4 Ship
O __! O mores!: 7 tempora
O, __ fortune's fool!: 3 I am
O, __ me the lass...: 3 gie
O-__: 4 ring, Zone 5 Cedar
'O' __ Outlaw: 5 Is for
__-O: 3 Day 4 Jell 6 double
oaf: 2 ox 3 ass, lug, nit, sap 4 boob, boor, bozo, clod, dolt, fool, hick, jerk, lout, lunk, rube, shmo, yo-yo 5 big ox, booby, chump, churl, clown, cluck, dummy, dunce, joker, klutz, looby, ninny, patsy, schmo, yokel 6 dimwit, duffer, galoot, lummox, nitwit, schmoe, sucker, turkey 7 boggler, botcher, buffoon, bumbler, bumpkin, bungler, dingbat, dullard, fathead, fumbler, galloot, half-wit, hayseed, jackass, palooka, pinhead, saphead, tomfool 8 bonehead, dumbbell, lardhead, lunkhead, meathead, numskull 9 bird-brain, blockhead, blunderer, ding-a-ling, harebrain, hillbilly, lamebrain, numbskull, schlemiel, simpleton 10 clodhopper, dunderhead, nincom-poop, stumblebum
oafish: 3 dim 5 dense, gawky, unapt 6 clumsy, gauche, klutzy 7 awkward, bearish, bestial, boorish, gawkish, loutish, uncouth 8 bumbling, bungling, churlish, cloddish, fumbling, impolite, ungainly 9 all thumbs, difficult, grace-less, lumbering, maladroit, stumbling, unskilled 10 unskillful
Oahu: 3 isl. 4 isle 6 island
city: 4 Aiea 6 Kailua 8 Honolulu
cookout: 4 luau
goose: 4 nene
greeting: 5 aloha
island near ~: 5 Kauai
locale: 6 Hawaii
souvenir: 3 lei
oak: 4 tree, wood 5 roble 7 quercus 8 hardwood 9 shade tree
evergreen ~: 4 holm, ilex
flower: 5 ament 6 catkin
leaf wearer: 3 maj. 5 lt. col., major
like an ~ leaf: 5 erose, lobed 7 rounded
live ~: 6 encina
nut: 5 acorn
oak __: 4 fern, gall 5 apple 7 leather
oak __ cluster: 4 leaf
__ oak: 3 bog, bur, pin, red, tan 4 cork, holm, jack, live, post, silk 5 black, Emory, holly, scrub, silky, water, white 6 laurel, poison, turkey, willow 7 shingle, tanbark
Oak __: 4 Park 5 Ridge
Oak __ Boys, The: 5 Ridge
__ Oak: 5 Royal 7 Charter
Oak Creek: 4 city, town
locale: 9 Wisconsin
Oakdale: 4 city, town
locale: 9 Minnesota
__ Oaken Bucket, The: 3 Old
Oakes: 5 Randi
Oak Forest: 4 city, town
locale: 8 Illinois
Oak Harbor: 4 city, town
locale: 10 Washington
Oakie: 4 Jack
Oakland: 4 city, port, town 5 Simon
county: 7 Alameda
locale: 10 California
newspaper: 7 Tribune
team: 5 The A's 7 Raiders 9 Athletics
Oakland Park: 4 city, town
locale: 7 Florida
Oak Lawn: 4 city, town
locale: 8 Illinois
oak leaf __: 7 cluster
Oakley: 4 city, town 5 Annie
locale: 10 California
Oakley, Annie: 4 pass 7 deadeye
emulate ~: 3 aim 5 shoot
Oak Park: 4 city, town
locale: 8 Illinois, Michigan
Oak Ridge: 4 city, town
agcy.: 3 AEC
locale: 7 Florida 9 Tennessee
Oak Ridge Boys song: Elvira (1981)
__ Oaks, CA: 7 Sherman 8 Thousand
Oakton: 4 city, town
locale: 8 Virginia
oakum: 4 rope 5 fiber
source: 4 jute
Oakville: 4 city, town
locale: 6 Canada 7 Ontario 8 Missouri
oar: 3 row 5 rower, scull 6 paddle, propel 7 paddler
combining form: 4 remi-
ender: 4 fish, lock
fulcrum: 5 thole
stroke: 4 pull
wood: 3 ash
oarlock: 5 thole
oars
boat with ~: 4 dory
both ~ in water: 4 sane
rest on one's ~: 4 idle 8 intermit
oarsmen: 4 crew 6 rowers
OAS: 8 alliance
birthplace: 6 Bogotá 8 Colombia
member: 3 Arg., Can., Col., Mex., Pan., Uru., USA 4 Cuba, Peru 5 Chile, Haiti 6 Belize, Brazil, Canada, Guyana, Mexico, Panama 7 Bahamas, Bolivia, Ecuador, Grenada, Jamaica, Uruguay 8 Bar-bados, Colombia, Dominica, Hon-duras, Paraguay, Suriname 9 Argentina, Costa Rica, Guatemala, Nicaragua, Venezuela 10 El Salvador, Saint Lucia
part of ~: 3 Org. 4 Amer. 6 States 8 American
predecessor: 3 PAU
oasis: 5 haven 6 asylum, refuge 7 retreat, sanctum 9 sanctuary
of a sort: 3 bar, pub 6 lounge, saloon, tavern 7 taproom
urban ~: 4 park 6 common 8 preserve 10 playground
view: 4 palm, sand, well
Oasis, The author: Mary McCarthy
oast: 4 kiln, oven 7 furnace
oat: 5 grain 6 cereal
eater of song: 3 doe 4 mare
ender: 4 cake, meal
genus: 5 avena
part: 3 awn 5 groat
oat __: 5 grass 6 burner
Oat Bran: 6 cereal
competitor: 3 Kix 4 Life, Trix 5 Kashi, Quisp, Total 6 Kaboom, Muesli, Oreo O's, Pablum, Smacks 7 All-Bran, Crispix, Harmony, Hunny B's, Mueslix, Pokemon 8 Boo Berry, Cheerios, Corn Chex, Corn Pops, Fiber One, Rice Chex, Special K, Uncle Sam, Wheaties 9 Alpha Bits, Apple Zaps, Grape Nuts, Honey Comb, Just Right, Wheat Chex 10 Apple Jacks, Bran Flakes, Cap'n Crunch, Cocoa Puffs, Froot Loops, Mini-Wheats, Nutri-Grain, Puffed Rice, Quaker Oats, Smart Start 11 Cocoa Blasts, Cookie Crisp, Golden Crisp, Lucky Charms, Puffed Wheat, Sweet Crunch, Waffle Crisp
oatcake: 5 bread
oater: 5 flick 7 western 9 shoot-'em-up 10 horse opera
affirmative: 3 yep, yup
ammo: 6 blanks
character: 5 posse 6 cowboy, outlaw 7 marshal, sheriff
command: 4 draw, whoa 7 giddyap
locale: 4 fort, mesa 5 cañon, ranch 6 canyon
meal: 4 chow, grub 7 vittles
name: 4 Duke, Hoot, Lash 5 Gabby
prop: 3 gun 4 Colt 5 rifle 10 six-shooter
salutation: 3 how 5 howdy
sound: 4 bray, clop 5 neigh 6 whinny
Oates: 4 John 6 Warren
partner: 4 Hall
Oates, Joyce Carol: 6 author, writer
work: American Appetites
Angel of Light
Bellefleur
Crossing the Border
Expensive People
Foxfire
A Garden of Earthly Delights
Last Days
Man Crazy
Mysteries of Winterthurn
Solstice
Them
Unholy Loves
Oates, Warren: 5 actor
film: 92 in the Shade (1975)
The Border (1982)
The Brink's Job (1978)
Cockfighter (1974)
Dillinger (1973)
The Hired Hand (1971)
In the Heat of the Night (1967)
Stripes (1981)
Tom Sawyer (1973)
Two-Lane Blacktop (1971)
The Wild Bunch (1969)
oath: 3 I do, vow 4 damn, darn, drat, gawd, heck, word 5 curse 6 avowal, dang it, pledge 7 promise 8 averment, cussword 9 assertion, assurance, expletive, guarantee, profanity, swear-word 10 adjuration, avouchment, engagement
British ~: 3 cor, gor 5 blimy 6 blimey
French: 8 zut alors 9 sacre bleu
lie under ~: 7 falsify, perjure 8 for-swear
mild ~: 3 gad 4 dang, darn, drat, gosh, heck, jeez 5 by gum, nerts, nertz 6 by gosh, cripes
old ~: 3 fie 4 egad 5 egads 6 by Jove 10 ods bodkins
say under ~: 6 attest, depone, depose 7 witness 8 attest to
take an ~: 5 swear 7 promise, warrant
taker's need: 5 Bible
__ oath: 5 under
oath of __: 6 office
oath of God, name meaning: 9 Eliza-beth
oatmeal: 5 gruel 6 cereal, cookie 8 flum-mery
clot: 4 lump
like cooked ~: 4 soft 5 mushy, soggy 7 squishy
porridge: 6 burgoo
Oatmeal Crisp: 6 cereal
competitor: 3 Kix 4 Life, Trix 5 Kashi, Quisp, Total 6 Kaboom, Muesli, Oreo O's, Pablum, Smacks 7 All-Bran, Crispix, Harmony, Hunny B's, Mueslix, Oat Bran, Pokemon 8 Boo Berry, Cheerios, Corn Chex, Corn Pops, Fiber One, Rice Chex, Special K, Uncle Sam, Wheaties 9 Alpha Bits, Apple Zaps, Grape Nuts, Honey Comb, Just Right, Wheat Chex 10 Apple Jacks, Bran Flakes, Cap'n Crunch, Cocoa Puffs, Froot Loops, Mini-Wheats, Nutri-Grain, Puffed Rice, Quaker Oats, Smart Start 11 Cocoa Blasts, Cookie Crisp, Golden Crisp, Lucky Charms, Puffed Wheat, Sweet Crunch, Waffle Crisp
Oatmeal Squares: 6 cereal
competitor: 3 Kix 4 Life, Trix 5 Kashi, Quisp, Total 6 Kaboom, Muesli,

Oreo O's, Pablum, Smacks **7** All-Bran, Crispix, Harmony, Hunny B's, Mueslix, Oat Bran, Pokemon **8** Boo Berry, Cheerios, Corn Chex, Corn Pops, Fiber One, Rice Chex, Special K, Uncle Sam, Wheaties **9** Alpha Bits, Apple Zaps, Grape Nuts, Honey Comb, Just Right, Wheat Chex **10** Apple Jacks, Bran Flakes, Cap'n Crunch, Cocoa Puffs, Froot Loops, Mini-Wheats, Nutri-Grain, Puffed Rice, Quaker Oats, Smart Start **11** Cocoa Blasts, Cookie Crisp, Golden Crisp, Lucky Charms, Puffed Wheat, Sweet Crunch, Waffle Crisp

oats: 4 feed **5** grain **6** cereal, fodder, groats, silage
feeling one's ~: 5 happy, jolly, merry **6** frisky, impish, lively **7** coltish, naughty, playful, puckish, teasing, waggish **8** mirthful, prankish, skittish, sportive **9** fun-loving, lightsome, sprightly, vivacious, whimsical **10** frolicsome, rollicking
sow wild ~: 3 err, sin **5** act up, be bad, cut up, stray **7** carry on, do wrong, go wrong **8** go astray **9** misbehave **10** fool around

__ oats: 3 sea **4** wild **5** water **6** rolled, winter

__ Oats: 6 Quaker

oats and nuts cereal: 7 granola

OAU, part of: 3 Afr., Org. **5** Unity **7** African

Oaxaca: 4 city, town **5** state **7** Mexican
city: 6 Atempa **7** Ixtepec, Ocotlán **8** Juchitán, Pochutla, Tlaxiaco, Tuxtepec, Zaachila **9** Huajuapan **10** Loma Bonita, Salina Cruz, Xoxocotlan
language: 6 Mixtec
ruins site near ~: 5 Mitla
see also Spanish

ob-__: 3 gyn

Ob: 5 river
feeder: 6 Irtysh
locale: 6 Russia

OB: 2 MD **6** doctor **9** physician

Obadiah: 4 book **7** prophet
follower: 5 Jonah
preceder: 4 Amos

obdt. __: 4 serv.

obdurate: 4 firm, iron **5** balky, onery, rigid, stony, tough **6** flinty, mulish, narrow, ornery, severe, stoney, wilful **7** adamant, hard-set, wayward, willful **8** contrary, hardened, indocile, indurate, perverse, pitiless, stubborn **9** immovable, impliable, obstinate, tenacious, unbending, unfeeling **10** hard-bitten, headstrong, inexorable, inflexible, persistent, relentless, unyielding

OBE: 6 honour
awarder: 4 Brit., Gr. Br. **5** the U.K.

obeah: 5 charm **6** fetich, fetish, voodoo

obeche: 4 tree

Obed
parent of ~: 4 Boaz, Ruth

obedience: 7 loyalty **9** deference, servitude **10** allegiance, compliance, conformity, observance, submission
class command: 3 beg, sit **4** heel, stay

obedient: 4 easy, good, meek, tame, true **5** mousy **6** broken, docile, filial, mousey, pliant **7** duteous, dutiful, orderly, passive, servile, subdued, subject, trained, willing **8** faithful, flexible, lamblike, obliging, resigned, yielding **9** adaptable, agreeable, assenting, compliant, malleable, prostrate, tractable **10** governable, law-abiding, manageable, respectful, submissive
one: 5 robot, sheep **6** heeder

obeisance: 6 homage, praise **7** respect **9** deference, reverence **10** admiration
pay ~: 3 bow **5** kneel **6** kowtow, salaam **9** genuflect, prostrate

obeisant: 4 oily **7** fawning, servile, slavish **8** toadyish, unctuous **9** adulatory **10** obsequious

obelisk: 5 pylon, tower **6** column, dagger, pillar **8** memorial, monument, pinnacle

Oberammergau: 4 city, town
locale: 7 Germany

Oberhausen: 4 city, town
locale: 7 Germany

Oberlin locale: 4 Ohio

Oberon: 4 moon **5** Merle **6** sprite **8** language
alternative: 3 ADA, APL, SQL **4** Alef, html, Icon, Java, LISP, Logo, Orca, Perl **5** Algol, Basic, Cecil, COBOL, Dylan, SISAL **6** Delphi, Eiffel, Erlang, Pascal, Prolog, Sather, Scheme, Snobol **7** Fortran
planet: 6 Uranus

Oberon, Merle: 7 actress
film: Beloved Enemy (1936)
Berlin Express (1948)
Folies Bergère (1935)
The Lodger (1944)
Lydia (1941)
The Private Life of Henry VIII (1933)
The Scarlet Pimpernel (1935)
That Uncertain Feeling (1941)
These Three (1936)
Wuthering Heights (1939)
spouse: Alexander Korda

Oberto composer: 5 Verdi

obese: 5 beefy, fubsy, heavy, plump, pudgy, pursy, stout, thick, tubby **6** chubby, fleshy, portly, pyknic, rotund, stocky, zaftig, zoftig **7** adipose, paunchy, weighty **8** roly-poly, thickset **9** corpulent **10** abdominous, overweight, well-padded

obey: 4 heed, mind **5** act on, bow to **6** accept, bend to, comply, follow, fulfil, listen, submit **7** abide by, act upon, agree to, defer to, fulfill, observe, respect, stick to **8** adhere to, carry out, listen to **9** conform to, consent to, prostrate, truckle to **10** comply with, keep in step, toe the line
refuse to ~: 4 balk **5** baulk, rebel **6** mutiny, resist
the clock: 4 rise, wake **5** arise, awake, get up, waken **6** awaken

obfuscate: 3 dim, fog **4** hide **5** bedim, befog, cloud, muddy **6** darken **7** becloud **8** disguise **9** adumbrate, blindfold **10** camouflage, overshadow

obfuscated: 3 dim **4** hazy **5** foggy, fuzzy, misty, muddy, murky, muzzy, smoky, vague **6** addled, bleary, blurry, cloudy, in a fog, opaque **7** blurred, clouded, muddled, obscure, shadowy, unclear **8** confused, nebulous **9** befuddled, imprecise, uncertain **10** bewildered, indistinct

obi: 4 band, belt, sash **8** Japanese
companion: 4 inro **6** kimono
wearer: 6 geisha

Obie: 5 award, prize **6** reward, trophy
contender: 4 play **5** actor

Obihiro: 4 city, town
locale: 5 Japan

obiter dictum: 6 remark **7** comment **9** assertion, statement, utterance **10** observance

Obi-Wan: 4 hero **6** Kenobi
AKA ~: 3 Ben
foe: 5 Darth, Vader
portrayer: 4 Alec **8** Guinness

object: 3 aim, end **4** care, goal, item, kick, mind, noun **5** demur, drift, point, thing **6** entity, intent, motive, reason, target **7** article, dissent, meaning, mission, protest, purport, purpose, reality **8** function **9** commodity, frown upon, give a darn, intention, something **10** disapprove, make a stand
of a joke: 4 dupe, gull **5** chump, patsy **7** fall guy
of ridicule: 4 butt **5** sport **6** effigy
of worship: 3 god **4** icon, idol, ikon **5** deity, eikon
to: 4 mind **5** fight **6** oppose, resent **7** contest, deplore, dislike, quarrel
ultimate ~: 5 be-all **6** end-all

object __: 4 ball, code, lens **5** glass **6** lesson

__ object: 5 found **6** direct **7** cognate

objection: 3 but **4** beef, fuss **5** cavil, qualm, query **6** outcry, plaint **7** dissent, quarrel **8** question **9** challenge, complaint, criticism, grievance
vocal ~: 2 no **3** nah, naw, nay, nix, non **4** nein, nope, nyet, uh-uh, veto **5** I won't, ixnay, never, no how, no way **6** indeed, no deal, nowise **7** I refuse, opposed **8** forget it, I will not, negative, negatory, to be sure **9** by no means, fat chance, I think not **10** count me out, not a chance, thumbs down

objectionable: 4 foul, grim, poor, ugly **5** awful, lousy, nasty, woful **6** crumby, crummy, dismal, horrid, odious, rotten, woeful **7** accurst, baleful, baneful, beastly, doleful, ghastly **8** accursed, annoying, dreadful, God-awful, grievous, horrible, inferior, shameful, stinking, terrible, unsavory, wretched **9** abhorrent, appalling, atrocious, defective, execrable, frightful, insidious, loathsome, miserable, offensive, repugnant, repulsive, revolting, unwelcome **10** abominable, despicable, detestable, disastrous, horrendous

objective: 3 aim, end, job **4** case, fair, goal, just, mark, open, sake **5** cause, equal, point, quest **6** design, honest, intent, square, target **7** mission, purport, purpose, resolve **8** ambition, balanced, detached, function, physical, rational, tangible, unbiased **9** corporeal, direction, equitable, impartial, uncolored, unslanted **10** aspiration, even-handed, ground zero, impersonal, reasonable, scientific
not ~: 6 biased, skewed **7** bigoted **8** partisan **10** intolerant, subjective
ultimate ~: 3 aim, end **4** goal **5** be-all **6** end-all, payoff, reason, target **7** mission, outcome, purpose **8** terminus **10** aspiration, conclusion

objective __: 4 case, lens, test **5** prism **6** spirit

Objective, Burma! (1945 film)
cast: James Brown, Errol Flynn, George Tobias
director: Raoul Walsh

objectless: 5 fluky, stray **6** casual, chance, random **7** aimless, oddball, unaimed **8** isolated, sporadic **9** haphazard, hit-or-miss, unplanned **10** accidental, fortuitous, incidental, unintended

Object of Beauty, The (1991 film)
cast: Lolita Davidovich, Andie MacDowell, John Malkovich

Object of My Affection, The (1998 film)
cast: Alan Alda, Jennifer Aniston, Nigel Hawthorne

objector: 5 NIMBY, rebel **7** fanatic, leftist, liberal, radical **8** maverick, militant, nihilist, pacifist, reformer, renegade **9** anarchist, extremist, firebrand, insurgent **10** immoderate, left-winger

objects: 5 stuff **6** things
inability to name ~: 6 anomia
nearby ~: 5 these
remote ~: 5 those

objet __: 4 d'art **6** trouvé

objet d'art: 5 curio **7** trinket **8** nicknack **9** curiosity **10** knickknack

objets d'art: 5 vertu, virtu

objurgate: 4 rail, ream **5** abuse, baste, blame, chide, scold **6** berate, jump on, preach **7** bawl out, censure, chew out, lecture, tell off, upbraid **8** chastise, denounce, lace into, lambaste, sail into, tear into **9** castigate, dress down, excoriate, find fault, light into **10** take to task, tongue-lash, vituperate

objurgation: 5 abuse **6** earful, rebuke **7** censure, chiding, reproof **8** hard time, reproach, scolding **9** reprimand, talking-to **10** bawling-out, chewing-out, telling-off, upbraiding

oblation: 4 alms, gift **7** charity, worship **8** donation, libation, offering **9** sacrifice

obligate: 4 bind **5** force **6** adjure, hold to **7** promise, require

obligated: 5 bound **6** in hock, liable **8** beholden, indebted **10** answerable, honor-bound
be ~: 4 must **6** have to

obligation: 3 job, tie **4** bond, call, debt, duty, must, need, onus, task **5** score, trust **6** charge, red ink **7** arrears, promise **8** contract, pressure, protocol **9** gratitude, liability, necessity **10** allegiance, commission, commitment, compulsion, engagement
be under ~: 3 owe **5** incur **6** borrow, charge **9** run up a tab
charge an ~: 5 debit
fulfill an ~: 5 pay up, repay **6** square **7** satisfy **10** remunerate
under an ~: 5 bound **6** in debt, liable **8** beholden, grateful, indebted, thankful **10** answerable, honor-bound
word of ~: 4 must **5** ought

__-obligation bond: 7 general

obligatory: 6 forced **7** binding **8** required **9** mandatory, necessary, requisite **10** compulsory, imperative, inevitable, peremptory
in French: 9 de rigueur
make ~: 5 exact, force, order **6** charge, compel, decree, demand, enjoin, impose **7** command, dictate, inflict **9** establish, institute, prescribe, stipulate **10** promulgate

oblige: 4 bind, lend, make, push **5** favor, force, serve, spoil, stoop **6** compel **7** cater to, gratify, require **9** constrain, legislate

obliged: 5 bound **6** in hock, liable **8** beholden, grateful, impelled, indebted **10** honor-bound
be ~: 3 owe **4** must **5** thank **6** have to **10** appreciate
much ~: 5 danke, merci **6** grazie, thanks **7** gracias, spasibo **8** beholden, grateful, indebted, thankful, thank you
not ~: 4 free **6** exempt, let off **7** excused **8** released **10** off the hook

obliging: 4 easy, good, kind, mild, nice **5** civil, suave **6** aidful, benign, decent, kindly, polite, urbane **7** affable, amiable, gallant, heedful, helpful, lenient, mindful, tactful **8** flexible, gracious, obedient, pleasant **9** agreeable, attentive, compliant, sensitive, unselfish **10** charitable, hospitable, neighborly, thoughtful

oblique: 4 skew 5 askew, bevel 6 aslant, biased, skewed, zigzag 7 devious, evasive, lateral 8 diagonal, indirect, slanting 9 equivocal, underhand 10 roundabout, unexplicit

combining form: 3 lox- 4 loxo- 5 plagi- 6 plagio-

cut: 5 bevel, miter

direction: 4 bias, skew 5 slant

line: 3 zig 4 bias, cant, diag. 8 diagonal

oblique __: 5 angle 6 motion 7 sailing, section

obliquely: 6 askant, aslant 7 asquint, athwart, sideway 8 sideways, sidewise 9 slantways, slantwise 10 diagonally

obliqueness: 4 bias 5 slant, slope

obliterate: 4 rase, raze, ruin, wipe, x out 5 crush, erase 6 defeat, delete, efface, remove, rub off, rub out 7 abolish, expunge, pluck up, wipe out 8 demolish, stamp out 9 eradicate, sponge out 10 annihilate, extinguish

obliterated: 4 gone, lost 5 ended 7 extinct 8 finished, vanished, wiped out 9 destroyed 10 demolished, devastated, eradicated

oblivion: 5 limbo

river of ~: 5 Lethe

oblivious: 3 lax 4 deaf, rapt 5 blind 7 unaware 8 careless, heedless, mindless 9 forgetful, unmindful 10 unthinking

be ~ to: 4 miss 6 forget, ignore 7 neglect, tune out 8 brush off, discount, laugh off, lay aside, overlook, pass over, pooh-pooh, shrug off 9 disregard

oblong: 4 oval, rect. 5 ovate 9 rectangle 10 elliptical

oblongata, medulla: 5 brain

Oblong Box, The author: Edgar Allan Poe

obloquy: 3 dig, lie 4 barb, gibe, jibe, slam, slap, slur, snub 5 abuse, blame, libel, odium, scorn, taunt 6 infamy, insult, rebuff, slight 7 affront, calumny, catcall, censure, disdain, mockery, offense, put-down, slander 8 contempt, derision, disgrace, dishonor, ridicule 9 aspersion, cheap shot, contumely, disrepute, ill repute, invective, notoriety 10 backbiting, defamation, disrespect, impugnment, opprobrium, reflection

obnoxious: 4 loud, mean, rude, ugly, vile 5 nasty, pesky, pesty, pushy 6 odious 7 hateful 8 annoying, horrible, sinister, terrible 9 execrable, loathsome, offensive, repellant, repellent, repugnant, unpopular, unwelcome 10 abominable, detestable, disgusting, in one's hair, unpleasant

find ~: 4 hate 6 detest, loathe 7 despise 8 execrate 9 abominate

one: 4 jerk, pest 5 creep, schmo, skunk 6 schmoe

oboe: 3 cor 4 reed, wind 7 arghool, hautboy 8 woodwind 10 double-reed

ancestor: 5 shawm

like an ~: 5 reedy

oboe __: 6 d'amore, d'amour

obol: 4 coin 5 money

place: 5 agora

Oboler: 4 Arch

Obote foe: 4 Amin

Obregón: 4 city, town

locale: 6 Mexico, Sonora

O'Brian: 4 Hugh 7 Patrick

O'Brian, Hugh: 5 actor

film: The Lawless Breed (1952)
Red Ball Express (1952)
The Shootist (1976)

TV: The Life and Legend of Wyatt Earp

O'Brien: 3 Dan, Pat 4 Edna 5 Conan, Flann 6 Edmond, George 8 Margaret

O'Brien, Edmond: 5 actor

film: 1984 (1956)
An Act of Murder (1948)
The Barefoot Contessa (1954, AA)
The Bigamist (1953)
D.O.A. (1950)
A Double Life (1947)
Fantastic Voyage (1966)
The Great Impostor (1961)
Julius Caesar (1953)
The Killers (1946)
Moon Pilot (1962)
Rio Conchos (1964)
The Third Voice (1960)
The Web (1947)
White Heat (1949)
The Wild Bunch (1969)

O'Brien, Edna: 5 Irish 6 writer

O'Brien, Flann: 5 Irish 6 writer

O'Brien, Margaret: 7 actress

film: The Canterville Ghost (1944)
Jane Eyre (1944)
Meet Me in St. Louis (1944)
Our Vines Have Tender Grapes (1945)
The Secret Garden (1949)

O'Brien, Pat: 5 actor

film: Airmail (1932)
American Madness (1932)
Angels With Dirty Faces (1938)
Bombardier (1943)
Boy Meets Girl (1938)
The Boy With the Green Hair (1948)
Broadway (1942)
Castle on the Hudson (1940)
Ceiling Zero (1935)
Crack-Up (1946)
Escape to Glory (1940)
The Fireball (1950)
The Front Page (1931)
Knute Rockne, All American (1940)
Oil for the Lamps of China (1935)
Perilous Holiday (1946)
Riffraff (1947)
Secret Command (1944)
Torrid Zone (1940)

Obringa today: 3 Aar 4 Aare

O Brother, Where Art Thou? (2000 film)

cast: George Clooney, Holly Hunter, John Turturro

director: Joel Coen

obscene: 3 raw 4 blue, lewd 5 bawdy, dirty, nasty 6 coarse, ribald, risqué, smutty, vulgar 7 naughty, profane 8 indecent, shameful 9 low-minded, monstrous, revolting 10 indelicate, lascivious, scurrilous, suggestive

obscenity: 8 lewdness, ribaldry 9 indecency, profanity

__ obscura: 6 camera

obscuration: 5 shade 6 shadow 7 eclipse

obscure: 3 dim, fog 4 blur, dark, deep, hazy, hide, mask, mist, veil 5 bedim, befog, blear, cache, cloak, cloud, couch, cover, faint, foggy, fuzzy, lowly, mirky, misty, muddy, murky, runic, shade, thick, vague 6 arcane, cloudy, darken, gloomy, hidden, ill-lit, lonely, occult, opaque, remote, screen, secret, shadow, somber, unseen, unsung 7 becloud, conceal, confuse, cryptic, dubious, eclipse, lowborn, secrete, unclear, unfamed, unknown 8 abstruse, darkened, disguise, esoteric, nameless, nebulous, oracular, puzzling, ulterior 9 adumbrate, blindfold, confusing, cryptical, difficult, enigmatic, hard to see, illegible, insoluble, recondite, tenebrous, unheard-of 10 camouflage, extinguish, indistinct, keep secret, lackluster, mysterious, perplexing, unfamiliar, unreadable, unrenowned

obscured: 3 dim 4 hazy, lost 5 blind, foggy 6 covert, hidden, secret, unseen 7 furtive, private 8 hush-hush, ulterior 9 invisible 10 undercover, under wraps, unviewable

Obscure Destinies author: Willa Cather

obscurity: 4 dark, haze 5 gloom, shade 6 shadow 8 darkness 9 ambiguity

leave ~: 6 arrive, emerge 7 succeed

obsequious: 4 meek, oily 5 lowly 6 menial 7 fawning 8 unctuous 9 adulatory, groveling 10 complacent

be ~: 4 fawn 5 kotow 6 grovel, kowtow 8 fawn over

observable: 4 open 5 clear, overt, plain 6 in view, patent, public 7 evident, exposed, obvious, outward, visible 8 apparent, clear-cut, explicit, manifest, palpable, sensible, tangible, unhidden, unveiled 10 unshrouded

observance: 4 form, heed, rite, rule, wont 6 custom, regard, remark, ritual 7 heeding, keeping, liturgy, lookout, service 8 ceremony, fidelity, honoring, localism, practice, religion 9 acquittal, adherence, awareness, discharge, formality, obedience, tradition 10 compliance, conformity

observant: 4 keen, live 5 alert, alive, awake, aware, fussy, quick, sharp 6 bright, wise to, with it 7 careful, finicky, heedful, mindful, prudent, tactful, wakeful 8 cautious, deducing, exacting, finiking, finnicky, keen-eyed, lynx-eyed, rigorous, sentient, thorough, vigilant, watchful 9 assiduous, attentive, au courant, cognizant, designing, detecting, eagle-eyed, judicious, on the ball, receptive, regardful, searching, sensitive, sharp-eyed, surveying, wide-awake 10 discerning, fastidious, interested, meticulous, on one's toes, particular, perceptive, reflective, responsive, scrupulous, sensible of, thoughtful

one: 4 eyer, seer 5 noter 7 watcher

observation: 3 mot 4 heed, look, view 5 check, crack, probe, sight, study 6 espial, regard, remark, review, saying 7 comment, finding, lookout, mention, opinion, thought 8 comeback, mouthful, noticing, once-over, research, scrutiny, watching 9 attention, cognition, detection, knowledge, statement, utterance, wisecrack 10 empiricism

observation __: 3 car 4 deck, post

observatory: 7 lookout

structure: 4 dome 6 cupola

__ Observatory: 4 Lick 5 Naval 6 Lowell, Yerkes 7 Arecibo, Palomar

observe: 3 say, see, spy 4 espy, find, heed, hold, keep, look, mark, mind, note, obey, read, spot, view 5 adopt, audit, bow to, catch, guard, honor, input, opine, scout, sense, sight, spy on, state, study, watch 6 accept, advert, behold, bend to, comply, detect, follow, fulfil, listen, look at, notice, peek at, regard, remark, revere, survey, take in 7 abide by, agree to, comment, conform, declare, defer to, discern, examine, eyeball, fulfill, inspect, make out, mention, monitor, pay heed, perform, respect, satisfy, sit in on, witness 8 adhere to, carry out, discover, eagle-eye, mouth off, perceive, pick up on, practice, remember, venerate 9 celebrate, consent to, recognize, solemnize, wisecrack 10 commentate, comply with, eyewitness, get a load of, scrutinize, toe the line

observer: 3 spy 4 eyer, seer 5 noter, spier 6 looker, viewer 7 student, witness 8 beholder, onlooker 9 spectator 10 eyewitness

__ observer: 3 air 6 ground

Observer: 5 paper 9 newspaper

locale: 9 Charlotte

__ Observer: 4 Mars

observers: 5 crowd 8 audience 10 attendance

observing: 4 live 5 alert, alive, awake, aware 6 wilful, with it 7 mindful, studied, willful 8 rational, sensible, sentient 9 attentive, au courant, cognizant, conscious, reasoning, regardful, sensitive 10 acquainted, calculated, conversant, deliberate, discerning, perceiving, perceptive, percipient, purposeful, reasonable, reflective, responsive

obsess: 5 haunt 6 absorb, fixate, plague, rankle 7 bedevil, consume, engross 8 dominate 9 infatuate, preoccupy

obsessed: 4 held, into 5 beset, rabid 6 dogged, driven, hooked, hung up, seized, tied up 7 fixated, gripped, haunted, plagued, touched, zealous 8 consumed, fiendish, hellbent, troubled, turned on 9 bedeviled, bewitched, dominated, engrossed, fanatical, possessed, taken over, tormented 10 captivated, controlled, infatuated

by: 4 into 9 far gone on

combining form: 6 -ridden

obsession: 3 bug 4 case, must 5 craze, crush, fancy, mania, thing 6 desire, fantom, fetich, fetish, hang-up, monkey, phobia 7 complex, passion, phantom 8 delusion, fixation, idée fixe, neurosis 9 addiction, ax to grind, monomania 10 attraction, compulsion, enthusiasm

in French: 8 idée fixe

Obsession: 5 scent 7 perfume

obsessive: 8 haunting 9 fanatical 10 compulsive

fan: 3 nut 4 nerd, nurd

obsidian: 4 lava, rock 7 mineral

obsolescence: 3 age 6 disuse

__ obsolescence: 7 built-in, planned

obsolescent: 3 out 5 dated, passé, stale 6 old-hat 8 outmoded

obsolete: 3 old, out 4 dead, gone, past 5 dated, dusty, fusty, kaput, moldy, musty, passé, stale 6 bygone, fossil, old-hat 7 ancient, antique, archaic, disused, done for, extinct, fogyish, outworn 8 dinosaur, outdated, outmoded, out of use, timeworn, unusable 9 discarded, moth-eaten, old-school, out-of-date 10 antiquated, back-number, out of style, superseded

become ~: 3 die, end 4 pass 5 cease, lapse 6 expire 7 decline 9 terminate

diction: 8 archaism 10 archaicism

obstacle: 3 bar, rub 4 bump, clog, dike, jump, snag, wall 5 block, catch, check, crimp, hitch, joker, minus, snarl 6 hang-up, hazard, hurdle, kicker, logjam 7 barrier, problem, setback, trammel 8 blockade, drawback, handicap, hardship, mountain, weakness 9 booby trap, deterrent, detriment, hindrance, impedance, liability 10 bottleneck, difficulty, impediment

teamwork ~: 3 ego

obstacle __: 4 race 6 course

obstetric adjective: 5 fetal 6 foetal

obstinacy: 8 defiance, firmness, rigidity, tenacity 10 fanaticism

obstinate: **3** set **4** firm, hard **5** balky, fusty, onery, rigid, stiff, tough **6** dogged, mulish, ornery, sullen, wilful **7** adamant, defiant, hard-set, piggish, restive, wayward, willful **8** contrary, dogmatic, factious, hardened, indocile, indurate, like iron, locked in, obdurate, perverse, resolved, stubborn **9** convinced, crotchety, dead set on, difficult, fanatical, immovable, impliable, insistent, pigheaded, steadfast, tenacious, unbending **10** determined, dogmatical, hard-bitten, headstrong, inexorable, inflexible, persistent, rebellious, refractory, relentless, self-willed, unamenable, unyielding
  be ~: **4** balk, don't **5** baulk **6** refuse
  one: **3** ass **4** mule
obstreperous: **4** loud, wild **5** noisy, onery, rowdy **6** brassy, ornery, unruly **7** defiant, naughty **9** crotchety, unbridled **10** rebellious
obstruct: **3** bar, dam, jam, tie **4** bolt, clog, cork, curb, halt, lock, plug, seal, shut, stay, stop **5** block, check, choke, close, cramp, cross, dam up, delay, deter, latch, stall, stimy, stymy, tie up **6** arrest, clog up, cut off, forbid, foul up, hamper, hang up, hinder, hold up, impede, lock up, oppose, plug up, retard, seal up, secure, stop up, stymie, thwart **7** congest, inhibit, occlude, prevent, sandbag, seal off, shut off, shut out, shutter, trammel **8** blockade, button up, encumber, prohibit, restrain, restrict, sabotage, slow down, throttle **9** barricade, foreclose, forestall, frustrate, hamstring, intercept, interfere, interrupt, stonewall, terminate, weigh down **10** discourage, monkey with
obstructed: **5** blind, tight **10** impassable
obstruction: **3** bar, dam, jam **4** clog, dike, lock, plug, snag, stop, wall **5** block, check, limit **6** arrest, hamper, holdup, hurdle **7** barrier, trammel, trouble **8** blockade, blockage, blocking, gridlock, mountain, obstacle, stoppage **9** barricade, booby trap, checkmate, hindrance, restraint, roadblock **10** resistance
obstruction of ___: **7** justice
obstructive: **7** counter, opposed **8** opposing
obtain: **3** buy, cop, get, nab, win **4** earn, find, gain, grab, have, land, reap, save, snag, take **5** annex, fetch, get at, glean, go get, hoard, lay up, order, reach, seize, stand **6** accept, access, attain, come by, corral, derive, drum up, effect, elicit, enlist, gather, line up, occupy, pick up, pocket, secure, wangle **7** achieve, acquire, capture, chalk up, collect, compass, conquer, extract, inherit, persist, possess, preempt, prevail, procure, realize, receive, recover, recruit, salvage, scare up **8** come into, gobble up, invest in, purchase, retrieve, scrape up **9** get hold of **10** accomplish, fall heir to, get hands on
  again: **4** find **6** ransom, recoup, redeem, regain, retake **7** get back, reclaim, recover, win back **8** reoccupy, retrieve, take back **9** bring back, reacquire, recapture, repossess
  as support: **5** draft **6** enlist, muster **7** recruit **8** mobilize
  as vengeance: **5** exact, force **6** demand, direct **7** call for, command, inflict
  by force: **3** pry **5** bully, exact, gouge, wrest, wring **6** coerce, extort, wrench **7** squeeze **9** blackmail, shake down
  by fraud: **3** con **4** bilk, rook, scam **5** cheat, grift **6** fleece
  in Dogpatch: **3** git
  the services of: **3** use **4** book, hire **5** enrol **6** employ, engage, enlist, enroll, line up, secure, sign up, take on **7** appoint, charter, recruit, reserve **8** contract **10** commission
obtainable: **4** open **5** on tap, ready **6** at hand, on deck **7** in stock, no sweat, to be had **8** gettable, possible **9** available, derivable, no problem, ready to go, securable **10** accessible, attainable, up for grabs
obtrude: **3** pry **6** butt in, impose, insert, meddle **7** barge in, break in, pry into, push out **8** butt into, horn into, nose into, stick out, trespass **9** break into, interfere, intervene
obtrusive: **4** loud, nosy **5** nosey, pushy **6** prying **7** blatant, bulging, forward, glaring, jutting, obvious, salient, visible **8** meddling **9** bumptious, intrusive, officious, prominent **10** meddlesome, noticeable, projecting, protruding
obtund: **4** dull **5** blunt, slake **6** deaden, muffle, soften **8** moderate, tone down
obtuse: **3** dim **4** dopy, dull **5** blunt, crass, dense, dopey, thick **6** bovine, opaque, stolid, stupid **7** doltish, foolish, lumpish, rounded, witless **8** ignorant, lubberly, mindless **9** dim-witted
  not ~: **4** keen **5** acute, canny, quick, sharp, smart **6** astute, clever, shrewd **8** vigilant **9** intuitive, sagacious **10** discerning, insightful, perceptive
obtuse ___: **5** angle
Obuasi: **4** city, town
  locale: **5** Ghana
obukano: **4** lyre **6** string
  origin: **6** Africa
obverse: **5** front **8** flip-side, opposite
obviate: **5** avert, block, deter **6** remove **7** counter, forfend, prevent, rule out, ward off **8** forefend, preclude, prohibit, stave off **9** forestall **10** anticipate, counteract, do away with
obvious: **4** easy, open **5** clear, gross, lucid, naked, overt, plain, vivid **6** bright, cogent, in view, limpid, marked, patent, public **7** blatant, evident, exposed, express, glaring, logical, outward, precise, salient, visible **8** apparent, clear-cut, definite, distinct, explicit, flagrant, luminous, manifest, palpable, tangible, unhidden, unsubtle, unveiled **9** axiomatic, barefaced, graspable, obtrusive, prominent **10** accessible, conclusive, in evidence, noticeable, observable, pronounced, spelled out, unarguable, undeniable, unshrouded, well-marked
obviously: **5** by far **6** openly **7** clearly **8** of course **10** far and away
O.C.: **5** Smith
Ocala: **4** city, town
  locale: **7** Florida
O Canada: **6** anthem
O Captain! My Captain!: **4** poem
  author: Walt Whitman
ocarina: **4** wind **10** instrument
Ocasek, Ric
  group: The Cars
  spouse: Paulina Porizkova
O'Casey, Sean: **5** Irish **10** playwright
  home: **4** Eire, Erin
  work: Juno and the Paycock
    The Plough and the Stars
    Purple Dust
    Within the Gates **4** play **5** drama
___ o' cat: **3** one, two **4** four **5** three
Occam's ___: **5** razor
occasion: **3** use **4** call, case, luck, need, room, shot, time **5** basis, cause, event, evoke, nonce, state, thing **6** affair, chance, create, demand, effect, elicit, excuse, induce, lead to, moment, motive, prompt, reason **7** episode, grounds, inspire, opening, produce, provoke, warrant **8** engender, goings-on, incident, instance, juncture, milepost **9** happening, milestone, originate **10** antecedent, bring about, foundation, give rise to, inducement, make happen, motivation
  grand ~: **4** ball, bash, fete, gala, prom **5** anniv., feast, party **6** affair, dinner, fiesta **7** blowout, jubilee, pageant, shindig **8** birthday, festival, function, wingding
  have ~ for: **3** use **4** need, want **6** desire **7** require
  on ~: **7** at times **8** sometime **9** sometimes **10** now and then
  on any ~: **4** ever **6** always **10** at all times, invariably
  on no ~: **5** never **7** not ever **8** not at all **9** nevermore
  on that ~: **4** then, when **9** thereupon
occasional: **3** few, odd **4** rare **5** stray **6** casual, fitful, random, scarce, seldom, sparse **7** oddball, special, unusual **8** especial, far apart, off and on, periodic, specific, sporadic, uncommon **9** desultory, irregular **10** incidental, infrequent, sporadical, unfrequent
occasionally: **6** hardly, rarely, seldom **7** at times **8** at random, scarcely, sometime **9** sometimes **10** hardly ever, now and then
Occident: **4** West
occipital: **4** bone
  locale: **4** head **5** skull **7** cranium
  point: **5** inion
occipital ___: **4** bone, lobe **7** condyle
occlude: **3** dam **4** clog, plug, seal, shut, stop **5** block, choke, close, dam up **6** hinder, impede, stop up **7** congest, lock out, prevent, shut out, stopper **8** close off, obstruct, throttle
occluded ___: **5** front
occlusion: **4** clog **8** blockage, stoppage **9** exclusion, impedance
  combining form: **6** -clisis **7** -cleisis
occult: **4** dark, deep, eery **5** eerie, magic, weird **6** arcane, hidden, mystic, orphic, secret, unseen, veiled **7** magical, obscure, psychic, unknown **8** abstruse, esoteric, hermetic, mystical, oracular, profound **9** concealed, invisible, prophetic, recondite, unearthly **10** cabalistic, mysterious, unknowable, unrevealed, witchcraft
  philosophy: **6** cabala, kabala **7** cabbala, kabbala
  sign: **5** sigil
occultism: **5** magic **6** cabala, kabala **7** cabbala, kabbala **10** necromancy
Occult, The author: Colin Wilson
occupancy: **3** use **4** deed, term **5** title **6** tenure **7** control, holding, tenancy **8** presence **9** ownership, residence, retention **10** habitation, possession, settlement
___ occupancy: **6** double, single
___-occupancy vehicle: **4** high
occupant: **5** liver **6** holder, lessee, lodger, renter, tenant **7** denizen, dweller, resider **8** occupier, resident **9** addressee, incumbent, possessor **10** inhabitant
  agreement: **5** lease **8** contract, sublease
occupation: **3** job **4** line, slot, work **5** clerk, craft, field, pilot, place, trade **6** career, doctor, lawyer, living, métier, racket, tenure **7** calling, capture, control, pursuit, seizure, station, tenancy **8** activity, business, conquest, entering, function, invasion, lifework, position, takeover, vocation **9** avocation, moonlight, ownership, residence, specialty **10** department, employment, livelihood, profession, walk of life
  outmoded ~: **6** iceman **9** town crier
  suffix: **3** -eer, -eur, -ier, -ist **4** -euse, -ster **5** -arian
  tame ~: **5** McJob
occupation ___: **5** layer, level
occupational ___: **6** hazard **7** therapy
occupied: **4** busy, full **5** in use, taken **6** active, intent, leased, rented, tied up **7** engaged, lived-in, peopled, settled, working **8** employed, utilized **9** engrossed, inhabited, on the move, populated
  keep ~: **4** hold **5** delay, tie up **6** divert, engage, hinder, impede **8** encumber, obstruct, slow down
  not ~: **4** open **5** empty **6** lonely, vacant **7** vacated **8** deserted, desolate **9** abandoned, available
  with: **4** into, up to **7** taken by **8** obsessed, turned on **10** involved in
___-occupied: **5** owner
occupy: **3** man, own, sit, use **4** fill, hold, keep, live, stay **5** amuse, dwell, seize, sit at, spend, stand, tie up **6** absorb, attend, divert, employ, engage, invade, live at, live in, obtain, people, remain, reside, take up, tenant **7** capture, conquer, engross, immerse, inhabit, involve, overrun, pervade, possess, utilize **8** ensconce, garrison, interest, keep busy, maintain, permeate, populate, take over **9** entertain, establish, preoccupy **10** monopolize
  an abandoned building: **5** squat
  temporarily: **3** let **4** rent **5** lease
  time and space: **2** be **4** last, live **5** exist **7** breathe **8** continue
occur: **2** be, go **3** hit **4** come, dawn, fall, jell, show **5** arise, break, ensue, exist, pop up **6** appear, befall, betide, chance, crop up, dawn on, happen, result, strike, turn up **7** come off, develop, turn out **8** come to be, come true, manifest **9** come about, eventuate, intervene, take place, transpire **10** come to mind, come to pass
  again: **6** repeat **7** iterate
  subsequently: **5** ensue **6** follow, result **9** arise from, eventuate, transpire
  to: **4** dawn **6** befall, strike
  with: **9** accompany
occurrence: **3** hap **4** case, luck, show **5** event, scene, state, thing **6** affair **7** episode **8** accident, exigence, exigency, incident, instance, juncture **9** adventure, condition, emergency, existence, happening, incidence, situation **10** experience
occurring: **5** afoot **7** going on, ongoing **8** underway **9** happening **10** in progress
occurs, as it: **4** live
ocean: **3** Atl., lot, Pac., sea, ton **4** blue, deep, gobs, heap, host, main, pile, slew, tide, tons **5** briny, drink, heaps, water **6** Arctic, Indian, legion, seaway **7** numbers, Pacific, zillion **8** Atlantic, high seas, plethora **9** abundance, Antarctic, multitude, profusion, salt water, seven seas
  across an ~: **6** abroad **7** far away, foreign, oversea **8** overseas

area: 4 deep 5 abyss 7 benthos
compound: 4 NaCl, salt
craft: 3 str. 4 boat, ship 5 liner 6 vessel 7 steamer
cross the ~: 4 sail 5 pilot 6 cruise, voyage 7 captain, journey 8 navigate
dweller: 3 cod 4 alga, fish, hake, mako, mola, opah, salp 5 algae, porgy, salpa, squid
edge: 4 sand 5 beach, coast, shore 8 littoral, seacoast 10 waterfront
Egyptian god of the ~: 4 Nunu
ender: 4 aria 5 front, going, ology
enjoy the ~: 4 surf, swim, wade 5 bathe 7 hang ten
explorer: 5 Beebe 8 Cousteau
flier: 4 tern
floor fissure: 4 vent
hail: 4 ahoy
in Tibetan: 5 Dalai
like an ~: 4 deep, wavy 7 aqueous
liner name: 6 Cunard
motion: 4 tide, wave 5 swell
on the ~: 4 asea 5 asail, at sea 7 en route
on the ~ floor: 5 below
pollution: 5 slick
re ~ depths: 5 hadal
rescuer: 4 USCG 10 Coast Guard
ring in the ~: 5 atoll
route: 4 lane 7 passage, sea lane
sound: 4 boom, roar, roll 5 crash
spot in the ~: 3 isl. 4 isle 5 islet 6 island
spray: 4 foam, surf, wave 5 froth, spume 8 breakers 9 spindrift
treat ~ water: 6 desalt 10 desalinate, desalinize
ocean ___: 4 pout 5 liner, perch 7 farming, sunfish
Ocean ___: 5 Spray
___ Ocean: 6 Arctic, German, Indian 7 Pacific, Western 9 Antarctic
Ocean, Billy
homeland: Trinidad
song: Caribbean Queen (1984)
The Colour of Love (1988)
Get Outta My Dreams...(1988)
Love Is Forever (1986)
Loverboy (1984)
Love Zone (1986)
Suddenly (1985)
There'll Be Sad Songs (1986)
When the Going Gets Tough...(1985)
oceangoing: 5 naval 6 marine 7 pelagic 8 maritime, nautical
Oceania: 4 isls. 5 isles 7 islands
republic: 4 Fiji 9 Australia
___ Oceania: 6 French
oceanic: 4 huge 5 naval 6 marine 7 aquatic 8 maritime, natatory, nautical
oceanid: 6 Nereid
Oceanid: 4 Asia 5 nymph
oceanographic: 5 naval 6 marine 8 maritime, nautical
oceanography: 7 science
oceans: 4 a lot, gobs, lots, slew, tons 5 heaps, loads, piles, scads 9 Seven Seas
Ocean's Eleven (1960 film)
cast: Joey Bishop, Richard Conte, Sammy Davis Jr., Angie Dickinson, Peter Lawford, Dean Martin, Cesar Romero, Frank Sinatra
director: Lewis Milestone
Ocean's Eleven (2001 film)
cast: George Clooney, Matt Damon, Andy Garcia, Brad Pitt, Carl Reiner, Julia Roberts
director: Steven Soderbergh
Oceanside: 4 city, town
locale: 7 New York 10 California
Oceanus: 5 giant, Titan
daughter of ~: 4 Asia 5 Argia, Metis
parent of ~: 4 Gaea 6 Uranus
wife of ~: 6 Tethys
ocelot: 3 cat 5 felid 6 animal, big cat, feline 7 wildcat
relative: 4 eyra, lion, lynx, puma 5 chita, liger, ounce, tiger, tigon 6 bobcat, cheeta, chetah, cougar, jaguar, margay, serval, tiglon 7 bay lynx, caracal, cheetah, leopard, panther 9 catamount 10 jaguarundi
ocher: 3 sil 5 brown, color 6 yellow 7 mineral, reddish 8 orangish 9 earth tone
Egyptian source of ~: 6 Dakhla
relative: 4 buff, corn, gold, lime, rust, sand 5 blond, brass, coral, cream, flaxy, lemon, maize, peach, rusty, straw 6 blonde, canary, chammy, citron, crocus, flaxen, shammy, shamoy 7 apricot, chamois, citrine, jasmine, mustard, nankeen, old gold, saffron, xanthic 8 daffodil, primrose 9 champagne, goldenrod, jessamine
___ ocher: 3 red 6 yellow
ochlophobe fear: 6 crowds
ocho: 5 eight 7 Spanish
follower: 5 nueve
preceder: 5 siete
Ocho ___, Jamaica: 4 Rios
Ochoa, Severo: 8 Nobelist
ochre
see ocher
Ochs: 4 Phil 6 Adolph
Ocicat: 3 cat 5 felid 6 feline
Ockham's ___: 5 razor
___ O'Clock High: 6 Twelve
___ O'Clock Jump: 3 One
...___ o'clock scholar: 4 a ten
___ o'clock shadow: 4 five
Ocmulgee, city on the: 5 Macon
Ocoee: 4 city, town
locale: 7 Florida
O Come, All Ye Faithful: 4 noel 5 carol
O come, let us ___ Him: 5 adore
O'Connell: 5 Helen 6 Arthur
O'Connor: 3 Des, Pat, Una 5 Edwin, Frank, Renee 6 Donald, Sinéad 7 Carroll, Glynnis 8 Flannery
O'Connor, Carroll: 5 actor
film: Law and Disorder (1974)
Marlowe (1969)
Not With My Wife You Don't! (1966)
Return to Me (2000)
TV: All in the Family, Archie Bunker's Place, In the Heat of the Night
O'Connor, Donald: 5 actor 6 dancer
film: Call Me Madam (1953)
Out to Sea (1997)
Singin' in the Rain (1952)
Sing, You Sinners (1938)
Walking My Baby Back Home (1953)
O'Connor, Flannery: 6 writer
work: Everything That Rises Must Converge
A Good Man is Hard to Find
The Violent Bear It Away
Wise Blood
O'Connor, Frank: 5 Irish 6 writer
O'Connor, Sinéad
homeland: Ireland, Eire, Erin
song: Nothing Compares 2 U (1990)
Ocosingo: 4 city, town
locale: 6 Mexico 7 Chiapas
ocotillo: 5 shrub
Ocotlán: 4 city, town
locale: 6 Mexico, Oaxaca 7 Jalisco
Ocoyoacac: 4 city, town
locale: 6 Mexico
Ocozocoautla: 4 city, town
locale: 6 Mexico 7 Chiapas
OCS
candidate: 3 NCO
grad: 2 lt. 5 lieut.
Oct.: 2 mo.
follower: 3 Nov.
it ends in ~: 3 DST
preceder: 3 Sep. 4 Sept.
see also October
octa-: 5 eight
half of ~: 5 tetra-
minus one: 5 septi-
octagon: 5 shape
word: 4 Stop
octagon ___: 5 house, scale
Octagon: 9 detergent
alternative: 3 All, Biz, Era, Fab, Yes 4 Bold, Dash, Gain, Surf, Tide, Wisk 5 Cheer, Dreft, Purex 6 Calgon, Dynamo, Oxydol 9 Ivory Snow
octane ___: 6 number, rating
___-octane: 4 high
octave: 6 eighth
plus one: 5 ninth
Octavia: 6 Butler
husband: 4 Nero
Octavian: 5 Roman
see also Latin
Octavio: 3 Paz
___ octavo: 4 demy 5 crown 6 medium
octet: 5 combo, group 8 ensemble 9 vocalists
fraction: 6 eighth
in Spanish: 4 ocho
plus one: 5 nonet
October: 5 month
announcement: 5 Nobel
birthstone: 4 opal
observance: 5 UN Day
position of ~: 5 tenth
sign: 5 Libra 6 Scales 7 Balance, Scorpio 8 Scorpion
where Thanksgiving is in ~: 6 Canada
October 1964 author: David Halberstam
October Revolution name: 5 Lenin
October 7: 5 nones
October Sky (1999 film)
cast: Chris Cooper, Laura Dern, Jake Gyllenhaal, Chris Owen
director: Joe Johnston
Octobre: 4 mois 5 month 6 French
octogenarian milestone: 6 eighty
Octoot composer: 4 Bach 7 PDQ Bach
Octopan: 4 city, town
locale: 6 Mexico 10 Guanajuato
octopus
defense: 3 ink
female ~: 3 hen
home: 3 sea 5 ocean
octet: 4 arms, legs 9 tentacles
Octopussy: 4 film 5 novel
author: Ian Fleming
cast: Maud Adams, Louis Jourdan, Roger Moore
director: John Glen
Octopus, The author: Frank Norris
octyl ___: 6 phenol 7 alcohol
ocular: 4 lens 6 visual 7 sensory 9 sensorial
device: 6 eyecup
layer: 4 uvea
socket: 6 eyepit
oculist: 9 eye doctor
ocupado: 5 in use 7 Spanish
Oda ___ Brown: 3 Mae
odaiko: 4 drum
origin: 5 Japan
odalisque: 5 haram, harem, harim 6 hareem
oda locale: 5 haram, harem, harim 6 hareem
Odawara: 4 city, town
locale: 5 Japan
O'Day: 4 Alan 5 Anita
O'Day, Alan song: Undercover Angel (1977)
odd: 3 one 4 eery, lone, rare, sole 5 alien, eerie, flaky, fluky, freak, funny, kinky, kooky, queer, spare, wacky, weird, wiggy 6 atypic, chance, cranky, exotic, far-out, flakey, flukey, freaky, kookie, quaint, quirky, random, single, spacey, sundry, uneven, unique, varied, way-out, whacky 7 bizarre, curious, deviant, erratic, offbeat, strange, surplus, unalike, uncanny, unequal, unusual, various 8 aberrant, abnormal, atypical, freakish, leftover, mateless, peculiar, periodic, seasonal, singular, solitary, sporadic, uncommon, unpaired 9 anomalous, different, divergent, eccentric, fantastic, grotesque, irregular, ludicrous, off-center, quizzical, remaining, unheard-of, unmatched, unnatural, whimsical 10 avant-garde, fortuitous, incidental, occasional, off-the-wall, outlandish, remarkable, sporadical, unexpected, unfamiliar, unorthodox
ender: 4 ball, ment 6 jobber
job: 4 task 5 chore 6 errand
not ~: 4 even 6 normal 7 regular 8 matching 10 true to type
notion: 4 whim 5 fancy 6 vagary 7 caprice 8 crotchet
one: 4 kook 5 crank, flake 6 codger, weirdo 7 oddball 9 character, eccentric 10 individual
one out: 8 newcomer, outsider, stranger
odd ___: 3 job, lot 5 trick
odd ___ out: 3 man
Odd ___: 4 John 6 Fellow
oddball: 4 geek, kook, nerd, nurd, rare 5 crazy, flake, flaky, fluky, freak, funny, kinky, kooky, queer, weird 6 atypic, chance, far-out, flakey, flukey, freaky, kookie, misfit, quaint, random, sundry, unique, weirdo 7 bizarre, curious, deviant, erratic, offbeat, strange, uncanny, unusual 8 abnormal, atypical, freakish, maverick, original, peculiar, rara avis, singular, solitary, uncommon 9 character, different, eccentric, fantastic, irregular 10 avant-garde, fortuitous, individual, occasional, off-the-wall, outlandish
Odd Couple, The: 4 film, play
author: Neil Simon
cast: Jack Lemmon, Walter Matthau
director: Gene Saks
game: 5 poker
role: 3 Roy 5 Felix, Oscar, Speed, Unger 6 Cecily, Murray, Pigeon, Vinnie 7 Madison 9 Gwendolyn
Odd Couple, The (ABC sitcom)
cast: Jack Klugman (Oscar Madison) Tony Randall (Felix Unger)
oddity: 3 tic 5 quirk, trait, twist 6 foible, rarity 7 anomaly, paradox 8 original, rara avis 9 curiosity, exception 10 aberration, phenomenon
carnival ~: 4 geek 5 freak
Oddjob creator: 3 Ian
Odd John author: Olaf Stapledon
odd man ___: 3 out
Odd Man Out (1947 film)
cast: James Mason, Kathleen Ryan
director: Carol Reed
oddment: 3 bit 5 scrap 6 snatch 7 remnant, snippet 8 fragment, leftover 9 remainder
oddments: 5 trash 6 excess, scraps 7 remnant, rummage 8 leavings 9 remainder
odd-numbered page: 5 recto
odd or ___: 4 even
odds: 4 edge 5 ratio 6 chance 7 chances 8 handicap, ten to one, two to one

9 advantage, allowance 10 likelihood
and ends: 4 bits, misc., olio, rest 5 melee, scrap, trash 6 debris, job lot, jumble, litter, medley, scraps, things 7 mélange, remnant, rubbish, rummage 8 et cetera, leavings, leftover, remnants, snatches, snippets 9 fragments, leftovers, potpourri, remainder 10 miscellany
at ~: 7 opposed 8 battling, clashing, opposing 9 differing, on the outs 10 in conflict, poles apart
at ~ with: 3 con 7 loath to 8 averse to, opposing 9 counter to, hostile to
be at ~: 4 feud 5 clash 8 conflict
ender: 5 maker, to one
give ~: 3 bet, fix, lay 5 wager 6 gamble 8 make book, take bets 9 speculate
set at ~: 6 divide 7 break up, disrupt, quarrel 8 alienate, disunite, estrange 9 disaffect
taker: 6 better, bettor, player 7 gambler, wagerer 8 gamester
take the ~: 3 bet 5 wager 6 gamble
Odds ___...: 3 are
Odds Against author: Dick Francis
Odds Against Tomorrow (1959 film)
cast: Harry Belafonte, Robert Ryan, Shelley Winters
director: Robert Wise
odds and ___: 4 ends
odds-on: 6 liable, likely 8 expected, favorite, probable 9 promising, seemingly 10 in the cards
ode: 4 hymn, poem, rime 5 rhyme, verse 7 canzona, canzone, writing 8 canticle 9 epinicion
like an ~: 5 lyric 6 poetic
Old French ~: 3 lai
subject: 3 urn
___ ode: 7 regular, Sapphic
Ode ___ Grecian Urn: 3 on a
Ode ___ Nightingale: 3 to a
Ode ___ West Wind: 5 to the
Ode: Intimations of Immortality
author: William Wordsworth
Odense: 4 city, font, port, town 8 typeface
island: 3 Fyn
locale: 7 Denmark
Odenton: 4 city, town
locale: 8 Maryland
odeon: 7 theater, theatre 9 music hall, playhouse
Ode on a Grecian Urn author: John Keats
Ode on Indolence author: John Keats
Ode on Melancholy author: John Keats
Oder: 5 river
locale: 6 Poland 7 Germany
river to the ~: 5 Warta 6 Neisse
Oder-___ Line: 6 Neisse
Odes author: Horace
Odessa: 4 city, port, town 6 Turner
locale: 5 Texas 7 Ukraine
river: 8 Dniester
___ Odessa: 6 Little
Odessa File, The (1974 film)
cast: Derek Jacobi, Maria Schell, Maximilian Schell, Jon Voight
director: Ronald Neame
Ode to a Nightingale author: John Keats
Ode to Autumn author: John Keats
Ode to Billy Joe (1967 song) artist: Bobbie Gentry
Ode to Duty author: William Wordsworth
Ode to Liberty author: Percy Bysshe Shelley
Ode to Psyche author: John Keats
Ode to the Confederate Dead author: Allen Tate
Ode to the West Wind author: Percy Bysshe Shelley
Odets, Clifford: 10 playwright
spouse: Luise Rainer
work: Awake and Sing!
The Big Knife
Clash by Night
The Country Girl
The Flowering Peach
Golden Boy
Night Music
None But the Lonely Heart
Paradise Lost
Sweet Smell of Success
Till the Day I Die
The Time Is Ripe
Waiting for Lefty
odeum: 7 theater, theatre 9 music hall, playhouse
odic: 7 lyrical 8 Horatian, Pindaric
Odi et ___: 3 Amo
Odin: 3 god 5 Norse, Wotan
horse: 8 Sleipner, Sleipnir
son of ~: 3 Tyr 5 Baldr 6 Balder
wife of ~: 5 Frigg
O Dio Mio (1960 song) artist: Annette Funicello
odious: 4 base, foul, grim, mean, poor, ugly, vile 5 awful, lousy, nasty, onery, woful 6 crumby, crummy, dismal, horrid, ornery, rotten, woeful 7 accurst, baleful, baneful, beastly, doleful, ghastly, hateful, heinous, hideous 8 accursed, annoying, dreadful, Godawful, grievous, horrible, infamous, inferior, shameful, shocking, stinking, terrible, wretched 9 abhorrent, appalling, atrocious, defective, execrable, frightful, insidious, invidious, loathsome, miserable, monstrous, nefarious, obnoxious, offensive, repellant, repellent, repugnant, repulsive, revolting 10 abominable, despicable, detestable, disastrous, disgusting, forbidding, horrendous, outrageous, unpleasant
one: 3 cad, cur, rat 4 heel, toad, worm 5 knave, rogue, scamp, skunk, snake, sneak, swine 6 wretch 7 stinker 9 scoundrel 10 blackguard
Odishaw: 4 peak 5 mount 8 mountain
locale: 10 Antarctica
odist: 4 bard, poet, scop 6 rhymer 8 minstrel 9 poetaster, rhymester, versifier
Muse: 5 Erato
odium: 4 blot, hate, slur, spot 5 blame, brand, shame, stain 6 animus, enmity, hatred, infamy, malice, rancor, stigma 7 censure, disgust, dislike, ill will, obloquy 8 acrimony, aversion, black eye, contempt, disfavor, disgrace, dishonor, ignominy, loathing 9 animosity, antipathy, discredit, disrepute, ill repute, repulsion, revulsion 10 abhorrence, opprobrium, repugnance
odometer
abbr.: 3 mph
new ~ reading: 4 OOOO 5 OOOOO
rig an ~: 5 reset
unit: 4 mile
O'Donnell: 5 Cathy, Chris, Rosie 7 Lillian
O'Donnell, Chris: 5 actor
film: Batman Forever (1995)
Batman & Robin (1997)
Circle of Friends (1995)
Cookie's Fortune (1999)
Scent of a Woman (1992)
School Ties (1992)
The Three Musketeers (1993)
O'Donnell, Lillian: 6 writer
odontophobe fear: 7 dentist
odor: 3 air 4 musk, nose, reek, tang 5 aroma, savor, scent, smell, stink, whiff 6 breath, flavor, repute, stench 7 bouquet, essence, perfume 8 pungency, tincture 9 effluvium, emanation, fragrance, redolence 10 exhalation, reputation
combining form: 3 osm- 4 osmo-
detector: 4 nose
foul ~: 4 reek 5 smell, stink 6 stench 9 effluvium
give off an ~: 4 reek 5 stink
having a bad ~: 4 foul, rank 5 fetid, musty, reeky 6 putrid, rancid, rotten, smelly, stinky, strong 7 noisome, reeking 8 mephitic, stinking
offensive ~: 5 fetor, stink 6 foetor
slight ~: 4 hint 5 sniff, trace, whiff 6 breath 9 suspicion
Odor ___: 6 Eaters
Odor of Sanctity, An author: Frank Yerby
odorous: 4 dank, foul, gamy, rank 5 fetid, gamey, moldy, musty, reeky, sharp, spicy 6 foetid, rotten, skunky, smelly, spicey, stinky, strong 7 miasmic, noisome, noxious, pungent, reeking, scented, squalid 8 aromatic, fragrant, mephitic, redolent, stagnant, stinking, unsavory 9 offensive, olfactory 10 effluvious
starter: 3 mal
___ O. Douglas: 7 William
Ods bodkins!: 4 egad 5 egads 6 zounds
ODU locale: 7 Norfolk 8 Virginia
OD wearer: 2 GI 7 private, recruit, soldier
Odysseus: 4 hero 6 Elytis 7 warrior
advisor: 6 Athena, Athene
dog: 5 Argus
emulate ~: 4 roam, rove 5 drift, range, stray 6 travel, wander 7 journey, meander 9 gallivant
home: 6 Greece, Ithaca
lover of ~: 5 Aeaea, Circe, Kirke 6 Evippe 7 Calypso 9 Callidice
parent: 7 Laertes 8 Anticlea, Sisyphus
son: 5 Romus 6 Agrius 7 Latinus, Romanus 8 Euryalus 9 Acusilaus, Telegonus 10 Polypoetes, Telemachus
wife: 8 Penelope
odyssey: 4 trek, trip 6 hejira 7 journey 8 long haul
Odyssey: 3 van 5 Honda
Odyssey, The: 4 epic, epos, poem 6 epopee
author: 5 Homer
character: 4 Irus, Maro, Zeus 5 Arete, Circe, Helen, Kirke, Medon, siren 6 Athena, Athene, Hermes, Mentor, Nestor, Noëmon, Scylla 7 Calypso, Elpenor, Eumaeus, Laertes, Phemius 8 Alcinous, Antinous, Eurynome, Melantho, Menelaus, Nausicaä, Odysseus, Peiraeus, Penelope, Poseidon, Tiresias 9 Charybdis, Eurycleia 10 Eurylochus, Eurymachus, Melanthius, Philoetius, Polyphemus, Telemachus
herb: 4 moly
peak: 4 Ossa
___ Odyssey, The: 6 Talbot
___ Oe: 5 Aloha
OED: 4 dict. 10 dictionary
ender: 3 zed
info: 3 def., wds. 5 words
unit: 3 vol. 6 volume
Oedipus
daughter of ~: 6 Ismene 8 Antigone
parent of ~: 5 Laius 7 Jocasta
son of ~: 8 Eteocles 9 Polynices
victim of ~: 5 Laius
wife of ~: 7 Jocasta
Oedipus ___: 3 Rex, Tex 7 complex
Oedipus at Colonus author: Sophocles
Oedipus Rex author: Sophocles
Oedipus Tex composer: PDQ Bach
oeil-de-___: 5 boeuf
Oe, Kenzaburo: 6 writer 8 Japanese, Nobelist
oenochoe: 3 jug 4 ewer 6 vessel 7 pitcher 9 container
oenology topic: 4 Napa, wine 5 aroma
oenomel: 5 drink 8 beverage
ingredient: 4 wine 5 honey
Oenone: 5 nymph
husband: 5 Paris
Oenone author: Alfred Tennyson
o'er: 4 thru 7 finish'd
opposite: 5 neath
o'er ___ and dale: 4 hill
Oersted, Hans: 6 Danish 9 physicist
Oerter: 2 Al
forte: 4 shot 7 shot put
oeuf layer: 5 poule
oeuvre: 4 opus, work 5 canon 6 corpus 10 opera omnia
of ___: 4 late, note 5 a kind, a sort, sorts 6 choice, course
of ___ proportions: 4 epic
of ___ words: 3 few
___ of: 3 all, off 4 back, fond, hear, kind, sort 5 ahead, aware, by way, on top, short, think 6 become, inside 7 apropos, because, dispose, outside, upwards
___-of: 7 unheard
Of ___ and Men: 4 Mice
Of ___ and the River: 4 Time
Of ___ Bondage: 5 Human
Of ___ I Sing: 4 Thee
of a ___: 4 kind, sort 5 piece
___ of Abraham: 6 Plains
___ of absence: 5 leave
___ of a chance: 5 ghost
___ of a Clown: 5 Tears
___ of a different color: 5 horse
___ of admissions: 4 dean
___ of a Doubt: 6 Shadow
___ of a Drag: 4 Kind
___ of Adrian Messenger, The: 4 List
___ of a feather: 5 birds
___ of affairs: 5 state
___ of Africa: 3 Out
___ of Age in Samoa: 6 Coming
___ of Ages: 4 Rock
___ of a gun: 3 son
___ of a kind: 3 one, two 4 four 5 three
___ of Alcatraz: 7 Birdman
___ of ale: 4 yard
___ of a Lifetime: 4 Love 6 Chance
___ of all: 5 least
___ of Allegiance: 6 Pledge
___ of All Fears, The: 3 Sum
___ of All Flesh, The: 3 Way
O'Fallon: 4 city, town
locale: 8 Illinois, Missouri
___-of-all-trades: 4 jack
___ of America: 3 Men 4 Bank 5 Voice
___ of Amontillado, The: 4 Cask
___ of a Nation, The: 5 Birth
___ of an era, the: 3 end
___ of a New Day, The: 7 Promise
___ of Angels: 4 City, Rage, Talk 6 Battle
___ of an idea: 4 germ
___ of Anxiety, The: 3 Age
O'Faolain, Sean: 5 Irish 6 author, writer
work: A Nest of Simple Folk
The Talking Trees
___ of appeals: 5 court
___ of approval: 4 seal 5 stamp
___ of a Preacher Man: 3 Son
___ of Aquarius: 3 Age
___ of Aquitaine: 7 Eleanor
___ of Arabia: 8 Lawrence
___ of Araby, The: 5 Sheik
___ of Aragon: 9 Catherine
___ of Arc: 4 Joan
___ of arms: 4 coat 5 place 7 officer

___ of art: 4 work
___ of articulation: 5 basis, place, point 6 manner
___ of a Salesman: 5 Death
___ of Assisi: 5 Clara, Clare 7 Francis
___ of assistance: 4 writ
___ of a sudden: 3 all
___ of Athens: 5 Timon
___ of Atonement: 3 Day
___ of attack: 4 plan 5 angle
___ of attainder: 4 bill
___ of attorney: 5 power
___ of August, The: 4 Guns 6 Whales
___ of Austria: 4 Anne, John
___ of averages: 3 law
___ of Avila: 6 Teresa 7 Theresa
___ of Avon: 4 Bard
___ of a Wayside Inn: 5 Tales
___ of a Woman: 5 Scent
___ of Babel: 5 Tower
___ of Baghdad, The: 5 Thief
___ of baloney: 4 full
___ of Base: 3 Ace
___ of beans: 4 full, hill
___ of beasts: 4 king
___ of beef: 4 side 5 baron, round
___ of Bernadette, The: 4 Song
___ of Bethlehem: 4 Star
___ of Biscay: 3 Bay
___ of bounds: 3 out
___ of breath: 3 out
___ of burden: 5 beast
___ of business: 5 order, piece
___ of cake: 5 piece
___ of call: 4 port
___ of Cancer: 6 Tropic
___ of Capricorn: 6 Tropic
___ of cards: 4 deck 5 house
___ of Cassini: 4 oval
___-of-center: 4 left 5 right
___ of ceremonies: 6 master
___ of certiorari: 4 writ
___ of chance: 4 game
___ of character: 3 out
___ of claims: 5 court
___ of clay: 4 feet
___ of Cleves: 4 Anne
___ of command: 5 chain
___ of commission: 3 out
___ of Concord: 4 Sage
___ of Confusion: 4 Ball, Land, Year
___ of Congress: 7 Library
___ of consciousness: 6 stream
___ of contention: 4 bone
___ of Corinth: 4 Gulf 7 Isthmus
Of course!: 2 ay 3 aha, aye, yes 4 fine, I see, okay, sure 5 natch, oh yes
___ of Court: 4 Inns
___ of credit: 4 line 6 letter
___ of curvature: 6 center, circle, radius
___ of Damocles: 5 sword
___ of Darkness: 4 Edge 5 Color, Heart 6 Prince
___ of date: 3 out
___ of David: 4 City, Star 6 Shield
___ of dawn: 5 crack
___ of day: 4 time 5 break
___ of Day: 5 Break
___ of Decision: 5 Years
___ of defeat: 5 agony
___ of departure: 5 point
___ of Divorcement: 5 A Bill
___ of Dog: 6 Beware
___ of do or die: 5 a case
___-of-doors: 3 out
___ of Dover: 6 Strait
___ of drawers: 4 nest 5 chest
___ of Dreams: 5 Field 6 Burden, Street
___ of duty: 4 tour
___ of 1812: 3 War
___ of Earl: 4 Duke
___ of Eden: 4 East 6 Garden
___ of education: 5 board
___ of eight: 5 piece
___ of Elea: 4 Zeno
___ of elections: 5 board
___ of Enchantment: 4 Land
___ of Endearment: 5 Terms
___ of Engineers: 5 Corps
___ of England: 6 Church 7 Primate
___ of entry: 4 bill, port
___ of errors: 6 Comedy
___ of ethics: 4 code
___ of Evil: 5 Force, Touch
___ of exchange: 4 bill, rate 5 piece 6 medium
off: 3 bad, far, out 4 afar, away, awry, gone, over, poor, rank, slim, slow, sour 5 apart, aside, askew, atilt, flaky, not on, small 6 absent, astray, behind, flakey, murder, rancid, remote, rotten, slight, spoilt, untrue 7 gone bad, inexact, outside, removed, slender, spoiled, strange, tainted 8 canceled, inferior, not right, sluggish 9 divergent, elsewhere, imprecise, incorrect, on one's way, out of here, out of sync, postponed, to one side, vanishing 10 decomposed, low-quality, malodorous, not working, on vacation
  ender: 3 key, set 4 beat, hand, load, side 5 print, shoot, shore, sides, stage 6 handed, screen, spring 7 setting 8 scouring
  in Italian: 3 via
  prefix: 3 apo-
  starter: 3 cut, lay, pay, put, rub, run, set, tee 4 blow, boil, cast, dust, fall, hand, kick, lead, lift, pick, play, sell, send, show, shut, spin, take, turn 5 blast, break, brush, check, knock, stand, trade
off ___: 4 year 5 and on, guard, plumb, stump
off ___ good start: 3 to a
off ___ tangent: 3 on a
off-___: 3 air, key 4 base, duty, hour, line, load, mike, peak, ramp, site 5 board, brand, glide, price, white 6 budget, camera, campus, center, island, limits, screen, season 7 putting
off-___ betting: 5 track
off-___ pitch: 5 speed
off-___ vehicle: 4 road
off.
  aide: 4 asst.
  assistant: 4 secy.
  church ~: 4 msgr.
  city ~: 3 ald.
  main ~: 5 hdqrs.
  military ~: 2 lt. 3 col., cpl., gen., maj., sgt. 4 MSgt., SSgt., TSgt. 5 lieut., lt. gen.
  naval ~: 3 CPO 4 bo's'n, cmdr., lt. jg., RAdm., VAdm. 5 lieut.
  police ~: 3 sgt. 4 capt. 5 lieut.
  see also office, officer, official
___ off: 3 bad, beg, bug, buy, cry, cut, fob, get, lay, let, log, lop, mid, nod, pay, pop, put, rip, run, set, tap, tee, top 4 back, blow, buzz, call, cast, come, dash, doze, drop, dust, ease, face, fair, fall, fend, fire, give, hand, haul, head, hold, kick, kiss, lead, lift, make, pack, palm, pass, peel, pick, pull, push, rake, reel, ring, rope, seal, sell, send, show, shut, sign, spin, step, stop, tail, take, tear, tell, tick, toss, turn, ward, wear, whip, wipe, work 5 a ways, blast, break, bring, brown, brush, carry, choke, clear, dusts, fight, first, hit it, knock, laugh, leave, level, mouth, on and, right, round, shake, shove, shrug, slack, smart, sound, split, spout, stand, stave, swear, taper, throw, touch, write 6 better, change, polish, square, switch 7 squeeze
___-off: 3 far, ill, rip, tip 4 bake, cook, face, goof, spin, well 5 angle, fence, sawed, trade
Off ___ Comet: 3 on a
Off ___ into the wild...: 4 we go
Off ___, on...: 5 again
___-Off: 4 Bake, Easy
___ of '42: 6 Summer
___ of fact: 5 point 6 matter
___ of faculty: 4 dean
___ off after: 4 take
___ of faith: 3 act 4 leap 6 breach 7 article
___ of Faith: 4 Leap 6 Breach
offal: 4 junk 5 swill, trash, waste 6 debris, litter, refuse 7 carrion, garbage, rubbish
___ of Fame: 4 Hall
off and ___: 7 running
___ of fare: 4 bill
___ of fate: 5 quirk, twist
off-balance: 6 uneven 7 unequal 8 lopsided 9 irregular
off-base: 6 all wet, errant, risqué 7 inexact 8 aberrant, abnormal, improper
offbeat: 3 odd 4 eery, luny 5 alien, eerie, fresh, funky, loony, loopy, novel, outré, weird 6 atypic, far out, freaky, looney, quaint, quirky, unique, unlike, way-out 7 bizarre, deviant, oddball, strange, unalike, unusual 8 aberrant, atypical, bohemian, freakish, peculiar, uncommon 9 anomalous, different, divergent, eccentric, fantastic, irregular, quizzical, unheard-of 10 unorthodox
off-Broadway ___: 4 show 5 stage
off-Broadway trophy: 4 Obie
off-center: 3 odd 4 awry, side 5 askew, atilt, wacky 6 whacky 7 strange 9 eccentric, irregular
off-color: 4 blue, lewd, racy, rank 5 bawdy, dirty, salty, shady, spicy 6 coarse, earthy, ribald, risqué, sickly, smutty, spicey, vulgar 7 naughty 8 indecent 9 offensive, tasteless 10 indelicate, lascivious, suggestive
___-off coupon: 5 cents
off-course: 4 awry, lost, wide 6 errant
  go ~: 3 yaw 4 veer 7 deviate
off-duty: 4 free, idle, open 7 resting 8 inactive, released 9 at leisure, at liberty, available 10 disengaged, unoccupied
  outfit: 5 mufti 7 civvies
___ of Fear, The: 4 Face 5 House 6 Valley
Offenbach: 4 city, town 7 Jacques
  locale: 7 Germany
Offenbach, Jacques: 6 French 8 composer
  work: Orpheus in the Underworld Tales of Hoffmann
offend: 3 jar, sin, vex 4 fret, gall, gibe, hurt, jeer, jibe, miff, mock, pain, rile, slam, slur, snub, zing 5 abuse, anger, annoy, chafe, decry, libel, pique, repel, scorn, shock, spite, spurn, sting, taunt, upset, wound, wrong 6 defame, deride, dump on, heckle, impugn, insult, malign, nettle, rebuff, revolt, sicken, slight, vilify 7 affront, asperse, degrade, disdain, disgust, disturb, fend off, hold off, horrify, outrage, provoke, put down, rank out, repulse, slander, tick off, traduce, turn off 8 aggrieve, alienate, belittle, denounce, distress, drive off, gross out, irritate, ridicule, trespass, vilipend 9 denigrate, discredit, disoblige, disparage, displease, humiliate, misbehave 10 antagonize, calumniate, disgruntle, disrespect, exasperate, transgress
  the eye: 5 clash
  the nose: 4 reek 5 smell, stink
  unlikely to ~: 4 kind, nice, warm 5 homey 6 decent, genial, gentle, kindly, modest, polite, proper, seemly 7 affable, amiable, amusing, cordial, correct, genteel, helpful, likable, refined, winsome 8 charming, cheerful, cultured, decorous, friendly, generous, gracious, ladylike, obliging, pleasant, pleasing, tasteful, very good, virtuous, wellbred 9 admirable, agreeable, befitting, courteous, exemplary, simpatico 10 attractive, meticulous, personable, scrupulous
offended: 4 hurt, sore 5 huffy, livid, moody 7 injured
  be ~ by: 4 mind 6 resent
  easily ~: 5 huffy 6 touchy 7 bristly
  easily ~ one: 4 prig 5 prude 7 Puritan
offender: 4 perp 5 felon 6 bad guy 7 runaway, villain 8 criminal, internee, prisoner 10 delinquent
  mil. ~: 4 AWOL 6 absent
offense: 3 cut, dig, hit, ire, sin 4 barb, foul, gibe, harm, hurt, jibe, quip, slam, slap, slur, snub, tort 5 abuse, anger, blitz, crime, fault, guilt, lapse, libel, pique, scorn, taunt, wrath, wrong 6 attack, breach, felony, injury, insult, rebuff, slight, zinger 7 affront, assault, battery, calumny, catcall, disdain, flare-up, misdeed, mockery, mugging, obloquy, outrage, put-down, slander, umbrage 8 contempt, derision, ridicule, trespass 9 annoyance, aspersion, cheap shot, contumely, indignity, injustice, offensive, onslaught, veniality, violation 10 aggression, blitzkrieg, defamation, disrespect, illegality, infraction, irritation, misconduct, opprobrium, peccadillo, resentment, wrongdoing
  beat the ~: 5 parry, repel 6 defeat, rebuff, resist 7 hold off, repulse 8 push back, turn back 9 force back, keep at bay, withstand
  deprive of ~: 5 unarm 6 disarm
  Inquisition ~: 6 heresy
  serious ~: 4 tort 5 arson, crime, heist, theft 6 felony, holdup, murder 7 assault, robbery, treason 8 burglary, delictum 10 kidnapping
  show ~: 4 mind, slap 6 resent
offensive: 4 base, evil, foul, grim, loud, poor, push, raid, rude, ugly, vile 5 awful, blitz, gross, lousy, nasty, onset, pushy, sally, seamy, woful 6 attack, biting, crumby, crummy, dismal, horrid, odious, rancid, risqué, rotten, sortie, vulgar, woeful 7 abusive, accurst, assault, baleful, baneful, beastly, cutting, doleful, ghastly, hateful, heinous, hideous, noisome, odorous, offense, squalid, uncivil 8 accursed, annoying, campaign, dreadful, God-awful, grievous, horrible, inferior, insolent, invasion, off-color, shameful, shocking, stinking, terrible, unsavory, wretched 9 abhorrent, appalling, atrocious, defective, execrable, frightful, insidious, insulting, invidious, loathsome, low-minded, miserable, monstrous, obnoxious, onslaught, repellant, repellent, repugnant, repulsive, revolting, sarcastic, unsightly 10 abominable, aggression, aggressive, derogatory, despicable, detestable, disastrous, disgusting, forbidding, horrendous, impossible, indelicate, irritating, lascivious, malodorous, outrageous, scandalous, scurrilous, unbecoming, unmannerly, unpleasant
  starter: 7 counter
  take the ~: 4 lead 6 attack 7 aggress

offensive ___: 3 end 4 line 6 tackle
___ offensive: 3 Tet 5 peace
offer: 3 bid 4 cite, give, hand, move, pass, pose, show 5 bring, grant, pitch, press, yield 6 afford, donate, extend, feeler, hand in, submit, tender 7 furnish, hold out, present, produce, proffer, propose, provide, request, suggest 8 endeavor, overture, proposal, put forth 9 hold forth, introduce, sacrifice, volunteer 10 administer, invitation, make a pitch, put forward
an opinion: 3 say 5 guide, opine 7 comment, counsel, observe, suggest, suppose, surmise 8 point out 9 recommend
assurance: 4 aver, avow 6 attest
evidence: 5 quote 6 attest 8 attest to
for a price: 4 hawk, sell, vend 5 put up 6 market, peddle
starter: 7 counter
temporarily: 4 lend, loan 7 advance
up: 4 cede, give 5 endow, grant 6 bestow, devote, donate, impart, render, tender 7 let have, proffer 8 fork over, heap upon, immolate, renounce, shell out 9 sacrifice, surrender 10 contribute, relinquish
___ offer: 5 final 6 tender
offering: 3 bid 4 alms, gift 5 tithe 7 charity, present, release, tribute, worship 8 donation, gratuity, libation, oblation 9 atonement, sacrifice
___ offering: 5 burnt, peace, stock 6 public
of few ___: 5 words
off-guard: 5 aback, short 6 unwary 7 napping 8 careless, reckless, sleeping 9 negligent 10 by surprise, unthinking
catch ~: 5 shock 8 surprise
put ~: 6 disarm 10 disconcert
offhand: 4 cool, curt, glib, rude 5 ad-lib, aloof, brusk 6 abrupt, breezy, casual, chance, mellow 7 brusque, cursory 8 careless, cavalier, laid-back, slapdash 9 arbitrary, easygoing, extempore, haphazard, impromptu, impulsive, negligent, throwaway, unguarded, unheedful, unstudied, whipped up 10 improvised, nonchalant, unagitated, uncritical, unprepared, unprompted, willy-nilly
do ~: 5 ad-lib 6 wing it 7 dash off 9 improvise
in Latin: 9 brevi manu
office: 3 job 4 duty, part, post, role, room, shop, work 5 place, suite, trust 6 agency, branch, bureau, center, charge 7 factory, foundry, station 8 benefice, building, business, capacity, facility, function, position, province, vocation 9 personnel, salt mines, situation, workplace 10 commission, department, profession
acronym: 4 ASAP
asst.: 4 secy.
away from the ~: 3 out 5 not in 9 elsewhere
break time: 5 ten a.m.
building area: 6 atrium
communication: 4 memo 5 e-mail
connection: 3 LAN 5 modem
copy of yore: 5 mimeo 6 carbon 10 mimeograph
crew: 5 staff 9 employees
do an ~ job: 4 file, sort, type 5 index 6 docket, record 7 arrange, catalog 8 classify, register 10 pigeonhole
dupe: 2 cc. 4 copy
ender: 6 holder
expense: 4 rent 5 lease 8 overhead
freebie: 4 perc, perk, plus 5 bonus 7 benefit 8 dividend 10 perquisite
front ~: 5 board 8 official 9 directors 10 executives, management
furniture: 4 desk, sofa 5 couch, divan, table 6 lounge, settee 7 rolltop 9 davenport, secretary, sectional 10 escritoire
hold ~: 5 serve 6 act for 7 serve as 8 speak for 9 represent 10 administer
home ~: 3 den 5 study 7 station
length of ~: 4 span, term 6 period, tenure 8 duration, interval 9 occupancy
note: 4 memo 7 message, missive, tickler 8 reminder 9 directive
phone: 3 ext. 9 extension
plant: 4 fern
put in ~: 4 seat, vote 5 elect 6 enseat
remove from ~: 4 oust 5 purge 6 depose
return to ~: 6 recall 7 reelect 9 bring back, reinstate
rooms: 5 suite
seek ~: 3 run 5 stump 7 contend 8 politick
seeker: 3 pol 9 candidate 10 politician
skills stat.: 3 wpm
stamp: 4 null, paid, recd. 7 invalid 9 cancelled
suffix: 3 -dom 4 -ship
supply: 2 PC 3 fax 4 pads, pens 5 dater, paper, Xerox 6 copier 7 erasers, pencils 8 computer
symbol of ~: 4 mace
wear: 3 tie 4 suit 6 outfit 7 uniform 8 ensemble
withdraw from ~: 4 quit 5 demit, leave
worker: 4 asst., boss, page, temp 5 clerk, filer, gofer, steno 6 gopher 7 manager 9 assistant
office ___: 3 boy 4 girl, park 5 block, hours, plaza 6 seeker
___ office: 3 box, DA's 4 back, home, land, loan, post 5 assay, front, night 6 divine, little, patent, ticket 7 booking, foreign
Office ___: 5 Depot
___ Office: 4 Holy, Oval
___-office business: 4 land
officeholder: 2 in 8 minister, official 10 politician
officer: 3 arm, cop 4 head 5 agent, badge, chief 6 captor, deputy, leader, mounty, shamus, warden 7 captain, manager, marshal, sheriff, soldier 8 director, sergeant 9 appointee, detective, dignitary, executive, policeman, president 10 bureaucrat, lieutenant, magistrate
antidrug ~: 4 narc, nark
career ~: 5 lifer
church ~: 5 elder, prior
Church of England ~: 6 beadle
command: 4 halt
company ~: 2 VP 3 CEO, CFO, COO 4 pres., secy. 5 treas. 9 president, secretary, treasurer
corrections ~: 6 jailer, warden 7 turnkey
financial: 2 tr. 3 CFO 5 treas. 9 treasurer
junior ~: 5 cadet 7 soldier
mil. ~: 2 lt. 3 cdr. 4 adjt., SSgt.
military ~: 2 lt. 3 adm., col., ens., gen., maj., sgt. 4 capt., mate 5 bosun, lieut., lt. col., major 6 ensign, gunner 7 admiral, captain, colonel, general 8 sergeant
Ottoman ~: 3 aga 4 agha 5 vizir
peace ~: 3 cop 6 lawman 7 marshal, sheriff
petty ~: 3 yeo. 4 rank 5 bosun 6 sailor, yeoman
police ~: 3 cop, law 4 bear, fuzz, heat, narc, nark 5 badge, bobby 6 copper, patrol 7 officer 8 bluecoat, gendarme 9 constable, detective
presiding ~: 4 head 5 chief 6 leader, top dog, warden 7 manager 8 director, governor 9 executive, president 10 supervisor
undercover ~ at times: 4 bait, lure 5 shill 6 come-on
___ officer: 4 deck, flag, line, loan 5 field, first, peace, petty, staff, third 6 flight, health, police, public, second, truant 7 company, general, orderly, reserve, warrant
Officer and a Gentleman, An (1982 film)
cast: Richard Gere, Louis Gossett Jr., Debra Winger
character: 4 Emil
director: Taylor Hackford
setting: 3 OCS
___, Officer Krupke: 3 Gee
officer of the ___: 3 day 4 deck 5 guard, watch
officers: 5 brass, staff
Officers and Gentlemen author: Evelyn Waugh
offices: 4 help 7 service 10 assistance
official: 3 CEO 4 boss, exec, OKed, true 5 agent, brass, mayor, valid 6 formal, gerent, lawful, leader, top dog 7 big shot, cleared, correct, manager, marshal, premier, regular 8 approved, bona fide, director, endorsed, governor, higher-up, licensed, minister, orthodox, rightful, standard, top brass, verified 9 canonical, certified, dignitary, executive, incumbent, president, secretary, treasurer 10 accredited, authorized, bureaucrat, chancellor, conclusive, ex cathedra, legitimate, magistrate, panjandrum, recognized, sanctioned, unarguable, unmistaken
church ~: 5 vicar 6 cleric, deacon, warden 8 minister 9 monsignor
college ~: 4 dean 6 bursar 9 registrar
ender: 3 dom
government ~: 5 envoy 6 legate 8 delegate, diplomat, emissary, minister 10 ambassador
Muslim ~: 3 aga 4 agha, amir, emir 5 ameer, emeer
proceedings: 4 acta
sports ~: 3 ref, ump 5 judge, timer, zebra 6 umpire 7 referee 8 linesman
officiate: 3 run, sit 4 boss 5 chair, emcee, serve 6 direct, govern, handle, manage, umpire 7 command, conduct, oversee, preside, referee
officious: 4 busy, rude 5 bossy, pushy 7 forward 8 impudent, meddling 9 intrusive, obtrusive, pragmatic 10 meddlesome
offing: 6 coming, future 7 by and by 8 imminent 9 impending, potential
be in the ~: 4 loom 6 impend 8 approach, threaten
in the ~: 4 near 6 coming 7 pending 8 imminent
___ of fire: 4 ball, line, zone 5 field 7 baptism
___ of Fire: 4 Ball, Face, Ring 7 Streets
offish: 3 icy 4 cold, cool 5 aloof 6 chilly, frigid, remote 7 distant, glacial, haughty 8 detached, reserved 9 withdrawn 10 antisocial, unfriendly, unsociable
___ of fish: 6 kettle
___ off it!: 4 Come
off-key: 4 flat, sour 5 harsh, sharp 7 deviant, grating, jarring 8 abnormal, jangling, strident 9 anomalous, dissonant, divergent, irregular, out of tune, unmusical, unnatural 10 discordant
___ of Flanders: 4 A Dog
off-limits: 4 tabu 5 taboo 9 forbidden
activity: 4 no-no, tabu 5 taboo
off-load: 4 dump 6 unlade
___ of Flubber: 3 Son
___ of Flying: 4 Fear
off on a ___: 7 tangent
Off on a Comet author: Jules Verne
off one's ___: 4 feed 5 guard, hands
___ off one's back, the: 5 shirt
___ off one's feet: 5 sweep
___ of Fools: 4 Ship 5 Chain, Feast
___ of force: 4 line 5 field
___ of fortune: 5 wheel 7 soldier
___ of Four, The: 4 Gang, Sign
off-peak time: 4 lull 5 letup 6 hiatus 8 breather
off-putting: 4 dour, grim, ugly, vile 5 nasty, stern 6 odious, severe, strict 7 hateful, hideous, hostile, noisome, ominous, squalid 8 daunting, menacing, shocking, sinister 9 abhorrent, execrable, loathsome, offensive, repellent, repugnant, repulsive, revolting, unsightly 10 abominable, detestable, disgusting, forbidding, unfriendly, unpleasant
not ~: 4 nice
off-ramp: 4 exit 6 egress
___ of Frankenstein: 3 Son 5 Bride 7 Revenge
___ of Freedom: 5 Medal
___ of Friends: 6 Circle 7 Society
off-road vehicle: 3 ATV 4 jeep
offset: 4 undo 5 cover, hedge, repay, stamp 6 cancel, negate, redeem 7 balance, counter, imprint, nullify, recover, redress 8 allow for, equalize, outweigh 9 cancel out, make up for, reimburse 10 compensate, counteract, invalidate, neutralize, recompense
offshoot: 3 arm 4 cion, limb, spur, twig 5 scion 6 branch, colony, result, sprout 7 adjunct, faction, product 9 affiliate, appendage, by-product, outgrowth 10 derivative, descendant
offshore: 4 asea, wind 5 alien, at sea 7 foreign, oversea 8 overseas
activity: 5 scuba 6 diving
lodging: 5 botel 6 boatel
structure: 3 rig 6 oil rig
offspring: 3 cub, kid, pup, son 4 baby, cion, desc., heir, kids, seed 5 brood, child, issue, kiddy, puppy, scion, spawn, young 6 family, litter 7 bambino, kinfolk, lineage, progeny 8 children, daughter, kinfolks, kinsfolk 9 posterity, successor 10 descendant, generation
combining form: 4 toco-, toko- 5 proli-
of ~: 6 filial
offstage area: 4 wing
___ off steam: 4 blow
off-target: 4 wide 6 errant
off the ___: 3 bat 4 cuff, face, hook, rack, wall 5 books, shelf, track 6 ground, record
off the ___ end: 4 deep
off the ___ of one's head: 3 top
off the ___ path: 6 beaten
___ off the bat: 5 right
Off the Court author: 4 Ashe
off-the-cuff: 5 ad-lib 6 casual, improv, vamped 8 informal 9 extempore, impromptu, whipped up 10 unscripted
___ off the fat of the land: 4 live
___ off the handle: 3 fly
___ off the hog: 4 high
___ off the old block: 5 a chip
off-the-rack: 3 RTW
off-the-wall: 3 odd 4 daft, zany 5 batty, dotty, flaky, loopy, manic, nutty, outré, wacky 6 absurd, flakey, insane, way-out, whacky 7 bizarre, comical, oddball

8 peculiar 9 eccentric, illogical 10 irrational
Off the Wall (1980 song) artist: Michael Jackson
__ **Off to See the Wizard:** 4 We're
__ **of Fugue, The:** 3 Art
__ **of fun:** 5 loads 6 barrel
off-white: 4 bone 5 pearl 6 pearly
__ **off with:** 3 run 4 make, walk
__ **of gab:** 4 gift
__ **of Galilee:** 3 Man, Sea
__ **of gas:** 3 out
__ **of Gibraltar:** 4 Rock
__ **of Gilead:** 4 balm
__ **of glasses:** 4 pair
__ **of Glory:** 5 Blaze, Paths, Price, Times 6 Depths
__ **of God:** 3 act, man, Son 4 A Man, City, John, Lamb, Word 5 Agnes, house 6 Church, Mother
__ **of gold:** 3 pot 5 heart
__ **of Good Feeling:** 3 Era
__ **of Good Hope:** 4 Cape
__ **of goods:** 4 bill
... __ **of good will:** 5 to men
__ **of grace:** 4 days, year 5 state
__ **of gratitude:** 4 debt
__ **of gravity:** 3 law 6 center
__ **of Green Gables:** 4 Anne
__ **of habit:** 5 force 6 change
__ **of Hammurabi:** 4 Code
__ **of hand:** 3 out 4 note 7 sleight
__ **of hands:** 4 show
__ **of Hazzard, The:** 5 Dukes
__ **of health:** 4 bill 5 board
__ **of heart:** 6 change
__ **of Heaven:** 4 Days, rose 5 Gates, Queen
__ **of Helen Trent, The:** 7 Romance
__ **of Hercules:** 6 labors 7 Pillars
__ **of Hiawatha, The:** 4 Song
__ **of Hoffmann:** 5 Tales
__ **of Honey, A:** 5 Taste
__ **of honor:** 4 debt, maid, word 5 court, field, guard, guest, point 6 matron
__ **of Honor:** 3 Men 4 Word 5 Guard, Medal 6 Legion 7 Capable
__ **of hope:** 3 ray
__ **of Hormuz:** 6 Strait
Of Human Bondage: 4 film 5 novel
author: W. Somerset Maugham
cast: Bette Davis, Frances Dee, Leslie Howard
character: 5 Carey, Fanny, Norah 6 Louisa, Nesbit 7 Mildred
__ **of human kindness:** 4 milk
__ **of humor:** 5 sense
__ **of Id, The:** 6 Wizard
__ **of incidence:** 5 angle, plane
__ **of Independence:** 3 War
__ **of industry:** 4 czar 7 captain
__ **of iniquity:** 3 den
__ **of Innocence, The:** 3 Age, End
__ **of inquiry:** 5 court
__ **of intent:** 6 letter
__ **of Iron:** 3 Man 5 Cross
__**-O-Fish:** 5 Filet
__ **of it?:** 4 What
__ **of itself:** 5 in and
__ **of ivy:** 5 halls
__ **of Iwo Jima:** 5 Sands
__ **of Japan:** 3 Sea
__ **of Jericho:** 4 rose
__ **of joint:** 3 out
__ **of Judah:** 4 Lion
__ **of July:** 6 Fourth
__ **of justice:** 6 scales
__ **of Kilimanjaro, The:** 5 Snows
__ **of kin:** 4 next
__ **of knowledge:** 4 tree
__ **of lading:** 4 bill
O'Flaherty, Liam: 5 Irish 6 author, writer
work: The Informer
__ **of La Mancha:** 3 Man
__ **of lamb:** 3 leg 4 rack
__ **of Langerhans:** 5 islet 6 island, islets 7 islands
__ **of Laredo:** 7 Streets
__ **of large numbers:** 3 law
__ **of laughs:** 6 barrel
__ **of Laura Mars:** 4 Eyes
__ **of law:** 5 court 6 matter, school
__ **of least resistance:** 4 path
__ **of Lepanto:** 4 Gulf
__ **of letters:** 3 man 5 woman
__ **of Liberty:** 4 Sons 6 Statue
__ **of life:** 4 fact, full, tree, walk 5 prime, slice, staff, wheel 6 elixir 7 quality
__ **of Life:** 4 Jaws, Love, Walk 5 Proof 7 Secrets
__ **of Life, The:** 4 Road 5 Bloom, Facts, House
__ **of Light:** 3 Ray 4 City 5 Angel
__ **of Lights:** 5 Feast
__ **of Lima:** 4 Rose
__ **of limitations:** 7 statute
__ **of line:** 3 out
__ **of little faith:** 3 O ye
__ **of living:** 4 cost
__ **of Living Dangerously, The:** 4 Year
__ **of Livin' to Do:** 4 A Lot
__ **of London:** 5 Tower 6 Lloyd's
__ **of Lords:** 5 House
__ **of Lots:** 5 Feast
__ **of love:** 5 labor 6 tunnel
__ **of Love:** 3 Sea 4 Book, Game 5 Glory, Power, Price, Words 6 Chains, Chapel, Cradle, Melody, Priest, Vision 7 Aspects, Because, Freeway, Soldier
Of Love and Shadows author: Isabel Allende
__ **of Love, The:** 3 Art, Way 4 Look 5 Place, Power, Works 6 Colour, Desert, Elixir, Tunnel 7 Pursuit
__ **of Loving, The:** 3 Art
__ **of luck:** 3 out
__ **of luxury, the:** 3 lap
__ **of Macedon:** 6 Philip
__ **of Madelon Claudet, The:** 3 Sin
__ **of Magellan:** 6 Strait
__ **of magnesia:** 4 milk
__ **of magnitude:** 5 order
__ **of mail:** 4 coat
__ **of Malacca:** 6 Strait
__ **of Malta, The:** 3 Jew
__ **of Man:** 3 Son 4 Isle
__ **of manners:** 6 comedy
__ **of Man, The:** 4 Tree 6 Ascent, Rights
__ **of many colors:** 5 a coat
__ **of March:** 4 Ides
__ **of Marmara:** 3 Sea
__ **of Me:** 3 All
__ **of means by no means...:** 4 a man
__ **of measure:** 4 unit
__ **of Melos:** 5 Venus
__ **of Merit:** 6 Legion
__ **of Mexico:** 4 Gulf
Of Mice and Men
author: John Steinbeck
character: 4 Slim 5 Candy, Small 6 Crooks, Curley, George, Lennie, Milton
Of Mice and Men (1939 film)
cast: Lon Chaney Jr., Burgess Meredith
director: Lewis Milestone
Of Mice and Men (1992 film)
cast: Alexis Arquette, Sherilyn Fenn, John Malkovich, Gary Sinise
director: Gary Sinise
__ **of milk:** 4 pint 5 quart 6 gallon
__ **of milk and honey:** 4 land
__ **of Miss Jean Brodie, The:** 5 Prime
__ **of mistaken identity:** 5 a case
__ **of Money, The:** 5 Color
__ **of Monte Cristo, The:** 3 Son 5 Count
__ **of Montreal:** 4 Bank
__ **of Mormon:** 4 Book
__ **of Moses:** 3 Law
__ **of motion:** 3 law
__ **of mouth:** 4 word
__ **of Music, The:** 5 Sound
__**-of-mutton:** 3 leg
__ **of My Heart:** 5 Music, Piece 6 Rhythm
__ **of Myself:** 4 Song
__ **of nails:** 3 bed
__ **of Nantes:** 5 Edict
__ **of Napoleon, The:** 3 Age
__ **of nations:** 3 law 6 comity
__ **of Nations, The:** 6 League, Wealth
__ **of nature:** 5 freak 7 balance
__ **of Naval Operations:** 5 Chief
__ **of Navarone, The:** 4 Guns
__ **of nerves:** 3 war 6 bundle
__ **of New Orleans, The:** 4 City 5 Flame 6 Battle
__ **of newt:** 3 eye
__ **of Night, The:** 4 Edge
__ **of Nod:** 4 land
__ **of no return:** 5 point
__ **of nowhere:** 3 out
__ **of office:** 4 oath
__ **of Okhotsk:** 3 Sea
__ **of Olay:** 3 Oil
__ **of Old Smokey:** 5 On Top
__ **of Omaha:** 6 Mutual
__ **of Oman:** 4 Gulf
__ **of one's brow:** 5 sweat
__ **of oneself:** 4 give
__ **of one's existence:** 4 bane
__ **of one's eye:** 5 apple
__ **of one's heart:** 7 cockles
__ **of one's life:** 4 time
__ **of One's Own:** 5 A Room
__ **of Opportunity:** 4 Land
__ **of Orange:** 7 William
__ **of order:** 3 out 5 point, rules
__ **of Orléans:** 4 Maid
... __ **of others:** 5 a host
__ **of Otranto:** 6 Strait
__ **of Our Discontent, The:** 6 Winter
__ **of Our Lives:** 4 Days
__ **of Ours:** 3 One
__ **of Our Teeth, The:** 4 Skin
__ **of Oz:** 4 Land 6 Wizard
__ **of pace:** 6 change
__ **of Padua:** 7 Anthony 9 Marsilius
__ **of Paleface:** 3 Son
__ **of palm:** 5 heart
__ **of Panama:** 4 Gulf 7 Isthmus
__ **of pants:** 4 pair
__ **of paradise:** 4 bird 6 grains
__ **of Paris:** 4 Joan 6 Treaty 7 Matthew, plaster
__ **of parsimony:** 3 law
__ **of particulars:** 4 bill
__ **of passage:** 4 bird, rite
__ **of Passage, The:** 6 Plains
__ **of Pauline, The:** 6 Perils
__ **of payments:** 7 balance
__ **of peace:** 4 bird, kiss, pipe
__ **of Peace:** 6 Prince
__**-of-pearl:** 6 mother
__ **of Penzance, The:** 7 Pirates
__ **of Peter Rabbit, The:** 4 Tale
__ **of phase:** 3 out
__ **of Philadelphia:** 7 Streets
__ **of Philosophy:** 6 Doctor
__ **of Philosophy, The:** 5 Story
__ **of Picardy:** 5 Roses
__ **of Pigs:** 3 Bay
__ **of Pines:** 4 Isle
__ **of play:** 3 out
__ **of plenty:** 4 horn
__ **of plumb:** 3 out
__ **of pocket:** 3 out
__ **of Pooh, The:** 3 Tao
__ **of pottage:** 4 mess
__ **of power:** 7 balance
__ **of Power:** 5 Tower
__ **of prayer:** 5 house
__ **of premium:** 6 waiver
__ **of prevention:** 5 ounce
__ **of prey:** 4 bird 5 beast
__ **of print:** 3 out
__ **of promise:** 6 breach
__ **of proof:** 6 burden
__ **of purchase:** 5 point, proof
__ **of Pythias:** 7 Knights
__ **of Queensberry rules:** 7 Marquis
__ **of Queens, The:** 4 King
__ **of Rain, A:** 6 Hatful
__ **of Ranchipur, The:** 5 Rains
__ **of Reading Gaol, The:** 6 Ballad
__ **of Reason:** 3 Age
__ **of Rebellion:** 3 War
__ **of reckoning:** 3 day
__ **of record:** 4 date 5 court 6 matter
__ **of Red Chief, The:** 6 Ransom
__ **of Red Gap:** 7 Ruggles
__ **of reference:** 5 frame
__ **of reflection:** 3 law 5 angle
__ **of refraction:** 3 law 5 angle, index
__ **of relativity:** 6 theory
__ **of Representatives:** 5 House
__ **of resolution:** 5 limit
__ **of rest:** 3 day
__ **of revolution:** 4 axis 5 solid 6 period 7 surface
__ **of Riga:** 4 Gulf
__ **of right:** 4 writ
__ **of Rights:** 4 Bill 7 Charter
__ **of Riley, the:** 4 life
__ **of Roaring Camp, The:** 4 Luck
__ **of robins...:** 5 A nest
__ **of Rome:** 6 Church
__ **of Rome, The:** 5 Pines
__ **of roses:** 3 bed 5 attar
__ **of rotation:** 6 period
__ **of Rothschild:** 5 House
__**-of-round:** 3 out
__ **of '76:** 6 Spirit
__ **of safety:** 6 factor, margin
__ **of Saint Agnes:** 5 Feast
__ **of Saint James's:** 5 Court
__ **of Saint Lawrence:** 4 Gulf
__ **of sale:** 4 bill 5 point
__ **of Salisbury:** 4 Earl, John
__ **of Samothrace:** 4 Nike 7 Victory
__ **of San Antone:** 4 Rose
__ **of Sandwich:** 4 Earl
__ **of San Francisco, The:** 7 Streets
__ **of San Luis Rey, The:** 6 Bridge
__ **of Saros:** 4 Gulf
__ **of schedule:** 5 ahead
__ **of Science:** 6 Master 8 Bachelor
__ **of Scone:** 5 Stone
__ **of scrimmage:** 4 line
__ **of season:** 3 out
__ **of Seven Gables, The:** 5 House
__ **of Seville, The:** 6 Barber
__ **of Shalott, The:** 4 Lady
__ **of Sharon:** 4 rose
__ **of Sheba:** 5 Queen
__ **of Sheila, The:** 4 Last
__ **of Shoals:** 5 Isles
__ **of shock:** 5 state
__ **of Siam:** 4 Gulf
__ **of Sidra:** 4 Gulf
__ **of siege:** 5 state
__ **of Siena:** 9 Catherine
__ **of Sighs:** 6 Bridge
__ **of sight:** 3 out 4 line
__ **of significance:** 5 level
__ **of Silas Lapham, The:** 4 Rise
__ **of silence:** 4 code, cone 5 tower
__ **of Silence, The:** 6 Sounds
__ **of sines:** 3 law
__ **of skill:** 4 game
__ **of Skye:** 4 Isle
__ **of Sleepy Hollow, The:** 6 Legend
__ **of sole:** 5 filet
__ **of Solomon:** 4 Odes, Song 6 Wisdom
__ **of sorts:** 3 out

__ of South Africa: **5** Union
__ of Spain: **4** Lady
__-of-Spain: **4** Port
__ of Species, The: **6** Origin
__ of speech: **4** part **6** figure **7** freedom
__ of Spring, The: **4** Rite
__ of square: **3** out
__ of staff: **5** chief
__ of St. Agnes, The: **3** Eve
__ of star-cross'd lovers: **5** a pair
__ of state: **3** out **4** head, ship **5** chief **7** council
__ of State: **5** O Ship
__ of steel: **6** nerves
__ of Steel: **3** Abs, Man
__ of step: **3** out
__ of Steve, The: **3** Tao
__ of St. James's: **5** Court
__ of St. Louis: **6** Spirit
__ of St. Mark, The: **3** Eve
__ of St. Mary's, The: **5** Bells
__ of stock: **3** out
__ of Stone: **5** Heart **6** Hearts **7** Gardens
__ of straw: **3** man
__ of strength: **4** test **5** tower
__ of students: **4** dean
__ of study: **5** house
__ of style: **3** out **5** go out
__ of sublimation: **4** heat
__ of Suez: **4** Gulf **7** Isthmus
__ of sugar: **4** lump
__ of Sulu, The: **6** Sultan
__ of Summer, The: **4** Boys
__ of summons: **4** writ
__ of Sundays: **5** month
__ of sunlight: **3** ray
__ of supervisors: **5** board
__ of Swat: **6** Sultan
__ of Swells, A: **6** Couple
__ of symmetry: **4** axis **6** center
__ of sync: **3** out
oft: 4 a lot, much **7** usually **8** commonly **9** generally, regularly **10** frequently, habitually, repeatedly
ender: **5** times
__ of Tabernacles: **5** Feast
__ of Tarsus: **4** Saul
__ of tartar: **5** cream
__ of tea: **3** cup **4** spot
__ of tears: **4** vale
often: 4 a lot, much **6** hourly, mostly **7** usually **9** generally, many a time, quite a bit, regularly **10** frequently, repeatedly
ender: **5** times
__ of Terror: **5** Reign, Tales
__ of Texas..., The: **4** eyes
of the __: **7** essence
of the __ dye: **7** deepest
__ of the Aar: **5** Gorge
__ of the above: **4** none
__ of the absurd: **7** theater, theatre
__ of the action: **5** piece
__ of the Air Force: **7** General
__ of the American Revolution: **4** Sons **9** Daughters
__ of the Americas: **3** Ave. **6** Avenue
__ of the Ancient Mariner, The: **4** Rime
__ of the Apes: **6** Planet
__ of the Apostles: **4** Acts
__ of the Army: **7** General
__ of the art: **5** state
__ of the arts: **6** patron
__ of the Ball: **5** Belle
__ of the band: **6** leader
__ of the Baskervilles, The: **5** Hound
__ of the Bath: **6** Knight
__ of the Bay, The: **4** Dock
__ of the beast: **4** mark
__ of the big-time spenders: **4** last
of the blackest __: **3** dye
__ of the blue: **3** out
__ of the Blues, The: **5** Birth
__ of the Brave: **4** Home
__ of the bride: **6** father, mother
__ of the Budget: **6** Bureau
__ of the Bulge: **6** Battle
__ of the Cat: **4** Year
__ of the Cat People, The: **5** Curse
__ of the Cave Bear, The: **4** Clan
__ of the Census: **6** Bureau
__ of the Century: **4** Sale
__ of the Circus: **4** A Son
__ of the city: **7** freedom
__ of the City: **4** Edge **6** Prince
__ of the Class: **4** Head
__ of the clear blue sky: **3** out
__ of the cloth: **3** man
__ of the community: **6** pillar
__ of the County: **6** Coward
__ of the court: **6** friend
__ of the Covenant: **3** Ark
__ of the crime: **5** scene
__ of the crop: **5** cream
__ of the cross: **3** way **4** sign
... __ of the Crowd, the: **5** Smell
__ of the day: **4** word **5** catch, order **7** officer
__ of the Day, The: **7** Remains
__ of the Deal, The: **3** Art
__ of the deck: **7** officer
of the deepest __: **3** dye
__ of the Desert: **4** Sons **5** Simon
__ of the dog: **4** hair
__ of the Dolls: **6** Valley
__ of the doubt: **7** benefit
__ of the draw: **4** luck
__ of the d'Urbervilles: **4** Tess
... __ of thee: **3** 'tis
__ of the earth: **4** ends, salt
Of Thee I Sing: 7 musical
author: George S. Kaufman
composer: **8** Gershwin
__ of the evening: **5** shank
__ of the Field: **6** Lilies
__ of the Fisherman, The: **5** Shoes
__ of the flame: **6** keeper
__ of the Fleet: **7** Admiral
__ of the Flies, The: **4** Lord
__ of the forest: **4** king
__ of the Fugue, The: **3** Art
__ of the future: **4** wave
__ of the game: **4** name
__ of the Game: **4** Name **5** Rules **6** Master
__ of the Garter: **5** Order
__ of the gods: **4** food **6** nectar
__ of the Golden West: **4** Girl
__ of the Greasepaint..., The: **4** Roar
__ of the guard: **6** yeoman **7** officer
__ of the Heart: **5** Music **6** Affair, Crimes
__ of the Hesperides: **6** Apples
__ of the Hesperus, The: **5** Wreck
__ of the hill: **4** king
__ of the Hop: **5** Queen
__ of the hour: **3** man
__ of the Hours: **5** Dance
__ of the house: **3** man **4** lady **5** woman
__ of the House of Usher, The: **4** Fall
__ of the iceberg: **3** tip
__ of the Iguana, The: **5** Night
__ of the Irish: **4** luck
__ of Their Lives, The: **4** Time
__ of Their Own, A: **6** League
__ of the Islands: **4** Song **7** Outcast
__ of the Jackal, The: **3** Day
__ of the Jedi: **6** Return
__ of the jungle: **3** law **4** king
__ of the Jungle: **5** Ramar **6** George
__ of the King: **6** Idylls, Sailor
__ of the Kings: **6** Valley
__ of the Lake, The: **4** Lady
__ of the Lambs, The: **7** Silence
__ of the land: **3** fat, law, lay
__ of the Last Minstrel, The: **3** Lay
__ of the Light Brigade: **6** Charge
__ of the line: **3** end **4** ship
__-of-the-line: **3** top **6** bottom
__ of the litter: **4** pick
__ of the Living Dead: **5** Night
__ of the Lock, The: **4** Rape
__ of the Locust, The: **3** Day
__ of the Lonesome Pine, The: **5** Trail
__ of the Loom: **5** Fruit
__ of the Lost Ark: **7** Raiders
__ of the Magi, The: **4** Gift
__ of the mark: **4** wide
__ of the matter: **5** heart
__ of the mean: **3** law **7** theorem
__ of the Midnight Sun: **4** Land
__-of-the-mill: **3** run
__ of the minds: **7** meeting
__-of-the-mine: **3** run
__ of the Mohicans, The: **4** Last
__ of the moment: **4** heat, spur
__ of the month: **6** flavor
__ of the Moon: **4** Dark **5** A Tour **7** Craters
__ of the morning: **3** top **5** pride
__ of the Morning: **5** Angel, Child
__ of the Native, The: **6** Return
__ of the Needle: **3** Eye
__ of the Nibelung, The: **4** Ring
__ of the Night: **4** Dark, Heat **5** Heart **6** Armies, Middle, Rhythm, Voices
__ of the Night, The: **5** Music, Voice **6** Armies
__ of the Nile: **5** Queen
__ of the Nile, The: **5** Jewel
__ of the Nineties: **5** Belle
__ of the North: **5** Spawn **6** Nanook **7** Emperor
__ of the Open Road: **4** Song
__ of the Opera, The: **7** Phantom
__ of the Pack: **6** Leader
__-of-the-pants: **4** seat
__ of the party: **4** life
__ of the past: **3** out
__ of the peace: **6** breach **7** justice
__ of the People, An: **5** Enemy
__ of the Perverse, The: **3** Imp
__ of the Phoenix: **6** Flight
__ of the Pioneers: **4** Sons
__ of the Plague Year: **7** Journal
__ of the Plainsmen, The: **4** Last
__ of the Potomac: **4** Army
__ of the President, The: **6** Making
__ of the press: **7** freedom
__ of the pudding: **5** proof
__ of the Purple Sage: **6** Riders
__ of the question: **3** out
__ of the realm: **4** coin, peer
__ of the Red Death, The: **6** Masque
__ of the Red Hot Lovers: **4** Last
__ of the Red Hot Mamas: **4** Last
__ of the Rings, The: **4** Lord
__ of the Rising Sun: **4** Land **5** House
__ of thermodynamics: **3** law
__ of the road: **4** rule
__-of-the-road: **6** middle
__ of the Road: **3** End **4** King **5** Kings **6** Middle
__ of the Roses: **4** Wars
__ of the Rose, The: **4** Name
__ of the Round Table: **7** Knights
__ of the running: **3** out
__ of the Sad Cafe, The: **6** Ballad
__ of the Screw, The: **4** Turn
__ of the Sea: **7** Chicken
__ of the seas: **7** freedom
__ of the Season: **4** Time
__ of These Days: **4** Some
__ of these days, Alice...: **3** One
__ of the Seven Gables, The: **5** House
__ of the sexes: **6** battle
__ of the Sheik: **3** Son
__ of the Shrew, The: **6** Taming
__ of the Sixth Happiness, The: **3** Inn
__ of the Snark, The: **7** Hunting
__ of the South: **4** Song
__ of the South Pacific: **5** Tales
__ of the spheres: **5** music
__ of the Spider Woman: **4** Kiss
__ of the Spirit: **7** Triumph
__ of the State: **5** Enemy
__ of the Sun: **4** Dark, East **6** Empire, Island, Valley
__ of the Thousand Days: **4** Anne
__ of the Tiger: **3** Eye
__ of the Titans: **5** Clash
__ of the tongue: **4** slip
__ of the Toreadors: **5** Waltz
__ of the Town, The: **4** Talk **5** Woman
__ of the trade: **5** tools **6** tricks
__ of the Triffids, The: **3** Day
__ of the Turtle, The: **5** Voice
__ of the Union: **5** State **7** Council
__ of the Unknown Soldier: **4** Tomb
__ of the valley: **4** lily
__ of the Vampire: **4** Mark **6** Shadow
__ of the Vanities, The: **7** Bonfire
__ of the walk: **4** cock
__ of the way: **3** out
__ of the Wedding, The: **6** Member
__ of the West: **3** Man **4** Code **6** Hearts
__ of the Western World: **7** Playboy
__ of the Whistler: **4** Mark **5** Voice **6** Secret
__ of the Wild, The: **4** Call
__ of the Will: **7** Triumph
__ of the Wind: **6** Colors
__ of the woods: **3** hen, out **4** bull, cock, neck
__ of the Woods: **4** Lake
__ of the woodwork: **3** out
__ of the world: **3** man, map, way **5** on top, state, woman
__ of the World: **3** Top **4** A Map
__ of the Worlds, The: **3** War
__ of the World, The: **3** End **4** Edge **6** Center, Master
__ of the Yankee Navy, The: **5** Glory
__ of the Yankees, The: **5** Pride
__ of the Year: **3** Man **5** Woman **6** Rookie
__ of the zodiac: **4** sign
__ of thieves: **3** den **4** a den **5** a nest
__ of things to come, the: **5** shape
__ of This Earth: **3** Not
__ of this world: **3** out
__ of thorns: **5** crown
__ of Thoth, The: **4** Ring
__ of thought: **3** law **6** school
__ of thousands: **5** a cast
__ of thumb: **4** rule
__ of thunder: **4** clap
__ of Thunder: **4** Days
__ of Tides, The: **6** Prince
__ of time: **5** ahead, sands
Of Time and the River
author: Thomas Wolfe
character: **3** Abe, Ann **4** Gant, Joel **5** Eliza **6** Elinor, Esther, Eugene, Oliver **10** Eugene Gant
__ of Times, The: **4** Best
__ of Time, The: **4** Care **5** March, Sands
__ of Titus: **4** Arch
__ of Tomorrow, The: **5** World
__ of touch: **3** out
__ of Tours: **6** Martin **7** Gregory
__-of-town: **3** out
__-of-Towners, The: **3** Out
__ of trade: **5** board **7** balance
__ of traitors!: **5** A nest
__ of Tralee: **4** Rose
__ of Tranquillity: **3** Sea
__ of tricks: **3** bag
__ of trim: **3** out
__ of Tripoli: **6** shores
__ of Triumph: **4** Arch
... __ of troubles: **4** a sea
__ of Troy: **5** Helen
__ of truce: **4** flag
__ of trust: **4** deed **6** breach
__ of trustees: **5** board
__ of truth: **6** moment

offtimes: 4 much 7 as a rule 9 generally, quite a bit, regularly 10 frequently, habitually, ordinarily, repeatedly
__ of Turin: 6 Shroud
__ of turn: 3 out
__ of turpentine: 3 oil 6 spirit
__ of Two Cities: 5 A Tale
__ of two evils: 6 lesser
__ of Us All, The: 6 Mother
__ of Usher: 5 House
__ of vantage: 5 coign
__ of Venezuela: 4 Gulf
__ of venue: 6 change
__ of Venus, The: 5 Delta
__ of view: 5 angle, field, point
__ of vision: 4 line 5 field
__ of vitriol: 3 oil
__ of voice: 4 tone
__ of Wakefield, The: 5 Vicar
__ of Wales: 6 Prince
__ of war: 3 act, law, tug 4 ship 5 sloop, state 6 honors 7 council, theater, theatre
__-of-war: 3 man
__ of War, The: 3 Art 4 Dogs 5 Winds
__ of wax: 4 ball
__ of Wax: 5 House
__ of way: 5 right
__ of Wellington: 4 Duke
__ of Wells Fargo: 5 Tales
__ of whack: 3 out
__ of Wheat: 5 Cream
__ of whole cloth: 3 out
__ of Wight: 4 Isle
__ of wind: 3 bag
__ of Wine and Roses: 4 Days
__ of wintergreen: 3 oil
__ of wisdom: 5 pearl
__ of woe: 4 tale
__ of Women Voters: 6 League
__ of wonder: 5 sense
__ of work: 3 out 5 a lick, piece
__ of worms: 3 can
__ of Worms: 4 Diet
__ of worship: 5 house
__ of Wrath, The: 6 Grapes
__ of yore: 4 days 7 knights
__ of You: 3 All 4 I Beg 7 Because
__ of your beeswax!: 4 none
__ of your business!: 4 none
__ of Your Life: 5 Times
__ of Your Life, The: 4 Time
__ of Your Smile, The: 6 Shadow
__ of You, The: 6 Wonder
__ of Zorro, The: 4 Mark, Mask, Sign
Ogaki: 4 city, town
  locale: 5 Japan
Ogden: 4 city, Nash, town
  locale: 4 Utah
__ Ogden Stiers: 5 David
ogee: 4 arch 5 curve
  shape: 3 ess
ogive: 3 rib 4 arch 7 molding
Ogives composer: 5 Satie
Oglala: 5 tribe 6 Indian 7 Amerind
ogle: 3 eye 4 gaup, gawk, gawp, leer, look 5 stare 6 gaze at, goggle, leer at, look at 7 stare at 8 check out 9 flirt with 10 give the eye, make eyes at, rubberneck, scrutinize
ogler: 4 eyer, rake, wolf 5 flirt 6 masher, starer
OGPU, like the: 3 Sov. 6 Soviet 7 Russian
O'Grady: 4 Gail, Lani 5 Rosie 7 Desmond
O'Grady, Desmond: 4 poet 5 Irish
ogre: 5 brute, demon, devil, fiend, giant, meany, Shrek, troll 6 bad guy, daemon, daimon, meanie, tyrant 7 bugbear, Grendel, monster 8 bogeyman, gargoyle, martinet 9 archfiend, barbarian
ogreish: 4 mean 9 irascible
ogress: 5 harpy, scold, shrew, vixen 6 beldam, virago 8 fishwife, harridan 9 henpecker, termagant, Xanthippe
oh: 3 cry 4 I see
  boy: 3 wow 4 whee 5 great, zowie
  dear: 4 alas, darn, egad, gosh, heck, my my, pooh 5 alack, egads, fudge, lordy 6 dash it 7 heavens, woe is me 8 goodness
  in German: 3 ach
  so: 4 very 5 quite 9 extremely 10 remarkably
__-oh: 4 good
Oh: 8 Sadaharu
Oh __: 4 Girl, My My 5 Julie 6 Father, Sheila 7 Sherrie
Oh __ can you see...: 3 say
Oh __ Day: 5 Happy
Oh __ Young: 4 Very
Oh! __: 5 Carol 7 Susanna
Oh! __ danced...: 5 how we
Oh, __!: 3 Boy, God, Kay 4 dear, Mama
Oh, __ a Beautiful Mornin': 4 What
Oh, __ a Night: 4 What
Oh, __ Beautiful Doll: 3 You
Oh, __ Beautiful Mornin': 5 What a
Oh, __ Golden Slippers: 3 Dem
Oh, __ in England...: 4 to be
Oh, __ Woman: 6 Pretty
Oh.
  neighbor: 3 Ind., Ken. 4 Penn.
  see also Ohio
O'Hair: 7 atheist, Madalyn
O'Hanlon: 6 George 8 Virginia
O'Hara: 3 Kim 4 John, Mary 5 Frank 7 Maureen 8 Scarlett 9 Catherine
  estate: 4 Tara
O'Hara, Frank: 4 poet 10 playwright
O'Hara, John: 6 author, writer
  work: Appointment in Samarra
    Butterfield 8
    Elizabeth Appleton
    The Ewings
    From the Terrace
    Lovey Childs
    Pal Joey
    A Rage to Live
    Ten North Frederick
O'Hara, Mary: 6 author, writer
  work: The Green Grass of Wyoming
    My Friend Flicka
O'Hara, Maureen: 7 actress
  film: The Black Swan (1942)
    How Green Was My Valley (1941)
    The Long Gray Line (1955)
    McLintock! (1963)
    Miracle on 34th Street (1947)
    Only the Lonely (1991)
    The Parent Trap (1961)
    The Quiet Man (1952)
    Rio Grande (1950)
    Sinbad the Sailor (1947)
    Sitting Pretty (1948)
    Ten Gentlemen From West Point (1942)
O'Hara's Choice author: Leon Uris
O'Hare: 7 airport
  departure: 6 flight
  info: 3 arr., ETA, ETD
  locale: 3 Chi. 7 Chicago
  on luggage tags: 3 ORD
Oh, Boy! (1957 song) artist: Buddy Holly and the Crickets
Oh, But __: 3 I Do
Oh! Carol (1959 song) artist: Neil Sedaka
Oh, come on now!: 6 really
O Henry, __ thine eyes!: 3 ope
O. Henry: 5 alias 6 Porter
O'Herlihy, Dan: 5 actor
  film: Home Before Dark (1958)
    MacArthur (1977)
    Macbeth (1948)
    RoboCop (1987)
Oh Father (1989 song) artist: Madonna
Oh Girl (song) artist: Chi-Lites, Paul Young
Oh, give __ home: 3 me a
Oh, God! (1977 film)
  cast: George Burns, John Denver, Teri Garr, Paul Sorvino
  director: Carl Reiner
Oh, Heavenly Dog dog: 5 Benji
Oh Henry: 5 candy 8 candy bar 9 chocolate
  alternative: 4 Mars, Twix 5 Clark, Heath 6 Kit Kat, Mounds, PayDay, Reese's, Zagnut 7 Krackel 8 Baby Ruth, Hershey's, Milky Way, Snickers 9 Almond Joy, Mr. Goodbar 10 NutRageous
Oh, How __ to Get Up...: 5 I Hate
  composer: 6 Berlin
ohia lehua: 5 plant 6 flower
O'Higgins: 8 Bernardo
Ohio: 5 river, state
  capital: 8 Columbus
  city: 3 Ada 4 Avon, Kent, Lima, Stow, Troy 5 Akron, Berea, Green, Mason, Miami, Niles, Parma, Piqua, Solon, Xenia 6 Athens, Canton, Dayton, Dublin, Elyria, Euclid, Hudson, Lorain, Marion, Medina, Mentor, Newark, Oxford, Sidney, Toledo, Warren 7 Ashland, Findlay, Gahanna, Norwood, Wooster 8 Alliance, Boardman, Columbus, Delaware, Eastlake, Fairborn, Hamilton, Hilliard, Lakewood, Sandusky, Trotwood, Westlake 9 Ashtabula, Barberton, Brook Park, Brunswick, Cleveland, Fairfield, Grove City, Kettering, Lancaster, Mansfield, Massillon, Riverside, Whitehall 10 Austintown, Cincinnati, Middletown, Portsmouth, Rocky River, Willoughby, Youngstown, Zanesville
  city on the ~: 10 Cincinnati, Pittsburgh
  college: 5 Hiram 6 Kenyon, Xavier 9 Kent State
  conference: 3 MAC
  county: 4 Erie 6 Scioto 7 Wyandot
  Indian: 4 Erie
  neighbor: 7 Indiana 8 Kentucky, Michigan
  political name: 4 Taft
  river to the ~: 5 Miami 6 Scioto, Wabash 8 Kentucky 9 Tennessee 10 Cumberland
  state bird: 8 cardinal
  state flower: 9 carnation
  state fossil: 9 trilobite
  state gemstone: 5 flint
  state insect: 7 ladybug
  state reptile: 5 racer
  state tree: 7 buckeye
Ohio __: 7 buckeye, Express, Players
Ohio Express
  song: Chewy Chewy (1968)
    Yummy Yummy Yummy (1968)
Ohio State
  athletes: 8 Buckeyes
  conference: 6 Big Ten
  locale: 8 Columbus
Ohio University
  athletes: 7 Bobcats
  locale: 6 Athens
Oh, Kay!: 7 musical
  songwriter: 8 Gershwin
Oh, Lady Be Good composer: 8 Gershwin
Ohlin, Bertil: 8 Nobelist 9 economist
Oh Lonesome Me (1958 song) artist: Don Gibson
Oh, Look __ Now: 4 at Me
ohm ender: 5 meter
Ohm, Georg: 6 German 9 physicist
Ohm's __: 3 law
Oh, my __ back!: 6 aching
Oh My My (1974 song) artist: Ringo Starr
Oh! My Pa-pa (1953 song) artist: Eddie Fisher
Oh no!: 4 darn, drat, rats, yipe 5 yikes, yipes
Oh No (1981 song) artist: Commodores
Oh, no! Not __!: 5 again
Oholibamah, husband of: 4 Esau
__-o-Honey: 3 Bit
Oh, Pretty Woman (1964 song) artist: Roy Orbison
Ohre: 4 Eger 5 river
  locale: 7 Germany
Oh Say Can You Say author: Dr. Seuss
Oh sure!: 4 As if, I bet
Oh! Susanna: 4 song 6 sitcom
  composer: 6 Foster
  instrument: 5 banjo
  star: 5 Storm
Oh, the Places You'll Go! author: Dr. Seuss
Oh, the Thinks You Can Think! author: Dr. Seuss
Oh to __ England: 4 be in
Oh Very Young (1974 song) artist: Cat Stevens
Oh! What __ Was Mary: 4 a Pal
Oh, What a Beautiful Mornin': 5 waltz
  composer: 7 Rodgers 11 Hammerstein
Oh What a Paradise It Seems author: John Cheever
Oh, what a relief __!: 4 it is
Oh what fun __ to...: 4 it is
...oh where can __?: 4 he be
Oh yeah? response: 6 sez who
Oh, You Beautiful __: 4 Doll
-oid relative: 3 -ish 4 -like
oil: 3 lub. 4 coal, corn, fuel, lard, lube, tung 5 crude, fluid, lipid, slick, tempt 6 anoint, buy off, canola, canvas, castor, grease, lipide, pomade 7 coconut, lanolin, lantern, picture, unguent, wheedle 8 cocoanut, cod-liver, flattery, kerosene, kerosine, kickback, lanoline, painting 9 black gold, lubricant, lubricate, petroleum, safflower 10 cottonseed, fossil fuel
  additive: 3 STP
  alternative: 3 gas
  aromatic ~: 5 anise 6 bay rum
  banana ~: 3 gas, rot 4 blah, bosh, bull, bunk, guff, jazz, jive, pooh, tosh 5 bilge, ester, fudge, hokum, hooey, prate, stuff, trash, tripe 6 bunkum, bushwa, drivel, footle, gabble, gammon, gibber, havers, hot air, humbug, jabber, jargon, kibosh, piffle 7 baloney, blarney, blather, blether, boloney, bushwah, eyewash, flannel, flubdub, fustian, garbage, hogwash, inanity, rubbish, twaddle 8 buncombe, claptrap, falderal, falderol, flimflam, flummery, folderal, folderol, nonsense, slipslop, tommyrot, trumpery 9 gibberish, goofiness, kidstakes, moonshine, poppycock, rigmarole 10 applesauce, balderdash, bilge water, codswallop, double-talk, flapdoodle, galimatias, Jabberwock, mumbo jumbo, rigamarole, taradiddle
  baron: 5 sheik 6 shaikh, sheikh
  boil in ~: 3 fry 5 sauté
  burn the midnight ~: 4 cram 5 learn, study
  -can letters: 3 SAE
  cartel: 4 OPEC
  combining form: 3 ole- 4 eleo-, olei-, oleo- 5 elaeo-, elaio-, petro-

company: 3 Oxy 4 Arco, Esso, Gulf, Hess 5 Amoco, Exxon, Getty, Mobil 6 Texaco 7 Chevron
container: 4 lamp 5 cruse 6 barrel
cooking ~: 4 corn 6 canola
cosmetic ~: 6 jojoba
ender: 3 can 4 bird, skin 5 cloth, paper, stone
exporter: 4 Iran, Iraq 5 Katar, Qatar 6 Arabia, Brunei, Kuwait 7 Nigeria 9 Venezuela
flow like an ~ well: 4 gush
holy ~: 6 chrism 7 chrisom
man, perhaps: 5 Texan
name in ~ filters: 4 Fram
need ~: 5 creak, grate 6 squeak, squeal
oil-field ~: 5 crude
painting: 3 art 6 canvas 7 picture 8 portrait 9 still life
part of an ~ lamp: 4 wick
perfume ~: 4 atar, otto 5 athar, attar, nerol, ottar
pour ~ on: 4 calm, ease 5 allay, salve 6 defuse, pacify, smooth, soften, soothe, stroke 7 appease, assuage, mollify, placate, relieve, sweeten 8 calm down 9 alleviate, untrouble 10 conciliate, smooth over
problem: 5 slick, spill
prospect for ~: 5 drill 7 wildcat
rose-scented ~: 5 nerol 6 neroli
sacramental ~: 6 chrism 7 chrisom
source: 3 cod, soy 4 corn, fish, palm, soya, well 5 copra, shale 6 sesame 8 copperah
unit: 2 qt. 3 bbl. 5 quart 6 barrel
varnish ~: 4 tung
well: 6 gusher

oil __: 3 can, pan 4 cake, lamp, meal, palm, sand, well 5 color, field, paint, patch, shale, slick, spill 6 beetle, burner, tanker 7 derrick, gilding, varnish
__ oil: 3 bay, ben 4 bone, coal, corn, fuel, holy, lamp, lard, oleo, palm, rock, rose, soya, tall, tung 5 anise, chile, chili, China, clove, colza, crude, fatty, fixed, fusel, kapok, lemon, maize, motor, olive, range, rosin, salad, shale, snake, stand, sweet, train, whale 6 almond, banana, betula, boiled, bunker, carron, castor, chilli, croton, Danish, diesel, drying, mowrah, neroli, peanut, sesame, strike, suntan 7 aniline, aniseed, arachis, babassu, camphor, coconut, copaiba, cutting, juniper, linseed, mineral, mustard, perilla, ricinus, soybean 8 cocoanut
Oil __: 4 City 6 Rivers
Oil __ Boyd: 3 Can
__ Oil: 4 Gulf 5 Ewing, Mobil
oil and vinegar: 8 dressing
Oil! author: Upton Sinclair
Oil Capital of the World: 5 Tulsa
oilcloth: 4 lino 6 fabric 8 linoleum
Oildale: 4 city, town
locale: 10 California
oiled: 4 waxy 5 slick, tipsy 6 greasy 8 slippery 9 lubricous
oiler: 4 boat, ship 6 tanker 7 garment
Oiler rival: 4 Blue, King, Star, Wild 5 Bruin, Devil, Flame, Flyer, Sabre, Shark 6 Canuck, Coyote, Ranger 7 Capital, Panther, Penguin, Red Wing, Senator 8 Canadien, Islander, Predator, Thrasher 9 Avalanche, Blackhawk, Hurricane, Lightning, Maple Leaf 10 Blue Jacket, Mighty Duck
Oilers: 3 six 4 team
home: 8 Edmonton
milieu: 3 ice 4 rink
org.: 3 NHL
sport: 6 hockey
Oil for the Lamps of China (1935 film)
cast: Josephine Hutchinson, Jean Muir, Pat O'Brien
director: Mervyn LeRoy
oil of __: 4 cade 5 anise 6 cloves 7 vitriol
Oil of __: 4 Olay
oils: 3 art 5 media, paint
oilskin: 4 coat 6 fabric, jacket 7 slicker 8 raincoat
oilstone, use an: 4 hone, whet 7 sharpen
oily: 4 glib, rich, waxy 5 fatty, lardy, sleek, slick, suave 6 creamy, greasy, smarmy, smooth 7 adipose, buttery, coaxing, fawning, fulsome, gushing, servile 8 cajoling, polished, slippery, unctuous 9 adulatory, lubricous, wheedling 10 flattering, lubricious, obsequious
liquid: 5 olein 6 oleine
oinker: 3 hog, pig, sow 5 swine
home: 3 pen, sty 6 pigpen, pigsty
ointment: 4 aloe, balm, nard, ungt. 5 cream, salve 6 balsam, Ben-Gay, cerate, lotion 7 unction, unguent 8 dressing, lenitive, liniment, medicine 9 demulcent, emollient 10 medication
apply ~: 5 rub on
bit of ~: 3 dab
fly in the ~: 3 rub 4 flaw, kink, snag 5 catch, hitch, snafu 6 defect, kicker 7 problem 8 drawback
holder: 4 tube
Oise: 5 river
locale: 6 France 7 Belgium
river to the ~: 5 Aisne
oiseau: 4 bird 6 French
feature: 3 bec 4 aile
'O' Is for Outlaw author: Sue Grafton
Oistrakh, David: 7 Russian 9 violinist
Oita: 4 city, town
locale: 5 Japan 6 Kiushu, Kyushu
oiticica: 3 oil 4 tree
relative: 4 pear, plum, rose 5 apple, peach 6 almond, cherry, medlar, quince 7 apricot 8 hawthorn 10 blackthorn
O.J.: 5 juice 7 Simpson
Ojai: 4 city, town
locale: 10 California
O'Jays
hometown: Canton
song: Back Stabbers (1972)
For the Love of Money (1974)
I Love Music (1975)
Livin' for the Weekend (1976)
Love Train (1973)
Put Your Hands Together (1974)
Use Ta Be My Girl (1978)
Ojibwa: 5 tribe 6 Indian 7 Amerind 8 language
language akin to ~: 4 Cree
Ojinaga: 4 city, town
locale: 6 Mexico 9 Chihuahua
Ojo de Agua: 4 city, town
locale: 6 Mexico
Ojos del Salado: 4 peak 5 mount 8 mountain
locale: 9 Argentina
Ojus: 4 city, town
locale: 7 Florida
OK
see okay, Oklahoma
O.K. __: 6 Corral
Oka: 5 river
city on the ~: 4 Orel
locale: 6 Russia
okapi: 6 animal, mammal
Okara, Gabriel: 4 poet 8 Nigerian
Okavango: 5 river
locale: 6 Africa, Angola 8 Botswana
okay: 2 ay, da, ja, si 3 aye, nod, oui, yea, yep, yes, yup 4 fair, fine, good, jake, nice, pass, safe, sign, so-so, sure, yeah 5 admit, adopt, allow, go for, good-o, great, leave, legit, licit, moral, natch, noble, quite, roger, say-so, uh-huh, valid, yield 6 accede, accept, agreed, aright, assent, comply, decent, enable, gladly, good-oh, indeed, just so, kasher, kosher, not bad, pass on, permit, proper, rather, ratify, righto, signal, surely, you bet, yowzah 7 agree to, approve, certify, confirm, consent, correct, endorse, ethical, exactly, go ahead, go along, include, indeedy, indorse, in order, license, mais oui, mandate, popular, quite so, ten-four, up to par, welcome 8 accredit, accurate, adequate, all right, approval, approved, assent to, as you say, blessing, laudable, middling, notarize, not great, of course, passable, pleasant, pleasing, sanction, say yes to, splendid, stand for, suitable, superior, thumbs up, validate, very well 9 admirable, agreeable, agreement, allowable, authorize, be my guest, certainly, certified, clearance, consent to, darn right, excellent, naturally, permitted, precisely, put up with, recognize, reputable, sign off on, sure thing, tolerable, undamaged, wonderful, you betcha, you said it 10 absolutely, acceptable, acceptance, admissible, beneficial, by all means, concur with, creditable, definitely, give the nod, green light, permission, personable, positively, reasonable, sure enough, that's right, unmistaken
in French: 3 oui
Okayama: 4 city, town
locale: 5 Japan
Okazaki: 4 city, town
locale: 5 Japan
O.K. Corral name: 3 Doc, Ike 4 Earp 5 Wyatt 6 Morgan, Virgil 7 Clanton 8 Holliday
okedo: 4 drum
origin: 5 Japan
Okeechobee: 4 lake
locale: 7 Florida
O'Keefe: 5 Danny 6 Dennis
O'Keeffe, Georgia: 6 artist 7 painter
spouse: Alfred Stieglitz
Okefenokee: 5 swamp
Okemos: 4 city, town
locale: 8 Michigan
okey-__: 4 doke 5 dokey
okey-dokey
see okay
Okhotsk: 3 sea 7 current
feeder: 4 Amur
islands: 6 Kurile 8 Sakhalin
locale: 6 Russia
Okinawa: 3 isl. 4 isle 6 island
town: 4 Nago, Naha
Okla.
campus: 3 OSU
football rival: 3 Neb. 4 Nebr.
neighbor: 3 Ark., Kan., Tex. 4 Kans., N. Mex.
once: 3 ter. 4 terr.
Oklahoma: 5 state
Air Force base: 5 Vance
capital: Oklahoma City
city: 3 Ada 4 Enid 5 Altus, Moore, Tulsa, Yukon 6 Duncan, Edmond, El Reno, Lawton, Norman 7 Ardmore, Bethany, Del City, Guthrie, Shawnee 8 Fort Sill, Muskogee 9 Ponca City 10 Stillwater
conference: 9 Big Twelve
fort: 4 Sill
Indian: 3 Kaw, Oto, Sac 4 Otoe, Sauk 5 Caddo, Erick, Kansa, Osage, Ponca, Sayre 6 Pawnee, Quapaw 7 Arapaho, Choctaw, Wichita 8 Arapahoe, Cherokee, Cheyenne, Comanche, Kickapoo, Muskogee, Seminole 9 Chickasaw 10 Chiricahua
neighbor: 5 Texas 6 Kansas 8 Arkansas, Colorado, Missouri 9 New Mexico
range: 6 Ozarks
state animal: 7 buffalo
state beverage: 4 milk
state bird: 10 flycatcher
state fish: 4 bass
state flower: 9 mistletoe
state furbearing animal: 7 raccoon
state game bird: 10 wild turkey
state insect: 8 honeybee
state musical instrument: 6 fiddle
state percussion instrument: 4 drum
state rock: 10 rose quartz
state tree: 6 redbud
Oklahoma __: 5 Crude
Oklahoma __, The: 3 Kid
Oklahoma! (1955 film): 7 musical
cast: Eddie Albert, Gloria Grahame, Shirley Jones, Gordon MacRae, Rod Steiger, James Whitmore
character: 3 Fry, Ike, Jud 4 Cord, Elam, Fred, Slim, Will 5 Curly, Eller 6 Carnes, Gertie, Laurey, Parker 8 Ado Annie, Ali Hakim 9 Aunt Eller
director: Fred Zinnemann
producer: 4 Todd
prop: 3 hay 4 bale 6 surrey
songwriter: 7 Rodgers 11 Hammerstein
Oklahoma Crude (1973 film)
cast: Faye Dunaway, John Mills, George C. Scott
director: Stanley Kramer
Oklahoma Kid, The (1939 film)
cast: Humphrey Bogart, James Cagney, Rosemary Lane
director: Lloyd Bacon
Oklahoma State
athletes: 7 Cowboys
conference: 9 Big Twelve
locale: 10 Stillwater
okle-__: 5 dokle
okra: 5 shrub 6 veggie 9 vegetable
dish: 5 gumbo
family: 6 mallow
relative: 5 urena 8 abutilon
Oksana: 5 Baiul
see also Russian
Oktoberfest
need: 3 keg 4 beer, bier, brew, suds, tent 5 lager, stein 7 brewski
tune: 5 polka
Oku: 7 volcano
locale: 6 Africa 8 Cameroon
Ol' __ River: 3 Man
Ola: 7 Ullsten, Winslow
Olaf: 4 Bull 5 saint 9 Stapledon
Olaf Liljekrans author: Henrik Ibsen
Olaf's Saga author: Snorri Sturluson
Olah, George: 7 chemist 8 Nobelist
Olajuwon: 5 Akeem 6 Hakeem
milieu: 5 court
org.: 3 NBA
sport: 10 basketball
__ O'Lakes: 4 Land
Olan: 5 Soule
Oland, Warner: 5 actor
film: Charlie Chan at the Opera (1936)
Charlie Chan in Egypt (1935)
Charlie Chan in London (1934)
Charlie Chan on Broadway (1937)
Shanghai Express (1932)
__-o'-lantern: 4 jack
Olathe: 4 city, town
locale: 6 Kansas
__ Olay: 5 Oil of

Olay competitor: 5 Nivea 7 Jergens
Olazabal, Jose Maria: 6 golfer
__ ol' boy: 4 good
old: 4 aged, done, gray, grey, late, once, past, used, worn 5 dated, early, hoary, musty, passé, rusty, stale, tired 6 bygone, démodé, former, fossil, infirm, mature, of yore, rancid, remote, senior 7 ancient, antique, archaic, decayed, elderly, lasting, matured, onetime, quondam, run-down, veteran, vintage, wizened, worn-out 8 decrepit, enduring, familiar, grizzled, hardened, inactive, lifelong, obsolete, original, outdated, outmoded, out of use, overripe, previous, primeval, seasoned, skillful, sometime, timeworn, well-used 9 crumbling, enfeebled, erstwhile, geriatric, getting on, hackneyed, long-lived, moth-eaten, out-of-date, perennial, perpetual, primaeval, primitive, twice-told, venerable, vestigial 10 aboriginal, antiquated, back-number, gray-haired, immemorial, inveterate, oldfangled, primordial, threadbare, time-tested, unoriginal
combining form: 4 pale- 5 palae-, paleo- 6 archeo-, geront-, palaeo-, palaio- 7 archaeo-, geronto-
ender: 4 ster
old __: 3 boy, hat, man 4 Adam, chap, fogy, girl, gold, hand, maid, moon, rose, shoe, tale 5 field, flame, fogey, guard, money, river, style 6 fellow, fustic, growth, master, school, sledge, stager 7 country
old __ hills: 5 as the
old __ tale: 5 wives'
old __ tie: 6 school
old-__: 4 line, time 5 timer
old-__ network: 3 boy 4 girl
__-old: 3 age
Old __: 3 Sod, Vic 4 Days, Maid, Miss, Navy, Nick, Stoa, Test., West 5 Delhi, Dutch, Glory, Guard, Harry, Ionic, Irish, Latin, Norse, Saxon, South, Spice, Times, Welsh, World 6 Bailey, Comedy, Danish, French, Gringo, Permic, Rivers, Slavic, Turkic, Yeller 7 British, Castile, English, Flemish, Frisian, Hickory, Italian, Kingdom, Persian, Russian, Scratch, Spanish
Old __ and the Sea, The: 3 Man
Old __ at Home: 5 Folks
Old __ Bucket, The: 5 Oaken
Old __ Cod: 4 Cape
Old __ Cole: 4 King
Old __, CT: 4 Lyme
Old __ Moon: 5 Devil
Old __, The: 4 Maid 5 Glory, Manse, Songs 6 Devils, Gringo
Old __ Trail: 7 Spanish
Old __ Tray: 3 Dog
Old Acquaintance (1943 film)
cast: Bette Davis, Miriam Hopkins, Gig Young
__ old age: 4 ripe
old as the __: 5 hills
Old Bailey: 5 bench, court 8 tribunal
Old Black Joe composer: 6 Foster
__ Old Black Magic: 4 That
Old Blue __: 4 Eyes
old-boy __: 7 network
__ old boy: 4 good
Old Bridge: 4 city, town
locale: 9 New Jersey
Old Cape Cod (1957 song) artist: Patti Page
__ old cat: 3 one, two 4 four 5 three
__, old chap...: 4 I say
old college __, the: 3 try
__ Old Cowhand: 4 I'm an
Old Crow: 4 city, town
locale: 6 Canada
Old Curiosity Shop, The
author: Charles Dickens
character: 3 Jem, Kit 4 Abel, Davy, Matt, Nell 5 Isaac, Quilp, Sally, Trent 6 Betsey 7 Melissa
Old Dark House, The (1932 film)
cast: Melvyn Douglas, Boris Karloff, Charles Laughton
Old Days (1975 song) artist: Chicago
__ old days, the: 4 good
Old Devil __: 4 Moon
Old Devils, The author: Kingsley Amis
Old Dog Tray composer: 6 Foster
Old Dominion: 8 Virginia
__ olde England: 6 merrie
olde establishment: 6 shoppe
Old El __: 4 Paso
olden: 6 bygone, former 7 ancient, archaic 8 outmoded 10 antiquated, immemorial
days: 4 past, yore 7 history 9 antiquity
in ~ days: 3 ago 4 once, then 6 before 7 earlier, long ago 8 back then, back when, formerly 9 at one time, in the past 10 heretofore, previously
not ~: 3 now 5 fresh, today 6 modern, recent 7 current, just out 8 contempo, up-to-date 10 avant-garde, newfangled, present-day
Oldenbourg, Zoé: 6 French, writer
work: The World Is Not Enough
Oldenburg: 4 city, town
locale: 7 Germany
Old English: 5 Saxon 6 polish
alternative: 6 Behold, Endust, Pledge 10 Liquid Gold
conger: 3 ele
festival: 6 lammas
laborer: 4 esne
letter: 3 edh, eth, wen 4 wynn
money: 3 ora 4 orae
writer: 7 Aelfric
older: 5 elder, first, prior 6 former, senior 7 earlier 9 first-born, preceding
grow ~: 3 age 4 grow 6 mature 7 develop
older but __: 5 wiser
Oldest Living Confederate Widow Tells All author: Allan Gurganus
Old Faithful: 6 geyser
Old Familiar Faces poet: 4 Elia
old-fashioned: 3 odd, out 4 dead 5 corny, dated, dowdy, drink, fusty, hoary, moldy, mossy, musty, passé 6 bygone, démodé, quaint, square, stuffy 7 antique, archaic, vintage 8 beverage, cocktail, medieval, obsolete, outdated, outmoded 9 mediaeval, not with it, out-of-date, unstylish 10 antiquated, out of style
get the ~ way: 4 earn
ingredient: 7 bitters, whiskey
one: 4 fogy, marm 5 fogey 6 square
Old Fashioned Love Song, An (1971 song) artist: Three Dog Night
Old-Fashioned Way, The (1934 film)
cast: W.C. Fields, Baby LeRoy
Oldfield, Barney: 5 racer 9 auto racer
milieu: 5 track
Oldfield, Mike
homeland: England
song: Tubular Bells (1974)
Old Folks at Home
composer: 6 Foster
river: 6 Swanee
Old Fuss and Feathers: 5 Scott
__ Old Gang of Mine: 4 That
old-girl __: 7 network
Old Glory: 4 flag
Old Glory, The author: Robert Lowell
old gold: 6 yellow
relative: 4 buff, corn, lime, rust, sand 5 blond, brass, coral, cream, flaxy, lemon, maize, ocher, ochre, peach, rusty, straw 6 blonde, canary, chammy, citron, crocus, flaxen, shammy, shamoy 7 apricot, chamois, citrine, jasmine, mustard, nankeen, saffron, xanthic 8 daffodil, primrose 9 champagne, goldenrod, jessamine
Old Gray __, The: 4 Mare
Old Gringo (1989 film)
cast: Jane Fonda, Gregory Peck, Jimmy Smits
Old Gringo, The author: Carlos Fuentes
Oldham: 4 city, town
locale: 7 England
Old Harry: 5 Satan
old-hat: 3 out 5 passé 8 obsolete, outdated, outmoded, timeworn 9 out-of-date
__ Old House: 4 This
oldie: 4 song, tune 6 melody
often: 5 goody 6 goodie
__ oldie: 5 moldy 6 golden
Old Ironsides: 4 boat, ship
author: Oliver Wendell Holmes
Old Ironsides (1926 film)
cast: Wallace Beery, Charles Farrell
Old King __: 4 Cole
old-line: 7 diehard, fogyish 8 mossback
Old Lyme: 4 city, town
locale: 4 Conn.
Old MacDonald
animal: 3 cat, cow, dog, pig 5 horse
refrain: 5 EIEIO
Old MacDonald had ___...: 5 a farm
old maid: 4 game 8 card game
Old Maid, The (1939 film)
cast: George Brent, Bette Davis, Miriam Hopkins
__ old man: 5 grand
Old Man and the Sea, The: 4 film 5 novel
author: Ernest Hemingway
cast: Spencer Tracy
character: 7 Manolin 8 Santiago
composer: 7 Tiomkin
director: John Sturges
fish: 6 marlin
Old Man Down the Road, The (1985 song) artist: John Fogerty
Oldman, Gary: 5 actor
film: Air Force One (1997)
Bram Stoker's Dracula (1992)
The Fifth Element (1997)
Immortal Beloved (1994)
JFK (1991)
Lost in Space (1998)
Prick Up Your Ears (1987)
Sid and Nancy (1986)
State of Grace (1990)
True Romance (1993)
We Think the World of You (1988)
film (voice): Quest for Camelot (1998)
spouse: Uma Thurman
Old Manse, The author: Nathaniel Hawthorne
Old Man's Winter Night, An poet: 5 Frost
Old Man, Woman and Flower painter: 5 Ernst
__ Old Men: 6 Grumpy
Old Mortality author: Katherine Anne Porter
oldness: 3 age 5 years 6 dotage 8 lifespan 10 senescence
Old New York author: Edith Wharton
Old Nick: 5 Satan
Old North __: 6 Church
Old Oaken Bucket, The artist: 5 Moses
old one in German: 4 alte
__ Old Party: 5 Grand
Old Patagonian Express, The author: Paul Theroux
Old Rivers (1962 song) artist: Walter Brennan
Olds: 3 car 4 auto, city, town 6 Ransom 10 automobile
locale: 6 Canada 7 Alberta
middle name: 3 Eli
old ~: 3 Reo
see also Oldsmobile
__ Old Saturday Night: 4 Same
old school __: 3 tie
old-school: 5 fusty, musty 7 fogyish 8 obsolete
Old Scratch: 5 Satan
specialty: 4 evil
old sledge: 4 game 8 card game
alias: 5 pitch 7 seven-up 11 high-low-jack
Oldsmobile: 3 car 4 auto
like an ~ of song: 5 merry
model: 5 Alero, Ciera, Delta, Omega 6 Aurora, Calais, Fiesta, Royale 7 Achieva, Bravada, Cutlass, Delmont, Firenza, Holiday, Jetfire, Jetstar 8 Intrigue, Starfire, Toronado 9 Celebrity, Futuramic 10 Silhouette 11 Eighty-Eight, Ninety-Eight
Old Smokey topper: 4 snow
Old Sod, from the: 5 Irish
old soft __, the: 4 shoe
Old Songs, The (1981 song) artist: Barry Manilow
Old Spanish __: 5 Trail
oldsquaw: 4 duck, fowl
relative: 4 smew, teal 5 eider, Pekin, Rouen, scaup 6 Cayuga, scoter 7 gadwall, mallard, pintail, pochard, redhead, sea duck, widgeon 8 garganey, gray duck, mandarin, musk duck, shoveler, surf duck, wood duck 9 black duck, broadbill, goldeneye, goosander, greenhead, merganser, ruddy duck, sprigtail 10 bufflehead, canvasback, surf scoter, tufted duck
old-style: 4 late 5 areek, prior 6 bygone, former, whilom 7 earlier, one-time, quondam 8 previous 9 erstwhile, foregoing, preceding
Old Swimmin' Hole, The: 4 poem
author: James Whitcomb Riley
Old Testament
book: 3 Bar., Ezr., Gen., Hab., Hos., Isa., Jer., Job, Lam., Lev., Mac., Mic., Nah., Neh., Num., Psa. 4 Amos, Deut., Eccl., Exod., Ezek., Ezra, Joel, Macc., Obad., Prov., Ruth, Zech. 5 Hosea, Jonah, Kings, Levit., Micah, Nahum 6 Daniel, Eccles., Esther, Exodus, Haggai, Isaiah, Joshua, Judges, Psalms, Samuel 7 Ezekiel, Genesis, Malachi, Numbers, Obadiah 8 Habakkuk, Jeremiah, Nehemiah, Proverbs 9 Leviticus, Zechariah, Zephaniah 10 Chronicles 11 Deuteronomy
city: 4 Lehi 5 Babel, Sodom
judge: 3 Eli
kingdom: 4 Aram, Edom 5 Sheba
mountain: 4 Nebo 5 Sinai
patriarch: 4 Enos 5 Isaac 7 Abraham
tower: 5 Babel
verb: 5 begat, beget, smite
see also Bible
old-time: 4 past 5 passé 6 bygone, former, quaint 7 quondam 8 outmoded, previous 9 erstwhile, graybeard
old-timer: 3 vet 6 senior 7 veteran
Old Time Rock & Roll (1989 song) artist: Bob Seger
Old Time Saloon, The author: George Ade
Old Times author: Harold Pinter
Oldtown Folks author: Harriet Beecher Stowe

Old Uncle __: 3 Ned
Olduvai Gorge locale: 6 Africa 8 Tanzania
Old Vic city: 6 London
Old West
conveyance: 3 nag 4 mare, pony 5 bronc, horse, mount, stage, wagon 6 bronco, cayuse, equine 7 gelding, mustang 8 stallion 10 stagecoach
walk in the ~: 4 poke 5 amble, drift, mosey
warrior: 6 Apache, Paiute
weapon of the ~: 4 Colt 5 rifle
oldwife: 4 fish
old wives' __: 4 tale
Old Wives' Tale, The
author: 5 Peele
character: 5 Delia
Old Yeller (1957 film)
cast: Tommy Kirk, Dorothy McGuire, Fess Parker
Ole: 4 Bull 5 Olsen 7 Rölvaag
Ole __: 4 Miss
Olé!: 3 cry, rah
accompaniment: 4 clap
oleaceous tree: 3 ash 5 olive
oleaginous: 4 oily 5 lardy, slick 6 greasy 8 slippery, unctuous 9 lubricous
Olean: 4 city, town
locale: 7 New York
oleander: 5 plant, shrub 6 flower
relative: 7 dogbane, karanda 10 frangipani
oleaster: 4 tree 5 shrub
oleate: 5 ester
__ ole boy: 4 good
Ole Buttermilk __: 3 Sky
olecranon: 4 bone, ulna
locale: 3 arm 7 forearm
Oleg: 7 Cassini
__ Ole Man: 6 Little
Ole Miss student: 5 Rebel
olent: 7 scented 8 aromatic, fragrant
oleo: 6 spread 9 margarine
holder: 3 tub
in Britain: 5 marge
serving: 3 pat
oleo __: 3 oil 5 strut
__ Ole Opry: 5 Grand
oleoresin: 5 elemi
Olerud, John sport: 8 baseball
Olesha, Yury: 6 writer 7 Russian
Olestra
lack: 3 fat
org. that approved ~: 3 FDA
Oleta: 5 Adams
olfactory: 7 odorous, sensory 9 sensorial
organ: 4 nose 5 snoot, snout 7 schnozz 9 proboscis 10 schnozzola
stimulus: 4 odor, reek 5 aroma, smell, stink
olfactory __: 4 bulb, lobe 5 nerve
Olga: 5 James 6 Korbut 9 Baclanova
sister of ~ in Chekhov: 5 Irina
olid: 4 rank 5 fetid 6 foetid, smelly, stinky 10 malodorous
oligarch: 5 ruler 6 gerent
oligarchic group: 4 bloc, ring 5 junta 7 council 9 coalition
Oligocene preceder: 6 Eocene
Olimpiade composer: 4 Arne
Olin: 3 Ken 4 Lena 5 Dutra
Olinda: 4 city, town
locale: 6 Brazil
Olin, Ken spouse: Patricia Wettig
Olin, Lena: 7 actress
film: Chocolat (2000)
Enemies, A Love Story (1989)
Havana (1990)
Polish Wedding (1998)
The Unbearable Lightness of Being (1988)
olio: 5 blend 6 jumble, medley 7 collage, mélange 8 mishmash, mixed bag, pastiche 9 pasticcio, patchwork, potpourri 10 assortment, crazy quilt, hodgepodge, miscellany, salmagundi
Oliphant: 3 Pat
Oliva, Tony sport: 8 baseball
olive: 3 tan 4 tree 5 color, fruit, green 6 veggie 8 brownish 9 evergreen, vegetable, yellowish
branch: 5 truce 7 amnesty 9 armistice, cease-fire 10 moratorium
drab: 4 garb 5 dress, khaki 6 attire 7 uniform
family shrub: 5 lilac 7 jasmine 9 forsythia, jessamine
genus: 4 olea
product: 3 oil
relative: 3 pea 4 cyan, jade, sage 5 beryl, breen, virid 6 myrtle, reseda 7 avocado, celadon, emerald, verdant 9 pistachio, turquoise 10 aquamarine, chartreuse
tree cousin: 3 ash
olive __: 3 oil 4 drab, wood 5 drabs, green, shell 6 branch
__ olive: 4 wild 5 black, queen 7 Russian
Olive: 3 Oyl 9 Schreiner
Olive Branch: 4 city, town
locale: 4 Miss.
Olive Oyl's parent: 4 Cole, Nana
Oliver: 3 cat 4 Reed 5 Evans, Hardy, North, Perry, Platt, Sacks, Stone, Susan, Twist 7 Edna May, La Farge 8 Cromwell 9 Goldsmith
partner: 4 Stan
song: Good Morning Starshine (1969) Jean (1969)
Oliver __ Holmes: 7 Wendell
Oliver __ Perry: 6 Hazard
Oliver! (1968 film)
cast: Ron Moody, Oliver Reed, Shani Wallis
director: Carol Reed
Oliver & Company
cat: 6 Oliver
dog: 4 Rita, Tito 6 DeSoto, Dodger, Roscoe 7 Francis 8 Einstein
Oliver, Edna May: 7 actress
film: David Copperfield (1935)
Drums Along the Mohawk (1939)
The Last Gentleman (1934)
Little Women (1933)
Lydia (1941)
Murder on a Honeymoon (1935)
Murder on the Blackboard (1934)
Nurse Edith Cavell (1939)
The Penguin Pool Murder (1932)
Pride and Prejudice (1940)
Romeo and Juliet (1936)
The Story of Vernon & Irene Castle (1939)
A Tale of Two Cities (1935)
Oliver's Story author: 5 Segal
Oliver Twist
author: Charles Dickens
character: 4 Bill, Fang, Jack, Mann, Noah, Rose, Toby 5 Bates, Fagin, Harry, Monks, Nancy, Sally, Sikes 6 Bedwin, Bumble, Corney, Dodger, Edward, Maylie 7 Charley, Crackit, Dawkins, Grimwig, Leeford 8 Brownlow, Claypole, Losberne 9 Charlotte 10 Sowerberry
dog: 8 Bull's-eye
Oliver Twist (1922 film)
cast: Lon Chaney, Jackie Coogan
director: Frank Lloyd
Oliver Twist (1948 film)
cast: John Howard Davies, Sir Alec Guinness, Robert Newton
director: David Lean
Oliver Wendell __: 6 Holmes
Olivia: 4 d'Abo 6 Hussey 10 Newton-John 11 de Havilland
Olivier: 8 Laurence, Messiaen
emulate ~: 3 act
Olivier, Laurence: 3 Sir 4 Lord 5 actor
film: As You Like It (1936)
The Beggar's Opera (1953)
The Betsy (1978)
The Bounty (1984)
Dance of Death (1968)
The Demi-Paradise (1943)
The Devil's Disciple (1959)
The Entertainer (1960)
Hamlet (1948, AA)
Henry V (1945)
A Little Romance (1979)
Marathon Man (1976)
Othello (1965)
Pride and Prejudice (1940)
Rebecca (1940)
Richard III (1955)
Sleuth (1972)
Spartacus (1960)
That Hamilton Woman (1941)
Three Sisters (1970)
Wuthering Heights (1939)
The Yellow Ticket (1931)
spouse: Vivien Leigh, Joan Plowright
olivine: 7 mineral 10 chrysolite
transparent green ~ gem: 7 peridot
olla podrida: 4 olio, stew 5 blend 6 jumble, medley 7 collage, farrago, mélange 8 mishmash, mixed bag, pastiche 9 pasticcio, patchwork, potpourri 10 assortment, crazy quilt, hodgepodge, miscellany, salmagundi
Ollie: 5 Hardy, North 6 Matson
friend: 4 Fran, Stan 5 Kukla
Olly olly __ free!: 4 oxen
olm: 9 amphibian 10 salamander
Ol' Man __: 4 Mose
Ol' Man River composer: 4 Kern 11 Hammerstein
Olmec descendant: 4 Maya
Olmos, Edward James: 5 actor
film: The Ballad of Gregorio Cortez (1983)
Blade Runner (1982)
My Family/Mi Familia (1995)
Selena (1997)
Stand and Deliver (1987)
Triumph of the Spirit (1989)
Wolfen (1981)
The Wonderful Ice Cream Suit (1999)
Zoot Suit (1981)
spouse: Lorraine Bracco
Olmsted, Frederick: 9 architect
Olney: 4 city, town
locale: 5 Texas 8 Maryland
Olof: 5 Palme
ology: 7 science
olor: 4 swan
__ o' Love: 5 Light
olpe: 3 jug 4 ewer 6 carafe, flagon, vessel 9 container
Olsen: 3 Mrs., Ole 5 Jimmy, Susan 6 Ashley, Merlin, Tillie 8 Mary-Kate
coworker: 4 Kent, Lane 5 White
Olsen, Merlin sport: 8 football
Olsen, Ole: 8 comedian
film: Crazy House (1943)
Ghost Catchers (1944)
Hellzapoppin' (1941)
Olson: 4 Lute 5 Nancy 7 Charles
Olson, Charles: 4 poet
work: The Maximus Poems
Olson, Charles work: The Maximus Poems
Olson, Lute: 5 coach
milieu: 5 court
org.: 3 NBA
sport: 10 basketball
Olson, Nancy: 7 actress
film: The Absent-Minded Professor (1961)
Smith! (1969)
So Big (1953)
Son of Flubber (1963)
Sunset Blvd. (1950)
Oluta: 4 city, town
locale: 6 Mexico 8 Veracruz
Olympia: 4 city, nude, town 7 Dukakis
artist: 5 Manet
county: 8 Thurston
locale: 10 Washington
rival: 5 Coors
Olympia (1936 film) director: Leni Riefenstahl
Olympian: 4 Ares, Hera, Zeus 5 Greek 6 Apollo
matchmaker: 4 Eros
troublemaker: 4 Eris
what an ~ breathed: 6 aether
Olympic: 4 park
locale: 10 Washington
Olympic __: 5 Games 7 Village
Olympics
ceremony song: 6 anthem
chant: 3 USA
contest: 4 dash, épée 5 event, relay 6 boxing, discus 7 fencing, shot put
first ~ site: 4 Elis
gear: 4 disc, disk, épée, shot 5 saber, scull
Jr. ~ sponsor: 3 AAU
L.A. ~ boycotter: 4 USSR
perfection: 3 ten
quest: 4 gold 5 medal
race unit: 5 meter
regulatory gp.: 3 IOC
site: 5 venue
symbol: 5 flame, torch
__ Olympics: 6 Junior, Summer, Winter 7 Special
Olympics sites (Summer):
2008 - Beijing, China
2004 - Athens, Greece
2000 - Sydney, Australia
1996 - Atlanta, Georgia
1992 - Barcelona, Spain
1988 - Seoul, South Korea
1984 - Los Angeles, USA
1980 - Moscow, USSR
1976 - Montreal, Canada
1972 - Munich, West Germany
1968 - Mexico City, Mexico
1964 - Tokyo, Japan
1960 - Rome, Italy
1956 - Melbourne, Australia
1952 - Helsinki, Finland
1948 - London, England
1936 - Berlin, Germany
1932 - Los Angeles, USA
1928 - Amsterdam, Holland
1924 - Paris, France
1920 - Antwerp, Belgium
1912 - Stockholm, Sweden
1908 - London, England
1904 - St. Louis, USA
1900 - Paris, France
1896 - Athens, Greece
Olympics sites (Winter):
2006 - Turin, Italy
2002 - Salt Lake City, USA
1998 - Nagano, Japan
1994 - Lillehammer, Norway
1992 - Albertville, France
1988 - Calgary, Canada
1984 - Sarajevo, Yugoslavia
1980 - Lake Placid, USA
1976 - Innsbruck, Austria
1972 - Sapporo, Japan
1968 - Grenoble, France
1964 - Innsbruck, Austria
1960 - Squaw Valley, USA
1956 - Cortina d'Ampezzo, Italy

1952 - Oslo, Norway
1948 - St. Moritz, Switzerland
1936 - Garmisch, Germany
1932 - Lake Placid, USA
1928 - St. Moritz, Switzerland
1924 - Chamonix, France
Olympics stars (Summer)
1912: 6 Thorpe
1920: 5 Nurmi
1924: 5 Nurmi
1932: 6 Crabbe
1936: 5 Owens
1948: 7 Mathias
1952: 7 Mathias, Zátopek 8 Richards
1956: 6 Fraser, Oerter 8 Richards
1960: 6 Bikila, Fraser, Oerter 7 Johnson, Rudolph
1964: 4 Tyus 5 Hayes 6 Bikila, Brumel, Fraser, Oerter
1968: 4 Tyus 5 Keino 6 Beamon, Oerter, Toomey 7 Fosbury, Seagren
1972: 5 Gould, Spitz 6 Korbut 7 Shorter
1976: 5 Ender 6 Jenner 8 Comaneci
1980: 3 Coe 5 Ovett
1984: 3 Coe 5 Lewis 6 Benoit, Retton 7 Ashford 8 Louganis
1988: 4 Otto 5 Bubka, Evans, Flo-Jo, Lewis 6 Biondi 8 Louganis
1992: 5 Evans, Lewis 6 Devers
1996: 5 Dyken, Lewis 6 Devers
Olympics stars (Winter)
1928: 5 Henie
1932: 5 Henie
1936: 5 Henie
1948: 6 Button
1952: 6 Button
1956: 8 Albright
1960: 5 Heiss
1968: 5 Killy 7 Fleming
1976: 6 Hamill 7 Klammer
1980: 4 Enke 6 Heiden 7 Cousins
1984: 4 Enke, Witt 5 Mahre 8 Hamilton
1988: 4 Witt 5 Tomba 7 Boitano
1992: 5 Blair, Tomba 9 Yamaguchi
1994: 3 Moe 5 Baiul, Blair
1998: 5 Kulik 6 Street 8 Lipinski
2002: 6 Hughes
Olympus: 4 peak 5 mount 6 camera 8 mountain
alternative: 4 Fuji 5 Canon, Kodak, Leica, Nikon 6 Konica, Pentax, Rollei 7 Minolta, Vivitar, Yashica 8 Polaroid
locale: 6 Europe, Greece
neighbor: 4 Ossa
resident: 3 god
sight from ~: 5 Egean 6 Aegean
see also Olympian
om: 6 mantra 7 mantram
Omaha: 4 city, town 5 tribe 6 Indian 7 Amerind
athletes: 8 Bluejays
county: 7 Douglas
home: 4 tipi 5 tepee 6 teepee
institution: 8 Boys Town
locale: 3 Neb. 4 Nebr. 8 Nebraska
river: 8 Missouri
school: 9 Creighton
Oman: 4 gulf 6 nation 7 country 9 sultanate
capital: 6 Muscat
coin: 5 baisa, baiza
group: 10 Arab League
locale: 6 Arabia
money: 4 rial
neighbor: 3 UAE 5 Saudi, Yemen
resident: 4 Arab
title: 4 amir, emir 5 ameer, emeer
Omar: 4 Epps 6 Sharif 7 Bradley, Gooding, Khayyám 8 Torrijos
grandfather of ~: 4 Esau
Omar Khayyám: 4 poet 7 Persian 9 tentmaker 10 astronomer
work: Rubáiyát
omber: 4 game 8 card game
alias: 6 hombre
variety: 9 quadrille
ombrophobe fear: 4 rain
ombu: 4 tree
'ome: 4 'ouse
Ome: 4 city, town
locale: 5 Hondo, Japan 6 Honshu
O'Meara, Mark: 6 golfer
milieu: 5 links 6 course
org.: 3 PGA
omega: 3 end 4 last 5 Greek 6 ending, letter
counterpart: 3 zee
in physics: 3 ohm
opposite: 5 alpha
preceder: 3 psi
Omega: 3 car 4 auto, Olds, Opel 5 watch 10 automobile, Oldsmobile, wristwatch
alternative: 4 Ebel, Rado 5 Casio, Elgin, Lorus, Rolex, Seiko, Timex 6 Bulova, Fossil, Movado, Pulsar, Swatch 7 Citizen 8 Longines, Tag Heuer, Tourneau
omega-3 __ acid: 5 fatty
O Mein __: 4 Papa
omelet: 8 frittata
cooker: 3 pan 5 grill 7 skillet
ingredient: 3 egg, ham 4 yolk 5 onion 6 cheese
__ omelet: 6 Denver 7 Spanish, western
omen: 4 sign 5 augur, token 6 augury, herald, signal, threat 7 auspice, bad sign, portent, presage, promise, warning 8 black cat, foreshow 9 foretoken, harbinger, indicator, predictor 10 foreboding, indication, prediction
be an ~ of: 4 bode, mean 5 augur 6 herald 7 betoken, point to, portend, presage, promise, signify 8 foreshow, foretell, indicate, prophesy 9 foretoken 10 foreshadow
good ~: 7 promise
interpreter: 4 seer 5 augur 6 auspex
Omerta author: Mario Puzo
Ometepec: 4 city, town
locale: 6 Mexico 8 Guerrero
omicron: 5 Greek 6 letter
follower: 2 pi
preceder: 2 xi
Omigosh!: 4 egad, yipe 5 egads, yikes, yipes
ominous: 4 dark, dire, grim, ugly 5 black, grave 6 creepy, dismal, doomed, gloomy, spooky 7 baleful, baneful, fateful, fearful, hostile, malefic, unlucky, warning 8 ill-fated, lowering, menacing, minatory, perilous, sinister 9 dangerous, frightful, ill-boding, impending, monstrous, prophetic 10 forbidding, foreboding, out of joint, portentous
sound: 4 toll 5 knell
O mio babbino __: 4 caro
omission: 3 gap 4 lack, miss, skip, slip 5 blank, break, error, lapse, space 6 hiatus, lacuna 7 absence, default, elision, mistake, neglect 9 disregard, exception, exclusion, oversight
omit: 3 cut 4 drop, edit, jump, miss, shun, skip 5 avoid, elide, leave, let go 6 bypass, cut out, delete, except, forget, go past, ignore, pass up, slight 7 discard, dismiss, exclude, forbear, mistake, neglect, scissor 8 count out, leave off, leave out, let slide, overlook, pass over, preclude 9 disregard, eliminate, gloss over
in fast-food lingo: 4 hold
prefix: 3 for-
omitted: 6 absent 7 missing 9 forgotten
omitting: 3 bar 4 save 6 except 9 except for
none: 3 all 4 full 5 fully 6 entire, wholly 7 totally 8 complete, entirely, everyone 9 everybody 10 completely, everything
not ~: 4 incl., with 9 including
Omiya: 4 city, town
locale: 5 Japan
__ omnes: 6 exeunt
Omni: 3 car 4 auto 5 arena, Dodge, hotel 10 automobile
alternative: 5 Hyatt 6 Hilton, Westin 7 Wyndham 8 Marriott, Radisson, Sheraton 10 DoubleTree
omnia __ amor: 6 vincit
omnia, opera: 4 body 5 whole 6 corpus, oeuvre 8 entirety 10 collection
__ omnia vincit: 5 labor
omnibus: 4 book, tome, work 6 volume 10 compendium, cyclopedia
omnibus __: 6 clause
omni ender: 3 bus 4 vore 6 potent
omnifarious: 5 mixed 6 divers, sundry, unlike, varied 7 diverse, unalike, various 8 assorted, distinct, manifold 9 different, disparate 10 dissimilar
omnipotence: 5 might, power
omnipotent: 6 divine, mighty 7 godlike 8 almighty, powerful
omnipresent: 6 divine 8 almighty 9 pervasive, universal, worldwide
omniscient: 4 wise 6 divine 7 all-wise, learned 8 almighty 9 all-seeing 10 all-knowing, infallible
omnium-gatherum: 4 olio 6 medley 7 grab bag, mélange, mixture 8 mish-mash, pastiche 9 pasticcio, potpourri 10 hodgepodge, miscellany
omnivore: 4 bear, goat 6 eat-all
omnivorous: 8 ravenous 9 insatiate, voracious 10 gluttonous
Omoo: 5 novel 7 romance
author: Herman Melville
dog: 9 Boatswain
__-o'-mountain: 3 cat
omphalos: 5 navel 9 umbilicus
omphaloskepsis
find: 4 lint
focus: 5 navel
Omri, son of: 4 Ahab
Omsk: 4 city, port, town
locale: 6 Russia
river: 6 Irtysh
Omuta: 4 city, town
locale: 5 Japan
__-o'-mutton: 3 leg
__ o' My Heart: 3 Peg
O, my luve is like __...: 4 a red
__-o'-my-thumb: 3 hop
on: 3 lit 4 as of, atop, near, over, upon 5 about, above, along, forth 6 aboard, airing 7 ahead of, close to, forward 8 adjacent, covering, touching 9 astraddle, supported
prefix: 3 epi-
on __: 3 end, ice, tap, top 4 call, deck, duty, edge, file, fire, hand, high, hold, line, spec, time, view 5 a dare, a diet, a lark, and on, a roll, a tear, a whim, draft, earth, order, paper, sight, the go, top of, trial 6 a leash, a spree, demand, report, stream, strike, target, tiptoe 7 balance, purpose, request, standby
on __ and a prayer: 5 a wing
on __ and needles: 4 pins
on __ ear: 3 its
on __ fours: 3 all
on __ knee: 6 bended
on __ of: 3 top 4 pain 6 behalf 7 account
on __ of the world: 3 top
on __-to-know basis: 5 a need
on __ with: 4 a par
on-__: 3 air, dit 4 line, mike, peak, ramp, seam, site 5 board, glide, stage 6 camera, limits, record, screen, season, stream
on-__ catalog: 4 line
__ on: 3 big, egg, get, has, hit, lay, let, log, mid, pin, put, rat, run, sit, spy, try 4 bear, dote, down, draw, fall, goof, hand, hang, harp, have, hold, jump, lead, lean, lock, look, move, pick, play, push, rely, sail, sign, sold, spur, step, take, trod, turn, wait, work 5 and so, bring, build, carry, catch, check, count, dwell, early, key in, let in, on and, pitch, stand, sweet, touch, trade 6 chance, figure, freeze, switch 7 bargain, reflect
__-on: 3 add 4 come, dead, head, odds, slip 5 blush, brush 6 goings, hanger
On __: 5 My Own 7 Liberty, Nothing
On __ Blindness: 3 His
On __ Boat to China: 5 a Slow
On __ Majesty's Secret Service: 3 Her
On __ of Old Smokey: 3 Top
On __ Pond: 6 Golden
On __ Toes: 4 Your
On __ Zebra: 6 Beyond
__ On: 4 Hold, Rave, Rock 5 Dream, Float, Get It 7 Holding
on a __: 4 dare, lark, roll, tear, whim 5 hunch, spree 6 string 7 rampage
on a __ basis: 5 trial
on a __ budget: 5 tight
on a __ errand: 5 fool's
on a __-name basis: 5 first
on a __ notice: 7 moment's
on a __ of one to ten: 5 scale
on a __ platter: 6 silver
on a __-to-know basis: 4 need
Ona: 6 Munson
On a __ Day...: 5 Clear
__ on a bet!: 3 not
On a Clear Day You Can See Forever (1970 film)
cast: Larry Blyden, Yves Montand, Bob Newhart, Barbra Streisand
director: Vincente Minnelli
__ on a dime: 4 stop
__ on a Feeling: 6 Hooked
on a first-__ basis: 4 name
on a fool's __: 6 errand
on-again, off-again: 6 spotty 8 periodic, sporadic 9 spasmodic 10 sporadical
onager: 3 ass 6 donkey, equine 7 jackass
relative: 5 burro, horse, kiang, zebra 6 quagga 7 jackass 8 chigetai 9 dziggetai
On Aggression author: Konrad Lorenz
__ on a Grecian Urn: 3 Ode
__ on a Happy Face: 3 Put
__ on a high note: 3 end
__ on a Hot Tin Roof: 3 Cat
__ on air: 4 walk 7 walking
on-air personality: 2 DJ 6 deejay
__ on airs: 3 put
__ on a Jet Plane: 7 Leaving
__ on a limb: 3 out
on all __: 5 fours
__ on a Match: 5 Three
on a moment's __: 6 notice
__ on-a My House: 4 Come
on an __: 7 average, impulse, upswing
on an __ keel: 4 even
on an __ of mercy: 6 errand
__ on an act: 3 put
on-and-off: 6 random, spotty 7 erratic 8 periodic 9 irregular, spasmodic
device: 3 tap 5 valve 6 faucet, spigot, switch 7 hydrant
On and On (song) artist: Gladys Knight and the Pips, Stephen Bishop
on a need-to-__ basis: 4 know
on an errand of __: 5 mercy
on an even __: 4 keel

On an Island With You (1948 film)
cast: Jimmy Durante, Peter Lawford, Ricardo Montalban, Esther Williams
__ on a rock: 4 duck
__ on a Rooftop: 4 Love
on a scale of __ to ten: 3 one
__ on a show: 3 put
on a silver __: 7 platter
__ on assets: 6 return
Onassis: 3 Ari 8 Cristina 9 Aristotle, Christina 10 Jacqueline
__ on a String: 3 Man 6 Puppet
__ on a tangent: 3 off
on a tight __: 6 budget
on a trial __: 5 basis
__ on a true story: 5 based
...__ on a tuffet...: 3 sat
...on a wing __ prayer: 4 and a
__ on a Wire: 4 Bird
__-on baggage: 5 carry
__ on Bald Mountain, A: 5 Night
__ on balls: 4 base
on bended __: 4 knee
On Bended Knee (1994 song) artist: Boyz II Men
On Beyond Zebra author: Dr. Seuss
__ on board: 4 free
On Borrowed Time (1939 film)
cast: Lionel Barrymore, Beulah Bondi, Cedric Hardwicke, Una Merkel
On Boxing author: 5 Oates
On Broadway (song) artist: Drifters, George Benson
__ On By: 4 Walk
once: 3 old 4 erst, late, past 6 before, bygone, erenow, whilom 7 ages ago, already, earlier, long ago, quondam, time was, way back 8 as soon as, back then, back when, formerly, sometime, until now, years ago 9 a while ago, erstwhile, in the past 10 back in time, heretofore, previously
called: 3 née
once __: 4 a day 5 a week, a year
once __ a time: 4 upon
once __ blue moon: 3 in a
once __ lightly: 4 over
once __ twice shy: 6 bitten
once __ while: 3 in a
once-__: 4 over
once-__-lightly: 4 over
__ once: 5 all at
Once __ a Mattress: 4 Upon
Once __ a midnight...: 4 upon
Once __ a time...: 4 upon
Once __ Enough: 5 Is Not
Once __ Lifetime: 3 in a
Once __ Pacific: 5 by the
once and __ all: 3 for
Once and Future King, The author: T.H. White
Once a Thief star: 5 Havoc
once-a-year: 6 annual 8 periodic
Once by the Pacific author: Robert Frost
once in __ moon: 5 a blue
once in a __: 5 while
Once in a Lifetime
author: Danielle Steel, George S. Kaufman, Moss Hart
__ once in a while: 5 every
Once in Love With __: 3 Amy
__ Once in My Life: 3 For 4 Just
once more: 4 anew 5 again
Once more unto the __: 6 breach
once, not even: 4 ne'er 5 never
once over __: 7 lightly
once-over: 4 look 6 gander, regard 10 inspection
give the ~: 3 eye 4 ogle, peek, scan, skim 7 inspect 8 check out
once upon __: 5 a time
Once Upon a Crime (1992 film)
cast: James Belushi, John Candy, Cybill Shepherd, Sean Young
director: Eugene Levy
Once Upon a Mattress prop: 3 pea
once upon a time: 3 ago
Once Upon a Time in America (1984 film)
cast: Robert De Niro, Elizabeth McGovern, Tuesday Weld, James Woods
director: Sergio Leone
Once Upon a Time in the West (1968 film)
cast: Charles Bronson, Claudia Cardinale, Henry Fonda, Jason Robards
director: Sergio Leone
__ once was a man...: 5 There
Once You Get Started (1975 song)
artist: Chaka Khan
__ on Classics: 6 Hooked
oncle: 5 uncle 6 French
brother: 4 père
wife: 5 tante
__ Oncle: 3 Mon
oncoming: 5 ahead 7 looming, nearing 8 expected, imminent 9 advancing, impending, onrushing
__ on Criticism, An: 5 Essay
On Dangerous Ground (1952 film)
cast: Ward Bond, Ida Lupino, Robert Ryan
director: Nicholas Ray
__ on deaf ears: 4 fall
__ on delivery: 4 cash 7 collect
__ On Down the Road: 4 Ease
one: 3 ace, odd 4 buck, folk, lone, only, sole, unit 5 monad, whole 6 dollar, number, person, single, unique, united 7 pronoun, unified, wee hour 8 separate, singular, solitary, somebody, together 9 connected, undivided 10 dollar bill, individual
and only: 4 lone, sole
at least ~: 3 any 4 some
combining form: 3 mon-, uni- 4 heno-, mono-
ender: 4 self
in French: 2 un 3 une
in German: 3 ein 4 eins
in Italian: 3 uno
in Japanese: 4 ichi
in Latin: 3 una
in Scottish: 3 ane
in Spanish: 3 una, uno
starter: 3 any 4 some 5 every
to Mohs: 4 talc
one __: 4 o' cat 5 to ten 7 another
one __ at a time: 3 day 4 step 5 thing
one __ cat: 3 old
one __ customer: 3 to a
one __ fits all: 4 size
one __ kind: 3 of a
one __ million: 3 in a
one __ or the other: 3 way
one __ other: 5 or the
one __ the books: 3 for
one __ the road: 3 for
one __ time: 3 at a
one __ two..., A: 4 and a
one-__: 4 a-cat, many, shot, spot, star, step, time 5 acter, liner, piece, sided, track 6 bagger, eighty, handed, reeler, suiter 7 worlder
one-__ band: 3 man
one-__ bandit: 5 armed
one-__ car: 5 owner
one-__ chance: 5 in-ten
one-__ deal: 4 shot
one-__ hit: 4 base
one-__ mind: 5 track
one-__ play: 3 act
one-__ punch: 3 two
one-__ shopping: 4 stop
one-__ show: 3 man 5 woman
one-__ street: 3 way
one-__ town: 5 horse
__ one: 3 big, day 4 cold, fast, long, not a, tall 5 admit, loved, nary a, young 6 number, square
__-one: 4 many 5 all-in, ten-to
One __: 4 of Us, Week 5 Night 6 Basket
One __ Apple: 3 Bad
One __ at a Time: 3 Day
One __ a Time: 5 Day at
One __ at McCool's: 5 Night
One __ Baby: 5 for My
One __ Bell to Answer: 4 Less
One __ Beyond: 4 Step
One __ Chance: 4 More
One __ Day: 4 Fine 5 Sweet
One __ Family: 4 Man's
One __ in the Tropics: 5 Night
One __ in Time: 6 Moment
One __ Jump: 6 O'Clock
One __ land...: 4 if by
One __ Mind: 5 Track
One __ Move: 5 False
One __ My Baby: 3 for
One __ Night: 4 More 6 Lonely, Summer
One __ of Venus: 5 Touch
One __ or two?: 4 lump
One __ Over the Cuckoo's Nest: 4 Flew
One __ Photo: 4 Hour
One __, The: 5 I Love
One __ the Heart: 4 From
One __ to Live: 4 Life
One, __, Three: 3 Two
One-__ Jacks: 4 Eyed
One-__ vitamins: 4 a-Day
__ One: 3 Act 4 Bank, Holy, Wild 5 Fiber, One on
one-a-__: 3 cat
one-acter: 4 play
O'Neal: 4 Ryan, Shaq 5 Tatum 7 Patrick 9 Shaquille
O'Neal, Ryan: 5 actor
film: Barry Lyndon (1975)
Chances Are (1989)
The Driver (1978)
Irreconcilable Differences (1984)
Love Story (1970)
Nickelodeon (1976)
Paper Moon (1973)
So Fine (1981)
What's Up, Doc? (1972)
Wild Rovers (1971)
Zero Effect (1998)
TV: Peyton Place
O'Neal, Shaquille
milieu: 5 court
org.: 3 NBA
sport: 10 basketball
O'Neal, Tatum: 7 actress
film: The Bad News Bears (1976)
Nickelodeon (1976)
Paper Moon (1973, AA)
spouse: John McEnroe
one and __: 3 all 4 only
one and a half, combining form: 6 sesqui-
one-armed bandit feature: 4 bell, slot 6 wheels
__ on Ears, A: 7 Chapter
On earth __ is in heaven: 4 as it
one at __: 5 a time
One Bad Apple (1971 song) artist: Osmonds
one-base __: 3 hit
One Basket author: Edna Ferber
One Big Happy dog: 5 Rowdy
one-billionth (prefix): 4 nano-
One Broken Heart for Sale (1963 song) artist: Elvis Presley
one by one, taken: 4 each 6 apiece
one-celled organism: 4 alga 5 ameba 6 amoeba
one-D: 6 linear
one day __ time: 3 at a
One Day at a Time (CBS sitcom)
cast: Valerie Bertinelli (Barbara Cooper)
Bonnie Franklin (Ann Romano)
Pat Harrington Jr. (Dwayne Schneider)
Mackenzie Phillips (Julie Cooper)
One Day of the Year, The author: Alan Seymour
one-dimensional: 6 linear
One-Dimensional Man author: Herbert Marcuse
One Door Away From Heaven author: Dean Koontz
one-eighty: 3 uey 5 U-turn 8 reversal 9 inversion, turnabout
__ one-eighty: 3 do a
One-Eyed Jacks (1961 film)
cast: Marlon Brando, Ben Johnson, Katy Jurado, Karl Malden, Slim Pickens
director: Marlon Brando
One False Move (1992 film)
cast: Bill Paxton, Billy Bob Thornton, Cynda Williams
One Fine Day (1963 song) artist: Chiffons
One Flew Over the Cuckoo's Nest: 4 film 5 novel
author: Ken Kesey
cast: Brad Dourif, Louise Fletcher, Jack Nicholson
director: Milos Forman
One Foot in Heaven (1941 film)
cast: Beulah Bondi, Fredric March, Martha Scott
director: Irving Rapper
One for My Baby
composer: 5 Arlen 6 Mercer
singer: 5 Horne
one-for-one deal: 4 swap, swop 5 trade 6 change
one for the __: 4 road 5 books
...__ one for the Gipper: 3 win
Oneg __: 7 Shabbat
Onega: 3 bay 4 lake 5 river
locale: 6 Russia
One Generation After author: Elie Wiesel
__ on eggs: 4 walk
...one giant __ for mankind: 4 leap
Onegin: 6 Eugene
One Good Woman (1988 song) artist: Peter Cetera
__ one hand: 5 on the
One Happy Island: 5 Aruba
One Heartbeat (1987 song) artist: Smokey Robinson
one-horse __: 4 town
one-horse carriage: 3 gig 5 buggy, sulky
one-hoss shay owner: 6 deacon
One Hour Photo (2002 film)
cast: Connie Nielsen, Dylan Smith, Michael Vartan, Robin Williams
One Hour With You (1932 film)
cast: Maurice Chevalier, Jeanette MacDonald
director: George Cukor, Ernst Lubitsch
One Human Minute author: 3 Lem
One Hundred Men and a Girl (1937 film)
cast: Deanna Durbin, Adolphe Menjou, Leopold Stokowski
director: Henry Koster
One Hundred Poems of Kabir author: Rabindranath Tagore
One Hundred Years of Solitude
author: Gabriel García Márquez
Oneida: 4 lake 5 tribe 6 Indian 7 Amerind 8 language 9 Iroquoian
ally: 6 Cayuga, Mohawk, Seneca 8 Onondaga 9 Tuscarora

cousin: 4 Erie
locale: 7 New York
One I Gave My Heart to, The (1997 song) artist: Aaliyah
O'Neill: 2 Ed 3 Tip 4 Oona 6 Eugene 8 Jennifer
O'Neill, Ed: 5 actor
film: K-9 (1989)
Lucky Numbers (2000)
TV: Married...With Children
O'Neill, Eugene: 6 writer 8 Nobelist
daughter: 4 Oona
forte: 4 play 5 drama
work: Ah, Wilderness!
All God's Chillun Got Wings
Anna Christie
Beyond the Horizon
Bound East for Cardiff
Days Without End
Desire Under the Elms
The Emperor Jones
The Great God Brown
The Hairy Ape
The Haunted
Homecoming
Hughie
The Hunted
The Iceman Cometh
Ile
In the Zone
Lazarus Laughed
Long Day's Journey Into Night
The Long Voyage Home
Marco Millions
A Moon for the Misbegotten
The Moon of the Caribbees
Mourning Becomes Electra
The Rope
Strange Interlude
A Touch of the Poet
O'Neill, Jennifer: 7 actress
film: The Carey Treatment (1972)
The Innocent (1976)
Rio Lobo (1970)
Such Good Friends (1971)
Summer of '42 (1971)
O'Neill, Oona spouse: Charles Chaplin
One I Love, The (1987 song) artist: R.E.M.
one-in-a-million: 4 rare 6 choice, superb, unique 7 special, unusual 8 peerless, singular, uncommon 9 a cut above, matchless, priceless 10 at a premium, hard to find, inimitable, invaluable, phenomenal, remarkable
One in a Million (1936 film)
cast: Don Ameche, Sonja Henie, Adolphe Menjou
One in a Million (1957 song) artist: Platters
oneiromancy: 10 divination
subject: 5 dream 6 vision 9 nightmare
oneiromancy subject: 5 dream
One Is a Lonely Number (1972 film)
cast: Janet Leigh, Monte Markham, Trish Van Devere
One Is Enough author: Flora Nwapa
One L author: Scott Turow
One Less Bell to Answer (1970 song)
artist: Fifth Dimension
One Life to Live: 4 soap 9 soap opera
network: ABC
one-liner: 3 gag 4 jest, joke, quip 9 sound bite, witticism
response: 4 ha-ha
one-liners, quick with: 5 witty
One-L lama poet: 4 Nash
One Lonely Night (1985 song) artist: REO Speedwagon
One Magic Christmas (1985 film)
cast: Harry Dean Stanton, Mary Steenburgen
one-man __: 4 band, show
One man's ___...: 4 meat
One man's __ is another man's
Persian: 4 Mede
One Man's Family: 9 radio show
One Man's San Francisco author: 4 Caen
One Man's Way (1964 film)
cast: Veronica Cartwright, Diana Hyland, Don Murray
One Man Woman...(1974 song) artist: Paul Anka
One Million Years B.C. (1966 film)
cast: John Richardson, Raquel Welch
One Mint Julep (1961 song) artist: Ray Charles
One Minute Man (2001 song) artist: Missy Elliott
One Moment in Time (1988 song)
artist: Whitney Houston
One More Chance (1995 song) artist: Notorious B.I.G.
One More Night (1985 song) artist: Phil Collins
One More Try (song) artist: George Michael, Timmy -T-
__ on empty: 7 running
One must __ live: 5 eat to
oneness: 5 unity, whole 7 harmony 8 sameness 9 unanimity 10 solidarity
One never knows, __?: 5 do one
One Night (1958 song) artist: Elvis Presley
One Night at McCool's (2001 film)
cast: Matt Dillon, John Goodman, Paul Reiser, Liv Tyler
One Night in the Tropics (1940 film)
cast: Bud Abbott, Lou Costello, Allan Jones
One Note __: 5 Samba
__ One Note: 6 Johnny
one o' __: 3 cat
one of __: 5 a kind
One of __: 4 Ours
One of __ days...: 5 these
one-of-a-kind: 6 unique 10 unexampled
One of a Kind (1973 song) artist: Spinners
One of Ours author: Willa Cather
One of These Nights (1975 song)
artist: Eagles
__ One of Those Things: 4 Just
__ One of Us: 7 Neither
One of Us (1995 song) artist: Joan Osborne
one old __: 3 cat
__ one on: 3 tie
one-on-one
participant: 5 tutee, tutor 6 dueler
One on One (1977 film)
cast: Robby Benson, Annette O'Toole, G.D. Spradlin
One on One (1983 song) artist: Hall and Oates
Oneonta: 4 city, town
locale: 7 New York
one or the __: 5 other
__ one over on: 4 slip
one-percent alternative: 4 skim
One Potato, Two Potato (1964 film)
cast: Barbara Barrie, Bernie Hamilton, Richard Mulligan
__ on equity: 6 return
oner: 4 lulu 5 beaut, dilly, doozy 8 rara avis, rare bird, standout 9 humdinger, nonpareil
__ one red cent: 3 not
onerous: 4 hard 5 grave, harsh, heavy, hefty, rough, tough 6 leaden, severe, taxing, thorny, tiring, trying, uphill 7 arduous, galling, irksome, painful, weighty 8 crushing, exacting, grievous, grinding, grueling, pressing, tiresome, toilsome 9 demanding, difficult, excessive, herculean, laborious, merciless, ponderous, strenuous, vexatious 10 burdensome, cumbersome, enervating, exhausting, formidable, oppressive, overtaxing
make ~: 3 tax
not ~: 4 easy 5 light
ones
column next to ~: 4 tens
the ~ here: 5 these
the ~ there: 5 those
unnamed ~: 4 they
__ one's act together: 3 get
__ one's all: 4 give
__ one's arm: 5 twist
__ one's back on: 4 turn
__ one's belt: 5 under 7 tighten
__ one's blessings: 5 count
__ one's bluff: 4 call
__ one's brain: 4 pick, rack
__ one's breath: 4 save 5 catch, under, waste
__ one's breath away: 4 take
__ one's bridges: 4 burn
__ one's cap for: 3 set
__ one's cards on the table: 3 lay, put
__ one's cards right: 4 play
__ one's case: 4 make
__ one's chin up: 4 keep
__ one's chops: 4 bust, lick
__ one's clock: 5 clean
__ one's cool: 4 blow, keep
__ one's door: 5 lay at
__ one's ducks in a row: 3 get
__ one's dues: 3 pay
__ one's ear: 4 bend
__ one's ears: 4 up to
__ one's elbows: 4 up to
__ oneself: 5 all by 6 beside, forget
oneself, by: 9 alone. solo
__ oneself go: 3 let
__ oneself of: 5 avail
__ oneself scarce: 4 make
__ oneself thin: 6 spread
__ oneself to: 4 help
__ oneself together: 4 pull
__ one's eye: 5 catch
__ one's eye on: 4 have
__ one's eyes: 4 open
__ one's eyes on: 3 lay, set 5 feast
__ one's eyes open: 4 keep, with
__ one's eyes out: 3 cry
__ one's eyes over: 3 run
__ one's eyes peeled: 4 keep
__ one's eyes to: 4 shut
__ one's eyeteeth on: 3 cut
__ one's face: 4 show 5 egg on, stuff
__ one's feathers: 6 ruffle
__ one's feed: 3 off
__ one's feet: 4 drag 5 lay at
__ one's finger on: 3 lay, put
__ one's fingers: 5 cross
__ one's fingers crossed: 4 have, keep
__ one's foot down: 3 put
__ one's foot in it: 3 put
__ one's foot in the door: 3 get
__ One's for You: 4 This
__ one's goat: 3 get
__ one's goose: 4 cook
__ one's ground: 4 hold 5 stand
__ one's guard: 3 off
__ one's guts: 5 spill
__ one's hackles up: 3 get
__ one's hair: 4 curl, tear 5 get in
__ one's hair down: 3 let
__ one's hair out: 4 tear
__ one's hand: 3 tip, try 4 show 5 force
__ one's hands: 3 off 5 sit on
__ one's hands of: 3 rub 4 wash
__ one's hand to: 4 turn
__ one's hash: 6 settle
__ one's hat: 5 under
__ one's hat in the ring: 5 throw
__ one's hat off to: 4 take
__ one's head: 4 go to, hide, keep, lose, over, turn 5 shake
__ one's head above water: 4 keep
__ one's head off: 4 snap
__ one's heart: 4 from 5 break, cross, steal
__ one's heart on: 3 set
__ one's heart out: 3 cry, eat
__ one's heart set on: 4 have
__ one's heart to: 4 lose
__ one's heels: 4 cool, drag, show 5 nip at
__ one's hide: 3 tan
__ one's high horse: 5 get on 6 get off
__ one's horses: 4 hold
one-shot __: 4 deal
__ one's house in order: 3 put, set
one-sided: 6 biased, uneven, unfair, unjust 7 partial, unequal 8 partisan 9 arbitrary 10 ill-matched, prejudiced, unbalanced
one-sidedness: 4 bias 5 slant 9 prejudice
one size __ all: 4 fits
__ one's leave: 4 take
__ one's leg: 4 pull
__ one's legs: 7 stretch
one's level __: 4 best
__ one's lid: 4 flip
__ one's lip: 4 bite, curl 6 button
__ one's lips: 4 pass 5 smack
__ one's loins: 4 gird
__ one's losses: 3 cut
__ one's lot with: 4 cast
__ one's luck: 3 try 4 push
__ one's lucky stars: 5 thank
One small __ for a man...: 4 step
__ one's mark: 4 make
__ one's match: 4 meet
__ one's mind: 4 blow, slip 5 cross 6 change
__ one's mouth water: 4 make
__ one's muscles: 4 flex
__ one's neck: 4 up to 5 break
__ one's neck out: 5 stick
__ one's nerves: 5 get on
__ one's nest: 7 feather
__ one's nose: 5 under 6 follow
__ one's nose at: 5 thumb
__ one's nose clean: 4 keep
__ one's nose in: 3 rub
__ one's nose into: 4 poke
__ one's number: 3 get 4 have
__ one's oar in: 3 put
__ one's oats: 4 feel, know 7 feeling
__ one's old tricks: 4 up to
One (song) artist: Backstreet Boys, Bee Gees, Elton John, Three Dog Night, U2
__ one's onions: 4 know
__ one's own: 4 hold
__ one's own business: 4 mind
one's own, combining form: 7 proprio-
__ one's own heart: 5 after
__ one's own horn: 4 blow, toot
__ one's own mind: 4 know
__ one's own ticket: 5 write
__ one's palm: 5 cross 6 grease
__ one's part: 4 take
__ one's path: 5 cross
__ one's peace: 4 hold, keep
__ one's place: 4 keep, know
__ one's pockets: 4 line
one-spot: 3 ace 4 bill, buck 6 dollar, single 9 greenback
__ one's powder dry: 4 keep
__ one's praises: 4 sing
__ one's punches: 4 pull
__ one's sails: 4 trim
__ one's salt: 5 worth
One's-Self I Sing: 4 poem
author: Walt Whitman
__ one's shirt: 4 lose
__ one's shirt on: 4 keep
__ one's shoes: 4 fill
__ one's shoulder: 5 cry on

__ one's sights on: 3 set
__ one's socks off: 5 knock
__ one's soul: 4 bare
__ one's spleen: 4 vent
__ one's spurs: 4 earn
__ one's stack: 4 blow
__ one's step: 5 watch
__ one's stride: 3 hit
__ one's stuff: 5 strut
__ one's style: 5 cramp
__ one's teeth: 4 bare, grit, show
__ one's teeth into: 3 get 4 sink
__ one's teeth on: 3 cut
one step __ time: 3 at a
one-step: 5 dance
One Step Up (1988 song) artist: Bruce Springsteen
__ Ones, The: 5 Loved 7 Defiant
__ one's thumb: 5 under
__ one's thumbs: 7 twiddle
__ one's thunder: 5 steal
__ one's time: 4 bide, take
__ one's tongue: 4 bite, hold, lose
__ one's top: 4 blow
__ one's tracks: 5 cover
__ one straight: 3 set
one-striper: 3 ens., PFC
__ one's troth: 6 plight
__ one's tune: 6 change
One Sunday Afternoon (1933 film)
  cast: Gary Cooper, Neil Hamilton, Fay Wray
__ one's wagon: 3 fix
__ one's Waterloo: 4 meet
__ one's way: 3 pay 4 come, make, pick, wend
__ one's way clear: 3 see
__ one's ways: 5 set in
One Sweet Day (1995 song)
  artist: Boyz II Men, Mariah Carey
__ one's weight: 4 pull
__ one's weight around: 5 throw
__ one's wheels: 4 spin
__ one's whistle: 3 wet
__ one's wig: 4 flip
__ one's wild oats: 3 sow
__ one's wing: 5 under
__ one's word: 4 keep
__ one's words: 3 eat 5 weigh
__ one's wounds: 4 lick
one that got __, the: 4 away
One That You Love, The (1981 song)
  artist: Air Supply
__ One, The: 4 Wild 5 Brave, Loved, Other 7 Strange
one thing __ time: 3 at a
One Thing Leads to Another (1983 song) artist: Fixx
one-time: 3 old 4 late, past 5 prior 6 bygone, former, whilom 7 earlier, quondam 8 previous 9 erstwhile, preceding
one to __: 3 ten
one to __ on: 4 grow
__ one to grow on: 3 and
One Touch of Venus: 7 musical
  composer: 4 Nash 5 Weill
  Venus in ~: 3 Ava
one-track: 4 mono
  mind: 5 mania 6 hang-up 8 fixation, idée fixe 9 monomania, obsession
One-Trick __: 4 Pony
One True Thing (1998 film)
  cast: William Hurt, Meryl Streep, Renée Zellweger
one-two: 3 hit, jab 4 belt, biff, blow, clip, cuff, slam, slug, sock 5 clout, punch, smack, smash, whomp 6 wallop 8 haymaker, uppercut 10 roundhouse
One, Two, Three (1961 film)
  cast: Horst Buchholz, James Cagney, Arlene Francis, Pamela Tiffin
  director: Billy Wilder
one-up: 3 top 4 best 5 outdo, trump
On Everything author: Hilaire Belloc
one way __ other: 5 or the
one-way __: 6 street
one way or the __: 5 other
One Way Passage (1932 film)
  cast: Kay Francis, Aline MacMahon, William Powell
  director: Tay Garnett
one-way symbol: 5 arrow
one-wheel vehicle: 6 barrow 8 unicycle
One Who Really Loves You, The (1962 song) artist: Mary Wells
One with Nineveh and __: 4 Tyre
one-woman __: 4 show
__-on favorite: 4 odds
__ on Film: 4 Agee
__ on fire: 3 set
__ on Fire: 5 Rooms, Souls 6 Hearts
__ on first?: 4 Who's
On First Looking Into Chapman's Homer author: John Keats
on foot (French): 5 à pied
__ on for size: 3 try
On Glory's Course author: James Purdy
ongoing: 6 extant, living, with us 7 current, growing 8 evolving, marching, underway 9 advancing, open-ended, unfolding 10 continuing, continuous, developing, in progress, successful, unfinished
On Golden Pond (1981 film)
  bird: 4 loon
  cast: Dabney Coleman, Henry Fonda, Jane Fonda, Katharine Hepburn, Doug McKeon
  director: Mark Rydell
Ongole: 3 cow 4 bull 6 bovine, cattle
__ on, Harvest Moon: 5 Shine
__ on Heaven's Door: 7 Knockin'
__ on her fingers...: 5 Rings
On Her Majesty's Secret Service: 4 film 5 novel
  author: Ian Fleming
  cast: George Lazenby, Diana Rigg
  director: 4 Hunt
On His Blindness author: John Milton
__ on horseback: 3 man
__ on Horseback: 6 Beggar, Sailor
ONI
  grp.: 3 USN
  part of ~: 3 Nav., Off. 5 Naval 6 Office
__ on Ice: 4 Soul
Onida: 4 city, town
  locale: 4 S. Dak.
__ on Indolence: 3 Ode
__-o'-nine-tails: 3 cat
__ on investment: 6 return
onion: 4 bulb 6 allium, veggie 7 shallot 9 condiment, vegetable
  cousin: 4 leek 5 chive 6 garlic
  cover: 4 skin
  ender: 4 skin
  martini with an ~: 6 Gibson
  outgrowth: 6 bulbel, bulbil 7 bulblet
  product: 4 ring
onion __: 4 dome, roll 5 rings 6 powder
__ onion: 3 sea 5 green, pearl 7 Bermuda, Spanish, Vidalia
Onion Field, The (1979 film)
  cast: John Savage, Franklyn Seales, James Woods
onions
  partner: 5 liver
  prepare ~: 4 chop, dice 5 mince, sauté
  react to ~: 3 cry 4 weep
onionskin: 5 paper
__ onion soup: 6 French
__ on it: 4 step 5 sleep
__ on it!: 3 Sit
on its __: 3 ear
__-on label: 5 stick
On Liberty author: 4 Mill
onliest: 4 lone 6 unique 8 solitary
on-line
  back ~: 5 fixed
  bookseller: 6 Amazon
  browse ~ without posting: 4 lurk
  choice: 3 AOL
  convenience: 4 link 5 e-mail 6 hookup 7 network 9 interface 10 attachment
  conversation: 2 IM 4 chat
  info: 3 FAQ
  investing service: 6 E-Trade
  marketing: 5 e-tail
  marketplace: 4 eBay
  need: 5 modem
  one ~: 4 user
  publication: 4 e-mag 5 e-book, e-zine
  response to an ~ joke: 3 LOL
  site: 5 forum 9 newsgroup
  VIP: 5 sysop
on-line __: 7 catalog 9 catalogue
__ Online: 7 America
onlooker: 4 seer 6 viewer 7 watcher, witness 8 beholder, observer 9 bystander, sightseer, spectator 10 eyewitness
onlookers: 7 gallery 8 audience 10 attendance
only: 3 all, but, one 4 just, lone, sole 6 at most, barely, hardly, merely, purely, simply, single, solely, unique, wholly 7 totally, utterly 8 entirely, isolated, peerless, separate, singular, solitary, uniquely 9 matchless, unequaled, unrivaled 10 nothing but, unrivalled
only __ in town, the: 4 game
__-only: 4 eyes
Only __: 3 You 5 a Curl, a Rose 7 Sixteen
__ only a bird...: 4 She's
Only a Curl author: Elizabeth Barrett Browning
Only Angels Have Wings (1939 film)
  cast: Jean Arthur, Cary Grant, Rita Hayworth
  director: Howard Hawks
only animal that blushes: 3 man
__ Only a Paper Moon: 3 It's
__ only as directed: 3 use
Only Children author: Alison Lurie
Only Game in Town, The (1970 film)
  cast: Warren Beatty, Elizabeth Taylor
  director: George Stevens
...only God can make __: 5 a tree
__ Only Had a Brain: 3 If I
only have __ for: 4 eyes
__ Only Have Love: 4 If We
Only in America (1963 song) artist: Jay and the Americans
Only in My Dreams (1987 song) artist: Debbie Gibson
__ Only Just Begun: 4 We've
__ Only Live Once: 3 You
__ Only Live Twice: 3 You
Only Love Can Break a Heart (1962 song) artist: Gene Pitney
__-only memory: 4 read
__ Only Money: 3 It's
__ Only Old Once!: 5 You're
Only Sixteen (1976 song) artist: Dr. Hook
Only the Good Die Young (1978 song)
  artist: Billy Joel
Only the Lonely (1991 film)
  cast: James Belushi, John Candy, Maureen O'Hara, Ally Sheedy
  director: Chris Columbus
Only the Lonely (song) artist: Motels, Roy Orbison
Only the Strong Survive (1969 song)
  artist: Jerry Butler
Only Time singer: 4 Enya
Only Wanna Be With You (1995 song)
  artist: Hootie and the Blowfish
Only When I Laugh (1981 film)
  cast: James Coco, Marsha Mason, Kristy McNichol
...only with __ eyes: 5 thine
Only Yesterday (1933 film)
  cast: John Boles, Billie Burke, Margaret Sullavan
Only Yesterday (1975 song) artist: Carpenters
Only You (1994 film)
  cast: Robert Downey Jr., Bonnie Hunt, Marisa Tomei, Billy Zane
  director: Norman Jewison
Only You (song)
  artist: Franck Pourcel's French Fiddles, Hilltoppers, Platters, Ringo Starr
Only you can prevent __ fires: 6 forest
__ on Man, An: 5 Essay
__ on Me: 4 Call, Lean, Take 5 Count
__ on Melancholy: 3 Ode
On Moonlight __: 3 Bay
On My __: 3 Own
__ on My Mind: 6 Always, Gentle 7 Georgia
On My Own (1986 song)
  artist: Michael McDonald, Patti LaBelle
On My Own author: Eleanor Roosevelt
__ on My Pillow: 5 Tears
__ on My Shoulder: 5 Angel
On My Word of Honor (1957 song)
  artist: Platters
on no __: 7 account
On Nothing author: Hilaire Belloc
__ Ono Band: 7 Plastic
on/off __: 6 switch
__ on of hands: 6 laying
Onofredo in English: 8 Humphrey
onomastician's concern: 4 name
onomatopoeic: 6 echoic 9 imitative
  word: 3 bam, pow 4 wham
Onondaga: 5 tribe 6 Indian 7 Amerind 8 language
  ally: 6 Cayuga, Mohawk, Oneida, Seneca 9 Tuscarora
  enemy: 4 Erie
on one's __: 3 ear, own, way 4 feet, mind, part, toes 5 guard, hands, knees 6 mettle, uppers
on one's __ account: 3 own
on one's __ horse: 4 high
on one's __ initiative: 3 own
on one's __ legs: 4 last
__ on one's back: 4 flat
__ on one's escutcheon: 5 a blot
__ on one's face: 3 egg
__ on one's feet: 4 land
__ on one's hands: 3 sit 4 time
on one's high __: 5 horse
__ on one's high horse: 3 get
on one's last __: 4 legs
__ on one's luck: 4 down
__ on one's nerves: 3 get
__ on one's oars: 4 rest
on one's own __: 7 account
__ on one's own two feet: 5 stand
__ on one's shoulder: 3 cry 4 chip
__ on one's toes: 4 step 5 tread
on or __: 5 about
Onorati: 5 Peter
On Our Own (1989 song) artist: Bobby Brown
__ on over: 4 come
Onoway: 4 city, town
  locale: 6 Canada 7 Alberta
Ono, Yoko spouse: John Lennon
on-paper: 8 unproved
__ on parle français: 3 ici
__-on part: 4 walk
__-on patch: 4 iron
on pins and __: 7 needles
__ on Pop: 3 Hop
on-ramp sign: 5 merge
onrush: 4 flow, wave 5 flood, onset,

river, sally, surge, swash **6** deluge, stream **7** cascade, torrent **8** stampede **9** avalanche, onslaught, upwelling **10** outpouring
emotional ~: 5 throe
onrushing: 7 looming, nearing **8** imminent, oncoming, upcoming **9** advancing, impending
__ on rye: 3 ham **4** tuna
Onsager, Lars: 7 chemist **8** Nobelist
On Seeing the Elgin Marbles: 4 poem
author: 5 Keats
__-on sentence: 3 run
onset: 4 dawn, rise **5** birth, get-go, start, storm **6** advent, attack, charge, day one, onrush, source **7** assault, dawning, genesis, kickoff, leadoff, opening **8** exordium, outbreak **9** beginning, first sign, inception, offensive, onslaught **10** aggression, incipience, initiation
__-on shoes: 4 slip
onshore: 4 wind
on short __: 6 notice
onside __: 4 kick
onslaught: 4 raid, rush **5** blitz, onset, sally, storm **6** attack, battle, charge, inroad, onrush, sortie, thrust **7** assault, barrage, battery, offense **8** invasion, violence **9** broadside, incursion, offensive **10** aggression
__ on Sloopy: 4 Hang
__ on Solitude: 3 Ode
on speaking __: 5 terms
onstage
prop: 5 phone, stool
walk ~: 5 enter
__ on strong: 4 come
__ on Sunday: 5 Never
Ont.: 4 prov.
neighbor: 3 Man., Que. **4** Minn.
__ on 34th Street: 7 Miracle
Ontake: 7 volcano
locale: 4 Asia **5** Japan **6** Honshu
__ on tap: 4 beer
Ontario: 4 city, lake, town **8** province
capital: 7 Toronto
city: 4 Ajax **5** Elgin **6** Aurora, Barrie, Dundas, Guelph, Kanata, London, Milton, Nepean, Oshawa, Ottawa, Sarnia, Scugog, Whitby **7** Caledon, Chatham, Grimsby, La Salle, Lincoln, Markham, Orillia, Sudbury, Timmins, Toronto, Vaughan, Welland, Windsor **8** Ancaster, Bradford, Brampton, Cornwall, Fort Erie, Georgina, Hamilton, Kingston, North Bay, Oakville, St. Thomas, Waterloo **9** Brantford, Cambridge, Haldimand, Innisfail, Kitchener, Nanticoke, Newmarket, Owen Sound, Pickering, Stratford, Woodstock **10** Belleville, Brockville, Burlington, Clarington, Cumberland, Gloucester, Thunder Bay, Whitchurch
Indian: 4 Cree **5** Huron **9** Saulteaux
lake: 5 Rainy **6** Simcoe **7** Nipigon
locale: 6 Canada **10** California
neighbor: 4 Erie
river: 5 Trent
school: 4 York **5** Brock, Trent **6** Queen's **7** Ryerson **8** Carleton, Lakehead, McMaster
waterfall: 7 Niagara
__-on-Thames: 6 Henley
on the __: 3 dot, fly, job, lam, run, sly, way **4** ball, beam, cuff, dole, edge, hoof, hook, line, mend, move, nose, outs, rack, road, side, spot, take, town, wane, wing **5** alert, blink, brain, cheap, fence, fritz, house, level, loose, march, money, prowl, rocks, ropes, scene, shelf, skids, table, whole **6** button, carpet, double, inside, market, record, square, street **7** surface
on the __ chance: 3 off
on the __ foot: 5 right, wrong
on the __ hand: 3 one **5** other
on the __ of: 4 edge, part **5** heels, order
on the __ of a dilemma: 5 horns
on the __ of it: 4 face
on the __ of one's tongue: 3 tip
on the __ of the moment: 4 spur
on the __ vive: 3 qui
on the __ wavelength: 4 same
On the __: 4 Road
On the __ hand...: 5 other
On the Avenue (1937 film)
cast: Madeleine Carroll, Alice Faye, Dick Powell
director: Roy Del Ruth
__ on the back: 3 pat **4** a pat
__ on the barrelhead: 4 cash
On the Beach: 4 film **5** novel
author: Nevil Shute
cast: Fred Astaire, Ava Gardner, Gregory Peck
director: Stanley Kramer
__ on the block: 3 put
__ on the Bounty: 6 Mutiny
__ on the cake: 5 icing
__ on the cob: 4 corn
__ on the dog: 3 put
On the double!: 4 ASAP, stat **6** move it
On the Double (1961 film)
cast: Wilfrid Hyde-White, Danny Kaye, Dana Wynter
__ on the draw: 5 quick
__ on the escutcheon: 4 blot
on the face __: 4 of it
__ on the feedbag: 3 put
on-the-fence: 9 undecided **10** irresolute
__-on-the-floor: 4 four
__ on the Floss, The: 4 Mill
__ on the Flying Trapeze, The: 3 Man
__ on the Fourth of July: 4 Born
On the Frontier author: W.H. Auden
__ on the gas: 4 step
On the Good __ Lollipop: 4 Ship
__ on the ground floor: 5 get in, got in
__ on the hand may be...: 5 A kiss
__ on the Hill, The: 4 Fool **5** House **7** Heather
__ on the hog: 4 high
on the horns of a __: 7 dilemma
__ on the Hudson: 6 Castle, Moscow
On the Idle Hill of Summer author: A.E. Housman
__ on the Keys: 6 Kitten
on-the-level: 5 legit **6** square **7** serious
__ on the line: 5 lay it
__ on the market: 4 drug
__ on the money: 5 right
__ on the Moon: 3 Man **5** A Walk, Blood, Shame
__ on the Mount: 6 Sermon
On the Nature of Things author: Lucretius
__ on the Nile: 5 Death
on the off __: 6 chance
on the one __: 4 hand
__ on the Orient Express: 6 Murder
on the other __: 4 hand
on the qui __: 4 vive
On the Radio (1980 song) artist: Donna Summer
__ on the Range: 4 Home
On the Rebound (1961 song) artist: Floyd Cramer
__ on the Rhine: 5 Watch
on the right __: 4 foot
__ on the ritz: 3 put
__ on the Ritz: 6 Puttin'
__ on the River: 6 Rhythm
On the Riviera (1951 film)
cast: Corinne Calvet, Danny Kaye, Gene Tierney
director: Walter Lang
On the Road: 5 novel
author: Jack Kerouac
character: 3 Sal **4** Dean, Inez **8** Paradise
On the Road Again (1980 song) artist: Willie Nelson
__ on the rock: 4 duck
__ on the Rocks: 4 Love
__ on the Roof: 4 Rain **7** Fiddler
__ on the Run: 3 Fox **4** Band, Nuns **5** Woman
__ on the Side: 4 Boys
on-the-spot: 6 snappy **7** instant, present
TV report: 4 nemo
__-on-the-spot: 6 Johnny
on the spur of the __: 6 moment
__ on the stick: 3 get
__ On The Storm: 6 Riders
__ on the street: 3 man
On the Street Where You Live: 4 song **5** novel
artist: Andy Williams, Vic Damone
author: Mary Higgins Clark
songwriter: 5 Loewe **6** Lerner
On the Third Day band: 3 ELO
on the tip of one's __: 6 tongue
On the Town (1949 film)
cast: Betty Garrett, Gene Kelly, Ann Miller, Jules Munshin, Frank Sinatra, Vera-Ellen
director: Stanley Donen, Gene Kelly
__ on the trail: 3 hot
__ on the wall: 7 writing
__ on the Wall: 6 Shadow **7** Flowers
On the Waterfront (1954 film)
cast: Marlon Brando, Lee J. Cobb, Karl Malden, Eva Marie Saint, Rod Steiger
director: Elia Kazan
__ on the Wild Side: 4 Walk **5** A Walk
__ on the Wind: 6 Kisses **7** Written
__ on the wrist: 4 slap
on the wrong __: 4 foot
__ on thick: 5 lay it
__ on thin ice: 7 skating
on this side prefix: 3 cis-
__-on tie: 4 clip
__ on Tight: 4 Hold
Ontkean, Michael: 5 actor
film: Just the Way You Are (1984)
Maid to Order (1987)
Slap Shot (1977)
Willie and Phil (1980)
TV: The Rookies
onto: 3 hep **4** upon, wise **5** aware **7** aware of **8** informed **9** in the know, mindful of
__ on to: 4 glom, hang **5** latch **6** freeze
ontologist's concern: 5 being **7** essence, reality **9** existence
on top __ world: 5 of the
On Top of Old __: 6 Smokey
__-on-Trent: 5 Stoke
__ on Truckin': 4 Keep
onus: 3 job **4** duty, load, slur, task **5** blame, fault, guilt **6** burden, charge, weight **7** incubus **9** liability, millstone **10** dead weight, imposition, obligation, oppression
__ on Venice: 3 Ode
__ on Walkin': 4 Keep
onward: 5 ahead, along, forth, going, hence **6** beyond, moving **7** forward, in front
combining form: 5 proso-
move ~: 2 go **4** pass **5** impel, shlep **6** schlep **7** advance, schlepp **8** progress **9** go forward
__ on water: 4 walk
On Wenlock Edge author: A.E. Housman
__ on wheels: 5 meals
__ on wood: 5 knock
__ on words: 4 play
__ on you!: 5 Shame
__ on You: 4 High **5** Crush, Stuck
On Your __: 4 Toes
__ on your life!: 3 Not
On your mark! follower: 6 get set
__ on Your Mind: 3 Man **5** What's
On Your Toes: 7 musical
songwriter: 4 Hart **7** Rodgers
onyx: 3 gem **5** black **6** marble **8** gemstone **10** chalcedony
decoration: 5 cameo
relative: 3 jet **4** inky **5** ebony, raven, sable, sooty
slipper: 5 shell **8** seashell
starter: 4 sard
white ~ gem: 8 sardonyx
__ onyx: 4 blue **7** Mexican
Onyx song: Slam (1993)
__-oo: 6 toodle
OO __: 5 gauge
oodles: 3 lot, ton **4** a lot, lots, many, much, peck, pile, raft, tons, wads **5** heaps, loads, scads **6** hoards, myriad, plenty, scores **7** numbers **8** jillions **9** a whole lot, multitude, truckload
of: 5 lotsa **6** divers, myriad, umteen, untold **7** copious, profuse, umpteen **8** abundant, manifold, numerous, umpsteen **9** bountiful, countless, quite a few
oof: 4 cash, gelt, jack, kail, kale, loot, peag, pelf **5** bills, bread, bucks, dough, funds, lucre, money, moola, mopus, pesos, rhino, sewan **6** dinero, do-re-mi, mammon, mazuma, moolah, seawan, silver, specie, wampum, wealth **7** cabbage, capital, dollars, lettuce, scratch, shekels **8** bankroll, cold cash, currency, hard cash, smackers **9** banknotes, frogskins, long green, simoleons **10** greenbacks, green stuff
ooh: 3 wow **4** gosh **5** golly
ooh __: 4 la la
ooh and __: 3 aah
Ooh Baby Baby (1978 song) artist: Linda Ronstadt
O-o-h Child (1970 song) artist: Five Stairsteps
Ooh! My Soul (1958 song) artist: Little Richard
ooid: 4 oval **5** ovate **9** egg-shaped
Oola boyfriend: 3 Oop **5** Alley
oolite: 7 mineral
oology subject: 4 eggs
oolong: 3 tea **8** beverage
Oom __: 4 Paul
oom-pah instrument: 4 tuba
oomph: 2 go **3** pep, vim, zip **4** dash, élan, life, zeal, zest, zing **5** ardor, flair, verve, vigor **6** energy, fervor, pizazz, spirit **7** pizzazz **8** vitality **9** animation, sex appeal **10** enthusiasm, get up and go
Oona: 6 O'Neill **7** Chaplin
father: 6 Eugene
Ooo Baby Baby (1965 song) artist: Miracles
Oola's boyfriend: 3 Oop **5** Alley
__-oop: 5 alley
Oop __ Sh'Bam: 3 Bop
oopak: 3 tea **8** black tea
Oop, Alley kingdom: 3 Moo
oops: 5 sorry **6** pardon **8** excuse me, pardon me
Oops!: 4 oh oh, uh-oh **6** oh dear
Oort __: 5 cloud
oospore: 3 egg
ooze: 3 goo, mud **4** drip, drop, emit, flow, glop, gook, guck, gunk, leak, mire, muck, seep, silt, weep, well **5** bleed, drain, exude, fluid, issue, leach, slime, spirt, spurt, sweat **6** effuse, escape, filter, sludge, strain **7** dribble, exudate,

seep out, trickle **8** alluvium, overflow, perspire **9** discharge, exudation, percolate
oozing: 5 moist, seepy, undry **9** emanation
oozy: 4 damp, ropy **5** gooey, gunky, mucky, muddy, ropey, slimy, undry **6** drippy, sludgy **7** squishy, wettish **8** swampish
op __: 3 art
op. __: 3 cit.
__ op: 5 photo
__-op: 3 pre **4** coin, post
Opa-__, FL: 5 Locka
opah: 4 fish **8** moonfish
opal: 3 gem **7** girasol, hyalite, mineral **8** gemstone, girasole
ender: 3 ine
like an ~: 5 milky **6** porous
month: 3 Oct. **7** October
__ opal: 4 fire **5** black, noble
opalescence: 4 glow **5** gleam, sheen **6** luster **7** shimmer **8** lambency **10** brilliance, effulgence, refulgence
opalescent: 5 milky **6** pearly **7** whitish **10** iridescent
opaleye: 4 fish
opaline: 7 whitish
opaque: 3 dim **4** dark, dull, hazy **5** milky, mirky, misty, muddy, murky, thick **6** cloudy, obtuse, turbid **7** muddied, obscure, unclear **8** abstruse, darkened **9** adumbrate, difficult, tenebrous **10** lusterless
combining form: 5 glauc- **6** glauco-
op art pattern: 5 moiré
Opatoshu: 5 David
O patria mia: 4 aria
opera: 4 Aïda
op. cit.: 8 notation
cousin: 4 ibid.
part of ~: 5 opere **6** citato
OPEC: 4 bloc, pact **6** cartel
concern: 3 oil
delegate: 5 Iraki, Irani, Iraqi
headquarters: 6 Vienna
leader: 4 amir, emir **5** ameer, emeer
member: 3 UAE **4** Arab, Irak, Iran, Iraq **5** Katar, Libya, Qatar **6** Kuwait **7** Algeria, Nigeria **9** Indonesia, Venezuela **11** Saudi Arabia
part: 3 Org. **9** Countries, Exporting, Petroleum
unit: 3 bbl. **4** drum **6** barrel
vessel: 5 oiler
Op-Ed __: 4 page
Op-Ed piece: 5 essay **6** column **7** article
Opel: 3 car **4** auto **10** automobile
like an ~: 6 German
model: 2 GT **5** Astra, Corsa, Manta, Omega, Tigra **6** Kadett, Vectra **7** Calibra
Opelika: 4 city, town
locale: 7 Alabama
Opelousas: 4 city, town
locale: 9 Louisiana
open: 3 gap, pop, tap **4** airy, ajar, bare, fair, free, gape, lacy, lead, moot, naif, rent, slit, tear, undo, vent, wide **5** agape, begin, burst, clear, crack, force, frank, jimmy, known, lance, naive, naked, on tap, overt, plain, split, start, unbar, unbox, uncap, unhid, unpeg, unpin, untie, unzip **6** broach, bust in, candid, direct, expand, free up, gaping, honest, in view, kick in, launch, let out, liable, mellow, on deck, patent, pierce, public, reveal, ring in, spread, trusty, turn on, unbolt, uncork, unfold, unfurl, unlock, unroll, unseal, unshut, unstop, unwrap, usable, vacant **7** artless, at issue, blatant, break in, cleared, convene, dubious, evident, exposed, glaring, kick off, lead off, natural, obvious, outside, outward, plenary, release, rolling, rupture, sincere, suspect, to be had, unblock, unclose, uncover, unlatch, untaken, up-front, useable, vacated, visible, yawning **8** amenable, apparent, break out, clear-cut, commence, disclose, doubtful, exoteric, explicit, extended, flagrant, flexible, get going, initiate, innocent, lacerate, manifest, outdoors, outgoing, passable, puncture, revealed, spacious, truthful, unartful, unbarred, unbiased, unbolted, unbuckle, unburden, unclosed, uncorked, unfasten, unfolded, unfurled, unhidden, unlidded, unlocked, unsealed, unveiled **9** agreeable, ambiguous, available, barefaced, come apart, debatable, dehiscent, disclosed, downright, dubitable, enter upon, equivocal, expansive, extensive, guileless, impartial, ingenuous, institute, navigable, objective, operative, originate, outspoken, penetrate, perforate, permitted, receptive, set up shop, spread out, unblocked, uncertain, uncovered, uncrowded, undecided, unguarded, unimpeded, unsettled, unstopped, ventilate, veracious, welcoming **10** aboveboard, accessible, come undone, flat-footed, forthright, free-spoken, from the hip, hospitable, inaugurate, in question, observable, obtainable, on the level, point-blank, responsive, unfastened, unhindered, unobstruct, unoccupied, unreserved, unresolved, unreticent, unshrouded, up for grabs, up in the air, ventilated
air: 6 nature **7** outside
and shut: 5 clear, plain, vivid **6** cogent, patent, simple **7** evident, express, obvious **8** apparent, distinct, explicit, manifest, palpable **9** graspable **10** spelled out
be ~: 4 tell **5** level **9** come clean
bring into the ~: 3 air **4** vent **7** freshen, publish **9** make known, talk about, ventilate
combining form: 6 phaner- **7** phanero-
cut ~: 4 slit, torn **5** lance
don't ~: 4 pass, shut **5** close, stick
door: 6 access, entrée
doors for: 3 aid **4** ease, help **6** assist **10** facilitate
ender: 4 work **6** handed **7** hearted
force ~: 3 pry **4** bust, rift **5** burst, crack, force, jimmy, lever **7** crowbar
for consideration: 4 iffy **8** doubtful, not final **9** dependent, provisory, tentative, uncertain, undecided, unsettled **10** contingent, indefinite
in the ~: 5 overt, unhid **7** outdoor, visible **8** apparent **10** aboveboard
lay ~: 4 tell **6** expose, unveil **7** uncover **8** endanger
not ~: 3 sly **4** shut **6** closed
one's eyes: 4 wake **5** awake, edify, waken **6** awaken
one's mouth: 4 blab, talk **5** speak
out: 5 widen **6** expand, spread **7** broaden
sesame: 6 ticket **8** password **10** hocus-pocus
space: 5 glade **8** clearing, headroom **9** clearance, elbowroom
the door for: 5 let go, let in, usher **6** accept, let out
the eyes of: 5 edify **7** educate **8** disabuse, illumine
to attack: 9 unguarded **10** undefended, vulnerable
to new ideas: 7 pliable **8** amenable, tolerant **9** acceptive, sensitive **10** hospitable, responsive
up: 4 stab, tell, thaw **5** admit, bloom, shoot, slash, unbar, widen, wound **6** broach **7** broaden, pioneer, profess, release, uncover **8** unfreeze **9** originate, spread out **10** accelerate
wide: 4 gape, yawn **5** agape
wide ~: 5 agape **6** gaping **7** yawning **9** unlimited **10** undefended, vulnerable
with ~ arms: 6 warmly **8** friendly **9** cordially **10** graciously
with eyes ~: 4 wary **5** awake, leery **10** suspicious
wrench ~: 3 rip **4** rive, tear **5** smash, split **6** sunder
open __: 3 air, bar, die, sea **4** book, call, door, plan, shop **5** chain, cover, field, flash, frame, house, order, quote, sight, space, stock, union **6** dating, letter, market, policy, quotes, season, secret, sesame, stance, string, system **7** account, circuit, cluster, couplet, housing, primary, trailer
open __ of worms: 4 a can
open-__: 3 air, cut, end, pit, web **4** cast, eyed **5** ended, faced, shelf, sided, stack **6** hearth, letter, minded **7** hearted, mouthed
open-__ policy: 4 door
open-__ sandwich: 5 faced
__ open: 3 lay
__-open: 4 wide
Open: 4 sign
Open __: 4 Arms, City, wide **5** House **6** Season, sesame
Open __ Heart: 4 Your
open-air: 7 outdoor, outside **8** alfresco **10** out-of-doors
open-and-shut __: 4 case
__ open arms: 4 with
Open Arms (1982 song) artist: Journey
Open Boat, The author: Stephen Crane
Open Conspiracy, The author: H.G. Wells
open-door: 6 public **9** available **10** accessible, responsive
Open Door Policy proponent: 3 Hay
opened: 4 ajar **7** abroach
just ~: 3 new **8** brand-new
open-ended: 5 broad **7** ongoing **8** optional **9** undefined
opener: 5 intro, start **6** lead-in
__ opener: 3 can, eye **4** door
__ openers: 3 for
open-eyed: 5 alert **6** astare **7** wakeful **8** vigilant, watchful
open 9 __ 5: 3 'til
openhanded: 6 giving, lavish **7** liberal, profuse **8** generous **9** unselfish **10** altruistic, munificent
move: 4 cuff, slap, swat **5** smack, spank, whack
open-hearted: 4 kind, open, warm **5** frank **6** candid, giving, honest, humane, kindly **7** liberal, sincere **10** benevolent, forthright
Open House author: Theodore Roethke
opening: 3 cut, gap, maw **4** dawn, door, exit, hole, leak, nook, pore, rent, rift, room, slit, slot, tear, time, vent, view, void **5** break, chink, cleft, crack, debut, first, hatch, intro, mouth, niche, onset, Part I, proem, space, split, spout, start **6** breach, cavity, cranny, eyelet, lacuna, opener, outlet, outset, pocket, portal, recess, refuge, source, window **7** crevice, fissure, ingress, initial, keyhole, kickoff, leadoff, orifice, passage, premier, rupture, vacancy, vacuity **8** aperture, big break, occasion, original, overture, preamble, premiere, puncture **9** beginning, inception, launching, threshold **10** initiation, initiatory, interspace, interstice, passageway
combining form: 5 -trema
grand ~: 5 debut **7** kickoff **8** premiere
have an ~ for: 4 need
jacket ~: 4 slit
staff ~: 3 job **4** slot **7** vacancy **8** position
word: 5 hello **7** welcome **8** greeting **10** salutation
words: 5 intro **6** prolog **7** prelude **8** foreword, preamble, prologue
opening __: 3 day **5** night
__ opening: 5 grand **7** winning
__-opening: 3 eye
opening-night
attendee: 6 critic **8** reviewer
memento: 4 stub **6** ticket
Opening Night (1977 film)
cast: John Cassavetes, Ben Gazzara, Gena Rowlands
director: John Cassavetes
openly: 5 fully **6** simply **7** frankly, naively, plainly, readily **8** brazenly, candidly, directly, honestly, in public, publicly, straight, wantonly **9** artlessly, blatantly, naturally, willingly **10** aboveboard, face-to-face, flagrantly, in full view, point-blank
oppose ~: 4 deft **5** cross, decry
open-minded: 8 amenable, catholic, tolerant, unbiased **9** impartial, receptive, unslanted **10** hospitable
open-mouthed: 4 agog **5** agape, agasp, in awe **6** amazed, gaping **7** shocked **8** startled **9** astounded, awestruck
leave ~: 3 awe, wow **4** stun **5** amaze **8** surprise
stand ~: 4 gape, gawk, ogle **5** stare **6** goggle
openness: 4 risk **6** candor **7** honesty, naiveté **8** veracity **9** liability, sincerity
open one's __: 4 eyes
open-sandwich topper: 5 gravy
Open Season (1996 film)
cast: Helen Shaver, Rod Taylor, Robert Wuhl
director: Robert Wuhl
open sesame sayer: 3 Ali **4** Baba
Open thine eyes __: 6 eterne
open weave fabric: 4 leno, mesh **5** scrim
Open wide!: 5 say ah
response: 3 aah
Open Window, The author: 4 Saki
openwork: 3 net **4** lace, mesh **5** grill **6** grille **7** lattice
do ~: 3 tat
Open Your Heart (1986 song) artist: Madonna
opera: 3 art **4** play, song **5** drama, genre, music, piece **9** singspiel
American ~ role: 4 Bess **5** Amahl, Porgy
cheer: 5 brava, bravo
comic ~: 6 bouffe
comic ~ singer: 5 buffo
division: 3 act **5** scene
extra, for short: 4 supe
horse ~: 5 drama, oater **7** western
house: 5 odeon, odeum **7** theater, theatre **10** auditorium
house section: 3 row **4** loge, tier
NYC ~ house: 3 Met
omnia: 4 body **5** whole **6** corpus, oeuvre **8** entirety **10** collection
opener: 4 Act I **6** act one
passage: 4 aria **5** scena **6** arioso
performer: 4 bass, diva **5** basso, mezzo, tenor **6** chorus, etoile **7** soprano **8** baritone **10** coloratura
perform in an ~: 4 sing **6** intone **7** belt out **8** vocalize

prince: 4 Igor
princess: 4 Aïda 8 Turandot
prop: 5 lance, spear
set in Egypt: 4 Aïda
slave: 4 Aïda
soap ~: 5 drama, story 6 series 9 imbroglio
opera __: 3 hat 5 buffa, glass, house, seria 6 bouffe, window 7 glasses
__ opera: 4 soap 5 comic, grand, horse, light, space 6 ballad, number 7 chamber
opéra __: 6 bouffe 7 comique
operable: 4 live 5 going 6 usable 7 running, working 10 functional
operand, having one: 5 unary
operandi
modus ~: 3 way 5 means 6 method, recipe 7 process 9 procedure, technique
Opera of Operas composer: 4 Arne
__ operas: 5 Savoy
operate: 2 do, go 3 hum, man, ply, run, use 4 hold, keep, play, roll, tick, work 5 drive, pilot, steer, treat, wield 6 behave, direct, employ, handle, manage 7 conduct, perform 8 engineer, exercise, function, maneuver, navigate, transact 10 manipulate
__-operated: 3 gas 4 coin 6 recoil
operatic: 5 vocal 7 lyrical 10 theatrical
operating: 5 alive, in use 6 active 7 engaged, rolling, running, working 10 performing
computer ~ system: 4 Unix 5 MSDOS 7 Windows
not ~: 3 off
operating __: 4 room 6 income, system
__ operating system: 4 disk
operation: 3 job, use 5 doing, force, usage 6 action, affair, effort, system 7 mission, process, project, running, surgery, working 8 activity, campaign, exercise, function, maneuver, practice 9 execution, mechanism, procedure, treatment 10 dissection, employment, enterprise, management
in ~: 5 going 6 moving 7 engaged, running 9 operative
loc.: 2 ER, OR
police ~: 4 raid 5 front, sting
sting ~: 3 con 4 trap 5 bunco, setup
__ operation: 5 unary 6 binary, covert, parity 7 Boolean, Lempert, ternary
Operation Crossbow (1965 film)
cast: Trevor Howard, Sophia Loren, George Peppard
Operation Dumbo Drop elephant: 3 Tai
Operation Overlord
when ~ began: 4 D-day
Operation Pacific (1951 film)
cast: Ward Bond, Patricia Neal, John Wayne
Operation Petticoat (1959 film)
cast: Tony Curtis, Cary Grant, Dina Merrill
director: Blake Edwards
operations
base of ~: 7 station
like some ~: 6 covert 8 hush-hush 10 undercover, under wraps
Operation Thunderbolt (1977 film)
cast: Assaf Dayan, Klaus Kinski
director: Menahem Golan
operative: 3 key, spy 4 aide, live, open 5 agent, alive, ninja, spook, valid 6 living, shamus, usable, worker 7 crucial, helpful, in force, running, staffer, useable, working 8 workable 9 detective, effective, important 10 accessible, functional, prevailing
operator: 4 doer, user 5 wheel 6 con man, driver, robber 7 employe 8 big wheel, employee, merchant, swindler
__ operator: 6 linear 7 logical
__-operator: 5 owner
__ Operator: 6 Smooth
Operator (1975 song) artist: Manhattan Transfer
opere __: 6 citato
operetta: 5 music
composer: 5 Lehár 7 Gilbert 8 Sullivan
operose: 4 hard 6 boring, taxing, uphill 7 arduous, labored, tedious 8 tiresome, toilsome 9 difficult, laborious, strenuous
Ophelia: 4 Dane, moon
brother: 7 Laertes
love: 6 Hamlet
planet: 6 Uranus
ophidian: 3 asp 5 adder, krait, snake 6 animal, uraeus 7 reptile
ophidiophobe fear: 6 snakes
ophiology: 7 science
study: 6 snakes
ophite: 7 mineral
ophthalmic: 5 optic 6 ocular, visual 7 sensory 9 sensorial
ophthalmologist: 9 eye doctor
concern: 4 iris 6 cornea, retina
need: 6 eyecup
ophthalmo- relative: 5 oculo-
Ophuls: 3 Max 6 Marcel
opiate: 4 drug 6 codeia 7 anodyne, codeine 8 narcotic, sedative 9 soporific 10 anesthetic
Opie: 4 Alan 6 Taylor
aunt: 3 Bee
father: 4 Andy
portrayer: 3 Ron 5 Ronny 6 Howard
opine: 3 say 4 aver 5 guess, voice 6 ideate 7 comment, observe, suggest, suppose, surmise 8 look upon
opinion: 3 say 4 idea, mind, side, take, view 5 guess, input, say-so, slant, stand, voice 6 advice, belief, notion, regard, theory, thesis 7 comment, feeling, surmise, theorem, thought, verdict 8 analysis, attitude, estimate, judgment, position, reaction 9 criticism, editorial, postulate, sentiment, suspicion, utterance, viewpoint 10 assessment, assumption, conception, conclusion, conjecture, contention, conviction, estimation, evaluation, hypothesis, impression, persuasion, reflection, standpoint
be of the ~: 4 feel 5 think 6 reckon 7 believe
difference of ~: 4 rift, spat, tiff 5 break, clash 7 dispute, quarrel 8 argument, squabble, variance
give an ~: 3 say 5 argue, speak, state, voice 6 assert, remark 7 chime in, observe 8 maintain, propound
good ~: 6 esteem, regard 7 respect 8 approval, prestige 10 reputation
have another ~: 4 vary 6 differ 7 deviate, dissent, diverge 8 disagree
high ~: 6 regard 7 respect 9 reverence 10 admiration
in French: 4 avis
offer an ~: 5 guide 6 advise 7 counsel, suggest 8 point out 9 recommend
of the same ~: 3 one 5 joint 6 agreed, united 8 in accord 9 concerted, unanimous, undivided 10 like-minded
piece: 4 Op-Ed 5 essay, tract 6 thesis 8 critique
public ~ gauge: 4 poll 6 survey 9 straw poll
seek the ~ of: 3 ask 4 talk 5 refer 6 call in, confer, huddle, parlay, powwow, turn to 7 consult 9 negotiate, touch base 10 brainstorm
unorthodox ~: 6 heresy 7 dissent 9 blasphemy, sacrilege
__ opinion: 6 public 8 matter of
opinionated: 5 bossy, cocky, vocal 6 biased 7 adamant, bigoted 8 cocksure, dogmatic, hard-line, indocile, locked in, obdurate, one-sided, positive, stubborn, vehement 9 arbitrary, assertive, conceited, obstinate, officious, pigheaded, pragmatic 10 dogmatical
O Pioneers!: 5 novel
author: Willa Cather
character: 3 Lou 4 Carl, Emil, Ivar 5 Marie, Nelse, Oscar, Sadie, Signa 6 Stella
opium: 4 drug 7 anodyne 8 hypnotic, laudanum, narcotic, nepenthe, sedative 9 calmative, soporific 10 painkiller, palliative
Opium: 5 scent 9 fragrance
Opium __: 3 War
Oporto: 4 city, port, town
city near ~: 6 Lisbon
locale: 6 Europe 8 Portugal
river: 5 Douro
opossum: 5 yapok 6 animal 9 marsupial
female: 4 jill
male: 4 jack
relative: 4 euro 5 bilbi, bilby, koala 6 numbat, wombat 7 bettong, dasyure, wallaby 8 kangaroo, wallaroo 9 bandicoot, phalanger
young: 4 joey
__ opossum: 5 mouse, water 6 murine
opp.: 3 ant. 8 opposite
O.P.P. (1991 song) artist: Naughty by Nature
Oppenheimer, J. Robert: 9 physicist
opponent: 3 con, foe 4 anti 5 enemy, match, rival 6 bandit, bidder, player 7 nemesis 8 litigant 9 adversary, assailant, candidate, dark horse, disputant, ill-wisher 10 antagonist, challenger, competitor, contestant
opportune: 3 apt, fit, pat 4 good, meet, ripe 5 happy, lucky, right 6 golden, proper, timely 7 apropos, fitting, helpful, hopeful 8 suitable 9 expedient, favorable, fortunate, well-timed 10 auspicious, convenient, felicitous, fortuitous, propitious, prosperous, seasonable, time-saving
time: 4 shot 6 chance 8 occasion
opportunist: 3 cad 4 user 5 cheat, knave, rogue 6 rascal 9 cardsharp, charlatan, scoundrel 10 blackguard, black sheep, scapegrace
opportunistic: 7 selfish, worldly 8 ulterior 10 exploitive
opportunity: 2 go 3 way 4 luck, risk, room, shot, time, turn 5 break, crack, means, scope, start, whack 6 chance, excuse 7 leisure, liberty, opening, vacancy 8 good luck, occasion 9 elbowroom, fair shake, privilege 10 good chance
at the first ~: 4 anon, soon 7 shortly 8 directly, promptly 9 forthwith, presently, right away 10 before long
__ opportunity: 5 equal, photo 6 golden
Opportunity: 4 city, town
locale: 10 Washington
opposable digit: 5 thumb
oppose: 3 bar, pit, vie 4 buck, defy, deny, stem 5 argue, check, cross, fight, flout, rebel, rebut, rival 6 assail, attack, battle, combat, debate, hinder, ignore, impugn, negate, rebuff, rebuke, refute, resist, revolt, take on, thwart 7 assault, compare, contest, counter, dispute, frown at, gainsay, play off, prevent, protest, reverse, vie with, violate 8 confront, contrast, disagree, face down, obstruct, question 9 disregard, frown upon, stand up to, take issue, withstand 10 antagonize, contradict, contravene, controvert, counteract, disapprove, neutralize, set against, take a stand
opposed: 4 agin, anti, loth 5 loath, polar 6 at odds, averse 7 adverse, against, counter, denying, hostile, warring 8 battling, clashing, contrary, crossing, indocile, inimical, rivaling 9 combating, defending, defensive, disputing, objecting, repelling, unwilling, up against 10 antithetic, antonymous, facing down, gainsaying, protesting
be ~: 4 mind 5 demur, rebel 6 object 7 dispute
diametrically ~: 5 polar 7 counter 8 contrary 9 antipodal 10 antipodean
to: 4 agin 6 gainst, versus 7 against, athwart
opposer: 3 foe 4 anti 5 enemy, rival 9 adversary, ill-wisher 10 antagonist
opposing: 3 con 4 anti 5 rival 6 at odds, averse, head-on, versus 7 against, counter, denying, hostile, loath to, warring 8 averse to, battling, clashing, contrary, crossing, disputed, inimical, negative, rivaling 9 combating, counter to, defending, defensive, disputing, hostile to, objecting, repelling, up against 10 antonymous, at odds with, facing down, gainsaying, protesting
prefix: 4 anti- 6 contra-
vote: 3 nay
opposite: 5 other, polar 6 contra, facing, gainst, unlike 7 abreast, adverse, against, antonym, counter, diverse, inverse, obverse, reverse, unalike, vis-à-vis 8 antipode, contrary, converse, flip-side, fronting, inimical, reversed 9 antipodal, crossways, crosswise, different, differing, inversion, other side, vice versa 10 antipodean, antithesis, antithetic, dissimilar, face-to-face
prefix: 3 dis- 4 anti- 7 counter-, enantio-
opposite __: 3 sex 6 number, prompt
oppositely: 9 in reverse, inversely, vice versa 10 conversely
Opposite of Fate, The author: Amy Tan
Opposite of Sex, The (1998 film)
cast: Lisa Kudrow, Lyle Lovett, Christina Ricci
director: Don Roos
Opposites Attract (1990 song) artist: Paula Abdul
Opposite Sex, The (1956 film)
cast: June Allyson, Joan Collins
opposition: 3 foe 4 flak 5 enemy, fight, flack, rival 6 combat, rebuff 7 defense, dissent, rivalry, warfare 8 aversion, conflict, defiance, friction, negation 9 adversary, antipathy, hostility, other side, rebellion 10 antagonism, antithesis, comparison, competitor, contention, difference, filibuster
check out the ~: 5 recon, scout
in direct ~: 6 head-on 10 face-to-face, unmediated
in ~ to: 3 con 4 anti 7 against, athwart
__ opposition: 5 loyal, polar 6 binary
oppositionist: 3 foe 4 anti
oppress: 3 tax 4 load, rack, ride, rule 5 abuse, bully, crush, force, grind, harry, hound, press, tread, weary, worry, wrong 6 burden, harass, pick on, plague, prey on, punish, sadden, saddle, subdue 7 afflict, depress, dragoon, put upon, smother, squeeze, squelch, torment, torture, trample 8 aggrieve, beat down, browbeat, dispirit, distress, domineer, encumber,

handicap, keep down, maltreat, overload, suppress 9 despotize, overpower, overwhelm, persecute, subjugate, terrorize, trample on, tyrannize, weigh down 10 dishearten

oppressed: 5 laden 9 aggrieved 10 despairing

oppression: 4 onus, yoke 5 abuse, force, wrong 6 injury, misery, stress 7 control, cruelty, fascism, torment, tyranny 8 coercion, hardship, iron hand, severity, subduing 9 autocracy, brutality, despotism, extortion, harshness, injustice, suffering 10 difficulty, domination

oppressive: 4 firm, hard, mean 5 bleak, bossy, close, cruel, harsh, heavy, hefty, muggy, picky, rigid, rough, stern, stiff, tough 6 brutal, dismal, gloomy, leaden, severe, somber, steamy, sticky, strict, stuffy, sultry, taxing, thorny, torrid, trying, unjust, uphill 7 airless, arduous, austere, exigent, inhuman, onerous, Spartan, unhappy, weighty 8 despotic, exacting, exigeant, grievous, grinding, grueling, hard-line, overcast, rigorous, stifling, tiresome, toilsome 9 cheerless, confining, demanding, draconian, imperious, laborious, ponderous, saddening, strenuous, stringent, unbending, unsparing 10 burdensome, cumbersome, depressing, despotical, enervating, formidable, inflexible, iron-fisted, no-nonsense, tenebrific, tyrannical
- **not ~:** 4 easy, mild 5 light, loose 6 gentle 8 moderate 9 easygoing 10 unexacting

oppressor: 4 tsar 5 bully 6 despot, tyrant 8 dictator 10 inquisitor

opprobriate: 4 slam 5 decry 6 vilify 7 asperse, censure, condemn, run down 8 badmouth, denounce, derogate 9 criticize, disparage 10 calumniate

opprobrious: 4 evil, ugly, vile 7 abusive, damning 8 damaging, reviling, shameful 9 malicious, maligning, nefarious, offensive, vitriolic 10 censorious, scurrilous

opprobrium: 3 dig 4 barb, evil, gibe, jibe, slam, slap, slur, snub 5 abuse, libel, odium, scorn, shame, taunt 6 infamy, insult, rebuff, slight 7 affront, calumny, catcall, disdain, mockery, obloquy, offense, put-down, slander 8 contempt, derision, disgrace, dishonor, ignominy, ridicule 9 aspersion, cheap shot, contumely, criticism, disrepute, ill repute, indignity 10 defamation, disrespect

oppugn: 3 pan 5 blast, knock 6 assail, attack 7 confute, put down, rip into 8 lace into, tear into 9 blaspheme, criticize, light into 10 controvert, prove wrong

oppugnant: 3 icy 5 nasty, stony 6 averse, bitter, chilly 7 adverse, hateful, hostile, opposed, scrappy 8 clashing, contrary, inimical, militant, opposing, venomous, virulent 9 bellicose, vitriolic 10 antagonist, pugnacious, unfriendly

Oprah: 7 Winfrey
- **emulate ~:** 4 diet, host 6 reduce
- **former rival:** 4 Phil 5 Rosie
- **production company:** 5 Harpo
- **stock-in-trade:** 4 chat, talk 8 dialogue 9 interview 10 discussion

Opry
- **greeting:** 5 howdy
- **instrument:** 5 banjo 6 guitar
- **locale:** 9 Nashville, Tennessee

Ops: 3 god
- **brother of ~:** 6 Saturn
- **daughter of ~:** 4 Juno 5 Ceres, Vesta 8 Euryclea
- **equivalent:** 4 Rhea
- **husband of ~:** 6 Saturn
- **son of ~:** 5 Pluto 7 Jupiter, Neptune

opt: 4 cull, mark, pick, take, vote, will 5 elect 6 choose, decide, prefer, select 9 single out
- **for:** 2 go 4 pick, take 5 elect, favor, key on 6 choose, prefer, select 7 pick out 8 decide on 9 single out 10 settle upon
- **out:** 4 quit 5 leave, rebel 7 abandon, retreat 8 abdicate, renounce 9 disengage 10 relinquish

opt __: 3 for, out

optic: 5 nerve 6 visual 7 sensory 9 sensorial
- **cover:** 6 eyelid

optic __: 4 axis, disk 5 nerve 6 center 7 chiasma

__ optic: 5 fiber

optical: 6 visual
- **device:** 4 lens 5 loupe 7 monocle 8 eyeglass, eyepiece 9 magnifier
- **illusion:** 6 mirage
- **organ:** 3 eye

optical __: 3 art 4 disc, disk, path 5 bench, fiber, glass, maser, sound, track, wedge 6 center, isomer 7 effects, printer, pumping, tooling

optician product: 4 lens 6 frames 7 glasses 8 contacts

optics: 6 vision 7 science
- **adjective:** 5 focal
- **device:** 5 prism
- **study:** 5 light
- **verb in ~:** 4 lase

__ optics: 5 fiber 7 quantum

Optima: 3 car, Kia 4 auto, font 8 typeface

optimal: 4 best 5 first, ideal 6 superb 7 in front 9 just right

optimally: 6 at best, at most

optimism: 4 hope 5 cheer, trust 6 morale 7 elation 8 buoyance, buoyancy, calmness, easiness, idealism, sureness 9 assurance, certainty, good cheer, happiness, lightness 10 brightness, confidence, enthusiasm, positivism

optimist: 5 hoper 7 dreamer 8 idealist, romantic 9 Pollyanna
- **Wall Street ~:** 4 bull

optimistic: 3 gay 4 high, rosy, sure 5 happy, jolly, merry, perky, sunny 6 blithe, bright, cheery, elated, hoping, joyful, upbeat 7 buoyant, certain, hopeful, radiant, utopian 8 carefree, cheerful, cheering, grooving, jubilant, laughing, positive, sanguine, trusting 9 believing, confident, convinced, expectant, overjoyed, promising, satisfied, sprightly 10 flying high, heartening, inspirited
- **about:** 6 high on
- **be ~:** 4 hope, wish 5 dream 6 aspire, expect 7 believe, look for 8 daydream 10 anticipate
- **phrase:** 4 I can 5 I hope

optimistically: 6 at best

Optimist's Daughter, The author: Eudora Welty

Optimists, The (1973 film)
- **cast:** Donna Mullane, Peter Sellers

optimum: 4 A-one, best, peak 5 first, ideal 6 all-out, choice 7 capital, highest, maximum, perfect 8 choicest, flawless, gilt-edge, greatest, peerless 9 excellent, matchless, solid gold 10 world-class

option: 5 spare, voice 6 choice, voting 7 refusal 8 druthers, election, flip side, free will, recourse, volition 9 privilege, selection 10 discretion, first claim, preference, supplement

__ option: 3 put 4 call 5 local, stock 6 spread 7 seller's

optional: 3 req. 5 extra, minor 8 elective, needless, possible, unforced, unneeded 9 allowable, open-ended, redundant, voluntary 10 additional

options list: 4 menu

__ Option, The: 5 Paris

optometría concern: 3 ojo

optométrie concern: 4 oeil

optometrist: 7 oculist 9 eye doctor
- **concern:** 4 iris, lens 5 pupil 6 cornea, frames, retina 7 glasses

opulence: 4 luxe 6 luxury, plenty, riches, wealth 7 comfort, fortune 8 grandeur 9 abundance, affluence 10 prosperity

opulent: 4 lush, luxe, posh, rich 5 fancy, flush, grand, plush, ritzy, showy, swank 6 deluxe, flashy, frilly, glitzy, lavish, ornate 7 copious, elegant, moneyed, profuse, riotous, stately, wealthy, well-off 8 affluent, luscious, palatial, well-to-do 9 decorated, elaborate, exuberant, luxuriant, luxurious, plentiful, profusive, sumptuous 10 ornamented, prosperous, well-heeled

opuntia: 5 plant 6 cactus

opus: 4 tome, work 5 piece 6 oeuvre 7 product, writing 8 creation, symphony 9 great work 10 production
- **magnum ~:** 4 tome, work 7 classic 8 monument 9 specialty

opus __: 3 Dei

or: 4 else 9 connector, otherwise
- **in music:** 5 ossia

or __: 4 else

__-or: 6 either

...or __ Memorex?: 4 is it

...or __ to be...: 3 not

OR
- **workers:** 3 Drs., RNs
- *see also* Oregon

ora __ nobis: 3 pro

orach: 7 potherb 8 saltbush

oracle: 4 sage, seer 5 augur, sibyl 6 answer, augury, vision 7 adviser, diviner, fortune, prophet 8 prophecy 9 divinator 10 divination, forecaster, prediction, revelation, soothsayer
- **site:** 6 Delphi, Phocis
- **words:** 4 I see

oracular: 4 wise 5 vague, vatic 6 arcane, occult, secret 7 cryptic, obscure, vatical 8 Delphian, divining, mystical 9 ambiguous, cryptical, presaging, prescient, prophetic, sibylline, vaticinal 10 auspicious, cabalistic, mysterious, portending, portentous, predicting, unknowable

Oradea: 4 city, town
- **locale:** 7 Romania, Rumania 8 Roumania

oral: 4 exam, said, test, told 5 vocal 6 buccal, phonic, spoken, verbal, voiced 7 lingual, related, sounded, uttered 8 narrated, phonetic, viva-voce 9 outspoken, recounted, unwritten, vocalized 10 articulate, verbalized
- **cavity:** 5 mouth
- **communication:** 4 talk 6 debate, homily, sermon, speech 7 address, lecture 8 dialogue, rhetoric 9 discourse 10 discussion
- **history:** 4 lore, myth 5 sagas, tales 7 beliefs, customs, legends, sayings 8 folklore 10 traditions

oral __: 4 exam 7 history, hygiene, surgeon, vaccine

orale: 4 cape 5 fanon 7 maniple
- **wearer:** 4 Pope 6 bishop 7 pontiff, prelate

orally: 5 aloud, parol 8 viva voce

Oral Roberts University
- **locale:** 5 Tulsa 8 Oklahoma

oral surgeon deg.: 3 DDS

Oran: 4 city, port, town 5 Jones
- **locale:** 7 Algeria

orang: 3 ape 6 animal, simian 7 primate
- **relative:** 3 ape 4 saki, titi 5 chimp, drill, jocko, lemur, loris, magot, potto, shrew 6 aye-aye, baboon, Bandar, galago, gelada, gibbon, grivet, guenon, howler, langur, macaco, monkey, rhesus, uakari, vervet 7 colobus, gorilla, guereza, hoolock, macaque, sapajou, siamang, tamarin, tarsier 8 bush baby, capuchin, mandrill, mangabey, marmoset, talapoin 10 Barbary ape, chimpanzee

orange: 4 soda, tree 5 coral, fruit, Jaffa, Osage, peach 6 carrot, citrus, flavor, salmon, tangor, titian 7 apricot, Seville 8 bergamot, Valencia 9 cantaloup, tangerine 10 cantaloupe
- **brownish ~:** 10 terra cotta
- **coating:** 4 rust
- **color:** 5 flame, henna 7 pumpkin, saffron 8 hyacinth 9 tangerine 10 terra cotta
- **container:** 3 box 4 case 5 crate 6 carton
- **derivative:** 6 citral
- **drink:** 3 ade 5 Crush, Fanta
- **ender:** 3 ade 4 root, wood
- **feature:** 5 navel
- **flower:** 5 poppy, tulip 6 cosmos 7 day lily 8 hawkweed, marigold 9 calendula 10 nasturtium, wallflower
- **gem:** 4 sard 5 balas 7 sardine, sardius
- **like ~ juice:** 5 tangy
- **like ~ traffic markers:** 5 conic 7 conical
- **make ~ juice:** 4 bore, ream
- **part:** 4 peel, pulp, rind, skin
- **pekoe:** 3 tea 4 brew 5 drink
- **reddish ~:** 5 flame, henna 8 hyacinth 9 tangerine
- **relative:** 4 lime, Ugli 5 lemon, navel 6 pomelo, tangor 7 kumquat, satsuma, Seville, tangelo 8 bergamot, mandarin, shaddock, Valencia 9 tangerine 10 calamondin, grapefruit
- **seed:** 3 pip
- **seedless ~:** 5 navel
- **vegetable:** 3 yam
- **yellowish ~:** 7 saffron
- **zircon:** 6 ligure

orange __: 4 lily, rust 5 crate, pekoe, stick 6 sulfur 7 blossom

__ orange: 4 gold, mock, sour, wild 5 blood, Jaffa, Natal, navel, Osage, sweet 6 bitter, methyl, pastel, temple 7 cadmium, Mexican, Seville

Orange: 4 city, town 5 river
- **locale:** 5 Texas 9 New Jersey 10 California
- **River locale:** 7 Lesotho
- **river to the ~:** 4 Vaal
- **William of ~ foe:** 6 De Witt

Orange __: 4 Bowl 6 Julius

Orange __ State: 4 Free

__ Orange: 4 Fort 5 Agent

orangeade: 5 drink 8 beverage

orange-and-black bird: 6 oriole

orange-and-white rental: 5 U-Haul

orange-billed bird: 5 mynah

orange blossom: 5 drink 8 beverage, cocktail
- **derivative:** 5 nerol 6 neroli
- **ingredient:** 3 gin

Orange Blossom Special: 5 train

Orange Bowl
locale: 5 Miami 7 Florida
org.: 4 NCAA
Orange County Register: 5 paper 9 newspaper
locale: 8 Santa Ana 10 California
Orange Free __: 5 State
__ or Angel: 5 Devil
__ Orange, NJ: 4 East
orange pekoe: 8 beverage
__ Orange Pips, The: 4 Five
orange-red
flower: 9 safflower
mineral: 4 sard 7 sardine, sardius
orange-roof eatery: 4 HoJo
oranges, apples and: 6 unlike 9 different
Oranges & Lemons artist: 3 XTC
Orangevale: 4 city, town
locale: 10 California
Orangeville: 4 city, town
locale: 6 Canada 7 Ontario
orange-yellow: 5 amber
orangish: 5 ocher, ochre, poppy 6 crocus 7 saffron
orangutan: 3 ape 5 biped 6 animal 7 primate
relative: 4 saki, titi 5 chimp, drill, jocko, lemur, loris, magot, potto, shrew 6 aye-aye, baboon, Bandar, galago, gelada, gibbon, grivet, guenon, howler, langur, macaco, monkey, rhesus, uakari, vervet 7 colobus, gorilla, guereza, hoolock, macaque, sapajou, siamang, tamarin, tarsier 8 bush baby, capuchin, mandrill, mangabey, marmoset, talapoin 10 Barbary ape, chimpanzee
Orani: 8 Algerian
Oranjestad: 4 city, town
locale: 5 Aruba
orant: 4 icon, ikon 5 eikon
ora pro nobis: 9 pray for us
orarion: 5 stole
orate: 3 jaw, say 4 rant, talk 5 Bryan, speak, spout 6 preach 7 address, declaim, expound, lecture 8 bloviate, harangue, homilize, sound off 9 discourse, hold forth, sermonize, speechify
oration: 4 talk 5 eloge, pitch, spiel 6 eulogy, homily, sermon, speech 7 address, lecture, pep talk, soapbox 8 harangue, rhetoric 9 chalk talk, discourse, panegyric, utterance 10 apostrophe, recitation, vocalizing
give an ~: 4 talk 5 speak, spout 7 declaim 9 hold forth
orator: 4 Cato, Clay 6 Cicero, rhetor 7 reciter, speaker 8 lecturer, Pericles, preacher 9 declaimer, Isocrates 10 Protagoras, sermonizer
contest: 6 debate 8 polemics
device: 5 irony
perch: 4 dais 6 podium 7 rostrum 8 platform
Orator: 4 font 8 typeface
oratorio: 5 music, piece
melody: 4 aria
singers: 5 choir 6 chorus
Orators, The author: W.H. Auden
oratory: 4 rhet. 6 chapel, speech 7 diction 8 rhetoric, sacellum 9 elocution, eloquence 10 vocalizing
orb: 3 eye, sph., sun 4 ball, moon 5 globe, world 6 planet, sphere 8 baby blue, baseball 10 basketball
edible ~: 3 pea
Orbach, Jerry: 5 actor
film: Dirty Dancing (1987)
Prince of the City (1981)
TV: Law & Order
orbed: 5 round 7 circled, rounded 8 circular 9 encircled, spherical
Orbison, Roy: 5 tenor 6 singer
song: Blue Angel (1960)
Blue Bayou (1963)
Crying (1961)
Dream Baby (1962)
Falling (1963)
Goodnight (1965)
In Dreams (1963)
It's Over (1964)
Leah (1962)
Mean Woman Blues (1963)
Oh, Pretty Woman (1964)
Only the Lonely (1960)
Pretty Paper (1963)
Running Scared (1961)
You Got It (1989)
orbit: 3 lap, way 4 path, turn 5 ambit, curve, field, limit, range, reach, realm, round, scope, sweep, track, wheel 6 bounds, circle, course, domain, length, radius, sphere, travel 7 circuit, compass, ellipse, expanse, purview, revolve 8 confines, dominion, encircle, province, rotation 9 influence 10 boundaries, revolution, trajectory
lose ~: 5 decay
period: 4 year
point: 4 apse 5 apsis 6 apogee 7 perigee
segment: 3 arc 5 curve
shape: 4 oval
transmission station: 6 Comsat
__ orbit: 5 lunar, polar 7 parking
Orbit: 3 gum 10 chewing gum
alternative: 5 Extra 7 Dentyne, Trident 8 Carefree, Chiclets, Freedent 10 Doublemint, Juicy Fruit
orbital __: 5 index 6 sander
orbiter: 4 moon 6 planet 9 satellite
solar ~: 4 Mars 5 comet, Earth, Pluto, Venus 6 Saturn, Uranus 7 Jupiter, Mercury
__ Orbiter: 5 Lunar
Orbiter org.: 4 NASA
__-or-break: 4 make
__-or-bust: 4 boom
orc: 5 whale 7 grampus 8 cetacean
relative: 3 sei 5 whale 6 beluga, narwal 7 cowfish, dolphin, finback, grampus, narwhal, rorqual 8 narwhale, porpoise
orca: 5 Shamu, Willy
Orca: 8 language
alternative: 3 ADA, APL, SQL 4 Alef, html, Icon, Java, LISP, Logo, Perl 5 Algol, Basic, Cecil, COBOL, Dylan, SISAL 6 Delphi, Eiffel, Erlang, Oberon, Pascal, Prolog, Sather, Scheme, Snobol 7 Fortran
orch.
Instrument: 2 vc.
section: 3 str. 4 perc.
union: 3 AFM
work: 3 sym.
see also orchestra
orchard: 5 grove, stand
device: 6 fogger
former ~ spray: 4 Alar
pest: 5 borer
product: 3 nut 4 pear, tree 5 apple, fruit, peach 6 cherry
tend an ~: 3 lop, mow, top 4 clip, crop, snip, trim 5 prune, shear
unit: 6 bushel
__ orchard: 3 sap 5 apple, peach, sugar 6 cherry, marble
__ Orchard, The: 6 Cherry
orchestra: 4 band 8 ensemble, symphony
arrange for an ~: 5 score
be in an ~: 4 play
cheer for an ~: 5 bravo
funding org.: 3 NEA
locale: 3 pit 4 row B, row C
member: 3 sax 4 gong, harp, horn, oboe, reed, tuba, wind 5 cello, flute, piano, viola 6 violin 7 bassoon 8 clarinet 9 saxophone 10 French horn 11 English horn
movement: 4 trio 5 largo, rondo 6 adagio 7 allegro
output: 5 music
practice: 3 reh. 9 rehearsal
section: 3 str. 5 brass 7 strings
VIP: 3 ldr. 7 maestro, soloist 9 conductor
work: 5 fugue, music, rondo, score, suite 6 sonata 7 cantata, chorale, scherzo, toccata 8 concerto, nocturne, oratorio, overture, symphony 9 pastorale
orchestra __: 3 pit
__ orchestra: 7 chamber 8 symphony
orchestrate: 5 score, set up, stage 6 direct, manage 7 arrange, control 8 organize 9 harmonize 10 manipulate
orchid: 5 plant 6 bluish, flower, purple 7 blueish, calypso, reddish 9 swamp pink
product: 5 salep
relative: 4 plum, puce 5 lilac, mauve 6 dahlia, damson 7 heather, petunia 8 amethyst, burgundy, eggplant, lavender, mulberry 9 raspberry 10 heliotrope
orchid __: 4 tree 6 cactus
__ orchid: 4 moth 5 pansy 7 fringed, peacock
orchidlike flower: 4 iris
__ or Consequences: 5 Truth
Orcus: 4 hell 5 abyss, Hades, limbo 7 inferno 9 perdition 10 lower world, underworld
__ or cut bait: 4 fish
Orcutt: 4 city, town
locale: 10 California
Orczy, Emmuska: 6 writer 7 English
work: The Scarlet Pimpernel
Ord: 4 Fort
ORD: 5 O'Hare
abbr.: 3 arr., ETA
locale: 3 Chi. 15 Chicago. Illinois
ordain: 3 fix, run, set 4 make, rule, will 5 bless, enact, frock 6 anoint, decree, enjoin, instal, invest 7 command, destine, dictate, install, instate 8 delegate, legalize 9 legislate, prescribe, pronounce 10 commission, consecrate, constitute
ordained: 5 fated 6 doomed, lawful 7 assured, certain, decided, decreed 8 destined, mandated 9 impending, statutory 10 determined, inevitable, inexorable, prescribed
one: 4 abbé 5 abbot, padre, rabbi, vicar 6 clergy, cleric, deacon, parson, pastor, priest 8 chaplain, minister, preacher
__ or Dare: 5 Truth
ordeal: 4 hell, test 5 agony, cross, curse, trial 6 misery, trauma 7 anguish, torment, torture, trouble 8 calamity, crucible, distress, irritant 9 martyrdom, nightmare, suffering 10 affliction, difficulty, infliction, visitation
ordeal __: 4 bean, tree
Ordeal of Gilbert Pinfold, The author: Evelyn Waugh
Ordeal of Richard Feverel, The author: George Meredith
order: 3 bid, buy, law, lot, set, sys. 4 book, calm, cite, club, fiat, file, form, gild, kind, rank, rule, sect, sort, syst., tell, tidy, tier, trim, type, warn, wish, word 5 align, aline, array, caste, class, edict, enact, force, genre, genus, goods, group, guild, index, peace, queue, range, ready, say-so, setup, ukase 6 adjure, amount, assign, behest, charge, codify, decree, degree, demand, dictum, direct, divide, engage, enjoin, impose, insist, kilter, league, lineup, nature, neaten, obtain, rating, ruling, secure, series, settle, stripe, summon, system 7 arrange, bidding, booking, catalog, command, dictate, dispose, harmony, mandate, marshal, pattern, precept, request, require, reserve, routine, society, sort out, species, station, variety 8 classify, graduate, instruct, neatness, organize, priority, purchase, quantity, regiment, regulate, sentence, sequence, shipment, sodality, sorority, subclass, symmetry, tabulate, tidiness 9 authorize, catalogue, direction, directive, gradation, hierarchy, legislate, materials, methodize, ordinance, prescribe, propriety, structure 10 categorize, discipline, distribute, fraternity, injunction, lawfulness, permission, pigeonhole, procession, regularity, regulation, sisterhood, succession, uniformity
absence of ~: 4 mess, riot 5 chaos, havoc, snarl 6 bedlam, mayhem, tumult, uproar 7 anarchy, clutter, discord, turmoil 8 disarray, shambles 9 confusion 10 unruliness
around: 4 boss 9 trample on, tyrannize 10 lord it over
be out of ~: 5 act up 9 misbehave
blank: 4 form 6 coupon
change the ~: 5 mix up 6 jumble, muddle 7 shuffle 8 disarray, scramble 9 rearrange 10 disarrange
combining form: 3 tax- 4 taxi-, taxo-, -taxy 5 -taxis
court ~: 4 rise, stay, writ 5 paper 7 all rise
for dinner: 3 eat, get 4 have 5 enjoy 7 procure
handle an ~: 4 fill, lade, load, pack 6 make up, supply 7 process, satisfy
in ~: 2 OK 4 neat, okay, okeh, okey, tidy 5 clean, ready 6 aright, proper, spruce, usable 7 orderly, regular, useable 8 prepared, straight
in short ~: 4 anon, fast, soon
in the ~ given (abbr.): 4 resp.
in ~ (to): 4 so as
king ~: 3 act 4 fiat 5 ukase 6 decree, dictum, ruling 7 dictate, mandate, precept 9 manifesto
make to ~: 6 tailor
member: 4 lama, monk 5 abbot, friar 6 priest, sensei 7 ascetic, bhikshu, brother 8 cenobite, monastic, rinpoche 9 religious
name meaning ~: 5 Cosmo
of business: 6 agenda 7 program 8 schedule
on the ~ of: 4 like 5 about 9 similar to 10 resembling
out of ~: 4 down 5 amiss, mussy, unapt, wrong 6 blooey, blooie, broken, busted, faulty 7 haywire, jumbled 8 improper 9 defective, disrepair, irregular 10 broken-down, nongermane, on the fritz
partner: 3 law
pecking ~: 4 rank 5 class, order, place 6 regime
put in ~: 4 sort, tidy 6 assort, settle 7 correct 8 organize, regulate, untangle
taker: 6 garçon, server, waiter
to go: 4 fire, mail, oust, post, send, ship 5 eat in, expel, route 6 assign, banish, deport, direct, put out 7 cast out, consign, turn out 8 dispatch,

displace, drive out, transfer 9 dismissal, ostracize, transport 10 expatriate
written ~: 3 req.
order ___: 4 arms, code, port 5 blank
___ order: 3 gag, job, new 4 back, bunt, mail, open, peck, stop, tall, word, work 5 a tall, court, Doric, Ionic, limit, major, minor, money, short 6 market, postal, sacred, Tuscan 7 batting, matched, pecking, working
___-order: 5 march 6 custom
Order ___ Garter: 5 of the
___ & Order: 3 Law
___-order cook: 5 short
___-order drill: 5 close
ordered: 4 bade, neat, tidy 6 lawful 7 regular 8 methodic 10 methodical
ordered ___: 4 pair 5 field 6 n-tuple
ordering: 5 array 6 system 8 sequence 9 placement
orderliness: 3 law 4 calm, form 5 order, peace 7 harmony 8 neatness, symmetry, tidiness 10 discipline, uniformity
orderly: 4 aide, calm, good, neat, tidy, trim 5 clean, crisp, kempt, quiet 6 docile, formal, spruce 7 in shape, regular, uniform 8 coherent, decorous, methodic, obedient, readable, straight, thorough, to rights, tranquil, well-kept 9 attendant, organized, peaceable, regulated, shipshape 10 controlled, fastidious, law-abiding, methodical, neat as a pin, nonviolent, submissive, systematic
British army ~: 6 batman
make ~: 4 tidy 5 clean 6 neaten 8 spruce up 10 straighten
thinking: 5 logic, sense 6 reason, sanity, thesis 9 coherence, deduction, dialectic, good sense, induction, inference, rationale, reasoning, syllogism 10 philosophy
___ order of: 5 on the
Order of ___: 5 Lenin, Merit
___ Order of Moose: 5 Loyal
Order of the ___: 6 Garter
orders
follow ~: 4 heed, mind, obey 5 act on, bow to 6 accept, bend to, listen, submit 7 abide by, agree to, defer to, observe, stick to 8 adhere to, carry out 9 conform to, consent to, truckle to 10 comply with, keep in step, toe the line
give ~: 4 boss, head, lead, rule, tell 5 steer 6 advise, charge, direct, enjoin, govern, manage 7 command, dictate, oversee, preside 8 dominate 9 officiate, prescribe, supervise 10 administer, mastermind, ride herd on, run the show
holy ~: 9 sacrament
not following ~: 5 rogue 10 rebellious
prone to giving ~: 5 bossy, pushy 8 arrogant, despotic 9 imperious 10 commanding, ironhanded, oppressive, peremptory, tyrannical
___ orders: 4 holy 6 sealed 7 general, special
___ ordinaire: 3 vin
ordinal: 2 no. 6 number
imprecise ~: 3 nth
suffix: 3 -eth
ordinal ___: 6 number 7 numeral
ordinance: 3 act, law 4 code, fiat, rule 5 bylaw, canon, edict, order, ukase 6 assize, decree, dictum, ruling 7 command, mandate, precept, statute 9 direction, directive, enactment, prescript 10 regulation
ordinarily: 6 simply 7 as a rule, usually 8 commonly, normally 9 generally, in general, most often, naturally, regularly 10 by and large, frequently
ordinary: 4 dull, fair, mean, so-so 5 banal, daily, lowly, plain, prosy, stock, trite, typic, usual 6 cleric, common, humble, jejune, medium, modest, normal, public, simple, vulgar, wonted 7 average, general, generic, humdrum, ignoble, insipid, mundane, natural, popular, prosaic, regular, routine, typical, vanilla 8 everyday, familiar, frequent, habitual, homespun, inferior, mediocre, middling, moderate, orthodox, plebeian, standard, workaday 9 customary, generical, household, prosaical, quotidian, tolerable, unnotable 10 accustomed, dullsville, fairly good, pedestrian, prevailing, second-rate, uneventful, uninspired, white-bread, widespread
out of the ~: 3 odd 4 rare 5 novel, queer, weird 7 bizarre, curious, oddball, special, strange, unusual 8 striking, uncommon 9 different
ordinary ___: 3 ray 4 wave 5 point, share, stock 6 income, seaman 7 jubilee
Ordinary Life, An author: Karel Capek
___ Ordinary Man: 4 I'm an
Ordinary People (1980 film)
cast: Judd Hirsch, Timothy Hutton, Mary Tyler Moore, Donald Sutherland
director: Robert Redford
Ordinary World (1993 song) artist: Duran Duran
ordination: 9 induction 10 delegation
ordnance: 4 arms 6 cannon 7 weapons 8 armament, materiel, weaponry 9 artillery, munitions
___ Ordo Seclorum: 5 Novus
ore: 4 lode, rock 5 borax, metal, money, prill, stone 6 barite, blende, galena, pyrite, raddle, reddle, ruddle, rutile 7 azurite, barytes, bauxite, bonanza, bornite, cuprite, kernite, mineral, pay dirt, realgar, sylvite, thorite, zincite 8 autunite, cinnabar, dolomite, galenite, goethite, hematite, ilmenite, limonite, monazite, siderite, smaltite, stannite, stibnite, taconite 9 argentite, carnotite, celestite, cerussite, columbite, covellite, magnetite, malachite, millerite, mispickel, niccolite, proustite, scheelite, sylvanite, tantalite, uraninite, willemite, wulfenite 10 calaverite, carnallite, chalcocite, garnierite, lepidolite, mother lode, polybasite, pyrolusite, sphalerite, vanadinite, yellowcake
aluminum ~: 7 bauxite
analyze ~: 5 assay
antimony ~: 8 stibnite
arsenic ~: 7 realgar
boron ~: 7 kernite
carrier: 4 scow, tram 5 barge
cobalt ~: 8 smaltite
copper ~: 7 azurite 9 malachite
diggers' org.: 3 UMW
gold ~: 9 sylvanite
iron ~: 8 hematite, limonite, siderite, taconite 9 magnetite
lead ~: 6 galena 10 vanadinite
lithium ~: 10 lepidolite
mixture: 4 flux
molybdenum ~: 9 wulfenite
nickel ~: 9 millerite, niccolite
niobium ~: 9 columbite
potassium ~: 7 sylvite
process ~: 5 smelt 6 reduce, refine
science: 10 metallurgy
seeker: 5 miner 6 digger 7 collier
silver ~: 9 argentite, sylvanite 10 polybasite
source: 4 lode, mine, seam, vein
splinter: 5 spall
strontium ~: 9 celestite
suffix: 3 -ite
tin ~: 8 stannite
titanium ~: 8 ilmenite
tungsten ~: 9 scheelite
zinc ~: 7 zincite 9 willemite 10 sphalerite
ore ___: 6 bridge, hearth, tanker 7 rotundo
öre: 4 coin
word on an ~: 5 Norge
Ore-___: 3 Ida
Ore.
campus: 3 OSU
neighbor: 3 Cal., Ida., Nev. 4 Wash. 5 Calif.
zone: 3 PDT, PST
see also Oregon
oread: 4 Echo 5 nymph 6 Daphne
Oreck: 3 vac 6 vacuum
rival: 5 Kirby 6 Eureka, Hoover 10 Electrolux
orectic: 7 athirst 8 desirous
Oreg.
see Oregon
oregano: 4 herb 9 seasoning
Oregon: 5 state, trail
campus: 3 OSU
capital: 5 Salem
city: 4 Bend 5 Aloha, Salem 6 Albany, Eugene, Keizer, Tigard 7 Ashland, Gresham, Medford 8 Altamont, Portland, Roseburg, Tualatin, West Linn, Woodburn 9 Beaverton, Corvallis, Hillsboro, Milwaukie 10 Grants Pass, Lake Oswego, Oregon City
conference: 6 Pac-Ten
county: 4 Coos 5 Wasco 7 Clatsop, Klamath
Indian: 5 Modoc 6 Cayuse 7 Klamath, Takelma 8 Sahaptin
lake: 6 Crater
mountain: 4 Hood
national park: 10 Crater Lake
native: 6 Beaver
neighbor: 3 Cal., Ida., Nev. 4 Wash. 5 Idaho 6 Nevada 10 California, Washington
river: 5 Rogue
start of ~ motto: 4 Alis
state animal: 6 beaver
state beverage: 4 milk
state bird: 10 meadowlark
state flower: 5 grape
state gemstone: 8 sunstone
state nut: 8 hazelnut
state rock: 5 geode
state tree: 10 Douglas fir
University of ~ locale: 6 Eugene
zone: 3 PDT, PST
Oregon ___: 3 fir 4 pine 5 cedar, grape, maple, Trail 6 myrtle
Oregonian: 5 paper 9 newspaper
locale: 8 Portland
Oregon State
athletes: 7 Beavers
conference: 6 Pac-Ten
locale: 9 Corvallis
Oregon Trail city: 5 Boise
Oregon Trail, The author: Francis Parkman
O'Reilly: 4 Bill 5 Radar
Orel: 4 city, town 9 Hershiser
locale: 6 Russia
river: 3 Oka
or else, in music: 5 ossia
Orem: 4 city, town
locale: 4 Utah
Orenburg: 4 city, town
locale: 6 Russia
river: 4 Ural
Oreo: 5 cooky 6 cookie
alternative: 7 Droxies 9 Chips Ahoy! 10 Fig Newtons, Lorna Doone
component: 5 cream, creme, wafer
Oreo O's: 6 cereal
competitor: 3 Kix 4 Life, Trix 5 Kashi, Quisp, Total 6 Kaboom, Muesli, Pablum, Smacks 7 All-Bran, Crispix, Harmony, Hunny B's, Mueslix, Oat Bran, Pokemon 8 Boo Berry, Cheerios, Corn Chex, Corn Pops, Fiber One, Rice Chex, Special K, Uncle Sam, Wheaties 9 Alpha Bits, Apple Zaps, Grape Nuts, Honey Comb, Just Right, Wheat Chex 10 Apple Jacks, Bran Flakes, Cap'n Crunch, Cocoa Puffs, Froot Loops, Mini-Wheats, Nutri-Grain, Puffed Rice, Quaker Oats, Smart Start 11 Cocoa Blasts, Cookie Crisp, Golden Crisp, Lucky Charms, Puffed Wheat, Sweet Crunch, Waffle Crisp
Oresteia author: Aeschylus
Orestes
father of ~: 9 Agamemnon
lover of ~: 7 Erigone
nurse of ~: 7 Arsinoe
sister of ~: 7 Electra 9 Iphigenia
son of ~: 9 Penthilus, Tisamenus
wife of ~: 8 Hermione
Orestes author: Euripides
___ or even: 3 odd
orf: 4 carp, fish
___-or-famine: 5 feast
orfe: 4 carp, fish
Orfeo: 5 opera
composer: 5 Rossi
Orfeo ed Euridice role: 4 Amor
Orff, Carl: 6 German 8 composer
___-or-flight: 5 fight
___ or foe?: 6 friend
org.: 2 co., gp. 3 CIA, grp., NSA, soc. 4 agcy., assn., corp. 5 assoc., group
part: 3 div. 4 dept.
.org alternative: 3 com, edu, gov, net
organ: 3 ear, eye 4 gill, leaf, lung, nose, skin, tool, wing 5 agent, brain, chela, forum, gland, heart, liver, means, paper, voice 6 agency, feeler, kidney, medium, member, review, spinet, spleen, stamen, tongue 7 antenna, channel, gizzard, journal, pincers, stomach, vehicle 8 body part, magazine, pinchers, tentacle 9 flagellum, machinery, newspaper, spinneret 10 instrument, periodical
ender: 3 ism
insect sense ~: 4 palp 6 palpus
largest ~: 4 skin
lever: 4 stop 5 pedal
lining: 6 intima
meat: 5 liver, tripe
mouth ~: 9 harmonica
olfactory ~: 5 snoot, snout 7 schnozz 9 proboscis 10 schnozzola
opening: 5 hilum
part: 3 key 4 pipe, stop 5 pedal
rudimentary ~: 6 anlage
stop: 4 oboe 5 quint
organ ___: 4 pipe 5 point 6 screen 7 grinder, whistle
___ organ: 3 end 4 hand, pipe, reed 5 chord, house, mouth, sense, steam, vital 6 barrel, speech, spinet 7 baroque, Hammond, storage
organdy: 6 fabric 8 material
organic: 4 live 5 basal, basic, vital 6 biotic, bodily, innate, living 7 animate, natural, plasmic, radical 8 anatomic, biotical, cellular, inherent, integral 9 elemental, essential, innermost 10 anatomical, biological, structural
compound: 4 enol 5 aldol, amide, amine, azole, ester, imide, imine, tolan 6 acetal, ethene, hexane,

isomer, ketone **9** acetaldol
compound suffix: 3 -ene, -ine
dye: 3 azo **6** kermes
material: 5 humus, mulch **7** compost **10** fertilizer
not ~: 9 inanimate, insensate **10** insentient
radical: 4 amyl
unit: 3 egg **4** cell, germ **5** spore

organism: 4 body, life **5** being, plant, whole **6** animal, entity, person **8** creature **9** structure
body of an ~: 4 soma
combining form: 3 bio-, -zoa **4** -zoon
infectious ~: 3 bug **4** germ **5** virus **7** microbe
modified by environment: 4 ecad
of a blue-green ~: 5 algal
simple ~: 5 monad **6** amoeba

organization: 2 co., gp. **3** grp., set **4** band, body, clan, club, crew, firm, form, gild, team **5** group, guild, house, lodge, order, party, setup, staff, trust, union **6** agency, cartel, circle, clique, design, format, layout, league, makeup, outfit, system, troupe **7** brigade, combine, company, concern, concord, conduct, coterie, harmony, machine, network, pattern, society **8** alliance, assembly, business, disposal, grouping, industry, movement, planning, sodality, sorority, symmetry **9** coalition, formation, framework, institute, structure, syndicate
part: 3 div. **4** dept. **8** division **10** department

organization ___: 5 chart
___ organization: 5 block **6** social
organizational div.: 4 dept.
Organization, The (1971 film)
cast: Barbara McNair, Sheree North, Sidney Poitier

organize: 3 run **4** form, plan, sort **5** array, found, frame, group, mount, order, rally, ready, set up, stage **6** codify, create, embody, format, get set, imbody, line up, tidy up **7** arrange, catalog, compile, compose, conduct, dispose, marshal **8** classify, engineer, get going, mobilize, regulate, schedule **9** catalogue, correlate, establish, formulate **10** coordinate, pigeonhole

organized: 4 neat, tidy **5** ready **6** social **7** orderly, regular **8** coherent, methodic **9** efficient **10** methodical, systematic
get ~: 4 plan, plot **5** chart, frame, set up **6** lay out, map out **7** outline, prepare, project, propose, work out **8** engineer, rough out, schedule, think out **9** formulate **10** mastermind
group: 4 team **7** machine **9** task force

organized ___: 5 crime, labor **7** ferment, militia

organizer: 4 boss, head **5** chair, chief, super **6** honcho, leader, regent, tycoon **7** curator, founder, kingpin, manager **8** director, governor, overseer **9** commander, executive, principal **10** mastermind, supervisor

organ of ___: 5 Corti
organ-pipe ___: 5 coral **6** cactus
organs: 6 vitals
___ Organum: 5 Novum

organza: 5 cloth **6** fabric **8** material
like ~: 4 fine, thin **5** filmy, gauzy, light, sheer **8** delicate, gossamer **10** diaphanous, see-through

Oriani, Alfredo: 4 poet **7** Italian **10** playwright

oribi: 6 animal **8** antelope
relative: 3 gnu, kob **4** guib, kudu, oryx, puku, topi **5** addax, bongo, chiru, eland, goral, korin, nyala, saiga, serow **6** chammy, dik-dik, duiker, impala, koodoo, lechwe, nilgai, rhebok, shammy, shamoy **7** blaubok, blesbok, chamois, defassa, gazelle, gemsbok, gerenuk, grysbok, nylghai, nylghau, sassaby **8** blesbuck, bontebok, bushbuck, gemsbuck, reedbuck, steenbok, steinbok **9** blackbuck, pronghorn, sitatunga, springbok, waterbuck **10** hartebeest, wildebeest

oriel: 6 recess, window **9** bay window
like an ~: 5 paned

orient: 3 set **4** turn **5** adapt, align, aline **6** adjust, direct, locate, relate **7** conform **8** accustom **9** determine, orientate

Orient: 4 Asia, east **5** Henry **7** Far East
Orient ___: 7 Express
Oriental: 3 cat **5** felid **6** feline **7** Eastern
Oriental ___: 3 rug **5** poppy **6** carpet **7** cat's-eye

orientation: 3 fix **8** bearings, location, position **9** direction, placement
orienteer need: 3 map **5** atlas, chart **7** compass

Orient Express: 5 coach, train **9** transport
stop: 5 Paris **6** Calais **8** Istanbul
unit: 3 car

orifice: 4 hole, pore, vent **5** mouth **6** outlet **7** opening
leaf ~: 5 stoma

orig.
not an ~: 4 dupl., imit. **5** repro.

origami: 3 art **8** Japanese
feature: 4 bend, fold **6** crease **7** fluting
need: 5 paper, sheet

Origami: 4 font **8** typeface

origin: 3 egg **4** base, dawn, font, germ, head, rise, root, seed, well **5** agent, basis, birth, blood, cause, fount, git-go, roots, start, stock **6** author, cradle, day one, family, father, matrix, mother, motive, outset, parent, source, spring **7** creator, dawning, descent, genesis, lineage, nucleus **8** ancestor, ancestry, creation, fountain, heritage, nativity, pedigree, producer **9** beginning, causation, emergence, etymology, generator, inception, parentage, principle, square one, threshold **10** antecedent, beginnings, conception, derivation, envisaging, extraction, foundation, incipience, initiation, mainspring, progenitor, provenance, wellspring
combining form: 4 -geny

original: 3 new, old **4** card, mint, real **5** early, first, fresh, model, novel, prime, valid, witty **6** clever, infant, master, native, oddity, quaint, single, virgin, weirdo **7** anomaly, coinage, fertile, genuine, initial, novelty, oddball, opening, paragon, pattern, pioneer, primary, radical, seminal, untried, unusual **8** creation, creative, earliest, exemplar, inspired, paradigm, primeval, pristine, singular, starting, uncommon, virginal **9** aborigine, archetype, authentic, beginning, character, demiurgic, eccentric, embryonic, firsthand, formative, inceptive, ingenious, inspiring, inventive, precursor, primaeval, primitive, prototype, realistic, underived **10** archetypal, avant-garde, commencing, conceiving, elementary, forerunner, generative, innovative, primordial, productive, refreshing, unfamiliar
at the ~ place: 6 in situ
combining form: 4 arch- **5** arche-, archi-
in ~ form: 5 uncut
not ~: 5 deriv. **6** copied **8** borrowed, rehashed **9** imitative **10** derivative
production: 5 debut **7** opening **8** premiere **10** first night
strategy: 5 plan A

original ___: 3 gum, sin
Original Amateur Hour, The host: Major Bowes, Ted Mack

originality: 6 daring **7** newness, novelty **8** boldness **9** freshness, ingenuity **10** uniqueness

Original Kings of Comedy, The (2000 film)
cast: Cedric the Entertainer, Steve Harvey, D.L. Hughley, Bernie Mac
director: Spike Lee

originally: 5 first **7** at first, by birth **8** by origin, formerly **9** basically, initially, primarily

Original Sin (2001 film)
cast: Pedro Armendariz, Antonio Banderas, Angelina Jolie

originate: 4 coin, come, dawn, flow, form, make, open, rise, stem **5** arise, begin, build, cause, found, hatch, issue, pop up, set up, spark, spawn, start **6** create, derive, design, emerge, evolve, invent, launch, make up, open up, parent, spring **7** compose, concoct, descend, develop, emanate, kick off, lead off, pioneer, proceed, produce, think up, usher in **8** come from, commence, conceive, discover, engineer, generate, get going, initiate, innovate, occasion **9** enter upon, establish, formulate, germinate, grow out of, institute, introduce **10** bring about, come up with, inaugurate, mastermind
(from): 4 hail **6** derive, result

origination: 4 dawn **6** origin, source **8** creation **9** causation
combining form: 4 -gony

origination ___: 3 fee

originator: 5 cause **6** father, parent, source **7** creator, founder **8** designer, inventer, inventor **9** architect, artificer, fashioner **10** forebearer, forerunner, mastermind

Origin, The author: Irving Stone

Orillia: 4 city, town
locale: 6 Canada **7** Ontario

Orinda: 4 city, town
locale: 10 California

O-ring: 4 seal **6** gasket

Orinoco: 3 río **5** river
feeder: 4 Meta **6** Caroni
locale: 6 Brazil **8** Colombia **9** Venezuela
tributary: 3 Aro **5** Apure

Orinoco Flow artist: 4 Enya

oriole: 4 bird **8** songbird
___ oriole: 6 golden **7** orchard

Oriole: 6 Ripken **9** Cal Ripken
Hall of Famer: 6 Palmer **8** Robinson
rival: 3 Cub, Met, Red **4** Expo, Twin **5** Angel, Astro, Brave, Giant, Padre, Rocky, Royal, Tiger **6** Brewer, Dodger, Indian, Marlin, Philly, Pirate, Ranger, Red Sox, Yankee **7** Blue Jay, Mariner **8** Athletic, Cardinal, Devil Ray, White Sox

Orioles: 3 ten **4** team
home: 9 Baltimore
org.: 3 ALE, MLB
sport: 8 baseball

Orion: 3 cat **5** giant **6** hunter, nebula
daughter of ~: 7 Menippe **8** Metioche
dog of ~: 6 Sirius **10** Canis Major, Canis Minor
has one: 4 belt
lover: 3 Eos
parent of ~: 4 Gaea **7** Euryale **8** Poseidon
star in ~: 5 Rigel

orison: 4 plea **5** grace **6** appeal, litany, prayer, rosary **7** service, worship **8** devotion, entreaty, petition, rogation **10** invocation
ending: 4 amen

Orissa language: 5 Oriya

Orizaba: 4 city, town **7** volcano
locale: 6 Mexico **8** Veracruz

Orkan, bit of: 4 nanu **5** bleem **7** shazbot

Orkhon: 5 river
River locale: 8 Mongolia

Orkin: 4 Ruth
target: 3 ant, bug **4** pest **6** insect

Orkney Islands
ancient ~ dweller: 4 Pict
locale: 8 Scotland

Orlando: 4 city, Tony, town **6** Cepeda
attraction: 5 Epcot
character: 5 Sasha
composer: 6 Handel
locale: 7 Florida
newspaper: 8 Sentinel
pro team: 5 Magic
school: 3 UCF
stadium: 5 Orena

Orlando author: Virginia Woolf

Orlando Furioso: 4 epic, poem
author: Lodovico Ariosto

Orlando, Tony
song: Bless You (1961)
Candida (1970)
He Don't Love You (1975)
Knock Three Times (1970)
Look in My Eyes Pretty Woman (1975)
Make Believe (1969)
Mornin' Beautiful (1975)
Say, Has Anybody Seen My Sweet Gypsy Rose (1973)
Steppin' Out (1974)
Tie a Yellow Ribbon Round the Ole Oak Tree (1973)

Orland Park: 4 city, town
locale: 8 Illinois

___ or later: 6 sooner

Orleans: 6 battle
song: Dance With Me (1975)
Love Takes Time (1979)
Still the One (1976)

___ Orleans: 3 New

Orléans: 4 city, town
city southeast of ~: 6 Nevers
department: 6 Loiret
locale: 6 France
river: 5 Loire

___ or less: 4 more
orlo: 6 plinth
Orlon: 5 fiber **6** fabric **8** material

Orlons
song: Don't Hang Up (1962)
South Street (1963)
The Wah Watusi (1962)

orlop: 4 deck
___ or lose...: 5 Use it

Orly: 4 city, town **7** airport
locale: 6 France

Ormandy, Eugene: 9 conductor
___ or miss: 3 hit

ormolu: 5 alloy, metal
component: 4 zinc **6** copper

Ormond Beach: 4 city, town
locale: 7 Florida

Ormond, Julia: 7 actress
film: First Knight (1995)
Sabrina (1995)
Smilla's Sense of Snow (1997)

ornament: 3 art, gem **4** deck, gild, lace, ring, trim **5** adorn, array, beads, bijou, dodad, dress, fix up, frill, grace, honor, jewel, pride, primp, prink **6** anklet, bangle, bauble, bedaub, bedeck, design, doodad, emboss, enrich, finial, flower, geegaw, gewgaw, polish **7** bedizen, corsage, dress up, encrust, festoon, flatter, garnish, incrust,

jewelry, smarten, trinket **8** accouter, accoutre, beautify, bracelet, brighten, decorate, emblazon, figurine, froufrou, furbelow, necklace, nicknack, prettify, spruce up, trapping, trimming, wristlet **9** accessory, adornment, embellish, embroider **10** decoration, knickknack
Christmas ~: **4** ball, cane, tree **5** angel
head ~: **5** crown, tiara **6** wreath **7** coronet
roof ~: **3** epi **6** finial
showy ~: **4** gaud **6** bauble, geegaw, gewgaw
__ ornament: **4** hood
ornamental: **5** fancy, plant, showy, shrub **6** azalea, dressy, frilly **7** for show **8** delicate, justicia **9** beautiful, elaborate, enhancing, exquisite **10** decorative
band: **4** sash **6** armlet, frieze
plant: **5** pilea **6** azalea, coleus
ornamentation: **4** trim **5** decor, frill **9** arabesque
ornamented: **5** fancy, showy **6** flashy, florid, frilly, glitzy, inlaid, lavish **7** baroque, flowery, opulent **9** decorated, elaborate, garnished, luxurious, sumptuous
not ~: **4** bare **5** basic, naked, plain, stark **6** modest, severe, simple **7** austere, natural, Spartan, vanilla **9** unadorned
ornate: **4** busy, fine, lacy, rich **5** fancy, fussy, gaudy, plush, showy **6** chichi, dressy, flashy, florid, frilly, gilded, glitzy, lavish, rococo, tawdry **7** aureate, baroque, elegant, flowery, for show, opulent, splashy **8** dazzling, overdone, splendid **9** bejeweled, brilliant, elaborate, high-flown, luxuriant, luxurious, sumptuous, tasteless **10** convoluted, flamboyant, rhetorical
not ~: **5** plain, stark **6** chaste
Orne, city on the: **4** Caen
__ Orne Jewett: **5** Sarah
ornery: **4** cold, cool, mean **5** aloof, balky, cross, huffy, nasty, rigid, sharp, surly, testy **6** chilly, crabby, cranky, crusty, feisty, grumpy, mulish, odious, remote, snappy, sullen, touchy, unruly, wilful **7** adverse, bearish, bilious, defiant, fretful, glacial, grouchy, hateful, hostile, loutish, naughty, peevish, restive, waspish, wayward, willful **8** choleric, churlish, contrary, fretsome, growling, grumpish, inimical, obdurate, perverse, snappish, snarling, spiteful, stubborn **9** bellicose, crotchety, fractious, irascible, irritable, malicious, obstinate, pigheaded, sarcastic, splenetic, truculent, withdrawn **10** hard-bitten, headstrong, ill-natured, inflexible, malevolent, out of sorts, pugnacious, rebellious
mood: **3** pet **4** huff, snit, stew **5** pique **6** temper **9** surliness
one: **4** cuss, mule **10** curmudgeon
Ornette: **7** Coleman
__ or never: **3** now
ornithological: **5** avian
ornithologist: **6** birder
ornithology: **7** science
study: **5** birds
ornithophobe fear: **4** fowl **5** birds
__ or no: **7** whether
__ or none: **3** all
__ or not...: **4** to be **5** Ready
__ or nothing: **3** all **6** double
__ Oro: **5** Rio de
oroide: **5** alloy
component: **3** tin **4** zinc **6** copper
orology: **7** science
study: **9** mountains
Oromo
home: **5** Kenya **6** Africa **8** Ethiopia
Orono: **4** city, town
athletes: **10** Black Bears
locale: **5** Maine
Orontes: **5** river
River locale: **5** Syria **6** Turkey **7** Lebanon
Oropa: **3** cow **4** bull **6** bovine, cattle
Orosco, Jesse sport: **8** baseball
__ or other: **7** somehow
orotund: **4** deep, full **5** round, tumid **6** strong **7** booming, fustian, hyped up, pompous **8** globular, powerful, resonant, sonorous **9** bombastic, grandiose, overblown
O'Rourke: **2** P.J. **3** sgt. **6** Morgan **7** Heather **8** sergeant
Oro Valley: **4** city, town
locale: **7** Arizona
Oroville: **3** dam
oro y __: **5** plata
Orozco: **4** José
Orpah, mother-in-law of: **5** Naomi
or partner: **6** either
orphan: **4** waif, ward **5** Annie **9** foundling **10** ragamuffin
ender: **3** age
herd ~: **4** dogy **5** dogey, stray **6** doggie
orphan __: **4** drug
__ Orphan Annie: **6** Little
Orphan, The author: **4** Rabe **5** Otway
Orphée artist: **5** Corot
Orpheus: **4** poet **6** ballet **8** Argonaut
brother of ~: **5** Linus
composer: **10** Stravinsky
father of ~: **7** Oeagrus
instrument: **4** lyre
parent of ~: **7** Oeagrus **8** Calliope
son of ~: **7** Musaeus
wife of ~: **8** Eurydice
__ Orpheus: **5** Black
Orpheus Descending author: Tennessee Williams
Orpheus in the Underworld composer: **9** Offenbach
orphic: **6** occult **8** esoteric, profound **9** recondite
orphica: **5** piano **8** keyboard
Orpington: **4** fowl **7** chicken
relative: **6** Bantam, Brahma, Houdan, Sussex **7** Cornish, Dorking, Leghorn **8** Araucana, Langshan, Shanghai **9** Dominique, Wyandotte
Orr: **5** Bobby, James **8** Benjamin
Orr, Bobby
emulate ~: **5** skate
milieu: **3** ice **4** rink **5** arena **6** hockey
org.: **3** NHL
Orrie's Story author: Thomas Berger
Orrin: **5** Hatch
orris: **5** braid
ender: **4** root
root extract: **5** irone
Orr, John Boyd: **7** British **8** Nobelist
__ or shine: **4** rain
__ or shut...: **5** put up
Orsk: **4** city, town
locale: **6** Russia
river: **4** Ural
__ or Something Like It: **4** Life
Orson: **4** Bean **5** Orkan **6** Welles
ex: **4** Rita
__ or swim: **4** sink
ort: **5** crumb, scrap **7** leaving, remnant **8** leftover
__ or tails: **5** heads
__ or take: **4** give
Ortegal: **4** cape
locale: **5** Spain
Ortega y Gasset, José: **6** writer **7** Spanish **8** essayist
__ or the other: **3** one
__ or the Tiger?, The: **4** Lady
__-orthicon tube: **5** image
orth- kin: **4** rect-
orthoclase to Mohs: **3** six
orthodontist
concern: **4** bite
deg.: **3** DDS, DMD
org.: **3** ADA
orthodox: **4** good, true **5** pious, right, sound, typic, usual **6** common, devout, in line, narrow, normal, proper, square, wonted **7** correct, diehard, limited, regular, routine, typical **8** accepted, approved, dogmatic, everyday, habitual, hard-line, official, ordinary, rightful, standard, straight **9** by the book, canonical, customary, doctrinal, religious **10** accustomed, conformist, dogmatical, legitimate, prevailing, recognized, sanctioned
opener: **3** neo
Orthodox __: **3** Jew **6** Church **7** Judaism
__ Orthodox Church: **5** Greek **7** Eastern, Russian
orthodoxy: **4** tune **7** harmony, keeping **8** likeness, religion, symmetry **9** agreement, coherence, congruity, obedience **10** allegiance, compliance, conformity, consonance, exactitude, observance, similarity, submission
orthopedist tool: **4** X-ray **10** radiograph
ortolan: **4** bird
Orton, Joe: **7** British **10** playwright
work: Loot
What the Butler Saw
Or to take __ against a sea...: **4** arms
__ or treat: **5** trick
orts: **4** rest **5** waste **7** residue
Oruro: **4** city, town
locale: **7** Bolivia
Orvieto: **4** wine **5** white
origin: **5** Italy
Orville: **5** Moody **6** Wright **11** Redenbacher
Orwell, George: **5** alias **6** author, writer **7** British
alma mater: **4** Eton
birthplace: **5** India
real name: Eric Blair
work: 1984
Animal Farm
Down and Out in Paris and London
Keep the Aspidistra Flying
Shooting an Elephant
__ or When: **5** Where
__ Ory: **5** Comte
Ory, Kid: **10** trombonist
genre: **4** jazz
oryx: **6** animal **8** antelope
relative: **3** gnu, kob **4** guib, kudu, puku, topi **5** addax, bongo, chiru, eland, goral, korin, nyala, oribi, saiga, serow **6** chammy, dik-dik, duiker, impala, koodoo, lechwe, nilgai, rhebok, shammy, shamoy **7** blaubok, blesbok, chamois, defassa, gazelle, gemsbok, gerenuk, grysbok, nylghai, nylghau, sassaby **8** blesbuck, bontebok, bushbuck, gemsbuck, reedbuck, steenbok, steinbok **9** blackbuck, pronghorn, sitatunga, springbok, waterbuck **10** hartebeest, wildebeest
orzo: **5** pasta
alternative: **4** ziti **5** penne **6** noodle **7** lasagna, lasagne, pastina, ravioli **8** bucatini, couscous, farfalle, linguine, linguini, macaroni, rigatoni **9** agnolotti, angelhair, cavatelli, manicotti, spaghetti **10** cannelloni, fettuccini, tortellini, vermicelli
Os: **4** elem. **6** osmium **7** element
76 for ~: **4** at. no.
Osa: **6** Massen **7** Johnson
Osage: **5** river, tribe **6** Indian, orange **7** Amerind **8** language
River locale: **6** Kansas **8** Missouri
Osaka: **4** city, port, town
city near ~: **4** Nara **5** Kioto, Kyoto, Sakai
locale: **5** Japan **6** Honshu
Osaka Bay, port on: **4** Kobe
Osario author: Coleridge
Osbert: **7** Sitwell
Osborne: **4** Joan, John **7** Jeffrey
Osborne, Joan song: One of Us (1995)
Osborne, John: **7** British **10** playwright
work: Look Back in Anger
Osbourne, Ozzy
group: Black Sabbath
homeland: England
song: Close My Eyes Forever (1989)
Oscan: **8** language
Oscar: **4** slob **5** Arias, award, Lewis, Mayer, Wilde **6** grouch, Levant, Muppet **7** Handlin, Homolka **8** de la Hoya, Hijuelos, Peterson **9** de la Renta, Pettiford, Robertson **10** Charleston
colleague: **4** Bert **5** Ernie, Piggy **6** Kermit **7** Big Bird
cousin: **4** Emmy, Obie, Tony
French ~: **5** César
night rental: **4** gown **7** costume
nominee: **4** star **5** actor **8** director
org.: **5** AMPAS
Oscar __ Hoya: **4** de la
Oscar __ Renta: **4** de la
Oscar __ Sanchez: **5** Arias
Oscar Mayer: **5** frank **6** hot dog, wiener
alternative: **5** Kahn's **6** Armour **8** Ball Park
Oscar winners (Actor):
2003 - Sean Penn
2002 - Adrien Brody
2001 - Denzel Washington
2000 - Russell Crowe
1999 - Kevin Spacey
1998 - Roberto Benigni
1997 - Jack Nicholson
1996 - Geoffrey Rush
1995 - Nicolas Cage
1994 - Tom Hanks
1993 - Tom Hanks
1992 - Al Pacino
1991 - Anthony Hopkins
1990 - Jeremy Irons
1989 - Daniel Day-Lewis
1988 - Dustin Hoffman
1987 - Michael Douglas
1986 - Paul Newman
1985 - William Hurt
1984 - F. Murray Abraham
1983 - Robert Duvall
1982 - Ben Kingsley
1981 - Henry Fonda
1980 - Robert De Niro
1979 - Dustin Hoffman
1978 - Jon Voight
1977 - Richard Dreyfuss
1976 - Peter Finch
1975 - Jack Nicholson
1974 - Art Carney
1973 - Jack Lemmon
1972 - Marlon Brando
1971 - Gene Hackman
1970 - George C. Scott
1969 - John Wayne
1968 - Cliff Robertson
1967 - Rod Steiger
1966 - Paul Scofield
1965 - Lee Marvin
1964 - Rex Harrison
1963 - Sidney Poitier
1962 - Gregory Peck
1961 - Maximilian Schell
1960 - Burt Lancaster
1959 - Charlton Heston
1958 - David Niven

1957 - Alec Guinness
1956 - Yul Brynner
1955 - Ernest Borgnine
1954 - Marlon Brando
1953 - William Holden
1952 - Gary Cooper
1951 - Humphrey Bogart
1950 - José Ferrer
1949 - Broderick Crawford
1948 - Laurence Olivier
1947 - Ronald Colman
1946 - Fredric March
1945 - Ray Milland
1944 - Bing Crosby
1943 - Paul Lukas
1942 - James Cagney
1941 - Gary Cooper
1940 - James Stewart
1939 - Robert Donat
1938 - Spencer Tracy
1937 - Spencer Tracy
1936 - Paul Muni
1935 - Victor McLaglen
1934 - Clark Gable
1932/33 - Charles Laughton
1931/32 - Fredric March
1931/32 - Wallace Beery
1930/31 - Lionel Barrymore
1929/30 - George Arliss
1928/29 - Warner Baxter
1927/28 - Emil Jannings

Oscar winners (Actress):
2003 - Charlize Theron
2002 - Nicole Kidman
2001 - Halle Berry
2000 - Julia Roberts
1999 - Hilary Swank
1998 - Gwyneth Paltrow
1997 - Helen Hunt
1996 - Frances McDormand
1995 - Susan Sarandon
1994 - Jessica Lange
1993 - Holly Hunter
1992 - Emma Thompson
1991 - Jodie Foster
1990 - Kathy Bates
1989 - Jessica Tandy
1988 - Jodie Foster
1987 - Cher
1986 - Marlee Matlin
1985 - Geraldine Page
1984 - Sally Field
1983 - Shirley MacLaine
1982 - Meryl Streep
1981 - Katharine Hepburn
1980 - Sissy Spacek
1979 - Sally Field
1978 - Jane Fonda
1977 - Diane Keaton
1976 - Faye Dunaway
1975 - Louise Fletcher
1974 - Ellen Burstyn
1973 - Glenda Jackson
1972 - Liza Minnelli
1971 - Jane Fonda
1970 - Glenda Jackson
1969 - Maggie Smith
1968 - Barbra Streisand, Katharine Hepburn
1967 - Katharine Hepburn
1966 - Elizabeth Taylor
1965 - Julie Christie
1964 - Julie Andrews
1963 - Patricia Neal
1962 - Anne Bancroft
1961 - Sophia Loren
1960 - Elizabeth Taylor
1959 - Simone Signoret
1958 - Susan Hayward
1957 - Joanne Woodward
1956 - Ingrid Bergman
1955 - Anna Magnani
1954 - Grace Kelly
1953 - Audrey Hepburn
1952 - Shirley Booth
1951 - Vivien Leigh
1950 - Judy Holliday
1949 - Olivia de Havilland
1948 - Jane Wyman
1947 - Loretta Young
1946 - Olivia de Havilland
1945 - Joan Crawford
1944 - Ingrid Bergman
1943 - Jennifer Jones
1942 - Greer Garson
1941 - Joan Fontaine
1940 - Ginger Rogers
1939 - Vivien Leigh
1938 - Bette Davis
1937 - Luise Rainer
1936 - Luise Rainer
1935 - Bette Davis
1934 - Claudette Colbert
1932/33 - Katharine Hepburn
1931/32 - Helen Hayes
1930/31 - Marie Dressler
1929/30 - Norma Shearer
1928/29 - Mary Pickford
1927/28 - Janet Gaynor

Oscar winners (Director):
2003 - Peter Jackson
2002 - Roman Polanski
2001 - Ron Howard
2000 - Steven Soderbergh
1999 - Sam Mendes
1998 - Steven Spielberg
1997 - James Cameron
1996 - Anthony Minghella
1995 - Mel Gibson
1994 - Robert Zemeckis
1993 - Steven Spielberg
1992 - Clint Eastwood
1991 - Jonathan Demme
1990 - Kevin Costner
1989 - Oliver Stone
1988 - Barry Levinson
1987 - Bernardo Bertolucci
1986 - Oliver Stone
1985 - Sydney Pollack
1984 - Milos Forman
1983 - James L. Brooks
1982 - Richard Attenborough
1981 - Warren Beatty
1980 - Robert Redford
1979 - Robert Benton
1978 - Michael Cimino
1977 - Woody Allen
1976 - John G. Avildsen
1975 - Milos Forman
1974 - Francis Ford Coppola
1973 - George Roy Hill
1972 - Bob Fosse
1971 - William Friedkin
1970 - Franklin Schaffner
1969 - John Schlesinger
1968 - Carol Reed
1967 - Mike Nichols
1966 - Fred Zinnemann
1965 - Robert Wise
1964 - George Cukor
1963 - Tony Richardson
1962 - David Lean
1961 - Robert Wise, Jerome Robbins
1960 - Billy Wilder
1959 - William Wyler
1958 - Vincente Minnelli
1957 - David Lean
1956 - George Stevens
1955 - Delbert Mann
1954 - Elia Kazan
1953 - Fred Zinnemann
1952 - John Ford
1951 - George Stevens
1950 - Joseph L. Mankiewicz
1949 - Joseph L. Mankiewicz
1948 - John Huston
1947 - Elia Kazan
1946 - William Wyler
1945 - Billy Wilder
1944 - Leo McCarey
1943 - Michael Curtiz
1942 - William Wyler
1941 - John Ford
1940 - John Ford
1939 - Victor Fleming
1938 - Frank Capra
1937 - Leo McCarey
1936 - Frank Capra
1935 - John Ford
1934 - Frank Capra
1932/33 - Frank Lloyd
1931/32 - Frank Borzage
1930/31 - Norman Taurog
1929/30 - Lewis Milestone
1928/29 - Frank Lloyd
1927/28 - Frank Borzage
1927/28 - Lewis Milestone

Oscar winners (Picture):
2003 - The Lord of the Rings: The Return of the King
2002 - Chicago
2001 - A Beautiful Mind
2000 - Gladiator
1999 - American Beauty
1998 - Shakespeare in Love
1997 - Titanic
1996 - The English Patient
1995 - Braveheart
1994 - Forrest Gump
1993 - Schindler's List
1992 - Unforgiven
1991 - The Silence of the Lambs
1990 - Dances With Wolves
1989 - Driving Miss Daisy
1988 - Rain Man
1987 - The Last Emperor
1986 - Platoon
1985 - Out of Africa
1984 - Amadeus
1983 - Terms of Endearment
1982 - Gandhi
1981 - Chariots of Fire
1980 - Ordinary People
1979 - Kramer vs. Kramer
1978 - The Deer Hunter
1977 - Annie Hall
1976 - Rocky
1975 - One Flew Over the Cuckoo's Nest
1974 - The Godfather Part II
1973 - The Sting
1972 - The Godfather
1971 - The French Connection
1970 - Patton
1969 - Midnight Cowboy
1968 - Oliver!
1967 - In the Heat of the Night
1966 - A Man for All Seasons
1965 - The Sound of Music
1964 - My Fair Lady
1963 - Tom Jones
1962 - Lawrence of Arabia
1961 - West Side Story
1960 - The Apartment
1959 - Ben-Hur
1958 - Gigi
1957 - The Bridge on the River Kwai
1956 - Around the World in 80 Days
1955 - Marty
1954 - On the Waterfront
1953 - From Here to Eternity
1952 - The Greatest Show on Earth
1951 - An American in Paris
1950 - All About Eve
1949 - All the King's Men
1948 - Hamlet
1947 - Gentleman's Agreement
1946 - The Best Years of Our Lives
1945 - The Lost Weekend
1944 - Going My Way
1943 - Casablanca
1942 - Mrs. Miniver
1941 - How Green Was My Valley
1940 - Rebecca
1939 - Gone With the Wind
1938 - You Can't Take It With You
1937 - The Life of Emile Zola
1936 - The Great Ziegfeld
1935 - Mutiny on the Bounty
1934 - It Happened One Night
1932/33 - Cavalcade
1931/32 - Grand Hotel
1930/31 - Cimarron
1929/30 - All Quiet on the Western Front
1928/29 - Broadway Melody
1927/28 - Wings

Oscar winners (Supp. Actor):
2003 - Tim Robbins
2002 - Chris Cooper
2001 - Jim Broadbent
2000 - Benicio Del Toro
1999 - Michael Caine
1998 - James Coburn
1997 - Robin Williams
1996 - Cuba Gooding Jr.
1995 - Kevin Spacey
1994 - Martin Landau
1993 - Tommy Lee Jones
1992 - Gene Hackman
1991 - Jack Palance
1990 - Joe Pesci
1989 - Denzel Washington
1988 - Kevin Kline
1987 - Sean Connery
1986 - Michael Caine
1985 - Don Ameche
1984 - Haing S. Ngor
1983 - Jack Nicholson
1982 - Louis Gossett Jr.
1981 - John Gielgud
1980 - Timothy Hutton
1979 - Melvyn Douglas
1978 - Christopher Walken
1977 - Jason Robards
1976 - Jason Robards
1975 - George Burns
1974 - Robert De Niro
1973 - John Houseman
1972 - Joel Grey
1971 - Ben Johnson
1970 - John Mills
1969 - Gig Young
1968 - Jack Albertson
1967 - George Kennedy
1966 - Walter Matthau
1965 - Martin Balsam
1964 - Peter Ustinov
1963 - Melvyn Douglas
1962 - Ed Begley
1961 - George Chakiris
1960 - Peter Ustinov
1959 - Hugh Griffith
1958 - Burl Ives
1957 - Red Buttons
1956 - Anthony Quinn
1955 - Jack Lemmon
1954 - Edmond O'Brien
1953 - Frank Sinatra
1952 - Anthony Quinn
1951 - Karl Malden
1950 - George Sanders
1949 - Dean Jagger
1948 - Walter Huston
1947 - Edmund Gwenn
1946 - Harold Russell
1945 - James Dunn
1944 - Barry Fitzgerald
1943 - Charles Coburn
1942 - Van Heflin
1941 - Donald Crisp
1940 - Walter Brennan
1939 - Thomas Mitchell
1938 - Walter Brennan
1937 - Joseph Schildkraut
1936 - Walter Brennan

Oscar winners (Supp. Actress):
2003 - Renée Zellweger
2002 - Catherine Zeta-Jones
2001 - Jennifer Connelly
2000 - Marcia Gay Harden
1999 - Angelina Jolie
1998 - Judi Dench
1997 - Kim Basinger
1996 - Juliette Binoche
1995 - Mira Sorvino
1994 - Dianne Wiest
1993 - Anna Paquin
1992 - Marisa Tomei
1991 - Mercedes Ruehl
1990 - Whoopi Goldberg
1989 - Brenda Fricker
1988 - Geena Davis
1987 - Olympia Dukakis
1986 - Dianne Wiest
1985 - Anjelica Huston
1984 - Peggy Ashcroft
1983 - Linda Hunt
1982 - Jessica Lange
1981 - Maureen Stapleton
1980 - Mary Steenburgen
1979 - Meryl Streep
1978 - Maggie Smith
1977 - Vanessa Redgrave
1976 - Beatrice Straight
1975 - Lee Grant
1974 - Ingrid Bergman
1973 - Tatum O'Neal
1972 - Eileen Heckart
1971 - Cloris Leachman
1970 - Helen Hayes
1969 - Goldie Hawn
1968 - Ruth Gordon
1967 - Estelle Parsons
1966 - Sandy Dennis
1965 - Shelley Winters
1964 - Lila Kedrova
1963 - Margaret Rutherford
1962 - Patty Duke
1961 - Rita Moreno
1960 - Shirley Jones
1959 - Shelley Winters
1958 - Wendy Hiller
1957 - Miyoshi Umeki
1956 - Dorothy Malone
1955 - Jo Van Fleet
1954 - Eva Marie Saint
1953 - Donna Reed
1952 - Gloria Grahame
1951 - Kim Hunter
1950 - Josephine Hull
1949 - Mercedes McCambridge
1948 - Claire Trevor
1947 - Celeste Holm
1946 - Anne Baxter
1945 - Anne Revere
1944 - Ethel Barrymore
1943 - Katina Paxinou
1942 - Teresa Wright
1941 - Mary Astor
1940 - Jane Darwell
1939 - Hattie McDaniel
1938 - Fay Bainter
1937 - Alice Brady
1936 - Gale Sondergaard

oscillate: **3** bob, wag **4** beat, rock, spin, sway, turn, vary, wave **5** pivot, pulse, shake, swing, waver **6** change, dangle, quiver, seesaw, switch, swivel, teeter, totter, wabble, waggle, wobble, zigzag **7** librate, pulsate, tremble, vibrate **8** fishtail, hesitate **9** alternate, come and go, fluctuate, vacillate **10** ebb and flow, equivocate
oscillation: **4** beat, vibe **6** motion **9** vibration **10** hesitation
oscine: **4** crow, lark **6** bulbul, shrike **8** trembler, tremblor **9** bowerbird **10** honeyeater
oscitate: **4** gape, yawn
osculate: **4** buss, kiss, lick, neck, peck **5** touch **6** smooch
osculation: **4** buss, kiss, peck **5** smack **6** smooch
-ose: **4** like **5** sugar
__ O. Selznick: **5** David
Osgood: **7** Charles, Conklin
Osh: **4** city, town
  locale: **10** Kyrgyzstan
OSHA
  department: **5** Labor
  part: **5** Admin. **6** Health, Safety
__-o'-shanter: **3** tam
Oshawa: **4** city, town
  locale: **6** Canada **7** Ontario
O'Shea: **4** Milo **6** Tessie **7** Michael
Osheroff, Douglas: **8** Nobelist **9** physicist
Oshima: **7** volcano
  locale: **4** Asia **5** Japan **8** Hokkaido
O Ship of State author: Henry Wadsworth Longfellow
Oshkosh: **4** city, town
  locale: **9** Wisconsin
OshKosh __: **5** B'Gosh
osier: **4** tree **6** willow
Osijek: **4** city, town
  locale: **7** Croatia
Osiris: **3** god **8** Egyptian
  brother of ~: **3** Set
  parent of ~: **3** Geb, Nut
  sister of ~: **4** Isis
  slayer of ~: **3** Set
  son of ~: **5** Horus **6** Anubis
  wife of ~: **4** Isis
Oskar: **6** Werner **9** Kokoschka, Schindler
Oslin: **2** K.T.
Oslo: **4** city, port, town **7** capital
  locale: **6** Norway
  sight: **5** fiord, fjord
Osman: **4** amir, emir **5** ameer, emeer
Osment, Haley Joel: **5** actor
  film: AI: Artificial Intelligence (2001)
    Forrest Gump (1994)
    Pay It Forward (2000)
    The Sixth Sense (1999)
osmics: **7** science
  study: **5** smell
osmium: **5** metal **7** element
  alloy: **7** platina
Osmond: **3** Ken **4** Alan **5** Donny, Marie
Osmond, Donny
  song: Are You Lonesome Tonight (1973)
    Go Away Little Girl (1971)
    Hey Girl (1971)
    Lonely Boy (1972)
    A Million to One (1973)
    My Love Is a Fire (1990)
    Puppy Love (1972)
    Sacred Emotion (1989)
    Soldier of Love (1989)
    Sweet and Innocent (1971)
    Too Young (1972)
    The Twelfth of Never (1973)
    Why (1972)
Osmond, Donny and Marie
  song: I'm Leaving It Up to You (1974)
    Morning Side of the Mountain (1974)
Osmond, Marie song: Paper Roses (1973)
Osmonds
  home: **4** Utah **5** Ogden
  members: Alan, Wayne, Merrill, Jay, Donny
  song: Crazy Horses (1972)
    Double Lovin' (1971)
    Down by the Lazy River (1972)
    Hold Her Tight (1972)
    Love Me for a Reason (1974)
    One Bad Apple (1971)
    Yo-Yo (1971)
osmose: **4** seep **5** drain, sop up **6** absorb, draw in, filter, gather, ingest, soak up, suck up, take in **7** drink in, swallow **10** assimilate
osmunda: **4** fern
Osnabrück: **4** city, town
  locale: **7** Germany
oso __: **6** blanco
O sole __: **3** mio
Osorno: **4** city, town
  locale: **5** Chile
Osoyoos: **4** city, town
  locale: **6** Canada
osprey: **4** bird **8** fish hawk
  cousin: **3** ern **4** erne
O.S.S. (1946 film)
  cast: Geraldine Fitzgerald, Patric Knowles, Alan Ladd
Ossa: **2** mt. **3** mtn. **4** peak **8** mountain
  locale: **6** Greece **8** Tasmania
osseous: **4** bony **5** boney
Ossett: **4** city, town
  locale: **7** England **9** Yorkshire
ossia: **2** or **6** or else **9** otherwise
Ossie: **5** Davis
  wife: **4** Ruby
ossified: **3** set **5** rigid, stiff **6** frozen **8** hardened **9** hidebound, petrified, unpliable **10** inflexible
ossifrage: **4** bird
ossify: **6** freeze, harden **7** petrify, stiffen **8** indurate, rigidify **9** fossilize, stabilize
Ossining: **4** city, town
  locale: **7** New York
osso __: **4** buco
OSS successor: **3** CIA
OS/2 company: **3** IBM
osteal: **4** bony **5** boney
Ostend: **4** port
  locale: **7** Belgium
ostensible: **5** quasi **6** avowed, likely **7** alleged, nominal, outward, reputed, seeming **8** apparent, illusive, illusory, knowable, manifest, palpable, probable, so-called, specious, supposed **9** pretended, professed, purported
ostensibly: **7** for show **8** to the eye **9** doubtless, evidently, outwardly, seemingly **10** apparently
Ostenso: **4** peak **5** mount **8** mountain
  locale: **10** Antarctica
ostentation: **4** fuss, pomp, ritz, show **5** array, flash, glitz, shine **6** parade, vanity **7** bravado, display, swagger **8** boasting, bragging, pretense, vaunting **9** flaunting, pageantry, showiness, spectacle, vainglory **10** pretension
ostentatious: **3** gay **4** loud, tony, vain **5** crass, fancy, fussy, gaudy, grand, proud, ritzy, showy, stagy, swank, toney **6** chichi, classy, flashy, garish, glitzy, ornate, solemn, stagey, swanky, tinsel, uptown, vulgar **7** blatant, dashing, opulent, pompous, splashy **8** affected, boastful, flaunted, glittery, pedantic, snobbish, specious **9** egotistic, grandiose, luxurious, tasteless **10** pedantical
  be ~: **5** boast, strut **6** flaunt, parade **7** show off, trot out
Osterizer, use an: **3** mix **5** blend
Osterman Weekend, The author: Robert Ludlum
Österreich, capital of: **4** Wien
Osterwald: **4** Bibi
Ostia: **4** port **7** seaport
  neighbor: **4** Roma
  river: **5** Tiber
  see also Latin
ostracism: **5** exile **6** rebuke **9** dismissal, exclusion, expulsion, isolation **10** punishment
ostracize: **3** ban, bar, cut **4** drop, oust, shun, snub, tabu **5** avoid, exile, expel, scorn **6** banish, deport, reject **7** boycott, cast out, censure, exclude, expulse, isolate, seclude, shut off, shut out **8** displace, relegate, throw out **9** blackball, blacklist, order to go **10** expatriate
ostracized: **5** rogue **9** unpopular **10** friendless
Ostrava: **4** city, town
ostrich: **4** bird, fern **5** biped **8** escapist
  cousin: **3** emu, moa **4** emeu, rhea
Ostwald, Wilhelm: **7** chemist **8** Nobelist
OSU
  conference: **6** Big Ten, Pac-Ten **9** Big Twelve
  part of ~: **3** Ore. **4** Ohio, Okla., Oreg., Univ. **6** Oregon **8** Oklahoma
  see also Ohio State, Oklahoma State, Oregon State
O'Sullivan: **7** Gilbert, Maureen
O'Sullivan, Gilbert
  homeland: Ireland
  song: Alone Again (Naturally) (1972)
    Clair (1972)
    Get Down (1973)
    Out of the Question (1972)
O'Sullivan, Maureen: **7** actress
  daughter: Mia Farrow
  film: The Big Clock (1948)
    A Connecticut Yankee (1931)
    David Copperfield (1935)
    A Day at the Races (1937)
    The Devil-Doll (1936)
    Hannah and Her Sisters (1986)
    Payment Deferred (1932)
    Skyscraper Souls (1932)
    The Tall T (1957)
    Tarzan and His Mate (1934)
    Tarzan Escapes (1936)
    Tarzan Finds a Son! (1939)
    Tarzan, the Ape Man (1932)
    The Thin Man (1934)
    A Yank at Oxford (1938)
  role: **4** Jane
Oswald: **4** Gerd **8** Spengler
Oswego: **4** lake
  locale: **6** Oregon
  tea: **5** plant **6** flower
O.T.
  book: **3** Bar., Ezr., Gen., Hab., Hos., Isa., Jer., Job, Lam., Lev., Mac., Mic., Nah., Neh., Num., Psa. **4** Deut., Eccl., Exod., Ezek., Macc., Obad., Prov., Zech. **5** Levit. **6** Eccles.
  passage: **3** ver.
  see also Bible, Old Testament
Ota: **4** city, town
  locale: **5** Japan
Otaheite __: **5** apple **6** orange
O Tannenbaum: **5** carol
  subject: **3** fir **4** tree
Otaru: **4** city, town
  locale: **5** Japan
otary: **4** seal **9** eared seal
OTB
  activity: **5** wager **6** exacta **8** perfecta, quinella, trifecta
  part of: **3** off **5** track **7** betting
  posting: **4** odds **7** winners
OTC
  buy: **5** stock
  part: **4** over **7** counter
  source: **4** phar. **5** pharm.
Oteapan: **4** city, town
  locale: **6** Mexico **8** Veracruz
Otello: **5** opera
  composer: **5** Verdi
  librettist: **5** Boito
  role: **4** Iago
  song: **4** aria
Otello (1986 film)
  cast: Justino Diaz, Plácido Domingo, Katia Ricciarelli
  director: Franco Zeffirelli
O tempora! O __!: **5** mores
O-T filler: **4** PQRS

O the Chimneys author: Nelly Sachs
Othello: **4** Moor, play **7** tragedy
  author: William Shakespeare
  character: **4** Iago **6** Bianca, Cassio, Emilia **7** Michael, Montano, Othello **8** Gratiano, Lodovico, Roderigo **9** Brabantio, Desdemona
Othello (1952 film)
  cast: Suzanne Cloutier, Micheal MacLiammoir, Orson Welles
  director: Orson Welles
Othello (1965 film)
  cast: Frank Finlay, Laurence Olivier, Maggie Smith
Othello (1995 film)
  cast: Kenneth Branagh, Laurence Fishburne, Irène Jacob
__ o' the mornin': **3** top
other: **3** new **4** else, more **5** added, extra, fresh, spare **6** unlike **7** another, distant, diverse, farther, further, unalike, unequal, variant **8** distinct, opposite, separate **9** alternate, auxiliary, different, disparate, divergent, unrelated **10** additional, dissimilar, substitute
  combining form: **3** all- **4** allo- **5** heter- **6** hetero-
  ender: **4** wise **5** world **7** worldly
  in Spanish: **4** otra, otro
  people: **4** them
other __: **4** half, than
other __ of the coin, the: **4** side
other __ to fry: **4** fish
__ other: **4** each **5** every
Other __, The: **3** Guy **5** Woman **6** Sister
other fish __: **5** to fry
__ other hand: **5** on the
otherness: **8** contrast, variance **9** departure, deviation, disparity, diversity, variation **10** aberration, difference, dissonance, divergence
Other People's Money (1991 film)
  cast: Danny DeVito, Piper Laurie, Penelope Ann Miller, Gregory Peck
  director: Norman Jewison
Other People's Money author: Jerome Weidman
others: **4** alii, rest, them, they **6** extras **7** the rest **9** leftovers, outsiders
  and ~: **6** et alia, et alii
  how ~ see us: **5** image **9** depiction **10** appearance, conception, impression, perception, projection
  in Durango: **5** otras, otros
  in Spanish: **5** otras, otros
  not ~: **2** us **5** these **6** myself
others': **5** their
__ others...: **6** Do unto
...others __!: **5** see us
Other Side of Midnight, The author: Sidney Sheldon
Other Side of the Rainbow, The
  author: **5** Torme
Other Sister, The (1999 film)
  cast: Diane Keaton, Juliette Lewis, Tom Skerritt
  director: Garry Marshall
Others, The (2001 film)
  cast: Christopher Eccleston, Fionnula Flanagan, Nicole Kidman
Other, The (1972 film)
  cast: Uta Hagen, Diana Muldaur
  director: Robert Mulligan
Other, The author: Thomas Tryon
Other Voices, Other Rooms author: Truman Capote
other white meat, the: **4** pork
__ Other Wife: **5** John's
otherwise: **4** else **5** if not **6** or else, or then **7** besides, unalike **9** different **10** contrarily
  called: **3** AKA **5** alias
  in music: **5** ossia
  literally: **5** alias
  show ~: **4** deny **5** belie, quash, rebut **6** negate, refute **7** confute, dispute **8** confound, disprove, overturn **9** discredit, shoot down **10** contradict, disconfirm, prove false, prove wrong
otherworldly: **3** fey **4** eery **5** eerie **7** magical, utopian **9** spiritual, visionary
__-o'-the-wisp: **4** will
otic: **5** aural **8** auditory **9** auricular
otiose: **4** idle, lazy **6** futile **7** languid, useless **8** dallying, inactive, indolent, slothful **9** apathetic, at leisure, donothing, for naught, lethargic, negligent, pointless, shiftless, to no avail, unhurried **10** neglectful, unavailing
otiosity: **5** sloth **6** acedia, torpor **7** inertia, languor **8** idleness, laziness **9** faineance, indolence, torpidity **10** stagnation
Otis: **4** Amos, Miss **5** Carré **6** Elisha, Johnny **7** Redding, Skinner **8** Birdsong, Chandler, Williams **9** Armstrong
  friend of ~: **4** Milo
Otis, Amos sport: **8** baseball
__ Otis Regrets: **4** Miss
__ Otis Skinner: **8** Cornelia
otitis site: **3** ear
Oto: **5** tribe **6** Indian, Siouan **7** Amerind **8** language
  prey: **5** bison
Otoe: **5** tribe **6** Indian, Siouan **7** Amerind
otolaryngology: **3** ENT
  focus: **3** ear **4** nose **6** throat
otologist concern: **3** ear
Otomi: **6** Indian **7** Amerind
O'Toole: **5** Peter **7** Annette
O'Toole, Peter: **5** actor
  film: Becket (1964)
    Brotherly Love (1969)
    Creator (1985)
    The Dark Angel (1991)
    How to Steal a Million (1966)
    The Last Emperor (1987)
    Lawrence of Arabia (1962)
    The Lion in Winter (1968)
    Lord Jim (1965)
    Murphy's War (1971)
    My Favorite Year (1982)
    Phantoms (1998)
    The Ruling Class (1972)
    The Stunt Man (1980)
    Zulu Dawn (1979)
otra __: **3** vez
Otranto: **3** str. **6** strait
OTS grad: **2** lt. **5** lieut.
Otsu: **4** city, town
  locale: **5** Japan
Ott: **2** Ed **3** Mel
ottava __: **4** rima
Ottawa: **4** city, town **5** river **6** Indian **7** Amerind, capital
  locale: **3** Ont. **6** Canada **7** Ontario
  network: **3** CBC
  newspaper: **3** Sun **7** Citizen, Le Droit
  pro team: **8** Senators
  River locale: **6** Quebec **7** Ontario
  school: **8** Carleton
otter: **3** fur **6** animal, mammal, weasel
  milieu: **3** sea, zoo **5** ocean
  relative: **4** mink **5** fitch, ratel, sable, skunk, stoat, tayra **6** badger, ermine, ferret, marten **7** foumart, polecat **8** carcajou, foulmart, kolinsky, muishond **9** wolverine
  secretion: **4** musk
otter __: **5** board, shrew, trawl
__ otter: **3** sea **5** giant, river
otterhound: **3** dog **5** canid **6** canine
Ott, Mel: **5** Giant **7** slugger **10** outfielder
otto: **5** eight **7** Italian
  follower: **4** nove
  preceder: **5** sette
Otto: **3** dog, Jim **4** Hahn, Kahn **5** Diels, Loewi, Stern **6** Graham, Kruger, Soglow **7** bulldog, Harbach, Kristin, Nicolai, Wallach, Warburg **8** Bismarck, Meyerhof, Nikolaus **9** Klemperer, Preminger **10** Lilienthal
  see also German
Otto __ Bismarck: **3** von
Otto, Kristin: **6** German **7** swimmer
ottoman: **4** seat **5** divan, stool **6** fabric **7** hassock **8** footrest **9** footstool
  occupy an ~: **3** sit **5** perch **6** hunker
  relative: **4** pouf
Ottoman: **4** Turk **8** language
  court: **5** porte
  inn: **6** imaret
  peasant: **4** raya
  sultan: **5** selim
  title: **3** aga, bey **4** agha **5** calif, kalif, pacha, pasha, vizir **6** caliph, kaliph, khalif, vizier
Ottoman __: **6** Empire
Ottone composer: **6** Handel
otto of __: **5** roses
Ottorino: **8** Respighi
Ottumwa: **4** city, town
  locale: **4** Iowa
Ouachita: **5** range, river **6** Indian **7** Amerind
  River locale: **8** Arkansas **9** Louisiana
Ouagadougou: **4** city, town **7** capital
  locale: Burkina Faso
oubliette: **5** vault **6** prison **7** dungeon
ouch: **3** cry, yow **4** hurt, yipe **9** that hurts
Ouche, city on the: **5** Dijon
oud: **4** lute **6** string
  origin: **6** Africa
Oue, Eiji: **9** conductor
Ouémé: **5** river
  locale: **5** Benin **6** Africa
ought: **4** duty, have, must, need, zero **6** should
  to: **6** should **7** had best **9** had better
__ Oughta Be in Pictures: **3** You
__ Oughta Know: **3** You
oui: **2** ay, da, ja, sí **3** aye, yea, yep, yes, yup **4** fine, okay, sure, yeah **5** good-o, natch, quite, right, roger, uh-huh **6** agreed, gladly, good-oh, indeed, just so, rather, righto, surely, you bet, yowzah **7** exactly, go ahead, indeedy, quite so, ten-four **8** all right, as you say, of course, thumbs up, very well **9** be my guest, certainly, darn right, naturally, precisely, sure thing, you betcha, you said it **10** absolutely, by all means, definitely, positively, sure enough, that's right
  mais ~: **8** very well
  opposite: **3** non
__ oui!: **4** Mais
oui-dire: **4** buzz, news, talk, word **5** noise, rumor **6** gossip, report, tattle **7** hearsay, scandal **9** grapevine
Ouija: **4** game **5** board
  word: **3** yes
Ouimet, Francis: **6** golfer
  milieu: **5** links **6** course
  org.: **3** PGA
Oulu: **4** city, town **5** river
  locale: **7** Finland
ounce: **3** bit, cat **4** unit **5** felid, grain, shred **6** feline **7** modicum **8** molecule, particle
  cousin: **4** gram
  fraction: **4** dram **5** pound
  of whiskey: **3** nip **4** shot, slug **5** drink
  relative: **4** eyra, lion, lynx, puma **5** chita, liger, tiger, tigon **6** bobcat, cheeta, chetah, cougar, jaguar, margay, ocelot, serval, tiglon **7** bay lynx, caracal, cheetah, leopard, panther **9** catamount **10** jaguarundi
__ ounce: **5** fluid
ounces
  4 fluid ~: **4** gill
  8 fluid ~: **3** cup
  16 ~: **5** pound
ouphe: **3** elf **5** fairy, gnome, nixie, pixie **6** goblin, kobold **7** brownie, gremlin **9** hobgoblin
our: **4** poss., pron. **7** pronoun **10** possessive
  ender: **4** self **6** selves
  in French: **3** nos **5** notre
  not ~: **5** their
Our __: **4** Gang, Lady, Love, Time, Town **5** House **6** Father **7** Betters
Our __ Brooks: **4** Miss
Our __ Friend: **6** Mutual
Our __ of Guadalupe: **4** Lady
Our __ Sunday: **3** Gal
Our __ Will Come: **3** Day
Our Betters author: W. Somerset Maugham
Our Day Will Come (song) artist: Frankie Valli, Ruby and the Romantics
Our Father who __ heaven: **5** art in
Our Gal Sunday: **9** radio show
Our Gang
  affirmative: **4** otay
  author: **4** Roth
  dog: **4** Pete **5** Petey
  kid: **6** Rascal
  member: **5** Butch, Darla, Porky, Waldo **6** Chubby, Farina, Froggy **7** Alfalfa, Wheezer **9** Buckwheat
  producer: **5** Roach
Our Hearts Were Young and Gay: **4** book, film
  author: Cornelia Otis Skinner
  cast: Diana Lynn, Charlie Ruggles, Gail Russell
  director: **5** Allen
__, Our Help in Ages Past: **4** O God
Our House (song) artist: Crosby, Stills & Nash, Madness
  composer: **4** Nash
Our Lady of Guadalupe: **5** saint
Our Lady of Loreto: **5** saint
Our Lady of Lourdes: **5** saint
Our Lady of the Flowers author: Jean Genet
Our Love (1978 song) artist: Natalie Cole
Our Man Flint (1966 film)
  dog: **6** Caesar
  star: **4** Cobb **6** Coburn
Our Man in Havana: **4** book, film
  actor: **4** Ives **5** O'Hara **6** Kovacs
  author: Graham Greene
Our Miss Brooks (CBS sitcom)
  cast: Eve Arden (Connie Brooks) Richard Crenna (Walter Denton) Gale Gordon (Osgood Conklin) Robert Rockwell (Philip Boynton)
  cat: **7** Minerva
Our Modern Maidens (1929 film)
  cast: Joan Crawford, Douglas Fairbanks Jr.
Our Mutual Friend author: Charles Dickens
Our National Parks author: **4** Muir
__ Our Part: **4** We Do
Our Relations (1936 film)
  cast: Oliver Hardy, Stan Laurel
ours: **4** poss., pron. **7** pronoun **10** possessive
__ Ours: **5** One of
ourselves
  between ~: **8** in secret **9** entre nous, privately
  in Spanish: **3** nos
  not ~: **6** others
Our Time author: Tom Wolfe
Our Town: **4** film, play
  author: Thornton Wilder

cast: Frank Craven, William Holden, Martha Scott
character: **3** Joe **4** Webb **5** Emily, Gibbs, Howie, Simon, Wally **6** George **7** Crowell, Newsome, Rebecca, Stimson
director: Sam Wood
Our Vines Have Tender Grapes (1945 film)
cast: James Craig, Margaret O'Brien, Edward G. Robinson
'ouse: **3** 'ome
Ouse: **5** river
locale: **7** England
river to the ~: **3** Cam **4** Aire
ousel: **4** bird **6** dipper
emulate an ~: **4** dive
Ouspenskaya: **5** Maria
oust: **3** axe, can **4** boot, drop, fire, lose, sack **5** eject, evict, exile, expel, let go, purge **6** banish, bounce, depose, divest, lay off, remove, topple, unseat **7** boot out, cashier, cast out, deprive, dismiss, drum out, exclude, expulse, kick out, pack off, release, replace, subvert, turn out **8** dethrone, dislodge, displace, drive out, force out, furlough, get rid of, pink-slip, relegate, supplant, throw out **9** blackball, bundle off, chase away, discharge, drive away, eliminate, order to go, ostracize, overthrow, terminate, transport **10** disinherit, dispossess
ouster: **4** boot, coup **5** purge **9** exclusion, expulsion **10** deposition
out: **3** off **4** away, cold, dead, gone, plea **5** dated, ended, forth, not in, passé **6** absent, asleep, démodé, deport, doused, old hat, used up **7** all gone, archaic, at an end, expired, forward, not home, on a date, pretext, without **8** finished, obsolete, on strike **9** elsewhere, exhausted, make known, not at home, unpopular **10** antiquated, impossible, not working, unfeasible
ender: **3** age **5** cross, place
starter: **3** buy, cop, cut, dug, lay, pay, put, rub, run, set, try **4** bail, blow, burn, cook, drop, fade, fall, fold, hand, hang, hide, hold, lock, look, pull, rain, read, roll, sell, shut, sick, spin, take, turn, walk, wash, wipe, with, work **5** black, break, brown, carry, check, close, flame, flunk, freak, knock, phase, pitch, print, shake, shoot, stake, stand, white **6** ground, strike **7** through
out __: **4** loud, of it **5** front, of gas, to sea
out __ blue: **5** of the
out __ clear blue sky: **5** of the
out __ cold: **5** in the
out __ elbows: **5** at the
out __ heels: **5** at the
out __ light: **5** like a
out __ limb: **3** on a
out __ question: **5** of the
out __ running: **5** of the
out __ under: **4** from
out __ way: **5** of the
out __ woods: **5** of the
out __ woodwork: **5** of the
out-__: **3** box **5** front, group **6** basket **7** country, migrate
__ out: **3** act, ask, bow, bug, buy, cop, cut, dig, eke, fan, far, get, ice, lay, let, log, map, max, opt, pan, pay, pig, put, rub, run, see, set, sit, tog, try, veg, win **4** back, bail, bawl, bear, beat, blot, blow, burn, call, camp, cash, cast, chew, clip, come, conk, cool, dish, dope, draw, drop, drum, ease, edge, fake, fall, farm, feel, fill, find, fish, flat, give, hand, hang, hash, help, hide, hike, hold, iron, kick, lash, lock, look, lose, luck, make, mete, move, nose, pass, pick, play, poop, pull, rack, read, ream, ride, roll, rule, sack, sell, send, ship, shut, sign, sing, sort, spin, step, stop, take, talk, tear, trot, tune, turn, walk, wash, wear, weed, wink, wipe, work **5** black, bleep, bliss, block, break, bring, carry, check, chill, churn, clean, clear, close, count, crank, cross, cut it, flunk, freak, fresh, gross, knock, peter, phase, prove, psych, punch, round, scope, shell, smoke, sound, speak, spell, stake, stand, stick, storm, swear, sweat, tease, throw, watch, write **6** bottom, figure, follow, freeze, inside, lights, mellow, muster, strike, thrash, weasel **7** chicken, filling, infield, stretch
__ out!: **3** Far, Yer
__ out?: **4** In or
__-out: **3** all, far, way **4** comb, cook, fade, flat, iris, sold, time, worn **5** diner, flame, force, in-and **6** bombed, circle, washed **7** blitzed, chucker, clapped, falling, thought
Out!: **4** call, scat, shoo **5** leave, scram
Out, __ spot!: **6** damned
__ Out: **4** Blow, Wipe **5** Movin', No Way **6** Lights **7** School's, Steppin'
__ out a living: **3** eke
__ out all the stops: **4** pull
out-and-out: **4** pure, rank **5** gross, plumb, right, sheer, stark, total, utter **6** arrant, wholly **8** absolute, complete, flagrant, outright, positive, profound, straight, thorough **9** downright, full-dress, intensive **10** consummate, exhaustive
Outa-Space (1972 song) artist: Billy Preston
out at the __: **5** heels, plate **6** elbows
outback: **4** bush **5** wilds **8** frontier **9** backwater **10** wilderness
denizen: **3** emu, 'roo **4** emeu **5** dingo **8** kangaroo
mineral: **4** opal
native: **6** Aussie
youngster: **4** joey
see also Australia
Outback: **3** SUV **6** Subaru
outboard: **5** motor **6** engine
outbreak: **3** fit **4** gush, riot, wave **5** blast, brawl, burst, flash, onset, storm, surge **6** attack, blowup, émeute, mutiny, plague, tumult, volley **7** flare-up **8** disorder, epidemic, eruption, paroxysm, uprising **9** commotion, explosion, irruption, rebellion **10** disruption, epidemical, revolution
Outbreak: **4** film **5** novel
author: Robin Cook
cast: Morgan Freeman, Dustin Hoffman, Rene Russo, Kevin Spacey
director: Wolfgang Petersen
outbuilding: **4** barn, shed **6** lean-to
outburst: **3** cry, fit **4** gush, gust, rage, riot **5** blast, blaze, flare, flash, round, sally, salvo, scene, shout, spasm, spirt, spurt, storm, surge **6** access, attack, fantod, flurry, frenzy, temper, tirade **7** flare-up, tantrum, torrent **8** eruption, paroxysm, upheaval **9** discharge, explosion, hysterics **10** conniption, impugnment
outcast: **3** bum **4** hobo, nerd, nurd **5** exile, gypsy, rogue, tramp **6** abject, lonely, pariah, rascal, wretch **7** refugee, vagrant **8** castaway, deportee, derelict, forsaken, fugitive, vagabond **9** abandoned, miscreant, reprobate **10** expatriate
Outcast of the Islands (1951 film)
cast: Trevor Howard, Ralph Richardson
director: Carol Reed
Outcasts of Poker Flat, The author: Bret Harte
outclass: **3** top **4** beat **5** excel, one-up **6** defeat, exceed **7** surpass **10** put to shame, tower above
outcome: **3** end **4** fate **5** fruit, score **6** effect, ending, payoff, result, sequel, upshot, windup **7** payback, product **8** decision, reaction **9** aftermath, end result **10** conclusion, resolution
favorable ~: **3** win **7** success, victory
guarantee the ~: **3** fix, peg, rig **5** frame, set up **6** buy off, cement, doctor **8** nail down **9** formalize, plan ahead, preordain **10** manipulate, prearrange, tamper with
outcropping: **4** crag **5** ledge, shelf
outcry: **4** call, flak, howl, roar, yell **5** flack, hoo-ha, noise, shout, stink, storm, whoop **6** clamor, racket, scream, tumult, uproar **7** ferment, protest **9** commotion, complaint, objection **10** hubba-hubba, hullabaloo
outcurved: **6** arched, convex **7** bulging, rounded
Out, damned __!: **4** spot
outdated: **3** obs., old **4** dull **5** corny, dated, dowdy, dusty, fusty, hokey, musty, passé, stale, tired, trite, vapid **6** common, démodé, jejune, old-hat, square **7** antique, archaic, clichéd, fatuous, fogyish, has-been, humdrum, prosaic, vintage **8** bromidic, obsolete **9** hackneyed, moth-eaten, prosaical **10** antiquated, back-number, uninspired, unoriginal
not ~: **3** new, now **5** faddy, novel **6** latest, modern, modish, recent, red-hot **7** current, revived, topical **8** advanced, brand-new **9** au courant **10** innovative, newfangled, redesigned
outdistance: **3** top **4** beat, pass **6** defeat, exceed **7** succeed, surpass **8** overtake, throw off
outdistanced, be: **4** lose
outdistancing: **7** ahead of
outdo: **3** cap, top **4** beat, best, bury, cook, down, lead, lick, pass, snow **5** break, cream, excel, one-up, trash, trump **6** better, defeat, exceed, show up **7** eclipse, get past, surpass **8** bulldoze, overcome, overtake, shake off **9** rise above, transcend **10** put to shame, shoot ahead
outdoor: **6** casual, garden, rustic **7** hilltop, natural, open-air **8** alfresco, exterior, informal **9** healthful, in the open
area: **4** camp, deck, yard **5** patio
outdoors: **4** open, yard **5** hills, woods **6** garden, nature **7** country **8** alfresco, fresh air **9** mountains
ender: **3** man, men **5** woman, women
not ~: **6** inside **7** indoors
__ outdoors, the: **5** great
outdoorsy type: **5** hiker
outen: **10** extinguish
outer: **3** ext. **4** over **5** alien, ectal **6** beyond, remote **7** exposed, surface **8** exoteric, exterior, external **9** extrinsic **10** extraneous, peripheral
combining form: **2** ex- **3** ect-, epi-, exo- **4** ecto-
ender: **4** most, wear
garment: **3** fur **4** coat, robe **5** cloak, parka, stole **6** jacket **8** overcoat
layer: **4** bark, coat, hull, husk, rind, skin **5** crust, shell **6** cortex **7** coating **8** covering **10** integument
limit: **3** rim **4** edge **5** ambit, ether, verge **6** aether, apogee **8** boundary **9** periphery
not ~: **5** inner **6** middle, within **7** central
space: **3** sky **6** vacuum
visitor from ~ space: **5** alien, comet **6** meteor
outer __: **3** bar, ear **5** space **6** planet **7** product
Outer __, NC: **5** Banks
Outer Limits, The genre: sci-fi
outermost: **4** last **7** extreme
outer space: **3** sky **6** vacuum
prefix: **5** astro-
wear: **5** G-suit
outerwear: **3** fur **4** coat, robe **5** cloak, parka, stole **6** anorak, jacket **8** overcoat, raincoat
material: **5** loden
woolen ~: **5** cloak, ruana, shawl
outfield
boundary: **5** fence
hit: **3** fly **5** bloop
make ~ repairs: **5** resod
material: **3** sod **4** turf **5** grass
outfielder: **2** CF, LF, RF **7** athlete
call: **6** I got it
Hall of Fame ~: **3** Ott **4** Bell, Cobb, Doby, Mays, Rice, Ruth **5** Aaron, Brock, Combs, Flick, Irvin, Kiner, Klein, Roush, Waner, Wheat **6** Cuyler, Goslin, Kaline, Keeler, Mantle, Mel Ott, Musial, Snider, Ty Cobb, Wilson **7** Ashburn, Averill, Jackson, Medwick, Puckett, Sam Rice, Speaker, Stearns **8** Al Kaline, Babe Ruth, Clemente, DiMaggio, Edd Roush, Lou Brock, Robinson, Stargell, Williams, Winfield **9** Hank Aaron, Larry Doby, Slaughter, Zack Wheat **10** Chuck Klein, Duke Snider, Earle Combs, Elmer Flick, Hack Wilson, Henry Aaron, Joe Medwick, Kiki Cuyler, Monte Irvin, Ralph Kiner, Stan Musial, Willie Mays **11** Yastrzemski
pride: **3** arm
outfit: **3** arm, kit, rig, set, tie, tog **4** band, clan, club, crew, deck, firm, gang, garb, gear, pack, ring, suit, team, togs, unit **5** array, cater, corps, drape, dress, equip, getup, group, guise, hands, house, party, rig up, squad, stock, troop **6** attire, clique, clothe, gear up, league, livery, purvey, supply, tackle, troupe **7** apparel, appoint, bedrape, brigade, clothes, company, concern, costume, coterie, furnish, garment, in-group, platoon, prepare, provide, rigging, society **8** accouter, accoutre, business, clothing, ensemble, equipage, garments, materiel, supplies, wardrobe **9** apparatus, caparison, provision, trappings **10** enterprise, Sunday best
outfits: **7** apparel, clothes **8** clothing, wardrobe
outfitted: **4** clad **8** equipped, supplied **10** accoutered
outfitter: **6** tailor **8** clothier **9** couturier **10** dressmaker
outflank: **3** fox **4** foil **6** defeat, thwart **9** frustrate, overreach **10** circumvent
outflow: **3** ebb **5** issue, sally **6** efflux **9** effluence, emanation
opposite: **6** intake
outflux: **3** ebb
__ out for: **3** cut
outfox: **3** top **4** fool, have **5** outdo **6** outwit **8** outsmart
out from __: **5** under
out-front: **4** open **5** bluff, blunt, frank, plain **6** candid, direct, honest, square **7** artless, genuine, sincere **8** straight, truthful **9** guileless, ingenuous,

unguarded, veracious **10** aboveboard, flat-footed, forthright, foursquare, free-spoken, from the hip, on the level, point-blank, unaffected, unreserved
outgas: 4 vent
outgo: 7 expense, payment, produce **8** expenses, spending
outgoing: 4 easy, kind, open, past, warm **5** civil, close **6** chummy, clubby, former, genial, kindly **7** affable, amiable, cordial, leaving **8** amicable, friendly, informal, intimate, retiring, sociable **9** convivial, departing, expansive, extrovert **10** benevolent, buddy-buddy, gregarious, neighborly, personable, solicitous, unreserved
not ~: 3 coy, shy **4** meek **5** mousy, quiet, timid **6** demure, modest, silent **7** bashful, fearful, nervous, prudish **8** backward, hesitant, reserved, reticent, retiring **9** diffident, shrinking, unassured, withdrawn **10** unassuming, uneffusive, unsociable
one: 5 mixer **7** mingler
...__ outgrabe: 5 raths
outgrowth: 5 bulge **6** branch, effect, result, upshot **7** outcome, product, spin-off **8** offshoot **9** by-product **10** derivative
outgushing: 5 flood, spate, surge **6** deluge **7** cascade, freshet, torrent **8** downpour, drencher, overflow **9** avalanche **10** inundation
outhaul: 4 line, rope **5** cable **6** hawser **7** lanyard
outhit: 3 tan **4** beat, best, drub, edge, lick, whip **5** cream, crush, skunk, swamp, trash, upset **6** defeat, thrash **7** mow down, shellac, trounce **8** demolish **9** plow under, steamroll
outie: 5 navel
out in __ field: 4 left
outing: 3 run **4** date, hike, ride, spin, tour, trek, trip, turn **5** drive, jaunt, sally, spree **6** junket, picnic **7** journey, weekend **8** vacation **9** excursion **10** expedition, roundabout
out in the __: 4 cold
__ out in the wash: 4 come
Outland character: 4 Opus
outlander: 5 alien **7** incomer **8** outsider, stranger **9** foreigner
outlandish: 3 odd **4** eery, wild, zany **5** alien, campy, droll, eerie, kinky, outré, queer, ultra, weird **6** clumsy, exotic, far-out, gauche, quaint **7** awkward, bizarre, boorish, curious, erratic, foreign, oddball, strange, uncouth, unusual **8** barbaric, freakish, peculiar, singular **9** barbarous, eccentric, fantastic, graceless, grotesque, ludicrous, tasteless, unheard-of, unnatural, whimsical **10** incredible, ridiculous
not ~: 3 fit **4** sane, wise **5** sober, sound **6** normal **7** logical, prudent **8** moderate, rational, sensible **9** practical, pragmatic, realistic **10** reasonable
outlast: 6 endure, hang on, remain **7** survive
outlaw: 3 ban, bar, con **4** damn, hood, stop, tabu, thug, veto **5** crook, ex-con, felon, rogue, taboo, thief **6** bad guy, bad man, bandit, banish, forbid, mugger, pariah, robber **7** brigand, burglar, condemn, drifter, embargo, exclude, hoodlum, mobster, prevent **8** criminal, disallow, fugitive, gangster, hooligan, jailbird, marauder, prohibit, renegade, tough guy **9** buccaneer, desperado, interdict, miscreant, proscribe, racketeer **10** delinquent, gunslinger
Outlaw Blues (1977 film)
cast: John Crawford, Peter Fonda, Susan Saint James
outlawed: 4 tabu **5** taboo **6** banned **7** illegal, illicit **8** criminal, improper, unlawful, verboten, wrongful **9** felonious, forbidden, off-limits **10** not allowed, prohibited
blast: 5 N test
Outlaw Josey Wales, The (1976 film): 5 oater **7** western **10** horse opera
cast: Clint Eastwood, Chief Dan George, Sondra Locke
director: Clint Eastwood
Outlaw, The (1943 film)
cast: Jack Buetel, Walter Huston, Jane Russell
character: 3 Rio
director: Howard Hughes
studio: 3 RKO
outlay: 3 tab **4** bite, cost, tune **5** price, spend **6** amount, charge, damage, expend, upkeep **7** expense, payment, setback **8** expenses, overhead, price tag, spending **10** bottom line, investment
__ outlay: 7 capital
outlays, after: 3 net
outlet: 4 duct, exit, mart, pore, shop, vent **5** crack, drain, spout, store **6** avenue, egress, escape, market, nozzle, refuge **7** channel, opening, orifice **8** aperture, emporium, loophole, retailer, showroom **9** mill store
danger: 5 shock
insert: 4 plug
OK in any ~: 4 AC/DC
output: 5 power **7** voltage
outlet __: 3 box **4** mall
__ outlet: 7 factory
__ out like a bandit: 4 make
outline: 3 map **4** edge, form, limn, list, plan, plot **5** brief, chart, draft, frame, paint, shape, sum up, trace **6** aperçu, define, depict, design, figure, précis, report, résumé, scheme, sketch, survey **7** contour, diagram, drawing, profile, program, rundown, sketchy, summary, tracing **8** abstract, describe, proposal, scenario, skeleton, synopsis **9** adumbrate, bare facts, blueprint, delineate, depiction, floor plan, framework, perimeter, rough idea, summarize, synopsize **10** figuration, impression, rough draft, silhouette
make an ~: 5 trace
sharply: 4 etch **6** incise **8** inscribe
Outline of History author: H.G. Wells
outlive: 6 linger, remain **7** survive
outlook: 4 view **5** angle, scape, scene, sight, slant, state, vista **6** aspect, morale, nature, school, spirit, vision **7** chances, headset, mind-set **8** attitude, forecast, panorama, position, prospect, size of it **9** direction, landscape, mentality, prospects, viewpoint **10** likelihood, philosophy, standpoint
positive ~: 4 hope **5** trust **6** morale **7** elation **8** buoyancy, calmness, easiness, idealism, optimism **9** assurance, certainty, good cheer, happiness, lightness **10** brightness, confidence, enthusiasm
__ out loud: 5 think
outlying: 3 far **4** afar **6** far-off, remote **7** distant, faraway, removed **8** external, far-flung **9** backwoods **10** peripheral, provincial
area: 4 burb **5** exurb **6** suburb
outmaneuver: 4 undo **5** one-up **6** defeat **9** get around
outmatch: 4 beat **6** defeat **7** surpass
outmode: 7 replace **8** archaize, displace, supplant **9** antiquate, supersede
outmoded: 3 obs., old **4** dead, dull **5** corny, dated, dowdy, hokey, moldy, musty, olden, passé, stale, tacky, tired, trite, vapid **6** bygone, common, effete, jejune, old-hat **7** antique, archaic, clichéd, disused, extinct, fatuous, has-been, humdrum, old-time, prosaic, vintage **8** bromidic, obsolete, unusable **9** hackneyed, moth-eaten, prosaical, unstylish **10** antiquated, back-number, superseded, uninspired, unoriginal
title: 3 Mrs.
outmost: 4 last **5** outer **7** extreme **8** farthest, furthest
__ out nines: 7 casting
out of __: 3 gas **4** date, hand, hock, line, luck, play, step, sync, trim, turn, work **5** joint, phase, plumb, print, sight, sorts, stock, style, synch, whack **6** bounds, breath, kilter, pocket, season, square **7** nowhere
out of __ cloth: 5 whole
out of __ way: 5 harm's
out of __ world: 4 this
out-of-__: 4 date, sync, town **5** court, doors, print, round, state **6** pocket, towner
Out of Africa: 4 book, film
author: Isak Dinesen
cast: Robert Redford, Meryl Streep
character: 4 Bror **5** Karen **6** Blixen
director: Sydney Pollack
__ out of bed: 4 fall
out-of-bounds: 4 foul **6** vulgar **9** offensive, priceless **10** indelicate, scandalous
serve: 5 fault
Out of Control author: 5 Liddy
__ out of court: 5 laugh
out-of-date: 3 obs., old **4** past **5** dowdy, dusty, fusty, hoary, musty, passé, stale, tacky, tired **6** bygone, démodé, old-hat, square **7** antique, archaic, fogyish, has-been, vintage **8** obsolete, timeworn **9** hackneyed, moth-eaten **10** antiquated, back-number
__ out of gas: 3 run
__ out of house and home: 3 eat
__ out of it: 4 snap
out of line: 4 pert **5** saucy **6** risqué **8** impudent **10** disorderly, disruptive, irreverent
__ out of mind: 4 time
Out of Mulberry Street author: 4 Riis
Out of my dreams and __ your arms...: 4 into
__ Out of My Head: 4 Goin'
__ Out of My Life: 4 She's
__ out of one's hand: 3 eat
out-of-place: 5 messy, mussy **6** untidy **10** disjointed, disordered
out of sight: 4 neat **6** costly **9** expensive, priceless
Out of Sight (1998 film)
cast: George Clooney, Jennifer Lopez, Ving Rhames, Steve Zahn
director: Steven Soderbergh
out of sorts: 5 angry, cross, huffy, moody, surly, testy, vexed **6** crabby, cranky, grumpy, morose, ornery, sullen **7** annoyed, fretful, grouchy, peevish, waspish **8** churlish, petulant **9** crotchety, irascible, irritable **10** ill-humored
out of style: 5 dated, hoary, passé, tacky, tired **6** démodé, square **7** vintage
out of the __: 3 way **4** blue **5** woods **7** running
out of the __ blue sky: 5 clear
Out of the Blue (song) artist: Debbie Gibson, ELO
__ out of the box: 5 knock
Out of the Cellar artist: 4 Ratt
Out of the Cradle...: 4 poem
author: Walt Whitman
Out of the Dark author: Helen Keller
Out of the Deeps author: John Wyndham
Out of the Fog (1941 film)
cast: John Garfield, Ida Lupino, Thomas Mitchell
director: Anatole Litvak
Out of the frying pan, __ the fire: 4 into
Out of the Inkwell clown: 4 Koko
__ out of the market: 5 price
out-of-the-ordinary: 4 rare **8** singular, uncommon **9** arresting
Out of the Past (1947 film)
cast: Kirk Douglas, Rhonda Fleming, Jane Greer, Robert Mitchum
Out of the Silent Planet author: C.S. Lewis
out-of-the-way: 3 far **5** apart, aside **6** far-off, lonely, remote, secret **7** distant, private, removed, strange **8** desolate, far-flung, isolated, secluded, solitary, uncommon **9** reclusive, sheltered **10** cloistered, unexplored
not ~: 5 usual
out of this __: 5 world
Out of Time artist: 3 REM
Out of Touch (1984 song) artist: Hall and Oates
out-of-towner: 5 guest **6** caller **7** company, invitee, tourist, visitor **8** stranger, underdog **9** foreigner, sightseer, transient
Out-of-Towners, The (1970 film)
cast: Sandy Baron, Sandy Dennis, Jack Lemmon, Anne Meara
director: Arthur Hiller
Out-of-Towners, The (1999 film)
cast: John Cleese, Goldie Hawn, Steve Martin
out-of-uniform garb: 5 mufti **7** civvies
__ out of water: 4 fish
out-of-whack: 10 disorderly
out of whole __: 5 cloth
out on __: 5 a limb
__ out on: 3 run **4** lose, miss, walk
__ out one's welcome: 4 wear
outpace: 3 cap, top **4** beat, best, pass **6** better, exceed **7** eclipse, surpass **8** go beyond **10** put to shame
outpatient facility: 6 clinic **8** hospital **9** infirmary **10** dispensary
outperform: 4 beat **5** trump **6** defeat **7** surpass **10** tower above
outplay: 4 beat, best **5** upset **6** defeat
outpost: 4 base, camp, fort **5** scout **6** branch, colony **9** outskirts **10** settlement
maritime ~: 3 NAS
outpour: 4 flow, gush, spew **5** spate, spirt, spout, spurt, surge **6** stream **8** eruption **9** discharge
outpouring: 4 flow, gush, wave **5** flood, river, sally, spate, spirt, spurt, surge **6** deluge, efflux, onrush, stream **7** cascade, torrent **9** effluence
output: 4 crop, gain, take, work **5** yield **6** amount, profit **7** harvest, product **10** production
outrage: 3 ire **4** evil, fury **5** abuse, anger, appal, crime, shock, storm, wrath, wrong **6** appall, burn up, fire up, injury, insult, madden, misuse, offend **7** affront, disgust, incense, offense, scandal **8** aggrieve, atrocity, enormity, maltreat, mischief, misdoing, mistreat **9** barbarism, evildoing, infuriate, injustice **10** inhumanity, resentment, scandalize, wrongdoing
cry of ~: 4 well **6** I never
outraged: 3 hot, mad **4** ired, sore **5** angry, cross, huffy, irate, livid, riled, upset, wroth **6** fuming, ireful, peeved,

raging, raving, red-hot **7** furious, ranting **8** choleric, wrathful **9** disgusted, indignant, resentful, splenetic
outrageous: **3** mad **4** wild **5** crazy, gross, lousy, steep **6** brazen, odious, unholy, wanton, wicked **7** beastly, corrupt, extreme, glaring, heinous, ignoble, inhuman, rampant, too much, ungodly **8** barbaric, criminal, depraved, enormous, fabulous, flagrant, grievous, horrible, infamous, shameful, shocking **9** atrocious, barbarous, desperate, egregious, excessive, monstrous, nefarious, notorious, offensive, shameless, unnatural **10** detestable, disgusting, exorbitant, impossible, indelicate, inordinate, scandalous
Outrageous Fortune (1987 film)
cast: Peter Coyote, Shelley Long, Bette Midler
director: Arthur Hiller
outrageously: **3** too **4** much, very **5** quite, truly **6** hugely, really, unduly, vastly **7** only too **8** terribly **9** decidedly, downright, extremely, seriously **10** incredibly, sure-enough
outrank: **7** precede, surpass **8** antecede
outranking: **7** ahead of
outré: **5** queer, weird **7** bizarre, extreme, offbeat, unusual **8** freakish, shocking **9** eccentric **10** off-the-wall, outlandish
Outremont: **4** city, town
locale: **6** Canada, Québec
outrider: **3** spy **5** scout, watch **7** lookout, spotter
outrigger: **4** boat, prao, prau, proa **5** canoe, craft, prahu **6** vessel
outright: **4** flat, pure, rank **5** fully, gross, sheer, stark, total, utter **6** arrant, direct, entire **7** perfect **8** absolute, by itself, complete, positive, specific, straight, thorough **9** instantly, wholesale **10** consummate, undeniable, unmediated
__ Outright, The: **4** Gift
outrival: **4** beat, best **6** defeat **9** transcend
outrun: **4** beat, lose **5** elude **6** exceed **7** surpass **8** throw off
outrush: **4** gale, gust, puff, wind **5** blast, burst, draft, sally **7** flare-up **8** eruption **9** irruption
outs
ins and ~: **4** ways **5** bends, turns **6** curves, habits, traits, twists **7** customs, details **8** patterns, windings
on the ~: **5** at war, in bad **6** at odds **7** feuding **10** quarreling
six ~: **6** inning
__ outs: **5** on the
outscore: **3** win **4** beat, best **6** defeat
outset: **4** dawn, rise **5** birth, git-go, start **6** advent, origin **7** genesis, kickoff, leadoff, opening **8** exordium **9** beginning, inception, threshold **10** conception, incipience
at the ~: **5** first **9** in advance, initially **10** beforehand
outshine: **3** cap, top **4** beat, pass **5** excel **6** better, exceed, show up **7** eclipse, surpass **8** dominate **9** transcend **10** overshadow, put to shame, tower above
outside: **3** far, off **4** away, face, husk, open, over, skin, slim **5** alien, faint, front, shell, small **6** beyond, facade, remote, sheath, slight, veneer **7** distant, extreme, farther, foreign, maximum, open-air, seeming, slender, surface, topside, without **8** alfresco, covering, exoteric, exterior, external, farthest, furthest, marginal, unlikely **9** apart from, periphery **10** appearance, extraneous, integument, negligible
at the ~: **9** maximally
not ~: **6** indoor, within **7** indoors
of: **3** bar **4** save **6** except **7** besides **9** other than
prefix: **4** ecto- **5** extra-
the law: **4** tabu **5** taboo **6** banned **7** illegal, illicit **8** criminal, improper, unlawful, verboten, wrongful **9** felonious, forbidden **10** prohibited
outside __: **4** loop, shot **6** chance **7** caliper, forward
Outside Man, The (1973 film)
cast: Ann-Margret, Angie Dickinson
Outside Providence (1999 film)
cast: Jon Abrahams, Alec Baldwin, George Wendt
outsider: **5** alien **7** floater, incomer, refugee **8** intruder, newcomer, stranger **9** foreigner, layperson, odd man out, odd one out **10** interloper
Outsider in Amsterdam author: Janwillem van de Wetering
outsiders: **6** others
Outsiders song: Time Won't Let Me (1966)
Outsider, The (1961 film)
cast: Bruce Bennett, Tony Curtis, James Franciscus
director: Delbert Mann
Outsider, The (1979 film)
cast: Sterling Hayden, Patricia Quinn, Craig Wasson
Outsider, The author: Colin Wilson
outsize: **3** big **4** huge **5** giant, large **7** hulking, immense **10** overweight
outskirts: **3** rim **4** edge **5** exurb, limit **6** border, fringe, sticks, suburb **7** exurbia, purlieu **8** boundary, environs, purlieus, suburbia, vicinity **9** periphery
outsmart: **3** cap, con, fox, top **4** beat, dupe, gull, have, hoax, undo **5** cheat, goose, trick, worst **6** baffle, defeat, end-run, take in **7** confuse, deceive, defraud, finagle, mislead, swindle **8** bewilder, hoodwink **9** bamboozle, get around, overreach **10** circumvent, lead astray
outspoken: **4** bold, free, open, oral **5** bluff, blunt, brusk, frank, plain, vocal **6** abrupt, brassy, candid, direct, square **7** artless, brusque, sincere, upfront **8** explicit, impolite, strident, tactless, truthful **9** ingenuous **10** forthright, foursquare, from the hip, indelicate, point-blank, unreserved, unreticent
outspread: **3** big **4** long, wide **5** broad **6** expand
outstanding: **3** ace, bad, def, due, rad, wow **4** aces, A-one, boss, braw, cool, dece, fine, gear, keen, main, neat, nice, open, phat, star, tops, tuff **5** chief, dandy, ducky, grand, great, major, marvy, neato, nobby, owing, prime, primo, slick, super, swell **6** bang on, bang-up, banner, bonzer, bosker, choice, divine, dreamy, famous, far-out, gnarly, groovy, lovely, marked, peachy, signal, slap-up, spot on, superb, terrif, tiptop, unpaid, unreal, whizzo, wicked **7** amazing, awesome, capital, corking, eminent, exalted, leading, mostest, notable, ongoing, overdue, payable, pending, perfect, ripping, salient, skookum, special, stellar, sublime, unusual **8** dazzling, dominant, especial, eximious, fabulous, five-star, four-star, frabjous, glorious, greatest, heavenly, historic, jim-dandy, renowned, singular, slam-bang, smashing, splendid, sterling, striking, superior, terrific, top-level, topnotch, towering, uncommon, very good, wondrous **9** arresting, bodacious, Endsville, excellent, exemplary, exquisite, first-rate, high-grade, hunky-dory, important, marvelous, memorable, momentous, number one, principal, prominent, remaining, sol-licker, top-flight, unsettled, well-known, wonderful **10** first-class, hotsy-totsy, jack-a-dandy, peachy-keen, phenomenal, remarkable, stupendous, super-duper, world-class
amount: **4** debt **6** arrear **7** arrears
be ~: **4** star **5** excel, shine
person: **4** oner, star **5** adept, great **7** notable **9** superstar
outstep: **3** cap, top **4** beat, best, lead, lick **5** excel **6** better, exceed **7** eclipse, surpass **8** go beyond **10** put to shame
outstretch: **5** widen **6** spread
outstretched: **4** flat, long, wide
outstrip: **3** cap, top **4** beat, lead, lick, pass, race, zoom **5** break, excel **6** better, exceed **7** eclipse, get past, surpass **8** antecede, overtake **9** transcend **10** put to shame, tower above
outstripping: **6** beyond **7** ahead of, beating **10** superior to, surpassing
Outta here!: **4** scat, shoo **5** scram
__ out the clock: **3** run
__ out the red carpet: **4** roll
out to __: **3** sea **5** lunch
__ out to pasture: **3** put
__ out to sea: **3** put
Out to Sea (1997 film)
cast: Dyan Cannon, Jack Lemmon, Walter Matthau, Donald O'Connor, Brent Spiner, Elaine Stritch
director: Martha Coolidge
outvote: **4** rule **5** upset **8** dominate, override, overturn
outward: **4** open, over **5** forth, outer **7** evident, obvious, surface, visible **8** apparent, exoteric, exterior, external, to the eye **10** from within, noticeable, observable, ostensible
appearance: **4** face, look, mask, mien, pose **5** cloak, cover, front, guise, shape **6** aspect, facade, manner, veneer **7** bearing **8** demeanor, disguise, exterior **9** semblance **10** camouflage, false front, impression, masquerade
curved ~: **6** convex
extend ~: **3** jut **4** lean, poke **5** bulge **7** project **8** overhang, protrude
flow: **3** ebb **4** tide **6** efflux **9** abatement, discharge, recession
prefix: **5** extro-
project ~: **3** jut **5** bloat, bulge, swell **6** expand **7** balloon, distend **8** protrude
turn ~: **5** flare, splay
outward-__: **5** bound
Outward Bound (1930 film)
cast: Douglas Fairbanks Jr., Leslie Howard
outwardly: **8** to the eye **9** seemingly **10** officially
outweigh: **3** top **5** excel **6** exceed, offset, redeem, set off **7** balance, eclipse, prevail, surpass **8** atone for, overcome, override, overrule **9** make up for, transcend **10** compensate, overshadow
__ Out West: **3** Way
outwit: **3** cap, con, fox, get, top **4** beat, dupe, foil, gull, have, hoax **5** cheat, elude, goose, stump, trick, trump, worst **6** baffle, defeat, end-run, take in, thwart **7** confuse, conquer, deceive, defraud, finagle, mislead, swindle **8** bewilder, hoodwink **9** bamboozle, frustrate, get around, overreach **10** circumvent, lead astray
tough to ~: **3** hip, sly **4** foxy, keen, wily, wise **5** acute, canny, quick, ready, savvy, sharp, smart **6** astute, brainy, bright, clever, crafty, shrewd **7** cunning, knowing **8** sensible **9** astucious, farseeing, judicious, on the ball, realistic, sagacious **10** discerning, insightful, perceptive, thoughtful
__ out with: **4** come
__ Out With My Baby: **7** Steppin'
outworn: **5** dated, passé, stale **6** old hat **8** obsolete
outwrestle: **3** pin **6** pinion **8** hold down **10** immobilize
ouzel: **4** bird **6** dipper
emulate a ~: **4** dive
ouzo: **5** drink **8** beverage
flavoring: **5** anise
ova: **3** roe **6** caviar **7** caviare
oval: **4** ooid **5** round, shape **6** oblong **7** rounded **8** elliptic, roundish **9** cartouche, egg-shaped, ellipsoid, racetrack **10** elliptical, racecourse
Oval __: **6** Office
Oval Portrait, The author: Edgar Allan Poe
Ovambo: **3** cow **4** bull **6** bovine, cattle
ovate: **9** egg-shaped **10** elliptical
ovation: **4** hand **5** salvo **6** bravos, praise **7** acclaim, big hand, tribute, welcome **8** applause, cheering, clapping, plaudits **9** standing O
give an ~: **4** clap **5** cheer, honor **6** praise **7** acclaim, applaud
Ovation: **7** channel
alternative: **3** BET, CMT, MTV, PAX, TBS, TLC, TNN, TNT, USA **4** ESPN, HGTV **5** A and E, C-SPAN, Style **6** Noggin, Tech TV, TV Land **7** Court TV, SoapNet **8** Lifetime
oven: **4** kiln, lehr, oast **5** stove **7** broiler, tandoor **8** limekiln **9** brickkiln, microwave **10** rotisserie
accessory: **4** mitt **5** glove
emanation: **5** aroma, smell
ender: **4** bird, ware **5** proof
gadget: **5** timer
like an ~: **3** hot **4** warm **6** heated, sultry, sweaty, toasty, torrid **7** blazing, boiling, burning, summery, sweltry **8** broiling, parching, roasting, scalding, sizzling, steaming, tropical **9** scorching **10** blistering, sweltering
name: **5** Amana
use the ~: **4** bake, heat **5** broil, roast
oven __: **4** mitt
__ oven: **4** coke **5** Dutch **7** beehive, toaster **10** convection
Oven Bird, The author: Robert Frost
ovenware: **5** Pyrex
over: **3** off, too **4** anew, atop, done, gone, more, past **5** above, again, aloft, ended, extra, kaput, outer **6** across, afresh, beyond, bygone, closed, finito, lapsed, on high, unduly, unused, upward **7** at an end, on top of, outside, outward, settled, surplus, through **8** apparent, covering, done with, finished, in excess, in heaven, in the sky, once more, superior, upstairs **9** completed, concluded, excessive, extremely, immensely, instead of, remaining, upwards of **10** from the top, higher than, in addition, in excess of, rather than, straight up, terminated
ender: **3** age **4** much **6** master
in German: **4** über
not ~: **5** below, under **8** less than
prefix: **3** epi-, sur- **5** hyper-, super-
starter: **3** all, cut, lay, pop **4** hang,

hold, hung, left, make, more, pull, push, roll, slip, stop, take, turn, walk, wing **5** carry, cross, flash, sleep, spill, voice **6** change, strike, switch
over ___: **4** easy, with **5** again
___ over: **3** all, get, lay, put, run **4** blow, boil, bowl, come, give, hand, hold, keel, look, make, pass, pick, pore, roll, stop, talk, tide, turn, walk, work **5** carry, check, cross, gloss, scoot, skate, sleep, stand, throw, watch **6** bowled, maiden
___-over: **3** cab, fly **4** once **5** going, voice **6** warmed
Over ___: **4** Easy **5** There
Over 21 (1945 film)
cast: Charles Coburn, Irene Dunne, Alexander Knox
director: Charles Vidor
over a ___: **6** barrel
overabundance: **4** glut **6** excess **7** nimiety, satiety, surfeit, surplus, too much **8** plethora **9** plenitude, profusion
overact: **5** emote **7** ham it up
overacted: **5** hammy, stagy **6** stagey **10** histrionic, theatrical
overactive: **5** hyper **7** fidgety **8** fluttery, frenetic, frenzied, restless **10** high-strung
overage: **4** rest **6** excess **7** surplus **8** plethora
overall: **5** gross, total **6** global, mainly, mostly **7** blanket, general, largely **8** complete, long-term, sweeping, thorough, umbrella **9** inclusive, in general, long-range, primarily, wholesale **10** everywhere, on the whole, throughout
total: **3** all, sum **5** gross, whole **8** entirety, receipts **9** aggregate
overalls: **5** pants **8** trousers **10** protection
material: **5** denim
part: **3** bib
over and ___: **3** out **4** done **5** above
Over and Over (1965 song) artist: Dave Clark Five
___ over a new leaf: **4** turn
overanxious: **5** antsy, tense **7** nervous
overawe: **3** cow **5** daunt, deter **10** discourage, intimidate
___ over backward: **4** bend, fall, lean
overbalance: **3** tip **4** fall, roll **5** spill, upend, upset **6** go down, teeter, topple, totter **7** capsize
overbalanced: **6** uneven **7** unequal **8** lopsided
overbear: **5** bully **10** lord it over
overbearing: **4** hard **5** bossy, cocky, lofty, proud, pushy **6** lordly, severe, uppity **7** haughty, pompous **8** arrogant, assuming, cavalier, despotic, dogmatic, dominant, imperial, insolent, superior **9** bumptious, egotistic, imperious, officious, sovereign **10** despotical, dogmatical, peremptory, tyrannical
not ~: **3** shy **4** meek, mild, soft, tame, weak **5** lowly, quiet, timid **6** docile, gentle, humble, modest **7** lenient, passive, patient, subdued **8** lamblike, peaceful, retiring, tolerant, yielding **10** manageable, submissive, unassuming
one: **4** czar, tsar **5** bully **6** despot, tyrant **7** monarch **8** autocrat, dictator, martinet **9** oppressor
___ Over Beethoven: **4** Roll
overblown: **3** big **4** tall **5** tumid, undue, windy **6** turgid **7** flowery, fulsome, hyped up, orotund, pompous, profuse, stilted, too much, verbose **8** inflated **9** bombastic, excessive **10** immoderate, oratorical, rhetorical
praise: **4** hype, plug, puff **5** promo **7** puffery **9** publicity
overboard: **9** excessive **10** exorbitant
goods thrown ~: **5** lagan, ligan
throw ~: **4** dump, junk **5** chuck, ditch, heave, scrap **6** unload **7** abandon, cast off, deep-six, discard, lighten **8** jettison
___ overboard!: **3** Man
Overboard (1987 film)
cast: Goldie Hawn, Edward Herrmann, Kurt Russell
director: Garry Marshall
overbold: **6** brassy, brazen **7** blatant **8** impudent **9** daredevil
___ Over Broadway: **6** Angels **7** Bullets
overburden: **3** tax **4** load, tire **5** abuse, swamp **6** overdo **7** congest, oppress **9** weigh down
Overbury, Thomas: **4** poet **7** British
overcast: **4** dark, dull, gray, grey, hazy **5** dusky, foggy, mirky, misty, murky **6** cloudy, dismal, dreary, gloomy, leaden, shadow, somber **7** clouded, sunless **8** darkened, lowering **9** adumbrate **10** oppressive
overcharge: **4** bilk, soak **5** bleed, cheat, gouge, sting **6** fleece, rip off
for tickets: **5** scalp
overcloud: **3** dim **4** mist **7** obscure
overcoat: **5** capot, jemmy **6** capote, duffle, duster, jacket, raglan, ulster **7** kuletuk **8** benjamin **9** balmacaan, Inverness **10** fearnought, macfarlane
fabric: **9** cothamore
Japanese straw ~: **4** mino
Overcoat, The author: Nikolai Gogol
overcome: **3** awe, win **4** beat, best, down, lick, rush, stun **5** crush, drown, outdo, quash, quell, seize, shock, still, unarm, upset, whelm, worst **6** beaten, buried, defeat, hurdle, master, reduce, subdue **7** conquer, prevail, rebound, recover, shocked, stunned, succeed, survive, swamped, triumph, trounce, weather **8** affected, convince, defeated, gang up on, outweigh, suppress, surmount, vanquish **9** blown-away, conquered, get around, prostrate, rise above, subjugate **10** neutralize, speechless
adversity: **3** win **4** beat, cope **6** attain, manage **7** achieve, conquer, make out, prevail, pull off, realize, succeed, triumph **8** struggle **9** withstand **10** accomplish
illness: **6** revive **7** get well, rebound, recover, shape up **9** get better **10** bounce back, come around, recuperate, turn around
with fear: **3** cow **4** faze **5** bully, daunt **6** dismay, menace **7** terrify, unnerve **8** paralyze **10** demoralize, intimidate, scare stiff
overconfident: **4** rash, smug **5** brash, cocky, pushy **8** careless, cocksure, heedless, impudent, reckless **9** bumptious, foolhardy, hubristic, presuming
overcook: **4** burn, char **7** blacken
overcritical: **7** carping, finicky **8** captious, caviling, contrary, exacting **9** demanding **10** censorious, nitpicking
overcrowd: **3** jam **4** cram, pack **5** jam in, stuff, swamp **6** cram in, pack in **7** congest, squeeze, stuff in **9** squeeze in
overcrowded: **4** full **5** awash, close, dense, thick **6** jammed, packed **7** crammed, stuffed, teeming **8** brimming, bursting **9** chock-full, jam-packed
overcurious: **4** nosy **5** nosey **6** prying, snoopy **8** snooping **9** butting in, intrusive, obtrusive **10** meddlesome
overdecorated: **4** busy
overdo: **4** hype, puff **6** pile on, stress **7** amplify, belabor, fatigue, lay it on, magnify, run riot, stretch, talk big **8** pressure, wear down **9** embroider, luxuriate **10** exaggerate
it: **4** brag, fawn **5** boast **6** pander **7** lay it on, talk big **8** go too far
overdone: **4** arty **5** artsy, campy, hammy, sappy, showy, stagy, tough **6** garish, ornate, stagey **7** labored **8** affected, wasteful **9** contrived, excessive
overdraft letters: **3** NSF
overdramatic: **5** stagy **6** stagey **10** theatrical
overdramatize: **4** gush **5** emote **7** carry on, ham it up
overdub: **3** add **7** include **9** interject
unit: **5** track
overdue: **3** due **4** late, ripe **5** owing, tardy **6** behind, held up, hung up, unpaid **7** belated, delayed, payable **8** detained **9** unsettled **10** behindhand, behind time, delinquent
payment: **6** arrear **7** arrears
overeager: **5** antsy, itchy **7** anxious, zealous **9** impatient
overeagerness: **4** fire, zeal **6** fervor **9** intensity, vehemence **10** fanaticism
overeasy: **3** lax **7** lenient
overeat: **5** gorge, stuff **6** pig out **7** engorge **10** gormandize
overeater: **3** pig **7** glutton **8** gourmand
overelaborate: **4** busy, lacy **5** fancy, fussy, showy **6** flashy, frilly, gilded, glitzy, ornate, rococo **7** baroque, flowery, opulent, splashy **9** tasteless **10** convoluted, flamboyant
overemotional: **5** gooey, gushy, hammy, mushy, sappy, soppy, stagy, teary, weepy **6** slushy, syrupy **7** cloying, insipid, maudlin, mawkish, tearful **8** bathetic, cornball **9** schmaltzy, sniveling **10** lachrymose, theatrical
over-enthuse: **4** gush, rave **5** drool, emote **6** effuse
overenthusiastic: **4** wild **5** rabid, ultra **6** crazed **7** berserk, violent, zealous **8** frenzied, obsessed, wild-eyed **9** delirious, fanatical **10** hysterical
overestimate: **3** err **6** puff up **7** inflate, mistake **8** misjudge
overexcited: **5** irate, manic **8** maniacal
overexert: **3** tax **4** ache, push, tire, toil **5** drive, labor, sweat **6** strain, stress **7** fatigue, peg away **8** go all out
overexertion result: **4** ache
overextend: **3** tax **5** force, press **6** burden, strain, stress **7** stretch
overfamiliar: **5** banal, corny, stale, tired, trite **6** common **7** clichéd, worn-out **8** bathetic, bromidic, shopworn **9** hackneyed **10** pedestrian, unoriginal
overfeed: **4** glut, sate **6** fatten **7** surfeit
overfill: **4** clog, cloy, cram, glut, sate **5** spill, stuff **7** congest, satiate, surfeit **8** saturate
___ over fist: **4** hand
overflow: **4** brim, gush, ooze, slop, teem **5** cover, drown, flood, issue, slosh, spate, spill, spirt, spout, spurt, surge, swamp **6** abound, deluge, engulf, excess, ingulf, irrupt **7** cascade, pour out, surfeit, surplus, torrent **8** cataract, inundate, plethora, submerge **9** overcrowd **10** congestion, inundation, redundancy
point: **3** lip, rim **4** brim, edge **5** brink, limit, verge **6** margin **9** periphery
overflowing: **4** full, rife **5** awash, flush, laden, thick **6** filled, jammed, loaded, packed **7** copious, crammed, crowded, profuse, replete, stuffed, teeming **8** abundant, effusive, generous **9** chock-full, luxuriant, plentiful
overfly: **3** spy **5** recon
overfond of, be: **4** baby **5** spoil **6** coddle, cosset, dote on, pamper **7** idolize, indulge **8** dote upon
overfull: **5** awash **6** jammed, loaded **7** crammed, crowded, fraught, replete, stuffed **8** brimming
overgenerous: **6** lavish, wanton **8** prodigal, wasteful **9** excessive **10** immoderate, profligate
overgrow: **6** sprawl, spread **7** overrun **8** multiply, mushroom
overgrown: **4** lush, rank, wild **5** large, mossy, reedy, seedy, weedy **6** jungly
tend to an ~ plant: **5** repot
overhang: **3** jut **4** eave, loom, poke **5** bulge, cliff **6** beetle, canopy, dangle, extend, impend **7** project **8** endanger, protrude, stand out, stick out, threaten **10** projection, tower above
overhanging: **7** pendant, pendent **8** lowering, towering
overhasty: **4** rash **9** imprudent, premature **10** ill-advised
overhaul: **3** fix **4** mend, redo **5** check, debug, patch, refit, renew **6** doctor, repair, revamp, revise **7** examine, improve, inspect, ransack, rebuild, restore, retread, service **8** renovate, revision **9** modernize, reexamine, refurbish **10** fiddle with, reorganize
overhead: **4** atop, cost, over, rent, roof **5** above, aloft, upper **6** aerial, burden, on high, outlay, upkeep, upward **7** expense, hanging, skyward, up above, upwards **8** expenses, in the sky **9** insurance, utilities
overhead ___: **4** shot **7** railway
overhead-___ engine: **3** cam **5** valve
overhear: **6** listen **9** eavesdrop, intercept
overheat: **4** burn, char **5** singe **6** scorch
___ over heels: **4** head
Over here!: **3** hey, pst **4** psst **6** hey you, yoo-hoo
Over hill, over ___...: **4** dale
___ Over India: **5** Flame
overindulge: **4** baby, dote, sate, tope **5** binge, gorge, spoil, stuff **6** coddle, dote on, pamper **7** cater to, satiate, surfeit **8** dote upon **10** gormandize
overindulged: **4** soft **8** pampered **10** namby-pamby
overindulgence: **3** jag **4** bash, orgy, tear **5** binge, fling, spree **6** excess **7** blowout, license, nimiety, revelry, splurge, surfeit **8** carousal **9** bacchanal, decadence **10** immoderacy, saturnalia
overindulgent: **3** lax **4** fond, soft **6** lavish, wanton **8** prodigal **9** excessive **10** immoderate, profligate
one: **5** doter
overindulgently: **3** too **4** very **6** too-too
overinquisitive: **4** nosy **5** nosey
be ~: **3** pry **4** nose, peer
one: **5** yenta **6** gossip **7** meddler **8** busybody, quidnunc
overjoy: **5** elate **6** please, ravish
overjoyed: **4** glad **5** happy, merry **6** blithe, cheery, elated, jovial, joyful, upbeat, wallow **7** charmed, gleeful, pleased, tickled **8** blissful, cheerful, ecstatic, euphoric, exultant, jubilant, mirthful, ravished, thrilled **9** delighted, delirious, gladdened, rapturous, rejoicing, rhapsodic **10** flying high
be ~: **4** crow **5** cheer, exult, glory, revel **7** delight, rejoice, triumph **8** jubilate **9** celebrate, make merry **10** effervesce
overkill: **6** excess **7** surfeit **8** plethora
Overkill (1983 song) artist: Men at Work

overland __: 4 mail 5 stage
Overland: 3 car 4 auto 6 Willys
Overland __: 5 Trail
Overland Park: 4 city, town
locale: 6 Kansas
org.: 4 NCAA
overlap: 3 lap 4 flap 7 project, shingle, stagger, stretch 8 go beyond, overhang, protrude 9 imbricate
overlarge: 4 huge, vast 5 giant, great, jumbo 7 hulking, immense, mammoth, massive, sizable, titanic 8 colossal, enormous, gigantic, king-size, sizeable, towering, whapping, whopping 9 Herculean, humongous 10 gargantuan, monumental, prodigious, stupendous, tremendous
overlay: 4 coat, gild, wash 5 cover, glaze, plate, sheet, smear 6 lamina, spread, veneer 7 blanket, encrust, incrust, plaster 8 laminate
thin metal ~: 4 wash 7 coating
overleap: 4 jump, miss, omit, skip 5 scorn, shirk, vault 6 bypass, hurdle, ignore, spring 7 neglect 8 shrug off 9 disregard, pay no mind 10 brush aside
overlie: 3 lap 5 cover 7 envelop
__ over lightly: 4 once
overload: 3 tax 4 glut, lade 5 swamp 6 burden, deluge, excess, strain 7 congest, oppress 8 encumber, keep down 9 weigh down
protector: 4 fuse
overloaded: 4 busy 6 hectic, snowed 7 popping, swamped
overlong: 7 lengthy 8 dragging 10 protracted
overlook: 4 face, look, miss, omit, pass, skip, view 5 cliff, front, let go, waive 6 excuse, forget, ignore, pardon, pass by, regard, slight, slip up, survey, wink at 7 blink at, condone, forgive, front on, let pass, lookout, mistake, neglect, rule out, stomach, tune out 8 bear with, discount, laugh off, leave out, let slide, live with, play past, prospect, shrug off, stand for 9 check up on, disregard, look out on, mishandle, mismanage, pay no mind, put up with, supervise, whitewash
overlord: 4 czar, tsar, tzar 5 ruler 6 gerent, master 7 viceroy 8 autocrat
overly: 3 too 4 over 6 too-too, unduly 7 too much 8 overmuch 9 extremely 10 improperly
__ over matter: 4 mind
__ Over Miami: 4 Moon
overmodest: 3 coy 4 prim 7 prudish
overmuch: 3 too 4 over 5 undue 6 overly, unduly 8 needless, to a fault 9 excessive, extremely 10 inordinate
overnice: 6 prissy 7 prudish 8 pedantic, precious 10 pedantical
overnight: 4 tour, trip 6 travel 7 layover 8 meteoric 9 temporary
duds: 3 PJs 7 jammies, pajamas
gear: 6 kitbag
send ~: 4 rush 5 FedEx 6 hasten 7 speed up 8 expedite 10 accelerate, lose no time
stay ~: 4 rest 5 crash, sleep 6 repose, turn in 7 sack out, saw wood, shuteye, slumber, zonk out 9 hit the hay 10 hit the sack
stop: 4 camp 5 hotel, motel 6 hostel 8 campsite, motor inn 10 motor lodge
temperature, usually: 3 low
overnight __: 3 bag 4 case
overnighters: 7 baggage, luggage 8 carry-ons 9 suitcases
over one's __: 4 head
__ over oneself: 4 fall
over-ornament: 4 gild
overpack: 3 jam, ram 4 cram, tamp 5 crowd, crush, stuff 6 squash 7 squeeze
overpamper: 4 baby 5 humor, spoil 6 coddle, dote on 7 cater to, indulge 9 spoon-feed
__ Over Parador: 4 Moon
overparticular: 7 finicky 8 finnicky 9 finicking
overpass: 6 bridge 7 viaduct 8 crossing, traverse
abbr.: 3 max
overpermissive: 3 lax 4 easy, soft 5 loose, slack 6 casual 7 lenient 8 tolerant, yielding
overplay: 3 mug 5 ham up 7 ham it up, labor at, magnify, show off, stretch 8 maximize 9 dramatize 10 accentuate, exaggerate
overpower: 3 awe, get 4 beat, bury, drub, rout, stun 5 break, cream, crush, drown, quell, seize, smash, swamp, total, trash, upset, waste 6 defeat, lay low, obsess, reduce, subdue 7 clobber, conquer, oppress, put away, shut off, stagger, take out, torpedo, trounce 8 bear down, beat down, blow away, bulldoze, keep down, knock out, shellack, suppress, vanquish 9 fascinate, prostrate, subjugate 10 immobilize, take care of
overpowering: 4 hale, iron, wiry 5 beefy, burly, hardy, hefty, hunky, husky, lusty, stout, tough 6 brawny, hearty, mighty, potent, robust, rugged, sinewy, steely, stocky, strong, sturdy, virile 7 doughty, onerous 8 athletic, forceful, indurate, muscular, powerful, puissant, stalwart, vigorous 9 Atlantean, Herculean, strapping, well-built 10 able-bodied, red-blooded
overpraise: 4 puff 6 fawn on, puff up 7 blarney, flatter
overprecise: 4 nice, prim 5 fussy, stiff 6 choosy, demure, formal, prissy, proper, stuffy 7 genteel, prudish, stilted, uptight 8 decorous, priggish, starched 9 bluenosed, squeamish 10 fastidious, fuddy-duddy, goody-goody, nit-picking, particular
overpriced: 4 dear, high, rich 5 steep 9 expensive 10 at a premium
overprofusion: 4 glut 6 excess 7 nimiety, surfeit, surplus 8 plethora
overproud: 4 smug 7 pompous, stuck-up 8 arrogant, egoistic, priggish, puffed-up, snobbish, superior 9 conceited 10 big-talking, complacent
overrate: 6 exceed 7 build up, magnify 8 misjudge 10 exaggerate
overreach: 4 undo 6 outwit 8 outflank, outsmart 10 circumvent
overreact: 5 panic 6 lose it 8 freeze up, have a fit, stampede 9 come apart, run scared 10 chicken out, go to pieces
overrefined: 6 prissy 7 finicky 8 precious 10 fastidious
overregulate: 6 corset 9 hamstring
override: 3 lap 4 rule, veto 5 alter, annul, quash, upset 6 cancel, recall, repeal, revoke, thwart 7 nullify, outvote, rescind, reverse, trample 8 disallow, dominate, outweigh, set aside 9 disregard, influence, supersede 10 invalidate
overriding: 4 main 5 chief, final, focal, major, prime 6 ruling 7 central, pivotal, primary, supreme 8 cardinal, dominant, ultimate 9 number one, paramount, principal, uppermost
overripe: 3 bad, old 4 soft 5 musty 6 rotten 7 decayed 10 malodorous
overrule: 3 nix 4 veto 5 alter, annul, quash, upset 6 cancel, ignore, recall, repeal, revoke, thwart 7 nullify, prevail, rescind, reverse, trample 8 disallow, dominate, hold sway, outweigh, overturn, set aside 9 disregard, influence, supersede 10 invalidate
overrun: 3 mob, top 4 beat, drub, lick, raid, rife, rout, teem, trim, whip, wild 5 beset, choke, foray, seize, spill, surge, swamp, swarm, worst 6 defeat, deluge, engulf, exceed, infest, ingulf, inroad, invade, occupy, ravage, thrash 7 clobber, lambast, surpass, surplus 8 go beyond, inundate, lambaste, massacre 9 intrude on
__ overrun: 4 cost
oversatisfy: 4 cloy, glut, jade, pall, sate 5 gorge, stuff, weary 7 satiate, surfeit
overseas: 5 alien 6 abroad 7 far away, foreign 8 offshore
overseasoned: 5 salty
oversee: 3 eye, run 4 boss, head, herd, mind, tend 5 watch 6 direct, govern, manage, survey 7 baby-sit, captain, command, conduct, control, inspect, monitor, preside, skipper 8 chaperon, regulate, shepherd 9 chaperone, check up on, look after, officiate, supervise 10 administer, ride herd on, run the show, sit on top of
overseer: 3 mgr. 4 boss, head, mgmt., supt. 5 chief 6 bishop, gerent, keeper, master, top dog, warden 7 manager, monitor, pit boss 8 director, guardian, higher-up, watchdog 9 custodian, executive, inspector, organizer, straw boss 10 head honcho, management, supervisor
oversensitive: 5 huffy, wired 6 touchy 7 prickly, waspish
oversentimental: 5 sappy, soppy, soupy
one: 5 softy 6 softie
oversentimentality: 4 mush 5 slush 8 schmaltz 9 mushiness
overset: 3 tip 4 tilt, undo 5 spill, upend 6 careen, invert, renege, revert, revoke, switch, topple 7 capsize, counter, retract, reverse 8 flip-flop 9 about-face, back-pedal, volte-face 10 turn around
overshadow: 3 dim 4 haze, loom 5 bedim, cloud, dwarf, excel 6 darken, show up 7 becloud, eclipse, surpass 8 dominate, outshine, outweigh 9 adumbrate, obfuscate, transcend 10 put to shame, tower above
overshoe: 4 boot 5 wader 6 galosh, golosh, rubber 7 galoshe, hip boot
overshoot: 4 jump, miss 6 go past
oversight: 4 egis, miss, skip, slip 5 aegis, error, fault, lapse, watch 6 boo-boo, charge, lapsus, laxity, miscue, slip-up 7 blunder, conduct, control, custody, default, failure, keeping, mistake, neglect 8 handling, omission, tutelage 9 disregard 10 management
oversize: 3 big 4 huge, vast 5 baggy, giant, great, jumbo, large 7 hulking, immense, mammoth, massive, titanic 8 colossal, enormous, gigantic, towering, whapping, whopping 9 Herculean, humongous 10 gargantuan, monumental, prodigious, stupendous, tremendous
oversoon: 8 untimely 9 premature
overspend: 4 lose 5 drain, use up, waste 6 burn up, lavish, misuse 7 deplete, fribble, splurge 8 squander 9 throw away 10 gamble away, run through, trifle away
__ over spilled milk: 3 cry
overspread: 4 fill, teem 5 choke, cover, swamp, swarm 6 engulf, extend, infest, invade 7 pervade, suffuse 8 inundate, permeate 9 percolate
overstate: 5 color, fudge 6 blow up 7 inflate, magnify, stretch 8 misquote 9 dramatize, embellish, embroider 10 exaggerate
overstatement: 4 tale 8 tall tale
overstep: 6 exceed 7 surpass 8 go beyond, trespass
overstock: 4 cram, glut, load 5 extra, flood 6 excess 7 congest, surplus 8 saturate 9 remainder
overstrain: 3 sap, tax 4 bush, tire 5 drain, weary 7 burn out, exhaust, fatigue, give out, go stale, poop out, wear out 8 enervate 9 prostrate
overstress: 4 hype 6 hype up, play up, puff up, step up 7 magnify, promote 8 escalate, overplay 9 aggravate, intensify 10 exaggerate
overstrung: 4 edgy, taut 5 drawn, hyper, jumpy, tense, wired 6 on edge 7 anxious, excited, fidgety, fretful, jittery, keyed up, nervous, uptight, wound up 8 agitated, fluttery, in a tizzy, unnerved 9 unsettled, up the wall
overstuff: 3 jam 4 cram, fill 5 bloat
overstuffed: 5 tumid 7 bloated
oversupply: 4 glut, load, much, sate 5 flood 6 excess 7 nimiety, surfeit, surplus 8 plethora 9 profusion
oversweet: 6 sirupy, syrupy 10 saccharine
overt: 4 open 5 clear, naked, plain 6 patent, public 7 evident, glaring, obvious, visible 8 apparent, definite, manifest, unhidden, unsubtle, unveiled 9 in the open 10 aboveboard, observable, plain to see, unshrouded
overtake: 3 lap 4 beat, pass, trap 5 catch, outdo, reach 6 befall, engulf, gain on, ingulf, pursue 7 get past, run down 8 come upon, outstrip
overtask: 3 tax 6 strain 9 weigh down
overtax: 4 jade, tire 5 abuse 6 strain 9 weigh down
overtaxing: 4 hard 5 harsh, heavy 6 tiring, trying 7 arduous, galling, onerous, weighty 8 crushing, exacting, grievous, grinding, grueling, pressing, toilsome 9 demanding, difficult, excessive, herculean, laborious, ponderous, strenuous 10 burdensome, enervating, exhausting, formidable, oppressive
over the __: 3 top 4 edge, hill, hump, line 7 counter, transom
over-the-__: 3 air 4 road
Over the __-dark sea: 4 wine
__ Over, The: 6 Party's
__ over the coals: 4 haul, rake
over-the-counter: 5 goods, stock, store, wares 8 supplies
Over the Edge author: Jonathan Kellerman
Over the Rainbow: 4 song, tune
composer: 5 Arlen 7 Harburg
ending: 5 can't I
Over There: 4 song, tune
composer: 5 Cohan
era: 3 WWI
__ Over the River Kwai, The: 6 Bridge
__ over the traces: 4 kick
overthrow: 3 err, zap 4 beat, fall, oust, rout, tilt, undo 5 purge, quash, rebel, smash, upset 6 defeat, depose, everse, mutiny, ravage, refute, revolt, topple, unseat 7 abolish, conquer, reverse, subvert 8 conquest, dethrone, suppress, vanquish 9 abolition, bring down, landslide, prostrate 10 deposition, invalidate, put an end to, revolution
overtime situation: 3 tie
overtire: 4 bore, bush, flag, jade 5 drain

6 strain, stress 7 conk out, exhaust, fatigue, poop out 8 enervate, wear down 9 tucker out
overtired: 4 beat, shot, worn 5 all in, drawn, fed up, had it, jaded, spent, stale, taxed, trite, weary 6 bushed, done in, pooped, punchy, used up, zonked 7 clichéd, drained, haggard, worn out 8 drooping, fatigued, flagging, out of gas, wiped out, wrung out 9 burned out, enervated, exhausted, hackneyed, played out, prostrate 10 knocked out
overtone: 4 hint, tone 5 sense, tinge 6 flavor, nuance 7 meaning 8 innuendo 9 inference 10 intimation, suggestion
overtrusting: 4 easy, naif 5 green, naive 6 simple, unwary, unwise 7 artless 8 gullible, innocent, lamblike, wide-eyed 9 childlike, confiding, credulous, guileless, ingenuous, unguarded, unworldly 10 unschooled, unseasoned
overture: 3 bid 4 pass 5 intro, music, offer 6 feeler, prolog, tender 7 advance, opening, preface, prelude 8 approach, foreword, prologue, proposal 9 intrusion 10 invitation
follower: 4 Act I 6 act one
make an ~ to: 3 ask 8 approach
__ Overture: 5 Cuban 6 Tragic 7 Leonore, Manfred, Russian, Trumpet
__ Overtures: 7 Pacific
overturn: 3 tip 4 roll, undo, void 5 annul, rebel, rebut, smash, spill, upend, upset 6 invert, repeal, revolt, topple, tumble 7 abolish, capsize, confute, nullify, rescind, reverse, shake up, subvert 8 set aside, vanquish 9 bring down, knock down, prostrate 10 invalidate, prove wrong
overturned: 5 spilt, upset 7 spilled, toppled 8 capsized 10 in disarray, upside-down
overused: 4 worn 5 stale, stock, trite 7 worn-out 9 played out 10 threadbare
phrase: 6 cliché
overventuresome: 4 rash, wild 5 brash, hasty 6 daring, madcap, unwary, unwise 8 feckless, headlong, heedless, mindless, pell-mell, reckless 9 audacious, breakneck, daredevil, foolhardy, hotheaded, imprudent, unadvised, uncareful 10 ill-advised, incautious
overview: 6 digest, survey 7 outline 8 panorama 10 compendium
give an ~: 5 sum up 6 digest 7 outline 8 condense 9 synopsize
overwary: 5 chary, leery 9 skeptical 10 suspicious
overweening: 4 vain 6 lordly 8 egoistic 9 egotistic
overweight: 4 huge 5 ample, beefy, bulky, fubsy, gross, heavy, hefty, large, obese, plump, pudgy, pursy, stout 6 chubby, fleshy, portly, pyknic, rotund, stocky, zaftig, zoftig 7 adipose, massive, outsize, overfed, paunchy, weighty 8 roly-poly 9 corpulent 10 abdominous, well-padded
overwhelm: 3 awe, win, wow 4 beat, bury, do in, drub, lick, rout, sink, slay, snow, stun, whip 5 amaze, crush, drown, flood, floor, seize, shock, swamp, total, upset, wreck 6 boggle, dazzle, defeat, deluge, engulf, ingulf, puzzle, ravage, thrash 7 astound, confuse, conquer, destroy, disturb, oppress, shatter, smother, stagger, stupefy, triumph, trounce 8 astonish, bedazzle, bewilder, confound, inundate, keep down, submerge, surprise, vanquish 9 devastate, downgrade, dumbfound, fascinate, prostrate, snow under 10 demoralize
with noise: 5 drown 6 deafen 8 drown out
with work: 5 swamp 6 deluge 9 snow under
overwhelmed: 5 agape, cowed 6 aghast, amazed, beaten, buried 7 abashed, daunted, shocked, stunned, swamped 8 affected, appalled, defeated, dismayed 9 astounded, awestruck, blown-away, conquered, prostrate 10 astonished, bewildered, bowled over, overthrown, speechless
overwhelming: 6 solemn 7 awesome 8 imposing 9 thrilling 10 prodigious
victory: 4 rout 5 upset 6 defeat 7 beating, debacle, laugher, pasting, shutout, washout 8 conquest, disaster, drubbing, stampede 9 thrashing, trouncing
__ over with: 3 all
overwork: 3 tax 4 jade, tire 5 weary 6 strain 7 belabor, exhaust
overworked: 4 worn 5 tired, trite, weary 7 harried, worn-out 9 elaborate, hackneyed, pressured
phrase: 6 cliché, saying 7 bromide 8 chestnut 9 platitude
overwrought: 3 hot, mad 4 edgy, high, ired, sore 5 crazy, cross, huffy, hyper, irate, livid, manic, riled, showy, spent, tense, tired, upset, vexed, wired, wroth 6 fuming, ireful, on edge, ornate, peeved, raging, raving, red-hot, rococo, uneasy 7 anxious, enraged, excited, fired up, frantic, furious, keyed-up, labored, nervous, ranting, stirred, uptight, worried, wound-up 8 affected, agitated, choleric, feverish, frenetic, frenzied, in a state, incensed, inflamed, maddened, outraged, unstrung, worked-up, wrathful 9 emotional, excitable, indignant, irritated, resentful, splenetic, steamed up, strung-out 10 freaked out, infuriated
Over You (1968 song) artist: Gary Puckett and the Union Gap
overzealous: 5 pushy 9 obtrusive, officious
Oveta __ Hobby: 4 Culp
Ovett, Steve: 6 runner
rival: 3 Coe
Ovid: 4 poet 5 Roman
work: The Art of Love Metamorphoses
see also Latin
Oviedo: 4 city, town
locale: 5 Spain 7 Florida
oviform: 4 ooid 6 oblong 9 egg-shaped, ellipsoid 10 elliptical
Ovimbundu home: 6 Africa, Angola
ovine: 8 sheepish
creature: 3 ewe, ram 4 lamb 5 sheep
product: 4 wool 6 fleece
sound: 3 baa, maa 5 bleat
Ovitz: 7 Michael
ovo-__-vegetarian: 5 lacto
ovoid: 4 eggy 8 elliptic 9 egg-shaped 10 elliptical
ovule: 3 egg 4 seed 6 embryo
ovum: 3 egg 4 cell, seed
Owatonna: 4 city, town
locale: 9 Minnesota
owe: 5 incur 6 borrow, charge 7 run a tab 9 attribute
owed: 3 due 7 payable 8 indebted
money ~: 4 debt, levy 6 arrear 7 arrears
one ~ money: 5 payee 8 creditor
Owego's county: 5 Tioga
Owen: 3 Don 5 Davis, Randy, Spike, Steve 6 Bieber, Mickey, Robert, Wilson, Wister 7 Wilfred, Wilfrid 8 Reginald 10 Richardson
Owens: 4 Buck, Gary 5 Jesse 6 George
Owens __: 7 Corning
Owensboro: 4 city, town
locale: 8 Kentucky
Owens, Jesse: 6 runner 8 sprinter
Owen Sound: 4 city, town
locale: 6 Canada 7 Ontario
Owen Stanley: 5 range
locale: 4 Asia 9 New Guinea
Owen, Wilfrid: 4 poet 7 British
work: Dulce et Decorum Est
ower: 6 debtor 8 deadbeat
document: 3 IOU 4 chit, note 6 marker
owing: 3 due 6 in debt, mature, unpaid 7 overdue, payable 8 beholden 9 liability, unsettled
to: 7 because 9 because of, imputable 10 by reason of, by virtue of
owl: 4 bird 6 hooter, raptor
hangout: 4 barn
like an ~: 4 wise
like some ~ s: 5 eared
mouse, to an ~: 4 prey 6 quarry
sound: 3 hoo, who 4 hoot, whoo
__ owl: 3 elf 4 barn, hawk, hoot 5 eagle, night, pygmy, scops, snowy, tawny 6 barred, ground, horned, little 7 Acadian, prairie, saw-whet, screech, spotted
Owl and the Pussycat, The (1970 film)
cast: Robert Klein, George Segal, Barbra Streisand
director: Herbert Ross
Owl and the Pussycat, The author: Edward Lear
Owl's Clover author: Wallace Stevens
Owls school: 4 Rice 6 Temple
Owl went, where the: 5 to sea
owly: 7 big-eyed 10 starry-eyed
own: 3 buy, run 4 avow, have, hold, keep 5 admit, allow, boast, enjoy, grant, let on 6 assert, fess up, occupy, pay for, proper, retain 7 concede, confess, control, declare, inherit, possess, private, reserve 8 personal 9 come clean, intrinsic, recognize 10 fall heir to, individual, monopolize, particular, respective
all you ~: 5 means 6 assets, estate, wealth
doesn't ~: 5 hasn't, rents
do on one's ~: 5 offer 6 enlist, sign up 7 pitch in, proffer, recruit, stand up, venture 9 undertake, volunteer 10 put forward
hold one's ~: 4 cope 5 get by 6 manage 7 make out
make one's ~: 5 co-opt 6 borrow 7 espouse
of one's ~ accord: 6 at will, freely, gladly 7 happily, readily 8 by choice 9 agreeably, voluntary, willingly
on one's ~: 4 free, solo 5 alone, unled, unwed 6 single 9 unmarried
place of one's ~: 4 home, slot 5 niche
up: 3 own 4 avow 5 admit 7 concede, confess, profess 9 come clean
ownable property: 4 farm, home, land 5 acres, field, manor, ranch, tract 6 estate, parcel, realty 7 acreage, grounds, holding 9 farmstead 10 real estate
owned: 3 had 4 kept
apartment: 4 co-op 5 condo
be ~ by: 8 belong to
previously ~: 4 used, worn 10 hand-me-down, secondhand
__-owned: 3 pre
owner: 4 heir, host 5 buyer 6 dealer, holder, keeper, master, squire 7 heiress, legatee, partner 8 investor, landlady, landlord 9 landowner, possessor, purchaser 10 proprietor
property ~: 6 lienee, squire 8 landlord 10 freeholder
starter: 4 home, land 5 share, stock, store
__-owner car: 3 one
ownerless: 7 cast off 8 derelict 9 abandoned, discarded
Owner of a Lonely Heart (1983 song)
artist: Yes
ownership: 4 deed 5 claim, slice, title 6 buying, patent, tenure 7 control, holding, tenancy 8 dominion, monopoly, property 9 enjoyment, occupancy 10 occupation, possession, purchasing
proof of ~: 4 deed 5 paper, title 8 document
__ ownership: 4 home
owns, old-style: 4 hath
__ Own, The: 6 Devil's
ox: 3 lug, oaf, yak 4 anoa, Babe, bozo, clod, dolt, gaur, lout, male, urus, zebu 5 bovid, gayal, klutz, looby, steer 6 animal, bovine, duffer, galoot, lubber, lummox, mammal, mithan 7 banteng, banting, boggler, botcher, bumbler, bungler, fumbler, galloot, kouprey 9 blunderer, harebrain 10 clodhopper, stumblebum
Asian ~: 3 yak 4 anoa, zebu 5 gayal
attachment: 4 yoke
big ~: 3 oaf 4 bozo 6 lummox
Celebes ~: 4 anoa
prehistoric ~: 7 aurochs
team: 4 span
wild ~: 4 gaur, urus
__ ox: 4 gray, grey, musk 5 water
oxalate: 4 salt 5 ester
oxalis: 5 plant 6 flower 10 wood sorrel
oxblood: 3 red 5 color
oxbow __: 4 lake 5 chest, front
Ox-Bow Incident, The: 4 film 5 novel, oater 7 western
author: Walter van Tilburg Clark
cast: Dana Andrews, Henry Fonda, Anthony Quinn
character: 3 Art, Gil 4 Rose 5 Canby, Croft, Mapes
director: William Wellman
Oxbridge school: 4 Eton
Oxenberg, Catherine spouse: Robert Evans
oxeye: 4 bird, posy 5 bloom, daisy, plant 6 flower 7 blossom 9 perennial, sunflower
oxford: 4 shoe 5 cloth 6 fabric 8 footwear
part: 4 heel, sole 5 upper 6 insole
Oxford: 4 city, peak, town 5 mount, sheep 8 mountain
athletes: 6 Rebels 7 Ole Miss 8 RedHawks
college: 6 Exeter
locale: 4 Miss., Ohio 7 England, Rockies 8 Colorado
river: 6 Thames
teacher: 3 don
Oxford __: 3 tie 4 gray, grey, rule, shoe 5 frame, Group 6 theory 7 corners
Oxfordshire: 4 Oxon 6 county
city: 7 Banbury
locale: 7 England
oxheart: 6 cherry
relative: 4 Bing 7 marasca, morello
oxhide strap: 4 riem
oxidation: 4 film, rust 6 patina 7 coating, tarnish 9 corrosion
oxide: 4 calx, rust 5 water 6 patina, patine 7 tarnish 8 corundum 9 quicklime
component: 5 metal
iron ~: 4 rust 9 corrosion

__ oxide: **4** iron, lead **5** boric, boron, ethyl **6** barium, ferric, nickel, nitric, sodium, uranic **7** calcium, chromic, diethyl, ferrous, lithium, mesityl, nitrous, stannic, terbium, uranium, yttrium
__ oxide ointment: **4** zinc
oxidize: **4** rust **7** corrode, tarnish
oxidizing __: **5** agent
...ox is __: **5** gored
Oxnard: **4** city, town
  locale: **10** California
Oxon: **6** county
  locale: **7** England
Oxon Hill: **4** city, town
  locale: **8** Maryland
Oxonian: **4** Brit **6** Briton **7** student
  rival: **6** Cantab
oxpecker: **4** bird
oxtail: **4** soup
oxy: **9** lumbering
Oxydol: **9** detergent
  alternative: **3** All, Biz, Era, Fab, Yes **4** Bold, Dash, Gain, Surf, Tide, Wisk **5** Cheer, Dreft, Purex **6** Calgon, Dynamo **7** Octagon **9** Ivory Snow
oxygen: **3** air **5** ozone **7** element
  add ~ to: **6** aerate
  lack of ~: **6** anoxia
  producer: **4** leaf, tree **5** plant
  user: **6** aerobe
oxygen __: **4** acid, debt, mask **5** cycle, lance
__ oxygen: **5** heavy **6** liquid
oxygenate: **3** air **6** aerate, purify
Oy __!: **3** vay, vey
Oy!: **4** alas, oh no
Oyama: **4** city, town
  locale: **5** Japan
Oye Como Va (1971 song) artist: Santana
oyez: **6** hear ye
Oyl: **5** Olive **6** Castor
Oyo: **4** city, town
  locale: **7** Nigeria
oyster: **5** color, shell, white **7** grayish **8** seashell
  combining form: **5** ostre- **6** ostrei-, ostreo-
  home: **3** bed **5** culch **6** cultch
  lift, as an ~: **4** tong
  open, as an ~: **5** shuck
  product: **5** pearl
  relative: **4** bone, clam, milk, snow **5** cream, ivory, milky **6** argent, mussel, silver **8** eggshell
  young ~: **4** spat **5** culch **6** cultch
oyster __: **3** bed, cap **4** crab, farm, fork **5** plant, scale, white **7** cracker
__ oyster: **4** seed **5** pearl
Oyster __: **3** Bay
oystercatcher: **4** bird
__ Oyster Cult: **4** Blue
oysters __ season: **3** R in
oz.: **2** wt. **3** qty. **4** meas.
  fraction of an ~: **3** pwt., tsp. **4** tbsp.
  multiple: **2** lb., pt. **3** gal.
  sixteen ~: **2** lb. **5** one lb.
Oz: **4** Amos **5** Frank, Scott
  actor: **4** Lahr **5** Burke, Haley **6** Bolger, Morgan **7** Garland **8** Hamilton
  role: **4** lion, Toto **5** witch **7** Dorothy
Oz, Amos: **6** writer **7** Israeli
  work: A Perfect Peace
Ozark parent: **3** maw, paw
Ozarks: **5** range
  locale: **8** Arkansas, Missouri, Oklahoma
Ozawa, Seiji: **8** Japanese **9** conductor
  contemporary: **5** Mehta
Oz, Frank: **8** director **9** puppeteer
  film: Bowfinger (1999)
    The Dark Crystal (1982)
    Dirty Rotten Scoundrels (1988)
    The Indian in the Cupboard (1995)
    In & Out (1997)
    Little Shop of Horrors (1986)
    The Muppets Take Manhattan (1984)
    The Score (2001)
    What About Bob? (1991)
  TV: The Muppet Show
ozone: **3** air, gas **5** layer **6** oxygen **8** fresh air
  alert prompter: **3** fog **4** haze, murk, smog **5** brume, vapor **9** fogginess
  enemy: **3** CFC **5** Freon
ozone __: **4** hole **5** alert, layer
O-Zone author: Paul Theroux
Ozumba: **4** city, town
  locale: **6** Mexico
Ozymandias: **4** poem **6** sonnet
  author: Percy Bysshe Shelley
Ozzie: **5** Smith **6** Nelson **7** Newsome
Ozzie son: **4** Rick **5** David, Ricky
Ozzy: **8** Osbourne

P

p __ puzzle: 4 as in
P: 3 vit. 4 elem. 6 letter 7 element, vitamin 10 phosphorus
15 for ~: 4 at. no.
followers: 3 QRS 4 QRST 5 QRSTU
in phonetic alphabet: 4 Papa
preceders: 3 MNO 4 LMNO 5 KLMNO
vitamin ~: 5 rutin
P __: 4 and L, wave 6 marker
__ P: 4 A and 6 Master 7 vitamin
__ P.: 3 K. of
'P' __ Peril: 5 Is for
pa: 3 dad, pop 4 male 5 daddy, pappy 6 father, parent
pa's ~: 5 gramp 6 gramps
p.a. __: 6 system
Pa: 4 elem. 7 element 11 proactinium
91 for ~: 4 at. no.
Pa.
see Pennsylvania
PA
see Pennsylvania
PA __: 6 factor, system
Paar, Jack: 2 MC 4 host 5 emcee
follower: 4 Leno
preceder: 5 Allen
Paavo: 5 Nurmi 8 Haavikko
PABA, part of: 4 acid, para 5 amino
Pabellón de Arteaga: 4 city, town
locale: 6 Mexico
Pablo: 6 Casals, Cruise, Neruda 7 Picasso
in English: 4 Paul
__ Pablo, CA: 3 San
Pablo Cruise
song: Cool Love (1981)
Don't Want to Live Without It (1978)
I Want You Tonight (1979)
Love Will Find a Way (1978)
Whatcha Gonna Do? (1977)
Pablum: 6 cereal
competitor: 3 Kix 4 Life, Trix 5 Kashi, Quisp, Total 6 Kaboom, Muesli, Oreo O's, Smacks 7 All-Bran, Crispix, Harmony, Hunny B's, Mueslix, Oat Bran, Pokemon 8 Boo Berry, Cheerios, Corn Chex, Corn Pops, Fiber One, Rice Chex, Special K, Uncle Sam, Wheaties 9 Alpha Bits, Apple Zaps, Grape Nuts, Honey Comb, Just Right, Wheat Chex 10 Apple Jacks, Bran Flakes, Cap'n Crunch, Cocoa Puffs, Froot Loops, Mini-Wheats, Nutri-Grain, Puffed Rice, Quaker Oats, Smart Start 11 Cocoa Blasts, Cookie Crisp, Golden Crisp, Lucky Charms, Puffed Wheat, Sweet Crunch, Waffle Crisp
eater: 3 tot 4 baby 6 infant
Pabst: 2 G.W. 4 beer
alternative: 3 Bud 5 Becks, Coors 6 Amstel, Corona, Miller, Molson 7 Schlitz 8 Heineken, Michelob 9 Lowenbrau 10 Ballantine
pac: 4 boot, shoe 8 footwear, moccasin
Pac-__: 3 Man
Pac-__ Conference: 3 Ten
Pac.: 10 See Pacific
PAC
contributor: 6 fat cat 8 politico 10 politician
donee: 3 rep., sen. 7 senator
paca: 4 cavy 6 animal, mammal, rodent
relative: 3 rat 4 cavy, degu, jird, vole 5 coypu, gundi, mouse, xerus 6 agouti, beaver, gerbil, gopher, jerboa, marmot, murine 7 hamster, lemming, muskrat, visacha 8 chipmunk, cricetid, dormouse, squirrel, tuco-tuco 9 chickaree, groundhog, guinea pig, porcupine, woodchuck 10 chinchilla, prairie dog
Pacaya: 7 volcano
locale: 9 Guatemala
pace: 3 jog, run 4 gait, lope, rate, step, time, trot, walk 5 amble, march, speed, stalk, tempo, tread 6 canter, gallop, patrol, stride 7 mark out, measure 8 ambulate, footstep, galopade, momentum, rapidity, velocity 9 gallopade, swiftness
ender: 5 maker 6 setter 7 setting
fast ~: 4 clip
keep ~: 4 meet 5 equal, rival
keep ~ with: 3 tie 5 equal, match, rival 8 parallel
off: 7 measure
pick up the ~: 3 fly, hie, run 4 dash, race, tear 5 hurry, speed
set the ~: 4 lead
snail's ~: 3 lag 4 slow 5 crawl
starter: 4 foot
pace __: 3 car, lap
__ pace: 4 keep 5 great, Roman 6 snail's
paced: 6 steady 7 metered, regular, uniform 8 constant, measured 9 modulated, regulated 10 rhythmical
Pacella: 4 font 8 typeface
Pacemaker: 3 car 4 auto 5 Essex 6 Hudson 10 automobile
Pacem in __: 6 terris
pacer: 5 horse, mount, steed 6 equine, leader 7 trotter 9 racehorse 10 forerunner
burden: 5 sulky
Pacer: 3 AMC, car 4 auto 5 Edsel
rival: 3 Cav, Mav, Net, Sun 4 Buck, Bull, Hawk, Heat, Jazz, King, Spur 5 Knick, Laker, Magic 6 Celtic, Hornet, Nugget, Piston, Raptor, Rocket, Wizard 7 Clipper, Grizzly, Warrior 8 Cavalier, Maverick 10 SuperSonic, Timberwolf
Pacers: 4 five, team
former org.: 3 ABA
home: 7 Indiana
org.: 3 NBA
sport: 10 basketball
pacesetter: 6 leader
Pa Chin: 6 writer 7 Chinese
pachinko: 4 game
pachisi: 4 game 9 board game
form of ~: 4 ludo
Pachuca: 4 city, town
locale: 6 Mexico 7 Hidalgo
pachyderm: 5 hippo, rhino 6 animal, mammal 8 elephant 10 rhinoceros
tooth: 4 tusk
pacific: 4 calm, cool 5 quiet 6 gentle, irenic, low-key, mellow, placid, sedate, serene 7 amiable, at peace, equable, relaxed, restful, stoical, unmoved 8 amicable, composed, irenical, laid-back, lamblike, moderate, peaceful, tranquil 9 collected, easygoing, impassive, quiescent, temperate, unexcited, unruffled 10 unagitated, untroubled
Pacific: 5 ocean
archipelago: 4 Fiji, Riau 5 Malay
atoll: 6 Bikini, Tarawa 8 Funafuti 9 Eniewetok
bay: 5 Manta 8 Monterey
bird: 5 goony 6 gooney
fish: 5 sargo 6 beshow, bigeye, salmon, tomcod 7 cabezon, corbina, corvina, halibut, herring, nibbler, opaleye, pomfret, ronquil, sand dab, wolf-eel 8 baysmelt, flathead, mahimahi, palometa, topsmelt, tubenose 9 greenling, surfperch, tubesnout
former ~ alliance: 5 SEATO
fruit: 7 coconut 9 pineapple
goatfish: 5 Moana
goose: 4 nene
greeting: 5 aloha
gulf: 5 Davao, Papua, Penas 6 Alaska 7 Fonseca 8 Papagayo 9 Guayaquil 10 California
island: 4 Guam, Java, Wake 5 Nauru, Timor 6 Borneo, Easter, Honshu 7 Rapa Nui, Sumatra 8 Hokkaido, Sakhalin 9 New Guinea
islands: 4 Cook, Fiji, Truk 5 Banda, Bonin, Kuril, Palau, Samoa 6 Futuna, Midway, Ryukyu 7 Mariana, Marshal, Oceania, Society, Solomon 8 Friendly, Gilberts, Hawaiian, Moluccas, Sandwich, South Sea 9 Galapagos, Marquesas, Melanesia, Polynesia 10 Micronesia, New Zealand 11 Philippines
islands flower: 5 lehua 6 orchid 8 hibiscus
islands palm: 4 nipa 7 coconut
river to the ~: 5 Lempa, Santa 6 Bio-Bio 7 Klamath 8 Columbia
salmon: 4 chum, coho 5 cohoe
sea: 4 Sulu 5 Banda, Coral 6 Tasman, Yellow 7 Celebes 10 South China
South ~ capital: 4 Apia, Suva 5 Agana 6 Majuro, Manila, Nouméa, Tarawa 7 Honiara, Papeete 8 Funafuti, Pago Pago, Port-Vila 9 Nuku'alofa
Pacific __: 3 cod, rim 4 high, time 5 Ocean, Plate 6 salmon 7 dogwood, Heights, madrone
__ Pacific: 5 South, Union
__-Pacific: 4 Indo 7 Georgia
Pacifica: 3 SUV 4 city, town 8 Chrysler
locale: 10 California
Pacific Coast
fruit: 5 salal 9 manzanita
range: 5 Andes 11 Sierra Madre
state: 3 Cal., Ore. 4 Wash. 5 Calif. 6 Oregon 10 California, Washington
Pacific Coast explorer: 6 Balboa 9 Vancouver
Pacific Heights (1990 film)
cast: Melanie Griffith, Michael Keaton, Mako, Matthew Modine
director: John Schlesinger
Pacific Overtures: 7 musical
songwriter: 8 Sondheim
Pacific Princess: 4 boat, ship 5 liner
pacifier: 3 sop
in Britain: 5 dummy
pacifist: 4 dove 7 radical 8 ultraist 10 nonviolent
pacifists' protest: 5 march, sit-in, vigil
pacify: 4 calm, ease, lull, tame 5 allay, quell, quiet, slake 6 defuse, defuze, soothe, stroke, subdue, temper 7 appease, assuage, compose, mollify, placate, relieve, satisfy, sweeten 8 mitigate, moderate 9 alleviate, quiet down, reconcile, soft-pedal, untrouble 10 ameliorate, conciliate, propitiate, smooth over
pacing: 5 upset 6 uneasy 7 anxious, fearful, in a stew, nervous, uptight, worried 9 attentive, concerned, disturbed, exercised, in a lather, perturbed 10 distraught, distressed
Pacino, Al: 5 actor
film: ... And Justice for All (1979)
Any Given Sunday (1999)
Author! Author! (1982)
Carlito's Way (1993)
City Hall (1996)
The Devil's Advocate (1997)
Dick Tracy (1990)
Dog Day Afternoon (1975)
Donnie Brasco (1997)
Frankie and Johnnie (1991)
Frankie and Johnny (1991)
Glengarry Glen Ross (1992)
The Godfather (1972)
The Godfather Part II (1974)
The Godfather Part III (1990)
Heat (1995)
The Insider (1999)
Insomnia (2002)
The Panic in Needle Park (1971)
Scarecrow (1973)
Scarface (1983)
Scent of a Woman (1992, AA)
Sea of Love (1989)
Serpico (1973)
__ Pacis: 3 Ara
pack: 3 box, jam, kit, lot, lug, mob, ram, set 4 bale, band, bevy, case, cram, crew, deck, fill, gang, haul, heap, herd, lade, load, pile, plug, stow, take, tamp, tote, wrap 5 batch, bunch, carry, crate, crowd, drove, ferry, flock, group, horde, press, stack, stuff, swarm, troop, wedge 6 bundle, clique, decamp, encase, gear up, incase, kennel, kitbag, outfit, parcel, rabble, throng 7 cluster, company, congest, coterie, put away, squeeze 8 get ready, knapsack, rucksack, shoulder 9 haversack, overcrowd, piggyback, transport
again: 5 rebag
a heater: 4 tote 5 carry
animal: 3 ass 4 mule 5 burro, horse, llama 6 donkey
away: 3 eat 4 stow 5 store 6 ingest
Cub Scout ~ leader: 5 Akela
ender: 3 age 4 sack 5 horse 6 saddle
extra: 5 joker
it in: 3 eat, end 4 halt, quit 5 cease, close 6 finish, wind up, wrap up 7 adjourn, break up 8 conclude 9 terminate
leading the ~: 5 on top 7 winning
member: 4 wolf 5 hyena 6 hyaena
rat: 5 saver 6 animal, mammal, rodent, storer 7 amasser, hoarder 8 gatherer 9 collector
scavenger: 5 hyena 6 jackal
starter: 3 day, mud 4 back
toter: 5 hiker 6 camper 7 student 8 traveler 10 hitchhiker
pack __: 3 ice, off, rat 4 away, date, it in, mule 6 animal
__ pack: 3 hot, ice 4 cold, disk, film, wolf 5 power 6 bubble, shrink, vacuum 7 blister
__-pack: 3 jam, six
__ Pack: 3 Rat 4 Brat
package: 3 box, can, tin 4 bale, mail, wrap 5 box up, crate 6 bundle, carton, encase, incase, parcel 7 arrival 9 container 10 assortment
CARE ~: 3 aid
deliverer: 3 UPS 4 USPS 5 FedEx
letters: 3 COD, ppd
of paper: 4 ream
open a ~: 4 undo 6 unwrap
secure a ~: 3 tie 4 tape
send a ~: 4 mail, ship
wrapped ~: 4 gift 7 present
wrapper: 4 cord, tape 5 paper, twine 6 ribbon
package __: 4 deal, plan, tour 5 store
package store buy: 3 ale, gin, keg, rum, rye 4 beer, wine 5 vodka 6 brandy, liquor, whisky 7 spirits, whiskey
packaging material: 5 paper 9 cellulose, newspaper, Styrofoam 10 bubble wrap
Packard: 3 car 4 auto 5 David, Vance
competitor: 6 De Soto
Packard __: 4 Bell

__-Packard: 7 Hewlett
packed: 4 full, rife 5 awash, close, dense, laden, thick, tight 6 loaded, mobbed 7 brimful, compact, crowded, replete, stuffed, teeming 8 arranged, brimfull, brimming, swarming, thronged 9 chock-full, condensed, congested, to the roof 10 compressed, gridlocked, wall-to-wall
packer
pistol ~: 4 thug 6 bandit, gunman, hit man, outlaw, robber 7 marshal, mobster, sheriff 9 desperado
starter: 4 back, meat
Packer
rival: 3 Jet, Ram 4 Bear, Bill, Colt, Lion 5 Brown, Chief, Eagle, Giant, Raven, Saint, Texan, Titan 6 Bengal, Bronco, Cowboy, Falcon, Jaguar, Raider, Viking 7 Charger, Dolphin, Panther, Patriot, Redskin, Seahawk, Steeler 8 Cardinal 9 Buccaneer
Packers: 4 team 6 eleven
div.: 3 NFC
home: 3 Wis. 4 Wisc. 11 Green Bay
org.: 3 NFL
sport: 8 football
packet: 3 box 4 boat 5 ferry, pouch 6 bundle, carton, folder, parcel 8 envelope 9 container
nursery ~: 4 seed
packhorse: 6 equine
packing: 5 armed
a pistol: 5 armed
a wallop: 5 harsh 6 potent, strong 8 powerful
container: 3 box 4 case 5 crate
send ~: 2 ax 3 axe, can, rid 4 boot, drop, fire, oust, sack 5 eject, evict, exile, expel, let go 6 banish, bounce, depose, lay off 7 cashier, dismiss, drum out, release, turn out 8 chase out, furlough, get rid of, pink-slip 9 discharge, terminate
slip: 3 inv. 7 invoice
some weight: 10 hefty. heavy
__ Packin' Mama: 6 Pistol
packsack: 5 kyack 6 duffel, duffle
Pac-Man: 4 game 9 video game
blue ghost, in ~: 4 Inky
emulate ~: 3 eat 6 devour
home: 6 arcade
morsel: 3 dot
Paco
see Spanish
Pacquin: 6 lotion
alternative: 4 Keri 5 Curel, Nivea 6 Aveeno 7 Eucerin, Jergens 9 Lubriderm
pact: 4 bond, deal, SALT 5 SEATO 6 accord, league, pledge, treaty 7 bargain, charter, concord, entente, promise, tontine 8 alliance, contract, covenant, protocol 9 agreement, concordat 10 compromise, engagement, settlement
defunct ~: 5 SEATO
name: 6 Briand 7 Kellogg
party to a ~: 4 ally
since 1949: 4 NATO
tariff ~: 5 NAFTA
tenant's ~: 5 lease
US-USSR ~: 4 SALT
__ Pact: 6 Warsaw 7 Locarno
Pac-10
overseer: 4 NCAA
school: 3 ASU, Ore., OSU, UCB, USC, WSU 4 Ariz., UCLA, Wash. 6 Oregon 7 Arizona 8 Stanford 10 Washington 11 Oregon State
Pac Ten: 6 league 10 conference
rival: 3 SEC 6 Big Ten 7 Big East
Pacueco: 4 city, town
locale: 6 Mexico 10 Guanajuato
Pacula: 6 Joanna
pad: 3 mat, wad 4 digs, flat, foot, home, leaf, line, spot, trot, walk 5 abode, creep, fudge, house, paper, place, sneak, stuff, tread 6 bulk up, expand, extend, patter, tablet 7 amplify, augment, bolster, cushion, domicil, enlarge, fill out, habitat, housing, inflate, magnify, protect, shelter, shuffle, wadding, zabuton 8 domicile, dressing, dwelling, flesh out, lengthen, lodgment, mattress, notebook, stuffing 9 apartment, fingertip, upholster 10 exaggerate, supplement
brake ~: 4 shoe
combining form: 3 tyl- 4 tylo-
ender: 4 lock
engraver's ~: 6 dabber
freshen a stamp ~: 5 reink
hair ~: 3 rat
memo ~: 6 tablet
shoe ~: 6 insole
starter: 3 key 4 foot 6 sketch 7 scratch
tumbler's ~: 3 mat
__ pad: 4 knee, lily, soap 5 brake, crash, legal, stamp, steno 6 launch, yellow 7 heating, scratch
__ P. Adams: 8 Franklin
Padang: 4 city, port, town
locale: 9 Indonesia
padded: 4 soft 5 comfy, cushy 9 cushioned, redundant
padding: 5 straw 6 buffer, cotton, excess 7 bombast, cushion, filling, wadding 8 stuffing 9 Styrofoam 10 bubble wrap, protection
excess ~: 3 fat 4 flab
paddle: 3 oar 4 flog, pull, swim, wade 5 canoe, spank 6 cudgel, dabble, punish, racket, splash, thrash 7 flipper 8 navigate
dog ~: 4 swim
ender: 4 ball, boat, fish 5 board
pin: 5 thole
wheeler site: 4 lake 5 river
paddle __: 3 box 5 wheel 6 tennis 7 steamer, wheeler
paddleball: 4 game
paddler: 3 oar 6 rafter 7 oarsman 8 canoeist
milieu: 4 lake, pond 5 creek, river 6 stream
org: 3 ACA
paddlewheeler: 4 boat, ship 5 craft 6 vessel
paddock: 3 pen 6 corral
adjunct: 4 hasp
occupant: 4 colt, foal, mare 5 filly, horse 6 bronco, equine 8 stallion
papa: 4 sire
paddy
crop: 4 rice
wagon: 6 lockup 7 vehicle
Paddy: 9 Chayefsky
paddywhack: 5 spank
Paderewski, Ignace: 6 Polish 7 pianist
instrument: 5 piano
Padgett: 5 Lewis
__ Padilla Jr.: 6 Manuel
padlock: 5 latch 6 secure 7 closure
partner: 4 hasp
padouk: 4 tree
family: 6 legume
relative: 3 koa 5 carob 6 cassia, cercis, locust, redbud 7 araroba, mesquit 8 mesquite, tamarind 9 poinciana
Padova: 4 city, town
locale: 5 Italy
Padraic: 5 Colum
in English: 7 Patrick
padre: 4 abbé 5 friar 6 cleric, curate, father, parson, pastor, priest, rector 7 brother 8 chaplain, minister, preacher, reverend, sky pilot 9 clergyman, pulpiteer, sermonist 10 sermonizer
brother: 3 tio
daughter: 4 hija 5 chica 8 muchacha
sister: 3 tia
son: 4 hijo 5 chico 8 muchacho
wife: 5 madre 6 esposa
Padre Island locale: 5 Texas
Padre rival: 3 Cub, Met, Red 4 Expo, Twin 5 Angel, Astro, Brave, Giant, Rocky, Royal, Tiger 6 Brewer, Dodger, Indian, Marlin, Oriole, Philly, Pirate, Ranger, Red Sox, Yankee 7 Blue Jay, Mariner 8 Athletic, Cardinal, Devil Ray, White Sox
Padres: 4 nine, team
div.: 3 NLW
home: 8 San Diego
org.: 3 MLB
sport: 8 baseball
pads, work with: 5 scour
Padua: 4 city, town
locale: 5 Italy
town near ~: 4 Este
paduasoy: 6 fabric 8 material
Paducah: 4 city, town
locale: 3 Ken. 8 Kentucky
paean: 4 hymn, poem, song, tune 5 psalm 6 anthem, homage, melody 7 hosanna 8 alleluia, encomium 9 extolment, panegyric 10 hallelujah
paella: 6 entrée 7 Spanish
cooker: 4 olla
ingerdient: 4 rice 7 chicken, mussels, saffron, sausage
paenula: 5 cloak
__ Paese: 3 Bel
pagan: 7 atheist, heathen, infidel 8 agnostic, hedonist, idolator 9 pantheist 10 idolatrous, polytheist, unbeliever
ender: 3 ism
practice: 5 wicca 10 witchcraft
prefix with: 3 neo
Paganini composer: 5 Lehár
Paganini, Niccolò instrument: 6 violin
Pagan Love __: 4 Song
page: 4 aide, beep, call, leaf, Op-Ed 5 check, folio, gofer, recto, sheet, usher, verso 6 gopher, lackey, number, summon 7 bellhop, call for, equerry, lacquey, send for, servant 8 announce, document 9 attendant
book ~: 4 leaf 5 recto, verso
cal. ~: 2 mo.
calendar ~: 5 month
calendario ~: 3 mes
commentators ~: 4 Op-Ed
fold: 6 dog-ear
home ~ address: 3 URL
job: 6 errand
last ~: 6 ending
like left-hand ~ numbers: 4 even
like right-hand ~ numbers: 3 odd
manuscript ~: 5 folio
web ~ access: 4 link
__ page: 3 web 4 home, Op-Ed 5 front, title
Page: 2 P.K. 3 Jim 4 Alan 5 Jimmy, Patti, Tommy 6 Hannah 7 Anthony, LaWanda 9 Geraldine
pageant: 4 gala, play, show 5 sight 6 parade, ritual 7 display 8 splendor 9 festivity, motorcade, spectacle 10 exhibition, procession
prop: 5 tiara 7 bouquet
winner: 5 queen 6 beauty
pageantry: 4 pomp, show 7 glitter 8 heraldry
page-bottom info: 6 footer
pageboy: 4 coif 6 hairdo 8 coiffure 9 hairstyle
relative: 3 bob
__ Page Farrell: 5 Front
Page, Geraldine: 7 actress
film: The Beguiled (1970)
Dear Heart (1964)
Hondo (1953)
Interiors (1978)
J W Coop (1972)
My Little Girl (1986)
Summer and Smoke (1961)
Sweet Bird of Youth (1962)
The Trip to Bountiful (1985, AA)
Whatever Happened to Aunt Alice? (1969)
You're a Big Boy Now (1966)
spouse: Rip Torn
Page, Patti: 6 singer
song: Allegheny Moon (1956)
Another Time, Another Place (1958)
Belonging to Someone (1958)
Go On with the Wedding (1956)
Hush, Hush, Sweet Charlotte (1965)
Left Right Out of Your Heart (1958)
Let Me Go, Lover! (1954)
Mama from the Train (1956)
Old Cape Cod (1957)
A Poor Man's Roses (1957)
Wondering (1957)
pager: 6 beeper
signal: 4 beep 9 vibration
pages, turn: 4 flip, scan, skim 9 speedread
Paget, Debra: 7 actress
film: Les Miserables (1952)
Love Me Tender (1956)
The River's Edge (1957)
Seven Angry Men (1955)
The Ten Commandments (1956)
Pagliacci: 5 opera
Canio in ~: 5 tenor
role: 5 Beppe, Canio, Nedda, Tonio 6 Silvio
setting: 5 Italy 8 Calabria, Montalto
__ Pagliaccio: 4 Ridi
pagne: 5 skirt
pagoda: 6 shrine, temple
Chinese ~: 3 taa
feature: 4 gong 6 statue 7 incense
land: 5 China
Pago Pago: 4 city, port, town
locale: 5 Samoa
__-pah: 3 oom 6 oompah
pahlavi: 4 coin
Pahlavi: 4 Reza 5 Irani
realm, once: 4 Iran
title: 4 shah
pahoehoe: 4 lava
Pahouin home: 5 Gabon, Gabun 6 Africa 8 Cameroon
Pahrump: 4 city, town
locale: 6 Nevada
paid
get ~: 4 earn, work
marker: 5 stamp
notice: 2 ad
performer: 3 pro
something ~: 5 visit 9 attention 10 compliment
starter: 4 post
to be ~: 3 due
work: 3 job 4 post 6 employ 8 position
__-paid: 4 well
Paige: 5 Janis, Turco 7 Satchel 8 Jennifer
Paige, Janis: 7 actress
film: Please Don't Eat the Daisies (1960)
Romance on the High Seas (1948)
Silk Stockings (1957)
Wallflower (1948)
Paige, Satchel: 6 hurler 7 pitcher
real first name: 5 Leroy
pail: 6 bailer, bucket, vessel 7 scuttle 9 container 10 receptacle
pain: 3 ail, irk, vex, woe 4 ache, bore,

burn, drag, gall, harm, hurt, kink, pang, pest, pill, rack, rile, tire **5** agony, catch, cramp, crick, grief, gripe, smart, spasm, sting, throb, throe, trial, upset, worry, wound **6** aching, bother, effort, grieve, harass, harrow, injure, injury, misery, offend, rankle, sadden, sorrow, stitch, strain, trauma, twinge, twitch **7** anguish, anxiety, malaise, sadness, torment, torture, travail, trouble **8** aggrieve, distress, irritate, nuisance, soreness, vexation **9** annoyance, heartache, suffering **10** bitterness, difficulty, discomfort, imposition, tenderness
be a ~: **3** nag **4** bore, carp **5** tease **6** bother, yammer **8** complain
cause ~: **4** hurt **6** injure **10** discomfort
combining form: **3** alg- **4** algo-, -algy, noci- **5** -algia **6** -odynia
draw back, as in ~: **5** wince **6** cringe, flinch
exclamation ~: **2** ow **3** oof, yow **4** ouch, yeow, yipe **5** yipes
express ~: **3** cry, sob **4** howl, mewl, wail, weep **5** whine **6** scream **7** whimper
feeling no ~: **4** numb **5** tipsy
in ~: **4** hurt **6** aching **7** hurting, unhappy **9** miserable, sorrowful
in the neck: **4** ache, bore, kink, pest, pill **5** crick, trial **6** bother, hassle **8** headache, irritant **9** annoyance
in the side: **5** thorn
reliever: **5** Advil, Aleve, salve **6** Ben-Gay, Motrin, opiate **7** anodyne, aspirin, Ecotrin, hot pack, Tylenol **8** Bufferin, cold pack, narcotic, ointment, sedative **9** analgesic **10** anesthetic
Pain and the Great One, The author: Judy Blume
Paine __: **6** Webber
Paine Field: **4** city, town
locale: **10** Washington
Paine, Thomas: **6** writer **7** British, radical **8** essayist
work: The Age of Reason
Common Sense
The Rights of Man
painful: **3** bad, raw, sad **4** achy, dire, hard, sore **5** nasty **6** aching, bitter, sticky, tender, tragic, trying **7** arduous, burning, hurting, onerous, tedious **8** dolorous, grievous, inflamed, piercing, stinging, terrible, tragical **9** agonizing, difficult, harrowing, irritated, laborious, sensitive, sorrowful, throbbing, vexatious **10** unpleasant
be ~: **4** ache, burn, itch **5** smart, throb
make less ~: **6** soothe **7** relieve
painless: **4** easy, snap **5** cinch, cushy **6** breeze, picnic, simple **8** duck soup, pushover **9** innocuous **10** child's play, effortless, unexacting
pains: **3** TLC **4** care, toil **5** labor **6** effort **7** trouble **8** exertion, struggle
partner: **5** aches
take ~: **6** bother **7** trouble
__ pains: **7** growing
painstaking: **5** exact, fussy **6** minute **7** careful, earnest, finicky, precise, prudent **8** cautious, diligent, exacting, finiking, finnicky, methodic, rigorous, sedulous, thorough **9** assiduous, attentive, by the book, judicious, laborious, observant **10** fastidious, meticulous, particular, scrupulous
paint: **3** dye, oil **4** coat, daub, draw, kohl, limn, oils, tint, wash **5** color, cover, horse, latex, pinto, rouge, stain **6** depict, enamel, equine, makeup, poster, redden, veneer **7** acrylic, blusher, encrust, gouache, incrust, outline, pigment, portray, stipple, tempera, touch up, varnish **8** colorant, cosmetic, decorate, emulsion, lipstick **9** adumbrate, delineate, represent, whitewash **10** illustrate, watercolor
additive: **5** drier, water **7** thinner **10** turpentine
apply ~: **4** coat, roll **5** brush, spray
base: **5** latex
container: **3** can **4** tube
crudely: **4** daub **5** smear
ender: **5** brush
fluorescent ~: **6** Day-Glo
glossy ~: **6** enamel
remove ~: **5** strip
splotch: **4** blob
starter: **3** war **6** finger, grease
surface: **4** coat **5** layer
the town red: **5** party, revel **6** barhop **7** carouse, roister **8** cut loose, let loose, live it up **9** celebrate, raise Cain, whoop it up
paintbrush
devil's ~: **5** plant **6** flower
material: **4** foam **5** nylon **8** bristles
paint-drier ingredient: **5** rosin
painted
freshly ~: **3** wet
lady: **3** bug **6** insect **9** butterfly
metal: **4** tole
Painted __, The: **4** Bird, Mesa, Veil
Painted Bird, The author: Jerzy Kosinski
Painted Desert feature: **4** mesa, rock, sand
painter: **3** Arp **4** Dali, Dufy, Goya, Gris, Hals, Kent, Klee, Lely, Miró, Reni, Sert, Wood **5** Bosch, Corot, Degas, Dürer, Ensor, Ernst, Homer, Johns, Kahlo, Klimt, Léger, Manet, Monet, Moses, Munch, Peale, Shahn, Sloan, Steen, Wyeth **6** artist, Benton, Braque, Copley, Eakins, Giotto, Hassam, Hopper, Ingres, Inness, Leutze, Man Ray, Renoir, Rivera, Rothko, Rubens, Seurat, Stuart, Tanguy, Tissot, Titian **7** Bonheur, Bruegel, Cassatt, Cézanne, Chagall, da Vinci, Duchamp, El Greco, Gauguin, Hogarth, Holbein, Matisse, O'Keeffe, Picasso, Pisarro, Pollock, Raphael, Sargent, Tiepolo, Utrillo, van Dyck, van Eyck, van Gogh, Vermeer **8** Angelico, Dubuffet, Magritte, Mondrian, Reynolds, Rockwell, Ter Borch, Whistler **9** Constable, de Kooning, Delacroix, Kandinsky, Rembrandt, Remington, Velázquez **10** Botticelli, Modigliani, Tintoretto **12** Gainsborough, Michelangelo
abstract ~: **6** Cubist
Abstractionist ~: **4** Klee **8** Mondrian **9** Kandinsky
American ~: **4** Kent, Wood **5** Homer, Johns, Moses, Peale, Shahn, Sloan, Wyeth **6** Benton, Copley, Eakins, Hassam, Hopper, Inness, Leutze, Man Ray, Rothko, Stuart **7** Cassatt, O'Keeffe, Pollock, Sargent **8** Rockwell, Whistler **9** Remington
Austrian ~: **5** Klimt **7** Schiele
Baroque ~: **6** Rubens **9** Velázquez
Belgian ~: **5** Ensor **8** Magritte
British ~: **7** Hogarth **8** Reynolds **9** Constable **12** Gainsborough
coverall: **5** smock
Cubist ~: **6** Braque
Dada ~: **6** Man Ray **7** Duchamp, Hans Arp, Jean Arp
deg.: **3** MFA
Dutch ~: **4** Hals, Lely **5** Steen **7** van Gogh, Vermeer **8** Mondrian, Ter Borch **9** de Kooning, Rembrandt
Fauvist ~: **4** Dufy **7** Matisse
Flemish ~: **5** Bosch **6** Rubens **7** Bruegel, van Dyck, van Eyck
French ~: **3** Arp **4** Dufy **5** Corot, Degas, Léger, Manet, Monet **6** Braque, Ingres, Renoir, Seurat, Tanguy, Tissot **7** Bonheur, Cézanne, Duchamp, Gauguin, Matisse, Utrillo **8** Dubuffet **9** Delacroix
from Iowa: **4** wood
German ~: **5** Dürer, Ernst **7** Holbein
Impressionist ~: **5** Monet **6** Renoir **7** Cassatt, Utrillo
Italian ~: **4** Reni **6** Giotto, Titian **7** da Vinci, Raphael, Tiepolo **8** Angelico **10** Botticelli, Modigliani, Tintoretto **12** Michelangelo
Japanese ~: **6** Sesshu
Mexican ~: **5** Kahlo **6** Rivera
mishap: **4** glob, spot **5** smear, stain **7** splotch
Norwegian ~: **5** Munch
Renaissance ~: **5** Dürer **6** Titian **7** Raphael **8** Angelico **10** Botticelli
Russian ~: **7** Chagall **9** Kandinsky
Spanish ~: **4** Dali, Goya, Gris, Miró, Sert **7** El Greco, Picasso, Pisarro **9** Velázquez
stand: **5** easel
surface: **4** wood **5** gesso, metal, paper **6** canvas
Surrealist ~: **4** Dali **6** Tanguy
Swiss ~: **4** Klee
tool: **5** brush **6** airgun, ladder, roller **7** palette
Western ~: **9** Remington
__ painter: **5** house
Painter, William: **6** author **7** British
painting: **3** art, oil **4** work **5** mural **6** canvas, fresco **7** picture **8** acryllic, portrait, seascape **9** aquarelle, landscape, still life, work of art **10** watercolor
combining form: **6** -chromy
family name: **5** Peale
holder: **3** mat **4** nail **5** frame
illusional ~: **5** op art
medium: **3** oil **6** pastel **8** acryllic **10** watercolor
oil ~: **3** art **6** canvas **7** picture **8** portrait **9** still life
on dry plaster: **5** secco
rock ~ symbol: **5** glyph
round ~: **5** tondo
Sistine Chapel ~: **6** fresco
subject: **3** jug **4** nude, vase **5** model **6** nature **7** flowers, pitcher
work on an old ~: **7** restore
Paint It, Black (1966 song) artist: Rolling Stones
Paint the Sky with Stars singer: **4** Enya
Paint Your Wagon (1969 film): **7** musical
cast: Clint Eastwood, Lee Marvin, Harve Presnell, Jean Seberg, Ray Walston
character: **5** Elisa
composer: **5** Loewe **6** Lerner
director: Joshua Logan
pair: **3** duo, two **4** duad, duet, dyad, join, span, team, yoke **5** brace, match, mates, twain, twins **6** couple, hook up **7** doublet, match up, twosome
au ~: **4** amah **5** nanny **6** nannie **8** domestic **9** nursemaid
connector: **2** no **3** and
matched ~: **4** team
one of a ~: **4** half, mate, twin
pair __: **4** bond **7** bonding
paired: **4** dual **6** double, duplex, dyadic **8** matching
combining form: **4** dipl- **5** diplo-
pair of __: **5** pants, socks **6** slacks **7** glasses **8** trousers
pairs skating: **5** event, sport
__ pais: **5** mal du, vin de
paisa: **5** money
100: **5** rupee
paisley: **3** tie **5** print, scarf **6** fabric **8** neckwear
Paisley: **4** city, town
locale: **8** Scotland
Paiute: **5** tribe **6** Indian **7** Amerind **8** language
pajama __: **5** party
Pajama Game, The (1957 film): **7** musical
cast: Doris Day, Carol Haney, John Raitt
character: **3** Mae, Sid **4** Babe **5** Mabel **6** Brenda, Gladys, Hasler
composer: **4** Ross **5** Adler
director: George Abbott, Stanley Donen
Pajama Party (1964 film)
cast: Annette Funicello, Tommy Kirk, Dorothy Lamour, Elsa Lanchester
director: Don Weis
pajamas: **3** PJ's **7** jammies **8** lingerie, sleepers **9** nightwear **10** loungewear
alternative: **7** nightie **9** nightgown
coverer: **4** robe **8** bathrobe
material: **4** silk **5** nylon **6** cotton **7** flannel
part: **3** top **4** tops **7** bottoms
__ pajamas: **4** cat's
Pakistan: **6** nation **7** country
bovine: **6** Channi, Dhanni, Lohani **7** Sahiwal
capital: **9** Islamabad
city: **6** Lahore **7** Karachi **9** Islamabad
crocodile: **6** gavial
desert: **4** Tahr, Thar, Tuhr
garment: **4** sari **5** lungi, saree **6** lungee, lungyi
language: **4** Urdu
location: **4** Asia
money: **4** anna, pice **5** paisa, rupee
mountain: **9** Broad Peak, Istoro Nal, Kanjut Sar, Rakaposhi, Tirich Mir **10** Gasherbrum
neighbor: **4** Iran **5** China, India **11** Afghanistan
Nobelist in Physics: **5** Salam
port: **7** Karachi
province of ~: **4** Sind
region of ~: **5** Tirah
river: **5** Indus
symbol on flag: **4** lune
Pak, Se Ri: **6** golfer, Korean
milieu: **5** links **6** course
org.: **4** LPGA
Pakula, Alan J.: **8** director
film: All the President's Men (1976)
The Devil's Own (1997)
Klute (1971)
Love and Pain... (1972)
The Parallax View (1974)
The Pelican Brief (1993)
Presumed Innocent (1990)
Sophie's Choice (1982)
Starting Over (1979)
The Sterile Cuckoo (1969)
pal: **3** bro, cuz **4** ally, chum, mate, pard **5** amiga, amigo, buddy, crony **6** cohort, frater, friend **7** brother, compeer, comrade, homeboy, pardner, partner **8** alter ego, confrere, homegirl, intimate, roommate, sidekick, soulmate **9** associate, colleague, companion, confidant, good buddy **10** bosom buddy, compatriot, well-wisher
in French: **3** ami **4** amie
in Spanish: **5** amiga, amigo **9** compañera, compañero
pal __: **6** around
__ pal: **3** gal, pen
palace: **4** hall, home **5** manor **6** castle

7 alcazar, chateau, lodging, mansion 8 dwelling 9 residence
dweller: 4 king 5 queen, royal 6 prince 7 monarch 8 princess
French ~: 6 Elysée
ice ~: 4 rink 5 arena
in Florence: 5 Pitti
Mideast ~ area: 5 haram, harem, harim 6 hareem
palace __: 4 coup 5 guard
__ palace: 3 ice
__ Palace: 3 Cow 5 White 7 Crystal, Lambeth, Lateran
Palade, George: 8 Nobelist, Romanian
paladin: 8 advocate, champion, defender, guardian 9 paraclete
Paladin portrayer: 5 Boone
palaestra: 5 arena
Palais des Nations home: 6 Geneva
Palamas, Koster: 4 poet 5 Greek
Palance: 4 Jack 5 Holly
Palance, Jack: 5 actor
film: Attack! (1956)
Bagdad Cafe (1988)
The Big Knife (1955)
City Slickers (1991, AA)
Contempt (1963)
The Lonely Man (1957)
Monte Walsh (1970)
Shane (1953)
Sudden Fear (1952)
palatable: 4 fair, good 5 sapid, tasty, yummy 6 divine, edible, savory, toothy 8 luscious, pleasant, pleasing, tempting 9 agreeable, ambrosial, delicious, enjoyable, flavorful, nectarous, nutritive, toothsome 10 acceptable, appetizing, attractive, delectable, delightful, flavorsome
palate: 5 taste 6 liking
combining form: 8 staphylo-
of the soft ~: 5 velar
part of the soft ~: 5 uvula
soft ~: 5 velum
palatial: 4 lush, posh, rich 5 grand, plush, regal, ritzy, swank 6 deluxe, swanky 7 opulent, stately 8 imposing, majestic, splendid 9 luxuriant, luxurious, sumptuous 10 impressive, majestical
dwelling: 5 manor 6 castle, estate 7 chateau
palatine: 4 bone, cape
locale: 5 mouth
Palatine: 4 city, hill, town
garb: 4 toga
locale: 4 Rome 8 Illinois
Palatino: 4 font 8 typeface
Palau: 4 city, isls., town 5 isles 7 islands
capital: 5 Koror
locale: 6 Mexico 8 Coahuila
palaver: 3 gab, rap, yak 4 chat, talk 5 clack, prate 6 confer, gibber, gossip, huddle, jargon, parley, powwow 7 blather, blether, chatter, coaxing 8 babbling, cajolery, chitchat, claptrap, converse, flattery, language, nonsense, soft soap 9 gibberish, loquacity, small talk, sweet talk, table talk
palaverous: 4 long 5 gabby, windy, wordy 6 prolix 7 diffuse, lengthy, verbose, voluble 8 rambling 9 bombastic, garrulous, talkative 10 discursive, long-winded, loquacious
Palazzo Pubblico site: 5 Siena
pale: 3 dim, wan 4 ashy, fade, gray, grey, post, soft, weak 5 ashen, bourn, faded, faint, light, livid, lurid, mealy, pasty, stake, stave, waxen, white 6 anemic, blanch, bounds, chalky, doughy, flaxen, pallid, pastel, peaked, picket, sallow, sickly, silver, watery, whiten 7 anaemic, ghastly, grayish, greyish, haggard, tail off, whitish 8 blanched, bleached, decrease, diminish, liverish, untanned 9 albescent, bloodless, colorless, ghostlike, lily-white, washed out 10 exsanguine, indistinct, lackluster, lusterless, white-faced
beyond the ~: 4 tabu 5 taboo 8 improper, unseemly 9 forbidden, impolitic, out of line
color: 4 tint 6 pastel
combining form: 7 palladi-
ender: 4 face
not ~: 4 rosy 5 ruddy 8 red-faced
turn ~: 6 blanch
pale __: 3 ale
pale __ ghost: 3 as a
pale-__ ginger ale: 3 dry
palea: 5 chaff
__ Paleface: 5 Son of
Paleface, The (1948 film)
cast: Robert Armstrong, Bob Hope, Jane Russell
director: Norman Z. McLeod
Pale Horse, Pale Rider author: Porter
Pale Horse, The author: Agatha Christie
Palenque: 4 city, town
builder: 4 Maya
locale: 6 Mexico 7 Chiapas
Paleocene follower: 6 Eocene
Paleolithic: 8 Stone-age
paleontologist: 9 scientist
find: 5 bones 6 fossil 8 artefact, artifact, skeleton
paleontology: 7 science
branch of ~: 9 ichnology
paleo- opposite: 3 neo-
Paleozoic: 3 Era
Pale Rider (1985 film)
cast: Clint Eastwood, Michael Moriarty, Carrie Snodgress
director: Clint Eastwood
Palermo: 4 city, peak, port, town 5 mount 8 mountain
locale: 5 Andes, Italy 9 Argentina
party: 5 festa
spa near ~: 4 Enna
Palestine
ancient ~ city: 3 Dan 6 Bethel
ancient district: 6 Gilead
ancient dweller: 6 Essene
ancient region: 6 Bashan, Judaea
area: 4 Gaza
group: 10 Arab League
Nobelist in Peace: 6 Arafat
peak in ancient ~: 4 Nebo
region near ancient ~: 4 Edom
region of ancient ~: 5 Judea 6 Judaea
seaport: 5 Haifa
Palestrina: 8 Giovanni
paletot: 4 cape, coat 6 jacket
palette
partner: 5 brush, easel, knife
pigment: 5 ocher, ochre, umber
shape: 4 oval
user: 6 artist 7 painter
Paley: 5 Grace 7 William
Paley, Grace: 6 writer
Paley, William
company: 3 CBS 5 CBS-TV
palfrey: 5 horse, mount, steed 6 equine 7 charger 8 warhorse
Pal, George: 8 director
film: 7 Faces of Dr. Lao (1964)
The Time Machine (1960)
tom thumb (1958)
The Wonderful World of the Brothers Grimm (1962)
Pali: 8 language
relative: 8 Sanskrit
Palikir: 4 city, town
locale: 10 Micronesia
Palillo: 3 Ron
Palin: 7 Michael
palindromic
address: 3 dad, mom, pop 4 ma'am 5 madam
animal: 3 ewe
bird: 3 tit
city: 3 Ada, Ede
computer language: 3 Ada
constellation: 3 Ara
emperor: 4 Otto
exclamation: 3 aha, hah, oho, tut, wow
Indian: 3 Oto
name: 3 Ada, Ava, Bob, Eve, Lil, Nan 4 Anna, Otto 6 Hannah
periodical: 4 Elle
pop group: 3 Aha 4 ABBA
potentate: 3 aga
principle: 5 tenet
time: 4 noon
verb: 3 tat
paling: 4 rail 5 fence, stake, stave 6 picket 7 railing
palisade: 4 post, wall 5 fence 6 picket 7 defense 9 barricade, precipice
Palisades Park (1962 song) artist: Freddy Cannon
Pal Joey (1957 film): 4 play 7 musical
author: John O'Hara
cast: Rita Hayworth, Kim Novak, Frank Sinatra
character: 3 Max 4 Vera 5 Agnes, Linda 6 Ernest, Gladys
composer: 4 Hart 7 Rodgers
director: George Sidney
pall: 4 bore, cloy, haze, jade, tire, veil 5 gloom, weary 6 mantle, shadow, shroud 7 dimness, satiate, surfeit 8 peter out 10 black cloud, depression, desolation, melancholy
cast a ~ over: 6 dampen, rain on
Pall __: 4 Mall
palladium: 5 metal 7 element
alloy: 7 platina 9 white gold
Palladium portrayal: 6 Athena, Athene
Pallas: 8 asteroid
daughter: 4 Nike
father: 6 Triton 8 Heracles
Pallas __: 6 Athena, Athene
pallet: 3 bed 4 skid 8 mattress, platform
palliate: 4 cure, ease, help 5 abate, allay, gloze, mince, quiet, salve, slake 6 hush up, lessen, remedy, smooth, soften, soothe, temper 7 assuage, justify, lighten, mollify, relieve, varnish 8 minimize, mitigate, moderate 9 alleviate, extenuate, gloss over, underplay, whitewash
palliative: 4 balm 5 salve 6 lotion, relief 7 anodyne 9 demulcent 10 corrective
pallid: 3 wan 4 ashy, pale, soft 5 ashen, livid, lurid, pasty, waxen, white 6 anemic, chalky, doughy, peaked, sallow, sickly 7 ghastly, grayish, greyish 8 untanned 9 albescent, bloodless, innocuous, lily-white
pallor: 6 anemia 7 anaemia, wanness 8 grayness, paleness
palm: 4 nipa, sago, tree 5 areca, assai, honor 6 pilfer, raffia, raphia, rattan, thenar 7 babassu, conceal, coquito, secrete, success, triumph, victory 8 carnauba, cocoanut, fishtail, ivorynut, piassava, umbrella 9 coco-de-mer 10 decoration
Asian ~: 4 nipa 5 areca, betel
basketry ~: 4 nipa
betel ~: 5 areca
Brazilian ~: 5 assai
cat's ~: 3 pad
Central American ~: 6 cohune
ceremonial ~ branch: 5 lulab, lulav
East Indian ~: 4 nipa
examine a ~: 4 read
fermented ~ sap: 4 arak 6 arrack
genus: 5 areca
grease a ~: 5 bribe, get to 6 buy off, pay off, suborn 7 corrupt 9 lubricate
itching ~: 5 greed
leaf: 3 fan 5 frond
nipa ~: 4 atap
nut: 5 betel
off: 3 fob 5 foist 7 pass off
of the ~: 5 volar
of the hand: 4 vola
Pacific ~: 4 nipa
product: 4 date 5 copra 6 thatch 7 coconut 8 copperah
reader: 4 seer 7 psychic
thatch: 4 atap, nipa
tropical ~: 4 nipa 5 betel
trunk: 6 caudex
palm __: 3 off, oil 4 chat, crab, leaf, wine 5 civet, sugar 6 reader 7 cabbage, warbler
__ palm: 3 fan, oil, sea, wax 4 date, doom, doum, lady, sago, wine 5 betel, curly, honey, ivory, peach, pindo, queen, royal, snake, sugar, toddy 6 cohune, gomuti, kentia, parlor, potted, raffia, rattan, sentry, thatch 7 cabbage, coconut, feather, talipot
Palm __: 5 Beach 6 Sunday 7 Springs
Palma: 4 city, port, town 7 Ricardo 8 asteroid
locale: 5 Spain
see also Spanish
Palma, Ricardo: 6 writer 8 Peruvian
work: Tradiciones Peruanas
__ Palmas: 3 Las
Palm Bay: 4 city, town
locale: 7 Florida
Palm Beach: 4 city, town
diversion: 4 golf, polo
locale: 7 Florida
residence: 5 condo 6 estate
Palm Beach Story, The (1942 film)
cast: Claudette Colbert, Joel McCrea, Rudy Vallee
director: Preston Sturges
Palm City: 4 town
locale: 7 Florida
Palm Coast: 4 city, town
locale: 7 Florida
Palmdale: 4 city, town
locale: 10 California
Palm Desert: 4 city, town
locale: 10 California
Palme __: 3 d'Or
Palmeiro, Rafael sport: 8 baseball
Palmer: 3 Jim 5 Arnie, Betsy, Lilli, Vance 6 Arnold, Robert
Palmer, Arnold: 6 golfer
followers: 4 army
milieu: 5 links 6 course
org.: 3 PGA
Palmer, Betsy: 7 actress
film: Friday the 13th (1980)
The Last Angry Man (1959)
Queen Bee (1955)
The Tin Star (1957)
Palmer, George Herbert: 11 philosopher
Palmer, Jim: 6 hurler, Oriole 7 pitcher
Palmer, Lilli: 7 actress
film: Body and Soul (1947)
Conspiracy of Hearts (1960)
The Counterfeit Traitor (1962)
The Four Poster (1952)
The Pleasure of His Company (1961)
spouse: Rex Harrison
Palmer, Robert
song: Addicted to Love (1986)
Bad Case of Loving You (1979)
Early in the Morning (1988)
Every Kinda People (1978)
I Didn't Mean to Turn You On (1986)

Mercy Mercy Me (1991)
Simply Irrestible (1988)
Palmer, Vance: 4 poet **6** author, writer **10** Australian, playwright
work: The Passage
Palm Harbor: 4 city, town
locale: 7 Florida
Palminteri: 5 Chazz
Palmira: 4 city, town
locale: 6 Mexico **8** Colombia, Veracruz
palmlike conifer: 5 cycad
Palmolive: 4 soap
alternative: 3 Joy, Lux **4** Ajax, Dawn, Dial, Dove, Lava, Tone, Zest **5** Camay, Coast, Ivory, Lever **6** Boraxo, Caress, Shield **7** Cascade **8** Lifebuoy, Sunlight **9** Safeguard **10** Electrasol **11** Irish Spring
palm reader phrase: 4 I see
palms-down call: 4 safe
Palm Springs: 4 city, town
former ~ mayor: 4 Bono
locale: 10 California
neighbor: 5 Indio
Palm Sunday
mount: 3 ass
period: 4 Lent
palmy: 4 rosy **7** booming, halcyon **8** glorious, thriving **9** bounteous **10** prosperous, successful
Palo Alto: 4 city, town
college near ~: 5 Menlo
locale: 10 California
Palomar: 4 peak **5** mount **8** mountain
locale: 10 California
palomino: 5 horse **6** equine
pride: 4 mane
palooka: 3 oaf, pug **4** lout **5** boxer **6** galoot **8** pugilist
Palooka: 3 Joe
bride: 3 Ann
Palooka (1934 film)
cast: Jimmy Durante, Stuart Erwin, Lupe Velez
palp: 6 feeler
palpable: 5 clear, naked, plain, solid, stark, vivid **6** cogent, patent **7** blatant, evident, express, obvious, visible **8** apparent, concrete, definite, distinct, explicit, knowable, manifest, tangible **9** barefaced, graspable, touchable **10** detectable, noticeable, observable, ostensible, spelled out
palpate: 4 feel **5** touch
palpitate: 4 beat, pant **5** pound, pulse, shake, throb **6** quiver, shiver **7** flutter, pitapat, pulsate, tremble
palsy-walsy: 5 close, thick **6** chummy **8** familiar
palter: 3 lie **5** waver **6** higgle, trifle
paltering: 5 lying **10** mendacious
Paltrow, Gwyneth: 7 actress
film: Bounce (2000)
Emma (1996)
Great Expectations (1998)
Jefferson in Paris (1995)
A Perfect Murder (1998)
The Royal Tenenbaums (2001)
Se7en (1995)
Shakespeare in Love (1998, AA)
Sliding Doors (1998)
The Talented Mr. Ripley (1999)
mother: Blythe Danner
paltry: 3 low **4** mean, mere, poor, puny **5** minor, petty, scant, small, sorry **6** feeble, humble, little, meager, measly, minute, shabby, shoddy, sleazy, slight, stingy, yeasty **7** limited, pitiful, shallow, trivial **8** beggarly, exiguous, pathetic, picayune, piddling, trifling, wretched **9** miserable, worthless **10** pathetical
paludal: 3 low, wet **6** marshy, swampy **8** low-lying
Pam: 4 Gems **5** Ewing, Grier **6** Dawber, Tillis **7** Shriver
__-pamby: 5 namby
Pamela: 4 Reed **5** Mason **6** Tiffin **7** Britton, Hensley, Johnson **8** Anderson, Harriman
Pamela __ Anderson: 3 Lee
Pamela __ Martin: 3 Sue
Pamela author: Samuel Richardson
Pamlico __: 5 Sound
Pampa: 4 city, town
locale: 5 Texas
pampas: 3 lea, ley **5** plain, veldt **7** lowland, prairie **9** grassland
bird: 4 rhea
cousin: 5 llano
cow catcher: 4 bola
rider: 6 gaucho
pamper: 3 pet **4** baby **5** favor, humor, nurse, spoil **6** coddle, cosher, cosset, dandle, dote on, lavish, please **7** cater to, gratify, indulge **8** dote upon, give in to **9** spoon-feed
Pampers: 6 diaper
alternative: 4 Luvs **7** Drypers, Huggies
pamphlet: 5 flier, flyer, tract **6** folder **7** booklet, handout, leaflet, writing **8** brochure, bulletin, circular **9** broadside, throwaway **10** literature
Pamplona: 4 city, town
hazard: 4 bull, toro
locale: 5 Spain
pan: 3 pot, rap, wok **4** flay, mine, scan, sift, slam, zoom **5** decry, knock, scale, scoff, smear, sweep, track **6** boiler, defame, demean, deride, follow, kettle, kisser, oppugn, review, swivel, vessel, vilify **7** degrade, griddle, lambast, put-down, roaster, skillet, slander, utensil **8** badmouth, belittle, features, lambaste, minimize, saucepan, talk down **9** container, criticize, disparage, find fault, pick apart
baking ~: 3 tin **5** sheet
ender: 3 fry **4** cake, pipe **5** dowdy **6** handle **7** handler **8** handling
expand in the ~: 4 rise
for gold: 8 prospect
frying ~: 6 vessel **7** skillet
opposite: 4 rave
out: 2 go **3** win **5** click, prove, solve **6** go over, happen, make it, result, thrive **7** prevail, prosper, resolve, succeed, triumph **8** flourish, get ahead, go places, make good **9** culminate, eventuate **10** come to pass
starter: 4 dead, dish, dust, hard **5** brain, patty, sauce
stir-fry ~: 3 wok
__ pan: 3 oil, pie **4** cake, drip, loaf, salt, tube **5** Bundt **6** frying, muffin, vacuum **7** warming
Pan: 4 moon **5** Peter, satyr **6** Hermes
daughter: 4 Lynx
father: 4 Zeus **6** Hermes
lover: 3 Aex **4** Echo **7** Eupheme
mother: 8 Penelope
planet: 6 Saturn
son of ~: 6 Crotus **7** Aegipan
Pan-__ makeup: 4 Cake
__-Pan: 3 Tai
panacea: 4 cure **6** elixir, potion, remedy **7** arcanum, cure-all, nostrum **10** catholicon
panache: 4 brio, dash, élan, snap **5** flair, plume, spunk, style, verve **7** sparkle
having ~: 4 chic, posh, tony **5** ritzy, sharp, swank, swish, toney **6** classy, dapper, dressy, modish, snappy, spruce, swanky **7** dashing, elegant, in vogue, stylish **9** exclusive, glamorous, high-toned
lacking ~: 4 blah **6** boring
Panache: 4 font **8** typeface
Panaji: 4 city, town **7** capital
locale: 3 Goa **5** India
__ Pan Alley: 3 Tin
Pan-Am: 7 airline
Panama: 3 hat **4** gulf **5** canal **6** nation, Norman **7** country, isthmus
capital: 10 Panama City
gulf: 7 San Blas
Indian: 4 Cuna **7** San Blas
lake: 5 Gatún
money: 6 balboa **9** centesimo
neighbor: 8 Colombia **9** Costa Rica
org.: 3 OAS
pest: 5 aedes **8** mosquito
port: 6 Balboa **9** Cristobal
see also Spanish
Panama __: 3 hat **5** Canal **6** Hattie
Panama (1984 song) artist: Van Halen
Panama Canal
dam: 5 Gatún
island near the ~: 4 Naos
ocean: 7 Pacific **8** Atlantic
terminus: 5 Colón
Panama City: 4 city, town **7** capital
locale: 6 Panama **7** Florida
Panama Deception, The director: 5 Trent
Panama Hattie: 7 musical
name: 4 Cole **5** Ethel
songwriter: 6 Porter
Panama, Norman: 8 director
film: Above and Beyond (1952)
Court Jester (1956)
Knock on Wood (1954)
Not With My Wife You Don't! (1966)
The Road to Hong Kong (1962)
Pan American __: 5 Games, Union
Pan-American __: 7 Highway
Pan American Union successor: 3 OAS
Panamint: 5 range
locale: 10 California
Panasonic: 2 TV **3** VCR **5** TV set **10** television
alternative: 3 JVC, NEC, RCA **4** Sony **5** Sanyo **6** Quasar, Zenith **7** Emerson, Hitachi, ProScan, Toshiba **8** Magnavox, Sylvania
panatela: 5 cigar
Panay: 4 isle **6** island
city: 6 Iloilo
native: 3 Ati
pan-broil: 3 fry
pancake: 5 bread, crash **6** blintz, makeup **7** blintze **8** flapjack
breakfast: 7 benefit
deli ~: 5 latke
Hanukkah ~: 5 latke
ingredient: 3 egg **4** milk **5** flour
mix: 6 batter
order: 5 stack
palace: 4 IHOP
Russian ~: 5 blini, bliny
thin ~: 5 blini, bliny, crape, crepe
topper: 5 sirup, syrup
pancake __: 7 landing
Pan-Cake __: 6 makeup
Panchen Lama: 4 monk **6** cleric
Pancho: 5 Villa **6** Segura **8** Gonzales
see also Spanish
__ Pan collar: 5 Peter
pancreas: 5 gland
enzyme: 6 lipase
hormone: 7 insulin
neighbor: 5 liver
panda: 6 animal, mammal **8** Ling-Ling
female: 3 sow
food: 6 bamboo
habitat: 5 China
male: 4 boar
young: 3 cub
__ panda: 3 red **5** giant **6** lesser
pandect: 5 brief **6** digest **7** summary **8** synopsis **10** abridgment, compendium
pandéiro: 10 percussion, tambourine
origin: 6 Brazil
pandemic: 4 rife **7** rampant **8** catching **9** extensive, worldwide **10** widespread
pandemonium: 3 din **4** riot, stir **5** babel, chaos, havoc, noise **6** bedlam, clamor, hubbub, mayhem, racket, ruckus, rumpus, tumult, uproar **7** anarchy, turmoil **8** madhouse **9** commotion, confusion, craziness, hue and cry **10** hurly-burly, turbulence
pander: 6 cajole, please **7** cater to, gratify, indulge, lay it on, satisfy **8** give in to, play up to, soften up, suck up to
P and L column heading: 3 YTD
pandora: 4 lute **6** string
Pandora: 4 moon
daughter of ~: 6 Pyrrha
husband of ~: 9 Epimethus
lover of ~: 4 Zeus
planet: 6 Saturn
what ~ unleashed: 4 ills
Pandora author: Anne Rice
Pandora's __: 3 box
pandowdy: 7 dessert
__ pandowdy: 5 apple
pane: 5 glass, sheet **9** partition
adhesive: 5 putty
holder: 4 sash
piece: 5 shard, sherd
starter: 5 march **6** window **7** counter
panegyric: 4 pean **5** eloge, honor, kudos, paean **6** eulogy, homage, praise, salute **7** acclaim, oration, plaudit, tribute **8** accolade, encomium, flattery **9** extolment, laudation **10** compliment, exaltation
panegyrical: 7 glowing **9** laudatory
panegyrize: 4 hail, laud **5** bless, exalt, extol, honor **6** extoll, praise, salute **7** acclaim, applaud, commend, flatter, glorify **8** eulogize, sanctify
panel: 4 gore, jury, wall **5** board, sheet **6** jurors **7** council, divider, inquest **8** bulkhead, trustees, wainscot **9** committee, grand jury, partition
dress ~: 4 gore **5** inset
focus: 5 issue, topic
member: 5 judge, juror
triptych ~: 5 volet
panel __: 3 saw **5** house, patch, point, strip, thief, truck **7** heating
__ panel: 4 drop **5** linen, solar **6** rocker **7** control, modesty
Panetta: 4 Leon
pang: 4 ache, hurt, kink, pain, stab **5** cramp, gripe, qualm, shame, spasm, sting, throb, throe **6** injury, misery, regret, stitch, twinge, wrench **8** distress **9** misgiving
Pangborn: 8 Franklin
pangolin: 6 animal, mammal
snack: 3 ant
pangs of conscience: 7 remorse
panguingue: 4 game **8** card game
Pangwe home: 5 Gabon, Gabun **6** Africa **8** Cameroon
panhandle: 3 beg **5** cadge, mooch **7** solicit **8** freeload, scrounge **9** impetrate
state with a ~: 3 Fla., Ida., Tex., W. Va. **4** Okla. **5** Idaho, Texas **6** Alaska **7** Florida **8** Oklahoma
Panhandle Cowboy author: McMurtry
panhandler: 3 bum **5** tramp **6** beggar **10** ragamuffin
request: 4 alms **5** coins, money
panic: 4 fear, flap, funk, rush **5** alarm, crash, dread, scare, slump **6** dismay, frenzy, fright, lose it, scream, terror **7** mad rush, unnerve **8** cold feet,

downturn, freeze up, frighten, have a fit, hysteria, stampede **9** come apart, confusion, go berserk, overreact, run scared, trepidity **10** chicken out, depression, go to pieces
button: **5** alarm
in a ~: **6** scared **7** alarmed **9** terrified **10** frightened
PC ~ button: **3** ESC
panic __: **3** bar **4** bolt **5** grass **6** attack, button
Panic (2000 film)
cast: Neve Campbell, William H. Macy, Donald Sutherland, Tracey Ullman
director: Henry Bromell
panic button, push the: **5** alarm, alert
Panic in Needle Park, The (1971 film)
cast: Al Pacino, Alan Vint, Kitty Winn
director: Jerry Schatzberg
Panic in the Streets (1950 film)
cast: Barbara Bel Geddes, Paul Douglas, Richard Widmark
director: Elia Kazan
panicky: **5** jumpy, timid **6** afraid, scared, trepid **7** abashed, alarmed, anxious, chicken, daunted, fearful, jittery, nervous, spooked **8** cowardly, fearsome, hesitant, timorous **9** petrified, terrified, tremulous **10** frightened
Panic Room (2002 film)
cast: Jodie Foster, Jared Leto, Forest Whitaker, Dwight Yoakam
director: David Fincher
panic-stricken: **6** afraid, scared **9** terrified **10** frightened
panicum: **5** grass
panjandrum: **7** pooh-bah **8** official
__-panky: **5** hanky
panned, it's often: **4** gold, play **5** movie
panner: **6** critic **9** sourdough **10** prospector
pannier: **6** basket, dosser
panophobe fear: **3** all **10** everything
panoply: **4** pomp **5** armor, array **6** parade **9** trappings
panorama: **4** view **5** gamut, scape, scene, sweep, vista **6** length **7** diorama, display, lookout, outlook, picture, scenery, tableau **8** overview, prospect **9** landscape
panoramic: **3** big **4** wide **6** scenic
panoramic __: **4** view **5** sight **6** camera
Panotla: **4** city, town
locale: **6** Mexico **8** Tlaxcala
Panova, Vera: **6** writer **7** Russian
panpipe: **4** wind **6** syrinx
Pansies author: D.H. Lawrence
pansophic: **4** sage, wise **7** learned
pansy: **5** plant, viola **6** flower **10** heart's-ease
combining form: **4** viol-
Pansy: **5** Yokum
pant: **4** blow, gasp, gulp, huff, puff, sigh **5** chuff, crave, heave, snort, yearn **6** breath, desire, wheeze **7** breathe **9** palpitate
ender: **4** suit
(for): **4** ache, burn, itch, long, lust, pine, wish **5** yearn **6** hunger, thirst
Pantagruel: **5** giant
Pantene: **7** shampoo
alternative: **4** Flex, Pert **5** Prell, Suave, Wella **7** Finesse
pantheist: **5** pagan
pantheon: **6** temple
panther: **3** cat **4** puma **5** felid **6** animal, cougar, feline **7** leopard, wildcat **9** catamount
kin: **6** jaguar
literary ~: **4** pard
perch: **4** tree
relative: **4** eyra, lion, lynx **5** chita, liger, ounce, tiger, tigon **6** bobcat, cheeta, chetah, jaguar, margay, ocelot, serval, tiglon **7** bay lynx, caracal, cheetah, panther **10** jaguarundi
Panther: **5** Falls, NHLer **10** footballer
rival: **3** Jet, Ram **4** Bear, Bill, Blue, Colt, King, Lion, Star, Wild **5** Brown, Bruin, Chief, Devil, Eagle, Flame, Flyer, Giant, Oiler, Raven, Sabre, Saint, Shark, Texan, Titan **6** Bengal, Bronco, Canuck, Cowboy, Coyote, Falcon, Jaguar, Packer, Raider, Ranger, Viking **7** Capital, Charger, Dolphin, Patriot, Penguin, Redskin, Red Wing, Seahawk, Senator, Steeler **8** Canadien, Cardinal, Islander, Predator, Thrasher **9** Avalanche, Blackhawk, Buccaneer, Hurricane, Lightning, Maple Leaf **10** Blue Jacket, Mighty Duck
__ Panther: **3** Joe **4** Gray **5** Black
Panthers: **3** six **4** team **6** eleven
div.: **3** NFC
home: **5** Miami **7** Florida **8** Carolina
milieu: **3** ice **4** rink
org.: **3** NFL, NHL
sport: **6** hockey **8** football
__ Panther, The: **4** Pink
Pantin: **4** city, town
locale: **6** France
panting: **7** excited, gasping, gulping, heaving **10** breathless
Pantoliano: **3** Joe
pantologist: **4** sage
pantomime: **3** ape, mum **5** mimic **6** act out **7** charade, gesture
actor: **4** Tati
dance: **4** hula
pantothenic __: **4** acid
pantry: **5** store **6** larder **8** cupboard
boat ~: **5** cuddy
feature: **3** bin, can, jar, tin **4** food **5** flour, shelf, sugar **6** closet **8** canister
keep in the ~: **5** store
old ~ supply: **4** lard
stock the ~: **5** lay in
pants: **5** chaps, cords, ducks, jeans, Levi's, trews **6** breeks, briefs, Capris, chinos, denims, khakis, shorts, slacks, tweeds **7** bikinis, drawers, gauchos, kerseys, panties, peg tops, shalwar, shulwar **8** bermudas, bloomers, breeches, britches, culottes, flannels, jodhpurs, knickers, leggings, overalls, trousers **9** blue jeans, corduroys, dungarees, moleskins, plus fours **10** hiphuggers, lederhosen **12** pedal-pushers
adjust ~: **5** rehem
alternative: **5** skirt
and jacket: **4** suit **6** outfit **8** ensemble
beat the ~ off: **5** cream, crush, tromp **7** trounce
British ~: **6** breeks
calf-length ~: **6** Capris
cuff in Britain: **6** turnup
cut: **4** full, slim **5** husky **7** regular
feature: **4** cuff, seam **5** pleat **6** crease
India ~: **7** shalwar, shulwar
inhabitants: **4** ants
material: **4** duck, wool **5** denim, nylon, tweed, twill **6** cotton **8** corduroy **9** polyester
measure: **4** hips **5** waist **6** inseam, length
part: **3** leg **4** knee, seat
riding ~: **8** jodhpurs
Scottish ~: **5** trews
slangily: **4** slax
smarty ~: **4** snob **8** wiseacre
starter: **5** sweat
unit: **4** pair
pants __: **4** suit
__ pants: **3** hot, ski **4** knee **5** Capri, harem **6** gaucho
__-pants: **5** fancy **6** smarty
pantyhose: **8** lingerie
brand: **5** Hanes, Leggs
color: **3** tan **4** ecru **5** beige, black, flesh, taupe
part: **3** leg **4** foot
ruin one's ~: **3** jag, run **4** snag
pantywaist: **5** sissy **6** coward **7** chicken **9** jellyfish **10** scaredy-cat
Pánuco: **4** city, town **5** river
locale: **6** Mexico **8** Veracruz
Pan With Us author: Robert Frost
__ Panza: **6** Sancho
panzer: **4** tank
Paola locale: **6** Kansas
Paolo: **7** Uccello **8** Veronese
in English: **4** Paul
see also Italian
pap: **3** gas, rot **4** blah, bosh, bull, bunk, guff, jazz, jive, mash, pooh, tosh **5** bilge, fudge, hokum, hooey, prate, stuff, trash, tripe **6** bunkum, bushwa, drivel, footle, gabble, gammon, gibber, havers, hot air, humbug, jabber, jargon, kibosh, piffle **7** baloney, blarney, blather, blether, boloney, bushwah, eyewash, flannel, flubdub, fustian, garbage, hogwash, inanity, rubbish, twaddle **8** baby food, buncombe, claptrap, falderal, falderol, flimflam, flummery, folderal, folderol, nonsense, slipslop, tommyrot, trumpery **9** banana oil, gibberish, kidstakes, moonshine, poppycock, rigmarole **10** applesauce, balderdash, bilge water, codswallop, double-talk, flapdoodle, galimatias, Jabberwock, mumbo jumbo, rigamarole, taradiddle
papa: **3** dad, pop **4** dada, male, mate, pops, sire **5** daddy, pappy, pater **6** father, parent **8** baby talk
paddock ~: **4** sire
partner: **4** mama **5** mamma
Papa __: **3** Doc **4** Bear, Joe's
__ Pa-pa: **4** Oh! My
Papa Bear: **5** Halas
__ Papa Bell: **4** Cool
Papa Doc country: **5** Haiti
Papa Don't Preach (1986 song) artist: Madonna
Papago: **5** tribe **6** Indian **7** Amerind **8** language
papal: **3** fig **4** tree **6** popish **8** clerical, pontific **10** pontifical
bull: **6** decree
cape: **5** fanon
diplomat: **6** legate
document: **4** bull
hat: **5** miter
headdress: **5** tiara
letter: **5** brief
name: **3** Leo **4** John, Paul, Pius **5** Caius, Conon, Donus, Felix, Linus, Peter, Soter, Urban **6** Adrian, Agatho, Albert, Cletus, Eugene, Fabian, Hilary, Julius, Landus, Lucius, Marcus, Martin, Philip, Sixtus, Victor **7** Anterus, Clement, Damasus, Eulabus, Gregory, Hyginus, Marinus, Paschal, Pontian, Romanus, Sergius, Stephen, Ursinus, Zachary, Zosimus **8** Agapitus, Anicetus, Benedict, Boniface, Eusebius, Formosus, Gelasius, Honorius, Innocent, John Paul, Lawrence, Liberius, Nicholas, Novatian, Pelagius, Sabinian, Siricius, Theodore, Vigilius, Vitalian **9** Adeodatus, Alexander, Anacletus, Callistus, Celestine, Cornelius, Dionysius, Dioscorus, Eutychian, Evaristus, Hormisdas, Marcellus, Severinus, Silverius, Sisinnius, Sylvester, Symmachus, Theodoric, Valentine **10** Anastasius, Hippolytus, Melchiades, Simplicius, Zephyrinus **11** Christopher, Constantine, Eleutherius, Marcellinus, Telesphorus
seal: **5** bulla
vestment: **5** orale
papal __: **4** bull **5** cross
Papa Loves Mambo (1954 song) artist: Perry Como
Papantla: **4** city, town
locale: **6** Mexico **8** Veracruz
paparazzo
creation: **3** pic **4** snap **5** photo **8** snapshot **10** photograph
need: **6** camera, tripod
quarry: **5** celeb **9** celebrity
papas __: **6** fritas
Papa's Got a Brand New Bag (1965 song) artist: James Brown
Papas, Irene: **7** actress
film: Anne of the Thousand Days (1969)
The Brotherhood (1968)
A Dream of Kings (1969)
Eboli (1979)
Z (1969)
Zorba the Greek (1964)
Papasquiaro: **4** city, town
locale: **6** Mexico **7** Durango
papaw: **4** tree **5** fruit **9** fruit tree
Papa Was a Rollin' Stone (1972 song)
artist: Temptations
papaya: **4** tree **5** fruit, shrub
Papeete: **4** city, port, town
location: **6** Tahiti
paper: **3** pad, rag **4** bond, deed, leaf, news, pass, will, writ **5** daily, essay, organ, press, sheet, stock, study, theme **6** letter, manila, poster, record, report, thesis, ticket, tissue, vellum, weekly **7** diploma, gazette, journal, monthly, notepad, papyrus, summons, tabloid, voucher, warrant, writing **8** contract, document, gift wrap, subpoena, treatise **9** affidavit, cardboard, monograph, onionskin **10** assignment, court order, exposition, instrument, periodical, stationery
bureaucrat's ~: **4** form
business owner's ~: **4** deed **5** lease, title **7** charter **8** contract
chem-lab ~: **6** litmus
chief: **6** editor
commit to ~: **3** jot, pen **4** note **5** write **6** record **8** scribble **9** chronicle
corrugated ~ feature: **5** ridge
covering: **5** emery
decorative ~: **5** crape, crepe **6** tissue **8** giftwrap
deliverer's way: **5** route
doll: **6** cutout
edge: **6** deckel, deckle
ender: **3** boy **4** back, clip, girl, work **5** board, bound, knife, maker **6** hanger, making, weight **7** hanging
holder: **3** pad **4** clip **6** binder
legal ~: **4** deed, will **5** lease, title **7** charter **8** contract **9** agreement
medical ~: **5** chart
mill commodity: **4** pulp, wood
money: **4** bill **8** currency
nest builder: **4** wasp
ower's ~: **3** IOU **4** note **8** mortgage
part of a ~ towel roll: **4** tube
party ~: **5** crape, crepe
piece of ~: **4** leaf, slip **5** sheet
quantity of ~: **4** ream **5** quire, sheaf
research ~: **6** thesis **8** treatise **9** monograph
school ~: **5** essay, theme **6** thesis
size: **4** demy, post, pott **5** atlas, crown, folio, legal, royal, sexto **6** medium,

octavo, quarto 8 elephant, foolscap, imperial, twelvemo, twentymo, vigesimo 9 duodecimo, sixteenmo 10 octodecimo, super-royal
starter: 3 end, fly, oil, tar 4 news, sand, wall 5 waste
strong brown ~: 5 kraft
trail: 5 proof 6 record 7 red tape
wrapping ~: 5 kraft 6 tissue 8 giftwrap
paper __: 3 bag 4 clip, doll, gold, mill, tape, wasp 5 birch, chase, knife, match, money, tiger, trail 6 cutter, profit
paper-__: 4 thin 5 mâché 6 pusher 7 shelled
__ paper: 3 end, rag, wax 4 bank, bond, copy, curl, laid, rice, silk, term, test, wove 5 Bible, crepe, flock, funny, graph, shelf, trade, waxed, white 6 carbon, filter, ledger, litmus, Manila, tissue 7 butcher, contact, scratch, tracing, writing
Paper __: 4 Doll, Lace, Lion, Mate, Moon 5 Roses
paperback: 4 book 5 novel
ID: 4 ISBN
publisher: 4 Avon, Dell 6 Bantam
__ paperback: 5 trade 7 quality
Paperback Writer (1966 song) artist: Beatles
Paper Chase, The: 4 film 5 novel
author: Hal Porter, John Jay Osborn
cast: Timothy Bottoms, John Houseman, Lindsay Wagner
director: James Bridges
student: 4 one-L
subject: 3 law
paper doll: 3 toy
dress part: 3 tab 4 slot
Paper in Fire (1987 song) artist: John Cougar Mellencamp
Paper Lion (1968 film)
cast: Alan Alda, Lauren Hutton, Alex Karras
director: Alex March
PaperMate: 3 pen
alternative: 3 Bic 5 Pilot 7 Uni-Ball
Paper Moon (1973 film)
cast: Madeline Kahn, Ryan O'Neal, Tatum O'Neal
director: Peter Bogdanovich
Paper Roses (song) artist: Anita Bryant, Marie Osmond
papers: 2 ID 4 visa 7 dossier 8 passport
funny ~: 6 comics
mark ~: 5 grade
pup without ~: 3 mut 4 mutt
walking ~: 5 the ax
__ papers: 5 ship's 7 walking, working
__ Papers, The: 6 Aspern, Biglow, Rachel
Paper, The (1994 film)
cast: Glenn Close, Robert Duvall, Michael Keaton, Jason Robards, Marisa Tomei
director: Ron Howard
paper towel brand: 4 Viva 5 Scott 6 Bounty, Brawny
paperwork: 4 form 5 forms 7 red tape
insurance ~: 5 claim
processor: 5 clerk
papier-__: 5 mâché
papillon: 3 dog 5 canid 6 canine
Papillon (1973 film)
cast: Dustin Hoffman, Victor Jory, Steve McQueen
director: Franklin Schaffner
papoose: 4 baby 6 infant 7 newborn
Papp: 6 Joseph
Pappas: 3 Ike 4 Milt
Pappas, Milt sport: 8 baseball
pappy: 2 pa 3 dad, pop 4 male, papa, soft 6 father, old man, parent
Pappy: 9 Boyington
paprika: 5 spice 9 condiment
Papua New Guinea: 4 isls. 5 isles 6 nation 7 country, islands
capital: Port Moresby
city: 3 Lae
coin: 4 toea
currency: 4 kina
neighbor: 9 Indonesia
port: 4 daru
volcano: 5 Manam 6 Bagana, Rabaul, Ulawun 7 Langila
papyrus: 4 reed 5 paper, sedge
noted ~ raft: 3 Ra I 4 Ra II
papyrus-swamp lake: 5 kioga
Paquin, Anna: 7 actress
film: Finding Forrester (2000) The Piano (1993, AA) A Walk on the Moon (1999)
par: 3 avg., std. 4 mean, norm 5 level, usual 6 median, medium, normal, parity 7 average, balance 8 equality, sameness, standard
beater: 5 eagle 6 birdie
below ~: 3 ill, off 4 poor 5 unfit 6 ailing, sickly 7 lacking, run-down, wanting 9 imperfect 10 inadequate, indisposed
for the course: 4 norm 5 typic, usual 7 typical 8 expected
neither under nor over ~: 4 even
on a ~: 4 akin, even, like, same, such, tied 5 alike, equal, level 7 cognate, similar 8 matching, parallel 9 analogous, consonant 10 comparable, equivalent, homogenous, tantamount
one over ~: 5 bogey
one under ~: 6 birdie
two under ~: 5 eagle
up to ~: 2 OK 4 hale, okay, well 7 healthy 8 all right 10 acceptable
par __: 5 avion, value
par __ the course: 3 for
__ par: 4 up to 5 issue 7 nominal
para: 4 aide 5 money
para-: 2 by 4 near, past
parable: 4 tale 5 fable, story 8 allegory
feature: 5 moral 6 lesson
parabola: 3 arc 5 curve 9 sinuosity
make a ~: 3 arc
peak: 6 apogee
Paracelsus author: Robert Browning
Paracho: 4 city, town
locale: 6 Mexico 9 Michoacán
parachute: 4 drop, jump 6 drogue
material: 5 nylon
part: 4 cord 6 canopy
strap: 5 riser
parachute __: 4 jump 5 brake 6 rigger
__ parachute: 3 tin 4 drag 6 drogue, golden
Parachutes and Kisses author: Jong
parachuting: 5 sport
parachutist: 6 bailer, jumper
paraclete: 7 paladin 8 advocate, champion, defender
parade: 3 air 4 brag, line, show, walk 5 array, boast, march, model, sight, strut, swash, troop, vaunt 6 column, flaunt, prance, review, series, stream 7 cortege, display, exhibit, fanfare, pageant, panoply, show off, swagger, trot out 8 autocade, brandish 9 cavalcade, festivity, promenade, spectacle 10 procession, wave around
Chinese ~ feature: 6 dragon
command: 4 halt
day: 6 Easter, Fourth 10 July Fourth 12 Thanksgiving
feature: 4 band 5 float, march 8 confetti 9 majorette
sponsor: 5 Macy's
stopper: 4 rain
__ parade: 3 hit
Parade: 6 ballet
composer: 5 Satie
__ Parade: 6 Easter, Spring 7 Pigskin
__ Parade, The: 3 Big 4 Love
paradigm: 4 type 5 guide, ideal, model 7 example, paragon, pattern 8 exemplar, original, standard 9 archetype, beau ideal, criterion, prototype 10 touchstone
paradigmatic: 5 ideal, model 7 typical
paradise: 4 Eden 5 bliss 6 heaven, utopia 7 Arcadia, ecstasy, Elysium, nirvana, rapture 8 empyrean, Valhalla 9 cloud nine, next world, Shangri-la
Arthurian ~: 6 Avalon
bird of ~ feature: 5 plume
Celtic ~: 6 Avalon
dweller: 3 god 5 angel, houri 7 goddess 8 Valkyrie 9 archangel
evictee: 3 Eve 4 Adam
fool's ~: 7 fantasy, reverie 8 delusion
Muslim bridge to ~: 5 sirat
opposite: 4 hell 10 underworld
paradise __: 4 fish 6 flower
Paradise: 3 Sal 4 city, town
Bird of ~ constellation: 4 Apus
locale: 6 Nevada 10 California
Paradise (1991 film)
cast: Thora Birch, Melanie Griffith, Don Johnson, Elijah Wood
director: Mary Agnes Donoghue
Paradise __: 4 City, Lost
__ Paradise: 3 Sal 6 Almost
Paradise (1988 song) artist: Sade
Paradise author: Larry McMurtry
Paradise by the Dashboard Light (1978 song) artist: Meat Loaf
Paradise, Hawaiian Style (1966 film)
cast: Suzanna Leigh, Elvis Presley, James Shigeta
director: Michael Moore
Paradise is where __: 3 I am
Paradise Lost: 4 epic, poem
author: Clifford Odets, John Milton
character: 3 Eve, Sin 4 Adam 5 Ariel, Satan, Uriel 6 Abdiel, Belial, Mammon, Moloch 7 Gabriel, Michael, Raphael 8 Mulciber 9 Beelzebub
Paradise of exiles: 5 Italy
Paradise Regained author: John Milton
__-Paradise, The: 4 Demi
paradisical: 6 divine 8 beatific, heavenly
__ Paradiso: 4 Gran 5 Hotel 6 Cinema
Paradiso writer: 5 Dante
paradox: 4 koan 6 enigma, oddity, puzzle, riddle 7 anomaly, mystery
__ paradox: 4 liar 5 Zeno's
paradoxical: 5 polar 6 ironic, unlike 7 adverse, counter, reverse 8 clashing, contrary, opposite 9 different 10 antithetic
paraffin __: 3 oil, wax
paraffin-based: 5 waxen
paragon: 3 gem 4 hero 5 angel, ideal, light, model 7 epitome, example, pattern 8 cynosure, exemplar, original, paradigm, standard, treasure, ultimate 9 archetype, beau ideal, criterion, nonpareil, prototype 10 apotheosis
Paragould: 4 city, town
locale: 8 Arkansas
paragraph: 4 text 6 clause 7 passage
start a ~: 6 indent
unit: 8 sentence
Paraguay: 5 river 6 nation 7 country
capital: 8 Asunción
from ~: 6 Latino
Indian: 6 Lengua 7 Guarani
money: 7 centimo, guarani
neighbor: 6 Brazil 7 Bolivia 9 Argentina
see also Spanish
Paraíso: 4 city, town
locale: 6 Mexico 7 Tabasco
parakeet: 3 pet 4 bird 6 budgie 10 budgerigar, budgerygah
home: 4 cage
seat: 5 perch
treat: 4 seed 8 bird seed
parallactic __: 6 motion 7 ellipse
__ parallax: 6 annual 7 diurnal
Parallax View, The (1974 film)
cast: Warren Beatty, William Daniels, Paula Prentiss
director: Alan J. Pakula
parallel: 3 tie 4 akin, echo, even, like, such 5 agree, alike, equal, level, match 6 allied, analog, equate, on a par 7 aligned, analogy, cognate, compare, imitate, kindred, related, similar 8 matching, relative, resemble 9 alongside, analogous, collimate, collocate, correlate 10 comparable, coordinate, equivalent, resembling, side-by-side, similarity
draw a ~: 6 equate 7 compare
make ~: 5 align, aline
parallel __: 3 top 4 bars 5 axiom 6 cousin, forces, motion, rulers 7 sailing
Parallel Lives author: Plutarch
parallelogram: 5 rhomb 6 square 7 rhombus 9 rectangle
paralyze: 4 daze, halt, lame, numb, stun 5 daunt, scare, shock 6 arrest, bemuse, benumb, freeze, weaken 7 destroy, nonplus, petrify, stupefy, terrify 8 shut down, transfix 9 indispose 10 immobilize
paralyzed: 6 torpid 9 enervated, powerless 10 motionless
Paramaribo: 4 city, port, town 7 capital
locale: 8 Suriname
paramatta: 6 fabric 7 textile 8 material
paramecium: 9 protozoan
like a ~: 6 apodal 7 apodous
paramedic
job: 3 aid 4 help 6 rescue 10 resusitate
letters: 3 EMT
org.: 3 EMS
skill: 3 CPR
parameters: 5 range, scope 6 bounds, limits 8 boundary, criteria 10 guidelines
set ~: 5 limit 6 define 7 delimit
paramnesia: 6 déjà vu
paramount: 3 big, top 4 best, main, star, tops 5 chief, first, prime, vital 6 urgent, utmost 7 capital, central, in front, leading, premier, primary, supreme, topmost 8 cardinal, crowning, dominant, foremost, headmost, powerful, superior, towering, ultimate 9 governing, high-level, immediate, important, necessary, prevalent, principal, sovereign, topflight, unequaled, uppermost 10 overriding, preeminent
Paramount: 4 city, town 6 studio
competitor: 3 Fox, MGM 6 Disney 7 Miramax, New Line 8 Columbia 9 Universal 10 Dreamworks, Warner Bros.
creation: 4 film 5 flick, movie
locale: 10 California
workplace: 3 lot, set 10 soundstage
paramour: 2 jo 3 pet 4 baby, dear, jill, love 5 angel, chéri, cooky, cutey, cutie, deary, ducky, flame, honey, leman, lover, lovey, novia, novio, sugar, sweet, wooer 6 bon ami, chérie, cookie, dautie, dearie, steady, suitor, sweets 7 beloved, dearest, dear one, pigsney, schatzi, squeeze, sweetie, tootsie 8 chou-chou, cutie pie, dowsabel, dulcinea, ladylove, lovebird, macushla, precious, snookums, sugar

pie, sweetums, truelove 9 bonne amie, boyfriend, dreamboat, inamorata, inamorato, petit chou, valentine 10 girlfriend, heartthrob, honeybunch, mavourneen, sweetheart, sweetie pie, turtledove
Paramus: 4 city, town
locale: 9 New Jersey
Paraná: 4 city, port, town
locale: 6 Brazil 8 Paraguay 9 Argentina
paranormal: 4 eery 5 eerie 6 mystic 7 psychic 8 mystical
ability: 3 ESP
parapet: 4 wall 7 bastion, defense, rampart 10 battlement
fortification: 5 redan
notch: 6 crenel 8 crenelle
paraphernalia: 3 rig 4 gear 5 goods, items, means, stuff, thing 6 outfit, tackle, things 7 baggage, effects, luggage, regalia 8 material 9 apparatus, equipment, machinery, trappings
paraphrase: 5 quote 6 digest, rehash, render, reword 7 reading, restate, version 8 rephrase 9 interpret, translate
paraprofessional: 4 aide 6 helper 9 assistant, secretary
parapsychology: 3 psi 9 telepathy
pioneer: 5 Rhine
subject: 3 ESP 10 sixth sense
paraquet: 4 bird
parasite: 4 flea, lice 5 drone, idler, leech, louse, toady 6 cadger, jackal, loafer, sponge 7 moocher, shirker, slacker, sponger 8 deadbeat 9 goldbrick, scrounger, sycophant 10 freeloader
animal ~: 4 flea, lice, mite, tick 5 ameba, louse
need: 4 host
plant ~: 5 aphid 9 mistletoe
worm: 4 nema
Parasite, The author: Doyle
parasol: 8 sunshade, umbrella
paratrooper: 7 soldier
gear: 5 chute 9 parachute
__ paratus: 6 semper
parboil: 4 cook 5 scald 6 blanch, simmer
parcel: 3 cut, lot, pak. 4 area, bale, deal, give, land, load, mail, mete, pack, part, plat, plot, sort 5 allot, chunk, group, piece, share, slice, split, tract 6 bundle, carton, divide, packet, ration 7 acreage, arrival, carve up, divvy up, dole out, package, portion, section, segment, split up 8 allocate, delegate, division, freehold, property 9 apportion, house site, partition 10 distribute
auction ~: 3 lot
land ~: 3 lot 4 acre
marking: 3 COD, ppd 4 rush 7 fragile
protector: 4 tape 5 paper, twine 9 cellulose, Stryofoam 10 bubble wrap
send a ~: 4 mail, ship
service: 3 UPS 4 USPS 5 FedEx
parcel __: 4 post 6 tanker 7 gilding
Parcells, Bill: 5 coach
nickname: 4 Tuna
sport: 8 football
parch: 3 dry 4 burn, sear 5 dry up, toast 6 dry out, scorch, wither 7 shrivel, torrefy, torrify 9 anhydrate, dehydrate, desiccate, exsiccate
parched: 3 dry 4 arid, sere 5 stale, unwet 6 barren, torrid 7 athirst, dried up, thirsty 8 dried out, droughty, scorched, withered 9 juiceless, shriveled, waterless 10 dehydrated
Parcheesi: 4 game 9 board game
feature: 3 die 4 dice 5 board
parching: 3 hot 6 sultry, torrid 8 stifling
parchment __: 4 worm 5 paper
pard: 3 cat, pal 6 cowboy 7 cowpoke, panther, pardner, partner
pardalis, felis: 6 ocelot
pardalote: 4 bird
pardner: 3 pal 6 cowboy 7 cowpoke
Pardo: 3 Don
pardon: 4 free, pity 5 clear, grace, mercy, remit, spare 6 accept, acquit, assoil, excuse, let off, spring 7 absolve, amnesty, commute, forgive, justify, release 8 clemency, overlook, reprieve, write off 9 acquittal, discharge, exculpate, exonerate, indemnity, remission, salvation 10 absolution
beg ~: 9 apologize
pardonable: 6 venial 9 excusable 10 defensible, forgivable, remittable, vindicable
pardoning: 7 lenient 8 merciful 9 forgiving
Pardon me!: 4 ahem 5 sorry
Pardon my __: 6 French
Pardon My English: 7 musical
songwriter: 8 Gershwin
Pardon My Past (1945 film)
cast: Marguerite Chapman, Fred MacMurray, Akim Tamiroff
Pardon My Sarong (1942 film)
cast: Bud Abbott, Lionel Atwill, Virginia Bruce, Lou Costello
director: Erle C. Kenton
Pardonnez-__: 3 moi
pare: 3 cut, lop 4 clip, crop, dock, flay, peel, skin, slow, trim 5 carve, lower, prune, shave, slash 6 cut off, lessen, reduce, scrape 7 abridge, curtail, cut away, cut back, shorten, whittle 8 decrease, diminish, downsize, minimize, truncate 9 cut back on, scale down 10 abbreviate
Paré: 7 Michael 8 Ambroise
__ Paree: 3 Gay
parent: 3 dad, mom 4 make, mama, papa, rear 5 cause, mamma, pappy 6 author, chider, father, mother, origin, source 7 kinsman, produce 8 ancestor, begetter, guardian, relative 9 architect, originate 10 forerunner, originator, progenitor
admonition: 3 eat 4 don't, quit, stop 6 behave
backwoods ~: 2 ma, pa 3 maw, paw 5 mammy, pappy
barnyard ~: 3 cow, dam, ewe, hen, ram, sow 4 boar, bull, duck, mare, sire 5 billy, drake, goose, nanny 6 gander 7 rooster 8 stallion
British ~: 5 mater, pater
cub ~: 4 bear, lion 5 panda, tiger 7 lioness, tigress
ender: 3 age
female ~: 2 ma 3 mom 4 mama 5 momma, mommy 6 mother
gen-Xer ~: 6 boomer
in French: 4 mère, père
in Spanish: 5 madre, padre
male ~: 2 pa 3 dad 4 dada, papa, sire 5 daddy, poppa 6 father
mule ~: 3 ass 4 mare
new ~: 5 namer
org.: 3 PTA 4 MADD
quadruped ~: 3 dam 4 sire
responsibility: 3 son, tot 4 baby, teen 5 child, minor 6 infant 8 daughter, teen-ager 9 youngster
restriction: 6 curfew
starter: 3 god 4 step 5 grand, trans
__ parent: 5 birth 6 foster
Parent-__ Association: 7 Teacher
parentage: 4 line 5 stock 6 origin 7 lineage 9 genealogy 10 extraction
parental: 4 fond, kind, warm 6 benign, caring, gentle, lineal, loving, tender 7 devoted 8 fatherly, maternal, motherly, paternal, watchful 9 indulgent 10 benevolent, comforting, forbearing, protective, supportive
parental __: 5 leave 7 consent
Parent, Bernie
milieu: 3 ice 4 rink 5 arena
org.: 3 NHL
parenthesis shape: 3 arc
parenthetical: 4 side 10 qualifying
parenthood: 9 maternity, paternity
Parenthood (1989 film)
cast: Tom Hulce, Steve Martin, Rick Moranis, Martha Plimpton, Jason Robards, Mary Steenburgen, Dianne Wiest
director: Ron Howard
parentless child: 6 orphan 9 foundling
parents: 5 folks
Parent Trap, The (1961 film)
cast: Brian Keith, Hayley Mills, Maureen O'Hara
director: David Swift
dog: 9 Andromeda
kid: 4 twin
Parent Trap, The (1998 film)
cast: Elaine Hendrix, Lindsay Lohan, Dennis Quaid, Natasha Richardson
director: Nancy Myers
parer: 4 tool 6 cutter, device, gadget, peeler
user: 4 chef, cook
Paretsky,Sara: 6 author, writer
pareu: 4 wrap 5 skirt 8 lavalava
par excellence: 3 ace 4 A-one, best, only, rare, tops 5 alone, great 6 single, superb, unique 7 in front, optimum, perfect, supreme 8 flawless, peerless, splendid, superior 9 faultless, matchless, nonpareil, solid-gold, topflight, unequaled, unmatched, unrivaled, virtuosic 10 consummate, inimitable, preeminent, unexampled, unrivalled, world-class
parfait: 7 dessert 8 ice cream
alternative: 6 gelati, gelato, sundae 7 spumone, spumoni, tortoni
par for the __: 6 course
pargo: 4 fish
pari __: 5 passu
pari-__: 6 mutuel
Paria: 4 gulf
pariah: 5 exile, Jonah 6 outlaw, wretch 7 outcast 8 anathema
campus ~: 4 nerd, nurd, wonk 5 dweeb 7 egghead
social ~: 4 bore, jerk 5 creep
treat like a ~: 3 cut 4 shun 5 avoid 6 slight 9 blackball
__ paribus: 7 ceteris
parietal: 4 bone
locale: 5 skull 7 cranium 9 braincase
parietal __: 3 eye 4 bone, cell, lobe 5 rules
Parigi, o cara: 4 duet
Parillaud: 4 Anne
pari-mutuel
listing: 4 odds
transaction: 3 bet 5 wager
Parinacota: 4 peak 5 mount 8 mountain
locale: 5 Andes, Chile 7 Bolivia
__-paring: 6 cheese
Parini, Giuseppe: 4 poet 7 Italian
pari passu: 6 evenly, fairly
Paris: 4 city, Mica, town 5 Jerry 6 Trojan 7 capital, musical
abductee: 5 Helen
airport: 4 Orly 8 de Gaulle
attraction: 4 arch 5 musée 6 cancan, Louvre 8 Left Bank 11 Eiffel Tower
brother: 6 Hector, Pammon 7 Helenus, Polites, Troilus 8 Antiphus 9 Deiphobus, Hipponous, Polydorus
city near ~: 5 Lille, Melun 6 Amiens, Sèvres
cop: 4 flic
designer: 4 Dior
home: 4 Troy
hotel: 4 Ritz
locale: 5 Texas 6 France
lover: 5 Helen 6 Oenone
money: 3 sou 4 euro 5 franc
palace: 6 Elysée
paper: 7 Le Monde
parent: 5 Priam 6 Hecuba 7 Priamus
plaster of ~: 6 gypsum
river: 5 Seine
ruffian: 6 apache
sister: 6 Creusa, Iliona 7 Laodice 8 Polyxena 9 Cassandra
songwriter: 6 Porter
son of ~: 6 Aganus, Idaeus 7 Bunomus 8 Corythus
subway: 5 Metro
to Romeo: 5 rival
to Ulysses: 3 foe 5 enemy
victim: 6 Eetion, Evenor 7 Mosynus, Phorcys 8 Achilles, Cleolaus, Deiochus, Demoleon, Euchenor 9 Cleodorus 10 Menesthius
see also French
Paris __: 5 Blues, daisy, green, Trout 7 Calling, Commune, Sisters
__ Paris: 5 I Love 6 Forget, Savage
Paris Blues (1961 film)
cast: Diahann Carroll, Paul Newman, Joanne Woodward
director: Martin Ritt
Paris Calling (1941 film)
cast: Basil Rathbone, Randolph Scott
director: Edwin L. Marin
parish: 4 fold, ward 5 flock, laity, local 6 church 8 brethren, district 9 community, territory 10 worshipers
donation: 5 tithe
hall shout: 5 bingo
Louisiana ~: 6 Acadia
official: 4 abbé 5 padre, vicar 6 beadle, curate, father
Parish: 5 Peggy 6 Robert
parishioner: 4 laic 5 laity 9 layperson
Parish, Robert: 5 cager
milieu: 5 court
org.: 3 NBA
sport: 10 basketball
__ parisienne: 3 à la
Parisienne: 3 mme. 4 mlle. 5 femme 6 madame
Parisina author: Byron
Parisina composer: 8 Mascagni
Paris in the Twentieth Century author: Jules Verne
Paris Option, The author: Ludlum
Paris Symphony composer: 6 Mozart
Paris Trout (1991 film)
cast: Ed Harris, Barbara Hershey, Dennis Hopper
parity: 3 par 7 balance, isonomy 8 equality, likeness, sameness 9 congruity 10 similarity, uniformity
parity __: 3 bit 5 check
park: 3 put, set, sit 4 lawn, stop 5 field, green, grove, leave, lodge, oasis, place, plaza, woods 6 common, curb it, estate, forest, locate, meadow, pull in, settle, square 7 commons, deposit, grounds, reserve, stadium, station 8 preserve, pull over, woodland 9 sanctuary 10 playground
activity: 4 hike, walk 6 picnic 7 camping, cookout
alcove: 5 arbor
amusement ~ ride: 5 flume 7 coaster 8 carousel 9 bumper car
animal ~: 3 zoo
carefully: 4 ease
ender: 3 way 4 land
feature: 5 bench, grass, shade, slide, swing, trail 6 gazebo, seesaw 8 fountain

in the ball ~: 4 near 5 about, close 7 roughly
Kenya ~: 5 Tsavo
London ~: 4 Hyde
municipal ~: 6 square
national ~: 4 Zion 5 Banff 6 Acadia, Arches, Denali, Katmai 7 Big Bend, Glacier, Olympic, Redwood, reserve, Saguaro, Sequoia 8 Badlands, Biscayne, preserve, Wind Cave, Yosemite 9 Haleakala, Lake Clark, Mesa Verde, sanctuary, Voyageurs 10 Crater Lake, Everglades, Glacier Bay, Grand Teton, Great Basin, Hot Springs, Isle Royale, Joshua Tree 11 Yellowstone
one way to ~: 6 back in, head-in
South Africa ~: 6 Kruger
visitor: 5 hiker, nanny 6 camper 7 tourist 8 stroller 9 sightseer
__ park: 4 ball, game 5 theme 6 pocket 7 trailer
__-park: 6 double
Park: 4 Brad 5 Linda, Mungo
in Monopoly: 5 Place
Park __: 3 Row 4 City 5 Range 6 Avenue
__ Park: 3 Oak 4 Echo, Hyde 5 Estes, Gorky 6 Bullet 7 Battery, Central, Gosford 10 Golden Gate
parka: 4 coat 6 anorak, jacket 7 skiwear 9 outerwear 10 protection
feature: 4 hood 6 lining, pocket, zipper
lining: 4 down 10 Thinsulate
wearer: 5 hiker 6 Eskimo
park-and-__: 4 ride
Park Avenue: 3 car 4 auto 5 Buick 10 automobile
Parkay: 9 margarine
alternative: 6 Shedd's 7 Promise 8 Imperial
Park, Brad: 8 puckster
milieu: 3 ice 4 rink 5 arena
org.: 3 NHL
__ Park, CA: 5 Buena, Menlo
Park Chung __: 3 Hee
Park City author: Ann Beattie
__ Park, CO: 5 Estes
parked: 7 garaged 10 not running, stationary
Parker: 3 Ace, Jim, Ray, Tom, wit 4 Alan, city, Dave, Fess, Jean, Suzy, town, Trey 5 Cecil, Posey 6 Bonnie, Graham 7 Charlie, Dorothy, Eleanor, Gilbert, Jameson 9 Stevenson 10 Mary-Louise
end ~: 3 nib
fluid: 3 ink
locale: 8 Colorado
Nosy ~: 5 prier, pryer, snoop
partner: 6 Barrow
Parker __ roll: 5 House
__ Parker: 4 Nosy 5 Nosey
Parker, Alan: 8 director
film: Angela's Ashes (1999)
Birdy (1984)
The Commitments (1991)
Evita (1996)
Midnight Express (1978)
Mississippi Burning (1988)
The Road to Wellville (1994)
Shoot the Moon (1982)
Parker-Bowles: 7 Camilla
Parker, Charlie: 11 saxophonist
genre: 3 bop 4 jazz
instrument: 3 sax 4 alto
nickname: 4 Bird
Parker, Dorothy: 3 wit 6 writer
work: After Such Pleasures
Enough Rope
Here Lies
Parker, Eleanor: 7 actress
film: Above and Beyond (1952)
Caged (1950)
Detective Story (1951)
Escape From Fort Bravo (1953)
Home From the Hill (1960)
Interrupted Melody (1955)
The Man With the Golden Arm (1955)
A Millionaire for Christy (1951)
The Naked Jungle (1954)
Pride of the Marines (1945)
Scaramouche (1952)
The Sound of Music (1965)
Three Secrets (1950)
The Voice of the Turtle (1947)
The Woman in White (1948)
Parker, Fess: 5 actor
film: Davy Crockett... (1955)
The Great Locomotive Chase (1956)
Hell Is for Heroes (1962)
The Light in the Forest (1958)
Old Yeller (1957)
song: Ballad of Davy Crockett (1955)
TV: Daniel Boone
Parker, Gilbert: 6 writer 8 Canadian
work: The Seats of the Mighty
Parker House: 4 roll 5 hotel
Parker Jr., Ray
song: Ghostbusters (1984)
I Still Can't Get Over Loving You (1983)
Jack and Jill (1978)
Jamie (1984)
The Other Woman (1982)
A Woman Needs Love (1981)
You Can't Change That (1979)
Parker Lewis Can't Lose (Fox sitcom)
cast: Corin Nemec (Parker Lewis)
Parker, Mary-Louise: 7 actress
film: Boys on the Side (1995)
Fried Green Tomatoes (1991)
Let the Devil Wear Black (2000)
Parker, Sarah Jessica: 7 actress
film: Dudley Do-Right (1999)
Ed Wood (1994)
Honeymoon in Vegas (1992)
Somewhere Tomorrow (1983)
State and Main (2000)
spouse: Matthew Broderick
Parkersburg: 4 city, town
locale: 3 W. Va.
Park Forest: 4 city, town
locale: 8 Illinois
__ Park, IL: 3 Oak
parking
airport ~: 5 apron
attendant: 5 valet
garage section: 5 level
lights: 6 dimmer
lot sight: 3 bus, car, van 4 auto 5 truck 7 minibus, vehicle 10 automobile
lot sign: 4 Exit, Full 5 Enter
mishap: 4 dent 7 scratch
place: 3 lot 6 garage, street
railroad ~ space: 4 yard
scofflaw stopper: 4 boot 6 ticket
parking __: 3 lot 4 ramp 5 brake, meter, orbit, space, strip
__ parking: 5 valet 8 parallel
__ Parkington: 3 Mrs.
Parkins, Barbara: 7 actress
film: Asylum (1972)
The Mephisto Waltz (1971)
TV: Peyton Place
Parkinson: 4 Dian
Parkinson's __: 3 law
Parkland: 4 city, town
locale: 10 Washington
Park Lane: 3 car 4 auto 7 Mercury
Parkman, Francis: 6 writer 9 historian
work: The Oregon Trail
Park, Mungo: 4 Scot 8 explorer
Park Near Lucerne artist: 4 Klee
__ Park, NJ: 5 Menlo 6 Asbury
__ Park, NY: 4 Hyde, Rego 6 Tuxedo
Park Place neighbor: 6 Chance
Park Ridge: 4 city, town
locale: 8 Illinois
Parks: 4 Bert, Rosa 5 Larry 6 Gordon 7 Michael, Van Dyke
Parks, Bert successor: 3 Ely
Parks, Gordon: 8 director
film: Aaron Loves Angela (1975)
Leadbelly (1976)
Shaft (1971)
Shaft's Big Score! (1972)
The Super Cops (1974)
Superfly (1972)
Parks, Larry: 5 actor
film: Freud (1962)
Jolson Sings Again (1949)
The Jolson Story (1946)
spouse: Betty Garrett
Parkville: 4 city, town
locale: 8 Maryland
Park Ward: 3 car 4 auto 10 Rolls-Royce
parkway: 4 pike, road 5 route 6 avenue, street 8 turnpike 9 boulevard
Parkway: 4 city, town
locale: 10 California
Parkwood: 3 car 4 auto 5 Chevy 9 Chevrolet 10 automobile
parlance: 4 cant, talk 5 argot, idiom, lingo 6 jargon, patois, speech, tongue 7 wording 8 language, verbiage 10 vernacular
parlay: 3 bet 5 wager
parley: 3 gab, rap, yak 4 chat, talk 5 speak 6 caucus, confer, dialog, huddle, powwow, speech 7 commune, meeting, palaver, schmoos 8 chitchat, colloquy, converse, dialogue, schmoose, schmooze 9 discourse, gathering, negotiate, touch base 10 chew the rag, conference, deliberate, discussion, round table
Parley: 4 Baer
parliament: 5 house
czar's ~: 4 Duma
Ireland ~: 4 Dail
Japan ~: 4 Diet
Poland: 4 Sejm
Parliament
first female in ~: 5 Astor
member: 4 lord, peer
VIP: 2 P.M.
__ Parliament: 4 Long, Rump 5 Act of
parliamentary
activity: 6 debate
phrase: 5 I move 7 I second
program: 6 agenda
vote: 3 aye, nay
parlor: 5 salon 6 lounge 8 anteroom 10 living room
beauty ~: 5 salon 9 hair salon
beauty ~ item: 3 net 4 clip 5 drier, dryer, razor 6 curler, roller 7 hairpin 8 bobby pin, scissors
beauty ~ treatment: 3 cut, set 4 perm, trim 5 rinse 6 dye job, facial 8 manicure, pedicure 9 permanent
piece: 4 lamp, sofa 5 chair, couch, divan 6 settee 8 armchair, loveseat, recliner 9 easy chair, floor lamp
parlor __: 3 car 4 game, palm 5 grand, house
__ parlor: 3 sun 5 horse 6 beauty 7 milking, tanning
parlous: 5 hairy, risky 6 chancy, unsafe, wicked 7 unsound, vicious 8 menacing, perilous, unstable 9 dangerous, desperate, harrowing, hazardous, unhealthy 10 jeopardous, touch-and-go, vulnerable
Parma: 4 city, town
locale: 4 Ohio 5 Italy
Parma Heights: 4 city, town
locale: 4 Ohio
Parmenides: 5 Greek 11 philosopher
specialty: 7 Eleatic
Parmesan __: 6 cheese
__ parmigiana: 4 veal
Parnaiba: 5 river
locale: 6 Brazil
Parnassus: 4 peak 5 mount 8 mountain
town near ~: 6 Delphi
Parnassus on Wheels author: Morley
Parnell: 5 Emory 6 Thomas
__ Parnell: 6 Lee Roy
Parnelli: 5 Jones
Parnell, Thomas: 4 poet 5 Irish
parochial: 5 local, petty 6 biased, little, narrow 7 bigoted, insular, limited, topical 8 regional 9 hidebound, localized, sectarian, small-town 10 prejudiced, provincial
parochial __: 6 school
parody: 3 ape 4 copy, mock, skit 5 farce, genre, mimic, put-on, revue, roast, spoof 6 deride, review, satire, send-up 7 burlesk, imitate, lampoon, mockery, portray, takeoff 8 ridicule, satirize, travesty 9 burlesque, imitation 10 caricature, impression
parol: 6 orally, verbal 8 verbally 9 utterance
parole: 4 free, word 7 freedom, promise 8 password 9 discharge
parolee: 5 ex-con 8 jailbird
paronomasia: 3 pun 8 wordplay
paroquet: 4 bird
Paros, neighbor of: 5 Naxos
parotitis: 5 mumps
paroxysm: 3 fit 4 rage 5 furor, spasm, throe 6 frenzy, tumult 7 seizure, tantrum 8 eruption, outbreak, outburst 9 hysterics 10 convulsion
parquet __: 4 tile 6 circle
parquetry: 5 inlay 10 decoration
installer: 5 tiler
wood: 3 oak
parr: 4 fish 6 salmon
Parr: 4 John 9 Catherine
Parra, Nicanor: 4 poet 7 Chilean
Parrilla: 4 city, town
locale: 6 Mexico 7 Tabasco
Parris: 4 isle 6 island
Parrish: 5 Lance, Larry
Parris Island: 4 city, town
grp.: 4 USMC
locale: 4 S. Car.
parrot: 3 ape, kea, pet 4 aper, bird, copy, echo, kaka, lory, mime 5 macaw, mimic, mouth, quote, resay 6 conure, echoer, kakapo, recite, repeat 7 copycat, imitate 8 imitator, lorikeet, lovebird 9 reiterate
Australian ~: 4 lory
cry: 3 awk 5 hello
emulate a ~: 3 ape 4 copy 5 mimic
ender: 4 fish
genus: 3 ara
home: 4 cage 6 aviary, jungle 7 tropics
kin: 8 cockatoo, parakeet, paraquet, paroquet, parroket 9 cockateel, cockatiel, parrakeet, parroquet
monk ~: 4 loro
name: 5 Polly
New Zealand ~: 3 kea 4 kaka 6 kakapo
nostril: 4 cere
seat: 5 perch
parrotfish: 4 loro
parry: 4 duck, shun 5 avoid, block, dodge, elude, evade, fence, rebut, repel, shirk 6 refute 7 confute, counter, deflect, fend off, hold off, repulse, ward off 8 sidestep, stave off 9 forestall, hold at bay, turn aside 10 anticipate, circumvent
alternative: 5 lunge

Parry, William: 8 explorer
Parsees: 4 sect
Parseghian: 3 Ara
parse, something to: 6 clause 8 sentence
Parsifal: 5 opera
character: 6 Kundry 7 Titurel 8 Amfortas, Klingsor 9 Gurnemanz
composer: 6 Wagner
setting: 5 Spain 8 Pyrenees
Parsifal Mosaic, The author: Ludlum
parsimonious: 4 mean 5 close, tight 6 frugal, greedy, saving, skimpy, stingy 7 chintzy, miserly, scrimpy, selfish, sparing, thrifty 8 tightwad 9 illiberal, penurious 10 avaricious, skinflinty
be ~: 3 eke 4 mete, save 5 skimp, stint 8 begrudge, keep back 9 economize
one: 5 miser 7 Scrooge 8 tightwad 9 skinflint 10 cheapskate, pinchpenny
parsimony: 6 thrift 9 frugality 10 stinginess
Parsippany: 4 city, town
locale: 9 New Jersey
parsley: 4 herb
piece: 5 sprig
relative: 4 dill 5 anise, cumin 6 fennel, lovage
with ~: 5 garni
Parsley, ___, Rosemary and Thyme: 4 Sage
parsnip: 4 root 6 veggie 9 vegetable
parson: 5 padre, vicar 6 cleric, curate, father, pastor, priest, rector 8 chaplain, minister, preacher, reverend 9 churchman, clergyman
bird: 3 tui
ender: 3 age
expletive: 4 amen
home: 5 manse 8 vicarage
parsonage: 5 manse 8 vicarage
Parsons: 4 Alan, Gram 7 Estelle, Louella
Parsons ___: 5 table
Parsons, Estelle Oscar: Bonnie and Clyde
Parsons Project, Alan
song: Don't Answer Me (1984)
Eye in the Sky (1982)
Games People Play (1981)
Parsons School of ___: 6 Design
part: 2 go 3 any, bit, cut, job, leg, lot 4 chip, duty, fork, hero, hunk, item, lead, limb, link, lump, role, side, sift, some, task, tear, unit, yawn 5 cameo, chunk, divvy, extra, leave, lines, piece, quota, scrap, sever, share, shred, slice, split, voice 6 aspect, behalf, branch, cleave, cut off, detach, detail, divide, factor, member, moiety, morsel, office, parcel, ration, region, sample, sector, spread, sunder, unlink, walk-on 7 break up, concern, deviate, disjoin, ease out, element, excerpt, faction, fitting, helping, portion, pull out, push off, quarter, radiate, scatter, section, segment, ship out, split up, take off, villain 8 break off, disunite, division, fraction, fragment, function, interest, location, province, separate, shove off, specimen, splinter, uncouple, withdraw 9 allotment, bifurcate, character, component, cut and run, dismantle, partition, take a hike 10 antagonist, disconnect, ingredient, proportion
combining form: 4 -mere, -plex
starter: 3 ram 7 counter
part ___: 4 song, with 5 music 7 singing
part-___: 4 time 5 timer
___ part: 3 bit 4 act a, real, take 5 spare, voice 6 walk-on
partake: 3 eat, sip 4 have 5 eat of, quaff, savor, share, taste, touch 6 accept, devour, ingest, join in, sample 7 consume, receive, share in 8 deal with 9 enter into
part and ___: 6 parcel
___-part harmony: 4 four
Parthe: 5 river
city on the ~: 7 Leipsic, Leipzig
locale: 7 Germany
Parthenon
goddess: 6 Athena, Athene, Pallas
site: 6 Athens, Greece
style ~: 5 Doric
Parthenope: 5 siren
lover of ~: 6 Apollo 8 Heracles
Parthian: 8 language
parti-___: 7 colored
partial: 3 cut 5 gonzo 6 biased, fond of, narrow, unfair, unjust 7 bigoted, colored, halfway, limited, reduced, sketchy 8 abridged, disposed, one-sided 9 arbitrary, condensed, curtailed, jaundiced, qualified, shortened 10 diminished, expurgated, fractional, incomplete, prejudiced, unbalanced, unfinished
be ~ to: 4 like 5 favor 6 prefer
prefix: 4 demi-, hemi-, semi-
refund: 6 rebate
to: 6 keen on
partial ___: 3 sum 4 tone 5 score 6 vacuum
partiality: 4 bias, love 5 fancy, mania, slant, taste 6 liking, relish 7 leaning 8 affinity, druthers, fondness, nepotism, penchant, tendency, velleity, weakness 9 appetence, injustice, prejudice, sentiment 10 attachment, fanaticism, favoritism, friendship, indulgence, proclivity, propensity
partially: 6 partly 7 halfway 8 somewhat 9 by degrees, piecemeal
participant: 5 actor, party 6 helper, member, player, sharer 7 entrant, partner 8 follower 9 associate, attendant, colleague
participate: 3 aid 4 play 5 enter, get in, share 6 accept, attend, chip in, join in, take on 7 compete, pitch in 8 deal with, engage in 9 cooperate, enter into, lend a hand
as a visitor: 5 audit, sit in
chance to ~: 4 turn 5 break
participation: 5 voice 8 interest
___ participle: 4 past 7 perfect, present
participle suffix: 3 ing
particle: 3 bit, dot, jot, ray 4 atom, drop, hoot, iota, mite, mote, seed, spot, whit 5 crumb, fleck, grain, minim, ounce, piece, scrap, shred, speck, trace 6 little, morsel, stitch, trifle 7 dribble, granule, modicum, smidgen, smidgin 8 fragment, molecule, smidgeon 10 smithereen
atomic ~: 6 proton 7 neutron 8 electron
burning ~: 4 coal 5 ember, spark
charged ~: 3 ion 5 anion 6 cation, kation
dirt ~: 4 grit, mote 5 speck
ender: 5 board
hypothetical ~: 5 axion
subatomic ~: 2 xi 4 kaon, muon, pion 5 axion, boson, gluon, meson, quark, tauon 6 baryon, hadron, K meson, lepton, photon 7 fermion, hyperon, neutron, pi meson, tachyon 8 deuteron, electron, graviton, neutrino, positron
particle ___: 4 beam 7 physics
___ particle: 3 eta, psi, tau 4 beta 5 alpha, delta, Higgs, sigma, Z-zero 6 lambda 7 cascade, charged, strange, upsilon, virtual
parti-colored: 6 calico, dapple 7 dappled
particular: 3 own 4 fact, item, nice, prim, sole, spec 5 exact, fussy, picky, point, thing 6 choosy, dainty, detail, prissy, proper, regard, single, strict, unique 7 careful, certain, choosey, element, express, feature, finicky, limited, precise, prudent, respect, several, special, topical 8 accurate, cautious, critical, definite, distinct, especial, exacting, finiking, finnicky, personal, rigorous, separate, singular, specific, thorough 9 assiduous, attentive, demanding, exclusive, judicious, observant, punctilio, selective, squeamish 10 fastidious, individual, meticulous, respective, scrupulous
particularize: 4 list 6 denote, detail, relate 7 specify, spec out 8 describe 9 stipulate
particularly: 5 extra 6 mostly, singly 7 notably 8 markedly 9 decidedly, expressly, specially, unusually
particulars: 5 terms 7 details
particulate matter: 3 ash 4 dust, grit, smut, soot
parting: 4 last 5 adieu, final, going, leave 6 schism 7 breakup, fission, goodbye, split-up 8 division, farewell 9 departure 10 crossroads, divergence, separation, withdrawal
shot: 5 taunt 6 retort, zinger
words: 3 bye 4 ciao, ta-ta, vale 5 adieu, adios, aloha, later, peace, see ya 6 bye-bye, shalom, sholom, so long 7 cheerio, good-bye 8 farewell, sayonara 10 hasta luego
parting ___: 4 line, shot
parting ___ ways: 5 of the
Parting ___ we know of heaven: 5 is all
Parting is such sweet ___: 6 sorrow
parting of the ___: 4 ways
parti pris: 9 prejudice
partisan: 3 fan 4 ally 5 blind 6 backer, biased, rooter, unfair, unjust, votary 7 admirer, booster, colored, devotee, diehard, fanatic, slanted, zealous 8 adherent, exponent, follower, guerilla, loyalist, militant, one-sided 9 arbitrary, factional, guerrilla, jaundiced, proponent, satellite, sectarian, supporter 10 enthusiast, prejudiced, unbalanced
be ~: 4 root, side
Partita ___ Minor: 3 in E
partition: 4 pane, wall 5 cut up, panel, sever, share, split 6 divide, screen 7 barrier, divider, divvy up, portion, rope off, section, split up, wall off 8 division, fence off, separate 9 apportion, parcel out, subdivide 10 distribute, separation
biological ~: 6 septum
court ~: 3 net
Japanese ~: 6 fusuma
ship ~: 8 bulkhead
partly: 5 quasi 7 halfway 8 slightly, somewhat 9 partially, to a degree 10 to an extent, up to a point
partner: 3 pal 4 ally, chum, date, mate, wife 5 buddy, crony, owner, unite 6 cohort, co-mate, friend, helper, spouse 7 coequal, comrade, consort, husband 8 coworker, helpmate, playmate, sidekick, teammate 9 accessory, affiliate, assistant, associate, colleague, companion 10 accomplice
___ partner: 6 secret, silent
partnerless: 4 stag 5 alone 8 solitary
partners, go: 5 unite 6 hook up, team up 9 affiliate 10 join up with
partnership: 3 tie 4 bond, firm, link 5 house, joint, match, nexus, union 6 cahoot, cartel, hookup, league 7 cahoots, combine, company, liaison 8 affinity, alliance, business, coupling, relation 9 ownership 10 connection
word: 3 and, son
Partnership for Peace org.: 4 NATO
part of ___: 6 speech
Parton, Dolly: 6 singer
song: 9 to 5 (1980)
Here You Come Again (1977)
Islands in the Stream (1983)
Two Doors Down (1978)
theme park: Dollywood
___ partout: 5 passe
partridge: 4 bird, fowl 5 quail 6 chukar, grouse 8 pheasant 9 francolin
family: 5 covey
relative: 5 poult, snipe 6 peahen, turkey 7 peacock, peafowl 8 curassow, moorfowl, woodcock 10 guinea fowl, wild turkey
...partridge ___ pear tree: 3 in a
Partridge, Eric: 6 writer 7 British
concern: 5 slang
Partridge Family
lead singer: David Cassidy
song: Doesn't Somebody Want to Be Wanted (1971)
I'll Meet You Halfway (1971)
I Think I Love You (1970)
I Woke Up in Love This Morning (1971)
Partridge Family, The (ABC sitcom)
cast: Danny Bonaduce (Danny Partridge)
David Cassidy (Keith Partridge)
Susan Dey (Laurie Partridge)
Shirley Jones (Shirley Partridge)
dog: 6 Simone
...___ partridge in a pear tree: 4 and a
parts
auto ~ brand: 4 Fram, NAPA
it had three ~: 4 Gaul
remove vital ~: 3 gut 4 sack 5 rifle 6 ravage 7 destroy, pillage, plunder, ransack 8 clean out, decimate
sum of the ~: 5 whole
unknown: 5 about 6 around 9 scattered, somewhere
___ parts: 4 auto
Part-Time Lover (1985 song) artist: Stevie Wonder
parturition: 5 birth
party: 2 do 3 bee, GOP, set, tea 4 ball, band, bash, bloc, body, crew, fest, fete, gala, luau, prom, ring, side, team, unit 5 actor, agent, blast, cabal, dance, feast, group, junta, junto, revel, salon, spree, squad, treat, troop, Whigs 6 affair, dinner, fiesta, league, outfit, person, regale, social, soiree, troupe 7 banquet, blowout, carry on, combine, company, coterie, faction, jubilee, Liberal, potluck, revelry, shindig 8 barbecue, function, jamboree, litigant, luncheon, visitors, wingding 9 amusement, Bull Moose, celebrate, coalition, coming-out, defendant, diversion, festivity, gathering, have a ball, make merry, plaintiff, reception, whoop it up 10 contractor, Democratic, detachment, electorate, have a blast, individual, persuasion
bachelor ~: 4 stag
be a ~ to: 4 abet, plot 8 conspire
big shot: 4 whip 9 candidate
birthday ~ item: 4 cake, gift 6 candle 7 present
British political ~: 6 Labour
cheese: 4 Brie, Edam 5 Gouda
costume ~: 10 masquerade
debutante's ~: 4 ball
dinner ~: 5 feast 7 banquet
drink: 4 beer, wine 5 punch 9 champagne

elephant ~: 3 GOP
evening ~: 4 ball 6 soiree
food: 3 dip 4 cake, nuts, pâté 5 chips, salsa, tarts 6 caviar, olives, pastry 7 canapés, cashews, Cheetos, peanuts, popcorn 8 brownies, crackers, crudités, pretzels 10 macadamias
frat ~: 4 stag 5 mixer
give a ~ for: 4 fete 5 honor 7 lionize 9 celebrate, entertain
hearty: 5 revel 9 have a ball, whoop it up
injured ~: 6 sucker, victim 9 scapegoat
Israeli political ~: 5 Likud, Mapam
join the ~: 4 be at 6 appear, attend, drop in, make it, show up 9 accompany
leader's goal: 5 unity
life of the ~: 3 wag, wit 4 card 5 mixer 6 joiner
line: 8 platform
memento: 5 favor
19th-century ~: 4 Whig
old-fashioned ~: 3 bee 6 social 7 potluck
Palermo ~: 5 festa
paper: 5 crape, crepe
pick: 5 slate 9 candidate
Polynesian ~: 4 luau
pooper: 4 bore, drip 10 wet blanket
quilting ~: 3 bee
search ~: 5 posse
site: 5 yacht 8 ballroom 9 frat house
staple: 3 keg
supply a ~: 5 cater
throw a ~: 4 host 6 regale 7 splurge 9 celebrate, entertain
thrower: 4 host 6 cohost
thrower plea: 4 RSVP
to: 4 in on
wedding ~ member: 5 bride, groom, usher 7 best man 10 bridesmaid, flower girl, ring bearer 11 maid of honor
wedding ~ members: 6 family 7 kinfolk
wild ~: 4 bash 5 blast 6 bustup 7 blowout 8 wingding
party __: 3 man 4 girl, line, whip 6 animal, pooper
__ party: 3 hen, keg, tea, war 4 frat, lawn 5 block, Green, house, major, minor, press, third 6 bridal, garden, pajama, search 7 costume, people's, slumber
Party __: 4 Doll, Girl, Wire 6 Lights
__ Party: 4 Don's 5 Beach, House, It's My 6 Pajama
Party Doll (1957 song)
artist: Buddy Knox with the Rhythm Orchids, Steve Lawrence
Party Girl (1958 film)
cast: Cyd Charisse, Lee J. Cobb, Robert Taylor
director: Nicholas Ray
partygoer: 5 guest 7 invitee 8 attendee
Party Lights (1962 song) artist: Claudine Clark
Partyman (1989 song) artist: Prince
Party of Five (Fox drama)
cast: Neve Campbell (Julia Salinger) Lacey Chabert (Claudia Salinger) Matthew Fox (Charlie Salinger) Jennifer Love Hewitt (Sarah Reeves) Jacob Smith (Owen Salinger) Scott Wolf (Bailey Salinger)
Party's Over, The composer: 5 Styne
__-party system: 3 two
Party, The (1968 film)
cast: Marge Champion, Claudine Longet, Peter Sellers
director: Blake Edwards
__ Party, The: 4 Last 6 Dinner, Garden
Party Wire (1935 film)
cast: Jean Arthur, Victor Jory
director: Erle C. Kenton
parula: 4 bird
Parvati: 7 goddess
consort: 4 Siva 5 Shiva
devotee: 5 Hindu 6 Hindoo
parvenu: 5 yahoo 6 nobody 7 upstart, wannabe 9 arriviste, latecomer, nonentity, vulgarian
pas: 4 step 9 dance step
de deux: 5 dance
faux ~: 4 slip 5 boner, error, gaffe, wrong 6 bêtise, boo-boo, howler, slip-up 7 blooper, blunder, misstep, mistake 8 indecoru 9 gaucherie
make a faux ~: 3 err 4 flub, goof, muff, slip, trip 5 botch, lapse, stray 6 booboo, bungle, foul up, fumble, mess up, slip up 7 blunder, go wrong, louse up, misstep, stumble 8 go astray
seul: 5 dance
pas __: 4 allé, d'âne, seul 6 marche 7 d'action
__ pas: 4 faux
__ pas?: 6 n'est-ce
__ pasa?: 3 Qué
__ Pasa: 8 El Condor
Pasadena: 4 city, town
happening: 6 parade
locale: 5 Texas 10 California
parade flower: 4 rose
Pascagoula: 4 city, town
locale: 4 Miss.
Pascal: 8 language
alternative: 3 ADA, APL, SQL 4 Alef, html, Icon, Java, LISP, Logo, Orca, Perl 5 Algol, Basic, Cecil, COBOL, Dylan, SISAL 6 Delphi, Eiffel, Erlang, Oberon, Prolog, Sather, Scheme, Snobol 7 Fortran
predecessor: 5 Algol
Pascal, Blaise: 6 French, writer 11 philosopher
work: Pensées
Pascal's __: 3 law 7 limaçon, theorem
Pasch: 5 Pesah 6 Easter, Pesach 8 Passover
season: 6 spring
paschal __: 4 lamb 6 candle, letter
Pasco: 4 city, town
locale: 10 Washington
Pascoli, Giovanni: 4 poet 7 Italian
Pasdar: 6 Adrian
pas de __: 4 chat, côté, deux 5 trois 6 basque, cheval, quatre 7 bourrée
Pas de Deux artist: 4 Erté
pas-de-deux sequence: 6 adagio
Pas de 'Duke' choreographer: 5 Ailey
pas du __: 4 tout
pase: 8 veronica
paseo: 4 walk 6 avenue, stroll 9 boulevard, promenade
Paseo: 3 car 4 auto 6 Toyota
pasha: 5 ruler 6 gerent
Tunis ~: 3 dey
__ Pasha: 3 Ali 5 Enver
pashka: 7 dessert
Pashto: 8 language
Pasiphae: 4 moon
daughter: 7 Ariadne, Phaedra
father: 6 Helios
husband: 5 Minos
planet: 7 Jupiter
sister: 5 Aeaea, Circe, Kirke
paso __: 5 doble
Paso __, CA: 6 Robles
__ Paso: 5 Old El
paso doble: 5 dance
Pasolini, Pier Paolo: 7 Italian 8 director
paspalum: 5 grass
__ Pasquale: 3 Don
pasquinade: 7 lampoon 10 caricature
pass: 2 go, OK 3 bye, gap 4 comp, fade, fare, flow, go by, jump, okay, skip, visa 5 adopt, badge, bandy, enact, excel, fly by, gorge, lapse, lunge, offer, outdo, paper, pinch, reach, serve, shoot, spend, stage, state 6 accept, aerial, befall, crisis, defile, elapse, exceed, hack it, perish, permit, plight, ratify, ravine, roll on, strait, ticket, vote in 7 advance, approve, decline, excrete, freebee, freebie, glide by, go ahead, let have, license, proceed, promote, qualify, refrain, refusal, run over, sneak by, succeed, suffice, surpass 8 blow over, exigence, exigency, free ride, furlough, go beyond, graduate, hand over, juncture, outshine, outstrip, overlook, overtake, overture, sanction, surmount, transfer, transmit 9 admission, emergency, get around, legislate, rejection, situation, transcend, transpire 10 free ticket, transferal
a bill: 5 adopt, enact
allow to ~: 5 let by
along: 4 send 5 relay
as: 7 imitate 9 represent
as time: 5 spend, while
bring to ~: 5 cause 6 ask for 7 achieve 10 effectuate
by: 2 go 3 fly 4 tick 5 spurn 6 elapse, ignore, reject, roll on 7 neglect 8 overlook 9 disregard
catcher: 3 end
come to ~: 2 be 4 fall 5 break, ensue, occur 6 befall, betide, happen, pan out, turn up 9 eventuate, intervene, take place, transpire
easily: 3 ace
ender: 3 ade, age, ion, ive, key 4 book, port, word
for: 8 look like, resemble
free ~: 4 comp 6 ticket
gambler's ~: 5 no bet
in baseball: 4 walk
in football: 4 bomb 6 aerial, looper, spiral 7 lateral
judgment: 4 jail, rule 6 punish 7 censure, condemn, convict, put away 8 imprison, penalize, sentence
let ~: 5 allow 6 wink at 7 forgive, neglect 8 overlook 9 disregard
matador ~: 5 faena
mountain ~: 3 col, gap 4 ghat 5 ghaut, notch 6 defile
mountain ~ info: 4 elev. 8 altitude 9 elevation
muster: 4 suit 6 hack it 7 qualify, satisfy
not ~: 4 fail 5 flunk
off: 5 foist 7 palm off
on: 4 veto, will 5 forgo, refer, relay, spurn 6 convey, forego, hand in, impart, perish, rebuff, reject, report 7 dismiss, exclude, kick off 8 disallow, hand down, relegate, transfer, transmit, turn down, turn over 9 blackball, cast aside, repudiate
out: 4 deal, give, zonk 5 faint, issue, sleep, swoon 6 assign, go limp, ration 7 divvy up 8 black out, disburse, dispense, fall over, keel over 10 distribute
over: 4 jump, lick, miss, omit, skip, snub, span 5 clear, cross, elide 6 except, forget, ignore 7 exclude, lose out, neglect 8 discount, go across, leave out, overlook 9 disregard
pretty ~: 4 mess, spot 5 pinch 6 crisis, pickle 7 trouble 8 hot water, quandary 10 difficulty 11 predicament
quietly: 5 creep, slink, steal 6 tiptoe 7 slither
slowly: 3 lag 4 drag
starter: 3 sur 4 over 5 under
take a ~ at: 3 try 7 attempt
the buck: 5 blame, refer 6 accuse
the hat: 3 beg 7 collect, solicit 9 fundraise
the time idly: 4 bask, laze, loaf 6 trifle 8 vegetate
the word: 4 tell 6 inform
through: 4 seep, sift 6 filter 8 permeate, traverse 9 negotiate, penetrate, percolate
tournament ~: 3 bye
up: 4 lose, miss, omit, shun, skip, snub 5 forgo, spurn, waive 6 forego, ignore, rebuff, refuse, reject 7 abstain, decline, dismiss, lose out, refrain 8 brush off, forswear, keep from 9 foreswear
Pass __: 4 it on, Me By
__ Pass: 3 Ute 5 Bolan, Mitla, White 6 Beilan, Donner, Khyber, Shipka, Sunset 7 Bernina, Brenner, Grimsel, Khaibar, Simplon 9 Wolf Creek
passable: 2 OK 4 fair, okay, open, so-so, tidy 6 decent, medium 7 average, livable 8 adequate, all right, drivable, liveable, mediocre, middling, moderate, traveled, very well 9 navigable, tolerable, unblocked, unnotable 10 acceptable, accessible, admissible, fairly good
passably: 8 very well
passacaglia: 5 dance
passage: 3 run, way 4 duct, exit, fare, flow, hall, lane, lift, line, path, road, text, trek, trip, visa, walk 5 aisle, alley, canal, lapse, lobby, piece, quote, route, shaft, verse 6 access, artery, avenue, clause, course, motion, strait, street, ticket, travel, tunnel, voyage 7 channel, conduit, excerpt, extract, freedom, hallway, ingress, journey, opening, section, transit, warrant 8 alleyway, citation, corridor, crossing, entrance, sentence 9 concourse, enactment, paragraph, quotation, transport, vestibule 10 acceptance, admittance, recitation, transition
air ~: 4 duct, flue, vent 7 chimney
brain ~: 4 iter
drainage ~: 5 ditch 6 trench
elevator ~: 5 shaft
ender: 3 way 4 work
horizontal ~: 4 adit 6 tunnel
literary ~: 5 quote 8 citation 9 quotation
mine ~: 4 adit 5 shaft 6 tunnel
monk's ~: 4 slip 5 slype
musical ~: 4 coda
nasal ~: 5 sinus
right of ~: 6 access
theater ~: 5 aisle
to the sea: 3 ria 5 creek, inlet, river 6 stream 9 tributary
trolley ~: 4 fare 5 token
underground ~: 4 cave, pipe 5 drain, sewer 6 cavern, grotto 7 conduit, culvert 8 lava tube
water ~: 4 duct, hose, pipe 8 aqueduct
white-water ~: 5 chute, rapid
__ Passage: 4 Dark, Mona 5 Drake, Night 6 Canyon, Inside
Passage of Arms, A author: Eric Ambler
Passage, The author: Vance Palmer
Passage to India, A: 4 film 5 novel
author: E.M. Forster
cast: Dame Peggy Ashcroft, Victor Banerjee, Judy Davis
character: 4 Aziz 5 Adela, Cecil 6 Stella

director: David Lean
subject: 3 Raj
passageway: 3 gap 4 door, duct, exit, gate, hall, lane, path 5 aisle, alley, canal, lobby, shaft, track, trail 6 access, arcade, strait, tunnel 7 channel, ingress, opening 8 corridor, entrance 9 concourse, vestibule
covered ~: 4 stoa 6 arcade, bridge 7 gallery
vertical ~: 3 rod 4 axis, beam, pole, post 5 pylon, stalk 6 column, pillar
Passaic: 4 city, town
locale: 9 New Jersey
Passamaquoddy __: 3 Bay
passant
en ~: 7 by the by 8 by the way 9 in passing
en ~ capture: 4 pawn
Passat: 2 VW 3 car 4 auto 10 automobile, Volkswagen
passbook
holder: 5 saver
information: 7 account, balance, deposit 8 interest 10 withdrawal
passe-__: 7 partout
passé: 3 old, out 4 dull 5 corny, dated, dowdy, fusty, hoary, hokey, musty, stale, trite, vapid 6 bygone, common, démodé, jejune, old hat 7 ancient, antique, archaic, clichéd, disused, extinct, fatuous, fogyish, has-been, humdrum, old-time, outworn, prosaic 8 bromidic, movement, obsolete, outdated, outmoded, out of use, timeworn, unusable 9 forgotten, hackneyed, moss-grown, out of date, prosaical 10 antiquated, gone to seed, out of style, superseded, uninspired, unoriginal
passel: 3 lot 4 lots, many, raft, slew 5 batch, bunch, crowd, group, horde 6 divers, myriad, umteen, untold 7 copious, profuse, umpteen 8 abundant, manifold, numerous 9 bountiful, countless, quite a few
passenger: 4 fare, ride 5 rider 7 arrival, voyager 8 commuter, traveler, wayfarer 9 journeyer 10 hitchhiker
limo ~: 3 VIP
payment: 4 fare, pass 5 token 6 ticket
rail company: 6 Amtrak 9 Via Canada
ship: 5 ferry, liner 7 steamer 9 freighter 10 cruise ship
taxi ~: 4 fare
vehicle: 3 bus, car, van 4 auto, boat, ship 5 ferry, train, truck 6 jitney
passenger __: 6 pigeon
Passenger 57 (1992 film)
cast: Bruce Payne, Tom Sizemore, Wesley Snipes
director: Kevin Hooks
passengers: 7 traffic
disgorge ~: 6 let off, unload 7 deplane, detrain
where ~ wait: 5 depot, lobby 6 lounge 7 bus stop 8 sidewalk, terminal
passe-partout: 3 key
Passepartout to Phileas Fogg: 5 valet
passepied: 5 dance
passer
baton ~ race: 5 relay
forged-check ~: 5 kiter
rush the ~: 5 blitz
touchdown ~: 11 quarterback
__ passer: 4 buck
Passer: 4 Ivan
passerby: 6 looker 10 pedestrian
passerine: 4 bird 5 finch, pitta, vireo 6 becard, drongo, oriole 7 bunting, manakin, swallow 8 leafbird, lyrebird, ovenbird, starling 9 broadbill, currawong, sharpbill 10 tailorbird
__ Passes: 5 Pippa
passes, informally: 3 tix
__ pass GO: 5 Do not
__ passim: 3 sic
passing: 3 end 5 brief, short 6 demise, mortal, slight 7 cursory 8 fleeting, fugitive, temporal 9 ephemeral, momentary, temporary, transient 10 evanescent, pro tempore, short-lived, transition, transitory, unenduring
fancy: 3 fad 4 rage, urge, whim 5 craze, mania, quirk 6 notion, vagary 7 caprice, impulse 8 crotchet
grade: 3 cee
in ~: 7 by the by 8 by the way
through: 7 migrant, nomadic 9 migratory
passing __: 4 lane, shot 5 fancy
passion: 3 yen 4 fire, fury, heat, itch, love, rage, urge, will, zeal, zest 5 amour, anger, ardor, craze, crush, drive, fancy, fever, flame, gusto, mania, storm, wrath 6 desire, fervor, frenzy, liking, misery, spirit, temper, thirst, warmth 7 beloved, craving, ecstasy, emotion, feeling, impulse, rapture, romance 8 ambition, appetite, delirium, devotion, fervency, fondness, interest, lyricism, rabidity, violence, weakness 9 adoration, affection, appetence, intensity, life force, obsession, sensation, sentiment, suffering, transport, vehemence 10 attachment, dedication, enthusiasm
ender: 3 ate 4 less, tide 5 fruit 6 flower
feel ~ for: 4 love, want 5 adore 6 desire 7 idolize
goddess of ~: 5 Venus 9 Aphrodite
god of ~: 4 Amor, Eros
infuse with ~: 4 vamp 5 charm, flirt 6 enamor 7 beguile, enchant 8 entrance 9 transport
without ~: 5 icily 6 calmly, coldly, coolly
passion __: 4 play
Passion: 7 musical
songwriter: 8 Sondheim
Passion __: 4 Fish, Play, Week 6 Sunday
Passion (1980 song) artist: Rod Stewart
Passion According to St. John composer: 4 Bach
Passion According to St. Matthew composer: 4 Bach
passionate: 3 hot 4 avid, deep, keen, warm, wild 5 eager, fiery, heavy 6 ardent, devout, fervid, fierce, gung-ho, hearty, heated, loving, red-hot, steamy, stormy, strong, sultry, torrid, urgent 7 amatory, amorous, aroused, blazing, burning, earnest, excited, fervent, flaming, furious, glowing, hugging, intense, kissing, lyrical, violent, zealous 8 desirous, eloquent, forceful, frenzied, headlong, inflamed, romantic, spirited, stirring, turned-on, vehement, wild-eyed 9 amatorial, emotional, excitable, exuberant, heartfelt, hotheaded, impetuous, impulsive, inspiring, thrilling 10 compulsive, expressive, hot-blooded
Passion Fish (1992 film)
cast: Mary McDonnell, David Strathairn, Alfre Woodard
director: John Sayles
passionflower fruit: 10 granadilla
passionfruit: 6 maypop
passionless: 3 icy 4 cold, cool 6 frigid 7 ice-cold
Passion of Anna, The (1969 film)
cast: Bibi Andersson, Liv Ullmann, Max von Sydow
director: Ingmar Bergman
Passion of Molly T, The author: Lawrence Sanders
Passion Play author: Jerzy Kosinski
passive: 3 lax 4 idle, lazy, logy, meek 5 inert, moony, slack, voice 6 asleep, docile, draggy, frigid, latent, static, stolid, torpid 7 dormant, servile 8 enduring, inactive, indolent, lamblike, lifeless, listless, obedient, resigned, slothful, sluggish, stagnant, yielding 9 apathetic, compliant, lethargic, quiescent, receptive, sedentary, tractable 10 disengaged, nonviolent, phlegmatic, submissive, unreactive
be ~: 5 sit by 6 ignore, submit 7 tune out 8 vegetate
protest: 5 sit-in
restraint: 6 airbag
passiveness: 8 laziness, lethargy, meekness 10 compliance, submission
passivity: 7 laxness
__ Passos: 3 Dos 7 John Dos
Passover: 5 Pasch
beverage: 4 wine
bread: 5 matzo 6 matzah, matzoh
meal: 5 seder
prayer: 6 Hallel
time from ~ to Shavuoth: 4 omer
passport: 2 ID 6 entrée, ID card, papers, permit, ticket
automobile ~: 6 carnet
department: 5 State
entry: 5 stamp
requirement: 5 photo 7 picture 8 snapshot 10 photograph
stamp: 4 visa
Passport: 3 SUV 5 Honda
pass the __: 3 hat 4 buck, time 5 torch
password: 3 key 4 word 6 parole, signal 9 watchword 10 open sesame
enter one's ~: 5 log in
know the ~: 5 enter, get in 6 access
Password: 8 game show
host: Allen Ludden
Passy, Frédéric: 6 French 8 Nobelist
past: 3 ago, eld, old 4 done, gone, late, lost, once, over, time, yore 5 ended, prior 6 beyond, bygone, former, gone by, lapsed, recent 7 defunct, earlier, elapsed, history, long ago, old-time, one-time, quondam, through 8 anterior, back then, back when, finished, foregone, long gone, obsolete, old times, outgoing, previous, years ago 9 antiquity, erstwhile, foregoing, forgotten, olden days, out-of-date, preceding, yesterday 10 historical, out of style, yesteryear
behavior: 4 file 6 record 7 dossier
brush ~: 5 graze, touch
combining form: 6 preter- 7 praeter-
dig into the ~: 6 recall 8 remember
due: 4 late 5 tardy 6 behind, unpaid
edge ~: 4 inch 5 sidle, skirt
events: 6 annals 7 account, history 9 chronicle, olden days, posterity, recountal
from ages ~: 3 old 5 early, hoary, of old, olden 7 ancient 8 primeval 9 primitive, venerable 10 primordial
from years ~: 3 old 6 bygone 7 archaic 8 outmoded
get ~: 3 ace 4 beat 5 clear, outdo, score, steer 6 detour 7 resolve 8 maneuver, outstrip, overtake 9 negotiate
go ~: 4 omit, skip 6 exceed 9 overshoot
graze ~: 5 brush, touch
in the ~: 3 ago, ere 4 once, then 6 before, erenow 7 long ago 8 formerly 9 at one time, a while ago 10 heretofore, previously
it flows ~ the Winter Palace: 4 Neva
it may be ~: 5 tense
its prime: 3 old 5 moldy, passé, stale 7 has-been
master: 4 guru 5 adept 6 expert, old pro
object from the ~: 4 idol 5 mummy, relic, stele 6 fossil, scroll 7 antique 8 artifact
play ~: 6 forget, ignore 8 overlook
prefix: 4 para- 6 preter-
recent ~: 7 just now 8 last week, last year 9 last month, yesterday 10 not long ago
slip ~: 4 edge
story of the ~: 4 epic, myth, saga, tale 6 legend
the deadline: 4 late
past __: 3 due 5 tense 6 master 7 perfect
pasta: 4 carb, orzo, ziti 5 carbo, penne, tubes, zitti 6 ditali, elbows, noodle, rigati, shells 7 fusilli, gnocchi, lasagna, lasagne, noodles, pastina, ravioli, rotelle, spirals 8 bucatini, couscous, farfalle, linguine, linguini, macaroni, rigatoni 9 agnolotti, alphabets, angelhair, cavatelli, maccaroni, manicotti, spaghetti 10 cannelloni, conchiglie, fettuccine, fettuccini, tagliarini, tortellini, vermicelli
alternative: 4 rice 6 potato 8 potatoes
bow tie ~: 8 farfalle
flat ~: 6 noodle 7 lasagna, lasagne 8 linguine, linguini 10 fettuccini
granular ~: 4 orzo 8 couscous
half-moon ~: 9 agnolotti
in brand names: 4 Roni
Japanese ~: 5 ramen 6 larmen
long ~: 9 angelhair, spaghetti 10 vermicelli
maker's need: 5 flour
maker's wheat: 5 durum
on a Chinese menu: 4 mein
pellet-sized ~: 6 farfel
ricelike ~: 4 orzo
ring-shaped ~: 10 tortellini
shape: 5 elbow, shell 6 bowtie
shell ~: 9 cavatelli
square pocket ~: 7 ravioli
tiny piece ~: 7 pastina
topping: 5 herbs, pesto, sauce 6 cheese 8 marinara, Parmesan 9 meatballs
tube ~: 4 ziti 5 penne, zitti 9 manicotti 10 cannelloni
pasta __: 6 fazool
pasta al __: 5 dente
pasta sauce: 4 Ragu 5 Prego 6 Prince 8 Classico 10 Newman's Own 11 Aunt Millie's
paste: 2 KO 3 fix, gem, goo, gum 4 bash, belt, bond, glue, mall, maul, pulp, rout, slug, sock, tack, verb, whup 5 affix, pound, stick 6 adhere, batter, cement, fasten, thrash, thwack, wallop 7 clobber, stickum, trounce 8 adhesive, fixative, mucilage
artist's ~: 5 gesso
edible ~: 5 guava 6 tomato
ender: 5 board
fruit used for ~: 5 guava
liver ~: 4 pâté
soybean ~: 4 miso, tofu
starter: 5 tooth
__ paste: 4 hard, puff, soft 6 almond, sesame 7 library, Turkish
pastel: 4 pale, soft 5 light, muted 8 delicate
artist's ~: 5 chalk
color: 4 aqua, pink 5 lilac 8 baby-blue, lavender
Pasternak, Boris: 4 poet 6 writer 7 Russian 8 Nobelist
heroine: 4 Lara
work: Doctor Zhivago
Safe Conduct

paste-up: 5 model
pasteurized: 4 pure 7 sterile
not ~: 3 raw
product: 4 milk 5 honey
pasteurizing
plant: 5 dairy 8 creamery
Pasteur, Louis: 7 chemist
pasticcio: 4 olio 6 medley 7 mélange 8 mishmash 9 potpourri 10 hodgepodge, miscellany, salmagundi
pastiche: 4 olio 6 jumble, medley 7 collage, lampoon, mélange 8 mishmash 9 patchwork, potpourri, synthesis, work of art 10 assortment, collection, cumulation, hodgepodge, miscellany, salmagundi
pastille: 6 troche 7 lozenge
pastime: 3 fun 4 game, play 5 hobby, sport 6 escape 7 pursuit 8 activity, interest, jump rope 9 amusement, avocation, diversion 10 recreation, relaxation
__ past is prologue: 5 What's
Pasto: 4 city, town
locale: 8 Colombia
pastor: 4 abbé 5 padre, vicar 6 cleric, father, parson, priest, rector 8 chaplain, minister, preacher, reverend, shepherd 10 missionary
flock: 5 laity 8 faithful 9 laypeople
pastoral: 4 calm, idyl 5 idyll, rural 6 rustic, serene, silvan, simple, sylvan 7 bucolic, country, eclogue, idyllic, nomadic 8 agrarian, Arcadian, clerical, farmlike, tranquil 9 bucolical, episcopal 10 provincial
deity: 3 Pan 4 faun 8 Silvanus
far from ~: 5 urban 8 citified
poem: 4 idyl 5 idyll
spot: 3 lea, ley 5 field, glade 6 meadow
pastoral __: 5 staff 6 letter, prayer
pastorale: 5 music
Pastorale d'__: 3 Été
Pastorals author: Alexander Pope
Pastoral Symphony composer: 9 Beethoven
pastorate: 6 clergy
__ Pastore: 4 Il re
pastrami: 4 meat
partner: 3 rye
seller: 4 deli
pastry: 4 puff, tart 5 donut, scone, torte, twist 6 cornet, Danish, éclair, kuchen, phyllo, quiche 7 baklava, bear paw, beignet, cannoli, cruller, crumpet, fritter, popover, strudel, timbale 8 clafouti, crescent, doughnut, meringue, napoleon, roly-poly, turnover 9 cream puff, madeleine, petit four, schnecken, sweet roll 10 baba au rhum, coffee roll, confection, feuilletée, frangipane, sopaipilla
cheese ~: 6 Danish
chef, at times: 4 icer
custard-filled ~: 6 éclair
filler: 3 jam 5 creme, fruit, jelly 7 custard
Mexican ~: 6 churro
pro: 4 chef, cook 5 baker
prune ~ filling: 6 lekvar
Queen of Hearts' ~: 4 tart
seller: 4 café 5 diner 6 bakery, eatery 10 coffee shop
tissue-thin ~: 4 filo
pastry __: 4 chef, tube 5 brush 7 blender
__ pastry: 4 chou, puff 6 Danish, French 7 toaster
pasturage: 3 hay 4 feed 7 verdure
pasture: 3 lea, ley, sod 5 field, grass, range, veldt 6 meadow 7 prairie, verdure 9 grassland
crop: 5 grass 6 clover, forage 7 alfalfa
divider: 5 fence 8 barb-wire 10 barbed wire
entry: 4 gate 5 stile
grass: 5 grama 6 fescue, redtop 7 festuca
grazer: 3 cow, ewe, ram 4 bull, calf, colt, foal, goat, mare, mule, pony 5 burro, filly, horse, llama, sheep 6 donkey 8 stallion
in poetry: 3 lea 4 mead
lands: 5 acres
plaint: 3 baa, maa, moo 5 bleat, neigh 6 hee-haw 7 whinney
pasty: 3 wan 4 ashy, dull, pale 5 ashen, gluey, livid, waxen, white 6 anemic, clayey, doughy, pallid, sallow, sickly 7 anaemic, clayish, greyish, meat pie 9 bloodless, unhealthy 10 exsanguine
pasty-__: 5 faced
P.A. system component: 3 amp
pat: 3 apt, dab, pet, rub, set, tap 4 daub, glib, lump, mold 5 flick, shape, slick, touch 6 caress, dollop, facile, fondle, smooth, soothe, stroke, tickle, timely 7 apropos, exactly, fitting 8 apposite, suitable 9 contrived, opportune, perfectly, precisely, rehearsed 10 flawlessly, stationary, understood
an infant: 4 burp
down: 4 tamp 5 frisk
dry: 4 blot
gently: 3 dab
get down ~: 4 know 5 learn 6 master 8 memorize
oneself on the back: 4 brag 5 boast, gloat 7 swagger
on the back: 4 hail, kudo, laud 5 exalt, extol, honor, kudos 6 credit, extoll, homage, praise, salute 7 acclaim, applaud, commend, flatter, glorify, plaudit, tribute 8 accolade, approval, encomium, flattery, good word 9 laudation, panegyric, patronize 10 compliment, exaltation, panegyrize
stand ~: 4 stay 6 endure, remain, resist 7 persist
pat __: 4 down, hand
pat-__: 5 a-cake
__ pat: 5 stand
Pat: 3 Day 4 Cash, host 5 Boone, emcee, Nixon, Riley, Sajak 6 Conroy, Cooper, Corley, Hingle, Morita, O'Brien, Priest 7 Benatar, Buttram, Carroll, Crowley, Garrett, Lawford, Metheny, O'Connor, Paulsen 8 Buchanan, Moynihan, Oliphant, Sullivan 9 Robertson, Schroeder, Summerall
Pat __ Mike: 3 and
pataca fraction: 3 avo
Patagonia
cowboy: 6 gaucho
locale: 9 Argentina
plain: 5 pampa 6 pampas
steer stopper: 4 bola
Pat and Mike (1952 film)
cast: Katharine Hepburn, Aldo Ray, Spencer Tracy
director: George Cukor
Pata Pata (1967 song) artist: Miriam Makeba
Patapsco, city on the: 9 Baltimore
patch: 3 bed, fix, lot, sew 4 area, blob, blot, darn, mend, plot, spot, vamp 5 clump, cover, field, piece, resew, scrap, spell, strip, tract 6 cobble, doctor, emblem, garden, ground, iron-on, repair, stitch 7 cover up, insigne, restore, retread, stretch, touch up 8 appliqué, insignia, overhaul
berry ~ hazard: 4 bear 5 briar, brier, thorn 7 prickle
ender: 4 work
item in a ~: 3 pea 5 melon 10 watermelon
pavement: 5 retar
place for a ~: 4 knee
site: 3 jag, rip 4 hole, tear 5 split
starter: 5 cross
things up: 6 soothe 7 mollify, placate 9 reconcile 10 conciliate
up: 7 retouch
patch __: 4 cord, reef, test 6 pocket
__ patch: 3 oil 4 skin 5 brood, panel 6 cinder, iron-on, router 8 shoulder
Patch: 3 Dan
Patch Adams (1998 film)
cast: Philip Seymour Hoffman, Daniel London, Monica Potter, Robin Williams
director: Tom Shadyac
patched: 3 old 4 worn 6 ragged 7 worn out
Patchen, Kenneth: 4 poet
Patches (song) artist: Clarence Carter, Dickey Lee
patching compound: 5 putty
__ Patch Kids: 7 Cabbage
Patch of Blue, A (1965 film)
cast: Elizabeth Hartman, Sidney Poitier, Shelley Winters
director: Guy Green
patchwork: 4 hash, olio 5 quilt 6 calico, jumble, medley, muddle, tangle 7 grab bag, mélange 8 disorder, mishmash, pastiche 9 checkered, confusion, makeshift, potpourri 10 hodgepodge, improvised, miscellany, salmagundi
product: 5 quilt
Patchwork Planet author: Anne Tyler
patchy: 4 pied 6 fitful, random, spotty, uneven 7 erratic, sketchy, varying 8 speckled, variable 9 imperfect, irregular, piecemeal 10 nonuniform
pate: 4 head 5 crown 6 noggin
topper: 3 wig 4 fall, hair 6 toupee 7 tresses 9 hairpiece
pâte __: 4 dure 5 à chou 6 tendre
pâté: 4 meat 5 paste 6 spread 9 appetizer
base: 4 foie 5 liver
Patek: 7 Freddie
Patek Philippe competitor: 5 Rolex
patella: 4 bone 7 kneecap
locale: 4 knee
neighbor: 5 femur, tibia 6 fibula
paten: 5 plate
patent: 4 open 5 clear, gross, naked, overt, plain, stark 6 in view, marked, permit, public 7 blatant, evident, exposed, glaring, license, obvious, visible 8 apparent, clear-cut, distinct, explicit, flagrant, knowable, manifest, monopoly, palpable, registry, unhidden, unsubtle, unveiled 9 franchise, ownership 10 concession, monopolize, observable, undeniable, unshrouded
kin: 9 copyright, trademark
medicine: 5 tonic 6 elixir, remedy 7 panacea 8 snake oil
office: 3 PTO
subject: 6 device, gadget 9 discovery, invention
patent __: 3 log 4 slip 5 flour, right 6 hammer, office 7 leather
patently: 8 markedly
true: 9 axiomatic
pater: 3 dad, pop 4 papa, pops 5 daddy, poppa 6 father 9 family man
daughter: 5 filia
partner: 5 mater
son: 6 filius
paternal: 4 male 6 agnate 8 fatherly, parental 10 protective
paternity: 6 source 10 fatherhood
paternity __: 5 leave
Paterno, Joe: 5 coach
sport: 8 football
Paterson: 4 city, town
locale: 9 New Jersey
Paterson author: William Carlos Williams
Pater, Walter: 6 writer 7 British 8 essayist
path: 3 way 4 lane, line, road, slog, tack, walk 5 aisle, alley, byway, means, orbit, route, steps, track, trail 6 access, avenue, course 7 bikeway, footway, ingress, passage, walkway 8 approach, shortcut 9 concourse, direction, esplanade, itinerary
alternative ~: 5 shunt 6 detour
ball's ~: 3 arc
beaten ~: 3 rut 5 track, trail
bike ~: 4 lane
bridal ~: 5 aisle
bridle ~: 5 trail
car's ~: 4 lane, pike, road 5 alley 6 avenue, street 7 highway 8 turnpike 9 boulevard 10 expressway
Chinese ~: 3 Tao
circular ~: 3 arc 5 orbit
dirt ~: 5 track, trail
ender: 3 way 6 finder
flight ~: 6 airway, ascent 8 jet route
go off the beaten ~: 4 rove 5 stray 6 wander 7 explore
hiking ~: 5 trace, track, trail
in a glacier's ~: 5 stoss
lawnmower ~: 5 swath 6 swathe
lead up the garden ~: 7 deceive 8 misguide
lob ~: 3 bow 5 curve 8 crescent, half-moon
moon ~: 3 arc 5 orbit
off the ~: 4 lost 6 astray
off the beaten ~: 6 afield, remote
perplexing ~: 4 maze 9 labyrinth
planetary ~: 3 arc 4 oval 5 orbit
raised ~: 4 berm, dike 5 berme, levee 8 causeway 10 embankment
river ~: 4 flow 6 course 7 channel
satellite ~: 3 arc 5 orbit
scythe ~: 5 swath 6 swathe
sprinter's ~: 4 lane
starter: 3 tow, war 4 foot, tele 5 osteo
to success: 5 rungs 6 ladder
user: 5 hiker 6 walker 7 tourist 9 sightseer
wilderness ~: 5 trace, track, trail
__ path: 4 bike 5 glide 6 beaten, bridle, flight 7 bicycle, optical
Pathet __: 3 Lao
pathetic: 3 sad 4 lame, poor, puny, weak 5 sorry, woful 6 crumby, crummy, feeble, meager, measly, moving, paltry, tragic, woeful 7 piteous, pitiful, tearful, useless 8 pitiable, poignant, touching, tragical, unusable, wretched 9 affecting, miserable, plaintive, sniveling, third-rate, worthless 10 deplorable, inadequate, lamentable
Pathétique Sonata composer: 9 Beethoven
Pathétique Symphony composer: 11 Tchaikovsky
pathfinder: 5 guide, scout 7 pioneer 8 explorer 10 discoverer
Pathfinder: 3 SUV 5 probe 6 Nissan
destination: 4 Mars
launcher: 4 NASA
Pathfinder, The
author: James Fenimore Cooper
character: 5 Mabel, McNab, Natty 6 Bumppo, Jasper
path of __ resistance: 5 least
Path of Dalliance author: Auburon Waugh
pathogen: 4 germ 5 staph, toxin 7 microbe 9 bacterium
pathophobe fear: 7 disease

pathos: 4 pity 5 drama 7 emotion, feeling, sadness 8 sympathy 9 poignancy, sentiment 10 compassion, desolation, heavy heart
sign of ~: 4 sigh, tear
Paths of Glory (1957 film)
cast: Kirk Douglas, Ralph Meeker, Adolphe Menjou
director: Stanley Kubrick
Path to Rome, The author: Hilaire Belloc
pathway: 4 lane, path, road, walk 5 alley, trace, track, trail 6 artery, avenue 7 channel, ingress 8 crossing
blood ~: 4 vein 6 artery 9 capillary
sloped ~: 4 ramp
supermarket ~: 5 aisle
winding ~: 4 maze 9 labyrinth
patience: 4 game, legs 5 poise 6 lenity, starch 8 calmness, card game, kindness, lenience, stoicism 9 diligence, endurance, fortitude, restraint, tolerance 10 equanimity, even temper, indulgence, moderation
cultivate ~: 4 wait 7 refrain 8 restrain
in America: 9 solitaire
lost one's ~: 5 had it 6 blew up 8 exploded 9 blew a fuse 10 came down on
out of ~: 5 fed up 6 fuming
strain one's ~: 3 irk, try 5 weary 7 provoke
patience __ saint: 3 of a
Patience (1989 song) artist: Guns N' Roses
Patience composer: 7 Gilbert 8 Sullivan
Patience of a Saint author: Andrew Greeley
Patience & Prudence song: Tonight You Belong to Me (1956)
patient: 4 calm, case, meek, mild 5 stoic, type B 6 client, dogged, gentle, inmate, serene, shut-in, steady 7 stoical, subject 8 enduring, resigned, resolute, sufferer, tolerant, untiring 9 easygoing, forgiving, unruffled 10 forbearing, outpatient, unflagging
attendant: 2 RN 4 aide 5 nurse 6 doctor, medico 7 orderly 9 physician
be ~: 3 sit 4 wait 5 await 6 endure, hang on 7 refrain, stand by
pediatrician ~: 3 kid, tot 4 baby 5 child, minor 6 infant 9 youngster
place: 6 clinic 8 hospital 9 ambulance
response: 2 ow 3 aah, yow 4 ouch 6 aaargh
vet ~: 3 cat, cow, cur, dog, ewe, hog, pet, pig, pup, ram, sow 4 bull, calf, colt, foal, goat, lamb, mare, mutt, pony 5 horse, hound, kitty, pooch, puppy, pussy, sheep, tabby 6 animal, canine, feline, kitten, parrot 7 mongrel 8 stallion
patient-care group: 3 HMO
Patientia: 8 asteroid
__ Patient, The: 7 English
patina: 4 film, rust 5 glaze, oxide, sheen, shine 6 finish 7 coating
Patinkin, Mandy: 5 actor
film: The Adventures of Elmo in Grouchland (1999)
Daniel (1983)
Impromptu (1991)
Maxie (1985)
The Princess Bride (1987)
Squanto: A Warrior's Tale (1994)
Yentl (1983)
TV: Chicago Hope
patio: 4 yard 5 court 9 courtyard, peristyle
appliance: 5 grill 6 hot tub 7 hibachi
block: 5 paver
cousin: 4 deck 5 lanai
enclosed ~: 5 court 6 atrium 9 courtyard
furniture: 5 chair, swing, table 6 chaise, glider 8 umbrella
on the ~: 7 outside 8 al fresco, outdoors
server: 4 cart
site: 4 lawn, yard
patisserie: 6 bakery
offering: 4 tart 5 tarte 6 éclair, gateau, pastry 9 cream puff
Patmore, Coventry: 4 poet
Pátmos: 3 isl. 4 isle 6 island
locale: 6 Greece
Patna: 4 city, town
locale: 5 India
river: 6 Ganges
state: 5 Behar, Bihar
patois: 4 cant, talk 5 argot, gumbo, idiom, lingo, slang 6 jargon, patter, tongue 7 dialect 8 language, localism, parlance 9 academese 10 vernacular
Paton, Alan: 6 writer 12 South African
work: Cry, the Beloved Country
pat on the __: 4 back
Patras: 4 gulf, port
location: 6 Greece
__ Patri: 6 Gloria
__ patriae: 4 amor
patriarch: 4 male, rank 5 elder, title 6 bishop, cleric, father, senior 9 graybeard 10 forebearer
deputy: 6 exarch
patriarchal: 6 lineal 9 ancestral
Patric: 5 Jason 7 Knowles
Patricia: 4 Neal 5 Ellis, Nixon 6 Heaton, Wettig 8 Arquette, Clarkson, Cornwell, Kalember 9 Highsmith, Schroeder 10 Richardson
Patricia (1958 song) artist: Perez Prado
patrician: 4 peer 5 baron, noble, royal 6 aristo 8 highborn, nobleman, wellborn, well-bred 9 blue blood, gentleman 10 aristocrat, upper-class, upper-crust
opposite: 4 pleb 5 slave 6 common, humble 7 plebian 8 commoner 10 lower-class
patricians: 5 lords 6 gentry 7 peerage 8 nobility 10 upper class 11 aristocracy
Patrick: 4 Gail, John 5 Butch, Duffy, Ewing, Henry, Leahy, Magee, Nigel, O'Neal, saint, White 6 Dennis, Macnee, O'Brian, Rafter, Robert, Swayze 7 Cassidy, Dempsey, Stewart 8 Blackett, McGoohan 9 Kavanaugh
in Irish: 7 Padraic, Padraig
Patrick, Gail: 7 actress
film: The Lone Wolf Returns (1935)
Mad About Music (1938)
My Favorite Wife (1940)
My Man Godfrey (1936)
Up in Mabel's Room (1944)
Patrick, Saint
land: 4 Eire, Erin 7 Ireland
service: 4 Mass
Patrick's Day, Saint
color: 5 green
dance: 3 jig
month: 5 March
musician: 5 piper
patrimony: 6 estate, legacy 7 bequest
patriot: 4 hawk 8 jingoist, loyalist 9 flag-waver
ender: 3 ism
Patriot
rival: 3 Jet, Ram 4 Bear, Bill, Colt, Lion 5 Brown, Chief, Eagle, Giant, Raven, Saint, Texan, Titan 6 Bengal, Bronco, Cowboy, Falcon, Jaguar, Packer, Raider, Viking 7 Charger, Dolphin, Panther, Redskin, Seahawk, Steeler 8 Cardinal 9 Buccaneer
Patriot Day's month: 5 April
Patriot Games (1992 film)
cast: Anne Archer, Patrick Bergin, Harrison Ford
character: 4 Ryan
director: Phillip Noyce
org.: 3 IRA
patriotic: 4 true 5 loyal 7 hawkish 9 right-wing 10 flag-waving, jingoistic
organization: 3 DAR, SAR
song: 6 anthem
symbol: 4 flag
Patriotic Gore author: Edmund Wilson
patriotism: 7 loyalty 8 jingoism
Patriot missile: 3 ABM
target: 4 Scud
Patriots: 4 team 6 eleven
home: 6 Boston 10 New England
org.: 3 AFC, NFL
sport: 8 football
Patriot, The (2000 film)
cast: Chris Cooper, Mel Gibson, Heath Ledger, Joely Richardson
director: Roland Emmerich
patrol: 3 spy 4 beat, pace, walk 5 guard, scout, watch 6 cruise, defend, detail, picket, police, rounds 7 inspect, lookout, protect 8 sentinel, squadron 9 keep watch, safeguard 10 detachment
boat: 5 aviso
ender: 3 man, men 5 woman, women
one on ~: 3 cop 6 sentry 7 lookout, officer 9 policeman 11 policewoman
what a ~ car might get: 3 APB
patrol __: 3 car 5 wagon
__ patrol: 5 shore 7 highway
__ Patrol: 3 Rat
patrolman: 3 cop 4 fuzz 6 Smokey 7 trooper
__ Patrol, The: 4 Dawn, Lost
patron: 4 user 5 angel, buyer, donor, urger 6 backer, client, friend, helper, vendee, votary 7 admirer, booster, grantor, habitué, shopper, sponsor 8 champion, customer, financer 9 guarantor, proponent, purchaser, supporter 10 benefactor, frequenter, well-wisher
diner ~: 5 eater
ender: 3 age, ess
patron __: 5 saint
patronage: 3 aid 4 egis, help 5 aegis, grant, trade 6 buying, custom 7 backing, funding, keeping, subsidy, support, traffic 8 auspices, business, commerce, cronyism, regulars, shopping 9 clientele, financing, following, promotion 10 assistance, pork barrel, protection
political ~: 4 pork
patronize: 3 use 4 back, fund 5 buy at, deign, favor, stoop, trust 6 foster, shop at 7 buy from, promote, sponsor, stoop to, support 8 deal with, frequent, purchase 9 cultivate, hang out at, shine up to, trade with 10 condescend, look down on, talk down to
a restaurant: 3 eat 4 dine 5 order
patronizing: 5 lofty 6 lordly, snobby, snooty 7 haughty, high-hat 8 snobbish, superior
patron of the __: 4 arts
patrons: 8 habitués, regulars 9 clientele, following
soup-kitchen ~: 4 poor 5 needy 8 homeless
patron saints
accountants: Matthew
actors: Genesius
airline passengers: Joseph of Cupertino
Americas: Rose of Lima
anesthetists: Rene Goupil
animals: Francis of Assisi
archers: Sebastian
architects: Barbara, Thomas
arthritis: James the Greater
astronauts: Joseph of Cupertino
astronomers: Dominic
aviators: Our Lady of Loreto, Therese of Lisieux
bachelors: Casimir of Poland
bad weather: Medard, Scholastica
bakers: Elizabeth of Hungary, Nicholas of Myra
bankers: Matthew
barbers: Cosmas, Damian, Louis IX, Martin de Porres
basket makers: Anthony the Abbot
bee keepers: Ambrose
beggars: Giles
bellringers: Agatha
blackbirds: Kevin
blacksmiths: Dunstan
blood banks: Januarius
bodily ills: Our Lady of Lourdes
bookbinders: Peter Celestine
booksellers: John of God
boys: John Bosco
brewers: Augustine
bricklayers: Stephen
brides: Nicholas of Myra
business women: Margaret of Clitherow
butchers: Anthony the Abbot
charities: Vincent de Paul
Chile: James the Greater
civil servants: Thomas More
comedians: Vitus
computer users: Isidore of Seville
contemplatives: John of the Cross
cooks: Lawrence, Martha
cows: Perpetua
dancers: Vitus
dentists: Apollonia
disasters: Genevieve
dogs: Hubert, Roch
domestic animals: Antony
doves: David
drought relief: Godeberta, Herbert
earaches: Polycarp
ecologists: Francis of Assisi
embroiderers: Clare
England: George
epidemics: Godeberta
farmers: Isidore the Farmer
fear of rats and mice: Gertrude
fear of snakes: Patrick
firefighters: Florian
fire prevention: Lawrence
fishermen: Andrew, Peter
florists: Rose of Lima, Therese of Lisieux
flyers: Michael
foreign missions: Francis Xavier
France: Denis, Denys
gardeners: Adelard
glassworkers: Luke
goldsmiths: Dunstan
gout: Maurice
hairdressers: Martin de Porres
headaches: Denis, Denys, Teresa of Avila
horsemen: Martin of Tours
hospitals: John of God
housewives: Anne, Martha
Hungary: Elizabeth of Hungary
hunters: Eustachius, Hubert
in-law problems: Elizabeth Ann Seton
innkeepers: Amand
Ireland: Brigid, Patrick
Italy: Catherine of Siena
jewelers: Eligius
judges: John of Capistrano
jury members: John of Capistrano

knee problems: Roch
lambs: John the Baptist
lawyers: Mark
learning: Thomas Aquinas
librarians: Jerome
lions: Mark
longevity: Peter
lost articles: Anthony of Padua
lost causes: Jude
lost keys: Zita
lovers: Valentine
maids: Zita
marble workers: Clement
marriages: Edward the Confessor
married women: Monica
medical technicians: Albertus Magnus
metalworkers: Eligius
Mexico: Our Lady of Guadalupe
mothers: Anne
music: Cecilia, Gregory
Naples: Januarius
orators: John Chrysostom
painters: Luke
paratroopers: Michael
Paris: Genevieve
pawnbrokers: Nicholas of Myra
pharmacists: Cosmas, Damian
Philippines: Rose of Lima
philosophers: Catherine of Alexandria
physicians: Cosmas, Damian, Luke
plasterers: Bartholomew
poets: David
Poland: Florian
poor: Giles
postal workers: Gabriel the Archangel
pregnant women: Margaret
priests: John Vianney
prisoners: Dismas
racial harmony: Martin de Porres
radio: Gabriel the Archangel
resolving of schisms: Cyril, Methodius
rheumatism: James the Greater
sailors: Elmo
Scandanavia: Ansgar
schools: Thomas Aquinas
scientists: Albertus Magnus
sculptors: Claude
Serbia: Sava
servants: Martha
shepherds: Bernadette
shoemakers: Crispin
silversmiths: Andronicus
sinners: Mary Magdalene
skaters: Lidwina
skiers: Bernard
snake bite victims: Hilary, Paul
soldiers: Ignatius, Joan of Arc, Martin of Tours
stonemasons: Stephen
students: Benedict
swordsmiths: Maurice
tax collectors: Matthew
taxi drivers: Fiacre
teenagers: Aloysius
television: Clare
theater: Genesius
thunderstorms: Barbara
travelers: Anthony of Padua, Christopher
undertakers: Joseph of Arimathea
volcanoes: Januarius
volunteers: Vincent de Paul
Wales: David
weavers: Maurice
winegrowers: Vincent of Saragossa
writers: Francis de Sales, John the Apostle
young girls: Agnes
patronymic: 4 name 7 surname 8 cognomen
patroons: 6 gentry
Patros: 4 city, town
locale: 6 Greece
Pats
see Patriots
patsy: 3 ass, oaf, sap 4 boob, butt, clod, dolt, dupe, foil, fool, goat, gull, lamb, mark, pawn, prey, tool 5 chump, clown, cluck, dummy, dunce, joker, ninny 6 dimwit, hunted, lummox, nitwit, pigeon, puppet, stooge, sucker, target, turkey, victim 7 buffoon, cat's-paw, dingbat, doormat, dullard, fall guy, fathead, half-wit, jackass, nebbish, pinhead, saphead 8 bonehead, dumbbell, easy mark, meathead, numskull, pushover 9 birdbrain, blockhead, born loser, lamebrain, numbskull, scapegoat, schlemiel, simpleton 10 dunderhead
Patsy: 5 Cline, Kelly 6 Kensit
patten: 4 boot, shoe 8 footwear
patter: 3 gab, pad, tap, yak 4 beat, blab, cant, drum, jive, line, pelt, rain, talk 5 argot, lingo, pitch, prate, sound, spiel, spout 6 babble, jabber, jargon, patois, rustle, tattoo 7 chatter, pitapat, prattle, rat-a-tat 8 fast talk, hard sell 9 yakety-yak 10 chew the rag, vernacular
glib ~: 4 jive, line 5 pitch, spiel 6 come-on
prideful ~: 4 brag 5 boast
provider: 4 host 5 emcee 6 deejay, vee-jay 10 disc jockey
__-patter: 6 pitter
pattern: 3 rut 4 form, kind, mold, norm, plan, type 5 array, guide, model, motif, order, shape, style 6 custom, design, figure, follow, format, rhythm, sample, scheme, symbol, system 7 emulate, example, fashion, imitate, paragon, stencil, templet, variety 8 exemplar, markings, original, paradigm, specimen, standard, template 9 archetype, prototype 10 decoration, impression, stereotype, touchstone
behavior ~: 5 habit, type A, type B 8 syndrome
fabric ~: 4 dots 5 plaid, print 6 checks 9 polka dots 13 stripes. Argyle
holding ~: 5 delay
intricate ~: 4 maze 9 labyrinth
machine ~: 3 die
oneself after: 4 copy 5 model 6 follow 7 imitate
repetitive ~: 3 rut 5 cycle 6 series 7 routine
rhythmic ~ for a poet: 5 meter
Scottish ~: 5 plaid
speech ~: 6 accent, stress
statistical ~: 5 trend
transfer: 5 rub-on 6 iron-on
wavelike ~: 5 moiré
wood ~: 5 grain
__ pattern: 4 test 5 dress 7 holding, traffic
patterns: 4 ways
Patterns (1956 film)
cast: Ed Begley, Van Heflin, Everett Sloane
director: Fielder Cook
Patterns author: Amy Lowell
Patterson: 5 Floyd, James 6 Melody
Patterson, Floyd: 5 boxer
milieu: 4 ring
Patti: 4 Page 5 Davis, Smith 6 Austin, Hansen, LuPone 7 Adelina, LaBelle
Patti, Adelina: 6 singer 7 soprano
specialty: 5 opera
Patton: 4 Will 6 George
Patton (1970 film)
cast: Karl Malden, George C. Scott, Stephen Young
director: Franklin Schaffner
Patton, George: 7 general
dog: 6 Willie
superior: 3 DDE
vehicle: 4 tank
Patton, Will: 5 actor
film: Entrapment (1999) Remember the Titans (2000) Tollbooth (1994)
patty __: 3 pan 5 shell
patty-__: 4 cake
Patty: 4 Berg, Duke 5 Smyth 6 Hearst 7 Andrews, Sheehan 8 Loveless
Patty Duke Show, The dog: 5 Tiger
pattypan: 6 squash, veggie 9 vegetable
Patuca: 5 river
locale: 8 Honduras
Patwin: 6 Indian 7 Amerind
Pátzcuaro: 4 city, town
locale: 6 Mexico 9 Michoacán
Pau: 4 city, town
locale: 6 France
paucis verbis: 7 briefly
paucity: 4 lack, need, want 6 dearth, famine 7 absence, fewness, poverty 8 exiguity, scarcity, shortage, sparsity 10 deficiency, inadequacy, meagerness, scantiness, sparseness
Pauhunri: 4 peak 5 mount 8 mountain
locale: 4 Asia 5 India, Tibet 6 Thibet, Xizang 7 Sitsang 9 Himalayas
Paul: 3 Fix, Les 4 Anka, Berg, Ford, John, Klee, Leni, Muni, pope, Rudd, Sand, tsar 5 Billy, Boyer, Brown, Burke, Celan, Davis, Dirac, Drake, Dukas, Evans, Flory, Fusco, Green, Hayne, Heyse, Hogan, LeMat, Lukas, Lynde, Nurse, saint, Silas, Simon, Waner, Wylie, Young 6 Adrian, Almond, Annett, Auster, Bartel, Bogart, Bowles, Bunyan, Dooley, Dunbar, Éluard, Erdman, Harvey, Horgan, Karrer, Krasny, Kruger, Masson, Müller, Newman, Powell, Reiser, Revere, Valéry 7 apostle, Azinger, Balluet, Bourget, Carrack, Cézanne, Claudel, Creston, Crutzen, Czinner, Desmond, Douglas, Ehrlich, Gallico, Gauguin, Henreid, Hornung, Kantner, Mauriat, Molitor, pontiff, Reubens, Robeson, Shaffer, Sorvino, Stookey, Theroux, Tillich, Wendkos 8 Benedict, Brickman, Brinegar, Mazursky, Nicholas, Petersen, Sabatier, Schrader, Scofield, Verlaine, Warfield, Whiteman, Williams, Winchell, Winfield, Wolfgang 9 Alexandra, Greengard, Hindemith, McCartney, Morrissey, Prudhomme, Samuelson, Schneider, Verhoeven 10 Hindenburg
companion of ~: 5 Demas, Silas, Titus 7 Artemas 8 Crescens
in Italian: 5 Paolo
in Russian: 5 Pavel
in Spanish: 5 Pablo
Paul __ Glaser: 7 Michael
Paul __ Hindenburg: 3 von
__ Paul: 3 Oom 4 Tall
Paula: 4 Cole, Zahn 5 Abdul 6 Devicq 8 Prentiss 10 Poundstone
__ Paula: 3 Hey
Paula author: Isabel Allende
__, Paul and Mary: 5 Peter
Paul and Mary Ford, Les song: Hummingbird (1955)
Paul and Paula
song: Hey Paula (1963) Young Lovers (1963)
__-Paul Belmondo: 4 Jean
Paul, Billy song: Me and Mrs. Jones (1972)
Paulette: 7 Goddard
Pauley, Jane spouse: Garry Trudeau
__ Paul Getty: 4 Jean
Paulie (1998 film)
cast: Bruce Davison, Cheech Marin, Gena Rowlands, Tony Shalhoub
director: John Roberts
__ Paul II: 4 John
Paulina: 9 Porizkova
Pauline: 4 Kael 7 Collins
adventure: 5 peril
Pauline author: Robert Browning
Pauling, Linus: 7 chemist 8 Nobelist
Paulinus: 5 saint
Paulista: 4 city, town
locale: 6 Brazil
Pauli, Wolfgang: 8 Nobelist 9 physicist
__ Paul Jones: 4 John
__ Paul Kruger: 3 Oom
Paul, Les: 9 guitarist
tune: 4 Nola
__ Paul Marat: 4 Jean
Paul Michael __: 6 Glaser
__ Paulo: 3 Sao
Paul Pry: 7 meddler 8 quidnunc 9 buttinsky
Paul Revere's Ride author: Longfellow
__ Paul Rubens: 5 Peter
__-Paul Sartre: 4 Jean
Paul's Case author: Willa Cather
Paulsen: 3 Pat 4 Axel 6 Albert
Pauly: 5 Shore
__-Pauncefote Treaty: 3 Hay
paunch: 3 gut 5 belly, bulge, tummy 7 abdomen, stomach 8 potbelly 9 bay window, beer belly, spare tire
paunchy: 5 beefy, fubsy, obese, plump, pudgy, pursy, stout 6 chubby, fleshy, portly, pyknic, rotund, stocky, zaftig, zoftig 7 adipose 8 roly-poly 9 corpulent 10 abdominous, overweight
pauper: 6 beggar 7 have-not 8 bankrupt, indigent 9 mendicant 10 supplicant
pauperism: 7 beggary 10 bankruptcy
pauperize: 5 break 6 reduce 8 straiten 10 impoverish
pauperized: 5 broke, needy 6 bad off, hard up, in need, in want 7 pinched 8 bankrupt, beggarly, homeless, indigent, strapped 9 destitute, insolvent, moneyless, penniless, penurious 10 down and out, straitened
Pausanias: 5 Greek 9 historian 10 geographer
pause: 3 gap 4 halt, hush, lull, rest, stay, stop, wait 5 break, cease, comma, delay, hitch, hover, lapse, letup, stand, tarry, truce, waver 6 boggle, breath, cesura, desist, freeze, hiatus, lacuna, loiter, recess 7 caesura, interim, leisure, reflect, respite, scruple, take ten, time out 8 abeyance, breather, call time, downtime, hesitate, intermit, interval, reprieve, take five 9 cessation, hesitancy, interlude, stalemate, vacillate 10 deliberate, hesitation, moratorium, standstill, suspension, take a break, think twice
Biblical ~: 5 selah
continue without ~: 5 segue 9 keep going
give ~: 3 cow 4 faze 5 alarm, daunt, deter, shake, worry 6 bemuse, dismay 7 overawe, unnerve 8 bewilder, dispirit, frighten 10 demoralize, discourage, dishearten, intimidate
indicator: 5 colon, comma 6 period 9 semi-colon
in music: 7 fermata
speaker's ~: 2 er, uh, um 3 hmm
that refreshes: 3 nap 6 catnap, siesta, snooze
__ pauvre: 7 nouveau
Pavan: 6 Marisa
pavane: 5 dance, music
accompaniment: 4 lute

Pavarotti, Luciano: 5 tenor 6 singer 7 Italian
milieu: 5 opera
piece: 4 aria
pave: 3 tar 4 tile 7 encrust, incrust, surface 8 blacktop 9 resurface 10 macadamize
anew: 5 retar, retop 9 resurface
the way: 4 ease 5 ready, usher 6 enable, get set, smooth 9 introduce 10 facilitate
Pavel: 9 Cherenkov
in English: 4 Paul
pavement: 4 road 6 street 7 highway 8 concrete, shoulder, sidewalk
pound the ~: 4 walk 7 job-hunt
Pavese, Cesare: 4 poet 7 Italian
work: The House on the Hill
pavid: 5 timid 6 afraid, scared 7 fearful, quaking, shaking 9 terrified, trembling 10 frightened
pavilion: 4 tent 6 canopy, gazebo 7 pergola 9 bandshell
__ Pavilions, The: 3 Far
Pavin, Corey: 6 golfer
milieu: 5 links 6 course
org.: 3 PGA
paving
flaw: 3 rut 4 bump 5 crack 7 pothole
hexagonal ~ stone: 5 favus
hexagonal ~ stones: 4 favi
job: 4 road 6 street 7 highway 8 shoulder, sidewalk
letters: 3 SLO 4 stop 6 detour 7 one-lane 10 lane closed
material: 3 tar 5 rebar 6 cement, gravel 7 asphalt 8 concrete
stone: 4 sett 5 favus 6 cobble
Pavlof: 7 volcano
locale: 6 Alaska
Pavlova, Anna: 6 dancer 8 danseuse
specialty: 6 ballet
Pavlov, Ivan: 7 Russian 8 Nobelist
Pavo: 7 Peacock 13 constellation
neighbor of: 3 Ara
paw: 3 pad, pes 4 foot, hand, hoof, maul, mitt 5 touch 6 claw at, molest 8 forefoot 9 manhandle
bottom: 3 pad 4 palm
starter: 4 cat's 5 south
__-paw: 4 cat's 5 bear's
pawl: 3 bar 5 catch 6 detent
pawn: 4 bond, dupe, gage, hock, mark, tool 5 agent, patsy, token 6 flunky, hunted, lackey, minion, pigeon, pledge, puppet, stooge, sucker, victim 7 cat's-paw, earnest, flunkey, forfeit, hostage, lacquey 8 borrow on, creature, guaranty, henchman, mortgage 9 assurance, guarantee, underling 10 chesspiece, collateral, instrument
ender: 4 shop 6 broker
pawn __: 6 ticket
pawnbroker: 6 lender
Pawnbroker, The (1965 film)
cast: Geraldine Fitzgerald, Brock Peters, Rod Steiger
director: Sidney Lumet
pawned: 6 in hock
Pawnee: 5 Caddo, tribe 6 Indian 7 Amerind 8 language
cousin: 4 Erie
home: 4 tipi 5 tepee 6 teepee
Indian: 7 Arikara
pawpaw: 4 tree 5 fruit
family: 6 annona
relative: 7 soursop
Paw Paw: 4 city, town
locale: 8 Michigan
Pawtucket: 4 city, town
Pax
counterpart: 5 Irene
father of ~: 7 Jupiter
Pax __: 6 Romana
PAX alternative: 3 BET, CMT, MTV, TBS, TLC, TNN, TNT, USA 4 ESPN, HGTV 5 A and E, C-SPAN, Style 6 Noggin, Tech TV, TV Land 7 Court TV, Ovation, SoapNet 8 Lifetime
Paxinou, Katina: 7 actress
Oscar: For Whom the Bell Tolls
Paxton, Bill: 5 actor
film: Apollo 13 (1995)
The Evening Star (1996)
Mighty Joe Young (1998)
One False Move (1992)
A Simple Plan (1998)
Titanic (1997)
Trespass (1992)
Twister (1996)
U-571 (2000)
Weird Science (1985)
pay: 3 fee 4 give, hire, wage 5 atone, bacon, bread, clear, fruit, money, put up, remit, spend, wages, yield 6 adjust, answer, ante up, chip in, defray, expend, fork up, income, kick in, lay out, pony up, profit, rebuke, refund, render, reward, salary, settle 7 bring in, cough up, dish out, fork out, redress, requite, revenue, satisfy, stipend, sweeten 8 be a sport, disburse, earnings, fork over, hand over, kick back, make good, pittance, proceeds, settle up, shell out, square up, take-home 9 allowance, discharge, emolument, indemnify, indemnity, liquidate, make money, plunk down, reimburse, retaliate 10 commission, compensate, emoluments, honorarium, make amends, perquisite, recompense, remunerate, reparation, take care of, underwrite
a call: 3 see 5 visit 6 drop by 10 come around
a premium for: 6 ensure, insure
as a bill: 4 foot
attention: 4 hark, hear, mark, mind, note 5 study, watch 6 harken, listen, notice, regard 7 hearken, look out, observe, respect
attention to: 3 sue, woo 4 tend 5 charm, court, flirt, spark 6 listen 9 visit with
back: 3 fix 5 repay 6 avenge, punish, refund, render, return 7 get even, revenge 8 make good, square up 9 indemnify, reimburse, retaliate 10 recompense
blackmail: 6 ransom
by mail: 5 remit
court to: 3 sue, woo 5 flirt, spark 6 call on
deduction: 3 tax 4 FICA
dirt: 3 ore 4 lode
ender: 3 day, off, ola, out 4 back, load, roll 5 check 6 master
extra ~: 5 bonus 8 overtime
for: 3 buy, own 4 fund, take 5 treat 6 afford, defray 7 finance, redress, support 8 answer to, make good, purchase, shell out 10 recompense
for services: 4 hire, rent 6 employ, engage 7 charter 8 contract
for the use of: 4 hire, rent 5 lease 6 engage 7 charter 8 sublease
heed: 6 attend, beware, listen, notice 7 hearken, observe, respect 8 watch out
hell to ~: 7 censure, penalty 10 punishment
hike: 5 raise 8 increase
hit ~ dirt: 5 score 7 succeed 8 get lucky
homage: 3 bow 4 hail 5 kneel 6 attend, curtsy, revere, salaam, salute 7 curtsey 9 genuflect, prostrate
increase: 4 COLA 5 raise
in kind: 6 avenge 7 get even, requite 9 get back at, retaliate
into the pot: 4 pool 6 ante up, chip in 7 cough up 10 contribute
it doesn't ~: 5 crime
no attention to: 4 snub 6 ignore, slight 7 disobey, neglect, tune out 8 overlook, sneeze at 9 disregard
obeisance: 6 kowtow 9 genuflect
off: 5 bribe 6 grease, redeem, settle, square 7 benefit, satisfy, succeed 8 square up 9 discharge, liquidate
part of: 6 defray
period: 4 week 5 month
promise to ~: 3 IOU 4 debt 9 debenture
the initiation fee: 4 join
the penalty: 5 atone 6 do time
tribute: 5 exalt, extol, honor 6 praise 7 glorify 8 eulogize
TV: 5 cable
two weeks with ~: 7 benefit 8 vacation
up: 4 ante 5 spend 6 settle, square 7 satisfy 8 make good 10 remunerate
with plastic: 3 owe 6 charge
pay __: 3 off, out 4 dirt 5 phone, raise 6 in full, period 7 station
pay __ the nose: 7 through
pay-__-go: 5 as-you
pay-__-view: 3 per
__ pay: 3 net 4 base, half, sick 5 merit 6 flight, strike
payable: 3 due 4 owed 5 owing 6 mature, unpaid 7 overdue 9 unsettled
to: 9 in favor of
when ~: 5 as due
__ payable: 8 accounts
payback: 6 rebate, return 7 outcome
paycheck
amount: 3 net 5 gross
get a ~: 4 earn, work
letters: 3 hrs., YTD 4 FICA
plus: 5 bonus 8 overtime
remainder: 4 stub
Paycheck: 6 Johnny
Paycock partner: 4 Juno
PayDay: 5 candy 9 chocolate
alternative: 4 Mars, Twix 5 Clark, Heath 6 Kit Kat, Mounds, Reese's, Zagnut 7 Krackel, Oh Henry 8 Baby Ruth, Hershey's, Milky Way, Snickers 9 Almond Joy, Mr. Goodbar 10 NutRageous
payee: 6 winner 8 creditor, receiver 9 recipient
April ~: 3 IRS
check ~: 6 bearer
item: 3 pot 4 cash 5 check, kitty 6 refund 7 voucher 10 money order
payer: 5 buyer, loser 8 remitter
dues ~: 3 mem. 6 member
fee ~: 6 client, patron 7 patient 8 customer
mortgage ~: 4 ower 5 buyer
rent ~: 6 lessee, tenant
starter: 3 tax
paying: 9 lucrative 10 profitable, successful, worthwhile
attention: 5 alert, aware 7 mindful
guest: 5 liver 6 lodger, patron 7 boarder
interest: 5 owing 6 in debt
leave without ~: 5 stiff
no mind: 3 lax 4 lazy 6 sleepy 8 uncaring 9 apathetic
stop ~ attention: 4 moon 5 dream, drift 8 daydream 9 fantasize 10 woolgather
__-paying: 4 dues
Pay It Forward (2000 film)
cast: Helen Hunt, Haley Joel Osment, Kevin Spacey
director: Mimi Leder
payload: 4 load 5 cargo 7 freight
paymaster: 7 cashier
payment: 3 fee, sum 4 wage 5 money, outgo, price, terms, wages 6 amends, charge, outlay, payoff, ransom, refund, reward 7 alimony, annuity, expense, pension, premium, redress, subsidy, support 8 defrayal, requital 9 discharge, emolument 10 honorarium, recompense, remittance, reparation, settlement
acknowledgment: 7 receipt
banque ~: 5 rente
club ~: 4 dues
demand ~: 3 dun, sue
details: 5 terms
down ~: 7 advance, deposit
freelance ~: 3 fee
homeowner's ~: 8 mortgage
hound for ~: 3 dun 9 keep after
insurance ~: 7 premium
Madison Avenue ~: 5 ad fee
mail ~: 5 remit
means: 4 cash 5 check 10 money order
monthly ~: 3 gas 4 rent 5 water 8 electric 9 utilities
overdue ~: 7 arrears
poker ~: 4 ante
rider's ~: 4 fare
time ~: 4 loan
unlawful ~: 3 sop 5 bribe, graft 8 kickback 9 blackmail
yearly ~: 3 tax 4 dues
__ payment: 4 down, stop 5 token 7 balloon, lump-sum
Payment Deferred (1932 film)
cast: Charles Laughton, Maureen O'Sullivan
Payment on Demand (1951 film)
cast: Bette Davis, Barry Sullivan
Paymer, David: 5 actor
film: Focus (2001)
Mighty Joe Young (1998)
Mr. Saturday Night (1992)
Nixon (1995)
Quiz Show (1994)
Payne: 4 John 5 Freda 7 Stewart
__ Payne: 5 Major
Payne, Freda
song: Band of Gold (1970)
Bring the Boys Home (1971)
Payne, John: 5 actor
film: 99 River Street (1953)
The Boss (1956)
Footlight Serenade (1942)
Kansas City Confidential (1952)
Miracle on 34th Street (1947)
The Razor's Edge (1946)
Remember the Day (1941)
The Saxon Charm (1948)
Springtime in the Rockies (1942)
Sun Valley Serenade (1941)
Week-end in Havana (1941)
spouse: Gloria De Haven
pay no __: 4 mind
payoff: 3 end 5 bribe, graft, prize 6 climax, grease, income, ransom, result, reward, sequel, upshot 7 outcome, payment, rake-off, revenue 8 clincher, earnings, high spot, kickback, venality 9 hush money, punch line 10 adjustment, bottom line, conclusion, corruption, percentage, settlement
political ~: 4 pork 5 graft 10 pork barrel
payola: 3 sop 5 bribe, graft, lucre 7 jobbery, rake-off 8 kickback, venality 10 corruption
pay one's __: 3 way 4 dues

payout ratio: 4 odds
pay-per-___: 4 view
pay phone
feature: 4 slot
word: 6 insert 7 deposit
payroll: 7 expense
addition: 5 hiree
deduction: 3 tax 4 FICA
ID: 3 SSN
ones on the ~: 5 staff
on the ~: 7 working 8 employed
put on the ~: 4 hire 6 employ, engage
Pays, Amanda: 7 actress
spouse: Corbin Bernsen
pay the ___: 5 piper
pay through the ___: 4 nose
Payton, Walter: 4 back
sport: 8 football
pay TV: 5 cable
letters: 3 HBO
Paz, Octavio: 4 poet 6 critic, writer 7 Mexican 8 Nobelist
work: The Labyrinth of Solitude
Pb: 4 elem., lead 7 element
82 for ~: 4 at. no.
PBA
area: 4 lane 5 alley
member: 3 cop 6 bowler, kegler
members: 6 police
PBJ alternative: 3 BLT
PbS: 6 galena 8 galenite
PBS: 7 network
affiliate: 3 NPR
affiliate in NYC: 4 WNET
benefactor: 3 NEA
funding: 5 grant
no-no: 2 ad
onetime ~ kids' show: 5 Rebop
program: 3 POV
science program: 4 Nova
supplier: 3 BBC
PBX number: 3 ext. 9 extension
PC: 2 AT, XT 3 CPU 4 mini 5 clone, micro 6 laptop 8 computer, notebook
alternative: 3 Mac 5 Apple
ancestor: 5 Eniac
attachment: 7 printer
attacker: 5 virus
capacity: 3 meg, MHz, RAM
chip maker: 5 Intel
clicker: 5 mouse
command: 4 copy, edit, move, save, sort 5 erase
communication: 5 E-mail
component: 3 CPU, ROM
data-exchange standard: 3 FTP
data medium: 2 CD 6 floppy
device: 5 CD-ROM, modem 6 floppy 7 printer 8 CD burner, keyboard 9 hard drive
early ~: 2 AT, XT
enthusiast: 4 user 6 hacker
flasher: 6 cursor
food: 4 byte, data 5 bytes
hookup: 3 LAN
image: 4 icon 6 bit map 7 graphic
image file format: 4 jpeg
innards: 3 ROM
insert: 2 CD 4 disk 6 floppy
key: 3 Alt, Del, End, Esc, Tab 4 Home 5 Enter, Shift 6 Insert, Page Up 7 Control 8 Page Down 9 Backspace
maker: 2 HP 3 IBM 4 Dell, Sony 7 Gateway
menu selection: 4 Help
monitor: 3 LCD
operating system: 3 DOS 5 MS/DOS 7 Windows
panic button: 3 ESC
portable ~: 6 laptop 8 notebook
reseller: 3 OEM
scanning ability: 3 OCR
screen: 3 CRT
screen image: 4 icon 7 graphic
timesaver: 5 macro
World rival: 4 Byte
see also computer
PC ___: 4 card 5 board
P.C.: 4 Wren
PC-based learning: 3 CAI
PCB regulator: 3 EPA
___ P. Chase: 6 Salmon
___ P. Cosmatos: 6 George
PCV ___: 5 valve
Pd: 4 elem. 7 element 9 palladium
46 for ~: 4 at. no.
PD
broadcast: 3 APB
employee: 4 insp.
member: 3 cop
rank: 2 lt. 3 det., sgt. 4 capt. 5 lieut.
see also police
P.D.: 5 James
PDQ: 3 now 4 ASAP, fast, stat 5 apace 6 at once, in a sec, presto, pronto 7 fleetly, hastily, quickly, rapidly, swiftly 8 in a flash, in a jiffy, in no time, pell-mell, promptly, right now, right off, speedily 9 forthwith, hurriedly, instantly, like a shot, posthaste, right away
P.D.Q.: 4 Bach
PDR
user: 2 GP, MD
pe: 6 Hebrew, letter
predecer: 4 ayin
successor: 4 sadi 5 sadhe, tsade, tsadi
P.E.: 3 gym
pea: 6 legume, veggie 8 spheroid 9 vegetable
container: 3 pod 4 hull
ender: 3 hen, nut 4 cock, fowl, king 7 shooter
soup: 3 fog
starter: 3 cow 5 chick
sweet ~: 5 plant 6 flower
pea ___: 4 coal, coat, crab, soup 5 aphid, green 6 jacket 7 shooter
___ pea: 4 snap, snow 5 beach, field, green, sugar, sweet 6 garden, ground 7 crowder, English
___ Pea: 4 Swee'
Peabo: 6 Bryson
peabody: 5 dance
peabrain: 3 ass, nit, oaf, sap 4 boob, clod, dolt, fool 5 chump, clown, cluck, dummy, dunce, goose, idiot, joker, klutz, ninny, patsy 6 dimwit, lummox, nitwit, sucker, turkey 7 buffoon, dingbat, dullard, half-wit, jackass, pinhead, saphead 8 dumbbell, numskull 9 blockhead, numbskull, simpleton 10 nincompoop
peace: 4 calm, ease, hush, rest 5 amity, order, quiet, truce, unity 6 accord, repose, shalom, sholom, solace, treaty 7 concord, harmony, silence 8 calmness, quietude, serenity, solitude 9 agreement, armistice, stillness, unanimity 10 equanimity, friendship, placidness, relaxation
break the ~: 4 riot
ender: 4 time 5 maker 6 keeper
gesture: 3 vee 5 V sign
goddess: 3 Pax 5 Irene
in Russian: 3 mir
keeper: 7 bailiff, officer, sheriff
make ~: 6 settle, soothe 7 mediate 8 moderate 9 negotiate, reconcile 10 conciliate, smooth over
name meaning ~: 5 Irene 6 Salome 7 Solomon
offering: 10 reparation
officer: 3 cop 6 lawman 7 marshal, sheriff 9 policeman 11 policewoman
of mind: 4 ease 8 security, serenity
symbol: 4 dove 11 olive branch
temporary ~: 5 truce 9 ceasefire
peace ___: 4 dove, pipe, sign 6 treaty
Peace: 5 river
locale: 6 Canada 7 Alberta
Peace ___: 5 Corps, Train
Peace!: 3 pax 6 shalom, sholom
peaceable: 4 calm, mild 5 quiet, still 6 gentle, irenic, serene 7 amiable, orderly, restful 8 amicable, dovelike, friendly, lamblike, moderate, peaceful, resigned, tranquil 10 nonviolent
___ Peace a Chance: 4 Give
peace and ___: 5 quiet
Peace Corps counterpart: 5 VISTA
peaceful: 4 calm, cool, easy, even, meek, mild 5 quiet, still 6 gentle, irenic, low-key, mellow, placid, sedate, serene, smooth 7 amiable, at peace, content, easeful, equable, halcyon, neutral, pacific, relaxed, restful, stoical, unmoved 8 amicable, carefree, composed, friendly, irenical, laid-back, tranquil 9 collected, easygoing, impassive, peaceable, quiescent, temperate, unexcited, unruffled 10 harmonious, nonchalant, nonviolent, pacifistic, rippleless, unagitated, untroubled
name meaning ~ friend: 7 Winfred 8 Winifred
period: 4 lull 5 truce 9 ceasefire
protest: 4 be-in 5 march, sit-in, vigil 6 love-in
Peaceful (1973 song) artist: Helen Reddy
peacefulness: 4 hush 5 order, quiet 7 comfort 8 serenity
Peace Garden: 4 park
locale: North Dakota
Peace in Our Time (1989 song) artist: Eddie Money
Peacekeeper: 4 ICBM
peacekeeper, international: 4 NATO
peacemaker: 8 diplomat, mediator 9 go-between 10 ambassador, arbitrator, interceder, negotiator
peacenik: 4 dove
peace of ___: 4 mind
Peace Train (1971 song) artist: Cat Stevens
peach: 3 pie, pip 4 tree 5 cling, color, drupe, fruit, honey, prize 6 flavor, looker, orange, yellow 7 delight, pinkish 8 ice cream 9 freestone 10 clingstone
butter: 3 jam 9 preserves
center: 3 pit 5 stone
dessert: 3 pie 7 cobbler 8 ice cream
family: 4 rose
fuzzless ~: 9 nectarine
pulp: 5 flesh
skin: 4 fuzz
peach ___: 4 moth 5 Melba 6 brandy 7 blossom
___ Peach: 4 Miss
peaches and ___: 5 cream
Peaches and Herb
song: Close Your Eyes (1967)
For Your Love (1967)
Let's Fall in Love (1967)
Love Is Strange (1967)
Reunited (1979)
Shake Your Groove Thing (1979)
peach Melba: 7 dessert
alternative: 5 bombe 6 frappe 7 parfait
ingredient: 8 ice cream 9 raspberry
Peachtree City: 4 town
locale: 7 Georgia
Peachum: 5 Polly
peachy: 3 def, rad 4 aces, A-one, boss, braw, cool, dece, fine, gear, keen, neat, nice, phat, tuff 5 dandy, ducky, grand, great, marvy, neato, nifty, nobby, prime, slick, super, swell 6 bang on, bang-up, bonzer, bosker, choice, divine, dreamy, far-out, gnarly, groovy, lovely, slap-up, spot on, superb, terrif, tiptop, unreal, whizzo, wicked 7 amazing, awesome, capital, corking, perfect, ripping, skookum, stellar, sublime 8 dazzling, especial, eximious, fabulous, five-star, four-star, frabjous, glorious, heavenly, jim-dandy, slam-bang, smashing, splendid, standout, sterling, stickout, superior, terrific, top-level, topnotch, very good, wondrous 9 admirable, agreeable, bodacious, Endsville, excellent, exemplary, exquisite, first-rate, high-grade, hunky-dory, marvelous, sollicker, top-flight, wonderful 10 first-class, hotsy-totsy, jack-a-dandy, out of sight, peachy-keen, phenomenal, remarkable, stupendous, super-duper
peacoat: 6 jacket
peacock: 3 fop 4 bird, blue, cyan, fowl, male, teal 5 azure, strut 6 indigo 7 swagger 8 greenish, pheasant 10 jack-a-dandy
act like a ~: 5 preen, strut
blue: 4 paon
feather spot: 3 eye
feature: 3 eye, fan 5 plume
like a ~: 4 vain 5 proud, showy
NBC ~: 4 logo
network: 3 NBC 5 NBC-TV
relative: 5 quail, snipe 6 chukar, grouse 8 curassow, moorfowl, pheasant, woodcock 9 partridge 10 guinea fowl
peacock ___: 3 ore 4 blue 6 orchid
Peacock constellation: 4 Pavo
Peacock, Thomas: 4 poet 6 writer 7 British
work: Crotchet Castle
Headlong Hall
Nightmare Abbey
Peacock Throne country: 4 Iran
peag: 5 sewan 6 seawan, wampum
pea-green boat passenger: 3 owl 8 pussycat
peahen: 4 bird, fowl 6 female
relative: 5 poult, quail, snipe 6 chukar, grouse 8 curassow, moorfowl, pheasant, woodcock 9 partridge 10 guinea fowl
peak: 3 alp, tip, top 4 acme, apex, best, brow, crag, head, pink, roof, time 5 crest, crown, mount, prime, spire 6 apogee, climax, height, heyday, heydey, max out, summit, tipoff, tiptop, top out, vertex, zenith 7 maximum, optimum, volcano 8 aiguille, high spot, meridian, mountain, pinnacle 9 crescendo, culminate, highlight, high point 10 prominence
at the ~: 4 atop 5 on top
covering: 4 snow
place: 5 graph 9 mountains
round mountain ~: 4 dome
scale a ~: 5 climb 6 ascend
tall ~: 5 spire 6 needle 8 pinnacle
time: 6 season
see also mountain
___ peak: 6 widow's
___ Peak: 5 Borah, Cloud, Grays, Kings, Lenin, Longs, Pikes, Scott 6 Blanca, Castle, Dante's, Franks, Harney, Lassen, Maroon, Pobeda, Sandia, Windom 7 Capitol, Culebra, Gannett, Glacier, Granite, La Plata, Pyramid, San Luis, Shavano, Torreys, Wheeler 8 Arapahoe, Boundary, Crestone, El Diente, Humboldt, Quandary, Redcloud, Sunlight 9 Humphreys, Telescope 10 San Antonio, Wetterhorn

peaked: 3 ill, wan 4 pale, sick, thin 5 ashen, drawn, sharp, spiky, white 6 pallid, pointy, sallow, sickly 7 bilious, haggard, run-down, starved 9 emaciated, unhealthy
roof: 6 A-frame, chalet
Peak Freans: 6 cookie
alternative: 7 Archway, Keebler, Nabisco 8 Sunshine 9 Mrs. Fields 10 Famous Amos
__ Peak Observatory: 4 Kitt
__ Peak or bust!: 5 Pikes
__ Peaks: 4 Twin
peal: 4 bong, clap, gong, ring, roar, roll, toll 5 blast, chime, clang, crack, crash, knell, noise 6 clamor, rumble 7 resound, ringing, ring out, thunder 8 laughter, resonate
mournful ~: 4 toll 5 knell
of laughter: 4 gale
Peale: 7 Charles 9 Rembrandt
Peale, Rembrandt: 6 artist 7 painter
peanut: 4 seed 5 snack 6 goober
brittle: 5 candy, sweet 10 confection
butter: 6 spread
butter brand: 3 Jif 6 Skippy 8 Peter Pan
butter companion: 5 jelly
product: 3 oil
shell: 4 husk
type of ~ butter: 6 chunky, creamy
peanut __: 3 oil 6 butter 7 brittle, gallery
peanut brittle: 5 candy
peanuts: 8 pittance 10 slave wages
Peanuts: 10 comic strip
character: Charlie Brown, Franklin, Linus, Lucy, Marcie, Peppermint Patty, Pig Pen, Rerun, Sally, Schroeder, Snoopy, Woodstock
creator: Charles Schulz
exclamation: 4 Rats 9 Good grief
lack: 6 adults
pea-picking machine: 5 viner
pear: 4 pome, tree 5 fruit, shape
family: 4 rose
fermented ~: 5 perry
prickly ~: 5 nopal, sabra 6 cactus
relative: 4 plum 5 apple, peach 6 almond, cherry, medlar, quince 7 apricot 8 hawthorn
thrips: 3 bug 4 pest 6 insect
type of ~: 4 Bosc 5 Anjou 6 Comice, Seckel 7 Kieffer 8 Bartlett, Bergamot
__ pear: 4 sand, snow 5 Asian, melon 6 balsam, cactus 7 anchovy, prickly
Pearce, Richard: 8 director
film: Country (1984)
Heartland (1979)
Leap of Faith (1992)
The Long Walk Home (1990)
pearl: 3 gem 4 gray, grey 5 color, prize 8 off-white, treasure
Japanese ~ diver: 3 ama
month: 4 June
name meaning ~: 8 Margaret
seeker: 5 diver
source: 3 sea 4 grit, sand 6 oyster
pearl __: 4 blue, gray, grey 5 danio, diver, onion, perch 6 barley, hominy, millet, oyster 7 molding, tapioca
__ pearl: 4 mabe, mobe, seed 8 cultured
Pearl: 4 Buck 5 river 6 Bailey, Minnie
city on the ~: 7 Jackson 8 Hong Kong
Pearl __: 3 Jam 6 Harbor
Pearl City: 4 town
locale: 6 Hawaii
Pearl Drops: 10 toothpaste
alternative: 3 Aim 5 Crest, Gleem, Topol 7 Close-Up, Colgate, Viadent 9 Aquafresh, Mentadent, Pepsodent, Rembrandt, Sensodyne 10 Ultra Brite 11 Tom's of Maine
pearleye: 4 fish
Pearl Fishers, The: 5 opera
composer: 5 Bizet
Pearl Harbor: 4 port
code word: 4 Tora
locale: 4 Oahu 6 Hawaii
Pearl Harbor (2001 film)
cast: Ben Affleck, Kate Beckinsale, Cuba Gooding Jr., Josh Hartnett, Jon Voight
director: Michael Bay
Pearl Jam
hometown: Seattle
lead singer: Eddie Vedder
song: Better Man (1994)
I Got Id (1995)
Last Kiss (1999)
Tremor Christ (1994)
Pearl Mosque
locale: 4 Agra 5 India
Pearl of Death, The (1944 film)
cast: Evelyn Ankers, Nigel Bruce, Basil Rathbone
director: Roy William Neill
Pearl S. __: 4 Buck
pearls before __: 5 swine
Pearl, The author: John Steinbeck
pearly: 5 milky, white 6 silver 7 frosted, opaline, whitish 8 lustrous, nacreous, off-white 10 iridescent, opalescent
pearly __: 5 white
Pearly __: 5 Gates
pear-shaped: 5 round
fruit: 3 fig
gem: 5 boule
instrument: 4 lute 5 rebec 6 cither, guitar, rebeck
sound: 2 oh
vessel: 6 aludel
Pearson: 4 Drew 6 Lester
Pearson, Lester: 2 P.M. 8 Canadian, Nobelist
predecessor: 11 Diefenbaker
successor: 7 Trudeau
Pears, Peter: 5 tenor 6 singer 7 British
milieu: 5 opera
piece: 4 aria
Peary, Robert: 8 explorer
of interest to ~: 4 pole 6 arctic 9 North Pole
peasant: 4 boor, hind, peon, pleb, serf 5 churl, yahoo, yokel 6 rustic, worker 7 bumpkin 8 commoner, plebeian 9 vulgarian 10 clodhopper
commune: 5 artel
dress: 6 bodice, dirndl
Egyptian ~: 6 fellah
girl: 5 wench
of India: 4 ryot
Ottoman ~: 4 raya
Russian ~: 5 mujik
peasantry: 3 mob 4 herd 5 crowd, plebs 6 masses, proles, rabble 8 canaille, riffraff 9 hoi polloi, multitude 10 lower class
pease __: 7 pudding
peashooter: 3 toy
__ peas in a pod: 4 like
__-pea soup: 5 split
pea-souper: 3 fog
peat: 4 fuel, moss 8 sphagnum
source: 3 bog 4 moor 5 swamp
peat __: 3 bog, pot 4 moss
peau de soie: 6 fabric 7 textile 8 material
peba: 6 mammal
pebble: 4 rock 5 stone
pebble __: 4 dash 6 heater 7 leather
Pebble Beach
event: 5 pro-am
game: 4 golf
peg: 3 tee
warning: 4 fore
Pebbles: 10 Flintstone
parent: 4 Fred 5 Wilma
pet: 4 Dino
__ Pebbles, The: 4 Sand
pebbly: 5 rocky 8 gravelly
pecan: 3 nut, pie 4 tree 7 hickory
pecan __: 3 pie 5 patty
Pecan Sandies: 6 cookie
alternative: 4 Oreo 7 Droxies 9 Chips Ahoy! 10 Fig Newtons, Lorna Doone
peccability: 5 guilt
peccadillo: 3 sin 7 misdeed, offense 9 veniality
peccant: 6 erring
peccary: 3 hog, pig 5 swine 6 animal, mammal
peccatophobe fear: 3 sin 7 sinning
pêche __: 5 Melba
__ pêcheurs de perles: 3 Les
Pechora: 5 river
locale: 6 Russia
peck: 3 jab, rap, tap 4 gobs, heap, kiss, lots, lump, much, pile 5 slews 6 nibble, oodles, plenty, strike 8 osculate 10 osculation
at: 3 nag 4 carp 6 harp on 9 criticize
hunt and ~: 4 type
starter: 3 hen
Peck, Annie Smith: 8 explorer
__ Peck Dam: 4 Fort
Peck, Gregory: 5 actor
film: Arabesque (1966)
The Big Country (1958)
The Bravados (1958)
Cape Fear (1962)
Captain Horatio Hornblower (1951)
Captain Newman, M.D. (1963)
Designing Woman (1957)
Duel in the Sun (1946)
Gentleman's Agreement (1947)
The Gunfighter (1950)
The Guns of Navarone (1961)
How the West Was Won (1962)
The Keys of the Kingdom (1944)
MacArthur (1977)
The Macomber Affair (1947)
The Man in the Gray Flannel Suit (1956)
Mirage (1965)
Moby Dick (1956)
Night People (1954)
Old Gringo (1989)
On the Beach (1959)
Other People's Money (1991)
Pork Chop Hill (1959)
The Purple Plain (1954)
Roman Holiday (1953)
The Sea Wolves (1980)
The Snows of Kilimanjaro (1952)
Spellbound (1945)
To Kill a Mockingbird (1962, AA)
Twelve O'Clock High (1949)
The Valley of Decision (1945)
The World in His Arms (1952)
The Yearling (1946)
Yellow Sky (1948)
film, with The: 4 Omen
role: 4 Ahab
pecking order: 4 rank 5 class, order, place 6 regime
Peckinpah, Sam: 8 director
film: The Ballad of Cable Hogue (1970)
Cross of Iron (1977)
The Getaway (1972)
Junior Bonner (1972)
Ride the High Country (1962)
Straw Dogs (1971)
The Wild Bunch (1969)
peckish: 5 unfed 7 starved 8 edacious, esurient, famished, ravenous 9 voracious
Peck of Gold, A author: Robert Frost
Peck's __ Boy: 3 Bad
pecks, four: 6 bushel
Pecksniff: 4 Seth
pecorino: 6 cheese
Pecos: 5 river
locale: 5 Texas 9 New Mexico
Pecos __: 4 Bill
pecs: 7 muscles
relative: 3 abs 6 glutes
show off the ~: 4 flex
Pécs: 4 city, town
locale: 7 Hungary
pectin, react to: 3 gel 4 jell
pectoral __: 3 fin 5 cross 6 girdle
peculate: 5 steal 6 pilfer 8 embezzle
peculation: 5 theft 9 pilfering
peculator: 5 thief 8 pilferer 9 embezzler
peculiar: 3 odd 4 eery 5 eerie, flaky, funny, kinky, kooky, queer, wacky, weird 6 atypic, creepy, flakey, freaky, kookie, quaint, quirky, unique, way-out, whacky 7 bizarre, curious, deviant, erratic, oddball, offbeat, special, strange, touched, unalike, unusual 8 aberrant, abnormal, atypical, freakish, personal, separate, singular, specific, uncommon 9 anomalous, different, divergent, eccentric, fantastic, intrinsic, irregular, quizzical, whimsical 10 individual, off-the-wall, outlandish, suspicious, unfamiliar, unorthodox
combining form: 4 idio-
peculiarity: 4 kink, mark, sign 5 quirk, trait, twist 6 foible, manner, oddity 7 anomaly, earmark, feature, quality, schtick 8 crotchet, property 9 attribute, mannerism, queerness
peculiarly: 5 oddly 9 strangely, unusually 10 especially
Peculiar Treasure, A author: Edna Ferber
pecuniary: 6 fiscal 8 economic, monetary 9 financial 8 commercial
sum: 5 money
pecunious: 4 rich 5 flush 6 loaded 7 wealthy 8 affluent 9 properous, well-fixed 10 in the money
Ped __: 4 Xing
pedagogic: 7 bookish, donnish 8 academic, didactic, pedantic, tutorial 9 scholarly 10 didactical, pedantical
pedagogue: 6 lector, master 7 teacher, trainer 8 lecturer 9 abecedary, professor 10 instructor
org.: 3 AFT, NEA
pedagogy: 8 teaching, training 9 education
pedal: 4 bike 5 cycle
car ~: 3 gas 5 brake 6 clutch
extremity: 3 toe 4 foot
foot ~: 5 lever
piano ~: 6 damper
pusher: 4 foot 5 biker
pushers: 5 pants 6 Capris
put the ~ to the metal: 3 rev, zip 4 zoom 5 speed 6 barrel
pedal __: 4 boat 7 pushers
__ pedal: 3 gas 5 brake
__-pedal: 4 back, soft
pedaling, ride without: 5 coast
pedal to the __: 5 metal
pedantic: 3 dry 4 arid, dull 5 fussy 6 stodgy 7 bookish, donnish, erudite, learned, pompous, stilted 8 abstruse, academic, affected, didactic, overnice, priggish 9 pedagogic, ponderous, recondite 10 didactical, nit-picking, scholastic
peddle: 4 hawk, push, sell, vend 5 trade 6 market, monger, unload 7 solicit 9 dispose of, liquidate 10 auction off
peddler: 5 crier 6 hawker, seller, vender, vendor
goal: 4 sale, sell
Pedernales: 5 river
locale: 5 Texas
Pedersen, Charles: 7 chemist 8 Nobelist

pedestal: **4** foot, post, rest **6** column, podium
bowl: **5** tazza
figure: **4** bust, idol **9** sculpture
part: **4** base, dado **5** socle
put on a ~: **5** adore, exalt, extol **6** esteem, extoll, praise **7** adulate, ennoble, glorify, idolize, worship **8** canonize, idealize, venerate
pedestal __: **5** table
pedestrian: **3** dim **4** blah, dull, flat, so-so **5** banal, hiker, inane, trite, unfun **6** ambler, boring, common, dreary, footer, jejune, stodgy, walker **7** humdrum, mundane, prosaic **8** banausic, everyday, mediocre, ordinary, passerby, plebeian, plodding, stroller **9** hackneyed, jaywalker, prosaical
haven: **4** curb **6** island
help for a ~: **3** arm **4** lift, ride
pediatrician: **2** MD **6** doctor **9** physician
patient: **3** kid, tot **4** baby **5** child, minor **6** infant **7** toddler **9** youngster
pedicle: **4** stem **5** stalk
pedicurist
coat: **6** enamel
target: **3** toe **4** nail **7** cuticle, toenail
pedigree: **4** line **5** birth, blood, breed, class, roots, stock **6** origin, strain **7** descent, lineage **8** ancestry, heritage, purebred **9** genealogy **10** derivation, extraction, family tree
org.: **3** AKC
pedigreed: **8** pure-bred
pediment: **5** gable **8** triangle
pedometer
new ~ reading: **3** OOO
reading: **5** miles **8** distance
Pedro: **6** Cabral **7** Salinas **8** Calderón, card game, Guerrero **9** Almodóvar **10** Armendariz
in English: **5** Peter
see also Spanish
__ Pedro: **3** San
Peds: **7** hosiery
peduncle: **4** stem **5** scape, stalk
Pee __ King: **3** Wee
Pee __ Reese: **3** Wee
Pee-__ Herman: **3** Wee
Pee Dee: **5** river
locale: **4** N. Car., S. Car.
peek: **3** eye, pry, see, spy **4** gaze, look, peep, peer, view **5** snoop **6** behold, gander, glance, squint **7** eyeshot, glimpse, look-see, observe **10** get a load of, sneak a look
at the cards: **5** cheat
peek-__: **4** a-boo
Peek __: **6** Freans
Peek-a-boo: **4** game
Peek-a-boo, __ you!: **4** I see
Peekskill: **4** city, town
locale: **7** New York
peel: **4** bark, flay, hull, husk, molt, pare, rind, skin **5** cover, flake, shave, shell, shuck, strip **6** cortex, denude, scrape **7** coating, disrobe, epicarp, exocarp, surface, undress **8** covering, flake off, get out of, unclothe **9** exfoliate **10** delaminate, desquamate
fruit ~: **4** rind, skin, zest
in a drink: **5** twist
off: **4** molt **5** flake, strip
precursor: **4** burn **7** blister, sunburn
rubber: **3** rev **4** zoom **5** speed **10** accelerate
something to ~: **4** pear, spud **5** apple, fruit, peach **6** potato
peel __: **3** off
Peel: **4** Emma **6** Robert
partner: **5** Steed
peel-and-__: **5** stick
peeled: **4** bare **5** naked
keep one's eyes ~: **5** watch **8** watch out **9** be careful
with eyes ~: **7** mindful **8** vigilant, watchful
Peele, George: **4** poet **7** British **10** playwright
peeler: **4** tool **5** parer **6** gadget
spud ~: **2** GI, KP **7** private, recruit
peeling: **4** rind, skin **10** integument
potatoes, perhaps: **4** on KP
tool: **5** parer
Peel me a grape lady: **3** Mae **4** West
Peene: **5** river
locale: **7** Germany
__-peen hammer: **4** ball
peep: **3** coo, pry, see, spy **4** call, gaze, look, peek, peer, pipe **5** cheep, chirp, snoop, tweet **6** appear, emerge, gander, glance, squint **7** chirrup, glimpse, look-see, twitter **8** bird call **10** get a load of, sneak a look
ender: **4** hole
out: **6** emerge, sprout **9** germinate
show: **5** raree
Peep at Polynesian Life, A: **5** Typée
peeper: **3** eye, spy **4** frog **9** amphibian
farm ~: **5** chick
plaint: **5** croak
protector: **3** lid **4** lash **6** eyelid **7** eyelash
spring ~: **4** frog, hyla **9** amphibian
peephole: **4** slit **5** Judas **6** eyelet
peeping __: **3** Tom
Peeples, Nia song: Street of Dreams (1991)
peer: **3** pry, see, spy **4** gape, gawk, gaze, look, lord, mate, peek, peep, scan, view **5** baron, equal, juror, match, noble, rival, snoop, stare, watch **6** appear, emerge, fellow, squint **7** coequal, compeer, examine, eyeball, glimpse, inspect, ransack **8** nobleman **9** associate, classmate, patrician **10** aristocrat, get a load of, rubberneck, scrutinize, sneak a look
ender: **3** age, ess
group: **4** jury
recognition: **5** honor
sheik's ~: **4** amir, emir **5** ameer, emeer
social ~: **5** equal
without ~: **5** alone **6** unique **7** perfect **9** unequaled, unmatched
peer __: **5** group **6** review
peer __ realm: **5** of the
Peer __: **4** Gynt
peerage: **5** lords **8** nobility **10** upper class, upper crust
member: **4** dame, duke, earl, lady, lord **5** baron **7** duchess, marquis **8** baroness, countess, viscount **11** marchioness
Peer and the __, The: **4** Peri
Peerce: **3** Jan **5** Larry
Peerce, Jan: **5** tenor **6** singer
milieu: **5** opera
peeress: **4** dame, lady **5** noble **7** duchess **8** countess **10** noblewoman **11** marchioness
Peer Gynt
author: Henrik Ibsen
character: **3** Ase **4** Aase, Huhu, Kari **5** Aslak, Brosë, troll **6** Anitra, Ingrid **7** Solveig **8** Mads Moën **9** Troll King
composer: **5** Grieg
peering: **4** nosy **5** nosey **6** snoopy **7** curious **9** quizzical
peerless: **3** ace **4** A-one, best, only, rare, tops **5** alone, great **6** single, superb, unique **7** in front, optimum, perfect, supreme **8** flawless, splendid, superior **9** excellent, faultless, matchless, nonpareil, solid-gold, topflight, unequaled, unmatched, unrivaled, virtuosic **10** consummate, inimitable, preeminent, unexampled, unrivalled, world-class
peer of the __: **5** realm
Peet: **6** Amanda
Peete: **6** Calvin
peetweet: **4** bird
peeve: **3** bug, get, irk, vex **4** burn, fret, gall, miff, rile, roil **5** anger, annoy, get to, grate, gripe, pique, spite, steam, upset **6** bother, bum out, hector, madden, needle, nettle, put out, rankle, ruffle, tee off, work up **7** disturb, enflame, incense, perturb, provoke, tick off, trouble **8** distress, irritate **9** aggravate, annoyance, displease **10** exasperate
pet ~: **7** bugbear **9** hot button
__ peeve: **3** pet
peeved: **3** hot, mad **4** ired, sore **5** angry, cross, huffy, irate, livid, riled, upset, wroth **6** fuming, in a pet **7** in a stew **8** choleric, in a pique **9** aggrieved, indignant, resentful
peevish: **4** mean, sour, ugly **5** cross, huffy, moody, onery, spiky, sulky, surly, techy, testy, upset **6** crabby, cranky, crusty, cussed, grumpy, ireful, morose, ornery, snappy, sullen, tetchy, touchy **7** bearish, carping, crabbed, fretful, grouchy, huffish, prickly, waspish, whining **8** captious, childish, choleric, churlish, critical, fretsome, grousing, growling, grumpish, petulant, snappish **9** crotchety, excitable, fractious, irascible, irritable, querulous, splenetic **10** ill-natured, out of sorts
mood: **4** huff, snit
peevishness: **4** bile **6** spleen, temper **8** asperity
pee-wee: **4** baby, puny, runt, tiny **5** bitty, teeny **6** atomic, bantam, little, minute, petite, pocket, teensy **7** stunted **8** halfpint **9** itsy-bitsy, itty-bitty, miniature, pint-sized, undersize **10** diminutive, homunculus, teeny-weeny, vest-pocket
Pee-wee __: **6** Herman
Pee Wee __: **4** King **5** Reese
Pee Wee's Big Adventure dog: **5** Speck
peewit: **4** bird
peg: **3** fix, pin, see, tee **4** cast, hurl, name, rank, rate, sort, type **5** dowel, fling, pitch, place, point, throw **6** assess, fasten, select, verify **7** look out, measure, specify **8** identify, indicate, make fast, work away **9** designate, recognize **10** categorize, clothespin
away: **4** toil, work **6** strain
driver's ~: **3** tee
ender: **5** board
quoits ~: **3** hob
replacer: **4** hook, nail **5** screw
take down a ~: **5** abase, lower, shame **6** demean, demote, humble, reduce **7** degrade, mortify **8** belittle **9** downgrade
wooden ~: **5** dowel
__-peg: **6** mumbly **7** clothes
Peg: **5** Bundy **7** Bracken
Peg __ Heart: **3** o' My
Peg-__: **5** Board
pega: **4** fish
Pegasus: **5** horse, steed **6** equine
brother: **8** Chrysaor
father: **8** Poseidon
feature: **5** wings
mother: **6** Medusa
neighbor: **6** Cygnus **8** Aquarius
Pegeen: **10** Fitzgerald
Peggy: **3** Dow, Lee, Rea **4** Cass, Ryan, Wood **5** Rosen **6** Lennon, Lipton, Parish **7** Cummins, Fleming **8** Ashcroft **10** Guggenheim
Peggy __: **3** Sue
Peggy __ Garner: **3** Ann
Peggy-Ann: **7** musical
songwriter: **4** Hart **7** Rodgers
Peggy from Paris author: George Ade
Peggy Hopkins __: **5** Joyce
Peggy Sue (1957 song) artist: Buddy Holly and the Crickets
Peggy Sue Got Married (1986 film)
cast: Nicolas Cage, Catherine Hicks, Barry Miller, Kathleen Turner
director: Francis Ford Coppola
__ peg in a round hole: **6** square
Pegler: **9** Westbrook
Peg o' My __: **5** Heart
Péguy, Charles: **4** poet **6** French **8** essayist
Peg Woffington author: **5** Reade
peh: **6** Hebrew, letter
follower: **4** sadi **5** sadhe, tsade, tsadi
preceder: **4** ayin
Pei: **2** I.M. **5** Mario
__-Pei: **4** Shar
PEI: **4** prov. **8** province
clock setting: **3** AST
locale: **6** Canada
part of ~: **3** Edw. **6** Edward, Island, Prince
peignoir: **6** kimono **8** negligee
Peignot: **4** font **8** typeface
Pei, I.M.: **7** Chinese **9** architect
Peirce, Charles Sanders: **6** writer **11** philosopher
specialty: **10** pragmatism
pejorative: **8** debasing, derisive, libelous, negative, scornful **9** degrading, demeaning, slighting **10** derogatory, detraction, minimizing
pekan: **6** fisher, marten
peke: **3** dog, pet, toy **5** canid **6** canine, lap dog, toy dog
alternative: **3** pom **6** poodle
pekin: **4** silk **6** fabric **7** textile **8** material
Pekin: **4** city, duck, fowl, town
locale: **8** Illinois
relative: **4** smew, teal **5** eider, Rouen, scaup **6** Cayuga, scoter **7** gadwall, mallard, pintail, pochard, redhead, sea duck, widgeon **8** garganey, gray duck, mandarin, musk duck, oldsquaw, shoveler, surf duck, wood duck **9** black duck, broadbill, goldeneye, goosander, greenhead, merganser, ruddy duck, sprigtail **10** bufflehead, canvasback, surf scoter, tufted duck
Peking: **4** city, town **7** capital
ender: **3** ese
locale: **5** China
Peking __: **3** man **4** duck
Pekingese: **3** dog, pet, toy **5** canid **6** canine, lap dog, toy dog
__-Pekka Salonen: **3** Esa
pekoe: **3** tea **4** brew **5** drink **8** beverage
__ pekoe: **6** orange
pelage: **3** fur **4** coat, hair, wool **6** fleece
pelagic: **5** naval **6** marine **8** maritime, nautical
Pelagius: **4** pope **7** pontiff
Pelee: **7** volcano
flow: **4** lava
locale: **9** Caribbean **10** Martinique
Peleg
father: **4** Eber
son: **3** Reu
pelerine: **4** cape
Pelew __: **7** Islands
pelf: **3** oof **4** cash, gelt, jack, kail, kale, loot, peag **5** bills, booty, bread, bucks, dough, funds, lucre, money, moola, mopus, pesos, rhino, sewan **6** dinero, do-re-mi, mammon, mazuma, moolah, riches, seawan, silver, specie, spoils,

wampum, wealth **7** cabbage, capital, dollars, lettuce, ooftish, scratch, shekels **8** bankroll, cold cash, currency, hard cash, smackers **9** banknotes, frogskins, long green, simoleons **10** greenbacks, green stuff
Pelham: **3** car **4** auto **10** Studebaker
Pelham author: Edward Bulwer-Lytton
pelican: **4** bird
feature: **5** pouch
relative: **6** gannet
Pelican Brief, The (1993 film)
cast: Tony Goldwyn, John Heard, Julia Roberts, Sam Shepard, Denzel Washington
director: Alan J. Pakula
Pelion base: **4** Ossa
pelisse: **4** cape **5** cloak
pell-__: **4** mell
Pell: **9** Claiborne
Pella: **4** city, town
locale: **4** Iowa
pellet: **2** BB **4** ammo, pill, shot **7** granule, missile
rifle ~: **2** BB
shooter: **5** BB gun **6** airgun
Pelle the Conqueror: **4** film **5** novel
author: Martin Andersen Nexö
cast: Pelle Hvenegaard, Max von Sydow
director: Bille August
Pelletier, Wilfrid: **9** conductor
pellets: **3** BBs
ice ~: **4** hail **5** sleet
lead ~: **4** ammo, shot
pistol ~: **4** ammo
Pelli, Cesar: **9** architect
pell-mell: **3** PDQ **4** rash **5** apace, hasty **6** abrupt, presto, rashly **7** blindly, chaotic, fleetly, hastily, hurried, mixed up, muddled, quickly, rapidly, swiftly, tangled **8** abruptly, careless, confused, headlong, in a flash, in a jiffy, in no time, reckless, slapdash, speedily **9** forthwith, haphazard, hurriedly, instantly, like a shot, posthaste, scrambled, uncareful **10** at full tilt, carelessly, disordered, disorderly, heedlessly, recklessly, topsy-turvy, willy-nilly
go ~: **3** hie, run, zip **4** bolt, leap, race, rush, tear, whiz, zoom **5** hurry, lunge, speed **6** charge, gallop, hurtle **8** scramble
pellucid: **4** pure **5** clear, lucid, sheer **6** limpid **8** knowable **9** unobscure **10** diaphanous
pelon: **4** bald **8** hairless
Peloponnesian
city: **5** Argos **7** Amalias
region: **4** Elis **6** Achaea
valley: **5** Nemea
Peloponnesian __: **3** War
Peloponnesus: **5** Morea
pelota: **5** sport **7** jai alai
basket: **5** cesta
Pelotas: **4** city, town
locale: **6** Brazil
pelt: **3** fur, hie, hit, run **4** beat, coat, hair, hide, hurl, race, rain, rush, skin, wool **5** hurry, pound, speed, stone, throw **6** assail, batter, beetle, ermine, fleece, hammer, patter, pepper, pummel, shower, strike, thrash, wallop **7** bombard, krimmer, lambast **8** fur piece, lambaste **9** epidermis
beaver ~: **3** plu **4** plew
peludo: **6** mammal
pelvic
bones: **4** ilia **5** sacra
joint: **3** hip
of the ~ region: **5** ileal
prefix: **5** sacro-
pelvic __: **3** fin **6** girdle
pelvis: **4** bone **7** hip bone
combining form: **4** pyel- **5** pyelo-
of the ~: **5** iliac
Pemberton: **4** John
Pembroke Pines: **4** city, town
locale: **7** Florida
pemmican: **4** food, meat **6** staple
Pemmican language: **4** Cree
pen: **3** Bic, box, nib, she, sty **4** bird, cage, coop, fold, jail, lair, poky, reed, stir, swan **5** draft, fence, Flair, hedge, hem in, hutch, pokey, quill, write **6** author, cooler, coop up, corral, female, indite, intern, lockup, marker, pigsty, prison, shut in, stylus **7** close in, compose, confine, enclose, felt-tip, fence in, hoosgow, impound, inclose, interne, jot down, paddock, piggery, put down, shelter, slammer, Uni-Ball **8** big house, hoosegow, inscribe **9** autograph, ball point, enclosure, handwrite, PaperMate **10** put on paper, stylograph
brand: **3** Bic **5** Flair **7** Uni-Ball **9** PaperMate
chicken ~: **4** coop
dweller: **3** hen, hog, pig, sow **4** boar, fowl **5** swine **6** rabbit **7** chicken **9** livestock
ender: **5** knife, light **6** holder
fluid: **3** ink
fountain ~: **3** pen
have a ~ pal: **5** write **10** correspond
holding ~: **9** detention
livestock ~: **6** corral
mate: **3** cob
name: **5** alias **6** anonym **9** pseudonym **10** nom de plume
old-fashioned ~: **5** plume, quill
one in a ~: **5** felon **7** convict **8** criminal
point: **3** nib
problem: **4** leak
sheep ~: **4** fold
starter: **3** pig **4** bull, play
young: **6** cygnet
pen __: **3** pal **4** name **5** point
__ pen: **3** sea **4** felt **5** fiber, light **6** poison **7** felt-tip
Peña: **4** Tony **9** Alejandro, Elizabeth
penal: **8** punitive **9** punishing **10** corrective, inflictive
institution: **3** can, jug, pen **4** gaol, jail, stir **5** clink **6** cooler, lockup, prison **7** slammer **8** bastille, big house, hoosegow **9** calaboose
penal __: **4** code **6** colony
penalize: **4** dock, fine **5** judge, mulct **6** amerce, punish **7** condemn, correct **8** chastise, handicap, sentence, slap with **9** castigate **10** discipline
penalties, like some: **5** stiff
penalty: **3** rap **4** cost, fine, toll **5** price **6** diktat, ticket **7** damages, forfeit **8** handicap, sanction, sentence **9** hell to pay **10** discipline, forfeiture, infliction, punishment
caller: **3** ref **7** referee
non-payer's ~: **4** repo
pay the ~: **5** atone **6** do time
speeder's ~: **4** fine **6** ticket
penalty __: **3** box **4** area, kick, shot **6** double, killer, stroke
penance: **9** atonement, expiation, hair shirt, sacrament **10** contrition, punishment, reparation
do ~: **5** atone **7** expiate
Penang: **4** city, isle, port, town **6** island
locale: **8** Malaysia
Penas: **4** gulf
locale: **5** Chile
Penates partners: **5** Lares
pence: **6** copper
starter: **3** six, two **4** half **5** three
__ pence: **6** Peter's
penchant: **4** bent, bias, gift, wont **5** fancy, habit, taste **6** liking, relish **7** faculty, leaning **8** affinity, appetite, druthers, fondness, tendency, velleity, weakness **9** appetence, proneness, sentiment **10** partiality, proclivity, propensity
pencil: **3** jot **5** write **8** scribble
blue ~: **4** edit, trim, void **5** amend **6** censor, revise **7** abridge, shorten **10** censorship
end: **5** point **6** eraser
eye ~: **5** liner
filler: **4** lead **8** graphite
holder: **3** ear **4** hand **6** finger
in: **7** program **8** schedule
maker: **5** Faber
partner: **3** pad **5** paper **6** tablet
pusher: **5** clerk
wax ~: **6** crayon
wood: **5** cedar
worn-down ~: **3** nub **4** knub, stub
pencil __: **3** box **4** beam, case **6** pusher, stripe
__ pencil: **4** lead **5** light **6** grease **7** eyebrow, styptic
__-pencil: **3** red **4** blue
pencil-and-paper game: **5** Jotto
pencil box item: **5** ruler **6** eraser **7** compass
pend: **4** hang **5** await **6** dangle **7** suspend **8** hang fire
__ pend.: **3** pat.
pendant: **6** locket **7** jewelry **8** lavalier
place: **4** neck **6** throat
Pendennis author: William Makepeace Thackeray
pendent: **7** hanging, jutting **8** dangling **9** undecided **10** protruding
Pendergrass, Teddy: **6** singer
song: Close the Door (1978)
pending: **5** until **7** hanging, on board **8** awaiting, imminent **9** in the wind, undecided, unsettled **10** continuing, in the works, unresolved, up in the air
in law: **4** nisi
Pendleton: **4** camp **5** Terry **6** Austin
Pend Oreille: **4** lake
locale: **5** Idaho
Pendragon: **5** Uther
son: **6** Arthur
pendulous: **6** droopy **7** hanging, sagging **8** dangling, drooping, swinging
pendulum
direction: **3** fro
move like a ~: **5** swing **9** oscillate
path: **3** arc
__ pendulum: **4** mock **6** simple **7** conical, torsion
Penelope: **8** Gilliatt, Mortimer, Spheeris
husband: **8** Odysseus
lover: **6** Hermes **8** Antinous **9** Telegonus
son: **3** Pan **6** Italus **9** Acusilaus **10** Telemachus
suitor: **6** Elatus, Liodes **7** Agelaus, Polybus **8** Antinous, Euryades, Pisander **9** Ctesippus, Eurydamas, Eurynomus, Liocritus **10** Eurymachus
Penelope __ Miller: **3** Ann
Penélope: **4** Cruz
Pénélope composer: **5** Fauré
penetrable: **6** liable **8** vincible **9** absorbent, permeable
penetrate: **3** jab, see **4** bore, gore, open, ream, seep, soak, stab **5** crack, drill, enter, grasp, knife, lance, plumb, prick, probe, stick **6** access, affect, empale, fathom, filter, impale, invade, pierce, sink in, soak in, thrust, tunnel **7** break in, discern, ingress, pervade, suffuse, unravel **8** decipher, encroach, filter in, permeate, puncture, saturate, transfix, trespass **9** ferret out, figure out, go through, percolate, perforate **10** comprehend, eat through, encroach on, infiltrate, see through, understand
slowly: **4** leak, ooze, seep **6** filter
penetrating: **4** cold, keen **5** acute, crisp, quick, sharp, witty **6** astute, biting, cogent, shrewd, shrill, subtle **7** cutting, pointed, pungent **8** carrying, clear-cut, critical, incisive, piercing, poignant, profound, stinging **9** astucious, observant, pervasive, sagacious, searching, trenchant **10** perceptive
beam: **4** X-ray **5** laser
penetration: **5** depth **6** wisdom **7** insight **8** infusion, keenness
pengo: **5** money
penguin: **4** bird
kind of ~: **4** king **6** Adelie **7** emperor
locale: **3** zoo **9** Antarctic, South Pole **10** Antarctica
Outland ~: **4** Opus
Penguin: **3** Cey **6** iceman
foe: **6** Batman
rival: **4** Blue, King, Star, Wild **5** Bruin, Devil, Flame, Flyer, Oiler, Sabre, Shark **6** Canuck, Coyote, Ranger **7** Capital, Panther, Red Wing, Senator **8** Canadien, Islander, Predator, Thrasher **9** Avalanche, Blackhawk, Hurricane, Lightning, Maple Leaf **10** Blue Jacket, Mighty Duck
Penguin Island author: Anatole France
Penguin Pool Murder, The (1932 film)
cast: Mae Clarke, James Gleason, Edna May Oliver
Penguins: **3** six **4** team
home: **10** Pittsburgh
milieu: **3** ice **4** rink
org.: **3** NHL
sport: **6** hockey
Penguins song: Earth Angel (1954)
__ Penh: **4** Pnom **5** Phnom
penicillin: **4** drug **10** antibiotic
source: **4** mold
target: **4** germ **5** strep **8** bacteria **9** infection
penicillium: **6** fungus
Penick, Harvey: **6** golfer
peninsula
Adriatic ~: **6** Istria
Alaskan ~: **5** Kenai
Asian ~: **5** Malay **6** Arabia
Canadian ~: **5** Gaspé
European ~: **5** Italy **6** Iberia
Greek ~: **5** Morea
Indian ~: **6** Deccan
Luzon ~: **6** Bataan
Mexican ~: **4** Baja
Mideast ~: **4** Aden **5** Sinai **6** Arabia
Philippine ~: **6** Bataan
Québec ~: **5** Gaspé
small ~: **4** spit
two-nation ~: **6** Iberia
Ukraine ~: **6** Crimea
world's largest ~: **6** Arabia
__ Peninsula: **4** Door, Eyre, Kola **5** Eyre's, Gaspé, Kenai, Lower, Malay, Sinai, Upper **6** Alaska, Avalon, Azuero, Balkan, Nicoya, Seward, Taimyr, Ungava **7** Arabian, Boothia, Chukchi, Iberian **8** Delmarva
Peniston, Ce Ce
hometown: Dayton
song: Finally (1991)
Keep on Walkin' (1992)
We Got a Love Thing (1992)
penitence: **5** shame **6** regret, sorrow **7** remorse **9** attrition, hair shirt **10** contrition, ruefulness
penitent: **5** sorry **6** abject, rueful, shamed **7** ashamed, humbled **8** contrite **9** regretful **10** apologetic, remorseful

be ~: 3 rue 4 weep 5 atone 6 regret
penitential period: 4 Lent
penitentiary: 3 can, jug, pen 4 gaol, jail, poky, stir 5 clink, joint, pokey 6 cooler, inside, lockup, prison 7 bastile, hoosgow, slammer 8 bastille, big house, hoosegow 9 calaboose
Pénjamo: 4 city, town
locale: 6 Mexico 10 Guanajuato
penmanship: 6 script 7 writing 8 longhand
Penn: 4 Sean 6 Arthur 7 William 8 Jillette
Penn __: 3 Ave., Sta. 5 State 6 Relays 7 Station
Penn __, NY: 3 Yan
Penn.
see Pensylvania
penna: 5 plume 7 feather
pennant: 4 flag, jack 6 banner, burgee, colors, cornet, emblem, ensign 7 bunting 8 screamer, standard, streamer 9 banderole 10 decoration
Penn, Arthur: 8 director
film: Alice's Restaurant (1969)
Bonnie and Clyde (1967)
Dead of Winter (1987)
Four Friends (1981)
Little Big Man (1970)
The Miracle Worker (1962)
Night Moves (1975)
penne: 5 pasta
alternative: 4 orzo, ziti 5 zitti 6 ditali, elbows, rigati, shells 7 fusilli, gnocchi, lasagna, lasagne, pastina, ravioli, rotelle, spirals 8 bucatini, couscous, farfalle, linguine, linguini, macaroni, rigatoni 9 agnolotti, alphabets, angelhair, cavatelli, maccaroni, manicotti, spaghetti 10 cannelloni, conchiglie, fettuccine, fettuccini, tagliarini, tortellini, vermicelli
Penney, J.C. middle name: 4 Cash
Penney rival: 5 Kmart, Sears 6 Target 7 Wal-Mart
Pennies From Heaven (1981 film)
cast: Steve Martin, Bernadette Peters, Christopher Walken
director: Herbert Ross
penniless: 4 flat, poor 5 broke, needy 6 bad off, hard up, ill off, in need, in want, ruined 7 lacking, pinched 8 badly off, bankrupt, beggarly, deprived, dirt poor, indigent, stranded, strapped 9 dead broke, destitute, flat broke, insolvent, miserable, moneyless, penurious, tapped out 10 cleaned out, down-and-out, pauperized, straitened
in Britain: 5 skint
Pennines: 4 Alps 5 range
locale: 5 Italy 6 Europe 11 Switzerland
Pennock: 4 Herb
pennon: 4 flag 6 banner
Pennsauken: 4 city, town
locale: 9 New Jersey
Penn, Sean: 5 actor
film: At Close Range (1986)
Bad Boys (1983)
Before Night Falls (2000)
Carlito's Way (1993)
Colors (1988)
Dead Man Walking (1995)
Fast Times at Ridgemont High (1982)
The Game (1997)
I Am Sam (2001)
The Indian Runner (1991)
The Pledge (2001)
Racing With the Moon (1984)
State of Grace (1990)
Sweet and Lowdown (1999)
The Thin Red Line (1998)
U Turn (1997)
spouse: Madonna, Robin Wright
Penn State: 3 PSU
conference: 6 Big Ten
Penn Station: 5 depot 8 terminal
carrier: 4 LIRR 6 Amtrak
posting: 4 sked 8 schedule
Pennsylvania: 5 state 6 avenue
capital: 10 Harrisburg
city: 4 Erie, Plum, Ross, York 6 Donora, Easton, Radnor, Shaler 7 Altoona, Baldwin, Chester, Latrobe, Lebanon, Reading 8 Hazleton, Scranton 9 Allentown, Bethlehem, Johnstown, Lancaster, Levittown, New Castle, Penn Hills, Pottstown 10 Bethel Park, Drexel Hill, Harrisburg, Norristown, Pittsburgh
county: 3 Elk 4 Erie, York 5 Berks, Bucks, Tioga 6 McKean 7 Dauphin, Wyoming 10 Schuylkill
Indian: 9 Nanticoke
league: 3 Ivy
mountains: 7 Poconos
neighbor: 4 Ohio 7 New York 8 Delaware, Maryland 9 New Jersey
people: 5 Amish
port: 4 Erie
school: 5 Thiel 6 Drexel, Lehigh, Temple 8 Bucknell, Duquesne 9 Lafayette, Penn State, Villanova
state bird: 6 grouse
state dog: 9 Great Dane
state fish: 10 brook trout
state flower: 6 laurel
state fossil: 9 trilobite
state tree: 7 hemlock
Pennsylvania __: 5 Dutch, Polka, rifle 6 German
Pennsylvania Dutch: 4 sect 5 Amish, style
barn symbol: 3 hex 7 hex sign
__ Penn Warren: 6 Robert
penny: 4 cent, coin 5 money 6 copper
ante: 4 game 5 poker 8 card game
bad ~: 4 slug
black: 5 stamp
down to one's last ~: 5 broke 6 busted 8 strapped
dreadful: 5 novel
ender: 4 wise, wort 5 cress, royal, worth 6 weight 7 whistle
like a new ~: 5 shiny
onetime ~ depiction: 5 wheat
pretty ~: 4 dear, high 5 bucks, pricy, steep 6 bundle, costly, pricey 8 big bucks, precious 9 expensive, priceless 10 exorbitant, high-priced, overpriced
starter: 3 six, two 4 half, true 5 catch, pinch, three
word on a ~: 3 God, one 4 cent, unum 5 trust 6 States, United 7 America, liberty 8 pluribus
penny __: 4 ante, post 5 stock 6 arcade, loafer 7 pincher, whistle
penny-__: 4 wise
Penny: 3 Joe 6 Sydney 8 Marshall 9 Singleton
to Sky King: 5 niece
Penny __: 4 Lane 5 Lover
__ Penny: 4 Will 5 Henny
penny-a-__: 5 liner
Penn Yan: 4 city, town
locale: 7 New York
penny-ante: 5 petty 8 picayune, trifling
pennycress: 4 weed
__ penny earned: 3 is a
Penny Lover (1984 song) artist: Lionel Richie
__ Penny Opera: 5 Three
penny pincher: 5 miser, piker 6 cheapo 7 Scrooge 8 el cheapo, tightwad 9 skinflint 10 cheapskate
penny-pinching: 4 mean 5 cheap, tight 6 greedy, skimpy, stingy 7 miserly, selfish, thrifty 8 grasping 9 penurious, provident 10 avaricious, skinflinty
pennyroyal: 5 plant 6 flower
Penny Serenade (1941 film)
cast: Beulah Bondi, Irene Dunne, Cary Grant
director: George Stevens
penny-wise: 6 frugal, stingy 8 ungiving 10 economical
Penny wise, pound foolish: 5 adage
Penobscot: 3 bay 5 river 6 Indian 7 Amerind
city on the ~: 5 Orono 6 Bangor
river locale: 5 Maine
Penrod author: Booth Tarkington
Penrod friend: 3 Sam
Pensacola: 3 bay 4 city, port, town
initials at ~: 3 NAS
locale: 7 Florida
Pensées author: Blaise Pascal
pen-shaped instrument: 6 stylus
pension: 5 grant, hotel 6 reward 7 annuity, payment, premium, stipend, subsidy, support 9 allowance
federal ~: 3 SSA
plan: 3 IRA 5 ERISA, Keogh
pensive: 3 sad 5 grave, moody, sober 6 dreamy, musing 7 serious, wistful 8 absorbed, thinking 9 pondering 10 abstracted, meditative, melancholy, reflective, ruminating, thoughtful
sound: 3 hmm
pent: 5 caged 6 shut in 7 boxed in, encaged, immured 8 closed in, confined, cooped up, fenced in, hedged in, hemmed in, interned, walled in 9 corralled 10 cloistered, imprisoned
penta-: 4 five
pentacle: 4 star
pentad: 7 quintet 9 quintette
Pentagon
bigwigs: 5 brass
org.: 3 DoD
VIP: 3 gen. 7 general
pentameter
iambic ~: 4 rime 5 meter, rhyme
unit: 4 foot, iamb
__ pentameter: 6 iambic 7 elegiac
pentane derivative: 4 amyl
Pentateuch: 4 Tora 5 Torah
author: 5 Moses
book: 6 Exodus 7 Genesis, Numbers 9 Leviticus 11 Deuteronomy
pentathlon: 5 sport
modern ~ event: 4 épée
Pentax: 6 camera
alternative: 4 Fuji 5 Canon, Kodak, Leica, Nikon 6 Konica, Rollei 7 Minolta, Olympus, Vivitar, Yashica 8 Polaroid
Pente: 4 game 9 board game
Pentecost: 5 feast 7 Holy Day
penthouse: 5 suite 9 apartment
feature: 4 view
in the ~: 4 atop
like a ~: 4 posh 5 plush, swank 6 swanky 9 expensive, luxurious
of a sort: 4 aery, eyry 5 aerie, eyrie
Penthouse (1933 film)
cast: Warner Baxter, Charles Butterworth, Myrna Loy
director: W.S. Van Dyke
Penticton: 4 city, town
locale: 6 Canada
Pentimento author: Lillian Hellman
Pentium: 4 chip
manufacturer: 5 Intel
unit: 3 GHz, MHz
pentlandite: 3 ore 7 mineral
pent-up: 6 curbed, shut in 7 bridled, checked, stifled 8 confined, held back, reined in 9 bottled-up, inhibited, repressed, smothered 10 restrained, restricted, suppressed
penuche: 5 candy
penultimate: 10 next-to-last
penumbra: 5 shade 6 shadow
penurious: 4 mean, near, poor 5 broke, cheap, close, needy, tight 6 bad off, greedy, hard up, ill off, in need, in want, skimpy, stingy 7 miserly, pinched, selfish 8 badly off, bankrupt, beggarly, deprived, grasping, indigent, strapped 9 destitute, flat broke, insolvent, moneyless, penniless 10 avaricious, down and out, economical, pauperized, skinflinty, straitened
state: 4 need 7 poverty
penuriousness: 5 greed 7 avarice
penury: 4 need, ruin, want 6 misery 7 beggary, poverty 9 indigence, privation 10 insolvency
Penza: 4 city, town
locale: 6 Russia
Penzance: 4 port
locale: 7 England
Penzias, Arno: 8 Nobelist 9 physicist
peon: 4 esne, hand, serf 5 slave 6 drudge, thrall 7 laborer, peasant 9 field hand
peonage: 4 yoke 7 slavery 9 servitude
peony: 5 plant, shrub 6 flower
people: 3 kin, mob 4 cats, clan, folk, herd, race, they 5 crowd, folks, plebs, tribe 6 bodies, family, humans, masses, nation, occupy, public, rabble 7 kinfolk, mankind, mortals, persons, society 8 citizens, humanity, kinfolks, kinsfolk, populace, riffraff 9 bourgeois, citizenry, hoi polloi, human race, multitude, plebeians, residents, vox populi 10 population
additional ~: 6 others
beautiful ~: 5 elite 6 jet set 7 society 8 nobility 10 blue bloods, upper crust
combining form: 3 dem- 4 demo- 5 ethno-
common ~: 4 herd 5 plebs 6 masses, rabble 8 plebians, riffraff 9 hoi polloi
full of ~: 5 dense 7 crowded 8 populous
let ~ know: 3 air 4 tell, vent 7 publish 8 proclaim 9 broadcast, publicize
many ~: 3 mob 4 gang, mass 5 crowd, crush, troop 9 multitude
values of a ~: 5 ethos
where most ~ live: 4 Asia
working ~: 5 labor 9 employees
people __: 5 mover 6 person
__ people: 3 lay 4 boat 6 little
People: 3 mag 4 song, tune 8 magazine
composer: 5 Styne 7 Merrill
person: 4 star 5 celeb 6 editor 9 celebrity
People __ Strange: 3 Are
__ People: 3 Cat 4 Show, Used 5 Night, Plain, Short, We the 6 Chosen, Listen, Lonely 7 Smiley's, Village
People (1964 song) artist: Barbra Streisand
People Are Funny: 8 game show
host: Art Linkletter
peopled: 7 settled 8 occupied 9 colonized
__ People Eater, The: 6 Purple
__ people go: 5 Let my
People Got to Be Free (1968 song)
artist: Rascals
People of the Deer author: Farley Mowat
__ People Play: 5 Games
people's
minding other ~ business: 4 nosy 5 nosey 6 prying, snoopy 7 gossipy
people's __: 5 court, front 7 commune
People's __: 5 Party 7 Charter
People's Choice, The
author: 4 Agar
dog: 4 Cleo

People's Court, The judge: Joseph Wapner
People's Liberation ___: 4 Army
___ People's Money: 5 Other
___ People, The: 4 Rain
People Will Say We're in Love composer: 7 Rodgers 11 Hammerstein
People Will Talk (1951 film)
cast: Jeanne Crain, Cary Grant
director: Joseph L. Mankiewicz
People, Yes, The: 4 poem
author: Carl Sandburg
Peoria: 4 city, town
athletes: 6 Braves
city near ~: 5 Pekin
locale: 7 Arizona 8 Illinois
school: 7 Bradley
pep: 2 go 3 vim, zip 4 kick, push, snap, zest, zing 5 drive, gusto, moxie, oomph, punch, spice, verve, vigor 6 bounce, energy, spirit, starch 8 buoyance, buoyancy, vitality, vivacity 9 animation 10 exuberance, friskiness, get up and go, liveliness
full of ~: 4 spry 5 agile, alive, vital 6 lively 7 playful, zestful
give a ~ talk: 4 urge 6 charge, exhort 7 cheer on, enliven 8 admonish, motivate 9 encourage
lack of ~: 6 anemia, apathy 7 anaemia 8 lethargy
lose ~: 4 flag, tire 5 weary 7 exhaust 8 slow down
rally shout: 3 rah, yay, yea 6 go team
up: 4 wake 5 cheer, liven, waken 6 turn on, vivify 7 animate, enliven, quicken 8 activate, energize, vitalize 9 encourage, stimulate 10 exhilarate, invigorate
pep ___: 4 talk 5 rally
Pep: 6 Willie
Pep Boy: 3 Moe 4 Jack 5 Manny
Pepcid: 7 antacid
alternative: 4 Tums 6 Maalox, Riopan, Zantac 7 Gelusil, Lactaid, Mylanta, Rolaids 8 Gaviscon 11 Alka-Seltzer, Pepto-Bismol
Pepe: 5 Le Pew 6 Le Moko
Pepe Le Pew defense: 4 odor
Pepin the ___: 5 Short
pepita: 5 snack
pepo: 5 gourd, melon 6 squash, veggie 7 pumpkin 8 cucumber 9 cantaloup, muskmelon, vegetable 10 cantaloupe, watermelon
Peppard, George: 5 actor
film: Breakfast at Tiffany's (1961)
Home From the Hill (1960)
How the West Was Won (1962)
Operation Crossbow (1965)
The Strange One (1957)
The Victors (1963)
spouse: Elizabeth Ashley
TV: The A-Team
pepper: 3 dot 4 pelt, spot 5 cover, spice, throw 6 flavor, season, veggie 7 spice up 8 jalapeño, sprinkle 9 condiment, punctuate, seasoning, vegetable
companion: 4 salt
dispenser: 4 mill 6 shaker
ender: 3 box, oni 4 corn, mint 5 grass
family shrub: 4 kava 5 cubeb
hot ~: 3 aji 5 chile, chili 6 chilli 7 cayenne, tabasco
kind of ~: 3 hot, red 4 bell 5 black, chile, green, sweet, white 6 cherry 7 cayenne, stuffed, tabasco
picker: 5 Peter
pot: 4 stew
pot ingredient: 4 meat, okra 5 tripe
rings: 9 appetizer
use a ~ mill: 5 grind 6 season
pepper ___: 3 pot, rat 4 game, mill, tree 5 steak
pepper-___: 5 upper
Pepper: 2 Dr. 3 Art, Sgt. 6 Martin
pepper-and-___: 4 salt
Pepperdine: 6 school 10 university
athletes: 5 Waves
locale: 6 Malibu 10 California
Pepper-Hot Baby (1955 song) artist: Jaye P. Morgan
Pepperidge ___: 4 Farm
peppermint: 4 herb 5 candy, sweet
candy: 5 patty, stick 6 pattie
peppermint ___: 3 oil 5 stick
Peppermint Patty to Marcie: 3 sir
Peppermint Twist (1961 song) artist: Joey Dee and the Starliters
pepperoni: 7 cold cut, sausage
place: 5 pizza 8 pizzeria
peppershrike: 5 vireo
pepperwort: 4 fern
peppery: 3 hot 4 gray, grey, sour 5 cross, fiery, sharp, spicy, testy 6 cranky, red-hot, snappy, spicey, touchy 7 piquant, pungent, zestful 8 choleric, snappish, spirited, stinging 9 irascible, irritable, trenchant, with a kick
Pepper Young's Family: 9 radio show
peppy: 4 spry 5 alert, brisk, perky, vital, zesty, zippy 6 active, bright, bubbly, feisty, frisky, lively 7 dashing, dynamic, piquant, rocking, romping, vibrant, zestful 8 animated, grooving, skittish, spirited, vigorous 9 energetic, sparkling, sprightly, vivacious
Pepsi: 3 pop 4 cola, soda 9 soft drink
competitor: 4 Coke 8 Diet Rite, Dr. Pepper
___ Pepsi: 4 Diet
pepsin: 6 enzyme
Pepsodent: 10 toothpaste
alternative: 3 Aim 5 Crest, Gleem, Ipana, Topol 7 Close-Up, Colgate, Viadent 9 Aquafresh, Mentadent, Rembrandt, Sensodyne 10 Pearl Drops, Ultra Brite 11 Tom's of Maine
peptide hormone: 5 kinin
Pepto-Bismol: 7 antacid
alternative: 4 Tums 6 Maalox, Pepcid, Riopan, Zantac 7 Gelusil, Lactaid, Mylanta, Rolaids 8 Gaviscon 11 Alka-Seltzer
Pep, Willie: 5 boxer
milieu: 4 ring
Pepys, Samuel: 6 writer 7 British, diarist
destination: 3 bed
Pequod: 4 boat, ship 6 whaler
captain: 4 Ahab
Pequot: 6 Indian 7 Amerind 8 language
per: 3 via 4 a pop, each 5 a head, every 6 apiece 7 for each, through
ender: 4 cent 5 force 6 chance, sister
per ___: 4 cent, diem, mill 5 annum 6 capita, centum, contra, curiam, mensem
perambulate: 4 rove, step, walk 5 amble, leg it, mosey 6 foot it, ramble, stroll 7 saunter 8 traverse, walk over
Per ardua ad ___: 5 astra
percale: 6 fabric 8 material, sheeting
per capita: 4 each 6 apiece
___ Percé: 3 Nez
perceivable: 7 obvious, visible 8 apparent, palpable
perceive: 3 get, see 4 feel, find, know, mark, note, spot, tell, view 5 catch, grasp, sense, sight, smell, think 6 behold, deduce, descry, divine, fathom, intuit, look on, notice, regard, remark, take in 7 cognize, discern, make out, observe, realize, receive 8 discover 9 apprehend, recognize 10 appreciate, comprehend, understand
ability to ~: 5 sight 7 empathy, insight 8 sympathy 9 intuition
fail to ~: 4 miss
with the nose: 5 sniff, whiff
perceiver: 4 eyer 6 viewer 7 witness 9 spectator
perceiving: 8 sentient 9 conscious, intuitive, sensitive 10 insightful
percent: 5 ratio 8 fraction 10 proportion
ender: 3 age, ile
fifty ~: 4 half 6 moiety
hundred ~: 3 all 5 fully 6 in full, in toto, purely, wholly 7 cap-a-pie, totally, utterly 8 entirely, from A to Z 9 all the way, every inch, to the hilt 10 absolutely, completely, thoroughly, to the limit
ten ~: 5 tithe
percent ___: 4 sign
percentage: 3 cut, lot 4 bite, gain, rate 5 bonus, chunk, juice, piece, quota, ratio, share, slice, split 6 payoff, profit 7 benefit, portion 8 discount, interest, kickback 9 advantage, allowance, brokerage 10 commission
percenter, ten: 5 agent
___-Per-Cent Solution, The: 5 Seven
perceptible: 4 real 5 clear, plain, vivid 6 cogent, visual 7 audible, evident, express, obvious, outward, sensory, visible 8 apparent, distinct, explicit, manifest, palpable, tangible 9 graspable, sensorial 10 noticeable, spelled out
perception: 3 ear, eye, ken, wit 4 grip, idea, plan, tact, wits 5 grasp, image, sense, sight 6 acumen, vision 7 concept, culture, feeling, hearing, insight, picture, thought 8 epiphany, eyesight, judgment, keenness 9 awareness, discovery, foresight, intuition, sensation 10 cognizance, horse sense, impression
extrasensory ~: 3 ESP 9 telepathy
keen ~: 5 grasp 6 acuity, acumen, wisdom 7 insight 8 judgment, lucidity 9 acuteness, awareness 10 astuteness, brainpower, brilliance, cleverness, shrewdness
___ perception: 5 depth, sense
___-perception: 4 self
perceptive: 4 keen, wise 5 acute, alert, aware, quick, ready, sharp 6 astute, shrewd, subtle, wise to 7 knowing, logical, tactful, tuned in 8 keen-eyed, lynx-eyed 9 astucious, cognizant, conscious, intuitive, judicious, observant, sagacious, sensitive 10 conversant, discerning, farsighted, insightful, responsive
perch: 3 sit 4 aery, eyry, fish, land, nest, pole, post, seat, stay 5 aerie, eyrie, light, lodge, roost, squat, stool 6 alight, branch, remain, settle 7 balance, seafood, sojourn 9 touch down
find a ~: 4 land 5 light 6 settle
high ~: 4 aery, eyry 5 aerie, eyrie
returned to the ~: 3 lit 4 alit 7 settled
___ perch: 4 sand, tule 5 black, ocean, pearl, white 6 golden, pirate, shiner, silver, yellow 7 rainbow
___-percha: 5 gutta
perchance: 4 lest 5 maybe 6 in case 7 perhaps 8 feasibly, possibly, probably
Percheron: 5 horse 6 animal, equine
repast: 3 hay 4 oats 5 grass 6 forage
perciatelli: 5 pasta
alternative: 4 orzo, ziti 5 penne, zitti 6 ditali, elbows, rigati, shells 7 fusilli, gnocchi, lasagna, lasagne, pastina, ravioli, rotelle, spirals 8 bucatini, couscous, farfalle, linguine, linguini, macaroni, rigatoni 9 agnolotti, alphabets, angelhair, cavatelli, macaroni, manicotti, spaghetti 10 cannelloni, conchiglie, fettuccine, fettuccini, tagliarini, tortellini, vermicelli
percipience: 3 wit 6 acumen
percipient: 5 aware, sharp 9 conscious, intuitive, observant 10 discerning
percolate: 4 drip, leak, ooze, seep, soak, weep 5 bleed, drain, exude, froth, leach, sweat 6 bubble, filter, ramble, strain 7 pervade, trickle 8 filter in, filtrate, permeate 9 lixiviate, penetrate, transfuse 10 impregnate, infiltrate
percussion: 5 crash 6 impact 9 collision, explosion
instrument: 3 riq, zil 4 bell, drum, gong, harp, trap 5 mbira, spoon, vibes 6 cabasa, caxixi, chimes, chimta, claves, cymbal, densho, ipu ipu, kenong, piatti, rattle, tam-tam 7 balafon, bonnang, cymbals, kalimba, maracas, marimba, mokugyo, sanh sua, shekere, sistrum 8 amadinda, angklung, carillon, ceng ceng, chocalho, clappers, gankogui, hyoshigi, Jew's harp, pandeíro, triangle 9 castanets, vibraharp 10 vibraphone
percussion ___: 3 cap 4 lock 7 flaking, welding
Percy: 5 Adlon, Faith, Henry 6 Sledge, Walker 7 Shelley 8 Bridgman, Kilbride 9 Rodrigues
Percy ___ Shelley: 6 Bysshe
Percy author: Hannah Moore
Percy, Thomas: 4 poet
Percy, Walker: 6 author, writer
work: Love in the Ruins
The Message in the Bottle
The Moviegoer
The Thanatos Syndrome
per diem: 4 a day 5 daily 7 diurnal 9 circadian, quotidian
Perdita's partner: 5 Pongo
perdition: 4 fall, hell, ruin 5 Hades 8 downfall 9 damnation
consign to ~: 4 damn 5 curse 9 imprecate
perdu: 6 hidden 9 concealed, invisible, unnoticed 10 out of sight, unviewable
père: 6 cleric, father, French
Père ___: 4 Noël 6 Goriot 8 Duchesne 9 Marquette
peregrinate: 4 hike, roam, rove, trek, walk 5 jaunt, march 6 ramble, travel, wander 7 journey, meander, wayfare 8 ambulate, traverse, walk over 9 itinerate 10 travel over
peregrination: 4 hike, tour, trek, trip, walk 5 jaunt 6 ramble, travel 7 journey 9 excursion
peregrine: 4 bird 5 alien 6 falcon 7 foreign 9 migrating, traveling, wandering
cover a ~'s eyes: 4 hood, seel
peregrine ___: 6 falcon
Peregrine Pickle author: Tobias Smollett
Pereira: 4 city, town
locale: 8 Colombia
Perelman, S.J.: 6 author, writer 8 humorist
peremptorily: 9 summarily
peremptory: 4 curt, firm, rude 5 bossy, final 6 lordly 7 binding 8 absolute, decisive, despotic, dogmatic 9 arbitrary, assertive, imperious, insistent, mandatory 10 aggressive, autocratic, commanding, despotical, dogmatical, high-handed, imperative, obligatory, tyrannical
peremptory ___: 4 plea
perennial: 3 old 5 plant 6 flower, steady, yearly 7 abiding, chronic, endless, eternal, lasting, nonstop, undying 8 constant, enduring, immortal, life-

long, long-term, timeless, unending, unwaning 9 ceaseless, chronical, continual, incessant, permanent, perpetual, recurrent, sustained, unabating, unceasing, unfailing 10 continuing, inveterate, persistent, unchanging
garden ~: 4 iris, lily, rose 5 aster, daisy, peony, phlox 7 daylily 9 coreopsis, oneflower 10 delphinium
Peres, Shimon: 2 P.M. 7 Israeli 8 Nobelist
predecessor: 5 Rabin 6 Shamir
successor: 6 Shamir 9 Netanyahu
Peretti: 4 Elsa
Perez: 4 Tony 5 Prado, Rosie 7 Vincent
__ Pérez de Cuellar: 6 Javier
Pérez Galdós, Benito: 6 author, writer 7 Spanish 10 playwright
Perez, Rosie: 7 actress
film: Fearless (1993)
It Could Happen to You (1994)
White Men Can't Jump (1992)
Perez, Tony: 3 Red
Perez, Vincent: 5 actor
film: Cyrano de Bergerac (1990)
Talk of Angels (1998)
Time Regained (1999)
perfect: 3 A-OK, def, rad, ten 4 aces, A-one, best, boss, braw, cool, dece, fine, gear, hone, keen, neat, nice, phat, pure, tops, tuff 5 clean, crown, dandy, ducky, exact, grand, great, ideal, marvy, model, neato, nobby, prime, right, sheer, slick, sound, super, swell, total, utter, whole 6 bang on, bang-up, better, bonzer, bosker, choice, dead-on, divine, dreamy, entire, evolve, far-out, finish, gnarly, groovy, intact, lovely, mature, peachy, polish, refine, revise, slap-up, smooth, spot on, strict, superb, terrif, tiptop, unreal, whizzo, wicked 7 achieve, amazing, awesome, capital, corking, correct, develop, improve, optimum, precise, realize, ripping, skookum, stellar, sublime, supreme, to a turn, touch up, utopian 8 absolute, accurate, complete, dazzling, especial, eximious, fabulous, five-star, flawless, four-star, frabjous, glorious, heavenly, jim-dandy, outright, peerless, polish up, round off, round out, slam-bang, smashing, splendid, standout, sterling, stickout, suitable, superior, terrific, textbook, thorough, top-level, topnotch, unbroken, unerring, unharmed, unmarred, very good, wondrous 9 bodacious, Endsville, excellent, exemplary, exquisite, faultless, first-rate, foolproof, high-grade, hunky-dory, just right, marvelous, matchless, sollicker, top-flight, unalloyed, undamaged, unrivaled, unspoiled, untouched, virtuosic, wonderful 10 accomplish, complement, consummate, first-class, hotsy-totsy, immaculate, impeccable, infallible, inimitable, jack-a-dandy, on the money, out of sight, peachy-keen, phenomenal, remarkable, stupendous, super-duper, unimpaired, unrivalled
at NASA: 3 AOK 5 a-okay
condition: 4 mint 7 like new
example: 7 epitome
4.0 is a ~ one: 3 GPA
game: 7 shutout 8 no-hitter
game spoiler: 3 hit 4 walk
in a ~ world: 7 ideally
it can be ~: 5 tense
not ~: 6 faulty, flawed 7 lacking 8 mediocre 10 incomplete
pair: 5 match
place: 4 Eden 6 heaven, Utopia 8 Paradise
rating: 3 ten
serve: 3 ace
perfect __: 3 gas 4 game, ream, year 5 pitch, rhyme, stage 6 number, square 7 binding, cadence
__ perfect: 4 past 6 future 7 present
__-perfect: 6 letter
Perfect (1985 film)
cast: Jamie Lee Curtis, John Travolta
director: James Bridges
Perfect __: 5 World 6 Recall
Perfect __, A: 5 Peace, World 6 Couple, Murder
Perfect __, The: 3 Spy 5 Storm
perfecta: 3 bet 5 wager
kin: 6 exacta
Perfect Couple, A (1979 film)
cast: Paul Dooley, Marta Heflin
director: Robert Altman
Perfect Day for Bananafish, A author: J.D. Salinger
perfection: 4 pink 5 ideal, prime, worth 6 purity 7 quality 8 fruition, maturity, ripeness 9 evolution, exactness, integrity, precision, sublimity, supremacy, wholeness 10 completion, excellence
standard of ~: 5 ideal
perfectionist: 5 type A 8 stickler
perfectly: 3 pat 4 to a T, well 5 fully, quite, right 6 dead-on, wholly 7 rightly, totally, utterly 8 entirely, laudably, superbly, very well, worthily 9 correctly, just right, on the nose, supremely 10 absolutely, altogether, completely, flawlessly, impeccably, thoroughly, to the limit
Perfect Murder, A (1998 film)
cast: Michael Douglas, Viggo Mortensen, Gwyneth Paltrow
director: Andrew Davis
perfecto: 5 cigar
Perfect Peace, A author: Amos Oz
Perfect Recall author: Ann Beattie
Perfect Sleeper maker: 5 Serta
Perfect Spy, A author: John le Carré
Perfect Storm, The (2000 film)
cast: George Clooney, Diane Lane, John C. Reilly, Mark Wahlberg
director: Wolfgang Petersen
setting: 3 sea
Perfect Strangers (ABC sitcom)
cast: Mark Linn-Baker (Larry Appleton)
Bronson Pinchot (Balki Bartokomous)
setting: Chicago, Illinois
Perfect World (1988 song) artist: Huey Lewis and the News
Perfect World, A (1993 film)
cast: Kevin Costner, Laura Dern, Clint Eastwood
director: Clint Eastwood
perfidious: 4 evil 5 false, lying 6 untrue 7 corrupt 8 disloyal, recreant 9 dishonest, faithless, insidious, insincere, two-timing 10 inconstant, traitorous
perfidy: 7 falsity, treason 8 bad faith, betrayal 9 dirty work, duplicity, treachery 10 disloyalty, untrueness, wickedness
perforate: 3 cut, pit 4 bore, open, stab 5 drill, prick, punch 6 pierce, riddle 8 puncture 9 honeycomb, penetrate
perforation: 4 hole 7 opening 8 puncture
perform: 2 do 3 act 4 sing 5 dance, emote, enact, serve, stage 6 acquit, commit, comply, effect, finish, fulfil, recite, render 7 achieve, execute, fulfill, ham it up, observe, operate, playact, produce, pull off, realize, satisfy 8 appear as, bring off, carry out, complete, function, generate, practice, transact 9 discharge, dramatize, implement, interpret 10 accomplish, effectuate
alone: 4 solo
a marriage: 3 wed 5 unite
in an opera: 4 sing 6 intone 7 belt out 8 vocalize
well: 5 excel, shine 7 surpass
with a baton: 5 twirl 7 conduct
without words: 4 mime 7 gesture 9 pantomime
performance: 3 act, gig 4 play, rite, show, work 5 dance, doing, drama, event, opera, revue, stunt 6 acting, action, ballet, record, rescue, review 7 burlesk, concert, matinee, pageant, pursuit, recital, special 8 ceremony, exercise, practice 9 burlesque, discharge, execution, operation, portrayal, rehearsal, rendition, spectacle, stage show, technique 10 recitation
acknowledge a ~: 4 clap 5 cheer 7 applaud
added ~: 6 encore
date: 7 booking
diva's ~: 4 aria 5 opera
extemporaneous ~: 6 improv
first ~: 7 opening 8 premiere
for charity: 7 benefit
jazz ~: 3 gig, set
mount a ~: 5 put on, stage
prepare for a ~: 8 practice, rehearse
short ~: 4 skit
virtuoso ~: 5 éclat
performance __: 3 art 4 bond, test
__ performance: 6 repeat 7 command
performed: 7 wrought
performer: 4 mime 5 actor, comic 6 artist, player 7 actress, trouper 8 comedian, musician, thespian, virtuoso
bit-part ~: 5 extra
carnival ~: 4 geek
circus ~: 3 dog 4 flea, pony, seal 5 clown, horse 7 acrobat, juggler 8 elephant 9 lion tamer
coffeehouse ~: 4 poet
extra: 6 encore
gesturing ~: 4 mime 5 clown, mimer, mimic
improv ~: 5 comic 8 comedian
kabuki ~: 4 male
monologue ~: 6 diseur
nightclub ~: 5 comic 6 singer 8 comedian
operatic ~: 4 alto, bass 5 basso, mezzo, tenor 7 soprano
paid ~: 3 pro
platform: 5 stage
rodeo ~: 5 roper 6 cowboy 7 cowgirl 8 cow belle 9 bullrider
solo ~: 4 diva 6 skater 7 danseur 9 ballerina, ice skater 10 prima donna
stunt ~: 5 clown 7 acrobat, juggler
symphony ~: 9 conductor, orchestra
top ~: 3 ace 4 star 9 headliner
union: 3 SAG 5 AFTRA
performing __: 4 arts, seal
perfume: 4 atar, balm, odor, otto 5 aroma, athar, attar, cense, ottar, scent, smell 6 sachet 7 bouquet, cologne, essence, incense 9 fragrance
amount: 3 dab 6 squirt
apply ~: 3 dab 5 spray
base: 4 atar, musk, otto 5 athar, attar, civet, orris, ottar
holder: 4 vial 5 phial 6 bottle, flacon
ingredient: 4 atar, musk, otto 5 athar, attar, civet, ester, myrrh, nerol, orris, ottar 6 acetal, citral, ionone
Japanese ~ source: 5 rasse
measure: 4 dram 5 ounce
name: 5 Estée 6 Chanel, Lanvin
scent: 4 lily, musk 7 jasmine 8 gardenia
solvent: 5 aldol 9 acetaldol
source: 5 civet, petal 6 flower
test spot: 5 wrist
__ perfumed sea: 4 o'er a
perfumy: 5 sweet 8 fragrant
perfunctory: 3 lax 4 cool 5 hasty, quick, stock, token 6 casual, remiss, sloppy, wooden 7 cursory, hurried, offhand, routine, sketchy, summary 8 careless, listless, lukewarm, slapdash, slipshod 9 apathetic, automatic, imprudent, negligent, unmindful 10 incautious, mechanical, nonchalant, uncritical, unthinking
pergola: 5 arbor, bower 8 pavilion 9 colonnade
perhaps: 4 lest 5 maybe 8 feasibly, possibly, probably 9 perchance 10 imaginably
peri: 3 fay 5 fairy 6 sprite
ending: 5 scope
Peri: 6 Gilpin
perianth part: 5 tepal
periapt: 5 charm 6 amulet, scarab 8 talisman
Peribán: 4 city, town
locale: 6 Mexico 9 Michoacán
pericarp: 4 aril 5 shell
Pericles: 5 Greek 6 orator
father: 10 Xanthippus
foe: 5 Cleon
mother: 8 Agariste
Pericles author: William Shakespeare
peridot: 3 gem 8 gemstone
color: 5 green
month: 6 August
perigee's opposite: 6 apogee
__ Pérignon: 3 Dom
peril: 4 risk 5 stake 6 danger, hazard, menace, threat 7 pitfall 8 endanger, exposure, jeopardy, unsafety 9 adventure, liability 10 insecurity, jeopardize
in ~: 6 at risk 7 at stake, exposed
perilous: 5 dicey, grave, hairy, risky, rocky, shaky, tight 6 chancy, loaded, touchy, unsafe, wicked 7 ominous, parlous, unsound 8 delicate, dynamite, menacing, slippery, ticklish 9 dangerous, hazardous, on thin ice, uncertain, unhealthy 10 precarious, touch and go
__ Perilous: 5 Siege
Perilous Holiday (1946 film)
cast: Alan Hale, Pat O'Brien, Ruth Warrick
perilousness: 4 risk 6 danger 7 gravity
Perils of Pauline, The: 6 serial
Perils of Pauline, The (1947 film)
cast: Constance Collier, Betty Hutton, John Lund
director: George Marshall
perimeter: 3 hem, rim 4 edge, side 5 ambit, limit, skirt, verge 6 border, bounds, circle, fringe, limits, margin 7 circuit, compass, outline 8 boundary, confines 9 periphery 10 boundaries
period: 3 age, day, dot, end, eon, era, run 4 aeon, halt, span, stop, term, time 5 close, cycle, epoch, limit, phase, point, shift, space, spell, stage, while 6 course, length, lesson, season, spread, streak 7 session, stretch 8 duration, interval, lifetime 9 cessation 10 conclusion, generation
brief ~: 5 spell
busy ~: 4 rush
calendar ~: 3 day 4 week, year 5 month
census ~: 6 decade
cooling-off ~: 4 stay 5 delay, grace, truce
galactic time ~: 3 age
geologic ~: 3 age, era 5 epoch
historical ~: 3 age, era 5 epoch 6 decade 7 century

lunch: 4 hour, noon
of decline: 3 ebb 5 slump 9 downswing 10 depression
off-peak ~: 4 lull 5 letup 6 hiatus 8 breather
of inactivity: 4 calm, lull 6 hiatus, layoff, recess, stasis 7 respite, timeout 8 downtime 9 interlude
of office: 4 term
of stability: 3 pax 5 peace
of time: 3 age, day, eon 4 aeon, hour, week 5 month, space 6 minute, moment, second 7 century 9 chilicosm 10 nanosecond
orbital ~: 4 year
pay ~: 4 week 5 month
probationary ~: 5 trial
prolonged ~ of trouble: 5 siege
prosperous ~: 4 boom 7 upswing
quiet ~: 4 lull
school ~: 4 term 8 semester
sports ~: 4 half 5 round 6 inning 7 chukker, quarter
work ~: 3 day 4 week 5 shift
period ___: 5 piece
___ period: 3 pay 5 grace 6 Sothic 7 waiting 10 breaking-in
periodic: 3 odd 4 eral 5 daily 6 annual, cyclic, hourly, random, spotty, weekly, yearly 7 epochal, erratic, monthly, regular, routine 8 cyclical, frequent, on-and-off, repeated, seasonal, sporadic 9 alternate, irregular, recurrent, recurring, spasmodic 10 occasional, sporadical
periodic ___: 3 law 4 acid 5 table 6 motion, system 7 decimal
periodical: 3 mag, rag 4 zine 5 daily, organ, paper, press, print, slick 6 review, weekly 7 journal, monthly 8 magazine 9 newspaper, quarterly
for short: 3 mag 4 zine
palindromic ~: 4 Elle
www. ~: 5 e-zine
periodically: 7 at times 9 sometimes 10 now and then
periodicals: 5 media
periodicity: 6 rhythm 10 regularity
periodic table
category: 3 gas 5 metal
datum: 4 at. no., at. wt.
member: 7 element
table suffix: 3 -ium
Periodic Table, The author: 4 Levi
Period of Adjustment: 4 film, play
author: Tennessee Williams
cast: Jane Fonda, Tony Franciosa, Jim Hutton
director: George Roy Hill
periodontist
concern: 3 gum
degree: 3 DDS
org.: 3 ADA
plea: 5 floss
peripatetic: 5 rover 6 mobile, roving 7 migrant, nomadic, roaming, vagrant 8 ambulant, gadabout, vagabond 9 itinerant, migratory, traveling, wandering, wayfaring
one: 4 goer 5 nomad, rover 8 gadabout, wanderer
peripheral: 5 add-on, minor, outer 7 surface 8 exterior, external, marginal, outlying 9 component, extrinsic, secondary 10 extraneous
peripheral ___: 6 vision
periphery: 3 hem, rim 4 brim, edge, side 5 limit, skirt, verge 6 border, fringe, limits, margin 7 outside, surface 8 boundary, confines 9 outskirts, perimeter 10 boundaries
periphrastic: 5 wordy 6 prolix 7 verbose 8 rambling 10 long-winded
periscope part: 4 tube 5 prism 6 mirror
perish the ___: 7 thought
peristyle: 5 patio 6 arcade, atrium 8 cloister 9 courtyard
periwinkle: 4 blue 5 plant, shell, vinca 6 flower 8 seashell
perjure oneself: 3 lie 7 falsify 8 forswear 9 foreswear
perjurer: 4 liar
confession: 5 I lied
perjury: 3 lie 5 lying
perk: 3 tip 4 brew, plus 5 bonus, extra, gravy 6 tipoff 7 benefit, largess, premium 8 dividend, gratuity, largesse 9 advantage, lagniappe
up: 4 gain 5 cheer, elate, extra, liven, rally, renew 6 revive, reward 7 elevate, enliven, improve, inspire, lighten, recover, refresh 8 brighten, interest, reassure 9 stimulate, take heart 10 convalesce, exhilarate, invigorate 16 recuperate. vivify
worker's ~: 4 ESOP 5 bonus 7 holiday 8 vacation
Perkins: 4 Carl, Tony 6 Marlin, Millie 7 Anthony, Frances 9 Elizabeth
Perkins, Anthony: 5 actor
film: Catch-22 (1970)
Fear Strikes Out (1957)
ffolkes (1980)
The Fool Killer (1965)
Friendly Persuasion (1956)
Goodbye Again (1961)
Green Mansions (1959)
The Lonely Man (1957)
The Matchmaker (1958)
Murder on the Orient Express (1974)
Pretty Poison (1968)
Psycho (1960)
Remember My Name (1978)
The Tin Star (1957)
WUSA (1970)
role: 5 Bates 6 Norman
Perkins, Carl song: Blue Suede Shoes (1956)
Perkins, Elizabeth: 7 actress
film: About Last Night ... (1986)
Avalon (1990)
Big (1988)
The Doctor (1991)
Enid Is Sleeping (1990)
He Said, She Said (1991)
Moonlight and Valentino (1995)
Sweet Hearts Dance (1988)
Perkins, Maxwell: 6 editor
Perkin, William: 7 chemist
perky: 4 busy, cute, pert, spry 5 alert, astir, brisk, happy, light, peppy, sunny 6 active, at work, bouncy, bright, bubbly, cheery, jaunty, lively 7 buoyant, chipper, dynamic, rocking, working 8 animated, bubbling, bustling, cheerful, grooving, spirited, tireless, untiring 9 assiduous, energetic, sprightly, vivacious
Perl: 8 language
alternative: 3 ADA, APL, SQL 4 Alef, html, Icon, Java, LISP, Logo, Orca 5 Algol, Basic, Cecil, COBOL, Dylan, SISAL 6 Delphi, Eiffel, Erlang, Oberon, Pascal, Prolog, Sather, Scheme, Snobol 7 Fortran
Perle: 5 Mesta
Perlea, Jonel: 9 conductor
Perlman: 3 Ron 4 Rhea 6 Itzhak
Perlman, Itzhak: 7 Israeli 9 violinist
Perlman, Rhea: 7 actress
spouse: Danny DeVito
Perl, Martin: 8 Nobelist 9 physicist
perm: 4 curl, wave
follow-up: 3 set 4 trim
part of a ~ kit: 6 curler
Perm: 4 city, town
locale: 6 Russia
permafrost: 3 ice
permanence: 6 fixity 9 constancy, endurance, existence, fixedness, stability 10 durability
permanent: 4 coif, firm 5 fixed 6 hairdo, rooted, stable, static 7 abiding, lasting, settled, undying 8 coiffure, constant, definite, enduring, immortal, ironclad, lifelong, long-term, standing, unfading, unwaning 9 continual, immutable, indelible, perennial, perpetual, steadfast 10 changeless, inerasable, inveterate, stationary, unchanging, undecaying
be ~: 4 last, stay 6 endure
make ~: 3 fix, set 6 lock in
marker: 3 pen
place: 5 salon 10 beauty shop
result: 4 curl, wave
permanent ___: 3 way 4 echo, lens, mold, wave 5 press, tooth 6 magnet, record
permanently: 6 always 7 forever, for good 8 evermore, for keeps 9 for always 10 for all time
Permanent Midnight (1998 film)
cast: Maria Bello, Elizabeth Hurley, Ben Stiller, Owen Wilson
director: David Veloz
permanent-press feature: 5 pleat 6 crease
Permanent Record (1988 film)
cast: Alan Boyce, Michelle Meyrink, Keanu Reeves
director: Marisa Silver
permeable: 4 thin 6 porous 8 bibulous, pervious 9 absorbent 10 penetrable, spongelike
permeate: 4 fill, seep, soak 5 imbue, steep 6 charge, drench, embrue, filter, imbrue, infuse, invade, occupy 7 pervade, suffuse 8 filter in, saturate 9 go through, penetrate, percolate 10 impregnate, infiltrate
permed: 4 wavy 5 curly 6 frizzy 7 frizzly
per mensum: 7 monthly
permissible: 2 OK 4 good, okay 5 legal, legit, licit 6 kasher, kosher, lawful, proper 8 all right, approved, bearable, endorsed 9 allowable, permitted, tolerable, tolerated
permission: 2 OK 3 nod 4 okay 5 leave, order, right, the OK 6 assent, permit 7 consent, freedom, go-ahead, liberty, license, warrant 8 approval, blessing, sanction 9 admission, agreement, authority 10 acceptance, concession
give ~: 3 let 5 agree, allow, grant, yield 6 accede, enable, permit 7 approve, certify, concede, empower, endorse, entitle, license 8 sanction 9 acquiesce, authorize
refuse ~: 3 nix 4 veto 6 forbid
word of ~: 2 ay, ja 3 aye, oui, yea, yep, yes, yup 4 fine, okay, sure, yeah 5 uh-huh 6 agreed, gladly, surely 7 go ahead, mais oui, ten-four 8 all right, of course, thumbs up, very well 9 be my guest, certainly 10 by all means, sure enough
written ~: 4 pass
permissive: 3 lax 4 easy, free, kind, mild, soft 5 loose, slack 6 gentle, kindly 7 clement, lenient, liberal, ruthful, sparing 8 allowing, flexible, laid-back, merciful, placable, tolerant, unstrict 9 agreeable, approving, assuasive, compliant, easygoing, forgiving, indulgent 10 forbearing, unexacting, unhardened
word: 3 may, yes
permissiveness: 6 laxity, lenity 8 lenience 9 tolerance
permit: 2 OK 3 let 4 bear, have, okay, pass, visa 5 agree, allow, bless, brook, grant, humor, leave, say OK, yield 6 accede, accept, enable, endure, patent, say yes, suffer, ticket, wink at 7 approve, consent, empower, endorse, entitle, go-ahead, indorse, indulge, intitle, liberty, license, qualify, receive, warrant 8 accede to, assent to, legalize, passport, sanction, stand for, thumbs-up, tolerate, variance 9 acquiesce, approve of, authorize, franchise, give leave, let happen, put up with, sign off on 10 green light, permission
travel ~: 4 visa 6 carnet 8 passport
Permit Me Voyage author: 4 Agee
permitted: 2 OK 4 able, okay, open 5 legit, licit 6 kosher, lawful, proper 8 rightful 9 by the book 10 admissible
permutable: 6 in flux 8 changing, shifting 10 changeable
permutation: 5 shift 6 change 8 mutation
permute: 4 vary 5 alter, shift 6 change, modify
Pernell: 7 Roberts
pernicious: 3 bad 4 evil 5 fatal, toxic 6 deadly, lethal, malign, nocent, wicked 7 baleful, baneful, harmful, hurtful, miasmic, nocuous, noxious, ruinous 8 damaging, sinister, venomous, virulent 9 dangerous, injurious, malicious, nefarious, pestilent, poisonous 10 calamitous, evil-minded
Pernod: 5 drink 7 liqueur 8 beverage
ingredient: 5 anise
Perón: 3 Eva 4 Juan 5 Evita 6 Isabel
perorate: 4 rant 6 preach 7 declaim, descant, discant, lecture 8 bloviate, harangue 9 discourse, expatiate, hold forth, sermonize, speechify
Perot: 4 Ross 5 H. Ross
Perote: 4 city, town
locale: 6 Mexico 8 Veracruz
___ peroxide: 6 barium, sodium 7 benzoyl
peroxide user: 6 blonde
perp: 5 felon 7 accused, suspect 8 criminal 9 wrongdoer 10 lawbreaker
catcher: 3 cop 6 police 9 detective, policeman
pick up a ~: 3 nab 4 bust 5 catch, pinch 6 arrest, collar 7 capture
perpendicular: 5 erect, on end, plumb, sheer, steep 7 upright 8 standing, straight, vertical
almost ~: 5 sheer, steep
off the ~: 5 alist 7 leaning, tilting 9 at an angle
to the keel: 5 abeam
perpetrate: 2 do 3 act 5 enact, wreak 6 commit, effect 7 execute, pull off 8 carry out 9 force upon, succeed in
perpetrator: 5 felon, thief 6 robber 8 criminal
___ perpetua: 4 esto
Perpetua: 4 font 5 saint 8 typeface
perpetual: 3 old 4 same 6 eterne, steady 7 abiding, endless, eternal, lasting, nonstop, undying 8 constant, enduring, immortal, infinite, long-term, repeated, standing, timeless, unbroken, unending, unwaning 9 ceaseless, continual, immutable, incessant, perennial, permanent, recurrent, recurring, repeating, unceasing, unfailing 10 continuous, invariable, unchanging, without end
perpetual ___: 5 check 6 motion
perpetually: 4 ever 6 always 7 forever 8 evermore 9 for always
Perpetual Peace author: 4 Kant
perpetuate: 6 secure 7 prolong, support, sustain 8 continue, maintain, preserve

9 keep going
perpetuity: 8 duration, sequence 9 constancy, continuum, extension, stability 10 continuity
in ~: 6 always 7 forever 9 eternally
perplex: 4 balk, faze 5 addle, amaze, baulk, cloud, floor, mix up, snarl, stump 6 baffle, bemuse, boggle, fuddle, muddle, puzzle, rattle 7 astound, buffalo, confuse, fluster, mystify, nonplus, perturb, stagger, trouble 8 astonish, befuddle, bewilder, confound, encumber, entangle, surprise 9 discomfit, dumbfound 10 discompose, disconcert
perplexed: 4 asea, lost 5 at sea 6 in a fog 7 at a loss, in a daze, puzzled 9 flummoxed 10 bewildered
perplexing: 4 hard 5 funny, mirky, murky, tough, vague 6 arcane, knotty, thorny, tricky 7 complex, cryptic, obscure, strange, unclear 8 abstruse, nebulous, puzzling 9 confusing, cryptical, difficult, enigmatic, intricate 10 indistinct, unsettling
perplexity: 4 knot, maze 5 worry 6 enigma, strait 8 quandary 9 amazement, confusion, labyrinth 10 difficulty
state of ~: 3 fog 4 daze
perquisite: 3 pay, tip 5 bonus, extra, gravy, right 6 tipoff 7 benefit, premium, revenue 8 dividend, gratuity 9 lagniappe, privilege
Perrault, Charles: 6 author, French, writer
Perreau: 4 Gigi
Perrier alternative: 4 Naya 5 Evian 8 Aquafina 9 Arrowhead
Perrine: 4 city, town 7 Valerie
locale: 7 Florida
Perrine, Valerie: 7 actress
film: The Border (1982)
The Electric Horseman (1979)
The Last American Hero (1973)
Lenny (1974)
Maid to Order (1987)
Superman (1978)
W.C. Fields and Me (1976)
Superman role: 3 Eve
Perrin, Jean: 7 chemist 8 Nobelist 9 physicist
__ & Perrins: 3 Lea
Perris: 4 city, town
locale: 10 California
perry: 5 drink 8 beverage
Perry: 3 Joe 4 Como, King, Luke 5 Ellis, Frank, Mason, Steve, White 6 Botkin, Oliver 7 Gaylord, Matthew 10 Antoinette
victory site: 4 Erie
Perry, Frank: 8 director
film: Compromising Positions (1985)
David and Lisa (1962)
Diary of a Mad Housewife (1970)
Hello Again (1987)
Ladybug Ladybug (1963)
Last Summer (1969)
Mommie Dearest (1981)
Rancho Deluxe (1975)
The Swimmer (1968)
Perry, Gaylord: 6 hurler 7 pitcher
Perry Hall: 4 city, town
locale: 8 Maryland
Perry Mason (CBS drama)
cast: Raymond Burr (Perry Mason)
Barbara Hale (Della Street)
William Hopper (Paul Drake)
William Talman (Hamilton Burger)
creator: Erle Stanley Gardner
feature: 5 trial 6 murder 9 courtroom
Perry, Ralph Barton: 11 philosopher
Persa daughter: 5 Aeaea, Circe, Kirke
perscrutation: 5 probe
perse: 4 blue 6 purple
persecute: 3 dog, rag 4 bait, ride 5 abuse, bully, grind, harry, hound, spite, tease, worry, wrong 6 badger, harass, hector, pester, pick on, plague, pursue 7 afflict, oppress, torment, torture 8 aggrieve, ill-treat, keep down, maltreat 9 beleaguer, tyrannize, victimize
persecutor: 3 foe 5 bully, enemy
Persephone
equivalent: 10 Proserpina
husband of ~: 5 Hades, Pluto
love of ~: 4 Zeus 6 Adonis
parent of ~: 4 Zeus 7 Demeter
son of ~: 7 Zagreus
Persepolis locale: 4 Iran
Perse, St.-John: 4 poet 6 French 8 diplomat, Nobelist
Perseus
daughter of ~: 10 Gorgophone
father of ~: 4 Zeus
mother of ~: 5 Danae
neighbor of ~: 5 Aries
son of ~: 6 Heleus, Mestor, Perses 7 Alcaeus, Cynurus 9 Electyron, Sthenelus
star in ~: 5 Algol
victim of ~: 6 Medusa
wife of ~: 9 Andromeda
perseverance: 4 cool, grit, guts, zeal 5 drive, moxie, pluck, spunk 7 stamina 8 backbone, hard work, patience, sedulity, tenacity 9 constancy, diligence, endurance, stability
persevere: 4 go on, hold, plod 5 abide, retry 6 endure, hang in, hold on, insist, keep on, pursue, remain, resist 7 carry on, go for it, persist, press on, proceed, survive 8 continue, go on with, maintain, plug away, work hard 9 hang tough, keep going, stand firm 10 go for broke
persevering: 4 at it 6 dogged 7 patient 8 diligent, hellbent, resolute, sedulous, stubborn, tireless, untiring 9 laborious, steadfast, tenacious
Pershing: 4 John
colleague: 4 Foch
Pershing II: 4 ICBM 7 missile
Persia
ancient city: 4 Susa
ancient native: 4 Mede
astronomer: 4 Omar 7 Khayyám
bird: 6 bulbul
lamb: 3 fur
language: 5 Farsi, Parsi 8 Parthian
mathematician: 4 Omar 7 Khayyám
money: 5 daric
mythology angel: 3 mah
poet: 4 Omar, Sa'di 5 Hafez, Hafiz 7 Khayyám
queen: 6 Esther
religion: 5 Baha'i
ruler: 4 Shah
siren: 5 houri
sprite: 4 peri
tiger: 4 sher
title: 5 sophy
today: 4 Iran
Persian: 3 cat 4 Gulf 5 felid, Irani 6 feline 8 language
remark: 3 mew 4 meow 5 miaou, miaow, miaul
rug: 5 kilim 6 Kirman
Persian __: 3 cat, rug 4 Gulf, knot, lamb 5 lilac, melon 6 blinds, carpet, Empire, violet, walnut
Persian Gulf
ancient kingdom: 4 Elam
capital: 4 Doha
city: 5 Basra, Busra 6 Busrah
country: 5 Katar, Qatar 6 Koweit, Kuwait
federation: 3 UAE
island: 7 Bahrain, Bahrein
port: 5 Dibai, Dubai
region: 4 Hasa
strait: 5 Ormuz 6 Hormuz
vessel: 5 oiler 6 tanker
Persians, The author: Aeschylus
persiflage: 4 talk 6 banter 7 ribbing 8 badinage, raillery, repartee, wordplay
persimmon: 4 tree 5 fruit
family: 5 ebony
Japanese ~: 4 kaki
Persion Boy, The author: Mary Renault
Persis: 9 Khambatta
persist: 2 go 4 go on, hold, last 5 abide, recur, stick 6 endure, hang it, hold on, insist, linger, obtain, pursue, remain, resist 7 carry on, survive 8 continue, go on with, maintain, plug away 9 hang tough, keep going, persevere, stand firm 10 go the limit, tough it out
persistence: 7 purpose 8 patience, tenacity 10 resolution
Persistence of Memory: 8 painting
artist: 4 Dali
persistent: 4 firm 5 fixed, pushy 6 dogged, steady, wilful 7 abiding, chronic, endless, undying, willful 8 constant, diligent, enduring, frequent, habitual, haunting, hellbent, lifelong, obdurate, repeated, resolute, sedulous, stubborn, tireless, untiring, unwaning 9 assiduous, chronical, continual, incessant, insistent, obstinate, perennial, steadfast, tenacious, unabating, unfailing 10 consistent, determined, inveterate, undeterred, unflagging, unwearying
persisting: 6 living 7 lasting 8 unwaning 9 continual 10 inveterate
combining form: 4 meno-
Persius: 4 poet 5 Roman
Persky: 4 Bill
persnickety: 5 fussy, picky 6 choosy, dainty, prissy 7 choosey, finicky, mincing, precise 8 exacting, finiking, finnicky, snobbish 9 selective 10 fastidious, nitpicking
Persoff: 8 Nehemiah
person: 3 gal, guy, man 4 body, self, sort, soul 5 being, human, joker, party, woman 6 feller, mortal 7 grown-up 8 customer, organism, somebody, specimen 9 character, earthling, personage 10 human being, individual, living soul
artificial ~: 5 droid, robot
beautiful ~: 6 vision
boat ~: 7 refugee
busy ~: 4 doer 6 dynamo
charitable ~: 5 donor
cleaning ~: 4 maid 7 janitor, servant
clumsy ~: 3 oaf 4 clod 5 klutz 7 bumbler
combining form: 6 prosop- 7 prosopo-
contemptible ~: 3 cad 4 jerk, worm 9 no-good-nik, sleazebag
crafty ~: 3 fox 8 slyboots
delivery ~: 6 driver 7 mailman 9 messenger
different ~: 5 other 7 another
displaced ~: 5 exile 6 émigré 7 outcast, refugee 8 emigrant
enlisted ~: 7 private, recruit, soldier
experienced ~: 3 pro 6 old pro 7 old hand, veteran
famous ~: 4 star 5 celeb 6 phenom 7 notable 8 luminary 9 celebrity, dignitary, headliner 10 phenomenon
funny ~: 3 wag 4 card, riot, zany 5 comic 6 scream
gifted ~: 3 wiz 6 genius 10 precocious
gullible ~: 3 sap 4 butt, dupe, tool 5 chump, patsy 6 pigeon, sucker, victim 7 fall guy 8 pushover
haughty ~: 4 snob 5 snoot
head ~: 4 boss 5 chief 7 foreman, manager 8 official
important ~: 3 VIP 4 czar, lion, name, star, tsar 5 mogul, mover, nabob, titan 6 shaker, tycoon 7 magnate, notable 8 luminary, somebody 9 celebrity, dignitary, plutocrat
in custody: 4 ward 5 felon 6 orphan 8 detainee
learned ~: 4 prof, sage 5 brain 7 scholar 9 professor
little ~: 3 elf 5 dwarf, faery, fairy, troll 6 faerie, midget 10 leprechaun
mean ~: 4 ogre 5 brute, bully
messy ~: 4 slob 5 frump
middle ~: 5 agent 6 broker, jobber 8 mediator 9 go-between
named derived from a ~: 6 eponym
new ~: 4 baby 5 hiree 6 novice 7 recruit 9 greenhorn 10 tenderfoot
newspaper ~: 6 editor 8 reporter 10 journalist
odd ~: 4 kook 5 crank, flake 6 weirdo 7 oddball 9 character, eccentric 10 individual
outgoing ~: 5 mixer 9 extrovert
per ~: 4 a pop, each 6 apiece
PR ~: 5 flack 8 promoter
repair ~: 5 fixer 8 mechanic 9 carpenter, craftsman
retired ~: 6 senior
rich ~: 6 fat cat 9 financier, moneybags
right-hand ~: 4 aide, asst. 6 helper 8 henchman, mainstay 9 assistant, gal Friday, man Friday 10 girl Friday
starter: 3 lay 4 news, wait 5 chair, sales 6 anchor, spokes 8 business
surly ~: 4 crab 5 churl, crank 6 grouch 10 curmudgeon
swell ~: 5 brick, honey, peach 7 sweetie 10 sweetheart
tiresome ~: 4 bore, pain, pest, pill
unfashionable ~: 4 geek, wonk 7 egghead
watch ~: 5 guard, scout 6 sentry 7 lookout
young ~: 3 boy, imp, kid, lad, son 4 babe, baby, brat, cion, teen, ward 5 bairn, child, minor, scion, youth 6 cherub, infant, moppet, nipper, squirt 7 bambino, neonate, newborn, preteen, sapling 8 daughter, juvenile, small fry, teenager 9 offspring, stripling 10 adolescent, descendant
__ person: 5 first, night, stunt, third 6 people, second 7 advance
persona
cast ~: 4 role 9 character
Halloween ~: 5 ghost, ghoul, haunt, spook, witch 7 vampire
opposite: 5 anima
public ~: 5 image 6 facade
persona __ grata: 3 non
Persona (1966 film)
cast: Bibi Andersson, Liv Ullmann
director: Ingmar Bergman
personable: 2 OK 4 nice, okay, warm 7 affable, amiable, cordial, likable, winning 8 all heart, all right, amicable, charming, friendly, likeable, outgoing, pleasant, pleasing, sociable 9 agreeable, easygoing 10 gregarious
personae, dramatis: 4 cast
personage: 3 VIP 4 name, soul 5 brass, celeb 6 bigwig, figure, person, top dog, worthy 7 big shot, hotshot, notable 8 eminence, luminary, somebody 9 celebrity, character, dignitary, superstar 10 individual

personal: 3 own 5 inner, privy 6 bodily, direct, inward, proper, secret 7 private, special 8 intimate, peculiar, ulterior 9 exclusive, innermost, nonpublic 10 individual, particular, respective, subjective
ad letters: 3 SWF, SWM
advisor: 4 guru 6 lawyer 7 teacher, trainer 8 attorney 9 counselor
asset: 4 pull 5 charm, magic 6 allure, appeal, glamor 7 charism, glamour 8 charisma, mystique, presence 9 magnetism
atmosphere: 4 aura 5 vibes 8 charisma
attendant: 4 aide 5 valet 9 chauffeur, secretary
combining form: 4 idio-
effects: 5 stuff 6 things 8 property
get too ~: 3 spy 5 snoop, stare 6 butt in, horn in, meddle 7 intrude, obtrude, wiretap 8 question 9 interfere
history: 3 bio 6 memoir, résumé 7 autobio, memoirs, profile 9 biography
interest: 5 share 10 investment
viewpoint: 4 bias 5 slant 7 opinion
personal __: 4 best, care, foul 5 space, staff 7 effects, pronoun, trainer
Personal __: 4 Best, Foul
Personal Best (1982 film)
cast: Scott Glenn, Mariel Hemingway
director: Robert Towne
Personal Finance rival: 5 Money
personal flotation __: 6 device
Personal Foul (1987 film)
cast: Adam Arkin, Susan Wheeler Duff, David Morse
director: Ted Lichtenfield
Personal Injuries author: Scott Turow
personality: 3 VIP, way 4 name, self, star 5 brass, celeb, charm 6 bigwig, figure, makeup, nature, psyche, temper, top dog, traits, worthy 7 big shot, charism, hotshot, notable 8 charisma, dynamism, eminence, identity, luminary, presence, selfhood, somebody 9 celebrity, dignitary, magnetism, mentality, superstar
asset: 4 tact 5 charm, poise
kind of ~: 5 type A, type B
part: 2 id 3 ego 5 anima 7 persona 8 superego
__ personality: 5 split
Personality (1959 song) artist: Lloyd Price
Personality composer: 5 Burke 9 Van Heusen
personalize: 7 initial 8 monogram
Personal Witness author: 4 Eban
persona non __: 5 grata
personate: 7 imitate
personify: 6 embody, imbody, mirror, typify 7 express 8 manifest, stand for 9 exemplify, incarnate, represent, symbolize 10 illustrate
personnel: 4 crew 5 cadre, corps, staff, troop 6 office, troops 7 faculty, helpers, members, workers 8 manpower 9 employees, work force 10 associates
datum: 3 age, sex
enlisted ~: 3 GIs 6 grunts 8 privates, recruits, soldiers
hire ~: 3 man 5 reman, staff 6 take on
key ~: 4 core
slot: 3 job 4 post 8 position
Person, place, and Thing author: Karl Shapiro
Persons and Places author: George Santayana
__ Person Singular: 6 Absurd
Person to Person (CBS) host: Edward R. Murrow
perspective: 4 view 5 angle, scene, slant, vista 6 aspect 7 context, horizon, mindset, outlook 8 attitude, overview, panorama, prospect 9 landscape, viewpoint
perspicacious: 4 keen, wise 5 acute, alert, canny, quick, savvy, sharp, smart 6 astute, clever, shrewd 7 politic 8 incisive, luminous, rational 9 astucious, observant, sagacious
perspicacity: 3 wit 4 wits 6 acumen, wisdom 7 insight 8 judgment, keenness
perspicuous: 5 clear, lucid 6 limpid 7 graphic, logical 8 apparent, clear-cut, luminous 9 graphical
perspiration: 5 sweat 6 egesta 8 moisture
combining form: 4 hidr- 5 hidro-
perspire: 4 drip, glow, ooze 5 egest, exude, sweat 6 lather 7 excrete, secrete, swelter
perspiring: 3 hot 4 warm 6 sweaty 10 overheated
Persson: 4 Nina
persuadable: 4 meek 6 docile 8 amenable 9 receptive, tractable 10 indecisive
persuade: 3 con, get, win, woo 4 bend, coax, draw, hook, lead, lure, move, push, sell, sway, talk, turn, urge 5 budge, impel, lobby, tempt 6 advise, affect, assure, cajole, compel, enlist, entice, exhort, incite, induce, prompt, reason 7 convert, counsel, impress, incline, involve, satisfy, wheedle, win over 8 blandish, convince, inveigle, motivate, talk into, wear down 9 argue into, brainwash, influence, instigate, prevail on
more than ~: 5 force 6 compel 8 armtwist, pressure
to marry: 3 win, woo 5 court
persuasion: 4 cult, sect, type, urge, view 5 creed, faith, party 6 advice, belief, church, school 7 coaxing, faction, opinion, snow job 8 cajolery, hard sell, pressure, religion, soft soap 9 dialectic, incentive, sentiment, sweet talk, wheedling 10 conviction, enticement
Persuasion author: Jane Austen
persuasive: 5 slick 6 cogent, moving, potent, smooth, strong 7 logical, telling, weighty 8 alluring, credible, eloquent, enticing, forceful, inviting, luculent, powerful 9 dialectic, disarming, effective, effectual, impelling, plausible 10 believable, convincing
pert: 4 bold, cute, flip, rude, spry 5 brash, brisk, fresh, lippy, nervy, perky, sassy, saucy, smart 6 awless, brazen, breezy, bright, cheeky, dapper, jaunty, lively, nimble, snappy, snippy 7 aweless, chipper, forward, uncivil 8 animated, cheerful, flippant, impolite, impudent, insolent, snippety, spirited 9 audacious, out of line, sprightly, vivacious 10 ungracious
female: 4 minx 5 hussy
Pert: 6 Kelton 7 shampoo
competitor: 4 Flex 5 Prell, Suave, Wella 7 Finesse, Pantene
pertain: 5 apply, refer, touch 6 affect, bear on, belong, regard, relate 7 concern, connect, touch on 8 bear upon, belong to 9 touch upon
pertaining: 4 as to 8 relative 9 pertinent 10 concerning, in regard to
Perth: 4 city, town
locale: 9 Australia
river: 3 Tay
Perth Amboy: 4 city, town
locale: 9 New Jersey
pertinacious: 5 onery, rigid 6 dogged, mulish, ornery, wilful 7 adamant, staunch, willful 8 contrary, obdurate, resolute, stalwart, stubborn, untiring 9 obstinate, pigheaded, steadfast, unbending 10 determined, headstrong, inflexible, persistent, unyielding
pertinent: 3 apt 5 ad rem, valid 6 cogent, proper, timely 7 apropos, fitting, germane, logical, on point, pointed, related, salient 8 apposite, material, relative, relevant, suitable, verified 9 competent, connected 10 admissible, applicable, felicitous, pertaining, to the point
be ~: 5 apply, refer 6 bear on, regard, relate 7 concern, touch on
pertness: 5 sauce 9 flippancy, impudence, insolence
perturb: 3 ail, bug, get, irk, vex 4 faze, miff 5 alarm, anger, annoy, harry, peeve, shake, upset, worry 6 affect, bother, dismay, flurry, needle, pester, put out, rattle, ruffle 7 agitate, chagrin, confuse, disturb, fluster, perplex, provoke, shake up, trouble, unnerve 8 bewilder, confound, disquiet, exercise, irritate, unsettle, unstring 9 discomfit 10 discomfort, discompose, disconcert, disgruntle
perturbed: 5 het up, upset 6 on edge, pacing, uneasy 7 shook up, worried 8 in a tizzy, restless 9 concerned, in a lather, unsettled 10 distraught, distressed, up in the air
Peru: 6 nation 7 country
ancient culture: 4 Inca 5 Nazca
beast: 5 llama 6 alpaca, vicuña
brandy: 5 pisco
capital: 4 Lima
cereal: 6 quinoa
city: 3 Ica 5 Cusco, Cuzco, Piura, Tacna 8 Arequipa, Trujillo
desert: 7 Sechura
explorer: 7 Pizarro
lake: 8 Titicaca
language: 6 Aymara, Jivaro, Kechua 7 Spanish
money: 3 sol 4 inti
mountain: 5 Cusco, Cuzco 6 Ampato 7 Huandoy 8 Coropuna, Solimana, Yerupaja 9 Huascarán, Pumasillo, Salcantay
mountains: 5 Andes
native: 4 Inca 6 Aymara, Jivaro, Kechua 7 Kechuan, Quechua, Quichua 8 Quechuan
neighbor: 5 Chile 6 Brazil 7 Bolivia, Ecuador 8 Colombia
org.: 3 OAS
poet: 4 Moro 6 Eguren
port: 5 Paita 6 Callao
river: 5 Purus 6 Amazon, Javari
saint: 10 Rose of Lima
tanager: 4 yeni
volcano: 7 El Misti
wind: 4 puna
writer: 5 Palma 7 Alegría 8 Arguedas
see also Spanish
Perugia: 4 city, town
locale: 5 Italy
town near ~: 6 Assisi
Perugina: 5 candy 9 chocolate
peruke: 3 wig 6 toupee
perusal: 5 study 6 review, survey 7 reading 8 scrutiny 10 inspection
peruse: 3 con 4 pore, read, scan, skim 5 learn, study 6 browse, look up 7 analyze, examine, inspect 8 check out, look over, pore over 10 glance over, scrutinize
Perutz, Max: 7 chemist 8 Nobelist
pervade: 4 fill 5 imbue, steep 6 charge, extend, infuse, occupy, riddle, spread 7 suffuse 8 permeate, saturate 9 penetrate, percolate 10 overspread
pervasive: 4 rife 6 common 7 all over, general 8 infested, profound 9 extensive, prevalent, universal 10 ubiquitous, widespread
quality: 4 aura, odor 5 vibes 10 atmosphere, vibrations
perverse: 3 wry 5 balky, onery, rigid, surly, wrong 6 dogged, morose, mulish, ornery, sullen, unruly, wanton, wilful 7 corrupt, naughty, vicious, wayward, willful 8 contrary, factious, indocile, obdurate, sadistic, sinister, stubborn, untoward 9 fractious, miscreant, nefarious, obstinate, pigheaded, unhealthy, unnatural 10 headstrong, ill-natured, inflexible, rebellious, refractory, self-willed
__-per-view: 3 pay
pervious: 6 porous 9 permeable, pregnable 10 vulnerable
pes: 3 paw 4 foot, hoof
pesante: 7 heavily
Pescadores: 4 isls. 5 isles 7 islands
locale: 6 Taiwan
Pesci, Joe: 5 actor
film: Betsy's Wedding (1990)
Casino (1995)
GoodFellas (1990, AA)
Home Alone (1990)
Home Alone 2: Lost in New York (1992)
JFK (1991)
Lethal Weapon 2 (1989)
Lethal Weapon 3 (1992)
Lethal Weapon 4 (1998)
My Cousin Vinny (1992)
Raging Bull (1980)
Pescow: 5 Donna
peseta: 5 money
word: 6 España
pesewa: 5 money
pesky: 7 irksome, nagging 8 annoying, worrying 9 loathsome, maddening, obnoxious, provoking, unwelcome, vexatious 10 bothersome, in one's hair, irritating, nettlesome
insect: 3 ant, fly 4 flea, gnat, wasp 5 midge 6 hornet 8 mosquito
plant: 4 weed
Pesky: 6 Johnny
peso: 5 money
ancestor: 4 tlac 5 tlaco
repository: 5 banco
pesos: 3 oof 4 cash, gelt, jack, kail, kale, loot, peag, pelf 5 bills, bread, bucks, dough, funds, lucre, money, moola, mopus, rhino, sewan 6 dinero, do-re-mi, mammon, mazuma, moolah, seawan, silver, specie, wampum, wealth 7 cabbage, capital, dollars, lettuce, ooftish, scratch, shekels 8 bankroll, cold cash, currency, hard cash, smackers 9 banknotes, frogskins, long green, simoleons 10 greenbacks, green stuff
Pessac: 4 city, town
locale: 6 France
pessimism: 5 gloom 7 despair, sadness 8 cynicism, dark side, distrust, glumness 9 dejection 10 depression, gloominess, melancholy, woefulness
pessimist: 5 cynic 6 downer 7 killjoy, sceptic, scoffer, skeptic, worrier 8 sourpuss 9 defeatist, gloomy Gus, worrywart 10 complainer, wet blanket
pessimistic: 3 sad 4 dark, glum, grim 5 bleak 6 gloomy, morbid, morose, sullen 7 bearish, cynical, worried 8 dejected, downbeat, hopeless, negative, resigned, troubled 9 depressed
investor: 4 bear
phrase: 5 I can't

pest: 3 ant, bug, fly, nag 4 bane, bore, drag, drip, flea, gnat, mite, pain, pill, slug, tick, wasp, weed 5 creep, mouse, roach, tease, trial, twerp, twirp, worry 6 bother, gadfly, hornet, insect, noodge, nudnik, plague, teaser, weevil 7 annoyer, heckler, no-see-um, scourge, termite 8 harasser, headache, horse fly, housefly, irritant, mosquito, nuisance, vexation 9 annoyance, buttinsky, cockroach, tormentor 10 irritation
closet ~: 4 moth
control: 3 cat 4 D Con, Raid 7 swatter 8 fumigant
cornfield ~: 4 coon, crow, deer 7 raccoon
ender: 4 hole
garden ~: 4 lice, mole, slug 5 aphid, aphis, borer, louse 6 earwig
hotel ~: 6 bedbug
household ~: 3 ant, fly 5 mouse, roach 6 insect, rodent 7 termite 8 mosquito
picnic ~: 3 ant
tiny ~: 3 ant 4 flea, gnat, mite 5 midge
winged ~: 3 fly 4 gnat, wasp 6 hornet 8 mosquito
pester: 3 bug, dog, dun, irk, nag, rag, vex 4 ride, wear 5 annoy, devil, get to, harry, hound, nag at, nudge, stalk, tease, worry 6 badger, bother, harass, hassle, heckle, hector, insist, madden, needle, nettle, noodge, pick at, plague, pother, put out, rankle, remind, work on 7 afflict, bedevil, bombard, disturb, henpeck, perturb, provoke, torment, trouble 8 disquiet, distress, irritate, mess with 9 aggravate, importune, persecute 10 drive crazy
pesthole: 3 sty 7 fleabag
pesticide: 5 spray
banned ~: 3 DDT
pestiferous: 8 annoying 9 vexatious 10 bothersome
pestilence: 6 plague 7 scourge 9 contagion
pestilent: 9 epizootic
pestilential: 5 toxic 7 baneful, harmful, noisome, noxious, ruinous 9 dangerous, injurious 10 contagious, infectious, pernicious
pestle: 4 mash 5 grind, pound 6 masher 7 grinder, pounder 9 pulverize 10 pulverizer
pesto: 5 sauce
ingredient: 5 basil
partner: 5 pasta
seasoning: 6 garlic
pet: 2 jo 3 cat, dog, hug, pat 4 baby, dear, huff, jill, kiss, love, neck, pony, tiff 5 amour, angel, bunny, chéri, cooky, Corgi, cutey, cutie, deary, ducky, flame, honey, leman, lover, lovey, novia, novio, pique, puppy, spoil, spoon, sugar, sweet, touch 6 adored, bon ami, canary, caress, chérie, cookie, cosset, cuddle, dandle, dautie, dearie, feline, ferret, fondle, kitten, pamper, parrot, rabbit, smooch, steady, stroke, sweets, tickle, toucan, turtle 7 beloved, darling, dearest, dear one, favored, hamster, pigsney, schatzi, special, squeeze, sweetie, tootsie 8 canoodle, chou-chou, cutie pie, dowsabel, dulcinea, favorite, foul mood, goldfish, housecat, ladylove, lovebird, loved one, macushla, parakeet, paramour, paraquet, paroquet, parroket, precious, snookums, sugar pie, sweetums, treasure, truelove 9 best-liked, bonne amie, boyfriend, cherished, dreamboat, guinea pig, inamorata, inamorato, keep close, parrakeet, parroquet, petit chou, preferred, valentine 10 fair-haired, girlfriend, heartthrob, honeybunch, mavourneen, sweetheart, sweetie pie, turtledove
big-eared ~: 5 bunny, burro, hound 6 basset, donkey, rabbit 9 dachshund
chatty ~: 4 mina, myna 5 minah, mynah 6 parrot
common ~ name: 4 Fido, Spot 5 Rover 6 Fluffy
cuddly ~: 5 bunny, puppy 6 kitten
exotic ~: 3 boa 6 iguana
food brand: 4 Alpo, Iams 6 Purina 7 Kibbles 9 Nine Lives
house ~: 3 cat, dog 4 bird, fish, myna 5 bunny, kitty, mouse, mynah, puppy 6 canary, ferret, kitten, parrot, rabbit, toucan, turtle 7 hamster 8 goldfish, parakeet
in a ~: 4 sore 5 irate, irked, testy, upset 6 peeved 7 annoyed, grouchy, sulking 8 snappish 9 irritated
lover org.: 4 SPCA
name: 3 hon 4 dear, name 5 deary, honey 6 dearie, sweets 7 darling, sweetie 8 nickname, sweetums 10 endearment, sweetie-pie
of nursery rhyme: 4 lamb
owner's need: 4 cage 5 leash 6 collar 8 aquarium
pampered ~: 6 lap dog
peeve: 7 bugbear 9 bête noire, hot button
problem: 5 mange, worms 8 parasite
project: 3 job 7 venture 10 enterprise
protection org.: 5 ASPCA
shop buy: 3 pup 4 bird, bone, cage, fish 5 bunny, leash, mouse, puppy, snake 6 canary, collar, gerbil, kitten, parrot, rabbit, turtle 7 hamster 8 parakeet 9 cat litter, doggy chew, guinea pig
small ~: 3 pup 5 bunny, mouse, puppy 6 gerbil, kitten, lap dog, turtle 7 hamster 9 guinea pig
pet __: 4 name 5 peeve 6 sitter
Pet __: 4 Rock
Pet __ Boys: 4 Shop
__ Pet: 4 Chia
PET __: 4 scan 7 scanner
Peta: 6 Wilson
PETA cousin: 5 ASPCA
petal: 4 leaf
base: 5 sepal
oil: 4 atar, otto 5 athar, attar, ottar
Petaluma: 4 city, town
locale: 10 California
petasus: 3 hat
Petatlán: 4 city, town
locale: 6 Mexico 8 Guerrero
petcock: 3 tap 6 faucet
__ pete: 6 sneaky
Pete: 4 Best, Rose 6 Hamill, Reiser, Seeger, Wilson 7 Rozelle, Sampras 8 Fountain, Maravich 9 Townshend 10 Incaviglia
__ peter: 4 blue
Peter: 3 Max, Pan 4 Arno, Cook, Falk, Funt, Gunn, Hall, Hunt, Lely, Nero, pope, Tork, tsar, Weir, Wolf 5 Adler, Allen, Boyle, Breck, Brook, Brown, Davis, Debye, Deuel, Finch, Fonda, Guber, Hyams, Lorre, Lupus, Medak, Noone, Osnos, Pears, Roget, saint, Sasdy, Sykes, Weiss, Yates 6 Bonerz, Cetera, Coyote, Duchin, Faiman, Gordon, Graves, Handke, Hertel, Horton, Markle, McCann, O'Toole, Rabbit, Serkin, Straub, Weller, Werner, Wimsey, Yarrow 7 Abelard, apostle, Behrens, Cushing, DeLuise, Doherty, Drucker, Gabriel, Gennaro, Godfrey, Hammond, Jackson, Kastner, Lawford, Martins, Medawar, Nichols, Onorati, pontiff, Riegert, Scolari, Sellers, Shaffer, Strauss, Ustinov, Watkins 8 Abrahams, Benchley, Farrelly, Frampton, Goldmark, Jennings, MacNicol, Marshall, McCarthy, Mitchell, Newbrook, Quennell, Strastny 9 Celestine, Gallagher, Glenville, Greenaway, Masterson, Tewksbury, Ueberroth 10 Cottontail, Stuyvesant
in French: 6 Pierre
in Italian: 6 Pietro
in Russian: 5 Pyotr
in Spanish: 5 Pedro
partner: 4 Mary
successor of ~: 4 pope
Peter __ collar: 3 Pan
Peter __ Fabergé: 4 Carl
Peter __ Hayes: 4 Lind
Peter __ Rubens: 4 Paul
__ Peter: 5 Simon
Peter and Gordon
members: Asher, Waller
song: I Go to Pieces (1965)
Knight in Rusty Armour (1967)
Lady Godiva (1966)
Nobody I Know (1964)
True Love Ways (1965)
Woman (1966)
A World Without Love (1964)
Peter and the Wolf
animal: 3 cat 4 bird, duck, wolf
bird: 5 flute, Sasha
character: 5 Sonia
composer: 9 Prokofiev
duck: 4 oboe
__ Peter Blatty: 7 William
Peterborough: 4 city, town
locale: 6 Canada 7 England, Ontario
school: 5 Trent
__ Peter Dunne: 6 Finley
Peter Grimes: 5 opera
composer: 7 Britten
song: 4 aria
Peter Gunn (NBC/ABC drama)
cast: Lola Albright (Edie Hart)
Craig Stevens (Peter Gunn)
hangout: Mother's
Peter Gunn (1959 song) artist: Ray Anthony
Peter Gunn guitarist: 4 Eddy
Peter Ibbetson (1935 film)
cast: Gary Cooper, John Halliday, Ann Harding
director: Henry Hathaway
Peter Lind __: 5 Hayes
peterman: 4 yegg
Peter O'__: 5 Toole
peter out: 3 die, ebb 4 burn, conk, curb, drop, fade, fail, flag, give, pall, slow, stop, tire, wane 5 abate, droop, lower 6 lessen, reduce, run dry, shrink, weaken 7 curtail, cut down, decline, dwindle, fall off, fatigue, run down, subside, tail off 8 decrease, diminish, get tired, slack off, slow down, taper off 9 evaporate, grow weary
Peter Pan
alternative: 3 Jif 6 Skippy
author: James M. Barrie
beast: 4 croc
character: 5 Wendy
collar kin: 4 Eton
dog: 4 Nana
friends' nickname: 4 Tink
pirate: 4 Smee
Peter Pan (1953 film)
director: Clyde Geronimi, Wilfred Jackson, Hamilton Luske
Peter Pan __: 6 collar
Peter Paul __: 6 Rubens
Peter, Paul and Mary
members: Yarrow, Stookey, Travers
song: Blowin' in the Wind (1963)
Don't Think Twice, It's All Right (1963)
I Dig Rock and Roll Music (1967)
If I Had a Hammer (1962)
Leaving on a Jet Plance (1969)
Lemon Tree (1962)
Puff (The Magic Dragon) (1963)
Peter, Peter, pumpkin __: 5 eater
Peter Piper picked __...: 5 a peck
Peter Quince at the Clavier: 4 poem
author: Wallace Stevens
Peter Rabbit and __ of Beatrix Potter: 5 Tales
Peter Rabbit sibling: 5 Mopsy 6 Flopsy 10 Cottontail
Peters: 3 Jon 4 Jean 5 Brock 7 Roberta 10 Bernadette
Peter's __: 5 pence 7 Friends
Peters, Brock: 5 actor
film: Black Girl (1972)
Lost in the Stars (1974)
The L-Shaped Room (1963)
The Pawnbroker (1965)
To Kill a Mockingbird (1962)
Petersburg: 4 city, town
locale: 8 Virginia
Petersen: 4 Paul 8 Wolfgang
Petersen, Paul song: My Dad (1962)
Petersen, Wolfgang: 8 director
film: Air Force One (1997)
Das Boot (1981)
Enemy Mine (1985)
In the Line of Fire (1993)
Outbreak (1995)
The Perfect Storm (2000)
Peter's Friends (1992 film)
cast: Kenneth Branagh, Rita Rudner, Emma Thompson
director: Kenneth Branagh
petersham: 4 coat 6 jacket
Peter Simple author: Frederick Marryat
Peters, Jean: 7 actress
film: Broken Lance (1954)
Captain From Castile (1947)
It Happens Every Spring (1949)
A Man Called Peter (1955)
Niagara (1953)
Pickup on South Street (1953)
Three Coins in the Fountain (1954)
Viva Zapata! (1952)
Wait 'Til the Sun Shines, Nellie (1952)
spouse: Howard Hughes
Peters, Jon spouse: Lesley Ann Warren
Peterson: 3 Ray 5 Oscar
Peterson, Oscar: 7 pianist 8 Canadian
genre: 4 jazz
Peters, Roberta: 6 singer 7 soprano
milieu: 5 opera
piece: 4 aria
peter starter: 4 salt
Peter the Great: 4 czar, tsar 7 Russian
__ Pete's Sake: 3 For
petiole: 5 stipe
petit: 5 minor, small
petit __: 3 feu 4 four, jury 5 juror, point 6 beurre 7 larceny
petit chou: 2 jo 3 pet 4 baby, dear, jill, love 5 amour, angel, chéri, cooky, cutey, cutie, deary, ducky, flame, honey, leman, lover, lovey, novia, novio, sugar, sweet 6 bon ami, chérie, cookie, dautie, dearie, steady, sweets 7 beloved, dearest, dear one, pigsney, schatzi, squeeze, sweetie, tootsie 8 chou-chou, cutie pie, dowsabel, dulcinea, ladylove, lovebird, macushla, paramour, precious, snookums, sugar pie, sweetums, truelove 9 bonne amie, boyfriend, dreamboat, inamorata, inamorato, valentine 10 girlfriend,

heartthrob, honeybunch, mavourneen, sweetheart, sweetie pie, turtledove
petite: 3 wee 4 baby, puny, size, tiny 5 bitty, dwarf, elfin, short, small, teeny 6 atomic, bantam, dainty, little, minute, peewee, teensy 8 atomical, atomlike, delicate 9 dress size, itsy-bitsy, itty-bitty, miniature, pint-sized, undersize 10 diminutive, teeny-weeny, vest-pocket
Petite __: 5 Fleur, Suite
__ Petite: 4 Reet
Petite Suite composer: 6 Bartók
petit four: 4 cake 6 cookie, pastry 10 confection
petition: 3 ask, beg, sue 4 case, plea, pray, seek, suit, urge 5 apply, claim, plead, press 6 appeal, demand, invite, invoke, litany, prayer 7 beseech, entreat, implore, request, solicit 8 entreaty, press for, put in for, question 10 invitation, round robin, supplicate
petits __: 4 pois
peto: 4 fish 5 wahoo 8 mackerel
Peto: 4 city, town
locale: 6 Mexico 7 Yucatán
Petraeus: 5 satyr 7 centaur
Petrarch: 4 poet 7 Italian, scholar
beloved: 5 Laura
opus: 6 sonnet
petrel: 4 bird 5 cahow 10 shearwater
lair: 4 aery, eyry 5 aerie, eyrie
relative: 6 fulmar
__ petrel: 5 giant, storm 6 diving, stormy 7 Bermuda
petri __: 4 dish
Petri: 4 Elio
petri dish contents: 4 agar 7 culture 8 agar-agar, bacteria
Petrie: 3 Ann, Rob 5 Laura 6 Daniel, Donald 7 Ritchie 8 Flinders
Petrie, Daniel: 8 director
film: The Betsy (1978)
Fort Apache, The Bronx (1981)
Lassie (1994)
A Raisin in the Sun (1961)
Resurrection (1980)
Rocket Gibraltar (1988)
Petrie, Laura husband: 3 Rob
petrified: 5 rocky, stiff, timid 6 afraid, frozen, scared, trepid 7 anxious, chicken, fearful, lithoid, nervous, panicky 8 cowardly, fearsome, hesitant, timorous 9 lithoidal, nerveless, unpliable 10 frightened, motionless, spellbound
sap: 5 amber
stand ~: 6 freeze
Petrified Forest: 4 park 8 monument
locale: 7 Arizona
Petrified Forest, The (1936 film)
cast: Bette Davis, Dick Foran, Leslie Howard
director: Archie Mayo
petrify: 3 set 4 numb, stun 5 alarm, amaze, appal, chill, scare, spook 6 appall, benumb, dismay, harden, ossify 7 astound, horrify, stiffen, stupefy, terrify 8 astonish, frighten, indurate, lapidify, paralyse, paralyze, transfix 9 dumbfound, fossilize, terrorize 10 immobilize, mineralize, scare stiff
petrifying: 5 scary 8 terrible 9 appalling
Pet Rocks: 3 fad 5 craze
petrographer specimen: 4 rock 5 stone 7 mineral
petrol: 3 gas 4 fuel 8 gasoline
measure: 5 litre
petroleum: 3 oil 8 crude oil, resource
byproduct: 3 tar 6 alkane, benzol, butene, ethane 8 dimethyl
exporter: 4 Iran, Iraq, OPEC 5 Libya 6 Mexico 7 Nigeria 8 Colombia 9 Venezuela 11 Saudi Arabia
measure: 3 bbl. 6 barrel
source: 4 well 5 shale 8 oil shale
petroleum __: 5 ether, jelly
petrology: 7 science
study: 5 rocks
Petrosian, Tigran forte: 5 chess
Petrouchka: 6 ballet
composer: 10 Stravinsky
Petrovic, Drazen: 5 cager
milieu: 5 court
org.: 3 NBA
sport: 10 basketball
Petrozavodsk: 4 city, town
locale: 6 Russia
Petruchio: 5 lover, tamer
emulate ~: 4 tame
intended: 4 Kate
Petrushka composer: 10 Stravinsky
Pet Sematary: 4 book 5 novel
author: Stephen King
cat: 6 Church
Pet Shop Boys
homeland: England
members: Tennant, Lowe
song: Always on My Mind (1988)
It's a Sin (1987)
Opportunities (1986)
West End Girls (1986)
What Have I Done to Deserve This? (1987)
Pettet: 6 Joanna
petticoat: 4 slip 8 lingerie 10 underskirt
antebellum ~: 4 hoop
Petticoat Junction (CBS sitcom)
cast: Bea Benaderet (Kate Bradley)
Edgar Buchanan (Joe Carson)
Frank Cady (Sam Drucker)
pettifog: 3 con 4 fool, jive, snow 5 cavil, trick 6 bicker, delude, niggle 7 deceive, nitpick, quibble 8 flimflam, hoodwink 9 bamboozle, disinform 10 split hairs
pettifogger: 6 lawyer 7 shyster 8 quibbler 10 fussbudget
Pettiford, Oscar: 7 bassist
genre: 4 jazz
petting zoo attraction: 3 boa 4 calf, colt, deer, pony 5 horse
Pettit, Bob: 5 cager
milieu: 5 court
org.: 3 NBA
sport: 10 basketball
Pettitte: 4 Andy
__ Pet Tricks: 6 Stupid
petty: 4 mean, puny, vain 5 catty, cheap, light, minor, small 6 little, measly, paltry, shabby, slight, stingy, two-bit, unfair, yeasty 7 shallow, trivial 8 niggling, picayune, piddling, spiteful, trifling 9 frivolous, malicious, parochial, penny-ante, secondary, valueless 10 negligible, nitpicking
be ~: 4 carp 5 cavil 7 nitpick, quibble
criminal: 4 punk 10 pickpocket, shoplifter
criminal, in Britain: 4 spiv
officer: 4 bo's'n 5 bosun 6 yeoman
quarrel: 4 fuss, huff, spat, tiff 5 set-to
sum: 7 peanuts
petty __: 4 cash, jury 5 juror, theft 7 larceny, officer
Petty: 3 Tom 4 Lori 7 Richard
Petty and the Heartbreakers, Tom
song: Change of Heart (1983)
Don't Come Around Here No More (1985)
Don't Do Me Like That (1979)
Free Fallin' (1989)
I Won't Back Down (1989)
Jammin' Me (1987)
Learning to Fly (1991)
Mary Jane's Last Dance (1994)
Refugee (1980)
Runnin' Down a Dream (1989)
Stop Draggin' My Heart Around (1981)
The Waiting (1981)
You Don't Know How It Feels (1994)
You Got Lucky (1982)
__ petty officer: 5 chief
Petty, Richard: 9 auto racer
milieu: 5 track
org.: 6 NASCAR
petulance: 5 anger 6 spleen, temper 9 surliness
show ~: 4 pout
petulant: 5 cross, huffy, irate, moody, sulky, testy, waspy, whiny 6 crabby, cranky, grumpy, ireful, snappy, sullen, touchy, whiney 7 crabbed, fretful, grouchy, peevish, pouting, prickly, waspish, whining 8 captious, fretsome, grumpish, snappish 9 fractious, grumbling, impatient, irascible, irritable, querulous, splenetic 10 ill-humored, ill-natured, out of sorts, ungracious
mood: 4 fret, huff, pout, snit, sulk
Petulia (1968 film)
cast: Richard Chamberlain, Julie Christie, George C. Scott
director: Richard Lester
petunia: 5 plant 6 flower
Petunia Pig: 3 sow 4 toon
friend: 5 Porky
peut-__: 4 être
Pevney: 6 Joseph
pew: 4 seat 5 bench
book: 6 hymnal
escort to a ~: 4 seat 5 usher
locale: 4 nave 6 church
separator: 5 aisle
use a ~: 3 sit
pewee: 4 bird 6 phoebe 10 flycatcher
pewit: 4 bird 6 phoebe, plover 7 lapwing
pewter: 3 ley 5 alloy
component: 3 tin 4 lead
peyote: 6 cactus
Peyton Place: 4 book 5 novel
author: Grace Metalious
street in ~: 3 Elm
Peyton Place (1957 film)
cast: Arthur Kennedy, Hope Lange, Lloyd Nolan, Lana Turner
director: Mark Robson
Peyton Place (ABC drama): 4 soap 9 soap opera
cast: Mia Farrow (Allison Mackenzie)
Dorothy Malone (Constance Mackenzie)
Ed Nelson (Dr. Michael Rossi)
Ryan O'Neal (Rodney Harrington)
Barbara Parkins (Betty Anderson)
PEZ: 4 nosh 5 candy, snack
PFC: 2 GI
address: 3 APO
boss: 3 sgt. 5 sarge
hangout: 2 PX 3 USO
rank above ~: 3 cpl.
see also private
Pfeiffer: 5 Dedee 8 Michelle
Pfeiffer, Michelle: 7 actress
film: The Age of Innocence (1993)
Batman Returns (1992)
Dangerous Liaisons (1988)
Deep End of the Ocean (1999)
The Fabulous Baker Boys (1989)
Frankie and Johnnie (1991)
Frankie and Johnny (1991)
I Am Sam (2001)
Into the Night (1985)
Ladyhawke (1985)
Married to the Mob (1988)
A Midsummer Night's Dream (1999)
The Russia House (1990)
Scarface (1983)
Sweet Liberty (1986)
Tequila Sunrise (1988)
To Gillian on Her 37th Birthday (1996)
Up Close & Personal (1996)
What Lies Beneath (2000)
White Oleander (2002)
The Witches of Eastwick (1987)
Wolf (1994)
film (voice): The Prince of Egypt (1998)
spouse: David E. Kelley
pfennig: 4 coin 5 money
multiple: 4 mark
pfft, go: 4 fail 6 vanish 7 conk out 8 collapse 9 disappear
Pfizer competitor: 5 Lilly, Merck
Pflug, Jo Ann: 7 actress
spouse: Chuck Woolery
pfui: 4 drat, rats, yuck 6 darn it
PG: 6 rating
issuer: 4 MPAA
P.G.: 9 Wodehouse
PGA
event: 5 Doral, pro-am
member: 3 pro 6 golfer
part: 4 Assn., Golf 5 Assoc.
PG-13: 6 rating
issuer: 4 MPAA
pH: 4 meas. 7 measure
high ~ substance: 3 alk. 4 base 8 alkaline
low ~ substance: 4 acid
tester: 6 litmus
Phact: 4 star
Phaedra
parent of ~: 5 Minos 8 Pasiphae
sister of ~: 7 Ariadne
son of ~: 6 Acamas 8 Demophon
phaeton: 3 car 4 auto 5 coach 7 vehicle 8 carriage 10 automobile
Phair: 3 Liz
phalanger: 9 marsupial
relative: 4 euro 5 bilbi, bilby, koala 6 numbat, wombat 7 bettong, dasyure, opossum, wallaby 8 kangaroo, wallaroo 9 bandicoot
phalanx: 4 bone 6 legion 7 brigade, platoon 8 division, regiment 9 battalion
phalarope: 4 bird
phantasm: 5 ghost, haunt, shade, spook 6 mirage, spirit, wraith 7 eidolon, phantom, specter 8 delusion, presence 10 apparition
phantasmagorical: 4 eery 5 eerie 6 unreal 7 ghostly 9 imaginary
phantasmal: 7 eidolic
phantasy: 6 revery 7 fantasy, reverie 8 daydream
phantom: 4 soul 5 ghost, haunt, shade, shape, spook 6 mirage, shadow, spirit, vision, wraith 7 bugbear, chimera, eidolon, specter 8 chimaera, delusion, illusive, illusory, revenant 9 obsession, unearthly 10 apparition, fictitious
Phantom: 3 car 4 auto 10 Rolls-Royce
Phantom Lady (1944 film)
cast: Alan Curtis, Ella Raines, Franchot Tone
Phantom Menace, The planet: 5 Naboo
Phantom of Paradise (1974 film)
cast: William Finley, Jessica Harper, Paul Williams
director: Brian De Palma
Phantom of the Opera (1943 film)
cast: Nelson Eddy, Susanna Foster, Claude Rains
director: Arthur Lubin
Phantom of the Opera, The: 7 musical
instrument: 5 organ
prop: 4 mask
role: 5 Raoul
setting: 5 Paris
songwriter: 11 Lloyd Webber
Phantom Regiment, The composer: 8 Anderson

Phantoms: 4 film 5 novel
author: Dean Koontz
cast: Joanna Going, Rose McGowan, Peter O'Toole, Liev Schreiber
director: Joe Chappelle
Phantom, The: 10 comic strip
character: 4 Sala
horse: 4 Hero
pharaoh: 3 Tut 4 king 5 ruler, title 6 Cheops, gerent, Ramses 7 Rameses 8 Egyptian, Thutmose 9 Akhenaton, Amenhotep 10 Hatshepsut 11 Tutankhamen
amulet: 4 ankh
city: 6 Amarna, Thebes 7 Memphis
deity: 3 Set 4 Amon, Aten, Aton, Bast, Isis, Ptah, Seth 5 Horus 6 Amen-Ra, Amon-Ra, Osiris 7 Sekhmet
fabric: 5 linen
headdress: 6 uraeus
perhaps: 5 mummy
river: 4 Nile
Pharaoh ___: 3 ant
pharisaism: 10 lip service
Pharisees: 4 sect
Phar Lap (1983 film)
cast: Tom Burlinson, Martin Vaughan
director: Simon Wincer
pharmaceutical: 4 drug 6 remedy 8 medicine 10 medication
giant: 5 Lilly, Merck 6 Pfizer
watchdog: 3 FDA
pharmacist: 8 druggist 10 apothecary
concern: 4 dose 6 dosage 7 formula 8 medicine 10 medication
container: 4 vial 5 phial 7 capsule
in Britain: 7 chemist
measure: 4 dram 5 minim
pharmacology: 7 science
study: 5 drugs 9 medicines
pharmacy: 5 store 7 chemist, science 9 drug store 10 apothecary, dispensary
Pharos: 6 beacon 10 lighthouse
Pharr: 4 city, town
locale: 5 Texas
Pharsalia: 4 epic
pharynx: 6 gullet
neighbor: 5 uvula
prefix for ~: 4 naso
phase: 4 side, step, term 5 angle, cycle, facet, point, slant, stage, state 6 aspect, degree, period 7 chapter, feature, process 8 juncture, position 9 condition 10 appearance
moon ~: 3 new 4 full 7 gibbous 8 crescent
out: 6 remove 8 obsolete, withdraw 9 eliminate
phaser setting: 4 stun
phat: 3 def, rad 4 aces, A-one, boss, braw, cool, dece, fine, gear, keen, neat, nice, tuff 5 dandy, ducky, grand, great, marvy, neato, nobby, prime, slick, super, swell 6 bang on, bang-up, bonzer, bosker, choice, divine, dreamy, far-out, gnarly, groovy, lovely, peachy, slap-up, spot on, superb, terrif, tiptop, unreal, whizzo, wicked 7 amazing, awesome, capital, corking, perfect, ripping, skookum, stellar, sublime 8 dazzling, especial, eximious, fabulous, five-star, four-star, frabjous, glorious, heavenly, jim-dandy, slam-bang, smashing, splendid, standout, sterling, stickout, superior, terrific, top-level, topnotch, very good, wondrous 9 bodacious, excellent, exemplary, exquisite, first-rate, high-grade, hunky-dory, marvelous, sollicker, top-flight, wonderful 10 first-class, hotsy-totsy, jack-a-dandy, out of sight, peachy-keen, phenomenal, remarkable, stupendous, super-duper
Ph.D.: 3 deg. 6 degree, doctor 8 graduate 9 doctorate
at times: 4 prof
exam: 5 orals
submission: 6 thesis
test for ~ entrants: 3 GRE
pheasant: 4 bird, fowl
Asian ~: 8 tragopan
brood: 3 nid 4 nide
dish: 5 salmi 6 salmis
female ~: 3 hen
relative: 5 poult, quail, snipe 6 chukar, grouse, peahen, turkey 7 peacock, peafowl 8 curassow, moorfowl, woodcock 9 partridge 10 guinea fowl, jungle fowl, wild turkey
young ~: 5 poult
Phecda: 4 star
Phèdre author: Jean Racine
Phèdre composer: 8 Massenet
Phelps: 4 Babe 6 Digger
Phenix City: 4 town
locale: 7 Alabama
Phenix City Story, The (1955 film)
cast: Kathryn Grant, Richard Kiley, John McIntire
phenol compound: 5 ester
phenom: 4 name, star 5 celeb 7 big name 9 celebrity, headliner
phenomenal: 3 def, rad 4 aces, A-one, boss, braw, cool, dece, fine, gear, keen, neat, nice, phat, rare, tuff 5 dandy, ducky, grand, great, marvy, neato, nobby, prime, slick, super, swell 6 bang on, bang-up, bonzer, bosker, choice, divine, dreamy, far-out, gnarly, groovy, lovely, peachy, slap-up, spot on, superb, terrif, tiptop, unique, unreal, whizzo, wicked 7 amazing, awesome, capital, corking, perfect, ripping, skookum, stellar, sublime, unusual 8 dazzling, especial, eximious, fabulous, five-star, four-star, frabjous, glorious, heavenly, jim-dandy, material, physical, singular, slam-bang, smashing, splendid, standout, sterling, stickout, superior, terrific, top-level, topnotch, very good, wondrous 9 bodacious, corporeal, Endsville, excellent, exemplary, exquisite, fantastic, first-rate, high-grade, hunky-dory, marvelous, sollicker, top-flight, unheard-of, unrivaled, wonderful, wunderbar 10 first-class, hotsy-totsy, jack-a-dandy, out of sight, peachy-keen, remarkable, stupendous, super-duper, unrivalled
phenomenon: 4 fact 5 event, thing 6 marvel, matter, oddity, rarity, wonder 7 anomaly, miracle, prodigy, reality 8 incident 9 actuality, curiosity, happening, nonpareil, sensation, spectacle 10 appearance
Phenomenon (1996 film)
cast: Robert Duvall, Kyra Sedgwick, John Travolta, Forest Whitaker
director: Jon Turteltaub
dog: 6 Attila
Phenomenon of Man, The author: Pierre Teilhard de Chardin
Pherkad: 4 star
Phffft! (1954 film)
cast: Jack Carson, Judy Holliday, Jack Lemmon
director: Mark Robson
phi: 5 Greek 6 letter
follower: 3 chi
preceder: 7 upsilon
phial: 6 bottle
Phi Beta Kappa concern: 3 GPA
Phil: 3 May 4 Fish, Lesh, Mogg, Ochs 5 Gramm, Mahre, Simms 6 Everly, Foster, Harris, Joanou, Lynott, Morris, Niekro, Nowlan 7 Collins, Donahue, Hartman, Jackson, Karlson, Rizzuto, Silvers, Spector 8 Esposito 9 Esterhaus, Mickelson
Philadelphia: 4 city, town
athletes: 4 Owls 7 Dragons, Quakers
city near ~: 6 Camden, Easton
clock setting: 3 EDT, EST
locale: 4 Penn.
newspaper: 4 News 8 Inquirer
pro team: 6 Eagles, Flyers, Sixers 8 Phillies
river: 8 Delaware 10 Schuylkill
school: 4 Penn 6 Drexel, Temple
transit system: 5 SEPTA
Philadelphia (1993 film)
cast: Tom Hanks, Jason Robards, Mary Steenburgen, Denzel Washington
director: Jonathan Demme
Philadelphia ___: 6 lawyer 7 Freedom
Philadelphia Freedom (1975 song)
artist: Elton John
___ Philadelphians, The: 5 Young
Philadelphia Story, The: 4 film, play
author: Philip Barry
cast: Cary Grant, Katharine Hepburn, Ruth Hussey, James Stewart
director: George Cukor
Philae: 3 isl. 4 isle 6 island
her temple was at ~: 4 Isis
Philanderer, The author: Shaw 4 Shaw
philanthropic: 4 good, kind 6 giving, humane, kindly 7 liberal 8 generous, gracious 9 bountiful, unselfish, unsparing 10 altruistic, beneficent, charitable, free-handed, munificent, unstinting
be ~: 4 fund, give 6 do good, donate 10 contribute
philanthropist: 5 donor 6 patron 10 benefactor
no ~: 5 miser 9 skinflint 10 pinchpenny
philanthropy: 7 largess 8 donation, kindness, largesse
philatelist concern: 5 stamp
abbr.: 4 perf.
need: 5 album, hinge
Philbin, Regis: 2 MC 4 host 5 emcee
partner: Kathie Lee Gifford, Kelly Ripa
Philby, Kim: 3 spy 4 mole
philemaphobe fear: 7 kissing
Philemon: 4 book
follower: 7 Hebrews
preceder: 5 Titus
philharmonic: 9 orchestra
philibeg: 4 kilt 5 skirt
Philip: 3 Ahn 4 Dorn, Hale, Neri, pope, Roth 5 Barry, Bosco, Dunne, Glass, Hench 6 Abbott, Bailey, Knight, Larkin, McKeon, Sidney 7 Freneau, Johnson, Kaufman, Leacock, Marlowe, pontiff 8 Anderson 9 Massinger, Noel-Baker
in Spanish: 6 Felipe
Philip ___: 4 Neri 7 of Hesse
Philip ___-Baker: 4 Noel
Philip K. ___: 4 Dick
Philip Michael ___: 6 Thomas
Philip of ___: 5 Hesse 6 Swabia 7 Macedon
Philippe: 5 Pinel 6 Noiret 7 Gaubert 8 Soupault 9 Desportes
see also French
___ Philippe: 5 Patek
Philippi: 4 city, town 6 battle
locale: 6 Greece 9 Macedonia
Philippians
follower: 10 Colossians
preceder: 9 Ephesians
philippic: 6 screed, tirade 8 diatribe, harangue, jeremiad 9 invective
Philippines: 4 isls. 5 isles 6 nation 7 country, islands
banana: 4 Saba
bay: 5 Subic 6 Manila
bivalve: 5 capiz
bovine: 7 carabao, tamarao, tamarau, timarau
capital: 6 Manila
city: 4 Cebu, Oton 5 Davao 6 Bacoor, Baguio, Iloilo, Manila 7 Bacolod
deer: 6 sambar, sambur 7 sambhar, sambhur
fish: 9 martinico
guerrilla: 3 huk
gulf: 5 Davao, Panay
island: 4 Cebu 5 Bohol, Leyte, Luzon, Panay, Samar 6 Negros 7 Mindoro 8 Mindanao, Visayans
islands near ~: 8 Marianas 9 Carolines
knife: 4 bolo 6 barong
language: 4 Moro, Sama 7 Bisayan, Tagalog, Visayan 8 Filipino
mahogany: 5 lauan
money: 4 peso 7 centavo
Moslem: 4 Moro
native: 3 Ati 4 Aeta 6 Igorot
palm: 4 nipa
peak: 3 Apo, Iba 8 Mount Apo
peninsula: 6 Bataan
plant: 5 abaca
port: 3 Iba 4 Cebu 5 Davao 6 Aparri, Iloilo, Manila
primate: 7 tarsier
river: 5 Pasig
sea: 4 Sulu 7 Celebes, Sibuyan 10 Philippine
seashell: 5 capiz
stew: 5 adobo
tree: 3 tua 4 acle, ipil, pili 5 almon, lauan 6 amugis
volcano: 4 Taal 5 Mayon 7 Bulusan, Canlaon 8 Pinatubo
writer: 5 Rizal
___ Philip Randolph: 3 Asa
Philips: 3 Emo
Philips, Ambrose: 4 poet
Philip Seymour ___: 7 Hoffman
___ Philip Sousa: 4 John
Philip the ___: 4 Fair
philistine: 4 boor 5 yahoo 9 barbarian, bourgeois
Philistine
ancient city-kingdom: 4 Gaza
city: 4 Gath
Phillies: 4 nine, team
org.: 3 MLB, NLE
sport: 8 baseball
Phillip: 5 Noyce, Sharp
___ Phillip Law: 4 John
Phillippe, Ryan spouse: Reese Witherspoon
Phillips: 3 Sam 4 John, Loud, Sian 5 Ethan, Julia, screw, Stone 6 Chynna, Esther 7 William 8 Julianne, Michelle 9 Mackenzie
Phillips ___: 4 head
Phillips ___ Academy: 6 Exeter
___ Phillips: 6 Wilson
Phillips, Chynna spouse: William Baldwin
Phillips, Julianne spouse: Bruce Springsteen
Phillips, Lou Diamond: 5 actor
film: The Big Hit (1998)
La Bamba (1987)
Stand and Deliver (1987)
Young Guns (1988)
Phillips, Michelle: 6 singer
once: 4 Mama
spouse: Dennis Hopper
Phillips University, home of: 4 Enid
Phillips, William: 8 Nobelist 9 physicist
Phillpotts: 4 Eden
Philly rival: 3 Cub, Met, Red 4 Expo, Twin 5 Angel, Astro, Brave, Giant, Padre, Rocky, Royal, Tiger 6 Brewer, Dodger, Indian, Marlin, Oriole, Pirate,

Ranger, Red Sox, Yankee 7 Blue Jay, Mariner 8 Athletic, Cardinal, Devil Ray, White Sox
dog: 5 dance
Hall of Famer: 7 Ashburn, Carlton, Roberts, Schmidt
philodendron: 5 aroid
family: 4 arum
Philo Judaeus: 11 philosopher
philosopher: 4 Hook, Hume, Kant, Mach, Marx, Mead, Mill, Reid, Ryle, sage, Weil 5 Adler, Bacon, Bayle, Bruno, Buber, Camus, Cohen, Comte, Croce, Dewey, Digby, Fiske, Hegel, Hu Shi, James, Jones, Lewes, Locke, Lully, Moore, Paley, Perry, Plato, Renan, Royce, Smith, Sorel, Taine, Wolff 6 Alcott, Anselm, Besant, Cicero, Colden, Eucken, Fichte, Harris, Herder, Hobbes, Langer, Lao-tse, Lao-tzu, Littré, Ockham, Origen, Palmer, Pascal, Peirce, Popper, pundit, Sartre, Seneca, Thales 7 Abelard, Aquinas, Beattie, Bentham, Bergson, Bradley, Calkins, Diderot, Driesch, Edwards, Emerson, Erastus, Erigena, Haeckel, Haldane, Herbart, Husserl, Jaspers, Marcuse, Mencius, Proclus, Russell, scholar, Spencer, Spinoza, Steiner, Stewart, Tillich, Tolstoy, Unamuno 8 Alembert, Apuleius, Averroës, Avicenna, Berdyaev, Berkeley, Boethius, Cassirer, Diogenes, Epicurus, highbrow, Leibnitz, Longinus, Maritain, Plotinus, Plutarch, Rousseau, Schlegel, Socrates, Spengler, Voltaire 9 Aristotle, Augustine, Cleanthes, Condorcet, Confucius, Descartes, Epictetus, Feuerbach, Heidegger, Helvétius, Jefferson, Kropotkin, Lucretius, Nietzsche, Plekhanov, Santayana, Schelling, Whitehead 10 Anaxagoras, Bonhoeffer, Democritus, Empedocles, Heraclitus, Maimonides, Mandeville, Parmenides, Parrington, Protagoras, Pythagoras, Saint-Simon, Schweitzer, Xenophanes, Zeno of Elea 11 Anaximander, Antisthenes, Kierkegaard, Malebranche, Mendelssohn, Montesquieu
Austrian ~: 4 Mach 5 Buber 7 Steiner
British ~: 4 Hume, Mill, Ryle 5 Bacon, Digby, Lewes, Locke, Moore, Paley 6 Anselm, Besant, Hobbes, Ockham, Popper 7 Bentham, Bradley, Russell, Spencer, Stewart 9 Stapledon, Whitehead
Chinese ~: 4 Mo Ti 5 Hu Shi 6 Lao-tse, Lao-tzu 7 Mencius 9 Confucius
Danish ~: 11 Kierkegaard
Dutch ~: 7 Spinoza 10 Mandeville
French ~: 4 Weil 5 Bayle, Camus, Comte, Renan, Sorel, Taine 6 Littré, Pascal, Sartre 7 Abelard, Bergson, Diderot 8 Alembert, Maritain, Rousseau, Voltaire 9 Condorcet, Descartes, Helvétius 10 Saint-Simon, Schweitzer 11 Malebranche, Montesquieu
German ~: 4 Kant, Marx 5 Hegel, Wolff 6 Eucken, Fichte, Herder 7 Driesch, Haeckel, Herbart, Husserl, Jaspers, Marcuse 8 Cassirer, Leibnitz, Schlegel, Spengler 9 Feuerbach, Heidegger, Nietzsche, Schelling 10 Bonhoeffer 11 Mendelssohn
Greek ~: 5 Plato 6 Origen, Thales 7 Proclus 8 Diogenes, Epicurus, Longinus, Plotinus, Plutarch, Socrates 9 Aristotle, Cleanthes, Epictetus 10 Anaxagoras, Democritus, Empedocles, Heraclitus, Parmenides, Protagoras, Pythagoras, Xenophanes, Zeno of Elea 11 Anaximander, Antisthenes
Irish ~: 6 Colden 7 Erigena, Murdoch 8 Berkeley
Italian ~: 5 Bruno, Croce 7 Aquinas
Jewish ~: 10 Maimonides
Marxist ~: 4 Hook
North African ~: 9 Augustine
Persian ~: 8 Avicenna
Quaker ~: 5 Jones
Roman ~: 6 Cicero, Seneca 8 Apuleius, Boethius, Plotinus 9 Lucretius
Russian ~: 7 Tolstoy 8 Berdyaev 9 Kropotkin, Plekhanov
Scottish ~: 4 Mill, Reid 5 Smith 7 Beattie, Haldane
Spanish ~: 5 Lully 6 Marías 7 Unamuno
Spanish-Moslem ~: 8 Averroës
Swedish ~: 10 Swedenborg
Swiss ~: 7 Erastus
philosopher's __: 5 stone
philosophical: 4 calm, cool, deep, wise 6 serene 7 erudite, learned, logical, patient, stoical, unmoved 8 abstract, composed, profound, rational, resigned, tranquil 9 impassive, judicious, sagacious, unruffled
philosophize: 6 reason
philosophy: 3 art, ism 4 idea, view 5 credo, creed, logic 6 reason, system, theory, wisdom 7 beliefs, outlook, thought 8 doctrine, ideology, ontology, thinking 9 knowledge, rationale, reasoning, viewpoint 10 hypothesis
mind, in ~: 4 nous
moral ~: 6 ethics
New Age ~: 6 holism
occult ~: 6 cabala, kabala 7 cabbala, kabbala
things, in ~: 5 entia
__ philosophy: 5 moral 7 natural
Philosophy of Composition, The author: Edgar Allan Poe
Philosophy of Furniture author: Edgar Allan Poe
Philosophy of Right, The man: 5 Hegel
Phil Silvers Show, The (CBS sitcom)
cast: Phil Silvers (M.Sgt. Ernie Bilko)
setting: Kansas
philter: 6 potion 10 love potion
Phineas: 6 Barnum
Phineas __: 4 Finn 5 Redux
Phineas Finn author: Anthony Trollope
Phineas Redux author: Anthony Trollope
Phineus: 4 seer
brother of ~: 6 Cadmus
father of ~: 8 Poseidon
sister of ~: 6 Europa
phiz: 3 mug, pan 4 face, puss 6 kisser
phlegm: 7 inertia 8 lethargy 9 lassitude
phlegmatic: 4 calm, cool, logy, slow 5 aloof, stoic 6 bovine, poised, steady, stolid 7 equable, languid, lumpish, passive, stoical 8 listless, lukewarm, sluggish, together 9 apathetic, collected, impassive, lethargic, temperate, unexcited, unruffled 10 unagitated
phloem locale: 4 tree, wood
phlox: 5 plant 6 flower 9 perennial
Phnom Penh: 4 city, town 7 capital
locale: 8 Cambodia
phobia: 4 fear 5 dread, thing 6 hang-up, hatred, horror, terror 7 anxiety 8 aversion, loathing, neurosis 9 obsession
phobic: 7 fearful
Phobos: 3 god 4 moon 5 deity
brother of ~: 6 Deimos
parent of ~: 4 Ares 9 Aphrodite
planet: 4 Mars
sister of ~: 8 Harmonia
phoebe: 4 bird 5 pewee
Phoebe: 4 moon, Snow 5 Cates, giant, nymph, Titan 6 Amazon, Gordon
planet: 6 Saturn
Phoebus __: 6 Apollo
Phoenicia: 7 country
city: 4 Tyre, Yafo 5 Jaffa, Saida, Sayda, Sidon, Zidon 6 Byblos
deity: 4 Baal 7 Astarte
phoenix: 4 bird
origin: 4 pyre 5 ashes
Phoenix: 3 car 4 auto, city, Rain, town 5 Dodge, River 6 Summer 7 Joaquin, Pontiac 10 automobile
brother of ~: 6 Cadmus
city near ~: 4 Mesa 5 Tempe
county: 8 Maricopa
locale: 7 Arizona
pro team: 4 Suns 6 D-Backs 7 Coyotes
river: 4 Salt
sister of ~: 6 Europa
Phoenix, Joaquin: 5 actor
film: Clay Pigeons (1998)
Gladiator (2000)
Quills (2000)
Return to Paradise (1998)
To Die For (1995)
Phoenix, River: 5 actor
film: Dogfight (1991)
The Mosquito Coast (1986)
My Own Private Idaho (1991)
Running on Empty (1988)
Stand by Me (1986)
Phoenix-to-Boise dir.: 3 NNW
Phoenix-to-Seattle dir.: 3 NNW
phone: 4 buzz, call, horn, ring 6 blower, call up, dial up, notify, ring up 7 contact, headset 8 receiver 9 extension, telephone, touch base 10 get a hold of
2, on a ~: 3 ABC
3, on a ~: 3 DEF
4, on a ~: 3 GHI
5, on a ~: 3 JKL
6 on a ~: 3 MNO
7 on a ~: 3 PRS
8, on a ~: 3 TUV
9, on a ~: 3 WXY
ABC, on a ~: 3 two
bug: 3 tap 4 mike
bulk-rate ~ line: 4 WATS
button: 4 hold, star
call beginning: 5 hello
cord shape: 4 coil
DEF, on a ~: 5 three
feature: 4 dial 6 button, cradle 8 receiver
GHI, on a ~: 4 four
grab the ~: 6 answer
hold the ~: 4 wait 6 cool it 7 stand by 8 mark time, sit tight
hook-up: 4 jack
JKL, on a ~: 4 five
line: 4 cord 5 trunk
London ~ booth: 5 kiosk
mind the ~: 3 man
MNO, on a ~: 3 six
office ~ line: 3 ext. 9 extension
onstage ~: 4 prop
PRS, on a ~: 5 seven
put the ~ down: 6 hang up
signal: 4 busy 8 dial tone
starter: 3 ear 4 head, mega, tele, xylo 5 micro, radio
system: 3 PBX
temporary ~ hookup: 5 patch
transmission: 3 fax
TUV, on a ~: 5 eight
WXY, on a ~: 4 nine
see also telephone
phone __: 3 tag 4 book, call, card 5 booth
__ phone: 3 pay 4 cell 6 mobile 8 cellular
phone book
home, in the ~: 3 res
listing: 2 ad 4 name 6 number
put in the ~: 4 list
Phone Call From a Stranger (1952 film)
cast: Bette Davis, Gary Merrill, Shelley Winters
director: Jean Negulesco
phone-line attachment: 3 fax 5 modem
phonemes, sequence of: 5 morph
phonetic: 4 oral 5 vocal 6 spoken
alphabet: 3 IPA
notation method: 5 romic
punctuation creator: 5 Borge
phonetic alphabet:
A - Alpha
B - Bravo
C - Charlie
D - Delta
E - Echo
F - Foxtrot
G - Golf
H - Hotel
I - India
J - Juliet
K - Kilo
L - Lima
M - Mike
N - November
O - Oscar
P - Papa
Q - Quebec
R - Romeo
S - Sierra
T - Tango
U - Uniform
V - Victor
W - Whiskey
X - X-ray
Y - Yankee
Z - Zulu
phonetics
smooth, in ~: 4 lene
weak, in ~: 5 lenis
phonic: 4 oral 5 vocal 6 spoken 7 sensory 8 acoustic 9 sensorial 10 acoustical
starter: 6 stereo
phoniness: 3 act 4 sham 6 facade 8 quackery 9 hypocrisy 10 lip service
phonograph: 4 hi-fi 6 stereo 8 Victrola
inventor: 6 Edison
inventor's monogram: 3 TAE
needle: 6 stylus
needles: 5 styli
part: 3 arm 7 tonearm 9 turntable
record: 2 LP 4 disc, disk 5 album
phony: 3 lie 4 fake, imit., liar, mock, sham 5 bogus, faker, false, fraud, hokey, knave, put-on, quack, spoof, trick 6 bad guy, ersatz, forged, poseur, pseudo, unreal 7 assumed, feigned, forgery, plastic 8 affected, imitator, imposter, impostor, simulate, spurious 9 charlatan, contrived, deceptive, hypocrite, imitation, imposture, insincere, pretended, pretender, simulated, synthetic, unnatural 10 artificial, fabricated, fallacious, fictitious, fraudulent, mountebank, suspicious
front: 6 facade
handle: 5 alias 9 pseudonym 10 nom de plume
not ~: 4 real 5 legit 7 genuine, sincere 9 heartfelt
up: 4 hoke 5 feign, forge 6 tamper 7 distort, falsify
phony-__: 7 baloney
phony as a __-dollar bill: 5 three
phooey: 2 aw 3 bah, fie 4 dang, darn, drat, nuts, pooh, rats 5 nerts, nertz 6 dang it, darn it, drat it, durn it
phosphate: 4 salt

phosphoresce: 4 glow 5 shine 7 shimmer
phosphorescence: 4 glow 5 light, shine 7 shimmer
phosphorus: 7 element
Photina: 4 font 8 typeface
photinia: 4 rose, tree 5 shrub
relative: 4 sloe 6 kerria, spirea 7 bramble, jetbead, spiraea 8 hardhack, ninebark 9 firethorn, raspberry
photo: 2 ID 3 pic 4 snap 5 print, shoot 6 candid, glossy 7 picture 8 likeness, snapshot 10 photograph
document: 6 ID card 7 license 8 passport
ender: 3 map, mat 4 copy, play, stat 5 drama 6 copier, setter 10 journalist
enlargement: 6 blowup
finish: 5 gloss, matte 9 semi-gloss
finish margin: 4 nose 5 a nose
frame a ~: 3 mat 5 remat
holder: 5 frame
locker ~: 5 pin-up
magazine of yore: 4 Life, Look
movie-ad ~: 5 still
physician's ~: 4 X-ray
session: 5 shoot
snapper: 3 SLR 6 camera
starter: 4 tele
take a ~ of: 4 snap 5 shoot
tint: 5 sepia
transparency: 5 slide
trim a ~: 4 crop
photo __: 2 ID 3 lab, ops 5 essay, shoot 6 layout
photocopier: 6 imager
ancestor: 5 mimeo
company: 4 Mita 5 Canon, Xerox
input: 8 original
photocopy: 4 copy, dupe, stat 5 clone, ditto, image, repro, Xerox 6 double, ectype 7 replica 8 knockoff, likeness 9 duplicate, facsimile, imitation, reproduce
photoelectric
cell component: 6 cesium 7 caesium
photoelectric __: 4 cell, tube 5 meter 6 effect 7 current
Photo Finish author: Ngaio Marsh
photograph: 3 pic 4 copy, film, shot, snap, x-ray 5 image, Kodak, pin-up, print, shoot, slide 6 blowup, poster, record 7 capture, close-up, picture, portray 8 likeness, negative, Polaroid, portrait, positive, snapshot 9 landscape, microfilm, reproduce
Photograph (1973 song) artist: Ringo Starr
photographer: 4 Capa 5 Adams, Arbus, Brady, Karsh, press 6 Abbott, Avedon 9 Stieglitz 11 Bourke-White, Eisenstaedt
choice: 3 SLR 7 instant
concern: 4 blur 5 glare, light 9 film speed
need: 4 film, lens 6 camera, filter, tripod
output: 3 pix 4 snap 5 print, proof, slide 6 blowup 7 picture 8 negative, snapshot
pose for a ~: 3 sit
ratio: 5 f-stop
word: 5 smile 6 cheese
photographic: 5 exact, vivid 6 visual 8 accurate, detailed, faithful 9 cinematic, realistic
photography
powder: 6 amidol
primary color in ~: 4 cyan 6 yellow 7 magenta
__ photography: 5 flash, spark 6 aerial 7 digital, instant, Kirlian
photogravure process: 4 roto
photo-lab print: 5 proof
photon: 8 particle
stream: 4 x-ray
photophobe fear: 5 light
photoplay: 4 cine, film 5 flick, movie 6 cinema, script
Photostat: 4 copy 5 repro 6 ectype 9 duplicate, facsimile
Phouma, Souvanna country: 4 Laos
phrase: 3 put 4 term, word 5 couch, frame, idiom, maxim, motto, voice 6 byword, cliché, remark, saying, slogan, truism 7 diction, express, proverb, wording 8 aphorism, subtitle 9 catchword, formulate, platitude, utterance, verbalize, watchword 10 expression, shibboleth
descriptive ~: 3 tag 5 label
phraseology: 6 syntax 7 grammar 8 language, locution, parlance, verbiage
phrasing: 5 style, usage 7 diction 8 locution, verbiage
Phrygia: 7 country, kingdom
king: 5 Midas
locale: 6 turkey 9 Asia Minor
Phrygian: 8 language
Phyfe: 6 Duncan
Phylicia: 6 Rashad
Phyllis: 4 Kirk 6 Coates, Diller, George 7 McGuire, Whitney 8 McGinley, Schlafly
phyllo: 6 pastry
phylum subdivision: 5 class
phys ed: 3 gym
physical: 4 exam, real 5 solid 6 actual, bodily, manual 7 natural, somatic, worldly 8 concrete, corporal, existent, material, sensible, tangible, temporal, visceral 9 corporeal, incarnate, objective, touchable 10 phenomenal, unimagined
activity: 4 game, work 5 sport 7 workout 8 exercise, training
arrangement: 6 design, layout
boundary: 3 lip, rim 4 edge 5 limit 6 margin
condition: 6 fettle, health
setting: 4 site 6 locale 8 locality
starter: 4 meta
strength: 4 main 5 might, thews
world: 6 matter 8 universe
physical __: 4 exam 7 science, therapy 8 exercise
Physical (1981 song) artist: Olivia Newton-John
physical science: 7 geology, physics 9 astronomy, chemistry
physician: 2 GP, MD 3 doc 5 bones, medic, quack 6 doctor, extern, healer, intern, medico 7 interne, surgeon 8 sawbones 10 specialist
advice: 4 rest 5 relax
ancient Greek ~: 5 Galen
clinic ~: 4 Mayo
Danish ~: 6 Finsen
group: 3 HMO 6 clinic
military ~: 5 medic
Muslim ~: 5 hakim
org.: 3 AMA
photo: 4 X-ray 7 CAT scan
request: 5 say ah 8 open wide
turned wordsmith: 5 Roget
see also doctor
__ physician: 5 house 6 family
Physician, __ thyself: 4 heal
physicist: 3 Ohm 4 Bohr, Born, Hess, Rabi 5 Boyle, Bragg, Dewar, Dirac, Esaki, Fermi, Fitch, Gamow, Henry, Hertz, Hooke, Joule, Pauli, Raman, Ruska, Stern, Tesla, Volta 6 Ampère, Binnig, Franck, Kelvin, Nernst, Newton, Perrin, Planck, Rohrer, Stokes, Yukawa 7 Compton, Coulomb, Crookes, Doppler, Faraday, Fourier, Fresnel, Goddard, Huygens, Marconi, Maxwell, Meitner, Oersted, Piccard, Réaumur, Thomson, Tyndall 8 Ångström, Avogadro, Blackett, Chadwick, Einstein, Foucault, Friedman, Millikan, Rayleigh, Roentgen, Sakharov, Van Allen 9 Arrhenius, Cavendish, Eddington, Gay-Lussac, Kirchhoff, Michelson 10 Archimedes, Fahrenheit, Fraunhofer, Heisenberg, Rutherford, Torricelli 11 Joliot-Curie, Oppenheimer, van der Waals
Austrian ~: 5 Pauli 7 Doppler, Meitner
British ~: 5 Boyle, Bragg, Dirac, Hooke, Joule 6 Kelvin, Newton, Stokes 7 Crookes, Faraday, Thomson, Tyndall 8 Blackett, Chadwick, Rayleigh 9 Cavendish, Eddington 10 Rutherford
Danish ~: 4 Bohr 7 Oersted
Dutch ~: 7 Huygens 11 van der Waals
French ~: 6 Ampère, Franck, Perrin 7 Coulomb, Fourier, Fresnel, Réaumur 8 Foucault 9 Gay-Lussac 11 Joliot-Curie
German ~: 3 Ohm 4 Born 5 Hertz, Ruska, Stern 6 Binnig, Nernst, Planck 8 Einstein, Roentgen 9 Kirchhoff 10 Fahrenheit, Fraunhofer, Heisenberg
Greek ~: 10 Archimedes
Indian ~: 5 Raman
Italian ~: 5 Fermi, Volta 7 Marconi 8 Avogadro 10 Torricelli
Japanese ~: 5 Esaki 6 Yukawa
particle: 3 ion
Scottish ~: 5 Dewar 7 Maxwell
Soviet ~: 8 Sakharov
Swedish ~: 8 Ångström 9 Arrhenius
Swiss ~: 6 Rohrer 7 Piccard
physics: 7 science
branch of: 6 optics 9 acoustics, mechanics
calculation: 4 mass 8 velocity
degree: 3 Ph.D., Sc.D.
F, in ~: 5 farad
particle: 3 ion 4 atom, beta, kaon, muon, pion 5 alpha, boson, charm, gluon, meson, quark 6 baryon, lepton, photon, proton 7 neutron, pi meson 8 electron, molecule, neutrino
research center: 4 CERN
starter: 3 geo 4 meta 5 astro
state: 3 gas 5 solid 6 liquid
study: 5 chaos 6 energy, matter, motion
unit: 3 erg, ion, rad 4 atom, dyne 8 molecule, particle
workplace: 3 lab 10 laboratory
__ physics: 5 cloud 7 nuclear 8 particle
physiognomy: 3 mug 4 face, look, puss 6 kisser
physique: 3 bod 4 body, form 5 build, frame, shape 6 figure
phytology: 6 botany
pi: 5 Greek, ratio 6 letter
preceder: 7 omicron
successor: 3 rho
__, p.i.: 6 Magnum
P.I.: 3 tec 4 dick, tail 6 shadow, shamus, sleuth 7 gumshoe 9 detective
job: 4 case
see also detective
pia __: 5 mater
Pia: 6 Zadora 9 Lindstrom
Piaf, Edith: 6 French, singer 9 chanteuse
Piaget, Jean: 5 Swiss 6 writer 8 educator 12 psychologist
pianissimo: 4 soft
pianist: 2 Ax 4 Hess, List, Monk, Nero, Tesh, Wild 5 Arrau, Basie, Blake, Borge, Bülow, Corea, Gould, Hines, Hyman, Lewis, Short, Tatum, Watts 6 Bolcom, Cortot, Duchin, Garner, Gilels, Iturbi, Kapell, Kenton, Levant, Morath, Morton, Serkin, Simone, Waller 7 Allison, Brendel, Brubeck, Cliburn, Connick, Dichter, Fischer, Hancock, Hofmann, Istomin, Teicher 8 Ferrante, Graffman, Guaraldi, Helfgott, Horowitz, Larrocha, Liberace, Marsalis, Peterson, Schnabel, Shearing, Williams 9 Ashkenazy, Ellington, Feinstein, Henderson, Hollander, Strayhorn 10 McPartland, Paderewski, Rubinstein
Austrian ~: 7 Brendel 8 Schnabel
British ~: 4 Hess 8 Helfgott
Canadian ~: 5 Gould 8 Peterson
Chilean ~: 5 Arrau
Danish ~: 5 Borge
German ~: 5 Bülow
Grammy-winning ~: 4 Nero
jazz ~: 4 Monk 5 Blake, Hines, Hyman, Lewis, Tatum 6 Garner, Kenton, Morton, Simone, Waller 7 Allison, Brubeck, Hancock 8 Guaraldi, Marsalis 9 Ellington, Henderson, Strayhorn 10 McPartland
New Age ~: 4 Tesh
Polish ~: 7 Hofmann 10 Paderewski, Rubinstein
Russian ~: 6 Gilels 9 Ashkenazy
Spanish ~: 6 Iturbi 8 Larrocha
Swiss ~: 6 Cortot 7 Fischer
Pianist, The (2002 film)
cast: Adrien Brody, Frank Finlay, Thomas Kretschmann, Maureen Lipman
director: Roman Polanski
piano: 3 low 4 soft 5 bated, faint, grand, muted, quiet 6 hushed, spinet 7 Baldwin, ivories, muffled, subdued, upright 8 dampened, deadened, keyboard, murmured, Steinway, virginal 9 baby grand, toned down, whispered 10 turned down
easiest ~ scale: 6 C major
ender: 5 forte
exercise: 5 étude, scale
fix a ~: 4 tune
four-handed ~ piece: 4 duet
hammer material: 4 felt
instructor's degree: 3 BME
key: 4 note
key material: 5 ebony, ivory
like a frontier ~: 5 tinny
note: 5 A flat, B flat, C flat, D flat, E flat, F flat, G flat 6 A sharp, B sharp, C sharp, D sharp, E sharp, F sharp, G sharp 7 middle C
opposite: 5 forte
output: 5 music
part: 3 key, leg 5 pedal 6 hammer
pedal: 6 damper
piece: 3 rag 4 duet, solo 5 étude 8 rhapsody 9 arabesque
seat: 5 bench, stool
size: 5 grand 6 spinet 7 upright 9 baby grand
tuner's tool: 5 wrest
piano __: 3 bar 4 duet, roll, solo, wire 5 bench, hinge, score, stool, tuner 6 nobile, player
__ piano: 5 grand, mezzo, thumb 6 player, spinet, square, stride 7 console, upright
Piano Man (1974 song) artist: Billy Joel
Piano, The (1993 film)
cast: Holly Hunter, Harvey Keitel, Sam Neill, Anna Paquin
director: Jane Campion
heroine: 3 Ada
piassava: 4 palm, tree
piaster: 5 money
piastre: 5 money

piatti: 7 cymbals 10 percussion
Piave: 5 river
  locale: 5 Italy
piazza: 5 court, lanai, porch 7 balcony, veranda 8 verandah
Piazza: 3 Ben 4 Mike
  del Campo site: 5 Siena
Piazza, Mike sport: 8 baseball
Piazzi, Giuseppi: 10 astronomer
pic: 4 film, snap 5 flick, movie, photo 6 cinema 8 snapshot 10 photograph
  ender: 4 king
pica: 4 font, type
  alternative: 5 elite
  fraction: 5 point
  widths: 3 ems
Pica: 4 font 8 typeface
Picabo: 6 Street
picador
  opponent: 4 bull, toro
  weapon: 5 lance
Picard: 5 Henry 7 Jean-Luc
Picard, Henry: 6 golfer
Picardo, Robert: 5 actor
picaresque: 6 rakish 7 raffish, roguish 8 rascally
picaroon: 5 knave, rogue, scamp 6 bad hat, pirate, rascal, rotter 7 brigand, so and so 8 scalawag 9 buccaneer, miscreant, reprobate, scallawag, scallywag, scoundrel 10 blackguard, ne'er-do-well
Picasso, Pablo: 6 artist 7 painter, Spanish 8 sculptor
  cap: 5 beret
  contemporary: 4 Miró 6 Braque
  daughter: 6 Paloma
  sister: 4 Lola
  specialty: 6 cubism
picayune: 4 puny 5 dinky, minor, money, petty, small 6 measly, minute, paltry, trifle, two-bit 7 trivial 8 piddling, trifling 9 penny-ante, rinky-dink
Piccadilly ___: 6 Circus
Piccadilly statue: 4 Eros
piccalilli: 6 relish
Piccard, Auguste: 5 Swiss 9 physicist
___ piccata: 4 veal
___ Picchu: 5 Machu
piccolo: 4 wind 10 instrument
  relative: 4 fife 5 flute
Piccolo: 5 Brian
pice: 5 money
pich: 4 tree 5 shrub
Pichel, Irving: 8 director
  film: Life Begins at Eight-Thirty (1942)
    The Man I Married (1940)
    A Medal for Benny (1945)
    The Moon Is Down (1943)
    The Most Dangerous Game (1932)
    O.S.S. (1946)
    The Pied Piper (1942)
    She (1935)
    They Won't Believe Me (1947)
    Tomorrow Is Forever (1946)
pick: 3 opt, tag 4 best, cull, name, pull, sort, take, tool 5 adopt, cream, elect, elite, glean, key on, pluck, prize 6 accept, choice, choose, finger, gather, opt for, prefer, select, vote in, winnow 7 excerpt, fix upon, harvest, jerk out 8 decide on, draw lots, nominate, plectrum, settle on 9 designate, selection, single out 10 decide upon, preference, settle upon
  apart: 3 pan 5 probe, roast, study, trash 6 assess, review 7 analyze, examine, run down 8 evaluate 9 criticize, cut to bits, find fault 10 scrutinize
  at: 3 nag 4 carp 5 cavil 6 badger, nibble, pester 7 quibble 9 criticize, find fault
  bone to ~: 4 feud, spat, tiff 5 gripe 7 dispute, quarrel 8 argument, conflict, squabble 9 exception 10 contention, difference
  ender: 3 axe 4 lock 6 pocket
  from a lineup: 2 ID 3 tag 6 finger 8 identify
  on: 3 nag, rib 4 bait 5 blame, bully, tease, upset 6 badger, bother, harass, hector, needle 7 henpeck, oppress, torment 8 distress, keep down 9 aggravate, persecute, victimize
  one with a ~: 5 miner 7 convict 9 guitarist
  out: 4 cull, spot 5 elect, glean 6 choose, gather, opt for, screen, select 7 discern, excerpt 8 decide on, identify, settle on
  party ~: 5 slate 7 nominee 9 candidate
  starter: 3 nit, nut 4 hand 5 tooth 6 finger
  the brains of: 4 pump, quiz 7 consult 8 question
  through: 4 cull, sift 5 glean 6 screen 7 examine
  top ~: 4 fave 5 A-list 8 favorite
  up: 3 buy, get, nab, win 4 book, bust, earn, gain, have, hear, lift, take 5 cheer, glean, grasp, hoist, learn, raise, rally, run in, scoop, score, seize, sense 6 arrest, collar, detain, detect, gather, handle, invite, master, obtain, pull in, resume, secure, take in 7 acquire, call for, capture, collect, enliven, improve, procure, realize, rebound, receive, recover, rectify, restart, stop for 8 continue, go on with, increase, invest in, purchase, reassure 9 apprehend, extradite, get better, get word of, reinforce 10 gain ground, invigorate, recommence, recuperate
  up a lease: 5 renew
  up a perp: 3 nab 4 bust 5 catch 6 arrest, collar 7 capture
  up a stitch: 3 tat 4 knit 7 crochet
  up furtively: 4 palm 5 filch, steal
  up on: 3 see 4 note 6 listen, notice, remark 7 observe
  up the pace: 3 hie, run, zip 4 race, zoom 5 hurry, speed
  up the tab: 3 pay 4 fund 5 spend, treat 6 defray 7 finance 9 subsidize
  use a ~: 5 strum
pick-___: 4 me-up
___ pick: 3 ice, toe
Pick ___, any...: 5 a card
pickaback: 9 astraddle
pick and ___: 6 choose, shovel
pickaxe: 4 hack
  cousin: 3 adz 4 adze
picked: 6 chosen, select
  it may be ~: 4 bone, lock
  just ~: 4 ripe 5 crisp, fresh
Pickens: 4 Fort, Slim
picker-___: 5 upper
___ picker: 3 rag 4 corn 6 cherry, cotton
___-picker: 3 nit
Pickering: 4 city, town
  locale: 6 Canada 7 Ontario
picker starter: 3 nit
picker-upper
  see pick-me-up
picket: 4 pale 5 fence, guard, scout, stake, stave, watch 6 paling, patrol, sentry, strike, tether 7 boycott, lookout, protest, striker, upright, walk out 8 blockade, palisade, sentinel 9 keep guard, protester, stanchion
picket ___: 4 boat, line 5 fence
Picket Fences (CBS drama)
  cast: Kathy Baker (Jill Brock)
    Fyvush Finkel (Douglas Wambaugh)
    Tom Skerritt (Jimmy Brock)
    Ray Walston (Judge Henry Bone)
  setting: Rome, Wisconsin
picket line crosser: 4 scab
Pickett: 5 Bobby 6 Wilson
Pickett, Bobby song: Monster Mash (1962)
Pickett, Wilson
  song: Don't Knock My Love (1971)
    Don't Let the Green Grass Fool You (1971)
    Engine Number 9 (1970)
    Funky Broadway (1967)
    In the Midnight Hour (1921)
    Land of 1000 Dances (1966)
    Mustang Sally (1966)
    She's Lookin' Good (1968)
Pickford, Mary: 7 actress
  Oscar film: Coquette
  spouse: Douglas Fairbanks Sr., Buddy Rogers
pickings: 4 loot 5 prize 6 spoils 7 jobbery, plunder
  easy ~: 6 breeze 8 kid stuff, pushover 10 child's play
  slim ~: 3 few 6 little
pickle: 3 can, fix, jam 4 bind, cure, hole, keep, mess, salt, snag, spot 5 pinch, souse, state, steep 6 corner, plight, scrape, veggie 7 dilemma, gherkin, problem, trouble 8 hot water, marinade, preserve, quagmire, quandary 9 deep water, inebriate, tight spot, vegetable 10 difficulty, intoxicate
  brand: 5 Heinz 6 Vlasic
  container: 3 jar 6 barrel
  flavoring: 4 dill 5 cumin, sugar 6 garlic
  ingredient: 4 alum
  measure: 3 jar 5 quart
  piece: 5 slice, spear
  solution: 5 brine
  source: 4 cuke 8 cucumber
  type: 4 dill 6 garlic 7 gherkin
___ pickle: 3 in a 4 dill
pickled: 4 high 5 tight, tipsy 6 stewed 7 smashed 9 plastered
  flower bud: 5 caper
  pepper measure: 4 peck
  veggie: 4 beet, cuke 8 cucumber
pickled ___: 5 beets 7 herring
pickled ___ feet: 4 pigs'
pickled-pepper picker: 5 Peter, Piper
Pickles: 5 comic 10 comic strip
  cat: 6 Muffin
  dog: 6 Roscoe
pick-me-up: 4 lift 5 boost, snack, tonic 6 bracer, elixir 7 revival 8 stimulus 9 energizer, eyeopener, stimulant 10 invigorant
pickpocket: 3 dip 4 lift 5 Fagin, taker, thief 6 robber 8 cutpurse 9 miscreant
pickup: 5 tonic, truck
  enclosure: 3 cab
  for ~: 4 to go
  garbage ~ place: 4 curb
Pickup on South Street (1953 film)
  cast: Jean Peters, Thelma Ritter, Richard Widmark
  director: Samuel Fuller
pick-up-sticks game: 3 nim
Pick up the Pieces (1974 song) artist: AWB
Pickwick Papers
  author: Charles Dickens
  character: 4 Fogg, Pott 5 Emily 6 Buzfuz, Rachel, Wardle, Weller, Winkle 8 Arabella, Isabella
picky: 4 nice 5 bossy, fussy, rigid 6 choosy, prissy 7 carping, choosey, finicky, precise 8 critical, exacting, finiking, finnicky, rigorous 9 demanding, difficult, selective, stringent 10 fastidious, inflexible, particular
Pick Yourself Up composer: 4 Kern 6 Fields
picnic: 3 eat 4 easy, lark, meal, snap 5 cinch, cushy, jaunt 6 breeze, junket, outing, simple 7 cookout, fish fry 8 barbecue, clambake, duck soup, kid stuff, painless, walkover 9 excursion, no problem, no trouble, sure thing 10 child's play, effortless, recreation
  days: 6 summer
  drink: 3 ade, pop 4 beer, soda, wine 6 ice tea 7 iced tea, Kool-Aid 8 lemonade
  fare: 4 cola, slaw, soda 5 chips, salad 8 sandwich
  gear: 6 basket, cooler, hamper
  go to a family ~: 5 reune
  no ~: 4 hard 5 bumpy, harsh, rough, tough 6 brutal, severe, taxing, thorny, trying, woolly 7 arduous, complex, painful, serious 8 terrible 9 difficult, strenuous 10 formidable, unpleasant
  pest: 3 ant, bug, fly 4 gnat 6 insect 8 mosquito
  spoiler: 4 rain 6 clouds 7 drizzle 8 overcast
  spot: 4 deck, park, yard 5 patio 7 grounds
Picnic: 4 film, play
  author: William Inge
  cast: William Holden, Kim Novak, Rosalind Russell
  character: 3 Flo, Hal 4 Alan, Irma, Owen 5 Madge, Potts 6 Millie
  director: Joshua Logan
Picnic (1956 song) artist: McGuire Sisters
Picnic Point: 4 city, town
  locale: 10 Washington
Pico de ___: 5 Aneto
Picon: 5 Molly
___-Picone: 4 Evan
Pico Rivera: 4 city, town
  locale: 10 California
picot: 4 lace, trim 6 edging, ribbon
Pict foe: 5 Roman
pictograph: 5 glyph 8 artifact
  computer ~: 4 icon
Pictou: 4 city, town
  locale: 6 Canada 10 Nova Scotia
picture: 3 art, map, oil, see 4 film, icon, ikon, limn, plot, show, view 5 eikon, fancy, flick, illus., image, movie, photo, print, proof, scape, scene, tanka 6 canvas, depict, effigy, ideate, looker, lovely, recite, render, scheme, sketch 7 cartoon, diagram, drawing, etching, gouache, imagine, portray, recount, replica, tableau, thangka, tintype 8 daydream, describe, envisage, envision, likeness, painting, panorama, portrait, seascape, snapshot 9 blueprint, delineate, engraving, fantasize, landscape, look-alike, portrayal, represent, situation, spectacle, statement, visualize 10 conceive of, dead ringer, embodiment, illustrate, perception, photograph, reflection, watercolor, woolgather
  barracks ~: 5 pin-up
  be the very ~ of: 8 look like, resemble
  big ~: 4 plan 5 mural, whole 6 blowup, fresco 8 time line
  book: 5 album
  enter the ~: 5 arise 6 appear 7 develop
  eye-fooling ~: 5 op art
  frame juncture: 5 bevel, miter, slant 8 diagonal
  get the ~: 3 see 5 sense 7 catch on, realize 8 perceive 9 visualize
  holder: 3 mat 4 nail, tack 5 frame

iron-on ~: **5** decal, patch
medical ~: **4** X-ray **7** CAT scan
mental ~: **4** idea **5** image **6** memory, vision **7** concept
motion ~: **3** pic **4** cine, film, show **5** flick, movie **6** cinema, silent, talkie
mount a ~: **4** hang
postcard ~ often: **5** vista
religious ~: **4** icon, ikon **5** eikon, tanka **7** thangka
take a ~: **4** snap **5** shoot
taker: **3** SLR **6** camera **7** tourist **9** sightseer
within a picture: **5** inset
picture __: **3** hat **4** book, card, mold, sash, show, tube **5** plane **6** layout, puzzle, spread, window **7** writing
__ picture: **3** big **4** word **5** flash **6** living, motion, moving **7** cabinet, program, talking
Picture of Dorian Gray, The: **4** film **5** novel
author: Oscar Wilde
cast: Hurd Hatfield, Angela Lansbury, Donna Reed, George Sanders
character: **4** Alan, Vane **5** Basil, Sibyl
director: Albert Lewin
Pictures at an Exhibition composer: **10** Mussorgsky
__ Picture Show, The: **4** Last
Picture Snatcher (1933 film)
cast: Ralph Bellamy, James Cagney, Alice White
director: Lloyd Bacon
picturesque: **5** vivid **6** quaint, rustic, scenic **7** graphic **8** artistic, charming, colorful, romantic, scenical, striking **9** arresting, beautiful, graphical **10** artistical
Picturing Will author: Ann Beattie
piddle around: **4** loaf **5** delay **6** putter
piddling: **4** puny **5** least, minor, petty, small **6** measly, minute, paltry, skimpy, slight, yeasty **7** shallow, trivial **8** beggarly, niggling, picayune, trifling **9** worthless
Pidgeon, Walter: **5** actor
film: Big Red (1962)
Blossoms in the Dust (1941)
Command Decision (1948)
Dark Command (1940)
Forbidden Planet (1956)
Holiday in Mexico (1946)
How Green Was My Valley (1941)
Julia Misbehaves (1948)
Madame Curie (1943)
Man Hunt (1941)
Men of the Fighting Lady (1954)
Million Dollar Mermaid (1952)
Mrs. Miniver (1942)
Mrs. Parkington (1944)
The Rack (1956)
Soldiers Three (1951)
Too Hot to Handle (1938)
Voyage to the Bottom of the Sea (1961)
Weekend at the Waldorf (1945)
pidgin __: **7** English
pie: **4** bird, tart **5** money, pizza **6** quiche **7** cobbler, dessert
Canadian ~: **5** rappe **6** rappie
chart: **5** graph
chart line: **6** radius
chart lines: **5** radii
cooling place: **4** rack, sill **5** ledge **6** fridge, window
crust: **5** shell
crust ingredient: **4** lard **6** Crisco
cutie ~: **4** doll
easy as ~: **4** snap **6** simple **7** no sweat
eat humble ~: **6** grovel **9** apologize
ender: **4** bald
filling: **3** mud **4** lime **5** apple, fruit, lemon, mince, peach, pecan **6** cherry **7** chiffon, custard, pumpkin, rhubarb, spinach **10** strawberry
finish a ~ crust: **5** crimp, flute
in apple ~ order: **4** neat, tidy, trim **9** shipshape
in the sky: **5** dream **7** fantasy
like ~ crust: **5** flaky **6** flakey
maker's device: **3** tin **5** corer, parer **6** peeler
meat ~: **5** pasty **8** empanada, turnover
piece of the ~: **3** cut **5** share
serving: **5** piece, slice, wedge
shepherd's ~ ingredient: **4** meat, spud **6** potato
small ~: **4** tart
starter: **3** pot **4** pork
store: **6** bakery **10** patisserie
sweetie ~: **3** hon **4** doll, love **5** cutey, cutie, deary **6** dearie
pie __: **3** bed, pan, tin **5** chart, graph, plant, plate
pie __ mode: **3** à la
__ pie: **5** cutie **6** easy as, humble **7** shoo-fly, sweetie **8** deep-dish **9** shepherd's
__-pie: **4** cap-à
Pie: **7** Traynor
__ Pie: **6** Eskimo, Tweety
piebald: **4** pony **5** horse, pinto **6** dapple, equine **7** dappled **8** brindled
marking: **4** spot **6** dapple
piece: **3** bit, cut, gat, gun, rod, sew **4** bite, chip, clip, coin, half, hank, hunk, item, join, link, lump, mend, opus, part, slab, song, tune, unit **5** chunk, music, opera, patch, queen, quilt, quota, scrap, shard, share, sherd, shred, slice, snack **6** bishop, column, dollop, factor, gobbet, heater, knight, length, morsel, parcel, pistol, rasher, roscoe, sample, sketch, sliver, snatch, statue **7** article, element, example, extract, firearm, fitting, flinder, passage, portion, remnant, section, segment, writing **8** assemble, chessman, clipping, division, fraction, fragment, instance, interest, nocturne, oratorio, particle, specimen, symphony **9** allotment, component, editorial, sound bite **10** percentage, recitation, smithereen
ender: **4** meal, work **6** worker
playing ~: **3** man **4** king, pawn, tile **5** queen **6** bishop, knight
starter: **3** ear, eye **4** hair, nose, show, time **5** cross, mouth **6** center, mantel, master **7** chimney
together: **4** mend **5** patch, quilt, solve **8** assemble **9** figure out
piece __ action: **5** of the
__ piece: **3** far, of a, set **4** Op-Ed, puff **5** think **6** joggle, museum, period, pocket **7** chimney, fowling
pièce de résistance: **4** dish **8** ultimate **9** specialty
piecemeal: **6** patchy, slowly, spotty **7** gradual **8** bit by bit, fitfully, one by one **9** by degrees, gradually, partially **10** fractional, one at a time, step by step
gather ~: **5** glean **7** collect **8** scrounge
piece of __: **4** cake, work **5** eight
piece of cake: **4** easy **5** can do **6** no prob, simple **7** no sweat **8** kid stuff **9** no problem **10** child's play
Piece of My Mind, A author: Edmund Wilson
Piece of the Action, A (1977 film)
cast: Bill Cosby, James Earl Jones, Denise Nicholas, Sidney Poitier
director: Sidney Poitier
pieces
bits and ~: **6** scraps
break into ~: **5** smash, stave **6** shiver **7** shatter **8** splinter
chop into small ~: **4** cube, dice **5** mince
fly to ~: **5** burst **7** explode
go to ~: **3** rot **5** decay, panic **7** crumble **8** collapse **9** break down **10** degenerate, tumble down
in ~: **6** broken **7** smashed **8** crumbled **9** shattered **10** fragmented
pick to ~: **3** pan **9** criticize, excoriate, find fault
Pieces of April (1972 song) artist: Three Dog Night
Pieces of Eight band: **4** Styx
__-piece suit: **3** two **5** three
pieceworker: **6** jobber **8** handyman
pied: **6** motley, patchy **7** dappled, spotted **8** brindled **10** variegated
changement de ~: **4** leap
pied-à-terre: **3** pad **4** flat **7** lodging **9** apartment, residence
pied-billed bird: **5** grebe
Piedmont
city: **4** Asti **5** Turin **6** Torino
Pied Piper
city: **6** Hamlin **7** Hamelin
emulate the ~: **3** rid
follower: **3** rat
Pied Piper author: Nevil Shute
Pied Piper of Hamelin, The author: Robert Browning
Pied Piper, The (1942 film)
cast: Roddy McDowall, Otto Preminger, Monty Woolley
Pied Piper, The (1972 film)
cast: Donovan, Donald Pleasence
director: Jacques Demy
Piedras Negras: **4** city, town
locale: **6** Mexico **8** Coahuila
__ Piedras, PR: **3** Rio
Piegan: **5** tribe
pie in the __: **3** sky
__-pie order: **5** apple
pier: **4** anta, dock, mole, pile, port, post, quay, slip, walk **5** berth, jetty, levee, pylon, wharf **6** column, harbor, piling, pillar **7** harbour, landing, support, upright **8** buttress, pilaster **9** anchorage **10** breakwater
architectural ~: **4** anta **6** column, pillar
foundation: **4** pile **6** piling
glass: **6** mirror
support: **6** gabion
Pier: **6** Angeli
pierce: **3** cut **4** bore, gore, open, slit, stab **5** drill, enter, knife, lance, prick, punch, slash, slice, spear, spike, stick, wound **6** broach, empale, impale, riddle, thrust **8** puncture, transfix **9** penetrate, perforate, stick into **10** cut through, laceration, run through
Pierce: **3** car **4** auto, Egan, Webb **7** Brosnan, Hawkeye, Mildred **8** Franklin
on M*A*S*H: **4** Alda
Pierce Arrow contemporary: **3** Reo
pierced
object: **3** ear, lip **4** lobe, nose **6** eyelid
Pierce, David Hyde: **5** actor
film: Nixon (1995)
Wet Hot American Summer (2001)
TV: Frasier
Pierce, Franklin: **9** president
alma mater: **7** Bowdoin
former occupation: **6** lawyer
home: **7** Concord
opponent: **5** Scott
veep: **4** King
wife: **4** Jane
piercing: **3** raw **4** cold, high, keen, loud, stab **5** acute, forte, noisy, sharp, witty **6** biting, bitter, fierce, shrewd, shrill, treble **7** blaring, blatant, booming, glacial, intense, jarring, numbing, painful, pealing, probing, pungent, rackety, raucous, reboant, roaring **8** crashing, freezing, incisive, plangent, poignant, rumbling, sonorous, stabbing, strident, turned up **9** agonizing, big-voiced, clamorous, deafening, exquisite, knifelike, searching **10** boisterous, resounding, stentorian, strepitous, thundering, uproarious, vociferant, vociferous
tool: **3** awl **5** auger, borer **6** needle
Pierre: **4** city, Loti, town **5** Bayle, Curie **6** Boulez, Boulle, Cardin, Laclos **7** Bonnard, Fresnay, L'Enfant, Monteux, Reverdy, Trudeau **8** Gringore, Proudhon, Salinger **9** Beauchamp, Berthelot, Corneille **10** Beauregard
in English: **5** Peter
locale: **4** S. Dak.
river: **8** Missouri
see also French
Pierre-Auguste: **6** Renoir
__-Pierre Aumont: **4** Jean
Pierre de __: **6** Fermat **7** Laplace, Ronsard **9** Coubertin
Pierrefonds: **4** city, town
locale: **6** Canada, Québec
__-Pierre Rampal: **4** Jean
pierrot: **4** fool, mime **5** clown **6** jester, mummer **7** buffoon, farceur **9** harlequin
Piers __: **7** Plowman
Piersall, Jimmy sport: **8** baseball
Pierson: **4** Kate
Piet: **8** Mondrian
Pieta: **6** statue **9** sculpture
Pieter: **6** Zeeman **7** Bruegel
Pietermaritzburg: **4** city, town **7** capital
locale: **5** Natal
pietistic: **5** godly, pious **7** devoted **9** dedicated, religious **10** goody-goody
pietoso: **8** tenderly
Pietrain: **3** hog, pig **5** swine
Pietro: **7** Aretino **8** Mascagni
in English: **5** Peter
piety: **4** zeal **5** faith **7** respect **8** devotion, fidelity, holiness, religion, sanctity **9** godliness, reverence **10** devoutness, veneration
false ~: **4** cant, show **6** facade **9** hypocrisy
piffle: **3** bah, gas, rot **4** blah, bosh, bull, bunk, guff, jazz, jive, pooh, tosh **5** bilge, fudge, hokum, hooey, prate, stuff, trash, tripe **6** bunkum, bushwa, drivel, footle, gabble, gammon, gibber, havers, hot air, humbug, jabber, jargon, kibosh **7** baloney, blarney, blather, blether, boloney, bushwah, eyewash, flannel, flubdub, fustian, garbage, hogwash, inanity, rubbish, twaddle **8** buncombe, claptrap, falderal, falderol, flimflam, flummery, folderal, folderol, nonsense, slipslop, tommyrot, trumpery **9** banana oil, gibberish, kidstakes, moonshine, poppycock, rigmarole **10** applesauce, balderdash, bilge water, codswallop, double-talk, flapdoodle, galimatias, Jabberwock, mumbo jumbo, rigamarole, taradiddle
pig: **3** hog, sow **4** boar, gilt, Kele, mold **5** Bazna, Duroc, Hezuo, piggy, shoat, shote, shott, swine, Welsh **6** farrow, Jinhua, mammal, Minzhu, Mukota, oinker, piggie, piglet, porker, rooter, sloven **7** glutton, grunter, Iberian, Lacombe, Meishan, Mong Cai, peccary, Suffolk **8** Hereford, Landrace, Pietrain, Potbelly, squealer, Tamworth **9** barbarian, Berkshire, chowhound, Hampshire, litterbug, overeater, razorback, Yorkshire
***Animal Farm* ~:** **8** Napoleon, Old Major, Snowball, Squealer

calling shout: 5 sooey
cartoon ~: 5 Porky 7 Hampton, Petunia
combining form: 3 hyo- 7 -choerus
digs: 3 pen, sty
ender: 3 nut, pen 4 skin, tail, weed 6 headed
food: 4 mast, slop 5 swill
guinea ~: 3 pet 4 cavy 6 animal, mammal, rodent 7 subject
hair: 7 bristle
hoof: 5 cloot 7 dewclaw
Indian ~: 8 babirusa
jungle ~: 4 boar 5 tapir
kiddie-lit ~: 6 Wilbur
Latin turndown: 5 ixnay
litter: 6 farrow
movie ~: 4 Babe
noise: 4 oink 5 grunt
out: 3 eat 5 binge, gorge 7 indulge, overeat
product: 3 ham 4 pork 5 bacon 7 chitlin, sausage 8 chitling
Scottish ~: 5 grice 7 grumphy 8 grumphie
thief of rhyme: 3 Tom
TV ~: 6 Arnold
young: 4 gilt 5 shoat, shote, shott 6 farrow

pig __: 3 out 4 iron 5 Latin
pig __ blanket: 3 in a
pig __ poke: 3 in a
pigeon: 3 sap 4 bird, butt, dupe, fool, gull, pawn, prey 5 chump, cooer, patsy, squab 6 culver, hunted, sucker, target, victim 7 fall guy, schnook 8 easy mark, pushover 9 soft touch
clay ~: 6 target
ender: 4 hole
home: 4 cote, loft
relative: 4 dove
sound: 3 coo
stool ~: 3 rat 4 fink, tool 5 namer 7 tattler, traitor 8 informer, turncoat 9 informant 10 tattletale
walk like a ~: 3 bob

pigeon-__: 4 toed 7 hearted, livered
__ pigeon: 4 clay, rock, wood 5 stool 6 homing 7 carrier
Pigeon Feathers author: John Updike
Pigeon Forge: 4 city, town
locale: 9 Tennessee

pigeonhole: 4 file, nook, rank, rate, slot, sort, tier, type 5 defer, group, niche, order, table 6 assort, league, put off, recess, shelve 7 arrange, catalog, cubicle, suspend 8 category, classify, file away, lay aside, organize, postpone, set apart, set aside 9 catalogue 10 categorize
locale: 4 desk

piggish: 5 balky 6 greedy, mulish, wilful 7 adamant, hoggish, lustful, willful 8 contrary, edacious, ravenous, stubborn 9 impliable, insatiate, obstinate, unbending, voracious 10 gluttonous, headstrong, implacable, inflexible
piggy: 3 pig, toe 5 swine 6 greedy, piglet 8 slovenly 9 voracious 10 gluttonous
ender: 4 back
fourth ~ portion: 4 none
little ~: 3 toe 5 digit
third ~ portion: 9 roast beef
where the first ~ went: 6 market
where the second ~ stayed: 4 home

__ Piggy: 4 Miss
piggy bank
deposit: 4 coin, dime 5 penny 6 nickel 7 quarter
opening: 4 slot

pigheaded: 5 balky, dense, onery, rigid 6 mulish, ornery, stupid, wilful 7 adamant, froward, hard-set, willful 8 contrary, dogmatic, indocile, perverse, stubborn 9 impliable, insistent, obstinate, unbending 10 dogmatical, hard-bitten, headstrong, implacable, inflexible, refractory, self-willed, unyielding
pig in a __: 4 poke 7 blanket
__ pig in a poke: 4 buy a
Piglet
creator: 5 Milne
pal of ~: 3 Owl 4 Pooh 6 Eeyore

Pigmeat: 7 Markham
pigment: 3 dye 4 tint, woad 5 color, paint, stain, tinct, tinge 6 litmus 8 colorant, dyestuff, tincture
combining form: 5 chrom- 6 -chrome, chromo-
containing iron: 4 heme
earth ~: 5 ocher, ochre, umber 6 bister, bistre, sienna
lacking ~: 5 white 6 albino 8 pink-eyed
natural ~: 4 bice, lake 6 ceruse

pignoli: 3 nut
pignut: 4 tree 7 hickory
pigpen: 3 sty 4 dump, mess 5 hovel 7 rathole
__ Pigs: 5 Bay of
__ pig's eye!: 3 In a
__ pigs fly!: 4 When
Pigs in Heaven author: Barbara Kingsolver
pigskin: 4 ball 7 leather 8 football
carry the ~: 3 run 4 rush
give up the ~: 4 punt
prop: 3 tee

Pigskin Parade (1936 film)
cast: Stuart Erwin, Judy Garland, Patsy Kelly

pigsney: 2 jo 3 pet 4 baby, dear, jill, love 5 amour, angel, chéri, cooky, cutey, cutie, deary, ducky, flame, honey, leman, lover, lovey, novia, novio, sugar, sweet 6 bon ami, chérie, cookie, dautie, dearie, steady, sweets 7 beloved, dearest, dear one, schatzi, squeeze, sweetie, tootsie 8 chouchou, cutie pie, dowsabel, dulcinea, ladylove, lovebird, macushla, paramour, precious, snookums, sugar pie, sweetums, truelove 9 bonne amie, boyfriend, dreamboat, inamorata, inamorato, petit chou, valentine 10 girlfriend, heartthrob, honeybunch, mavourneen, sweetheart, sweetie pie, turtledove
pigtail: 5 braid, plait, queue
pika: 4 cony 5 coney 6 animal, mammal
pike: 4 fish, road 5 route 7 highway, javelin, parkway 8 autobahn, tollgate, toll road 10 expressway, interstate
come down the ~: 6 appear, emerge
ender: 5 staff
starter: 4 turn

pikeblenny: 4 fish
pikeperch: 4 fish
piker: 8 tightwad 9 skinflint 10 cheapskate
Pikes Peak: 4 peak 5 mount 8 mountain
locale: 7 Rockies 8 Colorado

Pikesville: 4 city, town
locale: 8 Maryland

Pike, Zebulon: 8 explorer
pilaf: 4 dish
base: 4 rice
partner: 5 kebab

pilar: 5 hairy 7 hirsute
pilaster: 4 anta, pier 5 pylon 6 column, pillar
__ Pilate: 7 Pontius
Pilatus: 3 Alp
pilchard: 4 fish 7 sardine
pile: 3 gob, lot, nap, wad 4 bank, down, heap, load, lump, mass, mint, much, pack, peck, pier, post, raft, rush, shag 5 amass, batch, bunch, chunk, crowd, crush, drift, flock, hoard, money, mound, ocean, plush, press, shock, stack, store 6 boodle, bundle, fleece, gather, heap up, jumble, load up, oodles, pillar, riches, wealth 7 collect, fortune, javelin, lay away, pyramid, upright 8 mountain, quantity, treasure 9 aggregate, congeries, great deal, profusion, stanchion, stockpile 10 accumulate, assemblage, assortment, collection, cumulation
of hay: 4 rick 5 stack
of stones: 4 carn 5 cairn
rubbish ~: 4 dump 7 ash heap 8 junkyard, landfill
starter: 4 wood 5 stock
up: 5 amass, hoard, mount, score, stack 6 gather, rake in 7 collide 8 hold on to, salt away 9 stash away 10 accumulate

pile __: 6 driver
__ pile: 4 sand 5 slush 6 atomic, batter 7 voltaic
pile-driver head: 3 tup
Pileggi: 5 Mitch 8 Nicholas
pileous: 5 hairy 7 hirsute
piles: 4 a lot, lots 5 reams
of: 4 many 6 divers, myriad, plenty, umteen, untold 7 copious, profuse, umpteen 8 abundant, manifold, numerous, umpsteen 9 bountiful, countless, quite a few
put in ~: 4 sort 6 assort 8 classify

pile-up: 5 crash, smash, wreck 6 logjam 8 accident 9 collision, rear-ender
pilewort: 5 plant 6 flower
pilfer: 3 cop, rob 4 crib, glom, hook, lift, palm, take 5 boost, filch, heist, pinch, snare, steal, swipe 6 finger, pirate, pocket, rip off, snatch, thieve 7 purloin, ransack 8 embezzle, liberate, scrounge 10 run off with
pilferage: 5 heist, theft 8 burglary, thievery
pilferer: 5 crook, thief 6 robber 7 burglar 9 purloiner
pilgrim: 5 hadji, rover 7 pioneer, rambler, tourist 8 traveler, wanderer, wayfarer 9 journeyer
destination: 4 Puri 5 Kaaba, Mecca, stupa 6 Ganges, shrine, temple 7 Kailash, Lourdes 8 Bodh-gaya 9 Jerusalem

Pilgrim
memorable ~: 5 Alden 9 Priscilla
pronoun: 4 thee, thou

pilgrimage: 3 haj 4 hadj, hajj, trek, trip 5 quest 6 hejira 7 crusade, journey, sojourn 8 long haul
Pilgrim at Sea author: Pär Lagerkvist
Pilgrim's Progress: 8 allegory
author: John Bunyan
character: 4 Pope 5 Pagan 7 Hopeful, Pliable, Sincere 8 Watchful

pili: 3 nut 4 tree
pill: 4 bore, dose, drag, pain, pest 5 bolus, creep, trial 6 caplet, nudnik, pellet, remedy, tablet, troche 7 capsule, lozenge, placebo 8 medicine, nuisance 10 medication
allotment: 4 dose 6 dosage
bitter ~: 4 blow 6 misery 7 letdown, setback 8 comedown
bug: 6 isopod
ender: 3 box
large ~: 5 bolus

pillage: 3 gut, rob 4 loot, raid, ruin, sack 5 booty, harry, rifle, spoil, steal, strip, waste 6 devour, harrow, invade, maraud, prey on, ravage, spoils 7 despoil, destroy, plunder, predate, ransack 8 desolate, freeboot, lay waste, spoliate, trespass 9 depredate, desecrate, devastate
pillager: 6 pirate, raider, vandal, Viking 7 brigand 10 freebooter
pillar: 4 beam, pier, pile, post, prop, rock 5 pylon, shaft, tower 6 column, piling 7 obelisk, support, upright 8 mainstay, memorial, monument, pilaster 9 reinforce, stanchion
ancient ~: 5 pylon, stele 6 column
combining form: 4 clon-, styl- 5 clono-, stylo-
engraved ~: 5 stele
go from ~ to post: 4 roam, rove 5 drift 6 ramble, wander
memorial ~ of India: 5 minah
of heaven, to Pindar: 4 Etna 5 Aetna

Pillars of __: 5 Islam
Pillars of Society author: Henrik Ibsen
__ Pillars of Wisdom: 5 Seven
__ pillar to post: 4 from
pillbox: 3 hat
pillow: 4 seat 7 beanbag, bedding, cushion, protect
candy: 4 mint
casing: 4 tick
cover: 4 sham, slip 5 linen
plump the ~: 5 fluff
stuffing: 4 down, foam 5 hulls, kapok 6 cotton 7 batting 9 buckwheat

pillow __: 4 lava, sham, talk 5 block
Pillow Talk (1959 film)
cast: Doris Day, Rock Hudson, Tony Randall, Thelma Ritter

Pillow Talk (1973 song) artist: Sylvia
Pilos: 4 city, port, town 6 battle
locale: 6 Greece

pilose: 5 hairy 6 haired, shaggy 7 hirsute
pilot: 3 ace, fly 4 land, lead, sail, take 5 flier, flyer, guide, steer, trial 6 airman, aviate, direct, fly boy, govern, jockey, leader, manage 7 aviator, birdman, captain, conduct, control, operate, war hero 8 aeronaut, coxswain, helmsman, maneuver, navigate 9 navigator, sky jockey
affirmative: 3 A-OK 5 roger
aid: 4 gyro 5 LORAN, radar 9 gyroscope
assignment: 6 flight
bomber ~ concern: 4 flak 5 flack 7 missile
button: 5 eject
concern: 3 ice 4 drag 5 birds, geese, icing 9 wind shear
control: 4 helm 5 stick 6 tiller
expert ~: 3 ace
guidepost: 5 pylon
insignia: 5 wings
light: 3 jet 5 flame 6 gas jet
maneuver: 4 bank, dive 5 climb
milestone: 4 solo
military ~ award: 3 DFC
org.: 3 ADF, FAA, NAA
place: 3 jet 4 helm, port, ship 5 plane 6 hangar, tiller 7 airport, cockpit 8 jetliner
plane without a ~: 5 drone
shuttle ~ wear: 5 G-suit
sky ~: 5 padre
starter: 4 auto
the shuttle: 5 orbit
UFO ~: 2 ET 5 alien

pilot __: 4 boat, cell, film, fish, flag, lamp, tape 5 bread, chart, light, plant, raise, whale 6 burner, engine, ladder, signal, waters 7 balloon, biscuit, station
__ pilot: 3 cow, sky 4 bush, test 5 robot
Pilot: 3 pen, SUV 5 Honda
alternative: 3 Bic 7 Uni-Ball 9 Paper-Mate

pilotage: 10 leadership
pilous: 5 hairy 7 hirsute
pilsner: 4 beer, brew, suds 5 lager
Piltdown man: 4 hoax
pilum: 5 lance, spear 6 weapon

pilus: **4** hair
Pima: **5** tribe **6** Indian **7** Amerind
Pima __: **6** cotton
pimento: **3** red **5** spice
color kin: **4** rose, ruby, rust, wine **5** brick, coral, grape, poppy **6** cerise, cherry, claret, garnet, maroon **7** carmine, crimson, fuchsia, magenta, scarlet, sultana, vermeil **8** cardinal, geranium **9** cranberry, vermilion **10** strawberry
pimiento: **5** spice
holder: **5** olive
__-piminy: **6** niminy
Pimlico
event: **4** race **9** horse race
racer: **5** filly, horse
sound: **5** neigh **7** whinney
transaction: **3** bet **5** wager
Pim, Mr. creator: **5** Milne
__ Pimpernel, The: **7** Scarlet
pimple: **3** zit **7** blemish
__ pimples: **5** goose
pin: **3** fix, peg, rod, tag **4** bind, join, limb, nail, tack **5** affix, badge, clasp, spike, stick **6** attach, broach, brooch, fasten, hatpin, secure, skewer **7** jewelry, sticker **8** hold down, restrain **9** thumbtack **10** immobilize, keep in line, outwrestle
a crime on: **5** frame, set up **6** accuse
bowling ~: **5** maple
combining form: **6** perono-
down: **4** bind, nail, name **5** force, point, press **6** locate, select **7** specify **8** home in on, indicate, restrict, zero in on **9** determine
ender: **4** ball, head, hole, tail, worm **5** point, prick, wheel **6** stripe **7** cushion, feather
hard to ~ down: **4** eely **5** dodgy, vague **7** evasive **8** slippery
holder: **4** etui **5** etwee **7** cushion
metalworker's ~: **5** rivet
neat as a ~: **4** tidy, trim **7** orderly **9** shipshape
place for a ~: **5** lapel
rowboat ~: **5** thole
starter: **3** hat, ten **4** duck, hair, king, nine, push **5** crank, stick **6** candle **7** clothes **8** thorough
wooden ~: **3** peg **4** nogg **5** dowel
pin __: **3** boy, oak **4** curl, down, knot, mark, rail, seal, spot **5** money, plate **6** cherry, clover, wrench
__ pin: **3** bar **4** head **5** bobby, crank, dowel, guard, lapel, wrest, wrist **6** center, cotter, county, firing, piston, safety, shadow **7** banking, drawing, gudgeon, rolling, scatter
piña colada: **5** drink **8** beverage, cocktail
ingredient: **3** rum **9** grenadine, pineapple
pinafore: **5** apron, dress
Pinafore: **4** boat, ship
__ Pinafore: **3** HMS
piñata occasion: **6** fiesta
Pinatubo: **7** volcano
emulate ~: **5** erupt
locale: **4** Asia **5** Luzon **11** Philippines
output: **3** ash **4** lava
pinball: **4** game
foul: **4** tilt
palace: **6** arcade
pinball __: **7** machine
Pinball author: Jerzy Kosinski
Pinball Wizard (1969 song) artist: Who
Pincay, Laffit: **6** jockey
milieu: **5** track **9** racetrack
pince-nez: **7** glasses **10** eyeglasses
part: **4** lens
pincer: **4** claw **5** chela
pinch: **3** bit, cop, jot, nab, nip, rob **4** bust, crib, dash, hurt, iota, lift, mite, nail, pass, spot, take, whit **5** cramp, crumb, filch, purse, run in, seize, spare, speck, steal, swipe, theft, tinge, trace, tweak **6** arrest, collar, crisis, detain, little, pickle, pilfer, plight, pocket, pucker, pull in, rip off, scrape, snatch, strait, thieve, trifle, twinge **7** capture, jailing, larceny, modicum, purloin, ransack, smidgen, smidgin, soupçon, squeeze, tighten **8** compress, exigence, exigency, quagmire, smidgeon, thievery **9** apprehend, deep water, emergency, necessity, tight spot, tough spot, vellicate **10** difficulty, limitation, run off with
a pooch: **6** dognap, petnap
ender: **5** penny
hitter: **3** sub **9** surrogate **10** substitute
pennies: **3** eke **4** save **5** skimp **6** scrape, scrimp
reaction: **2** ow **3** yow **4** ouch, yeow
pinch __: **3** bar, hit **5** pleat **6** effect, hitter, of salt, roller, runner **7** pennies
__ pinch: **3** in a
Pinchas: **8** Zukerman
pinchbeck: **5** alloy
component: **4** zinc **6** copper
pinched: **4** poor, thin, worn **5** broke, needy, ran in **6** bad off, hard up, ill off, in need, in want, narrow **7** starved, worn-out **8** badly off, bankrupt, beggarly, indigent, starving, strapped **9** destitute, insolvent, moneyless, penniless, penurious **10** down and out, pauperized, straitened
__ pincher: **5** penny
pinchers: **6** pliers **7** forceps
pinch-hit: **3** sub **5** cover **6** act for, fill in **7** stand-in **8** cover for **10** substitute
Pinchot: **7** Bronson, Gifford
pinchpenny: **5** miser **6** stingy **8** tightwad, ungiving **9** skinflint
pin curls: **4** coif **6** hairdo **8** coiffure
Pindar: **4** poet **5** Greek
work: **3** ode
Pindus: **5** range
locale: **6** Europe, Greece
pine: **4** ache, fret, long, moon, mope, sigh, tree, want, wish, wood **5** brood, mourn, yearn **6** desire, grieve, hanker **7** conifer, dream of, long for **8** languish, loblolly, longleaf **9** evergreen, ponderosa
Australian ~: **5** bunya
cone projection: **4** umbo
ender: **5** apple
extract: **5** furan, resin, rosin **10** turpentine
Inut: **5** pinon
New Zealand: **5** kauri
product: **3** nut, tar **4** cone **6** needle
red ~: **4** rimu
relative: **3** fir **4** mugo **5** larch, mugho **6** spruce **7** hemlock **8** tamarack
sauce made with ~ nuts: **5** pesto
Tasmanian ~: **4** huon
pine __: **3** nut, tar **4** cone, vole **5** finch, mouse, snake **6** barren, marten, needle, siskin **7** barrens, warbler
__ pine: **3** fat, nut, red **4** gray, grey, hoop, jack, mugo **5** bunya, kauri, mugho, pitch, screw, scrub, slash, stone, sugar, white **6** Aleppo, Digger, ground, Jersey, knotty, limber, Norway, Oregon, pinyon, Scotch, spruce, Torrey, yellow **7** big-cone, cluster, Coulter, Douglas, Georgia, hickory, Jeffrey, Norfolk, parasol, prince's, running
Pine __: **5** Bluff **7** Barrens
pineal __: **3** eye **5** gland
pineapple: **5** fruit **7** grenade **8** ice cream **9** explosive **11** hand grenade
ice cream alternative: **5** lemon, mocha, peach **6** banana, coffee, Jamoca, toffee **7** caramel, coconut, vanilla **8** cinnamon, hazelnut **9** bubblegum, chocolate, pistachio, raspberry, rocky road, rum raisin **10** blackberry, cheesecake, Neapolitan, peppermint, strawberry
name: **4** Dole
source: **4** Maui **5** Lanai **6** Hawaii
pineapple __-down cake: **6** upside
Pineapple Island, The: **5** Lanai
Pine Bluff: **4** city, town
locale: **8** Arkansas
Pine Hills: **4** city, town
locale: **7** Florida
Pinellas Park: **4** city, town
locale: **7** Florida
Piñero (2001 film)
cast: Benjamin Bratt, Giancarlo Esposito, Talisa Soto
director: Leon Ichaso
Pinero, Arthur Wing: **5** actor **7** British **8** essayist **10** playwright
Pines of Rome, The composer: **8** Respighi
Pine Sol: **7** cleaner
competitor: **5** Brite, Lysol **6** Top Job **7** Lestoil, Mr. Clean **9** Fantastik, Step Saver
Pine Tree State: **5** Maine
Pinewood: **4** city, town
locale: **7** Florida
ping: **5** knock, sound, whine **6** signal
Ping-Pong: **4** game **5** sport
need: **3** net **4** ball **5** table **6** paddle
pinhead: **3** ass, nit, oaf, sap **4** boob, clod, dolt, fool **5** chump, clown, cluck, dummy, dunce, goose, joker, klutz, ninny, patsy **6** dimwit, lummox, nitwit, sucker, turkey **7** buffoon, dingbat, dullard, half-wit, jackass **8** dumbbell, numskull **9** birdbrain, harebrain, lamebrain, numbskull, simpleton **10** nincompoop
pinhole: **7** opening **8** aperture
pinhole __: **6** camera
Piniella: **3** Lou
pining: **3** sad **6** dreamy, morose **7** languid **10** melancholy
pinion: **4** bind, gear, limb, wing **5** plume, tie up **6** fetter, hogtie **7** feather, manacle, shackle, tie down **8** handcuff, restrain
partner: **4** rack
pink: **3** cut, hue **4** acme, peak, rose, rosy **5** bloom, blush, coral, notch, plant, prime, ruddy **6** ablush, flower, heyday, heydey, redden, salmon **7** flushed, fuchsia, roseate, scallop, scollop **8** blushing, cold duck **9** carnation **10** good health, perfection
and white flower: **8** dianthus **9** carnation
city of India: **6** Jaipur
color: **4** rose **5** coral, flesh, melon **6** damask, salmon **7** apricot **8** flamingo **9** carnation
flower: **4** lily **5** aster, lotus, peony, phlox, poppy **6** cosmos, lupine, mallow, mimosa, spirea, thrift **7** arbutus, begonia, dog rose, dogwood, freesia, rambler, spiraea, tea rose **8** arethusa, asphodel, camellia, geranium, hawthorn, larkspur, moss rose, oleander, tamarisk, wild rose **9** amaryllis, candytuft, corydalis, eglantine, hollyhock, hydrangea, mayflower, snowberry, water lily **10** bitterroot, cornflower, damask rose, delphinium, poinsettia, sweetbriar, sweetbrier
in the ~: **3** fit **4** hale, well **5** hardy, sound **6** robust **7** healthy **8** vigorous
not in the ~: **3** ill **4** sick **6** ailing **9** unhealthy
swamp ~: **5** plant **6** flower
tickle ~: **5** charm **6** please **9** titillate
tickled ~: **4** glad **5** happy **9** overjoyed
turn ~: **5** blush, flush **6** redden **7** sunburn
yellowish ~: **5** coral, peach **6** salmon **7** apricot
pink __: **3** gin, tea **4** coat, lady, root, slip **5** noise, stern **6** salmon
__ pink: **3** sea **4** fire, rose **5** bunch, clove, coral, grass, in the, marsh, shell, swamp **6** ground, maiden, salmon, tickle **7** cheddar, cushion, hunter's, mullein
Pink __: **4** Lady **5** Floyd, Marsh **6** Houses
Pink Cadillac (1989 film)
cast: Clint Eastwood, Bernadette Peters
director: Buddy Van Horn
Pink Cadillac (1988 song) artist: Natalie Cole
Pinkerton: **5** Allan
logo: **3** eye
Pinkett, Jada spouse: Will Smith
pink-eyed one: **3** rat **6** albino
Pink Floyd
homeland: England
members: Gilmour, Waters, Wright, Mason
song: Another Brick in the Wall (1980) Money (1973)
__ Pinkham's Medicine: **5** Lydia
Pink Houses (1983 song) artist: John Cougar Mellencamp
pinkie: **5** digit **6** finger
pinking __: **4** iron **6** shears
Pink Lady: **5** drink **8** beverage, cocktail
ingredient: **3** gin **4** lime **5** lemon **6** brandy
Pink Marsh author: George Ade
pinko: **4** left **7** leftist, radical
Pink Panther Strikes Again, The (1976 film)
cast: Colin Blakely, Herbert Lom, Peter Sellers
director: Blake Edwards
Pink Panther, The (1964 film)
cast: Capucine, David Niven, Peter Sellers
composer: Henry Mancini
director: Blake Edwards
pink-slip: **3** axe, can **4** boot, drop, fire, oust, sack **5** let go **6** bounce, lay off **7** cashier, dismiss, drum out, release **8** furlough, get rid of **9** discharge, terminate
pinky: **5** digit **6** finger
Pinky: **3** Lee
Pinky (1949 film)
cast: Ethel Barrymore, Jeanne Crain, Ethel Waters
director: Elia Kazan
pinna: **3** fin **4** wing **7** auricle, feather, flipper
locale: **3** ear
pinnace: **4** boat **8** sailboat
pinnacle: **3** top, tor **4** acme, apex, crag, peak **5** crest, crown, ridge, spire, tower **6** apogee, belfry, climax, flèche, height, heyday, heydey, needle, summit, vertex, zenith **7** maximum, obelisk, steeple **8** high spot, meridian **9** bell tower, campanile, crescendo **10** prominence
combining form: **5** apico-
glacial ice ~: **5** serac
pinned: **8** held down
Pinocchio: **4** liar
author: Carlo Collodi
cat: **6** Figaro
goldfish: **4** Cleo

polygraph: 4 nose
undoing: 3 lie
Pinochet: 7 Augusto
pinochle: 4 game 8 card game
card: 3 ten 4 jack, nine
holding: 4 meld
lowest ~ card: 4 nine
term: 5 trick
___ pinochle: 7 auction
piñon: 3 nut 4 tree 7 pine nut
Pinot: 3 vin 4 wine 5 grape 7 red wine 8 Burgundy 9 white wine
relative: 5 Gamay, Tokay 6 Merlot 7 Catawba, Concord, Niagara 8 Cabernet, malvasia, muscatel 9 muscadine, Sauvignon, zinfandel 10 Chardonnay
Pinot ___: 4 Noir 5 Blanc
Pinotta composer: 8 Mascagni
pinpoint: 3 dot, set 4 find, mark, spot 5 place, speck 6 define, denote, detect, finger, home in, locate 8 diagnose, home in on, identify, indicate, localize, smell out, zero in on 9 determine, get a fix on, recognize
PIN prompter: 3 ATM
pins and needles, on: 4 edgy 5 antsy, itchy, jumpy, tense 6 uneasy 7 anxious, jittery, keyed up, nervous, restive, uptight, worried 8 agitated, restless, skittish, troubled 9 concerned, excitable, ill at ease 10 high-strung, sweating it
pinsetter
company: 3 AMF 9 Brunswick
place: 4 lane 5 alley
Pinsk: 4 city, town
locale: 7 Belarus
river: 6 Pripet
Pinsky, Robert: 4 poet
Pinson, Vada sport: 8 baseball
pint: 3 ale 4 unit
enjoy a ~: 5 drink
fraction: 3 cup 4 gill 5 ounce
one-half ~: 3 cup
one-quarter ~: 4 gill
place for a ~: 3 bar, pub 6 tavern 8 alehouse
starter: 6 cuckoo
two ~ s: 5 quart
pint-___: 4 size 5 sized
___-pint: 4 half
Pinta: 4 boat, ship 7 caravel
companion: 4 Niña 10 Santa Maria
pintail: 4 duck, fowl
relative: 4 smew, teal 5 eider, Pekin, Rouen, scaup 6 Cayuga, scoter 7 gadwall, mallard, pochard, redhead, sea duck, widgeon 8 garganey, gray duck, mandarin, musk duck, oldsquaw, shoveler, surf duck, wood duck 9 black duck, broadbill, goldeneye, goosander, greenhead, merganser, ruddy duck, sprigtail 10 bufflehead, canvasback, surf scoter, tufted duck
Pintauro: 5 Danny
Pinter, Harold: 7 British 10 playwright
work: The Birthday Party
The Caretaker
The Collection
The Dumb Waiter
The Homecoming
Landscape
The Lover
Monologue
No Man's Land
Old Times
The Room
Silence
A Slight Ache
pin the ___ on the donkey: 4 tail
pinto: 4 bean 5 horse, paint, Scout 6 equine 9 chili bean
Pinto: 3 car 4 auto, Ford 10 automobile
pint-sized: 3 wee 4 baby, puny, tiny 5 bitty, short, small, teeny 6 atomic, bantam, little, minute, peewee, petite, teensy 7 stunted 8 atomical, atomlike 9 itsy-bitsy, itty-bitty, miniature 10 diminutive, teeny-weeny, vest-pocket
pin-up: 3 art 5 photo 6 poster 10 photograph
pinwheel: 3 toy
sound: 4 whir 5 whirr
piny: 5 spicy 8 fragrant 10 coniferous
Pinza, Ezio: 4 bass 5 basso 6 singer
specialty: 5 opera
pion: 5 boson, meson 8 particle
pioneer: 4 lead 5 early, first, found, guide, start 6 create, invent, launch, leader, map out, open up 7 develop, explore, founder, go first, initial, pilgrim, settler 8 colonist, discover, explorer, initiate, inventer, inventor, original, squatter 9 developer, establish, immigrant, inaugural, inceptive, innovator, institute, introduce, originate, spearhead 10 avant-garde, lead the way, pathfinder, show the way, trailblaze
place: 3 hut 5 cabin, shack 9 homestead
transport: 4 mule 5 horse, wagon 9 buckboard, Conestoga 10 wagon train
Pioneer: 3 car 4 auto 5 Dodge, probe
pioneering: 7 new wave 8 advanced 10 avant-garde
Pioneer Press: 5 paper 9 newspaper
locale: 6 St. Paul
Pioneers, The author: James Fenimore Cooper
pious: 4 holy 5 godly 6 devout, sacred 7 angelic, devoted, saintly 8 clerical, orthodox, priestly, reverent, seraphic, virtuous 9 angelical, born-again, prayerful, religious, righteous 10 goody-goody, seraphical, worshipful
ending: 4 amen
pip: 3 dot 4 lulu, seed 5 beaut, dandy, dilly, doozy, peach, prize 6 beauty, corker 9 humdinger
domino ~: 3 ace
pipa: 4 lute 6 string
origin: 5 China
pipal: 4 tree 6 bo tree
pipe: 3 cob 4 duct, flue, hose, line, main, peep, play, sing, toot, tube, vent, wind 5 cheep, chirp, drain, sewer, speak, spout, trill, tweet 6 convey, regard, siphon, squeak, syphon, warble 7 bring in, conduit, corncob, twitter, whistle 8 aqueduct, bird call, cylinder, transmit 9 water main 10 meerschaum
Asian ~: 5 hooka
clay ~: 6 dudeen
clean a ~: 4 ream
cleaner: 3 lye 5 Drano, snake
collar: 6 flange
combining form: 3 aul- 4 aulo- 5 solen- 6 soleno-
curved ~: 4 trap
cutter: 3 saw
down: 3 shh 4 hush 5 shush 6 shut up 7 be quiet, silence 9 keep still
dream: 5 fancy 6 revery, vision 7 chimera, fantasy, reverie 8 chimaera, delusion
ender: 4 line 5 stone
enjoy a ~: 4 puff 5 smoke
feature: 5 valve
hole: 5 crack, drain
Indian ~: 5 plant 6 flower
joint: 3 ell, wye
material: 3 cob, PVC 4 clay 5 briar, brier 6 copper 7 corncob, plastic 10 meerschaum
opening: 6 intake
part: 4 bowl, stem 5 shank
problem: 4 drip, leak
put down ~: 3 lay
rainwater ~: 5 spout
residue: 6 dottel, dottle
sealer: 5 putty
short ~: 4 spud
starter: 3 bag, pan 4 blow, horn, tail, wind 5 drain, stand, stove
stove ~: 3 hat 6 top hat
tobacco ~: 3 cob 4 clay 5 briar, brier 7 corncob 10 meerschaum
up: 3 say 5 speak, utter
water ~: 4 main 5 hooka 6 hookah 7 conduit 8 aqueduct
pipe ___: 4 clay, down, rack, vine 5 dream, organ, snake 6 batten, cutter, fitter, wrench 7 cleaner, fitting
___ pipe: 3 Pan 4 flue, reed, soil, vent 5 drill, light, organ, peace, pitch, waste, water 6 bustle, Indian, tuning 7 bleeder, corncob, exhaust, service
___-pipe cactus: 5 organ
___-pipe cinch: 4 lead
Pipe Dream: 7 musical
songwriter: 7 Rodgers 11 Hammerstein
pipeline: 4 main, pipe 7 channel, conduit 8 aqueduct
piper: 4 Scot 6 tooter 8 flautist 10 Highlander
mythical ~: 3 Pan
starter: 3 bag 4 sand
the ~ 's son: 3 Tom
Piper: 6 Laurie
pipestone: 7 mineral
pipette: 4 tube 5 pipet 7 lab tube 9 glassware
unit: 2 cc.
piping: 3 hot 4 high, trim 5 reedy 6 shrill
pipistrelle: 3 bat
pipit: 4 bird 7 titlark 8 songbird
pad: 4 nest
relative: 4 lark
Pippa: 5 Scott
Pippa Passes: 4 poem
author: Robert Browning
Pippen, Scottie: 5 cager
milieu: 5 court
org.: 3 NBA
sport: 10 basketball
Pippig: 3 Uta
Pippin: 5 apple
relative: 4 crab, Gala, Lodi, Rome 5 Mutsu 6 Empire, Ida Red, medlar, russet 7 Baldwin, Bramley, costard, Freedom, Liberty, Spartan, Wealthy, Winesap 8 Cortland, Jonathan, McIntosh 10 Rome Beauty
pips
piece with ~: 6 domino
with the ~ showing: 6 face-up
pipsqueak: 4 runt 5 scrub, twerp, twirp, weeny
Piqua: 4 city, town
locale: 4 Ohio
piquancy: 3 nip 4 bite, tang, zest 5 spice, taste 10 bitterness
piquant: 3 hot 4 racy, sour, tart 5 juicy, minty, peppy, salty, sharp, spicy, tangy, tasty, zesty, zingy 6 biting, lively, red-hot, savory, spicey, strong 7 peppery, pungent, zestful 8 poignant, spirited, stinging 9 flavorful, sparkling, trenchant
flavor: 3 zip 4 bite, tang, zest, zing
not ~: 4 blah, mild
pique: 3 get, irk, pet, vex 4 fret, gall, goad, huff, hurt, miff, rile, roil, snit, spur, step, stir, tiff, whet 5 anger, annoy, goose, grate, peeve, prick, rouse, sting, upset, wound 6 arouse, dander, excite, fire up, hatred, kindle, needle, nettle, offend, pother, put out, rancor, ruffle 7 affront, dudgeon, enflame, incense, offense, provoke, quicken, umbrage 8 interest, intrigue, irritate, slow burn, vexation 9 aggravate, annoyance, displease, galvanize, stimulate 10 conniption, exasperate, irritation, resentment
fit of ~: 3 ire 4 huff, pout, snit
piqué: 6 fabric 8 material
piqued: 3 hot, mad 4 hurt, ired, sore 5 angry, huffy, irate, livid, moody, upset 6 galled, put out 7 excited 8 steaming 9 indignant, irritated, resentful
piquet: 4 game 8 card game
Piraeus: 4 city, port, town
locale: 6 Greece
Pirandello, Luigi: 6 writer 7 Italian 8 Nobelist 10 playwright
work: Six Characters in Search of an Author
piranha: 4 fish 6 caribe
Piranha (1978 film)
cast: Bradford Dillman, Kevin McCarthy, Heather Menzies
director: Joe Dante
Piranha author: Harold Robbins
pirate: 4 copy, lift, raid 5 forge, steal, thief, usurp 6 bandit, borrow, kidnap, looter, pilfer, ravage, robber, sailor, vandal 7 brigand, corsair, jack tar, sea wolf, smuggle 8 freeboot, marauder, picaroon, rapparee, sea rover, simulate, spurious 9 buccaneer, depredate, reproduce 10 freebooter
drink: 3 rum 4 grog
feature: 5 patch 6 peg leg 8 eyepatch
fictional ~: 4 Hook, Smee
flag: 10 Jolly Roger
flag emblem: 5 skull 10 crossbones
haul: 4 loot, pelf, swag 5 booty 7 plunder 8 treasure
noted: 4 Kidd 5 Teach 6 Morgan 7 Lafitte 10 Blackbeard
ship: 5 rover, xebec, zebec 7 corsair 8 sea rover
shout: 6 yo-ho-ho
trunk: 5 chest
Pirate
Hall of Famer: 5 Kiner, Waner 6 Wagner 7 Averill, Vaughan 8 Clemente, Stargell 9 Mazeroski, Paul Waner 10 Lloyd Waner, Ralph Kiner
rival: 3 Cub, Met, Red 4 Expo, Twin 5 Angel, Astro, Brave, Giant, Padre, Rocky, Royal, Tiger 6 Brewer, Dodger, Indian, Marlin, Oriole, Philly, Ranger, Red Sox, Yankee 7 Blue Jay, Mariner 8 Athletic, Cardinal, Devil Ray, White Sox
Pirate author: Harold Robbins
Pirate Jenny composer: 5 Weill
Pirates: 4 nine, team 9 Seton Hall
home: 3 PGH 10 Pittsburgh
org.: 3 MLB, NLC
sport: 8 baseball
Pirates of Penzance, The: 8 operetta
character: 4 Kate, Ruth 5 Edith, Mabel 6 Isabel
composer: 7 Gilbert 8 Sullivan
Pirates of Penzance, The (1983 film)
cast: Kevin Kline, Angela Lansbury, Linda Ronstadt
director: Wilford Leach
Pirate, The (1948 film)
cast: Judy Garland, Gene Kelly, Walter Slezak
director: Vincente Minnelli
piratical: 7 lawless 8 thieving 9 predatory

Pire, Georges: 7 Belgian 8 Nobelist
Pirelli product: 4 tire
pirogi cousin: 5 knish
pirogue: 4 boat 5 canoe, skiff
need: 4 pole
waters: 5 bayou
pirouette: 4 jink, spin, turn 5 pivot, twirl, wheel, whirl 6 gyrate, rotate, swivel 7 revolve 8 gyration
Pisa: 4 city, town
attraction: 5 tower
city near ~: 5 Lucca
locale: 5 Italy 6 Italia
river: 4 Arno
Pisarro, Camille: 6 artist 7 painter, Spanish 8 sculptor
piscator: 6 angler 9 fisherman
Pisces: 4 fish, sign
follower: 5 Aries
month: 3 Feb., Mar. 5 March 8 February
preceder: 8 Aquarius
unit: 4 star
piscivore, flying: 3 ern 4 erne
Piscopo, Joe: 8 comedian
'P' Is for Peril author: Sue Grafton
Pisgah: 4 peak 5 mount 8 mountain
locale: 4 Asia 6 Jordan
summit: 4 Nebo
pismire: 3 ant, bug 5 emmet 6 insect
pismo __: 4 clam
Pismo Beach: 4 city, town
locale: 10 California
pistachio: 3 nut 4 tree 5 color, green 8 ice cream
color alternative: 3 pea 4 cyan, jade, Nile, sage 5 beryl, mango, olive 7 avocado, celadon, emerald, verdant 9 turquoise 10 aquamarine, chartreuse
family: 6 cashew
ice cream alternative: 5 lemon, mocha, peach 6 banana, coffee, Jamoca, toffee 7 caramel, coconut, vanilla 8 cinnamon, hazelnut 9 bubblegum, chocolate, pineapple, raspberry, rocky road, rum raisin 10 blackberry, cheesecake, Neapolitan, peppermint, strawberry
pistareen: 5 money
piste: 6 ski run 8 ski trail
pistil part: 5 ovary, style 6 stigma
pistol: 3 gat, gun, rod 4 Colt 5 piece 6 heater, roscoe 7 firearm, handgun 8 revolver 9 derringer, humdinger 10 six-shooter
ammo: 4 slug 6 bullet
German ~: 5 Luger
handle: 5 stock
packer: 6 gunman, outlaw, robber 7 marshal, sheriff 9 desperado 10 bank robber, gunfighter
packing a ~: 5 armed 8 carrying
point a ~: 3 aim 4 warn 8 threaten
starter ~ ammo: 5 blank
water ~: 3 toy 8 squirter
__ pistol: 3 air, cap 5 horse, water
pistole: 4 coin 5 money
Pistol Packin' __: 4 Mama
pistol-packing: 5 armed
pistols: 8 weaponry
Pistol, The author: James Jones
piston
location: 3 cyl. 6 engine 8 cylinder
sealer: 6 gasket
piston __: 3 rod 4 ring 6 engine
Piston rival: 3 Cav, Mav, Net, Sun 4 Buck, Bull, Hawk, Heat, Jazz, King, Spur 5 Knick, Laker, Magic, Pacer, Sixer, Sonic 6 Celtic, Hornet, Nugget, Raptor, Rocket, Wizard 7 Clipper, Grizzly, Warrior 8 Cavalier, Maverick 10 SuperSonic, Timberwolf
Pistons: 4 five, team
home: 7 Detroit
org.: 3 NBA
sport: 10 basketball
Piston, Walter: 8 composer
pit: 3 vie 4 dent, gulf, hole, mine, seed, tomb, well 5 abyss, chasm, ditch, fossa, gouge, match, shaft, stone, vault 6 cavity, crater, dimple, dugout, hollow, oppose, quarry, riddle, take on, trench, tunnel 7 foxhole, play off, pothole, vie with 9 perforate 10 depression, excavation, set against
boss: 8 overseer
bottomless ~: 5 abysm, abyss, chasm
ceremonial ~: 4 kiva
cherry ~: 5 stone
combining form: 5 bothr- 6 bothro-
ender: 4 cher, fall
grape ~: 6 acinus
luau cooking ~: 3 imu
make a ~ stop: 5 gas up
starter: 3 arm 4 cess, cock, flea, sand
pit __: 4 boss, bull, stop 5 viper 6 sample
__ pit: 4 coal, mosh, salt 5 rifle, snake, storm 6 barrow
pita: 5 bread
sandwich: 4 gyro
pitahaya: 5 fruit
Pit and the Pendulum (1961 film)
cast: John Kerr, Vincent Price, Barbara Steele
director: Roger Corman
Pit and the Pendulum, The (1991 film)
cast: Frances Bay, Jonathan Fuller, Lance Henriksen, Rona De Ricci
director: Stuart Gordon
Pit and the Pendulum, The author: Edgar Allan Poe
pitapat: 5 throb 6 patter 9 palpitate
go: 4 beat 5 pound 7 flutter 9 palpitate
pit bull: 3 dog 5 canid 6 canine
sound: 3 arf, yap 4 bark, gnar, yelp 5 gnarr, growl
Pitcairn: 3 isl. 4 isle 6 island
pitch: 2 ad 3 bid, dip, key, lob, peg, tar, yaw 4 buck, cant, cast, dive, fall, fire, flip, game, hurl, keel, lean, line, puff, rate, reel, rock, roll, sell, talk, tilt, tone, toss, trip 5 angle, chuck, drive, erect, fling, grade, heave, level, lobby, lunge, lurch, offer, plant, point, put up, raise, resin, set up, slant, sling, slope, slump, sound, speak, spiel, state, throw 6 billow, careen, degree, height, launch, let fly, locate, patter, plunge, scheme, seesaw, settle, slider, speech, submit, thrash, timbre, topple, tumble, wallow, welter 7 asphalt, deliver, incline, lecture, oration, present, proffer, project, promote, stagger, station 8 beanball, card game, change-up, fastball, flounder, forkball, gradient, heel over, proposal, spitball, splitter 9 advertise, curveball, frequency, promotion, publicity, publicize, sales talk, screwball, steepness 10 commercial, inflection, modulation, suggestion, turpentine
advertising ~: 5 try it
a tent: 4 camp 6 encamp 7 bivouac, rough it
baseball ~: 5 fader 6 sinker, slider 8 change-up, forkball, spitball, splitter 9 curve ball
detector: 3 ear
ender: 4 fork 6 blende
hay: 4 fork
in: 3 aid 4 give, help, join, pool 5 set to 6 assist, donate, fall to, go to it, pony up, tackle, tee off 7 get busy, hop to it 8 get going 9 cooperate, lend a hand, subscribe, undertake, volunteer 10 buckle down, contribute
indicator: 4 clef
into: 5 fly at 6 tackle
lacking ~: 6 atonal
make a ~: 3 bid 5 lobby, offer 6 submit 7 present, proffer, propose 9 advertise
of voice ~: 5 tonal
sales ~: 2 ad 4 line 5 spiel 8 hard sell, soft sell 10 commercial
slow ~: 3 lob
source: 3 tar 4 pine
water: 4 bail
woo: 3 hug 4 kiss, neck 5 spoon 6 caress
pitch __: 3 woo 4 cone, into, line, pine, pipe, shot, upon 5 a tent, chain, plane 6 chisel, circle 7 surface
pitch-__: 4 dark 5 black
__ pitch: 3 low 4 wild 5 fever, tough
__-pitch: 3 slo
pitch-black: 3 jet 4 dark, inky 5 sable, unlit 8 lowering 9 unlighted
pitchblende: 3 ore 7 mineral 9 uraninite
pitch-dark: 4 inky 5 black, sable, unlit 8 lowering 9 unlighted
pitched
it may be ~: 3 woo 4 tent
steeply ~: 6 gabled
too high: 5 sharp
too low: 4 flat
pitched __: 6 battle
__-pitched: 3 low 4 high
pitcher: 3 jug 4 ewer 5 adman 6 carafe, hurler, seller, vendor, vessel 7 amphora, athlete, creamer 8 decanter, sales rep 9 gravy boat 10 advertiser
asset: 3 arm
bag: 5 rosin
big-mouthed ~: 3 jug 4 ewer
coup: 4 save 7 shutout 8 no-hitter
dread: 3 hit 4 walk 5 homer
error: 4 balk
face the ~: 3 bat
facing the ~: 5 at bat
feature: 3 ear, lip 5 spout 6 handle
goal: 3 out, win 4 save 8 no-hitter
Greek wine ~: 4 olpe 7 amphora
Hall of Fame ~: 4 Dean, Ford, Hoyt, Ryan, Wynn 5 Gomez, Grove, Lemon, Paige, Perry, Rixey, Rusie, Spahn, Vance, Young 6 Bender, Feller, Gibson, Hunter, Koufax, Niekro, Palmer, Seaver, Sutton 7 Bunning, Carlton, Cy Young, Fingers, Hubbell, Jenkins, Johnson, Roberts, Ruffing, Waddell, Wilhelm 8 Bob Lemon, Drysdale, Marichal, Marquard 9 Alexander, Amos Rusie, Bob Feller, Bob Gibson, Dizzy Dean, Don Sutton, Early Wynn, Eppa Rixey, Jim Hunter, Jim Palmer, Mathewson, Newhouser, Nolan Ryan, Radbourne, Tom Seaver 10 Dazzy Vance, Jim Bunning, Lefty Gomez, Lefty Grove, Phil Niekro, Red Ruffing, Whitey Ford
mate: 5 basin
relief ~: 6 closer
Roman wine ~: 4 olpe 7 amphora
spot for a ~: 4 slab 5 mound
stat: 3 ERA 5 saves 8 shutouts 10 strikeouts
target: 4 mitt 5 plate
Pitcher: 5 Molly
pitchfork part: 4 tine 5 prong, tooth
pitchman: 6 barker
aide: 5 shill
payoff: 4 sale
__-pitch softball: 3 slo
piteous: 3 sad 5 woful 6 moving, woeful 7 doleful 8 grievous, pathetic, poignant, touching, wretched 9 affective, miserable, plaintive, sorrowful 10 deplorable, lamentable, pathetical
pitfall: 3 web 4 flaw, risk, snag, trap 5 catch, peril, setup, snare 6 danger, hazard 8 drawback 9 booby trap, mousetrap, quicksand
Pitfall (1948 film)
cast: Raymond Burr, Dick Powell, Lizabeth Scott, Jane Wyatt
director: Andre de Toth
pith: 4 core, crux, gist, meat 5 focus, heart, point, tenor 6 center, kernel, marrow, moment, thrust, upshot 7 essence, keynote, meaning, nucleus, purport 8 solidity 9 innermost, main point, substance 10 focal point, importance
helmet: 3 hat 4 topi 5 topee
pithecanthropus: 6 apeman
Pithecanthropus relative: 3 ape
pithecologist study: 3 ape
pithless: 4 puny 5 frail, wimpy 6 anemic, atonic, effete, feeble, flabby, flimsy 7 anaemic, fragile, wimpish 8 delicate, helpless 9 faltering, powerless, spineless 10 vulnerable
pithy: 4 curt, soft 5 brief, crisp, meaty, short, terse 6 cogent, gnomic 7 compact, concise, laconic, pointed, summary 8 succinct, vigorous 9 axiomatic, forceable, trenchant 10 meaningful, to the point
saying: 3 mot, saw 5 adage, gnome, motto 7 epigram 9 witticism
pitiable: 3 sad 5 woful 6 abject, tragic, woeful 7 forlorn 8 pathetic, tragical, wretched 9 miserable 10 deplorable
pitiful: 3 sad 4 mean, poor, vile 5 small, sorry, woful 6 abject, dismal, humble, measly, moving, paltry, scurvy, shabby, tragic, woeful 7 doleful, forlorn 8 beggarly, grievous, mournful, pathetic, poignant, touching, tragical, wretched 9 affecting, miserable, suffering, worthless 10 deplorable, despicable, inadequate, in bad shape, lamentable, pathetical
pitiless: 4 cold, hard, mean 5 cruel, harsh, nasty, stiff, stony 6 animal, brutal, fierce, savage, severe, stoney, unkind, wanton 7 austere, beastly, callous, hurtful, inhuman, vicious 8 barbaric, fiendish, inhumane, obdurate, ruthless, sadistic, vengeful 9 barbarous, cutthroat, dog-eat-dog, ferocious, heartless, impliable, inclement, merciless, monstrous, truculent, unfeeling 10 implacable, inexorable, insensible, relentless, unmerciful, vindictive
pitilessly: 9 viciously
Pitman: 5 Isaac
pupil: 5 steno 9 secretary
topic: 9 shorthand
Pitney __: 5 Bowes
Pitney, Gene
song: Half Heaven - Half Heartache (1963)
I'm Gonna Be Strong (1964)
It Hurts to Be in Love (1964)
Last Chance to Turn Around (1965)
Looking Through the Eyes of Love (1965)
Mecca (1963)
Only Love Can Break a Heart (1962)
She's a Heartbreaker (1968)
(The Man Who Shot) Liberty Valance (1962)
Town Without Pity (1961)
Twenty Four Hours from Tulsa (1963)
pitons: 6 spikes
use ~: 5 climb 6 ascend
pits
in the ~: 3 low 6 broody 7 way down

8 dejected, wretched **9** depressed, miserable **10** despairing, despondent
remove ~: 6 deseed
tar ~ locale: 6 La Brea
the ~: 5 awful, nadir, worst **10** rock bottom
pit stop item: 3 air, gas, gum, oil, pop **4** fuel, soda, tire **5** candy, chips, juice, snack **6** diesel **8** fast food, gasoline
Pitt: 4 Brad, Dirk
pitta: 4 bird
pittance: 3 bit, sou **4** mite **5** crumb, scrap **6** little **7** driblet, minimum, modicum, peanuts **10** slave wages
__ pittance: 4 mere
Pitt, Brad: 5 actor
film: Cool World (1992)
The Devil's Own (1997)
Interview With the Vampire: The Vampire Chronicles (1994)
Johnny Suede (1991)
Kalifornia (1993)
Meet Joe Black (1998)
Ocean's Eleven (2001)
A River Runs Through It (1992)
Se7en (1995)
Snatch (2000)
Twelve Monkeys (1995)
spouse: Jennifer Aniston
pitter-__: 6 patter
Pit, The: 5 novel
author: Frank Norris
__ Pit, The: 5 Money, Snake
Pittsburg: 4 city, town
locale: 10 California
Pittsburgh: 4 city, town
city north of ~: 4 Erie
conference: 7 Big East
county: 9 Allegheny
locale: 4 Penn.
product: 4 coal **5** steel
pro team: 7 Pirates **8** Panthers, Penguins, Steelers
river: 4 Ohio **9** Allegheny **11** Monongahela
school: 8 Duquesne
Pittsfield: 4 city, town
locale: 4 Mass.
Pitts, ZaSu: 7 actress
film: Dames (1934)
Greed (1925)
Let's Face It (1943)
Life With Father (1947)
Mrs. Wiggs of the Cabbage Patch (1934)
Ruggles of Red Gap (1935)
The Wedding March (1928)
TV: The Gale Storm Show
__ Pittypat: 4 Aunt
pituitary: 5 gland
output: 4 ACTH **7** hormone
pituri: 4 tree **5** shrub
pity: 4 ruth **5** crime, mercy, shame, spare **6** lenity, mishap, pardon, pathos, relent, sorrow, warmth **7** ache for, bad luck, charity, comfort, console, empathy, feel for, forgive, quarter, weep for **8** bleed for, clemency, go easy on, goodness, kindness, lenience, sympathy **9** grieve for, mischance **10** compassion, grieve with, kindliness, misfortune, ruefulness, sympathize, tenderness
exclamation: 4 alas **5** alack **8** lackaday
feel ~: 3 cry **4** ache, weep
have ~: 6 excuse, relent, soften **7** forgive
without ~: 4 hard **5** cruel **8** ruthless **10** relentless
Pity This Busy Monster...: 4 poem
author: e.e. cummings
piu: 4 more
Piura: 4 city, town
locale: 4 Peru
Pius: 4 pope **7** pontiff
pivot: 4 axis, axle, jink, slew, slue, spin, turn, veer **5** hinge, round, swing, twirl, wheel, whirl **6** center, circle, depend, hang on, rely on, rotate, slough, swivel, teeter **7** fulcrum, librate, revolve **9** oscillate, pirouette
ballet ~: 3 toe
pivotal: 3 key **5** focal, major, polar, vital **6** needed, ruling **7** central, crucial, primary **8** cardinal, critical, decisive, pregnant, required **9** essential, important, mandatory, momentous, necessary, principal **10** overriding, portentous
factor: 5 hinge **7** fulcrum
point: 3 toe **4** crux
pix: 5 films, snaps **6** flicks, movies, photos **9** snapshots
pixel: 3 dot
term: 6 low-res **7** graphic, high-res **8** graphics
pixie: 3 elf, imp **5** fairy, gnome, nisse, troll **6** goblin, sprite **7** brownie **10** leprechaun
Pixie: 4 toon **5** mouse
pixyish: 3 fey **5** elfin **6** impish
Pizarro, Francisco: 7 Spanish **8** explorer **9** conqueror
capital: 4 Lima
conquest: 4 Peru **5** Incas
quest: 3 oro **4** gold **8** treasure
pizazz: 3 vim, zip **4** brio, dash, élan, zest **5** class, flair, flash, oomph, punch, style, verve, vigor **6** energy **8** vitality, vivacity
lacking ~: 4 blah, drab, flat
Piz Bernina: 3 Alp
pizza: 3 pie **8** fast food
base: 5 crust
frozen: 5 Jeno's, Tony's **6** Ellio's **7** Celeste, Totino's **8** DiGiorno **9** Tombstone **10** Freschetta
go for ~: 6 eat out
order: 4 to-go
portion: 5 sixth, slice **6** eighth
slices per ~ often: 3 six **5** eight
topping: 5 bacon, olive, onion, sauce **6** cheese, pepper **7** anchovy, sausage **8** eggplant, meat ball, mushroom **9** pepperoni
pizza __: 6 parlor
__ Pizza: 6 Mystic
Pizza Hut rival: 7 Domino's
pizzazz
see pizazz
pizzeria: 10 restaurant
appliance: 4 oven
pizzicato: 4 note **7** plucked
P.J.: 7 O'Rourke
PJs: 7 pajamas **9** Dr. Dentons, nightwear, sleepwear **10** bedclothes
pkg.
see package
P.L.: 7 Travers
placable: 3 lax **4** easy, kind, mild, soft **5** loose **6** gentle, kindly **7** clement, ruthful, sparing **8** flexible, laid-back, merciful, tolerant **9** assuasive, compliant, easygoing, forgiving, indulgent **10** forbearing, permissive, unexacting
placard: 4 bill, sign **6** poster **9** broadside
placate: 4 calm **6** pacify, soothe **7** appease, assuage, compose, mollify, satisfy, sweeten **8** mitigate **9** reconcile, untrouble **10** conciliate, propitiate
place: 3 fix, job, lay, lie, pad, peg, put, set **4** area, city, duty, home, know, levy, lieu, nail, name, nook, park, post, rank, role, room, seat, site, slot, spot, stow, town, zone **5** abode, berth, house, joint, locus, lodge, niche, plant, posit, scene, stand, stead, stick, store, venue, where **6** assign, corner, hamlet, insert, instal, locale, locate, métier, milieu, office, reckon, region, settle, status, street, suburb **7** appoint, arrange, country, deposit, domicil, habitat, hangout, install, lay down, lodging, quarter, section, set down, situate, station, village **8** classify, diagnose, district, domicile, dwelling, function, identify, locality, location, lodgings, pinpoint, position, property, province, quarters, remember, standing, vicinity **9** apartment, bailiwick, community, designate, determine, recognize, recollect, residence, situation **10** categorize, commission, employment, occupation
combining form: 3 top- **4** loco-, topo- **5** -orium
on a pedestal: 5 adore **7** idolize, worship **8** idealize
starter: 3 any, dis, mis, out **4** fire, show, some, work **5** birth, every **6** common, market
place __: 3 mat **4** a bet, an ad, card, kick **7** setting
__ place: 4 high, take, ten's **5** run in, unit's **7** chimney, decimal, polling
Place: 4 Etta **7** Mary Kay
Place __ Arts: 3 des
__ Place: 6 Peyton **7** Melrose
__ Place, A: 6 Far-Off, Summer
Place de l'Opera artist: 4 Erté
__ Place I Hang My Hat Is Home: 3 Any
place in the __: 3 sun
Place in the Sun, A (1951 film)
cast: Montgomery Clift, Elizabeth Taylor, Shelley Winters
director: George Stevens
Place in the Sun, A (1966 song) artist: Stevie Wonder
place-kicker: 7 athlete **10** footballer
pride: 3 toe
prop: 3 tee
Place, Mary Kay: 7 actress
film: The Big Chill (1983)
Modern Problems (1981)
Sweet Home Alabama (2002)
TV: Mary Hartman, Mary Hartman
placement: 4 form **8** sequence **9** situation
placement __: 4 test
Placentia: 4 city, town
locale: 10 California
Place of Love, The author: Karl Shapiro
places: 4 loca, loci
go ~: 3 win **4** rise **6** hack it, make it, pan out, thrive **7** advance, luck out, make out, prevail, prosper, succeed, triumph, work out **8** flourish, get ahead, get along, hit it big, make good **10** do all right
trade ~: 4 swap **5** shift
__ Places: 7 Far-Away, Trading
Places in the Heart (1984 film)
cast: Lindsay Crouse, Sally Field, Danny Glover, Ed Harris, Amy Madigan, John Malkovich
director: Robert Benton
__ Places You'll Go!: 5 Oh the
placid: 4 calm, cool, even, mild, tame **5** quiet, staid, still, stoic **6** at ease, gentle, low-key, mellow, sedate, serene **7** amiable, at peace, easeful, equable, pacific, relaxed, restful, stoical, unmoved **8** amicable, carefree, composed, in repose, laid-back, peaceful, reserved, tranquil **9** collected, easygoing, impassive, quiescent, temperate, unexcited, unruffled, unworried **10** complacent, nonchalant, unagitated, untroubled
placidity: 4 calm **5** peace, quiet **8** calmness, serenity **9** composure **10** equanimity, sedateness
__ Placid, NY: 4 Lake
plack: 5 money
plagiarism: 5 fraud, theft **6** piracy **8** cribbing, stealing, thievery **9** borrowing
plagiarist: 6 copier **7** usurper **8** imitator
plagiarize: 4 copy, crib, lift **5** steal, usurp **6** borrow **8** arrogate **10** infringe on
plague: 3 bug, dog, dun, irk, nag, pox, rag, try, vex **4** bane, gall, pest, ride, roil **5** annoy, curse, grind, harry, haunt, hound, press, tease, worry **6** badger, blight, bother, gnaw at, harass, hassle, heckle, hector, needle, noodge, obsess, pester, pursue, rankle **7** afflict, disease, disturb, oppress, scourge, torment, trouble **8** aggrieve, calamity, disaster, distress, epidemic, nuisance, outbreak **9** beleaguer, contagion, detriment, importune, infection, nightmare, persecute, ruination **10** affliction, discompose, epidemical, pestilence
unit: 6 locust
__ Plague: 5 Black
plagued: 5 beset **8** besieged, obsessed
Plague Dogs, The (1982 film) director: Martin Rosen
Plague, The: 5 novel
author: 5 Camus
setting: 4 Oran
plaice: 4 fish
plaid: 6 fabric, tartan **9** checkered **10** Black Watch
fabric: 6 Madras, tartan
garment: 4 kilt
plain: 3 dry **4** bare, dull, easy, moor, naif, open, pure **5** basic, blunt, clean, clear, field, frank, heath, level, llano, lowly, lucid, mousy, naive, naked, overt, pampa, sober, stark, usual, vivid **6** candid, cogent, direct, folksy, honest, humble, in view, meadow, modest, mousey, pampas, patent, public, rustic, severe, simple, smooth, steppe, tundra, valley **7** audible, austere, clearly, evident, exposed, express, flat-out, insipid, legible, literal, lowland, natural, obvious, prairie, regular, sincere, Spartan, unfussy, vanilla, visible **8** apparent, clear-cut, definite, distinct, everyday, explicit, flatland, homespun, informal, knowable, manifest, moorland, no-frills, ordinary, out-front, palpable, readable, straight, unhidden, unsubtle, unveiled **9** big as life, downright, graspable, grassland, ingenuous, outspoken, tasteless, unadorned, unsightly **10** elementary, explicitly, forthright, from the hip, manifestly, monotonous, noticeable, noticeably, observable, spelled out, unaffected, unassuming, unshrouded, well-marked
African ~: 4 veld **5** veldt
alluvial ~: 5 delta
Asian ~: 6 steppe **7** steppes
combining form: 4 pedi- **5** pedio-
elevated ~: 4 mesa **5** butte **7** plateau **9** altiplano
ender: 4 song **5** chant **6** spoken
in ~ view: 5 overt **7** obvious, visible **8** apparent
Latin American ~: 5 campo, llano **6** pampas **7** el campo
lunar ~: 3 sea **4** mare
make ~: 4 show **6** evince **7** clarify, exhibit, speak up **8** manifest, simplify, speak out **9** bring home, elucidate, explicate **10** illustrate
name meaning ~: 6 Sharon
not ~: 4 lacy **5** fancy, fussy **6** frilly, ornate, rococo **7** ruffled **9** elaborate

starter: 5 flood
upland ~: 4 moor, wold
plain ___: 5 as day, table, to see, weave 7 dealing, sailing
___ Plain: 9 Mullarbor, Serengeti
___, Plain and Tall: 5 Sarah
plain as ___: 3 day
Plain Dealer: 5 paper 9 newspaper
locale: 9 Cleveland
Plain Dealer, The author: William Wycherley
plain-dealing: 6 honest 7 upfront 8 straight
___ Plaines, IL: 3 Des
Plainfield: 4 city, town
locale: 9 New Jersey
plainly: 5 by far 6 easily
Plain People: 5 Amish
Plains: 4 city, town
Amerind: 3 Ute 4 Cree, Crow 5 Teton 6 Apache, Dakota, Lakota 7 Lakhota
animal: 4 deer 5 bison, steer 6 coyote 7 buffalo 8 antelope 10 prairie dog
locale: 4 Iowa 7 Georgia
___ Plains: 5 Great
___ Plains Drifter: 4 High
Plainsman, The (1936 film)
cast: Jean Arthur, Gary Cooper
character: 3 Del
director: Cecil B. DeMille
Plains of ___: 7 Abraham
Plains of Passage, The: 5 novel
author: Jean Auel
plainsong: 5 chant, music 9 Gregorian
notation: 4 neum 5 neume
plainspoken: 5 bluff, blunt, brusk, frank, vocal 6 abrupt, candid, direct, honest 7 brusque, sincere, upfront 8 impolite, tactless, truthful 9 outspoken 10 forthright, foursquare, indelicate
plaint: 4 beef, moan 5 elegy, gripe, groan, whine 6 grouse, lament, squawk 9 grievance, objection
cat's ~: 3 mew 4 meow 5 miaou, miaow, miaul
coyote's ~: 4 howl
farm ~: 3 baa, low, moo 5 bleat, neigh, quack 6 gobble, squawk 7 whinney
peeper's ~: 5 croak
pound ~: 3 arf, yip 4 bark, woof, yelp
Shakespearean ~: 4 alas 8 lackaday
Yiddish ~: 2 oy
plaintiff: 4 suer 5 party 8 litigant
plaintive: 3 sad 5 sorry 6 woeful 7 doleful, hangdog, piteous, wistful 8 dolorous, grievous, mournful, pathetic 9 lamenting, querulous, sorrowful, woebegone 10 lamentable, melancholy, pathetical
cry: 5 whine
poem: 5 elegy
sound: 4 sigh
plain-vanilla: 5 basic 6 simple 7 humdrum, prosaic
Plainview: 4 city, town
locale: 5 Texas 7 New York
___ plaisir: 4 avec
plait: 4 coif, fold 5 braid, queue, tress, weave 6 hairdo, splice 7 cornrow, entwine, intwine, pigtail 8 coiffure 9 interlace 10 intertwine, interweave
s'il vous ~: 6 kindly, please
plakat: 4 fish
plan: 3 aim, lay, map, way 4 brew, idea, mean, mold, plot, spec 5 chart, draft, frame, hatch, setup, shape 6 agenda, cook up, design, devise, format, gambit, ideate, intend, intent, layout, map out, method, scheme, sketch, system 7 agendum, concoct, diagram, drawing, mark out, outline, pattern, prepare, program, project, propose, purpose, tactics, thought, work out 8 ambition, approach, block out, conceive, conspire, contrive, engineer, envisage, figure on, intrigue, maneuver, organize, proposal, reckon on, rough out, scenario, schedule, strategy, syllabus, think out, time line 9 blueprint, calculate, expedient, formulate, framework, intention, itinerary, look ahead, procedure, provision, visual aid 10 aspiration, bargain for, big picture, enterprise, mastermind, perception, prospectus, rough draft, strategize, suggestion
ahead: 3 fix 5 set up 6 budget 7 arrange, project 8 schedule
fiscal ~: 6 budget
floor ~: 5 chart 6 design, layout, sketch 7 diagram, drawing, outline 9 blueprint
food ~: 4 diet 7 regimen
game ~: 4 idea, ruse 5 model 6 design, scheme 8 scenario, strategy, time line 9 blueprint
ground ~: 3 map 5 chart, draft 6 design, layout, scheme, sketch, survey 7 diagram, program, rundown 8 proposal, scenario 9 blueprint, framework, rough idea 10 rough draft
in Britain: 4 rede
lurker's ~: 4 trap
on: 6 expect, reckon 7 wait for 9 calculate 10 anticipate
retirement ~: 3 IRA 5 Keogh
travel ~: 9 itinerary
___ plan: 4 game 5 floor 6 battle, budget, flight, ground, master 7 layaway, package, pension
___ Plan, A: 6 Simple
___ plan, a canal...: 1 a 4 A man
planate: 4 flat 5 level 6 planar, smooth
planchette, board with a: 5 Ouija
Planck, Max: 8 Nobelist 9 physicist, scientist
contemporary: 4 Bohr
plane: 3 jet, MiG, SST 4 bird, even, face, flat, prop, STOL, tool, tree, trim, VTOL 5 AWACS, craft, facet, level, liner, shave 6 Airbus, bomber, degree, ramjet, smooth, sphere, steppe 7 flatten, footing, pontoon, prairie, propjet, regular, stratum, surface, uniform, vehicle 8 aircraft, Concorde, flatland, jetliner, turbojet 9 transport, turboprop 10 crop duster, horizontal, twin-engine
alternative: 3 bus, car 4 auto, boat, ship 5 liner, train 9 freighter 10 cruise ship
area: 4 hold 5 cabin 7 cockpit
booster: 4 jato
bring the ~ in: 4 land 9 touch down
builders' org.: 3 UAW
crew: 5 pilot 6 airman 7 copilot, steward 9 navigator 10 stewardess
crystal ~: 4 face
datum: 3 arr., ETA
engine: 3 jet 6 fanjet 9 turboprop
European ~: 6 Airbus
fast ~: 3 jet, SST 8 Concorde
former Air France ~: 3 SST
gemstone ~: 5 facet
German ~: 5 Stuka
go by ~: 3 fly 6 aviate
grab a ~: 6 hijack 8 highjack
inspection agency: 3 FAA
jumping out of a ~: 4 feat 7 exploit
leave the ~: 4 jump 5 eject 7 deplane 9 parachute
left the ~: 3 lit 4 alit
light ~: 6 Cessna, glider
load: 5 cargo 7 baggage 10 passengers
locale: 3 sky 5 apron 6 hangar, runway 8 airstrip
military ~: 4 STOL, VTOL 5 AWACS
on a high ~: 5 lofty, noble
onetime enemy ~: 3 MIG
part: 3 fin 4 flap, tail, wing 5 aisle, cabin, strut 6 engine, galley 7 cockpit 8 bulkhead, fuselage
pontoon ~: 5 hydro
remote-controlled ~: 5 drone
reservation: 4 seat 6 flight
route: 6 airway
seating choice: 5 aisle 6 window 8 bulkhead
Soviet ~: 3 MiG
spotter: 5 LORAN, radar
spray: 6 deicer
stabilizer: 3 fin
starter: 2 bi 3 air, sea, tri, war 4 aero, aqua, jack, mono, sail 5 float
take a ~: 3 fly 6 aviate, travel
unidentified ~: 5 bogey, bogie
plane ___: 4 tree 5 angle, table
___ plane: 3 jet 5 fault, focal, glide, rotor 6 astral, badger, median, rabbet, rocket, router 7 jointer, molding
Planes, Trains & Automobiles (1987 film)
cast: John Candy, Steve Martin, Michael McKean, Laila Robins
director: John Hughes
planet: 3 orb 4 Mars 5 Earth, globe, Pluto, Venus, world 6 Saturn, sphere, Uranus 7 Jupiter, Mercury, Neptune, orbiter
circuit: 4 year
course: 3 arc 5 orbit
ender: 3 oid
fictional ~: 3 Ork 6 Vulcan
red ~: 4 Mars
reflecting power: 6 albedo
shadow: 5 umbra
___ planet: 5 inner, major, minor, outer
planetarium, Chicago: 5 Adler
Planet of the Apes (1968 film)
cast: Charlton Heston, Kim Hunter, Roddy McDowall
director: Franklin Schaffner
Planet of the Apes (2001 film)
cast: Helena Bonham Carter, Michael Clarke Duncan, Tim Roth, Mark Wahlberg
director: Tim Burton
role: 4 Nova
savage: 5 human
setting: 5 Earth 6 future
Planet of the Apes author: Pierre Boulle
Planets, The composer: 5 Holst
plangent: 5 forte, noisy 7 blaring, booming, jarring, pealing, rackety, raucous, reboant, roaring 8 crashing, piercing, rumbling, sonorous, strident, turned up 9 big-voiced, clamorous, deafening 10 boisterous, resounding, stentorian, strepitous, thundering, uproarious, vociferous
planimeter measurement: 4 area
plank: 5 board 6 timber 8 platform
material: 4 wood
ship ~: 3 sny 4 wale
slopes ~: 3 ski 4 skee
starter: 4 gang
Plank: 5 Eddie
___, Plank, Plunk: 5 Plink
planks: 4 wood 6 lumber
plankton: 4 brit 5 algae
component: 4 alga 6 diatom 9 protozoan
strainer: 6 baleen
Plan 9 From Outer Space
director: 4 Wood
role: 4 Eros
planned: 5 meant 6 wilful 7 studied, willful 8 intended, prepared 9 strategic, voluntary 10 deliberate, methodical, preplanned, purposeful, volitional
as ~: 5 slick 7 perfect 10 swimmingly
planner: 6 framer 8 designer, engineer 9 architect, developer, fashioner, tactician 10 mastermind, strategist
urban ~: 5 zoner
___ Planner, The: 7 Wedding
Plano: 4 city, town
locale: 5 Texas
plan of ___: 6 attack
plant: 3 fix, lay, pot, put, set, sow, spy 4 alga, bury, bush, cane, chia, farm, grow, herb, mill, mold, mole, moss, reed, seat, seed, shop, slip, till, tree, vine, weed, yard 5 embed, found, grass, imbed, lodge, pitch, place, put in, raise, shoot, shrub, stick, stock, works 6 anchor, annual, clover, croton, enroot, flower, fungus, hybrid, insert, instal, instil, set out, sprout, tamper 7 climber, creeper, cutting, deposit, factory, foundry, implant, install, instill, potherb, seaweed, station 8 biennial, cultivar, cyclamen, engender, ensconce, entrench, organism, seedling 9 accessory, equipment, establish, inculcate, machinery, perennial, toadstool, vegetable 10 accomplice, ornamental, transplant, vegetation
again: 5 resow
anchor: 4 bulb, root 7 rhizome, taproot
aquatic ~: 4 alga, iris 5 lotus, sedge 6 elodea 7 cattail, papyrus 9 water lily
aromatic ~: 4 herb, nard 5 spice 9 evergreen
century ~: 4 aloe 5 agave, plant 6 flower
climbing ~: 3 ivy, pea 4 rose, vine 5 grape, liana, liane 8 clematis, sweet pea
combining form: 4 phyt- 5 -phyte, phyto-
desert ~: 5 agave, sotol, yucca 6 cactus
disease: 4 rust 6 blight
dwarfed ~: 6 bonsai
dye-yielding ~: 4 anil 5 henna
fiber ~: 4 jute 5 agave, istle, ixtle
fit to ~: 4 rich 5 loamy 6 arable 7 fertile
flowering ~: 5 dicot 7 dicotyl
flowerless ~: 4 fern, moss
fluid: 3 sap 5 latex, resin
forage ~ of Asia: 3 urd
future ~: 4 bulb, seed 7 cutting, rhizome
gum-yielding ~: 4 guar
landscaping ~: 4 bush 5 shrub 9 perennial
life: 5 flora 10 vegetation
locale: 3 bed 6 garden 7 nursery 8 orangery 9 herbarium, terrarium 10 greenhouse
manufacturing ~: 4 mill 5 works 7 factory
marsh ~: 4 reed, rush 5 ament, calla, sedge 7 cattail 8 arum lily
medicinal ~: 4 aloe, herb 5 jalap 6 arnica, croton, ipecac
microscopic ~: 4 alga 6 diatom
moor ~: 5 gorse 7 heather
pasteurizing ~: 5 dairy 8 creamery
pest: 4 lice 5 aphis, louse 6 fungus
Polynesian ~: 2 ti 5 lehua 6 orchid
pore: 5 stoma
power ~: 5 hydro
protection: 5 mulch, straw
salad ~: 3 udo 5 cress 6 borage, carrot, celery, tomato 7 lettuce 8 cucumber 10 watercress
science: 6 botany
shade-loving ~: 5 hosta 9 impatiens
stalk: 4 stem 5 stipe

starter: 3 egg 5 house
sticker: 3 bur 5 briar, brier, spine, thorn 7 prickle
succulent ~: 4 aloe 5 sedum 6 cactus
surveillant's ~: 3 bug 4 mike 7 wiretap
terrarium ~: 4 fern, moss
tissue: 5 xylem 6 cambia
unwanted ~: 4 weed
__ plant: 3 air, bee, cup, dew, gas, gum, ice, pie, wax 4 bead, cone, corn, inch, iron, jade, life, musk, rock, seed, snow, soap, wind 5 batch, coral, money, pilot, poker, power, snake, stone, water, zebra 6 anchor, gopher, locker, mirror, oyster, prayer, ribbon, rubber, shrimp, spider, velvet 7 bedding, century, compass, foliage, packing, peacock, pitcher
Plant: 6 Robert
plantain: 4 weed 6 banana
lily: 5 hosta
pudding: 6 foofoo
plantation: 4 farm 5 manor 6 estate, spread 8 hacienda
drink: 5 julep 9 mint julep
fictional ~: 4 Tara
Plantation: 4 city, town
locale: 7 Florida
Plante, Jacques: 8 puckster
milieu: 3 ice 4 rink 5 arena
org.: 3 NHL
planter: 6 grower
planter's punch: 5 drink 8 beverage, cocktail
ingredient: 3 rum 7 bitters 9 grenadine, lime juice 10 lemon juice
Plantin: 4 font 8 typeface
planting
area: 3 bed 4 park 5 field 6 garden, meadow 7 orchard
backyard ~: 5 shrub
fall ~: 4 bulb, corm
garden ~: 3 row
lawn ~: 4 bush, tree 5 grass, shrub
medium: 4 dirt, loam, peat, soil 5 earth
tool: 3 hoe 4 rake 5 spade 6 dibble, shovel
plants: 5 flora 10 vegetation
regional ~ and animals: 5 biota
Plant, The author: Stephen King
plant-to-be: 4 seed
plaque: 5 award 8 memorial
plash: 3 lap 5 froth, slosh 6 ripple, splash 7 spatter
plasm starter: 4 ecto, endo, meta 5 proto
plaster: 4 cast, coat, daub, lime 5 cover, grout, smear 6 bedaub, cement, gypsum, smudge, stucco 7 encrust, incrust, overlay, spackle 8 dressing 10 intoxicate
art: 5 mural, secco 6 fresco
coat with ~: 5 parge
mold: 4 cast
of Paris: 5 gesso 6 gypsum
overhead: 4 ceil
support: 4 lath
plaster __: 4 cast
__ plaster: 7 mustard
plastered: 4 high 5 drunk, tight, tipsy 10 inebriated
plastic: 4 limp, soft 5 false, phony 6 clayey, credit, ersatz, giving, limber, phoney, pliant, pseudo, supple 7 clayish, ductile, elastic, pliable 8 flexible, formable, workable, yielding 9 insincere, malleable, resilient, shapeable, synthetic, tractable 10 artificial, substitute
building block: 4 Lego
clear ~: 5 Saran 6 Lucite
component: 4 urea 5 resin
hose ~: 3 PVC
pay with ~: 3 owe 6 charge
shiny ~: 5 vinyl
substitute: 4 cash 5 money
plastic __: 4 wrap 7 surgery
Plastic __: 4 Wood
Plastic __ Band: 3 Ono
plastron: 5 armor
plat: 3 lot, map 4 lace, plot 5 tract 6 parcel 10 interweave
make a new ~: 5 remap
portion: 4 acre
__ plata: 4 oro y
plat du __: 4 jour
plate: 4 coat, disc, dish, disk, meal, slab, tray 5 metal, scale, sheet 6 lamina, saucer, silver 7 anodize, encrust, helping, incrust, overlay, platter, serving, woodcut 8 choppers, dentures, laminate, trencher 10 escutcheon, lithograph
armadillo ~: 5 scute 6 scutum
armor ~: 4 tace 5 tasse
blue ~ special: 4 meal 8 luncheon
boundary hazard: 5 quake 6 tremor 7 temblor 8 slippage 10 earthquake
church ~: 5 paten
combining form: 4 plac- 5 elasm-, placo- 6 elasmo-
cross the ~: 5 score
dental ~: 5 lower, upper
fashion ~: 3 fop 4 dude 5 dandy 7 coxcomb
fish ~: 5 scale
flue ~: 6 damper
home ~: 4 base
insect ~: 5 notum
license ~: 2 ID 3 tag
scraping: 3 ort 5 scrap
starter: 4 book, name 6 boiler, breast, copper
thin ~: 6 lamina
tin ~: 4 tain
plate __: 4 mark 5 armor, glass, proof 6 girder
__ plate: 3 dry, end, hot, key, pie, pin, tie, tin 4 bite, butt, cell, deck, gold, home, kick, pole, push, race, soup, spot, wall, zone 5 angle, armor, chain, index, match, salad, sieve, swash, touch, wrist 6 batten, boiler, center, charge, dental, dinner, ground, ledger, nickel, purlin, quartz, silver, strike, switch, vanity 7 albumen, bearing, bolster, crustal, fashion, license, locking, raising, reverse, surface
__ Plate: 5 Cocos, Nazca 7 African, Pacific
plateau: 4 mesa, puna 5 butte, level, stage, table 6 upland 7 lowland 8 highland 9 elevation, tableland 10 high ground
Scandinavian ~: 5 fjeld
South African ~: 6 karroo
__ Plateau: 5 Ozark 7 Edwards, Iranian
__-plated: 4 gold 5 armor 6 chrome, silver
__ platelet: 5 blood
__ plate special: 4 blue
platform: 4 dais, shoe, walk 5 plank, stage, stand, stump 6 podium, policy, pulpit, tenets 7 balcony, landing, lectern, program, rostrum, soapbox, support, terrace 8 scaffold 9 elevation, manifesto, party line 10 objectives
by the water: 4 dock, pier, quay, slip 5 berth, jetty
Chinese sleeping ~: 4 kang
emcee ~: 6 podium 7 rostrum 8 platform
floating ~: 4 raft 5 barge
gas-pump ~: 6 island
nautical ~: 7 maintop
raised ~: 4 dais 5 altar, riser, stage 6 podium
synagogue ~: 4 bema
theater ~: 5 stage
warehouse ~: 4 skid
platform __: 3 bed 4 shoe 5 frame, scale 6 diving, tennis, ticket 7 balance
platforms: 5 podia
synagogue ~: 6 bemata
Plath, Sylvia: 4 poet
spouse: Ted Hughes
work: Ariel
The Bell Jar
The Colossus
Lady Lazarus
platina: 5 alloy
component: 6 osmium 7 iridium 9 palladium
Platinite: 5 alloy
component: 4 iron 6 nickel
platinoid: 5 alloy
component: 4 zinc 6 copper, nickel
platinum: 4 gray, grey 5 color, metal 6 blonde, bluish 7 blueish, element
alloy: 9 white gold
color kin: 3 ash 4 dove, drab 5 beige, dusty, merle, pearl, putty, slate, taupe 6 silver 7 grizzly 8 charcoal, gunmetal
platinum __: 5 blond 6 blonde
Platinum Blonde (1931 film)
cast: Jean Harlow, Robert Williams, Loretta Young
director: Frank Capra
platitude: 3 saw 5 maxim, motto, truth 6 cliché, phrase, saying, truism 7 bromide, proverb 8 buzzword, chestnut 10 shibboleth
platitudinous: 4 dull 5 corny, hokey, passé, stale, trite, vapid 6 common, jejune, old hat 7 clichéd, fatuous, humdrum, prosaic 8 bromidic, outdated, outmoded 9 hackneyed, prosaical 10 uninspired, unoriginal
Plato: 3 cat 4 Dana 5 Greek 11 philosopher
dialogue: 3 Ion
hangout: 4 stoa
parent of ~: 7 Ariston 10 Perictione
subject of ~'s Symposium: 4 Eros
work: Apology
Critias
Ion
Laches
Letters
Lysis
Meno
The Republic
The Sophist
Platonic __: 4 love, year 5 solid
platoon: 4 army, team, unit 5 group, squad, troop 6 outfit 7 company, phalanx 8 squadron 10 detachment
leader: 3 NCO 8 sergeant 10 lieutenant
member: 2 GI 7 recruit, soldier
subdivision: 5 squad
Platoon (1986 film)
cast: Tom Berenger, Willem Dafoe, Charlie Sheen, Forest Whitaker
director: Oliver Stone
extras: 6 troops
setting: 3 Nam 7 Vietnam
studio: 5 Orion
Platte: 5 river
locale: 8 Nebraska
tribe: 3 Oto 4 Otoe
tributary: 4 Loup
platter: 2 LP 4 disc, dish, disk, tray 5 plate 6 salver 7 charger
bottom: 5 B-side, side B
now: 2 CD
player: 4 hi-fi 6 stereo 10 phonograph
spinner: 2 DJ 6 deejay
top: 5 A-side, side A
__ Platter: 5 Pluto
Platters
members: Williams, Lynch, Robi, Reed, Taylor
song: Enchanted (1959)
The Great Pretender (1955)
Harbor Lights (1959)
He's Mine (1957)
I'm Sorry (1957)
It Isn't Right (1956)
My Prayer (1956)
One in a Million (1957)
Only You (1955)
On My Word of Honor (1957)
Smoke Gets in Your Eyes (1958)
To Each His Own (1960)
Twilight Time (1958)
With This Ring (1967)
You'll Never Never Know (1956)
(You've Got) The Magic Touch (1956)
Platt, Oliver: 5 actor
film: Bulworth (1998)
Dangerous Beauty (1998)
Doctor Dolittle (1998)
Gun Shy (2000)
The Imposters (1998)
Indecent Proposal (1993)
Simon Birch (1998)
Plattsburgh: 4 city, town
locale: 7 New York
platy: 3 pet 4 fish
platypus: 6 mammal
plaudits: 4 hand 5 éclat, honor, kudos 6 eulogy, homage, praise, salute 7 acclaim, big hand, ovation, tribute 8 accolade, applause, approval, encomium, flattery, good word 9 extolment, laudation, panegyric 10 exaltation
plausibility: 10 likelihood
plausible: 5 sound 6 doable, likely, viable 7 logical, tenable 8 apparent, credible, feasible, luculent, possible, probable, rational, specious, workable 9 deceptive, excusable, potential, practical 10 achievable, attainable, believable, convincing, defensible, imaginable, persuasive, reasonable
be ~: 4 wash 9 make sense
Plautus: 5 Roman 10 playwright
Plax: 9 mouthwash
competitor: 3 Act 5 Scope 6 Signal 7 Lavoris 9 Listerine 10 Fluorigard
play: 2 do 3 act, bet, fun, toy, vie 4 flop, game, give, jest, joke, lark, lick, pipe, ploy, risk, romp, room, show, skip, skit, trip, turn, work 5 caper, drama, farce, frisk, opera, prank, range, reach, revel, scope, serve, slack, smash, sound, space, sport, stage, stake, sweep, wager 6 cavort, comedy, fiddle, frolic, gamble, gambol, hazard, leeway, margin, one-act, render, tickle, tinker, trifle, turkey 7 carouse, compete, contend, disport, fribble, ham it up, musical, operate, pageant, pastime, portray, pretend, skylark, tragedy, writing 8 latitude, let loose, maneuver, movement, pleasure, simulate 9 amusement, diversion, elbowroom, enjoyment, free space, happiness, have a ball, make merry, melodrama, spectacle, stage show 10 fool around, manipulate, mess around, production, recreation, relaxation, roughhouse
again: 5 rerun
against: 3 pit 5 rival 6 oppose 7 compete
along: 5 agree, humor 6 comply 9 acquiesce, cooperate
a role: 3 act 5 emote, enact
around: 5 dally 6 trifle
a round: 4 golf

around (with): 6 dabble, fiddle, monkey, putter, tinker
at: 4 fake 5 feign 7 pretend 8 simulate
at full volume: 5 blast
at love: 3 toy 4 vamp 5 dally, flirt, tease 6 trifle 8 coquette
back: 6 repeat 7 recount 9 reiterate
ball: 5 agree 6 comply 9 acquiesce, cooperate
beginning of a ~: 4 Act I 6 act one
bring into ~: 3 use 5 apply, exert 6 entail, resort
by ear: 5 ad-lib 6 invent, make up, whip up, wing it 7 offhand 9 extempore, impromptu, improvise 10 improvised, off the cuff
caller: 2 QB 3 ref, ump 5 coach 6 umpire 7 referee
cards: 3 bet, gin 4 ante, deal, meld, pass, ruff 5 stake, trump, wager 6 gamble 7 shuffle
chance to ~: 4 turn
child's ~: 4 easy, snap 5 cinch, cushy 6 facile, no prob, picnic, simple 7 no sweat 8 duck soup, painless, pushover 9 no problem, uncomplex 10 effortless, elementary
device: 5 aside
direction: 4 exit 5 enter 6 exeunt
down: 6 soften 8 belittle, derogate, minimize, moderate, shrug off 9 deprecate, disparage, gloss over, soft-pedal, underrate, whitewash 10 understate
ender: 3 boy, let, off, pen 4 back, bill, book, girl, goer, list, mate, room, suit, time, wear 5 going, house, maker, thing 6 ground, making, wright
fair ~: 6 equity 7 justice 8 equality
false: 4 sell 6 betray, renege 7 sell out 8 go back on
favorites: 4 side 8 side with
footsie: 5 dally, flirt 6 trifle
for a fool: 3 con, use 4 bilk, dupe, gull, hoax, rook, snow, take 5 cheat 6 delude, entrap, outwit, rip off, take in 7 deceive, defraud, ensnare, fake out, finagle, mislead, snooker, swindle 8 flimflam, hoodwink, outsmart, sucker in 9 bamboozle, victimize 10 manipulate
for time: 5 delay, stall
foul ~: 4 harm 5 wrong 6 dupery, murder 8 inequity, violence
free ~: 5 range, scope, space 9 elbow room
games: 3 toy, use 5 abuse 6 expoit, manage, misuse, trifle 8 maneuver 9 machinate 10 manipulate, stragegize
hooky: 3 cut 4 skip 6 go AWOL 7 abscond
host: 5 ask in, emcee, treat 6 invite
humorous ~: 4 skit 5 farce 6 comedy
in ~: 4 fair 5 alive
in the water: 4 swim, wade 5 float, slosh 6 paddle, splash
it by ear: 5 ad-lib 6 invent, make up, wing it
Japanese ~: 3 noh
keep in ~: 4 pass 5 shoot, throw 6 assist, joggle, juggle 7 dribble, shuffle
matchmaker: 5 set up
music: 3 bow 4 blow, pick, toot 5 pluck, segue, skirl, strum, thrum
nongamblers ~ for it: 5 kicks, sport 9 enjoyment
on words: 3 pun 9 equivoque
out of ~: 4 dead, foul
part: 3 act 4 Act I, Act V 5 Act II, Act IV, scene 6 Act III, Act One
past: 6 endure, ignore 7 persist 8 overlook 9 hang tough
politics: 6 pander 8 maneuver 9 machinate 10 manipulate, strategize
possum: 4 sham 6 freeze 7 pretend 9 dissemble
put in ~: 4 pass, toss 5 serve, throw 7 dribble, kick off
roster: 4 cast
serious ~: 5 drama 7 tragedy
short ~: 4 skit
something to ~: 3 uke 4 game, harp 5 bugle, drums, flute, organ, piano, sport 6 fiddle, guitar, violin 7 trumpet 9 accordion
stoolie: 3 rat 4 blab, sing 5 rat on, spill 8 inform on
successful ~: 3 hit 5 boffo, smash
the game: 5 yield 6 accept, comply 7 conform, go along 9 acquiesce, cooperate 10 keep in step
the market: 3 buy 4 sell 5 trade 6 invest 7 venture 9 speculate
the odds: 3 bet 5 wager 6 gamble
to the crowd: 3 ham 5 emote 7 ham it up, swagger, upstage
unsuccessful ~: 4 bomb, flop
up: 6 accent, stress 7 feature, magnify, promote 8 reassert 9 embroider, emphasize, highlight, publicize, punctuate, spotlight, underline 10 accentuate, underscore
up to: 4 fawn 5 cater 6 cajole, pander 7 flatter, wheedle 8 blandish, fawn over
with fire: 4 dare, risk 6 chance 7 venture 9 take a risk
play ___: 3 hob 4 ball, date, down, up to 5 along, games, havoc, hooky, money 6 doctor, hookey, possum
play ___ and loose: 4 fast
play ___ ear: 4 it by
play ___ fiddle: 6 second
play ___ one's hands: 4 into
play ___ time: 3 for
___ play: 4 draw, fair, foul, long 5 force, match, medal, out of, power 6 child's, double, one-act, shadow, stroke, triple 7 miracle, mystery, passion, squeeze
___-play: 4 role
Play-___: 3 Doh
Playa Azul locale: 6 Ixtapa, Mexico
play-act: 4 play, pose 5 feign 6 fake it 7 perform, pretend 8 simulate
Playa del Carmen: 4 city, town
locale: 6 Mexico
Play a Simple Melody composer: Irving Berlin
Playback author: Raymond Chandler
playback machine: 3 VCR
playbill: 7 program
listing: 3 bio 4 cast, role
playbook: 6 script
playboy: 4 rake, roué 7 swinger 8 sybarite 9 jet setter, libertine
Playboy (1962 song) artist: Marvelettes
Playboy nickname: 3 Hef
Playboy of the Western World author: John Synge
played
down: 6 low-key
out: 4 beat, worn 5 all in, banal, stale, tired, trite, weary 6 dished, done in, old hat 8 fatigued, overused 9 destitute, hackneyed 10 dissipated
___ Played On, The: 4 Band
player: 3 ham, pro 4 jock, lead, mime, star 5 actor, extra, mimic 6 artist, better, bettor, goalie, mummer, walk-on 7 actress, athlete, ingénue, soloist, stand-in, trouper 8 opponent, thespian, virtuoso 9 contender, performer, superjock 10 competitor, contestant, understudy
excellent ~: 3 ace, pro 4 whiz 5 crack 6 expert, master, talent 8 virtuoso 9 first-rate 10 A number one, specialist
intermediary: 3 rep 5 agent 9 go-between 10 negotiator
key ~: 3 CEO, VIP 4 boss, czar, exec, suit 5 brass, mogul, titan, wheel 6 honcho, leader, top dog, tycoon 7 big shot, magnate, witness 8 big wheel, director, governor, higher-up, kingfish, top brass 9 commander, executive 10 head honcho
minor ~: 3 cog 5 extra
music ~: 2 DJ 4 band, hi-fi, juke 5 combo, phono, radio 6 deejay, stereo 7 boombox, juke box 8 tape deck 9 orchestra 10 phonograph
nonvarsity ~: 5 scrub
paid ~: 3 pro 4 jock 5 actor 7 actress 8 thespian
player ___: 5 piano
___ player: 3 bit 4 disc, disk, tape, team 5 piano 6 record, string
Player, Gary: 6 golfer
milieu: 5 links 6 course
org.: 3 PGA
players: 4 cast, team
first-string ~: 5 A-team 7 varsity
reserve ~: 5 bench
Player, The (1992 film)
cast: Peter Gallagher, Whoopi Goldberg, Tim Robbins, Greta Scacchi, Fred Ward
director: Robert Altman
play fast and ___: 5 loose
play for ___: 4 time 5 a fool, keeps
___ play for: 5 make a
playful: 3 fey 5 funny, happy, jolly, merry 6 frisky, impish, jocose, lively, unruly 7 coltish, jesting, naughty, puckish, teasing, waggish 8 humorous, mirthful, prankish, skittish, spirited, sporting, sportive 9 facetious, fun-loving, gamboling, lightsome, sprightly, vivacious, whimsical 10 capricious, frolicsome, rollicking
animal: 3 dog, pet, pup 4 seal 5 otter, puppy 6 kitten
talk: 4 jive 6 banter 8 chit-chat
playfully: 5 in fun
playfulness: 3 fun 5 humor 7 jollity 8 jocosity, mischief
playgoer: 6 viewer 9 spectator
playgoers: 8 audience
playground: 4 park, yard 5 field
apparatus: 5 slide, swing 6 see-saw 10 monkey bars
cry: 4 whee
game: 3 tag
purpose: 3 fun 8 exercise
retort: 4 is so 5 am not, is too 6 are too
play hard ___: 5 to get
playhouse: 5 odeon, odeum 7 theater, theatre 10 auditorium
playhouses, Greek: 4 odea
play in ___: 6 Peoria
playing
hard ball: 8 ruthless 10 determined, relentless
hooky: 6 absent
it safe: 7 careful 8 cautious
marble: 3 mib, mig 4 migg 5 aggie, immie
with a full deck: 4 sane
with fire: 4 bold, rash 6 daring, unwise 8 reckless 10 indiscreet
playing card: 3 ace, six, ten, two 4 club, five, four, jack, king, nine, trey 5 deuce, eight, heart, joker, queen, seven, spade, three 7 diamond
Playing for Keeps (1957 song) artist: Elvis Presley
Playing for Keeps author: David Halberstam
___ Playing Our Song: 6 They're
___-playing record: 4 long
play into one's ___: 5 hands
play it ___: 4 cool, safe 5 by ear
Play It Again, Sam (1972 film)
cast: Woody Allen, Diane Keaton, Tony Roberts
director: Herbert Ross
Play It as It Lays author: Joan Didion
play it close to the ___: 4 vest
Play it, Sam! speaker: 4 Ilsa
Play It to the Bone (1999 film)
cast: Antonio Banderas, Lolita Davidovich, Woody Harrelson, Tom Sizemore
director: Ron Shelton
Playland author: Athol Fugard
Playmaker, The author: Thomas Keneally
playmate: 4 chum 6 friend 7 partner 9 companion
nursery ~: 4 baby 6 infant 9 youngster
Playmates
song: Beep Beep (1958)
Jo-Ann (1958)
What is Love? (1959)
Play Me (1972 song) artist: Neil Diamond
Play Misty for Me (1971 film)
cast: Clint Eastwood, Donna Mills, Jessica Walter
director: Clint Eastwood
play on ___: 5 words
play one's ___ right: 5 cards
playpen
amusement: 3 toy
occupant: 3 tot 4 baby 6 infant
plays, call the: 4 boss 6 direct, manage
play second ___: 6 fiddle
PlayStation
maker: 4 Sony
rival: 4 Xbox
Play That Funky Music (song) artist: Vanilla Ice, Wild Cherry
play the ___: 4 fool, game 5 field 6 horses, ponies
___ Play, The: 6 Insect
plaything: 3 top, toy 4 ball, doll, kite 6 blocks, teaset
playtime: 6 recess 10 recreation
Play Time (1967 film)
cast: Jacques Tati
director: Jacques Tati
play to the ___: 4 hilt
play with ___: 4 fire
playwright: 6 author, writer 9 dramatist, wordsmith 10 librettist
American ~: 4 Hart, Inge, Rabe, Rice 5 Akins, Albee, Hecht, Kanin, Mamet, Odets, O'Hara, Simon 6 Abbott, Crouse, Henley, Miller, O'Neill 7 Hellman, Kaufman, Lindsay, Shepard 8 Anderson, Connelly, Sherwood, Williams 9 Chayefsky, Fierstein, Hansberry, Van Druten
Australian ~: 6 Palmer, Porter 7 Seymour, Stewart
Austrian ~: 10 Schnitzler 11 Grillparzer
award: 4 Obie, Tony
British ~: 3 Fry, Gay, Kyd 4 Bolt, Gray 5 Arden, Brome, Eliot, Frayn, Nashe, Orton, Peele 6 Cibber, Coward, Dekker, Dryden, Jonson, Morgan, Pinero, Pinter, Rowley, Rudkin, Savage, Steele, Storey, Wesker 7 Barstow, Chapman, Delaney, Heywood, Marlowe, Nichols, Osborne, Shaffer, Shirley, Webster, Whiting 8 Congreve, Far-

quhar, Fielding, Rattigan, Sheridan, Stoppard **9** Ayckbourn, Middleton, Priestley, Wycherley **10** Galsworthy **11** Shakespeare
Czech ~: 5 Capek, Havel **7** Jirásek
existentialist ~: 5 Genet
French ~: 5 Camus, Genet, Hardy, Jarry, Sagan **6** Gréban, Grévin, Musset, Racine, Sardou, Scribe **7** Anouilh, Feydeau, Garnier, Ionesco, Molière, Régnard, Rolland, Romains, Rostand, Sedaine **8** Salacrou, Sarraute **9** Corneille
German ~: 4 Holz **5** Sachs **6** Brecht, Grabbe, Hebbel, Kaiser **7** Büchner, Freytag, Gutzkow, Horvath **8** Gryphius, Schiller **9** Hauptmann, Sudermann, Zuckmayer
Greek ~: 8 Menander **9** Aeschylus, Euripides **12** Aristophanes
Indian ~: 8 Kalidasa
Irish ~: 4 Shaw **5** Colum, Friel, Synge, Wilde, Yeats **6** O'Casey **8** Donleavy
Italian ~: 5 Betti, Gozzi **6** Oriani **7** Giacosa, Goldoni, Rovetta **10** Pirandello
Japanese ~: 7 Abe Kobo
New Zealand ~: 8 Sargeson
Nigerian ~: 7 Soyinka
Norwegian ~: 5 Ibsen
offering: 5 drama
Polish ~: 6 Fredro **8** Rózewicz
Puerto Rican ~: 6 Arrivi
Roman ~: 6 Seneca **7** Plautus
Russian ~: 7 Chekhov
Scottish ~: 6 Barrie
Spanish ~: 4 Vega **6** Encina, Mihura, Sastre **7** Alberti **8** Calderón **9** Benavente **11** Pérez Galdós
Swedish ~: 9 Söderberg **10** Strindberg
Uruguayan ~: 7 Sánchez
plaza: 4 mall, park **5** court, green **6** common, square
Plaza: 3 car **4** auto **8** Plymouth
de la Revolución locale: 6 Havana
Plaza __: 5 Suite
plaza de __: 5 toros
Plaza Suite: 4 film, play
author: Neil Simon
cast: Lee Grant, Barbara Harris, Walter Matthau, Maureen Stapleton
director: Arthur Hiller
plea: 3 out **4** call, suit **5** alibi, claim, story **6** appeal, demand, excuse, orison, prayer **7** apology, defense, pretext, request **8** argument, entreaty, petition
defendant's ~: 4 nolo
enter a ~: 3 sue
for help: 3 SOS **6** Mayday
plea-__: 7 bargain
__ plea: 4 cop a
plead: 3 ask, beg, sue **4** pray, urge **5** argue, crawl, press, speak **6** appeal, enjoin, reason **7** beseech, declare, entreat, implore, request, solicit **8** appeal to, petition **9** impetrate, importune **10** supplicate
for: 4 back **7** support **8** advocate, champion
pleader: 3 att. **4** atty. **6** lawyer **7** accused **8** advocate, attorney **9** apologist, counselor, defendant
Pleading Guilty author: Scott Turow
plead the __: 5 Fifth
pleasant: 3 fun **4** cool, easy, fine, good, homy, mild, nice, okay, soft, warm **5** balmy, bland, civil, clear, great, homey, jolly, legit, moral, noble, suave, sunny, sweet **6** genial, gentle, jovial, kindly, lovely, polite, proper, smooth, social, urbane **7** affable, amiable, amusing, cordial, easeful, ethical, likable, welcome **8** all right, charming, cheerful, engaging, friendly, gladsome, gracious, heavenly, laudable, likeable, moderate, obliging, readable, splendid, superior **9** admirable, agreeable, congenial, convivial, enjoyable, excellent, favorable, palatable, reputable, temperate, unextreme, wonderful **10** acceptable, beneficial, creditable, delightful, diplomatic, enchanting, gratifying, personable, refreshing, satisfying, unagitated
combining form: 4 hedy-
name meaning ~: 5 Myron, Naomi
odor: 5 aroma **7** incense, perfume **9** fragrance, redolence
surprise: 4 gift **5** treat **7** present
Pleasant Grove: 4 city, town
locale: 4 Utah
Pleasant Hill: 4 city, town
locale: 10 California
Pleasant Island, today: 5 Nauru
Pleasanton: 4 city, town
locale: 10 California
pleasantries, exchange: 4 chat, talk **5** greet **7** speak to **8** converse
pleasantry: 3 wit **4** jest, joke, quip **5** sally **6** bon mot **8** greeting, repartee **9** witticism **10** salutation
Pleasant Valley Sunday (1967 song) artist: Monkees
Pleasantville (1998 film)
cast: Joan Allen, Jeff Daniels, William H. Macy, Tobey Maguire
director: Gary Ross
please: 3 wow **4** grab, like, send, suit, want, will, wish **5** amuse, charm, cheer, elate, humor, score **6** appeal, divert, kindly, pamper, pander, regale, see fit, thrill, tickle, turn on **7** cater to, content, delight, enchant, gladden, gratify, hearten, indulge, overjoy, satisfy **8** interest **9** entertain, go over big, titillate **10** hit the spot, tickle pink
as you ~: 6 at will, freely
easy to ~: 3 lax **8** laid-back
hard to ~: 5 fussy, picky **6** choosy **7** choosey, finicky **8** exacting, finiking, finnicky **9** demanding, querulous
in Japan: 4 dozo
power to ~: 5 charm **8** charisma **9** magnetism
Please Come to Boston (1974 song) artist: Dave Loggins
pleased: 4 glad **5** happy, merry, proud **6** blithe, cheery, elated, jovial, joyful, joyous, upbeat **7** content, gleeful, willing **8** blissful, cheerful, ecstatic, euphoric, exultant, jubilant, mirthful, relieved, thankful **9** rejoicing **10** complacent, flying high
be ~ by: 4 like, love **5** enjoy **9** delight in
look ~: 4 grin **5** smile
sounds: 3 ahs, ohs **4** aahs, oohs
with oneself: 4 smug, vain **5** proud **7** haughty **8** arrogant **9** conceited **10** complacent
pleased as __: 5 Punch
Please Don't Eat the Daisies (1960 film)
cast: Doris Day, David Niven, Janis Paige
director: Charles Walters
dog: 4 Hobo
Please Don't Go Girl (1988 song) artist: New Kids on the Block
Please Don't Go (song) artist: KC and the Sunshine Band, K.W.S., No Mercy
Please do preceder: 4 May I **6** Shall I
Pleased to __ you: 4 meet
Please Love Me Forever (1967 song) artist: Bobby Vinton
Please Mr. Please (1975 song) artist: Olivia Newton-John
Please Mr. Postman (1961 song) artist: Carpenters, Marvelettes
Pleasence, Donald: 5 actor
film: Cul-de-Sac (1966)
Escape From New York (1981)
Fantastic Voyage (1966)
The Great Escape (1963)
Halloween (1978)
Hearts of the West (1975)
The Pied Piper (1972)
Telefon (1977)
Will Penny (1968)
Please Please Me (1964 song) artist: Beatles
__ pleaser: 5 crowd
Please Remember Me (1999 song) artist: Tim McGraw
__ please the court: 4 If it
pleasing: 4 fine, good, nice, okay, rosy **5** ducky, great, legit, light, moral, nifty, noble, suave, sweet **6** comely, lovely, polite, pretty, proper, quaint, savory **7** amiable, easeful, ethical, likable, lilting, lovable, lyrical, musical, popular, welcome, winning, winsome **8** adorable, all right, alluring, charming, engaging, esthetic, fetching, gladsome, gorgeous, gracious, handsome, inviting, laudable, loveable, readable, splendid, stunning, suitable, superior, tasteful **9** admirable, agreeable, beautiful, congenial, enjoyable, excellent, palatable, reputable, rewarding, wonderful **10** acceptable, attractive, beneficial, creditable, delightful, enchanting, gratifying, personable, satisfying
name meaning ~: 4 Hedy
to the ear: 5 on key **6** dulcet **7** lyrical, melodic, tuneful **9** melodious
to the palate: 5 tasty, yummy **9** delicious, flavorful **10** delectable
pleasurable: 4 nice **6** social **7** welcome **9** agreeable, enjoyable, luxurious **10** gratifying
pleasure: 3 fun, joy **4** buzz, ease, glee, kick, play, will, wish, zest **5** bliss, fancy, gusto, kicks, mirth, spice, sport, treat **6** choice, desire, gaiety, gayety, liking, relish, thrill, turn-on **7** command, delight, jollies, pursuit, rapture, revelry **8** felicity, gladness, radiance **9** amusement, diversion, enjoyment, festivity, happiness, jocundity, merriment **10** jubilation, preference, propensity, recreation, regalement, relaxation
at one's ~: 6 freely
boat: 5 yacht **7** cruiser **8** trimaran **9** catamaran
exclamation: 3 aah, gee, hey, ooh, wow, yes **4** gosh, yeah **5** golly, zowie **6** whizzo, yippee **7** whoopee, whoopie **8** all right
get ~ from: 3 dig **4** like, love, want **5** enjoy, fancy, go for, savor **6** desire, dote on, relish **9** delight in, indulge in **10** appreciate, be mad about
give ~: 5 amuse **6** thrill **7** enchant, gladden, gratify, satisfy **8** enthrall **9** enrapture
obvious ~: 5 gusto **10** enthusiasm
show ~: 3 hum **4** glow, grin **5** laugh, smile **7** light up, whistle
sigh of ~: 3 aah
take ~: 4 live **5** enjoy, revel **6** relish, wallow **9** luxuriate
trip: 5 jaunt **6** cruise, junket, outing **9** excursion
with ~: 6 gladly **7** happily **9** willingly
Pleasure of His Company, The: 4 film, play
author: Cornelia Otis Skinner
cast: Fred Astaire, Lilli Palmer, Debbie Reynolds
director: George Seaton
Pleasure Ridge Park: 4 city, town
locale: 8 Kentucky
Pleasures of Helen, The author: Lawrence Sanders
pleat: 4 fold, tuck **5** crimp **6** crease, gusset, pucker, ruffle
alternative: 4 slit, vent **6** gather
__ pleat: 3 box **4** kick, kilt, reet **5** knife, pinch **7** crystal
plebe: 4 tiro, tyro **5** cadet, newie **7** recruit
academy: 4 USMA, USNA
answer: 3 sir **5** no sir **6** yes sir
plebeian: 3 low **4** base, mean, rude **5** banal, lowly, small **6** coarse, common, humble, vulgar **7** ignoble, lowborn, peasant, popular **8** baseborn, commoner, ordinary **9** bourgeois, unrefined **10** lower-class, pedestrian, uncultured
plebeians: 4 herd **6** masses **8** riffraff **9** hoi polloi **10** lower class
plebiscite: 4 vote **6** ballot
plectrum: 4 pick
use a ~: 4 pick **5** plink, pluck, strum, thrum
pledge: 3 vow **4** avow, bail, bond, gage, hock, oath, pact, pawn, word **5** stake, swear, toast, token, troth, vouch, wager **6** assure, avowal, commit, devote, plight, surety **7** bargain, earnest, promise, warrant **8** contract, covenant, dedicate, guaranty, security, warranty **9** agreement, assurance, guarantee, liability, stipulate, subscribe, undertake **10** collateral, commitment, engagement
medieval ~: 4 gage
name meaning ~: 5 Homer **6** Arlene
of fidelity: 5 troth
oneself: 3 vow **5** swear **7** promise
take the ~: 7 abstain, refrain
to wed: 5 troth **10** engagement
Pledge: 6 polish
alternative: 6 Behold, Endust **10** Liquid Gold, Old English
pledged: 5 bound, sworn **9** betrothed
Pledge of Allegiance last word: 3 all
Pledge, The (2001 film)
cast: Benicio Del Toro, Jack Nicholson, Vanessa Redgrave, Robin Wright
director: Sean Penn
Pledge, The author: Howard Fast
Pleiades: 4 Maia **6** Merope **7** Alcyone, Celaeno, Electra, Halcyon, Sterope, Taygete **8** Halcyone
father: 5 Atlas
one of the ~: 4 star
pursuer: 5 Orion
Pleione: 4 star
Pleistocene: 5 Epoch **6** Ice Age
Plekhanov, Georgi: 7 Russian **11** philosopher
plenary: 4 full, open **5** total, uncut, whole **6** entire **7** general **8** absolute, complete, finished, sweeping, thorough **9** inclusive, unreduced **10** exhaustive, unabridged
plenipotentiary: 5 envoy **6** legate **8** diplomat, minister
plenish: 5 stock **6** fill up
plenitude: 3 lot **4** glut **6** argosy, bounty, wealth **9** abundance, amplitude, profusion, repletion **10** cornucopia, exuberance
plentiful: 4 full, lush, many, much, rich, rife **5** ample, large **6** bumper, enough, galore, lavish **7** copious, fertile, flowing, liberal, opulent, profuse, replete, teeming **8** abundant, complete, fruitful, generous, handsome, princely **9** abounding, bounteous, bountiful, capacious, chock-full, exu-

berant, lousy with, luxuriant, unsparing **10** sufficient
be ~: **4** teem **5** swarm **6** abound
plenty: **3** lot **4** a lot, ease, lots, many, much, peck, tons **5** ample, heaps, loads, piles **6** armful, enough, highly, lavish, masses, oodles, riches, stacks, wealth **7** but good, copious, liberal, profuse, volumes **8** abundant, generous, good deal, opulence, opulency **9** abounding, abundance, affluence, bounteous, bountiful, extremely, great deal, mountains, profusion **10** prosperity, sufficient
in ~ of time: **5** early
of nothing: 3 OOO **4** OOOO **5** OOOOO
old-style: **4** enow
Roman goddess of ~: **3** Ops
slangily: **4** enuf
__ Plenty o' Nuthin': **4** I Got
pleonasm: **8** verbiage
pleonastic: **5** wordy **7** gushing, verbose
Pleshette, Suzanne: **7** actress
film: The Adventures of Bullwhip Griffin (1967)
The Birds (1963)
If It's Tuesday, This Must Be Belgium (1969)
The Power (1968)
The Shaggy D. A. (1976)
Support Your Local Gunfighter (1971)
spouse: Troy Donahue, Tom Poston
TV: The Bob Newhart Show
Plessy opponent: **8** Ferguson
plethora: **3** sea **4** glut, much **5** flood, ocean **6** deluge, excess **7** barrage, nimiety, overage, satiety, surfeit, surplus **8** overflow, overkill **9** abundance, profusion **10** exuberance, oversupply, redundancy
Pleven: **4** city, town
locale: **8** Bulgaria
Plexiglas: **6** Lucite
component: **6** ketone
plexus: **4** rete **7** network
solar ~: **5** belly **7** stomach **10** midsection
__ plexus: **5** solar **6** celiac, lumbar, sacral
pliable: **4** limp, soft **5** lithe, waxen **6** docile, gentle, limber, lissom, supple **7** elastic, lissome, plastic, rubbery, springy **8** amenable, bendable, flexible, formable, yielding **9** adaptable, lithesome, malleable, receptive, resilient, tractable **10** adjustable, responsive, submissive, unhardened
pliant: **4** limp, tame **5** lithe **6** broken, docile, limber, lissom, supple **7** lissome, plastic, subdued, trained **8** flexible, lamblike, obedient, resigned, yielding **9** formative, lightsome, lithesome, malleable, tractable **10** manageable, submissive
plica: **4** fold **5** ridge
plicate: **6** folded **7** pleated
plié: **4** bend
pliers: **4** tool **7** forceps
plight: **3** fix, jam, lot, vow **4** case, hole, mess, pass, spot, word **5** pinch, state **6** corner, crisis, muddle, pickle, pledge, scrape, strait **7** dilemma, impasse, promise, straits, trouble **8** exigence, exigency, position, quagmire, quandary **9** betrothal, condition, deep water, emergency, extremity, situation **10** difficulty
light: **5** flare
one's troth: **3** wed **5** marry **10** tie the knot
Plimpton: **6** George, Martha **7** Shelley
plimsoll: **4** shoe **7** sneaker **8** footwear
Plimsoll __: **4** line, mark
plink: **5** pluck, strum, thrum
Plink, Plank, Plunk! composer: Leroy Anderson
plinth: **4** base, foot, orlo, slab **5** block, socle
Pliny the Elder: **5** Roman **6** writer
work: Natural History
Pliny the Younger: **5** Roman **6** orator
where ~ served: **6** senate
plissé: **6** fabric **7** textile **8** material
plod: **3** lag **4** drag, grub, moil, plug, slog, toil, trek, wade, walk **5** clump, crawl, grind, labor, slave, stump, sweat, trail, tramp, tread, tromp **6** drudge, go slow, linger, lumber, trudge, waddle **7** galumph, schlepp, shuffle **8** keep at it, struggle **9** drag along, grind away, persevere
plodder: **4** hack **6** drudge
plodding: **4** poky, slow **6** draggy, stodgy **7** gradual, halting, humdrum, impeded, languid **8** dilatory, drawn-out, hesitant, slothful, sluggish, toddling **9** leisurely, lethargic, ponderous, prolonged, snail-like, unhurried **10** deliberate, monotonous, pedestrian, protracted
Plomer, William: **4** poet **12** South African
plop: **3** set, sit **4** drip, fall **5** plunk, thump **6** settle **7** deposit
down: **3** sit **4** flop
plot: **3** bed, fix, lot, way **4** brew, draw, land, mark, mold, plan, plat, ruse, scam, site, trap **5** chart, dodge, draft, frame, graph, hatch, patch, story, tract, trick **6** action, cook up, device, devise, gambit, garden, lay out, locate, map out, parcel, racket, scheme, sketch, survey, thread, wangle **7** acreage, collude, compute, concoct, connive, finagle, frame-up, outline, picture **8** conspire, contrive, engineer, home site, intrigue, maneuver, navigate, property, scenario, suspense **9** calculate, collusion, delineate, flower bed, machinate, narrative, story line, stratagem, visual aid **10** complicity, conspiracy
a course: **5** chart **8** navigate
again: **5** remap
device: **5** twist **10** red herring
element: **4** clue, love **5** humor, irony **6** climax, murder **7** mystery, revenge **8** suspense
garden ~: **3** bed
mathematically: **5** graph
measure: **4** acre
starter: **7** counter
plot __: **4** line
Plot __ Harry, The: **7** Against
Plotinus: **5** Greek, Roman **11** philosopher
Plott __: **5** hound
plottage: **4** area **5** acres
plotter: **9** intriguer
literary ~: **4** Iago
plotters: **5** cabal, junta
deed: **4** coup **9** coup d'état, overthrow
Plot That Thickened, The author: P.G. Wodehouse
plotz: **5** faint, swoon **8** collapse
Plough and the Stars, The author: Sean O'Casey
Plovdiv: **4** city, town
locale: **8** Bulgaria
plover: **4** bird **5** pewit, wader **6** peewit **7** dottrel, lapwing **8** dotterel, killdeer
pad: **4** nest
relative: **9** sandpiper
plow: **4** farm, till **6** furrow **8** reinvest, turn over **9** cultivate **10** cultivator
blade: **6** colter **7** coulter
ender: **3** boy, man, men **4** back **5** share
fit to ~: **4** rich **5** loamy **6** arable **7** fertile
follower: **6** harrow
into: **5** crash **7** collide
part: **4** sole **5** blade
puller: **2** ox **4** mule **5** horse
sole: **5** slade
starter: **4** snow
steel ~ inventor: **5** Deere
through: **4** plod, slog, wade
plow __: **4** back, into **5** steel, under
plowboy: **4** hick **5** yokel **6** rustic **7** bumpkin, hayseed **10** clodhopper, provincial
plowed land: **5** tilth
__ Plowman: **5** Piers
plowman, name meaning: **8** Ackerman
Plowright, Joan: **7** actress
film: 101 Dalmatians (1996)
Dance With Me (1998)
Drowning by Numbers (1987)
Enchanted April (1991)
The Entertainer (1960)
The Summer House (1993)
Three Sisters (1970)
spouse: Laurence Olivier
ploy: **4** game, move, play, ruse, trap, wile **5** dodge, feint, shift, trick **6** device, gambit, scheme, tactic **7** gimmick, pretext, sleight, tactics **8** artifice, maneuver, strategy **9** chicanery, imposture, stratagem **10** red herring, subterfuge
advertising ~: **4** hype **5** promo **6** coupon, rebate
baseball ~: **4** bunt **5** steal **7** squeeze **8** pitchout
legal ~: **4** stay **5** alibi **6** appeal
pluck: **3** rob, tug **4** bilk, cull, draw, grab, grit, guts, jerk, pick, pull, rook, sand, take, tear, will, yank **5** cheat, heart, moxie, nerve, seize, spine, spunk, strum, thrum, twang, tweak, valor **6** chisel, clutch, daring, gather, mettle, rip out, snatch, spirit, starch, uproot **7** bravado, bravery, courage, defraud, extract, harvest, heroism, jerk out, prowess, swindle, take out, tear out, yank out **8** backbone, boldness, flimflam, gameness, gumption, temerity, tenacity, true grit, wrest out, yank away **9** derring-do, endurance, extirpate, fortitude, gallantry, gutsiness **10** confidence, enterprise, feistiness, moral fiber, resolution
up: **6** muster, summon
plucked in music: **4** pizz. **9** pizzicato
pluckiness: **4** grit **5** spunk **10** feistiness
plucky: **4** bold, game **5** brave, gutsy, nervy, stout **6** awless, daring, feisty, gritty, heroic, spunky, strong **7** aweless, dashing, defiant, doughty, gallant, impavid, staunch, valiant **8** fearless, heroical, intrepid, resolute, spirited, stalwart, unafraid, valorous **9** audacious, dauntless, dreadless, undaunted, unfearful, unfearing **10** courageous, mettlesome, undismayed, unflagging
plug: **2** ad **3** dam, nag, ram, wad **4** bung, clog, cork, fill, hype, lure, pack, plod, puff, push, seal, stop, toil, tout **5** block, boost, close, dam up, horse, lobby, promo, punch, study, wedge **6** equine, hype up, impede, stop up, talk up **7** advance, block up, closure, congest, hydrant, mention, occlude, promote, stopper, stopple **8** advocate, blockade, good word, obstruct **9** advertise, get behind, promotion, publicity, publicize, recommend, reference, sparkplug
along: **4** moil, slog **6** schlep, trudge
away: **4** work **5** labor **7** address, persist **8** keep at it, struggle **9** persevere
into: **3** tap **4** link **5** tie in, unite **6** hook up, link up, relate **7** connect **9** affiliate, interface
kind of electrical ~: **4** male **6** female
pull the ~ on: **3** end **4** halt, stop **5** drain **9** terminate
starter: **3** ear **4** fire
up: **3** dam **4** clog, seal **5** block **7** seal off **8** obstruct
__ plug: **5** spark
Plug and __: **4** Play
plugged: **5** tight
in: **3** hep, hip **4** wise **5** aware, savvy **6** posted, versed, wise to, with it **7** knowing, mindful **8** apprised, hooked up, informed **9** cognizant **10** conversant
plugged __: **6** nickel
plugugly: **4** hood **5** rowdy, tough **7** hoodlum, ruffian
plum: **4** sloe, tree **5** bonus, color, cream, cushy, drupe, fruit, prize, prune **6** bluish, carrot, choice, damson, nugget, prized, purple, reward **7** blueish, premium, reddish **8** dividend, valuable, windfall **9** greengage, myrobalan
cherry ~: **9** myrobalan
dried ~: **5** prune
family: **4** rose
Japanese ~: **6** loquat
like a ~ job: **5** cushy
product: **4** duff **6** brandy **7** pudding
relative: **4** pear, puce **5** apple, lilac, mauve, peach **6** almond, cherry, dahlia, damson, medlar, orchid, quince **7** apricot, heather, petunia **8** amethyst, burgundy, eggplant, hawthorn, lavender, mulberry, oiticica **9** raspberry **10** blackthorn, heliotrope
starter: **5** sugar
sugar ~: **9** sweetmeat
wild ~: **4** sloe
plum __: **4** duff **6** tomato **7** pudding
__ plum: **3** hog **5** beach, nanny, Natal **6** cherry, damson, ground **7** bullace, Spanish **9** greengage
plumage: **4** down, tuft **6** plumes **8** feathers
grow ~: **6** fledge
soft ~: **4** down
plumb: **4** true **5** delve, erect, fully, gauge, probe, quite, smack, solve, sound **6** fathom, weight **7** dig into, exactly, examine, explore, measure, totally, unravel, upright **8** absolute, complete, directly, entirely, straight, vertical **9** delve into, downright, out-and-out, penetrate, precisely **10** absolutely, completely, thoroughly, to the limit
bob: **6** weight
crazy: **4** loco
make ~: **10** straighten
material: **4** lead
out of ~: **5** atilt **6** aslant **7** crooked, tilting **8** slanting **9** at an angle
plumb __: **3** bob **4** line, loco, rule **5** joint
__ plumb: **3** off **5** out of
Plumb: **3** Eve
plumbago: **7** mineral **8** graphite
plumber
concern: **4** clog, drip, leak, main, pipe **5** drain, pipes **8** freeze-up
connection: **3** ell, tee **4** trap **5** elbow, joint
filler: **5** oakum
supply: **3** PVC **4** pipe
tool: **5** snake **7** plunger
plumber's __: **5** snake **6** friend, helper
plumbiferous: **4** lead **6** leaden
plumbing: **8** fixtures, hardware

inlet: 3 tap 4 cock, main 6 faucet
outlet: 5 drain
__ plumbing: 6 indoor
Plum Blossom artist: 4 Erté
plumbum: 4 lead
plumcot: 4 tree 6 hybrid
plume: 5 crest, penna, quill, remex 6 aigret, pinion 7 feather, panache, tectrix 8 aigrette
helmet ~: 5 crest 7 panache
nom de ~: 4 name 5 alias, title 6 anonym 7 pen name 8 cognomen 9 pseudonym
owner: 5 tante
source: 5 egret 7 ostrich
__ plume: 5 nom de
plumed cap: 5 shako
Plumed Serpent, The author: D.H. Lawrence
Plum Island author: Nelson Demille
Plummer: 6 Amanda 11 Christopher
Plummer, Amanda: 7 actress
film: Cattle Annie and Little Britches (1980)
Courtship (1987)
The Fisher King (1991)
mother: Tammy Grimes
Plummer, Christopher: 5 actor
film: Aces High (1977)
Dragnet (1987)
Dreamscape (1984)
Inside Daisy Clover (1965)
The Insider (1999)
The Man Who Would Be King (1975)
The Pyx (1973)
The Royal Hunt of the Sun (1969)
The Silent Partner (1978)
Somewhere in Time (1980)
The Sound of Music (1965)
Twelve Monkeys (1995)
spouse: Tammy Grimes
plummet: 3 dip 4 dive, drop, fall, sink, skid 5 crash, slide, slump, swoop 6 go down, plunge, tumble 7 decline, descend 8 collapse, decrease, downturn, nose-dive
plump: 4 full, ripe 5 beefy, bulky, burly, buxom, fubsy, large, obese, pudgy, pursy, round, stout, swell, tubby 6 chubby, chunky, fatten, fleshy, portly, pyknic, rotund, sprawl, stocky, zaftig, zoftig 7 adipose, paunchy 8 roly-poly 9 corpulent, filled-out 10 abdominous, overweight, well-padded
down: 4 drop, fall 5 plonk, plotz 8 collapse
not ~: 4 lean, slim, thin 6 skinny, svelte 7 slender
the pillows: 5 fluff
Plum, Professor game: 4 Clue
plum pudding ingredient: 4 suet
__ Plumr: 6 Liquid
plumule: 7 feather
plumy: 9 feathered
plunder: 3 gut, rob 4 haul, loot, raid, sack, swag, take 5 booty, harry, rifle, spoil, steal, strip, theft 6 fleece, forage, harrow, hijack, invade, maraud, prey on, rapine, ravage, snatch, spoils 7 despoil, jobbery, pillage, ransack 8 freeboot, highjack, lay waste, pickings, spoliate 9 depredate, devastate 10 run off with
old-style: 5 reave
plunderer: 5 thief 6 bandit, pirate, raider, robber, vandal, Viking 7 brigand, rustler 10 freebooter
plundering: 9 piratical, predatory, rapacious, vulturous
plunge: 3 dip 4 cast, dash, dive, drop, duck, dunk, fall, heel, jump, leap, push, rush, sink, stab, tear, toss, trip 5 forge, heave, lunge, lurch, pitch, slide, slump, stick, swoop, wager 6 career, charge, go down, header, hurtle, thrust, topple, tumble 7 descend, descent, dunking, immerse, mad rush, plummet, venture 8 downturn, flounder, nosedive, submerge 9 hit bottom 10 go the limit, go whole hog
ahead: 3 ram 4 race, rush, tear 6 hurtle, thrust
forward: 4 jump, leap 5 lunge, swoop 6 hurtle, pounce
into: 5 begin 6 attack, tackle 7 pitch in
take the ~: 3 wed 4 dare, risk 5 marry, start 6 chance, hazard 7 venture
take the ~ again: 5 rewed
plunk: 3 set 4 plop, thud 5 pluck, plump, twang
down: 3 pay, put 7 deposit
Plunkett, Jim: 2 QB 10 footballer
plural: 3 few 4 many, some 7 several
pronoun: 4 them, they 5 these, those
verb: 3 are 4 have
plurality: 4 bulk, mass, most 8 majority
plus: 3 and, too 4 also, boon, gain, perc, perk 5 add-on, asset, bonus, extra 6 virtue 7 added to, benefit, besides, surplus 8 addition, positive 9 advantage, along with, including, lagniappe, what's more 10 additional, in addition
fours: 5 pants 8 breeches, knickers, trousers
in Spanish: 3 más
net ~ expenses: 3 sum 8 sum total
ne ~ ultra: 4 acme, A-one, apex, best, peak, tops 5 crest, crown, elite, prime 6 apogee, choice, far-out, finest, select, superb, unique, zenith 7 highest, maximum, optimal, optimum, paragon, perfect, stellar, sublime, supreme 8 choicest, exemplar, five-star, foremost, four-star, greatest, high spot, lodestar, nonesuch, paradigm, peerless, pinnacle, superior, topnotch, ultimate, very good 9 beau ideal, Endsville, excellent, exemplary, first-rate, high point, matchless, nonpareil, top-flight, unequaled, unrivaled 10 consummate, first-class, inimitable, out of sight, phenomenal, preeminent, touchstone
number next to a ~ sign: 6 addend
starter: 3 non
plus __: 4 sign 5 fours
plush: 4 lush, luxe, pile, posh, rich, soft 5 downy, furry, nappy, ritzy, silky, swank, swell, swish 6 costly, deluxe, fabric, fleecy, fluffy, lavish, ornate, snazzy, swanky 7 elegant, opulent, refined, squishy, velvety 8 cushiony, gorgeous, palatial, splendid 9 luxuriant, luxurious, sumptuous
item: 4 sofa 6 carpet 8 armchair
like a ~ toy: 4 soft 5 fuzzy 6 cuddly
Plutarch: 5 Greek 6 author, writer
subject: 4 Cato
work: Moralia
Parallel Lives
Pluto: 3 dog, god, orb 5 deity, Hades 6 planet
alias: 5 Orcus
brother of ~: 7 Jupiter, Neptune
equivalent: 5 Hades
moon of ~: 6 Charon
owner: 6 Mickey
parent of ~: 3 Ops 6 Saturn
sister of ~: 4 Juno 5 Ceres, Vesta
wife of ~: 10 Proserpina
plutocrat: 5 nabob 6 fat cat 7 Croesus, magnate 9 moneybags 10 capitalist, man of means
plutonium: 5 metal 7 element
Plutus author: Aristophanes
pluvial: 5 rainy 6 hyetal
pluviometer input: 4 rain
pluvious: 5 rainy 6 hyetal
ply: 3 run, use 4 fold, sail, work 5 beset, exert, ferry, hound, layer, sheet, twist, wield 6 assail, attack, badger, employ, handle, harass, lamina, manage, pursue, regale, strand, work at 7 besiege, carry on, operate, utilize, wheedle 8 dispense, engage in, maneuver 9 persist in, thickness 10 manipulate
a needle: 3 sew 5 baste 6 stitch 9 embroider
one's trade: 4 work
the oars: 3 row 5 scull
__-ply: 3 two 5 three
Plymouth: 3 car 4 auto, city, port, town 10 automobile
landmark: 4 rock
locale: 4 Mass. 5 Devon 7 England 9 Minnesota
model: 3 GTX 4 Fury, Neon 5 Laser, Plaza, Savoy 6 Breeze, DeLuxe, Duster, Volare 7 Acclaim, Concord, Horizon, Prowler, Reliant, Valiant, Voyager 8 Gran Fury, Roadking, Suburban, Sundance 9 Barracuda, Belvedere, Cambridge, Cranbrook, Satellite, Sport Fury 10 Road Runner
Plymouth __: 4 Rock 6 Colony 7 Company
Plymouth Rock: 3 hen 4 fowl 7 chicken
relative: 6 Bantam, Brahma, Houdan, Sussex 7 Cornish, Dorking, Leghorn 8 Araucana, Langshan, Shanghai 9 Dominique, Orpington, Wyandotte
Plymouth Township: 4 city, town
locale: 8 Michigan
Plympton: 4 Bill
Plywood: 5 panel
component: 5 layer
Plzen: 4 city, town
from ~: 5 Czech
Pm: 4 elem. 7 element 10 promethium
61 for ~: 4 at. no.
P.M.: 3 aft.
PMG employer: 4 USPS
__ P. Morgan: 4 Jaye
__ P. Morton: 4 Levi
pneuma: 4 soul 6 psyche
pneumatic __: 4 duct, pile, tire 5 drill 6 trough
Pnin author: Vladimir Nabokov
Po: 5 river 7 element 8 polonium
Basin city: 5 Milan
city on the ~: 5 Turin 6 Torino 7 Cremona
84 for ~: 4 at. no.
locale: 5 Italy
tributary: 4 Adda 7 Trebbia
PO
box item: 3 ltr. 4 card 6 letter, packet 8 postcard
branch ~: 3 sta. 7 station
busy mo. at the ~: 3 Dec. 8 December
competitor: 3 UPS 5 FedEx
concern: 3 pkg. 4 mail 6 letter 7 package
designation: 2 st. 3 RFD, rte., zip 4 addr., city 5 route, state 6 street 7 address, country, zip code
directive: 3 COD
stamp: 8 postmark
unit: 2 lb., oz. 5 ounce, pound
poa: 5 grass
poach: 3 rob 4 boil, cook 5 filch, steal 6 coddle 7 intrude, ransack 8 encroach, trespass 10 run off with
something to ~: 3 egg
poached egg foundation: 5 toast
Poanas: 4 city, town
locale: 6 Mexico 7 Durango
Póas: 7 volcano
locale: 9 Costa Rica
Pobble Who Has No Toes, The author: Edward Lear
Pobeda __: 4 Peak
po boy: 3 sub 4 hero 5 hoagy 6 hoagie 9 submarine
Po' Boy Blues author: Langston Hughes
pobre: 4 poor 7 Spanish
Pocahontas: 6 Indian
husband: 5 Rolfe
shelter: 4 tipi 5 tepee 6 teepee
transport: 5 canoe
Pocatello: 4 city, town
campus: 3 ISU
locale: 5 Idaho
pochard: 4 bird, duck, fowl
relative: 4 smew, teal 5 eider, Pekin, Rouen, scaup 6 Cayuga, scoter 7 gadwall, mallard, pintail, redhead, sea duck, widgeon 8 garganey, gray duck, mandarin, musk duck, oldsquaw, shoveler, surf duck, wood duck 9 black duck, broadbill, golden-eye, goosander, greenhead, merganser, ruddy duck, sprigtail 10 bufflehead, canvasback, surf scoter, tufted duck
Pochutla: 4 city, town
locale: 6 Mexico, Oaxaca
pocket: 3 bag, wee 4 hide, hole, lift, lode, sack, take, tiny, vein 5 filch, pinch, pouch, small, steal, swipe, teeny 6 cavity, hollow, little, midget, minute, obtain, peewee, pilfer, streak, teensy 7 chamber, compact, conceal, opening, purloin, receive 8 portable, shoplift 9 miniature, undersize 10 diminutive, receptacle, vest-pocket
billiards: 4 pool
bread: 4 pita
container: 5 flask
contents: 4 keys, lint 5 hanky 6 change, hankie 8 billfold
edition: 9 miniature
ender: 4 book, size 5 knife
money: 4 cash, cent, dime 5 bills, coins, fiver, penny 6 change, nickel, single 7 coinage, quarter, ten-spot
protector: 4 flap, snap 6 button, zipper
starter: 4 pick
warm in the ~: 4 rich 5 flush 6 loaded 7 wealthy 8 well-to-do 9 well-fixed
pocket __: 3 rat 4 book, door, park, veto 5 money, mouse, piece 6 chisel, gopher 7 borough, edition
pocket-__: 4 size 6 square
__ pocket: 3 air 4 side 5 cargo, out of, patch, slash, stage, watch
__-pocket: 4 vest
pocketbook: 3 bag 4 tote 5 means, pouch, purse 6 clutch 7 handbag 8 reticule
__-pocket expenses: 5 out-of
pocketful of __, A: 3 rye
Pocketful of Miracles: 4 film, song
cast: Bette Davis, Glenn Ford, Hope Lange, Arthur O'Connell
composer: 4 Cahn 9 Van Heusen
director: Frank Capra
Pocket Money (1972 film)
cast: Strother Martin, Lee Marvin, Paul Newman
__ pockets: 4 deep
pocket-size: 4 tiny 5 small, teeny 6 teensy 9 miniature
poco: 4 a bit 6 little
Poco
song: Call It Love (1989)
Crazy Love (1979)
Heart of the Night (1979)

Poconos: **5** range
locale: **4** Penn.
__-pocus: **5** hocus
pod: **4** case, hull, husk **5** shell, shuck **6** jacket, school, sheath **7** capsule **8** seedcase **9** container **10** integument
contents: **3** pea **4** seed
cotton ~: **4** boll
edible ~: **5** cacao, carob, chili, okram **8** sugar pea
flax ~: **4** boll
member: **4** seal **5** whale
pungent ~: **5** chili
starter: **3** tri **4** mega, octo, seed
Podhoretz, Norman: **6** writer **8** essayist
podia: **6** rostra
podiatrist concern: **3** toe **4** arch, foot
podium: **4** dais, foot **5** stage, stump **6** pulpit **7** lectern, rostrum, soapbox **8** platform
feature: **4** mike
speaker: **6** lector, orator **7** honoree **8** lecturer
take the ~: **4** talk **5** orate, speak
Podunk: **4** town **6** sticks
one from ~: **5** yokel
Poe, Edgar Allan: **4** poet **6** author
cat: **8** Caterina
night visitor: **5** raven
work: Al Aaraaf
Alone
The Angel of the Odd
Annabel Lee
The Assignation
Astoria
The Balloon Hoax
The Bells
Berenice
The Black Cat
Bon-Bon
Bridal Ballad
The Business Man
The Cask of Amontillado
City in the Sea
The City in the Sea
The Coliseum
The Colloquy of Monos and Una
The Conqueror Worm
The Conversation of Eiros and Chamion
A Descent Into the Maelstrom
The Devil in the Belfry
Diddling
The Domain of Arnheim
A Dream
Dream-Land
Dreams
A Dream Within a Dream
The Duc de l'Omelette
Eldorado
Eleonora
An Enigma
Eulalie
Eureka
Evening Star
The Facts in the Case of M. Valdemar
Fairy-Land
The Fall of the House of Usher
For Annie
The Gold Bug
The Happiest Day
The Haunted Palace
Hop-Frog
How to Write a Blackwood Article
Imitatation
The Imp of the Perverse
In Youth I Have Known One
The Island of the Fay
Israfel
King Pest
Landor's Cottage
Lenore
Ligeia
Lionizing
The Literary Life of Tingum Bob, Esq.
Loss of Breath
Maelzel's Chess-Player
A Man of the Crowd
The Man That Was Used Up
The Masque of the Red Death
Mellonta Tauta
Mesmeric Revelation
Metzengerstein
Morella
MS. Found in a Bottle
The Murders in the Rue Morgue
The Mystery of Marie Roget
Mystification
Narrative of A. Gordon Pym
Never Bet the Devil Your Head
The Oblong Box
The Oval Portrait
The Philosophy of Composition
Philosophy of Furniture
The Pit and the Pendulum
The Power of Words
A Predicament
The Premature Burial
The Purloined Letter
The Quacks of Helicon
The Raven
Romance
Shadow—A Parable
Silence
Silence—A Fable
The Sleeper
Some Words With a Mummy
Song
Sonnet—To Science
The Spectacles
The Sphinx
Spirits of the Dead
A Tale of Jerusalem
A Tale of the Ragged Mounains
Tamerlane
The Tell-Tale Heart
Thou Art the Man
The Thousand-and-Second Tale of Scheherazade
Three Sundays in a Week
To F.S.O.
To Helen
To Isadore
To M.L.S.
To My Mother
To One in Paradise
To Zante
Ulalume
The Unparalleled Adventure of One Hans Pfaall
A Valentine
The Valley of Unrest
Von Kempelen and His Discovery
William Wilson
X-ing a Paragrab
poem: **3** lai, ode **4** epic, hymn, pean, rime, rune, song, waka **5** elegy, haiku, paean, rhyme, tanka, verse **6** ballad, sonnet **7** ballade, sestina, sextain, writing **8** clerihew, limerick, rondelet **9** free verse **10** blank verse, villanelle
Christmas ~ opener: **4** 'Twas
closing stanza: **5** envoi
collection: **5** divan
division: **4** line **5** canto, envoi, stave, verse **6** stanza
epic ~: **5** Iliad **6** Aeneid **7** Beowulf **8** Oddyssey
heroic ~: **4** epic, saga **5** epode **6** epopee **8** epopoeia
Japanese ~: **4** waka **5** haiku, tanka
liturgical ~: **5** psalm
long ~: **4** epic, saga
lyric ~: **3** ode **6** sonnet
medieval ~: **3** lai, lay **6** aubade, ballad **7** ballade
morning ~: **6** aubade
mournful ~: **5** dirge, elegy
narrative ~: **4** idyl **5** idyll
of lament: **5** dirge, elegy **6** monody **8** threnody
pastoral ~: **4** idyl **5** idyll
17-syllable ~: **5** haiku
3-line ~: **5** haiku
poem lovely as a __: **4** tree
__ Poems, The: **7** Maximus
poesy: **4** poem, rime **5** rhyme, verse **6** poetry, rhymes
poet: **4** bard **5** odist, rimer **6** author, rhymer, writer **7** imagist **8** laureate, lyricist **9** balladist, rhymester, versifier
adverb for a ~: **3** e'en, e'er, ere, o'er, oft, 'tis, yon **4** enow, ne'er, nigh, 'twas **5** afore, anear, 'neath
American ~: **4** Dove, Hass, Tate **5** Benét, Plath, Pound, Wylie **6** Cullen, Dunbar, Kilmer, Kunitz, Lanier, Lowell, McKuen, Millay, Pinsky, Strand, Warren, Wilbur, Wilcox **7** Brodsky, Collins, Emerson, Jeffers, Kinnell, Lazarus, Markham, Nemerov, Rexroth, Roethke, Van Duyn, Whitman **8** Ginsberg, Levertov, MacLeish, Robinson, Rukeyser, Sandburg, Teasdale, Whittier **9** Dickinson **10** Longfellow
Argentine ~: **6** Storni
Australian ~: **4** Hope, Stow **6** Palmer, Porter, Wright **7** Brennan, Slessor, Stewart
Austrian ~: **7** Bachman
beat for a ~: **5** meter
Brazilian ~: **7** Andrade **8** Bandeira
British ~: **3** Gay, Pye **4** Gray, Gunn, Hood, Hunt, Owen, Pope, Read, Rowe, Tate **5** Blake, Byron, Carew, Clare, Davie, Donne, Eliot, Gower, Hardy, Keats, Monro, Peele, Powys, Raine, Rowse, Smart, Smith, Swift, Wyatt **6** Arnold, Austin, Brontë, Brooke, Bryher, Cibber, Cotton, Cowley, Cowper, Crabbe, Daniel, Dryden, Empson, Eusden, Fuller, Henley, Hughes, Jonson, Morris, Motion, Sidney, Symons, Waller, Warton **7** Bridges, Campion, Chapman, Chaucer, Collins, Crashaw, Drayton, Herrick, Heywood, Hopkins, Housman, Johnson, Marlowe, Marvell, Peacock, Quarles, Raleigh, Sassoon, Shelley, Sitwell, Skelton, Southey, Spender, Spenser **8** Betjeman, Browning, Day Lewis, de la Mare, Lovelace, Overbury, Richards, Rossetti, Shadwell, Suckling, Tennyson **9** Cleveland, Coleridge, Masefield, Sackville, Southwell, Swinburne, Whitehead **10** Chatterton, FitzGerald, Wordsworth **11** Shakespeare
Canadian ~: **4** Page **5** Blais, Dudek, Klein, Pratt, Purdy, Scott, Smith **6** Avison, Carman, Hébert **7** Garneau, Newlove, Service, Souster **8** Sangster **9** Choquette, Fréchette, Grandbois, Gustafson
Chilean ~: **5** Parra **6** Neruda **7** Mistral
Chinese ~: **4** Li Po, Tufu **7** Wang Wei
Chuvash ~: **4** Aigi
Colombian ~: **5** Silva **6** Rivera
Cuban ~: **5** Diego **7** Guillén
Czech ~: **5** Havel, Holub **6** Neruda **7** Seifert
Danish ~: **11** Stuckenberg
eye, to a ~: **3** orb
Finnish ~: **8** Runeberg
Flemish ~: **7** Gezelle
foot for a ~: **4** iamb **6** dactyl **7** spondee
French ~: **4** Char **5** Bodel, Jacob, Jouve, Marot, Péguy, Perse, Scève **6** Breton, Desnos, Éluard, France, Grévin, Musset **7** Boileau, Chénier, Heredia, Michaux, Mistral, Prévert, Queneau, Régnier, Reverdy, Rimbaud, Ronsard **8** Chartier, Soupault **9** Corneille, Deschamps, Desportes, Froissart, Lamartine, Prudhomme **10** Baudelaire
German ~: **4** Holz **5** Brant, Celan, Heine, Hesse, Rilke, Sachs, Storm **6** Brecht, Dehmel, George, Hebbel, Mörike **7** Fontane, Rückert **8** Brentano, Chamisso, Gryphius, Schiller, Schlegel **9** Nietzsche
Ghanaian ~: **8** Anyidoho
Greek ~: **5** Homer **6** Cavafy, Elytis, Pindar, Ritsos, Sappho **7** Palamas, Seferis **9** Aeschylus, Simonides
Hebrew ~: **6** Bialik **8** Alterman **9** Greenberg
Hindu ~: **5** Rishi
Hoosier ~: **5** Riley
Hungarian ~: **6** József
Indian ~: **5** Iqbal **6** Moraes **7** Bharati **8** Kalidasa
inspiration for a ~: **4** Muse **5** Erato
Ireland, to a ~: **4** Erin
Irish ~: **5** Colum, Moore, Wilde, Yeats **6** Boland, O'Grady **7** Parnell **8** MacNeice **9** Kavanaugh
Italian ~: **5** Belli, Berni, Dante, Tasso **6** Marino, Oriani, Parini, Pavese **7** Ariosto, Boiardo, Colonna, Folengo, Foscolo, Montale, Morante, Pascoli, Pontano **8** Carducci, Pasolini, Petrarch **9** Boccaccio, D'Annunzio, Quasimodo, Sacchetti **10** Cavalcanti, Sannazzaro
Japanese ~: **4** Issa **5** Basho, Buson, Ikkyu, Shiki **6** Hakuin, Ryokan **11** Akiko Yosano, Yosano Akiko
Lebanese ~: **5** Accad, Adnan
Lycian ~: **4** Olen
Martinican ~: **7** Césaire
Mexican ~: **3** Paz **4** Cruz **5** Nervo, Reyes
New Zealand ~: **6** Adcock, Baxter, Curnow
Nicaraguan ~: **5** Darío **8** Cardinal
Nigerian ~: **5** Okara **7** Soyinka
Norman ~: **4** Wace
of yore: **4** bard, scop **5** scald, skald **8** minstrel
Old Norse ~: **5** scald, skald
Persian ~: **4** Omar, Sa'di **5** Hafez, Hafiz **7** Khayyám
Peruvian ~: **4** Moro **6** Eguren
Polish ~: **7** Herbert **8** Krasicki, Rózewicz **10** Mickiewicz
Portuguese ~: **6** Camoes
pugilistic ~: **3** Ali **11** Muhammad Ali
Roman ~: **4** Ovid **6** Horace, Vergil **7** Juvenal, Persius **8** Catullus **9** Lucretius
Russian ~: **3** Fet **4** Bely, Blok **5** Bedny, Bunin **6** Esenin **7** Nabokov, Sologub **8** Nekrasov, Sloukhin **9** Akhmatova, Pasternak, Zhukovsky **10** Mayakovsky, Zabolotsky **11** Akhmadulina, Yevtushenko
Scottish ~: **4** Hogg, Muir **5** Burns, Scott, Spark **6** Dunbar **8** Campbell
Senegalese ~: **7** Senghor
South African ~: **6** Brutus, Plomer
Spanish ~: **4** Mena, Ruiz, Vega **6** Berceo, Boscán, Encina **7** Alberti, Bousoño, Góngora, Guillén, Herrera, Jiménez, Salinas **8** Manrique **11** Altoaquirre
Swedish ~: **6** Ekelöf **7** Bellman,

Fröding 9 Karlfeldt 10 Gustafsson, Strindberg
Swiss ~: 6 Keller 9 Spitteler
Turkish ~: 6 Hikmet
Urdu ~: 6 Ghalib
Venezuelan ~: 5 Bello
Welsh ~: 7 Herbert
poetic: 5 lyric 6 metric 7 idyllic, lilting, lyrical, musical 8 metrical, rhythmic, romantic, songlike 9 inspiring, melodious
poetic __: 7 justice, license
Poetica: 4 font 8 typeface
__ Poetica: 3 Ars
poetry: 3 art 4 rime 5 haiku, rhyme, verse 8 doggerel, limerick 10 literature
Poetry in Motion (1960 song) artist: Johnny Tillotson
Poetry Man (1975 song) artist: Phoebe Snow
__ Poets: 4 Lake
poets laureate (American):
2003– Louise Glück
2001–2003 Billy Collins
2000–2001 Stanley Kunitz
1997–2000 Robert Pinsky
1995–1997 Robert Hass
1993–1995 Rita Dove
1992–1993 Mona Van Duyn
1991–1992 Joseph Brodsky
1990–1991 Mark Strand
1988–1990 Howard Nemerov
1987–1988 Richard Wilbur
1986–1987 Robert Penn Warren
poets laureate (British):
1999– Andrew Motion
1984–1998 Ted Hughes
1972–1984 John Betjeman
1968–1972 Cecil Day Lewis
1930–1967 John Masefield
1913–1930 Robert Bridges
1896–1913 Alfred Austin
1850–1892 Alfred Tennyson
1843–1850 William Wordsworth
1813–1843 Robert Southey
1790–1813 Henry Pye
1785–1790 Thomas Warton
1757–1785 William Whitehead
1730–1757 Colley Cibber
1718–1730 Lawrence Eusden
1715–1718 Nicholas Rowe
1692–1715 Nahum Tate
1689–1692 Thomas Shadwell
1668–1689 John Dryden
Poet's Notebook, A author: Edith Sitwell
__ Poets Society: 4 Dead
poëtti: 4 drum
origin: 9 Polynesia
pogo: 5 dance
Pogo: 5 comic, strip
artist: 5 Kelly
dog: 10 Beauregard
pogonophobe fear: 6 beards
pogo stick: 3 toy
pogs: 3 fad
pogy: 4 fish 8 menhaden 9 surfperch
Pohl, Frederik: 6 editor, writer
genre: 5 sci-fi
poi
base: 4 eddo, taro
party: 4 luau
poignancy: 6 pathos
poignant: 3 sad 4 keen 5 sharp, woful 6 biting, moving, tender, woeful 7 intense, piquant, piteous, pitiful, tearful 8 eloquent, pathetic, piercing, touching 9 affecting, emotional, exquisite, sorrowful, trenchant 10 expressive, pathetical
poil: 4 silk, yarn 6 thread
poilu: 6 French 7 soldier
ally: 5 Tommy
cap: 4 kepi
Poincaré, Raymond: 6 French 9 statesman
poinciana: 4 tree
family: 6 legume
relative: 3 koa 5 carob 6 cassia, cercis, locust, padauk, padouk, redbud 7 araroba, mesquit 8 mesquite, tamarind
__ poinciana: 5 dwarf, royal 6 yellow
poinsettia: 5 plant 6 flower
point: 3 aim, dot, end, nib, nub, peg, set, tip, use 4 apex, barb, cape, crux, cusp, east, gist, goal, hint, idea, knub, lead, meat, pith, site, snag, spot, step, tend, text, time, tine, turn 5 drift, fleck, guide, heart, imply, issue, level, locus, moral, north, phase, pitch, prong, refer, score, sense, slant, south, speck, spike, spine, spire, stage, steer, sword, thing, thorn, train, where 6 burden, chakra, dagger, detail, direct, extent, finger, import, intent, kicker, marrow, moment, motive, nicety, object, period, reason, regard, signal, summit, thrust, tipoff, zero in 7 essence, feature, instant, meaning, message, minimum, pin down, purport, purpose, quality, quarter, respect, signify, sticker, suggest 8 argument, flyspeck, foreland, headland, indicate, interval, juncture, location, question, stiletto 9 designate, objective, punch line, situation, threshold 10 bottom line, particular, promontory, show the way
at any ~: 4 ever
at issue: 5 topic 8 argument
at that ~: 4 then 5 there
at the boiling ~: 3 hot 5 angry 6 fuming, raging 7 furious 8 bubbling, scalding, steaming
at this ~: 3 now 4 here 9 currently
a weapon: 3 aim
beside the ~: 4 moot 9 unrelated 10 extraneous, irrelevant
blue ~: 3 cat 7 Siamese
break ~: 5 ad out
breaking ~: 5 brink, limit 6 crisis 8 showdown
cardinal ~: 4 east, west 5 north, south
come to a ~: 5 taper
compass ~: 3 ENE, ESE, NNE, NNW, SSE, SSW, WNW, WSW 4 east, west 5 north, rhumb, south
crucial ~: 6 crisis, crunch 8 deadline
end ~: 3 cap 5 limit 7 ceiling
farthest ~: 3 end 5 brink 6 apogee, border, fringe 7 extreme 8 frontier 9 extremity, periphery
fine ~: 6 detail, nicety, nuance 9 condition, punctilio
focal ~: 3 hub 4 node, pith 5 focus, locus 6 center 8 cynosure 9 highlight
from this ~: 6 hereon
furthest ~: 4 edge 7 extreme 8 boundary 9 extremity
game ~: 3 run 4 goal 5 homer, score 6 basket 7 home run 9 field goal, touchdown
geometrical ~: 5 locus
get off the ~: 5 drift, stray 6 ramble, wander 7 deviate, digress, diverge 8 divagate
get the ~: 3 see 5 grasp 7 catch on 10 understand
halfway ~: 5 midst 6 center, median, middle
high ~: 3 tip, top 4 acme, apex, peak 5 crest, crown, limit 6 apogee, climax, summit, zenith 7 ceiling, maximum 8 pinnacle 10 prominence
in ~ of: 2 re 4 in re 5 as for 10 concerning
in ~ of fact: 6 indeed, really 8 actually
in question: 4 case 5 issue, theme, topic 6 affair, matter, thesis 7 problem, subject 8 business
joining ~: 4 link 5 ridge 8 juncture 9 stitching 10 connection
leading by a ~: 5 one up
low ~: 4 foot, pits, zero 5 abyss, chasm, floor, nadir 6 bottom, canyon, trough
main ~: 3 nub 4 core, crux, gist, knub, meat, pith 5 drift, heart 6 kernel, marrow, thrust, upshot 7 essence 9 substance 10 bottom line
make a ~ of: 6 repeat, stress 9 emphasize, stipulate, underline 10 underscore
of departure: 4 door, exit, gate, port 5 depot 8 terminal 9 threshold
of interest: 5 scene, vista 6 vision 7 display, exhibit 9 spectacle
of view: 4 mind, side, view 5 angle, light, slant 6 aspect, vision 7 feeling, opinion, outlook, posture
out: 4 cite, note, show, spot 5 input 6 adduce, advise, assert, denote, reason, record 7 comment, mention, specify, touch on 8 identify, indicate, register 9 touch upon
pen ~: 3 nib
rotating ~: 5 hinge 7 fulcrum
seal ~: 3 cat 7 Siamese
selling ~: 4 plus 5 asset, forte 6 virtue 7 benefit
starter: 3 end, gun, pin 4 view 5 check, flash, knife, stand 6 needle 7 counter
starting ~: 4 base 5 basis, git-go 6 origin, source 8 base camp 9 beginning, threshold
sticking ~: 3 rub 4 beef 7 impasse
stopping ~: 3 end 5 limit 7 ceiling
strong ~: 5 asset, forte
the finger at: 5 blame 6 accuse, charge
the way: 4 lead 5 guide, spark, steer, teach, train, tutor, usher 6 orient 7 conduct 8 instruct 9 spearhead
to the ~: 3 apt 4 curt 5 ad rem, blunt, brief, crisp, frank, pithy, short, terse, tight 6 direct, gnomic 7 apropos, compact, concise, germane, laconic, summary, well-put 8 apposite, relevant, succinct 9 pertinent, trenchant 10 applicable
to this ~: 3 yet 5 so far 6 to date
turning ~: 3 hub 4 axis, axle, crux 5 hinge, pivot, rally 6 climax, crisis 8 juncture, landmark, zero hour 9 milestone
up: 3 toe 4 mark 6 accent, stress 9 highlight, italicize, punctuate, spotlight, underline 10 accentuate, illustrate, underscore
up to a ~: 6 partly 8 somewhat 9 partially
weak ~: 4 flaw, vice 5 fault 6 defect
point __: 3 man 4 lace, tiré 5 count, coupé, group, guard, woman 6 charge, source, spread, system 7 d'esprit, shaving
point __ return: 4 of no
point-__: 5 blank 6 of-sale 8 and-shoot
__ point: 3 ace, dew, eye, pen, set 4 at no, blue, flex, game, gold, pass, sore 5 color, extra, flash, focal, frost, grade, honor, limit, match, nodal, petit, price, steam, to the, vowel 6 access, chisel, collar, Folsom, master, median, saddle, silver, triple, vernal 7 boiling, Brownie, cluster, control, decimal, diamond, melting, quarter, selling, talking, turning, vantage
Point __: 4 Ilio 5 Break, Reyes 6 Barrow
__ Point: 4 West 5 Pelee 6 Grosse 7 Montauk
point-and-shoot result: 3 pic 4 snap 5 photo 7 picture 8 snapshot 10 photograph
__ point average: 5 grade 7 quality
point-blank: 4 open 5 blunt, frank, smack 6 candid, direct, honest, openly 7 bluntly, frankly, sincere, up-front 8 candidly, directly, explicit, honestly, straight, truthful 9 outspoken, sincerely 10 explicitly, no-nonsense, truthfully, unmediated, unreticent
Point Blank (1967 film)
cast: Angie Dickinson, Lee Marvin, Keenan Wynn
director: John Boorman
Point Break (1991 film)
cast: Gary Busey, Lori Petty, Keanu Reeves, Patrick Swayze
director: Kathryn Bigelow
point-by-point: 8 detailed 10 spelled out
Point Counter Point
author: Aldous Huxley
character: 4 Lucy 5 Hilda 6 Elinor, Webley 7 Bidlake
Pointe __: 5 Noire
Pointe Claire: 4 city, town
locale: 6 Canada, Québec
pointed: 4 keen 5 pithy, sharp, short, smart, spiky, spiny, terse 6 acuate, barbed, spiked 7 cutting, prickly, pronged, pungent, right-on, telling 8 accurate, incisive, relevant, scathing 9 pertinent, sarcastic, trenchant 10 meaningful
arch: 5 ogive
as wit: 4 acid
comment: 4 barb 6 zinger
end: 4 cusp
not ~: 5 blunt 7 rounded
roof: 5 spire 7 steeple
tool: 3 awl 5 punch
weapon: 4 dart, shiv, snee 5 arrow, knife, lance, spear, sword 6 dagger 7 bayonet
pointer: 3 dog, rod, tip 4 clew, clue, dial, hint 5 arrow, canid, gauge, index 6 advice, canine, finger, hunter, needle, tipoff 7 warning 8 lodestar 9 indicator 10 suggestion
compass ~: 6 needle
CRT ~: 6 cursor
Pointer Sisters
hometown: Oakland
members: Ruth, Anita, June, Bonnie
song: American Music (1982)
Automatic (1984)
Dare Me (1985)
Fairytale (1974)
Fire (1978)
He's So Shy (1980)
How Long (1975)
I'm So Excited (1982)
Jump (For My Love) (1984)
Neutron Dance (1984)
Should I Do It (1982)
Slow Hand (1981)
Yes We Can Can (1973)
pointillism detail: 3 dot
__-point landing: 5 three
pointless: 4 dull, flat, idle, vain 5 blunt, inane, no use, no-win, nutty, silly, vapid 6 absurd, futile, hollow, jejune, otiose 7 aimless, insipid, useless 8 bootless, ill-spent, needless 9 for naught, frivolous, fruitless, illogical, senseless, worthless 10 extraneous, irrelevant, ridiculous, unavailing
point of __: 4 view 5 honor, order 7 sailing
__ point of: 5 make a
point of no __: 6 return
__ point Siamese: 4 blue, seal
__ Point, The: 7 Turning

pointy shoes wearer: 3 elf
poise: 4 calm, cool, ease, tact, wait 5 asset, grace, hover 6 aplomb, polish, stasis, temper 7 balance, bearing, dignity, suspend 8 calmness, demeanor, elegance, patience, presence, serenity 9 assurance, composure, diplomacy, gallantry, sangfroid, stability, stabilize 10 confidence, equanimity, moderation, sedateness, self-esteem, steadiness
starter: 4 equi 7 counter
poised: 4 calm, cool 5 ready, suave 6 sedate, serene, stable, steady, urbane 7 assured, tactful 8 composed, graceful, mannered, polished, tranquil 9 collected, unruffled 10 phlegmatic, unagitated
remain ~: 5 hover
poisha: 5 money
poison: 4 bane, evil, harm, kill, warp 5 ricin, taint, toxic, toxin, venom 6 infect 7 corrupt, henbane, pollute, subvert 8 impurity 9 herbicide, infection, prejudice, undermine 10 adulterate
animal ~: 5 venom
another's ~: 4 meat
arrow ~: 4 inee, upas 5 urare 6 antiar, curara, curare
hemlock ~: 5 conin
ivy genus: 4 rhus
ivy symptom: 4 itch, rash
poison ___: 3 haw, ivy, oak, pen 4 pill 5 sumac 7 hemlock
Poison (1989 song) artist: Alice Cooper
Poison Belt, The author: Arthur Conan Doyle
Poisoned Stream, The author: 4 Habe
Poison Ivy (1959 song) artist: Coasters
poisonous: 5 nasty, toxic 6 septic 7 baleful, baneful, corrupt, harmful, hurtful, nocuous, noisome, noxious, vicious 8 venomous, viperous, virulent 9 injurious, malicious, unhealthy 10 contagious, malevolent, pernicious
combining form: 5 toxic- 6 toxico-
mulberry tree: 4 upas
plant: 5 sumac 6 sumach 7 henbane 8 mandrake 9 snakeroot 10 belladonna, jimsonweed, nightshade
snake: 3 asp 5 adder, cobra, krait, mamba, viper 7 rattler 10 copperhead
poison-pen ___: 6 letter
Poissy: 4 city, town
locale: 6 France
Poitiers: 4 city, town
locale: 6 France
Poitier, Sidney: 5 actor
film: All the Young Men (1960)
The Bedford Incident (1965)
Brother John (1970)
Cry, the Beloved Country (1951)
The Defiant Ones (1958)
Duel at Diablo (1966)
Edge of the City (1957)
Guess Who's Coming to Dinner (1967)
In the Heat of the Night (1967)
The Jackal (1997)
Let's Do It Again (1975)
Lilies of the Field (1963, AA)
The Organization (1971)
A Patch of Blue (1965)
A Piece of the Action (1977)
Porgy and Bess (1959)
Pressure Point (1962)
A Raisin in the Sun (1961)
Something of Value (1957)
Stir Crazy (1980)
To Sir, With Love (1967)
The Wilby Conspiracy (1975)
poke: 3 bag, dig, jab, jut, lag, pry 4 butt, idle, prod, push, root, slap, stab, stir 5 amble, annoy, dally, delay, elbow, goose, impel, lunge, mosey, nudge, pouch, probe, punch, purse, rouse, shlep, shove, snoop, stick, tarry 6 arouse, bonnet, dawdle, fiddle, fillip, jostle, justle, linger, loiter, meddle, propel, putter, schlep, shlepp, thrust 7 dawdler, intrude, laggard, project, shamble 8 hang back, knapsack, overhang, protrude, slugabed, stand out, stick out, straggle 9 drag along, gunnysack, interfere, lazybones, sunbonnet 10 dillydally, incitement
along: 5 crawl, dally, trail 6 dawdle, loiter 7 saunter, shuffle
around: 3 pry 5 snoop 7 rummage
full of holes: 6 riddle 8 disprove, puncture 9 discredit, perforate 10 prove false
fun at: 3 kid, rag, rib 4 jeer, mock, ride, twit 5 fleer, roast, scoff, taunt, tease 6 deride, needle 7 put down 8 ridicule
one's nose in: 3 pry 5 snoop 6 meddle 7 intrude 9 eavesdrop, interfere
out: 3 jut 5 bulge 7 project
starter: 3 cow 4 slow
poke ___: 5 fun at 6 bonnet
Pokemon: 4 game 8 card game
poker: 4 game, tool 8 card game
action: 3 see 4 call, deal, fold 5 raise
bullet: 3 ace
call: 5 no bet
card: 3 ace, six, ten, two 4 five, four, jack, king, nine, trey 5 deuce, eight, joker, queen, seven, three 6 bullet
chip quantity: 5 stack
holding: 4 hand, pair 5 flush 6 aces up 10 royal flush
like some ~ hands: 3 pat
meet a ~ bet: 3 see
need: 4 deck, dice 5 chips, table
phrase: 4 I'm in 5 I call, I fold, I'm out 6 ante up
place: 5 stove 6 casino, hearth 8 fireside
ploy: 5 bluff
quit, in ~: 4 fold
raise, in ~: 4 bump
red-hot ~: 5 plant 6 flower
use a ~: 4 stir 5 stoke
variety: 4 brag, draw, stud 6 hold 'em 7 high-low, lowball 8 anaconda, baseball 9 freezeout, penny ante
wager: 3 bet 4 ante, chip 5 kitty, money, stake
winnings: 3 pot 5 kitty
poker-faced: 5 blank, stoic, stony 6 glassy, stoney, wooden 7 neutral 9 impassive
Poker Flat chronicler: 5 Harte
___-pokery: 7 jiggery
pokey: 3 can, jug, pen 4 jail, slow, stir 5 clink 6 cooler, lockup, prison 7 hoosgow, slammer 8 hoosegow, sluggish 9 calaboose
___-pokey: 5 hokey
Pokey: 5 Reese
poky: 4 jail, slow 5 tardy 6 cooler, draggy, lockup 7 gradual, halting, hoosgow, impeded, lagging, languid, slammer, tedious 8 crawling, creeping, dawdling, dilatory, dragging, drawn-out, hesitant, hoosegow, plodding, slothful, sluggish, toddling 9 leisurely, lethargic, prolonged, puttering, snail-like, unhurried 10 deliberate, protracted
pol: 10 ward heeler
concern: 4 vote 5 image
often: 6 orator 7 debater 9 sleazebag
Pol ___: 3 Pot
Pola: 5 Negri
Poland: 6 nation 7 country
astronomer: 10 Copernicus
capital: 6 Warsaw
chemist: 5 Curie
city: 4 Lódz 5 Posen, Radom 6 Gdansk, Kalisz, Kraków, Lublin, Poznan 7 Wroclaw
dance: 7 mazurka 8 mazourka 9 polonaise
export: 4 coal
gulf: 6 Danzig
harpsichordist: 9 Landowska
lancer: 4 ulan 5 uhlan
legislature: 4 Sejm
length measure: 4 mila
money: 5 grosz, zloty
mountain: 4 Rysy 5 Tatra
neighbor: 6 Russia 7 Belarus, Germany, Ukraine 8 Slovakia 9 Lithuania
Nobelist in Literature: 6 Milosz 7 Reymont 10 Szymborska 11 Sienkiewicz
Nobelist in Peace: 6 Walesa 7 Rotblat
Nobelist in Physics: 7 Charpak
org.: 4 NATO
pianist: 7 Hofmann 10 Paderewski, Rubinstein
playwright: 6 Fredro 8 Rózewicz
poet: 7 Herbert 8 Krasicki, Rózewicz 10 Mickiewicz
port: 6 Danzig, Gdansk, Gdynia 8 Szczecin
river: 4 Oder, Odra 5 Narew
saint: 7 Florian
soprano: 5 Raisa
stew: 5 bigos
writer: 6 Milosz, Mrozek 8 Borowski, Konwicki 10 Gombrowicz 11 Sienkiewicz
Poland author: James A. Michener
Poland China: 3 hog, pig 5 swine
Poland Spring: 5 water
competitor: 4 Naya 5 Evian 7 Perrier 8 Aquafina 9 Arrowhead
Polaner: 5 jelly
competitor: 5 Kraft 6 Knott's, Welch's 8 Smucker's
Polanski, Roman: 8 director
film: Chinatown (1974)
Cul-de-Sac (1966)
Death and the Maiden (1994)
Knife in the Water (1962)
Macbeth (1971)
The Pianist (2002, AA)
Repulsion (1965)
Rosemary's Baby (1968)
The Tenant (1976)
Tess (1979)
spouse: Sharon Tate
Polanyi, John: 7 chemist 8 Nobelist
polar: 3 icy 4 cold 5 chill, nippy 6 arctic, biting, chilly, frigid, frosty, frozen, wintry 7 central, counter, extreme, glacial, guiding, ice-cold, numbing, opposed, pivotal, reverse, shivery, wintery 8 contrary, freezing, opposite 9 antipodal 10 antipodean
bear country: 6 Alaska, Arctic
departure point for ~ expeditions: 4 Etah
feature: 6 aurora, icecap
wear: 3 pac 5 parka 6 mukluk
polar ___: 3 cap 4 axis, bear, body, star 5 angle, front, orbit 6 circle, lights 7 nucleus, valence
Polara: 3 car 4 auto 5 Dodge
Polaris: 4 ICBM, star 8 lodestar
Polaroid: 4 film, lens 6 camera
competitor: 4 Fuji 5 Canon, Kodak, Leica, Nikon 6 Konica, Pentax, Rollei 7 Minolta, Olympus, Vivitar, Yashica
inventor: 4 Land
Polaroid ___ Camera: 4 Land
pole: 3 bar, rod, xat 4 axle, beam, bean, cane, mast, post, rail, spar, stud 5 perch, ridge, shaft, sprag, staff, stake, stave, stick, stilt 6 timber 7 railing 8 baluster, flagpole, terminus 9 extremity, flagstaff
along: 3 ski 4 raft, skee
antenna ~: 4 mast
bean ~: 5 stalk
boat to ~: 4 punt, raft 5 barge, ferry 7 gondola
clothes ~: 4 tree
dance with a ~: 5 limbo
ender: 3 axe, cat 4 star
Eskimo's ~: 3 xat 5 totem
fishing ~: 3 rod
make a totem ~: 5 carve
one with a striped ~: 6 barber
ship's ~: 4 boom, mast, spar 5 sprit
sport with a ~: 5 caber, kendo, vault
starter: 3 May, tad 4 bean, flag 5 catch, ridge
to pole: 10 everywhere
vaulter: 5 Bubka 7 Seagren 8 Richards
pole ___: 4 bean, jump, lamp, mast 5 horse, piece, plate, vault 6 hammer 7 compass
___ pole: 3 ski 4 cold, fish, foul, pike 5 range, totem 6 animal, barber, simple 7 clothes, fishing, liberty, utility, whisker
Pole: 4 Slav
___ Pole: 5 North, South
polecat: 5 fitch, skunk
relative: 4 mink 5 otter, ratel, sable, stoat, tayra 6 badger, ermine, ferret, marten 7 foumart 8 carcajou, foulmart, kolinsky, muishond 9 wolverine
polemic: 6 debate 7 dispute 8 argument
polemical: 8 juristic
polemics: 6 debate 8 argument 9 bickering, dialectic, wrangling
polenta: 5 grain
poles apart: 5 split 6 at odds, unlike 7 unalike, unequal 9 different, disparate, divergent 10 antithetic, dissimilar
poles connector: 4 axis
polestar: 3 hub 5 focus 7 Polaris 8 cynosure
police: 3 law 4 heat, tidy 5 guard, watch 6 patrol 7 control, protect
baton: 4 cosh 5 billy 9 billy club
blotter info: 2 MO 3 aka, DWI 5 alias 6 arrest
brass: 5 chief 7 marshal
bulletin: 3 APB 5 alert
car device: 5 siren
chase object: 5 felon 7 suspect
club, in India: 5 lathi 6 lathee
East German secret ~: 5 Stasi
ecol. ~: 3 EPA
headquarters: 7 station 8 precinct
insignia: 5 badge
line: 6 cordon
name on a ~ blotter: 3 Doe, Roe
officer: 3 cop, law 4 bear, fuzz, narc, nark 5 badge, bobby 6 copper, patrol 7 officer 8 bluecoat, gendarme 9 constable, detective
operation: 4 bust, raid, trap 5 sting 10 undercover
order: 4 halt 6 freeze 7 hands up
org.: 3 FOP, PBA
patrol: 4 beat
procedure: 6 lineup
Russian secret ~: 3 KGB 4 NKVD, OGPU
school: 4 acad. 7 academy

slangily: **4** fuzz, heat **6** Smokey
squad: **4** vice
station: **4** jail, poky **6** lockup
target: **4** gang, perp **5** felon **7** suspect
team: **4** SWAT **5** squad
police __: **3** car, dog **5** court, force, power, state, wagon **6** action **7** officer, station, village
__ police: **5** state **6** secret **7** kitchen
Police
homeland: England
lead singer: Sting
song: De Do Do Do, De Da Da Da (1980)
Don's Stand So Close to Me (1981)
Every Breath You Take (1983)
Every Little Thing She Does Is Magic (1981)
King of Pain (1983)
Roxanne (1979)
Spirits in the Material World (1982)
Synchronicity II (1983)
Wrapped Around Your Finger (1984)
Police __: **5** Story, Woman
Police Story (1985 film)
cast: Jackie Chan, Bridget Lin
director: Jackie Chan
Police Woman (NBC drama)
cast: Angie Dickinson (Sgt. Pepper Anderson)
Earl Holliman (Lt. Bill Crowley)
employer: L.A.P.D.
policy: **3** way **4** code, line, rule, tact **5** stand, tenet **6** course, custom, system **7** posture, process, program, red tape, tactics **8** approach, behavior, channels, contract, doctrine, document, platform, practice, protocol, strategy **9** guideline, procedure **10** ground rule, management
hold a ~: **6** ensure, insure
noted ~ issuer: **6** Lloyd's
postscript: **5** rider
seller: **5** agent
__ policy: **4** open, term **5** debit **6** income, master, public, valued **7** foreign, limited
polio vaccine
developer: **4** Salk **5** Sabin
polis: **6** Athens, Sparta **9** city-state
polish: **3** rub, wax **4** buff, edit **5** class, clean, fix up, glaze, gloss, grace, poise, scour, scrub, sheen, shine, style, taste **6** better, enamel, enrich, finish, luster, redact, refine, reform, revise, smooth **7** brush up, burnish, correct, culture, develop, enhance, finesse, furbish, manners, perfect, retouch, shape up, sharpen, suavity, touch up, upgrade, varnish **8** breeding, brighten, cleanser, elegance, ornament, practice, spruce up, urbanity **9** gentility, meliorate, politesse, suaveness **10** ameliorate, brilliance, refinement, smoothness
apple ~: **4** fawn **5** toady **7** flatter **8** bootlick, butter up, suck up to
fingernail ~: **5** glaze, paint **6** enamel **7** lacquer, varnish
fingernail ~ brand: **5** Cutex
lacking ~: **5** crude **6** coarse, gauche **9** unrefined
off: **3** eat **4** down, wolf **5** eat up, scarf, use up, worst **6** devour, finish **7** consume, feast on, put away, scarf up **8** dispatch **9** dispose of, eliminate, liquidate, scarf down **10** consummate
prose: **4** edit **6** redact, revise
up: **4** cram **5** study **6** bone up, review
wood: **3** wax **4** sand **7** shellac
Polish: **8** language
see also Poland
Polish __: **3** ham **5** wheat **7** sausage, Wedding
polished: **3** ace **4** nice, oily **5** level, light, shiny, sleek, slick, suave **6** bright, glassy, glossy, poised, polite, smooth, social, urbane, versed **7** courtly, elegant, genteel, refined, stylish, tactful **8** cultured, debonair, esthetic, highbred, ladylike, lettered, lustrous, mannerly, slippery, tasteful, well-bred **9** debonaire, processed **10** cultivated, debonnaire
polished __: **4** rice
Polish Wedding (1998 film)
cast: Mili Avital, Gabriel Byrne, Claire Danes, Lena Olin
director: Theresa Connelly
polite: **4** good, kind, mild, nice **5** bland, civil, suave **6** decent, formal, gentle, kindly, proper, smooth, social, subtle, urbane **7** affable, amiable, cordial, courtly, gallant, genteel, heedful, mindful, refined, tactful **8** amenable, amicable, cultured, discreet, friendly, gracious, highbred, ladylike, likeable, mannerly, obliging, pleasant, pleasing, polished, sociable, well-bred **9** attentive, civilized, concerned, courteous, judicious, sensitive, unselfish **10** chivalrous, diplomatic, neighborly, respectful, solicitous, thoughtful
address: **2** Ms. **3** Mrs., sir **4** ma'am, Miss **5** madam **6** Mister
fit for ~ society: **5** civil **7** genteel, refined
gesture: **3** bow **6** curtsy, salaam
language: **4** may I **6** if I may, pardon, please, thanks **8** excuse me, thank you
mot: **5** merci
not ~: **4** curt, rude **5** surly **7** brusque **9** impatient
remark: **10** pleasantry
politeness: **4** tact **7** amenity, manners **8** ceremony, civility, courtesy, niceties **9** deference, etiquette, gallantry, gentility, propriety **10** attentions
politesse: **6** polish **7** manners **8** niceties, protocol **9** etiquette, formality, propriety **10** refinement
politic: **4** cool, sane, wise **5** canny, sharp, smart, suave **6** adroit, artful, shrewd, smooth, subtle, urbane **7** prudent, tactful **8** cautious, delicate, discreet, sensible, suitable **9** advisable, courteous, expedient, judicious, provident, sagacious, sensitive, strategic **10** diplomatic, reasonable, thoughtful
body ~: **4** weal **5** state **6** nation, people **10** population
political
alliance: **4** bloc **5** junta
battlefield: **5** arena
benefactor: **6** fat cat
British ~ party: **4** Tory **6** Labour
campaign: **4** race
Canada ~ party: **7** Liberal **12** Conservative
cartoonist: **4** Nast
division: **4** ward **5** state
escapee: **6** émigré **7** refugee
event: **5** rally **6** caucus, debate **8** election **10** convention, referendum
faction: **5** cadre, lobby, party
football: **5** issue **7** problem
former ~ party: **4** Whig
gathering: **6** caucus **10** convention
housecleaning: **5** purge
illegal ~ money: **5** slush
influence: **4** pull
initials: **3** GOP
Israeli ~ party: **5** Likud, Mapam
Mexican ~ party: **3** PRI
organization: **7** machine
party offering: **5** slate
party VIP: **4** whip
patronage: **4** pork **10** pork barrel
payoff: **5** graft
platform part: **5** plank
ploy: **5** smear
position: **4** left **5** right, stand **8** platform
scandal suffix: **4** gate
symbol: **6** donkey **8** elephant
upset: **4** coup **5** purge **6** revolt, stroke **10** revolution
U.S. ~ party: **9** Socialist **10** Democratic, Republican **11** Independent, Libertarian
venue for ~ coverage: **5** CSPAN
political __: **5** party **6** asylum **7** economy, refugee, science
Political Fictions author: Joan Didion
politically __: **7** correct
Politically Incorrect (Comedy Central)
host: Bill Maher
politician: **4** boss **6** heeler, leader **8** inflamer, lawmaker **9** demagogue, incumbent, statesman **10** campaigner, handshaker, legislator
picker: **5** voter
politick: **3** run **5** lobby, stump **8** campaign
politics: **6** civics **9** diplomacy **10** government, statecraft
play ~: **5** lobby, toady **6** pander **8** bootlick, maneuver **10** manipulate, strategize
__ politics: **4** play **5** party, power **6** office
Politics of Ecstasy author: **5** Leary
polka: **5** dance, music
polka __: **3** dot
Polk, James K.: **9** president
former occupation: **6** lawyer
middle name: **4** Knox
opponent: **4** Clay
veep: **6** Dallas
wife: **5** Sarah
__ Polk, LA: **4** Fort
poll: **4** list, vote **5** count, tally **6** ballot, census, number, sample, survey, voting **7** canvass, figures, returns **8** question, register, sampling **9** interview, straw vote **10** count noses
exit ~ participant: **5** voter
finding: **5** trend
starter: **3** red **5** catch
poll __: **3** tax **6** parrot **7** watcher
__ poll: **4** exit **5** straw **6** Gallup
pollack: **4** fish
cousin: **3** cod
Pollack, Sydney: **8** director
film: Absence of Malice (1981)
Changing Lanes (2002)
The Electric Horseman (1979)
Eyes Wide Shut (1999)
The Firm (1993)
Havana (1990)
Husbands and Wives (1992)
Jeremiah Johnson (1972)
Out of Africa (1985, AA)
Sabrina (1995)
They Shoot Horses, Don't They? (1969)
Three Days of the Condor (1975)
Tootsie (1982)
The Way We Were (1973)
The Yakuza (1975)
Pollak: **5** Kevin
pollan: **4** fish
Pollan, Tracy spouse: Michael J. Fox
pollen
bearer: **3** bee **4** wind **5** theca **6** anther, flower, stamen **7** blossom
grain: **5** spore
outer coat of a ~ grain: **5** exine
reaction to ~: **6** ah choo, sneeze **7** allergy
pollen __: **3** sac **4** tube **5** brush, count, grain **6** basket
pollera: **5** skirt
Polleras: **4** peak **5** mount **8** mountain
locale: **5** Andes **9** Argentina
pollex: **5** thumb
Pollin: **3** Abe
pollinate: **9** fertilize
__-pollinate: **5** cross
pollinator: **3** bee **4** wind
polling __: **5** booth, place
polliwog: **7** tadpole
finally: **4** frog
pollock: **4** fish
kin: **3** cod
Pollock: **6** George **7** Jackson
Pollock (2000 film)
cast: Jennifer Connelly, Marcia Gay Harden, Ed Harris, Val Kilmer, Amy Madigan
director: Ed Harris
Pollock, Jackson: **6** artist **7** painter
spouse: Lee Krasner
pollutant: **5** toxin **8** impurity
pollute: **4** foul, ruin, soil **5** alloy, dirty, spoil, stain, sully, taint **6** befoul, crud up, damage, debase, defile, infect, poison, smudge **7** begrime, blacken, corrupt, tarnish, vitiate **8** besmirch **9** desecrate, inebriate **10** adulterate, intoxicate
polluted: **4** foul **5** dirty, grimy, nasty, sooty **6** filthy, grubby, grungy, impure, rancid, rotten **7** corrupt, unclean **8** maculate, slovenly, vitiated **10** insanitary, unsanitary
not ~: **4** pure **5** clean **8** pristine
pollution: **4** ruin, smog **5** filth, smoke, taint **6** blight, damage, misuse **8** foulness, impurity **9** contagion, dirtiness **10** corruption, defilement, spoliation
air ~: **4** haze, smog **5** smaze
control org.: **3** EPA
ear ~: **4** roar, stir **5** blare, hoo-ha, noise **6** bedlam, clamor, hubbub, jangle, racket, scream, shriek, tumult, uproar **7** clangor, clatter, discord **8** brouhaha, disquiet **9** commotion, hue and cry **10** hullabaloo
ocean ~: **5** slick **8** oil slick **9** petroleum
__ pollution: **5** light, noise, sound **7** thermal
Pollux: **4** star
parent of ~: **4** Leda, Zeus
sister of ~: **5** Helen
to Castor: **4** twin
Polly: **5** Adler **6** Bergen, Draper, parrot **8** Holliday
pad: **4** cage
to Tom: **4** aunt
Pollyanna: **5** novel **8** optimist
author: **6** Porter
Pollyanna (1920 film)
cast: Katherine Griffith, Mary Pickford, Herbert Ralston
director: Paul Powell
Pollyanna (1960 film)
cast: Richard Egan, Hayley Mills, Jane Wyman
director: David Swift
Polly playwright: **3** Gay
polo: **4** game **5** shirt, sport **10** water sport
like the ~ set: **5** horsy **6** horsey
need: **4** pony
period: **7** chukker
shirt brand: **4** Izod
team complement: **4** four
water ~ need: **3** net
__ polo: **5** water
Polo Grounds star: **3** Ott
Polo, Marco: **7** Italian **8** explorer
locale: **4** Asia **5** China **6** Orient

polonaise: 5 dance, dress, music
polonium: 5 metal 7 element
Polonius
hiding place: 5 arras
son: 7 Laertes
victim: 6 Hamlet
Poltava: 4 city, town
locale: 7 Ukraine
poltergeist: 5 ghost 6 spirit 7 specter
Poltergeist (1982 film)
cast: Craig T. Nelson, Beatrice Straight, JoBeth Williams
director: Tobe Hooper
dog: 5 E. Buzz
poltroon: 4 wimp 5 sissy 6 coward, craven 7 chicken, dastard 8 recreant 9 fraidy-cat, jellyfish 10 scaredy-cat
poly: 6 fabric
ender: 4 math 5 ester
kin: 5 multi
see also polyester
poly ___: 3 sci
___-poly: 4 roly
___ Poly: 3 Cal
polyacrylonitrile: 5 Orlon
polybasite: 3 ore 7 mineral
Polycarp: 5 saint
polychromatic: 6 motley 8 colorful 10 multi-color
polyester: 6 fabric 8 material 9 synthetic
fabric: 5 Kodel, nylon, rayon 6 Dacron
film: 5 Mylar
polyglot: 8 linguist
polygon corner: 5 angle
Polyhymnia: 4 Muse
domain: 4 song
parent of ~: 4 Zeus 9 Mnemosyne
sister: 4 Clio 5 Erato 6 Thalia, Urania 7 Euterpe 8 Calliope 9 Melpomene 11 Terpsichore
polymath: 7 learned 10 generalist
___ polymerase: 3 DNA, RNA
polymerization
candidate: 5 ester
product: 5 latex
Polynesia: 4 isls. 5 isles 7 islands 9 South Seas
beer: 4 kava
carving: 4 tiki
celebration: 4 luau
chestnut: 4 rata
dance: 4 hula
fabric: 4 tapa
farewell: 5 aloha
flower: 5 lehua 6 orchid
food: 3 poi 4 taro 6 lau lau
garment: 5 pareo, pareu 6 sarong 8 lavalava 10 grass skirt
greeting: 5 aloha
plant: 2 ti
porch: 5 lanai
shrub: 4 kava
stone marker: 3 ahu
supernatural force: 4 mana
tongue: 5 Maori
tree: 4 palm 5 lehua
tuber: 4 taro
woman: 6 wahine
see also Hawaii
___ Polynesia: 6 French
polyp: 5 coral, hydra 10 sea anemone
Polyphemus: 5 giant 7 Cyclops
father: 8 Poseidon
polyphonic composition: 5 motet
polypody: 4 fern
polytech grad: 4 engr. 8 engineer
___ Polytechnique: 5 École
polyvinyl ___: 5 resin 6 acetal, formal 7 acetate, alcohol, butyral
pom: 6 canine, lap dog
pomace: 4 pulp
pomade: 8 ointment
apply ~: 5 slick
pome: 4 pear 5 apple, fruit 6 quince
pomegranate: 4 tree 5 fruit 6 purple

pomelo: 4 tree 5 fruit 6 citrus
relative: 4 lime, Ugli 5 lemon, navel 6 orange, tangor 7 kumquat, satsuma, Seville, tangelo 8 bergamot, mandarin, shaddock, Valencia 9 tangerine 10 calamondin, grapefruit
Pomeranc: 3 Max
Pomeranian: 3 dog, pet, toy 5 canid, spitz 6 canine, lap dog
pomfret: 4 fish
Pommard: 3 red 4 wine 7 red wine
origin: 6 France
pomme de ___: 5 terre
pommel: 3 zap 4 beat, belt, club, drub, hurt 5 flail, knock, pound, punch, smite, thump 6 batter, beat up, buffet, defeat, hammer, strike, thrash, thwack, wallop 7 trounce
pommel ___: 5 horse
pommes ___: 6 frites
Pomo: 6 Indian 7 Amerind
pomology: 6 botany 7 science
study: 6 fruits
Pomona: 4 city, town
locale: 10 California
pomp: 4 ritz, show 5 éclat, state 7 display, fanfare, panoply 8 ceremony, grandeur, heraldry, splendor 9 formality, pageantry, solemnity, vainglory
pompadour: 4 coif 6 hairdo 7 upsweep 8 coiffure
Pompadour: 3 Mme. 6 Madame
Pomp and Circumstance composer: 5 Elgar
pompano: 4 fish 8 palometa
Pompano Beach: 4 city, town
locale: 7 Florida
Pompeii: 4 city, town
art: 5 mural 6 fresco
city near ~: 6 Naples
court: 6 atrium
covering: 3 ash
heroine: 4 Ione
undoing: 7 volcano 8 eruption, Vesuvius
Pompey: 5 Roman
to Caesar: 3 foe 5 enemy
___ Pompilius: 4 Numa
pompom place: 3 cap, tam 4 shoe 7 curtain
pomposity: 4 airs, ritz 6 hubris, hybris 7 bombast, bravado, hauteur 9 arrogance, euphemism 10 floridness
pompous: 3 big 4 smug, vain 5 cocky, grand, proud, showy, stiff, tumid, windy 6 ritual, stuffy, turgid 7 courtly, flowery, fustian, haughty, hyped up, orotund, stately, stilted, stuck-up 8 affected, arrogant, boastful, decorous, inflated, pedantic, puffed up, snobbish, sonorous 9 big-headed, bombastic, conceited, dignified, egotistic, grandiose, high-flown, hubristic, imperious, overblown 10 big-talking, euphuistic, hoity-toity, pedantical, rhetorical
Ponca: 6 Indian 7 Amerind
Ponca City: 4 town
locale: 8 Oklahoma
Ponce: 4 city, town
locale: 10 Puerto Rico
Ponce de León: 7 Spanish 8 explorer
Ponchielli, Amilcare: 7 Italian 8 composer
work: Dance of the Hours
poncho: 8 rain gear
relative: 6 sarape, serape
pond: 4 lake, mere, pool, tarn 5 basin, lough 6 lagoon 8 millpond 9 backwater, reservoir, water hole
big ~: 3 sea 5 ocean
blossom: 5 lotus 9 water lily
covering: 4 scum 5 algae

denizen: 3 eft, koi 4 alga, carp, fish, frog 7 tadpole
ender: 4 weed
floater: 3 pad
maker: 3 dam 6 beaver
salt ~: 9 backwater, tidewater
sound: 5 croak
starter: 4 fish, mill
___ Pond: 6 Walden
ponder: 3 see 4 mull, muse 5 brood, study, think, weigh 6 debate, digest, figure, ideate, puzzle, wonder 7 dwell on, examine, reflect, revolve 8 cogitate, consider, evaluate, look back, meditate, mull over, pore over, question, ruminate, turn over 9 brood over, dwell upon, reason out, speculate, sweat over 10 brainstorm, deliberate, introspect, meditate on, puzzle over, think about
Ponder Heart, The author: Eudora Welty
ponderosa: 4 pine
Ponderosa: 5 ranch
brother: 3 Joe 4 Adam, Hoss 9 Little Joe
cook: 7 Hop Sing
patriarch: 3 Ben
ponderous: 3 big, dry 4 arid, dull, huge, slow 5 bulky, grave, heavy, hefty, large 6 boring, clumsy, dreary, leaden, prolix, stodgy, stuffy, taxing, wooden 7 awkward, hulking, humdrum, labored, lumpish, massive, onerous, stilted, tedious, verbose, weighty 8 cumbrous, lifeless, pedantic, plodding, sluggish, unwieldy 9 corpulent, graceless, important, laborious, lumbering, unwieldly 10 burdensome, cumbersome, enervating, galumphing, long-winded, monotonous, oppressive, pedantical, uninspired, well-padded
Pondicherry: 4 city, port, town
locale: 5 India
Pond in Winter, The work: 6 Walden
Pond's competitor: 5 Nivea 7 Jergens
pone: 9 corn bread 10 johnnycake
starter: 4 corn
___-Pong: 4 Ping
pongee: 4 silk 5 Honan 6 fabric
pongid: 3 ape
Pong producer: 5 Atari
poniard: 5 knife 6 dagger 7 sidearm 8 stiletto
ponies, play the: 3 bet 5 wager 6 gamble
Poni-Tails song: Born Too Late (1958)
Ponselle, Rosa: 6 singer 7 soprano
role: 4 Aïda
specialty: 5 opera
Pons, Lily: 6 singer 7 soprano
specialty: 5 opera
spouse: André Kostelanetz
Ponta Delgada: 4 city, town
locale: 6 Azores
Ponta Grossa: 4 city, town
locale: 6 Brazil
Pontano, Giovanni: 4 poet 7 Italian
Pontchartrain: 4 lake
locale: 9 Louisiana
Ponte di ___: 6 Rialto
Ponte Vecchio river: 4 Arno
Pontiac: 3 car 4 auto, city, town 10 automobile
locale: 8 Michigan
model: 3 GTO 4 Vibe 5 Astre, Fiero 6 LeMans, Safari 7 Montana, Phoenix, Sunbird, Sunfire, Tempest, Torpedo, Trans Am, Ventura 8 Catalina, Firebird 9 Chieftain, Executive, Grand Prix, Star Chief 10 Bonneville, Grand Ville, Super Chief 11 Streamliner

Pontic: 3 mts. 4 mtns. 5 range 9 mountains
locale: 4 Asia 6 Turkey
Ponti, Carlo: 7 Italian 8 producer
spouse: Sophia Loren
pontiff: 4 pope 6 bishop, priest 7 prelate
of the ~: 5 papal
vestment: 5 fanon, orale
pontifical: 5 papal 7 fustian 8 clerical, dogmatic
Pontifical ___: 4 Mass 7 College
pontificate: 5 orate, spout 6 preach 7 address, declaim, lecture 8 harangue, perorate 9 hold forth, sermonize
Pontius ___: 6 Pilate
Pont l'Évêque: 6 cheese, French
pontoon: 4 boat, game 6 bridge 8 card game
alias: 9 blackjack, twenty-one, vingt-et-un
plane: 5 hydro
Pontoppidan, Henrik: 6 writer 8 Nobelist
Ponwar: 3 cow 4 bull 6 bovine, cattle
pony: 3 pet 4 crib, ride, trot 5 dance, horse, money, mount 6 animal, equine 7 mustang 8 Shetland 9 racehorse
cow ~: 5 paint, pinto 6 cayuse 7 mustang
ender: 4 tail
foot: 4 hoof
frat ~: 4 crib
Indian ~: 6 cayuse
reply: 5 neigh, snort 7 whinney
spotted ~: 5 paint, pinto
up: 3 pay 4 ante, give 5 put up 6 chip in, donate, kick in, settle, supply 7 pitch in 9 do one's bit 10 contribute
see also horse
___ pony: 3 cow 4 polo 5 paint, Welsh 7 painted 8 Shetland
Pony Express
load: 4 mail 7 letters
station: 4 Elko
Pony Express (1953 film)
cast: Rhonda Fleming, Charlton Heston, Jan Sterling
ponytail: 2 do 4 coif 5 braid 6 hairdo 8 coiffure 9 hairstyle
site: 4 nape
___ Pony, The: 3 Red
Pony Time (1961 song) artist: Chubby Checker
Ponzi scheme: 4 scam
___-poo: 5 cock-a 6 cutesy
pooch: 3 dog, mut 4 mutt 5 canid, doggy 6 beagle, bowwow, canine, doggie
comment: 3 arf, yip 4 bark, woof, yelp
lift a ~: 6 dognap
name: 4 Fido, Fifi, Spot 5 Rover
see also dog
poodle cut: 4 coif 6 hairdo 8 coiffure
poof, go: 6 vanish 9 disappear
pooh: 3 bah, rot 4 bosh, bull, tosh 5 fudge, pshaw 6 bushwa, humbug, phooey, piffle 7 baloney, bushwah, fustian, hogwash, oh fudge, rubbish, twaddle 8 nonsense, tommyrot 9 banana oil, moonshine, poppycock
Pooh: 4 bear
creator: 5 Milne
pal of ~: 3 Owl, Roo 6 Eeyore
Pooh ___: 3 Bah 6 Corner
pooh-bah: 6 fat cat
Pooh Goes Visiting author: A.A. Milne
pooh-pooh: 5 decry, scoff, scorn 6 deride, ignore, reject, slight 7 disdain, dismiss 8 minimize, ridicule 9 disregard, underplay
pool: 3 pot 4 bank, bath, fund, game, lake, mere, pond, ring, tank, tarn, well

5 basin, funds, group, immix, kitty, merge, share, sport, unite 6 lagoon, league, mingle, puddle, raffle, stakes 7 combine, jackpot, snooker 8 millpond, monopoly 9 billiards, reservoir 10 amalgamate, consortium, coordinate, join forces, natatorium
accessory: 3 cue 4 rack 5 chalk 6 bridge
amenity: 6 cabana, chaise 9 bath house
clean the ~: 4 skim
coral-reef ~: 6 lagoon
dimension: 5 depth, width 6 length
dirty ~: 5 guile 6 deceit, racket 7 knavery, swindle 9 duplicity
distance: 3 lap
division: 4 lane
ender: 4 room, side
enjoy the ~: 4 dive, swim, wade 5 float 6 paddle 9 dogpaddle
fix a ~ cue: 5 retip
hustler: 5 shark
item in a ~: 4 gene
money ~: 5 kitty
mountain ~: 4 tarn
open-air ~: 4 lido
place: 3 bar, spa 4 hall, park, YMCA, YWCA 6 resort, saloon, tavern
prepare for ~: 5 cue up
problem: 5 algae
resources: 5 unite 9 cooperate 10 join forces
shot: 5 carom, massé 6 carrom
starter: 4 cess 5 whirl
table covering: 4 felt 5 baize
wear: 6 bikini, trunks 7 maillot 8 swimsuit
worker: 5 steno
pool __: 4 hall 5 shark, table, train
__ pool: 3 car 4 gene 5 dirty, motor, tidal 6 bumper, indoor, wading 7 outdoor
Poole: 4 city, town
locale: 6 Dorset 7 England
__ Pool Murder, The: 7 Penguin
poolside
area: 4 deck 5 patio
recliner: 6 chaise
turban: 5 towel
pools, like some: 6 heated
__ Pool, The: 4 Dead 6 Devil's
poon: 4 tree 8 hardwood
poop: 4 deck, info, news, tire 5 facts 6 gossip, notice 7 exhaust, fatigue, frazzle, lowdown 10 fuddy-duddy
out: 4 fail, jade, tire 7 exhaust, fatigue, frazzle
poop __: 3 out 4 deck 5 cabin, sheet
pooped: 4 beat, worn 5 all in, spent, tired, weary 6 bushed 7 drained, worn out 9 exhausted, prostrate 10 knocked out
__ pooped to pop: 3 too
poor: 3 bad, low, off 4 bare, flat, foul, grim, junk, lame, mean, puny, slim, thin, weak 5 awful, broke, crude, lousy, lowly, needy, scant, seedy, small, sorry, spare, woful 6 bad off, barren, crumby, crummy, dismal, faulty, feeble, flimsy, hard up, horrid, humble, in need, in want, meager, measly, modest, odious, paltry, ragged, rotten, scanty, shabby, shoddy, skimpy, sleazy, slight, sloppy, sordid, sparse, woeful 7 accurst, baleful, baneful, beastly, doleful, ghastly, ill-done, lacking, limited, lowborn, pinched, pitiful, reduced, squalid 8 accursed, bankrupt, beggarly, below par, depleted, deprived, dreadful, exiguous, God-awful, grievous, horrible, ill-fated, indigent, inferior, low-grade, luckless, mediocre, pathetic, shameful, stinking, strapped, terrible, trifling, wretched 9 abhorrent, appalling, atrocious, defective, deficient, destitute, execrable, fifth-rate, flat broke, frightful, imperfect, insidious, insolvent, loathsome, miserable, moneyless, offensive, penniless, penurious, revolting, third-rate, unfertile, worthless 10 abominable, deplorable, despicable, detestable, disastrous, down and out, fourth-rate, horrendous, inadequate, lamentable, low-quality, low-ranking, negligible, pathetical, second-rate, stone-broke, straitened, threadbare
devil: 6 wretch
in ~ health: 3 ill 4 sick 6 ailing, sickly, unwell 7 unsound
in ~ shape: 4 torn, worn 5 ratty, unfit 6 beat-up, flabby, ragged, shabby 10 overweight, ramshackle
in ~ taste: 4 loud 5 crude, tacky 6 coarse, flashy, vulgar 8 unseemly
like a ~ excuse: 4 thin, weak 6 feeble 10 inadequate
use ~ judgment: 4 flub, goof, muff 5 botch 6 bungle, foul up, mess up, slip up 7 blunder, go wrong, louse up, snarl up, stumble 9 mishandle, mismanage
poor __ church mouse: 3 as a
__-poor: 4 dirt, land
poor-box contents: 4 alms
Poor Clare: 3 nun
poor dog
what the ~ had: 4 none
__ poor example: 4 set a
Poor Folk author: Fyodor Dostoyevsky
Poor Little Fool (1958 song) artist: Ricky Nelson
Poor Little Rich Girl (1936 film)
cast: Alice Faye, Jack Haley, Shirley Temple
poorly: 3 ill, low 4 sick 5 badly 6 adverb, ailing, sickly, unwell 7 failing 10 indisposed
lit: 3 dim 4 dark 5 dusky, murky 6 gloomy, somber 7 shadowy 9 tenebrous
Poor Man's Roses, A (1957 song)
artist: Patti Page
poor-mouth: 5 smear 8 minimize 9 deprecate
Poor People of Paris, The (1956 song)
artist: Les Baxter
Poor Richard's Almanack feature: 3 saw 5 adage, maxim 6 saying
Poor Side of Town (1966 song) artist: Johnny Rivers
__! poor Yorick: 4 Alas
pop: 3 dad, hit, put, try 4 bang, Coke, leap, male, open, papa, shot, snap, sock, soda 5 burst, crack, daddy, drink, music, pappy, Pepsi, shoot, whack 6 appear, father, uncork 7 explode 8 beverage, Coca-Cola, Dr. Pepper, relative, shoot off 9 explosion, Pepsi-Cola, soft drink
a ~: 3 per 4 each 6 apiece, for one
artist: 6 Warhol 7 Indiana
a top: 5 uncap
container: 3 can 6 bottle
ender: 3 gun 4 corn, over
fly: 5 bloop 6 looper
in: 3 see 4 call, come 5 enter, visit 6 appear, arrive, drop by, show up, stop by 7 go to see, turn out
off: 2 go 3 gab 5 leave 6 depart 7 chatter
partner: 3 mom
preppie's ~: 5 pater
star: 4 idol
starter: 3 may 5 lolli, lolly
the cork: 4 open
the question: 3 ask 7 propose
to a toddler: 4 dada
up: 4 come, show 5 arise, occur 6 appear, attend, blow in, emerge, happen, make it, roll in, sign in, spring 7 check in, clock in, hit town, punch in 8 breeze in 9 originate
pop __: 3 art, fly, for, off, top 4 quiz, wine 5 psych 7 concert
Pop: 4 Iggy 6 Warner
Pop-__: 4 Tart
__ Pop: 3 Vox 5 Hop on, Jiffy
Popayán: 4 city, town
locale: 8 Colombia
popcorn: 4 nosh 5 dance, snack
holder: 3 tub
how some ~ is popped: 5 in oil
nuisance: 4 hull
topper: 4 salt 6 butter
unit: 6 kernel
popcorn __: 6 flower, shrimp
Popcorn: 5 Faith
Popcorn (1972 song) artist: Hot Butter
pope: 4 male, rank 6 bishop, cleric 7 pontiff, prelate 10 Holy Father
calendar: 4 ordo
cape: 5 orale
council: 5 curia
emissary: 6 legate
headdress: 5 miter, tiara
rite: 4 Mass
teachings: 5 dogma
who crowned Charlemagne: 3 Leo
WWII ~: 4 Pius
Pope, Alexander: 4 poet 7 British 8 essayist, satirist
work: The Dunciad
Eloisa to Abelard
Epistle to Dr. Arbuthnot
An Essay on Criticism
An Essay on Man
Imitations of Horace
Pastorals
The Rape of the Lock
Solitude
Pope John __ II: 4 Paul
Pope of Greenwich Village, The (1984 film)
cast: Daryl Hannah, Eric Roberts, Mickey Rourke
director: Stuart Rosenberg
popes (with highest number):
Adeodatus (II)
Adrian (VI)
Agapitus (II)
Agatho
Albert
Alexander (VIII)
Anacletus (II)
Anastasius (IV)
Anicetus
Anterus
Benedict (XV)
Boniface (IX)
Caius
Callistus (III)
Celestine (V)
Christopher
Clement (XIV)
Cletus
Conon
Constantine
Cornelius
Damasus (II)
Dionysius
Dioscorus
Donus
Eleutherius
Eugene (IV)
Eulabus
Eusebius
Eutychian
Evaristus
Fabian
Felix (V)
Formosus
Gelasius (II)
Gregory (XVI)
Hilary
Hippolytus
Honorius (IV)
Hormisdas
Hyginus
Innocent (XIII)
John Paul (II)
John (XXIII)
Julius (III)
Landus
Lawrence
Leo (XIII)
Liberius
Linus
Lucius (III)
Marcellinus
Marcellus (II)
Marcus
Marinus (II)
Martin (V)
Melchiades
Nicholas (V)
Novatian
Paschal (III)
Paul (VI)
Pelagius (II)
Peter
Philip
Pius (XII)
Pontian
Romanus
Sabinian
Sergius (IV)
Severinus
Silverius
Simplicius
Siricius
Sisinnius
Sixtus (V)
Soter
Stephen (X)
Sylvester (IV)
Symmachus
Telesphorus
Theodore (II)
Theodoric
Urban (VIII)
Ursinus
Valentine
Victor (IV)
Vigilius
Vitalian
Zachary
Zephyrinus
Zosimus
Popeye: 3 gob, tar 4 salt 6 sailor
affirmative: 3 aye
Bluto, to ~: 5 rival
cartoonist: 5 Segar
girlfriend: Olive Oyl
greeting: 4 ahoy
prop: 4 pipe
to Pipeye: 5 uncle
verb: 3 yam
Popeye (1980 film)
cast: Paul Dooley, Shelley Duvall, Ray Walston, Robin Williams
director: Robert Altman
Popeye (1962 song) artist: Chubby Checker
popgun: 3 toy
Popi (1969 film)
cast: Miguel Alejandro, Alan Arkin, Rita Moreno
director: Arthur Hiller
Pop, Iggy
real name: James Jewel Osterberg
song: Candy (1991)
popinjay: 3 fop 4 dude 5 dandy 7 coxcomb 9 pretty boy 10 jack-a-dandy

popish: 5 papal
Popish Plot fabricator: 5 Oates
Popkin: 3 Leo
poplar: 4 tree 5 abele, alamo
family: 6 willow
relative: 5 aspen 10 cottonwood
Poplars painter: 5 Monet
Pople, John: 7 chemist 8 Nobelist
Pop Life (1985 song) artist: Prince
poplin: 6 fabric 8 material
Popo: 7 volcano
locale: 6 Mexico
Popov: 5 vodka
competitor: 5 Stoli 8 Smirnoff
popover: 6 pastry
Popp: 5 Lucia
poppa: 2 pa 3 dad 4 papa, pops 5 daddy 6 father, old man
partner: 5 momma
__ Poppa?: 6 Where's
Poppaea husband: 4 Nero, Otho
Popper, Karl: 7 British 11 philosopher
popping: 4 busy
one's buttons: 5 proud
__-popping: 3 eye
Poppins: 4 Mary
Popp, Lucia: 6 singer 7 soprano
specialty: 5 opera
poppy: 3 red 4 seed 5 color, plant 6 flower 7 anodyne 8 orangish
color kin: 4 rose, ruby, rust, wine 5 brick, coral, grape, rusty, sandy 6 cerise, cherry, claret, garnet, maroon 7 carmine, crimson, fuchsia, magenta, pimento, scarlet, sultana, vermeil 8 amaranth, cardinal, dubonnet, geranium, rubicund 9 carnation, cranberry, vermilion 10 strawberry
ender: 4 cock
Poppy (1936 film)
cast: W.C. Fields
director: A. Edward Sutherland
poppycock: 3 gas, rot 4 blah, bosh, bull, bunk, guff, jazz, jive, pooh, tosh 5 bilge, fudge, hokum, hooey, prate, stuff, trash, tripe 6 bunkum, bushwa, drivel, footle, gabble, gammon, gibber, havers, hot air, humbug, jabber, jargon, kibosh, piffle 7 baloney, blarney, blather, blether, boloney, bushwah, eyewash, flannel, flubdub, fustian, garbage, hogwash, inanity, malarky, rubbish, twaddle 8 buncombe, claptrap, falderal, falderol, flimflam, flummery, folderal, folderol, malarkey, nonsense, slipslop, tommyrot, trumpery 9 banana oil, gibberish, goofiness, kidstakes, moonshine, rigmarole 10 applesauce, balderdash, bilge water, codswallop, double-talk, flapdoodle, galimatias, Jabberwock, mumbo jumbo, rigamarole, taradiddle
pops: 2 pa 3 dad 4 papa 5 daddy 6 father
Popsicle: 3 ice 4 nosh 5 snack
eat a: 4 lick
flavor: 5 grape 6 banana, cherry, orange
Popsicles and Icicles (1973 song) artist: Murmaids
Pop Singer (1989 song) artist: John Cougar Mellencamp
pop-top beverage: 4 beer, cola, soda 9 soft drink
populace: 3 mob 5 plebs 6 masses, people, public, voters 7 country 9 commoners, hoi polloi, multitude, residents
popular: 3 big, hot, mod, now 4 chic, okay, tony 5 known, liked, stock, toney, vogue 6 chi-chi, common, famous, modish, public, ruling, staple, trendy 7 à la mode, current, faddish, favored, general, in favor, in style, in vogue, leading, likable, selling, stylish, topical, voguish 8 accepted, approved, embraced, familiar, favorite, in demand, ordinary, pleasing, plebeian, run-after, societal, standard, up-to-date 9 customary, in fashion, preferred, prevalent, prominent, well-known, well-liked 10 all the rage, attractive, celebrated, fair-haired, mainstream, marketable, newfangled, prevailing, ubiquitous, widespread
place: 6 in spot
popular __: 4 song, vote 5 front 6 prices, singer
Popular __: 7 Science
popularity: 4 fame 5 favor, kudos, vogue 6 demand, esteem, renown 7 acclaim 8 approval, currency 9 celebrity 10 admiration
popularize: 6 revive, spread 7 promote 8 simplify
popularly: 9 generally
populate: 5 dwell 6 live in, occupy, settle 7 dwell in, inhabit 8 reside in
populated
heavily ~: 5 dense, thick 7 crowded, teeming 8 crawling, swarming
thinly ~: 6 sparse
population: 4 folk, size 6 people, public 7 natives 8 citizens, denizens 9 residents
center: 3 urb 4 burb, city, town 5 exurb 6 suburb 10 metropolis
survey: 6 census
__ population growth: 4 zero
__ populi: 3 vox
populist: 9 socialist 10 democratic, self-ruling
populous: 5 dense, thick 6 jammed 7 crowded, peopled, teeming 8 crawling, swarming, thronged
populus tremula: 5 aspen
pop-up: 3 fly 5 bloop 6 looper
breakfast item: 4 Eggo
por __: 3 qué 5 favor
porcelain: 5 china 7 Limoges, pottery 8 ceramics, clayware, crockery 10 dinnerware
base: 4 clay, frit 6 kaolin 7 kaoline
British ~: 5 Spode
Chinese ~: 4 Ming
flower: 4 hoya
French ~: 6 Sèvres
Japanese ~: 5 Imari
__ porcelain: 4 bone 6 Canton 7 Dresden, Meissen, Nankeen
porch: 4 stoa 5 lanai, lobby, stoop 6 piazza 7 balcony, ingress, veranda 8 verandah
classical ~: 4 stoa
furniture: 5 chair, swing 6 glider, rocker
Polynesian ~: 5 lanai
urban ~: 5 stoop
__ porch: 3 sun
porcine: 5 stout 7 hoggish, weighty
animal: 3 hog, pig 5 swine
home: 3 pen, sty
meal: 4 slop 5 swill
Muppet: 9 Miss Piggy
parent: 3 sow 4 boar
sound: 4 oink 5 grunt
youngster: 5 piggy, shoat, shote, shott 6 piggie, piglet
porcupine: 6 animal, mammal, rodent
female: 3 sow
like a ~: 5 spiny
male: 4 boar
part: 5 quill
relative: 3 rat 4 cavy, degu, jird, paca, vole 5 coypu, gundi, mouse, xerus 6 agouti, beaver, gerbil, gopher, jerboa, marmot, murine 7 hamster, lemming, muskrat, visacha 8 chipmunk, cricetid, dormouse, squirrel, tuco-tuco 9 chickaree, groundhog, guinea pig, woodchuck 10 chinchilla, prairie dog
young: 3 pup
pore: 4 read, scan 5 stoma, study 6 outlet, peruse 7 dig into, foramen, opening, orifice 8 aperture, look over, meditate 9 delve into 10 scrutinize
leaf ~: 5 stoma
over: 4 look, mull, read, sift 5 learn, study, think 6 peruse, ponder, regard 7 examine 8 consider 9 lucubrate 10 scrutinize
Porfirio: 4 Diaz
porgy: 4 fish, scup 5 bream, pargo 8 sea bream
Porgy and Bess: 5 opera
author: DuBose Heyward
composer: 8 Gershwin
Porgy and Bess (1959 film)
cast: Pearl Bailey, Dorothy Dandridge, Sammy Davis Jr., Sidney Poitier
director: Otto Preminger
Porgy author: DuBose Heyward
Porizkova, Paulina: 5 model
spouse: Ric Ocasek
pork
barrel: 9 patronage
ender: 3 pie
fat: 4 lard
prepare ~ for wonton: 5 mince
rind: 4 nosh 5 snack
source: 3 hog, pig
pork __: 4 chop, loin 5 belly 6 barrel 7 sausage
__ pork: 4 salt 5 roast
Pork Chop Hill (1959 film)
cast: Harry Guardino, Gregory Peck, Rip Torn
director: Lewis Milestone
porker: 3 hog, pig 5 swine
hangout: 3 pen, sty
nose: 5 snout
young ~: 5 shoat, shote, shott
porkpie: 3 hat
material: 4 felt
Porky, friend of: 5 Darla 6 Spanky 7 Alfalfa, Petunia 9 Buckwheat
porous: 5 holey, leaky, light 6 leachy, spongy 8 pervious 9 absorbent, permeable, sievelike
rock: 4 tufa, tuff
porphyry: 4 rock 7 mineral
like ~: 7 igneous
porpoise: 6 animal, mammal 8 cetacean
relative: 3 orc, sei 5 whale 6 beluga, narwal 7 cowfish, dolphin, finback, grampus, narwhal, rorqual 8 narwhale
porridge: 4 mush, samp 5 gruel 6 burgoo, cereal 7 oatmeal
portion: 4 mess
__ Porridge Hot: 5 Pease
Porrima: 4 star
Porsche: 3 car 4 auto 6 German 9 Ferdinand 10 automobile
model: 5 Targa 7 Boxster, Carrera, Cayenne
Porsena: 4 Lars
port: 3 red 4 left, wine 5 docks, haven, wharf 6 harbor, refuge 9 anchorage
holder: 5 glass 6 bottle, carafe
home ~: 4 base
in ~: 6 ashore, docked
kind of computer ~: 3 USB 4 game, SCSI 6 serial 8 parallel
leave ~: 4 sail 6 embark 7 set sail 8 go aboard
not in ~: 4 asea 5 at sea 7 en route 8 cruising
source: 5 grape 8 Portugal
starter: 3 air, car, jet, rap, sea 4 pass, tele 5 space, trans
when sailing north: 4 west
when sailing south: 4 east
__ port: 4 free, home
Port-__: 5 Salut
Port.
see Portugal
portable: 5 handy, light 6 mobile, pocket 7 compact, folding, movable 8 haulable, moveable 10 convenient, conveyable, manageable
portage: 3 fee 5 track, trail 9 transport
item: 5 canoe
Portage: 4 city, town
locale: 7 Indiana 8 Michigan
portal: 4 adit, arch, door, gate 5 entry, way in 7 doorway, gateway, ingress, opening 8 entrance, entryway, hatchway 9 threshold
Shinto ~: 5 torii
Port Arthur: 4 city, port, town
locale: 5 Texas
Port-au-Prince: 4 city, town 7 capital
locale: 5 Haiti
Port Charlotte: 4 city, town
locale: 7 Florida
Port Chester: 4 city, town
locale: 7 New York
Port Coquitlam: 4 city, town
locale: 6 Canada
port de __: 4 bras
Port du __: 5 Salut
porte-__: 7 cochere
Port Elgin: 4 city, town
locale: 6 Canada
portend: 4 bode, hint, loom, mean 5 augur, spell 6 herald, menace, warn of 7 bespeak, betoken, point to, predict, presage, promise, signify 8 forebode, foreshow, foretell, forewarn, indicate, prophesy, threaten 9 adumbrate, foretoken 10 foreshadow
portent: 4 omen, sign 5 hunch, vibes 6 augury, marvel, threat, wonder 7 caution, presage, warning 9 foretoken, harbinger, predictor 10 foreboding, forerunner, indication, prediction
portentous: 5 grave, vatic, vital 6 solemn 7 bodeful, charged, crucial, fateful, ominous, pivotal, serious, weighty 8 critical, decisive, ill-fated, oracular, sinister 9 dangerous, important, momentous, prophetic 10 meaningful
porter: 3 ale 4 brew 5 drink 6 bearer, redcap, skycap 7 bellhop, carrier, janitor 8 beverage 10 doorkeeper, gatekeeper
ender: 5 house
Mideast ~: 5 hamal 6 hammal
relative: 4 beer 5 lager, stout
__-porter: 5 prêt-à
Porter: 3 Don, Hal 4 Cole 6 George, Quincy, Rodney, Sylvia 7 Eleanor, Wagoner
Porter, Cole: 8 composer
alma mater: 4 Yale
film score: Born to Dance
Broadway Melody of 1940
The Gay Divorcee
High Society
Les Girls
Night and Day
The Pirate
Rosalie
Something to Shout About
You'll Never Get Rich
hometown: 4 Peru
musical: Anything Goes
Can-Can
Du Barry Was a Lady
Fifty Million Frenchmen
Gay Divorce
Jubilee
Kiss Me, Kate

Leave It to Me!
Let's Face It
Mexican Hayride
The New Yorkers
Panama Hattie
Paris
Red, Hot and Blue!
Seven Lively Arts
Silk Stockings
Something for the Boys
Wake Up and Dream
song: Always True to You in My Fashion
Another Op'nin', Another Show
Anything Goes
At Long Last Love
Be a Clown
Begin the Beguine
Bingo Eli Yale
Blow, Gabriel, Blow
Brush Up Your Shakespeare
But in the Morning, No
Can-Can
C'est Magnifique
Don't Fence Me in
Easy to Love
Friendship
From This Moment on
Go Into Your Dance
I Concentrate on You
I Get a Kick out of You
I Hate Men
I Love Paris
It's De-Lovely
I've Got You Under My Skin
Just One of Those Things
Katie Went to Haiti
Let's Do It
Let's Misbehave
Love for Sale
Miss Otis Regrets
My Heart Belongs to Daddy
Night and Day
So in Love
Too Darn Hot
True Love
Well, Did You Evah!
What Is This Thing Called Love
Wunderbar
You'd Be So Nice to Come Home to
You Do Something to Me
You're the Top
Porter, Don: 5 actor
film: The Candidate (1972)
Live a Little, Love a Little (1968)
TV: Private Secretary
Porter, George: 7 British, chemist **8** Nobelist
Porter, Hal: 4 poet **6** author, writer **10** Australian, playwright
work: Criss-Cross
The Extra
The Paper Chase
porterhouse: 4 beef, meat **5** steak
alternative: 5 T-bone **6** rib-eye **7** sirloin
Porter, Katherine Anne: 6 author, writer
work: Flowering Judas
The Leaning Tower
Noon Wine
Old Mortality
Pale Horse, Pale Rider
Ship of Fools
Porter, Rodney: 7 British **8** Nobelist
__ Porter Stomp: 4 King
Porterville: 4 city, town
locale: 10 California
portfolio: 3 bag **4** case, file **5** album **6** folder **7** dossier **8** envelope **9** briefcase, container
item: 4 bond **5** asset, share, stock
option: 3 IRA **4** bond **5** stock
porthole: 4 vent **6** window
Porthos: 9 musketeer
partner: 5 Athos **6** Aramis **9** d'Artagnan
weapon: 5 sword
Port Hueneme: 4 city, town
locale: 10 California
Port Huron: 4 city, town
locale: 8 Michigan
Portia: 4 moon
planet: 6 Uranus
Portia Faces Life: 9 radio show
portico: 4 stoa **5** porch **6** arcade **7** balcony, ingress
church ~: 6 parvis
seat: 6 exedra **7** exhedra
portiere: 5 arras **7** curtain, drapery
Portinari, Beatrice admirer: 5 Dante
__ port in a storm: 3 any
portion: 3 bit, cut, gob, leg, lot **4** deal, dole, doom, dose, fate, hunk, luck, lump, mete, part, slab, some, unit **5** allot, chunk, divvy, piece, quota, scrap, share, slice, split, taste **6** divide, dollop, factor, kismat, kismet, length, moiety, morsel, parcel, ration, sample **7** destiny, divvy up, dole out, element, excerpt, extract, fortune, helping, measure, mete out, prorate, quarter, section, segment, serving **8** allocate, dispense, dividend, division, fraction, fragment, interest, quantity, spoonful **9** allotment, apportion, partition **10** allocation, distribute, percentage
Portland: 4 city, port, town **5** Hoffa
bay: 5 Casco
county: 9 Multnomah
locale: 5 Maine **6** Oregon
newspaper: 9 Oregonian
river: 10 Willamette
time zone: 3 EDT, EST, PDT, PST
Portland __ Blazers: 5 Trail
Portland cement ingredient: 5 shale
Port Louis: 4 city, town **7** capital
locale: 9 Mauritius
portly: 5 ample, beefy, broad, bulky, burly, fubsy, heavy, hefty, husky, large, obese, plump, pudgy, pursy, stout **6** chubby, fleshy, pyknic, rotund, stocky, zaftig, zoftig **7** adipose, paunchy, stately, weighty **8** roly-poly **9** corpulent, filled-out **10** abdominous, overweight, well-padded
Portman: 4 Eric **6** Rachel **7** Natalie
Portman, Eric: 5 actor
film: A Canterbury Tale (1944)
The Colditz Story (1957)
Corridor of Mirrors (1948)
portmanteau: 3 bag **5** trunk **6** valise
Port Moody: 4 city, town
locale: 6 Canada
Portmore: 4 city, town
locale: 7 Jamaica
Port Moresby: 4 city, port, town **7** capital
locale: Papua New Guinea
Portnoy's Complaint author: Philip Roth
Porto: 4 city, town
city near ~: 6 Lisboa, Lisbon
locale: 8 Portugal
Pórto Alegre: 4 city, town
locale: 6 Brazil
port of __: 4 call **5** entry
Portoferraio island: 4 Elba
Port of Spain: 4 city, town **7** capital
locale: 8 Trinidad
Porto Novo: 4 city, town **7** capital
locale: 5 Benin
Port Orange: 4 city, town
locale: 7 Florida
Pórto Velho: 4 city, town
locale: 6 Brazil
Portoviejo: 4 city, town
locale: 7 Ecuador
Port Philip: 3 bay
locale: 9 Australia
portrait: 3 art **5** image **6** canvas, figure, sketch **7** account, drawing, picture, profile **8** likeness, painting, snapshot, vignette **9** depiction, lineation, portrayal **10** photograph, silhouette
do a ~: 4 draw **5** paint **10** photograph
have a ~ done: 3 sit **4** pose
medium: 3 oil **4** film **7** pastels **8** charcoal **10** watercolor
__-portrait: 4 self
Portrait in Brownstone author: Louis Auchincloss
Portrait in Sepia author: Isabel Allende
Portrait of a Lady author: T.S. Eliot
Portrait of a Lady, The: 5 novel
author: Henry James
character: 5 Merle, Pansy, Ralph **6** Archer, Caspar, Gemini, Isabel, Osmond, Rosier **8** Goodwood
dog: 7 Bunchie
Portrait of Bascom Hawke, A author: Thomas Wolfe
Portrait of Berthe Morisot artist: 5 Manet
Portrait of Jennie (1948 film)
cast: Ethel Barrymore, Joseph Cotten, Jennifer Jones
director: William Dieterle
Portrait of My Love (1961 song) artist: Steve Lawrence
Portrait of the Artist as a Young Man, A: 4 film **5** novel
author: James Joyce
cast: John Gielgud, Bosco Hogan, T.P. McKenna
character: 5 Dante, Davin, Dolan, Nasty, Roche, Simon, Vance **6** Arnall, Cranly, Eileen **7** Dedalus, Stephen
director: Joseph Strick
portray: 2 do **3** act **4** copy, draw, limn, play, tell **5** enact, mimic, model, paint **6** depict, detail, parody, recite, render, sculpt, sketch **7** imitate, narrate, picture, recount **8** describe, simulate **9** adumbrate, delineate, interpret, represent **10** illustrate, photograph
portrayal: 4 role **6** acting, sketch **7** picture, recital, version **8** portrait **9** depiction, enactment, rendition
__ Ports: 6 Cinque
Port Said: 4 city, port, town
locale: 5 Egypt
Port Salut: 6 cheese
ports, between: 4 asea **5** at sea
portside: 4 left
portsider: 5 lefty **6** leftie **8** southpaw
Portsmouth: 4 city, port, town
locale: 4 Ohio **8** Virginia
town near ~: 5 Poole
Ports of Call composer: 5 Ibert
Port Stanley: 4 city, port, town
locale: 9 Falklands
Port St. Lucie: 4 city, town
locale: 7 Florida
Portugal: 6 nation **7** country
bay: 7 Setúbal
cape: 4 Roca
capital: 6 Lisboa, Lisbon
city: 4 Nisa **5** Braga, Évora, Olhao, Porto **6** Lisboa, Lisbon, Oporto **7** Amadora
explorer: 6 Cabral, da Gama **8** Magellan
folksong: 4 fado
former colony: 3 Goa **5** Macao, Macau, Timor
island: 6 Azores **7** Madeira
length measure: 4 vara
locale: 6 Europe, Iberia
money: 3 rei **5** conto **6** escudo **7** centavo, cruzado, milreis, moidore **8** johannes
neighbor: 5 Spain
Nobelist in Literature: 8 Saramago
Nobelist in Medicine: 5 Moniz
org.: 4 NATO
pilgrimage site: 6 Fatima
poet: 6 Camoes
port: 5 Porto **6** Lisbon, Oporto
river: 4 Miño **5** Minho, Tagus
wine: 4 port **7** Madeira, malmsey
Portuguese: 8 language
no, in ~: 3 nao
pronoun: 3 mim
title: 3 dom **4** dona
toast: 5 saude
wine, in ~: 5 vinho
Portuguese __ dog: 5 water
Portuguese __-of-war: 3 man
Portuguese West Africa today: 6 Angola
portulaca: 5 plant **6** flower **8** moss rose
Port-Vila: 4 city, town
locale: 7 Vanuatu
posada: 3 inn
pose: 3 act, air, ask, sit **4** mask, mien, sham **5** feign, front, guise, mince, model, offer, put to, query, stand, strut **6** affect, facade, fake it, stance, submit, tender **7** advance, arrange, bearing, charade, playact, posture, present, pretend, profess, proffer, show off, suggest **8** attitude, carriage, pretense, propound, question, set forth, simulate **9** mannerism, put on airs, say cheese **10** false front, grandstand, masquerade, put forward
a question: 3 ask **6** baffle **7** inquire
for more pictures: 5 resit
for the camera: 3 mug **5** smile **9** say cheese
strike a ~: 5 model
Poseidon: 3 god **5** Greek
brother of ~: 4 Zeus **5** Hades
Celtic ~: 3 Ler, Lir
child of ~: 4 Abas, Eryx, Idas, Otus, Urea **5** Arion, Belus, Chios, Lamia, Lelex, Lycus, Melas, Orion, Rhode **6** Aeolus, Agelus, Agenor, Aloeus, Amycus, Anthas, Asopus, Athena, Athene, Augeas, Cromus, Cycnus, Dictys, Eirene, Eleius, Evadne, Leches, Minyas, Mygdon, Neleus, Nireus, Pelias, Phaeax, Phocus, Rhodus, Sciron, Thasus, Triton **7** Aethusa, Ancaeus, Antaeus, Boeotus, Busiris, Chryses, Cteatus, Epopeus, Erginus, Eurytus, Hopleus, Hyrieus, Nycteus, Oeoclus, Pegasus, Peratus, Phineus, Phthius, Proteus, Taphius, Theseus **8** Achaneus, Althepus, Aspledon, Celaenus, Chrysaor, Cychreus, Dercynus, Despoina, Eumolpus, Euphemus, Ialebion, Megareus, Messapus, Nauplius, Pelasgus **9** Charybdis, Corynetes, Cymopolea, Ephialtes, Eurypylus, Hyperenor, Parnassós, Parnassus **10** Hippothous, Polyphemus, Procrustes
domain: 3 sea **5** ocean
epithet: 5 Soter **7** Hippios **10** Phytalmios
equivalent: 7 Neptune
lover of ~: 4 Arne, Leis, Pero, Tyro **5** Alope, Arene, Ascra, Beroe, Halia, Libya, Melie **6** Aethra, Anippe, Calyce, Canace, Celusa, Chione, Cleito, Euryte, Larisa, Medusa, Mideia, Oenope, Pirene, Pitana, Thoosa **7** Agamede, Alcyone, Althaea, Amymone, Antiope, Celaeno, Corcyra, Demeter, Euryale, Halcyon, Molione, Salamis **8** Arethusa, Cleodora, Eurycyda, Halcyone, Periboea, Thalatta,

Themisto, Tritonis **9** Astypalea, Calchinia, Iphimedia, Theophane **10** Lysianassa, Melantheia
parent of ~: **6** Cronos, Cronus
sculptor: **6** Milles
sister of ~: **6** Hestia **7** Demeter
wife of ~: **10** Amphitrite
Poseidon Adventure, The (1972 film)
cast: Jack Albertson, Ernest Borgnine, Red Buttons, Gene Hackman, Carol Lynley, Pamela Sue Martin, Roddy McDowall, Leslie Nielsen, Stella Stevens, Shelley Winters
director: Ronald Neame
poser: **4** koan **5** asker, dilly, model **6** enigma, puzzle, riddle, teaser, toughy **7** problem, stumper, toughie **9** conundrum, cover girl, pretender
give a ~ to: **5** throw **6** puzzle **7** buffalo, mystify, perplex **8** confound
Posets: **4** peak **5** mount **8** mountain
locale: **5** Spain **6** Europe **8** Pyrenees
poseur: **4** fake **5** phony **6** phoney **8** imposter, impostor **9** hypocrite, pretender
Posey: **5** Sandy **6** Parker
posh: **4** chic, lush, luxe, rich **5** fancy, grand, plush, ritzy, smart, swank, swell, swish **6** classy, deluxe, la-de-da, la-di-da, lavish, lordly, luxury, modish, swanky, trendy **7** elegant, opulent, refined, upscale **8** lah-di-dah, palatial, splendid **9** exclusive, expensive, high-class, luxurious, sumptuous **10** upper-class
accommodations: **5** suite, villa **9** penthouse
posies: **8** bouquets
place for ~: **4** vase
posit: **3** put **5** place **6** affirm, assert, assume, thesis **7** premise, presume, proffer, situate, suggest **8** put forth, question **9** assertion, postulate, stipulate **10** assumption, contention, hypothesis, presuppose
position: **3** fix, job, lay, put **4** case, move, pose, post, rank, role, seat, side, site, slot, spot, view, work **5** angle, berth, caste, class, level, locus, mount, niche, phase, place, set at, situs, stand, state, stead, stick, terms, where **6** aspect, belief, billet, branch, cachet, career, instal, locale, locate, office, plight, sphere, stance, status, theory, thesis **7** arrange, echelon, footing, install, opinion, outlook, posture, quality, quarter, setting, station, stature, straits, vacancy **8** attitude, bearings, doctrine, judgment, locality, location, prestige, standing **9** condition, sentiment, situation, viewpoint **10** employment, importance, nine-to-five, occupation, profession, reputation, standpoint
combining form: **5** stasi-
___ position: **4** pole **5** fetal, lotus
positioned: **3** set **5** fixed
as originally ~: **6** in situ
___ Positioning System: **6** Global
positive: **4** cold, firm, good, plus, real, sure **6** actual, aidful, benign, cheery, direct, upbeat, useful **7** assured, certain, decided, factual, genuine, helpful, settled **8** absolute, concrete, decisive, definite, explicit, forceful, in the bag, outright, remedial, resolved, salutary, sanguine, specific, verified **9** believing, confident, convinced, effectual, favorable, out-and-out, practical, satisfied **10** beneficial, conclusive, determined, guaranteed, inarguable, optimistic, photograph, productive, purposeful, undeniable, undisputed, worthwhile
be ~: **4** aver **5** swear **6** affirm, assert
make a ~ from a negative: **5** print
outlook: **4** hope **5** trust **6** morale **7** elation **8** buoyancy, calmness, easiness, idealism, optimism **9** assurance, certainty, good cheer, happiness, lightness **10** brightness, confidence, enthusiasm
sign: **4** plus
thinker: **5** Peale
vote: **3** aye, yea, yes
___ positive: **5** proof
___-positive: **4** Gram **5** false
positively: **3** aye, oui, yea, yep, yes, yup **4** amen, fine, okay, sure, yeah **5** good-o, natch, quite, right, roger, uh-huh **6** agreed, and how, easily, gladly, good-oh, indeed, it is so, just so, rather, really, righto, surely, wholly, you bet, yowzah **7** exactly, flat out, for sure, go ahead, indeedy, mais oui, quite so, right on, ten-four **8** all right, as you say, for a fact, of course, thumbs up, very well **9** assuredly, be my guest, certainly, darn right, decidedly, doubtless, expressly, favorably, hands down, naturally, no mistake, on the nose, precisely, sure thing, you betcha, you said it **10** absolutely, by all means, definitely, far and away, inevitably, sure as hell, sure enough, that's right
Positively ___!: **3** not
Positively 4th Street (1965 song)
artist: Bob Dylan
positron: **8** particle
posologist: **8** druggist **10** pharmacist
posse: **3** mob **4** crew, gang **7** pursuer
member: **6** deputy
movie: **5** oater **7** western
quest: **6** outlaw, robber **9** desperado
Posse (1975 film)
cast: Bruce Dern, Kirk Douglas, Bo Hopkins
director: Kirk Douglas
possess: **3** hog, own **4** bear, grab, have, hold, keep **5** boast, enjoy, seize, wield **6** lock up, madden, obtain, occupy, retain **7** acquire **8** hold on to, maintain **9** get hold of, latch onto **10** monopolize
old-style: **4** hath
possessed: **5** curst **6** cursed, raving **7** berserk, far gone, haunted, zealous **8** composed, consumed, fiendish, frenzied, obsessed **9** bedeviled, bewitched, collected, enchanted, fanatical **10** enthralled, hysterical, infatuated, spellbound
___-possessed: **4** self
Possessed (1931 film)
cast: Joan Crawford, Wallace Ford, Clark Gable
Possessed (1947 film)
cast: Joan Crawford, Van Heflin, Raymond Massey
Possessed, The author: Fyodor Dostoyevsky
possession: **4** grip, hold **5** title **6** colony, effect, tenure **7** chattel, control, custody, tenancy **8** clutches, dominion, property **9** commodity, enjoyment, furniture, occupancy, ownership, territory
be in ~ of: **3** own **4** have
gain ~: **4** take
gain ~ again: **6** redeem
prized ~: **3** gem **5** jewel **8** heirloom, treasure, valuable
valuable ~: **5** asset
Possession author: A.S. Byatt
Possession of Joel Delaney, The (1972 film)
cast: Perry King, Lisa Kohane, Shirley MacLaine
director: Waris Hussein
possessions: **4** gear **5** goods, stuff **6** assets, estate, things, wealth **7** baggage, effects **8** chattels, property **10** belongings
possessive: **6** greedy **7** jealous, pronoun **9** tenacious
Dogpatch ~: **8** his'n her'n **9** our'n your'n
French ~: **3** mes, tes, toi **5** notre, votre
German ~: **3** mie **4** mein **5** meine
Italian ~: **3** mia, mio
Latin ~: **3** sua, suo
pronoun: **3** his, its, our **4** hers, mine, ours, your **5** their, whose
Quaker ~: **3** thy **5** thine
Spanish ~: **3** mia, mio, tua, tuo **7** nuestra, nuestro
possessor: **5** owner **6** tenant **8** occupant **10** proprietor
posset: **5** drink **8** beverage
ingredient: **3** ale **4** milk, wine
possibilities: **7** promise **9** potential
possibility: **2** if **4** hope, odds, risk **5** break, fluke, maybe **6** chance, gamble, hazard, prayer, resort, toss-up **7** latency, opening, promise, surmise **8** fortuity, occasion, prospect **9** fair shake, liability **10** likelihood, lucky break
strong ~: **10** likelihood
within ~: **6** likely, viable **8** feasible
possible: **6** doable, latent, likely, viable **7** earthly, hopeful **8** apparent, credible, feasible, optional, probable, workable **9** available, plausible, potential, practical, promising, thinkable, uncertain **10** accessible, achievable, attainable, believable, contingent, imaginable, obtainable, realizable
least ~: **7** minimal, minimum
make ~: **5** set up **6** enable **7** approve, arrange
quite ~: **6** likely **8** feasible, probable
possibly: **5** maybe **7** perhaps **8** feasibly, probably **9** perchance
possum
comic-strip ~: **4** Pogo
honey ~: **4** tait
play ~: **4** fake, sham **5** feign **7** pretend **9** dissemble
___ possum: **4** play
post: **3** job, leg, set **4** base, beam, beat, fort, mail, mast, pale, pier, pile, pole, prop, race, rail, ride, seat, send, site, spot, stud, warn **5** after, brief, newel, perch, place, pylon, ready, remit, shaft, stake, stave, stilt **6** advise, assign, billet, column, fill in, inform, notify, office, pillar, record, update **7** forward, lookout, quarter, railing, situate, station, support, upright, vacancy **8** acquaint, baluster, banister, garrison, handrail, location, palisade, pedestal, position, province, quarters, register, transfer, vocation **9** make known, situation **10** assignment, employment, profession
ancient Roman racing ~: **4** meta
Army ~: **4** fort
banister ~: **5** newel
ender: **3** age, man **4** card, date, hole, mark, paid, pone **5** haste **6** master
go from pillar to ~: **3** gad **4** roam, rove **5** drift **6** ramble, wander **7** traipse
nautical ~: **4** bitt **7** bollard
starter: **3** bed, out **4** door, gate, lamp, mile, sign **5** guide
vertical ~: **4** beam **8** doorpost **9** doorframe
wooden ~: **3** rod **5** stake **6** picket, timber
post ___: **3** hoc **4** card, road, time **5** entry, horse, house **6** chaise, factum, office
post-___: **3** ops **4** free **6** modern, season
___ post: **4** goal **5** crown, miter, newel, penny **6** finger, parcel **7** command, staging, trading, winning
Post: **3** Ted **4** Mike **5** Emily, paper, Wiley **6** Markie, Wilbur **9** newspaper
cereal: **6** Oreo O's **9** Alpha Bits, Grape Nuts, Honey Comb **10** Bran Flakes **11** Golden Crisp, Waffle Crisp
newspaper locale: **6** Denver **7** New York **10** Cincinnati
postage ___: **3** due **5** meter, stamp
postal: **4** amok **6** raging **8** unhinged **9** murderous
abbr.: **3** APO, RFD, rte.
address word: **3** box
code: **3** zip
delivery: **2** ad **4** card, mail **6** letter **7** package **8** circular, junk mail, magazine
equipment: **5** dater, scale
postaxial bone: **4** ulna
postcard: **4** mail **7** memento **8** souvenir
cost, once: **5** penny
message: **4** note
picture: **5** vista
___ postcard: **7** picture
Postcards From the Edge (1990 film)
cast: Richard Dreyfuss, Gene Hackman, Shirley MacLaine, Dennis Quaid, Meryl Streep
director: Mike Nichols
postdate: **6** follow **7** succeed
Post-Dispatch: **5** paper **9** newspaper
locale: **7** St. Louis
posted: **3** hep, hip **5** aware **6** au fait, versed **7** knowing, learned, located **8** familiar, informed **9** au courant, cognizant, conscious, on the beam, plugged in **10** conversant
it may be ~: **4** bail
keep ~: **4** tell **6** advise, inform
poster: **4** bill, sign **5** paper **6** banner **7** affiche, placard **9** billboard, broadside **10** broadsheet, photograph
GI ~: **5** pin-up
holder: **4** tack **7** push pin **9** thumbtack
info: **3** aka **5** alias **6** reward
Marine ~ words: **4** a few
surety ~: **6** bailor
Uncle Sam ~ words: I Want You
poster ___: **5** child, color, paint
___-poster bed: **4** four
posterity: **4** kids, seed **5** brood, heirs, issue, stock **6** family, future, scions **7** kinfolk, lineage, progeny **8** children, kinfolks, kinsfolk **9** offspring **10** descendant, successors
postern: **4** door, gate **7** gateway, ingress **8** back door, entrance, entryway
Postern of ___: **4** Fate
postgame discussion: **5** recap **7** summary
Post-Gazette: **5** paper **9** newspaper
locale: **10** Pittsburgh
postgraduate
degree: **2** MA **3** MBA, MFA, PHD
requirement: **5** orals **6** thesis
posthaste: **3** PDQ **4** ASAP, fast, soon, stat **5** apace, quick, swift **6** at once, presto, pronto, speedy **7** fleetly, quickly, rapidly, swiftly **8** directly, in a flash, in a jiffy, in no time, pell-mell, promptly, speedily **9** forthwith, hurriedly, instantly, like a shot, on the spot
post hoc: **9** afterward
post hoc, ___ propter hoc: **4** ergo
Post-it ___: **4** note
postlarval: **5** pupal
Postlethwaite: **4** Pete
postman
assignment: **5** route
challenge: **3** dog, ice **4** rain, snow **5** sleet

Postman Always Rings Twice, The: 4 film 5 novel
author: James M. Cain
cast: Hume Cronyn, John Garfield, Cecil Kellaway, Lana Turner
director: Tay Garnett
Postman, The (1994 film)
cast: Philippe Noiret, Massimo Troisi
director: Michael Radford
Postman, The author: Roger Martin du Gard
Post, Markie: 7 actress
TV: Hearts Afire, Night Court, The Fall Guy
Postmaster General's org.: 4 USPS
Post, Mike: 8 composer
song: The Rockford Files (1975)
The Theme from Hill Street Blues (1981)
postnasal __: 4 drip
post office: 4 game
buy: 5 stamp
creed word: 3 nor 4 rain, snow 5 sleet
do ~ work: 4 sort 5 weigh 7 collect, deliver
machine: 5 scale
poster datum: 3 aka 5 alias 6 reward
symbol: 5 eagle
unit: 5 ounce, pound
post-office __: 3 box
__ post office: 7 general
Poston, Tom: 5 actor
film: Cold Turkey (1971)
spouse: Suzanne Pleshette
TV: Mork & Mindy, Newhart
post-op destination: 3 ICU
postpone: 4 slow, stay 5 defer, delay, remit, sit on, stall, table, waive 6 hold up, put off, retard, shelve 7 adjourn, hold off, lay over, neglect, put back, suspend 8 hold over, prorogue 10 pigeonhole, reschedule
as a deadline: 6 extend
postponement: 4 stay 5 delay 7 respite 8 abeyance, reprieve
postprandial quaff: 4 port 6 brandy 7 liqueur
post-Reformation council: 5 Trent
postscript: 6 epilog 7 codicil 8 addendum, addition, appendix, epilogue 9 afterword 10 supplement
musical ~: 4 coda
write a ~: 3 add
post-season game: 4 bowl
post-shower sight: 6 fogbow 7 rainbow
post-tax profit: 3 net
postulant: 3 nun 9 applicant
postulate: 3 law 5 axiom, claim, given, posit 6 assert, assume, hazard, theory, thesis 7 believe, opinion, premise, solicit, suppose, theorem 8 theorize 9 predicate, speculate 10 assumption, conjecture, generalize, hypothesis, presuppose, put forward
postulation: 5 claim 6 belief 8 argument 9 assertion 10 allegation, assumption, contention
posture: 3 act, sit 4 mask, mien, pose 5 guise, mince, state 6 fake it, policy, stance 7 bearing, conduct, feeling, show off 8 attitude, carriage, position, presence 9 condition, sentiment, viewpoint 10 deportment, masquerade, standpoint
have poor ~: 3 sag 5 droop, slump, stoop
posturing: 8 pretense
Post, Wilbur pal: 4 Mr. Ed
posy: 5 bloom 6 flower 7 blossom, bouquet, nosegay
portion: 4 leaf, stem 5 petal
pot: 3 jar, jug, pan 4 bank, mint, olla, pool 5 basin, belly, crock, grass, kitty, plant, stake, wager 6 kettle, vessel 7 abdomen, amphora, caldron, stomach, tankard 8 cauldron, saucepan 9 container 10 jardiniere, receptacle
booster: 3 bet 4 ante 5 stake, wager
ender: 3 pie 4 herb, hole, hook, luck, shot 5 belly, bound, latch 6 boiler, holder, hunter 7 bellied
fragment: 5 shard, sherd
gambler's ~: 5 kitty, stake
go to ~: 4 rust 8 vegetate
hot ~: 4 stew 9 casserole
item: 3 IOU 4 cash, chip 5 money
lobster ~: 4 trap
monkey ~: 4 tree
pepper ~: 4 stew
protector: 6 enamel
starter: 3 tea 4 fuss, jack, toss 5 crack, flesh, sauce, stink, stock 6 coffee, flower
start the ~: 6 ante up
take the ~: 3 win
top: 3 lid 5 cover
pot __: 4 luck, shot 5 metal, roast 6 cheese, liquor 7 sticker
pot-__: 5 au-feu
__ pot: 3 hot, mud 4 bean, fire, go to, peat 5 paint 6 monkey, pepper, smudge 7 chimney, lobster, melting
__ Pot: 3 Pol 5 Crock
potable: 4 kava 5 drink, juice 6 liquor 8 beverage, libation, vermouth 9 aqua vitae, drinkable, inebriant
make ~: 6 desalt, filter, purify 10 desalinate, desalinize
nonpotent ~: 3 ade, pop, tea 4 soda 5 juice 6 coffee 7 herb tea, soda pop
potent ~: 3 ale, gin, rum, rye 4 beer, mead, port, sake, saki, wine 5 lager, stout, vodka 6 brandy, liquor, sherry, whisky 7 liqueur, whiskey
potage: 4 soup
potash: 3 lye 6 alkali
chemically: 3 KOH
potassium: 5 metal 7 element
hydroxide: 3 KOH, lye
nitrate: 5 niter
ore: 7 sylvite
potassium __: 4 alum 6 iodide 7 acetate, bromate, bromide, hydrate, nitrate, oxalate, sulfate
potation: 5 draft, drink, quaff 8 beverage, libation 10 intoxicant
potato: 4 carb, spud 5 carbo, tuber 6 veggie 9 vegetable
alternative: 4 rice
baking ~: 5 Idaho
couch ~: 5 sloth 6 loafer 9 lazybones
dish: 4 soup 5 baked, fries, salad 8 au gratin 9 home fries, scalloped 10 hash browns
emulate a couch ~: 3 lie, veg 4 laze 6 veg out 7 recline
hot ~: 5 issue 7 problem
in Spanish: 4 papa
pancake: 5 latke
part: 3 eye 4 skin
preparer: 5 parer, ricer 6 peeler
salad ingredient: 3 egg 4 mayo 6 celery, pepper 10 mayonnaise
skin: 6 jacket 9 appetizer
sweet ~: 3 yam 7 ocarina
turnover: 5 knish
potato __: 3 bug 4 bean, chip, moth, race, skin, vine, worm 5 knish, salad 6 beetle
__ potato: 3 air, hot 4 wild 5 baked, couch, Idaho, Irish, sweet, white 7 prairie
...potato and __ potahto: 4 I say
potato chip: 4 nosh 5 snack 7 munchie
Brit's ~: 5 crisp
feature: 5 ridge
flavor: 5 chive 6 cheese
partner: 3 dip
Potato Eaters, The: 3 oil 8 painting
artist: 7 Van Gogh
potatoes
brand: 6 Ore-Ida
partner: 4 meat
peeling ~ perhaps: 4 on KP
portion: 5 scoop
prepare ~: 4 bake, dice, mash, pare, peel, whip 5 grate
unit: 6 bushel
__ potatoes: 5 small 6 O'Brien 7 duchess
potatoes au __: 6 gratin
pot-au-feu: 4 meat, stew
Potawatomi: 6 Indian 7 Amerind
potbelly: 3 gut 6 paunch 7 stomach 9 spare tire
potbelly __: 5 stove
Potbelly: 3 pig 5 swine
potboiler: 4 yarn 5 novel, story 7 fiction 9 narrative
author: 4 hack
Potemkin __: 7 village
Potemkin (1925 film) director: Sergei Eisenstein
Potemkin mutiny site: 5 Odesa 6 Odessa
potency: 3 vim, zip 4 dint, kick, sway, thew, zing 5 brawn, force, juice, might, power, punch, sinew, thews, vigor 6 energy, muscle 7 command, control, fitness, muscles, stamina 8 capacity, dominion, efficacy, strength, vitality 9 authority, beefiness, endurance, fortitude, hardiness, huskiness, influence, intensity, puissance, stoutness, toughness 10 brawniness, brute force, capability, horsepower, mightiness, robustness, sturdiness
lacking ~: 4 weak 6 feeble
potent: 4 hale, iron, male, wiry 5 beefy, burly, hardy, hefty, hunky, husky, lusty, solid, stiff, stout, tough 6 brawny, cogent, hearty, mighty, robust, rugged, sinewy, steely, stocky, strong, sturdy, virile 7 doughty, dynamic, telling, violent 8 athletic, forceful, indurate, muscular, powerful, puissant, stalwart, vigorous 9 Atlantean, effective, Herculean, strapping, well-built 10 able-bodied, commanding, compelling, convincing, formidable, full-bodied, impressive, persuasive, red-blooded
starter: 4 omni
potentate: 3 aga 4 agha, amir, czar, emir, king, raja, shah, tsar, tzar 5 ameer, emeer, mogul, queen, rajah, ruler 6 gerent, sultan, tyrant 7 emperor, empress, monarch, pharaoh 8 maharaja 9 maharajah, sovereign
Mideast ~: 3 aga 4 agha, amir, emir 5 ameer, emeer 6 sultan
of yore: 4 czar, shah, tsar, tzar 7 pharaoh
Punjab ~: 4 raja 5 rajah 8 maharaja 9 maharajah
potential: 5 power 6 covert, doable, future, hidden, latent, likely, viable 7 ability, budding, dormant, earthly, lurking, makings, promise 8 aptitude, capacity, credible, feasible, implicit, inherent, possible, upcoming, workable 9 concealed, embryonic, plausible, practical, quiescent, thinkable 10 achievable, attainable, capability, imaginable, unrealized
client: 8 prospect
has the ~ to: 3 can, may
potential __: 6 energy 7 divider
__ potential: 6 action, biotic, evoked 7 contact, kinetic
potentiality: 5 power 7 ability, latency 9 potential
pother: 3 bug, vex 4 flap, fret, fuss, gall, rile, stir, to-do 5 annoy, chafe, harry, pique, upset, worry 6 bother, flurry, harass, hector, hubbub, nettle, pester, ruckus, rumpus, tumult, uproar 7 disturb, provoke, trouble, turmoil 8 irritate 9 commotion 10 hullabaloo
potherb: 4 mint 5 basil, orach, plant, thyme 6 catnip, orache, savory 7 oregano 8 rosemary 9 chamomile, spearmint 10 peppermint
pothole: 3 pit, rut
locale: 4 road 7 highway 8 pavement
pothook shape: 3 ess
potion: 4 balm, brew 5 drink, tonic 6 elixir, remedy 7 arcanum, mixture, philter 8 medicine 10 medication
__ potion: 4 love
potlatch: 5 feast
potluck: 4 meal 6 social 10 fund-raiser
potluck __: 6 dinner, supper
Pot Luck author: Emile Zola
pot metal: 5 alloy
component: 4 lead 6 copper
pot of __: 4 gold
Potok, Chaim: 6 author, writer
work: The Book of Lights
The Chosen
In the Beginning
My Name Is Asher Lev
The Promise
Potomac: 4 city, town 5 river
city locale: 8 Maryland
city on the ~: 10 Washington
river locale: 8 Maryland, Virginia
river to the ~: 9 Anacostia 10 Shenandoah
potoo: 4 bird
Potosí: 4 city, town
locale: 7 Bolivia
potpie: 9 casserole 10 frozen food
veggie: 6 carrot, celery, potato
potpourri: 3 mix 4 hash, olio, stew 5 blend, combo 6 jumble, medley 7 farrago, goulash, mélange, mixture, variety 8 mishmash, mixed bag, pastiche 9 patchwork 10 assortment, collection, cumulation, hodgepodge, miscellany, salmagundi
Potsdam: 4 city, town
locale: 7 Germany
river: 5 Havel
potsherd: 8 artifact
potshot: 4 barb, slam
take a ~: 5 snipe
potsy: 4 game 9 hopscotch
pottage: 4 soup
buyer: 4 Esau
potter: 6 trifle 7 artisan 10 mess around
at times: 5 firer 6 hunter
clay: 5 argil 6 kaolin 7 kaoline 10 terra cotta
device: 4 kiln 5 wheel
mix: 4 slip 5 glaze, paste
name meaning ~: 7 Crocker
wheel kin: 5 lathe
work at a ~'s wheel: 5 throw
Potter: 2 H.C. 5 Carol 6 Dennis, Israel, Monica 7 Beatrix
Potter, Beatrix: 6 author, writer 7 British
work: Jemima Puddleduck
The Roly-Poly Pudding
The Tale of Benjamin Bunny
The Tale of Peter Rabbit
The Tale of Tom Kitten
Potter, Colonel: 7 Sherman
aide: 5 Radar 7 Klinger
program: 4 MASH
Potter, H.C.: 8 director
film: Beloved Enemy (1936)
The Farmer's Daughter (1947)
Hellzapoppin' (1941)

Mr. Blandings Builds His Dream House (1948)
Mr. Lucky (1943)
The Shopworn Angel (1938)
The Story of Vernon & Irene Castle (1939)
Potter, Monica: 7 actress
film: A Cool, Dry Place (1999)
Patch Adams (1998)
Without Limits (1998)
pottery: 3 art 4 clay, ware 6 jasper 8 ceramics, clayware, crockery 9 porcelain, stoneware 10 terra cotta
bake ~: 4 fire
blue ~ of Holland: 4 delf 5 delft
finish: 4 slip 5 glaze
flaw: 4 nick 5 crack
fragment: 5 shard, sherd 8 artifact
Iron Age ~ of Africa: 5 Urewe
Italian ~: 6 Faenza
material: 4 clay 5 argil 6 kaolin 7 kaoline 10 terra cotta
potto: 7 primate
relative: 3 ape 4 saki, titi 5 chimp, drill, jocko, lemur, loris, magot, orang, shrew 6 aye-aye, baboon, Bandar, galago, gelada, gibbon, grivet, guenon, howler, langur, macaco, monkey, rhesus, uakari, vervet 7 colobus, gorilla, guereza, hoolock, macaque, sapajou, siamang, tamarin, tarsier 8 bush baby, capuchin, mandrill, mangabey, marmoset, talapoin 9 orangutan 10 Barbary ape, chimpanzee, orangutang
Potts: 5 Annie, Cliff
Pottstown: 4 city
locale: 4 Penn.
Potvin, Denis
milieu: 3 ice 4 rink 5 arena
org.: 3 NHL
pou ___: 3 sto
pouch: 3 bag, sac 4 poke, sack 5 purse, swell 6 kitbag, packet, pocket 7 bladder, handbag, satchel, vesicle 8 carryall, knapsack, reticule, rucksack 9 container 10 pocketbook, receptacle
contents: 4 mail
pouched
animal: 3 roo 6 possum 7 hamster, opossum, pelican 8 chipmunk, kangaroo 9 marsupial
pouf: 4 coif 5 quilt 6 hairdo 7 hassock 8 coiffure
Poughkeepsie: 4 city, town
locale: 7 New York
Pouilly-___: 4 Fumé 6 Fuissé
Pouilly-___-Loire: 3 sur
pouilly-fuissé: 4 wine
poulard: 3 hen
Poulenc, Francis: 6 French 8 composer
contemporary of ~: 5 Satie
poule product: 4 oeuf
poult: 4 fowl 6 turkey 7 chicken 8 pheasant
relative: 5 quail, snipe 6 chukar, grouse, peahen 7 peacock, peafowl 8 curassow, moorfowl, woodcock 9 partridge 10 guinea fowl
poult-de-soie: 6 fabric 8 material
poultice: 4 balm 6 remedy 8 dressing
poultry: 3 hen 4 duck, fowl, hens, meat 5 capon, ducks, fryer, geese, goose, quail 6 pullet, turkey 7 chicken, turkeys 8 chickens, pheasant, roosters 10 Cornish hen
housing: 4 coop
part: 4 wing 5 thigh 6 breast 8 dark meat 9 drumstick, white meat
plant worker: 5 sexer
product: 3 egg
seasoning: 4 sage
pounce: 4 dive, jump, leap 5 bound, fly at, lunge, seize, surge, swoop 6 ambush, attack, snatch, spring 8 drop down, fall upon
on: 3 nab 5 catch 6 ambush, snap up, waylay 10 buttonhole
pound: 3 hit, ram 4 bang, bash, beat, cake, club, drub, drum, lash, mall, mash, maul, mill, nail, pelt, pint, slam, thud, unit 5 baste, clout, crush, drive, grind, knock, money, paste, pulse, punch, smash, smite, stamp, stomp, throb, thump, tramp, whack, whang, whomp 6 batter, beetle, buffet, cudgel, defeat, hammer, kennel, larrup, pestle, pommel, powder, pummel, squash, strike, thrash, thwack, wallop 7 clobber, lambast, pulsate, thunder, trounce 8 give it to, lambaste, levigate 9 palpitate, pulverize, triturate
British ~: 4 quid
dweller: 3 cat, cur, dog 4 mutt 5 stray 6 canine
fraction: 5 ounce
fractions: 5 pence
into: 5 teach 7 ingrain 9 brainwash 10 evangelize
metric ~: 4 kilo
sound: 3 arf, grr, mew, yip 4 bark, meow, woof, yelp
the pavements: 5 tramp 7 job-hunt
pound ___: 4 cake, sign
pound-___: 7 foolish
___-pound: 4 foot, half, inch
poundage: 6 weight
extra ~: 3 fat 4 flab 9 spare tire
pounder: 6 pestle 10 pile-driver
Pounder: 3 CCH
Pound, Ezra: 4 poet
birthplace: 5 Idaho
work: Cantos
pound-foolish: 8 wasteful
pounding: 4 ache 5 thump 6 athrob
pound of ___: 5 flesh
pounds: 4 heft
about 2200 ~: 5 tonne
1000 ~: 3 kip
shillings, and pence: 3 LSD
take off ~: 4 diet, lose, slim
unwanted ~: 4 flab 9 spare tire
Poundstone: 5 Paula
___ Poupon: 4 Grey
pour: 3 jet, run, tip 4 emit, flow, gush, pump, rain, roll, rush, spew, spue, teem 5 crowd, drain, flood, issue, spill, spout, storm, surge, swarm 6 course, decant, deluge, drench, effuse, lavish, shower, splash, stream, throng 7 cascade, gush out, proceed, radiate, spew out, torrent 8 inundate 9 discharge
down the drain: 5 waste
forth: 4 emit, flow, gush, shed 5 erupt 6 effuse 9 discharge
oil on: 4 calm, ease 5 allay, salve 6 defuse, pacify, smooth, soften, soothe, stroke 7 appease, assuage, mollify, placate, relieve, sweeten 8 calm down 9 untrouble 10 conciliate, smooth over
out: 4 gush, spew, vent 5 empty, spill, spurt 6 decant, effuse, unload 7 confide
starter: 4 down
pour ___: 4 it on
pour ___ troubled waters: 5 oil on
pourboire: 3 tip 8 gratuity
pouring: 3 wet 5 rainy 6 stormy
aid: 6 funnel
sound: 4 glug
Pour Some Sugar on Me (1988 song)
artist: Def Leppard
pousse-___: 4 café
Poussin: 7 Nicolas
pout: 4 fume, mope, moue, sulk 5 brood, frown 6 glower
starter: 3 eel 4 horn
pouter: 4 bird 6 pigeon
pouting: 5 sulky 6 sullen
Po Valley city: 5 Parma
poverty: 4 debt, lack, need, want 6 dearth, famine, misery, penury 7 beggary, paucity, squalor 8 exiguity, hardship, scarcity, shortage, sparsity 9 indigence, necessity, privation 10 bankruptcy, deficiency, inadequacy, insolvency, meagerness, starvation
poverty ___: 4 line 5 level
poverty-stricken: 4 poor 5 broke, needy, short 6 bad off, hard up, ill off, in need, in want, shabby 7 pinched, squalid, wanting 8 badly off, bankrupt, beggarly, dirt poor, indigent, stranded, strapped 9 destitute, insolvent, miserable, moneyless, penniless, penurious 10 down and out, pauperized, straitened
Povich, Maury: 2 MC 4 host 5 emcee
spouse: Connie Chung
POV network: 3 PBS
pow: 3 bam, bop 4 sock, wham 5 noise, punch, whack 6 kaboom
response: 3 oof
POW: 2 GI
Poway: 4 city, town
locale: 10 California
powder: 4 dust, film, grit, meal, snow, talc 5 crush, flour, grate, grind, pound, smash 6 crunch, makeup, reduce 7 crumble, scatter 8 cosmetic, levigate, sprinkle 9 granulate, pulverize, triturate
baking ~: 6 leaven
bath ~: 4 talc 6 talcum
container: 4 horn
glass-polishing ~: 5 ceria
lover: 5 skier
needing ~: 5 shiny
photography ~: 6 amidol
reduce to ~: 5 grind 9 pulverize
room: 2 WC 3 lav 4 bath, john 8 lavatory
starter: 3 gun
take a ~: 2 go 3 run 4 blow, bolt 5 leave 6 decamp, escape 8 run for it, skip town 10 make tracks
powder ___: 3 boy, keg 4 blue, horn, puff, room 10 snow monkey
___ powder: 3 Goa 4 face, soap 5 black, chili, curry, onion, take a, tooth 6 baking, chilli, talcum 7 dusting
powdered ___: 4 milk 5 donut, sugar
powder puff, use a: 3 dab
powdery: 3 dry 4 fine 5 dusty, loose, mealy 6 chalky, floury, grainy, gritty, ground, milled 7 friable 8 granular 9 crumbling 10 pulverized
residue: 3 ash 4 dust
Powell: 4 Adam, Boog, Dick, Jane, Paul 5 Cecil, Colin, Jesse 7 Anthony, Eleanor, Michael, William
Powell, Anthony: 6 author, writer 7 British
work: A Dance to the Music of Time
Powell, Cecil: 8 Nobelist 9 physicist
Powell, Colin: 7 general
Powell, Dick: 5 actor
film: 42nd Street (1933)
The Bad and the Beautiful (1952)
Blessed Event (1932)
Christmas in July (1940)
Colleen (1936)
Cornered (1945)
Cry Danger (1951)
Dames (1934)
The Enemy Below (1957)
Footlight Parade (1933)
Gold Diggers of 1935 (1935)
Hard to Get (1938)
In the Navy (1941)
It Happened Tomorrow (1944)
A Midsummer Night's Dream (1935)
Murder, My Sweet (1944)
On the Avenue (1937)
Pitfall (1948)
Station West (1948)
The Tall Target (1951)
Thanks a Million (1935)
To the Ends of the Earth (1948)
True to Life (1943)
Varsity Show (1937)
You Never Can Tell (1951)
spouse: June Allyson, Joan Blondell
Powell, Eleanor: 6 dancer 7 actress
film: Born to Dance (1936)
Broadway Melody of 1936 (1935)
Broadway Melody of 1940 (1940)
Lady Be Cool (1941)
Rosalie (1937)
spouse: Glenn Ford
Powell, Jane: 7 actress
film: The Girl Most Likely (1957)
Royal Wedding (1951)
Seven Brides for Seven Brothers (1954)
Powell, Michael: 8 director
film: Black Narcissus (1947)
A Canterbury Tale (1944)
Contraband (1940)
The Edge of the World (1937)
I Know Where I'm Going! (1945)
Life and Death of Colonel Blimp (1943)
The Red Shoes (1948)
The Small Back Room (1949)
The Spy in Black (1939)
Stairway to Heaven (1946)
The Thief of Bagdad (1940)
Powell, William: 5 actor
costar: 3 Loy
film: After the Thin Man (1936)
Another Thin Man (1939)
Crossroads (1942)
Double Wedding (1937)
The Ex-Mrs. Bradford (1936)
Fashions (1934)
The Great Ziegfeld (1936)
High Pressure (1932)
I Love You Again (1940)
Jewel Robbery (1932)
The Kennel Murder Case (1933)
The Last Command (1928)
The Last of Mrs. Cheyney (1937)
Lawyer Man (1932)
Libeled Lady (1936)
Life With Father (1947)
Manhattan Melodrama (1934)
Mister Roberts (1955)
My Man Godfrey (1936)
One Way Passage (1932)
The Senator Was Indiscreet (1947)
Shadow of the Thin Man (1941)
The Thin Man (1934)
The Thin Man Goes Home (1944)
Ziegfeld Follies (1946)
spouse: Carole Lombard
power: 3 arm, law, vim 4 beef, cube, dint, gift, kick, pull, rule, sway, thew 5 brawn, clout, force, juice, means, might, punch, reach, right, say-so, sinew, skill, steam, thews, title, vigor 6 agency, energy, muscle, propel, square, talent, virtue, weight 7 ability, command, faculty, fitness, freedom, license, mastery, muscles, potence, potency, prowess, regency, stamina, strings, utility, voltage 8 capacity, dominion, dynamism, efficacy, energize, exponent, hegemony, imperium, kingship, leverage, momentum, prestige, strength, violence, vitality 9 authority, beefiness, endurance, for-

titude, hardiness, huskiness, influence, intensity, magnetism, potential, privilege, puissance, stoutness, supremacy, toughness **10** ascendance, ascendancy, ascendence, ascendency, brawniness, brute force, capability, competence, government, horsepower, leadership, management, mightiness, robustness, ruggedness, sturdiness
colonial ~: **5** Spain **6** France **7** England
combining form: **4** dyna- **5** dynam- **6** dynamo-
decision-making ~: **4** veto **5** say-so
ender: **4** boat **5** house **6** broker
enforcement ~: **5** teeth **8** iron hand
exercise ~: **4** rule **5** wield **6** govern
friendly ~: **4** ally
give ~ to: **7** entitle, license **9** authorize
high ~: **3** nth
in Taoism: **3** teh
magic ~: **3** hex **4** mojo **5** spell
mental ~: **4** will **7** resolve
metaphorically: **5** reins
of choice: **7** freedom, liberty
org.: **3** REA, TVA
PA ~ plant: **3** TMI
paranormal ~: **3** ESP **10** sixth sense
personal ~: **8** clutches
plant: **5** hydro
problem: **5** surge **8** blackout, brownout
put in ~ again: **7** reelect **9** reinstate
put out of ~: **4** oust, vote **5** exile, usurp **6** depose
Roman emblem of ~: **6** fasces
run without ~: **5** coast, glide
sea ~: **4** navy **5** fleet **6** armada
second ~: **6** square
source: **3** gas, oil, sun **4** atom, elec., fuel, wind **5** motor, steam **6** engine
starter: **3** man **4** fire, will **5** brain, horse, super, water **6** candle
staying ~: **5** might, vigor **7** stamina **8** patience, strength **9** tolerance
supernatural ~: **5** magic **6** voodoo
third ~: **4** cube
to please: **5** charm **8** charisma **9** magnetism
train: **6** engine
unit: **2** hp, kw **4** watt **8** kilowatt, megawatt
up: **5** start **6** turn on
voting ~: **5** agent, proxy **8** delegate **9** franchise
water ~: **5** hydro
power __: **3** saw, set **4** base, dive, line, pack, play, tool, trip **5** brake, cable, chain, drill, elite, mower, plant, press, train **6** assist, broker, series, shovel, supply **7** forward, loading, station, takeoff
__ power: **3** air, man, nth, sea **4** gray, grey, land, veto, will, wind **5** green, solar, stock, water, world **6** atomic, buying, candle, flower, motive, police **7** nuclear, staying
Power, __ and Politics: **5** Pasta
Power and Glory author: Karel Capek
Power and the Glory, The (1933 film)
cast: Colleen Moore, Ralph Morgan, Spencer Tracy
PowerBook maker: **5** Apple
power-control mechanism: **5** servo
power-driven: **8** electric **10** electrical
__-powered: **4** high
powerful: **3** big, fit **4** able, hale, high, iron, loud, wiry **5** beefy, burly, hardy, hefty, hunky, husky, lusty, nervy, solid, stiff, stout, tough, vivid **6** brawny, cogent, hearty, mighty, potent, robust, rugged, ruling, sinewy, steely, stocky, strong, sturdy, virile **7** capable, doughty, dynamic, intense, orotund, supreme, telling, violent, weighty **8** athletic, dominant, dramatic, emphatic, forceful, indurate, muscular, puissant, stalwart, striking, vigorous **9** Atlantean, effective, effectual, energetic, extremely, heavy-duty, herculean, in control, paramount, sovereign, strapping, trenchant, well-built **10** able-bodied, commanding, compelling, convincing, formidable, impressive, omnipotent, overruling, persuasive, preeminent, prevailing, privileged, red-blooded
not ~: **4** puny, weak
one: **4** czar, lion, tsar **5** baron, mogul, mover, nabob, titan **6** shaker **7** magnate
__-powerful: **3** all
powerful eagle, name meaning: **6** Arnold
powerhouse: **6** dynamo **8** live wire, stalwart, tough guy
powerless: **4** puny, weak **5** at bay, frail, wimpy **6** anemic, atonic, effete, feeble, flabby, flimsy, infirm, unable **7** anaemic, fragile, unarmed, wimpish **8** delicate, helpless, pithless **9** dependant, dependent, faltering, incapable, prostrate **10** handcuffed, impuissant, unequipped, vulnerable
render ~: **2** KO **4** kayo, slug **5** unarm **7** capture
Powermaster: **3** car **4** auto **6** DeSoto
Power of Good-Bye, The (1998 song)
artist: Madonna
Power of Love (1972 song) artist: Celine Dion, Huey Lewis and the News, Joe Simon, Luther Vandross
Power of Positive Thinking, The
author: **5** Peale
Power of Words, The author: Edgar Allan Poe
Power Politics author: Margaret Atwood
Powers: **4** Joey, Mala **5** Hiram **6** Boothe **8** Stefanie
Powers, Austin: **3** spy **5** agent
Powers, Stefanie spouse: Gary Lockwood
powers that be: **3** ins
Powers That Be, The author: David Halberstam
Power, The (1968 film)
cast: Richard Carlson, George Hamilton, Suzanne Pleshette
power-tool name: **4** Skil **5** Black **6** Decker
Power to the People (1971 song)
artist: John Lennon
power train part: **4** gear
Power, Tyrone: **5** actor
film: Abandon Ship (1957)
Alexander's Ragtime Band (1938)
The Black Swan (1942)
Blood and Sand (1941)
Captain From Castile (1947)
Diplomatic Courier (1952)
In Old Chicago (1938)
Jesse James (1939)
Johnny Apollo (1940)
The Long Gray Line (1955)
The Mark of Zorro (1940)
Nightmare Alley (1947)
The Razor's Edge (1946)
Son of Fury (1942)
Suez (1938)
The Sun Also Rises (1957)
This Above All (1942)
Untamed (1955)
Witness for the Prosecution (1957)
A Yank in the RAF (1941)
Powhatan: **5** chief
daughter: **10** Pocahontas
son-in-law: **5** Rolfe
POW information: **4** name, rank **5** ser. no.
Pow, right in the __!: **6** kisser
Powter: **5** Susan
powwow: **4** chat, meet, talk **5** forum, rally **6** confab, confer, dialog, huddle, parley **7** consult, council, meeting, palaver **8** conclave, dialogue **9** gathering, touch base **10** conference, convention, discussion, round table
hold a ~: **6** huddle, parley **7** commune, palaver **8** converse **10** deliberate
Powys, J.C.: **4** poet **5** Welsh **6** author, writer
work: Wolf Solent
Powys, T.F.: **6** author, writer **7** British
work: The Left Leg
Mr Weston's Good Wine
The Two Thieves
Unclay
pox: **6** plague
starter: **3** cow **5** small, swine **7** chicken
Poza Rica: **4** city, town
locale: **6** Mexico **8** Veracruz
Poznan: **4** city, town
locale: **6** Poland
Pozzuoli: **4** city, port, town
locale: **5** Italy **8** Campania
ppd., not: **3** COD
Pr: **4** elem. **7** element **12** praseodymium
59 for ~: **4** at. no.
PR: **9** promotion, publicity
concern: **3** rep **5** image
gimmick: **2** ad **4** gift **5** promo **6** coupon, rebate **7** freebie, premium
job: **4** hype
person: **5** agent, flack **8** promoter **9** publicist **10** spin doctor
P.R.
see Puerto Rico
__ Prabang: **5** Luang
practicable: **3** fit **5** handy, utile **6** doable, likely, useful, viable **8** feasible, possible, workable
practical: **4** sane **5** handy, of use, sober, solid, sound, utile **6** doable, earthy, likely, usable, useful, viable **7** earthly, empiric, helpful, stopgap, useable, working, worldly **8** credible, feasible, positive, possible, rational, salutary, sensible, skillful, workable, workaday **9** effective, efficient, empirical, expedient, plausible, potential, pragmatic, realistic **10** achievable, attainable, economical, functional, hard-bitten, hard-boiled, hardheaded, imaginable, profitable, reasonable, unromantic
for all ~ purposes: **8** in effect **9** virtually
having ~ value: **5** handy, utile **6** usable, useful
joke: **4** dido, hoax **5** prank, trick **7** hotfoot
joker: **3** wag **4** zany **5** cutup, scamp
practical __: **4** joke **5** nurse **6** reason
practicality: **7** utility **10** horse sense
practically: **4** most, near, nigh **5** about **6** all but, almost, nearly **7** close to, morally **8** as good as, as much as, in effect, not quite, well-nigh **9** basically, in essence, in the main, just about, virtually
Practical Magic (1998 film)
cast: Sandra Bullock, Stockard Channing, Nicole Kidman, Aidan Quinn
director: Griffin Dunne
practice: **2** do **3** ism, job, use, way **4** form, hone, mode, rite, rule, wont, work **5** apply, drill, habit, study, train, trick, usage **6** action, career, custom, dry run, follow, go over, lesson, manner, method, policy, polish, praxis, pursue, repeat, ritual, system, tune-up, warmup **7** carry on, clients, fashion, iterate, observe, perform, prepare, process, routine, sharpen, workout **8** business, engage in, exercise, function, habitude, live up to, localism, patients, rehearse, training, transact, vocation **9** clientele, operation, procedure, rehearsal, shake-down, specialty, tradition, treatment, undertake **10** convention, discipline, experience, observance, profession, repetition, run through, specialize
current ~: **5** vogue **7** fashion
customary ~: **4** rite **9** tradition
diligently: **3** ply **5** exert, sweat
expel from ~: **6** disbar
out of ~: **5** rusty
prohibited ~: **4** no-no, tabu **5** taboo
__ practice: **5** choir, group **6** family **7** general, private
practiced: **3** ace **4** able, deft, neat **5** adept, crack **6** expert, versed **7** capable, skilled, veteran **8** habitual, masterly, seasoned, skillful **9** efficient, masterful, qualified **10** consummate, conversant, proficient, well-versed
Practice, The (ABC drama)
cast: Lara Flynn Boyle (Helen Gamble)
Steve Harris (Eugene Young)
Camryn Manheim (Ellenor Frutt)
Dylan McDermott (Bobby Donnell)
Kelli Williams (Lindsay Dole)
role: **6** lawyer
setting: Boston
Practice What You Preach (1994 song)
artist: Barry White
practitioner, general: **2** dr., MD **3** doc **5** medic **6** doctor, medico **8** sawbones **9** physician
__ Pradesh, India: **5** Uttar
Prado: **5** Perez **6** museum
display: **3** art **9** paintings
locale: **5** Spain **6** Madrid
Prado, Perez
nickname: The King of the Mambo
song: Cherry Pink and Apple Blossom White (1955)
Patricia (1958)
Praetorian
employer: **6** caesar **7** emperor
Praetorian __: **5** guard
praetor superior: **5** edile
pragmatic: **4** sane **5** sober, sound **6** cogent, useful **7** empiric, logical, tenable **8** analytic, coherent, methodic, rational, sensible **9** empirical, expedient, officious, practical, realistic **10** analytical, consistent, hard-bitten, hard-boiled, hardheaded, unromantic
believer: **5** deist
Prague: **4** city, town **5** Praha **7** capital
city near ~: **5** Plzen, Tabor
resident: **5** Czech
river: **6** Moldau **7** Vlatava
Prague Symphony composer: **6** Mozart
Praia: **4** city, town **7** capital
locale: **9** Cape Verde
prairie: **5** campo, llano, plain, plane, range **6** meadow, pampas **7** lowland, pasture, steppes **9** grassland
African ~: **4** veld **5** veldt
animal: **4** deer **6** coyote, ferret, rabbit **8** antelope **10** jackrabbit
predator: **6** coyote
schooner: **5** wagon
South American ~: **5** campo, pampa **6** pampas
prairie __: **3** dog, owl **4** fowl, lily, rose, wolf **5** skirt, smoke **6** clover, falcon, grouse, potato, turnip **7** breaker, chicken, pointer, warbler

prairie chicken: **4** fowl
relative: **5** poult, quail, snipe **6** chukar, grouse, peahen, turkey **7** peacock, peafowl **8** curassow, moorfowl, pheasant, woodcock **9** partridge **10** guinea fowl, jungle fowl, wild turkey
prairie dog: **6** rodent
female: **3** sow
male: **4** boar
predator: **6** ferret
relative: **3** rat **4** cavy, degu, jird, paca, vole **5** coypu, gundi, mouse, xerus **6** agouti, beaver, gerbil, gopher, jerboa, marmot, murine **7** hamster, lemming, muskrat, visacha **8** chipmunk, cricetid, dormouse, squirrel, tuco-tuco **9** chickaree, groundhog, guinea pig, porcupine, woodchuck **10** chinchilla
young: **3** pup
Prairie State: **3** Ill. **8** Illinois
Prairie, The author: James Fenimore Cooper
Prairie Village: **4** city, town
locale: **6** Kansas
praisable: **6** worthy **7** fitting **8** laudable **9** admirable, deserving, estimable, righteous **10** creditable
praise: **4** cite, clap, hail, hymn, laud, puff, rave, sing, tout **5** adore, bless, boost, cheer, cry up, éclat, ensky, exalt, extol, glory, honor, kudos, thank **6** admire, cajole, credit, esteem, eulogy, extoll, homage, honors, puff up, regard, salute, stroke, thanks **7** acclaim, adulate, applaud, approve, big hand, bow down, build up, commend, dignify, elevate, endorse, ennoble, flatter, glorify, hosanna, indorse, laurels, lay it on, lionize, ovation, plaudit, smile on, tribute, worship **8** accolade, advocate, applause, approval, citation, encomium, eulogize, flattery, good word, gush over, hand it to, plaudits, proclaim, sanctify, sanction **9** adoration, adulation, celebrate, encourage, extolment, laudation, obeisance, panegyric, pay homage, recommend, reverence, warm fuzzy **10** admiration, aggrandize, appreciate, be gracious, compliment, exaltation, give thanks, make much of, panegyrize, pay tribute, sycophancy
ender: **6** worthy
from the audience: **5** brava, bravo **6** encore **9** standing O
high ~: **4** kudo **5** kudos **8** emcomium
hymn of ~: **3** ode **4** pean **5** paean, psalm
name meaning ~: **5** Judah **8** Thaddeus
offer faint ~: **4** damn
oneself: **4** brag, crow **5** boast
opposite of ~: **5** knock **8** belittle
overblown ~: **4** hype, plug, puff, rave **5** promo **7** puffery **9** publicity
overly: **4** gush, hype, rave
shout of ~: **7** hosanna **10** hallelujah
word of ~: **4** good
Praise Singer, The author: Mary Renault
Praise to the End author: Theodore Roethke
praiseworthy: **4** fine, good, nice, okay **5** great, legit, moral, noble **6** proper **7** ethical, stellar **8** all right, laudable, pleasant, pleasing, splendid, superior, virtuous **9** admirable, agreeable, estimable, excellent, exemplary, honorable, reputable, righteous, wonderful **10** acceptable, beneficial, creditable
praline: **4** nosh **5** candy, snack, sweet
ingredient: **3** nut **5** pecan, sugar **6** almond **10** brown sugar
pram: **5** buggy **7** vehicle **8** carriage
pusher: **4** nana **5** nanny **6** nannie
Pran: **4** Dith
prance: **4** jump, leap, romp, skip, step, walk **5** bound, caper, dance, frisk, mince, strut, vault, waltz **6** cavort, frolic, gambol, parade, sashay, spring **7** flounce, show off, swagger **9** have a ball
Prancer: **8** reindeer
colleague: **5** Comet, Cupid, Vixen **6** Dancer, Dasher, Donder **7** Blitzen
Prancer (1989 film)
cast: Sam Elliott, Cloris Leachman
director: John Hancock
prank: **3** gag **4** dido, game, hoax, jape, jest, joke, lark, play, quiz, trap, trim **5** antic, caper, put-on, spoof, sport, trick **6** frolic **7** hotfoot **8** escapade, mischief **9** capriccio, high jinks, horseplay, vandalism **10** shenanigan, tomfoolery
prankster: **3** wag **4** brat, zany **5** clown, cutup, joker, scamp **6** jester, rascal **8** funnyman
praseodymium: **7** element **9** rare earth
prate: **3** gab, gas, rot, yak, yap **4** blab, blah, bosh, bull, bunk, carp, chat, guff, gush, jazz, jive, pooh, talk, tosh **5** bilge, bleat, fudge, hokum, hooey, run on, stuff, trash, tripe **6** babble, bunkum, bushwa, drivel, footle, gabble, gammon, gibber, gossip, havers, hot air, humbug, jabber, jargon, kibosh, patter, piffle, rattle, tattle, yammer **7** baloney, blarney, blather, blether, boloney, bushwah, chatter, eyewash, flannel, flubdub, fustian, garbage, hogwash, inanity, palaver, rubbish, twaddle **8** babbling, blabbing, buncombe, chitchat, claptrap, falderal, falderol, fast talk, flimflam, flummery, folderal, folderol, idle talk, nonsense, ramble on, slipslop, talk idly, tommyrot, trumpery **9** banana oil, gibberish, gossiping, jabbering, kidstakes, moonshine, poppycock, prattling, rigmarole, table talk **10** applesauce, balderdash, bilge water, blathering, chattering, chew the rag, codswallop, double-talk, empty words, flapdoodle, galimatias, Jabberwock, mumbo jumbo, rigamarole, taradiddle, yackety-yak
pratfall, do a: **4** slip, trip **6** topple
pratincole: **4** bird
Prato: **4** city, town
locale: **5** Italy
Pratt, E.J.: **4** poet **8** Canadian
prattle: **3** gab, jaw, yak, yap **4** blab, chat, gush, talk **6** babble, drivel, footle, gabble, gibber, gossip, jabber, patter, rattle, speech, tattle **7** blather, blether, chatter, twaddle **8** babbling, nonsense, ramble on, rattle on **9** gibberish **10** chew the rag, vocalizing
prattler: **6** gossip **10** chatterbox, motor mouth
Prattville: **4** city, town
locale: **7** Alabama
Pravda: **9** newspaper
cofounder: **5** Lenin
source: **4** Tass **8** ITAR-Tass
__ Prawer Jhabvala: **4** Ruth
prawn: **6** shrimp **7** seafood **10** crustacean
combining form: **5** -caris
praxis: **3** use **4** wont **5** habit, usage **6** custom **8** practice **10** convention
Praxis: **4** font **8** typeface
pray: **3** ask, beg, sue **4** urge **5** plead **6** adjure, appeal, cry for, invoke **7** beseech, entreat, implore, request, solicit, worship **8** call upon, petition, say grace **9** importune **10** supplicate
in Latin: **3** ora
place to ~: **5** altar **6** chapel, church, shrine, temple **8** prie-dieu **9** cathedral
__ pray: **5** let us
Pray (1990 song) artist: M.C. Hammer
prayer: **4** plea, suit **5** chant, grace **6** appeal, litany, mantra, orison, rosary **7** request, service, worship **8** devotion, entreaty, petition, rogation **9** adoration, communion **10** invocation
beads: **4** mala **6** rosary
beginning: **5** O Lord
Catholic ~: **3** ave **6** novena, rosary
ending: **4** amen **5** svaha
Hopi ~ stick: **4** paho
hour: **4** sext **5** lauds, nones, prime **6** matins, tierce **7** complin, vespers **8** compline
house of ~: **4** shul **5** schul, zendo **6** chapel, church, shrine, temple **8** lamasery **9** cathedral, monastery, synagogue
Islamic ~: **4** raka **5** salah, salat
liturgical ~: **3** ave **5** kyrie **6** mantra **10** invocation
meal ~: **5** grace
not a ~: **8** high-risk, hopeless **10** impossible
start of a children's ~: **4** now I
synagogue ~: **5** shema **6** Hallel
vestment: **4** wrap **5** cloak
wear: **5** robes, shawl **8** vestment
prayer __: **3** rug **4** book, flag **5** beads, plant, shawl, wheel **7** meeting, service
Prayer for Owen Meany, A author: John Irving
prayerful: **5** pious **9** religious
prayer wheel user: **4** lama **5** geshe, tulku **6** khenpo
praying
figure: **5** orans, orant **6** orante
mantis: **3** bug **6** insect
Praying for Rain author: Jerome Weidman
Praying for Time (1990 song) artist: George Michael
pre-__ show: **4** game
pre-__ student: **3** law, med
__ Pré: **5** Grand
preach: **4** talk **5** orate, scold **6** advise, exhort **7** address, lecture **8** admonish, harangue, homilize, moralize, perorate, prophesy **9** exprobate, preachify, sermonize **10** evangelize
preacher: **5** padre, vicar **6** cleric, curate, divine, father, orator, parson, pastor **7** apostle **8** chaplain, minister, reverend **10** evangelist, missionary
bird: **5** vireo
degree: **3** Th.D.
spot: **5** altar **6** church
word: **4** amen
Preacher: **3** Roe
__ Preacher Man: **6** Son-of-a
Preacher's Wife, The (1996 film)
cast: Gregory Hines, Whitney Houston, Courtney B. Vance, Denzel Washington
director: Penny Marshall
Preakness: **4** race **9** horse race
competitor: **4** pony **5** horse **9** racehorse
prize: **5** purse
preamble: **5** intro, proem **6** prolog **7** opening, preface, prelude **8** exordium, foreword, prologue **9** beginning
prearrange: **3** fix, rig **5** set up **7** bespeak, reserve **10** foreordain
prearranged: **3** set **5** meant **8** intended **10** purposeful, volitional
prebend: **8** benefice
prebendary: **6** cleric
Precambrian: **3** Era
precarious: **4** iffy **5** dicey, hairy, risky, rocky, shaky, tight **6** chancy, jiggly, loaded, touchy, tricky, unfirm, unsafe, unsure, wabbly, wobbly **7** dubious, rickety **8** delicate, doubtful, dynamite, insecure, perilous, ticklish, unstable, unsteady **9** dangerous, hazardous, on thin ice, sensitive, uncertain **10** touch-and-go, unreliable
precariousness: **4** risk **6** danger **8** jeopardy
precaution: **4** care **7** defense **8** prudence, security, wariness **9** canniness, foresight, insurance, provision, safeguard **10** discretion, protection
as a ~: **6** in case **10** just in case
precede: **4** lead **5** usher **6** forego, lead to, ring in **7** go first, predate, preface, presage **8** announce, antedate, run ahead **9** come first, go ahead of, introduce **10** anticipate, come before
precedence: **4** lead, rank **8** priority **9** advantage, immediacy, seniority **10** importance, right of way
take ~: **8** outweigh
precedent: **4** rule **5** model **6** custom **7** example **8** exemplar, instance **9** authority, criterion, foregoing
__ precedent: **4** set a
preceding: **3** ere **4** late, past **5** older, prior, supra **6** before, former **7** ahead of, earlier, leading, one-time, prior to **8** anterior, long gone, previous, until now **9** aforesaid, erstwhile, foregoing, in advance **10** heretofore
precentor: **6** cleric
precept: **3** ism, law **4** rule **5** adage, axiom, bylaw, canon, dogma, edict, maxim, moral, motto, order, tenet, truth **6** behest, belief, byword, decree, dictum, lesson, ruling, saying **7** bidding, command, dictate, formula, mandate, statute **8** aphorism, doctrine **9** direction, guideline, ordinance, principle, teachings **10** convention, ground rule, injunction, regulation
cultural ~: **5** ethic, ethos **9** moral code
preceptor: **4** guru **5** tutor **6** expert, lector, master, sensei **7** teacher **9** abecedary, principal, professor **10** instructor
pre-Christmas period: **6** Advent
precinct: **4** area, ward, zone **5** field, limit **6** region, sector, sphere **7** quarter, section **8** district, division, vicinity **10** department
worker: **3** cop **9** policeman **11** policewoman
precious: **2** jo **3** pet **4** baby, cute, dear, jill, love, rare, rich **5** amour, angel, chéri, cooky, cutey, cutie, deary, ducky, flame, honey, leman, loved, lover, lovey, novia, novio, sugar, sweet **6** adored, bon ami, chérie, cookie, costly, cutesy, dainty, dautie, dearie, golden, prissy, prized, steady, sweets, valued **7** beloved, darling, dearest, dear one, finicky, lovable, mincing, pigsney, schatzi, squeeze, sweetie, tootsie **8** adorable, chou-chou, cutie pie, dowsabel, dulcinea, finiking, finnicky, idolized, ladylove, loveable, lovebird, macushla, overnice, paramour, snookums, sugar pie, sweetums, truelove, uncommon, valuable **9** bonne amie, boyfriend, cherished, dreamboat, expensive, exquisite, inamorata, inamorato, petit chou, priceless, recherché, treasured, valentine **10** fastidious, girlfriend, heartthrob, high-priced, honeybunch, invaluable, mavourneen, sweetheart,

sweetie pie, turtledove
gem: 4 opal, ruby 5 jewel, pearl, stone, topaz 7 diamond, emerald 8 sapphire
metal: 4 gold 6 silver 8 platinum
resource: 4 time 5 water 6 health
Precious and Few (1972 song) artist: Climax
precipice: 4 crag, edge 5 bluff, brink, cliff, scarp 6 height 8 mountain, palisade 10 escarpment, prominence
precipitance: 4 rush 5 haste, hurry, speed 8 rapidity 10 expedition
precipitate: 4 drop, hail, hurl, rain, rash, snow, spur 5 brash, cause, fling, hasty, hurry, sleet, spark, swift, throw 6 abrupt, hasten, launch, let fly, rushed, shower, sudden 7 advance, bring on, distill, drizzle, frantic, hurried, provoke, quicken, speed up, trigger 8 catapult, dizzying, engender, expedite, headlong, heedless, previous, reckless, sediment, sprinkle 9 breakneck, foolhardy, impatient, impetuous, impulsive 10 accelerate, uncautious
heavily: 4 pour, teem 5 flood
precipitateness: 4 rush 5 haste, hurry, speed 8 rapidity 10 expedition
precipitation: 4 hail, rain, snow 5 sleet, storm 7 drizzle, wetness 8 moisture, rainfall 9 hailstorm, rainstorm
that doesn't reach the ground: 5 virga
winter ~: 4 snow 5 sleet
precipitiously: 7 in a rush 8 pell-mell 9 headfirst
precipitous: 4 rash 5 hasty, rapid, sharp, sheer, steep, swift 6 abrupt, craggy, rushed, sudden 7 cragged, hurried 8 dizzying, headlong, heedless, plunging, reckless, straight 9 impetuous, impulsive
précis: 5 brief, recap 6 aperçu, digest, report, résumé, sketch, survey 7 outline, rundown, summary 8 abstract, syllabus, synopsis 10 abridgment, compendium, literature
Precis: 3 car 4 auto 10 Mitsubishi
precise: 4 fine, just, neat, nice, true 5 clean, clear, exact, fixed, fussy, level, picky, right, rigid, short, sound, valid 6 direct, minute, proper, strict 7 bookish, careful, correct, express, factual, finicky, graphic, limited, obvious, perfect, prudish, refined, regular, specify 8 absolute, accurate, clear-cut, concrete, decisive, definite, delicate, detailed, distinct, exacting, explicit, faithful, finiking, finnicky, flawless, incisive, methodic, on the dot, readable, rigorous, specific, truthful, unerring 9 definable, errorless, graphical, sensitive, stringent 10 definitive, fastidious, impeccable, inflexible, methodical, meticulous, on the money, particular, scientific, scrupulous, systematic, unmistaken, well-marked
don't be ~: 5 guess, round 8 estimate
precisely: 3 aye, oui, pat, yea, yep, yes, yup 4 fine, just, okay, sure, to a T, yeah 5 good-o, natch, plumb, quite, right, roger, sharp, smack, spang, uh-huh 6 agreed, dead-on, gladly, good-oh, indeed, just so, rather, really, righto, surely, to a tee, you bet, yowzah 7 exactly, go ahead, indeedy, mais oui, quite so, right on, ten-four 8 all right, as you say, directly, of course, smack-dab, squarely, thumbs up, verbatim, very well 9 be my guest, carefully, certainly, correctly, darn right, doubtless, expressly, just right, literally, literatim, naturally, on the nose, sure thing, you betcha, you said it 10 absolutely, accurately, by all means, definitely, delicately, positively, sure enough, that's right, unerringly
precision: 4 care 5 rigor, truth 7 clarity 8 accuracy, fidelity, veracity 9 attention, clockwork, exactness 10 exactitude, factuality, perfection, refinement
preclude: 3 bar 4 curb, foil, omit, veto 5 avert, check, debar, deter 6 enjoin, forbid, hamper, hinder, impede, thwart 7 exclude, forfend, head off, inhibit, obviate, prevent, rule out, ward off 8 forefend, prohibit, stave off 9 foreclose, forestall, frustrate, interdict
precocious: 3 apt 5 early, quick, smart 6 bright, gifted, mature 7 forward 8 advanced, talented 9 brilliant 10 beforehand
precognition: 3 ESP 4 vibe 5 hunch, vibes 8 prophecy 9 intuition
pre-college: 4 el-hi
pre-Columbian: 3 old 7 ancient
civilization: 4 Inca, Maya 5 Aztec, Olmec 6 Mixtec 7 Zapotec
preconception: 4 bias, tilt 5 slant 6 notion 7 bigotry, leaning 8 delusion, illusion 9 prejudice 10 partiality
precondition: 2 if 4 must 9 condition, determine, necessity, requisite
precursor: 4 sign 6 herald, leader 7 symptom 8 ancestor, forebear, original, vanguard 9 harbinger, messenger, prototype 10 antecedent, forebearer, forefather, forerunner, progenitor
precursory: 10 antecedent
predacious: 6 fierce 8 ravaging 9 ferocious, on the hunt, vulturous 10 aggressive
predate: 7 precede 8 antecede
predating life, in geology: 5 azoic
predator: 3 cat, man, owl 4 hawk, lion, mako, puma, wolf 5 dingo, eagle, harpy, human, shark, tiger 6 coyote, hunter 7 brigand, panther 9 carnivore, meat-eater, polar bear 10 highwayman
move like a ~: 5 prowl
nocturnal ~: 3 owl
quarry: 4 prey
Predator (1987 film)
cast: Elpidia Carrillo, Arnold Schwarzenegger, Carl Weathers
director: John McTiernan
Predator rival: 4 Blue, King, Star, Wild 5 Bruin, Devil, Flame, Flyer, Oiler, Sabre, Shark 6 Canuck, Coyote, Ranger 7 Capital, Panther, Penguin, Red Wing, Senator 8 Canadien, Islander, Thrasher 9 Avalanche, Blackhawk, Hurricane, Lightning, Maple Leaf 10 Blue Jacket, Mighty Duck
Predators
home: 9 Nashville
org.: 3 NHL
sport: 6 hockey
Predators, The author: Harold Robbins
predatory: 6 greedy, lupine 7 wolfish 8 ravaging, ravening, ravenous, thieving, thievish 9 ferocious, marauding, on the hunt, pillaging, piratical, rapacious, raptorial, voracious, vulturine, vulturous 10 aggressive, plundering
predecessor: 6 father, mother 8 forebear 9 precursor
predestination: 3 lot 4 doom, fate 5 karma 6 kismet 7 fortune
predestine: 4 doom, fate 9 determine, preordain 10 foreordain
predestined: 5 fated 6 doomed 7 certain
predetermined: 3 set 5 fated, fixed 7 decided, planned 8 destined 10 deliberate
predicament: 3 fix, jam, rub 4 bind, hole, mess, node, pass, soup, spot, stew 5 event, pinch, state 6 clutch, corner, crisis, matter, muddle, pickle, plight, scrape, strait 7 dilemma, impasse, problem, rough go, trouble 8 exigence, exigency, hardship, headache, hot water, juncture, position, quagmire, quandary 9 deep water, imbroglio
Predicament, A author: Edgar Allan Poe
predicate: 4 aver, base, rest 5 imply 6 affirm, assert 7 bespeak, connote, declare, express, profess, signify, suggest 8 indicate, intimate, maintain, proclaim, put forth, set forth 9 establish, postulate, represent
part: 4 verb
predict: 4 call, warn 5 augur, guess 6 divine, figure, gather, size up 7 betoken, foresee, portend, presage, project, surmise 8 envisage, envision, estimate, forebode, forecast, foreshow, foretell, prophesy, soothsay, theorize 9 adumbrate, see coming 10 anticipate, conjecture, foreshadow, have a hunch, vaticinate
predictability: 8 sameness
predictable: 4 sure 5 usual 6 likely 7 certain 8 expected, foreseen, probable, reliable, sure-fire
prediction: 3 tip 4 omen, sign 5 guess, hunch 6 augury, oracle, tipoff 7 portent, warning 8 estimate, forecast, prophecy 9 horoscope, indicator, palmistry, prognosis 10 divination, expectancy, foreboding
weather ~: 3 dry 4 fair, gale, hail, rain, snow 5 clear, gusty, rainy, sleet, storm, sunny, windy 6 breezy, cloudy 7 tornado 8 overcast
predictor: 4 omen, seer, sign 5 augur, sibyl 6 shaman 7 diviner, portent, prophet 9 harbinger 10 forecaster, soothsayer
predilection: 4 bent, bias, dish 5 fancy, slant, taste 6 liking, relish 7 faculty, leaning 8 appetite, aptitude, attitude, cup of tea, druthers, fondness, penchant, tendency, weakness 9 proneness, sentiment 10 partiality, proclivity, propensity
predispose: 4 bend, bias, sway 5 prime 6 affect, govern, induce, prompt 7 dispose, impress, incline, inspire, prepare 8 activate, motivate 9 determine, encourage, influence, prejudice, stimulate
predisposed: 5 prone, ready 6 biased, liable, likely 7 partial, subject, tending, willing 8 amenable, inclined, prepared 9 agreeable
predisposition: 4 bent, bias 5 slant 6 liking 7 leaning 8 instinct, penchant, tendency, weakness 9 proneness
predominance: 4 sway 5 power 9 supremacy
predominant: 4 best, main, star 5 chief, first, major, prime 6 ruling, staple 7 central, leading, primary, rampant, supreme, weighty 8 forceful, powerful, reigning, superior 9 ascendant, governing, important, paramount, prevalent, principal, prominent, sovereign, uppermost
part: 4 bulk 8 majority 9 plurality 10 lion's share
predominantly: 6 mainly, mostly 7 largely, overall 9 primarily
predominate: 4 rule 5 reign 6 govern 7 command, prevail, surpass 8 hold sway, outweigh, overrule 9 sovereign
pre-election event: 4 poll 6 debate 8 campaign 10 convention
preemie: 4 baby 6 infant
preeminence: 4 fame 6 renown 8 dominion, prestige, priority 9 supremacy 10 precedence
preeminent: 3 top 4 A-one, arch, best, head, main, star, tops 5 chief, famed, first, grand, major, noble, noted 6 famous, ruling, utmost 7 honored, in front, leading, stellar, supreme 8 absolute, cardinal, dominant, foremost, greatest, peerless, powerful, renowned, superior, towering, ultimate 9 governing, important, matchless, number one, paramount, principal, prominent, topflight, unequaled, unrivaled, uppermost, virtuosic, worthiest 10 celebrated, consummate, unequalled, unrivalled
preeminently: 8 above all
preempt: 4 bump, take 5 co-opt, seize, usurp 6 assume, obtain 7 acquire 8 arrogate, take over 10 anticipate, commandeer, confiscate
preempted: 5 not on
preemptive __: 5 right 6 strike
preen: 5 gloat, groom, pride, primp, prink 6 doll up, dude up 7 dress up, gussy up, swank up 8 titivate 9 tittivate
preener: 3 fop 4 bird 5 dandy 7 peacock
pre-engage: 4 book 7 charter, reserve
preening, prone to: 4 smug, vain 5 proud 9 conceited 10 complacent
pre-entrée course: 4 soup 5 salad 9 appetizer
preestablished: 3 set 5 fixed
preexisting: 5 prior
preface: 5 begin, intro, proem, usher 6 launch, prolog 7 precede, prelude 8 commence, exordium, foreword, lead into, overture, preamble, prologue 9 beginning, introduce
prefer: 3 opt, put 4 cull, lean, like, love, pick, take, want 5 adopt, elect, fancy, favor, go for 6 choose, desire, opt for, select 7 elevate, fix upon 9 single out
charges: 3 sue 9 prosecute
preferable: 6 better 8 superior
preferably: 6 rather, sooner 7 instead 10 just as soon
preference: 4 bent, bias, pick, will 5 fancy, taste, voice 6 choice, desire, liking, option 7 leaning 8 cup of tea, decision, druthers, favorite, fondness, pleasure, priority, volition 9 advantage, proneness, selection, seniority 10 favoritism, propensity
preferment: 8 benefice 9 elevation
preferred: 3 pet 5 liked, named, taken 6 choice, chosen, culled, picked, select 7 elected, fancied, favored, popular 8 approved, endorsed, favorite, selected, set apart, superior 10 fair-haired, handpicked
group: 5 A-list, elite
item: 4 fave
prefigure: 8 foreshow 9 adumbrate, foretoken 10 foreshadow
pre-film feature: 5 short
prefixes (by meaning)
about: 4 peri-
above: 3 sur- 5 hyper-, super-, supra-
absence: 3 dis-, non-
accurate: 4 docu-
across: 3 dia- 5 trans-
adverse: 7 counter-
advocating: 3 pro-
Africa: 4 Afro-
after: 3 epi- 4 meta-, post- 5 infra-
again: 3 ana-
against: 3 cat- 4 anti-, cata-, cath- 6 contra-
all: 4 omni-
alone: 4 mono-
among: 5 inter-
around: 4 peri- 6 circum-
Austria: 6 Austro-

away: 3 apo-
backward: 3 ana- 5 retro-
bad: 3 dys-, mal-
before: 3 pre-, pro- 4 ante-, fore-
behind: 4 meta-, post- 5 retro-
below: 3 sub- 5 infra-, under- 6 contra-
beneath: 4 hypo- 5 under-
beside: 4 para-
besides: 3 epi-
between: 5 inter-
beyond: 3 out- 4 meta-, para- 5 extra-, hyper-, trans-, ultra- 6 preter-
billion: 4 giga-
both: 4 ambi- 5 amphi-
center: 3 mid-
Chinese: 4 Sino-
computer: 5 cyber-
contrary: 5 retro- 7 counter-
culture: 5 ethno-
double: 3 twi-
down: 3 cat- 4 cata-, cath-, hypo-
during: 3 dia- 5 intra-
earlier: 3 pre-, pro- 4 ante-, fore-
earth: 3 geo-
eight: 4 octa-, octo-
English: 5 Anglo-
environment: 3 eco-
equal: 3 iso-
Europe: 4 Euro-
excessive: 3 sur- 5 hyper-
excessively: 4 over- 5 ultra-
exclude: 3 dis-, for-
extra: 5 super-
fail: 3 for-
false: 6 pseudo-
farming: 4 agri-
Finnish: 5 Finno-
first: 5 archi-, proto-
fluorine: 6 fluoro-
foremost: 5 proto-
four: 5 tetra- 6 quadri-
French: 6 Franco-
front: 4 fore-
great: 4 maxi- 5 macro-
half: 4 demi-, hemi-, semi-
heat: 6 thermo-
higher: 5 super-, supra-
hundred: 5 centi-, hecto-
ill: 3 dys-, mal-, mis-
immunity: 6 immuno-
incorrect: 3 mis-
India: 4 Indo-
into: 5 intro-
inward: 5 intro-
itself: 4 self-
jointly: 3 col-, com-, con-
large: 4 maxi- 5 macro-
later: 4 meta-, post- 5 infra-
lesser: 5 under-
life: 3 bio-
light: 5 photo-
like: 3 sym-, syn-
long: 5 macro-
lower: 3 sub- 5 infra-
machine: 7 mechano-
magnetic: 7 magneto-
many: 4 poly- 5 multi-
mercury: 7 mercuro-
metal: 7 metallo-
methyl: 4 meth-
million: 4 mega-
modified: 3 neo-
more: 5 super-
much: 4 poly-
mutual: 5 inter-
nature: 3 eco-
near: 3 epi- 4 peri-, pros-
nearer: 3 cis-
nerve: 5 neuro-
new: 3 neo-
nitrogen: 5 nitro-
not: 3 dis-, non-
nucleus: 6 nucleo-
off: 3 apo-
oil: 5 petro-
omit: 3 for-
one: 3 uni- 4 mono-
one and a half: 6 sesqui-
oneself: 4 self-
on this side: 3 cis-
opposite: 3 dis- 4 anti- 7 counter-
outside: 5 extra-
outward: 5 extro-
over: 3 epi-, sur- 5 hyper-, super-
past: 4 para- 6 preter-
principal: 5 archi-
prior: 3 pre-, pro- 4 ante-
prohibit: 3 for-
quadrillionth: 5 femto-
quintillionth: 4 atto-
race: 5 ethno-
radiation: 5 radio-
recent: 3 neo-
reciprocal: 5 inter-
related by remarriage: 4 step-
resembling: 5 quasi-
reverse: 3 dis-, non-
round: 4 peri- 6 circum-
Russia: 5 Russo-
same: 4 auto-, equi-
secondary: 3 sub-
self: 4 auto-
separate: 3 apo-
seven: 5 hepta-, septi-
since: 3 cis-
single: 4 mono-
six: 4 hexa-
small: 4 mini- 5 micro-
society: 5 socio-
solid: 6 stereo-
spectrum: 7 spectro-
stars: 5 astro-
sulfur: 5 sulfo-
supporting: 3 pro-
surpass: 3 out-
surround: 6 circum-
synchronized: 7 synchro-
ten: 4 deca-, deka-
tenth: 4 deci-
thoroughly: 3 per-
thousand: 4 kilo-
thousandth: 5 milli-
three: 3 tri-
through: 3 dia-, per- 5 trans-
together: 3 col-, com-, con-, sym-, syn-
too: 4 over-
toward: 4 pros-
transcending: 5 ultra-
true: 4 docu-
turbine: 5 turbo-
two: 3 twi- 5 amphi-
under: 3 sub- 4 hypo-
underneath: 5 intra-
unreal: 6 pseudo-
upon: 3 epi-
upward: 3 ana-
water: 4 aqua- 5 hydro-
with: 3 col-, com-, con-, sym-, syn-
within: 5 infra-, intra-, intro-
wrong: 3 mis-
wrongful: 3 mal-
see also combining forms

prefixes (by root)
Afro-: 6 Africa
agri-: 7 farming
ambi-: 4 both
amphi-: 3 two 4 both
ana-: 5 again 6 upward 8 backward
Anglo-: 7 English
ante-: 5 prior 6 before 7 earlier
anti-: 7 against 8 opposite
apo-: 3 off 4 away 8 separate
aqua-: 5 water
archi-: 5 first 9 principal
astro-: 5 stars
Austro-: 7 Austria
auto-: 4 same, self
bio-: 4 life
cat-: 4 down 7 against
cata-: 4 down 7 against
cath-: 4 down 7 against
centi-: 7 hundred
circum-: 5 round 6 around 8 surround
cis-: 5 since 6 nearer
col-: 4 with 7 jointly 8 together
com-: 4 with 7 jointly 8 together
con-: 4 with 7 jointly 8 together
contra-: 5 below 7 against
counter-: 7 adverse 8 contrary, opposite
cyber-: 8 computer
deca-: 3 ten
deci-: 5 tenth
deka-: 3 ten
demi-: 4 half
dia-: 6 across, during 7 through
dis-: 3 not 7 absence, exclude, reverse 8 opposite
docu-: 4 true 8 accurate
dys-: 3 bad, ill
eco-: 6 nature
epi-: 4 near, over, upon 5 after 7 besides
equi-: 4 same
ethno-: 4 race 7 culture
Euro-: 6 Europe
extra-: 6 beyond 7 outside
extro-: 7 outward
Finno-: 7 Finnish
fluoro-: 8 fluorine
for-: 4 fail, omit 7 exclude 8 prohibit
fore-: 5 front 6 before 7 earlier
Franco-: 6 French
geo-: 5 earth
giga-: 7 billion
hecto-: 7 hundred
hemi-: 4 half
hepta-: 5 seven
hexa-: 3 six
hydro-: 5 water
hyper-: 4 over 5 above 6 beyond 9 excessive
hypo-: 4 down 5 under 7 beneath
immuno-: 8 immunity
Indo-: 5 India
infra-: 5 after, below, later, lower 6 within
inter-: 5 among 6 mutual 7 between 10 reciprocal
intra-: 6 during, within 10 underneath
intro-: 4 into 6 inward, within
iso-: 5 equal
kilo-: 8 thousand
macro-: 4 long 5 great, large
magneto-: 8 magnetic
mal-: 3 bad, ill 8 wrongful
maxi-: 5 great, large
mechano-: 7 machine
mega-: 7 million
mercuro-: 7 mercury
meta-: 5 after, later 6 behind, beyond
metallo-: 5 metal
meth-: 6 methyl
micro-: 5 small
mid-: 6 center
milli-: 10 thousandth
mini-: 5 small
mis-: 3 ill 5 wrong 9 incorrect
mono-: 3 one 5 alone 6 single
multi-: 4 many
neo-: 3 new 6 recent 8 modified
neuro-: 5 nerve
nitro-: 8 nitrogen
non-: 3 not 7 absence, reverse
nucleo-: 7 nucleus
octa-: 5 eight
octo-: 5 eight
omni-: 3 all
out-: 6 beyond 7 surpass
over-: 3 too
para-: 4 past 6 beside, beyond
per-: 7 through 10 thoroughly
peri-: 4 near 5 about, round 6 around
petro-: 3 oil
photo-: 5 light
poly-: 4 many, much
post-: 5 after, later 6 behind
pre-: 5 prior 6 before 7 earlier
preter-: 4 past 6 beyond
pro-: 5 prior 6 before 7 earlier 10 advocating, supporting
pros-: 4 near 6 toward
proto-: 5 first 8 foremost
pseudo-: 5 false 6 unreal
quadri-: 4 four
quasi-: 10 resembling
radio-: 9 radiation
retro-: 6 behind 8 backward, contrary
Russo-: 6 Russia
self-: 6 itself 7 oneself
semi-: 4 half
septi-: 5 seven
Sino-: 7 Chinese
socio-: 7 society
spectro-: 8 spectrum
stereo-: 5 solid
sub-: 5 below, lower, under 9 secondary
sulfo-: 6 sulfur
super-: 4 more, over 5 above, extra 6 higher
supra-: 5 above 6 higher
sur-: 4 over 5 above 9 excessive
sym-: 4 like, with 8 together
syn-: 4 like, with 8 together
tetra-: 4 four
thermo-: 4 heat
trans-: 6 across, beyond 7 through
tri-: 5 three
turbo-: 7 turbine
twi-: 3 two 6 double
ultra-: 6 beyond
under-: 5 below 6 lesser 7 beneath
uni-: 3 one

pre-game __: 4 show
Pregl, Fritz: 7 chemist 8 Austrian, Nobelist
pregnancy: 9 gestation, gravidity
pregnant: 6 gravid 7 pivotal 8 critical, decisive, enceinte, eventful 9 expectant, expecting, important, momentous, with child 10 meaningful
Prego: 10 pasta sauce
competitor: 4 Ragu 6 Prince 8 Classico 10 Newman's Own 11 Aunt Millie's
prehistoric: 7 ancient, antique 8 primeval 9 primaeval
axe head: 4 Celt
discovery: 4 fire
dwelling: 4 cave
Great Plains culture: 6 Folsom
invention: 5 wheel
shelter: 4 abri
stone tower: 6 chulpa 7 chullpa
tool: 3 axe 4 adze 5 burin 6 eolith
pre-holiday night: 3 eve
pre-Inca culture: 5 Chimu
preindication: 4 omen, sign 6 herald
pre-intermission period: 4 Act I 5 Act II
prejudge: 8 misjudge 9 prejudice
prejudice: 4 bias, harm, hurt, skew, sway 5 slant, spoil 6 ageism, damage, enmity, hinder, impair, injure, poison 7 bigotry, distort, incline, mindset 8 aversion, jaundice, prejudge 9 animosity, antipathy, detriment, influence, injustice 10 chauvinism, compromise, disservice, fanaticism, favoritism, inequality, narrowness, partiality, predispose, unfairness, unjustness
prejudiced: 6 biased, narrow, unfair, unjust 7 bigoted, insular, partial 8 one-sided, partisan 9 arbitrary, fanatical, jaundiced, parochial 10 interested, intolerant

Prejudices author: H.L. Mencken
prejudicial: 6 biased, unjust 7 bigoted, harmful, hurtful 8 damaging 9 injurious
prelacy: 3 see 6 clergy 7 diocese 9 bishopric 10 episcopate
prelate: 4 pope 6 bishop, cleric 7 pontiff 8 cardinal, minister 10 archbishop
headdress: 5 miter
tribunal: 4 rota
pre-law exam: 4 LSAT
prelection: 4 talk 7 lecture 9 discourse
prelim: 5 event, intro 6 lead-in
preliminary: 4 test 5 basic, first, pilot, prior, rough, trial 7 initial, opening, prelude, sketchy 9 beginning, elemental, preceding, prefatory, requisite
race: 4 heat 5 trial
text: 5 draft
Prell: 7 shampoo
competitor: 4 Flex, Pert 5 Suave, Wella 7 Finesse, Pantene
Prelog, Vladimir: 7 chemist 8 Nobelist 11 Yugoslavian
prelude: 5 intro, music, proem, start 6 prolog 7 preface 8 exordium, foreword, overture, preamble, prologue 9 beginning
Prelude: 3 car 4 auto 5 Honda
__ Préludes: 3 Les
Prelude to a Kiss (1992 film)
cast: Alec Baldwin, Kathy Bates, Ned Beatty, Meg Ryan
director: Norman René
pre-marriage: 3 née
premature: 4 rash 5 early, hasty 6 unripe 7 forward, too soon 8 abortive, oversoon, previous, too early, untimely 9 overhasty, unfledged 10 half-cocked
Premature Burial, The author: Edgar Allan Poe
prematurely: 5 early, short 7 betimes, too soon 8 too early 9 in advance 10 beforehand
premaxilla: 4 bone
locale: 3 jaw
Prem Chand: 6 author, Indian, writer
work: The Gift of a Cow
premed class: 4 anat., chem. 7 anatomy 9 chemistry
exam: 4 MCAT
premeditated: 5 fixed, meant, set-up 6 wilful 7 laid-out, planned, plotted, studied, willful 8 intended 9 contrived, voluntary 10 deliberate, purposeful, volitional
premier: 4 head, main 5 chief, first, prime 6 top dog 7 highest, initial, leading, opening, primary 8 champion, earliest, foremost, headmost, minister, official 9 beginning, inaugural, paramount, principal, topflight
premiere: 4 lead 5 debut 7 opening 9 beginning 10 first night
__ premiere: 5 world
Premiere: 3 car 4 auto 7 Lincoln
Preminger, Otto: 8 director
brother: 4 Ingo
film: Advise & Consent (1962)
Anatomy of a Murder (1959)
Bonjour Tristesse (1958)
Carmen Jones (1954)
The Court-Martial of Billy Mitchell (1955)
Exodus (1960)
Forever Amber (1947)
Laura (1944)
The Man With the Golden Arm (1955)
The Pied Piper (1942)
Porgy and Bess (1959)
Stalag 17 (1953)
Such Good Friends (1971)
Tell Me That You Love Me, Junie Moon (1970)
Where the Sidewalk Ends (1950)
Whirlpool (1949)
premise: 5 basis, given, posit, terms 6 ground, theory, thesis 7 grounds, thought 8 argument 9 assertion, postulate, reasoning 10 assumption, hypothesis
logical ~: 5 lemma
premises: 4 site 5 scene 6 bounds 7 grounds 8 property, vicinity
force off the ~: 4 boot, oust 5 evict
premium: 3 fee, gas 4 gift, perc, perk, plum 5 bonus, extra, price, prize, value 6 bounty, carrot, costly, reward, select 7 freebee, freebie, payment, pension, subsidy 8 dividend, gasoline, giveaway, splendid, superior 9 excellent, unrivaled 10 perquisite, unrivalled
at a ~: 4 dear, high, rare 5 pricy, steep 6 costly, pricey, scarce 8 in demand, uncommon 9 expensive 10 exorbitant, high-priced, overpriced
currency ~: 4 agio
pay a ~ for: 6 ensure, insure
__ premium: 3 at a
premolar: 5 tooth
neighbor: 6 canine
premonition: 4 omen, sign 5 hunch, sense, vibes 7 feeling, inkling, portent, presage, warning 9 intuition, misgiving 10 foreboding
Prendergast school: 6 Ashcan
prenomen: 4 name
Prentiss, Paula: 7 actress
film: The Black Marble (1979)
Buddy Buddy (1981)
Catch-22 (1970)
Last of the Red Hot Lovers (1972)
The Parallax View (1974)
The Stepford Wives (1975)
The World of Henry Orient (1964)
spouse: Richard Benjamin
preoccupation: 5 mania, thing 6 fetich, fetish, hang-up 8 fixation 9 immersion, obsession
preoccupied: 4 busy, lost, rapt 6 intent 7 bemused, engaged, faraway, pensive, unaware 8 absorbed, heedless, immersed, obsessed 9 engrossed, forgetful, oblivious, wrapped-up 10 distracted
preoccupy: 5 rivet 6 absorb, bemuse, divert, engage, fixate, obsess, occupy 7 consume, engross, enthral, immerse, inthral 8 distract, enthrall, inthrall
preordain: 3 fix, set 4 doom 5 impel, judge 6 choose, decide 7 destine, dictate, specify 8 identify 9 determine, establish 10 predestine
preordained: 5 fated 7 decided 8 destined
pre-owned: 4 used 6 resold 10 hand-me-down, secondhand
not ~: 3 new
prep: 5 groom, ready 6 get set, warm-up 8 get ready, rehearse 9 make ready, rehearsal
British ~ school: 4 Eton
school: 7 academy
school attire: 6 blazer
prepaid, not: 3 COD
preparation: 4 plan 5 basis, study 6 lotion 7 build-up, measure, mixture, prelude, workout 8 homework, lead time, medicine, practice, training 9 alertness, decoction, education, foresight, provision, readiness, rehearsal, safeguard
preparatory: 5 basic
prepare: 2 do 3 arm, fix, set 4 cook, gear, gird, make, plan, till, warm, warn 5 adapt, brace, coach, draft, endow, equip, frame, groom, hatch, learn, prime, ready, sauté, set up, shape, teach, train 6 adjust, devise, draw up, fill in, fit out, gear up, get set, ground, make up, outfit, school, season, supply, warm up 7 arrange, break in, build up, concoct, develop, dispose, fashion, fortify, furnish, look for, process, provide, psych up, qualify 8 assemble, contrive, get ready, mobilize, practice 9 condition, construct, fabricate, formulate 10 anticipate, predispose, square away, strengthen
in advance: 4 plan 7 arrange, charter, reserve
prepared: 3 fit, set 4 able, ripe, up on 5 fixed, handy, ready, set-up, wired 6 all set, primed, rigged 7 adapted, groomed, in order, on guard, planned, willing 8 adjusted, arranged, disposed, educated, inclined, skillful, watchful 9 available, psyched-up, qualified, rehearsed 10 accustomed
__-prepared: 3 ill 4 well
prepayment: 7 advance, deposit
preplanned: 5 meant 6 wilful 7 willful 9 voluntary 10 purposeful, volitional
preponderance: 4 bulk, glut, mass, most 6 excess 8 majority, plethora 9 plurality, supremacy 10 lion's share
preponderant: 6 ruling 8 dominant 9 paramount, prevalent, sovereign
preposition: 3 à la, bar, ere, for, fro, o'er, off, out, per, 'til, via 4 amid, as of, as to, atop, fore, in re, into, less, like, near, onto, over, pace, past, sans, save, than, till, unto, upon, word 5 about, above, after, aloft, along, among, après, midst, neath, since, under, until 6 across, amidst, mongst 7 amongst
poetic ~: 3 e'en, ere, o'er 5 neath
prepossessing: 4 nice 6 lovely, taking 7 likable, winsome 8 alluring, charming, engaging, fetching, handsome, magnetic, pleasant, pleasing, striking 9 appealing, beautiful, beguiling 10 attractive, bewitching, enchanting, impressive
preposterous: 3 mad 4 rich, tall, wild 5 balmy, goofy, inane, outré, sappy, silly, thick, wacky 6 absurd, far-out, whacky 7 asinine, bizarre, extreme, fatuous, foolish, too much 8 cockeyed, shocking 9 fantastic, laughable, ludicrous, monstrous, senseless, unheard-of 10 irrational, outrageous, ridiculous
preppie
parent: 5 mater, pater
wear: 5 tweed 6 blazer
prepupal phase: 5 larva
prerecord: 4 tape
pre-release software version: 4 beta
prerequisite: 4 must, need 5 state, vital 8 demanded, required 9 called for, de rigueur, essential, mandatory, necessary, necessity, provision, requisite 10 imperative, sine qua non
prerogative: 3 due 5 claim, droit, place, power, right, title 6 choice, option 7 freedom, liberty, warrant 8 immunity 9 advantage, authority, exemption, privilege
presidential ~: 4 veto
pres.
see president
presage: 4 bode, lead, mean, omen, sign, warn 5 augur, token 6 herald, threat 7 auspice, betoken, point to, portend, portent, precede, predict, promise, signify, warning 8 antecede, forebode, forecast, foreshow, foretell, forewarn, prophesy, threaten 9 adumbrate, foretoken, harbinger, introduce 10 come before, foreboding, foreshadow, indication, vaticinate
presbyter: 5 elder
preschooler: 3 kid, tot 9 youngster
prescience: 6 vision 9 foresight
prescient: 7 fatidic 8 oracular 9 farseeing, prophetic, vaticinal 10 farsighted
Prescott: 4 city, town
locale: 7 Arizona
prescribe: 3 set 4 bind, rule 5 enact, limit, order, treat 6 advise, assign, decree, direct, enjoin, impose, ordain 7 appoint, command, dictate, lay down, require, specify 8 instruct, proclaim 9 designate, establish, institute, legislate, recommend, stipulate
prescribed: 3 set 5 legal 6 formal 8 required 9 requisite 10 inevitable
amount: 4 dose
not ~: 3 OTC
prescript: 4 writ 9 ordinance 10 regulation
prescription: 3 law 4 dose, drug, rule 5 edict 6 decree, recipe, remedy 7 formula, mixture 8 medicine 9 direction, ordinance, treatment
abbr.: 2 cc. 3 alb., b.d.s., bib., cib., cuj., d.t.d., ead., gtt., liq., pil., p.r.n., q.i.d, Sig., t.d.s., t.i.d., ung., vin. 4 agit., coch., elix., ferv., filt., garg., quat., quor., trid., ungt. 5 calef., emuls., qq. hor., quinq., utend.
data: 4 dose 6 dosage 10 expiration
org.: 3 FDA
prescriptions
four times a day, in ~: 3 q.i.d.
shake, in ~: 4 agit.
such, in ~: 3 tal.
the same, in ~: 3 ead.
three times a day, in ~: 3 t.i.d.
presence: 3 air, set 4 aura, ease, look, mien, wits 5 front, ghost, midst, poise, shade 6 entity, manner, shadow, spirit, troops, ubiety, wraith 7 bearing, charism, company, fantasm, posture, reality, specter 8 calmness, carriage, charisma, demeanor, nearness, phantasm, ubiquity, vitality 9 closeness, composure, existence, life force, occupancy, proximity, sangfroid 10 apparition, appearance, attendance, sedateness
in the ~ of: 6 before
of mind: 5 poise 6 aplomb 8 calmness 9 alertness, composure, sangfroid, stability
presence of __: 4 mind
present: 3 lay, now, put 4 gift, give, hand, here, lend, look, pose, show, time 5 award, favor, grant, in use, lay on, nonce, offer, pitch, put on, serve, stage, stake, state, there, today, voice 6 accord, at hand, at home, bestow, confer, donate, extant, extend, goodie, hand in, kick in, modern, nearby, on deck, on hand, relate, render, submit, tender, unfold, with us 7 current, declare, deliver, display, drop off, entrust, exhibit, expound, going on, handout, hold out, intrust, largess, on board, produce, proffer, propose, provide, recount, roll out, trot out 8 acquaint, donation, gratuity, hand over, largesse, nominate, nowadays, offering, put forth, up-to-date 9 attending, endowment, immediate, introduce, on-the-spot, time being 10 contribute, promulgate, put forward
a case: 5 argue
arms: 6 salute
at ~: 3 now 5 today 7 already 8 promptly, right now, right off 9 forthwith, presently, right away

10 here and now, this minute
in its ~ state: 4 as is 6 as it is
itself: 5 occur 6 happen 7 develop
not ~: 4 away, gone 6 absent 9 elsewhere
prepare a ~: 4 wrap 8 decorate
starter: 4 omni
topper: 3 bow 6 ribbon
up to the ~: 5 as yet, so far 6 to date
present ___: 4 arms 5 tense 7 perfect
present-___: 3 day
Present: 4 font 8 typeface
presentable: 2 OK 3 fit 4 okay, so-so 6 decent, not bad 8 adequate, all right, becoming, passable, suitable 9 tolerable 10 acceptable, good enough
make ~: 4 dust, tidy 5 clean, groom, sweep 6 neaten
Present Arms: 7 musical
songwriter: 4 Hart 7 Rodgers
presentation: 3 act 4 face, show 5 award, debut, offer, pitch 7 display, exhibit, present, program, recital, staging 8 bestowal, delivery, donation, offering, overture, proposal 9 coming out, conferral, launching, reception, rendition, statement
end a ~: 5 recap, sum up 9 summarize
present-day: 6 modern, recent 7 current
presentiment: 4 fear, sign 5 hunch, qualm, sense, vibes, worry 7 feeling, portent, presage 8 mistrust 9 intuition, misgiving 10 foreboding
Present Indicative author: Noël Coward
presently: 3 now 4 anon, nigh, soon 5 today 6 at once 7 by and by, shortly 8 directly, hereupon, nowadays, promptly, right now, right off 9 following, forthwith, in a minute, in a moment, right away 10 at this time, before long, here and now, in good time, this minute, ultimately
preservation: 4 care 6 curing, saving, upkeep 7 canning, defense, tanning 8 freezing, pickling 9 salvation, upholding 10 conserving, protection
___-preservation: 4 self
preservative: 3 BHA, BHT 4 agar, EDTA, salt 5 brine, sugar 8 agar-agar
preserve: 3 can, dry, tin 4 corn, cure, jerk, keep, park, salt, save 5 guard, lay up, put up, smoke, souse, store 6 bottle, bronze, defend, encase, freeze, incase, keep up, kipper, pickle, record, refuge, rescue, retain, season, secure, shield, uphold 7 care for, mummify, process, protect, shelter, sustain 8 conserve, continue, maintain, mothball 9 dehydrate, safeguard, sanctuary, stabilize 10 perpetuate, protection
again: 5 recan
fodder: 6 ensile
nature ~: 4 park 9 sanctuary
veggies: 3 can, dry, ice 4 corn 5 frost 6 freeze, pickle 7 ice over
Preserve and Protect author: Allen Drury
___ preserver: 4 life
Preserver, Hindu: 6 Vishnu
preserves: 3 jam 5 jelly 6 spread 7 compote 8 conserve 9 confiture, conserves, marmalade 10 confection
container: 3 jar
preside: 3 run, sit 4 lead, rule 5 chair 6 advise, direct, govern, handle, head up, manage 7 conduct, control, oversee 8 moderate 9 officiate, supervise 10 administer
over: 4 head, hold, lead 6 direct 7 conduct 9 supervise
president: 4 exec, head, suit 5 chief 6 leader, top dog 7 officer 9 executive
advisory group: 3 NSC
first one-term ~: 5 Adams
four years, for a ~: 4 term
honest ~: 3 Abe
initials: 3 CAA, DDE, FDR, GRF, GWB, HCH, HST, JAG, JEC, JFK, JKP, JQA, LBJ, MVB, RBH, RMN, RWR, USG, WGH, WHH, WHT, WJC 4 GHWB
maybe: 3 CEO 8 chairman
military title: 4 C in C
nickname: 3 Abe, Cal, Ike 4 Bill
pet: 3 Her, Him 4 Fala 5 Socks
prerogative: 4 veto
terse ~: 3 Cal
___ president: 4 vice
President: 3 car 4 auto 10 Studebaker
presidential ___: 5 suite 7 primary
Presidential Papers, The author: Norman Mailer
President of the U.S.: 4 Bush, Ford, Polk, Taft 5 Adams, Grant, Hayes, Nixon, Tyler 6 Arthur, Carter, Hoover, Monroe, Pierce, Reagan, Taylor, Truman, Wilson 7 Clinton, Harding, Jackson, Johnson, Kennedy, Lincoln, Madison 8 Buchanan, Coolidge, Fillmore, Garfield, Harrison, McKinley, Van Buren 9 Cleveland, Jefferson, John Adams, John Tyler, Roosevelt 10 Eisenhower, Gerald Ford, Washington
president pro ___: 3 tem 7 tempore
President's Analyst, The (1967 film)
cast: Godfrey Cambridge, James Coburn, Severn Darden
director: Theodore J. Flicker
Presidents' Day event: 4 sale
President's Lady, The (1953 film)
cast: Susan Hayward, Charlton Heston, John McIntire
director: Henry Levin
presiding officer: 4 head 5 chief 6 leader, top dog, warden 7 manager 8 director 9 executive 10 supervisor
presidio: 4 fort 8 fastness, fortress 10 stronghold
Presley: 4 Lisa 5 Elvis 9 Priscilla
Presley, Elvis: 5 actor 6 singer
contemporary: 5 Darin
film: Blue Hawaii (1961)
Change of Habit (1969)
Charro! (1969)
Clambake (1967)
Double Trouble (1967)
Easy Come, Easy Go (1967)
Flaming Star (1960)
Follow That Dream (1962)
Frankie and Johnny (1966)
Fun in Acapulco (1963)
G.I. Blues (1960)
Girl Happy (1965)
Girls! Girls! Girls! (1962)
Harum Scarum (1965)
It Happened at the World's Fair (1963)
Jailhouse Rock (1957)
Kid Galahad (1962)
King Creole (1958)
Kissin' Cousins (1964)
Live a Little, Love a Little (1968)
Love Me Tender (1956)
Loving You (1957)
Paradise, Hawaiian Style (1966)
Roustabout (1964)
Speedway (1968)
Spinout (1966)
Stay Away, Joe (1968)
Tickle Me (1965)
The Trouble With Girls (1969)
Viva Las Vegas (1964)
Wild in the Country (1961)
hometown: Tupelo, Mississippi
middle name: 4 Aron
nickname: The King
song: Ain't That Loving You Baby (1964)
All Shook Up (1957)
Any Way You Want Me (1956)
Are You Lonesome Tonight? (1960)
Ask Me (1964)
Big Boss Man (1967)
A Big Hunk O' Love (1959)
Blue Suede Shoes (1956)
Bossa Nova Baby (1963)
Burning Love (1972)
Can't Help Falling in Love (1961)
Crying in the Chapel (1965)
Devil in Disguise (1963)
Doncha' Think It's Time (1958)
Don't (1958)
Don't Be Cruel (1956)
Don't Cry Daddy (1969)
Do the Clam (1965)
Fame and Fortune (1960)
Flaming Star (1961)
Follow That Dream (1962)
A Fool Such As I (1959)
Frankie and Johnny (1966)
Good Luck Charm (1962)
Hard Headed Woman (1958)
Heartbreak Hotel (1956)
His Latest Flame (1961)
Hound Dog (1956)
I Beg of You (1958)
I Feel So Bad (1961)
If I Can Dream (1968)
If You Talk in Your Sleep (1974)
I Got Stung (1958)
I Gotta Know (1960)
I'm Yours (1965)
I Need Your Love Tonight (1959)
In the Ghetto (1969)
I Really Don't Want to Know (1971)
It's Now or Never (1960)
I Want You, I Need You, I Love You (1956)
I Was the One (1956)
Jailhouse Rock (1957)
Kentucky Rain (1970)
Kissin' Cousins (1964)
(Let Me Be Your) Teddy Bear (1957)
Little Sister (1961)
Love Letters (1966)
Love Me (1956)
Love Me Tender (1956)
Loving You (1957)
My Boy (1975)
My Wish Came True (1959)
One Broken Heart for Sale (1963)
One Night (1958)
Playing for Keeps (1957)
Promised Land (1974)
Puppet on a String (1965)
Return to Sender (1962)
Separate Ways (1972)
She's Not You (1962)
Steamroller Blues (1973)
Stuck on You (1960)
(Such an) Easy Question (1965)
Such a Night (1964)
Surrender (1961)
Suspicious Minds (1969)
Tell Me Why (1966)
Too Much (1957)
Treat Me Nice (1957)
U.S. Male (1968)
Viva Las Vegas (1964)
Way Down (1977)
Wear My Ring Around Your Neck (1958)
What'd I Say (1964)
When My Blue Moon Turns to Gold Again (1956)
The Wonder of You (1970)
You Don't Have to Say You Love Me (1970)
spouse: Priscilla Presley
Presley, Lisa Marie
spouse: Nicolas Cage, Michael Jackson
Presley, Priscilla spouse: Elvis Presley
Presnell, Harve: 5 actor
film: Fargo (1996)
Paint Your Wagon (1969)
The Unsinkable Molly Brown (1964)
Presque Isle: 4 city, town
locale: 5 Maine
press: 3 beg, dun, get, hug, jam, jog, mob, nag, ram, sue, vex 4 cram, herd, hold, host, iron, lock, make, mash, mass, milk, mill, pack, pile, prod, push, rush, sell, spur, urge, vise 5 beset, bunch, clasp, cramp, crowd, crush, drove, egg on, flock, force, haste, horde, hurry, impel, level, lobby, media, offer, paper, plead, shove, sqush, steam, stuff, swarm, worry 6 assert, bustle, coerce, compel, demand, enfold, enjoin, estate, exhort, harass, harp on, hassle, hasten, infold, insist, lean on, mangle, plague, push on, reduce, smooth, squash, squish, squush, strain, stress, throng, thrust, work on 7 beseech, besiege, embrace, entreat, extrude, flatten, implore, newsmen, pin down, scrunch, squeeze, squoosh, torment, trouble, urgency 8 appeal to, bear down, blandish, bulldoze, compress, condense, insist on, petition, railroad, reporter, shoulder 9 columnist, confusion, emphasize, importune, magazines, multitude, news media, newspaper, promotion, publicist, publicity, publisher, unwrinkle, weigh down 10 buttonhole, journalism, journalist, newspapers, periodical
agent: 5 flack 8 promoter 9 advertise
charges: 8 litigate
coverage: 3 ink
down: 4 tamp 7 depress
ender: 3 run, ure 4 gang, mark, room, work 5 board
for: 4 urge 6 demand, exhort 8 advocate, petition
for details: 4 pump
for money: 3 dun, sue 4 bill
for political action: 5 lobby
go to ~: 5 print 7 let roll
hot off the ~: 3 new 5 fresh 6 recent
into service: 3 use 5 avail 6 enlist 7 recruit
member: 6 editor, photog 8 reporter 10 journalist
on: 7 advance, proceed 8 continue 9 go forward, persevere
one's luck: 4 dare, push
one's suit: 3 sue, woo 5 court 7 propose
prepare a ~: 3 ink 5 reink
release: 4 news, word 5 aviso 6 notice, report 7 handout, message 8 bulletin, dispatch 9 statement 10 communiqué
secretary: 4 aide 9 assistant
starter: 4 wine 6 letter 7 clothes
the flesh: 5 lobby, stump 8 campaign, politick 10 shake hands
together: 5 purse
press ___: 3 bed, box, fit, kit, run 4 gang, lord, stud, time 5 agent, baron, brake, corps, party, proof 6 bureau 7 gallery, release, section
___ press: 3 web 4 body, drop, duck, free, go to, hand, wine 5 bench, cider, cooky, drill, power, punch, screw 6 cookie, cotton, rotary, vanity, web-fed 7 durable, flat-bed
___-press: 3 hot 5 perma
Press: 4 peak 5 mount 8 mountain
locale: 10 Antarctica

Pressburger: **6** Emeric
press conference
format: **5** Q and A
gear: **4** mike **6** camera **10** microphone
pressed ___: **4** duck **5** brick, glass
___-pressed: **4** hard
pressing: **4** dire, live, sore **5** acute, vital **6** crying, urgent **7** burning, crucial, exigent, hurry-up, instant, onerous, serious **8** critical, exigeant **9** demanding, immediate, important, insistent, necessary **10** compelling, imperative
situation: **4** crux, need **6** crisis **7** urgency **9** emergency
___ Press International: **6** United
press the ___: **5** flesh
pressure: **4** heat, load, prod, pull, push, rush, sell, sway, urge **5** clout, drive, force, hurry, impel **6** burden, coerce, compel, crunch, demand, duress, hassle, insist, lean on, overdo, strain, stress, thrust, weight, work on **7** squeeze, straits, tension, tighten, trouble, urgency **8** coercion, deadline, exigence, exigency, politick, strength, threaten **9** adversity, constrain, heaviness, influence, necessity, strong-arm **10** compulsion, insistence, obligation, persuasion
apply ~: **4** push, urge **5** force **6** coerce, compel, lean on **7** squeeze **8** arm-twist **9** strong-arm
combining form: **3** bar- **4** baro-, tono- **5** piezo-
decrease ~: **4** ease
give in to ~: **4** obey **5** crack, yield **6** submit
grace under ~: **4** cool, tact **5** poise **6** aplomb **7** dignity **8** presence **9** assurance, composure, diplomacy, sang-froid **10** confidence, equanimity
measure: **3** atm., PSI
NASA ~ unit: **4** one G
put ~ on: **3** tax **5** crowd, lobby **6** strain
so to speak: **6** screws
unit: **3** bar **4** torr **6** pascal **8** millibar **10** atmosphere
pressure ___: **3** ice **4** cone, head, hull, suit **5** cabin, gauge, group, point, ridge **6** center, cooker **7** flaking, welding
___ pressure: **3** air **4** peer, root **5** blood, fluid, pulse, vapor **7** osmotic
___-pressure: **3** low **4** high
pressured: **5** tense **7** harried **10** overworked
Pressure Point (1962 film)
cast: Bobby Darin, Peter Falk, Sidney Poitier
pressurize: **3** bar **4** bind, curb, make **5** check, cramp, force, hem in, impel, stint **6** coerce, compel, hogtie, oblige, rein in, stifle **7** abstain, confine, control, harness, inhibit, require, squeeze, trammel **8** bottle up, hold back, moderate, pressure, prohibit, restrain **9** constrain, constrict **10** intimidate
Press Your Luck: **8** game show
host: Peter Tomarken
pre-stereo system: **4** hi-fi **5** phono **10** phonograph
prestidigitation: **5** magic, trick **7** sorcery **8** wizardry **9** conjuring
prestidigitator: **4** mage **6** wizard **8** conjurer, conjuror, magician, sorcerer
prestige: **4** fame, rank, sway **5** clout, éclat, glory, honor, power, state **6** cachet, credit, esteem, regard, renown, repute, status, weight **7** control, dignity, laurels, stature **8** eminence, good name, position, standing **9** authority, celebrity, influence **10** importance, prominence, reputation
prestigious: **5** famed, great **6** famous **7** eminent, exalted, notable **8** esteemed, imposing, renowned **9** important, prominent, reputable, respected
presto: **3** PDQ **4** ASAP, fast, stat **5** apace, quick, tempo **6** at once **7** fleetly, hastily, quickly, rapidly, swiftly **8** in a flash, in a jiffy, in no time, pell-mell, right now, speedily **9** forthwith, hurriedly, instantly, like a shot, posthaste
slower than ~: **7** allegro
presto ___: **6** chango
Presto!: **4** poof, ta-da **5** ta-dah, there, voilà
Preston: **3** Sgt. **5** Billy, Kelly **6** Foster, Johnny, Robert **7** Sturges
Preston, Billy
song: Nothing From Nothing (1964)
Outa-Space (1972)
Space Race (1973)
Will It Go Round in Circles (1973)
With You I'm Born Again (1980)
Preston, Johnny
song: Cradle of Love (1960)
Feel So Fine (1960)
Running Bear (1959)
Preston, Kelly: **7** actress
film: For Love of the Game (1999)
Jack Frost (1998)
Jerry Maguire (1996)
Twins (1988)
spouse: John Travolta
Preston, Robert: **5** actor
film: All the Way Home (1963)
Beau Geste (1939)
The Dark at the Top of the Stairs (1960)
How the West Was Won (1962)
Junior Bonner (1972)
The Lady Gambles (1949)
The Macomber Affair (1947)
The Music Man (1962)
This Gun for Hire (1942)
Tulsa (1949)
Union Pacific (1939)
Victor/Victoria (1982)
Wake Island (1942)
When I Grow Up (1951)
Preston, Sergeant
beat: **5** Yukon
horse: **3** Rex
org.: **4** RCMP
presumable: **6** likely **8** probable, specious **10** believable, convincing
presumably: **6** likely, surely **8** probably **9** assumably, doubtless, seemingly
presume: **4** dare, deem, feel, hold, take **5** guess, infer, posit, think, trust **6** assume, bank on, expect, figure, gather, impose, take it **7** believe, count on, imagine, intrude, suppose, surmise, suspect, venture **8** conclude, consider, infringe, misjudge, theorize **9** count upon, speculate, undertake **10** conjecture, jump the gun, presuppose, understand
presumed: **7** seeming **8** probable, putative, unproved **10** understood
truth: **5** axiom, given
Presumed Innocent: **4** film **5** novel
author: Scott Turow
cast: Brian Dennehy, Harrison Ford, Raul Julia
director: Alan J. Pakula
presuming: **4** bold, sure **5** brave **6** secure, upbeat **7** assured, certain, hopeful, valiant **8** cocksure, fearless, intrepid, positive, sanguine, unafraid **9** assertive, collected, confident, convinced, dauntless, expectant, expecting, satisfied, undaunted **10** complacent, counting on, courageous, optimistic
presumption: **4** gall **5** basis, brass, cheek, guess, nerve, pride **6** belief, daring, theory, thesis **7** conceit, egotism, opinion, premise, surmise **8** audacity, boldness, chutzpah, rudeness, temerity **9** arrogance, brashness, contumely, impudence, insolence **10** assumption, conjecture, effrontery, likelihood
presumptive: **7** a priori **8** putative, specious
___ presumptive: **4** heir
presumptuous: **3** big **4** bold, pert, rude, smug **5** brash, cocky, fresh, lofty, nervy, proud, pushy, saucy **6** brassy, brazen, cheeky, lordly, uppity **7** forward, haughty, pompous, unasked **8** arrogant, assuming, cocksure, familiar, impudent, insolent, snobbish **9** audacious, conceited, egotistic, imperious, obtrusive, shameless **10** disdainful
presumptuousness: **5** brass, cheek, nerve **7** license **8** audacity
presuppose: **5** imply, infer, posit **6** assume **7** believe, presume **8** misjudge **9** postulate
presupposition: **5** given **6** belief, thesis **7** opinion, premise
prêt-à-___: **6** porter
pre-taped, not: **4** live
preteen: **3** kid **5** kiddy, minor **9** youngster **10** adolescent
school: **4** elem. **10** elementary, junior high
pretend: **3** act **4** dupe, fake, fool, play, pose, sham **5** bluff, cheat, claim, cozen, feign, fudge, let on, mimic, put on **6** affect, allege, assume, delude, fake it, play at, pseudo, sucker **7** act as if, act like, beguile, deceive, fake out, imagine, imitate, mislead, playact, profess, purport, suppose **8** hoodwink, lay claim, malinger, simulate, spurious **9** disinform, dissemble, represent, whitewash **10** masquerade, play possum, put on an act
to be: **8** disguise, double as
___ Pretend: **4** Let's
pretended: **4** fake, mock, sham **5** bogus, false, lying, phony, put-on, quack, quasi **6** phoney, pseudo, unreal **7** alleged, assumed, feigned, nominal **8** affected, so-called, spurious, strained, supposed **9** imaginary, insincere, professed, purported, vicarious **10** artificial, factitious, fictitious, ostensible
pretender: **4** fake **5** faker, fraud, knave, phony, poser, quack **6** phoney, poseur, rascal **7** upstart, wannabe **8** imposter, impostor **9** hypocrite
Pretenders
song: Back on the Chain Gang (1983)
Brass in Pocket (1980)
Don't Get Me Wrong (1986)
I'll Stand by You (1994)
Middle of the Road (1984)
vocalist: Chrissie Hynde
Pretenders, The author: Henrik Ibsen
___ Pretender, The: **5** Great
Pretend You Don't See Her author: Mary Higgins Clark
pretense: **3** act, gag **4** airs, cant, hoax, mask, pose, ritz, ruse, sham, show, veil, wile **5** bluff, claim, cloak, cover, decoy, feint, fraud, guise, put-on, shill, stall, stunt, title, trick **6** acting, deceit, dupery, excuse, facade, fakery, humbug, posing, veneer **7** charade, display, evasion, mockery, pretext, routine, schtick, snow job, swindle **8** artifice, disguise, feigning, trickery **9** deception, falsehood, hypocrisy, imposture, invention, posturing, semblance, shuffling **10** appearance, lip service, masquerade, pretension, simulation, subterfuge
without ~: **4** open **5** naive **7** artless **8** innocent, trusting **9** ingenuous
___ pretenses: **5** false
pretension: **4** airs, ritz, show **5** claim, front, pride, title **6** hubris, hybris, vanity **7** big talk, bombast, bravado, conceit, display **8** ambition, pretense, snobbery **9** arrogance, hypocrisy, imposture, mannerism, vainglory **10** lip service, narcissism
pretentious: **3** big **4** arty, smug, vain **5** artsy, cocky, gaudy, lofty, proud, ritzy, showy, stagy, swank **6** flashy, garish, hollow, la-de-da, la-di-da, ornate, stagey, swanky, tawdry, too-too, turgid **7** fatuous, flowery, fustian, haughty, mincing, opulent, pompous, splashy, stilted, stuck-up **8** affected, arrogant, assuming, boastful, imposing, inflated, lah-di-dah, mannered, overdone, puffed up, snobbish, specious, superior **9** big-headed, bombastic, conceited, flaunting, grandiose, high-flown, high-toned, insincere, luxurious, overblown, tasteless, unnatural **10** hoity-toity, theatrical
preterit: **5** tense
preternatural: **3** odd **4** eery **5** eerie, weird **6** arcane, atypic, freaky, mystic, occult, quirky **7** bizarre, deviant, ghostly, offbeat, psychic, strange, uncanny, unusual **8** aberrant, abnormal, atypical, esoteric, freakish, mystical, peculiar, uncommon **9** anomalous, divergent, eccentric, fantastic, irregular, unearthly, unnatural **10** mysterious, unorthodox
pretext: **3** out **4** mask, plea, ploy, show, veil **5** alibi, basis, bluff, cloak, cover, feint, front, guise **6** cop-out, excuse **7** cover-up, evasion, grounds **8** pretense **9** deception, semblance **10** cover story, masquerade, subterfuge
Pretoria: **4** city, town **7** capital **8** asteroid
coin: **4** rand
locale: **3** RSA **11** South Africa
prettify: **4** deck **5** adorn, groom, preen, primp **6** bedeck **8** beautify, decorate, ornament **9** glamorize
pretty: **4** boss, cute, fair, fine, foxy, neat, nice **5** bonny, dishy, quite **6** bonnie, comely, dainty, dreamy, eyeful, fairly, kind of, lovely, rather, sort of **7** darling, winsome **8** adorable, alluring, becoming, charming, delicate, engaging, fetching, gorgeous, graceful, handsome, pleasing, skillful, somewhat, striking, stunning, tasteful **9** appealing, beauteous, beautiful, ravishing **10** attractive, delightful, moderately, reasonably
boy: **3** fop **4** buck, dude **5** blade, dandy, spark, swell **7** coxcomb **8** popinjay **10** jack-a-dandy
good: **4** fair, okay, tidy
name meaning ~: **5** Linda, Lynda
nice: **4** okay **6** not bad
one: **5** cutey, cutie **8** cutie-pie
penny: **4** dear, high **5** pricy, steep **6** bundle, costly, pricey **8** big bucks, precious **9** expensive, priceless **10** exorbitant, high-priced, overpriced
sitting ~: **4** rich **6** loaded **7** wealthy, well-off **8** affluent, in clover, well-to-do **9** well-fixed **10** in the money, well-heeled
pretty ___: **4** much **5** penny

pretty __ pretty does: 4 is as
__ pretty: 7 sitting
Pretty __: 4 Baby 5 Paper, Woman 6 Poison
__ Pretty: 5 I Feel 7 Sitting
pretty as a __: 7 picture
Pretty Baby (1978 film)
  cast: Keith Carradine, Susan Sarandon, Brooke Shields
  director: Louis Malle
Pretty Blue Eyes (1959 song) artist: Steve Lawrence
Pretty Boy: 5 Floyd
Pretty Girl Is Like a Melody, A composer: Irving Berlin
Pretty in Pink (1987 film)
  cast: Jon Cryer, Andrew McCarthy, Molly Ringwald
  director: Howard Deutch
Pretty Little Angel Eyes (1961 song)
  artist: Curtis Lee
Pretty Maids All in a Row (1971 film)
  cast: Angie Dickinson, Rock Hudson, Telly Savalas
  director: Roger Vadim
Pretty Paper (1963 song) artist: Roy Orbison
pretty please, say: 3 beg 7 implore
Pretty Poison (1968 film)
  cast: Beverly Garland, Anthony Perkins, Tuesday Weld
__ pretty sight: 4 not a
Pretty Woman (1990 film)
  cast: Ralph Bellamy, Richard Gere, Julia Roberts
  director: Garry Marshall
pretzel: 4 nosh 5 snack
  topping: 4 salt 7 mustard
prevail: 3 win 4 lead, live, rule 5 carry, reign, stand 6 abound, endure, make it, obtain, pan out, remain, thrive 7 conquer, luck out, make out, prosper, succeed, triumph, work out 8 dominate, flourish, get ahead, go places, hold sway, make good, outweigh, overcome, overrule, prove out, surmount
  against: 6 endure 7 survive, weather 9 withstand
  on: 3 get 4 coax, make, move, sway 6 induce, prompt, reason, suck in 7 impress, win over 8 convince, motivate, persuade, talk into 9 argue into, get around, influence
  over: 4 beat, whip 5 outdo 6 defeat 8 override, overrule
prevailing: 3 set 4 main 5 fixed, typic, usual 6 common, normal, ruling, wonted 7 current, general, in style, popular, rampant, regnant, regular, routine, supreme, typical 8 dominant, everyday, habitual, ordinary, orthodox, powerful, standard, superior 9 customary, operative, principal, universal, worldwide 10 accustomed
prevalence: 9 frequency
prevalent: 4 rife 5 in use, typic, usual 6 common, normal, ruling, wonted 7 current, general, popular, rampant, regular, typical 8 dominant, familiar, frequent, habitual, infested, numerous 9 customary, extensive, paramount, pervasive, sovereign, universal 10 accustomed, prevailing, ubiquitous, widespread
prevaricate: 3 fib, lie 4 jive 5 dodge, evade, hedge 6 garble, invent, palter 7 deceive, distort, falsify, mislead, perjure, phony up, quibble 8 misquote, misspeak 9 dissemble, fabricate, misinform
prevarication: 3 fib, lie 4 tale 5 story 7 untruth 9 falsehood 10 taradiddle
prevaricator: 4 liar 6 fibber 8 deceiver, perjurer
prevent: 3 bar, dam 4 balk, cork, foil, halt, keep, stay, stem, stop 5 avert, avoid, baulk, block, check, debar, deter, limit, stimy, stymy 6 arrest, baffle, forbid, hamper, hinder, impede, muzzle, oppose, outlaw, retard, stifle, stymie, thwart 7 counter, exclude, forfend, head off, hold off, inhibit, obviate, occlude, repress, rule out, shut out, ward off 8 dissuade, forefend, handicap, hold back, obstruct, preclude, prohibit, restrain, restrict, sabotage, stave off 9 foreclose, forestall, frustrate, hamstring, intercept, interdict, interrupt, turn aside 10 anticipate, counteract, put an end to, put a stop to
  from seeing: 4 hide, veil 6 screen 9 blindfold
  in legalese: 5 estop
preventive: 4 drug 5 serum 9 defensive, deterrent 10 antiseptic
preventive __: 7 measure
Prévert, Jacques: 4 poet 6 French
Previa: 3 van 6 Toyota
__ preview: 5 sneak
previewer, movie: 5 rater 6 critic
Previn: 4 Dory 5 André
Previn, André: 9 conductor
  spouse: Mia Farrow
previous: 3 old 4 last, late, past 5 prior 6 bygone, former 7 beloved, earlier, old-time, one-time, quondam 8 anterior, foregone, oversoon, sometime 9 erstwhile, foregoing, preceding, premature 10 antecedent
  to: 3 ere 6 before
previously: 3 ere, née 4 once, then 5 ahead 6 before, erenow 7 already, earlier, long ago, time was 8 back when, formerly, hitherto, until now 9 at one time, a while ago, erstwhile, in advance, in the past 10 beforehand, beforetime, heretofore
Prévost, Abbé: 6 French, writer
  work: Manon Lescaut
prewarn: 5 alert 6 inform, tip off 7 caution
pre-weekend cry: 4 TGIF
prexy: 4 boss, exec 6 leader 9 president 10 head honcho
  often: 3 CEO 8 chairman
  subordinate: 4 dean, veep
prey: 4 dupe, game, gull, kill, mark 5 patsy, ravin 6 hunted, martyr, pigeon, quarry, ravage, spoils, sucker, target, victim 7 cat's-paw, fall guy
  bird of ~: 3 ern, owl 4 erne, hawk, kite 5 eagle 6 elanet, falcon, lanner 7 kestrel
  grabber: 4 claw, fang 5 talon, tooth
  move towards ~: 4 inch 5 bound, crawl, slink 6 pounce
  on: 3 eat, mug, tax 4 hunt, raid 5 bleed, bully, haunt, seize, worry 6 attack, devour, fleece, ravage 7 consume, exploit, oppress, pillage, plunder, trouble 8 distress, freeboot 9 blackmail, depredate, strong-arm, subjugate, terrorize, victimize 10 intimidate
  on one's mind: 6 obsess, plague 9 preoccupy
  search for ~: 5 prowl
__ prey: 6 bird of
__ prey to: 4 fall
prez
  see president
Priam: 4 king 6 Trojan
  daughter of ~: 6 Creusa 7 Laodice 8 Polyxena 9 Cassandra
  lover of ~: 6 Arisbe 7 Laothoe 8 Alexiroe 10 Castianira
  parent of ~: 6 Strymo 8 Laomedon
  sister of ~: 5 Cilla
  son of ~: 4 Bias, Isus 5 Axion, Paris 6 Aretus, Dryops, Hector, Lycaon, Mestor, Pammon 7 Aesacus, Helenus, Polites, Troilus 8 Antiphus, Chromius, Democoon, Doryclus, Echemmon 9 Cebriones, Deiopites, Deiphobus, Hipponous, Polydorus 10 Antiphonus, Gorgythion, Hippodamas, Melanippus
  wife of ~: 6 Arisbe, Hecuba
Pribilofs: 4 isls. 5 isles 7 islands
  locale: 6 Alaska 9 Bering Sea
price: 3 fee, fix, set, tab 4 bill, cost, dues, fare, hire, rate, toll, tune 5 quote, value, wages, worth 6 amount, bounty, charge, damage, demand, figure, mark up, outlay, ransom, reduce, retail, return, reward, tariff, ticket, upkeep 7 ceiling, damages, expense, payment, penalty, premium, sticker, tuition 8 appraise, discount, estimate, evaluate, mark down 9 appraisal, quotation, reckoning, sacrifice, valuation, wholesale 10 assessment
  add-on: 3 tax 4 duty
  again: 5 retag
  beyond ~: 8 precious
  ceiling: 3 cap
  cut: 4 deal, sale 6 rebate, saving 7 bargain 8 discount 9 reduction
  discuss ~: 4 deal 6 dicker 7 bargain
  fixer: 6 cartel
  give a ~: 5 quote
  good ~: 4 deal 7 bargain
  lower the ~: 3 cut 4 trim 5 slash 6 reduce
  market ~: 5 quote, value 9 quotation
  of admission: 3 fee 6 ticket
  offer for a ~: 4 sell, vend 6 peddle 7 auction
  pay the ~: 3 buy, get 8 purchase
  raise the ~: 2 up 4 hike 5 bid up, run up
  reducer: 6 coupon
  remove ~ supports: 5 unpeg
  set a ~: 3 ask
  suggest a ~: 3 bid 5 offer
  tag: 6 amount, outlay, ticket
  ticket ~: 4 fare
  word: 3 per 4 each 6 apiece
price __: 3 cut, tag, war 4 list 5 index, point, range 6 fixing 7 control, cutting, support
price __ of the market: 3 out
__ price: 3 at a, bid 4 base, list, spot, stop, unit 5 fixed, floor, upset 6 asking, beyond, market 7 closing, factory, reserve, sticker, support
Price: 3 Ray 4 Marc, Nick 5 Kelly, Lloyd 7 Anthony, Vincent 8 Leontyne, Reynolds
__ Price: 5 T. Rowe
__-Price: 6 Fisher
Price Above Rubies (1998 film)
  cast: Christopher Eccleston, Glenn Fitzgerald, Julianna Margulies, Allen Payne, Renée Zellweger
  director: Boaz Yakin
priced
  be ~ at: 4 cost 5 run to
  reasonably ~: 6 budget
__-priced: 3 low 4 high
price-earnings __: 5 ratio
__ Price Glory?: 4 What
__ Price Hollywood?: 4 What
Price Is Right, The: 8 game show
  announcer: 5 Olson, Pardo, Roddy
  host: Bill Cullen, Bob Barker
  prop: 3 tag
  shout: 5 lower 6 higher
Price, Leontyne: 6 singer 7 soprano
  forte: 5 opera
  role: 4 Aïda
priceless: 4 dear, rare, rich 5 droll 6 absurd, costly, prized, scream, valued 7 amusing, riotous 8 humorous, precious, valuable 9 cherished, excellent, expensive, hilarious, treasured 10 gut-busting, invaluable, out-of-sight, ridiculous
  individual: 3 gem
Price, Lloyd
  song: I'm Gonna Get Married (1959)
    Personality (1959)
    Stagger Lee (1959)
Price, Nick: 6 golfer 12 South African
  milieu: 5 links 6 course
  org.: 3 PGA
Price of Glory (2000 film)
  cast: Clifton Collins Jr., Maria del Mar, Jon Seda, Jimmy Smits
  director: Carlos Avila
price out of the __: 6 market
Prices may __: 4 vary
Price, Vincent: 5 actor
  film: The Abominable Dr. Phibes (1971)
    Champagne for Caesar (1950)
    The Comedy of Terrors (1964)
    The Conquerer Worm (1968)
    Edward Scissorhands (1990)
    The Fly (1958)
    His Kind of Woman (1951)
    The House of Seven Gables (1940)
    House of Usher (1960)
    House of Wax (1953)
    House on Haunted Hill (1958)
    The Invisible Man Returns (1940)
    The Keys of the Kingdom (1944)
    Laura (1944)
    The Masque of the Red Death (1964)
    Master of the World (1961)
    Pit and the Pendulum (1961)
    The Raven (1963)
    Tales of Terror (1962)
    The Ten Commandments (1956)
    Theatre of Blood (1973)
    Twice-Told Tales (1963)
    The Whales of August (1987)
    Wilson (1944)
pricey: 4 dear, high 5 steep 6 costly 9 expensive 10 at a premium, exorbitant
Prichard: 4 city, town
  locale: 7 Alabama
prick: 3 jab, jag 4 bore, goad, hurt, prod, spur, stab 5 pique, punch, smart, spike, sting, thorn, wound 6 needle, pierce, twinge, whip up 7 pinhole, prickle, scratch 8 puncture 9 penetrate, perforate 10 incitement
  starter: 3 pin
  up one's ears: 6 listen
prickle: 4 barb 5 briar, brier, prick, smart, sting, thorn 6 nettle, tingle 7 bristle
prickly: 5 sharp, spiky, spiny 6 barbed, crabby, grumpy, knotty, thorny, touchy, tricky, trying 7 brambly, bristly, fretful, peevish, pointed, waspish 8 annoying, fretsome, grumpish, involved, petulant, snappish, ticklish 9 difficult, irritable 10 nettlesome, unamenable
  combining form: 5 echin- 6 echino-
prickly __: 3 ash 4 heat, pear 5 poppy
prickly pear: 5 fruit 6 cactus
  locale: 6 desert
Prick Up Your Ears (1987 film)
  cast: Alfred Molina, Gary Oldman, Vanessa Redgrave
  director: Stephen Frears
pricy
  see pricey
pride: 3 ego 4 airs, brag, crow, face 5 boast, cream, preen, strut, vaunt

6 egoism, hubris, hybris, puff up, vanity 7 conceit, egotism, ego trip, emotion, hauteur, swagger, triumph 8 ornament, smugness, snobbery 9 arrogance, cockiness, gasconade, immodesty, insolence, loftiness, vainglory 10 narcissism, pretension, self-esteem
and joy: 8 treasure
burst with ~: 4 brag 5 boast, gloat, glory, kvell, strut 7 swagger
member: 3 cub 4 lion 7 lioness
successor: 4 fall
__ pride: 5 civic 6 ethnic
Pride: 7 Charley, Charlie, Hofstra
Pride __...: 5 goeth
pride and __: 3 joy
Pride and Joy (1963 song) artist: Marvin Gaye
Pride and Prejudice: 4 film 5 novel
author: Jane Austen
cast: Greer Garson, Edmund Gwenn, Edna May Oliver, Laurence Olivier
character: 5 Darcy, Kitty, Lydia 6 Bennet
director: Robert Z. Leonard
Pride, Charley: 6 singer
song: Kiss an Angel Good Mornin' (1971)
Pride of the Marines (1945 film)
cast: Dane Clark, John Garfield, Eleanor Parker
director: Delmer Daves
Pride of the Yankees, The (1942 film)
cast: Walter Brennan, Gary Cooper, Teresa Wright
director: Sam Wood
prie-__: 4 dieu 5 dieux
prie-dieu, use a: 4 pray 5 kneel
prier: 5 snoop 7 crowbar 9 buttinsky 10 Nosy Parker
priest: 4 abbé, imam, lama, monk, rank 5 druid, friar, geshe, padre, roshi, tulku, vicar 6 bishop, cleric, curate, divine, father, khenpo, parson, pastor, rector, sensei, shaman 7 adviser, advisor, holy man, pontiff 8 chaplain, minister, rinpoche 9 monsignor 10 archbishop
ancient Roman ~: 6 flamen
Asian ~: 4 lama 5 geshe, roshi, tulku 6 khenpo, sensei 8 rinpoche
calendar: 4 ordo
Celtic ~: 5 druid
cup: 7 chalice
ender: 3 ess
flock: 4 fold 5 laity 6 parish
French ~: 4 abbé
garment: 3 alb, zen 4 cope 5 amice, orale, robes 6 rakasu 8 vestment
headdress: 5 miter, mitre
in a Nash verse: 4 lama
item: 6 censer 7 incense
mantle: 4 cope
Muslim ~: 4 imam
name meaning ~: 5 Cohen
one-L ~: 4 lama
plate: 5 paten
school: 8 lamasery, seminary 9 monastery
stole: 5 amice
subordinate: 6 curate, deacon
__ priest: 4 high
Priest: 3 Pat
__ Priest: 5 Judas, Judge
Priest director: 4 Bird
__ priestess: 4 high
priesthood: 6 clergy
Priestley: 2 J.B. 5 Jason 6 Joseph
Priestley, J.B.: 6 writer 7 British 8 essayist 10 playwright
Priestley, Joseph: 7 British, chemist
priestly: 5 pious 8 clerical, hieratic 9 religious
combining form: 4 hier- 5 hiero-
not ~: 4 laic 6 laical
prig: 5 dandy, prude, snoot 6 carper, purist 7 caviler, fusspot, puritan 8 bluenose 9 formalist, nice Nelly, nitpicker, Victorian 10 fuddy-duddy, goody-goody
priggish: 4 prim, smug 5 staid, stiff 6 proper, stuffy 7 prudish 8 pedantic 10 goody-goody, pedantical
Prigogine, Ilya: 7 Belgian, chemist 8 Nobelist
prill: 3 ore
prim: 3 coy 4 nice, smug, tidy 5 fussy, rigid, stiff 6 choosy, demure, formal, prissy, proper, sedate, stuffy 7 choosey, correct, genteel, prudish, stilted, upright, uptight 8 decorous, priggish, reserved, starched 9 bluenosed, squeamish, Victorian 10 fastidious, fuddy-duddy, goody-goody, nit-picking, overmodest, particular, unassuming
ender: 4 rose
prima __ pares: 5 inter
Prima and Keely Smith, Louis
song: That Old Black Magic (1958) Wonderland by Night (1960)
prima ballerina: 6 dancer, étoile
Prima Ballerina artist: 5 Degas
primacy: 4 lead, rank 7 command 8 hegemony 9 supremacy 10 ascendance, ascendancy, ascendence, ascendency, leadership
prima donna: 4 diva 6 artist, singer 7 actress, artiste 8 vocalist
problem: 3 ego
prima facie: 6 likely 7 obvious
Primal Fear (1996 film)
cast: Richard Gere, Laura Linney, John Mahoney, Edward Norton, Alfre Woodard
director: Gregory Hoblit
Prima, Louis: 6 singer 9 trumpeter
spouse: Keely Smith
prim and __: 6 proper
primarily: 5 first 6 mainly, mostly 7 at first, chiefly, largely, overall 8 above all 9 basically, generally, in essence, initially 10 at the start, especially, on the whole, originally
primary: 3 key, top 4 arch, main 5 basal, basic, chief, first, major, vital 6 needed, simple, staple, urgent 7 central, crucial, highest, initial, leading, pivotal, premier, radical, special 8 cardinal, dominant, earliest, election, foremost, greatest, headmost, original, required, superior, ultimate 9 beginning, elemental, essential, governing, immediate, important, mandatory, necessary, number one, paramount, principal, uppermost 10 aboriginal, elementary, overriding, underlying
color: 3 red 4 blue, cyan 5 green 6 yellow 7 magenta
participant: 5 voter
school: 4 elem., el-hi 10 elementary
primary __: 4 beam, care, cell, root, type, wave 5 color, group, metal, tooth, xylem 6 accent, letter, memory, phloem, school, stress, tissue 7 contact, quality, rainbow
__ primary: 4 open 6 closed, direct, runoff
Primary Colors: 4 book, film
author: 5 Klein
cast: Kathy Bates, Emma Thompson, John Travolta
director: Mike Nichols
primate: 3 ape, man 4 saki, titi 5 biped, chimp, drill, human, jocko, lemur, loris, magot, orang, potto, shrew 6 aye-aye, baboon, Bandar, bishop, galago, gelada, gibbon, grivet, guenon, howler, langur, macaco, mammal, monkey, rhesus, simian, uakari, vervet 7 colobus, gorilla, guereza, hoolock, macaque, sapajou, siamang, tamarin, tarsier 8 bush baby, capuchin, mandrill, mangabey, marmoset, talapoin 9 orangutan 10 Barbary ape, chimpanzee, orangutang
African ~: 5 chimp, drill, indri, lemur, potto 6 aye-aye, baboon, galago, gelada, grivet, guenon, vervet 7 colobus, gorilla, guereza 8 bush baby, mandrill, mangabey, talapoin 10 Barbary ape, chimpanzee
arboreal ~: 5 lemur, orang 6 gibbon 7 tarsier 9 orangutan
Asian ~: 5 orang 6 gibbon, langur 7 macaque, siamang, tarsier 9 orangutan 10 orangutang
Borneo ~: 5 orang 9 orangutan
Central American ~: 7 sapajou 8 capuchin, marmoset
genus: 4 homo
Gibraltar ~: 10 Barbary ape
hypothetical ~: 6 apeman
Indian ~: 5 loris 6 Bandar, rhesus 7 hoolock
nocturnal ~: 5 lemur, loris 6 aye-aye, galago 7 tarsier 8 bush baby
South American ~: 4 saki, titi 6 uakari 7 tamarin 8 capuchin, marmoset
tailless ~: 3 ape 4 lori
__ primavera: 5 pasta
prime: 3 def, fab, fit, rad 4 aces, A-one, best, boss, braw, cool, dawn, dece, fine, gear, good, head, hour, keen, main, morn, move, neat, nice, peak, phat, pink, ripe, tops, tuff 5 bloom, brief, chief, coach, dandy, ducky, elite, first, grade, grand, great, groom, heavy, marvy, neato, nobby, primo, prize, ready, slick, start, sunup, super, swell, train, vigor, youth 6 bang on, bang-up, bonzer, bosker, choice, direct, divine, dreamy, excite, far-out, fill in, flower, get set, gnarly, goodly, grade A, groovy, heyday, heydey, inform, lovely, master, notify, peachy, school, select, simple, slap-up, spot on, spring, superb, terrif, tiptop, unreal, utmost, whizzo, wicked, zenith 7 amazing, awesome, capital, central, corking, highest, initial, leading, morning, perfect, premier, prepare, provoke, ripping, skookum, stellar, sublime, sunrise, supreme, vintage 8 best days, cardinal, champion, daybreak, dazzling, deciding, dominant, earliest, especial, eximious, fabulous, five-star, foremost, four-star, frabjous, glorious, greatest, headmost, heavenly, jim-dandy, majority, maturity, motivate, original, rehearse, slam-bang, smashing, splendid, standout, sterling, stickout, superior, terrific, top-level, topnotch, ultimate, very good, vitality, wondrous 9 bodacious, essential, excellent, exemplary, exquisite, first-rate, flowering, full-grown, galvanize, governing, high-grade, hunky-dory, make ready, marvelous, matchless, nonpareil, number one, paramount, principal, sollicker, top-drawer, topflight, unrivaled, uppermost, uttermost, wonderful 10 first-class, hotsy-totsy, jack-a-dandy, out of sight, overriding, peachy-keen, perfection, phenomenal, predispose, remarkable, springtime, stupendous, super-duper, underlying, unrivalled, world-class
first ~: 3 two
for the picking: 4 ripe
in one's ~: 4 ripe 6 mature 8 vigorous
mover: 5 cause
not quite ~: 6 choice
of life: 8 fullness, maturity
past its ~: 3 old 5 moldy, passé, stale
the pump: 4 fund 9 subsidize
time: 3 ten 4 nine 5 eight, night, seven, ten p.m. 6 nine p.m. 7 eight p.m., evening, seven p.m.
prime __: 3 rib 4 cost, rate, ribs, time 5 field, ideal, mover 6 number
Prime Cut (1972 film)
cast: Gene Hackman, Lee Marvin, Angel Tompkins
director: Michael Ritchie
primed: 3 set 5 ready 6 all set 7 groomed 8 prepared 9 rehearsed
prime lending __: 4 rate
Prime of Life, The author: Simone de Beauvoir
Prime of Miss Jean Brodie, The: 4 film 5 novel
author: Muriel Spark
cast: Pamela Franklin, Maggie Smith, Robert Stephens
director: Ronald Neame
primer: 4 book, coat, text 6 manual 8 handbook 10 schoolbook
topic: 4 ABCs 6 lesson
primero: 4 game 8 card game
prime the __: 4 pump
primeval: 3 old 5 early, first 6 native, virgin 7 ancient 8 earliest, original, virginal 9 ancestral, unevolved 10 aboriginal
upheaval: 5 chaos
primitive: 3 old, raw 4 rude, wild 5 basic, crude, early, first, rough 6 animal, coarse, native, savage, simple 7 ancient, archaic, artless, austere, bestial, natural, radical, Spartan, untamed 8 barbaric, earliest, original, pristine 9 atavistic, barbarian, barbarous, childlike, inelegant, makeshift, unevolved, unrefined, vestigial 10 aboriginal, amateurish, elementary, indigenous, underlying, unpolished
primo: 4 A-one, best, fine, good, tops 5 first, great, prime 6 unique 8 fabulous, topnotch, top-rated 9 excellent, first-rate, principal, topflight 10 first-class
Primo: 4 Levi 7 Carnera
__ primo cit.: 3 loc.
__ primo citato: 4 loco
primogenitary: 6 eldest
primordial: 3 old 5 basic, early, first 7 ancient 8 earliest, original 9 elemental, unevolved 10 aboriginal
primordial __: 4 soup
primp: 4 deck 5 fix up, groom, preen, prink 6 doll up, dude up 7 deck out, dress up, gussy up, smarten, spiff up, swank up 8 beautify, ornament, pretty up, spruce up, titivate 9 smarten up, tittivate
primrose: 5 color, oxlip, plant 6 flower, yellow
color kin: 4 buff, corn, gold, lime, rust, sand 5 blond, brass, coral, cream, lemon, maize, ocher, ochre, peach, rusty, straw 6 blonde, canary, chammy, citron, crocus, flaxen 7 apricot, chamois, citrine, mustard, nankeen, old gold, saffron, xanthic 8 daffodil 9 champagne, goldenrod
primrose __: 4 path 6 yellow 7 jasmine
__ primrose: 5 fairy 7 British, Chinese, evening
Primrose: 7 musical
songwriter: 8 Gershwin
Primrose Lane (1959 song) artist: Jerry Wallace
primus __ pares: 5 inter

prince: **4** amir, emir, male, raja **5** ameer, emeer, Harry, Henry, mogul, noble, rajah, royal, ruler **6** Andrew, dynast, Edward, gerent **7** Charles, monarch, William **8** maharaja **9** maharajah, sovereign
Abyssinian ~: **3** ras
Bard's ~: **3** Hal
in disguise: **4** frog
Islamic ~: **4** amir, emir **5** ameer, emeer
of darkness: **5** devil, Satan **7** Lucifer
of India: **4** raja **5** rajah **8** maharaja **9** maharajah
operatic ~: **4** Igor
Trojan ~: **5** Paris
word for a TV ~: **5** fresh
prince __: **5** royal **6** regent **7** consort
__ prince: **5** crown
Prince: **10** pasta sauce
competitor: **4** Ragu **5** Prego **8** Classico **10** Newman's Own **11** Aunt Millie's
Prince (singer)
born: Prince Roger Nelson
song: 1999 (1983)
7 (1992)
Alphabet St. (1988)
Batdance (1989)
Cream (1991)
Delirious (1983)
Diamonds and Pearls (1991)
Gett Off (1991)
I Could Never Take the Place of Your Man (1987)
I Hate U (1995)
I Wanna Be Your Lover (1979)
I Would Die 4 U (1984)
Kiss (1986)
Let's Go Crazy (1984)
Little Red Corvette (1983)
The Most Beautiful Girl in the World (1994)
Partyman (1989)
Pop Life (1985)
Purple Rain (1984)
Raspberry Beret (1985)
Sign 'O' the Times (1987)
Thieves in the Temple (1990)
U Got the Look (1987)
When Doves Cry (1984)
Prince __: **3** Ali, Hal **4** Igor **7** Valiant
Prince __ Island: **6** Edward
Prince __ Sound: **7** William
Prince Albert: **4** city, town
locale: **6** Canada
Prince Albert __: **4** coat
Prince and the Pauper, The: **4** film **5** novel
author: Mark Twain
cast: Errol Flynn, Billy Mauch, Bobby Mauch, Claude Rains
character: **3** Tom **4** Hugo **5** Canty, Edith **6** Edward, Hendon
director: William Keighley
Prince Edward Island: **8** province
capital: Charlottetown
city: **6** Souris **8** Alberton, Cornwall
locale: **6** Canada
Prince George: **4** city, town
locale: **6** Canada
Prince Harry brother: **5** Wills
Prince Igor: **5** opera
composer: **7** Borodin
princely: **5** noble, regal, ritzy, royal, swank **6** lavish, lordly, swanky **7** copious, liberal, profuse **8** abundant, generous, handsome, imperial, splendid **9** bountiful, luxurious, plentiful, sumptuous **10** altruistic, beneficent, benevolent, bighearted, unstinting
Prince of __: **5** Peace, Wales
__ Prince of Bel Air: **5** Fresh
Prince of Egypt, The (1998 film)
voice cast: Sandra Bullock, Ralph Fiennes, Val Kilmer, Michelle Pfeiffer
Prince of the City (1981 film)
cast: Jerry Orbach, Treat Williams
director: Sidney Lumet
Prince of Tides, The (1991 film)
cast: Blythe Danner, Nick Nolte, Barbra Streisand
director: Barbra Streisand
Prince of Wales: **4** heir **7** Charles
game: **4** polo
motto: **6** I serve **7** Ich Dien
Prince Rupert: **4** city, port, town
locale: **6** Canada
princess: **4** rani **5** noble, royal, ruler, woman **6** gerent **7** monarch **9** sovereign
adornment: **5** tiara
British ~: **4** Anne
disturber: **3** pea
Golden Fleece ~: **5** Medea
of India: **4** rani **5** ranee **8** maharani
opera ~: **4** Aïda
Raj ~: **5** begum
princess __: **4** post, tree **5** royal **6** flower, regent
__ princess: **5** crown
Princess __: **3** Ida **5** Daisy, Diana, phone **7** Caraboo, Cruises
Princess __, The: **5** Bride **7** Diaries
Princess and the Pea, The author: Hans Christian Andersen
Princess and the Pirate, The (1944 film)
cast: Bob Hope, Virginia Mayo, Walter Slezak
Princess Bride, The (1987 film)
cast: Billy Crystal, Cary Elwes, Peter Falk, Christopher Guest, Carol Kane, Mandy Patinkin, Chris Sarandon, Robin Wright
director: Rob Reiner
Princess Caraboo (1994 film)
cast: Jim Broadbent, Phoebe Cates, Wendy Hughes
director: Michael Austin
Princess Casamassima, The author: Henry James
Princess Comes Across, The (1936 film)
cast: Douglass Dumbrille, Carole Lombard, Fred MacMurray
Princess Daisy author: Judith Krantz
Princess Diaries, The (2001 film)
cast: Julie Andrews, Hector Elizondo, Anne Hathaway, Heather Matarazzo
director: Garry Marshall
Princess Ida: **8** operetta
composer: **7** Gilbert **8** Sullivan
Princess of Power: **5** She-Ra
__ Princess, The: **6** Jungle, Little
__ Prince, The: **6** Little
Princeton: **4** city, peak, town **5** mount **8** mountain
athletes: **6** Tigers
league: **3** Ivy
locale: **7** Rockies, Sawatch **8** Colorado **9** New Jersey
Prince Valiant: **5** comic **10** comic strip
Aleta's kingdom, in ~: **10** Misty Isles
Arn's domain, in ~: **3** Orr
son: **3** Arn
wife: **5** Aleta
Prince William __: **5** Sound
Princip: **7** Gavrilo
principal: **3** key, top **4** arch, dean, head, lead, main, star **5** basic, chief, first, grand, major, money, prime **6** assets, leader, master, rector, ruling, staple, top dog **7** capital, central, highest, leading, pivotal, premier, primary, stellar, supreme **8** cardinal, champion, crowning, deciding, director, dominant, foremost, greatest, headmost, superior **9** essential, governing, important, organizer, paramount, preceptor, sovereign, uppermost **10** headmaster, overriding, preeminent, prevailing
combining form: **4** arch-
dish: **6** entrée
in music: **5** primo
part: **4** bulk **8** majority **10** lion's share
principal __: **3** sum **4** axis **5** focus, ideal, parts, plane, point, value **6** clause, rafter, series
Principal: **8** Victoria
principality: **6** nation **7** country
principally: **6** mainly, mostly **7** chiefly, largely, notably, overall **8** above all **9** basically, eminently, generally, in the main, primarily, supremely
Principal, The (1987 film)
cast: James Belushi, Rae Dawn Chong, Louis Gossett Jr.
director: Christopher Cain
Principia Mathematica author: Alfred North Whitehead
principle: **3** ism, law **4** code, fact, rule, sake, soul **5** axiom, basis, canon, credo, creed, dogma, ethic, ideal, maxim, tenet, truth **6** belief, dictum, ground, origin **7** dictate, formula, precept, probity, scruple, theorem **8** doctrine, morality, rudiment, standard, teaching **9** beginning, criterion, discovery, essential, integrity, knowledge, rationale **10** conviction, foundation, generality, honestness, hypothesis, principium, regulation
guiding ~: **3** saw **5** adage, axiom, credo, maxim, moral, motto, tenet **6** belief, byword, dictum, saying, slogan, war cry **7** epigram, precept, proverb **8** aphorism **9** battle cry, platitude, watchword
in ~: **7** ideally
palindromic ~: **5** tenet
universal ~: **3** law **5** axiom, given
__ principle: **5** first, Mach's, vital **6** bitter **7** banking, duality, Fermat's, Huygens, maximum
__ Principle: **5** Peter
principled: **4** fair, just **5** moral, noble, right **6** trusty **7** ethical, upright **8** virtuous **10** scrupulous
principles: **4** code **5** creed, dogma, faith **6** ethics, morals, values **7** conduct, probity **8** ideology, morality, superego **9** character, integrity, rectitude **10** conscience
Principles and Practices of Medicine author: **5** Osler
Prine: **4** John
Pringle: **6** Aileen
Pringle's competitor: **4** Lay's, Wise **7** Doritos
prink: **4** trim **5** preen, primp **6** doll up, dude up **7** deck out, dress up, gussy up, spiff up **8** ornament, spruce up **9** smarten up
print: **4** book, copy, font, mark, step, type **5** issue, litho, photo, stamp, write **6** glossy, letter, medium, put out, run off **7** engrave, etching, impress, imprint, journal, let roll, letters, picture, publish, reissue, reprint, writing **8** halftone, magazine, put to bed, snapshot, typeface **9** engraving, go to press, lettering, newspaper, newsprint, reproduce **10** characters, impression, lithograph, newsletter, periodical, photograph, typescript
check the fine ~: **4** pore **5** study **8** pore over
ender: **3** out
fine ~: **5** terms **7** details, strings **8** provisos **10** conditions, provisions
fit to ~: **5** newsy **7** topical
indelibly: **4** etch
photographic ~: **3** pos. **5** proof **8** positive
starter: **3** off **4** blue, foot, hand, news, wood **5** thumb, voice **6** finger
see also fingerprint
print __: **3** run **4** shop **5** wheel
__ print: **3** gum **4** fine, Jouy **5** block, India, out of, small **6** answer **7** contact, married, paisley, release
__-print: **5** large, out-of
printed __: **6** matter **7** circuit
printed material: **4** book, text, tome **6** manual, volume
printemps: **6** French, spring
Printemps sculptor: **4** Erté
printer
apprentice: **5** devil
goof: **4** typo **7** erratum
goofs: **6** errata
mark: **4** dele, fist, stet **5** caret, obeli **6** dagger, obelus
measure: **2** em, en **4** pica, quad **6** em dash, em quad, en dash, en quad
need: **3** ink **5** paper, press **9** cartridge
option: **4** font **8** font size, typeface
part: **4** drum **6** feeder, roller **9** cartridge
speed: **3** cps, lpm
__ printer: **5** color, laser **6** ink-jet **7** contact, optical, thermal
printing: **3** run **4** type **5** issue **7** edition
compose for ~: **3** set **7** typeset
flourish: **5** swash **6** paraph
fluid: **3** ink
mold: **3** mat
process: **4** roto
printing __: **3** ink **5** frame, paper, press **6** office
__ printing: **3** bat, jet **6** blotch, offset, relief, resist **7** contact, extract, process
Prinze Jr., Freddie: **5** actor
film: I Know What You Did Last Summer (1997)
I Still Know What You Did Last Summer (1998)
Scooby-Doo (2002)
She's All That (1999)
spouse: Sarah Michelle Gellar
prior: **4** abbé, monk, past, prev. **5** ahead, older **6** before, former **7** advance, brother, earlier, one-time **8** anterior, foregone, previous **9** foregoing, in advance, preceding **10** antecedent
combining form: **4** arch- **5** arche-, archi- **6** yester-
concern: **4** monk **7** brother
prefix: **3** pre-, pro- **4** ante-
superior: **5** abbot
to: **3** ere **5** afore, until **6** before, erenow **7** ahead of **9** in advance, preceding
prioress: **3** nun **6** sister
priority: **4** lead, rank **5** order **7** urgency **8** emphasis **9** immediacy, seniority, supremacy **10** ascendency, importance, precedence, preference, right of way
Priority __: **4** Mail
priory: **5** abbey **8** cloister **9** monastery
Pripet: **5** river
city on the ~: **5** Pinsk
locale: **7** Belarus, Ukraine
__ pris: **5** parti
Priscilla: **4** Lane **6** Barnes **7** Presley
prism: **7** rainbow
prismatic: **10** iridescent
prison: **3** can, jug, pen **4** bars, brig, coop, gaol, jail, keep, poky, stir **5** clink, gulag, joint, pokey, tower **6** cooler, lockup **7** dungeon, slammer **8** bastille, big house, stockade **9** captivity **10** guardhouse

head: 6 warden
in Britain: 4 gaol
related: 5 penal
send to ~: 7 convict 8 sentence
unit: 4 cell
__ Prison Blues: 6 Folsom
prisoner: 3 con 5 felon, lifer 6 inmate 7 captive, convict, hostage 8 criminal, detainee, internee, jailbird, offender, yardbird 10 lawbreaker
take ~: 3 nab 4 bust 5 pinch, run in, seize 6 arrest, collar 7 capture 9 apprehend
wear: 5 irons 7 manacle, shackle, stripes
prisoner of __: 3 war
Prisoner of Chillon, The author: Byron
Prisoner of Second Avenue, The: 4 film, play
author: Neil Simon
cast: Anne Bancroft, Jack Lemmon, Gene Saks
character: 3 Mel 4 Edna 6 Edison
director: Melvin Frank
Prisoner of Shark Island, The (1936 film)
cast: Warner Baxter, Gloria Stuart
director: John Ford
Prisoner of Zenda, The: 4 film 5 novel
author: Anthony Hope
cast: Madeleine Carroll, Ronald Colman, Douglas Fairbanks Jr.
character: 4 Rose, Sapt 5 Josef 6 Flavia, Rudolf, Rupert
director: John Cromwell
prisoner's base: 4 game
Prisoner, The (1955 film)
cast: Alec Guinness, Jack Hawkins
director: Peter Glenville
Prison of Ice author: Dean Koontz
priss: 5 prude 8 bluenose 10 goody-goody
prissy: 4 prim 5 fussy, picky, sissy 6 demure, proper, stuffy 7 finicky, genteel, prudish 8 finiking, finnicky, overnice, precious 9 sissified, squeamish, Victorian 10 fastidious, goody-goody, párticular, tight-laced
Pristina's province: 6 Kosovo
pristine: 4 pure 5 clean 6 unused, virgin, washed 7 aseptic 8 germ-free, hygienic, innocent, original, sanitary, spotless, unmarred, unsoiled, virginal 9 primitive, stainless, undefiled, unspoiled, unsullied 10 antiseptic, immaculate, unpolluted
Pritchett, V.S.: 6 writer 7 British
work: Mr. Beluncle
__ prius: 4 nisi
privacy: 5 quiet 7 retreat, secrecy 8 solitude 9 aloneness, isolation, seclusion 10 retirement
allow some ~: 5 let be 10 leave alone
invade ~: 3 pry 4 nose, poke 5 mix in, snoop 6 horn in, impose, kibitz, meddle, worm in 7 barge in, break in, intrude, obtrude 9 eavesdrop, interfere, intervene
private: 2 GI 3 own 4 rank 5 inner, privy, quiet 6 covert, hidden, inside, inward, lonely, masked, remote, secret, unseen, untold, veiled 7 cloaked, furtive, soldier, special 8 desolate, discreet, esoteric, hush-hush, interior, intimate, isolated, obscured, personal, reserved, secluded, separate, shrouded, solitary 9 concealed, disguised, exclusive, innermost, legionary, nonpublic, reclusive, secretive, withdrawn 10 classified, first-class, individual, restricted, tucked away, unattended, undercover, under wraps, unofficial
eye: 3 tec 4 dick, tail 6 shadow, shamus, sleuth 7 gumshoe 9 detective
having ~ knowledge: 4 in on
hoard: 5 stash 7 reserve 9 stockpile
make ~: 4 lock 5 fence 7 exclude, seclude 10 soundproof
not ~: 6 public
reply: 3 sir 5 no sir 6 yes sir
school: 4 acad. 7 academy
source: 5 cache, hoard, stash
teacher: 5 coach, tutor 7 trainer
private __: 3 eye 4 bill 5 brand, label, trust 6 school, sector, treaty 7 company
private __ class: 5 first
Private __: 4 Eyes 5 Lives 6 Dancer, Member
Private Affairs of Bel Ami, The (1947 film)
cast: Ann Dvorak, Angela Lansbury, George Sanders
director: Albert Lewin
Private Benjamin (1980 film)
cast: Armand Assante, Eileen Brennan, Goldie Hawn
director: Howard Zieff
Private Dancer (1985 song) artist: Tina Turner
privateer: 4 ship 6 pirate 7 brigand, corsair 8 rapparee, sea rover 9 buccaneer 10 freebooter
Private Eyes (1981 song) artist: Hall and Oates
__ Private Idaho: 5 My Own
Private Life of Henry VIII, The (1933 film)
cast: Binnie Barnes, Robert Donat, Elsa Lanchester, Charles Laughton, Merle Oberon
director: Alexander Korda
Private Life of Sherlock Holmes, The (1970 film)
cast: Colin Blakely, Genevieve Page, Robert Stephens
director: Billy Wilder
Private Lives: 4 film, play
author: Noël Coward
cast: Una Merkel, Robert Montgomery, Norma Shearer
character: 5 Chase, Elyot, Sibyl 6 Amanda, Prynne, Victor
director: Sidney Franklin
Private Lives of Elizabeth and Essex, The (1939 film)
cast: Bette Davis, Olivia de Havilland, Errol Flynn
director: Michael Curtiz
privately: 5 alone, aside 6 inward 7 inwards, sub rosa 8 secretly 9 between us, entre nous, off-camera
privately-owned business: 5 indie
Private Pleasures author: Lawrence Sanders
__ Private Ryan: 6 Saving
__ Privates: 4 Buck
Private Secretary (CBS/NBC sitcom)
cast: Don Porter (Peter Sands) Ann Sothern (Susie McNamara)
Private's Progress (1956 film)
cast: Jill Adams, Richard Attenborough
director: John Boulting
Private View, A author: 5 Havel
privation: 4 lack, loss, need, want 6 misery, penury 7 absence, poverty 8 distress, hardship 9 indigence 10 bankruptcy, deficiency
privet: 5 hedge, shrub
privilege: 3 due 4 boon, rank 5 claim, favor, grant, honor, power, right, title 6 chance, option 7 benefit, charter, entitle, freedom, intitle, liberty, license 8 immunity, sanction 9 advantage, authority, exception, exemption, franchise, indemnity 10 birthright, concession, indulgence, perquisite
privileged: 4 free, rich 5 elite, flush, privy 6 exempt, immune, loaded, monied, secret, select, vested 7 excused, favored, moneyed, special, wealthy, well-off 8 affluent, eligible, entitled, in clover, indulged, licensed, powerful, well-to-do 9 empowered, exclusive, qualified, well-fixed 10 fair-haired, in the dough, in the money, propertied, prosperous, well-heeled
group: 5 elite, haves 6 jet set
privy: 6 covert, hidden, secret 7 latrine, private 8 hush-hush, outhouse, personal, secluded 9 concealed, innermost
to: 4 in on 5 aware 7 aware of, wised up 8 apprised, informed 9 cognizant, in the know 10 acquainted
privy __: 4 coat, seal 5 purse 7 chamber, council
prix __: 4 fixe
__ Prix: 5 Grand
prize: 3 cup, gem, pip, pry, top 4 haul, like, loot, love, pick, plum, swag 5 adore, award, catch, crown, dandy, honey, honor, jewel, kitty, medal, peach, pearl, prime, purse, stake, title, value 6 choice, esteem, honors, payoff, revere, reward, ribbon, spoils, trophy 7 care for, cherish, guerdon, jackpot, laurels, premium 8 accolade, citation, dividend, gold star, hold dear, pickings, topnotch, treasure, windfall, winnings 9 care about, first-rate, humdinger, medallion, recommend, rejoice in 10 appreciate, blue ribbon, decoration, first place, inducement, set store by
carnival ~: 6 kewpie 9 teddy bear
ender: 5 fight 6 winner 7 fighter
fighting: 4 ring 6 boxing
game-show ~: 3 car 4 cash, trip 6 cruise
take the ~: 3 win
prize __: 4 ring 5 money
__ prize: 4 door 5 booby, first, third 6 second
__ Prize: 5 Nobel 8 Pulitzer
prized: 4 dear 7 beloved, darling 8 precious, valuable 9 priceless
possession: 3 gem 5 asset 8 treasure, valuable
prizefighter: 3 pug 5 boxer 7 bruiser
org.: 3 WBA
wear: 4 robe 6 gloves, trunks
Prizefighter and the Lady, The (1933 film)
cast: Max Baer, Otto Kruger, Myrna Loy
director: W.S. Van Dyke
prizefighting: 5 sport 6 boxing
Prize of Gold, A (1955 film)
cast: Nigel Patrick, Richard Widmark, Mai Zetterling
director: Mark Robson
Prize, The (1963 film)
cast: Paul Newman, Edward G. Robinson, Elke Sommer
director: Mark Robson
prizewinner: 5 champ 6 victor 8 champion, medalist
prizing: 7 valuing
Prizm: 3 car, Geo 4 auto 10 automobile
Prizzi's Honor (1985 film)
cast: Anjelica Huston, Robert Loggia, Jack Nicholson, Kathleen Turner
director: John Huston
pro: 3 ace, for 4 whiz 5 crack, maven, mavin 6 behind, expert, master, player, wizard 7 old hand, veteran 8 favoring, skillful 9 big-league, endorsing, in favor of 10 big leaguer, past master, specialist
bono: 4 free 6 gratis
opposite: 3 con 4 anti 6 contra
tem: 6 acting 7 interim
vote: 3 aye, yea, yes
pro __: 3 tem 4 bono, rata 5 forma 6 patria 7 memoria, tempore
Pro __: 4 Bowl
proa: 4 boat 9 outrigger
pro-am: 5 event 7 tourney 10 tournament
game: 4 golf
holder: 3 PGA
pro and __: 3 con
probability: 4 odds 6 chance, toss-up 7 chances, outlook 8 prospect 10 likelihood
probability __: 5 curve 6 theory 7 density
__ probability: 5 in all
probable: 3 apt 6 likely, odds-on 7 earthly, logical, regular, seeming 8 apparent, credible, expected, feasible, possible, presumed, rational 9 plausible, promising, thinkable 10 believable, contingent, in the cards, legitimate, ostensible, presumable, reasonable
not ~: 8 unlikely
probably: 5 maybe 6 adverb, likely 7 no doubt, perhaps 8 possibly 9 assumably, doubtless, like as not, perchance, seemingly 10 apparently, imaginably, most likely, presumably
__ probandi: 4 onus
probate concern: 4 will 6 estate
probationary: 5 trial 9 tentative
probe: 3 ask, dig 4 comb, hunt, poke, prod, pump, quiz, sift, test 5 delve, enter, grope, plumb, query, quest, study, touch 6 go into, search, verify 7 enquire, enquiry, examine, explore, fish for, inquire, inquiry, inspect, Pioneer, probing, pry into, ransack, rummage, Voyager 8 check out, follow up, look into, question, research, scrutiny, see about, sound out 9 catechize, criticize, delve into, feel about, penetrate, pick apart 10 inspection, poke around, scrutinize
__ probe: 3 DNA 5 space
Probe: 3 car 4 auto, Ford 10 automobile
probing, as a look: 6 shrewd 8 piercing 9 quizzical
probity: 4 good 5 honor 6 virtue 7 decency, honesty, loyalty 8 fairness, goodness, morality, veracity 9 character, good faith, innocence, integrity, principle, rectitude, sincerity 10 principles
problem: 3 rub, woe 4 mess, snag 5 delay, doubt, hitch, issue, mix-up, poser, query, snarl, topic, vexer, worry 6 bother, crunch, enigma, glitch, hang-up, hassle, holdup, matter, misery, pickle, puzzle, riddle, scrape, teaser, unruly 7 bad news, bugaboo, dilemma, dispute, example, mystery, puzzler, squeeze, stumper, trouble 8 headache, hot water, obstacle, quandary, question 9 annoyance, conundrum, deep water, difficult, labyrinth, situation 10 can of worms, difficulty
no ~: 4 easy 6 simple 8 duck soup, kid stuff 10 child's play
problematic: 4 iffy, moot, open 5 shaky, vague 6 chancy, knotty, thorny, tricky, unsure 7 dubious, suspect, unknown 8 arguable, doubtful, puzzling 9 ambiguous, debatable, enigmatic, uncertain, unsettled, worrisome
Problems (1958 song) artist: Everly Brothers

problem-solve: 5 think 8 consider, mull over 10 brainstorm
proboscis: 4 beak, nose 5 snoot, snout, trunk 6 beezer
Pro Bowl
contender: 3 AFC, NFC
site: 6 Hawaii
procedure: 3 way 4 mode, plan, step 5 setup, usage 6 action, agenda, course, custom, manner, method, policy, recipe, system 7 formula, measure, process, program, red tape, routine 8 approach, channels, practice, strategy 9 formality, mechanism, operation, technique 10 experiment, regulation, technology
according to ~: 4 duly
backup ~: 5 plan B
part: 4 step 5 phase, stage
question of ~: 3 how
usual ~: 4 wont 5 habit, usage 6 custom, policy, system 7 routine 8 practice 9 tradition 10 observance
proceed: 2 go 3 run 4 fare, move, pass, pour, rise, stem, wend 5 arise, ensue, get on, issue, march, start 6 derive, follow, happen, move on, pursue, push on, repair, result, resume, spring, take up, travel 7 advance, carry on, emanate, go ahead, journey, press on, push off 8 come from, continue, go on with, lengthen, progress 9 arise from, get to work, go forward, grow out of, originate, persevere 10 spring from, take action
briskly: 3 hie, jog, run 4 trot 5 hurry
(from): 4 flow 5 arise, issue 7 develop
laboriously: 4 plow, slog, wade 6 trudge
smoothly: 3 hum 4 flow, roll
proceedings: 4 acta 6 annals, doings, events 7 affairs, lawsuit, matters, minutes, records 8 archives, business, dealings, goings-on 9 documents 10 happenings
start legal ~: 3 sue 6 charge 8 litigate
proceeds: 3 pay 4 gain, gate, goes, take 5 funds, lucre, split, yield 6 income, profit, return, reward 7 returns, revenue 8 earnings, interest, receipts 9 royalties
process: 3 can, dry, way 4 fill, flow, flux, form, limb, mode, ship, step, wise, writ 5 candy, means, phase, smelt, smoke, stage, treat, trial 6 action, course, freeze, growth, handle, manner, method, policy, recipe, refine, screen, system 7 measure, prepare, program, routine, summons 8 channels, deal with, movement, practice, preserve, subpoena 9 dehydrate, evolution, freeze-dry, mechanism, operation, procedure, technique, transform, unfolding 10 litigation
due ~: 3 law 7 justice
due ~ championer: 4 ACLU
food: 3 can, fry 4 bake, boil, chew, cook, stew 5 broil, roast 6 digest, freeze 7 parboil 8 marinate, preserve 9 masticate
lumber: 3 cut, saw 4 mill
ore: 5 smelt 6 reduce, refine
part of a ~: 4 step 5 phase, stage
veggies: 4 chop, core, cube, dice, pare, peel 5 grate, slice
__ process: 3 due, oxo 4 Hall 5 basic, diazo, Haber, kraft, world 6 Benday, carbon, carbro, duplex, Frasch, Markov, social, Solvay 7 Bergius, bromoil, ciliary, contact, cyanide, lost-wax, Markoff, mastoid, spinous, styloid, sulfate, sulfite, trustee
processed __: 6 cheese
__ processing: 4 data, word 5 batch
procession: 3 run 4 file, line, rank 5 array, cycle, march, order, train 6 column, course, parade, review, series, string 7 caravan, cortege, pageant 8 movement, sequence 9 cavalcade, motorcade 10 succession
processor
food ~: 5 belly, corer, dicer, mixer, parer 6 enzyme, grater, peeler, slicer 7 blender, stomach
grain ~: 4 mill
wood ~: 3 saw 7 sawmill 8 chainsaw 10 lumberjack
word ~: 6 typist 8 software 9 secretary
__ processor: 4 data, food
Prochnow: 6 Jürgen
proclaim: 3 air 4 aver, avow, call, show, tell, vent 5 admit, break, spout, state, utter, voice 6 affirm, assert, blazon, clamor, evince, flaunt, herald, praise, spread 7 declare, deliver, divulge, expound, express, give out, profess, publish, purport, signify, trumpet 8 announce, antecede, disclose, manifest, shout out, sound off 9 advertise, broadcast, circulate, enunciate, make known, predicate, prescribe, pronounce, propagate 10 make public, promulgate
__-proclaimed: 4 self
proclaimer: 5 crier 6 hawker, herald, pedlar, pedler, vender, vendor 7 peddler 8 huckster 9 announcer
proclamation: 4 fiat 5 edict, order, ukase 6 decree, dictum, notice 7 release 9 broadcast, manifesto, statement
proclivity: 4 bent, bias, wont 5 taste 7 faculty, leaning 8 affinity, appetite, aptitude, attitude, druthers, instinct, penchant, tendency, weakness 9 direction, proneness 10 partiality, propensity
Proclus: 5 Greek 11 philosopher
Procol Harum song: A Whiter Shade of Pale (1967)
procrastinate: 3 lag 4 drag, idle, laze, loaf, poke, slow, stay, wait 5 amble, dally, defer, delay, mosey, stall, tarry 6 dawdle, linger, loiter, put off 7 adjourn, hold off, neglect, prolong, saunter, suspend 8 hang back, hesitate, let slide, lollygag, postpone, protract, slack off, straggle 9 goldbrick, temporize, waste time 10 dillydally
procrastinating: 4 lazy, poky, slow 6 draggy 7 gradual, halting, impeded, languid 8 dilatory, drawn-out, hesitant, slothful, sluggish, toddling 9 leisurely, lethargic, prolonged, snaillike, unhurried 10 deliberate, protracted
stop ~: 3 act 4 move 7 go ahead, proceed 9 get to work
procrastinator: 6 loafer 7 goof-off, slacker 9 goldbrick, lazybones
problem: 5 sloth 8 laziness
procreate: 5 beget, breed, spawn
Procter & Gamble
detergent: 3 Era
shampoo: 5 Prell
soap: 4 Lava 5 Ivory
toothpaste: 5 Crest
proctor: 7 monitor 8 look over
cry: 4 time
Proctor-__: 5 Silex
procure: 3 buy, cop, get, win 4 book, earn, find, gain, grab, have, land, take 5 annex, score, seize 6 attain, come by, derive, effect, enlist, gather, induce, line up, obtain, pick up, secure, wangle 7 acquire, compass, provide, receive, recruit, solicit 8 hold on to, purchase 9 latch onto 10 accumulate, commandeer
Procyon: 4 star
prod: 3 cue, egg, jab, jog, nag 4 coax, goad, poke, push, spur, urge, wake 5 crowd, drive, egg on, elbow, goose, hound, impel, liven, nudge, press, prick, probe, punch, rouse, shove, spark, stick, waken 6 excite, exhort, fillip, incite, needle, poke at, prompt, propel, remind, stir up, thrust, urge on, whip up 7 provoke, refresh, wheedle 8 mnemonic, motivate, persuade, pressure 9 encourage, galvanize, stimulate 10 incitement
gently: 4 coax 5 nudge 6 cajole 8 persuade
__ prod: 6 cattle
prodigal: 4 free, lush 5 ample, flush 6 lavish, myriad, rakish, rascal, wanton 7 copious, liberal, profuse, spender, teeming, wastrel 8 abundant, generous, misspent, numerous, rakehell, reckless, swarming, vagabond, wasteful 9 abounding, bounteous, bountiful, countless, excessive, exuberant, libertine, luxuriant, luxurious, sumptuous, unthrifty 10 big spender, high roller, immoderate, munificent, numberless, profligate, squanderer
prodigal __: 3 son
prodigality: 5 waste 6 excess 7 license
prodigally: 9 in a big way
Prodigal Summer author: Barbara Kingsolver
prodigious: 3 big 4 huge, vast 5 giant, great, jumbo, large 6 mighty 7 amazing, hulking, immense, mammoth, massive, sizable, titanic, uncanny, unusual 8 colossal, enormous, gigantic, king-size, oversize, singular, sizeable, striking, stunning, towering, uncommon, whapping, whopping 9 anomalous, elaborate, fantastic, herculean, humongous, marvelous, monstrous, overlarge, startling, voracious, wonderful 10 astounding, gargantuan, incredible, monumental, remarkable, stupendous, tremendous
prodigy: 3 ace 4 whiz 5 brain 6 expert, genius, marvel, rarity, wizard, wonder 7 egghead, miracle, stunner, thinker, whiz kid 8 Einstein, highbrow, rare bird, virtuoso 9 sensation 10 mastermind, phenomenon, wunderkind
Prodigy rival: 3 AOL
produce: 2 do 3 lay 4 bear, crop, form, give, make, reap, show 5 beget, breed, build, cause, crops, erect, fetch, forge, frame, fruit, goods, hatch, mount, offer, outgo, put on, put up, raise, shape, spawn, stage, stock, wares, write, yield 6 afford, author, create, design, devise, direct, effect, flower, fruits, greens, induce, invent, muster, parent, put out, render, return, secure, set off, supply, unfold, work up 7 advance, blossom, compose, deliver, develop, display, edibles, exhibit, fashion, furnish, harvest, perform, present, prosper, provide, provoke, pull off, realize, secrete, trigger, turn out 8 assemble, engender, generate, multiply, occasion, result in, set forth 9 construct, cultivate, establish, fabricate, foodstuff, originate, propagate, send forth, vegetable 10 accomplish, bring about, bring forth, contribute, effectuate, give rise to, put forward, regenerate, vegetables
a show: 5 stage
producer: 4 farm
seller: 6 grocer, market 7 grocery
unit: 4 peck, pint 5 bunch, pound, quart 6 bushel
produced, newly: 5 fresh 6 recent 7 just out
Producers, The (1968 film)
cast: Kenneth Mars, Zero Mostel, Gene Wilder
director: Mel Brooks
product: 4 line, opus, ware, work 5 brand, fruit, goods, issue 6 effect, legacy, output, result, upshot 7 outcome, results, spinoff 8 creation, offshoot 9 aftermath, commodity, handiwork, invention, outgrowth 10 derivative
production: 4 film, opus, play, show, work 5 drama, movie, revue 6 growth, output, sitcom 7 musical, program, staging, turnout 8 creation, game show 9 formation, melodrama, spectacle, stage show 10 exposition, generation, handicraft
make a ~ out of: 4 carp 5 argue 6 play up 7 nitpick 10 exaggerate
stage ~: 4 play, skit 5 drama, revue 6 comedy, review 9 melodrama
target: 5 quota
production __: 4 line 7 control
productive: 4 rich 6 aidful, arable, benign, fecund, useful 7 dynamic, fertile, gainful, helpful 8 creative, fruitful, original, positive, prolific, remedial, salutary, valuable 9 effective, effectual, efficient, energetic, favorable, inventive, lucrative, luxuriant, rewarding 10 profitable, worthwhile
starter: 7 counter
productivity: 5 yield 6 output 8 capacity
Product 19: 6 cereal
competitor: 3 Kix 4 Life, Trix 5 Kashi, Quisp, Total 6 Kaboom, Muesli, Oreo O's, Pablum, Smacks 7 All-Bran, Crispix, Harmony, Hunny B's, Mueslix, Oat Bran, Pokemon 8 Boo Berry, Cheerios, Corn Chex, Corn Pops, Fiber One, Rice Chex, Special K, Uncle Sam, Wheaties 9 Alpha Bits, Apple Zaps, Grape Nuts, Honey Comb, Just Right, Wheat Chex 10 Apple Jacks, Bran Flakes, Cap'n Crunch, Cocoa Puffs, Froot Loops, Mini-Wheats, Nutri-Grain, Puffed Rice, Quaker Oats, Smart Start 11 Cocoa Blasts, Cookie Crisp, Golden Crisp, Lucky Charms, Puffed Wheat, Sweet Crunch, Waffle Crisp
proem: 6 prolog 7 preface, prelude 8 foreword, preamble, prologue
prof: 3 don 5 tutor 7 teacher 9 professor 10 instructor
__ prof.: 4 asst. 5 assoc.
profanation: 6 misuse 9 violation
profane: 3 lay 4 cuss, foul, mock 5 abuse, crude, curse, dirty, nasty, swear, trash 6 befoul, coarse, debase, defile, filthy, impure, misuse, smutty, unholy, vulgar, wicked 7 abusive, godless, heathen, immoral, impious, mundane, obscene, raunchy, secular, ungodly, violate, worldly 8 indecent, temporal 9 atheistic, blaspheme, desecrate 10 irreverent
profanity: 4 no-no, oath 5 abuse, curse, filth, oaths 7 cursing, cussing, impiety 8 cussword, swearing 9 blasphemy, obscenity, sacrilege, swearword 10 execration
use ~: 4 cuss 5 curse, swear
profess: 4 aver, avow, pose, sing 5 admit, claim, feign, own up, teach, vouch 6 affirm, allege, assert, avouch, open up 7 declare, make out, pretend, promise, protest, purport 8 maintain, proclaim 9 dissemble, predicate
professed: 7 nominal 8 so-called 9 pretended 10 ostensible

profession: **3** art, biz, job, vow **4** game, line, post, slot, walk, work **5** craft, field, skill, trade **6** avowal, career, métier, office, sphere **7** calling, mission, pursuit, service **8** business, lifework, medicine, position, practice, vocation **9** admission, assertion, assurance, expertise, situation, specialty, statement, testimony **10** allegation, confession, contention, employment, livelihood, occupation, speciality, walk of life
professional: **3** ace **4** star, whiz **5** adept, brain, slick, yuppy **6** artist, doctor, expert, lawyer, wizard, yuppie **7** artiste, capable, hotshot, learned, old hand, skilled **8** licensed, polished, skillful, virtuoso **9** authority, competent, efficient, on the ball, practiced, qualified, superstar, technical, up to speed
 pursuit: **3** job **6** career **9** specialty
Professionals, The (1966 film)
 cast: Lee Marvin, Robert Ryan, Woody Strode
 director: Richard Brooks
Professional, The actor: **4** Reno
professor: **3** don **4** prof, rank **5** brain, tutor **6** fellow, lector, pundit, savant **7** egghead, pedagog, scholar, teacher **8** academic, educator, emeritus, lecturer, longhair **9** abecedary, authority, pedagogue **10** instructor
 aide: **2** TA **3** GTA
 concoction: **4** exam, lect., quiz, test **7** lecture
 degree: **3** Ph.D. **9** doctorate
 title: **4** emer. **8** emeritus
Professor Bernhardi author: Arthur Schnitzler
professorial: **7** learned **9** pedagogic, scholarly
Professor Irwin __: **5** Corey
professors: **7** faculty
__ Professor, The: **5** Nutty
Professor, The author: Charlotte Brontë
proffer: **3** bid **4** gift, give, hand, make, pose, show **5** posit, yield **6** extend, submit, tender **7** advance, commend, hold out, present, propose, provide, suggest **8** proposal **9** hold forth, volunteer **10** administer, contribute
proficiency: **5** craft, skill **6** talent **7** ability, know-how, mastery, sleight **8** artistry, facility, learning, literacy **9** expertise, technique
proficient: **3** ace, apt **4** able, deft, good, upon **5** adept, crack, handy, quick, ready, savvy, sharp, slick **6** adroit, at home, au fait, clever, expert, facile, gifted, good at, habile, nimble, up to it, versed, with it **7** capable, skilled, trained **8** aptitude, delicate, dextrous, graceful, masterly, seasoned, skillful, talented **9** competent, dexterous, effective, efficient, masterful, on the beam, practiced, qualified, up to speed **10** conversant
 become ~: **5** excel **6** master
profile: **3** bio **4** face, form, vita **5** shape, study **6** figure, résumé, sketch, survey **7** contour, diagram, dossier, drawing, outline, skyline **8** analysis, likeness, portrait, side view, vignette **9** biography, lineament, lineation **10** silhouette
 keep a low ~: **4** hide, lurk **6** hole up, lay low, lie low **7** conceal **8** lie doggo **9** take cover
__ profile: **3** low **4** high, soil **7** Grecian
Profiler (NBC drama) cast: Ally Walker (Dr. Sam Waters)
Profiles in Courage: **4** book
 author: John F. Kennedy
 character: **4** Ross, Taft **5** Adams, Lamar **6** Benton, Norris **7** Houston, Webster
profit: **3** net, pay, use **4** earn, gain, gate, help, luck, reap, sake, skim, take **5** avail, clear, fruit, gravy, gross, lucre, score, serve, split, value, yield **6** income, output, return, reward, thrive **7** benefit, clean up, harvest, improve, prosper, realize, results, revenue, savings, surplus, takings, utility, welfare **8** earnings, interest, proceeds, receipts, winnings **9** advantage, increment, make money, well-being **10** bottom line, emoluments, percentage, prosperity
 ender: **3** eer
 for no ~: **6** at cost **9** wholesale
 from: **3** use **5** learn **7** utilize
 make a ~: **3** net **4** turn **7** realize
 opposite: **4** loss
profit __: **6** center, margin, motive, taking **7** sharing, squeeze
__ profit: **3** net **5** gross, paper, turn a
profitable: **5** sweet **6** paying, useful **7** gainful, helpful **8** fruitful, salutary, valuable **9** covetable, desirable, efficient, expedient, fortunate, lucrative, practical, rewarding **10** beneficial, commercial, high-income, productive, well-paying, worthwhile
 be ~: **3** pay
profitless: **4** vain **6** barren, futile **7** useless **8** bootless, misspent **9** fruitless, worthless
profligacy: **4** riot, vice **7** license **8** hedonism **9** depravity **10** corruption, indulgence
profligate: **4** fast, lewd, rake, roué, wild **5** loose **6** bad guy, lavish, rakish, rascal, wanton, wicked **7** corrupt, immoral, swinger, vicious, villain, wastrel **8** depraved, prodigal, rakehell, reckless, shameful, uncurbed, wasteful **9** abandoned, corrupted, dissolute, excessive, libertine, reprobate, shameless, unthrifty **10** dissipated, immoderate, licentious
profound: **4** deep, keen, sage, vast, wise **5** acute, great, heavy, meaty, sound, total, utter **6** occult, orphic, secret, shrewd, subtle **7** abysmal, erudite, extreme, intense, knowing, learned, radical, serious, sincere, weighty, yawning **8** absolute, abstruse, esoteric, hermetic, incisive, informed, mystical, thorough, unbroken **9** extensive, full-dress, heartfelt, innermost, intensive, out-and-out, pervasive, recondite, sagacious, scholarly **10** bottomless, consummate, deep-seated, discerning, exhaustive, fathomless, impressive, insightful, mysterious, pronounced, reflective, thoughtful, unknowable
profundity: **4** gulf **5** depth **6** wisdom **7** insight **8** deepness, sagacity **9** intellect
__ profundo: **5** basso
profuse: **4** full, lush, many, much, rank, rife **5** ample, thick **6** a lot of, divers, effuse, galore, gobs of, hearty, lavish, lots of, myriad, plenty, umteen, untold **7** a host of, aplenty, a slew of, copious, extreme, fulsome, heaps of, liberal, no end of, opulent, piles of, rampant, scads of, teeming, umpteen **8** a bunch of, abundant, an army of, effusive, frequent, fruitful, generous, infested, manifold, numerous, oodles of, princely, prodigal, prolific, scores of, swarming, umpsteen **9** abounding, alive with, a passel of, bounteous, bountiful, countless, excessive, exuberant, luxuriant, overblown, plentiful, profusive, quite a few, sumptuous, unsparing **10** dime a dozen, immoderate, inordinate, munificent, openhanded, unstinting, zillions of
profusely: **9** in a big way
profusion: **3** lot, sea, ton **4** glut, heap, host, load, mass, mess, pile, slew **5** flood, ocean, stack **6** bounty, excess, galore, plenty, spread, wealth **7** barrage, legions, nimiety, surfeit, surplus **8** lushness, mountain, plethora, quantity **9** abundance, multitude, plenitude **10** congestion, cornucopia, exuberance, generosity, oversupply
profusive: **6** lavish **7** gushing, opulent, profuse **9** luxuriant
progenitor: **4** sire **6** mother, origin, parent **7** forbear **8** ancestor **9** archetype, precursor, prototype **10** antecedent, forebearer, forefather, forerunner
progenitors: **7** lineage **8** ancestry **10** family tree
progeny: **3** get, kin **4** cion, kids, race, seed, sons **5** heirs, issue, scion, spawn, stock, young **6** family, litter, scions **7** kindred, kinfolk, lineage **8** children, kinfolks, kinsfolk **9** inheritor, offspring, posterity **10** descendent
prognosis: **7** surmise **8** forecast **9** diagnosis **10** prediction, projection
prognostic: **4** omen, sign **7** fatidic, portent **9** vaticinal **10** indication, indicative
prognosticate: **5** augur **6** divine, herald **7** betoken, portend, predict, presage **8** forecast, foretell, prophesy, soothsay **9** adumbrate
prognostication: **4** omen, sign **6** oracle **7** portent **8** prophecy
prognosticator: **4** seer **5** augur **6** medium, oracle, shaman **7** diviner, prophet **9** predictor **10** forecaster, palm reader
program: **4** bill, book, card, plan, show **5** revue, set up, slate **6** agenda, budget, course, design, docket, lay out, line up, map out, method, policy, recipe, roster, series **7** catalog, details, listing, outline, process, project, work out **8** bulletin, calendar, pencil in, platform, playbill, proposal, schedule, sequence, strategy, syllabus **9** broadcast, catalogue, itinerary, procedure, timetable **10** curriculum, production, prospectus
 business ~: **6** agenda **8** schedule
 computer ~: **3** DOS **5** MS-DOS **7** Windows
 interrupter: **2** ad **8** bulletin **9** news flash **10** commercial
 regular ~: **4** soap **6** series, sitcom **7** regimen
__ program: **4** quiz **5** crash **6** system **7** systems, utility
programming
 command: **4** go to
 language: **3** Ada, APL, SQL **4** Alef, html, Icon, Java, LISP, Logo, Orca, Perl **5** Algol, Basic, Cecil, COBOL, Dylan, SISAL **6** Delphi, Eiffel, Erlang, Oberon, Pascal, Prolog, Sather, Scheme, Snobol **7** Fortran
 web ~ language: **4** html, Java
Program, The actor: **4** Caan
Progreso: **4** city, town
 locale: **6** Mexico **7** Hidalgo, Yucatán
progress: **4** fare, gain, grow, hike, rate, work **5** forge, get on, go far, march, sweep **6** course, evolve, growth, inroad, look up, mature, motion, move on, thrive, travel **7** achieve, advance, blossom, build up, develop, headway, impetus, improve, journey, proceed, prosper, shape up, success, upgrade **8** continue, get ahead, increase, momentum, movement **9** evolution, flowering, go forward, keep going, unfolding **10** accomplish, betterment, forge ahead, gain ground, shoot ahead, transition
 in ~: **5** afoot, begun **6** at work **7** current, going on, ongoing **8** underway **9** happening, occurring
 prevent ~: **5** stymy **6** hinder, impede **8** obstruct, sabotage
 slight ~: **4** dent
progressing: **6** better **7** en route, ongoing **8** thriving **9** on the move **10** on the march
 not ~: **5** stuck **8** moribund
progression: **3** run **4** flow, step **5** chain, order, scale, swing, train **6** course, growth, sequel, series **7** advance, current, headway **8** movement, progress, sequence **9** gradation **10** locomotion
progressive: **5** broad **6** modern **7** dynamic, gradual, growing, leftist, liberal, ongoing, radical **8** activist, advanced, positive, tolerant, unbroken, up-to-date **9** advancing, reformist
progressive __: **4** jazz, lens **6** dinner
__ Progress, The: **5** Rake's
prohibit: **3** ban, bar, nix **4** cork, deny, halt, kill, stay, stop, tabu, veto **5** block, debar, delay, estop, spike, stimy, stymy, taboo, tie up **6** abjure, censor, enjoin, forbid, freeze, hamper, hinder, hold up, impede, lock up, outlaw, reject, stymie **7** abolish, exclude, forfend, inhibit, obviate, prevent, put down, rule out, shut out **8** disallow, forefend, gridlock, obstruct, preclude, restrain, restrict **9** constrain, interdict, proscribe **10** keep in line
prohibited: **4** tabu **5** shady, taboo **6** banned, vetoed **7** illegal, illicit, wildcat **8** criminal, improper, outlawed, smuggled, unlawful, verboten, wrongful **9** felonious, forbidden, off-limits, out of line **10** contraband, not allowed
 practice: **4** no-no, tabu **5** taboo
prohibition: **3** ban, bar **4** don't, no-no, tabu, veto **5** taboo **6** denial **7** embargo, refusal **8** negation **9** abatement, exclusion, interdict, restraint
 word: **2** no **3** not **4** don't
Prohibition backer: **3** Dry **9** abstainer **10** teetotaler
prohibitive: **5** steep **7** sky-high **9** excessive, expensive **10** burdensome
project: **3** job, jut **4** baby, butt, cast, deal, hurl, plan, poke, task, toss, work **5** bulge, chore, draft, exude, fling, frame, gauge, heave, pitch, shoot, think, throw **6** affair, beetle, design, devise, launch, map out, matter, propel, reckon, scheme **7** ascribe, concern, overlap, predict, program, venture **8** activity, business, contrive, envision, estimate, forecast, overhang, proposal, protrude, see ahead, stand out, stick out, strategy, theorize, transmit **9** calculate, plan ahead, visualize **10** assignment, enterprise, stretch out
Project A (1983 film)
 cast: Yuen Biao, Jackie Chan
 director: Jackie Chan
projectile: **4** bolt, shot, slug **5** arrow **6** bullet **7** missile
 game ~: **4** dart, puck **6** discus **7** Frisbee
 long-range ~: **4** ICBM **7** missile
 path: **3** arc **5** curve
projecting: **7** beetled, salient **9** obtrusive, prominent
projection: **3** jut, map, rim, tab **4** bump,

eave, hump, knob, limb, lobe, sill, spur **5** bulge, guess, image, ledge, ridge, shelf, spine, tooth **8** estimate, forecast, overhang **9** appendage, extension, outthrust, prognosis **10** elongation
room unit: **4** reel
rounded ~: **4** dome, lobe
sharp ~: **3** jag **5** quill, spike, spine, thorn
projection —: **4** room **5** booth, paper, print **7** machine, printer
— projection: **4** rear **5** conic, front **7** central, conical, oblique
projectionist concern: **5** focus
projector
insert: **5** slide
part: **4** lens
screen: **4** wall **5** sheet
Prokhorov, Aleksandr: **7** Russian **8** Nobelist **9** physicist
Prokne: **8** asteroid
Prokofiev, Sergei: **7** Russian **8** composer
work: Alexander Nevsky
The Love for Three Oranges
Peter and the Wolf
Russian Overture
Scythian Suite
War and Peace
— prole: **4** sine
prolegomenon: **7** preface, prelude
proletarian: **4** pleb **5** lowly, prole **6** worker **7** popular **8** baseborn, commoner, plebeian
proletariat: **3** mob **4** herd **5** labor **6** masses, people, rabble **8** riffraff **9** hoi polloi, multitude **10** lower class
proliferate: **4** boom, rise, teem **5** breed, hatch, spawn, swarm **6** abound, expand, spread, step up **7** burgeon, enlarge, radiate, run riot, shoot up **8** bourgeon, escalate, increase, multiply, mushroom, snowball **9** propagate, reproduce, skyrocket, spread out **10** accelerate
proliferation: **6** growth, spread **8** increase
prolific: **4** lush, rank, rich **6** breedy, fecund, lavish **7** copious, fertile, profuse, teeming **8** abundant, creative, fruitful, swarming, thriving **9** abounding, bountiful, exuberant, luxuriant **10** generative, productive
be ~: **4** teem **5** swarm **7** run riot
prolix: **4** glib, long **5** gabby, windy, wordy **7** diffuse, lengthy, unterse, verbose, voluble **8** inflated, rambling **9** bombastic, garrulous, ponderous, redundant, talkative **10** bigmouthed, discursive, long-winded, loquacious, palaverous
not ~: **4** curt **5** brief, crisp, short, terse **10** to the point
prolixity: **8** verbiage **9** garrulity, wordiness
prolog
see prologue
Prolog: **8** language
alternative: **3** ADA, APL, SQL **4** Alef, html, Icon, Java, LISP, Logo, Orca, Perl **5** Algol, Basic, Cecil, COBOL, Dylan, SISAL **6** Delphi, Eiffel, Erlang, Oberon, Pascal, Sather, Scheme, Snobol **7** Fortran
prologue: **5** intro, proem **7** preface, prelude **8** foreword, overture, preamble
prolong: **5** delay, renew, stall **6** expand, extend, retard, shelve **7** carry on, drag out, draw out, let ride, spin out, stretch, sustain **8** continue, hold back, hold over, increase, lengthen, maintain, protract, slow down **9** string out **10** perpetuate, stretch out
prolonged: **4** poky, slow, vast **6** draggy **7** gradual, halting, impeded, lagging, languid, lengthy **8** crawling, creeping, dawdling, dilatory, dragging, drawn-out, hesitant, plodding, slothful, sluggish, toddling **9** leisurely, lethargic, snaillike, unhurried **10** continuous, deliberate
account: **5** spiel **6** litany
prom: **4** ball, gala **5** dance, party **9** festivity
attendee: **4** teen **5** dater **6** junior, senior **8** chaperon **9** chaperone
attire: **3** tie, tux **4** gown, suit **6** formal, tuxedo **7** corsage
locale: **3** gym
partner: **4** date **6** escort
transport: **4** limo
unlikely ~ king: **4** nerd, nurd
promenade: **4** mall, stoa, turn, walk **5** amble, dance, march, paseo **6** flaunt, parade, ramble, stroll **7** display, exhibit, saunter, show off **8** ambulate **9** cavalcade
area: **4** deck
Promethea —: **4** moth
Prometheus: **4** moon **5** giant, Titan
brother of ~: **5** Atlas **10** Epimetheus
parent of ~: **7** Clymene, Iapetus
planet: **6** Saturn
punisher of ~: **4** Zeus **5** eagle
son of ~: **9** Deucalion
Prometheus —: **5** Bound **7** Unbound
Prometheus author: André Maurois
Prometheus Bound: **4** play **9** sculpture
author: Aeschylus
sculptor: **3** Ney
Prometheus Deception, The author: Robert Ludlum
promethium: **7** element **9** rare earth
emission: **7** beta ray
Promethus Unbound: **5** drama
author: Percy Shelley
character: **4** Asia, Ione **5** Earth **7** Jupiter
prominence: **3** tor **4** bump, crag, fame, hill, mesa, name, note, peak, rank, rise, spur **5** bluff, bulge, cliff, crest, knoll, kudos, mound **6** height, renown, status, summit, weight **7** hillock, stature **8** emphasis, headland, mountain, pinnacle, prestige, salience, standing, swelling **9** celebrity, elevation, greatness, high point, influence, precipice **10** high ground, importance, promontory, reputation
give ~: **6** play up **7** feature **9** publicize, spotlight
prominent: **3** big, top **4** high, main, star **5** chief, famed, great, large, noted **6** famous, marked, signal **7** big-name, bulging, evident, glaring, jutting, leading, notable, obvious, popular, salient **8** apparent, aquiline, beetling, foremost, renowned, stand-out, striking **9** arresting, big-league, brilliant, important, obtrusive, respected, topflight, well-known **10** celebrated, noticeable, preeminent, projecting, pronounced, protruding, protrusive, remarkable
feature: **3** jaw **4** nose
person: **3** VIP **4** lion, star **5** celeb, mover, nabob, titan **6** shaker, tycoon **7** magnate **9** celebrity
promise: **3** vow **4** avow, bind, bode, bond, hint, hope, oath, omen, pact, word **5** agree, augur, flair, say-so, spell, swear, token, troth, vouch **6** assure, avowal, engage, ensure, insure, parole, pledge, plight, talent **7** bargain, bespeak, betoken, betroth, compact, consent, declare, earnest, portend, presage, profess, warrant **8** affiance, aptitude, contract, covenant, forebode, foreshow, good omen, indicate, obligate, prospect, security, warranty **9** agreement, assurance, betrothal, foretoken, guarantee, insurance, potential, stipulate, subscribe, undertake **10** capability, commitment, engagement, foreshadow, likelihood, obligation, underwrite
break a ~: **6** betray, renege **7** violate
keep a ~: **4** meet **6** please **7** fulfill, gratify, perform **8** make good, reassure **9** discharge
partner: **4** lick
solemn ~: **3** vow **4** oath
to marry: **5** troth
to pay: **3** IOU **4** debt **9** debenture
word: **4** soon **5** later **8** tomorrow
written ~: **8** warranty **9** guarantee
Promise: **9** margarine
alternative: **6** Parkay, Shedd's **8** Imperial
Promise — New Day, The: **3** of a
Promised Land: **4** Sion, Zion **6** Canaan
Promised Land (1974 song) artist: Elvis Presley
Promise her anything perfume: **6** Arpege
Promise of a New Day, The (1991 song) artist: Paula Abdul
Promise of Joy, The author: Allen Drury
Promises (1978 song) artist: Eric Clapton
promises, like some: **4** kept **5** empty
Promises, Promises author: Neil Simon
Promise, The author: Chaim Potok
promising: **3** apt **4** able, rosy **5** happy, lucky **6** bright, gifted, golden, likely, rising, timely, upbeat **7** budding, hopeful **8** cheerful, cheering, possible, probable, talented **9** favorable, fortunate **10** auspicious, inspirited, optimistic, propitious, prosperous, reassuring
promissory note: **3** IOU **4** chit **5** T-bill, T-bond
receiver: **6** drawee **8** creditor
Prom Night (1980 film)
cast: Antoinette Bower, Jamie Lee Curtis, Leslie Nielsen
director: Paul Lynch
promo: **2** ad **4** hype, plug, puff **5** blurb **6** teaser **7** gimmick **9** publicity **10** commercial
promontory: **4** cape, head, hill, ness, spit **5** bluff, point **8** foreland, headland, landmark **10** prominence
promote: **3** aid **4** back, bump, flog, help, hype, lift, pass, plug, puff, push, sell, tout, urge **5** avail, boost, exalt, favor, lobby, pitch, raise, serve, speed, tempt **6** anoint, assist, better, foment, foster, hype up, incite, move up, second, talk up, uphold **7** advance, benefit, bolster, build up, develop, display, elevate, endorse, ennoble, espouse, feature, forward, further, improve, indorse, magnify, make for, nurture, push for, quicken, solicit, sponsor, support, trumpet, upgrade, work for **8** advocate, befriend, campaign, champion, graduate, increase, speak for **9** advertise, cooperate, cultivate, encourage, get behind, influence, patronize, publicize, recommend, stimulate, subsidize **10** aggrandize, contribute, facilitate, popularize, promulgate, rally round
aggressively: **4** flog, hype
another: **4** back **7** sponsor, support
in checkers: **5** crown
promoter: **5** agent, flack, PR man **7** handler, sponsor **8** advocate, exponent **9** expounder, publicist **10** missionary, press agent
Promoter, The (1952 film)
cast: Alec Guinness, Glynis Johns
director: Ronald Neame
promotion: **3** ads **4** hype, plug, rise **5** blurb, boost, pitch, press, raise, squib **6** brevet, hoopla **7** advance **8** advocacy, ballyhoo, espousal **9** elevation, patronage, publicity **10** betterment, exaltation, propaganda
basis: **5** merit
objective: **4** gate, take **5** sales **6** profit
promotive: **9** accessory, conducive, efficient **10** convenient
prompt: **3** cue, get, jog, tip **4** goad, hint, lead, move, prod, spry, spur, stir, urge, warn **5** alert, brisk, cause, eager, early, egg on, hasty, impel, nudge, quick, rapid, ready, swift **6** elicit, exhort, fillip, incite, induce, on time, propel, remind, speedy, timely, tipoff **7** bring up, counsel, inspire, instant, provoke, refresh, suggest, trigger, willing **8** activate, mnemonic, motivate, occasion, on the dot, persuade, punctual, reminder, vigilant, watchful **9** efficient, immediate, instigate, on the ball, on the nose, prevail on, stimulate, wide-awake **10** give rise to, in good time, predispose, responsive
more than ~: **5** early **7** too soon **8** too early **9** premature
not ~: **4** late **5** tardy **7** overdue
prompting: **6** behest **10** invitation
promptly: **3** now, PDQ **4** anon, fast, soon **5** right, sharp, today **6** at once, on time, pronto **7** flat out, hastily, quickly, rapidly, readily, swiftly **8** directly, on the dot, right now, right off, speedily **9** at present, forthwith, instantly, like a shot, posthaste, presently, right away, summarily **10** at this time, here and now, punctually, this minute
promptness: **5** haste, hurry **8** alacrity, celerity, dispatch, rapidity, velocity **9** eagerness, fleetness, readiness **10** expedition
promulgate: **3** sow **5** issue, strew, teach **6** decree, impose, spread **7** declare, display, expound, present, promote, publish, trumpet **8** announce, proclaim **9** advertise, broadcast, circulate, enunciate, make known, propagate
prone: **3** apt **4** flat **5** ready **6** liable, likely, supine **7** exposed, subject, tending, willing **8** disposed, face down, inclined **9** lying down, prostrate, reclining, recumbent **10** accustomed, horizontal
(to): **3** apt **7** of a mind, subject **8** disposed
proneness: **6** liking **7** leaning **8** penchant, tendency, weakness **9** liability **10** preference, proclivity, propensity
prong: **4** spur, tine **5** point **6** branch **7** stabber
ender: **4** horn
pronghorn: **6** animal **8** antelope
relative: **3** gnu, kob **4** guib, kudu, oryx, puku, topi **5** addax, bongo, chiru, eland, goral, korin, nyala, oribi, saiga, serow **6** chammy, dik-dik, duiker, impala, koodoo, lechwe, nilgai, rhebok, shammy, shamoy **7** blaubok, blesbok, chamois, defassa, gazelle, gemsbok, gerenuk, grysbok, nylghai, nylghau, sassaby **8** blesbuck, bontebok, bushbuck, gemsbuck, reedbuck, steenbok, steinbok **9** blackbuck, sitatunga, springbok, waterbuck **10** hartebeest, wildebeest
— pro nobis: **3** ora

pronoun: **3** all, any, few, her, him, his, its, one, our, she, thy, who, why, you **4** both, hers, mine, none, ours, some, that, thee, them, this, thou, what, whom **5** their, there, these, thine, those **6** itself **7** herself, himself **10** themselves
Brooklyn ~: **3** dem **4** dose **5** youse
demonstrative ~: **4** that, this **5** these, those
Dixie ~: **4** y'all **6** you all
feminine ~: **3** her, she **4** hers **7** herself
French ~: **3** lui, mes, qui, soi, tes, toi **4** nous, tien, vous **5** notre
German ~: **3** mie, sie **4** mein **5** einer, meine, unser
interrogative ~: **3** who, why **4** what, whom
Italian ~: **2** io, tu **3** mia, mio, noi **4** ella, esse, esso
Latin ~: **3** sua **4** quis
masculine ~: **3** him, his **7** himself
nonstandard ~: **3** yer **4** hern, his'n, ourn **5** yourn
Portuguese ~: **2** eu, tu **3** ela, ele, mim, nós, vós **4** elas, eles
possessive ~: **3** her, his, its, our **4** hers, ours, your **5** their, whose **10** themselves
Quaker ~: **3** thy **4** thee, thou **5** thine
reflexive ~: **6** itself **7** herself, himself **8** yourself **10** themselves
relative ~: **4** that **5** which
sharer's ~: **3** our **4** ours
Spanish ~: **2** tu, yo **3** esa, eso **4** ella **5** ellas, ellos, quien, usted **7** ustedes **8** nosotros
pronounce: **3** say **4** read, rule, talk **5** judge, speak, state, utter, voice **6** affirm, assert, decree, intone, ordain **7** declare, deliver, trumpet **8** proclaim, vocalize **9** emphasize, enunciate, verbalize **10** articulate
pronounced: **4** bold **5** acute, clear, vocal **6** marked, signal, strong **7** decided, evident, notable, obvious, salient, visible **8** clear-cut, definite, distinct, emphatic, profound, striking, vehement **9** prominent
pronouncement: **4** word **5** edict, ukase **6** decree, dictum, ruling **8** decision, judgment, sentence **9** manifesto, statement, utterance
__ pronounce you...: **4** I now
pronto: **3** now, PDQ **4** anon, ASAP, fast, soon, stat **5** quick, swift **6** at once **7** quickly **8** directly, promptly, right now, right off **9** posthaste, right away
pronunciation: **6** accent, speech **8** delivery
omit in ~: **4** slur **5** elide
symbol: **4** shwa **5** acute, grave, schwa, tilde **6** macron, umlaut **7** cedilla
proof: **4** data, lead, mark, sign, test **5** facts, goods, tight, title, token, trace, trial **6** galley, reason, skinny **7** grabber, grounds, picture, records, warrant, witness **8** acid test, argument, clincher, evidence, scrutiny, specimen **9** affidavit, documents, proofread, reasoning, testament, testimony **10** deposition, indication, paper trail, smoking gun, validation
cite as ~: **6** adduce, attest **7** certify
ender: **4** read **6** reader **7** reading
find: **4** typo **5** error, typos **6** errata **7** erratum
give ~: **4** aver **5** prove, swear **6** assure, depone, verify **7** bear out, certify, confirm, declare, stand by, testify, warrant, witness **8** vouch for
mark: **4** dele, stet **5** caret
math ~ abbr.: **3** QED
of employment: **5** badge **6** ID card
of ownership: **4** deed **5** paper, title **8** document
of purchase: **6** boxtop **7** receipt
printer's ~: **5** repro
starter: **4** bomb, fire, fool, goof, heat, leak, moth, oven, pick, rust **5** child, flame, light, shell, shock, sound, water **6** bullet, grease **7** burglar, scratch, shatter, weather
word: **4** ergo **9** therefore
__ proof: **6** galley **7** foundry
Proof author: Dick Francis
Proof of Life (2000 film)
cast: Russell Crowe, David Morse, Pamela Reed, Meg Ryan
director: Taylor Hackford
proof of the __: **7** pudding
prop: **3** leg, set **4** beam, buoy, cane, hold, lean, post, rest, stay **5** brace, shore, staff, stand, strut **6** crutch, hold up, pillar, uphold **7** bolster, bracket, fortify, shore up, stiffen, support, sustain **8** buttress, mainstay **9** reinforce, stabilize, stanchion **10** strengthen
ender: **3** jet
prop __: **4** root, wash
propaganda: **4** hype, lies **7** handout, hogwash, release **8** doctrine, newspeak **9** diffusion, promotion, publicity
US ~ source: **3** VOA **4** USIA
propagandize: **3** lie **4** push **7** promote **8** persuade **9** brainwash, publicize
propagate: **3** sow **4** bear, grow, sire **5** beget, breed, raise **6** father, spread **7** diffuse, produce, publish, radiate **8** disperse, engender, generate, increase, multiply, proclaim, transmit **9** broadcast, circulate, cultivate, fertilize, make known, publicize, reproduce **10** distribute, promulgate
in a way: **5** clone
propane: **4** fuel
form of ~: **3** LPG **5** LP gas
propel: **3** oar, row, tow **4** goad, hurl, move, poke, pole, prod, push, send, spur, toss, urge **5** drive, eject, fling, force, heave, impel, power, scull, shoot, shove, slide, sling, spark, throw **6** launch, let fly, prompt, thrust **7** actuate, advance, project **8** activate, catapult, mobilize, motivate
propellant: **4** fuel **8** stimulus **9** explosive **10** rocket fuel
remove ~: **6** defuel
__ propellant: **5** solid **6** liquid
__-propelled: **3** jet **4** self **6** rocket
propeller: **3** fan, oar **5** screw
arm: **5** blade
site: **5** plane **6** beanie **8** aircraft, airplane
sound: **4** whir **5** whirr
propeller __: **4** head, wash **5** shaft
__ propeller: **5** screw
__-propeller engine: **5** turbo
propeller-head: **4** nerd, nurd **5** dweeb
propensity: **4** bent, bias, turn **5** fancy, habit, knack, taste **6** liking **7** faculty, leaning **8** affinity, aptitude, capacity, penchant, pleasure, tendency, weakness **9** affection, appetence, proneness, sentiment **10** partiality, preference, proclivity
proper: **3** apt, due, fit, own **4** fair, fine, good, just, meet, nice, okay, prim, true, well **5** exact, great, legal, legit, licit, moral, noble, per se, pucka, pukka, right, sound, usual **6** au fait, august, comely, decent, demure, formal, honest, in line, kasher, kosher, lawful, modest, polite, prissy, seemly, stuffy, suited, timely **7** allowed, apropos, condign, correct, elegant, ethical, express, fitting, genteel, germane, in order, precise, prudish, refined, regular, special, stately **8** accepted, all right, apposite, assigned, becoming, decorous, highbrow, ladylike, laudable, mannerly, orthodox, personal, pleasant, pleasing, priggish, relevant, rightful, specific, splendid, straight, suitable, superior **9** admirable, agreeable, allowable, befitting, by the book, courteous, customary, de rigueur, equitable, excellent, opportune, permitted, pertinent, qualified, reputable, wonderful **10** acceptable, applicable, authorized, beneficial, creditable, defensible, individual, legitimate, particular, reasonable, respective, sanctioned, vindicable
be ~: **5** befit **6** beseem
in ~ style: **4** duly **6** aright
overly ~ one: **5** priss, prude **7** puritan **10** goody-goody
proper __: **4** name, noun
Proper Bostonians, The author: **5** Amory
properly: **7** rightly **8** laudably, worthily **9** honorably
propertied: **4** rich **5** flush **6** loaded, monied **7** moneyed, wealthy, well-off **8** affluent, in clover, well-to-do **9** well-fixed **10** in the dough, in the money, privileged, prosperous, well-heeled
property: **3** lot **4** farm, home, land, plot **5** acres, claim, goods, house, means, money, place, stuff, thing, title, tract, trait, worth **6** assets, equity, estate, parcel, realty, riches, wealth **7** acreage, capital, chattel, effects, feature, grounds, quality **8** chattels, freehold, hallmark, holdings, premises **9** attribute, buildings, ownership, resources, substance **10** belongings, possession, real estate
attachment: **4** lien **8** mortgage
be the ~ of: **8** belong to
demarcation: **5** fence, stake
Federal ~ overseer: **3** GSA
hot ~: **5** asset **8** valuable
landed ~: **5** acres **6** estate
one with ~: **5** owner **6** squire **10** freeholder
ownable ~: **4** farm, home **5** acres, field, manor, ranch, tract **6** estate, parcel, realty **7** acreage, grounds, holding **9** farmstead **10** real estate
personal ~: **4** gear **5** goods, stuff **6** things **8** chattels
piece of ~: **3** lot **5** asset **6** spread **7** holding
stolen ~: **4** loot, swag **6** spoils **7** plunder
strip of ~: **6** devest
title: **4** deed **6** papers
property __: **3** tax **5** right
__ property: **4** real **6** common **7** private
prophecy: **6** augury, oracle, vision **8** forecast **10** divination, foreboding, prediction, revelation
prophesy: **4** warn **5** augur **6** divine, preach **7** betoken, foresee, portend, predict, presage **8** forebode, forecast, foreshow, foretell, forewarn, soothsay **9** adumbrate, see coming **10** foreshadow, vaticinate
combining form: **5** -mancy
prophet: **4** seer **5** augur, druid, magus, sibyl **6** auspex, herald, medium, oracle, reader, shaman, wizard **7** aruspex, diviner, palmist, seeress **8** haruspex, sorcerer **9** Cassandra, geomancer, messenger, predictor **10** astrologer, forecaster, prophesier, soothsayer
Biblical ~: **4** Amos, Ezra, Osee **5** Elias, Hosea, Micah, Moses **6** Daniel, Isaiah **8** Jeremiah
female ~: **5** sibyl **9** Cassandra
of a ~: **5** vatic **7** vatical
of doom: **9** pessimist
prophetic: **5** vatic **6** mantic, occult **7** fatidic, ominous **8** Delphian, oracular, pythonic, sibyllic **9** prescient, sibylline, vaticinal, visionary **10** portentous, prognostic
Prophet, The
author: Kahlil Gibran, Sholem Asch
propinquity: **8** nearness, presence, relation, vicinity **9** closeness, proximity
propitiate: **4** calm **5** allay **6** pacify **7** assuage, mediate, mollify, placate, satisfy, sweeten **9** reconcile **10** recompense
propitiatory: **6** irenic **8** irenical **9** peaceable
propitious: **3** fit **5** happy, lucky, right **6** benign, golden, timely **7** hopeful **8** gracious, suitable **9** favorable, fortunate, opportune, promising, well-timed **10** auspicious, beneficial, felicitous, prosperous
propjet: **5** plane **6** engine **8** airplane
proponent: **5** urger **6** backer, friend, patron, votary **7** apostle, booster **8** advocate, champion, defender, endorser, espouser, exponent, partisan, upholder, votarist **9** apologist, protector, supporter **10** enthusiast, subscriber, vindicator
proportion: **3** cut, pct. **4** part, rate, size **5** allot, quota, ratio, scale, share **6** degree, ration **7** balance, harmony, measure, percent, segment **8** division, equation, fraction, symmetry **9** agreement, congruity, harmonize, integrate, magnitude **10** classicism, coordinate
blow out of ~: **6** play up **7** magnify **8** overplay **10** exaggerate
words: **4** is to
proportional: **4** even, just **7** uniform **8** balanced, relative **9** equitable
share: **3** cut **5** quota **9** allotment
proportionate: **4** even, just **5** equal, level **7** uniform **8** balanced, relative **9** equitable
proportions: **4** area, bulk, mass, size, span **5** range, scale, scope, width **6** extent, volume **7** breadth, expanse **9** amplitude, magnitude **10** dimensions
of epic ~: **3** big **4** huge, vast **5** giant, grand, great, gross, heavy, jumbo, large **6** cosmic **7** immense, mammoth, massive, monster, titanic **8** colossal, enormous, gigantic, oversize, spacious, terrific, towering, whopping **9** extensive, herculean, humongous, monstrous, walloping **10** gargantuan, monumental, overweight, prodigious, tremendous
proposal: **3** bid **4** bill, call, idea, plan, spec, suit **5** draft, offer, pitch, quote, terms, toast **6** appeal, feeler, layout, motion, scheme, tender, thesis **7** measure, outline, proffer, program, project **8** overture, question **10** brainchild, hypothesis, invitation, nomination, resolution, suggestion
starter: **7** counter
__ Proposal, A: **6** Modest
Proposals author: Neil Simon
propose: **3** aim, ask, bid, put, woo **4** hope, mean, move, name, plan, urge **5** offer, posit **6** advise, aspire, broach, design, expect, intend, submit, tender **7** advance, counsel, present, proffer, purpose, request, resolve, suggest **8** nominate, propound, put forth, set forth **9** determine, introduce, recom-

mend, undertake **10** come up with, put forward
prepare to ~: 5 kneel
proposition: 3 ask, bid **4** deal, plan **5** offer, terms **6** motion, scheme, thesis **7** bargain, measure, proffer, propose, solicit, theorem, venture **8** contract, overture, question **9** agreement, principle, reasoning **10** resolution, suggestion
logical ~: 5 axiom, lemma **6** if-then
losing ~: 3 dog **4** bomb, diet, flop, no-go **6** bummer, fiasco **7** clinker, debacle, failure, washout
propound: 3 put **4** pose **5** state **6** assert, submit **7** declare, propose, suggest **8** advocate, set forth, theorize **10** put forward
__-propre: 5 amour
proprietary __: 6 colony, school
proprietary rights: 9 ownership
proprieties: 8 protocol
proprietor: 4 host **5** owner **6** holder **7** manager **8** landlady, landlord **9** possessor
proprietorship: 6 tenure **8** monopoly, property **9** ownership
__ proprietorship: 4 sole
propriety: 4 form **5** mense, mores, order, right **6** reason **7** concord, decency, decorum, dignity, fitness, modesty **8** breeding, ceremony, courtesy, delicacy, meetness, niceties, protocol **9** amenities, etiquette, formality, gentility, politesse, punctilio, rectitude, rightness **10** accordance, civilities, classicism, convention, politeness, properness, refinement, seemliness
proprio __: 4 motu
propter __: 3 hoc
propulsion: 6 thrust **8** momentum
__ propulsion: 3 ion, jet **5** ionic **6** rocket
Propus: 4 star
propyl __: 7 alcohol
propylene __: 6 glycol
propylene derivative: 5 allyl
__ pro quo: 4 quid
prorate: 5 allot, scale, share **6** divide, ration **7** portion **9** apportion
pro re __: 4 nata
prorogue: 5 waive **6** put off, recess **8** postpone **9** terminate
prosaic: 3 dry **4** blah, drab, dull, flat, tame **5** banal, corny, ho-hum, hokey, lowly, passé, stale, trite, vapid **6** boring, common, jejune, old hat **7** clichéd, fatuous, humdrum, insipid, literal, mundane, routine, tedious **8** bromidic, everyday, lifeless, ordinary, outdated, outmoded, unlively, workaday **9** colorless, hackneyed **10** lackluster, monotonous, pedestrian, uneventful, uninspired, unoriginal
pros and __: 4 cons
ProScan: 2 TV **5** TV set **10** television
competitor: 3 JVC, NEC, RCA **4** Sony **6** Quasar, Zenith **7** Emerson, Hitachi, Toshiba **8** Magnavox, Sylvania **9** Panasonic
proscenium: 5 apron
proscenium __: 4 arch
prosciutto: 3 ham **4** meat
purveyor: 4 deli
proscribe: 3 ban, bar, nix **4** damn, tabu, veto **5** debar, exile, taboo **6** abjure, banish, enjoin, forbid, outlaw, reject **7** boycott, censure, condemn, enforce, exclude, rule out **8** denounce, disallow, prohibit, sentence **9** blacklist, interdict, repudiate **10** expatriate
proscribed: 4 tabu **5** taboo **7** illegal **8** smuggled **9** forbidden **10** contraband, not allowed
act: 4 no-no, tabu **5** taboo
proscription: 3 ban **4** tabu, veto **5** exile, taboo **7** embargo, refusal **8** negation **9** expulsion **10** banishment
prose: 4 book, talk, text **5** essay, novel, story **6** letter, ramble, satire, speech, thesis **7** article, fiction, romance, writing **8** language, whodunit, workbook **10** bestseller, exposition, literature, nonfiction, short story
art of ~: 4 rhet. **8** rhetoric
improve ~: 4 edit **5** emend **6** revise **7** rewrite
__ prose: 6 purple
Prose __: 4 Edda
prosecute: 3 sue, try **4** wage **6** accuse, indict, pursue, summon **7** arraign, conduct, contest, wage war **8** litigate **9** go to court **10** put on trial
prosecution: 4 suit **5** trial **7** lawsuit **10** litigation
prosecutor: 2 DA **3** att. **5** trier **6** lawyer **8** attorney, litigant **9** detective
chief ~: 2 AG
phrase: 5 I rest
__ prosecutor: 6 public **7** special
proselyte: 7 recruit **8** disciple, follower **9** layperson **10** catechumen
proselytize: 7 convert, recruit, win over **8** persuade
__ prosequi: 5 nolle
__ prosequitur: 3 non
Proserpina
equivalent: 10 Persephone
husband of ~: 5 Pluto
mother of ~: 5 Ceres
Proserpina author: John Ruskin
pro-shop purchase: 3 peg **4** club, iron, tees **5** visor, wedge **6** driver, putter **7** golf bag **8** golf club
prosit: 5 salud, skoal, toast **6** cheers, kampai, saluté **9** bene vobis
Prosky: 6 Robert
prosody, dictionary of: 6 gradus
prospect: 3 dig, pan **4** hope, seek, sift, view **5** drill, scene, sight, vista **6** chance, search, survey **7** chances, nominee, outlook, promise, scenery **8** look into, overlook, panorama **9** candidate, job-hunter, landscape **10** likelihood
prospective: 6 coming, future, likely **7** looming, pending, planned, would-be **8** destined, eventual, expected, hoped-for, imminent, intended, possible, proposed, soon-to-be **9** impending, in the wind, looked-for, potential, promising
prospector: 5 miner **9** sourdough **10** forty-niner
aid: 3 map, pan **4** pick **6** shovel
find: 3 ore **4** lode **6** nugget
property: 4 mine **5** claim
test: 5 assay
prospects: 7 outlook
good ~: 4 hope **7** promise
like some ~: 5 bleak
__ Prospect, The: 5 Urban
prospectus: 4 list, plan **7** catalog, program, summary **8** brochure, document, syllabus, synopsis **9** catalogue
prosper: 3 win **4** boom, gain, grow, live, rise **5** bloom, score, yield **6** arrive, do well, flower, hack it, make it, pan out, profit, thrive **7** advance, blossom, catch on, develop, luck out, make out, prevail, produce, succeed, triumph, work out **8** fare well, flourish, get ahead, go places, go to town, grow rich, hit it big, increase, make good, multiply, progress **9** bear fruit, luxuriate, make money **10** strengthen
Prosper: 7 Mérimée **9** Buranelli
prospering: 7 booming, roaring **8** thriving **9** doing well
prosperity: 4 boom, ease, gain, luck **6** bounty, growth, luxury, plenty, profit, riches, wealth **7** comfort, fortune, success, welfare **8** good life, good luck, increase, interest, opulence, opulency, thriving **9** abundance, affluence, expansion, good times, happiness, inflation, well-being **10** betterment
general ~: 4 weal
Prospero: 8 magician, sorcerer
play: The Tempest
servant: 5 Ariel
prosperous: 4 rich **5** flush, lucky, palmy **6** loaded, monied, timely **7** booming, moneyed, opulent, roaring, wealthy, well-off **8** affluent, blooming, in clover, thriving, well-to-do **9** doing well, favorable, fortunate, opportune, promising, well-fixed **10** auspicious, in the dough, in the money, privileged, propertied, propitious, successful, well-heeled
time: 4 boom **6** uptick **7** upswing
Prost: 5 Alain
prostrate: 3 low, sap **4** deck, fell, flat, obey, tire, weak **5** drain, floor, kneel, kotow, level, prone, spent, tired, weary **6** abject, broody, fallen, grovel, kowtow, pooped, ravage, submit, supine **7** bow down, drained, exhaust, fatigue, flatten, frazzle, wearied, wear out, worn out **8** dejected, frazzled, helpless, obedient, overcome, overturn, paralyse, paralyze, tuckered **9** bring down, enervated, exhausted, knock down, lying down, overpower, overthrow, overwhelm, powerless, reclining, recumbent, tucker out **10** beseeching, debilitate, discourage, horizontal, knocked out, submissive
be ~: 3 lie **7** recline
oneself: 3 bow **5** kneel **9** pay homage
prostration: 3 bow **6** homage **9** reverence, weariness
prosy: 4 dull **5** vapid **6** common **7** humdrum, prosaic, tedious **8** lifeless, ordinary **9** prosaical **10** dullsville
Prot.: 4 Bapt., Epis., Luth., Meth. **5** Episc., Presb.
see also Protestant
protactinium: 7 element
discoverer: 4 Hahn
protagonist: 4 hero, lead, part, star **6** leader **7** heroine **8** champion, exponent **9** headliner, principal, title role
Protagoras: 5 Greek **6** orator **11** philosopher
specialty: 7 Sophism
protean: 5 fluid **6** labile **7** erratic, mutable **8** shifting, unstable, variable, wavering **9** mercurial, uncertain, versatile **10** changeable
protea tree: 7 banksia
protect: 3 pad **4** hide, save, tend, veil, wrap **5** cover, guard, shade, watch **6** assure, convoy, cradle, defend, embank, encase, ensure, foster, harbor, incase, insure, patrol, pillow, police, rescue, screen, secure, shield **7** bulwark, care for, cover up, cushion, fortify, harbour, shelter, store up, support, ward off **8** champion, chaperon, conserve, insulate, maintain, preserve, scrimp on, shepherd **9** chaperone, guarantee, look after, safeguard, vaccinate, watch over **10** take care of
protected: 4 alee, safe **5** legal **6** immune, inside, lawful, secure **9** unanxious **10** guaranteed
place: 5 haven **6** cocoon, refuge **8** preserve
species: 4 nene **5** panda
protection: 3 lee, mac, net **4** care, coat, egis, ward **5** aegis, apron, armor, cover, guard, haven, parka **6** buffer, escrow, harbor, jacket, mantra, refuge, safety, shield **7** barrier, bulwark, custody, defense, harbour, keeping, lodging, mantram, padding, rampart, shelter, slicker, support, sweater **8** auspices, covering, immunity, overalls, preserve, raincoat, security, tutelage, umbrella **9** armaments, assurance, blackmail, extortion, insurance, patronage, safeguard, sanctuary, tarpaulin **10** mackintosh, precaution
from harm: 6 asylum, refuge, safety **7** shelter **9** sanctuary
money: 3 ice
name meaning ~: 6 Warren
__ protection factor: 3 sun
protective: 7 careful, heedful, jealous **8** fatherly, maternal, motherly, parental, paternal, vigilant, watchful **9** avuncular, custodial, defensive **10** solicitous
covering: 4 tarp **5** armor, shell
garment: 3 bib **5** apron, G-suit, smock **7** lab coat **8** overalls
glasses: 6 shades **7** goggles
insert: 5 liner **6** insole
layer: 5 ozone, paint
protective __: 7 custody
protector: 5 guard **6** escort, keeper, knight, savior **7** saviour, shelter **8** champion, defender, guardian, watchdog, watchman **9** bodyguard, caretaker, companion, custodian, proponent **10** benefactor
__ protector: 5 check, chest, surge
__ Protector: 4 Lord
protectorate: 6 colony **7** outpost **8** province **9** territory **10** dependency, possession, settlement
former British ~: 4 Aden **6** Gambia
protégé: 4 ward
Protege: 3 car **4** auto **5** Mazda
protein
acid: 5 amino
blood ~: 6 globin
castor bean ~: 5 ricin
coagulation ~: 6 fibrin
corn ~: 4 zein
digestive ~: 6 enzyme
milk ~: 6 casein
muscle ~: 5 actin
shell: 6 capsid
source: 3 egg, soy **4** bean, beef, fish, food, meat, soya, tofu **6** legume, lentil **7** seafood
starter: 4 meta
synthesis need: 3 RNA
wheat ~: 6 gluten
protest: 4 beef, buck, flak, kick, riot, yowl **5** argue, demur, fight, flack, gripe, knock, march, rally, rebel, say no, sit-in **6** affirm, assert, attest, avouch, clamor, differ, grouse, insist, love-in, object, oppose, outcry, picket, refuse, resist, revolt, squawk, squeal, strike, unrest **7** boycott, dissent, grumble, inveigh, quibble **8** back-talk, complain, disagree, maintain, question, sound off **9** bellyache, challenge, complaint, fulminate, grievance, make a fuss **10** asseverate, make a stand, make a stink
dummy: 6 effigy
kid's ~: 5 did so, not me **6** did not
non-violent ~: 5 chant, march, sit-in, vigil **6** love-in
under ~: 8 forcibly
protester: 5 rebel **6** picket **7** heretic **8** maverick, militant, renegade **9** dissident **10** iconoclast, malcontent
__ protest too much: 4 doth
Proteus: 4 moon, seer

daughter of ~: 6 Cabiro 7 Idothea 8 Eidothea
father of ~: 8 Poseidon
planet: 7 Neptune
son of ~: 9 Polygonus, Telegonus
protoavis: 6 fossil
protocol: 4 form, pact 6 policy, ritual, treaty 7 compact, concord, customs, decorum, manners, red tape 8 behavior, ceremony, civility, courtesy, covenant, niceties 9 agreement, amenities, concordat, etiquette, formality, politesse, propriety, rigmarole 10 obligation, rigamarole
___ Protocol, The: 5 Sigma
proto ender: 3 zoa 4 zoan 5 plasm
proton site: 4 atom 7 nucleus
protoplasm: 5 cells 6 matter
component: 5 lipid 6 lipide
protoprogenitor: 3 Eve 4 Adam
prototype: 4 norm 5 first, ideal, model 6 mock-up 7 example, paragon, pattern 8 ancestor, exemplar, original, paradigm, standard 9 criterion, precursor 10 antecedent, forerunner, progenitor
prototypical: 5 ideal, model 7 classic
protozoan: 5 ameba, monad 6 amoeba 10 paramecium
propeller: 6 cilium 9 pseudopod
protract: 5 delay 6 drag on, expand, extend, ramble 7 draw out, prolong, spin out, stretch, suspend, sustain 8 continue, hold over, increase, lengthen 9 keep going, string out 10 stretch out
protracted: 4 long, poky, slow 6 draggy 7 gradual, halting, lagging, languid, lengthy 8 crawling, creeping, dawdling, dilatory, dragging, drawn-out, hesitant, marathon, overlong, plodding, slothful, sluggish, toddling 9 extensive, leisurely, lethargic, snaillike, strung-out, unhurried 10 deliberate
not ~: 5 brief, short, terse 8 succinct 10 to the point
protractedness: 6 length
protractor
measure: 5 angle
unit: 6 degree
protrude: 3 jut 4 poke 5 bulge, swell 6 beetle, extend 7 butt out, overlap, project 8 overhang, stand out, stick out
protruding: 7 beetled, pendant, pendent, salient 8 aquiline 9 obtrusive, prominent
edge: 6 flange
protrusion: 3 nub 4 bump, hump, knob, knot, knub, lump, node 5 bulge, gnarl 6 nodule 8 swelling 10 projection
protrusive: 9 prominent
protuberance: 3 nub 4 bump, hump, knob, knot, knub, lump, node 5 bulge, gnarl 6 nodule 8 swelling
protuberant: 5 nodal 6 bunchy 7 bulging 9 obtrusive, prominent
proud: 3 big 4 smug, vain 5 cocky, fiery, grand, lofty, noble, regal 6 august, chesty, lordly, snooty, superb 7 haughty, honored, pleased, pompous, stately, stuck-up, sublime, upright 8 arrogant, boastful, cavalier, egoistic, gloating, glorious, imposing, majestic, puffed up, scornful, snobbish, spirited, splendid, superior 9 conceited, dignified, gratified, hubristic, imperious, red-letter 10 big-talking, disdainful, dismissive, egoistical, high-handed, hoity-toity, majestical, triumphant
do one ~: 3 win 7 achieve, succeed 10 accomplish
proud ___ peacock: 3 as a
Proud ___: 4 Mary
Proud ___, The: 4 Ones 5 Rebel
proud as a peacock
network: 3 NBC 5 NBC-TV
Proud Mary (song) artist: Creedence Clearwater Revival, Ike and Tina Turner
Proud Rebel, The (1958 film)
cast: Olivia de Havilland, Dean Jagger, Alan Ladd
director: Michael Curtiz
proustite: 3 ore
Proust, Marcel: 6 author, French, writer
work: The Captive
Cities of the Plain
The Guermantes Way
The Past Recaptured
Remembrance of Things Past
Swann's Way
The Sweet Cheat Gone
Within a Budding Grove
prove: 3 fix, try 4 find, show, test 5 add up, assay, check, end up 6 affirm, attest, back up, evince, pan out, reason, result, settle, try out, uphold, verify 7 analyze, bear out, certify, confirm, examine, explain, justify, sustain, testify, turn out, warrant, witness 8 check out, document, evidence, indicate, manifest, validate 9 ascertain, determine, establish, make stick 10 experiment
out: 4 wash 7 prevail
something to ~: 6 theory, thesis 7 theorem
wrong: 5 belie, parry, rebut 6 debunk, negate, oppugn, refute 7 confute, explode 8 disprove, overturn 10 contradict, controvert, invalidate
Prove It All Night (1978 song) artist: Bruce Springsteen
proven: 5 sound, tried, valid 7 genuine 8 reliable, verified 9 qualified 10 undeniable
provenance: 4 root 6 origin, source 9 etymology, inception 10 derivation
Provençal: 8 language
___ provençale: 3 à la
Provence
city in ~: 3 Aix 5 Arles
dance: 9 tambourin
department in ~: 3 Var
locale: 6 France
___-Provence: 5 Aix-en
provender: 4 chow, eats, feed, food, grub, meat 6 ration, viands 7 aliment, eatable, edibles, vittles 8 victuals 10 provisions, sustenance
preparer: 4 chef, cook
provide ~: 4 cook, feed 5 cater, serve 7 nourish
proverb: 3 saw 4 word 5 adage, axiom, gnome, maxim, moral, motto, truth 6 byword, dictum, phrase, saying, slogan, truism 7 epigram 8 aphorism, apothegm 9 platitude 10 apophthegm
proverbial: 5 known 6 famous 8 familiar 9 axiomatic, well-known
follower: 4 Eccl.
preceder: 6 Psalms
Proverbs: 4 book
Prove Your Love (1988 song) artist: Taylor Dayne
provide: 3 fit 4 feed, give, keep, lend 5 allow, bring, cater, equip, fix up, grant, offer, put up, ready, serve, spare, stake, stock, treat, yield 6 afford, bestow, donate, fit out, impart, outfit, purvey, ration, render, supply 7 advance, appoint, deliver, furnish, prepare, present, procure, produce, proffer, require, satisfy, specify, support, sustain 8 accouter, accoutre, dispense, maintain, turn over 9 look after, replenish, stipulate 10 administer, contribute, take care of
for: 4 feed, keep 7 shelter, support, sustain 8 maintain 9 stipulate
more: 3 add 6 top off 9 replenish
temporarily: 4 lend, loan
provided: 8 granting 9 given that
that: 4 so as 6 in case 8 as long as
providence: 4 fate 5 karma 6 kismat, kismet 7 caution, fortune 9 foresight, frugality 10 discretion
Providence: 4 city, port, town 5 river
athletes: 5 Bears
conference: 7 Big East
locale: Rhode Island
school: 5 Brown
school south of ~: 3 URI
Providence (NBC drama)
cast: Mike Farrell (Dr. Jim Hansen)
Melina Kanakaredes (Dr. Sydney Hansen)
Concetta Tomei (Lynda Hansen)
provident: 4 wise 5 canny, chary, sober 6 frugal, saving, shrewd 7 careful, politic, prudent, sparing, thrifty 8 cautious, discreet, vigilant 9 judicious 10 deliberate, discerning, economical, farsighted, thoughtful
providential: 4 well 5 blest, happy, lucky 7 blessed, charmed, favored, on a roll 9 fortunate, on a streak 10 auspicious, felicitous, fortuitous, propitious
providing: 8 as long as, assuming, provided 9 given that, subject to, supposing 10 in the event
province: 3 job 4 area, duty, land, line, part, post, role, zone 5 arena, field, orbit, place, range, realm, shire, world 6 canton, charge, colony, county, domain, office, region, sphere 7 concern, demesne, purview, quarter, section 8 business, capacity, district, division, dominion, function 9 bailiwick, territory 10 department
Provincetown: 4 city, town
locale: 4 Mass. 7 Cape Cod
provincial: 4 hick, rude 5 local, rough, rural, yokel 6 common, little, narrow, rustic 7 bucolic, bumpkin, country, insular, limited, plowboy 8 homespun, outlying, pastoral 9 backwoods, bucolical, hidebound, home-grown, parochial, sectarian, small-town 10 clodhopper
language: 6 patois 7 dialect
___ Provincial: 6 French
Provine: 7 Dorothy
proving ___: 6 ground
provision: 3 rig 4 plan, term 5 catch, equip, joker, rider, stock, store, terms 6 clause, demand, fit out, kicker, outfit, ration, supply 7 article, furnish, strings, support 8 accouter, accoutre, catering 9 agreement, condition, endowment, fine print, foresight, insurance, requisite 10 limitation, precaution, small print
home contract ~: 6 escrow
make ~ for: 5 allow, set up 7 arrange, prepare
provisional: 4 test 5 trial 6 acting, pro tem 7 interim, limited, passing, stopgap, subject 9 dependant, dependent, ephemeral, makeshift, provisory, qualified, temporary, tentative, transient
government: 5 junta
worker: 4 temp
provisionary: 9 tentative
provisions: 3 kit 4 eats, fare, food, grub, meat 5 board, items 6 stores, viands 7 aliment, eatable, edibles, strings, victual, vittles 8 eatables, supplies, victuals 9 equipment, groceries, provender 10 sustenance
proviso: 4 term 5 catch, joker, rider, state 6 clause, demand, kicker 7 strings 9 agreement, condition, fine print, requisite 10 limitation, small print
provisory: 9 dependant, dependent, temporary, tentative
Provo: 4 city, town
athletes: 7 Cougars
locale: 4 Utah
neighbor: 4 Orem
school: 3 BYU
town near ~: 4 Lehi
___ provocateur: 5 agent
provocation: 4 spur 5 cause 6 injury, insult, reason, slight 7 affront, grounds, offense 8 occasion, vexation 9 annoyance, challenge, incentive, indignity
provocative: 5 heady, juicy, pushy 6 erotic, lively, risqué, sultry, trying 7 defiant, irksome 8 alluring, annoying, exciting, inviting, tempting 9 insulting, offensive, provoking, ravishing, vexatious 10 irritating
provoke: 3 bug, egg, get, ire, irk, nag, vex 4 bait, defy, fire, fret, gall, goad, miff, move, prod, rile, roil, spur, stir 5 anger, annoy, cause, chafe, egg on, evoke, grate, hop up, hound, incur, peeve, pique, prime, raise, rouse, roust, spark, spite, start, taunt, tease, tempt, upset, waken 6 arouse, ask for, bother, elicit, enrage, excite, foment, incite, induce, insult, kindle, lead to, madden, needle, nettle, offend, pester, pother, prompt, put out, ruffle, stir up, whip up, work up 7 affront, aggress, bedevil, disturb, enflame, ferment, incense, inflame, inspire, perturb, produce, torment, trigger 8 engender, exercise, irritate, motivate, occasion 9 aggravate, call forth, challenge, displease, draw forth, galvanize, impassion, infuriate, instigate, stimulate, tantalize, titillate 10 exasperate
as a fight: 4 pick
provoked: 3 mad 5 huffy, irate, upset
easily ~: 5 fiery, short 7 grouchy 8 snappish 9 irascible
provoker: 5 tease 6 gadfly 9 aggressor
provolone: 6 cheese 7 Italian
provost ___: 5 court, guard 7 marshal
___ Provost: 4 Lord
prow: 3 bow 4 stem 5 front
away from the ~: 3 aft 6 astern
locale: 4 hull
opposite: 5 stern
part of the ~: 5 hawse 10 figurehead
prowess: 4 grit, guts 5 heart, might, nerve, pluck, power, skill, spunk, valor, vigor 6 daring, genius, mettle, starch, talent 7 ability, bravery, courage, heroism, mastery, stamina, stomach 8 boldness, facility, strength 9 derring-do, endurance, expertise, fortitude, gallantry, hardihood, readiness 10 efficiency, right stuff, virtuosity
prowl: 4 hunt, lurk, roam, rove, seek 5 creep, range, sculk, skulk, slink, sneak, stalk, steal 6 cruise, forage, search, wander, waylay 7 slither 8 scavenge 10 nose around
on the ~: 5 loose 7 escaped
prowl ___: 3 car
prowler: 5 thief 6 robber 7 burglar 8 intruder
Prowler: 3 car 4 auto 8 Plymouth
Prowse: 6 Juliet
proximal: 4 near 9 immediate
opposite: 6 distal
proximate: 4 near, next, nigh 5 close, later 6 at hand, nearby 7 close by, closest, nearest 8 adjacent, imminent 9 bordering, following, immediate,

impending, secondary **10** convenient, subsequent
proximity: **8** nearness, presence, vicinity **9** closeness, immediacy **10** contiguity
in close ~: **4** near **5** anear **6** hard by
place in ~: **6** appose
Proxmire: **7** William
proxy: **3** agt., rep, sub **5** agent, vicar **6** deputy **7** stand-in **8** delegate **9** alternate, appointee, go-between, surrogate **10** lieutenant, substitute
be ~ for: **7** stand in **9** represent **10** substitute
Proyas: **4** Alex
PRS, on the phone: **5** seven
prude: **4** prig **7** puritan **8** bluenose **9** nice Nelly, Victorian **10** goody-goody
prudence: **4** care, wits **5** sense **6** sanity, thrift, virtue, wisdom **7** caution, economy **8** judgment, sapience **10** discretion, expediency, horse sense, precaution
___ Prudence: **4** Dear
prudent: **4** safe, sage, sane, wary, wise **5** canny, chary, fussy, leery, sound **6** frugal, shrewd **7** careful, finicky, guarded, heedful, politic, sapient, sparing, tactful, thrifty **8** cautious, discreet, exacting, finiking, finnicky, keen-eyed, rational, rigorous, sensible, tactical, thorough, vigilant **9** advisable, assiduous, attentive, expedient, farseeing, judicious, observant, provident, realistic, sagacious **10** diplomatic, discerning, economical, farsighted, fastidious, longheaded, meticulous, particular, reasonable, scrupulous, thoughtful
be ~: **3** eke **5** skimp, stint **6** budget **7** refrain **9** economize
prudential: **10** economical
Prudential competitor: **5** Aetna
prudery: **7** modesty
Prudhoe Bay
craft: **5** kayak, oiler **6** tanker
dwelling: **4** iglu **5** igloo
locale: **6** Alaska
product: **3** oil **9** petroleum
Prudhomme: **4** Paul **5** Sully
Prudhomme, Paul: **4** chef
Prudhomme, Sully: **4** poet **6** French **8** Nobelist
prudish: **4** prim, smug **5** fussy, rigid, stern, timid **6** demure, prissy, proper, strict, stuffy **7** finicky, genteel, mincing, precise, stilted, uptight **8** affected, finiking, finnicky, overnice, priggish, starched **9** simpering, squeamish, Victorian **10** fastidious, goody-goody, overmodest
Pruett: **6** Jeanne
Prufrock creator: T.S. Eliot
prune: **3** cut, lop, mow, top **4** clip, crop, dock, pare, plum, snip, thin, trim **5** fruit, lower, shape, shave, shear **6** lop off, reduce, remove **7** abridge, curtail, cut back, scissor, shorten, snip off, thin out **8** condense, diminish, minimize, truncate **9** summarize **10** abbreviate
formerly: **4** plum
pastry filling: **6** lekvar
prunella: **6** fabric **8** material
pruning ___: **4** hook **6** shears
pruning candidate: **4** tree **5** hedge, shrub
Prusiner, Stanley B.: **8** Nobelist
Prussia: **5** state
cavalryman: **4** ulan **5** uhlan
locale: **7** Germany
Prussian ___: **4** blue
___-Prussian War: **6** Austro, Franco
Prut: **5** river
locale: **7** Moldova, Romania, Rumania, Ukraine **8** Roumania
prutah: **4** coin
pry: **3** spy **4** nose, peek, peep, peer, poke, root **5** force, heave, jimmy, lever, raise, snoop, stare, wrest, wring **6** butt in, elicit, extort, horn in, kibitz, meddle, search **7** crowbar, disjoin, enquire, extract, inquire, intrude, obtrude, ransack, wiretap **8** jerk away, listen in, question, quidnunc **9** disengage, eavesdrop, ferret out, force open, interfere, interpose **10** scrutinize
pry ___: **3** bar
___ Pry: **4** Paul
Pryce: **8** Jonathan
prying: **4** busy, nosy **5** nosey **7** curious, ferrety **8** invasive **9** curiosity, intrusive, obtrusive **10** meddlesome, snoopiness
tool: **5** jimmy, lever **7** crowbar
Prynne, Hester daughter: **5** Pearl
Pryor: **7** Richard
Pryor, Richard: **5** actor **8** comedian
film: The Bingo Long Traveling All-Stars & Motor Kings (1976)
Blue Collar (1978)
Bustin' Loose (1981)
California Suite (1978)
Hit! (1973)
Lady Sings the Blues (1972)
Silver Streak (1976)
Stir Crazy (1980)
psalm: **4** hymn, pean, song **5** chant, paean, verse **6** eulogy **7** chorale, introit **8** canticle
address: **5** O Lord
word: **3** yea **5** selah
___ Psalm Book: **3** Bay
Psalms: **4** book
follower: **8** Proverbs
preceder: **3** Job
singer: **6** cantor
psaltery: **6** string, zither
origin: **6** Europe
Psamathe: **6** Nereid
lover: **6** Apollo
p's and q's: **7** manners **8** protocol **9** etiquette
mind one's ~: **6** behave **10** toe the line
PSAT: **4** exam, test
provider: **3** ETS
taker: **2** jr. **6** junior
pseudo: **4** fake, mock, sham **5** bogus, faked, false, phony, put-on, quack, quasi **6** ersatz, forged, phoney, unreal **7** assumed, feigned, plastic, pretend, suspect **8** spurious **9** imitation, imitative, pretended, simulated, synthetic, unnatural **10** artificial, fabricated, fictitious, fraudulent
pseudoaesthetic: **4** arty **5** artsy
pseudonym: **4** name **5** alias, title **6** anonym **7** pen name **8** cognomen **10** nom de plume
letters: **3** AKA
pseudopod possessor: **5** ameba **6** amoeba
pshaw: **3** bah, tut **4** drat, pooh **9** expletive
psi: **5** Greek **6** letter **9** telepathy
preceder: **3** chi
successor: **5** omega
P.S. I ___ U: **3** Luv
psilomelane: **3** ore **7** mineral
P.S. I Love You (1964 song) artist: Beatles
psoas site: **3** hip
psst!: **3** hey **6** hey you
cousin: **4** ahem
follower: **6** in here, listen
PSU
conference: **6** Big Ten
see also Penn State
psych: **4** stir **5** rouse, upset **6** arouse **7** agitate, enthuse **10** intimidate
out: **5** bluff, spook **6** rattle, unglue **7** disrupt, disturb, fluster, unnerve **8** unsettle **9** speculate **10** demoralize, discompose, disconcert, intimidate
up: **5** ready **6** incite **7** enthuse, hearten, inspire, prepare **8** embolden, enspirit, get ready, imbolden, inspirit, motivate **9** encourage
___ psych: **3** pop
psyche: **4** mind, self, soul **5** anima **6** pneuma, spirit **9** élan vital **10** inner child
component: **2** id **3** ego **8** superego
Psyche: **8** asteroid
daughter of ~: **7** Volupta
lover of ~: **4** Eros
___ Psyche: **5** Ode to
Psychedelic Shack (1970 song) artist: Temptations
psyched up: **4** agog, high **5** eager, ready **6** on edge **8** prepared **10** inspirited
Psyche knot: **4** coif **6** hairdo **8** coiffure
psychiatrist: **7** analyst
Austrian ~: **5** Adler, Freud
org.: **3** APA
Swiss ~: **4** Jung
psychic: **4** seer **6** medium, mental, mystic, occult **8** mystical **9** sensitive, spiritual **10** palm reader, responsive, soothsayer, telepathic
power: **3** ESP **9** telepathy
sight: **4** aura
Psycho (1960 film)
cast: Martin Balsam, John Gavin, Janet Leigh, Vera Miles, Anthony Perkins
director: Alfred Hitchcock
locale: **5** motel
psycho ender: **6** babble
psychological: **6** mental **9** emotional
threshold: **5** limen
psychological ___: **5** novel **6** moment **7** warfare
psychology: **7** science
appetite, in ~: **6** orexis
branch of ~: **7** haptics
starter: **4** meta, para
study: **4** mind
___ psychology: **3** ego **4** mass **5** depth **6** social **7** dynamic, Gestalt, reverse
psychrophobe fear: **4** cold
pt.: **3** amt., qty. **4** meas.
compass ~: **3** dir., ENE, ESE, NNE, NNW, SSE, SSW, WNW, WSW
fraction: **2** oz.
high ~: **3** mtn. **4** elev.
multiple: **2** qt. **3** gal.
of speech: **2** vb **3** adj., adv. **4** conj.
see also point
Pt: **4** elem. **7** element **8** platinum
78 for ~: **4** at. no.
P.T.: **6** Barnum
P.T. 109 (1962 song) artist: Jimmy Dean
PTA
member: **3** dad, mom **7** teacher
part of ~: **4** assn. **5** assoc. **6** parent **7** teacher
ptarmigan: **4** bird **6** grouse
PT boat: **7** warship
P-T connection: **3** QRS
PT Cruiser: **3** car **4** auto **8** Chrysler
pteriodsperm: **4** fern **5** plant
pterodactyl: **7** reptile
of film: **5** Rodan
Ptolemy: **8** Egyptian **10** astronomer
ptui: **3** fie **4** pooh **6** bunkum **8** nonsense
Pu: **4** elem. **7** element **9** plutonium
94 for ~: **4** at. no.
pub: **3** bar, inn **4** dive **5** joint **6** lounge, saloon, tavern **7** barroom, gin mill, taproom **8** alehouse, grogshop, taphouse **9** bierstube, roadhouse
expression: **5** on tap
fixture: **3** tap **9** dartboard, pool table
game: **4** pool **5** darts
order: **3** ale **4** beer, pint, suds **5** draft, lager, round, stein, stout **8** schooner
perch: **5** stool **8** barstool
projectile: **4** dart
pub-crawl: **6** barhop
puberty: **5** youth **8** minority **9** childhood **10** immaturity, pubescence
combining form: **4** hebe-
past ~: **5** adult **7** grown-up
pubescent: **5** young **8** immature **10** adolescent
public: **3** mob **4** city, folk, free, open **5** civic, civil, clear, known, overt, plain, state, urban **6** buyers, common, in view, masses, nation, patent, people, shared, social, voters, vulgar **7** country, exposed, federal, general, obvious, popular, society, visible **8** apparent, audience, citizens, clear-cut, communal, everyone, exoteric, explicit, manifest, national, ordinary, populace, societal, subjects, unhidden, unveiled **9** clientele, community, following, hoi polloi, multitude, municipal, published, statewide, universal, well-known **10** accessible, electorate, observable, population, recognized, supporters, unshrouded, widespread
announcer, formerly: **5** crier **9** town crier
area: **4** mall, park **5** plaza **6** square **7** commons
assembly: **4** diet **5** forum **7** meeting
figure: **3** VIP **4** lion, name, star **5** celeb **7** big name, notable **8** eminence, luminary, somebody **9** celebrity, dignitary, personage, superstar
general ~: **3** mob **4** folk, herd **5** world **6** masses, people, rabble **7** society **8** populace, riffraff **9** bourgeois, citizenry, hoi polloi, multitude, plebeians
good: **4** weal
house: **3** bar, inn, pub **5** lodge **6** saloon, tavern **7** barroom
in ~: **6** openly **7** overtly
land: **4** park **5** plaza **6** square **7** commons
make ~: **3** air **4** bare, leak, talk, vent **5** admit, break, speak, spill, voice **6** betray, expose, report, reveal, spread, unmask, unveil **7** come out, divulge, exhibit, lay bare, let slip, publish, uncover **8** announce, disclose, give away, proclaim **9** broadcast
notices: **2** ad
outcry: **5** stink **7** scandal
performance: **4** play **5** drama, opera, raree **6** ballet **7** concert
persona: **5** image
regard: **5** éclat **6** renown, repute **7** acclaim, stardom **8** eminence **9** celebrity, notoriety **10** popularity, prominence, reputation
sentiment: **5** pulse
servant: **3** rep **4** veep **5** mayor **7** officer, senator **8** alderman, governor **9** president, town clerk **10** politician
spat: **5** scene
speaker: **6** orator **10** campaigner, politician
transport: **2** el **3** bus, cab, jet **4** hack, taxi **5** ferry, metro, plane, train **6** subway **7** autobus, minibus **8** airplane
public ___: **3** act, bar, eye, law **4** bill, debt, life, room, sale **5** enemy, house,

image, trust, works **6** charge, domain, figure, health, policy, school, sector **7** affairs, company, housing, library, officer, opinion, servant, service, statute, utility
__ public: 6 notary
Public __ Administration: 5 Works
__ Public: 3 Joe **5** John Q.
__ publica: 3 res
public-address __: 6 system
publication: 4 book, text, tome **5** issue, novel, organ, print **6** annals, volume **7** booklet, edition, journal, leaflet, release, reprint, romance, writing **8** brochure, handbill, magazine, pamphlet, printing, whodunit **9** anthology, broadcast, newspaper, paperback, statement **10** bestseller, newsletter, periodical
book before ~: 2 ms. **10** manuscript
online ~: 5 e-book, e-zine
prepare for ~: 4 edit **6** censor, redact, revise **10** blue-pencil
slick ~: 3 mag **8** magazine
Public Citizen, Inc. founder: 5 Nader
public defender: 3 att. **4** atty. **6** lawyer **8** attorney **9** counselor
Public Enemy, The (1931 film)
cast: James Cagney, Mae Clarke, Jean Harlow, Eddie Woods
director: William Wellman
__ public eye: 5 in the
publicity: 2 ad **3** ink **4** hype, plug, puff **5** blurb, boost, flack, pitch, press, promo **6** hoopla, report, spread **7** billing, build-up, fanfare, handout, puffery, release, write-up **8** ballyhoo **9** attention, billboard, limelight, notoriety, promotion, spotlight **10** commercial, propaganda
generator: 4 sale **5** press, PR man, stunt **6** come-on **7** freebie **8** promoter
piece: 2 ad **5** promo **6** come-on, review **10** commercial
publicize: 3 air **4** bare, bill, flog, hype, plug, puff, push, sell, tout **5** boost, extol, pitch **6** extoll, herald, hype up, play up, spread, talk up **7** build up, promote, trumpet, write up **8** announce, headline, skywrite **9** advertise, billboard, broadcast, celebrate, circulate, make known, propagate, spotlight
publicized: 6 famous **8** renowned **9** notorious, well-known **10** celebrated
Public Men author: Allen Drury
public-opinion __: 4 poll
publish: 3 air **4** bare, vend **5** issue, print, write **6** get out, put out, report, reveal, spread **7** lay bare **8** disclose, proclaim **9** circulate, propagate, ventilate **10** distribute, promulgate
publisher: 5 press **8** magazine **9** newspaper
ad: 5 blurb **6** review
crime: 5 libel
DC ~: 3 GPO
org.: 3 ABA
__ publisher: 6 vanity
publishing: 5 media, press
employee: 6 editor **7** proofer **8** reporter **9** columnist **10** journalist
exec: 2 ed. **6** editor
problem: 6 errata **7** erratum
publishing __: 5 house
__ publishing: 7 desktop
Pucci, Emilio: 7 Italian **8** designer
Puccini, Giacomo: 7 Italian **8** composer
piece: 4 aria, opus, tema **5** opera
work: Edgar
Girl of the Golden West
La Boheme
La Rondine
Le Villi
Madame Butterfly
Manon Lescaut
Tosca
Turandot
puce: 5 color **6** purple **8** brownish, purplish
kin: 4 plum **5** lilac, mauve **6** dahlia, damson, orchid **7** heather, petunia **8** amethyst, burgundy, eggplant, lavender, mulberry **9** raspberry **10** heliotrope
puck: 4 disc, disk
game: 6 hockey **9** ice hockey
stopper: 6 goalie
Puck: 4 moon **6** sprite
master: 6 Oberon
planet: 6 Uranus
pucka: 4 good **6** proper **7** genuine **8** reliable **9** authentic
pucker: 4 fold, knit, ruck, tuck **5** pinch, plait, pleat, purse **6** cockle, crease, furrow, gather, ruffle, rumple, shrink **7** crinkle, crumple, squeeze, wrinkle **8** compress, contract
up: 4 kiss **5** purse
puckered fabric: 6 plisse
Puckett: 4 Gary **5** Kirby
Puckett and the Union Gap, Gary
song: Lady Willpower (1968)
Over You (1968)
This Girl Is a Woman Now (1969)
Woman, Woman (1967)
Young Girl (1968)
Puckett, Kirby: 4 Twin **10** outfielder
puckish: 3 fey **5** elfin **6** impish **7** playful
creature: 3 elf **4** pixy **5** pixie **6** sprite **10** leprechaun
expression: 4 grin
puckster: 6 skater
org.: 3 NHL
sport: 6 hockey **9** ice hockey
P-U connection: 4 QRST
pudding: 4 flan **5** sweet **6** junket, mousse **7** custard, dessert, tapioca **8** flummery
ingredient: 3 egg **4** milk, plum
plantain ~: 6 foofoo
thickened, as ~: 3 set
__ pudding: 4 plum, snow, suet **5** black, blood, bread, hasty, pease **6** frozen, Indian **7** cabinet, cottage
...pudding __ the eating: 4 is in
puddle: 4 pool
contents: 3 mud **4** rain **5** water
walk through a ~: 4 wade **5** slosh **6** splash
__ puddle: 3 mud
Puddleduck: 6 Jemima
puddle-jumper: 5 plane **8** airplane
take a ~: 3 fly
Pudd'nhead Wilson author: Mark Twain
...puddy __!: 3 tat
pudgy: 5 beefy, buxom, dumpy, fubsy, hefty, obese, plump, pursy, round, squat, stout, thick, tubby **6** chubby, chunky, fleshy, portly, pyknic, rotund, stocky, zaftig, zoftig **7** adipose, paunchy **8** roly-poly, thickset **9** corpulent, filled-out **10** abdominous, overweight
not ~: 4 lean, slim, thin, wiry **5** rangy **6** skinny, svelte **7** slender, willowy
pudu: 4 deer
relative: 3 elk, roe **4** axis, shou, sika **5** moose **6** chital, guemal, hangul, huemul, sambar, sambur, thamin, wapiti **7** brocket, caribou, muntjac, muntjak, sambhar, sambhur **8** reindeer **9** barasingh
Puebla: 4 city, town **5** state **7** Mexican
city: 5 Canoa **6** Amozoc, Chilac, Izúcar, Libres, Serdán **7** Acajete, Acatlán, Ajalpán, Atlixco, Cholula, Tepeaca **8** Altepexi, Chiautla, Tehuacán, Zacatlán **9** Acatzingo, Sanctórum, Teziutlán, Xicotepec **10** Moyotzingo, Texmelucan
Pueblo: 4 city, town **5** tribe **6** Indian **7** Amerind
ancestor: 7 Anasazi
enemy: 3 Ute
locale: 8 Colorado
material: 5 adobe
New Mexico ~: 5 Acoma
people: 4 Hopi, Taos, Zuñi
site: 5 cliff
sunken chamber: 4 kiva
Puente Alto: 4 city, town
locale: 5 Chile
Puente, Tito: 7 drummer **10** bandleader
genre: 4 jazz **5** salsa
Puenzo: 4 Luis
puerile: 3 raw **4** weak **5** green, inane, silly, vapid, young **6** callow, infant, jejune, simple, stupid **7** babyish, fatuous, foolish, kiddish, trivial **8** childish, immature, juvenile, youthful **9** childlike, frivolous, infantile, senseless, unfledged **10** adolescent, nonserious, ridiculous, sophomoric
puerility: 5 youth **9** frivolity **10** callowness, immaturity
Puerto __: 4 Rico
Puerto Montt: 4 city, town
locale: 5 Chile
Puerto Peñasco: 4 city, town
locale: 6 Mexico, Sonora
Puerto Rico: 3 isl. **4** isle **6** island
capital: 7 San Juan
city: 4 Moca **5** Ponce **6** Caguas **7** Bayamón **8** Carolina
clock setting: 3 AST
instrument: 6 cuatro
writer: 5 Ferré **6** Arrivi
Puerto Rico __: 6 Trench, Trough
Puerto Vallarta: 4 city, town
locale: 6 Mexico **7** Jalisco
__-Puf: 3 Sta
puff: 3 air **4** blow, drag, gasp, gulp, gust, huff, hype, pant, plug, pull, waft, wind, wisp **5** blast, bloat, blurb, boost, draft, heave, pitch, promo, quilt, smoke, swell, whiff **6** breath, breeze, exhale, hairdo, inhale, overdo, pastry, praise, wheeze **7** breathe, distend, draught, enlarge, flatter, inflate, promote, upsweep **9** advertise, comforter, publicity, publicize **10** exaggerate, overpraise
along: 4 chug
ender: 4 ball
huff and ~: 4 blow, gasp, pant **6** wheeze
move on a ~ of air: 4 waft
of smoke: 4 wisp
out: 5 bulge **6** billow, blouse **7** balloon, inflate
piece: 5 blurb
up: 4 laud **5** bloat, elate, exalt, extol, pride, swell **6** billow, expand, extoll, praise **7** balloon, distend, enlarge, fill out, flatter, inflate, magnify **9** embroider, intumesce **10** exaggerate, overpraise
puff __: 5 adder, piece
__ puff: 5 cream **6** powder
Puff: 3 cat **6** dragon
puffball: 6 fungus **9** dandelion
Puff Daddy
real name: Sean Combs
song: All Night Long (1999)
Been Around the World (1998)
Can't Nobody Hold Me Down (1997)
Come With Me (1998)
I'll Be Missing You (1997)
It's All About the Benjamins (1997)
Lookin' at Me (1998)
Mo Money Mo Problems (1997)
No Time (1996)
Satisfy You (1999)
Someone (1997)
Victory (1998)
Puffed Rice: 6 cereal
competitor: 3 Kix **4** Life, Trix **5** Kashi, Quisp, Total **6** Kaboom, Muesli, Oreo O's, Pablum, Smacks **7** All-Bran, Crispix, Harmony, Hunny B's, Mueslix, Oat Bran, Pokemon **8** Boo Berry, Cheerios, Corn Chex, Corn Pops, Fiber One, Rice Chex, Special K, Uncle Sam, Wheaties **9** Alpha Bits, Apple Zaps, Grape Nuts, Honey Comb, Just Right, Wheat Chex **10** Apple Jacks, Bran Flakes, Cap'n Crunch, Cocoa Puffs, Froot Loops, Mini-Wheats, Nutri-Grain, Quaker Oats, Smart Start **11** Cocoa Blasts, Cookie Crisp, Golden Crisp, Lucky Charms, Puffed Wheat, Sweet Crunch, Waffle Crisp
puffed-up: 4 smug, vain **5** proud, tumid **6** stuffy **7** fustian, pompous, swollen **8** gloating **9** conceited **10** big-talking
Puffed Wheat: 6 cereal
competitor: 3 Kix **4** Life, Trix **5** Kashi, Quisp, Total **6** Kaboom, Muesli, Oreo O's, Pablum, Smacks **7** All-Bran, Crispix, Harmony, Hunny B's, Mueslix, Oat Bran, Pokemon **8** Boo Berry, Cheerios, Corn Chex, Corn Pops, Fiber One, Rice Chex, Special K, Uncle Sam, Wheaties **9** Alpha Bits, Apple Zaps, Grape Nuts, Honey Comb, Just Right, Wheat Chex **10** Apple Jacks, Bran Flakes, Cap'n Crunch, Cocoa Puffs, Froot Loops, Mini-Wheats, Nutri-Grain, Puffed Rice, Quaker Oats, Smart Start **11** Cocoa Blasts, Cookie Crisp, Golden Crisp, Lucky Charms, Sweet Crunch, Waffle Crisp
puffer: 4 fish, fugu **9** globefish
puffery: 4 hype **6** hoopla **8** ballyhoo, flattery **9** publicity
puffin: 3 auk **4** bird
puffiness: 5 bloat, edema **6** oedema **8** swelling
puff-of-smoke sound: 4 poof
__ Puffs: 5 Cocoa
Puff (The Magic Dragon) (1963 song)
artist: Peter, Paul and Mary
puffy: 4 full **7** billowy, bloated, bulging, swollen **8** enlarged, inflamed, inflated **9** distended
__ Puffy Combs: 4 Sean
pug: 3 dog, toy **4** nose **5** boxer **6** canine **7** fighter **9** gladiator
ender: 4 mark
pug __: 4 mill, nose
Puget Sound: 5 inlet
locale: 7 Pacific **10** Washington
puggaree: 4 band **5** scarf
pugilism: 4 ring **6** boxing **10** fisticuffs
pugilist: 5 boxer **7** fighter, palooka **9** gladiator
asset: 5 reach
garb: 4 robe **6** gloves, trunks
milieu: 4 ring **5** arena
org.: 3 WBA, WBC
pay: 5 purse
punch: 2 KO **3** jab, TKO **6** one-two
seat: 5 stool
weapon: 4 fist
see also boxer
pugmark: 5 trace, trail
pugnacious: 4 mean, ugly **5** irate, nasty, onery, salty, surly, tough **6** feisty, ornery **7** defiant, hateful, hawkish,

hostile, martial, scrappy, warlike 8 contrary, fighting, inimical, menacing, militant, ructious, spiteful 9 bellicose, combative, malicious, truculent 10 aggressive, malevolent, unfriendly

pugnacity: 5 fight 6 temper 9 surliness 10 aggression

Pugni: 5 Cesar 6 Cesare

Pugsley: 6 Addams

puisne: 6 junior 7 younger

puissance: 3 vim 4 dint, thew 5 brawn, force, might, power, thews, vigor 6 energy, muscle 7 fitness, muscles, potence, potency, stamina 8 vitality 9 beefiness, endurance, fortitude, hardiness, huskiness, stoutness, toughness 10 browniness, brute force, mightiness, robustness, ruggedness, sturdiness

puissant: 4 hale, iron, wiry 5 beefy, burly, hardy, hefty, hunky, husky, lusty, stout, tough 6 brawny, hearty, mighty, potent, robust, rugged, sinewy, steely, stocky, sturdy, virile 7 doughty 8 almighty, athletic, forceful, indurate, muscular, powerful, stalwart, vigorous 9 Atlantean, herculean, strapping, well-built 10 able-bodied, red-blooded

Pujols, Albert sport: 8 baseball

pukka: 4 good 6 proper 7 genuine 8 reliable 9 authentic

pukka ___: 5 sahib

puku: 8 antelope

relative: 3 gnu, kob 4 guib, kudu, oryx, topi 5 addax, bongo, chiru, eland, goral, korin, nyala, oribi, saiga, serow 6 chammy, dik-dik, duiker, impala, koodoo, lechwe, nilgai, rhebok, shammy, shamoy 7 blaubok, blesbok, chamois, defassa, gazelle, gemsbok, gerenuk, grysbok, nylghai, nylghau, sassaby 8 blesbuck, bontebok, bushbuck, gemsbuck, reedbuck, steenbok, steinbok 9 blackbuck, pronghorn, sitatunga, springbok, waterbuck 10 hartebeest, wildebeest

pul: 5 money

pula: 5 money

Pular: 4 peak 5 mount 8 mountain

locale: 5 Andes, Chile

___ Pulaski: 4 Fort

pulchritude: 6 beauty

pulchritudinous: 4 cute, fair 5 bonny 6 bonnie, comely, lovely, pretty 7 winsome 8 alluring, gorgeous, handsome, striking, stunning 9 beautiful, ravishing 10 attractive

pule: 3 sob 4 bawl, mewl, wail, weep 5 whine 6 boohoo, snivel 7 blubber, grumble, whimper

puli: 3 dog 5 canid 6 canine

Pulitzer: 5 award, prize 6 Joseph

category: 5 drama, music 10 journalism, literature

rival: 4 Ochs 6 Hearst

pull: 3 lug, row, tow, tug 4 cull, drag, draw, haul, jerk, lure, pick, puff, tear, weed, yank 5 clout, heave, labor, pluck, power, trail, troll, truck, tug at, tweak, twist 6 allure, appeal, entice, entrée, evulse, gather, paddle, remove, snatch, sprain, strain, twitch, uproot, weight, wrench 7 attract, charism, extract, receive, stretch 8 charisma, intrigue, leverage, pressure, strength, traction 9 dislocate, influence, magnetism 10 attraction

a fast one: 3 con 4 fool 5 cheat, cozen, outdo, trick 6 delude, outwit 7 deceive, defraud, mislead, swindle 8 flimflam, hoodwink, outsmart 9 bamboozle

ahead of: 4 pass

a hoax: 5 bluff, cheat, feign, put on 7 mislead, pretend

an all-nighter: 4 cram

apart: 4 rend, tear 5 split 7 split up 9 find fault

a punch: 5 mince 6 soften

a switcheroo: 6 change 7 reverse 9 back-pedal

away: 4 lead 5 wrest 6 secede

back: 5 quail 6 recoil, retire 7 retract, retreat 8 hesitate, withdraw

down: 3 get, net 4 earn, fell, make, rase, raze 5 gross, level, lower, wreck 6 humble, ravage, reduce, remove 7 destroy, receive, subvert, unbuild 8 bulldoze, collapse, demolish, take home 9 dismantle, humiliate, knock over

for: 7 support 9 encourage 10 rally round

hard: 3 tug 4 jerk 5 pluck 6 wrench

in: 3 nab 4 bust, curb, draw, hook, lure, nail, park, rein, rope 5 check, pinch, snare, tempt 6 allure, arrest, arrive, bridle, collar, detain, entice, pick up 7 attract, tighten 8 appeal to, get there, restrain 9 apprehend

off: 2 do 3 win 4 skin 5 score 6 commit, detach, effect, manage, wangle 7 achieve, execute, perform, produce, succeed 8 conclude 10 accomplish, perpetrate, put through

one's leg: 3 guy, kid, rag, rib 4 fool, razz, twit 5 chaff, tease, trick 6 banter, take in 7 deceive, mislead

out: 2 go 4 exit, move, part, quit 5 leave, scram, split 6 beat it, be gone, decamp, defect, depart, go away, remove, renege, retire, secede 7 abandon, abscond, go south, retreat, ride off, take off 8 evacuate, hightail, separate, shove off, withdraw

out of: 8 give up on

over: 4 park

strings: 5 lobby, order, pluck 8 maneuver 10 manipulate

the lever: 3 opt 4 vote 5 elect 6 decide

the plug on: 3 end 4 stop 5 drain 6 cancel 7 rescind

the strings: 4 rule 6 govern

the trigger: 4 fire 5 shoot

the wool over: 3 con, lie, rob, sap 4 bilk, butt, dupe, have, hoax, jerk, prey, scam, trap 5 cheat, fraud, shaft, trick 6 delude, fleece, lead on, outwit, rip off, rope in, suck in, take in 7 beguile, buffalo, chicane, deceive, defraud, mislead, swindle, two-time, wheedle 8 bulldoze, flimflam, hoodwink, inveigle, outsmart, sucker in 9 bamboozle, disinform, scapegoat

through: 4 heal, mend 5 rally 6 make it 7 get over, get well, rebound, recover, survive, triumph, weather 10 recuperate

together: 4 tidy 5 amass, unite 6 gather 7 collect

up: 4 halt, hike, stop 5 brake, raise 6 arrive 9 extirpate

up stakes: 4 move 5 leave 6 decamp

pull ___: 3 for, off, out 4 away, back, date, down, rank 7 strings

pull ___ all the stops: 3 out

pull ___ one: 5 a fast

pull-___: 3 tab, top

___ pull: 4 bell 5 candy, taffy 7 drawbar, tractor

___-pull: 3 leg 4 push

pull a rabbit out of ___: 4 a hat

...pulled out ___: 5 a plum

pullet: 3 hen 4 bird, fowl 5 biddy, layer 7 chicken, poultry

pull in one's ___: 5 horns

Pullman: 4 Bill, city, town

amenity: 5 berth

athletes: 7 Cougars

choice: 5 lower, upper

locale: 10 Washington

school: 3 WSU

Pullman ___: 3 car 4 case

Pullman, Bill: 5 actor

film: Independence Day (1996)
The Last Seduction (1994)
Malice (1993)
Mr. Wrong (1996)
Sleepless in Seattle (1993)
Sommersby (1993)
Spaceballs (1987)
While You Were Sleeping (1995)
Zero Effect (1998)

pull one's ___: 3 leg 6 weight 7 punches

pull-out: 7 retreat 10 withdrawal

pullover: 3 tee 6 anorak, blouse, jersey 7 sweater

pull the ___ on: 4 plug

pull the ___ out from under: 3 rug

pullulate: 3 bud 4 teem 7 burgeon 8 bourgeon, increase 9 germinate

pull up ___: 6 stakes

pull-ups: 8 exercise

do ~: 4 chin

___ Pull Your Love: 4 Don't

pulmonary ___: 4 tree, vein 5 valve 6 artery

pulmonary organ: 4 lung

pulp: 4 mash, mush, tree 5 crush, paste, purée 6 pomace, squash 7 tabloid 8 magazine 9 cellulose, dime novel, sarcocarp

ender: 4 wood

fruit ~: 5 flesh

like ~ fiction: 5 lurid

pulp ___: 7 fiction, plaster

___ pulp: 4 wood 6 dental 7 sulfate, sulfite

Pulp (1972 film)

cast: Michael Caine, Mickey Rooney, Lionel Stander

director: Mike Hodges

pulper: 6 logger 10 lumberjack

Pulp Fiction (1994 film)

cast: Samuel L. Jackson, Harvey Keitel, Uma Thurman, John Travolta

director: Quentin Tarantino

like ~: 6 R-rated

Uma in ~: 3 Mia

pulpit: 4 ambo 5 ambon, table 6 podium 7 lectern, rostrum 8 platform

address: 6 homily, sermon

pulpiteer: 5 padre, vicar 6 parson 8 minister, preacher

pulpy: 4 soft 5 mushy 6 liquid, spongy

fruit: 5 drupe, mango, peach 6 orange 7 apricot 10 grapefruit

pulque: 4 beer 5 drink, quaff 8 beverage 10 potato beer

drinker's place: 4 Peru 5 Andes

pulsar: 4 Mira, star

___ pulsar: 6 binary

Pulsar: 3 car 4 auto 5 watch 6 Nissan 10 wristwatch

watch rival: 4 Ebel, Rado 5 Casio, Elgin, Lorus, Omega, Rolex, Seiko, Timex 6 Bulova, Fossil, Movado, Swatch 7 Citizen 8 Longines, Tag Heuer, Tourneau

pulsate: 4 beat, drum, pump, roar, tick, wave 5 pound, quake, throb, thrum, thump 6 quaver, quiver, shiver 7 flutter, tremble, vibrate 9 oscillate, palpitate

pulsating: 6 athrob 7 vibrant

pulsation: 4 beat, tick 5 throb 9 frequency, vibration

pulse: 4 beat, drum, pump, thud, tick, wave 5 plant, pound, tempo, throb, thrum, thump 6 hammer, quiver, rhythm 7 cadence, cadency, shudder, tremble, vibrate 9 consensus, fluctuate, heartbeat, oscillate, palpitate, vibration, vital sign

combining form: 7 sphygmo-

pulsejet ___: 6 engine

pulverize: 4 mash, mill 5 crush, grate, grind, mince, pound, smash, wreck 6 crunch, defeat, ground, pestle, powder 7 atomize, break up, crumble, shatter 8 demolish, levigate 9 comminute, granulate, triturate

pulverized: 4 fine 7 powdery

pulverizer: 4 mano 6 metate, mortar, pestle

Pulver rank: 3 ens. 6 ensign

pulverulent: 5 dusty

puma: 3 cat 5 felid 6 animal, big cat, cougar, feline 7 panther

relative: 4 eyra, lion, lynx 5 chita, liger, ounce, tiger, tigon 6 bobcat, cheeta, chetah, jaguar, margay, ocelot, serval, tiglon 7 bay lynx, caracal, cheetah, leopard 9 catamount 10 jaguarundi

Puma: 4 shoe 7 sneaker

competitor: 4 Nike 6 Adidas, Reebok

Pumasillo: 4 peak 5 mount 8 mountain

locale: 4 Peru 5 Andes

pumice: 4 rock 5 stone

feature: 4 pore

source: 4 lava

use ~: 6 abrade, smooth

pummel: 4 bang, beat, club, cuff, hurt, lash, mall, maul, pelt 5 baste, flail, knock, pound, punch, smite 6 beat on, beat up, beetle, buffet, hammer, strike, thrash, thwack, wallop 7 lambast 8 lambaste 9 fisticuff

pump: 3 ask 4 milk, pour, quiz, shoe 5 drain, eject, empty, grill, probe, pulse, shoot 6 siphon, syphon 7 draw out, inflate, pulsate 8 drive out, energize, footgear, footwear, force out, high heel, question

chamber: 4 sump

choice: 6 diesel 7 premium, regular

circulatory ~: 5 heart

fix a ~: 4 sole 6 resole

gas: 4 fill 6 fill up, fuel up, tank up

get a ~ flowing: 5 prime

iron: 4 lift 7 work out 8 exercise

ornament: 3 bow 4 clip

part: 6 insole, instep

prime the ~: 4 fund 5 stake 9 grubstake, subsidize

purchase: 3 gas 4 shoe 8 gasoline

unit: 3 gal. 5 liter, litre 6 gallon

up: 4 fill 5 bloat, liven, swell 6 expand, turn on, vivify 7 animate, balloon, distend, enlarge, enliven, inflate 8 activate, energize, vitalize 9 stimulate

pump ___: 3 box, gun 4 iron, room 7 priming

___ pump: 3 air, gas 4 beer, gear, heat, lift, sump, wind 5 bilge, chain, force 6 duplex, rotary, sodium, vacuum, wobble 7 lobular, stirrup, suction

Pump ___ Jam: 5 Up the

pumpernickel: 5 bread

relative: 3 rye 5 wheat, white 10 whole wheat

Pump House Gang, The author: Tom Wolfe

Pumping Iron (1977 film)

cast: Lou Ferrigno, Robert Fiore, Arnold Schwarzenegger

director: George Butler

pumpkin: 3 pie 4 pepo 5 color, fruit 6 orange, veggie 9 vegetable

color kin: 7 saffron 9 tangerine 10 terra cotta

ender: 4 seed
field: 5 patch
kin: 5 gourd
pie ingredient: 3 egg 4 milk 5 spice 6 ginger, nutmeg
smashing ~ sound: 5 splat
pumpkin __: 3 pie 4 head
pumpkin eater of rhyme: 5 Peter
Pumpkin Eater, The: 4 film 5 novel
author: Penelope Mortimer
cast: Anne Bancroft, Peter Finch, James Mason
director: Jack Clayton
pun: 3 mot 4 joke, quip 7 groaner 8 wordplay 9 equivoque, wisecrack, witticism
feedback: 2 ow 3 yow 4 ha-ha, ouch, yeow 5 groan, laugh, wince 7 chuckle
puna: 4 wind
punch: 3 awl, bop, box, hit, jab, pep, rap, zip 4 bash, beat, belt, biff, bite, blow, brio, clip, cuff, hook, hurt, kick, left, plug, poke, prod, shot, slam, slap, slug, sock, tang, tool, whop, zest 5 clout, cross, drill, drink, drive, force, knock, nudge, pound, power, prick, right, smack, smash, smite, spark, spice, stamp, taste, thump, verve, vigor, whang, whomp 6 batter, buffet, energy, impact, lollop, one-two, pierce, pizazz, pommel, pummel, strike, thrash, thrust, thwack, wallop 7 cogency, lambast, potence, potency 8 beverage, haymaker, knock out, lambaste, puncture, uppercut, validity, vitality 9 fisticuff, haul off on, perforate 10 excitement, fruit drink, initiative, roundhouse
a clock: 4 work 8 report in
add ~ to: 5 pep up 7 enliven
boxer's ~: 3 jab 4 chop, hook, kayo 5 cross, right 6 one-two 8 haymaker, uppercut
competitively: 3 box
ender: 5 board
get the ~ line: 4 grin, howl, roar 5 groan, laugh 6 giggle, guffaw 7 chortle, chuckle, crack up, snicker, snigger
in: 4 come 5 enter, pop up 6 appear, arrive, attend, turn up
kin: 3 ade 5 juice
line: 5 point 6 climax, payoff
maker: 4 fist
out: 2 go 4 exit, quit 5 leave
pull a ~: 5 mince 6 soften
server: 4 bowl 5 ladle
sound: 3 pow 4 wham 5 kapow
spike the ~: 4 lace
starter: 3 key 4 gang 7 counter
without ~: 4 tame
punch __: 3 out 4 bowl, card, line, list 5 press, spoon
__ punch: 4 card, milk 5 Roman 6 center, one-two, rabbit, sucker, Sunday
Punch: 5 clown 6 puppet
Judy, to ~: 4 wife
Punch-and-Judy __: 4 show
punchbowl: 5 jorum
partner: 5 ladle
puncheon: 3 tub
__ puncher: 5 clock 6 ticket
punches
pulling no ~: 5 frank 6 candid 8 straight
rolling with the ~: 5 stoic 7 stoical 8 flexible, resolute 9 resilient
roll with the ~: 4 cope 5 adapt 6 adjust, manage
punching __: 3 bag
punching tool: 3 awl
Punchline (1988 film)
cast: Sally Field, John Goodman, Tom Hanks
director: David Seltzer
punchy: 5 dizzy, giddy, weary 6 addled 7 reeling 8 confused 10 bewildered, knocked out
punctilio: 6 detail, nicety, nuance 8 loose end, niceties 9 fine point, propriety 10 particular
punctilious: 5 exact, fussy, right, rigid 6 formal, minute, polite, proper, strict 7 careful, correct, finicky, precise, prudent, refined, upright 8 accurate, cautious, exacting, finiking, finnicky, orthodox, pedantic, rigorous, thorough 9 assiduous, attentive, judicious, observant 10 fastidious, meticulous, particular, pedantical, scrupulous
punctiliously: 4 to a T
punctual: 5 early, quick, ready 6 on time, prompt, steady, timely 7 regular 8 on the dot, reliable 10 dependable, on schedule, scrupulous
not ~: 4 late 5 tardy 7 delayed, overdue
punctually: 4 duly 5 sharp 6 on time 8 promptly
punctuate: 4 lace, mark 5 break 6 accent, divide, pepper, play up, stress 7 point up, scatter 8 separate, sprinkle 9 emphasize, highlight, interject, interrupt, spotlight, underline 10 accentuate, underscore
punctuation mark: 4 dash 5 colon, comma 6 hyphen, period 9 semicolon
puncture: 3 cut, jab, pit 4 bore, flat, hole, leak, nick, open, slit, stab 5 break, burst, drill, knife, prick, punch, stick 6 broach, debunk, empale, go flat, impale, pierce, riddle 7 deflate, flatten, opening, rupture 8 disprove, lacerate 9 penetrate, perforate
combining form: 5 -nyxis
result: 4 flat
sound: 4 hiss
pundit: 4 guru, sage 5 guide, solon, swami, swamy 6 critic, expert, master, mentor, savant, wizard 7 idea man, scholar, teacher, thinker 9 abecedary, authority, intellect, professor 10 specialist
like a ~: 7 learned 9 scholarly
pundits: 8 literati
puneca: 4 fish
pung: 4 sled 6 sledge, sleigh
relative: 4 luge 8 toboggan
pungency: 3 nip 4 bite, kick, odor, tang, zest 5 spice, sting 7 acidity 9 spiciness
pungent: 3 hot 4 acid, keen, racy, rank, rich, sour, tart 5 acrid, acute, salty, sharp, spicy, tangy, zesty 6 biting, bitter, red-hot, savory, spicey, strong 7 caustic, mordant, odorous, peppery, piquant, pointed, telling, zestful 8 aromatic, incisive, piercing, poignant, stinging, stinking, vinegary 9 flavorful, trenchant 10 astringent
Punic: 8 language
Punic War city: 5 Utica 8 Carthage
punish: 3 fix, tar 4 beat, cane, damn, fine, flog, hurt, jail, lash, whip 5 abuse, debar, exile, expel, mulct, spank 6 amerce, avenge, ground, immure, misuse, paddle, strike, switch, thrash 7 chasten, correct, defrock, dismiss, execute, lambast, lecture, oppress, pay back, reprove, scourge, torment 8 admonish, chastise, imprison, lambaste, penalize, sentence 9 blacklist, castigate, dress down, exprobate 10 discipline, take to task
by fine: 6 amerce 8 penalize
punishing: 5 penal, tight 6 severe, uphill 7 arduous 8 grueling, punitive 10 relentless
stick: 6 ferula, ferule, switch
punishment: 3 rap, rod 4 fine 5 abuse, lumps 6 desert, lesson, rebuke, reward 7 beating, damages, deserts, forfeit, penalty, penance, redress 8 flogging, reprisal, sanction, sentence, spanking, whipping 9 execution, hell to pay, ostracism 10 correction, discipline, reparation
decide ~: 8 sentence
just ~: 6 desert
light ~: 4 slap
monetary ~: 4 fine
of ~: 5 penal
teen ~ perhaps: 4 no TV
punitive: 5 harsh, penal 8 vengeful 9 punishing 10 corrective, inflictive, vindictive
punitive __: 7 damages
Punjab
boss: 8 Warbucks
capital: 6 Lahore
friend: 3 Asp 5 Annie 6 The Asp
native: 4 Sikh
river: 5 Indus
royalty: 4 raja, rani 5 rajah, ranee 8 maharaja 9 maharajah
wild sheep of ~: 5 urial
punk: 2 JD 4 blah, brat, coif, hood, runt 5 dinky, lousy, rowdy, thief, tough, twerp, twirp 6 crumby, crummy, hairdo, rotten, shabby, trashy 7 haircut, hoodlum, lowlife, ruffian, tinhorn 8 coiffure, hooligan, inferior 10 jackanapes
like ~ hairdos: 5 spiky
punk __: 4 rock
punkie: 4 gnat
punky: 6 rotten
Punky Brewster (NBC sitcom)
cast: Soleil Moon Frye (Punky Brewster)
dog: 7 Brandon
punster: 3 wag, wit 4 card 5 joker 8 funnyman
punt: 4 boat, kick
propeller: 5 poler
spender: 5 Irish
Punta Arenas: 4 city, port, town
locale: 5 Chile
Punta del __, Uruguay: 4 Este
punting game: 5 rugby 6 soccer 8 football
puny: 3 wee 4 baby, poor, thin, tiny, vain, weak 5 bitty, frail, light, petty, runty, small, teeny, wimpy 6 anemic, atomic, atonic, bantam, effete, feeble, flabby, flimsy, humble, infirm, little, meager, measly, minute, paltry, peewee, petite, sickly, skimpy, slight, teensy, two-bit 7 anaemic, fragile, shrimpy, stunted, trivial, wimpish 8 atomical, atomlike, delicate, helpless, niggling, pathetic, picayune, piddling, pithless, sawed-off, trifling, underfed 9 brawnless, emaciated, faltering, itsy-bitsy, itty-bitty, miniature, pint-sized, powerless, undersize, worthless 10 diminutive, inadequate, pathetical, teeny-weeny, undersized, vest-pocket, vulnerable
not ~: 6 strong
pup: 3 dog, pet 4 runt 5 canid, doggy, whelp, youth 6 canine, doggie, urchin 9 offspring, youngling, youngster 10 jackanapes
see also puppy
pup __: 4 tent
pupa: 3 bug 6 insect 9 chrysalis
eventually: 4 moth 9 butterfly
preceder: 5 imago, larva
protection: 6 cocoon
pupil: 4 tiro, tyro 5 tutee, youth 6 intern, junior, novice, senior 7 learner, scholar, student, trainee 8 academic, adherent, beginner, bookworm, disciple, follower, freshman, neophyte 9 sophomore, youngster 10 apprentice, catechumen, tenderfoot
chore: 5 essay 6 lesson 8 homework
contraction: 6 miosis, myosis
covering: 4 uvea 6 cornea
gift: 5 apple
in French: 5 élève
locale: 3 eye 4 desk, iris 6 school 9 classroom
surrounder: 6 areola, areole
puppet: 3 toy 4 doll, dupe, pawn, tool 5 patsy 6 jackal, lackey, stooge, victim 7 cat's-paw, lacquey, manikin, nominal, servant 8 creature, mannikin, pushover 9 sycophant 10 figurehead, instrument, marionette, mouthpiece
rudimentary ~: 4 sock
puppet __: 4 show
__ puppet: 4 hand 6 finger
Puppet on a String (1965 song) artist: Elvis Presley
puppy: 3 dog, pet 5 canid, whelp 6 canine
family: 6 litter
like a ~: 6 cuddly 10 cuddlesome
love: 5 ardor, crush 8 devotion, fondness 9 adoration, affection 10 admiration, attachment
pickup point: 4 nape
protest: 3 nip, yip 4 yelp 5 whine 7 whimper
smallest ~: 4 runt
starter: 3 mud 4 hush
without papers: 3 mut 4 mutt 5 stray
puppy __: 3 dog 4 love
__ puppy: 3 mud 4 hush, sand
Puppy Love (song) artist: Donny Osmond, Paul Anka
__ pura: 4 aqua
Puracé: 7 volcano
locale: 8 Colombia
Purcell: 5 Henry, range, Sarah 6 Edward
locale: 6 Canada 7 Montana
Purcell, Edward: 8 Nobelist 9 physicist
purchase: 3 buy, get 4 edge, gain, hold, sale, shop, take 5 order, steal 6 charge, come by, deal in, invest, obtain, pay for, pick up, redeem, secure 7 acquire, bargain, footing, procure, toehold 8 customer, foothold, invest in, leverage 9 advantage, influence, patronize 10 investment
alternative: 5 lease 6 rental
offer: 3 bid
__ Purchase: 6 Alaska 7 Gadsden 9 Louisiana
purchased, just: 3 new 5 fresh 8 brand-new
purchaser: 5 buyer, owner 6 patron 8 consumer, customer
boon: 4 sale 5 no tax 6 coupon, rebate 8 discount
purchasing __: 5 agent, power
purdah: 4 veil 6 screen 7 curtain 9 seclusion
Purdue: 6 school 10 university
athletes: Boilermakers
conference: 6 Big Ten
locale: 7 Indiana
Purdy: 2 Al 5 James
Purdy, Al: 4 poet 8 Canadian
Purdy, James: 6 author, writer
work: Color of Darkness
Dream Palace
Malcolm
Mourners Below
Narrow Rooms
The Nephew
On Glory's Course
pure: 4 good, mere, neat 5 clean, clear, fresh, lucid, moral, naked, plain, sheer,

snowy, solid, stark, sweet, uncut, utter **6** chaste, devout, kasher, kosher, limpid, modest, sacred, simple, strong, unmixt, virgin **7** genuine, natural, perfect, refined, saintly, sterile, unmixed, upright **8** absolute, abstract, celibate, flawless, germfree, innocent, maidenly, outright, pellucid, pristine, sanitary, spotless, straight, thorough, unsoiled, virginal, virtuous **9** blameless, continent, downright, exemplary, faultless, guileless, guiltless, healthful, inviolate, lily white, out-and-out, pedigreed, righteous, spiritual, stainless, unalloyed, unclouded, uncorrupt, undefiled, undiluted, unsullied, untainted, untouched, wholesome **10** antiseptic, immaculate, impeccable, sterilized, unpolluted
ender: **4** bred **5** blood
name meaning ~: **7** Kathryn **9** Catherine, Katharine, Katherine
__-pure: **5** simon
Pure __ and Drug Act: **4** Food
pure as the __ snow: **6** driven
purebred: **8** pedigree
not a ~: **3** cur, mut **4** mutt **5** stray **8** alley cat
purée: **4** pulp, soup **6** bisque
purely: **3** all **4** just, only **5** quite **6** merely, simply, solely, wholly **7** totally, utterly **8** entirely **10** absolutely, altogether, completely, nothing but
Purépero: **4** city, town
locale: **6** Mexico **9** Michoacán
Pure Reason exponent: **4** Kant
Purex: **6** bleach **9** detergent
competitor: **3** All, Biz, Era, Fab, Yes **4** Bold, Dash, Gain, Surf, Tide, Wisk **5** Cheer, Dreft, Snowy, Vivid **6** Calgon, Clorox, Dynamo, Oxydol **7** Octagon **8** Borateem **9** Ivory Snow
purfle: **5** adorn **6** finish **8** decorate, ornament **9** embellish
purgation: **8** emptying **9** catharsis, cleansing **10** evacuation
Purgatorio author: **5** Dante
Purgatory author: William Butler Yeats
purge: **3** rid **4** coup, oust **5** atone, eject, empty, erase, expel **6** banish, delete, ouster, purify, remove, uproot **7** cleanse, cleanup, dismiss, expiate, expunge, forgive, root out, rout out, shake up, wipe out **8** clean out, clear out, empty out, evacuate, exorcise, exorcize, flush out, get rid of, sweep out, wash away **9** catharsis, cathartic, eliminate, eradicate, expulsion, expurgate, overthrow, witch hunt **10** do away with
purification: **5** grace **7** baptism, rebirth **8** ablution **9** atonement, catharsis, cleansing, expiation, salvation
purified: **5** clean **6** washed **7** refined **8** sanitary
purifier: **6** filter **7** alembic **10** antiseptic
purify: **4** free, sift, wash **5** atone, clean, clear, purge **6** aerate, censor, desalt, filter, rarify, redeem, refine, shrive, strain **7** absolve, clarify, cleanse, deterge, distill, expiate, freshen, improve **8** exorcise, exorcize, fumigate, sanctify, sanitize **9** deodorize, disinfect, oxygenate, sterilize, sublimate **10** desalinate, desalinize
Purim
month: **4** Adar
queen: **6** Esther
Purina: **7** cat food, dog food
competitor: **4** Alpo, Iams **5** Amore, Nutro **6** Figaro **7** Whiskas **8** Eukanuba, Friskies **10** Chef's Blend, Fancy Feast, Ken-L Ration
__ Purina: **7** Ralston
Purísima de Bustos: **4** city, town
locale: **6** Mexico **10** Guanajuato
purist: **8** stickler **9** formalist **10** taskmaster
puritan: **4** prig **5** priss, prude **9** nice Nelly **10** goody-goody
Puritan: **10** cooking oil
alternative: **6** Crisco, Mazola, Wesson
Puritan __: **5** ethic, spoon
puritanical: **4** prim **5** sober **6** prissy, proper, severe, strict, stuffy **7** ascetic, austere, prudish **9** squeamish
Puritanism: **9** austerity
purity: **6** virtue **7** modesty **8** morality **9** innocence, integrity **10** perfection, simplicity
purl: **3** lap **4** knit, loop **6** gurgle, murmur, ripple, stitch **7** lapping
Purl: **5** Linda
purlieu: **4** area, land, site **5** haunt, limit **7** hangout
purlieus: **4** area **6** milieu **8** environs, vicinage, vicinity **9** outskirts
purloin: **3** rob **4** lift, take **5** filch, pinch, steal, swipe **6** pilfer, pocket, rip off, thieve **7** ransack **8** embezzle **10** run off with
Purloined Letter, The author: **3** Poe
character: **5** Dupin
purloiner: **5** crook, felon, thief **6** bandit, robber **7** burglar, filcher **8** criminal, pilferer
puro: **5** cigar
purple: **5** livid **6** ornate **10** apoplectic, rhetorical
bluish ~: **4** plum **5** mauve **6** orchid **8** lavender
brownish ~: **4** puce
color: **4** plum, puce **5** grape, lilac, mauve **6** dahlia, orchid, violet **7** heather **8** amethyst, burgundy, eggplant, hyacinth, lavender, mulberry **9** raspberry **10** heliotrope
combining form: **7** purpuri-
flower: **3** mum **4** flag, iris **5** aster, lilac, tulip, vetch **6** betony, crocus, maypop, orchid, violet **7** figwort, fuchsia, heather, petunia, saffron, thistle **8** amaranth, boltonia, cyclamen, erigeron, foxglove, hepatica, hyacinth, lavender, wistaria, wisteria **9** candytuft, cockscomb, monkshood, wolfsbane **10** bluebottle, coneflower, cornflower, heliotrope, motherwort, pennyroyal
fruit: **4** plum, sloe **5** grape
grayish ~: **8** mulberry
in heraldry: **7** purpure
pinkish ~: **7** heather
reddish ~: **4** plum, ruby **5** lilac, murex **6** claret, orchid **7** carmine, crimson, fuchsia, magenta, petunia **8** cyclamen **9** cranberry, raspberry **10** heliotrope
purple __: **4** sage **5** beech, finch, heron, prose **6** martin, mombin **7** boneset, grackle, passion **8** broccoli
__ purple: **5** royal **6** banded, Tyrian, visual
Purple __: **4** Dust, Haze, Rain **5** Heart
Purple __, The: **5** Heart, Plain **7** Decades
__ Purple: **4** Deep
Purple Decades, The author: Tom Wolfe
Purple Dust author: Sean O'Casey
Purple Heart: **5** award, medal
like a ~ recipient: **3** WIA
Purple Heart, The (1944 film)
cast: Dana Andrews, Farley Granger, Sam Levene
director: Lewis Milestone
Purple People Eater, The (1958 song)
artist: Sheb Wooley
Purple Plain, The (1954 film)
cast: Bernard Lee, Gregory Peck
director: Robert Parrish
Purple Rain (1984 song) artist: Prince
Purple Rose of Cairo, The (1985 film)
cast: Danny Aiello, Jeff Daniels, Mia Farrow, Dianne Wiest
director: Woody Allen
__ Purple, The: **5** Color
purport: **3** aim, nub **4** gist, idea, knub, mean, meat, pith **5** claim, drift, heart, imply, point, score, sense, tenor **6** allege, assert, burden, convey, denote, effect, hint at, import, intend, intent, matter, object, pose as, spirit, thrust, upshot **7** bearing, connote, contend, express, meaning, message, point to, pretend, profess, purpose, signify, suggest **8** allude to, indicate, intimate, maintain, proclaim **9** intention, objective, substance
purported: **7** nominal **8** so-called **9** pretended **10** ostensible
purpose: **3** aim, end, job, use **4** goal, hope, idea, plan, sake, will **5** angle, avail, cause, point, scope, sense **6** animus, design, desire, import, intend, intent, layout, method, motive, object, reason, spirit, target **7** meaning, mission, propose, purport, resolve, thought, utility **8** ambition, firmness, function, lifework, nominate, tenacity **9** direction, intention, objective, rationale **10** aspiration, motivation, resolution
answer the ~: **4** work **5** avail, serve
devious ~: **5** angle
lack of ~: **5** anomy **6** anomie
on ~: **9** expressly, willfully, wittingly **10** deliberate, designedly
serving a ~: **5** utile **6** useful
strength of ~: **4** will **7** resolve **8** tenacity **9** will power **10** resolution
to no ~: **4** vain **7** inutile **8** bootless
to the ~: **3** apt **8** relevant **9** pertinent
ultimate ~: **3** end **6** end-all, end use
without ~: **4** idly **7** blindly
__ purpose: **4** to no
__-purpose: **3** all **4** dual **7** general
purposeful: **4** firm **5** bound, can-do, fixed, meant, telic **6** intent, steady, wilful **7** dead set, decided, earnest, intense, planned, settled, staunch, studied, willful **8** intended, positive, resolute, stalwart **9** ambitious, committed, conscious, dedicated, iron-jawed, observant, steadfast, tenacious, voluntary **10** deliberate, determined, preplanned, volitional
purposeless: **4** idle, vain **5** empty, inane **6** adrift, random **7** aimless, inutile, useless **8** bootless, drifting, feckless, goalless, needless **9** desultory, haphazard, hit-or-miss, pointless, senseless, unhelpful, worthless
purposely: **8** by design **9** expressly, knowingly, willfully, wittingly **10** designedly, explicitly
purposes
at cross ~: **7** opposed
for all practical ~: **8** in effect **9** virtually
purr: **3** hum **6** murmur
it may ~: **3** cat **5** kitty **6** engine, feline, kitten
__ Purr-ee: **3** Gay
purse: **3** bag **4** knit, poke, sack, tote **5** award, bursa, funds, kitty, means, money, pinch, pouch, prize, stake **6** clutch, crease, pucker, reward **7** handbag, sporran, tighten, wrinkle **8** bankroll, billfold, carryall, finances, moneybag, pucker up, reticule, treasury, winnings **9** affluence, container, exchequer **10** pocketbook, receptacle
big ~: **4** tote **8** carryall
carrier: **5** strap **10** drawstring
contents: **2** ID **3** pen **4** cash, coin, comb, Mace **5** coins, hanky, money **6** hankie, powder **7** compact **8** billfold, lipstick **9** checkbook **10** credit card
ender: **7** strings
fastener: **4** snap **5** clasp **6** zipper **10** drawstring
geisha's ~: **4** inro
keeper of the ~ strings: **9** treasurer **10** controller
loosen the ~ strings: **3** buy **5** spend
snatcher: **5** thief
starter: **3** cut
purse __: **4** crab **5** seine **7** strings
purse-__: **5** proud
__ purse: **3** sea **4** coin **5** privy **6** clutch **7** beggar's
purser: **6** bursar **7** cashier **9** treasurer
purslane: **4** weed **5** plant
pursue: **3** bug, dog, ply, sue, tag, woo **4** call, date, hunt, rush, seek, tail, wage **5** chase, chivy, court, harry, haunt, hound, quest, spark, stalk, trace, track, trail **6** aim for, aspire, badger, desire, follow, gun for, harass, hold to, keep on, plague, shadow, tackle, try for **7** attempt, bird-dog, carry on, conduct, fish for, go after, persist, proceed, run down **8** continue, engage in, follow up, hunt down, maintain, overtake, practice, quest for, run after, scout out **9** cultivate, persecute, persevere, prosecute, search out, shine up to, strive for, track down **10** prowl after, specialize, work toward
romantically: **3** woo **4** date **5** court **7** propose **9** send roses, sweet-talk
Pursued (1947 film)
cast: Judith Anderson, Robert Mitchum, Teresa Wright
director: Raoul Walsh
pursuit: **3** biz, job **4** game, hunt, line, race, work **5** chase, hobby, quest, trail **6** career, racket, search, wooing **7** attempt, calling, enquiry, inquiry, mission, pastime, venture **8** activity, business, interest, lifework, pleasure, vocation **9** avocation, courtship, following, specialty **10** employment, enterprise, occupation, profession
in ~ of: **5** after **7** chasing **9** following
Pursuit of Happiness, The (1971 film)
cast: Barbara Hershey, Robert Klein, Michael Sarrazin
director: Robert Mulligan
Pursuit of Love, The author: Nancy Mitford
pursy: **5** beefy, fubsy, obese, plump, pudgy, stout **6** chubby, fleshy, portly, pyknic, rotund, stocky, zaftig, zoftig **7** adipose, paunchy **8** roly-poly **9** corpulent **10** overweight
Puruándiro: **4** city, town
locale: **6** Mexico **9** Michoacán
Purús: **5** river
locale: **4** Peru **6** Brazil
purvey: **5** cater, equip **6** outfit, supply **7** furnish, provide
purveyor: **6** grocer, source **8** supplier
Purviance: **4** Edna
purview: **3** ken **4** area **5** field, grasp, orbit, range, reach, realm, scope, sweep **6** length, radius, sphere **7** compass, horizon **8** confines, province **9** bailiwick, territory **10** boundaries, walk of life
Pusan: **4** city, port, town
locale: **10** South Korea
push: **2** go **3** jam, jog, pep, ram, tie **4** bump, goad, hawk, hype, jolt, move,

plug, poke, prod, rush, sell, spur, sway, tout, urge, work, worm, zeal **5** boost, crowd, drive, egg on, elbow, exert, force, forge, goose, impel, labor, lobby, lunge, nudge, press, shove, spunk, stick, stuff, vigor, wedge **6** charge, coerce, effort, energy, fillip, harp on, hasten, hustle, hype up, incite, jostle, justle, lean on, muscle, oblige, peddle, plunge, propel, racket, sprout, squash, strain, strive, talk up, thrust, wiggle **7** advance, crusade, depress, further, inspire, promote, smuggle, speed up, squeeze, try hard **8** ambition, campaign, expedite, gumption, momentum, motivate, persuade, pressure, railroad, scramble, shoulder, stick out, stimulus, vitality **9** advertise, encourage, fast-track, get behind, go forward, influence, offensive, publicize, steamroll, strong-arm **10** enterprise, get up and go, go whole hog, incitement, initiative
ahead: **4** nose **7** advance
and shove: **5** crowd, elbow **8** shoulder
around: **5** bully **8** mistreat, threaten **10** intimidate
away: **5** shove **7** repulse
back: **5** repel **6** rebuff
back the boundaries: **5** widen **6** extend
button predecessor: **4** dial
down: **4** tamp **5** lower, press **6** squash **7** depress
ender: **3** pin **4** ball, cart, over **6** button
for: **4** urge **5** lobby **6** talk up **7** promote **8** advocate
forward: **4** goad, move, prod, push, spur, urge **5** boost, drive, press, shove, speed **6** attack, incite, induce, prompt, propel, stir up **7** actuate, inspire **8** motivate **9** influence, instigate, stimulate **10** accelerate
gentle ~: **3** jog **5** nudge
hard: **4** slam
in: **4** dent **5** barge, stave **7** intrude
off: **2** go **4** exit, part, quit **5** leave, start **6** beat it, begone, depart, repair, set out **7** get lost, head out, journey, proceed, set sail **8** hightail, light out, set forth **10** hit the road
on: **2** go **5** press **7** advance, proceed **8** continue **9** keep going
oneself: **4** toil **5** exert, slave **6** overdo **8** overwork
out of bed: **4** wake **5** awake, roust, waken **6** awaken, wake up
the buttons: **7** control
too far: **3** tax **4** task, tire, wear **6** exceed, impose, strain, weaken **7** oppress, wear out **8** overload, overtask, overwork **9** weigh down **10** overburden
to the limit: **3** tax **4** test
push __: **3** off **4** shot **5** broom, cycle, plate **6** around, button **7** bicycle
__ push: **4** bell
pushball: **4** game
pushcart
in Britain: **6** barrow
purchase: **3** ice **6** hot dog **7** flowers, pretzel **8** ice cream
__ push comes to shove: **4** when
pushed aside: **7** ignored, snubbed **9** unnoticed **10** overlooked
__-pusher: **5** paper **6** pencil
pusher nemesis: **4** narc, nark
__ pushers: **5** pedal
Pushing Tin (1999 film)
cast: Cate Blanchett, John Cusack, Angelina Jolie, Billy Bob Thornton
director: Mike Newell
Push It (1987 song) artist: Salt-n-Pepa
Pushkin, Aleksandr: **6** author, writer **7** Russian
hero: **5** Boris
work: The Bronze Horseman
The Captain's Daughter
Eugene Onegin
The Queen of Spades
push one's __: **4** luck
pushover: **4** dupe, easy, fool, lamb, snap, wimp **5** chump, cinch, cushy, patsy **6** breeze, picnic, pigeon, puppet, simple, stooge, sucker, victim **7** triumph **8** duck soup, easy mark, kid stuff, painless, weakling **9** jellyfish, no problem, receptive, soft touch **10** child's play, effortless
pushpin: **4** tack
push to the __: **4** wall
push-up: **8** exercise
muscle: **3** pec **4** pecs
pushy: **4** bold, loud, rude **5** bossy, brash, nervy **6** strong **7** forward, zealous **8** assuming, invasive, militant **9** ambitious, assertive, bumptious, insistent, obnoxious, obtrusive, offensive, officious **10** aggressive, meddlesome
be ~: **5** elbow **6** impose
pusillanimous: **5** timid **6** afraid, craven, yellow **7** chicken, fearful **8** cowardly, recreant, timorous **9** dastardly **10** frightened
puss: **3** cat, mug, yap **4** face **5** bazoo, felid, kitty, mouth, tabby **6** feline, kisser, kitten, mouser, tomcat, visage **8** features **9** grimalkin
starter: **4** sour
__ puss: **3** sea **7** glamour
Puss-in-Boots: **3** cat
Pussy-Cat
boat: **8** pea-green
suitor: **3** owl
where the ~ went: **5** to sea
pussyfoot: **5** avoid, creep, dodge, evade, hedge, shirk, slink, sneak, steal, waver **6** tiptoe, weasel **7** shuffle, slither, whiffle **8** hesitate, sidestep **9** dissemble, hem and haw, vacillate **10** equivocate
pussy-toes: **5** plant **6** flower
pussy willow: **4** tree **5** ament, shrub **6** catkin
put: **3** lay, pop, set **4** give, levy, park, rest, word **5** couch, embed, imbed, place, plant, posit, rivet, stand, state, stick, utter, voice **6** assign, commit, employ, enjoin, impose, induce, insert, instal, invest, locate, phrase, prefer, reckon, render, settle, submit, tender **7** advance, consign, deposit, express, inflict, install, present, propose, require, set down, situate, station, suggest **8** position, propound **9** formulate, plunk down, translate, transpose **10** motionless
a crimp in: **5** block **6** hinder **8** obstruct
across: **6** convey, effect **7** explain **8** convince, spell out **9** make clear
a damper on: **5** quash **6** sadden **10** discourage, dishearten
a gloss on: **3** rub, wax **4** buff **5** shine **6** polish **7** burnish, varnish
a line through: **4** x out
a lock on: **6** ensure, secure **9** safeguard
a mark on: **3** tag **5** label
a match to: **3** lit **5** light, relit **6** ignite, kindle, set off **8** enkindle
an edge on: **4** hone **7** sharpen
an end to: **3** nix **4** stop **5** cease, sever **6** arrest, scotch, settle **7** abolish, prevent **8** abrogate, stamp out, suppress **9** close down, overthrow **10** do away with
another way: **5** resay **8** rephrase
a point on: **4** hone **7** sharpen
a question: **3** ask **4** pose **5** query **7** inquire
aside: **4** hold, keep, save **5** cache, defer, lay in, on ice, store, table, waive **6** shelve **7** deposit **8** hold on to, salt away, stow away **9** in reserve, stockpile
a spell on: **3** hex, zap **4** jinx **5** charm, curse **7** enchant **9** hypnotize
asunder: **5** sever, split **8** separate
at ease: **5** allay **6** assure **7** satisfy
at one's disposal: **5** offer **9** volunteer
at risk: **3** bet, lay **4** dare **5** stake, wager **6** chance, gamble, menace **7** imperil, venture **8** endanger, threaten **9** undermine **10** jeopardize
a value on: **3** tag **4** deem, rank, rate **5** gauge, grade, guess, judge, quote, scale, value, weigh **6** assess, charge, esteem, figure, regard, size up, survey **7** measure, valuate **8** appraise, classify, estimate, evaluate **9** determine
away: **3** box, eat, pen, tie **4** bind, cage, file, hold, jail, keep, pack, save, shut, stow **5** amass, bound, cache, chain, cramp, fence, hedge, hem in, hoard, lay by, lay in, lay up, limit, set by, stash, store, tie up **6** commit, coop up, detain, devour, fetter, garner, gobble, ground, hinder, hogtie, imbibe, immure, intern, lock up, murder, retain, save up, shut in, shut up **7** certify, confine, consume, deposit, enclose, feast on, impound, inclose, interne, isolate, reserve, scarf up, seclude, swallow, trounce **8** bottle up, hang onto, hold back, hold onto, imprison, maintain, salt away, sentence, set apart, set aside, straiten, surround, wolf down **9** constrain, grab a bite, overpower, polish off, scarf down, stockpile **10** accumulate
back: **6** return **7** replace, restore **8** postpone
back into service: **5** reuse
back on one's feet: **4** cure, heal, mend **5** treat
back to zero: **5** reset
between: **6** insert
by: **4** keep, save **5** cache, lay in, spare, stash, store **7** deposit, reserve, store up **8** hold on to, salt away, set aside, stow away **9** stockpile
down: **3** cut, dig, dis, hit, log, pan, pen **4** barb, gibe, gybe, jeer, jibe, land, mock, sink, slam, slap, slur, snub, stop, veto, zing **5** abase, abuse, crush, decry, enter, knock, libel, quash, quell, quiet, roast, scold, scorn, shame, sneer, spurn, still, taunt, tease, write **6** berate, debase, defame, defeat, demean, depone, deride, dump on, heckle, humble, ignore, impugn, insult, jibe at, malign, negate, offend, oppugn, quench, rebuff, rebuke, record, reject, slight, squash, subdue, vilify, zinger **7** affront, asperse, calumny, catcall, deflate, degrade, disdain, dismiss, mockery, obloquy, offense, rank out, repress, sarcasm, silence, slander, sneer at, specify, traduce **8** badmouth, belittle, contempt, denounce, derision, derogate, diminish, discount, minimize, prohibit, ridicule, stamp out, suppress, vanquish, vilipend **9** aspersion, blaspheme, cheap shot, contumely, denigrate, deprecate, discredit, disparage, find fault, humiliate, lash out at, poke fun at, subjugate **10** calumniate, defamation, disrespect, extinguish, opprobrium, transcribe
down, as money: **5** plunk **7** deposit
down for: **3** tag **4** slot **6** assign **7** earmark **8** allocate, delegate, set aside **9** apportion, designate
down for the count: **2** KO **4** deck, kayo **5** floor
down roots: **4** stay **6** linger, remain, settle **8** colonize
forth: **3** use **5** exert, offer, posit, voice **6** assert, submit **7** burgeon, present, propose **8** bourgeon, exercise **9** predicate
forward: **3** lay, say **4** move, pose **5** exert, issue, offer, raise **6** assert, submit, turn in **7** advance, declare, present, produce, propose, suggest, support **8** propound **9** introduce, postulate, recommend, volunteer
hard ~: **5** taxed **8** strained
in: **3** add, use **4** ante, dock, give, land **5** plant, spend, use up **6** devote, expend, instal, invest **7** consume, install, utilize **8** dedicate, exercise **9** interject, introduce **10** contribute
in a call: **4** dial, ring **5** phone
in a good word for: **4** laud, plug **8** champion **9** recommend
in an appearance: **4** come, show **6** attend, show up
in a nutshell: **4** trim **5** recap, sum up **6** digest **7** abridge, shorten **8** simplify **9** summarize
in a row: **4** even **5** align, aline, array, order **10** straighten
in a snit: **3** irk **4** miff, rile **5** anger, peeve, upset
in for: **5** apply **7** request **8** petition
in good shape: **5** fix up **6** neaten **10** straighten
in irons: **6** fetter **7** enchain, manacle, shackle, trammel **8** handcuff
in jeopardy: **3** bet **4** dare, risk **5** brave, stake, wager **6** chance, gamble, hazard
in mothballs: **5** store
in motion: **3** set **5** begin, start **8** commence
in office: **4** vote **5** elect
in order: **4** sort, tidy **6** assort **7** correct **8** organize, regulate, untangle
in place: **3** fix, set **6** instal **7** install
in play: **5** serve
in power again: **7** reelect **9** reinstate
in service: **3** use **5** avail **6** deploy **7** utilize
in something extra: **3** add, tip **7** augment
in the closet: **4** hang
in the hold: **4** lade, load, stow
into a funk: **6** bum out, deject **7** depress **8** dispirit, distress **10** discourage, dishearten
into circulation: **5** issue
into effect: **4** vote **5** enact, order **8** legalize **9** establish, institute, legislate
in touch: **5** refer **9** introduce
into words: **3** say **4** limn, talk **5** speak, state, utter, vocal, voice **6** phrase, relate, spoken **7** express **8** vocalize
in writing: **3** log **4** mark **5** enter **6** record **7** catalog, jot down, set down **8** mark down, take down **10** transcribe
money on: **3** bet **5** wager **6** gamble **7** venture
not ~ off: **9** undaunted
off: **3** lag **4** late, stay **5** dally, defer, delay, deter, evade, remit, repel, sit on, stall, table, tarry, waive **6** dawdle, dismay, linger, loiter, rattle, rebuff, retard, shelve **7** abeyant, adjourn,

hold off, lighten, suspend **8** file away, hold over, lay aside, postpone, prorogue **10** dillydally, pigeonhole, reschedule
off-guard: 5 charm **6** disarm
on: 3 act, add, don, kid, lie **4** fake, fool, hire, hoax, jest, levy, mock, ruse, sham, wear, worn **5** affix, apply, bluff, bogus, faked, farce, feign, fraud, front, light, phony, prank, spoof, stage, stake, tease, trick **6** affect, assume, ersatz, facade, forged, humbug, parody, phoney, pseudo, satire, unreal **7** assumed, confuse, deceive, feigned, lampoon, mislead, mockery, present, pretend, produce **8** activate, confound, mannered, pretense, simulate, spurious **9** activated, high-toned, imitation, imposture, pretended, simulated, synthetic, unnatural **10** artificial, caricature, fabricated, fictitious, fraudulent, masquerade
on account: 6 charge
on a happy face: 4 beam, glow, grin **5** smile
on airs: 4 pose **5** mince, strut **6** fake it **7** swagger
on an act: 4 fake **6** fake it **7** pretend **8** simulate **9** dissemble, misinform
on a pedestal: 5 adore, exalt, extol **6** esteem, extoll, praise **7** adulate, ennoble, glorify, idolize, worship **8** canonize, idealize, venerate
on a show: 3 act **5** amuse, stage
on board: 4 lade, load, ship, stow
on cloud nine: 5 cheer, elate, exult **6** buck up, perk up, uplift **7** delight, gladden, hearten **8** inspirit **9** make happy **10** exhilarate
on display: 4 show **5** array, shown
one over on: 3 con, get **4** fool, have **5** trick **6** delude, outwit **8** outsmart
one's cards on the table: 6 reveal **8** disclose
oneself out: 3 try **4** care **5** exert **6** bother **7** attempt
one's feet up: 4 laze, loaf, loll, rest **5** relax **6** repose, rest up, unwind **7** lay back, lie down, recline, sit back, take ten **8** take five **10** settle back, take a break, take it easy
one's finger on: 4 find **5** place **6** locate, recall **7** find out **8** discover, identify, remember **9** bring back
one's foot down: 4 step, walk **5** stamp, stomp, tread **6** demand, insist **7** protest **9** stand firm
one's hands on: 4 find **6** locate, turn up
ones' heads together: 6 confer
one's John Henry on: 3 ink **7** endorse, initial **9** formalize
one's mind to rest: 4 buoy **5** cheer **7** cheer up, comfort, console, hearten, satisfy **8** inspirit
one's two cents in: 3 add **5** opine **6** meddle **9** interfere
on guard: 4 warn **5** alarm, alert, awake, scare **6** arouse, clue in, inform, notify, tip off **7** apprise, caution, forearm, prepare **8** acquaint, forewarn
on hold: 5 defer, table **6** recess, shelve **7** suspend **8** postpone
on ice: 5 chill, delay, table **6** assure, shelve **7** confine, suspend **8** sentence
on notice: 4 warn **5** alert **6** inform, remind, signal, tip off **7** caution **8** admonish, forewarn, threaten
on one's feet: 5 boost **6** assist, buck up **7** bolster, support, sustain **10** facilitate
on one's thinking cap: 4 mull, muse **5** solve **7** analyze **8** consider, meditate **9** figure out
on paper: 3 pen **5** write **6** record
on tape: 6 record
on the back burner: 5 delay, table **6** shelve **7** suspend **8** postpone
on the dog: 6 flaunt **7** show off
on the feedbag: 3 eat
on the fire: 4 heat, warm **6** heat up, warm up
on the market: 4 sell, vend **5** offer **6** peddle **7** auction
on the payroll: 4 hire **5** staff **6** employ
on the radio: 3 air **8** transmit **9** broadcast
on the spot: 4 trap **5** abash **6** entrap **9** embarrass
on the tab: 4 bill **6** charge
on trial: 3 sue **9** prosecute
on view: 3 air **4** bare, show **6** expose, flaunt, lay out, parade, reveal **7** display, exhibit, present, show off, trot out **8** showcase **10** illustrate
out: 3 bug, irk, vex **4** emit, gall, make, miff, rile, send **5** annoy, cross, douse, dowse, evict, exert, huffy, issue, peeve, pique, print, reach, snuff, spite, upset **6** badger, bother, harass, nettle, pester, piqued, quench, rattle, retire **7** disturb, go to sea, perturb, produce, provoke, publish, smother, torment, trouble **8** distress, irritate, squander **9** aggravate, disoblige, displease, eliminate, incommode **10** discommode, dispossess, exasperate, extinguish, impose upon, recompense
out a runner: 3 tag
out feelers: 3 ask **4** fish **5** probe, query **9** ask around
out of commission: 4 hurt **5** smash **6** injure **7** disable **8** sabotage
out of power: 4 oust **5** exile **6** depose
out with: 5 angry, irate, irked, vexed **9** indignant
over one's knee: 3 tan **4** lick, whip **5** smack, spank **6** punish, thrash, wallop **8** chastise **10** paddywhack
pen to paper: 5 write
pep into: 7 enliven, hearten **8** energize **10** exhilarate
pressure on: 3 tax **5** crowd, force, lobby
right: 3 fix **6** remedy **7** rectify, redress
starter: 3 out **7** through
stay ~: 3 fix **4** hold **5** stick
the arm on: 5 run in **9** shake down
the brakes on: 4 slow **6** slow up **8** slow down **10** decelerate
the chill on: 4 shun, snub **6** ignore, rebuff
the collar on: 3 nab **4** bust **5** run in **6** arrest **7** capture
the finger on: 4 name, tell **6** betray, inform, snitch, squeal, tattle
the kibosh on: 3 ban, end, nix, zap **4** curb, halt, stop, veto **5** check, quash, quell **6** forbid **7** abolish, contain, repress, squelch **8** cut short, suppress
the lid on: 3 gag **4** cork **5** cover, quash, quell **6** muffle, stifle **7** cover up
the pedal to the metal: 5 speed **6** barrel
the screws to: 5 force **6** coerce, compel **7** oppress **8** pressure
the top on: 3 cap **4** cork, seal **5** close, cover **7** stopper
the whammy on: 3 hex **4** damn, jinx **5** curse **7** bedevil, bewitch, condemn **9** imprecate
through: 3 end **6** effect, finish, wind up **7** achieve, execute, get done, pull off **8** bring off, complete, conclude, engineer **10** accomplish, bring about
through the wringer: 5 grill **7** torment **8** question **9** challenge
to bed: 5 close, print **6** finish **7** let roll **8** complete **10** consummate
to flight: 4 rout **5** panic, repel **7** overrun, repulse, scatter **8** chase out, stampede
together: 3 add, mix **4** form, join, make, mold **5** amass, build, frame, piece, rig up, set up **6** create, derive, hook up, make up **7** combine, compile, prepare, work out **8** assemble
together again: 5 refit
to ~ it another way: 5 I mean
to rights: 4 tidy **5** clean, order **6** neaten, spruce **7** ordered, orderly **9** smarten up **10** straighten
to sea: 4 sail **6** launch **7** set sail, ship out **8** shove off **10** lift anchor
to shame: 4 beat, best **5** abase, outdo **6** exceed, humble, show up **7** eclipse, surpass **8** outclass, outshine, outstrip **9** humiliate **10** overshadow
to sleep: 4 bore, lull, rock, tire **9** hypnotize
to the proof: 3 try **4** test **5** assay
to the test: 3 try **5** prove
to use: 5 apply, avail, wield **7** utilize
to work: 3 use **4** hire **5** apply **6** employ, engage
two and two together: 3 add **5** solve **8** conclude
under a spell: 3 hex **5** charm **7** bewitch **9** hypnotize
under observation: 3 eye **4** tail **5** spy on **6** shadow **10** scrutinize
up: 3 bet, can, pay **4** ante, bunk, lift, make, rear, stay **5** board, build, built, erect, forge, house, lodge, pitch, raise, stake, wager **6** billet, canned, create, harbor, invest, lay out, lodged, supply, take in **7** auction, harbour, produce, provide, quarter, venture **8** assemble, domicile, nominate, preserve, ventured **9** construct, entertain, establish, fabricate, subscribe **10** contribute
up a fight: 6 oppose, resist **7** dissent **8** struggle
up a front: 3 lie **4** pose, sham **7** pretend
up a fuss: 4 balk, carp **5** baulk, demur **6** grouse, insist, refuse, resist **8** complain
up a smoke screen: 7 deceive **9** misinform
up for sale: 5 offer **7** auction
up money for: 4 back, fund **7** finance, sponsor **9** grubstake
upon: 7 oppress **8** bothered, keep down **9** disturbed, exploited
up to: 3 sic **4** abet, spur, urge **6** incite
up with: 3 let **4** bear, have, lump, okay, take **5** abide, admit, adopt, allow, brook, go for, stand, stick **6** accept, assent, comply, endure, permit, suffer, wink at **7** condone, include, let ride, stomach, sustain, swallow, undergo, welcome **8** accede to, assent to, overlook, sanction, stand for, submit to, tolerate **9** approve of, authorize, recognize, reconcile, sign off on **10** concur with, give the nod
well ~: 3 apt **6** cogent, timely **8** apposite, relevant, suitable **10** to the point
put __: 3 off, out **4** away, down, it to, over, upon **5** about, aside, forth, to bed, to use **6** across, option **7** forward, through
put __ act: 4 on an
put __ and two together: 3 two
put __ block: 5 on the
put __ disadvantage: 3 at a
put __ dog: 5 on the
put __ face on: 5 a bold
put __ fight: 3 up a
put __ good word for: 3 in a
put __ in: 5 a dent, stock
put __ in it: 5 a sock
put __ in one's ear: 4 a bug
put __ in the water: 4 a toe
put __ on: 5 money
put __ on it: 4 a lid
put __ roots: 4 down
put __ sea: 5 out to
put __ show: 3 on a
put __ shut up: 4 up or
put __ to: 5 an end, a stop
put __ together: 5 heads, it all
put __ to pasture: 3 out
put __ writing: 4 it in
put-__: 4 down, upon
__-put: 4 hard, well
Put
father of ~: 3 Ham
grandfather of ~: 4 Noah
Put __ Hands Together: 4 Your
Put __ Happy Face: 3 on a
put a __ in: 5 crimp
put a __ in one's ear: 3 bug
put a bold __ on: 4 face
Put a Light in the Window (1957 song)
artist: Four Lads
Put a Little Love in Your Heart (song)
artist: Al Green, Annie Lennox, Jackie DeShannon
put an __ to: 3 end
put a tiger in your tank company: **4** Esso
putative: 7 alleged, assumed, imputed, reputed, seeming **8** presumed, reported, supposed
Put 'er __!: 5 there
put in __ word for: 5 a good
Put-in-Bay lake: 4 Erie
Putin, Vladimir: 7 Russian **9** statesman
put it __ together: 3 all
Putnam: 6 George, Israel
Putney Swope (1969 film)
cast: Pepi Hermine, Ruth Hermine, Arnold Johnson
director: Robert Downey
put on __: 4 airs **5** an act, a show
put one's __ down: 4 foot
put one's __ in: 3 oar
put one's __ in order: 5 house
put one's __ on: 6 finger
put one's cards on the __: 5 table
put one's foot __: 4 down, in it
put on the __: 3 dog, map **4** ritz **5** block **7** feedbag
put out to __: 3 sea **7** pasture
putrefied: 6 rancid, rotten
putrefy: 3 rot **5** decay, go bad, spoil
putrescent: 6 rancid, rotten
putrid: 3 bad **5** awful, nasty **6** rancid, rotten, smelly **8** inedible, terrible
putsch: 4 coup **6** revolt **10** revolution
put something __ on: 4 over
putt: 4 shot **5** swing
easy ~: 5 gimme, tap-in
first to ~: 4 away
__ putt: 5 hole a
puttee: 6 gaiter **7** gambado, legging
putter: 4 club, fool, poke **6** dabble, diddle, doodle, fiddle, linger, piddle, tinker, trifle **7** fritter **8** golf club **10** goof around, mess around, play around
org.: 3 PGA

__-putter: 4 shot
putterer: 4 tiro, tyro 6 novice 7 amateur 8 beginner 9 greenhorn 10 dilettante
put the __ on: 3 arm 4 bite 5 skids 6 finger, kibosh 7 squeeze
put the __ to: 6 screws
put the __ to the metal: 5 pedal
__ Put the Bomp: 3 Who
putting __: 5 green
__-putting: 3 off
Puttin' on the Ritz: 4 song, tune
  composer: Irving Berlin
putto: 5 Cupid 6 cherub, infant
put to __: 3 bed, use 4 rest 5 shame 6 flight
put to the __: 4 test
putty: 4 gray, grey 6 cement 8 brownish 9 yellowish
  kin: 3 ash 4 dove, drab 5 beige, dusty, merle, pearl, slate, taupe 6 silver 7 grizzly 8 charcoal, gunmetal, platinum
  like: 8 yielding 9 malleable, tractable
  user: 5 tiler
putty __: 5 knife
__ Putty: 5 Silly
Putumayo: 5 river
  locale: 6 Brazil 8 Colombia
put-up job: 4 ploy 5 frame 6 scheme 8 maneuver 9 strategem
put up or __ up: 4 shut
put up your __: 5 dukes
Put Your Hand in the Hand (1971 song) artist: Ocean
Put Your Head on My Shoulder (1959 song) artist: Paul Anka
Puyallup: 4 city, town 6 Indian 7 Amerind
  locale: 10 Washington
Puy-de-__: 4 Dôme
__ P'u Yi: 5 Henry
Puzo, Mario: 6 author, writer
  work: The Dark Arena
    Fools Die
    The Fortunate Pilgrim
    Fourth K, The
    The Godfather
    The Last Don
    Omerta
    The Sicilian
puzzle: 4 beat, faze, knot, maze, muse, snow 5 addle, floor, mix up, poser, rebus, stump, throw, vexer 6 baffle, bemuse, enigma, fuddle, jigsaw, marvel, ponder, riddle, secret, wonder 7 becloud, buffalo, confuse, flummox, mystery, mystify, nonplus, paradox, perplex, problem, stagger, trouble 8 befuddle, bewilder, confound, entangle, mull over, quandary 9 bamboozle, brood over, conundrum, crossword, dumbfound, labyrinth, overwhelm 10 disconcert
  direction: 4 down 6 across
  do a ~: 4 work 5 solve
  element: 4 clew, clue
  fodder: 3 wds. 5 clues, words
  help: 4 hint
  need: 6 eraser, pencil
  out: 5 crack, solve 6 decode 7 resolve, unravel 8 decipher, get right
  over: 4 muse 6 ponder 8 meditate, question
  part: 4 clue, grid, word 5 piece 7 picture
__ puzzle: 6 jigsaw, monkey 7 Chinese, picture
puzzled: 4 asea, lost 5 at sea, stuck 6 hung up, in a fog, thrown 7 at a loss, baffled, stumped 8 bollixed, clueless, confused, doubtful 9 buffaloed, flummoxed, mystified, perplexed 10 bewildered, nonplussed
  exclamation: 3 duh, gee 4 gosh 5 golly 6 jiminy 7 jeepers 8 excuse me 9 beg pardon, come again
puzzlement: 4 koan 5 vexer 6 riddle, wonder 7 mystery 9 confusion, conundrum
puzzler: 4 snag 6 enigma, riddle 7 mystery, problem 9 conundrum
puzzling: 4 dark, hard 5 funny, mirky, murky, queer, tough, vague 6 arcane, knotty 7 cryptic, curious, elusive, elusory, obscure, unclear 8 abstruse, baffling, involved, nebulous, singular 9 ambiguous, confusing, cryptical, difficult, enigmatic, insoluble 10 indistinct, misleading, mysterious, mystifying, perplexing, surprising, unsettling
P-V connection: 5 QRSTU
PVC part: 4 poly 5 vinyl 8 chloride
pvt.: 2 GI
  boss: 3 cpl., NCO, sgt.
  like a ~: 3 enl.
  see also private
P.W.: 5 Botha
pwr.: 4 elec.
  source: 3 TVA 5 hydro
  see also power
PX
  part: 4 post 8 exchange
  patron: 2 GI 3 NCO, PFC, sgt.
pya: 5 money
Pye, Henry: 4 poet 7 British
Pyewacket: 3 cat
__-pye weed: 3 joe
Pygmalion: 4 film, play 5 drama 8 sculptor
  author: George Bernard Shaw
  cast: Wendy Hiller, Leslie Howard, Wilfrid Lawson
  director: Anthony Asquith, Leslie Howard
  love: 7 Galatea
  sister of ~: 4 Dido 6 Elissa
pygmy: 3 wee 5 small 9 miniature, undersize 10 diminutive, homunculus
pyknic: 5 beefy, fubsy, obese, plump, pudgy, pursy, stout 6 chubby, fleshy, portly, rotund, stocky, zaftig, zoftig 7 adipose, paunchy 8 roly-poly 9 corpulent 10 overweight
Pylades wife: 7 Electra
Pyle: 5 Ernie, Gomer 6 Denver
pylon: 4 cone, pier, post 5 shaft, tower 6 column, marker, pillar 7 obelisk, support, upright 8 memorial, monolith, monument, pilaster
Pym: 4 John 7 Barbara
Pym, Barbara: 6 author, writer 7 British
  work: Excellent Woman
    A Few Green Leaves
    Glass of Blessings
    Quartet in Autumn
    Some Tame Gazelle
    A Very Private Eye
__ Pym Disposes: 4 Miss
Pynchon, Thomas: 6 author, writer
  work: The Crying of Lot 49
    Gravity's Rainbow
    Low-Lands
    Mason and Dixon
    The Secret Integration
    The Small Rain
    V.
    Vineland
Pyongyang: 4 city, town 7 capital
  locale: 10 North Korea
Pyotr: 7 Kapitsa 9 Kropotkin
  in English: 5 Peter
pyramid: 4 mass, pile, tomb 5 raise, stack 8 monument
  builder: 5 Aztec, Mayan 8 Egyptian
  find: 4 gold 5 mummy 7 jewelry, Pharaoh 8 artifact
  glass ~ architect: 3 Pei
  glass ~ site: 5 Paris 6 France, Louvre
  part: 4 apex, base 5 shaft, steps
  site: 4 Giza, Nile 5 Egypt, Uxmal 6 Mexico, Thebes 7 Memphis 11 Chichén Itzá
pyramid __: 3 bet 6 letter, scheme
Pyramus lover: 6 Thisbe
pyrargyrite: 7 mineral
Pyrenees: 3 mts. 4 mtns. 5 range 9 mountains
  bovine: 7 Alberes
  chamois: 5 Izard
  city: 3 Pau
  locale: 5 Spain 6 Europe, France
  native: 6 Basque
  peak: 5 Aneto 6 Estats, Posets
  region south of the ~: 6 Iberia
__-Pyrénées: 6 Basses, Hautes
pyrethrum: 5 plant 6 flower
pyretic: 3 hot 7 febrile 8 feverish
Pyrex: 5 glass 8 ovenware 9 glassware
pyrexia: 5 fever
pyrite: 3 ore 7 mineral
__ pyrite: 3 tin 4 iron 6 copper
pyro: 5 torch 7 firebug 8 arsonist 10 incendiary
pyrolusite: 3 ore
pyromaniac: 5 torch 7 firebug 8 arsonist 10 incendiary
  crime: 5 arson
pyrope: 3 gem 8 gemstone
pyrophobe fear: 4 fire
Pyrrha mother: 7 Pandora
pyrrhic: 4 foot
  relative: 4 iamb 6 dactyl 7 anapest, spondee, trochee
Pyrrhic __: 7 victory
P.Y.T. (1983 song) artist: Michael Jackson
Pythagoras: 5 Greek 11 philosopher 13 mathematician
Pythia: 5 sibyl 9 priestess
Pythian Games site: 6 Delphi
Pythias to Damon: 3 pal 6 friend
python: 5 snake 6 animal 7 reptile
  relative: 3 asp, boa 5 aboma, adder, cobra, krait, mamba, racer, viper 6 dhaman, taipan 7 markhor, rattler 8 anaconda, moccasin, ringhals 9 boomslang, coachwhip 10 bushmaster, copperhead, sidewinder
__ Python: 5 Monty
pythonic: 9 prophetic
Pyx, The (1973 film)
  cast: Karen Black, Christopher Plummer
  director: Harvey Hart

Q: 6 letter
and A: 7 enquiry, inquiry
followers: 3 RST 4 RSTU 5 RSTUV
in phonetic alphabet: 6 Quebec
neighbor: 3 Tab
preceders: 3 NOP 4 MNOP 5 LMNOP
Q ___: 4 and A 5 gauge
Q ___ queen: 4 as in
Q-___: 3 Tip 4 boat, ship, Tips 5 ratio 6 Celtic, factor
___ Q: 4 John 6 Stacey
'Q' ___ Quarry: 5 Is for
___-Q: 4 Bar-B
Q&A
part of ~: 3 ans. 4 ques.
Q & A actor: 5 Nolte 6 Hutton
director: 5 Lumet
Qaddafi: 7 Muammar
qanun: 6 string, zither
origin: 7 Mideast
Qara ___: 3 Qum
qat: 5 shrub
Qatar: 6 nation 7 country
capital: 4 Doha
group: 10 Arab League
leader: 4 amir, emir 5 ameer, emeer
locale: 4 Asia 6 Arabia
money: 4 rial 5 riyal 6 dirham
org.: 4 OPEC
Qatari: 4 Arab
neighbor: 5 Saudi
Qattara Depression: 6 desert
QB
armchair ~ channel: 4 ESPN
attacker: 2 LT, RT
bad ~ pass result: 3 int.
objective: 2 TD
org.: 3 NFL
protector: 2 LT, RT 3 end
see also football, quarterback
QB VII author: 4 Uris
QED part: 4 erat, quod
QE2: 4 ship 5 liner
letters: 3 HMS
line: 6 Cunard
Qingdao: 4 city, town
locale: 5 China
Qinghai Hu: 4 lake
formerly: 7 Koko Nor
locale: 5 China
qintar: 4 coin 5 money
100 ~s: 3 lek
qirsh: 5 money
20 ~s: 5 riyal
'Q' Is for Quarry author: Sue Grafton
Qom: 4 city, town 5 river
locale: 4 Iran
qoph: 6 Hebrew, letter
follower: 4 resh
preceder: 4 sadi 5 sadhe, tsade, tsadi
___ Q. Public: 4 John
q's, p's and: 7 manners 9 etiquette, formality
mind one's ~: 6 behave 10 toe the line
qt.: 3 amt. 4 meas.
half: 2 pt.
multiple: 3 gal.
Q-Tip: 4 swab, swob
target: 3 wax 6 earwax 7 cerumen
QT, on the: 5 close, slily, slyly 6 covert, hidden, secret 8 secretly 9 furtively, secretive, underhand 10 stealthily, undercover
qtr., first: 3 spr.
qty.: 3 amt., num. 4 meas.
food package ~: 3 doz. 4 nt. wt.
lab ~: 2 cc.
least ~: 3 min.
liquid ~: 2 oz., pt. 3 gal.
of the same ~: 5 equiv.
qua: 2 as 5 Latin
sine ~ non: 4 must, need 9 condition, essential, necessity, requisite
quab: 4 fish
quack: 4 fake, sham 5 cheat, faker, fraud, knave, phony 6 humbug, phoney, pseudo 7 sharper, sharpie 8 imposter, impostor, swindler 9 charlatan, con artist, hypocrite, physician, pretended, pretender, simulator 10 medicaster, mountebank
ender: 6 salver
grass: 4 weed
quackery: 4 sham 5 fraud 8 pretense 9 deception, duplicity, hypocrisy, imposture, phoniness
Quackser Fortune ... (1970 film)
cast: Margot Kidder, Gene Wilder
Quacks of Helicon, The author: 3 Poe
___ quack, there...: 5 Here a
quad: 4 four 5 court, space 6 campus 7 quarter 9 courtyard
building: 4 dorm
celeb: 4 BMOC
Quad ___: 6 Cities
quadr-: 4 four
predecessor: 3 tri-
successor: 4 pent-
quadrangle: 4 yard 5 court 6 square 9 courtyard, enclosure
setting: 6 campus
quadratic: 6 square
quadratic ___: 4 form 7 formula, residue 8 equation
quadriceps muscle: 6 vastus
quadrilateral: 5 rhomb 6 square 7 diamond, lozenge, rhombus 8 tetragon 9 trapezoid
type: 4 rect., rhom., trap. 7 rhombus 9 rectangle
quadrille: 4 game 5 dance 8 card game
quadrillion prefix: 4 peta-
quadrillionth prefix: 5 femto-
quadri- plus one: 5 penta-
quadrireme: 4 boat 5 craft 6 vessel 10 watercraft
quadruped: 3 ape, cat, cow, dog, elk, fox, gnu, pig, rat, sow, yak 4 bear, bull, deer, goat, hare, lion, lynx, mink, mole, puma, wolf 5 camel, hippo, horse, hyena, koala, lemur, llama, moose, mouse, panda, sheep, shrew, skunk, sloth, tapir, tiger, zebra 6 animal, badger, beaver, donkey, ermine, ferret, gerbil, gopher, jackal, jaguar, monkey, ocelot, rabbit, weasel, wombat 7 buffalo, echidna, gazelle, giraffe, hamster, leopard, muskrat, opossum, panther, raccoon 8 aardvark, anteater, antelope, chipmunk, dormouse, elephant, hedgehog, kangaroo, kinkajou, mongoose, platypus, reindeer, squirrel 9 bandicoot, groundhog, guinea pig, porcupine, woodchuck 10 rhinoceros
parent: 4 sire
quads kin: 3 abs 4 lats 5 traps
quaestor subordinate: 5 edile 6 aedile
quaff: 3 ade, ale, nog, rum, sip, sup 4 beer, down, grog, gulp, mead, swig, toss 5 draft, drink, lager, stout, toddy 6 brandy, eggnog, guzzle, imbibe, liquor 7 iced tea, liqueut, partake, swallow 8 hot toddy, potation
quantity: 4 pint
see also beverage, drink
quag: 3 bog 5 swamp 9 marshland, quicksand
ender: 4 mire
quagga: 6 equine
relative: 3 ass 5 burro, horse, kiang, zebra 6 donkey, onager 7 jackass 8 chigetai 9 dziggetai
quagmire: 3 bog, fen, fix, jam 4 hole, mire, trap 5 marsh, pinch, swamp, waste 6 corner, morass, muddle, pickle, plight, scrape, slough 7 dilemma, impasse 8 headache, quandary 9 imbroglio, marshland, quicksand 10 difficulty, pretty pass
quahog: 4 clam 5 shell 7 bivalve, mollusc, mollusk 8 seashell 10 littleneck
Quaid, Dennis: 5 actor
film: Any Given Sunday (1999)
The Big Easy (1987)
Breaking Away (1979)
D.O.A. (1988)
Dreamscape (1984)
Enemy Mine (1985)
Everybody's All-American (1988)
Far From Heaven (2002)
Innerspace (1987)
The Long Riders (1980)
The Parent Trap (1998)
Postcards From the Edge (1990)
The Right Stuff (1983)
The Rookie (2002)
The Savior (1998)
Suspect (1987)
Wyatt Earp (1994)
spouse: Meg Ryan
Quai d'Orsay, view from the: 5 Seine
Quaid, Randy: 5 actor
film: Bye Bye, Love (1995)
Days of Thunder (1990)
Hard Rain (1998)
Independence Day (1996)
Kingpin (1996)
The Last Detail (1973)
The Last Picture Show (1971)
The Long Riders (1980)
National Lampoon's Christmas Vacation (1989)
Quick Change (1990)
quail: 4 bird, fear, fowl 5 colin, cower, droop, faint, quake, shake, start, wince 6 blanch, blench, cringe, falter, flinch, recoil, shrink 7 shudder, tremble 8 bobwhite, coturnix, draw back, game bird, pull back 9 lose heart 10 chicken out
group: 4 bevy 5 covey
hunter: 6 fowler
relative: 5 poult, snipe 6 chukar, grouse, peahen, turkey 7 peacock, peafowl 8 curassow, moorfowl, pheasant, woodcock 9 partridge 10 guinea fowl, jungle fowl, wild turkey
quaint: 3 odd, rum 4 cute 5 droll, funny 6 freaky, Gothic 7 antique, baroque, bizarre, curious, erratic, oddball, offbeat, old-time, strange, unusual 8 adorable, charming, colonial, fanciful, old-timey, original, peculiar, pleasing, singular 9 eccentric, nostalgic, Victorian, whimsical 10 antiquated, enchanting, outlandish
in Britain: 4 twee
quake: 4 jerk, rock 5 cower, quail, seism, shake, shock 6 jitter, jounce, quiver, recoil, shiver, shrink, totter, tremor, wabble, wobble 7 pulsate, shudder, temblor, tremble, vibrate 8 upheaval 9 vibration 10 aftershock, convulsion
locale: 5 fault 9 fault line
make ~: 5 alarm, panic, scare 6 rattle 7 horrify, petrify, shake up, startle, terrify 8 frighten 10 intimidate
starter: 3 sea 4 moon 5 earth
Quaker ___: 3 gun 4 Oats 7 meeting
Quaker cereal: 4 Life 5 Quisp 7 Oat Bran 9 Apple Zaps 10 Cap'n Crunch, Puffed Rice, Quaker Oats
Quaker Oats: 6 cereal
competitor: 3 Kix 4 Life, Trix 5 Kashi, Quisp, Total 6 Kaboom, Muesli, Oreo O's, Pablum, Smacks 7 All-Bran, Crispix, Harmony, Hunny B's, Mueslix, Oat Bran, Pokemon 8 Boo Berry, Cheerios, Corn Chex, Corn Pops, Fiber One, Rice Chex, Special K, Uncle Sam, Wheaties 9 Alpha Bits, Apple Zaps, Grape Nuts, Honey Comb, Just Right, Wheat Chex 10 Apple Jacks, Bran Flakes, Cap'n Crunch, Cocoa Puffs, Froot Loops, Mini-Wheats, Nutri-Grain, Puffed Rice, Smart Start 11 Cocoa Blasts, Cookie Crisp, Golden Crisp, Lucky Charms, Puffed Wheat, Sweet Crunch, Waffle Crisp
Quakers: 4 sect 7 Friends
pronoun: 3 thy 4 thee, thou 5 thine
st.: 5 Penna.
verb: 3 art
Quaker State: Pennsylvania
quaking ___: 5 aspen, grass
qualification: 4 need, term 5 goods, skill, stuff 6 caveat, string 7 ability, fitness, makings, proviso, stature 8 aptitude, capacity 9 attribute, condition, criterion, endowment, essential, exception, exemption, provision, requisite
form: 4 exam, test
without ~: 6 flatly
qualified: 3 apt, fit 4 able, good 5 adept, ready, tried 6 au fait, expert, fitted, proper, proven, tested, up to it, versed 7 bounded, capable, limited, partial, trained, veteran 8 adequate, eligible, equipped, licensed, modified, prepared, skillful, talented 9 certified, competent, cut out for, efficient, practiced, up to snuff, up to speed 10 contingent, instructed, privileged, proficient, restricted
become ~ for: 8 grow into
no longer ~: 5 rusty, stale 10 out of shape
qualifier: 2 if 3 but 6 adverb 9 adjective
qualify: 3 fit 4 lull, meet, name, pass, suit, vary 5 adapt, alter, cut it, endow, equip, get by, limit, ready, score, train 6 assign, change, enable, ground, hack it, impute, lessen, make it, modify, permit, reduce, season, soften, temper, weaken 7 ascribe, assuage, certify, empower, entitle, intitle, prepare, satisfy, suffice 8 check out, describe, diminish, mitigate, moderate, modulate, regulate, restrain, restrict, sanction 9 attribute, authorize, condition, designate, measure up 10 capacitate, commission, make the cut, pass muster
for: 3 get, win 4 earn, gain, rate, reap 5 merit 6 attain, come by, derive, obtain, pick up, secure 7 deserve, procure, receive, warrant
quality: 3 air 4 aura, kind, make, mark, rank, sort, tone 5 asset, class, fiber, grade, merit, point, state, thing, trait, value, worth 6 aspect, factor, flavor, goodly, nature, repute, status, virtue 7 caliber, earmark, essence, feature, footing, station, stature, texture, variety 8 position, property, standing, superior 9 attribute, character, condition, endowment, parameter 10 excellence, perfection, superbness
characteristic ~: 4 aura, odor 5 aroma, savor, smell
of poor ~: 3 bad 5 cheap, tacky, tatty 6 ragged, shabby, shoddy 8 mediocre
star ~: 5 charm 6 glamor 7 charism, glamour 8 charisma
suffix: 3 -ism 4 -ness, -ship
quality ___: 4 time 5 point 6 circle 7 control

__-quality: 5 first 6 letter
Quality Inn: 5 motel
alternative: 7 Days Inn 9 Ramada Inn 10 Comfort Inn, Econo Lodge, Hampton Inn, Holiday Inn, Red Roof Inn, Travelodge 11 Best Western
quality of __: 4 life
Quality of Mercy, The author: Faye Kellerman
quality point __: 7 average
Quality Street (1937 film)
cast: Fay Bainter, Katharine Hepburn, Franchot Tone
director: George Stevens
Quality Street author: James M. Barrie
qualm: 3 rue 4 fear, pang 5 doubt, worry 6 regret, repent, twinge, unease 7 anxiety, scruple 8 disquiet, distrust, wariness 9 leeriness, misgiving, objection, suspicion 10 conscience, foreboding, hesitation, indecision, reluctance, skepticism, solicitude, uneasiness
have ~ s: 5 doubt, worry 6 regret, repent
qualmish: 4 sick 6 queasy, queazy 9 squeamish
qualmless: 3 bad 5 wrong 6 amoral, wicked 10 licentious
__ quam videri: 4 esse
quandary: 3 fix, jam 4 bind, mess, spot 5 doubt 6 clutch, corner, muddle, pickle, plight, puzzle 7 dilemma, impasse, problem 8 exigence, exigency, juncture, quagmire 9 deep water 10 difficulty, perplexity
in a ~: 6 unsure 7 at a loss
Quang __: 3 Tri 4 Binh, Ngai
Quang Tri locale: 3 Nam 7 Vietnam
__ qua non: 4 sine
Quant: 4 Mary
Quantico: 4 city, town
initials: 3 FBI 4 USMC
locale: 8 Virginia
quantify: 4 rate 5 gauge 7 measure
quantitative target: 5 quota
quantity: 3 lot, sum 4 bulk, deal, dose, hunk, load, mass, pile, size 5 batch, bunch, order, quota, store, total 6 amount, figure, length, number, supply, volume 7 measure, portion, variety 8 capacity 9 abundance, aggregate, allotment, multitude, profusion 10 collection, complement, cumulation
fixed ~: 4 unit
large ~: 3 gob, lot, sea, ton 4 acre, mass, much, peck, pile, raft, yard 5 ocean 6 boodle, galore, oodles 9 wholesale
liquid ~: 3 cup 4 pint 5 quart 6 gallon
miscellaneous ~: 6 job lot
small ~: 3 dab 4 dash, dram, drib, drop, iota, spot 5 ounce
__ quantity: 5 known
Quant, Mary: 7 British 8 designer
design: 3 mod 4 mini 9 miniskirt
Quanto è bella: 4 aria
Quanto rapita in estasi: 4 aria
quantum: 6 amount, ration
quantum __: 4 jump, leap 5 state 6 number, optics, theory
quantum __ theory: 5 field
Quantum Leap (NBC sci-fi)
cast: Scott Bakula (Sam Beckett) Dean Stockwell (Al Calavicci)
computer: Ziggy
quantum mechanics: 7 science
Quapaw: 6 Indian 7 Amerind 8 language
quarantine: 4 seal 6 cut off, enisle, shut in 7 isolate, seclude 8 solitude 9 detention, seclusion, segregate
in ~: 4 lone 5 alone, apart, aside 8 isolated, secluded, separate, solitary 9 by oneself
Quare Fellow, The author: 5 Behan
quark: 8 particle
+ antiquark: 5 meson
binder: 5 gluon
container: 4 atom
__ quark: 3 top 4 down 5 truth 6 beauty, bottom 7 charmed, strange
Quarles, Francis: 4 poet 7 British
Quarnero: 4 gulf
locale: 6 Europe 7 Croatia
quarrel: 3 row, war 4 beef, carp, feud, fray, fuss, rift, spar, spat, tiff, to-do 5 argue, brawl, broil, cavil, clash, fight, run-in, scrap, set-to, snarl 6 affray, barney, battle, bicker, breach, debate, differ, divide, dustup, fracas, haggle, hassle, jangle, ruckus, rumpus, strife, strive, take on, tangle, tumult 7 collide, contend, contest, discord, dispute, dissent, dustups, embroil, fall out, mix it up, quibble, rhubarb, wrangle 8 argument, catfight, complain, conflict, disagree, friction, object to, skirmish, squabble, struggle, vendetta 9 altercate, bickering, brannigan, break with, commotion, complaint, encounter, find fault, have it out, have words, imbroglio, lock horns, make a fuss, objection, take issue 10 bone to pick, contention, difference, difficulty, disapprove, dissension, dissidence, falling-out, fisticuffs
quarreling: 9 on the outs 10 discordant
quarrelsome: 4 ugly 5 cross, fiery, hasty, huffy, onery, surly, testy 6 crabby, feisty, ornery, snappy, touchy, unruly 7 defiant, naughty, peevish, pettish, violent, warlike, wayward 8 brawling, choleric, churlish, contrary, fighting, militant, petulant, ructious, snappish, stubborn 9 bellicose, cat-and-dog, combative, excitable, fractious, hotheaded, irascible, irritable, litigious, querulous, splenetic, truculent, turbulent 10 out of sorts, pugnacious, rebellious
quarry: 3 pit 4 game, land, mine, prey, rock 6 source, target, victim 8 excavate 10 excavation
granite ~ locale: 5 Barre 7 Vermont
perhaps: 5 hider
yield: 3 gem, ore 4 rock 5 jewel, stone 6 gravel 7 crystal, mineral
quart: 4 unit
buy: 4 milk
eight ~ s: 4 peck
ender: 3 ile
fraction: 2 pt. 3 cup 4 peck, pint
metric ~: 5 liter, litre
not quite a ~: 5 fifth
quarter: 4 area, bunk, coin, part, pity, post, quad, slum, spot, term, turf, ward, zone 5 board, cut up, grace, house, lodge, mercy, money, place, point, put up, tract 6 barrio, billet, canton, domain, fourth, ghetto, harbor, instal, lenity, locale, region, season, sector, take in 7 domicil, harbour, install, portion, section, shelter, station, two bits 8 clemency, district, domicile, lenience, leniency, locality, location, position, precinct, province, quadrant 9 direction, dismember, inner city, one-fourth, territory 10 compassion
bad ~: 4 slug
ender: 3 age, saw 4 ages, back, deck, tone 5 final, staff 6 master 8 finalist
give ~: 4 pity 5 spare 6 relent
half a ~: 3 bit 6 eighth
like a new ~: 5 shiny 6 agleam, bright 8 gleaming
note: 8 crotchet
of a quart: 3 cup
of eight: 3 two
starter: 4 fore, head, hind
third of a ~: 5 month
word on a ~: 3 God 4 unum 5 trust 6 dollar, States, United 7 America, liberty 8 pluribus
quarter __: 3 bar, day 4 bend, note, rest, tone 5 eagle, grain, horse, point, round 6 dollar, hollow, nelson 7 binding, blanket, section
__ quarter: 4 last 5 ask no, first, grand
__-quarter: 5 three
__ Quarter: 5 Latin 6 French
quarterback: 4 lead 5 guide 6 direct 7 athlete, control, oversee 9 supervise
colleague: 6 center
great: 5 Baugh, Fouts, Kelly, Starr 6 Blanda, Dawson, Graham, Griese, Marino, Namath, Tittle, Unitas 7 Luckman, Montana 8 Bradshaw, Dan Fouts, Jim Kelly, Staubach, Y.A. Tittle 9 Bart Starr, Bob Griese, Dan Marino, Jurgensen, Len Dawson, Tarkenton 10 Joe Montana, Otto Graham, Sammy Baugh, Sid Luckman
move: 4 fade, pass 5 sneak
resource: 3 arm
signal: 3 hup 4 hike
tackle the ~: 4 sack
target: 3 end 8 receiver
the ~ takes it: 4 snap
quarterly: 8 magazine 10 periodical
Quartermaster __: 5 Corps
quarter-pint: 4 gill
Quarter Pounder: 6 burger 9 hamburger
part: 5 patty 6 pattie
quarters: 4 digs, dorm, flat, home, post, room, tent, yurt 5 abode, cabin, condo, house, lodge, money, place, ranch, roost, suite 6 billet, change 7 cottage, domicil, habitat, housing, lodging, shelter, station 8 barracks, chambers, domicile, dwelling, lodgment, sorority 9 apartment, residence 10 fraternity, habitation
at close ~: 4 near 6 nearby
cramped ~: 4 cell, coop 5 booth 6 alcove, recess 7 chamber, cubicle, dungeon 8 cloister
give ~ to: 4 rent 5 board, house, lodge, put up 6 billet, harbor, take in 7 shelter 9 entertain
in a sultan's palace: 5 haram, harem, harim 6 hareem
living ~: 4 home 5 abode, place
private ~: 5 house
sailor's ~: 5 cabin 6 fo'c's'le
squalid ~: 3 sty 4 dump, slum 5 hovel 6 pigsty 8 cesspool, pesthole
starter: 4 head, hind
take up ~: 4 live, stay 5 abide, dwell, lodge, roost 6 occupy, reside, settle 7 inhabit, sojourn
temporary ~: 4 tent 7 bivouac
two ~: 4 half
winter ~: 3 den 4 lair
__ quarters: 5 close 6 call to 7 general
quartet: 4 four 5 combo, group 8 ensemble, foursome
alphabet ~: 4 ABCD, BCDE, CDEF, DEFG, EFGH, FGHI, GHIJ, HIJK, IJKL, JKLM, KLMN, LMNO, MNOP, NOPQ, OPQR, PQRS, QRST, RSTU, STUV, TUVW, UVWX, VWXY, WXYZ
deck ~: 4 aces, tens, twos 5 fives, fours, jacks, kings, nines, sixes 6 deuces, eights, queens, sevens, threes
double ~: 5 octet
half a ~: 3 duo, two 4 pair
member: 4 alto, bass 5 basso, tenor 7 soprano
minus one: 4 trio
plus five: 5 nonet
string ~ member: 5 cello, viola 6 violin
__ quartet: 5 piano 6 string
Quartet in Autumn author: Barbara Pym
__ Quartet, The: 3 Raj
__ quartile: 5 first, third 6 second
__ quarto: 4 demy 5 crown 6 medium
quarto, larger than: 5 folio
quartz: 4 rock 5 flint 7 mineral
deep-orange ~: 4 sard 5 agate, chert, topaz 6 jasper 7 sardine, sardius
fine-grained ~: 5 flint
grains: 4 sand
like ~: 4 hard 5 rocky, solid, stony
mineral in ~: 6 silica
pale yellow: 7 citrine
smoky ~: 3 gem
to Mohs: 5 seven
translucent ~: 10 chalcedony
violet: 8 amethyst
quartz __: 4 lamp 5 clock, glass, plate, watch 7 crystal
__ quartz: 4 rose 5 fused, smoky, topaz
quartzite: 7 mineral
Quasar: 2 TV 5 TV set 10 television
alternative: 3 JVC, NEC, RCA 4 Sony 6 Zenith 7 Emerson, Hitachi, ProScan, Toshiba 8 Magnavox, Sylvania 9 Panasonic
quash: 3 end, nix 4 kill, stop, undo, veto, void 5 abate, annul, crush, estop, quell, rebut, sit on, sqush, trash 6 cancel, defeat, hush up, negate, quench, refute, repeal, revoke, scotch, squish, squush, subdue 7 abolish, blow out, destroy, nullify, put down, repress, rescind, reverse, scrunch, silence, smother, squeeze, squelch, squoosh, vitiate 8 abrogate, bottle up, dissolve, overcome, override, overrule, set aside, shut down, stamp out, suppress 9 extirpate, overthrow 10 annihilate, extinguish, invalidate
quasi: 4 as if, fake, mock, near, semi-, sham 6 almost, in part, kind of, partly, pseudo 7 nominal, seeming, virtual, would-be 8 apparent, so-called 9 pretended, synthetic 10 ostensible, resembling, supposedly
Quasimodo
creator: 4 Hugo
portrayer: 3 Lon 5 Quinn 6 Chaney 8 Laughton
voice: 5 Hulce
Quasimodo, Salvatore: 4 poet 6 writer 7 Italian 8 Nobelist
quassia: 4 tree 5 shrub 9 ailanthus
Quatermain: 4 hero 5 Allan
Quaternary division: 6 ice age
__ Quatorze: 5 Louis
quatrain: 4 poem 5 verse
scheme: 4 ABAB, ABBA
__ quatrain: 6 heroic 7 elegiac
quatrainist, famous: 4 Omar
quatre: 4 four 6 French
follower: 4 cinq
preceder: 5 trois
__ quatre: 5 pas de
Quatre Evangiles author: Emile Zola
quatri-
twice: 4 octa-, octo-
Quatro: 4 Suzi
quattordici: 7 Italian 8 fourteen
half of: 5 sette
quattro: 4 four 7 Italian
preceder: 3 tre
tre + ~: 5 sette
- tre: 3 una, uno
Quattro: 3 car 4 Audi, auto 10 automobile
quaver: 4 note 5 shake, trill 6 shiver, tremor, twitch, wabble, wobble 7 pulsate, tremble 10 eighth note
quavering: 5 reedy 6 shrill

quay: 4 dock, pier, port 5 berth, jetty, levee, wharf 7 landing 9 anchorage
ender: 3 age
Quayle: 2 VP 3 Dan 4 veep 7 Anthony
home: 3 Ind. 7 Indiana
predecessor: 4 Bush
successor: 4 Gore
Quayle, Anthony: 5 actor
film: Anne of the Thousand Days (1969)
The Guns of Navarone (1961)
Lawrence of Arabia (1962)
The Tamarind Seed (1974)
Woman in a Dressing Gown (1957)
The Wrong Man (1957)
__-que: 4 bar-b
Que __...: 4 sera
Que.: 4 prov.
neighbor: 2 NH 3 Ont. 4 Newf.
see also Québec
Qué __?: 4 pasa
Qué __ es?: 4 hora
queasiness: 5 upset 6 nausea 8 sickness
queasy: 3 ill 4 sick 5 queer, rocky, upset 6 uneasy, unwell 7 anxious, bilious, nervous 8 qualmish, troubled 9 squeamish, uncertain 10 indisposed
Québec: 4 city, prov., town 8 province
city: 4 Alma, Amos, Baie, Hull 5 Laval, Lévis, Rouyn, Sorel 6 Aylmer, Comeau, Granby, La Baie, Ste.-Foy, Val-d'Or, Verdun 7 Chambly, Lachine, La Salle, Mirabel, Noranda 8 Beauport, Brossard, Gatineau, Montréal, Rimouski, Sept-Iles, Ste.-Julie, St.-Hubert, St.-Jérôme 9 Côte-St.-Luc, Jonquière, Longueuil, Mascouche, Outremont, St.-Georges, St.-Lambert, St.-Laurent, St.-Léonard, Val-Belair, Westmount 10 Blainville, Boisbriand, Chicoutimi, Repentigny, Sherbrooke, St.-Constant, Ste.-Thérèse, St.-Eustache, St. Luc Anjou, Terrebonne
Indian: 6 Abnaki, Micmac 7 Abenaki, Naskapi 8 Wabanaki
locale: 6 Canada
neighbor: 5 Maine 7 New York
newspaper: 8 Le Soleil
peninsula: 5 Gaspé
school: 5 Laval 6 McGill 7 Bishop's 9 Concordia
see also French
Quechua: 4 Inca 5 Incan 6 Indian 7 Amerind 8 language
Queeg ship: 5 Caine
queen: 3 ant, HRH, sov. 4 card 5 noble, piece, ruler, title, woman 6 dynast, victor 7 czarina, empress, monarch, sultana, tsarina, tzarina 8 face card 9 potentate, sovereign 10 chesspiece, Her Majesty
address: 4 ma'am
beater: 3 ace 4 king
ender: 4 side
fit for a ~: 5 regal, royal 9 luxurious
future ~ maybe: 4 pawn
home: 4 hive, nest 6 apiary, castle
in French: 5 reine
mate: 5 drone
name meaning ~: 6 Regina
Old Testament ~: 6 Esther
subject: 3 bee
topper: 5 crown, tiara
queen __: 3 bee 4 palm, post 5 olive, truss 6 closer, mother, regent 7 consort, dowager, regnant
queen-__ bed: 4 size 5 sized
Queen: 4 Anne, band, Bess 6 Ellery 7 Beatrix, Latifah 8 Victoria 9 Elizabeth
homeland: England
Queen (rock group)
members: Mercury, May, Deacon, Taylor
song: Another One Bites the Dust (1980)
Body Language (1982)
Bohemian Rhapsody (1976)
Crazy Little Thing Called Love (1980)
Killer Queen (1975)
Somebody to Love (1976)
Under Pressure (1981)
We Are the Champions (1977)
You're My Best Friend (1976)
Queen __: 3 Mab, Mum 4 Anne, Bess, City, Mary 5 Kelly 6 Margot 7 Latifah
Queen __ a Day: 3 for
Queen __ Damned, The: 5 of the
Queen __ Hop: 5 of the
Queen __ lace: 5 Anne's
Queen __ Land: 4 Maud
Queen __ Nile: 5 of the
Queen __ War: 5 Anne's
__ Queen: 5 Dairy 6 Killer, Virgin 7 Dancing
Queen Anne: 5 style
Queen Anne's
lace: 5 plant 6 flower
Queen Anne's __: 3 War 4 lace
Queen-Anne's-Lace: 4 poem
author: William Carlos Williams
Queen Bee (1955 film)
cast: Joan Crawford, Betsy Palmer, Barry Sullivan
Queen Charlotte __: 7 Islands
Queen Christina (1933 film)
cast: Greta Garbo, John Gilbert
director: Rouben Mamoulian
Queen City of the Rockies: 6 Helena
Queen Elizabeth: 4 boat, ship 5 liner
Queen, Ellery creator: 3 Lee 6 Dannay
__ Queene, The: 6 Faerie
Queen for a Day (game show) host: Jack Bailey
Queenie author: 5 Korda
queenly: 5 noble, regal, royal 7 stately 8 imperial
Queen Mab author: 7 Shelley
Queen Mary: 4 boat, ship 5 liner
Queen Maud __: 4 Land 5 Range
Queen Maud Range locale: 9 Antartica
Queen of __: 5 Sheba 6 Heaven
Queen of Hearts (1981 song) artist: Juice Newton
__, Queen of Scots: 4 Mary
Queen of Spades, The author: Aleksandr Pushkin
Queen of the __: 4 Nile
Queen of the Damned, The author: Anne Rice
Queen of the Hop (1958 song) artist: Bobby Darin
Queen of the West, The: 4 Dale 5 Evans
Queen (rock group) (rock group)
song: Radio Ga-Ga (1984)
queen's __: 4 ware 5 scout 6 bounty 7 English, highway
queen's-__ openings: 4 pawn
Queens: 3 bor. 7 borough
locale: 3 NYC 7 New York
stadium: 4 Ashe, Shea
team: 4 Mets
Queen's __: 5 Bench 6 speech 7 Counsel, pattern, Proctor
Queensberry __: 5 rules
queens, game of: 5 chess
queenside castle, in chess: 3 OOO
queen-size __: 3 bed
Queensland: 5 state
capital: 8 Brisbane
city: 6 Cairns 8 Brisbane 10 Townsville
neighbor: 3 NSW
Queen's University
location: 6 Canada 7 Ontario 8 Kingston
__ Queen, The: 3 May 4 Beet, Snow 6 Virgin 7 African
Queequeg captain: 4 Ahab
Queirós, Rachel de: 6 writer 9 Brazilian
Quela: 4 peak 5 mount 8 mountain
locale: 5 Andes 9 Argentina
Queler: 3 Eve
quell: 4 calm, dull, ease, kill, lull, stop 5 abate, allay, check, crush, quash, queer, quiet, sit on, slake, still 6 becalm, defeat, hush up, pacify, quench, reduce, settle, soften, soothe, squash, stifle, subdue 7 appease, assuage, compose, conquer, control, head off, mollify, put down, repress, silence, smother 8 beat down, mitigate, moderate, overcome, shut down, stamp out, suppress, vanquish 9 alleviate, overpower, subjugate 10 extinguish
quelque-__: 5 chose
Quemoy: 4 isle 6 island
neighbor: 4 Mazu 5 Matsu
quena: 5 flute 6 string
__ Que Nada: 3 Mas
quench: 3 end 4 cool, ruin, sate 5 allay, crush, douse, dowse, quash, quell, slake, wreck 6 dampen, put out, stifle 7 assuage, blow out, destroy, moisten, put down, relieve, satisfy, smother, squelch 8 decimate, demolish, mitigate, snuff out, suppress 9 alleviate 10 extinguish
quencher
thirst ~: 3 ade, ale, tea 4 beer 5 drink, juice, water
quenchless: 10 gluttonous, insatiable
Queneau, Raymond: 4 poet 6 French
work: The Bark Tree
Zazie
quenelle: 4 meat
Quennell, Peter: 6 writer 7 English
Quentin: 5 Crisp 6 Massys 9 Tarantino
__ Quentin: 3 San
Quentin Durward author: Walter Scott
Quentins author: Maeve Binchy
Qué pasa? reply: 4 nada
quercus: 3 oak 4 tree
Querétaro: 4 city, town 5 state
city: 8 Jauregui 10 El Pueblito
locale: 6 Mexico
querulous: 4 edgy, sour 5 cross, fussy, huffy, testy, waspy, whiny 6 crabby, cranky, crusty, crying, grumpy, snappy, sullen, touchy, whiney 7 bearish, carping, finical, finicky, fretful, grouchy, nervous, peevish, scrappy, uptight, wailing, waspish, whining 8 captious, caviling, choleric, critical, finiking, finnicky, fretsome, grousing, grumpish, petulant, snappish 9 bemoaning, crotchety, demanding, deploring, fractious, grumbling, irascible, irritable, lamenting, plaintive, splenetic 10 censorious, out of sorts, whimpering
querulousness: 4 rage 5 spite, venom, wrath 6 enmity, malice, rancor, spleen 8 acrimony, ill humor 9 hostility, petulance, testiness 10 crabbiness, grumpiness, irritation, touchiness
query: 2 eh 3 ask, how, who, why 4 pose, quiz, seek, what, when 5 doubt, grill, issue, probe, where, which, whose 6 impugn, wonder 7 concern, dispute, enquire, enquiry, examine, inquire, inquiry, problem, request, solicit, suspect 8 distrust, mistrust, question, sound out 9 catechize, challenge, objection 10 disbelieve
mock-innocent ~: 5 who me
reporter's ~: 3 how, who, why 4 what, when 5 where
response: 5 reply 6 answer 8 comeback 9 rejoinder
ques.: 3 inq.
response: 3 ans.
Que Sera, Sera (1956 song) artist: Doris Day
quest: 4 hunt, seek 5 chase, probe 6 pursue, search, voyage 7 crusade, enquiry, inquest, inquiry, journey, mission, pursuit 8 ambition, campaign, research 9 adventure, objective 10 enterprise, expedition, pilgrimage
object: 5 Grail 9 Holy Grail
__ quest: 6 vision
Quest: 3 van 6 Nissan
Quest __ Camelot: 3 for
__ Quest: 6 Galaxy
Questa notte: 4 aria
Quest for Camelot (1998 film)
voice cast: Cary Elwes, Eric Idle, Gary Oldman, Don Rickles, Jane Seymour
Quest for Fire (1981 film)
cast: Rae Dawn Chong, Ron Perlman
role: 3 Gaw, Ika 4 Faum, Matr, Mikr, Naoh, Tsor 5 Aghoo, Hourk, Lakar, Modoc, Morah, Rouka 6 Gammla
questing: 6 errant
question: 3 ask, how, pry, who, why 4 mull, poll, pose, pump, quiz, seek, what, when 5 demur, doubt, grill, hit up, issue, point, posit, probe, query, topic, where, which 6 debate, enigma, go over, impugn, matter, motion, needle, oppose, ponder, riddle, search, wonder 7 contest, dispute, enquire, enquiry, examine, impeach, inquire, inquiry, mystery, problem, protest, request, solicit, suspect 8 argument, ask about, distrust, hesitate, mistrust, petition, proposal, sound out 9 catechize, challenge, confusion, fight over, interview, misgiving, objection, speculate, suspicion 10 contention, controvert, difficulty, disbelieve, discussion, puzzle over
answer the ~: 5 field, reply 7 respond
anticipatory ~: 3 and
baffling ~: 5 poser 6 enigma, riddle 7 stumper, toughie
beyond ~: 4 sure, true 5 plain 6 surely
call into ~: 5 doubt 6 impugn, oppose 7 dispute 9 challenge
child's ~: 3 why
computer ~: 4 fail 5 abort, retry
French ~: 5 quand
gift recipient's ~: 5 for me
in ~: 4 open 7 at issue 10 suspicious
journalist's ~: 3 how, who, why 4 what, when 5 where
kind of ~: 5 essay, trick, yes/no
lamenter's ~: 5 why me
loaded ~: 4 bait, ruse, trap 6 ambush, come-on, device 8 maneuver 9 booby trap, deception 10 enticement, subterfuge
out of the ~: 2 no 3 nah, naw, nay, nix, non 4 nein, nope, nyet, uh-uh 5 I won't, ixnay, never, no how, no way 6 absurd, no deal, noways, nowise 7 I refuse 8 forget it, hopeless, I will not, negative, negatory 9 by no means, fat chance, forbidden, I think not 10 count me out, impossible, infeasible, not a chance, ridiculous, thumbs down
point in ~: 4 case 5 issue, theme, topic 6 affair, matter, thesis 7 problem, subject 8 business
pop the ~: 3 ask 7 propose
scientist's ~: 3 why
Spanish ~: 3 qué
tourist's ~: 5 where
question __: 4 mark, time 5 of law
__ question: 3 tag 4 echo 5 essay, trick, yes-no 6 beyond, loaded 7 leading
__ Question, A: 6 Lover's

questionable: 4 iffy, moot, open, thin 5 fishy, queer, shady, shaky, vague 6 chancy, occult, unsure 7 cryptic, dubious, obscure, suspect, tenuous 8 arguable, doubtful, oracular, unlikely, unproven 9 ambiguous, cryptical, debatable, dubitable, enigmatic, equivocal, uncertain, undefined, unsettled 10 indefinite, unresolved, up for grabs, up in the air
questionables: 3 ifs 6 issues
questioner: 5 cynic 7 doubter, sceptic, scoffer, skeptic 8 examiner
conference ~: 5 media, press 8 reporter
motive ~: 5 cynic 7 doubter, skeptic
questioning: 7 curious, enquiry, inquiry 9 observant, quizzical, skeptical
sound: 2 eh 3 huh
questionnaire: 4 form, test
datum: 3 age, sex 4 name
question of ___: 3 law 4 fact
Question of Mercy, A author: 4 Rabe
___ questions: 4 four 6 twenty
___ questions?: 3 Any
quetzal: 4 bird 5 money
Quetzalcoatl: 3 god
worshiper: 5 Aztec 6 Toltec
queue: 3 row 4 coif, file, line, rank, tier 5 braid, chain, order, plait, train 6 column, hairdo, line up, series, string 7 pigtail 8 coiffure 10 succession
airport ~: 4 cabs 5 taxis
call to a ~: 4 next
queued up: 4 arow 6 in line, on line
queuing ___: 6 theory
Quezon City's island: 5 Luzon
quibble: 4 carp, spar, spat 5 argue, avoid, cavil, clash, dodge, evade, fudge, gripe, stall, whine 6 bicker, differ, hassle, niggle, pick at, waffle 7 dispute, evasion, nitpick, protest, quarrel, shuffle, sophism, wrangle 8 conflict, disagree, flip-flop, pettifog, squabble 9 altercate, argue over, chicanery, complaint, criticism, criticize, find fault, hem and haw, take issue 10 equivocate, split hairs
quibbler: 6 critic 10 fussbudget
quiche: 3 pie 6 pastry
alternative: 6 omelet 8 omelette
base: 5 crust
ingredient: 3 egg 5 bacon, Swiss 6 cheese 7 Gruyère
quick: 3 apt 4 able, anon, ASAP, curt, deft, fast, keen, rush, soon, spry 5 acute, adept, agile, alert, alive, brief, brisk, canny, fleet, hasty, nifty, rapid, ready, savvy, sharp, slick, smart, swift, tight 6 abrupt, active, adroit, astute, bright, clever, facile, flying, in a sec, liquid, lively, marrow, nimble, presto, prompt, pronto, racing, shrewd, snappy, speedy, sudden, winged 7 capable, cursory, express, hastily, hurried, instant, knowing 8 all there, dextrous, flitting, headlong, punctual, skillful, spirited 9 astucious, breakneck, competent, dexterous, effective, effectual, energetic, immediate, impatient, impetuous, mercurial, momentary, observant, on the ball, posthaste, rapid-fire, receptive, sprightly, whirlwind 10 discerning, double-time, hypersonic, insightful, perceptive, precocious, proficient, responsive, supersonic
be ~: 3 fly, hie, rip, run, zip 4 dart, dash, flit, move, race, rush, tear, whiz 5 hurry, scoot, smoke, speed, whisk 6 barrel, gallop, hasten, hustle, rocket, scurry 7 floor it, scamper 8 make time, step on it 9 make haste, shake a leg 10 accelerate, get a move on, lose no time, make tracks
ender: 3 set 4 lime, sand, step 6 silver
look: 4 peek, peep 6 aperçu
meal: 4 bite, nosh
on the uptake: 3 apt 4 glib 5 quick, sharp, smart, witty 6 adroit, astute, bright 9 astucious, receptive
too ~: 4 rash 5 hasty 10 headstrong
to the ~: 6 deeply, highly
to the helm: 3 yar 4 yare
turn: 3 zag, zig 4 jink
quick ___: 3 fix 4 draw, fire, kick, time 5 bread, grass, march, study, trick 6 assets
quick ___ draw: 5 on the
quick ___ wink: 3 as a
quick-___: 6 freeze, witted 7 setting
quick-___ artist: 6 change
___-quick: 6 double
Quick, ___, the Flit!: 5 Henry
quick-and-dirty: 6 make-do 7 stopgap 8 slapdash 9 expedient, makeshift, temporary 10 improvised, pro tempore
Quick and the Dead, The (1995 film)
cast: Russell Crowe, Leonardo DiCaprio, Gene Hackman, Sharon Stone
director: Sam Raimi
Quick Change (1990 film)
cast: Geena Davis, Bill Murray, Randy Quaid, Jason Robards
Quick Draw: 3 dog 6 McGraw 7 sheriff
quicken: 3 fly, hie, rip, run, zip 4 dart, dash, flit, goad, grow, move, race, rush, spur, stir, tear, urge, wake, whet, zoom 5 hurry, impel, liven, pep up, pique, rouse, scoot, speed, touch, waken 6 arouse, awaken, barrel, excite, gallop, hasten, hustle, incite, kindle, move it, revive, rocket, scurry, step up, thrill, vivify 7 actuate, animate, enliven, floor it, hop to it, inspire, promote, refresh, scamper, speed up 8 activate, dispatch, energize, enspirit, expedite, increase, inspirit, motivate, step on it, vitalize 9 galvanize, hotfoot it, intensify, make haste, shake a leg, skedaddle, stimulate 10 accelerate, get a move on, hightail it, invigorate, revitalize, strengthen
Quicken company: 6 Intuit
quickener, heartbeat: 6 crisis
quickening: 7 revival 8 kindling
quicker-than-the-eye movement: 4 blur
Quick, Henry, the ___!: 4 Flit
quicklime: 4 calx 5 oxide
quickly: 3 PDQ 4 ASAP, fast, soon, stat 5 apace, madly, right 6 adverb, presto, pronto 7 briefly, rapidly, readily, swiftly 8 directly, in a flash, in a jiffy, in no time, on the fly, on the run, pell-mell, promptly, right now, right off, suddenly, very soon 9 forthwith, instantly, like a shot, on the spot, posthaste, right away 10 here and now, swimmingly
quickness: 4 rush 5 haste, hurry, speed 8 alacrity, celerity, dispatch, legerity, rapidity, velocity 9 briskness, dexterity, diligence, eagerness, fleetness, readiness, smartness, swiftness 10 cleverness, expedition, nimbleness
quick on the ___: 4 draw 6 uptake
Quick Pick: 6 tomato
relative: 4 Roma 6 Big Boy 9 beefsteak, Better Boy, Early Girl
quicksand: 4 mire, quag, trap 5 snare 7 pitfall 8 quagmire
Quicksand (1963 song) artist: Martha & the Vandellas
quicksilver: 5 azoth, metal 6 fickle 7 mercury 9 mercurial
quick-tempered: 5 angry, cross, fiery, testy 6 cranky, snappy, touchy 7 grouchy, peppery, waspish 8 choleric, petulant, shrewish, snappish, wrathful 9 excitable, impatient, irascible, irritable, sensitive, splenetic
quick-witted: 3 apt 4 keen 5 acute, agile, alert, canny, quick, ready, savvy, sharp, slick, smart, witty 6 astute, brainy, bright, clever, nimble, prompt, shrewd 7 jesting, knowing 8 humorous 9 astucious, brilliant, facetious, ingenious, inventive, on the ball, sprightly
quid: 4 chaw 5 money 9 sovereign
pro quo: 6 barter 8 exchange, reprisal 10 substitute
Quidde, Ludwig: 8 Nobelist, pacifist
quiddity: 6 entity, nicety, nuance 7 essence 8 badinage, subtlety
quidnunc: 3 pry 5 snoop, yenta 6 gossip 7 meddler, Paul Pry, snooper 8 busybody 10 nosy Parker
like a ~: 4 nosy 5 nosey
quid pro quo: 4 swap, swop 5 trade
Quién ___?: 4 sabe
quiescence: 4 ease, lull, rest 6 repose, stasis 7 latency, silence 8 abeyance 10 inactivity
quiescent: 4 calm, cool 5 inert, quiet, still 6 at rest, latent, low-key, mellow, placid, sedate, serene 7 abeyant, amiable, at peace, dormant, equable, pacific, passive, relaxed, stoical, unmoved 8 amicable, composed, inactive, laid-back, peaceful, tranquil, unmoving 9 collected, easy-going, immovable, impassive, inanimate, potential, temperate, unexcited, unruffled 10 motionless, stationary, unagitated, untroubled
quiet: 3 gag, ice, lay, low, mum, shy 4 calm, cool, dumb, ease, easy, hush, lick, lull, meek, mild, mute, rest, soft, stop 5 allay, bated, can it, choke, close, faint, inert, light, muted, peace, piano, quell, relax, shush, slack, sober, still 6 becalm, clam up, cool it, deaden, docile, gentle, hushed, lonely, low-key, mellow, modest, muffle, muzzle, pacify, placid, repose, secret, sedate, serene, settle, shut up, silent, simple, smooth, soften, soothe, squash, stable, subdue 7 amiable, appease, assuage, at peace, console, cool out, dead air, easeful, equable, halcyon, harmony, leisure, mollify, muffled, orderly, pacific, privacy, private, put down, relaxed, relieve, restful, retired, satisfy, silence, squelch, stilled, stoical, subdued, unmoved 8 amicable, becalmed, calm down, calmness, composed, dampened, deadened, hushed up, inactive, isolated, laid-back, mitigate, moderate, murmured, palliate, peaceful, reserved, reticent, retiring, secluded, serenity, stagnant, stealthy, taciturn, tasteful, tone down, tranquil 9 cessation, clammed up, collected, contented, easy-going, impassive, inaudible, noiseless, peaceable, placidity, quiescent, reconcile, seclusion, secretive, soft-pedal, soundless, stillness, temperate, toned down, unexcited, unruffled, unuttered, voiceless, whispered 10 ameliorate, buttoned up, coolheaded, hold it down, low-pitched, motionless, nonviolent, relaxation, restrained, speechless, turned down, unagitated, unassuming, uneventful, unspeaking, untroubled
be ~: 3 sit 4 hush 5 bag it, can it, shush 6 clam up, hush up, shut up 7 silence 8 pipe down
become ~: 4 lull 5 abate, cease 6 recede 7 die down, subside 8 moderate
down: 4 calm, hush, lull 5 abate 6 pacify, subdue, unwind 7 silence
exclamation of ~: 3 shh 4 hush 5 shush 7 hushaby, silence
greeting: 3 nod 4 wave
in music: 5 tacet
make ~: 6 muffle, shut up 7 silence
one: 4 clam 5 mouse
on the ~: 7 sub rosa 8 secretly
partner: 5 peace
peace and ~: 6 relief 8 solitude
period: 4 calm, lull
suffix for ~: 3 ude
quiet ___: 3 sun 4 time
Quiet ___: 4 City, Riot 7 Village
Quiet ___, The: 3 Don, Man 4 Dust
Quiet!: 3 shh 4 hush 5 bag it, can it, shush 6 hush up, shut up 7 silence 8 pipe down
quiet as a ___: 4 lamb 5 mouse
Quiet City composer: 7 Copland
Quiet Don, The author: 9 Sholokhov
Quiet Dust, The author: William Styron
quieten: 6 muffle 7 subside
quietly: 7 lightly 8 secretly
move ~: 5 slink, steal 7 slither
very ~ in music: 3 ppp
Quiet Man, The (1952 film)
cast: Barry Fitzgerald, Victor McLaglen, Maureen O'Hara, John Wayne
director: John Ford
quietness: 4 calm, ease 7 reserve, silence 8 calmness, serenity
Quiet on the ___!: 3 set
___ Quiet on the Western Front: 3 All
quietude: 4 calm, hush, rest 5 peace, quiet 6 repose 8 serenity
quietus: 3 end 4 rest 7 silence
Quiet Village singer: 5 Denny
Quigley Down Under (1990 film)
cast: Alan Rickman, Laura San Giacomo, Tom Selleck
quill: 3 pen 5 plume, spine 7 calamus, feather
ender: 4 back, work, wort
partner: 6 inkpot
tip: 3 nib
Quiller-Couch, Anthony: 6 author, writer 7 British
Quiller Memorandum, The (1966 film)
cast: Sir Alec Guinness, George Segal, Max von Sydow
Quills (2000 film)
cast: Michael Caine, Joaquin Phoenix, Geoffrey Rush, Kate Winslet
Quilmes: 4 city, town
locale: 9 Argentina
Quilpué: 4 city, town
locale: 5 Chile
quilt: 3 sew 4 pouf, puff 5 cover, duvet, piece 6 spread 7 bedding, blanket 8 bedcover, coverlet, coverlid 9 comforter, eiderdown, patchwork
crazy ~: 4 olio 6 jumble, medley 7 mélange 8 mishmash, mixed bag, pastiche 9 pasticcio, patchwork, potpourri 10 assortment, hodgepodge, miscellany, salmagundi
material: 4 batt, down 5 cloky, eider, patch 6 calico, cloque
quilting ___: 3 bee
___-Quilt, The: 5 Crazy
quince: 4 pome, tree 5 fruit
family: 4 rose
relative: 4 pear, plum 5 apple, peach 6 almond, cherry, medlar 7 apricot 8 hawthorn, oiticica 10 blackthorn
Quincy: 4 city, town 5 Jones, Magoo 6 Josiah, Porter
locale: 3 Ill. 4 Mass. 8 Illinois
___ Quincy Adams: 4 John
Quincy, M.E. (NBC drama)
cast: Robert Ito (Sam Fujiyama) Jack Klugman (Dr. Quincy)
Quindlen: 4 Anna

Quine: 7 Richard
quinella: 3 bet 5 wager
  kin: 6 exacta 8 perfecta
Qui Nhon: 4 city, town
  locale: 7 Vietnam
quinine: 7 bitters
  like ~: 4 sour, tart 5 acerb 6 bitter 7 acerbic
  water: 5 tonic
Quinlan, Kathleen: 7 actress
  film: Apollo 13 (1995)
    The Doors (1991)
    I Never Promised You... (1977)
    My Giant (1998)
Quinn: 5 Aidan 6 Martin 7 Anthony 8 Cummings
___ Quinn: 6 Mighty
Quinn, Aidan: 5 actor
  film: At Play in the Fields... (1991)
    Avalon (1990)
    Benny & Joon (1993)
    Crusoe (1988)
    Desperately Seeking Susan (1985)
    Michael Collins (1996)
    Music of the Heart (1999)
    Practical Magic (1998)
    Songcatcher (2001)
    Stakeout (1987)
    Stolen Summer (2002)
Quinn, Anthony: 5 actor
  film: Across 110th Street (1972)
    Back to Bataan (1945)
    Barabbas (1962)
    The Brave Bulls (1951)
    The Buccaneer (1958)
    The Destructors (1974)
    A Dream of Kings (1969)
    The Guns of Navarone (1961)
    La Strada (1954)
    Last Train From Gun Hill (1959)
    Lawrence of Arabia (1962)
    Lost Command (1966)
    Lust for Life (1956, AA)
    The Ox-Bow Incident (1943)
    Requiem for a Heavyweight (1962)
    Revenge (1990)
    The Ride Back (1957)
    The River's Edge (1957)
    Road to Morocco (1942)
    Sinbad the Sailor (1947)
    Viva Zapata! (1952, AA)
    A Walk in the Clouds (1995)
    Warlock (1959)
    Zorba the Greek (1964)
quinoa: 3 nut 6 cereal
Quintana Roo: 5 state 7 Mexican
  city: 6 Cancún 7 Cozumel 8 Chetumal
  see also Spanish
quintessence: 4 core, gist, meat, pith, root, soul, type 5 heart, model, stuff 6 kernel, marrow, spirit 7 epitome, essence, extract 8 quiddity 9 lifeblood, substance
quintessential: 5 ideal, model, typic 6 innate 7 classic, typical 9 necessary
quintet: 4 five 5 combo, group 6 pentad 8 ensemble, fivesome
  alphabet ~: 5 ABCDE, AEIOU, BCDEF, CDEFG, DEFGH, EFGHI, EIEIO, FGHIJ, GHIJK, HIJKL, IJKLM, JKLMN, KLMNO, LMNOP, MNOPQ, NOPQR, OPQRS, PQRST, QRSTU, RSTUV, STUVW, TUVWX, UVWXY, VWXYZ 6 vowels
  string ~ member: 4 bass 5 cello, viola 6 violin 10 double-bass
___ quintet: 5 piano
___ Quintet: 5 Trout
quintillion prefix: 3 exa-
quintillionth prefix: 4 atto-
quinto: 4 drum
  origin: 4 Cuba 6 Africa
quinton: 4 viol 6 string
Quint's boat: 4 Orca
___ Quinze: 5 Louis
quip: 3 gag, mot, pun 4 barb, gibe, jape, jeer, jest, jibe, joke 5 ad-lib, crack, sally, spoof 6 banter, bon mot, insult, japery, retort, ripost, satire, zinger 7 epigram, mockery, offense, riposte 8 badinage, drollery, laconism, one-liner, repartee 9 wisecrack, witticism 10 pleasantry
  ender: 4 ster
  quick with a ~: 4 glib 5 witty
quipster: 3 wag, wit 4 card 5 clown, comic, joker 8 comedian, humorist 9 jokesmith 10 smart aleck
quipu maker: 4 Inca
quirk: 3 tic 4 kink, turn, whim 5 fancy, fluke, habit, thing, trait, trick, twist 6 fetich, fetish, foible, hang-up, oddity, vagary, whimsy 7 anomaly, caprice, conceit, whimsey 8 crotchet 9 aberrance, attribute, exception, mannerism 10 aberration
quirky: 3 odd 4 eery 5 eerie, funky, weird 6 atypic, freaky, tricky 7 bizarre, deviant, offbeat, strange, unusual 8 aberrant, atypical, freakish, peculiar, uncommon 9 anomalous, divergent, eccentric, fantastic, irregular 10 capricious, unorthodox
Quiroga: 4 city, town
  locale: 6 Mexico 9 Michoacán
quirt: 4 lash, whip
Quisenberry: 3 Dan
quisling: 5 snake, viper 7 traitor 8 turncoat 10 subversive
Quisp: 6 cereal
  competitor: 3 Kix 4 Life, Trix 5 Kashi, Total 6 Kaboom, Muesli, Oreo O's, Pablum, Smacks 7 All-Bran, Crispix, Harmony, Hunny B's, Mueslix, Oat Bran, Pokemon 8 Boo Berry, Cheerios, Corn Chex, Corn Pops, Fiber One, Rice Chex, Special K, Uncle Sam, Wheaties 9 Alpha Bits, Apple Zaps, Grape Nuts, Honey Comb, Just Right, Wheat Chex 10 Apple Jacks, Bran Flakes, Cap'n Crunch, Cocoa Puffs, Froot Loops, Mini-Wheats, Nutri-Grain, Puffed Rice, Quaker Oats, Smart Start 11 Cocoa Blasts, Cookie Crisp, Golden Crisp, Lucky Charms, Puffed Wheat, Sweet Crunch, Waffle Crisp
quit: 2 go 3 end 4 drop, exit, fold, gone, halt, kick, part, stop 5 cease, close, forgo, leave, let up, yield 6 bow out, cop out, cut out, decamp, depart, desert, desist, expire, finish, forego, get out, give up, lay off, relent, resign, retire, secede, strike, vacate, wind up, wrap up 7 abandon, abscond, adjourn, bail out, break up, concede, conk out, drop out, forsake, pull out, push off, refrain, satisfy, scuttle, succumb, suspend, take off, walk out 8 abdicate, break off, check out, conclude, cut it out, give over, hang it up, kick over, knock off, leave off, light out, pack it in, renounce, run out on, say uncle, shove off, skip town, step down, swear off, withdraw 9 leave flat, liquidate, pull out of, stand down, surrender, take a hike, terminate, throw over, walk out on 10 call it a day, chicken out, give notice, go away from, knock it off, relinquish
  ender: 4 rent 5 claim
.... ___ quit!: 3 or I
quitch: 5 grass
quitclaim: 4 deed 8 abdicate
quite: 2 ay, da, ja, sí, so 3 all, aye, far, oui, yea, yep, yup 4 fine, just, oh so, okay, sure, very, well, yeah 5 fully, good-o, natch, plumb, right, roger, sheer, stark, truly, uh-huh 6 agreed, ever so, fairly, gladly, good-oh, highly, hugely, indeed, in fact, in toto, just so, pretty, purely, rather, really, righto, surely, wholly, you bet, yowzah 7 assuage, exactly, go ahead, greatly, indeedy, in truth, largely, mais oui, ten-four, totally, utterly 8 actually, all right, as you say, entirely, for a fact, of course, somewhat, thumbs up, very well 9 be my guest, certainly, darn right, decidedly, extremely, in reality, naturally, perfectly, precisely, seriously, sure thing, you betcha, you said it 10 absolutely, altogether, by all means, completely, definitely, moderately, more or less, noticeably, positively, reasonably, relatively, remarkably, sure enough, that's right, thoroughly
  a while: 3 eon 4 aeon, days
quite ___: 4 a few 6 enough
Quito: 4 city, town 7 capital
  locale: 7 Ecuador
  see also Spanish
quits, call it: 4 halt, stop 5 cease, yield
quittance: 7 receipt, redress
quitter: 4 wimp 5 mouse 6 coward 7 chicken 8 deserter, weakling 9 fraidy-cat, jellyfish 10 scaredy-cat
  toss: 5 towel
  word: 4 can't 5 uncle 6 cannot
quitting time for some: 3 six 4 five
quiver: 3 tic, wag 4 beat, jerk, lick, rock, stir 5 nidge, pulse, quake, shake, sheaf, spasm, throb 6 cringe, jitter, shiver, teeter, thrill, totter, tremor, twitch 7 pulsate, shimmer, shudder, sparkle, tremble, vibrate 8 convulse 9 oscillate, palpitate, vibration
  carrier: 6 archer, bowman 9 Robin Hood 10 longbowman
  item: 5 arrow
quivering: 5 jumpy, shaky 7 jittery 9 tremulous, vibration
  motion: 3 tic 6 tremor
  tree: 5 aspen
Quivers: 5 Robin
quivery: 7 fearful 9 tremulous
qui vive, on the: 4 wary 5 alert, aware, sharp 6 uneasy 7 heads-up, heedful, wakeful 8 keen-eyed, vigilant, watchful
Quixote, Don: 6 knight
  horse: 9 Rocinante, Rosinante
  see also Don Quixote
quixotic: 6 dreamy 7 utopian 8 chimeric, delusive, fanciful, romantic 9 imaginary, visionary 10 chimerical, idealistic
quiz: 3 ask 4 exam, hoax, pump, test 5 check, grill, prank, probe, query 6 lesson 7 enquire, examine, inquire 8 blue book, querying, question 9 catechize, check up on, interview
  answer: 4 true 5 false
quiz ___: 3 kid 4 show 7 program
___ quiz: 3 pop
Quiz Kids, The: 9 radio show
quiz show: 4 game
  need: 5 booth 6 buzzer 10 contestant
  radio ~: 4 Dr. IQ
  VIP: 2 MC 4 host 5 emcee
Quiz Show (1994 film)
  cast: Ralph Fiennes, Rob Morrow, Paul Scofield, John Turturro
  character: 4 Herb 5 Barry 7 Enright, Goodwin, Stempel 8 Van Doren
  director: Robert Redford
quizzical: 3 odd 4 arch 5 droll 6 show-me 7 amusing, comical, curious, mocking, off-beat, peering, probing, teasing 8 confused, derisive, peculiar, sardonic 9 bantering, eccentric, inquiring, laughable, searching, skeptical, whimsical 10 suspicious
quizzing: 7 enquiry, inquiry
Q-U link: 3 RST
Qum: 4 city, town 5 river
  country: 4 Iran
___ Qum: 4 Qara 5 Qizil
Qumran inhabitant: 6 Essene
quo
  quid pro ~: 6 barter 8 exchange, reprisal 10 substitute
  status ~: 8 reaction 9 condition, situation
___ quo: 6 status
Quo ___?: 5 Vadis
quod ___ demonstrandum: 4 erat
quod ___ faciendum: 4 erat
quodlibet, like a: 4 moot
quoin: 4 nook 5 wedge 8 keystone
quoits: 4 game 7 pastime
  peg: 3 hob
  play ~: 4 toss 5 throw
quondam: 3 old 4 erst, late, once, past 6 bygone, former 7 old-time, one-time 8 previous 9 erstwhile
Quonset hut: 8 barracks, quarters
Quorum: 4 font 8 typeface
quota: 3 cut, lot 4 goal, part, rate 5 chunk, floor, limit, piece, ratio, share, slice 6 ration 7 ceiling, measure, portion 8 quantity 9 allotment, allowance 10 allocation, assignment, complement, contingent, percentage, proportion
  meeting the ~: 6 enough 8 adequate 10 acceptable, sufficient
  off one's ~: 4 slow 6 behind 7 lagging 8 trailing 9 in arrears 10 delinquent
quota ___: 6 system
quotation: 3 bid 4 cost, rate, text 5 price 6 charge, citing, figure, saying, tender 7 cutting, excerpt, extract, passage 8 bid price, citation 9 reference, selection 10 recitation
  attribution: 4 anon., Shak. 9 anonymous
quotation ___: 4 mark
quotations: 8 analecta, analects
quote: 3 bid 4 cite, cost, rate 5 price, refer 6 adduce, attest, charge, figure, parrot, recite, repeat, retell, saying, tender 7 excerpt, extract, mention, passage, refer to 8 allude to, bid price, citation 9 recollect, reference, selection 10 paraphrase
  quote ___: 4 mark
  source: 3 ASE, OTC 4 NYSE 9 Bartlett's
___ quotes: 4 open 5 close 6 double, single
Quoth the ___...: 5 raven
quotidian: 5 daily, usual 6 common 7 diurnal, per diem, routine 8 everyday, ordinary 9 hackneyed
quotient: 5 share 6 result
quotient ___: 4 ring 5 group, space
Quo Vadis? (1951 film)
  cast: Deborah Kerr, Robert Taylor, Peter Ustinov
  character: 4 Nero 5 Actea, Aulus, Croto, Lygia, Peter, Ursus 6 Eunice, Seneca
  director: Mervyn LeRoy
  garb: 4 toga
qurush: 5 money
QVC: 7 channel
  alternative: 3 HSN 7 ShopNBC
Q-V connection: 4 RSTU
q.v., part of: 4 quod, vide
Q-W connection: 5 RSTUV
QWERTY alternative: 6 Dvorak

R: 6 letter, rating
and B: 4 soul 5 music
and R: 5 leave 7 time off 8 down time, furlough, vacation 10 recreation
followers: 3 STU 4 STUV 5 STUVW
in phonetic alphabet: 5 Romeo
issuer: 4 MPAA
preceders: 3 OPQ 4 NOPQ 5 MNOPQ
R ___: 4 and B, and D, and R 6 factor 7 horizon
R ___ rat: 4 as in
R-___: 5 rated, value
Ra: 3 god 4 boat, elem., ship 6 radium, sun god 7 element
88 for ~: 4 at. no.
enemy: 7 Apophis
symbol of ~: 4 Aten, Aton
___-Ra: 4 Amen, Amon
Raabe, Wilhelm: 6 German, writer
raad: 4 fish 7 catfish
Rabat: 4 city, port, town 7 capital
locale: 7 Morocco
rabbet: 6 furrow, groove, joiner
rabbet ___: 5 joint, plane
rabbi: 3 Jew 6 cleric 8 chaplain, minister 10 theologian
detective: 5 Small
place: 4 shul 5 schul 9 synagogue
Rabbi Ben Ezra author: Robert Browning
rabbinate: 6 clergy 8 ministry
rabbinical: 8 clerical
sch.: 3 sem.
rabbit: 3 fur, pet 4 cony 5 bunny, coney 6 animal, hopper, jumper, mammal 10 cottontail
breed: 6 angora
cousin: 4 hare
ears: 6 aerial, dipole 7 antenna
feature: 3 ear
female ~: 3 doe
fictional ~: 4 Br'er, Bugs 5 Mopsy, Peter, Roger 6 Flopsy 8 Crusader 9 Bugs Bunny 10 Cottontail
food: 5 salad 6 carrot, greens
foot: 3 paw
fur: 4 cony 5 coney, lapin
home: 5 hutch 6 burrow
like some ~ ears: 4 alop
male ~: 4 buck
starter: 4 jack
tail: 4 scut
Welsh ~ ingredient: 6 cheese
young: 5 bunny 6 kitten
rabbit ___: 4 ball, ears, food, test 5 punch 6 warren
___ rabbit: 4 rock, wood 5 swamp, Welsh 6 Angora
Rabbit: 2 VW 3 car 4 auto 10 automobile, Maranville, Volkswagen
Rabbit ___: 5 Redux
Rabbit, ___: 3 Run
___ Rabbit: 4 Br'er 5 Peter, White
Rabbit at Rest author: John Updike
rabbit-eared bandicoot: 5 bilbi, bilby
Rabbit is Rich author: John Updike
rabbitlike mammal: 4 mara, pika 6 agouti
___ rabbit out: 5 pull a
Rabbit Redux author: John Updike
Rabbit, Run author: John Updike
rabbit's foot: 5 charm 6 amulet 8 talisman
Rabbitt, Eddie
song: Drivin' My Life Away (1980)
I Love a Rainy Night (1980)
Step by Step (1981)
Suspicions (1979)
You and I (1982)
rabble: 3 mob 4 gang, herd, mass, pack, raff, ring, riot, scum 5 crowd, dregs, drove, flock, horde 6 masses, people, throng 7 beggary 8 riffraff 9 commoners, gathering, hoi polloi, multitude 10 lower class
in French: 8 canaille
Rabble in Arms author: Kenneth Roberts
rabble-rouser: 7 inciter 8 agitator, inflamer 9 demagogue, firebrand 10 instigator
Rabe, David: 9 dramatist 10 playwright
spouse: Jill Clayburgh
work: The Basic Training of Pavlo Hummel
The Crossing Guard
Goose and Tomtom
Hurlyburly
I'm Dancing as Fast as I Can
In the Boom Boom Room
The Orphan
A Question of Mercy
Recital of the Dog
Sticks and Bones
Streamers
Those the River Keeps
Rabelais, François: 6 French, writer 8 humanist
work: Gargantua and Pantagruel
rabid: 3 mad 4 wild 5 feral, manic, ultra 6 crazed, ferine, raging, savage 7 beastly, berserk, bigoted, hog-wild, radical, untamed, violent, zealous 8 frenzied, in a furor, maniacal, obsessed, unbroken, vehement, white-hot, wild-eyed 9 delirious, fanatical, ferocious, unbridled, wrought-up 10 hysterical, infuriated
rabidity: 4 fury 5 wrath 6 frenzy 7 passion 8 ferocity 9 intensity, vehemence 10 fierceness
rabidly: 4 very 5 madly 7 acutely, greatly 9 devotedly, fervently, intensely, like crazy, zealously 10 thoroughly
rabies: 5 lyssa
like ~: 5 viral
Rabi, Isidor: 8 Nobelist 9 physicist, scientist
Rabindranath: 6 Tagore
Rabin, Yitzhak: 7 Israeli 8 Nobelist
predecessor: 4 Meir 6 Shamir
successor: 5 Begin, Peres
___-Ra-Boom-De-Ré: 4 Ta-Ra
raccoon: 3 fur 6 animal, mammal
cousin: 5 coati, panda
male ~: 4 boar
marking: 4 mask
to farmers: 6 bandit
Raccoon, city on the: 9 Des Moines
race: 3 fly, hie, rip, run, zip 4 bolt, clan, dart, dash, drag, flit, heat, meet, pelt, post, rill, rush, scud, sort, tear, tide, whiz, zoom 5 blood, breed, brook, chase, color, creek, derby, event, hurry, match, relay, rille, river, scoot, scram, shoot, spank, speed, tribe, whisk 6 barrel, careen, career, course, family, gallop, hasten, hurtle, hustle, Le Mans, move it, nation, people, rocket, runlet, runnel, scurry, slalom, sluice, sprint, stream 7 channel, compete, contest, culture, current, floor it, hop to it, lineage, progeny, pursuit, quicken, rivulet, scamper, scuttle, species, tear off 8 campaign, election, hightail, light out, make time, marathon, outstrip, scramble, step on it, undertow, waterway 9 go quickly, hotfoot it, shake a leg, skedaddle, streamlet, whip along 10 get a move on, go pell-mell, hightail it, lose no time, make tracks
an engine: 3 rev
auto ~: 4 Indy 5 rally 6 enduro, Le Mans 7 Daytona
combining form: 4 geno-, phyl- 5 ethno-, phylo-
competitor: 5 entry
course: 4 oval
downhill: 3 ski 4 skee
ender: 3 car, way 5 horse, track 6 course, runner
fabled ~ loser: 4 hare
human ~: 3 man 5 world 6 people 7 mankind
join the rat ~: 4 moil, slog, toil 5 labor, slave, sweat 6 drudge, hustle, strive 7 achieve, peg away 8 plug away 9 freelance, grind away, moonlight 10 buckle down
marker: 5 pylon
mythical ~: 7 Amazons
official: 5 timer
out of the rat ~: 4 retd. 7 retired
place: 4 gate, tape
preliminary ~: 4 heat
prize: 5 medal, purse
rat ~: 3 rut 5 grind 7 society 8 drudgery 10 livelihood
starter: 3 gun 4 foot, head, mill, tail 5 horse
Triple Crown ~: 5 Derby 7 Belmont 9 Preakness
type of ~: 4 ten K 5 derby, relay 8 marathon
unit: 3 lap 4 mile, yard 5 meter
race ___: 5 plate 7 walking
race-___: 4 walk
___ race: 3 rat 4 arms, drag, flat, foot, post, road, sack 5 horse, human, relay, stake 6 barrel, potato, stakes 7 bicycle, harness, produce, selling
Race: 4 cape
locale: 6 Canada
race against ___: 4 time
racecar: 3 GTO 6 hot rod
engine: 5 turbo
sound: 5 vroom 6 varoom
sponsor: 3 STP
racehorse: 3 nag 4 pony 5 pacer
certain ~: 4 mare 5 filly
racer: 5 miler, snake, yacht 6 animal, hot rod, jockey, runner 7 harrier, hurdler, reptile, speeder, trotter 8 dragster, sprinter 9 greyhound 10 speed demon
Aesop ~: 4 hare 8 tortoise
downhill ~: 3 ski 4 luge, skee, sled 5 skier
gauge: 4 tach
kid's ~: 4 kart 6 go-cart, go-kart
Olympics ~: 4 luge 5 rower, scull 10 marathoner
relative: 3 asp, boa 5 aboma, adder, cobra, krait, mamba, viper 6 dhaman, python, taipan 7 markhor, rattler 8 anaconda, moccasin, ringhals 9 boomslang, coachwhip 10 bushmaster, copperhead, sidewinder
track ~: 4 kart 5 horse 6 equine 8 sprinter
___ racer: 4 blue, slot 5 black
Racer's Edge, The: 3 STP
racetrack: 4 oval, turf 6 course
alternative: 3 OTB
Ancient Greek ~: 6 dromos
ancient Roman ~ marker: 4 meta
boundary: 4 rail
British ~: 5 Ascot, Epsom
California ~: 6 Del Mar 10 Santa Anita
circuit: 3 lap
combining form: 5 -drome
figure: 4 odds, tout 6 jockey
like ~ curves: 6 banked
margin: 4 neck, nose
NYC: 4 Big A 8 Aqueduct
painter of ~ scenes: 5 Degas
prop: 4 gate
wager: 6 exacta 8 perfecta, quinella 9 quiniella
Rachael Leigh ___: 4 Cook
Rachel: 4 Ward 5 Field, Weisz 6 Carson, Hunter 7 Jackson, Roberts, Ticotin 9 de Queiròs
father of ~: 5 Laban
husband of ~: 5 Jacob
in Spanish: 6 Raquel
sister of ~: 4 Leah
son of ~: 6 Joseph 8 Benjamin
Rachel and the Stranger (1948 film)
cast: William Holden, Robert Mitchum, Loretta Young
director: Norman Foster
Rachel Papers, The author: Martin Amis
Rachel, Rachel (1968 film)
cast: Kate Harrington, James Olson, Joanne Woodward
director: Paul Newman
Rachins: 4 Alan
rachis: 5 spine
Rachmaninoff: 5 Serge 6 Sergei, Sergey 7 pianist, Russian 8 composer
racial: 6 ethnic, lineal, tribal 7 genetic 8 national 9 ancestral, genetical 10 hereditary
Racine: 4 city, Jean, town
locale: 9 Wisconsin
see also French
Racine, Jean: 6 French 10 playwright
work: Andromaque
Britannicus
Esther
Iphigenie En Aulide
Phedre
racing: 4 fast 5 brisk, fleet, hasty, quick, rapid, sport, swift 6 speedy 7 express, hurried, instant 9 breakneck 10 double-time, supersonic
ancient Roman ~ post: 4 meta
car ~ org.: 4 NHRA 6 NASCAR
starter: 5 horse
vehicle: 4 bike, luge 5 scull, shell, yacht 6 hot rod 7 bicycle
world: 4 turf
see also race
racing ___: 3 car 4 flag, form 5 skate
___ racing: 4 auto, drag, road, slot 5 horse 6 barrel 7 harness
Racing With the Moon (1984 film)
cast: Nicolas Cage, Elizabeth McGovern, Sean Penn
director: Richard Benjamin
racism: 4 bias 7 bigotry 9 apartheid, prejudice 10 unfairness
rack: 3 try 4 lamb, pain, tear 5 frame, shelf, stand, wring 6 clouds, harrow, holder, siphon, strain, stress, syphon, wrench 7 afflict, antlers, oppress, stretch, torment, torture, trestle 8 aggrieve, distress 10 excruciate
and ruin: 5 havoc 7 debacle 8 calamity, shambles 9 cataclysm
element: 6 antler
for fodder: 4 crib
one's brains: 4 mull 5 think 6 puzzle 8 ruminate
partner: 4 ruin
starter: 3 hat, hay 4 book, coat
up: 3 get, win 4 gain 5 incur, reach, score 6 attain, secure 7 achieve, acquire, realize 8 hold on to 10 accumulate
rack ___: 3 car, out 4 rail, rate 7 railway
rack-___: 4 rent
___ rack: 3 ski 4 bomb, pipe 5 cloud,

hotel, on the, spice, towel, trash **7** clothes, helical, mooring
rack-and-__: **6** pinion
racket: **3** ado, din, job, lay, row **4** fuss, game, plot, push, riot, roar, scam, stir, talk, to-do, work **5** babel, blare, brawl, cheat, clash, crash, crime, dodge, fight, fraud, graft, hoo-ha, noise, sound, storm, theft, trick **6** battle, career, clamor, fracas, hoopla, hubbub, jangle, outcry, paddle, rip-off, rumpus, scheme, squall, tumult, uproar **7** calling, clangor, clatter, con game, discord, jobbery, pursuit, ruction, shuffle, squeeze, swindle, turmoil, wrangle **8** artifice, cheating, intrigue, shouting, squabble, thievery, vocation **9** agitation, commotion, dirty pool, extortion, shakedown, specialty, swindling **10** clattering, conspiracy, corruption, dishonesty, free-for-all, hullabaloo, hurly-burly, illegality, livelihood, occupation, turbulence, underworld
  ender: **3** eer
  game: **6** squash, tennis **8** lacrosse, Ping-Pong **9** badminton
  make a ~: **5** shout
  making a ~: **5** noisy
  sports ~: **6** crosse, paddle
  see also tennis
racketeer: **4** thug **5** crook, fraud **6** gunsel, outlaw **7** hoodlum, mobster **8** criminal, gangster **9** miscreant
racketeering statute: **4** RICO
Racket, The (1951 film)
  cast: Robert Mitchum, Robert Ryan, Lizabeth Scott
rackety: **5** forte, noisy **7** blaring, booming, jarring, pealing, raucous, reboant, roaring **8** crashing, piercing, strident, plangent, rumbling, sonorous, strident, turned up **9** big-voiced, clamorous, deafening **10** boisterous, resounding, stentorian, strepitous, thundering, uproarious, vociferous
racking: **5** acute **8** grueling **9** harrowing
__-racking: **5** nerve
rack of __: **4** lamb
rack one's __: **5** brain
Rackstraw, Ralph: **3** gob, tar
Rack, The (1956 film)
  cast: Wendell Corey, Paul Newman, Walter Pidgeon
raconteur: **7** reciter **10** anecdotist
racquet
  see racket
racquetball: **4** game **5** sport
  target: **4** wall
racy: **4** blue, lewd **5** bawdy, heady, lurid, salty, spicy, witty **6** erotic, lively, purple, ribald, risqué, smutty, snappy, spicey, vulgar **7** naughty, piquant, pungent, zestful **8** exciting, immodest, indecent, off-color, vigorous **9** energetic, sparkling, sprightly **10** indelicate, suggestive
  hardly ~: **4** dull, flat, tame **5** bland **6** boring, jejune **7** humdrum, insipid, prosaic, routine, subdued, tedious **9** colorless **10** dullsville
rad: **3** def **4** aces, A-one, boss, braw, cool, dece, fine, gear, good, keen, neat, nice, phat, tuff, wild **5** dandy, ducky, grand, great, marvy, neato, nobby, prime, slick, super, swell **6** bang on, bang-up, bonzer, bosker, choice, divine, dreamy, far out, gnarly, groovy, lovely, peachy, slap-up, spot on, superb, terrif, tiptop, unreal, whizzo, wicked **7** amazing, awesome, capital, corking, perfect, ripping, skookum, stellar, sublime **8** dazzling, especial, eximious, fabulous, five-star, four-star, frabjous, glorious, heavenly, jim-dandy, slam-bang, smashing, splendid, standout, sterling, stickout, superior, terrific, top-level, topnotch, very good, wondrous **9** bodacious, Endsville, excellent, exemplary, exquisite, extremist, first-rate, high-grade, hunky-dory, marvelous, sollicker, top-flight, wonderful **10** first-class, hotsy-totsy, jack-a-dandy, out of sight, peachy-keen, phenomenal, remarkable, stupendous, super-duper
rad.
  doubled: **3** dia. **4** diam.
Rada locale: **7** Ukraine
Radames' love: **4** Aïda
radar
  beacon: **5** racon
  ender: **5** scope
  flying ~ station: **5** AWACS
  image: **3** pip **4** blip, echo, scan
  laser ~: **5** lidar
  measure: **3** mph
radar __: **4** trap **6** beacon, picket
__ radar: **7** Doppler, weather
Radar: **7** O'Reilly
  home: **4** Iowa **7** Ottumwa
  milieu: **4** MASH
Radarange maker: **5** Amana
Radbourne, Hoss: **6** hurler **7** pitcher
Radcliff: **4** city, town
  locale: **8** Kentucky
Radcliffe: **3** Ann **7** college
  most ~ grads: **5** women
Radcliffe, Ann: **6** writer **7** English
  work: The Mysteries of Udolpho
Radford: **5** Basil **7** Michael
Radford, Michael: **8** director
  film: Nineteen Eighty-Four (1984)
    The Postman (1994)
    White Mischief (1988)
radial: **4** tire
  British ~: **4** tyre
  feature: **3** air **5** tread
  opposite of ~: **5** ulnar
  perpendicular to ~: **5** axial
radial __: **3** saw **4** tire **6** engine, motion
radiance: **3** joy **4** glow **5** blaze, glare, gleam, light, sheen, shine **6** beauty, dazzle, gaiety, gayety, luster, warmth **7** aureola, aureole, delight, glitter, rapture, sparkle **8** gloriole, pleasure, splendor **9** happiness **10** brightness, brilliance, effulgence, loveliness, luminosity
  surround with ~: **6** enhalo
radiant: **3** gay, lit **4** glad **5** aglow, happy, light, lucid, nitid, shiny, sunny **6** ablaze, agleam, bright, cheery, flashy, joyful, joyous, lucent **7** beaming, blazing, fulgent, glowing, lambent, shining **8** beatific, blissful, blooming, cheerful, dazzling, ecstatic, gleaming, glorious, luminous, lustrous, splendid **9** beautiful, brilliant, delighted, effulgent, gladdened, radiating, rapturous, refulgent, sparkling **10** flying high, glittering
  be ~: **4** glow **5** gleam, shine **7** glisten, shimmer, sparkle **9** luminesce
radiant __: **4** flux, heat **6** energy **7** heating
radiate: **4** beam, cast, emit, glow, part, pour, send, shed, spew, spue **5** eject, expel, exude, flash, gleam, issue, shine, split, strew, yield **6** afford, branch, expand, ramble, ramify, spread **7** bestrew, cast out, deviate, diffuse, diverge, emanate, give off, give out, glitter, light up, scatter, send out **8** illumine, separate, shoot out, sprinkle, throw off, throw out, transmit **9** bifurcate, branch out, broadcast, circulate, irradiate, luminesce, propagate, send forth, spread out **10** distribute
radiation: **4** aura **5** light **6** spread **8** emission **9** emanation **10** divergence
  cosmic ~ particle: **4** muon
  emit ~: **5** decay
  generator: **5** maser
  give off focused ~: **4** lase
  infrared ~: **4** heat
  monitoring org.: **3** EPA
  unit: **3** rem **5** curie **8** roentgen
radiation __: **3** fog **4** belt
__ radiation: **5** alpha **7** nuclear, thermal
radiator: **6** heater
  output: **4** heat **5** steam
  part: **4** coil, vane **5** grill **6** grille
  sound: **3** sss **4** ssss
radiator __: **5** grill **6** grille
radical: **5** basal, basic, rabid, rebel, ultra, vital **6** bottom, entire, far-out, innate, native, new-ave, primal, severe, way out **7** drastic, extreme, fanatic, lawless, leftist, liberal, natural, organic, primary, restive, riotous, violent **8** advanced, cardinal, complete, inherent, maverick, militant, mutinous, nihilist, objector, original, pacifist, profound, recusant, reformer, renegade, sweeping, thorough, ultimate, ultraist **9** anarchist, essential, excessive, extremist, fanatical, firebrand, insurgent, intrinsic, primitive, seditious **10** avant-garde, deep-seated, immoderate, left-winger, nihilistic, rebellious, refractory, stupendous, underlying
  change: **7** shake-up **8** upheaval **10** revolution
  onetime ~ grp.: **3** SDS, SLA **4** SNCC
  organic ~: **4** acyl, amyl, aryl **5** alkyl **6** acetyl
  politically ~: **4** left
radical __: **4** axis, chic, sign
__ radical: **4** acid, acyl, free **5** amino, vinyl **6** acetyl **7** acrylyl
Radical Chic author: Tom Wolfe
Radical, The author: George Eliot
radicle: **4** root
radii: **4** rays **5** bones **6** spokes
radio: **2** AM, CB, FM **5** media **7** boombox, Walkman **8** receiver, transmit, wireless **9** shortwave
  adjunct: **6** aerial **7** antenna
  AMC series ~ station: **4** WENN
  antenna: **6** dipole
  band: **2** AM, CB, FM **3** VLF
  broadcaster: **3** sta., stn. **7** station
  button: **5** on/off
  CB ~ knob: **3** vol. **6** volume **7** squelch
  control: **4** knob **5** tuner
  detecting and ranging: **5** radar
  discoverer of ~ waves: **5** Hertz
  ender: **3** man, men **4** thon **5** meter, phone **9** broadcast, telegraph, telephone
  enjoy a ~: **6** listen, tune in **8** listen in
  first all-sports ~ station: **4** WFAN
  first commercial ~ station: **4** KDKA
  format: **4** news, rock, talk **6** call-in, oldies, sports
  frequency band: **6** airway
  freq. unit: **3** MHz
  kind of ~: **4** AMFM
  London ~: **3** BBC
  message: **3** SOS
  network: **3** ABC, CBS, MBS, NBC, NPR **6** Mutual
  old ~ part: **4** tube
  operator: **3** ham **4** Cber
  overseer: **3** FCC
  part: **4** dial **5** diode
  put on the ~: **3** air **9** broadcast
  receiver: **3** set
  reply: **3** out **4** copy, over **5** roger, wilco
  spots: **3** ads
  stations: **5** media
  studio need: **4** mike
  studio sign: **5** on air
  talk-show participant: **6** caller
  transmitter: **5** tower
  tube gas: **5** argon, xenon
  type of ~ channel: **6** diplex
  US ~ service: **3** VOA
  worker: **2** DJ **6** deejay **8** engineer
radio __: **3** car **4** beam, star, taxi, tube, wave **6** beacon, galaxy, source, window **7** compass, horizon, station
__ radio: **4** AM FM, talk **5** clock, shock **7** college, crystal
Radio __: **4** Days, Ga-Ga **5** Flyer, Shack **7** Liberty
Radio __ Europe: **4** Free
__ Radio: **4** Talk **5** On the
radioactive: **3** hot
  element: **5** radon **6** curium, radium **7** bohrium, dubnium, fermium, hassium, thorium, uranium **8** actinium, astatine, francium, nobelium, polonium **9** americium, berkelium, neptunium, plutonium **10** lawrencium, meitnerium, promethium, seaborgium, technetium **11** californium, einsteinium, mendelevium **12** protactinium **13** rutherfordium
  gas: **5** radon
  particle: **4** beta
radioactive __: **5** decay **6** dating
radiocarbon-dating developer: **5** Libby
Radio Days (1987 film)
  cast: Jeff Daniels, Mia Farrow, Seth Green, Julie Kavner, Josh Mostel
  director: Woody Allen
  studio: **5** Orion
Radio Flyer: **5** wagon
Radio Flyer (1992 film)
  cast: Lorraine Bracco, John Heard, Elijah Wood
  director: Richard Donner
  dog: **5** Shane
Radio Free Europe artist: **3** R.E.M.
Radio Ga-Ga (1984 song) artist: Queen
radiogram: **4** wire **5** cable, telex **7** message
radiograph: **4** x-ray
radioman's nickname: **6** Sparks
radio shows (old-time):
  The Aldrich Family
  Amos 'n' Andy
  The Breakfast Club
  Burns and Allen
  Can You Top This?
  Double or Nothing
  Dr. I.Q.
  Duffy's Tavern
  Easy Aces
  Fibber McGee and Molly
  First Nighter
  Front Page Farrell
  The Great Gildersleeve
  The Green Hornet
  I Love a Mystery
  Information, Please!
  The Inner Sanctum Mysteries
  It Pays to Be Ignorant
  Jack Armstrong, the All-American Boy
  John's Other Wife
  Let's Pretend
  Life Can Be Beautiful
  Lights Out
  Lora Lawton
  Lorenzo Jones
  Lum and Abner
  Lux Radio Theatre
  Ma Perkins
  The March of Time
  Mary Noble, Backstage Wife

Meet Corliss Archer
Melody Ranch
Mr. Keen, Tracer of Lost Persons
Myrt and Marge
One Man's Family
Our Gal Sunday
Pepper Young's Family
Portia Faces Life
The Quiz Kids
The Right to Happiness
The Road of Life
The Romance of Helen Trent
The Shadow
The Story of Mary Marlin
Suspense
Today's Children
Valiant Lady
Vic and Sade
Vox Pop
When a Girl Marries
Young Dr. Malone
Young Widder Brown
Your Hit Parade
__ Radio Theatre: 3 Lux
radish: 4 root 6 veggie 9 appetizer, vegetable
Japanese ~: 6 daikon
starter: 5 horse
Radisson: 5 hotel
alternative: 4 Omni 5 Hyatt 6 Hilton, Westin 7 Wyndham 8 Marriott, Sheraton 10 DoubleTree 11 Crowne Plaza, Four Seasons
radium: 5 metal 7 element
radius: 4 bone, span 5 ambit, limit, orbit, range, reach, scope, space, spoke, sweep 6 extent, length 7 compass, expanse, purview 8 boundary, interval 9 extension
companion: 4 ulna
locale: 3 arm 7 forearm
radius __: 3 rod 6 vector
radix: 4 root
RAdm employer: 3 USN
Radner, Gilda spouse: Gene Wilder
Radnor: 4 city, town
locale: 4 Penn.
Rado: 5 watch 10 wristwatch
alternative: 4 Ebel 5 Casio, Elgin, Lorus, Omega, Rolex, Seiko, Timex 6 Bulova, Fossil, Movado, Pulsar, Swatch 7 Citizen 8 Longines, Tag Heuer, Tourneau
radon: 3 gas 7 element 8 noble gas
former name: 5 niton
like ~: 5 inert
Radziwill: 3 Lee
sister: 6 Jackie 10 Jacqueline
Rae: 3 Bob 4 John 9 Charlotte
Rae __: 6 Strait
__ Rae: 5 Norma
Rae Dawn __: 5 Chong
Rae, John: 8 explorer
Raf: 7 Vallone
RAF
auxiliary: 4 WAAF
award: 3 DFM
flyer: 4 Brit 6 airman
Rafael: 7 Alberti, Kubelik 8 Palmeiro
__ Rafael, CA: 3 San
Rafelson, Bob: 8 director
film: Black Widow (1987)
Five Easy Pieces (1970)
Head (1968)
The King of Marvin Gardens (1972)
Mountains of the Moon (1990)
Stay Hungry (1976)
Rafer: 7 Johnson
raff: 6 masses, rabble 9 commoners, hoi polloi, multitude
raffee: 4 sail
Rafferty: 5 Gerry
raffia: 4 palm
Raffin: 7 Deborah
raffish: 3 gay 4 fast, wild 5 cheap, crude 6 casual, coarse, jaunty, rakish, sporty, tawdry, trashy, vulgar 7 boorish, dashing, ill-bred, loutish, uncouth 8 bohemian, careless, unseemly 9 dissolute, tasteless, unrefined 10 picaresque
raffle: 4 game, lots, pool 5 flier, flyer 7 benefit, drawing, lottery 10 sweepstake
offering: 5 prize 6 chance
Raffles (1930 film)
cast: Ronald Colman, Bramwell Fletcher, Kay Francis
rafflesia: 5 plant 6 flower
Rafsanjani: 5 Irani
raft: 3 lot, ton 4 boat, heap, host, pile, slew 5 bunch, craft, scads 6 oodles, passel 7 vehicle
noted papyrus ~: 3 Ra I 4 Ra II
propel a ~: 4 pole
user: 5 poler
wood: 5 balsa
__ raft: 4 life
rafter: 4 beam 5 brace, joist 6 girder, timber 9 crossbeam
locale: 4 roof
thrill: 5 chute 6 rapids
__ rafter: 4 jack, knee 5 crook 6 common 7 binding, compass, cushion
Rafter, Patrick: 7 netster 9 tennis pro
milieu: 5 court
Raft, George: 5 actor
film: Background to Danger (1943)
The Bowery (1933)
Broadway (1942)
Each Dawn I Die (1939)
Follow the Boys (1944)
The Glass Key (1935)
If I Had a Million (1932)
Invisible Stripes (1939)
Johnny Angel (1945)
Manpower (1941)
Nocturne (1946)
Rogue Cop (1954)
Scarface (1932)
She Couldn't Take It (1935)
Some Like It Hot (1959)
Souls at Sea (1937)
Spawn of the North (1938)
They Drive by Night (1940)
rafting: 5 sport
whitewater ~ site: 5 cañon 6 canyon
rafts: 4 a lot, much 5 no end, reams 6 highly 7 greatly
rag: 3 kid, rib 4 bait, gibe, jibe, mock, ride, twit 5 abuse, annoy, beset, blame, chide, cloth, harry, paper, roast, scoff, scold, scrap, shred, taunt, tease, tweak, wiper 6 badger, berate, bother, deride, duster, harass, heckle, noodge, pester, plague, rebuke, tatter 7 censure, chew out, lecture, reprove, tabloid, torment, toy with, upbraid 8 admonish, badinage, chastise, irritate, magazine, reproach, ridicule 9 castigate, dishcloth, dress down, dustcloth, make fun of, newspaper, persecute, poke fun at, reprimand 10 hand-me-down, make game of, periodical, take to task, tongue-lash, trifle with
chew the ~: 3 gab, jaw, rap, yak, yap 4 chat, talk 5 prate 6 gossip, jabber, parley, patter 7 blabber, blather, chatter, prattle 8 chitchat, schmooze 10 yakkety-yak
doll: 3 Ann 4 Andy
ender: 3 bag, man, men, tag, top 4 time, weed, wort
like a wet ~: 4 limp
man: 6 Joplin
starter: 4 dish, wash
use a ~: 4 wipe
rag __: 3 rug 4 bolt, doll 5 gourd, paper, trade 6 picker
Rag __: 3 Mop 4 Doll
__ Rag: 5 Tiger
raga: 5 music
name: 4 Ravi 7 Shankar
ragamuffin: 3 bum 4 hobo, waif 5 gamin, tramp 6 beggar, gamine, orphan, sloven, urchin 7 vagrant 8 derelict, vagabond 9 foundling 10 panhandler
Ragdoll: 3 cat 5 felid 6 feline
Rag Doll (1964 song) artist: Four Seasons
rage: 3 bug, fad, ire 4 boil, fume, fury, gall, heat, huff, mode, rant, rave, tear, yell 5 anger, chafe, craze, erupt, freak, furor, go ape, mania, steam, storm, style, trend, vogue, wrath 6 blow up, choler, dander, frenzy, latest, lose it, rail at, scream, seethe, simmer, spleen, temper, uproar 7 bluster, bristle, carry on, dudgeon, emotion, explode, fashion, flare up, go crazy, in thing, madness, passion, rampage, run amok, run riot, run wild, tantrum, umbrage 8 boil over, ferocity, go postal, have a fit, outburst, paroxysm, run amuck, violence 9 blow a fuse, fireworks, fulminate, go bananas, go berserk, throw a fit, vehemence 10 bitterness, dernier cri, hit the roof, kick up a row, make a scene, resentment, turbulence
all the ~: 2 in 3 hip, hot, mod 4 tony 5 faddy, toney 6 chi-chi, modish, trendy 7 a la mode, current, in style, popular, stylish, voguish 8 up-to-date 9 in fashion
be all the ~: 4 rule
filled with ~: 3 hot, mad 4 ired, sore, wild 5 angry, cross, huffy, irate, livid, rabid, riled, rough, upset, wroth 6 ablaze, fierce, fuming, heated, ireful, peeved, raving, red-hot, savage, stormy 7 furious, rampant, ranting, violent 8 blustery, choleric, frenzied, going ape, incensed, inflamed, maddened, seething, wrathful 9 indignant, irritated, resentful, seeing red, splenetic, turbulent 10 blustering, boiling mad, freaked out, hysterical, infuriated, tumultuous
__ rage: 4 road
Rage author: Stephen King
Rage of Angels author: Sidney Sheldon
Rage of Paris, The (1938 film)
cast: Mischa Auer, Danielle Darrieux, Douglas Fairbanks Jr.
director: Henry Koster
Rage to Live, A author: John O'Hara
R-A-G-G-__...: 4 M-O-P-P
ragged: 4 fray, mean, poor, rent, torn, worn 5 badly, crude, dingy, erose, rough, seedy, tacky, tatty 6 broken, frayed, jagged, rugged, shabby, shaggy, shoddy, uneven 7 dressed, in holes, notched, patched, scraggy, scruffy, unkempt, worn-out 8 battered, frazzled, ill-kempt, in shreds, serrated, shredded, tattered 9 desultory, in tatters, irregular, lacerated, moth-eaten, ungroomed, unpressed 10 fragmented, threadbare, unfinished
become ~: 4 fray 5 shred
robin: 5 plant 6 flower
run ~: 4 tire 7 exhaust
ragged __: 4 edge 5 robin 6 jacket
Ragged Dick author: Horatio Alger
raggedy: 4 worn 5 erose
Raggedy __: 3 Ann, Man 4 Andy
Raggedy Ann or Andy: 4 doll
Raggedy Man (1981 film)
cast: Eric Roberts, William Sanderson, Sissy Spacek
director: Jack Fisk
Raggedy Man, The: 4 poem
author: James Whitcomb Riley
raggee: 5 grain, grass
raggle-__: 6 taggle
ragi: 5 grain, grass
Ragin' __: 6 Cajuns
raging: 3 hot, mad 4 ired, sore, wild 5 angry, cross, huffy, irate, livid, rabid, riled, rough, upset, wroth 6 ablaze, fierce, fuming, heated, ireful, peeved, raving, red-hot, savage, stormy 7 enraged, furious, rampant, ranting, violent 8 blustery, choleric, frenzied, going ape, in a furor, incensed, inflamed, maddened, outraged, seething, volcanic, white-hot, wild-eyed, wrathful 9 indignant, irritated, resentful, seeing red, splenetic, turbulent 10 blustering, boiling mad, freaked out, hysterical, infuriated, tumultuous
Raging Bull (1980 film)
cast: Robert De Niro, Cathy Moriarty, Joe Pesci
director: Martin Scorsese
raglan: 4 coat 6 jacket, sleeve 8 overcoat
Rag Mop (1950 song) artist: Ames Brothers
Ragnar: 6 Frisch, Granit
ragout: 4 hash, meat, stew 5 salmi 6 salmis
ingredient: 5 onion
rags: 4 garb, gear, togs 5 array 6 attire, finery 7 clothes 8 castoffs, wardrobe 9 caparison
in ~: 4 poor 5 needy 8 tattered
like some ~: 5 linty
__ rags: 4 glad
Ragsdale: 7 William
Rags to Riches (1953 song) artist: Tony Bennett
rags-to-riches author: 5 Alger
ragtag: 5 mangy 6 motley, shoddy 7 scruffy
ragtag and __: 7 bobtail
ragtime: 5 music
dance: 6 shimmy 10 turkey trot
master: 6 Joplin
Ragtime: 4 film 5 novel
author: E.L. Doctorow
cast: James Cagney, Elizabeth McGovern, Howard Rollins, Mary Steenburgen
director: Milos Forman
Ragu: 10 pasta sauce
alternative: 5 Prego 6 Prince 8 Classico 10 Newman's Own 11 Aunt Millie's
ragweed: 8 allergen
reaction: 5 achoo 6 ahchoo, hachoo 7 kerchoo
react to ~: 5 sniff 6 sneeze 7 sniffle
ragwort: 5 plant 6 flower
rah: 3 olé 4 yell 5 cheer, huzza 6 hooray, hurrah, hurray, huzzah
Rahal, Bobby: 5 racer 9 auto racer
milieu: 5 track
rah-rah: 4 keen 5 eager 6 ardent, gung-ho 7 anxious, excited, fired up, keyed up, zealous 8 enthused, spirited 9 fanatical 10 passionate
Rahway: 4 city, town
locale: 9 New Jersey
Raiatea: 3 isl. 4 isle 6 island
locale: 9 Polynesia
raid: 3 rob 4 bust, loot, sack 5 blitz, foray, harry, rifle, sally, shell, storm, sweep, swoop 6 arrest, attack, forage, inroad, invade, maraud, pirate, prey

on, ravage, sortie, strafe, strike **7** assault, break in, descent, despoil, overrun, pillage, plunder, ransack, round up, sacking, torpedo **8** fall upon, freeboot, invasion, lay waste, spoliate **9** air strike, depredate, descend on, devastate, incursion, intrude on, irruption, offensive, onslaught **10** plundering
site: **6** fridge
the fridge: **3** eat **4** nosh **5** munch, snack **6** nibble
__ raid: **3** air
Raid
competitor: **4** D Con
target: **3** ant **5** roach **6** insect
__ Raid: **7** Ulzana's
raider: **6** bandit, robber **7** brigand, corsair, invader **8** attacker **9** aggressor **10** freebooter
of old: **3** Hun
__ Raider: **4** Tomb
Raider rival: **3** Jet, Ram **4** Bear, Bill, Colt, Lion **5** Brown, Chief, Eagle, Giant, Niner, Raven, Saint, Texan, Titan **6** Bengal, Bronco, Cowboy, Falcon, Jaguar, Packer, Viking **7** Charger, Dolphin, Panther, Patriot, Redskin, Seahawk, Steeler **8** Cardinal **9** Buccaneer
Raiders: **4** team **6** eleven **7** Colgate
home: **7** Oakland
org.: **3** AFC, NFL
sport: **8** football
__ Raiders: **6** Nader's
Raiders of the Lost Ark (1981 film)
cast: Karen Allen, Harrison Ford
composer: John Williams
director: Steven Spielberg
snake: **3** asp
villain: **4** Nazi
Raiders, The author: Harold Robbins
Raid on Entebbe
airline: **4** El Al
setting: **6** Uganda
weapon: **3** Uzi
__-raid shelter: **3** air
Raid, The (1954 film)
cast: Anne Bancroft, Richard Boone, Van Heflin
director: Hugo Fregonese
Ra II home: **4** Oslo
rail: **3** bar, jaw **4** bird, carp, pole, post, rant, rate, rave, rest, sora **5** blast, crake, fence, scold, train **6** berate, paling, revile, siding **7** barrier, censure, chew out, declaim, inveigh, lampoon, tell off, thunder, upbraid **8** banister, bloviate, complain, denounce, footrest **9** castigate, criticize, fulminate, go on about, make a fuss, marsh bird, transport **10** balustrade, tongue-lash, vituperate, wading bird
at: **3** hit, jaw **4** jeer, rage **5** abuse, blast, decry, scold **6** assail, attack, berate, hit out **7** condemn **8** denounce **9** criticize, fustigate **10** denunciate
ballet ~: **3** bar **5** barre
company: **6** Amtrak
connection: **3** tie
crossing sign: **4** STOP
ender: **3** car, way **4** bird, head, road
end of a ~: **5** newel
like a ~: **4** lank, lean, slim, thin **5** lanky, rangy, reedy **6** gangly, skinny, svelte, twiggy **7** scraggy, scrawny, slender, willowy **8** raw-boned
lip: **6** flange
nautical: **6** gunnel **7** bulwark, gunwale
relative: **4** coot **7** finfoot
rider: **4** hobo **5** tramp
starter: **4** hand, mono **5** guard
strike a ~: **5** carom **6** carrom
rail __: **4** bead **5** fence **6** anchor
__ rail: **3** fly, pin **4** fife, king, land, lash, lock, rack, sora, trim **5** altar, chair, check, crest, guide, plain, plate, split, third, water **6** toggle **7** bearing, clapper, meeting, working
__-rail: **4** slip **5** light
railing: **3** bar **4** pole, post, rest **5** abuse, fence **6** paling, siding **7** barrier **8** banister **10** balustrade
raillery: **3** wit **4** jest, joke, talk **5** chaff, humor, sport **6** banter, joking **7** jesting, joshing, ribbing **8** badinage, repartee, ridicule **9** funniness **10** jocoseness, persiflage
railroad: **4** line, push, tube **5** impel, metro, press **6** subway, tracks **7** lantern **9** train line
beam: **3** tie
branch ~: **6** feeder
car: **5** diner **6** engine **7** caboose **10** locomotive
cars: **5** train
device: **5** shunt
flare: **5** fusee, fuzee
mine ~: **4** tram
parking space: **4** yard
siding: **5** lie-by
station: **4** stop
stop: **3** sta., stn. **5** depot **7** station
switch: **3** wye
system: **6** Amtrak
terminal: **5** depot
unit: **3** car
railroad __: **3** pen **4** flat, worm
Railroaded! (1947 film)
cast: Hugh Beaumont, John Ireland
director: Anthony Mann
rails: **5** track
distance between ~: **5** gauge
riding the ~: **6** aboard
Railsback: **5** Steve
railsplitter, famous: **3** Abe **7** Lincoln
railway: **5** track, train
overhead: **2** el
__ railway: **3** cog **4** rack, tube **5** cable **6** aerial, marine, scenic, street
raiment: **4** duds, garb, togs **5** dress **6** attire, livery, things **7** apparel, clothes, garment, threads **8** clothing, garments **9** trappings **10** Sunday best
in ~: **4** clad
Raimi: **3** Sam, Ted
Raimi, Sam: **8** director
film: Darkman (1990)
For Love of the Game (1999)
The Gift (2000)
The Quick and the Dead (1995)
A Simple Plan (1998)
Spider-Man (2002)
rain: **4** fall, hail, mist, pelt, pour, spit **5** flood, sleet, spate, storm, water **6** deluge, lament, lavish, patter, precip, shower, stream, volley **7** drizzle, monsoon, torrent **8** downpour, drencher, moisture, sprinkle **10** cloudburst
anti-acid ~ org.: **3** EPA
bit of ~: **4** drop
cats and dogs: **4** pelt, pour, teem **5** flood, spate
check: **4** stub **10** invitation
clearer: **5** wiper
collector: **4** eave, pond **9** reservoir
combining form: **4** hyet- **5** hyeto-, ombro-, pluvi- **6** pluvia-, pluvio-
dancer: **4** Hopi
delay coverup: **4** tarp **9** tarpaulin
drain: **4** sump
drain locale: **4** curb
ender: **3** bow, out **4** coat, drop, fall, wear **5** maker, spout, storm, water **6** making, squall
fine ~: **4** mist **7** drizzle
forest: **5** biome, selva **6** jungle
frozen ~: **4** hail **5** sleet
gear: **3** mac **7** slicker **10** mackintosh
give a ~ check: **5** defer, delay **6** put off **7** suspend **8** postpone
in Japanese: **3** ame
like ~: **5** right
on: **4** soak **6** dampen, drench **7** moisten
or shine: **6** surely **10** definitely, for certain
out of the ~: **6** inside **7** indoors
right as ~: **5** sound
sign of ~: **5** cloud **6** nimbus
signs of ~: **5** nimbi
that doesn't reach the ground: **5** virga
without ~: **3** dry **4** arid, sere **7** parched
rain __: **4** date, frog, tree **5** check, cloud, dance, delay, gauge **6** forest, shadow, shower
rain __ and dogs: **4** cats
__ rain: **3** ice **4** acid, land **6** yellow **7** driving, pouring
...rain, __ sleet...: **3** nor
Rain: **7** Phoenix
role: **5** Sadie **8** Thompson
setting: **5** Samoa **8** Pago Pago
Rain __: **3** Man
__ Rain: **4** Hard **5** Black, Candy, In the **6** Purple, Summer
Rain author: W. Somerset Maugham
rainbow: **3** arc, bow **4** iris **5** curve, prism **6** motley **8** crescent
fish: **5** smelt, trout
goddess: **4** Iris
like a ~: **5** arced **6** arcing
producer: **5** prism
segment: **3** hue, red **4** blue **5** color, green **6** indigo, orange, violet, yellow
rainbow __: **4** fish, roof **5** perch, snake, trout **6** cactus, darter, runner
__ rainbow: **5** lunar, white **7** primary
__ Rainbow: **4** Neon **5** Black, She's a **6** Broken **7** Finian's **8** Gravity's
Rainbow Falls site: **4** Hilo **6** Hawaii
Rainbow's End author: James M. Cain
Rainbow, The author: D.H. Lawrence
character: **4** Anna **5** Anton, Inger, Lydia, Tilly **6** Ursula
Rainbow Trail, The author: Zane Grey
rain cats and __: **4** dogs
raincheck: **6** ticket
take a ~: **4** wait
raincoat: **3** mac **6** jacket, poncho **7** cagoule, oilskin, slicker **9** sou'wester **10** mackintosh, protection
feature: **6** lining
Raindrops (1961 song) artist: Dee Clark
Raindrops Keep Fallin' on My Head (1969 song) artist: B.J. Thomas
raindrop sound: **4** plop
Raine, Kathleen: **4** poet **7** British
Rainer: **4** Iris **5** Luise, Rilke
Rainer __ Fassbinder: **6** Werner
Rainer __ Rilke: **5** Maria
Rainer, Luise
Oscar: The Good Earth, The Great Ziegfeld
Oscar role: **4** O-lan
spouse: Clifford Odets
Raines: **3** Tim **4** Ella
Raines, Ella: **7** actress
film: Corvette K-225 (1943)
Hail the Conquering Hero (1944)
Impact (1949)
Phantom Lady (1944)
The Senator Was Indiscreet (1947)
The Strange Affair of Uncle Harry (1945)
The Suspect (1944)
Tall in the Saddle (1944)
The Walking Hills (1949)
The Web (1947)
Raines, Tim sport: **8** baseball
Rainey: **2** Ma
rainfall measure: **4** inch
Rainier: **2** mt. **4** peak **5** mount **8** mountain
locale: **8** Cascades **10** Washington
rain in ___, The: **5** Spain
raining: **3** wet **7** showery
quit ~: **5** let up
Rain in Spain, The: **4** song **5** tango
composer: **5** Loewe **6** Lerner
place: **5** plain **8** Hartford, Hereford **9** Hampshire
rainless: **3** dry **4** arid, sere **5** unwet **6** desert
expanse: **6** desert
Rainmaker, The (1956 film)
cast: Wendell Corey, Katharine Hepburn, Burt Lancaster
director: Joseph Anthony
Rainmaker, The (1997 film)
cast: Matt Damon, Claire Danes, Danny DeVito, Jon Voight
director: Francis Ford Coppola
Rain Man (1988 film)
cast: Tom Cruise, Valeria Golino, Dustin Hoffman
director: Barry Levinson
__ Rain on My Parade: **4** Don't
Rain on the Roof (1966 song) artist: Lovin' Spoonful
rain or __: **5** shine
__ Rain or Come Shine: **4** Come
Rain People, The (1969 film)
cast: James Caan, Robert Duvall, Shirley Knight
director: Francis Ford Coppola
Rains __, The: **4** Came
Rains, Claude: **5** actor
film: The Adventures of Robin Hood (1938)
Angel on My Shoulder (1946)
Casablanca (1942)
The Clairvoyant (1934)
Crime Without Passion (1934)
Daughters Courageous (1939)
Deception (1946)
Four Daughters (1938)
Here Comes Mr. Jordan (1941)
The Invisible Man (1933)
The Last Outpost (1935)
Lawrence of Arabia (1962)
The Man Who Reclaimed His Head (1934)
Mr. Skeffington (1944)
Mr. Smith Goes to Washington (1939)
Mystery of Edwin Drood (1935)
Notorious (1946)
Now, Voyager (1942)
Phantom of the Opera (1943)
The Prince and the Pauper (1937)
The Sea Hawk (1940)
They Won't Forget (1937)
The Wolf Man (1941)
rainspout: **6** gutter
rainstorm: **8** downpour, drencher **10** cloudburst
Rain, the Park & Other Things, The (1967 song) artist: Cowsills
Rain, The (song) artist: Madonna, Oran Jones
Raintree County (1957 film)
cast: Walter Abel, Montgomery Clift, Eva Marie Saint, Elizabeth Taylor
character: **4** Nell **6** Esther, Stiles
director: Edward Dmytryk
Rainwater: **3** Leo **6** Marvin
Rainwater, Leo: **8** Nobelist **9** physicist

Rain Without Thunder (1992 film)
cast: Betty Buckley, Jeff Daniels, Frederic Forrest
rainy: 3 wet 4 foul 5 moist, undry 6 hyetal, stormy 7 drizzly, pluvial, showery 8 pluvious 9 drizzling, inclement, showering
day fund: 7 nest egg, reserve, savings
days: 5 slump 9 recession 10 depression
not ~: 3 dry 4 arid, fair 5 clear, sunny
prepare for a ~ day: 4 plan, save 8 salt away
wind direction: 4 east
rainy ___: 3 day
Rainy: 4 lake
locale: 6 Canada 7 Ontario 9 Minnesota
Rainy Day People (1975 song) artist: Gordon Lightfoot
Rainy Days and Mondays (1971 song) artist: Carpenters
Rainy Day Women (1966 song) artist: Bob Dylan
Rainy Night in ___, A: 3 Rio
Rainy Night in Georgia (1970 song) artist: Brook Benton
Raisa: 4 Rosa 9 Gorbachev
see also Russian
Raisa, Rosa: 6 singer 7 soprano
specialty: 5 opera
raise: 2 up 3 pry, set, sow 4 bump, buoy, grow, heft, hike, incr., jack, levy, lift, rear, whet 5 add to, boost, breed, build, cause, dig up, erect, exalt, goose, heave, hoist, honor, lever, mount, pitch, plant, put up, rally, run up, set up, upend 6 better, broach, bump up, call up, drag up, draw up, emboss, foment, foster, gather, haul up, hike up, hold up, incite, jack up, jerk up, jump up, kindle, mark up, move up, muster, pick up, pull up, step up, stir up, uphold, uplift 7 advance, augment, bring up, care for, collect, dignify, elevate, enhance, enlarge, improve, inflate, magnify, nourish, nurture, produce, promote, provoke, pyramid, recruit, scale up, shoot up, support, upgrade, upheave 8 addition, dredge up, escalate, heighten, increase, mobilize, multiply, snowball, summon up 9 conjure up, construct, cultivate, elevation, increment, instigate, intensify, introduce, promotion, propagate 10 accelerate, invigorate, put forward, strengthen
a finger for: 3 aid 4 help 6 assist
a fuss: 5 act up
a red flag: 4 warn 5 alert 6 tip off 7 caution
Cain: 4 rave, riot 5 brawl, clash 6 clamor, squawk 7 carouse
hackles: 3 irk 4 rile 5 anger, peeve, upset
hell: 5 party 9 make merry
high: 4 heft, hike 5 extol 6 hike up 7 build up, elevate, ennoble, glorify, idolize, lionize, worship
meet a ~: 3 see 4 call
one's hackles: 3 bug, get, try, vex 4 fret, gall, miff, rile 5 annoy, chafe, grate, harry, peeve, pique 6 abrade, bother, harass, hector, needle, nettle, pester, plague, rankle, ruffle 7 disturb, provoke 8 irritate 9 aggravate, displease
one's spirits: 4 buoy 5 cheer, elate 6 buck up, buoy up, solace 7 cheer up, comfort, console, enliven, gladden, hearten 8 brighten 9 encourage
one's voice: 3 cry 4 howl, roar, yell 5 shout, whoop 6 bellow, cry out, holler, scream, shriek, squeal 7 exclaim, screech
reason: 5 merit
starter: 4 fund
the roof: 5 gripe, revel, shout, storm 6 clamor, holler, squawk 7 grumble 8 complain 9 bellyache
raise ___: 3 hob 4 Cain, hell
___ raise: 3 pay 5 merit, pilot
raise a ___: 5 stink
raised: 5 lofty, steep, upped 7 upright
make a ~ design: 6 emboss
path: 4 berm, dike 5 berme, levee 8 causeway 10 embankment
Raise High the Roof-Beam, Carpenters author: J.D. Salinger
___ raiser: 7 curtain
___-raiser: 4 fund, hair, hell
raise the ___: 4 roof 5 devil 6 stakes
raisin: 4 blue 5 fruit 6 purply 8 purplish
center: 6 Fresno
originally: 5 grape
relative: 4 anil, cyan, navy, Nile, teal 5 Alice, azure, slate 6 cobalt, indigo, violet 7 peacock 8 cerulean, sapphire 9 turquoise 10 aquamarine, periwinkle
Raisin ___: 4 Bran
raisin-and-rum cake: 5 babka
raisin bran: 6 cereal
Raisinets: 5 candy
alternative: 7 Goobers 8 Milk Duds
raising
goose bumps: 5 scary, weird 6 creepy, occult, spooky 7 ghostly, macabre, uncanny 9 unearthly 10 mysterious
hell: 4 wild 5 noisy 6 unruly 7 lawless, naughty, raucous 9 turbulent 10 boisterous, disorderly, tumultuous
the roof: 4 loud 7 blaring, booming, raucous, riotous, yelling 8 blasting, piercing, shouting 9 bellowing, clamorous, screaming 10 boisterous, uproarious, vociferous
___ raising: 4 barn 5 stock
___-raising: 4 fund, hair 5 house
Raising Arizona (1987 film)
cast: Nicolas Cage, Holly Hunter, Trey Wilson
director: Joel Coen
raising the roof: 5 noisy
Raisin in the Sun, A: 4 film, play
author: Lorraine Hansberry
cast: Ruby Dee, Claudia McNeil, Sidney Poitier
character: 4 Bobo, Karl, Lena, Ruth 5 Asagi 6 Joseph, Travis, Walter 7 Lindner, Younger 8 Beneatha
director: Daniel Petrie
setting: 7 Chicago 8 Illinois
Raisin Nut Bran: 6 cereal
competitor: 3 Kix 4 Life, Trix 5 Kashi, Quisp, Total 6 Kaboom, Muesli, Oreo O's, Pablum, Smacks 7 All-Bran, Crispix, Harmony, Hunny B's, Mueslix, Oat Bran, Pokemon 8 Boo Berry, Cheerios, Corn Chex, Corn Pops, Fiber One, Rice Chex, Special K, Uncle Sam, Wheaties 9 Alpha Bits, Apple Zaps, Grape Nuts, Honey Comb, Just Right, Wheat Chex 10 Apple Jacks, Bran Flakes, Cap'n Crunch, Cocoa Puffs, Froot Loops, Mini-Wheats, Nutri-Grain, Puffed Rice, Quaker Oats, Smart Start 11 Cocoa Blasts, Cookie Crisp, Golden Crisp, Lucky Charms, Puffed Wheat, Sweet Crunch, Waffle Crisp
raisins, soak: 5 plump
raison ___: 5 d'état, d'être
raison d'être: 3 end 5 basis, cause 7 purpose 8 function 9 rationale
Raitt: 4 John 6 Bonnie
Raitt, Bonnie
song: I Can't Make You Love Me (1992)
Love Sneakin' Up on You (1994)
Something to Talk About (1991)
You Got It (1995)
Raj
headquarters: 5 Delhi
princess: 5 begum
servant: 3 ama 4 amah
rajah: 5 Hindu, noble, ruler 6 gerent 7 monarch
land: 5 India
starter: 4 maha
wife: 4 rani 5 ranee
Rajiv: 6 Gandhi
mother: 6 Indira
see also India
Rajput
see India
Raj Quartet, The title: 5 sahib
Rajshahi: 4 city, town
locale: 10 Bangladesh
Rakaposhi: 4 peak 5 mount 8 mountain
locale: 4 Asia 7 Kashmir
rake: 3 cad 4 comb, hunt, roué, scan, tilt, tool, weed 5 clear, graze, ogler, scour, sweep 6 gather, harrow, rebuke, search, smooth, wanton 7 clean up, collect, ransack, rummage 8 lothario 9 libertine, scoundrel 10 garden tool, profligate
cousin: 3 hoe
in: 5 amass 6 gather, pile up 7 collect, round up
over the coals: 4 flay 5 roast, scold 6 berate 7 lambast, tell off 8 lambaste
part: 4 tine
starter: 4 muck
through: 5 rifle, scour 7 pillage, plunder, ransack
rake ___: 3 off 4 it in
___ rake: 3 hay 4 drag 5 horse
rakehell: 3 cad 5 knave, rogue, scamp, skunk 6 rascal 7 wastrel 8 prodigal, scalawag, sybarite 9 libertine, miscreant, reprobate, scoundrel 10 blackguard, jackanapes, ne'er-do-well, profligate, scapegrace
rake-off: 5 bribe 6 grease, payoff, payola 7 jobbery 8 kickback
rake over the ___: 5 coals
raker starter: 4 muck
Rake's Progress, The: 5 opera
composer: 10 Stravinsky
raki: 5 drink 8 beverage
raking: 5 chore
starter: 4 muck
raking ___: 4 bond 5 piece 6 course 7 cornice
rakish: 3 gay 4 airy, chic, fast, lewd, wild 5 dandy, loose, natty, saucy, sleek, smart, swank 6 breezy, dapper, flashy, jaunty, sinful, snazzy, spiffy, sporty, swanky, wanton 7 dashing, raffish 8 cavalier, charming, debonair, depraved, prodigal, uncurbed 9 abandoned, debauched, debonaire, dissolute, lecherous 10 debonnaire, dissipated, licentious, picaresque, profligate
Rakosi, Carl: 4 poet
Raleigh: 4 city, town 6 Walter
athletes: 8 Wolfpack
county: 4 Wake
locale: 4 N. Car.
neighbor: 6 Durham
school: 4 NCSU
Raleigh, Walter: 3 Sir 4 poet 7 English 8 courtier, explorer
rival: 5 Essex
work: Cynthia
rally: 4 call, fire, herd, meet, mock, spur, stir, urge, wake, whet 5 bandy, raise, renew, rouse, sit-in, steel, surge, unite, waken 6 arouse, awaken, bestir, charge, gather, kindle, muster, perk up, pick up, pow-wow, reform, revive, stir up, summon 7 brace up, collect, convene, enliven, fortify, get well, improve, marshal, meeting, protest, rebound, recover, refresh, regroup, renewal, restore, revival, round up, session, shape up 8 assemble, assembly, auto race, clambake, comeback, enspirit, inspirit, jamboree, mobilize, organize, recovery, redouble 9 challenge, come about, come along, encourage, gathering, get better, resurrect 10 assemblage, bounce back, call to arms, close ranks, come around, congregate, convention, invigorate, make a stand, reassemble, recuperate, rejuvenate, reorganize, resurgence, strengthen, turn around
pep ~ shout: 3 yay
road ~: 4 meet, race 7 contest
round: 4 back, help 5 boost, favor 6 assist, defend 7 bolster, endorse, promote, pull for, stand by, stick by, support 8 champion, side with 9 encourage, get behind 10 go to bat for, stand up for, stick up for
Wall Street ~: 5 runup
___ rally: 3 pep 4 road
rallying cry: 5 motto 6 slogan
Ralph: 4 Houk 5 James, Kiner, Nader, Smart, Waite 6 Bakshi, Branca, Bunche, Lauren, Meeker, Nelson, Thomas 7 Bellamy, Edwards, Ellison, Fiennes, Guldahl, Kramden, Macchio 8 Tresvant 9 Gustafson 10 Richardson
Ralph ___ Abernathy: 5 David
Ralph ___ Doister: 7 Roister
Ralph ___ Emerson: 5 Waldo
Ralph ___ Williams: 7 Vaughan
Ralph Roister Doister author: 5 Udall
Ralston: 6 Dennis, Jobyna
Ralston ___: 6 Purina
Ralston, Dennis: 7 netster 9 tennis pro
milieu: 5 court
ram: 3 hit, jam 4 beat, butt, cram, dash, male, plug, push, sink, slam, stab, tamp 5 Aries, crash, drive, force, pound, press, sheep, smash, stick, stuff, wedge 6 animal, batter, beetle, butter, hammer, hurtle, pack in, thrust 7 jam-pack, rear-end, run into, squeeze 8 bang into 9 barge into, broadside, crash into, smash into 10 barrel into, crunch into
battering ~: 6 engine
ender: 3 jet, rod 7 shackle
in: 4 cram 5 crowd, stuff 9 overcrowd
(in): 4 pack 5 shove
in Britain: 3 tup
mate: 3 ewe
remark: 3 baa, maa 5 bleat
sign of the ~: 5 Aries
young ~: 4 lamb
ram ___ one's throat: 4 down
Ram: 4 Dass, sign 5 Aries, Singh
month: 3 Apr., Mar. 5 April, March
predecessor: 4 Fish
rival: 3 Jet 4 Bear, Bill, Colt, Lion 5 Brown, Chief, Eagle, Giant, Niner, Raven, Saint, Texan, Titan 6 Bengal, Bronco, Cowboy, Falcon, Jaguar, Packer, Raider, Viking 7 Charger, Dolphin, Panther, Patriot, Redskin, Seahawk, Steeler 8 Cardinal 9 Buccaneer

successor: 4 Bull
RAM
computer program: 3 TSR
counterpart: 3 ROM
part of ~: 6 access, memory, random
thing with ~: 2 PC 3 CPU, Mac 6 laptop 8 computer
Rama
wife: 4 Sita
ramada: 5 arbor
Ramada Inn: 5 motel
alternative: 4 HoJo 5 Motel 7 Days Inn 10 Comfort Inn, Econo Lodge, Hampton Inn, Holiday Inn, Quality Inn, Red Roof Inn, Travelodge 11 Best Western
offering: 2 rm. 4 room
Ramadan: 5 month
observance: 4 fast
Rama Lama Ding Dong (1961 song) artist: Edsels
Raman, Chandrasekhara: 8 Nobelist 9 physicist, scientist
__ Rama Rau: 6 Santha
Ramayana: 4 epic, poem, saga
reader: 5 Hindu 6 Hindoo
setting: 5 India
ramble: 3 gad 4 fork, hike, roam, rove, tour, trip, turn, walk, wind 5 amble, climb, drift, jaunt, prose, range, run on, snake, spout, stray, trail, tramp, twist 6 babble, cruise, depart, drivel, extend, gossip, harp on, jabber, loiter, mumble, roving, sprawl, spread, stroll, trapes, travel, wander, zigzag 7 amplify, blather, blether, chatter, clamber, descant, digress, discant, diverge, dwell on, enlarge, excurse, journey, maunder, meander, radiate, roaming, saunter, traipse 8 ambulate, divagate, go astray, protract, rattle on, scramble, straddle, straggle 9 bat around, branch off, dwell upon, excursion, expatiate, gallivant, go on and on, percolate, promenade 10 knock about
on: 3 gab, jaw, yak, yap 4 blab 5 prate, speak, spout 6 gabble, gibber, jabber, yammer 7 blather, chatter, prattle
rambler: 4 rose 5 nomad, plant, rover 6 flower 7 pilgrim 8 gadabout, runagate, traveler, vagabond, wanderer 9 itinerant, journeyer
Rambler: 3 car 4 auto 6 Hudson 10 automobile
manufacturer: 3 AMC 4 Nash
model: 5 Rebel, Rogue 6 Marlin 7 Classic 8 American 10 Ambassador
Ramblers: 6 Loyola
rambling: 4 long 5 gabby, loose, windy, wordy 6 errant, gangly, prolix, random, strewn, zigzag 7 diffuse, erratic, lengthy, unterse, verbose, voluble 8 at length, confused, covering, episodic, gangling, rootless, trailing, vagabond 9 bombastic, desultory, excursive, garrulous, irregular, itinerant, scattered, sprawling, spreading, spread out, talkative, unplanned, vagarious, wayfaring 10 circuitous, digressive, discursive, disjointed, episodical, incoherent, long-winded, loquacious, palaverous, straggling
one: 5 nomad
Rambling __: 4 Rose 5 Wreck
Ramblin' Gamblin' Man (1969 song) artist: Bob Seger
Rambling Rose (1991 film)
cast: Laura Dern, Robert Duvall, Diane Ladd
director: Martha Coolidge
__ rambling wreck...: 3 I'm a
Ramblin Man (1973 song) artist: Allman Brothers Band
Ramblin' Rose (1962 song) artist: Nat King Cole
Rambo - First Blood Part II (1985 film)
cast: Richard Crenna, Charles Napier, Sylvester Stallone
director: George P. Cosmatos
setting: 3 Nam 7 Vietnam
Rambo III (1988 film)
cast: Richard Crenna, Sylvester Stallone
Rambouillet: 5 sheep
rambunctious: 4 loud 5 noisy, rough, rowdy 6 unruly 7 raucous 9 energetic, turbulent
become ~: 5 act up
rambutan: 4 tree 5 fruit
ram down one's __: 6 throat
rame: 6 branch
ramen: 4 soup
Ramey, Samuel: 4 bass 6 singer
specialty: 5 opera
rami: 8 branches
ramie: 5 shrub
family: 6 nettle
relative: 6 feijoa
ramification: 6 result, upshot 8 offshoot
ramiform: 8 arboreal
ramify: 6 branch 7 radiate
Ramirez, Manny sport: 8 baseball
Ramis, Harold: 5 actor 8 director
film: Analyze This (1999)
Baby Boom (1987)
Bedazzled (2000)
Caddyshack (1980)
Ghostbusters (1984)
Ghostbusters II (1989)
Groundhog Day (1993)
National Lampoon's Vacation (1983)
Stripes (1981)
Ramiz: 4 Alia
ramjet: 5 plane 6 engine 8 airplane
__-ramjet: 5 turbo
ramkie: 6 guitar, string
ramon: 4 tree
relative: 3 fig 4 upas 5 ficus 6 antiar, fustic 18 breadfruit. mulberry
Ramón: 7 Novarro
in English: 7 Raymond
see also Spanish
Ramona author: Helen Hunt Jackson
Ramón y Cajal, Santiago: 8 Nobelist
Ramos __ fizz: 3 gin
Ramos Arizpe: 4 city, town
locale: 6 Mexico 8 Coahuila
ramose: 8 arboreal 10 branchlike
Ramos, Graciliano: 6 writer 9 Brazilian
Ramos-Horta, José: 8 Nobelist
Ramos, Joao de Deus: 4 poet
ramous: 10 branchlike
ramp: 4 adit 5 chute, grade, slant, slope 6 access, way off 7 gangway, incline, walkway 8 gradient 9 gangplank
alternative: 5 stair 8 elevator 9 escalator
ender: 3 age
highway ~: 4 exit 8 entrance
__ ramp: 4 exit 7 parking
__-ramp: 3 off
rampage: 3 mad 4 fury, rage, riot, tear 5 binge, fling, spree, storm 6 blowup, frenzy, ruckus, tumult, uproar 7 ferment, go crazy, run riot, run wild, splurge, tantrum, tempest, turmoil 8 run amuck, violence, wingding 9 go berserk
on a ~: 4 amok 7 berserk, haywire
__ rampage: 3 on a
Rampal, Jean-Pierre: 6 French 7 flutist 8 flautist
rampant: 4 rank, rife, wild 6 raging, ruling, unruly, wanton 7 furious, growing, profuse, riotous, violent 8 dominant, epidemic, flagrant, infested, pandemic, vehement 9 clamorous, excessive, exuberant, fanatical, impetuous, impulsive, luxuriant, out of hand, prevalent, rampaging, spreading, tumultous, turbulent, unbridled, unchecked 10 aggressive, blustering, boisterous, epidemical, outrageous, prevailing, tumultuous, widespread
be ~: 4 rule
run ~: 4 rage, rant, rave 5 erupt, freak, storm 7 explode 8 freak out 9 go berserk 10 hit the roof
rampart: 4 fort, hill, wall 5 fence, guard, mound, redan, ridge 6 shield 7 barrier, bastion, bulwark, defense, parapet, support 8 fastness, security 9 barricade, earthwork, elevation, vallation 10 battlement, breastwork, embankment, protection, stronghold
ramparts
assail the ~: 5 arise, rebel 6 attack, charge
surrounder: 4 moat
Rampling, Charlotte: 7 actress
film: Rotten to the Core (1965)
Stardust Memories (1980)
The Verdict (1982)
ramrod: 4 ogre 6 tyrant 8 martinet, stickler 10 taskmaster
ram's __: 4 horn
Rams: 4 team 6 eleven 7 Fordham
div.: 3 NFC
home: 3 St. L. 7 St. Louis
org.: 3 NFC, NFL
sport: 8 football
Ramsay: 4 Alec 7 William
Ramsay, William: 7 chemist 8 Nobelist
Ramses II, father of: 4 Seti
Ramses I, son of: 4 Seti
Ramses river: 4 Nile
Ramsey: 4 Anne 5 Clark, Lewis, Logan 6 Norman
__ Ramsey: 3 Hec
Ramsey, Norman: 8 Nobelist 9 physicist
ramshackle: 5 shaky 6 flimsy, shabby, unfirm, unsafe 7 rickety, run-down, squalid 8 decrepit, derelict, timeworn, unsteady, untended 9 crumbling, tottering 10 broken-down, jerry-built, tumbledown
ram's horn: 6 shofar 7 shophar
ram's-horn: 5 shell 8 seashell
ramus: 6 branch
Ramuz, Charles-Ferdinand: 5 Swiss 6 writer
ran
at: 7 charged, set upon 8 attacked
ender: 4 sack
in: 6 busted, nabbed 7 pinched 8 arrested, collared 9 dropped by
on: 6 gabbed, prated 7 babbled, rambled 8 jabbered, prattled 9 blabbered, chattered, continued
to: 7 reached, totaled
up: 5 added 7 amassed 8 incurred 9 increased
__-ran: 4 also
Ran (1985 film) director: Akira Kurosawa
rana: 4 frog
Rancagua: 4 city, town
locale: 5 Chile
see also Spanish
Rance: 6 Howard
ranch: 4 farm, King, land 5 finca 6 estate, spread 7 acreage 8 dressing, estancia, hacienda, quarters 9 farmstead, homestead, Ponderosa, Southfork
beast: 4 calf, dogy 5 dogey, dogie, horse, steer
beasts: 4 cows, herd 5 bulls, stock 6 calves, cattle, dogies 9 livestock, longhorns
do a ~ job: 5 brand 6 dehorn 7 round up
hand: 6 drover 8 buckaroo, wrangler
menace: 4 puma 6 bobcat, coyote 7 bay lynx
quarters: 4 bunk 9 bunkhouse
rope: 5 lasso, reata, riata
unit: 4 acre
vacationer: 4 dude
worker: 4 hand 6 cowboy, herder
ranch __: 4 mink 5 house
__ ranch: 4 dude 5 fruit
Ranch: 3 car 4 auto, Ford 10 automobile
__ Ranch: 6 Melody
rancher: 6 cowboy, cowman 7 cowpoke 8 wrangler
need: 3 hay 5 lasso, water
perhaps: 5 Texan
tool: 4 prod 5 brand
__ Rancher: 5 Jolly
__ rancheros: 6 huevos
ranchero wrap: 6 sarape, serape
ranchland: 5 field
Rancho Cordova: 4 city, town
locale: 10 California
Rancho Cucamonga: 4 city, town
locale: 10 California
Rancho Deluxe (1975 film)
cast: Elizabeth Ashley, Jeff Bridges, Sam Waterston
director: Frank Perry
Rancho Mirage: 4 city, town
locale: 10 California
__ Rancho, NM: 3 Rio
Rancho Notorious (1952 film)
cast: Marlene Dietrich, Mel Ferrer, Arthur Kennedy
director: Fritz Lang
Rancho Palos Verdes: 4 city, town
locale: 10 California
Rancho San Diego: 4 city, town
locale: 10 California
Rancho Santa Margarita: 4 city, town
locale: 10 California
Ranch, The author: Danielle Steel
Ranch Wagon: 3 car 4 auto, Ford 10 automobile
rancid: 3 bad, off, old 4 foul, gamy, high, rank, sour 5 fetid, fusty, gamey, moldy, musty, nasty, reeky, sharp, stale 6 foetid, frowsy, frowzy, impure, putrid, rotten, smelly, soured, strong, turned 7 carious, curdled, gone bad, noisome, noxious, reeking, tainted, unclean 8 feculent, polluted, stinking, unsavory 9 loathsome, offensive, putrefied, repulsive, unhealthy 10 disgusting, malodorous, putrescent
become ~: 4 sour, turn
rancor: 4 bile, gall, hate 5 odium, pique, spite, venom, wrath 6 animus, enmity, grudge, hatred, malice, spleen 7 discord, dudgeon, ill will, sarcasm, umbrage 8 acerbity, acrimony, aversion, bad blood, variance 9 animosity, antipathy, harshness, hostility, malignity, mordacity, nastiness, vengeance, virulence 10 antagonism, bitterness, grumpiness, resentment, unkindness
rancorous: 4 evil 5 catty 6 bitter, malign 7 hateful, hostile 8 scathing, spiteful, vengeful, venomous, virulent 9 malicious, resentful, splenetic 10 implacable, malevolent, vindictive
rand: 5 money
starter: 6 Kruger
Rand: 3 Ayn 5 Sally
Rand __: 7 McNally
Randa: 6 Haines
Randal: 7 Kleiser
Randall: 4 Tony 7 Jarrell

Randallstown: 4 city
locale: 8 Maryland
Randall, Tony: 5 actor 8 comedian
film: 7 Faces of Dr. Lao (1964)
The Adventures of Huckleberry Finn (1960)
Boys' Night Out (1962)
Let's Make Love (1960)
Lover Come Back (1961)
The Mating Game (1959)
Pillow Talk (1959)
Send Me No Flowers (1964)
Will Success Spoil Rock Hunter? (1957)
TV: The Odd Couple
Rand, Ayn: 6 author, writer
work: Atlas Shrugged
The Fountainhead
We the Living
Randi: 5 James, Oakes
Rand McNally
product: 3 map 5 atlas, globe
Randolph: 4 city, John, Ross, Stow, town 5 Boots, Joyce, Scott 8 Mantooth
locale: 4 Mass.
Randolph, Boots instrument: saxophone
___ Randolph Hearst: 7 William
random: 3 odd 4 spot 5 fluky, stray 6 casual, chance, flukey, patchy, spotty 7 aimless, erratic, oddball, unaimed 8 isolated, on-and-off, periodic, rambling, slapdash, sporadic 9 arbitrary, desultory, driftless, haphazard, hit or miss, irregular, spasmodic, unplanned 10 accidental, contingent, designless, disorderly, fortuitous, incidental, nonuniform, objectless, occasional, sporadical, unintended, willy-nilly
at ~: 7 blindly 8 by chance
notion: 4 whim 5 fancy, quirk 6 vagary 7 caprice, impulse 8 crotchet
random ___: 4 line, walk 5 error 6 access, number
random-___ memory: 6 access
Random Harvest: 4 film 5 novel
author: James Hilton
cast: Ronald Colman, Philip Dorn, Greer Garson
director: Mervyn LeRoy
Rand, Sally, gear: 3 fan
randy: 7 lustful 9 lubricous 10 lascivious
Randy: 4 Owen, Ross 5 Quaid 6 Newman, Shilts, Travis 7 Johnson, Meisner 9 Vanwarmer
skating partner: 3 Tai
Randy & the Rainbows song: Denise (1963)
ranee's wrap: 5 saree
___ rang?: 3 You
range: 3 Erz, ken, Mts., row, run 4 Alai, Alps, area, band, Harz, Jura, oven, play, rank, roam, room, rove, site, size, span, sway, tier, trek, vary 5 align, aline, Altai, ambit, Andes, array, Atlas, Baird, Black, chain, class, drift, field, float, gamut, Ghats, Green, James, Lewis, orbit, order, prowl, reach, realm, ridge, Sayan, scale, scope, space, stove, stray, sweep, Tatra, tenor, tramp, Uinta, Urals, White, width 6 Anadir, assort, Balkan, bounds, Brooks, cruise, degree, differ, domain, Elburz, extend, extent, Kjölen, Kolyma, Kunlun, leeway, length, limits, line up, Ozarks, Pindus, Pontic, radius, ramble, region, series, sphere, spread, Taurus, Tetons, trapes, travel, wander, Zagros 7 Ala Dagh, Bighorn, bracket, breadth, Cariboo, compass, Darling, earshot, expanse, explore, freedom, habitat, horizon, Laramie, leisure, meander, migrate, Mitumba, Mustagh, Nan Ling, pasture, Poconos, prairie, Purcell, purview, Rhodope, Rockies, San Juan, Sawatch, Selkirk, soprano, St. Elias, stretch, Sudeten, Torngat, traipse, variety, Wasatch 8 ambulate, Cardamom, Cascades, Catoctin, Caucasus, Cevennes, classify, confines, distance, Flinders, latitude, Mogollon, mountain, Panamint, province, Pyrenees, spectrum, Stanovoi, straggle, Tian Shan, Tien Shan, traverse, vicinity, Wrangell 9 Admiralty, Aleutians, Apennines, Blue Ridge, dimension, diversity, Dolomites, Edsel Ford, encompass, fluctuate, gallivant, globe-trot, Himalayas, Hindu Kush, incidence, Karakoram, largeness, Mackenzie, magnitude, Queen Maud, repertory, Savoy Alps, selection, territory, Trans Alai 10 assortment, boundaries, Carnic Alps, Carpathian, categorize, dimensions, knock about, meadowland, parameters, Serra do Mar, St. Gotthard
Africa: 5 Atlas
animal: 4 calf, dogy 5 bison, dogey, dogie, steer 6 cayuse
Asia: 4 Alai, Ural 5 Altai, Urals 6 Kunlun 7 Kuenlun
ender: 4 land 6 finder
Europe: 4 Alps, Jura, Rhon, Ural 5 Alpes, Tatra, Urals 6 Cadore, Kjölen, Ortles, Pindus
feature: 5 timer
full ~: 4 A to Z 5 gamut, scope, sweep 6 extent 7 breadth, compass 8 spectrum
home on the ~: 5 tepee 6 wigwam
North America: 5 Lasal, Ozark, Teton, Uinta 7 Cascade, Rockies, Wasatch 10 Adirondack
of vision: 3 ken 4 view 5 sight 8 eyesight
out of ~: 3 far 4 away 6 remote 7 distant
out of ~ of: 6 beyond
over: 4 hike 5 cover, scout 6 search, survey, travel 7 explore 8 traverse
part: 3 mtn. 6 burner 8 mountain
South America: 5 Andes
starter: 4 down
within ~: 4 near 5 close 6 at hand, nearby 7 close-by 9 proximate
see also mountain
range ___: 3 oil 4 line, pole, wool 5 table 6 finder
___ range: 3 gas 4 home 5 basin, price, rifle 6 firing, visual 7 driving, dynamic
___-range: 4 free, long 5 short
Rangeley: 5 lakes
locale: 5 Maine
ranger: 6 warden
forest ~ at times: 5 guide
starter: 4 bush
___ ranger: 6 forest
Ranger: 3 car 4 auto 5 Edsel, NHLer 10 automobile, baseballer
rival: 3 Cub, Met, Red 4 Blue, Expo, King, Star, Twin, Wild 5 Angel, Astro, Brave, Bruin, Devil, Flame, Flyer, Giant, Oiler, Padre, Rocky, Royal, Sabre, Shark, Tiger 6 Brewer, Canuck, Coyote, Dodger, Indian, Marlin, Oriole, Philly, Pirate, Red Sox, Yankee 7 Blue Jay, Capital, Mariner, Panther, Penguin, Red Wing, Senator 8 Athletic, Canadien, Cardinal, Devil Ray, Islander, Predator, Thrasher, White Sox 9 Avalanche, Blackhawk, Hurricane, Lightning, Maple Leaf 10 Blue Jacket, Mighty Duck
___ Ranger: 4 Lone 5 Night, Texas 6 Sloane
Rangers: 3 six, ten 4 team
home: 5 Texas 7 New York
milieu: 3 ice 4 rink
org.: 3 ALW, MLB, NHL
sport: 6 hockey 8 baseball
___ Ranger, The: 4 Dude, Lone
ranginess: 4 size 5 sweep 6 length 7 breadth, compass, expanse
ranging: 6 mobile 7 migrant, nomadic 9 itinerant, migratory, transient
___-ranging: 4 wide
Rangoon: 4 city, port, town 6 Yangon 7 capital
locale: 5 Burma 7 Myanmar
royalty: 4 raja 5 rajah
rangy: 4 lank, lean, long, slim, tall, thin, wiry 5 lanky, leggy, reedy, weedy 6 gangly, skinny 7 slender, spindly 8 gangling 9 spindling 10 long-legged, long-limbed
___ Ranh Bay: 3 Cam
rani: 5 noble, ruler 6 gerent 8 princess
servant: 3 ama 4 amah, ayah
spouse: 4 raja 5 rajah
wear: 4 sari 5 saree
ranid: 4 frog 9 amphibian
rank: 3 bad, fix, off, peg, row, tab 4 duke, earl, foul, gamy, high, line, lush, olid, rate, rich, sort, sour, step, tier, type, wild 5 acrid, align, aline, array, baron, birth, caste, class, count, dense, fetid, funky, fusty, gamey, grade, gross, group, judge, level, major, moldy, musty, nasty, order, place, queue, range, sheer, stale, stand, stark, state, thick, total, utter 6 arrant, assign, assort, belong, column, estate, esteem, foetid, frowsy, frowzy, league, rancid, rating, rotten, series, size up, smelly, sphere, squire, status, stinky, string, strong, turned 7 arrange, blatant, colonel, dignity, duchess, echelon, extreme, footing, general, glaring, gone bad, measure, noisome, noxious, odorous, primacy, profuse, pungent, quality, rampant, reeking, station, stature, tainted, unclean 8 absolute, category, classify, complete, countess, estimate, evaluate, flagrant, graduate, immodest, leverage, mephitic, nobility, off-color, outright, position, prestige, priority, prolific, sergeant, standing, stinking, thorough, tropical, unsavory 9 authority, commander, downright, egregious, excessive, exuberant, gradation, hierarchy, low-minded, luxuriant, nefarious, out-and-out, overgrown, privilege, repellent, seniority, situation 10 categorize, consummate, disgusting, importance, indecorous, junglelike, malodorous, pigeonhole, precedence, procession, prominence, scurrilous
and file: 5 crowd, plebs 6 masses, people, public, rabble 8 plebeian
Army: 2 lt. 3 cpl., gen., maj., PFC, SFC, sgt 4 capt., corp. 5 lieut., lt. col., major 6 maj. gen. 7 captain, colonel, general, private 8 corporal, sergeant 10 lieutenant
Boy Scout ~: 4 Life, Star 5 Eagle
contestants: 4 seed
equal in ~: 5 level 10 comparable
front ~: 4 lead
grow ~: 3 rot
Navy: 3 cdr., CPO, ens., yeo. 4 capt., cmdr., RAdm. 5 lieut., lt. com. 6 ensign, seaman, yeoman 7 admiral, captain 10 lieutenant
of higher ~: 5 above, finer 6 better, senior 7 grander, greater 8 superior
out: 4 gibe, jeer, jibe, mock, slam, slur, snub 5 abuse, decry, libel, scorn, spurn, taunt 6 defame, deride, dump on, heckle, impugn, malign, offend, rebuff, slight, vilify 7 affront, asperse, degrade, disdain, put down, slander, traduce 8 belittle, denounce, ridicule, vilipend 9 denigrate, discredit, disparage, humiliate 10 calumniate, disrespect
partner: 4 file, name
raise in ~: 5 exalt 7 promote
reduce in ~: 4 bust 5 abase, break 6 demote 7 degrade 8 take down 9 downgrade
suffix: 4 -ship
with: 5 equal, match, rival 7 emulate 9 compare to
___ rank: 4 flag, pull 5 break
___-rank: 5 front
rank and ___: 4 file
ranking: 5 first 6 status 7 echelon 9 hierarchy, seniority
Rankin, Judy: 6 golfer
milieu: 5 links 6 course
org.: 4 LPGA
rankle: 3 get, irk, vex 4 fret, gall, hurt, pain, rile 5 anger, annoy, chafe, grate, peeve, upset 6 bother, fester, harass, nettle, obsess, pester, plague 7 enflame, inflame, mortify, torment 8 embitter, imbitter, irritate 9 aggravate 10 exasperate
ranks
close ~: 4 ally 5 merge, rally, unite 8 assemble, coalesce, converge 9 integrate
in ~: 4 arow
ransack: 3 gut, pry, rob, see, spy 4 comb, hunt, lift, loot, peer, raid, rake, rape, rout, scan, seek 5 filch, harry, pinch, poach, probe, rifle, scour, seize, sound, spoil, steal, strip 6 ferret, forage, maraud, pilfer, ravage, ravish, rustle, search, thieve 7 despoil, explore, pillage, plunder, purloin, rummage 8 freeboot, lay waste, look into, overhaul, spoliate, take away 9 depredate, go through, shake down 10 scrutinize
ransom: 4 free, save 5 bribe, price 6 payoff, redeem, regain, rescue 7 deliver, payment, recover, release, set free 8 liberate 9 expiation 10 redemption
hold for ~: 6 abduct, hijack, kidnap, pirate
pay ~: 6 redeem
___ ransom: 5 king's
Ransom (1996 film)
cast: Mel Gibson, Delroy Lindo, Rene Russo, Gary Sinise
director: Ron Howard
Ransom ___ Chief, The: 5 of Red
Ransom ___ Olds: 3 Eli
Ransom, John: 4 poet
Ransom of Red Chief, The author: O. Henry
rant: 4 fume, rage, rail, rave, yell 5 go ape, orate, shout, spiel, spout, storm 6 bellow, blow up, gibber, holler, scream, tirade 7 bluster, bombast, carry on, declaim, fustian, go crazy 8 bloviate, diatribe, go postal, harangue, have a fit, perorate, rhetoric 9 go bananas, go bonkers, go on about, make a fuss, throw a fit, utterance 10 hit the roof, make a scene
and rave: 6 ramble
___ Ran the Circus: 3 If I
___ Ran the Zoo: 3 If I
ranting: 3 hot, mad 4 ired, sore 5 cross,

huffy, irate, livid, riled, upset, wroth **6** ireful, peeved, raging, raving, red-hot, stormy, tirade **7** enraged, furious **8** choleric, harangue, incensed, inflamed, maddened, outraged, wrathful **9** bombastic, indignant, irritated, resentful, splenetic **10** freaked out, infuriated, vociferous
ranunculus: **5** plant **6** flower
Rao, Raja: **6** Indian, writer
work: The Serpent and the Rope
Raoul: **4** Dufy **5** Walsh
__ Raoul: **6** Eating
rap: **3** gab, hit, pan, say, tap, yak **4** bark, beat, blow, cane, chat, chin, conk, drum, flak, peck, slur, talk, tick, yarn **5** blame, clout, crack, decry, flack, genre, idiom, knock, music, punch, smear, speak, swipe, thump, whack **6** gabble, hip-hop, jabber, malign, parley, rebuke, strike, vilify, yammer **7** censure, chatter, condemn, palaver, penalty, schmoos, slander **8** admonish, badmouth, chitchat, converse, denounce, schmoose, schmooze, sentence, vocalize **9** criticism, criticize, disparage, table talk, tête-à-tête, touch base **10** chew the fat, chew the rag, punishment, yackety-yak
beat the ~: **4** walk **6** go free
bum ~: **5** frame **7** raw deal
ender: **8** scallion
give a ~: **4** care
music fan: **4** b boy, teen
on the knuckles: **5** scold **6** berate, punish, rebuke **7** censure, tell off, upbraid **8** admonish **9** reprimand
outlet: **3** MTV
sheet datum: **5** prior
starter: **3** rip
rap __: **4** full **5** group, music, sheet **7** session
__ rap: **3** bad, bum **7** gangsta
rapacious: **5** feral, venal **6** greedy, lupine, savage **7** furious, hoggish, lustful, preying **8** grasping, ravaging, ravening, ravenous, thieving, thievish **9** ferocious, marauding, murderous, predatory, raptorial, voracious, vulturous **10** aggressive, avaricious, gluttonous, insatiable, plundering
one: **3** hog **5** miser
rapacity: **5** greed **7** avarice **8** cupidity **9** esurience **10** grabbiness
Rapa Nui: **3** isl. **4** isle **6** Easter, island
Rape of the Lock, The author: **4** Pope
rapeseed __: **3** oil
Raph: **4** Alan
Raphael: **5** angel **6** artist, Sanzio **7** painter
homeland: **5** Italy
raphe: **4** seam **5** ridge
rapid: **4** fast, rush **5** brisk, fleet, hasty, quick, ready, swift **6** flying, prompt, racing, snappy, speedy, sudden, winged **7** cursory, express, hurried, instant **8** flitting, meteoric **9** breakneck, galloping, whirlwind **10** celeritous, double-time, harefooted, hypersonic, supersonic, ultrasonic
be ~: **3** hie **4** dash, race, tear **5** hurry, speed
growth environment: **3** den **4** nest **6** cradle
in music: **5** mosso
not ~: **4** poky, slow **6** draggy **7** gradual, halting, lagging **8** crawling, creeping, dawdling, dilatory, indolent, plodding, slothful, sluggish **9** leisurely, lethargic, ponderous, prolonged, snaillike, unhurried **10** protracted
pace: **4** clip
succession: **5** whirl **6** flurry
rapid __: **7** transit
rapid __ movement: **3** eye
rapid-__: **4** fire
Rapid __: **5** Shave
Rapidan: **5** river
locale: **8** Virginia
Rapid City: **4** town
locale: **4** S. Dak.
rapid-fire: **4** fast **5** hasty, quick, swift **6** speedy **7** hurried **9** breakneck **10** harefooted
rapidity: **3** bat, vel. **4** gait, pace, rush **5** haste, hurry, speed **8** alacrity, celerity, dispatch, velocity **9** briskness, fleetness, quickness, readiness, swiftness **10** expedition, promptness, speediness
rapidly: **3** PDQ **4** fast, soon **5** apace, madly **6** presto **7** briskly, flat out, fleetly, hastily, in a rush, in haste, quickly, swiftly **8** full tilt, in a flash, in a hurry, in a jiffy, in no time, pell-mell, promptly, speedily **9** forthwith, hurriedly, instantly, like a shot, posthaste **10** in high gear
rapids: **5** sault **6** chutes, dalles **10** white water
conveyance: **4** raft **5** kayak
__ Rapids, IA: **5** Cedar
rapier: **4** foil **5** blade, sword
cousin: **4** épée
rapierlike: **4** keen **5** honed, sharp **8** incisive
rapine: **7** looting, plunder, sacking, seizure
Rappahannock: **5** river
locale: **8** Virginia
Rappaport: **5** David
__ Rappaport: **5** I'm Not
rapparee: **6** pirate **7** brigand, corsair, sea wolf **8** marauder **9** buccaneer, privateer
rappel site: **5** cliff
rapper
bench ~: **5** gavel
friend: **3** bro
knock a ~: **3** dis
rave: **3** def, rad **4** phat
skill: **4** rime **5** rhyme
Rapper, Irving: **8** director
film: The Adventures of Mark Twain (1944)
The Brave One (1956)
The Corn Is Green (1945)
Deception (1946)
Forever Female (1953)
Marjorie Morningstar (1958)
Now, Voyager (1942)
One Foot in Heaven (1941)
Rhapsody in Blue (1945)
The Voice of the Turtle (1947)
rapport: **4** bond, link, soul **5** unity **6** accord, cotton, groove **7** concord, empathy, harmony **8** affinity, goodwill, sympathy **9** agreement, belonging, communion, consensus, good vibes, simpatico, unanimity **10** friendship
rapprochement: **7** détente, harmony **9** agreement, softening
rapscallion: **3** cur, imp **4** heel, worm **5** churl, knave, rogue, scamp **6** rascal, wretch **7** lowlife, villain **8** picaroon, scalawag **9** miscreant, reprobate, scallawag, scallywag, scoundrel, vulgarian **10** blackguard, ne'er-do-well, scapegrace
rap sheet
datum: **5** theft **6** arrest
word: **3** AKA **5** alias
rapt: **4** awed, deep, lost **5** in awe, taken **6** dreamy, intent **7** all ears, bemused, charmed, focused, gripped **8** absorbed, beguiled, ecstatic, held fast, immersed, involved, ravished **9** awestruck, delighted, engrossed, entranced, gladdened, oblivious **10** blissed out, captivated, enraptured, enthralled, fascinated, hypnotized, mesmerized, moonstruck, spellbound, thoughtful, transfixed
ender: **3** ure
hold ~: **5** charm **6** absorb, allure, engage, occupy **7** enchant, engross, immerse **8** enthrall, entrance **9** fascinate, preoccupy
raptor: **3** owl **5** eagle **6** eaglet
nest: **4** aery, eyry **5** aerie, eyrie
victim: **4** prey
raptorial: **5** feral **8** ravaging **9** on the hunt, predatory, rapacious
Raptor rival: **3** Net, Sun **4** Buck, Bull, Hawk, Heat, Jazz, King, Spur **5** Knick, Laker, Magic, Pacer, Sixer **6** Celtic, Hornet, Nugget, Piston, Rocket, Wizard **7** Clipper, Grizzly, Warrior **8** Cavalier, Maverick **10** SuperSonic, Timberwolf
Raptors: **4** five, team
home: **7** Toronto
org.: **3** NBA
sport: **10** basketball
rapture: **3** joy **4** cool, love **5** bliss, cheer, glory, spell **6** gaiety, gayety, heaven, trance **7** delight, ecstasy, elation, Elysium, nirvana, passion **8** buoyance, buoyancy, euphoria, felicity, gladness, lyricism, paradise, pleasure, radiance, radiancy, rhapsody **9** atoneness, beatitude, cloud nine, communion, enjoyment, happiness, transport, well-being **10** ebullience, enthusiasm, exaltation, jubilation, ravishment
Rapture, The (1991 film)
cast: David Duchovny, Mimi Rogers
rapturous: **6** elated, joyful, joyous **7** excited, radiant **8** beatific, blissful, ecstatic, euphoric, heavenly, in heaven, jubilant, ravished, thrilled **9** delirious, overjoyed, rhapsodic **10** delightful
become ~: **5** faint, swoon
raptus: **5** bliss **7** delight, ecstasy **8** euphoria **10** excitement
Rapunzel pride: **4** hair **5** tress
Raquel: **5** Welch
in English: **6** Rachel
rara avis: **3** gem **4** oner **6** oddity, wonder **7** oddball
rarae __: **4** aves
rare: **3** odd, red **4** thin **6** choice, exotic, lovely, scarce, select, single, sparse, superb, unique **7** extreme, oddball, several, special, strange, unusual, vintage **8** far apart, peerless, precious, singular, splendid, sporadic, uncommon, unlikely, unwonted **9** a cut above, exquisite, matchless, priceless, recherché, scattered, unheard of, unrivaled **10** at a premium, endangered, hard to find, improbable, infrequent, inimitable, invaluable, occasional, phenomenal, remarkable, sporadical, unexampled, unfrequent, unrivalled
earth: **5** metal **6** cerium, cesium, erbium **7** caesium, holmium, terbium, thulium, yttrium **8** europium, lutetium, samarium, scandium **9** neodymium, ytterbium **10** dysprosium, gadolinium, promethium **12** praseodymium
ender: **3** bit **4** ripe
like a ~ day in hell: **4** cool **6** chilly **8** freezing
not ~: **6** common **7** routine **8** familiar, frequent, ordinary **10** widespread
rarer than ~: **3** raw
rare __: **4** book **5** earth
rare as __ teeth: **4** hen's
__ rarebit: **5** Welsh
raree: **4** show **8** carnival, peep show
rarefaction: **6** vacuum
rarefied: **4** thin **5** lofty **6** select **7** exalted, refined, sublime, tenuous **8** eclectic, elevated, esoteric **9** selective, spiritual **10** unphysical
rarefy: **5** clean **6** purify, refine **7** cleanse, freshen
rarely: **6** little, seldom **7** notably **8** not often, scarcely **9** extremely, unusually **10** hardly ever, now and then, singularly, uncommonly
raring to go: **4** avid, keen **5** eager, itchy, ready **6** all set, on edge **9** hot to trot **10** inspirited
Raritan: **5** river **6** valley
locale: **9** New Jersey
rarity: **6** luxury, oddity, wonder **7** miracle, prodigy **9** curiosity **10** phenomenon
Rarotonga: **4** isle **6** island
island near ~: **4** Atiu
ras: **4** cape **8** headland
__ rasa: **6** tabula
Rasalas: **4** star
rascal: **3** bum, cad, cur, imp **4** heel, liar, worm **5** bully, cheat, churl, demon, devil, felon, fraud, ganef, gonef, gonif, idler, knave, losel, rogue, rowdy, scamp, skunk, sneak, tough, tramp **6** bad guy, bad hat, beggar, daemon, daimon, goniff, loafer, monkey, robber, sinner, wretch **7** grafter, outcast, ruffian, varment, varmint, villain, wastrel **8** disgrace, hooligan, picaroon, prodigal, rakehell, recreant, scalawag, swindler **9** cardsharp, charlatan, hypocrite, miscreant, prankster, pretender, reprobate, scallawag, scallywag, scoundrel, trickster, vulgarian **10** blackguard, black sheep, delinquent, holy terror, jackanapes, ne'er-do-well, profligate, scapegrace
rascality: **7** devilry, roguery **8** deviltry, mischief **10** dishonesty, impishness
rascally: **6** impish **7** knavish, naughty **9** miscreant **10** picaresque
Rascals
song: A Beautiful Morning (1968)
A Girl Like You (1967)
Good Lovin' (1966)
Groovin' (1967)
How Can I Be Sure (1967)
I've Been Lonely Too Long (1967)
People Got to Be Free (1968)
Rasche: **5** David
Ras Dashan: **4** peak **5** mount **8** mountain
locale: **6** Africa **8** Ethiopia
rash: **4** wave, wild **5** blind, brash, hasty, hives, spate **6** daring, litter, madcap, stupid, sudden, unwary, unwise, wanton **7** torrent **8** careless, eruption, headlong, heedless, immature, mindless, pell-mell, reckless **9** audacious, daredevil, desperate, foolhardy, hotheaded, impatient, impetuous, imprudent, impulsive, overhasty, premature, unadvised, unbridled, uncareful, unchecked, unguarded, unhearing, whirlwind **10** headstrong, ill-advised, incautious, indiscreet, regardless, succession, unthinking
act: **5** folly
not ~: **4** sane **5** lucid, sober, sound **6** steady **7** careful, logical, politic, prudent, tactful **8** cautious, discreet, moderate, rational, sensible, together **9** judicious, practical, pragmatic, provident, realistic, temperate **10** diplomatic, restrained, thoughtful

Rashad: 5 Ahmad 8 Phylicia
rasher: 5 bacon, piece, slice
rashly: 5 madly 8 pell-mell 9 headfirst
rashness: 5 folly, haste 7 courage 8 audacity 10 impatience, imprudence
goddess of ~: 3 Ate
Rashomon (1950 film)
cast: Machiko Kyo, Toshiro Mifune
director: Akira Kurosawa
Raskolnikov's love: 5 Sonya
Rasmussen, Knud: 6 Danish 8 explorer
rasophore: 4 monk 5 Greek 9 religious
rasp: 3 rub 4 bray, file, tool 5 grate, grind 6 abrade, scrape, squeal, wheeze 7 grate on, scratch 9 grate upon
ender: 5 berry
raspberry: 3 boo 4 jeer, twit 5 color, fruit, shrub 6 purple 7 reddish 8 ice cream 10 Bronx cheer
alternative: 5 lemon, mocha, peach 6 banana, coffee, Jamoca, toffee 7 caramel, coconut, vanilla 8 cinnamon, hazelnut 9 bubblegum, chocolate, pineapple, pistachio, rocky road, rum raisin 10 blackberry, cheesecake, Neapolitan, peppermint, strawberry
bit: 4 seed
cousin: 4 hoot
give the ~: 3 boo 4 hiss, hoot, mock 5 fleer, taunt 6 deride, heckle 7 catcall 9 make fun of
relative: 4 plum, puce, rose, sloe 5 lilac, mauve 6 dahlia, damson, kerria, orchid, spirea 7 bramble, heather, jetbead, petunia, spiraea 8 amethyst, burgundy, eggplant, hardhack, lavender, mulberry, ninebark, photinia 9 firethorn 10 heliotrope
sauce: 5 Melba
stem: 4 cane
raspberry ___: 4 tart 6 sawfly
___ raspberry: 5 black 7 boulder
Raspberry Beret (1985 song) artist: Prince
rasping: 5 husky, roupy 7 grating, raucous 8 friction, gravelly, guttural, strident
sound: 5 skirr
Rasputin and the Empress (1932 film)
cast: Ethel Barrymore, John Barrymore, Lionel Barrymore
raspy: 5 gruff, harsh, husky, rough, roupy, testy 6 coarse, froggy, hoarse 7 grating, throaty 8 gravelly, guttural 9 irritable 10 laryngitic
not ~: 6 smooth
rasse: 5 civet
Rastaban: 4 star
Rasulala: 7 Thalmus
rat: 3 cur 4 degu, fink, nark, sing, tell, toad, turn 5 knave, namer, scamp 6 animal, bad guy, mammal, rodent, snitch, squeal, tattle 7 stoolie, tattler, traitor 8 apostate, fat mouth, informer, inform on, squeaker, turncoat 9 informant, miscreant, no-goodnik, scoundrel 10 taleteller, tattletale
catcher: 4 trap 6 ferret
ender: 4 a-tat, fink, fish, line, tail, trap
female: 3 doe
join the ~ race: 4 moil, slog, toil 5 labor, slave, sweat 6 drudge, hustle, strive 7 achieve, peg away 8 plug away 9 freelance, grind away, moonlight 10 buckle down
male: 4 buck
milieu: 3 lab 4 maze 5 sewer, wharf
of film: 3 Ben 7 Willard
on: 4 sell 6 betray, give up, snitch, squeal, tattle, turn in 7 sell out 9 implicate
out of the ~ race: 4 retd. 7 retired
pack ~: 5 saver 6 animal, mammal, rodent, storer 7 amasser, hoarder 8 gatherer 9 collector
race: 3 rut 4 work 5 grind 7 society 8 drudgery 10 livelihood
race result: 6 stress
relative: 4 cavy, degu, jird, paca, vole 5 coypu, gundi, mouse, xerus 6 agouti, beaver, gerbil, gopher, jerboa, marmot, murine 7 hamster, lemming, visacha 8 chipmunk, cricetid, dormouse, squirrel, tucotuco 9 chickaree, groundhog, guinea pig, porcupine, woodchuck 10 chinchilla, prairie dog
rug ~: 3 kid, tot 4 babe, baby 6 infant
smell a ~: 5 doubt 7 suspect 8 distrust, mistrust 10 disbelieve
starter: 4 musk
young: 3 pup 6 kitten
rat ___: 4 pack, race 5 guard, snake 6 cheese 7 terrier
rat-___: 4 a-tat
rat-___ cactus: 4 tail
___ rat: 4 mole, pack, rice, rink, roof, sand, wood 5 black, brown, sewer, spiny, trade, water, wharf, white 6 desert, Norway, pepper, pocket 7 pouched
___ Rat: 4 King
___ rata: 3 pro
rat!, A: 3 eek
ratafia: 5 drink 6 cookie 7 biscuit 8 beverage
ingredient: 4 wine 5 fruit, juice 6 almond, brandy 10 grape juice
ratal: 5 value, worth
rat-a-tat: 4 roll 5 spiel 6 babble, jabber, patter 7 chatter 9 yakety-yak
ratatouille: 4 stew
ratchet: 5 wheel 6 detent
partner: 4 pawl
ratchet ___: 4 down, jack 5 wheel 6 effect
rate: 3 fee, jaw, pct., peg, set, tab, tag, tax 4 clip, cost, deem, dues, earn, gait, pace, rail, rank, time, toll 5 chide, count, grade, judge, merit, pitch, price, quota, quote, scale, score, set at, speed, tempo, terms, value, weigh 6 assess, assort, charge, degree, esteem, figure, reckon, regard, size up, survey, tariff, towage 7 adjudge, deserve, lecture, measure, percent, upbraid 8 appraise, classify, estimate, evaluate, progress, velocity 9 determine, incidence, quotation 10 have coming, percentage, pigeonhole, proportion
at any ~: 3 yet 10 all the same, in any event
ender: 5 payer 6 making
high: 3 dig 4 like, love 5 adore, enjoy, exalt, favor, go for 6 admire, prefer, relish, revere 7 cherish, idolize 8 hold dear, venerate 10 appreciate
of motion: 3 vel. 4 clip, pace 5 speed 8 velocity
poorly: 3 pan, rap 4 slam 5 knock 6 deride, oppugn 7 put down 8 lambaste 9 criticize, disparage
starter: 3 pro 5 birth
rate ___: 4 base, card
___ rate: 3 cut, tax 4 bank, base, call, rack 5 at any, basic, birth, decay, heart, lapse, piece, prime, pulse, short, space 6 church, coupon 7 milline
___-rate: 3 cut, low 5 first, third 6 fourth, second
rated
highly ~: 3 AAA 4 A-one, best, one A, tops
X: 4 lewd, racy 5 spicy 6 erotic, risqué, sultry, torrid
ratel: 6 weasel
relative: 4 mink 5 fitch, otter, sable, skunk, stoat, tayra 6 badger, ermine, ferret, marten 7 foumart, polecat 8 carcajou, foulmart, kolinsky, muishond 9 wolverine
___-rate mortgage: 5 fixed
rater: 5 judge 6 critic 8 assessor 9 appraiser
film ~: 4 MPAA 6 critic
film ~ unit: 4 star
ratfink: 5 crumb 6 snitch 7 traitor 8 betrayer, informer, renegade, turncoat 10 tattletale
Rath: 3 cow 4 bull 6 bovine, cattle
Rathbone, Basil: 5 actor
costar: Nigel Bruce
film: The Adventures of Robin Hood (1938)
The Adventures of Sherlock Holmes (1939)
Bathing Beauty (1944)
Confession (1937)
Court Jester (1956)
David Copperfield (1935)
The Dawn Patrol (1938)
Frenchman's Creek (1944)
The Hound of the Baskervilles (1939)
The House of Fear (1945)
If I Were King (1938)
The Last Days of Pompeii (1935)
The Mark of Zorro (1940)
Paris Calling (1941)
The Pearl of Death (1944)
Rhythm on the River (1940)
Romeo and Juliet (1936)
The Scarlet Claw (1944)
Sherlock Holmes and the Secret Weapon (1942)
Sherlock Holmes Faces Death (1943)
Son of Frankenstein (1939)
The Spider Woman (1944)
Tales of Terror (1962)
Tovarich (1937)
The Woman in Green (1945)
rather: 2 ay, da, ja, sí 3 aye, oui, yea, yep, yup 4 a bit, fine, lief, okay, some, so-so, sure, very, well, yeah 5 first, good-o, kinda, natch, quite, right, roger, sorta, uh-huh 6 agreed, enough, fairly, gladly, good-oh, indeed, just so, kind of, pretty, righto, sooner, sort of, surely, you bet, yowzah 7 a little, exactly, for sure, go ahead, indeedy, instead, mais oui, quite so, ten-four 8 a good bit, all right, as you say, by choice, of course, passably, slightly, somewhat, thumbs up, very well 9 averagely, be my guest, certainly, darn right, naturally, precisely, ratherish, something, sure thing, to a degree, tolerably, willingly, you betcha, you said it 10 absolutely, by all means, definitely, just as soon, moderately, more or less, much sooner, noticeably, positively, preferably, reasonably, relatively, sure enough, that's right
suffix: 3 -ish
than: 4 over 8 in lieu of
would ~: 5 elect, favor 6 choose, opt for, prefer, select 10 like better
Rather: 3 Dan
bailiwick: 4 news
network: 3 CBS 5 CBS-TV
rival: 6 Brokaw 8 Jennings
___ Rather Be With Me: 4 She'd
Rather you ___ me: 4 than
Rathi: 3 cow 4 bull 6 bovine, cattle
rathole: 3 hut 4 slum 5 hovel 6 pigpen
rathskeller: 3 bar, inn 6 eatery 10 restaurant
order: 3 ale 4 beer 5 lager, stein, wurst
...___ raths outgrabe: 4 mome
ratification: 6 assent 7 passage 8 adoption, sanction
ratify: 2 OK 4 bind, okay, pass, seal, sign 5 bless, go for 6 accept, affirm, attest, uphold 7 approve, bear out, certify, confirm, consent, endorse, indorse, license, sustain 8 accredit, sanction, validate 9 authorize, establish, make legal 10 commission
ratiné: 8 material 14 fabric. material
rating: 2 PG 3 TV-G, TV-M, TV-Y 4 mark, rank, tier, TV-PG 5 class, grade, level, order, score 6 degree, rebuke, status 8 category, judgment, standard 9 appraisal, valuation 10 assessment, evaluation
beef ~: 5 grade, prime 6 choice
bond ~: 3 AAA, Baa, BBB, CCC
dairy ~: 6 grade A
draft ~: 4 one A, two A 5 four F
film ~: 2 PG
film ~ org.: 4 MPAA
gasoline ~: 6 octane
high ~: 4 fine 5 prime 6 choice, superb 8 five-star, four-star, very good 9 excellent
perfect ~: 3 ten
sitcom ~: 4 TVPG
top ~: 4 A-one, one A 5 A plus
unit: 4 star
___ rating: 6 cetane, credit, octane 7 Nielsen
ratio: 4 sine 5 quota, scale 6 cosine 7 measure, tangent 8 equation, fraction, ten to one, two to one 10 comparison, percentage, proportion
indicator: 5 colon
math ~: 2 pi 3 cos, cot, sin, tan 4 sine 6 cosine 7 tangent 8 cosecant, fraction 9 cotangent
payout ~: 4 odds
phrase: 4 is to
___ ratio: 4 gear, loss 5 cross, focal 6 aspect, common, mixing, payout 7 current, fatigue
ratiocinate: 5 think 6 reason, reckon
ratiocination: 5 logic 6 reason 8 thinking 9 deduction, reasoning, reckoning
ratiocinator: 8 logician
ration: 3 bit, cut, lot 4 deal, dole, drag, food, give, meed, mete, part, save 5 allot, divvy, issue, limit, quota, share, store 6 assign, budget, divide, parcel, supply 7 control, deal out, dish out, divvy up, dole out, give out, hand out, helping, measure, mete out, pass out, portion, prorate, provide, quantum 8 allocate, conserve, disburse, dispense, division, restrict 9 allotment, allowance, apportion, parcel out, provender, provision 10 allocation, assignment, distribute, measure out, proportion, sustenance
slip: 6 coupon
___ ration: 5 field
___-Ration: 4 Ken-L
rational: 4 calm, cook, cool, sane, wise 5 lucid, right, sober, sound 6 cogent, likely, mental, normal, stable 7 knowing, liberal, logical, prudent, regular, sapient, tenable 8 all there, analytic, balanced, cerebral, coherent, credible, luculent, methodic, probable, sensible, thinking, together 9 cognitive, collected, conscious, deductive, impartial, judicious, objective, observant, plausible, practical, pragmatic, realistic, reasoning, sagacious, synthetic, unslanted 10 analytical, believable, consis-

tent, convincing, deliberate, discerning, farsighted, reasonable, reflective, thoughtful, unagitated
ender: 3 ism
mind: 3 ego
rational __: 4 form 6 number
rationale: 5 logic, story 6 excuse, motive, reason, theory, whyfor 7 account, big idea, grounds, purpose, reasons, whatfor 9 incentive, principle, reasoning 10 definition, exposition, hypothesis, motivation, philosophy, sour grapes
rationalism: 5 sense 6 reason, sanity 8 judgment, sapience 9 intellect, mentality, soundness 10 moderation, philosophy
rationalist: 5 cynic 7 doubter, sceptic, skeptic 10 questioner
rationality: 4 wits 5 sense 6 reason, sanity 8 sapience
rationalization: 4 plea 6 reason 7 defense, pretext, thought 9 rationale
rationalize: 5 think 6 cop out, defend, reason, renege 7 explain, justify 9 extenuate, whitewash
rationing agcy., WWII: 3 OPA
rations: 4 chow, fare, food, grub 5 items 7 aliment 8 supplies, victuals
ratite: 3 emu, moa 4 emeu, kiwi, rhea 9 cassowary
extinct ~: 3 moa
ratlike rodent: 4 vole
ratline: 4 rope
Ratner, Brett: 8 director
film: The Family Man (2000)
Red Dragon (2002)
Rush Hour (1998)
Rush Hour 2 (2001)
Ratoff, Gregory: 8 director
film: The Corsican Brothers (1941)
Footlight Serenade (1942)
Intermezzo (1939)
Lancer Spy (1937)
Sing, Baby, Sing (1936)
Skyscraper Souls (1932)
Something to Shout About (1943)
Wife, Husband and Friend (1939)
ratón chaser: 4 gato
__ Raton, FL: 4 Boca
Rat Pack member: 4 Dean, Dino, Joey 5 Frank, Peter, Sammy 6 Bishop, Martin 7 Lawford, Sinatra 10 Dean Martin, Joey Bishop
Rat Race (2001 film)
cast: Rowan Atkinson, Whoopi Goldberg, Cuba Gooding Jr., Jon Lovitz
director: Jerry Zucker
Rat Race author: Dick Francis
Rat Race, The (1960 film)
cast: Tony Curtis, Jack Oakie, Debbie Reynolds
director: Robert Mulligan
rat's __: 4 nest
Rats!: 3 fie 4 dang, darn, drat, heck, oath, oh no, pfui 5 pshaw 6 darn it, oh crud, phooey, shucks
ratskeller serving: 4 bier
Ratso: 5 Rizzo 6 Dustin
__ Rats, The: 6 Desert
rats, to cats: 4 prey
rat-tail __: 4 file 6 cactus
rattan: 4 cane, palm
artisan: 5 caner
ratter: 4 fink 5 snake 7 stoolie, tattler, traitor 8 betrayer, quisling, squealer, turncoat
Rat, The author: Günter Grass
Rattigan, Terrence;: 7 British 9 dramatist 10 playwright
work: French Without Tears
Separate Tables
While the Sun Shines
The Winslow Boy
rattle: 3 cow, gab, jar, jaw, toy, yak 4 bang, chat, drum, faze, gush, jolt, list, rock, verb 5 abash, addle, adodo, clack, clank, get to, knock, prate, run on, scare, shake, sound, throw, upset 6 axatse, babble, baffle, bicker, bother, bounce, cackle, caxixi, dismay, flurry, gabble, harass, heckle, jabber, jangle, jiggle, jounce, judder, muddle, noodge, put off, put out, unglue 7 chatter, clatter, confuse, disrupt, disturb, flummox, fluster, nonplus, perplex, perturb, prattle, reel off, shake up, shatter, unnerve, vibrate 8 bewilder, confound, distract, frighten, irritate, psych out, unsettle, unstring 9 discomfit, embarrass, give a turn 10 demoralize, discompose, disconcert, percussion, run through
chest ~: 4 rale
ender: 3 box 4 trap 5 brain, snake
off: 6 recite
on: 3 gab, yak, yap 4 blab, talk 5 prate 6 babble, jabber, ramble 7 blather, chatter, prattle 8 divagate
__, Rattle and Roll: 5 Shake
rattlebrain: 3 ass, oaf, sap 4 boob, clod, dolt, fool 5 chump, clown, cluck, dummy, dunce, joker, ninny, patsy 6 dimwit, lummox, nitwit, sucker, turkey 7 buffoon, dingbat, dullard, fathead, half-wit, jackass, pinhead, saphead 8 bonehead, dumbbell, meathead, numskull 9 blockhead, numbskull, simpleton 10 dunderhead, nincompoop
rattlebrained: 5 giddy, goofy, inane, silly 7 foolish
rattled: 5 shook, upset 6 addled 7 abashed, fuddled 9 unsettled
it may get ~: 5 saber
rattleheaded: 3 mad 4 daft, soft 5 balmy, dotty, flaky, inane, nutty, silly, wacky 6 absurd, flakey, whacky 7 asinine, doltish, foolish, touched, unsound, witless 9 brainless, half-baked, senseless 10 off-the-wall, ridiculous
rattlepate: 3 ass, oaf, sap 4 boob, clod, dolt, fool 5 chump, clown, cluck, dummy, dunce, joker, ninny, patsy 6 dimwit, lummox, nitwit, sucker, turkey 7 buffoon, dingbat, dullard, fathead, half-wit, jackass, pinhead, saphead 8 bonehead, dumbbell, lunkhead, meathead, numskull 9 blockhead, harebrain, numbskull, simpleton 10 dunderhead, nincompoop, noodlehead 11 chucklehead, knucklehead
rattler: 5 snake 6 animal 7 reptile
defense: 4 fang 5 venom
position: 4 coil
relative: 3 asp, boa 5 aboma, adder, cobra, krait, mamba, racer, viper 6 dhaman, python, taipan 7 markhor 8 anaconda, moccasin, ringhals 9 boomslang, coachwhip 10 bushmaster, copperhead, sidewinder
rattles: 6 sistra 7 sistrum
rattlesnake __: 4 fern, root, weed 6 master
__ rattlesnake: 6 banded, timber 7 prairie
rattlesnakes do it: 4 molt
rattletrap: 3 car 4 auto, heap 5 crate, lemon, wreck 6 jalopy, junker 7 clunker, flivver
rattling: 5 shaky 8 clashing 9 talkative
__-rattling: 5 saber
Rattray: 7 Heather
ratty: 4 torn, worn 5 cheap, seedy, tacky 6 shabby 7 run-down, unkempt 8 dog-eared, tattered, wretched 9 moth-eaten 10 disheveled, gone to seed, in bad shape, threadbare
Ratzenberger: 4 John
raucous: 3 dry 4 loud 5 acute, brusk, forte, gruff, harsh, husky, noisy, rough, rowdy, sharp, thick 6 atonal, coarse, hoarse, shrill, unruly 7 blaring, blatant, booming, braying, brusque, grating, jarring, pealing, rackety, rasping, reboant, roaring 8 absonant, crashing, grinding, piercing, plangent, rumbling, sonorous, strident, turned up 9 big-voiced, clamorous, deafening, dissonant, squawking, tumultous, turbulent, unmelodic, unmusical 10 boisterous, discordant, disorderly, resounding, stentorian, stertorous, strepitous, thundering, tumultuous, uproarious, vociferant, vociferous
sound: 4 blat 5 blare 6 clamor, racket
Raul: 5 Julia
see also Spanish
Raunchy (1957 song)
artist: Bill Justis, Billy Vaughan and His Orchestra, Ernie Freeman
Raung: 7 volcano
locale: 4 Asia, Java 9 Indonesia
rauwolfia: 4 tree
RAV: 3 SUV 6 Toyota
ravage: 3 gut, rob 4 loot, prey, raid, rase, raze, ruin, sack, sink 5 cream, crush, erode, foray, harry, seize, smash, spoil, strip, total, trash, waste, wreck, wrest 6 damage, forage, harrow, impair, invade, maraud, pirate, prey on, waster 7 break up, capture, consume, corrupt, despoil, destroy, disrupt, overrun, pillage, plunder, ransack, shatter, trample 8 demolish, desolate, freeboot, lay waste, mutilate, pull down, spoliate, stamp out 9 depredate, desecrate, devastate, dismantle, overthrow, overwhelm, prostrate, sweep away 10 annihilate, extinguish, wreak havoc
ravager: 3 Hun 6 bandit, vandal
ravaging: 6 lupine 7 wolfish 8 ravenous 9 ferocious, predatory, rapacious, raptorial, voracious, vulturous 10 aggressive, predacious
rave: 4 boil, flip, fume, gush, rage, rail, rant 5 cry up, freak, go ape, go mad, kudos, shout, storm 6 babble, bubble, jabber, praise, review, scream, wander 7 acclaim, bluster, carry on, declaim, enthuse, explode, flare up, go crazy, thunder 8 bloviate, freak out, harangue, have a fit, splutter 9 blow a fuse, go bananas, go bonkers, raise Cain, throw a fit 10 effervesce, hit the roof, rhapsodize
at: 4 slam 8 lace into 10 vituperate
partner: 4 rant
ravel: 6 loosen, unwind 7 unravel, untwine, untwist, unweave 8 entangle, untangle 9 come apart
ravell'd __ of care..., The: 6 sleave
Ravel, Maurice: 6 French 8 composer
work: Bolero
Daphnis and Chloe
Jeux d'eau
La Valse
Rhapsodie Espagnole
Tzigane
Ravelstein author: Saul Bellow
raven: 3 jet 4 bird 5 black, sable 7 engorge
call: 3 caw 5 croak
combining form: 5 -corax
cousin: 3 daw 4 crow
haven: 4 nest
relative: 3 jet 4 inky, onyx 5 ebony, sable, sooty
__ raven: 3 sea 5 night
ravening: 6 lupine 7 lustful 9 predatory, rapacious, voracious
Ravenna: 4 city, town
locale: 5 Italy
ravenous: 5 empty, feral, unfed 6 greedy, hungry, lupine 7 longing, peckish, piggish, starved, wolfish 8 covetous, desirous, edacious, esurient, famished, grasping, ravaging, starving 9 devouring, ferocious, insatiate, predatory, rapacious, voracious 10 avaricious, gluttonous, insatiable, omnivorous, very hungry
ravenousness: 6 hunger 7 craving, edacity, longing 8 appetite, cupidity, voracity 9 appetence, esurience
Raven rival: 3 Jet, Ram 4 Bear, Bill, Colt, Lion 5 Brown, Chief, Eagle, Giant, Niner, Saint, Texan, Titan 6 Bengal, Bronco, Cowboy, Falcon, Jaguar, Packer, Raider, Viking 7 Charger, Dolphin, Panther, Patriot, Redskin, Seahawk, Steeler 8 Cardinal 9 Buccaneer
Ravens: 4 team 6 eleven
home: 9 Baltimore
org.: 3 AFC, NFL
sport: 8 football
Raven's Wing author: 5 Oates
Raven, The: 4 poem
author: Edgar Allan Poe
emulate ~: 3 rap
goddess: 6 Pallas
opener: 4 once
word: 4 upon 5 quoth 9 nevermore
Raven, The (1935 film)
cast: Boris Karloff, Bela Lugosi, Irene Ware
director: Lew Landers
Raven, The (1963 film)
cast: Boris Karloff, Peter Lorre, Vincent Price
director: Roger Corman
raver: 6 ranter 7 windbag 8 blowhard 9 loudmouth
Ravi: 7 Shankar
ravin: 4 prey
ravine: 3 cut, gap 4 gulf, pass, rift, wadi, wady, wash 5 abyss, break, cañon, chasm, clove, ditch, flume, gorge, gulch, gully, notch 6 arroyo, canyon, coulee, defile, gullet, gulley, valley 7 crevice, fissure 8 crevasse
South African ~: 5 kloof
raving: 3 hot, mad 4 ired, sore, wild 5 cross, huffy, irate, livid, manic, riled, upset, wroth 6 fierce, ireful, peeved, raging, red-hot, stormy 7 enraged, furious 8 choleric, harangue, incensed, inflamed, maddened, maniacal, outraged, white-hot, wrathful 9 fanatical, indignant, irritated, possessed, resentful, splenetic, wrought-up 10 freaked out, hysterical, infuriated
ravioli: 5 pasta 6 entrée
alternative: 4 orzo, ziti 5 penne 6 noodle 7 lasagna, lasagne, pastina 8 bucatini, couscous, farfalle, linguine, linguini, macaroni, rigatoni 9 agnolotti, angelhair, cavatelli, manicotti, spaghetti 10 cannelloni, fettuccini, tortellini, vermicelli
kin: 6 dim sum, wonton 8 dumpling, kreplach
ravish: 4 ruin 5 charm, seize 6 abduct 7 bewitch, delight, enchant, enthral, inthral, overjoy, ransack, violate 8 enthrall, entrance, inthrall 9 captivate, enrapture, fascinate, spellbind, transport
ravished: 4 rapt 6 elated, joyful 7 gleeful, gripped 8 beguiled, ecstatic,

euphoric, exultant, immersed, jubilant, thrilled **9** delighted, engrossed, entranced, overjoyed, rapturous, rhapsodic **10** captivated, enraptured, enthralled, fascinated, moonstruck, spellbound

ravishing: 4 cute **5** bonny **6** bonnie, comely, lovely, pretty **7** lovable, winsome **8** alluring, dazzling, gorgeous, handsome, loveable, striking, stunning **9** beautiful **10** attractive, delightful, enchanting

raw: 3 icy, new **4** cold, damp, dank, gory, nude, rude, sore **5** basic, bleak, chill, crass, crisp, crude, fresh, green, gross, harsh, naked, rough, seamy, stark, windy, young **6** biting, bitter, bloody, breezy, callow, chafed, chilly, coarse, earthy, frigid, frosty, frozen, grazed, ribald, risqué, smutty, tender, unclad, vulgar, wintry **7** abraded, bruised, cutting, exposed, fibrous, glacial, natural, numbing, obscene, painful, puerile, scraped, unbaked, uncouth, wintery **8** blustery, freezing, ignorant, immature, piercing, uncooked, untested, unversed **9** au naturel, blistered, inclement, irritated, primitive, roughhewn, scratched, sensitive, unclothed, uncovered, underdone, unrefined, unskilled, untrained, untutored **10** lascivious, uncultured, unfinished, unpolished, unschooled, unseasoned
  ender: 4 hide **5** boned
  in the ~: 4 bare, nude **5** naked **6** unclad **7** exposed **8** disrobed, stripped **9** unattired, unclothed, uncovered, undressed
  nearly ~: 4 rare

raw __: 4 data, deal, silk **5** score, umber **6** fibers, sienna

rawboned: 4 lank, lean, thin **5** gaunt, lanky, spare **6** gangly, meager, skinny **8** gangling
  animal: 5 scrag

Raw Deal (1948 film)
  cast: Marsha Hunt, Dennis O'Keefe, Claire Trevor
  director: Anthony Mann

rawhide: 4 whip **7** leather

Rawhide (CBS western)
  cast: Paul Brinegar (Wishbone)
    Clint Eastwood (Rowdy Yates)
    Eric Fleming (Gil Favor)
    Sheb Wooley (Pete Nolan)
  prop: 5 lasso, reata, riata **6** lariat
  theme singer: Laine

Rawlings, Marjorie Kinnan: 6 author, writer
  work: The Yearling

Rawls: 3 Lou **5** Betsy

Rawls, Betsy: 6 golfer
  milieu: 5 links **6** course
  org.: 4 LPGA

Rawls, Lou
  song: Lady Love (1978)
    Love Is a Hurtin' Thing (1966)
    A Natural Man (1971)
    You'll Never Find Another Love Like Mine (1976)
    Your Good Thing (1969)

Raw Material author: Oliver La Farge

rawness: 4 cold **5** chill **10** immaturity, inclemency

ray: 4 beam, fish **5** flash, gleam, glint, light, manta, shaft, shred, skate, spark, spoke, trace **6** streak **7** flicker, glimmer, glitter, sunbeam **8** flatfish, moonbeam, particle **9** scintilla
  combining form: 5 actin- **6** actino-
  starter: 5 sting

ray __: 3 gun **6** floret, flower

__ ray: 3 bat, fin **4** beta, pith, wood **5** alpha, anode, canal, delta, devil, eagle, gamma, manta, xylem **6** cosmic, phloem **7** actinic, cathode

Ray: 3 Amy, Man **4** Aldo, John, Kroc **5** Bloch, Evans, Floyd, Hamel, Meyer, Price **6** Bolger, Danton, Eberle, Liotta, Parker, Romano, Schalk **7** Anthony, Charles, Conniff, Enright, Johnnie, Mancini, Milland, Sharkey, Stevens, Walston **8** Bradbury, Goulding, Manzarek, Nicholas, Nitschke, Peterson, Satyajit **9** Dandridge

Ray, Aldo: 5 actor
  film: Battle Cry (1955)
    The Day They Robbed the Bank of England (1960)
    Dead Heat on a Merry-Go-Round (1966)
    God's Little Acre (1958)
    Haunts (1977)
    Let's Do It Again (1953)
    The Marrying Kind (1952)
    Miss Sadie Thompson (1953)
    The Naked and the Dead (1958)
    Nightfall (1956)
    Pat and Mike (1952)

Rayburn: 3 Sam **4** Gene

__ Ray Cyrus: 5 Billy

Raye: 6 Collin, Martha

Raye, Martha: 7 actress **8** comedian
  film: The Big Broadcast of 1938 (1938)
    Billy Rose's Jumbo (1962)
    College Swing (1938)
    Hellzapoppin' (1941)
    Keep 'em Flying (1941)
    Monsieur Verdoux (1947)
    Navy Blues (1941)
    Never Say Die (1939)
    Waikiki Wedding (1937)
  spouse: David Rose
  TV: Alice

ray gun, use a: 3 zap

__ Ray Hutton: 3 Ina

Ray, Johnnie
  song: Cry (1951)
    Just Walking in the Rain (1956)
    You Don't Owe Me a Thing (1957)

Rayleigh, John: 7 British **8** Nobelist **9** physicist

__ Ray Leonard: 5 Sugar

Raymond: 4 Alex, Burr, Gene **5** Davis, Flynn, Lully **6** Bailey, Carver, Massey **7** Queneau, Souster **8** Chandler, Poincaré **9** St. Jacques
  in Spanish: 5 Ramón

Raymond, Gene: 5 actor
  film: Flying Down to Rio (1933)
    Hooray for Love (1935)
    Mr. and Mrs. Smith (1941)
    Sadie McKee (1934)
    Zoo in Budapest (1933)

Ray, Nicholas: 8 director
  film: 55 Days at Peking (1963)
    Bigger Than Life (1956)
    The Flying Leathernecks (1951)
    In a Lonely Place (1950)
    Johnny Guitar (1954)
    King of Kings (1961)
    The Lusty Men (1952)
    On Dangerous Ground (1952)
    Party Girl (1958)
    Rebel Without a Cause (1955)
    They Live by Night (1949)

ray of __: 4 hope

Ray of Light (1998 song) artist: Madonna

__ rayon: 4 spun **7** acetate, butcher, viscose

rayon fabric: 3 rep **4** repp **5** moire, piqué, satin, surah, tulle, voile **6** chally, faille, jersey, pongee, poplin, velvet **7** challie, challis, charvet, chiffon, duvetyn, foulard, Mogador, organza, ottoman, silesia, taffeta **8** Celanese, chenille, marocain, Milanese, popeline, shantung **9** grenadine, sharkskin **10** seersucker

__ Ray Robinson: 5 Sugar

rays: 5 radii
  catch some ~: 3 sun, tan **4** bask

Raytown: 4 city
  locale: 8 Missouri

__-ray tube: 7 cathode

__ Ray Vaughan: 6 Stevie

Raz: 4 Kavi

raze: 4 bomb, ruin **5** level, smash, total, waste, wreck **6** efface, ravage, remove, topple **7** destroy, flatten, mow down, unbuild, wipe out **8** bulldoze, demolish, dynamite, pull down, take down, tear down **9** devastate, eradicate, extirpate, knock down **10** obliterate

razee: 4 ship **5** craft **6** vessel **7** warship

razing: 8 leveling **10** bulldozing, demolition
  remains: 5 ruins **6** debris, rubble

razor: 3 Bic **4** Atra **6** cutter, Schick, shaver **7** trimmer **8** Gillette
  alternative: 4 Nair, Neet **10** depilatory
  asset: 4 edge
  cut: 2 do **8** coiffure **9** hairstyle
  ender: 4 back, bill
  filler: 5 blade
  like a ~: 5 sharp
  mishap: 3 cut **4** nick
  ready a ~: 4 hone, whet **7** sharpen
  sharpener: 5 strop
  use a ~: 3 cut **5** shave

razor __: 4 clam, wire **5** blade

razor-__ auk: 6 billed

__ razor: 4 band **6** Occam's, safety **7** Ockham's

razorback: 3 hog, pig **4** boar **5** swine

Razorbacks: 3 Ark. **8** Arkansas

razor-billed bird: 3 auk **5** murre **6** auklet

razorlike: 4 keen **5** sharp

Razor's Edge, The: 4 film **5** novel
  author: W. Somerset Maugham
  cast: John Payne, Tyrone Power, Gene Tierney
  director: Edmund Goulding

razz: 3 kid, rib **4** hiss, jeer, twit **5** chaff, taunt, tease **6** banter, deride, heckle **8** ridicule **9** make fun of **10** Bronx cheer

razzing: 8 derision **9** raspberry **10** Bronx cheer

razzle-dazzle: 5 éclat **8** trickery **10** virtuosity

Rb: 4 elem. **7** element **8** rubidium
  37 for ~: 4 at. no.

RBI: 4 stat

R. Buckminster __: 6 Fuller

RC: 4 cola, soda **9** soft drink
  competitor: 4 Coke **5** Pepsi

RCA: 2 TV **3** VCR **5** TV set **10** television
  alternative: 3 JVC, NEC **4** Sony **6** Quasar, Zenith **7** Emerson, Hitachi, ProScan, Toshiba **8** Magnavox, Sylvania **9** Panasonic
  dog: 6 Nipper

RCA __: 4 Dome **6** Victor

RCMP: 8 Mounties
  part of ~: 3 Mtd. **5** Royal **6** Police **7** Candian, Mounted
  patrol zone: 3 NWT **5** Yukon
  rank: 3 sgt.

rcpt.: 3 vou.

rct.: 2 GI
  employer: 3 USN **4** USMC

rd.: 2 ln. **3** ave., hwy., rte., tpk. **4** pkwy., tnpk.

R.D.: 5 Laing

RDA formulator: 3 FDA

re: 4 as to, note **5** about, anent, as for **6** toward **7** towards **9** apropos of, as regards **10** concerning, in regard to

Re: 4 elem. **7** element, rhenium
  75 for ~: 4 at. no.
  see also rhenium

__ rea: 4 mens

Rea: 5 Chris, Peggy **7** Gardner, Stephen

Rea __: 6 Silvia

reach: 2 go, to **3** end, get, hit, ken, win **4** buck, come, drop, fall, gain, go on, go to, hand, join, land, lead, make, meet, move, pass, play, rise, room, show, sink, span, sway **5** ambit, climb, enter, equal, gamut, get at, get in, get to, grasp, lunge, orbit, power, range, realm, run to, scale, scope, score, seize, shoot, space, stand, sweep, swing, total, touch, width **6** affect, amount, arrive, attain, come at, come to, derive, extend, extent, gain on, land at, land on, length, make it, obtain, put out, rack up, radius, ring in, roll in, roll on, show up, sign in, spread, strain, strike, tamper, turn up **7** ability, achieve, breadth, carry to, check in, climb to, clock in, command, compass, contact, expanse, feel for, hit town, hold out, horizon, mastery, measure, purview, realize, stretch **8** amount to, approach, arrive at, capacity, come up to, distance, dominion, extend to, get there, go across, latitude, lengthen, maintain, overtake, wind up at **9** catch up to, dimension, encompass, extension, get hold of, get to know, go as far as, influence, largeness, magnitude, pass along, set foot in **10** accomplish, continue to, get a hold of, get as far as, get in touch, get through, shake hands
  across: 4 span **6** bridge **8** traverse
  a limit: 3 max **4** peak **6** max out
  for: 6 grab at **9** stretch to
  new heights: 4 grow, soar **5** bloom, climb **6** ascend, evolve, expand, rocket, sprout, thrive **7** burgeon, enlarge, prosper **8** increase, multiply, progress **9** skyrocket
  out: 4 talk **6** extend **9** touch base
  out blindly: 5 grope
  out of ~: 3 far **7** distant **8** hopeless **10** infeasible
  out of ~ of: 4 past **6** beyond
  the top: 4 rise **5** climb **6** arrive, ascend **7** prosper, succeed, triumph **8** flourish, get ahead, surmount
  within ~: 4 near, nigh, open **5** close, handy **6** at hand, doable, likely, nearby, viable **8** adjacent, credible, feasible, imminent, possible, workable **9** bordering, impending, plausible, potential, practical, proximate **10** achievable, attainable, convenient, imaginable
  within ~ of: 4 near **6** nearby **7** close by, close to **10** adjacent to

__ reach: 3 sea **4** beam, free **5** broad, close **6** within

reachable: 9 available **10** accessible, attainable

reached, not: 5 unmet

__ reaches: 5 outer, upper

__-reaching: 3 far

Reach Out I'll Be There (1966 song)
  artist: Four Tops

reacquire: 6 recoup, regain **7** get back, reclaim, recover, win back **8** retrieve **9** recapture

react: 4 feel, take **5** reply, start **6** behave, recoil **7** counter, hit back, respond **8** backfire, talk back

9 boomerang, get back at 10 answer back, bounce back
to a bad joke: 4 moan 6 flinch 7 grimace 9 make a face
to funniness: 4 howl, roar 6 giggle, titter 7 chuckle, crack up
to onions: 3 cry 4 weep
to ragweed: 6 sneeze 7 sniffle
toward: 5 treat 6 handle, regard
unlikely to ~: 4 calm, cool 5 inert 6 serene
__-react: 5 chain
reactant: 8 catalyst
reaction: 3 hit, lip 4 echo, kick, sass, take 5 reply, right, vibes 6 answer, recoil, reflex, retort, return 7 feeling, opinion, outcome, rebound, relapse, retreat, Toryism 8 attitude, backfire, backlash, back talk, comeback, feedback, kickback, knee-jerk, response 9 boomerang, reception, rejoinder, revulsion, status quo, wisecrack 10 double-take, impression, reflection, regression, withdrawal
atomic ~: 6 fusion 7 fission
chemical ~: 5 redox 9 oxidation, reduction
combining form: 4 trop- 5 tropo-
critical ~: 3 pan 4 rave
get a ~ from: 6 arouse
hostile ~: 4 flak 5 flack 6 outcry 7 dissent, protest 9 criticism
reaction __: 4 time 5 motor 6 engine 7 turbine
__ reaction: 3 gut, oxo 4 dark 5 alarm, chain 7 nuclear
reactionaries: 5 right 9 right wing
reactionary: 4 tory 5 right 6 narrow 7 diehard, hard-hat 8 loyalist, orthodox, renegade, rightist, royalist 9 old-school
__ reactor: 5 chain 6 atomic, fusion 7 breeder, nuclear
reactor, nuclear: 4 pile
element: 5 boron
part: 3 rod
PA ~ site: 3 TMI
read: 4 look, pore, scan, skim, view 5 learn, sense, study 6 browse, decode, devour, go over, locate, peruse, rebuke, recite, record, regard, survey 7 deliver, dictate, dip into, make out, measure, observe 8 audition, bone up on, check out, construe, decipher, discover, look over, pore over, register 9 get to know, grind away, interpret, pronounce, translate 10 crack a book, understand
ability to ~: 8 literacy
able to ~: 8 literate
back: 6 repeat
between the lines: 3 bet 5 glean, guess, infer, judge, wager, weigh 6 assume, call it, deduce, figure, gather, intuit, reckon, size up, wonder 7 imagine, make out, presume, suppose, surmise, suspect 8 arrive at, conclude, construe, intimate 9 figure out, interpret, postulate, speculate 10 conjecture, have a hunch, understand
easily ~: 5 clear, lucid, plain 7 legible 8 distinct
ender: 3 out
inability to ~: 6 alexia 10 illiteracy
it may be ~: 4 lips, mind, palm 7 riot act
make hard to ~: 6 encode
one way to ~: 5 aloud
out loud: 6 recite 7 narrate, perform
starter: 5 proof
the riot act to: 3 hit 4 flay, flog, slam 5 blast, chide, scold 6 berate, rebuke 7 bawl out, censure, chasten, chew out, condemn, lecture, reprove, upbraid 8 admonish, chastise, denounce, lambaste, reproach, sail into, tear into, threaten 9 castigate, criticize, dress down, excoriate, reprehend, reprimand 10 come down on, discipline, take to task, vituperate
up on: 5 study 8 research 9 delve into
read __: 3 out 4 up on 5 out of
read __ the lines: 7 between
read __ weep: 5 'em and
read-__: 7 through
read-__ memory: 4 only
__-read: 3 lip 4 must, well 5 sight, speed
readable: 4 easy, tidy 5 clean, clear, lucid, plain 6 clever, fluent, simple, smooth 7 amusing, flowing, graphic, legible, orderly, precise, regular 8 coherent, distinct, eloquent, engaging, exciting, explicit, gripping, inviting, pleasant, pleasing, relaxing 9 absorbing, appealing, brilliant, enjoyable, graphical, ingenious, rewarding 10 engrossing, gratifying, satisfying, worthwhile
make ~: 5 crack 6 decode 7 decrypt 8 decipher 9 interpret, translate
__-readable: 7 machine
Read all __ it: 5 about
read between the __: 5 lines
Reade, Charles: 6 author, writer 7 British
work: The Cloister and the Hearth
Read 'Em and Weep (1983 song)
artist: Barry Manilow
reader: 4 book, text 6 cleric, lector 7 prophet 8 lecturer 10 schoolbook
avid ~: 8 bookworm
manuscript ~: 6 editor
need: 4 lamp 5 light
omen ~: 4 seer 5 augur 6 auspex 7 prophet, psychic
starter: 4 copy 5 proof
__ reader: 3 lay, lip 4 mind, palm, wand 6 script
Reader's Digest lack, until 1955: 3 ads
Reader's Encyclopedia editor: 5 Benét
__ Reader, The: 4 Utne
Read, Herbert: 4 poet 7 British
readily: 4 lief 5 lieve 6 at once, easily, freely, gladly, openly 7 eagerly, quickly 8 in a jiffy, in no time, promptly, speedily 9 naturally, right away, summarily, willingly 10 cheerfully, swimmingly
readiness: 4 ease, zeal 5 skill, speed 7 address, aptness, fitness, fluency, prowess, sleight 8 alacrity, capacity, deftness, dispatch, facility, good will, keenness, maturity, rapidity, ripeness, tendency 9 dexterity, eagerness, eloquence, handiness, quickness 10 adroitness, efficiency, enterprise, expedience, expedition, generosity, promptness, volubility
in ~: 5 on tap 6 all set, on call, on hand 8 geared up, prepared, warmed up
state of ~: 5 alert 7 caution
reading: 5 grasp, study 6 lesson, review 7 account, perusal, recital, version 8 audition, learning, scrutiny 9 education, erudition, knowledge, narration, rehearsal, rendering, rendition, treatment 10 commentary, conception, impression, inspection, paraphrase, recitation
compact ~: 5 brief 6 digest 7 summary 8 abstract, synopsis
compass ~: 3 ENE, ESE, NNE, NNW, SSE, SSW, WNW, WSW 7 heading
course ~: 4 text 8 textbook
desk: 7 lectern
gauge ~: 6 status 8 altitude 9 elevation
give a ~: 6 recite, render 7 narrate 9 dramatize, interpret
hold a ~: 5 drill 6 review, warm up 8 practice, rehearse 9 go through 10 run through
light: 4 lamp
light ~: 5 novel
material: 3 mag 4 book, text, tome 5 novel, paper 8 magazine 9 newspaper
required ~: 4 text 8 syllabus
room: 3 den 5 study 7 library
starter: 5 proof
reading __: 4 desk, room 5 chair 6 notice 7 glasses
__ reading: 3 lip 4 mind 5 first, light, third 6 finger, second 7 thought
Reading: 2 RR 4 city, town 8 railroad
locale: 4 Penn. 7 England 9 Berkshire
readjust: 4 suit 6 modify, revise, tailor 8 regulate
Read my __!: 4 lips
read-only __: 6 memory
readout: 3 LCD, LED
__ readout: 7 digital
Read, Piers Paul book: 5 Alive
read the __ act: 4 riot
ready: 3 apt, fit, fix, fox, get, set 4 deft, done, fain, game, gird, glad, keen, live, make, near, post, prep, ripe, spry 5 acute, adept, alert, brace, brief, cando, eager, equip, fixed, groom, handy, happy, on tap, order, prime, prone, quick, rapid, sharp, smart, steel, tutor, wired 6 active, adroit, all set, ardent, astute, at hand, braced, bright, clever, cooked, expert, fill in, fit out, gear up, get set, in gear, in line, liquid, make up, mature, minded, nearby, on call, on hand, poised, primed, prompt, speedy, usable, warm up, wise up 7 arrange, covered, dynamic, equal to, fortify, heedful, incline, in order, in place, in shape, let in on, paratus, prepare, prepped, provide, psyched, psych up, put on to, qualify, skilled, useable, waiting, willing, zealous 8 adjusted, arranged, dextrous, disposed, equipped, geared up, get ready, inclined, masterly, mobilize, organize, prepared, punctual, rehearse, skillful, watchful 9 agreeable, astucious, available, brilliant, completed, dexterous, expectant, fitted out, on the ball, organized, psyched up, qualified, receptive, rehearsed 10 accessible, convenient, in position, keep posted, obtainable, on the brink, pave the way, perceptive, proficient, raring to go, square away, strengthen, time-saving
be ~: 4 wait
be ~ for: 5 await
companion: 4 able 7 willing
follower: 3 set
(for): 4 game
for action: 3 arm, fit 4 game 5 alert, eager
for use: 9 available
get ~: 3 fix, set 4 gird, pack, prep 5 brace, equip, groom, prime, ripen, train 6 gear up 7 arrange, prepare, psych up 8 mobilize 9 condition 10 square away
(to): 4 open
to fight: 7 hawkish, martial 8 militant 9 bellicose, combative 10 aggressive, pugnacious
to fire: 5 armed
to go: 7 in store 9 available 10 obtainable
ready __: 4 room 5 money, or not, to eat
ready, __, and able: 7 willing
ready-__: 3 mix 4 made 6 witted
__ ready: 3 get 4 make 5 at the
__-ready: 4 make 5 cable 6 camera, combat
Ready, __!: 5 set go
Ready, __, fire!: 3 aim
__ Ready: 3 Get 4 We're 5 Yes I'm
Ready or not, here __!: 5 I come
ready-to-__: 4 wear
Ready to Take a Chance Again (1978 song) artist: Barry Manilow
Ready to Wear (1994 film)
cast: Danny Aiello, Anouk Aimée, Lauren Bacall, Kim Basinger, Harry Belafonte, Cher, Rupert Everett, Teri Garr, Linda Hunt, Sally Kellerman, Sophia Loren, Lyle Lovett, Marcello Mastroianni, Stephen Rea, Tim Robbins, Julia Roberts, Lili Taylor, Tracey Ullman, Forest Whitaker
director: Robert Altman
ready, willing, and __: 4 able
reaffirm: 5 renew 6 stress
Reagan: 3 Ron 5 Nancy 6 Ronald 7 Maureen
Reagan, Ronald: 5 actor 9 president
alma mater: 6 Eureka
birthplace: 7 Tampico 8 Illinois
cabinet member: 4 Bell, Dole, Haig, Lyng, Watt 5 Baker, Block, Bowen, Brady, Brock, Clark, Hodel, Lewis, Meese, Regan, Smith 6 Pierce, Verity 7 Bennett, Burnley, Cavazos, Donovan, Edwards, Heckler, Schultz 8 Carlucci 9 Baldridge
child: 3 Ron 5 Patti 7 Maureen, Michael
film: Bedtime for Bonzo (1951)
Kings Row (1942)
Louisa (1950)
This Is the Army (1943)
The Voice of the Turtle (1947)
home: 10 California
middle name: 6 Wilson
opponent: 6 Carter 7 Mondale 8 Anderson
parent: 4 Jack 5 Nelle
previous occupation: 5 actor
program: 3 SDI
spouse: Jane Wyman, Nancy
V.P.: 4 Bush
was its pres.: 3 SAG
Reagle: 4 Merl
real: 4 coin, good, live, sure, true 5 basic, legit, money, right, solid, valid 6 actual, bodily, dinkum, kasher, kosher, native 7 certain, de facto, evident, factual, genuine, natural, sincere 8 bona fide, concrete, definite, embodied, existing, explicit, material, original, physical, positive, rightful, tangible, verified 9 authentic, corporeal, decidedly, heartfelt, in earnest, intrinsic, touchable, unfeigned, veracious, veritable 10 legitimate, sure-enough, true-to-life, undeniable, unimagined, verifiable
be ~: 4 live 5 exist 7 breathe
ender: 3 ism, ist
for ~: 2 so 4 true 6 honest, indeed, surely 7 genuine 9 seriously
get ~: 6 come on
McCoy: 5 legit
not ~: 3 bad 5 phony 6 ersatz, phoney, pseudo
world: 7 reality 9 actuality, existence

real __: **4** axis, line, part, time **5** McCoy, wages, world **6** estate, income, memory, number **7** storage
real __ agent: **6** estate
real-__: **4** life
__ real: **3** for, get
Real __, The: **5** Glory **6** Blonde, McCoys
__ Real: **6** Camino
Real Blonde, The (1998 film)
cast: Maxwell Caulfield, Daryl Hannah, Catherine Keener, Matthew Modine
director: Tom DiCillo
real estate: **3** lot **4** bldg., home, land **5** asset, house **6** assets, ground, spread **7** acreage, grounds **8** building, property
abbr.: **2** BR, LR, rm. **3** blk., EIK, fpl., gar., MLS **4** bdrm., bsmt.
account: **6** escrow
chart: **4** plat
document: **4** deed **5** lease, title
investment: **4** REIT
seller: **5** agent **6** agency, broker
sign: **4** sold **5** to let **10** in contract
term: **4** relo
transaction: **6** resale
unit: **3** lot **4** acre, home **5** house **8** building, property
realgar: **3** ore **7** mineral
Real Glory, The (1939 film)
cast: Gary Cooper, David Niven
director: Henry Hathaway
__ realism: **5** magic, naive **6** social **7** natural
__ Realism: **3** New
Real is rational man: **5** Hegel
realistic: **4** hard, sane, true **5** sober, sound **6** astute, earthy, shrewd **7** genuine, graphic, natural, prudent **8** faithful, lifelike, original, rational, sensible, truthful **9** astucious, authentic, graphical, practical, pragmatic **10** hard-bitten, hard-boiled, reasonable, true-to-life, unromantic
reality: **4** deed, esse, fact **5** being, facts, score, truth **6** entity, matter, object, verity **8** like it is, presence, realness, solidity, validity **9** actuality, certainty, existence, phenomena, substance, what's what **10** bottom line, brass tacks, phenomenon
in ~: **5** quite, truly **6** au fond, indeed, really **7** at heart, de facto **8** actually
old-style: **5** sooth
reality __: **5** check
reality-__: **5** based
__ reality: **7** virtual
Reality Bites (1994 film)
cast: Janeane Garofalo, Ethan Hawke, Winona Ryder, Ben Stiller
director: Ben Stiller
realizable: **6** liquid **8** feasible, knowable, possible **9** available **10** attainable
realization: **4** grip, life **5** grasp **7** success, thought **8** fruition
cry: **3** aha
__-realization: **4** self
realize: **2** do **3** get, net, see, win **4** earn, gain, know, make **5** catch, clear, fancy, fetch, get it, go for, grasp, image, reach, reify, score, sense, think **6** attain, awaken, effect, finish, follow, fulfil, intuit, obtain, pick up, profit, rack up, take in, vision **7** achieve, acquire, bring in, catch on, compass, develop, discern, feature, fulfill, imagine, perfect, perform, produce, receive, sell for, succeed **8** bring off, carry out, complete, conceive, discover, envisage, envision, make good, perceive **9** actualize, apprehend, implement, learn from, liquidate, recognize, visualize **10** accomplish, appreciate, bring about, comprehend, consummate, effectuate, make good on, make happen, understand
realized: **4** done **8** finished
be ~: **5** occur **6** happen **8** come true
not ~: **5** unwon
realizing, without: **9** unwitting
Real Love (song) artist: Doobie Brothers, Jody Watley, Mary J. Blige
really: **4** very, well **5** quite, truly **6** easily, honest, indeed, in fact, simply, surely, verily **7** at heart, de facto, in truth **8** actually, for a fact, honestly, in effect, of course **9** assuredly, certainly, genuinely, literally, precisely, sincerely **10** absolutely, admittedly, positively
Really!: **5** no lie **6** do tell, so true
really big __: **4** show
__ Really Going Out With Him?: **5** Is She
__ Really Want to Do: **4** All I
realm: **3** job **4** land, turf, zone **5** arena, bourn, field, orbit, range, reach, scope, state, sweep, world **6** domain, empire, length, nation, region, sphere **7** compass, country, expanse, grounds, kingdom, purview **8** dominion, monarchy, province **9** dimension, territory **10** department, walk of life
suffix: **3** -dom
Real McCoys, The (ABC/CBS sitcom)
cast: Walter Brennan (Amos McCoy) Richard Crenna (Luke McCoy) Kathy Nolan (Kate McCoy)
Realms of Being author: George Santayana
__ real nowhere man: **4** He's a
Real Peace author: **5** Nixon
Realtor
see real estate
realty
see real estate
Real War, The author: **5** Nixon
ream: **3** wad **4** bore, skim **5** scold, widen **7** defraud **9** penetrate
fraction: **5** quire, sheet
ream __: **3** out
reams: **5** piles, rafts, scads **6** masses, oceans, oodles, scores, stacks **7** bunches
reanimate: **6** revive **7** recruit, refresh **10** regenerate
reap: **3** cut, get, mow **4** earn, gain, take **5** clear, glean **6** derive, garner, gather, obtain, profit, secure, take in **7** bring in, collect, harvest, produce, receive **8** gather in
reaped row: **5** swath **6** swathe
reaper: **6** farmer **7** machine **9** harvester
follow the ~: **5** glean **6** garner, gather **7** collect, harvest
reaping: **4** crop **6** profit **7** farming, harvest
stalks left after ~: **4** halm **5** haulm
reappear: **6** return **8** come back
Reap the Wild Wind (1942 film)
cast: Paulette Goddard, Ray Milland, John Wayne
director: Cecil B. DeMille
dog: **7** Romulus
rear: **3** aft, end **4** back, form, heel, hind, lift, seat, side, tail **5** breed, build, erect, hoist, put up, raise, set up, stern, teach, tower, train **6** astern, behind, bottom, breech, dorsal, foster, parent, rise up, tag end **7** bring up, care for, educate, nourish, nurture, raise up, reverse, tail end, upheave **8** back seat, hindmost **9** construct, cultivate **10** hindermost
bringing up the ~: **4** last **6** behind, in back **7** lagging **8** trailing
bring up the ~: **3** lag **5** trail **6** follow
combining form: **7** opistho-
in the ~: **3** aft **4** last **5** aback, abaft **6** astern
up: **6** bridle, get mad, see red **7** bristle **8** get angry
rear __: **3** end **4** deck **5** guard, sight **7** admiral, echelon
rear-end: **3** ram **5** total **6** strike **7** wrack up **8** slam into **9** smash into
rear-ender: **5** crash, wreck **6** impact, pileup **7** smashup **8** accident **9** collision
rearing up in heraldry: **7** rampant
rearmost: **3** end **4** hind, last **5** after **6** latter
rearrange: **5** alter, shift **6** change, reform, switch **7** reorder, shuffle **9** transpose **10** reposition
rearrangement: **5** shift **6** change
rearview mirror decoration: **4** dice
Rear Window (1954 film)
cast: Raymond Burr, Wendell Corey, Grace Kelly, Thelma Ritter, James Stewart
director: Alfred Hitchcock
remake star: **5** Reeve
reason: **3** aim, end, use, why, wit **4** call, case, goal, idea, mind, move, nous, root, sake, soul, talk, urge, wits **5** argue, basis, brain, cause, cover, infer, logic, point, proof, prove, sense, solve, study, think **6** acumen, adduce, bounds, brains, debate, decide, deduce, deduct, design, excuse, gather, ground, limits, motive, noesis, notion, object, sanity, senses, spring, target, whyfor, wisdom **7** account, apology, contend, defense, discuss, dispute, examine, grounds, impetus, justify, make out, marbles, purpose, reflect, resolve, suppose, warrant, whatfor, win over, work out **8** apologia, argument, cogitate, conclude, dissuade, draw from, judgment, lucidity, occasion, persuade, point out, saneness, sapience, talk into **9** causation, cerebrate, deduction, discourse, establish, figure out, incentive, induction, inference, intellect, intention, mentality, propriety, rationale, reasoning, soundness, speculate, syllogize, talk out of, thresh out, wherefore **10** antecedent, deliberate, dialectics, exposition, generalize, horse sense, inducement, moderation, motivation, philosophy
alleged ~: **5** alibi, bluff, cover, guise **6** excuse **7** cover-up, pretext **8** pretense **10** cover story
by ~ of: **5** due to **7** owing to
by ~ (of): **7** because
for any ~: **5** at all
for no ~: **4** idly
for this ~: **4** ergo, then, thus **5** hence **6** hereat **9** therefore
for what ~: **3** why
give a ~ for: **4** show **6** defend **7** clarify, clear up, explain, justify **8** spell out **9** expound on, make clear
having a ~: **6** causal
out: **5** educe, infer **6** deduce, derive, ponder
partner: **5** rhyme
rhyme or ~: **5** cause, logic, sense **6** motive
the ~ for: **6** behind **7** causing
(with): **5** plead
within ~: **4** fair **5** legit **7** logical **8** credible, rational, sensible **9** plausible, tolerable **10** legitimate
without ~: **4** idle **6** wanton **8** baseless, needless **9** causeless, illogical, senseless **10** gratuitous, groundless, unprovoked
without rhyme or ~: **4** idle **5** inane, nutty, silly, wacky **6** absurd **7** asinine, foolish, puerile **8** mindless **9** frivolous, half-baked, illogical, ludicrous, pointless **10** irrational, ridiculous
__ reason: **4** pure, with **6** active, within **7** passive
Reason: **3** Rex **6** Rhodes
reasonable: **2** OK **3** fit, low **4** cool, fair, just, okay, sane, wise **5** cheap, legit, lucid, right, sober, sound, sweet, valid **6** decent, earned, honest, humane, likely, modest, on sale, proper, viable **7** average, bargain, cut-rate, knowing, liberal, logical, low-cost, natural, politic, prudent, sapient, tenable **8** arguable, cerebral, clear-cut, credible, deserved, discreet, feasible, luculent, moderate, probable, rational, sensible, suitable, together, tolerant, unbiased, uncostly **9** advisable, cognitive, conscious, equitable, excusable, half-price, impartial, judicious, low-priced, objective, plausible, practical, realistic, temperate, tolerable, unextreme **10** acceptable, admissible, analytical, believable, consequent, consistent, controlled, convincing, economical, legitimate, perceiving, percipient, reflective, restrained, thoughtful, thought-out, unagitated
seem ~: **5** add up **9** make sense
reasonableness: **6** sanity **10** likelihood
reasonably: **5** quite **6** enough, pretty, rather **10** apparently
reason-based
believer: **5** deist
faith: **5** deism
reasoned: **8** coherent, dogmatic **10** dogmatical
reasoner: **7** casuist, sophist **8** logician
Reasoner: **5** Harry
reason for war in Latin: **10** casus belli
Reason in Art author: George Santayana
reasoning: **5** logic, proof, sense **6** acumen, mental, noesis **7** premise, thought **8** analysis, argument, judgment, rational **9** conscious, deduction, dialectic, rationale, syllogism **10** dialectics, exposition, hypothesis, philosophy, thoughtful
valid ~: **5** sense **6** sanity **7** thought **9** coherence, deduction, good sense, induction, inference, rationale, syllogism
Reason in Science author: George Santayana
Reason in Society author: George Santayana
reasonless: **10** fallacious, gratuitous, irrational
__ Reason, The: **5** Age of
Reason to Believe (song) artist: Carpenters, Rod Stewart
reassemble: **5** rally, reune
reassert: **6** accent, play up, stress **7** dwell on, iterate **9** emphasize, underline **10** accentuate, underscore
reassess: **6** review **10** reconsider, think twice
reassign: **5** shift **6** demote
reassignment: **5** shift
reassurance: **4** lift **5** boost **6** succor **7** comfort **10** comforting
reassure: **4** buoy, calm **5** brace, cheer **6** perk up, pick up, settle, uphold **7** bolster, cheer up, comfort, console, hearten, inspire, relieve, satisfy **8** convince, enspirit, inspirit **9** encourage, give a lift, guarantee

reassuring: **9** favorable, promising **10** comforting, supportive
words: **4** I'm OK **5** it's OK
Rea, Stephen: **5** actor
film: Angie (1994)
The Crying Game (1992)
Danny Boy (1982)
Interview With the Vampire: The Vampire Chronicles (1994)
Michael Collins (1996)
reata: **4** rope **5** lasso **6** lariat
kin: **4** bola
user: **5** roper **6** cowboy, gaucho
Reatta: **3** car **4** auto **5** Buick **10** automobile
Réaumur, René Ade: **6** French **9** physicist
reawaken: **5** renew **6** come to **8** rekindle **10** regenerate
Reb: **4** gray, grey
general: **3** Lee **5** Early **6** Stuart **7** Forrest, Jackson **10** Beauregard, Longstreet
letters: **3** CSA
state: **3** Ala., Fla., Tex. **4** Miss., N. Car., S. Car. **5** Texas **7** Alabama, Ark. Tenn., Florida, Georgia **8** Arkansas, Virginia **9** Louisiana, Tennessee **11** Mississippi **13** North Carolina, South Carolina
Yank, to a ~: **3** foe **5** enemy
__ Reb: **6** Johnny
Reba: **6** sitcom **8** McEntire
rebab: **6** string, violin
origin: **7** Mideast
rebate: **5** bonus, repay **6** deduct, reduce, refund, return **7** payback **8** decrease, diminish, discount, kickback **9** allowance, deduction, reduction
rebec: **6** string, violin
kin: **5** crwth
origin: **6** Europe
Rebecca: **4** film, West **5** novel **6** Romijn **8** DeMornay **9** Schaeffer
author: Daphne du Maurier
cast: Judith Anderson, Joan Fontaine, Laurence Olivier, George Sanders
director: Alfred Hitchcock
Rebekah
brother of ~: **5** Laban
father of ~: **7** Bethuel
husband of ~: **5** Isaac
son of ~: **4** Esau **5** Jacob
rebel: **4** defy, riot, rise **5** arise, fight, flout **6** defier, ignore, mutiny, oppose, opt out, resist, revolt, rise up, secede **7** boycott, disobey, dissent, drop out, heretic, protest, radical, traitor, violate **8** agitator, frondeur, maverick, mutineer, nihilist, overturn, renegade, resister, turncoat, ultraist **9** anarchist, break with, disregard, dissenter, dissident, fight back, insurgent, make waves, overthrow, protester, young Turk **10** go on strike, iconoclast, malcontent, schismatic, separatist, subversive
African ~ org.: **5** SWAPO, UNITA
1850s ~: **5** Sepoy
1898 ~: **5** Boxer
Nicaragua: **6** Contra
rebel __: **4** yell
Rebel: **3** AMC, car **4** auto **7** Rambler **10** automobile
Rebel __ a Cause: **7** Without
__ Rebel: **4** He's a
rebellion: **6** heresy, revolt, rising, schism, unrest **7** dissent **8** apostasy, civil war, defiance, disorder, outbreak, uprising **9** commotion, defection, sundering **10** insurgence, insurgency, opposition, revolution
incite ~: **5** rouse **6** arouse, foment, stir up, whip up, work up **7** agitate **9** instigate
__ Rebellion: **5** Dorr's, Great, Sepoy, War of **6** Bacon's **7** Whiskey
rebellious: **4** wild **5** onery **6** feisty, ornery, unruly **7** defiant, lawless, naughty, radical, wayward **8** contrary, disloyal, factious, indocile, mutinous, perverse, stubborn **9** alienated, bellicose, dissident, insurgent, obstinate, turbulent **10** disorderly, refractory, subversive, traitorous, unpeaceful
one: **6** defier
Rebel-Rouser (1958 song) artist: Duane Eddy
__ Rebels: **7** Running
Rebels song: Wild Weekend (1963)
Rebel, The (ABC/NBC western)
cast: Nick Adams (Johnny Yuma)
theme singer: Johnny Cash
Rebel, The author: Albert Camus
Rebel Without a Cause (1955 film)
cast: Jim Backus, James Dean, Ann Doran, Sal Mineo, Natalie Wood
director: Nicholas Ray
Rebel Yell singer: **4** Idol
reboant: **5** forte, noisy **7** blaring, booming, jarring, pealing, rackety, raucous, roaring **8** crashing, piercing, plangent, rumbling, sonorous, strident, turned up **9** big-voiced, clamorous, deafening **10** boisterous, resounding, stentorian, strepitous, thundering, uproarious, vociferous
reboot, require a: **5** crash
rebound: **4** echo, heal, mend **5** carom, rally **6** bounce, carrom, glance, pick up, recoil, return, revive, spring **7** get well, recover, reflect **8** backfire, comeback, kick back, overcome, reaction, ricochet, snap back **9** boomerang, get better **10** bounce back, convalesce, recuperate, rejuvenate, spring back
shot after a ~: **5** tip-in
__ rebound: **5** on the
rebounding: **9** resilient
rebozo: **5** scarf
Rebozo: **4** Bebe
rebuff: **2** no **3** cut, dig, nix **4** barb, deny, gibe, go-by, jeer, jibe, mock, shun, slam, slap, slur, snub, veto **5** abuse, check, chide, decry, knock, libel, repel, scorn, spurn, taunt **6** bounce, defame, defeat, denial, deride, dump on, heckle, ignore, impugn, insult, malign, offend, oppose, pass on, pass up, put off, rebuke, refuse, reject, resist, slight, vilify **7** affront, asperse, beat off, calumny, catcall, censure, decline, degrade, disdain, dismiss, exclude, fend off, hold off, mockery, neglect, obloquy, offense, put-down, rank out, refusal, reprove, repulse, say no to, setback, slander, tell off, traduce **8** belittle, brush-off, contempt, denounce, derision, disallow, hard time, ignoring, push back, ridicule, send away, stave off, turn away, turn back, turndown, vilipend **9** aspersion, blackball, cast aside, cheap shot, contumely, denigrate, discredit, disparage, disregard, humiliate, lash out at, rejection, reprimand, repudiate **10** calumniate, defamation, discourage, disrespect, nonconsent, opposition, opprobrium, resistance, thumbs down
rebuild: **3** fix **6** reform **7** restore **8** overhaul
rebuilt: **5** fixed **9** good as new
rebuke: **3** fry, pay, rag, rap, rip, row, zap **4** flay, rake, read, slap, snub, twit **5** blame, chide, scold, sit on **6** berate, carp on, earful, jump on, lean on, lesson, monish, oppose, rating, rebuff **7** bawl out, censure, chew out, chiding, correct, go after, jawbone, lambast, lay into, lecture, put-down, refusal, reproof, reprove, repulse, rip into, tell off, tick off, upbraid **8** admonish, berating, denounce, hard time, lambaste, reproach, reproval, scolding, sound off **9** castigate, criticize, dress down, excoriate, exprobate, going-over, lash out at, ostracism, reprehend, reprimand, talking-to, tear apart **10** admonition, affliction, bawling-out, chewing-out, correction, punishment, take to task, telling-off, upbraiding
rebuker: **5** scold, shrew **6** chider **9** henpecker, termagant
rebus: **6** puzzle
rebut: **4** deny **5** belie, parry, quash **6** answer, negate, oppose, refute, retort **7** confute, counter, dispute, ward off **8** confound, disprove, overturn **9** discredit, shoot down **10** contradict, controvert, disconfirm, prove false, prove wrong
rebuttal: **6** answer, retort, ripost **7** riposte **8** comeback, feedback, response **9** rejoinder **10** refutation
rec __: **4** room
rec. __: **3** sec.
recalcitrance: **4** sass **7** bravado **8** back talk, defiance **10** opposition, resistance
recalcitrant: **4** wild **5** onery **6** ornery, unruly, wilful **7** defiant, naughty, piggish, radical, wayward, willful **8** contrary, indocile, opposing, stubborn, untoward **9** fractious, obstinate, pigheaded, reluctant, resistant, resisting, unwilling **10** rebellious, refractory
be ~: **4** balk **5** demur **6** refuse, resist
recalibrate: **5** alter, right, shift **7** rectify, redress
recall: **4** cite, lift, mind, stir **5** annul, educe, evoke, flash, renew, rouse, think, unsay, waken **6** abjure, arouse, awaken, cancel, elicit, memory, recant, remind, repeal, retain, revive, revoke, summon **7** bethink, dismiss, extract, flash on, nullify, rescind, retract, reverse, suspend, think of **8** forswear, hark back, look back, nail down, override, overrule, palinode, recision, remember, take back, withdraw **9** anamnesis, annulment, discharge, dismantle, foreswear, hindsight, recognize, recollect, reinstate, reminisce, think back **10** bear in mind, disqualify, keep in mind, rescission, retraction, retrospect, revocation, withdrawal
cause: **6** defect
in Britain: **5** rub up
__ recall: **5** total
__ recall...: **3** As I
__ Recall: **5** Total **7** Perfect
recant: **4** deny, void **5** annul, unsay, welsh **6** abjure, cancel, disown, recall, renege, repeal, revoke **7** back off, back out, disavow, nullify, rescind, retract **8** abnegate, abrogate, back down, call back, dial back, disclaim, forswear, renounce, take back, withdraw **9** back-pedal, backtrack, foreswear, repudiate, weasel out, worm out of **10** apostatize, contradict
recap: **4** tire **5** sum up **6** précis, review, wrap-up **7** recount, rundown, run over, summary **8** condense, synopsis **9** reiterate, summarize **10** highlights
recapitulate: **5** brief, sum up **6** detail, recite, rehash, repeat, replay, review, reword **7** iterate, outline, recount, restate, run over **8** hark back, rehearse, rephrase **9** epitomize, reiterate, summarize **10** paraphrase
recapitulation: **6** résumé **7** outline, recital, rundown, summary
recapture: **6** redeem, regain, rescue **7** get back, recover **8** retrieve, take back **9** reacquire
recast: **5** alter **6** modify, revise, reword **8** innovate **9** translate
recede: **3** die, dip, ebb **4** back, drop, fade, fall, sink, wane **5** abate, close, lapse, taper **6** depart, die off, go away, go back, lessen, narrow, reduce, retire, return, shrink **7** abridge, compact, curtail, decline, die down, dwindle, regress, relapse, retract, retreat, shorten, subside, tail off **8** compress, condense, contract, decrease, diminish, draw back, fall back, flow back, head away, level off, slack off, taper off, withdraw **9** disappear, drain away **10** abbreviate, retrograde, retrogress
receding: **9** on the wane
receipt: **3** vou. **4** chit, slip, stub **5** scrip **6** letter, notice, taking, ticket **7** arrival, getting, release, revenue, voucher **8** delivery, intaking **9** accession, acquiring, admission, admitting, discharge, quittance, sales slip
word: **4** paid
__ receipt: **5** sales **6** return
receipts: **3** get, net **4** gain, gate, take, wage **5** gross, lucre, money, wages **6** handle, income, profit, return, take-in, taking **7** revenue, royalty **8** cash flow, earnings, proceeds **9** royalties **10** bottom line
receivable: **3** due **4** owed **5** owing **6** coming
__ receivable: **8** accounts
receivables: **6** income, inflow
receive: **3** cop, get, see, win **4** bear, draw, earn, gain, grab, have, hear, hold, host, make, meet, pull, reap, snag, take **5** admit, catch, clear, greet, learn, let in, seize **6** accept, assume, come by, corral, derive, endure, gather, incept, induct, instal, invite, listen, obtain, permit, pick up, pocket, redeem, secure, show in, suffer, take in **7** acquire, bring in, collect, inherit, install, partake, procure, realize, sustain, undergo, usher in, welcome **8** arrogate, come into, initiate, meet with, perceive, pull down **9** apprehend, encounter, entertain, get hold of, go through, introduce, latch onto **10** experience, fall heir to, let through, shake hands
as news: **5** catch, learn **6** pick up **7** find out **8** discover **9** get wind of
a visitor: **4** mark, view **5** greet, pop in **6** attend, behold **7** receive **9** recognize **10** anticipate
enthusiastically: **5** lap up
likely to ~: **5** in for
__-received: **4** well
receiver: **3** set **4** dish **5** donee, payee, phone, radio **9** inheritor
holder: **6** cradle
wide ~: **3** end **7** gridder **10** footballer
__ receiver: **4** wide
receiving
area: **5** foyer, lobby **8** anteroom
receiving __: **3** end, set **4** line **7** blanket
recent: **3** new **4** late, past **5** fresh, novel, today, young **6** latter, modern **7** current, just out, newborn **8** contempo, neoteric, up-to-date **9** immediate, latter-day **10** newfangled, present-day
combining form: **2** ne- **3** neo- **4** ceno-

more ~: 5 later 6 latter 9 following
most ~: 4 last 6 latest, newest 8 up-to-date
not ~: 5 olden
past: 9 yesterday 10 not long ago

recently: 4 anew, just 5 newly 6 afresh, lately, of late 7 freshly, just now 8 latterly 9 currently, yesterday 10 not long ago

receptacle: 3 bin, box, can, cup, jug, pot, vat 4 bowl, case, pail, slot, tray, vase 5 pouch, purse, stein 6 ashcan, basket, bunker, hamper, holder, hopper, pocket, vessel 7 humidor 8 trash can 9 container, reservoir 10 repository
combining form: 7 -clinium
water ~: 5 basin

reception: 2 do 3 tea 4 ball 5 levee, party, salon 6 affair, at home, buffet, dinner, lounge, soiree, supper 7 banquet, matinee, meeting, receipt, welcome 8 function, greeting, reaction, response 9 accession, admission, encounter, enrolment, festivity, gathering, induction, treatment 10 absorption, acceptance, enrollment, salutation
aid: 4 dish 6 aerial 10 rabbit ears
area: 5 foyer, lobby, salon 6 lounge, parlor
in India: 6 durbar
interference: 4 snow 6 static
offering: 5 punch 6 canapé

reception __: 4 desk, room

receptionist's call: 4 next

receptive: 4 open 5 alert, quick, ready 6 bright 7 liberal, passive, pliable, sensory 8 amenable, catholic, friendly, pushover, swayable, tolerant 9 acceptant, favorable, observant, sensitive, sensorial, welcoming 10 accessible, hospitable, interested, open-minded, responsive

__ receptor: 4 beta 5 alpha 7 stretch

recess: 3 bay, gap 4 apse, cell, cove, dent, drop, fork, halt, hole, lull, nook, rest, rise, slot, stop 5 angle, arbor, bower, break, crypt, heart, inlet, letup, mouth, niche, oriel, pause, shake, space 6 alcove, ambush, carrel, cavity, closet, corner, cranny, crutch, cutoff, depths, drop it, grotto, hiatus, hollow, indent, layoff, socket 7 adjourn, break up, carrell, closure, cubicle, holiday, interim, leisure, opening, reaches, respite, retreat, take ten, time-out 8 abeyance, break off, breather, call time, dissolve, downtime, free time, intermit, playtime, prorogue, sideline, take five, vacation 9 cessation, embrasure, happy hour, interlude, put on hold, terminate 10 depression, penetralia, pigeonhole, suspension, take a break

recession: 3 ebb 4 bust, slip 5 lapse, slide, slump 7 decline 8 bad times, collapse, downturn, reversal, shakeout 9 bottom-out, deflation, departure, hard times, inflation, rainy days 10 bankruptcy, depression, stagnation

Recessional author: Rudyard Kipling

recessive __: 4 gene

recharging, in need of: 4 dead

recherché: 4 rare 6 arcane, exotic, unique 7 special, unusual 8 precious, singular, uncommon

recidivate: 5 lapse 6 revert 7 regress, relapse 8 fall back, slip back 10 retrogress

recidivism: 8 apostasy

Recife: 4 city, port, town
city near ~: 5 Natal
locale: 6 Brazil

recipe: 4 dish 6 design, method 7 formula, process, program 8 compound 9 direction, procedure, technique 10 directions
abbr.: 3 tbs., tsp. 4 tbsp.
amount: 3 cap 4 dash 5 pinch 6 cupful
direction: 3 add 4 bake, beat, boil, chop, dice, heat, stir 5 add in, sauté, scald
part: 4 step
phrase: 3 à la 8 au gratin

recipient: 5 donee, payee 7 legatee

reciprocal: 6 common, double, fellow, mutual, shared 7 related, similar 8 matching, relative, requited 9 alternate, bilateral, companion, dependant, dependent, duplicate, exchanged 10 changeable, coordinate, equivalent
combining form: 6 allelo-

reciprocally: 7 by turns, jointly 8 mutually, together 9 in concert
prefix: 5 inter-

reciprocate: 4 swap, swop 5 equal, match, repay, reply 6 return 7 requite, respond 8 exchange 9 alternate, retaliate

reciprocated: 6 mutual

reciprocity: 5 trade 8 exchange 9 tit for tat 10 quid pro quo

recision: 6 recall 7 voiding 9 canceling

recital: 3 gig 4 tale 5 fable, story 6 litany, report 7 account, concert, musical, reading, telling 8 delivery, musicale, relation 9 detailing, narration, narrative, portrayal, recountal, rehearsal, rendering, rendition, statement 10 recounting, repetition
give a ~: 4 play, sing 5 dance 7 perform
hall: 5 odeon, odeum 7 theater, theatre
instrument: 4 harp 5 organ, piano
offering: 4 duet, solo 5 piece 6 encore, sonata

Recital of the Dog author: David Rabe

recitation: 3 say 4 talk 5 piece 6 appeal, lesson, litany, report, speech 7 address, lecture, monolog, oration, passage, telling 8 delivery, exercise, speaking 9 discourse, monologue, narrating, narration, quotation, rehearsal, rendering, selection, statement, utterance 10 confession, declaiming, discussion, recounting, vocalizing

recitative kin: 4 aria 6 arioso

recite: 3 say 4 read, tell 5 chant, enact, quote, reply, speak, state, utter 6 answer, convey, detail, impart, incant, intone, parrot, relate, render, repeat, report, retell 7 address, declaim, deliver, enlarge, explain, itemize, lecture, mention, narrate, perform, picture, portray, recount, reel off 8 describe, rehearse, set forth 9 delineate, discourse, dramatize, enumerate, expatiate, hold forth, interpret, rattle off 10 account for
dramatically: 3 act 5 emote, orate 7 perform, playact
in a monotone: 5 thrum

reciter: 6 orator
verse ~: 4 poet 8 poetizer 9 sonneteer, versifier

reckless: 4 rash, wild 5 blind, brash, hasty, kooky 6 daring, kookie, madcap, unwary, unwise, wanton 7 lawless 8 carefree, careless, feckless, headlong, heedless, hopeless, mindless, off-guard, pell-mell, prodigal 9 audacious, breakneck, daredevil, desperate, foolhardy, haphazard, hotheaded, imprudent, negligent, unadvised, uncareful, unhearing, unheedful, venturous 10 ill-advised, incautious, indiscreet, profligate, regardless, sophomoric, unbothered, willy-nilly
activity: 5 stunt
one: 5 darer

Reckless Ecstasy author: Carl Sandburg

recklessly: 5 madly 8 pell-mell 9 fervently, headfirst, like crazy

Reckless Moment, The (1949 film)
cast: Joan Bennett, Geraldine Brooks, James Mason
director: Max Ophuls

recklessness: 5 folly, haste 7 abandon 8 audacity

reckon: 3 add, put, sum, tot 4 call, cast, deem, foot, hold, make, rate, take, tell, tote, view 5 add up, count, fancy, gauge, guess, infer, judge, place, tally, think, total, tot up 6 assess, assume, bank on, cipher, esteem, expect, figure, gather, number, plan on, regard, rely on, size up, square, take it, tote up 7 account, believe, build on, compute, count on, imagine, measure, project, suppose, surmise, suspect, think of, tick off, trust in 8 appraise, conclude, consider, depend on, estimate, evaluate, keep tabs, look upon, theorize 9 build upon, calculate, count upon, enumerate, figure out, keep score 10 bargain for, conjecture, count heads, count noses, understand
with: 4 face 5 treat 6 handle 7 foresee 8 consider 10 bear in mind, take note of
(with): 4 cope, deal

__ reckoner: 5 ready

reckoning: 3 due, fee, IOU, sum, tab 4 bill, cost, debt 5 check, count, grunt, guess, price, score, tally 6 adding, charge, reward 7 account, bad news, invoice, working 8 addition, counting, estimate, figuring 9 appraisal, ciphering, dependant, dependent, statement, summation 10 arithmetic, assessment, estimation, settlement
final ~: 3 end 6 payoff, result, upshot 7 outcome 9 punch line 10 bottom line, conclusion, settlement

__ reckoning: 4 dead 5 day of

Reckoning, The author: David Halberstam

reclaim: 6 redeem, reform, regain, rescue 7 get back, recover, salvage 8 retrieve, take back 9 reacquire 10 rejuvenate, repurchase

recline: 3 lay, lie, tip 4 cant, heel, lean, list, loll, rest, tilt 5 relax, slant, slope 6 lounge, repose, sprawl, unwind 7 lay down, lie down, stretch 10 stretch out

recliner: 4 lier, seat 5 chair 6 chaise, rocker 9 furniture

reclining: 5 prone 6 at rest 9 prostrate, recumbent

recluse: 3 nun 4 monk 5 friar, loner 6 hermit 7 ascetic, eremite, isolato 8 anchoret, cenobite, eremitic, hermetic, homebody, isolated, monastic, reserved, retiring, secluded, solitary 9 anchorite, religious, solitaire, withdrawn 10 antisocial, cloistered, hermitlike, monastical, troglodyte, unsociable

reclusive: 3 shy 5 aloof, loner 6 lonely, modest 7 ascetic, bashful, distant, private 8 eremitic, hermetic, isolated, monastic, reserved, reticent, retiring, secluded, shielded, solitary 9 diffident, nonpublic, withdrawn 10 antisocial, cloistered, hermitlike, monastical, unsociable

reclusiveness: 7 secrecy 8 solitude 9 hermitage, isolation, seclusion

recognition: 3 ken 4 fame, plum, puff, rave 5 award, honor, kudos, sense 6 avowal, credit, esteem, memory, notice, praise, recall, regard, renown, salute, thanks, tumble 7 acclaim, laurels, respect, strokes, tribute 8 approval, greeting, high sign, noticing 9 admission, allowance, attention, awareness, detection, discovery, gratitude, reception 10 acceptance, double take, perception
sound: 2 oh
words: 4 I see 5 got it

__ recognition: 5 voice 6 speech 7 pattern

recognizable: 5 clear, plain, vivid 6 cogent 7 evident, express, obvious 8 apparent, distinct, explicit, knowable, manifest, palpable 9 graspable 10 spelled out

recognize: 3 nod, own, peg, see, tab, tag 4 avow, cite, espy, find, hail, know, make, nail, name, note, okay, spot, tell 5 admit, adopt, agree, allow, catch, go for, grant, greet, honor, place, sight, thank 6 accept, assent, comply, descry, detect, fess up, finger, notice, recall, remark, salute, verify 7 approve, bethink, concede, confess, discern, flash on, include, make out, mention, observe, realize, respect, welcome 8 accredit, diagnose, identify, perceive, pinpoint, remember, sanction, stand for 9 apprehend, entertain, put up with, recollect, sign off on 10 appreciate, bear in mind, comprehend, concur with, give the nod, keep in mind, understand
as an undercover cop: 4 name 6 finger
don't ~: 5 scorn 6 ignore

recognized: 5 known, noted, sound 6 public 8 official, orthodox, standard 9 canonical, customary, well-known
to be: 6 seen as

recoil: 4 balk, jerk, jump, kick, reel, turn 5 baulk, blink, carom, cower, demur, dodge, quail, quake, react, shake, shirk, start, stick, waver, wince 6 blanch, blench, bounce, carrom, cringe, falter, flinch, resile, return, shrink, spring, swerve, writhe 7 rebound, shudder, shy away, stickle, tremble 8 backfire, draw back, hesitate, pull back, reaction, step back, turn away, withdraw 10 shrink away, spring back
from: 4 duck, hate 5 abhor, avoid, dodge, skirt 6 detest, eschew, loathe 7 deplore, despise, disdain 8 execrate, sidestep 9 abominate

recollect: 4 cite, mind, stir 5 flash, place, quote, rouse, think, waken 6 arouse, awaken, recall, relive, remind, retain, revive, summon 7 bethink, flash on 8 hark back, remember 9 conjure up, recognize, reminisce 10 bear in mind, call to mind, keep in mind, look back on

recollection: 3 bio 6 memoir, memory 9 biography, life story

recolor: 3 dye

recombinant __: 3 DNA

recommence: 5 renew 6 pick up, reopen, resume, take up 7 restart 8 continue, go on with

recommend: 4 back, laud, move, plug, tout, urge 5 exalt, extol, favor, prize, refer, steer, value 6 advise, enjoin,

esteem, exhort, extoll, hold up, praise, second, uphold **7** acclaim, advance, applaud, approve, confirm, counsel, endorse, glorify, indorse, justify, magnify, promote, propose, put on to, stand by, suggest **8** advocate, eulogize, front for, nominate, sanction, speak for, vouch for **9** celebrate, introduce, prescribe **10** come up with, compliment, felicitate, put forward
recommendation: **3** tip **4** plug **5** order **6** advice, motion, praise **7** counsel **8** advocacy, approval, blessing, good word, guidance, proposal, sanction **9** direction, reference
form of ~: **3** ltr. **6** letter
recompense: **3** due, fee, fix, pay **4** comp, wage **5** atone, repay, right, wages **6** amends, ante up, grease, make up, offset, pay for, put out, recoup, refund, return, reward, salary, square **7** balance, cough up, deserts, expiate, justice, pay back, payment, recover, redress, requite, satisfy **8** atone for, equalize, make good, retrieve, swing for **9** allowance, atonement, emolument, indemnify, make up for, reimburse, repayment, spring for **10** make amends, propitiate
old-style: **4** meed
recon: **3** spy **6** patrol **7** overfly
one on ~: **3** spy **5** scout **7** spotter
plane: **5** AWACS
reconcile: **3** fit, fix **4** cool, suit, tune **5** adapt, atone, fix up, quiet, yield **6** accept, accord, adjust, attune, make up, pacify, resign, settle, square, submit **7** appease, arrange, assuage, balance, compose, conform, correct, mediate, patch up, placate, rectify, resolve, reunite, win over **8** accustom, mitigate, regulate **9** acquiesce, arbitrate, get used to, harmonize, integrate, intercede, intervene, make peace, put up with **10** conciliate, coordinate, propitiate
reconciliation: **5** peace, truce **9** mediation
recondite: **4** dark, deep, hard **5** heavy **6** arcane, hidden, mystic, occult, orphic, secret **7** cryptic, learned, obscure **8** abstract, abstruse, academic, esoteric, hermetic, involved, mystical, pedantic, profound **9** concealed, cryptical, difficult, scholarly **10** far-fetched, mysterious, pedantical, unfamiliar, unknowable
recondition: **3** fix **4** mend **5** renew **6** change, revive **7** furbish, restore **8** overhaul **9** refurbish
reconnaissance: **4** look **6** survey **8** scouting
run ~: **3** spy **5** scout **6** patrol, survey **7** bird-dog
__ reconnaissance: **6** aerial
reconnoiter: **3** spy **5** range, scout, spy on, watch **6** survey **7** explore, inspect, observe **8** check out, scout out, stake out
reconnoiterer: **5** scout
reconsider: **6** rehash, review **7** revisit, reweigh, sleep on **8** mull over, reassess **9** reexamine, think over **10** think twice
reconstruct: **3** fix **4** copy, do up **5** alter, fix up, patch **6** deduce, doctor, recast, reform, remake, remold, repair, retool, revamp, rework **7** build up, correct, rebuild, remodel, replace, restore **8** make over, overhaul, recreate, renovate, reorient **9** modernize, replicate, reshuffle
Recontres writer: **4** Gide
record: **3** can, cut, dub, log, say, wax **4** book, copy, disk, file, film, list, mark, memo, note, post, read, show, tape **5** diary, enrol, enter, entry, paper, reign, score, story, table, tally, trace, video, write **6** annals, career, enroll, indite, insert, jacket, legend, memoir, notate, report, résumé, roster, script, scroll, ticket **7** almanac, archive, catalog, ceiling, chalk up, conduct, contain, dossier, explain, history, itemize, jot down, journal, lay down, maximum, minutes, monitor, point to, put down, set down, studies, witness, writing **8** archives, document, evidence, indicate, inscribe, mark down, memorial, monument, notation, point out, preserve, register, registry, tabulate, take down **9** audiotape, catalogue, chronicle, designate, directory, enumerate, inventory, keep count, keep score, put on file, statement, testimony, videotape, way of life, write down **10** background, experience, journalize, manuscript, memorandum, paper trail, photograph, put on paper, report card, tabulation, transcribe, transcript
academic ~: **6** grades
adjust the ~ book: **5** relog
as a complaint: **5** lodge
big ~ label: **3** MCA, RCA **6** Arista **7** Elektra **8** Atlantic, Columbia
break the ~ of: **3** top **4** beat, best, pass **5** outdo **6** better, exceed **7** eclipse, surpass **8** outshine, outstrip, surmount
British ~ label: **3** EMI
company: **5** label
cutter: **6** stylus
gold ~: **3** hit **5** smash **7** success, triumph **9** sensation
holder: **4** file **6** jacket, sleeve
jazz ~ label: **5** Verve
keeper: **5** clerk **6** scribe **9** archivist, historian **10** amanuensis
legal ~ book: **5** liber
like some ~ labels: **5** indie
mail-order ~ label: **4** K-Tel
make a ~: **3** cut **5** press
material: **5** vinyl
off the ~: **5** privy **6** secret **7** private, sub rosa **9** entre nous **10** unofficial
old ~ label: **4** Atco, Okeh, Stax **5** Decca
org.: **4** RIAA
phonograph ~: **2** LP **4** disc, disk **5** album
player: **2** DJ **4** hi-fi, juke **5** phono **6** deejay, stereo **9** turntable **10** phonograph
producer's work: **3** mix
sample ~: **4** demo
speed: **3** rpm
surface: **4** side **5** A-side, B-side, side A, side B
track: **6** groove
without a ~: **5** clean
record __: **6** player **7** changer
__ record: **4** go on, unit **5** on the, stock, track
__-record: **4** tape **5** video
record book: **5** annal **6** annals
entry: **4** stat
suffix: **3** est
recorder: **4** wind **9** historian **10** bookkeeper, chronicler
cassette ~ letters: **3** mic
fodder: **4** tape
plug: **6** fipple
__ recorder: **4** film, tape, wire **6** flight
recording: **2** CD, LP **4** tape **10** transcript
combining form: **4** disc- **5** disci-, disco-
go back to the ~ studio: **5** remix
medium: **3** DAT **4** disc, disk, tape
studio apparatus: **5** mixer
tool: **4** mike
vinyl ~ type: **2** EP
recording __: **4** head
__ recording: **4** tape, wire **6** analog **7** digital
recordings: **4** trax
recording-tape
material: **5** Mylar
name: **3** TDK **6** Maxell **7** Memorex
__ recordist: **5** sound
records: **5** files, proof **6** annals **7** archive
book of public ~: **5** liber
check of ~: **5** audit
historical ~: **7** archive **9** chronicle
like old ~: **4** mono
place for ~: **5** shelf **7** cabinet
recount: **4** cite, echo, tell **5** cover, recap, state, track, voice **6** convey, depict, detail, recite, rehash, relate, repeat, report, set out, unload **7** itemize, iterate, mention, narrate, picture, portray, present, run down **8** describe, play back, rehearse **9** chronicle, delineate, enumerate, verbalize **10** run through
recountal: **4** saga, tale **5** diary, story **6** annals, memoir, report **7** history, journal, recital **9** chronicle, narration, narrative
recounted: **4** oral **5** vocal **6** spoken, verbal, voiced **7** uttered **9** vocalized
recounting: **7** recital **9** narration, narrative **10** recitation
recoup: **5** repay **6** redeem, refund, regain **7** get back, get well, recover, recruit, requite, satisfy, win back **8** make good, retrieve **9** make up for, reacquire, reimburse, repossess **10** compensate, recompense, remunerate
recourse: **3** aid, out **4** help **5** shift **6** appeal, option, refuge, remedy, resort, way out **8** resource **9** expedient
recover: **4** find, gain, grow, heal, mend, save **5** rally, renew **6** better, obtain, offset, perk up, pick up, ransom, recoup, redeem, regain, repair, rescue, resume, retake, revive **7** balance, catch up, get back, get over, get well, rebound, reclaim, recruit, refresh, replevy, restore, salvage, survive, win back **8** increase, make good, overcome, reoccupy, replevin, retrieve, snap back, take back **9** bring back, extricate, get better, reacquire, recapture, reimburse, repossess **10** bounce back, come around, compensate, convalesce, forge ahead, get in shape, recompense, recuperate, rediscover, rejuvenate
quick to ~: **9** resilient
recovered: **4** well **5** sound, whole **7** healthy
from: **4** over, past
recovering: **6** better **8** improved **9** healthier, improving, on the mend
recovery: **5** rally **7** revival **8** comeback
regiment: **5** rehab
recovery __: **4** room
recreancy: **9** defection, desertion **10** disloyalty
recreant: **5** false, knave, sissy, timid **6** afraid, bad hat, coward, craven, rascal, scared, untrue, yellow **7** chicken, crybaby, dastard, fearful, hellion, milksop, wimpish **8** apostate, betrayer, cowardly, defector, deserter, disloyal, poltroon, renegade, turncoat, two-faced **9** dastardly, faithless, fraidy-cat, jellyfish, spineless, two-timing **10** delinquent, frightened, perfidious, scaredy-cat, traitorous, unfaithful
recreate: **4** rest **5** enact, relax, revel **6** divert, unwind **7** refresh **9** replicate **10** regenerate
recreation: **3** fun **4** ball, ease, game, play, rest **5** games, hobby, mirth, R and R, sport **6** frolic, laughs, picnic, relief, repose, sports **7** disport, holiday, jollity, leisure, pastime, rollick **8** exercise, field day, free time, hilarity, interest, playtime, pleasure, vacation **9** amusement, athletics, avocation, diversion, enjoyment, festivity
place: **3** gym **4** park, YMCA, YMHA, YWCA, YWHA **9** gymnasium
recreation __: **4** room
recreational
activity: **4** game **5** sport **7** pastime **9** athletics
vehicle: **3** ATV **5** canoe
recreational __: **7** vehicle
recrimination: **5** blame
recriminatory: **8** vengeful
rec room: **3** den
item: **2** TV **3** VCR **5** TV set
recruit: **2** GI **4** gain, levy, pleb, tiro, tyro **5** draft, enrol, newie, plebe, raise, renew **6** airman, better, call up, engage, enlist, enroll, fill up, greeny, helper, induct, muster, novice, obtain, recoup, regain, repair, revive, rookie, sailor, select, sign on, sign up, supply, take in, take on **7** augment, build up, convert, deliver, draftee, impress, improve, jack tar, learner, new hand, procure, recover, refresh, restore, round up, soldier, store up, trainee, win over **8** beginner, initiate, mobilize, neophyte, newcomer, retrieve, selectee, shanghai **9** conscript, fledgling, greenhorn, layperson, legionary, novitiate, proselyte, reanimate, reinforce, replenish, repossess, volunteer **10** apprentice, call to arms, recuperate, strengthen, tenderfoot
like a new ~: **5** green
see also army, soldier
recruited, be: **6** enlist
recruiter: **5** hirer, scout
goal: **5** quota
regulating org.: **4** NCAA
recruiting poster word: **3** you **4** want
recruit-to-be: **4** one A
rect-
kin: **4** orth-
__ recta: **4** cyma
rectangle: **6** isogon **7** polygon
shaped state: **3** Wyo. **4** Colo. **7** Wyoming **8** Colorado
rectangular: **2** ob. **6** oblong
dimension: **5** width **6** length
groove: **4** dado
rectification: **7** redress
rectifier, TV: **5** diode
rectify: **3** fix **4** cure, mend **5** amend, debug, emend, fix up, right, scrub **6** adjust, doctor, go over, pick up, reform, remedy, repair, revise, settle, square **7** clean up, correct, expiate, improve, launder, redress, shape up **8** dial back, make good, put right, regulate, set right **9** do justice, make right, make up for, reconcile **10** counteract, straighten
rectilinear: **6** in a row **8** straight **10** horizontal
rectitude: **4** good **5** honor **6** virtue **7** decency, honesty, justice, probity **8** goodness, morality, veracity **9** character, integrity, propriety **10** honestness, principles
recto: **4** page
opposite: **5** verso

rector: 5 padre 6 cleric, leader, parson, pastor, priest 8 minister 9 principal
assistant: 6 curate
representative: 5 vicar
Rector of Justin, The author: Louis Auchincloss
rectory: 5 manse
rectus: 6 muscle
locale: 3 eye
recumbent: 4 flat 5 level, prone 6 supine 8 resupine 9 decumbent, lying down, prostrate, reclining, sprawling 10 horizontal, procumbent
be ~: 3 lie 4 laze, loll, rest 6 repose 7 lie down, recline
one: 4 lier
recuperate: 4 gain, heal, mend 5 rally 6 look up, perk up, pick up 7 get well, rebound, recover, recruit 9 come along, get better 10 ameliorate, bounce back, convalesce
recuperating: 9 on the mend
recur: 4 echo 5 cycle 6 repeat, return 7 persist 8 continue, intermit 9 come and go
recurrence: 6 return 7 atavism 9 duplicate, frequency
recurrent: 6 cyclic 7 regular 8 cyclical, frequent, habitual, haunting, iterated, periodic, unwaning 9 alternate, continual, continued, irregular, perennial, perpetual 10 monotonous, repetitive
recurrently: 4 much 5 again, often 8 ofttimes 10 oftentimes
recurring: 6 cyclic 8 periodic 9 perpetual
idea: 5 motif, theme 9 leitmotif
melody: 5 motif, thema
music with a ~ theme: 5 rondo
recurring ___: 7 decimal
recusant: 7 lawless, radical 8 indurate
recyclable item: 3 can 5 empty, scrap 6 bottle 9 newspaper
recycle: 5 reuse
recycled: 4 used 10 hand-me-down, secondhand
recycling ___: 3 bin
recycling station: 8 landfill
red: 3 hot 4 gory, Marx, port, rare, rose, rosy, ruby, rust, wine 5 aglow, brick, Gamay, Lenin, Médoc, Pinot, Rioja, ruddy 6 ablush, Barolo, bloody, blowsy, blowzy, cerise, cherry, claret, florid, garnet, Maoist, maroon, russet, Soviet, Stalin, titian 7 Amarone, Barbera, blowsed, blowzed, carmine, Chianti, Concord, crimson, flaming, flushed, fuchsia, glowing, magenta, Musigny, Pommard, scarlet, Trotsky 8 blushing, burgundy, Cabernet, cardinal, chestnut, Dolcetto, geranium, inflamed, Leninist, muscatel, portwine, rubicund, sanguine 9 Bardolino, bloodshot, Bolshevik, Communist, irritated, lambrusco, rubescent, Stalinist, sunburned, table wine, vermilion, Zinfandel 10 Beaujolais, Chambertin
and yellow: 6 orange
be in the ~: 3 owe
bluish ~: 9 cranberry
brownish ~: 5 brick 6 maroon
color: 4 rose, ruby, rust, wine 5 brick, coral, grape, poppy, rusty, sandy 6 cerise, cherry, claret, garnet, maroon 7 carmine, crimson, fuchsia, magenta, pimento, scarlet, sultana, vermeil 8 amaranth, cardinal, dubonnet, geranium, rubicund 9 carnation, cranberry, vermilion 10 strawberry
combining form: 5 pyrrh-, pyrro- 6 erythr-, pyrhho- 7 erythro-
dark ~: 4 puce, winy 5 brick, winey
dog in football: 5 blitz
dwarf: 4 star
dye: 3 azo 5 eosin, henna 6 eosine, kermes
ender: 3 bud, bug, cap, eye, top 4 bait, bird, coat, fish, head, line, poll, root, wing, wood 5 brick, shank, shirt, start 6 breast, headed
entry in ~: 4 debt 5 debit
flag: 5 alarm 6 caveat 7 caution, warning
flower: 3 mum 4 lily 5 lehua, peony, poppy, tulip 6 cosmos, salvia 7 day lily, rambler 8 camellia, geranium, japonica, marigold, oleander, rockrose, tamarisk 9 amaryllis, candytuft, cockscomb, hollyhock, ohia lehua, Oswego tea, snow plant, woundwort 10 nasturtium, poinsettia
giant: 4 Mira, star 5 S star 7 Antares
herring: 4 ploy, ruse 5 decoy 9 diversion 10 camouflage
hot: 5 zesty 7 peppery, piquant, pungent 8 seasoned
in heraldry: 5 gules
ink: 4 debt, loss 7 arrears, deficit 8 mortgage 9 arrearage, debenture, liability 10 obligation
in the ~: 9 insolvent
in the face: 6 ablush
it turns ~: 6 litmus
letters: 4 USSR
light: 4 flag 6 signal 7 caution, warning
make see ~: 3 irk 4 rile 5 anger, peeve, upset 6 enrage, madden
man in ~: 5 Santa 10 Santa Claus
meat: 4 beef 5 steak
name meaning ~: 3 Roy 4 Roth 7 Russell
one in the ~: 4 ower
on the inside: 4 rare
orangish ~: 5 poppy
paint the town ~: 5 revel 6 barhop 7 carouse, roister 8 cut loose, let loose, live it up 9 celebrate, raise Cain, whoop it up
pinkish ~: 4 rose
preceder: 5 amber
purplish ~: 4 rose, ruby 5 grape, murex 6 claret 7 carmine, crimson, fuchsia, magenta, sultana 8 amaranth, dubonnet 9 cranberry
raise a ~ flag: 4 warn 5 alert 6 tip off 7 caution
roll out the ~ carpet: 5 greet, honor 7 lionize, receive, welcome
see ~: 4 boil, fume 6 rear up, seethe 7 bristle, flame up 8 get angry 9 blow a fuse 10 hit the roof
seeing ~: 3 mad 5 angry, irate, livid, upset 6 raging 7 furious 9 indignant
tape: 4 maze 5 delay 6 policy, system 8 protocol 9 paperwork, procedure, rigmarole 10 impediment
turn ~: 5 blush, flush
turning litmus ~: 6 acidic
vegetable: 4 beet
wave a ~ flag: 6 enrage 7 caution 8 forewarn
what ~ means: 4 stop
wine: 4 port, rosé 5 gamay, Médoc, pinot, Rioja, tavel 6 barolo, claret 7 Chianti, Concord, Musigny, Pommard 8 burgundy, Cabernet, Dolcetto, muscatel 9 Bardolino, lambrusco, Zinfandel 10 Beaujolais, Chambertin
wrap in ~ tape: 5 sit on 8 withhold
yellowish ~: 4 rust 5 brick, coral, rusty, sandy
red ___: 3 ant, bay, dog, eft, fir, fox, gum, hat, ink, oak, rag, rot, tag, tai 4 card, cell, cent, clay, deer, drum, feed, fire, flag, heat, hind, lead, line, meat, pine, rose, sage, snow, star, tape, tide, wine, wolf, worm 5 alder, alert, algae, birch, brass, cedar, coral, count, dwarf, flash, giant, heart, label, light, maids, maple, ocher, ochre, osier, panda, rover, stuff 6 carpet, clover, duster, fescue, grouse, kowhai, liquor, mombin, mullet, pepper, ribbon, salmon, shanks, spider, spruce, squill 7 admiral, cabbage, currant, dogwood, herring, seaweed, snapper
red ___ beet: 3 as a
red ___ cell: 5 blood
red-___: 3 dog, eye, hot, wat 5 faced, short 6 figure, handed, headed, letter, pencil 7 blooded
red-___ day: 6 letter
red-___ gravy: 3 eye
red-___ sale: 3 tag
___ red: 3 see 4 fire, Mars 5 blood, brick, Congo, in the, poppy 6 cherry, chrome, claret, Indian, Levant, methyl, turkey 7 cadmium, Chinese, English, oxblood
Red: 3 sea 5 Adair, Foley, Norvo, river, Smith 6 Barber, Grange, Sovine 7 Buttons, Holzman, Nichols, Ruffing, Skelton 8 Auerbach 10 baseballer
Hall of Famer: 5 Bench, Perez, Roush
jet: 3 MiG
leader: 3 Mao
rival: 3 Cub, Met 4 Expo, Twin 5 Angel, Astro, Brave, Giant, Padre, Rocky, Royal, Tiger 6 Brewer, Dodger, Indian, Marlin, Oriole, Philly, Pirate, Ranger, Red Sox, Yankee 7 Blue Jay, Mariner 8 Athletic, Cardinal, Devil Ray, White Sox
River locale: 5 China, Texas 7 Vietnam 8 Oklahoma 9 Louisiana
role for ~: 4 Clem
Sea locale: 6 Africa, Arabia
see also Russia
Red ___: 3 Sea, Sox 4 Army, Dust, Hats, Heat, Mass, Poll, Spot, Wing 5 Alert, Angus, Baron, China, Cloud, Cross, Guard, River, Ryder, Sonja 6 Branch, Desert, Dragon, Jacket, Sindhi, Square 7 Chamber, Lobster
Red ___ at Morning: 3 Sky
Red ___ Chili Peppers: 3 Hot
Red ___ for a Blue Lady: 5 Roses
Red ___ in the Sunset: 5 Sails
Red ___ Morning: 5 Sky at
Red ___ of Courage, The: 5 Badge
Red ___, The: 4 Lily, Pony, Room 5 Baron, House, Shoes
Red, ___ and Blue!: 3 Hot
Red-___ League, The: 6 Headed
Red-___ Woman: 6 Headed
___ Red: 3 Big 4 I Saw 5 Beach 6 Simply 7 Eric the, Erik the
redact: 4 edit 5 emend 6 polish, refine, revise 7 correct, tighten, touch up 8 fine-tune 10 blue-pencil
jointly: 6 coedit
redaction: 6 change 7 editing, rewrite 8 revision 10 emendation
redactor: 6 editor
word: 4 dele, stet
redan: 4 fort 7 rampart 9 fieldwork 10 battlement
Redan: 4 city, town
locale: 7 Georgia
Red and the Black, The author: Stendhal
character: 4 Abbé 5 Sorel 6 Julien 7 de Rênal 8 de La Mole
Red and White Domes artist: 4 Klee
red as ___: 5 a beet
Red Badge of Courage, The: 4 film 5 novel
author: Stephen Crane
cast: Douglas Dick, Bill Mauldin, Audie Murphy
director: John Huston
setting: 8 Civil War
Red Ball Express (1952 film)
cast: Jeff Chandler, Hugh O'Brian
Red Balloon artist: 4 Klee
Red Bank Boogie composer: 5 Basie
red-blooded: 4 hale, iron, wiry 5 beefy, burly, hardy, hefty, hunky, husky, lusty, stout, tough 6 brawny, hearty, mighty, potent, robust, rugged, sinewy, steely, stocky, sturdy, virile 7 doughty 8 athletic, forceful, indurate, muscular, powerful, puissant, stalwart, vigorous 9 Atlantean, energetic, Herculean, strapping, well-built 10 able-bodied, courageous
redbone: 3 dog 5 hound 6 canine
Redbone: 4 Leon
redbreast: 4 bird 5 robin
redbud: 4 tree
family: 6 legume
relative: 3 koa 5 carob 6 cassia, cercis, locust, padauk, padouk 7 araroba, mesquit 8 mesquite, tamarind 9 poinciana
redcap: 6 porter
burden: 3 bag 7 luggage 8 suitcase
domain: 5 depot
red-carpet treader: 3 VIP 7 bigshot, notable 8 luminary 9 celebrity, dignitary
Red Cedar, city on the: 7 Lansing
Red Cloud: 6 Indian
residence: 4 tipi 5 tepee 6 teepee
Redcoat: 4 Tory
Continental, to a ~: 3 foe 5 enemy
general: 4 Howe
red-complexioned: 5 ruddy
Red Cross
concern: 6 famine
supply: 4 sera 5 blood, serum
volunteer: 5 donor
Redd: 4 Foxx
Red Deer: 4 city, town
locale: 6 Canada 7 Alberta
Red Delicious: 5 apple
relative: 4 crab, Gala, Lodi, Rome 5 Mutsu 6 Empire, medlar, Pippin, russet 7 Baldwin, Bramley, costard, Freedom, Liberty, Spartan, Wealthy, Winesap 8 Cortland, Jonathan, McIntosh 10 Rome Beauty
redden: 3 dye 4 chap, glow, pink, rose, ruby, rust, tint 5 blush, color, flush, paint, rouge, ruddy 6 bloody, mantle, pinken, raddle, rubify, rubric, ruddle 7 crimson, roughen, suffuse 8 irritate 9 encarmine, rubricate
crack and ~: 4 chap
reddened: 4 sore 5 angry, ruddy 6 florid, tender 7 bruised 8 inflamed, rubicund 9 indignant
Reddi ___: 3 Wip
Redding: 4 city, Otis, town
locale: 10 California
Redding, Otis song: (Sittin' On) The Dock of the Bay (1968)
reddish: 5 ruddy 6 rufous 8 sanguine
color: 3 bay 4 bole, foxy, plum, rust, sand 5 brass, cocoa, coral, flame, henna, lilac, ocher, ochre, rusty, umber 6 auburn, copper, ginger, orchid, russet, sorrel, walnut 7 petunia 8 chestnut, cinnamon, hyacinth, mahogany, rubicund 9 raspberry, tangerine 10 heliotrope
red dog: 4 game 8 card game
Red Dragon (2002 film)
cast: Ralph Fiennes, Anthony

Hopkins, Harvey Keitel, Edward Norton
director: Brett Ratner
Red Dust (1932 film)
cast: Mary Astor, Clark Gable, Jean Harlow
director: Victor Fleming
Reddy, Helen
homeland: Australia
song: Ain't No Way to Treat a Lady (1975)
Angie Baby (1974)
Delta Dawn (1973)
I Am Woman (1972)
I Don't Know How to Love Him (1971)
Keep On Singing (1974)
Leave Me Alone (1973)
Peaceful (1973)
Somewhere in the Night (1975)
You and Me Against the World (1974)
You're My World (1977)
redecorate: 4 redo **6** do over **8** make over
redeem: 4 cash, free, meet, save **5** cover, loose, repay **6** acquit, buy off, call in, cash in, change, defray, fulfil, offset, pay off, purify, ransom, recoup, reform, refund, regain, rescue, set off, settle, take in, unbind **7** abide by, absolve, balance, buy back, deliver, fulfill, get back, manumit, perform, receive, reclaim, recover, redress, release, replevy, restore, salvage, satisfy, set free, trade in, unchain, win back **8** adhere to, atone for, carry out, exchange, liberate, make good, outweigh, purchase, replevin, retrieve, unfetter **9** discharge, extricate, make up for, recapture, reinstate, repossess **10** compensate, emancipate, make amends, repurchase
redeemer: 6 savior **7** messiah, saviour **9** liberator
redemption: 6 cash-in, ransom **7** freedom **9** atonement, salvation
slip: 6 coupon, ticket **7** voucher
Redemption author: Leon Uris
Redenbacher: 7 Orville
redesigned: 3 new **7** updated
redeye: 5 gravy, hooch **6** flight, hootch, whisky **7** alcohol, whiskey
gravy source: 3 ham
red-faced: 4 rosy **5** ruddy **6** blowsy, blowzy **7** blowsed, blowzed
Redford: 4 city, town **6** Robert
locale: 8 Michigan
Redford, Robert: 5 actor **8** director
film: All the President's Men (1976)
Barefoot in the Park (1967)
Brubaker (1980)
Butch Cassidy and the Sundance Kid (1969)
The Candidate (1972)
The Chase, (1966)
Downhill Racer (1969)
The Electric Horseman (1979)
The Great Gatsby (1974)
The Great Waldo Pepper (1975)
Havana (1990)
The Horse Whisperer (1998)
The Hot Rock (1972)
Indecent Proposal (1993)
Inside Daisy Clover (1965)
Jeremiah Johnson (1972)
Legal Eagles (1986)
The Legend of Bagger Vance (2000)
The Milagro Beanfield War (1988)
The Natural (1984)
Ordinary People (1980, AA)
Out of Africa (1985)
Quiz Show (1994)
A River Runs Through It (1992)
Sneakers (1992)
The Sting (1973)
Tell Them Willie Boy Is Here (1969)
Three Days of the Condor (1975)
Up Close & Personal (1996)
The Way We Were (1973)
Redgrave: 4 Lynn **7** Michael, Vanessa
Redgrave, Lynn: 7 actress
film: All I Wanna Do (1998)
Georgy Girl (1966)
Getting It Right (1989)
Gods and Monsters (1998)
How to Kill Your Neighbor's Dog (2001)
The Simian Line (2001)
Redgrave, Michael: 5 actor
film: 1984 (1956)
The Browning Version (1951)
Captive Heart (1946)
The Dam Busters (1955)
Dead of Night (1945)
The Innocents (1961)
The Lady Vanishes (1938)
The Loneliness of the Long Distance Runner (1962)
The Night My Number Came Up (1955)
The Stars Look Down (1939)
Thunder Rock (1942)
Time Without Pity (1956)
The Way to the Stars (1945)
Redgrave, Vanessa: 7 actress
film: Agatha (1979)
Blowup (1966)
Deep Impact (1998)
Déjà Vu (1998)
The Devils (1971)
Howards End (1992)
Isadora (1968)
Julia (1977, AA)
Mary, Queen of Scots (1971)
Mission: Impossible (1996)
Morgan! (1966)
Murder on the Orient Express (1974)
The Pledge (2001)
Prick Up Your Ears (1987)
A Rumor of Angels (2002)
The Seven-Per-Cent Solution (1976)
Yanks (1979)
red-handed: 6 guilty **8** blamable, culpable, in the act **9** blameable **10** censurable, delinquent
catch ~: 3 bag, get, nab, net **4** bust, grab, nail, trap **5** catch, pinch, run in, seize **6** arrest, collar, snatch **7** capture, startle **8** surprise **9** apprehend, burst in on
redhead: 4 Ball, duck, Eric, Erik, fowl, Lucy
become a ~: 3 dye
dye: 5 henna
relative: 4 smew, teal **5** eider, Pekin, Rouen, scaup **6** Cayuga, scoter **7** gadwall, mallard, pintail, pochard, sea duck, widgeon **8** garganey, gray duck, mandarin, musk duck, oldsquaw, shoveler, surf duck, wood duck **9** black duck, broadbill, goldeneye, goosander, greenhead, merganser, ruddy duck, sprigtail **10** bufflehead, canvasback, surf scoter, tufted duck
Red-Headed League, The author: Arthur Conan Doyle
red-headed, name meaning: 5 Rufus
Red-Headed Woman (1932 film)
cast: Jean Harlow, Una Merkel, Chester Morris
director: Jack Conway
Red Heat (1988 film)
cast: James Belushi, Peter Boyle, Arnold Schwarzenegger
director: Walter Hill
red-hot: 3 mad, new **4** avid, ired, sore **5** afire, angry, candy, cross, eager, faddy, fresh, huffy, irate, livid, riled, surly, testy, wroth **6** aflame, ardent, baking, fervid, fuming, gung-ho, ireful, peeved, piqued, raging, raving, snappy, sultry, torrid **7** angered, blazing, boiling, burning, enraged, fervent, flaming, furious, grouchy, in a stew, intense, peevish, ranting, teed off, uptight, zealous **8** brand-new, broiling, choleric, in a pique, incensed, inflamed, maddened, outraged, seething, sizzling, up-to-date, volcanic, wrathful **9** indignant, irritable, irritated, querulous, rancorous, resentful, scorching, splenetic **10** blistering, freaked out, infuriated, oppressive, passionate, sweltering
Red, Hot and Blue!: 7 musical
songwriter: 6 Porter
Red Hot Chili Peppers
lead singer: Kiedis
song: Scar Tissue (1999)
Soul to Squeeze (1993)
Under the Bridge (1992)
Red House Mystery, The author: 5 Milne
Red House, The (1947 film)
cast: Lon McCallister, Allene Roberts, Edward G. Robinson
director: Delmer Daves
redingote: 4 coat **5** dress **6** jacket
red-ink amount: 4 debt, loss **5** debit **7** deficit
redirect: 5 alter, deter **6** divert **7** reroute
Redlands: 4 city, town
locale: 10 California
red-letter: 5 proud **6** banner **7** special **8** historic **9** memorable
sign: 4 Exit
red-letter ___: 3 day
Red Light Special (1995 song) artist: TLC
Red Lily, The author: Anatole France
redline: 4 drop, omit, snip, trim, X out **5** erase, scrub **6** cancel, delete, efface, excise, remove, rub off, rub out **7** blot out, exclude, expunge, scissor, scratch, wipe out **8** cross off, cross out **9** eliminate, expurgate, strike out **10** obliterate
___ Red Line, The: 4 Thin
redly: 6 ablush
Redmond: 4 city, town
locale: 10 Washington
redness: 5 flush
exemplar of ~: 4 beet
redo: 4 edit **5** fix up **6** change, modify, revise, update **7** remodel **8** make over, overhaul, renovate, work over **9** modernize, refurbish, replicate **10** redecorate
Red October: 3 sub **7** Russian **9** submarine
Red Oleanders author: Tagore
redolence: 4 odor **5** aroma, scent, smell **6** stench **7** bouquet **9** balminess, fragrance
redolent: 5 spicy, sweet **6** spicey **7** odorous, scented **8** aromatic, fragrant **10** suggestive
Redondo Beach: 4 city, town
locale: 10 California
___ Red One, The: 3 Big
redouble: 5 rally **7** magnify **9** intensify
redoubt: 4 fort **7** citadel, defense **8** fastness, fortress **10** stronghold
Redoubt: 7 volcano
locale: 6 Alaska
redoubtable: 4 hale, iron, wiry **5** beefy, burly, hardy, hefty, hunky, husky, lusty, stout, tough **6** brawny, hearty, mighty, potent, robust, rugged, sinewy, steely, stocky, strong, sturdy, virile **7** awesome, doughty, valiant **8** athletic, fearsome, forceful, indurate, muscular, powerful, puissant, stalwart, vigorous **9** Atlantean, Herculean, strapping, well-built **10** able-bodied, red-blooded
red-pencil: 4 dele **5** bleep **6** censor, delete, excise, remove **8** cross off, cross out **9** expurgate, strike out **10** bowdlerize
Red Planet: 4 Mars
redpoll: 4 bird
Red Poll: 3 cow **4** bull **6** bovine, cattle
Red Pony, The: 4 film **5** novel
author: John Steinbeck
cast: Myrna Loy, Peter Miles, Robert Mitchum
director: Lewis Milestone
redraft: 6 revise **8** revision
Red Raiders: 9 Texas Tech
Red, Red Rose, A author: Robert Burns
redress: 3 aid, pay **4** cure, ease, help, mend **5** amend, annul, atone, right **6** adjust, amends, avenge, cancel, change, make up, negate, offset, pay for, redeem, reform, refund, relief, remedy, repair, return, revise, reward, square **7** balance, correct, even out, expiate, justice, payment, rectify, relieve, renewal, restore **8** dial back, negative, put right, regulate, reprisal, requital, revision **9** amendment, atonement, balancing, do justice, expiation, frustrate, indemnity, make up for, quittance, remission, reworking, vengeance, vindicate **10** assistance, compensate, correction, counteract, make amends, neutralize, offsetting, punishment, recompense, remodeling, reparation, turn around
seek ~: 3 sue **8** litigate **9** prosecute
___ Red Riding Hood: 6 Little
Red River (1948 film): 5 oater **7** western
cast: Walter Brennan, Montgomery Clift, Joanne Dru, John Wayne
director: Howard Hawks
role: 4 Tess
Red River ___: 3 War **6** Valley
Red River of the North locale: 8 Manitoba **9** Minnesota
Red River Valley locale: 4 N. Dak.
Red Rock West (1993 film)
cast: Lara Flynn Boyle, Nicolas Cage, Dennis Hopper
director: John Dahl
Red Roof Inn: 5 motel
alternative: 4 HoJo **7** Days Inn **9** Ramada Inn **10** Comfort Inn, Econo Lodge, Hampton Inn, Holiday Inn, Quality Inn, Travelodge **11** Best Western
Red Room, The author: August Strindberg
Red Rose: 3 tea
alternative: 6 Lipton, Nestea, Salada, Tetley **7** Bigelow **8** Twinings
Red Roses for a Blue Lady (1965 song) artist: Vic Dana
Reds: 4 nine, team
home: 10 Cincinnati
org.: 3 MLB, NLC
sport: 8 baseball
Reds (1981 film)
cast: Warren Beatty, Edward Herrmann, Diane Keaton, Jack Nicholson, Paul Sorvino, Maureen Stapleton
director: Warren Beatty
role: 4 Emma, Reed **7** Goldman

Red Sea
access: **4** Suez **9** Suez Canal
ancient ~ kingdom: **5** Nubia
arm: **5** Akaba, Aqaba
boat: **3** dau, dow **4** dhow
country: **5** Egypt, Sudan, Yemen **7** Eritrea
gulf: **4** Suez
island: **5** Tiran
port: **5** Jedda, Jidda
region: **4** Asir **5** Hejaz, Hijaz, Negeb, Negev **6** Arabia, Hedjaz
strait: **5** Tiran
town: **4** Elat **5** Eilat, Elath
redshank: **4** bird
Red Shoes, The (1948 film)
cast: Marius Goring, Moira Shearer, Anton Walbrook
Redskin rival: **3** Jet, Ram **4** Bear, Bill, Colt, Lion **5** Brown, Chief, Eagle, Giant, Niner, Raven, Saint, Texan, Titan **6** Bengal, Bronco, Cowboy, Falcon, Jaguar, Packer, Raider, Viking **7** Charger, Dolphin, Panther, Patriot, Seahawk, Steeler **8** Cardinal **9** Buccaneer
Redskins: **4** team **6** eleven
home: **10** Washington
org.: **3** NFC, NFL
sport: **8** football
Red Sky at Morning (1970 film)
cast: Desi Arnaz Jr., Catherine Burns, Richard Crenna, Richard Thomas
red snapper: **4** fish
Red Sox: **3** ten **4** team
Hall of Famer: **5** Doerr **6** Cronin **8** Williams **11** Yastrzemski
home: **6** Boston
nickname: **3** Yaz
org.: **3** ALE, MLB
rival: **3** Cub, Met, Red **4** Expo, Twin **5** Angel, Astro, Brave, Giant, Padre, Rocky, Royal, Tiger **6** Brewer, Dodger, Indian, Marlin, Oriole, Philly, Pirate, Ranger, Yankee **7** Blue Jay, Mariner **8** Athletic, Cardinal, Devil Ray, White Sox
sport: **8** baseball
__ Red Spot: **5** Great
Red Square figure: **5** Lenin
redstart: **4** bird
residence: **4** nest
Red Storm: **10** Saint John's
red-tag __: **4** sale
redtop: **3** hay **5** grass
reduce: **3** cut, sag, sap **4** bant, bate, bump, bust, chop, clip, crop, curb, dice, diet, drop, ease, flag, mute, pare, ruin, slim, slow, thin, tire, trim, wane **5** abase, abate, allay, blunt, break, bring, crush, drain, drive, force, limit, lower, press, price, prune, quell, relax, shave, slash, smelt, taper **6** deaden, debase, deduct, defeat, demote, derate, digest, dilute, humble, impair, lessen, master, modify, narrow, powder, rebate, recede, shrink, soften, subdue, weaken **7** abridge, cheapen, compact, conquer, cripple, curtail, cut back, cut down, declass, deflate, degrade, demerit, deplete, depress, detract, disable, disrate, dwindle, exhaust, fall off, fatigue, lighten, mollify, qualify, scissor, shorten, thin out, whittle **8** bankrupt, bear down, beat down, bring low, close out, compress, condense, contract, decrease, diminish, discount, disgrade, downsize, enervate, enfeeble, mark down, minimize, mitigate, moderate, modulate, overcome, peter out, pull down, restrict, roll back, simplify, slim down, slow down, step down, take away, taper off, tone down, truncate, turn down, vanquish, wind down **9** attenuate, downgrade, go on a diet, humiliate, knock down, lose speed, overpower, pauperize, scale down, subjugate, telescope, undermine **10** abbreviate, debilitate, depreciate, devitalize, impoverish, lose weight
in rank: **4** bust **5** break **6** demote **7** degrade **8** take down **9** downgrade
speed: **4** slow **5** brake **8** slow down **10** decelerate
reduced: **3** cut, low **4** less, poor, slow **5** cheap, lower **6** on sale **7** limited, partial, sketchy **8** lessened, uncostly **9** condensed, half-price **10** compressed, synopsized, unfinished
in ~ circumstances: **5** needy
in value: **7** debased **8** degraded **9** worthless
reduce to __ of rubble: **5** a pile
reducing __: **5** agent, glass
reduction: **3** cut **4** dent, drop, fall, lack, sale **5** let up **6** rebate, saving **7** bargain, cutback, decline, summary **8** decrease, discount, rollback **9** abatement, allowance, decrement, deduction, lessening, remission, shrinkage **10** diminution
redundancy: **6** excess **8** overflow, plethora, verbiage
redundant: **5** extra, windy, wordy **6** de trop, excess, padded, prolix **7** surplus, verbose **8** needless, unneeded **9** bombastic, excessive **10** extraneous, inordinate, long-winded, loquacious
redux: **4** back **9** resurgent
__ Redux: **6** Rabbit **7** Phineas
Red Wheelbarrow, The author: William Carlos Williams
redwing: **4** bird
Red Wing rival: **4** Blue, King, Star, Wild **5** Bruin, Devil, Flame, Flyer, Oiler, Sabre, Shark **6** Canuck, Coyote, Ranger **7** Capital, Panther, Penguin, Senator **8** Canadien, Islander, Predator, Thrasher **9** Avalanche, Blackhawk, Hurricane, Lightning, Maple Leaf **10** Blue Jacket, Mighty Duck
Red Wings: **3** six **4** team
home: **7** Detroit
milieu: **3** ice **4** rink
org.: **3** NHL
sport: **6** hockey
redwood: **4** tree
like a ~: **4** tall
relative: **7** sequoia
__ redwood: **4** dawn **5** coast, giant
Redwood City: **4** town
locale: **10** California
Ree: **5** tribe **6** Indian **7** Amerind, Arikara
Reebok: **6** sneaks **8** sneakers
rival: **4** Avia, Keds, Nike **6** Adidas
reecho: **4** ring, roll
reed: **3** pen, sax **4** oboe, rush **5** grass, plant, stalk **6** bamboo **7** bassoon, bulrush, cattail, hautboy, papyrus **8** reed mace, woodwind **9** saxophone
combining form: **5** calam- **6** calami-, calamo-
ender: **3** man, men **4** bird, buck
giant ~: **3** nal
hollow ~: **6** bamboo
like a ~: **4** slim **6** skinny
weaver's ~: **4** slay, sley **6** sleigh
reed __: **4** mace, pipe, stop **5** organ **7** bunting, warbler
__ reed: **3** bur **4** cane **5** giant **6** double
Reed: **3** Lou, Rex **4** Alan, John **5** Carol, Donna, Jerry, Jimmy **6** Alaina, Oliver, Pamela, Robert, Shanna, Walter, Willis **7** Ishmael
reedbuck: **8** antelope
relative: **3** gnu, kob **4** guib, kudu, oryx, puku, topi **5** addax, bongo, chiru, eland, goral, korin, nyala, oribi, saiga, serow **6** chammy, dikdik, duiker, impala, koodoo, lechwe, nilgai, rhebok, shammy, shamoy **7** blaubok, blesbok, chamois, defassa, gazelle, gemsbok, gerenuk, grysbok, nylghai, nylghau, sassaby **8** blesbuck, bontebok, bushbuck, gemsbuck, steenbok, steinbok **9** blackbuck, pronghorn, sitatunga, springbok, waterbuck **10** hartebeest, wildebeest
Reed, Carol: **3** Sir **8** director
film: Odd Man Out (1947)
Oliver! (1968, AA)
Outcast of the Islands (1951)
The Running Man (1963)
The Stars Look Down (1939)
The Third Man (1949)
Trapeze (1956)
The Way Ahead (1944)
Reed, Donna: **7** actress
film: From Here to Eternity (1953, AA)
It's a Wonderful Life (1946)
The Last Time I Saw Paris (1954)
The Picture of Dorian Gray (1945)
Scandal Sheet (1952)
See Here, Private Hargrove (1944)
They Were Expendable (1945)
Three Hours to Kill (1954)
TV: Dallas, The Donna Reed Show
TV surname: **5** Stone
Reed-Hall: **6** Alaina
Reed, Ishmael: **4** poet **6** writer
Reed, Jerry
song: Amos Moses (1971)
When You're Hot, You're Hot (1971)
Reed, John: **6** writer **10** journalist
movie about ~: **4** Reds
work: Ten Days That Shook the World
Reedley: **4** city, town
locale: **10** California
Reed, Lou song: Walk on the Wild Side (1973)
Reed, Oliver: **5** actor
film: The Assassination Bureau (1969)
The Devils (1971)
The Four Musketeers (1975)
Gladiator (2000)
I'll Never Forget What's 'is Name (1967)
Oliver! (1968)
The Three Musketeers (1974)
The Trap (1966)
Women in Love (1969)
__ Reeds: **5** Lip My
Reed, Willis
milieu: **5** court
org.: **3** NBA
sport: **10** basketball
reedy: **4** slim, thin, weak **5** frail, rangy **6** piping, shrill, slight **7** slender **9** overgrown, quavering
reef: **3** bar, cay, key **4** bank, rock **5** atoll, ledge, ridge, shelf, shoal **7** barrier, sand bar
material: **5** coral
__ reef: **5** coral, patch **7** barrier
reefer: **4** coat **6** jacket **9** outerwear
reek: **4** emit, fume **5** exude, fetor, smell, smoke, steam, stink **6** foetor, stench **7** malodor **9** effluvium, fetidness
reeked: **5** stank, stunk
__ Reekie: **4** Auld
reeking: **4** foul, rank **5** fetid, stale **6** foetid, rancid, rotten, smelly, stinky **7** noisome, noxious, odorous, squalid **8** mephitic, stinking **10** malodorous
reel: **4** keel, rock, roll, spin, sway, wind **5** dance, lurch, music, pitch, shake, spool, swing, swirl, twirl, waver, weave, wheel, whirl **6** careen, falter, recoil, rotate, teeter, totter, unwind, wabble, wobble **7** stagger, stumble **9** folk dance **10** spin around
contents: **4** film **5** movie
film ~ holder: **3** can
fishing ~ in Britain: **4** pirn
in: **4** land **6** entrap **7** retract
like a fly ~: **5** aspin
off: **4** tell **6** rattle, recite
out: **6** uncoil, unfold, unfurl, unwind
starter: **4** news
reel __: **3** off
reelect: **6** return **9** reinstate
reelection runners: **3** ins
__-reeler: **3** one, two
reeling: **5** dazed, dizzy, shaky, tipsy, woozy **6** addled, punchy, wobbly **8** confused **9** befuddled **10** bewildered
Reeling in the Years (1973 song)
artist: Steely Dan
reel-to-reel __: **4** tape
reenergize: **6** revive
reentry: **6** return
reentry __: **4** card **7** vehicle
reequip: **9** refurbish
Rees: **5** Jerry, Roger
Reese: **5** Della, Mason, Pokey **6** Pee Wee **7** Lizette **11** Witherspoon
Reese, Della
real name: Delloreese Patricia Early
song: And That Reminds Me (1957)
Don't You Know (1959)
Not One Minute More (1959)
Reese, Pee Wee: **6** Dodger **9** shortstop
Reese, Pokey sport: **8** baseball
Reese's: **5** candy **9** chocolate
alternative: **4** Mars, Twix **5** Clark, Heath **6** Kit Kat, Mounds, PayDay, Zagnut **7** Krackel, Oh Henry **8** Baby Ruth, Hershey's, Milky Way, Snickers **9** Almond Joy, Mr. Goodbar **10** NutRageous
Reese's __: **6** Pieces
Reese's Peanut Butter Puffs: **6** cereal
competitor: **3** Kix **4** Life, Trix **5** Kashi, Quisp, Total **6** Kaboom, Muesli, Oreo O's, Pablum, Smacks **7** All-Bran, Crispix, Harmony, Hunny B's, Mueslix, Oat Bran, Pokemon **8** Boo Berry, Cheerios, Corn Chex, Corn Pops, Fiber One, Rice Chex, Special K, Uncle Sam, Wheaties **9** Alpha Bits, Apple Zaps, Grape Nuts, Honey Comb, Just Right, Wheat Chex **10** Apple Jacks, Bran Flakes, Cap'n Crunch, Cocoa Puffs, Froot Loops, Mini-Wheats, Nutri-Grain, Puffed Rice, Quaker Oats, Smart Start **11** Cocoa Blasts, Cookie Crisp, Golden Crisp, Lucky Charms, Puffed Wheat, Sweet Crunch, Waffle Crisp
reestablish: **5** renew **6** recall **9** reinstate
reet __: **5** pleat
reevaluate: **6** review **7** revisit
Reeve, Christopher: **5** actor
costar: **6** Kidder
film: Deathtrap (1982)
Noises Off (1992)
The Remains of the Day (1993)
Somewhere in Time (1980)
Speechless (1994)
Superman (1978)
Superman II (1980)
Switching Channels (1988)
role: **4** Kent
Reeves: **3** Del, Jim **5** Keanu **6** George, Martha

Reeves, George role: 4 Kent 8 Superman
Reeves, Keanu: 5 actor
  film: Bill & Ted's Excellent Adventure (1989)
    Bram Stoker's Dracula (1992)
    Dangerous Liaisons (1988)
    The Devil's Advocate (1997)
    The Gift (2000)
    Hardball (2001)
    The Matrix (1999)
    Much Ado About Nothing (1993)
    My Own Private Idaho (1991)
    Permanent Record (1988)
    Point Break (1991)
    River's Edge (1986)
    Speed (1994)
    Sweet November (2001)
    A Walk in the Clouds (1995)
reexamine: 6 review 7 revisit 8 overhaul 10 reconsider
ref: 6 umpire 10 arbitrator
  see also referee
ref.: 2 bk.
  book: 3 gaz. 4 dict., ency. 5 encyc. 6 encycl
  multivolume ~ book: 3 OED
refashion: 5 alter 6 modify, reform
refection: 4 fare, meal 6 repast 7 aliment 8 victuals
refectory: 10 dining room
refer: 4 cite, send 5 apply, guide, point, quote 6 advert, allude, direct, look up, pass on, relate, resort, submit, turn to 7 concern, connect, consult, iterate, mention, pertain, speak of, suggest, touch on 8 accredit, relegate, turn over 9 appertain, recommend, touch upon
  ender: 3 ent 4 ence
  to: 4 cite, name, note 5 quote, touch 6 advert, regard, resort 7 bring up, mention, speak of, specify, touch on 9 touch upon
  (to): 4 turn
referee: 3 try, ump 5 judge, zebra 6 umpire 7 adjudge, arbiter, mediate 8 moderate 9 arbitrate, go-between, interpose, negotiate, officiate 10 adjudicate, arbitrator, interceder
  call: 3 TKO 4 foul, time 7 time out
  count: 3 ten
  employer: 3 NBA, NFL, NHL
  order: 5 break
  signal: 3 tee
reference: 4 cite, hint, note, plug, text 5 quote 6 look up, regard, remark, source 7 bring up, mention, stating, tribute, writing 8 allusion, archives, citation, evidence, good word, innuendo, relating, resource, workbook 9 attribute, character, quotation, thesaurus 10 connecting, cyclopedia, delegation, dictionary, indicating, mentioning, suggestion
  book: 4 text, tome 6 manual
  center: 7 library
  field of ~: 3 run 4 area, play, span, sway, view 5 ambit, gamut, orbit, range, reach, realm, scale, scope, space, sweep, width 6 extent, margin, radius, sphere 7 breadth, compass, expanse, horizon, purview, subject 8 confines, latitude 9 amplitude, dimension
  frame of ~: 4 idea, side, view 5 angle, light, slant, stand 6 aspect, stance, system 7 horizon, opinion, outlook, posture 8 attitude, position 9 viewpoint 10 estimation, philosophy, standpoint
  have ~ to: 5 touch 6 bear on 7 concern, involve 8 deal with
  indirect ~: 4 hint 8 allusion, innuendo 10 imputation, intimation, suggestion
  in ~ to: 5 about, as for 9 apropos of, as regards
  make ~: 5 refer 6 allude
  mark: 6 obelus
  marks: 5 obeli
  quick ~: 5 index
  use as a ~: 4 cite 6 quotee
reference ___: 4 book, mark 5 frame, group
___ reference: 5 cross
reference book: 5 atlas 7 almanac, lexicon 9 gazetteer 10 dictionary
  direction: 3 see
  name: 5 Roget 7 Webster
referendum: 4 vote 6 ballot, voting 8 election
  choice: 2 no 3 yes
referring: 8 relative 10 delegation
  to: 5 about 10 concerning
refill: 7 restock 9 replenish
  in need of a ~: 3 dry 5 empty 7 drained 8 depleted 9 exhausted
refine: 4 edit, hone, thin 5 clean, round, sleek, slick 6 better, filter, finish, polish, purify, rarefy, rarify, redact, smooth, strain, temper 7 clarify, cleanse, develop, distill, elevate, explain, improve, perfect, process 8 civilize, polish up, round off, round out 9 cultivate, make clear
  metal: 5 smelt
refined: 4 nice, posh, pure, thin 5 civil, clean, couth, exact, haute, noble, plush, ritzy, suave 6 classy, dainty, polite, proper, snazzy, spiffy, subtle, swanky, urbane, washed 7 aerated, courtly, drained, elegant, genteel, precise, sublime 8 cleansed, cultural, cultured, debonair, decorous, delicate, esthetic, filtered, graceful, gracious, highbred, highbrow, ladylike, lettered, mannerly, polished, purified, rarefied, strained, tasteful, well-bred 9 aesthetic, civilized, clarified, courteous, debonaire, dignified, distilled, processed, sensitive, spiritual, uplifting 10 boiled down, cultivated, debonnaire, discerning, expurgated, fastidious, high-minded, restrained
  it's ~: 3 oil, ore
  not ~: 3 raw 5 crass, rough 6 coarse, gauche
refinement: 4 chic, lore, tact 5 class, grace, style, taste 6 beauty, change, finish, nicety, nuance, polish 7 amenity, culture, dignity, finesse, manners, suavity 8 breeding, civility, cleaning, courtesy, delicacy, draining, elegance, fineness, literacy, niceties, noblesse, subtlety, urbanity 9 education, erudition, gentility, knowledge, politesse, precision, propriety, suaveness 10 classicism
refinery: 7 factory
  output: 5 metal
  residue: 4 slag 5 dross
refinish furniture: 5 stain
refit: 5 renew 8 overhaul 9 refurbish
refitting: 10 adaptation, adjustment, alteration, conversion, remodeling
reflect: 4 cast, copy, echo, muse, show, stew 5 catch, flash, match, pause, reply, shine, sound, study, think, weigh 6 chew on, evince, follow, mirror, ponder, reason, repeat, return, reveal, revert, wonder 7 bear out, bespeak, display, emulate, exhibit, express, imitate, rebound, resound, reverse 8 cogitate, consider, give back, indicate, look back, manifest, meditate, mull over, register, resonate, ruminate 9 cerebrate, give forth, repercuss, reproduce, speculate, take after, throw back 10 deliberate, introspect, think about
  light: 4 beam, glow 5 blaze, gleam, glint, shine 6 dazzle 7 flicker, glimmer, glisten, glitter, radiate, sparkle 8 illumine 9 coruscate, luminesce 10 incandesce
  on: 4 mull 5 weigh 8 consider, mull over, turn over
  time to ~: 4 lull, rest 5 break, pause 6 hiatus 7 respite 8 breather
reflection: 4 echo, idea, slam, slur, view 5 blame, image, light, study 6 glance, musing, remark, shadow 7 censure, obloquy, opinion, picture, thought 8 likeness, reaction, reproach, thinking 9 aspersion, brainwork, criticism, deduction, discredit, duplicate, imitation, stricture 10 appearance, cogitation, derogation
reflection ___: 5 plane 6 nebula
___ reflection: 4 upon 5 Bragg, law of, space, total
Reflections ___ Life: 4 of My
Reflections (1967 song) artist: Supremes
Reflections in a Golden Eye author: Carson McCullers
Reflections on Ice-Breaking poet: 4 Nash
Reflections on the Death of a Porcupine author: D.H. Lawrence
Reflections on Violence author: 5 Sorel
reflective: 4 wise 5 shiny 6 glassy, solemn 7 pensive, wistful 8 profound, rational, studious, thinking 9 conscious, emulative, imitative, observant 10 reasonable, thoughtful
reflector: 5 glass 6 mirror
reflex: 6 hiccup 8 hiccough, knee-jerk, reaction 9 automatic
  ending: 3 ive 5 ology
  testing site: 4 knee
reflex ___: 3 act, arc 5 angle 6 action, camera
___ reflex: 3 gag 4 bass 6 diving 7 corneal, plantar
Reflex author: Dick Francis
reflexive pronoun: 6 itself, myself 7 herself, himself, oneself 9 ourselves 10 themselves
Reflex, The (1984 song) artist: Duran Duran
refluence: 3 ebb
reflux: 3 ebb
reform: 4 cure, mend 5 alter, amend, emend, fix up, rally, renew 6 better, change, enrich, modify, polish, redeem, remake, remedy, repair, revise, rework, uplift 7 clean up, convert, correct, enhance, improve, rebuild, reclaim, rectify, redress, remodel, resolve, restore, shape up, sharpen, upgrade 8 make over, renovate, spruce up, swear off 9 amendment, meliorate, rearrange, refashion, transform 10 ameliorate, conversion, go straight, make amends, regenerate, reorganize
reform ___: 6 school
___ reform: 4 land, tort
Reform ___: 3 Act, Jew 4 Bill 5 flask 7 Judaism
Reforma: 4 city, town
  locale: 6 Mexico 7 Chiapas
reformation: 7 redress
  starter: 7 counter
Reformation center: 6 Geneva
reformative: 8 remedial
reformatory: 3 pen 4 stir 5 joint, penal 6 lockup, prison 7 slammer 8 big house
reformer: 6 zealot 7 liberal, radical 8 advocate, champion, crusader, ultraist 10 campaigner
  target: 4 slum
refractor, light: 5 prism 7 crystal, rainbow
refractory: 5 balky, tough 6 mulish, unruly, wilful 7 defiant, naughty, radical, wayward, willful 8 contrary, factious, indocile, perverse, stubborn 9 difficult, fractious, obstinate, pigheaded 10 bullheaded, disorderly, headstrong, rebellious, unamenable
refrain: 4 curb, halt, keep, pass, quit, song, stop, tune 5 avoid, cease, check, forgo, music, remit, verse 6 arrest, burden, chorus, desist, eschew, forego, give up, melody, pass up, resist, sit out, strain 7 abstain, back off, decline, forbear, inhibit 8 keep from, leave off, renounce, restrain, withhold 9 do without, interrupt, undersong
  end of a childhood ~: 3 EIO 5 EIEIO
  from: 4 duck, shun 5 avoid, defer, dodge, evade, forgo, shirk, spare, spurn 6 bypass, desist, eschew, forego 7 boycott, forbear 10 circumvent
  mountaineer's ~: 5 yodel, yodle
  part: 3 tra 4 fa la, la la 5 la-la's, tra la 6 fa la la 7 tra la la
  please ~: 4 don't
refresh: 3 air, jog 4 cool, prod 5 brace, cheer, rally, renew, slake 6 perk up, prompt, regain, regale, repair, revive, update, vivify 7 brush up, disport, enliven, fortify, quicken, recover, recruit, restock, restore 8 enspirit, inspirit, recreate, renovate, revivify 9 deodorize, modernize, reanimate, refurbish, replenish, restitute, stimulate 10 exhilarate, invigorate, regenerate, rejuvenate, revitalize, strengthen
refresher course, take a: 6 bone up
refreshing: 3 new 4 cool 5 balmy, brisk, crisp, novel 6 lively, unique 7 bracing, cooling, welcome 8 original, pleasant 9 different, restoring 10 comforting, delightful, energizing, fortifying
refreshment: 3 ade 4 bite, eats, food, kick, meal, rest 5 drink, snack, treat 6 spread, tidbit, viands 8 pick-me-up, victuals
  liquid ~: 5 drink, juice 8 beverage
  stand: 5 kiosk
refried ___: 5 beans
refrigerant: 6 dry ice, ethane 8 dimethyl
  cryogenic ~: 4 neon
refrigerate: 3 ice 4 cool 5 chill 6 freeze 7 air-cool 8 preserve
refrigerated: 3 icy 4 cool, iced 5 algid, gelid 6 chilly, frosty, frozen 7 chilled 8 freezing
refrigeration: 4 cold 10 chilliness
refrigerator: 6 icebox
  gas: 5 Freon
  jar: 4 mayo 5 jelly
  name: 5 Amana 6 Maytag 7 Kenmore 9 Whirlpool
refrigerator ___: 3 car
refrigerator-___: 7 freezer
___ refrigerator: 6 Carnot, walk-in
Refrigerator, The: 5 Perry
refuel: 3 eat 5 gas up
refueling area: 3 pit
refuge: 3 den, lee 4 aery, exit, eyry, fort, hole, home, lair, nest, port 5 aerie, cover, eyrie, haven, oasis, shift 6 ambush, asylum, covert, escape, harbor, outlet, resort, safety, shield, way out 7 asylums, harbour, hideout, opening, retreat, shelter, stopgap 8 fastness, fortress, hideaway, immunity, preserve, recourse, resource,

security **9** anchorage, expedient, harborage, hermitage, makeshift, safe house, sanctuary **10** ivory tower, protection, stronghold
give ~: **4** hide, save **6** foster, harbor, rescue, shield **7** protect, shelter **8** insulate, keep safe **9** look after, safeguard
place of ~: **3** ark **4** fort, lair **5** haven, oasis **6** asylum **7** shelter **8** fortress **9** sanctuary
wayfarer ~: **5** hotel, lodge, motel **6** hostel **9** roadhouse
refugee: **2** DP **5** alien, exile **6** émigré **7** escapee, evacuee, outcast **8** defector, deserter, emigrant, outsider **9** foreigner **10** boat person, expatriate
request: **6** asylum
Refugee (1980 song) artist: Tom Petty
Refugees, The author: Arthur Conan Doyle
refulgence: **4** glow **5** light, shine **6** luster
refulgent: **5** aglow, light, lucid, nitid, shiny **6** ablaze, bright **7** beaming, glowing, radiant, shining **8** aglitter, dazzling, gleaming, luminous, lustrous, splendid **9** brilliant, sparkling **10** glistening, glittering
refund: **3** pay **5** remit, repay **6** adjust, give-up, rebate, recoup, redeem, return, reward, settle **7** balance, pay back, payment, redress, replace, restore **8** discount, give back, kickback, make good **9** allowance, discharge, indemnify, make up for, money back, reimburse, repayment **10** compensate, make amends, recompense, relinquish, remunerate, settlement
reason: **6** damage
refurbish: **4** do up, mend, redo **5** fix up, refit, rehab, renew **6** repair, revamp, spruce, update **7** clean up, gussy up, reequip, refresh, remodel, restore, retouch, retread, touch up, upgrade **8** overhaul, renovate, spruce up **9** modernize, restitute **10** rejuvenate
refusal: **2** no **3** ban, nix **4** pass, veto, writ **6** choice, denial, option, rebuff, rebuke **7** dissent, regrets, repulse **8** defiance, disfavor, negation, reversal, turndown **9** disavowal, exclusion, knockback, rejection, repulsion **10** abnegation, declension, disclaimer, enjoinment, forbidding, nonconsent, refutation, resistance, thumbs down
emphatic ~: **5** never, no how, no way
formal ~: **3** nay **4** veto
informal ~: **3** nah, naw **4** nope, uh-uh
in German: **4** nein
in Scottish: **3** nae
military ~: **5** no sir
words of ~: **4** not I **5** I won't, no how, no way **6** no deal **8** forget it **9** by no means, fat chance **10** count me out, not a chance
refuse: **3** nix **4** balk, deny, dump, dust, junk, muck, scum, shun, slag, slop **5** baulk, chaff, demur, dodge, dregs, dross, evade, filth, offal, repel, say no, scorn, spurn, swill, trash, waste **6** beg off, debris, desist, ignore, litter, loathe, pass up, rebuff, regret, reject, resist, scraps **7** abstain, decline, dissent, garbage, hogwash, hold off, hold out, protest, remains, repulse, residue, rubbish, send off, shut off, shut out **8** brush off, disallow, hold back, keep from, leavings, sediment, set aside, turn away, turn down, turn from, withdraw, withhold **9** disaccord, foreclose, frown upon, reprobate, repudiate, sweepings **10** disapprove
admission: **3** bar **5** block **6** forbid **7** exclude, keep out **9** freeze out
consent: **4** deny, veto **6** forbid, reject **7** decline **8** disallow, prohibit, turn down **9** interdict, proscribe **10** disapprove
hauler: **6** ashman **7** junkman
heap: **4** dump **8** junkyard, landfill
I ~: **2** no **3** nah, naw, nay, nix, non **4** nein, nope, nyet, uh-uh **5** ixnay, never, no how, noway **6** no deal, noways, nowise **8** forget it, negative, negatory **9** by no means, fat chance **10** count me out, not a chance, thumbs down
old-style: **4** nill
receptacle: **6** ashcan **8** trash can **10** garbage can
to deal with: **4** shun, snub **5** scorn, spurn **6** ignore, rebuff, reject **7** disavow, disdain, neglect, scoff at **8** turn down
to go: **5** demur **6** recoil **9** stop short
to obey: **4** balk **5** baulk, rebel **6** mutiny
refusenik word: **4** nyet
refuses: **4** won't
refutation: **2** no **6** answer, denial **7** refusal **8** rebuttal
refute: **3** top **4** burn, deny **5** belie, break, crush, evert, parry, quash, rebut **6** answer, cancel, debate, expose, impugn, naysay, negate, oppose, show up **7** confute, contend, convict, counter, dispute, explode, gainsay, reply to, silence, squelch **8** abnegate, burn down, demolish, disagree, disclaim, disprove, tear down **9** cancel out, disaffirm, discredit, dispose of, overthrow, repudiate, shoot down, vindicate **10** contradict, contravene, controvert, disconfirm, invalidate, prove false, prove wrong
reg.: **3** std.
Reg: **4** Owen **6** Grundy
Reg. __ Dept. Agr.: **5** Penna.
Reg. __ Off.: **5** U.S. Pat.
regain: **6** ransom, recoup, redeem **7** get back, reclaim, recover, recruit, refresh, salvage, win back **8** make back, retrieve, take back **9** reacquire, recapture, repossess
consciousness: **4** stir, wake **5** waken **6** awaken, come to, return, revive **7** recover **10** come around
one's health: **4** heal **5** rally **7** get well, rebound, recover **8** snap back **9** get better **10** convalesce, recuperate
regal: **5** grand, noble, proud, royal **6** august, kingly, lordly **7** courtly, haughty, queenly, stately **8** imperial, imposing, kinglike, majestic, palatial, princely, splendid **9** dignified, sovereign **10** majestical, statuesque
home: **6** castle, palace
letters: **3** HRH
Regal: **3** car **4** auto **5** Buick **10** automobile, Studebaker
__ Regal: **6** Chivas
Regalbuto: **3** Joe
regale: **3** ply **4** grab **5** amuse, feast, party, serve, treat **6** divert, please, spread **7** delight, gratify, have fun, nurture, refresh, satisfy **8** fracture **9** entertain, knock dead, laugh it up
regalement: **3** fun **5** cheer, mirth **7** delight **8** pleasure **9** amusement, diversion
regalia: **6** attire, finery, livery, symbol **7** clothes, uniform **10** Sunday best
item: **3** orb **5** tiara
Regan's father: **4** Lear
regard: **3** eye, see, spy **4** beam, care, deem, gaze, heed, hold, item, look, love, mark, mind, note, pipe, rate, read, sake, scan, take, view **5** assay, count, favor, flash, honor, judge, point, stare, store, think, treat, value, watch **6** admire, advert, aspect, assess, attend, behold, credit, detail, esteem, gaze at, homage, liking, look at, look on, matter, notice, praise, reckon, remark, repute, revere **7** account, apply to, bearing, believe, concern, dignity, eyeball, feature, observe, opinion, pertain, prizing, refer to, respect, stare at, suppose, surmise, thought, valuing, witness, worship **8** approval, bear upon, consider, devotion, estimate, fondness, good name, interest, listen to, look upon, once-over, overlook, perceive, pore over, prestige, relate to, relation, scrutiny, sympathy **9** advertise, affection, attention, curiosity, deference, pertain to, reference, relevance, reverence, think of as **10** admiration, attachment, cherishing, cognizance, connection, estimation, get a load of, observance, particular, reputation, scrutinize, self-esteem, solicitude, veneration
critical ~: **8** analysis, scrutiny **10** inspection
hastily: **4** peek, peep **6** glance, peek at, peep at **8** glance at
high ~: **4** love **6** esteem **10** attachment
highly: **5** adore, favor, prize **6** admire, revere **8** look up to
in high ~: **5** great **6** adored **7** beloved
public ~: **4** fame **5** éclat **6** renown, repute **7** acclaim, stardom **8** eminence **9** celebrity, notoriety **10** popularity, prominence, reputation
with interest: **4** gape, gawk **5** stare **10** rubberneck
with ~ to: **4** in re **5** about, anent, as for **6** toward **7** towards **9** apropos of
__-regarded: **4** well
regarded to be: **6** seen as
regardful: **5** aware **7** careful, duteous, dutiful, heedful, mindful **8** watchful **9** advertent, attentive, observant, observing **10** respectful, solicitous, thoughtful
regarding: **4** as to, look **5** about, anent, as for **6** toward **7** towards **9** apropos of
this: **6** hereto **8** hereunto
Regarding Henry (1991 film)
cast: Annette Bening, Harrison Ford
director: Mike Nichols
dog: **5** Buddy
Regarding Wave author: Gary Snyder
regardless: **3** but, lax **4** deaf, rash, rude **5** altho, blind, crude, slack, still **6** anyhow, anyway, coarse, remiss **7** against **8** although, careless, derelict, heedless, listless, mindless, reckless **9** aside from, at any cost, in any case, negligent, unfeeling, unheeding, unmindful **10** for all that, in any event, incautious, neglectful
of: **7** despite
regards: **4** love **7** devoirs **8** greeting, respects **9** deference, greetings **10** best wishes, good wishes, salutation
as ~: **4** in re **5** about, anent **6** toward **7** towards **8** relative, relevant **10** concerning
__ regard to: **4** with
regatta: **4** race
entrant: **4** crew **5** racer, rower, scull, shell, yacht **6** boater
locale: **6** Henley
regency: **5** power **7** command **8** dominion **9** authority **10** leadership
__ Regency: **5** Hyatt
regenerate: **5** renew **6** change, reform, revive, uplift **7** produce, refresh, restore **8** enspirit, inspirit, reawaken, recreate, renovate, revivify **9** modernize, reanimate **10** rejuvenate
regent: **6** deputy **8** delegate, director **9** organizer
__ regent: **5** queen **6** prince
__-regent: **4** vice
regent of the sun: **5** Uriel
Regents song: Barbara-Ann (1961)
reggae: **5** music
musician, perhaps: **5** rasta
relative: **3** ska
Reggie: **7** Jackson
__ regia: **4** aqua
regime: **4** rule, sway **5** reign **6** system, tenure **7** dynasty **8** kingship **10** government, incumbency, leadership, management
__ régime: **6** ancien
regimen: **4** diet **6** course **9** treatment **10** discipline, weight plan
regiment: **4** army **5** corps, force, order, squad, troop **7** phalanx
regimentals: **7** uniform
regimentation: **8** severity **9** sternness **10** discipline, strictness
__ Regiment, The: **5** Rifle **7** Phantom
Regina: **4** city, town **7** capital
locale: **4** Sask. 6 Canada
__ Regina Coelorum: **3** Ave
Reginald: **4** Owen **5** Denny **8** Gardiner **10** VelJohnson
author: **4** Saki
region: **3** ter. **4** area, belt, land, part, soil, terr., turf, walk, ward, zone **5** arena, block, field, place, range, realm, scene, scope, shire, tract, world **6** domain, ground, locale, sector, sphere, suburb **7** country, demesne, expanse, quarter, section, stretch, terrain **8** clearing, confines, district, division, dominion, environs, locality, location, precinct, province, vicinity **9** bailiwick, territory
regional: **5** local **6** native **7** endemic, topical **9** endemical, localized, parochial, sectional **10** indigenous
plants and animals: **5** biota
__ regions: **6** nether
__ Regions: **5** Polar
Regis: **6** Toomey **7** Philbin
__ Regis: **5** Curia
register: **3** log, say **4** book, file, join, list, mark, note, poll, post, read, roll, rota, show, tell, till **5** diary, enrol, enter, entry, log in, scale, score, table, tally **6** annals, betray, dawn on, enlist, enroll, ledger, record, reveal, roster, scroll, sign on, sign up, sink in, strike **7** account, bespeak, catalog, check in, display, exhibit, express, impress, journal, point to, reflect, set down, weigh in, who's who **8** archives, disclose, indicate, inscribe, manifest, point out, roll call, schedule, take down **9** catalogue, chronicle, directory, inventory, keep count, keep score, sign up for, subscribe, write down **10** come home to, memorandum, tabulation, understand
as a complaint: **5** lodge
cash ~ calculation: **3** tax
cash ~ co.: **3** NCR
ringer: **4** sale
signer: **5** guest **6** lodger, roomer **7** boarder, visitor
__ register: **4** cash, head, thin **5** chest, sales, thick **6** church, parish
Register: **5** paper **9** newspaper
locale: **6** Mobile **9** Des Moines

__ Register: 6 Lloyd's, Social **7** Federal
registered __: 4 bond, mail **5** nurse
registration: 6 sign-up **10** enlistment, enrollment
registry: 6 patent, record
regnant: 6 ruling **7** supreme **8** dominant, in charge **9** sovereign **10** prevailing
__ regnant: 5 queen
Régnard, Jean François: 6 French **10** playwright
regnat __: 7 populus
__ regni: 4 anno
Régnier, Henri de: 4 poet **6** French
Regor: 4 star
regress: 3 ebb **4** sink **5** lapse **6** go back, recede, revert **7** fall off, relapse, retreat, setback **8** fall away, fall back, return to, roll back, turn back **9** backslide, throw back **10** degenerate, lose ground, recidivate
ender: 3 ion, ive
regression: 3 ebb **5** lapse **7** setback **8** movement, reaction **9** decadence
__ regression: 6 linear
regret: 3 rue, woe **4** care, dole, miss, moan, mope, pang, weep **5** demur, grief, mourn, qualm, worry **6** bemoan, bewail, grieve, lament, qualms, refuse, repent, repine, sorrow **7** anguish, apology, concern, cry over, deplore, remorse, scruple **8** weep over **9** annoyance, apologies, apologize, deprecate, heartache, misgiving, nostalgia, penitence **10** affliction, bitterness, conscience, contrition, disapprove, discomfort, heartbreak, misgivings, repentance, ruefulness, uneasiness
exclamation: 3 och **4** alas, rats **5** alack, sorry **6** shucks **7** Odzooks **8** Gadzooks, lackaday
express ~: 4 sigh
with ~: 5 sadly **8** grudging **9** reluctant
regretful: 3 sad **5** sorry **6** afraid, rueful **7** ashamed, humbled **8** contrite, mournful, penitent **9** repentant, sorrowful **10** apologetic, lamentable, remorseful
one: 4 ruer **6** atoner
regretfulness: 3 rue **6** qualms, regret **7** remorse **10** contrition, misgivings
regrets: 7 refusal **8** turndown
send ~: 5 say no **6** beg off, refuse **7** decline
with ~: 5 sadly
regrettable: 3 sad **4** dire **5** woful, wrong **6** woeful **7** pitiful, unhappy **8** dreadful, grievous, pitiable, shameful **10** afflictive, calamitous, deplorable, ill-advised, lamentable
regroup: 5 rally
regular: 3 gas, set **4** even, flat **5** daily, exact, fixed, level, paced, plain, plane, stock, typic, usual **6** client, common, cyclic, formal, lawful, no-lead, normal, proper, serial, smooth, stated, steady, wonted **7** classic, correct, general, in order, natural, ordered, orderly, precise, routine, sincere, typical, uniform **8** accepted, approved, arranged, balanced, bona fide, clean-cut, constant, everyday, expected, frequent, gasoline, habitual, measured, official, ordinary, orthodox, periodic, probable, punctual, rational, readable, rhythmic, standard, straight, unbroken, unwaning **9** accordant, automatic, congruous, consonant, continual, customary, efficient, momentary, organized, patterned, prevalent, recurrent, regulated, unvarying **10** accustomed, classified, consistent, dependable, frequenter, harmonious, invariable, legitimate, mechanical, methodical, prevailing, sanctioned, successive, systematic, true to type, unchanging, uneventful
fellow: 3 Joe
hangout: 5 haunt
regular __: 3 lay, ode **4** year **5** bevel
Regular __: 4 Army
regularity: 5 order **6** rhythm **8** symmetry **9** clockwork, constancy, exactness, fixedness, frequency **10** classicism
regularly: 3 oft **4** a lot, much **5** often **6** mostly, yearly **7** usually **9** eternally, generally, gradually, quite a bit, routinely **10** frequently, ordinarily, repeatedly
regulars: 5 trade **7** patrons **9** clientage, clientele, following, patronage
regulate: 3 fit, fix, run, set **4** rule, slow, time, true, tune **5** adapt, align, aline, guide, order, reset, shape **6** adjust, direct, govern, handle, manage, settle, square, temper, tune up **7** arrange, balance, conduct, control, correct, dispose, improve, measure, monitor, oversee, qualify, rectify, redress, shape up **8** allocate, classify, legalize, moderate, modulate, organize, readjust, restrict **9** determine, legislate, methodize, normalize, reconcile, supervise **10** coordinate, put in order, stereotype
Regulate (1994 song)
artist: Nate Dogg, Warren G
regulated: 5 paced **7** orderly, regular
be ~ by: 4 mind, obey **6** follow **7** observe, respect **8** adhere to **9** conform to
company: 4 util. **7** utility
item: 4 drug **8** narcotic
__ regulated militia...: 5 a well
regulation: 3 law **4** book, code, form, rule, tabu **5** bible, bylaw, canon, edict, no-nos, order, taboo **6** decree, tuning **7** control, dictate, numbers, precept, statute **8** guidance, handling, managing, standard **9** customary, direction, directive, enactment, ordinance, prescript, principle, procedure **10** adjustment, discipline, government
regulations: 4 code **5** canon **6** policy **7** charter **9** etiquette **10** directions, guidelines
__ regulator: 7 voltage
regulator combining form: 4 -stat
Regulus: 4 star
constellation: 3 Leo
regurgitate: 4 spew, spue **5** eject, erupt, expel **8** disgorge **9** discharge
Reg. U.S. Pat. __: 3 Off.
rehab: 6 repair **7** restore **8** renovate **9** refurbish **10** rejuvenate
center: 6 clinic
rehabilitate: 4 cure, mend, save **5** clear, fix up, renew, right **6** adjust, better, change, enrich, polish, redeem, reform **7** convert, enhance, furbish, improve, rebuild, reclaim, recover, restore, salvage, shape up, sharpen, upgrade **8** make good, renovate, spruce up **9** meliorate, reeducate, refurbish, reinstate **10** ameliorate
rehabilitation: 7 redress, therapy
Rehan: 3 Ada
rehash: 5 weigh **6** repeat, review, rework **7** belabor, discuss, iterate, recount, rewrite, summary **9** reiterate, summarize **10** paraphrase, reconsider
rehashed: 9 imitative **10** derivative, unoriginal
rehearsal: 4 call, prep **5** drill **6** dry run, tryout **7** reading, recital, workout **8** practice, readying, relation **9** going-over, retelling, shakedown **10** experiment, recitation, repetition, run-through
__ rehearsal: 5 dress
Rehearsal of a Ballet painter: 5 Degas
rehearse: 3 act **4** hone, tell, test **5** drill, prime, ready, state, study, train **6** depict, do over, dry run, get set, go over, recite, relate, repeat, review, try out, tune up, warm up **7** iterate, narrate, recount, reenact, work out **8** describe, exercise, practice **9** go through, reiterate **10** experiment, prepare for, run through
rehearsed: 3 pat **4** glib **5** ready **6** primed **7** prepped **8** prepared
rehearsing, without: 5 ad-lib
reheat perhaps: 4 nuke
Rehnquist: 5 judge **7** Justice, William
Rehoboth Beach: 4 city, town
locale: 8 Delaware
Reichstein, Tadeus: 8 Nobelist
Reid: 3 Tim **4** Kate **5** Britt **6** Thomas
Reid, Thomas: 8 Scottish **11** philosopher
reign: 4 rule, sway **6** govern, record, regime, tenure **7** command, prevail **8** dominate, dominion, hold sway, kingship, monarchy **9** influence, supremacy **10** ascendance, ascendancy, ascendence, ascendency, incumbency, leadership
of terror: 5 purge **7** tyranny **9** despotism **10** oppression
over: 4 boss, head, helm, lead, rule **6** govern, head up, manage **7** command, control **8** dominate, domineer **9** supervise
reigning: 5 on top **8** dominant **9** sovereign
Reign of Terror (1949 film)
cast: Robert Cummings, Arlene Dahl
director: Anthony Mann
Reilly, John C.: 5 actor
film: For Love of the Game (1999)
Magnolia (1999)
The Perfect Storm (2000)
reimburse: 3 pay **5** repay **6** offset, recoup, refund, return, square **7** balance, pay back, recover, replace, requite, restore **8** make good, square up **9** indemnify, liquidate, make up for **10** compensate, recompense, remunerate
reimbursement: 6 rebate, refund **7** payment
reimpose: 7 put back, restore
Reims: 4 city, town
locale: 6 France
rein: 4 curb, slow, stop **5** check, leash, strap **6** bridle, halter, hamper, hinder, hold up, impede, muzzle, pull in, slow up, tether **7** contain, control, harness, smother, trammel **8** hold back, restrain, slow down **9** constrain, deterrent, restraint **10** constraint, keep a lid on
in: 10 keep in line
__ rein: 4 free **7** bearing
reina: 5 queen **7** Spanish
mate: 3 rey
reindeer: 4 deer **5** Comet, Cupid, octet, Vixen **6** Dancer, Dasher, Donder **7** Blitzen, Prancer, Rudolph
driver: 5 Santa **10** Santa Claus
herder: 4 Lapp **5** Yurak
part: 4 hoof **6** antler
relative: 3 elk, roe **4** axis, pudu, shou, sika **5** moose **6** chital, guemal, hangul, huemul, sambar, sambur, thamin, wapiti **7** brocket, caribou, muntjac, muntjak, sambhar, sambhur **9** barasingh
reined in: 6 curbed, pent-up **7** bridled, checked, stifled **8** held back **9** bottled-up, inhibited, repressed **10** restrained, restricted, suppressed
Reiner: 3 Rob **4** Carl **5** Fritz
Reiner, Carl: 5 actor **8** director
film: All of Me (1984)
Dead Men Don't Wear Plaid (1982)
The Gazebo (1959)
The Jerk (1979)
The Man With Two Brains (1983)
Ocean's Eleven (2001)
Oh, God! (1977)
son: 3 Rob
TV: Your Show of Shows
Reiner, Fritz: 7 maestro **9** conductor
Reiner, Rob: 5 actor **8** director
father: 4 Carl
film: The American President (1995)
A Few Good Men (1992)
Ghosts of Mississippi (1996)
Misery (1990)
The Princess Bride (1987)
Stand by Me (1986)
This Is Spinal Tap (1984)
When Harry Met Sally ... (1989)
spouse: Penny Marshall
Reines, Frederick: 8 Nobelist **9** physicist
reinforce: 4 gird, hype, line, prop, tone **5** add to, boost, brace, build, carry, cover, shore, steel **6** anneal, back up, beef up, harden, heat up, pick up, pillar, prop up, soup up, stress, stroke, temper, tone up **7** augment, bolster, brace up, build up, burgeon, develop, empower, enhance, enlarge, fortify, punch up, recruit, shore up, stiffen, support, sustain, toughen **8** bourgeon, buttress, energize, increase, indurate, multiply, vitalize **9** emphasize, encourage, intensify, undergird, underline **10** contribute, invigorate, strengthen, supplement
reinforced: 5 tough **6** rugged, strong, sturdy **7** durable **8** well-made **9** well-built
reinforcement: 3 aid **4** stay **5** brace **6** facing **7** buildup, support **8** buttress
steel ~ rod: 5 rebar
Reinhart in Love author: Thomas Berger
Reinhold: 5 Judge **6** Glière **7** Niebuhr
Reinhold, Judge: 5 actor
film: Beverly Hills Cop (1984)
Enid Is Sleeping (1990)
Fast Times at Ridgemont High (1982)
Ruthless People (1986)
The Santa Clause (1994)
Vice Versa (1988)
Reinking: 3 Ann
reins: 4 helm
hold the ~: 4 rule **5** guide, reign, steer **6** direct, govern **7** command, control, oversee
reinstate: 6 recall, redeem, return **7** put back, reelect, restore **9** bring back
reintroduce: 6 recall **7** put back, restore **9** bring back
reinvent the __: 5 wheel
reinvest: 4 plow **8** plow back, roll over
reinvigorate: 6 revive **7** refresh **8** vitalize
Reiser: 4 Paul, Pete
Reiser, Paul: 5 actor
costar: 4 Hunt
film: Bye Bye, Love (1995)
Diner (1982)
One Night at McCool's (2001)
TV: Mad About You, My Two Dads
Reis, Irving: 8 director
film: All My Sons (1948)
The Bachelor and the Bobby-Soxer (1947)
Crack-Up (1946)

Enchantment (1948)
The Falcon Takes Over (1942)
The Four Poster (1952)
Hitler's Children (1943)
Reisterstown: 4 city
locale: 8 Maryland
Reisz, Karel: 8 director
film: The French Lieutenant's Woman (1981)
Isadora (1968)
Morgan! (1966)
Saturday Night and Sunday Morning (1960)
Sweet Dreams (1985)
Who'll Stop the Rain (1978)
__ Reiter: 5 Blaue
reiterate: 3 rpt. **4** echo **5** ditto, recap, renew, resay, rub in **6** go over, harp on, parrot, rehash, repeat, retell **7** recheck, reprise, restate **8** play back, rehearse **9** come again, emphasize
reiterated: 4 many **7** regular **8** frequent, habitual, numerous, repeated **9** recurrent
reiteration: 4 echo
reiteratively: 4 anew **5** again **8** once more **10** repeatedly
Reitman, Ivan: 8 director
film: Dave (1993)
Ghostbusters (1984)
Ghostbusters II (1989)
Junior (1994)
Kindergarten Cop (1990)
Legal Eagles (1986)
Meatballs (1979)
Six Days Seven Nights (1998)
Stripes (1981)
Twins (1988)
REIT part: 4 real **5** trust **6** estate **10** investment
Reivers, The: 4 film **5** novel
author: William Faulkner
cast: Sharon Farrell, Will Geer, Steve McQueen
character: 3 Ned **4** Bobo, Boon, Otis, Reba **5** Maury, Sarah **6** Alison, Minnie
director: Mark Rydell
music: John Williams
reject: 3 ban, bar, nix **4** burn, deny, jilt, kill, shed, shun, veto **5** chuck, debar, ditch, repel, scoff, scorn, scout, scrap, spurn **6** abjure, bounce, disown, except, forbid, ignore, loathe, pass by, pass on, pass up, rebuff, refuse, second, slight, slough **7** abandon, cashier, cast off, cast out, decline, despise, disavow, discard, disdain, dismiss, exclude, forsake, kiss off, put down, repulse, rule out, say no to, toss out **8** abrogate, brush off, castaway, disallow, disclaim, discount, forswear, jettison, lay aside, pooh-pooh, prohibit, renounce, throw out, turn down **9** blackball, cast aside, discredit, eliminate, foreclose, foreswear, ostracize, proscribe, reprobate, repudiate, shoot down, throw away **10** contravene, disapprove, disbelieve
old-style: 4 nill
rejectamenta: 5 trash
rejected: 6 lonely **9** unpopular, unwelcome
rejecting: 6 except **8** negative **10** disdainful
rejection: 2 no **3** nix **4** no go, pass, veto **5** no way, spurn **6** bounce, denial, no dice, rebuff, slight **7** refusal, repulse **8** brush-off, hard time, negation, nihilism, turndown **9** defection, desertion, disbelief, dismissal, exception, exclusion, sundering **10** abdication, abnegation, nonconsent, thumbs down
exclamation: 3 nay, ugh **4** heck, pfui, phoo **6** phooey
rejection __: 4 slip **6** region
rejects: 4 junk **6** debris **8** castoffs, discards, leavings **9** sweepings
rejoice: 5 enjoy, exult, glory, revel **7** beatify, delight, satisfy, triumph **8** jubilate **9** celebrate, make merry **10** effervesce
in: 4 like **5** prize, savor **6** relish **8** hold dear **9** gloat over
name meaning ~: 3 Kay
rejoicing: 4 glad **5** happy, merry, mirth **6** blithe, cheery, elated, jovial, upbeat **7** gleeful, pleased, tickled, triumph **8** blissful, cheerful, ecstatic, euphoric, exultant, jubilant, laughter, mirthful, thrilled **9** delighted, happiness **10** exultation, risibility, triumphant
rejoin: 6 answer **7** respond
rejoinder: 3 ans. **5** reply **6** answer, retort, return, ripost **7** defense, riposte **8** comeback, reaction, rebuttal, repartee, response **9** wisecrack
rejuvenate: 4 do up **5** rally, rehab, renew **6** revive, spruce, update **7** enliven, rebound, reclaim, recover, refresh, restore, retread **8** renovate, revivify, spruce up, vitalize **9** modernize, refurbish, restitute **10** invigorate, regenerate
rejuvenation: 7 revival
name meaning ~: 4 Edna
rekindle: 6 revive **8** reawaken **10** revitalize
rel.: 3 bro., unc.
deg.: 3 Th.D.
school: 3 sem.
rel. __: 4 pron.
relapse: 4 fade, fail, sink **6** recede, return, revert, weaken, worsen **7** regress, setback **8** fall back, reaction, slip back, turn back **9** backslide, slide back **10** recidivate, retrogress
relate: 3 say **4** link, talk, tell **5** apply, cover, refer, spill, state, tie to, unite **6** clue in, cohere, convey, depict, detail, impart, orient, recite, report, reveal, set out **7** ascribe, concern, connect, divulge, express, itemize, narrate, pertain, present, recount **8** advise of, bear upon, belong to, describe, disclose, interact, rehearse **9** analogize, appertain, associate, chronicle, expound on, make sense, touch base, verbalize
to: 3 dig **4** grok **5** grasp **6** inform, regard **7** concern, involve **9** tie in with **10** comprehend, sympathize, understand
well: 2 go **4** jibe **5** fit in **6** cohere **7** conform
related: 3 kin **4** akin, like, oral **5** alike, joint **6** agnate, allied, enmesh, immesh, inmesh, linked, mutual, tied up **7** cognate, connate, germane, kindred, similar **8** incident, parallel, relevant **9** analogous, bracketed, connected, dependant, dependent, fraternal, pertinent **10** affiliated, associated, collateral, connatural, correlated, incidental, interwoven, reciprocal
item: 5 tie in
maternally: 5 enate
paternally: 6 agnate
relating to: 5 about
suffix: 3 -ile, -ine
relation: 3 dad, kin, mom, pop **4** aunt, bond, tale **5** niece, uncle **6** cousin, father, mother, nephew, regard, sister **7** bearing, brother, grandma, grandpa, kindred, kinship, kinsman, liaison, recital, sibling **8** affinity, alliance, grandson **9** great-aunt, rehearsal, statement **10** connection, great-uncle, kinsperson, similarity
in ~ to: 5 about **7** against, vis-à-vis **8** opposite
mathematical ~: 5 ratio **8** equation, fraction
with ~ to: 4 as to **5** anent, as for **9** regarding **10** concerning
__ relation: 5 blood
relations: 3 kin **5** terms **7** kinfolk **8** dealings, kinfolks, kinsfolk **9** coherence
break in ~: 4 rift **6** breach, schism **7** quarrel **10** falling-out
good ~: 5 amity, peace **6** comity **7** concord, harmony **8** goodwill **10** cordiality, fellowship, friendship
__ relations: 5 human, labor **6** public **7** foreign
relationship: 3 tie **4** bond, link **5** logic, ratio, tie in, tie-up **6** accord, affair, hookup, ration **7** analogy, contact, kinship, liaison, network, rapport, romance **8** affinity, alliance, exchange, likeness, marriage, nearness, parallel **9** relevance **10** connection
end a ~: 4 part **5** leave, split **7** break up, split up
relative: 3 bro, dad, kin, mom, pop, sib, sis, son **4** aunt, folk, near **5** about, blood, folks, in-law, niece, uncle **6** agnate, allied, cousin, father, in-laws, mother, nephew, parent, sister **7** apropos, brother, cognate, germane, grandma, grandpa, kinsman, reliant, sibling **8** apposite, parallel **9** analogous, as regards, connected, dependant, dependent, kinswoman, pertinent, referring **10** applicable, associated, concerning, connection, contingent, great-uncle, in regard to, kinsperson, pertaining, reciprocal, respective, stepfather, stepmother, stepparent, stepsister
through marriage: 5 in-law
relative __: 4 wind **5** major, minor, pitch **6** clause **7** bearing, density, maximum, minimum, pronoun
__ relative: 5 blood
relatively: 5 quite **6** rather **8** somewhat
Relatively Speaking author: Alan Ayckbourn
relatives: 3 fam., kin **5** folks **6** family **7** kindred, kinfolk **8** kinfolks, kinsfolk
relax: 3 ebb, lax, nap, sit, veg **4** bask, calm, ease, give, idle, laze, lift, loaf, loll, rest, slow **5** abate, coast, let go, let up, loose, lower, quiet, remit, slack, yield **6** cool it, ease up, go easy, lessen, loosen, lounge, modify, reduce, relent, repose, rest up, settle, soften, unbend, unwind, veg out, weaken **7** compose, cool off, ease off, goof off, lay back, let up on, lie down, lighten, recline, relieve, sit back, sit down, slacken, take ten **8** calm down, chill out, diminish, kick back, knock off, loosen up, mitigate, moderate, modulate, recreate, slack off, slow down, take five, tone down, wind down **9** hang loose, lie around, lighten up, mellow out, sit around, soft-pedal, untighten **10** liberalize, settle back, settle down, simmer down, take a break, take it easy
as rules: 4 bend
place to ~: 3 den
Relax!: 6 at ease
relaxation: 3 fun **4** ease, play, rest **5** peace, quiet **6** relief, repose **7** comfort, leisure, liberty, license, pastime, resting **8** free time, pleasure **9** amusement, diversion, enjoyment
relaxed: 4 calm, clam, cool, easy, homy, limp **5** homey, let up, loose, quiet, slack, staid, stoic **6** at ease, casual, low-key, mellow, placid, sedate, serene **7** amiable, at peace, easeful, equable, pacific, stoical, unmoved **8** amicable, carefree, composed, familiar, informal, laid-back, lounging, peaceful, tranquil **9** collected, easygoing, impassive, leisurely, quiescent, temperate, unexcited, unruffled **10** nonchalant, unagitated, untroubled
not ~: 4 edgy, taut **5** rigid, tense
relaxedness: 4 ease **5** peace, poise, quiet **6** aplomb **7** comfort, leisure, license **8** serenity **9** composure
relaxing: 4 cosy, cozy, easy **6** at ease, dreamy **7** easeful
relay: 4 race, send **5** carry **6** fork up, hand on, pass on, spread **7** deliver, hand off **8** hand down, hand over, transfer, transmit, turn over **9** broadcast, pass along, send forth
relay __: 4 race
__ relay: 6 medley
relay race
hand-off: 5 baton
length: 4 mile
portion: 3 leg
release: 3 axe, can, rid **4** boot, drop, emit, free, leak, news, open, oust, sack, undo, vent **5** clear, flash, issue, let go, let up, loose, slack, spare, spell, story, unbar, unmew, unpen, untie, yield **6** acquit, bounce, charge, excuse, exempt, lay off, let off, let out, loosen, notice, open up, pardon, ransom, redeem, relief, report, rescue, spring, unbind, unhand **7** absolve, bail out, cashier, commute, deliver, dismiss, drum out, floater, forgive, freedom, freeing, give off, give out, handout, let up on, liberty, manumit, receipt, set free, slacken, take out, turn out, unchain, unleash, unloose **8** clemency, delivery, dispense, furlough, get rid of, go easy on, liberate, lifeboat, offering, pink-slip, set loose, unfasten, unfetter **9** acquittal, cast loose, discharge, disengage, dismissal, exculpate, exemption, exonerate, extricate, lifesaver, publicity, salvation, surrender, terminate, turn loose, unshackle **10** abreaction, absolution, emancipate, liberation, propaganda, relinquish
press ~: 4 news, word **5** aviso **6** notice, report **7** handout, message **8** bulletin, dispatch **9** statement **10** communiqué
software ~: 3 ver. **7** version
upon: 5 let at
release __: 4 copy, date, time **5** print
__ release: 4 news **5** cable, press **7** shutter
__-release: 4 slow, time, work **5** timed
released: 4 free **5** let go, loose **6** exempt, untied
be ~: 6 go free
just ~: 3 new
Release Me (song) artist: Engelbert Humperdinck, Esther Phillips, Wilson Phillips
relegate: 3 lag **4** oust **5** eject, exile, expel, refer **6** assign, banish, charge, commit, credit, demote, deport, pass on, remove **7** commend, confide, consign, dismiss, entrust, expulse, intrust **8** accredit, displace, hand over, throw out, transfer, turn over **9** downgrade, ostracize, transport **10** expatriate
relegation: 9 dismissal, exclusion, expulsion

relent: **3** bow, ebb **4** drop, ease, fall, fold, give, melt, pity, quit, slow, wane **5** let go, let up, relax, spare, yield **6** cave in, comply, cool it, ease up, give in, give up, go soft, soften, weaken **7** back off, die away, die down, ease off, forbear, give way, lay back, slacken, subside **8** ease up on, go easy on, have pity, loosen up, moderate, say uncle **9** acquiesce, lighten up, mellow out **10** capitulate, come around
  don't ~: **5** press **6** demand, insist **7** persist **9** stand firm
relentless: **4** grim, hard, iron **5** bound, cruel, harsh, rigid, stern, stiff **6** dogged, fierce, hang in, savage, severe, strict **7** adamant, dead set, inhuman, nonstop **8** constant, obdurate, pitiless, rigorous, ruthless, sedulous, stubborn, unabated, unbroken, untiring, unwaning **9** continual, cutthroat, ferocious, hang-tough, incessant, merciless, obstinate, punishing, steadfast, stringent, sustained, tenacious, unbending, unpitying **10** implacable, inexorable, inflexible, iron-willed, undeterred, unflagging
relentlessly: **4** ever, hard **6** always **7** forever **8** evermore, for keeps **9** eternally **10** at all times, unendingly
relet: **8** sublease
relevance: **3** use **5** tie-in **6** regard **7** aptness, bearing, concern, fitness, utility **8** interest **10** connection, importance
  have ~: **5** apply **6** relate **7** concern, pertain **8** bear upon **9** appertain, make sense
  show ~: **5** tie in **7** connect **9** correlate
relevant: **3** apt, fit **5** ad rem **6** cogent, proper, tied in, timely **7** apropos, cognate, fitting, germane, logical, on point, pointed, related, well-put **8** apposite, material, suitable, valuable **9** as regards, bearing on, congruous, consonant, important, pertinent **10** applicable, concerning, felicitous, to the point
  be ~: **5** apply, tie in **6** belong, relate **7** pertain **9** appertain
  be ~ to: **6** bear on, regard **8** bear upon, belong to
  not ~: **5** unapt **9** ill-suited **10** inapposite, malapropos, nongermane, out of order, out of place, unsuitable
  not ~ to: **6** beside
reliability: **5** trust **7** loyalty **8** fidelity **9** sincerity
reliable: **4** firm, good, just, safe, sane, sure, true **5** loyal, pucka, pukka, solid, sound, tried **6** honest, proven, secure, stable, steady, trusty, worthy **7** careful, certain, devoted, durable, sincere, staunch, upright, willing **8** constant, credible, fail-safe, faithful, inerrant, punctual, straight, true-blue, truthful, unerring **9** foolproof, goofproof, honorable, incorrupt, reputable, rock solid, steadfast, unfailing, veracious **10** definitive, dependable, impeccable, infallible, inviolable, legitimate
  not ~: **5** shaky **7** erratic
reliance: **5** faith, stock, trust **6** belief, credit **8** credence, security **9** assurance **10** confidence, conviction, dependance, dependence
__-reliance: **4** self
reliant: **8** relative **9** dependant, dependent
__-reliant: **4** self
Reliant: **3** car **4** auto **8** Plymouth **10** automobile
relic: **5** curio, scrap, token, trace, wreck **6** fossil, shadow **7** antique, memento, remnant, vestige **8** archaism, artefact, artifact, fragment, heirloom, keepsake, monument, souvenir, survival **9** antiquity **10** archaicism
relics: **5** ashes, ruins
relied upon, to be: **6** honest
relief: **3** aid **4** alms, balm, dole, ease, hand, help, lift, rest **5** break, let up, model, spell **6** remedy, solace, succor **7** charity, comfort, redress, release, respite, support **8** breather, easement **9** abatement, diversion, softening **10** assistance, lightening, mitigation, palliative, recreation, relaxation, substitute, sustenance
  cry of ~: **2** ah **3** aah **4** phew, sigh, whew, whoo **6** at last **7** finally **8** gracious
  on ~: **5** needy
  org.: **3** ARC **4** CARE, FEMA
  source of ~: **4** balm **5** salve **6** lotion, remedy **7** anodyne, comfort, unguent **8** liniment, medicine, ointment **9** analgesic, emollient **10** medication, palliative
relief __: **3** map **5** valve **7** pitcher
__ relief: **3** low **4** half, high, sunk **5** comic
__-relief: **3** bas
relieve: **3** aid, rid, rob **4** calm, cure, dull, ease, free, help, loot, vent **5** abate, allay, clear, quiet, relax, salve, slake, spare, spell **6** assist, exempt, let off, pacify, quench, rip off, rotate, soften, solace, soothe, succor, temper, unload **7** absolve, anodyne, appease, assuage, bail out, comfort, console, dismiss, let up on, lighten, mollify, redress, slacken, support, sustain **8** brighten, mitigate, moderate, palliate, reassure, unburden **9** alleviate, give a hand, untrouble **10** ameliorate, stand in for, substitute
  from: **5** spare **6** excuse, exempt, pardon **7** bail out, forgive
  of doubt: **6** assure **7** certify **8** convince **9** guarantee
  of responsibility: **2** ax **4** fire, oust **5** let go **7** dismiss, suspend **8** furlough **9** discharge
relieved: **8** grateful, thankful **9** gratified
reliever: **6** hurler **7** pitcher
  goal: **4** save
  inning: **5** ninth **6** eighth **7** seventh
__-relievo: **4** alto, cavo **5** basso, mezzo
relig.: **4** Bapt., Cath., Prot. **5** theol.
religion: **3** Zen **4** Cath., cult, myth, Prot., sect **5** Baha'I, creed, deism, dogma, faith, Islam, piety, tenet **6** belief, church, Shinto **7** Jainism, Judaism, pietism, Rom. Cath. **8** Buddhism, doctrine, Hinduism, theology **9** Mormonism, mythology, orthodoxy **10** observance, persuasion
__ religion: **5** pagan, state **7** natural
Religion and Science author: Bertrand Russell
religion of Abraham, The: **5** Islam
religious: **3** dom, Fra, nun **4** holy, lama, monk, yogi **5** abbot, bonze, fakir, friar, godly, moral, pious, prior, rigid, sadhu, swami, tulku, yogin **6** abbess, cleric, devout, divine, father, hermit, mother, novice, sacred, sister, solemn, vestal, votary **7** ascetic, brother, caloyer, deistic, dervish, recluse, saintly, starets **8** Capuchin, cenobite, clerical, monastic, orthodox, priestly, prioress, reverent, theistic, Ursuline **9** anchorite, born-again, canonical, Carmelite, doctrinal, gyrovague, hesychast, pietistic, Poor Clare, postulant, prayerful, rasophore, righteous, sectarian, spiritual **10** Cistercian, cloistress, God-fearing, pontifical, sacerdotal, sacrosanct, scriptural, unswerving
  art figure: **5** orans, orant **6** orante
  building: **5** abbey **6** ashram, asrama, chapel, church, mosque, pagoda, priory, temple **7** convent **8** basilica, cloister, lamasery **9** cathedral, monastery, synagogue
  ceremony: **4** Mass, rite **6** ritual **7** baptism, liturgy, service **9** communion, Eucharist, sacrament **10** observance
  deg.: **3** SSD, STB, std., STM, Th.D.
  dissent: **6** heresy **9** blasphemy, sacrilege
  donation: **5** tithe
  leader: **3** rev. **4** msgr., pope **5** rabbi **6** abbess, bishop, pastor, priest **8** cardinal, reverend **9** monsignor **10** archbishop
  offshoot: **4** cult, sect
  sayings: **5** logia
  school: **3** sem. **7** yeshiva **8** seminary
  scroll: **4** Tora **5** Torah
  song: **4** hymn **5** psalm
  symbol: **4** icon, ikon **5** eikon
  very ~: **4** orth. **8** orthodox
  virtue: **4** zeal **5** faith **8** devotion **9** reverence **10** devoutness, veneration
religiousness: **5** faith, piety **8** devotion, holiness **9** godliness, reverence **10** devoutness
relinquish: **3** end **4** cede, drop, dump, give, lose, quit, sell, shed **5** chuck, demit, ditch, forgo, leave, let go, spare, waive, yield **6** forego, fork up, give up, opt out, refund, render, resign, vacate **7** abandon, discard, forfeit, forsake, kiss off, lay down, let go of, release **8** abdicate, abnegate, forswear, get rid of, hand over, jettison, lay aside, part with, renounce, sign away, throw out, turn over **9** cast aside, dispose of, foreswear, sacrifice, stand down, surrender, throw away
relinquishment: **6** waiver **7** cession **9** surrender **10** abdication
reliquary: **9** container **10** receptacle, repository
relish: **3** dig, zip **4** like, love, take, tang, zeal, zest **5** eat up, enjoy, fancy, go for, gusto, revel, savor, spice, taste **6** accept, catsup, desire, devour, flavor, liking, wallow **7** catchup, chutnee, chutney, ketchup, stomach **8** appetite, dressing, fondness, penchant, pleasure **9** condiment, delight in, enjoyment, flavoring, get high on, gloat over, luxuriate, rejoice in **10** appreciate, chili sauce, enthusiasm, love of life, partiality, piccalilli
  excessively: **4** brag, crow **5** gloat **7** rub it in, swagger **9** whoop it up
  fish ~: **4** alec
  maker: **5** Heinz
  with ~: **6** gladly **7** eagerly, happily
relish tray item: **5** olive **6** carrot, celery, pepper, pickle
relive: **8** remember, summon up **9** recollect, reminisce, think back
__ relleno: **5** chile
relocate: **4** move **5** carry, shift **7** migrate **8** displace, resettle, transfer **9** transpose **10** transplant
relocation: **4** move **5** shift **6** exodus **10** emigration, resettling
  expert: **5** mover
reluctance: **5** qualm **8** aversion **9** timidness **10** diffidence, hesitation
reluctant: **3** coy, shy **4** loth, slow, wary **5** balky, chary, loath **6** afraid, averse, gun-shy **7** adverse, uneager **8** backward, grudging, hesitant **9** demurring, diffident, flinching, laggardly, tentative, uncertain, unwilling **10** indisposed, uneffusive, uninclined, unobliging
  be ~: **4** balk **5** dally, demur, hedge, waver **6** recoil, waffle **7** hold off, shy away **8** hesitate, hold back, pull back **9** hem and haw, pussyfoot, vacillate **10** dillydally, equivocate, think twice
  be more than ~: **5** dread
  one: **6** balker
rely
  on: **5** pivot, swear, trust **6** accept, assume, credit, expect, look to, reckon **7** believe, swear by **8** be sure of **9** believe in, calculate **10** set store by
  (on): **4** bank, lean, rest **5** build, count, hinge **6** depend, gamble
  too much: **7** presume
REM
  engaged in ~: **6** asleep **8** sleeping
  experience ~: **5** dream, sleep **7** slumber
  part: **3** eye **5** rapid **8** movement
REM __: **5** sleep
R.E.M.
  hometown: Athens, Georgia
  lead singer: Michael Stipe
  song: Bang and Blame (1995)
    Drive (1992)
    Everybody Hurts (1993)
    Losing My Religion (1991)
    Man on the Moon (1993)
    The One I Love (1987)
    Shiny Happy People (1991)
    Stand (1989)
    What's the Frequency, Kenneth? (1994)
remain: **3** lie, sit **4** bide, halt, hold, last, live, stay, wait **5** abide, cling, delay, dwell, exist, hover, lodge, perch, roost, squat, stand, stick, tarry, visit **6** endure, keep on, linger, occupy, reside **7** hang out, outlast, outlive, persist, prevail, sojourn, survive **8** continue, go unused, sit tight **9** persevere **10** hang around, sit through, stay a while, stick it out, wait around
  undone: **4** hang **5** await, delay, stall
remainder: **3** end **4** rest, stub **5** dregs, scrap **6** excess **7** balance, oddment, remnant, residue, salvage, surplus **8** leavings, leftover, residuum **9** aftermath, carry-over, liability **10** complement
  leaving no ~: **6** evenly
remaining: **3** net, odd **4** left, over, sole **6** extant, with us **7** uneaten **8** leftover, residual **9** vestigial **10** unconsumed
  combining form: **4** meno-
  ones: **4** rest **6** others
remains: **4** rest **5** ashes, chaff, ruins, trace **6** refuse, shards **7** remnant, residue, vestige **8** leavings
remains __ seen: **4** to be
Remains of the Day, The (1993 film)
  cast: James Fox, Anthony Hopkins, Christopher Reeve, Emma Thompson
  director: James Ivory
Remains to Be Seen (1953 film)
  cast: June Allyson, Van Johnson, Angela Lansbury
  director: Don Weis
remake: **6** change, reform **9** modernize, replicate
remand: **4** jail **6** detain, immure, intern, lock up **7** confine **8** imprison
remark: **3** mot, say, see **4** barb, espy, mind, note, quip, word **5** ad lib, aside, crack, gloss, input, speak, state **6** advert, behold, bon mot, notice, phrase, regard **7** comment, declare,

mention, observe **8** comeback, perceive, pick up on **9** assertion, recognize, reference, statement, utterance, wisecrack **10** observance, reflection

remarkable: **3** ace, def, odd, rad **4** aces, A-one, boss, braw, cool, dece, fine, gear, keen, neat, nice, phat, rare, tuff **5** dandy, ducky, grand, great, marvy, neato, nobby, noble, prime, queer, slick, super, swell **6** bang on, bang-up, bonzer, bosker, choice, divine, dreamy, famous, far-out, gnarly, groovy, lovely, peachy, signal, slap-up, spot on, superb, terrif, tiptop, unique, unreal, whizzo, wicked **7** amazing, awesome, capital, corking, curious, notable, perfect, ripping, salient, skookum, stellar, strange, sublime, uncanny, unusual **8** dazzling, especial, eximious, fabulous, five-star, four-star, frabjous, glorious, heavenly, historic, jim-dandy, singular, slam-bang, smashing, splendid, standout, sterling, stickout, striking, stunning, superior, terrific, top-level, topnotch, uncommon, very good, wondrous **9** arresting, bodacious, Endsville, excellent, exemplary, exquisite, first-rate, high-grade, hunky-dory, important, marvelous, memorable, prominent, sollicker, top-flight, unrivaled, wonderful **10** first-class, hotsy-totsy, impressive, jack-a-dandy, out of sight, peachy-keen, phenomenal, prodigious, stupendous, super-duper, unrivalled
person: **4** oner **6** corker
thing: **4** lulu **5** dilly

remarkably: **4** oh so, very **5** extra, quite, right **6** highly, vastly **7** greatly **8** markedly, terribly **9** eminently, extremely, unusually **10** especially, incredibly

remarks: **6** speech **8** analysis **9** voice-over **10** commentary

Remarque, Erich Maria: **6** author, German, writer
spouse: Paulette Goddard
work: All Quiet on the Western Front
A Time to Love and a Time to Die

remarriage: **6** digamy

Rembrandt: **5** Peale **6** artist, van Ryn **7** painter, van Rijn **10** toothpaste
alternative: **3** Aim **5** Crest, Gleem, Topol **7** Close-Up, Colgate, Viadent **9** Aquafresh, Mentadent, Pepsodent, Sensodyne **10** Pearl Drops, Ultra Brite **11** Tom's of Maine
homeland: **7** Holland
work: **3** oil **8** portrait

Rembrandt (1936 film)
cast: Elsa Lanchester, Charles Laughton, Gertrude Lawrence
director: Alexander Korda

remedial: **6** aidful, benign, iatric, useful **7** healing, helpful **8** curative, positive, salutary, sanative **9** effectual, favorable, medicinal **10** beneficial, corrective, productive, worthwhile
assistant: **5** coach, tutor **7** trainer
procedure: **7** therapy
workshop: **6** clinic

remedial ___: **7** reading

remediless: **9** unfixable

remedy: **3** aid, fix **4** balm, cure, drug, ease, heal, help, pill **5** right, salve **6** doctor, elixir, physic, potion, reform, relief, repair, soothe **7** assuage, cure-all, expiate, panacea, rectify, redress, therapy **8** antidote, medicine, mitigate, palliate, put right, recourse, solution **9** alleviate, do justice, expiation, treatment **10** ameliorate, corrective, make good on, medication
old-fashioned ~: **5** tonic **6** elixir, potion **7** nostrum
secret ~: **7** arcanum

remember: **4** cite, mind **5** learn, place, think **6** call up, recall, relive, retain **7** bethink, observe **8** enshrine, hold dear, inshrine, look back, memorize, summon up, treasure **9** brood over, conjure up, dwell upon, give a darn, recognize, recollect, reminisce, think back **10** bear in mind, call to mind, keep in mind
a time to ~: **3** age, era **5** epoch
don't ~: **6** forget
thing to ~: **5** Alamo, Maine
words to ~: **3** saw **5** adage, axiom, maxim, motto **6** dictum, saying, slogan **7** epigram, precept, proverb **8** aphorism, apothegm

Remember ___: **4** WENN

___ Remember: **3** I'll **5** This I, Try to

Remember (1964 song) artist: Shangri-las

remembered, easily: **6** catchy

Remember Me (1971 song) artist: Diana Ross

Remember Me author: Mary Higgins Clark

Remember My Name (1978 film)
cast: Geraldine Chaplin, Moses Gunn, Anthony Perkins
director: Alan Rudolph

Remember the ___!: **5** Alamo, Maine

Remember the Day (1941 film)
cast: Claudette Colbert, John Payne
director: Henry King

Remember the Night (1940 film)
cast: Beulah Bondi, Fred MacMurray, Barbara Stanwyck
director: Mitchell Leisen

Remember the Time (1992 song)
artist: Michael Jackson

Remember the Titans (2000 film)
cast: Donald Faizon, Wood Harris, Will Patton, Denzel Washington
director: Boaz Yakin

Remember WENN network: **3** AMC

Remember You're Mine (1957 song)
artist: Pat Boone

remembrance: **4** gift **5** favor, relic, token **6** memory, recall, record **7** memento, present **8** keepsake, monument, reminder, souvenir **9** hindsight

Remembrance ___: **3** Day

Remembrance of Things Past author: Marcel Proust

remembrances: **7** regards **8** respects **9** greetings **10** best wishes

remex: **5** plume **7** feather

Remick, Lee: **7** actress
film: Anatomy of a Murder (1959)
Baby The Rain Must Fall (1965)
The Competition (1980)
Days of Wine and Roses (1962)
The Detective (1968)
The Europeans (1979)
Experiment in Terror (1962)
A Face in the Crowd (1957)
No Way to Treat a Lady (1968)
The Running Man (1963)
A Severed Head (1971)
Telefon (1977)
These Thousand Hills (1959)
The Wheeler Dealers (1963)
Wild River (1960)

remind: **4** hint, prod, warn **5** nudge **6** pester, prompt, recall **7** bethink, caution, suggest **9** recollect, reminisce
one of: **8** resemble
too often: **3** bug, nag **4** carp, harp **5** annoy, cavil, harry **6** badger, berate, harass, hector, needle, pester **7** henpeck, nitpick **8** browbeat, irritate **9** aggravate, importune

reminder: **3** cue **4** hint, memo, note, sign **5** nudge, token **6** notice, prompt **7** jotting, memento, trinket, warning **8** keepsake, mnemonic, souvenir **10** admonition, indication, memorandum, suggestion

remindful: **8** symbolic **9** evocative **10** suggestive

___ reminds me...: **4** That

Remington: **5** razor **6** shaver, Steele **8** Frederic
alternative: **5** Braun **6** Schick **7** Norelco

Remington-___: **4** Rand

Remington, Frederic: **6** artist **7** painter **8** sculptor

Remington Steele (NBC drama)
cast: Pierce Brosnan (Remington Steele)
Stephanie Zimbalist (Laura Holt)
cat: **4** Nero
producer: MTM

reminisce: **5** think **6** recall, relive, remind **8** hark back, look back, remember **9** recollect, think back

reminiscence: **6** memory, recall

reminiscent: **8** mnemonic, redolent **9** evocative, nostalgic, remindful

remiss: **3** lax **4** lazy, loth, slow **5** hasty, loath, loose, slack **6** sloppy **7** belated **8** careless, derelict, dilatory, heedless, slapdash, slipshod, slothful **9** forgetful, imprudent, negligent, unmindful **10** delinquent, incautious, neglectful, nonchalant, regardless, unthinking, unthorough
be ~: **4** omit **5** shirk **6** ignore, pass by **7** neglect, slacken **8** overlook, pass over **9** disregard, gloss over

remission: **3** ebb **4** stay **5** letup **6** easing, ebbing, pardon, waning **7** amnesty, anodyne, decline, redress **8** abeyance, decrease **9** abatement, cessation, dwindling, lessening, reduction **10** diminution, subsidence, suspension

remissness: **6** laxity **7** laxness, neglect **8** laziness

remit: **3** pay **4** give, mail, post, send, ship **5** abate, defer, delay, relax, waive **6** cancel, excuse, modify, pardon, put off, refund, return, settle **7** absolve, deliver, forbear, forgive, forward, refrain, slacken, tail off **8** decrease, dispatch, fork over, mitigate, postpone, set right, transmit **9** exonerate

remittable: **9** allowable, excusable **10** condonable, defensible, forgivable, pardonable

remittance: **3** pmt. **7** payment **9** allowance, discharge

remitted in advance: **3** ppd. **7** prepaid

remitter: **5** payer

remnant: **3** bit, end **4** butt, dreg, heel, lees, orts, rest, snip, stub **5** crumb, dregs, dross, piece, relic, scrap, shard, sherd, shred, trace **6** excess **7** balance, frazzle, oddment, remains, residue, surplus, vestige **8** fragment, landmark, leavings, leftover, residuum **9** remainder
grill ~: **3** ash **6** cinder

remnants: **5** ruins **8** leavings **9** leftovers

Remo: **8** Williams

remodel: **4** redo **5** adapt, alter, renew, shape **6** change, do over, modify, reform **8** innovate, make over, renovate **9** modernize, refurbish, transform

remodeling: **6** change **7** redress **9** refitting **10** adaptation, alteration, correction
project: **3** ell **5** annex, attic **7** kitchen **8** basement

___ Remo, Italy: **3** San

remold: **5** alter

remonstrance: **5** blame **6** rebuke **7** censure **8** question

remonstrate: **4** warn **5** argue, chide, demur, scold **6** differ, object, reason **7** censure, contend, dispute, dissent, inveigh, protest **8** complain, reproach **9** take issue

remora: **4** fish, pega
ride: **5** shark

remorse: **3** rue **5** grief, guilt, shame **6** regret, sorrow **7** anguish, emotion **9** penitence **10** contrition, repentance, ruefulness
feel ~: **3** rue **6** regret, repent
sign of ~: **4** pang, tear

remorseful: **5** sorry **6** rueful **7** ashamed, humbled **8** contrite, penitent **9** chastened, regretful, repentant **10** apologetic
one: **4** ruer

remorseless: **4** grim, hard, mean **5** cruel, harsh **6** brutal, mortal, savage **7** callous, inhuman **8** hardened, indurate, inhumane, obdurate, pitiless, ruthless **9** merciless, murderous, shameless

remote: **3** far, icy, off, old **4** away, cold, cool, slim, wild **5** alien, alone, aloof, apart, outer **6** chilly, far-off, lonely, slight, uppity, yonder **7** distant, far away, foreign, glacial, obscure, outside, private, slender, strange, stuck-up, unknown **8** detached, far-flung, frontier, isolated, lonesome, outlying, reserved, secluded, snobbish, solitary, unlikely **9** bellicose, withdrawn **10** abstracted, antisocial, impersonal, improbable, insociable, negligible, out of range, unagitated, unamicable, unfamiliar
area: **6** Podunk **7** boonies **9** boondocks
button: **3** rec **4** mute, play **5** on-off, pause **6** record, vol. off, volume. **7** channel
more ~: **7** farther, further
most ~: **4** last **7** extreme **8** farthest
target: **2** TV **3** VCR **5** TV set **8** CD player **9** DVD player
TV ~ control: **4** nemo

remote ___: **7** control, sensing

remoteness: **6** length **8** distance **9** seclusion **10** alienation, detachment

removal: **8** excision, transfer **9** departure, dismissal, exclusion, expulsion, uprooting **10** deposition, extraction, transferal, unfrocking, withdrawal
combining form: **6** -ectomy
unlawful ~: **5** heist, theft **6** holdup, piracy **7** larceny, looting, robbery, robbing, swiping **8** burglary, poaching, stealing, thievery **9** pilferage, pilfering **10** plundering

remove: **3** rid **4** dele, doff, do in, drop, junk, kill, lift, oust, pull, rase, raze, shed, snip, take, undo, wean, wipe, x out **5** clear, drain, eject, erase, evict, expel, prune, purge, scoop, shear, strip, sweep **6** banish, bounce, censor, cut out, delete, depose, detach, dig out, divest, evulse, excise, exsect, lop off, rip out, unlade, unload, unseat, uproot **7** cart off, cashier, dismiss, drag off, exclude, excrete, expunge, exscind, extract, lighten, obviate, off with, pull out, root out, scratch, shake up, take off, take out, tear off, tear out, wipe out **8** cross off, cross out, dethrone, dislodge, dis-

place, evacuate, exorcise, exorcize, get rid of, phase out, pull down, relegate, shake off, subtract, take away, throw out, transfer, white out, withdraw **9** carry away, clear away, discharge, dispose of, eliminate, eradicate, extirpate, liquidate, red-pencil, slip out of, transport **10** do away with, obliterate, transplant
a renter: **4** boot **6** bounce **7** boot out, kick out, toss out **8** force out **10** dispossess
feeling: **4** dull **6** deaden
gradually ~: **4** wean
oneself: **7** leave. go
(oneself): **6** absent
opposite of ~: **5** put in **7** include, install
prefix: **3** dis-
rind: **4** pare, peel, skin
vital parts: **3** gut **4** sack **5** rifle **6** ravage **7** destroy, pillage, plunder, ransack **8** clean out, decimate
removed: **3** off **5** aloof **6** lonely **7** distant, missing **8** outlying, secluded, separate **9** withdrawn
__ remover: **5** paint **6** staple
remover, dirt: **8** cleanser **9** detergent
Remsen, Ira: **7** chemist
remuda: **6** horses, mounts **7** cayuses
remunerate: **3** pay **5** pay up, repay **6** ante up, recoup, refund, reward **7** guerdon, satisfy **8** shell out **9** indemnify, reimburse **10** compensate
remuneration: **3** fee, pay **4** wage **5** wages **6** profit, refund, reward, salary **7** payment **8** earnings **9** emolument
not taking ~: **6** unpaid **9** volunteer
remunerative: **7** gainful **9** lucrative, rewarding **10** good-paying, profitable, well-paying
Remus: **4** twin **5** Roman
parent of ~: **4** Ares, Mars **10** Rhea Silvia
twin of ~: **7** Romulus
Remus, Uncle
character: **3** Fox **4** Bear, Br'er **6** Rabbit **7** Br'er Fox **8** Br'er Bear **10** Br'er Rabbit
Remy: **4** wine
Ren: **3** dog **4** toon **5** Woods **9** Chihuahua
renaissance: **7** revival
Renaissance: **5** style
composition: **5** motet
engraver: **5** Dürer
headdress: **6** cornet
instrument: **4** lute **5** rebec **6** rebeck
man: **10** generalist
painter: **5** Dürer **6** Titian **7** Raphael **9** Donatello **10** Botticelli **11** Fra Angelico
sword: **5** estoc
Renaissance __: **3** man **5** woman **7** Revival
__ Renaissance: **4** High **5** Black, Early **6** Harlem
Renaissance Man (1994 film)
cast: Danny DeVito, Gregory Hines, Cliff Robertson
director: Penny Marshall
renal: **7** hepatic, nephric
Renaldo: **6** Duncan
Ren and Stimpy: **3** duo **4** pair
cat: **6** Stimpy
dog: **3** Ren
Renan, Ernest: **6** French, writer
renascence: **7** revival
Renascence and Other Poems
author: Edna St. Vincent Millay
__ re nata: **3** pro
Renata: **7** Tebaldi
Renault: **3** car **4** auto, Mary **5** Louis **10** automobile
model: **4** Clio **5** Le Car **6** Laguna, Megane **8** Dauphine
Renault, Louis: **8** Nobelist
Renault, Mary: **6** writer **7** English
work: The Charioteer
Fire from Heaven
The King Must Die
The Last of the Wine
The Persion Boy
The Praise Singer
Renay, Diane song: Navy Blue (1964)
rend: **3** rip **4** rive, tear **5** break, rip up, sever, slash, split **6** cleave, harrow, mangle, sunder **7** afflict, break up, disjoin, disturb, shatter, split up **8** distress, disunite, fracture, lacerate, rip apart, separate **9** pull apart, tear apart **10** break apart
old-style: **5** reave
Rendell: **4** Ruth
render: **2** do **3** bid, pay, put, say **4** cede, deal, give, melt, play **5** allot, grant, repay, yield **6** accord, afford, depict, donate, effect, fork up, hand in, impart, recite, return, sketch, supply, tender **7** furnish, pay back, perform, picture, portray, present, produce, provide, restore **8** dispense, fork over, hand down, hand over, melt down, shell out, turn over **9** interpret, translate **10** contribute, paraphrase, relinquish, transcribe
helpless: **4** bind **6** fetter, hamper, hobble **8** restrain **9** hamstring
speechless: **3** awe, wow **4** stun **5** amaze, floor **9** overwhelm
unconscious: **2** KO **4** drug, stun **5** floor, punch **7** flatten
rendered: **4** done **7** wrought
rendering: **7** reading, recital, version **9** depiction, execution **10** definition, recitation
rendering __: **5** plant, works
Render therefore __ Caesar...: **4** unto
rendezvous: **4** date **5** haunt, tryst **6** gather, join up, liaise **7** hangout, meeting **9** encounter, forgather, get to know, heavy date, tête-à-tête **10** congregate, engagement
with: **3** see **4** meet
Rendezvous artist: **4** Erté
Rendezvous With Rama author: Arthur C. Clarke
__-rending: **5** heart
rendition: **7** reading, recital, version **8** delivery **9** depiction, portrayal **10** definition, expression
Rene: **5** Russo **6** Goupil **7** Lacoste
René: **4** Char, Coty **5** Clair, Dubos **6** Cassin, Norman **7** Lacoste, Lalique **8** Favaloro, Levesque, Magritte **9** Descartes, Leibowitz
see also French
René __ Réaumur: **3** Ade
Renee: **6** Adoree, Taylor **7** Daalder, O'Connor **8** Richards
Renée: **7** Fleming **9** Zellweger
see also French
renegade: **5** exile, rebel, snake, stray **6** outlaw **7** escapee, hellion, heretic, radical, ratfink, runaway, traitor **8** apostate, betrayer, defector, derelict, deserter, disloyal, forsaker, frondeur, fugitive, maverick, mutineer, mutinous, recreant, resister, turncoat **9** dissenter, dissident, insurgent, protester **10** iconoclast, malcontent, schismatic
renege: **4** turn **6** cop out, recant **7** back out, pull out, retract, reverse, worm out **8** abrogate, go back on, withdraw **9** back-pedal, weasel out
renew: **4** mend **5** fix up, rally, refit, waken **6** extend, perk up, recall, reform, repair, resume, revive, take up, update **7** enliven, fortify, freshen, furbish, prolong, recover, recruit, refresh, remodel, restart, restore, retread, touch up **8** continue, overhaul, reaffirm, reawaken, renovate, spruce up **9** modernize, refurbish, reiterate, replenish, restitute, start over, transform **10** invigorate, recommence, regenerate, rejuvenate, revitalize, strengthen
renewable __: **6** energy
renewal: **5** rally **7** healing, redress **8** comeback, recovery
candidate: **4** slum
card: **6** insert
require ~: **5** lapse **6** expire, run out
__ renewal: **5** urban
renewed, not get: **5** lapse
Renfrew: **4** city, town
locale: **8** Scotland
Renfro: **3** Mel **4** Brad
Renfro, Mel sport: **8** football
Reni: **5** Guido **7** Santoni
Reni, Guido: **6** artist **7** painter
homeland: **5** Italy
Rennes: **4** city, town
locale: **6** France
river: **4** Ille **7** Vilaine
Rennie, Michael: **5** actor
film: 5 Fingers (1952)
The Day the Earth Stood Still (1951)
Les Miserables (1952)
Sailor of the King (1953)
Soldier of Fortune (1955)
Third Man on the Mountain (1959)
Renny: **6** Harlin
Reno: **4** city, Mike, town **5** Janet, Kelly
alternative: **5** Vegas **8** Las Vegas
city near ~: **4** Elko **6** Sparks
locale: **3** Nev. **6** Nevada
zone: **3** PDT, PST
see also casino
Renoir, Jean: **6** French **8** director
film: A Day in the Country (1946)
Grand Illusion (1937)
La Chienne (1931)
Nana (1926)
The River (1951)
Rules of the Game (1939)
The Southerner (1945)
film heroine: **5** Elena
Renoir, Pierre-Auguste: **6** artist, French **7** painter
associate: **5** Degas, Monet
subject: **4** nude
renounce: **4** deny, drop, dump, quit, turn **5** annul, demit, forgo, leave, spurn, waive **6** abjure, defect, desert, disown, eschew, forego, give up, opt out, recant, reject, resign **7** abandon, abstain, cast off, disavow, forbear, forsake, let go of, refrain, retract **8** abdicate, abnegate, disclaim, forswear, keep from, lay aside, part with, swear off, toss over **9** foreswear, repudiate, sacrifice, surrender **10** relinquish
renounced: **6** lonely **7** outcast **8** forsaken, isolated **9** by oneself
renouncement: **6** denial **7** refusal **8** apostasy **10** abdication
renovate: **4** mend, redo **5** alter, fix up, rehab, renew **6** change, reform, repair, revamp, update **7** furbish, refresh, remodel, restore, touch up **8** overhaul, spruce up **9** modernize, refurbish **10** regenerate, rejuvenate
renown: **4** fame, name **5** éclat, glory, honor **6** credit, luster, repute, status **7** acclaim, laurels, stardom **8** eminence, prestige, splendor **9** celebrity, notoriety **10** popularity, prominence, reputation
renowned: **4** star **5** famed, great, lofty, noted **6** famous, mighty, of note, signal **7** big-name, eminent, notable, storied **8** esteemed, extolled, glorious, historic, laureate, splendid **9** acclaimed, legendary, prominent, superstar, topflight, well-known **10** celebrated, preeminent
__-renowned: **5** world
rent: **3** let, rip **4** gash, hire, open, rift, slit, take, tear, torn **5** break, cleft, crack, lease, lodge, slash, split **6** borrow, breach, engage, income, ragged, ripped, schism, sublet, tatter **7** charter, crevice, fissure, hire out, opening, rupture **8** fracture, overhead, sundered **9** lacerated **10** interspace
accommodation for ~: **2** rm. **3** inn **4** room **5** B and B, hotel, motel, suite **6** marina **7** lodging **10** motor lodge
apartment without ~: **5** condo
collector: **6** lessor **8** landlady, landlord
for ~: **5** to let, unlet **6** vacant
out again: **5** relet
payer: **6** lessee, tenant
rent __: **4** seck **5** party, table **6** strike **7** control
rent-__: **4** a-car, free
__ rent: **3** dry, for **6** ground
__-rent: **4** rack
rental: **4** flat **5** suite **7** vacancy
see also apartment
rental __: **7** library
__-rent district: **3** low **4** high
rented: **5** in use **7** lived-in **8** occupied
renter: **5** guest, liver **6** lessee, lodger, tenant **8** occupant **10** inhabitant, vacationer
paper: **5** lease
remove a ~: **4** boot **5** evict **6** bounce **7** boot out, kick out, toss out **8** force out **10** dispossess
Renton: **4** city, town
locale: **10** Washington
rent-to-__: **3** own
renunciation: **6** denial **7** refusal **8** apostasy **10** abdication
Renuzit alternative: **5** Glade **6** Wizard **7** Airwick, Stick-Up
__ reo: **7** absente
Reo: **3** car **4** auto **10** automobile
maker: **4** Olds
model: **5** Elite **6** Royale **11** Flying Cloud, Silver Cloud
part: **3** Eli **4** Olds **6** Ransom
rival: **5** Essex
reoccupy: **6** retake **7** recover
reoccur: **6** repeat **9** come again
reoccurring: **8** repeated, unending **9** continual, perpetual
reopen: **6** resume **7** restart **8** continue **10** recommence
reorder: **4** move **5** alter, shift **6** change, invert, switch **7** reverse **9** rearrange, transpose
reorganize: **5** rally **6** change, modify, reform **7** shake up **8** make over, overhaul
REO Speedwagon
lead singer: Cronin
song: Can't Fight This Feeling (1985)
Here With Me (1988)
In My Dreams (1987)
In Your Letter (1981)
Keep On Loving You (1980)
Keep the Fire Burnin' (1982)
One Lonely Night (1985)
Take It on the Run (1981)
That Ain't Love (1987)
rep: **3** agt., att. **4** atty., name **5** agent, proxy **6** cravat, deputy, fabric **8** attor-

ney, good name **9** deal maker, middleman **10** mouthpiece, negotiator
see also representative
__ rep: 5 sales
Rep.: 3 pol.
counterpart: 3 Dem., Sen.
epithet: 3 GOP
not ~ or Dem.: 3 Ind.
see also Republican
__ Rep.: 3 Dom.
repair: 2 go **3** fix, hie, sew **4** cure, darn, mend, trim, vamp **5** amend, debug, emend, fixup, leave, patch, rehab, renew, resew, right **6** adjust, betake, doctor, modify, reform, remedy, revamp, stitch, tinker, travel **7** correct, journey, patch up, proceed, push off, recover, recruit, rectify, redress, refresh, replace, restore, retouch, retread, touch up **8** overhaul, renovate, retrieve **9** do justice, refurbish **10** adjustment
anew: 5 refix
beyond ~: 4 shot **5** kaput
bill part: 5 labor, parts
do a makeshift ~: 5 rig up
ender: 3 man, men **5** woman, women **6** people, person
needing ~: 6 broken, busted, faulty **7** cracked, damaged, haywire **9** defective, fractured, in the shop **10** inoperable, not working, on the blink, on the fritz, out of order
state of ~: 4 trim **5** shape **6** fettle **7** fitness **9** condition
to: 7 head for
repairer: 4 mech **5** fixer **8** mechanic
repairs: 6 upkeep
without ~: 4 as is
repair-shop substitute: 6 loaner
reparation: 3 pay **4** dues, fine **6** amends **7** apology, damages, payment, penance, redress **9** atonement, expiation, repayment **10** correction, punishment
make ~: 5 atone **7** redress, satisfy **9** reimburse
maker: 6 atoner
repartee: 3 wit **4** quip **5** sally **6** banter, bon mot, retort, ripost **7** riposte **8** badinage, chitchat, comeback, raillery, wordplay **9** rejoinder, table talk, witticism **10** persiflage, pleasantry
bit of ~: 3 mot **4** quip **5** crack **6** bon mot, retort, zinger **7** riposte **8** one-liner **9** wisecrack
repast: 4 meal **5** feast **6** dinner **7** aliment, banquet **8** victuals **9** collation, refection
enjoy a ~: 3 eat, sup **5** feast
quite a ~: 4 fete, gala **5** feast **6** spread **7** banquet **8** clambake
repay: 6 avenge, offset, rebate, recoup, redeem, refund, render, return, reward **7** get even, replace, requite, satisfy **8** give back, make good, settle up, square up **9** get back at, indemnify, liquidate, reimburse, retaliate **10** compensate, make amends, make good on, recompense, remunerate
must ~: 3 owe
repayment: 3 due **6** refund, reward **9** vengeance **10** recompense, reparation
repeal: 3 nix **4** kill, lift, void **5** annul, quash, scrub **6** cancel, negate, recall, recant, revoke **7** abolish, nullify, rescind, retract, reverse **8** abrogate, dissolve, override, overrule, overturn, set aside, withdraw **9** annulment, repudiate **10** invalidate
repeat: 3 say **4** copy, echo **5** clone, ditto, quote, recur, rerun, resay **6** do over, encore, harp on, parrot, recite, rehash, replay, retell, return, stress **7** imitate, iterate, narrate, recount, reflect, reoccur, reprise, restate, run over, stammer **8** drum into, multiply, play back, play over, practice, read back, reappear, rehearse **9** come again, duplicate, reiterate, replicate, reshowing
in music: 3 bis
performance: 6 déjà vu, encore
sign, in music: 5 segno
verbatim: 4 cite, copy, echo **5** mimic, quote **6** parrot, recite, repeat, retell **7** excerpt, extract
without ~: 4 once
repeated: 6 afresh **8** frequent, habitual, periodic, standing **9** perpetual **10** persistent, reiterated
exercises: 5 drill
repeatedly: 3 oft **4** much **5** again, often **8** ofttimes **9** many times, regularly **10** frequently
repeated pattern in heraldry: 4 semé
repeating __: 7 decimal, firearm
repeating, keep: 5 chant **6** intone
Repeat Performance (1947 film)
cast: Tom Conway, Louis Hayward, Joan Leslie
director: Alfred Werker
repel: 4 buck, defy **5** fight, parry, spurn **6** defeat, offend, put off, rebuff, refuse, reject, resist, revolt, sicken **7** disgust, fend off, hold off, repulse, turn off, ward off **8** beat back, drive off, fight off, frighten, gross out, push back, shake off, stave off, turn back, vanquish **9** chase away, displease, drive away, drive back, hold at bay, keep at bay, turn aside, withstand **10** antagonize
repellence: 4 hate **6** hatred, horror **7** disgust, dislike **8** aversion, distaste, loathing **9** antipathy, repulsion, revulsion **10** abhorrence, repugnance
repellent: 4 foul, icky, rank, ugly, vile **5** awful, gross, nasty, seamy **6** creepy, odious, sordid **7** beastly, ghastly, hateful, heinous, hideous, squalid **8** horrible, terrible, wretched **9** abhorrent, appalling, execrable, frightful, loathsome, monstrous, obnoxious, offensive, repugnant, revolting, unsightly **10** abominable, despicable, detestable, disgusting, forbidding, uninviting, unpleasant
__ repellent: 5 shark **6** insect
__-repellent: 5 water
repeller combining form: 4 -fuge
repeller, evil: 5 charm, spell **7** periapt **8** talisman
repent: 5 atone **6** bewail, lament
of: 3 rue **6** regret **7** deplore **8** weep over
repentance: 5 guilt **6** regret, sorrow **7** penance, remorse **9** attrition, penitence **10** contrition
repentant: 5 sorry **7** subdued **8** contrite, penitent **9** regretful **10** apologetic, remorseful
one: 4 ruer **6** atoner
Repentigny: 4 city, town
locale: 6 Canada, Québec
repercussion: 4 echo, flak **5** flack, waves **6** effect, impact, recoil, result, upshot **7** fallout, outcome **8** backlash, backwash, follow-up, reaction **9** aftermath
repertoire: 4 list **5** stock **6** dramas, operas, pieces **7** catalog **9** catalogue, inventory
repertory: 3 rep **5** range, shtik, stock, store **6** shtick, supply **10** collection, depository, repertoire
repertory __: 7 catalog, company, theater, theatre **9** catalogue
__ repetatur: 3 non
repetition: 4 copy, echo, rote **5** chant, drill **6** chorus, encore, litany, rhythm **7** recital **8** practice, sameness **9** duplicate, frequency, iteration, rehearsal, tautology
mark of ~: 5 ditto
rapid ~ in music: 7 tremolo
request for ~: 4 what
rhetorical ~: 5 ploce
repetitious: 4 dull **5** stale, windy, wordy **6** boring, prolix **7** tedious, verbose **8** habitual **9** iterative, redundant, wearisome
repetitive: 7 verbose **8** unwaning **9** continual, recurrent
pattern: 5 cycle **6** series **7** routine
repetitiveness: 3 rut **5** ennui **6** tedium **7** boredom, routine **8** dullness, monotony, sameness **10** insipidity, uniformity
rephrase: 4 edit **5** amend **6** reword **9** translate **10** paraphrase
repine: 4 beef, fret, kick, moan, mope, wail **5** gripe, groan, whine **6** lament, regret, squawk **7** grumble **8** complain, languish **9** bellyache, make a fuss
replace: 3 sub **4** oust **5** alter, repay, shift, spell **6** change, fill in, follow, refund, repair, return, switch **7** put back, restock, restore, succeed **8** displace, exchange, give back, supplant **9** antiquate, reimburse, replenish, supersede **10** compensate, substitute
ready to ~: 4 worn **6** broken, ruined
replacement: 3 sub **4** temp **6** change, fill-in **9** surrogate **10** substitute
vehicle: 6 loaner
Replacement Killers, The (1998 film)
cast: Jürgen Prochnow, Michael Rooker, Mira Sorvino, Chow Yun-Fat
director: Antoine Fuqua
replacing: 7 instead **8** in lieu of **9** instead of
replay: 6 do over, repeat
instant ~ technique: 5 slo-mo **10** slow motion, stop-action
__ replay: 6 action **7** instant
replenish: 4 fill **5** renew, stock **6** load up, make up, refill, reload, supply, top off **7** provide, recruit, refresh, replace, restock, restore
replenishments: 6 stores **7** rations **8** supplies **10** provisions
replete: 4 full, rife **5** alive, awash, laden, sated, thick **6** filled, full up, gorged, heaped, jammed, lavish, loaded, packed **7** charged, crammed, crowded, fraught, glutted, overfed, stuffed, teeming **8** abundant, brimming, infested, satiated, swarming **9** abounding, chock-full, jam-packed, plenteous, plentiful
repletion: 4 glut **7** satiety, surfeit **8** plethora **9** plenitude
replevin: 4 writ **6** redeem **7** lawsuit, recover
replevy: 6 redeem **7** recover
replica: 4 copy, dupe **5** clone, ditto, image, match, model, repro, xerox **6** carbon, double, ectype **7** picture **8** knockoff, likeness **9** duplicate, facsimile, imitation, look-alike, miniature, photocopy **10** carbon copy, mimeograph
crude ~: 6 effigy
__ replicase: 3 RNA
replicate: 4 copy, redo **5** clone **6** do over, remake, repeat **7** imitate **8** recreate, simulate **9** reproduce
reply: 3 ans., lip, say **4** RSVP, sass **5** react **6** answer, letter, recite, retort, return, ripost **7** counter, defense, hit back, reflect, respond, riposte **8** antiphon, back talk, comeback, feedback, reaction, response **9** get back to, rejoinder, retaliate, utterance, wisecrack, write back
defiant ~: 5 never, no way
hedging ~: 5 maybe **7** perhaps **8** possibly **9** it could be, it might be
roll-call ~: 3 aye, nay, yea, yes **4** here **7** present
sarcastic ~: 4 I bet, sure
to: 5 field, rebut **6** answer, refute **7** counter, dispute **8** disclaim
wishy-washy ~: 7 perhaps **8** possibly **9** it could be, it might be, perchance
reply __: 4 card
Repo Man (1984 film)
cast: Emilio Estevez, Vonetta McGee, Harry Dean Stanton
director: Alex Cox
répondez __ vous plaît: 3 s'il
report: 3 air, say **4** bang, boom, buzz, come, dirt, info, list, name, news, note, tale, talk, tell, wire, word **5** blast, brief, cable, crack, paper, rumor, scoop, sound, state, story, telex, theme **6** advise, cahier, canard, detail, digest, earful, exposé, gossip, impart, inform, letter, notice, notify, pass on, précis, recite, record, relate, repute, résumé, reveal, rumble, show up, tattle, tell on, turn up **7** account, article, check in, clock in, dossier, hearsay, history, itemize, mention, message, missive, narrate, outline, publish, recital, recount, release, rundown, scandal, summary, tidings, trumpet, version, weigh in, whisper, write-up **8** advise of, announce, describe, disclose, dispatch, document, telegram **9** broadcast, chronicle, circulate, discharge, explosion, expound on, grapevine, make known, narration, narrative, publicity, recountal, statement, telephone, term paper, touch base **10** communiqué, detonation, exposition, literature, make public, memorandum, recitation, reputation, whispering
ender: 3 age
false ~: 3 lie **5** libel, smear **7** calumny, slander, untruth **10** imputation
maker: 3 gun **7** firearm
on: 5 cover **6** relate, tell of **7** write up **9** talk about
unfounded ~: 3 lie **4** buzz, dirt, tale, talk, word **5** bruit, rumor **6** canard, earful, gossip, tattle **7** fiction, hearsay, whisper **9** falsehood, grapevine, invention **10** suggestion
weather ~ word: 3 dry, hot, wet **4** cold, cool, fair, hail, hazy, mild, rain, snow, warm **5** clear, foggy, humid, misty, sleet, storm, sunny **6** chilly, cloudy
report __: 4 card
__ report: 6 annual **7** weather
report card: 6 record
datum: 3 GPA **4** mark **5** grade
mark: 2 ef **3** bee, cee, dee **5** A plus, B plus, C plus, D plus **6** A minus, B minus, C minus, D minus
word: 5 tardy **6** absent
reported: 7 alleged, reputed **8** believed, putative, supposed
reporter: 3 cub **4** corr. **5** press **6** anchor, author, legman, writer **8** stringer **9** announcer, columnist, newshound, wordsmith **10** journalist, newscaster, newsperson, newswriter
angle: 5 focus, slant **9** viewpoint **10** standpoint
boss: 6 editor

coup: **5** scoop **9** exclusive
credit: **6** byline
news ~ of yore: **5** crier
often: **5** asker
question: **3** how, who, why **4** what, when **5** where
rookie ~: **3** cub
staple: **5** quote
__ reporter: **3** cub **5** court **6** action, police
reporting to: **5** under
__ Report, The: **4** Hite
repose: **3** lie **4** calm, ease, loaf, loll, rest **5** peace, quiet, relax, sleep **6** lounge, settle **7** leisure, lie down, recline, respite, slumber **8** calmness, free time, quietude **9** stillness **10** inactivity, quiescence, recreation, relaxation, stretch out, take it easy
in ~: **4** calm **5** quiet, still **6** at rest, placid, serene **7** dormant **9** quiescent
reposing: **6** at rest **8** lounging **9** incumbent
reposition: **4** move **5** alter, shift **6** change **7** shuffle **8** displace, maneuver, transfer **9** rearrange **10** move around
repository: **4** fund, safe, stge. **5** booth, depot, store, vault **6** closet, coffer, museum **7** arsenal, lockbox, storage **8** magazine, treasury **9** container, reservoir, warehouse **10** receptacle
repossess: **6** recoup, redeem, regain **7** get back, recover, recruit **8** retrieve, take back **9** reacquire
repp: **4** silk, wool **5** rayon **6** cotton, fabric **8** material
repp __: **3** tie
Repp: **8** Stafford
reprehend: **4** trim **5** chide, decry, knock, scold **6** berate, charge, rebuke **7** bawl out, censure, chew out, condemn, lecture, reprove, upbraid **8** chastise, denounce, reproach **9** castigate, criticize, dress down, fustigate **10** disapprove, take to task, tongue-lash
reprehensible: **4** vile **5** nasty, wrong **6** wicked **7** heinous, ignoble, low-down, very bad **8** shameful, unseemly, unworthy, wrongful **9** miscreant, offensive **10** despicable, scandalous, villainous
most ~: **5** worst
reprehension: **5** blame **6** rebuke
represent: **4** limn, mean, show, tell **5** enact, paint **6** act for, denote, depict, embody, imbody, mirror, pass as, sketch, typify **7** betoken, express, picture, portray, pretend, serve as, signify, suggest **8** appear as, describe, speak for, stand for **9** adumbrate, epitomize, exemplify, interpret, personify, predicate, symbolize **10** illustrate
representation: **3** map **4** icon, ikon, show, sign **5** eikon, image, totem **6** effigy, emblem, figure, sketch, statue, symbol **7** tableau **8** likeness, specimen **9** spectacle
representational: **7** graphic **9** graphical, realistic
representative: **3** agt., rep **5** agent, envoy, model, proxy, typal, typic **6** consul, deputy, jobber, legate, member, sample **7** example, officer, proctor, senator, typical **8** delegate, emissary, lawmaker, official, specimen, symbolic **9** appointee, councilor, depictive, messenger, realistic, surrogate **10** councillor, emblematic, mouthpiece
foreign ~: **3** amb. **5** envoy **6** consul, legate **8** delegate, diplomat, emissary, minister **10** ambassador
legal ~: **6** jurist, lawyer **7** adviser, advisor, counsel **8** advocate, attorney **9** barrister, solicitor **10** mouthpiece
Representative locale: **5** House
representatives: **4** gild **5** guild, union **6** caucus, league **7** chamber, council, meeting **8** assembly, conclave, congress **9** committee, delegates, gathering **10** conference, convention, delegation
representing: **3** for **9** acting for **10** in behalf of, on behalf of
repress: **3** gag **4** bury, cork, curb, hold, stop, tame **5** check, crush, quash, quell **6** bottle, bridle, censor, deaden, fetter, hold in, keep in, muffle, muzzle, stifle, subdue **7** confine, contain, control, inhibit, prevent, put down, smother, squelch, swallow **8** blank out, restrain, stamp out, vanquish **9** interdict **10** discourage, keep a lid on, keep in line
repressed: **6** pent-up **7** subdued **9** forgotten, inhibited **10** unrecalled
repression: **9** abatement, restraint **10** constraint, domination
reprieve: **4** free, lull, stay **5** delay, grace, letup, pause, truce **6** pardon **7** forgive, respite **8** abeyance, breather **9** deferment, salvation **10** suspension
reprimand: **3** rag **4** slap **5** blame, chide, scold **6** berate, jump on, lesson, rebuff, rebuke **7** censure, chew out, lambast, lecture, reprove, tell off, upbraid, what for **8** admonish, denounce, lambaste, reproach, reproval, scolding **9** castigate, criticize, dress down, exprobate, lash out at, light into, talking-to **10** bawling-out, come down on, take to task, upbraiding
reprint: **4** copy **5** print **6** ectype **7** edition **9** reproduce
reprisal: **7** redress, revenge **9** tit for tat, vengeance **10** punishment, quid pro quo
reprise: **6** encore, repeat **9** reiterate, reshowing
repro: **3** fax **4** copy, dupe, stat **6** ectype **7** replica **9** photocopy, Photostat
of yore: **5** mimeo **6** carbon **10** carbon copy, mimeograph
repro.
not a ~: **4** orig.
reproach: **3** rag, tax **4** slam, slur, twit **5** abuse, blame, chide, scold, shame, stain **6** berate, charge, rebuke, stigma **7** asperse, calumny, censure, condemn, reproof, reprove, scandal, tell off, upbraid **8** denounce **9** criticize, discredit, excoriate, frown upon, invective, reprehend, reprimand **10** impugnment, imputation, reflection, take to task
above ~: **5** clean **6** chaste **8** flawless, innocent, spotless, virtuous **9** blameless, faultless, guiltless
exclamation: **3** tch, tsk, tut **4** tush, well **5** shame **6** tsk tsk, tut-tut
oneself: **5** atone **6** repent
__ reproach: **6** beyond
__-reproach: **4** self
reproachful: **7** injured, nagging **8** caviling, critical **9** querulous **10** derogatory, detractive
reprobate: **3** cur **4** heel, worm **5** churl, knave, losel, rogue, rowdy, scamp, spurn **6** bad guy, bad hat, rascal, refuse, reject, varlet, wretch **7** lowlife, outcast, so-and-so, villain **8** picaroon, rakehell, scalawag, shameful **9** corrupted, criticize, debauched, dissolute, miscreant, scallawag, scallywag, scoundrel, shameless, vulgarian **10** blackguard, delinquent, disapprove, licentious, ne'er-do-well, profligate, scapegrace
reprobation: **5** blame **7** censure **9** criticism, reprimand
reproduce: **4** bear, copy, dupe, echo, sire **5** beget, breed, clone, hatch, mimeo, print, spawn, trace, xerox **6** carbon, father, pirate **7** produce, reflect, reprint **8** multiply, simulate **9** duplicate, photocopy, Photostat, propagate, replicate **10** mimeograph, photograph, transcribe
reproduction: **3** fax **4** copy, dupe, fake **5** clone, ditto, image, mimeo, model, xerox **6** carbon, double, ectype **7** replica **8** knockoff, likeness **9** duplicate, facsimile, imitation, look-alike, photocopy, Photostat **10** mimeograph
reproof: **3** rag, tax **4** slam, slur, twit **5** abuse, blame, chide, scold, shame, stain **6** berate, charge, lesson, rebuke, stigma **7** asperse, calumny, censure, condemn, lecture, scandal, tell off, upbraid **8** denounce, reproach, scolding **9** criticism, criticize, discredit, excoriate, frown upon, invective, reprehend, reprimand **10** imputation, reflection, take to task, upbraiding
reproval: **6** rebuke **7** censure, lecture **8** scolding **9** reprimand, talking-to **10** admonition, bawling-out, chewing-out, upbraiding
reprove: **3** rag, tax **4** warn **5** blame, chide, scold **6** berate, punish, rebuff, rebuke **7** censure, condemn, lecture, tell off, upbraid **8** admonish, denounce, reproach **9** criticize, excoriate, exprobate, lash out at, reprehend, reprimand **10** take to task
reptile: **3** asp, boa, uta **4** croc, T-Rex **5** aboma, adder, agama, anole, cobra, gator, gecko, krait, mamba, racer, skink, snake, teiid, viper **6** agamid, caiman, cooter, dhaman, dragon, elapid, gavial, goanna, iguana, lizard, moloch, python, ridley, taipan, turtle **7** markhor, rattler, serpent, snapper **8** anaconda, dinosaur, moccasin, ophidian, ringhals, stinkpot, tortoise **9** alligator, boomslang, chameleon, coachwhip, crocodile, hawksbill **10** bushmaster, copperhead, loggerhead, sidewinder
Africa: **5** mamba **8** ringhals **9** boomslang
Asia: **5** krait **6** dhaman, gavial
Australia: **6** goanna, moloch, taipan
combining form: **4** -saur **6** herpet-, -saurus **7** herpeto-
extinct ~: **4** T-Rex **8** dinosaur
like a ~: **5** scaly
Mexico: **3** uta **9** coachwhip
mythical ~: **6** dragon
New Guinea: **6** taipan
republic: **5** state **6** nation **9** democracy *see also* country
__ republic: **6** banana
__ Republic: **5** Czech, Fifth, First, Khmer, Third **6** Fourth, Plato's, Second, Slovak, Weimar **7** People's
Republican: **3** GOP **5** party, river
forerunner: **4** Whig
Party birthplace: **3** Wis. **4** Wisc. **5** Ripon **9** Wisconsin
River locale: **6** Kansas **8** Colorado, Nebraska
Republican, Mr.: Robert Taft
__ Republic of Egypt: **4** Arab
Republic, The author: **5** Plato
repudiate: **4** deny, drop, dump, shun, veto, void **5** annul, flout, spurn **6** abjure, bounce, cancel, disown, loathe, pass on, rebuff, recant, refuse, refute, reject, repeal, revoke **7** abandon, abolish, cast off, disavow, disdain, dismiss, exclude, forsake, gainsay, let go of, nullify, rescind, retract, reverse **8** disallow, disclaim, forswear, go back on, renounce, take back, turn down **9** blackball, blacklist, break with, cast aside, foreswear, proscribe **10** contradict, contravene, disbelieve, disinherit
repudiated: **7** cast off, outcast **8** forsaken
repudiation: **5** blame, spurn **6** denial **7** refusal **8** apostasy, negation **10** abdication
exclamation: **4** pfui, phoo **6** phooey
repugnance: **4** hate **5** odium **6** hatred, horror **7** disgust, dislike **8** aversion, distaste, loathing **9** antipathy, repulsion, revulsion **10** ill feeling, repellence
exclamation: **3** ack, ick, ugh **4** yuck **5** yecch
feel ~: **4** hate **5** abhor **6** detest, loathe **7** despise **8** execrate **9** abominate
repugnant: **4** base, evil, foul, icky, ugly, vile **5** nasty, seamy, yucky **6** horrid, odious **7** hateful, hideous, noisome **8** gruesome, inimical, unsavory **9** abhorrent, invidious, loathsome, obnoxious, offensive, repellant, repellent, repulsive, revolting **10** abominable, detestable, disgusting
repulse: **4** defy, rout, snub **5** parry, repel, spurn **6** defeat, offend, rebuff, rebuke, refuse, reject, revolt, sicken, thwart **7** disgust, fend off, hold off, refusal, turn off, ward off **8** alienate, drive off, fight off, hold back, nauseate, push away, stave off, turn away, turn back **9** drive back, force back, hold at bay, rejection
repulsion: **5** odium **6** hatred **7** disgust, refusal **8** aversion, distaste, loathing **9** antipathy, revulsion **10** abhorrence, repellence, repugnance
Repulsion (1965 film)
cast: Catherine Deneuve, John Fraser, Ian Hendry
director: Roman Polanski
repulsive: **4** foul, icky, ugly, vile **5** nasty, slimy **6** creepy, odious, rancid **7** hateful, hideous, noisome, squalid **8** shocking, terrible **9** abhorrent, atrocious, execrable, loathsome, offensive, repellent, repugnant, revolting, unsightly **10** abominable, detestable, disgusting, forbidding, off-putting, unpleasant
measure of ~ force: **3** ESU
repurchase: **6** redeem **7** buy back, get back, reclaim **8** retrieve
reputability: **6** ethics, virtue **7** honesty, probity **9** integrity, rectitude **10** trustiness
reputable: **4** fine, good, nice, okay **5** great, legit, moral, noble, sound, tried **6** honest, proper, savory, worthy **7** ethical, upright **8** all right, esteemed, laudable, pleasant, pleasing, reliable, splendid, superior **9** admirable, agreeable, estimable, excellent, honorable, well-known, wonderful **10** acceptable, beneficial, creditable, dependable
reputation: **4** fame, name, odor **5** glory, state **6** credit, esteem, regard, renown, report **7** stature **8** eminence, good name, position, prestige, standing **9** celebrity, character, condition, influence, notoriety **10** importance, prominence
harm a ~: **5** smear

repute: 4 fame, name, odor 5 éclat, value 6 credit, esteem, regard, renown, report 7 quality 8 eminence, good name, prestige, standing 9 celebrity, character
  high ~: 4 fame 5 glory 6 renown 7 acclaim 8 eminence, prestige 9 celebrity
  ill ~: 5 odium, shame 6 infamy 7 obloquy 8 disfavor, disgrace, dishonor, ignominy 9 disesteem, disrepute, notoriety 10 opprobrium
  of ill ~: 5 shady 7 crooked 8 infamous, shameful, unsavory 9 dishonest, notorious, unethical 10 inglorious, scandalous
reputed: 4 held, said 6 deemed 7 alleged, assumed, seeming, thought 8 believed, reckoned, regarded, reported, supposed 10 considered, ostensible
request: 3 ask, beg, bid, sue 4 call, plea, pray, seek, suit, urge 5 apply, hit up, lobby, offer, order, plead, query, touch 6 appeal, ask for, behest, demand, desire, hustle, invite, prayer, summon 7 beseech, bespeak, call for, enquire, enquiry, entreat, inquire, inquiry, propose, solicit 8 entreaty, petition, put in for, question 10 commercial, invitation, supplicate
  again: 5 reask
  polite ~: 4 may I 6 please
__ request: 4 upon
requiem: 4 Mass 5 dirge, elegy 6 lament
__ Requiem: 3 War 6 German
Requiem for a Heavyweight (1962 film)
  cast: Jackie Gleason, Anthony Quinn, Mickey Rooney
  director: Ralph Nelson
Requiem for a Nun author: William Faulkner
requiescence: 4 ease, rest 7 leisure
require: 3 ask, bid, put 4 bind, cost, lack, miss, need, take, tell, want, wish 5 crave, exact, force, order 6 adjure, compel, demand, desire, direct, enjoin, entail, expect, insist, oblige 7 command, involve, look for, provide, push for 8 call upon, instruct, obligate 9 constrain, prescribe, stipulate 10 depend upon, have use for, insist upon
required: 3 due, set 5 bound, major, vital 6 needed, urgent 7 binding, crucial, needful, pivotal, primary 8 impelled 9 called for, essential, important, mandatory, necessary 10 compulsory, imperative, obligatory, prescribed
  beyond what's ~: 4 more 5 extra 8 optional 10 additional
  is ~ to: 4 must 5 has to
  reading: 4 text 8 syllabus, textbook
requirement: 4 must, need, want 5 state, terms 6 demand 7 dictate, proviso, urgency 8 exigence, exigency 9 condition, essential, extremity, necessity, provision 10 sine qua non
  in Latin: 10 sine qua non
requirements: 5 terms 7 strings 10 conditions, provisions
  meet ~: 2 do 4 pass, suit 5 serve 7 fulfill, qualify, satisfy, suffice
requisite: 3 due 4 must, need 5 terms, vital 6 demand 7 binding, needful, proviso 8 adequate, exigence, exigency, integral 9 condition, essential, extremity, mandatory, necessary, necessity, provision, right-hand 10 compulsory, imperative, obligatory, prescribed, sine qua non
requisition: 3 rob 5 claim, exact, order, seize 6 ask for, demand 7 request, require, solicit 8 apply for, put in for
requital: 6 amends 7 payment, redress, revenge 9 vengeance
requite: 3 pay 5 repay, right 6 avenge, recoup, reward 7 get even, revenge, satisfy 9 do justice, reimburse, retaliate 10 compensate, make amends, recompense
requited: 6 mutual, shared 8 conjoint, returned 9 bilateral 10 reciprocal
reroute: 6 detour, divert 8 redirect 9 sidetrack
rerun: 6 encore, repeat 9 reshowing
res __: 6 gestae 7 alienae, publica
res __ loquitur: 4 ipsa
__-res: 3 low
resale __: 5 value
__ Resartus: 6 Sartor
resay: 4 echo 6 parrot, repeat 7 iterate, restate 9 reiterate
__ Res. Bd.: 3 Fed.
reschedule: 5 defer, table 6 put off 8 postpone
rescind: 4 lift, void 5 annul, quash, scrub 6 cancel, negate, recall, recant, repeal, revoke 7 abolish, nullify, retract, reverse 8 abrogate, override, overrule, overturn, set aside 9 backpedal, repudiate 10 invalidate
rescission: 6 recall 9 abolition, annulment
rescue: 3 aid 4 free, save 6 ransom, redeem, snatch, spring 7 bailout, deliver, freedom, heroics, heroism, protect, reclaim, recover, release, restore, salvage, set free, unloose 8 delivery, liberate, preserve, retrieve 9 extricate, recapture, safeguard, salvation
  vehicle: 6 copter 8 aircraft 9 ambulance 10 helicopter
rescued: 6 untied 9 liberated
Rescue Me (song) artist: Fontella Bass, Madonna
Rescue 911 (CBS) host: William Shatner
rescuer: 4 hero 6 savior 7 heroine, saviour 9 liberator
  ocean ~: 4 USCG 10 Coast Guard
rescues, like some: 6 air-sea
research: 5 delve, dig up, probe, quest, study 6 look up, survey 7 enquiry, explore, inquiry, legwork, science 8 analysis, findings, learning, look into, read up on, scrutiny 10 groundwork, literature
  aid: 5 index
  do ~: 3 dig 4 seek 5 crack, delve, probe, study
  funds: 5 grant 9 endowment 10 fellowship
  govt. ~ sponsor: 3 NSF
  paper: 6 thesis 8 treatise 9 monograph
  place: 3 lab
  project: 5 probe 6 thesis
  subject: 6 lab rat
research __: 4 park 7 library
__ research: 6 market
resect: 6 excise
resection: 8 excision
reseda: 5 green 7 grayish
  relative: 3 pea 4 cyan, jade, sage 5 beryl, breen, olive, virid 6 myrtle 7 avocado, celadon, emerald, verdant 9 pistachio, turquoise 10 aquamarine, chartreuse
resemblance: 7 analogy, kinship 8 affinity, likeness, parallel, sameness 9 closeness
resemble: 4 look, seem 5 match, mimic, rival 6 be like, mirror 7 pass for, smack of 8 look like, parallel, seem like, simulate 9 come close, take after 10 appear like, correspond
resembling: 3 à la 4 like 6 akin to 7 similar 8 parallel 9 analogous
  combining form: 4 para- 5 quasi-
  suffix: 3 -ine 4 -eous
resent: 4 mind 7 dislike 8 object to
resentful: 3 hot, mad 4 hurt, ired, sore 5 angry, cross, huffy, irate, irked, livid, riled, wroth 6 bitter, fuming, ireful, miffed, peeved, piqued, raging, raving, red-hot 7 angered, annoyed, enraged, envious, furious, hostile, jealous, ranting, teed off 8 choleric, incensed, inflamed, maddened, outraged, virulent, wrathful 9 indignant, irritable, irritated, jaundiced, malicious, rancorous, splenetic, ticked off 10 aggravated, freaked out, frustrated, infuriated, vindictive
resentment: 3 ire 4 fury, hate, huff, hurt, rage 5 anger, pique, spite, venom, wrath 6 animus, choler, grudge, malice, rancor, temper 7 dudgeon, ill will, offense, outrage, umbrage 8 acrimony, friction, vexation 9 animosity, annoyance, grievance, hostility, nastiness, surliness 10 sour grapes, unkindness
  cause ~: 3 vex 4 miff, roil 5 anger, annoy, peeve, pique, upset 6 nettle, offend, put out 7 provoke 8 irritate 9 displease
  show ~: 6 bridle 7 bristle
reservation: 5 doubt, order, place, qualm, query, terms 7 booking, enclave, proviso, scruple, strings 8 preserve 9 condition, hesitancy, misgiving, provision, territory 10 settlement
  make a ~: 4 book
  without ~: 5 fully 6 wholly 7 totally, utterly 8 entirely 10 absolutely, completely, thoroughly
reservations, with: 8 grudging
reserve: 3 own 4 book, fund, hold, mine, park, save, stow, take 5 cache, extra, hoard, lay up, order, put by, spare, stash, stock, store 6 assets, devote, engage, retain, secure, supply 7 bespeak, capital, caution, charter, earmark, lay away, modesty, nest egg, put away, rope off, savings, shyness, silence, store up 8 backbone, calmness, coldness, contract, distance, gold mine, hold back, keep back, maintain, schedule, set apart, set aside, stow away, withhold 9 aloofness, formality, insurance, inventory, quietness, reservoir, resources, restraint, reticence, sanctuary, secondary, stockpile, timidness 10 constraint, diffidence, prearrange, substitute
  financial ~: 6 buffer 7 cushion
  in ~: 5 apart, aside, extra, on ice, on tap, spare 8 held back, kept back, put aside, set aside 9 held aside, kept aside
  keep in ~: 5 put by, store 7 put away 8 put aside
  without ~: 6 openly, wholly 7 frankly, plainly, readily, totally 8 candidly, directly, entirely, honestly, straight 9 all the way, to the hilt 10 completely, point-blank
reserve __: 4 bank 5 price 6 clause 7 officer
__ reserve: 4 gold 5 legal 6 forest
__ Reserve Bank: 7 Federal
reserved: 3 coy, icy, shy 4 cold, cool, kept, mild, prim 5 aloof, close, quiet, sober, staid, taken 6 booked, demure, formal, humble, modest, placid, remote, sedate, serene, silent, steady 7 bashful, claimed, distant, engaged, limited, private, recluse 8 cautious, composed, detached, laid away, moderate, retained, reticent, retiring, set apart, set aside, solitary, specific, taciturn 9 collected, diffident, reclusive, secretive, spoken for, unbending, withdrawn 10 antisocial, insociable, restricted, soft-spoken, unagitated, unamicable, unassuming, uneffusive, unsociable
  in a ~ manner: 5 shyly
reserves: 5 means 6 assets 7 backlog, savings 9 resources
reservoir: 4 fund, lake, pond, pool, tank, tarn, well 5 basin, lough, stock, store 6 source, spring, supply 7 backlog, cistern 8 fountain 9 container, inventory, stockpile 10 receptacle, repository
  filler: 4 rain 5 water
Reservoir Dogs (1992 film)
  cast: Harvey Keitel, Michael Madsen, Tim Roth
  director: Quentin Tarantino
reset: 5 adapt, align, fix up 6 adjust, modify 7 balance 8 fine-tune, modulate, regulate 9 calibrate
resettle: 4 move 8 emigrate, relocate 9 immigrate 10 transplant
resettling: 6 exodus 10 emigration, relocation
resew: 4 darn, mend 5 alter, patch 6 repair
res gestae: 4 acts 5 deeds 8 exploits
resh: 6 Hebrew, letter
  predecessor: 4 koph, qoph
  successor: 3 sin
reshape: 5 alter 6 change, modify 8 make over 9 customize, transform
reshaping: 6 change 8 revision 10 adjustment, alteration
reshowing: 5 rerun 6 repeat 7 reprise
reside: 3 lie 4 bide, live, nest, rest, stay 5 abide, dwell, exist, lodge, squat 6 belong, billet, inhere, locate, occupy, remain, settle, tenant 7 inhabit, sojourn
  in: 6 occupy 7 inhabit 8 populate
residence: 4 co-op, digs, dorm, flat, hall, home, roof, seat 5 abode, condo, dacha, house, lease, manor, place, villa 6 datcha, estate, palace, tenure 7 address, domicil, embassy, habitat, housing, lodging, mansion, sojourn 8 domicile, dwelling, fireside, location, lodgment, quarters 9 apartment, dormitory, occupancy, townhouse 10 habitation, occupation, pied-à-terre, settlement
  afterthought: 4 wing 5 add-on
  change ~: 4 move 6 uproot 7 migrate 8 relocate
  in one's ~: 4 home 6 at home
  stately ~: 5 manor, villa 6 castle, estate, palace 7 chateau
  tumbledown ~: 3 hut 5 shack 6 lean-to, shanty
  see also home
Residence Inn: 5 motel
  alternative: 7 Days Inn 9 Ramada Inn 10 Comfort Inn, Econo Lodge, Hampton Inn, Holiday Inn, Quality Inn, Red Roof Inn, Travelodge 11 Best Western
resident: 5 liver, local, voter 6 inmate, intern, lodger, native, tenant 7 citizen, denizen, dweller, interne 8 habitant, occupant, squatter, urbanite 9 indweller 10 inhabitant
  a ~ of: 4 from
  big house ~: 3 con 5 crook, lifer 7 convict 8 criminal, jailbird, prison-

er, yardbird **10** lawbreaker
future ~: **6** intern **7** interne
kennel ~: **3** dog, pet **5** doggy, whelp **6** canine
nearby ~: **8** neighbor
suffix: **3** -ese, -ite, -ote
temporary ~: **6** lodger, renter, roomer, tenant **7** boarder
resident __: **5** alien
residential area: **5** exurb **6** suburb
residents: **4** folk **6** people **8** populace **9** citizenry, community **10** population
resider: **5** liver **6** native **7** citizen, denizen, dweller **8** habitant, occupant **10** inhabitant
residual: **3** net **4** left **5** extra **6** unused **7** balance, surplus **8** enduring, leftover **9** aftermath, lingering, remaining, vestigial **10** continuing, unconsumed
residual __: **3** oil **5** power **6** stress
residue: **3** end **4** dreg, gunk, heel, orts, rest, rmdr., scum, silt, slag **5** dregs, dross, extra, trash **6** cinder, excess, refuse, scraps, sewage **7** balance, garbage, grounds, parings, remains, remnant, surplus **8** leavings, leftover, sediment, sewerage, shavings **9** leftovers, remainder, scourings, sweepings
grate ~: **3** ash **5** ember
greasy ~: **4** ooze **5** grime, slime
remove ~: **4** sift
volcano ~: **5** ember **6** cinder
residuum: **4** orts, slag **5** dregs, dross **6** scraps **7** remnant **8** leavings, leftover, sediment **9** leftovers, remainder, sweepings
resign: **4** quit **5** demit, leave, waive, yield **6** bow out, retire, secede, vacate **7** abandon, bail out, drop out, sign off, walk out **8** abdicate, hand over, hang it up, renounce, step down **9** reconcile, surrender, terminate **10** give notice, relinquish, stand aside
force to ~: **7** relieve
oneself: **3** bow **4** bend, fold **5** adapt, defer **6** accept, adjust, buckle, comply, give in, submit **7** truckle **9** acquiesce, get used to, make peace, reconcile, surrender **10** capitulate, come around
oneself to: **5** allow **6** permit, suffer **7** condone **8** stand for, tolerate
resignation: **6** notice **8** docility, meekness, patience, quitting, stoicism **9** departure, endurance, fortitude, passivity **10** abdication, equanimity, retirement, withdrawal
resigned: **4** calm, meek **5** stoic **6** docile, pliant **7** adapted, passive, patient, stoical, subdued **8** amenable, biddable, obedient, yielding **9** agreeable, compliant, peaceable, tractable **10** reconciled, submissive
resile: **6** recoil
resilience: **4** give, snap, tone **5** sinew **6** bounce, spring **7** stamina **9** tolerance
resilient: **5** hardy, tough **6** bouncy, limber, lissom, sinewy, spongy, strong, supple **7** buoyant, elastic, lissome, plastic, pliable, rubbery, springy **8** flexible, stretchy, yielding **9** adaptable, expansive **10** rebounding
be ~: **4** give **10** bounce back
resin: **3** gum, lac **4** glue **5** alkyd, amber, anime, copal, epoxy, myrrh, pitch **6** Dammar, guaiac, Lucite, mastic **7** shellac **8** shellack
component: **6** indene
fossil ~: **5** amber, copal
fragrant ~: **4** tolu **5** elemi **6** balsam
gum ~: **4** kino **5** myrrh **6** copalm
varnish ~: **5** anime, copal, damar **6** dammar
resin __: **4** duct **5** canal
__ resin: **3** ABS, gum **4** tolu **5** alkyd, allyl, amino, epoxy, kauri, vinyl **7** acaroid, acrylic, styrene
resist: **4** balk, buck, defy, stay, stem **5** baulk, demur, fight, flout, forgo, rebel, repel **6** assail, battle, bear up, combat, endure, forego, hinder, ignore, mutiny, oppose, rebuff, refuse, revolt, strike, suffer, thwart **7** abstain, contend, counter, dispute, forbear, hit back, hold out, protest, refrain, weather **8** confront, keep from, maintain, turn down **9** disregard, fight back, frustrate, persevere, stand up to, stonewall, withstand **10** antagonize, contravene, go on strike, leave alone, strike back
resistance: **5** fight, stand **6** battle, combat, mutiny, rebuff **7** defense, dissent, refusal **8** defiance, fighting, friction, struggle, traction **9** endurance, tolerance **10** antagonism
air ~: **4** drag
of ~: **5** ohmic
symbol: **5** omega
unit: **3** ohm **5** abohm
__ resistance: **4** fire **5** anode, ohmic, plate, sales **7** lateral, natural
résistance, pièce de: **9** specialty
resistant: **5** stiff, tough **6** immune, stable **7** defiant **8** indocile **9** unwilling **10** impervious
combining form: **5** -proof
make ~: **8** immunize **9** stabilize
__-resistant: **4** fire **5** child, shock, water **6** crease, tamper **7** weather
resister: **5** rebel **8** frondeur, renegade **9** insurgent
__ resister: **7** passive
resistive: **5** balky **7** adverse, cynical **8** contrary, negative **9** defensive
Resnais: **5** Alain
resolute: **3** set **4** bent, bold, fast, firm, game, grim, hard, true **5** brave, fixed, gutsy, loyal, nervy, rigid, set on, stern, stout, tough **6** all-out, ardent, awless, daring, dogged, gritty, heroic, intent, plucky, severe, spunky, stable, steady, steely, strong, sturdy **7** adamant, aweless, dead-set, decided, defiant, doughty, earnest, gallant, hard-set, patient, serious, staunch, valiant **8** constant, decisive, diligent, emphatic, faithful, fearless, forceful, hellbent, heroical, intrepid, sedulous, spirited, stalwart, stubborn, tireless, unafraid, unshaken, untiring, valorous **9** audacious, dauntless, dreadless, hard-nosed, immovable, impliable, iron-jawed, masterful, steadfast, strenuous, tenacious, unbending, undaunted, unfearful, unfearing **10** conclusive, courageous, deliberate, determined, foursquare, hard-bitten, inexorable, inflexible, iron-willed, persistent, purposeful, undeterred, unflagging, unshakable, unswerving, unwavering, unwearying, unyielding
be ~: **4** last **6** endure, hold on, insist, linger **7** persist **8** plug away **9** hang tough, keep going, persevere, stand firm **10** tough it out
resolutely: **7** sternly **8** for keeps, intently **9** fervently, intensely, seriously, zealously **10** vigorously
resoluteness: **4** grit **8** decision **9** stability
resolution: **3** act, end **4** guts, will **5** close, heart, nerve, pluck, spunk, valor **6** ending, energy, finale, finish, intent, mettle, motion, ruling, spirit, upshot, windup, wrap-up **7** finding, loyalty, measure, outcome, purpose, verdict **8** backbone, decision, firmness, judgment, proposal, strength, tenacity, terminus, volition **9** breakdown, constancy, endurance, fixedness, fortitude, gallantry, hardiness, intention, willpower **10** conclusion, confidence, conversion, denouement, moral fiber
weaken the ~ of: **5** daunt **6** unglue **7** unnerve **8** dispirit **10** demoralize, discourage, dishearten, intimidate
__ resolution: **5** joint **6** budget
__-resolution: **3** low **4** high
resolve: **2** do **3** end, fix **4** grit, rule, will **5** agree, steel, think **6** answer, decide, fathom, finish, intend, mettle, morale, pan out, reason, reform, settle, spirit, unfold **7** achieve, clear up, explain, impulse, iron out, mediate, propose, purpose, unravel, work out **8** conclude, decision, firmness, nail down, tenacity **9** determine, elucidate, intention, objective, puzzle out, reconcile, willpower **10** commitment, have in view
lacking ~: **4** weak **5** timid, wimpy **6** craven, scared, yellow **7** chicken, fearful, gutless **8** cowardly, recreant, timorous **9** dastardly, fraidy-cat, weak-kneed
resolved: **3** set **4** sure **5** clear **6** intent **7** assured, decided, serious **8** definite, hellbent, in the bag, positive **9** obstinate **10** conclusive, foursquare
be ~: **6** intend **9** persevere
resonance: **4** ring, tone, vibe **5** sound **9** vibration
resonant: **4** deep, full, loud, rich **6** in tune, mellow **7** booming, echoing, orotund, ringing, vibrant **9** melodious, throbbing **10** stentorian, thundering, thunderous
effect: **4** echo
not ~: **5** tinny
resonate: **4** peal, ring **5** sound, throb **7** reflect, vibrate
resort: **3** inn, spa, use **4** camp, hope, lido **5** apply, haven, hotel, lodge, motel, refer, shift **6** chance, course, employ, harbor, refuge **7** fat farm, hangout, harbour, lodging, measure, retreat, solicit, utilize **8** exercise, frequent, hideaway, recourse, resource **9** expedient, hot spring, make use of, sanctuary **10** expediency
accommodation: **5** cabin, condo, suite
activity: **4** golf **6** skiing, tennis **8** swimming
place: **4** isle
to: **6** invoke **7** utilize **10** fall back on
(to): **2** go **4** look, turn **5** refer, stoop
__ resort: **3** ski **4** last
resound: **4** boom, echo, gong, peal, ring, roar, roll, sing **5** clang **6** bellow, rumble **7** reflect, thunder, vibrate
resounding: **4** loud **5** boomy, forte, noisy **6** echoic **7** blaring, jarring, rackety, raucous, reboant **8** crashing, emphatic, piercing, plangent, sonorous, strident, turned up **9** big-voiced, clamorous, deafening **10** boisterous, stentorian, strepitous, uproarious, vociferant, vociferous
resource: **4** coal **5** asset, shift **6** refuge, resort **7** measure, mineral **8** recourse **9** expedient, ingenuity, petroleum, reference **10** capability, expediency, initiative, natural gas
natural ~: **3** oil, ore **4** coal **5** water **6** timber
precious ~: **4** time
shared ~: **4** pool
__ resource: **7** natural
resourceful: **4** able **5** ready, sharp, smart **6** active, adroit, artful, bright, clever, shifty, strong **7** capable **8** creative, dextrous, original, talented **9** dexterous, ingenious, inventive, versatile
resourcefulness: **7** ability **8** gumption **10** initiative
resources: **5** funds, kitty, lucre, means, money **6** assets, basics, budget, income, riches, wealth **7** backing, capital, nest egg, reserve, revenue, savings **8** bankroll, holdings, property, reserves **10** collateral, livelihood
financial ~: **5** means, purse **10** pocketbook
gather ~: **6** enlist, enroll, muster **7** procure, recruit, round up **8** mobilize
having the ~: **4** able
human ~: **5** staff **7** members, workers **9** employees, personnel, work force
pool ~: **5** unite **6** club up **9** cooperate **10** join forces
sans ~: **4** poor **5** broke, needy **8** beggarly, dirt poor, indigent **9** dead broke, destitute, penniless, penurious **10** down and out, down at heel, straitened
__ resources: **5** human
resp.: **3** ans.
respect: **3** awe **4** fear, heed, keep, mind, obey, sake **5** bow to, defer, facet, favor, honor, piety, point, spare, value **6** accept, admire, bend to, comply, detail, esteem, follow, fulfil, hallow, homage, regard, revere, uphold **7** abide by, agree to, dignity, fulfill, observe, pay heed, tribute, worship **8** adhere to, carry out, courtesy, listen to, look up to, venerate **9** conform to, consent to, deference, obeisance, recognize, reverence **10** admiration, appreciate, estimation, particular, self-esteem, set store by, toe the line, veneration
in any ~: **5** at all
in every ~: **4** to a T **6** to a tee, wholly **7** exactly
show ~: **3** bow **5** kneel **7** lionize
term of ~: **3** sir **4** abba, ma'am, miss, sire **5** madam
with ~ to: **4** in re **5** about, as for **6** toward **7** towards **8** relative **9** apropos of, as regards, regarding **10** concerning
with ~ to this: **5** in hoc
__-respect: **4** self
Respect (1967 song) artist: Aretha Franklin
respectability: **6** virtue **7** dignity **9** propriety
respectable: **4** done, fair, fine, good, nice, okay, so-so, tidy **5** clean, great, legit, moral, noble **6** decent, goodly, honest, modest, proper, savory, seemly, worthy **7** ethical, sizable, upright **8** all right, decorous, laudable, moderate, passable, pleasant, pleasing, sizeable, splendid, straight, suitable, superior, virtuous **9** admirable, agreeable, dignified, estimable, excellent, high-toned, honorable, reputable, tolerable, wholesome, wonderful **10** aboveboard, acceptable, beneficial, creditable
respected: **5** noted **9** dignified, estimable, prominent, venerable
one, maybe: **5** elder
Respect for Acting author: **5** Hagen
respectful: **4** good **5** civil **6** filial, humble, polite **7** courtly, duteous, dutiful **8** admiring, gracious, highbred, man-

nerly, obedient **9** attentive, courteous, regardful
address: **3** sir **4** abba, ma'am **5** madam
not ~: **4** flip, pert, rude **5** brash, fresh, nervy, sassy, saucy **6** brassy, brazen, cheeky, snippy **7** defiant, forward **8** flippant, impudent, insolent **9** intrusive, out-of-line, sarcastic, shameless **10** irreverent
respecting: **4** as to **7** valuing
respective: **3** own **4** each **6** proper **7** several **8** personal, relative, separate, singular **9** bilateral **10** individual, particular
respects: **7** devoirs, regards **9** greetings
in all ~: **5** fully, quite **6** wholly
pay ~ to: **6** salute
Respect Yourself (1987 song) artist: Bruce Willis
Respighi, Ottorino work: The Pines of Rome
respiration: **6** breath, eupnea **8** exhaling, inhaling **9** breathing **10** exhalation
combining form: **4** -pnea **5** -pnoea
respiratory: **9** breathing
organ: **4** gill, lung
passage: **6** airway
sound: **4** rale
woe: **6** asthma
respiratory __: **5** chain **6** system
respire: **4** sigh **6** exhale, inhale **7** breathe
respite: **3** gap, nap **4** lull, rest, stay **5** break, delay, letup, pause, R and R, truce **6** breath, easing, hiatus, recess, relief, repose **7** anodyne, leisure, time out **8** breather, downtime, furlough, reprieve, vacation **9** cessation, deferment, happy hour, interlude **10** moratorium, suspension
resplendence: **6** luster **8** radiance, radiancy **10** effulgence
resplendent: **4** rich **5** fancy, light, lucid, nitid, regal, royal, showy, vivid **6** bright, ornate, superb **7** beaming, blazing, flaming, glowing, lambent, radiant, shining, sublime **8** dazzling, gleaming, glorious, gorgeous, luminous, lustrous, splendid **9** brilliant, effulgent, refulgent, sparkling **10** glittering
respond: **3** act, nod, say **5** react, reply **6** answer, behave, retort **7** counter, get back **8** talk back **10** get in touch
ender: **3** ent
to: **5** act on **6** answer **7** confirm **9** write back
response: **3** lip **4** echo, sass **5** reply, vibes **6** action, answer, retort, ripost **7** defense, riposte **8** antiphon, back talk, comeback, feedback, kickback, knee jerk, reaction, rebuttal **9** reception, rejoinder, sensation, utterance, wisecrack **10** double take
fence-sitting ~: **7** perhaps **8** possibly **9** it could be, it might be
military ~: **3** aye **5** no sir **6** aye aye, yes sir **9** aye aye sir
negative ~: **3** nah, nay **4** nope
noncommittal ~: **7** perhaps **8** possibly, probably **9** it could be, it might be
roll-call ~: **3** aye, nay, yea, yes
time: **3** lag
uncertain ~: **4** shot, stab **5** hunch **6** notion, theory **7** feeling, opinion, surmise, venture **9** suspicion **10** conjecture, hypothesis, prediction, projection
unequivocal ~: **2** no **3** nah, naw, nay, nix, non **4** nein, nope, nyet, uh-uh **5** ixnay, never, no how, no way **6** no deal, nowise **7** not ever **8** at no time, forget it, negative, not at all **9** by no means, fat chance **10** count me out, impossible, not a chance, thumbs down
unsure ~: **5** guess, maybe **6** I guess **7** maybe so, perhaps
response __: **4** time
__ response: **4** bass **6** immune
responsibility: **3** job **4** beat, care, duty, load, onus, part, spot, task, work **5** blame, fault, guilt, place, power, trust **6** burden, charge, office, weight **7** concern, honesty, mission **8** contract, function, maturity, province **9** albatross, authority, liability **10** obligation
denial of ~: **7** refusal
duck ~: **5** evade **6** cop out, renege
relieve of ~: **2** ax **4** fire, oust **5** let go **6** lay off **7** dismiss, suspend **8** furlough **9** discharge
take ~: **5** own up **6** fess up **7** confess
responsible: **5** adult, loyal, right, sober, sound **6** bonded, guilty, honest, liable, mature, stable, steady, trusty **7** at fault, capable, obliged, pledged, to blame, willing **8** blamable, culpable, in charge, indebted, reliable, sensible **9** at the helm, blameable, competent, duty-bound, efficient, important, in control, incumbent, obligated, on the hook, qualified **10** chargeable
be ~ for: **3** own **4** lead **5** see to **7** sponsor **8** organize, shoulder
for: **6** behind
hold ~: **5** blame, thank **6** assign
not ~: **6** exempt **7** cleared **9** acquitted **10** exonerated, off the hook, vindicated
responsive: **3** yar **4** open, warm, yare **5** alive, awake, aware, quick, sharp **6** prompt, tender **7** pliable, psychic, vibrant **8** empathic, sentient **9** agreeable, conscious, emotional, observant, receptive, sensitive **10** empathetic, expressive, hospitable, interested, perceptive
rest: **3** gap, lay, lie, nap, nod, put, set, sit **4** calm, doze, ease, halt, idle, laze, lean, loaf, loll, lull, orts, prop, rail, rely, stay, stop, wait **5** break, hinge, letup, lie by, light, pause, peace, quiet, relax, roost, shelf, sleep, stand, truce **6** at ease, breath, cesura, depend, drowse, ease up, excess, lay off, lounge, others, recess, relief, repose, reside, settle, siesta, snooze, turn in, unwind **7** balance, caesura, holiday, leisure, liberty, lie down, overage, quietus, railing, recline, remains, remnant, residue, respite, sack out, silence, sit back, sit down, slumber, sojourn, support, surplus, take ten, time off **8** be seated, breather, calm down, calmness, downtime, interval, leavings, lie still, pedestal, pediment, quietude, recreate, reside in, stand for, take a nap, take five, vacation **9** cessation, do nothing, go to sleep, hang loose, hibernate, idle hours, interlude, leftovers, predicate, remainder, stillness **10** fall asleep, forty winks, inactivity, quiescence, recreation, relaxation, standstill, stretch out, take a break, take it easy
against: **6** lean on
area: **6** lounge
at ~: **4** idle **5** still **6** halted **7** napping **8** inactive, in repose, reposing, unmoving **9** not moving, quiescent, reclining **10** motionless, stationary
atop: **5** lie on
came to ~: **3** lit **4** alit
come to ~: **4** land **5** light, lodge **6** alight, settle
day of ~: **3** Sab. **7** Sabbath **8** vacation
give one's feet a ~: **5** relax
name meaning ~: **4** Noah
next to: **4** abut **5** touch **6** adjoin, border
(on): **4** base, hang, lean, rely **5** hinge **6** depend
put one's mind to ~: **4** buoy **5** allay, cheer **7** cheer up, comfort, console, hearten, satisfy **8** inspirit, reassure
room: **2** WC **3** lav **4** bath, john **6** lounge **7** latrine **8** lavatory
room sign: **5** in use
starter: **3** arm **4** back, foot, head
stop: **3** inn **5** hotel, lodge, motel **6** hostel **7** auberge, lodging **8** hostelry **9** roadhouse **10** motor court
the ~: **6** others
rest __: **4** area, mass, room, stop **6** energy
__ rest: **3** bed **4** chin, half **5** day of, knife, lance, lay to, put to, whole **6** eighth, parade **7** quarter
restart: **5** renew **6** pick up, reopen, resume **8** continue, return to **10** recommence
restate: **5** resay **6** repeat **7** iterate **9** reiterate **10** paraphrase
restaurant: **3** bar, inn **4** café, dive **5** diner, grill, joint **6** bistro, eatery, in spot, saloon **7** canteen, drive-in **8** pizzeria, teahouse **9** brasserie, cafeteria, chophouse, hash house, lunchroom, nightclub **10** steakhouse
area: **9** food court
bill: **3** tab **5** check
chain: **3** KFC **4** IHOP **6** Wendy's **8** Pizza Hut **9** Applebee's, McDonald's **10** Burger King, TGI Friday's
choice: **5** order
employee: **4** chef, cook **5** valet **6** busboy, waiter **7** cashier, maître d' **10** dishwasher
forgo the ~: **5** eat in
freebie: **4** roll, salt **5** bread, sugar, water **6** catsup, pepper
furnishing: **5** table **10** tablecloth
go to a ~: **4** dine **6** eat out
group: **5** party
list: **4** menu **5** carte **10** bill of fare
offering: **5** lunch **6** brunch, buffet, dinner, supper **8** salad bar **9** breakfast
order: **4** to go
patron: **5** diner, eater, guest
requirement, maybe: **3** tie **5** shirt **6** jacket
work in a ~: **3** bus
__ Restaurant: **6** Alice's
rested: **5** fresh **7** revived
__-rested: **4** well
restful: **4** calm, cosy, cozy, snug **5** cozey, cozie, quiet **6** placid, serene **7** easeful, pacific **8** peaceful, tranquil **9** leisurely, peaceable
restfulness: **4** calm **6** repose **7** comfort **8** calmness
resting: **4** idle **5** in bed **6** asleep, at ease **7** abeyant **8** lounging **9** incumbent, unengaged **10** relaxation, unemployed
combining form: **5** stato-
on: **4** atop, over **5** above **8** touching
place: **3** bed, inn **4** lair, seat **5** perch **6** settee
restitute: **5** renew **7** refresh, restore **9** refurbish **10** rejuvenate
restitution: **6** amends, rebate, refund, return **7** redress **9** expiation, indemnity, repayment **10** paying back
exact ~: **6** avenge
make ~: **5** atone, repay **6** render **7** redress **8** square up
restive: **4** edgy **5** antsy, balky, itchy, jumpy, onery, tense **6** ornery, uneasy, unruly **7** anxious, fidgety, fretful, froward, jittery, keyed up, nervous, radical, uptight **8** agitated, contrary, fluttery, fretsome, indocile, skittish, stubborn, troubled **9** concerned, excitable, ill at ease, impatient, obstinate, unsettled **10** high-strung
be ~: **4** fret **5** brood, worry
restiveness: **4** care **5** angst **6** dismay **7** anxiety, concern, fidgets **8** disquiet, distress
restless: **4** edgy **5** antsy, hyper, itchy, jumpy, nervy, tense **6** fitful, mobile, on edge, uneasy **7** anxious, fidgety, fretful, jittery, keyed up, nervous, on the go, uptight, wakeful, worried **8** agitated, feverish, fretsome, skittish, troubled **9** concerned, excitable, footloose, ill at ease, impatient, perturbed, strung out, turbulent, unsettled **10** highstrung
feeling: **3** yen **4** itch, urge **7** craving, longing **8** yearning **9** hankering
__ restless as a willow...: **4** I'm as
restlessness: **5** fever **6** nerves **7** anxiety, ferment, jitters, tension **8** disquiet, edginess, insomnia **9** agitation, antsiness, jumpiness **10** uneasiness
restock: **6** refill **7** refresh, replace **9** replenish
Reston: **4** city, town **5** James
locale: **8** Virginia
rest on one's __: **4** oars **7** laurels
restoration: **7** revival **8** comeback, recovery **9** salvation **10** renascence, resurgence
Restoration (1995 film)
cast: Robert Downey Jr., Sam Neill, David Thewlis
director: Michael Hoffman
restorative: **4** cure **5** tonic **6** potion, remedy **7** bracing, healthy **8** curative, pick-me-up, remedial **9** stimulant
restore: **3** fix **4** cure, heal, mend, undo **5** fix up, rally, rehab, renew, right **6** redeem, reform, refund, render, repair, rescue, return, revive, update **7** fortify, freshen, furbish, improve, patch up, put back, rebuild, recover, recruit, redress, refresh, replace, retouch, salvage, touch up, win back **8** give back, overhaul, reimpose, renovate, retrieve, revivify **9** bring back, modernize, refurbish, reimburse, reinstate, replenish, restitute **10** regenerate, rejuvenate, revitalize, strengthen
to health: **4** cure, heal **5** fix up, treat **6** doctor, remedy **7** patch up
restrain: **3** bar, dam, gag, pin, tie **4** bate, bind, curb, hold, jail, rein, rule, stem, stop, tame **5** chain, check, cramp, deter, hem in, leash, limit, sit on, tie up **6** arrest, bridle, dampen, detain, enjoin, fetter, forbid, govern, hamper, hinder, hogtie, impede, lock up, muzzle, pinion, pull in, rein in, slow up, stifle, subdue, temper, tether, thwart **7** confine, contain, control, curtail, harness, impound, inhibit, manacle, prevent, qualify, refrain, repress, smother, squelch, tie down, trammel **8** handcuff, handicap, hold back, imprison, moderate, obstruct, prohibit, restrict, slow down, straiten, suppress, tone down **9** constrain, crack down, hamstring, interdict **10** discourage, hold it down, keep a lid on, keep in line
restrained: **4** calm, cool, mild **5** muted,

quiet, sober **6** low-key, pent-up, silent **7** limited, refined, subdued, uptight **8** closed in, discreet, esthetic, hemmed in, moderate, on a leash, reined in, reticent, retiring, tasteful **9** classical, continent, temperate, unextreme, withdrawn **10** abstemious, reasonable, unagitated, unspeaking
restraining __: **5** order
restraint: **3** ban, bar **4** curb, rein, tabu, yoke **5** brake, check, irons, leash, limit, taboo, taste **6** arrest, bridle, chains, fetter, halter, tether **7** barrier, bondage, caution, control, economy, embargo, measure, reserve, squeeze, trammel **8** coercion, coolness, eschewal, patience **9** abatement, avoidance, captivity, detention, deterrent, endurance, hindrance **10** abstinence, classicism, compulsion, deterrence, discipline, government, impediment, imposition, inhibition, limitation, moderation, repression, self-denial, temperance
passive ~: **6** airbag
use ~: **6** go easy
without ~: **5** ad lib **6** at will, freely
__ restraint: **4** head **5** prior **7** passive
__-restraint: **4** self
restraint of __: **5** trade
restrict: **3** ban, tie **4** bind, curb, slow **5** bound, check, cramp, fence, hem in, limit, pen in, stint, tie up **6** arrest, define, fetter, forbid, ground, hamper, hang up, hobble, impede, intern, modify, narrow, ration, reduce, shut in, temper, tether **7** abridge, confine, contain, inhibit, pin down, prevent, qualify, trammel **8** handcuff, handicap, hold down, moderate, obstruct, prohibit, regulate, restrain, straiten **9** constrict, hamstring **10** abbreviate, come down on, keep a lid on, keep in line
restricted: **5** light, local, scant **6** closed, inside, narrow, pent-up, secret, single **7** insular, limited, private, special, topical **8** hemmed in, hush-hush, reined in, reserved, shielded, specific **9** confining, exclusive, nonpublic, qualified, technical **10** cloistered
not ~: **4** free, open **6** public **8** passable **9** unblocked **10** accessible, unreserved
restricted __: **4** area, code **5** class, stock
restriction: **4** curb, no-no, rule, tabu **5** limit, taboo **6** bounds, lock-in **7** control, embargo, proviso, trammel **8** obstacle **9** condition, fine print, provision, restraint **10** regulation
restrictive: **5** tight **6** narrow **7** cramped, opposed **8** limiting, opposing **9** confining
restyle: **5** adapt, alter **6** adjust, change, modify **8** innovate **9** modernize, transform
result: **3** end **4** stem **5** arise, end up, ensue, fruit, occur, prove, score, total **6** accrue, answer, appear, come of, derive, effect, emerge, finish, follow, go well, happen, pan out, payoff, sequel, upshot **7** develop, fallout, outcome, proceed, product, succeed, turn out, work out **8** backwash, decision, flow from, fruition, offshoot, solution **9** aftermath, arise from, by-product, come about, culminate, eventuate, grow out of, outgrowth, terminate, transpire **10** completion, conclusion, denouement, impression, spring from
as a ~: **4** ergo **5** hence **6** hereby **7** through **9** therefore
as a ~ of: **5** due to **7** because, owing to
expected ~: **3** par **4** mean, norm **7** average **8** standard **9** benchmark, yardstick
from: **6** attend **9** originate
(from): **5** arise, issue
in: **5** beget, bring, cause **6** lead to, tend to **7** produce, redound
without ~: **4** vain **6** in vain **7** inutile, useless **8** bootless **9** for naught, pointless, to no avail, worthless **10** unavailing
resultant: **7** ensuing **9** derivable, secondary **10** consequent
resulting: **8** eventual **9** following **10** consequent, subsequent
resultingly: **4** ergo, thus **5** hence **9** therefore
results: **5** fruit **6** profit, return, reward **7** benefit, outcome, product
resume: **4** go on **5** renew **6** keep on, pick up, reopen, revert, take up **7** carry on, proceed, recover, restart **8** continue, go on with, return to **10** recommence
résumé: **3** bio **4** vita **6** digest, précis, record, report, review **7** outline, rundown, summary **8** abstract, synopsis
accent: **5** acute
detail: **4** jobs **7** address, hobbies **9** reference **10** experience
resupine: **9** recumbent
resurface: **3** tar **4** pave
resurgence: **5** rally **7** revival **8** comeback
resurgent: **5** redux
resurgently: **4** anew
resurrect: **5** rally **6** araise **9** bring back
resurrection __: **4** fern, gate **5** plant
Resurrection (1980 film)
cast: Ellen Burstyn, Richard Farnsworth, Sam Shepard
director: Daniel Petrie
__ Resurrection: **5** Alien
Resurrection Mass time: **6** Easter
Resurrection of Zachary Wheeler, The (1971 film)
cast: James Daly, Angie Dickinson, Bradford Dillman
Resurrection Symphony composer: **6** Mahler
resuscitate: **4** wake **5** rally **6** revive **7** refresh
Reta: **4** Shaw
retail: **4** sell, vend **6** handle, market
big ~ season: **4** Xmas
business: **4** mart, shop **5** store **8** boutique
grouping: **4** line
ID: **3** SKU
retailer: **6** dealer, grocer, outlet, seller, trader **8** merchant **10** franchisee
concern: **4** sale **5** sales
retain: **3** own **4** have, hire, hold, keep, save **5** amass, cache, hoard, put by, store **6** absorb, clutch, employ, engage, garner, recall, save up, sign on, sign up, take on **7** cling to, husband, lay away, possess, put away, reserve **8** hang on to, hold on to, maintain, memorize, preserve, put aside, remember, withhold **9** recollect **10** accumulate
don't ~: **4** cede, fire **5** let go, loose, yield **6** lay off **7** abandon, dismiss, manumit, release, set free **8** cut loose **9** discharge, surrender
retainer: **3** fee **4** dike, wall **6** flunky **7** advance, deposit, flunkey, servant **8** follower **9** attendant
retainers: **5** staff, suite, train **6** escort **7** company, retinue **9** entourage, following, hangers-on **10** attendants
retaining __: **4** wall
retake: **7** get back, recover
retaliate: **3** pay **5** repay, reply, wreak **6** answer, return **7** counter, get even, hit back, pay back **9** get back at, pay in kind **10** strike back
for: **6** avenge **7** requite
retaliation: **6** rancor **7** revenge **8** reprisal **9** vengeance **10** punishment
bit of ~: **3** tit
retaliatory: **8** punitive, vengeful **10** vindictive
retard: **3** lag **4** balk, clog, slow **5** baulk, block, brake, check, delay, stall **6** arrest, baffle, dampen, detain, hamper, hang up, hinder, hold up, impede, put off, slow up **7** draw out, inhibit, prevent, prolong, set back, slacken, suspend **8** obstruct, postpone, slow down **10** decelerate
__-retardant: **4** fire **5** flame
rete: **4** mesh **6** plexus
retell: **5** quote **6** recite, repeat **7** iterate **9** reiterate
retem: **5** shrub
retention: **6** memory **9** detention, occupancy **10** absorption
retentive: **9** absorbent, tenacious
retentiveness: **6** memory, recall
retest, require a: **4** fail **5** flunk
reticence: **7** modesty, reserve, secrecy, silence **10** inhibition
reticent: **3** coy, shy **4** mute **5** aloof, close, quiet **6** modest, silent **7** bashful, distant **8** reserved, retiring, taciturn **9** diffident, reclusive, secretive, withdrawn **10** restrained, uneffusive
not ~: **4** bold **5** brash, gutsy, nervy **6** brassy, brazen, daring, heroic **7** defiant, doughty, forward, valiant **8** fearless, intrepid, resolute **9** audacious, dauntless, undaunted **10** courageous
reticulation: **3** web **7** lattice, network
reticule: **3** bag **5** pouch, purse **7** handbag **10** pocketbook
retina
cell: **3** rod **4** cone
neighbor: **4** lens
Retinta: **3** cow **4** bull **6** bovine, cattle
retinue: **4** crew **5** court, suite, train **6** escort **7** company, cortege, escorts **9** entourage, hangers-on, retainers **10** attendants
retire: **4** exit, quit **5** leave, sleep **6** decamp, depart, go away, put out, recede, resign, secede, turn in **7** give way, go to bed, pull out, retreat, sack out, saw logs, seclude, take off **8** abdicate, draw back, fall back, pull back, run along, withdraw **9** antiquate, go to sleep, hit the hay, rusticate **10** call it a day, give ground, hit the sack
signal to ~: **4** Taps **9** lights out
retired: **4** abed **5** in bed, quiet **6** lonely **9** withdrawn
retiree: **3** snr. **6** senior
benefits org.: **3** SSA
kitty: **3** IRA **7** nest egg, pension
residence: **5** condo
retirement: **4** exit **7** leisure, privacy **9** departure, seclusion **10** abdication
community caveat: **6** no kids
plan: **3** IRA **5** Keogh **7** pension, Roth IRA **8** Roth plan
retiring: **3** coy, shy **4** meek **5** aloof, lowly, quiet, timid **6** demure, humble, modest **7** bashful, distant, recluse **8** outgoing, reserved, reticent, sheepish, timorous **9** diffident, reclusive, shrinking, withdrawn **10** abdication, restrained, unassuming, uneffusive, unsociable
hardly ~: **4** bold **5** brash, nervy, pushy **7** forward **9** assertive, insistent, obtrusive **10** aggressive, meddlesome
retort: **3** ans., say **4** quip, snap **5** rebut, reply, sally **6** answer, ripost **7** alembic, counter, defense, respond, riposte **8** comeback, crucible, fire back, reaction, rebuttal, repartee, response **9** rejoinder, witticism
kid's ~: **4** is so **5** can so, did so, is too
retouch: **3** fix **4** edit, mend **5** emend, fix up, patch **6** doctor, modify, polish, repair, revise **7** brush up, enhance, improve, patch up, restore **9** refurbish
retrace steps: **6** return **8** turn back
retract: **4** turn **5** unsay **6** abjure, cancel, draw in, negate, recall, recant, recede, reel in, repeal, revoke, secede **7** call off, disavow, rescind, reverse, rule out, sheathe **8** abrogate, disclaim, forswear, go back on, pull back, renege on, renounce, take back, withdraw **9** back-pedal, foreswear, repudiate
as words: **5** unsay **6** recant
retraction: **6** denial, recall **9** annulment **10** withdrawal
retread: **4** tire **5** patch, renew **6** lubber, repair **8** overhaul **9** refurbish **10** rejuvenate
retreading, in need of: **4** bald
retreat: **3** den, ebb **4** aery, exit, eyry, flee, lair, nest, nook, rout **5** aerie, cover, elude, eyrie, haunt, haven, leave, lodge, oasis **6** asylum, beat it, corner, decamp, depart, escape, flight, go back, harbor, opt out, recede, recess, refuge, resort, retire, return, secede, shrink, vacate **7** back off, convent, harbour, privacy, pull out, regress, ride off, shelter **8** cloister, downturn, draw back, fall back, hideaway, log cabin, pull back, reaction, run for it, solitude, turn tail, withdraw **9** back-pedal, backtrack, departure, disappear, disengage, hermitage, safe house, safe place, sanctuary, seclusion, sequester **10** evacuation, give ground, ivory tower, withdrawal
beat a hasty ~: **3** hie, rip, run **5** hurry, lam it **7** dash off
hasty ~: **3** lam **6** escape, flight **7** getaway
__ retreat: **5** beat a
retrench: **6** reduce **7** cut down **8** conserve **9** economize **10** cut corners
retribution: **6** payoff, refund, reward **7** justice, penalty, penance, redress, revenge **8** reprisal **9** reckoning, repayment, vengeance **10** punishment, recompense
bit of ~: **3** tit
divine ~: **5** wrath
exact ~: **5** repay **6** avenge **7** get even, hit back, pay back **9** retaliate **10** strike back
goddess of ~: **3** Ate
matter for ~: **3** tat
retributive: **5** penal **8** spiteful, vengeful **10** corrective, vindictive
retrieve: **3** get **5** fetch, field, go get **6** obtain, recoup, redeem, regain, repair, rescue **7** get back, reclaim, recover, recruit, restore, salvage, win back **9** reacquire, recapture, repossess **10** recompense
retriever: **3** dog, lab **5** canid **6** canine
__ retriever: **6** golden
retrocede: **3** die, ebb **4** ease, fade, fall, wane **5** let up **6** ease up, lessen, reflux **7** decline, die down, dwindle, ease off, slacken, subside, tail off **8** decrease, diminish, fade away, fall away, fall back, moderate, slack off, taper off, withdraw

retrograde: 4 sink 5 lapse 6 recede 7 decline 8 backward 10 degenerate
retrogress: 4 sink, slip 5 decay, slide 6 recede, revert, worsen 7 relapse 9 aggravate 10 degenerate, exacerbate, recidivate
retrogression: 5 lapse 7 relapse 8 apostasy, reaction 9 backslide 10 withdrawal
retrospect: 6 memory, recall 9 hindsight
retry: 6 hang in, hold on, keep on 7 persist, press on 8 continue, keep at it, plug away 9 hang tough, persevere
retsina: 4 wine
origin: 6 Cyprus, Greece
Rettig: 5 Tommy
Retton, Mary Lou: 7 gymnast
return: 3 net 4 earn, gain, wage 5 bring, fruit, lapse, price, recur, remit, repay, reply, wages, yield 6 bestow, come to, go back, income, profit, rebate, recede, recoil, refund, render, repeat, reseat, revert, reward 7 accrual, benefit, bring in, pay back, produce, put back, rebound, redress, reenter, reentry, reflect, relapse, replace, restore, results, retreat, revenue, revisit 8 comeback, dividend, earnings, give back, hand back, interest, move back, proceeds, reaction, reappear, receipts, roll back, send back, take back 9 carry back, come again, indemnify, reimburse, reinstate, rejoinder, retaliate 10 bounce back, circle back, double back, homecoming, recompense, recurrence
get in ~: 4 earn, gain, reap 5 clear 6 derive, garner, profit, secure, take in 7 bring in, collect, harvest, receive 8 gather in
give in ~: 3 pay 6 avenge, reward 7 get even, requite 9 retaliate
investment ~: 5 yield 6 income, profit 7 revenue 8 earnings, proceeds
involuntary ~: 4 repo
never to ~: 4 gone 7 extinct 8 departed, vanished
the favor: 7 pay back, requite
to: 6 resume, revert 7 iterate, regress, restart 8 continue, go on with
to form: 4 heal, mend 5 rally 7 get well, rebound, recover 8 snap back 9 get better 10 bounce back, come around, convalesce, recuperate, rejuvenate, spring back
to office: 6 recall 7 reelect 9 bring back, reinstate
return __: 4 bend, trip 6 ticket 7 receipt
__ return: 3 sea, tax 5 joint 6 I shall 7 current
Return __ Jedi: 5 of the
Return __ Native, The: 5 of the
return-address word: 4 from
returned: 8 requited
Return From the Ashes (1965 film)
cast: Samantha Eggar, Maximilian Schell, Ingrid Thulin
director: J. Lee Thompson
Return From Witch Mountain (1978 film)
cast: Bette Davis, Christopher Lee
Return of Buck Gavin, The author: Thomas Wolfe
Return of Frank James, The (1940 film)
cast: Jackie Cooper, Henry Fonda, Gene Tierney
director: Fritz Lang
Return of the Jedi (1983 film)
beast: 4 Ewok
cast: Carrie Fisher, Harrison Ford, Mark Hamill, Billy Dee Williams
composer: John Williams
director: Richard Marquand
role: 3 Han 4 Leia, Luke, Oola, Solo, Yoda 5 Darth, Lando, Vader 7 Han Solo 9 Skywalker 10 Darth Vader
Return of the Native, The
author: Thomas Hardy
character: 3 Vye 4 Clym, Venn 5 Damon 6 Tamsin 7 Clement, Diggory, Wildeve 8 Eustacia, Thomasin 9 Yeobright
return on __: 6 assets, equity
returns: 4 poll, take 8 proceeds
calculation: 3 tax
expert: 3 CPA 4 acct. 7 auditor 10 accountant
org.: 3 IRS
__ Returns: 6 Batman, Topper
Return to Mars author: 4 Bova
Return to Me (2000 film)
cast: Minnie Driver, David Duchovny, Robert Loggia, Carroll O'Connor
director: Bonnie Hunt
Return to Me (1958 song) artist: Dean Martin
Return to Paradise (1998 film)
cast: Anne Heche, Joaquin Phoenix, Vince Vaughn
director: Joseph Ruben
Return to Sender (1962 song) artist: Elvis Presley
Reuben: 8 sandwich
brother of ~: 3 Dan, Gad 4 Levi 5 Asher, Judah 6 Joseph, Simeon 7 Zebulun 8 Benjamin, Issachar, Naphtali
ingredient: 3 rye 5 kraut 6 cheese 8 rye bread 10 corned beef, sauerkraut
parent of ~: 4 Leah 5 Jacob
sister of ~: 5 Dinah
son of ~: 5 Carmi 6 Hanoch, Hezron
Reuben, Reuben (1983 film)
cast: Tom Conti, Kelly McGillis
Reubens: 4 Paul
Reuel, father of: 4 Esau
reunion: 7 meeting 8 assembly, conclave 9 gathering 10 convention
attendee: 3 rel., unc 4 alum, aunt, grad 5 niece, uncle 7 alumnus 8 relative
greeting: 3 hug
group: 3 fam., kin 4 clan 5 class 6 family
__ reunion: 5 class 6 family
Réunion: 3 isl. 4 isle 6 island
Reunion in Vienna (1933 film)
cast: John Barrymore, Frank Morgan, Diana Wynyard
reunite: 6 gather 8 assemble 9 reconcile 10 conciliate
Reunited (1979 song) artist: Peaches and Herb
reuse: 7 recycle
Reuters rival: 3 UPI
rev: 3 gun 4 race 5 crank 7 crank up 10 accelerate
up: 6 excite 8 increase 9 intensify
rev.
address: 3 ser.
training: 5 theol.
Rev. __: 3 Ver.
revamp: 3 fix 4 mend 5 alter, fix up 6 repair, revise 7 improve, touch up 8 overhaul, renovate 9 modernize, refurbish, transform
reveal: 3 air, ope, say 4 bare, blab, leak, open, show, talk, tell 5 admit, break, let on, spill, unrip, utter 6 betray, decode, detail, evince, expose, fess up, impart, let out, relate, report, show up, turn up, unfold, unmask, unveil 7 add up to, bespeak, concede, confess, confide, declare, display, divulge, exhibit, express, give out, lay bare, let slip, mention, reflect, uncover, unearth 8 announce, decipher, disclose, evidence, give away, indicate, manifest, register, unburden, unclothe 9 make known, put on view 10 make public
oneself: 4 show 5 arise 6 appear, emerge 7 come out, peep out, surface
one's feelings: 4 avow, tell 5 admit, allow 6 fess up 7 concede, confess, divulge 8 disclose 9 make known
one's hunger: 8 salivate
revealed: 4 open 5 naked 7 visible 8 knowable, manifest
revealing: 6 low-cut 8 telltale 10 conclusive, expressive
Rêve author: Emile Zola
reveille: 4 call 6 signal
opposite: 4 Taps
player: 5 bugle 6 bugler
respond to ~: 4 rise, wake 5 awake, get up 6 awaken
sound ~: 4 wake 5 awake, rouse, waken 6 arouse, awaken, wake up
__ Reveille: 3 'Til
revel: 4 gala, lark, play 5 binge, enjoy, exult, gloat, glory, party, spree 6 bask in, cavort, frolic, gaiety, gambol, gayety, relish, wallow 7 blowout, carouse, delight, indulge, jollity, rejoice, roister, rollick, skylark, triumph 8 cut loose, hilarity, live it up, recreate 9 bacchanal, celebrate, festivity, have a ball, luxuriate, make merry, whoop it up 10 go on a spree, have a blast, have a fling, masquerade, saturnalia
cry: 4 evoe
in: 4 like, love 5 eat up, enjoy 6 devour 9 luxuriate
(in): 4 bask 7 delight
revelation: 3 tip 4 find, idea, info, jolt, leak, news, show, talk 5 augur, dream, scoop, shock, state, story 6 airing, answer, augury, avowal, baring, earful, espial, exposé, oracle, report, tipoff, vision, whammy 7 account, adviser, display, exhibit, finding, hearsay, insight, lowdown, message, miracle, outlook, release, scandal, shake-up, shocker, showing, stunner, tidings 8 betrayal, bulletin, exposure, forecast, prophecy, surprise 9 admission, assertion, bombshell, broadcast, detection, discovery, exclusive, eyeopener, foresight, intuition, news flash, statement, testimony, unmasking, unveiling, utterance 10 appearance, astuteness, communiqué, confession, deposition, disclosure, divination, divulgence, exhibition, exposition, expression, foreboding, prediction, prescience, profession, recitation, unbosoming, uncovering, unearthing, unexpected, wonderment
response: 3 aha
Revelation
name in ~: 3 Gog 5 Magog
preceder: 4 Jude
reveler: 9 wassailer
revelry: 3 fun, joy 5 mirth, party, spree 6 fiesta, gaiety, gayety 7 gayness, jollity, jubilee 8 carousal, festival, goings-on, hilarity, pleasure 9 festivity, high jinks, merriment, whoop-de-do 10 liveliness, risibility, saturnalia, sybaritism
revenant: 6 fantom 7 phantom, specter 10 apparition
revenge: 5 spite 6 avenge 7 get even, hit back, pay back, requite 8 reprisal, requital 9 get back at, stick it to, tit for tat, vengeance, vindicate
get ~: 9 retaliate
get ~ on: 3 fix, get 5 repay, set up 6 punish 7 pay back
Revenge (1990 film)
cast: Kevin Costner, Sally Kirkland, Anthony Quinn, Madeleine Stowe
director: Tony Scott
revengefulness: 4 hate 6 animus, enmity, grudge, hatred, malice, rancor 7 ill will 8 acrimony, bad blood 9 animosity, antipathy, hostility 10 antagonism
Revenge of the Nerds (1984 film)
cast: Timothy Busfield, Robert Carradine, Anthony Edwards
director: Jeff Kanew,
revenue: 3 net, pay 4 gain, gate, take 5 funds, gravy, lucre, means, money, split, wages, yield 6 income, payoff, profit, return, reward, salary, wealth 7 annuity, receipt 8 benefice, cash flow, earnings, interest, proceeds, receipts 9 dividends, emolument, resources 10 bottom line
deduction from ~: 5 debit
less outlays: 3 net 6 profit
of ~: 6 fiscal 8 economic, monetary 9 budgetary, financial, pecuniary
source: 4 sale 8 receipts
revenue __: 4 bond 5 agent, stamp 6 cutter, tariff 7 sharing
__ revenue: 5 gross 7 accrued, average
revenuer: 4 T-man
quest: 5 still
reverb __: 5 pedal
reverberant: 6 echoic 8 resonant
reverberate: 4 boom, echo, peal, ring, roar, roll 5 clang, sound 6 reecho 7 reflect, resound, thunder, vibrate
reverberation: 4 boom, echo, ring 5 clang, sound 6 report 8 reaction 9 vibration
Reverdy, Pierre: 4 poet 6 French 8 essayist
revere: 4 laud, like, love 5 adore, ensky, exalt, go for, honor, prize, value 6 admire, esteem, hallow, regard 7 beatify, care for, cherish, defer to, glorify, idolize, magnify, observe, respect, worship 8 enshrine, hold dear, inshrine, look up to, treasure, venerate 9 care about
Revere: 4 Anne, city, Paul, town
emulate ~: 4 ride 6 arouse
locale: 4 Mass.
Revere and the Raiders, Paul
song: Good Thing (1966)
Him or Me-What's It Gonna Be? (1967)
Hungry (1966)
Indian Reservation (1971)
Just Like Me (1965)
Kicks (1966)
vocalist: Mark Lindsay
Revere, Anne Oscar: National Velvet
revered: 5 hoary 6 sacred 7 beloved 9 venerable 10 celebrated
object: 4 icon, idol, ikon 5 eikon
reverence: 3 awe 4 fear 5 honor, piety, value 6 esteem, homage, praise, regard, wonder 7 respect, worship 8 devotion 9 adoration, deference, obeisance 10 admiration, devoutness, exaltation, veneration
show ~: 3 bow 5 kneel 9 genuflect
reverend: 5 padre 6 cleric, father, parson, pastor 8 minister, preacher
mother: 3 nun
residence: 5 manse
__ Reverend: 4 Most, Very 5 Right
Reverend Mr. Black (1963 song)
artist: Kingston Trio
reverent: 4 holy 5 pious 6 devout, loving 9 awestruck, religious, righteous
not ~: 6 unholy 7 godless, impious,

ungodly 8 agnostic 9 atheistic
reverential: 5 lowly 6 loving 7 dutiful 9 awestruck
__ Revere's Ride: 4 Paul
reverie: 5 dream, study 6 musing, trance 7 fantasy, thought 8 daydream, head trip, phantasy 9 pipe dream 10 brown study, meditation
in ~: 5 moony 6 adream
indulge in ~: 4 muse 5 dream 7 reflect 8 daydream, meditate, ruminate 10 introspect
revers: 5 lapel
__ reversa: 4 cyma
reversal: 4 jolt 6 change, switch 7 licking, refusal, setback, tragedy, undoing 8 apostasy, flip-flop 9 about-face, inversion, one-eighty, recession, turnabout
auto ~: 3 uey 5 U-turn
reversal __: 4 film 5 plate 7 process
Reversal of Fortune (1990 film)
cast: Glenn Close, Jeremy Irons, Ron Silver
director: Barbet Schroeder
role: 5 Claus, Sunny 8 von Bülow
reverse: 4 back, bath, blow, gear, lift, rear, turn, undo, void 5 annul, check, evert, polar, quash, shift, slump, upend, upset, verso, wrong 6 cancel, change, contra, invert, mishap, negate, oppose, recall, renege, repeal, revoke, switch 7 bad luck, counter, failure, inverse, nullify, overset, reflect, rescind, retract, setback 8 antipode, contrary, converse, exchange, flip-flop, flip side, negation, opposite, override, overrule, overturn, turn over 9 about-face, adversity, back-pedal, mischance, other side, overthrow, repudiate, transpose, turnabout, underside, volte-face 10 antithesis, antithetic, double back, invalidate, misfortune, turn around
a decision: 8 override, overrule
go into ~: 4 back 5 shift 6 back up
in ~: 9 vice versa
oneself: 6 recant, renege 7 retract, retreat 8 flip-flop 9 back-pedal
prefix: 3 dis-, non-
reverse __: 3 bar, bid 4 shot, side, snob 5 bevel, curve, fault, plate, video 7 English, osmosis
reversed: 8 opposite 9 inside out 10 upside-down
reversible: 9 revocable 10 changeable
Reversible Errors author: Scott Turow
reversion: 7 atavism
revert: 4 turn 5 lapse 6 go back, resume, return 7 reflect, regress, relapse 9 backslide, throw back 10 change back, recidivate, retrogress
review: 3 pan 4 look, mull, rate, rave, slam 5 audit, blurb, check, drill, learn, organ, recap, study, sum up, trash, weigh 6 assess, bone up, column, go over, parade, rehash, résumé, survey 7 analyze, article, brush up, canvass, checkup, debrief, discuss, examine, hearing, inspect, journal, perusal, reading, revisit, rundown, run over, summary, touch on, write-up, writing 8 abstract, analysis, appraise, bone up on, critique, evaluate, hash over, look back, magazine, peculate, reassess, rehearse, scrutiny, synopsis 9 appraisal, comment on, criticism, criticize, newspaper, pick apart, reexamine, summarize, think over, touch upon 10 call to mind, commentary, discussion, inspection, look back on, periodical, procession, reconsider, reevaluate, run through, scrutinize, second look
bad ~: 3 pan 9 broadside
board: 5 panel 7 inquest 9 committee
good ~: 4 rave
legal ~: 6 appeal
__ review: 4 book, peer
reviewer: 5 rater 6 critic 8 examiner 9 evaluator, inspector
Review-Journal: 5 paper 9 newspaper
locale: 8 Las Vegas
revile: 3 jaw 4 hoot, rail 5 abuse, baste, libel, scoff, scorn, sully 6 assail, malign, vilify 7 despise, inveigh, run down, slander, tell off 8 backbite, denounce 9 blaspheme, denigrate, lash out at 10 blackguard, calumniate, villainize, vituperate
revilement: 5 abuse 6 tirade 7 calumny 9 invective 10 detraction, muckraking
reviler: 5 shrew 8 vilifier 9 detractor, henpecker
Revill, Clive: 5 actor
film: Avanti! (1972)
Fathom (1967)
The Legend of Hell House (1973)
revisal: 6 change 7 editing 9 amendment 10 adjustment, alteration, correction, emendation
revise: 3 cut, fix 4 edit, mend, redo, suit 5 adapt, alter, amend, debug, emend 6 change, doctor, modify, polish, recast, redact, reform, revamp, rework, update 7 clean up, correct, improve, perfect, rectify, redraft, redress, retouch, rewrite, scissor, touch up 8 emendate, overhaul 9 tighten up 10 blue-pencil
jointly: 6 coedit
Revised Standard __: 7 Version
reviser: 6 editor
revision: 6 change, update 7 editing, redraft, redress, rewrite 8 overhaul 9 amendment, redaction, reshaping 10 adjustment, alteration, correction, emendation
revisionist starter: 3 neo
revisit: 6 go back, return, review 8 come back 9 come again, reexamine 10 reconsider, reevaluate
revitalize: 5 renew 6 revive 7 freshen, inspire, quicken, refresh, restore 8 embolden, imbolden, rekindle 9 encourage 10 invigorate
revival: 5 rally 8 comeback, pick-me-up, recovery 9 awakening 10 quickening, renascence, resurgence
setting: 4 tent
shout: 4 amen
technique: 3 CPR
__ Revival: 5 Greek
revivalist: 3 neo
revive: 4 wake 5 awake, cheer, rally, renew, rouse, slake, waken 6 awaken, come to, perk up, recall 7 bring to, freshen, lighten, quicken, rebound, recover, recruit, refresh, restore 8 brighten, rekindle 9 bring back, modernize, reanimate, recollect 10 bounce back, come around, come to life, exhilarate, popularize, reenergize, regenerate, rejuvenate, revitalize
revived: 3 new 5 fresh 6 rested 7 like new
revivify: 7 hearten, refresh, restore 9 encourage 10 regenerate, rejuvenate
Revlon: 6 makeup
alternative: 4 Avon 5 Almay 7 Lancome, Mary Kay 8 Clinique 9 Cover Girl, Max Factor 10 Maybelline 11 Estée Lauder, Merle Norman
revocable: 5 fluid 9 adaptable, temporary 10 changeable, reversible
revocation: 6 recall 9 abolition, annulment 10 withdrawal
revoir, au: 7 goodbye 8 farewell
revoke: 4 kill, lift, void 5 annul, erase, quash, scrub 6 cancel, negate, recall, recant, repeal 7 abolish, dismiss, expunge, nullify, rescind, retract, reverse 8 abrogate, disallow, disclaim, override, overrule, set aside, take back, withdraw 9 repudiate 10 invalidate
a legacy: 5 adeem
revolt: 4 coup, defy, riot, rise, turn 5 appal, flout, rebel, repel, shock 6 appall, ignore, loathe, mutiny, offend, oppose, putsch, resist, rise up, sicken 7 disgust, disobey, dissent, horrify, protest, repulse, treason, turn off, violate 8 civil war, defiance, gross out, overturn, sedition, uprising 9 break away, displease, disregard, make waves, overthrow, rebellion 10 insurgency, revolution
leader: 6 anarch 9 insurgent
__ revolt: 6 palace
revolting: 4 base, evil, foul, grim, icky, poor, ugly, vile 5 awful, gross, lousy, nasty, seamy, woful 6 crumby, crummy, dismal, horrid, odious, rotten, sickly, woeful 7 accurst, baleful, baneful, beastly, doleful, ghastly, hateful, heinous, hideous, noisome, obscene 8 accursed, dreadful, God-awful, grievous, horrible, inferior, shameful, shocking, stinking, terrible, wretched 9 abhorrent, appalling, atrocious, defective, execrable, frightful, insidious, insurgent, loathsome, low-minded, miserable, monstrous, offensive, repellant, repellent, repugnant, repulsive, unsightly 10 abominable, despicable, detestable, disastrous, disgusting, horrendous, uninviting, unpleasant, virtueless
find ~: 4 hate 5 abhor, scorn 6 detest, loathe 7 deplore, despise 8 execrate 9 abominate
revolution: 4 coup, spin, turn 5 cycle, golpe, orbit, round, storm, upset 6 change, circle, mutiny, putsch, revolt, strife 7 anarchy, circuit, shake-up 8 civil war, gyration, outbreak, rotation, upheaval, uprising, violence 9 bloodshed, coup d'état, overthrow, rebellion
line: 4 axis
starter: 7 counter
time for one ~: 4 year
__ Revolution: 5 Texas 6 French 7 Chinese, English, October, Russian
Revolution (1968 song) artist: Beatles
revolutionary: 3 new 4 left 5 novel, rebel, ultra 6 anarch 7 lawless, radical 8 renegade 9 different, extremist, insurgent 10 avant-garde, innovative, subversive
Chinese ~: 3 Mao
core: 5 cadre
French ~: 5 Marat
Irish ~: 6 Fenian
path: 5 orbit
Russian ~: 5 Lenin
Revolutionary __: 3 War 5 Étude
Revolutionary Étude composer: 6 Chopin
Revolutionary, The (1970 film)
cast: Seymour Cassel, Jennifer Salt, Jon Voight
director: Paul Williams
Revolutionary War
general: 4 Howe 5 Gates, Wayne 6 Arnold, de Kalb, Greene, Marion, Putnam 7 Clinton, Pulaski, Steuben 9 Lafayette 10 Cornwallis, von Steuben, Washington
hero: 5 Allen 10 Ethan Allen
spy: 4 Hale 10 Nathan Hale
revolutionize: 6 change, reform 8 innovate 9 transform
Revolutions of the Viaducts artist: 4 Klee
revolve: 4 mull, muse, roll, spin, turn 5 orbit, pivot, swing, think, twirl, twist, wheel, whirl 6 circle, gyrate, ponder, rotate, swivel 8 go around, mull over, ruminate, turn over 9 pirouette 10 deliberate, think about
around: 5 orbit
revolver: 3 arm, gun 6 pistol 7 firearm
inventor: 4 Colt
revolving: 6 rotary
part: 5 rotor
revolving __: 4 door, fund 5 stage 6 charge, credit
revue: 4 show, skit 6 parody 7 program 10 production
line: 6 chorus
place: 6 casino
segment: 4 skit
revulsion: 4 hate 5 odium 6 hatred, horror 7 disgust, dislike 8 aversion, distaste, loathing, reaction 9 antipathy, repulsion 10 abhorrence, repellence, repugnance
revved up: 5 hyper
reward: 3 due, pay, tip 4 gift, meed, plum, wage 5 award, bonus, crown, favor, fruit, grant, gravy, honor, lucre, medal, merit, perks, price, prize, purse, repay, wages 6 bounty, carrot, desert, grease, payoff, profit, refund, return, tipoff, trophy 7 garland, goodies, guerdon, jackpot, laurels, payment, pension, premium, redress, requite, revenue, satisfy, strokes, subsidy 8 accolade, dividend, gratuity, kickback, proceeds 9 indemnify, lagniappe, reckoning, repayment, sweetener 10 compensate, inducement, punishment, recompense, remunerate, take care of
old-style: 4 meed
rewarding: 7 gainful 8 edifying, fruitful, pleasing, readable, valuable 9 well-spent 10 beneficial, fulfilling, gratifying, productive, profitable, satisfying, successful, worthwhile
reword: 5 alter 6 recast 7 clarify 9 translate 10 paraphrase
rework: 4 edit 6 modify, reform, rehash, revise
reworking: 6 rehash 7 redress 10 adaptation
rewrite: 4 copy, edit 6 rehash, revise 8 revision 9 redaction 10 emendation
rex: 4 king
Rex: 3 cat 4 Reed 5 Allen, felid, Smith, Stout 6 Barney, feline, Ingram, Morgan, Reason, Warner 7 Humbard 8 Harrison
colleague of ~: 4 Erle 6 Agatha
__ Rex: 6 Arthur 7 Oedipus
Rexroth, Kenneth: 4 poet
rey: 6 Felipe 7 Alfonso 9 Ferdinand 10 Juan Carlos
mate: 5 reina
Rey: 6 Alvino 8 Fernando, Margaret 9 Alejandro
Reyes, Alfonso: 4 poet 7 Mexican 8 essayist
Rey, Fernando: 5 actor
film: The Discreet Charm of the Bourgeoisie (1972)
The French Connection (1971)
Seven Beauties (1976)
Reykjavik: 4 city, town 7 capital
locale: 4 Icel. 7 Iceland
Reyles, Carlos: 6 writer 9 Uruguayan

Reymont, Wladyslaw: **6** writer **8** Nobelist
Reynard, like: **3** sly **4** foxy
Reynard the Fox author: John Masefield
Reynolds: **4** Burt, Jody, Lynn **5** Allie, Price **6** Debbie, Freddy, Joshua **8** Marjorie
alternative: **4** Glad **5** Alcoa, Hefty **6** Ziploc **9** Saran Wrap
Reynoldsburg: **4** city, town
locale: **4** Ohio
Reynolds, Burt: **5** actor
film: Boogie Nights (1997)
Breaking In (1989)
The Cannonball Run (1981)
City Heat (1984)
The Crew (2000)
Deliverance (1972)
The End (1978)
Hooper (1978)
The Longest Yard (1974)
The Man Who Loved Cat Dancing (1973)
Nickelodeon (1976)
Semi-Tough (1977)
Shamus (1973)
Smokey and the Bandit (1977)
Starting Over (1979)
Switching Channels (1988)
spouse: Loni Anderson, Judy Carne
TV: Evening Shade, Gunsmoke
Reynolds, Debbie: **7** actress
daughter: Carrie Fisher
film: The Affairs of Dobie Gillis (1953)
The Catered Affair (1956)
Divorce American Style (1967)
The Gazebo (1959)
How the West Was Won (1962)
The Mating Game (1959)
The Pleasure of His Company (1961)
The Rat Race (1960)
Singin' in the Rain (1952)
Tammy and the Bachelor (1957)
The Tender Trap (1955)
This Happy Feeling (1958)
The Unsinkable Molly Brown (1964)
What's the Matter With Helen? (1971)
musical revival: **5** Irene
song: Tammy (1957)
spouse: Eddie Fisher
Reynolds, Joshua: **6** artist **7** British, painter
Reynolds, Marjorie: **7** actress
film: Holiday Inn (1942)
Ministry of Fear (1944)
The Time of Their Lives (1946)
Up in Mabel's Room (1944)
TV: The Life of Riley
Reynosa: **4** city, town
locale: **6** Mexico **10** Tamaulipas
see also Spanish
Reza: **7** Pahlavi
Rezé: **4** city, town
locale: **6** France
Reznor: **5** Trent
RF: **3** pos.
RFD part: **4** Free **5** Rural **8** Delivery
RFK, Mrs.: **5** Ethel
Rh: **4** elem. **7** element, rhodium
45 for ~: **4** at. no.
what the ~ factor is named for: **6** monkey, rhesus
Rh ___: **6** factor
rhabdomantists do, what: **5** dowse
Rhaetian ___: **4** Alps
Rhaiadr: **5** falls **9** waterfall
locale: **5** Wales
Rhames, Ving: **5** actor
film: Bringing Out the Dead (1999)
Con Air (1997)
Entrapment (1999)
Mission: Impossible II (2000)
Out of Sight (1998)
rhapsodic: **6** elated **7** glowing, lilting, lyrical **8** blissful, ecstatic, in heaven, ravished, thrilled **9** bombastic, delighted, gladdened, overjoyed, rapturous
Rhapsodie Espagnole composer: **5** Ravel
rhapsodize: **4** rave, talk **5** orate **7** enthuse **9** go on about, hold forth
rhapsody: **5** music **7** rapture **8** lyricism **10** jubilation
___ Rhapsody: **4** Alto **6** Second
Rhapsody for Orchestra composer: **6** Dvorák
Rhapsody in Blue (1945 film)
cast: Robert Alda, Joan Leslie, Alexis Smith
director: Irving Rapper
subject: **8** Gershwin
rhatany: **5** shrub
rhea: **4** bird **6** ratite
cousin: **3** emu **4** emeu
Rhea: **4** moon **5** giant, Titan **7** Perlman **8** Caroline
brother of ~: **6** Cronos, Cronus
daughter of ~: **4** Hera **6** Hestia **7** Demeter
equivalent: **3** Ops
husband of ~: **6** Cronos, Cronus
parent of ~: **4** Gaea **6** Uranus
planet: **6** Saturn
son of ~: **4** Zeus **5** Hades, Pluto **8** Poseidon
Rhea ___: **6** Silvia
rhebok: **6** animal **8** antelope
relative: **3** gnu, kob **4** guib, kudu, oryx, puku, topi **5** addax, bongo, chiru, eland, goral, korin, nyala, oribi, saiga, serow **6** chammy, dik-dik, duiker, impala, koodoo, lechwe, nilgai, shammy, shamoy **7** blaubok, blesbok, chamois, defassa, gazelle, gemsbok, gerenuk, grysbok, nylghai, nylghau, sassaby **8** blesbuck, bontebok, bushbuck, gemsbuck, reedbuck, steenbok, steinbok **9** blackbuck, pronghorn, sitatunga, springbok, waterbuck **10** hartebeest, wildebeest
Rhee: **7** Syngman
Rheem alternative: **5** Trane **6** Lennox **7** Carrier, Fedders **9** Friedrich
Rheims: **4** city, town
locale: **6** France
___ Rheingold: **3** Das
Rhein port: **4** Köln
rhenium: **5** metal **7** element
rhesus: **6** animal, Bandar **7** macaque, primate
relative: **3** ape **4** saki, titi **5** chimp, drill, jocko, lemur, loris, magot, orang, potto, shrew **6** aye-aye, baboon, Bandar, galago, gelada, gibbon, grivet, guenon, howler, langur, macaco, uakari, vervet **7** colobus, gorilla, guereza, hoolock, macaque, sapajou, siamang, tamarin, tarsier **8** bush baby, capuchin, mandrill, mangabey, marmoset, talapoin **9** orangutan **10** Barbary ape, chimpanzee, orangutang
rhesus ___: **6** monkey
Rhesus ___: **6** factor
rhetor: **6** orator
rhetoric: **4** bunk, rant **5** hooey **6** bunkum, hot air, speech **7** address, bombast, fustian, oration, oratory **8** buncombe **9** discourse, elocution, eloquence, gift of gab, hyperbole, verbosity, wordiness **10** balderdash, vocalizing
rhetorical: **4** glib **5** showy, tumid, windy, wordy **6** florid, mouthy, ornate, purple, turgid **7** flowery, pompous, stilted, unterse, verbose, voluble **8** eloquent, forensic, inflated, sonorous **9** bombastic, grandiose, high-flown, overblown **10** euphuistic, flamboyant
device: **5** ploce, trope **7** imagery
rhetorician: **6** orator
Rhett: **5** Akins **6** Butler
daughter: **6** Bonnie **10** Bonnie Blue
rival: **6** Ashley
rheum: **4** cold **7** catarrh
___-Rhin: **3** Bas **4** Haut
rhinal: **5** nasal
Rhine: **2** J.B. **4** wine **5** river
branch of the ~: **6** Ijssel
city on the ~: **4** Bonn, Köln **5** Basel, Basle, kleve, Mainz, Worms **6** Arnhem **7** Cologne **10** Düsseldorf
ender: **4** land
feeder: **3** Aar **4** Aare, Main, Ruhr **5** Mosel **6** Neckar **7** Moselle
in Holland: **4** Rijn
locale: **7** Germany, Holland
region: **6** Alsace
wine: **4** hock
wine center: **5** Mainz
Rhine, J.B. field: **3** ESP
Rhinemann Exchange, The author: Robert Ludlum
Rhinestone Cowboy (1975 song)
artist: Glen Campbell
rhino: **3** oof **4** cash, gelt, jack, kail, kale, loot, peag, pelf **5** bills, bread, bucks, dough, funds, lucre, moola, mopus, pesos, sewan **6** dinero, do-re-mi, mammon, mazuma, moolah, seawan, silver, specie, wampum, wealth **7** big game, cabbage, capital, dollars, lettuce, ooftish, scratch, shekels **8** bankroll, cold cash, currency, hard cash, smackers **9** banknotes, frogskins, leviathan, long green, pachyderm, simoleons **10** greenbacks, green stuff
rhinoceros: **5** beast **6** animal, mammal
beetle: **4** uang
cousin: **5** hippo, tapir
feature: **4** horn
female: **3** cow
home: **3** zoo **6** Africa
male: **4** bull
young: **4** calf
Rhinoceros author: Eugène Ionesco
rhizome: **4** root
rho: **5** Greek **6** letter
predecessor: **2** pi
successor: **5** sigma
Rhoda (CBS sitcom)
cast: David Groh (Joe Gerard)
Valerie Harper (Rhoda Morgenstern)
Julie Kavner (Brenda Morgenstern)
Nancy Walker (Ida Morgenstern)
producer: MTM
Rhoda Fleming author: George Meredith
Rhode: **5** nymph
brother of ~: **6** Triton
father of ~: **8** Poseidon
lover of ~: **6** Helios
Rhode Island: **5** state
capital: **10** Providence
city: **7** Bristol, Newport, Warwick **8** Coventry, Cranston, Johnston, Westerly **9** Pawtucket **10** Cumberland, Providence, Woonsocket
Indian: **9** Wampanoag
motto: **4** Hope
nickname: **10** Ocean State
region: **4** N. Eng. **10** New England
school: **5** Brown
state flower: **6** violet
state mineral: **8** bowenite
state motto: **4** Hope
state shell: **6** quahog
state tree: **8** red maple
Rhode Island ___: **3** Red **4** bent **5** White
Rhode Island Red: **3** hen **4** fowl **7** chicken
relative: **6** Bantam, Brahma, Houdan, Sussex **7** Cornish, Dorking, Leghorn **8** Araucana, Langshan, Shanghai **9** Dominique, Orpington, Wyandotte
Rhodes: **3** isl. **4** city, Hari, isle, port, town **5** Cecil **6** island
locale: **6** Greece
Rhodes ___: **5** grass **7** scholar
Rhodesian Ridgeback: **3** dog **5** canid **6** canine
rhodium: **5** metal **7** element
rhodochrosite: **3** ore **7** mineral
rhododendron: **5** plant **6** flower
relative: **6** azalea
___ rhododendron: **4** pink **5** coast, great
rhodolite: **3** gem **6** garnet **8** gemstone
Rhodope: **5** range
locale: **6** Europe **8** Bulgaria
rhodora: **5** shrub
relative: **5** heath, salal **6** azalea, kalmia **7** arbutus **8** cassiope, cowberry **9** blueberry, deerberry
Rhody: **4** aunt
___ Rhody: **6** Little
rhombus: **5** shape
rhonchus: **5** snore
Rhonda: **7** Fleming
Rhondda: **4** city, town
locale: **5** Wales
Rhone: **4** wine **5** river
city on the ~: **4** Lyon **5** Arles, Lyons **6** Geneva **7** Avignon
feeder: **5** Isère, Saône
locale: **6** France
tributary: **3** Ain
rhubarb: **3** pie **5** brawl, set-to **6** barney, fracas, hassle, rumpus **7** quarrel **8** argument **10** donnybrook
unit: **5** stalk
Rhubarb (1951 film)
cast: Gene Lockhart, Ray Milland, Jan Sterling
Rhue: **6** Madlyn
rhumb ___: **4** line **7** sailing
rhumba: **5** dance
Rhumba Is My Life author: **5** Cugat
rhum cake: **4** baba
Rhyl: **4** city, town
locale: **5** Wales
rhyme: **3** ode **4** beat, poem, rune **5** ditty, meter, poesy, verse **6** poetry, rhythm, sonnet **7** cadence, cadency, couplet, measure, versify **8** doggerel, limerick, rondelet
maker: **4** bard, poet
or reason: **5** cause, logic, sense **6** motive
scheme: **4** AABA, AABB, ABAA, ABAB, ABBA, ABCA **6** ABACAB
without ~ or reason: **4** idle **5** inane, nutty, silly, wacky **6** absurd **7** asinine, foolish, puerile **8** mindless **9** frivolous, half-baked, illogical, ludicrous, pointless, senseless **10** irrational, ridiculous
rhyme ___: **5** royal **6** scheme
___ rhyme: **3** end, eye **4** full, half, head, near, rich, true **5** sight, slant, vowel **6** double, female, linked, single, triple **7** initial, nursery, perfect
Rhyme Pays artist: **4** Ice-T
rhymer: **4** bard, poet
rhymes: **5** poesy, verse **6** poetry
___ Rhymes: **5** Busta
rhymester: **4** bard, poet **6** rhymer **9** sonneteer, versifier

Rhymes to Be Traded for Bread
author: Vachel Lindsay
rhyming __: 5 slang
rhyming game: 6 crambo
rhyolite: 4 lava 7 mineral
Rhys, Jean: 6 author, writer 7 British
work: Good Morning, Midnight
The Left Bank and Other Stories
Sleep It Off, Lady
Tigers are Better-Looking
Wide Sargasso Sea
rhythm: 4 beat, lilt, rime, time 5 meter, pulse, rhyme, swing, tempo, throb 6 accent, stress 7 cadence, cadency, measure, pattern 8 downbeat, symmetry 10 regularity, repetition
and blues: 5 music
body ~: 5 pulse
graceful ~: 4 lilt
instrument: 4 drum
rhythm __: 4 band 5 stick 7 section
__ rhythm: 4 beta, body 5 alpha, delta, duple, theta 6 common, gallop, rising, sprung, triple 7 falling, rocking, running
Rhythm __ Heart: 4 of My
__ Rhythm: 4 I Got
rhythm and __: 5 blues
Rhythm Heritage song: Theme from S.W.A.T. (1976)
rhythmic: 4 even 5 paced 6 cadent, poetic, smooth, steady 7 lilting, lyrical, musical, regular 8 poetical 10 harmonious
movement: 5 dance
Rhythm Is Gonna Get You (1987 song) artist: Gloria Estefan
Rhythm Nation (1989 song) artist: Janet Jackson
Rhythm 'N' Blues (1955 song) artist: McGuire Sisters
Rhythm of My Heart (1991 song) artist: Rod Stewart
Rhythm of the Night (1985 song) artist: DeBarge
Rhythm on the River (1940 film)
cast: Bing Crosby, Mary Martin, Basil Rathbone
__ Rhythm Section: 7 Atlanta
R.I.
neighbor: 4 Conn., Mass.
see also Rhode Island
ria: 5 creek, inlet 7 estuary, rivulet
RIAA, part of: 4 Amer., Assn. 5 Assoc 6 Record 7 America 8 Industry
rial: 5 money
locale: 4 Iran, Oman
Rialto: 4 city, town
locale: 10 California
Rialto Ripples composer: 8 Gershwin
riant: 3 gay 7 gleeful, smiling 8 cheerful, laughing, mirthful
riata: 4 rope 5 lasso 6 lariat
end: 5 noose
rib: 3 kid, rag 4 bone, jape, joke, josh, mock, razz, twit, wale 5 chaff, costa, ridge, roast, taunt, tease 6 banter, deride, flange, needle, pick on, timber 8 ridicule 9 make fun of, poke fun at
combining form: 4 cost- 5 costo-, pleur- 6 pleuro-
ender: 4 wort 5 grass
leaf ~: 4 vein
order: 4 rack
relinquisher: 4 Adam
skyscraper ~: 6 girder
slangily: 4 slat
vault ~: 5 ogive 6 lierne
rib __: 4 cage 5 roast, steak, vault
rib-__ steak: 3 eye
__ rib: 4 true 5 false, prime
__ Rib: 5 Adam's
ribald: 3 raw 4 blue, lewd, racy 5 bawdy, crude, gross, juicy, nasty, salty, spicy 6 coarse, earthy, purple, risqué, smutty, spicey, unmeet, vulgar 7 naughty, obscene, raunchy 8 indecent, off-color, shameful 9 low-minded, salacious 10 indecorous, licentious, scurrilous
ribaldry: 8 lewdness 9 grossness, indecency, lubricity
riband: 4 cord, sash 5 badge 6 cordon
ribbed fabric: 3 rep 4 repp 5 pique, twill 6 faille, poplin, tricot 7 épinglé 8 corduroy 9 grosgrain
ribbing: 4 jest 5 roast 6 banter 8 badinage, raillery, ridicule 10 persiflage
ribbon: 4 band, belt, tape 5 medal, prize, shred, strip, title 6 cordon, edging, stripe, trophy 9 audiotape 10 decoration
blue ~: 5 prize 6 trophy 7 laurels
combining form: 4 taen-, -tene 5 taeni- 6 taenio-
earn a blue ~: 3 win 7 succeed, triumph
hair ~: 6 fillet
holder: 5 spool
trim: 9 picot, gimp
ribbon __: 4 copy, worm 5 plant, snake, strip 6 window
__ ribbon: 3 red 4 blue, sash 6 yellow
Ribbon: 5 falls 9 waterfall
locale: 8 Yosemite 10 California
__ ribbons: 5 cut to
ribbons, cut into: 5 shred
rib-eye: 3 cut 4 beef, meat 5 steak
Ribisi, Giovanni: 5 actor
film: The Boiler Room (2000)
The Gift (2000)
The Mod Squad (1999)
The Other Sister (1999)
riboflavin: 3 vit. 7 vitamin 8 B vitamin, nutrient
ribonucleic __: 4 acid
ribosomal __: 3 RNA
ribs: 4 beef, meat
elbow in the ~: 3 jab 4 poke, prod 5 goose, nudge 6 tickle
source: 3 pig
spot: 5 grill 8 barbecue
__ ribs: 5 prime, short
rib-tickler: 4 hoot, jest, joke 6 gasser
rib-tickling: 4 rich 5 comic, funny 9 hilarious, priceless
Ric: 6 Ocasek
__ Rica: 5 Costa
__ Rican: 5 Costa 6 Puerto
rica, not: 5 pobre
Ricardo: 4 Lucy 5 David, Palma, Ricky 6 Cortez 9 Güiraldes, Montalban
costar: 5 Hervé
in English: 7 Richard
portrayer: 4 Ball, Desi, Lucy 5 Arnaz 7 Lucille
see also Spanish
Riccardo: 4 Muti 5 Drigo 8 Giacconi
in English: 7 Richard
Ricci: 4 Nina 6 Matteo 9 Christina
Ricci, Christina: 7 actress
film: The Addams Family (1991)
Addams Family Values (1993)
Desert Blue (1999)
The Ice Storm (1997)
The Opposite of Sex (1998)
Sleepy Hollow (1999)
rice: 4 carb 5 carbo, grain 6 cereal, Minute 7 Success 8 Carolina, side dish 9 Uncle Ben's
cake: 4 nosh 5 mochi, snack 6 nibble 7 munchie
combining form: 4 oryz- 5 oryzi-, oryzo-
cooker: 3 wok
dirty ~ cuisine: 5 Cajun
dish: 5 pilaf, pilau, pilaw 6 pilaff
field: 5 paddy
wine: 4 sake, saki
rice __: 3 rat 4 bean, cake, coal, wine 5 blast, paddy, paper 6 weevil
__ rice: 4 wild 5 brown, dirty, water 6 Indian 7 Spanish
Rice: 3 Sam, Tim 4 Anne, univ. 5 Elmer, Jerry 8 Rosemary 9 Grantland 10 university
athletes: 4 Owls
conference: 3 WAC
locale: 5 Texas 7 Houston
Rice __: 4 Chex 8 Krispies
Rice-__: 5 a-Roni
__ Rice: 6 Minute
Rice, Anne: 6 author, writer
work: Beauty's Punishment
Beauty's Release
Belinda
Blackwood Farm
Blood and Gold
The Claiming of Sleeping Beauty
Cry to Heaven
Exit to Eden
Feast of All Saints
Interview With the Vampire
Lasher
Memnoch the Devil
Merrick
The Mummy
Pandora
The Queen of the Damned
Servant of the Bones
The Tale of the Body Thief
Taltos
The Vampire Armand
The Vampire Chronicles
The Vampire Lestat
Violin
Vittorio the Vampire
The Witching Hour
__ Rice Burroughs: 5 Edgar
Rice Chex: 6 cereal
competitor: 3 Kix 4 Life, Trix 5 Kashi, Quisp, Total 6 Kaboom, Muesli, Oreo O's, Pablum, Smacks 7 All-Bran, Crispix, Harmony, Hunny B's, Mueslix, Oat Bran, Pokemon 8 Boo Berry, Cheerios, Corn Chex, Corn Pops, Fiber One, Special K, Uncle Sam, Wheaties 9 Alpha Bits, Apple Zaps, Grape Nuts, Honey Comb, Just Right, Wheat Chex 10 Apple Jacks, Bran Flakes, Cap'n Crunch, Cocoa Puffs, Froot Loops, Mini-Wheats, Nutri-Grain, Puffed Rice, Quaker Oats, Smart Start 11 Cocoa Blasts, Cookie Crisp, Golden Crisp, Lucky Charms, Puffed Wheat, Sweet Crunch, Waffle Crisp
Rice, Elmer: 6 writer 10 playwright
work: The Adding Machine
Street Scene
We, the People
Rice Krispies: 6 cereal
competitor: 3 Kix 4 Life, Trix 5 Kashi, Quisp, Total 6 Kaboom, Muesli, Oreo O's, Pablum, Smacks 7 All-Bran, Crispix, Harmony, Hunny B's, Mueslix, Oat Bran, Pokemon 8 Boo Berry, Cheerios, Corn Chex, Corn Pops, Fiber One, Rice Chex, Special K, Uncle Sam, Wheaties 9 Alpha Bits, Apple Zaps, Grape Nuts, Honey Comb, Just Right, Wheat Chex 10 Apple Jacks, Bran Flakes, Cap'n Crunch, Cocoa Puffs, Froot Loops, Mini-Wheats, Nutri-Grain, Puffed Rice, Quaker Oats, Smart Start 11 Cocoa Blasts, Cookie Crisp, Golden Crisp, Lucky Charms, Puffed Wheat, Sweet Crunch, Waffle Crisp
sound: 3 pop 4 snap 7 crackle
ricelike pasta: 4 orzo
Rice, Sam: 7 Senator 10 outfielder
Rice, Tim musical: 4 Aida 5 Chess, Evita
rich: 3 fat 4 deep, full, lush, luxe, oily, posh, rank, warm 5 droll, fancy, fatty, flush, funny, grand, haves, heavy, juicy, light, meaty, plush, ritzy, spicy, swank, sweet, tasty, vivid 6 absurd, bright, classy, costly, creamy, deluxe, fecund, gilded, landed, lavish, loaded, mellow, ornate, savory, spicey, strong, swanky, toothy, uptown 7 amusing, comical, copious, fertile, intense, liberal, moneyed, opulent, pungent, upscale, vibrant, wealthy, well-off 8 abundant, affluent, farcical, fruitful, gorgeous, humorous, in clover, luscious, old money, palatial, precious, prolific, resonant, sonorous, splendid, thriving, valuable, well-to-do 9 abounding, bounteous, bountiful, deep-toned, delicious, diverting, doing well, elaborate, excessive, expensive, exuberant, flavorful, high-class, hilarious, laughable, ludicrous, luxuriant, luxurious, plentiful, priceless, succulent, sumptuous, very funny 10 exorbitant, expressive, full-bodied, gut-busting, high-priced, in the chips, in the dough, in the money, meaningful, nourishing, nutritious, overpriced, privileged, productive, propertied, prosperous, ridiculous, upper class, upper crust, well-heeled
as land: 7 fertile 8 farmable, tillable 10 cultivable
be ~ (in): 6 abound
be too ~: 4 cloy
grow ~: 4 gain 5 get on, score 6 arrive, batten, do well, profit, thrive 7 burgeon, make out, prosper, succeed 8 flourish, get ahead, go places, hit it big, make good 9 make money
not ~: 4 poor 8 indigent
one: 6 fat cat
one way to get ~: 5 lotto 7 inherit, lottery
striking it ~: 5 lucky 9 fortunate 10 fortuitous, prosperous, successful
supply: 4 lode, mine, vein
__ rich: 6 filthy
Rich: 4 Adam 5 Buddy, Irene 6 Little 7 Charlie 8 Adrienne
Rich, Adrienne: 4 poet
Rich and Famous (1981 film)
cast: Candice Bergen, Jacqueline Bisset, Hart Bochner, David Selby
director: George Cukor
Rich and Famous author: John Guare
Rich and Famous host: 5 Leach
Richard: 3 Dix, Roe 4 Bach, Byrd, Egan, Ford, Gere, Kiel, Kind, Kuhn, Long, Marx, Moll, Todd 5 Adams, Arlen, Boone, Brome, Cliff, Conte, Daley, Ernst, Haydn, Kiley, Kline, Lewis, Masur, Nixon, Petty, Pryor, Quine, Simon, Stone, Synge 6 Armour, Avedon, Belzer, Beymer, Brooks, Burton, Condon, Crenna, Dawson, Deacon, Dehmel, Donner, Dysart, Greene, Grieco, Harris, Jordan, Leakey, Lester, Maltby, Pearce, Savage, Scarry, Steele, Taylor, Thomas, Thorpe, Tucker, Wagner, Wilbur, Wright 7 Branson, Carlson, Crashaw, Denning, Ellmann, Feynman, Gatling, Haldane, Jaeckel, Maurice, Roberts, Rodgers, Sanders, Simmons, Smalley, Strauss, Wallace, Widmark 8 Anderson, Basehart, Benjamin, Cromwell, Dreyfuss, Eberhart, Gephardt, Lovelace,

Marquand, Matheson, Mulligan, Sarafian, Sheridan **9** Carpenter, Fleischer, Linklater, Llewellyn, Lockridge, Roundtree, Silvestri, Zsigmondy **10** Castellano, Clayderman, D'Oyly Carte, Farnsworth, Hofstadter
in Italian: **8** Riccardo
in Spanish: **7** Ricardo
Richard ___: **3** III, Roe **4** Cory
Richard ___ Anderson: **4** Dean
Richard ___ Carte: **5** D'Oyly
Richard ___ Dana: **5** Henry
Richard ___ de Lion: **5** Coeur
___ Richard: **4** Poor **6** Little
Richard, Cliff
song: Devil Woman (1976)
Dreaming (1980)
A Little in Love (1981)
We Don't Talk Anymore (1979)
Richard Coeur de ___: **4** Lion
Richard Cory author: Edward Arlington Robinson
Richard Dean ___: **8** Anderson
Richard Henry ___: **4** Dana
Richard II author: Shakespeare
Richard III (1955 film)
cast: Sir John Gielgud, Laurence Olivier, Ralph Richardson
director: Laurence Olivier
Richard III (1995 film)
cast: Annette Bening, Jim Broadbent, Ian McKellen
director: Richard Loncraine
Richard III author: Shakespeare
Richard III need: **5** horse
Richard, Maurice
milieu: **3** ice **4** rink **5** arena
org.: **3** NHL
Richards: **2** I.A. **3** Ann, Bob **4** Mary **5** Keith, Renee **6** Denise **7** Michael **8** Theodore **9** Dickinson
___ Richard's Almanack: **4** Poor
Richards, Bob: **7** athlete **8** Olympian **11** pole vaulter
Richards, Denise spouse: Charlie Sheen
Richards, Dickinson: **8** Nobelist
Richards, I.A.: **4** poet **7** British **8** linguist
Richards, Keith: **5** Stone
Richards, Mary player: **5** Moore
Richardson: **3** Ian **4** city, Owen, Tony, town **5** Bobby, Joely, Ralph **6** Robert, Samuel **7** Dorothy, Miranda, Natasha **8** Patricia
locale: **5** Texas
___ Richardson, AK: **4** Fort
Richardson, Dorothy: **6** writer **7** British
work: Fortunes of Richard Mahony
Richardson, Miranda: **7** actress
film: The Apostle (1997)
The Bachelor (1993)
The Crying Game (1992)
Dance With a Stranger (1985)
Empire of the Sun (1987)
Enchanted April (1991)
The Evening Star (1996)
Get Carter (2000)
Sleepy Hollow (1999)
Tom & Viv (1994)
film (voice): The King and I (1999)
Richardson, Natasha: **7** actress
film: Nell (1994)
The Parent Trap (1998)
mother: Vanessa Redgrave
spouse: Liam Neeson
Richardson, Owen: **8** Nobelist **9** physicist
Richardson, Ralph: **3** Sir **5** actor
film: Breaking the Sound Barrier (1952)
Bulldog Jack (1934)
The Citadel (1938)
Dragonslayer (1981)
Exodus (1960)
The Four Feathers (1939)
Greystoke: The Legend of Tarzan, Lord of the Apes (1984)
The Heiress (1949)
Long Day's Journey Into Night (1962)
Outcast of the Islands (1951)
Richard III (1955)
South Riding (1938)
The Wrong Box (1966)
Richardson, Robert: **8** Nobelist **9** physicist
Richardson, Samuel: **6** writer **7** British
work: Clarissa Harlowe
Pamela, or Virtue Rewarded
wrote: first modern English novel
Richardson, Tony: **8** director
film: Blue Sky (1994)
The Border (1982)
The Entertainer (1960)
The Hotel New Hampshire (1984)
The Loneliness of the Long Distance Runner (1962)
Look Back in Anger (1958)
The Loved Ones (1965)
A Taste of Honey (1961)
Tom Jones (1963, AA)
Richards, Theodore: **7** chemist **8** Nobelist
Richard the ___-Hearted: **4** Lion
Rich, Buddy: **7** drummer
genre: **4** jazz
Rich, Charlie
nickname: The Silver Fox
song: Behind Closed Doors (1973)
The Most Beautiful Girl (1973)
A Very Special Love Song (1974)
___ riche: **4** rime **7** nouveau
Richelieu: **5** river **8** Cardinal
locale: **6** Canada, Quebec
riche, nouveau: **7** parvenu, upstart **9** arriviste
riches: **4** cash, gold, pelf, pile **5** lucre, means, money, worth **6** assets, clover, mammon, plenty, wealth **7** fortune **8** opulence, opulency, property, treasure **9** abundance, affluence, resources, substance **10** prosperity
hidden ~: **5** trove
Richest Girl in the World, The (1934 film)
cast: Miriam Hopkins, Joel McCrea, Fay Wray
Richet, Charles: **8** Nobelist **12** physiologist
Richfield: **4** city, town
locale: **9** Minnesota
rich friend
name meaning ~: **5** Edwin **6** Edwina
Rich Girl (1977 song) artist: Hall and Oates
rich guardian
name meaning ~: **6** Edward
rich hall
name meaning ~: **5** Edsel
Rich Harbor artist: **4** Klee
Richie: **4** Rich **6** Havens, Lionel **7** Ashburn, Sambora
portrayer: **3** Ron
Richie, Lionel
lead singer of: The Commodores
song: All Night Long (1983)
Ballerina Girl (1987)
Dancing in the Ceiling (1986)
Endless Love (1981)
Hello (1984)
Love Will Conquer All (1986)
My Love (1983)
Penny Lover (1984)
Running with the Night (1983)
Say You, Say Me (1985)
Se La (1987)
Stuck on You (1984)
Truly (1982)
You Are (1983)
Richie Rich dog: **6** Dollar
Rich Kids (1979 film)
cast: Trini Alvarado, Jeremy Levy, John Lithgow
Richland: **4** city, town
locale: **10** Washington
Richler: **8** Mordecai
Rich Man, Poor Man: **5** novel **10** miniseries
actor: **5** Asner, Bixby, Nolte **7** Blakely, Ed Asner, McGuire, Milland, Strauss **9** Bill Bixby, Nick Nolte
author: Irwin Shaw
role: **3** Sue, Tom **4** Axel, Berg, Joey, Mary, Rudy **5** Asher, Julie **6** Abbott, Quales, Smitty, Willie **8** Jordache
Richmond: **4** city, town
county: **7** Henrico
locale: **6** Canada **7** Georgia, Indiana **8** Kentucky, Virginia **10** California
river: **5** James
was its cap.: **3** CSA
Richmond-___-Thames: **4** upon
Richmond Hill: **4** city, town
locale: **6** Canada **7** Ontario
Richmond West: **4** city, town
locale: **7** Florida
richness: **4** luxe **6** luxury, wealth **8** grandeur, splendor, treasure **9** fecundity, fertility **10** exuberance, lavishness
Rich Project, Tony song: Nobody Knows (1996)
rich protection
name meaning ~: **6** Edmond, Edmund
rich spear, name meaning: **5** Edgar
Richter: **6** Burton, Conrad **7** Charles
concern: **5** quake, seism **6** tremor **10** earthquake
Richter ___: **5** scale
Richter, Burton: **8** Nobelist **9** physicist
Richter, Conrad: **6** author, writer
work: The Fields
The Light in the Forest
The Sea of Grass
The Town
The Trees
The Water of Kronos
Richter, Jean Paul Friedrich: **6** German, writer
Richter, Mordecai: **6** author, writer **8** Canadian
work: The Apprenticeship of Duddy Kravitz
Richthofen: **3** ace **5** Baron, flier, flyer, pilot **6** German **7** aviator, Manfred
rich war
name meaning ~: **5** Edith **6** Edythe
ricin: **5** toxin **6** poison
rick: **4** pile **8** haystack
starter: **3** hay
Rick: **4** Dees **5** Barry, Jason, Mears **6** Astley, Ocasek **7** Moranis, Nielsen **8** Newcombe, Schroder
Rickenbacker: **3** ace **5** Eddie, flier, flyer, pilot **7** aviator
rickety: **4** sick, thin, weak **5** frail, rocky, shaky **6** flimsy, infirm, jiggly, shabby, unfirm, wabbly, wobbly **7** fragile, rundown, unsound **8** decrepit, delicate, insecure, unstable, unsteady, untended **9** breakable, dangerous, frangible, tottering **10** broken-down, jerry-built, precarious, ramshackle, tumbledown
not as ~: **5** safer
sound ~: **5** creak
rickey: **5** drink **8** beverage, cocktail
ingredient: **3** gin **4** lime
Rickey: **6** Branch **9** Henderson
Ricki: **4** Lake
Rickie ___ Jones: **3** Lee
Rickles: **3** Don
Rickman, Alan: **5** actor
film: Close My Eyes (1991)
Die Hard (1988)
Dogma (1999)
Galaxy Quest (1999)
Judas Kiss (1999)
Quigley Down Under (1990)
Sense and Sensibility (1995)
Rickover: **5** Hyman **7** admiral
rickrack: **6** fringe
Rick's: **4** café
end of ~ toast: **3** kid
pianist: **3** Sam
rickshaw: **4** cart
Rickshaw Boy author: Lao She
Ricky: **3** Jay **5** Zahnd **6** Martin, Nelson, Skaggs **7** Ricardo
landlord: **4** Fred **10** Ethel. Mertz
portrayer: **4** Desi **5** Arnaz
wife: **4** Lucy
rico: **4** rich **7** Spanish
not ~: **5** pobre
___ Rico: **6** Puerto
ricochet: **4** skip **5** carom **6** bounce, careen, carrom, glance **7** deflect, rebound **10** bounce back
Ricochet actor: **4** Ice-T **6** Pollak **7** Lithgow
Ricoh: **6** camera, copier
competitor: **5** Nikon, Xerox
ricotta: **6** cheese **7** Italian
rictus: **4** gape **5** mouth **6** gaping **7** opening
rid: **4** dump, fire, free, junk, lose, shed **5** clear, eject, expel, purge, scrap **6** dispel, divest, remove, unload, uproot **7** abolish, release, relieve, shake up, toss out **8** disabuse, liberate, shake off, stamp out, unburden **9** disburden, dispose of, eliminate, eradicate, extirpate, liberated, throw away **10** do away with, unhindered
get ~ of: **2** ax **3** axe, can, zap **4** boot, cede, drop, dump, junk, oust, sack, sell, shed **5** chuck, ditch, drain, eject, erase, expel, forgo, let go, purge, scrap, shake, yield **6** banish, bounce, depose, forego, give up, lay off, remove, unload **7** abandon, cashier, discard, dismiss, drum out, exclude, forfeit, forsake, release, wipe out **8** exorcise, exorcize, forswear, furlough, hand over, jettison, part with, pink-slip, shake off, stamp out, throw out, unburden **9** cast aside, discharge, eliminate, foreswear, liquidate, surrender, terminate, throw away **10** do away with, relinquish
of: **8** done with, free from
(of): **4** free **5** empty
___ Riddance: **3** Bed
ridden starter: **3** bed
Riddick: **4** Bowe
riddle: **3** pit **4** maze, sift **5** poser, rebus, vexer **6** damage, enigma, impair, infest, pepper, pierce, puzzle **7** charade, mystery, paradox, pervade, problem, puzzler, stumper **8** puncture, question **9** conundrum, honeycomb, labyrinth, perforate **10** cryptogram, puzzlement
explanation: **3** key
starter: **4** what
Zen ~: **4** koan
Riddle: **6** Nelson
Riddle-me-___: **3** ree
Riddle, Nelson song: Lisbon Antigua (1955)
Riddler foe: **6** Batman
ride: **3** bug, fly, nag, rag, run, vex **4** bait, fare, hack, lift, post, spin, taxi, trot,

waft, whip 5 abuse, annoy, drift, drive, flume, get on, harry, hitch, hound, jaunt, motor, roast, taunt, tease, whirl 6 airing, badger, berate, bother, cruise, depend, Dodgem, gallop, go-cart, go-kart, harass, heckle, hector, jockey, junket, needle, outing, pester, plague, travel 7 bicycle, commute, henpeck, journey, joyride, mount up, oppress, torment, unnerve 8 carousel, log flume, ridicule, saddle up, travel on 9 excursion, hitchhike, move along, passenger, persecute, poke fun at, transport, tyrannize 10 Tilt-a-Whirl, tool around
ahead: 5 scout
allow to ~: 5 let on
free ~: 4 comp, lift, pass 7 license
go for a ~: 4 bike 5 motor 6 travel
herd on: 3 run 4 mind, tend 5 drive 6 direct 7 conduct, oversee 9 supervise, trample on, tyrannize 10 administer
let ~: 6 excuse, wink at 7 condone, forgive 8 overlook, shrug off, tolerate 9 put up with
off: 2 go 4 exit, flee 5 leave, split 6 beat it, be gone, decamp, depart 7 abscond, head out, move out, pull out, retreat, ship out, skip out 8 clear out, light out, run along, withdraw
(on): 4 rely 5 hinge 6 depend
out: 4 bear, take 5 brave 6 endure 7 subsist, survive, sustain, weather 8 navigate 9 withstand 10 see through
roughshod over: 5 bully 7 trample 9 trample on, tyrannize
seek a ~: 5 thumb
short ~: 3 hop 4 spin
shotgun: 5 watch 6 assist, defend, patrol, shield 7 protect 9 safeguard
starter: 3 hay
take for a ~: 3 gyp 4 bilk, dupe, gull, hoax, take 5 cheat, cozen, trick 6 fleece 7 deceive, defraud, mislead, swindle 8 flimflam, hoodwink 9 bamboozle
there for the ~: 5 along
thumb a ~: 5 hitch 9 hitchhike
to hounds: 4 hunt 5 chase, track 9 track down
via gravity: 5 coast
ride __: 3 out 4 down, high 7 shotgun
ride __ fall: 4 for a
ride __ on: 4 herd
__ ride: 4 free 5 Roman
__ Ride: 4 Free, Let's 6 Sleigh
Ride! (1962 song) artist: Dee Dee Sharp
Rideau Canal terminus: 6 Ottawa
Ride Back, The (1957 film)
cast: William Conrad, Lita Milan, Anthony Quinn
director: Allen H. Miner
Ride Captain Ride (1970 song) artist: Blues Image
Ride 'em Cowboy (1942 film)
cast: Bud Abbott, Lou Costello
ride for __: 5 a fall
Ride Like the Wind (1980 song) artist: Christopher Cross
Ride Lonesome (1959 film)
cast: Pernell Roberts, Randolph Scott, Karen Steele
rider: 4 fare 5 add-on, biker 6 cowboy, jockey 7 codicil, proviso 8 addendum, addition, commuter, horseman 9 amendment, bicyclist, passenger, provision 10 attachment, equestrian, hitchhiker, horsewoman, supplement
assistance: 5 leg up
attire: 5 habit 8 jodhpurs
command: 4 whoa 6 giddap 7 giddyap, giddyup
goad: 4 crop, spur 5 quirt
mishap: 4 buck 5 spill
payment: 4 fare
rail ~: 5 tramp
stance: 4 seat
strap: 4 rein
throw the ~: 4 buck
__ rider: 3 low 4 free 7 circuit, freedom
__ Rider: 3 Low 4 Easy, Pale 6 Knight, Uneasy
__ Riders: 3 Sky 5 Rough
Riders of the Purple Sage author: Zane Grey
Riders to the Sea author: John Synge
__ Rides Again: 6 Destry
Ride, Sally: 9 astronaut
Ride the High Country (1962 film)
cast: Mariette Hartley, Joel McCrea, Randolph Scott
director: Sam Peckinpah
Ride With the Devil (1999 film)
cast: Jim Caviezel, Tobey Maguire, Jonathan Rhys Meyers, Skeet Ulrich
director: Ang Lee
ridge: 3 rib, rim 4 apex, dune, fold, hill, line, nurl, pole, reef, rise, ruck, seam, wale, weal, welt 5 arête, arris, bluff, chain, chine, crest, esker, knoll, knurl, ledge, mound, range, scarp, spine, stria 6 crease, cuesta, flange, furrow, sierra, upland 7 crinkle, hillock, hogback, moraine, parapet, rampart, wrinkle 8 backbone, mountain, pinnacle, swelling 9 elevation 10 high ground, projection
anatomical ~: 4 ruga 5 gyrus
botanical ~: 5 raphe 6 carina
button ~: 4 nurl 5 knurl
corduroy ~: 3 rib 4 wale
depression: 3 col
ender: 4 back, line, pole
fingerboard ~: 4 fret
fingerprint ~: 5 whorl
glacial ~: 4 kame 5 arete, esker
ice ~: 7 hummock
rock ~: 4 crag
sand ~: 4 dune
seashell: 5 varix
__ ridge: 4 brow 5 basal, beach
__ Ridge Boys: 3 Oak
__ Ridge Boys, The: 3 Oak
Ridgecrest: 4 city, town
locale: 10 California
ridged: 5 rough 6 craggy, jagged, spiked 7 grooved, serrate, unlevel 8 crinkled, furrowed, serrated 10 corrugated
__ Ridge Mountains: 4 Blue
ridges: 5 rugae
glacial ~: 4 osar
__ Ridge, TN: 3 Oak
Ridgewood: 4 city, town
locale: 9 New Jersey
ridgy: 6 craggy, jagged, rugged, uneven 7 serrate 9 irregular
ridicule: 3 dig, kid, rag, rib 4 bait, barb, defy, gibe, haze, hiss, hoot, jape, jeer, jibe, jive, josh, lash, mock, razz, ride, slam, slap, slur, snub, twit 5 abuse, chaff, decry, farce, fleer, libel, mimic, roast, scoff, scorn, shame, sneer, spurn, taunt, tease 6 banter, debunk, defame, deride, dump on, expose, heckle, impugn, jeer at, jibe at, malign, needle, offend, parody, rebuff, satire, send-up, slight, vilify 7 affront, asperse, burlesk, calumny, catcall, deflate, degrade, disdain, lampoon, laugh at, mockery, mortify, obloquy, offense, putdown, rank out, ribbing, run down, sarcasm, slander, take off, traduce 8 belittle, contempt, denounce, derision, laugh off, pooh-pooh, raillery, satirize, sneeze at, vilipend 9 aspersion, burlesque, cheap shot, contumely, denigrate, discredit, disparage, humiliate, make fun of, poke fun at 10 calumniate, caricature, defamation, disrespect, make game of, opprobrium
Greek god of ~: 5 Momus
hold up to ~: 4 mock, twit 5 taunt 6 dump on, insult 7 disdain, lampoon, put down 8 belittle, satirize 9 burlesque 10 caricature
object of ~: 4 butt 5 sport 6 effigy
ridiculing: 7 jeering, satiric 8 derisive 9 satirical
ridiculous: 4 daft, rich 5 antic, crazy, daffy, droll, funny, goofy, goony, inane, nutty, sappy, silly, wacky 6 absurd, screwy, stupid, whacky 7 asinine, bizarre, comical, fatuous, foolish, puerile, suspect 8 cockeyed, farcical 9 facetious, fantastic, fatuitous, grotesque, hilarious, laughable, ludicrous, pointless, priceless, senseless, unearthly 10 hysterical, incredible, irrational, outlandish
idea: 5 folly 6 lunacy 7 fatuity, madness 8 nonsense 9 absurdity, silliness
riding: 5 sport 6 ahorse 9 annoyance
see also rider
riding __: 4 boot, crop, sail 5 habit, light, mower 6 master, school
...riding on __: 5 a pony
ridley: 6 animal, turtle 7 reptile 9 amphibian, sea turtle
Ridley: 5 Scott
__ rid of: 3 get
Riefenstahl: 4 Leni
Rieger: 4 Alex
Riegert: 5 Peter
riel: 5 money
rien __ plus: 4 ne va
Rienzi author: Edward Bulwer-Lytton
Rienzi composer: 6 Wagner
Riesa: 4 city, town
locale: 6 Saxony 7 Germany
Riesling: 4 wine 5 white
rife: 4 many 5 alive, awash, laden 6 common, filled, jammed, loaded, packed 7 copious, crammed, crowded, general, overrun, profuse, rampant, replete, stuffed, teeming 8 abundant, brimming, bursting, epidemic, infested, numerous, pandemic, swarming, thronged 9 abounding, chock-full, extensive, pervasive, plentiful, prevalent, universal 10 epidemical, ubiquitous, widespread
be ~: 4 rule 6 abound
(with): 5 alive, lousy
with vegetation: 4 rich, wild 5 dense, green 6 lavish 7 fertile, teeming, verdant 8 abundant, tropical 9 plentiful, succulent
riff: 6 melody
jazz ~: 4 vamp
Riff: 6 Berber
home: 6 Africa 7 Morocco
riffle (through): 4 leaf, scan, skim 5 thumb 6 browse
riffraff: 3 mob 4 scum 5 dregs 6 masses, people, rabble 7 beggary 9 commoners, hoi polloi, peasantry 10 lower class, underworld
associate with ~: 4 slum
Riffraff (1947 film)
cast: Anne Jeffreys, Pat O'Brien, Walter Slezak
Rifkin: 3 Ron
rifle: 3 arm, gun, gut, rob, Uzi 4 loot, M one, raid, sack 5 BB gun, steal, strip, yager 6 burgle, Garand, musket, rip off, search 7 despoil, firearm, pillage, plunder, ransack, rummage, shotgun 9 flintlock, go through 10 burglarize, Winchester
carrying a ~: 5 armed
ender: 3 man, men 4 bird 5 scope
mount: 5 bipod
part: 4 bead, butt 5 scope, sight, stock 6 barrel, breech
pellet: 2 BB 6 beebee
ready a ~: 3 aim
sight a ~ again: 5 reaim
rifle __: 3 pit 4 bird 5 range 7 grenade
__ rifle: 3 air 4 long 6 Garand, target 7 assault, Enfield, express, machine
rifled __: 4 slug
Rifleman, The (ABC western)
cast: Chuck Connors (Lucas McCain) Johnny Crawford (Mark McCain) Paul Fix (Micah Torrance)
Rifle Regiment, The composer: 5 Sousa
rifles: 4 arms 8 weaponry 9 firepower
rift: 3 cut, gap 4 feud, gape, gash, gulf, rent, tear 5 abyss, break, chasm, chink, cleft, crack, fault, gorge, gulch, gully, split 6 breach, cranny, gulley, hiatus, ravine, schism 7 crevice, fissure, opening, quarrel, rupture 8 aperture, cleavage, crevasse, division, fracture, squabble 10 alienation, falling-out, separation
rift __: 3 saw 4 zone 6 valley
__ Rift Valley: 5 Great
rig: 3 arm, fit, fix, kit 4 fake, gear, semi, team 5 array, dress, equip, getup, lorry, set up, sulky, truck 6 attire, clothe, doctor, fit out, gear up, juggle, outfit, square, supply, tackle, tamper 7 appoint, bedrape, costume, falsify, furnish, trump up, turnout 8 accouter, accoutre, carriage, contrive, engineer, equipage, maneuver 9 apparatus, buckboard, caparison, equipment, improvise, machinery, provision 10 fiddle with, manipulate, prearrange, tamper with
as a sports event: 3 fix
big ~: 4 mack, semi 5 truck 9 transport
renter: 5 Ryder, U-Haul
starter: 7 thimble
up: 3 fix 4 garb 5 equip 6 attire, outfit 7 furnish 8 accouter, accoutre 9 caparison
__ rig: 3 cat 4 gaff 5 drill, sloop 6 jackup 7 Bermuda, jackass, Marconi
__-rig: 4 jury
Rig-__: 4 Veda
Riga: 4 city, gulf, port, town 7 capital
locale: 6 Latvia
resident: 4 Lett
river: 5 Dvina
rigadoon: 5 dance
rigamarole: 9 goofiness
rigati: 5 pasta 7 noodles 8 macaroni
rigatoni: 5 pasta 7 noodles 8 macaroni
alternative: 4 orzo, ziti 5 penne 6 noodle 7 lasagna, lasagne, pastina, ravioli 8 bucatini, couscous, farfalle, linguine, linguini, macaroni 9 agnolotti, angelhair, cavatelli, manicotti, spaghetti 10 cannelloni, fettuccini, tortellini, vermicelli
sauce: 5 pesto 6 tomato 8 marinara
__ Rigby: 7 Eleanor
Rigby, Cathy: 7 gymnast
Rigel: 4 star
constellation: 5 Orion
Rigg, Diana: 4 Dame 7 actress
film: The Assassination Bureau (1969)
The Hospital (1971)

On Her Majesty's Secret Service (1969)
Theatre of Blood (1973)
role: 4 Emma, Peel
TV: The Avengers
__-rigged: 3 lug 4 full, jury, ship, yawl 5 ketch, sloop 6 cutter, lateen, square
rigger starter: 3 out 4 down
rigging: 4 gear 6 outfit, tackle 9 caparison, trappings
make over the ~: 5 refit
overseer: 4 bo's'n 5 bosun
part of a ship's ~: 4 bibb
support: 4 mast, spar
Riggs, Bobby: 7 netster 9 tennis pro
milieu: 5 court
right: 2 ay, da, ja, sí 3 apt, aye, due, fit, fix, oui, yea, yep, yes, yup 4 cure, fair, fine, good, hale, just, meet, mend, nice, okay, real, sane, sure, true, very, well, wise, yeah 5 aptly, claim, emend, exact, fixed, good-o, hardy, ideal, legal, licit, lucid, moral, natch, power, punch, quite, roger, smack, sound, spang, title, truly, truth, uh-huh, utter, valid 6 actual, agreed, avenge, dead-on, decent, dexter, direct, equity, evenly, gladly, good-oh, honest, indeed, justly, just so, lawful, normal, proper, rather, remedy, repair, seemly, spot on, square, surely, virtue, wholly, you bet, yowzah 7 condign, correct, ethical, exactly, factual, fitting, freedom, genuine, go ahead, honesty, indeedy, justice, legally, liberty, license, licitly, logical, mais oui, merited, morally, perfect, precise, quickly, quite so, rectify, redress, requite, restore, sort out, ten-four, totally, utterly 8 accuracy, accurate, all there, as you say, bona fide, deserved, directly, discreet, entirely, fairness, faithful, flawless, for suree, goodness, honestly, interest, lawfully, morality, of course, on target, on the dot, orthodox, promptly, properly, rational, reaction, reliably, sensible, smack-dab, squarely, straight, suitable, suitably, thumbs up, truthful, unerring, validity, veracity, very well, virtuous 9 actuality, authentic, authority, befitting, be my guest, certainly, clockwise, correctly, equitable, errorless, ethically, exactness, exemption, faultless, favorable, favorably, fittingly, franchise, honorable, honorably, instantly, integrity, judicious, make up for, naturally, on the beam, on the mark, on the nose, opportune, out-and-out, perfectly, precisely, privilege, propriety, sure thing, undoubted, veracious, veritable, vindicate, you betcha, you said it 10 aboveboard, absolutely, accurately, admissible, by all means, completely, definitely, exactitude, factuality, felicitous, infallible, lawfulness, legitimacy, legitimate, on the money, permission, perquisite, positively, principled, propitious, reasonable, recompense, remarkably, scrupulous, sure enough, unimagined, unmistaken, virtuously, watertight
angle: 2 el 3 ell
as rain: 5 sound
at ~ angles: 4 orth., perp. 5 plumb 10 orthogonal
at ~ angles to the keel: 5 abeam
at the ~ time: 3 apt 5 on cue 6 prompt 7 fitting 8 apposite, punctual 9 expedient 10 auspicious, convenient, felicitous
away: 3 now, PDQ 4 anon, ASAP, soon, stat 5 today 6 at once, pronto 7 quickly, readily, swiftly 8 directly, promptly 9 at present, forthwith, instantly, on the spot, presently 10 at this time, here and now, this minute
a wrong: 5 repay 6 avenge 7 get even, pay back, redress, requite 9 retaliate, retribute
be ~ for: 3 fit 4 suit 5 befit, match 6 become 7 apply to 9 agree with
by ~: 6 de jure
combining form: 4 orth-, rect- 5 dextr-, ortho-, recti- 6 dextro-
do all ~: 3 win 6 hack it, make it, manage, thrive 7 make out, prevail, prosper, succeed, triumph 8 flourish, go places, make good
ender: 3 ist 4 most, ness, ward
forgo a ~: 4 cede 5 forgo, waive 6 give up 8 sign away 10 relinquish
from the factory: 3 new 5 fresh 6 unused 8 brand-new 9 untouched
get ~: 5 solve 6 unlock 7 explain, unravel, work out 8 decipher 9 figure out, puzzle out
good ~ arm: 8 backbone, linchpin, mainstay
hand: 6 dexter
hang a ~: 4 turn
have a ~ to: 4 earn 5 merit 7 deserve
having the ~ stuff: 5 adept 6 suited, up to it 7 capable 8 skillful, talented 9 competent, efficient, qualified, up to snuff, up to speed 10 proficient
hitting the ~ notes: 5 on key
if all goes ~: 6 at best
ignorant of ~ and wrong: 6 amoral
in French: 9 n'est-ce pas?
in heraldry: 6 dexter
in one's ~ mind: 4 sane 5 lucid 8 sensible 10 reasonable
just ~: 4 to a T 5 ideal 6 to a tee 7 optimal, perfect, utopian 8 flawless 9 beautiful, correctly, exemplary, faultless, nonpareil, on the nose, perfectly, precisely 10 accurately, consummate
legal ~: 5 droit
look ~ through: 3 cut 4 shun, snub 5 scorn, spurn 6 ignore, insult, rebuff, slight 7 disdain, neglect, put down, tune out 8 brush off 9 blackball, disregard, humiliate, ostracize
make ~: 3 fix 5 atone, remit 6 adjust, remedy 7 correct, rectify, redress 8 disabuse
maker: 5 might
name meaning ~: 6 Dexter
not ~: 3 off 4 awry, left 5 amiss, wrong
now: 3 PDQ 4 anon, ASAP 5 as yet, today 6 at once, pronto 7 quickly, swiftly 8 promptly 9 at present, forthwith, instantly, on the spot, presently 10 at this time, the present, this minute
of access: 6 entrée 7 ingress, passage 10 admittance
off the bat: 6 at once, pronto 7 quickly, rapidly, swiftly 8 in a flash, in no time, on the fly 9 instantly, like a shot
of way: 8 priority 10 precedence
on: 3 yes 4 amen 5 exact 6 it is so 8 for a fact, specific 9 certainly, precisely 10 acceptable, positively
on the map: 4 east
party of the ~: 3 GOP
ship's ~ side: 4 stbd. 9 starboard
starter: 4 copy, down 5 birth, forth
stuff: 5 goods, knack, savvy, skill 6 talent 7 ability, faculty, know-how, prowess 8 aptitude, capacity, facility 9 dexterity, expertise 10 capability, competence, competency
to buy: 6 option
to the ~: 3 gee 4 away 5 aside
to vote: 9 franchise
right __: 3 off 4 away, face, hand, wing 5 angle, brain, field, guard, of way, stage, stuff, whale 6 tackle 7 fielder, section
right __ and there: 4 then
right __ money: 5 on the
right __ the bat: 3 off
right __ the horse's mouth: 4 from
right __ up: 4 side
right-__: 4 laid, wing 6 handed, hander, minded
right-__ man: 4 hand
__ right: 3 all 4 acre, eyes, quad, shop 5 flush, guide, hang a, stage, water 6 patent, timber 7 natural
__, right!: 4 Yeah
__-right: 3 all 4 half
Right __: 4 Bank 5 Guard
Right __, The: 5 Stuff
right and wrong, uncaring of: 6 amoral
right-angled: 4 boxy 6 square
right as __: 4 rain
Right Back Where We Started From (1976 song) artist: Maxine Nightingale
Right Bank attraction: 6 Louvre
Right Bank author: 4 Neal
right circular __: 4 cone
righteous: 4 fair, good, holy, just, pure, smug 5 godly, moral, pious 6 devout, honest, trusty, worthy 7 angelic, dutiful, ethical, saintly, sincere, sinless, upright 8 elevated, innocent, reverent, virtuous 9 angelical, blameless, deserving, exemplary, guiltless, honorable, praisable, religious, veracious, wholesome 10 charitable, law-abiding, scrupulous
indignation: 4 fury 5 anger, pique 6 choler, dander 7 dudgeon, offense, outrage, umbrage 10 resentment
__-righteous: 4 self
Righteous Brothers
members: Medley, Hatfield
song: Ebb Tide (1965)
He (1967)
Just Once in My Life (1965)
Rock and Roll Heaven (1974)
Soul and Inspiration (1966)
Unchained Melody (1965)
You've Lost That Lovin' Feelin' (1964)
righteousness: 4 good 5 honor 6 virtue 7 justice, probity 8 goodness, morality
right from the __ mouth: 6 horse's
rightful: 3 apt, due, fit 4 fair, just, real, true 5 jural, legal, legit, licit, valid 6 earned, kasher, kosher, lawful, proper, vested 7 allowed, condign, fitting, merited 8 bona fide, deserved, official, orthodox, suitable 9 befitting, by the book, canonical, permitted 10 authorized, legitimate, sanctioned
rightfully: 8 lawfully
Right Guard: 9 deodorant
alternative: 3 Ban 4 Sure 5 Arrid, Tussy 6 Degree, Secret 7 Dry Idea, Mitchum 10 Soft and Dri, Speed Stick
right-hand: 3 key 5 basic, vital 6 needed 7 crucial 9 important, necessary, requisite
person: 4 aide, asst. 6 helper 7 adviser, advisor 8 henchman, mainstay
__ Right In: 4 Walk
rightly: 4 ably, fine, well 6 nicely 7 adeptly, capably 8 expertly, properly, suitably 9 admirably, correctly, perfectly 10 accurately, adequately, splendidly
right-minded: 4 true 5 sound 6 worthy 7 ethical 8 virtuous
Right, Mr., not: 3 cad 4 heel
rightness: 8 justness, morality 9 propriety
righto: 2 ay, da, ja, sí 3 aye, oui, yea, yep, yup 4 fine, okay, sure, yeah 5 good-o, natch, quite, roger, uh-huh 6 agreed, gladly, good-oh, indeed, just so, rather, surely, you bet, yowzah 7 exactly, go ahead, indeedy, mais oui, quite so, ten-four 8 all right, as you say, of course, thumbs up, very well 9 be my guest, certainly, naturally, precisely, sure thing, you betcha, you said it 10 absolutely, by all means, definitely, positively, sure enough
right of __: 3 way 6 asylum, search
right-of-__: 6 center
right off the __: 3 bat
__ right of kings: 6 divine
Right on!: 4 amen, okay
right on the __: 5 money
rights: 4 dibs 5 claim, title
by ~: 6 fairly, justly
have ~ to: 3 own 6 retain 7 control, possess
movement word: 3 lib
org.: 3 ADL 4 ACLU, EEOC, NLRB, SCLC 5 NAACP
put to ~: 5 clean, order 6 neaten, spruce 7 ordered, orderly 9 smarten up 10 straighten
set to ~: 6 remedy 7 restore 9 refurbish
strip of ~: 6 divest
to ~: 4 tidy, trim 7 orderly
__ rights: 3 air 5 civil, human 6 animal, serial, states', women's
Rights __, The: 5 of Man
__ Rights Amendment: 5 Equal
Rights of Man, The author: Thomas Paine
Right Stuff , The: 4 book, film
author: Tom Wolfe
cast: Kathy Baker, Scott Glenn, Ed Harris, Barbara Hershey, Dennis Quaid, Sam Shepard, Kim Stanley, Fred Ward
director: Philip Kaufman
org: 4 NASA
role: 3 LBJ 5 Glenn 6 Cooper, Yaeger 7 Grissom, Schirra, Shepard, Slayton 9 Carpenter
right then and __: 5 there
__ Right Thing: 5 Do the
right-thinking: 4 good 5 sound, valid 6 cogent, proper 7 correct, ethical, logical 8 accurate, credible, rational, sensible 9 competent, honorable 10 reasonable
Right Time of the Night (1977 song) artist: Jennifer Warnes
right-to-__: 4 know
right-to-__ law: 4 work
Right to Happiness, The: 9 radio show
Right Turn __: 4 Only
__ right up!: 4 Step
__ right with the world: 4 All's
Right you __!: 3 are
rigid: 3 set 4 firm, hard, iron, prim, snug, taut 5 balky, bossy, cruel, exact, fixed, harsh, onery, picky, rocky, solid, stern, stiff, stony, tense, tight, tough 6 flinty, mulish, ornery, severe, static, steely, stoney, strict, stuffy, wooden 7 adamant, austere, dead set, diehard, hard-set, literal, precise, prudish, Spartan 8 absolute, concrete, contrary, despotic, exacting, hard-line, immobile, indurate, ironclad,

locked in, obdurate, perverse, resolute, stubborn **9** demanding, difficult, draconian, hidebound, immovable, impliable, inelastic, obstinate, pigheaded, religious, sectarian, steadfast, stringent, unbending, unpliable, unsparing, unvarying **10** bullheaded, despotical, determined, hard-bitten, implacable, inexorable, inflexible, invariable, iron-fisted, iron-willed, nononsense, oppressive, relentless, tyrannical, unamenable, unchanging, unswerving, unyielding
not ~: **3** lax **5** slack **7** bending, relaxed
rigidify: **3** fix, set **7** tighten
rigidity: **6** starch **8** firmness, hardness
lose ~: **3** dip, sag **4** wilt **5** droop
rigmarole: **3** gas, rot **4** blah, bosh, bull, bunk, guff, jazz, jive, pooh, tale, tosh **5** bilge, fudge, hokum, hooey, prate, stuff, trash, tripe **6** bunkum, bushwa, drivel, footle, gabble, gammon, gibber, havers, hot air, humbug, jabber, jargon, kibosh, piffle **7** baloney, blarney, blather, blether, boloney, bushwah, eyewash, flannel, flubdub, fustian, garbage, hogwash, inanity, red tape, rubbish, twaddle **8** buncombe, claptrap, falderal, falderol, flimflam, flummery, folderal, folderol, nonsense, protocol, slipslop, tommyrot, trumpery **9** banana oil, gibberish, goofiness, kidstakes, moonshine, poppycock **10** applesauce, balderdash, bilge water, codswallop, double-talk, flapdoodle, galimatias, hocus-pocus, Jabberwock, mumbo jumbo, taradiddle
Rigney: **4** Bill
Rigoberta: **3** Tum
Rigoletto: **5** opera
character: **4** Duke **5** Borsa, Gilda **7** Ceprano, Marullo **8** Giovanna **9** Maddalena, Monterone
composer: **5** Verdi
piece: **4** aria
sculptor: **4** Erté
setting: **5** Italy **6** Mantua
rigor: **8** asperity, fidelity, hardness, hardship, iron hand, severity **9** austerity, diligence, exactness, harshness, precision, sternness **10** discipline, exactitude, inclemency, severeness, strictness, stringency
ending: **3** ous
rigorous: **4** firm, hard **5** bossy, cruel, exact, fussy, harsh, picky, stern, stiff, tough **6** bitter, Lenten, rugged, severe, strict, trying **7** austere, careful, correct, finicky, precise, prudent, Spartan **8** accurate, cautious, despotic, exacting, finiking, finnicky, hard-line, thorough **9** assiduous, attentive, demanding, draconian, inclement, judicious, observant, stringent, unbending, unsparing **10** despotical, fastidious, inflexible, iron-fisted, meticulous, nononsense, oppressive, particular, relentless, scrupulous, tyrannical
rigorously: **4** hard **6** keenly **8** severely **9** carefully
__ rigueur: **3** à la
rigueur, de: **6** proper **9** mandatory, necessary **10** compulsory
Rig-Veda god: **4** Agni
Riis, Jacob: **6** Danish, writer **8** reformer
work: How the Other Half Lives
The Making of an American
Rijeka: **4** city, port, town
locale: **7** Croatia
Rijksmuseum artist: **4** Hals
Rikki Don't Lose That Number (1974 song) artist: Steely Dan
Rikki-tikki-__: **4** Tavi
Riksdag locale: **6** Sweden
rile: **3** bug, get, irk, vex **4** fret, gall, pain, stir **5** anger, annoy, get to, grate, peeve, pique, rouse, upset **6** arouse, bother, enrage, excite, fire up, hassle, madden, needle, nettle, offend, pother, put out, rankle, stir up, tee off, work up **7** agitate, disturb, enflame, grate on, incense, inflame, provoke, steam up, tick off **8** irritate **9** aggravate, displease, infuriate **10** exasperate, run afoul of
riled: **3** hot, mad **4** ired, sore, warm **5** angry, cross, het up, huffy, irate, livid, upset, wroth **6** fuming, galled, ireful, raging, raving, red-hot **7** enraged, furious, ranting **8** choleric, wrathful **9** indignant, irritated, resentful, splenetic **10** infuriated
riler: **7** inciter **8** agitator, fomenter **10** instigator
Riley: **3** Pat **7** Chester **8** Jeannine
life of ~: **4** ease
Riley, James Whitcomb
nickname: Hoosier Poet
work: Little Orphant Annie
The Old Swimmin' Hole
The Raggedy Man
When the Frost Is on the Punkin
Riley, Jeannie C. song: Harper Valley P.T.A. (1968)
__ Riley, KS: **4** Fort
Riley, Mrs. Chester: **3** Peg
__-rilievo: **4** alto
Rilke, Rainer Maria: **4** poet **6** German
work: The Duino Elegies
The Sonnets to Orpheus
rill: **4** race **5** bourn, brook, creek, crick **6** runlet, runnel, stream **7** rivulet **9** streamlet
rille: **6** trench, valley
rim: **3** hem, lip, top **4** brim, brow, curb, edge, hoop, line, side **5** brink, frame, ledge, limit, mouth, ridge, skirt, verge **6** border, flange, margin **8** boundary, surround **9** extremity, outskirts, perimeter, periphery **10** projection
basketball ~: **4** hoop
circular ~: **5** felly **6** felloe
watch ~: **5** bezel
wheel ~: **6** flange
rim __: **3** man **4** lock, shot
__ Rim: **7** Pacific
__ rima: **5** terza **6** ottava
Rímac, city on the: **4** Lima
Rima's beloved: **4** Abel
Rimbaud, Arthur: **4** poet **6** French
rime: **4** hoar, poem **5** frost **9** hoarfrost, Jack Frost
rime __: **3** ice **5** riche
Rime of the Ancient Mariner, The: **4** poem
author: Samuel Taylor Coleridge
rimer: **4** bard, poet **5** odist **9** versifier
__-rimés: **5** bouts
Rimes, LeAnn
song: How Do I Live (1997)
Looking Through Your Eyes (1998)
Written in the Stars (1999)
Rimini: **4** city, town
locale: **5** Italy
__-rimmed glasses: **4** horn
rimose: **7** cracked
Rimouski: **4** city, town
locale: **6** Canada, Québec
rimple: **6** furrow
rims, horn: **7** glasses **8** cheaters **10** spectacles
Rimsky-Korsakov, Nikolai: **7** Russian **8** composer
work: Capriccio Espagnol
Le Coq d'Or
Scheherazade
The Snow Maiden
The Tsar's Bride
rimu: **4** pine **7** red pine
rimy: **3** icy **5** gelid **6** frozen
rin
ten ~: **3** sen
Rinaldo: **5** opera
composer: **6** Handel
Rinaldo author: Torquato Tasso
Rincón de Romos: **4** city, town
locale: **6** Mexico
rind: **4** bark, coat, hull, husk, peel, skin **5** cover, crust **6** albedo, casing, cortex **7** coating, peeling, surface **8** covering **10** integument
remove ~: **4** pare, peel, skin
remover: **5** parer **6** peeler
__ rinds: **4** pork
Rinehart, Mary Roberts: **6** author, writer
work: The Circular Staircase
The Door
The Man in Lower Ten
The Swimming Pool
Tish
The Yellow Room
ring: **3** mob **4** band, belt, bloc, bong, buzz, call, clan, dial, echo, gang, gird, gong, gyre, halo, hoop, link, loop, peal, pool, rink, toll, wind **5** arena, bunch, cabal, chime, clang, cycle, go off, hedge, hem in, junta, junto, knell, noise, party, phone, round, sound, torus, troop, wheel **6** call up, cartel, circle, clique, corona, engird, flange, gasket, girdle, jangle, jingle, league, outfit, rabble, reecho, summon, tinkle, troupe, wreath **7** annulet, bandlet, circuit, clangor, combine, compass, coterie, enclose, environ, faction, inclose, in-group, jewelry, resound, seal off, sing out, society, stadium, vibrate **8** alliance, bandelet, cincture, encircle, gloriole, ornament, resonate, surround **9** coalition, encompass, enwreathe, resonance, syndicate, telephone **10** federation, hippodrome
a bell: **6** recall **8** remember **9** recognize
anatomical ~: **6** areola, areole
bearer: **4** wife **5** bride, groom
boundary: **4** rope
combining form: **3** gyr- **4** cycl-, gyro- **5** cyclo-
competitor: **3** pug **5** boxer **7** fighter **8** pugilist
decision: **2** KO **3** TKO **4** draw, kayo
ender: **3** let **4** bolt, bone, dove, side, tail, toss, worm **6** leader, master
event: **4** bout **5** fight, match
face off in the ~: **3** box
foul: **4** butt, knee
in: **4** come, open **5** reach, start, usher **7** precede, welcome
(in): **5** usher
off: **6** hang up
official ~: **3** ref **7** referee
of light: **4** halo **7** aureola, aureole
org.: **3** WBA, WBC
out: **4** peal, toll **8** resonate
part: **3** gem **5** bezel, jewel
practice in the ~: **4** spar
Roman ~: **6** anello
rubber ~: **6** gasket
site: **3** ear **5** arena, pinky **6** big top, circus, finger
starter: **3** ear **4** bull
surface: **3** mat
tactic: **5** feint **6** clinch
thing on a ~: **3** key
three minutes in the ~: **3** rnd. **5** round
up: **4** call **5** phone, total **9** telephone, touch base
see also boxing
ring __: **3** man, off, rot, taw **4** buoy, gage, gate, gear, spot, toss, true **5** a bell, dance, frame, gauge, shout, snake, stone **6** binder, finger, galaxy **7** machine, seizing
ring __ curtain: **5** up the
ring __ new year: **5** in the
ring __ the curtain: **4** down
ring-__: **6** porous, tailed
ring-__-the-rosey: **6** around
__ ring: **3** key **4** bird, flan, mood, nose, seal, slip, snap, snow, tree **5** black, brass, fairy, guard, prize **6** anchor, annual, boxing, coffee, dinner, growth, napkin, piston, signet **7** benzene, Bishop's, Boolean, chapter, diamond, lantern, packing, squared, storage, wedding
Ring: **7** Lardner
composer: **6** Wagner
goddess: **4** Erda
Ring __: **5** Cycle, Dings **6** Nebula
ring a __: **4** bell
ring-a-levio: **4** game
Ring and the Book, The: **4** poem
author: Robert Browning
character: **5** Guido
Ring and the Rose, The author: Thackeray
ring around the __: **6** collar
ring-around-the-__: **5** rosey
Ring Around the Moon author: Jean Anouilh
__-ring circus: **5** three
__ Ring des Nibelungen: **3** Der
ringdove: **4** bird
ringer: **4** bell **8** doorbell **9** accessory, imitation
bell ~: **6** caller **7** visitor
dead ~: **4** twin **5** image, match **6** double **7** picture **8** likeness **9** duplicate, facsimile, identical, look-alike **10** equivalent
register ~: **4** sale
__ ringer: **4** bird, dead
Ringer, The (1952 film)
cast: Herbert Lom, Mai Zetterling
director: Guy Hamilton
ringhals: **5** snake **6** animal **7** reptile
relative: **3** asp, boa **5** aboma, adder, cobra, krait, mamba, racer, viper **6** dhaman, python, taipan **7** markhor, rattler **8** anaconda, moccasin **9** boomslang, coachwhip **10** bushmaster, copperhead, sidewinder
ringing: **4** loud, peal **5** knell, sound **7** vibrant **8** resonant
sound: **4** bong, ding, peal, ting
ring in the __: **3** new
ringlet: **4** curl, lock **5** tress **10** lock of hair
ringlets: **4** coif **6** hairdo **8** coiffure
make ~: **4** coil, curl **5** swirl, twine, twirl, twist
ringlike: **5** curvy, round **6** curved **8** circular
Ringling: **4** John, Otto **5** Henry **6** Albert, Alfred, August **7** Charles
see also circus
Ringling __: **4** Bros.
ringmaster: **4** host **5** emcee
Ring My Bell (1979 song) artist: Anita Ward
Ring Nebula constellation: **4** Lyra
ring-necked __: **4** duck **5** snake
Ringo: **3** Jim **5** Starr
colleague: **4** John, Paul **6** George
son: **3** Zak
Ringo (1964 song) artist: Lorne Greene
Ring of Bright Water (1969 film)
cast: Virginia McKenna, Bill Travers
pet: **5** otter

Ring of Fire (1963 song) artist: Johnny Cash
Ring of Thoth, The author: Arthur Conan Doyle
rings: 4 tori 7 jewelry
mood ~: 3 fad 5 craze
run ~ around: 3 top 4 beat, best 5 outdo 7 surpass
tree ~: 6 annuli
___ rings: 5 onion, smoke 7 Newton's
___ rings around: 3 run
ring-shaped: 5 toric
Rings on ___ fingers...: 3 her
ring-tailed animal: 4 coon 5 coati, genet 6 monkey
Ring, The (1927 film) director: Alfred Hitchcock
ringtoss: 4 game
game piece: 5 quoit
target: 3 peg
Ringwald, Molly: 7 actress
film: Betsy's Wedding (1990)
The Breakfast Club (1985)
Pretty in Pink (1987)
Sixteen Candles (1984)
ringworm: 5 tinea
rink: 5 arena
see also hockey
rink ___: 3 rat
___ rink: 6 roller
rinky-dink: 5 cheap 6 flimsy 8 picayune
Rinna, Lisa spouse: Harry Hamlin
rinpoche: 4 monk 6 cleric
rinse: 3 dip, wet 4 soak, tint, wash 5 bathe, clean, flush, henna 6 dampen, gargle 7 cleanse, dunking, immerse, launder, moisten, wash off 8 flush out 9 hair color
needing a ~: 5 foamy, soapy, sudsy 6 frothy 7 lathery
salon ~: 5 henna
Rinso rival: 3 Duz, Fab 4 Tide
Rin Tin Tin: 3 dog 6 canine 8 shepherd
see also Adventures of Rin Tin Tin
Rinzai ___: 3 Zen
río: 4 Ebro 5 river 7 Orinoco, Spanish
Rio: 3 car, Kia 4 auto, port 10 automobile
see also Rio de Janeiro
Rio ___: 4 Lobo, Rita 5 Bravo, de Oro, Negro 6 Blanco, Cuarto, Grande 7 Conchos, Piedras
Rio ___ Plata: 4 de la
___ Rio: 3 Del 5 I Go to
Rio Bravo (1959 film): 5 oater
cast: Dean Martin, Ricky Nelson, John Wayne
composer: 7 Tiomkin
director: Howard Hawks
Río Bravo: 4 city, town
locale: 6 Mexico 10 Tamaulipas
Rio Conchos (1964 film)
cast: Richard Boone, Tony Franciosa, Edmond O'Brien, Stuart Whitman
Rio de ___: 3 Oro 7 Janeiro
Rio de Janeiro: 4 city, port, town
airline: 5 Varig
airport: 6 Galeao
dance: 5 samba
locale: 6 Brasil, Brazil
Rio de la Plata: 5 river
locale: 3 Arg., Uru. 7 Uruguay 9 Argentina
Rio Grande: 5 river
capital of ~ do Norte: 5 Natal
city on the ~: 6 El Paso, Laredo 11 Albuquerque
locale: 5 Texas 8 Colorado 9 New Mexico
river to the ~: 5 Pecos 7 Conchos
Rio Grande (1950 film): 5 oater
cast: Ben Johnson, Maureen O'Hara, John Wayne
director: John Ford
Río Grande: 4 city, town
locale: 6 Mexico 9 Zacatecas
Rioja: 3 red 4 wine 5 Pilar
like ~ wine: 4 seco
origin: 5 Spain
Rio Lobo (1970 film): 5 oater
cast: Jack Elam, Jennifer O'Neill, John Wayne
director: Howard Hawks
Rion ___: 6 Strait
Riopan: 7 antacid
alternative: 4 Tums 6 Maalox, Pepcid, Zantac 7 Gelusil, Lactaid, Mylanta, Rolaids 8 Gaviscon 11 Alka-Seltzer, Pepto-Bismol
Rio Rancho: 4 city, town
locale: 9 New Mexico
Rio Rita (1942 film)
cast: Bud Abbott, Lou Costello, Kathryn Grayson
___ Rios, Jamaica: 4 Ocho
riot: 3 mob, row 4 card, flap, fray, howl, rise, to-do 5 blast, brawl, chaos, mix-up, rebel, scene 6 bedlam, émeute, fracas, gasser, mutiny, rabble, racket, revolt, rise up, ruckus, rumble, rumpus, scream, strife, tumult, uproar 7 clutter, protest, rampage, ruction, run wild, triumph, turmoil 8 carousal, disorder, foofaraw, live it up, outbreak, run amuck, upheaval, uprising, violence 9 brannigan, commotion, confusion, go berserk, imbroglio, laughable, luxuriate, mobocracy, raise Cain, whoop it up 10 donnybrook, free-for-all, profligacy
cause a ~: 5 rouse 6 arouse, foment, incite, set off, whip up, work up 7 agitate, inflame 9 instigate
ending: 3 ous
read the ~ act to: 3 hit 4 flay, flog, slam 5 blast, chide, scold 6 berate, rebuke 7 bawl out, censure, chasten, chew out, condemn, lambast, lecture, reprove, upbraid 8 admonish, chastise, denounce, lambaste, reproach, sail into, tear into, threaten 9 castigate, criticize, dress down, excoriate, reprehend, reprimand 10 come down on, discipline, take to task, vituperate
run ~: 4 rage 6 abound, overdo 7 rampage 9 luxuriate
spray: 4 mace
stop a ~: 5 quash, quell 6 pacify 7 put down 8 beat down
riot ___: 3 act, gun 5 squad
___ riot: 3 run 5 laugh
rioting: 5 brawl, chaos 6 fracas, mayhem, uproar 7 turmoil 8 disorder, violence 9 imbroglio
riotous: 4 lush, wild 5 funny, noisy 6 hectic, lavish 7 chaotic, lawless, opulent, radical, rampant, roaring 8 anarchic 9 insurgent, luxuriant, priceless, turbulent 10 anarchical, boisterous, disorderly, topsy-turvy, tumultuous
group: 3 mob 5 horde
___ Rio, TX: 3 Del
Ríoverde: 4 city, town
locale: 6 Mexico
rip: 3 cut, fly, hie, jag, run, zip 4 claw, dart, dash, flit, hack, hole, race, rend, rent, rive, rush, slit, snag, tear, tide, zoom 5 burst, hurry, scoot, shred, slash, speed, split, spree 6 barrel, cleave, deride, gallop, hasten, hustle, move it, rebuke, rocket, scurry, wrench 7 blacken, disjoin, floor it, hop to it, quicken, scamper, yank off 8 badmouth, belittle, lacerate, mistreat, separate, step on it 9 castigate, criticize, denigrate, deprecate, hotfoot it, humiliate, shake a leg, skedaddle 10 come undone, get a move on, hightail it, laceration
ender: 3 rap, saw 4 cord
fix a ~: 5 resew
into: 5 abuse, roast 6 assail, attack, harass, impugn, malign, oppugn, rebuke, vilify 7 besiege, bombard, lambast 8 lambaste 9 lash out at 10 calumniate, vituperate
let ~: 5 begin, start 6 launch, set off, set out 7 kick off, lead off, take off, usher in 8 commence, get going, initiate, set about, set forth 10 inaugurate
off: 3 con, cop, gyp, nab, rob, use 4 dupe, flay, lift, loot, rook, soak, take 5 boost, cheat, filch, pinch, rifle, steal, swipe, trick 6 detach, fleece, pilfer, thieve 7 defraud, exploit, mislead, purloin, relieve, swindle 8 flimflam 10 overcharge, run a game on
on: 3 dis, rap 4 slam 5 knock 6 malign, vilify 7 asperse, put down, traduce 8 backbite, bad-mouth 9 criticize, denigrate, disparage
out: 5 pluck, unsew 6 remove, uproot 9 extirpate
up: 4 rend 5 shred, smear 6 vilify 7 destroy 9 tear apart
rip ___: 3 off 4 cord, into, tide 7 current
rip-___: 3 off 7 roaring
Rip: 4 Torn 6 Sewell, Taylor 9 Van Winkle
ripe: 3 due 4 aged 5 adult, plump, prime, ready 6 mature, mellow, stinky, timely 7 matured, overdue, ripened, skilled 8 blooming, prepared, seasoned, suitable 9 developed, favorable, filled out, full-grown, opportune, perfected 10 auspicious, well-versed
not ~: 5 green
starter: 4 rare
ripen: 3 age 4 grow 5 bloom 6 evolve, mature, mellow, season 7 blossom, develop 8 maturate 9 bear fruit
ripened: 5 adult 6 mature, mellow 9 full-grown
ripener: 4 ager
fruit ~: 6 ethene
ripeness: 8 fruition, maturity 9 readiness 10 perfection
ripening early: 4 rath 5 rathe
Riperton, Minnie song: Lovin' You (1975)
Rip It Up (1956 song) artist: Little Richard
Ripken: 3 Cal 6 Oriole
sport: 8 baseball
Ripley: 6 Robert 9 Alexandra
Ripley's Believe It or ___: 3 Not
rip-off: 3 con 4 scam 5 cheat, fraud, heist, steal, theft, thief, trick 6 racket 7 robbery, swindle 8 swindler, thievery
artist: 5 cheat, shark 6 bilker, con man 7 grifter, hustler, scammer 8 swindler 9 defrauder
riposte: 4 barb, quip 5 reply 6 answer, retort, zinger 8 comeback, rebuttal, repartee, response, wordplay 9 rejoinder, witticism
ripped: 4 rent, torn 7 asunder
ripping: 3 def, rad 4 aces, A-one, boss, braw, cool, dece, fine, gear, keen, neat, nice, phat, tuff 5 dandy, ducky, grand, great, marvy, neato, nobby, prime, slick, super, swell 6 bang on, bang-up, bonzer, bosker, choice, divine, dreamy, far-out, gnarly, groovy, lovely, peachy, slap-up, spot on, superb, terrif, tiptop, unreal, whizzo, wicked 7 amazing, awesome, capital, corking, perfect, skookum, stellar, sublime 8 dazzling, especial, eximious, fabulous, five-star, four-star, frabjous, glorious, heavenly, jim-dandy, slam-bang, smashing, splendid, standout, sterling, stickout, superior, terrific, top-level, topnotch, very good, wondrous 9 bodacious, Endsville, excellent, exemplary, exquisite, first-rate, high-grade, hunky-dory, marvelous, sollicker, top-flight, unrivaled, wonderful 10 first-class, hotsy-totsy, jack-a-dandy, out of sight, peachy-keen, phenomenal, remarkable, stupendous, super-duper, unrivalled
good time: 3 gas 5 blast
ripple: 3 lap 4 beat, lick, purl, wave 5 surge, swell 6 billow, gurgle, murmur, ruffle, rustle, tremor 7 flutter, vibrate 8 undulate
design: 5 moiré
rippleless: 4 calm 6 serene, smooth 8 peaceful, tranquil
___ Ripples: 6 Rialto
rippling: 4 wavy 9 vibrating
riprap: 5 revet
rip-roaring: 5 noisy 6 hectic, stormy 8 exciting 9 thrilling
ripsnorter: 4 lulu 5 dilly, doozy 9 humdinger
Riptide (1934 film)
cast: Herbert Marshall, Robert Montgomery, Norma Shearer
Rip Van Winkle author: Washington Irving
Rip Van Winkle dog: 4 Wolf
riq: 10 percussion, tambourine
origin: 7 Mideast
rise: 3 wax 4 dawn, go up, grow, hike, hill, incr., jump, leap, lift, loom, riot, soar, stem, upgo, wake 5 add to, awake, begin, bob up, boost, build, climb, crest, debut, get up, issue, knoll, mound, mount, onset, reach, rebel, ridge, scale, sit up, slope, stand, start, surge, swell, tower, waken, way up 6 appear, ascend, ascent, awaken, billow, crop up, derive, double, emerge, expand, gather, glacis, growth, height, jump up, move up, mutiny, origin, outset, pile up, recess, revolt, rocket, source, spiral, spring, step-up, upturn, wake up, well up 7 advance, augment, balloon, build up, burgeon, climb up, develop, elevate, emanate, flare up, hillock, hummock, improve, incline, infancy, mount up, proceed, prosper, roll out, speed up, stack up, stand up, start up, succeed, turn out, upclimb, upgrade, upslope, upsurge, upswing, uptrend 8 bourgeon, commence, eminence, escalate, flourish, go places, gradient, heighten, increase, levitate, mounting, multiply, surmount, upgrowth 9 acclivity, ascension, beginning, elevation, emergence, eventuate, inception, increment, inflation, intensify, originate, promotion, upwelling 10 appearance, appreciate, escalation, high ground, incipience, levitation, move upward, prominence, spring from, supplement
above: 5 outdo, tower 6 exceed 7 weather 8 overcome, surmount 9 cut across, transcend
and fall: 4 toss 6 billow, rhythm
and shine: 4 wake 5 get up, waken 6 awaken 7 turn out
cause to ~: 6 leaven
give ~ to: 5 beget, breed, cause, spawn 6 effect, induce, prompt 7 inspire, produce, trigger 8 engender, generate, occasion 10 bring about

in waves: 5 pitch, surge, swell 6 billow
on a wave: 5 scend
sharply: 4 zoom 5 surge 6 rocket 7 shoot up 9 skyrocket
starter: 3 sun 4 moon 5 earth
to the occasion: 4 cope 5 get by 6 manage
up: 4 rear, riot 5 rebel 6 mutiny, revolt
rise ___ occasion: 5 to the
___-rise: 3 low, mid 4 dead, high
Risë: 7 Stevens
Rise (1979 song) artist: Herb Alpert
Rise and ___!: 5 shine
Rise and Fall of Legs Diamond, The (1960 film)
cast: Ray Danton, Karen Steele, Elaine Stewart
Rise, Glory, Rise composer: 4 Arne
risen: 2 up 5 aloft, awake 6 high up 7 skyward 8 overhead, skywards 10 up in the air, up in the sky
not ~: 4 abed 5 in bed
Rise of Silas Lapham, The
author: William Dean Howells
character: 4 Anna, Lily 5 Corey, Irene, Nanny 6 Milton, Persis 7 Zerilla 8 Penelope
riser: 4 step
cousin: 5 tread
plus tread: 5 stair
___ riser: 5 early
rises
it ~ to the top: 5 cream
where hair ~: 4 nape
___ rise to: 4 give
Rise up so early in the ___: 4 morn
rishi: 4 guru, poet, sage
risibility: 3 fun, joy 4 glee 5 cheer, mirth 6 gaiety, laughs, levity 7 revelry 8 gladness 9 amusement, happiness, merriment, rejoicing 10 jocularity
risible: 5 comic, droll, funny 6 har-har 7 comical 9 laughable, ludicrous
rising: 6 source, uphill 9 promising, rebellion
ground: 4 bank, hill 7 incline 8 gradient
in heraldry: 7 issuant
star: 5 comer
time: 4 dawn, morn 5 sunup
rising ___: 4 sign, star 5 hinge 6 action, rhythm
___-rising flour: 4 self
Rising Sun: 4 film 5 novel
author: Michael Crichton
cast: Sean Connery, Harvey Keitel, Wesley Snipes
Rising Sun, Land of the: 5 Japan
risk: 3 bet, try 4 dare, face, play 5 brave, peril, stake, wager 6 chance, danger, gamble, hazard, menace, threat 7 imperil, pitfall, venture 8 endanger, exposure, jeopardy, long shot, openness, unsafety 9 adventure, liability, speculate 10 compromise, go for broke, insecurity, jeopardize, take a flyer
assessor: 5 rater
at ~: 6 liable 7 exposed, in peril 8 in danger 9 imperiled, on the line 10 endangered, in jeopardy
coverage: 3 ins. 9 insurance
not at ~: 4 safe 6 secure 9 protected
put at ~: 3 lay 5 stake, wager 6 chance, gamble 7 imperil, venture 8 endanger, threaten 9 undermine 10 jeopardize
take a ~: 3 bet 4 dare, defy 5 wager 6 gamble, hazard 7 presume, venture 9 challenge, speculate
taker: 4 doer 5 darer 6 better, bettor 7 gambler
underwrite a ~: 5 cover 6 ensure, insure, shield 7 protect, warrant 9 guarantee, indemnify
risk ___: 6 factor 7 capital
risk-___: 7 benefit
___ risk: 3 sea 6 credit
___-risk: 4 high
Risk: 4 game 9 board game
Risk author: Dick Francis
risked: 7 at stake, in peril 9 on the line 10 in jeopardy
risker: 7 gambler 9 daredevil 10 adventurer, speculator
riskless: 4 safe 6 secure 8 harmless
Risk, The (1960 film)
cast: Ian Bannen, Tony Britton, Peter Cushing
risky: 4 bold, iffy 5 dicey, hairy, rocky 6 chancy, daring, thorny, touchy, tricky, unsafe 7 fraught, parlous, unsound 8 insecure, perilous, ticklish, wide-open 9 dangerous, daredevil, desperate, difficult, foolhardy, hazardous, on thin ice, uncertain, unhealthy 10 jeopardous, out on a limb, precarious, touch-and-go, unreliable
business: 4 dare, spec 5 wager 6 hazard
Risky Business (1983 film)
cast: Curtis Armstrong, Tom Cruise, Rebecca De Mornay
director: Paul Brickman
risotto: 4 rice
risqué: 3 raw 4 blue, gamy, lewd, racy 5 bawdy, crude, gamey, lurid, salty, spicy 6 daring, purple, ribald, spicey, unmeet, vulgar, X-rated 7 naughty, obscene, off-base 8 immodest, improper, indecent, off-color 9 lubricous, offensive, out-of-line, salacious, unrefined 10 indecorous, indelicate, suggestive
rissole: 6 pastry 8 turnover
ristorante: 9 trattoria
offering: 4 vino, ziti 5 pasta, pollo, squid, zuppa 6 gelati, gelato 7 Chianti, lasagna, lasagne, spumoni, tortoni 8 linguine, linguini 9 antipasto
sauce: 5 pesto 6 tomato 8 marinara
Rit: 3 dye
Rita: 3 Gam 4 Dove 6 Moreno, Rudner, Wilson 7 Johnson 8 Coolidge, Hayworth 10 Tushingham
Rita ___ Brown: 3 Mae
___ Rita: 3 Rio
ritardando: 4 slow 6 slower
opposite: 5 accel.
undoer: 6 a tempo
Ritchie: 3 Guy 6 Petrie, Valens 7 Michael
Ritchie, Guy: 8 director
film: Snatch (2000)
spouse: Madonna
Ritchie, Michael: 8 director
film: The Bad News Bears (1976)
The Candidate (1972)
Downhill Racer (1969)
The Fantasticks (2000)
Fletch (1985)
Prime Cut (1972)
Semi-Tough (1977)
Smile (1975)
Wildcats (1986)
rite: 4 form, Mass 7 baptism, liturgy, service 8 ceremony, exorcism, marriage, practice 9 communion, Eucharist, formality, sacrament, solemnity 10 bar mitzvah, ceremonial, observance
site: 5 altar
___ rite: 4 York 5 Greek, Roman 7 Eastern
Rite ___: 3 Aid
___ Rite: 5 Latin 6 Stride
Ritenour, Lee: 9 guitarist
rite of passage, teen: 4 prom
Rite of Spring author: Andrew Greeley
Rite of Spring, The: 6 ballet
composer: 10 Stravinsky
Ritorna vincitor singer: 4 Aïda
Ritsos, Yannis: 4 poet 5 Greek
Ritter: 3 Tex 4 John 6 Thelma
Ritter, John: 5 actor 8 comedian
father: 3 Tex
film: Noises Off (1992)
They All Laughed (1981)
TV: 8 Simple Rules for Dating My Teenage Daughter, Hearts Afire, Three's Company
Ritter, Thelma: 7 actress
film: Birdman of Alcatraz (1962)
Daddy Long Legs (1955)
The Misfits (1961)
The Model and the Marriage Broker (1951)
Pickup on South Street (1953)
Pillow Talk (1959)
Rear Window (1954)
Ritt, Martin: 8 director
film: The Brotherhood (1968)
Conrack (1974)
Cross Creek (1983)
Edge of the City (1957)
The Front (1976)
The Great White Hope (1970)
Hombre (1967)
Hud (1963)
The Long Hot Summer (1958)
Murphy's Romance (1985)
No Down Payment (1957)
Norma Rae (1979)
Nuts (1987)
Paris Blues (1961)
Sounder (1972)
The Spy Who Came in From the Cold (1965)
Stanley & Iris (1990)
ritual: 4 form, rote 6 custom, formal, solemn 7 baptism, courtly, liturgy, pageant, pompous, service, stately 8 ceremony, decorous, exercise, exorcism, practice, protocol 9 dignified, formality, sacrament, solemnity, tradition 10 ceremonial, liturgical, observance
like some ~ s: 5 pagan 9 religious
Ritual Bath, The author: Faye Kellerman
ritualistic: 6 formal, proper, solemn 7 courtly, stately 8 decorous 9 dignified 10 ceremonial
ritualize: 4 keep 5 extol 7 glorify 8 adhere to 9 celebrate
ritz: 4 pomp 5 style 8 elegance, pretense 9 pageantry, pomposity 10 flashiness, peacockery, pretension
Ritz: 5 César, hotel 7 cracker
alternative: 5 Zesta 6 Krispy 7 Cheez-It 8 Triscuit 10 Cheese Nips 14 Wheat Thins. Hi-Ho
home of The ~: 5 Paris
locale: 5 Paris
Ritz ___: 7 Carlton 8 Brothers
ritzy: 4 chic, lush, posh, rich, tony 5 fancy, plush, sharp, showy, swank, swell, swish, toney 6 chichi, classy, deluxe, dressy, flashy, lavish, lordly, luxury, snazzy, swanky, urbane 7 elegant, opulent, refined, stylish 8 palatial, princely 9 elaborate, exclusive, expensive, high-class, high-toned, luxurious, sumptuous
group: 5 elite
not ~: 4 non-U 5 seedy
rival: 3 foe, tie, vie 4 meet, peer, side, vier 5 enemy, equal, match, touch 6 oppose 7 compete, contend, emulate, nemesis, opposer, vie with 8 approach, emulator, keep pace, opponent, opposing, rank with, resemble 9 adversary, challenge, contender, disputant, emulative, ill-wisher, measure up 10 antagonist, challenger, competitor, equivalent, keep up with, opposition
rivalry: 4 feud 5 fight, match 6 strife 7 contest 8 conflict, friction 10 contention, opposition
Rivals, The author: Richard Sheridan
character: 5 Acres, Lydia 6 Lucius 8 Malaprop
rive: 3 rip 4 rend, tear 5 break, sever, smash, split 6 cleave, harrow, shiver, sunder 7 rupture, shatter 8 distress, fracture, separate 9 tear apart
riven: 4 torn 5 cleft, split 7 asunder 8 sundered
river: 3 Aar, Apa, Bug, Cam, Dal, Dee, Don, Fly, Han, Inn, Lek, Lot, Lys, Oka, Qom, Qum, Red, San, Tay, Ume, Usk, Wye 4 Aare, Adda, Aire, Amur, Arno, Aube, Avon, Bear, Beni, Bomu, Cher, Coco, Doon, Drin, East, Ebro, Eder, Eger, Elbe, flow, Geba, Gila, gush, Ille, Iowa, Isar, Juba, Juru, Kama, Kura, Lena, Liao, Maas, Main, Miño, Napo, Neva, Nile, Oder, Odra, Ohio, Ohre, Oise, Oulu, Ouse, Prut, race, Ruhr, Saar, Salt, Sava, Styr, Styx, Taff, Tana, Tees, Tyne, Uele, Ulúa, Ural, Vaal, Waal, Yalu, Yser, Yüen 5 Adige, Aisne, Apure, Argun, Atrak, Atrek, Benin, Benue, Boyne, Cauca, Chari, Clyde, Congo, Desna, Doubs, Douro, Drava, Drina, Dvina, Grand, Hondo, Indus, Isère, James, Japur, Jumna, Kabul, Kafue, Karun, Kasai, Kuban, Lempa, Lethe, Liard, Loire, Marne, Mbomu, Memel, Meuse, Miami, Minho, Murat, Mures, Narew, Negro, Neman, Niger, Onega, Osage, Ouémé, Paran, Peace, Pearl, Pecos, Peene, Piave, Purús, Rhine, Rhone, Santa, Saône, Seine, Shari, Siret, Slave, Snake, Somme, spate, Stone, Tagus, Tarim, Tiber, Tisza, Tobol, Trent, Tsana, Tumen, Tweed, Volga, Volta, Warta, Weser, White, Xingú, Yampa, Yaqui, Yazoo, Yukon, Zaire 6 Allier, Amazon, Angara, Atbara, attach, Bio-Bio, Brazos, Chenab, Clutha, Copper, Cuiabá, Cydnus, Danube, Donets, feeder, Fraser, Gambia, Ganges, Glomma, Harlem, Hudson, Humber, IJssel, Irtish, Irtysh, Isonzo, Javari, Javary, Jhelum, Jordan, Kagera, Kansas, Khabur, Kolyma, Lehigh, Liffey, Mamoré, Maumee, Mekong, Mersey, Mobile, Mohawk, Moldau, Molopo, Morava, Murray, Neckar, Neisse, Nelson, Niemen, Nueces, onrush, Orange, Orkhon, Ottawa, Pánuco, Patuca, Pee Dee, Platte, Pripet, Rovuma, Ruvuma, Sabine, Sambre, Santee, Scioto, Severn, Seyhan, Shashi, St. John, stream, Struma, Sutlej, Tanana, Thames, Thelon, Thjórs, Tigris, Ubangi, Ussuri, Vardar, Vltava, Wabash, Yakima, Yamuna, Yarmuk, Yarrow, Yellow 7 Alabama, Aruwimi, Ausuble, Berbice, Bermejo, Bighorn, Calabar, Catawba, Cauvery, Chagres, Charles, Conchos, Darling, Derwent, Detroit, Dnieper, Durwent, Garonne, Genesee, Guaporé, Helmand, Hooghly, Huang He, Iguassú, Karkheh, Klamath, Krishna, Limpopo, Livenza, Lualaba, Luapula, Madeira, Mangoky, Mantaro, Marañón, Maritsa, Moselle, Motagua, Narbada, Niagara,

Orinoco, Orontes, Pechora, Potomac, Rapidan, Roanoke, Rubicon, Salween, Schelde, Scheldt, Selenga, Senegal, Shannon, Songhua, St. Clair, St. Croix, St. Johns, St. Marys, Taoajós, Trebbia, Truckee, Ucayali, Vistula, Wateree, Xi Jiang, Yenisei, Zambezi **8** Amu Darya, Araguaya, Arkansas, Berezina, Big Muddy, Blue Nile, Canadian, Cheyenne, Chindwin, Cimarron, Colorado, Columbia, Congaree, Delaware, Demerara, Dniester, Dordogne, Godavari, Granicus, Guadiana, Hamilton, Illinois, Kennebec, Kentucky, Klondike, Kootenay, Menderes, Nerbudda, Niobrara, Okavango, Ouachita, Paraguay, Parnaiba, Putumayo, Rio Bravo, Saguenay, Savannah, Shoshone, Suwannee, Syr Darya, Volturno, waterway **9** Allegheny, Anacostia, Aroostook, Churchill, Deschutes, Des Moines, Euphrates, Irrawaddy, Mackenzie, Macquarie, Magdalena, Merrimack, Minnesota, Penobscot, Richelieu, Rio Grande, Roosevelt, Tennessee, tributary, Wisconsin **10** Appomattox, Chao Phraya, Coppermine, Cumberland, Housatonic, inundation, outpouring, Pedernales, Republican, Schuylkill, Shenandoah, St. Lawrence, Tippecanoe, Willamette
Afghanistan: **5** Farah
Africa: **4** Nile, Tana, Uele, Vaal **5** Benue, Congo, Ebola, Niger, Tsana, Tsavo, Volta, Zaire **6** Atbara, Orange
Alaska: **5** Yukon
Albania: **4** Drin
Alps: **3** Aar **4** Aare **5** Isère, Rhone
area: **3** bed **4** fork **5** bayou, delta, mouth, oxbow, shore **6** rapids, source
Argentina: **5** Negro, Plata
Arizona: **4** Gila, Salt **8** Colorado
Asia: **4** Amur, Liao, Oxus, Yalu **6** Tigris
Australia: **5** Tamar
Austria: **3** Mur **4** Enns, Isar, Raab, Raba **5** Donau
barrier: **3** dam **4** dike **5** levee **10** embankment
Belgium: **3** Lys **4** Leie, Oise, Yser **5** Meuse, Senne
bend: **5** bight, elbow
Bolivia: **4** Beni
branch: **4** trib. **9** tributary
Brazil: **4** Acre **5** Negro, Purus, Xingu **6** Javari
Canada: **4** Nass **5** Liard, Trent, Yukon **6** Fraser, Ottawa **10** St. Lawrence
Caucasus: **4** Rion **5** Rioni
Chile: **6** Bíobío
China: **3** Han, Hsi, Ili **4** Liao, Yalu, Yuan, Yuen **5** Siang, Tarim
Colombia: **4** Meta
Colorado: **5** Yampa
combining form: **5** fluvi-, potam- **6** fluvio-, potamo-
Connecticut: **6** Thames
Croatia: **4** Sava
crosser: **5** ferry **6** bridge
crossing: **4** ford
curve: **4** bend
Czech: **4** Eger, Elbe, Hron, Iser, Oder, odra, Ohre
deity: **4** nais **5** nymph
depth measure: **3** fth. **10** fath.. fath-om
Ecuador: **4** Napo
Egypt: **4** Nile
ender: **3** bed **4** bank, boat, head, side, ward, weed **5** front, wards
England: **3** Cam, Exe, Ure, Usk, Wye **4** Aire, Avon, Leam, Ouse, Tyne **5** Leame, Tamar, Trent **6** Thames
Europe: **4** Eder, Eger, Elbe, Oder, Odra, Oise, Saar **5** Meuse, Siret, Volga
feeder: **6** stream
fictional: **4** Kwai
France: **3** Lys **4** Aude, Eure, Ille, Leie, Oise, Orne, Saar, Yser **5** Aisne, Isère, Loire, Marne, Meuse, Rhone, Saône, Sarre, Seine, Selle, Somme, Yonne **6** Escaut
Georgia: **4** Rion **5** Coosa, Rioni
Germany: **3** Ems **4** Eder, Eger, Elbe, Isar, Naab, Oder, Odra, Ohre, Oste, Ruhr, Saar **5** Fulda, Rhine, Weser
Greece: **4** Arta
Guatamala: **5** Hondo
Hungary: **4** Eger, Raab, Raba **5** Tisza **6** Danube
Iberia: **4** Ebro, Miño **5** Douro, Minho, Tagus
Idaho: **5** Snake
India: **5** Indus, Jumna, Purna, Sarda **6** Ganges, Yamuna
in Spanish: **3** río
Iraq: **6** Tigris
Ireland: **4** Erne, Nore **5** Boyne
island: **3** ait **4** eyot
Italy: **4** Arno, Nera **5** Adige, Oglio, The Po, Tiber
Japan: **3** Ota
Kansas: **5** Osage
Kashmir: **5** Indus
Kazakhstan: **3** Ili **4** Ural **5** Tobol
Korea: **4** Yalu
Latvia: **5** Dvina
like a ~ bed: **5** silty, stony **6** stoney
Maine: **4** Saco
Malaysia: **5** Perak
mammal: **5** otter
Mexico: **5** Yaqui
Michigan: **5** Huron
Mississippi: **5** Yazoo
Nebraska: **4** Loup **6** Platte
Netherlands: **3** Lek **4** Maas, Rijn, Waal **5** Issel, Yssel **6** Ijssel
New York: **4** East **5** Tioga **6** Hudson
Norway: **4** Tana **5** Tsana
of forgetfulness: **5** Lethe
Oregon: **5** Rogue
overflow: **5** flood
Pakistan: **5** Indus
path: **4** flow **6** course **7** channel
Pennsylvania: **4** Ohio **6** Lehigh **8** Delaware **9** Allegheny
Peru: **5** Purus **6** Javari
Philippines: **5** Pasig
Poland: **4** Oder, Odra **5** Narew
Portugal: **4** Miño **5** Douro, Minho
rapids: **5** chute **6** dalles
Romania: **3** Olt **4** Prut **5** Siret
Russia: **3** Don, Oka, Oma **4** Lena, Neva, Seim, Seym, Yana **5** Aldan, Onega, Tobol **6** Angara, Kolima, Kolyma
Scotland: **3** Ayr, Dee, Esk, Tay **4** Doon, Lyon, Spey **5** Afton, Clyde, Devon, Lyons, Nairn, Tweed
sell down the ~: **5** rat on **6** betray, expose, fink on, give up, snitch, squeal, tattle, turn in **8** give away
Serbia: **4** Sava
Siberia: **4** Lena, Yana **5** Aldan
Slovenia: **4** Sava
source: **4** head
South America: **5** Negro, Plata **6** Amazon, Bíobío
Spain: **4** Ebro **5** Douro, Tinto
structure: **5** levee
Sweden: **3** Dal, Ume **4** Gota **5** Torne
Switzerland: **3** Aar **4** Aare **5** Reuss, Rhone, Seuss
Tasmania: **5** Tamar
terminus: **5** mouth
Texas: **5** Pecos **6** Brazos, Nueces **9** Rio Grande **10** Pedernales
transport: **4** raft **5** barge, canoe, ferry **6** packet **7** steamer
Turkey: **4** Aras **5** Murat **6** Tigris
Turkmenistan: **4** Oxus
Ukraine: **4** Prut, Seim, Seym **5** Seret, Siret, Tisza
underworld: **4** Styx **5** Lethe
Uzbekistan: **4** Oxus
Venezuela: **3** Aro **5** Apure
vessel: **4** boat **5** craft, kayak **6** vessel **9** outrigger
Virginia: **5** James
Wales: **3** Dee, Usk, Wye
Wheeling's ~: **4** Ohio
world's longest ~: **4** Nile
Xanadu: **4** Alph
Yugoslavia: **4** Sava **5** Tisza
river __: **5** basin, birch, horse, otter, wheat
__ river: **3** old **4** lost **5** up the
River __ Return: **4** of No
River __ Through It, A: **4** Runs
__ River: **4** Moon **5** Ol' Man
Rivera: **4** José **5** Chita, Diego **7** Geraldo
__ Rivera, CA: **4** Pico
Rivera, Diego: **6** artist **7** painter
homeland: **6** Mexico
spouse: Frida Kahlo
Rivera, José: **4** poet **6** writer **9** Colombian
__ River Anthology: **5** Spoon
riverbank: **5** shore
plant: **4** reed **5** sedge
steps, in India: **4** ghat **5** ghaut
riverbed: **6** canada
dry ~: **4** wadi, wady, wash
item: **5** stone
riverboat offering: **6** casino
Riverby author: John Burroughs
River City locale: **4** Iowa
Riverdale High student: **5** Betty, Moose **6** Archie **7** Jughead **8** Veronica
__ River, MA: **4** Fall
River Niger, The (1976 film)
cast: James Earl Jones, Glynn Turman, Cicely Tyson
director: Krishna Shah
__ River, NJ: **4** Toms
River of Dreams, The (1993 song)
artist: Billy Joel
__ River of the North: **3** Red
River Runs Through It, A (1992 film)
cast: Emily Lloyd, Brad Pitt, Craig Sheffer, Tom Skerritt
director: Robert Redford
Rivers: **4** Joan **6** Johnny, Mickey **7** Melissa
__ River school: **6** Hudson
River's Edge (1986 film)
cast: Crispin Glover, Keanu Reeves, Ione Skye
director: Tim Hunter
River's Edge, The (1957 film)
cast: Ray Milland, Debra Paget, Anthony Quinn
director: Allan Dwan
riverside: **5** shore
Riverside: **4** city, town
locale: **4** Ohio **10** California
Rivers, Johnny
real last name: Ramistella
song: Baby I Need Your Lovin' (1967)
Maybelline (1964)
Memphis (1964)
Midnight Special (1965)
Mountain of Love (1964)
Muddy Water (1966)
Poor Side of Town (1966)
Rockin' Pneumonia (1972)
Secret Agent Man (1966)
Seventh Son (1965)
Slow Dancin' (1977)
Summer Rain (1967)
Swayin' to the Music (1977)
The Tracks of My Tears (1967)
Rivers to the Sea author: Sara Teasdale
River, The (1951 film) director: Jean Renoir
Riverton: **4** city, town
locale: **4** Utah
River Town, A author: Thomas Keneally
River Wild, The (1994 film)
cast: Kevin Bacon, David Strathairn, Meryl Streep
director: Curtis Hanson
rivet: **3** fix, put, tie **4** bolt, grip, stud **5** affix, infix, stare **6** absorb, anchor, arrest, attach, fasten, fixate, secure, thrill **7** enchain, engrain, engross, enthral, ingrain, inthral **8** bolt down, enthrall, fastener, interest, inthrall, intrigue, look hard, make fast, transfix **9** fascinate, preoccupy, spellbind
one's eyes: **5** focus **6** obsess, zero in **9** preoccupy
riveted: **4** firm **6** intent, rooted **7** focused **8** immobile
riveter: **5** drill
Riviera: **3** car **4** auto **5** Buick **6** resort **10** automobile
acquisition: **3** tan
locale: **6** France, Monaco
resort: **3** Eze **4** Biot, Nice **6** Cannes, Frejus, Gassin, Menton **7** Antibes, Cap d'Ail, Cogolin, Grimaud, Mougins **8** Beaulieu, St. Tropez **9** Mandelieu, Ste. Maxime, St. Raphael **10** Beausoleil, Monte Carlo, Ramatuelle
wear: **6** bikini
Riviera Beach: **4** city, town
locale: **7** Florida
__-Rivières, Que.: **5** Trois
__ Rivoli: **5** Rue de
rivulet: **3** ria **4** race, rill **5** bourn, brook, creek, rille **6** stream **9** streamlet
Rixey, Eppa: **6** hurler **7** pitcher
Riyadh: **4** city, town **7** capital
district: **4** Nejd
resident: **4** Arab **5** Saudi
riyal: **4** coin **5** money
fraction: **6** halala
spender: **6** Qatari
Rizal, José: **6** writer **10** Philippine
Rizzo: **5** Ratso **6** Enrico
of the Muppets: **3** rat
Rizzuto, Phil: **6** Yankee **7** Scooter **9** shortstop
rival: **5** Reese **6** Pee Wee
RKO: **6** studio
R.L.: **5** Stine
RLS part: **4** Robt. **5** Louis **6** Robert **9** Stevenson
rm. cooler: **2** AC
RMN: **4** pres.
opponent: **3** JFK
predecessor: **3** LBJ
successor: **3** GRF
VP: **3** NAR, STA
was his Vice President: **3** DDE
see also Nixon
__ R. Murrow: **6** Edward
Rn: **4** elem. **5** radon **7** element
86 for ~: **4** at. no.
RN: **5** nurse
asset: **3** TLC
asst.: **3** LPN
colleague: **2** dr., GP, MD
employer: **3** HMO **4** hosp.
org.: **3** ANA

responsibility: 2 IV
station: 2 ER, OR 3 CCU, ICU
unit: 2 cc
RNA
ender: 3 ase
part of ~: 4 acid, ribo 7 nucleic
RNC org.: 3 GOP
rnd., not: 3 sqr.
roach: 4 pest 6 insect 7 sunfish
starter: 4 cock
Roach: 3 Hal, Jay, Max
Roach __: 5 Motel
Roach, Jay: 8 director
film: Austin Powers in Goldmember (2002)
Austin Powers: International Man of Mystery (1997)
Austin Powers: The Spy Who Shagged Me (1999)
Meet the Parents (2000)
Roach, Max: 7 drummer
genre: 4 jazz
road: 3 hwy., rte., way 4 belt, drag, lane, path, pike, walk 5 alley, byway, drive, means, route, track, trail 6 access, artery, avenue, by-path, course, street 7 freeway, highway, impetus, ingress, parkway, passage, thruway, viaduct 8 driveway, main drag, pavement, turnpike 9 boulevard, concourse 10 back street, expressway, Interstate, switchback, throughway
alternate ~: 6 detour
bend: 3 ess 4 turn 5 curve
burn up the ~: 4 race, rush, zoom 5 spank, speed
caution: 4 bump
charge: 4 toll
country ~ feature: 3 rut
covering: 3 tar 6 gravel 7 asphalt
crew member: 5 paver
do a ~ job: 3 tar 4 pave 5 retar, widen 6 repave
down the ~: 4 anon, soon, then 5 after, later 6 in a bit, in time 7 by and by, later on, someday 8 in a while, sometime 9 afterward, hereafter, presently 10 before long, eventually
ender: 3 bed, map, way 4 side, ster, work 5 block, house, stead 6 runner, worthy
get the show on the ~: 5 begin 6 launch 7 lead off 8 commence
go on the ~: 4 tour
guide: 3 map
hazard: 3 ice, rut 7 pothole
hit the ~: 2 go 4 blow, hike, rove, scat, walk, went 5 leave, scram, start 6 beat it, decamp, depart, set off, set out 7 push off, take off 8 hightail, set forth
inclination: 5 grade, slope
in Italian: 3 via
in Latin: 3 via 4 iter
junction: 4 fork, turn 6 branch
king of the ~: 4 hobo 5 tramp 7 drifter, vagrant 8 vagabond, wanderer
like some ~ s: 3 icy 5 curvy, laned, rutty, stony 7 one-lane
noise: 4 honk, horn 5 siren
not on the ~: 4 home 6 at home
on the ~: 4 away 7 driving, en route, touring 9 traveling 10 journeying
rally: 4 meet 7 contest
service: 3 tow
service org.: 3 AAA
shoulder: 4 berm 5 berme
side ~: 4 lane 5 byway 6 by-path
sign: 3 dip, gas, slo 4 exit, slow, stop 5 merge, yield 6 danger, detour
signal: 5 flare
sign shape: 5 arrow 7 octagon 8 triangle
sign word: 4 thru, xing 5 ahead
situate back from the ~: 5 set in
split in the ~: 4 fork
starter: 4 rail 5 cross
take the wrong ~: 3 err 4 flub, goof, muff, slip 5 lapse, stray 6 boo-boo, bungle, foul up, fumble, mess up, slip up, wander 7 blunder, deviate, louse up, stumble 8 go astray 10 transgress
toll ~: 4 pike 7 highway 8 turnpike
treat an icy ~: 4 salt, sand
road __: 3 hog, map 4 gang, race, rage, show, test 5 agent, atlas, metal, rally 6 hockey, racing, roller 7 company, warrior
__ road: 3 big, low 4 back, bush, dirt, grid, high, post, toll, tote 5 on the, royal 6 access, feeder 7 service, surface, winding
Road __: 4 Trip 5 House, to Rio 6 Runner 7 Scholar
Road __ Taken, The: 3 Not
__ Road: 4 Silk, Tara 5 Abbey, Burma, Glory, On the 7 Freedom, Thunder, Tobacco
__ Road Again: 5 On the
roadblock: 3 bar 4 snag, stop, wall 9 barricade 10 impediment
__ roadblock: 4 hit a
Road film
destination: 3 Rio 4 Bali 6 Utopia 7 Morocco 8 Hong Kong, Zanzibar 9 Singapore
name: 3 Bob 4 Bing, Hope 6 Crosby, Lamour 7 Dorothy
roadhouse: 3 inn, pub 5 hotel, lodge 6 tavern 8 rest stop, taphouse 9 nightclub
of yore: 4 inne
Road House (1948 film)
cast: Celeste Holm, Ida Lupino, Cornel Wilde
director: Jean Negulesco
roadie equipment: 3 amp
Roadking: 3 car 4 auto 8 Plymouth 10 automobile
Road Less Traveled, The author: 4 Peck
road map
see map
Roadmaster: 3 car 4 auto 5 Buick 10 automobile
Road Not Taken, The: 4 poem
author: Robert Frost
Road of Life, The: 9 radio show
road rally: 4 race
need: 3 map
Road Runner: 3 car 4 auto, bird, toon 8 Plymouth 10 automobile
cartoon backdrop: 4 mesa
foe: 5 Wile E. 6 coyote
sound: 4 beep
__ Roads: 7 Hampton
road-safety org.: 4 MADD, SADD
Road Scholar (1993 film) director: Roger Weisberg
roadside
establishment: 3 inn 5 diner, motel, stand
offer: 5 hop in
problem: 6 litter
sign: 4 eats
warning: 5 flare
Roadside Prophets (1992 film)
cast: David Carradine, John Doe, Adam Horovitz
director: Abbe Wool
roadster: 3 car 4 auto 10 automobile
Roads to Freedom, The author: Jean-Paul Sartre
road-test task: 5 U-turn 7 parking
Road, The author: Harry Matinson
Road to Bali (1952 film)
cast: Bing Crosby, Bob Hope, Dorothy Lamour
Road to Gandolfo, The author: Robert Ludlum
__ Road to Glory: 5 A Hard
Road to Glory, The (1936 film)
cast: Lionel Barrymore, Warner Baxter, Fredric March
director: Howard Hawks
Road to Hong Kong, The (1962 film)
cast: Joan Collins, Bing Crosby, Bob Hope, Dorothy Lamour
director: Norman Panama
__ Road to Mandalay: 5 On the
Road to Mecca, The author: Athol Fugard
Road to Morocco (1942 film)
cast: Bing Crosby, Bob Hope, Dorothy Lamour, Anthony Quinn
music: 5 Burke 9 Van Heusen
talker: 5 camel
Road to Omaha, The author: Robert Ludlum
Road to Perdition (2002 film)
cast: Tom Hanks, Jennifer Jason Leigh, Paul Newman
director: Sam Mendes
Road to Rio (1947 film)
cast: Bing Crosby, Bob Hope, Dorothy Lamour
Road to Rome, The author: Robert E. Sherwood
Road to Singapore (1940 film)
cast: Charles Coburn, Bing Crosby, Bob Hope, Dorothy Lamour
Road to Utopia (1945 film)
cast: Bing Crosby, Bob Hope, Dorothy Lamour
Road to Wellville, The (1994 film)
cast: Matthew Broderick, John Cusack, Bridget Fonda, Anthony Hopkins
director: Alan Parker
Road to Xanadu, The author: 5 Lowes
Road to Yesterday, The (1925 film)
director: Cecil B. DeMille
Road to Zanzibar (1941 film)
cast: Bing Crosby, Bob Hope, Dorothy Lamour, Una Merkel
__-road vehicle: 3 off
roadway: 4 road 5 route 6 street 7 ingress
Roadwork author: Stephen King
Roald: 4 Dahl 8 Amundsen, Hoffmann
roam: 3 gad 4 hike, rove, trek, walk 5 amble, drift, prowl, range, stray, tramp 6 ramble, trapes, travel, wander 7 digress, journey, maunder, meander, migrate, saunter, traipse 8 ambulate, gad about, nomadize, straggle, vagabond 9 bat around, bum around, gallivant, globetrot, run around 10 knock about
roamer: 5 nomad, rover 8 runagate, traveler, wanderer, wayfarer
roaming: 5 loose 6 astray, errant, ramble 7 nomadic 8 rootless, vagabond 9 itinerant, wayfaring
roan: 5 horse 6 equine, sorrel 8 chestnut
Roanne: 4 city, town
locale: 6 France
Roanoke: 3 isl. 4 city, isle, town 5 river 6 island
locale: 8 Virginia
roar: 3 bay, cry, din 4 bark, bawl, boom, call, drum, hoot, howl, peal, roll, yell 5 blast, crash, growl, laugh, noise, shout, sound, storm, voice 6 bellow, clamor, guffaw, holler, outcry, racket, rumble, scream, uproar 7 bluster, exclaim, explode, pulsate, resound, thunder, trumpet 8 laughter 9 explosion 10 belly laugh, clattering, detonation, hit the roof, horse laugh, vociferate
roaring: 4 loud 5 brisk, forte, noisy 6 active 7 booming, jarring, pealing, rackety, raucous, reboant, riotous 8 crashing, laughing, piercing, plangent, sonorous, strident, thriving, turned up 9 big-voiced, clamorous, deafening, turbulent 10 boisterous, prospering, prosperous, stentorian, strepitous, successful, uproarious, vociferous
__-roaring: 3 rip
Roaring Fork River, town on the: 5 Aspen
Roaring Girl, The author: Thomas Middleton
Roaring Twenties: 3 era
Roaring Twenties, The (1939 film)
cast: Humphrey Bogart, James Cagney, Priscilla Lane
director: Raoul Walsh
roast: 3 kid, rag, rib 4 bake, burn, cook, flay, gala, gibe, haze, heat, jibe, meat, mock, ride, slur, twit 5 abuse, blast, broil, grill, knock, taunt, tease, toast 6 defame, deride, entrée, malign, parody, picnic, scorch, sizzle, vilify 7 lambast, lampoon, put down, ribbing, rip into, slander, swelter 8 badinage, badmouth, barbecue, belittle, denounce, lace into, lambaste, ridicule, tear into, travesty 9 criticize, denigrate, disparage, excoriate, festivity, light into, pick apart, poke fun at
device: 4 spit 6 baster
host: 2 MC 5 emcee, Friar
place: 4 oven 5 grill 8 barbecue
seasoning: 4 sage
table: 4 dais
wiener ~: 6 picnic 7 cookout
__ roast: 3 pot, rib 4 loin, rump 5 crown 6 French, rolled, weenie
__-roasted: 3 dry
roaster: 3 pan 7 chicken 8 barbecue
roasting: 3 hot 6 steamy
rob: 3 con, cop, mug, sap 4 lift, loot, raid, roll, sack, take 5 cheat, filch, harry, heist, pinch, pluck, poach, rifle, steal, strip, swipe 6 burgle, divest, fleece, hijack, hold up, hustle, pilfer, ravage, rip off, snitch, thieve 7 bereave, break in, defraud, deprive, despoil, do out of, pillage, plunder, promote, purloin, ransack, relieve, stick up, swindle 8 embezzle, highjack, liberate, spoliate 9 break into, depredate, knock over, strong-arm 10 burglarize, disinherit, dispossess
old-style: 5 reave
rob __: 5 blind
Rob: 4 Lowe 5 Cohen, Estes 6 Morrow, Petrie, Reiner 7 Epstein, Minkoff 9 Camiletti, Schneider
Rob __: 3 Roy
roband: 4 yarn
Robards, Jason: 5 actor
film: All the President's Men (1976, AA)
Any Wednesday (1966)
The Ballad of Cable Hogue (1970)
Black Rainbow (1991)
Divorce American Style (1967)
The Good Mother (1988)
Isadora (1968)
The Journey (1959)
Julia (1977, AA)
Long Day's Journey Into Night (1962)
Magnolia (1999)
Max Dugan Returns (1983)
Melvin and Howard (1980)
The Night They Raided Minsky's

(1968)
Once Upon a Time in the West (1968)
The Paper (1994)
Parenthood (1989)
Philadelphia (1993)
A Thousand Clowns (1965)
spouse: Lauren Bacall

Robb: 3 Nen
robbed: 6 bereft
old-style: 4 reft
Robbe-Grillet, Alain: 6 French, writer
robber: 4 thug 5 cheat, crook, felon, fence, fraud, thief 6 bandit, looter, mugger, outlaw, pirate, raider, rascal 7 brigand, burglar, corsair, grafter, prowler, rustler, stealer 8 chiseler, hijacker, marauder, operator, pilferer, pillager, swindler 9 buccaneer, con artist, desperado, despoiler, plunderer, purloiner 10 cat burglar, pickpocket, shoplifter
accomplice: 5 fence
Asian ~: 6 dacoit, dakoit
chaser: 3 cop 6 lawman 7 officer
robber __: 3 fly 4 frog 5 baron
__ robber: 3 sea 4 camp
Robber Bride, The author: Margaret Atwood
Robbers' Roost author: Zane Grey
Robbers, The author: Friedrich von Schiller
robbery: 3 job 5 caper, heist, theft 6 felony, holdup, rip-off 7 break-in, larceny, mugging, stickup 8 burglary, thievery
__ robbery: 5 armed 7 highway
Robbie: 5 Nevil 6 Dupree
Robbins: 3 Tim, Tom 5 Marty 6 Harold, Jerome 9 Frederick
partner: 6 Baskin
Robbins, Frederick: 8 Nobelist
Robbins, Harold: 6 author, writer
work: 79 Park Avenue
The Adventurers
The Betsy
The Carpetbaggers
Descent from Xanadu
The Dream Merchants
Dreams Die First
Goodbye, Janette
The Inheritors
The Lonely Lady
Memories of Another Day
Never Enough
Never Leave Me
Never Love a Stranger
Piranha
Pirate
The Predators
The Raiders
The Secret
Sin City
Spellbinder
The Stallion
Stiletto
A Stone for Danny Fisher
The Storyteller
Tycoon
Where Love Has Gone
Robbins, Jerome Oscar: West Side Story
Robbins, Marty
song: Don't Worry (1961)
El Paso (1959)
A White Sport Coat (1957)
Robbins, Tim: 5 actor 8 director
film: Antitrust (2001)
Bob Roberts (1992)
Bull Durham (1988)
Cadillac Man (1990)
Cradle Will Rock (1999)
Dead Man Walking (1995)
Five Corners (1988)
The Hudsucker Proxy (1994)
Human Nature (2001)
I.Q. (1994)
Miss Firecracker (1989)
The Player (1992)
The Shawshank Redemption (1994)

Robby: 5 robot 6 Benson
robe: 3 aba 4 abba, gown, vest 5 cloak, dress, kanzu, simar, stola, talar 6 bertha, caftan, chimar, chimer, cyclas, dolman, kaftan, kimono, mantua, yukata 7 chimere, chrisom, garment, lounger, wrapper 8 bathrobe, covering, peignoir, vestment 9 djellabah, housecoat
African ~: 5 kanzu 9 djellabah
Arab ~: 3 aba 4 abba
church ~: 3 alb 6 chimar, chimer 7 chimere, chrisom
Japanese ~: 6 kimono, yukata
Roman ~: 5 stola, tunic 6 cyclas
starter: 4 bath, ward
Turkish ~: 6 dolman
woman's ~ of old: 5 simar
robe __: 5 de bal
__ robe: 3 lap 5 cedar, night, terry 7 buffalo, hunter's
robed: 4 clad
Robert: 3 Bly, Ito 4 Adam, Alda, Bolt, Bork, Capa, Culp, Curl, Davi, Dole, Gray, Hass, Hays, John, Koch, Moog, Owen, Peel, Reed, Ryan, Shaw, Wise, Wuhl 5 Blake, Boyle, Burns, Clary, Clive, Crumb, Donat, Evans, Fiore, Fogel, Frost, Hamer, Henry, Hooke, Huber, Klein, Lucas, Mills, Moore, Morse, Musil, Novak, Noyce, Peary, Plant, Ruark, Scott, Solow, Stack, Towne, Urich, Vesco, Young 6 Altman, Bárány, Benton, Bochsa, Bunsen, Conrad, Coover, De Niro, Desnos, Downey, Duncan, Duvall, Florey, Fowler, Fuller, Fulton, Goulet, Graves, Greene, Hayden, Hegyes, Holley, Horton, Hutton, Jarvik, Loggia, Lowell, Ludlum, Mandan, Merton, Morley, Mugabe, Newton, Palmer, Parish, Pinsky, Prosky, Ripley, Rossen, Shayne, Taylor, Vaughn, Wagner, Walden, Walker, Webber, Wilder, Wilson 7 Aldrich, Beltran, Bridges, Creeley, Englund, Forster, Francis, Fulghum, Garnier, Goddard, Herrick, Horvitz, Indiana, Joffrey, Kennedy, Leonard, MacNeil, McNeill, Merrill, Mitchum, Mundell, Parrish, Patrick, Picardo, Preston, Redford, Service, Siodmak, Southey, Swanson, Walpole, Woolsey 8 Anderson, Benchley, Browning, Cummings, Flaherty, Foxworth, Heinlein, Laughlin, McNamara, Millikan, Mulligan, Mulliken, Robinson, Rockwell, Schuller, Schumann, Stephens, Sterling, Townsend, Woodward, Zemeckis 9 Armstrong, Carradine, Choquette, Furchgott, Guillaume, Rodriguez, Southwell, Stevenson 10 Hofstadter, La Follette, Merrifield, Montgomery, Richardson, Silverberg
Robert __: 4 E. Lee
Robert __ Leonard: 4 Sean
Robert __-Powell: 5 Baden
Robert __ Scott: 6 Falcon
Robert __ Stevenson: 5 Louis
Robert __ Waller: 5 James
Robert __ Warren: 4 Penn
Roberta: 5 Flack 6 Peters
Roberta (1935 film): 7 musical
cast: Fred Astaire, Irene Dunne, Ginger Rogers
songwriter: 4 Kern 7 Harbach
Robert Baden-__: 6 Powell
Robert De __: 4 Niro
Robert E. __: 3 Lee 8 Sherwood
Robert Edward __: 3 Lee
Robert F. __: 7 Kennedy
__ Robert Feller: 5 Rapid
Robert James __: 6 Waller
Robert Louis __: 9 Stevenson
Roberto: 5 Duran 6 Alomar 7 Benigni 8 Clemente 10 Rossellini
see also Spanish
Robert Penn __: 6 Warren
Roberts: 4 Eric, Oral, Tony 5 Cokie, Doris, Julia, Robin, Tanya 6 Austin, Rachel 7 Kenneth, Pernell, Richard
Robert's __ of Order: 5 Rules
__ Roberts: 3 Bob 6 Mister
Roberts, Eric: 5 actor
film: The Coca-Cola Kid (1984)
Final Analysis (1992)
The Pope of Greenwich Village (1984)
Raggedy Man (1981)
Runaway Train (1985)
Wildflowers (1999)
sister: 5 Julia
Roberts, Julia: 7 actress
brother: 4 Eric
film: America's Sweethearts (2001)
Conspiracy Theory (1997)
Erin Brockovich (2000, AA)
Everyone Says I Love You (1996)
Flatliners (1990)
Hook (1991)
Michael Collins (1996)
My Best Friend's Wedding (1997)
Mystic Pizza (1988)
Notting Hill (1999)
Ocean's Eleven (2001)
The Pelican Brief (1993)
Pretty Woman (1990)
Runaway Bride (1999)
Sleeping With the Enemy (1991)
Steel Magnolias (1989)
spouse: Lyle Lovett
Roberts, Kenneth: 6 author, writer
work: Arundel
March to Quebec
Northwest Passage
Rabble in Arms
Robertson: 3 Don, Pat 4 Dale 5 Cliff, Oscar 6 Davies
Robertson, Cliff: 5 actor
film: The Best Man (1964)
Charly (1968, AA)
The Girl Most Likely (1957)
The Interns (1962)
J W Coop (1972)
The Naked and the Dead (1958)
Renaissance Man (1994)
Sunday in New York (1963)
Three Days of the Condor (1975)
Too Late the Hero (1970)
Wild Hearts Can't Be Broken (1991)
spouse: Dina Merrill
__ Robertson Justice: 5 James
Robertson, Oscar
milieu: 5 court
org.: 3 NBA
sport: 10 basketball
Roberts, Oral city: 5 Tulsa
Roberts, Pernell: 5 actor
film: Ride Lonesome (1959)
TV: Bonanza, Trapper John, M.D.
Roberts, Rachel: 7 actress
film: Murder on the Orient Express (1974)
O Lucky Man! (1973)
Saturday Night and Sunday Morning (1960)
This Sporting Life (1963)
Roberts, Richard: 8 Nobelist
__ Roberts Rinehart: 4 Mary
Roberts, Robin: 7 Phillie 13 pitcher, hurler
Roberts, Tony: 5 actor
film: 18 Again! (1988)
Annie Hall (1977)
A Midsummer Night's Sex Comedy (1982)
Play It Again, Sam (1972)
__ Roberts University: 4 Oral
Robert the Bruce: 4 Scot
where ~ was crowned: 5 Scone
Robert Z. __: 7 Leonard
robes: 4 duds, garb, gear 5 getup 6 attire 7 apparel, clothes, costume, garment 8 clothing, garments 9 trappings
Robeson: 4 Paul
Robespierre: 10 Maximilien
foe: 6 Danton
Robic: 3 Ivo
robin: 4 bird 6 herald, nester 9 redbreast
ragged ~: 5 plant 6 flower
round ~: 4 plea 6 series 7 tourney 8 petition 10 conference, tournament
__ robin: 3 sea 5 round 6 flying, ground, ragged
Robin: 4 Cook, Gibb, Luke 5 Leach, Moore, Yount 6 Givens, Trower, Wright, Zander 7 Cousins, Quivers, Roberts, Ventura 8 McNamara, Williams
accessory: 3 bow 4 cape 5 arrow 6 quiver
partner: 6 Batman
portrayer in 1938: 5 Errol
Robin __: 4 Hood
Robin __ Penn: 6 Wright
__ Robin: 6 Rockin'
Robin and Marian (1976 film)
cast: Sean Connery, Richard Harris, Audrey Hepburn, Robert Shaw
director: Richard Lester
Robin and the Seven Hoods (1964 film)
cast: Victor Buono, Bing Crosby, Sammy Davis Jr., Peter Falk, Dean Martin, Barbara Rush, Frank Sinatra
character: 3 sot
Robin, Christopher creator: 5 Milne
__ Robin Gray: 4 Auld
Robin Hood: 6 archer
beneficiaries: 4 poor
like ~ 's men: 5 merry 6 merrie
quarry: 4 rich
Robin Hood - Men in Tights (1993 film): Cary Elwes, Richard Lewis, Roger Rees
director: Mel Brooks
Robin Hood - Prince of Thieves (1991 film)
cast: Kevin Costner, Morgan Freeman, Mary Elizabeth Mastrantonio, Alan Rickman, Christian Slater
...robins __ hair: 5 in her
Robins: 5 Laila
robin's-egg: 4 blue 5 color 8 greenish
Robinson: 4 Bill 5 Chris, David, Frank 6 Brooks, Crusoe, Jackie, Robert, Smokey 7 Jeffers
Mrs. ~ 's daughter: 6 Elaine
__ Robinson: 3 Mrs.
Robinson, Bill: 5 actor 6 dancer
film: Hooray for Love (1935)
The Little Colonel (1935)
The Littlest Rebel (1935)
Stormy Weather (1943)
Robinson, Brooks: 6 Oriole 9 infielder
Robinson Crusoe author: Daniel Defoe
Robinson, Edward Arlington: 4 poet
work: Luke Havergal

The Man Against the Sky
The Man Who Died Twice
Miniver Cheevy
Richard Corey
Tristram
Two Men
Robinson, Edward G.: 5 actor
film: All My Sons (1948)
The Amazing Doctor Clitterhouse (1938)
Barbary Coast (1935)
Black Tuesday (1954)
A Boy Ten Feet Tall (1963)
Brother Orchid (1940)
Bullets or Ballots (1936)
The Cincinnati Kid (1965)
Double Indemnity (1944)
Dr. Ehrlich's Magic Bullet (1940)
Five Star Final (1931)
Flesh and Fantasy (1943)
The Glass Web (1953)
Good Neighbor Sam (1964)
House of Strangers (1949)
Key Largo (1948)
Kid Galahad (1937)
Larceny, Inc. (1942)
The Last Gangster (1937)
Little Caesar (1930)
The Little Giant (1933)
Manpower (1941)
Our Vines Have Tender Grapes (1945)
The Prize (1963)
The Red House (1947)
Scarlet Street (1945)
The Sea Wolf (1941)
Seven Thieves (1960)
A Slight Case of Murder (1938)
The Stranger (1946)
The Ten Commandments (1956)
Thunder in the City (1937)
Tiger Shark (1932)
Tight Spot (1955)
Two Weeks in Another Town (1962)
Unholy Partners (1941)
The Whole Town's Talking (1935)
The Woman in the Window (1944)
Robinson, Frank: 3 Red 6 Oriole 10 outfielder
Robinson, Jackie: 6 Dodger
Robinson, Robert: 7 chemist 8 Nobelist
Robinson, Smokey
lead singer of: The Miracles
song: Being With You (1981)
Cruisin' (1979)
Just to See Her (1987)
One Heartbeat (1987)
Robinson, Sugar Ray: 5 boxer
milieu: 4 ring
Robinson, Vicki Sue song: Turn the Beat Around (1976)
Robin Wright ___: 4 Penn
Robitussin
alternative: 5 Afrin 6 Contac, Nyquil, Tavist 7 Actifed, Comtrex, Dayquil, Dristan, Sinutab, Sudafed 8 Benadryl, Dimetapp, Drixoral, TheraFlu 9 Coricidin, Triaminic
target: 5 cough
roble: 3 oak 4 tree
Robles, Alfonso García: 8 Nobelist
___ Robles, CA: 4 Paso
RoboCop (1987 film)
cast: Nancy Allen, Dan O'Herlihy, Peter Weller
director: Paul Verhoeven
robot: 5 droid, golem 7 machine 9 automaton
cousin: 6 cyborg
folklore ~: 5 golem
play: 3 R.U.R.
robot ___: 3 arm 4 bomb 5 pilot
robotics cousin: 7 bionics
rob roy: 5 drink 8 beverage, cocktail
ingredient: 6 Scotch 7 bitters 8 vermouth
Rob Roy: 4 Scot
Rob Roy (1995 film)
cast: John Hurt, Jessica Lange, Liam Neeson
director: Michael Caton-Jones
Rob Roy author: Walter Scott
Robson: 3 May 4 Mark, peak 5 Flora, mount 8 mountain
locale: 6 Canada 7 Rockies
Robson, Mark: 8 director
film: Bedlam (1946)
The Bridges at Toko-Ri (1955)
Bright Victory (1951)
Champion (1949)
Daddy's Gone A-Hunting (1969)
From the Terrace (1960)
The Ghost Ship (1943)
Happy Birthday, Wanda June (1971)
The Harder They Fall (1956)
Home of the Brave (1949)
The Inn of the Sixth Happiness (1958)
Isle of the Dead (1945)
I Want You (1951)
Lost Command (1966)
My Foolish Heart (1949)
Peyton Place (1957)
Phffft! (1954)
The Prize (1963)
A Prize of Gold (1955)
The Seventh Victim (1943)
Trial (1955)
Von Ryan's Express (1965)
Robson, May: 7 actress
film: Bringing Up Baby (1938)
Dancing Lady (1933)
Lady for a Day (1933)
Strange Interlude (1932)
Robt. ___: 4 E. Lee
Robur the Conqueror author: Jules Verne
robust: 3 fit 4 hale, iron, spry, well, wiry 5 beefy, burly, hardy, hefty, hunky, husky, large, lusty, sound, stout, tough 6 brawny, earthy, hearty, mighty, potent, rugged, sinewy, steely, stocky, strong, sturdy, virile 7 doughty, healthy 8 athletic, forceful, indurate, muscular, powerful, puissant, stalwart, thriving, vigorous 9 Atlantean, heavy-duty, Herculean, in the pink, strapping, well-built 10 able-bodied, boisterous, full-bodied, red-blooded
not ~: 4 weak 5 frail 6 dainty, feeble, flimsy, infirm, slight 7 brittle, fragile, rickety, tenuous, unsound 8 delicate 9 breakable, frangible 10 vulnerable
robusta: 6 coffee
Robustelli, Andy sport: 8 football
robustness: 3 vim 4 dint, thew 5 brawn, force, might, power, sinew, thews, vigor 6 energy, health, muscle 7 fitness, muscles, potence, potency, stamina 8 strength, vitality 9 endurance, fortitude, hardiness, puissance 10 brute force
robustus, dinornis: 3 moa
Robyn: 5 Smith
roc: 4 bird
Roc (Fox sitcom)
cast: Charles S. Dutton (Roc Emerson)
Ella Joyce (Eleanor Emerson)
Roca: 4 cape
locale: 6 Europe, Iberia 8 Portugal
rocambole: 9 condiment
Rocco: 4 Alex 7 Mediate
Roch: 5 saint
Roche: 6 Eugene
Rochelle: 6 Hudson
Rochester: 4 city, town
clinic: 4 Mayo
company: 5 Kodak
county: 6 Monroe
locale: 7 New York 9 Minnesota
love: 4 Eyre
to Benny: 5 valet
ward: 5 Adele
Rochester Hills: 4 city, town
locale: 8 Michigan
Rochon: 4 Lela
rock: 3 gem, jar, ore, wag 4 crag, jolt, lava, mica, reef, reel, roll, spar, stun, sway, talc, toss 5 agate, crust, dance, flint, genre, geode, jewel, lurch, magma, music, pitch, prase, quake, shake, shale, shelf, shock, solid, stone, swing 6 careen, gneiss, gravel, jasper, jiggle, jounce, mantle, marble, ophite, pebble, pillar, quarry, quartz, quiver, rattle, rubble, seesaw, teeter, totter, wabble, wobble 7 agitate, bastion, bedrock, boulder, bowlder, disturb, granite, igneous, librate, mineral, shake up, stagger, startle, stupefy, support, tremble, trinket, vibrate 8 feldspar, mainstay, surprise, unstring 9 oscillate 10 kryptonite
and roll: 5 genre, music, pitch 6 boogie
between a ~ and a hard place: 6 in a fix, in a jam
bottom: 4 zero 5 nadir, worst
cavity: 3 vug 4 vugg, vugh
climber's gear: 5 piton
coating: 6 lichen
collapse: 6 cave-in
combining form: 4 petr-, saxi- 5 petri-, petro-
concert need: 3 amp
crystals: 5 druse
detritus: 4 sand 5 scree
don't ~ the boat: 3 bow 4 mind 5 agree, yield 6 accede, accept, assent, comply, give in, relent, submit 7 go along, respect 8 play ball 9 acquiesce, cooperate 10 come around
ender: 4 fish, rose, weed, work 5 bound, shaft, slide 8 hounding
flowing ~: 4 lava
fracture: 5 fault
genre: 3 rap 4 acid, hard, punk 5 metal 6 grunge
igneous ~: 4 sima 6 basalt, gabbro, pumice 8 obsidian
igneous ~ source: 4 lava
inscribed ~: 5 stela, stele
isolated ~: 4 scar
jagged ~: 3 tor 5 arête 8 pinnacle 10 escarpment
layer: 4 vein 5 shelf 6 mantle
like a ~: 4 hard 5 solid 6 firmly 7 lithoid 9 lithoidal
name meaning ~: 5 Craig, Peter
partner: 4 roll
porous ~: 4 tufa, tuff
ridge: 4 crag 5 arete
rugged ~: 3 tor 4 crag
salt: 4 NaCl 6 halite
scratch: 5 stria
sheet: 5 nappe
shelf: 5 ledge
shelter: 4 abri
solid: 5 loyal 6 honest, trusty 7 certain, ethical, staunch 8 faithful, reliable, surefire 9 honorable, steadfast, unfailing 10 consistent, dependable, infallible
starter: 3 bed 4 sham
steep ~: 3 tor 4 crag 5 arête, bluff, cliff, scarp 8 overhang, pinnacle 9 precipice 10 escarpment, prominence
suffix: 3 -ite
the boat: 5 rebel, upset 6 revolt
thin layers of ~: 5 folia
valueless ~: 6 gangue
volcanic ~: 4 lava, tuff 5 magma
rock ___: 3 cod, elm, oil 4 bass, bolt, crab, dove, dust, hind, milk, salt, wall, wool, wren 5 candy, cress, fence, flour, hound, hyrax, maple, 'n' roll, plant, spray, tripe 6 beauty, blenny, bottom, flower, garden, gunnel, pigeon, rabbit, steady, thrush 7 crystal, glacier, jasmine, lobster, wallaby
rock-___: 3 eel 4 a-bye 5 bound, faced, 'n'-roll 6 ribbed 7 shelter
___ rock: 3 art, cap 4 acid, folk, glam, hard, punk, soft, wall 5 grind 6 alkali, mantle 7 asphalt, chimney, country, igneous
___-rock: 4 jazz 5 blues
Rock: 5 Chris 6 Hudson 7 Blossom
30 ~ occupant: 3 NBC 5 NBC-TV
Rock ___ game hen: 7 Cornish
Rock ___ Line: 6 Island
Rock ___ the Clock: 6 Around
Rock-___: 3 ola
Rock-___ baby...: 4 a-bye
___ Rock: 3 Cop, Pet 4 I Am a 5 Ayers, Like a, Limbo 7 Thunder
Rock-A-Billy (1957 song) artist: Guy Mitchell
Rock-a-Bye Baby (1958 film)
cast: Jerry Lewis, Marilyn Maxwell, Connie Stevens
director: Frank Tashlin
Rock-a-Bye Your Baby With a Dixie Melody (song) artist: Al Jolson, Jerry Lewis
rock and ___: 3 rye 4 roll
rock and roll classic: 4 oldy 5 oldie
Rock and Roll Dreams Come Through (1994 song) artist: Meat Loaf
Rock and Roll Heaven (1974 song) artist: Righteous Brothers
Rock and Roll Is ___ to Stay: 4 Here
___ Rock and Roll Music: 4 I Dig
Rock and Roll Music (1976 song) artist: Beach Boys
Rock and Roll Part 2 (1972 song) artist: Gary Glitter
Rock and Roll Waltz (1956 song) artist: Kay Starr
rock and rye: 5 drink 8 beverage, cocktail
ingredient: 7 whiskey 9 rock candy
Rock Around the Clock (1955 song) artist: Bill Haley and His Comets
___ Rock, Australia: 5 Ayers
rock brake: 4 fern
___ Rock Cafe: 4 Hard
Rockcliffe: 8 Fellowes
rock climbing: 5 sport
Rock Cornish: 3 hen 4 fowl 7 chicken
relative: 6 Bantam, Brahma, Houdan, Sussex 7 Dorking, Leghorn 8 Araucana, Langshan, Shanghai 9 Dominique, Orpington, Wyandotte
Rock Cornish ___ hen: 4 game
Rock Creek: 4 Park
Rockefeller: 4 John 5 David 6 Nelson 8 Winthrop
handout: 4 dime
___ Rockefeller: 7 oysters
rocker: 4 seat 5 chair 6 cradle 8 recliner 9 furniture
part: 3 arm 4 back, seat, slat
place: 5 porch
rocker ___: 3 arm, cam 5 panel
rocket: 3 fly, hie, rip, run, zip 4 bomb, dart, dash, flit, leap, race, rise, rush, soar, tear, Thor, zoom 5 climb, hurry,

scoot, speed **6** Ariane, barrel, gallop, hasten, hustle, move it, scurry **7** floor it, hop to it, missile, quicken, scamper, shoot up **8** step on it **9** hotfoot it, shake a leg, skedaddle **10** get a move on, hightail it
booster ~: **5** Agena, Atlas
deviation: **3** yaw
ender: **3** eer
French ~: **6** Ariane
fuel ingredient: **3** LOX **5** nitro
gasket: **5** O-ring
housing: **4** silo
interceptor: **3** ABM
launch: **4** shot **7** liftoff, takeoff **8** blastoff
no ~ scientist: **3** dim, oaf **4** ditz, fool, jerk, simp, slow **5** dense, dopey, dummy, dunce, ninny, thick **6** lubber, nitwit, oafish, obtuse **7** boorish, doltish, dullard, jackass, loutish **8** dumbbell **9** blockhead, simpleton **10** nincompoop
org.: **4** NASA
path: **3** arc
scaffold: **6** gantry
scientist: **5** brain **6** genius **7** egghead, scholar
section: **5** stage
starter: **3** sky **5** retro
top: **4** nose **5** ogive **8** nose cone
rocket __: **3** gun **4** bomb, ship, sled **5** motor, plane, salad **6** engine **7** science
__ rocket: **3** ion **4** step **5** dame's, dyer's **7** control
rocketeer: **7** Goddard **9** astronaut, cosmonaut
Rocketeer, The (1991 film)
cast: Alan Arkin, Jennifer Connelly, Timothy Dalton
director: Joe Johnston
Rocket Gibraltar (1988 film)
cast: Suzy Amis, Patricia Clarkson, Burt Lancaster
director: Daniel Petrie
Rocket Man (1972 song) artist: Elton John
Rocket rival: **3** Net, Sun **4** Buck, Bull, Hawk, Heat, Jazz, King, Spur **5** Knick, Laker, Magic, Pacer, Sixer **6** Celtic, Hornet, Nugget, Piston, Raptor, Wizard **7** Clipper, Grizzly, Warrior **8** Cavalier, Maverick **10** SuperSonic, Timberwolf
Rockets: **4** five, team
home: **7** Houston
org.: **3** NBA
sport: **10** basketball
Rockette: **6** dancer
Rocket, The: Rod Laver
rockfish, California: **4** rena
Rockford: **4** city, town
city near ~: **6** De Kalb
locale: **8** Illinois
Rockford Files, The (NBC drama)
cast: Noah Beery Jr. (Joseph Rockford)
James Garner (Jim Rockford)
theme song: Mike Post
rockhound science: **4** geol. **7** geology
Rockies: **3** mts. **4** mtns., nine, team **5** range
beast: **3** elk **4** dall, pika, puma **6** cougar **7** bighorn, panther **8** cimarron
brew: **5** Coors
city: **6** Denver, Helena
explorer: **4** Pike
highest of the ~: **6** Elbert
hrs.: **3** MDT, MST
locale: **3** Ida., Mex., Nev., Wyo. **4** Alta., Ariz., Colo., Mont., Utah **5** Idaho, Yukon **6** Alaska, Canada, Mexico, Nevada **7** Alberta, Arizona, Montana, Wyoming **8** Colorado **9** New Mexico
mountain: **4** Yale **5** Bross, Eolus, Evans **6** Antero, Elbert, Oxford, Robson, Wilson **7** Belford, Cameron, Harvard, Lincoln, Shavano, Sherman **8** Columbia, Democrat, Sneffels **9** Bierstadt, Pikes Peak, Princeton
org.: **3** MLB, NLW
park: **5** Banff
range: **5** Teton, Uinta
ski resort: **4** Vail **5** Aspen
sport: **8** baseball
team home: **8** Colorado
tribe: **3** Ute
wind: **7** chinook
zone: **3** MDT, MST
Rockin' Around the Christmas Tree (1960 song) artist: Brenda Lee
rocking: **4** spry **5** brisk, merry, peppy, perky, vital, zesty **6** active, bouncy, jaunty **7** vibrant, zestful **8** animated, spirited, vigorous **9** energetic, exuberant, vivacious
rocking __: **5** chair, horse, shear, stone, valve **6** rhythm
rocking chair: **5** dance
rocking horse: **3** toy
Rocking Horse Winner, The (1949 film)
cast: Valerie Hobson, John Mills
Rockin' Good Way (song), A artist: Brook Benton, Dinah Washington
Rocking the Boat author: Gore Vidal
Rockin' Pneumonia (1972 song) artist: Johnny Rivers
Rockin' Robin (song) artist: Bobby Day, Michael Jackson
word: **5** tweet
Rock in the Casbah (1982 song) artist: Clash
R.O.C.K. in the U.S.A. (1986 song) artist: John Cougar Mellencamp
Rock Island: **4** city, town
locale: **8** Illinois
Rock Island Line (1956 song) artist: Lonnie Donegan
Rockledge: **4** city, town
locale: **7** Florida
rocklike: **4** firm, hard **5** solid **6** rugged, strong
Rocklin: **4** city, town
locale: **10** California
Rock Me (1969 song) artist: Steppenwolf
Rock Me Gently (1974 song) artist: Andy Kim
rock-'n'-__: **4** roll
Rockne: **5** Knute
Rock'n Me (1976 song) artist: Steve Miller Band
Rock 'n' Roll High School (1979 film)
cast: Clint Howard, P.J. Soles, Vincent Van Patten
director: Allan Arkush
Rock 'n' Roll Is King artist: **3** ELO
Rock of Ages: **4** hymn
Rock On (song) artist: David Essex, Michael Damian
Rock & Roll Music (1957 song) artist: Chuck Berry
rockrose: **5** plant **6** flower
rocks: **3** ice **5** cubes
growth on ~: **4** moss
hot ~: **4** lava **5** magma **6** basalt, pumice, scoria **8** obsidian
like some ~: **5** mossy
not on the ~: **4** neat **8** straight
on the ~: **4** iced **8** deprived, stranded **9** destitute, insolvent
science of ~: **9** petrology
__ rocks: **5** on the
rock salt: **6** halite **7** mineral
rockslide: **9** earthfall
Rock Star (2001 film)
cast: Jennifer Aniston, Jason Flemyng, Mark Wahlberg
director: Stephen Herek
Rock Steady (song) artist: Aretha Franklin, Whispers
rock-strewn: **5** stony **6** stoney
rock the __: **4** boat
Rock, The (1996 film)
cast: Michael Biehn, Nicolas Cage, Sean Connery, Ed Harris
director: Michael Bay
__ Rock, The: **3** Hot
Rock the Boat (1974 song) artist: Hues Corporation
rock video award: **3** Ava
Rockville: **4** city, town
locale: **8** Maryland
Rockville Centre: **4** city, town
locale: **7** New York
Rockwell: **4** font, Kent **6** Norman, Robert **8** typeface
Rockwell, Norman: **6** artist **7** painter **11** illustrator
Rock Wit'cha (1989 song) artist: Bobby Brown
Rock With You (1979 song) artist: Michael Jackson
rocky: **3** ill **4** firm, hard, iffy, sick **5** dizzy, rigid, risky, rough, shaky, solid, stony **6** chancy, craggy, flinty, jagged, jouncy, lithic, pebbly, queasy, queazy, rugged, steady, steely, stoney, tricky, wabbly, wobbly **7** arduous, cragged, dubious, rickety, unlevel **8** concrete, doubtful, gravelly, indurate, perilous, ticklish, unsteady **9** difficult, hazardous, petrified, uncertain **10** precarious, unyielding
debris: **5** scree, talus
height: **3** tor **4** crag **5** cliff
ledge: **3** tor **5** arête, cliff **8** pinnacle **9** precipice **10** escarpment, prominence
not ~: **6** smooth
Rocky: **3** SUV **8** Burnette, Daihatsu, Graziano, Marciano, squirrel
enemy: **5** Boris **7** Natasha
rival: **3** Cub, Met, Red **4** Expo, Twin **5** Angel, Astro, Brave, Giant, Padre, Royal, Tiger **6** Apollo, Brewer, Dodger, Indian, Marlin, Oriole, Philly, Pirate, Ranger, Red Sox, Yankee **7** Blue Jay, Mariner **8** Athletic, Cardinal, Devil Ray, White Sox
to Bullwinkle: **3** pal
Rocky (1976 film)
cast: Burgess Meredith, Talia Shire, Sylvester Stallone, Carl Weathers, Burt Young
character: **5** Creed **6** Adrian, Apollo, Balboa, Mickey, Paulie
composer: **5** Conti
director: John G. Avildsen
dog: **6** Butkus
Rocky __ Friends: **6** and His
Rocky __ Picture Show, The: **6** Horror
Rocky and His Friends dog: **9** Mr. Peabody
Rocky Horror Picture Show, The (1975 film)
cast: Barry Bostwick, Tim Curry, Susan Sarandon
hero: **4** Brad
Rocky II (1979 film): **6** sequel
cast: Burgess Meredith, Talia Shire, Sylvester Stallone, Carl Weathers, Burt Young
director: Sylvester Stallone
Rocky III (1982 film)
cast: Burgess Meredith, Mr. T, Talia Shire, Sylvester Stallone, Carl Weathers, Burt Young,
director: Sylvester Stallone
villain: **4** Lang
Rocky IV (1985 film)
cast: Dolph Lundgren, Mr. T, Brigitte Nielsen, Talia Shire, Sylvester Stallone, Burt Young
director: Sylvester Stallone
setting: **6** Russia
villain: **4** Ivan **5** Drago
Rocky Mount: **4** city, town
locale: **4** N. Car.
Rocky Mountain: **4** park
see also Rockies
Rocky Mountain __: **4** goat, High **5** sheep **6** locust, States **7** bighorn, juniper
Rocky Mountain High (1973 song) artist: John Denver
Rocky Mountain News: **5** paper **9** newspaper
locale: **6** Denver
Rocky River: **4** city, town
locale: **4** Ohio
rocky road: **6** flavor **8** ice cream
alternative: **5** lemon, mocha, peach **6** banana, coffee, Jamoca, toffee **7** caramel, coconut, vanilla **8** cinnamon, hazelnut **9** bubblegum, chocolate, pineapple, pistachio, raspberry, rum raisin **10** blackberry, cheesecake, Neapolitan, peppermint, strawberry
rococo: **5** style **6** florid, ornate **7** flowery **10** flamboyant
too ~: **4** arty **5** artsy
rod: **3** bar, gat, gun, pin **4** axle, bolt, cane, pole, rung, spit, wand, whip **5** baton, birch, dowel, piece, poker, shaft, spike, staff, stake, stave, stick, swish **6** cudgel, heater, pistol, roscoe, switch **7** pointer, scepter **8** baluster, cylinder **9** truncheon **10** discipline, punishment
combining form: **6** -bacter, rhabdo-
construction ~: **5** rebar
divining ~: **4** twig **6** dowser
hot ~: **4** auto **5** racer **6** go fast **7** fast car **8** dragster **9** drive fast, racing car **10** speed demon
item on a ~: **5** towel
nautical: **7** bobstay
of authority: **4** mace
punishing ~: **6** ferula, ferule
starter: **3** ram **4** push **6** golden, silver
wheel ~: **4** axle **5** spoke
__ rod: **3** fly, hot, sag, tie **4** fuel, jack, king **5** lease, reach, stair, truss, withe **6** Aaron's, ground, piston, radius, square, stadia, street **7** casting, control, curtain, dowsing, fishing
Rod: **5** Carew, Laver **6** McKuen, Taylor **7** Gilbert, Langway, Serling, Steiger, Stewart
Rodan (1956 film)
like ~: **6** dubbed
setting: **5** Japan, Tokio, Tokyo
rod and __: **4** reel
Rodari: **8** asteroid
Rodbell, Martin: **8** Nobelist
Rodd: **6** Marcia
Roddenberry: **4** Gene
__ rodder: **3** hot
Roddy: **3** Rod **8** McDowall
rodent: **3** rat **4** cavy, degu, hare, jird, mara, paca, vole **5** coypu, gundi, mouse, shrew, xerus **6** agouti, animal, beaver, gerbil, gopher, jerboa, mammal, marmot, murine, suslik **7** hamster, lemming, mole rat, muskrat, pack rat, rice rat, sand rat, souslik, visacha, wood rat **8** capibara, capybara, chip-

munk, cricetid, dormouse, spiny rat, squirrel, trade rat, tuco-tuco, water rat, wharf rat **9** chickaree, groundhog, guinea pig, porcupine, woodchuck **10** chinchilla, prairie dog
Africa: **4** jird **5** gundi, xerus **6** gerbil, jerboa **7** mole rat
aquatic ~: **5** coypu **6** beaver **7** muskrat
Asia: **4** jird **6** gerbil, jerboa, suslik **7** hamster, souslik
burrowing: **4** degu, jird, mole **6** gerbil, gopher **7** hamster, mole rat, visacha **8** tuco-tuco **9** groundhog, woodchuck **10** prairie dog
Central America: **4** paca **6** agouti **8** spiny rat
desert ~: **5** gundi
Europe: **6** suslik **7** hamster, lemming, mole rat, souslik
Mexico: **7** rice rat
mouselike: **4** vole **6** jerboa **7** lemming
rabbitlike ~: **4** mara **6** agouti
reaction to a ~: **3** eek
South America: **4** cavy, mara, paca **5** coypu **6** agouti **7** rice rat, visacha **8** capibara, capybara, spiny rat, tuco-tuco **9** guinea pig **10** chinchilla
rodents, old-style: **5** meece
rodeo: **5** sport
compete in a ~: **4** ride, rope
mount: **4** bull **5** bronc, steer **6** Brahma, bronco **7** broncho
need: **5** chute, lasso, noose, reata, riata **6** barrel, lariat
performer: **5** rider, roper
yell: **5** wahoo, whoop
Rodeo: **3** SUV **5** Isuzu **6** ballet
composer: **7** Copland
Rodeo __: **5** Drive
Rodeo author: Larry McMurtry
Roderick
in Italian: **7** Rodrigo
in Spanish: **7** Rodrigo
Roderick __: **6** Hudson, Random
Roderick Hudson author: Henry James
Roderick Random author: Tobias Smollett
Roderick, the Last of the __: **5** Goths
Rodez: **4** city, town
locale: **6** France
Rodgers: **4** Bill **6** Jimmie **7** Richard
Rodgers, Jimmie
song: Are You Really Mine (1958)
Honeycomb (1957)
Kisses Sweeter Than Wine (1957)
Oh-Oh, I'm Falling in Love Again (1958)
Secretly (1958)
Rodgers, Richard: **8** composer
collaborator: **4** Hart **8** Sondheim **11** Hammerstein
musical: Allegro
Babes in Arms
The Boys From Syracuse
By Jupiter
Carousel
A Connecticut Yankee
Dearest Enemy
Do I Hear a Waltz?
Flower Drum Song
The Garrick Gaieties
The Girl Friend
Heads Up!
Higher and Higher
I'd Rather Be Right
I Married an Angel
Jumbo
The King and I
Me and Juliet
No Strings
Oklahoma!
On Your Toes
Pal Joey
Peggy-Ann
Pipe Dream
Present Arms
Simple Simon
The Sound of Music
South Pacific
Spring Is Here
Too Many Girls
Two by Two
song: Bali Ha'i
Bewitched, Bothered and Bewildered
Blue Moon
Climb Ev'ry Mountain
A Cockeyed Optimist
Do-Re-Mi
Edelweiss
The Gentleman Is a Dope
Getting to Know You
Happy Talk
Hello, Young Lovers
I Cain't Say No
I Could Write a Book
I Enjoy Being a Girl
If I Loved You
Isn't It Romantic
It Might as Well Be Spring
It's a Grand Night for Singing
I Whistle a Happy Tune
I Wish I Were in Love Again
Johnny One Note
June Is Bustin' Out All Over
The Lady Is a Tramp
Little Girl Blue
Manhattan
Many a New Day
Mimi
The Most Beautiful Girl in the World
Mountain Greenery
My Favorite Things
My Funny Valentine
My Heart Stood Still
Oh, What a Beautiful Mornin'
Oklahoma
People Will Say We're in Love
Shall We Dance?
Some Enchanted Evening
The Sound of Music
The Surrey With the Fringe on Top
The Sweetest Sounds
Ten Cents a Dance
There Is Nothin' Like a Dame
There's a Small Hotel
This Can't Be Love
Thou Swell
Where or When
With a Song in My Heart
A Wonderful Guy
You'll Never Walk Alone
Younger Than Springtime
__ Rodham Clinton: **7** Hillary
Rodin, Auguste: **6** artist **8** sculptor
homeland: **6** France
work: **4** Adam, nude **6** St. John **7** The Kiss, Ugolino **9** Le Penseur, The Bather **10** The Thinker
Rodman, Dennis
milieu: **5** court
org.: **3** NBA
sport: **10** basketball
spouse: Carmen Electra
Rodney: **6** Caesar, Porter
Rodolfo in English: **7** Rudolph
Rodolfo's beloved: **4** Mimi
rodomontade: **6** hot air **7** bluster, bombast **8** boasting, bragging, claptrap **9** gasconade, vainglory
Rodrigo in English: **8** Roderick
Rodrigues: **5** Percy
Rodriguez, Robert: **8** director
film: El Mariachi (1992)
The Faculty (1998)
Spy Kids (2001)
Rodzinski, Artur: **9** conductor
roe: **3** egg, ova **4** buck, deer, eggs, hind, stag **6** animal, caviar **7** caviare, seafood
ender: **4** buck
lobster ~: **5** coral
relative: **3** elk **4** axis, pudu, shou, sika **5** moose **6** chital, guemal, hangul, huemul, sambar, sambur, thamin, wapiti **7** brocket, caribou, muntjac, muntjak, sambhar, sambhur **8** reindeer **9** barasingh
source: **4** shad **8** sturgeon
roe __: **4** deer
Roe: **4** Jane **5** Tommy **7** Allison, Richard **8** Preacher
Roebling: **4** John
roebuck: **4** deer, male
Roebuck partner: **5** Sears
Roeg, Nicolas: **8** director
film: Don't Look Now (1973)
Insignificance (1985)
The Man Who Fell to Earth (1976)
The Witches (1990)
spouse: Theresa Russell
roentgenogram: **4** x-ray
Roentgen, Wilhelm: **6** German **9** physicist
discovery: **4** X-ray
Roethke, Theodore: **4** poet
work: The Far Field
Open House
Praise to the End
The Waking
Words for the Wind
Roe, Tommy
hometown: Atlanta
song: Dizzy (1969)
Everybody (1963)
Hooray for Hazel (1966)
Jam Up Jelly Tight (1969)
Sheila (1962)
Sweet Pea (1966)
Roe vs. __: **4** Wade
__ rogas: **3** uti
rogation: **6** prayer
roger: **2** ay, da, ja, OK, sí **3** aye, oui, yea, yep, yup **4** fine, okay, okeh, okey, sure, yeah **5** good-o, natch, quite, right, uh-huh **6** agreed, gladly, good-oh, indeed, just so, rather, righto, surely, you bet, yowzah **7** exactly, go ahead, indeedy, mais oui, quite so, ten-four **8** all right, as you say, of course, thumbs up, very well **9** be my guest, certainly, darn right, naturally, precisely, sure thing, you betcha, you said it **10** absolutely, by all means, definitely, positively, sure enough, that's right, understood
follower: **5** wilco
Roger: **4** Mudd, Rees **5** Bacon, Ebert, Maris, Moore, Smith, Taney, Vadim **6** Allers, Corman, du Gard, Miller, Mosley, Rabbit, Sperry **7** Clemens, Daltrey, Livesey, Maltbie, McGuinn, Zelazny **8** Staubach, Weisberg, Williams **9** Bannister, Bresnahan, Christian, Donaldson, Guillemin, Whittaker
in German: **6** Rutger
in Italian: **7** Ruggero **8** Ruggiero
Roger __: **5** and Me
__ Roger: **5** Jolly
Roger and Me (1989 film) director: Michael Moore
Roger B. __: **5** Taney
Roger E. __: **6** Mosley
Rogers: **3** Roy **4** Buck, city, Fred, Mimi, peak, town, Will **5** Buddy, Kenny, mount, Wayne **6** Ginger **7** Hornsby **8** mountain
locale: **8** Arkansas, Virginia
partner: **5** Evans **7** Astaire
Rogers, Buddy spouse: Mary Pickford
Rogers, Ginger: **7** actress
film: Bachelor Mother (1939)
The Barkleys of Broadway (1949)
Carefree (1938)
Dreamboat (1952)
Flying Down to Rio (1933)
Follow the Fleet (1936)
Forever Female (1953)
The Gay Divorcee (1934)
Kitty Foyle (1940, AA)
The Major and the Minor (1942)
Monkey Business (1952)
Roberta (1935)
Romance in Manhattan (1934)
Shall We Dance (1937)
Stage Door (1937)
The Story of Vernon & Irene Castle (1939)
Swing Time (1936)
Tight Spot (1955)
Tom, Dick and Harry (1941)
Top Hat (1935)
Upperworld (1934)
Vivacious Lady (1938)
Weekend at the Waldorf (1945)
We're Not Married (1952)
You Said a Mouthful (1932)
spouse: Lew Ayres
__ Rogers in the 25th Century: **4** Buck
Rogers, Kenny
member of: New Christy Minstrels
song: But You Know I Love You (1969)
Coward of the County (1979)
Don't Fall in Love With a Dreamer (1980)
The Gambler (1978)
I Don't Need You (1981)
Islands in the Stream (1983)
Just Dropped In (1968)
Lady (1980)
Love Will Turn You Around (1982)
Lucille (1977)
Ruby, Don't Take Your Love to Town (1969)
She Believes in Me (1979)
Something's Burning (1970)
We've Got Tonight (1983)
You Decorated My Life (1979)
Rogers, Mimi: **7** actress
film: Austin Powers: International Man of Mystery (1997)
Lost in Space (1998)
The Mirror Has Two Faces (1996)
Monkey Trouble (1994)
The Rapture (1991)
Someone to Watch Over Me (1987)
spouse: Tom Cruise
Rogers, Roy: **6** cowboy
dog: **6** Bullet
horse: **7** Trigger
spouse: Dale Evans
__ Rogers St. Johns: **5** Adela
Rogers, Wayne: **5** actor
film: The Gig (1985)
Once in Paris ... (1978)
TV: MASH
Rogers, Will: **5** actor **6** writer **8** humorist
film: A Connecticut Yankee (1931)
Doubting Thomas (1935)
Dr. Bull (1933)
Judge Priest (1934)
Life Begins at Forty (1935)
State Fair (1933)
Steamboat 'Round the Bend (1935)
horse: **8** Soapsuds
prop: **4** rope **5** lasso
work: The Cowboy Philosopher on Prohibition
The Illiterate Digest
Sanity is Where You Find It
Roget: **5** Peter
entry: **3** syn. **7** synonym

rogue: **3** cad, cur **4** heel, toad, worm **5** cheat, churl, crook, demon, devil, fraud, knave, losel, scamp, stray **6** bad egg, bad guy, con man, daemon, daimon, goonda, outlaw, rascal, rotter **7** bad news, bounder, brigand, dastard, lowlife, outcast, stinker, varment, varmint, villain, wastrel **8** blighter, criminal, deceiver, hooligan, picaroon, rakehell, scalawag, spalpeen, swindler **9** charlatan, con artist, defrauder, miscreant, reprobate, scallawag, scallywag, scoundrel, trickster, vulgarian **10** blackguard, black sheep, mountebank, ne'er-do-well, scapegrace
Rogue: **3** car **4** auto **7** Rambler **10** automobile
Rogue Cop (1954 film)
 cast: Janet Leigh, George Raft, Robert Taylor
Rogue River Feud author: Zane Grey
roguery: **7** devilry, knavery **8** deviltry, mischief **9** rascality
rogues' __: **7** gallery
roguish: **3** sly **4** arch, base **5** rowdy **6** shifty **7** jesting, jocular, knavish **8** sporting, sportive **9** deceitful, deceptive **10** frolicsome, picaresque
 one wit: **3** wag **6** gamine
Roh __ Woo: **3** Tae
Rohmer: **3** Sax **4** Eric
Rohmer, Eric: **8** director
 film: Autumn Tale (1998)
  Chloe in the Afternoon (1972)
  Claire's Knee (1971)
Rohmer, Sax: **6** author, writer
Rohnert Park: **4** city, town
 locale: **10** California
Rohrer, Heinrich: **8** Nobelist **9** physicist, scientist
roi: **4** king **5** Louis **6** French **7** Louis IV **8** Louis XIV, Louis XVI, monarque
 spouse: **5** reine
__ Roi: **3** Ubu
roil: **3** irk, vex **4** bait, gall, miff **5** anger, annoy, chafe, churn, muddy, peeve, pique, swirl **6** badger, harass, hector, plague, ruffle, stir up, tee off **7** agitate, becloud, bedevil, churn up, cloud up, disturb, enflame, incense, inflame, provoke, tick off **8** disquiet, irritate **9** aggravate, displease **10** exasperate
roiled: **5** mirky, muddy, murky, rough **6** turbid **9** turbulent
roister: **4** romp **5** revel **6** gambol **7** carouse **9** have a ball
__ Roister Doister: **5** Ralph
Rojas, Manuel: **6** writer **7** Chilean
Rojhan: **3** cow **4** bull **6** bovine, cattle
Roker: **2** Al **5** Roxie
Rolaids: **7** antacid
 alternative: **4** Tums **6** Maalox, Pepcid, Riopan, Zantac **7** Gelusil, Lactaid, Mylanta **8** Gaviscon **11** Alka-Seltzer, Pepto-Bismol
Roland: **4** hero **5** Joffe, Young **7** Gilbert **8** Emmerich
 love: **4** Aude
Roland, Gilbert: **5** actor
 film: Beneath the 12 Mile Reef (1953)
  Bullfighter and the Lady (1951)
  The Last Train From Madrid (1937)
  The Miracle of Our Lady of Fatima (1952)
  My Six Convicts (1952)
  She Done Him Wrong (1933)
  Thunder Bay (1953)
role: **3** bit, job **4** duty, hero, lead, part, star, task **5** cameo, extra, guise, place, stint, super, title **6** aspect, office, status, walk-on **7** ingénue **8** business, capacity, function, position, province **9** character, portrayal, situation **10** appearance
 assign a ~: **4** cast
 brief ~: **5** cameo
role __: **3** set **5** model **6** strain
__ role: **5** cameo, title **6** gender
roleo, compete in a: **4** birl
role-playing __: **4** game
Rolex: **5** watch **10** wristwatch
 alternative: **4** Ebel, Rado **5** Casio, Elgin, Lorus, Omega, Seiko, Timex **6** Bulova, Fossil, Movado, Pulsar, Swatch **7** Citizen **8** Longines, Tag Heuer, Tourneau
 rival: **5** Casio
Rolfe, Frederick: **6** writer **7** British
rolfing: **7** massage
roll: **3** bun, hum, rob, wad, yaw **4** bolt, boom, bowl, coil, echo, flow, furl, hank, keel, list, loop, peal, pour, reel, roar, rock, spin, sway, toss, turn, verb, wind, wrap **5** bagel, bialy, bread, drive, glide, growl, heave, level, lurch, money, pitch, spool, surge, swirl, table, trill, twirl, twist, wheel, whirl, whirr **6** billow, census, gyrate, kaiser, lumber, muster, reecho, roster, rotate, rumble, scroll, stream, swivel, totter, tumble, waddle, wallow **7** catalog, operate, rat-a-tat, resound, revolve, thunder, trundle **8** cylinder, drumbeat, get going, gyration, overturn, register, schedule, turn over, undulate **9** cannonade, catalogue, directory, get moving, luxuriate **10** somersault, tabulation
 back: **5** lower, skimp **6** deduct, lessen, reduce, return **7** regress, tail off **8** decrease, downsize **10** underspend
 bakery ~: **3** bun **5** bagel, bialy
 by: **6** elapse
 call: **6** muster **8** register
 ender: **3** mop, out, way **4** away, back, over
 expert: **5** baker
 in: **4** come **5** enter, pop up, reach **6** appear, arrive, show up, wallow **7** turn out **8** get there **9** luxuriate
 in the aisles: **4** howl, roar **5** laugh **6** guffaw **7** break up, crack up **8** convulse
 jelly ~: **7** dessert **10** confection
 let ~: **5** print **6** run off **8** put to bed **9** go to press
 on: **2** go **3** fly **4** flow, go by, pass **6** pass by **7** glide by **8** tick away **9** transpire
 on a ~: **3** hot **5** blest, lucky **7** blessed, charmed, favored **9** fortunate **10** auspicious, felicitous, fortuitous
 out: **4** rise, wake **5** arise, get up, waken **6** awaken, smooth, spread, unfurl **7** exhibit, flatten, present, turn out **9** introduce
 out of bed: **4** rise, wake **5** awake, get up, rouse, waken **6** awaken, bestir
 out the red carpet: **5** greet, honor **7** lionize, receive
 over: **8** reinvest **9** overpower, surrender
 (over): **4** mull **5** think
 starter: **3** bed, log, pay **4** bank **5** jelly, steam
 the eyes: **4** leer, look, ogle **5** stare **6** goggle
 topping: **5** onion **6** sesame **10** sesame seed
 up: **4** furl, wrap **5** amass, lay up **6** arrive, garner
 with the punches: **4** cope **5** adapt **6** adjust, manage **8** overlook
roll __: **3** bag, bar, out, top **4** back, book, cage, call, film, over **5** cloud
roll __ the punches: **4** with
roll __ the red carpet: **3** out
roll-__ desk: **3** top
__ roll: **3** egg, on a **4** snap, warp, whip **5** cloth, couch, dandy, honor, jelly, music, onion, piano, split, sweet **6** barrel, French, kaiser, muster, shadow, spring **7** aileron, blanket, chicken, lobster
__-roll: **5** rock-'n'
Roll __ Beethoven: **4** Over
Roll __ bones!: **3** dem
Rolla: **4** city, town
 locale: **8** Missouri
Rolland, Romain: **6** French, writer **8** essayist, Nobelist **10** playwright
rollaway feature: **6** caster
rollback: **6** saving **8** discount **9** reduction **10** concession
__-roll bar: **4** anti
roll call
 response: **3** aye, nay, yea, yes **4** here
Rolle: **6** Esther
rolled __: **4** gold, oats **5** glass, roast **6** collar
Rollei: **6** camera
 alternative: **4** Fuji **5** Canon, Kodak, Leica, Nikon **6** Konica, Pentax **7** Minolta, Olympus, Vivitar, Yashica **8** Polaroid
roller: **4** bird, wave **5** surge, wheel **6** caster
 ender: **5** skate
 high ~: **7** spender **8** prodigal **10** big spender
 starter: **5** steam, stone
roller __: **4** gate, mill, rink **5** chain, derby, skate, towel **6** hockey **7** bearing, coaster
__ roller: **4** high, leaf, road **5** blind, paint, pinch
Rollerball (1975 film)
 cast: Maud Adams, James Caan, John Houseman
 director: Norman Jewison
rollerblader's wear: **5** skate **6** helmet
roller coaster: **4** ride **5** dance
 cry: **4** whee
 feature: **3** dip
 like a ~: **4** fast **5** loopy
 operator: **5** carny **6** carney
roller derby: **5** sport
 track: **4** oval
rollers: **4** dice
 use ~: **3** set
__ Rollers: **4** High
roller skating: **5** sport
 accessory: **3** key
 place: **4** rink
rollick: **4** lark, romp **5** caper, frisk, revel **6** cavort, frolic, gambol **9** have a ball, luxuriate **10** recreation
rollicking: **3** gay **4** glad **5** happy, jolly, merry **6** frisky, hearty, jaunty, jovial, joyful, joyous, lively **7** jesting, playful, romping **8** carefree, cheerful, spirited, sporting, sportive **9** exuberant, fun-loving, hilarious, sprightly **10** boisterous, frolicsome
Rollie: **7** Fingers
Rollin: **4** Hand **5** Betty
rolling: **4** open **5** hilly **6** active **8** gyration, thriving
 get things ~: **4** open **5** begin, cause, start **6** launch, tackle **8** commence **10** lead the way
 in dough: **4** rich **5** flush **6** loaded, monied **7** moneyed, wealthy, well-off **8** affluent, well-to-do **9** well-fixed **10** privileged, propertied, prosperous, well-heeled
 really ~: **4** fast **5** brisk, fleet, quick, rapid, swift **6** flying, speedy
 starter: **3** log **5** steam
 stone: **5** rover **7** drifter, vagrant **8** wanderer
 stone lack: **4** moss
 with the punches: **5** stoic **7** stoical **9** resilient
rolling __: **3** pin **4** in it, mill, stop **5** hitch, stock **7** kitchen
__ rolling: **3** egg, ply **4** pack
__-rolling: **4** high
Rolling __: **5** Stone **6** Stones
rolling in the __: **6** aisles
Rolling Meadows: **4** city, town
 locale: **8** Illinois
Rolling Rock rival: **5** Coors
rolling stock repository: **4** yard
Rolling Stone: **3** mag **8** magazine
__ Rolling Stone: **5** Like a
Rolling Stones
 members: Jagger, Richards, Jones, Wyman, Watts, Wood
 song: 19th Nervous Breakdown (1966)
  Ain't Too Proud to Beg (1974)
  Angie (1973)
  As Tears Go By (1966)
  Beast of Burden (1978)
  Brown Sugar (1971)
  Dandelion (1967)
  Emotional Rescue (1980)
  Fool to Cry (1976)
  Get Off My Cloud (1965)
  Happy (1972)
  Harlem Shuffle (1986)
  Have You Seen Your Mother, Baby? (1966)
  Heart of Stone (1965)
  Honky Tonk Women (1969)
  (I Can't Get No) Satisfaction (1965)
  It's All Over Now (1964)
  It's Only Rock 'n Roll (1974)
  Jumpin' Jack Flash (1968)
  Lady Jane (1966)
  The Last Time (1965)
  Miss You (1978)
  Mixed Emotions (1989)
  Mothers Little Helper (1966)
  Paint It, Black (1966)
  Ruby Tuesday (1967)
  She's a Rainbow (1968)
  Start Me Up (1981)
  Time Is on My Side (1964)
  Tumbling Dice (1972)
  Undercover of the Night (1983)
  Waiting on a Friend (1981)
  Wild Horses (1971)
Rollins: **4** Easy **5** Sonny **6** Howard
Rollins, Sonny: **11** saxophonist
 genre: **4** jazz
__ Roll Morton: **5** Jelly
roll-on: **9** deodorant
 alternative: **5** spray **7** aerosol
rollout: **6** launch
roll out the __ carpet: **3** red
Roll Out the __: **6** Barrel
Roll Over Beethoven (1956 song)
 artist: Chuck Berry
rollover subj.: **3** IRA
rolls
 like ~: **5** crisp **6** crusty
 remove from the ~: **6** delist
 shop: **6** bakery **10** patisserie
Rolls-Royce: **3** car **4** auto **7** British **10** automobile
 model: **7** Phantom **8** Camargue, Corniche, Park Ward **10** Silver Dawn, Silver Spur **11** Silver Cloud, Silver Ghost
 part: **4** boot, tyre **6** bonnet
__ Roll Symphony: **4** Drum
rolltop: **4** desk **9** furniture, secretary **10** escritoire
Roll With It (1988 song) artist: Steve Winwood
roll with the __: **7** punches

Rolonda: **5** Watts
Rölvaag, Ole: **6** author, writer
work: Giants in the Earth
roly-poly: **5** beefy, fubsy, obese, plump, pudgy, pursy, round, stout, tubby **6** chubby, fleshy, portly, pyknic, rotund, stocky, zaftig, zoftig **7** adipose, paunchy **9** corpulent **10** overweight
Roly-Poly Pudding, The author: Beatrix Potter
ROM
medium: **2** CD **4** disc, disk
part: **3** mem. **4** only, read **6** memory
Roma: **4** city, town **6** Downey, tomato
hill count in ~: **5** sette
locale: **5** Italy **6** Italia
relative: **6** Big Boy **9** beefsteak, Better Boy, Early Girl, Quick Pick
Roma composer: **5** Bizet
__-Romagna, Italy: **6** Emilia
Romain: **4** Gary **7** Rolland
romaine: **3** cos **7** lettuce
Romains, Jules: **6** French, writer **8** essayist **10** playwright
roman __: **5** à clef
roman-__: **6** fleuve
Roman: **4** Ruth, type **6** Horace **8** aquiline, Polanski **9** classical
not ~: **4** Ital. **6** Italic
see also Latin, Rome
Roman __: **3** law **4** arch, mile, nose, pace, ride, rite **5** brick, Curia, peace, punch, shade **6** candle, collar, Empire, strike **7** holiday, liturgy, numeral
__-Roman: **5** Greco **6** Graeco
__ romana: **4** alla
Romana: **4** font **8** typeface
__ Romana: **3** Pax **5** Curia
roman à clef: **4** book **5** novel **7** fiction
__ Romana Rota: **5** Sacra
romance: **3** woo **4** book, idyl, love, tale **5** amour, fling, genre, idyll, novel, prose, story **6** affair, glamor, legend, wooing **7** fantasy, fiction, glamour, liaison, mystery, passion **8** intrigue **9** adventure, courtship, fairy tale, love story, melodrama, narrative, sentiment **10** attachment, flirtation, tearjerker
in French: **5** amour
language: **6** French, Ladino **7** Italian, Spanish **8** Romanian, Rumanian **9** Provençal, Sardinian **10** Portuguese
of yore: **4** gest **5** geste
__ Romance: **4** True **5** A Fine **7** Crimson, Murphy's
__ Romance, A: **4** Fine **6** Little
Romance author: Edgar Allan Poe
Romance in Manhattan (1934 film)
cast: Francis Lederer, Ginger Rogers
Romance of Helen Trent, The: **9** radio show
Romance of Rosy Ridge, The (1947 film)
cast: Van Johnson, Janet Leigh, Thomas Mitchell
Romance on the High Seas (1948 film)
cast: Jack Carson, Don DeFore, Janis Paige
director: Michael Curtiz
Romancero gitano poet: **5** Lorca
romances name: **5** Steel **8** Cartland
Romancing the Stone (1984 film)
cast: Danny DeVito, Michael Douglas, Kathleen Turner
cat: **5** Romeo
director: Robert Zemeckis
Roman Curia office: **6** datary
Roman de Brut author: Wace
__ Roman Empire: **4** Holy **7** Eastern, Western
Romanesque: **5** style
Roman/Greek god equivalents:
Amor - Eros
Apollo - Apollo
Aurora - Eos
Bacchus - Dionysus
Cupid - Eros
Demeter - Ceres
Diana - Artemis
Jove - Zeus
Juno - Hera
Jupiter - Zeus
Mars - Ares
Mercury - Hermes
Minerva - Athena
Neptune - Poseidon
Ops - Rhea
Pax - Irene
Pluto - Hades
Proserpina - Persephone
Saturn - Cronos
Sol - Helios
Venus - Aphrodite
Vesta - Hestia
Vulcan - Hephaestus
Roman Holiday (1953 film)
cast: Eddie Albert, Audrey Hepburn, Gregory Peck
director: William Wyler
Romania: **6** nation **7** country
ancient: **5** Dacia
capital: **9** Bucharest
city: **4** Arad, Iasi **5** Bacau, Sibiu **6** Braila, Brasov, Galati, Oradea **9** Bucharest, Constanta
conductor: **6** Perlea **10** Comissiona
dance: **4** hora **5** horah
gymnast: **8** Comaneci
locale: **3** Eur. **6** Europe **7** Balkans
money: **3** ban, leu, ley
neighbor: **7** Hungary, Moldova, Ukraine **8** Bulgaria **10** Yugoslavia
Nobelist in Medicine: **6** Palade
Nobelist in Peace: **6** Wiesel
port: **6** Braila **9** Constanta
region: **5** Banat
river: **3** Olt **4** Prut **5** Siret
tennis pro: **7** Nastase
violinist: **6** Enesco
Romanian: **8** language
Romano: **3** Ray **6** cheese
source: **3** ewe **5** sheep
Romanoff and Juliet (1961 film)
cast: Sandra Dee, John Gavin, Peter Ustinov
director: Peter Ustinov
__ Romanorum: **5** Gesta
Romanov: **7** Mikhail
title: **4** tsar
see also Russian
Roman, Ruth: **7** actress
film: The Far Country (1955) Strangers on a Train (1951) Three Secrets (1950)
Romans, book before: **4** Acts
Roman Scandals (1933 film)
cast: Eddie Cantor, Ruth Etting, Gloria Stuart
director: Frank Tuttle
Romansh language: **5** Ladin
Roman Spring of Mrs. Stone, The: **4** film **7** novella
author: Tennessee Williams
cast: Warren Beatty, Vivien Leigh, Lotte Lenya
romantic: **4** fond, wild **5** corny, mushy, soppy **6** ardent, dreamy, erotic, exotic, loving, poetic, sirupy, sloppy, syrupy, tender **7** amatory, amorous, hugging, idyllic, kissing, maudlin, utopian **8** charming, colorful, enamored, exciting, idealist, poetical, quixotic **9** amatorial, fairy-tale, fantastic, glamorous, legendary, nostalgic, visionary **10** chivalrous, enchanting, idealistic, lovey-dovey, mysterious, passionate, quixotical, starry-eyed
beginning: **3** neo
ender: **3** ist
inspiration: **4** moon
offering: **4** rose
one: **5** lover, Romeo **6** suitor **8** lothario
outing: **4** date
work: **4** poem **5** novel **6** ballad
Romantic Englishwoman, The (1975 film)
cast: Helmut Berger, Michael Caine, Glenda Jackson
director: Joseph Losey
Romanus: **4** pope **7** pontiff
__-Roman wrestling: **5** Greco **6** Graeco
Romany: **8** language
Rombauer: **4** Irma
Romberg: **7** Sigmund
Rom. Cath. off: **3** mgr. **4** msgr.
Rome: **4** city, town **5** apple **6** Harold **7** capital
Bishop of ~: **4** pope **7** pontiff
city near ~: **5** Terni **6** Naples
fountain: **5** Trevi
lake near ~: **6** Albano
like ~: **5** hilly **7** eternal
locale: **5** Italy **7** Georgia, New York
relative: **4** crab, Gala, Lodi **5** Mutsu **6** Empire, Ida Red, medlar, Pippin, russet **7** Baldwin, Bramley, costard, Freedom, Liberty, Spartan, Wealthy, Winesap **8** Cortland, Jonathan, McIntosh
river: **5** Tiber
see also Italy, Latin
Rome (ancient)
amphitheaters: **6** arenae
army: **6** legion
augur: **6** auspex
bathtub: **6** labrum
biographer: **9** Suetonius
boxing glove: **6** cestus
bronze: **3** aes
bust: **4** herm
calendar date: **4** ides **5** nones **7** calends, kalends
carriage: **5** rheda
censor: **4** Cato
commoner: **4** pleb
council: **6** Senate
emblem of power: **6** fasces
emperor: **4** Nero, Otho **5** Galba, Nerva, Titus **6** Caesar, Julius, Trajan **7** Hadrian **8** Augustus, Caligula, Claudius, Tiberius **9** Vitellius
festivals: **4** ludi
foe: **4** Goth, Pict
games: **4** ludi
garment: **4** toga **5** stola, tunic **6** abolla, birrus, byrrus, cyclas **7** paenula
god: **3** Dis **4** Jove, Mars **5** Cupid, Janus, Pluto **6** Saturn, Vulcan **7** Bacchus, Jupiter, Mercury, Neptune **8** Silvanus
goddess: **3** Nox, Ops **4** Juno, Spes **5** Ceres, Diana, Flora, Parca, Salus, Venus, Vesta **6** Aurora **7** Fortuna, Minerva
historian: **4** Cato, Livy **7** Sallust, Tacitus **9** Suetonius
household god: **3** lar
household gods: **5** lares
initials: **4** SPQR
language: **5** Latin
marketplace: **5** forum
money: **2** as **3** aes **5** libra, semis, uncia **6** aureus, talent, triens **7** denarii, sextans **8** denarius, sesterce **9** dupondius, sestertia, sestertii **10** sestertium, tripondius
official: **5** edile **6** aedile, lictor
orator: **4** Cato
philosopher: **6** Seneca
pitcher: **4** olpe
playwright: **6** Seneca **7** Plautus, Terence
poet: **4** Ovid **6** Horace, Vergil **7** Juvenal, Persius **8** Catullus **9** Lucretius
port: **5** Ostia
priest: **6** flamen
province: **4** Gaul **5** Dacia, Lycia
racetrack marker: **4** meta
racing post: **4** meta
resort: **5** Gaeta
road: **4** iter
rooms: **5** atria
saint: **5** Agnes **6** Agatha **7** Cecilia, Clement, Crispin **8** Paulinus **9** Dionysius, Valentine **11** Christopher
satirist: **6** Horace **7** Juvenal
shield: **6** ancile
spear: **4** pila **5** pilum
spectacles: **4** ludi
statuary: **4** herm
theaters: **4** odea
trumpets: **5** tubae
underworld: **5** Orcus
vase stone: **5** murra **6** murrha
vessel: **6** bireme, galley **7** trireme **10** quadrireme
victory site: **4** Zama
wars: **5** Punic
writer: **4** Livy **5** Pliny **7** Martial, Sallust, Tacitus **9** Suetonius
see also Latin
Rome __ apple: **6** Beauty
Rome __ built...: **5** wasn't
__ Rome: **4** Tony
Rome Adventure (1962 film)
cast: Rossano Brazzi, Angie Dickinson, Troy Donahue
director: Delmer Daves
Rome Beauty: **5** apple
relative: **4** crab, Gala, Lodi **5** Mutsu **6** Empire, Ida Red, medlar, Pippin, russet **7** Baldwin, Bramley, costard, Freedom, Liberty, Spartan, Wealthy, Winesap **8** Cortland, Jonathan, McIntosh
Romeo: **4** roué **5** lover, swain **6** suitor **7** Don Juan **8** Casanova, lothario, lover boy **9** inamorato
rival: **5** Paris
__ Romeo: **4** Alfa
Romeo and Juliet: **4** play **7** tragedy
author: Shakespeare
character: **4** John **5** Friar, Paris, Peter **6** Samson, Tybalt **7** Capulet, Escalus, Gregory **8** Benvolio, Lawrence, Mercutio, Montague **9** Balthasar, Friar John
emulate ~: **5** elope
event: **5** tryst
scene: **4** tomb
setting: **5** Italy **6** Verona
Romeo and Juliet (1936 film)
cast: John Barrymore, Leslie Howard, Edna May Oliver, Basil Rathbone, Norma Shearer
director: George Cukor
Romeo and Juliet (1968 film)
cast: Olivia Hussey, Leonard Whiting
director: Franco Zeffirelli
Rome of Hungary, The: **4** Eger
Romeo Is Bleeding star: **4** Olin
Romeo & Juliet (1996 film)
cast: Claire Danes, Brian Dennehy, Leonardo DiCaprio, John Leguizamo
director: Baz Luhrmann

Romeo Must Die (2000 film)
cast: Aaliyah, Jet Li, Delroy Lindo, Henry O
director: Andrzej Bartkowiak
Romeoville: 4 city, town
locale: 8 Illinois
Romero: 5 Cesar 6 George
Romero (1989 film)
cast: Ana Alicia, Richard Jordan, Raul Julia
Romero, Cesar: 5 actor
film: Charlie Chan at Treasure Island (1939)
Coney Island (1943)
Frontier Marshal (1939)
Ocean's Eleven (1960)
Show Them No Mercy! (1935)
TV: Batman
Romero, George A.: 8 director
film: Dawn of the Dead (1978)
Knightriders (1981)
Martin (1978)
Night of the Living Dead (1968)
Rome wasn't built __: 6 in a day
Romic: 4 font 8 typeface
Romijn, Rebecca spouse: John Stamos
Romita: 4 city, town
locale: 6 Mexico 10 Guanajuato
Rommel: 5 Erwin 9 Desert Fox
Romney: 4 Mitt 5 sheep 6 George
Romola author: George Eliot
character: 4 Tito 5 Nello, Piero, Tessa
romp: 3 fun 4 lark, play, skip 5 antic, caper, cut up, frisk, spree 6 cavort, frolic, gambol, prance 7 carouse, disport, roister, rollick, scamper 8 cakewalk, good time, recreate 9 have a ball, make merry, whoop it up
romper: 6 jumper
romper __: 4 room
romping: 3 gay 5 happy, merry, peppy, zesty 6 bouncy, feisty, frisky, jaunty, jovial, joyful, joyous, lively 7 coltish 8 carefree, cheerful, spirited 9 exuberant, fun-loving 10 frolicsome
Romulan: 5 alien
Romulo: 6 Carlos 8 Gallegos
Romulus: 4 city, town, twin 5 Roman 6 eponym
daughter of ~: 5 Prima
locale: 8 Michigan
parent of ~: 4 Ares, Mars, Rhea 10 Rhea Silvia
son of ~: 7 Aollius
twin of ~: 5 Remus
wife of ~: 8 Hersilia
Romy: 9 Schneider
Ron: 3 Cey, Ely, Mix 4 Gant, Mann, Wood 5 Brown, Glass, Kovic, Moody, Santo 6 Guidry, Holden, Howard, Nessen, Reagan, Rifkin, Silver 7 Leflore, Leibman, Palillo, Perlman, Shelton, Swoboda, Winston 8 Clements, Turcotte 9 Greschner, Underwood
Rona: 5 Jaffe 7 Barrett
Ronald: 4 Ross 5 Coase, Isley, Neame 6 Colman, Reagan, Searle 7 Firbank, Norrish
rond de __: 5 jambe
rondelet: 4 poem 5 rhyme, verse
rondo: 5 music
Ronee: 7 Blakley
Ronettes song: Be My Baby (1963)
__-Roni: 5 Rice-a
Roni (1988 song) artist: Bobby Brown
Ronkonkoma: 4 city, town
locale: 7 New York
Ronne __ Shelf: 3 Ice
Ronnie: 4 Lott 5 Dyson 6 Milsap 7 Van Zant 8 McDowell, Montrose
Ronnie (1964 song) artist: Four Seasons
Ronny: 3 Cox 6 Howard
Ronny & the Daytonas song: G.T.O. (1964)
ronquil: 4 fish
__ Ron Ron: 5 Da Doo
Ronsard, Pierre de: 4 poet 6 French
Ronson competitor: 3 Bic 5 Zippo
Ronstadt, Linda
song: All My Life (1990)
Blue Bayou (1977)
Different Drum (1967)
Don't Know Much (1989)
Heat Wave (1975)
How Do I Make You (1980)
Hurt So Bad (1980)
It's So Easy (1977)
Ooh Baby Baby (1978)
Somewhere Out There (1987)
That'll Be the Day (1976)
When Will I Be Loved (1975)
You're No Good (1975)
Röntgen, Wilhelm: 8 Nobelist 9 physicist
Ronzoni __ buoni: 4 sono
roo: 4 joey 6 jumper
Roo
creator: 5 Milne
friend: 3 Owl 4 Pooh 6 Eeyore, Piglet, Winnie
parent: 5 Kanga
rood: 5 cross 7 measure 8 crucifix
four ~ s: 4 acre
rood __: 4 arch 5 spire 6 screen 7 steeple
__ Rood: 4 Holy
roof: 3 top 4 dome, peak 6 shield, summit, zenith 7 ceiling, gambrel, lodging, mansard, shelter 8 covering, housetop, overhead, top level 9 residence
attachment: 4 dish 6 aerial, gutter, leader
beam: 6 header
curved ~: 4 dome 6 cupola
ender: 3 top 4 line, tree
fix a ~: 5 retar
go through the ~: 4 grow, rise, soar 5 mount, surge 6 ascend 7 burgeon, mount up 8 escalate, increase 9 intensify, skyrocket 10 appreciate
hanging: 6 icicle
hit the ~: 4 flip, rage, rant, rave, roar, snap 5 storm 6 blow up, bridle, get mad, see red 7 explode 8 have a fit 9 blow a fuse, throw a fit
nester: 5 stork
problem: 4 drip, leak
projection: 4 eave
raise the ~: 5 gripe, revel, shout, storm 6 clamor, holler, squawk 7 grumble 8 complain 9 bellyache
raising the ~: 4 loud 5 noisy 7 blaring, booming, raucous, riotous, yelling 8 blasting, piercing, shouting 9 bellowing, clamorous, screaming 10 boisterous, uproarious, vociferous
runoff: 4 rain
send through the ~: 5 anger 6 enrage, fire up, madden 7 incense, inflame, provoke 9 infuriate 10 exasperate
starter: 3 sun
support: 5 truss
topper: 3 epi 4 vane 6 aerial
to the ~: 6 loaded, packed 7 crowded, replete, stuffed 9 chock-full, jam-packed
type of ~: 5 gable 6 A-frame
under the ~: 6 indoor, inside 7 indoors
worker: 5 tiler
roof __: 3 rat 4 iris 5 guard, prism 6 garden
__ roof: 3 fan, hip 4 curb, shed, span 5 gable, wagon 6 barrel, cradle, French, saddle, trough 7 built-up, gambrel, lamella, mansard, rainbow
roofer
material: 3 tar 4 tile 5 nails, slate
need: 3 adz, zax 4 adze 6 ladder
Roof of the World, The: 5 Tibet
rooftop
tell from the ~: 5 shout
Rooftop Singers song: Walk Right In (1963)
rook: 3 con 4 bilk, bird, burn, crow, dupe, gull, have, hoax, nick 5 cheat, cozen, gouge, pluck, sting, trick 6 castle, chisel, fleece, rip off 7 beguile, defraud, mislead, swindle 8 flimflam, swindler 9 blackbird 10 chess piece, run a game on
place: 6 corner
Rook: 5 Susan
Rooker, Michael: 5 actor
film: The Bone Collector (1999)
Cliffhanger (1993)
The Replacement Killers (1998)
__ Rookh: 5 Lalla
rookie: 4 tiro, tyro 5 newie 6 novice 7 recruit 8 freshman, neophyte, newcomer 9 fledgling 10 apprentice, first-timer, tenderfoot
like a ~: 5 green
military ~: 4 pleb 5 plebe 10 rct. Recruit
promising ~: 5 comer
Rookie of the Year: 5 award
Rookie of the Year (1993 film)
cast: Gary Busey, Albert Hall, Thomas Ian Nicholas
director: Daniel Stern
Rookie, The (2002 film)
cast: Rachel Griffiths, Jay Hernandez, Dennis Quaid
director: John Lee Hancock
room: 3 den, way 4 cave, cell, dorm, flat, hall, play 5 attic, cabin, lodge, niche, place, range, reach, salon, scope, slack, space, study, vault 6 alcove, cellar, chance, garret, leeway, lounge, margin, office, parlor, volume 7 boudoir, chamber, compass, cubicle, expanse, library, license, lodging, nursery, opening, vacancy 8 basement, capacity, latitude, lodgment, occasion, quarters, vastness 9 allowance, apartment, clearance, cubbyhole, free space, largeness 10 auditorium
and board: 4 keep 7 lodging, pension
asset: 4 view
at the top: 4 loft 5 attic 6 garret
book ~: 3 den 5 study 7 library
British ~: 6 bed-sit
college ~: 4 dorm, hall 7 commons
connector: 4 hall 5 foyer 8 corridor
cooler: 3 fan 9 window fan 10 ceiling fan
decorate a ~: 5 panel, paper
dining ~: 4 mess 8 chow hall, mess hall 9 cafeteria, refectory 10 triclinium
divider: 4 wall 9 partition
ender: 4 ette, mate
extension: 3 ell 5 add-on
furnace ~: 6 cellar
furnishings: 5 decor
home ~: 3 den, lav 4 bath, loft 5 attic, study 6 cellar, parlor 7 boudoir, kitchen 8 basement
in French: 5 salle
in Latin: 6 camera
in Spanish: 4 sala
lecture ~: 10 auditorium
make ~ for: 3 add 5 admit 6 append, edge in, insert 7 include 9 interject
measure: 4 area, sq. ft. 5 width 6 length
out of ~: 4 full
partner: 5 board
place to rent a ~: 3 inn 5 hotel, motel
powder ~: 4 john
rest ~: 4 john
starter: 3 bar, bed, gun, leg, sun, tap, tea 4 ante, back, ball, bath, bunk, club, coat, dark, head, home, mail, mush, news, play, pool, rest, sick, ward, ware, wash, work 5 board, check, class, cloak, court, elbow, green, grill, guard, house, lunch, press, sales, state, stock, store 6 school
storage ~: 5 attic 6 cellar 8 basement
strong ~: 5 vault
take a ~: 4 stay 5 lodge 7 sojourn 8 stop over
temple ~: 6 adytum
to move: 4 give 5 space, width 6 leeway 8 latitude
underground ~: 8 basement
unfinished ~: 4 loft 6 garret
visitor ~: 6 parlor 7 gallery 10 living room
wiggle ~: 4 play 5 space 7 freedom 8 latitude
with ~ to spare: 4 vast, wide 5 ample, broad 7 sizable 8 spacious 9 capacious, expansive 10 voluminous
work the ~: 3 mix 6 hobnob, mingle 9 circulate 10 fraternize
room __: 5 clerk 6 father, mother 7 divider, service
__ room: 3 box, day, gun, mud, rec, sea, war 4 back, chat, city, game, jury, mail, men's, pump, shed, tack, twin 5 board, chart, clean, elbow, front, guest, ready, squad, steam 6 boiler, common, dining, double, family, living, locker, lumber, powder, public, romper, rumpus, sample, throne, trophy, wiggle 7 banquet, control, cutting, drawing, fitting, Florida, keeping, orderly, reading, running, sitting, utility, waiting
Room __: 5 to Let 7 Service
Room __ One More: 3 for
Room __ Top: 5 at the
Room __ View, A: 5 With a
__ Room: 4 East, In My 5 Panic, White 6 Jacob's
room and __: 5 board
Room at the Top (1959 film)
cast: Laurence Harvey, Simone Signoret
Room at the Top singer: Adam Ant
__-room comedy: 7 drawing
roomer: 5 guest, liver 6 lessee, lodger, tenant 10 inhabitant, vacationer
Room for One More (1952 film)
cast: Betsy Drake, Cary Grant, Lurene Tuttle
director: Norman Taurog
roominess: 5 space, width 7 breadth 9 amplitude
rooming house: 3 inn 5 hotel 7 lodging
British: 3 kip
roommate: 3 pal 4 mate 5 buddy, crony 6 cohort, escort, fellow, friend 7 compeer, consort 8 intimate, sidekick 9 associate, companion, confidant
Room of One's Own, A author: Virginia Woolf
rooms: 5 lodge, suite 6 billet 7 housing, lodging 8 quarters
Room Service (1938 film)
cast: Lucille Ball, Chico Marx, Groucho Marx, Harpo Marx, Ann Miller

studio: 3 RKO
room-service prop: 4 cart, tray
Rooms on Fire (1989 song) artist: Stevie Nicks
Room 222 (ABC sitcom)
cast: Michael Constantine (Seymour Kaufman)
Lloyd Haynes (Pete Dixon)
Denise Nicholas (Liz McIntyre)
Karen Valentine (Alice Johnson)
__ Room, The: 3 Red, War 5 Black, Small 6 Boiler, Yellow 7 L-Shaped
Room, The author: Harold Pinter
room to swing __: 4 a cat
Room With a View, A: 4 film 5 novel
author: E.M. Forster
cast: Helena Bonham Carter, Denholm Elliott, Maggie Smith
character: 4 Lucy, Vyse 5 Cecil
director: James Ivory
setting: 5 Italy 8 Florence
view: 4 Arno
roomy: 3 big 4 wide 5 ample, broad, large, loose 7 sizable 8 far-flung, generous, sizeable, spacious, sweeping 9 capacious, cavernous, expansive, extensive, spread out, uncrowded 10 commodious, voluminous, widespread
Roone: 7 Arledge
Rooney: 3 Art 4 Andy 5 Annie 6 Mickey
Rooney, Mickey: 5 actor
film: The Black Stallion (1979)
The Bold and the Brave (1956)
Boys Town (1938)
A Family Affair (1937)
The Fireball (1950)
Girl Crazy (1943)
Huckleberry Finn (1939)
The Human Comedy (1943)
It's a Mad Mad Mad Mad World (1963)
Killer McCoy (1947)
Life Begins for Andy Hardy (1941)
Love Finds Andy Hardy (1938)
National Velvet (1944)
Pulp (1972)
Requiem for a Heavyweight (1962)
The Secret Invasion (1964)
Young Tom Edison (1940)
spouse: Ava Gardner
Roosevelt: 5 Grier, river 7 Eleanor 8 Theodore
River locale: 6 Brazil
Roosevelt __: 3 Dam 6 Island
Roosevelt, Eleanor
work: My Days
On My Own
This I Remember
This Is My Story
Roosevelt, Franklin Delano: 9 president
alma mater: 6 Groton 7 Harvard
cabinet member: 4 Hull, Knox 5 Ickes, Roper 6 Edison, Farley 7 Hopkins, Perkins, Stimson, Wallace
child: 4 Anna, John 5 James 7 Elliott
film portrayer: 7 Bellamy 8 Herrmann
home: 7 New York 8 Hyde Park
mother: 4 Sara
opponent: 5 Dewey 6 Hoover, Landon 7 Willkie
predecessor: 6 Hoover
successor: 6 Truman
V.P.: 6 Garner, Truman 7 Wallace
wife: 7 Eleanor
__ Roosevelt Longworth: 5 Alice
Roosevelt, Theodore: 8 Nobelist 9 president
alma mater: 7 Harvard
child: 5 Alice, Ethel 6 Archie, Kermit 7 Quentin
home: 7 New York
opponent: 4 Debs 6 Parker
predecessor: 8 McKinley
successor: 4 Taft
V.P.: 9 Fairbanks
wife: 5 Alice, Edith
roost: 3 sit 4 home, live, nest, rest, seat, stay 5 dwell, house, light, lodge, perch, squat 6 alight, remain, settle 7 domicil, habitat, housing, shelter, sojourn 8 domicile, henhouse, quarters 9 birdhouse
rule the ~: 4 boss, head, lead 5 order 6 direct, manage 7 command, control 8 dominate
sitter: 3 hen
rooster: 4 cock, fowl, male 6 bantam 7 chicken, poultry
mate: 3 hen
name meaning ~: 4 Hahn
pride: 4 comb 5 crest
replacement: 5 alarm 10 alarm clock
sound: 4 crow
time: 4 dawn 5 sunup
walk like a ~: 5 strut
Rooster Cogburn (1975 film)
cast: Katharine Hepburn, Strother Martin, John Wayne, Anthony Zerbe
director: Stuart Millar
root: 3 dig, fix, nub, pry 4 base, beer, beet, core, font, germ, grub, hunt, knub, nose, poke, seek, soul, stem, stub, well 5 amole, basis, cause, delve, embed, imbed, lodge, orris, radix, tuber 6 bottom, burrow, carrot, center, ferret, forage, ground, insert, jicama, marrow, motive, origin, radish, reason, search, source, spring, turnip 7 essence, grounds, implant, keynote, parsnip, radicle, rhizome, rummage, unearth 9 beginning, causation, etymology, substance, vegetable 10 derivation, foundation, mainspring, provenance, underlying
chopper: 3 adz 4 adze
combining form: 4 rhiz- 5 -rhiza, rhizo- 6 -rrhiza
edible ~: 3 oca, oka, yam 4 beet, eddo, taro 5 tuber 6 carrot, jicama
ender: 3 age 4 hold, worm 5 stalk, stock
for: 5 cheer, favor 7 applaud 8 advocate 9 encourage
hair: 6 fibril
malady: 3 rot
out: 5 purge 6 remove, uproot 7 abolish, unearth 9 eradicate, extirpate 10 do away with
starter: 3 red, tap 4 alum, beet, musk, pink, poke, rose 5 arrow, birth, blood, bread, briar, colic, coral, orris, putty, snake 6 balsam, bitter, canker, dragon, ginger, orange 7 crinkle
take ~: 6 settle, sprout 7 develop 8 spring up 9 germinate
word: 6 etymon
root __: 3 rot 4 beer, crop, hair, knot, test 5 field, graft 6 cellar, doctor, system 7 climber
__ root: 4 cube, pink, prop, take 5 brace, motor, nerve 6 bitter, celery, dorsal, fungus, square 7 bowman's, Culver's, primary, sensory, ventral
Root: 5 Elihu
root beer: 4 soda 5 drink 8 beverage 9 soft drink
alternative: 4 cola
brand: 4 Dad's 5 Barqs
plus ice cream: 5 float
rooted: 3 set 4 firm 5 fixed, solid 6 frozen, inborn, inbred, stable, static 7 riveted, settled 8 constant, definite, embedded, immobile, ironclad 9 immovable, ingrained, permanent 10 deep-seated, inveterate, motionless, stationary, unchanging
__-rooted: 4 deep
Root, Elihu: 8 diplomat, Nobelist
rooter: 3 fan, pig 4 buff 7 admirer, booster, devotee, fancier 8 follower, partisan 9 supporter 10 aficionado, enthusiast
cry: 3 rah, yay
__-Rooter: 4 Roto
rooters: 6 claque
rootless: 5 shaky 6 roving 7 nomadic, roaming 8 drifting, rambling, vagabond 9 itinerant, wandering, wayfaring 10 journeying
plant: 4 alga
rootlessness: 5 anomy 6 anomie
roots: 6 origin 7 descent, genesis, lineage 8 ancestry, heritage, homeland, pedigree 9 ancestors, bloodline, forebears, genealogy 10 extraction, family tree, fatherland, motherland, native land, native soil
put down ~: 4 stay 6 linger, remain, settle 8 colonize
__ roots: 5 grass
Roots (ABC miniseries): 4 saga
cast: John Amos (Kunta Kinte)
LeVar Burton (Kunta Kinte)
Leslie Uggams (Kizzy)
Ben Vereen (Chicken George)
Emmy winner: 5 Asner
historian: 5 griot
Roots author: Alex Haley
rope: 3 tie 4 bind, bond, cord, lace, line, vang 5 cable, lasso, leash, twine 6 hawser, lariat, pull in, ratlin, secure, strand, string, tether 7 cordage, lanyard, ratline 8 ligature
at the end of one's ~: 7 frantic, panicky 8 frenzied, strained, wretched 9 desperate, miserable
climber: 5 faker, fakir, faqir 6 faquir
cowboy ~: 5 lasso, reata, riata 6 lariat
ender: 4 walk
fasten a ~: 3 tie 4 bind, knot 5 belay
feature: 4 knot 5 bight, noose
horse guiding ~: 5 longe
in: 4 coax, dupe, fool, gull, hoax, hook, lure, trap 5 cheat, decoy, lasso, shill 6 delude, entice, entrap, fleece 7 attract, beguile, ensnare, mislead 8 inveigle 9 captivate, disinform, victimize
injury: 4 burn
jump ~: 3 toy 4 game, skip
knot: 4 loop 5 noose, snare
nautical ~: 3 tye 4 vang 6 cablet, earing, gilguy, hawser 7 bobstay, bowline, outhaul, ratline 8 buntline, gantline, girtline
off: 5 fence 6 divide 7 reserve 8 set apart 9 partition
open a ~: 5 unrig, untie 6 loosen
separate strands of ~: 5 feaze, feeze, unlay
source: 4 bast, coir, hemp, jute, riem 5 abaca, istle, ixtle, oakum, sisal 6 baobab
starter: 3 man 4 bolt, foot 5 tight
target: 4 calf, dogy 5 dogey, steer 6 doggie
twist: 4 kink
rope __: 3 off, tow 4 yarn 6 bridge, socket, stitch
rope-__: 5 a-dope
__ rope: 4 bolt, bull, grab, jack, jump, skip, wire 5 guide, leech, trail 6 Manila, thread 7 armored
Rope (1948 film)
cast: John Dall, Farley Granger, James Stewart
director: Alfred Hitchcock
Rope-a-dope boxer: 3 Ali
Rope of Sand (1949 film)
cast: Corinne Calvet, Paul Henreid, Burt Lancaster
Roper: 4 Elmo
report: 4 poll
ropes
learn the ~: 5 adapt, study, train 6 adjust, bone up, master 9 acclimate
on the ~: 5 at bay, spent, tired 6 in a fix, in a jam 7 in a mess, run-down, trapped, up a tree, worn out 9 enervated, exhausted 10 in hot water
show the ~: 5 coach, teach, train, tutor 6 school 7 educate 8 instruct
__ ropes: 5 on the
ropy: 4 oozy 5 thick, tough 6 viscid 7 fibrous, stringy, viscose, viscous 8 cordlike 9 glutinous
roque: 4 game
need: 6 mallet
Roquefort: 6 cheese
hue: 4 bleu, blue
roquelaure: 5 cloak
Rorem: 3 Ned
rorqual: 3 sei 5 whale 6 animal, mammal 8 cetacean
relative: 3 orc, sei 5 whale 6 beluga, narwal 7 cowfish, dolphin, finback, grampus, narwhal 8 narwhale, porpoise
Rorschach: 4 test
image: 4 blot 7 ink blot
Rory: 7 Calhoun
Rosa: 5 Parks, Raisa 6 Chacel 7 Bonheur 8 Ponselle
see also Spanish
__ Rosa: 5 Monte, Santa
Rosalie (1937 film)
cast: Nelson Eddy, Eleanor Powell
composer: 6 Porter
director: W.S. Van Dyke
Rosalind: 4 moon 7 Russell
planet: 6 Uranus
role for ~: 4 Mame
Rosalyn: 5 Yalow
Rosalynn: 6 Carter
child: 3 Amy 4 Chip
to Jimmy: 4 wife
Rosamund composer: 4 Arne
Rosanna: 8 Arquette
Rosanna (1982 song) artist: Toto
Rosanne: 4 Cash
Rosa Parks Day month: 3 Dec. 8 December
Rosario: 4 city, port, town 5 Ferré
locale: 9 Argentina
Rosarito: 4 city, town
locale: 6 Mexico
rosary: 3 ave 5 beads 6 prayer
part: 3 ave 4 bead, gaud
Rosary, The composer: 5 Nevin
rosa, sub: 7 furtive, illegal 8 hush-hush, on the sly, secretly 9 entre nous, furtively, privately
roscoe: 3 gat, gun, rod 5 piece 6 heater, pistol 7 firearm
Roscoe: 4 Ates 5 Karns 8 Conkling
Roscoe Lee __: 6 Browne
rose: 3 red 4 pink 5 color, got up, plant, sat up, shrub 6 damask, flower, redden, went up 7 climbed, crimson, rambler, stood up 9 table wine, vermilion 10 floribunda, multiflora, sweetbrier
chafer: 3 bug 6 insect
combining form: 4 rhod- 5 rhodo-
ender: 3 bay, bud, hip 4 bush, fish, root, wood
enjoy a ~: 5 smell
extract: 4 atar, otto 5 athar, attar,

ottar
family plant: **4** sloe **5** avens **6** kerria, spirea **7** bramble, jetbead, spiraea **8** hardhack, ninebark, photinia **9** firethorn, raspberry
family tree: **4** pear, plum **5** apple, peach **6** almond, cherry, medlar, quince **7** apricot **8** hawthorn, oiticica, photinia **10** blackthorn
fruit: **3** hip
holder: **4** stem
locale: **3** bed
of Sharon: **6** althea
oil: **5** nerol **6** neroli
pest: **5** aphid
protection: **5** thorn
relative: **4** ruby, rust, wine **5** brick, coral, grape, poppy, rusty, sandy **6** burnet, cerise, cherry, claret, garnet, maroon **7** carmine, crimson, fuchsia, magenta, pimento, scarlet, sultana, vermeil **8** amaranth, cardinal, dubonnet, geranium, rubicund **9** carnation, cranberry, vermilion **10** strawberry
starter: **4** prim, rock
rose __: **3** box, hip, oil **4** comb, hips, moss, pink, slug **5** aphid, apple, noble, water **6** acacia, beetle, chafer, madder, mallow, quartz, weevil, window **7** campion, d'Anvers, pogonia
rose-__ glasses: **7** colored
__ rose: **3** dog, old, red, tea **4** moss, musk, wild, wind, wood **5** China, swamp, white **6** Bengal, burnet, canker, damask, French, golden, mallow, rugosa, Scotch, winter **7** banksia, bourbon, cabbage, compass, guelder, pasture, prairie
rosé: **4** pink, wine **5** tavel
alternative: **6** claret
Rose: **3** Axl **4** Pete **5** Billy, David, Marie, Tokyo **7** Bernard, Charlie, Kennedy **8** Macaulay
like Abie's ~: **5** Irish
Rose __: **4** Bowl **5** Marie, Royce **6** Garden, Madder, of Lima
Rose __ rose...: **3** is a
__ Rose: **4** Jack, Lida **5** Only a, Tokyo **7** Ramblin'
Roseanne: **4** Barr
like ~ 's speech: **5** nasal
Roseanne (ABC sitcom)
cast: Sara Gilbert (Darlene Conner)
John Goodman (Dan Conner)
Laurie Metcalf (Jackie Harris)
Roseanne (Roseanne Conner)
Roseanne spouse: Tom Arnold
roseate: **4** pink **6** bright **9** promising **10** optimistic
Roseau: **4** city, town **7** capital
locale: **8** Dominica
__ Rose Benét: **7** William
Rose, Billy spouse: Fanny Brice
Rose Bowl
kickoff: **6** parade
org.: **4** NCAA
Rosebud: **4** sled
owner: **4** Kane
...rosebuds while __: **5** ye may
Roseburg: **4** city, town
locale: **6** Oregon
rose-colored: **7** hopeful **8** sanguine **10** optimistic
glasses: **4** hope **8** idealism, optimism **10** positivism
Rose, David: **8** composer **9** conductor
song: The Stripper (1962)
spouse: Judy Garland, Martha Raye
Rose Garden (1970 song) artist: Lynn Anderson
Rose is a rose... writer: **5** Stein
Roseland (1977 film)
cast: Geraldine Chaplin, Lou Jacobi, Teresa Wright
director: James Ivory
__ Rose Lee: **5** Gypsy
Roselle: **4** city, town
locale: **8** Illinois **9** New Jersey
Rose Madder author: Stephen King
Rose Marie (1936 film)
cast: Nelson Eddy, Jeanette MacDonald, Reginald Owen
director: W.S. Van Dyke
org.: **4** RCMP
Rose Marie (1954 film)
cast: Ann Blyth, Howard Keel, Bert Lahr, Fernando Lamas, Marjorie Main
director: Mervyn LeRoy
rosemary: **4** herb **5** shrub, spice
family: **4** mint
relative: **4** sage **8** lavender
Rosemary: **4** Lane, Rice **6** Casals, De Camp **7** Clooney
portrayer: **3** Mia
Rosemary's Baby: **4** film **5** novel
author: Ira Levin
cast: John Cassavetes, Mia Farrow, Ruth Gordon
director: Roman Polanski
Rosemead: **4** city, town
locale: **10** California
Rosemont: **4** city, town
locale: **10** California
Rosen: **2** Al
Rosenberg: **4** Alan, city, town **6** Stuart
locale: **5** Texas
Rosenberg, Stuart: **8** director
film: Brubaker (1980)
Cool Hand Luke (1967)
Murder, Inc. (1960)
Pocket Money (1972)
The Pope of Greenwich Village (1984)
Voyage of the Damned (1976)
WUSA (1970)
Rosenbloom: **5** Maxie
Rosencrantz and Guildenstern Are Dead author: Tom Stoppard
Rosencrantz, friend of: **6** Hamlet
__ Rosenkavalier: **3** Der
Rosenthal: **5** china **8** Emmanuel
competitor: **5** Lenox **6** Mikasa
Rosenthal, Emmanuel: **9** conductor
rose of __: **5** China **6** Heaven, Sharon **7** Jericho
Rose of __: **4** Lima **6** Tralee
__ Rose of Cairo, The: **6** Purple
Rose of Lima: **5** saint
__ Rose of Texas, The: **6** Yellow
Rose, Pete
forte: **4** hits **7** singles
sport: **8** baseball
roses
bed of ~: **4** ease **6** luxury **7** comfort **8** good life, opulence
coming up ~: **5** lucky
gather ~: **3** cut **4** clip, snip
run for the ~: **5** Derby
__ roses: **5** bed of
Roses __ red...: **3** are
__ Roses: **5** Bed of, Guns N', Paper
Roses Are Red (1962 song) artist: Bobby Vinton
__ Roses for a Blue Lady: **3** Red
__ Rose's Jumbo: **5** Billy
Rose Tattoo, The: **4** film, play
author: Tennessee Williams
cast: Burt Lancaster, Anna Magnani
director: Daniel Mann
Rose, The (1979 film)
cast: Alan Bates, Frederic Forrest, Bette Midler, Harry Dean Stanton
director: Mark Rydell
__ Rose, The: **4** Sick **5** Black **7** Charnel
Rose, The (1980 song) artist: Bette Midler
Rosetta locale: **4** Nile **5** Egypt
Rosetta Stone
language: **5** Greek
material: **6** basalt
Roseville: **4** city, town
locale: **8** Michigan **9** Minnesota **10** California
Rosewall, Ken: **7** netster **9** tennis pro
milieu: **5** court
rosewood: **4** tree
Rosey: **5** Grier
Rosh __: **6** Hodesh **7** Chodesh, Hashana, Hashono
roshi: **6** cleric
Rosie: **5** Daley, Perez **6** Casals **8** O'Donnell
fastener: **5** rivet
former rival: **5** Oprah
Rosie! (1967 film)
cast: Brian Aherne, Sandra Dee, Rosalind Russell
__ Rosie O' Grady: **5** Sweet
rosin: **9** colophony
ender: **4** weed
source: **4** pine
rosin __: **3** oil
Rosinante: **5** horse **6** equine
rosiness: **5** blush, flush
Rosmersholm author: Henrik Ibsen
Ross: **3** sea, Ted **4** city, John, town **5** Betsy, Diana, James, Lanny, Perot **6** Hunter, Marion, Martin, Nellie, Ronald **7** Herbert, McElwee **9** Katharine, Macdonald, McWhirter
locale: **10** Antarctica, New Zealand
Ross __: **3** Sea **6** Island
Ross __ Shelf: **3** Ice
Rossano: **6** Brazzi
Ross, Betsy: **10** seamstress
emulate ~: **3** sew
need: **6** needle, thread
product: **4** flag
Ross, Diana
born: Diane Earle
lead singer of: The Supremes
song: Ain't No Mountain High Enough (1970)
All of You (1984)
Endless Love (1981)
I'm Coming Out (1980)
It's My Turn (1980)
Love Hangover (1976)
Mirror, Mirror (1982)
Missing You (1985)
Muscles (1982)
Remember Me (1971)
Swept Away (1984)
Theme from Mahogany (1975)
Touch Me in the Morning (1973)
Upside Down (1980)
Why Do Fools Fall in Love (1981)
You're a Special Part of Me (1973)
Rossellini: **7** Roberto **8** Isabella
Rossellini, Isabella: **7** actress
film: Blue Velvet (1986)
Cousins (1989)
Death Becomes Her (1992)
Fearless (1993)
Immortal Beloved (1994)
mother: Ingrid Bergman
Rossellini, Roberto spouse: Ingrid Bergman
Rossen, Robert: **8** director
film: Alexander the Great (1956)
All the King's Men (1949)
Body and Soul (1947)
The Brave Bulls (1951)
The Hustler (1961)
Rossetti: **5** Dante **9** Christina
Rossetti, Christina: **4** poet **7** British
Rossetti, Dante Gabriel: **4** poet **7** British
work: The Blessed Damozel
The House of Life
Rosshalde author: **5** Hesse
Ross, Herbert: **8** director
film: Boys on the Side (1995)
California Suite (1978)
Footloose (1984)
The Goodbye Girl (1977)
The Last of Sheila (1973)
Max Dugan Returns (1983)
My Blue Heaven (1990)
The Owl and the Pussycat (1970)
Pennies From Heaven (1981)
Play It Again, Sam (1972)
The Secret of My Success (1987)
The Seven-Per-Cent Solution (1976)
Steel Magnolias (1989)
The Sunshine Boys (1975)
The Turning Point (1977)
Rossini, Gioacchino: **7** Italian **8** composer
genre: **5** opera
work: The Barber of Seville
Comte Ory
Mosè
Tancredi
William Tell
Ross Island volcano: **6** Erebus
Rossiya
see Russian
Ross, James: **7** British **8** explorer
Ross, John: **8** explorer, Scottish
Ross, Katharine: **7** actress
film: The Betsy (1978)
Butch Cassidy and the Sundance Kid (1969)
The Final Countdown (1980)
The Graduate (1967)
The Stepford Wives (1975)
Tell Them Willie Boy Is Here (1969)
spouse: Sam Elliott
Rossner: **6** Judith
Ross, Ronald: **8** Nobelist
Ross Sea bay: **6** Whales
__ Ross Trophy: **3** Art
Rostand, Edmond: **6** French **10** playwright
work: Cyrano de Bergerac
Rosten, Leo: **6** writer **8** humorist
specialty: **7** Yiddish
roster: **4** bill, list, roll, rota **5** index **6** agenda, lineup, muster, record **7** catalog, listing, program **8** register, schedule **9** catalogue, directory, inventory
listing: **4** name **6** member **7** surname
on the ~: **6** active
Rostock: **4** city, port, town
locale: **7** Germany
Rostov: **4** city, port, town
locale: **6** Russia
Rostov-__: **5** on-Don
Rostropovich, Mstislav: **7** cellist, Russian
rostrum: **4** dais **5** stage **6** podium, pulpit **7** lectern **8** platform
Roswell: **4** city, town
locale: **7** Georgia **9** New Mexico
rosy: **3** red **4** pink **5** coral, fresh, palmy, ruddy **6** bright, upbeat **7** flushed, glowing, hopeful **8** blooming, blushing, cheerful, pleasing, red-faced, rubicund, sanguine **9** favorable, hunky-dory, promising **10** auspicious, optimistic
feature: **5** cheek
hardly ~: **3** wan **4** ashy, pale **5** ashen
make ~: **5** flush **6** redden
not ~: **4** dire, dour, glum, grim **5** bleak, harsh **6** gloomy, morose, somber, woeful **7** ominous **8** hopeless **9** cheerless, depressed, frightful
opposite of ~: **4** grim **5** bleak **6** dismal, gloomy **8** hopeless
rosy-cheeked: **3** fit **4** hale, well **5** hardy,

ruddy, sound **6** robust **7** healthy **8** vigorous **9** in the pink
rosy-fingered goddess: **6** Aurora
rot: **3** eat, gas **4** blah, bosh, bull, bunk, guff, jazz, jive, mold, pooh, rust, sink, talk, tosh, turn **5** bilge, decay, fudge, go bad, hokum, hooey, prate, spoil, stuff, taint, trash, tripe **6** blight, bunkum, bushwa, canker, drivel, fester, footle, gabble, gammon, gibber, havers, hot air, humbug, jabber, jargon, kibosh, molder, perish, piffle, wither **7** baloney, blarney, blather, blether, boloney, bushwah, compost, corrode, corrupt, crumble, decline, degrade, eyewash, flannel, flubdub, fustian, garbage, go stale, hogwash, inanity, malarky, rubbish, twaddle **8** buncombe, claptrap, falderal, falderol, flimflam, flummery, folderal, folderol, go to seed, languish, malarkey, nonsense, slipslop, stagnate, trumpery **9** banana oil, break down, corrosion, decompose, fall apart, gibberish, goofiness, kidstakes, lie fallow, moonshine, overripen, poppycock, rigmarole, silliness **10** applesauce, balderdash, bilge water, codswallop, degenerate, double-talk, empty words, flapdoodle, galimatias, go to pieces, Jabberwock, mumbo jumbo, rigamarole, taradiddle
  ender: **3** gut
  starter: **5** tommy
__ rot: **3** dry, red **4** ring, ripe, root, soft, soil, stem **5** black, brown, crown, white **6** bitter, collar **7** oak-root, stem-end
rota: **6** roster **8** register
Rotanev: **4** star
Rota, Nino: **7** Italian **8** composer
rotary: **7** turning **8** spinning, whirling **9** revolving
  motion: **5** twirl, twist
  tool: **5** auger, drill
rotary __: **3** hoe **4** dial, plow, pump, wing **5** press, valve **6** beater, engine, tiller **7** shutter
Rotary __: **4** Club
rotate: **4** eddy, jink, reel, roll, spin, turn **5** pivot, spell, swing, twirl, twist, wheel, whirl **6** circle, follow, gyrate, switch, swivel **7** relieve, revolve, succeed **8** exchange, go around, turn over **9** alternate, change off, pirouette, take turns
  to an astronaut: **3** yaw
rotating: **6** awhirl
  piece: **3** cam
  point: **5** hinge, pivot **7** fulcrum
rotation: **4** spin, turn **5** orbit **8** gyration **10** revolution
  line: **4** axis
__ rotation: **4** crop **7** optical
rotational: **5** axial
  device: **4** pawl
  speed: **3** rps
rotator __: **4** cuff
Rotblat, Joseph: **8** Nobelist
ROTC relative: **3** OCS, OTC, OTS
rote: **5** habit **6** groove, ritual **7** routine **10** repetition
  by ~: **10** from memory
Rote, Kyle: **2** QB
  sport: **8** football
rotelle: **5** pasta **7** noodles
rotgut: **5** booze **6** whisky **7** alcohol, whiskey **10** intoxicant
Roth: **3** Tim **4** Mark **6** Philip **7** Lillian, William
Roth __: **3** IRA
Roth, David Lee
  lead singer of: Van Halen
  song: California Girls (1985)
    Just Like Paradise (1988)
Rotherham: **4** city, town
  locale: **7** England **9** Yorkshire
Rothko, Mark: **6** artist **7** painter
Roth, Mark: **6** bowler
  milieu: **5** alley
  org.: **3** PBA
Roth, Philip: **6** author, writer
  spouse: Claire Bloom
  work: The Anatomy Lesson
    The Ghost Writer
    Goodbye, Columbus
    Letting Go
    My Life as a Man
    Portnoy's Complaint
    When She Was Good
    Zuckerman Bound
    Zuckerman Unbound
Rothstein: **6** Arnold
Roth, Tim: **5** actor
  film: Little Odessa (1994)
    Lucky Numbers (2000)
    Planet of the Apes (2001)
    Reservoir Dogs (1992)
    Vincent & Theo (1990)
rotini: **5** pasta **8** macaroni
rotisserie: **4** oven **5** grill **8** barbecue
Rotisserie __: **8** Baseball
roto-__: **6** tiller
Roto-__: **6** Rooter
rotor
  ender: **5** craft
  noise: **4** whir **5** whirr
rotor __: **5** blade, cloud, plane
Roto-Rooter alternative: **5** Drano
rotte: **5** crwth
rotten: **3** bad, bum, off **4** foul, grim, mean, poor, punk, rank, sick, sour, vile **5** amiss, awful, dirty, fetid, gross, lousy, moldy, nasty, punky, reeky, sorry, woful, wrong **6** crumby, crummy, dismal, filthy, foetid, horrid, odious, putrid, rancid, scurvy, shabby, smelly, spoilt, strong, wicked, woeful **7** accurst, baleful, baneful, beastly, bruised, corrupt, crooked, decayed, doleful, ghastly, gone bad, noisome, noxious, odorous, spoiled, tainted, unclean, vicious **8** accursed, depraved, dreadful, God-awful, grievous, horrible, inedible, infamous, inferior, overripe, polluted, shameful, stinking, terrible, two-faced, wretched **9** abhorrent, appalling, atrocious, crumbling, dastardly, deceitful, defective, dishonest, execrable, faithless, frightful, insidious, loathsome, mercenary, miserable, moldering, nefarious, offensive, putrefied, revolting, unhealthy, worm-eaten **10** abominable, deplorable, despicable, detestable, disastrous, disgusting, horrendous, lamentable, malodorous, scurrilous, unpleasant, villainous
  be ~: **4** reek **5** smell, stink
  bunch: **6** bad lot
  combining form: **4** sapr- **5** sapro-
  feeling ~: **3** ill
  kid: **3** imp **4** brat, punk **5** demon, rowdy, scamp, tough **6** rascal **7** hellion, hoodlum, ruffian **8** hooligan
  luck: **6** mishap **7** setback **8** bad break, calamity **9** adversity, mischance
  spoil ~: **4** baby **6** pamper
rotten __ core: **5** to the
Rotten: **6** Johnny
__ Rotten Scoundrels: **5** Dirty
rotter: **3** cad **4** heel, roué **5** rogue **6** bad egg, bad guy **8** picaroon **9** scoundrel **10** blackguard
Rotterdam: **3** spt. **4** city, port, town **7** seaport
  locale: **7** Holland, New York
  river: **4** Maas **5** Meuse
  see also Netherlands
Rottweiler: **3** dog **5** canid **6** canine
rotund: **5** beefy, fubsy, obese, plump, pudgy, pursy, round, stout **6** chubby, chunky, fleshy, portly, pyknic, stocky, zaftig, zoftig **7** adipose, paunchy **8** globular, roly-poly **9** corpulent, filled-out **10** abdominous, overweight, well-padded
Roubaix: **4** city, town
  locale: **6** France
Rouben: **9** Mamoulian
roué: **3** cad **4** rake, wolf **5** Romeo **6** masher, rotter **7** bounder, Don Juan, playboy, swinger **8** Casanova, lothario, lover boy, sybarite **9** ladies' man, libertine **10** profligate, sensualist, voluptuary
Rouen: **4** city, duck, fowl, town
  locale: **6** France
  relative: **4** smew, teal **5** eider, Pekin, scaup **6** Cayuga, scoter **7** gadwall, mallard, pintail, pochard, redhead, sea duck, widgeon **8** garganey, gray duck, mandarin, musk duck, oldsquaw, shoveler, surf duck, wood duck **9** black duck, broadbill, goldeneye, goosander, greenhead, merganser, ruddy duck, sprigtail **10** bufflehead, canvasback, surf scoter, tufted duck
  river: **5** Seine
  town near ~: **6** Dieppe
Rouen Cathedral artist: **5** Monet
rouge: **3** bet, red **5** blush, paint **6** French, makeup, redden **7** blusher **8** cosmetic **9** beauty aid
  apply ~: **6** redden
__ rouge: **3** vin **6** bonnet **7** mordant
__ Rouge: **5** Baton, Khmer **6** Moulin
rouge et noir: **4** game **8** card game
rough: **3** raw **4** curt, hard, mean, rude, ugly, wild **5** brash, brusk, bumpy, crass, crude, cruel, gruff, hairy, harsh, heavy, husky, jaggy, nasty, nubby, raspy, rocky, rowdy, rutty, scaly, seamy, short, stern, stony, surly, tight, tough, uncut, vague, wooly **6** abrupt, biting, bitter, broken, brutal, choppy, coarse, craggy, crusty, fierce, gauche, hackly, hoarse, hubbly, jagged, jouncy, knobby, knotty, ragged, raging, ridged, roiled, rugged, rustic, rutted, savage, severe, shaggy, smutty, sticky, stoney, stormy, thorny, trying, tufted, uneven, unmeet, uphill, vulgar, woolly **7** arduous, austere, bearish, bristly, brusque, brutish, chapped, cragged, crinkly, crudely, drastic, extreme, gnarled, grating, grouchy, hard-won, harshly, inexact, jarring, loutish, naughty, onerous, raucous, ruffled, scraggy, scruffy, sketchy, Spartan, stubbly, uncivil, uncouth, unlevel, vicious, violent **8** abrasive, churlish, grueling, homemade, impolite, impudent, leathery, no picnic, scabrous, scratchy, strident, tactless, toilsome, ungently, unshaven **9** demanding, difficult, draconian, estimated, ferocious, graceless, imperfect, imprecise, inclement, inelegant, irregular, laborious, makeshift, primitive, strenuous, stringent, tasteless, turbulent, uncourtly, unfeeling, ungroomed, unrefined, untrained, untutored, unwrought, violently **10** amateurish, corrugated, disordered, disorderly, formidable, indecorous, indelicate, laryngitic, nonuniform, oppressive, provincial, tumultuous, unbecoming, uncultured, unfinished, ungracious, unmannerly, unpleasant, unpolished, unprepared
  combining form: **6** trachy-
  draft: **6** sketch **7** outline
  ender: **3** age, dry **4** back, cast, neck, shod **5** dried, house, rider **6** caster **7** casting
  handling: **4** harm **5** abuse **6** misuse
  it: **4** camp **7** camp out **10** pitch a tent
  not ~: **4** calm, easy, kind, mild, pure **5** balmy, civil, exact, suave **6** benign, classy, docile, genial, gentle, kindly, mellow, placid, serene, smooth, tender, urbane **7** amiable, clement, courtly, genteel, lenient, pacific, precise, refined, subdued **8** cultured, gracious, laid back, mannerly, merciful, moderate, pleasant, polished, purified **9** civilized, courteous, dignified, easygoing, leisurely, processed, temperate **10** cultivated
  out: **4** plan **5** draft **6** sketch **7** outline, suggest **8** block out **9** adumbrate
  partner: **5** ready **6** tumble
  sketch: **4** plan **5** draft **7** croquis, outline
  time: **5** slump **6** downer **8** dry spell, tailspin
  up: **3** hit **4** bash, hurt, mall, maul **5** abuse **6** batter, beat up **8** maltreat, mistreat **9** manhandle **10** slap around
rough __: **3** cut **4** fish **5** lemon, stuff
rough-__: **3** dry, hew **4** hewn, sawn **6** spoken, voiced
Rough __: **6** Riders
roughage: **4** bran **5** fiber
rough-and-__: **5** ready **6** tumble
Rough Boy artist: **5** ZZ Top
rough-cut: **4** hewn
roughen: **4** chap **5** crack **6** abrade, redden **7** callous, coarsen, wrinkle **9** corrugate
rough-hew: **5** shape
rough-hewn: **3** raw **4** rude **5** wooly **6** rugged, woolly **7** lowbred **10** unfinished
roughhouse: **4** play **5** abuse, brawl **8** mistreat **9** misbehave
Roughing It author: Mark Twain
Roughing It in the Bush author: Susanna Moodie
roughly: **4** hard, or so **5** about, circa **6** approx., around, nearly **8** severely **9** generally
Roughly Speaking (1945 film)
  cast: Jack Carson, Rosalind Russell
  director: Michael Curtiz
rough-mannered: **4** curt, rude **5** blunt, gruff, harsh, surly **6** coarse, crabby, crusty, grumpy **7** bearish, boorish, brusque, grating, grouchy, loutish, uncivil **8** churlish, impolite, inurbane, tactless **10** unfriendly, ungracious, unmannerly
roughneck: **4** bozo, goon, thug **5** rowdy, tough **7** ruffian
roughness: **4** chop, woof **7** texture **8** violence **10** coarseness
roughrider: **5** tamer
roughshod, ride: **5** bully **6** defeat **7** trample **9** overpower, trample on, tyrannize
rough-sounding: **6** hoarse
roughy: **4** fish
roulade: **4** meat **6** entrée
roulette: **4** game
  bet: **3** odd, red **4** even, noir
  need: **5** wheel
  opponent: **5** house
  play ~: **3** bet
round: **3** cut, lap, run **4** bout, full, oval, ring, turn **5** bowed, curvy, cycle, orbed, orbit, pivot, plump, pudgy,

route, salvo, semis, stage, steak, tubby, wheel, whirl, whole **6** arched, around, chubby, coiled, course, curled, curved, curvey, entire, finals, looped, nearly, refine, rotund, series, sphere **7** bulbous, circuit, concave, globule, gunshot, orotund **8** circular, disklike, division, globular, outburst, ringlike, roly-poly, schedule, sequence **9** discharge, egg-shaped, filled-out, globelike, spherical **10** abdominous, ball-shaped, curvaceous, disk-shaped, elliptical, pear-shaped, revolution, succession
ender: **4** bell, worm **5** about, house
not perfectly ~: **4** oval **5** ovoid **8** elliptic **10** elliptical
off: **3** cap, end, top **6** beef up, finish **7** augment, touch up **8** conclude, estimate, finalize **9** culminate
out: **3** cap, end **5** close, swell **6** fatten, fill in, finish, refine, top off **7** perfect **8** complete, conclude, finalize **9** culminate, terminate **10** complement, supplement
prefix: **4** peri- **6** circum-
rally ~: **4** back, help **5** boost, favor **6** assist, defend **7** bolster, endorse, promote, pull for, stand by, stick by **8** champion, side with **9** encourage, get behind **10** go to bat for, stand up for, stick up for
robin: **4** plea **6** series **7** tourney **8** petition **10** conference, tournament
starter: **4** bell
table: **5** forum **6** parley, powwow **9** symposium **10** conference
thing: **3** orb **4** ball **5** globe **6** circle, sphere
trip: **4** tour **5** jaunt **6** junket, travel **7** circuit, journey **9** excursion
up: **4** bead, cull, herd, raid **5** amass, drive, group, rally, snare **6** arrest, corral, gather, muster, rake in **7** capture, cluster, collect, convene, convoke, marshal, recruit, wrangle **8** assemble **10** accumulate, congregate
round __: **3** lot, off, out **4** arch, clam, file, hand, trip, turn **5** angle, dance, robin, steak, table **6** barrow, window **7** herring, kumquat
round-__: **5** faced
__ round: **3** top **4** come **5** bring **6** bottom **7** beehive, quarter
__-round: **3** all **4** year **5** out-of
roundabout: **5** wordy **6** outing **7** devious, evasive, oblique, winding **8** indirect, tortuous **10** circuitous, collateral
not ~: **5** blunt, clear, frank, plain **6** candid, direct, head-on **7** express, precise **8** explicit, straight **10** forthright, point-blank, to the point
way: **6** detour
Roundabout (1972 song) artist: Yes
Round and Round (song) artist: Perry Como, Ratt
__-Round-a-Rosie...: **5** Ring-a
roundball
see basketball
round-bellied: **5** obese, plump, pudgy, tubby **6** chubby, portly, rotund **7** paunchy **9** corpulent **10** abdominous
rounded: **4** full, oval **5** blunt, lobar, lobed, orbed **6** convex, obtuse **7** bulbous, shapely **8** globular **9** spherical
protuberance: **4** knop
__-rounded: **4** well
rounders: **5** sport
Rounders (1998 film)
cast: Matt Damon, Gretchen Mol, Edward Norton, John Turturro
director: John Dahl
round hill, name meaning: **6** Gordon
roundhouse: **5** punch **8** uppercut
roundish: **4** oval **5** ovate, ovoid **8** elliptic **9** egg-shaped **10** elliptical
Round Lake Beach: **4** city, town
locale: **8** Illinois
round of __: **4** beef, golf
Round Rock: **4** city, town
locale: **5** Texas
rounds: **4** ammo, beat, tour **5** route **6** patrol **10** ammunition
go a few ~: **3** box **4** spar **5** fight
make the ~: **3** mix **4** walk **5** watch **6** hobnob, mingle, patrol, police **7** inspect **9** socialize
Rounds for Squares composer: PDQ Bach
Round Table
adventure: **5** quest
member: **3** Kay, Tor **4** Bors, Eric **5** Driam, Ector, Floll, Lucan, Yvain, Ywain **6** Acolon, Brunor, Ewaine, Gareth, Gawain, Hector, knight, Lanval, Lavain, Manier, Morolt, Ryence, Sagrid, Torres **7** Belvour, Bersunt, Caradoc, Dinadam, Dodynas, Gaheris, Galahad, Grislet, Ladynas, Lionell, Marhaus, Mordred, Pelleas, Peredur, Tristan, Wigamor **8** Agravain, Beaumans, Bevidere, Galohalt, Lancelot, Meliadus, Palamede, Percival, Tristram, Turquine, Wigalois **9** Ballamore, Brandiles, Launcelot, Pellinore
quest: **5** Grail **9** Holy Grail
title: **3** sir
...Round the __ Oak Tree: **3** Ole
round-the-clock: **6** steady **7** nonstop **8** constant, unending **9** ceaseless, incessant **10** continuous, relentless
__ Round the Mountain: **5** Comin'
Roundtree, Richard: **5** actor
film: Q (1982)
Shaft (1971)
Shaft in Africa (1973)
Shaft's Big Score! (1972)
roundup: **4** herd **5** drive **6** muster **7** summary **9** gathering
group: **4** herd **6** beeves, cattle, strays
need: **4** prod **5** brand, lasso **6** herder
site: **5** range
Roundup: **3** car **4** auto **5** Edsel **10** automobile
Round up the __ suspects: **5** usual
roundworm: **4** nema
roup: **9** huskiness **10** hoarseness
roupy: **5** husky, raspy **6** hoarse **7** grating, rasping **8** gravelly, scratchy
Rourke, Mickey: **5** actor
film: Animal Factory (2000)
Barfly (1987)
Diner (1982)
The Pope of Greenwich Village (1984)
Rumble Fish (1983)
White Sands (1992)
rouse: **4** call, fire, goad, move, poke, prod, rile, spur, stir, wake, whet **5** awake, drive, get up, hop up, liven, pique, rally, start, tempt, waken **6** awaken, bestir, buck up, excite, fire up, foment, incite, kindle, recall, revive, stir up, thrill, vivify, wake up, work up **7** actuate, agitate, animate, disturb, enflame, enliven, ferment, fortify, freshen, hearten, inflame, inspire, provoke, quicken, startle, trigger **8** activate, embolden, engender, enkindle, enspirit, get going, heighten, imbolden, inspirit, interest, motivate, psyche up, summon up **9** electrify, encourage, enhearten, galvanize, impassion, influence, instigate, recollect, stimulate **10** exhilarate, intoxicate, invigorate
roused: **5** astir, awake **8** up in arms **9** wrought up
__-rouser: **6** rabble
Roush, Edd: **3** Red **10** outfielder
rousing: **5** brisk **6** lively **7** bracing, dashing **8** animated, spirited, vigorous **9** energetic, thrilling **10** fortifying, impressive
Rous, Peyton: **8** Nobelist
Rousseau and Revolution author: Will Durant
Rousseau, Jean Jacques: **6** French, writer **11** philosopher
work: Confessions
Emile
The Social Contract
roust: **4** stir **5** waken **6** awaken, stir up **7** disturb, drag out, kick out, provoke, shake up, yank out **8** drive out
ender: **5** about
(from): **5** drive, heave
roustabout: **4** hand **7** laborer
Roustabout (1964 film)
cast: Leif Erickson, Joan Freeman, Elvis Presley, Barbara Stanwyck
director: John Rich
rout: **3** zap **4** beat, best, bury, do in, drub, lick, stir, whip **5** cream, crush, eject, expel, score, skunk, swamp, total, trash, upset, whomp, worst **6** defeat, dispel, finish, legion, thrash, wallop **7** beating, conquer, debacle, failure, overrun, pasting, ransack, repulse, retreat, rummage, scatter, shutout, torpedo, trounce, washout, wipeout **8** conquest, disaster, drive off, drive out, drubbing, gouge out, stampede, vanquish, walkover **9** chase away, landslide, overpower, overthrow, overwhelm, slaughter, thrashing, trouncing **10** demoralize
out: **4** find **5** dig up, purge **7** uncover, unearth **8** discover
route: **3** run, way **4** beat, lane, line, path, pike, road, send, ship **5** byway, guide, means, round, steer, steps, track, trail **6** access, artery, avenue, byroad, course, detour, direct, rounds, street **7** address, beeline, channel, circuit, consign, forward, freeway, heading, highway, ingress, parkway, passage, roadway **8** dispatch, shepherd, short cut, transmit, turnpike **9** boulevard, direction, itinerary **10** Interstate, throughway
alternate ~: **6** bypass, detour
direct ~: **7** beeline
en ~: **6** aboard, coming, midway **7** driving **8** embarked, motoring, on the way **9** advancing, in transit, on the road, traveling
en ~ in a way: **4** asea **5** at sea
go the ~: **6** finish **9** culminate
in Latin: **3** via
in Spanish: **3** vía
jet ~: **3** arc **4** lane **6** airway, flyway, skyway **7** airlane
narrow ~: **6** strait
ocean ~: **4** lane **6** seaway **7** passage, sea lane
recommender: **3** AAA **8** Auto Club
secondary ~: **4** lane **6** byroad
__ route: **3** air **4** star **5** rural, trade
router: **4** tool
router __: **5** patch, plane
Route 66 (CBS adventure)
cast: George Maharis (Buz Murdock) Martin Milner (Tod Stiles)
routine: **3** act, job, rut, way **4** dull, rote, rule, tack, tame, wont **5** cycle, daily, drill, grind, habit, ho-hum, order, spiel, stock, trite, typic, usage, usual **6** boring, common, custom, groove, method, normal, system, tedium, wonted **7** formula, general, generic, humdrum, mundane, process, prosaic, regular, schtick, tedious, typical, workout **8** everyday, familiar, frequent, habitual, habitude, monotony, ordinary, orthodox, periodic, practice, pretense, standard, workaday **9** customary, generical, procedure, prosaical, quotidian, technique, treadmill, unvarying **10** accustomed, daily grind, dullsville, mechanical, prevailing, uneventful, widespread
dull ~: **3** rut **4** rote **5** chore, grind
fixed ~: **7** rat race **8** monotony **9** treadmill
routine-bound: **6** in a rut
routinely: **5** often **7** as a rule, usually **8** commonly, normally **9** generally, in general, in the main, regularly **10** by and large, frequently, habitually, ordinarily
Rouyn: **4** city, town
locale: **6** Canada, Québec
rove: **3** gad **4** roam, trek, walk **5** amble, drift, prowl, range, stray, tramp **6** ramble, travel, wander **7** explore, journey, maunder, meander, migrate, saunter **8** ambulate, gad about, nomadize, straggle, traverse **9** bum around, gallivant, itinerate, run around **10** hit the road, knock about
rover: **5** gypsy, nomad **6** roamer **7** drifter, pilgrim, rambler, voyager **8** fugitive, gadabout, runagate, traveler, vagabond, wanderer, wayfarer **9** itinerant, journeyer, meanderer, sojourner, transient **10** adventurer
sea ~: **6** pirate **7** corsair **8** freeboot **9** buccaneer **10** freebooter
__ rover: **3** red, sea **5** lunar
Rover: **3** dog **5** pooch **6** canine
doc: **3** DVM, vet
friend: **4** Fido, Spot
remark: **3** arf **4** bark, woof **6** bowwow
Rover __: **3** Boy
__ Rovers: **4** Wild **5** Irish
Rovetta, Gerolamo: **6** writer **7** Italian **10** playwright
roving: **6** errant, ramble **7** erratic, migrant, nomadic **8** rootless, vagabond **9** itinerant, migratory, wayfaring
Rovuma: **5** river
locale: **8** Tanzania **10** Mozambique
row: **4** feud, file, fray, fuss, line, pull, rank, riot, spat, stir, tier, tiff, to-do **5** aisle, brawl, chain, clash, fight, furor, melee, mix-up, noise, queue, range, run-in, scene, scrap, scull, set-to, storm, train, words **6** affray, barney, blowup, clamor, column, dustup, fracas, frenzy, furrow, hassle, kickup, lineup, racket, rebuke, ruckus, rumpus, series, string, tumult, uproar **7** contest, dispute, ferment, quarrel, scuffle, trouble, wrangle **8** argument, ballyhoo, brouhaha, catfight, conflict, sequence, skirmish, squabble, struggle **9** altercate, commotion, hue and cry, imbroglio **10** difference, donnybrook, falling-out, free-for-all, hullabaloo, succession
ender: **4** boat, lock
in a ~: **6** alined, linear, unbent **7** aligned, lined up, unbowed **8** straight **10** single-file, unswerving
kick up a ~: **5** anger **6** burn up, fire up, madden, offend **7** incense **9** infuriate, instigate
long ~ to hoe: **4** task, toil **5** chore, grind, labor **6** burden **8** headache
put in a ~: **4** even **5** align, aline,

array, order 10 straighten
starter: 4 corn, shed, wind 5 fence, hedge
row ___: 5 house 6 vector
___ row: 3 in a 4 home, note, skid, tone 6 ground
___ Row: 4 Park, Skid 5 Kings 7 Cannery
rowan: 3 ash 4 tree
fruit: 4 sorb
Rowan: 3 Dan 4 Carl 8 Atkinson
Rowan and Martin's Laugh-In (NBC comedy)
cast: Ruth Buzzi
Judy Carne
Henry Gibson
Goldie Hawn
Arte Johnson
Dick Martin
Gary Owens
Dan Rowan
Alan Sues
Jo Anne Worley
rowboat: 3 gig 4 dory 5 scull, skiff 6 dinghy, vessel
need: 3 oar
pin: 5 thole
problem: 4 leak
rowdy: 4 goon, loud, lout, punk, thug, wild 5 brute, bully, fiend, noisy, rough, tough, wooly, yahoo 6 heller, hoiden, hoyden, mugger, rascal, unruly, vandal, woolly 7 brawler, brutish, hellion, hoodlum, lawless, naughty, raucous, roguish, ruffian 8 hooligan 9 miscreant, out of hand, reprobate, roughneck, scoundrel, turbulent 10 boisterous, disorderly, hopping mad, tumultuous, unpeaceful, vociferant
be ~: 5 act up
rowdydow: 3 ado 4 flap, to-do 5 melee 6 hubbub 10 hullabaloo
rowed combining form: 8 -stichous
Rowe, Nicholas: 4 poet 7 British
rower: 3 oar 5 racer 7 oarsman, sculler
craft: 5 canoe, kayak, skiff
foremost ~: 6 bow oar
rowing: 5 sport
muscles used in ~: 5 delts
team: 4 crew 5 eight, octad
team member: 3 oar
rowing ___: 4 boat 7 machine
Rowland: 3 Roy 4 Hill 5 Evans 8 Sherwood
Rowland Heights: 4 city, town
locale: 10 California
Rowland, Roy: 8 director
film: The 5,000 Fingers of Dr. T. (1953)
Killer McCoy (1947)
Our Vines Have Tender Grapes (1945)
Rogue Cop (1954)
The Romance of Rosy Ridge (1947)
Witness to Murder (1954)
Rowlands, Gena: 7 actress
film: Another Woman (1988)
A Child Is Waiting (1963)
Faces (1968)
Hope Floats (1998)
Lonely Are the Brave (1962)
The Mighty (1998)
Minnie and Moskowitz (1971)
Night on Earth (1991)
Opening Night (1977)
Paulie (1998)
son: Nick Cassavetes
spouse: John Cassavetes
Rowland, Sherwood: 7 chemist 8 Nobelist
Rowlett: 4 city, town
locale: 5 Texas
Rowley, William: 7 British 10 playwright
work: The Changeling

Rowlf of the Muppets: 3 dog
Rowling, J.K.: 6 author, writer 7 British
honour: 3 OBE
Row, Row, Row Your Boat: 5 round
end: 6 a dream
rows
combining form: 5 -stich
series of ~: 4 bank, tier 5 level 7 section, stratum
Rowse, A.L.: 4 poet 7 British
___ row to hoe: 4 hard, long
Roxana: 3 Zal
Roxann ___-Dawson: 5 Biggs
Roxanne: 4 Hart
Roxanne (1987 film)
cast: Shelley Duvall, Daryl Hannah, Steve Martin
director: Fred Schepisi
Roxanne (1979 song) artist: Police
Roxette
members: Fredriksson, Gessle
song: Dangerous (1990)
Dressed for Success (1989)
Fading Like a Flower (1991)
It Must Have Been Love (1990)
Joyride (1991)
Listen to Your Heart (1989)
The Look (1989)
Roxie: 4 Hart 5 Roker
Roxy Music co-founder: 3 Eno
Roy: 4 Bean, Cohn, Head 5 Acuff, Clark, Innis 6 Disney, Fuller, London, Rogers 7 Del Ruth, Emerson, Huggins, Orbison, Rowland, Thinnes, Wilkins 8 Boulting, Eldridge, Hamilton, Scheider 9 Firestone, Gabrielle 10 Campanella
royal: 4 blue, fern, king, palm, sail 5 grand, lofty, noble, regal, ruler 6 august, gerent, kingly, lordly, superb 7 courtly, exalted, queenly, stately, supreme, viceroy 8 dynastic, highborn, highbred, imperial, imposing, kinglike, majestic, princely, splendid 9 patrician, sovereign 10 autocratic, majestical
address: 4 sire
battle ~: 4 to-do 5 brawl, clash, fight, run-in, set-to 6 affray, dustup, fracas, ruckus, rumpus, tangle 7 quarrel, rhubarb, ruction, wrangle 8 brouhaha 9 imbroglio
command: 4 fiat 5 edict 6 decree
ender: 3 ist 4 mast
fur: 6 ermine
headgear: 5 crown, tiara 7 coronet
home: 6 castle, palace
letters: 3 HIH, HRH, HSH
name meaning ~: 5 Basil
part of a ~ flush: 3 ace, ten 4 jack, king 5 queen
starter: 5 penny
symbol: 3 orb
royal ___: 4 blue, fern, fizz, lily, mast, palm, road 5 flush, jelly 6 antler, colony, family, purple, tennis
___ royal: 4 bleu, pair 5 blood, rhyme 6 battle, coffee, prince 7 battles
Royal: 3 car 4 auto, Dano 5 Dodge 8 Chrysler 10 automobile
Hall of Famer: 5 Brett
rival: 3 Cub, Met, Red 4 Expo, Twin 5 Angel, Astro, Brave, Giant, Padre, Rocky, Tiger 6 Brewer, Dodger, Indian, Marlin, Oriole, Philly, Pirate, Ranger, Red Sox, Yankee 7 Blue Jay, Mariner 8 Athletic, Cardinal, Devil Ray, White Sox
Royal ___: 3 Oak 4 Anne 5 Flash, Teens 7 Academy, Society, Wedding
Royal ___ Hall: 6 Albert
Royal ___, MI: 3 Oak
Royal ___ of the Sun, The: 4 Hunt
Royal Ascot time: 4 June
Royal, Billy Joe song: Down in the Boondocks (1965)
Royal Crown: 4 cola, soda 9 soft drink
alternative: 3 TAB 4 Coke, Nehi 5 Fanta, Pepsi 6 Fresca, Sprite 8 Coca-Cola, Diet Rite, Dr Pepper 9 Canada Dry, Pepsi-Cola 10 Mello Yello 11 Mountain Dew
___ royale: 4 café
Royale: 3 car, Reo 4 auto, Olds 10 automobile, Oldsmobile
___ Royale: 6 Casino
___ Royale, MI: 4 Isle
___ Royale National Park: 4 Isle
Royal Family of Broadway, The (1930 film)
cast: Ina Claire, Cyril Gardner, Fredric March
director: George Cukor
Royal Family, The author: Edna Ferber
Royal Firewater Musick composer: 4 Bach 7 PDQ Bach
Royal Flash (1975 film)
cast: Alan Bates, Malcolm McDowell
director: Richard Lester
Royal Guardsmen song: Snoopy vs. the Red Baron (1966)
___ Royal Highness: 3 Her, His
Royal Hunt of the Sun, The: 4 film, play
author: Peter Shaffer
cast: Nigel Davenport, Christopher Plummer, Robert Shaw
director: Irving Lerner
royal jelly producer: 3 bee
Royal Oak: 4 city, town
locale: 8 Michigan
Royal Palm Beach: 4 city, town
locale: 7 Florida
Royals: 3 ten 4 team
home: 10 Kansas City
org.: 3 ALC, MLB
sport: 8 baseball
Royal Teens song: Short Shorts (1958)
Royal Tenenbaums, The (2001 film)
cast: Gene Hackman, Anjelica Huston, Gwyneth Paltrow, Ben Stiller
director: Wes Anderson
royalties: 6 income 8 earnings, proceeds, receipts
org.: 3 BMI 5 ASCAP
royalty: 5 crown, lords, noble 6 income 8 kingship, nobility, receipts
receiver: 6 author, singer 8 composer
Royal Wedding (1951 film)
cast: Fred Astaire, Peter Lawford, Jane Powell
director: Stanley Donen
Royce, Josiah: 6 writer 8 essayist 11 philosopher
Roy G. ___: 3 Biv
Roy, Gabrielle: 6 writer 8 Canadian
work: The Tin Flute
Roy G. Biv part: 3 hue, red 4 blue 5 color 6 indigo, orange, violet, yellow
___ Roy Hill: 6 George
Royko: 4 Mike
Roz: 4 Ryan 5 Chast
Rozanov, Vasily: 6 writer 7 Russian
Rozelle: 4 Pete
Rózewicz, Tadeusz: 4 poet 6 Polish 10 playwright
RPI: 6 school
locale: 4 Troy 7 New York
part of ~: 4 Inst., Poly
rival: 3 MIT
RPM
indicator: 4 tach
part of ~: 3 min., per, rev. 6 minute
step up the ~ s: 3 gun, rev 4 race
RPS part: 3 Per, Rev., Sec. 6 Second
RR
driver: 4 engr.
info: 3 ETA, ETD
mail place: 3 RPO
sign abbreviation: 4 xing
stop: 3 dep., sta., stn.
see also railroad, train
R&R: 5 leave 7 time off 8 furlough, vacation
locale: 3 USO
part of ~: 4 rest 10 recreation
R-rated
like some ~ movies: 4 gory
or higher: 5 adult
R's
have trouble saying ~: 4 lall
three ~ org.: 3 AFT, NEA, UFT
___ R's: 5 three
RSVP: 3 ans. 5 reply 6 answer
insert: 4 card, encl. 7 SASE. SAE
part: 3 s'il 4 vous 5 plaît 8 répondez
RSV, part of: 3 Rev., Ver. 7 Revised, Version 8 Standard
RSX: 3 car 4 auto 5 Acura 10 automobile
Rt. ___: 3 Hon., Rev.
R2-D2: 5 robot
rte.: 2 av., st. 3 ave., hwy., tpk. 4 hgwy., tnpk. 9 itinerary
where ~ s meet: 3 jct.
see also route
rt.-hand man: 2 lt. 3 ADC 4 asst.
RT quarry: 2 QB
rt. to left: 3 ccw
Ru: 4 elem. 7 element 9 ruthenium
44 for ~: 4 at. no.
ruan: 4 lute 6 string
origin: 5 China
Ruanda-___: 6 Urundi
Ruapehu: 7 volcano
locale: 10 New Zealand
Ruark: 6 Robert
rub: 3 mop, pat 4 bark, buff, fray, lick, rasp, snag, wear, wipe 5 apply, brush, catch, chafe, erase, gloss, grate, graze, grind, hitch, knead, scour, scrub, shine, smear, touch 6 abrade, caress, hangup, hurdle, polish, scrape, smooth, spread, stroke 7 burnish, dilemma, massage, problem, scratch 8 drawback, friction, irritate, levigate, obstacle 9 annoyance, hindrance, tight spot 10 difficulty, impediment
clean: 4 wipe 5 erase 6 delete, efface 7 expunge, wipe off 10 obliterate
down: 4 file, wear 5 erode 6 abrade 7 massage
elbows: 3 mix 6 hobnob, mingle 9 socialize 10 fraternize
ender: 3 off, out 4 down
in: 6 harp on, repeat, stress 7 belabor, iterate 9 emphasize, reiterate
it in: 4 crow 5 gloat 7 swagger
off: 5 erase 6 delete 7 blot out, expunge, wipe out 9 eradicate 10 obliterate
on: 3 dab 4 coat 5 apply, cover, smear 6 spread
the wrong way: 3 get, ire, irk, vex 4 fret, gall, miff, rack, rile, roil 5 annoy, chafe, grate, harry, hound, peeve 6 harass, offend, pester, pick on, plague, rankle 7 afflict, agonize, anguish, bedevil, oppress, torment, torture 8 aggrieve, distress, irritate 9 persecute
rub ___: 3 out 4 down, it in
rub ___ with: 6 elbows
rub-a-dub-dub craft: 3 tub
Rubáiyát, The: 4 poem
author: Omar Khayyám
word: 4 enow
Rub al Khali: 6 desert

locale: 4 Oman 5 Yemen 6 Arabia 7 Mideast
rubbed
be ~ wrong way: 4 mind 8 object to
rubber: 3 ule 4 shoe, tree 6 balata, caucho, eraser, galosh, golosh, lissom 7 galoshe, lissome 8 footwear, overshoe
burn ~: 3 hie, zip 4 bolt, dash, rush, zoom 5 hurry, speed 6 barrel, career, hasten, hustle, scurry 8 step on it 9 hotfoot it, make haste, shake a leg 10 accelerate
city: 5 Akron
ender: 4 neck
product: 4 ball, tire 6 eraser, gasket
synthetic ~: 4 buna 5 latex
tire ~: 5 tread
tree: 3 ule 7 seringa
tree mover of song: 3 ant
rubber ___: 4 ball, band, game, tree 5 check, latex, match, plant, stamp 6 bridge, cement
rubber-___: 5 faced
rubber-___ circuit: 7 chicken
___ rubber: 3 lay 4 burn, cold, foam, hard, Pará, wild 5 butyl, crepe, India 6 sponge 7 natural, nitrile
Rubber Ball (1960 song) artist: Bobby Vee
Rubberband Man, The (1976 song) artist: Spinners
Rubber Duckie singer: 5 Ernie
rubber-duck owner: 6 bather
rubberized canvas: 4 tarp
rubberneck: 3 eye 4 gawk, gaze, look, ogle, peer, view 5 ogler, stare, watch 6 gawker 7 witness 8 busybody 9 spectator
rubber stamp: 2 OK 4 okay, sign 6 accept, affirm, ratify 7 certify 8 validate
partner: 6 inkpad
word: 4 paid, void 8 received
rubber tree mover of song: 3 ant
rubbery: 5 mushy 6 bouncy, limber, spongy, supple 7 pliable 8 flexible 9 resilient
Rubbia, Carlo: 8 Nobelist 9 physicist
rubbing: 7 massage 8 abrasion, friction
liquid: 3 alc. 7 alcohol
out: 7 erasure
the wrong way: 5 nasty 7 caustic, galling 8 abrasive, annoying 10 irritating, unpleasant
rubbing ___: 7 alcohol
rubbish: 3 gas, rot 4 blah, bosh, bull, bunk, guff, jazz, jive, junk, pooh, talk, tosh 5 bilge, chaff, dregs, dross, fudge, hokum, hooey, offal, prate, scrap, stuff, swill, trash, tripe, waste 6 bunkum, bushwa, debris, drivel, footle, gabble, gammon, gibber, grunge, havers, hot air, humbug, jabber, jargon, kibosh, litter, piffle, refuse, rubble, shards 7 baloney, blarney, blather, blether, boloney, bushwah, eyewash, flannel, flubdub, fustian, garbage, hogwash, inanity, malarky, twaddle 8 buncombe, claptrap, falderal, falderol, flimflam, flummery, folderal, folderol, leavings, malarkey, nonsense, slipslop, tommyrot, trumpery 9 banana oil, gibberish, goofiness, kidstakes, moonshine, poppycock, rigmarole, sweepings 10 applesauce, balderdash, bilge water, codswallop, double-talk, flapdoodle, galimatias, Jabberwock, mumbo jumbo, rigamarole, taradiddle
pile: 4 dump, heap 7 ash heap 8 junkyard, landfill
rubble: 4 rock 5 ruins, trash, waste 6 debris 7 garbage, rubbish
reduced to ~: 7 in ruins
reduce to ~: 8 demolish
Rubble: 5 Betty 6 Barney
rubdown, require a: 4 ache
rube: 3 oaf 4 clod, hick 5 looby, yahoo, yokel 6 gaffer, rustic 7 bumpkin, hayseed 9 hillbilly
___ rube: 3 hey
Rube: 6 Foster 7 Waddell 8 Goldberg, Marquard
rubellite: 3 gem 8 gemstone
Ruben: 5 Dario 6 Blades, Joseph, Sierra
Rubenesque: 5 buxom
Ruben, Joseph: 8 director
film: Dreamscape (1984)
Return to Paradise (1998)
Sleeping With the Enemy (1991)
The Stepfather (1987)
True Believer (1989)
Rubens, Peter Paul: 6 artist 7 painter
homeland: 8 Flanders
subject: 4 nude
rubescent: 3 red
Rubicon: 5 river
crosser: 6 Caesar
land across the ~: 4 Gaul
locale: 5 Italy
rubicund: 3 red 4 rosy 5 ruddy 6 blowsy, blowzy, florid 7 blowsed, blowzed, flushed, reddish 8 reddened 9 rufescent
relative: 4 rose, rust, wine 5 brick, coral, grape, poppy, rusty, sandy 6 cerise, cherry, claret, garnet, maroon 7 carmine, crimson, fuchsia, magenta, pimento, scarlet, sultana, vermeil 8 amaranth, cardinal, dubonnet, geranium 9 carnation, cranberry, vermilion 10 strawberry
rubidium: 5 metal 7 element
Rubidoux: 4 city, town
locale: 10 California
rubify: 6 redden
Rubik: 4 Erno
Rubik's ___: 4 Cube
Rubinstein: 5 Anton, Artur 6 Arthur, Helena
rival: 4 Avon 5 Almay 6 Lauder 7 Mary Kay
Rubinstein, Anton: 7 pianist, Russian
Rubinstein, Artur: 6 Polish 7 pianist
ruble: 5 money
fraction: 5 kopek 6 copeck, kopeck
locale: 6 Russia
rub one's ___ in: 4 nose
rub one's ___ of: 5 hands
rubric: 5 title 6 legend, redden
rubricate: 6 redden
rub the ___ way: 5 wrong
ruby: 3 gem, red 5 color, jewel 6 redden 7 carmine, crimson, mineral 8 corundum, gemstone 9 vermilion
month: 4 July
relative: 4 rose, rust, wine 5 brick, coral, grape, poppy, rusty, sandy 6 cerise, cherry, claret, garnet, maroon 7 carmine, crimson, fuchsia, magenta, pimento, scarlet, sultana, vermeil 8 amaranth, cardinal, dubonnet, geranium 9 carnation, cranberry, vermilion 10 strawberry
synthetic ~: 5 boule
ruby ___: 5 glass, laser 6 silver, spinel
Ruby: 3 Dee 5 Harry 6 Keeler
hubby: 5 Ossie
Ruby ___: 4 Baby 7 Tuesday
Ruby and the Romantics song: Our Day Will Come (1963)
Ruby Baby (1963 song) artist: Dion
Ruby, Don't Take Your Love to Town (1969 song) artist: Kenny Rogers
Ruby, Harry: 8 composer
collaborator: 6 Kalmar
song: Ev'ryone Says I Love You
Hooray for Captain Spaulding
I Wanna Be Loved by You
Nevertheless
Three Little Words
Who's Sorry Now
Ruby in Paradise (1993 film)
cast: Todd Field, Ashley Judd, Bentley Mitchum
director: Victor Nunez
Ruby Tuesday (1967 song) artist: Rolling Stones
Ruchbah: 4 star
ruche: 4 fold, lace, trim 6 ruffle
ruck: 4 fold, mass 5 ridge 6 crease, pucker 7 wrinkle 9 hoi polloi
ender: 4 sack
up: 4 muss 6 rumple 7 crumple 8 dishevel
Ruck: 4 Alan
___ Rucker, AL: 4 Fort
Rückert, Friedrich: 4 poet 6 German
rucksack: 3 bag 4 pack 5 pouch 6 kitbag 8 backpack
ruckus: 3 ado, din, row 4 flap, fray, fuss, riot, stir, to-do 5 brawl, furor, hoo-ha, melee 6 clamor, frenzy, hoohah, hoopla, hubbub, pother, uproar 7 quarrel, rampage, scuffle, wrangle 8 argument, brouhaha, conflict, disorder, friction 9 commotion 10 hullabaloo
ruction: 4 riot, to-do 5 melee 6 fracas, frenzy, hubbub, racket, tumult, uproar 7 wrangle 8 skirmish 10 free-for-all, hullabaloo
ructious: 7 hawkish, hostile, martial, warlike 8 militant 9 bellicose, combative 10 aggressive, pugnacious
rudbeckia: 5 bloom, plant 6 flower
rudd: 4 carp, fish
Rudd: 4 Paul 6 Hughes
rudder: 4 helm 5 blade 7 control
ender: 4 fish, post 5 stock
locale: 3 aft 5 stern 6 astern
support: 4 skeg
toward the ~: 3 aft 5 abaft 6 astern 8 rearward
use the ~: 5 pilot, steer 6 direct 8 maneuver, navigate
rudderless: 8 unguided
Ruddigore composer: 7 Gilbert 8 Sullivan
ruddiness: 5 blush, flush
ruddle: 3 ore 6 redden
ruddy: 3 red 4 duck, pink, rosy 5 fresh 6 blowsy, blowzy, florid, redden 7 blowsed, blowzed, bronzed, crimson, flushed, glowing, reddish, scarlet 8 blooming, blushing, reddened, redfaced, rubicund, sanguine 9 rufescent
not ~: 3 wan 4 ashy, pale 5 ashen
ruddy duck: 4 fowl
relative: 4 smew, teal 5 eider, Pekin, Rouen, scaup 6 Cayuga, scoter 7 gadwall, mallard, pintail, pochard, redhead, widgeon 8 garganey, mandarin, oldsquaw, shoveler 9 broadbill, goldeneye, goosander, greenhead, merganser, sprigtail 10 bufflehead, canvasback, surf scoter
rude: 3 raw 4 bold, curt, flip, loud, mean, pert, wild 5 bawdy, blunt, brash, brusk, crass, crude, fresh, gross, gruff, harsh, nervy, pushy, rough, sassy, saucy, sharp, short, surly 6 abrupt, awless, brassy, brazen, cheeky, coarse, hoiden, hoyden, incult, rustic, savage, simple, snippy, vulgar 7 abusive, aweless, boorish, brusque, crabbed, forward, ill-bred, loutish, lowbred, offhand, selfish, uncivil, uncouth 8 assuming, churlish, flippant, heedless, impolite, impudent, indecent, insolent, inurbane, liverish, plebeian, snippety, tactless, unseemly, unsubtle 9 audacious, backwater, difficult, graceless, insulting, makeshift, obnoxious, offensive, officious, out of line, primitive, roughhewn, shameless, tasteless, truculent, ungallant, unrefined 10 indecorous, indelicate, peremptory, provincial, regardless, uncultured, ungracious, unmannerly, unthinking
be ~ to: 3 dis 6 insult
comment: 3 dig 4 barb, slam, slap, slur 5 crack, taunt 6 insult 7 affront, offense
look: 4 leer 5 sneer, stare
not ~: 4 kind, nice 6 genial, kindly, polite, proper 7 affable, amiable, cordial, likable, refined 8 charming, cultured, decorous, friendly, gracious, pleasant, pleasing, polished 9 civilized, courteous, exemplary, simpatico 10 fastidious, personable, scrupulous
one: 3 cad 4 boor, bozo, lout 5 churl
Rudel, Julius: 9 conductor
rudeness: 3 lip 4 sass 5 brass, cheek, mouth, nerve 6 insult 8 acerbity, acrimony, audacity, temerity 9 impudence, indecorum 10 disrespect, effrontery, indelicacy, inurbanity, misconduct, unkindness
reaction to ~: 4 slap
Rudge: 7 Barnaby
Rudi: 3 Joe 9 Gernreich
rudiment: 4 germ, seed 5 basis 6 embryo 9 principle
rudimentary: 5 basic, crude, early, prime, rough 6 coarse, larval, latent, simple 7 initial, primary 8 immature, original 9 beginning, elemental, embryonic, inelegant, makeshift, primitive, unrefined, vestigial 10 amateurish, unpolished
life: 4 germ, seed 5 virus 6 embryo 7 microbe 8 pathogen 9 bacterium
prefix: 3 pro-
rudiments: 4 ABCs 6 basics
Rudkin, David: 7 British 10 playwright
Rudner, Rita: 5 comic 8 comedian
Rudolf: 3 Max 4 Abel, Bing, Hess, lake 5 Friml 6 Diesel, Eucken 7 Nureyev, Steiner 9 Mössbauer
locale: 5 Kenya
Rudolf, Max: 9 conductor
Rudolph: 4 Alan, Mate 5 Dirks, Isley, Wilma 6 Marcus 8 Giuliani 9 Valentino
costar: 4 Lila
in Italian: 7 Rodolfo
in Spanish: 7 Rodolfo
master: 5 Santa
Rudolph the ___-Nosed Reindeer: 3 Red
Rudolph, Wilma: 6 runner 8 sprinter
Rudy: 4 Maté 5 Wiebe 6 Gatlin, Solari, Vallee 8 Giuliani, Huxtable
Rudy (1993 film)
cast: Sean Astin, Ned Beatty, Robert Prosky
director: David Anspaugh
Rudyard: 7 Kipling
rue: 4 herb 5 grief, mourn 6 bemoan, bewail, grieve, lament, qualms, regret, repent 7 deplore, remorse 8 repent of 10 contrition
family shrub: 7 skimmia 9 jaborandi
Rue: 10 McClanahan
costar: 3 Bea 5 Betty 7 Estelle
Rue de ___: 6 la Paix, Rivoli
rueful: 3 sad, wry 7 doleful 8 penitent 9 miserable, regretful 10 apologetic, lamentable, lugubrious, remorseful
sigh: 4 ah me

ruefulness: 4 pity 6 regret 7 remorse 9 penitence
Ruehl, Mercedes: 7 actress
film: The Fisher King (1991, AA)
Lost in Yonkers (1993)
Married to the Mob (1988)
Rue Morgue
creator: 3 Poe
culprit: 3 ape
__ Rue My Heart Is Laden: 4 With
ruer: 6 atoner
like a ~: 5 sorry 8 contrite, penitent 9 regretful, repentant 10 apologetic, remorseful
word: 4 alas
rue the __: 3 day
rufescent: 5 ruddy 8 rubicund
ruff: 4 bird, fish, mane 5 scarf 6 collar 9 sandpiper
female ~: 3 ree 5 reeve
in bridge: 5 trump
material: 4 lace
starter: 4 wood 5 cross
Ruff and Reddy: 5 toons 7 cartoon
cat: 4 Ruff
dog: 5 Reddy
ruffian: 4 goon, hood, punk, thug 5 brute, bully, knave, rowdy, scamp, tough, yahoo 6 apache, bad guy, goonda, heller, rascal 7 brigand, hoodlum 8 gangster, hooligan, plugugly, tough guy 9 miscreant, roughneck, scoundrel
Ruffin: 5 David, Jimmy
Ruffing, Red: 6 hurler, Yankee 7 pitcher
ruffle: 3 irk, vex 4 faze, fret, gall, miff, muss, roil, tuck, wave 5 abash, anger, annoy, chafe, frill, jabot, peeve, pique, plait, pleat, ruche, shake, tease, upset 6 bother, crease, excite, flurry, harass, mess up, muss up, needle, nettle, noodge, pucker, ripple, rumple, tangle, tousle, touzle 7 agitate, crinkle, disturb, flounce, fluster, flutter, perturb, provoke, shake up, wrinkle 8 dishevel, froufrou, furbelow, irritate, unsettle 9 corrugate, discomfit 10 disarrange, discompose, disconcert, intimidate
feathers: 3 irk, vex 5 annoy, peeve 6 bother, nettle 8 irritate
ruffled: 5 irate, rough, upset 6 shaggy 7 nervous, tousled 9 turbulent
Ruffles feature: 5 ridge
rufiyaa: 4 coin
rufous: 7 reddish
Rufus: 6 Sewell, Thomas
Rufus T. __: 7 Firefly
rug: 3 rya, wig 4 shag 5 kilim, Saruk 6 Berber, carpet, kaross, Kirman, runner, Sarouk, Saxony, toupee 8 bearskin 9 broadloom, carpeting, hairpiece
cleaner: 3 vac 6 beater, vacuum
color variation: 6 abrash
coverage: 4 area
cut a ~: 5 dance
exporter: 4 Iran
fabric: 5 frise, nylon
feature: 3 nap 4 pile
fiber: 5 sisal
knot: 5 sehna
like a bug in a ~: 4 snug
like some ~ s: 4 oval
make a ~: 5 weave
Persian ~: 5 kilim 6 Kirman
rat: 3 kid, tot 4 babe, baby 6 infant
Scandinavian ~: 3 rya
wear a hole in the ~: 4 pace
__ rug: 3 rag 4 area, cut a 5 grass, throw 6 hooked, prayer, Wilton 7 Bokhara, Bukhara, Kashmir, Persian, scatter, steamer, Turkish 8 Cashmere
ruga: 5 ridge 7 wrinkle
rugby: 5 shirt, sport
formation: 5 scrum 9 scrummage
kick: 4 punt
score: 3 try
Rugby: 4 city, town
locale: 7 England
Rugby __: 5 shirt 6 jersey
rugged: 3 big, fit 4 hale, hard, iron, wild, wiry, worn 5 beefy, bumpy, burly, hardy, harsh, hefty, hilly, hunky, husky, lusty, ridgy, rocky, rough, solid, sound, stony, stout, tough, wooly 6 brawny, craggy, hearty, jagged, mighty, potent, ragged, robust, savage, severe, shaggy, sinewy, steely, sticky, stocky, stoney, strong, sturdy, taxing, trying, uneven, virile, woolly 7 arduous, cragged, doughty, unlevel 8 athletic, forceful, furrowed, heavy-set, indurate, leathery, muscular, no picnic, powerful, puissant, rigorous, rocklike, stalwart, vigorous, well-made, wrinkled 9 Atlantean, demanding, difficult, energetic, heavy-duty, Herculean, inclement, irregular, roughhewn, strapping, strenuous, weathered, well-built 10 able-bodied, formidable, red-blooded, reinforced
rock: 3 tor
ruggedness: 5 brawn, force, might, power, vigor 6 muscle 7 stamina 8 strength 9 fortitude, puissance
Ruggero in English: 5 Roger
Ruggiero in English: 5 Roger
Ruggles: 6 Wesley 7 Charles, Charlie
Ruggles, Charlie: 5 actor 8 comedian
film: Anything Goes (1936)
Bringing Up Baby (1938)
Incendiary Blonde (1945)
Love Me Tonight (1932)
Murders in the Zoo (1933)
Our Hearts Were Young and Gay (1944)
Ruggles of Red Gap (1935)
Ruggles of Red Gap (1935 film)
cast: Mary Boland, Charles Laughton, ZaSu Pitts, Charlie Ruggles
director: Leo McCarey
Ruggles, Wesley: 8 director
film: Cimarron (1931)
College Humor (1933)
The Gilded Lily (1935)
I'm No Angel (1933)
See Here, Private Hargrove (1944)
Sing, You Sinners (1938)
Too Many Husbands (1940)
Rugrats kid: 3 Dil
Ruhr: 5 river 6 valley
city: 4 Hamm 5 Essen, Herne
locale: 7 Germany
ruin: 3 end, mar, sap, zap 4 bane, bust, dash, do in, doom, fall, harm, loss, maim, rase, raze, sack, sink, undo 5 blast, botch, break, crush, decay, havoc, level, queer, smash, spoil, taint, total, waste, wrack, wreck 6 beggar, blight, blow up, damage, debase, deface, defeat, finish, fleece, foul up, go sour, injure, mangle, mess up, penury, quench, ravage, ravish, reduce, topple 7 break up, butcher, consume, corrupt, debacle, debauch, degrade, despoil, destroy, disable, disrupt, failure, flatten, louse up, nemesis, pillage, pollute, scourge, screw up, scuttle, shamble, shatter, subvert, undoing, wipe out 8 bankrupt, bring low, bulldoze, calamity, clean out, cut short, decimate, demolish, desolate, disaster, dissolve, downfall, lay waste, spoilage, spoliate, straiten, take down, tear down, Waterloo, wreckage 9 bring down, cataclysm, desecrate, devastate, dismantle, knock down, overthrow, perdition, pollution, shoot down, take apart, undermine 10 annihilate, bankruptcy, corruption, desolation, disruption, extinction, impoverish, insolvency, invalidate, lead astray, obliterate, subversion
cause of ~: 4 bane 6 plague 7 scourge 8 anathema, calamity, downfall
in the kitchen: 4 char, sear 5 singe 6 scorch 9 carbonize
partner: 4 rack
rack and ~: 7 debacle 8 calamity, shambles 9 cataclysm
ruination: 3 end 4 bane, doom 5 havoc, waste 6 blight, plague 7 debacle, undoing 8 calamity, collapse, disaster, downfall 9 detriment, disrepair, nightmare, perdition 10 bankruptcy
ruined: 4 lost, shot, sunk, worn 5 broke, kaput 6 doomed, fallen, shabby, undone 7 injured, worn-out 8 bankrupt, ill-fated, in pieces 9 insolvent, penniless 10 irremedial
be ~: 4 bust, fail 7 founder 8 collapse
ruinous: 3 bad, ill 4 dire 5 fatal, sorry, toxic 6 costly, deadly, malign, shabby, tragic 7 adverse, baleful, baneful, fateful, harmful 8 damaging, luckless, negative, tragical, wasteful 9 dangerous, ill-omened, injurious, murderous, pestilent 10 calamitous, disastrous, immoderate, pernicious, shattering
ruins: 5 ashes, shell 6 debris, relics, rubble 7 remains 8 landmark, remnants, wreckage
fall into ~: 5 decay 7 crumble 8 collapse
in ~: 5 kaput 6 undone 9 destroyed 10 devastated
__ Ruins National Monument: 5 Aztec
Ruiz: 4 city, Juan, town 7 volcano
locale: 6 Mexico 7 Nayarit 8 Colombia
Ruiz, Juan: 4 poet 7 Spanish
Rukbat: 4 star
Rukeyser: 5 Louis 6 Muriel
Rukeyser, Muriel: 4 poet
rule: 3 law, run, reg. 4 code, find, head, lead, line, mode, no-no, norm, sway, wont 5 axiom, bylaw, canon, edict, gnome, judge, maxim, model, moral, order, power, reign, stick, tenet, usage 6 assize, custom, decide, decree, dictum, direct, empire, govern, manage, ordain, policy, regime, ruling, settle, system, truism 7 command, conduct, control, dictate, dynasty, formula, measure, oppress, precept, preside, prevail, resolve, routine, statute, theorem 8 aphorism, conclude, dominate, domineer, dominion, hegemony, hold sway, kingship, lord over, normalcy, override, practice, regulate, restrain, sentence, standard, take over 9 authority, be rampant, criterion, determine, directive, dominance, establish, guideline, influence, normality, ordinance, precedent, prescribe, principle, pronounce, reign over, supremacy, underline 10 adjudicate, administer, ascendance, ascendancy, ascendence, ascendency, domination, generality, government, leadership, observance, principium, regulation, run the show, suzerainty, take charge
against: 3 nix 4 veto 5 annul 6 revoke 8 disallow, override, overturn, set aside, turn down 10 invalidate
as a ~: 6 mostly 7 largely, usually 8 commonly, normally 9 generally, in general, in the main, most times, routinely 10 by and large, frequently, on the whole, ordinarily
combining form: 5 -archy, -cracy
ground ~: 6 policy 7 precept
mob ~: 7 anarchy 8 disorder, nihilism
out: 3 ban, bar, nix 4 tabu, veto 5 avert 6 bypass, except, forbid, ignore, reject 7 dismiss, exclude, forfend, obviate, prevent, retract, ward off 8 forefend, overlook, preclude, prohibit, stave off 9 disregard, eliminate, forestall, proscribe
the roost: 4 boss, head, lead 6 direct, manage 7 command, control
unwritten ~: 4 wont 5 usage 6 custom, policy 7 folkway 8 practice 9 etiquette, precedent 10 convention, observance
rule __: 3 out 5 joint
rule __ road: 5 of the
__ rule: 3 as a, gag, mob 4 foot, home, unit 5 board, chain, house, phase, plumb, slide 6 closed, golden, ground, Oxford, zigzag 7 caliper, Cramer's, folding, general, hearsay, sliding, special
__-rule: 4 self
Rule: 3 Ann 6 Janice
Golden ~ word: 4 unto 6 others
Rule, Britannia composer: 4 Arne
ruled: 4 liny 5 liney 8 governed
__ Ruled the World: 3 If I
Rule, Janice: 7 actress
film: 3 Women (1977)
The Ambushers (1968)
Bell, Book and Candle (1958)
The Swimmer (1968)
Welcome to Hard Times (1967)
spouse: Ben Gazzara
rule of __: 5 three, thumb 6 eleven
rule of the __: 4 road
ruler: 3 bey, dey, emp., oba, sov. 4 amir, boss, czar, doge, emir, khan, king, lord, raja, rani, shah, tsar, tzar 5 ameer, calif, chief, crown, emeer, kalif, mogul, nawab, pacha, pasha, queen, rajah, royal, scale, stick 6 archon, caesar, caliph, despot, dynast, exarch, gerent, kaiser, kaliph, khalif, leader, master, mikado, prince, satrap, shogun, sultan, top dog, tyrant 7 czarina, emperor, empress, headman, monarch, pharaoh, sultana, tsarina, T-square, tzarina, viceroy 8 dictator, governor, heptarch, kingfish, maharani, oligarch, overlord, princess, superior, suzerain 9 chieftain, commander, maharajah, potentate, sovereign, yardstick
absolute ~: 4 tsar 6 despot, tyrant
Arabian Nights ~: 5 calif, kalif 6 caliph, kaliph, khalif
combining form: 4 -arch, -crat 5 -ocrat
hereditary ~: 4 king
length: 4 foot
Moslem ~: 3 aga 4 agha, amir, emir 5 ameer, calif, emeer, kalif, mogul 6 caliph, kaliph, khalif
name meaning ~: 4 Eric, Erik 5 Cyril, Erich
part: 4 inch
ruler of peace
name meaning ~: 7 Fredric 8 Frederic 9 Frederick
...ruler of the Queen's __: 5 navee
rulers, interim: 5 junta
rules
break the ~: 4 defy 5 cheat, flout 7 disobey 9 disregard
government ~ to some: 6 jungle, morass 9 labyrinth
in the ~: 4 good 5 legal, legit, licit,

valid 6 kosher 9 allowable, warranted 10 acceptable, admissible, legitimate
__ rules: 4 work 6 ground
rules of __: 5 order
Rules of Engagement (2000 film)
cast: Samuel L. Jackson, Tommy Lee Jones, Ben Kingsley, Guy Pearce
director: William Friedkin
__ Rules of Games: 6 Hoyle's
Rules of the Game (1939 film) director: Jean Renoir
__ rules the gods...: 4 Love
rule the __: 5 roost
rule with peace, name meaning: 8 Vladimir
Rulfo, Juan: 6 writer 7 Mexican
ruling: 3 law 4 main 5 chief, edict, order, ukase 6 decree, dictum 7 central, current, finding, leading, pivotal, popular, precept, rampant, regnant, supreme, verdict 8 cardinal, decision, dominant, judgment, powerful, sentence 9 directive, executive, ordinance, prevalent, principal, sovereign 10 overriding, preeminent, prevailing, resolution, widespread
body: 4 govt. 10 government
class: 5 elite, lords 7 royalty 8 nobility
Ruling Class, The (1972 film)
cast: Peter O'Toole, Alastair Sim
director: Peter Medak
Ruling Voice, The (1931 film)
cast: Walter Huston, Doris Kenyon, Loretta Young
director: Rowland Lee
ruly: 4 tame 10 manageable
rum: 5 drink, quaff, tafia 6 liquor, taffia 7 Bacardi 8 beverage 10 intoxicant
bay ~: 10 aftershave
brand: 7 Bacardi
cake: 4 baba
drink: 4 grog
ender: 6 runner
mixer: 4 Coke, cola 8 Coca-Cola
run ~: 7 bootleg, smuggle
source: 4 Cuba 7 Jamaica
__ rum: 3 bay 5 demon 7 Jamaica
Rum __ Tugger: 3 Tum
rumaki: 8 Hawaiian 9 appetizer
rumal: 5 scarf
Rum and Coca-Cola (1945 song)
artist: Andrews Sisters
Rumania
see Romania
Ruman, Sig: 5 actor
film: Ninotchka (1939)
The Saint in New York (1938)
Think Fast, Mr. Moto (1937)
rumba: 4 step 5 dance, music
relative: 5 mambo
Rumba King: 5 Cugat
rumble: 4 boom, fray, peal, riot, roar, roll, talk, word 5 brawl, fight, growl, sound 6 frenzy, mumble, murmur, mutter, report 7 contest, ferment, grumble, resound, thunder, wrangle 8 violence 10 donnybrook
weapon: 4 shiv
rumble __: 4 seat 5 strip
Rumble Fish (1983 film)
cast: Matt Dillon, Dennis Hopper, Diane Lane, Mickey Rourke
director: Francis Ford Coppola
Rumble in the Jungle: 4 bout 5 fight, match
boxer: 3 Ali 7 Foreman
site: 5 Zaire
rumbling: 5 forte, noisy 7 jarring, rackety, raucous, reboant, roaring 8 piercing, plangent, sonorous, strident, turned up 9 big-voiced, clamorous, deafening 10 boisterous, stentorian, strepitous, uproarious, vociferous
Rumer: 6 Godden
ruminant: 3 cow, elk, gnu, kob, roe 4 axis, deer, guib, kudu, oryx, pudu, puku, shou, sika, topi 5 addax, bison, bongo, bovid, camel, chiru, eland, goral, korin, llama, moose, nyala, okapi, oribi, saiga, serow, steer 6 alpaca, animal, bovine, chammy, chital, dik-dik, duiker, guemal, hangul, huemul, impala, koodoo, lechwe, nilgai, rhebok, sambar, sambur, shammy, shamoy, thamin, vicuna, wapiti 7 blaubok, blesbok, brocket, buffalo, caribou, chamois, defassa, gazelle, gemsbok, gerenuk, giraffe, grysbok, muntjac, muntjak, nylghai, nylghau, sambhar, sambhur, sassaby 8 antelope, blesbuck, bontebok, bushbuck, gemsbuck, reedbuck, reindeer, steenbok, steinbok 9 barasingh, blackbuck, pronghorn, sitatunga, springbok, waterbuck 10 hartebeest, wildebeest
chew: 3 cud
stomach: 5 rumen 6 omasum
stomachs: 5 omasa
ruminate: 4 mull, muse 5 brood, study, think, weigh 6 chew on, digest, figure, look at, ponder 7 examine, reflect, revolve, sleep on 8 chew over, cogitate, consider, look back, meditate, mull over, see about, turn over 9 reflect on, speculate, sweat over, think over 10 deliberate, introspect, toss around
over: 4 call, deem, feel, heed, mull, muse, view 5 count, judge, study, think, weigh 6 credit, debate, digest, look at, ponder, reckon, regard, take up 7 balance, believe, examine, inspect, presume, reflect, sleep on, suppose, surmise, suspect 8 allow for, cogitate, consider, deal with, envisage, look upon, meditate, see about 9 enter into, reflect on, speculate 10 reckon with, toss around, understand
ruminater: 5 muser
rumination: 5 study 7 thought 9 deduction 10 cogitation
rummage: 4 comb, fish, grub, hunt, muss, rake, root, rout, seek 5 delve, probe, rifle, scour, upset, waste 6 dig out, forage, jumble, litter, search 7 explore, ransack 8 leavings 10 poke around
sale: 5 bazar 6 bazaar
rummage __: 4 sale
Rummies author: Peter Benchley
rummy: 3 gin 4 game 5 toper 8 card game
group: 4 meld
variety: 3 gin 4 tonk 7 canasta, cooncan 8 conquian 10 panguingue
__ rummy: 3 gin 5 knock
rumor: 3 lie, say 4 buzz, dirt, news, tale, talk, wind, word 5 bruit, on dit, story 6 canard, earful, gossip, report, tattle 7 fiction, hearsay, lowdown, scandal, whisper 9 circulate, falsehood, grapevine, invention, undertone 10 suggestion
ender: 6 monger
result, maybe: 5 panic, scare
starter: 5 I hear
rumor __: 4 mill
Rumor __...: 5 has it
rumormonger: 5 yenta 7 tattler 8 quidnunc
Rumor of Angels, A (2002 film)
cast: Ray Liotta, Catherine McCormack, Vanessa Redgrave
director: Peter O'Fallon
rumors: 4 talk 5 noise 6 gossip
spread ~: 3 pan 4 blab, slam, slur, talk 5 libel, smear, sully, taint 6 defame, gossip, malign, tattle, vilify 7 asperse, slander, tarnish, traduce 8 backbite, badmouth, besmirch 9 denigrate, discredit, disparage 10 calumniate, scandalize, stigmatize, throw mud at, vituperate
Rumors author: Neil Simon
Rumpelstiltskin: 5 troll
rumple: 4 fold, muss 5 crimp, crush 6 crease, muss up, pucker, ruck up, ruffle, tangle, tousle, touzle 7 crinkle, scrunch, wrinkle 8 dishevel, disorder 9 bedraggle
rumpled: 5 messy, mussy 6 matted, unneat, untidy 7 tousled, unkempt 10 disheveled
Rumpleteazer: 3 cat
creator: T.S. Eliot
rumpus: 3 ado, din, row 4 fray, riot, spat, tiff, to-do 5 brawl, clash, hoo-ha, melee, mix-up, scrap 6 affray, clamor, dustup, fracas, frenzy, hoo-hah, hoopla, hubbub, pother, racket, tumult, uproar 7 clatter, dispute, quarrel, rhubarb, scuffle, wrangle 8 argument, brouhaha, disorder, friction, squabble 9 commotion, encounter 10 hullabaloo
raising a ~: 5 noisy
room: 3 den
rumpus __: 4 room
rum raisin: 8 ice cream
alternative: 5 lemon, mocha, peach 6 banana, coffee, Jamoca, toffee 7 caramel, coconut, vanilla 8 cinnamon, hazelnut 9 bubblegum, chocolate, pineapple, pistachio, raspberry, rocky road 10 blackberry, cheesecake, Neapolitan, peppermint, strawberry
rum-running: 9 smuggling 10 contraband
run: 3 fly, hie, jog, own, ply, rip, use, zip 4 bolt, boss, dart, dash, flee, flit, flow, flux, gait, gush, hare, head, keep, last, leak, lift, lope, melt, move, oper., pace, pelt, pour, race, ride, rule, rush, sail, scud, shag, skim, skip, spin, step, sway, tear, ten K, thaw, tick, tide, tour, trip, trot, vary, verb, whiz, work, zoom 5 bleed, bound, carry, creek, cycle, dog it, drift, drive, elope, glide, hurry, issue, jaunt, lam it, leg it, range, round, route, scoot, scope, score, shoot, smoke, speed, spell, spill, spirt, spout, spurt, steer, stick, stump, trend 6 barrel, beat it, bustle, canter, career, course, cut out, decamp, depart, direct, escape, extend, flight, gallop, govern, handle, hasten, head up, hustle, ladder, manage, move it, ordain, outing, period, rocket, scurry, season, series, spread, sprint, streak, stream, string, whoosh 7 abscond, command, compete, conduct, contend, control, dash off, floor it, hop to it, journey, joy ride, keep fit, leak out, liquefy, liquify, make off, operate, oversee, passage, perform, preside, proceed, quicken, scamper, scuttle, skip out, skitter, stretch, take off, tear off 8 cheese it, clear out, continue, duration, function, hightail, latitude, light out, organize, politick, printing, regulate, scramble, sequence, skip town, ski slope, stampede, step on it, turn tail, unfreeze 9 excursion, flow along, get moving, go quickly, go swiftly, hotfoot it, look after, make haste, officiate, shake a leg, skedaddle, streamlet, supervise, transport 10 administer, coordinate, get a move on, get hopping, hightail it, kiss babies, lose no time, make a break, make tracks, procession, ride herd on, shake hands, succession, take flight
across: 4 find, meet 5 hit on 7 hit upon 8 bump into, chance on, come upon 9 encounter, stumble on 10 chance upon
afoul of: 3 irk 4 rile 5 peeve
after: 3 dog, woo 4 hunt, seek, tail 5 chase, hound 6 follow, pursue, shadow 8 hunt down
a game on: 2 do 3 con 4 bilk, burn, clip, dupe, fool, gull, hoax, rook, scam, snow 5 cheat, gouge, hocus, set up, shaft, sting, trick 6 fleece, hustle, rip off, rope in, take in 7 deceive, defraud, fake out, swindle 8 flimflam, hoodwink 9 bamboozle, four-flush, shake down, victimize
aground: 4 fail 5 wreck 8 stranded
ahead: 4 lead 5 scout 7 precede 8 antecede, go before 10 show the way, trail-blaze
along: 2 go 4 move 5 leave 6 be gone, depart, go away, retire 7 head out, ride off 8 shove off 9 get moving
amok: 4 rage, riot 5 storm 7 rampage 8 have a fit
around: 3 gad 4 roam, rove 9 gallivant 10 equivocate, knock about
at: 6 attack, charge
(at): 5 lunge
away: 2 go 3 fly 4 bail, bolt, flee, skip 5 break, elope 6 cop out, decamp, defect, escape, get out, go AWOL 7 abscond, make off, take off 8 fugitate, hightail, light out, turn tail 10 hightail it
away from: 4 jilt, skip 5 ditch, split 6 desert, escape, maroon, strand 7 abandon, forsake 9 leave flat
batted in: 3 RBI 5 ribby
circles around: 3 top 4 beat, best 5 outdo 6 outwit 8 outsmart 9 overwhelm
counter to: 4 vary 5 belie 6 differ, oppose 7 deviate, diverge 8 conflict, contrast, disagree
cut and ~: 7 go south 8 fugitate
down: 4 find, quit, slam, slur, stop 5 abase, abuse, cease, chase, decry, knock, seedy, trace, track 6 defame, impugn, malign, pursue, revile, search, vilify 7 asperse, degrade, detract, recount 8 backbite, badmouth, belittle, derogate, diminish, minimize, overtake, peter out, research, ridicule, throw mud 9 blaspheme, criticize, denigrate, deprecate, discredit, disparage, enumerate, frown upon, humiliate, make fun of, pick apart, search out, summarize 10 blackguard, calumniate, speak ill of, vituperate
dry ~: 4 test 5 trial 8 practice 9 rehearsal
end ~: 9 deviation, diversion, variation 10 aberration, deflection, red herring
ender: 3 off, out, way 4 away, back, down 5 about 6 around
(for): 7 compete 8 campaign
for it: 3 fly 4 blow, bolt, flee, skip 5 leave, scoot, scram, split 6 bug out, cut out, decamp, escape, skidoo 7 abscond, bail out, get away, make off, retreat, scamper, skip out, vamoose 8 clear out, fugitate, skip town, turn tail 9 skedaddle 10 fly the coop
help ~: 6 cohost 8 co-manage
hot and cold: 4 yo-yo 5 hedge

6 dither, seesaw, waffle, wobble 8 straddle 9 hem and haw, pussyfoot
in: 3 nab 4 bust, call, jail 5 pinch 6 arrest, collar, detain, pick up 7 capture 8 handcuff 9 apprehend
in neutral: 4 idle
interference for: 3 aid 4 help 6 assist, defend 7 support 8 advocate
in the long ~: 7 finally, overall 8 after all 10 eventually, ultimately
into: 3 ram, see 4 butt, find, meet, snag 5 total 6 accost, fall on, strike 8 come upon, fall upon, happen on, meet with 9 encounter, stumble on
(into): 5 empty
into the ground: 6 overdo 7 belabor, overuse 8 overplay
its course: 3 ebb 4 ease, fade, flag, stop, wane 5 abate, let up, relax 6 ease up, lessen, recede 7 die down, dwindle, ease off, slacken, subside, tail off 8 blow over, diminish, fade away, moderate, peter out, taper off 10 slacken off
last: 4 lose
leisurely ~: 3 jog 4 lope, trot
make a ~ at: 6 tackle 7 attempt 9 undertake
off: 2 go 3 fly, hie 4 bolt, flee, gone, skip 5 drain, elope, leave, print, split 6 escape 7 abscond 8 chase out, clear out, slip away 9 enumerate 10 break loose, mimeograph
off at the mouth: 3 gab, yak 4 blab 6 babble, jabber 7 blather, blether
off the page: 5 bleed
off with: 4 lift, take 5 heist, pinch, poach, steal, swipe 6 abduct, hijack, kidnap, pilfer, snatch, thieve 7 plunder, purloin 10 spirit away
on: 3 gab, yak, yap 4 talk 5 prate 6 rattle 7 chatter, maunder 8 continue
on the ~: 7 fleeing, hastily, in a rush, in haste, quickly, swiftly 8 escaping, in flight, speedily 9 hurriedly
out: 3 end 4 skip, stop 5 cease, dry up, end up, lapse, spill, use up 6 defect, elapse, escape, expire, finish, lapsed, wind up 7 deplete, exhaust, expired 8 conclude, finish up, jump bail 9 dissipate, terminate
(out): 4 give 5 peter
out of: 4 lack 5 use up 7 exhaust
out of gas: 3 sag 4 drop, flag, fold, tire, yawn 5 stall, weary 6 fizzle 7 dwindle, poop out 8 collapse, overwork
out of town: 4 oust 5 eject 6 depose, remove, unseat 7 cashier, drum out, kick out 9 overthrow
out on: 4 jilt, quit 6 desert 7 abandon, forsake 8 forswear 9 foreswear 10 go away from
over: 4 brim, echo, gush, lick, pass 5 recap, spill 6 exceed, repeat, review 7 do again, iterate, surpass, trample 8 go beyond 9 summarize
ragged: 7 exhaust
rampant: 4 rage, rant, rave 5 erupt, freak, storm 7 explode 8 freak out 9 go berserk 10 hit the roof
reconnaissance: 3 spy 6 patrol, survey 7 bird-dog
rings around: 4 best 5 outdo 7 surpass
riot: 4 rage 6 abound, overdo 7 rampage 9 luxuriate
rum: 7 bootleg
scared: 5 panic 10 chicken out
smoothly: 3 hum 4 purr 7 prosper
the show: 4 rule 6 direct, manage 7 oversee 8 dominate 9 supervise 10 administer
things: 4 lead 5 reign, steer
through: 3 reh., use 4 blow, leaf, lose, scan, skim, stab 5 spear, spend, use up, waste 6 empale, expend, finish, impale, infest, lavish, misuse, pierce, rattle, review 7 consume, exhaust, recount 8 look over, practice, rehearse, squander, transfix 9 dissipate, throw away 10 gamble away
to: 4 cost 5 reach, total
together: 3 mix 4 meld 5 blend, merge, unite 6 mingle 7 combine 8 intermix 9 integrate
trial ~: 4 test 5 trial, whirl 10 experiment
up: 3 sew 5 amass, incur, raise 6 stitch 7 magnify 8 increase 10 accumulate
up the flagpole: 5 raise
wild: 4 rage, riot 7 rampage 8 cut loose 9 go berserk
(with): 3 mix 6 hobnob, mingle 7 consort 9 associate, socialize 10 fraternize
words together: 6 garble, mumble
run __: 3 off, out 4 amok, away, down, into, over, riot, wild 5 after, along, amuck, out of, out on, short 6 across, scared 7 against, through
run __ around: 5 rings
run __ gas: 5 out of
run __ ground: 5 to the
run __ in: 6 batted
run __ of: 3 out 5 afoul, short
run __ on: 3 out
run __ the clock: 3 out
run __ the ground: 4 into
run __ with: 3 off 4 away
run-__-mill: 5 of-the
__ run: 3 dry, end, ice, ski 4 back, bomb, dead, home, long, milk 5 on the, press, print, split, trial 6 cattle, double, earned 7 bombing, chicken
__-run: 4 long 5 after, short
Run __, Run Deep: 6 Silent
Run __ Your Life: 3 for
Run, __, run!: 4 Spot
Run-__: 3 D.M.C. 6 Around
__ Run: 4 Bull 5 Trial 6 Logan's
__, Run: 6 Rabbit
run a __ ship: 5 tight
runabout: 4 auto, boat 5 craft
runagate: 5 nomad, rover 6 roamer 7 drifter, rambler 8 gadabout, vagabond, wanderer, wayfarer 9 itinerant, sojourner, transient
runaround: 5 delay, dodge, hedge 6 bypass 7 evasion 8 sidestep 9 avoidance
Runaround Sue (1961 song) artist: Dion
__ run average: 6 earned
runaway: 4 wild 6 bolter, truant 7 at large, escapee 8 deserter, forsaker, fugitive, offender, renegade 9 absconder 10 delinquent, lawbreaker, on the loose
of rhyme: 4 dish 5 spoon
Runaway Bride (1999 film)
cast: Joan Cusack, Hector Elizondo, Richard Gere, Julia Roberts
cat: 7 Italics
director: Garry Marshall
dog: 7 Skipper
Run Away Child, Running Wild (1969 song) artist: Temptations
Runaway (song) artist: Del Shannon
artist: Janet Jackson
Runaway Train (1985 film)
cast: Rebecca De Mornay, Eric Roberts, Jon Voight
Runaway Train (1993 song) artist: Soul Asylum

__ Run Baker: 4 Home
runcible spoon: 7 utensil
feature: 4 tine 5 prong
Runciman, Steven: 6 writer 7 British 9 historian
Rundgren, Todd: 6 singer
song: Hello It's Me (1973)
I Saw the Light (1972)
Rundi home: 5 Congo 6 Africa 7 Burundi
rundle: 4 rung, step
Run-D.M.C.
genre: 3 rap
members: Simmons, McDaniels
song: Down with the King (1993)
Walk This Way (1986)
rundown: 5 brief, recap 6 précis, report, résumé, review, sketch 7 account, outline, summary 8 briefing, scenario, synopsis 9 statement
dwelling: 4 dive, slum 5 hovel
give the ~: 6 fill in, inform, report, update 7 apprise
run-down: 3 old 4 drab, mean, sick, weak, worn 5 dingy, dumpy, mangy, ratty, seamy, seedy, tacky, tired, weary 6 ailing, beat-up, crumby, crummy, grungy, mangey, peaked, shabby, shoddy, sickly, sleazy, used up 7 drained, rickety, scruffy, squalid, worn-out 8 below par, decrepit, derelict, desolate, fatigued, forsaken, tattered, timeworn, untended 9 abandoned, crumbling, enervated, exhausted, neglected 10 in bad shape, on the ropes, ramshackle, threadbare, uncared-for
area: 4 slum 5 slurb 7 skid row
dwelling: 4 dump 5 hovel
rune: 4 poem, rime 5 rhyme, verse 6 letter
letter: 3 edh
Runeberg, Johan: 4 poet 7 Finnish
Run for the Sun (1956 film)
cast: Jane Greer, Trevor Howard, Richard Widmark
Run for Your Life (NBC drama) cast: Ben Gazzara (Paul Bryan)
rung: 3 bar, rod 4 step 5 level, spoke, stage, stave, tread 6 degree, rundle 10 crosspiece
runic: 7 magical, obscure 8 mystical
run-in: 3 row 4 tiff, to-do 5 brush, clash, fight, set-to 6 dustup, fracas, hassle, tussle 7 contest, dispute, quarrel 8 argument, conflict, skirmish 9 encounter, imbroglio 10 falling-out
run into the __: 6 ground
runlet: 5 brook 6 stream
run like __: 5 a deer
__-run movie: 5 first
runnel: 4 race, rill 5 creek, rille 6 stream 9 streamlet
runner: 3 Coe, rug, ski 4 skee, Tyus 5 Flo-Jo, Hayes, Keino, Lewis, loper, miler, Nurmi, Ovett, Owens, racer, scout 6 bearer, Benoit, Bikila, carpet, Devers 7 Ashford, athlete, carrier, courier, entrant, harrier, hurdler, nominee, Rudolph, Shorter, Zátopek 8 Bob Hayes, Kip Keino, sprinter 9 candidate, Carl Lewis, messenger 10 Gail Devers, Jesse Owens, Joan Benoit, Paavo Nurmi, Steve Ovett, Wyomia Tyus
British ~: 3 Coe 5 Ovett 10 Steve Ovett
concern: 4 pace
Czech ~: 7 Zátopek
distance ~: 5 miler 10 marathoner
downhill ~: 3 ski 4 skee 5 skier
Ethiopian ~: 6 Bikila
Finnish ~: 5 Nurmi 10 Paavo Nurmi
goal: 4 tape
Kenyan ~: 5 Keino 8 Kip Keino
put out a ~: 3 tag
starter: 3 gun, rum 4 fore, race, road 5 front
unit: 3 lap 4 mile, yard 5 meter 9 kilometer
__ runner: 3 art 4 base, blue, draw 5 front, joint, pinch 7 rainbow, scarlet, stretch
__ Runner: 4 Road 5 Blade 6 Indian
runners: 5 field, slate
carry it: 4 sled
of song: 4 mice
__ Runner, The: 6 Indian
runner-up: 5 loser 6 second
__ Runneth Over: 5 My Cup
Runnin' Down a Dream (1989 song) artist: Tom Petty
running: 4 live, on TV 5 alive, fluid, going, sport 6 active, flight, liquid, usable 7 cursive, flowing, useable, working 8 handling, straight, unbroken 9 continual, direction, incessant, operation, operative 10 continuous, management
a fever: 3 ill 4 sick 6 ailing, unwell 9 bedridden 10 indisposed
combining form: 4 drom- 5 -drome, dromo- 7 -dromous
hot and cold: 4 torn 7 not sure 8 hesitant, waffling, wavering 9 equivocal, uncertain, undecided, unsettled 10 ambivalent, indecisive, irresolute, of two minds, on the fence
in ballet: 5 couru
in the ~: 8 eligible 9 qualified
late: 5 tardy 6 behind, held up, hung up 7 delayed, overdue 8 detained 10 unpunctual
mate: 2 VP 4 veep 6 veepee
over: 4 full 5 awash, flush, laden 6 jammed 7 brimful, copious, crammed, crowded, profuse, replete, stuffed, teeming 8 brimming, bursting 9 bounteous, chock-full, plenteous, plentiful 10 voluminous
partner: 3 off
place: 4 oval 5 track
smoothly: 6 in sync
still in the ~: 5 alive
stop ~: 4 fail 6 unplug 7 conk out, go kaput, turn off 8 shut down 9 break down
together: 6 branch, feeder 7 joining, meeting 8 blending, mingling 9 confluent, tributary 10 concurrent
wild: 7 haywire
running __: 3 fix, gag 4 back, bond, gaff, gear, hand, head, joke, knot, mate, pine, room, shoe, text, time 5 board, light, start, story, title 6 myrtle, rhythm, stitch 7 English, rigging
running __ jump: 5 broad
Running __: 3 Dog 4 Bear, Wild 6 Rebels, Scared
__ Running: 4 Come 6 Silent
Running Bear (1959 song) artist: Johnny Preston
Running Dog author: Don DeLillo
running man: 5 dance
Running Man, The: 4 film 5 novel
author: Richard Bachman (Stephen King)
cast: Maria Conchita Alonso, Richard Dawson, Yaphet Kotto, Arnold Schwarzenegger
director: Paul Michael Glaser
Running Man, The (1963 film)
cast: Alan Bates, Laurence Harvey, Lee Remick
director: Carol Reed

Running on Empty (1988 film)
cast: Judd Hirsch, Christine Lahti, River Phoenix
director: Sidney Lumet
Running Rebels, The: 4 UNLV
__ Runnings: 4 Cool
Running Scared (1961 song) artist: Roy Orbison
Running Wild (1973 film)
cast: Lloyd Bridges, Pat Hingle, Dina Merrill
Running with the Night (1983 song) artist: Lionel Richie
Runnin' Rebels: 4 UNLV
runny: 4 thin, weak 5 fluid, soupy, unset 6 liquid, watery
not ~: 3 set 5 solid
Runnymede: 6 meadow
document: 10 Magna Carta
locale: 6 Surrey 7 England
run-of-__: 5 paper 7 the-mill
runoff __: 7 primary
runoff site: 4 eave, roof
run-of-the-mill: 4 dull, so-so 5 banal, plain, stock, trite, usual, vapid 6 common, medium, normal 7 average, general, generic, regular, routine, same old 8 everyday, familiar, frequent, mediocre, middling, ordinary, standard 9 generical, tolerable 10 dullsville
run one's __ over: 4 eyes
run out of __: 3 gas
run out the __: 5 clock
Run River author: Joan Didion
Run Silent, Run Deep (1958 film)
cast: Clark Gable, Burt Lancaster, Jack Warden
director: Robert Wise
__ Runs Through It, A: 5 River
runt: 3 lad, pup 4 punk 5 dwarf, puppy, scrub 6 midget, peewee, shrimp 8 half-pint 9 pipsqueak
run the __: 4 risk, show
run-through: 4 test 5 drill 9 rehearsal
run to __: 4 seed 5 earth
Run to Him (1961 song) artist: Bobby Vee
run to the __: 6 ground
Run to You (1984 song) artist: Bryan Adams
runty: 4 puny 5 small 7 stunted 8 pint-size, sawed-off
run up __: 4 a tab
runway: 5 strip 6 tarmac 7 landing
hit the ~: 3 lit 4 alit, land 6 alight
move on the ~: 4 taxi
work on the ~: 4 pave 6 repave
Run with the __ and hunt...: 4 Hare
Runyon, Damon: 6 author, writer
work: Blue Plate Special
Guys and Dolls
rupee: 4 coin 5 money
100 ~s: 4 lakh
fraction: 4 pice 5 paisa
ten million ~ s: 5 crore
Rupert: 6 Brooke, Holmes 7 Everett, Murdoch
Rupp, Adolph: 5 coach
milieu: 5 court
org.: 3 NBA
sport: 10 basketball
rupture: 4 feud, open, rent, rift, rive, tear 5 break, burst, clash, crack, erupt, sever, split 6 breach, divide, schism, sunder 7 disrupt, divorce, fissure, opening, shatter, split-up 8 disunion, division, fracture, puncture, separate 10 come undone, falling-out, separation
rural: 4 calm, farm, hick 6 rustic, silvan, sylvan 7 bucolic, country, georgic 8 agrarian, Arcadian, farmlike, outlying, pastoral 9 agronomic, backwoods, bucolical 10 provincial
addr.: 3 RFD
agcy.: 3 FCA, TVA
area: 7 boonies, country 9 backwoods
club: 3 FFA 5 four H
crossing: 5 stile
not ~: 5 civic, urban 9 municipal
road: 2 ln. 4 lane
sight: 3 inn 4 farm, well 5 field
structure: 3 pen, sty 4 barn, shed, silo 5 fence 9 farmhouse
rural __: 4 dean 5 route
rural __ delivery: 4 free
R.U.R. author: Karel Capek
character: 4 Gall 5 Domin 6 Helena, Primus 7 Alquist
language: 5 Czech
machine: 5 robot
__ R Us: 4 Toys
rusa: 4 deer
Rusalka: 5 opera
composer: 6 Dvorák
ruse: 3 jig 4 flam, game, hoax, juke, plot, ploy, sham, trap, wile 5 angle, blind, bluff, craft, dodge, feint, fraud, guile, put-on, shift, stunt, trick, twist 6 deceit, device, dupery, gambit, humbug, scheme, switch 7 chicane, evasion, gimmick, sleight, snow job, swindle 8 artifice, game plan, intrigue, maneuver, pretense, scenario 9 booby trap, chicanery, curveball, deception, imposture, stratagem 10 red herring, subterfuge
Ruse: 4 city, town
locale: 8 Bulgaria
rush: 3 fly, hie, rip, run, woo, zip 4 bolt, dart, dash, flit, flow, flux, gush, gust, leap, pelt, pile, pour, push, race, reed, scud, tear, tide, whiz, zoom 5 blitz, flood, haste, hasty, hurry, lunge, panic, plant, press, quick, rapid, scoot, sedge, shoot, sough, spate, speed, spirt, spurt, storm, surge, swash, swoop, whirl, whisk 6 action, attack, barrel, bustle, careen, career, charge, course, deluge, flurry, gallop, hasten, hurtle, hustle, influx, move it, plunge, pursue, rocket, scurry, sprint, streak, stream, thrash, thrill, urgent, whoosh 7 assault, besiege, dash off, floor it, hop to it, hotfoot, hurried, hurry-up, quicken, scamper, speed up, torrent, urgency 8 celerity, expedite, gang up on, hightail, outbreak, overcome, pressure, rapidity, scramble, step on it 9 avalanche, hastiness, horsetail, hotfoot it, make haste, onslaught, quickness, shake a leg, skedaddle 10 accelerate, burn rubber, get a move on, get hopping, go pell-mell, go whole hog, hightail it, lose no time, make tracks
give the bum's ~ to: 4 boot, oust 6 bounce 7 boot out, cast out, kick out, turn out 8 throw out 9 chase away
in: 5 enter 6 arrive
in a ~: 7 fleeing, hastily, quickly, rapidly, swiftly 8 escaping, on the run, speedily 9 hurriedly
mad ~: 4 dash 5 furor, hurry, panic 6 bustle, frenzy, plunge, scurry 7 ferment, scamper, turmoil 8 outburst, stampede
milieu: 3 bog, fen 5 marsh, swamp 7 wetland
together: 5 bunch, swarm 6 stream, throng 7 cluster 10 congregate
rush __: 4 hour 6 candle
__ rush: 3 in a 4 bum's, gold 5 Dutch
Rush: 7 Barbara 8 Geoffrey, Limbaugh 9 Merrillee
Rush!: 4 ASAP, stat 6 pronto
Rush and the Turnabouts, Merrillee song: Angel of the Morning (1968)
Rush, Barbara: 7 actress
film: Bigger Than Life (1956)
Captain Lightfoot (1955)
Flaming Feather (1951)
It Came From Outer Space (1953)
Magnificent Obsession (1954)
Robin and the Seven Hoods (1964)
When Worlds Collide (1951)
The Young Philadelphians (1959)
Rushdie, Salman: 6 critic, Indian, writer
work: Midnight's Children
Satanic Verses
rushed: 5 hasty 6 hectic 7 hurried 8 headlong
rusher, NFL: 2 FB 8 fullback
rushes, covered with: 5 sedgy
Rush, Geoffrey: 5 actor
film: Frida (2002)
Lantana (2001)
Les Misérables (1998)
Quills (2000)
Shakespeare in Love (1998)
Shine (1996, AA)
The Tailor of Panama (2001)
rush hour
component: 3 car 4 auto
problem: 3 jam 5 tie up 7 traffic
speed: 5 crawl
train: 3 exp. 7 express
Rush Hour (1998 film)
cast: Jackie Chan, Elizabeth Peña, Chris Tucker, Tom Wilkinson
director: Brett Ratner
Rush Hour 2 (2001 film)
cast: Jackie Chan, John Lone, Chris Tucker
director: Brett Ratner
rush-hour speed: 5 creep
__ Rush In: 5 Fools
rushing: 5 sough 6 abrupt 7 hurried 8 headlong 9 impetuous
sound: 5 whish 6 whoosh
Rushing: 5 Jimmy
Rushmore: 5 Mount
face: 7 Lincoln 9 Jefferson, Roosevelt 10 Washington
locale: 4 S. Dak.
Rushmore (1998 film)
cast: Seymour Cassel, Bill Murray, Jason Schwartzman, Olivia Williams
director: Wes Anderson
Rush, Rush (1991 song) artist: Paula Abdul
__ Rush, The: 4 Gold
Rusie, Amos: 5 Giant 6 hurler 7 pitcher
rusk: 5 bread, toast 8 zwieback
Rusk: 4 Dean
Ruska, Ernst: 8 Nobelist 9 physicist, scientist
Ruskin, John: 6 critic, writer 7 British
work: Deucalion
Modern Painters
Proserpina
Sesame and Lilies
The Seven Lamps of Architecture
The Stones of Venice
Russ: 3 Tim 5 Meyer 6 Morgan 7 Columbo, Tamblyn 8 Hamilton
Russ.: 4 lang.
neighbor of ~: 3 Est., Fin., Ukr
see also Russia
Russel: 6 Crouse
Russell: 3 Ken 4 Andy, Bill, Gail, Jane, John, Keri, Kurt, Leon, Mark, peak 5 Baker, Bobby, Crowe, Hulse, mount, Myers, rouse 6 Brenda, Harold, Nipsey 7 Johnson, Markert, Theresa 8 Bertrand, mountain, Rosalind
locale: 10 California
2000: 5 index 10 stock index
Russell __ College: 4 Sage
Russell, Bertrand: 6 writer 7 British 8 Nobelist, reformer 11 philosopher
work: The ABC of Relativity
Common Sense and Nuclear Warfare
Has Man a Future?
A History of Western Philosophy
Religion and Science
Unarmed Victory
Russell, Bill
milieu: 5 court
org.: 3 NBA
sport: 10 basketball
Russell, Gail: 7 actress
film: Angel and the Badman (1947)
Our Hearts Were Young and Gay (1944)
Salty O'Rourke (1945)
Seven Men From Now (1956)
Russell, Harold Oscar: The Best Years of Our Lives
Russell, Jane: 7 actress
film: Gentlemen Prefer Blondes (1953)
His Kind of Woman (1951)
The Outlaw (1943)
The Paleface (1948)
Son of Paleface (1952)
in The Outlaw: 3 Rio
Russell, Ken: 8 director
film: Altered States (1980)
Billion Dollar Brain (1967)
The Boy Friend (1971)
The Devils (1971)
Savage Messiah (1972)
Tommy (1975)
Women in Love (1969)
Russell, Kurt: 5 actor
film: 3000 Miles to Graceland (2001)
Backdraft (1991)
The Best of Times (1986)
Escape From New York (1981)
Executive Decision (1996)
Overboard (1987)
Silkwood (1983)
Stargate (1994)
Tequila Sunrise (1988)
Tombstone (1993)
Unlawful Entry (1992)
Used Cars (1980)
Vanilla Sky (2001)
role: 4 Earp 9 Wyatt Earp
__ Russell Lowell: 5 James
Russell, Mark: 8 humorist, satirist
instrument: 5 piano
Russell, Rosalind: 7 actress
film: Auntie Mame (1958)
The Citadel (1938)
Craig's Wife (1936)
The Guilt of Janet Ames (1947)
Gypsy (1962)
Hired Wife (1940)
His Girl Friday (1940)
Night Must Fall (1937)
Picnic (1955)
Rosie! (1967)
Roughly Speaking (1945)
Sister Kenny (1946)
Take a Letter, Darling (1942)
This Thing Called Love (1941)
Trouble for Two (1936)
A Woman of Distinction (1950)
The Women (1939)
role: 4 Mame
__ Russell terrier: 4 Jack
Russell, Theresa: 7 actress
film: The Believer (2002)
Black Widow (1987)
Impulse (1990)
Insignificance (1985)
Straight Time (1978)
Wild Things (1998)
spouse: Nicolas Roeg
Russellville: 4 city, town
locale: 8 Arkansas

Russell, William Howard: 6 writer 7 British 10 journalist
__ Russel Wallace: 6 Alfred
russet: 3 red 4 rust 5 apple, brown, color 6 veggie 7 reddish 9 vegetable, yellowish
relative: 3 bay, dun, tan 4 bole, crab, ecru, fawn, foxy, Gala, Lodi, nude, Rome, seal 5 amber, beige, camel, cocoa, hazel, khaki, mocha, Mutsu, sepia, tawny, umber 6 auburn, bister, bistre, bronze, coffee, copper, Empire, ginger, Ida Red, medlar, Pippin, sienna, sorrel, suntan, walnut 7 Baldwin, biscuit, Bramley, caramel, costard, dogwood, Freedom, Liberty, Spartan, Wealthy, Winesap 8 chestnut, cinnamon, Cortland, Jonathan, mahogany, McIntosh 9 butternut, chocolate 10 Rome Beauty
Russia: 6 nation 7 country
aircraft: 3 MiG
antelope: 5 saiga
auto: 3 Zil 4 Lada
ballet: 5 Kirov 7 Bolshoi
ballet dancer: 5 Lifar 7 Massine, Nureyev, Pavlova, Ulanova 8 Danilova, Nijinsky 11 Baryshnikov, Youskevitch
bass: 9 Chaliapin
bay: 5 Dvina, Onega
beer: 5 kvass, quass
bovine: 7 Istoben
capital: 6 Moscow
cellist: 12 Rostropovich
chemist: 9 Mendeleev
city: 3 Ufa 4 Omsk, Orel, Orsk, Perm, Tula 5 Kazan, Penza, Serov, Sochi, Tomsk 6 Kaluga, Moscow, Rostov, Samara 7 Irkutsk, Ulan-Ude
collective: 5 artel
commune: 3 mir
composer: 3 Cui 6 Glière, Glinka 7 Arensky, Borodin 8 César Cui 9 Prokofiev 10 Stravinsky 11 Moussorgsky 12 Shostakovich 19 Scriabin. Tchaikovsky
conductor: 8 Smallens 9 Goldovsky, Markevich 11 Kostelanetz 12 Koussevitzky
council: 4 Duma
country home: 5 dacha 6 datcha
czar: 4 Ivan, Paul 5 Ivan V, Paul I, Peter 6 Feodor, Ivan IV, Ivan VI, Peter I 7 Feodor I, Ivan III, Peter II, Romanov 8 Nicholas, Peter III 9 Alexander 10 Alexander I
distance unit: 5 verst 6 verste, werste
dog: 6 borzoi
drink: 5 vodka
dry measure: 3 lof
emperor: 4 czar, tsar, tzar
epic hero: 4 Igor
figure skater: 5 Kulik 9 Ilia Kulik
fur: 5 sable
girl's nickname: 5 Tasha
gulf: 8 Taganrog
gymnast: 6 Korbut 10 Olga Korbut
hemp: 4 rine
high jumper: 6 Brumel
John, in ~: 4 Ivan
journalist: 8 Sloukhin
lake: 5 Onega 6 Ladoga, Peipus
legislature: 4 Duma
log house: 4 isba, izba
money: 5 kopec, kopek, ruble 6 copeck, kopeck, rouble
mountain: 4 Alai 5 Altai, Sayan, Urals 6 Anadir, Elbrus, Elbruz, Kolyma 8 Caucasus
native: 5 Osset 6 Ossete
neighbor: 5 China 6 Latvia, Norway, Poland 7 Belarus, Estonia, Finland, Georgia, Ukraine 8 Mongolia 9 Lithuania 10 Azerbaijan, Kazakhstan, North Korea
Nobelist in Chemistry: 7 Semenov
Nobelist in Economics: 11 Kantorovich
Nobelist in Literature: 5 Bunin 7 Brodsky 9 Pasternak, Sholokhov 12 Solzhenitsyn
Nobelist in Medicine: 6 Pavlov
Nobelist in Peace: 8 Sakharov 9 Gorbachev
Nobelist in Physics: 4 Tamm 5 Basov, Frank 6 Landau 7 Alferov, Kapitsa 9 Cherenkov, Prokhorov
noble: 5 boyar 6 boyard
once: 4 USSR
painter: 7 Chagall 9 Kandinsky
pancake: 5 blini, bliny
peasant: 5 mujik
people: 4 Mari
pianist: 6 Gilels 9 Ashkenazy
place-name suffix: 4 grad
poet: 3 Fet 4 Bely, Blok 5 Bedny, Bunin 6 Esenin 7 Nabokov, Sologub 8 Nekrasov, Sloukhin 9 Akhmatova, Pasternak, Zhukovsky 10 Mayakovsky, Zabolotsky 11 Akhmadulina, Yevtushenko
pole vaulter: 5 Bubka
port: 4 Omsk 7 Yakutsk 8 Murmansk 9 Archangel, Leningrad
revolutionary: 3 Red 5 Lenin 9 Bolshevik, Menshevik
river: 3 Don, Oka, Oma 4 Lena, Neva, Seim, Seym, Yana 5 Onega, Tobol 6 Angara, Kolima, Kolyma
rodent: 6 gerbil
saint: 6 Nevski 8 Vladimir
scientist: 9 Mendeleev
sea: 4 Aral, Azov 5 White 6 Sivash 7 Okhotsk
secret police: 4 OGPU
spacecraft: 3 Mir 5 Lunik, Soyuz 6 Vostok 7 Sputnik, Voskhod
spy org.: 3 KGB
symbol: 4 bear
tennis pro: 10 Kournikova
tent: 4 yurt
typical ~: 4 Ivan
village: 3 mir
violinist: 5 Elman 8 Milstein, Oistrakh 9 Zimbalist
volcano: 5 Alaid 6 Tiatia 8 Karymsky 9 Tolbachik
weight: 4 pood
writer: 4 Grin 5 Babel, Gogol, Gorky 6 Daniel, Ivanov, Krylov, Kuprin, Olesha, Panova, Yashin 7 Aksakov, Amalrik, Bryusov, Chekhov, Fadayev, Gladkov, Katayev, Nabokov, Pushkin, Rozanov, Sologub, Tolstoy 8 Aksyonov, Andreyev, Bulgakov, Karamzin, Nekrasov, Saltykov, Sloukhin, Turgenev, Zamyatin 9 Goncharov, Sholokhov, Sinyavsky 10 Zoshchenko 11 Aleshkovsky, Dostoyevsky 12 Solzhenitsyn
__ Russia: 5 White 6 Little, Soviet
Russia House, The (1990 film)
cast: Sean Connery, Michelle Pfeiffer, Roy Scheider
director: Fred Schepisi
Russian: 8 dressing, language
neighbor: 4 Esth, Finn, Pole 6 Korean 7 Chinese, Latvian 8 Estonian, Georgian 9 Mongolian, Norwegian, Ukrainian 10 Lithuanian
no, in ~: 4 nyet
peace, in ~: 3 mir
yes, in ~: 2 da
Russian __: 5 olive 6 Church, Empire 7 thistle 8 dressing
__ Russian: 3 Old 5 Black, Great 6 Little
Russian America capital: 5 Sitka
Russian Bear ingredient: 5 vodka
Russian Blue: 3 cat 5 felid 6 feline
Russian Girl, The author: Kingsley Amis
Russian Overture composer: 9 Prokofiev
Russians __ Coming..., The: 3 Are
__ Russia $1200: 4 I Owe
__ Russia Today: 6 Inside
__ Russia With Love: 4 From
Russlan and Ludmilla composer: 6 Glinka
Russo-Japanese __: 3 War
Russo, Rene: 7 actress
film: The Adventures of Rocky and Bullwinkle (2000)
Big Trouble (2002)
Get Shorty (1995)
In the Line of Fire (1993)
Lethal Weapon 3 (1992)
Lethal Weapon 4 (1998)
Outbreak (1995)
Ransom (1996)
Showtime (2002)
The Thomas Crown Affair (1999)
Tin Cup (1996)
__-Russo War: 5 Finno
rust: 3 eat, red, rot 4 film, mold 5 brown, color, decay, eat at, erode, oxide 6 auburn, blight, fungus, patina, patine, redden, russet, wither, yellow 7 coating, corrode, crumble, eat away, go stale, go to pot, oxidize, reddish, tarnish 8 go to seed, stagnate 9 corrosion, iron oxide, lie fallow, oxidation, yellowish 10 brown shade, degenerate
ender: 5 proof
relative: 4 buff, corn, gold, lime, rose, ruby, sand, wine 5 blond, brass, brick, coral, cream, flaxy, grape, lemon, maize, ocher, ochre, peach, poppy, sandy, straw 6 blonde, canary, cerise, chammy, cherry, citron, claret, crocus, flaxen, garnet, maroon, shammy, shamoy 7 apricot, carmine, chamois, citrine, crimson, fuchsia, jasmine, magenta, mustard, nankeen, old gold, pimento, saffron, scarlet, sultana, vermeil, xanthic 8 amaranth, cardinal, daffodil, dubonnet, geranium, primrose, rubicund 9 carnation, champagne, cranberry, goldenrod, jessamine, vermilion 10 strawberry
rust __: 4 belt, mite 5 joint
rust-__: 7 colored, through
__ rust: 4 iron, leaf, stem 5 black, crown, wheat, white 6 orange, stripe, yellow 7 blister
Rustavi: 4 city, town
locale: 7 Georgia
rustic: 4 boor, hick, hind, homy, rube, rude 5 crude, homey, plain, rough, rural, yokel 6 coarse, farmer, folksy, gaffer, gauche, silvan, simple, sylvan 7 austere, boorish, bucolic, bumpkin, country, hayseed, loutish, outdoor, peasant, plowboy, redneck, uncouth 8 agrarian, Arcadian, churlish, farmlike, homemade, homespun, pastoral 9 backwoods, bucolical, hillbilly 10 clodhopper, provincial, unpolished
fellow: 5 swain
lodging: 3 inn 4 camp 5 B and B
poem: 4 idyl 5 idyll
structure: 4 barn 5 cabin, lodge
way: 4 lane
rustle: 4 sigh, stir 5 filch, sough, speed, steal, swipe, swish 6 gather, murmur, patter, ripple, thieve 7 crackle, crinkle, flutter, ransack, whisper 9 crepitate
up: 3 get 4 find 5 scout 6 gather
rustler: 5 crook, thief 6 bandit, outlaw, robber 7 stealer 8 criminal, marauder 9 larcenist, plunderer 10 bushranger
target: 4 herd 6 cattle
rustling: 5 sough, swish, theft 6 rustle 8 thievery
sound: 5 swish
Ruston: 4 city, town
athletes: 8 Bulldogs
locale: 9 Louisiana
school: 3 LTU
rustproof coating: 4 zinc
rusty: 3 old, red 4 soft, weak 5 stale, stiff 6 yellow 7 decayed, reddish 8 corroded, impaired, oxidized, sluggish 9 deficient, neglected, unpliable, yellowish 10 out of shape
relative: 4 buff, corn, gold, lime, rose, ruby, sand, wine 5 blond, brass, brick, coral, cream, flaxy, grape, lemon, maize, ocher, ochre, peach, poppy, sandy, straw 6 blonde, canary, cerise, chammy, cherry, citron, claret, crocus, flaxen, garnet, maroon, shammy, shamoy 7 apricot, carmine, chamois, citrine, crimson, fuchsia, jasmine, magenta, mustard, nankeen, old gold, pimento, saffron, scarlet, sultana, vermeil, xanthic 8 amaranth, cardinal, daffodil, dubonnet, geranium, primrose, rubicund 9 carnation, champagne, cranberry, goldenrod, jessamine, vermilion 10 strawberry
Rusty: 5 Hamer, Staub 6 Draper 8 Cundieff
rut: 3 job 5 ditch, gouge, grind, habit, slump, track, trail 6 custom, furrow, groove, hollow, trench 7 channel, pattern, pothole, rat race, routine 8 flatness, monotony 9 treadmill 10 daily grind
in a ~: 5 bored, stuck 8 stagnant 10 bogged down, stultified, uncreative
__ rut: 3 in a
Rutger: 5 Hauer
in English: 5 Roger
Rutgers
conference: 7 Big East
locale: 9 New Jersey
ruth: 4 pity 5 heart, mercy 6 lenity, pardon 7 ache for, console, empathy, feel for 8 bleed for, clemency, go easy on, kindness, lenience, sympathy 9 tolerance 10 compassion, humaneness, tenderness
Ruth: 2 Dr. 4 Babe 5 Buzzi, Orkin, Roman 6 Etting, Gordon, Hussey 7 McKenny, Rendell, slugger, Warrick 8 Ginsberg 10 Chatterton, Westheimer
follower: 6 Samuel
homeland: 4 Moab
husband of ~: 4 Boaz
mother-in-law of ~: 5 Naomi
preceder: 6 Judges
sister-in-law of ~: 5 Orpah
son of ~: 4 Obed
Ruth __ Ginsberg: 5 Bader
Ruth __ Jhabvala: 6 Prawer
__ Ruth: 4 Baby
Ruth, Babe: 6 George, Yankee 7 slugger 10 outfielder
rival: 4 Cobb 6 Gehrig, Ty Cobb 9 Lou Gehrig
stat: 3 HRs, RBI 6 homers
sultanate: 4 swat
topper: 5 Aaron
uniform number: 5 three

Ruth, Dr. subject: **3** sex
ruthenium: **5** metal **7** element
Rutherford: **3** Ann **5** Hayes, Kelly **6** Ernest **8** Margaret
concern: **4** atom
Rutherford, Ernest: **7** chemist **8** Nobelist **9** physicist, scientist
Rutherford, Margaret: **7** actress
film: Chimes at Midnight (1967)
The Mouse on the Moon (1963)
Murder Ahoy (1964)
Murder at the Gallop (1963)
Murder Most Foul (1965)
Murder, She Said (1961)
The V.I.P.s (1963, AA)
ruthful: **3** lax **4** easy, kind, mild, soft **5** loose **6** gentle, kindly **7** clement, sparing **8** flexible, laid-back, merciful, placable, tolerant **9** assuasive, compliant, easygoing, forgiving, indulgent, miserable **10** forbearing, permissive, unexacting
ruthless: **4** cold, grim, hard, mean **5** cruel, harsh, nasty, stern, stony, tough **6** animal, bitter, brutal, fierce, mortal, savage, stoney, unkind, wanton **7** beastly, callous, hurtful, inhuman, vicious **8** barbaric, fiendish, inhumane, pitiless, sadistic, vengeful **9** barbarian, barbarous, cutthroat, dog-eat-dog, ferocious, heartless, inclement, merciless, monstrous, murderous, truculent, unfeeling, unpitying **10** implacable, ironfisted, relentless, unmerciful, unyielding, vindictive
Ruthless (1948 film)
cast: Louis Hayward, Diana Lynn, Zachary Scott
director: Edgar G. Ulmer
ruthlessly: **4** hard **5** felly **9** viciously
ruthlessness: **5** venom **6** malice, rancor **7** cruelty, tyranny **8** coldness, ferocity, savagery, severity, violence **9** barbarism, brutality, depravity, despotism, harshness **10** inhumanity, oppression
Ruthless People (1986 film)
cast: Danny DeVito, Bette Midler, Judge Reinhold, Helen Slater
director: Jim Abrahams, David Zucker, Jerry Zucker
Ruth Prawer __: **8** Jhabvala
Ruth, Roy Del: **8** director
film: Blessed Event (1932)
Born to Dance (1936)
Broadway Melody of 1936 (1935)
DuBarry Was a Lady (1943)
Employees' Entrance (1933)
Folies Bergère (1935)
Kid Millions (1934)
Lady Killer (1933)
The Little Giant (1933)
The Maltese Falcon (1931)
On the Avenue (1937)
Thanks a Million (1935)
Topper Returns (1941)
Upperworld (1934)
Ruthville: **9** bleachers
rutile: **3** ore **7** mineral
synthetic ~: **7** titania
rutin: **8** vitamin P
Rutland: **4** city, town **6** county
locale: **7** England, Vermont
Rutledge: **3** Ann
Ruttan: **5** Susan
rutted: **5** bumpy, rough **8** potholed
ruvo __: **4** kale
Ruvuma: **5** river
locale: **8** Tanzania **10** Mozambique
Ruwenzori: **5** range **9** mountains
locale: **5** Congo **6** Africa, Uganda
Ruy __ chess opening: **5** Lopez
Ruy Blas Overture composer: **11** Mendelssohn
Ruy Díaz de Bivar: **3** Cid **5** El Cid
Ruzicka, Leopold: **7** chemist **8** Nobelist
RV: **6** camper **9** motor home, Winnebago
fuel: **3** LNG
haven: **3** KOA
park convenience: **6** hookup
park the ~: **6** encamp
part of ~: **3** rec., veh. **7** vehicle
R-V connectors: **3** STU
Rwanda: **6** nation **7** country
capital: **6** Kigali
lake: **4** Kivu
money: **5** franc
neighbor: **5** Congo **6** Uganda **7** Burundi **8** Tanzania
people: **4** Hutu, Tusi **5** Tussi, Tutsi **6** Watusi **7** Watutsi
Rx
abbr.: **2** cc. **3** alb., b.d.s., bib., cib., cuj., d.t.d., ead., gtt., liq., pil., p.r.n., q.i.d, sig., t.d.s., t.i.d., ung., vin. **4** agit., coch., elix., ferv., filt., garg., quat., quor., trid., ungt. **5** calef., emuls., qq. hor., quinq., utend.
amount: **4** dose **6** dosage
not needing an ~: **3** OTC
writer: **2** dr., GP, MD **3** doc **5** doser **6** doctor
writers org.: **3** AMA
Ry: **6** Cooder
rya: **3** rug **4** shag **6** carpet
Ryan: **3** Meg, Roz **4** Jeri **5** Irene, Nolan, O'Neal, Peggy **6** Robert, Sheila, Stiles **9** Cornelius, Phillippe
Ryan, Meg: **7** actress
film: City of Angels (1998)
Courage Under Fire (1996)
The Doors (1991)
Hanging Up (2000)
Innerspace (1987)
I.Q. (1994)
Joe Versus the Volcano (1990)
Kate and Leopold (2001)
Prelude to a Kiss (1992)
Proof of Life (2000)
Sleepless in Seattle (1993)
When a Man Loves a Woman (1994)
When Harry Met Sally ... (1989)
You've Got Mail (1998)
spouse: Dennis Quaid
Ryan, Nolan: **6** hurler **7** pitcher
once: **3** Met **5** Angel, Astro **6** Ranger
Ryan, Robert: **5** actor
film: About Mrs. Leslie (1954)
Act of Violence (1949)
Bad Day at Black Rock (1955)
Berlin Express (1948)
Billy Budd (1962)
The Boy With the Green Hair (1948)
Caught (1949)
Clash by Night (1952)
Crossfire (1947)
The Dirty Dozen (1967)
The Flying Leathernecks (1951)
God's Little Acre (1958)
The Iceman Cometh (1973)
King of Kings (1961)
Lawman (1971)
The Longest Day (1962)
Odds Against Tomorrow (1959)
On Dangerous Ground (1952)
The Professionals (1966)
The Racket (1951)
The Secret Fury (1950)
The Set-Up (1949)
The Wild Bunch (1969)
Ryan's __: **4** Hope
Ryan's daughter: **5** Tatum
Ryan's Daughter (1970 film)
cast: Trevor Howard, Leo McKern, Sarah Miles, John Mills, Robert Mitchum
director: David Lean
__ Ryan's Express: **3** Von
Ryan's Hope (ABC): **4** soap **9** soap opera
Rybinsk Reservoir site: **5** Volga
Ryde: **4** city, town
locale: **7** England
Rydell: **4** Mark **5** Bobby
Rydell, Bobby
born: Robert Ridarelli
song: The Cha-Cha-Cha (1962)
Forget Him (1963)
Kissin' Time (1959)
Swingin' School (1960)
Volare (1960)
We Got Love (1959)
Wild One (1960)
Rydell, Mark: **8** director
film: Cinderella Liberty (1973)
For the Boys (1991)
The Fox (1968)
On Golden Pond (1981)
The Reivers (1969)
The Rose (1979)
Ryder: **5** Mitch **6** Alfred, Winona
offering: **3** rig, van **5** truck
rival: **5** U-Haul
Ryder Cup: **6** trophy
sport: **4** golf
__ Ryder Open: **5** Doral
Ryder, Winona: **7** actress
film: The Age of Innocence (1993)
Bram Stoker's Dracula (1992)
Edward Scissorhands (1990)
Girl, Interrupted (1999)
Heathers (1989)
How to Make an American Quilt (1995)
Little Women (1994)
Mermaids (1990)
Night on Earth (1991)
Reality Bites (1994)
rye: **3** liq. **5** bread, drink, grain **6** cereal, liquor, whisky **7** whiskey **8** beverage
ender: **5** grass
grass: **6** darnel
mold: **5** ergot
partner: **3** ham
rye __: **5** bread, grass **6** whisky **7** whiskey
__ rye: **4** wild **5** ham on **6** Jewish
Rye: **4** city, town
locale: **7** New York
Ryeland: **5** sheep
Ryerson: **3** RPU **6** school
locale: **6** Canada **7** Ontario, Toronto
Ryle, Gilbert: **6** writer **7** British **11** philosopher
Ryle, Martin: **8** Nobelist **9** physicist, scientist **10** astronomer
Ryman Auditorium show: **4** Opry
Ryne: **5** Duren **8** Sandberg
ryokan: **3** inn **5** hotel **8** Japanese
Ryokan: **4** poet **8** Japanese
Rysy: **4** peak **5** mount **8** mountain
locale: **6** Europe, Poland
Ryukyus: **4** isls. **5** isles **7** islands
locale: **5** Japan
part: **4** Kume **5** Amami, Iheya **6** Kerama, Miyako, O-shima **7** Iishima, Okinawa **8** Iriomote, Ishigaki, Okierabu **9** Sakishima
port: **4** Naha
Ryun, Jim: **5** miler **6** runner

6 on a phone: 3 MNO
6th Day (2000 film), The
cast: Robert Duvall, Tony Goldwyn, Michael Rapaport, Arnold Schwarzenegger
director: Roger Spottiswoode
7-__: 6 Eleven
7 (1992 song) artist: Prince
7 Faces of Dr. Lao (1964 film)
cast: Barbara Eden, Arthur O'Connell, Tony Randall
director: George Pal
7 on a phone: 3 PRS
7th Voyage of Sinbad (1958 film), The
cast: Richard Eyer, Kathryn Grant, Kerwin Mathews
director: Nathan Juran
7UP: 9 soft drink
alternative: 3 TAB 4 Coke, Nehi 5 Fanta, Pepsi 6 Fresca, Sprite 8 Diet Rite, Dr Pepper 9 Canada Dry 10 Mello Yello, Royal Crown 11 Mountain Dew
16 Candles (1958 song) artist: Crests
__ 17: 6 Stalag
__ 60: 6 cobalt
60 Minutes (CBS news)
feature: 6 exposé
reporter: Ed Bradley
Steve Kroft
Dan Rather
Harry Reasoner
Andy Rooney
Morley Safer
Diane Sawyer
Lesley Stahl
Meredith Vieira
Mike Wallace
61* subject: 5 Maris
__ 66: 5 Route
__ '70s Show: 4 That
76er
rival: 3 Net, Sun 4 Buck, Bull, Hawk, Heat, Jazz, King, Spur 5 Knick, Laker, Magic, Pacer 6 Celtic, Hornet, Nugget, Piston, Raptor, Rocket, Wizard 7 Clipper, Grizzly, Warrior 8 Cavalier, Maverick 10 SuperSonic, Timberwolf
76ers: 4 five, team
org.: 3 NBA
sport: 10 basketball
__ '77: 7 Airport
77 Dream Songs author: John Berryman
77 Sunset Strip (ABC drama)
cast: Edd Byrnes (Kookie)
Roger Smith (Jeff Spencer)
Efrem Zimbalist Jr. (Stu Bailey)
restaurant: 5 Dino's
79 Park Avenue author: Harold Robbins
622 event: 6 hegira
704 Hauser star: 4 Amos
707: 3 jet
714
Badge ~ holder: 6 Friday
747: 3 jet
alternative: 6 Airbus
767: 3 jet
777: 3 jet
1776 (1972 film)
cast: William Daniels, Howard da Silva, Ken Howard
director: Peter H. Hunt
$64,000 Question, The (game show)
host: Hal March
s __: 5 quark
S: 3 dir. 4 elem., size 6 letter, sulfur 7 element
follower: 3 TUV 4 TUVW 5 TUVWX
in phonetic alphabet: 6 Sierra
mispronounce ~: 4 lisp
preceders: 3 PQR 4 OPQR 5 NOPQR
16 for ~: 4 at. no.
S __: 4 and L, star, wave 5 gauge, phase, sleep, twist
S __ 500: 4 and P
S __ Green Stamps: 4 and H
S __ Sam: 4 as in
S. __: 3 Afr., Sgt. 4 Amer.
__ 6: 5 Motel
S.A.: 4 cont.
country: 3 Arg., Bol., Col., Par., Uru. 4 Braz., Ecua. 5 Venez.
see also South America
Saab: 3 car 4 auto 7 Swedish 10 automobile
competitor: 5 Volvo
model: 4 Aero
Saale, city on the: 5 Halle
Saanich: 4 city, town
locale: 6 Canada
Saar: 5 basin, river
locale: 6 France 7 Germany
Saarinen, Eero: 7 Finnish 9 architect
Saarinen, Eliel: 7 Finnish 9 architect
Saatchi product: 3 ads
sabar: 4 drum
origin: 6 Africa
Sabatier, Paul: 7 chemist 8 Nobelist
Sabatini, Gabriela: 7 netster 9 tennis pro
Sábato, Ernesto: 6 author, writer 9 Argentine
Sabbath activity: 4 rest
sabbatical: 5 leave 6 hiatus 7 leisure 8 free time, vacation
sabbatical __: 4 year 5 leave
Sabbatical author: John Barth
__ Sabe: 4 Kemo
saber: 3 arm, saw 4 stab 5 blade, knife, sword
alternative: 4 épée, foil 6 rapier
deflect a ~: 5 parry
handle: 4 hilt
set-to: 4 duel
saber-__ tiger: 7 toothed
Saberhagen, Bret: 6 hurler 7 pitcher
Saberjet's erstwhile foe: 3 MiG
sabers: 8 weaponry
sabertooth: 3 cat 5 felid, tiger 6 feline
Sabik: 4 star
Sabin __: 7 vaccine
Sabin, Albert: 9 physician
contemporary: 4 Salk
Sabinas: 4 city, town 5 river
locale: 6 Mexico 8 Coahuila
Sabine: 4 cape, lake, peak 5 mount, river 8 mountain
Cape locale: 6 Canada 9 Ellesmere
Mount locale: 10 Antarctica
River/Lake locale: 5 Texas 9 Louisiana
Sabinian: 4 pope 7 pontiff
sable: 3 fur 4 dark 5 black, color 6 animal, weasel 9 pitch-dark 10 pitch-black
relative: 3 jet 4 inky, mink, onyx 5 ebony, fitch, otter, ratel, raven, skunk, sooty, stoat, tayra 6 badger, ermine, ferret, marten 7 foumart, polecat 8 carcajou, foulmart, kolinsky, muishond 9 wolverine
Sable: 3 car 4 auto, cape, Merc 7 Mercury 10 automobile
Sabon: 4 font 8 typeface
sabot: 4 clog, shoe 8 footwear 10 wooden shoe
ender: 3 age
sound: 4 clop
sabotage: 4 do in, harm 5 block, wreck 6 damage, hamper, hinder 7 destroy, disable, disrupt, subvert, take out, torpedo 8 mischief, obstruct, undercut 9 frustrate, treachery, undermine, vandalism, vandalize 10 demolition, disruption, subversion
Sabotage (1936 film)
cast: Oscar Homolka, John Loder, Sylvia Sidney
director: Alfred Hitchcock
saboteur: 5 enemy 9 ill-wisher 10 subversive
Saboteur (1942 film)
cast: Robert Cummings, Priscilla Lane, Norman Lloyd
director: Alfred Hitchcock
sabre: 5 sword
Sabre and Spurs composer: 5 Sousa
Sabre rival: 4 Blue, King, Star, Wild 5 Bruin, Devil, Flame, Flyer, Oiler, Shark 6 Canuck, Coyote, Ranger 7 Capital, Panther, Penguin, Red Wing, Senator 8 Canadien, Islander, Predator, Thrasher 9 Avalanche, Blackhawk, Hurricane, Lightning, Maple Leaf 10 Blue Jacket, Mighty Duck
Sabres: 3 six 4 team
home: 7 Buffalo
milieu: 3 ice 4 rink
org.: 3 NHL
sport: 6 hockey
Sabrina (1954 film)
cast: Humphrey Bogart, Audrey Hepburn, William Holden
director: Billy Wilder
Sabrina (1995 film)
cast: Harrison Ford, Greg Kinnear, Julia Ormond
director: Sydney Pollack
Sabrina the Teenage Witch (ABC sitcom)
cast: Beth Broderick (Zelda Spellman)
Melissa Joan Hart (Sabrina Spellman)
Caroline Rhea (Hilda Spellman)
cat: Salem
Sabu: 5 actor 6 Indian
film: Black Narcissus (1947)
Cobra Woman (1944)
Drums (1938)
Elephant Boy (1937)
Jungle Book (1942)
The Thief of Bagdad (1940)
sac: 3 wen 4 cyst 5 bursa, pouch, theca 7 bladder, blister, capsule, vesicle 8 follicle 9 container, marsupium
air ~: 8 alveolus
anatomical ~: 5 bursa
combining form: 3 asc- 4 asco-
fungus spore ~: 5 ascus 6 aecium
gland ~: 6 acinus
pollen ~: 5 theca
starter: 3 ovi
__ sac: 3 air 4 yolk 6 pollen
__-sac: 5 cul-de
Sac: 6 Indian 7 Amerind 9 Black Hawk
SAC
counterpart: 5 NORAD
headquarters: 5 Omaha
part: 3 Air 7 Command 9 Strategic
saccharin discoverer: Ira Remsen
saccharine: 5 mushy, sappy, sweet 6 honied, sirupy, sugary, syrupy 7 candied, cloying, honeyed, mawkish 9 disarming, oversweet
Sacchetti, Franco: 4 poet 7 Italian
sacellum: 6 chapel, shrine, temple 7 oratory
sacerdotal: 8 hieratic 9 religious
Sacha: 6 Guitry
in English: 9 Alexander
sachem: 5 chief
Sacher torte: 4 cake 7 dessert
sachet: 5 aroma 7 perfume
item: 5 petal
Sachs: 4 Hans 5 Nelly
__ Sachs: 7 Goldman
Sachs, Hans: 4 poet 6 German, writer 10 playwright
Sachs, Nelly: 4 poet 6 German, writer 8 Nobelist 10 playwright
work: Journey into a Dustless Room
O the Chimneys
sack: 2 ax 3 axe, bag, bed, can, gut, rob 4 base, boot, drop, fire, loot, oust, raid, ruin, wine 5 dress, harry, let go, pouch, purse, rifle, spoil, steal, strip, waste 6 bounce, harrow, lay off, maraud, pocket, ravage, tackle 7 cashier, despoil, destroy, dismiss, drum out, garment, pillage, plunder, ransack, release 8 demolish, desolate, displace, freeboot, furlough, get rid of, lay waste, pink-slip, spoliate 9 container, depredate, desecrate, devastate, discharge, terminate
a student: 5 expel
designer: 4 Dior
ender: 5 cloth
in the ~: 4 abed
leave the ~: 4 rise, wake 5 arise, awake, waken 6 awaken
material: 5 gunny 6 burlap
out: 4 rest 5 sleep 6 retire, turn in 7 go to bed, saw logs 9 go to sleep, hit the hay
remove from a ~: 5 unbag
sad ~: 5 schmo 6 schmoe, wretch
starter: 3 hop, ran 4 grip, knap, pack, ruck, wool 5 gunny
time: 5 sleep 7 slumber
sack __: 3 out 4 coat, race, suit, time 5 dress
__ sack: 3 sad 5 grass 6 crocus, croker
__ Sack: 4 Coal 5 Hacky
sackbut: 4 wind 8 trombone 10 instrument
sackcloth
and ashes: 7 penance
wearer: 6 atoner
sacked out: 4 abed 5 in bed 6 asleep, dozing 7 dormant, napping 8 dreaming, snoozing 9 somnolent 10 sawing logs, slumbering
sacker: 7 brigand
Rome ~: 4 Goth
Sackett: 5 Jubal
__ sack had seven cats...: 4 Each
Sacks: 6 Oliver
__ Sack, The: 3 Sad
Sackville: 4 city, town 6 Thomas
locale: 6 Canada 10 Nova Scotia
Sackville, Thomas: 4 poet 7 British 9 statesman
Sackville-West, Victoria: 4 poet 7 British
Saco: 4 city, town
locale: 5 Maine
sacque: 5 dress
sacra: 9 vertebrae
Sacra __ Rota: 6 Romana
sacral __: 5 nerve 6 plexus
sacrament: 4 rite 6 ritual 7 baptism, liturgy, penance 8 marriage 9 communion, Eucharist, matrimony 10 holy orders
__ Sacrament: 4 Holy 7 Blessed
sacramental __: 4 wine
sacramental oil: 6 chrism 7 chrisom
Sacramento: 3 mts. 4 city, mtns., town 5 range 6 valley 7 capital 9 mountains
arena: 4 Arco
locale: 3 Cal. 10 California
newspaper: 3 Bee
team: 5 Kings
Valley tribe: 5 Maidu
Sacra Romana __: 4 Rota

Sacre __!: 4 bleu
sacred: 4 holy, pure 5 blest, godly, pious 6 divine, iconic, solemn 7 blessed, revered, saintly 8 hallowed, iconical, numinous 9 cherished, dedicated, enshrined, inviolate, religious, spiritual, venerable 10 inviolable, sanctified
  combining form: 4 hier- 5 hiero-
  hold ~: 5 exalt 6 hallow 8 enshrine, inshrine, sanctify 10 consecrate
  image: 4 icon, idol, ikon 5 eikon
  make ~: 6 anoint
  spot: 5 altar 6 shrine
  writings: 4 Veda 5 Bible, Koran
sacred __: 3 cow 4 ibis 5 lotus, order 6 baboon, bamboo, thread 7 monster
Sacred __: 4 Nine, Writ 5 Heart 7 Emotion
Sacred __, The: 4 Wood 5 Fount
Sacred and Profane author: Faye Kellerman
Sacred Emotion (1989 song) artist: Donny Osmond
Sacred Fount, The author: Henry James
sacred name, name meaning: 6 Jerome
Sacred Wood, The
  author: T.S. Eliot
sacrifice: 4 cede, cost, lose, loss 5 forgo, let go, offer, price 6 forego, give up, victim 7 forbear, forfeit, offer up 8 libation, offering, part with, renounce 9 surrender 10 abnegation, contribute, relinquish
  diamond ~: 3 fly 4 bunt
  Hebrew ~: 6 corban, korban
  site: 5 altar
sacrifice __: 3 fly, hit 4 bunt
sacrificial __: 4 lamb 5 anode
sacrilege: 3 sin 5 crime 6 heresy 7 impiety, mockery 9 blasphemy, profanity, violation 10 disrespect
sacrilegious: 7 impious, profane
sacrosanct: 4 holy 6 sacred 9 immutable, inviolate, religious
sacrum: 4 bone
  locale: 6 pelvis
sad: 3 bad, low 4 blue, dark, dour, down, glum, mopy 5 bleak, funky, grave, heavy, moody, mopey, sorry, teary, woful 6 broody, dismal, dreary, gloomy, morose, rueful, shabby, somber, tragic, triste, woeful 7 crushed, doleful, elegiac, forlorn, grieved, hangdog, hurting, joyless, painful, pensive, piteous, pitiful, subdued, tearful, unhappy, wistful 8 bereaved, crushing, dejected, dolorous, downcast, grievous, mournful, pathetic, pitiable, poignant, touching, tragical, troubled, wretched 9 bummed out, cheerless, depressed, heartsick, long-faced, miserable, plaintive, regretful, saturnine, sorrowful, upsetting, woebegone 10 chapfallen, deplorable, depressing, despairing, despondent, dispirited, lachrymose, lamentable, lugubrious, melancholy, pathetical
  be ~: 5 mourn 6 grieve, sorrow
  expression: 4 ah me, pout
  in ~ shape: 6 bad off
  name meaning ~: 7 Tristan
  occurrence: 7 tragedy
  one: 5 moper, schmo 6 schmoe, wretch
  sound: 3 sob 4 sigh
sad __: 4 sack, tree
Sad __: 4 Eyes 5 Songs 6 Movies
Sad __, The: 4 Sack
Sada: 8 Thompson
Sadaharu: 2 Oh
Sadat: 5 Anwar, Jihan
Sadat, Anwar: 4 Arab 8 Egyptian, Nobelist
sadden: 4 hurt, pain 6 bum out, darken, deject, dismay, grieve 7 depress, oppress, trouble, turn off 8 dispirit, distress, drag down, keep down 9 bring down, weigh down 10 disappoint, discourage, dishearten
saddened: 5 sorry 7 unhappy 10 melancholy
saddening: 5 bleak 6 dismal, dreary, gloomy, somber 7 joyless 8 hopeless, mournful 9 cheerless, dejecting, upsetting 10 depressing, lugubrious, melancholy, oppressive
saddle: 3 lay, tan, tax 4 load, meat 5 blame 6 burden, lumber 7 oppress 8 encumber, keep down 9 weigh down
  be in the ~: 3 run 7 operate 9 supervise
  elephant ~: 6 houdah, howdah
  ender: 3 bag, bow 4 back, tree 5 cloth
  horse: 4 hack, pony 5 mount, steed 7 hackney, palfrey 9 Appaloosa
  irritant: 3 bur
  loop: 3 lug
  material: 7 leather
  part: 4 girt, horn 5 girth 6 cantle
  starter: 4 pack, side
  strap: 6 latigo
  tighten a ~: 5 cinch
  up: 4 ride
saddle __: 4 horn, roof, seat, shoe, soap, sore 5 horse, joint, point 6 oxford, stitch 7 blanket, leather
__ saddle: 5 stock 7 English, Western
saddlebag: 8 knapsack
saddlemaker tool: 3 awl
__ Saddles: 7 Blazing
Saddle the Wind (1958 film)
  cast: John Cassavetes, Donald Crisp, Julie London, Robert Taylor
  director: Robert Parrish
Sade
  born: Helen Folasade Adu
  homeland: Nigeria
  song: Paradise (1988)
    Smooth Operator (1985)
    The Sweetest Taboo (1985)
__/Sade: 5 Marat
Sade, Marquis de: 6 French, writer
  work: Justine
sadhe: 6 Hebrew, letter
  predecessor: 2 pe 3 peh
  successor: 4 koph, qoph
sadhu: 4 monk 5 friar
sadi: 6 Hebrew, letter
  predecessor: 2 pe 3 peh
  successor: 4 koph, qoph
Sa'di: 4 poet 7 Persian
Sadie: 5 Frost 7 Hawkins 8 Thompson
Sadie Hawkins Day creator: 4 Capp
Sadie McKee (1934 film)
  cast: Joan Crawford, Gene Raymond, Franchot Tone
  director: Clarence Brown
Sadie Thompson (1928 film)
  cast: Lionel Barrymore, Gloria Swanson, Raoul Walsh
  director: Raoul Walsh
__ Sadie Thompson: 4 Miss
sadist: 6 abuser
sadistic: 4 mean, sick 5 cruel, harsh, nasty 6 animal, brutal, fierce, savage, unkind, wanton 7 beastly, callous, hurtful, vicious 8 barbaric, fiendish, inhumane, perverse, pitiless, ruthless, vengeful 9 barbarous, cutthroat, ferocious, merciless, monstrous, truculent 10 vindictive
Sadler, Barry: 4 SSgt.
Sadler, Barry song: The Ballad of the Green Berets (1966)
__ Sad Love Song: 7 Another
sadly: 4 alas 9 unhappily
sadness: 3 woe 4 funk, pain 5 blahs, blues, dolor, gloom, grief, mopes 6 bummer, downer, misery, pathos, sorrow 7 anguish, dismals, emotion, letdown 8 blue funk, distress, glumness, mourning 9 bleakness, dejection, heartache, pessimism, poignancy 10 depression, desolation, gloominess, heartbreak, heavy heart, infelicity, loneliness, melancholy, woefulness
  show ~: 3 cry, sob 4 weep
Sadr: 4 star
Sad Sack girlfriend: 5 Sadie
__ Sad, Serbia: 4 Novi
Sad Songs (1984 song) artist: Elton John
SAE: 3 enc. 4 encl. 9 enclosure
__ sae weary...: 4 and I
safari: 4 tour, trek 5 jaunt 7 caravan, journey 9 excursion 10 expedition
  camp: 4 base
  concern: 5 spoor, trail
  helmet material: 4 pith
  leader: 5 bwana 6 hunter
  park: 3 zoo
  servant: 6 bearer
  sight: 3 gnu 5 hippo, okapi, rhino
  souvenir: 5 photo
safari __: 4 park, suit 5 shirt 6 jacket
Safari: 3 car, GMC, van 4 auto 7 Pontiac 10 automobile
__ Safari: 6 Surfin'
__ Safari, A: 7 Swingin'
safe: 2 OK 4 cosy, cozy, okay, snug, sure, till, wary 5 clear, cozey, cozie, sound, vault 6 secure, steady, tended, unhurt 7 careful, certain, checked, guarded, healthy, lockbox, prudent 8 cautious, discreet, harmless, homefree, nontoxic, reliable, risk-free, riskless, treasury, tucked in, unharmed, unmarked 9 foolproof, goofproof, innocuous, innoxious, preserved, protected, strongbox, unanxious, undamaged, uninjured, unscathed, untouched, wholesome 10 depository, impervious, in the clear, inviolable, repository, unhindered, unpolluted
  ender: 5 guard, light 7 cracker, keeping
  environmentally ~: 5 green
  from the elements: 6 inside 7 indoors
  house: 6 asylum 7 hideout, retreat 9 sanctuary
  keep ~: 4 hide 5 guard 6 assure, back up, defend, foster, harbor, patrol, police, screen, secure, shield 7 fortify, protect, shelter, ward off 8 chaperon, fight for, preserve, shepherd 9 look after, safeguard, watch over 10 take care of
  make ~: 6 declaw, ensure, secure
  not ~: 3 out
  partner: 5 sound
  place: 4 bank 6 refuge 7 retreat
  playing ~: 7 careful, prudent 8 cautious
  starter: 5 vouch
  to be ~: 6 in case 10 just in case
safe __: 5 haven, house 6 harbor 7 harbour
safe-__: 7 conduct
safe-__ box: 7 deposit
safe-__ pass: 7 conduct
__-safe: 4 fail
Safe __: 3 Men 7 Conduct
Safe!: 4 call
safe and __: 5 sound
safe-conduct: 4 pass 6 permit 7 passage 8 passport
Safe Conduct author: Boris Pasternak
safecracker: 4 yegg 5 thief 6 robber 7 burglar
  need: 4 soup 5 nitro
safe-deposit box: 5 vault
safeguard: 4 egis, fend, keep, tend 5 aegis, armor, cover, watch 6 buffer, convoy, defend, ensure, escort, harbor, insure, patrol, rescue, screen, secure, shield, surety 7 bulwark, defense, harbour, protect, shelter, store up 8 chaperon, conserve, preserve, scrimp on, security 9 chaperone, companion, cut back on, insurance, look after, watch over 10 precaution, protection
Safeguard: 4 soap
  alternative: 3 Lux 4 Dial, Dove, Lava, Tone, Zest 5 Camay, Coast, Ivory 6 Boraxo, Caress, Shield 8 Lifebuoy 9 Palmolive 11 Irish Spring
safekeeping: 4 care 5 trust 6 charge 7 custody 8 wardship 9 salvation 10 protection
Safe Men (1998 film)
  cast: Harvey Fierstein, Michael Lerner, Sam Rockwell, Steve Zahn
  director: John Hamburg
Safer, Morley: 8 reporter
  colleague of ~: 5 Kroft, Stahl 7 Bradley, Wallace
  network: 3 CBS 5 CBS-TV
__ safe than sorry: 6 better
safety: 5 cover 6 asylum, refuge 7 freedom, shelter 8 immunity, security 9 assurance, sanctuary 10 protection
  device: 3 net 6 airbag 8 seat belt
  hwy. ~ org.: 4 MADD, SADD
  measure: 10 precaution
  place of ~: 6 asylum
  provide ~: 7 shelter
  specifications: 4 code
  valve: 4 duct, vent 5 spout 6 nozzle, outlet 7 channel
safety __: 3 car, man, net, pin 4 belt, film, fuze, hook, lamp, lock 5 catch, glass, match, razor, valve 6 factor, island, lintel 7 circuit, curtain, lantern, squeeze
__ safety: 4 free, weak 6 strong
Safety __: 4 Last 5 First 7 Islands
Safety __, The: 5 Dance
safety-deposit __: 3 box
Safety Last (1923 film) cast: Harold Lloyd
safflower: 3 oil 5 plant 6 flower
saffron: 5 color, plant, spice 6 flower, orange, yellow 8 orangish 9 condiment
  dish: 4 rice 6 paella
  family: 4 iris
  relative: 4 buff, corn, gold, lime, rust, sand 5 blond, brass, coral, cream, flame, flaxy, henna, lemon, maize, ocher, ochre, peach, rusty, straw 6 blonde, canary, chammy, citron, crocus, flaxen, shammy, shamoy 7 apricot, chamois, citrine, jasmine, mustard, nankeen, old gold, pumpkin, xanthic 8 daffodil, hyacinth, primrose 9 champagne, goldenrod, jessamine, tangerine 10 terra cotta
  source: 6 crocus
Safi: 4 city, port, town
  locale: 7 Morocco
Safid __: 3 Rud
Safire, William: 6 author, writer
  concern: 5 usage
S. Africa
  see South Africa
sag: 3 bag, bow, dip, sap 4 bend, cant, drop, fail, fall, flag, flex, flop, give, lean, list, loll, sink, slip, tire, wane, wilt 5 blunt, bulge, curve, droop, lower, slump, stoop, yield 6 cave in, dangle, falter, go limp, impair, reduce, shrink, slouch, soften, tumble 7 decline, deplete, drop off, exhaust, fatigue, give

way 8 collapse, diminish, downturn, enervate, enfeeble, hang down, languish, sink down 9 attenuate, downslide, hang loose, undermine, worsening 10 debilitate, depression, devitalize
sag ___: 3 rod 5 wagon
Sag ___: 6 Harbor
SAG: 5 union
former ~ president: 4 Duke 5 Asner 6 Cagney, Heston, Reagan
member: 5 actor
part: 5 Guild 6 Actors, Screen
saga: 4 epic, tale, yarn 5 novel, story 6 legend 9 adventure, chronicle, narrative, recountal
Icelandic ~: 4 edda
like a ~: 6 epical
poetic ~: 4 epos
Saga: 4 city, font, town 8 typeface
locale: 5 Japan
___ Saga: 5 Olaf's
sagacious: 3 apt 4 cagy, foxy, keen, wise 5 acute, cagey, canny, savvy, sharp, smart 6 astute, shrewd, strong 7 knowing, politic, prudent, sapient 8 profound, rational, sensible 9 astucious, judicious 10 discerning, far-sighted, insightful, perceptive
sagacity: 3 wit 4 wits 5 depth, sense 6 acumen, sanity, wisdom 7 insight 8 judgment, sapience 9 intellect 10 profundity
Sagal: 5 Katey
Sagami: 3 bay, sea
locale: 5 Japan
Sagan: 4 Carl 9 Françoise
Sagan, Carl: 6 author 10 astronomer
Sagan, Françoise: 6 author, French, writer 10 playwright
work: Bonjour Tristesse
A Certain Smile
___ Saga, The: 7 Forsyte
sage: 4 guru, herb, wise 5 brain, green, magus, shrub, smart, Solon 6 expert, master, mentor, Nestor, oracle, pundit, savant 7 grayish, knowing, learned, mahatma, prudent, sapient, scholar, Solomon, thinker 8 harmless, high-brow, profound, sensible 9 authority, graybeard, intellect, judicious, pansophic, seasoning, Solomonic, venerable 10 discerning, specialist
ender: 5 brush
family: 4 mint
Hindu ~: 5 rishi
like a ~: 7 learned
relative: 3 pea 4 cyan, jade 5 beryl, breen, olive, virid 6 myrtle, reseda 7 avocado, celadon, emerald, verdant 8 lavender, rosemary 9 pistachio, turquoise 10 aquamarine, chartreuse
Roman ~: 4 Cato
scarlet ~: 5 plant 6 flower
sage ___: 3 hen 4 cock 5 green 6 grouse 7 sparrow
___ sage: 3 red 5 black, Texas, white 6 purple, yellow 7 scarlet
Sägebrecht: 8 Marianne
sagebrush: 5 plant, shrub
Sagebrush State: 3 Nev. 6 Nevada
___ Sage College: 7 Russell
sageness
see sagacity
Sage of Concord: Ralph Waldo Emerson
Sager, Carole Bayer spouse: Burt Bacharach
sages: 8 literati
Moslem ~: 5 ulema
New Testament ~: 4 Magi
Saget: 3 Bob
sagging: 4 limp 5 baggy, loppy, seedy, slack 6 adroop, broody, droopy, floppy 7 concave, flaccid 8 dangling, dejected 9 pendulous 10 ill-fitting
Sag Harbor: 4 city, town
locale: 7 New York 10 Long Island
___-saghyz: 3 kok
Saginaw: 3 bay 4 city, port, town
Bay lake: 5 Huron
locale: 8 Michigan
Sagittarius: 4 sign 6 archer
month: 3 Dec., Nov. 8 December, November
predecessor: 7 Scorpio
projectile: 5 arrow
successor: 9 Capricorn
sago: 4 palm
saguaro: 5 fruit, plant 6 cactus, flower
locale: 6 desert
part: 5 spine
Saguaro: 4 park
locale: 7 Arizona
Saguenay: 5 river
locale: 6 Quebec
Sagwa, the Chinese Siamese Cat author: Amy Tan
Sahagún: 4 city, town
locale: 6 Mexico 7 Hidalgo
Sahaptin: 6 Indian 7 Amerind
Sahara: 3 SUV 4 Jeep 6 desert
beast: 5 camel
like the ~: 3 dry 4 arid, sere, vast 5 sandy
massif: 5 Adrar
mountains: 5 Atlas
nation: 4 Mali 5 Libya, Niger
nomad: 6 Berber
region: 5 Sahel
robe: 3 aba 4 abba
scarcity: 4 rain 5 water
sight: 4 dune
stop-off: 5 oasis
wind: 6 simoom
Sahara (1943 film)
cast: Bruce Bennett, Humphrey Bogart, J. Carrol Naish
director: Zoltan Korda
___ Sahara: 7 Spanish, Western
Sahel: 6 desert
locale: 6 Africa
sahib
address: 3 sri
cousin: 5 bwana
land: 5 India
prefix: 3 mem
___ sahib: 5 pukka
Sahiwal: 3 cow 4 bull 6 bovine, cattle
Sahl, Mort: 5 comic 8 comedian, humorist, satirist
Sahuayo: 4 city, town
locale: 6 Mexico 9 Michoacán
said: 4 oral 5 vocal 6 spoken, verbal 7 reputed 9 vocalized
all ~ and done: 5 ended
old-style: 5 spake
you ~ it: 3 aye, oui, yea, yep, yup 4 fine, okay, sure, yeah 5 good-o, natch, quite, right, roger, uh-huh 6 agreed, and how, gladly, good-oh, indeed, just so, rather, righto, surely, yowzah 7 exactly, go ahead, indeedy, mais oui, quite so, ten-four 8 all right, of course, thumbs up, very well 9 be my guest, certainly, darn right, naturally, precisely, sure thing 10 absolutely, by all means, definitely, positively, sure enough, that's right
___ said: 4 'Nuff
___ said...: 3 as I
___ Said: 4 I Am...I, Mama, Port
___ Said a Mouthful: 3 You
___ Said and Done: 3 All
___ Said, 'HA!': 3 God
Said I Loved You...But I Lied (1994 song) artist: Michael Bolton
___ said it!: 3 You
___ Said Knock You Out: 4 Mama
Saidpur: 4 city, town
locale: 10 Bangladesh
Said, Sultan Qabus bin: 5 Omani
___ said than done: 6 easier
___ said there'd be days like this: 4 Mama
saiga: 6 animal 8 antelope
relative: 3 gnu, kob 4 guib, kudu, oryx, puku, topi 5 addax, bongo, chiru, eland, goral, korin, nyala, oribi, serow 6 chammy, dik-dik, duiker, impala, koodoo, lechwe, nilgai, rhebok, shammy, shamoy 7 blaubok, blesbok, chamois, defassa, gazelle, gemsbok, gerenuk, grysbok, nylghai, nylghau, sassaby 8 blesbuck, bontebok, bushbuck, gemsbuck, reedbuck, steenbok, steinbok 9 blackbuck, pronghorn, sitatunga, springbok, waterbuck 10 hartebeest, wildebeest
Saigon: 4 city, port, town
locale: 3 Nam 7 Vietnam
Saigon ___: 4 Kick
sail: 3 fly, ply, run 4 flit, skim, soar 5 drift, float, glide, leave, pilot, speed, sweep 6 cruise, embark, jigger, junket, travel, voyage 7 cast off, go to sea, head out, ship out 8 navigate, put to sea, shove off
adjust a ~: 4 trim 5 rerig
before the wind: 4 scud
combining form: 5 histi- 6 histio-
corner: 4 clew
edge: 4 luff
ender: 4 boat, fish 5 board, cloth, plane 6 planer 7 boarder
fit a ~ to: 3 rig
for home: 6 head in
holder: 4 mast 5 sprit
into: 4 lace 5 abuse, scold
into the wind: 4 luff
lash down a ~: 4 frap
over: 4 leap
raise a ~: 5 hoist
reduce ~: 4 reef
securer: 6 batten
set ~: 6 embark 7 push off, ship out 8 put to sea, shove off
small ~: 5 royal
starter: 3 lug, sky, top, try 4 head, main, stay 5 sprit 7 foretop 8 forestay, studding
support: 4 gaff, spar
through: 3 ace 6 breeze
triangular ~: 3 jib 5 raffe 6 lateen, raffee, raffie
type of ~: 3 jib 4 mule 5 mizen 6 gunter, jigger, lateen, mizzen, raffee 7 spanker, spencer 9 spinnaker
under ~: 4 asea 5 at sea
___ sail: 3 lug, set 4 drag, full, gaff, make, wind 5 plain, solar 6 lateen, riding, square 7 balloon, driving, lifting
Sail
constellation: 4 Vela
Sail ___ Ship of State!: 3 on O
Sail ___ Silvery Moon: 5 Along
___ Sail Away: 4 Come
sailboat: 3 cat 4 dory, yawl 5 ketch, skiff, sloop, yacht 6 galley 7 galleon, pinnace 8 schooner, tall ship, trimaran 9 catamaran 10 knockabout, windjammer
stabilizer: 4 keel
sailcloth: 6 canvas, fabric
...sailed the ___ blue...: 5 ocean
___ sailer: 3 day 5 motor
Sailfish: 4 boat 5 skiff
sailing: 4 asea 5 at sea, sport 6 cruise 10 navigation
maneuver: 4 tack
of ~: 8 nautical
smooth ~: 4 snap 6 picnic
starter: 4 wind 5 board
vessel: 4 bark, boat, ship, yawl 5 craft, ketch, skiff, sloop 6 barque
sailing ___: 4 boat, ship 6 length
___ sailing: 5 plain, plane, rhumb 7 oblique
Sailing (1980 song) artist: Christopher Cross
Sailing to Byzantium author: William Butler Yeats
Sail on (1979 song) artist: Commodores
sailor: 3 gob, hat, tar 4 bo's'n, hand, salt, swab, swob 5 bosun, middy 6 ensign, pirate, sea dog, seaman 7 boatman, captain, crewman, jack tar, mariner, matelot, matelow, old salt, recruit, skipper 8 coxswain, deckhand, helmsman, salty dog, seafarer, traveler, water dog 9 boatswain, first mate, yachtsman 10 midshipman
accommodation: 5 berth
depth measure: 6 fathom
direction: 4 alee, port 5 aport 6 astern 9 starboard
drink: 3 rum 4 grog
East Indian ~: 6 lascar 7 lashkar
exclamation ~: 3 aye 4 ahoy 5 avast 6 aye aye 7 heave ho
guide: 4 buoy 6 beacon, Pharos 10 lighthouse
like a ~ on leave: 6 ashore
line: 5 brail
name meaning ~: 6 Morgan
on standby: 3 RNR 4 USAR
pal: 5 matey
patron: 4 Elmo
pride: 4 knot
quarters: 6 fo'c's'le
shift: 5 watch
sighting: 4 land
song: 6 chanty
spy grp.: 3 ONI
unskilled ~: 6 lubber 10 landlubber
where a ~ goes: 5 to sea
wooden-shoe ~: 3 Nod 6 Wynken 7 Blynken
Sailor Beware (1951 film)
cast: Corinne Calvet, Jerry Lewis, Dean Martin
director: Hal Walker
sailorly: 5 naval 8 nautical
Sailor of the King (1953 film)
cast: Wendy Hiller, Jeffrey Hunter, Michael Rennie
Sailor on Horseback author: Irving Stone
sailors: 4 crew 5 hands
Sailor's Song start: 5 to sea
Sailor Who Fell from Grace with the Sea, The author: Yukio Mishima
sails: 6 canvas
___ Sails in the Sunset: 3 Red
sail the ___ seas: 5 seven
...sail the ___ blue: 5 ocean
Saimaa: 4 lake
locale: 7 Finland
saint: 5 angel, model
Alexandrian ~: 10 Athanasius
American ~: 5 Seton
Avila ~: 6 Teresa
Bohemian ~: 10 Wenceslaus
British ~: 4 Bede, More 5 Alban, Baeda 6 Anselm 7 Dunstan 8 Boniface, Cuthbert 10 Thomas More
combining form: 4 hagi- 5 hagio-
ender: 3 dom
French ~: 5 Denis, Denys, Giles 6 Ansgar, Fiacre 7 Bernard, Louis

IX, Vianney **8** Lawrence **9** Genevieve, Joan of Arc **10** Bernadette
Greek ~: **5** Cyril
Hungarian ~: **7** Stephen
Irish ~: **5** Aidan, Kevin **7** Patrick
Italian ~: **5** Paolo, Pius X **7** Ambrose, Gregory **8** Benedict **10** Philip Neri **11** Bonaventure
Moslem ~: **3** pir
North African ~: **7** Cyprian **9** Augustine
Peruvian ~: **10** Rose of Lima
Polish ~: **7** Casimir, Florian
Roman ~: **5** Agnes **6** Agatha **7** Cecilia, Clement, Crispin **8** Paulinus **9** Dionysius, Valentine **11** Christopher
Russian ~: **6** Nevski **8** Vladimir
Serbian ~: **4** Sava
Spanish ~: **7** Dominic **8** Ignatius
Welsh ~: **5** David
Saint: **10** footballer
rival: **3** Jet, Ram **4** Bear, Bill, Colt, Lion **5** Brown, Chief, Eagle, Giant, Raven, Texan, Titan **6** Bengal, Bronco, Cowboy, Falcon, Jaguar, Packer, Raider, Viking **7** Charger, Dolphin, Panther, Patriot, Redskin, Seahawk, Steeler **8** Cardinal **9** Buccaneer
Saint ___: **4** Jack, Joan, Pete **5** Maybe **6** Moritz
Saint ___ and Miquelon: **6** Pierre
Saint ___ and Nevis: **5** Kitts
Saint ___ Back, The: **7** Strikes
Saint ___ College: **4** Olaf
Saint ___ Cross: **7** Andrew's, George's
Saint ___ Day: **7** George's
Saint ___ de Paul: **7** Vincent
Saint ___ Eve: **5** Agnes'
Saint ___ fire: **5** Elmo's
Saint ___ Merici: **6** Angela
Saint ___ Mountains: **5** Elias
Saint-___: **5** Saens **6** Tropez
Saint-___, France: **4** Malo
Saint Agnes' ___: **3** Eve
Saint Andrews: **5** links **6** course **10** golf course
locale: **8** Scotland
Saint Andrew's ___: **5** Cross
Saint Anthony's ___: **4** fire **5** Cross
Saint Augustine: **4** city, town
locale: **3** Fla. **7** Florida
Saint Bernard: **3** dog **5** canid **6** canine
beat: **4** Alps
fictional ~: **4** Neil
Sainte-Beuve, Charles: **6** French, writer **9** historian
sainted: **4** holy
Saint Elias: **4** peak **5** mount **8** mountain
Saint Elmo's ___: **4** fire
Sainte-Marie, Buffy: **6** singer
Saint, Eva Marie: **7** actress
film: All Fall Down (1962)
Exodus (1960)
A Hatful of Rain (1957)
Loving (1970)
North by Northwest (1959)
Nothing in Common (1986)
On the Waterfront (1954, AA)
Raintree County (1957)
The Sandpiper (1965)
Saint-Exupéry, Antoine de: **6** French, writer **7** aviator
work: The Little Prince
Night Flight
Southern Mail
Wind, Sand, and Stars
Saint-Gaudens: **8** Augustus
Saint George's ___: **3** Day **5** Cross
Saint Helena: **3** isl. **4** isle **6** island
Saint Helens: **4** peak **5** mount **8** mountain
locale: **10** Washington
sainthood, fit for: **4** holy
Saint Jack (1979 film)
cast: Denholm Elliott, Ben Gazzara, James Villiers
director: Peter Bogdanovich
Saint James, Susan: **7** actress
film: Don't Cry, It's Only Thunder (1982)
Love at First Bite (1979)
Outlaw Blues (1977)
TV: Kate & Allie, McMillan and Wife, The Name of the Game
Saint Joan author: George Bernard Shaw
Saint-John: **5** Perse
Saint John Passion composer: **4** Bach
Saint John's: **4** city, port, town **10** university
athletes: **8** Red Storm
locale: **7** Jamaica, New York
Saint Kitts: **3** isl. **4** isle **6** island
Saint Kitts and Nevis org.: **3** OAS
Saint Laurent: **4** Yves
birthplace: **4** Oran
Saint Lawrence ___: **6** Seaway
saintliness: **5** piety **8** morality
Saint-Lô: **4** city, town
locale: **6** France
Saint Louis: **4** city, port, town
bridge: **4** Eads
landmark: **4** arch
pro team: **4** Rams **5** Blues **9** Cardinals
Saint Lucia: **3** isl. **4** isle **6** island, nation **7** country
money: **4** cent **6** dollar
org.: **3** OAS
saintly: **4** good, holy, pure **5** blest, godly, moral, pious **6** devout, divine, sacred **7** angelic, blessed, sincere **8** beatific, seraphic, virtuous **9** angelical, religious, righteous **10** benevolent, seraphical
Saint Mark, symbol of: **4** lion
Saint Maybe author: Anne Tyler
___-Saint-Michel: **4** Mont
Saint Nick
see Santa Claus
Saint Patrick's Day event: **6** parade
Saint Paul: **6** writer **9** cathedral **10** evangelist
architect of ~: **4** Wren
feature: **4** dome
locale: **6** London **7** England
longtime dean of ~: **4** Inge
once: **4** Saul
story of ~: **4** Acts
Saint Peter's
feature: **4** dome
locale: **4** Rome **7** Vatican
service: **4** Mass
Saint Petersburg: **4** city, port, town
Ballet once: **5** Kirov
locale: **6** Russia **7** Florida
neighbor: **5** Tampa
river: **4** Neva
setting: **3** EDT, EST
saint's ___: **3** day
Saints: **4** team **6** eleven
home: **10** New Orleans
org.: **3** NFC, NFL
sport: **8** football
Saints (patron):
Adelard (gardeners)
Agatha (bellringers)
Agnes (young girls)
Albertus Magnus (scientists)
Aloysius (teenagers)
Amand (innkeepers)
Ambrose (beekeepers)
Andrew (fishermen)
Andronicus (silversmiths)
Anne (mothers, housewives)
Ansgar (Scandinavia)
Anthony of Padua (lost articles, travelers)
Anthony the Abbot (basket makers, butchers)
Antony (domestic animals)
Apollonia (dentists)
Augustine (brewers)
Barbara (architects, thunderstorms)
Bartholomew (plasterers)
Benedict (students)
Bernadette (shepherds)
Bernard (skiers)
Blaise (throat ailments, wild animals)
Bridgid (Ireland)
Casimir of Poland (bachelors)
Catherine of Alexandria (philosophers)
Catherine of Siena (Italy)
Cecilia (music)
Christopher (travelers)
Clare (embroiderers, television)
Claude (sculptors)
Clement (marble workers)
Cosmas (barbers, pharmacists, physicians)
Crispin (shoemakers)
Cyril (resolving of schisms)
Damian (barbers, pharmacists, physicians)
David (doves, poets, Wales)
Denis (France)
Denys (France)
Dismas (prisoners)
Dominic (astronomers)
Dunstan (goldsmiths, blacksmiths)
Eligius (jewelers, metalworkers)
Elizabeth of Hungary (bakers)
Elmo (sailors)
Eustachius (hunters)
Fiacre (taxi drivers)
Florian (firefighters, Poland)
Francis de Sales (writers)
Francis of Assisi (animals, ecologists)
Francis Xavier (foreign missions)
Gabriel the Archangel (postal workers, radio)
Genesius (actors, theater)
Genevieve (disasters, Paris)
George (England)
Gertrude (fear of rats and mice)
Giles (the poor)
Godeberta (drought relief, epidemics)
Gregory (music)
Herbert (drought relief)
Hilary (snake bite victims)
Hubert (dogs, hunters)
Ignatius (soldiers)
Isidore of Seville (computer users)
Isidore the Farmer (farmers)
James the Greater (Chile)
Januarius (blood banks, Naples, volcanoes)
Jerome (librarians)
Joan of Arc (soldiers)
John Bosco (boys)
John Chrysostom (orators, speakers)
John of Capistrano (judges, jury members)
John of God (booksellers, hospitals)
John of the Cross (contemplatives)
John the Apostle (writers)
John the Baptist (lambs)
John Vianney (priests)
Joseph of Cupertino (astronauts, airline passengers)
Jude (lost causes)
Kevin (blackbirds)
Lawrence (cooks, fire prevention)
Lidwina (skaters)
Louis IX (barbers)
Luke (physicians, painters, glassworkers)
Margaret of Clitherow (business women)
Margaret (pregnant women)
Mark (lawyers, lions)
Martha (cooks, housewives, servants)
Martin de Porres (barbers, hairdressers)
Martin of Tours (horsemen, soldiers)
Mary Magdalene (sinners)
Matthew (accountants, bankers, tax collectors)
Maurice (swordsmiths, weavers)
Medard (bad weather)
Methodius (resolving of schisms)
Michael (flyers, paratroopers)
Monica (married women)
Nicholas of Myra (bakers, brides, pawnbrokers)
Our Lady of Guadalupe (Mexico)
Our Lady of Loreto (aviators)
Our Lady of Lourdes (bodily ills)
Patrick (fear of snakes, Ireland)
Paul (snake bite victims)
Perpetua (cows)
Peter Celestine (bookbinders)
Peter (fishermen, longevity)
Polycarp (earaches)
Rene Goupil (anesthetists)
Roch (dogs, dog lovers)
Rose of Lima (florists, the Americas, Philippines)
Sava (Serbia)
Scholastica (bad weather)
Sebastian (archers)
Stephen (bricklayers, stonemasons)
Teresa of Avila (headaches)
Therese of Lisieux (aviators, florists)
Thomas Aquinas (schools, learning)
Thomas (architects)
Thomas More (English, civil servants)
Valentine (lovers)
Vincent de Paul (charities, volunteers)
Vincent of Saragossa (winegrowers)
Vitus (comedians, dancers)
Walburga (famine)
Zita (lost keys, maids)
Saint-Saëns, Camille: **6** French **8** composer
___ Saints' Day: **3** All
Saint-Simon, Comte de: **6** French **11** philosopher
specialty: rationalism
___ Saints in Three Acts: **4** Four
saints, roll of: **5** canon
Saint Strikes Back, The (1939 film)
cast: Wendy Barrie, Jonathan Hale, George Sanders
director: John Farrow
Saint, The (1997 film)
cast: Val Kilmer, Elisabeth Shue
director: Phillip Noyce
Saint, The (NBC adventure) cast: Roger Moore (Simon Templar)
Saint-Tropez: **4** city, town **6** resort
locale: **6** France
Saint Vincent: **4** cape
locale: **10** Madagascar
Saint Vincent and the Grenadines: **4** isls. **5** isles **6** nation **7** country, islands
locale: **10** West Indies
money: **4** cent **6** dollar
org.: **3** OAS
Saint Vincent de ___: **4** Paul
Saipan: **3** isl. **4** isle **6** island
island near ~: **4** Guam
Saiph: **4** star
saison: **3** été
___ sais quoi: **4** je ne
saithe: **4** fish
Sajak, Pat: **2** MC **4** host **5** emcee
boss: **4** Merv **7** Griffin
colleague: **5** White
purchase from ~ perhaps: **3** an a, an e, an i, an o
Sajama: **4** peak **5** mount **8** mountain
locale: **7** Bolivia
Sakado: **4** city, town

locale: 5 Japan
Sakai: 4 city, town
locale: 5 Hondo, Japan 6 Honshu
Sakakawea: 4 lake 9 reservoir
dam: 8 Garrison
locale: 4 N. Dak.
river: 8 Missouri
Sakall: 2 S.Z.
Sakamoto, Kyu song: Sukiyaki (1963)
Sakata: 4 city, town 6 Harold
locale: 5 Japan
sake: 3 aim 4 gain, good, wine 5 cause, drink, score 6 behalf, motive, profit, reason, regard 7 benefit, concern, purpose, respect, welfare 8 beverage, interest 9 advantage, objective, principle, well-being
for the ~ of: 7 because
starter: 4 keep, name
see also saki
saker: 4 bird 6 falcon
__ sakes alive!: 4 Land
Sakhalin: 3 isl. 4 isle 6 island
locale: 6 Russia
Sakharov, Andrei: 8 Nobelist 9 physicist
saki: 4 wine 5 drink 7 primate 8 beverage
base: 4 rice
relative: 3 ape 4 titi 5 chimp, drill, jocko, lemur, loris, magot, orang, potto, shrew 6 aye-aye, baboon, Bandar, galago, gelada, gibbon, grivet, guenon, howler, langur, macaco, monkey, rhesus, uakari, vervet 7 colobus, gorilla, guereza, hoolock, macaque, sapajou, siamang, tamarin, tarsier 8 bush baby, capuchin, mandrill, mangabey, marmoset, talapoin 9 orangutan 10 Barbary ape, chimpanzee, orangutang
Saki: 5 alias 6 writer
pen name of: H.H. Munro
work: Beasts and Super Beasts
The Chronicles of Clovis
Esme
Reginald
The Square Egg
The Unbearable Bassington
Sakmann, Bert: 6 German 8 Nobelist
Saks, Gene: 8 director
film: Barefoot in the Park (1967)
Brighton Beach Memoirs (1986)
Cactus Flower (1969)
Last of the Red Hot Lovers (1972)
The Odd Couple (1968)
The Prisoner of Second Avenue (1975)
Sakura: 4 city, town
locale: 5 Japan
Sakutaro, Hagiwara: 4 poet 8 Japanese
sal __: 4 soda
Sal: 3 gal 4 mule 5 Bando, Mineo 6 Maglie 7 Viscuso
canal: 4 Erie
__ Sal: 5 My Gal
sala: 4 room 7 Spanish
site: 4 casa
salaam: 3 bow 5 greet 8 greeting
__ Salaam: 5 Dar es
Salaberry-de-Valleyfield: 4 city, town
locale: 6 Canada, Québec
Salacia, husband of: 7 Neptune
salacious: 4 lewd 6 ribald, risqué, smutty 8 uncurbed 10 lubricious, scurrilous, unbecoming
Salacrou, Armand: 6 French 10 playwright
salad: 4 slaw 5 mache 6 course 7 Waldorf 8 coleslaw, side dish 9 macédoine, tabbouleh 10 salmagundi
bowl wood: 4 teak
cheese: 4 bleu, blue
complete a ~: 5 dress
days: 5 youth
deli ~: 4 slaw
follower: 6 entrée
green: 5 cress 6 borage 7 spinach
help with the ~: 4 toss
ingredient: 3 udo 4 cuke, mayo 5 onion 6 carrot, celery, endive
like some ~ dressings: 5 zesty 6 creamy
order: 5 no oil
salad __: 3 bar, oil 4 bowl, days, fork 5 green, plate 6 basket, burnet, greens
__ salad: 3 egg 4 corn, tuna, word 5 chef's, fruit, Greek, pasta 6 Caesar, garden, potato, rocket, tossed 7 spinach, Waldorf
Salada: 3 tea
alternative: 6 Lipton, Nestea, Tetley 7 Bigelow, Red Rose 8 Twinings
__ Salad Annie: 4 Polk
salad-bar habitué: 5 vegan
salad dressing: 4 Roka 5 aioli, house, ranch 6 French 7 Italian, Russian 8 Wish-Bone 9 Seven Seas 10 bleu cheese, honey Dijon, mayonnaise 11 Good Seasons
bottle: 5 cruet
ingredient: 3 oil 7 vinegar
Saladin citadel site: 5 Cairo
salal: 5 fruit, shrub
family: 5 heath
relative: 6 azalea, kalmia 7 arbutus, rhodora 8 cassiope, cowberry 9 blueberry, deerberry
Salam, Abdus: 8 Nobelist 9 Pakistani, physicist
Salamanca: 4 city, town
locale: 6 Mexico 10 Guanajuato
salamander: 3 eft, olm 4 newt 6 mud eel 7 axolotl 8 mudpuppy 9 amphibian
__ salamander: 4 mole 5 blind, tiger 7 spotted
salami: 4 meat 5 Genoa 7 cold cut, sausage
salary: 3 fee, pay 4 take, wage 5 bacon, money, wages 6 income 7 revenue, stipend 8 earnings 9 emolument 10 recompense
get a ~: 4 earn, work
increase: 5 raise
less deductions: 3 net
limit: 3 cap
__ salary: 4 base
Salcantay: 4 peak 5 mount 8 mountain
locale: 4 Peru
Salchow: 4 jump, move
sport: 10 ice skating
Saldana: 7 Theresa
sale: 4 deal 7 auction, bargain, special 8 discount, disposal, markdown, purchase 9 clearance, reduction, vendition
bake ~: 7 benefit 10 fund-raiser
disclaimer: 4 as is
for ~: 9 available
incentive: 6 rebate
item for ~: 4 good, ware
item marking: 3 irr. 5 irreg. 9 imperfect, irregular
offer for ~: 5 put up 6 market
on ~: 3 low 5 cheap 7 cut-rate, good buy, low-cost, reduced, slashed, thrifty 8 uncostly 9 half-price 10 economical, marked down, reasonable
put up for ~: 5 offer
rummage ~: 5 bazar 6 bazaar 7 benefit 10 fund-raiser
starter: 5 whole
word: 3 off 4 only, save 5 limit
__ sale: 3 tag, tax 4 bake, fire, wash, yard 5 short, white 6 forced, garage, jumble, public, red-tag 7 rummage
salele: 4 fish
Salem: 3 cat 4 city, town
city near ~: 6 Eugene
county: 6 Marion
locale: 4 Mass. 6 Oregon 8 Virginia
river: 10 Willamette
Salem __: 4 desk
__-Salem: 7 Winston
salema: 4 fish
Salem's Lot author: Stephen King
Sale of the Century: 8 game show
Salerno: 4 city, port, town 8 province
commune: 5 Eboli
Gulf of ~ resort: 6 Amalfi
locale: 5 Italy
Salers: 3 cow 4 bull 6 bovine, cattle
sales: 5 trade
attraction: 6 come-on, rebate 8 discount 9 clearance
bonus: 5 spiff
ender: 3 man, men 4 girl, lady, room 5 clerk, woman, women 6 ladies, people, person
goal: 5 quota
group: 5 force
pitch: 2 ad 4 line 5 spiel
rep's client: 3 acc. 7 account
sample: 4 demo
slip: 4 rcpt. 7 receipt
slip entry: 3 tax 5 price
talk: 4 puff 5 pitch
venue: 4 mall, mart, shop 5 store 6 market 8 boutique
sales __: 3 rep, tax 4 slip, talk 5 check 7 receipt
salesperson: 3 rep 5 agent, clerk 6 closer, hawker, vender, vendor 7 employe 8 employee, merchant
lines: 4 puff, sell 5 offer, spiel 6 patter 9 promotion
Sales, Soupy: 4 host 5 comic 8 comedian
dog: 9 White Fang 10 Black Tooth
missile: 3 pie
Salic __: 3 law
salicylate: 5 ester
__ salicylate: 6 methyl, phenyl, sodium 7 isoamyl
salicylic __: 4 acid
salient: 5 sharp 6 famous, marked, signal 7 central, jutting, notable, obvious, weighty 8 striking 9 arresting, important, intrusive, obtrusive, pertinent, prominent, trenchant 10 impressive, noticeable, projecting, pronounced, protruding, remarkable
Salieri, Antonio: 7 Italian 8 composer
rival: 6 Mozart
Saliers: 5 Emily
Salina: 4 city, town
locale: 6 Kansas
Salinas: 4 city, town 5 Pedro
locale: 10 California
Salinas, Pedro: 4 poet 7 Spanish
saline: 5 salty 8 brackish
solution: 5 brine
symbol: 4 NaCl
Salinger, J.D.: 6 author, writer
work: The Catcher in the Rye
For Esme-with Love and Squalor
Franny and Zooey
A Perfect Day for Bananafish
Raise High the Roof-Beam, Carpenters
Salisbury: 4 city, town
locale: 8 Maryland, Rhodesia
today: 6 Harare
Salisbury __: 5 Plain, steak
Salisbury Plain river: 4 Avon
Salish: 6 Indian 7 Amerind
saliva: 4 spit 5 drool
antibody in ~: 3 IGA
combining form: 4 sial- 5 ptyal-, sialo- 6 ptyalo-
eject ~: 4 spit
salivary __: 5 gland 7 amylase
salivate: 5 drool 7 slobber
Salk, Jonas: 9 physician
contemporary: 5 Sabin
product: 5 serum 7 vaccine
salle: 4 room 6 French 7 chambre
salle à __: 6 manger
Sallie __: 3 Mae
sallow: 3 wan 4 dull, pale, waxy 5 ashen, mealy, pasty 6 anemic, chalky, pallid, peaked, sickly 7 anaemic, bilious 8 liverish 9 albescent, bloodless, jaundiced, unhealthy, yellowish 10 exsanguine
Sallust: 5 Roman 6 author, writer 9 historian
sally: 3 wit 4 joke, quip, raid 5 burst, foray, jaunt, leave 6 assail, attack, junket, onrush, outing, retort, sortie 7 assault, go forth, outflow, outrush 8 burst out, outburst, repartee 9 excursion, irruption, offensive, onslaught, stream out 10 expedition, outpouring, pleasantry
forth: 2 go 5 start 6 set off, set out
lunn: 4 cake
sally __: 4 lunn, port 5 forth
Sally: 4 Rand, Ride, song 5 Field 6 Bowles, Eilers 7 Hemings, musical 8 Kirkland 9 Kellerman, Struthers
composer: 4 Kern
Sally __ Alley: 5 in Our
Sally __ Raphael: 5 Jessy
__ Sally: 4 Aunt, Axis 7 Mustang
Sally Bowles author: Christopher Isherwood
Sally G (1974 song) artist: Paul McCartney
Sally Go Round the __: 5 Roses
Salma: 5 Hayek
salmagundi: 3 mix 4 hash, olio, stew 5 salad 6 jumble, medley 7 farrago, mélange, mixture 8 mishmash, mixed bag, pastiche 9 pasticcio, patchwork, potpourri 10 hodgepodge, miscellany
Salman: 7 Rushdie
salmi: 4 game 6 ragout
like ~: 5 spicy 6 spicey
salmon: 3 lox 4 chum, coho, fish, masu, pink, tyee 5 cohoe, color 6 kipper, orange 7 sockeye 9 yellowish
Chinook ~: 4 tyee
cured ~: 7 gravlax
emulate ~: 5 spawn
ender: 5 berry
mature ~: 4 kelt
Pacific ~: 4 chum, coho 5 cohoe
relative: 4 nude 5 melon 6 damask 7 apricot 8 flamingo 9 carnation
serving: 5 steak
smoked ~: 3 lox 4 nova
three-year-old ~: 4 mort
young: 4 jack, parr 5 smolt 6 grilse, samlet
salmon __: 4 pink 5 brick, trout, wheel
__ salmon: 3 dog, red 4 chum, coho, jack, king, lake, pink, tyee 5 cohoe, white 6 beaked, silver 7 chinook, Pacific, quinnat, sockeye
Salmon
son of: 4 Boaz
salmonberry: 5 fruit
salmonlike fish of Japan: 3 ayu
Salmon P. __: 5 Chase
Salome: 4 Jens 5 opera
composer: 7 Strauss
role: 5 Herod 8 Herodias, Jokanaan 9 Narraboth
setting: 7 Galilee
to Herod: 5 niece
Salomé author: Oscar Wilde
salon: 4 shop 6 parlor, soiree 7 gallery 8 assembly, boutique, tea party 9 reception 10 art gallery, living room

color: 5 henna
concern: 4 hair 5 nails
creation: 4 coif 6 hairdo
item: 6 curler
job: 3 dye, set 4 perm, tint 5 rinse 6 facial
product: 3 dye, gel 4 curl, wave 5 spray
sound: 4 snip
worker: 6 barber
__ salon: 3 art 6 beauty
Salonen, Esa-Pekka: 7 Finnish 9 conductor
Salonga: 3 Lea
Salonika: 4 gulf
locale: 6 Greece
saloon: 3 bar, inn, pub 4 dive 6 lounge, tavern 7 barroom, taproom 8 alehouse, taphouse 9 speakeasy 10 restaurant
chit: 3 tab 6 bar tab
entertainer: 5 B-girl
habitué: 6 barfly
light: 4 neon
order: 3 ale 4 beer 5 booze
seat: 5 stool
smashers assn.: 4 WCTU
__-Saloon League: 4 Anti
Salop: 6 county
locale: 7 England
salpinx: 4 wind 7 trumpet 10 instrument
origin: 6 Greece
salsa: 3 dip 4 salt 5 dance, gravy, music, sauce, spice 6 relish 8 dressing 9 condiment, flavoring, seasoning
club dance: 5 rumba 6 rhumba
holder: 4 chip 5 nacho
like ~: 3 hot 4 mild 5 tangy, zesty
salsify: 6 veggie 9 vegetable
salt: 3 gob, tar 4 cure, NaCl, swab, swob, zest 6 borate, deicer, flavor, iodate, kipper, living, pickle, sailor, sea dog, seaman, season 7 acetate, bromate, citrate, crewman, jack tar, mariner, matelot, matelow, nitrate, nitrite, sulfate, sulfite, swabbie 8 benzoate, deckhand, dry humor, fluoride, preserve, seafarer, stearate, tartrate 9 carbonate, condiment, cyclamate, phosphate, seasoning, shellback 10 bluejacket
acid ~: 5 ester
add ~: 6 flavor, season
away: 4 bank, hide, keep, save 5 amass, cache, hoard, lay by, lay up, put by, spare, stash, store 6 invest, pile up 7 deposit, store up 8 hold on to, lay aside, put aside, set aside 9 stockpile 10 accumulate
bit: 5 grain, pinch
combining form: 3 hal- 4 hali-, halo-, sali-
deposit: 4 lick
ender: 3 box 4 bush, wort 5 peter, water, works 6 cellar, shaker
his wife turned to ~: 3 Lot
in French: 3 sel
mines: 4 work 6 office
preserve with ~: 4 corn
rock ~: 4 NaCl 6 halite
rub ~ in the wound: 3 vex 4 fret, rack 5 harry, hound 6 harass, pester, pick on, plague, rankle 7 afflict, agonize, anguish, bedevil, oppress, torment, torture 8 aggrieve, distress, irritate 9 persecute
spread ~: 5 deice
treat ~: 6 iodize
tree: 4 atle
water: 3 sea 5 brine, ocean
see also sailor
salt __: 3 hay, pan, pit 4 away, cake, dome, down, flat, junk, lake, lick, mine, pork, tree, well 5 cedar, chuck, gland, glaze, grass, horse, marsh, shake, spoon, stick, water 6 shaker
salt __ earth: 5 of the
salt __ taffy: 5 water
salt-__: 3 box
__ salt: 3 bay, sea 4 acid, bile, rock, sour 5 attic, basic, Epsom, table 6 celery, common, double, garlic, sorrel
Salt: 5 river 8 Jennifer
city on the ~: 7 Phoenix
locale: 7 Arizona
Salt __ City: 4 Lake
SALT: 4 pact 6 treaty
concern: 3 ABM 4 ICBM, nuke 5 H-bomb
part: 4 Arms 5 Talks 9 Strategic 10 Limitation
participant: 3 USA 4 USSR
Salta: 4 city, town
locale: 9 Argentina
salt and __: 6 pepper
saltarello: 5 dance
saltate: 4 jump, leap
saltbox topper: 4 roof
saltbush: 5 orach, shrub 6 orache
__ Salt Desert: 5 Great
salted peanuts: 5 snack
Salten, Felix: 6 author, writer 9 Hungarian
work: Bambi
Saltillo: 4 city, town
locale: 6 Mexico 8 Coahuila
saltine: 5 bread 7 cracker 9 appetizer
brand: 5 Zesta 7 Premium
Salt, Jennifer: 7 actress
film: The Revolutionary (1970)
Sisters (1973)
TV: Soap
__ Salt Lake: 5 Great
Salt Lake City: 4 town
athlete: 3 Ute
city near ~: 4 Orem
grp.: 3 LDS
locale: 4 Utah
newspaper: 7 Tribune
river: 6 Jordan
saltlike: 6 haloid
salt-marsh shrub genus: 3 iva
Salt-n-Pepa: 4 trio
genre: 3 rap
members: James, Denton, Roper
song: Do You Want Me (1991)
Push It (1987)
Shoop (1993)
Whatta Man (1994)
Salto: 4 city, town
locale: 7 Uruguay
Salton Sea: 4 lake
locale: 10 California
saltpeter: 5 niter
source: 5 Chile
__ salts: 4 bath 5 Epsom
saltwater: 5 brine 6 marine 8 maritime
Salt-Water Ballads author: John Masefield
saltwater taffy: 5 candy
salty: 3 dry 4 blue, racy, tart 5 bawdy, briny, tangy, taste, witty 6 coarse, earthy, lively, ribald, risqué, saline 7 piquant, pungent 8 alkaline, brackish, off-color 10 indelicate, pugnacious
dog: 7 jack tar
salty dog: 5 drink 6 sailor 8 beverage, cocktail
ingredient: 3 gin 5 vodka
Saltykov, Mikhail: 6 writer 7 Russian
Salty O'Rourke (1945 film)
cast: William Demarest, Alan Ladd, Gail Russell
director: Raoul Walsh
salubrious: 4 good 7 healthy 8 hygienic, sanitary 9 healthful, wholesome 10 beneficial
salubrity: 8 wellness
Salud!: 5 skoal, toast 6 cheers, kampai
Saludos __!: 6 amigos
Saluki: 3 dog 5 canid 6 canine
__-Salut: 4 Port
salutary: 4 good 6 aidful, benign, useful 7 gainful, healthy, helpful 8 curative, positive, remedial, sanative, valuable 9 effectual, favorable, healthful, practical, wholesome 10 beneficial, productive, profitable, worthwhile
salutation: 3 bow 4 hail, kiss 5 hallo, hello, title 6 speech 7 address, regards, welcome 8 greeting 9 reception 10 apostrophe, good wishes, pleasantry
word: 3 sir 4 dear, sirs 6 madame
salutations: 7 regards 8 respects
salute: 3 bow, nod 4 hail, laud, wave 5 exalt, extol, greet, honor, kudos, toast 6 extoll, homage, kampai, praise 7 acclaim, address, applaud, commend, flatter, gesture, glorify, plaudit, tribute, welcome 8 accolade, encomium, flattery, good word, greeting 9 laudation, panegyric, pay homage, recognize 10 exaltation, panegyrize
Salvador: 4 city, Dali, town 5 Luria 7 Allende
formerly: 5 Bahia
locale: 6 Brasil, Brazil
__ Salvador: 3 San
Salvador author: Joan Didion
salvage: 4 junk, loot, save, take 5 glean 6 obtain, redeem, regain, rescue 7 get back, reclaim, recover, restore 8 retrieve 9 remainder
salvation: 6 escape, pardon, rescue 7 freedom, release 8 delivery, lifeline, reprieve 10 liberation, redemption
Salvation Army: 7 charity
temp: 5 Santa 10 bell-ringer
trainee: 5 cadet
Salvatore: 9 Quasimodo
salve: 4 balm, ease 5 cream 6 lotion, remedy, soothe 7 anodyne, assuage, comfort, mollify, relieve, unction, unguent 8 dressing, lenitive, liniment, medicine, ointment, palliate 9 alleviate, emollient, lubricant, mollifier, untrouble 10 medication, palliative
apply ~: 5 rub in
ingredient: 4 aloe
Salve __: 6 Regina
salver: 4 tray 7 platter
salvia: 5 plant 6 flower
cousin: 4 sage
salvo: 4 bang, fire, hail 5 blast, burst, shout 6 volley 7 barrage, ovation, tribute 8 outburst 9 broadside, cannonade, discharge, explosion, fusillade
Salween: 5 river
locale: 5 China 7 Myanmar
Salwen: 3 Hal
Salzburg: 4 city, town
environs: 4 Alps
locale: 3 Aus. 4 Aust. 7 Austria
river: 3 Mur
Sam: 4 Bass, Colt, Hill, Huff, Nunn, Rice, Wood 5 Adams, Cooke, Ervin, Jaffe, Neill, Raimi, Sills, Snead, Spade, uncle, Wyche 6 Levene, Malone, Mendes, Taylor, Walton 7 Bottoms, Clemens, Elliott, Houston, Kinison, McCloud, Rayburn, Shepard, Spiegel 8 Bischoff, Crawford, Levenson, Phillips 9 Donaldson, Peckinpah, Wanamaker, Waterston
Sam __: 4 Hill 7 the Sham
Sam __ belt: 6 Browne
Sam-__: 3 I-Am
__ Sam: 3 I Am 5 Uncle
sama: 4 fish
Sama: 8 language
Sam Adams product: 3 ale
__ Samaj: 6 Brahma, Brahmo
Samana __: 3 Cay
Sam and Dave
members: Moore, Prater
song: Hold On! I'm a Comin' (1966)
I Thank You (1968)
Soul Man (1967)
Samantha: 3 Fox 4 Sang 5 Eggar 6 Mathis
aunt: 5 Clara
mother: 6 Endora
Samar: 3 isl. 4 isle 6 island
island near: 5 Leyte
locale: Philippines
Samara: 3 car 4 auto, city, Lada, town 10 automobile
locale: 6 Russia
Samaria, south of: 5 Judea 6 Judaea
Samaritan
be a ~: 3 aid 4 help
__ Samaritan: 4 Good
samarium: 5 metal 7 element
Samarra: 4 city, town
locale: 4 Irak, Iraq
river: 6 Tigris
samba: 4 step 5 dance, music
variation: 7 carioca
sambal: 9 condiment
sambar: 4 deer
relative: 3 elk, roe 4 axis, pudu, shou, sika 5 moose 6 chital, guemal, hangul, huemul, thamin, wapiti 7 brocket, caribou, muntjac, muntjak 8 reindeer 9 barasingh
Sambora, Richie spouse: Heather Locklear
Sambre: 5 river
locale: 6 France 7 Belgium
same: 4 dupe, ibid., idem, like, twin 5 alike, clone, ditto, equal, exact, level, xerox 6 coeval, double, on a par 7 pronoun, similar, uniform 8 constant, likewise, matching, unvaried 9 aforesaid, analogous, congruous, duplicate, identical, perpetual, similarly, unaltered, unchanged, unfailing, unvarying 10 carbon copy, coincident, comparable, compatible, consistent, equivalent, invariable, synonymous, tantamount, true to type, two of a kind, unchanging
at the ~ time: 5 along 8 meantime 9 meanwhile
at the ~ time as: 5 while 6 during, whilst
be the ~: 4 gybe, jibe 5 agree, match, tally 6 concur, square 8 coincide, dovetail 10 correspond
combining form: 3 aut-, hom-, iso-, syn- 4 auto-, equi-, homo-, taut- 5 homeo-, tauto-
consider the ~: 6 equate
in prescriptions: 3 ead.
in the ~ way: 3 too 4 also 6 as well 8 likewise 9 similarly
In the ~ way: 9 similarly, uniformly 10 comparably
just the ~: 3 yet 5 still 6 anyhow, anyway, at that, even so, though 7 however 9 at any rate
make the ~: 8 equalize
of the ~ height: 4 even 6 square 8 parallel
of the ~ opinion: 3 one 5 joint 6 agreed 8 in accord 9 concerted, unanimous, undivided 10 like-minded
starter: 4 self
Same __ Me: 3 Ole
__ same boat: 5 in the
__ same breath: 5 in the
samech: 6 Hebrew, letter
predecessor: 3 nun
successor: 4 ayin

Same here!: 5 ditto, me too
samekh: 6 Hebrew, letter
predecessor: 3 nun
successor: 4 ayin
sameness: 3 par 5 unity 6 parity, tedium, unison 7 analogy, oneness 8 equality, likeness, monotony 9 alikeness 10 repetition, similarity, uniformity
same old __: 5 grind, story
Same Old Lang Syne (1980 song)
artist: Dan Fogelberg
same-old-same-old: 3 rut 4 dull 7 rat race, routine 9 treadmill
Same Old Saturday Night (1955 song)
artist: Frank Sinatra
__ same time: 5 at the
Same Time, Next Year: 4 film, play
author: Bernard Slade
cast: Alan Alda, Ellen Burstyn
director: Robert Mulligan
__ same token: 5 by the
__ same wavelength: 5 on the
Sami: 4 Lapp 9 Laplander
Samian __: 4 ware
samiel: 4 wind
samisen: 4 lute 6 string 10 instrument
origin: 5 Japan
samite: 6 fabric 8 material
Sammamish: 4 city, town
locale: 10 Washington
Sammee: 4 Tong
Sammi: 5 Davis, Smith
Samms: 4 Emma
Sammy: 4 Cahn, Fain, Kaye, Sosa 5 Baugh, Davis, Hagar, Johns 6 Turner
Sammy __: 6 Jo Dean
Sammy __ Jr.: 5 Davis
Samoa: 4 isls. 5 isles 7 islands
capital: 4 Apia
island: 5 Upolu 6 Hivaoa, Savaii
neighbor: 5 Tonga
port: 8 Pago Pago
studier of ~: 4 Mead
Samos: 3 isl. 4 isle 6 island
locale: 6 Aegean, Greece
site of ancient ~: 5 Ionia
storyteller of ~: 4 Esop 5 Aesop
samovar: 3 urn
serving: 3 tea
Samoyed: 3 dog, pet 5 canid, spitz 6 canine
burden: 4 sled
samp: 4 corn 6 hominy
sampan: 4 boat 5 skiff
sample: 3 bit, eat, sip, try 4 bite, case, clip, demo, lick, part, poll, test, unit 5 model, piece, savor, taste, token 6 morsel, survey, swatch 7 display, examine, example, handout, inspect, partake, pattern, portion, section, segment 8 fragment, instance, specimen, spoonful, standard 10 experience, experiment
sign by a free ~: 5 try me
__ sample: 3 pit 5 floor
sampler statement: 5 motto
sampling: 4 case, poll 8 instance, specimen
__ sampling: 6 random
Sampras, Pete: 7 netster 9 tennis pro
milieu: 5 court
rival: 6 Agassi
Sampson: 4 Will
Sam's Club rival: 3 BJ's 6 Costco
Samson: 5 he-man, opera
composer: 6 Handel
father of ~: 6 Manoah
Samson Agonistes author: John Milton
Samson and Delilah (1949 film)
cast: Hedy Lamarr, Victor Mature, George Sanders
director: Cecil B. DeMille
setting: 4 Gaza
Samsung country: 5 Korea

Sam the Sham and the Pharaohs song: Lil' Red Riding Hood (1966) Wooly Bully (1965)
Samuel: 4 Colt, Ting 5 Adams, Baker, Morse, Pepys, Ramey 6 Barber, Butler, Daniel, Fuller, Selvon 7 Beckett, Goldwyn, Gompers, Jackson, Johnson 9 Coleridge, Hahnemann 10 Duesenberg, Richardson
parent of ~: 6 Hannah 7 Elkanah
preceder: 4 Ruth
son of ~: 4 Joel 6 Abijah
teacher: 3 Eli
Samuel __ Coleridge: 6 Taylor
Samuel __ Morison: 5 Eliot
Samuel de __: 9 Champlain
Samuel F.B. __: 5 Morse
Samuel L. __: 7 Jackson
Samuelson, Paul: 8 Nobelist 9 economist
Samuelsson, Bengt: 7 Swedish 8 Nobelist
Samurai: 3 SUV 6 Suzuki
__ Samurai, The: 5 Seven
__ s'amuse: 5 Le roi
San: 5 river
locale: 6 Poland 7 Ukraine
San __: 4 Blas, José, Remo 5 Bruno, Diego, Dimas, Mateo, Pablo, Pedro 6 Angelo, Antone, Benito, Felipe, Isidro, Marcos, Marino, Martín, Rafael, Simeon, Ysidro 7 Agustín, Antonio, Gabriel, Gennaro, Lorenzo, Quentin
San __ Bay: 5 Pablo
San __ Capistrano: 4 Juan
San __ Chargers: 5 Diego
San __ Chicken: 5 Diego
San __ Day: 7 Jacinto
San __ fault: 7 Andreas
San __ Hill: 4 Juan
San __ Mountains: 4 Juan 7 Gabriel
San __ Obispo: 4 Luis
San __ Potosí: 4 Luis
San __ scale: 4 Jose
San __ Spurs: 7 Antonio
San __ Valley: 7 Joaquin
Sana: 4 city, town 7 capital
locale: 5 Yemen
San Agustín: 4 city, town
locale: 6 Mexico 7 Jalisco
__ sana in corpore sano: 4 mens
San Angelo: 4 city, town
locale: 5 Texas
San Antonio: 4 city, town
county: 5 Bexar
landmark: 5 Alamo
locale: 5 Texas
pro team: 5 Spurs
San Antonio (1945 film)
cast: Errol Flynn, S.Z. Sakall, Alexis Smith
director: David Butler
San Antonio Rose (1961 song) artist: Floyd Cramer
sanative: 5 tonic 6 iatric 7 healing 8 curative, remedial, salutary 9 healthful, medicinal 10 corrective
sanatorium: 8 hospital
sanatory: 7 healthy
San Benito: 4 city, town
locale: 5 Texas
San Bernardino: 3 mts. 4 city, mtns., town 5 range 6 valley 9 mountains
locale: 10 California
San Bernardo: 4 city, town
locale: 5 Chile
San Blas: 4 gulf 6 Indian 7 Amerind
San Bruno: 4 city, town
locale: 10 California
San Carlos: 4 city, town
locale: 10 California
Sancerre: 4 wine 5 white
origin: 6 France
Sánchez, Florencio: 9 Uruguayan 10 playwright

Sanchez, Oscar Arias: 8 Nobelist 10 Costa Rican
Sancho __: 5 Panza
San Clemente: 3 isl. 4 isle 6 island
locale: 10 California
sanctified: 4 holy 5 blest 6 divine, sacred, solemn
sanctify: 4 keep 5 adore, bless, deify, exalt, extol 6 anoint, devote, extoll, hallow, praise, purify 7 absolve, cleanse, glorify, worship 8 canonize, dedicate, enshrine, inshrine, set apart 10 consecrate, panegyrize
sanctimonious: 4 smug 5 false, pious 7 bigoted, prudish 8 unctuous 9 deceiving, insincere
sanction: 2 OK 3 ban, let, nod 4 abet, back, okay, pass, tabu, writ 5 allow, bless, brook, leave, taboo 6 accept, assent, decree, invest, permit, praise, ratify, suffer 7 approve, backing, boycott, certify, command, confirm, consent, embargo, empower, endorse, go-ahead, indorse, liberty, license, mandate, penalty, qualify, support, warrant 8 accede to, accredit, approval, assent to, blessing, legalize, sentence, stand for, tolerate, validate, vouch for 9 approve of, authorize, clearance, encourage, get behind, give leave, privilege, put up with, recognize, recommend, subscribe 10 commission, give the nod, green light, injunction, legitimize, permission, punishment, sufferance, underwrite
sanctioned: 5 jural, legal, legit, licit, sound, valid 6 kasher, kosher, lawful, proper 7 regular 8 official, orthodox, rightful, verified 9 by the book, canonical 10 legitimate
__ Sanction, The: 3 Loo 5 Eiger
sanctity: 5 piety 8 holiness
sign of ~: 4 halo
__ sanctorum: 4 acta 7 sanctum
Sanctórum: 4 city, town
locale: 6 Mexico, Puebla
sanctuary: 3 den 4 aery, bema, eyry, hole, lair, park, port 5 aerie, altar, cover, eyrie, haven, oasis, zendo 6 asylum, bethel, chapel, church, covert, harbor, hole-up, refuge, resort, safety, shrine, temple 7 chancel, convent, defense, harbour, hideout, reserve, retreat, shelter 8 cloister, hideaway, preserve 9 anchorage, cathedral, harborage, hermitage, safe house, seclusion 10 ivory tower, protection, tabernacle
African ~: 6 casbah
give ~: 7 protect
Greek ~: 5 secos, sekos
Sanctuary author: Faye Kellerman, William Faulkner
sanctum: 3 den 4 lair 5 haven, oasis 6 shrine
inner ~: 6 adytum
__ Sanctum Mysteries, The: 5 Inner
sand: 3 tan 4 dune, grit 5 pluck, scour, shore, valor 6 abrade, smooth, yellow 7 reddish 8 abrasive, brownish
bar: 4 reef 5 shoal
combining form: 3 amm- 4 ammo- 5 psamm- 6 psammo-
creation: 6 castle
dab: 4 fish
dune: 4 seif
ender: 3 bag, bar, box, bur, hog, lot, man, men, pit 4 bank, fish, spur, worm, wort 5 blast, paper, piper, stone, storm 6 bagger, castle 7 blaster
fine ~: 4 silt
hill: 4 dune

kind of ~: 4 slag
lance: 4 fish
product: 5 glass
relative: 4 buff, corn, gold, lime, rust 5 blond, brass, coral, cream, flaxy, lemon, maize, ocher, ochre, peach, rusty, straw 6 blonde, canary, chammy, citron, crocus, flaxen, shammy, shamoy 7 apricot, chamois, citrine, jasmine, mustard, nankeen, old gold, saffron, xanthic 8 daffodil, primrose 9 champagne, goldenrod, jessamine
starter: 5 green, quick
trap: 6 bunker, hazard
unit: 5 grain
sand __: 3 bar, dab, eel, rat 4 crab, dune, flea, jack, lily, pear, pike, pile, shoe, trap, wasp 5 chair, lance, perch, puppy, shark, table, tiger, viper, yacht 6 castle, cherry, dollar, grouse, hopper, launce, lizard, martin, myrtle 7 cricket, verbena
__ sand: 3 oil, tar
Sand: 4 Paul 6 George
Sandahl: 7 Bergman
sandal: 4 geta, shoe, zori 5 thong 8 footgear, footwear
ender: 4 wood
part: 5 strap
sandals: 5 flats
sandalwood: 4 tree
__, Sand, and Stars: 4 Wind
sandarac: 4 tree
family: 7 cypress
relative: 7 juniper 10 arborvitae
wood: 5 thuja, thuya
sandbag: 5 cheat, force 7 inhibit, swindle 8 obstruct, undercut 9 undermine
sandbank: 5 shelf, shoal
Sandberg, Ryne sport: 8 baseball
sandbox
need: 4 pail
patron: 3 kid, tot 4 tike, tyke
__ Sandbox: 5 Up the
Sandbox, The author: Edward Albee
sandbur: 5 grass
Sandburg, Carl: 4 poet 6 author, writer
work: Abraham Lincoln—The Prairie Years
Abraham Lincoln—The War Years
A.E.F.
The American Songbag
Chicago
Chicago Poems
Cornhuskers
Fog
Good Morning, America
Grass
Harvest Poems
Honey and Salt
The People, Yes
Reckless Ecstasy
Rootabaga Stories
Smoke and Steel
sand-castle
destroyer: 4 wave
locale: 5 beach
Sandcastle, The author: Iris Murdoch
Sande, Earl: 6 jockey
milieu: 5 track
Sandel, Cora: 6 writer 9 Norwegian
__ sander: 4 belt, disk 7 orbital
Sander: 7 Vanocur
sanderling: 4 bird
Sanders: 5 Deion 6 George 7 Harland, Richard 8 Lawrence
Sanders, Deion: 10 baseballer, footballer
nickname: 4 Neon
Sanders, George: 5 actor
film: All About Eve (1950, AA)

The Falcon Takes Over (1942)
Four Men and a Prayer (1938)
The Ghost and Mrs. Muir (1947)
Hangover Square (1945)
The House of Seven Gables (1940)
Jupiter's Darling (1955)
The King's Thief (1955)
Lancer Spy (1937)
The Last Voyage (1960)
The Lodger (1944)
Man Hunt (1941)
The Moon and Sixpence (1942)
Nurse Edith Cavell (1939)
The Picture of Dorian Gray (1945)
The Private Affairs of Bel Ami (1947)
Rebecca (1940)
The Saint Strikes Back (1939)
Samson and Delilah (1949)
A Shot in the Dark (1964)
Solomon and Sheba (1959)
Son of Fury (1942)
The Son of Monte Cristo (1940)
The Strange Affair of Uncle Harry (1945)
Summer Storm (1944)
That Kind of Woman (1959)
Thieves' Holiday (1946)
A Touch of Larceny (1959)
Village of the Damned (1960)
Witness to Murder (1954)
persona: 3 cad
spouse: Zsa Zsa Gabor
Sanders, Harland: 3 Col. 7 Colonel
company: 3 KFC
Sanders, Lawrence: 6 author, writer
work: The Anderson Tapes
Caper
Capital Crimes
The Case of Lucy Bending
The Dream Lover
The Eighth Commandment
The First Deadly Sin
The Fourth Deadly Sin
Guilty Pleasures
The Loves of Harry Dancer
Love Songs
The Marlow Chronicles
McNally's Alibi
McNally's Caper
McNally's Chance
McNally's Dilemma
McNally's Folly
McNally's Gamble
McNally's Luck
McNally's Puzzle
McNally's Risk
McNally's Secret
McNally's Trial
The Passion of Molly T
The Pleasures of Helen
Privat Pleasures
The Second Deadly Sin
The Seduction of Peter S
The Seventh Commandment
The Sixth Commandment
Stolen Blessings
Sullivan's Sting
Tales of the Wolf
The Tangent Factor
The Tangent Objective
The Tenth Commandment
The Third Deadly Sin
The Timothy Files
Timothy's Game
The Tomorrow File
Sand, George: 5 alias 6 author, French, writer
friend: 6 Chopin
work: Agendas
The Bagpipers
The Black City
Consuelo
Country Waif
The Devil's Pool
Elle et lui
François le Champi
The Gallant Lords of Bois-Dori
Histoire de Ma Vie
Horace
Indiana
La Mare au diable
La Petite Fadette
La Ville Noire
Lavinia
Lélia
Le Marquis de Villemer
Le menunier d'Angibault
Les Maîtres Mosaïstes
Les Maîtres Sonneurs
Lucrezia Floriani
Mademoiselle Merquem
Marianne
The Master Mosaic Workers
The Master Pipers
Mauprat
The Miller of Angibault
Nanon
Narcisse
Nohant
She & He
Simon
Valentine
A Winter on Majorca
sandhill: 5 crane
Sandhurst school: 3 RMA
San Diego: 4 city, port, town
athletes: 6 Aztecs
attraction: 3 zoo
city near ~: 6 Del Mar, La Mesa
locale: 10 California
newspaper: 7 Tribune
pro team: 6 Padres 8 Chargers
school: 4 SDSU
San Diego ___: 7 Chicken
San-Diego-to-Santa-Ana dir.: 3 NNW
San Dimas: 4 city, town
locale: 10 California
Sandinista foe: 6 Contra
Sandler, Adam: 5 actor
film: Big Daddy (1999)
The Waterboy (1998)
The Wedding Singer (1998)
song: The Chanukah Song (1995)
___ Sandman: 5 Enter 6 Mister
Sandoz, Mari: 6 author, writer
sandpaper: 4 buff 6 abrade
covering: 4 grit
like ~: 4 fine 5 rough 6 coarse, gritty
Sandpaper Ballet composer: Leroy Anderson
Sand Pebbles, The (1966 film)
cast: Richard Attenborough, Candice Bergen, Richard Crenna, Steve McQueen
director: Robert Wise
sandpiper: 4 bird, knot, ruff 5 snipe, stint 6 dunlin, willet 8 grayback, peetweet, redshank 10 sanderling
female ~: 3 ree 5 reeve
relative: 6 curlew
Sandpipers song: Guantanamera (1966)
Sandpiper, The (1965 film)
cast: Charles Bronson, Richard Burton, Eva Marie Saint, Elizabeth Taylor
director: Vincente Minnelli
Sandra: 3 Dee 6 Haynie 7 Bullock 8 Bernhard
Sandra ___ O'Connor: 3 Day
Sandrich: 3 Jay 4 Mark
Sandrich, Mark: 8 director
film: Buck Benny Rides Again (1940)
Carefree (1938)
Cockeyed Cavaliers (1934)
Follow the Fleet (1936)
The Gay Divorcee (1934)
Here Come the Waves (1944)
Hips, Hips, Hooray (1934)
Holiday Inn (1942)
Shall We Dance (1937)
Skylark (1941)
So Proudly We Hail! (1943)
Top Hat (1935)
A Woman Rebels (1936)
Sand Rivers author: Peter Matthiessen
Sandro: 10 Botticelli
sandroller: 4 fish
sands: 5 shore 8 littoral
Sands: 5 Diana, Tommy
___ Sands: 5 White 7 Goodwin
___ Sands Missile Range: 5 White
sands of ___: 4 time
Sands of Iwo Jima (1949 film)
cast: John Agar, Adele Mara, John Wayne
director: Allan Dwan
Sands of Time, The author: Sidney Sheldon
Sands, Tommy
song: Teen-Age Crush (1957)
spouse: Nancy Sinatra
sandstone: 5 wacke 7 mineral 9 graywacke
sandstorm: 4 wind
sand-trap club: 5 wedge
Sandusky: 4 city, town
lake: 4 Erie
locale: 4 Ohio
sandwich: 3 sub 4 gyro, hero 5 bread, po boy 6 hoagie, reuben 7 Dagwood 9 hamburger, interpose
bread: 3 rye 4 pita 5 white 9 sourdough 10 whole wheat
deli ~: 3 sub 4 hero 5 hoagy 6 hoagie
filler: 3 ham 4 tuna 5 jelly 6 cheese, salami, turkey 7 bologna, chicken 8 tuna fish 9 roast beef 10 corned beef
garnish: 5 caper
grilled ~: 4 melt
knuckle ~: 4 fist
need: 5 bread 7 filling
remnant: 5 crumb
shop: 4 deli
spread: 4 mayo 6 catsup 7 ketchup, mustard 10 mayonnaise
tiny ~: 6 canapé
wrapper: 4 foil 5 Saran 6 Baggie 7 tin foil
sandwich ___: 3 bag, man 4 beam, coin 5 board, panel 6 batten
___ sandwich: 4 club, hero, open 5 Cuban 6 Reuben 7 Dagwood, knuckle, western
sandwich-board: 2 ad
words: 5 eat at
Sandwich Islands: 6 Hawaii
sandy: 3 red 5 blond, flaxy, light 6 blonde, flaxen, gritty 7 arenose, arenous 8 gravelly 9 arenulous, towheaded, yellowish
area: 5 beach
islet: 5 atoll
relative: 4 rose, ruby, rust, wine 5 brick, coral, grape, poppy, rusty 6 cerise, cherry, claret, garnet, maroon 7 carmine, crimson, fuchsia, magenta, pimento, scarlet, sultana, vermeil 8 amaranth, cardinal, dubonnet, geranium, rubicund 9 carnation, cranberry, vermilion 10 strawberry
Sandy: 3 dog 4 city, Gary, Lyle, town 5 Posey 6 Dennis, Duncan, Koufax, Nelson
locale: 4 Utah
owner: 5 Annie
___ Sandy Desert: 5 Great
sandy-haired: 5 blond 6 blonde
Sandy Springs: 4 city, town
locale: 7 Georgia
sane: 3 fit 4 well, wise 5 lucid, right, sober, sound 6 normal, steady 7 healthy, logical, politic, prudent 8 all there, balanced, credible, feasible, moderate, oriented, rational, reliable, sensible, together 9 competent, judicious, practical, pragmatic, realistic 10 discerning, fair-minded, reasonable, thoughtful
San Felipe: 4 city, town
locale: 6 Mexico 10 Guanajuato
San Fernando: 4 city, town 6 valley
locale: 6 Mexico 10 California, Tamaulipas
neighbor: 6 Encino
Sanford: 4 city, peak, town 5 Clark, mount 6 Isabel 8 mountain
locale: 5 Maine 7 Florida
Sanford and Son (NBC sitcom)
cast: Redd Foxx (Fred Sanford)
Whitman Mayo (Grady Wilson)
LaWanda Page (Esther Anderson)
Demond Wilson (Lamont Sanford)
producer: Lear
___ Sanford Brown: 5 Georg
San Franciscan Nights (1967 song)
artist: Animals
San Francisco: 3 bay 4 city, port, town
Bay tribe: 5 Miwok
county north of ~: 5 Marin
district: 6 Castro
like ~: 5 hilly
locale: 10 California
1906 ~ event: 5 quake
newspaper: 8 Examiner 9 Chronicle
pro team: 6 Giants, Niners
setting: 3 PDT, PST
street: 6 Haight 7 Ashbury
tower: 4 Coit
transit system: 4 BART
San Francisco (1936 film)
cast: Clark Gable, Jeanette MacDonald, Spencer Tracy
director: W.S. Van Dyke
San Francisco (1967 song) artist: Scott McKenzie
sang-___: 5 froid
Sang: 8 Samantha
San Gabriel: 3 mts. 4 city, mtns., town 5 range 9 mountains
locale: 10 California
Sangay: 7 volcano
locale: 7 Ecuador
Sanger: 8 Margaret 9 Frederick
Sanger, Frederick: 7 chemist 8 Nobelist 10 biochemist
sang-froid: 5 poise 6 aplomb 8 calmness, coolness, presence 9 composure 10 equanimity, sedateness
San Giacomo, Laura: 7 actress
film: Quigley Down Under (1990)
sex, lies, and videotape (1989)
TV: Just Shoot Me
sanglier: 6 fabric 8 material
Sangre de Cristo: 3 mts. 4 mtns. 5 range 9 mountains
locale: 8 Colorado 9 New Mexico
sangria: 5 drink 8 beverage
container: 6 carafe
ingredient: 4 wine 10 fruit juice
Sangster, Charles: 4 poet 8 Canadian
sanguinary: 9 ferocious
sanguine: 3 red 4 rosy, sure 5 happy, ruddy 6 blowsy, blowzy, bright, elated, florid, upbeat 7 assured, blowsed, blowzed, buoyant, certain, crimson, flushed, glowing, hopeful, reddish, scarlet 8 cheerful, positive 9 believing, confident, convinced, presuming, satisfied 10 flying high, inspirited, optimistic
___ sanguinis: 3 jus
Sanhe: 3 cow 4 bull 6 bovine, cattle

sanh sua: 7 cricket 10 percussion
origin: 7 Vietnam
Sanibel: 6 island 7 isl. isle
locale: 7 Florida
San Isidro: 4 city, town
locale: 9 Argentina
___ sanitaire: 6 cordon
sanitary: 4 pure 5 clean 6 washed 7 aseptic, healthy, sterile 8 germfree, hygienic, pristine, purified, spotless, unsoiled 9 healthful, unsullied, untouched, wholesome 10 antiseptic, immaculate, salubrious, uninfected, unpolluted
sanitation: 7 hygiene
sanitize: 6 censor, degerm, purify 7 absolve, cleanse 9 deodorize, disinfect, expurgate, sterilize
sanitized: 5 clean
sanity: 3 wit 4 wits 5 logic, sense 6 acumen, reason, senses, wisdom 7 balance 8 lucidity, prudence, sagacity 9 lucidness, soundness, stability
Sanity is Where You Find It author: Will Rogers
San Jacinto: 4 city, town 6 battle
locale: 10 California
San Jacinto ___: 3 Day
San Joaquin Valley city: 6 Fresno
San Jorge: 4 gulf
locale: 9 Argentina
San Jose: 4 city, town
athletes: 8 Spartans
conference: 3 WAC
county: 10 Santa Clara
locale: 10 California
pro team: 6 Sharks
river: 6 Coyote 9 Guadalupe
San José: 4 city, town 7 capital
locale: 9 Costa Rica
see also Spanish
San Juan: 4 city, peak, port, town 5 mount, range 8 mountain
locale: 5 Andes, Chile, Texas 8 Colorado 9 Argentina, New Mexico 10 Puerto Rico
suburb: 6 Cataño
see also Spanish
San Juan Hill: 6 battle
locale: 4 Cuba
San Juan Mountains peak: 5 Eolus
Sanka: 4 java 5 decaf 6 coffee
alternative: 5 Yuban 7 Folgers, Melitta, Nescafe, Savarin 9 Hills Bros.
San Leandro: 4 city, town
locale: 10 California
San Lorenzo: 4 city, town
locale: 10 California
San Lucas: 4 cape
locale: 4 Baja 6 Mexico 10 California
___ San Lucas: 4 Cabo
San Luis Obispo: 4 city, town
locale: 10 California
San Luis Potosí: 4 city, town 5 state 7 Mexican
city: 5 Ébano 6 Tamuín 7 Charcas, Soledad 8 Cárdenas, Cerritos, Ríoverde 9 Fernández, Matehuala
San Marcos: 4 city, town
locale: 5 Texas 10 California
San Marino: 4 city, town 7 capital
currency: 4 lira, lire
locale: 9 Nicaragua
neighbor: 5 Italy 6 Italia
San Martín: 4 José
San Mateo: 4 city, town
locale: 10 California
San Matias: 4 gulf
locale: 9 Argentina
San Miguel: 4 city, town
locale: 10 El Salvador
Sannazzaro, Jacopo: 4 poet 7 Italian
San Pablo: 3 bay 4 city, town
locale: 10 California
neighbor: 4 Napa
San Pedro: 4 city, town
locale: 6 Mexico 8 Coahuila
San Pedro ___: 7 Channel
San Rafael: 4 city, town
county: 5 Marin
locale: 10 California
San Ramon: 4 city, town
locale: 10 California
San Remo: 4 city, port, town
locale: 5 Italy 7 Riviera
sans: 5 minus 6 French 7 lacking, needing, without
sans ___: 4 égal, gêne 5 doute, serif, souci
sans ___ et sans reproche: 4 peur
sans-___: 7 culotte
sansa: 10 percussion
origin: 6 Africa
San Salvador: 4 city, town 7 capital
locale: 10 El Salvador
see also Spanish
sansei: 8 Japanese
grandparent: 5 issei
parent: 5 nisei
sansevieria: 5 plant 6 flower
Sanskrit: 5 Indic 8 language
canon: 5 agama
classic: 4 Gita
cousin: 4 Pali
language: 5 Vedic
syllable: 2 om 3 aum
Sansom: 3 Art 7 William
Sansom, William: 6 writer 7 British
sans souci: 8 carefree
Santa: 5 river
locale: 4 Peru
see also Santa Claus
Santa ___: 3 Ana 4 Anna, Cruz, Rosa 5 Anita, Clara, Claus, Lucia, Maria, Tecla 6 Monica 7 Barbara
Santa ___ and Pooh Box: 3 Roo
Santa ___ Canyon: 5 Elena
Santa ___ Islands: 4 Cruz 7 Barbara
Santa ___ winds: 3 Ana
Santa Ana: 4 city, town, wind
base near ~: 6 El Toro
city near ~: 6 Irvine
county: 6 Orange
locale: 10 California, El Salvador
Santa Anita: 5 track 9 racetrack
locale: 10 California
transaction: 3 bet 5 wager
Santa Anna battleground: 5 Alamo
Santa Baby artist: 4 Kitt
Santa Barbara: 4 city, soap, town 7 islands
city near ~: 4 Ojai
locale: 10 California
Santa Catalina: 3 isl. 4 isle 6 island
locale: 10 California
Santa Catarina: 4 city, town
locale: 6 Mexico 9 Nuevo León
Santa Clara: 4 city, town
locale: 10 California
Santa Claus: 10 benefactor
artist: 4 Nast
bane: 4 soot
busy time: 3 Dec. 4 Xmas, yule 8 December 9 Christmas
delivery: 3 toy 4 gift 7 present
helper: 3 elf 8 reindeer
jingle: 5 reins
letter to ~: 4 list
prop: 4 pipe
reindeer, before Rudolph: 5 octet 7 octette
vehicle: 4 sled
Santa Clause, The (1994 film)
cast: Tim Allen, Wendy Crewson, Judge Reinhold
director: John Pasquin
Santa Claus Is Coming to Town composer: 5 Coots 9 Gillespie
Santa Cruz: 4 city, town 7 islands
city on the ~: 6 Tucson
locale: 7 Bolivia 10 California
Santa Fe: 3 SUV 4 city, town 5 trail 7 Hyundai
brick: 5 adobe
locale: 9 New Mexico
town near ~: 4 Taos
Santa Fe Trail, The author: Vachel Lindsay
Santa Gertrudis: 3 cow 4 bull 6 bovine, cattle
Santa Maria: 4 boat, city, ship, town
companion: 4 Niña 5 Pinta
locale: 10 California
Santa Marta: 4 city, town
locale: 8 Colombia
Santa Monica: 4 city, town
locale: 10 California
Santana, Carlos
homeland: Mexico
song: Black Magic Woman (1970)
Evil Ways (1970)
Oye Como Va (1971)
Smooth (1999)
Santa Paula: 4 city, town
locale: 10 California
Santarém: 4 city, town
locale: 6 Brazil
Santa Roo and Pooh Box author: A.A. Milne
Santa Rosa: 4 city, town
locale: 10 California
Santa's Twin author: Dean Koontz
Santayana, George: 6 author, writer 7 Spanish 11 philosopher
work: The Last Puritan
Persons and Places
Realms of Being
Reason in Art
Reason in Science
Reason in Society
The Sense of Beauty
Skepticism and Animal Faith
santé, A votre: 5 salud, skoal, toast 6 cheers, French
Santee: 4 city, town 5 river, tribe 6 Indian 7 Amerind
locale: 10 California
Santha ___ Rau: 4 Rama
Santiago: 4 city, port, town 7 capital, Saundra
locale: 4 Cuba 5 Chile 6 Mexico 9 Nuevo León
river: 7 Mapocho
see also Spanish
Santiago ___ Cajal: 6 Ramón y
santir: 6 string 8 dulcimer
origin: 7 Mideast
___ santo: 4 palo
Santo: 3 Ron
Santo André: 4 city, town
locale: 6 Brazil
Santo Domingo: 4 city, town 7 capital
locale: 6 Dom. Rep. 10 Hispaniola
see also Spanish
Santoni: 4 Reni
santonica: 5 plant 6 flower
Santorini: 4 isle 6 island 7 volcano
formerly: 5 Thera, Thira
locale: 6 Greece
Santos: 4 city, port, town
locale: 6 Brazil
product: 6 coffee
Sanyo
competitor: 4 Aiwa 5 Sharp
product: 3 VCR
Sanzio: 7 Raphael
Sao ___: 4 Luis 5 Jorge, Paulo 6 Miguel 7 Vicente
Sao ___ and Principe: 4 Tomé
Sao Francisco ___: 5 River
Saône: 5 river
city on the ~: 4 Lyon 5 Lyons, Mâcon
locale: 6 France
river to the ~: 5 Doubs
___-Saône: 5 Haute
Sao Paulo: 4 city, town
city near ~: 3 Itu
locale: 6 Brazil
river: 5 Tietê
Saorstát ___: 7 Éireann
Sao Tomé: 3 isl. 4 city, isle, town 6 island 7 capital
Sao Tomé and Principe: 6 nation 7 country
sap: 3 ass, oaf, rob, sag, tax 4 boob, butt, clod, cosh, dolt, dupe, flag, fool, gowk, gull, jerk, nerd, nurd, ruin, tire, wane 5 bleed, blunt, chump, clown, cluck, drain, dunce, erode, fluid, joker, ninny, patsy, schmo, trash, waste, weary, wreck 6 burn up, cudgel, dimwit, impair, liquid, lummox, nectar, nitwit, pigeon, reduce, schmoe, shrink, soften, sucker, turkey, weaken 7 buffoon, deplete, destroy, dingbat, dullard, exhaust, fall guy, fathead, fatigue, half-wit, jackass, pinhead, schnook, subvert, unnerve, vitiate 8 bludgeon, bonehead, dumbbell, easy mark, enervate, enfeeble, fool away, lunkhead, meathead, numskull, squander, weakling, wear down 9 attenuate, birdbrain, blockhead, dissipate, harebrain, lamebrain, numbskull, prostrate, schlemiel, simpleton, thickhead, undermine 10 debilitate, devitalize, dunderhead, noodlehead
as energy: 4 tire 5 leach 6 expend, lessen 7 deplete, exhaust, fatigue, suck dry, tire out 8 diminish, wear down 10 debilitate, devitalize, impoverish
collect ~: 3 tap
combining form: 3 opo-
derivative: 5 sirup, syrup
ender: 4 head, ling, wood 6 headed, sucker
fermented palm ~: 4 arak 6 arrack
petrified ~: 5 amber
source: 5 maple
spout: 5 spile
starter: 4 pine, wine
sucker: 5 aphid
sap ___: 4 bush 5 green 7 orchard
sapajou: 7 primate
relative: 3 ape 4 saki, titi 5 chimp, drill, jocko, lemur, loris, magot, orang, potto, shrew 6 aye-aye, baboon, Bandar, galago, gelada, gibbon, grivet, guenon, howler, langur, macaco, monkey, rhesus, uakari, vervet 7 colobus, gorilla, guereza, hoolock, macaque, siamang, tamarin, tarsier 8 bush baby, capuchin, mandrill, mangabey, marmoset, talapoin 9 orangutan 10 Barbary ape, chimpanzee, orangutang
sapele: 4 tree
family: 8 mahogany
relative: 4 neem 6 acajou, carapa 7 avodire 8 andiroba, crabwood
Saperstein: 3 Abe
saphead: 3 ass, oaf 4 boob, clod, dolt, fool 5 chump, clown, cluck, dummy, dunce, joker, ninny, patsy 6 dimwit, lummox, nitwit, sucker, turkey 7 buffoon, dingbat, dullard, half-wit, jackass 8 dumbbell, numskull 9 birdbrain, lamebrain, numbskull, simpleton
sapid: 5 tasty, yummy 6 savory, toothy 8 luscious 9 delicious, flavorful, nectarous, palatable, toothsome 10 appetizing, delectable
sapience: 3 wit 4 wits 5 sense 6 reason,

wisdom 7 insight 8 judgment, prudence, sagacity 9 knowledge
sapiens, homo: 3 man 4 race 5 biped, human 6 person
sapient: 4 sage, wise 5 smart 6 brainy 7 erudite, knowing, learned, prudent 8 rational, sensible 9 judicious, sagacious 10 reasonable
sapless: 3 dry 4 arid
sapling: 3 boy, kid 4 girl, tree 5 child, youth 8 juvenile 9 youngster
sapodilla: 4 plum, tree 5 fruit 6 sapota 9 evergreen
sap: 6 chicle
tree: 4 shea 6 balata 7 almique 8 alamiqui
saponaceous: 5 soapy
sapor: 4 tang 5 taste 6 flavor
sapota: 4 tree 5 fruit 9 sapodilla
sapped: 5 drawn 9 exhausted
Sapphic __: 3 ode
sapphire: 3 gem 4 blue 5 color, jewel 7 mineral 8 corundum, gemstone
month: 4 Sept. 9 September
relative: 4 anil, cyan, navy, Nile, teal 5 Alice, azure, slate 6 cobalt, indigo, raisin, violet 7 peacock 8 cerulean 9 turquoise 10 aquamarine, periwinkle
synthetic ~: 5 boule
__ sapphire: 4 star 5 water, white
Sappho: 4 poet 5 Greek
Sapporo: 4 city, town
city near ~: 5 Otaru
locale: 5 Japan
sappy: 4 zany 5 corny, goony, goosy, inane, mushy, silly 6 absurd, drippy, liquid, slushy, sticky, stupid 7 fatuous, foolish, maudlin, mawkish 8 overdone 9 illogical 10 ridiculous, saccharine, weak-minded
stuff: 5 sirup, syrup
sapsago: 6 cheese
Saps at Sea (1940 film)
cast: James Finlayson, Oliver Hardy, Stan Laurel, Ben Turpin
sapsucker: 4 bird
Sara: 3 Lee, Mia 7 Allgood, Gilbert 8 Paretsky, Teasdale
saraband: 4 step 5 dance
Sarabandes composer: 5 Satie
Sarabi: 3 cow 4 bull 6 bovine, cattle
Saracen: 4 Arab
to a Crusader: 3 foe 5 enemy
Sarafian, Richard C.: 8 director
film: Andy (1965)
Man in the Wilderness (1971)
The Man Who Loved Cat Dancing (1973)
The Next Man (1976)
Saragossa: 4 city, town
locale: 5 Spain
river: 4 Ebro
Sarah: 5 Miles 6 Fergie, Hughes 7 Purcell, Siddons, Vaughan 8 Caldwell, Ferguson 9 Bernhardt, Churchill, McLachlan
husband of ~: 7 Abraham
maid of ~: 5 Hagar
son of ~: 5 Isaac
Sarah __ Gellar: 8 Michelle
Sarah __ Hale: 7 Josepha
Sarah __ Jewett: 4 Orne
Sarah __ Parker: 7 Jessica
Sarah __ Siddons: 6 Kemble
Sarah Bishop author: 5 O'Dell
Sarah Lawrence: 7 college
grad: 5 woman 6 alumna
Sarajevo: 4 city, town 7 capital
locale: 6 Bosnia 7 Balkans
Sara Lee employee: 5 baker
Saramago, José: 6 writer 8 Nobelist 10 Portuguese
Sara, Mia spouse: Jason Connery
Saranac __: 5 Lakes
Sarandon: 5 Chris, Susan
Sarandon, Susan: 7 actress
film: Atlantic City (1981)
Bull Durham (1988)
The Client (1994)
Compromising Positions (1985)
Dead Man Walking (1995, AA)
The Great Waldo Pepper (1975)
Light Sleeper (1992)
Little Women (1994)
Lorenzo's Oil (1992)
Pretty Baby (1978)
The Rocky Horror Picture Show (1975)
Sweet Hearts Dance (1988)
Thelma & Louise (1991)
Twilight (1998)
White Palace (1990)
The Witches of Eastwick (1987)
role: 3 nun
Saran Wrap alternative: 4 foil, Glad 5 Hefty 6 Ziploc 8 Reynolds, wax paper
sarape: 5 scarf
__ sarà sarà: 3 che
Sara Smile (1976 song) artist: Hall and Oates
Sara (song) artist: Fleetwood Mac, Starship
Sarasota: 4 city, town
locale: 7 Florida
Saratoga: 3 car 4 auto, city, town 6 battle 8 Chrysler 10 automobile
event: 4 race
locale: 7 New York 10 California
Saratoga __: 4 chip 5 trunk 6 potato
Saratoga Springs: 3 spa 4 city, town
locale: 7 New York
Saratoga Trunk author: Edna Ferber
Sarawak
locale: 6 Borneo 8 Malaysia
people: 4 Iban
sultanate: 6 Brunei
tribe: 5 Dayak
Sarazen, Gene: 6 golfer
milieu: 5 links 6 course
org.: 3 PGA
sarcasm: 3 cut, dig 4 acid, gibe, jeer, jibe 5 irony, scorn, taunt 6 banter, rancor, satire 7 mockery, put-down 8 acerbity, acrimony, contempt, cynicism, derision, ridicule, scoffing 9 aspersion, criticism, wisecrack 10 bitterness, enantiosis, lampooning, unkindness
sarcastic: 3 dry, wry 4 acid, mean 5 acerb, edged, nasty, onery, saucy, sharp, snide 6 biting, bitter, ironic, ornery 7 abusive, acerbic, caustic, cutting, cynical, jeering, mocking, mordant, pointed, satiric 8 arrogant, captious, critical, derisive, incisive, sardonic, scornful, sneering, stinging, taunting 9 acidulous, corrosive, facetious, irascible, offensive, satirical, scorching 10 backhanded, derogatory, scurrilous
sarcenet: 6 fabric 8 material
sarcocarp: 4 pulp
sard: 3 gem 8 gemstone 9 carnelian 10 chalcedony
sardine: 4 fish, sild 5 sprat
holder: 3 tin
sardines
packed like ~: 5 in oil, solid 6 jammed
Sardinia: 3 isl. 4 isle 6 island
city: 8 Cagliari
locale: 5 Italy, Medit.
sheep: 7 mouflon 8 moufflon
sardonic: 3 dry, wry 5 sharp 6 bitter, ironic 7 caustic, cutting, cynical, mocking, mordant, satiric 8 derisive, incisive, scathing, scornful, sneering 9 quizzical, sarcastic, satirical, trenchant 10 disdainful
humor: 7 sarcasm
sardonyx: 3 gem 8 gemstone
Sardou, Victorien: 6 French 10 playwright
saree: 4 garb, gown, wrap
kin: 6 chadar, chador 7 chaddar, chuddar
wearer: 4 rani 5 ranee
Sarek: 5 alien 6 Vulcan
son: 5 Spock
Sarera: 3 bay
locale: 9 Indonesia
Sargasso: 3 sea
locale: 10 West Indies
__ Sargasso Sea: 4 Wide
sarge: 3 NCO
superior: 5 looey, looie, louie
Sargent: 4 Dick 6 Joseph 7 Malcolm
Sargent, John Singer: 6 artist 7 painter
Sargent, Joseph: 8 director
film: Colossus: The Forbin Project (1970)
MacArthur (1977)
The Taking of Pelham One Two Three (1974)
Sargent, Malcolm: 7 British 9 conductor
Sargeson, Frank: 6 writer 10 New Zealand, playwright
sargo: 4 fish
sari: 5 dress 7 garment
locale: 5 India
material: 6 Madras
use a ~: 5 drape
wearer: 4 rani 5 ranee
Sark: 3 isl. 4 isle 6 island
locale: 7 England
__ Sark: 5 Cutty
Sarmiento, Domingo: 6 writer 8 statesman 9 Argentine
work: Facundo
Sarnia: 4 city, town
locale: 6 Canada 7 Ontario
Sarnoff, David org.: 3 RCA
sarod: 4 lute
sarong: 5 skirt
Malaysian ~: 4 kain
relative: 4 sari 5 saree
Saros: 4 gulf
locale: 6 Aegean
Sarouk: 3 rug
Saroyan: 4 Aram 7 William
Saroyan, William: 6 author, writer
work: The Bicycle Rider in Beverly Hills
The Daring Young Man on the Flying Trapeze
The Human Comedy
The Laughing Matter
My Heart's in the Highlands
My Name Is Aram
The Time of Your Life
Sarraute, Nathalie: 6 French, writer 10 playwright
Sarrazin, Michael: 5 actor
film: The Flim Flam Man (1967)
For Pete's Sake (1974)
The Gumball Rally (1976)
Harry in Your Pocket (1973)
The Pursuit of Happiness (1971)
They Shoot Horses, Don't They? (1969)
sarsaparilla: 5 drink 8 beverage
sarsenet: 6 fabric 8 material
sarsnet: 6 fabric 8 material
Sarton, May: 4 poet
work: The Small Room
Sartoris author: William Faulkner
Sartre, Jean-Paul: 6 critic, French, writer 8 Nobelist 11 philosopher
contemporary: 5 Camus
work: Being and Nothingness
Dirty Hands
The Flies
Intimacy
Nausea
No Exit
The Roads to Freedom
Saruk: 3 rug
sarus __: 5 crane
SAS: 7 airline
competitor: 3 KLM
Sasdy: 5 Peter
SASE: 3 enc. 4 encl. 9 enclosure
part: 4 self 7 stamped 8 envelope 9 addressed
use an ~: 5 reply
Sasebo: 4 city, town
locale: 5 Japan
sash: 3 obi 4 belt, faja 5 scarf 6 cordon, girdle, riband 9 framework, waistband 10 cummerbund
filler: 4 pane
place: 5 waist
stopper: 4 sill
sash __: 3 bar 4 cord, line 5 chain 6 ribbon, weight
__ sash: 5 storm 6 cellar, window 7 picture
Sasha: 8 Mitchell
sashay: 5 amble, mince, mosey, strut 6 prance 7 saunter
sashayed: 4 went
sashimi: 4 fish
alternative: 5 sushi
sasin: 9 blackbuck
Sask.: 4 prov.
Saskatchewan: 8 province
capital: 6 Regina
city: 5 Craik, Unity 6 Regina 7 Avonlea, Eastend, Melfort, Nipawin, Tisdale, Weyburn, Wynyard, Yorkton 8 Moose Jaw 9 Saskatoon
Indian: 4 Cree 9 Saulteaux
lake: 9 Athabasca
locale: 6 Canada
neighbor: 3 Alb., Man. 4 Alta., Mont., N. Dak. 7 Alberta, Montana 8 Manitoba
Saskatoon: 4 city, town
locale: 6 Canada
Sasquatch: 5 giant 7 Bigfoot
kin: 4 yeti
sass: 3 lip 4 guff 5 cheek, mouth, reply, sauce 8 audacity, back talk, boldness, contempt, defiance, get fresh, get smart, mouth off, reaction, response, rudeness, talk back 9 brashness, flippancy, freshness, fresh talk, impudence, insolence, sauciness 10 answer back, brazenness, disrespect, effrontery, impishness, incivility, talk back to
Sass: 6 Sylvia
sassaby: 8 antelope
relative: 3 gnu, kob 4 guib, kudu, oryx, puku, topi 5 addax, bongo, chiru, eland, goral, korin, nyala, oribi, saiga, serow 6 chammy, dik-dik, duiker, impala, koodoo, lechwe, nilgai, rhebok, shammy, shamoy 7 blaubok, blesbok, chamois, defassa, gazelle, gemsbok, gerenuk, grysbok, nylghai, nylghau 8 blesbuck, bontebok, bushbuck, gemsbuck, reedbuck, steenbok, steinbok 9 blackbuck, pronghorn, sitatunga, springbok, waterbuck 10 hartebeest, wildebeest
sassafras: 4 tree
family: 6 laurel
relative: 7 avocado, camphor 8 cinnamon
sassafras __: 3 oil, tea
Sassanid: 3 Era
Sassari: 4 city, town

locale: 5 Italy
sassiness: 3 lip 5 sauce
Sassoon: 4 font 5 Vidal 8 typeface 9 Siegfried
Sassoon, Siegfried: 4 poet 6 author, writer 7 British
work: Counter-Attack and Other Poems
Memoirs of a Fox-Hunting Man
sassy: 4 bold, flip, pert, rude 5 brash, fresh, lippy, nervy, saucy, smart 6 awless, brazen, cheeky, jaunty, lively, snippy 7 aweless, defiant, forward, uncivil 8 derisive, flippant, impolite, impudent, insolent, snippety 9 out of line 10 irreverent, ungracious
girl: 5 missy
one: 4 snip
Sastre, Alfonso: 7 Spanish 10 playwright
...sat __ tuffet...: 3 on a
Sat.: 3 day
follower: 3 Sun.
preceder: 3 Fri.
SAT: 4 exam, test
college counterpart: 3 GRE
fill-in: 6 answer
part: 4 Test 8 Aptitude 10 Scholastic
preparer: 3 ETS
section: 4 math 7 English
taker: 2 sr. 4 teen 6 senior
Satan: 5 devil 6 diablo 7 Lucifer, Old Nick 8 evildoer, Old Harry 9 Beelzebub 10 Old Scratch
ally: 5 Magog
Satan Bug, The (1965 film)
cast: Richard Basehart, Anne Francis, George Maharis
director: John Sturges
satanic: 4 dark, evil, vile 6 horrid, wicked 7 demonic, hateful, heinous, hellish, malefic 8 daemonic, devilish, diabolic, fiendish, horrible, infernal, sinister 9 abhorrent, demonical, execrable, loathsome, monstrous, nefarious 10 abominable, despicable, detestable, diabolical, iniquitous, malevolent, villainous
satchel: 3 bag 5 pouch
binder: 5 strap
Satchel: 5 Paige
mom: 3 Mia
Satchmo
see Louis Armstrong
...sat down beside __...: 3 her
sate: 4 cloy, fill, glut 5 gorge, stuff 7 appease, engorge, satisfy, surfeit 8 overfeed, overfill 10 gormandize, oversupply
sated: 4 full 5 blasé 7 replete 8 cram-full 10 world-weary
sateen: 6 fabric 8 material
like ~: 6 glossy
satellite: 4 moon 8 partisan 9 ancillary 10 collateral
broadcast: 4 feed
community: 5 exurb
early ~: 3 OGO 4 Echo, ESSA 5 Tiros 6 Comsat
Earth ~: 4 moon
job: 3 spy 4 scan 5 recon 7 surveil
launcher: 4 NASA 6 Ariane
NASA ~ launcher: 5 Agena
path: 5 orbit
reconnaissance ~: 5 Samos
Soviet: 5 Lunik 7 Sputnik
tracker: 5 NORAD
see also moon
satellite __: 3 DNA 4 city, dish, town 7 station
__ satellite: 7 weather
Satellite: 3 car 4 auto 8 Plymouth
__ Satellites: 7 Georgia
Sather: 8 language
alternative: 3 ADA, APL, SQL 4 Alef, html, Icon, Java, LISP, Logo, Orca, Perl 5 Algol, Basic, Cecil, COBOL, Dylan, SISAL 6 Delphi, Eiffel, Erlang, Oberon, Pascal, Prolog, Scheme, Snobol 7 Fortran
satiate: 4 cloy, fill, glut, jade, pall 5 gorge, slake, stuff 7 gratify, indulge, satisfy, surfeit 8 overfill 10 gormandize
satiated: 3 fed 4 full, sick 5 blasé 7 replete 10 world-weary
Satie, Erik: 6 French 8 composer
work: Gymnopédies
Mercure
Ogives
Parade
Sarabandes
Socrate
satiety: 4 glut 7 surfeit 8 fullness, plethora 9 repletion
satin: 5 cloth, sleek 6 fabric 8 material
like ~: 4 soft 5 silky 6 smooth
satin __: 4 spar 5 glass, weave 6 stitch
Satin __: 4 Doll
satinet: 6 fabric 8 material
satins: 6 finery
satinwood: 4 tree
satiny: 4 soft 5 silky, sleek 6 flossy, glossy, smooth 8 lustrous, slippery
satire: 3 wit 4 quip, skit 5 farce, genre, irony, prose, put-on, spoof 6 comedy, parody, send-up 7 burlesk, lampoon, mockery, sarcasm, takeoff 8 ridicule, travesty 9 burlesque 10 caricature, enantiosis
magazine: 3 MAD
Satires author: Horace
satirical: 6 biting, bitter, ironic 7 burlesk, caustic, cutting, cynical, mocking, mordant 8 farcical, incisive, sardonic, spoofing, stinging, taunting 9 burlesque, facetious, parodying, sarcastic 10 lampooning, ridiculing
comedy: 5 sotie 6 sottie
production: 5 revue 6 review
satirist: 8 humorist
British ~: 4 Pope 5 Nashe, Swift 9 Thackeray
Roman ~: 6 Horace 7 Juvenal
satirize: 4 lash, mock, twit 5 sneer 6 parody 7 burlesk, lampoon 8 ridicule 9 burlesque 10 caricature
satisfaction: 3 joy 4 ease, zest 5 bliss, pride 6 luxury, refund, regard, relief, reward 7 comfort, content, damages, delight, emotion, justice, rapture, redress, revenge, satiety 8 fruition, gladness, pleasure, serenity 9 amusement, atonement, enjoyment, happiness, well-being
exact ~: 6 avenge
exclamation: 3 aah, ooh, yum 5 uh-huh, voilà 6 yum-yum
express smug ~: 5 gloat
get ~ from: 3 dig 4 like 5 boast, eat up, enjoy, go for, savor 6 dote on, wallow 7 revel in 8 flip over, thrill to 9 delight in 10 appreciate
seek ~ in court: 3 sue
Satisfaction (1965 song) artist: Rolling Stones
starter: 5 I can't
satisfactory: 2 OK 3 A-OK 4 fair, fine, good, jake, nice, okay, okeh, okey, so-so, tidy, well 5 ample, great, legit, moral, noble, right, solid, sound, valid 6 decent, enough, proper 7 average, ethical, up to par 8 adequate, all right, laudable, passable, pleasant, pleasing, splendid, suitable 9 admirable, agreeable, competent, excellent, palatable, reputable, sufficing, tolerable, up to grade, up to snuff, wonderful 10 acceptable, beneficial, creditable
satisfied: 4 full, sure 5 clear, happy 7 certain, content 8 positive, relieved, sanguine, thankful 9 believing, confident, contented, fulfilled 10 complacent, optimistic
not ~: 5 unmet
not easily ~: 5 picky
__-satisfied: 4 self
Satisfied (1989 song) artist: Richard Marx
satisfy: 2 do 3 pay 4 cloy, fill, glut, jade, meet, quit, sate, suit 5 amuse, atone, avail, elate, equip, get by, gorge, pay up, quiet, repay, score, serve, slake 6 answer, assure, fulfil, pacify, pander, pay off, please, quench, recoup, redeem, regale, reward, sell on, settle, square, supply 7 appease, assuage, cheer up, clear up, comfort, content, delight, enthral, fulfill, furnish, gladden, gratify, indulge, inthral, mollify, observe, perform, placate, provide, qualify, rejoice, requite, satiate, suffice, surfeit, win over, work out 8 come up to, complete, convince, enthrall, inthrall, make good, persuade, reassure, square up, tide over 9 conform to, discharge, indemnify, liquidate, put at ease 10 accomplish, compensate, comply with, conciliate, do the trick, exhilarate, hit the spot, pass muster, propitiate, recompense, remunerate
satisfying: 4 good, nice 5 solid, sound 6 cogent, worthy 7 welcome 8 pleasant, pleasing, readable 9 agreeable, enjoyable, rewarding 10 believable, convincing, delectable, delightful, gratifying
Satisfy You (1999 song)
artist: Puff Daddy, R. Kelly
S. Atlantic
see South Atlantic
Sato, Eisaku: 8 Japanese, Nobelist
Satori in Paris author: Jack Kerouac
satrap: 5 ruler 6 despot, gerent
satsuma: 5 fruit 6 citrus
relative: 4 lime, Ugli 5 lemon, navel 6 orange, pomelo, tangor 7 kumquat, Seville, tangelo 8 bergamot, mandarin, shaddock, Valencia 9 tangerine 10 calamondin, grapefruit
saturate: 3 sop, wet 4 dunk, glut, soak 5 bathe, douse, dowse, imbue, souse, steep, tinge, water 6 dampen, drench, embrue, imbrue, infuse 7 immerse, moisten, pervade, suffuse, surfeit 8 humidify, overfill, permeate, waterlog 9 penetrate 10 impregnate
saturated: 3 wet 4 damp 5 juicy, soggy, soppy, undry 6 sodden 7 wettish
saturated __: 3 fat 5 vapor 6 liquid
saturation: 4 glut 9 immersion 10 absorption
saturation __: 5 level, point 6 diving
Saturday
morning TV fare: 4 toon 7 cartoon
night ritual: 4 bath
night special: 3 gun
to some: 7 Sabbath
__ Saturday: 4 Holy 7 Violent
Saturday in the Park (1972 song)
artist: Chicago
Saturday Night __: 4 Live 5 Fever
__ Saturday Night: 7 Another
Saturday Night (1975 song) artist: Bay City Rollers
Saturday Night and Sunday Morning: 4 film 5 novel
author: Alan Sillitoe
cast: Albert Finney, Rachel Roberts
director: Karel Reisz
Saturday Night Fever (1977 film)
cast: Karen Lynn Gorney, Donna Pescow, John Travolta
director: John Badham
setting: 5 disco 7 New York 8 Brooklyn
Saturday Night Is the Loneliest Night of the Week composer: 4 Cahn 5 Styne
Saturday Night Live (NBC comedy)
bit: 4 skit
cat: 7 Toonces
Saturday Night Special (1975 song)
artist: Lynyrd Skynyrd
Saturn: 3 car, god, orb 4 auto 10 automobile
daughter of ~: 4 Juno 5 Ceres, Vesta
ender: 4 alia
equivalent: 6 Cronos
model: 3 Ion, Vue
moon: 3 Pan 4 Rhea 5 Atlas, Dione, Janus, Mimas, Titan 6 Helene, Phoebe, Tethys 7 Calypso, Iapetus, Pandora, Telesto 8 Hyperion 9 Enceladus 10 Epimetheus, Prometheus
neighbor: 6 Uranus
ring phenomenon: 4 ansa
sister of ~: 3 Ops
son of ~: 5 Pluto 7 Jupiter
wife of ~: 3 Ops
saturnalia: 5 blast, revel 7 revelry
saturniid: 3 bug 6 insect
saturnine: 3 sad 4 blue, dour, glum, ugly 5 moody, sulky, surly 6 broody, crabby, crusty, dismal, gloomy, morbid, morose, somber, sullen 7 unhappy 8 dejected, downcast, liverish 9 depressed, sorrowful 10 dispirited, lugubrious, melancholy
Satya __: 4 Yuga
Satyajit: 3 Ray
satyr: 3 Pan 4 faun 5 Gemon, Lamis, Lycon, Lycus, Maron 6 Cissus, lecher, Leneus, Pithos 7 Ampelos, Marsyas, Napaeus, Oestrus, Phereus, Scirtus, Silenos, Silenus, Thiasus 8 Astraeus, Lenobius, Petraeus, Pronomus, Pylaieus, Seilenos 9 Iobacchus, libertine, Onthyrius, Poemenius 10 Hypsicerus, Phlegraeus
in part: 4 goat
trait: 4 lust
sauce: 3 lip 4 gall, guff, sass 5 booze, brass, cheek, gravy, hooch, mouth, nerve, pesto 6 catsup, hootch, liquor, Mornay, whisky 7 alcohol, Alfredo, catchup, chutnee, chutney, ketchup, soubise, Tabasco, velouté, whiskey 8 audacity, back talk, béchamel, boldness, dressing, marinara, pertness 9 aqua vitae, béarnaise, brashness, condiment, flavoring, freshness, hard stuff, impudence, inebriant, insolence, sassiness 10 bordelaise, brassiness, brazenness, cheekiness, intoxicant
basil ~: 5 pesto
ender: 3 box, pan, pot 4 boat
fish ~: 4 alec
flavoring: 4 miso
hit the ~: 4 tope 5 booze, drink
holder: 3 can
Mexican ~: 4 mole
pasta ~: 5 pesto 7 Alfredo 8 marinara
raspberry ~: 5 Melba
source: 4 soya
starter: 5 apple
sundae ~: 5 fudge
tend the ~: 4 stir
Tex-Mex ~: 5 salsa
thickener: 4 roux
sauce __: 5 Bercy 7 suprême
__ sauce: 3 hot, soy 4 clam, hard, soya 5 Bercy, brown, chile, chili, cream, Melba, white 6 butter, chilli, hoisin,

Mornay, tartar, tomato **7** hunter's, soubise, Tabasco, velouté
saucepan: 3 pan, pot **6** boiler
saucer: 4 bowl, dish, disk **5** plate
emulate a flying ~: 5 hover
flying ~: 3 UFO
saucer __: 4 dome
__ saucer: 6 cup and, flying
Saucillo: 4 city, town
locale: 6 Mexico **9** Chihuahua
sauciness: 3 lip **4** gall, sass **5** mouth **7** license **9** flippancy **10** impishness
saucy: 4 bold, flip, pert, rude, smug **5** brash, fresh, nervy, sassy, smart **6** awless, bantam, brassy, brazen, cheeky, rakish, snippy **7** aweless, forward, uncivil **8** flippant, impolite, impudent, insolent, snippety, volatile **9** audacious, combative, intrusive, out-of-line, sarcastic, shameless, sprightly **10** irreverent, ungracious
miss: 4 minx
__ Saud: 3 Ibn
Saudi Arabia: 6 nation **7** country
capital: 6 Riyadh
city: 4 Taif **5** Jedda, Jidda, Mecca **6** Jiddah, Medina
desert: 5 Dahna, Nefud **6** Syrian
group: 4 OPEC **10** Arab League
gulf: 4 Aden **5** Akaba, Aqaba
money: 4 rial **5** girsh, gursh, qirsh, qursh, riyal **6** ghirsh, halala, qurush
neighbor: 3 UAE **4** Irak, Iraq, Oman **5** Katar, Qatar, Yemen **6** Jordan, Kuwait
port: 5 Jedda, Jidda **6** Jiddah
region: 4 Asir, Nejd
VIP: 5 sheik **6** shaikh, sheikh
sauerbraten: 4 meat **6** German **8** pot roast
Saugus: 4 city, town
locale: 4 Mass.
Sauk: 5 tribe **6** Indian **7** Amerind **8** language
Sauk Centre: 4 city, town
locale: 9 Minnesota
Saul: 4 king, poem **6** Bellow **7** Chaplin **8** oratorio
author: Robert Browning
composer: 6 Handel
cousin of ~: 5 Abner
daughter of ~: 6 Michal
father of ~: 4 Kish
grandfather of ~: 3 Ner
son of ~: 5 Ishvi **6** Armoni **8** Jonathan **10** Malchishua
wife of ~: 7 Ahinoam
Saul of __: 6 Tarsus
sault: 6 rapids **9** waterfall
Saulteaux: 6 Indian **7** Amerind
Sault Ste. Marie: 4 city, town
locale: 6 Canada **7** Ontario **8** Michigan
sauna: 6 hot tub **7** thermae **9** caldarium, steam bath **10** sudatorium
need: 5 towel
output: 5 steam
site: 3 spa
Saunders: 8 Jennifer
Saundra: 8 Santiago
saunter: 3 gad, lag **4** idle, laze, loaf, roam, rove, walk **5** amble, dally, drift, mosey, stall, tarry **6** airing, canter, dawdle, linger, loiter, lounge, ramble, sashay, stroll, toddle, trapes, wander **7** meander, traipse **8** ambulate, lollygag, straggle **9** poke along, promenade, waste time **10** dillydally
saurel: 4 fish
saurian: 6 lizard
-saurus starter: 5 stego **6** bronto
saury: 4 fish
sausage: 4 meat **5** wurst **6** banger, boudin, kishke, kiskha, salami **7** bologna **8** kielbasa **9** bratwurst, pepperoni **10** knockwurst, liverwurst
combining form: 6 allant- **7** allanto-
meat: 4 pork
seasoning: 4 sage **6** fennel
segment: 4 link
skin: 6 casing
sausage __: 4 curl, link, tree **7** turning
__ sausage: 5 blood, liver **6** Polish, summer, Vienna **7** bologna
Sausalito: 4 city, town
county: 5 Marin
locale: 10 California
saut de basque: 4 leap
sauté: 3 fry **4** cook, leap **5** brown **6** braise, panfry **7** prepare
Sauterne: 3 vin **4** wine **5** white **9** white wine
see also French
sautoir: 5 scarf
Sauvignon: 5 grape
relative: 5 Gamay, pinot, Tokay **6** Merlot **7** Catawba, Concord, Niagara **8** Cabernet, malvasia, muscatel **9** muscadine, zinfandel **10** Chardonnay
Sauvignon Blanc: 4 wine
Sava: 5 river, saint
city on the ~: 6 Zagreb **8** Belgrade
locale: 7 Croatia **8** Slovenia **10** Yugoslavia
river to the ~: 5 Drina
savage: 4 grim, mall, maul, mean, rude, wild **5** beast, brute, cruel, feral, fiend, harsh, nasty, rabid, rough, swine, tough **6** animal, bitter, brutal, crazed, ferine, fierce, lupine, raging, rugged, unkind, wanton **7** beastly, bestial, callous, furious, hellish, hurtful, inhuman, lawless, monster, untamed, vicious, violent, wolfish **8** barbaric, demoniac, fiendish, infernal, inhumane, pitiless, ruthless, sadistic, vengeful **9** atrocious, barbarian, barbarous, cutthroat, ferocious, heartless, hellhound, inclement, merciless, monstrous, primitive, rapacious, truculent, unpitying **10** infuriated, relentless, vindictive
Savage: 3 Ben, Doc **4** city, Fred, town **7** Richard
locale: 9 Minnesota
Savage __: 5 Paris **6** Garden, Island **7** Messiah
Savage Eye, The (1960 film)
cast: Barbara Baxley, Herschel Bernardi
Savage Island today: 4 Niue
Savage Messiah (1972 film)
cast: Scott Antony, Dorothy Tutin
director: Ken Russell
Savage Paris author: Emile Zola
Savage, Richard: 7 British **10** playwright
savagery: 4 fury **6** ferity **7** cruelty **8** ferocity, violence **10** inhumanity
__ Savages, The: 5 Young
Savaii: 3 isl. **4** isle **6** island
locale: 5 Samoa
Savalas, Telly: 5 actor
film: The Assassination Bureau (1969) The Dirty Dozen (1967) Kelly's Heroes (1970) Pretty Maids All in a Row (1971)
like ~: 4 bald
TV: Kojak
Savana: 3 GMC, van
savanna: 3 lea, ley **4** moor **5** plain, veldt **9** grassland
dweller: 3 gnu
kin: 5 campo, veldt
tree: 6 baobab
Savannah: 4 city, port, town **5** river
locale: 7 Georgia
savant: 4 sage **6** expert, master, pundit **7** scholar, thinker **8** highbrow **9** authority, literatus, professor **10** specialist
Savant: 4 Doug
savarin: 4 cake
ingredient: 3 rum
Savarin: 6 coffee
alternative: 5 Sanka, Yuban **7** Folgers, Melitta, Nescafe **9** Hills Bros.
save: 3 bar, but **4** balm, bank, free, hold, keep **5** amass, cache, guard, hoard, lay by, lay up, put by, set by, skimp, spare, stash, stint, stock, store **6** defend, except, garner, gather, obtain, pile up, ransom, ration, redeem, rescue, retain, scrimp, secure, shield, spring, unless **7** bail out, collect, deliver, deposit, husband, lay away, protect, put away, recover, reserve, salvage, sustain, unchain **8** conserve, file away, gather up, hang onto, hide away, hold back, hold onto, lay aside, liberate, maintain, omitting, preserve, put aside, retrench, salt away, set apart, set aside, sock away, stow away, treasure, withhold **9** economize, except for, excepting, extricate, outside of, safeguard, stash away, stockpile, unshackle **10** accumulate, cut corners, emancipate, underspend
alternative: 5 spend
as coupons: 4 clip
computer files: 6 back up
for: 3 but **6** except
one's neck: 4 free, save **6** let off, pardon, rescue **7** bail out, manumit, release, set free, unchain **9** extricate, unshackle
save __: 4 face
save __ a rainy day: 3 for
saved __ bell: 5 by the
Save It for Me (1964 song) artist: Four Seasons
save one's __: 6 breath
saver: 7 pack rat **9** depositor
like a ~: 6 frugal **7** thrifty
of fable: 3 ant
starter: 4 life, time
__ saver: 6 screen
__ Saver: 4 Step
saves, what a certain stitch: 4 nine
Save the Best for Last (1992 song) artist: Vanessa Williams
Save the Last Dance (2001 film)
cast: Fredro Starr, Julia Stiles, Sean Patrick Thomas, Kerry Washington
director: Thomas Carter
Save the Last Dance for Me (1960 song) artist: Drifters
Save the Tiger (1973 film)
cast: Jack Gilford, Jack Lemmon
director: John G. Avildsen
Save your __!: 6 breath
Save Your Heart for Me (1965 song) artist: Gary Lewis and the Playboys
__ Save Your Own Life: 5 How to
Saviano: 4 Josh
Saville, Victor film of 1950: 3 Kim
savin: 5 cedar **7** juniper **8** red cedar
saving: 6 stingy, thrift **7** economy, keeping, sparing **8** discount, price cut, rollback **9** deduction, provident, reduction
starter: 4 life, time
saving __: 5 grace
__-saving: 4 face **5** labor, space
Saving __ for You: 7 Forever
Saving All My Love for You (1985 song) artist: Whitney Houston
Saving Private Ryan (1998 film)
cast: Edward Burns, Matt Damon, Jeremy Davies, Vin Diesel, Tom Hanks, Tom Sizemore
composer: 8 Williams
craft: 3 LST
director: Steven Spielberg
setting: 4 D-day **6** France **8** Normandy
savings: 4 cash **5** cache, funds, kitty, means, stake, store **6** assets, profit **7** capital, deposit, nest egg, reserve **8** reserves **9** resources
account: 2 CD **3** IRA
account addition: 3 int. **8** interest
protector: 4 FDIC **5** FSLIC
savings __: 4 bank, bond **7** account
savings and __: 4 loan
__ savings bank: 6 mutual
Savion: 6 Glover
savior: 4 hero **5** freer **7** messiah, rescuer **8** defender, redeemer **9** deliverer, liberator, preserver, protector
Saviors of the Forest director: 3 Day
Savior, The (1998 film)
cast: Nastassja Kinski, Dennis Quaid
saviour: 5 freer **7** messiah, rescuer **8** redeemer **9** deliverer, liberator
Savoca: 5 Nancy
Savoie
see Savoy
__-Savoie: 5 Haute
savoir-__: 5 faire, vivre
savoir faire: 4 tact **5** grace, poise, skill, style **6** aplomb, polish **7** culture, finesse, know-how, suavity **8** breeding, urbanity **9** gentility, suaveness **10** refinement
savola: 4 fish
Savonarola: 5 chair **8** Girolamo
savor: 3 sip **4** bask, feel, like, live, mark, odor, tang, zest **5** enjoy, gloat, gusto, scent, smack, smell, spice, taste, tinge, verve **6** appeal, bask in, degust, flavor, relish, sample **7** cherish, dwell on, feast on, partake **9** degustate, delight in, dwell upon, get high on, gloat over, rejoice in **10** appreciate, attraction, enticement, experience
savory: 4 good, herb, nice, rich **5** sapid, spicy, tangy, tasty, yummy **6** spicey, toothy **7** piquant, pungent **8** fragrant, luscious, noshable, pleasing, tempting **9** ambrosial, delicious, flavorful, nectarous, palatable, reputable, toothsome **10** appetizing, delectable
__ savory: 6 summer, winter
Savoy: 3 car **4** auto, font **5** duchy, hotel **8** Plymouth, typeface **10** automobile
dance: 5 stomp
locale: 6 France
savvy: 3 apt, hep, hip **4** able, wise **5** adept, aware, get it, knack, quick, sense, sharp, skill **6** adroit, astute, clever, expert, shrewd, up to it, versed, wisdom, wise to, with it **7** ability, erudite, finesse, know-how, knowing, mindful, tuned in **8** apprised, informed, instinct, judgment, skillful **9** astucious, cognizant, competent, erudition, expertise, intellect, in the know, plugged in, sagacious **10** appreciate, competence, comprehend, horse sense, insightful, proficient, right stuff, streetwise, understand
about: 4 onto, up on
saw: 3 cut **4** lore, tool, word **5** adage, axiom, gnome, maxim, moral, motto **6** bisect, byword, cutter, dictum, saying, truism **7** bromide, epigram, proverb **8** aphorism, apothegm, Atticism, dissever, laconism **9** platitude **10** apophthegm, folk wisdom, shibboleth, woodcutter
combining form: 3 pri- **5** prion-, serri- **6** priono-
cut: 4 kerf
down: 4 fell
ender: 3 fly, yer **4** buck, dust, fish, mill **5** bones, dusty, horse

I ~: **4** vidi
logs: 3 nap **5** crash, sleep, snore, snort **6** nod off, retire, snooze, turn in **7** drop off, sack out, slumber, snuffle, zonk out **8** take a nap **9** hit the hay **10** hit the sack
part: 5 tooth
starter: 3 jig, pit, rip, see **4** back, buck, hack, hand, whip **5** sight **7** quarter
saw __: 3 log, pit, set **4** wood
saw-__: 7 toothed
saw-__ owl: 4 whet
__ saw: 3 bow, pad, pit **4** band, buzz, fret, gang, grub, hole, rift **5** chain, crown, miter, muley, panel, power, saber, table **6** coping, planer, radial, scroll **7** bracket, compass, keyhole, musical
__ saw a purple cow...: 6 I never
Sawatch: 3 mts. **4** mtns. **5** range **9** mountains
locale: 8 Colorado
mountain: 4 Yale **6** Antero **7** Harvard, Shavano **9** Princeton
sawbones: 2 dr., MD **6** doctor **7** surgeon **9** physician
sawbuck: 3 ten **4** bill **5** money **8** banknote, currency
fraction: 3 fin, one **5** fiver
sawbucks
a hundred ~: 4 one G **5** G-note
ten ~: 3 cee **5** C-note
Sawchuk, Terry: 8 puckster
milieu: 3 ice **4** rink **5** arena
org.: 3 NHL
sawdust __: 5 trail **7** circuit
Sawdust and Tinsel (1953 film) director: Ingmar Bergman
sawed-off: 4 puny **5** runty, short
...__ saw Elba: 4 ere I
sawing logs: 3 out **8** snoozing **9** sacked out
sawlike: 8 serrated
__-Saw, Margery Daw: 3 See
sawmill
machine: 5 edger
output: 5 board **6** lumber
sawn: 3 cut
__-sawn: 5 rough
sawtooth: 8 serrated
Sawyer: 3 Tom **5** Diane **7** Forrest
Sawyer, Diane spouse: Mike Nichols
Sawyer, Tom
craft: 4 raft
friend: 4 Finn, Huck
half brother: 3 Sid
sax: 4 reed, wind **8** woodwind **10** instrument
ender: 4 horn, tuba
__ sax: 4 alto, bass **5** tenor **7** soprano
Sax: 5 Steve **6** Rohmer **7** Adolphe
__ Sax: 6 Doctor
Sax by the Fire artist: 4 Tesh
Saxe-Coburg-__: 5 Gotha
saxhorn: 4 tuba, wind **10** instrument
saxifrage: 4 itea **6** willow **7** syringa
Saxo: 3 car **4** auto **7** Citroen **10** automobile
Saxon: 4 John
contemporary: 4 Jute
__ Saxon: 3 Old **4** West
__-Saxon: 5 Anglo **7** Hiberno
Saxon Charm, The (1948 film)
cast: Susan Hayward, Robert Montgomery, John Payne
saxony: 4 yarn **6** fabric **8** material
Saxony: 5 state
city: 5 Riesa
locale: 7 Germany
once: 5 duchy
river: 5 Weser
saxophonist: 4 Getz, Sims **5** Young **6** Barnet, Bechet, Beneke, Carter, Dorsey, Gordon, Herman, Kenny G, Parker **7** Coleman, Desmond, Hawkins, Rollins **8** Adderley, Coltrane, Marsalis, Mulligan, Stan Getz, Zoot Sims **9** Tex Beneke
saxtuba: 4 wind **8** woodwind **10** instrument
say: 3 add, bid, gab, jaw, rap, yak **4** aver, avow, talk, tell **5** about, claim, guess, imply, judge, let on, opine, orate, reply, rumor, speak, spiel, state, utter, voice **6** affirm, allege, answer, assert, attest, convey, decide, inform, intone, pipe up, recite, record, relate, remark, render, repeat, report, retort, reveal **7** breathe, bring up, control, declare, dictate, divulge, express, mention, observe, opinion, respond, suggest **8** announce, bring out, disclose, intimate, maintain, register, rephrase, set forth, throw out, vocalize **9** enunciate, give forth, insinuate, make known, pronounce, verbalize **10** articulate, asseverate, conjecture, for example, put forward, recitation
again: 4 echo **6** repeat **7** recount, run over **9** reiterate
as you ~: 3 aye, oui, yea, yep, yes, yup **4** fine, okay, sure, yeah **5** good-o, natch, quite, right, roger, uh-huh **6** agreed, gladly, good-oh, indeed, just so, rather, righto, surely, yowzah **7** exactly, go ahead, indeedy, mais oui, quite so, ten-four **8** all right, of course, thumbs up, very well **9** be my guest, certainly, darn right, naturally, precisely, sure thing **10** absolutely, by all means, definitely, positively, sure enough, that's right
cheese: 4 grin, pose **5** smile
dare ~: 7 venture
goodbye: 4 part **5** leave **6** go home
grace: 4 pray **6** invoke
have one's ~: 4 vote **5** speak **7** speak up **8** speak out
hello: 5 greet **7** welcome
I do: 3 wed **5** marry **10** tie the knot
imperfectly: 4 lisp, slur **6** mumble
inadvertently: 4 blab **5** blurt **7** let slip
indirectly: 5 couch
in fun: 3 kid **4** fool, gibe, jape, jest, joke, josh **5** clown, crack **9** kid around
it isn't so: 4 deny
it's so: 6 attest
loud and clear: 7 speak up **8** speak out
more: 3 add
needless to ~: 8 of course **9** naturally, obviously
no: 3 nix **4** deny, shun, veto **5** spurn **6** bounce, forbid, pass on, rebuff, refuse, reject, resist **7** decline, disdain, dismiss, exclude, protest **8** disallow, turn down **9** blackball
one with nothing to ~: 4 mime **5** mimer
over and over: 5 chant
pretty please: 3 beg
silently: 5 mouth
softly: 7 whisper
starter: 3 nay **4** dare, gain, hear **5** sooth
that is to ~: 3 viz. **5** to wit **6** namely
the word: 9 authorize, give leave
the wrong thing: 3 err
unable to ~ no: 5 timid **6** docile **7** lenient, servile, slavish **8** lamblike, yielding **9** spineless **10** obsequious, submissive
uncle: 4 quit **5** yield **6** fess up, give up, relent, submit **7** concede **9** acquiesce
under oath: 5 swear **6** attest, depone, depose **7** testify, witness
what they ~: 4 buzz, talk **5** rumor **6** gossip **7** hearsay **9** grapevine
what you think: 5 opine
wrongly: 3 lie
yea or nay: 4 vote
yes: 2 OK **3** nod **4** okay **5** agree, allow, yield **6** accede, accept, assent, permit **7** consent, go along
say __: 3 aah **4** no to, what, when **5** uncle
__ say!: 3 I'll
__ say...: 5 Sad to
Say __: 4 Si Si
Say __ My Girl: 5 You're
Say __ only a paper moon: 3 it's
Say __, Somebody: 4 Amen
Say __ Will: 3 You
Say again?: 3 huh **4** what
Sayama: 4 city, town
locale: 5 Japan
Sayan: 3 mts. **4** mtns. **5** range **9** mountains
locale: 6 Russia
Say Anything ... (1989 film)
cast: John Cusack, John Mahoney, Ione Skye, Lili Taylor
director: Cameron Crowe
__ Say a Word: 4 Don't
Say cheese!: 5 smile
__ Say Die: 5 Never
sayer: 7 speaker **8** declarer **9** announcer
Sayer, Leo
song: Long Tall Glasses (I Can Dance) (1975)
More Than I Can Say (1980)
When I Need You (1977)
You Make Me Feel Like Dancing (1976)
Sayers: 4 Gale **7** Dorothy
Sayers, Dorothy: 6 author, writer **7** British
sleuth: Lord Peter Wimsey
work: Busman's Honeymoon
The Nine Tailors
Strong Poison
Whose Body?
Sayers, Gale sport: 8 football
Say goodnight, __: 6 Gracie
...say goodnight till it be __: 6 morrow
Say, Has Anybody Seen My Sweet Gypsy Rose (1973 song) artist: Tony Orlando & Dawn
Say Hey Kid, The: Willie Mays
saying: 3 saw **4** word **5** adage, axiom, maxim, moral, motto, quote, squib **6** byword, cliché, dictum, homily, logion, phrase, slogan, truism **7** epigram, precept, proverb **8** aphorism, laconism **9** platitude, quotation, utterance
nothing: 3 mum **4** mute **5** quiet **6** silent **7** aphonic **8** nonvocal, taciturn, wordless **9** secretive, soundless, voiceless **10** pantomimic, speechless, tongue-tied
sayings: 4 lore **8** analecta, analects
collected ~: 3 ana
religious ~: 5 logia
Say It Isn't So (1983 song) artist: Hall and Oates
Say It Loud - I'm Black and I'm Proud (1968 song) artist: James Brown
__ Say It's Wonderful: 4 They
Say It With Music composer: 6 Berlin
Sayles, John: 8 director
film: Baby It's You (1982)
The Brother From Another Planet (1984)
City of Hope (1991)
Eight Men Out (1988)
Lianna (1983)
Limbo (1999)
Matewan (1987)
Men With Guns (1998)
Passion Fish (1992)
Return of the Secaucus Seven (1980)
The Secret of Roan Inish (1994)
__ say more?: 5 Need I
Say My Name (2000 song) artist: Destiny's Child
__ say, not...: 5 Do as I
...say, not __: 5 as I do
__ Say Nothin' Bad: 4 Don't
Sayonara (1957 film)
cast: Marlon Brando, Red Buttons, James Garner, Ricardo Montalban, Martha Scott, Miyoshi Umeki
director: Joshua Logan
Sayonara!: 3 bye **4** ta-ta **5** adieu, later **7** goodbye **8** farewell
in French: 5 adieu
in Hawaiian: 5 aloha
in Italian: 4 ciao
in Latin: 3 ave **4** vale
in Spanish: 5 adios
__ says: 5 Simon
Say Say Say (1983 song)
artist: Michael Jackson, Paul McCartney
say-so: 2 OK **4** okay, word **5** order, power, voice **6** dictum **7** opinion, promise **9** assertion, authority, clearance
says old-style: 5 saith
__ Say the Darndest Things: 4 Kids
Sayula: 4 city, town
locale: 6 Mexico **7** Jalisco **8** Veracruz
Say what?: 3 huh
Say You'll Be There (1997 song) artist: Spice Girls
Say You, Say Me (1985 song) artist: Lionel Richie
saz: 4 lute **6** string **10** instrument
origin: 6 Turkey
Sb: 4 elem. **7** element **8** antimony
51 for ~: 4 at. no.
SBA: 6 lender
part of ~: 5 Admin., Small **8** Business
SbE: 3 hdg.
SBLI part: 3 Ins. **4** Bank, Life **7** Savings **9** Insurance
__ S. Buck: 5 Pearl
__ S. Burroughs: 7 William
Sc: 4 elem. **7** element **8** scandium
21 for ~: 4 at. no.
S.C.
see South Carolina
scabbard insert: 5 sword
scabrous: 5 rough **10** licentious
Scacchi, Greta: 7 actress
film: The Coca-Cola Kid (1984)
Country Life (1995)
Defence of the Realm (1985)
Emma (1996)
Festival in Cannes (2002)
Jefferson in Paris (1995)
The Player (1992)
White Mischief (1988)
scad: 3 lot, ton **4** fish, load
__ scad: 6 bigeye
scads: 4 a lot, a ton, lots, many, much, raft, wads **5** acres **6** flocks, hoards, oodles, scores **7** bushels, legions **8** zillions
of: 6 divers, myriad, umteen, untold **7** copious, profuse, umpteen **8** abundant, manifold, numerous, umpsteen **9** bountiful, countless, quite a few
scaffold: 5 frame **8** platform, skeleton
rocket ~: 6 gantry
Scaggs, Boz
song: JoJo (1980)
Lido Shuffle (1977)
Lowdown (1976)
Scala: 3 Gia

scalare: 4 fish
scalawag: 5 knave, rogue, scamp 6 bad hat, rascal 7 bounder 8 blighter, picaroon, rakehell, spalpeen 9 miscreant, reprobate, scoundrel 10 blackguard, ne'er-do-well, scapegrace
scald: 4 burn, cook, heat 6 scorch 7 parboil 9 cauterize
starter: 3 sun 4 leaf
scalding: 3 hot 6 torrid
scale: 3 pan, top 4 film, go up, norm, rate, rise, size, skin 5 climb, flake, gamut, gauge, layer, mount, plate, range, ratio, reach, ruler, scope, shell, strip 6 adjust, ascend, degree, extent, ladder, lamina, series, shinny, spread 7 balance, breadth, clamber, coating, measure, prorate, shinney 8 register, spectrum, surmount 9 barometer, calibrate, continuum, dimension, gradation, hierarchy, sliderule, yardstick 10 proportion
allowance: 4 tare
bottom of a ~: 3 one
bump on the ~: 3 pip 4 blip
combining form: 5 lepid-, -lepis, squam- 6 lepido-, pholid-, squamo- 7 pholido-
down: 4 pare, trim 5 lower 6 lessen, reduce 7 cut back 8 downsize
drawing: 4 plan 9 blueprint
earthquake ~: 7 Richter
entire ~: 4 A to Z 5 field, gamut, range, reach, scope, sweep 6 extent 7 breadth 8 panorama, spectrum
hardness ~: 4 Mohs
hydrometer ~: 5 Baume
interval: 5 fifth, sixth, third 6 octave
kind of ~: 5 major, minor
note: 2 do, fa, la, mi, re, ti, ut 3 sol
off: 9 exfoliate
on a small ~: 8 slightly
part: 3 pan
segment: 4 note, tone
starter: 4 down
temperature ~: 3 Fah. 4 Fahr 6 Kelvin 7 Celsius 10 Fahrenheit
thin ~: 6 lamina
top of a ~: 3 ten
uncomfortability ~: 3 THI
unit: 2 lb., oz. 4 gram 5 ounce, pound
up: 5 boost, raise 7 augment, greaten 8 escalate, increase 9 intensify
scale ___: 4 leaf, moss 5 model 6 insect
___ scale: 3 bud, pit 4 Brix, gray, grey, Mach, mill, Mohs, rank, soft, wage, wind 5 Baumé, Binet, gypsy, Knoop, major, minor, union 6 Kelvin, oyster 7 armored, octagon, Richter, sliding, vernier
___-scale: 4 full 5 grand, large, small
scaled-down: 9 miniature
scaleless fish: 3 eel
___ scale of one to ten: 3 on a
scales
heavenly ~: 5 Libra
tip the ~: 5 weigh 8 outweigh
Scales: 4 sign 5 Libra
month: 3 Oct., Sep. 4 Sept. 7 October 9 September
predecessor: 6 Virgin
successor: 8 Scorpion
Scalia: 7 Antonin
scaling ___: 6 ladder
scall: 8 dandruff
scallion: 6 veggie 9 vegetable
cousin: 4 leek 5 onion
starter: 3 rap
scallop: 4 curl, loop, pink 5 curve, shell 8 seashell
___ scallop: 3 bay, sea 5 giant
scaloppine ingredient: 4 veal
scalp: 4 skin
scalpel: 5 knife 6 lancet
like a ~: 5 sharp
___ scalper: 6 ticket
scalp lock: 4 coif 6 hairdo 8 coiffure
scaly: 5 rough 7 scutate 8 lamellar, squamose, squamous
scam: 3 con, gyp 4 bilk, dupe, fool, hoax, plot 5 bunco, cheat, cozen, dodge, fraud, sting 6 con job, dupery, humbug, hustle, racket, rip-off 7 beguile, con game, deceive, defraud, mislead, swindle 8 artifice, flimflam, hoodwink, maneuver, trickery 9 deception 10 run a game on
artist: 3 con 5 cheat 6 conman 7 hustler
scamp: 3 bum, cad, cur, imp, rat 4 brat, heel, toad, worm 5 churl, knave, louse, rogue 6 bad boy, bad hat, monkey, rascal, urchin 7 bounder, dastard, lowlife, ruffian, stinker 8 blighter, picaroon, rakehell, scalawag, spalpeen 9 miscreant, no-goodnik, prankster, reprobate, scallawag, scallywag, scoundrel, vulgarian 10 blackguard, holy terror, jackanapes, malefactor, ne'er-do-well, scapegrace
scamper: 3 fly, hie, rip, run, zip 4 bolt, dart, dash, flee, flit, race, romp, rush, skip, tear, trot, whip, zoom 5 hurry, scoot, shoot, speed 6 barrel, bustle, gallop, hasten, hustle, move it, rocket, scurry, sprint 7 floor it, hop to it, mad rush, make off, quicken, scuttle 8 fugitate, run for it, step on it 9 hotfoot it, shake a leg, skedaddle, speed away 10 get a move on, hightail it
scampi ingredient: 5 prawn 6 garlic, shrimp
scan: 3 eye, pan 4 leaf, look, peer, pore, rake, read, skim, view 5 check, scour, study, sweep, watch 6 browse, look up, peruse, regard, riffle, screen, search, size up, survey 7 dip into, examine, inspect, monitor, ransack 8 digitize, look over, read over 9 speed-read 10 glance over, inspection, run through, scrutinize
___ scan: 3 CAT, MRI, NMR, PET 5 brain
Scand.
see Scandinavia
scandal: 3 mud 4 dirt, flap, news, tale, talk 5 crime, juice, libel, rumor, shame, stink 6 exposé, gossip, infamy, report 7 hearsay, outrage, slander 8 disgrace, dishonor, reproach 9 discredit, disrepute, improbity, sensation 10 dirty linen, wrongdoing
combining form: 4 -gate
ender: 3 ous 6 monger
sheet: 3 rag 9 newspaper
Scandal (1989 film)
cast: Bridget Fonda, John Hurt, Joanne Whalley
director: Michael Caton-Jones
Scandal in Bohemia, A author: Arthur Conan Doyle
scandalize: 4 slur 5 appal, shock 6 appall, defame 7 horrify, outrage, slander 9 denigrate
scandalmonger: 7 tattler 8 busybody
scandalous: 4 foul, lewd, ugly 5 juicy, lurid, seamy, shady, spicy 6 spicey, wicked 7 heinous 8 flagrant, horrible, improper, libelous, shameful, shocking 9 atrocious, desperate, egregious, gossiping, invidious, monstrous, offensive 10 defamatory, deplorable, disgusting, outrageous, scurrilous
city: 5 Sodom 8 Gomorrah
remark: 7 slander
___ Scandals: 5 Roman
Scandal Sheet (1952 film)
cast: Broderick Crawford, John Derek, Donna Reed
___ Scandal, The: 5 Age of
Scandinavia
bard: 5 scald, skald
city: 4 Oslo, Oulu 8 Helsinki 9 Stockholm 10 Copenhagen
country: 6 Norway, Sweden 7 Denmark, Finland
epic: 4 edda
flier: 3 SAS
folklore creature: 5 nisse, troll
god: 4 Odin, Thor 5 Othin
goddess: 4 Norn
gods: 5 Vanir
gulf: 7 Bothnia
land, to natives: 5 Norge, Suomi 7 Sverige
language, to natives: 5 Norsk
one of a trio in ~ myth: 4 Norn
plateau: 5 fjeld
range: 6 Kjölen
rodent: 7 lemming
royal name: 4 Erik, Olaf, Olav
rug: 3 rya
sea: 6 Baltic 7 Barents
sight: 5 fiord, fjord
toast: 5 skoal
Scandinavian: 4 Dane, Finn, Lapp 5 Norse, Swede 9 Norwegian
Scandinavian ___: 3 lox
scandium: 5 metal 7 element
scanner: 3 CAT, MRI, NMR, OCR, PET 7 monitor
checkout ~ ID: 3 UPC
scanning ___: 4 disk, line
___ scanning: 7 optical
scant: 3 low, shy 4 bare, mere, poor, slim, thin 5 short, skimp, spare, tight 6 little, meager, narrow, paltry, scarce, skimpy, sparse, spotty 7 cramped, limited, minimal, scrimpy, slender, sparing, wanting 8 one or two 9 confining, deficient, hardly any, scattered 10 a handful of, compressed, contracted, inadequate, restricted
scantiness: 4 lack, want 6 dearth 7 paucity 8 exiguity, scarcity, shortage, sparsity 10 deficiency, inadequacy
scantling: 4 stud
scantly: 6 hardly
scanty: 3 shy 4 bare, lean, poor, slim, thin 5 light, short, small, spare, tight 6 exotic, little, meager, measly, scarce, skimpy, slight, sparse, spotty 7 limited, minimal, scrimpy, slender, sparing, trivial, wanting 8 exiguous, uncommon 9 deficient, miserable, scattered 10 inadequate
Scapa ___: 4 Flow
scape
ender: 4 goat 5 grace
starter: 3 ice, sea 4 city, land, mind, moon, town 5 beach, cloud, dream, lunar, night, water 6 street
scapegoat: 4 butt, dupe, gull, mark 5 patsy 6 azazel, sucker, target, victim 7 fall guy 10 blame-taker
burden: 5 blame
scapegrace: 3 cur 5 knave, rogue, scamp 6 bad guy, bad hat, rascal 7 bounder 8 blighter, rakehell, scalawag, spalpeen 9 reprobate, scallawag, scallywag, scoundrel 10 blackguard, ne'er-do-well
scapula: 4 bone 5 blade
locale: 8 shoulder
neighbor: 7 humerus
scar: 3 mar 4 flaw, hurt, line, mark, nick, scab, welt 5 brand, slash, wound 6 crater, damage, deface, defect, fright, injure, stigma 7 blemish, scratch 8 cicatrix 9 cicatrice 10 traumatize
seed ~: 5 hilum
scarab: 3 bug 6 amulet, beetle, insect 7 periapt 8 talisman
scarabaeid: 6 chafer
Scaramouche (1952 film)
cast: Stewart Granger, Janet Leigh, Eleanor Parker
director: George Sidney
Scarborough ___: 4 Fair, lily
Scarborough Fair (1968 song)
artist: Sergio Mendes & Brasil '66, Simon and Garfunkel
herb: 4 sage 5 thyme 7 parsley 8 rosemary
scarce: 3 few, shy 4 bare, rare, slim, thin 5 scant, short 6 exotic, scanty, sparse 7 limited, slender, unusual 8 far apart, sporadic, uncommon, valuable 9 deficient 10 at a premium, inadequate, infrequent, occasional, sporadical
make oneself ~: 2 go 4 hide 5 scram 6 lie low 7 abscond, push off 8 withdraw
scarce as ___ teeth: 4 hen's
scarcely: 4 just 6 barely, hardly, little, rarely, seldom 8 narrowly, slightly 10 hardly ever
scarcity: 4 lack, want 6 dearth 7 paucity, poverty 8 exiguity, shortage, sparsity 10 deficiency, inadequacy, meagerness, scantiness
scare: 3 cow 4 funk, turn 5 alarm, alert, daunt, deter, panic, shock, spook, start, upset 6 dismay, fright, menace, rattle 7 horrify, petrify, shake up, startle, terrify 8 frighten, paralyse, paralyze, threaten 9 close call, give a turn, terrorize 10 close shave, discourage, intimidate
ender: 4 crow 6 monger
off: 4 shoo 5 deter 8 frighten
up: 3 get 4 find 5 amass, group 6 gather, obtain, secure 7 acquire, collect, convene 8 assemble, scrounge 10 accumulate
word: 3 boo
scare ___: 7 tactics
scarecrow
innards: 5 straw
wish: 5 brain
Scarecrow (1973 film)
cast: Gene Hackman, Al Pacino
director: Jerry Schatzberg
Scarecrow and Mrs. King (CBS drama)
cast: Bruce Boxleitner (Lee Stetson) Kate Jackson (Amanda King)
scared: 5 funky, jumpy, timid 6 afeard, afraid, aghast, craven, divine, gun-shy, shaken, trepid 7 afeared, anxious, chicken, fearful, nervous, panicky, spooked, wimpish 8 cowardly, fearsome, hesitant, recreant, startled, timorous 9 nerveless, petrified, terrified, tremulous 10 frightened
be ~ of: 4 fear 5 dread
looking ~: 4 ashy, pale 5 ashen
run ~: 5 panic 10 chicken out
scared ___: 5 stiff
___ Scared: 7 Running
___ Scared Stupid: 6 Ernest
scaredy-cat: 4 wimp 6 coward, craven, yellow 7 chicken, quitter, wimpish 8 poltroon, recreant
scarf: 3 boa, eat 4 gulp, ruff, sash, wolf, wrap 5 ascot, barbe, curch, do-rag, fichu, lungi, nubia, rumal, shawl, stole, throw 6 cravat, devour, fraise, gobble, guzzle, madras, pugree, rebosa, reboso, rebozo, riboso, ribozo, sarape, serape, tippet, wimple 7 bandana, consume, muffler, paisley, pugaree, sautoir 8 babushka, bandanna, covering, kaffiyeh, kerchief, mantilla, puggaree, wolf down 9 comforter, headcloth, headdress, neckpiece, polish off 10 fascinator

British ~: 5 ascot
crocheted ~: 5 nubia
down: 3 eat 4 bolt, gulp, wolf 5 eat up 6 devour, gobble, inhale 7 feast on 9 grab a bite, polish off
embroidered ~: 6 fraise
ender: 4 skin
feathery ~: 3 boa
liturgical ~: 5 amice, stole
make a ~: 4 knit
neck ~: 5 dicky 6 dickey, dickie
of India: 5 rumal
Scottish ~: 5 curch
starter: 4 head
support: 4 nape
scarf ___: 4 down 5 cloud, joint
Scarface (1932 film)
cast: Ann Dvorak, Paul Muni, George Raft
director: Howard Hawks
Scarface (1983 film)
cast: Steven Bauer, Mary Elizabeth Mastrantonio, Al Pacino, Michelle Pfeiffer
director: Brian De Palma
scarfpin: 7 jewelry
Scaria: 4 Emil
scaring-away shout: 4 scat, shoo 5 scram 6 begone 7 amscray 8 scramola
Scarlatti, Domenico: 7 Italian 8 composer
Scarlatti Inheritance, The author: Robert Ludlum
scarlet: 3 red 5 color, ruddy 8 sanguine
relative: 4 rose, ruby, rust, wine 5 brick, coral, grape, poppy, rusty, sandy 6 cerise, cherry, claret, garnet, maroon 7 carmine, crimson, fuchsia, magenta, pimento, sultana, vermeil 8 amaranth, cardinal, dubonnet, geranium, rubicund 9 carnation, cranberry, vermilion 10 strawberry
runner: 4 bean
sage: 5 plant 6 flower
the ~ letter: 4 red A
turn ~: 5 blush 6 redden
scarlet ___: 3 cup, hat 4 sage 5 gilia 6 runner 7 lobelia, lychnis, tanager
Scarlet ___, The: 4 Claw 6 Letter 7 Empress
scarlet bean: 6 veggie 9 vegetable
Scarlet Claw, The (1944 film)
cast: Nigel Bruce, Basil Rathbone
director: Roy William Neill
Scarlet Empress, The (1934 film)
cast: Marlene Dietrich, Louise Dresser
director: Josef von Sternberg
Scarlet Feather author: Maeve Binchy
Scarlet Knights: 7 Rutgers
Scarlet Letter, The: 5 novel
author: Nathaniel Hawthorne
character: 5 Pearl, Roger 6 Arthur, Hester, Prynne 10 Bellingham, Dimmesdale
Scarlet Pimpernel, The: 4 film 5 novel
author: Baroness Emmuska Orczy
cast: Nigel Bruce, Leslie Howard, Raymond Massey, Merle Oberon
director: Harold Young
scarlet runner: 6 legume, veggie 9 vegetable
Scarlet Street (1945 film)
cast: Joan Bennett, Dan Duryea, Edward G. Robinson
director: Fritz Lang
Scarlett: 5 belle, O'Hara 6 Sylvia
daughter: 4 Ella 10 Bonnie Blue
home: 4 Tara 7 Atlanta, Georgia
love: 5 Rhett 6 Ashley
mother: 5 Ellen
scarp: 5 cliff, ridge 9 declivity, precipice
like a ~: 5 steep
___-scarred: 6 battle
Scarry, Richard: 5 Swiss 6 author, writer
Scar Tissue (1999 song) artist: Red Hot Chili Peppers
___-scarum: 5 harum
Scarwid: 5 Diana
scary: 4 eery 5 eerie, hairy 6 creepy, spooky 7 macaber, macabre, uncanny 8 alarming, chilling, daunting, fearsome, menacing, shocking 9 frightful, unearthly, unnerving 10 disturbing, horrendous, horrifying, terrifying
feeling: 4 fear 5 alarm, angst, dread, panic 6 fright, horror, terror 7 anxiety
Scary Movie (2000 film)
cast: Jon Abrahams, Carmen Electra, Shannon Elizabeth
director: Keenen Ivory Wayans
scat: 4 flee, shoo 5 music, scram 6 beat it, begone 7 amscray, buzz off, get lost, vamoose 8 clear out 9 skedaddle, take a hike 10 hightail it, hit the road
do ~: 4 sing
queen: 4 Ella
scathe: 4 slam 7 lambast 8 lambaste 9 castigate, criticize, excoriate
scathing: 5 cruel, harsh, sharp 6 biting, bitter, severe 7 caustic, cutting, pointed, searing 8 critical, incisive, sardonic, stinging, virulent 9 rancorous, scorching, trenchant, truculent, vitriolic
Scatman: 8 Crothers
scatter: 3 sow 4 cast, flee, part, rout, shed, spew, spue 5 fling, spill, spray, strew, throw 6 dispel, divide, fan out, lavish, litter, powder, shower, spread 7 bestrew, diffuse, disband, diverge, migrate, radiate, spatter, split up 8 disorder, disperse, disunite, separate, sprinkle, squander 9 broadcast, dissipate, punctuate 10 besprinkle, distribute
ender: 3 gun 4 good, shot 5 brain 7 brained
scatter ___: 3 pin, rug 4 shot 7 diagram
scatter-___ housing: 4 site
scatterbrained: 4 daft 5 ditsy, ditzy, dizzy, giddy, silly 6 goosey, madcap 7 flighty 8 skittish 9 forgetful, illogical
scattered: 4 rare, sown, thin 5 scant 6 effuse, scanty, skimpy, sparse, spotty 7 diffuse 8 far apart, rambling, separate, sporadic 9 somewhere 10 disorderly, dissipated, infrequent, sporadical, unfrequent
scattering: 3 few 6 litter 7 handful 8 stampede 9 diffusion 10 dispersion
scaup: 4 bird, duck, fowl 8 bluebill
emulate a ~: 4 dive
relative: 4 smew, teal 5 eider, Pekin, Rouen 6 Cayuga, scoter 7 gadwall, mallard, pintail, pochard, redhead, sea duck, widgeon 8 garganey, gray duck, mandarin, musk duck, oldsquaw, shoveler, surf duck, wood duck 9 black duck, broadbill, goldeneye, goosander, greenhead, merganser, ruddy duck, sprigtail 10 bufflehead, canvasback, surf scoter, tufted duck
scavenge: 5 prowl 6 forage
scavenger
beach ~: 3 ern 4 erne, gull
canine ~: 5 hyena 6 hyaena, jackal
scavenger hunt: 4 game
Sc.D.: 3 deg.
sceat: 5 money
sceatta: 5 money
Scedrin: 6 Rodion
scena: 4 solo
scenario: 4 idea, plan, plot, ruse 5 setup 6 design, scheme, script, sketch 7 outline, rundown, summary 8 game plan, strategy, time line 9 story line 10 screenplay
scend: 5 heave
scene: 3 ado, row, set 4 fuss, riot, site, spot, to-do, view 5 arena, event, furor, hoo-ha, place, scape, sight, stage, venue, vista 6 hoo-hah, locale, milieu, region 7 episode, lookout, outlook, picture, setting, tableau, tantrum, theater, theatre, wrangle 8 backdrop, brouhaha, incident, locality, location, outburst, panorama, premises, prospect, squabble, standing, strategy 9 commotion, happening, landscape, situation, spectacle 10 background, exhibition, hullabaloo, occurrence
bad ~: 4 mess, riot 6 downer, uproar 10 unpleasant
do a ~: 3 act 7 perform
how to enter a ~: 5 on cue
locale: 3 set
make a ~: 3 act 4 rage, rant 5 act up, upset 7 trouble
make the ~: 4 come, show 5 reach, visit 6 appear, arrive, attend, emerge, stop by 7 turn out
of action: 5 arena, venue 6 sphere
quit the ~: 2 go 4 part 5 leave
shift, in a movie: 4 wipe
stealer: 3 ham 6 emoter
scene ___ crime: 5 of the
___ scene: 3 mob 4 drop 5 on the 6 street
scène, mise en: 5 stage
scenery: 3 set 4 view 5 scape, stage, vista 6 nature 7 terrain 8 backdrop, panorama, prospect, stage set 9 landscape, spectacle
bit of ~: 4 drop
chewer: 3 ham 6 emoter
suffix: 5 -scape
Scenes From a Mall star: 5 Allen
Scenes From a Marriage (1973 film)
cast: Bibi Andersson, Liv Ullmann
director: Ingmar Bergman
Scenes From Childhood composer: 8 Schumann
___ Scenes of Winter: 6 Chilly
scenic: 5 grand 8 dramatic, striking 9 beautiful, panoramic 10 impressive
scent: 4 aura, hint, nose, odor, tang 5 aroma, odour, savor, sense, smell, sniff, spoor, track, trail, whiff 6 detect 7 bouquet, cologne, essence, incense, perfume 9 fragrance, get wind of, redolence
air-freshener ~: 4 pine 5 lilac
animal ~: 5 spoor, trail
brand: 5 Opium 6 Chanel 9 Obsession
maker: 4 atar, otto 5 athar, attar, ottar
on the ~ of: 5 after 9 following
throw off the ~: 7 mislead
scented: 5 balmy, olent, sweet 7 odorous 8 aromatic, redolent 9 ambrosial
Scent of a Woman (1992 film)
cast: Gabrielle Anwar, Chris O'Donnell, Al Pacino
director: Martin Brest
scepter: 3 rod 4 wand 5 staff
hold the ~: 4 rule 6 govern 7 command
mock ~: 6 bauble
partner: 3 orb
wielder: 5 ruler 8 governor
Scève, Maurice: 4 poet 6 French
sch.
see school
Schacht: 2 Al
Schaech, Johnathon spouse: Christina Applegate
Schaeffer: 7 Rebecca
Schafer: 7 Natalie
Schaffner, Franklin: 8 director
film: The Best Man (1964)
Lionheart (1987)
Papillon (1973)
Patton (1970, AA)
Planet of the Apes (1968)
The War Lord (1965)
Schalk: 3 Ray
Schally, Andrew: 8 Nobelist 12 physiologist
Schatzberg, Jerry: 8 director
film: Honeysuckle Rose (1980)
The Panic in Needle Park (1971)
Scarecrow (1973)
The Seduction of Joe Tynan (1979)
schatzi: 2 jo 3 pet 4 baby, dear, jill, love 5 amour, angel, chéri, cooky, cutey, cutie, deary, ducky, flame, honey, leman, lover, lovey, novia, novio, sugar, sweet 6 bon ami, chérie, cookie, dautie, dearie, steady, sweets 7 beloved, dearest, dear one, pigsney, squeeze, sweetie, tootsie 8 chou-chou, cutie pie, dowsabel, dulcinea, ladylove, lovebird, macushla, paramour, precious, snookums, sugar pie, sweetums, truelove 9 bonne amie, boyfriend, dreamboat, inamorata, inamorato, petit chou, valentine 10 girlfriend, heartthrob, honeybunch, mavourneen, sweetheart, sweetie pie, turtledove
Schaumburg: 4 city, town
locale: 8 Illinois
schav: 4 soup
ingredient: 6 sorrel
Schawlow, Arthur: 8 Nobelist 9 physicist
Schayes, Dolph: 5 cager
milieu: 5 court
org.: 3 NBA
sport: 10 basketball
Scheat: 4 star
schedule: 4 bill, book, card, list, plan, roll 5 chart, round, set up, slate, table 6 agenda, docket, lineup, roster 7 appoint, arrange, program, reserve 8 calendar, organize, pencil in, register, time line 9 itinerary, timetable 10 tabulation
abbr.: 3 arr., dep., ETA, ETD, TBA
ahead of ~: 5 early
behind ~: 4 late 5 tardy 7 overdue
busy ~: 5 whirl
on ~: 6 timely 8 punctual
position: 4 slot
tough ~: 5 grind
scheduled: 3 due, set 5 on tap
schedules, like some: 5 light, tight
Scheele, Karl: 7 chemist, Swedish
scheelite: 3 ore 7 mineral
Scheherazade: 6 ballet
composer: Rimsky-Korsakov
hero: 3 Ali
specialty: 4 tale
subject: 3 roc
Scheib: 4 Earl
Scheider, Roy: 5 actor
film: 2010 (1984)
All That Jazz (1979)
The French Connection (1971)
Jaws (1975)
Last Embrace (1979)
Marathon Man (1976)
The Russia House (1990)
Schelde: 5 river
city on the ~: 5 Ghent 7 Antwerp
feeder: 3 Lys 4 Leie
locale: 6 France 7 Belgium
Scheldt
see Schelde
Schell: 5 Maria 10 Maximilian
Schelling, Friedrich von: 6 German 11 philosopher
Schell, Maria: 7 actress
film: The Brothers Karamazov (1958)

The Hanging Tree (1959)
The Magic Box (1951)
The Odessa File (1974)
Schell, Maximilian: 5 actor
film: The Castle (1968)
The Chosen (1981)
Cross of Iron (1977)
The Deadly Affair (1967)
Deep Impact (1998)
A Far Off Place (1993)
Festival in Cannes (2002)
The Freshman (1990)
Judgment at Nuremberg (1961, AA)
The Odessa File (1974)
Return From the Ashes (1965)
Topkapi (1964)
Schelomo composer: 5 Bloch
schema: 6 method
schematic detail, briefly: 4 spec
scheme: 3 aim, job, way 4 brew, form, hoax, idea, plan, plot, ploy, ruse 5 angle, cabal, cadre, craft, dodge, hatch, pitch, plan A, plan B, setup, shift, trick, twist 6 course, design, device, format, hookup, hustle, layout, method, racket, system 7 collude, connive, diagram, drawing, finagle, frame-up, gimmick, network, outline, pattern, picture, project, sleight, tactics, trump up, wrangle 8 conspire, game plan, intrigue, maneuver, proposal, put-up job, scenario, strategy 9 blueprint, cast about, framework, machinate, speculate, stratagem 10 brainchild, conspiracy, subterfuge, suggestion
color ~: 5 décor
crooked ~: 3 con 4 scam 5 setup 6 racket
in Britain: 4 rede
__ scheme: 5 color, Ponzi, rhyme 7 pyramid
Scheme: 8 language
alternative: 3 ADA, APL, SQL 4 Alef, html, Icon, Java, LISP, Logo, Orca, Perl 5 Algol, Basic, Cecil, COBOL, Dylan, SISAL 6 Delphi, Eiffel, Erlang, Oberon, Pascal, Prolog, Sather, Snobol 7 Fortran
schemer: 5 snake 6 con man 9 intriguer
schemers: 5 cabal
scheming: 3 sly 4 foxy, wily 5 slick 6 artful, crafty, shifty, shrewd, subtle, tricky 7 cunning, devious, furtive, knavish 8 slippery 9 conniving, deceitful, deceptive, designing, underhand
Schenectady: 4 city, town
locale: 7 New York
Schepisi, Fred: 8 director
film: Barbarosa (1982)
The Chant of Jimmie Blacksmith (1978)
A Cry in the Dark (1988)
The Devil's Playground (1976)
Fierce Creatures (1997)
Iceman (1984)
I.Q. (1994)
Roxanne (1987)
The Russia House (1990)
Six Degrees of Separation (1993)
Schertzinger, Victor: 8 director
film: The Birth of the Blues (1941)
The Fleet's In (1942)
The Mikado (1939)
One Night of Love (1934)
Rhythm on the River (1940)
Road to Singapore (1940)
Road to Zanzibar (1941)
scherzo: 5 music
Scherzo __ Flat Minor: 3 in E
Schiaparelli: 4 Elsa 8 Giovanni
Schiaparelli, Giovanni: 7 Italian 10 astronomer
Schick: 4 Bela 5 razor
alternative: 3 Bic 4 Atra 8 Gillette
Schick __: 4 test
Schiele, Egon: 7 painter 8 Austrian
Schiffer: 7 Claudia
Schifrin: 4 Lalo
Schildkraut, Joseph: 5 actor
film: The Cheaters (1945)
The Diary of Anne Frank (1959)
The Life of Emile Zola (1937, AA)
Orphans of the Storm (1922)
The Road to Yesterday (1925)
Schiller, Friedrich von: 4 poet 6 German 9 historian 10 playwright
collaborator: 6 Goethe
work: Don Carlos
The Maid of Orleans
The Robbers
Wilhelm Tell
schilling: 4 coin 5 money
Schilling, Curt sport: 8 baseball
Schindler: 5 Oskar
Schindler's List: 4 book, film
author: Thomas Keneally
cast: Ralph Fiennes, Ben Kingsley, Liam Neeson
composer: 8 Williams
director: Steven Spielberg
villain: 4 Nazi
schipperke: 3 dog 5 canid 6 canine
Schippers, Thomas: 9 conductor
Schirra, Wally: 9 astronaut
schism: 4 rent, rift 5 break, chasm, space, split 6 breach 7 dissent, faction, parting, rupture 8 cleavage, disunion, division, fracture 9 rebellion 10 disruption, divergence, separation
__ Schism: 5 Great
schismatic: 5 rebel 8 forsaker, renegade 9 dissident, heretical, sectarian
schist: 7 mineral
Schlafly: 7 Phyllis
Schlatter: 7 Charlie
Schlegel, August Wilhelm von: 4 poet 6 German 11 philosopher
Schlegel, Friedrich von: 4 poet 6 German
Schleiermacher, Friedrich: 6 German 11 philosopher
schlemiel: 3 oaf, sap 4 clod, fool, gull, jerk 5 looby, patsy
question: 5 why me
schlep: 3 lug 4 cart, drag, haul, plod, poke, tote, walk 5 carry, fetch 6 convey, trudge
Schleptet composer: PDQ Bach
Schlesinger, John: 8 director
film: Billy Liar (1963)
Cold Comfort Farm (1995)
Darling (1965)
The Day of the Locust (1975)
Far From the Madding Crowd (1967)
Madame Sousatzka (1988)
Marathon Man (1976)
Midnight Cowboy (1969, AA)
The Next Best Thing (2000)
Pacific Heights (1990)
Sunday, Bloody Sunday (1971)
Yanks (1979)
Schlesinger Jr., Arthur: 6 writer 9 historian
Schlessinger: 5 Laura
Schliemann, Heinrich: 6 German, writer 13 archaeologist
discovery: Troy, Mycenae
Schlitz: 4 beer
alternative: 5 Becks, Coors, Pabst 6 Amstel, Corona, Miller, Molson 8 Heineken, Michelob 9 Lowenbrau 10 Ballantine
schlocky: 5 cheap, junky, tacky 6 cheesy, shoddy, tawdry 7 chintzy
schmaltz: 4 corn 5 slush 6 bathos
schmaltzy: 5 corny, mushy 7 maudlin, mawkish 8 affected
Schmeling, Max: 5 boxer
milieu: 4 ring
Schmidt: 3 Joe 4 Mike 6 Helmut
__-Schmidt: 4 Gram
Schmidt, Mike: 7 Phillie
sport: 8 baseball
schmo: 3 oaf, sap 4 dolt, fool, jerk, nerd, nurd 5 dufus, klutz, yahoo 6 doofus 7 sad sack 9 blockhead 10 dunderhead, nincompoop, noodlehead
like a ~: 5 dense, inept 7 hapless
schmooze: 3 gab, rap 4 chat 6 gossip, hobnob, parley 8 causerie, converse 9 tête-à-tête 10 chew the rag
Schnabel, Artur: 7 pianist 8 Austrian
schnapper: 4 fish
schnapps: 3 gin 5 drink 8 beverage
schnauzer: 3 dog, pet 5 canid 6 canine
feature: 5 beard
like a ~ coat: 4 wiry
schnecken: 6 pastry
Schneider: 3 Rob 4 John, Paul, Romy
Schneitzhoeffer: 4 Jean
__ schnitzel: 6 Wiener
Schnitzler, Arthur: 8 Austrian 10 playwright
work: La Ronde
Leutnant Gustl
Light o' Love
Professor Bernhardi
schnook: 3 sap 6 pigeon, sucker
schnoz: 4 beak, nose 5 snoot, snout 6 beezer, honker
ender: 3 ola
Schoedsack, Ernest B.: 8 director
film: Grass (1925)
King Kong (1933)
The Last Days of Pompeii (1935)
Mighty Joe Young (1949)
The Most Dangerous Game (1932)
The Son of Kong (1933)
__ schoen: 5 danke
Schoenberg, Arnold: 8 composer
style: 6 atonal
Schoendienst, Red: 8 Cardinal
sport: 8 baseball
scholar: 4 coed, sage 5 brain, pupil 6 critic, pundit, savant 7 egghead, learner, student, teacher, thinker 8 academic, bookworm, highbrow, longhair, mandarin 9 abecedary, authority, intellect, literatus, professor, undergrad 10 specialist
assistant: 7 famulus
classical ~: 8 humanist
wish: 5 grant
__ scholar: 6 Rhodes
Scholar-Gipsy, The author: Matthew Arnold
scholarly: 4 wise 7 bookish, erudite, learned 8 academic, cerebral, cultured, educated, highbrow, lettered, literary, literate, longhair, profound, studious, well-read 9 pedagogic, recondite, technical
scholarship: 4 lore 5 award, grant, prize 7 letters, reading, subsidy 8 learning, literacy 9 erudition
criterion: 4 need
endower: 6 Rhodes
scholastic: 7 bookish 8 academic, pedantic 9 classical 10 pedantical
Scholastica: 5 saint
Scholastic Aptitude __: 4 Test
Scholes, Myron: 8 Canadian, Nobelist 9 economist
schook: 4 gull
school: 3 ism, pod 4 acad., coll., form, sect, univ. 5 class, coach, drill, edify, genre, group, guide, lycée, prime, swarm, teach, train, tutor, verse 6 belief, ground, inform, litter, lyceum 7 academy, break in, college, educate, nurture, outlook, prepare 8 devotees, instruct, seminary 9 adherents, alma mater, cultivate, disciples, enlighten, followers, following 10 discipline, halls of ivy, persuasion, university
absence from ~: 5 hooky 6 hookey
administrator: 4 dean, supt. 9 principal
aim: 9 education
boarding ~: 4 acad., prep 7 academy
clanger: 4 bell
closet: 6 locker
community ~: 2 JC
country ~ teacher: 4 marm
dance: 4 prom
division: 5 grade
do well in ~: 5 learn
ender: 3 bag, boy, man, men 4 book, girl, marm, mate, room, work, yard 5 child, house 6 fellow, master 7 teacher 8 children, mistress
essay: 6 thesis
founded in 1440: 4 Eton
French ~: 5 école, lycée
furniture: 4 desk
grade ~ subject: 3 Eng. 4 geog. 5 arith. 7 English 9 geography 10 arithmetic
grounds: 4 quad 6 campus
group: 3 PTA 4 fish 5 class, grade
issue: 6 busing
kid: 5 pupil 7 student
middle ~: 2 JH
not in ~: 6 absent
nursery ~: 4 pre-K
officers' ~: 3 OTC, OTS
of fish: 5 shoal
of the old ~: 5 passé 7 veteran
of thought: 3 ism
onetime ~ subject: 4 rhet. 8 rhetoric
ordeal: 4 exam, test
org.: 3 NEA, PTA
paper: 5 essay, theme
period: 4 term 7 quarter, session 8 semester
plebe ~: 4 USMA, USNA
police ~: 7 academy
prep ~: 7 academy
primary ~: 4 elem. 10 elementary
publication: 5 paper 8 yearbook 9 newspaper
spinner: 5 globe
sports org.: 4 NCAA
staffer: 2 TA 7 teacher 9 professor 10 instructor
subject: 3 alg., bio., Eng., ESL, mus., RRR, sci. 4 econ., geog., hist., math 5 arith., music 7 algebra, biology, English, history, science, three Rs 9 economics, geography 10 arithmetic
supply: 4 glue 5 paper, paste, ruler 7 binders, pencils, tablets
tabloid program for ~: 3 NIE
tech ~: 4 inst. 9 institute
tool: 2 PC 5 ruler
vehicle: 3 bus
work: 6 lesson
worker: 4 aide 5 nurse 7 teacher
school __: 3 age, bus, day, tie 4 ship, year 5 board, night 6 figure 7 edition
school __ walls: 7 without
__ school: 3 day, med, old 4 free, high, prep 5 Bible, charm, grade, Latin, lower, night, trade, upper 6 Ashcan, church, common, dental, hostel, junior, Lu-Wang, magnet, middle, normal, public, reform, riding, summer, Sunday 7 charity, evening, grammar, medical, nursery, primary, private, Sabbath
School __: 3 Day 4 Days, Daze, Ties 5 Is Out, of Law
__ School: 4 Lake 5 Charm 6 Prague 7 Chicago, Prairie, Swingin', Yin-Yang

schoolbook: 4 text 6 primer, reader 8 workbook
__ School Cadets, The: 4 High
schoolchild: 3 boy, lad 4 girl, miss 5 minor, pupil, youth 9 stripling, youngster
__ School Confidential: 4 High
Schoolcraft, Henry Rowe: 6 writer 8 explorer
School Day (1957 song) artist: Chuck Berry
schooldays: 9 childhood 10 juvenility
School Daze (1988 film)
cast: Tisha Campbell, Giancarlo Esposito, Laurence Fishburne
director: Spike Lee
schooled: 6 expert 8 literate 10 well-versed
be ~ in: 4 know
School for Scandal, The author: Richard Sheridan
School for Scoundrels (1960 film)
cast: Alastair Sim, Terry-Thomas
director: Robert Hamer
School for Wives, The author: Molière
schooling: 6 lesson 7 tuition 8 learning, training, tutelage 9 education, knowledge 10 upbringing
School Is Out (1961 song) artist: Gary U.S. Bonds
schoolmarm
reply to a: 4 yes'm
rod: 6 ferule
schoolmarmish: 4 prim
school of __: 7 thought
school of __ knocks: 4 hard
School of __: 3 Law 4 Mind
__ School of Design: 7 Parsons
schoolroom: 4 hall
schools, like most: 4 coed
School's Out (1972 song) artist: Alice Cooper
__ school tie: 3 old
School Ties (1992 film)
cast: Matt Damon, Brendan Fraser, Chris O'Donnell
director: Robert Mandel
schoolwork
do ~: 9 grind away
holder: 6 binder
School Zone: 4 sign
warning: 4 slow
schooner: 3 mug 4 boat 6 argosy 8 sailboat
contents: 3 ale 4 beer
feature: 4 mast
prairie ~: 5 wagon
team: 4 oxen
__ schooner: 7 prairie, topsail
Schopenhauer, Arthur: 6 German, writer 11 philosopher
schottische: 4 step 5 dance
Schrader: 4 Paul
Schreiber: 4 Liev 5 Avery
Schreiber, Liev: 5 actor
film: The Hurricane (1999)
Kate and Leopold (2001)
Phantoms (1998)
Spring Forward (2000)
The Sum of All Fears (2002)
A Walk on the Moon (1999)
Schreiner, Olive: 6 writer 12 South African
work: The Story of an African Farm
Schrieffer, John: 8 Nobelist 9 physicist
schrod: 4 fish
Schroder: 4 Rick 5 Ricky
Schrödinger, Erwin: 8 Nobelist 9 physicist
Schroeder: 3 Pat 6 Barbet 8 Patricia
Schroeder, Barbet: 8 director
film: Barfly (1987)
Before and After (1996)
Murder by Numbers (2002)
Reversal of Fortune (1990)
Single White Female (1992)
schtick: 7 routine 8 pretense
Schubert, Franz: 8 Austrian, composer
composition: 4 lied
string work: 5 octet 7 octette
work: Tragic Symphony
Trout Quintet
Unfinished Symphony
Schuck: 4 John
schul: 6 temple 7 synagog 9 synagogue
Schulberg, Budd: 6 author, writer
work: The Disenchanted
The Harder They Fall
What Makes Sammy Run?
Schuller, Robert: 10 evangelist
Schultz: 4 Carl 8 Theodore
Schultz, Dutch: 5 alias 8 gangster
Schultz, Theodore: 8 Nobelist 9 economist
Schulz: 4 Axel 7 Charles
Schumacher, Joel: 8 director
film: Batman Forever (1995)
Batman & Robin (1997)
The Client (1994)
Cousins (1989)
D.C. Cab (1983)
Flatliners (1990)
St. Elmo's Fire (1985)
Tigerland (2000)
A Time to Kill (1996)
Schuman __: 4 Plan
Schumann: 5 Clara 6 Robert
Schumann, Robert: 6 German 8 composer
wife: 5 Clara
work: Manfred Overture
Scenes From Childhood
schuss: 3 ski 4 skee
ender: 6 boomer
Schuster, Max: 9 publisher
partner: 5 Simon
Schütz, Heinrich: 6 German 8 composer
Schuyler: 5 James 6 Colfax, Philip
Schuyler, James: 4 poet 10 playwright
Schuylkill: 5 river
locale: 4 Penn.
schwa: 5 sound 6 symbol
Schwab: 7 Charles
Schwann, Theodor: 6 German 12 physiologist
Schwartz: 6 Melvin 7 Delmore 8 Berthold
Schwartz, Delmore: 4 poet 6 author, writer
work: Genesis
Shenandoah
Summer Knowledge
The World Is a Wedding
Schwartz, Melvin: 8 Nobelist 9 physicist
__ Schwarz: 3 FAO
Schwarzenegger, Arnold: 5 actor
film: The 6th Day (2000)
Batman & Robin (1997)
Commando (1985)
Conan the Barbarian (1982)
Eraser (1996)
Junior (1994)
Kindergarten Cop (1990)
Last Action Hero (1993)
Predator (1987)
Pumping Iron (1977)
Red Heat (1988)
The Running Man (1987)
Stay Hungry (1976)
The Terminator (1984)
Total Recall (1990)
True Lies (1994)
Twins (1988)
spouse: Maria Shriver
Schwarzkopf: 6 Norman 9 Elisabeth
biography collaborator: 5 Petre
like ~: 3 ret. 7 retired
rank: 3 gen. 7 general
Schweitzer, Albert: 6 German 8 Nobelist 9 physician
Schweppes: 9 soft drink
Schwimmer: 5 David
Schwinger, Julian: 8 Nobelist 9 physicist
sci.
see science
__ sci: 4 poli, poly
sciatic: 5 nerve
science: 3 bio., bot. 4 anat., biol., chem., geol., phys. 5 logic, ology, theol. 6 astron., botany, method, optics, osmics 7 anatomy, biology, ecology, geodesy, haptics, myology, orology, physics, zoology, zymurgy 8 agrology, avionics, bryology, forestry, gemology, genetics, horology, learning, medicine, mycology, pharmacy, pomology, research, taxonomy, theology, zymology 9 acoustics, astronomy, chemistry, cosmology, dentistry, economics, ethnology, geography, geoponics, hydrology, ichnology, knowledge, mechanics, ophiology, petrology, sociology, technique, telemetry, zoography 10 archeology, biophysics, demography, discipline, embryology, entomology, ergonomics, exobiology, geophysics, hydraulics, metallurgy, mineralogy, morphology, psychology, seismology, topography 11 aeronautics, agriculture, aquaculture, biodynamics, criminology, electronics, herpetology, ichthyology, lichenology, meteorology, myrmecology, ornithology, thermionics, volcanology 12 horticulture
behavioral ~: 5 psych. 10 psychology
builder's ~: 4 arch. 6 archit.
center: 3 lab
combining form: 4 -logy 5 -sophy
course cost: 6 lab fee
cyborg ~: 7 bionics
divine ~: 5 theol. 8 theology
earth ~: 4 geol. 7 geology
environmental ~: 4 ecol. 7 ecology 8 oecology
farming ~: 3 agr. 11 agriculture
gardener's ~: 4 hort. 12 horticulture
insect ~: 5 entom. 10 entomology
life ~: 3 bot. 4 biol., zool. 6 botany 7 biology, zoology
like ~: 6 amoral
magazine: 4 Omni
mapping ~: 5 topog. 10 topography
medieval ~: 7 alchemy
of reasoning: 5 logic
of selling: 4 mktg. 9 marketing
of smell: 6 osmics
of touch: 7 haptics
physical ~: 6 astron. 7 geology, physics 9 astronomy, mechanics
poison ~: 3 tox. 10 toxicology
program: 4 Nova
social ~: 3 eco. 4 econ. 9 economics
starter: 3 bio, con, pre 4 omni
the sweet ~: 6 boxing
science __: 7 fiction
__ science: 3 big 4 food, hard, life, soft, soil 5 earth, exact, space 6 rocket, social 7 library, natural
__ Science: 5 Weird 7 Popular
Science and the Modern World
author: Alfred North Whitehead
science fiction: 5 genre
award: 4 Hugo
character: 2 ET 5 alien, droid, robot 6 cyborg
father of ~: 5 Verne
film: 4 Tron 5 Alien 6 Aliens
magazine: 6 Analog
setting: 6 future
understand, in ~: 4 grok
vehicle: 3 UFO
weapon: 5 laser 6 phaser
Science Guy, The: 3 Nye
sciences partner: 4 arts
scientia __ potentia: 3 est
scientific: 7 learned, logical, precise 9 deductive, objective, technical
combining form: 5 -logic
scientific __: 6 method
scientist: 3 Ohm, Ray 4 Baer, Berg, Bohr, Born, Cohn, Davy, Gray, Hahn, Hess, Koch, Kuhn, Mead, Rabi, Ryle, Todd, Urey 5 Banks, Black, Boyle, Bragg, Brahe, Crick, Curie, Dewar, Dirac, Esaki, Euler, Evans, Fabre, Fermi, Fitch, Gamow, Gauss, Hedin, Henry, Hertz, Hooke, Joule, Libby, Lyell, Nobel, Pauli, Raman, Ruska, Sagan, Soddy, Stern, Tesla, Volta, Vries, Young 6 Adrian, Ampère, Binnig, Buffon, Bunsen, Carrel, Carter, Carver, Cuvier, Dalton, Darwin, Draper, Finsen, Franck, Frazer, Galton, Gesner, Halley, Hubble, Huxley, Kelvin, Kepler, Leakey, Mendel, Müller, Napier, Nernst, Newton, Pascal, Peirce, Perkin, Perrin, Piazzi, Planck, Ramsay, Remsen, Rohrer, Sanger, Sitter, Solvay, Stokes, Strabo, Susumu, Torrey, Watson, Yukawa 7 Agassiz, Borlaug, Celsius, Compton, Coulomb, Crookes, Doppler, Faraday, Fleming, Fourier, Fresnel, Galilei, Galvani, Goddard, Hodgkin, Hopkins, Huggins, Huygens, Lamarck, Laplace, Marconi, Maxwell, Meitner, Oersted, Pasteur, Pauling, Piccard, Ptolemy, Réaumur, Scheele, Thomson, Tyndall, Wallace, Wegener, Woolley 8 Ångström, Avogadro, Blackett, Breasted, Chadwick, Einstein, Foucault, Friedman, Herschel, Lagrange, Linnaeus, Mercator, Millikan, Rayleigh, Roentgen, Sakharov, Sorensen, Tombaugh, Van Allen, Weismann 9 Arrhenius, Berthelot, Berzelius, Cavendish, Eddington, Gay-Lussac, Kirchhoff, Lavoisier, Mendeleev, Michelson, Pausanias, Priestley 10 Archimedes, Copernicus, Fahrenheit, Fraunhofer, Heisenberg, Hipparchus, Malinowski, Rutherford, Schliemann, Torricelli 11 al-Khwarizmi, Aristarchus, Joliot-Curie, Omar Khayyám, Oppenheimer, Sherrington, van der Waals
Arabic ~: 11 al-Khwarizmi
association: 3 ACS
Austrian ~: 5 Pauli 6 Mendel 7 Doppler, Meitner
Belgian ~: 6 Solvay
British ~: 3 Ray 4 Davy, Ryle, Snow 5 Banks, Black, Boyle, Bragg, Crick, Dirac, Evans, Hooke, Joule, Lyell, Soddy, Young 6 Adrian, Dalton, Darwin, Galton, Halley, Huxley, Kelvin, Leakey, Newton, Perkin, Ramsay, Sanger, Stokes 7 Crookes, Faraday, Hodgkin, Hopkins, Huggins, Thomson, Tyndall, Wallace, Woolley 8 Blackett, Chadwick, Herschel, Rayleigh 9 Cavendish, Eddington, Priestley 10 Malinowski, Rutherford 11 Sherrington
Danish ~: 4 Bohr 5 Brahe 6 Finsen 7 Oersted 8 Sorensen
Dutch ~: 5 Vries 6 Sitter 7 Huygens 11 van der Waals
Egyptian ~: 7 Ptolemy
Flemish ~: 8 Mercator
French ~: 5 Curie, Fabre 6 Ampère, Buffon, Carrel, Cuvier, Franck,

Pascal, Perrin 7 Coulomb, Fourier, Fresnel, Lamarck, Laplace, Pasteur, Réaumur 8 Foucault, Lagrange 9 Berthelot, Gay-Lussac, Lavoisier 11 Joliot-Curie
German ~: 3 Ohm 4 Baer, Born, Cohn, Hahn, Koch, Kuhn 5 Gauss, Hertz, Ruska, Stern 6 Binnig, Bunsen, Kepler, Müller, Nernst, Planck 7 Wegener 8 Einstein, Roentgen, Weismann 9 Kirchhoff 10 Fahrenheit, Fraunhofer, Heisenberg, Schliemann
Greek ~: 6 Strabo 9 Pausanias 10 Archimedes, Hipparchus 11 Aristarchus
Indian ~: 5 Raman
Italian ~: 5 Fermi, Volta 6 Piazzi 7 Galilei, Galvani, Marconi 8 Avogadro 10 Torricelli
Japanese ~: 5 Esaki 6 Susumu, Yukawa
Kenyan ~: 6 Leakey
no rocket ~: 3 dim, oaf 4 ditz, fool, jerk, slow 5 dense, dopey, dummy, dunce, thick 6 lubber, nitwit, oafish, obtuse 7 boorish, doltish, dullard, jackass, loutish 8 dumbbell 9 blockhead, simpleton 10 nincompoop
Persian ~: 4 Omar 7 Khayyám
Polish ~: 5 Curie 10 Copernicus
question: 3 how, why
rocket ~: 5 brain 6 genius 7 scholar
Russian ~: 9 Mendeleev
Scottish ~: 4 Todd 5 Dewar 6 Frazer, Napier 7 Fleming, Maxwell
Soviet ~: 8 Sakharov
Swedish ~: 5 Hedin, Nobel 7 Celsius, Scheele 8 Ångström, Linnaeus 9 Arrhenius, Berzelius
Swiss ~: 5 Euler 6 Gesner, Rohrer 7 Piccard
workplace: 3 lab
__ scientist: 3 mad 6 rocket
sci-fi
see science fiction
scilicet: 6 namely
Scilly: 4 isls. 5 isles 7 islands
locale: 7 England
scimitar: 5 blade, sword
cousin: 5 saber
scintilla: 3 bit, jot, ray 4 atom, hint, iota, mite, mote, whit 5 gleam, glint, grain, shred, spark, speck, touch, trace 7 glimmer, minimum, modicum
scintillate: 5 blink, flare, flash, gleam, shine 6 dazzle 7 glimmer, glisten, glitter, shimmer, sparkle, twinkle 9 coruscate
scintillating: 5 brisk, smart, witty 6 bright, lively, lucent 7 beaming, buoyant, dynamic, piquant, radiant, shining 8 dazzling, exciting, flashing, gleaming, glinting, luminous, lustrous, shimmery, spirited 9 brilliant, ebullient, sparkling, sprightly, twinkling, vivacious
scintillation: 5 gleam, light, spark 7 shimmer, sparkle
scion: 3 kid, son 4 heir, seed, slip 5 child, graft, issue, sprig 6 branch, sprout 7 heiress, progeny 8 daughter, grandson, offshoot 9 inheritor, offspring, posterity, successor 10 descendant
Sciorra, Annabella: 7 actress
film: The Addiction (1995)
The Hand That Rocks the Cradle (1992)
Jungle Fever (1991)
Mr. Jealousy (1998)
True Love (1989)
What Dreams May Come (1998)
Scioto: 5 river
city on the ~: 8 Columbus
locale: 4 Ohio
Scipio: 5 Roman
rival of ~: 4 Cato
Scirocco: 2 VW 3 car 4 auto 10 automobile, Volkswagen
scissor: 2 ax 3 axe, cut, lop 4 chop, clip, crop, edit, hack, omit, pink, snip, trim 5 erase, prune, sever, shear, shred, slash 6 censor, cleave, delete, digest, excise, reduce, revise, shears 7 abridge, expunge 8 leave out 9 capsulize, expurgate
ender: 4 tail
__ Scissorhands: 6 Edward
scissors __: 4 hold, jack, kick 5 chair, truss
__ scissors: 4 nail
scissortail: 4 bird
sclaff outcome: 5 divot
__ S. Cobb: 5 Irvin
scoff: 3 boo, pan, rag 4 gibe, gybe, jeer, jibe, mock 5 fleer, flout, knock, laugh, scorn, sneer, spurn 6 deride, jibe at, reject, revile, slight 7 disdain, laugh at, poke fun 8 belittle, discount, pooh-pooh, ridicule 9 discredit, poke fun at
at: 5 flout, scorn, taunt 6 deride 8 belittle, discount 9 discredit, frown upon, make fun of 10 disbelieve, make game of
ender: 3 law
scoffer: 5 cynic 7 doubter, killjoy, sceptic, skeptic 9 pessimist 10 questioner
scoffing: 4 gibe, jibe 5 snide 7 jeering, mockery, sarcasm 8 derision, derisive 9 skeptical
scofflaw: 8 criminal
Scofield, Paul: 5 actor
film: Carve Her Name With Pride (1958)
Hamlet (1990)
King Lear (1971)
A Man for All Seasons (1966, AA)
Quiz Show (1994)
The Train (1965)
Scoggins: 5 Tracy
Scolari: 5 Peter
scold: 3 jaw, nag, rag 4 flay, lash, rail, ream, snub 5 abuse, baste, blame, chide, shrew 6 berate, chider, critic, hector, jump on, preach, rebuke, virago 7 bawl out, censure, chasten, chew out, henpeck, lambast, lecture, needler, put down, rebuker, reprove, tell off, upbraid 8 admonish, chastise, denounce, fishwife, harridan, lace into, lambaste, reproach, sail into, tear into 9 castigate, criticize, disparage, dress down, excoriate, exprobate, find fault, fustigate, henpecker, light into, objurgate, reprehend, reprimand, termagant, Xanthippe 10 castigator, denunciate, take to task, tongue-lash, vituperate
scolding: 5 abuse 6 earful, lesson, rebuke 7 censure, lecture, reproof 8 critical, reproval 9 reprimand 10 impugnment, upbraiding
words: 4 no-no
__'s Coming: 3 Eli
sconce: 4 head 5 skull 6 noggin, noodle 7 cranium 9 braincase
spot: 4 wall
scone: 6 pastry 7 biscuit, teacake
like ~: 4 oaty 5 oaten
partner: 3 tea
__ S. Connell Jr.: 4 Evan
Scooby-Doo: 3 dog 4 film 7 cartoon
cast: Linda Cardillini, Sarah Michelle Gellar, Matthew Lillard, Freddie Prinze Jr.
director: Raja Gosnell
scooch: 5 slide
scoop: 3 dip 4 bail, beat, dirt, info, lift, news, skim 5 empty, gouge, ladle, spade, spoon, story, truth 6 bailer, bucket, burrow, deepen, dig out, dipper, dredge, gather, hollow, pick up, remove, report, shovel, take up, trowel 7 lowdown, sweep up, utensil 8 excavate 9 clear away, exclusive 10 depression, revelation
get the ~: 5 learn
long-handled ~: 4 bail 5 ladle 6 dipper
receptacle: 4 cone
scoop __: 4 neck, seat
__ scoop: 3 air
Scoop author: Evelyn Waugh
scooped out: 5 round 6 curved, dented, dished, hollow, sunken 7 concave, sagging 8 indented 9 depressed, excavated
scoot: 3 fly, hie, rip, run, zip 4 bolt, dart, dash, flee, flit, race, rush, skip, tear, zoom 5 hurry, scram, shoot, spank, speed 6 barrel, gallop, hasten, hustle, move it, rocket, scurry, sprint, streak 7 floor it, hop to it, make off, quicken, rush off, scamper 8 fugitate, run for it, scramble, step on it 9 hotfoot it, make haste, shake a leg, skedaddle 10 get a move on, get hopping, hightail it, make tracks
scoot __: 4 over
scooter
Italian ~: 5 Vespa
kin: 5 moped 6 go-cart, go-kart
__ scooter: 5 motor
scop: 4 bard, poet 8 minstrel
scope: 3 run 4 area, play, room, size, span, sway, view 5 ambit, depth, field, gamut, orbit, range, reach, realm, scale, space, sweep, width 6 degree, extent, leeway, margin, radius, region, sphere, spread, survey, vision 7 breadth, compass, expanse, freedom, horizon, leisure, liberty, look out, measure, purpose, purview, stretch 8 capacity, confines, distance, latitude, wideness 9 amplitude, dimension, elbowroom, extension, full range, incidence, largeness 10 boundaries
camera lens ~: 5 field
of great ~: 3 big 4 vast 5 broad
out: 3 see 4 case 5 check, watch
starter: 3 oto 4 endo, peri, tele 5 fiber, micro, radar, rifle
use a ~: 3 aim
Scope: 9 mouthwash
alternative: 3 Act 4 Plax 6 Signal 7 Lavoris 9 Listerine 10 Fluorigard
use ~: 6 gargle
Scopes Trial
lawyer: 5 Bryan 6 Darrow
locale: 9 Tennessee
org.: 4 ACLU
scorch: 4 bake, burn, char, cook, heat, melt, sear, slur 5 broil, parch, roast, scald, singe, smear 6 vilify, wither 7 blacken, blister, frizzle, lambast, shrivel, slander, swelter 8 lambaste 9 carbonize
scorched: 3 dry 6 torrid 7 parched
scorched-__ policy: 5 earth
scorching: 3 hot 4 fire, warm 5 fiery 6 red-hot, sultry, torrid 7 burning 8 scathing, tropical 9 sarcastic 10 sweltering
score: 3 bag, cut, get, mar, run, sum, tab, win 4 bill, debt, earn, gain, gash, goal, mark, nick, rate, rout, sake, slit 5 chalk, count, facts, gouge, grade, notch, point, reach, slash, tally, theft, total, truth 6 basket, charge, deface, furrow, groove, grudge, incise, pick up, pile up, please, profit, rack up, rating, record, result, scrape, thrill, twenty 7 account, achieve, chalk up, luck out, outcome, procure, prosper, pull off, purport, qualify, reality, realize, satisfy, scratch, serrate, succeed, triumph 8 come home, conquest, lacerate, register, thievery 9 go over big, grievance, reckoning 10 crosshatch, hit pay dirt, obligation
baseball ~: 3 run
below D: 5 flunk
bowling ~: 3 pin 5 spare 6 strike
ender: 4 card 5 board 6 keeper 7 keeping
even the ~: 3 tie 5 repay 6 avenge 7 revenge 9 retaliate
exam ~: 4 mark, rank 6 rating
final ~: 5 total
football ~: 2 TD 3 PAT 6 safety 9 field-goal, touchdown
golf ~: 3 ace 5 bogey, bogie, eagle, one up 6 birdie
half a ~: 3 ten 6 decade
hockey ~: 4 goal
horseshoes ~: 6 leaner, ringer
in French: 5 vingt
keep ~: 3 add, sum 5 count, sum up, tally, total, tot up 6 figure, record 7 compute 8 register 9 enumerate
notation: 5 G clef, tacet 6 a tempo, da capo
settle the ~: 3 get 5 repay 6 avenge
starter: 4 four 5 three
tennis ~: 3 ace 4 ad in 5 ad out
unit: 5 point
__ score: 3 box, hog, raw 4 back, foot, line 5 Apgar, piano 7 partial
__-score: 4 part
scoreboard
division: 6 inning
heading: 3 RHE
statistic: 3 hit, out, run 5 error
scorecard
abbr.: 3 yds.
word: 3 out, par
scoreless, hold: 5 skunk 7 shut out
scores: 3 lot 4 army, lots, many, tons, wads 5 hosts, loads, reams, scads 6 clouds, crowds, divers, droves, flocks, hoards, legion, masses, myriad, oodles, swarms, umteen, untold 7 copious, legions, myriads, numbers, profuse, throngs, umpteen 8 abundant, billions, manifold, millions, numerous, umpsteen, very many 9 bountiful, countless, multitude, quite a few, trillions 10 multitudes
Score, The (2001 film)
cast: Angela Bassett, Marlon Brando, Robert De Niro, Edward Norton
director: Frank Oz
scoria: 4 lava, slag 7 mineral
scorn: 3 boo, dig, dis 4 barb, defy, gibe, hate, hoot, jeer, jibe, mock, shun, slam, slap, slur, snub, twit 5 abhor, abuse, decry, flout, libel, scoff, sneer, spurn, taunt, trash 6 defame, demean, deride, disown, dump on, hatred, heckle, hoot at, ignore, impugn, insult, jeer at, jibe at, malign, offend, rebuff, refuse, reject, revile, slight, vilify 7 affront, asperse, calumny, catcall, contemn, degrade, despise, disavow, disdain, high-hat, laugh at, mockery, neglect, obloquy, offense, put down, rank out, sarcasm, scoff at, slander, sneer at, sniff at, traduce 8 belittle, contempt, denounce, derision, pooh-pooh, ridicule, sneeze at, spit upon, turn down, vilipend 9 arrogance, aspersion, contumely, denigrate, deprecate, discredit, disparage, disregard, humiliate, invective, ostracize 10 calumniate, defamation, disbelieve, disrespect, look down on, opprobrium

scorned: **9** unpopular
scornful: **5** proud, snide **7** cynical, haughty, jeering, mordant **8** cavalier, derisive, sardonic **9** sarcastic, vitriolic **10** derogatory, minimizing, pejorative
Scorpio: **4** sign
  month: **3** Nov., Oct. **7** October **8** November
  predecessor: **5** Libra **6** Scales **7** Balance
  successor: **6** Archer **11** Sagittarius
Scorpio Illusion, The author: Robert Ludlum
scorpion: **3** bug **8** arachnid
  product: **5** venom
  water ~ genus: **4** nepa
__ scorpion: **3** sea **4** book, wind
Scorpius neighbor: **3** Ara
Scorsese, Martin: **8** director
  film: The Age of Innocence (1993)
    Alice Doesn't Live Here Anymore (1974)
    Bringing Out the Dead (1999)
    Cape Fear (1991)
    Casino (1995)
    The Color of Money (1986)
    GoodFellas (1990)
    The King of Comedy (1983)
    The Last Temptation of Christ (1988)
    The Last Waltz (1978)
    Mean Streets (1973)
    New York, New York (1977)
    Raging Bull (1980)
    Taxi Driver (1976)
    Who's That Knocking at My Door? (1968)
scot
  starter: **4** wain
scot-__: **4** free
Scot: **4** Celt, Gael **6** Newman **9** Dalrymple **10** Glaswegian, Highlander
  ancient ~ ally: **4** Pict
  see also Scotland
scot and __: **3** lot
scotch: **4** foil, kill **5** crush, quash **6** thwart **7** nullify, scuttle **8** stamp out **9** frustrate **10** neutralize, put an end to
  starter: **3** hop **6** butter
Scotch: **5** drink **6** liquor, whisky **7** whiskey **8** beverage
  like ~: **4** aged
  partner: **4** soda
  product: **4** tape
  relative: **3** rye
Scotch __: **3** egg **4** mist, pine, rose, tape **5** broom, broth **6** crocus, Gaelic, whisky **7** furnace, terrier, thistle, verdict
scotch and __: **4** soda
Scotch Plains: **4** city, town
  locale: **9** New Jersey
scoter: **4** bird, coot, duck, fowl
  relative: **4** smew, teal **5** eider, Pekin, Rouen, scaup **6** Cayuga **7** gadwall, mallard, pintail, pochard, redhead, sea duck, widgeon **8** garganey, gray duck, mandarin, musk duck, oldsquaw, shoveler, surf duck, wood duck **9** black duck, broadbill, goldeneye, goosander, greenhead, merganser, ruddy duck, sprigtail **10** bufflehead, canvasback, tufted duck
scot-free: **10** in the clear, on the loose
__ Scotia: **4** Nova
Scotland
  accent: **4** burr
  anthropologist: **6** Frazer
  bacteriologist: **7** Fleming
  ballet dancer: **7** Shearer
  bovine: **5** Angus, Luing **8** Ayrshire, Galloway
  boy: **3** lad **6** laddie
  capital: **9** Edinburgh
  cheese: **7** crowdie
  chemist: **4** Todd **5** Dewar
  city: **3** Ayr **4** Oban **5** Perth, Troon **6** Dundee, Irvine, Wishaw **7** Airdrie, Falkirk, Glasgow, Paisley, Renfrew **8** Aberdeen, Bearsden, Dumfries, Greenock, Stirling **9** Edinburgh
  dance: **4** reel **5** fling **9** écossaise **10** strathspey
  economist: **5** Smith
  explorer: **4** Park, Ross **11** Livingstone
  former county: **5** Nairn **6** Argyll
  game pole: **5** caber
  hat: **3** tam
  historian: **7** Carlyle
  household: **4** clan
  inventor: **4** Watt
  island: **4** Iona, Mull, Skye, Uist **5** Arran, Tiree, Tyree **8** Hebrides
  lake: **4** Ness **5** Maree **6** Lomond
  land tenure system: **4** udal
  language: **4** Erse **6** Celtic, Gaelic
  mathematician: **6** Napier
  miss: **4** lass **6** lassie
  money: **4** merk, rial, ryal **5** plack **6** bawbee **7** unicorn
  mountain: **8** Ben Nevis
  musician: **5** piper
  name prefix: **3** Mac
  neighbor: **3** Eng. **7** England
  Nobelist: **7** Macleod
  noble: **5** thane, thegn
  pattern: **5** plaid
  philosopher: **5** Smith
  physicist: **5** Dewar **7** Maxwell
  playwright: **6** Barrie
  poet: **4** Hogg, Muir **5** Burns, Scott, Spark **6** Dunbar **8** Campbell
  port: **3** Ayr **7** Glasgow **8** Greenock **9** Edinburgh, Scapa Flow
  pudding: **6** haggis
  river: **3** Awe, Ayr, Dee, Esk, Tay **4** Doon, Lyon, Spey **5** Afton, Clyde, Devon, Lyons, Nairn, Tweed
  scientist: **4** Todd **5** Dewar **6** Frazer, Napier **7** Fleming, Maxwell
  skirt: **4** kilt **7** filibeg **8** philibeg
  sound: **5** Sleat
  tartan: **4** kilt
  terrier: **5** cairn
  tongue: **4** Erse
  writer: **3** Tey **5** Scott, Smith, Spark **6** Buchan, Cronin **7** Boswell, Carlyle **8** Mitchell **9** Stevenson
Scotland, Pa. (2002 film)
  cast: James LeGros, Maura Tierney, Christopher Walken
  director: Billy Morrissette
Scotland Yard: **3** CID
Scots __: **6** Gaelic
__ Scots: **5** pound
Scotsman: **3** car **4** auto **10** automobile, Studebaker
Scott: **2** Oz, S.R. **4** Baio, Dred, Eric, Hoch, Jack, Tony, Wolf **5** Brady, Glenn, Linda, Pippa, Turow **6** Bakula, Gordon, Joplin, Martha, Ridley, Robert, Walter, Wilson **7** Cynthia, McGehee, Willard, Zachary **8** Campbell, Debralee, Hamilton, Lizabeth, McKenzie, Randolph, Winfield **9** Carpenter **10** paper towel
  alternative: **4** Viva **6** Bounty, Brawny, Marcal **7** Charmin **8** Northern, Soft Weve **10** Cottonelle, White Cloud
__ Scott: **4** Jock **5** Great
Scott, Dred: **5** slave
Scott, Duncan Campbell: **4** poet **8** Canadian
Scott, George C.: **5** actor
  film: Bank Shot (1974)
    The Changeling (1979)
    Dr. Strangelove (1964)
    Firestarter (1984)
    The Flim Flam Man (1967)
    The Hospital (1971)
    The Hustler (1961)
    The List of Adrian Messenger (1963)
    Movie Movie (1978)
    The New Centurions (1972)
    Not With My Wife You Don't! (1966)
    Oklahoma Crude (1973)
    Patton (1970, AA)
    Petulia (1968)
    They Might Be Giants (1971)
  spouse: Colleen Dewhurst, Trish Van Devere
Scott-Heron: **3** Gil
Scotti: **4** Vito
Scottie, FDR: **4** Fala
Scottie, Pippen sport: **10** basketball
Scottish __: **4** rite, star **6** Gaelic **7** terrier
Scottish Fold: **3** cat, pet **5** felid **6** feline
Scottish Symphony composer: **11** Mendelssohn
Scottish words
  adverb: **3** nae **4** syne
  ago: **4** syne
  alder: **3** arn
  askew: **4** agee
  church: **4** kirk
  estuary: **5** firth, frith
  exclamation: **3** och
  fish: **3** ged
  fishing boat: **6** baldie
  goblet: **4** tass
  have: **3** hae
  hill: **4** brae
  John: **3** Ian
  knife: **5** skean, skene
  lake: **4** loch
  no: **3** nae
  number: **3** ane, twa
  pants: **5** trews
  scarf: **5** curch
  shoe: **5** gilly **6** gillie
  since: **4** syne
  to: **3** tae
  turnip: **4** neep
  waterfall: **3** lin **4** linn
  yes: **2** ay **3** aye
__ Scott Key: **7** Francis
__ Scott King: **7** Coretta
__ Scott Lee: **5** Jason
Scott, Lizabeth: **7** actress
  film: Dead Reckoning (1947)
    Easy Living (1949)
    Loving You (1957)
    Pitfall (1948)
    The Racket (1951)
    The Strange Loves of Martha Ivers (1946)
Scott, Martha: **7** actress
  film: Ben-Hur (1959)
    Cheers for Miss Bishop (1941)
    One Foot in Heaven (1941)
    Our Town (1940)
    Sayonara (1957)
    So Well Remembered (1947)
    The Ten Commandments (1956)
    When I Grow Up (1951)
Scotto, Antonio: **6** singer **7** Italian
Scotto, Renata: **4** diva **6** singer **7** Italian, soprano
Scott, Randolph: **5** actor
  film: Abilene Town (1946)
    Badman's Territory (1946)
    Bombardier (1943)
    Buchanan Rides Alone (1958)
    Coroner Creek (1948)
    Corvette K-225 (1943)
    The Desperadoes (1943)
    Follow the Fleet (1936)
    Frontier Marshal (1939)
    Go West, Young Man (1936)
    The Last of the Mohicans (1936)
    Murders in the Zoo (1933)
    Paris Calling (1941)
    Ride Lonesome (1959)
    Ride the High Country (1962)
    Seven Men From Now (1956)
    She (1935)
    The Tall T (1957)
    Village Tale (1935)
    The Walking Hills (1949)
    Western Union (1941)
    When the Daltons Rode (1940)
Scott, Ridley: **8** director
  film: Alien (1979)
    Black Hawk Down (2001)
    Black Rain (1989)
    Blade Runner (1982)
    The Duellists (1977)
    G.I. Jane (1997)
    Gladiator (2000)
    Hannibal (2001)
    Someone to Watch Over Me (1987)
    Thelma & Louise (1991)
    White Squall (1996)
Scott, Robert Falcon: **7** British **8** explorer
Scottsdale: **4** city, town
  locale: **7** Arizona
Scott, S.R.: **4** poet **8** Canadian
Scott, Steve: **5** miler **6** runner
__ Scott Thomas: **7** Kristin
Scott, Tony: **8** director
  film: Crimson Tide (1995)
    Days of Thunder (1990)
    Enemy of the State (1998)
    The Fan (1996)
    The Last Boy Scout (1991)
    Revenge (1990)
    Top Gun (1986)
    True Romance (1993)
Scott, Walter: **3** Sir **4** poet **6** author, writer **8** Scottish
  work: The Antiquary
    The Bride of Lammermoor
    Guy Mannering
    The Heart of Midlothian
    Ivanhoe
    Kenilworth
    The Lady of the Lake
    The Lay of the Last Minstrel
    Marmion
    Quentin Durward
    Rob Roy
    The Talisman
    Waverley
Scotty: **7** Beckett
Scott, Zachary: **5** actor
  film: Bandido (1956)
    Flamingo Road (1949)
    It'$ Only Money (1962)
    The Mask of Dimitrios (1944)
    Mildred Pierce (1945)
    Ruthless (1948)
    Shadow on the Wall (1950)
    The Southerner (1945)
__ Scotus: **4** Duns
scoundrel: **3** cad, cur, rat **4** heel, rake, toad, worm **5** cheat, churl, creep, crook, devil, ganef, gonef, gonif, knave, losel, rogue, rowdy, scamp, sneak, swine, thief, viper **6** bad egg, bad guy, bad hat, goniff, maggot, rascal, rotter, varlet, weasel, wretch **7** bad news, bounder, lowlife, ruffian, varment, varmint, villain **8** picaroon, rakehell, scalawag, swindler **9** miscreant, reprobate, scallawag, scallywag, vulgarian **10** blackguard, black sheep, mountebank, ne'er-do-well, scapegrace
Scoundrel, The (1935 film)
  cast: Noël Coward, Julie Haydon
  director: Ben Hecht, Charles MacArthur
Scoupe: **3** car **4** auto **7** Hyundai **10** automobile

scour: 3 rub 4 buff, comb, find, grub, hunt, rake, sand, scan, seek, wash 5 brush, clean, flush, scrub 6 abrade, forage, polish, pumice, search 7 burnish, cleanse, enquire, inquire, ransack, rummage 9 ferret out, track down
Scourby: 9 Alexander
scourge: 3 tan 4 bane, beat, belt, cane, flog, lash, pest, ruin, slam, whip 5 blast, curse, flail, knout, whale 6 blight, plague, punish, terror, thrash 7 afflict, lambast, torment 8 calamity, lambaste 9 castigate, excoriate, horsewhip, terrorize 10 affliction, flagellate, infliction
  of mortals: 4 Ares
Scourge of God: 6 Attila
scouring
  need: 3 S.O.S. 6 Brillo 7 soap pad
  starter: 3 off
scouring ___: 3 pad 4 rush
scourings: 4 dirt 5 trash 7 residue
scouse: 4 stew
scout: 3 spy 4 case, look 5 guide, recce, recon, snoop, watch 6 escort, patrol, picket, reject, runner, search, survey 7 bird-dog, explore, lookout, observe, outpost, servant, soldier, spotter 8 check out, explorer, front man, outrider, rustle up, vanguard 9 ferret out, range over, recruiter 10 advance man, look down on
  act: 4 deed 8 good deed
  destination: 4 camp
  ender: 6 master
  handiwork: 4 knot
  out: 4 find, hunt, seek 6 pursue, search 7 hunt for, look for 8 hunt down 9 search for, track down
  pledge word: 4 duty
  recitation: 4 oath
  sew-on: 5 badge 10 merit badge
  shelter: 4 tent
  unit: 3 den 5 troop
scout ___: 3 car
___ scout: 5 king's 6 queen's, talent
Scout: 3 Cub 4 Life, Star 5 Eagle, horse, pinto, steed 6 equine 7 Brownie, Cadette 8 Explorer 10 Tenderfoot
  rider: 5 Tonto
___ Scout: 3 Boy, Cub, Sea 4 Girl 5 Eagle
scow: 4 boat, ship 5 barge 8 flatboat
scowl: 4 lour, sulk 5 frown, glare, lower 6 glower 7 grimace 8 threaten 9 dirty look, make a face
scrabble: 6 shinny 7 clamber, shinney
  starter: 4 hard
Scrabble: 4 game 9 board game
  inventor: 5 Butts
  maker: 6 Hasbro
  need: 4 rack, tile, word 5 board
  unit: 6 letter
  versatile ~ tile: 5 blank
scrag: 4 nape, neck 6 scruff 8 beanpole 10 string bean
scraggy: 4 lank, lean, slim, thin, wiry 5 gaunt, lanky, rough, spare 6 dainty, gangly, meager, ragged, skinny, slight, slinky, svelte, twiggy, uneven 7 gracile, scrawny, slender, spidery, willowy 8 gangling 9 sylphlike
scram: 2 go 3 hie 4 exit, flee, move, race, scat 5 leave, scoot, split 6 beat it, begone, bug out, decamp, depart, get out, go away 7 abscond, buzz off, get lost, make off, pull out, take off, vamoose 8 cheese it, clear out, fugitate, hightail, run for it, shove off 9 disappear, skedaddle, take a hike 10 go fly a kite, hightail it, hit the road, make tracks, take flight
Scram!: 3 git 4 away, blow, scat, shoo 5 leave 6 beat it, begone, get out
scramble: 3 run, vie 4 hash, push, race, rush 5 addle, climb, melee, mix up, scoot 6 bustle, encode, garble, hasten, jockey, jostle, jumble, justle, litter, muddle, muss up, ramble, scurry, shinny, strive, tussle 7 clamber, clutter, compete, scuffle, scuttle, shinney, shuffle, snarl up 8 mishmash, straggle, struggle 9 commotion, confusion, make haste, scrimmage 10 disarrange, free-for-all
  a message: 6 encode
  something to ~: 4 yolk
scrambled: 8 pell-mell 10 disorderly
scrambled ___: 4 eggs
Scranton: 4 city, town
  city near ~: 6 Elmira
  locale: 4 Penn.
scrap: 3 bit, ort, rag, rid, row 4 atom, bite, bout, chip, dump, fray, hunk, iota, junk, lump, mite, part, shed, spat, tiff, whit 5 abort, argue, brawl, brush, chuck, chunk, clash, crumb, ditch, fight, grain, patch, piece, relic, set-to, shard, sherd, shred, slice, spark, speck, trace, trash, waste 6 barney, bicker, fracas, hassle, morsel, reject, rumpus, sliver, tussle 7 abandon, contest, discard, dispute, fall out, garbage, modicum, oddment, portion, quarrel, remnant, rubbish, scuffle, snippet, toss out, uneaten, useless, vestige, wrangle 8 argument, conflict, demolish, fragment, get rid of, have at it, jettison, junkyard, leftover, mouthful, particle, pittance, skirmish, squabble, struggle, throw out 9 eighty-six, encounter, fistfight, have words, remainder, square off, throw away 10 difference, free-for-all, smithereen
  ender: 4 book, heap
scrapbook: 5 album
  need: 4 glue 5 paste, photo 7 memento
scrape: 3 eke, fix, jam, rub 4 bark, claw, file, gall, mess, pare, peel, rasp, skin, snag, spot, wear 5 chafe, clean, grate, graze, grind, pinch, score, shave, skimp, spare, stint, wound 6 abrade, boo-boo, bruise, corner, injury, lesion, pickle, plight, scrimp 7 dilemma, problem, scratch, shuffle, trouble 8 abrasion, exigence, exigency, irritate, quagmire, squeak by 9 economize, excoriate, tight spot 10 difficulty, underspend
  as a knee: 4 bark 5 graze 6 abrade, scrape
  away at: 5 erode 6 abrade
  bow and ~: 4 fawn 5 court, kneel, kotow, toady 6 grovel, kowtow 8 bootlick, fawn upon, suck up to 10 curry favor, pay court to
  by: 3 eke 5 exist 6 eke out, make do, manage 7 make out, subsist, survive
  treatment: 6 iodine 7 Band-Aid
  up: 5 amass, glean 6 garner, gather, obtain 7 acquire, collect 8 assemble
scraped: 3 raw 4 hurt
scraper: 4 tool
  starter: 3 sky
  use a ~: 5 deice
scraping: 5 trash, waste 6 refuse 7 garbage, grating, residue 8 friction, leftover
scrapple: 4 meat
scrappy: 6 feisty 7 hostile 8 militant 9 querulous, truculent 10 pugnacious, unflagging
scraps: 5 trash, waste 6 refuse 7 residue 8 leftover, residuum
scratch: 3 cut, eke, mar, oof, rub 4 cash, claw, drop, etch, flaw, gash, gelt, hurt, jack, kail, kale, loot, mark, nick, peag, pelf, rasp, scar, snub, tear, work, zero 5 abort, annul, bills, bread, bucks, dough, erase, funds, grate, graze, lucre, money, moola, mopus, pesos, prick, rhino, score, sewan, wound 6 boo-boo, cancel, damage, deface, defect, delete, dinero, do-re-mi, incise, injury, lesion, mammon, mazuma, moolah, remove, scrape, scrawl, seawan, silver, specie, wampum, wealth 7 blemish, cabbage, capital, dollars, engrave, lettuce, ooftish, redline, shekels 8 abrasion, bankroll, cold cash, currency, hard cash, lacerate, scribble, smackers, withdraw 9 banknotes, eliminate, frogskins, long green, simoleons, terminate 10 greenbacks, green stuff, laceration
  ender: 5 board, proof
  from ~: 4 anew, over 6 afresh
  not up to ~: 3 bad 4 poor, weak 5 rusty 6 faulty, flawed 7 lacking, wanting 8 impaired, inferior 9 defective, deficient, imperfect 10 inadequate, incomplete
  out: 5 erase 6 cancel, efface, excise
  out a living: 6 scrape
  pad: 6 tablet 8 foolscap
  rock ~: 5 stria
  without a ~: 4 safe 5 whole 8 unharmed 9 untouched
scratch ___: 3 awl, hit, pad, wig 4 coat, line, test 5 paper, sheet
___ scratch: 4 from, up to
___ Scratch: 3 Old
scratch and ___: 5 sniff
scratched out: 3 x'ed
___ scratcher: 4 back
___ scratches: 3 hen
scratching-post covering: 6 carpet
scratchy: 5 husky, itchy, rough, roupy 6 coarse, gritty 8 abrasive
scrawl: 5 write 6 doodle 7 scratch, writing 8 longhand, scribble, squiggle
scrawly: 6 sloppy 9 illegible 10 unreadable
scrawny: 4 bony, lank, lean, slim, thin, wiry 5 boney, gaunt, lanky, spare, weedy 6 dainty, gangly, ill-fed, meager, skinny, slight, slinky, svelte, twiggy 7 angular, gracile, scraggy, slender, spidery, willowy 8 angulose, angulous, gangling 9 sylphlike
scream: 3 cry, jar 4 bawl, card, hoot, howl, rage, rant, rave, riot, roar, wail, yell, yowl 5 blare, cheer, comic, joker, laugh, panic, shout, whoop 6 bellow, cry out, holler, outcry, shriek, squeal 7 screech, sing out 8 comedian, funnyman 9 caterwaul, character, laughable, priceless, sensation 10 comedienne, vociferate
  cartoon ~: 3 eek
Scream (1995 song)
  artist: Janet Jackson, Michael Jackson
Scream (1996 film)
  cast: David Arquette, Drew Barrymore, Neve Campbell, Courteney Cox, Jamie Kennedy, Matthew Lillard, Rose McGowan, Skeet Ulrich
  director: Wes Craven
screamer: 4 bird 7 pennant 8 headline
Screamin' ___ Hawkins: 3 Jay
screaming: 5 noisy, showy 7 blatant 9 deafening
screaming-___: 7 meemies
Screaming ___: 6 Eagles
Scream of Fear (1961 film)
  cast: Christopher Lee, Susan Strasberg
  director; Seth Holt
___ Screams: 6 Africa
scree: 5 talus 6 debris 8 detritus
screech: 3 cry 4 bawl, yell, yelp, yowl 5 groan, shout 6 holler, scream, shriek, squawk, squeak, squeal 9 caterwaul 10 vociferate
screech ___: 3 owl
screeching: 5 noisy 6 shrill 8 jangling, strident
screed: 4 talk 6 tirade 8 diatribe, harangue 9 philippic
screen: 3 net, VDT 4 cull, hide, mask, mesh, scan, sift, sort, veil, wall 5 blind, cloak, cover, gauge, grade, grill, guard, hedge, shade, shoji, sieve, unmix 6 awning, canopy, defend, enveil, filter, grille, mantle, select, shadow, shield, strain, winnow 7 conceal, curtain, divider, examine, lattice, obscure, pick out, process, protect, seclude, secrete, shelter, shut off, shut out, wall off 8 block out, evaluate, security, separate, terminal 9 eliminate, partition, safeguard 10 camouflage
  again: 5 rerun
  blinker: 6 cursor
  computer ~: 3 CRT, VDT 7 monitor 8 terminal
  ender: 4 land, play 5 saver 6 writer
  from view: 4 hide 6 enisle 7 conceal, confine, isolate 8 cloister, separate 9 keep apart, segregate, sequester 10 quarantine
  image unit: 5 pixel
  Japanese ~: 5 shoji
  local ~: 4 nabe
  partner: 5 stage
  perforated ~: 5 grill 6 grille
  silver ~: 5 films 6 cinema, flicks, movies 7 filmdom 8 pictures
  starter: 3 off, sun 4 silk, wind 5 smoke
screen ___: 4 grid, pass, test 5 saver 6 memory
___ screen: 4 fire, home, rood 5 delay, organ, sight, small, smoke, split, video 6 cheval, silver
___-screen: 3 off 4 wide, wind
Screen ___: 4 Gems
Screen ___ Guild: 6 Actors
screened: 5 shady 6 hidden, select 9 unexposed
screening device: 5 sieve, V-chip
screenplay: 5 movie 6 script 8 scenario
Screens, The author: Jean Genet
screenwriter: 6 writer 18 dramatist. scenarist
screw: 4 turn, wind 5 helix, twist, wring 6 fasten, spiral, wrench 7 contort 8 fastener, flathead 9 propeller
  backing: 6 cap nut
  ender: 4 ball, worm 6 driver
  starter: 3 air, set 4 cork, jack 5 thumb
  thread: 5 helix
  up: 4 blow, flub, goof, muff, ruin, undo 5 botch, louse, spoil 6 blow it, bobble, boggle, bungle 7 confuse 9 mishandle, mismanage
screw ___: 3 cap, eye, fly, log, nut 4 axis, bean, hook, jack, nail, pile, pine 5 auger, press 6 anchor, thread 7 mooring
screw-___: 3 top
___ screw: 3 cap, lag 4 hand, lead, wood 5 Allen, bench, coach, drive, stage 7 machine, mooring, tapping 8 Phillips
screwball: 4 kook, zany 5 flake, nutty, pitch
screw-cutting tool: 3 die
screwdriver: 4 tool 5 drink 8 beverage, cocktail
  impromptu ~: 4 dime
  ingredient: 5 vodka
screw-shaped: 6 spiral 7 helical

Screwtape Letters, The author: C.S. Lewis
screwup: **4** flub, mess, slip **5** lapse, snafu, upset **6** muddle **7** blunder, mistake
screwy: **4** zany **5** flaky, goofy, inane, silly, wacky **6** absurd, flakey, whacky **7** fatuous, unsound **8** cockeyed, specious **9** illogical, senseless, untenable **10** groundless, ridiculous
Scriabin, Alexsandr: **7** Russian **8** composer
scribble: **3** jot **5** write **6** doodle, scrawl **7** scratch, writing **8** longhand
scribbles: **8** graffiti
scribe: **5** clerk, write **6** author, copier, penner, writer **7** copyist **8** annalist, essayist **9** columnist, scrivener, secretary, wordsmith **10** amanuensis, chronicler, journalist
Biblical ~: **4** Ezra
Dead Sea Scrolls ~: **6** Essene
Scribe, Augustin: **6** French **10** playwright
Scribner: **7** Charles
scrim: **6** fabric **7** drapery **8** backdrop, material
scrimmage: **4** tilt **5** clash, fight, melee, mix-up **6** battle, fracas **8** scramble, skirmish
starter: **4** snap
scrimp: **4** save **5** hoard, spare, stint **6** meager, scrape **7** cut back **8** conserve **9** economize **10** cut corners, underspend
scrimping: **6** stingy **7** economy **9** frugality **10** economical
scrimpy: **5** scant **6** meager, scanty, skimpy, sparse
scrimshaw material: **5** ivory **6** baleen
Scripps: **2** E.W.
script: **4** book, copy, text **5** lines, story **6** dialog, record **7** letters, writing **8** dialogue, document, libretto, longhand, playbook, scenario **10** manuscript, penmanship, screenplay
alter a ~: **4** edit
as directed by the ~: **5** on cue
direction: **4** exit, fade **5** enter **6** fade in
ender: **3** ure **6** writer
ignore the ~: **5** ad-lib
lines: **6** dialog
starter: **4** Act I, manu, type
writer: **6** author **9** dramatist, scenarist **10** playwright
script __: **4** girl **6** doctor, reader
__ scripta: **3** lex
scriptural doctrine: **6** cabala, kabala **7** cabbala, kabbala
scripture: **5** Bible **7** the Word
excerpt: **5** verse
Hindu ~: **4** Veda
Moslem: **5** Koran
__ Scripture: **4** Holy
scrivener: **6** scribe **7** copyist **10** amanuensis, journalist
scrod: **4** fish **7** codfish, haddock, seafood
scroll: **4** coil, roll **6** record **8** register
ancient ~ writer: **6** Essene
holder: **3** ark
synagogue ~: **4** Tora **5** Torah
scroll __: **3** saw **4** foot
__ scroll: **4** hand, wave **7** Flemish, hanging
scrolled: **6** spiral
Scrooge: **5** miser, saver **8** tightwad **9** skinflint
comment: **3** bah
nephew: **6** Donald
play ~: **5** stint
Scrooge (1970 film)
cast: Albert Finney, Alec Guinness
director: Ronald Neame
Scrooged (1988 film)
cast: Karen Allen, John Forsythe, John Glover, Bill Murray
director: Richard Donner
scrounge: **3** beg, bum **4** grub, hunt **5** cadge, filch, leech, mooch **6** forage, pilfer, sponge **7** finagle, scare up, wheedle **8** freeload **9** panhandle
scrounger: **5** leech **6** beggar **8** parasite
scrub: **3** mop, mut, rub **4** buff, drop, mutt, runt, stop, wash **5** abort, bathe, brush, clean, erase, scour **6** abrade, cancel, delete, lather, polish, repeal, revoke, shelve **7** abandon, abolish, call off, cleanse, correct, deterge, launder, mongrel, rectify, rescind, stunted, thicket **8** abrogate, brighten, inferior **9** disinfect, pipsqueak, terminate **10** do away with
ender: **4** land
up: **4** lave, wash
scrub __: **3** jay, oak **4** fowl, pine, suit **5** brush, nurse
__ Scrub: **4** Soft
scrubber, back: **5** loofa, luffa **6** loofah
scrubbing: **4** bath
need: **3** S.O.S. **5** brush **6** Brillo **7** soap pad
scrubby: **5** small **6** humble **8** slipshod
scrubland: **5** heath
scrubs: **5** B team
scruff: **4** nape, neck **5** nucha, scrag
hair: **7** hackles
scruffy: **4** mean **5** mangy, messy, rough, seedy, sorry, tacky **6** mangey, ragged, ragtag, shabby, shoddy, unneat, untidy **7** run-down, unkempt **8** slipshod, slovenly, tattered, untended **9** ungroomed **10** bedraggled, threadbare
Scruggs, Earl: **8** banjoist
partner: **5** Flatt
scrum game: **5** rugby
scrumptious: **4** nice **5** sapid, tasty, yummy **6** lovely, savory **8** heavenly, luscious **9** ambrosial, delicious, exquisite, flavorful, palatable, succulent, toothsome **10** appetizing, delectable
scrunch: **4** mash **5** munch, press, quash, smash **6** rumple, squash, squint **7** squeeze, wrinkle
scruple: **4** balk **5** baulk, demur, doubt, grain, pause, qualm **6** falter, regret, twinge **7** anxiety, measure **8** hesitate **9** misgiving, principle **10** conscience, hesitation, solicitude, think twice, uneasiness
scruples: **6** morals **8** superego **10** conscience, inner voice
three ~: **4** dram
without ~: **6** amoral
Scruples author: Judith Krantz
scrupulous: **4** fair, just, nice, true **5** chary, exact, frank, fussy, legit, moral, right **6** honest, minute, square, strict **7** careful, correct, dutiful, earnest, ethical, factual, finicky, precise, prudent, sincere, upright **8** accurate, cautious, credible, exacting, finiking, finnicky, methodic, punctual, rigorous, sedulous, straight, thorough, truthful **9** assiduous, attentive, honorable, judicious, observant, righteous, squeamish, veracious **10** deliberate, fastidious, forthright, meticulous, on the level, particular, principled, upstanding
scrupulousness: **4** care **5** honor **7** honesty, loyalty
scrutinize: **3** eye, see, spy **4** case, comb, look, ogle, peer, pore, scan, sift, view **5** assay, audit, check, probe, study, watch, weigh **6** look at, peruse, regard, review, search, survey **7** compare, dissect, examine, explore, inspect, observe, pry into, ransack **8** look into, look over, peer into, pore over **9** criticize, enter into, pick apart, take stock
scrutiny: **4** look, test **5** audit, check, probe, proof, study, watch **6** regard, review, survey **7** enquiry, inquiry, perusal, reading, thought **8** analysis, eagle eye, research **9** attention, probation **10** inspection, weather eye
bear ~: **4** wash
combining form: **5** -scopy
SCTV
actor: **5** Candy, O'Hara
bit: **4** skit
scuba
diving: **5** sport
gear: **4** tank
tank supply: **3** air
user: **5** diver
weapon: **5** spear
Scuba Duba author: Bruce Jay Friedman
scud: **3** run **4** race, rush **5** glide, sweep
Scud downer: **3** ABM
Scudéry, Madeleine de: **6** author, French, writer
work: Clélie
scudo: **4** coin **5** money
scuff: **3** mar **4** gall, mule, walk, wear **6** abrade **7** shuffle **8** abrasion
scuffle: **3** row **4** bout, cuff, fray, fuss, tilt **5** brawl, clash, fight, melee, scrap **6** affray, barney, fracas, jostle, justle, ruckus, rumpus, tussle **7** grapple, mix it up, shuffle, wrangle, wrestle **8** brouhaha, scramble, skirmish, struggle **9** commotion **10** donnybrook, free-for-all
memento: **5** mouse **6** fat lip, shiner **8** black eye
scuffle __: **3** hoe
Scugog: **4** city, town
locale: **6** Canada **7** Ontario
scull: **3** row **4** boat **7** rowboat
ancient ~: **6** bireme **7** trireme
implement: **3** oar
squad: **4** crew
scullcap, ancient: **6** pileus
scullery: **7** kitchen
sculling: **5** sport
Scully: **3** Vin **4** Dana **5** agent
sculpin: **4** fish
sculpt: **4** mold **5** carve, model, shape **6** chisel, incise **7** portray, whittle **9** give shape
sculpted-heads island: **6** Easter
sculptor: **3** Arp **5** Moore, Rodin **6** artist, Calder, French, Giotto **7** Borglum, Cellini, Noguchi, Picasso, Pisarro **8** Dubuffet **9** Donatello, Remington **12** Michelangelo
American ~: **6** Calder, French **7** Borglum, Noguchi **9** Remington
British ~: **5** Moore
Dada ~: **3** Arp
deg.: **3** MFA
French ~: **3** Arp **5** Rodin **8** Dubuffet
funding source: **3** NEA
Greek ~: **5** Myron **6** Scopas
Italian ~: **6** Giotto **7** Cellini **9** Donatello **12** Michelangelo
material: **3** ice **4** clay, jade **5** stone
mobile ~: **6** Calder
need: **6** chisel
Renaissance ~: **9** Donatello
Spanish ~: **7** Picasso, Pisarro
subject: **4** head **5** torso
Western ~: **9** Remington
work: **4** bust
sculpture: **3** art, cut, hew **4** bust, cast, mold, work **5** carve, model, shape **6** incise, medium, mobile, statue **7** contour, fashion, whittle
1498 ~: **5** Pietà
kind of ~: **4** bust, head **5** torso
mineral: **9** alabaster
Parthenon ~: **6** Athena, Athene
scum: **3** mob **4** dirt, film **5** algae, crust, dregs, dross, froth, slime, trash, waste **6** rabble, refuse, vermin **7** lowlife, residue **8** riffraff **9** miscreant **10** lower class
scummy: **5** slimy, sorry **6** shabby
scup: **5** porgy
scuppernong: **5** fruit, grape
relative: **5** Gamay, pinot, Tokay **6** Merlot **7** Catawba, Concord, Niagara **8** Cabernet, malvasia, muscatel **9** muscadine, Sauvignon, zinfandel **10** Chardonnay
scurf: **8** dandruff
scurrility: **6** insult **9** blasphemy, invective **10** detraction, muckraking
scurrilous: **3** low **4** lewd, mean, rank **5** dirty, gross, nasty **6** coarse, filthy, ribald, rotten, smutty, vulgar **7** abusive, obscene, raunchy **8** indecent, libelous **9** insulting, offensive, salacious, sarcastic, shameless **10** scandalous
scurry: **3** fly, hie, rip, run, zip **4** dart, dash, flee, flit, race, rush, skim, tear, zoom **5** haste, hurry, scoot, spank, speed, whisk **6** barrel, bustle, gallop, hasten, hustle, move it, rocket, sprint **7** floor it, hop to it, mad rush, quicken, scamper **8** scramble, step on it **9** hotfoot it, shake a leg, skedaddle, tear along **10** burn rubber, get a move on, get hopping, hightail it
__-scurry: **5** hurry
scurvy: **3** low **6** rotten, sordid, stingy **7** pitiful **9** miserable
scut: **4** tail
ender: **4** work
Scutari: **4** lake
locale: **7** Albania **10** Yugoslavia
scutate: **5** scaly
scuttle: **3** run **4** pail, quit, race, ruin, sink **5** ditch, wreck **6** defeat, scotch **7** abandon, destroy, forsake, scamper **8** give up on, scramble **9** back out of, container, pull out of
coal ~: **3** hod
load: **4** coal
scuttlebutt: **4** buzz, dirt, poop, talk, word **5** rumor **6** gossip, report **7** hearsay
scuttled: **6** sunken **9** submerged
scuzzy: **5** gross
scythe: **3** mow **5** knife
handle: **5** snath **6** snathe
path: **5** swath **6** swathe
use a ~: **3** cut **4** reap
Scythian: **8** language
Scythian lamb: **4** fern
Scythian Suite composer: **9** Prokofiev
S. Dak.
see South Dakota
SDI
concern: **3** ABM **4** ICBM
part: **3** Def. **7** Defense **9** Strategic **10** Initiative
SDS protest target: **3** SSS
__ se: **3** per **5** inter
Se: **4** elem. **7** element **8** selenium
34 for ~: **4** at. no.
Se __: **5** Ri Pak
Se __ español: **5** habla
SE: **3** dir., hdg.
Se7en (1995 film)
cast: Morgan Freeman, Gwyneth Paltrow, Brad Pitt, Kevin Spacey
director: David Fincher
sea: **3** Red **4** Aral, Azov, Dead, deep, Java, Kara, main, Ross, Sulu **5** Banda, Black, briny, China, Coral, Egean, Irish, Japan, North, ocean, spate,

swell, Timor, waves, White 6 Aegean, Baltic, Bering, Inland, Ionian, Laptev, Sagami, Salton, Sivash, Tasman, Yellow 7 Andaman, Arabian, Arafura, Barents, Caspian, Celebes, Galilee, legions, Marmara, Okhotsk, Sibuyan, Weddell 8 Adriatic, Amundsen, Beaufort, Bismarck, Labrador, Ligurian, plethora, Sargasso 9 abundance, Caribbean, East China, Greenland, Hudson Bay, multitude, Norwegian, profusion 10 Philippine, South China, Tyrrhenian
Africa ~: 3 Red
Alaska ~: 6 Bering 8 Beaufort
anemone: 5 polyp 6 animal
Antarctica ~: 4 Ross 7 Weddell 8 Amundsen
Arabia ~: 3 Red
Arctic ~: 4 Kara 7 Barents
arm of the ~: 5 fiord, fjord, inlet
Asia ~: 4 Aral, Kara, Savu, Sawu, Sulu 5 Banda, China, Coral, Timor 6 Flores, Inland, Laptev, Sagami, Yellow 7 Andaman, Arafura, Marmara 8 Bismarck 9 East China 10 South China
at ~: 4 lost 6 addled, adrift, afloat, in a fog, unsure 7 at a loss, baffled, bemused, in a daze, muddled, out of it, puzzled, sailing, stumped 8 clueless, confused, cruising, drifting, floating, offshore, steaming, voyaging, yachting 9 befuddled, flummoxed, mystified, perplexed, sailoring, uncertain, under sail 10 bewildered, nonplussed
Australia ~: 5 Coral, Timor 6 Tasman 7 Arafura
away from the ~: 6 inland
barrier: 4 dike
bass: 4 fish 7 grouper 9 blackfish
be stationary at ~: 5 lie to
bottom: 3 bed 7 benthos
bream: 4 fish
Canada ~: 8 Labrador 9 Hudson Bay
change course, at ~: 4 tack
chicken of the ~: 4 tuna
color: 4 blue
combining form: 3 mer- 4 hali-, mari- 5 pelag- 6 pelago- 7 thalass- 8 thalasso-
cow: 6 dugong
creature: 4 salp 5 salpa, squid, whale, whelk
dog: 3 gob, tar 4 salt 6 sailor 7 jack tar, mariner
dog quaff: 3 rum 4 grog
dogs: 4 crew
eagle: 3 ern 4 erne
ender: 3 bed, man, men, way 4 bird, cock, food, fowl, girt, gull, jack, lift, mark, port, sick, side, wall, ward, ware, weed 5 board, borne, coast, farer, floor, going, mount, plane, quake, scape, shell, shore, train, wards, water 6 faring, jacker, strand, worthy
Eurasia ~: 5 Black 7 Caspian
Europe ~: 4 Azov 5 Egean, Irish, North 6 Aegean, Baltic, Ionian 7 Barents 8 Adriatic, Ligurian 10 Tyrrhenian
extension: 3 arm 4 gulf
foam: 5 spume
grape: 5 fruit
Greek personification of the ~: 6 Pontos, Pontus
greenery: 4 alga
Greenland ~: 8 Labrador
holly: 6 eryngo
horse: 4 fish
in French: 3 mer
inland ~: 4 Aral, lake
in Latin: 4 mare
lettuce: 4 ulva
like the ~: 5 briny, salty
lion: 6 animal, mammal
lunar ~: 4 mare
mean ~ level: 5 geoid
mew: 4 bird
Mideast ~: 4 Dead 7 Galilee
motion: 4 tide
mythical ~ nymph: 4 Ione
New Zealand ~: 4 Ross 6 Tasman
Norwegian ~ monster: 7 krakens
not at ~: 6 ashore
nymph: 5 siren 6 nereid
of the ~: 6 marine 8 maritime, nautical
Pacific ~: 5 Coral
Philippines ~: 4 Sulu 7 Celebes, Sibuyan
pollution: 5 slick
power: 6 armada
put to ~: 4 sail 6 launch 7 set sail, ship out 8 shove off
raven: 4 fish
resort: 4 Lido
robber: 6 pirate 7 brigand, corsair 8 freeboot 9 buccaneer 10 freebooter
Russia ~: 4 Aral, Azov 5 White 6 Sivash 7 Okhotsk
shocker: 3 eel
swell: 4 surf, wave
swirl: 4 eddy 9 maelstrom
treat ~ water: 6 desalt 10 desalinate, desalinize
urchin: 7 echinus
voyage: 4 sail, trip 6 cruise, junket, travel 7 journey 8 crossing
wall: 4 dike, mole 5 levee 10 breakwater
West Indies ~: 8 Sargasso 9 Caribbean
wolf: 8 rapparee
sea __: 3 bag, cow, dog, fan, fox, hog, mew, pen 4 bass, calf, duck, duty, fire, foam, gate, gull, hare, kale, king, lane, legs, lily, lion, mile, mist, moss, oats, palm, pink, puss, risk, room, salt, slug, star, wall, wasp, whip, wolf 5 blite, bread, bream, chest, devil, eagle, fight, floor, front, gauge, grape, green, holly, horse, level, mouse, onion, otter, poppy, power, purse, raven, reach, robin, rover, smoke, snail, snake, squab, stack, stock, trout, wrack 6 anchor, breeze, change, cradle, dahlia, ladder, lawyer, nettle, return, robber, spider, squill, squirt, stores, tangle, trials, turtle, urchin, walnut 7 anemone, biscuit, cabbage, captain, feather, lamprey, leather, lettuce, scallop, serpent, swallow
__ sea: 4 beam, head, open 5 all at, cross, green 6 hollow
__-sea: 4 deep
Sea __: 4 Calm, Hunt 5 Scout 6 Cruise 7 Islands
Sea __, The: 4 Hawk, Wolf 6 Wolves 7 Gypsies
Sea-__ Airport: 3 Tac
__ Sea: 3 Red 4 Aral, Dead, Java, Kara, Ross, Sulu 5 All at, Banda, Black, China, Coral, Irish, North, Out to, Timor, White 6 Aegean, Baltic, Bering, Euxine, Flores, Inland, Ionian, Laptev, Salton, Tasman, Yellow 7 Andaman, Arabian, Arafura, Barents, Caspian, Celebes, Chukchi, Icarian, Weddell
Sea and Sardinia author: D.H. Lawrence
Sea Around Us, The: 4 book, film
author: Rachel Carson
director: Irwin Allen
Seabee: 4 doer 7 builder
motto: 5 Can Do
organization: 3 USN 4 Navy
seabird: 3 auk, ern, mew 4 coot, erne, gull, skua, tern 5 booby, jager, solan, yager 6 auklet, bonxie, gannet, jaeger, petrel, puffin 7 dovekey, dovekie, pelican 9 albatross, cormorant, guillemot, mallemuck, mollymawk, mollymoke 10 sheathbill
Seabiscuit: 5 horse 9 racehorse
seaboard: 5 coast
Seaborg, Glenn: 7 chemist 8 Nobelist
Sea Breeze ingredient: 5 vodka
Sea Calm author: Langston Hughes
seacoast: 5 beach, shore 6 strand 9 shoreline
seacock: 5 valve
seadog: 6 fogbow
seafarer: 3 gob, tar 4 salt 6 sailor 7 jack tar, mariner 8 helmsman, traveler
seafaring: 5 naval 6 marine, travel 8 maritime, nautical 10 navigation
seafood: 3 cod, eel, roe 4 clam, crab, sole 5 gaper, perch, prawn, scrod 6 schrod, shrimp
course: 4 bisk 6 bisque
garnish: 5 lemon
how to pack ~: 5 in ice
Seagal, Steven: 5 actor
film: Above the Law (1988)
Executive Decision (1996)
Hard to Kill (1990)
Under Siege (1992)
spouse: Kelly LeBrock
seagirt land: 4 isle
seagoing: 5 naval 8 maritime, nautical
initials: 3 HMS, ONI, USS
see also nautical
sea grant __: 7 college
Seagren, Bob: 11 pole vaulter
seagull: 3 mew 4 bird
cousin: 4 tern
hangout: 4 pier
Seagulls artist: 4 Erté
Seagull, The author: Anton Chekhov
character: 4 Dorn, Ilia, Nina 5 Boris, Irina, Masha, Simon, Sorin
Seaham: 4 city, town
locale: 6 Durham 7 England
Seahawk rival: 3 Jet, Ram 4 Bear, Bill, Colt, Lion 5 Brown, Chief, Eagle, Giant, Raven, Saint, Texan, Titan 6 Bengal, Bronco, Cowboy, Falcon, Jaguar, Packer, Raider, Viking 7 Charger, Dolphin, Panther, Patriot, Redskin, Steeler 8 Cardinal 9 Buccaneer
Seahawks: 4 team 6 eleven
div.: 3 NFC
home: 7 Seattle
org.: 3 NFL
sport: 8 football
Sea Hawk, The (1940 film)
cast: Errol Flynn, Brenda Marshall, Claude Rains
director: Michael Curtiz
Sea Hunt (TV drama)
apparatus: 5 scuba
cast: Lloyd Bridges (Mike Nelson)
__ Sea Islands: 5 South
seal: 3 bar, cap, dam, gum 4 bolt, clog, cork, lock, mark, plug, sear, shut, stop, tape 5 block, brown, close, dam up, latch, sigil, stamp 6 animal, assure, attest, barker, cement, clinch, clog up, emblem, encase, ensure, fasten, gasket, lock up, mammal, plug up, ratify, secure, settle, signet, stop up, tape up 7 close up, closure, confirm, occlude, shutter, sticker, stopper, wall off 8 blockade, button up, finalize, hallmark, obstruct, validate 9 assurance, guarantee, medallion 10 coat of arms, escutcheon, imprimatur, quarantine, underwrite, waterproof
affix a ~: 5 stamp 8 validate
a tub: 4 calk 5 caulk, grout
baby ~: 3 pup 4 calf 5 whelp
break the ~: 6 launch
eared ~: 5 otary
ender: 4 skin
female: 3 cow
fur ~: 5 matka
group: 3 pod
home: 3 sea, zoo 5 ocean
in the juices: 4 sear
kin: 6 walrus
male: 4 bull
movie ~: 5 André
of approval: 2 OK 4 okay 6 cachet 8 sanction
papal ~: 5 bulla
point: 3 cat 5 felid 6 feline
prepare to ~: 4 lick
relative: 3 bay, dun, tan 4 bole, ecru, fawn, foxy, nude 5 amber, beige, camel, cocoa, hazel, khaki, mocha, sepia, tawny, umber 6 auburn, bister, bistre, bronze, coffee, copper, ginger, russet, sienna, sorrel, suntan, walnut 7 biscuit, caramel, dogwood 8 chestnut, cinnamon, mahogany 9 butternut, chocolate
seal __: 3 dog, off 4 ring 5 brown
seal __ Siamese: 5 point
__ seal: 3 fur, pin 4 hair, harp, monk, true 5 broad, eared, great, privy 6 Arctic, harbor, hooded, Hudson 7 bearded, earless, harbour, leopard
__-seal: 4 heat
Seal
org.: 3 USN
song: Crazy (1991)
Fly Like an Eagle (1996)
Kiss From a Rose (1995)
sealant: 6 cement
roofing ~: 3 tar
Seal Beach: 4 city, town
locale: 10 California
sealed: 5 tight 6 closed 7 assured 8 airtight, destined 9 leakproof, nonporous
with cement: 5 luted
sealed __: 3 bid 4 beam, book 6 orders
Sealed With a Kiss (1962 song) artist: Brian Hyland
sea-level: 4 flat 10 unelevated
sealing __: 3 wax
Seal in the Bedroom, The author: James Thurber
Seals: 3 Dan, Jim
__ Seals: 6 Easter 9 Christmas
Seals and Crofts
members: Jim Seals, Dash Crofts
song: Diamond Girl (1973)
Get Closer (1976)
Summer Breeze (1972)
sealskin
canoe: 5 kayak
mukluk: 5 kamik
wearer: 6 Eskimo
__ Seal, The: 6 Golden 7 Seventh
Sealy competitor: 5 Serta 7 Simmons
seam: 3 hem, sew 4 line, link, lode, tuck, vein 5 joint, layer, ridge 6 furrow, suture 7 closure, coal bed, deposit, stratum 8 junction, juncture, vinculum 9 stitching 10 connection
coal ~: 4 vein
filler: 5 grout
make a ~: 3 sew
open a ~: 5 unrip 6 let out
style: 4 welt
tapered ~: 4 dart
__ seam: 4 coal, lock 6 French
seaman: 3 gob, tar 4 rank, salt 6 sailor 7 jack tar, mariner, swabbie 8 deckhand 10 bluejacket
name meaning ~: 6 Morgan
saint: 4 Elmo
see also sailor

__ seaman: 4 able
Seaman's Friend, The author: 4 Dana
seamount, flat-topped: 5 guyot
seams
bursting at the ~: 4 full 7 crammed
join at the ~: 4 tack 5 baste 6 repair, stitch
seamstress: 6 tailor 10 dressmaker
inset: 6 gusset
strip: 4 welt
work: 6 edging
Seamus: 6 Heaney
in English: 5 James
seamy: 3 low, raw 4 base 5 rough 6 coarse, shabby, sordid 7 ignoble, run-down, squalid, unkempt 8 degraded, depraved, shameful, unsavory, wrinkled 9 execrable, offensive, repellent, repugnant, revolting 10 abominable, despicable, detestable, scandalous, unpleasant
Sean: 4 Penn 5 Astin, Young 6 Lennon, O'Casey 7 Connery 8 MacBride, O'Faolain
in English: 4 John
Sean __ Combs: 5 Puffy
Sean __ Flanery: 7 Patrick
Sean __ Lennon: 3 Ono
Seanad __: 7 Éireann
séance: 7 meeting, session, sitting
figure: 5 ghost
like a ~: 4 eery 5 eerie
sound: 3 rap
Séance on a Wet Afternoon (1964 film)
cast: Richard Attenborough, Patrick Magee, Kim Stanley
director: Bryan Forbes
__ Sean Leonard: 6 Robert
Sea of __: 4 Azov, Love 5 Crete, Japan 7 Galilee, Marmara, Marmora, Okhotsk
Sea of Azov
feeder: 3 Don
gulf: 8 Taganrog
Sea of Death author: Jorge Amado
Sea of Grass, The author: Conrad Richter
Sea of Japan feeder: 5 Tumen
Sea of Love (1989 film)
cast: Ellen Barkin, John Goodman, Al Pacino
director: Harold Becker
Sea of Love (song) artist: Phil Phillips With the Twilights
artist: Honeydrippers
Sea of Okhotsk feeder: 4 Amur
Sea of Tranquillity site: 4 Moon
seaplane: 8 aircraft
attachment: 5 float
seaport: 6 harbor 7 harbour
SeaQuest __: 3 DSV
sear: 3 dry, fry 4 burn, char, cook, heat, seal 5 brand, brown, dry up, grill, parch, singe 6 braise, scorch, sizzle, wither 7 blacken, frizzle, shrivel 8 barbecue 9 carbonize, cauterize, dehydrate, desiccate
search: 3 dig, pry, spy 4 comb, fish, grub, hunt, look, rake, root, scan, seek, sift 5 check, delve, frisk, grope, probe, prowl, quest, rifle, scour, scout, snoop, study, sweep 6 ferret, forage, lookup, survey 7 dragnet, examine, explore, inspect, legwork, look for, pursuit, ransack, rummage, run down 8 poke into, prospect, question, scout out 9 cast about, feel about, ferret out, go through, range over, shakedown, track down, witch hunt 10 inspection, scrutinize
blindly: 5 grope
diligently: 4 comb 5 delve, scour
ender: 5 light
engine find: 3 URL
for: 4 seek 5 trace 6 look up 7 scout up 8 scout out
for prey: 5 prowl
go in ~ of: 5 quest 6 aspire, gun for, pursue 7 hunt for, long for, look for 8 yearn for 9 track down
high heaven: 4 comb 6 forage 7 ransack
in ~ of: 5 after 9 following
in ~ of adventure: 6 errant
Internet ~ engine: 5 Yahoo 6 Google
out: 5 dig up 6 locate, pursue 9 challenge
party: 5 posse
thorough ~: 5 sweep
search __: 5 party 6 engine 7 warrant
Search __ Tomorrow: 3 for
__ Search: 4 Star
Searchers
homeland: England
song: Love Potion Number Nine (1964)
Needles and Pins (1964)
Searchers, The (1956 film)
cast: Jeffrey Hunter, Vera Miles, John Wayne
director: John Ford
__ Search for Meaning: 4 Man's
Search for Signs of Intelligent Life in the Universe, The (1991 film) cast: Lily Tomlin
Search for Tomorrow (CBS/NBC): 4 soap 9 soap opera
Searchin' (1957 song) artist: Coasters
searching: 7 in-depth 8 complete, piercing, thorough 9 full-dress, inquiring, observant, quizzical 10 exhaustive
__-searching: 4 soul
Searching for Bobby Fischer (1993 film)
cast: Joan Allen, Joe Mantegna, Max Pomeranc
director: Steven Zaillian
Searching for Caleb author: Anne Tyler
Searchin' So Long (1974 song) artist: Chicago
searchlight: 7 lantern
Search me!: 6 I dunno
Search, The (1948 film)
cast: Montgomery Clift, Ivan Jandl, Aline MacMahon
director: Fred Zinnemann
Search, The author: C.P. Snow
Searcy: 4 Nick
searing: 3 hot 8 scathing
Searle: 6 Ronald
Sears: 5 store 8 retailer
competitor: 5 K-Mart 6 Target 7 Penney's, Wal-Mart
partner: 7 Roebuck
Sears __: 5 tower
seas: 5 seven 6 heptad
__ seas: 4 high
seascape: 4 view 6 nature 7 picture 8 painting
artist: 5 Homer
Seascape author: Edward Albee
__ Sea Scrolls: 4 Dead
Sea Serpent constellation: 5 Hydra
seashell: 5 capiz, conch, cowry, murex, snail, whelk 6 chiton, cockle, cowrie, limpet, mussel, oyster, quahog, triton, volute, winkle 7 abalone, bivalve, crinoid, scallop 8 ammonite, argonaut, baculite, escallop, frustule, nautilus, ram's-horn, univalve 9 belemnite, giant clam, pink conch 10 blue mussel, crown conch, eyed cowrie, periwinkle, quahog clam
sharp point on a ~: 5 mucro
seashore: 5 beach, coast 6 strand
recess: 5 inlet
seasickness in French: 8 mal de mer
seaside: 5 coast, shore 7 coastal 8 littoral
resort: 4 lido
sidler: 4 crab
town: 4 port
Seaside: 4 city, town
locale: 10 California
season: 3 age, dry, run 4 fall, lace, salt, term, time 5 admix, drill, enure, inure, pep up, ripen, space, spell, spice, train 6 autumn, flavor, harden, length, mature, mellow, pepper, period, spring, summer, temper, winter 7 prepare, qualify, quarter, spice up, toughen, weather 8 accustom, indurate, interval, preserve 9 acclimate, condition
ticketholder: 6 abonne
__ season: 4 open 5 out of, silly 6 closed 7 monsoon
__-season: 3 off 4 post
Season: 6 Hubley
__ Season: 4 Open
seasonable: 6 timely 8 apposite, suitable 9 expedient, favorable, judicious, opportune 10 convenient, felicitous
seasonal: 3 odd 8 periodic 9 migratory
drink: 6 eggnog
song: 4 noel 5 carol
visitor: 5 Santa 6 St. Nick
worker: 7 migrant
seasoned: 3 old 4 deft, ripe 5 hardy, slick, spicy, tough 6 adroit, au fait, expert, mature, mellow, nimble, red-hot, spicey 7 capable, skilled, trained, veteran 8 dextrous, graceful, masterly, skillful 9 competent, dexterous, efficient, masterful, practiced 10 acclimated, proficient
become ~: 8 practice
highly ~: 5 spicy 6 spicey, strong 7 peppery, piquant
seasoning: 4 file, herb, mint, sage, salt, zest 5 curry, spice, thyme 6 fennel, flavor, garlic, ginger, pepper 8 dressing, jalapeño 9 condiment, flavoring 10 background, experience
German ~: 4 salz
Seasonings, The composer: PDQ Bach
seasons
four ~: 4 year 5 cycle
__ Seasons: 4 Four 5 Sweet, Three
season's growth: 5 yield 7 harvest
Seasons in the Sun (1974 song) artist: Terry Jacks
Seasons of the Soul poet: 4 Tate
__ Seasons, The: 4 Four
Seasons, The painter: 4 Erté
__-seas over: 4 half
Seastrom: 6 Victor
seat: 3 hub, pew, sit, ush 4 base, hold, post, sofa, spot, town 5 abode, bench, booth, cause, chair, couch, divan, heart, perch, place, plant, roost, see in, stool, usher 6 center, daybed, escort, estate, exedra, instal, locate, nestle, pillow, rocker, settee, settle 7 capital, cushion, install, instate, mansion, ottoman, situate, station 8 bleacher, enthrone, inthrone, location, position, recliner 9 davenport, easy chair, establish, footstool, lawn chair, residence, situation, wing chair 10 foundation
back ~: 4 rear
backless ~: 5 stool
be in the driver's ~: 3 run 5 steer 6 direct 7 operate, oversee 9 supervise
belt: 5 strap
bird ~: 5 perch
bishop's ~: 9 cathedral
booster ~ user: 5 child
bridge ~: 4 East, West 5 North, South
catbird ~: 7 lookout
cathedral ~: 7 diocese
church ~: 3 pew
court ~: 4 banc 5 bench
cover: 6 dosser
cushionlike ~: 4 pouf
elephant ~: 6 houdah, howdah
ender: 4 back, mate, work
for several: 4 sofa 6 settee 9 davenport
leave one's ~: 4 rise 5 arise, get up, stand 6 jump up
material: 4 cane
of government: 7 capital
piano ~: 5 stool
porch ~: 5 swing
portico ~: 6 exedra 7 exhedra
show to one's ~: 5 usher 6 lead in
starter: 4 love
sunbather's ~: 6 chaise
take a back ~ (to): 5 defer
theater ~: 3 box, row 4 loge 5 aisle
tot: 3 lap 4 knee
weave a chair ~: 4 cane
seat __: 4 back, belt 5 angle
seat-__-pants: 5 of-the
__ seat: 3 box, car, hot 4 back, bell, drop, flag, jump, love, slip 5 aisle, buddy, have a, house, mercy, scoop, take a, wagon 6 banana, bucket, county, deacon, rumble, saddle, window 7 anxious, balloon, bicycle, booster, catbird, driver's, dropped, ejector, sleeper, sliding
seat-belt feature: 6 buckle
__-seat driver: 4 back
seated: 9 sedentary
be ~: 4 rest
__-seated: 4 deep
__-seater: 3 two
__ Sea, The: 3 Big 5 Cruel
Sea, the Sea, The author: Iris Murdoch
SEATO: 4 pact
counterpart: 4 NATO
kin: 5 ASEAN
part: 3 Org. 4 Asia, East 5 South 6 Treaty
seat-of-the-__: 5 pants
Seaton, George: 8 director
film: Airport (1970)
Apartment for Peggy (1948)
The Counterfeit Traitor (1962)
The Country Girl (1954)
The Hook (1963)
Little Boy Lost (1953)
Miracle on 34th Street (1947)
The Pleasure of His Company (1961)
Teacher's Pet (1958)
seats
near the stage: 4 row A, row B, row C
section of ~: 4 tier
series of ~: 6 gradin 7 gradine
Seats of the Mighty, The author: Gilbert Parker
Seattle: 4 city, port, town
arena: 3 Key
athletes: 7 Huskies
county: 4 King
locale: 10 Washington
neighbor: 6 Tacoma
pro team: 6 Sonics 8 Mariners, Seahawks
sound: 5 Puget
suburb: 7 Lynwood
time zone: 3 PDT, PST
Seattle Slew: 5 horse 9 racehorse
to Swale: 4 sire
Seaver, Tom: 3 Met 6 hurler 7 pitcher
seawater mineral: 4 NaCl, salt
seaway: 5 canal, ocean
seaweed: 4 alga, kelp 5 algae, arame, dulse, fucus, laver, plant, sloke 6 hijiki, wakame 9 carrageen, Irish moss

brown ~: 5 fucus 6 wakame
combining form: 4 phyc- 5 phyco-
edible ~: 5 arame, dulse, laver
food wrapped in ~: 5 sushi
product: 4 agar, nori 5 kombu 8 agar-agar
red ~: 5 dulse, laver
Sea Wolf, The: 4 film 5 novel
author: Jack London
cast: John Garfield, Ida Lupino, Edward G. Robinson
director: Michael Curtiz
Sea Wolves, The (1980 film)
cast: Roger Moore, David Niven, Gregory Peck
director: Andrew V. McLaglen
Sea World attraction: 4 seal
sebaceous __: 5 gland
Sebastian: 3 Coe 4 crab, John 5 Brant, Cabot, saint
__ Sebastián: 3 San
__ Sebastian Bach: 6 Johann
Sebastian, John song: Welcome Back (1976)
Seberg, Jean: 7 actress
film: Airport (1970)
Bonjour Tristesse (1958)
Breathless (1959)
A Fine Madness (1966)
The Mouse That Roared (1959)
Paint Your Wagon (1969)
Sebring: 3 car 4 auto, race 8 auto race, Chrysler 10 automobile
sec: 3 dry 4 jiff 5 jiffy, trice 6 minute, moment 7 instant
drier than ~: 4 brut
in a ~: 3 PDQ 4 soon 5 quick 7 shortly 8 very soon
__ sec: 3 arc, in a 6 triple
__ sec.: 3 fin., rec.
__-sec: 4 demi
SEC: 8 agcy. conf.
part: 4 Comm., Exch. 5 South 7 Eastern 8 Exchange 10 Commission, Securities
school: 3 LSU 6 Auburn 7 Alabama, Florida, Georgia 8 Arkansas, Kentucky 9 Tennessee 10 Vanderbilt 11 Mississippi
Secada, Jon
song: Do You Believe in Us (1992)
If You Go (1994)
Just Another Day (1992)
__ secant: 3 arc 7 inverse
__ secco: 6 fresco
secede: 4 quit 5 leave, rebel, split 6 defect, depart, desert, resign, retire 7 drop out, pull out, retract, retreat 8 pull away, separate, withdraw 9 break away, break with
__ Secession: 5 War of
__-Secession: 5 Photo
sechs: 3 six 6 German
Sechura: 6 desert
locale: 4 Peru
sechzehn: 6 German 7 sixteen
Seckel: 4 pear 5 fruit
relative: 4 Bosc 5 Anjou 6 Comice 8 Bartlett
seclude: 4 hide 6 enisle, immure, retire, screen 7 conceal, confine, enclose, inclose, isolate, secrete, shut off, shut out 8 cloister, separate, withdraw 9 ostracize, segregate, sequester 10 quarantine
secluded: 4 lone 5 alone, privy, quiet 6 covert, cut off, hidden, lonely, remote, secret, single, unseen 7 cloaked, furtive, insular, private, recluse, removed, shut off 8 deserted, hermetic, hush-hush, isolated, lonesome, shielded, solitary 9 out of view, reclusive, sheltered, unexposed, withdrawn 10 cloistered, tucked away, undercover, under wraps
place: 3 den 4 cell, glen, lair, nest, nook, vale 5 abbey 6 alcove, ashram, asrama, friary, priory 7 convent, nunnery, retreat 8 cloister, lamasery 9 courtyard, hermitage, monastery, sanctuary
seclusion: 5 quiet 6 hiding 7 privacy, retreat, secrecy, shelter 8 hideaway, solitude 9 aloneness, hermitage, isolation, sanctuary 10 quarantine, remoteness, retirement, withdrawal
second: 4 aide, back, base, help, jiff, next, tick, time, twin, wink 5 extra, flash, jiffy, least, looie, lower, shake, trice 6 assist, back up, helper, latter, lesser, minute, moment, reject, uphold 7 another, approve, endorse, forward, further, indorse, instant, promote, support 8 inferior, runner-up 9 assistant, encourage, get behind, recommend, subscribe, twinkling 10 additional, bat of an eye, lieutenant, subsequent, substitute, succeeding
combining form: 4 deut- 5 deuto- 6 deuter- 7 deutero-
draft: 4 redo
finish ~: 4 fail, lose 5 place 9 fall short
go into ~: 5 shift
in a ~: 4 anon, soon 8 directly
in command: 2 VP 4 veep 6 veepee
man: 4 Cain
of two: 6 latter
person: 3 Eve, you
section: 5 part B
showing: 5 rerun
sight: 3 ESP 8 prophecy
sound of a ~: 4 tick
split ~: 4 jiff, wink 5 flash, jiffy, trice 6 minute, moment
starter: 4 nano 5 micro
this ~: 6 at once 8 right now
time: 4 anew 5 again
to none: 4 A-one, best, tops 5 first, prime 8 peerless 9 unequaled 10 preeminent
to the ~: 5 exact
second __: 4 base, best, gear, hand, home, lien, mate, self, unit, wind 5 class, floor, of arc, sheet, sight, story 6 banana, cousin, estate, fiddle, growth, nature, papers, person, string 7 baseman, officer, reading, service, thought
second __ motion: 5 law of
second-__: 4 foot, rate 5 class, guess
store-__ man: 5 story
__ second: 3 arc 4 leap 5 split
Second __: 4 Best, Wind 5 Birth, World 6 Advent, Chance, Coming, Empire, Reader 7 Chamber
Second __ Around, The: 4 Time
Second __ Council: 7 Vatican
Second __ Rose: 4 Hand
Second __, The: 3 Sex 5 Stage 6 Coming
Second __ War: 5 World
Second Amendment
supporter: 3 NRA
word: 4 arms
secondary: 4 less, side 5 lower, minor, petty, small 6 backup, junior, lesser 7 reserve, subject, trivial 8 inferior, ulterior 9 alternate, ancillary, auxiliary, dependant, dependent, proximate, resultant, small-time, tributary, vicarious 10 collateral, consequent, contingent, derivative, incidental, low-ranking, peripheral, subsequent, subsidiary
prefix: 3 sub-
to: 5 under
secondary __: 4 beam, cell, road, wave 5 color, group, metal, xylem 6 accent, market, memory, phloem, school, stress, tissue 7 battery, boycott, contact, process, quality, rainbow, storage
second baseman, Hall of Fame: 3 Fox 5 Carew, Doerr, Evers 6 Frisch, Lajoie, Morgan 7 Collins, Hornsby, Lazzeri 8 Robinson, Rod Carew 9 Joe Morgan, Mazeroski, Nap Lajoie, Nellie Fox 10 Bobby Doerr 12 Schoendienst
Second Best (1994 film)
cast: John Hurt, William Hurt, Chris Cleary Miles
director: Chris Menges
second-class: 4 hack, junk, poor 5 cheap, lower, tacky 6 common, shoddy, tawdry 8 inferior, low-grade, mediocre
Second Coming, The author: William Butler Yeats
Second Deadly Sin, The author: Lawrence Sanders
second-fiddle: 5 lower, minor 6 lesser
__ second fiddle: 4 play
Second Generation, The author: Howard Fast
secondhand: 4 used, worn 8 indirect, preowned, recycled 9 emulative, imitative, vicarious 10 derivative, indirectly
it may be ~: 5 smoke
second-hand
item: 5 timer
movement: 5 sweep
Second Hand Love (1962 song) artist: Connie Francis
second-in-command: 4 aide 5 agent 6 acting, deputy, helper 9 assistant 10 lieutenant
naval ~: 4 exec
__ second law: 7 Mendel's
second-nature: 6 inbred, rooted 9 ingrained
second of __: 3 arc
Second of May, The painter: 4 Goya
second-place finisher: 5 loser
second-quality: 3 irr. 5 irreg. 9 irregular
second-rate: 4 hack, junk, poor 5 cheap, dinky, lousy, minor, tacky 6 cheesy, common, crumby, crummy, lesser, shoddy, tawdry 8 déclassé, inferior, low-grade, mediocre, ordinary
material: 5 tripe
Second Rhapsody composer: 8 Gershwin
seconds: 10 irregulars
sixty ~: 6 minute
store: 6 outlet
Seconds (1966 film)
cast: Rock Hudson, Salome Jens, John Randolph
director: John Frankenheimer
second-sequel letters: 3 III
Second Sex, The author: Simone de Beauvoir
__ Seconds Over Tokyo: 6 Thirty
Second Stage, The author: Betty Friedan
second-story
job: 5 caper, crime, heist, theft 6 felony 7 break-in, larceny, robbery
man: 5 thief 6 robber 7 burglar
__-Second Street: 5 Forty
second-string: 5 lower, minor 6 lesser
second-stringer: 2 JV 3 sub 5 scrub 6 jayvee
Second Time Around, The composer: 4 Cahn 9 Van Heusen
second to __: 4 none
Second Wind author: Dick Francis
secours: 4 lift
secrecy: 4 hush 6 hiding 7 mystery, privacy, silence 8 darkness, muteness, solitude 9 isolation, reticence, seclusion 10 confidence, covertness
breach of ~: 4 leak
secret: 3 sly 4 dark, deep 5 close, inner, privy, quiet, trick 6 arcane, cabala, closet, covert, enigma, hidden, inmost, inside, inward, kabala, latent, lonely, masked, mystic, occult, puzzle, unseen, veiled 7 arcanum, cabbala, cloaked, cryptic, encoded, furtive, kabbala, mystery, obscure, on the QT, private, uncanny, unknown 8 abstruse, backdoor, esoteric, hush-hush, intimate, mystical, obscured, oracular, password, personal, profound, secluded, shrouded, stealthy, ulterior 9 concealed, cryptical, disguised, incognito, innermost, in the dark, nonpublic, recondite, underhand, unnoticed 10 classified, enshrouded, mysterious, privileged, restricted, tucked away, undercover, under wraps, undetected, undivulged, unrevealed
agent: 3 spy 5 spook
combining form: 5 crypt-, krypt- 6 crypto-, krypto-
divulge a ~: 4 blab, tell 5 spill 7 whisper
ender: 3 ive
govt. group: 3 CIA, NSA, ONI
in ~: 8 on the sly 9 entre nous
information: 3 tip 6 tipoff
keep ~: 4 hide, mask, veil 5 cache, cloak, couch, cover, sit on 6 hush up 7 conceal, cover up, obscure 8 disguise, suppress 10 camouflage
like an open ~: 5 known
make ~: 6 encode 7 encrypt
motive: 5 angle
not keep a ~: 3 gab 4 blab, leak, tell 5 blurt, let on, spill 6 squeal, tattle, tip off 7 divulge, let slip 8 blurt out, give away
observer: 3 spy 5 spier
one who can't keep a ~: 5 sieve
place: 6 recess
plan: 4 plot
self: 4 soul
society: 4 tong 5 cabal
writing: 4 code 10 cryptogram
secret __: 5 agent 6 ballot, police 7 partner, society
__ secret: 4 deep, open 5 in on a, state, trade
__-secret: 3 top
Secret: 9 deodorant
alternative: 3 Ban 4 Sure 5 Arrid, Tussy 6 Degree 7 Dry Idea, Mitchum 10 Right Guard, Soft and Dri, Speed Stick
Secret __: 4 Love 5 Agent, Honor 6 Garden, Lovers 7 Command, Service
Secret __, The: 4 Fury, Land 5 Storm 6 Garden, Sharer 7 Partner
__ Secret: 3 Pop 5 State
Secret (1994 song) artist: Madonna
Secret Agent Man (1966 song) artist: Johnny Rivers
secretary: 4 aide, asst., desk 5 clerk 6 helper, scribe, typist 7 copyist, rolltop 8 minister, official 9 assistant, attendant, gal Friday, man Friday 10 amanuensis, escritoire, girl Friday
at times: 5 filer, steno
slip: 4 typo
stat.: 3 wpm
work: 4 memo 6 letter
secretary-__: 7 general
__ secretary: 5 press, Salem 6 pocket, social 7 foreign, private
__ Secretary: 4 Home 7 Private
secretary of __: 5 labor, state 6 energy 7 defense

Secret Ceremony (1968 film)
cast: Mia Farrow, Robert Mitchum, Elizabeth Taylor
director: Joseph Losey
Secret Command (1944 film)
cast: Carole Landis, Chester Morris, Pat O'Brien
secrete: 4 bury, emit, hide, mask, palm, stow, veil **5** cache, cloak, couch, cover, exude, stash, sweat **6** effuse, harbor, screen, shroud **7** conceal, cover up, curtain, give off, harbour, obscure, produce, seclude, wall off **8** disguise, perspire, stow away **9** discharge, sequester, stash away **10** camouflage
Secret Fury, The (1950 film)
cast: Claudette Colbert, Robert Ryan
director: Mel Ferrer
Secret Garden (1997 song) artist: Bruce Springsteen
Secret Garden, The (1949 film)
cast: Herbert Marshall, Margaret O'Brien, Dean Stockwell
Secret Honor (1984 film)
cast: Philip Baker Hall
director: Robert Altman
Secret Integration, The author: Thomas Pynchon
Secret Invasion, The (1964 film)
cast: Stewart Granger, Mickey Rooney, Raf Vallone
director: Roger Corman
secretion: 6 liquid
odorous ~: 4 musk
skin ~: 5 sebum
toxic ~: 5 venom
secretive: 3 coy, mum **4** cagy **5** cagey, close, quiet **6** covert, hushed, silent, sneaky, zipped **7** cryptic, furtive, on the QT, private **8** reserved, reticent, stealthy, taciturn, thieving, thievish **9** clammed up, cryptical, enigmatic, in the dark, nonpublic, underhand, withdrawn **10** backstairs, buttoned up, in chambers, mysterious, undercover, unsociable, unspeaking
sort: 3 spy **5** hider
Secret Life of Walter Mitty, The: 4 film **5** novel
author: James Thurber
cast: Fay Bainter, Boris Karloff, Danny Kaye, Virginia Mayo
director: Norman Z. McLeod
Secret Love singer: 3 Day
secretly: 7 on the QT, quietly, sub rosa **8** covertly, hush-hush, inwardly, on the sly **9** between us, entre nous, furtively, obscurely, privately **10** intimately, on the quiet, personally, stealthily, under cover, unobserved
Secretly (1958 song) artist: Jimmie Rodgers
Secret of __, The: 4 Nimh
Secret of My Success, The (1987 film)
cast: Michael J. Fox, Helen Slater
director: Herbert Ross
Secret of Roan Inish, The (1994 film)
cast: Eileen Colgan, Jeni Courtney, Mick Lally
director: John Sayles
Secret Policeman's Other Ball, The (1982 film)
cast: John Cleese, Peter Cook
director: Roger Graef, Julien Temple
secrets: 6 arcana
__ Secret Senses, The: 7 Hundred
Secret Service agent: 4 G-man, T-man
Secret Sharer, The author: Joseph Conrad
Secret Storm, The (CBS): 4 soap **9** soap opera
Secret, The author: Harold Robbins
sect: 3 set **4** bloc, camp, cult, side, wing **5** faith, group, order **6** church, school **7** faction, Quakers, Shakers **8** division, religion **10** Mennonites, persuasion
Buddhist ~: 3 Zen
Hindu ~ member: 4 Jain, yogi **5** Jaina, yogin
Indian ~ members: 4 Sikh
Islam ~: 5 Sunni
Jamaican ~ member: 5 rasta
Jewish ~ member: 5 Hasid
Mennonite ~: 5 Amish
Moslem ~: 4 Sufi **5** Sunni
sectarian: 5 bigot, rigid **6** narrow, zealot **7** bigoted, fanatic, insular, limited **8** adherent, clannish, cliquish, dogmatic, partisan **9** dissident, dogmatist, exclusive, extremist, factional, heretical, parochial, religious **10** dogmatical, provincial, schismatic, separatist
suffix: 3 -ist, -ite
section: 3 cut, leg **4** area, belt, bite, hunk, link, lump, part, site, slot, spot, tier, unit, wing, zone **5** block, chunk, field, piece, place, share, slice, split, strip, tract **6** branch, clause, length, moiety, parcel, region, sample, sphere **7** bracket, chapter, element, passage, portion, quarter, segment **8** category, district, division, fraction, fragment, locality, location, precinct, province, vicinity **9** component, partition, territory **10** department
combining form: 4 tomo-
cross ~: 6 sample **8** specimen
first ~: 5 part A, part I **7** part one
prefix for ~: 3 mid
second ~: 5 part B **7** part two
section __: 4 boss, gang, hand, mark
__ section: 4 type **5** conic, cross, press, right, staff **6** golden, rhythm **7** oblique, quarter
sectional: 4 sofa **5** local, zonal **6** zonary **7** divided, limited **8** regional **9** factional **10** fractional
sections, divided into: 5 paned
sector: 4 area, part, side, spot, zone **5** arena, tract **6** locale, region **7** quarter, segment, stratum **8** category, district, division, locality, precinct **9** territory
__ sector: 4 warm **5** third **6** public **7** private
secular: 3 lay **4** laic **5** civil **6** laical **7** earthly, profane, worldly **8** temporal **9** layperson
__ secund.: 4 dieb.
securable: 9 available **10** attainable, obtainable
secure: 3 bag, bar, buy, dam, fix, get, ice, pin, tie, win **4** bind, bolt, clog, cork, cosy, cozy, earn, fast, firm, gain, gird, have, hook, know, land, lash, lock, moor, nail, plug, reap, rope, safe, save, seal, shut, sure, tack, take, tape, yoke **5** annex, block, bound, catch, chain, cinch, clamp, close, cover, cozey, cozie, dam up, fixed, grasp, guard, hitch, latch, leash, on ice, order, rivet, seize, solid, sound, tie up, tight, truss **6** accept, anchor, assure, at ease, attach, attain, batten, buy out, cement, clinch, clog up, collar, come by, defend, effect, embank, engage, enlist, ensure, fasten, harbor, insure, line up, locked, lock up, obtain, pick up, plug up, rack up, seal up, shield, stable, steady, stop up, strong, sturdy, tether **7** achieve, acquire, bespeak, bulwark, capture, certain, chalk up, collect, harbour, padlock, procure, produce, protect, receive, reserve, scare up, seal off, settled, shutter, staunch, succeed, tie down, tighten **8** anchored, blockade, button up, carefree, definite, entrench, fastened, harmless, home-free, in the bag, locked on, obstruct, preserve, purchase, reliable, riskless, shielded, tucked in, unharmed **9** confident, fortified, guarantee, immovable, indemnify, protected, safeguard, sheltered, stabilize, thumbtack, unanxious, undamaged, untouched **10** batten down, button down, dependable, nailed down, perpetuate, underwrite
a boat: 4 moor **6** anchor
a contract: 4 land
a package: 3 tie
a tent: 3 peg
by tying down: 5 belay
place: 4 nest
position: 8 foothold
together: 3 sew
secured: 4 firm **6** in hand
securely: 4 fast **9** immovably
securities: 5 means **8** holdings
dealer: 3 arb **6** broker, trader
like some ~: 3 OTC
offering: 3 IPO **4** bond **5** issue, stock
security: 4 bail, bond, ease, egis, gage **5** aegis, cover, guard, token **6** pledge, refuge, safety, screen, shield, surety, tenure, wealth **7** defense, earnest, freedom, hostage, promise, rampart, shelter, warrant **8** immunity, reliance, strength **9** assurance, certainty, guarantee, insurance, safeguard, stability **10** collateral, confidence, precaution, protection
equipment: 6 camera
give as ~: 4 hock, pawn **8** mortgage
government ~: 5 E bond, T-bill, T-bond, T-note
holder: 6 bailee
org.: 3 CIA, NSA, ONI, OSS
problem: 4 leak **6** breach
security __: 4 risk **5** guard **6** police, thread **7** analyst, blanket
__ security: 6 equity, social
__-security: 7 maximum
Security: 4 city, town
locale: 8 Colorado
Security Council
denial: 4 veto
former ~ member: 4 USSR
secy.
see secretary
Sedaine, Michel Jean: 6 French **10** playwright
Sedaka, Neil
hometown: Brooklyn
song: Bad Blood (1975)
Breaking Up Is Hard to Do (1962)
Calendar Girl (1960)
The Diary (1958)
Happy Birthday, Sweet Sixteen (1961)
Laughter in the Rain (1974)
Little Devil (1961)
Next Door to an Angel (1962)
Oh! Carol (1959)
Stairway to Heaven (1960)
Sedalia: 4 city, town
locale: 8 Missouri
sedan: 3 car **4** auto **7** carrier, hardtop **10** automobile, touring car
large ~: 4 limo **9** limousine
take in a ~: 4 bear
sedan __: 5 chair
Sedan: 4 city, town **6** battle
locale: 6 France
river: 4 Maas **5** Meuse
Sedan de Ville: 3 car **4** auto **8** Cadillac
sedate: 4 calm, cool, drug, prim **5** quiet, sober, staid, stoic **6** at ease, demure, gentle, low-key, mellow, placid, poised, serene, settle, somber, steady **7** amiable, at peace, equable, pacific, relaxed, serious, stoical, unmoved **8** amicable, carefree, composed, decorous, laid-back, peaceful, reserved, tranquil **9** collected, dignified, easy-going, impassive, quiescent, temperate, unexcited, unruffled **10** deliberate, nonchalant, unagitated, untroubled
sedateness: 4 calm, cool **5** poise **6** aplomb **7** balance, dignity **8** presence, serenity **9** assurance, composure, placidity, sang-froid, stability **10** dispassion, equanimity
sedative: 4 drug **6** opiate **7** anodyne **8** hypnotic, medicine **9** analgesic, calmative, soporific **10** anesthetic, medication, painkiller
sedentary: 3 lax **4** idle, lazy **5** inert, unfit **6** asleep, draggy, seated, torpid **7** dormant, passive, settled, sitting **8** inactive, indolent, slothful, sluggish **9** desk-bound, lethargic **10** disengaged, motionless, stationary
Seder: 5 feast
celebrant: 3 Jew
fare: 4 lamb **5** matzo **6** matzah, matzoh
sedge: 5 brush **7** bulrush, papyrus
Sedgwick: 4 Edie, Kyra **6** Edward
Sedgwick, Kyra spouse: Kevin Bacon
sedgy area: 3 fen **5** marsh, swamp
sediment: 4 dreg, gunk, lees, silt, slag **5** dregs, trash, waste **6** debris, refuse, solids **7** deposit, grounds, residue **8** residuum **9** settlings
sedimentary: 4 rock
sedition: 6 revolt, unrest **7** treason **8** civil war
seditious: 7 lawless, radical **8** disloyal **9** insurgent **10** incendiary, subversive
Sedona: 3 Kia, van **4** city, town
locale: 7 Arizona
Seduction of Joe Tynan, The (1979 film)
cast: Alan Alda, Barbara Harris, Meryl Streep, Rip Torn
director: Jerry Schatzberg
Seduction of Peter S, The author: Lawrence Sanders
__ Seduction, The: 4 Last
sedulous: 5 stout **7** earnest **8** diligent, resolute, studious, tireless, untiring **9** assiduous, laborious, motivated **10** determined, persistent, relentless, scrupulous, unflagging
sedulously: 4 hard
see: 3 eye, get, peg, spy **4** be at, date, espy, feel, gape, gawk, gaze, know, look, mark, meet, note, peek, peep, peer, show, spot, tell, view, wake **5** get it, grasp, greet, learn, pop in, sight, stare, think, usher, visit, waken, watch, weigh **6** advert, attend, behold, detect, drop by, escort, fathom, follow, gaze at, go with, intuit, look at, notice, peek at, peer at, ponder, regard, remark, stop in, survey, take in **7** catch on, cognize, consult, diocese, discern, examine, find out, glimpse, imagine, inspect, make out, observe, picture, prelacy, ransack, realize, receive, run into, so there, take out, unearth, witness **8** appraise, discover, drop in on, envision, foretell, identify, look upon, meet with, perceive, pick up on, scope out **9** accompany, ascertain, bishopric, encounter, figure out, go out with, interview, penetrate, recognize, visualize **10** anticipate, appreciate, comprehend, confer with, episcopacy, experience, eyewitness, get a load of, get the idea, I told you so, scrutinize, understand
about: 5 probe **6** tend to **8** attend to,

consider, look into 10 take care of
after: 4 tend 5 watch 8 shepherd
ahead: 7 portend, predict, project 8 prophesy 10 anticipate
cause to ~ red: 3 irk 4 rile 5 anger, peeve, upset 6 enrage, madden
come to ~: 5 visit
daylight: 5 get it 7 realize 9 recognize
ender: 3 saw
eye to eye: 4 gybe, jibe 5 agree 6 accede, accord, assent, comply, concur 7 approve, consent, go along 8 coincide 9 acquiesce, harmonize
face to face: 5 greet 7 run into 8 bump into, confront 9 run across
fit: 5 deign 6 please 10 condescend
go to ~: 5 pop in, visit 6 attend, call on, drop by, look up, stop in, travel 7 sojourn, swing by 8 pay a call, stay with
hard to ~: 3 dim 4 hazy 5 faint, fuzzy, murky, muzzy, vague 6 bleary, blurry, far-off, opaque 7 blurred, clouded, muddled, obscure, shadowy, unclear 8 nebulous 10 indistinct
how others ~ us: 5 image 9 depiction 10 appearance, conception, impression, perception, projection
in: 4 seat 5 admit, greet, usher 6 escort 7 welcome
in court: 3 sue 8 litigate
old friends: 5 reune
partner: 4 wait
plain to ~: 5 clear, overt 7 obvious
red: 4 boil, fume 6 rear up, seethe 7 bristle, flame up 8 get angry 9 blow a fuse 10 hit the roof
socially: 4 date
something to ~: 5 sight 6 eyeful
starter: 5 sight
the error of one's ways: 5 atone 6 repent
the light: 7 realize
through: 4 help, last, stay 5 stick 6 keep at, remain 7 achieve, persist, ride out, survive 8 tide over 9 penetrate, persevere
to: 2 do 3 fix 4 tend 6 advert, attend, handle 7 address, care for, monitor, sit with 9 look after 10 take care of
what you ~: 4 view 5 image, vista
you later: 3 bye 4 ciao, ta-ta 5 adieu, adios, aloha, later 6 bye-bye, shalom, so long 7 cheerio, goodbye 8 au revoir, farewell, sayonara, toodle-oo
see __: 3 out, red 4 to it 5 about, after, stars 6 double, things 7 through
see-__: 4 thru 7 through
__ see...: 5 Let me
__-see: 4 look, must
See __ care!: 3 if I
See __ Later, Alligator: 3 You
See __, pick it up...: 4 a pin
See __ run: 4 Spot
__ See: 4 Holy 5 You'll
seeable: 6 visual
__ See About Me: 4 Come
__ See Clearly Now: 4 I Can
seed: 3 egg, nut, pip, pit, sow 4 cion, core, germ, idea, kids, ovum 5 acorn, anise, benne, benny, cumin, grain, heirs, issue, ovule, plant, poppy, scion, spark, spawn, spore, start 6 embryo, fennel, gamete, kernel, origin, pippin, scions, sesame, source 7 caraway, concept, inkling, kinfolk, mustard, nucleus, progeny 8 germ cell, kinfolks, kinsfolk, particle, rudiment 9 beginning, broadcast, coriander, inheritor, offspring, posterity 10 successors
aromatic ~: 5 anise, cumin 6 fennel
bacteria ~: 5 spore
combining form: 4 cocc- 5 cocci-, cocco-
company: 6 Burpee
covering: 3 pod 4 aril, boll, hull, husk 5 testa
destination: 4 soil
dill ~: 4 anet
edible ~: 3 nut 4 chia 5 pinon
ender: 3 bed, pod 4 time 5 eater
fern ~: 5 spore
fit to ~: 6 arable
fruit ~: 3 pip
gone to ~: 4 soft 5 passé, ratty 9 enervated 10 dissipated
go to ~: 3 rot 4 rust 5 decay 8 stagnate, vegetate
grain: 6 kernel
hard-roll ~: 5 poppy 6 sesame
immature ~: 5 ovule
perk: 3 bye
plant with two ~ leaves: 5 dicot 7 dicotyl
remover: 3 gin
ridge: 5 raphe
scar: 5 hilum
scatter ~: 3 sow
starter: 3 all, hay 4 bird, flax, moon, tick, worm 5 stick 6 cotton 7 pumpkin
winged ~: 5 maple
seed __: 4 coat, corn, fern, leaf, tick 5 coral, money, pearl, plant, stock 6 beetle, oyster, shrimp, vessel, weevil
__ seed: 4 fern, go to 5 anise, blind, melon, Niger, poppy, run to 6 canary, fennel, sesame 7 caraway
__ Seed: 5 Demon 6 Dragon
seedbed: 4 soil
seedcase: 3 pod
seed-catalog offering: 6 hybrid
seedeater: 4 bird
__ seeding: 5 cloud
seedless orange: 5 navel
seedling: 4 tree 5 plant
container: 4 flat, tray
plant a ~: 5 unpot
seed-money
govt. ~ agency: 3 SBA
seedpod, clingy: 3 bur
seeds
plant ~: 3 sow 6 garden
sow the ~ of: 6 arouse
__ Seed, The: 3 Bad 4 Wild
seedtime: 6 spring
seedy: 4 mean, poor, torn, worn 5 dingy, faded, grody, mangy, ratty, tacky, tired 6 beat-up, crumby, crummy, grotty, grubby, mangey, ragged, shabby, shoddy, sickly, sleazy, sordid 7 run down, sagging, scruffy, squalid, unkempt 8 decaying, decrepit, flagging, slovenly, tattered, untended 9 neglected, overgrown, ungroomed 10 bedraggled, disheveled, threadbare
establishment: 4 dive 5 joint 9 flophouse, speakeasy
__ See for Miles: 4 I Can
Seeger: 4 Alan, Pete
Seeger, Alan: 4 poet
work: I Have a Rendezvous with Death
Seeger, Pete: 6 folkie 8 banjoist
__ see here!: 3 Now
See Here, Private Hargrove (1944 film)
cast: Donna Reed, Robert Walker, Keenan Wynn
director: Wesley Ruggles
See if __!: 5 I care
seeing: 5 sense, sight 6 vision
prevent from ~: 9 blindfold
red: 3 mad 4 sore 5 angry, irate, livid 6 raging 7 furious 9 indignant
starter: 3 far 5 sight
that: 5 since 7 because, whereas
Seeing __ dog: 3 Eye
__ seeing things?: 3 Am I
__ Seeing You: 5 I'll Be
__ See It: 3 As I 4 I Can
See It Now (CBS) host: Edward R. Murrow
seek: 3 aim, ask, beg, dig, try 4 comb, hunt, look, nose, root, want 5 chase, covet, crave, delve, essay, prowl, query, quest, scour, trace 6 aspire, beg for, bid for, desire, dig for, forage, gun for, invite, look up, pursue, search, strive 7 attempt, bird-dog, dragnet, enquire, entreat, explore, find out, fish for, go after, hunt for, inquire, long for, look for, ransack, request, rummage, scout up, solicit 8 endeavor, petition, plead for, probe for, prospect, quest for, question, run after, scout out, sniff out, yearn for 9 cast about, ferret out, hanker for, search for, track down
a handout: 3 beg 5 hit up
another opinion: 3 ask 4 talk 5 refer 6 call in, confer, huddle, look to, parlay, powwow, turn to 7 consult 9 negotiate, touch base 10 brainstorm
a ride: 5 thumb
charity: 3 beg
employment: 5 apply 8 petition
favor: 4 fawn 10 ingratiate
office: 3 run 5 stump 7 contend 8 politick
redress: 3 sue 8 litigate 9 prosecute
shelter: 9 take cover
(to): 6 aspire
to win: 5 chase, court, spark 6 pursue 10 bill and coo
Seek __ shall find: 5 and ye
seeker: 6 hunter 9 applicant, candidate, job-hunter
asylum ~: 5 alien 6 émigré
evade the ~: 4 hide, lurk 5 ditch 6 hole up, lie low 8 disguise, tuck away 9 hibernate, sequester, take cover 10 camouflage
information ~: 5 asker
office ~: 3 pol 9 candidate 10 politician
query: 3 how, who, why 4 what, when 5 where 7 how many, how much
target: 5 hider
thrill ~: 8 hedonist
__ seeker: 3 job 6 office, status
Seekers
homeland: Australia
song: Georgy Girl (1966)
I'll Never Find Another You (1965)
__ Seekers: 3 New
seeking: 5 after
combining form: 5 -petal
seem: 4 hint 5 feign, imply, sound 6 appear, assume, strike 7 suggest 8 feel as if, intimate, look as if, look like, resemble 9 insinuate, sound like
like: 7 smack of 8 resemble
See Me, Feel Me (1970 song) artist: Who
seeming: 4 look, show 5 quasi 6 likely 7 evident, nominal, outside, reputed 8 apparent, presumed, probable, putative, specious, supposed 9 semblance 10 ostensible
seemingly: 4 as if 6 likely 8 just like, probably 9 doubtless, evidently, outwardly 10 apparently, ostensibly, presumably
seemliness: 8 niceties 9 etiquette, propriety
seemly: 3 apt, fit 4 good, nice 5 moral, right 6 decent, modest, proper 7 correct, fitting 8 apposite, becoming, decorous, suitable 9 advisable, befitting
Seems Like Old Times (1980 film)
cast: Chevy Chase, Charles Grodin, Goldie Hawn
director: Jay Sandrich
seen: 6 visual 7 visible
as ~ fit: 4 duly
easily ~: 4 open 5 overt, plain 9 prominent
never before ~: 6 all-new 8 brand-new
seldom ~: 4 rare 6 exotic, scanty, scarce 8 uncommon
...seen and not __: 5 heard
See No __: 4 Evil
__ Seen Wearing: 4 Last
see one's __ clear: 3 way
seep: 4 drip, flow, leak, ooze, soak 5 drain, exude, leach, sweat 6 filter, osmose 7 dribble, trickle 8 filter in, filtrate, permeate, transude 9 penetrate, percolate
ender: 3 age
(into): 3 get
seepage: 9 discharge
collector: 3 pit 5 bilge
seer: 4 Demo, guru, Olen 5 augur, Crius, Iamus, Iapis, Idmon, Maeon, Manto, Sabbe, sibyl, swami, swamy, Vanus 6 Andros, Apollo, Asilas, Carnus, Daphne, medium, Merops, Mopsus, mystic, oracle, Pholus, Scirus, viewer, wizard 7 Aesacus, Ampycus, aruspex, Asbolus, Calchas, diviner, Ennomus, Glaucus, Helenus, Laocoon, Laokoon, Lavinia, palmist, Phineus, prophet, Proteus, psychic, Rhamnes, Telemus, Thestor, witness 8 Alcander, haruspex, Melampus, Munichus, observer, onlooker, Phrasius, Polyidus, presager, Tiresias 9 Amphiarus, Aristaeus, Cassandra, Herophile, predictor, spectator, theurgist, Thiodamas, Tolumnius, visionary, Xenocleia 10 eyewitness, forecaster, foreteller, mind reader, palm reader, Polyphides, soothsayer
asset: 3 ESP
card: 5 tarot
ender: 3 ess 6 sucker
need: 4 omen
pertaining to a ~: 5 vatic 7 vatical
site: 6 Delphi
starter: 5 sight
Seeress of __, The: 4 Kell
seersucker: 6 fabric 8 material
seesaw: 4 rock, tilt, toss 5 lurch, pitch, waver 6 teeter, totter 7 librate, whiffle 8 exchange, hesitate 9 alternate, fluctuate, oscillate, vacillate
quorum: 3 two
site: 4 park
See-saw, Margery __: 3 Daw
See See Rider (1966 song) artist: Animals
See Spot run textbook: 6 reader
seethe: 4 boil, burn, foam, fume, rage, soak, stew 5 churn, froth, souse, storm, surge 6 bubble, see red, simmer 7 bristle, ferment, flame up, smolder 8 smoulder
with activity: 3 hum
see the __: 5 light
See the Funny Little Clown (1964 song) artist: Bobby Goldsboro
seething: 5 aboil, irate, wroth 6 raging, red-hot, tumult
see-through: 4 thin 5 clear, gauzy, sheer 6 limpid 10 diaphanous
material: 5 glass
See You in September (1966 song) artist: Happenings
See You Later, Alligator (1956 song) artist: Bill Haley and His Comets
__ See You Smile: 5 When I
__ See You, The: 5 More I

Sefer ___: **5** Torah
Seferis: **6** George **7** Giorgos
Seferis, George: **4** poet **5** Greek **6** writer **8** diplomat, Nobelist
Segal: **4** Alex **5** Erich **6** George
Segal, George: **5** actor
film: Blume in Love (1973)
The Bridge at Remagen (1969)
The Cable Guy (1996)
For the Boys (1991)
The Hot Rock (1972)
King Rat (1965)
Lost Command (1966)
Loving (1970)
No Way to Treat a Lady (1968)
The Owl and the Pussycat (1970)
The Quiller Memorandum (1966)
The Terminal Man (1974)
A Touch of Class (1973)
Who Is Killing the Great Chefs of Europe? (1978)
Who's Afraid of Virginia Woolf? (1966)
TV: Just Shoot Me
Segar, E.C.: **10** cartoonist
character: **3** Oyl **5** Bluto, Olive, Wimpy **6** Popeye **7** Swee' Pea **8** Olive Oyl
Sega rival: **3** NES **5** Atari
Seger, Bob
song: Against the Wind (1980)
American Storm (1986)
Even Now (1983)
Fire Lake (1980)
Hollywood Nights (1978)
Like a Rock (1986)
Night Moves (1977)
Old Time Rock & Roll (1989)
Ramblin' Gamblin' Man (1969)
Shakedown (1987)
Shame on the Moon (1982)
Still the Same (1978)
Tryin' to Live My Life Without You (1981)
Understanding (1984)
We've Got Tonite (1978)
You'll Accomp'ny Me (1980)
Segin: **4** star
Seginus: **4** star
segment: **3** bit, cut, leg **4** part, unit, zone **5** block, piece, share, slice, strip, wedge **6** length, member, moiety, parcel, sample, sector **7** portion, section **8** division, fraction **9** component **10** proportion
combining form: **4** -mere
___ segment: **4** line
___ segno: **3** dal
sego lily state: **4** Utah
Ségou: **4** city, town
locale: **4** Mali
Segovia, Andrés: **7** Spanish **9** guitarist
Segrè, Emilio: **8** Nobelist **9** physicist
segregate: **5** sever, split **6** cut off, divide, island **7** isolate, seclude, split up **8** close off, insulate, separate, set apart **9** sequester, single out **10** disconnect, dissociate, quarantine
segregated: **5** apart **9** exclusive
segue: **4** link **6** lead-in **10** connection, transition
seguidilla: **5** dance
Seguin: **4** city, town
locale: **5** Texas
Segura, Pancho: **7** netster **9** Ecuadoran, tennis pro
milieu: **5** court
Se habla ___: **6** inglés
___ se habla Español: **4** Aquí
sehna: **4** knot
Sehorn, Jason spouse: Angie Harmon
sei: **5** whale **8** cetacean
relative: **3** orc **6** beluga, narwal **7** cowfish, dolphin, finback, grampus, narwhal, rorqual **8** narwhale, porpoise
Seidelman, Susan: **8** director
film: Cookie (1989)
Desperately Seeking Susan (1985)
Making Mr. Right (1987)
She-Devil (1989)
Smithereens (1982)
seif: **4** dune **8** sand dune
Seifert, Jaroslav: **4** poet **5** Czech **6** writer **8** Nobelist
Seiji: **5** Ozawa
Seiko: **5** watch **10** wristwatch
alternative: **4** Ebel, Rado **5** Casio, Elgin, Lorus, Omega, Rolex, Timex **6** Bulova, Fossil, Movado, Pulsar, Swatch **7** Citizen **8** Longines, Tag Heuer, Tourneau
Seiler: **5** Lewis
seine: **3** net **4** fish **7** fish net
like a ~: **5** meshy, netty
Seine: **5** river
city on the ~: **5** Melun, Paris, Rouen **6** Troyes
landscapist: **5** Monet
locale: **6** France
tributary: **4** Aube, Eure, Oise **5** Marne
seiner: **6** angler **9** fisherman
Seinfeld (NBC sitcom)
cast: Jason Alexander (George Costanza)
Estelle Harris (Estelle Costanza)
Wayne Knight (Newman)
Julia Louis-Dreyfus (Elaine Benes)
Michael Richards (Cosmo Kramer)
Jerry Seinfeld (Jerry Seinfeld)
Jerry Stiller (Frank Costanza)
seis: **3** six **7** Spanish
seism: **5** quake **6** tremor **10** earthquake
seismic ___: **3** gap
seismograph
part: **6** stylus
part of a ~ reading: **5** L wave
reading: **5** quake **6** tremor **10** earthquake
seismologist's field: **7** geology
Seiter, William A.: **8** director
film: Allegheny Uprising (1939)
Broadway (1942)
Diplomaniacs (1933)
Hired Wife (1940)
If You Could Only Cook (1935)
A Lady Takes a Chance (1943)
The Lady Wants Mink (1953)
Little Giant (1946)
Nice Girl? (1941)
The Richest Girl in the World (1934)
Roberta (1935)
Room Service (1938)
Sons of the Desert (1933)
This Is My Affair (1937)
You Were Never Lovelier (1942)
Seitz, George B.: **8** director
film: A Family Affair (1937)
Kit Carson (1940)
The Last of the Mohicans (1936)
Life Begins for Andy Hardy (1941)
Love Finds Andy Hardy (1938)
seize: **3** bag, get, nab **4** bust, fist, gain, glom, grab, grip, hold, jail, lift, nail, snag, snap, take, tear, trap **5** annex, catch, clasp, exact, force, grasp, pinch, pluck, reach, snare, usurp, wrest **6** abduct, ambush, arrest, assume, clench, clinch, clutch, collar, detain, hijack, intern, kidnap, obtain, occupy, pick up, pounce, prey on, ravage, ravish, secure, snap up, snatch, tackle, wrench **7** capture, embrace, grapple, impound, interne, overrun, possess, preempt, procure, ransack, receive **8** arrogate, carry off, highjack, hold fast, overcome, take over, throttle **9** apprehend, extradite, intercept, latch onto, overpower, overwhelm, pitch into **10** commandeer, comprehend, confiscate, spirit away, take hold of
eagerly: **6** jump at
old-style: **5** reave
power: **5** usurp
the day: **4** live
___ Seize: **5** Louis
seized
item: **4** repo
old-style: **4** reft
Seize the Day: **4** film **5** novel
author: Saul Bellow
cast: Jerry Stiller, Robin Williams, Joseph Wiseman
director: Fielder Cook
seize the day in Latin: **9** carpe diem
Seize the Night author: Dean Koontz
seizure: **4** bust, grab, loot, turn **6** collar, rapine, snatch **7** capture **9** abduction **10** annexation, assumption, kidnapping, occupation, usurpation
Seizure author: Robin Cook
Sejm: **10** parliament
locale: **6** Poland
Sekely: **5** Steve
Sekt: **4** wine **6** German
Sela: **4** Ward
Se La (1987 song) artist: Lionel Richie
Selassie: **5** Haile
country: **8** Ethiopia
Selby, David: **5** actor
film: Rich and Famous (1981)
The Super Cops (1974)
Up the Sandbox (1972)
TV: Falcon Crest
Selby Jr., Hubert
work: Last Exit to Brooklyn
Selden: **4** city, town
locale: **7** New York **10** Long Island
seldom: **6** hardly, little, rarely **8** far apart, scarcely, sporadic **9** sometimes **10** hardly ever, infrequent, occasional, sporadical, uncommonly, unfrequent
seen: **4** rare **6** exotic, scanty, scarce **8** uncommon
used: **5** dusty, rusty
select: **3** opt, peg, tab, tag, tap, top **4** A-one, best, cull, fine, mark, name, pick, rare, sort, take, tops **5** elect, elite, first, glean, key on, prime **6** assign, choice, choose, chosen, deluxe, gather, go into, goodly, opt for, picked, prefer, screen, weeded, winner **7** appoint, excerpt, extract, fix upon, limited, pick out, pin down, premium, recruit, sort out, special, vintage **8** bookmark, draw lots, handpick, identify, nominate, rarefied, screened, superior, topnotch **9** excellent, exclusive, exquisite, first-rate, number one, preferred, single out, unrivaled **10** first-class, handpicked, preferable, privileged, settle upon, unrivalled, world-class
at random: **4** draw
from a menu: **5** order
group: **5** A-list, elite
on a computer: **5** click
selectee: **7** recruit, soldier **9** appointee
selection: **3** cut **4** pick **5** quote, range, stock **6** choice, option **7** culling, excerpt, extract, picking **8** adoption, decision, election **9** anthology, quotation **10** assignment, assortment, collection, nomination, preference, recitation
___ selection: **7** natural
selective: **5** picky **6** choosy **7** careful, choosey **8** rarefied **9** judicious **10** discerning, particular
Selective ___ System: **7** Service
Selena (1997 film)
cast: Jennifer Lopez, Edward James Olmos, Jon Seda
director: Gregory Nava
Selena song: I Could Fall in Love (1995)
Selene: **7** goddess
brother of ~: **6** Helios
daughter of ~: **6** Pandia
equivalent: **4** Luna
lover of ~: **4** Zeus **8** Endymion
mother of ~: **4** Thia
realm: **4** moon
sister of ~: **3** Eos
son of ~: **9** Narcissus
Selenga: **5** river
locale: **6** Russia **8** Mongolia
selenium: **7** element
selenology: **9** astronomy
Seles, Monica: **7** netster **9** tennis pro
milieu: **5** court
self: **3** ego, you **4** atma, soul **5** anima, atman, being **6** nature, person, psyche **8** identity **9** character **10** individual
combining form: **3** aut- **4** auto-
ender: **3** dom **4** same
Hindu ~: **4** atma **5** atman
pride: **3** ego
starter: **3** her, him, one, our, thy **4** your
self-___: **4** help, made, pity, rule, will **5** doubt, image, study, worth **6** denial, esteem, styled, taught **7** assured, control, defense, evident, imposed, reliant, respect, service, serving, starter
self-___ flour: **6** rising
self-___ man: **4** made
self-___ millionaire: **4** made
self-___ turkey: **7** basting
self-___ watch: **7** winding
___ self: **6** second
self-absorption: **6** egoism **7** conceit, egotism
self-admiration: **5** pride **6** egoism **7** conceit, egotism
self-admiring: **4** vain **9** conceited
self-aggrandizing: **8** boastful
self-assertive: **5** brash, pushy **6** strong **9** bumptious
self-assurance: **5** brass, poise **6** aplomb, morale **8** presence
self-assured: **6** poised, secure **8** composed
self-basting: **5** moist
self-centered: **4** smug, vain **5** cocky **6** little, stuffy **7** fustian, haughty, pompous, selfish, stuck-up, worldly **8** arrogant, boastful, egoistic, snobbish **9** big-headed, egotistic **10** egoistical
one: **6** egoist **7** egotist
self-cleaning ___: **4** oven
self-command: **5** poise
self-concern: **6** egoism **7** egotism
self-condemnation: **6** regret
self-condemnatory: **5** sorry
self-confidence: **5** poise **6** aplomb, morale
destroy ~: **5** abash
self-confident: **4** sure **6** hotdog, poised, secure **7** assured, certain, hotshot **8** fearless
self-conscious: **3** shy **5** stiff **6** uneasy, unsure **7** anxious, awkward, bashful, nervous, stilted **8** mannered, sheepish, strained **9** ill-at-ease, uncertain
make ~: **5** abash
self-contained: **5** whole **6** closed **8** reserved, reticent
self-contented: **4** smug **8** arrogant
self-contradiction: **7** paradox
self-control: **4** will **5** poise **6** aplomb, temper **7** balance, reserve **8** patience, sobriety **9** restraint, reticence, sangfroid, stability, willpower **10** temperance
lose one's ~: **4** flip, slap, snap **5** crack, go ape, smack, smash, whack **6** injure, insult, lose it **7** thunder **9** go bonkers

Self Control (1984 song) artist: Laura Branigan
self-controlled: 4 cool 5 sober, stoic 7 stoical 9 temperate
self-defense
  art: 4 judo 6 aikido, karate, kung fu
  expert: 6 judoka
  school: 4 dojo
  spray: 4 mace
self-denial: 9 austerity, restraint 10 abnegation, abstinence
self-denying: 7 ascetic, austere
self-determination: 7 liberty, license
self-discipline: 4 will 9 restraint, willpower
self-disgust: 5 shame 6 regret
self-effacing: 3 coy, shy 5 mousy 6 demure, humble, modest, mousey 8 reserved, retiring 9 diffident 10 unassuming
self-employed: 5 indie
self-esteem: 3 ego 5 poise, pride 6 egoism, regard 7 dignity, egotism, hauteur, respect
self-evident: 5 clear, plain 6 patent 7 obvious, visible 8 apparent, manifest 9 axiomatic
self-explanatory: 5 clear, plain 6 simple 7 obvious, visible 8 apparent, manifest
self-government: 7 freedom, liberty
self-help category: 5 how-to
self-image: 3 ego
self-importance: 3 ego 5 pride 6 hubris, hybris 7 conceit, hauteur 10 pretension
self-important: 4 smug, vain 5 proud 6 snooty, stuffy 7 fustian, haughty, pompous, stuck-up 8 arrogant, snobbish 9 bigheaded, conceited, officious 10 hoity-toity
  one: 3 ass
self-indulgence: 7 license 8 pleasure
self-indulgent: 6 effete 9 luxurious
self-interest: 6 egoism
selfish: 3 big 4 mean, rude 5 brash, nervy, small, tight 6 grabby, greedy, little, sordid, stingy 7 boorish, hoggish, miserly, worldly 8 egoistic, grasping, heedless, impolite, tactless, ulterior, ungiving 9 egotistic, mercenary, penurious 10 avaricious, egocentric, egoistical, skinflinty, ungenerous, ungracious, ungrateful, unthinking
  one: 3 hog, pig 5 taker 6 egoist 7 egotist
selfishness: 5 greed 7 avarice
selfless: 3 big 10 altruistic, bighearted
self-love: 6 egoism, vanity 7 conceit, egotism 10 narcissism
self-loving: 10 egocentric, egoistical
self-named: 8 so-called
self-possessed: 4 calm, cool, sure 6 placid, poised, sedate, serene, steady 7 assured, patient, relaxed 8 balanced, composed, peaceful, tranquil 9 collected, easygoing, nerveless 10 untroubled
self-possession: 5 poise 6 aplomb 7 balance 8 calmness, presence 9 restraint
Self-Reliance: 5 essay
  author: Emerson
self-reliant: 4 sure 6 secure 7 assured, valiant 9 confident
self-reproach: 5 shame 6 regret 7 remorse 9 penitence 10 repentance
self-reproachful: 5 sorry
self-respect: 3 ego 5 pride 7 conceit, dignity
self-restraint: 4 will 7 control, reserve 9 sang-froid 10 discipline, temperance
self-righteous: 4 smug 5 pious 7 canting, preachy 8 superior
  person: 4 prig
self-ruling: 4 free 8 populist 10 autonomous, democratic
self-sacrificing: 5 chary 7 prudent, thrifty 9 provident 10 economical
selfsame: 4 like, twin, very 9 identical
self-satisfied: 4 smug, vain 5 proud 7 pleased 8 puffed up 9 conceited, egotistic
  act ~: 5 gloat
self-seeker: 6 egoist 7 egotist 10 narcissist
self-service
  ending: 4 -omat 5 -teria
self-serving: 8 ulterior
  one: 5 taker
self-styled: 7 nominal, wannabe, would-be 8 so-called 9 soi-disant
self-sufficient: 4 unit 5 proud 6 closed 9 competent, confident, on one's own
self-sustaining: 6 closed 7 insular 8 solitary
self-willed: 4 wild 7 wayward 8 indocile, perverse, stubborn 9 obstinate, pig-headed 10 headstrong
self-worship: 5 pride 6 egoism, vanity 7 egotism
Selick, Henry: 8 director
  film: James and the Giant Peach (1996)
    The Nightmare Before Christmas (1993)
Selkirk: 3 mts. 4 mtns. 5 range 9 Alexander, mountains
  locale: 6 Canada
Selkirk Rex: 3 cat 5 felid 6 feline
sell: 4 dump, fail, hawk, push, sham, shed, show, snow, vend 5 close, cross, lobby, pitch, press, rat on, spiel, spoof, trade 6 barter, betray, deal in, delude, give up, handle, hustle, market, peddle, retail, take in, unload 7 auction, beguile, deceive, dispose, mislead, promote, traffic, triumph, win over 8 contract, convince, exchange, get rid of, give away, hand over, part with, persuade, pressure, transact, transfer 9 deliver up, disinform, dispose of, influence, liquidate, move goods, play false, publicize, surrender, sweet talk, wholesale 10 auction off, relinquish
  a bill of goods: 2 do 3 con, rob 4 bilk, burn, clip, dupe, fool, gull, have, hoax, nick, rook, scam, take, trim 5 cheat, cozen, fraud, gouge, mulct, pluck, set up, shaft, stiff, sting, trick 6 diddle, extort, fleece, hustle, outwit, rip off, sucker 7 deceive, defraud, finagle, sandbag, swindle 8 flimflam, hoodwink, outsmart 9 bamboozle, four-flush, shake down, victimize 10 run a game on
  abroad: 6 export
  aggressively: 4 flog, hype
  buy and ~: 4 deal 5 trade 7 traffic 8 exchange
  cheap: 4 dump
  door to door: 6 peddle
  down the river: 5 rat on 6 betray, expose, fink on, give up, snitch, squeal, tattle, turn in 7 sell out 8 give away
  ender: 3 off, out 4 back
  for: 4 cost 5 bring, fetch, yield 6 charge 7 realize
  hard ~: 5 spiel 6 patter 8 cajolery 10 persuasion
  off: 6 divest 9 liquidate
  on: 5 lobby 7 satisfy
  out: 5 cross, rat on 6 betray, give up 7 deceive, mislead, violate 8 give away 9 deliver up, play false, surrender
  try to ~: 7 solicit
sell __: 3 off, out 4 date 5 short
sell __ hotcakes: 4 like
sell __ of goods: 5 a bill
sell __ the river: 4 down
__ sell: 4 hard, soft
Sellecca, Connie: 7 actress
  spouse: Gil Gerard, John Tesh
Selleck, Tom: 5 actor
  film: 3 Men and a Baby (1987)
    In & Out (1997)
    Quigley Down Under (1990)
  TV: Magnum, p.i.
seller: 5 agent 6 broker, dealer, grocer, hawker, pedlar, pedler, trader, vender, vendor 7 peddler 8 marketer, merchant, retailer 10 auctioneer, franchisee, shopkeeper
  caveat: 4 as is
  short ~: 4 bear
  spots: 3 ads
  starter: 4 book
  tip ~: 4 tout
__ seller: 4 best 5 short
seller's __: 6 market, option
Sellers, Peter: 5 actor
  film: The Battle of the Sexes (1960)
    Being There (1979)
    Casino Royale (1967)
    Dr. Strangelove (1964)
    I Love You, Alice B. Toklas (1968)
    Lolita (1962)
    The Mouse That Roared (1959)
    Murder by Death (1976)
    The Optimists (1973)
    The Party (1968)
    The Pink Panther (1964)
    The Pink Panther Strikes Again (1976)
    A Shot in the Dark (1964)
    There's a Girl in My Soup (1970)
    tom thumb (1958)
    Two Way Stretch (1960)
    Waltz of the Toreadors (1962)
    Woman Times Seven (1967)
    The World of Henry Orient (1964)
    The Wrong Arm of the Law (1962)
    Your Past Is Showing (1957)
  spouse: Britt Ekland
Sellery: 4 peak 5 mount 8 mountain
  locale: 10 Antarctica
selling __: 4 race 5 floor, point 6 climax
__-selling: 4 best
sell-off: 7 auction
sellout: 3 hit 6 throng 9 treachery
  notice: 3 SRO
__ sells seashells...: 3 She
Selma: 4 city, town 7 Diamond 8 Lagerlöf
  locale: 7 Alabama 10 California
Selman: 7 Waksman
Selten, Reinhard: 6 German 8 Nobelist 9 economist
seltzer: 4 fizz, soda 5 mixer 8 beverage
  make ~: 6 aerate
seltzer __: 5 water
__ Seltzer: 5 Bromo
__-Seltzer: 4 Alka
selva: 10 rain forest
selvage: 3 end 5 verge 6 margin
Selvon, Samuel: 6 writer 11 Trinidadian
Selwyn, Edgar: 8 director
  film: The Mystery of Mr. X (1934)
    The Sin of Madelon Claudet (1931)
    Skyscraper Souls (1932)
    Turn Back the Clock (1933)
Selznick, David O. spouse: Jennifer Jones
semana: 4 week 7 Spanish
semantic: 10 linguistic
semaphore: 4 code
  sender: 5 waver
Semarang: 4 city, port, town
  locale: 4 Java 9 Indonesia
__ Sematary: 3 Pet
Sembello, Michael song: Maniac (1983)
semblance: 3 air 4 aura, cast, face, feel, form, look, mask, mood, show, veil 5 front, guise, image, shape 6 aspect, facade, simile, veneer 7 analogy, bearing, feeling, pretext, seeming, showing 8 likeness, likening, pretense 9 imitation 10 appearance, atmosphere, comparison, complexion, similarity, similitude
semé: 4 sown
Semele: 8 oratorio
  composer: 6 Handel
  father of ~: 6 Cadmus
  lover of ~: 4 Zeus
  sister of ~: 3 Ino
  son of ~: 7 Bacchus 8 Dionysus
Semenov, Nikolay: 7 chemist, Russian 8 Nobelist
Semeru: 7 volcano
  locale: 4 Java 9 Indonesia
semester: 4 term
  ender: 4 exam, test 5 final
semester __: 4 hour
semesters, two: 4 year
semi: 3 rig 5 lorry, truck 6 big rig, hauler 9 transport
  British ~: 5 lorry
  compartment: 3 cab
  drive a ~: 4 haul
  fuel: 6 diesel
semi-: 4 half 5 quasi
semiautomatic rifle: 4 M one
semibreve: 4 note
semicircle: 3 arc, bow
semicircular: 5 round
semicircular __: 5 canal
semicolon: 4 dots, mark
semiconductor: 5 diode
  concentration: 3 LSI
  giant: 5 Intel
  impurity: 6 dopant
  metal: 6 indium 7 silicon 9 germanium
semidiameter: 6 radius
semidurable __: 5 goods
semiliquid: 3 gel 5 mushy
seminal: 8 original
seminar: 4 talk 5 class 6 course 8 elective 10 conference
  follower: 5 Q and A
seminary: 6 school 7 academy
  degree: 3 STB, STM, Th.D.
  subject: 3 rel. 8 religion
  text: 5 Bible
Seminole: 5 tribe 6 Indian 7 Amerind, athlete
Seminole __: 4 Wars
Seminoles' school: 3 FSU
semiprecious __: 5 stone
semiquaver: 4 note
semirural region: 5 exurb
semis: 4 coin 5 money
semisolid: 3 gel 5 mushy
Semite: 3 Jew 4 Arab
  ancient ~: 6 Essene
Semitic: 6 Jewish 8 language
  deity: 4 Baal
  kingdom: 4 Moab
  language: 6 Arabic, Hebrew 7 Amharic, Aramaic 8 Akkadian
Semi-Tough (1977 film)
  cast: Jill Clayburgh, Kris Kristofferson, Burt Reynolds
  director: Michael Ritchie
semolina: 5 grain, wheat
  product: 5 pasta 9 spaghetti
semper __: 4 idem 7 fidelis, paratus
Semper Fidelis: 5 march, motto
  composer: 5 Sousa
  org.: 4 USMC
  vower: 6 Marine
__ semper liberi: 7 montani
__ semper tyrannis: 3 sic
__ Semple McPherson: 5 Aimee

sempre: 6 always
__ sempre: 4 ora e
sen: 4 coin 5 money
Sen, Amartya: 6 Indian 8 Nobelist 9 economist
Senate: 10 upper house
airer: 5 CSPAN
ancient Roman ~ house: 5 curia
assistant: 4 aide, page
counterpart: 5 House
garb: 4 toga
influencer: 8 lobbyist
locale: 4 Rome 5 Italy 6 Canada, France, Mexico
member: 8 lawmaker 10 legislator
official: 4 whip
output: 3 law 4 bill
six years, for the ~: 4 term
vote: 3 aye, nay, yea
senator: 8 lawgiver
Senator: 6 iceman
Hall of Famer: 4 Rice 7 Johnson, Sam Rice
rival: 4 Blue, King, Star, Wild 5 Bruin, Devil, Flame, Flyer, Oiler, Sabre, Shark 6 Canuck, Coyote, Ranger 7 Capital, Panther, Penguin, Red Wing 8 Canadien, Islander, Predator, Thrasher 9 Avalanche, Blackhawk, Hurricane, Lightning, Maple Leaf 10 Blue Jacket, Mighty Duck
Senators: 3 six 4 team
home: 6 Ottawa
milieu: 3 ice 4 rink
org.: 3 NHL
sport: 6 hockey
Senator Was Indiscreet, The (1947 film)
cast: Peter Lind Hayes, William Powell, Ella Raines
director: George S. Kaufman
send: 3 fax 4 cast, drop, emit, fire, hurl, mail, move, post, ship, stir, wire 5 charm, drive, elate, fling, grant, issue, refer, relay, remit, route, shoot, sling, telex 6 assign, commit, convey, detail, direct, excite, impart, let fly, please, propel, put out, thrill, turn on 7 advance, consign, delight, deliver, dismiss, enchant, enthral, enthuse, forward, freight, give off, inthral, radiate 8 delegate, dispatch, enthrall, hurry off, inthrall, televise, transfer, transmit 9 broadcast, bundle off, circulate, electrify, enrapture, pass along, stimulate, titillate, transport 10 exhilarate, intoxicate
a letter: 4 mail 5 write 10 correspond, epistolize
a message to: 4 wire
a package: 4 ship
away: 6 banish, deport, rebuff 7 dismiss 8 chase out
away for: 5 order
back: 6 return
ender: 3 off
for: 4 page 6 muster, summon
forth: 4 bear, emit, gush, shed, spew, spue 5 eject, expel, exude, issue, relay, yield 6 launch 7 cast out, diffuse, emanate, give off, produce, radiate 8 generate, throw off 9 discharge
forward: 7 advance
hit ~: 5 e-mail
money: 5 remit
off: 4 beam 6 export, launch, refuse 7 dismiss 8 disperse
out: 4 emit 5 exude, issue 7 radiate
overnight: 4 rush 6 hasten 7 speed up 8 expedite 10 accelerate
packing: 2 ax 3 axe, can, rid 4 boot, drop, fire, oust, sack 5 eject, evict, exile, expel, let go 6 banish, bounce, depose, lay off 7 cashier, dismiss, drum out, release, turn out 8 chase out, furlough, get rid of, pink-slip 9 discharge, terminate
regrets: 5 say no 6 beg off, refuse 7 decline
skyward: 4 loft
starter: 3 god
through the roof: 5 anger 6 enrage, fire up, madden 7 incense, inflame, provoke 9 infuriate 10 exasperate
to another: 5 refer
to Coventry: 4 shun, tabu 5 taboo
to the bottom: 4 sink
up: 4 loft, mock 6 launch 7 imitate, lampoon 8 ridicule
word to: 6 inform, notify
send __: 3 for, off, out 5 forth 6 flying 7 packing
send-__: 2 up
Sendai: 4 city, town
locale: 5 Japan
Sendak, Maurice: 6 author, writer
Sender, Ramón José: 6 writer 7 Spanish
Send for Me (1957 song) artist: Nat King Cole
Sending __ Love: 5 All My
Send in the Clowns starter: 4 Isn't
__ Send Me: 3 You
Send Me No Flowers (1964 film)
cast: Doris Day, Rock Hudson, Tony Randall
director: Norman Jewison
Send Me the Pillow You Dream On (1965 song) artist: Dean Martin
sendoff: 5 start 8 farewell 9 launching
Send One Your Love (1979 song) artist: Stevie Wonder
send-up: 5 spoof 6 comedy, parody, satire 7 lampoon, mockery, takeoff 8 travesty 10 caricature, impression
Seneca: 3 car 4 auto, lake 5 Dodge, Roman, tribe 6 Indian 7 Amerind 8 language 10 playwright 11 philosopher
ally: 6 Cayuga, Mohawk, Oneida 8 Onondaga 9 Tuscarora
enemy: 4 Erie
locale: 7 New York
specialty: 8 Stoicism
student: 4 Nero
Seneca __ Conference: 5 Falls
Senegal: 5 river 6 nation 7 country
capital: 5 Dakar
city: 5 Dakar, Thiès
language: 5 Wolof 7 Malinke
locale: 6 Africa
money: 5 franc
neighbor: 4 Mali 6 Gambia, Guinea 10 Mauritania
people: 4 Fula 5 Wolof 6 Fulani
poet: 7 Senghor
port: 5 Dakar
River locale: 4 Mali
senescent: 4 aged 5 aging 6 ageing 7 ancient, elderly, wizened 8 grizzled 9 geriatric, getting on, up in years
Senghor, Léopold Sédar: 4 poet 9 statesman 10 Senegalese
__ Seng Index: 4 Hang
senhor: 3 man 5 title 6 mister 10 Portuguese
senhora: 4 dona, lady 5 title 10 Portuguese
daughter: 5 filha
senhorita: 4 miss 5 title 10 Portuguese
senior: 3 old 4 head, year 5 elder, major, older, pupil 6 higher 7 leading 8 oldtimer, superior 9 collegian, first-born, matriarch, patriarch 10 golden-ager
citizen group: 4 AARP
exam: 4 GMAT, LSAT
former ~: 4 alum, grad 6 alumna 7 alumnus
goal: 6 degree 7 diploma
member: 4 dean 5 doyen
year highlight: 4 prom
senior __: 4 debt, prom 7 citizen
senior __ school: 4 high
Senior Bowl team: 5 North, South
seniority: 4 rank 7 ranking 8 priority, standing 9 advantage 10 precedence, preference
greater in ~: 5 older 9 first-born
having more ~: 5 older
senna: 5 shrub
source: 6 cassia
Senne: 5 river
city on the ~: 8 Brussels
locale: 7 Belgium
sennet: 4 fish
Sennett: 4 Mack
__ sennit: 4 flat 6 common 7 English
señor: 3 man 5 title 6 Latino 7 Spanish
shawl: 6 sarape, serape
squiggle: 5 tilde
wife: 6 esposa, marida
señora: 4 lady, wife 5 title 6 Latina 7 Spanish
husband: 6 esposo, marido
shawl: 6 rebozo
squiggle: 5 tilde
señorita: 5 title 6 Latina 8 fräulein
squiggle: 5 tilde
sensa: 7 stimuli
sensation: 3 hit, wow 4 feel, kick, stir, vibe 5 flash, furor, smash, vibes 6 marvel, scream, splash, thrill, tingle, wonder 7 emotion, feeling, miracle, passion, prodigy, scandal, stunner, triumph 8 response, surprise 9 agitation, awareness, bombshell, commotion 10 excitement, gold record, impression, perception, phenomenon
causer: 5 nerve
combining form: 8 esthesio- 9 aesthesio-
without ~: 4 numb 9 unfeeling
__ Sensation: 3 New 5 Sweet
sensational: 3 def, rad 4 aces, A-one, boss, braw, cool, dece, fine, gear, keen, neat, nice, phat, tuff 5 dandy, ducky, grand, great, juicy, livid, lurid, marvy, neato, nobby, prime, rough, showy, slick, spicy, super, swell 6 bang on, bang-up, bonzer, bosker, choice, coarse, divine, dreamy, far-out, gnarly, groovy, lovely, moving, peachy, slap-up, spicey, spot on, sultry, superb, terrif, tiptop, unreal, vulgar, whizzo, wicked 7 amazing, awesome, capital, corking, perfect, pointed, ripping, salient, skookum, stellar, sublime 8 dazzling, dramatic, eloquent, especial, exciting, eximious, fabulous, five-star, four-star, frabjous, glorious, heavenly, jim-dandy, shocking, slam-bang, smashing, splendid, standout, sterling, stickout, stirring, stunning, superior, terrific, top-level, topnotch, very good, wondrous 9 agitating, arresting, bodacious, emotional, Endsville, excellent, exemplary, exquisite, first-rate, high-grade, hunky-dory, marvelous, prominent, revealing, sollicker, startling, thrilling, top-flight, wonderful 10 first-class, hotsy-totsy, jack-a-dandy, out of sight, peachy-keen, phenomenal, remarkable, scandalous, stupendous, super-duper
__ Sensational: 5 You're
sensationalism: 4 hype 6 hoopla
sensationless: 4 numb 9 unfeeling
Sensations song: Let Me In (1962)
Sens Cathedral artist: 5 Corot
sense: 3 get, use, wit 4 aura, core, feel, gist, hear, hold, know, meat, mind, read, soul, tact, wits 5 drift, grasp, logic, point, savvy, scent, sight, smell, stuff, taste, tenor, think, touch, value, worth 6 absorb, acuity, brains, detect, divine, import, intuit, matter, notice, nuance, pick up, reason, sanity, seeing, smarts, spirit, take in, thrust, upshot, wisdom 7 ability, believe, catch on, discern, faculty, feeling, hearing, insight, meaning, message, observe, purport, purpose, realize, summary 8 aptitude, capacity, function, instinct, judgment, keenness, overtone, perceive, prudence, sagacity, sapience 9 apprehend, awareness, intellect, intuition, knowledge, reasoning, sharpness, smartness, substance 10 anticipate, appreciate, atmosphere, cleverness, cognizance, definition, denotation, impression, perception, understand
a ~: 5 smell, taste, touch 6 seeing, vision 7 hearing
common ~: 3 wit 4 tact, wits 5 logic 6 sanity, wisdom 8 gumption, judgment 9 practical, pragmatic 10 discretion
general ~: 4 gist, tone, vein 5 drift, tenor, theme, trend 6 burden, intent 7 essence, meaning, purport 9 substance
horse ~: 5 savvy 6 acumen, brains, reason, wisdom 7 insight 8 judgment, prudence, sagacity 9 ingenuity, reasoning, sharpness 10 astuteness, perception, shrewdness
make ~: 4 jell 5 add up, fit in 6 cohere, figure, relate, square 7 conform, connect 8 dovetail 9 hold water 10 correspond
make ~ of: 6 decode 9 figure out
making ~: 10 reasonable
moral ~: 8 superego 10 conscience, small voice
not making ~: 9 illogical
of a ~: 4 otic 5 aural
of humor: 3 wit 9 wittiness 10 cleverness
organ: 3 ear, eye 4 nose, skin 6 tongue
sixth ~: 3 ESP 8 instinct 9 intuition, telepathy
__ sense: 3 in a 4 talk 5 horse, moral, sixth 6 common, muscle
__ Sense: 6 Common
Sense and Sensibility: 4 film 5 novel
author: Jane Austen
cast: Hugh Grant, Alan Rickman, Emma Thompson, Kate Winslet
character: 4 Anne, Lucy 5 Fanny 6 Elinor 8 Marianne
director: Ang Lee
sensei: 6 master 7 teacher
art: 3 Zen 4 judo 6 karate
locale: 5 Japan
milieu: 4 dojo
senseless: 3 mad 4 daft, dopy, idle, null, numb, vain 5 batty, blind, crazy, dopey, empty, flaky, goony, goosy, inane, no-win, nutty, silly, wacky 6 absurd, flakey, insane, jejune, screwy, simple, unwise, wanton, whacky 7 asinine, fatuous, foolish, puerile, trivial, unsound 8 cockeyed, headless, mindless, specious 9 frivolous, half-baked, illogical, ludicrous, pointless, unfeeling, unmeaning, untenable 10 groundless, irrational, ridiculous, unprofound, unthinking, weak-minded
knock ~: 4 kayo 5 floor 6 lay out 9 overpower
senselessness: 5 folly 6 idiocy 8 nonsense

sense of ___: 5 humor, smell
Sense of ___, A: 4 Loss
Sense of Beauty, The author: George Santayana
Sense of Wonder, The author: Rachel Carson
senses: 6 reason, sanity
bring to one's ~: 5 alert 6 wake up
Senses Working Overtime artist: 3 XTC
sensibility: 5 taste 7 feeling, finesse, insight, reality 8 attitude, judgment, keenness 9 awareness, intuition, rationale
sensible: 4 sage, sane, wise 5 aware, lucid, right, smart, sober, solid, sound 6 astute, cogent, shrewd, steady, trusty 7 knowing, logical, mindful, politic, prudent, sapient, tenable 8 all there, analytic, coherent, discreet, informed, methodic, physical, rational, together 9 advisable, astucious, attentive, cognizant, conscious, judicious, observant, practical, pragmatic, realistic, sagacious, temperate, unextreme 10 analytical, consistent, discerning, farsighted, legitimate, observable, reasonable, unromantic
be ~ of: 3 see 4 know 5 grasp 6 fathom 7 cognize, discern 8 perceive 9 apprehend 10 understand
of: 6 wise to
sensing device: 5 radar, sonar
sensitive: 3 raw 4 fine, keen, kind, soft, sore 5 sharp 6 gentle, kindly, liable, polite, subtle, tender, touchy, tricky, wise to 7 feeling, gallant, heedful, knowing, mindful, nervous, painful, politic, precise, psychic, refined, tactful, tuned in 8 delicate, discreet, gracious, obliging, reactive, skittish, ticklish, unstable 9 cognizant, conscious, courteous, emotional, excitable, formative, irritable, judicious, observant, receptive, unselfish 10 diplomatic, discerning, high-strung, perceiving, perceptive, precarious, responsive, thoughtful, unhardened, vulnerable
one: 6 empath
people get them: 5 vibes
sensitive to combining form: 5 -ergic
sensitivity: 3 ear 4 tact 5 heart 7 allergy, feeling, finesse 8 delicacy, keenness, subtlety, sympathy 9 awareness, tolerance
sensitivity ___: 5 group
Sensodyne: 10 toothpaste
alternative: 3 Aim 5 Crest, Gleem, Topol 7 Close-Up, Colgate, Viadent 9 Aquafresh, Mentadent, Pepsodent, Rembrandt 10 Pearl Drops, Ultra Brite 11 Tom's of Maine
sensor: 6 feeler
sensory: 5 aural, optic 6 neural, ocular, phonic, visual 7 audible, lingual, tactile 8 acoustic, afferent, auditory, hearable 9 olfactive, olfactory, receptive 10 acoustical, ophthalmic
sensory ___: 4 root 6 cortex, neuron
sensualist: 4 roué 8 hedonist 9 epicurean
___-sent: 6 heaven
Senta: 6 Berger
sentence: 3 rap 4 jail, rule, term, text, time 5 blame, edict, hitch, judge, order 6 dictum, punish, ruling, settle 7 adjudge, censure, condemn, confine, convict, impound, mete out, passage, penalty, put away, verdict 8 decision, imprison, judgment, penalize, sanction 9 proscribe, utterance 10 punishment
analyze a ~: 5 parse
break: 3 dot 4 dash 5 colon, comma 6 period 8 ellipsis
one whose ~ is complete: 5 ex-con
part: 4 verb, word 6 adverb, clause, object, phrase 7 subject 9 adjective, predicate
pass ~: 5 judge 7 convict
reduce a ~: 6 pardon 7 commute
serve a ~: 6 do time
server: 3 con 5 lifer 6 inmate 7 convict 8 jailbird, prisoner, yardbird
structure: 7 grammar
___ sentence: 4 full, open 5 cleft, fused, loose, minor, run-on, topic 6 kernel, matrix, simple 7 complex, nominal
sentences, like some: 5 run-on
sententious: 7 laconic 8 pedantic 9 axiomatic 10 pedantical
sentience: 4 life 9 awareness
sentient: 5 aware 7 knowing 9 conscious, observant 10 responsive
sentiment: 4 bias, love, view 5 slant, toast 6 belief, pathos 7 emotion, feeling, leaning, opinion, passion, posture, romance, thought 8 attitude, judgment, penchant, position 9 affection, inclining 10 compliment, conviction, partiality, persuasion, propensity
sentimental: 4 soft 5 corny, hokey, mushy, sappy, silly, soppy, sweet, vapid, weepy 6 dreamy, drippy, loving, sirupy, sugary, syrupy, tender 7 maudlin, mawkish, tearful 8 affected, dewy-eyed, effusive, poignant, romantic, schmalzy, shmaltzy, touching 9 emotional, nostalgic, schmaltzy
one: 5 softy 6 softie
overly ~: 4 icky 5 gushy, mushy, sappy, soupy, weepy
sentimentality: 3 goo 4 glop, mush 5 slush 6 bathos
Sentimental Journey, A author: Laurence Sterne
___ Sentimental Mood: 3 In a
sentinel: 5 guard, watch 6 patrol, picket, sentry 7 lookout 8 guardian, watchman 10 doorkeeper, gatekeeper
Sentinel: 5 paper 9 newspaper
locale: 7 Orlando
Sentra: 3 car 4 auto 6 Nissan
cousin: 6 Altima
sentry: 5 guard, watch 6 picket 7 lookout 8 sentinel 10 doorkeeper, gatekeeper
duty: 5 vigil, watch
like a good ~: 5 alert, awake
order: 4 halt
sentry ___: 3 box 4 palm
Senufo home: 4 Mali 6 Africa 10 Ivory Coast
___ Sen Yung: 6 Victor
Seoul: 4 city, town 7 capital
GI: 3 ROK
locale: 5 Korea
river: 3 Han
SEP: 3 IRA
sepals, flower: 5 calyx
separable: 10 dissoluble
separate: 3 one, rip 4 fork, free, lone, only, part, rend, rive, sift, skim, snap, sole, sort, tear, undo, vary, wean 5 alone, apart, break, fence, group, leave, loose, other, sever, split, unfix, unmix, unpeg 6 assign, assort, bisect, blouse, branch, cleave, cut off, depart, detach, divide, filter, go away, loosen, parted, screen, secede, single, spread, strain, sunder, unique, unlike, unlink, unwind, varied, winnow 7 asunder, break up, deviate, disjoin, dissect, distant, diverge, diverse, divided, divorce, insular, isolate, private, pull out, radiate, removed, rope off, rupture, scatter, seclude, several, severed, split up, tear off, unalike, unravel, variant, various 8 alienate, break off, classify, close off, come away, contrast, cut apart, cut in two, detached, discrete, disjoint, distinct, disunite, estrange, insulate, isolated, laminate, peculiar, set apart, singular, solitary, sundered, uncouple 9 bifurcate, come apart, different, disengage, divergent, draw apart, interrupt, intervene, partition, punctuate, scattered, segregate, sequester, single out, take leave, unrelated 10 autonomous, come undone, disconnect, disjointed, distribute, far between, individual, particular, respective, unattached
combining form: 4 idio-
go ~ ways: 4 fork, part 5 leave, split 7 break up, disband, diverge, pull out, scatter, split up
in a ~ place: 5 aside
prefix: 3 apo-
Separate ___: 4 Ways 5 Lives 6 Tables
Separate ___, A: 5 Peace
separated: 4 lone 5 alone, apart, cleft, in two 6 single 7 asunder 8 sundered 10 disjointed
combining form: 4 dich- 5 chori-, dialy-, dicho- 7 chorist- 8 choristo-
Separate Lives (1985 song)
artist: Marilyn Martin, Phil Collins
separately: 5 alone, apart, aside, per se 6 apiece, singly, solely 8 one by one
Separate Tables: 4 film, play
author: Terrence Rattigan
cast: Rita Hayworth, Deborah Kerr, Burt Lancaster, David Niven
director: Delbert Mann
Separate Ways (song) artist: Elvis Presley, Journey
separating: 7 between
separation: 3 gap 4 gape, rift 5 break, space, split 6 schism 7 breakup, divorce, parting, rupture, split-up, veering 8 cleavage, contrast, distance, disunion, division, farewell 9 defection, departure, exclusion, partition, severance, sundering 10 alienation, comparison, detachment, difference, disruption, divergence, extraction
separation ___: 5 layer 6 center, energy
separation of ___: 6 powers
separatist: 5 rebel 9 dissident, sectarian
Sephardic language: 6 Ladino
Sepher ___: 5 Torah
Sephia: 3 car, Kia 4 auto 10 automobile
sepia: 3 ink 5 brown, color 7 grayish
relative: 3 bay, dun, tan 4 bole, ecru, fawn, foxy, nude, seal 5 amber, beige, camel, cocoa, hazel, khaki, mocha, tawny, umber 6 auburn, bister, bistre, bronze, coffee, copper, ginger, russet, sienna, sorrel, suntan, walnut 7 biscuit, caramel, dogwood 8 chestnut, cinnamon, mahogany 9 butternut, chocolate
Sepoy Mutiny center: 5 Delhi
Sept-___: 4 Iles
septa-
predecessor: 4 hexa-
successor: 4 octa-, octo-
September: 5 month
birthstone: 8 sapphire
predecessor: 3 Aug. 6 August
sign: 5 Libra, Virgo 6 Scales, Virgin 7 Balance
successor: 3 Oct. 7 October
September 5: 5 nones
September Morn (1980 song) artist: Neil Diamond
septic: 5 germy, toxic 8 virulent 9 poisonous 10 insanitary
septic ___: 4 tank
Sept-Iles: 4 city, town
locale: 6 Canada, Québec
septillion combining form: 5 yotta-
septillionth combining form: 5 yocto-
Septuagesima ___: 6 Sunday
septum: 4 wall 8 membrane
sepulchral: 6 somber 9 cavernous, unearthly
sequel: 5 chain, issue, story 6 ending, epilog, payoff, result, series 7 closing, outcome, spin-off 8 epilogue, follow-up 9 aftermath, finishing 10 conclusion
title starter: 3 son 5 son of
sequence: 3 row, run 4 flow 5 array, chain, cycle, order, round, suite, train 6 course, series, streak, string 7 program 8 grouping, ordering 9 gradation, placement 10 catenation, continuity, graduation, perpetuity, procession, succession
sequential: 4 next 5 later 6 serial 9 following
sequential-___: 6 access
sequentially: 6 in turn
sequester: 4 hide 6 cut off, set off 7 isolate, retreat, seclude, secrete 8 cloister, close off, draw back, ensconce, hide away, insulate, separate, set apart, withdraw 9 segregate 10 commandeer, confiscate
sequestered: 5 quiet 6 hidden, lonely 7 insular, private, recluse 8 secluded, solitary 9 reclusive 10 cloistered
sequin: 5 money 7 spangle 10 decoration
sequins, apply: 5 sew on
___ sequitur: 3 non
sequoia: 4 tree
locale: 10 California
relative: 7 redwood
___ sequoia: 5 giant
Sequoia: 3 SUV 4 park 6 Toyota
locale: 10 California
ser.
see sermon
sera: 4 whey 8 vaccines 10 antitoxins, antivenins, inoculants
___ sera: 5 buona
Serafita composer: Leoncavallo
seraglio: 5 haram, harem, harim 6 hareem
chamber: 3 oda 4 odah
serai: 3 inn 6 imaret
site: 5 oasis
serape: 5 scarf, shawl
seraph: 5 angel
seraphic: 4 holy 5 pious 7 angelic, saintly 8 heavenly 9 angelical, celestial
___ será, será: 3 qué
Serb: 4 Slav 6 Balkan
Serbia: 6 nation 7 country
bovine: 4 Busa
capital: 8 Belgrade
city: 3 Nis 5 Vrsac 7 Novi Sad 8 Belgrade, Podorica, Subotica 10 Kragujevac
dance: 4 kolo
former capital: 3 Nis
neighbor: 6 Bosnia 7 Albania, Croatia, Hungary, Romania 8 Bulgaria
saint: 4 Sava
Serdán: 4 city, town
locale: 6 Mexico, Puebla
sere: 3 dry 4 arid 5 unwet 7 bone-dry, dried up, parched, wizened 8 dried out, droughty, rainless, withered 9 infertile, juiceless, shriveled, unfertile, waterless 10 dehydrated, desertlike, desiccated
Serena: 8 Williams
sister: 5 Venus
serenade: 4 sing 5 music 6 ballad
dawn ~: 4 alba

instrument: 4 lute
the moon: 3 bay 4 howl
Serenade
author: James M. Cain
__ Serenade: 5 Penny 7 Sunrise
Serenade painter: 5 Steen
__ Serenade, The: 6 Donkey
serenata: 5 music
serendipitous: 5 blest, lucky 6 casual 7 blessed, charmed, favored, helpful, on a roll 9 fortunate, on a streak 10 auspicious, felicitous, fortuitous
serendipity: 4 luck 6 chance 8 fortuity, good luck
Serendipity (2001 film)
cast: Kate Beckinsale, John Cusack, Jeremy Piven
director: Peter Chelsom
serene: 4 calm, cool, easy, even, fair, meek, mild 5 clear, quiet, sober, staid, still, stoic 6 at ease, gentle, low-key, mellow, placid, poised, sedate, smooth, steady 7 amiable, at peace, content, equable, halcyon, idyllic, pacific, patient, relaxed, restful, stoical, unfazed, unmoved 8 amicable, carefree, composed, in repose, laid-back, pastoral, peaceful, reserved, tranquil 9 collected, easygoing, impassive, peaceable, quiescent, temperate, unexcited, unruffled, unworried 10 Apollonian, nonchalant, rippleless, unagitated, untroubled
__ Serene Highness: 3 Her
Serengeti: 5 plain
animal: 4 lion 5 eland, hyena, zebra 6 hyaena, impala
dweller: 5 Masai 6 Maasai
group: 5 pride
locale: 6 Africa 8 Tanzania
Serenissima author: Erica Jong
__ Serenitatis: 4 Mare
serenity: 4 calm, ease 5 peace, poise, quiet 7 concord, harmony 8 calmness, quietude 9 composure, placidity, quietness, stillness 10 equanimity, sedateness
serf: 4 esne, hand, peon 5 helot, slave 6 thrall, vassal, worker 7 bondman, chattel, colonus, peasant, servant, subject, villain, villein
ender: 3 dom
of a ~: 6 feudal
serfdom: 4 yoke 7 slavery 9 servitude
serge: 5 cloth, twill 6 fabric 8 material
bane: 4 lint
Serge: 5 Lifar 8 Reggiani 9 Diaghilev
sergeant: 3 NCO 4 rank, York 6 Friday, noncom, Pepper 7 officer, Preston, Snorkel
address: 3 APO
call: 3 hep, hup
command: 4 halt 5 march 6 at ease
denial: 5 no sir
like a ~: 8 enlisted
major: 3 NCO
mess ~: 4 cook
subordinate: 3 PFC, pvt. 7 private 8 corporal
superior: 2 lt. 5 lieut. 10 lieutenant
voice: 4 bark, roar, snap, yell 5 growl, shout, snarl
sergeant __: 5 at law, major
__ sergeant: 3 top 5 color, drill, first, lance, staff 6 master 7 gunnery, platoon, provost
sergeant at __: 3 law 4 arms
Sergeant Preston of the Yukon (CBS drama)
cast: Richard Simmons (Sgt. Preston)
dog: 4 King
horse: 3 Rex
Sergeant Rutledge (1960 film)
cast: Jeffrey Hunter, Constance Towers
director: John Ford
Sergeant York (1941 film)
cast: Walter Brennan, Gary Cooper, Joan Leslie
composer: 7 Steiner
director: Howard Hawks
Sergei: 6 Esenin 7 Aksakov 9 Prokofiev 10 Eisenstein
see also Russian
Sergey: 5 Bubka 8 Korolyov 9 Diaghilev, Prokofiev
see also Russian
Sergio: 5 Leone 6 Garcia, Mendes 7 Franchi
Sergiu: 10 Comissiona
Sergius: 4 pope 7 pontiff
Seri: 6 Indian 7 Amerind
Se Ri __: 3 Pak
__ seria: 5 opera
serial: 5 story 7 ensuing, going on, regular, sequent 9 continual, continued, following 10 continuing, sequential, succeeding, successive
link: 5 nexus
serial __: 5 comma 6 number, rights
Serial (1980 film)
cast: Sally Kellerman, Martin Mull, Tuesday Weld
director: Bill Persky
Serial Mom (1994 film)
cast: Ricki Lake, Matthew Lillard, Kathleen Turner, Sam Waterston
director: John Waters
seriatim: 8 detailed
seriema: 4 bird
series: 3 row, run, set 4 file, flow, line, list, rank, suit, tier 5 array, chain, cycle, group, order, queue, range, round, scale, suite, train 6 catena, column, course, parade, sequel, sitcom, streak, string 7 battery, program 8 category, sequence 9 gradation, soap opera 10 continuity, procession, round robin, succession
connected ~: 5 nexus
ender: 3 etc.
last of a ~: 3 end
repeating ~: 5 cycle
separator: 5 comma
starter: 4 mini
__ Series: 5 World
__ serif: 4 sans 6 square
Serifa: 4 font 8 typeface
serin: 4 bird 8 songbird
seringa: 4 tree 6 rubber
serious: 3 bad, big 4 deep, dire, grim, hard, ugly 5 acute, grave, heavy, major, sober, solid, staid, stern, tough 6 devout, fervid, honest, no joke, sedate, severe, solemn, somber, urgent 7 arduous, crucial, deadpan, earnest, fervent, genuine, pensive, sincere, subdued, weighty 8 grievous, menacing, pressing, profound, resolute, resolved, sobering, studious, terrible 9 big-league, dangerous, difficult, humorless, important, laborious, momentous, strenuous, unamusing, unsmiling 10 deliberate, determined, formidable, inexpiable, meaningful, nononsense, portentous, thoughtful
offense: 4 tort 5 arson, crime, heist, theft 6 felony, holdup 7 assault, robbery, treason 8 burglary, delictum 10 kidnapping
Serious: 5 Yahoo
seriously: 4 hard, very 5 badly, quite 6 cool it, sorely 7 for real, gravely, soberly, sternly 8 actively, for keeps, intently, sedately, severely, solemnly, terribly, urgently 9 fervently, harmfully, intensely, sincerely, zealously 10 critically, deplorably, grievously, menacingly, perilously, resolutely, vigorously
not ~: 5 in fun
seriousness: 6 fervor, import, moment, weight 7 earnest, gravity, urgency 8 enormity, sobriety 9 heaviness, sincerity, solemnity, staidness, sternness
Serkin, Peter: 7 pianist
Serling, Rod: 2 MC 5 emcee
TV: Night Gallery, The Twilight Zone
sermon: 4 talk 6 advice, homily, lesson, speech, tirade 7 address, lecture, monolog, oration, service 8 harangue 9 discourse, monologue, preaching 10 vocalizing
Buddha ~: 5 sutra
deliver a ~: 6 preach
ender: 4 amen, ette
passage: 4 text
spot: 5 mount
Sermon __ Mount: 5 on the
sermonist: 5 padre 6 orator 8 preacher
sermonize: 5 orate, speak, spout, teach 6 preach 7 address, lecture 8 perorate 9 discourse, exprobate, pound into
serous: 5 fluid 6 liquid 7 aqueous
serow: 8 antelope
relative: 3 gnu, kob 4 guib, kudu, oryx, puku, topi 5 addax, bongo, chiru, eland, goral, korin, nyala, oribi, saiga 6 chammy, dik-dik, duiker, impala, koodoo, lechwe, nilgai, rhebok, shammy, shamoy 7 blaubok, blesbok, chamois, defassa, gazelle, gemsbok, gerenuk, grysbok, nylghai, nylghau, sassaby 8 blesbuck, bontebok, bushbuck, gemsbuck, reedbuck, steenbok, steinbok 9 blackbuck, pronghorn, sitatunga, springbok, waterbuck 10 hartebeest, wildebeest
Serpens: 13 constellation
neighbor: 5 Libra
star in ~: 4 Alya
serpent: 3 asp 5 adder, krait, snake, viper 6 animal, hisser 7 reptile, traitor
combining form: 4 ophi- 5 ophio-
ender: 3 ine
home: 4 Eden
like a ~: 5 scaly
name meaning ~: 6 Lilith
Pharaoh's ~: 6 uraeus
sound: 4 hiss
__ serpent: 3 sea
Serpent and the Rainbow, The setting: 5 Haiti
Serpent and the Rope, The author: Raja Rao
serpentine: 3 sly 4 arch, wavy, wily 5 slick, snaky 6 artful, crafty, curved, shifty, shrewd, tricky 7 crooked, cunning, mineral, sinuous, winding 8 tortuous, twisting, writhing 9 dangerous, deceptive 10 meandering
form: 3 ess
line: 9 arabesque
mottled ~: 4 verd 5 verde
serpentine __: 4 jade 5 front
serpent's mouth, name meaning: 7 Phineas
Serpent's Tooth author: Faye Kellerman
Serpico: 4 book, film
author: Peter Maas
cast: Jack Kehoe, Al Pacino, John Randolph
director: Sidney Lumet
dog: 5 Alfie
Serra: 4 city, town 8 Junípero
locale: 6 Brazil
Serra da Estrela: 3 mts. 4 mtns. 5 range 9 mountains
locale: 8 Portugal
Serra do Mar: 3 mts. 4 mtns. 5 range 9 mountains
locale: 6 Brazil
Serra, Junípero: 5 padre 10 missionary
serrate: 5 ridgy, score 6 jagged, ridged, uneven 7 unlevel 8 lacerate
serrated: 5 sharp 6 jagged, ragged, ridged, scored, zigzag 7 notched, sawlike, toothed 8 indented, sawtooth 10 saw-toothed
Serta competitor: 5 Sealy 7 Simmons
Sert, José: 6 artist 7 painter, Spanish
Serturner: 9 Friedrich
serum: 4 whey 7 vaccine 8 medicine 9 antitoxin 10 medication
give ~: 6 inject
milk ~: 4 whey
__ serum: 5 blood, truth 6 immune
serv.
see service
Servadac: 6 Hector
serval: 3 cat 5 felid 6 animal, feline
relative: 4 eyra, lion, lynx, puma 5 chita, liger, ounce, tiger, tigon 6 bobcat, cheeta, chetah, cougar, jaguar, margay, ocelot, tiglon 7 bay lynx, caracal, cheetah, leopard, panther 9 catamount 10 jaguarundi
servant: 4 cook, hand, help, maid, mozo, page, serf 5 slave, valet 6 drudge, flunky, helper, lackey, live-in, menial, minion, puppet, server, thrall 7 flunkey, lacquey, villein 8 domestic, factotum, follower, hireling, retainer 9 attendant, launderer
civil ~: 7 officer 8 official 10 politician
garb: 6 livery
name meaning ~: 5 Abdul
of India: 3 ama 4 amah, ayah, maty 5 matee
starter: 3 man 4 bond, maid
__ servant: 4 bond 5 civil 6 fellow, public
Servant of the Bones author: Anne Rice
servants: 4 help 5 staff
Servants of Twilight, The author: Dean Koontz
Servant, The (1963 film)
cast: Dirk Bogarde, James Fox, Sarah Miles
director: Joseph Losey
serve: 2 do 3 act, aid, fit, hit 4 feed, give, help, pass, play, suit, tend, toil, work 5 avail, do for, labor, nurse 6 accept, act for, answer, assist, attend, dish up, fulfil, handle, oblige, profit, regale, set out, squire, supply, wait on 7 benefit, care for, carry on, deliver, dish out, fulfill, perform, present, promote, provide, satisfy, suffice, work for 8 attend to, function, minister, wait upon 9 discharge, look after, officiate, put in play 10 administer, distribute, do one's duty, minister to
a meal: 4 feed, wait 6 wait on
as: 9 represent
a sentence: 6 do time
drinks: 4 pour
out-of-bounds ~: 5 fault
voided ~: 3 let
well: 3 ace
wine: 6 decant
served: 3 due
__-served: 4 well
serve one __: 5 right
server: 4 tray 6 carhop, waiter 7 servant 8 waitress 9 attendant, lazy Susan
handout: 4 menu
__ server: 4 file, list 7 process
service: 3 aid, job, use 4 duty, help, mass, mend, rite, sext, turn, wear, work 5 asset, avail, favor, labor, nones, prime, terce, value 6 action, combat, matins, prayer, ritual, sermon, supply, wait on 7 benefit, liturgy,

offices, station, utility, vespers, worship **8** business, ceremony, compline, courtesy, function, kindness, military, overhaul, wait upon **10** active duty, assistance, employment, observance, profession, usefulness
agency: **5** VISTA
area: **5** plaza
award: **3** tip
bad ~ result: **5** no tip
be of ~: **5** avail, stead
branch: **3** USA, USN **4** Army, Navy, USAF, USMC **7** Marines **8** Air Force
charge: **3** fee
church ~: **4** Mass **7** worship
club: **3** VFW **4** Elks, YMCA, YMHA, YWCA, YWHA **5** Lions **6** Amvets **7** Kiwanis
compel into ~: **9** conscript
end ~: **6** resign
error: **3** let **5** fault
game: **6** tennis
lip ~: **4** cant **7** mockery **8** pretense **9** hypocrisy, phoniness **10** pharisaism, pretension, sanctimony
morning ~: **5** terce **6** matins
of ~: **5** utile **6** aidful, useful
out of ~: **6** closed
paid ~: **6** employ
part of a ~: **3** cup **4** dish, fork **5** knife, plate, spoon
people: **8** military
perfect ~: **3** ace
press into ~: **3** use **6** enlist
put back into ~: **5** reuse
religious: **4** mass, sext **5** nones, prime, terce **6** matins **7** liturgy, vespers **8** compline
stay in the ~: **4** reup
tree fruit: **4** sorb
see also army, military
service __: **3** ace, cap **4** book, club, flat, line, mark, pipe, road, tree **5** break, clasp, court, medal **6** center, charge, module, stripe **7** station, uniform
service __ smile: **5** with a
__ service: **3** air, lip, tea **4** curb, debt, food, maid, news, room, wire **5** civil **6** active, divine, postal, prayer, public, second, silent, social **7** foreign, sunrise, yeoman's
__-service: **4** full, self
__ Service: **4** Room **6** Forest, Secret
serviceable: **4** good **5** handy, of use, utile **6** aiding, usable, useful **7** durable, helpful, useable **8** salutary, valuable **9** assistive, operative, practical
service-academy freshman: **4** pleb **5** plebe
serviceperson: **7** recruit, soldier, warrior
career ~: **5** lifer
Service, Robert: **4** poet **8** Canadian
work: The Shooting of Dan McGrew
__ services: **5** armed, human
services of, obtain the: **3** use **4** book, hire **5** enrol **6** employ, engage, enlist, enroll, line up, secure, sign up, take on **7** appoint, charter, recruit, reserve **8** contract **10** commission
service station: **6** garage
job: **3** LOF **4** lube **6** tune-up
purchase: **3** gas **8** gasoline
servicewoman: **3** WAC, WAF
serviette in America: **6** napkin
servile: **3** low **4** base, mean, meek, oily, ugly **5** lowly **6** abject, craven, humble, menial **7** fawning, ignoble, passive, slavish, subject, wimpish **8** beggarly, obedient, obeisant, unctuous **9** adulatory, groveling **10** despicable, submissive
be ~: **3** bow **4** fawn **5** kotow, slave **6** grovel, kowtow **8** fawn over
one: **5** toady **6** lackey **7** lacquey
servility: **8** humility **10** submission
serving: **5** piece, plate, share **6** active, entrée **7** portion
a purpose: **5** of use, utile
piece: **4** bowl, tray **5** plate
utensil: **5** ladle, spoon
__-serving: **4** self
servitor: **5** toady **6** fawner, flunky **7** flunkey **8** courtier, follower **9** attendant, flatterer, sycophant **10** bootlicker
servitude: **3** job **4** work, yoke **5** bonds **6** chains, thrall **7** bondage, peonage, serfdom, slavery **9** captivity, obedience, vassalage
symbol: **4** yoke
sesame: **3** til **4** teel
confection: **5** halva **6** halvah **7** halavah
open ~: **6** ticket **8** password **10** hocus-pocus
plant: **3** til **5** benne, benny
product: **4** seed
seeds: **5** benne, benny
sesame __: **3** oil **4** seed **5** paste
__ sesame: **4** open
Sesame and Lilies author: John Ruskin
Sesame Street
character: **3** Sam **4** Bert, Elmo **5** Ernie, Oscar **6** Kermit, Muppet **7** Big Bird
lesson: **4** ABCs
network: **3** PBS
__ Sese Seko: **6** Mobutu
sesi: **4** fish
sess.: **3** mtg.
Sesshu: **7** painter **8** Japanese
session: **4** meet, term **5** forum, rally **6** caucus, huddle, period **7** hearing, meeting, sitting, workout **8** assembly **9** concourse, gathering **10** conference, discussion
be in ~: **3** sit **4** meet **7** convene
bull ~: **3** gab, jaw, rap, yak **4** chat, talk **7** palaver **10** conference, discussion
court ~: **5** trial **6** assize
full-group ~: **6** plenum
returned to ~: **5** remet, resat
schedule: **6** agenda
training ~: **6** lesson
__ session: **3** jam, rap **4** bull **5** joint, skull **7** special
__ sessions: **5** petty **7** general, quarter
Sessue: **8** Hayakawa
sesterce: **4** coin **5** money
sestertia: **5** money
sestertii: **5** money
sestertium: **5** money
sestet: **8** ensemble
sestina: **4** poem **5** verse
set: **2** TV **3** aim, dip, fit, fix, gel, kit, lay, mob, pat, put **4** band, bent, body, camp, cast, clan, clot, crew, curl, drop, fast, firm, gang, jell, levy, make, mien, name, pack, park, plop, post, prop, rate, rest, sect, sink, sort, sure, team, tune, wave **5** affix, align, aline, allot, apply, array, batch, bunch, class, clump, covey, crowd, embed, fixed, given, group, imbed, inlay, limit, lodge, mount, order, party, place, plant, plunk, point, price, raise, ready, rigid, scene, sited, solid, stage, staid, stake, stand, stick, stiff, suite, telly, tight, trite, usual **6** adjust, agreed, anchor, assess, assign, braced, bundle, circle, clique, clutch, decide, decree, direct, fasten, firm up, gaggle, gelate, go down, harden, impose, incite, inlaid, insert, instal, intent, jelled, little, locate, narrow, ordain, orient, outfit, placed, primed, rooted, series, stable, stated, strict, whip up, zero in **7** arrange, assured, battery, certain, cluster, congeal, coterie, decided, deposit, descend, dictate, dispose, doublet, encrust, faction, implant, incrust, in-group, install, in stone, lay down, limited, located, petrify, prepare, regular, scenery, situate, special, specify, stiffen, subside, thicken **8** allocate, arranged, assembly, cemented, concrete, constant, decide on, decisive, definite, demeanor, embedded, ensconce, estimate, hardened, indurate, initiate, instruct, ironclad, locked in, pinpoint, prepared, presence, receiver, regulate, required, resolute, resolved, situated, solidify, specific, standard, stubborn **9** agree upon, appointed, coagulate, concluded, confirmed, customary, delineate, designate, determine, disappear, establish, immovable, in granite, instigate, introduce, iron-jawed, make ready, obstinate, preordain, prescribe, ready to go, scheduled, specified, stabilize, steadfast, stipulate, stringent, tenacious, unbending **10** assemblage, assortment, collection, compendium, decide upon, deportment, determined, entrenched, fraternity, gelatinize, inflexible, in position, positioned, prescribed, prevailing, sound stage, stipulated, television, undoubtful, unwavering, unyielding
about: **5** begin, enter, start **6** assume, launch, let rip, tackle, take up **8** approach, get going **9** undertake
against: **3** pit **6** down on, oppose **8** alienate
all ~: **5** ready **6** primed **7** groomed **8** prepared **10** raring to go
apart: **4** part, save **5** lay by, lay up, sever, split, store **6** cut off, detach, devote, divide, enisle, unlink **7** disjoin, earmark, isolate, lay away, put away, reserve, rope off, split up, store up **8** break off, dedicate, disunite, reserved, sanctify, separate, uncouple **9** preferred, segregate, sequester **10** disconnect, pigeonhole
aside: **4** hold, save **5** allot, allow, amass, annul, lay by, lay up, put by, quash, store, table, waive **6** cancel, devote, refuse, repeal, revoke **7** abeyant, abolish, earmark, lay away, put away, rescind, reserve, rope off, store up **8** allocate, laid away, override, overrule, overturn, reserved, salt away **9** designate, in reserve, supersede **10** pigeonhole
at: **4** rate **6** assail, attack **7** go after, lay into **8** appraise, assailed, attacked, position **9** appraised, establish, went after **10** positioned
at odds: **6** divide **7** break up, disrupt, quarrel **8** alienate, disunite, estrange **9** disaffect
back: **4** mire, slow **5** delay **6** detain, hang up, hinder, hold up, impede, retard, slow up **7** bog down, reverse **8** slow down **9** depressed
by: **7** lay away, put away
cry: **6** places
dead ~: **5** rigid **8** resolute, stalwart **9** immovable, obstinate **10** inexorable, purposeful, relentless, unwavering, unyielding
down: **3** lay, lit, put **4** alit, copy, land, note **5** enter, light, lower, place, write **6** record **8** register **9** chronicle, formulate
ender: **3** off, out **4** back, line **5** screw
eyes on: **3** see, spy **6** look at, regard
firmly: **5** posit **6** anchor
foot in: **5** enter, get to, reach **6** come to **8** arrive at
forth: **2** go **3** say **4** give, pose, show, tell **5** begin, couch, leave, speak, start, state, voice, write **6** depart, detail, embark, let rip, recite, travel **7** declare, expound, express, go ahead, head out, itemize, move out, narrate, produce, propose, push off **8** commence, describe, get going, propound, start out, vocalize **9** enunciate, expound on, introduce, predicate, verbalize **10** articulate, hit the road
free: **5** clear, let go, loose, unpen, untie **6** loosen, ransom, redeem, rescue, unbind, unhand **7** absolve, manumit, release **8** liberate **9** discharge, liberated **10** unhindered
get ~: **3** fix **4** prep **5** equip, prime, ready **6** fit out, gear up, warm up **7** arrange, prepare **8** mobilize, organize, rehearse **10** pave the way, square away
in: **5** began, begin, start **6** arrive, harden **7** arrived, implant, started **8** commence, hardened, take hold **9** commenced **10** take effect
in motion: **3** act **4** open, spur **5** begin, impel, shake, spark, start **6** launch **7** trigger **8** activate, mobilize, touch off **9** originate **10** lead the way
in one's ways: **4** firm, iron **5** balky, fixed, rigid, stern, stiff, stony **6** dogged, mulish, ornery **7** adamant, piggish, willful **8** contrary, indurate, obdurate, perverse, resolute, stubborn **9** fractious, hard-nosed, immovable, obstinate, pig-headed, tenacious, unbending **10** bullheaded, hard-bitten, hard-headed, headstrong, inflexible, refractory, unshakable, unyielding
in stone: **5** solid **6** steady **7** adamant **9** immovable, permanent, unbending **10** inexorable
jet ~: **5** elite, haves **7** in-crowd, society **8** well-to-do **9** beau monde **10** glitterati, haute monde, socialites, upper crust
leaders ~ it: **4** pace
matched ~: **4** pair
movie ~: **3** lot **10** sound stage
off: **2** go **4** fire **5** begin, grace, leave, shoot, start **6** depart, embark, ignite, incite, let rip, redeem **7** explode, garnish, go ahead, move out, produce, trigger **8** commence, contrast, detonate, get going, outweigh, start out **9** discharge, sequester **10** hit the road, sally forth
on: **6** affect, assail, attack **7** assault, lay into **8** resolute
(on): **8** hellbent
one back: **4** cost
on end: **5** tip up
one's cap for: **3** woo **4** date **5** court **6** pursue **7** take out **9** cultivate
one's hand to: **3** ink **4** sign
one's heart on: **4** pine, want, wish **5** yearn **6** desire
one's sights on: **3** see **6** aim for, behold, look at
on its way: **6** convey, propel **8** dispatch
out: **2** go **3** lay **4** show, tell **5** begin, leave, plant, serve, start **6** define, depart, detail, embark, let rip, relate, travel **7** display, explain, go ahead, itemize, push off, recount, specify, take off **8** commence, describe, get going **9** elucidate, undertake **10** hit the road, sally forth
out on: **5** enter
right: **3** fix **6** adjust **7** correct, rectify **8** disabuse **10** make good on
sail: **6** embark **7** push off, ship out

8 go aboard, put to sea, shove off 9 leave port
side by side: 5 check, liken, weigh **6** equate, oppose, size up **7** analyze, balance, compare, examine, inspect, stack up **8** contrast, parallel **9** correlate **10** correspond, scrutinize
start a ~: 5 serve
starter: 3 off, sun **4** back, bone, hand, head, lock, moon, type **5** heavy, quick, thick **6** tumble
store by: 5 prize, value **6** accept, bank on, esteem, rely on **7** count on, respect, trust in **8** depend on, hold with **9** count upon
straight: 3 fix **5** right **6** orient **7** correct **8** disabuse **9** reconcile
the pace: 4 lead
to: 7 pitch in, quarrel
to rights: 6 remedy **7** restore **9** refurbish
up: 3 fix, rig **4** back, book, form, hoax, rear **5** begin, build, erect, found, frame, mount, pitch, raise, start, trick **6** create, entrap, instal, launch, lay for **7** arrange, compose, elevate, install, prepare, program, swindle, usher in **8** assemble, engineer, generate, initiate, organize, schedule **9** construct, establish, institute, introduce, originate, subsidize, victimize **10** constitute, inaugurate, prearrange
(up): 4 line
upon: 3 mob **5** lunge, ran at **6** assail, attack, have at, waylay **7** assault, lay into
VIP: 4 star
set __: 3 off, out **4** back, down, free, sail, shot, upon **5** about, a date, apart, aside, a trap, forth, piece, point **6** chisel, theory **7** forward
set __ by: 5 store
set __ example: 4 a bad **5** a good, a poor
set __ for: 5 a date, a trap
set __ in: 4 foot
set __ standard: 5 a high
set __ to: 4 fire
__ set: 3 all, box, get, jet, saw, tea **4** data, dead, desk, love, nail, null, role **5** chess, fuzzy, horsy, index, power, rivet, smart, stage, steak **6** Cantor, closed, horsey, socket, square, toilet **7** crystal, dinette, dresser
__-set: 4 deep, hard, mind **5** point, sharp
Set
brother: 4 Isis **6** Osiris
victim: 6 Osiris
__ Set: 3 Tee **4** Desk **7** Erector
seta: 7 bristle
setaria: 5 grass
setback: 4 blow, jolt, loss, snag **5** delay, hitch **6** defeat, glitch, hiccup, holdup, mishap, outlay, rebuff **7** bad luck, letdown, licking, regress, relapse, reverse, tragedy, trouble **8** accident, hard luck, hiccough, obstacle, reversal, slowdown **9** about-face, hindrance **10** difficulty, impediment, misfortune, regression
Seth: 6 Kantor, Thomas **9** Pecksniff
brother of ~: 4 Abel, Cain
parent of ~: 3 Eve **4** Adam
son of ~: 4 Enos **5** Enosh
Setif: 4 city, town
locale: 7 Algeria
set in __: 6 motion
set-in __: 6 sleeve
set in one's __: 4 ways
Seto: 4 city, town
locale: 5 Hondo, Japan **6** Honshu
set on __: 4 fire
Seton: 4 Anya **6** Ernest **9** Elizabeth
Seton __ University: 4 Hall
Seton, Anya: 6 author, writer
work: Dragonwyck
Foxfire
My Theodosia
set one __: 4 back, wise
Seton, Elizabeth Ann: 5 saint
set one's __ for: 3 cap
set one's __ in order: 5 house
set one's __ on: 4 eyes **5** heart **6** sights
Seton Hall: 10 university
athletes: 7 Pirates
conference: 7 Big East
locale: 9 New Jersey
sètte: 5 seven **7** Italian
follower: 4 otto
preceder: 3 sei
settee: 4 seat, sofa **5** bench, couch, divan **7** seating **8** loveseat **9** furniture
__ settee: 7 Windsor
setter: 3 dog **5** canid **6** canine
starter: 3 pin **4** pace, type **5** photo, trend
__ setter: 3 jet, job **5** Irish **6** Gordon **7** English
set the __: 4 pace
set the __ for: 5 stage
set the __ on fire: 5 world
Set the Night to Music (1991 song)
artist: Maxi Priest, Roberta Flack
Set This House on Fire author: William Styron
setting: 4 site **5** scene, stage, venue **6** locale, medium, milieu **7** context, horizon **8** ambience, backdrop, distance, location, mounting, position **9** framework, situation **10** adjustment, background
starter: 3 off **4** film, pace, type **5** trend
switch ~: 2 on **3** off **4** stop
__ setting: 4 fire **5** gypsy, place, stage **7** Tiffany
__-setting: 5 quick
settle: 3 end, fix, lay, pay, put, sit **4** calm, land, live, lull, park, plop, rest, rule, seal, seat, sink, stay **5** abide, agree, allay, clear, droop, dwell, judge, light, lodge, order, pay up, perch, pitch, place, prove, quell, quiet, relax, remit, roost, solve, spend, squat, stand, still **6** adjust, alight, assure, belong, choose, clinch, decide, define, encamp, figure, finish, harden, instal, locate, make up, pay off, pony up, redeem, refund, repose, reside, sedate, soothe, square, verify **7** achieve, appoint, arrange, bed down, clean up, clear up, confirm, descend, dispose, inhabit, install, mediate, rectify, resolve, satisfy, specify, squelch, subside, work out **8** colonize, complete, conclude, dispatch, ensconce, finalize, make good, nail down, reassure, regulate, sentence, square up, take root, transact **9** arbitrate, determine, discharge, dispose of, establish, homestead, liquidate, make peace, negotiate, reconcile, stabilize, touch down **10** adjudicate, come to rest, compromise, put an end to
a deal: 3 ice
a debt: 3 pay **5** pay up, remit, repay **9** discharge
a score: 3 get **5** repay **6** avenge
back: 4 laze **5** relax
down: 5 light, marry, relax **6** gentle, mature, mellow, nestle **7** cool off **8** blow over
in: 4 nest **5** lodge **6** encamp, nestle **7** inhabit
on: 3 tap **4** cull, name, pick, take, vote **5** adopt, draft, elect, favor **6** assign, choose, decide, desire, opt for, prefer, select **7** appoint, pick out **8** delegate, draw lots, nominate **9** designate, determine, single out
upon: 4 name
settle __: 4 down, into
settled: 3 lit **4** alit, firm, over, sure **5** given, staid **6** intent, mature, secure, stable, static, steady **7** assured, certain, decided **8** constant, decisive, definite, in the bag, ironclad, occupied, positive **9** permanent, sedentary **10** conclusive, inevitable, inveterate, purposeful, unchanging, undoubtful
in: 10 accustomed
thickly ~: 5 dense, urban **8** populous
settlement: 4 base, deal, mise, pact, town **6** accord, colony, diktat, hamlet, payoff, refund, treaty **7** compact, outpost, payment **8** contract, covenant, decision, defrayal **9** agreement, community, discharge, occupancy, reckoning, residence **10** adjustment, compromise, conclusion, foundation
settlement __: 5 house **6** option, worker
settle one's __: 4 hash
settler: 7 pioneer **8** colonist, newcomer **9** colonizer **10** inhabitant
dispute ~: 6 umpire **7** arbiter
migration: 4 trek
settlings: 5 dregs **7** deposit, grounds
set-to: 3 row **4** bout, fray, spat, tiff, tilt **5** brawl, brush, clash, fight, melee, run-in, scrap, words **6** fracas, tussle **7** contest, quarrel, rhubarb, wrangle **8** argument, brouhaha, catfight, conflict, skirmish, squabble, struggle **9** encounter **10** contention, donnybrook
Setúbal: 3 bay **4** city, town
locale: 8 Portugal
setup: 4 form, plan, trap **5** order **6** design, entrap, format, layout, scheme, system **7** machine, pitfall **8** easy mark, scenario, strategy **9** framework, procedure, structure
set up __: 4 shop
Set-Up, The (1949 film)
cast: Robert Ryan, George Tobias, Audrey Totter
director: Robert Wise
Setzer: 5 Brian
__ seul: 3 pas
Seurat, Georges: 6 artist, French **7** painter
Seurat's Lunch artist: 5 Shahn
Seuss, Dr.
real name: Theodor Seuss Geisel
work: The 500 Hats of Bartholomew Cubbins
And to Think That I Saw It on Mulberry Street
The Butter Battle Book
The Cat in the Hat
The Foot Book
Fox in Socks
Green Eggs and Ham
Hop on Pop
Horton Hatches the Egg
Horton Hears a Who
How the Grinch Stole Christmas
Hunches in Bunches
I Can Read With My Eyes Shut
If I Ran the Circus
If I Ran the Zoo
I Had Trouble Getting to Solla Sollew
King's Stilts
The Lorax
McElligot's Pool
Norval the Great
Oh Say Can You Say
Oh, the Places You'll Go!
Oh, the Thinks You Can Think!
On Beyond Zebra
There's a Wocket in My Pocket!
Thidwick: The Big-Hearted Moose
What Was I Scared Of?
Yertle the Turtle
You're Only Old Once!
__ Seuss Geisel: 7 Theodor
Sevareid: 4 Eric
Sevastopol: 4 city, port, town
locale: 6 Crimea, Russia
seven: 3 VII **6** heptad, number
best of ~: 6 series
biggest of ~: 4 Asia **7** Pacific
combining form: 4 hept-, sept- **5** hepta-, septi-
days: 4 week
ender: 4 teen
in French: 4 sept
in German: 6 sieben
in Italian: 5 sette
in Japanese: 4 nana
in Portuguese: 4 sete
in Spanish: 5 siete
man has ~ of them: 4 ages
one of ~: 3 sea **9** continent
times a week: 7 diurnal
seven __ sins: 6 deadly
seven-__ boots: 6 league
seven-__ cake: 5 layer
seven-__ stud: 4 card
Seven __: 4 Seas **5** Sages **7** Chances, Thieves
Seven __ Arts: 6 Lively
Seven __ Itch, The: 4 Year
Seven __ Mystery, The: 5 Dials
Seven __ of Architecture, The: 5 Lamps
Seven __ of Rome: 5 Hills
Seven __ of the World: 7 Wonders
Seven __ of Wisdom: 7 Pillars
Seven __ to Baldpate: 4 Keys
Seven __ to Noon: 4 Days
Seven __ War: 5 Weeks', Years'
Seven Against Thebes author: Aeschylus
Seven Angry Men (1955 film)
cast: Jeffrey Hunter, Raymond Massey, Debra Paget
Seven Beauties (1976 film)
cast: Giancarlo Giannini, Fernando Rey
director: Lina Wertmuller
Seven Brides for Seven Brothers (1954 film)
cast: Howard Keel, Jane Powell, Russ Tamblyn
director: Stanley Donen
Seven Cities of __: 6 Cibola
Seven Days in May: 4 film **5** novel
author: Fletcher Knebel
cast: Kirk Douglas, Ava Gardner, Burt Lancaster, Fredric March
director: John Frankenheimer
Seven Days to __: 4 Noon
Seven Descents of Myrtle, The author: Tennessee Williams
Seven Dwarfs
any of the ~: 4 toon **5** miner
one of the ~: 3 Doc **5** Dopey, Happy **6** Grumpy, Sleepy, Sneezy **7** Bashful
workplace: 4 mine
Seven Gothic Tales author: Isak Dinesen
Seven Hills of __: 4 Rome
Seven Keys to Baldpate author: Earl Derr Biggers
Seven Lamps of Architecture, The author: John Ruskin
seven-league __: 5 boots
Seven Little Foys, The (1955 film)
cast: Bob Hope, George Tobias
director: Melville Shavelson

Seven Lively Arts: 7 musical
songwriter: 6 Porter
Seven Men From Now (1956 film)
cast: Lee Marvin, Gail Russell, Randolph Scott
Seven-Per-Cent Solution, The (1976 film)
cast: Alan Arkin, Robert Duvall, Vanessa Redgrave, Nicol Williamson
director: Herbert Ross
Seven Pillars of Wisdom author: T.E. Lawrence
sevens: 4 game 6 fan-tan
Seven Samurai, The (1954 film)
cast: Yoshio Inaba, Toshiro Mifune, Takashi Shimura
director: Akira Kurosawa
Seven Seas: 8 dressing
alternative: 8 Wish-Bone 11 Good Seasons
Seven Storey Mountain, The author: Thomas Merton
seventeen-___ locust: 4 year
Seventeen (1955 song)
artist: Boyd Bennett and his Rockets, Fontane Sisters
Seventeen author: Booth Tarkington
dog: 6 Flopit 8 Clematis
seventh
day activity: 4 rest
heaven: 6 utopia 7 rapture 8 empyrean, paradise
in ~ heaven: 4 glad 5 happy, merry 6 blithe, cheery, elated, jovial, joyful, joyous, upbeat 7 gleeful, pleased, tickled 8 blissful, cheerful, ecstatic, euphoric, exultant, jubilant, mirthful, thrilled 9 delighted, overjoyed, rejoicing
seventh ___: 5 chord 6 heaven
seventh-___ stretch: 6 inning
Seventh ___: 3 Son 6 Avenue, Heaven
Seventh ___, The: 4 Seal, Veil 5 Cross 6 Victim
Seventh-___ Adventist: 3 Day
Seventh Commandment, The author: Lawrence Sanders
Seventh Cross, The (1944 film)
cast: Hume Cronyn, Signe Hasso, Spencer Tracy
director: Fred Zinnemann
Seventh Heaven (1927 film)
cast: Charles Farrell, Janet Gaynor
director: Frank Borzage
Seven Thieves (1960 film)
cast: Joan Collins, Edward G. Robinson, Rod Steiger
director: Henry Hathaway
Seventh Seal, The (1957 film)
cast: Bibi Andersson, Gunnar Bjornstrand, Nils Poppe, Max von Sydow
director: Ingmar Bergman
Seventh Son (1965 song) artist: Johnny Rivers
___ Seventh, The: 7 Gallant
Seventh Veil, The (1945 film)
cast: Herbert Lom, James Mason, Ann Todd
Seventy-Six Trombones instrument: 6 cornet
seven-up: 4 game 5 pitch 8 card game 9 old sledge
Seven Wise Men home: 6 Greece
Seven Wonders ___ World: 5 of the
Seven Wonders site: 6 Rhodes
Seven Year Itch, The (1955 film)
cast: Tom Ewell, Evelyn Keyes, Marilyn Monroe
director: Billy Wilder
Seven Years in Tibet
setting: 4 Lasa 5 Lhasa
Seven Years' War loser: 6 Russia
sever: 3 cut, hew, lop 4 part, rend, rive, slit, tear 5 carve, slash, slice, split 6 bisect, cleave, cut off, detach, divide, lop off, sunder, unlink 7 abandon, abscind, chop off, disband, disjoin, dissect, divorce, hack off, rupture, scissor, split up, tear off 8 break off, cut apart, cut in two, disjoint, dissolve, disunite, separate, set apart, shear off, slice off, uncouple 9 interrupt, partition, segregate, terminate 10 disconnect, dissociate, put an end to, put asunder
severable: 10 dissoluble
several: 4 a few, many, rare, some 6 divers, legion, plural 7 diverse, handful, special, various 8 assorted, distinct, numerous, separate, specific 9 different 10 infrequent, particular, respective, sprinkling
ender: 4 fold
more than ~: 4 a lot, lots, many
severance: 7 fission 9 defection, sundering 10 separation
severance ___: 3 pay, tax
Severance: 4 Joan
severe: 3 bad 4 dour, firm, grim, hard, sore 5 acute, bleak, bossy, cruel, exact, grave, harsh, heavy, hefty, nasty, picky, plain, rigid, rough, sharp, sober, stark, stern, stiff, tough 6 barren, biting, bitter, brutal, fierce, mortal, rugged, strict, strong, taxing, trying, wicked 7 arduous, ascetic, austere, caustic, cutting, drastic, extreme, intense, mordant, onerous, radical, serious, Spartan, violent, weighty 8 critical, despotic, exacting, grievous, grueling, hard-line, incisive, obdurate, pitiless, resolute, rigorous, scathing, terrible, terrific, toilsome 9 bare-bones, dangerous, demanding, difficult, draconian, hard-nosed, inclement, intensive, merciless, punishing, strenuous, stringent, unadorned, unbending, unfeeling, unsmiling, unsparing 10 astringent, despotical, forbidding, implacable, inexorable, inflexible, iron-fisted, iron-handed, iron-willed, no-nonsense, oppressive, relentless, tyrannical, unpleasant
more ~: 5 worse
severed: 4 torn 8 separate
Severed Head, A: 4 film 5 novel
author: Iris Murdoch
cast: Richard Attenborough, Ian Holm, Lee Remick
severely: 4 hard 5 badly 6 firmly 7 acutely, gravely, harshly, roughly, sharply, sternly 8 forcibly, markedly, strictly, urgently 9 extremely, intensely, painfully, seriously, viciously 10 critically, powerfully, rigorously
Severinsen: 3 Doc 4 Carl
Severinus: 4 pope 7 pontiff
severity: 5 rigor 6 degree 7 cruelty, gravity, tyranny 8 iron hand, violence 9 intensity 10 inclemency, oppression
Severn: 4 city, town 5 river 6 Darden
city on the ~: 9 Annapolis
feeder: 3 Usk
locale: 8 Maryland
River locale: 5 Wales 7 England
tributary: 3 Wye 4 Avon
Severna Park: 4 city, town
locale: 8 Maryland
Severo: 5 Ochoa
Severus: 5 Roman 6 Caesar
Sevigny: 5 Chloë
Sevilla: 4 city, town
locale: 5 Spain
Seville: 3 car 4 auto, city, port, town 5 David 6 citrus, orange 8 Cadillac
locale: 5 Spain
orange: 6 bitter
relative: 4 lime, Ugli 5 lemon, navel 6 pomelo, tangor 7 kumquat, satsuma, tangelo 8 bergamot, mandarin, shaddock, Valencia 9 tangerine 10 calamondin, grapefruit
worker: 6 barber, Figaro
Seville and the Chipmunks, David
Chipmunks: Alvin, Simon, Theodore
song: Alvin's Harmonica (1959)
The Chipmunk Song (1958)
Witch Doctor (1958)
Sevran: 4 city, town
locale: 6 France
Sèvres: 4 city, town 5 china
locale: 6 France
___-Sèvres: 4 Deux
Se vuol ballare: 4 aria
sew: 3 hem 4 bind, darn, mend, seam, tack 5 baste, patch, piece, quilt, run up 6 fasten, repair, stitch, suture 9 embroider
loosely: 4 tack 5 baste
on: 5 affix
up: 3 end, ice 5 close 6 assure, clinch, finish, stitch 8 complete, conclude, finalize, nail down, transact 10 accomplish, consummate, make sure of, monopolize
sewan: 4 peag 5 beads 6 wampum
Seward: 4 city, town 7 William
locale: 6 Alaska
purchase: 6 Alaska
Seward Peninsula
cape: 4 Nome
city: 4 Nome
locale: 6 Alaska
Seward's Folly: 6 Alaska
Sewell: 3 Joe, Rip 4 Anna 5 Rufus
sewer: 3 sty 4 pipe 5 drain 7 conduit, culvert 10 storm drain
org.: 5 ILGWU
___ sewer: 5 storm
sewing: 9 housework
kit item: 3 awl 5 spool 6 button, needle
machine attachment: 6 hemmer
machine part: 6 bobbin
sewing kit: 4 etui 5 etwee
stitch: 4 purl
trim: 5 inkle
sewing ___: 3 awl, kit 4 silk 5 table 6 circle, cotton, needle 7 machine
___ sewing: 5 Smyth
sex: 6 gender
appeal: 5 oomph
___ sex: 4 fair
Sexagesima ___: 6 Sunday
Sex and the City network: 3 HBO
Sex and the Single Girl (1964 film)
cast: Lauren Bacall, Tony Curtis, Henry Fonda, Natalie Wood
director: Richard Quine
sexes, for both: 4 coed
sex, lies, and videotape (1989 film)
cast: Peter Gallagher, Andie MacDowell, Laura San Giacomo, James Spader
director: Steven Soderbergh
sext: 4 hour
sextans: 4 coin 5 money
Sextans: 13 constellation
sextant successor: 5 loran
sextet: 4 band 8 ensemble
sextillion combining form: 5 zetta-
sextillionth combining form: 5 zepto-
sexto: 5 paper
sexton: 6 beadle
Sexton, Anne: 4 poet
work: Live or Die
Sexton III, Brendan: 5 actor
film: Boys Don't Cry (1999)
Desert Blue (1999)
Hurricane Streets (1998)
Sexy Eyes (1980 song) artist: Dr. Hook
sey: 4 fish
Seychelles: 4 isls. 5 isles 6 nation 7 country, islands
capital: 8 Victoria
island: 4 Mahé 7 La Digue, Praslin
money: 4 cent 5 rupee
Seyhan: 5 river
locale: 6 Turkey
Seymour: 4 Alan, Anne, Cray, Jane 6 Cassel
Seymour, Alan: 10 Australian, playwright
work: The One Day of the Year
___ Seymour Hoffman: 6 Philip
Seymour, Jane: 7 actress
film: Live and Let Die (1973)
Somewhere in Time (1980)
TV: Dr. Quinn, Medicine Woman
Sez who?: 6 oh yeah
S.F.
see San Francisco
Sfax: 4 city, town
locale: 7 Tunisia
SFC: 3 NCO
SFO: 7 airport
SFX, part of: 7 effects, special
___ S. Gilbert: 7 William
___ S. Grant: 7 Ulysses
sgt.
see sergeant
___ sgt.: 4 tech.
Sgt. Bilko (1996 film)
cast: Dan Aykroyd, Phil Hartman, Steve Martin
director: Jonathan Lynn
Sha ___: 4 La La, Na Na
___ Shabbat: 4 Oneg
shabby: 3 sad 4 bare, drab, junk, mean, poor, punk, torn, worn 5 cheap, dingy, dinky, dowdy, faded, mangy, petty, ratty, seamy, seedy, shady, sorry, tacky, tatty, tired 6 crumby, crummy, frayed, frowsy, frowzy, frumpy, humble, mangey, meager, paltry, ragged, rotten, ruined, scummy, shoddy, sleazy, sordid, stingy, unjust, unkind, unneat 7 chintzy, decayed, ignoble, low-down, miserly, pitiful, rickety, ruinous, run-down, scruffy, squalid, unkempt, worn-out 8 beggarly, decaying, decrepit, desolate, shameful, slipshod, tattered, timeworn, untended, unworthy, wretched 9 miserable, moth-eaten, neglected, ungroomed 10 bedraggled, broken-down, despicable, ramshackle, threadbare, undeserved
dresser: 5 frump
shabby-___: 7 genteel
shack: 3 hut 4 shed 5 abode, bower, cabin, house, hovel, hutch, lodge 6 lean-to, shanty 7 cottage, shelter
like a ~: 5 crude
___ Shack: 4 Love 5 Radio, Sugar
Shackelford: 3 Ted
shackle: 3 tie 4 band, bind, bond, cuff, gyve, iron, yoke 5 chain, cramp, tie up 6 fetter, hamper, hogtie, pinion 7 enchain, manacle 8 enfetter, handcuff 9 hamstring 10 impediment
site: 5 ankle
starter: 3 ram
shackles: 8 trammels 9 bracelets
Shackleton, Ernest: 3 Sir 7 British 8 explorer
Shack Out on 101 (1955 film)
cast: Frank Lovejoy, Lee Marvin, Terry Moore
director: Edward Dein
shad: 4 fish 7 herring
ender: 3 fly 4 blow, bush 5 berry
product: 3 roe
shaddock: 5 fruit 6 citrus, pomelo
relative: 4 lime, Ugli 5 lemon, navel

6 orange, tangor **7** kumquat, satsuma, Seville, tangelo **8** bergamot, mandarin, Valencia **9** tangerine **10** calamondin, grapefruit
shade: 3 dim, hue **4** cast, dash, hide, hint, mask, tint, tone, veil **5** bedim, blind, bogey, color, cover, ghost, gloom, haunt, stain, tinct, tinge, touch, trace, umbra **6** amount, awning, breath, canopy, darken, deepen, degree, fantom, nuance, screen, shield, spirit, trifle, wraith **7** becloud, blacken, conceal, cover up, curtain, dimness, fantasm, obscure, phantom, protect, shelter, shutter, specter, umbrage **8** coolness, covering, darkness, disguise, penumbra, phantasm, presence, tone down **9** adumbrate, gradation, obscurity, suspicion, variation **10** apparition, camouflage, gloominess, suggestion
starter: 3 eye, sun **4** lamp **5** night
see also color
shade __: 4 deck, tree **5** cloth
shade-__: 5 grown
__ shade: 5 Roman, sleep **6** window **7** balloon
__ Shade: 7 Evening
shaded: 5 leafy
Shade of Difference, A author: Allen Drury
__ Shade of Pale, A: 6 Whiter
__ Shade of Winter: 5 A Hazy
shader: 4 tree
shades: 7 glasses **10** sunglasses
reason for ~: 5 glare
shadiness: 8 venality **10** corruption, illegality
shading: 4 tint **6** nuance
mark with ~: 5 hatch
shadow: 3 dim, dog, spy, tag **4** dark, dusk, gray, grey, haze, hint, kohl, pall, soul, tail, veil **5** bedim, cloud, cover, gloom, relic, shred, spare, spy on, stalk, tinge, touch, trace, trail, umbra, watch **6** darken, fantom, makeup, pursue, screen, shield, spirit **7** becloud, dimness, eclipse, epigone, minimum, obscure, phantom, shelter, specter, umbrage, vestige, whisper **8** darkness, imitator, overcast, penumbra, presence, run after **9** accompany, adumbrate, obscurity, suspicion, track down **10** intimation, reflection, silhouette, suggestion
astronomical ~: 5 umbra
beyond the ~ of a doubt: 6 surely
cast a ~: 8 overhang
combining form: 3 sci- **4** scia-, scio-, skia-
eliminator: 5 razor
ender: 3 box **5** graph
eye ~: 4 kohl **5** liner **6** makeup
five o'clock ~: 5 beard **7** stubble
locale: 3 lid **6** eyelid
shadow __: 3 pin **4** mask, play, roll, show **5** dance **7** cabinet, theater, theatre
shadow __ frame: 3 box
__ shadow: 3 eye **4** rain
Shadow: 3 car **4** auto **5** Dodge
Shadow __, The: 5 Flies, knows
Shadow and Act author: Ralph Ellison
Shadow–A Parable author: Edgar Allan Poe
shadowbox: 4 spar
Shadowboxer singer: 5 Apple
Shadow Dancing (1978 song) artist: Andy Gibb
Shadowfires author: Dean Koontz
Shadow Flies, The author: Rose Macaulay
shadowing: 7 eclipse
Shadowlands (1993 film)
cast: Anthony Hopkins, Debra Winger
director: Richard Attenborough
Shadowland singer: 4 Lang
Shadow of a Doubt (1943 film)
cast: Macdonald Carey, Joseph Cotten, Teresa Wright
director: Alfred Hitchcock
Shadow of a Sun, The author: A.S. Byatt
Shadow of the Thin Man (1941 film)
cast: Myrna Loy, Barry Nelson, William Powell
director: W.S. Van Dyke
Shadow of the Vampire (2000 film)
cast: Willem Dafoe, Cary Elwes, John Malkovich
director: E. Elias Merhige
shadow of Virtue, The: 4 fame
Shadow on the Trail author: Zane Grey
Shadow on the Wall (1950 film)
cast: Nancy Davis, Zachary Scott, Ann Sothern
__ Shadows: 4 Dark
Shadows and Fog (1992 film)
cast: Woody Allen, Kathy Bates, John Cusack, Mia Farrow
director: Woody Allen
Shadows on the Rock author: Willa Cather
shadows, remain in the: 4 lurk
Shadow, The: 9 radio show
garment: 4 cape
nemesis: 4 evil
Shadow, The (1994 film)
cast: Alec Baldwin, Peter Boyle, John Lone, Penelope Ann Miller
director: Russell Mulcahy
shadowy: 3 dim **4** dark, hazy **5** black, dusky, faded, fuzzy, mirky, murky, muted, vague **6** bleary, blurry, gloomy, hidden, ill-lit, somber **8** nebulous **9** hard to see, lightless, tenebrous, unlighted **10** indistinct
Shadrach (1998 film)
cast: Monica Bugajski, Harvey Keitel, Andie MacDowell, John Franklin Sawyer
director: Susanna Styron
Shadwell, Thomas: 4 poet **7** British
shady: 3 dim **4** dark, foul **5** dusky, leafy, queer, vague, wrong **6** cloudy, louche, shabby, shifty, shoddy, somber, tricky **7** corrupt, covered, crooked, devious, dubious, illegal, suspect **8** arboreal, darkened, infamous, off-color, screened, shameful, slippery, unsavory **9** dishonest, notorious, sheltered, tree-lined, underhand, unethical **10** fly-by-night, inglorious, prohibited, scandalous, suspicious, umbrageous
deal: 5 cheat **6** con job **10** corruption
place: 5 arbor, bower, grove **6** gazebo
walk: 4 mall
Shadyac, Tom: 8 director
film: Ace Ventura: Pet Detective (1994)
Dragonfly (2002)
Liar Liar (1997)
The Nutty Professor (1996)
Patch Adams (1998)
Shady Business, A author: Honoré de Balzac
SHAEF
commander: 3 DDE
sector: 3 ETO
Shaffer: 4 Paul **5** Peter **7** Anthony
Shaffer, Anthony spouse: Diane Cilento
Shaffer, Peter: 7 British **10** playwright
work: Amadeus
Black Comedy
Equus
Five Finger Exercise
The Royal Hunt of the Sun
shaft: 3 bar, pit, ray, rod **4** axis, axle, beam, duct, dupe, mine, pole, post, well **5** cheat, pylon, stalk **6** column, fleece, pillar, tongue, tunnel **7** defraud, javelin, mislead, passage, swindle, two-time, upright **8** flimflam **10** passageway, run a game on
air ~: 6 intake
auto: 3 cam **4** axle
column ~: 5 scape
combining form: 5 scapi-
end of a ~: 4 adit
feathered ~: 5 arrow
groove: 6 keyway
light ~: 3 ray **4** beam **7** sunbeam **8** moonbeam
mine ~: 3 pit **5** winze
starter: 3 cam **4** jack, mine, rock **5** crank, drive **7** counter
worker: 5 miner
__ shaft: 3 air **4** back, butt, main, wind **5** drive **7** balance, midwall
Shaft (1971 film)
cast: Charles Cioffi, Moses Gunn, Richard Roundtree
director: Gordon Parks
Shaft (2000 film)
cast: Christian Bale, Samuel L. Jackson, Jeffrey White, Vanessa Williams
director: John Singleton
Shaft in Africa (1973 film)
cast: Frank Finlay, Vonetta McGee, Richard Roundtree
director: John Guillermin
Shaft's Big Score! (1972 film)
cast: Moses Gunn, Richard Roundtree
director: Gordon Parks
Shaft Theme (1971 song) artist: Isaac Hayes
shag: 3 nap, rug, run, rya **4** bird, pile **5** chase, dance **6** carpet, hairdo
cousin: 3 bob
ender: 4 bark
shagbark: 3 nut **4** tree **7** hickory
shaggy: 5 bushy, furry, hairy, nappy, rough **6** pilose, pilous, ragged, rugged, unneat **7** hirsute, ruffled, unkempt, unshorn **8** uncombed **10** long-haired
animal: 3 yak **4** bear **5** bison, bruin
blossom: 6 dahlia
coat: 4 hair
combining form: 4 dasy-
__ Shaggybreeches: 6 Ragnar
shaggy cap: 8 mushroom
Shaggy D. A., The (1976 film)
cast: Tim Conway, Dean Jones, Suzanne Pleshette
director: Robert Stevenson
shaggy-dog
story: 4 joke
unlike a ~ story: 5 short
Shaggy Dog, The (1959 film)
cast: Annette Funicello, Jean Hagen, Tommy Kirk, Fred MacMurray
director: Charles Barton
dog: 7 Chiffon
shaggymane: 8 mushroom
shagreen: 7 leather
Shah: 5 exile, Jahan, Jehan, ruler, title **6** gerent **7** Krishna, monarch
land: 4 Iran
language: 5 Farsi
name: 4 Reza
Shah Jahan
building site: 4 Agra
wife: 5 Mahal
Shahn, Ben: 6 artist **7** painter
Shaka __: 4 Zulu
shake: 3 jar, jog, wag **4** bump, flap, flit, foil, jerk, jolt, lose, move, reel, rock, sway, tick, toss, wake, wave, whip, wink **5** alarm, avoid, churn, cower, dance, daunt, dodge, drink, elude, greet, quail, quake, swing, upset, waken, worry **6** bother, dismay, dither, dodder, frappe, jiggle, joggle, jostle, jounce, justle, minute, quaver, quiver, rattle, recess, recoil, ruffle, second, shimmy, shiver, stir up, totter, tremor, unglue, wabble, waggle, weaken, wobble **7** agitate, chatter, disturb, flicker, flitter, fluster, flutter, horrify, perturb, shimmer, shudder, stagger, startle, tremble, unnerve, vibrate **8** brandish, convulse, disquiet, distress, frighten, get out of, sprinkle, throw off, unsettle, unstring **9** discomfit, fluctuate, make waves, oscillate, palpitate, take aback **10** demoralize, discompose, disconcert, earthquake, intimidate
a fist at: 8 threaten
a leg: 3 fly, hie, rip, run, zip **4** dart, dash, flit, move, race, rush, stir, tear, zoom **5** hurry, scoot, speed **6** barrel, boogie, gallop, hasten, hustle, move it, rocket, scurry **7** floor it, hop to it, quicken, scamper, speed up **8** step on it **9** hotfoot it, skedaddle **10** burn rubber, get a move on, get hopping, hightail it
down: 4 bilk, test **5** bleed, bully, frisk **6** coerce, extort, lean on **7** ransack, squeeze **9** blackmail **10** experiment, run a game on
ender: 3 out **4** down
fair ~: 6 chance
hands: 6 make up
hands on: 4 seal **5** agree, close **6** clinch, settle **7** confirm **8** finalize
hands with: 4 meet **5** greet
ingredient: 4 milk
in prescriptions: 4 agit.
off: 3 rid **4** drop, foil, lose, shun **5** avoid, clear, dodge, elude, evade, outdo, repel **6** remove **7** discard **8** dislodge, get rid of, unburden **10** escape from, knock loose
starter: 4 hand, head
up: 3 jar, mix, rid **4** faze, jolt, stun **5** addle, alarm, churn, purge, roust, scare, shock, upset **6** rattle, remove, ruffle **7** agitate, disturb, perturb, startle, stupefy, trouble, unnerve **8** bewilder, clean out, clear out, convulse, disquiet, distress, mistreat, overturn, surprise, unsettle **10** disconcert, reorganize
violently: 5 upset **6** quiver **7** agitate, disturb **8** unsettle **10** discompose
shake __: 3 off **4** a leg, down **5** hands
__ shake: 3 cup **4** fair, milk, salt, wind **6** square
Shake __: 4 It Up **5** 'N Bake
Shake __ Down: 3 You
Shake (1965 song) artist: Sam Cooke
shake a __: 3 leg
shake a __ at: 5 stick
shakedown: 6 racket, search **7** jobbery, swindle **8** practice **9** blackmail, extortion, rehearsal **10** experiment
shakedown __: 6 cruise, flight
Shakedown (1988 film)
cast: Patricia Charbonneau, Sam Elliott, Peter Weller
Shakedown (1987 song) artist: Bob Seger
Shake Hands With the Devil (1959 film)
cast: James Cagney, Don Murray, Dana Wynter
director: Michael Anderson
Shake It Up (1981 song) artist: Cars
shake like __: 5 a leaf
shaken: 5 fazed **6** addled, scared, uneasy **8** unstrung **9** unsettled
it may be ~: 3 leg **4** fist

__-shaken: 4 wind
shake one's __: 4 head
shakeout: 8 upheaval 9 recession
shaker: 3 VIP 6 afuché, cabasa, dynamo 8 chocalho
contents: 4 NaCl, salt
mover and ~: 4 doer 5 mogul 6 leader
__ shaker: 4 bone, salt 6 pepper
__-shaker: 5 world
Shaker __: 3 Hts.
Shake, Rattle and Roll (1954 song) artist: Bill Haley and His Comets
Shaker Heights: 4 city, town
locale: 4 Ohio
Shakers: 4 sect
Shaker, Why Don't You Sing author: Maya Angelou
shakes: 7 jitters, tension, willies
have the ~: 6 shiver
in two ~ of a lamb's tail: 3 now 4 anon, soon 6 at once, in a sec, pronto 7 hastily, quickly, rapidly, shortly 8 directly, promptly, right now, speedily 9 forthwith, in a minute, in a second, right away 10 this moment
no great ~: 4 so-so 8 mediocre, ordinary
two ~ of a lamb's tail: 3 sec 4 jiff 5 jiffy, trice
Shakespearean __: 6 sonnet
Shakespeare in Love (1998 film)
cast: Dame Judi Dench, Joseph Fiennes, Gwyneth Paltrow, Geoffrey Rush
director: John Madden
Shakespeare, William: 4 bard, poet 7 British 10 playwright
adverb: 4 anon
contemporary: 5 Bacon
cry: 3 fie
device: 5 aside
edition: 5 Folio
forest: 5 Arden
forte: 5 drama
king: 4 Lear
muse: 5 Erato
plaint: 4 alas
prince: 3 Hal
product: 4 play
river: 4 Avon
segment: 3 act 5 scene
shrew: 4 Kate
sprite: 5 Ariel
suffix: 3 est, eth
teen: 5 Romeo 6 Juliet
theatre: 5 Globe
verb: 4 hast, hath 5 seest
very foolish fond old man: 4 Lear
villain: 4 Iago
wife: 4 Anne
work: All's Well That Ends Well
Antony and Cleopatra
As You Like It
The Comedy of Errors
Coriolanus
Cymbeline
Hamlet
Henry IV
Henry V
Henry VI
Julius Caesar
King John
King Lear
Love's Labour's Lost
Macbeth
Measure for Measure
The Merchant of Venice
The Merry Wives of Windsor
A Midsummer Night's Dream
Much Ado About Nothing
Othello
Pericles
Richard II
Richard III
Romeo and Juliet
The Taming of the Shrew
The Tempest
Timon of Athens
Titus Andronicus
Troilus and Cressida
Twelfth Night
Two Gentlemen of Verona
The Winter's Tale
shake-up: 5 purge, upset 10 revolution
Shake Your Body (1979 song) artist: Jackson 5
Shake Your Booty (1976 song) artist: KC and the Sunshine Band
Shake Your Groove Thing (1979 song) artist: Peaches and Herb
Shake Your Love (1987 song) artist: Debbie Gibson
Shakiest __ in the West, The: 3 Gun
shaking: 9 tremulous, vibration
hands: 6 custom, ritual 9 formality 10 convention
starter: 5 earth
shako: 3 hat 8 headgear
feature: 5 plume
Shakopee: 4 city, town
locale: 9 Minnesota
Shakur: 5 Tupac
shaky: 4 weak 5 dizzy, jumpy, rocky, tense, timid 6 aquake, flimsy, infirm, jiggly, uneasy, unfirm, unsafe, unsure, wabbly, wobbly 7 aquiver, dubious, jittery, nervous, quaking, reeling, rickety, suspect, tenuous, unclear, unsound 8 doubtful, insecure, perilous, rattling, rootless, unstable, unsteady, wavering, yielding 9 dangerous, faltering, jellylike, quivering, spasmodic, squeamish, teetering, tentative, tottering, trembling, tremorous, tremulous, uncertain, unsettled 10 frightened, indecisive, precarious, ramshackle, suspicious, unbalanced, unreliable, up in the air
Shalala: 5 Donna
Sha La La (song) artist: Al Green, Manfred Mann
shale: 7 mineral
product: 3 oil
rock formed from ~: 5 slate
Shaler: 4 city, town
locale: 4 Penn.
Shalhoub, Tony: 5 actor
film: A Civil Action (1998)
Galaxy Quest (1999)
Life or Something Like It (2002)
Paulie (1998)
The Siege (1998)
Shalimar Gardens locale: 6 Lahore
Shalit, Gene: 6 critic
shall: 4 will 6 plan to 8 intend to
ender: 4 owed 5 owing
__ Shall Be No Night: 5 There
...__ shall die: 3 or I
__ Shall Escape: 4 None
__ Shall Have Music: 4 They
Shall I compare thee to a summer's day?: 4 poem 6 sonnet
author: Shakespeare
...shall not __ from the earth: 6 perish
shalloon: 6 fabric 8 material
shallot: 5 onion 6 allium, veggie 9 vegetable
kin: 4 leek 6 garlic
shallow: 3 low 4 dull, flat, vain, weak 5 inane, petty, shelf, shoal 6 flimsy, narrow, paltry, simple, slight 7 cursory, sketchy, surface, trivial, unsound, vacuous 8 ignorant, piddling, skin-deep, trifling 9 frivolous, half-baked 10 nonserious, uncritical, unprofound, unthinking
Shall we? answer: 4 Let's
Shall We Dance (1937 film): 7 musical
cast: Fred Astaire, Eric Blore, Ginger Rogers
director: Mark Sandrich
music: George and Ira Gershwin
Shall We Dance? composer: 7 Rodgers 11 Hammerstein
__-shally: 6 shilly
shalom: 5 hello, peace 6 Hebrew 7 goodbye 8 greeting
Shalom: 6 Harlow 8 Aleichem
shalwar: 5 pants
sham: 3 act, ape, lie 4 cant, copy, fake, hoax, jive, mock, pose, ruse, sell, show 5 bluff, bogus, cheat, dummy, false, farce, feign, feint, fraud, lying, phony, put on, quack, quasi, shuck, spoof, trick 6 deceit, dupery, ersatz, facade, fake it, fakery, forged, humbug, phoney, pseudo, sucker, unreal, untrue 7 assumed, cover-up, falsity, feigned, forgery, imitate, mislead, mockery, pretend, snow job, swindle 8 artifice, flimflam, imposter, impostor, pretense, simulate, so-called, spurious, travesty 9 charlatan, contrived, deception, falsehood, hypocrisy, imitation, imposture, insincere, invention, mare's nest, phoniness, pretended, simulated, synthetic, ungenuine 10 artificial, caricature, fabricated, factitious, false front, fictitious, fraudulent, misleading, mountebank, play possum, substitute, subterfuge
__ sham: 6 pillow
Sham: 4 star
__ Sham: 6 Sam the
shama: 4 bird
Shamah, grandfather of: 4 Esau
shaman: 5 druid 6 cleric, healer, priest, wizard 7 prophet
find: 4 omen
specialty: 5 spell
wisdom: 4 lore
Shambala (1973 song) artist: Three Dog Night
shamble: 4 poke, ruin, walk 6 loiter, lumber 7 shuffle
shambles: 4 mess 5 babel, botch, chaos, havoc, mix-up, wreck 6 bedlam, mess-up, muddle 7 anarchy, clutter 8 disarray, disorder, madhouse 9 confusion, maelstrom 10 hodgepodge
shame: 3 fie 4 blot, pang, pity, soil 5 abase, abash, guilt, odium, smear, stain 6 debase, defile, humble, infamy, show up, stigma 7 chagrin, decency, degrade, emotion, modesty, mortify, put down, remorse, scandal 8 calamity, contempt, derision, disfavor, disgrace, dishonor, ignominy, reproach, ridicule, take down 9 abashment, discredit, disrepute, embarrass, frown upon, humiliate, penitence, shoot down 10 contrition, disconcert, disgruntle, opprobrium, stigmatize
ender: 5 faced
feel ~ over: 3 rue
put to ~: 4 beat, best 5 abase, outdo 6 exceed, humble, show up 7 eclipse, mortify, surpass 8 outclass, outshine, outstrip 9 humiliate 10 overshadow, tower above
Shame (1968 film)
cast: Gunnar Bjornstrand, Liv Ullmann, Max von Sydow
director: Ingmar Bergman
Shame __!: 5 on you
Shame!: 3 fie, tsk, tut 6 tsk tsk, tut-tut
__ Shame: 4 It's a
shamed: 5 sorry 6 fallen 7 abashed 8 penitent
be ~: 8 lose face
shamefaced: 3 shy 5 sorry 8 sheepish
shameful: 4 base, foul, grim, lewd, poor, vile 5 awful, gross, lousy, nasty, seamy, shady, sorry, woful, wrong 6 crumby, crummy, dismal, horrid, impure, odious, ribald, rotten, shabby, shoddy, sordid, vulgar, wicked, woeful 7 accurst, baleful, baneful, beastly, corrupt, doleful, ghastly, heinous, ignoble, immoral, obscene, unclean 8 accursed, degraded, dreadful, flagrant, God-awful, grievous, horrible, immodest, indecent, infamous, inferior, shocking, stinking, terrible, unworthy, wretched 9 abhorrent, appalling, atrocious, dastardly, defective, degrading, execrable, frightful, insidious, loathsome, miserable, nefarious, notorious, offensive, reprobate, revolting 10 abominable, deplorable, despicable, detestable, diabolical, disastrous, horrendous, inglorious, mortifying, outrageous, profligate, scandalous, unbecoming, villainous
shameless: 4 bold, lewd, mean, open, rude 5 brash, saucy, tacky 6 arrant, brassy, brazen, cheeky, wanton, wicked 7 blatant, corrupt, forward, immoral 8 depraved, flagrant, immodest, improper, impudent, indecent, insolent, unchaste 9 abandoned, audacious, barefaced, dissolute, graceless, reprobate, unabashed 10 disgusting, outrageous, profligate, scurrilous, unblushing
be ~: 6 flaunt
Shame on the Moon (1982 song) artist: Bob Seger
shames: 6 candle
Shamir, Yitzhak: 2 P.M. 7 Israeli
predecessor: 5 Begin, Peres
successor: 5 Peres, Rabin
shammes: 6 candle
shampoo: 4 Flex, lave, Pert, wash 5 Breck, clean, Prell, Suave, Wella 7 Finesse, Pantene
additive: 4 aloe 6 balsam
bottle word: 5 rinse
feature: 6 lather
measure: 2 pH
oil: 6 jojoba
Shampoo (1975 film)
cast: Warren Beatty, Julie Christie, Carrie Fisher, Lee Grant, Goldie Hawn
director: Hal Ashby
screenwriter: 5 Towne
shampoos, like some: 5 low pH
__ Shamra, Syria: 3 Ras
shamrock: 6 clover
isle: 4 Eire, Erin 7 Ireland
Shamsky: 3 Art
shams, pillow: 5 linen
Shamu: 4 orca
shamus: 2 PI 3 cop, tec 4 narc, nark 5 agent, snoop 6 sleuth 7 gumshoe, officer 9 constable, detective, operative 10 bloodhound, private eye
Shamus (1973 film)
cast: Dyan Cannon, Burt Reynolds, Giorgio Tozzi
director: Buzz Kulik
Shan: 8 language
__ Shan: 3 Tai 4 Tien 6 Qilian
Shana: 9 Alexander
in English: 4 Jane
Sha Na Na
number: 4 oldy 5 oldie
Shandling: 5 Garry
Shandong city: 4 Zibo 5 Tzepo, Tzupo
shandy: 5 drink 8 beverage
ingredient: 4 beer 8 lemonade
shandygaff: 5 drink 8 beverage
ingredient: 4 beer 10 ginger beer
Shane: 5 Gould 7 Maxwell 8 MacGowan

in English: 4 John
Shane (1953 film): 5 oater 7 western
cast: Jean Arthur, Brandon de Wilde, Van Heflin, Alan Ladd, Jack Palance
director: George Stevens
Shang Dynasty center: 6 Anyang
shanghai: 4 levy 5 draft, force 6 abduct, enlist, induct, kidnap 7 impress, recruit, soldier, warrior 8 inductee 9 conscript 10 commandeer
Shanghai: 4 city, fowl, port, town 7 chicken
locale: 5 China
relative: 6 Bantam, Brahma, Houdan, Sussex 7 Cornish, Dorking, Leghorn 8 Araucana, Langshan 9 Dominique, Orpington, Wyandotte
river: 7 Huangpu
Shanghai __: 4 Noon 7 Express
Shanghai Express (1932 film)
cast: Marlene Dietrich, Warner Oland, Anna May Wong
director: Josef von Sternberg
Shanghai Noon (2000 film)
cast: Jackie Chan, Lucy Liu, Brandon Merrill, Owen Wilson
director: Tom Dey
Shangri-la: 4 Eden 6 heaven, utopia 7 Elysium 8 paradise
cleric: 4 lama
creator: 6 Hilton
locale: 4 Asia 5 Tibet 6 Thibet, Xizang 7 Sitsang
Shangri-las
hometown: Queens
song: I Can Never Go Home Anymore (1965)
Leader of the Pack (1964)
Remember (Walkin' in the Sand) (1964)
Shani: 6 Wallis
Shania: 5 Twain
shank: 3 gam, leg 4 crus, meat, shin, stab
of the ~: 6 crural
__ shank: 4 hind 5 black
Shankar, Ravi: 6 Indian 8 sitarist
genre: 4 raga
instrument: 5 sitar
shanks'
by ~ mare: 5 afoot
go by ~ mare: 4 slog, walk 5 leg it, march 6 foot it, hoof it, trudge
Shanna: 4 Reed
Shannen: 7 Doherty
Shannon: 3 Del 4 city, font, town 5 river, Tweed 6 Miller 8 typeface 9 Elizabeth
locale: 4 Eire, Erin 7 Ireland
Shannon (1976 song) artist: Henry Gross
Shannon, Del
song: Hats Off to Larry (1961)
Keep Searchin' (We'll Follow the Sun) (1964)
Runaway (1961)
Shannon's __: 3 Way
__ Shan Range: 3 Nan
__-shanter: 4 tam-o'
shantung: 6 fabric 8 material
like ~: 5 nubby
shanty: 3 hut 4 dump, shed, song 5 cabin, house, hovel, lodge, shack 6 lean-to 7 cottage
Shanxi: 8 province
locale: 5 China
town: 6 Datong
shape: 3 fit, hew, pat 4 bend, body, case, cast, form, grow, look, make, mint, mold, oval, pear, plan, trim, turn, work 5 adapt, build, carve, forge, frame, guide, guise, knead, model, prune, rhomb, stamp, state, thing 6 beetle, chisel, circle, create, define, devise, embody, fantom, fettle, figure, format, health, imbody, modify, sculpt, sketch, square, tailor, work up 7 chassis, contour, develop, fashion, fitness, octagon, outline, pattern, phantom, prepare, produce, profile, remodel, rhombus, whittle 8 assemble, block out, jaundice, octangle, pentagon, physique, regulate, roughhew, symmetry, take form, triangle 9 condition, construct, curvature, fabricate, lineament, lineation, sculpture, semblance, structure, trapezoid 10 appearance, embodiment, manipulate, silhouette, streamline
beat into ~: 5 forge
bend out of ~: 4 warp
bent out of ~: 5 irate, upset 6 raging 7 furious
get in ~: 3 jog 4 hone, sort, tidy, tone 5 train 7 arrange, rebound, recover, work out 8 exercise, organize
give ~: 4 cast, form, mold 5 forge, model 6 design, sculpt 7 fashion, whittle
in bad ~: 4 soft 5 ratty, unfit 6 bad off, shabby, shoddy 7 pitiful, run-down 8 untended
in good ~: 3 fit 4 able, buff, hale, lean, neat, tidy, trim 5 hardy, ready, sound 6 robust, strong 7 healthy, orderly
lick into ~: 5 coach, groom 8 organize
out of ~: 4 bent, soft 5 rusty, stiff, unfit 6 flabby, sickly 7 untoned 8 lopsided 9 enervated, unhealthy
put in good ~: 5 fix up 6 neaten 10 straighten
starter: 4 ship
take ~: 3 gel 4 form, jell, loom
up: 3 fix 4 form, tidy 5 groom, rally 6 better, enrich, evolve, polish, reform 7 correct, develop, enhance, improve, rectify, sharpen, upgrade 8 progress, regulate 9 come along, condition, go forward, meliorate 10 ameliorate, go straight
__ shape: 4 take
shapeable: 7 plastic 8 formable
shaped combining form: 4 -form 7 -morphic 8 -morphous
__-shaped curve: 4 bell
__-Shaped Room: 4 The L
__-shaped tone: 4 pear
shapeless: 3 lax 5 baggy, vague 8 abnormal, amorphic, deformed, formless, nebulous, unformed 9 amorphous, anomalous, irregular, malformed 10 indefinite, indistinct
mass: 4 blob, glob
Shape Of My Heart (2000 song) artist: Backstreet Boys
SHAPE, org. that includes: 4 NATO
shaper: 4 adze, file, mold 5 swage
Shapes of Things (1966 song) artist: Yardbirds
Shape up or __ out!: 4 ship
Shaphat, son of: 6 Elisha
shaping: 10 adjustment
tool: 3 die 4 adze 5 gouge, lathe 6 chisel
Shapiro: 4 Karl 5 Artie
Shapiro, Karl: 4 poet 6 critic
work: Person, place, and Thing
The Place of Love
Trial of a Poet
V-Letter and Other Poems
shapu: 5 sheep
relative: 4 geep 5 argal 6 aoudad, argali, bharal, merino 7 bighorn, burrhel, mouflon 8 cimarron, moufflon
Shaq: 5 O'Neal
Shar-__: 3 Pei
shard: 3 bit 4 chip 5 piece, scrap 7 remnant 8 fragment, potsherd
starter: 3 pot
shards: 5 chaff, trash 6 debris 7 remains, rubbish
share: 3 cut, due, lot 4 bite, deal, dose, lend, mete, part, pool, take, wage 5 allot, chunk, claim, cut in, divvy, piece, quota, slice, split, stake, taste, wages, yield 6 assign, bestow, divide, parcel, ration 7 divvy up, dole out, give out, go Dutch, helping, measure, mete out, partake, percent, portion, prorate, section, segment, serving, split up 8 dispense, dividend, division, fraction, fragment, go in with, interest, kickback, pittance, quotient 9 allotment, allowance, apportion, parcel out, partake of, partition 10 allocation, commission, distribute, experience, percentage, proportion, take part in
a side with: 4 abut
a view: 5 agree, match 6 accord, concur 7 conform 9 harmonize 10 go together
biggest ~: 4 bulk
billing: 6 costar
don't ~: 3 hog 10 monopolize
earning: 8 dividend
ender: 4 crop 5 owner 6 holder
fair ~: 4 half
fifty-fifty: 5 halve
ideas: 10 brainstorm
lion's ~: 3 all 4 bulk, mass, most 8 majority
one unlikely to ~: 3 pig
proportional ~: 5 quota
starter: 4 plow, ride
the load: 4 ease, help 6 assist, join in 7 pitch in, relieve 9 cooperate, lend a hand 10 see through
share __: 5 draft 7 account
__ share: 4 book 5 lion's 6 market
__-share: 4 cost, time
sharecrop: 4 farm
sharecropper beast: 4 mule
shared: 5 joint 6 common, mutual, public 8 communal, requited 9 corporate, unanimous 10 collective, reciprocal
feeling: 5 unity 7 empathy, rapport 8 affinity, sympathy
resource: 4 pool
shareholder: 5 owner 8 investor
__ Sharer, The: 6 Secret
sharer word: 3 our 4 ours
shares: 5 slice, stock
how some ~ sell: 5 at par
Share the Land (1970 song) artist: Guess Who
Sharett, Moshe: 2 P.M. 7 Israeli
predecessor: 9 Ben-Gurion
successor: 9 Ben-Gurion
Shari: 5 Lewis, river 9 Belafonte
locale: 6 Africa
Sharif, Omar: 5 actor
film: Doctor Zhivago (1965)
Funny Girl (1968)
Lawrence of Arabia (1962)
The Tamarind Seed (1974)
__ sharing: 3 tax 6 profit 7 revenue
__-sharing: 3 job 4 code, time
Sharing the Night Together (1978 song) artist: Dr. Hook
shark: 4 fish, mako, tope 5 cheat, crook, fraud, knave, nurse 6 con man, usurer, wizard 7 cheater, dogfish, grifter, hustler, sharper, sharpie 8 chiseler, predator, swindler 10 hammerhead
ender: 4 skin
environment: 3 sea 5 ocean
feature: 3 fin
flick: 4 Jaws
Hawaiian ~: 4 mano
loan ~: 5 leech 6 lender, usurer 7 Shylock
nurse ~: 4 gata
__ shark: 3 cow, cub 4 blue, bull, card, loan, mako, pool, sand 5 angel, dusky, lemon, nurse, tiger, whale, white 6 bonnet, carpet, ground 7 basking, leopard, requiem, soupfin
Sharkey: 3 Ray
__ Sharkey: 3 C.P.O.
Shark rival: 4 Blue, King, Star, Wild 5 Bruin, Devil, Flame, Flyer, Oiler, Sabre 6 Canuck, Coyote, Ranger 7 Capital, Panther, Penguin, Red Wing, Senator 8 Canadien, Islander, Predator, Thrasher 9 Avalanche, Blackhawk, Hurricane, Lightning, Maple Leaf 10 Blue Jacket, Mighty Duck
Sharks: 3 six 4 gang, team
home: 7 San Jose
milieu: 3 ice 4 rink
org.: 3 NHL
sport: 6 hockey
shark's fin: 4 soup
sharkskin: 6 fabric 8 material
Shark Trouble author: Peter Benchley
Sharm al-__: 6 Sheikh
Sharman, Bill: 5 cager
Sharon: 4 Leal, Tate 5 Ariel, Gless, Stone 7 Farrell 8 Lawrence
rose of ~: 6 althea
Sharon, Ariel: 2 P.M. 7 Israeli
predecessor: 5 Barak
sharp: 3 apt, hot, sly 4 able, acid, chic, cold, curt, fast, fine, foxy, keen, rude, sore, sour, tart, wily, wise 5 acerb, acrid, acute, adept, alert, angry, brisk, class, clean, clear, crisp, edged, fresh, harsh, honed, natty, nifty, onery, quick, ready, ritzy, savvy, short, slick, smart, snaky, spiky, spiny, steep, stiff, swank, tined, vivid, windy 6 abrupt, acidic, acuate, adroit, apical, artful, astute, barbed, biting, bitter, brainy, briery, bright, classy, clever, crafty, dapper, dressy, expert, fierce, jagged, keenly, lively, marked, nimble, on time, ornery, peaked, pointy, rancid, severe, shrewd, shrill, snappy, spiked, square, strong, sudden, swanky, thorny, trendy, tricky 7 acerbic, acutely, austere, caustic, cunning, cutting, dashing, exactly, extreme, hurtful, in focus, in style, intense, knowing, learned, legible, odorous, peppery, piquant, pointed, politic, prickly, pungent, raucous, salient, stylish, tapered, violent, voguish, whetted 8 abrasive, abruptly, clear-cut, critical, definite, distinct, explicit, handsome, incisive, keen-eyed, lynx-eyed, on the dot, piercing, poignant, promptly, sardonic, scathing, serrated, shooting, skillful, slippery, spirited, squarely, stabbing, stinging, suddenly, swindler, tactless, vigilant, vigorous, vinegary, virulent 9 acidulous, acuminate, acuminous, agonizing, astucious, brilliant, excellent, ingenious, inventive, keen-edged, knifelike, observant, on the ball, on the nose, precisely, sagacious, sarcastic, sensitive, splintery, trenchant, underhand, unethical, vitriolic 10 accurately, astringent, discerning, first-class, insightful, knife-edged, needlelike, perceptive, proficient, punctually, rapierlike, responsive, ungracious, well-marked
combining form: 3 oxy-
corner: 5 angle
dresser: 5 dandy
end: 5 point, spike
ender: 7 shooter
flavor: 3 nip, zip 4 bite, kick, tang, zest 6 relish 8 piquancy, pungency

9 spiciness
make ~: 4 hone, whet
make a ~ turn: 4 veer
part: 3 jag 4 edge 5 thorn
practice: 7 swindle 8 trickery
starter: 4 card
turn: 3 jog, zag 6 dogleg
sharp __ tack: 3 as a
sharp-__: 3 cut, set 4 eyed 5 eared, edged, nosed 6 freeze, witted 7 sighted, tongued
__ sharp: 4 look 6 double
Sharp: 3 Don 6 Dee Dee 7 Phillip
competitor: 4 Sony
sharpbill: 4 bird
sharp-cornered: 7 angular, pointed 8 angulose, angulous
Sharp, Dee Dee
song: Do the Bird (1963)
Gravy (for My Mashed Potatoes) (1962)
Mashed Potato Time (1962)
Ride! (1962)
Slow Twistin' (1962)
Sharpe: 7 William
Shar-Pei: 3 dog 5 canid 6 canine 7 Chinese
sharpen: 4 file, hone, whet 5 fix up, grind, strop, taper 6 adjust, better, enrich, polish, reform 7 enhance, improve, shape up, upgrade 8 practice, spruce up 9 acuminate, condition, intensify, meliorate 10 ameliorate
sharpened: 4 keen 5 honed 6 acuate
sharpener: 4 hone 5 strop
sharper: 5 cheat, fraud, knave, quack, shark 6 con man 7 cheater 8 chiseler, swindler
Sharper __, The: 5 Image
Sharpe, William: 8 Nobelist 9 economist
sharp-eyed: 4 wary 5 alert 9 observant
sharp-flavored: 5 tangy
sharpie: 5 knave 6 bad guy
Sharpie: 3 pen 6 marker
Sharpless, Barry: 7 chemist 8 Nobelist
sharp-looking: 5 natty 6 spiffy
sharply: 4 hard 8 intently, severely
sharpness: 3 nip 4 edge, tang 5 depth, sense, spice 6 acuity, acumen 8 judgment, keenness 9 intensity, smartness 10 bitterness, cleverness, horse sense
Sharp, Phillip: 8 Nobelist
sharps
key with four ~: 6 E major
key with three ~: 6 A major
sharpshooter: 5 yager 6 archer 8 marksman
need: 5 rifle, scope
org.: 3 NRA
sharp-smelling: 5 acrid
Sharpsteen, Ben: 8 director
film: Dumbo (1941)
Pinocchio (1940)
Snow White and the Seven Dwarfs (1937)
sharp-tasting: 5 tangy 6 bitter 7 pungent
Sharpton: 2 Al
sharp-tongued: 4 acid 5 salty, sassy
one: 5 shrew
sharp-witted: 6 astute 9 astucious
__ S. Hart: 7 William
Shashi: 5 river
locale: 8 Botswana, Zimbabwe
Shasta: 3 mtn. 4 lake, peak 5 mount, tribe 8 mountain
daisy: 5 plant 6 flower
locale: 8 Cascades 10 California
Shatner, William: 5 actor
film: Big Bad Mama (1974)
Free Enterprise (1999)
The Intruder (1961)
Judgment at Nuremberg (1961)
Kingdom of the Spiders (1977)
Miss Congeniality (2000)
Star Trek Generations (1994)
Star Trek III: The Search for Spock (1984)
Star Trek II: The Wrath of Khan (1982)
Star Trek IV: The Voyage Home (1986)
Star Trek-The Motion Picture (1979)
Star Trek VI: The Undiscovered Country (1991)
TV: Rescue 911, Star Trek, T.J. Hooker
Shatt-al-Arab: 5 river
island in the ~: 6 Abadan
locale: 4 Irak, Iraq
port on the ~: 5 Basra, Busra 6 Busrah
shatter: 4 dash, rend, rive, ruin, snap, undo 5 blast, break, burst, crack, crash, crush, smash, split, total, upset, wreck 6 crunch, impair, madden, rattle, ravage, shiver 7 destroy, disable, explode, implode, rupture, smatter, stagger, torpedo, wrack up 8 demolish, dissolve, dynamite, fracture, fragment, splinter 9 devastate, dumbfound, overwhelm, pulverize
ender: 5 proof
shatterable: 7 fragile
shattered: 5 spent 6 broken, undone 8 in pieces
Shattered
author: Dean Koontz, Dick Francis
__-shattering: 5 earth
shatterproof __: 5 glass
Shaud: 5 Grant
Shaughnessy: 7 Maxwell
Shaula: 4 star
Shaun: 7 Cassidy
Shavano: 4 peak 5 mount 8 mountain
locale: 7 Rockies, Sawatch 8 Colorado
shave: 3 cut, mow 4 clip, crop, kiss, pare, peel, skim, skin, snip, thin, trim 5 brush, graze, lower, plane, prune, shear, shred, slash, slice, strip, touch 6 barber, cut off, reduce, scrape, sliver 7 cut away, cut back, cut down, shingle, snip off, tonsure, whittle
prepare to ~: 5 strop
__ shave: 5 close
__-shave: 5 after
Shave __ haircut...: 4 and a
__ Shave: 5 Burma, Rapid 7 Lectric
Shavelson, Melville: 8 director
film: Beau James (1957)
Houseboat (1958)
On the Double (1961)
The Seven Little Foys (1955)
Yours, Mine and Ours (1968)
shaven: 6 smooth 8 glabrous, hairless
__-shaven: 5 clean 6 smooth
shaver: 3 boy, kid, tad, tot 4 tike, tyke 5 child, razor, youth 6 barber
aid: 4 foam 6 lather
electric ~: 5 Braun 7 Norelco 9 Remington
insert: 5 blade
lotion: 6 bay rum
wood ~: 5 plane
Shaver: 5 Helen
shavetail: 2 lt. 5 lieut. 10 lieutenant
academy: 3 OCS, OTS
shaving: 3 bit 4 chip 5 flake 6 sliver 8 splinter
mishap: 4 nick
site: 4 sink
shaving __: 4 soap 5 brush, cream, horse
__ shaving: 5 point
shaving cream: 3 gel 4 foam
additive: 4 aloe
shavings: 5 trash 7 residue 8 kindling
Shaw: 4 Reta, Stan 5 Artie, Irwin 6 George, Robert 7 Bernard
Shaw, Artie: 11 clarinetist
genre: 4 jazz
spouse: Ava Gardner, Evelyn Keyes
Shaw, George Bernard: 5 Irish 6 author, critic, writer 8 Nobelist 10 playwright
contemporary: 5 Yeats
work: Androcles and the Lion
Arms and the Man
Back to Methuselah
Buoyant Billions
Caesar and Cleopatra
Candida
Captain Brassbound's Conversion
The Devil's Disciple
Fanny's First Play
Heartbreak House
John Bull's Other Island
Major Barbara
Man and Superman
The Man of Destiny
Mrs. Warren's Profession
The Philanderer
Pygmalion
Saint Joan
Widowers' Houses
You Never Can Tell
Shaw, Irwin: 6 author, writer
work: Bury the Dead
Love on a Dark Street
Mixed Company
Rich Man, Poor Man
The Young Lions
shawl: 4 wrap 5 cloak, manta, scarf, stole, throw 6 afghan, sarape, serape 8 covering, mantilla
Indian ~: 5 pattu
triangular ~: 5 fichu
shawl __: 6 collar, tongue
__ shawl: 6 prayer
shawm: 4 wind 10 instrument
descendant: 4 oboe
Shawn: 3 Ted 4 Dick 5 Estes 6 Colvin 7 Mullins, Wallace
Shawnee: 4 city, town 5 tribe 6 Indian 7 Amerind 8 language
locale: 6 Kansas 8 Oklahoma
Shaw, Robert: 5 actor
film: The Birthday Party (1968)
Black Sunday (1977)
The Deep (1977)
From Russia With Love (1963)
Jaws (1975)
The Luck of Ginger Coffey (1964)
A Man for All Seasons (1966)
Robin and Marian (1976)
The Royal Hunt of the Sun (1969)
The Sting (1973)
The Taking of Pelham One Two Three (1974)
Shawshank Redemption, The (1994 film)
cast: Morgan Freeman, Bob Gunton, Tim Robbins, William Sadler
director: Frank Darabont
extra: 5 lifer 6 inmate
highlight: 6 escape
setting: 5 Maine 6 prison
shay: 6 chaise 7 vehicle
one-hoss ~ owner: 6 deacon
Shayne: 6 Robert 7 Michael
Shayne, Michael portrayer: 5 Nolan
shazam: 6 presto
she: 3 gal, her 4 lady 5 woman 6 female, madame 7 pronoun 8 daughter
he and ~: 4 they
in French: 4 elle
in Spanish: 4 ella
she-__: 4 wolf 5 devil
she-__ soup: 4 crab
She (1935 film)
cast: Helen Gahagan, Helen Mack, Randolph Scott
She __: 3 Bop 5 Cried
She __ Say Yes: 5 Didn't
shea: 4 tree
family: 9 sapodilla
relative: 6 balata 7 almique 8 alamiqui
Shea: 4 John 7 stadium 8 ballpark
player: 3 Met 5 NY Met
sheaf: 5 batch, bunch, stack 6 bundle, quiver 10 collection
She Ain't Worth It (1990 song)
artist: Bobby Brown, Glenn Medeiros
shear: 3 cut, mow 4 chop, clip, crop, trim 5 prune, sever, shave 6 cut off, dehair, fleece, lop off, remove 7 cut back, scissor, snip off 8 truncate
ender: 5 water
__ shear: 4 wind 6 flying 7 rocking
Shear: 4 peak 5 mount 8 mountain
locale: 10 Antarctica
Shearer: 5 Harry, Moira, Norma
Shearer, Moira: 6 dancer 7 actress 8 danseuse 9 ballerina
film: The Red Shoes (1948)
The Story of Three Loves (1953)
Shearer, Norma: 7 actress
film: The Barretts of Wimpole Street (1934)
The Divorcée (1930, AA)
Escape (1940)
A Free Soul (1931)
He Who Gets Slapped (1924)
Idiot's Delight (1939)
Private Lives (1931)
Riptide (1934)
Romeo and Juliet (1936)
Smilin' Through (1932)
Strange Interlude (1932)
The Student Prince in Old Heidelberg (1927)
The Women (1939)
spouse: Irving Thalberg
shearing
candidate: 3 ewe, ram 5 sheep
output: 4 wool
Shearing, George: 7 pianist
shears: 7 cutters 8 clippers, scissors
use dressmaker's ~: 4 pink
__ shears: 5 grass 7 pinking, pruning
Shearson partner: 6 Lehman
shearwater: 4 bird
Shea Stadium: 8 ballpark
see also Shea
sheath: 3 pod 4 skin 5 dress, skirt 6 casing, jacket 7 outside 8 membrane 10 integument
combining form: 4 cole- 5 coleo-, -theca
plant ~: 5 ocrea 6 ochrea
sheath __: 4 pile 5 knife
__ sheath: 6 myelin
sheathbill: 4 bird
sheathe: 4 wrap 6 encase, incase 7 retract
with metal: 4 clad
sheathing: 4 case, skin
She author: H. Rider Haggard
sheaves, grain: 5 shock
Sheb: 6 Wooley
Sheba
creator: 4 Inge
locale: 5 Yemen 6 Arabia
shebang, the whole: 3 all 5 works 10 everything
Shebat: 5 month 6 Hebrew
follower: 4 Adar
She Believes in Me (1979 song) artist: Kenny Rogers
__ she blows!: 4 Thar
She Bop (1984 song) artist: Cyndi Lauper
Sheboygan: 4 city, town
locale: 9 Wisconsin
She Came to Stay author: Simone de Beauvoir
Shecky: 6 Greene

___ She Coo?: 4 Who'd
She Couldn't Take It (1935 film)
cast: Joan Bennett, Billie Burke, George Raft
director: Tay Garnett
she-crab ___: 4 soup
She Cried (1962 song) artist: Jay and the Americans
shed: 3 hut, rid 4 beam, cast, cede, doff, drop, dump, emit, lose, molt, sell, skin, slip 5 chuck, ditch, exude, forgo, scrap, shack, spill, strip, yield 6 forego, give up, hangar, lean-to, reject, remove, shanty, shower, slough 7 abandon, cast off, diffuse, discard, drop off, forfeit, forsake, let fall, let go of, radiate, scatter, shelter, take off, undress 8 exuviate, forswear, get out of, get rid of, hand over, jettison, part with, sprinkle, throw off, throw out 9 cast aside, disburden, dispose of, exfoliate, foreswear, give forth, pour forth, send forth, slough off, surrender, throw away, toolhouse 10 relinquish
feathers: 4 molt 5 moult
light: 5 shine
light on: 7 clarify, explain 8 illumine, simplify
pounds: 4 diet, slim
Shetland Islands ~: 4 skeo
something to ~: 4 tear
starter: 3 cow 4 wood 5 blood, water
tears: 3 cry, sob 4 bawl, mewl, pule, wail, weep 6 boohoo, snivel 7 blubber, whimper
shed ___: 4 roof, room 5 a tear
shed ___ on: 5 light
___ shed: 3 air 5 wharf 7 transit
Shedar: 4 star
___-shedding: 4 load
Shedd's: 6 spread 9 margarine
alternative: 6 Parkay 7 Promise 8 Imperial
She-Devil (1989 film)
cast: Roseanne Barr, Ed Begley Jr., Linda Hunt, Meryl Streep
director: Susan Seidelman
She Didn't Say Yes composer: 4 Kern 7 Harbach
She Done Him Wrong (1933 film)
cast: Cary Grant, Gilbert Roland, Mae West
She'd Rather Be With Me (1967 song)
artist: Turtles
shee: 5 fairy
Sheed, Wilfrid: 6 author, writer
Sheedy, Ally: 7 actress
film: Betsy's Wedding (1990)
The Breakfast Club (1985)
Maid to Order (1987)
Only the Lonely (1991)
Short Circuit (1986)
St. Elmo's Fire (1985)
WarGames (1983)
Sheehan: 4 Neil 5 Patty
Sheehan, Patty: 6 golfer
milieu: 5 links 6 course
org.: 4 LPGA
Sheehy: 4 Gail
sheen: 3 wax 4 glow 5 glaze, gleam, glint, gloss, light 6 finish, luster, patina, patine, polish 7 burnish, glitter, shimmer 8 radiance, radiancy 9 shininess 10 brightness, luminosity
give a ~: 5 shine
Sheen: 6 Fulton, Martin 7 Charlie
Sheena: 6 Easton
in English: 4 Jane
Sheena, Queen of the Jungle chimp: 4 Neal
Sheen, Charlie: 5 actor
brother: Emilio Estevez
father: Martin
film: The Arrival (1996)
Eight Men Out (1988)
Hot Shots! (1991)
Lucas (1986)
Major League (1989)
Platoon (1986)
Terminal Velocity (1994)
The Three Musketeers (1993)
Wall Street (1987)
Young Guns (1988)
spouse: Denise Richards
Sheen, Martin: 5 actor
film: The American President (1995)
Apocalypse Now (1979)
Catch-22 (1970)
The Final Countdown (1980)
Firestarter (1984)
Gettysburg (1993)
The Incident (1967)
Man, Woman and Child (1983)
O (2001)
The Subject Was Roses (1968)
Wall Street (1987)
son: Emilio, Charlie Estevez
sheep: 3 ram 4 geep, lamb, meat 5 argal, bovid, shapu, stock, toady, urial 6 animal, aoudad, argali, bharal, merino, yes man 7 Babbitt, bighorn, burrhel, Cheviot, mouflon 8 assenter, cimarron, Cotswold, emulator, follower, moufflon 9 followers, livestock 10 conformist
African ~: 6 aoudad, dorper
Asian ~: 5 argal, shapu, urial 6 argali, bharal 7 burrhel, Karakul
bear a ~: 4 yean
black ~: 5 rogue 6 bad guy, rascal 9 miscreant, scoundrel 10 delinquent
breed: 5 Devon 6 dorper, Oxford, Romney 7 Cheviot, Karakul, Lincoln, Ryeland, Suffolk 8 Columbia, Cotswold, Dartmoor 9 Hampshire, Leicester, Montadale, Southdown, Wiltshire 10 Corriedale, Dorset Horn, Shropshire
British ~: 5 Devon 6 Oxford, Romney 7 Cheviot, Lincoln, Ryeland, Suffolk 8 Cotswold, Dartmoor 9 Hampshire, Leicester, Southdown, Wiltshire 10 Dorset Horn, Shropshire
cloned ~: 5 Dolly
coat: 6 fleece
Corsican ~: 7 mouflon 8 moufflon
ender: 3 dog 4 cote, fold, skin 5 berry, shank 6 herder
female ~: 3 ewe
foot: 4 hoof
grease: 5 suint
group: 4 fold 5 drove, flock
hybrid ~: 4 geep
like a ~: 4 meek 6 docile, fleecy, lanose
like some ~: 5 shorn
male ~: 3 ram
New Zealand ~: 10 Corriedale
pen: 4 cote, fold
product: 4 wool
Rockies ~: 4 Dall 7 bighorn 8 cimarron
seeds for pottery ~: 4 chia
shave ~: 5 shear
sound: 3 baa, maa 4 blat 5 bleat
Spanish ~: 6 merino
young ~: 3 teg 4 lamb, tegg 8 yeanling
sheep ___: 3 ked 6 fescue, laurel, sorrel
sheep-___: 3 dip
___ sheep: 4 blue, Dall 5 black, Dall's 7 Barbary
sheepdog: 6 collie, herder
Hungarian ~: 4 puli 6 kuvasz
___ sheepdog: 7 Belgian, English
sheepfold: 4 cote
sheepish: 3 shy 4 tame 5 ovine, silly, sorry, timid 6 docile 7 abashed, ashamed, bashful, fearful 8 retiring 9 chagrined, diffident, flinching, mortified 10 shamefaced, uneffusive
Sheepman, The (1958 film)
cast: Glenn Ford, Shirley MacLaine, Leslie Nielsen
sheep's ___: 4 eyes
sheepshank: 4 knot
sheepskin: 3 fur 6 degree 7 diploma
alternative: 3 GED
cap: 6 calpac 7 calpack
holder: 4 alum, grad
leather: 4 roan
sheeptick: 3 ked
sheer: 4 airy, fine, lacy, main, mere, pure, rank, soft, thin, turn 5 erect, filmy, gauzy, gross, light, lucid, naked, quite, stark, steep, total, utter 6 arrant, fabric, flimsy, limpid, simple, slight, smooth, swerve, unmixt 7 chiffon, extreme, fragile, perfect, totally, unmixed, upright 8 absolute, complete, delicate, entirely, finespun, gossamer, outright, pellucid, straight, thorough, vertical 9 downright, out-and-out, undiluted 10 altogether, completely, confounded, diaphanous, see-through, to the limit
drop: 5 cliff 9 precipice
fabric: 4 lawn, leno 5 gauze, ninon, toile, voile 6 barege, dimity 7 batiste, chiffon 9 georgette
off: 4 veer 6 swerve
sheet: 3 ply 4 area, coat, film, leaf, page, pane, slab, slip 5 layer, panel, paper, plate, verso 6 lamina, veneer 7 bedding, blanket, coating, expanse, overlay, stratum, stretch, surface 8 bedcover, bed linen, covering, membrane 9 lightning, newspaper, tarpaulin
cheat ~: 4 crib, trot
four-page ~: 5 folio
glass ~: 4 pane
metal ~: 4 foil 5 plate 6 latten
paper ~: 4 leaf
scandal ~: 9 newspaper
starter: 3 fly 4 clip, main, spec, work 5 baker, broad 6 spread
thin ~: 6 lamina
sheet ___: 3 ice 4 bend, film, knot, pile 5 glass, metal, music 6 anchor, feeder 7 erosion
___ sheet: 3 cue, end, fly, ice, rap, tip 4 bath, buck, cost, crib, dope, flow, free, lead, poop, spec, tear, time, work 5 proof, style, tally 6 baking, cookie, ground, second 7 balance, blanket, contact, contour, scandal, scratch, swindle, winding
___-sheet: 5 short, smear
sheet-music feature: 5 lyric, notes 6 chords, lyrics
sheets: 5 linen 6 linens, tablet 10 scratch pad
come down in ~: 4 pour, rain
24 ~: 5 quire
Sheffer: 5 Craig
Sheffield: 4 city, town 6 Johnny
artisan: 6 cutler
city near ~: 5 Leeds
locale: 7 England 9 Yorkshire
She Gets Her Man (1945 film)
cast: Joan Davis, Leon Errol, William Gargan
director: Erle C. Kenton
She & He author: George Sand
sheik: 4 Arab, male 5 Saudi
ender: 3 dom
peer: 4 amir, emir 5 ameer, emeer
robe: 3 aba 4 abba
wives: 5 haram, harem, harim 6 hareem
sheikdom
group: 3 UAE
Mideast ~: 5 Dibai, Dubai
musical ~: 5 Araby
Sheik of ___, The: 5 Araby
Sheik, The (1921 film)
cast: Agnes Ayres, Adolphe Menjou, Rudolph Valentino
sheila: 4 girl 5 woman 6 Aussie
Sheila: 4 Ryan 5 James 6 Kelley, MacRae
in English: 7 Cecilia
Sheila (1962 song) artist: Tommy Roe
Sheila E.
last name: Escovedo
song: The Glamorous Life (1984)
Sheilah: 6 Graham
shekel: 4 coin 5 money
fraction: 5 agora
locale: 6 Israel
shekels: 3 oof 4 cash, gelt, jack, kail, kale, loot, peag, pelf 5 bills, bread, bucks, dough, funds, lucre, money, moola, mopus, pesos, rhino, sewan 6 dinero, do-re-mi, mammon, mazuma, moolah, seawan, silver, specie, wampum, wealth 7 cabbage, capital, dollars, lettuce, ooftish, scratch 8 bankroll, cold cash, currency, hard cash, smackers 9 banknotes, frogskins, long green, simoleons 10 greenbacks, green stuff
shekere: 5 gourd 10 percussion
origin: 4 Cuba 6 Africa
Shelagh: 7 Delaney
Shelby: 4 city, town 5 Foote, Lynne
locale: 4 Ohio
Sheldon: 6 Sidney 7 Glashow, Harnick, Leonard
Sheldon, Sidney: 6 author, writer
work: The Best Laid Plans
Bloodline
The Doomsday Conspiracy
If Tomorrow Comes
Master of the Game
Memories of Midnight
Morning Noon and Night
The Naked Face
Nothing Lasts Forever
The Other Side of Midnight
Rage of Angels
The Sands of Time
The Sky is Falling
The Stars Shine Down
Stranger in the Mirror
Tell Me Your Dreams
Toby
Windmills of the Gods
sheldrake: 4 bird
shelduck: 4 bird
shelf: 4 bank, berm, rack, reef, rest, rock 5 berme, layer, ledge, shoal 6 mantel, mantle 7 console, counter, shallow 8 cupboard, sandbank 10 projection
chimney ~: 3 hob
on a ~: 4 atop
on the ~: 4 idle 6 unused 7 dormant 8 inactive
starter: 4 book 6 mantel
take off the ~: 3 use
underwater ~: 4 reef
shelf ___: 3 ice 4 life, mark 5 angle, paper 6 talker
___ shelf: 3 ice 4 wind 5 on the, smoke 6 closed, simian, sulfur
___-shelf: 4 open
Sheliak: 4 star
shell: 3 pod 4 bark, boat, bomb, case, coat, face, fire, hull, husk, peel, raid, skin 5 conch, cowry, crust, frame, murex, ruins, scale, shuck, snail, whelk 6 chiton, cockle, cowrie, facade, limpet, mussel, oyster, quahog, triton, veneer, volute, winkle 7 abalone, bivalve, bombard, chassis, coating, crinoid, grenade, outside, scallop,

surface 8 ammonite, argonaut, baculite, carapace, covering, escallop, fire upon, frustule, magazine, nautilus, pericarp, piecrust, ram's-horn, skeleton, univalve 9 belemnite, cannonade, container, explosive, framework, giant clam, pink conch, structure 10 blue mussel, crown conch, eyed cowrie, integument, periwinkle, quahog clam, watercraft
abalone ~: 5 ormer
abandoned ~: 4 hulk
combining form: 5 conch- 6 concho-, ostrac- 7 ostraco-
ender: 4 back, bark, fire, fish 5 proof 6 flower 7 fishery, shocked
game: 5 cheat 7 swindle 8 trickery 9 collusion
lining: 5 nacre
necklace ~: 4 puka
out: 3 pay 4 ante, fork, give 5 spend 6 ante up, divide, expend, fork up, pay for, render 8 disburse, dispense, fork over, hand over 10 remunerate
peanut ~: 4 husk
pie ~: 5 crust
propel a ~: 3 oar, row 5 scull
protein ~: 6 capsid
put into a ~: 6 enhusk
ridge: 5 varix
ship ~: 4 hull
spiral ~: 5 conch
starter: 3 egg, nut, sea 4 band, bomb, clam, lamp 6 cockle 8 tortoise
shell __: 3 out 4 back, bean, game, pink, star 5 steak 6 jacket
__ shell: 3 ark 4 band, clam, cone, half, harp, horn, lamp, moon, star, tear, tusk 5 blank, heart, money, olive, patty, tooth 6 closed, helmet, jingle, needle, trough, turtle 7 lantern, pandora, slipper, spindle, sundial, trumpet, valence
__-shell: 4 hard, soft
Shell: 3 Art, gas 8 gasoline
former ~ rival: 4 Esso
rival: 5 Amoco, Exxon, Getty, Mobil 6 Conoco, Texaco 7 Chevron
shellac: 4 drub, lick, whip 5 cream, resin, tromp, worst 6 defeat, wallop 7 clobber, lambast, varnish 8 lambaste 9 overpower
shellacking: 4 bath, rout 6 defeat 7 beating, debacle, licking
Shell and Head sculptor: 3 Arp
Shell, Art sport: 8 football
shellback: 4 salt 7 veteran
__-shell clam: 4 hard, soft
__-shell crab: 4 hard, soft
Shelley: 4 Hack, Long, Mary, poet 6 Berman, Duvall 7 Fabares, Winters
Shelley, Mary: 6 author, writer 7 British
work: Frankenstein
Shelley, Percy Bysshe: 4 poet 7 British
alma mater: 4 Eton
biography by Maurois: 5 Ariel
contemporary: 5 Byron, Keats
work: Adonais
Alastor
The Cenci
The Cloud
Hymn to Intellectual Beauty
Ode to Liberty
Ode to the West Wind
Ozymandias
Prometheus Unbound
Promethus Unbound
Queen Mab
To a Skylark
shellfish: 4 clam, crab 6 limpet
eater: 5 otter
shelling: 4 fire 5 blitz 6 volley 7 barrage 9 cannonade
shells: 4 ammo 5 chaff, pasta 7 noodles 10 ammunition
alternative: 4 orzo, ziti 5 penne 7 lasagna, lasagne, pastina, ravioli 8 bucatini, couscous, farfalle, linguine, linguini, macaroni, rigatoni 9 agnolotti, angelhair, cavatelli, manicotti, spaghetti 10 cannelloni, fettuccini, tortellini, vermicelli
__ She Lovely?: 4 Isn't
she loves in Latin: 4 amat
She Loves Me Not (1934 film)
cast: Kitty Carlisle, Bing Crosby, Miriam Hopkins
She loves me... unit: 5 petal
She Loves You (1964 song) artist: Beatles
word: 4 yeah
shelter: 3 den, hut, lee, pad, pen 4 cave, co-op, cove, hide, home, keep, need, nest, port, roof, shed, tent, yurt 5 admit, condo, cover, guard, haven, house, joint, lodge, roost, shack, shade, tower 6 asylum, awning, billet, covert, defend, foster, hangar, harbor, hostel, kennel, lean-to, refuge, safety, screen, shadow, shield, take in, wigwam 7 chamber, conceal, cover up, defense, enclose, habitat, harbour, hideout, housing, inclose, lodging, protect, quarter, retreat 8 dwelling, ensconce, hideaway, hold on to, preserve, quarters, security, surround, umbrella 9 anchorage, apartment, harborage, hermitage, protector, safeguard, sanctuary, seclusion, watch over 10 protection, take care of
adoptee: 3 cat, dog 4 mutt 5 stray
animal ~: 4 barn, cote, fold, shed
as in a cove: 5 embay
crude ~: 3 hut 6 dugout, lean-to
farm ~: 4 barn, shed
give ~ to: 4 hide 5 house 6 billet, harbor, shield 7 conceal, protect
leafy ~: 5 arbor, bower 6 recess 7 pergola
marine ~: 4 cove
military ~: 4 tent 8 barracks
org.: 5 ASPCA
rustic ~: 5 cabin
seek ~: 9 take cover
shelter __: 4 deck, half, tent
__ shelter: 3 tax 4 bomb 6 animal 7 air-raid
__ Shelter: 5 Gimme
sheltered: 4 cosy, cozy, snug 5 cozey, cozie, shady 6 covert, inside, secure 7 indoors 8 secluded, shielded, tucked in 10 cloistered
nautically: 4 alee
spot: 4 cove, dale
Shelters of Stone, The author: Jean Auel
character: 4 Ayla
sheltie: 3 dog 5 canid 6 canine
charge: 5 sheep
Shelton: 3 Ron 4 city, town
locale: 4 Conn.
Shelton, Ron: 8 director
film: Blaze (1989)
Bull Durham (1988)
Cobb (1994)
Play It to the Bone (1999)
Tin Cup (1996)
White Men Can't Jump (1992)
shelve: 4 drop, hold, stay 5 delay, scrub, table, waive 6 freeze, hang up, hold up, put off, slow up 7 adjourn, dismiss, hold off, prolong, suspend 8 file away, hold over, lay aside, mothball, postpone, put aside, sideline 10 inactivate, pigeonhole
shelved: 7 abeyant
shelves, fill the: 5 stock
Shem
brother of ~: 3 Ham 7 Japheth
father of ~: 3 Noe 4 Noah
son of ~: 3 Lud 4 Aram, Elam 6 Asshur 10 Arpachshad
Shemoneh __: 5 Esreh
Shemp: 6 Howard
brother: 3 Moe 5 Curly
partner: 5 Larry
Shenandoah: 4 park 5 river 6 valley
locale: 8 Virginia
Shenandoah (1965 film)
cast: Glenn Corbett, Doug McClure, James Stewart
director: Andrew V. McLaglen
Shenandoah author: Delmore Schwartz
shenanigan: 3 gag 4 jape, lark 5 antic, caper, prank, stunt, trick 6 frolic 8 escapade
shenanigans: 7 foolery 8 jocosity, mischief 10 tomfoolery
__ Sheni: 4 Adar
Shensi: 8 province
capital: 4 Sian
city: 5 Yanan, Yenan
locale: 5 China
Shenyang: 4 city, town
locale: 5 China
Shep: 6 Fields
Shep and the Limelites song: Daddy's Home (1961)
Shepard: 3 Sam 4 Alan, Jean 5 Vonda
Shepard, Alan org.: 4 NASA
Shepard, Sam: 5 actor 10 playwright
film: Baby Boom (1987)
Country (1984)
Crimes of the Heart (1986)
Days of Heaven (1978)
Frances (1982)
The Pelican Brief (1993)
Resurrection (1980)
The Right Stuff (1983)
Steel Magnolias (1989)
Thunderheart (1992)
Shepeardes Calendar: 4 poem
author: 7 Spenser
shepherd: 3 dog, pet 4 herd, lead, show, tend 5 canid, guard, guide, route, steer 6 canine, collie, direct, leader, pastor 7 conduct, oversee, protect 8 chaperon, guardian, minister, see after 9 chaperone, look after, watch over
Biblical ~: 4 Abel
charge: 5 flock
god: 3 Pan
locale: 3 lea 6 meadow
staff: 5 crook
__ shepherd: 6 German
Shepherd: 4 Jean 6 Cybill
__ Shepherd: 4 Good
Shepherd, Cybill: 7 actress
film: Chances Are (1989)
The Heartbreak Kid (1972)
The Last Picture Show (1971)
Once Upon a Crime (1992)
Silver Bears (1978)
Special Delivery (1976)
Taxi Driver (1976)
Texasville (1990)
TV: Moonlighting
Shepherd Moons singer: 4 Enya
Shepherd of the Hills (1941 film)
cast: Harry Carey, Betty Field, John Wayne
director: Henry Hathaway
shepherd's __: 3 pie 5 check, plaid
shepherd's purse: 4 weed
__ sher!: 3 fer
Shera: 4 Mark
Sheratan: 4 star
Sheraton: 5 hotel, style
alternative: 4 Omni 5 Hyatt 6 Hilton, Westin 7 Wyndham 8 Marriott, Radisson 10 DoubleTree 11 Crowne Plaza, Four Seasons
sherbet: 3 ice 7 dessert
flavor: 4 lime 5 fruit, lemon 6 orange
Sherbrooke: 4 city, town
locale: 6 Canada, Québec
Shere: 4 Hite
Sheree: 5 North
Sheree J. __: 6 Wilson
Shere Khan: 5 tiger
Sheridan: 3 Ann 7 Richard 10 Nicollette
__ Sheridan: 4 Fort
Sheridan, Ann: 7 actress
film: City for Conquest (1940)
Come Next Spring (1956)
Dodge City (1939)
Edge of Darkness (1943)
I Was a Male War Bride (1949)
Kings Row (1942)
The Man Who Came to Dinner (1941)
Navy Blues (1941)
They Drive by Night (1940)
Torrid Zone (1940)
Woman on the Run (1950)
spouse: George Brent
Sheridan, Nicollette spouse: Harry Hamlin
Sheridan, Richard: 7 British 9 statesman 10 playwright
work: The Duenna
The Rivals
The School for Scandal
sheriff: 6 lawman 7 officer
aide: 6 deputy 7 bailiff
band: 5 posse
cry: 6 drop it
symbol: 4 star 5 badge
TV ~: 4 Lobo
__ sheriff: 6 deputy
Sherilyn: 4 Fenn
Sherlock: 6 Holmes 9 detective
Sherlock Holmes and the Secret Weapon (1942 film)
cast: Lionel Atwill, Nigel Bruce, Basil Rathbone
director: Roy William Neill
Sherlock Holmes Faces Death (1943 film)
cast: Hillary Brooke, Nigel Bruce, Basil Rathbone
director: Roy William Neill
Sherman: 4 city, peak, tank, town 5 Allan, Allie, Bobby, mount 6 Lowell 7 Hemsley, Vincent 8 mountain
locale: 5 Texas 7 Rockies 8 Colorado
Sherman, Allan song: Hello Mudduh, Hello Fadduh! (1963)
Sherman Antitrust __: 3 Act
Sherman, Bobby
song: Easy Come, Easy Go (1970)
Julie, Do Ya Love Me (1970)
La La La (1969)
Little Woman (1969)
Sherman Oaks: 4 city, town
locale: 10 California
town near ~: 6 Encino
Sherman, Vincent: 8 director
film: Adventures of Don Juan (1949)
All Through the Night (1942)
Flight From Destiny (1941)
Goodbye, My Fancy (1951)
The Hard Way (1942)
Harriet Craig (1950)
Mr. Skeffington (1944)
Old Acquaintance (1943)
Underground (1941)
The Young Philadelphians (1959)
Sherpa: 5 guide
home: 5 Nepal
sighting: 4 yeti
Sherr: 4 Lynn
Sherrill: 6 Milnes
Sherrington, Charles: 8 Nobelist 12 physiologist

sherry: 4 wine
city: 4 Xera 5 Jerez, Xeres
dry ~: 4 fino
sherry ___: 7 cobbler
Sherry: 7 Jackson, Lansing
Sherry (1962 song) artist: Four Seasons
Sherwood: 4 city, town 6 forest 7 Rowland 8 Anderson
locale: 7 England 8 Arkansas
Sherwood, Robert E.: 10 playwright
work: Abe Lincoln in Illinois
Idiot's Delight
The Road to Rome
There Shall Be No Night
Sheryl: 3 Lee 4 Crow
Sheryl ___ Ralph: 3 Lee
She's ___: 4 Gone, Mine 5 a Fool, a Lady
She's ___ Hard to Get: 7 Playing
She's ___ I Ever Had: 3 All
She's a Fool (1963 song) artist: Lesley Gore
She's a Heartbreaker (1968 song) artist: Gene Pitney
___, She Said: 6 Murder
She's a Lady (1971 song) artist: Tom Jones
composer: 4 Anka
___ She's a Lady, The: 5 Liner
She's All I Ever Had (1999 song) artist: Ricky Martin
She's All That (1999 film)
cast: Rachael Leigh Cook, Matthew Lillard, Freddie Prinze Jr., Paul Walker
director: Robert Iscove
She's Always a Woman (1978 song) artist: Billy Joel
She's a Rainbow (1968 song) artist: Rolling Stones
She's a Woman (1964 song) artist: Beatles
She's Gone (1976 song) artist: Hall and Oates
She's Got a Way (1981 song) artist: Billy Joel
She's Gotta Have It (1986 film)
cast: Tommy Redmond Hicks, Tracy Camilla Johns, Spike Lee, John Canada Terrell
character: 4 Nola
director: Spike Lee
She's Having a Baby (1988 film)
cast: Kevin Bacon, Alec Baldwin, Elizabeth McGovern
director: John Hughes
She's Just My Style (1965 song) artist: Gary Lewis and the Playboys
She's Like the Wind (1988 song) artist: Patrick Swayze
She's Lookin' Good (1968 song) artist: Wilson Pickett
She's Not There (1964 song) artist: Zombies
She's Not You (1962 song) artist: Elvis Presley
She's Out of My Life (1980 song) artist: Michael Jackson
She stood in tears amid the ___ corn: 5 alien
She Stoops to Conquer
author: Oliver Goldsmith
character: 4 Kate, Tony 6 Marlow
___ She Sweet?: 4 Ain't
Shetland: 4 isls., pony 5 horse, isles 7 islands
Shetland Islands
fishing grounds: 4 Haaf
hut: 4 skeo
neighbor: 5 Faroe 6 Faeroe
Shevardnadze: 6 Eduard
Shevat: 5 month 6 Hebrew
predecessor: 5 Tevet
successor: 4 Adar
She Walks in Beauty author: Byron
She Was a Phantom of Delight: 4 poem
author: William Wordsworth
___ She Was Good: 4 When
She Wore a Yellow Ribbon (1949 film): 5 oater 7 western
cast: John Agar, Joanne Dru, John Wayne
director: John Ford
She Works Hard for the Money (1983 song) artist: Donna Summer
___, She Wrote: 6 Murder
shh: 5 quiet 8 pipe down
Shiba Inu: 3 dog 5 canid 6 canine
shibboleth: 3 saw 5 motto 6 phrase 9 catchword, platitude
shield: 4 egis, fend, hide, keep, mail, roof, save, tend, veil 5 aegis, armor, badge, cover, guard, haven, house, shade 6 buffer, bumper, defend, embank, ensure, fender, harbor, insure, refuge, screen, secure, shadow 7 bulwark, conceal, cover up, defense, harbour, protect, rampart, shelter, ward off 8 absorber, armament, preserve, security 9 safeguard, stonewall 10 escutcheon, protection
archer's ~: 5 pavis 6 pavise
Athena's ~: 4 egis 5 aegis
border: 4 orle
camera-lens ~: 4 gobo
combining form: 4 scut- 5 aspid-, scuti- 6 aspido-
division in heraldry: 4 ente
in heraldry: 10 escutcheon
knob: 4 umbo
old ~: 3 écu 5 targe 6 ancile
starter: 4 wind
sun ~: 5 visor, vizor
shield ___: 3 law 4 back, fern 6 bearer
___ shield: 4 heat 5 water 7 Faraday
Shield: 4 soap
alternative: 3 Lux 4 Dial, Dove, Lava, Tone, Zest 5 Camay, Coast, Ivory 6 Boraxo, Caress 8 Lifebuoy 9 Palmolive, Safeguard 11 Irish Spring
___ Shield: 4 Blue 6 Desert
shielded: 6 hidden, secure 8 secluded 9 insulated, reclusive, sheltered, withdrawn 10 cloistered, restricted
Shield of ___: 5 David
Shields, Brooke: 7 actress
film: Black and White (2000)
The Blue Lagoon (1980)
Brenda Starr (1989)
Freeway (1996)
Pretty Baby (1978)
spouse: Andre Agassi
TV: Suddenly Susan
shift: 3 job, tip 4 bout, move, ploy, ruse, slip, stir, tack, tilt, time, tour, turn, vary, veer, wile 5 alter, budge, dodge, dress, drift, fault, slide, spell, stint, swing, trick, waver 6 change, gambit, manage, modify, period, refuge, resort, scheme, squirm, swerve, switch, waffle 7 chemise, deviate, disturb, evasion, lighten, replace, reverse, shuffle, stopgap, veering 8 artifice, camisole, displace, exchange, flip-flop, lingerie, maneuver, movement, move over, reassign, recourse, relocate, resource, transfer 9 about-face, deviation, dislocate, expedient, fluctuate, hem and haw, rearrange, transpose, vacillate, variation 10 alteration, changeover, conversion, deflection, expediency, move around, relocation, reposition, substitute, subterfuge, switch over, transition, turn around
starter: 4 down, gear, make
work ~: 4 days 6 nights
shift ___: 3 bid, key 4 lock 5 gears, lever
___ shift: 3 day, dog 4 blue 5 night, split, stick, swing 6 cyclic 7 lobster
___-shift: 4 jump
___ Shift: 5 Night
shifting: 5 fluid 7 erratic, mutable, protean 8 floating, unstable, variable 9 irregular, mercurial, momentary, uncertain, unsettled 10 changeable, nonuniform
___ shifting: 4 time
shiftless: 4 idle, lazy 5 slack 6 otiose 8 dallying, fainéant, feckless, indolent, slothful 9 apathetic, do-nothing, negligent 10 neglectful, unreliable
one: 5 idler 10 ne'er-do-well
shiftlessness: 5 sloth
Shift neighbor: 3 Alt, Tab 5 Enter
shifty: 3 sly 4 cagy, foxy, wily 5 cagey, lying, shady, slick, slimy 6 crafty, louche, shrewd, sneaky, tricky 7 crooked, cunning, devious, dodging, elusive, elusory, evasive, furtive, roguish 8 guileful, scheming, slippery, stealthy 9 conniving, deceitful, deceptive, dishonest, ingenious, insidious, insincere, inventive, shuffling, underhand 10 contriving, fly-by-night, fraudulent, mendacious, serpentine, unfaithful, unreliable, untruthful
one: 6 dodger
Shigeta: 5 James
Shih Tzu: 3 dog, pet, toy 5 canid 6 canine, lap dog
shiitake: 8 mushroom
Shi'ite: 4 Arab 5 Irani
caliph: 3 Ali
faith: 5 Islam
God: 5 Allah
holy city: 5 Najaf
holy man: 4 imam 5 imaum
Shijiazhuang province: 5 Hebei
shikari: 5 guide 6 hunter
Shikoku: 6 island
city: 5 Kochi
locale: 5 Japan
Shilh
home: 6 Africa 7 Morocco
shill: 4 bait, lure, tout 5 decoy, plant, tempt, trick 6 allure, come-on, entice, lead on, rope in, suck in 7 insider 8 inveigle, pretense 9 accessory, deception
shillelagh: 4 club 5 staff 6 cudgel 9 truncheon
land: 4 Eire, Erin 7 Ireland
shilling: 3 bob 4 coin 5 money
fraction: 5 penny
21 ~ s: 6 guinea
___ shilling: 5 king's 6 queen's
Shilling for Candles, A author: 3 Tey
Shillong region: 5 Assam
Shilluk: 8 language
locale: 5 Sudan 6 Africa
shilly-shally: 4 drag, poke, vary, yo-yo 5 hedge, waver 6 seesaw 7 dubiety 8 hesitate 9 dubiosity, hem and haw, oscillate, vacillate
Shiloh: 5 novel 6 battle
author: 5 Foote
locale: 9 Tennessee
Shilts: 5 Randy
shim: 5 strip, wedge
Shimazaki Toson: 4 poet 8 Japanese
___ Shimbun: 5 Asahi
Shimizu: 4 city, port, town
locale: 5 Japan
shimmer: 4 glow 5 blink, flare, flash, gleam, glint, gloss, shake, sheen, shine, spark 6 glance, luster, quiver 7 flicker, glimmer, glisten, glitter, spangle, sparkle, twinkle 8 blinking 9 irradiate, luminesce 10 incandesce, luminosity
shimmering: 5 aglow 6 bright 7 vibrant 8 lustrous 10 iridescent
shimmier of song: 4 Kate
shimmy: 4 step 5 dance, shake 6 jiggle, judder, totter, wabble, wiggle, wobble 7 shudder, vibrate 8 lingerie
Shimmy, Shimmy, Ko-Ko-Bop (1960 song) artist: Little Anthony and the Imperials
Shimon: 5 Peres
Shimura: 7 Takashi
shin: 4 calf, go up 5 climb, shank, tibia 6 Hebrew, letter 7 clamber, foreleg, leg bone
armor: 6 greave
ender: 3 dig 4 bone, leaf 7 plaster
neighbor: 5 ankle
predecessor: 3 sin
successor: 3 tau, tav, taw
topper: 4 knee
shin ___: 5 guard 6 splint
shinbone: 5 tibia
shindig: 4 ball, bash, fest, fete, gala, luau 5 party 6 affair 7 blowout, jubilee 8 clambake, jamboree 9 festivity
shine: 3 rub, wax 4 beam, buff, glow, show 5 blaze, brush, excel, flame, flare, flash, glare, glaze, gleam, glint, glitz, gloss, light, sleek 6 buff up, dazzle, finish, luster, mirror, patina, patine, polish 7 burnish, deflect, flicker, furbish, glimmer, glisten, glister, glitter, lighten, radiate, reflect, shimmer, sparkle, twinkle 8 bedazzle, brighten, illumine, radiance, radiancy, stand out 9 coruscate, freshness, irradiate, luminesce 10 brightness, brilliance, effulgence, illuminate, incandesce, luminosity, refulgence
alternative: 4 rain
in ad-speak: 3 glo
intermittently: 5 blink
lose ~: 4 dull 7 tarnish
partner: 4 rise
rain or ~: 6 surely 10 definitely, for certain
rise and ~: 4 wake 5 awake, waken 6 awaken 7 turn out
spoil a ~: 4 dull 5 scuff
starter: 3 sun 4 moon, shoe 5 earth 6 monkey
take a ~ to: 4 like
up to: 3 woo 5 court 6 pursue 7 flatter 8 butter up 9 cultivate, patronize 10 curry favor
___-shine: 4 spit
Shine (1996 film)
cast: Armin Mueller-Stahl, Geoffrey Rush, Noah Taylor
director: Scott Hicks
Shine a Little Love (1979 song) artist: ELO
___, shine, for thy light is come...: 5 Arise
shiner: 4 fish 5 mouse 6 bruise 8 black eye
___ Shines Bright, The: 3 Sun
___ shine to: 5 take a
shingle: 3 lap 5 shave 7 overlap
abbr.: 2 MD 3 DDS, esq.
hang up one's ~: 4 open
site: 4 roof
words: 5 at law
shining: 3 lit 5 aglow, clean, clear, light, lucid, nitid, sunny, vivid 6 ablaze, aglare, agleam, bright, flashy, golden, lucent, washed 7 fulgent, lambent, radiant 8 glorious, luminous, lustrous, spotless 9 brilliant, refulgent
combining form: 4 phen- 5 pheno-
Shining ___: 4 Star 7 Through
Shining Star (song) artist: Earth, Wind & Fire, Manhattans

Shining, The: 4 film 5 novel
author: Stephen King
cast: Scatman Crothers, Shelley Duvall, Jack Nicholson
director: Stanley Kubrick
mirrored word in ~: 6 redrum
Shining Through (1992 film)
cast: Michael Douglas, Melanie Griffith, Liam Neeson, Joely Richardson
Shinn: 4 peak 5 mount 8 mountain
locale: 10 Antarctica
Shinnecock Hills: 10 golf course
locale: 7 New York 10 Long Island
shinny: 5 climb, mount, scale, sport 6 ascend 7 clamber 8 scrabble, scramble
Shinto: 8 Japanese, religion
gateway: 5 torii
god: 4 Kami
shiny: 3 lit 5 aglow, clear, light, nitid, sleek, slick, sunny 6 ablaze, agleam, bright, flashy, glassy, glossy, smooth 7 beaming, blazing, fulgent, glowing, lambent, radiant 8 aglimmer, dazzling, gleaming, luminous, lustrous, polished 9 brilliant, burnished, refulgent, sparkling 10 glimmering, glistening, glittering, reflective, unpowdered
coating: 5 glaze 6 enamel
Shiny Happy People (1991 song)
artist: R.E.M.
ship: 3 dau, dow, tug 4 boat, brig, dhow, haul, move, scow, send, yawl 5 barge, craft, liner, oiler, razee, remit, route, xebec, zebec 6 caique, direct, drakar, embark, export, galley, lugger, tanker, tender, vessel, zebeck 7 chebeck, clipper, coaster, consign, deliver, felucca, forward, freight, frigate, process, vehicle 8 dispatch, ironclad, transfer, transmit 9 bundle off, destroyer, freighter, hydrofoil, submarine, transport 10 icebreaker, ocean liner, spacecraft, watercraft
abroad: 6 export
anchor a ~: 5 lay to
any ~: 3 her, she
auxiliary ~: 4 dory 6 tender 8 lifeboat
beam: 4 keel
bed: 4 bunk
bottom: 4 hull
canvas: 4 sail
capacity measure: 3 ton
cargo: 4 bulk
cargo ~: 5 oiler 6 argosy, coaler, tanker
clumsy ~: 3 ark, tub
colors: 6 ensign
crane: 5 davit
cruise ~: 5 liner 6 vessel
cruise ~ accommodation: 5 cabin
cruise ~ stop: 3 POC 10 port of call
Cunard ~: 4 QE II
curved plank: 3 sny
deck: 4 poop 5 orlop 6 fo'c's'le
drainage area: 5 bilge
ender: 3 lap, man, men, way 4 load, mate, side, worm, yard 5 board, borne, shape, wreck 6 master, wright 7 builder 8 building
engine part: 4 pump
en route on a ~: 4 asea 5 at sea
fictional ~: 5 Caine
floor: 4 deck
give up the ~: 6 resign
go by ~: 4 sail
guidance system: 5 loran, radar
holder: 6 anchor
in the ~ hold: 4 alow
journal: 3 log
leave the ~: 6 debark 9 disembark
line: 6 inhaul
loading area: 4 quay
Mediterranean ~: 5 xebec, zebec 6 caique, zebeck 7 chebeck
memorable ~: 5 Maine
merchant ~: 6 argosy
multimasted ~: 8 schooner
officer: 4 mate 5 bosun
off the ~: 6 ashore
of the desert: 5 camel
of the Middle Ages: 3 nao
on a ~: 6 aboard
origin: 4 port
out: 4 part, sail 5 leave 6 embark, export 7 abandon, ride off, set sail 8 go aboard, put to sea, shove off
personnel: 4 crew
pirate ~: 5 rover, xebec, zebec 6 zebeck 7 chebeck
plank: 4 wale
pole: 4 boom, mast, spar
post: 4 bitt 7 bollard
prison: 4 brig
prow: 4 nose
Roman ~: 6 bireme, galley 7 trireme
rope: 3 tye
rusted-out ~: 4 hulk
sailing ~: 4 bark 5 ketch, skiff
side: 4 port 9 starboard
slot: 4 slip 5 berth
stall a ~: 6 becalm
starter: 3 air, kin 4 amid, flag, head, king, lady, star 5 court, light, space, steam, troop 6 amidst, battle, fellow, friend, master 7 comrade, speaker
storage area: 4 hold
strip a ~: 5 unrig 6 demast
tall ~: 8 sailboat
three-masted ~: 5 xebec, zebec 6 zebeck 7 chebeck
timber: 4 mast
to a poet: 4 keel
turn a ~: 4 tack
wake of a ~: 5 track
wheel: 4 helm 6 tiller
wood: 4 teak
see also boat
ship __: 3 out 5 bread, canal, money, of war 7 biscuit
__ ship: 3 log 4 fire, wind 5 about, cargo, dress, solar 6 cruise, mother, packet, rocket, school 7 capital, clipper, factory, landing, Liberty, sailing, Victory, weather
__-ship: 3 air 4 drop
Ship __!: 4 ahoy
shipboard
buddy: 4 mate
romance: 4 idyl 5 fling, idyll
Shipka: 4 pass 8 asteroid
locale: 7 Balkans 8 Bulgaria
Shipley: 3 Tom
__ & Shipley: 6 Brewer
shipload: 5 cargo
shipmate: 6 sailor 7 mariner
shipmates: 4 crew
shipment: 4 load 5 batch, cargo, order 6 export, lading 7 arrival, freight 8 delivery 9 wagonload
ship of __: 3 war 5 state
Ship of Fools: 4 film 5 novel
author: Katherine Anne Porter
cast: José Ferrer, Vivien Leigh, Simone Signoret, Oskar Werner
character: 3 Rac, Ric 4 Elsa, Graf, Lola, Lutz, Pepe, Tito 5 Greta, Käthe, Lizzi 6 Theile
director: Stanley Kramer
ship of the desert: 5 camel
shipper: 8 merchant
shipping: 9 transport 10 navigation
abbr.: 3 COD, FOB, ppd. 4 recd.
hazard: 4 floe, reef
like some ~ rates: 5 zonal 6 zonary
paper: 7 invoice
route: 4 lane 5 canal
unit: 3 ton
shipping __: 3 out, ton 4 lane, room 5 clerk
Shipping News, The (2001 film)
cast: Cate Blanchett, Dame Judi Dench, Julianne Moore, Kevin Spacey
director: Lasse Hallström
ships
group of ~: 5 fleet 6 armada
of ~: 5 naval 8 nautical
starter: 4 amid
ship's __: 3 boy 5 store 6 papers, stores 7 company
Ships (1979 song) artist: Barry Manilow
shipshape: 4 good, neat, taut, tidy, trim 5 kempt 6 spruce 7 orderly 8 well-kept 10 fastidious
make ~ again: 5 refit
ship-shaped clock: 3 nef
ship-to-shore
vehicle: 6 amtrac 7 amtrack
shipworm: 5 borer
shipwreck: 4 hulk, sink 5 wreck 6 maroon, strand
cause: 4 reef
visitor: 5 diver
Shipwreck: 5 Kelly
shipwrecked: 7 aground
Shirakawa, Hideki: 7 chemist 8 Nobelist
Shiraz: 4 city, town
locale: 4 Iran
shire: 5 Devon, Essex 6 county, region, Surrey 8 province
starter: 3 Ayr 4 York 9 Worcester
Shirelles
hometown: Passaic
song: Baby It's You (1962)
Dedicated to the One I Love (1961)
Foolish Little Girl (1963)
Mama Said (1961)
Soldier Boy (1962)
Will You Love Me Tomorrow (1960)
Shirer, William L.: 6 author, writer 9 historian
Shire, Talia: 7 actress
brother: Francis Ford Coppola
film: The Godfather (1972)
The Godfather Part II (1974)
The Godfather Part III (1990)
Rocky (1976)
Rocky II (1979)
nephew: Nicolas Cage
shirk: 4 duck, loaf, lurk, shun, slip 5 avoid, cheat, dodge, dog it, elude, evade, parry, sculk, skulk, slack, slink, snake, sneak 6 bypass, cop out, eschew, recoil 7 abstain, default, goof off, neglect, shy from, slacken 8 flee from, get out of, malinger, sidestep 9 get around, goldbrick, pussyfoot, slough off 10 circumvent, malingerer, shuffle off
shirker: 3 bum 5 idler 6 truant 8 fainéant, layabout, parasite 9 goldbrick 10 malingerer, ne'er-do-well
like a ~: 4 lazy
Shirley: 4 Anne, city, Grau, town 5 Booth, Eaton, Ellis, James, Jones 6 Bassey, Knight, Manson, Temple 7 Jackson 8 Chisholm, MacLaine 9 Muldowney
locale: 7 New York 10 Long Island
__ & Shirley: 7 Laverne
Shirley, Anne: 7 actress
film: Anne of Green Gables (1934)
Murder, My Sweet (1944)
Steamboat 'Round the Bend (1935)
Stella Dallas (1937)
Vigil in the Night (1940)
Shirley author: Charlotte Brontë
Shirley, James: 7 British 10 playwright
Shirley Temple: 5 drink 8 beverage
Shirley Temple __: 5 Black
Shirley Valentine (1989 film)
cast: Pauline Collins, Tom Conti
director: Lewis Gilbert
shirr: 4 bake, cook
shirred item: 3 egg
shirt: 3 tee, top 4 polo 5 kurta, middy, rugby, tunic, V-neck 6 banian, banyan, blouse, camise, halter, Henley, jersey, khurta 7 blouson, bustier, chemise, cover-up, dashiki, hauberk, maillot, singlet, tank top 8 daishiki, guernsey 9 garibaldi 10 button-down
accessory: 3 tie
armor ~: 7 hauberk
athletic ~: 6 jersey
ender: 4 tail 5 dress, waist 6 sleeve
feature: 5 V-neck
hair ~: 7 penance 9 penitence 10 contrition
keep one's ~ on: 4 bide, wait 5 abide 6 cool it, hold on 7 stand by, sweat it 8 sit tight
like a stuffed ~: 5 stiff
loose ~: 6 camise
lose one's ~: 4 fold 6 go bust
measurement: 4 neck 6 sleeve
neaten a ~: 4 tuck
of India: 5 kurta 6 banian, banyan, khurta
part: 3 arm 6 button, collar, sleeve
preceder: 5 sport
ruffle: 5 jabot
size: 3 lge., med. 5 large, small 6 medium, x-large
sleep ~: 9 nightgown
starter: 3 red 5 brown, night, sweat, under
stuffed ~: 4 snob 5 snoot 7 elitist
shirt __: 5 front 6 jacket
shirt-__: 3 jac 5 dress 6 sleeve
__ shirt: 3 tee 4 body, bush, camp, hair, polo 5 aloha, dress, Rugby, sport 6 Basque, boiled, Henley, muscle, safari, skivvy 7 stuffed
shirtwaist: 5 dress
shish: 6 skewer
shish __: 5 kebab, kebob
shish kebab
necessity: 4 spit
shiv: 4 dirk 5 blade, knife 6 weapon
user: 4 hood, thug
Shiva: 9 Destroyer
believer: 5 Hindu 6 Hindoo
coequal: 6 Brahma, Vishnu
wife: 4 Kali
shiver: 4 jerk, rive 5 burst, crack, quake, shake, smash 6 dither, freeze, quaver, quiver, tingle, tremor, twitch 7 flutter, pulsate, shatter, shudder, smatter, tremble, vibrate 8 fragment, splinter 9 palpitate
shiverer's utterance: 3 brr
shivering, fit of: 4 ague
shiver me __: 7 timbers
shiver-producing: 4 eery 5 eerie
shivers: 7 jitters, willies
shivery: 3 icy 4 cold, cool 5 chill, nippy, polar 6 arctic, biting, chilly, frigid, frosty, frozen, wintry 7 numbing, wintery 8 freezing 10 frightened
shiwaya: 4 wind 5 flute 10 instrument
Shizuoka: 4 city, town
locale: 5 Japan
shlemiel: 3 oaf 5 klutz
shlep: 3 lug 4 drag, haul 5 carry, fetch
shmo: 3 oaf 4 jerk
Shmoo creator: 4 Capp
Shmuel: 5 Agnon
SHO: 7 channel
alternative: 3 AMC, HBO, IFC, TMC 4 Flix 5 Bravo, Starz 6 Encore 7 Cinemax 8 Sundance
shoal: 4 reef, spit 5 shelf 6 lagoon 7 sand bar, shallow 8 sandbank
__ Shoals: 6 Muscle

shoat: 3 hog, pig 5 swine
home: 3 pen, sty 6 pigpen, pigsty
shock: 3 awe, jar, mop, wow 4 blow, bump, daze, hair, jolt, mass, numb, pile, rock, stun, tuft, wisp 5 abash, amaze, anger, appal, clash, crash, flood, floor, mound, quake, scare, start, upset, wreck 6 appall, dismay, fright, impact, injury, insult, offend, revolt, sicken, stroke, stupor, terror, trauma, tremor, wallop, whammy 7 agitate, astound, disgust, disturb, horrify, jarring, outrage, shake up, stagger, startle, stupefy, terrify, tragedy 8 astonish, bowl over, collapse, disquiet, distress, frighten, hysteria, overcome, paralyse, paralyze, surprise, unsettle 9 bombshell, breakdown, buffeting, collision, displease, electrify, encounter, eyeopener, galvanize, overwhelm, terrorize, trepidity 10 antagonize, concussion, earthquake, excitement, scandalize, scare stiff, traumatize
absorber: 3 pad 6 buffer, bumper
exclamation: 2 oy 4 gasp, yipe 5 yikes, yipes 7 omigosh
in ~: 4 agog
partner: 3 awe
starter: 5 after, shell
shock __: 4 cord, wave 5 front, radio 6 troops
__ shock: 3 bow, hay 6 future 7 culture, sticker
Shock author: Robin Cook
Shock Corridor (1963 film)
cast: Peter Breck, Gene Evans, Constance Towers
shocked: 5 agasp, upset 6 aghast, jolted 8 overcome 10 dumbstruck, speechless
act ~: 5 start
in a ~ state: 5 agape
more than ~: 4 numb
shocker: 10 revelation
shocking: 4 ugly, vile 5 awful, gross, lurid, outré, scary, utter 6 grisly, odious, tragic, unholy 7 fearful, ghastly, glaring, hateful, heinous, hideous, ungodly 8 dreadful, flagrant, grievous, gruesome, horrible, horrific, infamous, shameful, terrible, terrific, tragical 9 appalling, atrocious, desperate, loathsome, monstrous, offensive, repulsive, revolting, unheard-of 10 abominable, detestable, disgusting, formidable, horrifying, outrageous, petrifying, scandalous, stupefying, surprising
shade: 4 pink
Shocking __: 4 Blue
Shockley, William: 8 Nobelist 9 physicist
shod: 6 booted
it may be ~: 4 hoof
starter: 4 slip 5 rough
shoddy: 3 low 4 base, junk, poor 5 cheap, dingy, gaudy, junky, lousy, mangy, seedy, shady, sorry, tacky, tinny 6 cheapo, cheesy, common, grungy, mangey, paltry, ragged, ragtag, shabby, sleazy, tawdry, trashy 7 run-down, scruffy, squalid 8 el cheapo, inferior, schlocky, shameful, untended 9 makeshift, ungroomed 10 broken-down, inglorious, jerry-built, second-rate
shoe: 3 pac 4 boot, cack, clog, flat, geta, mule, pump 5 gilly, heels, sabot, sling, sneak, spike, stogy, thong, wader 6 bootee, bootie, brogan, brogue, buskin, chopin, chukka, galosh, gillie, golosh, kiltie, loafer, oxford, patten, rubber, sandal, stogie, wedgie 7 chopine, galoshe, ghillie, gumboot, high-low, jodhpur, ski boot, slipper, sneaker, wingtip 8 balmoral, brake pad, elevator, flip-flop, footgear, footwear, high-heel, Mary Jane, moccasin, platform, plimsoll, sneakers, Top-Sider 9 ankle boot, high heels, sling-back, spike heel 10 clodhopper, wellington, white bucks
ankle-length ~: 3 bal 6 chukka 7 high-low, jodhpur
baby ~: 6 bootee, bootie
backless ~: 4 mule 5 thong 8 flip-flop
beach ~: 5 thong
blemish: 5 scuff
brand: 4 Avia, Nike 5 Bally 6 Adidas, Reebok 8 Converse 9 Florsheim 10 New Balance
calf-length ~: 7 gumboot
canted ~: 6 wedgie
canvas ~: 7 sneaker 8 plimsoll, Top-Sider
clerk query: 4 size
cowpuncher's ~: 4 boot
deerskin ~: 3 moc 8 moccasin
divided-toe ~: 5 thong 8 flip-flop
dressy ~: 5 heels, spike 6 oxford 7 wingtip 9 high heels, spike heel
ender: 3 box, pac 4 bill, horn, lace, pack, tree 5 maker, shine 6 string
fix a ~: 4 sole 6 cobble, resole
form: 4 last
gym ~: 5 sneak 7 sneaker
heavy ~: 5 stogy 6 stogie 10 clodhopper
insert: 4 foot, lift, tree
Japanese ~: 4 geta
knee-length ~: 10 wellington
light ~: 3 moc 7 slipper 8 moccasin
like a ~: 5 soled
liner: 3 pac
low-cut ~: 4 flat, pump 6 brogue, gillie, oxford, sandal 7 ghillie, slipper 9 ankle boot, Mary Janes
mark up a ~: 5 scuff
material: 5 suede 6 canvas 7 leather
part: 3 toe 4 arch, heel, sole, vamp, welt 5 shank, upper 6 eyelet, insole, instep 7 outsole
plastic ~: 7 ski boot
polish brand: 4 Kiwi
preserver: 4 tree
rubber ~: 7 gumboot, sneaker 8 plimsoll, Top-Sider
running ~: 6 jogger
salesperson, at times: 5 lacer
slip-on ~: 6 loafer
spike: 5 cleat
starter: 3 gum 4 over, snow 5 horse
stat: 4 size 5 width
strapless ~: 4 pump
string: 4 lace
suede ~: 6 chukka
thick-soled ~: 4 clog 5 sabot 6 buskin, chopin, patten 7 chopine
tighten a ~: 5 retie
tongueless ~: 6 gillie 7 ghillie
walking ~: 4 flat 8 balmoral
waterproof ~: 4 boot 5 wader 6 galosh, rubber
width: 3 AAA, EEE 4 AAAA, EEEE
woman's ~: 4 flat, heel, pump 5 sling 8 balmoral
wooden ~: 4 clog, geta 5 sabot
work ~: 4 boot 6 brogan
__ shoe: 3 gym, hot, old 4 jazz, sand 5 brake, court, track 6 Oxford, saddle, tennis, wooden 7 jodhpur, jogging, running
__-shoe: 4 soft 5 white
shoebill: 4 bird
shoebox
datum: 4 size 5 width
letters: 3 AAA, EEE
__ shoe fits...: 5 If the
shoehorn: 4 cram 6 insert
shoelace
feature: 4 knot
fix a ~: 5 retie
hole: 6 eyelet
tip: 5 aglet 6 aiglet
shoeless: 6 unshod 8 barefoot
Shoeless Joe author: W.P. Kinsella
shoemaker
at times: 5 soler
bottle: 3 dye
helper: 3 elf
mold: 4 last
tool: 3 awl
Shoemaker, Bill: 6 jockey
milieu: 5 track
Shoemaker-Levy: 5 comet
Shoemaker, Willie: 6 jockey
milieu: 5 track
shoer: 10 blacksmith
concern: 4 hoof
Shoeshine (1946 film) director: Vittorio De Sica
Shoes of the Fisherman, The author: Morris West 4 West
__ Shoes, The: 3 Red
shoestring: 5 light 6 little
shoestring __: 5 catch 6 tackle
__ shoestring: 3 on a
shoestrings: 6 lacing
shofar: 4 wind 8 ram's horn
origin: 6 Hebrew
shogi: 4 game 8 Japanese
master: 3 dan
shogun: 5 ruler 6 gerent 8 Japanese
capital: 3 Edo 4 Yedo 5 Yeddo
extra: 6 geisha
sash: 3 obi
vassal: 6 daimio, daimyo
warrior: 5 ninja
Shogun author: James Clavell
Sholem: 4 Asch
Sholokhov, Mikhail: 6 author, writer 7 Russian 8 Nobelist
work: The Quiet Don
Shona home: 6 Africa 8 Zimbabwe 10 Mozambique
Shondell: 4 Troy
sho' nuff: 3 yep, yup
shoo: 3 git 4 away, scat 5 scram 6 beat it, begone 8 wave away 9 chase away, drive away, scare away
shoo-__ pie: 3 fly
Shoo-Be-Doo-Be-Doo-Da-Day (1968 song) artist: Stevie Wonder
shooby-doo, go: 4 scat
shoo-fly pie: 6 pastry
shook: 4 agog 5 upset 6 aghast 7 gyrated, rattled, stunned 8 confused, got rid of, quivered, shimmied, trembled, vibrated 9 perturbed, unsettled 10 high-strung
__ Shook Up: 3 All
Shoop (1993 song) artist: Salt-n-Pepa
Shoop Shoop Song, The (1964 song)
artist: Betty Everett
refrain: 6 na na na
shoot: 3 bag, bud, gun, hie, hit, pop, run, zap 4 bolt, dart, dash, emit, film, fire, hurl, lick, pass, pump, race, rush, send, slip, snap, soar, stem, tear, twig, zoom 5 blast, chase, expel, flash, fling, graft, photo, plant, reach, scoot, sling, speed, spire, spirt, sprig, spurt, start, throw, whisk 6 charge, darn it, hasten, hurtle, ignite, launch, let fly, member, open up, propel, set off, spring, sprout, stolon, streak 7 barrage, bombard, cutting, explode, pick off, project, scamper, torpedo 8 catapult, dispatch, fire upon, open fire, spring up 9 bring down, discharge, germinate, new growth 10 photograph
ahead: 4 pass 5 outdo 8 progress
(at): 3 aim
at, as tin cans: 5 plink
director's ~: 4 take 5 scene
down: 3 nix 4 fell, flay, ruin, slam, veto 5 rebut, shame 6 debase, debunk, refute, reject 7 deflate, degrade, explode 8 belittle 9 disparage, eradicate, find fault, humiliate
ender: 3 out 4 down
for: 3 try 5 aim at 6 aspire, strive 8 aspire to
forth: 3 jet 4 spew, spue 5 erupt
for the green: 4 chip 5 slice
from ambush: 5 snipe
get ready to ~: 3 aim 5 focus, point
in and out: 6 dartle
off: 3 pop 4 fire 5 erupt 7 explode 8 detonate 9 discharge, fulminate
off one's mouth: 4 brag 5 spout 7 bluster
oneself in the foot: 3 err 4 flub, goof 5 gum up 6 blow it, bungle, foul up, fumble, goof up, mess up 7 blunder, louse up 9 mishandle, mismanage
out: 4 emit 5 eject, flash, spirt, spurt 7 burgeon, radiate 8 bourgeon
plant ~: 4 twig 5 spire
slender ~: 4 wand
starter: 3 off 4 crap, snap 7 trouble
the breeze: 3 gab, jaw, rap 4 blab, chat 5 prate, speak 6 gossip, jabber 7 blather, blether, chatter 8 chitchat, talk idly 10 chew the fat, chew the rag
the curl: 4 surf
the moon: 6 gamble
up: 4 soar, zoom 5 raise 6 mature, rocket, spring, sprout, thrive 7 burgeon 8 bourgeon, mushroom
shoot __: 3 for 4 down 5 hoops
shoot __ one's mouth: 3 off
shoot __ the hip: 4 from
__ shoot: 5 photo 6 bamboo, turkey
Shoot!: 3 ask 4 darn, drat 5 ask me
shoot-'em-up: 5 oater 7 western
shooter: 3 gun 6 gunman
ammo: 2 BB 3 pea
circus ~: 6 cannon
marble: 3 mib, taw 5 agate, aggie
need: 6 camera
pellet ~: 5 BB gun 6 airgun
request: 5 smile 9 say cheese
spot: 6 rapids
starter: 3 pea 4 trap 5 sharp 7 trouble
__ shooter: 3 pea 6 square
__-shooter: 3 six
shoot from the __: 3 hip
shooting: 5 sharp 6 murder
area: 5 range
clay-pigeon ~: 5 skeet
end of ~: 4 wrap
game: 5 skeet
position: 5 prone
range shout: 3 aim 4 fire 5 ready
star: 5 plant 6 flower, meteor
star path: 3 arc
shooting __: 3 box, war 4 iron, star 5 brake, match, stick 6 script 7 gallery
__ shooting: 4 trap, wing 5 skeet 6 flight
Shooting an Elephant author: George Orwell
Shooting of Dan McGrew, The author: Robert Service
Shooting, The (1967 film)
cast: Will Hutchins, Jack Nicholson, Millie Perkins
__ shootin' match, the: 5 whole
Shootist, The (1976 film): 5 oater 7 western
cast: Lauren Bacall, Richard Boone, Ron Howard, Hugh O'Brian, James Stewart, John Wayne
director: Don Siegel

__ Shoot Me: 4 Just
shootout: 4 duel
__ shoots: 6 bamboo
shoot the __: 5 works 6 breeze, chutes, rapids
Shoot the Moon (1982 film)
cast: Karen Allen, Albert Finney, Diane Keaton
director: Alan Parker
Shoot the Piano Player (1960 film)
cast: Charles Aznavour, Nicole Berger, Marie Dubois
director: François Truffaut
shop: 3 buy 4 deli, mart, mill 5 plant, salon, stand, store, trade 6 bakery, garage, market, office, outlet 7 factory, hunt for, look for, splurge 8 boutique, business, emporium, purchase, showroom
at: 9 patronize
chic ~: 5 salon
close up ~: 10 call it a day
ender: 4 lift, talk, worn 6 keeper
for: 3 buy
in the ~: 6 broken
machine: 5 lathe 6 jigsaw
set up ~: 4 open
specialty ~: 8 boutique
starter: 4 bake, book, hock, pawn, work 5 sweat, sweet 6 barber
talk: 4 cant 5 argot, lingo 6 jargon
tool: 3 awl 4 vise 6 hammer, pliers
without buying: 6 browse
shop __: 5 right 6 around 7 steward
__ shop: 3 job, pro, tea 4 body, chop, malt, open, swap, talk 5 cycle, fix-it, plate, print, set up, speed, union 6 agency, beauty, bottle, closed, coffee, thrift 7 betting, butcher, machine
__-shop: 3 pop 4 tuck 5 sweet 6 window
shopaholic hangout: 4 mall
Shop Around (song) artist: Captain & Tennille, Miracles
Shop Around the Corner, The (1940 film)
cast: Frank Morgan, James Stewart, Margaret Sullavan
director: Ernst Lubitsch
__ Shop Boys: 3 Pet
shopkeeper: 6 grocer, seller, trader 8 merchant
shoplift: 5 boost, steal, swipe 6 pocket, thieve
shoplifter: 5 thief 6 klepto
ShopNBC: 7 channel
alternative: 3 HSN, QVC
__ Shop of Horrors: 6 Little
shoppe descriptor: 4 olde
shopper: 6 patron 8 consumer, customer
aid: 3 bag 4 cart, list
channel: 3 HSN, QVC
clipping: 6 coupon
concern: 5 price
find: 3 buy 7 bargain
lure: 4 free, sale 5 no tax 6 rebate
often: 5 toter
stop: 4 mall, mart 5 salon, store 8 boutique
window ~: 4 eyer 7 browser
shopping: 9 patronage
center: 4 mall, mart 5 bazar, plaza, store 6 arcade, bazaar, market
extravaganza: 5 spree
go ~: 3 buy 5 spend
shopping __: 3 bag 4 cart, list, mall 5 plaza, spree 6 center
__ shopping: 6 window 7 one-stop
Shop 'Til You Drop: 8 game show
host: Pat Finn
shopworn: 5 corny, hokey, stale, trite 10 threadbare
Shopworn Angel, The (1938 film)
cast: James Stewart, Margaret Sullavan
director: H.C. Potter
Shor: 5 Toots
shore: 4 bank, brim, hold, land, prop, sand 5 beach, brace, brink, coast, sands 6 anneal, bear up, border, margin, uphold 7 bolster, bulwark, seaside, support, sustain 8 buttress, lakeside, littoral, seacoast, underpin 9 coastland, coastline, reinforce, riverbank, riverside, waterside 10 embankment, strengthen, waterfront
away from the ~: 6 inland
ender: 4 bird, line, ward 5 front, wards
feature: 3 bay 4 cove 5 bight, inlet
find: 5 conch, shell
leave: 8 furlough
leave ~: 4 sail 7 set sail 8 shove off
make ~: 4 land
starter: 3 off, sea 4 back, lake, long 5 along
up: 4 gird, hold, prop, tone 5 brace, build, shore, steel 6 anneal, harden, temper, uphold 7 bolster, burgeon, develop, empower, enhance, fortify, stiffen, support, sustain, toughen 8 bourgeon, buttress, energize, indurate, underpin, vitalize 9 intensify, reinforce, undergird 10 invigorate, strengthen
shore __: 3 bug, fly 4 bird, crab 5 leave 6 dinner, patrol 7 terrace
__ shore: 3 lee
Shore: 5 Dinah, Eddie, Ernie, Pauly
shorebird: 3 ern 4 erne, gull, tern 5 heron, oxeye, stilt, wader 6 avocet, curlew, dunlin, godwit, plover, willet 7 tattler 9 dowitcher, sandpiper, turnstone 10 greenshank, yellowlegs
Shore, Dinah
song: Love and Marriage (1955) Whatever Lola Wants (1955)
spouse: George Montgomery
Shoreline: 4 city, town
locale: 10 Washington
shoreline indentation: 3 bay 4 cove, gulf 5 basin, bayou, bight, fiord, firth, fjord, inlet 6 lagoon 7 estuary
Shoreview: 4 city, town
locale: 9 Minnesota
shorn: 3 cut 4 bare 7 clipped, fleeced 8 glabrous, hairless, tonsured
short: 3 low, shy, wee 4 curt, flat, rude, slim 5 blunt, brief, brusk, coast, crisp, gruff, huffy, needy, pithy, rough, scant, sharp, small, spare, squat, terse, testy, tight 6 abrupt, curtly, direct, gnomic, in need, little, meager, petite, scanty, scarce, skimpy, snappy, snippy, sparse, stocky, stubby, sudden 7 briefly, brusque, cartoon, compact, concise, cursory, failing, friable, hastily, hurried, lacking, laconic, limited, missing, needing, passing, pointed, precise, squatty, stunted, summary, tersely, uncivil, wanting 8 abridged, fleeting, flitting, impolite, knee-high, lessened, off-guard, sawed-off, sea-level, snippety, strapped, succinct, suddenly, travelog, unawares 9 brusquely, condensed, curtailed, decreased, deficient, ephemeral, hurriedly, irascible, minimovie, momentary, pint-sized, temporary, transient, truncated, two-reeler, undersize 10 boiled down, by surprise, compressed, diminished, diminutive, evanescent, inadequate, succinctly, summarized, to the point, travelogue, undersized, unelevated, unenduring, ungracious
and stocky: 5 squat
and sweet: 5 brief, pithy, terse 7 laconic
a ~ time ago: 6 lately, of late 8 recently 9 yesterday
at ~ notice: 9 summarily
be ~: 4 snap
be ~ of: 4 lack, need
combining form: 5 brevi- 6 brachy-
come up ~: 3 owe 4 fail, lack, lose
cut ~: 3 bob, end, nip 4 crop, ruin, stop 5 elide, shave 7 curtail, silence, suspend 8 compress, condense 9 interrupt, synopsize, telescope, terminate 10 unfinished
cut ~ as a tail: 4 dock
distance: 3 hop 4 inch
end: 4 stub 5 least
ender: 3 age, cut 4 cake, fall, hair, hand, horn, list, stop, wave 5 bread 6 change, coming, haired 7 sighted 8 changing
fall ~: 4 fail, lack, lose, miss 7 let down, lose out
haul: 3 hop, run 6 outing 7 day trip
in ~: 7 briefly 9 concisely
in a ~ time: 4 anon, fast, soon
in ~ supply: 6 exotic, scanty, scarce, sparse 8 uncommon
in the ~ term: 6 for now
of: 5 low on 6 except 10 leaving out
of cash: 4 poor 5 needy
period: 3 bit 5 spell, trice
seller: 4 bear
stop ~: 4 balk 5 baulk 10 abbreviate
supply: 6 dearth
time: 4 msec., nsec. 7 instant
trip: 5 jaunt, whirl 6 dayhop, errand, outing
version: 6 digest
short __: 3 con, run, ton 4 fuse, game, haul, iron, line, list, rate, ribs, sale, time 5 field, order, story, title 6 ballot, seller, shrift, splice 7 account, circuit, subject
short __ of the stick, the: 3 end
short-__: 3 cut, day, run 4 laid, term 5 lived, range, sheet 6 handed, spoken, winded 7 commons, waisted
short-__ cook: 5 order
short-__ memory: 4 term
__ short: 3 cut, for, run 4 fall, sell
__-short: 3 hot, red
Short: 5 Bobby 6 Martin
Short __: 4 Cuts, Eyes 6 People, Shorts 7 Circuit
shortage: 4 lack, need, want 5 lapse 6 dearth, famine 7 deficit, failure, paucity, poverty 8 leanness, scarcity, sparsity, weakness 9 tightness 10 deficiency, inadequacy, scantiness
Short, Bobby: 7 pianist
shortbread: 6 cookie
shortcake: 7 dessert
Short Circuit (1986 film)
cast: Steve Guttenberg, Ally Sheedy
director: John Badham
short-circuit sight: 5 spark
shortcoming: 3 sin 4 flaw, lack, need, vice, want 5 catch, debit, fault, lapse, minus 6 defect, foible, hurdle 7 barrier, demerit, failing, frailty 8 drawback, handicap, obstacle, weakness 9 detriment, hindrance, infirmity, liability, weak point 10 impediment
Short Cuts (1993 film)
cast: Bruce Davison, Jack Lemmon, Andie MacDowell, Julianne Moore
director: Robert Altman
shorten: 3 bob, lop 4 chop, clip, crop, dock, edit, pare, snip, trim 5 prune, slash 6 digest, lessen, narrow, recede, reduce, shrink 7 abridge, commute, compact, curtail, cut back, cut down 8 abstract, boil down, compress, condense, contract, decrease, diminish, minimize, simplify, truncate 9 capsulize, summarize, synopsize, telescope 10 abbreviate, blue-pencil
a garment: 3 hem 5 alter
grass: 3 mow
sideburns: 5 razor, shave
shortened: 3 cut 4 less 7 capsule, partial, sketchy 10 unfinished
shortening: 4 lard
brand: 6 Crisco
Shorter, Frank: 6 runner
shortfall: 4 lack, need 7 arrears, deficit 8 exiguity, underage 10 inadequacy
short-fused: 9 excitable, irritable 10 intolerant
shorthair: 3 cat 5 felid 6 feline
shorthand
expert: 5 steno
stat: 3 wpm
short-haul: 5 brief 7 passing 8 fleeting, flitting 9 momentary, temporary, transient 10 transitory
Short History of the World, A author: H.G. Wells
Shorthorn: 3 cow 4 bull 6 bovine, cattle
short-lived: 5 brief, swift 6 little 7 passing 8 fleeting, flitting, temporal, volatile 9 ephemeral, momentary, temporary, transient 10 fly-by-night, pro tempore, transitory
shortly: 4 anon, soon 6 awhile, in a bit, in a sec 7 briefly 8 directly, hereupon 9 presently 10 in good time
Short, Martin: 5 actor 8 comedian
film: Father of the Bride (1991) Innerspace (1987) Three Amigos! (1986)
TV: Saturday Night Live
shortness: 4 lack 10 impatience
__ short of: 3 run
short-order place: 5 diner
employee: 4 cook
Short People (1977 song) artist: Randy Newman
__ short run: 5 in the
shorts: 4 BVDs 5 pants 6 boxers, briefs, trunks, undies 7 cutoffs, drawers, jockeys 8 bermudas, bloomers, breeches, hot pants, knickers, skivvies 9 underwear 10 lederhosen
class: 3 gym
stat: 5 waist
__ shorts: 3 gym 4 walk 5 boxer 6 Jockey 7 Bermuda, Jamaica, walking
short-sheeting: 5 prank
Short Shorts (1958 song) artist: Royal Teens
shortsighted: 4 rash 6 myopic, unwary, unwise 7 foolish 8 careless 9 imprudent
one: 5 myope
short-spoken: 4 curt 5 brief, terse
shortstop: 7 athlete 9 intercept, interrupt 10 baseballer
gear: 5 glove
Hall of Fame ~: 5 Banks, Reese, Smith, Yount 6 Cronin, Wagner 7 Appling, Rizzuto, Vaughan 8 Aparicio, Boudreau 9 Joe Cronin 10 Ernie Banks, Ozzie Smith, Robin Yount
stat: 6 assist, putout
Short Symphony composer: 7 Copland
short-tempered: 5 huffy, irate, moody, onery, surly, testy 6 crabby, cranky, crusty, feisty, grumpy, ireful, ornery, snarly, touchy 7 bearish, bilious, crabbed, fretful, grouchy, peevish, waspish 8 choleric, fretsome, grumpish, petulant, snappish 9 fractious, irascible, irritable, querulous, splenetic
Short-Tempered Clavier, The composer: PDQ Bach
short-term: 5 brief 9 transient 10 transitory

short-term ___: 6 memory
shortwave: 4 band 5 radio
broadcaster: 3 ham
US ~ service: 3 VOA
short-winded: 5 brief, pursy, terse
___ short work of: 4 make
___ Shorty: 3 Get
Shoshone: 3 Ute 5 river, tribe 8 Comanche 9 waterfall
language family: 5 Numic
river locale: 7 Wyoming
structure: 4 tipi 5 tepee 6 teepee
Shoshone ___: 3 Dam 5 Falls 6 Cavern
Shoshone Falls locale: 5 Idaho
Shostakovich, Dmitri: 7 Russian 8 composer
work: The Age of Gold, Festival Overture, Leningrad Symphony, October Symphony
shot: 3 BBs, lob, nip, pop, try 4 ammo, ball, bang, dart, dram, gone, hypo, slap, slug, stab, time, turn, worn 5 blast, break, burst, crack, drink, fling, guess, kaput, noise, punch, smash, spent, tense, throw, whack, whirl 6 beebee, bullet, chance, effort, gamble, pellet, ruined, used up 7 attempt, damaged, far-gone, liftoff, missile, vaccine, venture, worn-out 8 endeavor, marksman, occasion, slam dunk, washed-up 9 discharge, fisticuff, injection, in tatters, wild guess 10 ammunition, conjecture, photograph, projectile
a ~: 4 each 6 apiece
bar ~: 5 snort
basketball ~: 4 dunk 5 lay up, tip-in 8 slam dunk
big ~: 3 VIP 4 king, lion, name 5 mogul, nabob, nawab, wheel 6 fat cat, kahuna, tycoon 7 notable 8 higher-up, official 9 authority, celebrity, dignitary, personage
billiards ~: 5 carom, massé 6 carrom
camera ~: 4 zoom 6 fade-in
cheap ~: 3 dig 4 barb, gibe, jibe, slam, slap, slur, snub 5 abuse, libel, scorn, taunt 6 insult, rebuff, slight 7 affront, calumny, catcall, disdain, low blow, mockery, obloquy, offense, put-down, slander 8 contempt, derision, ridicule 9 aspersion, contumely 10 defamation, disrespect, opprobrium
down: 8 dejected
ender: 3 gun
follower: 6 chaser
get a ~: 4 snap 10 photograph
give a ~: 8 immunize 9 vaccinate
glass: 6 jigger
golf ~: 4 chip, putt 5 drive, gimme, pitch, shank, tap-in
go like a ~: 3 hie, run 4 race, rush 5 speed 6 streak
hot ~: 6 dynamo, wizard 9 personage
in the arm: 4 lift 5 boost, tonic 8 pick-me-up, stimulus
in the dark: 3 bet 4 risk, stab 5 guess 6 gamble 9 guesswork
like a ~: 3 PDQ 4 fast 5 apace 6 presto 7 fleetly, hastily, quickly, rapidly, swiftly 8 in a flash, in a jiffy, in no time, pell-mell, promptly, speedily 9 forthwith, hurriedly, instantly, posthaste
prepare to be ~: 4 pose
put: 5 event, sport
short ~: 4 putt 5 lay-up
small ~: 4 dram
soccer ~: 4 kick 6 header
starter: 3 big, bow, ear, eye, gun, hot, out, pot 4 bird, buck, head, over, snap 5 blood, grape, sling, under 7 scatter, trouble
sure ~: 3 ace
take a ~: 3 try 5 guess 8 theorize 10 conjecture
tennis ~: 3 lob 4 dink 5 smash 6 volley 8 backhand, forehand
volleyball ~: 4 dink 5 spike
wide ~: 4 miss
shot ___: 3 put 4 hole 5 clock, glass, metal, noise, tower 6 effect
shot-___: 6 putter
___ shot: 3 big, hot, mug, pot, rim, set 4 bank, bean, bird, boom, case, chip, draw, drop, dunk, dust, foul, hook, jump, kill, long, moon, push, slap, trap, wing, wood, zoom 5 angle, chain, cheap, close, dolly, like a, massé, matte, pitch, slung, stock, stuff, tight, track 6 anchor, follow, medium, travel 7 booster, cutaway, feather, grapple, panning, parting, passing, penalty, reverse, scatter
___-shot: 3 one, two 5 guest 6 single
___ Shot: 3 Big 4 Bank, Slap 7 Warning
___ shot at: 5 have a, take a
___-shot deal: 3 one
shote: 3 hog, pig
shotgun: 3 arm 5 rifle 6 coerce 7 firearm
diameter: 5 gauge
ride ~: 5 watch 6 assist, defend, patrol, shield 7 protect 8 advocate 9 safeguard
___ shotgun: 4 ride
Shotgun ___: 5 Slade
shotguns: 8 weaponry
shot in the ___: 3 arm 4 dark
Shot in the Dark, A (1964 film)
cast: George Sanders, Peter Sellers, Elke Sommer
director: Blake Edwards
shot putter: Al Oerter
shots: 4 ammo 10 ammunition
call the ~: 4 boss, lead, rule 5 order 6 direct, govern, manage, settle 7 dictate, oversee 8 dominate 9 supervise
series of ~: 5 salvo
___ Shots!: 3 Hot
shou: 4 deer
relative: 3 elk, roe 4 axis, pudu, sika 5 moose 6 chital, guemal, hangul, huemul, sambar, sambur, thamin, wapiti 7 brocket, caribou, muntjac, muntjak, sambhar, sambhur 8 reindeer 9 barasingh
should: 4 must 5 ought 6 in case 7 had best 9 had better
Shoulda listened!: 6 told ya
___ Should Be Dancing: 3 You
shoulder: 4 bear, meat, pack, push, take 5 carry, elbow, nudge, press, shove 6 accept, assume, flange, hustle, take on 7 go about, support 9 push aside, undertake
bag: 5 purse 9 haversack
cold ~: 3 cut 4 snub 5 spurn 6 rebuff, slight 7 refusal, repulse 9 rejection
combining form: 2 om- 3 omo-
enhancer: 3 pad
gesture: 5 shrug
muscle: 4 delt
part: 5 blade
road ~: 4 berm 5 berme
something to ~: 5 blame
to shoulder: 7 abreast
with a chip on one's ~: 6 bitter 9 resentful
wrap: 5 shawl
shoulder ___: 3 bag, gun 4 arms, belt, knot, loop, mark 5 blade, board, patch, strap 6 season, weapon 7 harness, holster
___ shoulder: 4 cold, soft 6 picnic
___-shouldered: 5 round 6 square
___ shoulders with: 3 rub
shoulder to ___: 5 cry on
Should I Do It (1982 song) artist: Pointer Sisters
shout: 3 bay, cry, yap 4 bark, bawl, call, hoot, howl, rant, rave, roar, yell 5 cheer, hallo, huzza, salvo, sound, speak, utter, voice, whoop 6 bellow, clamor, cry out, halloa, halloo, holler, huzzah, outcry, scream, shriek, squawk, squeal, tumult, yammer 7 belt out, call out, exclaim, screech, sing out, thunder 8 laughter, let loose, outburst, vocalize 10 vociferate
shout ___: 4 down
shout ___ the rooftops: 4 from
shouting: 5 aroar, noise, noisy 6 racket 10 vociferous
match: 3 row 8 argument
within ~ distance: 4 near 6 nearby
Shout (song) artist: Joey Dee and the Starliters, Tears for Fears
shove: 3 jab, jam 4 cram, grub, move, poke, prod, push, tuck 5 boost, crowd, elbow, forge, impel, nudge, press, slide, stuff 6 hustle, insert, jostle, justle, propel, thrust 8 bulldoze, shoulder 9 strong-arm
it may come to ~: 4 push
off: 2 go 4 exit, part, quit, sail 5 leave, scram, split 6 beat it, be gone, decamp, depart, go away 7 head out, pull out, set sail, ship out, vamoose 8 clear out, hightail, put to sea, run along, start out
upward ~: 4 lift, push 5 heave, hoist 6 assist, thrust
shove ___: 3 off
shove ___ one's throat: 4 down
shovel: 4 tool 5 gouge, scoop, spade
ender: 4 head, nose
in: 3 eat
use a ~: 3 dig
___ shovel: 5 power, steam
shoveler: 4 bird, duck, fowl
relative: 4 smew, teal 5 eider, Pekin, Rouen, scaup 6 Cayuga, scoter 7 gadwall, mallard, pintail, pochard, redhead, sea duck, widgeon 8 garganey, gray duck, mandarin, musk duck, oldsquaw, surf duck, wood duck 9 black duck, broadbill, goldeneye, goosander, greenhead, merganser, ruddy duck, sprigtail 10 bufflehead, canvasback, surf scoter, tufted duck
show: 3 act, air, gig, see 4 bare, come, expo, face, fair, film, give, look, play, pomp, sell, sham, time, view 5 array, drama, flick, front, guide, guise, mount, movie, occur, offer, pop up, prove, reach, revue, shine, sight, sport, stage, steer, teach 6 adduce, appear, arrive, assert, attend, blow in, cinema, circus, comedy, confer, denote, depict, detail, direct, effect, emerge, escort, evince, expose, flaunt, lay out, mirror, parade, record, reveal, review, set out, splash, spread, turn up, unfold, unfurl, unveil, vanity 7 act with, bespeak, betoken, burlesk, clarify, concert, display, divulge, exhibit, explain, express, glitter, pageant, picture, present, pretext, produce, proffer, program, reflect, seeming, signify, sparkle, testify, trot out, turn out, uncover 8 brandish, bring out, carnival, disclose, discover, document, evidence, flourish, indicate, instruct, manifest, point out, pretense, proclaim, register, set forth, shepherd, spell out, splendor, stick out 9 accompany, burlesque, determine, elucidate, establish, fireworks, make clear, make known, make plain, pageantry, put on view, represent, semblance, spectacle, symbolize, testify to 10 appearance, evincement, exhibition, exposition, false front, grandstand, illustrate, impression, occurrence, pretension, production, vaudeville
affection: 4 kiss 5 spoon 6 caress
approval: 3 nod 4 buoy, clap, yell 5 cheer, shout, whoop 6 buck up, perk up, praise, scream, uplift 7 acclaim, applaud, elevate, enliven, gladden, hearten, root for, support 8 enspirit, inspirit, reassure 9 encourage 10 brighten up, exhilarate, strengthen
around: 5 usher 9 accompany
clearly: 6 detail 7 specify
contempt: 4 jeer, mock 5 scoff
curiosity: 3 ask 8 question
delight: 4 beam, glow, grin 5 smile
disapproval: 3 boo 4 hiss 5 frown
disdain: 4 jeer 5 shrug, sniff
displeasure: 4 pout 5 frown
disrespect: 4 snub 6 slight
do a ~: 3 act 4 sing 6 appear 7 perform
do better than ~: 5 place
elation: 4 beam 5 smile 7 light up
embarrassment: 5 blush 6 redden
ender: 3 biz, man, men, off 4 boat, case, down, girl, time 5 piece, place 6 finale 7 stopper
excitement: 4 rave 6 bubble 7 delight, enthuse, rejoice, sparkle 10 effervesce
failure: 4 bomb 6 turkey
false ~: 3 act 4 sham 8 pretense
fatigue: 3 nod 4 yawn
fear: 3 run 5 cower, quake, wince 6 cringe
feelings: 5 emote, react
for ~: 5 fancy 6 dressy, ornate 9 beautiful, elaborate, exquisite 10 decorative, ornamental, ostensibly
get the ~ on the road: 5 begin 6 launch 7 lead off 8 commence
give the ~ away: 4 blab, leak, talk 5 spill 6 tattle
glee: 4 grin 5 smile 7 sparkle
hesitation: 5 waver 6 falter, wobble 9 hem and haw, vacillate
improvement: 4 gain, mend 6 look up, pick up 7 advance, shape up 8 progress 9 come along, get better 10 recuperate
in: 5 usher 7 receive, welcome
industrial ~: 4 expo
irritation: 4 boil, fume, rage, rant, rave 5 chafe 6 blow up, seethe
need: 6 ticket
no ~: 4 AWOL 7 absence 8 absentee
off: 4 brag, pose, tout, wear 5 boast, flash, model, sport, strut 6 expose, fake it, flaunt, parade, prance 7 bluster, display, exhibit, posture, swagger, trot out 8 brandish, overplay 9 advertise, promenade 10 grandstand, wave around
one's face: 5 pop in, visit 6 appear, arrive, attend, blow in, drop in, emerge, roll in, turn up 7 check in, clock in, punch in, turn out 8 breeze in
one's heels: 3 hie, run
otherwise: 4 deny 5 belie, quash, rebut 6 negate, refute 7 confute, dispute 8 confound, disprove, overturn 9 discredit, shoot down 10 contradict, disconfirm
partner: 4 tell 6 cohost
patience: 5 abide, await
position: 5 third
put on a ~: 3 act 5 amuse, stage

relevance: 5 tie in 7 connect 9 correlate
respect: 3 bow 5 honor, kneel 7 lionize
run the ~: 4 rule 6 direct, manage 7 oversee 8 dominate 9 supervise 10 administer
sadness: 3 cry, sob 4 bawl, wail, weep 6 bewail
short ~: 3 act 4 skit
SRO ~: 3 hit 5 smash
stage ~: 4 play 5 drama, revue 6 review 10 production
starter: 4 Act I, side, song 5 floor
the ropes: 5 coach, teach, train, tutor 6 school 7 educate 8 instruct
the way: 4 lead 5 guide, point 6 direct, lead in, lead on 7 pioneer
to advantage: 7 flatter
to a seat: 5 usher 6 escort 7 usher in
traveling ~: 6 circus 8 carnival
up: 4 come 5 enter, get in, outdo, pop in, reach, shame, visit 6 appear, arrive, attend, blow in, defeat, drop in, expose, refute, report, reveal, roll in, unmask 7 eclipse, lay bare, turn out, uncloak, weigh in 8 belittle, breeze in, get there, outshine, unshroud 9 discredit, embarrass 10 invalidate, overshadow, put to shame
use: 4 fade, fray, wear 5 decay, erode, scuff 6 abrade, weaken 7 corrode, crumble, wear out, weather 8 wear down
venue: 5 stage 8 Broadway
Western ~: 5 oater, rodeo
show __: 3 biz, off 4 bill, card, girl 5 house 6 window
show __ order: 5 cause
show-__: 7 stopper, through
__ show: 3 dog, ice 4 chat, game, late, quiz, road, talk, tent 5 bench, floor, horse, light, raree, trade 6 best in, cattle, one-man, puppet, shadow, talent 7 picture, pre-game, variety
Show: 5 Grant
__ Show: 4 Quiz 6 Armory 7 Varsity
show and __: 4 tell
showboat: 4 brag 10 grandstand
Show Boat (1936 film): 7 musical
cast: Irene Dunne, Allan Jones, Helen Morgan, Paul Robeson
character: 3 Kim 4 Andy 5 Ellie, Julie 7 Gaylord, Ravenal
composer: 4 Kern 11 Hammerstein
director: James Whale
prop: 4 bale
tune: 4 Bill
Show Boat (1951 film): 7 musical
cast: Ava Gardner, Kathryn Grayson, Howard Keel
composer: 4 Kern 11 Hammerstein
director: George Sidney
Show Boat author: Edna Ferber
showcase: 4 expo 5 array 7 display, exhibit, feature 8 headline
showdown: 4 duel 5 clash 6 climax, crisis 7 meeting 8 skirmish 9 unfolding
Showdown author: Jorge Amado
__ Showed Me: 3 You
shower: 4 hail, lave, mist, pelt, pour, rain, shed, wash 5 spray, throw 6 lavish, splash 7 barrage, moisten, scatter, smother, spatter 8 ablution, sprinkle
affection: 4 dote 5 adore
alternative: 3 tub 4 bath
baby ~ gift: 7 bootees, booties
ender: 4 head
feature: 5 drain
kudos on: 4 laud 5 extol 6 extoll, praise, puff up 7 acclaim, applaud, commend 10 compliment
meteor ~: 5 Lyrid 6 Cygnid, Leonid
sealer: 5 grout
sponge: 5 loofa
starter: 7 thunder
take a ~: 4 lave, wash 5 bathe
shower __: 3 tea 5 stall
__ shower: 3 air 4 rain 5 Auger 6 bridal, meteor
__ Showers: 5 April
showery: 3 wet 5 rainy 6 hyetal 7 pluvial, raining
month: 3 Apr. 5 April
Show Girl tune: 4 Liza
showgoer: 6 viewer 9 spectator
showgoers: 8 audience
showiness: 5 glitz 7 glitter
showing: 7 display 9 semblance 10 exhibition
advance ~: 6 prevue 7 preview
cinema ~: 4 film 5 movie, short
first ~: 5 debut 8 premiere
second ~: 5 rerun
with more ~: 5 nuder
show-me: 9 quizzical, skeptical
Show Me State: 8 Missouri
Show Me the Meaning of Being Lonely (2000 song) artist: Backstreet Boys
Show Me the Way (song) artist: Peter Frampton, Styx
Show Must Go On, The (1974 song) artist: Three Dog Night
shown: 6 taught 8 manifest 9 on display
show of __: 5 hands
__ show of: 5 make a
showoff: 3 ham 4 zany 6 gascon, hotdog 7 boaster, egotist 8 braggart 9 daredevil, swaggerer
__ Show of Shows: 4 Your
show one's __: 4 face, hand 5 heels, teeth
show one the __: 4 door
Show People (1928 film)
cast: Marion Davies, William Haines, Del Henderson
director: King Vidor
showpiece: 3 art 8 nicknack 10 knickknack
showroom: 4 mart, shop 5 store 6 outlet 7 gallery
car: 4 demo
caveat: 4 as is
operator: 6 dealer
__ Show, The: 4 Gong, Late, Lucy, T.A.M.I. 5 Cosby 6 Muppet, Truman
__ showtime!: 3 It's
Showtime: 7 channel
alternative: 3 AMC, HBO, IFC, TMC 4 Flix 5 Bravo, Starz 6 Encore 7 Cinemax 8 Sundance
offering: 5 movie
Showtime (2002 film)
cast: Robert De Niro, Eddie Murphy, Rene Russo
director: Tom Dey
show to __: 5 a seat
showy: 4 arty, bold, gala, loud 5 artsy, fancy, gaudy, jazzy, ritzy, swank, vivid 6 chichi, flashy, florid, frilly, garish, glitzy, lavish, ornate, snazzy, swanky, tawdry, tinsel 7 dashing, flowery, glaring, opulent, pompous, splashy 8 gorgeous, imposing, overdone, peacocky, striking 9 decorated, elaborate, grandiose, high-flown, luxurious, screaming, sumptuous, tasteless 10 expressive, flamboyant, ornamental, ornamented, rhetorical, theatrical
ornament: 4 gaud 6 bauble, geegaw, gewgaw
something ~: 9 spectacle
shoyu ingredient: 3 soy
Shrapnel: 5 Henry
__ shrdlu: 6 etaoin
shred: 3 bit, cut, jot, rag, ray, rip 4 atom, fray, iota, part, snip, tear, whit, wisp 5 crumb, grain, grate, mince, ounce, piece, scrap, shave, slice, speck, strip, trace 6 ribbon, shadow, sliver, stitch, tatter 7 frazzle, modicum, remnant, scissor, smidgen, smidgin, snippet, vestige 8 fragment, particle, smidgeon 9 scintilla
shredded wheat: 6 cereal
shreds
cut to ~: 6 impugn
in ~: 4 torn 6 ragged
Shrek (2001 film)
voice cast: Cameron Diaz, John Lithgow, Eddie Murphy, Mike Myers
Shreveport: 4 city, town
county: 5 Caddo
locale: 9 Louisiana
school: 3 LSU
shrew: 3 nag 5 harpy, momus, scold, vixen 6 animal, beldam, blamer, chider, grouch, kvetch, mammal, nagger, noodge, ogress, virago, whiner 7 beldame, caviler, needler, primate, rebuker, reviler 8 fishwife, grumbler, harridan, spitfire 9 henpecker, termagant, Xanthippe 10 castigator, complainer
kin: 4 mole
__ shrew: 4 tree 5 least, otter
shrewd: 3 sly 4 cagy, cute, deep, foxy, keen, neat, wily, wise 5 acute, cagey, canny, quick, savvy, shark, sharp, slick, smart 6 artful, astute, brainy, clever, crafty, shifty, smooth, tricky 7 cunning, cutting, knowing, politic, probing, prudent 8 guileful, piercing, profound, scheming, sensible, slippery 9 astucious, designing, farseeing, ingenious, in the know, judicious, provident, realistic, sagacious, underhand 10 discerning, farsighted, insightful, longheaded, perceptive, serpentine, streetwise
shrewdness: 3 wit 4 wits 5 craft, wiles 6 acumen, wisdom 8 gumption, judgment 9 smartness 10 cleverness, discretion, horse sense
shriek: 2 ow 3 cry, eek, yow 4 bawl, howl, ouch, wail, yell, yeow 5 blare, laugh, shout, sound, whoop 6 bellow, holler, scream, shrill, squawk, squeal 7 screech 8 laughter 9 caterwaul 10 vociferate
__ shrift: 5 short
shrike: 4 bird 8 woodchat
shrill: 4 high, yell 5 acute, reedy, sharp, sound 6 brassy, piping, shriek, squeak, squeal, treble 7 blaring, blatant, clarion, grating, raucous 8 clanging, jangling, metallic, piercing, strident 9 deafening, unmusical 10 clangorous, discordant, screeching, vociferous
noise: 6 scream, shriek 7 whistle
shrimp: 4 runt
combining form: 5 -caris
prepare ~: 6 devein
relative: 5 prawn
sense organ: 4 palp 6 palpus
tiny ~: 5 krill
shrimp __: 5 plant, salad 6 creole, scampi
__ shrimp: 4 seed 5 brine, fairy, ghost, jumbo 6 mantis, mussel, pistol 7 opossum, popcorn
shrimp cocktail: 9 appetizer
shrimper gear: 3 net
Shrimpton: 4 Jean
shrimpy: 4 puny, tiny 5 small 6 little
shrine: 5 altar, zendo 6 adytum, chapel, church, temple 7 sanctum 8 monument, sacellum 9 sanctuary 10 tabernacle
Buddhist ~: 5 stupa 6 Ajanta
French ~: 7 Lourdes
innermost ~: 6 adytum
Moslem ~: 4 Kaba 5 Kaaba, Kabah 6 Kaabah
Texas ~: 5 Alamo
Shriner: 3 Wil 4 Herb
gathering: 5 lodge
hat: 3 fez
shrink: 3 ebb, sag, sap 4 curb, drop, fail, flag, tire, wane 5 blunt, cower, demur, lower, quail, quake, start, waste, wince, wizen 6 blanch, cringe, crouch, draw up, flinch, huddle, impair, lessen, narrow, pucker, recede, recoil, reduce, soften, wither 7 abridge, analyst, compact, curtail, cut down, decline, deflate, deplete, drop off, dwindle, exhaust, fall off, fatigue, retreat, shorten, shrivel, shudder, shy away, wrinkle 8 compress, condense, contract, decrease, diminish, downsize, draw back, enervate, enfeeble, hang back, hesitate, minimize, peter out, withdraw 9 attenuate, constrict, undermine 10 abbreviate, debilitate, devitalize
back: 5 wince 6 flinch
ender: 3 age 4 able
from: 4 shun 5 avoid, dread 6 blench, detest 7 retreat
shrink-__: 4 pack, wrap
shrinkage: 4 lack, loss 5 theft 8 decrease 9 reduction
shrinking: 3 coy, shy 4 lack 5 timid 6 averse, demure, modest 7 bashful, fearful, nervous 8 blushing, reserved, retiring 9 diffident, flinching, unwilling, withdrawn
shrinking __: 6 violet
shrive: 6 purify
shrivel: 3 dry 4 sear, wilt 5 decay, dry up, parch, stale, wizen 6 go limp, scorch, shrink, welter, wither 7 dwindle, mummify, wrinkle 8 contract, decrease, emaciate 9 dehydrate, desiccate
shriveled: 3 dry 4 sere, thin 5 unwet 6 little 9 juiceless
from heat: 7 parched 10 desiccated
Shriver: 3 Pam 5 Maria 7 Sargent
Shriver, Maria spouse: Arnold Schwarzenegger
Shropshire: 5 sheep 6 county
city: 7 Telford
locale: 7 England
Shropshire Lad, A: 4 poem
author: A.E. Housman
shroud: 4 hide, pall, veil, wrap 5 cloak, cover 6 enveil, enwrap, inwrap 7 conceal, secrete, shut off, shut out, smother 8 disguise 9 dissemble 10 camouflage
city: 5 Turin
shrouded: 5 misty 6 covert, hidden, masked, secret, unseen 7 furtive, private 8 hush-hush, ulterior 9 out of view, unexposed 10 undercover, under wraps, undetected
Shroud of __: 5 Turin
Shrove __: 6 Monday, Sunday 7 Tuesday
Shrove ender: 4 tide
Shrovetide Revelers artist: 4 Hals
Shrove Tuesday follower: 4 Lent
Shroyer, Sonny role: 4 Enos
shrub: 3 bay, box, fig, kat, qat 4 aloe, anil, bush, coca, gumi, hebe, ilex, itea, karo, kava, khat, ocra, okra, okro, pich, rose, sage, sloe, sola, sunn, titi, tree 5 aalii, akala, alder, birch, briar, brier, buchu, caper, cubeb, elder, erica, ficus, gorse, guava, hakea, hazel, heath, henna, holly, ixora, lilac, maqui, mulga, peony, plant, ramee, ramie,

retem, salal, senna, sumac, toyon, urena, yapon **6** abelia, acacia, annona, aucuba, azalea, cassia, cercis, cleome, coffee, cornel, dahoon, daphne, fatsia, feijoa, jojoba, kalmia, kerria, mimosa, myrtle, nardin, nettle, papaya, pawpaw, pituri, privet, spirea, storax, sumach, tobira, willow, yaupon **7** agarita, arbutus, banksia, boxwood, bramble, buckeye, cumquat, currant, deutzia, dogwood, figwort, filbert, fuchsia, geebung, goldcup, guarana, guayule, hoptree, jasmine, jetbead, juniper, karanda, kumquat, logania, mahonia, mahuang, mesquit, nandina, quassia, rhatany, rhodora, skimmia, spiraea, syringa **8** abutilon, albizzia, algerita, barbasco, barberry, bauhinia, bayberry, beverage, bignonia, bluewood, buddleia, camellia, caragana, cassiope, cat's-claw, cinchona, columnea, corkwood, cowberry, divi-divi, euonymus, evonymus, firebush, gardenia, guaiacum, hardhack, hornbeam, huisache, inkberry, justicia, lancepod, lavender, leadwort, magnolia, mangrove, mesquite, mezereon, mezereum, milkwort, myoporum, ninebark, ocotillo, oleander, oleaster, photinia, rosemary, saltbush, snowball, snowbush, sweetsop, tamarisk, wistaria, wisteria **9** blueberry, bouvardia, deerberry, firethorn, forsythia, hackberry, hydrangea, jaborandi, jessamine, kalanchoe, mistletoe, monacillo, raspberry, sagebrush, sugarbush **10** blackthorn, frangipani, gooseberry, ornamental
Arabian ~: **5** retem
Asian ~: **4** gumi **5** ramee, ramie
bog ~ fruit: **9** cranberry
desert ~: **5** retem **6** jojoba
evergreen ~: **5** erica, gorse, salal **6** dahoon
flowering ~: **5** lilac **6** abelia, acacia, azalea
fruit: **6** annona **8** barberry **9** bearberry, blueberry
Hawaiian ~: **5** olona
Indian hemp ~: **4** pooa **5** pooah
medicinal ~: **5** senna, sumac **6** sumach
miniature ~: **6** bonsai
New Zealand ~: **4** karo
of India: **4** sola, sunn
poisonous ~: **5** sumac **6** sumach
prickly ~: **5** briar, gorse **7** bramble **8** hawthorn
row: **5** hedge
South African ~: **6** narras
southern ~: **4** titi
spiny ~: **5** furze, gorse
see also plant
shrubbery: **5** brush, hedge **6** bushes, hedges **10** vegetation
maintain ~: **4** clip **5** prune
shrug: **7** gesture
indication: **6** apathy
off: **6** ignore, slight, wink at **7** let ride, neglect **8** minimize, overlook, play down, sneeze at **9** disregard, gloss over, underplay
__ Shrugged: **5** Atlas
shrunken: **3** dry **5** tight **6** narrow
shtick: **3** act **6** comedy **9** repertory
Shu __ dynasty: **3** Han
shuck: **3** pod **4** hull, husk, peel, sham, skin **5** shell, strip **7** uncover **9** throw away **10** integument
shuck and __: **4** jive
Shucks!: **4** darn, drat, durn, heck, rats **6** darn it
shudder: **4** fear, wave **5** pulse, quail, quake, shake **6** dither, gyrate, jitter, quiver, recoil, shimmy, shiver, shrink, tremor, twitch **7** tremble, twitter **8** convulse
shuddering: **9** tremulous
shuddersome: **6** creepy **7** fearful, hateful **8** dreadful
Shue: **6** Andrew **9** Elisabeth
Shue, Elisabeth: **7** actress
brother: **6** Andrew
film: Back to the Future Part II (1989)
Back to the Future Part III (1990)
Cocktail (1988)
Cousin Bette (1998)
The Karate Kid (1984)
Leaving Las Vegas (1995)
The Marrying Man (1991)
The Saint (1997)
Soapdish (1991)
shuffle: **3** lag, pad **4** drag, limp, plod, walk **5** bandy, dance, hedge, mix up, scuff, shift, trail **6** change, juggle, jumble, linger, litter, loiter, lumber, muddle, racket, scrape, waddle **7** confuse, disrupt, disturb, quibble, scuffle, shamble, stumble **8** disarray, disorder, exchange, intermix, scramble, straggle **9** dislocate, poke along, pussyfoot, rearrange **10** disarrange, discompose, reposition
along: **5** amble, mosey **7** saunter
ender: **5** board
fast ~: **5** fraud **7** swindle **8** trickery
follower: **3** cut **4** deal
off: **2** go **4** exit, move **5** leave, shirk **6** depart, go away
__ Shuffle: **4** Lido **6** Harlem
shuffleboard: **4** game **5** sport
locale: **4** deck
Shuffle Off to Buffalo composer: **5** Dubin **6** Warren
__-shuffler: **5** paper
shuffling: **6** shifty **8** pretense
Shu Han: **7** dynasty
__ shui: **4** feng
shul: **6** temple **7** synagog **9** synagogue
scroll: **4** Tora **5** Torah
teacher: **5** rabbi, rebbe
Shula, Don: **5** coach
sport: **8** football
Shull, Clifford: **8** Nobelist **9** physicist
Shulman: **3** Max
shulwar: **5** pants
Shumway, Gordon alias: **3** Alf
shun: **4** bilk, duck, omit, snub, veto **5** avoid, ditch, dodge, elude, evade, forgo, parry, scorn, shirk, spurn **6** beware, bounce, bypass, escape, eschew, forego, ignore, pass on, pass up, rebuff, refuse, reject **7** abstain, despise, disdain, dislike, dismiss, exclude, forbear, neglect, palm off, shy from **8** disallow, flee from, keep from, shake off, sidestep, turn away, turn down **9** blackball, cast aside, freeze out, get around, ostracize, repudiate **10** circumvent, shrink from
shunned: **9** abandoned, unpopular
shunt: **4** turn **5** avert **6** bypass, divert, switch **8** file away, lay aside **9** push aside, sidetrack, turn aside
__ shu pork: **3** moo
Shusaku: **4** Endo
shush: **5** quiet **6** shut up **7** be quiet, silence, squelch **8** pipe down, suppress **9** keep still
Shuster: **3** Joe
shut: **3** bar, dam **4** bolt, cage, clog, cork, draw, lock, plug, seal, slam **5** block, close, dam up, latch, tight **6** bolted, clog up, closed, fasten, fold up, lock up, plug up, seal up, secure, stop up **7** close up, confine, enclose, exclude, inclose, occlude, seal off, wall off **8** airtight, blockade, button up, closed up, close off, folded up, imprison, obstruct **9** close down **10** batten down
almost ~: **4** ajar
down: **3** end **4** fold, halt, stop **5** cease, close, quash, quell, stall **6** arrest, closed, finish, squash **7** conquer, suspend, turn off
ender: **3** eye, off, out **4** down
in: **3** pen **4** pent **6** begird, immure, pent-up **7** confine, enclose, impound, isolate **8** confined, imprison, restrict **9** barricade **10** quarantine
off: **3** bar **4** hide, kill, mask, stem, veil **5** block, close, cover, debar, evict **6** refuse, screen, shroud **7** conceal, exclude, keep out, lock out, seclude, tune out **8** blockade, block out, obstruct, secluded **9** beleaguer, ostracize, overpower
one's eyes to: **6** ignore, wink at **9** disregard
out: **3** ban, bar, top, win **4** mask, rout, tabu, veil **5** blank, close, cover, debar, evict, skunk **6** refuse, screen, shroud **7** boycott, conceal, exclude, occlude, prevent, seclude **8** blockade, disallow, fence off, obstruct, prohibit **9** beleaguer, foreclose, ostracize, unwelcome
up: **3** gag **4** cage, hush **5** box in, can it, choke, quiet, shush, still **6** immure, muzzle, stifle, stow it **7** be quiet, confine, impound, silence **8** imprison, pipe down **9** keep still
wouldn't ~ up: **5** ran on
shut __: **3** off, out **4** down
shut __ on: **4** down
shutdown: **8** stoppage
computer ~: **5** crash
Shute, Nevil: **6** author, writer **7** British
work: No Highway
On the Beach
Pied Piper
A Town Like Alice
shuteye: **3** nap **4** doze **5** sleep **6** catnap, snooze **7** slumber
getting some ~: **6** asleep, dozing **7** dormant, napping **8** dreaming, snoozing **9** sacked out, somnolent **10** slumbering
shut-in: **7** patient
shutoff: **5** valve
shut one's __ to: **4** eyes
shutout: **4** rout, zero
like a ~: **5** no-run
score, in Britain: **3** nil
shutter: **3** dam **4** bolt, clog, cork, lock, plug, seal **5** block, close, dam up, latch, shade **6** clog up, lock up, plug up, seal up, secure, stop up **7** seal off **8** blockade, button up, obstruct
ender: **3** bug
part: **6** louver, louvre
sound: **5** click
shutter __: **5** speed **7** release
shutterbug
see photographer
shut the __ on: **4** door
shuttle: **3** bus **5** ferry **6** flight, jitney **8** exchange
ender: **4** cock **5** craft
org.: **4** NASA
take a ~: **3** fly **4** ride
use a ~: **3** tat **5** weave
__ shuttle: **5** space
shuttlecock: **4** bird
Shut up!: **4** hush **5** Can it, quiet
shy: **3** coy **4** meek, slim, wary **5** aloof, chary, leery, loner, mousy, quiet, scant, short, start, throw, timid, wince **6** averse, demure, humble, modest, mousey, scanty, scarce, silent, skimpy **7** bashful, distant, failing, fearful, lacking, needing, nervous, uneager **8** backward, cautious, cowardly, hesitant, reserved, reticent, retiring, sheepish, skittish, unsocial **9** deficient, diffident, flinching, recessive, reclusive, reluctant, shrinking, unassured, unwilling, withdrawn **10** inadequate, indisposed, shamefaced, unassuming, uneffusive, unsociable
away: **4** turn **6** blench, flinch, recoil, shrink **8** hesitate
be ~: **3** owe **4** lack **7** wanting
ender: **4** lock, ness, ster
from: **4** duck, shun **5** avoid, dodge, evade, shirk **6** bypass, eschew **7** abstain **8** flee from **10** circumvent
make ~: **5** abash
__-shy: **3** gun **6** camera
__ Shy: **3** Gun, Too **4** Girl **5** He's So, Twice
Shyer, Charles: **5** actor
film: Baby Boom (1987)
Father of the Bride (1991)
Irreconcilable Differences (1984)
shylock: **6** lender, usurer **8** creditor **9** loan shark
Shylock's Daughter author: Erica Jong
shyness: **7** modesty, reserve **9** abashment, timidness **10** constraint, diffidence, insecurity
__ shy of: **5** fight
shyster: **5** knave **6** bad guy
sí: **2** ay, da, ja **3** aye, oui, yea, yep, yes, yup **4** fine, okay, sure, yeah **5** good-o, natch, quite, right, roger, uh-huh **6** agreed, gladly, good-oh, indeed, just so, rather, righto, surely, you bet, yowzah **7** exactly, go ahead, indeedy, mais oui, quite so, ten-four **8** all right, as you say, of course, thumbs up, very well **9** be my guest, certainly, darn right, naturally, precisely, sure thing, you betcha, you said it **10** absolutely, by all means, definitely, positively, sure enough, that's right
Si: **3** cat **4** elem. **7** element, silicon
14 for ~: **4** at. no.
S.I.: **3** mag **8** Hayakawa, Newhouse
siamang: **3** ape **7** primate
relative: **4** saki, titi **5** chimp, drill, jocko, lemur, loris, magot, orang, potto, shrew **6** aye-aye, baboon, Bandar, galago, gelada, gibbon, grivet, guenon, howler, langur, macaco, monkey, rhesus, uakari, vervet **7** colobus, gorilla, guereza, hoolock, macaque, sapajou, tamarin, tarsier **8** bush baby, capuchin, mandrill, mangabey, marmoset, talapoin **9** orangutan **10** Barbary ape, chimpanzee, orangutang
Siamese: **3** cat, Tai **4** Thai **5** felid **6** feline **8** language
coin: **4** baht
old ~ coin: **5** tical
remark: **3** mew **4** meow **5** miaou, miaow, miaul
twin: **3** Eng
weight: **3** pai
Siamese __: **3** cat **4** twin
Siamese fighting __: **4** fish
sib: **3** bro, kin, rel., sis **6** sister **7** brother **8** relative
see also sibling
Sibelius, Jean: **7** Finnish **8** composer
work: Finlandia
Siberia: **5** limbo
antelope: **5** saiga
city: **4** Omsk **5** Tomsk
feature: **5** taiga **6** tundra
lake: **6** Baikal
language: **5** Yakut
locale: **4** Asia **6** Russia

mountain: 6 Anadir, Kolyma
people: 5 Tatar, Yakut, Yupik, Yurak 6 Evenki
river: 4 Lena, Yana 5 Aldan
sea: 4 Kara 6 Laptev
Siberian: 3 cat 4 cold 5 felid 6 feline, frigid, frosty, frozen 7 ice-cold 8 freezing
Siberian __: 4 high, ruby 5 Husky 6 squill 7 mammoth
Siberian Husky: 3 dog 5 canid 6 canine
__-Siberian Railroad: 5 Trans
sibilance: 4 hiss, lisp
sibilant: 3 ess 4 hiss, soft
sound: 3 sss 5 swish
sibilate: 4 hiss, lisp 5 swish 7 whisper
Sibiu: 4 city, town
locale: 7 Romania, Rumania 8 Roumania
sibling: 3 bro, kin, sis 8 relation, relative
child: 5 niece 6 nephew
colt's ~: 5 filly
having no ~: 4 only
often: 6 coheir
starter: 4 step
victim of ~ rivalry: 4 Abel
__ Si Bon: 4 C'est
Sibuyan: 3 sea
locale: 11 Philippines
sibyl: 4 seer 5 augur 6 medium, oracle, Pythia 7 diviner, palmist, prophet, seeress 8 Amalthea 9 Cassandra, predictor 10 forecaster, prophetess, soothsayer
sibyllic: 7 fatidic 9 vaticinal
Sibyl, The author: Pär Lagerkvist
sic: 4 thus 6 attack 8 verbatim 9 literally
sic __: 6 passim
sic __ gloria mundi: 7 transit
sic __ tyrannis: 6 semper
Sichuan: 8 province
city: 6 Luchou, Luchow, Luzhou
Sicilian __: 5 pizza
siciliano: 5 dance
Sicilian, The author: Mario Puzo
Sicily: 3 isl. 4 isle 6 island
city: 4 Enna 7 Catania, Messina, Palermo 8 Siracusa
commune: 5 Riesi
islands off ~: 5 Egadi 6 Lipari
locale: 5 Italy
money: 4 tari 5 scudi, scudo
neighbor: 5 Malta
peak: 4 Etna 5 Aetna
port: 7 Trapani
sea off ~: 5 Medit. 6 Ionian
volcano: 4 Etna 5 Aetna
wine: 5 corvo 7 Marsala
sick: 3 bad, ill, low 4 down, weak 5 fed up, frail, green, gross, jaded, lousy, rocky, tired, upset, weary 6 ailing, feeble, infirm, laid up, morbid, morose, peaked, poorly, queasy, queazy, rotten, unwell, wabbly, wobbly 7 macaber, macabre, rickety, rundown, unsound 8 confined, delicate, feverish, ghoulish, impaired, infected, qualmish, sadistic 9 afflicted, bedridden, declining, defective, disgusted, imperfect, in a bad way, miserable, squeamish, suffering, tottering, unhealthy 10 broken-down, displeased, indisposed, out of sorts
and tired: 5 fed up, weary
at heart: 3 sad 4 blue, glum 5 moody, mopey 6 gloomy, morose, woeful 7 doleful 8 dejected, dolorous, downcast, grieving, mournful, troubled 9 cheerless, depressed, miserable, saturnine, sorrowful, woebegone 10 despondent, dispirited, melancholy
bay: 8 hospital 9 infirmary
become ~ with: 3 get
be ~ of: 4 hate 5 abhor 6 detest, loathe
ender: 3 bed, out 4 room
feel ~: 3 ail
(of): 5 bored, tired
partner: 5 tired
starter: 3 air, car, sea 4 home, love 5 green, heart, space
sick __: 3 bay, day, pay 4 call, list 5 leave
sick __ dog: 3 as a
sicken: 3 ail 4 tire 5 repel, shock, upset, weary 6 affect, offend, revolt 7 afflict, derange, disgust, fend off, hold off, repulse, turn off, unhinge 8 alienate, disorder, drive off, gross out, languish, unsettle 9 indispose
sickle: 4 tool 5 knife
ender: 4 bill
hammer and ~: 6 emblem
swing a ~: 4 reap
sicklebill: 4 bird
sickle-shaped: 5 arced, bowed 7 falcate 8 crescent, falcated, meniscus
sickly: 3 low, wan 4 down, pale, puny, weak 5 faint, pasty, seedy 6 ailing, feeble, infirm, laid up, morbid, morose, pallid, peaked, pining, poorly, sallow, unwell 7 cloying, languid, mawkish, noxious, run-down, unsound 8 below par, delicate, dragging, liverish, off-color 9 afflicted, bedridden, miserable, revolting, squeamish, unhealthy 10 indisposed, lackluster, out of shape
sickness: 3 bug, ill 6 malady 7 ailment, disease, illness, malaise 8 disorder, syndrome 9 complaint, condition, ill health, infirmity 10 affliction, queasiness, unwellness
__ sickness: 6 motion
Sick Rose, The: 4 poem
author: William Blake
Sic semper tyrannis shouter: 5 Booth
sic transit __ mundi: 6 gloria
Sicut __ in principio: 4 erat
Sid: 5 Bream, Levin, Stone 6 Caesar, Melton 7 Catlett, Gillman, Grauman, Luckman, Vicious
Sidamo home: 6 Africa 8 Ethiopia
Sid and Nancy (1986 film)
cast: Gary Oldman, Drew Schofield, Chloe Webb
director: Alex Cox
Siddhartha author: Hermann Hesse
Siddig: 9 Alexander
Siddons: 5 Sarah
side: 3 foe, lee, rim 4 camp, edge, face, hand, jamb, join, loin, part, rear, sect, team, view, wall 5 angle, cause, facet, flank, front, jambe, limit, minor, party, phase, rival, slant, stand, verge 6 aspect, behalf, belief, border, bottom, haunch, lesser, margin, sector, stance 7 faction, lateral, opinion, surface, version 8 attitude, boundary, coleslaw, division, flanking, indirect, interest, marginal, position, skirting 9 ancillary, auxiliary, combatant, direction, elevation, off-center, perimeter, periphery, secondary, viewpoint 10 appearance, collateral, contestant, hypotenuse, incidental, standpoint, subsidiary, tangential
at one ~ of (prefix): 4 para-
by side: 4 near 7 abreast, lateral 8 parallel, together
by the ~ of: 4 with 5 along
combining form: 5 later-, pleur- 6 lateri-, latero-, pleuro-
dark ~: 4 evil 9 pessimism
dish: 4 rice, slaw 5 salad 6 potato 8 coleslaw 9 vegetable
ender: 3 arm, bar, car, man, way 4 band, kick, line, long, rite, show, slip, spin, step, walk, wall, ward, ways, wise 5 board, burns, light, piece, swipe, track, wards 6 saddle, stroke, winder 9 splitting
flip ~: 6 option 7 reverse 9 inversion 10 antithesis
from ~ to side: 7 athwart
head for the other ~: 5 cross
larger on one ~: 4 awry 5 askew 6 canted, uneven 7 crooked, unequal 8 cockeyed, lopsided, top-heavy 9 irregular 10 off-balance, unbalanced
lean to one ~: 4 list
left ~: 4 port
move side to ~: 3 wag 6 zigzag
on one's ~: 5 loyal
on the ~: 5 extra 10 additional
on the far ~ of: 6 across 7 athwart
on the ~ of: 3 for, pro 6 behind 10 supporting
on the opposite ~: 6 across
other ~: 3 foe 5 enemy 7 reverse 8 opposite 9 ill-wisher, inversion 10 antithesis, opposition
port ~: 4 left
put to one ~: 7 isolate 8 separate
right ~: 9 starboard
set side by ~: 5 check, liken, weigh 6 appose, equate, oppose, size up 7 analyze, balance, compare, examine, inspect, stack up 8 contrast, parallel 9 correlate 10 correspond, scrutinize
starboard ~: 5 right
starter: 3 air, bay, bed, day, off, out, sea, sub, top, way 4 back, curb, dock, down, fire, hill, king, lake, land, pool, port, ring, road, ship, surf 5 along, beach, blind, broad, court, green, plane, queen, river, state, table, track, trail, under, water 6 ground, hearth, silver, stream 7 country, slicken 8 mountain
thorn in the ~: 4 bane, pain, pest 7 bugbear 8 nuisance 9 annoyance
to one ~: 2 by 3 off 5 apart, askew
to side: 6 across
view: 7 contour, profile 10 silhouette
with: 4 ally, back, join 5 agree, align, aline, favor 6 uphold 7 support 8 champion 9 cooperate, encourage 10 rally round, sympathize
side __: 3 arm, bet, pot 4 band, card, curl, dish, drum, meat, step, suit, trip, with 5 chain, chair, horse, money, table 6 effect, pocket, street 7 circuit
side-__: 5 dress, wheel 6 glance 7 wheeler
__ side: 4 felt, flip, weak, wire 5 blind, board, on the, spear, sunny 6 gospel, prompt, strong 7 distaff, epistle, reverse, spindle
__-side: 6 demand, supply
__ Side: 4 East, West 5 North, South
sidearm: 4 Colt, dirk 5 blade, knife, Luger 6 cutlas, dagger 7 cutlass, poniard 8 stiletto
sideboard: 5 table 9 furniture
sideburn: 4 hair
shortener: 5 razor
sidecar: 5 drink 8 beverage, cocktail
ingredient: 6 brandy 10 lemon juice
occupant: 5 rider
__-sided: 3 one, two 4 many, open, slab 5 crank, sober 6 double
sided starter: 3 lop
sidekick: 3 pal 4 aide, ally, chum, mate 5 amigo, buddy, crony 6 cohort, friend 7 compeer, comrade, partner 8 alter ego, follower, henchman, roommate 9 associate, colleague, companion, confidant 10 compatriot, well-wisher
cowboy's ~: 4 pard
Sidekick: 3 SUV 6 Suzuki
sideline: 5 hobby 6 recess, shelve 9 avocation, indispose
shout: 3 rah
sidelined: 4 lame 6 unable 7 dormant 8 stranded 9 abandoned
sidelines
on the ~: 7 neutral 8 inactive
put on the ~: 5 bench
sidelong: 7 asquint, athwart, lateral 9 laterally
sideman instrument: 3 axe
side of __: 4 beef
__ Side of Midnight, The: 5 Other
__ Side of Paradise: 4 This
__ side of the coin, the: 5 other
__ Side of Town: 4 Poor
sidepiece: 4 jamb 5 jambe
__-Sider: 3 Top
sidereal: 6 astral
sidereal __: 3 day 4 hour, time, year 5 month
siderite: 3 ore 7 mineral
constituent: 4 iron
sides
change ~: 4 turn 6 defect
slopping over the ~: 5 awash
starter: 3 off 5 sober
take ~: 6 choose
__ sides: 4 take
sideshow
attraction: 4 geek 5 freak
worker: 6 barker
sideslip: 4 skid, veer 6 swerve
__ Sides Now: 4 Both
sidesplitter: 4 hoot, joke, riot 6 scream
sidesplitting: 4 rich 5 funny 7 comical 8 humorous 9 priceless 10 uproarious
sidestep: 3 zig 4 duck, shun 5 avert, avoid, dodge, elude, evade, fence, hedge, parry, shirk, skirt 6 bypass, detour, swerve 8 get out of 9 pussyfoot, runaround 10 circumvent, work around
__ Side Story: 4 West
Side Street director: 4 Mann
sidestroke: 4 swim
sideswipe: 3 hit 5 crash 9 collision, criticism
__ Side, The: 3 Far
sidetrack: 4 turn 5 avert, shunt 6 divert 7 deflect, reroute 8 lead away
sidetracked, get: 5 stray 6 ramble, wander 7 digress, meander
__ side up: 5 right, sunny
sidewalk: 6 street 8 pavement
activity: 4 sale
amusement: 5 raree
artist need: 5 chalk
edge: 4 curb
game: 5 jacks, potsy 9 hopscotch
hazard: 5 grate
joint: 5 chink, crack 7 crevice
London ~: 4 kerb
material: 6 cement
stand: 5 kiosk
superintendent: 7 meddler 8 busybody
sidewalk __: 4 café, sale 5 Santa 6 artist
__ sidewalk: 6 moving
Sidewalks of London (1938 film)
cast: Rex Harrison, Charles Laughton, Vivien Leigh
Sidewalks of New York (2001 film)
cast: Edward Burns, Rosario Dawson, Heather Graham, Stanley Tucci
director: Edward Burns
Sidewalk Stories (1989 film)
cast: Nicole Alysia, Charles Lane, Sandye Wilson
director: Charles Lane
sidewall protection: 4 eave
sideward: 7 lateral
sideways: 6 aslant, aslope 7 asquint,

athwart, lateral, sloping **8** slanting **9** laterally, obliquely, slantwise, to the edge **10** indirectly, slantingly
sidewinder: **5** snake **6** animal **7** reptile
relative: **3** asp, boa **5** aboma, adder, cobra, krait, mamba, racer, viper **6** dhaman, python, taipan **7** markhor, rattler **8** anaconda, moccasin, ringhals **9** boomslang, coachwhip **10** bushmaster, copperhead
sidewise: **8** flanking
sidhe: **5** fairy
Sidi ___: **4** Ifni
siding: **4** rail, spur **7** railing
material: **4** wood **5** steel, vinyl **8** aluminum, tarpaper
producer: **5** Alcoa
railroad ~: **5** lie by
___ siding: **4** drop **5** bevel **7** novelty
sidle: **4** edge, inch **5** slink, sneak **7** slither
Sidley: **4** peak **5** mount **8** mountain
locale: **10** Antarctica
Sidney: **4** city, Hook, town **5** Furie, Lumet, Toler **6** Altman, Bechet, George, Hayers, Howard, Lanier, Philip, Sylvia **7** Gilliat, Poitier, Sheldon **8** Franklin, Kingsley, Lanfield
locale: **4** Ohio
Sidney, George: **8** director
film: Anchors Aweigh (1945)
Annie Get Your Gun (1950)
Bathing Beauty (1944)
Bye Bye Birdie (1963)
The Harvey Girls (1946)
Holiday in Mexico (1946)
Jupiter's Darling (1955)
Kiss Me Kate (1953)
Pal Joey (1957)
Scaramouche (1952)
Show Boat (1951)
Viva Las Vegas (1964)
Who Was That Lady? (1960)
Young Bess (1953)
Sidney J. ___: **5** Furie
Sidney, Philip: **3** Sir **4** poet **6** writer **7** British
work: Arcadia
Astrophel and Stella
Sidney, Sylvia: **7** actress
film: Blood on the Sun (1945)
City Streets (1931)
Dead End (1937)
Fury (1936)
Jennie Gerhardt (1933)
Mary Burns, Fugitive (1935)
Sabotage (1936)
Street Scene (1931)
Summer Wishes, Winter Dreams (1973)
The Trail of the Lonesome Pine (1936)
You Only Live Once (1937)
spouse: Bennett Cerf
Sido author: Colette
Sidra: **4** gulf
locale: **5** Libya
sieben: **5** seven **6** German
Siebert: **6** Muriel **7** Charles
siècle ___: **3** d'or
___-siècle: **5** fin-de
Siegbahn, Karl: **8** Nobelist **9** physicist
siege: **5** box in, storm **6** attack, battle **8** blockade, encircle, surround **9** cordon off
lay ~ to: **4** gird **5** beset, box in, hem in **6** begird, circle **7** fence in **8** blockade, encircle **9** beleaguer, close in on, encompass
___ Siege: **5** Under
Siegel: **3** Don **5** Bugsy, Jerry
Siegel, Don: **8** director
film: The Beguiled (1970)
Big Steal (1949)
Charley Varrick (1973)
Coogan's Bluff (1968)
Dirty Harry (1972)
Escape From Alcatraz (1979)
Flaming Star (1960)
Hell Is for Heroes (1962)
Hound-Dog Man (1959)
Invasion of the Body Snatchers (1956)
Madigan (1968)
Riot in Cell Block 11 (1954)
The Shootist (1976)
Telefon (1977)
Two Mules for Sister Sara (1970)
Siegen: **4** city, town
locale: **7** Germany
Siegena: **8** asteroid
Siege, The (1998 film)
cast: Annette Bening, Tony Shalhoub, Denzel Washington, Bruce Willis
director: Edward Zwick
___ siege to: **3** lay
Siegfried: **4** hero **5** opera **7** Sassoon
composer: **6** Wagner
role: **4** Erda, Mime **5** Wotan **6** Fafner **9** Sieglinde
setting: **5** Rhine **7** Germany
Siegfried ___: **4** Line
Siegfried and ___: **3** Roy
Siegmeister: **4** Elie
Siena: **4** city, town
locale: **5** Italy **7** Tuscany
Sienkiewicz: **6** Henrik, Henryk
Sienkiewicz, Henrik: **6** Polish, writer **8** Nobelist
sienna: **5** brown, color **9** yellowish
relative: **3** bay, dun, tan **4** bole, ecru, fawn, foxy, nude, seal **5** amber, beige, camel, cocoa, hazel, khaki, mocha, sepia, tawny, umber **6** auburn, bister, bistre, bronze, coffee, copper, ginger, russet, sorrel, suntan, walnut **7** biscuit, caramel, dogwood **8** chestnut, cinnamon, mahogany **9** butternut, chocolate
___ sienna: **3** raw **5** burnt
Sienna: **3** van **6** Toyota
Siepi, Cesare: **4** bass
sierra: **5** ridge **8** mountain
Sierra: **3** car **4** auto **5** Dodge, Ruben **7** Gregory
Sierra ___: **4** lily **5** Leone, Madre **6** Madres, Nevada
___ Sierra: **4** High
Sierra Club pioneer: **4** Muir
Sierra Leone: **6** nation **7** country
bovine: **5** n'dama
capital: **8** Freetown
city: **5** Koidu **6** Makeni **8** Freetown
lingua franca: **4** Krio
money: **4** cent **5** leone
neighbor: **6** Guinea **7** Liberia
people: **5** Mende, Temne
Sierra Madre: **3** mts. **4** mtns. **5** range **9** mountains
locale: **6** Mexico **7** Wyoming **8** Colorado **9** Guatemala
Sierra Maestra country: **4** Cuba
Sierra Nevada: **3** mts. **4** mtns. **5** range **9** mountains
locale: **10** California
mountain: **4** Muir, Sill **5** Lyell **7** Granite, Langley, Russell, Tyndall, Whitney **9** El Capitan **10** Williamson
resort: **5** Tahoe
Sierra Vista: **4** city, town
locale: **7** Arizona
siesta: **3** nap **4** doze, rest **5** sleep **6** catnap, snooze
end a ~: **4** wake **5** awake, get up, waken **6** awaken
unit: **4** wink
siete: **5** seven **7** Spanish
sieve: **4** sift **6** filter, screen, strain **8** colander, strainer
like a ~: **5** leaky **6** porous
Sif husband: **4** Thor
sift: **3** pan **4** comb, part, size, sort **5** drain, glean, grade, probe, sieve, unmix **6** assort, filter, go into, purify, riddle, screen, search, strain, winnow **7** analyze, dig into, enquire, examine, explore, inquire **8** colander, evaluate, look into, pore over, prospect, separate **9** delve into, go through **10** scrutinize
in Britain: **3** lue
through: **4** cull **7** examine
___ sifter: **5** flour, sugar
sifting, needing: **5** lumpy
Sig: **4** Arno **5** Ruman
sigh: **2** ah **3** aah, sob **4** ache, ah me, blow, gasp, howl, lust, moan, pant, pine **5** crave, dream, groan, mourn, sough, sound, whine, yearn **6** exhale, hanker, hunger, lament, murmur, rustle, sorrow, thirst, wheeze **7** long for, respire, suspire, whisper **8** aspirate, complain, languish **10** exhalation
for: **4** long, pine, want, wish **5** crave, yearn
sighing: **5** sough
sight: **3** aim, eye, ken, see **4** espy, eyes, find, look, mess, show, slob, spot, view **5** scene, sense, vista **6** aperçu, behold, descry, eyeful, fright, glance, parade, seeing, vision **7** discern, display, exhibit, eyeshot, eyesore, glimpse, make out, observe, outlook, pageant, viewing **8** perceive, prospect **9** great deal, recognize, spectacle **10** appearance, exhibition, inspection, perception, visibility
combining form: **4** -opia, opto- **5** -opsia
ender: **3** saw, see **4** line, seer **6** seeing
related: **5** optic
starter: **3** eye **4** bomb, hind
sight ___: **3** gag **5** draft, rhyme **6** screen, unseen
sight ___ sore eyes: **3** for
sight-___: **4** read
___ sight: **4** open, peep, plus, rear **5** minus, out of **6** second
___-sighted: **3** far **4** long **5** clear, sharp
sighted starter: **3** far **4** near **5** short
Sighted sub, sank ___: **4** same
sighting: **6** espial
___ sight of: **5** catch
sights
get in one's ~: **5** aim at
set one's ~ on: **6** aim for, behold
take in the ~: **4** look, tour
sightsee: **4** tour
sightseer: **7** tourist, visitor **8** onlooker, traveler **10** vacationer
need: **3** map **6** camera
sigil: **4** seal, sign **6** signet
sigma: **3** ess, sum **5** Greek **6** letter
predecessor: **3** rho
successor: **3** tau
Sigma: **3** car **4** auto **10** Mitsubishi
Sigma ___: **3** Chi
Sigma Protocol, The author: Robert Ludlum
sigmatism: **4** lisp
sigmoid: **6** curved
curve: **3** ess
Sigmund: **5** Freud **7** Romberg
daughter: **4** Anna
sign: **2** OK **3** cue, ink, nod **4** bell, clew, clue, flag, hint, lead, logo, mark, name, note, okay, omen, type, wave, wink **5** augur, badge, board, crest, index, light, proof, title, token, trace, track, write **6** augury, beacon, cipher, emblem, herald, letter, motion, notice, poster, ratify, symbol **7** auspice, caution, confirm, endorse, express, gesture, indorse, initial, inkling, insigne, placard, portent, presage, symptom, vestige, warning, whistle, witness **8** evidence, forecast, giveaway, hallmark, indicate, inscribe, insignia, landmark, lodestar, mnemonic, reminder **9** assurance, authorize, autograph, billboard, foretoken, formalize, guidepost, handwrite, harbinger, indicator, precursor, predictor, subscribe **10** denotation, divination, foreboding, indication, intimation, prediction, prognostic, suggestion, underwrite
a contract: **3** ink
advertising ~: **4** neon
arithmetic ~: **4** plus **5** minus, times **6** divide
away: **4** cede **5** forgo, waive **6** forego, give up **9** surrender **10** relinquish
bad ~: **4** omen
be a ~ of: **6** denote **7** suggest
combining form: **7** symbolo-
direction ~: **5** arrow
ender: **3** age **4** post **5** board
first ~: **5** onset
for: **6** accept
give the high ~: **3** tip **5** alert **6** advise, signal, tip off **7** caution **8** forewarn
high ~: **4** wink **5** alarm, alert **6** motion
in: **4** come **5** pop up, reach **6** arrive **8** get there
language: **3** ASL
large ~: **6** banner
off: **3** end **4** stop **6** resign
off on: **2** OK **4** okay **5** admit, adopt, allow, go for **6** accept, assent, comply, permit **7** approve, confirm, include, welcome **8** stand for, validate **9** put up with, recognize **10** concur with, give the nod
of the future: **4** omen **6** augury, herald **7** portent, presage **9** foretoken, harbinger
on: **4** hire, join **5** draft, enrol, enter, log in **6** employ, engage, enlist, enroll, join up, retain **7** recruit **8** register
on the dotted line: **5** agree
over: **4** cede **5** trust **8** transfer
starter: **7** counter
telltale ~: **4** odor
up: **4** hire, join **5** draft, enrol, enter **6** employ, engage, enlist, enroll, join up, muster, retain **7** recruit **8** register **9** volunteer
zodiac ~: **3** Leo, Ram **4** Bull, Crab, Fish, Goat, Lion **5** Aries, Libra, Twins, Virgo **6** Archer, Cancer, Gemini, Pisces, Taurus **7** Balance, Scorpio **8** Aquarius, Scorpion **9** Capricorn **11** Sagittarius
sign ___: **3** off, out **6** manual **8** language
sign ___ cross: **5** of the
___ sign: **3** air, hex, sun **4** call, cent, fire, hard, high, plus, soft, stop **5** earth, equal, fixed, minus, peace, pound, times, water **6** dollar, equals, number, rising **7** mutable, percent, radical
signal: **2** OK **3** cue, nod, SOS **4** beck, beep, bell, blip, call, feed, flag, hail, okay, omen, warn, wave, wink, word **5** alarm, alert, bleep, flare, flash, great, point, token **6** beacon, beckon, denote, famous, herald, marked, Mayday, motion, tocsin, wigwag **7** blinker, gesture, go-ahead, notable, salient, warning, whistle **8** indicate, language, lodestar, mnemonic, movement, password, red light, renowned, striking, wave down **9** harbinger, indicator, memorable, momentous, prominent **10** green light, indication, individual,

lighthouse, noteworthy, noticeable, pronounced, remarkable
at the ~: 5 on cue
booster: 3 amp
caller: 2 QB
danger ~: 3 red 5 alert
device: 5 pager 6 beeper
distress ~: 3 SOS 5 flare 7 warning
electronic ~: 4 blip 5 bleep
eye ~: 4 wink
fire ~: 4 bell
hand ~: 4 clap, wave
nautical ~: 4 bell
phone ~: 4 busy
receiver: 5 tuner
sonar ~: 4 echo
traffic ~: 4 honk, horn 5 green, light
transmit a ~: 4 beam
turn ~: 5 arrow
visual ~: 3 bat 5 blink, flick 6 squint 7 flutter, twinkle 8 high sign
signal __: 3 box 5 board, corps
__ signal: 3 fog 4 busy, hand, time, turn 5 block, pilot, storm 7 traffic, weather
Signal: 9 mouthwash
alternative: 3 Act 4 Plax 5 Scope 7 Lavoris 9 Listerine 10 Fluorigard
signalize: 9 celebrate
signally: 8 markedly 10 especially
signals
call the ~: 4 lead 6 direct 7 control, oversee 11 quarterback
signatory: 5 inker 7 witness
signature: 4 name 5 stamp 7 imprint, writing 8 longhand 9 autograph, John Henry
attestor: 2 NP
follower: 2 PS
imitate a ~: 5 forge
song: 5 theme
signature __: 4 loan, song, tune
__ signature: 3 key 4 time
Signe: 5 Hasso
signed __: 6 number 7 English
Signed, Sealed, Delivered I'm Yours (1970 song) artist: Stevie Wonder
signer: 5 inker 7 witness
need: 3 pen
signet: 4 seal 5 sigil
signet __: 4 ring
significance: 4 heft, meat, note, pith 5 drift, force, heart, merit, point, sense, stuff, value, worth 6 accent, credit, effect, impact, import, kicker, moment, stress, virtue, weight 7 bearing, gravity, meaning, message, purport 8 emphasis, interest, prestige 9 authority, influence, magnitude, punch line, relevance, substance 10 prominence
have ~ for: 6 bear on 7 concern
statistical ~ measure: 5 t-test
significance __: 5 level
significant: 3 big 4 high, rich 5 great, major, meaty, sound, valid, vital 6 cogent 7 central, fateful, helpful, knowing, notable, salient, serious, special, telling, weighty 8 critical, denoting, eloquent, forceful, historic, material, powerful, pregnant, relevant, symbolic, ultimate 9 important, memorable, momentous, operative
other: 4 love, mate, wife 5 hubby 7 beloved 9 boyfriend 10 girlfriend
significant __: 5 other 6 digits, symbol 7 figures
__ significant digit: 4 most 5 least
significantly: 3 far 5 quite 6 rather 8 somewhat
signification: 7 purport 9 magnitude
signifier: 10 indication
signify: 4 bear, bode, mark, mean, show, tell, wink 5 carry, imply, point, spell, weigh 6 convey, denote, evince, import, intend 7 add up to, bespeak, betoken, connote, exhibit, express, portend, presage, purport, suggest 8 announce, disclose, evidence, foreshow, indicate, intimate, manifest, proclaim, stand for 9 insinuate, predicate, represent, symbolize
signoff: 3 end 8 last word
word: 4 love, over 5 later, see ya
Sign of Four, The author: Arthur Conan Doyle
sign of the __: 5 cross, times 6 zodiac
signor: 2 Mr. 3 sir 5 title 6 mister 7 Italian 9 gentleman
signora: 3 Mrs. 4 lady 5 title 7 Italian
Signoret, Simone: 6 French 7 actress
film: Against the Wind (1948)
The Crucible (1957)
The Deadly Affair (1967)
Diabolique (1955)
Room at the Top (1959, AA)
Ship of Fools (1965)
spouse: Yves Montand
signorina: 2 Ms. 4 Miss 5 title 7 Italian
Sign o' the Times: 4 film, song
artist: Prince
cast: Sheena Easton, Prince, Sheila E.
director: Prince
__ signo vinces: 5 in hoc
signs
indicate by ~: 4 bode
read the ~: 7 predict
show ~ of: 7 promise
__ signs: 4 life 5 vital
Signs (song) artist: Five Man Electrical Band, Tesla
__ signum: 4 ecce
sign-up: 10 enlistment
Sigourney: 6 Weaver
uncle: 7 Doodles
Sigrid: 6 Undset
Sigurd
horse: 5 Grani
successor: 4 Atli
Sigurd the Volsung: 4 epic, poem
author: William Morris
sika: 4 deer
relative: 3 elk, roe 4 axis, pudu, shou 5 moose 6 chital, guemal, hangul, huemul, sambar, sambur, thamin, wapiti 7 brocket, caribou, muntjac, muntjak, sambhar, sambhur 8 reindeer 9 barasingh
Sikasso: 4 city, town
locale: 4 Mali
Sikes: 3 Dan 7 Cynthia
Sikh: 5 Hindu 6 Indian
dagger: 6 kirpan
founder: 5 Nanak
Sikkim: 5 state
bovine: 4 Siri
locale: 5 India
people: 6 Lepcha
Sikorsky: 4 Igor
s'il __ plaît: 4 vous
silage: 3 hay 4 feed, oats 6 fodder
Silao: 4 city, town
locale: 6 Mexico 10 Guanajuato
Silas: 4 Paul 5 Deane 10 evangelist
companion of ~: 4 Paul
Silas Marner: 4 film 5 novel
author: George Eliot
cast: Jenny Agutter, Ben Kingsley
character: 4 Cass, Dane 5 Aaron, Dolly, Eppie, Molly, Nancy
director: Giles Foster
sild: 7 herring, sardine
silence: 3 gag, nix 4 calm, dull, hush, lull, mute, stop, sulk 5 dry up, peace, quash, quell, quiet, shush, sit on, still 6 clam up, cool it, cut off, dampen, deaden, muffle, muzzle, refute, shut up, stifle, subdue 7 be quiet, close up, dead air, put down, quietus, reserve, secrecy, squelch 8 choke off, cut short, hush-hush, muteness, pipe down, suppress, throttle 9 keep still, quiet down, quietness, reticence, stillness, tongue-tie 10 censorship, extinguish, keep it down, quiescence, sullenness
break ~: 3 say 4 talk 5 speak
exclamation for ~: 4 hush 5 shush 7 hushaby
in music: 4 rest
Silence–A Fable author: Edgar Allan Poe
Silence author: Harold Pinter
silenced: 4 mute 5 quiet
Silence is Golden (1967 song) artist: Tremeloes
Silence of Colonel Bramble, The author: André Maurois
Silence of the Lambs, The (1991 film)
cast: Jodie Foster, Scott Glenn, Anthony Hopkins
character: 6 Lecter 7 Clarice 8 Hannibal, Starling
director: Jonathan Demme
studio: 5 Orion
silencer: 3 gag
court ~: 5 gavel
in America: 7 muffler
Silencers, The (1966 film)
cast: Victor Buono, Dahlia Lavi, Dean Martin, Stella Stevens
hero: 4 Helm
Silences author: 5 Olsen
__ Silence, The: 5 Angry
Silence, The (1963 film) director: Ingmar Bergman
silent: 3 mum, shy 4 hush, mute 5 faint, movie, muted, quiet, still, tacit 6 curbed, hushed, sullen, unsaid 7 aphonic, bashful, checked, implied, laconic, unheard 8 hushed up, implicit, nonvocal, reserved, reticent, stealthy, taciturn, unspoken, unvoiced, wordless 9 clammed up, inhibited, noiseless, secretive, soundless, voiceless, withdrawn 10 buttoned up, incoherent, indistinct, restrained, speechless, tongue-tied, unsociable, unspeaking
approval: 3 nod
be ~: 6 shut up 9 keep still
be ~ in music: 5 tacet
communication: 3 ESP
entertainer: 4 mime 5 Harpo, mimer
fall ~: 5 quiet 8 pipe down 9 keep still
film accompaniment: 5 organ
language: 3 ASL
make ~: 5 quiet
one: 4 clam
strike ~: 3 awe, wow 4 stun 5 amaze
silent __: 4 vote 5 alarm 6 barter, butler 7 auction, partner, service
Silent __: 3 Cal 5 Honor, Movie, Night 6 Spring 7 Partner, Running
Silent Clowns, The author: 4 Kerr
Silent Honor author: Danielle Steel
Silent Movie (1976 film)
cast: Mel Brooks, Dom DeLuise, Marty Feldman, Bernadette Peters
director: Mel Brooks
Silent Night: 4 noel 5 carol, novel
author: Mary Higgins Clark
word: 5 sleep
Silent Partner author: Jonathan Kellerman
Silent Partner, The (1978 film)
cast: Elliott Gould, Christopher Plummer
Silent Running (1971 film)
cast: Bruce Dern, Cliff Potts, Ron Rifkin
director: Douglas Trumbull
Silent Running (1986 song) artist: Mike + the Mechanics
Silent Spring
author: Rachel Carson
topic: 3 DDT
__ silent type, the: 6 strong
Silent, upon a peak in __: 6 Darien
Silent World, The (1956 film)
director: Jacques-Yves Cousteau, Louis Malle
silesia: 6 fabric 8 material
Silesian: 5 Czech
river: 4 Oder, Odra
__ Silesius: 7 Angelus
silex: 5 flint
__-Silex: 7 Proctor
silhouette: 4 form, line 5 shape 6 shadow 7 contour, outline, profile 8 likeness, portrait, side view 9 adumbrate, lineament, lineation
Silhouette: 3 van 4 Olds 10 Oldsmobile
Silhouettes (song)
artist: Herman's Hermits, Rays
Silhouettes song: Get a Job (1958)
silica: 5 flint 6 quartz 7 mineral
form of ~: 4 opal
trap, as ~ gel: 6 adsorb
silica __: 3 gel 5 glass
silicate: 4 mica, talc 6 garnet, zircon 9 rhodolite 10 tourmaline
__ silicate: 6 sodium 7 calcium
silicon: 7 element
alloy: 7 Everdur 9 barberite
slice: 5 wafer
silicon __: 7 carbide, dioxide
Silicon __: 5 Alley 6 Valley
silicone: 9 lubricant
Silicon Valley name: 5 Intel
silk: 5 cloth 6 damask, fabric 8 material
ancient ~ fabric: 6 byssus
combining form: 5 seric-
corn ~: 5 floss
cotton: 5 ceiba
dye: 5 eosin 6 eosine
ender: 4 weed, worm 6 screen
fabric: 3 rep 4 repp 5 crape, crepe, gazar, Honan, moire, pekin, piqué, plush, satin, surah, tulle, voile 6 armure, byssus, camaca, camaka, camoca, damask, faille, gloria, jersey, pongee, poplin, samite, tricot, tussah, tusseh, tusser, tussor, tussur, velvet 7 charvet, chiffon, duvetyn, foulard, grogram, Mogador, organza, ottoman, sarsnet, tabaret, tabinet, taffeta, tussore 8 chambray, chenille, marocain, Milanese, paduasoy, popeline, sarcenet, sarsenet, tabbinet 9 charmeuse, grenadine 10 peau de soie
French ~ center: 4 Lyon 5 Lyons
in French: 4 soie
replacement: 5 nylon
source: 4 worm 6 cocoon
thread: 4 poil
watered ~: 5 moiré
silk __: 3 gum, hat, oak 4 tree 5 gland, paper 6 cotton
silk-__: 6 tassel
__ silk: 3 net, raw 4 corn, spun, wild 5 China, floss, glove, India 6 Indian, reeled, sewing, souple, thread, thrown 7 schappe
Silk __: 4 Road
silkaline: 6 fabric 8 material
silk-cotton: 4 tree
tree: 5 ceiba
silken: 4 soft 5 plush, sleek 6 flossy, glossy, satiny, smooth, tender 7 velvety 8 delicate, lustrous, slippery 9 luxurious, satinlike
silklike fabric: 5 ramee, ramie
silk-making region: 5 Assam
silks: 6 finery

silkscreen ___: **7** process
Silk Stalkings (CBS/USA drama)
cast: Rob Estes (Sgt. Chris Lorenzo) Mitzi Kapture (Sgt. Rita Lance)
silk-stocking: **4** dude **5** elite, noble **6** gentry **8** nobleman, well-born **9** patrician **10** upper-class
Silk Stockings (1957 film): **7** musical
cast: Fred Astaire, Cyd Charisse, Janis Paige
director: Rouben Mamoulian
Silkwood: **5** Karen
Silkwood (1983 film)
cast: Cher, Kurt Russell, Meryl Streep
director: Mike Nichols
silkworm: **3** bug **5** larva **6** insect
Assam ~: **3** eri **4** eria
silky: **4** soft **5** plush, sleek **6** flossy, glossy, satiny, smooth, tender **7** velvety **8** delicate, lustrous, slippery **9** luxurious, satinlike
sound: **5** swish
silky ___: **3** oak **6** cornel **7** terrier
sill: **5** ledge **9** threshold **10** projection
opposite: **6** lintel
sitter: **5** plant
starter: **3** mud **4** door **6** ground, window
___ sill: **3** box **6** window
Sill: **4** peak **5** mount **8** mountain
locale: **10** California
___ Sill: **4** Fort
Silla: **5** Felix
Sillanpää, Frans Eemil: **6** writer **7** Finnish **8** Nobelist
Sillas: **5** Karen
silliness: **3** rot **4** bosh **5** folly **6** footle, humbug, levity, lunacy **7** fatuity, foolery, inanity **8** jocosity, nonsense **9** absurdity, frivolity, goofiness
Sillitoe, Alan: **6** author, writer **7** British
work: The Loneliness of the Long Distance Runner
Saturday Night and Sunday Morning
Sills: **3** Sam **7** Beverly
Sills, Beverly: **4** diva **6** singer **7** soprano
former company: **3** Met
specialty: **5** opera
silly: **4** daft, dopy, soft, zany **5** apish, daffy, dazed, dippy, dizzy, dopey, droll, empty, funny, giddy, goofy, goony, goose, goosy, inane, nutty, sappy, trite, wacky **6** absurd, cuckoo, giggly, gooney, jejune, jocose, looney, screwy, simple, unwise, whacky **7** amusing, asinine, comical, doltish, fatuous, flighty, foolish, jocular, puerile, unsound, vacuous, waggish, witless **8** anserine, anserous, bonehead, childish, cockeyed, farcical, humorous, ignorant, immature, mindless, sheepish, specious, trifling **9** brainless, dim-witted, facetious, fatuitous, foolhardy, frivolous, half-baked, illogical, ill-suited, imprudent, laughable, lightsome, ludicrous, nitwitted, pointless, senseless, untenable, whimsical **10** addlepated, boneheaded, cockamamie, groundless, half-witted, ill-advised, irrational, nonserious, ridiculous, unprofound, weak-minded
one: **3** ass **5** goose, idiot
silly ___: **5** billy **6** season
silly ___ goose: **3** as a
silly-___: **5** sider
Silly Love Songs (1976 song) artist: Paul McCartney
Silly Putty
handful: **4** glob
holder: **3** egg
___ silly question,...: **4** Ask a
Silly Symphony: **7** cartoon
silo
contents: **4** ICBM **5** grain **6** fodder, forage
neighbor: **4** barn
Silone, Ignazio: **6** author, writer **7** Italian
work: Bread and Wine
silt: **3** mud **4** ooze **7** deposit, residue **8** alluvium, sediment
deposit: **5** delta
depositor: **5** flood
remove ~: **6** dredge
windblown ~: **5** loess
silva: **5** trees **8** woodland
Silva: **4** José **5** Henry
Silva, José: **4** poet **9** Colombian
Silvana: **7** Mangano
Silvano composer: **8** Mascagni
silver: **3** oof **4** cash, coin, gelt, gray, grey, jack, kail, kale, loot, pale, peag, pelf **5** bills, bread, bucks, color, dough, funds, lucre, metal, money, moola, mopus, pesos, plate, rhino, sewan, white **6** argent, bright, change, dinero, do-re-mi, mammon, mazuma, moolah, pearly, plated, seawan, specie, wampum, wealth, whiten **7** cabbage, capital, dollars, element, lettuce, ooftish, scratch, shekels, whitish **8** bankroll, cold cash, currency, flatware, hard cash, lustrous, smackers, sterling **9** banknotes, frogskins, long green, simoleons, valuables **10** greenbacks, green stuff
alloy: **7** amalgam **8** electrum
bar: **5** ingot
braid: **5** orris
combining form: **5** argyr- **6** argent-, argyro- **7** argenti-, argento-
dollar: **6** cactus
ender: **3** eye, rod, tip **4** back, fish, side, ware, weed, work **5** berry, point, smith
fabric: **4** lamé
German ~: **6** albata
in heraldry: **6** argent
measure: **8** sterling
Navaho ~: **6** concha
ore: **9** argentite, sylvanite **10** polybasite
piece of ~: **4** fork **5** knife, spoon
relative: **3** ash **4** bone, dove, drab, milk, snow **5** beige, cream, dusty, ivory, merle, milky, pearl, putty, slate, taupe **6** argent, oyster **7** grizzly **8** charcoal, eggshell, gunmetal, platinum
source: **3** ore **4** mine, vein
starter: **5** quick
take the ~: **5** place
uncoined ~: **5** sycee
silver ___: **3** age, fir, fox **4** bass, bell, fizz, foil, gilt, gray, grey, hake, leaf, thaw, vine **5** frost, jenny, maple, medal, paper, perch, plate, point, spoon, trout **6** bullet, doctor, dollar, halide, iodate, iodide, lining, poplar, salmon, screen, wattle **7** bromide, jubilee, nitrate, wedding
silver-___: **6** plated **7** tongued
___ silver: **4** coin, flat, free, horn, ruby **5** sycee **6** German, nickel
Silver: **3** Ron **5** horse, steed **6** equine
companion: **5** Scout
State: **6** Nevada
Silver ___: **4** Bird, Star **5** Bears, Bells **6** Streak **7** Wedding
Silverado (1985 film)
cast: Rosanna Arquette, Kevin Costner, Scott Glenn, Danny Glover, Kevin Kline
director: Lawrence Kasdan
role: **3** Mal **4** Jake
___ Silver, away!: **4** Hi-yo
Silver Bears (1978 film)
cast: Michael Caine, Louis Jourdan, Cybill Shepherd
silverbell: **4** tree
Silverberg: **6** Robert
Silver Bow: **4** city, town
locale: **7** Montana
Silver Chalice, The author: Thomas Costain
Silver Cloud: **3** car, Reo **4** auto **10** automobile, Rolls-Royce
Silver Comet: **5** train
Silver Dawn: **3** car **4** auto **10** automobile, Rolls-Royce
Silverdome: **5** arena
Silver Firs: **4** city, town
locale: **10** Washington
silver fizz: **5** drink **8** beverage, cocktail
ingredient: **3** gin **4** soda **5** vodka **8** egg white **10** lemon juice
Silver Ghost: **3** car **4** auto **10** automobile, Rolls-Royce
silver-gray: **3** ash
Silverheels: **3** Jay
partner: **5** Moore
role: **5** Tonto
Silver Hill: **4** city, town
locale: **8** Maryland
Silverius: **4** pope **7** pontiff
Silver, Joan Micklin: **8** director
film: Between the Lines (1977)
Crossing Delancey (1988)
Hester Street (1975)
silver-lining locale: **5** cloud
Silverman: **5** Belle **8** Jonathan
___ silver platter: **3** on a
Silver, Ron: **5** actor
film: The Arrival (1996)
Enemies, A Love Story (1989)
Garbo Talks (1984)
Reversal of Fortune (1990)
___ Silver Sands: **5** White
Silver Seraph: **3** car **4** auto **10** automobile, Rolls-Royce
Silver Shadow: **3** car **4** auto **10** automobile, Rolls-Royce
silverside: **4** fish
Silvers, Phil: **5** actor **8** comedian
film: It's a Mad Mad Mad Mad World (1963)
A Thousand and One Nights (1945)
Top Banana (1954)
TV: The Phil Silvers Show
Silver Spirit: **3** car **4** auto **10** automobile, Rolls-Royce
Silver Spring: **4** city, town
locale: **8** Maryland
Silver Springs, city near: **5** Ocala
Silver Spur: **3** car **4** auto **10** automobile, Rolls-Royce
Silver Star: **5** medal
Silverstein: **4** Shel
Silverstone: **6** Alicia, estate
owner: **6** Tipton
Silverstone, Alicia: **7** actress
film: Batman & Robin (1997)
Blast From the Past (1999)
Clueless (1995)
Silver Streak (1976 film)
cast: Jill Clayburgh, Richard Pryor, Gene Wilder
director: Arthur Hiller
silvertip: **4** bear
silver-tongued: **4** glib **5** suave, sweet **8** eloquent **10** articulate, rhetorical, well-spoken
silverware: **4** fork **5** knife, spoon **7** utensil
Silver Wedding author: Maeve Binchy
Silver Wraith: **3** car **4** auto **10** automobilr, Rolls-Royce
silvery: **4** gray, grey **5** smoky, white **6** argent **7** melodic, musical **9** melodious
___ Silvia: **3** Rea **4** Rhea
silviculture: **8** forestry
s'il vous plait: **6** French, kindly, please
Sim, Alastair: **5** actor
film: The Belles of St. Trinian's (1953)
A Christmas Carol (1951)
Doctor's Dilemma (1958)
Green for Danger (1946)
The Littlest Horse Thieves (1977)
The Ruling Class (1972)
School for Scoundrels (1960)
Wee Geordie (1956)
simar: **4** coat, robe **6** jacket
Simba: **3** cat **4** lion
uncle: **4** Scar
Simba (1955 film)
cast: Dirk Bogarde, Virginia McKenna
tribesmen: **6** Mau Mau
___ Simbel: **3** Abu
Simchas ___: **5** Torah
Simcoe: **4** lake
locale: **6** Canada **7** Ontario
Si, me ne vo, Contessa: **4** aria
Simenon, Georges: **6** author, French, writer
sleuth: Inspector Maigret
Simeon: **5** saint
brother of ~: **3** Dan, Gad **4** Levi **5** Asher, Judah **6** Joseph, Reuben **7** Zebulun **8** Benjamin, Issachar, Naphtali
parent of ~: **4** Leah **5** Jacob
sister of ~: **5** Dinah
___ Simeon: **3** San
___ Simeone Chorale: **5** Harry
Simhat ___: **5** Torah
simian: **3** ape **5** jocko, orang **6** baboon, monkey **7** primate
Simian Line, The (2001 film)
cast: Harry Connick Jr., Cindy Crawford, Lynn Redgrave, Jamey Sheridan
director: Linda Yellen
Simic, Charles: **4** poet
similar: **3** kin **4** akin, like, same, such, twin **5** alike **6** akin to, allied, on a par **7** cognate, kindred, related, uniform **8** matching, parallel **9** analogous, congruent, congruous, consonant, identical **10** coincident, coinciding, comparable, equivalent, like-minded, reciprocal, resembling
be ~: **8** resemble
combining form: **5** homeo- **6** homeoe-, homoio-
prefix: **3** syn- **4** para-
think ~: **5** liken **6** equate
similarity: **6** parity **7** analogy, kinship **8** affinity, likeness, parallel, relation, sameness **9** agreement, alikeness, closeness, community, congruity, lookalike, semblance **10** comparison, conformity
suffix: **3** -oid
similarly: **4** also, same **5** alike **6** in kind **8** likewise
to: **4** like
simile: **5** image **8** likeness, likening **9** semblance **10** comparison
center: **3** as a **4** as an
start: **5** like a
___ simile: **4** epic **7** Homeric
similitude: **8** likeness, metaphor **9** semblance
Simi Valley: **4** city, town
locale: **10** California
Simmental: **3** cow **4** bull **6** bovine, cattle
simmer: **4** boil, burn, cook, foam, fume, heat, rage, stew, warm **5** churn, froth, smart **6** braise, bubble, seethe **7** ferment, parboil, smolder **8** smoulder **10** effervesce
down: **4** calm **5** relax **7** compose, cool off
simmer ___: **4** down
simmering: **5** aboil, on low

Simmons: **2** Al **4** Gene, Jean **7** Richard **8** mattress
competitor: **5** Sealy, Serta
Simmons, Jean: **7** actress
film: All the Way Home (1963)
Androcles and the Lion (1952)
The Blue Lagoon (1949)
Divorce American Style (1967)
Elmer Gantry (1960)
Guys and Dolls (1955)
Home Before Dark (1958)
So Long at the Fair (1950)
Spartacus (1960)
Young Bess (1953)
spouse: Stewart Granger
Simms: **4** Phil **7** William
Simms, Phil: **2** QB
sport: **8** football
Simms, William: **4** poet **6** author, writer
work: Beauchampe
Charlemont
Woodcraft
simnel ___: **4** cake
simoleon: **4** bill, buck, clam **6** dollar **7** smacker **8** banknote, frogskin **9** greenback
simoleons: **3** oof **4** cash, gelt, jack, kail, kale, loot, peag, pelf **5** bread, bucks, dough, funds, lucre, money, moola, mopus, pesos, rhino, sewan **6** dinero, do-re-mi, mammon, mazuma, moolah, seawan, silver, specie, wampum, wealth **7** cabbage, capital, lettuce, ooftish, scratch, shekels **8** bankroll, cold cash, currency, hard cash **9** long green **10** green stuff
simon-___: **4** pure
Simon: **3** Joe **4** Gray, Neil, Paul, Ward **5** Carly, Estes, Wells **6** Claude, Simone, Stevin, Wincer **7** Herbert, Kuznets, Oakland, Richard **10** Wiesenthal
brother: **5** Jesus
Simon ___: **4** says **5** Birch, Le Bon, Magus, Peter **6** Legree
___ Simon: **6** Simple
Simón: **7** Bolívar
Simon and Garfunkel: **3** duo
members: Paul Simon, Art Garfunkel
song: At the Zoo (1967)
The Boxer (1969)
Bridge Over Troubled Water (1970)
Cecilia (1970)
The Dangling Conversation (1966)
El Condor Pasa (1970)
Fakin' It (1967)
A Hazy Shade of Winter (1966)
Homeward Bound (1966)
I Am a Rock (1966)
Mrs. Robinson (1968)
My Little Town (1975)
Scarborough Fair (1968)
The Sounds of Silence (1965)
Wonderful World (1978)
Simon author: George Sand
Simon Birch (1998 film)
cast: Ashley Judd, Joseph Mazzello, Oliver Platt, Ian Michael Smith
Simon Boccanegra: **5** opera
composer: **5** Verdi
setting: **5** Genoa, Italy
Simon, Carly
song: Anticipation (1972)
Haven't Got Time for the Pain (1974)
Jesse (1980)
Mockingbird (1974)
Nobody Does It Better (1977)
That's the Way I've Always Heard It Should Be (1971)
You Belong to Me (1978)
You're So Vain (1972)
spouse: James Taylor
Simon, Claude: **6** French, writer **8** Nobelist
Simone: **4** Nina, Weil **5** Simon **8** Signoret **10** de Beauvoir
Simone, Nina: **7** pianist
genre: **4** jazz
Simon Fraser University
location: **6** Canada **7** Burnaby
Simon, Herbert: **8** Nobelist **9** economist
Simonides: **4** poet **5** Greek
Simoniz: **3** wax **6** car wax
Simon, Neil: **10** playwright
character: **5** Felix, Oscar
nickname: **3** Doc
spouse: Marsha Mason
work: Barefoot in the Park
Biloxi Blues
Brighton Beach Memoirs
Broadway Bound
California Suite
Chapter Two
Come Blow Your Horn
Fools
The Gingerbread Lady
The Good Doctor
I Ought to Be in Pictures
Jake's Women
Last of the Red Hot Lovers
Laughter on the 23rd Floor
London Suite
Lost in Yonkers
The Odd Couple
Plaza Suite
Prisoner of Second Avenue
Promises, Promises
Proposals
Rumors
The Star-Spangled Girl
The Sunshine Boys
Sweet Charity
They're Playing Our Song
Simon of the Desert (1965 film) director: Luis Buñuel
Simon, Paul
song: 50 Ways to Leave Your Lover (1976)
Kodachrome (1973)
Late in the Evening (1980)
Loves Me Like a Rock (1973)
Me and Julio Down by the Schoolyard (1972)
Mother and Child Reunion (1972)
Slip Slidin' Away (1977)
spouse: Edie Brickell, Carrie Fisher
Simon Says player: **4** aper
___-Simon scale: **5** Binet
Simon & Simon (CBS drama)
cast: Gerald McRaney (Rick Simon) Jameson Parker (A.J. Simon)
dog: **7** Marlowe
simoom: **4** wind
simp: **4** dolt, fool **5** dunce, ninny **6** dimwit **7** airhead, dullard, jackass **8** easy mark **9** birdbrain, harebrain, ignoramus, lamebrain, numbskull **10** bubblehead, dunderhead, nincompoop, noodlehead
simpatico: **4** nice **7** rapport **8** likeable **10** compatible, harmonious
simper: **4** grin **5** smile, smirk
simple: **4** bare, dull, easy, homy, mere, mild, naif, pure, rude, slow, snap, soft **5** basic, cinch, clean, clear, crude, cushy, dense, frank, goosy, green, homey, inane, light, lowly, lucid, naive, naked, plain, prime, quiet, sheer, silly, stark, thick **6** breeze, common, direct, earthy, facile, feeble, folksy, honest, humble, modest, picnic, rustic, single, unmixt **7** amateur, artless, asinine, austere, classic, foolish, literal, lowborn, natural, no sweat, primary, puerile, shallow, Spartan, unfussy, unmixed, witless **8** absolute, backward, childish, discreet, duck soup, gullable, gullible, homemade, homespun, ignorant, inexpert, informal, innocent, mindless, ordinary, painless, pastoral, pushover, readable, trusting, unartful, untaxing, walkover, workable **9** backwater, brainless, childlike, credulous, dimwitted, easy as pie, guileless, ingenuous, nitwitted, no problem, primitive, senseless, unadorned, unalloyed, unblended, uncomplex, unlabored, unstudied **10** child's play, effortless, elementary, half-witted, illiterate, manageable, soft-headed, unaffected, unassuming, uncombined, undeniable, uneducated, unexacting, uninvolved, unschooled
combining form: **4** hapl- **5** haplo-
ender: **6** minded **7** hearted
something ~: **4** snap **6** breeze
simple ___: **3** arc, vow **4** pole, time **5** as ABC, fruit, group, sugar, syrup **6** honors **7** machine, measure, protein
simple ___ curve: **6** closed
___ simple: **3** fee
Simple ___: **3** Men **5** Minds, Simon
___ Simple: **5** Blood, Peter
simple as ___: **3** ABC
___ Simple Melody: **5** Play a
simpleminded: **4** dopy, dull **5** dense, dopey, silly **6** obtuse **7** doltish, foolish, witless **9** dim-witted
one: **4** naif
Simple Plan, A (1998 film)
cast: Brent Briscoe, Bridget Fonda, Bill Paxton, Billy Bob Thornton
director: Sam Raimi
Simple Simon: **7** musical
songwriter: **4** Hart **7** Rodgers
treat: **3** pie
Simple Simon met a ___: **6** pieman
Simple Symphony composer: **7** Britten
simpleton: **3** ass, nit, oaf, sap **4** boob, clod, dodo, dolt, dope, fool, gowk, zany **5** chump, clown, cluck, dummy, dunce, goose, joker, klutz, looby, ninny, patsy **6** cuckoo, dimwit, lubber, lummox, nitwit, sucker, turkey **7** buffoon, dingbat, dullard, fathead, half-wit, jackass, pinhead, saphead **8** bonehead, dumbbell, lunkhead, meathead, numskull **9** birdbrain, blockhead, greenhorn, harebrain, lamebrain, numbskull **10** dunderhead, nincompoop
Simple Twist of Faith, A (1994 film)
cast: Stephen Baldwin, Gabriel Byrne, Steve Martin, Catherine O'Hara
director: Gillies MacKinnon
simplicity: **4** ease **6** candor, purity **7** clarity, modesty, naivety **8** chastity, easiness **9** austerity, clearness, ignorance, innocence, integrity, plainness **10** classicism
Simplicius: **4** pope **7** pontiff
simplified: **10** elementary
simplify: **4** ease **5** clear **6** lay out, reduce **7** abridge, clarify, clear up, cut down, explain, shorten **8** boil down, make easy, spell out **9** break down, elucidate, interpret, make clear, make plain, translate **10** facilitate, popularize, streamline, unscramble
Simplon ___: **4** Pass
simply: **4** just, mere, only **6** barely, easily, in fact, merely, openly, purely, really, solely, wholly **7** clearly, frankly, lightly, plainly, totally, utterly **8** candidly, commonly, directly, honestly, modestly **9** literally, naturally, sincerely **10** absolutely, completely, nothing but, ordinarily
Simpson: **2** O.J. **3** Abe **4** Alan, Bart, Lisa, Mona **5** Adele, Homer, Louis, Marge **6** desert, Maggie **7** Jessica, Valerie
Simpson, Jessica song: I Wanna Love You Forever (1999)
Simpson, Louis: **4** poet
Simpson, O.J. sport: **8** football
Simpsons, The (Fox sitcom)
bar: **4** Moe's
bartender: **3** Moe
bus driver: **4** Otto
cat: **8** Scratchy, Snowball
clerk: **3** Apu
grandfather: Abe
mouse: **5** Itchy
neighbor: **3** Ned
voice cast: Nancy Cartwright (Bart Simpson)
Dan Castellaneta (Homer Simpson)
Julie Kavner (Marge Simpson)
Yeardley Smith (Lisa Simpson)
Simpson, Valerie spouse: Nickolas Ashford
Sims: **3** Kym **4** Zoot
Sims, Zoot: **11** saxophonist
genre: **4** jazz
simulacrum: **4** copy, icon, ikon **5** eikon, image **9** imitation
simulate: **3** act, ape, lie **4** copy, fake, lift, mock, play, pose, sham **5** bluff, cheat, feign, fence, forge, mimic, phony, put on, steal **6** affect, assume, borrow, fake it, invent, mirror, phoney, pirate, play at **7** act like, concoct, deceive, imitate, playact, portray, pretend **8** disguise, knock off, resemble **9** fabricate, replicate, reproduce **10** equivocate, put on an act
simulated: **4** fake, mock, sham **5** bogus, false, phony, put-on, quack **6** ersatz, phoney, pseudo, unreal **7** assumed **8** spurious **9** emulative, imitation, imitative, synthetic **10** artificial, factitious, fictitious, fraudulent
simulation: **3** act **8** pretense **9** imitation
___ simulator: **6** flight
simultaneous: **10** concurrent
simultaneously: **5** along **6** at once, in sync **8** meantime, together **9** at one time, meanwhile
sin: **3** err **4** evil, lust, vice **5** anger, cheat, crime, error, fault, guilt, lapse, lying, stray, wrong **6** Hebrew, letter, offend, wander **7** avarice, demerit, deviate, do wrong, impiety, misdeed, offense **8** go astray, iniquity, peccancy, trespass **9** backslide, blasphemy, evildoing, misbehave, sacrilege, veniality, violation **10** immorality, infraction, misconduct, peccadillo, transgress, wickedness, wrongdoing
deadly ~: **4** envy, lust **5** pride, sloth, wrath **7** avarice **8** gluttony
lead into ~: **6** entice, entrap
predecessor: **4** resh
successor: **4** shin
sin ___: **3** tax
___ sin: **3** arc **6** actual, deadly, mortal, venial
Sinai: **4** peak **5** mount **8** mountain
city near ~: **4** Gaza
desert near ~: **5** Negeb, Negev
locale: **4** Asia **7** Mideast
Sinaloa: **5** state **7** Mexican
city: **5** Ahome **7** Guasave **8** Culiacán, Mazatlán, Navolato **9** El Rosario, Escuinapa, Guamúchil, Los Mochis **12** Juan José Ríos
Sinatra: **4** Tina **5** Frank, Nancy
Sinatra, Frank: **5** actor **6** singer
film: 4 for Texas (1963)
Anchors Aweigh (1945)
Can-Can (1960)
Come Blow Your Horn (1963)
The Detective (1968)
Dirty Dingus Magee (1970)

The First Deadly Sin (1980)
From Here to Eternity (1953, AA)
Guys and Dolls (1955)
High Society (1956)
The Joker Is Wild (1957)
Kings Go Forth (1958)
The Manchurian Candidate (1962)
The Man With the Golden Arm (1955)
Not as a Stranger (1955)
Ocean's Eleven (1960)
On the Town (1949)
Pal Joey (1957)
Robin and the Seven Hoods (1964)
Some Came Running (1959)
Step Lively (1944)
Suddenly (1954)
Take Me Out to the Ball Game (1949)
The Tender Trap (1955)
Tony Rome (1967)
Von Ryan's Express (1965)
Young at Heart (1954)
hometown: Hoboken
song: All the Way (1957)
Can I Steal a Little Love (1957)
Hey! Jealous Lover (1956)
High Hopes (1959)
How Little We Know (1956)
It Was a Very Good Year (1966)
Learnin' the Blues (1955)
Love and Marriage (1955)
My Way (1969)
Same Old Saturday Night (1955)
Somethin' Stupid (1967)
Strangers in the Night (1966)
The Tender Trap (1955)
That's Life (1966)
Witchcraft (1958)
spouse: Mia Farrow, Ava Gardner
Sinatra, Nancy
song: How Does That Grab You, Darlin'? (1966)
Somethin' Stupid (1967)
Sugar Town (1966)
These Boots Are Made for Walkin' (1966)
spouse: Tommy Sands
Sinbad: 4 hero
emulate ~: 4 rove
number of voyages of ~: 5 seven
transport: 3 roc
Sinbad the Sailor (1947 film)
cast: Douglas Fairbanks Jr., Maureen O'Hara, Anthony Quinn
since: 3 ago, for **4** as of **7** because, whereas **8** as long as, from then, until now **9** therefore **10** inasmuch as
in French: 3 des
in Scottish: 4 syne
prefix: 3 cis-
Since __ for You: 5 I Fell
Since __ Have You: 5 I Don't
Since __ You, Baby: 4 I Met
since Hector was __: 4 a pup
sincere: 4 dear, just, naif, open, real, true, warm **5** frank, meant, naive, plain **6** actual, candid, devout, direct, fervid, hearty, honest, infelt, square **7** artless, cordial, earnest, fervent, genuine, natural, regular, saintly, serious, up-front **8** bona fide, credible, faithful, innocent, like it is, out-front, profound, reliable, true-blue, truthful **9** dead-level, guileless, heartfelt, honorable, ingenuous, on the line, outspoken, righteous, unfeigned, unguarded **10** aboveboard, forthright, no-nonsense, on the level, point-blank, scrupulous, sure enough, unaffected, unimagined
sincerely: 4 true **5** truly **6** deeply, really, simply **7** frankly **8** candidly, for keeps, heartily, honestly **9** earnestly, genuinely, seriously **10** aboveboard, point-blank, profoundly, truthfully
in Latin: 7 ex animo
Sincerely (1955 song)
artist: McGuire Sisters, Moonglows
sincerity: 4 zeal **5** heart, honor, truth **6** candor, fervor, warmth **7** honesty, loyalty, probity **8** devotion, goodwill, openness, veracity **9** frankness, good faith, innocence, integrity **10** cordiality
Since you __...: 5 asked
Since You __ Me: 5 Asked
Since You've Been Gone (1968 song)
artist: Aretha Franklin
Since You Went Away (1944 film)
cast: Claudette Colbert, Joseph Cotten, Jennifer Jones
Sin City author: Harold Robbins
Sinclair: 5 Lewis, Madge, Upton
rival: 4 Esso **7** Flying A
Sinclair, Upton: 6 author, writer
work: Boston
The Jungle
King Coal
Oil!
World's End
sine: 5 ratio
reciprocal: 5 cosec
sine __: 3 die **4** wave **5** curve, prole
__ sine: 3 arc **6** versed **7** inverse
Sinéad: 7 O'Connor
__ sine numine: 3 nil
sine qua non: 4 gist, must, need **7** essence **9** condition, essential, necessity, requisite
sinew: 4 beef, thew **5** brawn, force, power, thews, vigor **6** muscle, tendon **7** potence, potency **8** strength **9** toughness **10** resilience, robustness
sinewy: 4 hale, iron, lean, wiry **5** beefy, burly, hardy, hefty, hunky, husky, lusty, nervy, stout, tough **6** brawny, hearty, mighty, potent, robust, rugged, steely, stocky, strong, sturdy, virile **7** doughty, stringy **8** athletic, forceful, indurate, muscular, powerful, puissant, stalwart, vigorous **9** Atlantean, Herculean, resilient, strapping, well-built **10** able-bodied, red-blooded
sinful: 3 bad **4** dark, evil **5** cruel **6** guilty, rakish **7** harmful, immoral **8** depraved **10** inexpiable, iniquitous, villainous
sing: 3 hum, pur, rat **4** belt, blab, fink, laud, pipe, purr, talk, tune **5** carol, chant, chirp, croon, honor, sound, trill, troll, tweet, whine, yodel, yodle **6** betray, depone, inform, intone, lament, praise, snitch, tattle, turn in, warble **7** belt out, confess, descant, discant, glorify, perform, profess, resound, tell all, testify **8** melodize, serenade, vocalize **9** celebrate, harmonize **10** cantillate
ender: 4 song **5** spiel
falsetto: 5 yodel, yodle
how to ~: 5 on key
one's own praises: 4 brag, crow **5** boast
out: 3 cry **4** call, ring, yell **5** shout **6** bellow, holler, scream
softly: 5 croon
the blues: 4 mope, wail **6** bemoan, lament, sorrow
the praises of: 4 laud **5** exalt, extol **6** extoll **7** glorify
without words: 3 hum
sing __: 3 out
sing-__: 4 song **5** along
Sing __ of sixpence...: 5 a song
Sing __ songs for me...: 5 no sad
Sing __ With Mitch: 5 Along
__ Sing: 3 Hop
Sing (1973 song) artist: Carpenters
sing a different __: 4 tune
Sing Along With Mitch (NBC music)
cast: Mitch Miller
Leslie Uggams
__ Sing and I'm Happy: 5 Let Me
Singapore: 3 isl. **4** city, isle, town **6** island, nation **7** capital, country
capital: 9 Singapore
language: 5 Malay
locale: 4 Asia
money: 4 cent **6** dollar
Singapore sling: 5 drink **8** beverage, cocktail
ingredient: 3 gin
Singapura: 3 cat **5** felid **6** feline
Singaraja: 4 city, town
locale: 4 Bali
Sing a Song (1975 song) artist: Earth, Wind & Fire
Sing, Baby, Sing (1936 film)
cast: Alice Faye, Adolphe Menjou, Gregory Ratoff
Sing Down the Moon author: 5 O'Dell
singe: 3 fry **4** burn, char, heat, sear **6** scorch **7** blacken, torrefy, torrify **8** overheat **9** carbonize
singer: 4 alto, bass, diva **5** basso, tenor **6** artist, canary **7** artiste, chanter, crooner, intoner, soloist, warbler, yodeler **8** melodist, minstrel, musician, songbird, songster, vocalist **9** chanteuse, choralist, chorister, serenader **10** troubadour
gig: 6 lounge
starter: 4 folk **6** master
work: 5 vocal
__ singer: 3 pop **4** folk, jazz **5** torch **7** country, popular
Singer: 4 Lori, Marc **5** Bryan, Isaac
Singer, Bryan: 8 director
film: The Usual Suspects (1995)
X-Men (2000)
Singer, Isaac Bashevis: 6 writer **7** Yiddish **8** Nobelist
work: Enemies, a Love Story
The Estate
The Family Moskat
The Magician of Lublin
The Manor
The Penitent
Satan in Goray
Shosha
The Slave
singers: 5 choir **6** chorus **8** ensemble
__ Singers: 6 Staple **7** Rooftop
__ Singer Sargent: 4 John
__ Singer, The: 4 Jazz **6** Praise **7** Wedding
Singh: 3 Ram **5** Vijay
Singhalese: 8 language
Singh, Vijay: 6 golfer
milieu: 5 links **6** course
org.: 3 PGA
singing: 5 music
group: 5 choir **6** chorus
style: 6 arioso, doo-wop
suitable for ~: 5 melic
syllables: 4 la la **5** tra la
the blues: 3 low **4** down **6** morose **8** downcast **9** sorrowful
voice: 4 alto, bass **5** basso, mezzo, tenor **7** soprano **8** baritone
singing __: 8 telegram
__ singing: 4 folk, part, scat
Singing Cowboy, The: 5 Autry
Singing Nun song: Dominique (1963)
Singing the Blues (1956 song) artist: Guy Mitchell
Singin' in the Rain (1952 film): 7 musical
cast: Cyd Charisse, Jean Hagen, Gene Kelly, Donald O'Connor, Debbie Reynolds
director: Stanley Donen, Gene Kelly
studio: 3 MGM
__ Sing in the Sunshine: 4 We'll
single: 3 hit, odd, one **4** lone, only, rare, sole, solo, unal **5** alone, loner, unwed **6** dollar, lonely, simple, unique, unmixt **7** unitary, unmixed **8** bachelor, distinct, divorced, eligible, especial, isolated, original, peerless, secluded, separate, solitary, specific, uncommon, unshared, wifeless **9** exclusive, on one's own, separated, unalloyed, unblended, undivided, unmarried, unrivaled **10** individual, particular, restricted, spouseless, unattached, unfettered, unrivalled
combining form: 3 mon- **4** hapl-, mono- **5** haplo-
entity: 4 item, unit **5** monad
having a ~ element: 5 unary
in ~ file: 4 arow
new ~: 2 ex
no more: 3 wed
out: 3 opt **4** cite, name, pick, take **5** elect, key on **6** choose, opt for, prefer, select **7** fix upon **8** decide on, handpick, identify, separate **9** designate, segregate **10** settle upon
softly-hit ~: 5 bloop
time: 4 once
single __: 3 cut, man, tax **4** bond, file, knot, tape, whip, wing **5** cross, modal, rhyme **6** combat, quotes, sculls, ticket, wicket **7** premium
single-__: 4 foot, knit, shot **5** blind, cross, digit, ended, phase, space, track **6** acting, action, barrel, family, handed, minded, suiter, valued **7** hearted
single-__ bookkeeping: 5 entry
single-__ reflex camera: 4 lens
__ single: 4 bunt
single-file: 6 in a row
single-minded: 5 rigid **6** intent, steady **8** stubborn **9** steadfast, unbending
single-mindedness: 4 will **7** loyalty, purpose **9** willpower
single-name
singer: 4 Cher **6** Prince **7** Madonna
supermodel: 4 Iman
singleness: 5 unity **7** loyalty
single-purpose: 5 ad hoc
singles __: 3 bar
singles party: 5 mixer
singlet: 5 shirt
in America: 10 undershirt
singleton: 5 loner **10** individual
Singleton: 4 John **5** Penny
__ Singleton Copley: 4 John
Single White Female (1992 film)
cast: Bridget Fonda, Jennifer Jason Leigh, Steven Weber
director: Barbet Schroeder
singly: 3 but **4** each **5** alone, apart **6** apiece, solely **8** one by one **10** one at a time, separately
sing one's __: 7 praises
__ Sings Again: 6 Jolson
Sing Sing: 6 prison
locale: 7 New York
resident: 3 con **5** felon **6** inmate **8** prisoner
singsong: 6 intone **10** monotonous
__ Sings the Blues: 4 Lady
sing the __: 5 blues
singular: 3 odd, one **4** lone, only, rare, sole, solo, unal **5** alone, loner, queer **6** atypic, quaint, unique **7** certain, curious, eminent, oddball, special, strange, uncanny, unusual **8** atypical, definite, especial, original, peculiar, puzzling, separate, solitary, striking, uncommon, unwonted **9** eccentric, exclusive, marvelous, recherché, unheard-of **10** individual, noteworthy, outlandish, particular, phenomenal,

prodigious, remarkable, respective, unexampled, unordinary
singularity: 5 quirk 6 oddity 8 identity 9 mannerism
Sing, You Sinners (1938 film): 7 musical
cast: Bing Crosby, Fred MacMurray, Donald O'Connor
director: Wesley Ruggles
Sinhalese: 5 Indic
Sinise, Gary: 5 actor
film: Apollo 13 (1995)
Bruno (2000)
Forrest Gump (1994)
Jack the Bear (1993)
Of Mice and Men (1992)
Ransom (1996)
sinister: 3 bad, ill 4 base, dark, evil, grim, left, ugly, vile 5 lurid, nasty, woful 6 creepy, malign, woeful 7 baleful, baneful, corrupt, doomful, harmful, hurtful, malefic, ominous, satanic, unlucky 8 lowering, menacing, perverse 9 dishonest, ill-boding, injurious, malignant, obnoxious, satanical 10 disastrous, forbidding, foreboding, malevolent, pernicious, portentous, villainous, virtueless
look: 4 leer
opposite: 6 dexter
__ sinister: 3 bar 4 bend
sinistral: 4 left
sink: 3 bog, dip, ebb, fen, lay, ram, rot, sag, set 4 dive, drop, fail, fall, flag, hole, mire, ruin, slip, stab, tire, verb, wane, wilt 5 abate, basin, decay, drill, drive, droop, drown, embed, imbed, lapse, lower, marsh, reach, slide, slope, slump, spoil, stick, stoop, swamp, swoop, waste, wreck 6 cave in, debase, defeat, demean, engulf, fall in, go down, hollow, ingulf, lessen, plunge, ravage, recede, settle, thrust, weaken, worsen 7 capsize, decline, degrade, depress, descend, destroy, drop off, dwindle, fatigue, founder, go broke, go under, immerse, let down, plummet, put down, regress, relapse, scuttle, subside, succumb, tail off, triumph, venture 8 bankrupt, cast down, collapse, decrease, demolish, diminish, excavate, flounder, submerge, submerse, vanquish, washbowl 9 aggravate, backslide, bring down, devastate, disappear, force down, humiliate, overwhelm, shipwreck 10 degenerate, depreciate, depression, exacerbate, go bankrupt, go downhill, impoverish, retrograde, retrogress
alternative: 4 swim
ender: 3 age 4 hole
feature: 4 trap 5 drain
in: 8 register 9 penetrate
like the kitchen ~: 5 soapy, sudsy
one's teeth into: 3 nip 4 bite
starter: 7 counter
to the bottom: 6 settle
trap shape: 3 ess
__ sink: 3 dry 4 heat, slop 7 kitchen
sinker: 5 donut, pitch 6 weight 8 doughnut
ender: 4 ball
material: 4 lead
sub ~: 6 ashcan
sinkhole: 6 hollow 10 depression
Sin Killer author: Larry McMurtry
sinking: 3 low 4 down 7 descent
sinking __: 4 fund 5 spell
sinking ship deserter: 3 rat
sink one's __ into: 5 teeth
sink or __: 4 swim
Sink the Bismarck! (1960 film)
cast: Kenneth More, Dana Wynter
director: Lewis Gilbert
Sink the Bismarck (1960 song) artist: Johnny Horton
Sink the Bismarck! author: C.S. Forester
sinless: 5 clean 6 chaste 8 innocent 9 faultless, guiltless, righteous 10 immaculate, impeccable
sinner: 6 rascal 8 criminal, evildoer
former ~: 6 atoner
Sinn Fein
land: 4 Eire 7 Ireland
org.: 3 IRA
Sino-: 7 Chinese
Sin of Father Mouret author: Emile Zola
Sin of Madelon Claudet, The (1931 film)
cast: Neil Hamilton, Helen Hayes, Lewis Stone
director: Edgar Selwyn
Sino-Japanese __: 3 War
Sinope: 4 moon
planet: 7 Jupiter
Sint __: 7 Maarten
__ Sin to Tell a Lie: 4 It's a
sinuate: 4 coil, curl, kink, loop, wind 5 crimp, curve, snake, swirl, twine, twirl, twist, whorl 6 spiral, tangle 7 entwine, intwine, meander, wreathe 9 convolute, corkscrew 10 intertwine
sinuosity: 3 arc, bow 4 arch, bend, coil, curl, loop, ogee, turn 5 crook, curve, orbit, twist, whorl 6 camber, circle, spiral 7 contour, ellipse, flexure, rainbow 8 parabola 9 arabesque, concavity, hyperbola 10 trajectory
sinuous: 4 bent, viny, wavy 5 curvy, lithe, snaky 6 curved, curvey, supple, zigzag 7 coiling, crooked, devious, turning, vagrant, winding 8 flexuous, indirect, tortuous, twisting, writhing 9 lithesome, meandrous 10 circuitous, convoluted, meandering, serpentine, undulating
shape: 3 ess
sinus: 6 cavity 10 depression
cavity: 6 antrum
Sinutab alternative: 5 Afrin 6 Contac, Nyquil, Tavist 7 Actifed, Comtrex, Dayquil, Dristan, Sudafed 8 Benadryl, Dimetapp, Drixoral, TheraFlu 9 Coricidin, Triaminic 10 Robitussin
Sinyavsky, Andrey: 6 author, writer 7 Russian
Siobhan: 7 McKenna
Siodmak, Robert: 8 director
film: Christmas Holiday (1944)
Cobra Woman (1944)
Crimson Pirate (1952)
Criss Cross (1949)
The Dark Mirror (1946)
The Killers (1946)
Phantom Lady (1944)
Son of Dracula (1943)
The Spiral Staircase (1946)
The Strange Affair of Uncle Harry (1945)
The Suspect (1944)
Sion: 4 city, town
locale: 6 Valais 11 Switzerland
Siouan: 8 language
Indian: 3 Oto 4 Crow, Otoe 5 Omaha 6 Mandan 8 Missouri 10 Assiniboin
language: 4 Iowa 5 Osage, Ponca
Sioux: 5 tribe 6 Dakota, Indian, Lakota 7 Amerind, Lakhota
Sioux __: 3 War 4 City 5 Falls
Sioux __ Sue: 4 City
Sioux City: 4 town
locale: 4 Iowa
Sioux Falls: 4 city, town
locale: 4 S. Dak.
sip: 3 lap, nip 4 test, toss 5 drink, quaff, savor, taste, touch 6 imbibe, sample 7 drink in, partake, swallow 8 spoonful 10 thimbleful
loudly: 5 slurp
more than a ~: 4 swig
siphon: 3 tap 4 draw, hose, pipe, pump, rack 5 drain 7 channel, extract 8 transmit
siphon __: 6 bottle
sipper: 5 straw
sir: 2 he 3 guy, him 4 chap, male, tuan 5 bloke, title 6 feller, fellow, knight, mister 7 effendi 9 gentleman
counterpart: 4 ma'am 5 madam
Hindu ~: 4 babu 5 baboo
Indian: 5 saheb, sahib
in Spanish: 5 señor
__, sir!: 3 Yes
Sir __: 4 Duke 5 Nigel 7 Mix-a-Lot
Sir __ Belch: 4 Toby
Siracusa: 4 city, town
locale: 5 Italy
Sir Duke (1977 song) artist: Stevie Wonder
sire: 3 dad 4 male, papa 5 beget, breed, spawn 6 father 7 creator 8 ancestor, stallion 9 propagate, reproduce 10 progenitor
mate: 3 dam
siren: 4 Bara, vamp 5 alarm, alert, houri, lurer, nymph, vixen 6 mud eel 7 Aglaope, enticer, Lorelei, manatee, Pisinoe, tempter, warning, whistle 8 alluring, Leucosia, sea nymph, tempting 9 beguiling, enchanter, temptress 10 bewitching, enchanting, Parthenope, Thelxiepia
sound: 4 wail
siren __: 4 song
Sirens sculptor: 4 Erté
__ Sirenum: 4 Mare
Siret: 5 river
locale: 7 Romania, Rumania, Ukraine 8 Roumania
Sir Galahad: 4 poem
author: 8 Tennyson
Siri: 3 cow 4 bull 6 bovine, cattle
Siricius: 4 pope 7 pontiff
Sirius: 4 star 6 Sothis 7 Dog Star
owner: 5 Orion
Sirk, Douglas: 8 director
film: All That Heaven Allows (1955)
Battle Hymn (1957)
Captain Lightfoot (1955)
The First Legion (1951)
Imitation of Life (1959)
Magnificent Obsession (1954)
Shockproof (1949)
Sleep My Love (1948)
Summer Storm (1944)
The Tarnished Angels (1958)
Thieves' Holiday (1946)
Thunder on the Hill (1951)
A Time to Love and a Time to Die (1958)
Written on the Wind (1956)
sirloin: 4 meat 5 steak
Sir Nigel author: Arthur Conan Doyle
sirocco: 4 wind
__, Sir, That's My Baby: 3 Yes
Sirtis: 6 Marina
sis
see sister
sisal: 5 agave, fiber
sisal __: 4 hemp
SISAL: 8 language
alternative: 3 ADA, APL, SQL 4 Alef, html, Icon, Java, LISP, Logo, Orca, Perl 5 Algol, Basic, Cecil, COBOL, Dylan 6 Delphi, Eiffel, Erlang, Oberon, Pascal, Prolog, Sather, Scheme, Snobol 7 Fortran
sise: 3 six
Sisinnius: 4 pope 7 pontiff
Siskel: 4 Gene
siskin: 4 bird 5 tarin
Sisler, George: 8 Cardinal 10 baseballer
sissified: 6 effete, prissy
sissonne: 4 leap
sissy: 4 nerd, nurd, wimp, wuss 5 nerdy, weeny 6 craven, moaner, prissy 7 chicken, crybaby, dastard, mincing 8 mama's boy, poltroon, recreant, weakling 9 fraidy cat, jellyfish 10 namby-pamby, pantywaist
lack: 5 spine
like a ~: 5 timid
sissy __: 3 bar
Sissy: 6 Spacek
sister: 3 kin, nun, rel., sib 6 female 7 kinsman, sibling 8 relation, relative 9 kinswoman 10 kinsperson
child: 5 niece 6 nephew
ender: 4 hood
group: 3 sor. 8 sorority
parent's ~: 4 aunt 5 aunty
sib: 3 bro
starter: 4 step
superior: 6 abbess
sister-__: 5 in-law
__ sister: 3 big, lay, sob 4 half, soul, weak 5 whole 6 foster
Sister __: 3 Act 5 Kenny, Sarah 6 Carrie, Sledge
__ Sister: 6 Little
Sister Act (1992 film)
cast: Whoopi Goldberg, Harvey Keitel, Maggie Smith
director: Emile Ardolino
role: 3 nun
setting: 4 Reno
Sister Carrie author: Theodore Dreiser
character: 3 Bod 4 Ames, Sven 6 Drouet, Hanson, Meeber, Minnie
Sister Golden Hair (1975 song) artist: America
sisterhood: 5 order
sister-in-law: 8 relative
Sister Kenny (1946 film)
cast: Dean Jagger, Alexander Knox, Rosalind Russell
sisterly: 4 kind 5 thick
Sister of __: 5 Mercy 7 Charity, Loretto
__ sisters: 5 weird
Sisters (1973 film)
cast: Charles Durning, Margot Kidder, Jennifer Salt
director: Brian De Palma
Sisters (NBC drama)
cast: Ashley Judd (Reed Halsey)
Patricia Kalember (Georgie Whitsig)
Swoosie Kurtz (Alex Barker)
Julianne Phillips (Frankie Reed)
Sela Ward (Teddy Reed)
__ Sisters: 3 Two 5 Paris, Three 6 DeJohn, Summer 7 Andrews, Fontane, McGuire, Pointer
Sisters artist: 4 Erté
Sister Sledge
song: He's the Greatest Dancer (1979)
We Are Family (1979)
Sisters of Charity founder: 5 Seton
Sisters, The (1938 film)
cast: Bette Davis, Errol Flynn, Anita Louise
director: Anatole Litvak
__ Sister, The: 5 Other 6 Little
Sistine __: 6 Chapel 7 Madonna
Sistine Chapel
locale: 4 Rome 7 Vatican
work: 5 mural 6 fresco
sistrum: 6 rattle 10 percussion
origin: 6 Africa
Sisyphean: 7 endless, eternal
Sisyphus: 4 king
brother of ~: 7 Athamas 9 Salmoneus
parent of ~: 6 Aeolus 7 Enarete
son of ~: 5 Almus 7 Glaucus

8 Odysseus, Ornytion 10 Thersander
wife of ~: 6 Merope
sit: 3 lie 4 meet, park, plop, pose, rest, seat, wait 5 brood, cover, light, model, perch, relax, roost, squat, usher 6 bear on, groove, hunker, instal, lounge, occupy, remain, settle, sprawl 7 convene, install, posture, preside 8 assemble, bear upon, ensconce, plop down 9 officiate, watch over 10 deliberate, take a chair, take it easy
around: 4 laze, loaf, rest 5 relax 6 linger, unwind
down: 4 land, rest 5 light, relax 6 strike
in: 6 attend, strike
in on: 5 audit, visit 7 observe
not ~ well: 3 irk, vex 4 gall, rile 5 anger, annoy, chafe, grate 6 bother, nettle, pester, rankle 8 irritate 10 exasperate
on: 5 hatch, quash, quell 6 put off, rebuke, squash, stifle 7 secrete, silence, squelch 8 hold back, incubate, postpone, restrain, suppress, withhold 10 keep in line, monopolize
on one's hands: 7 abstain
on the fence: 5 waver 7 abstain, quibble 8 hesitate 9 pussyfoot
out: 5 forgo 6 forego 7 abstain, refrain
place to ~: 3 lap 4 sofa 5 bench, chair, perch
spread out: 6 sprawl
starter: 5 house
still for: 3 let 5 abide, allow 6 accept 8 tolerate
through: 6 endure, remain
tight: 4 stay, wait 6 remain
unable to ~ still: 5 antsy 7 fidgety
up for: 5 await
sit __: 3 out 4 down, in on, spin, upon 5 tight 6 around
sit-__ strike: 4 down
__-sit: 3 bed 4 baby
Sita
husband: 4 Rama
sitar: 6 string 10 instrument
motif: 4 raga
origin: 5 India
sitarist: 7 Shankar
sitatunga: 8 antelope
relative: 3 gnu, kob 4 guib, kudu, oryx, puku, topi 5 addax, bongo, chiru, eland, goral, korin, nyala, oribi, saiga, serow 6 chammy, dik-dik, duiker, impala, koodoo, lechwe, nilgai, rhebok, shammy, shamoy 7 blaubok, blesbok, chamois, defassa, gazelle, gemsbok, gerenuk, grysbok, nylghai, nylghau, sassaby 8 blesbuck, bontebok, bushbuck, gemsbuck, reedbuck, steenbok, steinbok 9 blackbuck, pronghorn, springbok, waterbuck 10 hartebeest, wildebeest
sitcom: 6 series 10 production
award: 4 Emmy
demo: 5 pilot
material: 5 humor
sit-down: 6 strike 8 stoppage
affair: 6 dinner
site: 3 fix, lay 4 area, base, home, plot, post, slot, spot 5 haunt, locus, place, point, range, scene, venue, where 6 ground, layout, locale, locate 7 habitat, hangout, purlieu, section, setting, station, theater, theatre 8 locality, location, position, premises, wherever
starter: 4 camp, dump
__ site: 3 Web 6 active
__-site: 3 off 4 type
sited: 3 set
__-site housing: 7 scatter
sit-in: 5 rally 7 protest 10 substitute
Sitka: 4 city, Emil, town
locale: 6 Alaska
Sitka __: 6 spruce
sit on one's __: 5 hands
sitophobe fear: 4 food
sitter: 5 model 8 caretake, guardian, watchdog 9 attendant, caretaker, custodian
bane: 4 brat
__ sitter: 3 pet 4 baby 5 aisle, house
__-sitter: 3 bed 4 farm 5 fence
Sitter, Willem de: 5 Dutch 10 astronomer
sitting: 4 idle 7 session 9 sedentary
duck: 4 butt, dupe, goat, prey 6 pigeon, sucker, target, victim
on: 4 atop
place: 5 roost, stoop
pretty: 4 rich, safe 6 loaded 7 wealthy, well-off 8 affluent, in clover, thriving, well-to-do 9 well-fixed 10 well-heeled
room: 5 salon 6 lounge, parlor 7 boudoir
starter: 5 house
sitting __: 4 duck, room 6 pretty
Sitting __: 4 Bull 5 Ducks 6 Pretty
Sitting __ Back Seat: 5 in the
Sitting Bull: 5 chief, Sioux
foe: 6 Custer
Sitting Pretty (1948 film)
cast: Maureen O'Hara, Clifton Webb, Robert Young
director: Walter Lang
(Sittin' On) The Dock of the Bay (1968 song) artist: Otis Redding
Sittin' Up in My Room (1996 song) artist: Brandy
Sittwe: 4 port
locale: 5 Burma 7 Myanmar
situate: 3 put, set 4 post, seat 5 place, posit 6 locate 8 ensconce
situated, get: 3 set 5 dwell, lodge, perch, roost, set up 6 locate, orient, settle
situation: 3 job 4 case, hire, mode, pass, post, rank, role, seat, site, spot, trim 5 event, locus, place, point, scene, stage, state, thing, trade 6 billet, locale, matter, office, plight, sphere, status 7 footing, picture, problem, setting, station, vacancy 8 ball game, bearings, instance, latitude, like it is, locality, location, position, size of it, standing 9 adversity, condition, placement, status quo 10 employment, engagement, occurrence, profession, standpoint, walk of life
accept the ~: 4 cope 5 adapt 6 face it, manage
bad ~: 3 fix 4 bind, drag, mess, spot 5 pinch 6 scrape 8 quagmire
no-win ~: 4 bind 7 dilemma 8 dead heat, deadlock, quandary, standoff 9 stalemate
situation __: 4 room 6 comedy, ethics
__ situation: 5 no-win
__ sit under the apple tree...: 4 Don't
situs: 6 locale 8 position
Sitwell: 5 Edith 6 Osbert
Sitwell, Edith: 4 Dame, poet 7 British
work: A Poet's Notebook
Still Falls the Rain
Sitwell, Osbert: 4 poet 7 British
sitz __: 4 bath
Sivan: 5 month 6 Hebrew
predecessor: 4 Iyar
successor: 6 Tammuz
Sivash: 3 sea
locale: 6 Russia
Siva worshiper: 5 Hindu 6 Hindoo
Siwalik Hills: 3 mts. 4 mtns. 5 range 9 mountains
locale: 5 India, Nepal 9 Himalayas
six: 5 hexad 6 hexade, number
combining form: 3 hex-, sex- 4 hexa-, sexi- 5 sexti-
ender: 4 teen 5 pence, penny
feet: 6 fathom
games in tennis: 3 set
in dice: 4 sise
in French: 3 six
in German: 5 sechs
in Italian: 3 sei
in Japanese: 4 roku
in Portuguese: 4 seis
in Spanish: 4 seis
outs: 6 inning
to Mohs: 10 orthoclase
years, for senators: 4 term
six __ and half...: 5 of one
six-__: 3 gun 4 pack, spot 6 footer 7 shooter, wheeler
__-six: 4 deep 6 eighty
Six __: 6 Crises, O'Clock 7 Nations
Six __ a-laying...: 5 geese
Six __ Riv Vu: 3 Rms
Six Characters in Search of an Author
author: Luigi Pirandello
Six Crises author: 5 Nixon
Six Days Seven Nights (1998 film)
cast: Harrison Ford, Anne Heche, David Schwimmer
director: Ivan Reitman
Six-Day War site: 5 Sinai
Six Degrees of Separation: 4 film, play
author: John Guare
cast: Stockard Channing, Mary Beth Hurt, Ian McKellen, Will Smith, Donald Sutherland
director: Fred Schepisi
Sixers: 4 five, team 6 cagers
org.: 3 NBA
sixes
at ~ and sevens: 4 hazy 5 aback, dizzy, messy, muddy, upset, wooly 6 cloudy, hectic, punchy, woolly 7 abashed, chaotic, haywire, out of it, puzzled, shook up 8 anarchic, confused, mistaken, nebulous, pell-mell, rambling 9 misguided, quizzical, slaphappy, spaced out, unsettled 10 anarchical, disjointed, disorderly, indefinite, in disarray, indistinct, out to lunch, topsy-turvy, upside-down
double ~: 7 boxcars
pair of ~: 5 dozen
Six Feet Under network: 3 HBO
Six Flags attraction: 4 ride
Six Flags New England locale: 6 Agawam
six-mile
about a ~ run: 4 ten K
Six Million Dollar Man, The (ABC adventure)
cast: Richard Anderson (Oscar Goldman)
Martin E. Brooks (Dr. Rudy Wells)
Lee Majors (Col. Steve Austin)
employer: OSI
hometown: Ojai
Six O'Clock (1967 song) artist: Lovin' Spoonful
Six of a Kind (1934 film)
cast: Gracie Allen, George Burns, W.C. Fields
director: Leo McCarey
six-pack: 5 hexad
unit: 3 can
__ Six-pack: 3 Joe
six-packs, four: 4 case
sixpence: 4 coin 5 money
sixpenny __: 4 nail
six-pointer: 2 TD 9 touchdown
six-shooter: 3 arm, gun 6 pistol
six-sided
crystal: 4 snow
solid: 4 cube
sixteen
one of ~ in a game: 4 pawn
one of ~ teeth: 5 upper
oz.: 5 one lb.
tablespoons: 3 cup
__ sixteen: 5 sweet
Sixteen __: 4 Tons 7 Candles, Reasons
__ Sixteen: 4 Only 5 You're
Sixteen Candles (1984 film)
cast: Paul Dooley, Anthony Michael Hall, Molly Ringwald, Michael Schoeffling
director: John Hughes
sixteenpenny __: 4 nail
Sixteen Reasons (1960 song) artist: Connie Stevens
sixteenth __: 4 note, rest
Sixteen Tons (1955 song) artist: Tennessee Ernie Ford
sixth __: 3 man 5 chord, sense 6 column
Sixth Commandment, The author: Lawrence Sanders
sixth-grader: 5 'tween
sixth sense: 3 ESP 8 instinct 9 intuition, telepathy
Sixth Sense, The (1999 film)
cast: Toni Collette, Haley Joel Osment, Olivia Williams, Bruce Willis
director: M. Night Shyamalan
__-Six Trombones: 7 Seventy
Sixtus: 4 pope 7 pontiff
sixty: 10 threescore
grains: 4 dram
minutes: 4 hour
seconds: 6 minute
sixty-__-dollar question: 4 four
sixty-fourth __: 4 note, rest
Sixty Glorious Years (1938 film)
cast: Anna Neagle, Anton Walbrook
director: Herbert Wilcox
sixty-six: 4 game 8 card game
Six Weeks (1982 film)
cast: Dudley Moore, Mary Tyler Moore
director: Tony Bill
sizable: 3 big 4 good, huge, much, tall, tidy, vast 5 ample, burly, giant, great, gross, hefty, husky, jumbo, large, major, roomy 6 decent, goodly 7 hulking, immense, mammoth, massive, titanic 8 colossal, enormous, gigantic, handsome, spacious, towering, whapping, whopping 9 capacious, extensive, Herculean, humongous, overlarge, strapping 10 gargantuan, large-scale, monumental, prodigious, stupendous, tremendous, voluminous
size: 4 area, bulk, girt, mass, sift, tall 5 girth, jumbo, large, range, scale, scope, small, width 6 amount, extent, height, junior, length, medium, petite, spread, volume 7 bigness, breadth, caliber, content, stature, stretch, tonnage, tunnage 8 capacity, classify, enormity, hugeness, quantity, vastness 9 amplitude, dimension, extension, greatness, immensity, intensity, largeness, magnitude, ranginess, substance 10 dimensions, extra large, population, proportion
adjust the ~ of: 6 zoom in 7 zoom out
cut down to ~: 5 shame 6 demean, humble 7 deflate 8 belittle, minimize 9 humiliate
geometric ~: 4 area 6 volume
large ~: 9 greatness
starter: 3 mid 4 down
test for ~: 5 try on
the ~ of it: 7 outlook 8 position 9 situation
up: 3 eye 4 rank, rate, scan, sort

5 assay, gauge, judge 6 assess, reckon, survey, verify 7 compare, look out, measure, predict 8 appraise, check out, estimate, evaluate 9 determine, speculate
__ size: 4 half, trim
__-size: 3 lap, mid 4 bite, desk, full, king, life, pint, twin 5 legal, queen 6 letter, pocket 7 economy, Olympic
__-size car: 3 mid
__-sized: 3 man 4 bite, full, good, king, pint 6 medium, middle
__ size fits all: 3 one
Sizemore, Tom: 5 actor
film: Big Trouble (2002)
Black Hawk Down (2001)
Devil in a Blue Dress (1995)
Passenger 57 (1992)
Play It to the Bone (1999)
Saving Private Ryan (1998)
sizzle: 3 fry 4 cook, hiss, sear, spit, whiz 5 broil, grill, roast, swish 6 wheeze 7 crackle, frizzle, sputter, whisper
sizzling: 3 hot 4 warm 6 red-hot, sultry, toasty, torrid 7 burning, summery 8 ovenlike, tropical, white-hot 10 sweltering
S.J.: 8 Perelman
SJD: 6 degree
Sjöwall, Maj: 6 writer 7 Swedish
SJU
see Saint John's
ska: 5 music
kin: 7 calypso
Skagerrak
port: 4 Oslo
river to the ~: 6 Glomma
Skaggs: 5 Ricky
Skagway: 4 city, town
locale: 6 Alaska
Skala, Lilia: 7 actress
film: Charly (1968)
Flashdance (1983)
Lilies of the Field (1963)
skald: 4 poet 6 Viking
Skaneateles: 4 city, lake, town
locale: 7 New York
Skara __: 4 Brae
skat: 4 game 8 card game
low card: 5 seven
skate: 3 ray 4 fish, skim, slip 5 dance, glide, slide
bottom: 5 blade
ender: 5 board
kin: 5 manta
kind of ~: 6 in-line
on thin ice: 4 risk
starter: 5 cheap
__ skate: 3 big, bob, ice 4 gray, grey 5 speed 6 hockey, racing, roller 7 tubular
skate-boarding: 5 sport
skate on __ ice: 4 thin
skater: 6 carhop
fictional ~: 4 Hans 7 Brinker
figure: 5 eight
game: 6 hockey
leap: 4 axel, lutz 7 toe loop
need: 3 ice 4 rink 6 barrel
org.: 3 NHL
spin: 5 camel 7 layback
__ skater: 3 ice 6 figure
skating: 5 sport
figure ~ event: 3 men 5 pairs 6 ladies
__ skating: 4 pair 5 pairs, speed 6 figure, in-line
__ S. Kaufman: 6 George
Skaw: 4 cape
locale: 7 Denmark, Jutland
skean: 4 dirk 5 knife
sked
see schedule
skedaddle: 3 fly, git, hie, lam, rip, run, zip 4 bolt, dart, dash, flee, flit, race, rush, scat, shoo, skip, tear, zoom 5 leave, scoot, scram, spank, speed 6 barrel, cut out, decamp, gallop, get out, hasten, hustle, move it, rocket, scurry 7 abscond, floor it, go south, hop to it, make off, quicken, scamper 8 fugitate, run for it, step on it, turn tail 9 hotfoot it, shake a leg 10 get a move on, hightail it
Skee-Ball site: 6 arcade
skeet: 4 game 5 sport
Skeet: 6 Ulrich
skeeter __: 4 hawk
Skeeter: 5 Davis
skein: 4 hank, knot 6 tangle 9 labyrinth
call: 4 honk
grounded ~: 6 gaggle
material: 4 silk, wool
unit: 5 goose
skeleton: 4 bone, cage, slim 5 bones, draft, frame, shell 6 design, sketch, slight 7 outline, slender, summary, support 9 framework, structure
in the closet: 5 shame 6 secret 7 scandal
starter: 3 exo 4 endo
skeleton __: 3 car, key 4 crew
__-skelter: 6 helter
Skelton: 3 Red 4 John
Skelton, John: 4 poet 7 British
Skelton, Red: 5 actor 8 comedian
character: 4 Clem
film: Bathing Beauty (1944)
DuBarry Was a Lady (1943)
Neptune's Daughter (1949)
A Southern Yankee (1948)
Three Little Words (1950)
Whistling in Dixie (1942)
Whistling in the Dark (1941)
The Yellow Cab Man (1950)
Ziegfeld Follies (1946)
persona: 4 hobo
wife: 4 Edna
skep: 6 basket
skeptic: 5 cynic 7 atheist, doubter, infidel, killjoy, scoffer 8 apostate, nihilist 9 dissenter, pessimist, worrywart 10 questioner, unbeliever
skeptical: 4 wary 5 chary, leery 6 show-me, unsure 7 cynical, dubious, guarded 8 cautious, doubtful, doubting, hesitant, scoffing 9 faithless, heretical, jaundiced, quizzical, uncertain 10 dissenting, hesitating, suspicious
comment: 3 bah 4 as if, I bet 5 how so
skepticism: 5 doubt, qualm, query 6 wonder 7 dubiety 8 distrust, mistrust, nihilism, wariness 9 disbelief, dubiosity, leeriness, misgiving, suspicion 10 hesitation
Skepticism and Animal Faith author: George Santayana
Skerritt, Tom: 5 actor
film: Alien (1979)
Big Bad Mama (1974)
The Big Town (1987)
Contact (1997)
The Dead Zone (1983)
MASH (1970)
The Other Sister (1999)
A River Runs Through It (1992)
Steel Magnolias (1989)
TV: Picket Fences
sketch: 3 art, map 4 copy, draw, form, limn, plan, plot, skit 5 brief, cameo, chart, draft, piece, shape, trace 6 depict, design, detail, doodle, figure, lay out, map out, précis, render, survey 7 account, cartoon, croquis, develop, diagram, drawing, outline, picture, portray, profile, rundown, summary, version 8 block out, describe, likeness, portrait, rough out, scenario, skeleton, syllabus, synopsis, vignette 9 adumbrate, blueprint, delineate, depiction, floor plan, landscape, lineation, portrayal, represent, synopsize 10 compendium, figuration, illustrate
ender: 3 pad 4 book
literary ~: 5 cameo
thumbnail ~: 3 bio 7 outline, profile
__ Sketch: 5 Etch a
sketcher need: 6 eraser, pencil
Sketches by __: 3 Boz
sketchy: 3 cut 4 thin 5 crude, rough, vague 6 coarse, faulty, patchy, skimpy, slight 7 cursory, outline, partial, reduced, shallow, tenuous 8 abridged, half-done 9 condensed, curtailed, defective, depthless, imperfect, shortened 10 diminished, expurgated, inadequate, incomplete, unfinished
skew: 4 bias, skid, tilt, veer 5 slant, slope, twist 6 squint, squirm, swerve 7 deflect, distort, diverge, oblique 8 angle off, misquote, misstate 9 misrender, misreport, prejudice, turn aside 10 deflection, divergence
ender: 4 back, bald
skew __: 4 arch 5 field, lines 6 chisel
skewbald: 5 horse 6 equine
skewed: 3 wry 4 awry, bent 5 askew 6 angled, biased, warped 7 angular, beveled, crooked, oblique, on a bias, slanted, twisted 8 angulose, angulous, cockeyed, diagonal, lopsided, slanting, tortuous 9 contorted, crossways, crosswise, distorted, malformed 10 asymmetric, transverse
skewer: 3 pin 4 stab 5 spear, spike 6 empale, impale 8 transfix
meat ~: 5 shish
tidbit: 5 cabob, kabab, kabob, kebab, kebob
ski: 5 glide 6 runner, schuss
area: 3 run 5 piste, slope, trail
dwelling: 5 lodge 6 chalet
ender: 3 bob 4 wear 6 bobber, mobile
gear: 3 bib 4 mask, pole 7 goggles
instructor: 3 pro
jacket: 6 anorak
lift: 4 J-bar, T-bar
maneuver: 4 stem
need: 4 snow
part: 4 prow
position: 4 tuck
resort: 4 Alta, Vail 5 Aspen, Banff, Tahoe 6 Gstaad
slope bump: 5 mogul
slope machine: 3 tow 4 lift
wood: 3 ash
ski __: 3 bum, pro, run, tow 4 boot, jump, lift, mask, pole, rack, suit 5 pants 6 troops 7 touring
__ ski: 5 water
__-ski: 5 après, hydro
Ski-__: 3 Doo
__ Ski: 3 Jet
Skia: 4 font 8 typeface
skiagraph: 4 x-ray
skid: 4 skew, slew, slip, slue, veer 5 drift, glide, slide 6 sledge, slough, swerve 7 plummet 8 fishtail, sideslip
starter: 3 non 4 anti, tail
skid __: 3 fin, row 5 chain
skidoo: 3 fly 4 flee 5 scram 8 fugitate, run for it
skid-prone: 3 icy
skids, hit the: 4 fail, sink 5 slump 7 decline
skier: 3 Moe 5 Killy, Mahre, Tomba 6 Street 7 Klammer
Austrian ~: 7 Klammer
French ~: 5 Killy
Italian ~: 5 Tomba
Olympian ~: 3 Moe
showoff ~: 6 hotdog
see also ski
skies: 9 firmament
__ skies: 5 to the
__ Skies: 4 Blue
skies they were __ and sober, The: 5 ashen
skiff: 4 boat, dory 5 barca, canoe, kayak 6 dinghy, dugout, sampan 7 catboat, pirogue, rowboat, Sunfish 8 sailboat, Sailfish 9 catamaran
body: 4 hull
propel a ~: 3 row
tool: 3 oar
skiffle: 5 music
Ski Hall of Fame site: 4 Vail
skiing: 5 sport
see also ski
__ skiing: 5 grass 6 alpine
Skikda: 4 city, port, town
locale: 7 Algeria
skil: 4 fish
skill: 3 art, job 4 ease, gift, head, line, tact, work 5 clout, craft, goods, knack, moxie, power, savvy, stuff, touch, trade, trick 6 smarts, talent 7 ability, command, cunning, faculty, finesse, know-how, masonry, mastery, prowess, sleight 8 aptitude, artistry, capacity, deftness, facility, hang of it, juggling 9 adeptness, carpentry, dexterity, diplomacy, expertise, handiness, ingenuity, readiness, smartness, technique 10 capability, cleverness, competence, competency, efficiency, experience, green thumb, leadership, nimbleness, profession, right stuff, toolmaking, virtuosity
combining form: 6 techno-
having ~: 4 able
in Chinese: 6 kung fu
in Italian: 4 arte
to a sore loser: 4 luck
skilled: 3 ace, apt 4 able, deft, good, ripe 5 adept, crack, handy, ready, slick 6 adroit, au fait, expert, gifted, habile, nimble, up to it, versed 7 capable, learned, tactful, trained 8 delicate, dextrous, graceful, masterly, seasoned 9 competent, dexterous, efficient, masterful, practiced, versatile 10 conversant, proficient
in: 6 good at
occupation: 5 craft
one: 3 wiz 4 tech, whiz 6 master, techie
skilled __: 5 labor
skillet: 3 pan 6 frypan 9 frying pan
use a ~: 3 fry 5 sauté
skillful: 3 ace, apt, old, pro, vet 4 able, cool, deft, fine, good, neat, whiz 5 adept, canny, crack, great, handy, quick, ready, savvy, sharp, slick, smart 6 adroit, artful, au fait, brainy, clever, expert, facile, fluent, habile, nimble, pretty, primed, up to it, versed 7 capable, cunning, knowing, learned, tactful, trained, tuned in, versant, veteran 8 dextrous, graceful, masterly, prepared, seasoned, talented 9 competent, dexterous, efficient, excellent, ingenious, judicious, masterful, practical, practiced, qualified 10 proficient, well-versed
facetiously: 3 ept
skillfully: 4 neat, well 8 laudably, very well, worthily 10 delicately, swimmingly
skillfulness: 4 ease 5 knack 8 facility 9 dexterity
skills, basic: 4 ABCs
skim: 3 dip, fly, run, top 4 dart, film, kiss, leaf, milk, read, ream, sail, scan, skip, soar 5 coast, cream, defat, float, glide, graze, ladle, scoop, shave, skate,

skirr, slide, sweep 6 browse, low-fat, peruse, profit, riffle, scurry 7 fat-free, lightly, skitter 8 glance at, separate 9 brush over 10 glance over, go smoothly, hydroplane, run through
along: 4 flit, skip
milk lack: 3 fat
the cream: 5 defat
skimble-___: 7 scamble
skimmer: 3 hat 4 bird 5 A-line, dress
skimmia: 5 shrub
family: 3 rue
relative: 9 jaborandi
skimp: 3 eke 4 save 5 scant, screw, spare 6 scrape, slight 7 cut back, stretch 8 conserve, roll back, withhold 9 economize 10 cut corners, under-spend
on: 5 stint 7 cut down
skimpiness: 4 want 10 inadequacy
skimpy: 3 shy 4 poor, puny, thin, weak 5 brief, lousy, scant, short, spare, tight 6 faulty, feeble, frugal, little, meager, measly, scanty, scrimp, sparse, spotty, stingy 7 chintzy, failing, lacking, miserly, scrimpy, sketchy, wanting 8 exiguous, piddling 9 deficient, illiberal, penurious, scattered 10 inadequate, skinflinty, ungenerous
skin: 3 fur 4 bare, bark, coat, film, flay, hide, hull, husk, pare, peel, pelt, rind, shed, trim 5 cover, crust, derma, flesh, graze, layer, organ, scale, scalp, shave, shell, shuck, strip 6 abrade, casing, corium, cut off, defeat, dermis, jacket, scrape, sheath, slough 7 coating, leather, outside, pull off, surface, swindle 8 carapace, membrane 9 container, epidermis, excoriate, parchment, sheathing 10 integument
alive: 4 flay 6 vilify 9 criticize
and bones: 4 lank, thin 5 spare
animal ~: 3 rug 4 hide, pelt
bare ~: 4 buff
blemish: 3 wen, zit 4 wart
by the ~ of one's teeth: 6 barely 8 narrowly
combining form: 4 derm-, scyt- 5 -derma, dermo-, scyto- 6 dermat-, -dermis 7 dermato-
cream: 5 toner
damager: 3 sun 5 UV ray
diving: 5 sport
ender: 5 flint, tight
feature: 4 pore
fold: 6 dewlap
get under one's ~: 3 irk, vex 4 rile 5 annoy, peeve, pique, upset
hardened ~: 6 callus
irritation: 5 uredo
layer: 5 derma
lotion ingredient: 4 aloe
of the ~: 6 dermal, dermic
opening: 5 stoma
secretion: 5 sebum
sensation: 5 touch
shed ~: 4 molt
shrinker: 4 alum
soother: 5 salve
starter: 3 doe, kid, oil, pig 4 bear, buck, calf, cape, coon, deer, goat, lamb, mole, seal, swan, wine, wool 5 onion, scarf, shark, sheep, snake
tone: 4 look 5 flesh 6 aspect 8 coloring 10 appearance, complexion
skin ___: 4 care, game, test 5 diver, patch 6 diving, effect
skin-___: 4 deep, dive
___ skin: 5 goose 6 potato
Skin ___: 4 Game 5 Tight 6 Bracer
skin-and-bones: 7 scrawny
skin-deep: 7 shallow, trivial 8 external 10 unprofound
skin-dive: 4 swim
skin diving: 5 sport
skinflint: 5 miser, piker 7 miserly, Scrooge 8 tightwad 10 cheapskate, pinchpenny
skinflinty: 4 near 5 cheap, small, tight 6 greedy, skimpy, stingy 7 miserly, selfish 8 ungiving 9 penurious 10 avaricious
Skin Game (1971 film)
cast: Susan Clark, James Garner, Louis Gossett Jr.
skink: 6 animal, lizard 7 reptile
Skinnay: 5 Ennis
___-skinned: 4 thin 5 thick
skinned combining form: 9 -dermatous
___ skinner: 4 mule
Skinner: 2 B.F. 4 Otis
Skinner ___: 3 box
___ Skinner Blues: 4 Mule
Skinner, Cornelia Otis: 6 author, writer
work: The Ape in Me
Our Hearts Were Young and Gay
The Pleasure of His Company
skinny: 4 bony, dirt, info, lank, lean, slim, thin, wiry 5 boney, gaunt, lanky, proof, rangy, spare 6 dainty, gangly, latest, meager, skinny, slight, slinky, svelte, twiggy 7 gracile, lowdown, scraggy, scrawny, slender, spidery, starved, willowy 8 gangling, rawboned, starving 9 emaciated, sylphlike
one: 4 wisp
skinny-dip: 4 swim
Skinny Legs and All (1967 song)
artist: Joe Tex
___ skin of one's teeth: 5 by the
Skin of Our Teeth, The author: Thornton Wilder
'Skins
see Redskins
skintight: 4 snug 5 close
skip: 3 bob, cut, fly, hop, run 4 bolt, flee, flit, jump, leap, lope, miss, omit, pass, play, romp, skim, slur, snub, trip, verb 5 avoid, bound, caper, dance, forgo, frisk, graze, scoot, skirr, skirt 6 bounce, bypass, canter, cavort, desert, escape, eschew, forego, forget, gambol, glance, go past, hasten, ignore, pass up, prance, run off, run out, slight, spring, tiptoe 7 exclude, make off, neglect, run away, scamper, skitter 8 fugitate, jump over, leapfrog, leave out, omission, overlook, pass over, ricochet, run for it, skim over 9 disregard, exclusion, miss out on, oversight, play hooky, skedaddle 10 bounce over, fly the coop, hippety-hop
ender: 4 jack
meals: 4 fast
out: 2 go 3 fly, run 4 flee, move, quit 5 elope, leave 6 escape 7 abscond, go south, make off, ride off 8 jump bail, run for it
out on: 4 jilt 5 dodge 6 desert 7 abandon
past commercials: 3 zap
stones: 3 dap
sweets: 4 diet
syllables: 5 elide
skip ___: 3 car 4 bail, rope, town 5 a beat 6 tracer 7 welding
Skip: 7 Homeier
Skip ___ Lou: 4 to My
___ Skip: 5 My Dog
___, skip and a jump: 3 hop
skipjack: 4 fish
skipper: 4 boss 5 steer 6 leader, master, sailor 7 captain, headman, jack tar, oversee 8 director, helmsman, kingfish 9 commander
be a ~: 8 navigate
nickname: 4 cap'n
place: 4 helm 6 bridge
starter: 3 mud
Skipper's friend: 6 Barbie
Skippy (1931 film)
cast: Robert Coogan, Jackie Cooper, Mitzi Green
director: Norman Taurog
Skippy alternative: 3 Jif 8 Peter Pan
Skipworth: 6 Alison
skirmish: 3 row 4 fray, spat, tiff, tilt 5 brush, clash, fight, melee, mix-up, run-in, scrap, set-to 6 action, attack, battle, combat, dustup, fracas, tussle 7 contest, dispute, quarrel, ruction, scuffle 8 argument, conflict, showdown, squabble, struggle 9 encounter, scrimmage, square off 10 donnybrook, engagement
set for a ~: 5 armed
skirr: 3 fly 4 flee, skim, skip
skirt: 3 hem, rim 4 brim, duck, edge, hoop, kilt, maxi, midi, mini, skip, tutu 5 A-line, avoid, brink, dodge, dress, elude, evade, flank, hedge, pagne, pareu, verge 6 border, bypass, detour, dirndl, escape, fringe, hobble, ignore, margin, peplum, sarong, sheath 7 filibeg, pollera 8 culottes, go around, lavalava, lie along, philibeg, sidestep, surround 9 crinoline, get around, perimeter, periphery 10 circumvent, equivocate, fustanella, work around
accessory: 4 belt
African ~: 5 pagne
alter a ~: 3 sew 5 rehem
alternative: 5 pants 6 slacks 8 culottes
Balkan ~: 10 fustanella
edge: 3 hem
feature: 4 dart, gore, slit, vent 5 plait, pleat, waist
length: 4 maxi, midi, mini
movement: 5 swish
panel: 6 insert
partner: 6 bodice
Polynesian ~: 5 pareu 6 sarong 8 lavalava
Scottish ~: 4 kilt 7 filibeg 8 philibeg
short ~: 4 mini 6 peplum
South American ~: 7 pollera
strapped ~: 6 jumper
wearer: 4 lady 5 woman 6 female
skirt ___: 5 steak
___ skirt: 4 hoop, hula 6 hobble, poodle 7 prairie
Skirts ___: 4 Ahoy
skit: 4 play 5 revue, spoof 6 parody, satire 7 lampoon 8 blackout
collection: 5 revue 6 review
Skitch: 9 Henderson
skitter: 3 run 4 skid, skim, skip 5 slink 6 spring 7 slither
skittish: 3 coy, shy 4 edgy 5 antsy, dizzy, giddy, itchy, jumpy, leery, nervy, peppy, tense, timid 6 demure, fickle, lively, uneasy 7 anxious, excited, fearful, fidgety, flighty, jittery, keyed up, nervous, playful, restive, uptight 8 agitated, restless, troubled, volatile 9 alarmable, concerned, excitable, frivolous, ill at ease, sensitive, tremulous, whimsical 10 capricious, high-strung, unreliable
Skittle Players artist: 5 Steen
skittles: 4 game
Skittles: 5 candy
skivvies: 6 briefs, shorts, undies 8 lingerie 9 underwear
skiwear: 5 parka
skoal: 5 prost, toast 6 cheers, kampai, prosit
Skokie: 4 city, town
locale: 8 Illinois
skookum: 3 def, rad 4 aces, A-one, boss, braw, cool, dece, fine, gear, keen, neat, nice, phat, tuff 5 dandy, ducky, grand, great, marvy, neato, nobby, prime, slick, super, swell 6 bang on, bang-up, bonzer, bosker, choice, divine, dreamy, far-out, gnarly, groovy, lovely, peachy, slap-up, spot on, superb, terrif, tiptop, unreal, whizzo, wicked 7 amazing, awesome, capital, corking, perfect, ripping, stellar, sublime 8 dazzling, especial, eximious, fabulous, five-star, four-star, frabjous, glorious, heavenly, jim-dandy, slam-bang, smashing, splendid, standout, sterling, stickout, superior, terrific, top-level, topnotch, very good, wondrous 9 bodacious, Endsville, excellent, exemplary, exquisite, first-rate, high-grade, hunky-dory, marvelous, sollicker, top-flight, wonderful 10 first-class, hotsy-totsy, jack-a-dandy, out of sight, peachy-keen, phenomenal, remarkable, stupendous, super-duper
Skopje: 4 city, town 7 capital
locale: 9 Macedonia
skosh: 3 bit, tad 4 iota 7 smidgen, smidgin 8 smidgeon
Skou, Jens: 6 Danish 7 chemist 8 Nobelist
skua: 4 bird 6 bonxie
skulk: 4 lurk 5 creep, prowl, shirk, slink, sneak 6 lay for 7 slither 9 lie in wait 10 nose around
skull: 4 bone, head 6 noodle, sconce 7 cranium 9 braincase
cavity: 5 sinus
combining form: 5 crani- 6 cranio-
ender: 3 cap
protuberance: 5 inion
seam: 5 raphe
starter: 4 numb
skull ___: 7 session
skullcap: 6 beanie, pileus 8 yarmulke
___-skulled: 5 thick
skunk: 3 cur 4 rout, toad 5 grape, sneak 6 animal, bad hat, defeat, rascal, weasel 7 polecat, shut out, stinker 8 rakehell
African ~: 5 zoril 7 zorilla, zorille
Bambi ~: 6 Flower
cabbage family: 4 arum
defense: 4 odor 5 scent
ender: 4 weed
relative: 4 mink 5 fitch, otter, ratel, sable, stoat, tayra 6 badger, ermine, ferret, marten 7 foumart 8 carcajou, foulmart, kolinsky, muishond 9 wolverine
young: 3 kit
skunk ___: 5 works 7 cabbage
Skunk: 5 river
city on the ~: 4 Ames
locale: 4 Iowa
skunky: 7 odorous
___-skurry: 5 hurry
Skvorecky, Josef: 5 Czech 6 writer 8 essayist 9 publisher
sky: 5 azure, ether 6 aether, canopy, heaven 7 heavens 8 empyrean 9 firmament 10 atmosphere, outer space
battle: 6 air war
blow ~ high: 5 rebut 8 disprove 9 discredit, shoot down 10 invalidate
clear ~: 5 ether 6 aether
color: 4 blue 5 azure
Egyptian ~ goddess: 3 Nut
ender: 3 box, cap, way 4 dive, hook, jack, lark, line, sail, walk, ward 5 diver, light, wards, write 6 diving, rocket, writer 7 scraper
fall from the ~: 4 hail, rain, snow
hit the ~: 3 fly 4 soar 6 aviate

in the ~: 4 over 6 aerial 8 overhead
light: 3 sun 4 moon, star 6 albedo, aurora
maybe: 5 limit
path: 6 airway
pie in the ~: 5 dream
pilot: 5 padre 6 cleric, priest
science: 9 astronomy
tilt toward the ~: 5 tip up
traveler: 5 comet 6 meteor
up in the ~: 5 above, aloft, risen 6 aerial
sky ___: 3 cav 4 blue, wave 5 cover, diver, pilot, train 6 diving 7 cavalry, compass, marshal
sky-___: 3 cam 4 high, hook
___ sky: 5 to the
___-sky: 4 blue
Sky: 9 Masterson
___ Sky: 4 Blue 6 Liquid, Yellow 7 October, Vanilla
___ Sky at Morning: 3 Red
___ sky at night...: 3 Red
sky-blue: 5 azure, lapis
skycap: 5 toter 6 porter
concern: 3 bag 7 luggage
skydive: 4 jump
skydiving: 5 sport
need: 5 chute 9 parachute
Sky Dragon hero: 4 Chan
Skye: 4 lone, isle 6 island
Skye, lone: 7 actress
father: Donovan
film: River's Edge (1986)
Say Anything ... (1989)
Went to Coney Island...(2000)
Skyhawk: 3 car 4 auto 5 Buick 10 automobile
Sky Hawk: 3 car 4 auto 10 automobile, Studebaker
sky-high: 4 tall 5 aloft, lofty 9 excessive, expensive
Sky High (1975 song) artist: Jigsaw
Sky is Falling, The author: Sidney Sheldon
Skykje: 5 falls 9 waterfall
locale: 6 Norway
Skylab
org.: 4 NASA
sighting: 5 comet
skylark: 4 bird, play 5 revel, sport
Skylark: 3 car 4 auto 5 Buick 10 automobile
Skylark (1941 film)
cast: Brian Aherne, Claudette Colbert, Ray Milland
director: Mark Sandrich
___ Skylark: 3 To a
___-sky law: 4 blue
skylight site: 4 roof 7 ceiling
skyline: 7 profile
feature: 5 spire, tower
obscurer: 3 fog 4 haze, smog
Skyliner: 3 car 4 auto, Ford 10 automobile
skylit area: 6 atrium
___ Skynyrd: 6 Lynyrd
Sky Riders (1976 film)
cast: James Coburn, Robert Culp, Susannah York
director: Douglas Hickox
skyrocket: 4 leap, soar, zoom 5 mount, surge
skyscraper: 5 tower 7 edifice 9 structure
support: 5 I-beam 6 girder
Skyscraper Souls (1932 film)
cast: Maureen O'Sullivan, Gregory Ratoff, Warren William
director: Edgar Selwyn
skyscraping: 4 high, tall 5 lofty 7 soaring 8 elevated, towering, uplifted
Sky's the Limit, The (1943 film)
cast: Fred Astaire, Robert Benchley, Joan Leslie
___ Sky, The: 3 Big
Skywalker, Luke: 4 hero, Jedi
foe: 5 Vader
member of ~'s army: 4 Ewok
skyward: 5 above, aloft, lofty 6 uphill 8 overhead
skywrite: 9 advertise, publicize
S&L: Savings and Loan 4 bank
device: 3 ATM
offering: 2 CD 3 IRA 4 mtge.
payment: 3 int.
protector: 4 FDIC
unit: 3 acc. 4 acct.
slab: 3 bar, bit, cut 4 cake, hunk, lump 5 block, board, chunk, ingot, layer, piece, plate, sheet, slice, stave, stela, stick, stone, strip, table, wedge 6 billet 7 boulder, bowlder, cutting, portion 9 flagstone
slabber: 7 slobber
slack: 3 lax 4 dull, ease, idle, lazy, limp, play, room, slow, soft, wane, weak 5 abate, baggy, dodge, inert, let up, loose, quiet, relax, shirk, taper, tardy 6 droopy, excess, feeble, flabby, flimsy, floppy, infirm, leeway, lessen, loosen, remiss, sloppy, slow-up, supine 7 drop off, dwindle, ease off, flaccid, goof off, hanging, laggard, lay back, neglect, passive, relaxed, release, sagging, unready, untoned 8 careless, dangling, decrease, derelict, dilatory, diminish, flexible, heedless, inactive, indolent, listless, malinger, slothful, slovenly, slowdown, sluggish, stagnant, unsteady, unstrict 9 do-nothing, easygoing, forgetful, imprudent, leisurely, lethargic, loitering, negligent, shiftless, slow-paced, unheedful 10 delinquent, neglectful, permissive, regardless, slow-moving, sluggardly
cut some ~: 6 relent
off: 3 ebb 4 fade, idle, loaf, wane 5 abate, dally, let up, relax 6 cop out, dawdle, ease up, recede, soften 7 dwindle, lighten, subside 8 fade away, malinger, peter out, tone down, wind down 9 goldbrick, retrocede
slack ___: 3 off 4 suit 5 water
slack-___: 5 baked, jawed
slacken: 3 die, ebb, lag, lax 4 ease, idle, lull, slow, tire, wane 5 abate, delay, dodge, let up, loose, relax, remit, shirk, taper 6 dampen, lessen, loiter, loosen, modify, relent, retard, unwind 7 drop off, dwindle, ease off, goof off, lay back, neglect, release, relieve, subside, tail off 8 decrease, diminish, head away, level off, moderate, slow down 9 lighten up, retrocede 10 liberalize
slackened: 5 loose 9 leisurely
slackening: 3 ebb 5 letup 8 slowdown
slacker: 5 idler 6 loafer, truant 7 goof-off, shirker 8 layabout, parasite 9 do-nothing, goldbrick 10 malingerer
bane: 3 job 4 work
slack-jawed: 4 agog 5 agape 6 gaping
slackness: 6 laxity 7 laxness, license, neglect 8 laziness
slacks: 5 jeans, pants 6 chinos, khakis 8 breeches, flannels, trousers 10 hiphuggers
measure: 5 waist 6 inseam
slade: 4 sole
slag: 5 dregs, dross 6 cinder, scoria 7 residue 8 residuum, sediment
slake: 4 cool 5 allay, quell 6 obtund, pacify, quench, revive 7 appease, assuage, mollify, refresh, relieve, satiate, satisfy 8 palliate
slaked ___: 4 lime
slalom: 4 race 5 event
curve: 3 ess
marker: 4 gate
need: 3 ski
site: 5 slope
___ slalom: 5 canoe, giant
slam: 3 bat, dig, hit, jab, pan, ram 4 bang, barb, bash, beat, belt, blow, boom, clap, damn, dash, ding, flay, gibe, hurl, jeer, jibe, mock, shut, slap, slug, slur, snub, swat, wham 5 abuse, blast, burst, close, crack, crash, decry, fling, knock, libel, pound, punch, scorn, smack, smash, smear, sneer, sound, spurn, swipe, taunt, thump, whack 6 attack, batter, cudgel, defame, deride, dump on, hammer, heckle, impugn, insult, jibe at, malign, offend, rebuff, review, scathe, slight, strike, thwack, vilify, wallop 7 affront, asperse, banging, calumny, catcall, clobber, degrade, disdain, lambast, mockery, obloquy, offense, potshot, putdown, rank out, reproof, run down, scourge, slander, traduce 8 badmouth, belittle, contempt, denounce, derision, lace into, lambaste, lash into, reproach, ridicule, throw mud, uppercut, vilipend 9 aspersion, castigate, cheap shot, contumely, criticism, criticize, denigrate, discredit, disparage, humiliate, light into, shoot down 10 calumniate, defamation, disrespect, opprobrium, reflection, villainize
component: 5 trick
dance: 4 mosh
grand ~: 5 homer 7 home run, success, triumph, victory 9 landslide
into: 3 ram 7 rear-end
slam ___: 4 dunk 5 dance 7 dancing
___ slam: 4 body 5 belly, grand, small 6 little
slam-bang: 3 def, rad 4 aces, A-one, boss, braw, cool, dece, fine, gear, keen, neat, nice, phat, tuff 5 dandy, ducky, grand, great, marvy, neato, nobby, prime, slick, super, swell 6 bonzer, bosker, choice, divine, dreamy, far-out, gnarly, groovy, lovely, peachy, slap-up, spot on, superb, terrif, tiptop, unreal, whizzo, wicked 7 amazing, awesome, capital, corking, perfect, ripping, skookum, stellar, sublime 8 dazzling, especial, eximious, fabulous, five-star, four-star, frabjous, glorious, heavenly, jim-dandy, smashing, splendid, standout, sterling, stickout, superior, terrific, top-level, topnotch, very good, wondrous 9 bodacious, Endsville, excellent, exemplary, exquisite, first-rate, high-grade, hunky-dory, marvelous, sol-licker, top-flight, wonderful 10 first-class, hotsy-totsy, jack-a-dandy, out of sight, peachy-keen, phenomenal, remarkable, stupendous, super-duper
slam dunk: 4 shot 5 stuff
alternative: 5 lay-up
target: 4 hoop
Slamet: 7 volcano
locale: 4 Asia, Java 9 Indonesia
slammer: 3 can, pen 4 coop, jail, poky, stir 5 pokey 6 cooler, lockup, prison 8 hoosegow
Slammin' Sammy: 4 Sosa 5 Snead
rival: 6 Big Mac
Slam the Door Softly author: Clare Boothe Luce
slander: 3 dig, lie, mud, pan, rap 4 barb, blot, dirt, gibe, hurt, jeer, jibe, mock, slam, slap, slur, snub, tale 5 abuse, belie, curse, decry, libel, roast, scorn, slime, smear, sneer, spurn, sully, taunt, wrong 6 accuse, assail, attack, damage, defame, defile, deride, dump on, heckle, impugn, injure, insult, malign, offend, rebuff, revile, scorch, slight, smirch, vilify 7 affront, asperse, blacken, calumny, catcall, degrade, detract, disdain, mockery, obloquy, offense, put-down, rank out, scandal, tarnish, traduce 8 backbite, badmouth, belittle, besmirch, black eye, contempt, denounce, derision, derogate, dishonor, ridicule, sling mud, tear down, throw mud, vilipend 9 aspersion, blaspheme, cheap shot, contumely, denigrate, discredit, disparage, humiliate 10 backbiting, calumniate, defamation, depreciate, detraction, disrespect, impugnment, imputation, muckraking, opprobrium, scandalize, villainize
ammo: 3 mud
slanderous: 7 vicious 9 injurious, invidious 10 defamatory, derogatory
slang: 4 cant, talk 5 argot, lingo 6 jargon, patois, pidgin 7 dialect, neology 8 jive talk, language, localism 9 Briticism, neologism 10 street talk, vernacular
___ slang: 7 rhyming
slangy suffix: 3 -ese, -ola 4 -aroo, -eroo
slant: 3 tip 4 beam, bend, bent, bias, cant, heel, lean, list, look, ramp, side, skew, tilt, veer, view, warp 5 angle, bevel, color, focus, fudge, grade, level, light, phase, pitch, point, slope, splay, stand, twist 6 aspect, camber, direct, garble, stance, swerve, weight 7 decline, descend, deviate, distort, diverge, incline, leaning, opinion, outlook, recline 8 angle off, approach, attitude, diagonal, emphasis, gradient, judgment, misquote, skewness, strategy 9 direction, influence, prejudice, sentiment, viewpoint 10 conviction, deflection, diagonally, distortion, divagation, divergence, partiality, standpoint
ender: 4 ways, wise
slant ___: 5 board, front, rhyme 6 height
slant-___ desk: 3 top
slanted: 5 askew, bevel, leant 6 aslope, leaned, skewed 7 crooked 8 diagonal, partisan
type: 6 italic
slanting: 5 atilt 6 skewed 7 oblique, sideway 8 diagonal, sideways, sidewise
surface: 4 ramp
slantwise: 7 sideway 8 sideways 9 at an angle, obliquely, on the bias 10 diagonally
slap: 3 box, dig, hit, lap 4 bang, barb, bash, beat, blow, bust, chop, clap, cuff, gibe, hurt, jibe, lick, poke, shot, slam, slur, snub, sock, spat, swat, wham 5 abuse, crack, knock, libel, punch, scorn, smack, spank, swipe, taunt, thump, whack 6 insult, rebuff, rebuke, slight, strike, thwack, wallop 7 affront, calumny, catcall, disdain, lambast, mockery, obloquy, offense, put-down, slander 8 contempt, derision, lambaste, ridicule 9 aspersion, cheap shot, contumely, reprimand 10 defamation, disrespect, opprobrium
around: 7 rough up
ender: 4 dash, jack 5 happy, stick
in the face: 4 slam, slur 5 smear 6 rebuke, slight 7 affront, obloquy, offense, repulse 9 aspersion, cheap shot, rejection 10 backbiting, defamation, detraction, opprobrium
on: 3 add 4 link 5 affix 6 attach
on the wrist: 5 chide, scold 6 rebuke 7 lecture, reprove, upbraid 8 admon-

ish, reproach 9 reprehend, reprimand
starter: 4 back
the cuffs on: 3 nab 5 run in 6 arrest
together: 4 make 5 rig up 7 throw up
with: 8 penalize
slap __: 4 down, shot
slap __ wrist: 5 on the
slapdash: 5 hasty, messy 6 random, remiss, untidy 7 cursory, hurried, offhand 8 careless, pell-mell, slipshod, slovenly 9 haphazard, makeshift, negligent, temporary, unheedful 10 last-minute, unthinking, unthorough, willy-nilly
slaphappy: 5 dizzy, giddy 6 addled, spacey 7 out of it 8 confused 9 befuddled
slapjack: 4 game 8 card game
__-slapper: 4 knee 5 thigh
Slap Shot (1977 film)
cast: Lindsay Crouse, Paul Newman, Michael Ontkean
director: George Roy Hill
slap-shot projectile: 4 puck
Slapsie __ Rosenbloom: 5 Maxie
slapstick: 4 zany 5 farce, funny, genre 6 comedy
noise: 5 splat
prop: 3 pie
slap-up: 3 def, rad 4 aces, A-one, boss, braw, cool, dece, fine, gear, keen, neat, nice, phat, tuff 5 dandy, ducky, grand, great, marvy, neato, nobby, prime, slick, super, swell 6 bang on, bang-up, bonzer, bosker, choice, divine, dreamy, far-out, gnarly, groovy, lovely, peachy, spot on, superb, terrif, tiptop, unreal, whizzo, wicked 7 amazing, awesome, capital, corking, perfect, ripping, skookum, stellar, sublime 8 dazzling, especial, eximious, fabulous, five-star, four-star, frabjous, glorious, heavenly, jim-dandy, slam-bang, smashing, splendid, standout, sterling, stickout, superior, terrific, top-level, topnotch, very good, wondrous 9 bodacious, Endsville, excellent, exemplary, exquisite, first-rate, high-grade, hunky-dory, marvelous, sollicker, top-flight, wonderful 10 first-class, hotsy-totsy, jack-a-dandy, out of sight, peachy-keen, phenomenal, remarkable, stupendous, super-duper
slash: 3 axe, cut, rip 4 chop, clip, crop, drop, gash, hack, mark, pare, rend, rent, slit, tear 5 carve, lower, score, sever, shave, slant, slash, slice, split, wound 6 cleave, incise, injure, mangle, open up, pierce, reduce, streak, stroke 7 abridge, curtail, cut back, cut down, lambast, scissor, shorten, solidus, virgule, whittle 8 close out, decrease, diagonal, discount, incision, lacerate, lambaste, mark down 10 abbreviate, laceration, separatrix
slash-and-__: 4 burn
slashed: 3 low 4 torn 5 cheap 6 on sale 7 incised 9 lacerated
it may be ~: 5 price
slasher movie, like a: 4 gory
slat: 4 lath 5 board 6 batten, louver, louvre
slat-__ chair: 4 back
slate: 4 blue, gray, grey, list, sked 5 color 6 agenda, bluish, lineup, tablet 7 blueish, grayish, mineral, program, runners 8 blue-gray, nominate, schedule 10 blackboard
need: 5 chalk 6 eraser
once: 5 shale
relative: 3 ash 4 anil, cyan, dove, drab, navy, Nile, teal 5 Alice, azure, beige, dusty, merle, pearl, putty, taupe 6 cobalt, indigo, raisin, silver, violet 7 grizzly, peacock 8 cerulean, charcoal, gunmetal, platinum, sapphire 9 turquoise 10 aquamarine, periwinkle
tool: 3 zax
wipe the ~ clean: 5 erase 6 pardon 7 absolve, forgive, release 8 overlook
Slater: 5 Helen 9 Christian
slather: 6 spread
Slatkin, Leonard: 9 conductor
Slaughter: 4 Enos 5 Frank
Slaughter, Enos: 10 outfielder
Slaughterhouse-Five: 4 film 5 novel
author: Kurt Vonnegut Jr.
cast: Ron Leibman, Eugene Roche, Michael Sacks
director: George Roy Hill
Slaughter on Tenth Avenue (1957 film)
cast: Dan Duryea, Richard Egan, Jan Sterling
slauson: 5 dance
Slav: 4 Pole, Serb 5 Croat, Czech 6 Balkan, Slovak 7 Russian 8 Moravian 9 Bulgarian, Ukrainian
slave: 4 esne, grub, hand, help, moil, peon, plod, serf, slog, toil, work 5 grind, labor 6 drudge, jackal, menial, thrall, toiler, vassal, victim, worker 7 bondman, captive, chattel, laborer, servant, villein 8 liniment, struggle, work hard 9 Nat Turner, Spartacus, sycophant, workhorse
ancient ~: 4 esne
driver: 6 despot, master, tyrant 8 dictator, martinet 10 taskmaster
operatic ~: 4 Aïda
wages: 7 peanuts 8 pittance
slave __: 3 ant 6 driver
__ slave: 4 wage 6 galley
Slave: 5 river
locale: 6 Canada 7 Alberta
__ Slave: 6 Marche
__ Slave Lake: 5 Great
slaver: 5 drool 6 drivel 7 lay it on, slobber
slavery: 4 toil, work, yoke 5 grind 6 chains, drudge, thrall 7 bondage, peonage, serfdom 8 drudgery, serfhood, thraldom 9 captivity, feudalism, indenture, servitude, thralldom, vassalage 10 constraint
Slave Ship (1937 film)
cast: Elizabeth Allen, Warner Baxter, Wallace Beery
director: Tay Garnett
Slave, The sculptor: 4 Erté
Slavic
cake: 5 babka
cold soup: 5 schav
dance: 4 kolo 8 kazatsky
sovereign: 4 czar, tsar
__-Slavic: 5 Balto
slavish: 4 meek 6 menial 7 fawning, servile 9 adulatory, groveling 10 submissive
Slavonic Dances composer: 6 Dvorák
slaw: 5 salad 8 side dish
starter: 4 cole 7 cabbage
Slawomir: 6 Mrozek
slay: 3 zap 4 do in 5 smite 8 dispatch
__ Slayer, The: 4 Deer
Slay Ride author: Dick Francis
Slayton: 4 Deke
sleazebag: 4 crud, dirt 5 slime, trash
sleazy: 3 low 4 base, limp, mean, poor, vile 5 cheap, dirty, grody, mangy, seedy, tacky 6 common, flimsy, mangey, paltry, shabby, shoddy, sordid, tawdry, trashy 7 run-down, squalid 8 slovenly 9 loathsome 10 broken-down, disgusting
sled: 3 toy 4 luge, pung 6 sledge, sleigh, troika 7 coaster, go-devil, Rosebud, vehicle 8 toboggan
racing ~: 4 luge 8 skeleton
runner: 5 blade
starter: 3 bob
sled __: 3 dog
__ sled: 3 dog 6 rocket
sledding
go ~: 5 coast, glide, slide
need: 4 hill, snow 5 slope
__ sledding: 5 rough, tough
sled dog: 5 husky
command: 4 mush
heroic ~: 5 Balto
sledge: 4 dray, skid 6 hammer
ender: 6 hammer
__ Sledge: 6 Sister
sledgehammer: 4 mall, maul
Sledgehammer (1986 song) artist: Peter Gabriel
Sledge, Percy: 6 singer
song: When a Man Loves a Woman (1966)
sleek: 4 neat, oily, tidy, trim 5 natty, satin, shine, shiny, silky, slick, swank 6 dapper, glassy, glossy, jaunty, rakish, refine, satiny, silken, smooth, snazzy, spiffy, sporty, swanky 7 groomed 8 lustrous, polished, slippery, spruce up 9 lubricous 10 glistening
sleep: 3 nap, nod, zzz 4 doze, rest, yawn 5 crash, snore 6 catnap, drowse, nod off, repose, retire, siesta, snooze, torpor, trance, turn in 7 bed down, bedtime, conk off, drop off, fall out, latency, pass out, sack out, saw logs, saw wood, shuteye, slumber, zonk out 8 dormancy, dullness, languish, lethargy, take a nap 9 dreamland, hibernate, hit the hay, torpidity 10 catch a wink, estivation, forty winks, hit the sack
aid: 5 Nytol 6 Compoz, Unisom 7 Sominex
combining form: 4 hypn- 5 hypno-, somni-
cycle: 3 REM
deep ~: 4 coma 5 sopor
disorder: 5 apnea 6 apnoea
disturber: 5 light, noise
emerge from ~: 4 wake 5 awake, get up, waken 6 awaken
ender: 4 over, walk, wear
go to ~: 3 nap 4 rest 6 retire, turn in 7 lie down, sack out 8 abdicate 9 hit the hay 10 hit the sack
lightly: 4 doze 6 snooze
lose ~ (over): 4 fret 5 sweat
on: 8 consider, mull over 10 reconsider
place to ~: 3 bed, inn 8 quarters
put to ~: 4 bore, lull, tire 9 hypnotize
restlessly: 4 toss
scene: 5 dream
sound: 3 zzz 5 snore
spoiler: 5 alarm
unit: 4 wink
wear: 3 PJs 5 teddy 7 jammies, pajamas 9 nightgown 10 nightshirt
sleep __: 4 on it, over, sofa 5 shade
sleep __ a top: 4 like
sleep-__ camp: 4 away
sleep-__ cycle: 4 wake
__ sleep: 3 REM 4 NREM 6 beauty
sleeper: 3 car, spy 4 sofa
compartment: 5 berth
legendary ~: 3 Rip
upside-down ~: 5 sloth
sleeper __: 3 car 4 seat
Sleeper (1973 film)
cast: Woody Allen, John Beck, Diane Keaton
director: Woody Allen
dog: 4 Rags
role: 4 Erno
__ Sleeper: 5 Light
Sleepers (1996 film)
cast: Kevin Bacon, Robert De Niro, Dustin Hoffman, Jason Patric
director: Barry Levinson
Sleeper, The author: Edgar Allan Poe
sleep-inducing: 8 hypnotic 9 soporific
sleepiness: 8 laziness, lethargy 9 lassitude
sleeping: 4 abed 5 in bed, not up, under 6 latent 7 dormant 9 unmindful 10 unrealized
bag stuffing: 5 kapok
Chinese ~ platform: 4 kang
place: 3 bed, cot 4 bunk
stop ~: 4 wake 5 awake, get up, waken 6 awaken
sleeping __: 3 bag, car 5 chair, porch
Sleeping __: 6 Beauty
Sleeping __ to Trieste: 3 Car
Sleeping Bag (1985 song) artist: ZZ Top
__ Sleeping Beauty: 3 To a
Sleeping Beauty author: Ross Macdonald
Sleeping Beauty, The: 6 ballet
composer: 11 Tchaikovsky
__ sleeping dogs lie: 3 let
Sleeping Prophet, The: 5 Cayce
sleeping sickness carrier: 6 tsetse, tzetze 8 glossina
Sleeping Tiger, The (1954 film)
cast: Dirk Bogarde, Alexis Smith
Sleeping With the Enemy (1991 film)
cast: Kevin Anderson, Patrick Bergin, Julia Roberts
director: Joseph Ruben
__ Sleep in the Subway: 4 Don't
Sleep It Off, Lady author: Jean Rhys
Sleepless in Seattle (1993 film)
cast: Tom Hanks, Bill Pullman, Meg Ryan
director: Nora Ephron
role: 5 Annie
sleeplessness: 6 nerves 8 insomnia
sleep like __: 4 a log, a top
sleeplike state: 8 hypnosis
Sleep My Love (1948 film)
cast: Don Ameche, Claudette Colbert, Robert Cummings
director: Douglas Sirk
__ Sleeps Tonight, The: 4 Lion
__ Sleep, The: 3 Big
sleepy: 4 dopy, dozy, dull, lazy, logy, slow 5 dopey, heavy, tired, weary 6 draggy, drowsy, groggy, snoozy, torpid 7 nodding, out of it, yawning 8 fatigued, hypnotic, inactive, listless, sluggish 9 heavy-eyed, lethargic, somnolent, soporific 10 knocked out, slumberous
be ~: 3 nod 6 drowse
ender: 4 head
get ~: 4 doze 5 droop 6 drowse
make ~: 9 hypnotize
sign: 4 yawn
Sleepy: 5 dwarf
colleague: 3 Doc 5 Dopey, Happy 6 Grumpy, Sneezy 7 Bashful
Sleepy __ chair: 6 Hollow
sleepyhead
advice to a ~: 5 get up
sleepyheaded: 7 languid 8 sluggish 9 lethargic
Sleepy Hollow
schoolmaster: 5 Crane
Sleepy Hollow (1999 film)
cast: Johnny Depp, Christina Ricci, Miranda Richardson
director: Tim Burton
Sleepy John: 5 Estes

__ Sleepy People: 3 Two
Sleepy Time Gal lyricist: 4 Egan
sleet: 3 ice 4 rain 5 storm
sleeve
band: 6 armlet
end: 4 cuff
filler: 3 arm
it may be up one's ~: 3 ace
part: 5 wrist
type of ~: 6 dolman
__ sleeve: 3 air, cap 4 wind 5 set-in 6 dolman, raglan
__-sleeve: 5 shirt
sleeveless
blouse: 5 shell
cloak: 3 aba 4 abba
dress: 6 jumper
top: 4 vest
sleigh: 4 pung, sled
driver: 5 Santa
puller: 5 horse 8 reindeer
sleigh __: 3 bed 5 bells
Sleigh Ride composer: 8 Anderson
sleight: 4 ploy, ruse 5 knack, magic, skill, trick 6 gambit, scheme 7 gimmick 8 artifice, deftness, facility, maneuver 9 adeptness, dexterity, expedient, readiness, stratagem 10 adroitness, subterfuge
sleight-of-hand: 5 magic, trick
Sleipnir: 5 horse, steed 6 equine
owner: 4 Odin 5 Othin
slender: 3 off 4 bare, fine, lank, lean, slim, thin, trim, weak, wiry 5 faint, lanky, light, lithe, rangy, reedy, scant, small, spare, stick, wispy 6 dainty, feeble, gangly, little, meager, minute, narrow, remote, scanty, scarce, skinny, slight, slinky, stalky, svelte, twiggy 7 fragile, gracile, outside, scraggy, scrawny, spidery, tenuous, wanting, willowy, wispish 8 beanpole, exiguous, gangling 9 beanstalk, deficient, lithesome, sylphlike, waferlike 10 inadequate, negligible, threadlike
one: 4 wisp 5 sylph
slenderize: 4 slim
Slessor, Kenneth: 4 poet 10 Australian
sleuth: 2 PI 3 spy, tec 5 snoop 6 shamus 7 gumshoe 9 detective
cry: 3 aha 4 ah so
ender: 5 hound
find: 4 clew, clue
game: 4 Clue
job: 4 case 5 caper
Sleuth (1972 film)
cast: Michael Caine, Laurence Olivier
character: 4 Milo, Wyke 6 Tindle
director: Joseph L. Mankiewicz
slew: 3 wad 4 gobs, host, lots, raft, skid 5 bunch, ocean, pivot 6 myriad, passel 7 legions, numbers, zillion 9 multitude, profusion, turn about
a ~ of: 4 many 6 legion, myriad, umteen, untold 7 copious, profuse, umpteen 8 abundant, manifold, numerous, umpsteen 9 bountiful, countless, quite a few
__ Slew: 7 Seattle
__ Slew-Foot: 3 Ole
Slezak: 5 Erika 6 Walter
Slezak, Walter: 5 actor
daughter: 5 Erika
film: Bedtime for Bonzo (1951)
Born to Kill (1947)
Cornered (1945)
The Inspector General (1949)
Lifeboat (1944)
The Pirate (1948)
The Princess and the Pirate (1944)
Riffraff (1947)
The Yellow Cab Man (1950)
slice: 3 cut, lot 4 bite, chip, chop, gash, hack, hunk, part, slab, slit, stab 5 carve, knife, piece, quota, scrap, sever, share, shave, shred, slash, split, strip, wedge, wound 6 cleave, divide, incise, morsel, parcel, pierce, rasher, shares, sliver, sunder 7 dissect, helping, percent, portion, section, segment 8 division, fraction, fragment, triangle 9 allotment, allowance, ownership, subdivide 10 commission, laceration, percentage
destination, often: 5 rough
in four: 7 quarter
in two: 5 halve
off: 3 lop 4 trim 5 sever
pizza ~: 6 eighth
thick ~: 4 slab
thin: 5 shave 7 shaving
up: 5 split 6 divide 10 distribute
Slice: 4 soda 9 soft drink
maker: 5 Pepsi
slice of __: 4 life
slicer place: 4 deli
slick: 3 def, icy, oil, pat, rad, sly 4 aces, A-one, boss, braw, cagy, cool, dece, deft, fine, foxy, gear, glib, keen, neat, nice, oily, phat, slip, trim, tuff, waxy, wily, wise 5 adept, cagey, canny, dandy, ducky, grand, great, marvy, neato, nobby, prime, quick, sharp, shiny, sleek, slimy, smart, soapy, spill, super, swell 6 adroit, artful, au fait, bang on, bang-up, bonzer, bosker, choice, clever, crafty, divine, dreamy, expert, far-out, flossy, glassy, glazed, glossy, gnarly, greasy, groovy, lovely, nimble, peachy, refine, shifty, shrewd, slap-up, smooth, spot on, superb, terrif, tiptop, tricky, unreal, urbane, whizzo, wicked 7 amazing, awesome, capable, capital, corking, cunning, elegant, groomed, knowing, perfect, ripping, skilled, skookum, slither, stellar, stylish, sublime, trained 8 dazzling, dextrous, especial, eximious, fabulous, five-star, four-star, frabjous, glorious, graceful, guileful, heavenly, jim-dandy, masterly, polished, scheming, seasoned, skillful, slam-bang, slippery, slithery, smashing, splendid, spruce up, standout, sterling, stickout, superior, terrific, top-level, topnotch, unctuous, very good, wondrous 9 bodacious, brilliant, competent, deceitful, deceptive, dexterous, efficient, Endsville, excellent, exemplary, exquisite, first-rate, high-grade, hunky-dory, ingenious, insidious, insincere, inventive, lubricate, lubricous, marvelous, masterful, sollicker, talkative, top-drawer, top-flight, unethical, wonderful 10 first-class, hotsy-totsy, jack-a-dandy, lubricated, out of sight, peachy-keen, periodical, persuasive, phenomenal, proficient, remarkable, serpentine, streetwise, stupendous, super-duper, well-spoken
contents: 3 oil
get ~: 5 ice up
make ~: 9 lubricate
on top: 4 bald
opposite: 4 pulp
Slick: 5 Grace
slicker: 3 mac 4 coat 6 jacket 7 oilskin 8 raincoat 10 protection
__ slicker: 4 city
__ Slickers: 4 City
slide: 3 dip 4 dive, drop, fall, flow, lurk, sink, skid, skim, slip, tilt, trip, veer 5 coast, decay, drift, glide, lapse, lurch, shift, shove, skate, slink, slump, sneak, spill, steal, swoop 6 go down, plunge, propel, scooch, stream, thrust, tumble 7 decline, descend, descent, drop off, fall off, plummet, slither 8 downturn, move down, move over, toboggan 9 aggravate, move along, recession, worsening 10 degenerate, exacerbate, go smoothly, hit the dirt, lose ground, photograph, retrogress, take it easy
back: 7 relapse
by: 6 elapse
dye: 5 eosin 6 eosine
let ~: 4 omit 6 wink at 7 neglect 8 overlook
on snow: 3 ski 4 skee
over: 5 elide
prepare a ~: 5 stain
site: 4 park
starter: 3 mud 4 back, down, land, rock
water ~: 5 chute, flume
slide __: 4 knot, rule 5 valve 6 guitar
__ slide: 3 mud 4 dark, draw 6 alpine 7 gelatin, lantern
Slidell: 4 city, town
locale: 9 Louisiana
slider: 5 curve, pitch
objective: 4 base
__ Slidin' Away: 4 Slip
sliding
door: 6 fusuma
door groove: 5 regle
part: 4 bolt
sliding __: 4 seat 5 scale 6 vector
Sliding Doors (1998 film)
cast: John Hannah, Gwyneth Paltrow, Jeanne Tripplehorn
director: Peter Howitt
slight: 3 cut, dig, off 4 barb, defy, fail, gibe, jeer, jibe, lank, lean, mere, mock, omit, poor, puny, skip, slam, slap, slim, slur, snub, thin, tiny, weak, wiry 5 abuse, chill, decry, faint, frail, lanky, libel, light, lithe, minor, petty, reedy, scoff, scorn, sheer, skimp, small, sneer, spare, spurn, stick, taunt, teeny, wispy, wrong 6 dainty, defame, deride, dump on, feeble, flimsy, forget, gangly, heckle, ignore, impugn, insult, little, malign, meager, minute, modest, offend, paltry, rebuff, reject, remote, scanty, skinny, slinky, sparse, subtle, svelte, teensy, twiggy, vilify 7 affront, asperse, calumny, catcall, contemn, degrade, despise, disdain, fragile, gracile, mockery, neglect, obloquy, offense, outside, passing, put-down, rank out, scraggy, scrawny, shallow, sketchy, slander, slender, spidery, tenuous, traduce, trivial, willowy, wispish 8 belittle, brush-off, call-down, contempt, delicate, denounce, derision, discount, exiguous, feathery, gangling, marginal, overlook, piddling, pooh-pooh, ridicule, shrug off, trifling, unlikely, vilipend 9 aspersion, attenuate, cheap shot, contumely, denigrate, discredit, disparage, disregard, humiliate, lithesome, rejection, sylphlike, undersize 10 calumniate, defamation, diminutive, disrespect, negligible, opprobrium, weightless
amount: 4 hint, tint, wisp 5 tinge, touch, whiff
combining form: 4 lept- 5 lepto-
difference: 5 shade
lead: 9 advantage, head start
odor: 4 hint 5 sniff, trace 6 breath 9 suspicion
progress: 4 dent
Slight Ache, A author: Harold Pinter
Slight Case of Murder, A (1938 film)
cast: Jane Bryan, Allen Jenkins, Edward G. Robinson
director: Lloyd Bacon
slighter: 4 less 6 lesser
slightest: 5 least 7 minimal, minimum 8 littlest 9 narrowest
in the ~: 5 at all
not in the ~: 5 no how
slightly: 4 a bit 5 a mite 6 hardly, kind of, partly, rather 7 a little, faintly, lightly 8 somewhat 9 to a degree 10 marginally, moderately
Slightly Scarlet star: 4 Dahl
Sligo: 3 Bay 4 city, town
locale: 4 Eire, Erin 7 Ireland
slim: 3 off, shy 4 lank, lean, poor, thin, trim, weak, wiry 5 faint, lanky, lithe, rangy, reedy, scant, short, small, spare, stick 6 dainty, feeble, flimsy, gangly, meager, narrow, reduce, remote, scanty, scarce, skinny, slight, slinky, stalky, svelte, twiggy 7 fragile, gracile, outside, scraggy, scrawny, slender, spidery, tenuous, wanting, willowy 8 beanpole, gangling 9 attenuate, beanstalk, deficient, lithesome, sylphlike 10 improbable, inadequate, lose weight, negligible, slenderize, threadlike
down: 4 diet, lose 6 reduce
Slim: 7 Pickens, Whitman
Slim __: 3 Jim
Slimbach: 4 font 8 typeface
slime: 3 goo, mud 4 crud, glop, guck, gunk, mire, muck, ooze, scum 5 sloke 6 fungus, sludge 7 lowlife, slander 10 sleazeball
combining form: 3 myx- 4 myxo-
slime mold: 6 fungus
slimming device: 6 girdle
slim to __: 4 none
slimy: 3 wet 4 icky, miry, oozy, vile 5 dirty, gooey, mucky, muddy, slick, yucky, yukky 6 greasy, scummy, shifty 7 viscose, viscous 8 slippery 9 glutinous, loathsome 10 despicable
one: 4 slug 5 snail
sling: 3 lob 4 cast, fire, hurl, send, shoe, toss 5 chuck, drink, fling, heave, hoist, pitch, shoot, swing, throw 6 dangle, launch, let fly, propel 7 suspend 8 beverage, catapult, cocktail, footwear, hang over 9 throw over
ender: 4 shot
ingredient: 3 gin 9 lime juice 10 lemon juice
missile: 2 BB 4 rock
mud: 4 slur 5 smear 7 slander
part: 4 band 5 strap
shape: 3 wye
sling __: 5 chair
sling-back: 4 shoe 8 footwear
slinger
hash ~: 4 cook
ink ~: 6 writer 8 reporter 9 columnist 10 journalist, newswriter
starter: 3 gun, mud
...slings and ___: 6 arrows
slingshot alternative: 3 bow 5 BB gun
slink: 4 lurk, slip 5 coast, cower, crawl, creep, glide, prowl, sculk, shirk, sidle, skulk, slide, snake, sneak, steal 7 creep by, meander, skitter 8 glissade, undulate 9 pussyfoot 10 nose around
slinking: 5 snaky 7 furtive 8 stealthy
slinky: 4 lank, lean, slim, thin, wiry 5 lanky, spare 6 dainty, gangly, skinny, slight, svelte, twiggy 7 furtive, gracile, scraggy, scrawny, slender, spidery, willowy 8 gangling 9 sylphlike
Slinky: 3 toy 4 coil 6 spring
shape: 5 helix
slip: 3 err, sag, tag 4 bomb, bust, cion, dock, drop, fall, flop, flub, gaff, goof, knot, lose, lurk, miss, move, muff, pier, shed, sink, skid, trip 5 berth, decay, error, fault, fluff, flunk, gaffe, glide, jetty, lapse, lurch, plant, scion, sheet,

shift, shirk, shoot, skate, slick, slide, slink, slump, sneak, steal, strip, wharf **6** blow it, boo-boo, bungle, falter, flit by, foozle, foul-up, howler, lapsus, sliver, ticket, totter, tumble **7** abscond, blooper, blunder, chemise, decline, drop off, erratum, failure, fall off, faux pas, founder, go under, go wrong, landing, misdeed, misstep, mistake, receipt, screw-up, slither, stumble, wash out **8** fall flat, flounder, giveaway, glissade, lay an egg, lingerie, misjudge, omission **9** aggravate, backslide, indecorum, oversight, petticoat, recession, strike out, underwear **10** degenerate, diminution, exacerbate, imprudence, inaccuracy, infraction, lose ground, pillowcase, retrogress

away: **2** go **3** fly **4** exit, flee, lose **5** elope, fly by, leave **6** be gone, depart, elapse, escape, run off **7** head out **8** sneak out

back: **7** relapse **10** recidivate

by: **4** edge **5** drift **6** elapse

ender: **3** way **4** case, knot, over, page, shod, slop, ware **5** cased, cover **6** stitch, stream

exclamation: **4** oh-oh, oops, uh-oh

ferry ~: **4** pier **5** berth

give the ~: **4** foil, lose **5** avoid, dodge, elude, evade, leave, shake **8** shake off, throw off

give the pink ~: **2** ax **3** axe **4** fire, oust, sack **7** dismiss **9** discharge

in: **5** enter **6** arrive

into: **3** don **4** wear **5** put on

keyboard ~: **4** typo **7** erratum, mistake **8** misprint **10** inaccuracy

let ~: **4** blab, leak, miss, tell **5** blurt, spill **6** betray, expose, forget, reveal, unmask, unveil **7** divulge, exhibit, lay bare, uncover **8** disclose **9** make known **10** make public

off: **6** escape **7** undress **8** get out of

of the tongue: **5** gaffe **7** blunder, faux pas, mistake

one over on: **4** fool

one's mind: **6** forget

out: **2** go **5** leave

past: **4** edge **5** elude

redemption ~: **6** coupon, ticket **7** voucher

sales ~: **7** receipt

ship ~: **4** dock **5** wharf

starter: **3** cow **4** land, side

through one's fingers: **4** flee, skip **6** escape, pass by, run off, run out **7** abscond, bail out, duck out, get away, make off, run away **9** break away, steal away **10** fly the coop

up: **3** err **4** goof, trip **5** lapse **7** mistake **8** overlook

slip __: **3** top **4** a cog, away, form, hook, ring, seat, stem **5** joint **6** stitch **7** casting, tracing

slip __ the cracks: **7** between

slip-__ pliers: **5** joint

__ slip: **3** let **4** buck, call, draw, pink **5** cover, sales **6** camber, credit, patent, strike **7** deposit

slip a __: **3** cog

slipknot: **5** noose

slip-on: **3** moc **6** loafer **8** moccasin

slipover: **7** sweater

slipper: **8** footwear

backless ~: **4** mule **5** scuff

ender: **4** wort

lady's ~: **6** flower

material: **5** glass **7** leather

onyx ~: **5** shell **8** seashell

slipper __: **4** foot, sock **5** chair, shell

__ slipper: **5** house **6** ballet, carpet **7** bedroom

__-slipper: **5** fairy, lady's

Slipper and the Rose, The (1976 film)

cast: Richard Chamberlain, Gemma Craven

director: Bryan Forbes

slippers like Dorothy's: **4** ruby

slippery: **3** icy, wet **4** cagy, eely, foxy, glib, oily, waxy, wily **5** cagey, glacé, shady, sharp, silky, sleek, slick, slimy, soapy **6** crafty, glassy, glazed, greasy, louche, satiny, shifty, shrewd, smooth, sneaky, tricky, unsafe, wiggly **7** cunning, devious, elusive, elusory, evasive **8** guileful, insecure, perilous, polished, scheming, slithery, unctuous, unstable, unsteady, variable **9** deceptive, dishonest, lubricous, uncertain, underhand, unethical **10** changeable, glistening, lubricated, lubricious, unreliable

get ~: **5** ice up **6** freeze

make ~: **3** oil **9** lubricate

one: **3** eel **6** dodger

on ~ ground: **4** iffy **5** dicey, hairy, risky **6** chancy, daring, touchy, tricky, unsafe **7** fraught **8** ticklish **9** dangerous, desperate, foolhardy, hazardous **10** precarious, touch-and-go

slippery __: **3** elm **5** slope

slippery __ eel: **4** as an

Slippery When __: **3** Wet

Slippin' and Slidin' (1956 song) artist: Little Richard

Slipping-Down Life, A author: Anne Tyler

slipshod: **3** bad, lax **5** hasty, junky, loose, messy, tacky **6** faulty, remiss, shabby, sloppy, untidy **7** botched, ill-done, scrubby, scruffy, unkempt **8** careless, fouled-up, slapdash, slovenly, tattered **9** haphazard, hit-or-miss, imperfect, imprudent, neglected, negligent, screwed-up, unheedful, unmindful **10** bedraggled, disheveled, inaccurate, incautious, jerry-built, last-minute, nonchalant, uncritical, unthinking, unthorough, willy-nilly

Slip Slidin' Away (1977 song) artist: Paul Simon

slipslop: **3** gas, rot **4** blah, bosh, bull, bunk, guff, jazz, jive, pooh, tosh **5** bilge, fudge, hokum, hooey, prate, stuff, trash, tripe **6** bunkum, bushwa, drivel, footle, gabble, gammon, gibber, havers, hot air, humbug, jabber, jargon, kibosh, piffle **7** baloney, blarney, blather, blether, boloney, bushwah, eyewash, flannel, flubdub, fustian, garbage, hogwash, inanity, rubbish, twaddle **8** buncombe, claptrap, falderal, falderol, flimflam, flummery, folderal, folderol, nonsense, tommyrot, trumpery **9** banana oil, gibberish, kidstakes, moonshine, poppycock, rigmarole **10** applesauce, balderdash, bilge water, codswallop, double-talk, flapdoodle, galimatias, Jabberwock, mumbo jumbo, rigamarole, taradiddle

slip-up: **4** boot, flub, goof, muff **5** boner, botch, error, fault, fluff, gaffe, lapse **6** boo-boo, bungle, fumble, miscue **7** blunder, faux pas, misdeed, misstep, mistake **9** indecorum, oversight

slit: **3** cut, rip **4** gash, hole, nick, open, rent, slot, tear, torn, vent **5** cleft, crack, knife, lance, score, sever, slash, slice, split **6** crenel, incise, louver, pierce **7** crevice, cut open, fissure, incised, keyhole, opening **8** aperture, cleavage, crenelle, incision, peephole, puncture, sundered **9** lacerated, split open **10** buttonhole, interspace, interstice, laceration

garment ~: **4** vent

organ-pipe ~: **4** flue

slither: **4** lurk, slip, wind **5** coast, cower, creep, glide, prowl, sculk, sidle, skulk, slick, slide, snake, sneak, steal **7** creep by, meander, skitter **8** glissade, undulate **9** pussyfoot **10** nose around

Slither (1973 film)

cast: Peter Boyle, James Caan, Sally Kellerman

director: Howard Zieff

slitherer: **4** worm **5** snake

slithery: **4** eely **5** slick **8** slippery **9** lubricous

slithy

creatures: **5** toves

what the ~ toves did: **4** gyre

Sliven: **4** city, town

locale: **8** Bulgaria

sliver: **3** bit **4** chip, slip, snip **5** crumb, flake, piece, scrap, shave, shred, slice, thorn **6** paring **7** flinder, shaving, snippet **8** fragment, splinter

Sliver: **4** film **5** novel

author: Ira Levin

cast: William Baldwin, Tom Berenger, Sharon Stone

slivovitz: **5** drink **8** beverage

maker: **4** Serb

slo-__: **5** pitch

Sloan: **4** John **6** Alfred, Wilson

Sloane, Everett: **5** actor

film: Citizen Kane (1941)
The Lady From Shanghai (1948)
The Men (1950)
Patterns (1956)
Somebody Up There Likes Me (1956)

Sloan, John: **6** artist **7** painter

slob: **5** sight **6** lubber **9** litterbug

slobber: **4** drip, spit **5** drool, froth **6** drivel, slaver **7** dribble, slabber **8** salivate

__ Slobbovia: **5** Lower

sloe: **4** plum, tree **5** fruit, shrub **10** blackthorn

family: **4** rose

relative: **6** cherry, damson, kerria, spirea **7** bramble, jetbead, spiraea **8** hardhack, ninebark, photinia **9** firethorn, greengage, myrobalan, raspberry

sloe-__: **4** eyed

sloe gin fizz: **5** drink **8** beverage

slog: **4** grub, path, plod, toil, trek, wade, walk, work **5** slave, trail, tramp, tread **6** lumber, trudge, wallop

slogan: **4** word **5** idiom, motto **6** byword, jingle, phrase, saying, war cry **7** proverb **9** battle cry, catchword, trademark, watchword **10** expression

like a ~: **6** catchy

maker: **5** adman

repeated ~: **5** chant

sloke: **5** algae, slime **7** seaweed

sloop: **4** boat **5** craft, yacht **8** sailboat **10** knockabout, watercraft

sloop __: **3** rig **5** of war

Sloop John B (1966 song) artist: Beach Boys

slop: **4** drip **5** dance, slosh, slush, smear, spill, spray, swill, waste **6** liquid, refuse, smudge, splash, wallow **7** spatter **8** overflow, splatter **9** litterbug

slop __: **3** jar **4** bowl, pail, sink **5** basin, chest **6** bucket

slope: **3** dip, tip **4** bank, bend, bias, cant, drop, fall, hill, lean, list, ramp, rise, sink, skew, sway, tilt **5** angle, bevel, chute, grade, pitch, slant, splay, way up **6** ascend, ascent, cuesta **7** descend, descent, incline, leaning, recline **8** diagonal, drop away, gradient, hillside **9** declivity, deviation, downgrade, obliquity, steepness **10** declension, deflection

combining form: **4** clin- **5** -cline, clino- **6** -clinal

downward: **4** drop **7** descend

downward ~: **4** drop **7** descent **9** declivity

fortification ~: **5** talus

gentle ~: **6** glacis **9** acclivity

Hawaiian steep ~: **4** pali

Highlands ~: **4** brae

hollow: **6** corrie

rugged ~: **4** scar **6** escarp

steep ~: **5** chute, cliff, scarp

upward: **4** rise **5** climb **6** ascend

upward ~: **4** bank, hill, rise **5** grade **6** ascent, glacis **7** hillock, incline **8** gradient, hillside **9** acclivity, elevation

__ Slope: **5** North

slopes, hit the: **3** ski **4** skee, sled

sloping: **5** bevel **6** aslant, uphill **7** sideway **8** sideways, sidewise

sharply ~: **5** steep

slopping

over the sides: **5** awash

the hogs: **5** chore

sloppy: **3** lax **4** poor **5** dirty, hasty, loose, messy, muddy, mushy, mussy, slack, tacky **6** blowsy, blowzy, clumsy, frowsy, frowzy, grungy, remiss, sludgy, slushy, unneat, untidy **7** awkward, blowsed, blowzed, botched, mawkish, splashy, squalid, unclean, unkempt **8** careless, romantic, slipshod, slovenly **9** imprudent, negligent, unmindful **10** bedraggled, disheveled, incautious, nonchalant, unthinking, unthorough

stuff: **3** goo

Sloppy Joe: **4** beef **7** sweater **8** sandwich

slosh: **3** lap **4** slop, wade, wash **5** plash, spill **6** splash **8** overflow **9** spill over

around: **6** wallow

slot: **3** cut, job **4** file, hole, site, slit, spot, time, work **5** niche, notch, place, space **6** groove, recess, socket **7** channel, earmark, keyhole, opening, section, specify, station, vacancy **8** aperture, position, standing **9** designate **10** department, depository, interspace, job opening, letter drop, livelihood, occupation, pigeonhole, profession

filler: **3** tab **5** hirer

spot: **6** casino

slot __: **3** car, man **5** racer **6** racing **7** machine

sloth: **2** ai **3** sin **4** bear, unau **5** idler **6** acedia, animal, laxity, mammal, torpor **7** dawdler, inertia, languor, laxness **8** hebetude, idleness, laziness, lethargy, loginess, otiosity **9** fainéance, indolence, inertness, torpidity **10** inactivity, stagnation

act the ~: **4** laze

home: **4** tree

slothful: **3** lax **4** idle, lazy, logy, poky, slow **5** inert, slack, tardy **6** asleep, draggy, otiose, remiss, torpid **7** dormant, gradual, halting, impeded, lagging, languid, passive **8** crawling, creeping, dallying, dawdling, dilatory, dragging, drawn-out, fainéant, hesitant, inactive, indolent, lifeless, plodding, sluggish, toddling **9** apathetic, do-nothing, leisurely, lethargic, loitering, negligent, prolonged, sedentary, shiftless, snaillike, unhurried **10** deliberate, disengaged, neglectful, protracted, sluggardly

slot machine
city: 4 Reno 5 Tahoe, Vegas
feature: 3 arm
input: 4 coin
play the ~: 3 bet 5 wager 6 gamble
slotted ___: 5 spoon
slouch: 3 bow, lag, sag 4 bend, flex, lean, loaf, loll, tilt, wilt 5 droop, slump, stoop 6 crouch, linger, loafer, lounge, sprawl 8 loiterer 9 lazybones, slump over
Slouching Towards Bethlehem
author: Joan Didion
slough: 3 bog 4 molt, shed, skin 5 marsh, swamp 6 loiter, reject 8 quagmire
off: 4 shed 5 shirk
Slough: 4 city, town
locale: 7 England 9 Berkshire
Sloukhin, Vladimir: 4 poet 7 Russian
Slovakia: 6 nation 7 country
capital: 10 Bratislava
city: 6 Kosice 10 Bratislava
Danube, in ~: 5 Dunaj
mountain range: 5 Tatra
neighbor: 6 Poland 7 Austria, Hungary, Ukraine
tennis pro: 6 Hingis
sloven: 3 pig 9 litterbug 10 ragamuffin
Slovenia: 6 nation 7 country
capital: 9 Ljubljana
city: 7 Maribor 9 Ljubljana
neighbor: 5 Italy 7 Austria, Croatia, Hungary
river: 4 Sava
slovenly: 4 icky 5 dingy, dirty, dowdy, grimy, grody, loose, lousy, messy, mussy, piggy, seedy, slack, sooty, tacky 6 blowsy, blowzy, filthy, fouled, frowsy, frowzy, frumpy, grubby, grungy, piggie, pigpen, sleazy, sloppy, soiled, sordid, unneat, untidy 7 blowsed, blowzed, botched, raunchy, scruffy, smudged, squalid, stained, tainted, unclean, unkempt, unswept 8 befouled, begrimed, careless, heedless, maculate, messed up, polluted, slapdash, slipshod 9 blackened, negligent, tarnished, ungroomed 10 bedraggled, besmirched, disheveled, disordered, disorderly, topsy-turvy, unsanitary
slow: 3 dim, lag, off 4 beam, curb, damp, dull, late, lazy, poky, tame 5 abate, brake, check, choke, delay, dense, dunce, inert, pokey, relax, slack, stall, stunt, tardy, thick, unapt 6 adagio, arrest, behind, dampen, detain, draggy, dreamy, drowsy, ease up, hamper, hang up, hinder, hold up, impede, leaden, lessen, loiter, reduce, rein in, relent, remiss, retard, simple, sleepy, stolid, torpid 7 belated, bog down, curtail, cut back, cut down, delayed, ease off, fall off, glacial, gradual, halting, impeded, inhibit, laggard, lagging, languid, limited, lumpish, reduced, set back, slacken, tedious 8 backward, cautious, crawling, creeping, dawdling, decrease, delaying, detained, dilatory, diminish, hindered, hold back, inactive, indolent, lifeless, listless, moderate, peter out, plodding, postpone, regulate, restrict, road sign, slothful, sluggish, wind down 9 backwater, dimwitted, leisurely, lethargic, lighten up, lingering, loitering, negligent, ponderous, prolonged, reluctant, snaillike, unhurried 10 decelerate, deliberate, dull-witted, phlegmatic, postponing, protracted, uneventful, unpunctual, unreactive
burn: 5 pique 6 temper 9 surliness 10 irritation
combining form: 5 brady-
do a ~ burn: 4 fume, stew 5 react 6 seethe
down: 4 damp, loaf, rein, tire 5 brake, check, delay, deter, let up, relax, stall, tie up 6 arrest, dampen, detain, hamper, hang up, hinder, impede, lessen, reduce, rein in, retard, unwind, weaken 7 fall off, inhibit, prolong, set back, slacken, tail off 8 decrease, encumber, hold back, make late, obstruct, peter out, restrain 10 decelerate
ender: 4 down, poke
go ~: 4 plod 5 crawl
in music: 5 largo, lento, tardo 6 adagio
in retail: 4 dead
interval: 4 lull
one: 2 ox 4 poke, worm 5 sloth, snail
on the uptake: 3 dim 5 dense 6 obtuse
signal: 5 amber 6 yellow
take it ~: 4 laze 6 go easy
up: 3 lag 4 rein 5 abate, check, delay 6 impede, rein in, retard, shelve 7 set back 8 hold back, restrain 10 decelerate
slow ___: 4 burn, fire, gait, time, wave 5 loris, match 6 cooker, motion 7 neutron
slow-___: 6 footed, moving, witted 7 release
___ slow: 4 dead
Slow ___: 6 Dancin' 7 Twistin'
___ Slow Boat to China: 3 On a
Slow Dancin' (1977 song) artist: Johnny Rivers
slowdown: 3 jam 4 lull 5 delay, letup, slack, slump, tie-up 6 arrest, strike 7 decline, drop-off, falloff, setback 8 downturn, tarrying 9 downtrend, worsening 10 slackening
slower
in music: 3 rit. 4 rall. 8 ritenuto 10 ritardando
traffic ~: 4 bump 9 speed bump
Slow Hand (1981 song) artist: Pointer Sisters
slowly: 5 largo 6 adagio 7 loathly 8 bit by bit 9 languidly, leisurely, piecemeal
slow-moving: 4 lazy, logy 5 slack 6 torpid 8 sluggish 9 lethargic
slow on the ___: 6 uptake
slowpoke: 5 snail 6 lagger 7 dawdler, laggard 8 lingerer, loiterer 9 latecomer
Slow Twistin' (1962 song)
artist: Chubby Checker, Dee Dee Sharp
slow-witted: 4 dull 5 dense, thick
SLR: 6 camera
slub: 4 burl
sludge: 4 gook, guck, ooze, slop 5 slime
slue: 4 skid, veer 5 pivot 6 swerve 9 turn about
sluff
see slough
slug: 3 bat, hit, nip 4 bash, beat, belt, blow, deck, hurt, pest, shot, slam, sock, swat, swig, wham 5 clout, drink, drone, flail, paste, punch, smash, smite, thump, whack 6 bullet, strike, wallop 7 clobber 8 uppercut 9 gastropod, haul off on
cousin: 5 snail
ender: 4 fest
it out: 3 box 5 fight 6 battle
like a ~: 4 fake 5 bogus, slimy
___ slug: 3 sea 4 rose 6 rifled
slugabed: 4 poke 5 idler 7 dawdler 9 do-nothing, lazybones
slugfest: 4 fray 6 boxing 10 donnybrook
sluggard: 5 drone, idler, sloth 6 loafer, truant 7 dawdler, slacker 8 loiterer 9 do-nothing, lazybones 10 ne'er-do-well
bane: 3 job 4 work
slugged, old-style: 4 smit 5 smote
Slugger, Louisville: 3 bat
slugging ___: 5 it out 7 average
sluggish: 3 lax, off 4 blah, dopy, down, dull, idle, lazy, logy, poky, slow, weak 5 dopey, heavy, inert, leady, pokey, rusty, slack 6 asleep, bovine, draggy, drippy, drowsy, leaden, sleepy, stupid, sullen, torpid 7 dormant, gradual, halting, impeded, lagging, languid, lumpish, passive 8 crawling, creeping, dawdling, dilatory, dragging, drawn-out, hesitant, inactive, indolent, laid-back, lifeless, listless, plodding, slothful, stagnant, toddling 9 apathetic, leisurely, lethargic, lymphatic, ponderous, prolonged, sedentary, snaillike, unhurried 10 deliberate, disengaged, languorous, phlegmatic, protracted, slow-moving, slumberous, unreactive
one: 5 sloth
sluggishness: 5 sloth 7 languor, latency 8 laziness, lethargy 9 lassitude
sluice: 4 race, tide 5 flume, surge 6 gutter, stream
ender: 3 box, way
Sluiskin: 5 falls 9 waterfall
locale: 10 Washington
slum: 3 sty 4 dump 6 ghetto, pigsty, sordid 7 piggery, quarter, rathole, skid row 9 inner city
ender: 4 lord
outer city ~: 5 slurb
Sluman, Jeff: 6 golfer
milieu: 5 links 6 course
org.: 3 PGA
slumber: 3 nap 4 doze, rest 5 sleep 6 drowse, repose, snooze, stupor, torpor 7 languor, latency, saw logs, shut-eye 8 dormancy, lethargy, sack time 10 forty winks, inactivity
see also sleep
slumbering: 4 abed 6 asleep 7 dormant 9 sacked out, somnolent
slumberland: 5 sleep
slumberous: 6 drowsy, sleepy 8 sluggish 9 lethargic, somnolent
slumber-party attire: 3 PJs 7 pajamas
slumgullion: 4 hash, stew
slump: 3 dip, low, nod, rut, sag 4 bend, drop, fall, flag, flex, flop, funk, loll, sink, slip, wilt 5 crash, decay, droop, dumps, hunch, panic, pitch, slide, stoop 6 cave in, downer, go down, plunge, slouch, sprawl, topple, trough, tumble 7 decline, descend, descent, dessert, drop off, failure, falloff, plummet, reverse, tail off 8 bad times, blue funk, collapse, decrease, downturn, dry spell, keel over, nosedive, slowdown, tailspin 9 downslide, downswing, downtrend, hard times, recession, worsening 10 degenerate, depression, falling-off, go downhill, stagnation
slumping, stop: 5 sit up
Slums of Beverly Hills (1998 film)
cast: Alan Arkin, Kevin Corrigan, Natasha Lyonne, Marisa Tomei
director: Tamara Jenkins
slung: 6 hurled, tossed 9 suspended
slur: 3 cap, dig, rap 4 barb, blot, chop, gibe, jeer, jibe, mock, onus, skip, slam, slap, snub, zing 5 abuse, brand, cut up, decry, elide, knock, libel, odium, roast, scorn, smear, spurn, stain, taunt 6 defame, deride, dump on, expose, garble, heckle, impugn, insult, malign, mumble, offend, rebuff, scorch, slight, smirch, stigma, vilify, zinger 7 affront, asperse, blacken, blemish, blister, calumny, catcall, degrade, detract, disdain, mockery, obloquy, offense, putdown, rank out, run down, slander, spatter, stutter, traduce 8 backbite, belittle, besmirch, black eye, contempt, denounce, derision, disgrace, innuendo, reproach, ridicule, tear down, throw mud, vilipend 9 aspersion, black mark, cheap shot, contumely, denigrate, discredit, disparage, humiliate, insinuate, stricture 10 accusation, calumniate, defamation, disrespect, imputation, opprobrium, reflection, scandalize, villainize, vituperate
in music: 5 glide
slurp: 3 lap, sip 5 drink, lap up 6 guzzle 7 swallow
slush: 3 mud 4 mire, mush, slop 7 schmalz, shmaltz 8 schmaltz 9 mushiness, soppiness
slush ___: 4 fund, pile
slushy: 3 wet 5 muddy, mushy, sappy 6 sloppy 7 maudlin
beverage: 6 frappé
SLX: 3 SUV 5 Acura
sly: 3 coy 4 arch, cagy, foxy, wily 5 cagey, canny, sharp, slick, smart, snaky, sneak 6 artful, astute, clever, covert, crafty, feline, impish, secret, shifty, shrewd, smooth, sneaky, subtle, tricky 7 crooked, cunning, devious, elusive, elusory, evasive, furtive, knavish, roguish, vulpine 8 bluffing, delusive, guileful, plotting, scheming, sneaking, stealthy 9 astucious, conniving, deceitful, deceptive, designing, dishonest, ingenious, insidious, underhand 10 intriguing, serpentine
one: 3 fox 9 intriguer
on the ~: 7 sub rosa 8 covertly, in secret, secretly, sneakily 9 furtively 10 stealthily, undercover
sly ___ fox: 3 as a
___ sly: 5 on the
Sly: 5 Stone 8 Stallone
Sly and the Family Stone
song: Dance to the Music (1968)
Everyday People (1969)
Family Affair (1971)
Hot Fun in the Summertime (1969)
Stand! (1969)
Thank You (Falettinme Be Mice Elf Agin) (1970)
slyly: 7 asquint 10 guilefully
Slyne Head: 4 cape
locale: 4 Eire, Erin 7 Ireland
slyness: 3 art 4 wile 5 craft, guile 6 deceit
Sm: 4 elem. 7 element 8 samarium
62 for ~: 4 at. no.
sma: 3 wee
one: 5 bairn
smack: 3 box, hit 4 bang, beat, belt, blow, boat, buss, chop, clap, clip, cuff, kiss, lash, lick, slam, slap, sock, spat, swat, tang, thud 5 clout, crack, flail, knock, plumb, punch, right, savor, spank, swipe, taste, thump, tinge, touch, whack, whang 6 buffet, strike, trifle, wallop 7 clearly, clobber, exactly, lay into 8 directly, squarely, uppercut 9 fisticuff, precisely 10 accurately, osculation, point-blank, suggestion
dab: 8 directly
ender: 4 eroo
of: 5 smell 7 suggest 8 look like, resemble, seem like
one's lips: 5 eat up, enjoy, gloat, savor 6 devour, relish 7 feast on
smack-dab: 5 right 9 precisely
smacker: 4 bill, buck 6 dollar 8 banknote, frogskin 9 greenback
smackers: 3 oof 4 cash, gelt, jack, kail,

kale, loot, peag, pelf **5** bread, dough, funds, lucre, moola, mopus, pesos, rhino, sewan **6** dinero, do-re-mi, mammon, mazuma, moolah, seawan, silver, specie, wampum, wealth **7** cabbage, capital, lettuce, ooftish, scratch, shekels **8** bankroll, cold cash, currency, hard cash **9** long green, simoleons **10** green stuff
Smacks: 6 cereal
competitor: 3 Kix **4** Life, Trix **5** Kashi, Quisp, Total **6** Kaboom, Muesli, Oreo O's, Pablum **7** All-Bran, Crispix, Harmony, Hunny B's, Mueslix, Oat Bran, Pokemon **8** Boo Berry, Cheerios, Corn Chex, Corn Pops, Fiber One, Rice Chex, Special K, Uncle Sam, Wheaties **9** Alpha Bits, Apple Zaps, Grape Nuts, Honey Comb, Just Right, Wheat Chex **10** Apple Jacks, Bran Flakes, Cap'n Crunch, Cocoa Puffs, Froot Loops, Mini-Wheats, Nutri-Grain, Puffed Rice, Quaker Oats, Smart Start **11** Cocoa Blasts, Cookie Crisp, Golden Crisp, Lucky Charms, Puffed Wheat, Sweet Crunch, Waffle Crisp
small: 3 off, toy, wee **4** baby, base, mere, mini, poor, puny, size, slim, tiny **5** bitty, dinky, light, minor, petty, runty, short, sorry, teeny, weeny, young **6** atomic, bantam, elfish, elvish, humble, lesser, little, meager, midget, minute, modest, narrow, paltry, petite, pocket, scanty, shrimp, slight, teensy **7** cramped, ignoble, limited, nominal, outside, pitiful, scrubby, selfish, slender, stunted, trivial **8** atomical, atomlike, exiguous, immature, inferior, marginal, picayune, piddling, plebeian, trifling **9** lowercase, miniature, minuscule, pint-sized, secondary, undersize **10** bush-league, diminutive, humiliated, inadequate, low-ranking, negligible, skinflinty, undersized, ungenerous
combining form: 4 micr-, mini-, parv- **5** micro-, parvi-, parvo-
ender: 3 pox **4** time **5** timer
name meaning ~: 4 Paul **5** Klein **6** Vaughn **7** Vaughan
suffix: 3 -let, -ule **4** -ette
small __: 3 arm, cap, fry **4** beer, cane, game, slam, talk **5** hours, print, stuff, world **6** change, circle, screen, stores **7** calorie, capital, holding
small __ advisory: 5 craft
small-__: 4 bore, time, town **5** scale **6** minded
small-__ court: 5 debts **6** claims
Small __: 3 Fry **4** Town **5** Faces, World **6** Change, Wonder
Small Change (1976 film) director: François Truffaut
Small Craft Warnings author: Tennessee Williams
Smallens, Alexander: 7 Russian **9** conductor
smaller: 4 less **5** lower, minor
get ~: 3 ebb **4** wane **6** lessen, narrow, reduce, shrink **7** decline, deflate, drop off, dwindle, shrivel **8** contract, decrease, diminish **9** waste away
make ~: 6 lessen, shrink **7** dwindle **8** minimize
to a ~ extent: 5 fewer, lower, minor **7** limited, reduced, without **8** inferior **9** excepting, secondary, shortened **10** diminished
smallest: 5 least **7** minimal, minimum **8** littlest **9** narrowest
part: 8 molecule
Smallest Show on Earth, The (1957 film)
cast: Virginia McKenna, Bill Travers
director: Basil Dearden
Smalley, Richard: 7 chemist **8** Nobelist
small-fry: 5 minor **6** lesser
__ Small Hours: 3 Wee
Small, Millie song: My Boy Lollipop (1964)
small-minded: 5 petty **6** little, narrow, sordid **7** bigoted **9** parochial
smallmouth __: 4 bass
Small Rain, The author: Thomas Pynchon
small rock, name meaning: 8 Rochelle
Small Room, The author: May Sarton
small screen
see television
Small Soldiers (1998 film)
cast: Kirsten Dunst, Phil Hartman, Jay Mohr, Gregory Smith
director: Joe Dante
small-time: 5 dinky, local, minor **6** lesser **9** parochial, secondary **10** provincial
Small Time Crooks (2000 film)
cast: Woody Allen, Hugh Grant, Elaine May, Tracey Ullman
director: Woody Allen
Small Town (1985 song) artist: John Cougar Mellencamp
Small Town author: Sloan Wilson
Small Town Girl (1936 film)
cast: Binnie Barnes, Janet Gaynor, Robert Taylor
director: William Wellman
Smallville (WB sci-fi)
cast: Kristin Kreuk (Lana Lang) Michael Rosenbaum (Lex Luthor) Tom Welling (Clark Kent)
Small Wonder author: Barbara Kingsolver
Small world, __ it?: 4 isn't
__ Small World: 4 It's a
Small World composer: 5 Styne **8** Sondheim
smaltite: 3 ore **7** mineral
smarmy: 4 oily
smart: 3 apt, hip, sly **4** able, ache, bold, burn, chic, fine, good, hurt, keen, neat, pain, pert, posh, sage, trim, whiz, wise **5** acute, adept, agile, alert, brisk, canny, crisp, faddy, fresh, natty, nervy, nifty, prick, quick, ready, sassy, saucy, sharp, slick, sting, swank, swell, swish, throb **6** astute, brainy, brazen, bright, clever, crafty, dapper, dressy, genius, gifted, lively, modish, nimble, rakish, shrewd, simmer, snappy, spruce, suffer, swanky, trendy, twinge, with it **7** cunning, dashing, elegant, erudite, groomed, knowing, learned, pointed, politic, prickle, sapient, stylish, voguish **8** cerebral, cracking, flippant, impudent, insolent, masterly, sensible, skillful, spirited, vigorous, well-read **9** astucious, brilliant, effective, eggheaded, energetic, exclusive, in fashion, ingenious, inventive, judicious, on the ball, sagacious, sprightly **10** discerning, insightful, keen-witted, precocious
aleck: 7 wise guy **8** quipster, wiseacre
get ~: 4 sass **8** mouth off, talk back
group: 5 Mensa
one: 5 brain **6** genius **8** Einstein, wiseacre
talk: 4 sass
smart __: 3 off, set **4** bomb, card **5** aleck, money
smart __ whip: 3 as a
__-smart: 6 street
Smart: 5 Ralph **7** Maxwell
__ Smart: 3 Get
smart-alecky: 4 bold, flip, pert, wise **5** fresh, lippy, nervy, sassy, saucy **6** brazen **7** forward **8** cocksure, derisive, flippant, impudent **9** sarcastic
Smart, Christopher: 4 poet **7** British
smarten: 5 primp **8** ornament, spruce up
up: 4 tidy, trim **5** groom, primp, prink, spiff **6** neaten **7** get wise **8** beautify **9** glamorize
__ Smart Girls: 5 Three
smarting: 4 achy, sore **9** irritated
Smart, Maxwell: 3 spy **5** agent
portrayer: Don Adams
smartmouth: 5 sassy, saucy **8** back talk, impudent
smartness: 4 wits **5** craft, guile, sense, skill **6** acumen, brains **7** finesse **8** aptitude, keenness **9** canniness, ingenuity, quickness, sharpness **10** adroitness, astuteness, brightness, cleverness, shrewdness
smarts: 5 sense, skill **6** acumen **8** aptitude, keenness **9** intellect, mentality
__ smarts: 6 street
Smart Start: 6 cereal
competitor: 3 Kix **4** Life, Trix **5** Kashi, Quisp, Total **6** Kaboom, Muesli, Oreo O's, Pablum, Smacks **7** All-Bran, Crispix, Harmony, Hunny B's, Mueslix, Oat Bran, Pokemon **8** Boo Berry, Cheerios, Corn Chex, Corn Pops, Fiber One, Rice Chex, Special K, Uncle Sam, Wheaties **9** Alpha Bits, Apple Zaps, Grape Nuts, Honey Comb, Just Right, Wheat Chex **10** Apple Jacks, Bran Flakes, Cap'n Crunch, Cocoa Puffs, Froot Loops, Mini-Wheats, Nutri-Grain, Puffed Rice, Quaker Oats **11** Cocoa Blasts, Cookie Crisp, Golden Crisp, Lucky Charms, Puffed Wheat, Sweet Crunch, Waffle Crisp
Smart Woman (1948 film)
cast: Brian Aherne, Constance Bennett, Barry Sullivan
Smart Women author: Judy Blume
smarty: 8 wiseacre **9** know-it-all **10** jackanapes
smarty-__: 5 pants
smash: 3 hit, jar, ram, wow **4** bang, bash, belt, boom, clap, play, rase, raze, rive, ruin, shot, slam, slug, sock, swat, undo, welt, wham **5** blast, break, burst, crack, crash, crush, pound, punch, smite, sound, spoil, sqush, stave, trash, whack, wreck **6** bash in, batter, big hit, defeat, impact, pile-up, powder, ravage, shiver, squash, squish, squush, topple, tumble, wallop, winner **7** break up, clobber, collide, crackup, debacle, destroy, disrupt, failure, flatten, implode, scrunch, shatter, squoosh, success, triumph **8** accident, breaking, collapse, decimate, demolish, destruct, disaster, downfall, fracture, fragment, knockout, overturn, splinter, stampede, tear down, uppercut, vanquish **9** breakdown, collision, devastate, haul off on, knock down, overpower, overthrow, pulverize, sensation **10** annihilate, gold record, shattering
and grab: 4 loot **5** rifle **7** plunder
ender: 4 eroo
into: 3 hit, ram **4** bump **6** strike **7** rear-end
letters: 3 SRO
smash __: 3 hit
smashed: 5 tight **6** broken, undone **8** in pieces
__ smasher: 4 atom
__ Smasher: 3 Spy
smashing: 3 def, rad **4** aces, A-one, boss, braw, cool, dece, fine, gear, keen, neat, nice, phat, tuff **5** boffo, dandy, ducky, grand, great, marvy, neato, nobby, prime, slick, super, swell **6** bang on, bang-up, bonzer, bosker, choice, divine, dreamy, far-out, gnarly, groovy, lovely, peachy, slap-up, spot on, superb, terrif, tiptop, unreal, whizzo, wicked **7** amazing, awesome, boffola, capital, corking, perfect, ripping, skookum, special, stellar, sublime **8** dazzling, especial, eximious, fabulous, five-star, four-star, frabjous, glorious, heavenly, jim-dandy, slam-bang, splendid, standout, sterling, stickout, stunning, superior, terrific, top-level, topnotch, very good, wondrous **9** bodacious, Endsville, excellent, exemplary, exquisite, first-rate, high-grade, hunky-dory, marvelous, sollicker, top-flight, unrivaled, wonderful, wunderbar **10** first-class, hotsy-totsy, jack-a-dandy, out of sight, peachy-keen, phenomenal, remarkable, stupendous, super-duper, unrivalled
atom ~: 7 fission
find ~: 4 love **5** adore
Smashing __: 8 Pumpkins
smashup: 5 crash, wreck **6** impact **7** rear-end **8** accident
smatter: 6 shiver **7** shatter
smattering: 3 few **5** tinge, touch **6** snatch **7** handful
smaze: 3 fog
cousin: 4 smog
smear: 3 dab, mud, pan, rap, rub, tar **4** blob, blot, blur, coat, daub, foul, lick, slam, slop, slur, soil **5** abuse, apply, bribe, cover, dirty, libel, rip up, rub on, shame, spray, stain, sully, taint **6** bedaub, befoul, crud up, defame, defile, impugn, malign, mess up, scorch, smudge, spread, streak, vilify **7** asperse, blacken, blister, lambast, overlay, plaster, slander, spatter, tarnish, traduce **8** backbite, badmouth, belittle, besmirch, denounce, discolor, innuendo, lambaste, sling mud, throw mud **9** aspersion, denigrate, discredit, disparage, lubricate, poor-mouth **10** calumniate, defamation, imputation, spread over, stigmatize, villainize
on: 5 apply
smear-__: 5 sheet
smeared: 5 grimy, sooty **7** unclean
Smee: 4 mate **6** pirate
smell: 4 funk, odor, reek, tang **5** aroma, fetor, odour, savor, scent, sense, sniff, snuff, stink, trace, trail, whiff **6** breath, detect, foetor, inhale, stench **7** bouquet, essence, incense, perfume, suspect **8** identify, perceive **9** emanation, fetidness, fragrance, get wind of, redolence, suspicion
a rat: 5 doubt **7** suspect **8** distrust, mistrust **10** disbelieve
combining form: 3 osm-, ozo- **4** osmo-
detector: 4 nose
mask the ~ of: 6 purify **7** freshen, sweeten **8** sanitize **9** deodorize
(of): 5 smack
out: 3 spy **4** espy, find **5** catch, hit on, trace **6** detect, expose, locate, unmask **7** discern, uncover **8** discover, identify, pinpoint **9** ascertain, track down
science of ~: 6 osmics
sense of ~: 4 nose
smell __: 4 a rat
Smell! author: William Carlos Williams
smeller: 4 nose **5** snoot **6** beezer, honker, schnoz
smelling __: 5 salts **6** bottle
__ Smell of Success: 5 Sweet
smelly: 4 foul, olid, rank **5** fetid, funky,

musty, reeky, stale **6** foetid, frowsy, frowzy, putrid, rancid, rotten, stinky, strong **7** noisome, noxious, odorous, reeking **8** mephitic, stinking **10** malodorous
smelt: 4 fish **6** inanga, reduce **7** process **8** sparling
smeltery
input: 3 ore
leftover: 4 slag **5** dross
oxide: 4 calx
Smetana, Bedrich: 5 Czech **8** composer
work: The Bartered Bride
M Vlast
smew: 4 bird **9** merganser
relative: 4 teal **5** eider, Pekin, Rouen, scaup **6** Cayuga, scoter **7** gadwall, mallard, pintail, pochard, redhead, sea duck, widgeon **8** garganey, gray duck, mandarin, musk duck, oldsquaw, shoveler, surf duck, wood duck **9** black duck, broadbill, goldeneye, goosander, greenhead, ruddy duck, sprigtail **10** bufflehead, canvasback, surf scoter, tufted duck
smew: 4 duck, fowl
smidgen: 3 bit, dab, jot, tad **4** atom, dash, drop, iota, mite, snip, spot, whit, wisp **5** crumb, grain, pinch, shred, skosh, speck, trace **7** minimum, modicum **8** particle
Smight: 4 Jack
smilax: 5 plant **6** flower
smile: 4 beam, grin, luck **5** laugh, smirk **6** simper **9** say cheese **10** expression
bring a ~ to: 5 amuse
derisive ~: 5 sneer
feature: 6 dimple
sly ~: 4 leer **5** smirk
upon: 4 help **5** bless, favor, grace, shine **9** encourage
upside-down ~: 5 frown, scowl
Smile (1975 film)
cast: Bruce Dern, Barbara Feldon, Michael Kidd
director: Michael Ritchie
__ Smile: 4 Sara
__ Smile, A: 7 Certain
Smile a Little Smile for Me (1969 song)
artist: Flying Machine
__ Smile Be Your Umbrella: 4 Let a
Smiles of a Summer Night (1955 film)
director: Ingmar Bergman
Smile (song) artist: Tupac, Vitamin C
__ Smile Without You: 4 Can't
smiley __: 4 face
Smiley: 3 spy **5** agent
Smiley, Jane novel: 3 Moo
Smiley's People author: John le Carré
smiling: 5 riant, sunny **8** laughing **9** lightsome
keep ~: 5 cheer **6** divert, please, tickle **7** delight **9** entertain
Smiling Faces Sometimes (1971 song)
artist: Undisputed Truth
Smilin' Through (1932 film)
cast: Leslie Howard, Fredric March, Norma Shearer
director: Sidney Franklin
smilodon: 5 tiger
smirch: 4 slur **5** stain **6** bedaub **7** begrime, besmear, calumny, slander **8** backbite **10** calumniate, imputation
smirk: 4 grin, leer **5** fleer, smile, sneer **6** jibe at, simper **7** grimace, snicker, snigger **9** make a face **10** expression
cousin: 4 leer
Smirnoff: 5 vodka, Yakov
competitor: 5 Popov, Stoli
smite: 3 zap **4** bash, conk, flog, slay, slug, sock **5** flail, pound, punch, smash, visit, whack, whomp **6** batter, buffet, cudgel, hammer, pommel, pummel, strike, thrash, thwack, wallop **7** lambast, torment **8** bludgeon, lambaste **10** lay waste to, strike down
smith: 5 shoer **7** farrier **10** horseshoer
starter: 3 gun, tin **4** gold, iron, lock, song, tune, word **5** black, white **6** copper, silver
Smith: 2 E.E., O.C. **3** A.J.M., Bob, Hal, Ian, Lee, Liz, Red, Rex **4** Adam, John, Kate, Kent, Kerr, Lane, Seba, Stan, Will **5** Betty, Bubba, Dodie, Jacob, Keely, Kevin, Ozzie, Patti, Robyn, Roger, Sammi **6** Alexis, Bessie, Brooke, Cotter, Emmitt, Horton, Jaclyn, Joseph, Maggie, Stevie, Sydney, Thorne, Vernon **7** college, Lillian, Michael, Pinetop **8** Hamilton, Margaret, Yeardley
grad: 5 woman **6** alumna
partner: 6 Corona, Wesson
Smith! (1969 film)
cast: Glenn Ford, Dean Jagger, Nancy Olson
director: Michael O'Herlihy
__ Smith: 6 Granny, Nevada
Smith, Adam: 6 author, writer **8** Scottish **9** economist
work: The Wealth of Nations
Smith, A.J.M.: 4 poet **8** Canadian
Smith, Alexis: 7 actress
film: The Adventures of Mark Twain (1944)
The Constant Nymph (1943)
Gentleman Jim (1942)
The Horn Blows at Midnight (1945)
Night and Day (1946)
Rhapsody in Blue (1945)
San Antonio (1945)
The Sleeping Tiger (1954)
Tough Guys (1986)
The Woman in White (1948)
The Young Philadelphians (1959)
spouse: Craig Stevens
__ Smith and Jones: 5 Alias
Smith Brothers: 9 cough drop
competitor: 6 Luden's
feature: 5 beard
Smith, C. Aubrey: 3 Sir **5** actor
film: The Four Feathers (1939)
Little Lord Fauntleroy (1936)
Tarzan, the Ape Man (1932)
Wee Willie Winkie (1937)
Smith, Charles Martin: 5 actor
film: The Buddy Holly Story (1978)
Never Cry Wolf (1983)
The Untouchables (1987)
Smith, Emmitt sport: 8 football
smithereens: 5 atoms **6** pieces, scraps **8** flinders **9** particles
Smithereens (1982 film)
cast: Susan Berman, Richard Hell, Brad Rinn
director: Susan Seidelman
Smithers: 3 Jan
Smithfield __: 3 ham
Smith, H. Allen: 6 author, writer **8** humorist
Smith, Hamilton: 8 Nobelist
Smith, Hannibal group: 5 A-Team
Smith, Horton: 6 golfer
Smith, John perhaps: 5 alias
Smith, Kate film: The Big Broadcast (1932)
Smith, Keely spouse: Louis Prima
Smith, Kent: 5 actor
film: Cat People (1942)
Curse of the Cat People (1944)
Magic Town (1947)
My Foolish Heart (1949)
Smith, Lane: 5 actor
film: The Distinguished Gentleman (1992)
The Mighty Ducks (1992)
TV: Lois & Clark
Smith, Lee: 6 hurler **7** pitcher
Smith, Lillian
work: Strange Fruit
Smith, Maggie: 4 Dame **7** actress
film: California Suite (1978, AA)
The First Wives Club (1996)
Love and Pain (and the Whole Damn Thing) (1972)
Murder by Death (1976)
Othello (1965)
The Prime of Miss Jean Brodie (1969, AA)
A Room With a View (1986)
Sister Act (1992)
Young Cassidy (1965)
Smith, Michael: 7 chemist **8** Nobelist
Smith, O.C. song: Little Green Apples (1968)
Smith, Ozzie: 8 Cardinal **9** shortstop
Smith, Rex song: You Take My Breath Away (1979)
Smith, Robyn spouse: Fred Astaire
Smith, Roger spouse: Ann-Margret
Smiths: 4 city, town
locale: 7 Alabama
Smith, Sammi song: Help Me Make It Through the Night (1971)
Smith, Seba: 4 poet **8** humorist
Smithsonian: 6 museum
diamond: 4 Hope
locale: 10 Washington
smithsonite: 3 ore **7** mineral
Smith, Stan: 7 netster **9** tennis pro
milieu: 5 court
Smith, Stevie: 4 poet **7** British
Smith, Stuffy: 4 toon **5** comic **7** cartoon **10** comic strip
baby: 5 Tater
dog: 8 Ol' Bullet
__ Smith Surtees: 6 Robert
Smith, Thorne: 6 author, writer **8** humorist
creation: 6 Topper
Smithtown: 4 city
locale: 7 New York **10** Long Island
Smith, Vernon: 8 Nobelist **9** economist
Smith & Wesson: 3 gun
Smith, Will: 5 actor
film: Ali (2001)
Enemy of the State (1998)
Independence Day (1996)
The Legend of Bagger Vance (2000)
Men in Black (1997)
Men in Black II (2002)
Six Degrees of Separation (1993)
Wild Wild West (1999)
song: Gettin' Jiggy Wit It (1998)
Men in Black (1997)
Wild Wild West (1999)
spouse: Jada Pinkett
TV: Fresh Prince of Bel Air
smithy: 5 forge **9** ironworks
item: 4 shoe **9** horseshoe
tool: 5 anvil, tongs **6** hammer
Smitrovich: 4 Bill
Smits, Jimmy: 5 actor
film: My Family/Mi Familia (1995)
Old Gringo (1989)
Price of Glory (2000)
TV: L.A. Law, N.Y.P.D. Blue
smitten: 4 gaga **5** crazy, taken **6** in love **7** far gone **8** enamored **10** infatuated
smock: 4 coat **5** apron, frock **6** camise, duster **7** coverup, garment
smog: 3 fog **4** haze, mist **5** vapor **8** haziness **9** pollution
cousin: 5 smaze
smoke: 3 cig, run **4** cure, fume, puff, reek, tree **5** cigar, color, hurry, vapor **6** inhale, kipper, stogie **7** cheroot, incense, light up, process, smolder **8** fastball, preserve, smoulder **9** pollution
and mirrors: 6 deceit
bit of ~: 4 puff, wisp
detector: 5 alarm
emitter: 4 flue
ender: 5 house, stack **6** jumper, screen
go up in ~: 4 burn, fail **6** ignite
out: 4 find **5** learn **6** expose, locate
put up a ~ screen: 9 misinform
rid of ~: 6 air out
signal: 5 plume
tree: 6 fustet
smoke __: 3 out **4** bomb, dome, tree **5** alarm, shelf **6** screen **7** chamber
smoke-__: 3 dry
smoke-__ room: 6 filled
__ smoke: 3 sea **4** up in **5** frost **7** prairie
Smoke (1995 film)
cast: Stockard Channing, William Hurt, Harvey Keitel
director: Wayne Wang
Smoke __: 5 Rings **7** Signals
__ Smoke: 4 Up in **5** White
smoke and __: 7 mirrors
Smoke and Steel author: Carl Sandburg
smoked fish: 3 lox **6** salmon **7** herring
Smoke Gets in Your Eyes (1958 song)
artist: Platters
composer: 4 Kern **7** Harbach
smokehouse worker: 5 curer
smokejumper's need: 5 chute
smokeless __: 6 powder
Smoke on the Water (1973 song)
artist: Deep Purple
Smokeout sponsor: 3 ACS
smokescreen: 10 camouflage
Smokescreen author: Dick Francis
Smoke Signals (1998 film)
cast: Evan Adams, Adam Beach, Irene Bedard, Gary Farmer
director: Chris Eyre
smokestack: 4 flue **6** funnel
like a ~: 5 sooty
Smokey: 4 bear **6** Stover **8** Robinson
Smokey and the Bandit (1977 film)
cast: Sally Field, Jackie Gleason, Burt Reynolds
director: Hal Needham
dog: 4 Fred
__ Smokies: 5 Great
smoking: 3 hot **7** on a roll
smoking __: 3 gun **6** jacket
__-smoking: 3 non
Smoking or __?: 3 non
Smokin' in the Boys Room (song)
artist: Brownsville Station, Mötley Crüe
smoky: 4 fumy, gray, grey, hazy **5** black, dingy, grimy, mirky, murky, sooty, thick **6** fuming **7** burning, silvery **8** begrimed, vaporous **10** smoldering
smoky __: 5 topaz **6** quartz
Smoky (1946 film)
cast: Anne Baxter, Burl Ives, Fred MacMurray
__ Smoky Mountains: 5 Great
smoky quartz: 3 gem **8** gemstone
smolder: 4 boil, burn, fume, stir **5** smoke, steam **6** bubble, fester, seethe, simmer **7** consume, explode, ferment **9** fulminate
smoldering: 5 smoky **6** latent **10** unrealized
Smollett, Tobias: 6 writer **7** British
work: Peregrine Pickle
Roderick Random
smolt: 4 fish
smooch: 3 pet **4** buss, kiss, neck **5** spoon **8** osculate **10** osculation
__-Smoot: 6 Hawley
smooth: 3 pat, rub, sly **4** calm, ease, easy, even, file, flat, glib, iron, mild, nice, oily, rake, sand, soft, wily **5** adept, allay, bland, clear, fluid, flush,

glaze, gloss, grind, level, light, plain, plane, press, quiet, sheer, shiny, silky, sleek, slick, suave, sweet, touch 6 artful, crafty, creamy, facile, finish, flossy, fluent, genial, gentle, glassy, glazed, glossy, legato, liquid, mellow, polish, polite, refine, satiny, serene, shaven, shrewd, soften, stable, steady, stroke, tricky, urbane 7 appease, assuage, burnish, comfort, flatten, flowing, iron out, mollify, perfect, planate, politic, regular, roll out, uniform, varnish, velvety 8 dextrous, graceful, hairless, lustrous, mitigate, palliate, peaceful, pleasant, polished, readable, rhythmic, slippery, soothing, tranquil, unbroken, unctuous, untaxing 9 agreeable, alleviate, dexterous, lubricate, make peace, talkative, unruffled, unvarying 10 continuous, effortless, facilitate, horizontal, integrated, invariable, lubricated, mirrorlike, monotonous, nonchalant, pave the way, persuasive, rippleless, uneventful, untroubled, unwrinkled
along: 4 slip 5 slide
combining form: 3 lio- 4 leio-
in phonetics: 4 lene
make ~: 4 sand 5 shave 9 lubricate
on: 6 spread
out: 4 even, iron
over: 6 defuse, defuze, disarm, lessen, pacify, soften, soothe 7 mollify 8 moderate 9 untrouble
sailing: 4 snap 6 picnic
the way: 5 set up 6 loosen 7 further, lighten 8 expedite, mitigate, moderate, simplify
very ~: 5 silky
smooth-___: 4 talk 5 faced 6 shaven, spoken 7 tongued
Smooth (1999 song) artist: Santana
smooth as ___: 4 silk 5 satin
Smooth Criminal (1988 song) artist: Michael Jackson
smoothly: 4 even, well 6 legato 7 lightly 10 swimmingly
in music: 6 legato
smoothness: 4 ease, tact, woof 6 polish 7 fluency, texture 8 facility, fluidity 9 clockwork, dexterity
Smooth Operator (1985 song) artist: Sade
smooth-pated: 4 bald
smooth-shaven: 9 beardless
smooth-spoken: 4 glib, oily 5 slick, suave, vocal 6 fluent
smorgasbord: 4 meal 5 feast 6 buffet
enjoy a ~: 3 eat
item: 3 ham 5 pasta, roast, salad
smother: 4 heap, lick, rein, trim 5 cover, douse, dowse, quash, quell, snuff 6 hush up, muffle, put out, quench, shower, shroud, stifle 7 blow out, control, envelop, lambast, oppress, repress, squelch 8 inundate, keep down, lambaste, restrain, stamp out, suppress, surround 9 keep quiet, overwhelm 10 extinguish
smothered: 6 pent-up
Smothers: 3 Tom 4 Dick 5 Tommy
Smothers Brothers: 3 duo 4 pair
Smothers, Tom hobby: 4 yo-yo
SMU
athlete: 7 Mustang
conference: 3 WAC
locale: 5 Texas 6 Dallas
Smucker's: 3 jam 5 jelly
alternative: 5 Kraft 6 Knott's, Welch's 7 Polaner
smudge: 3 dab 4 blob, blot, blur, daub, foul, mark, slop, soil, spot 5 blear, dirty, grime, smear, stain, sully, taint 6 bedaub, befoul, blotch, crud up, defile 7 begrime, besmear, blacken, blemish, plaster, pollute, spatter, tarnish 8 besmirch
smudge ___: 3 pot
smudged: 5 dirty, grimy, sooty 6 filthy, grubby, grungy 7 unclean 8 maculate, slovenly, unwashed 10 unsanitary
smug: 4 prim, vain 5 cocky, proud, saucy 6 stuffy 7 content, fustian, haughty, hotshot, pompous, prudish, stuck-up 8 arrogant, boastful, cocksure, egoistic, gloating, priggish, puffed-up, snobbish, superior 9 bigheaded, conceited, hubristic, overproud, righteous 10 big-talking, complacent, egoistical
be ~: 5 gloat
look: 4 grin, leer 5 smirk, sneer 6 simper
one: 4 prig
smuggle: 4 deal, hide, push 5 sneak 6 export, pirate 7 bootleg, snake in
smuggled: 7 illegal 9 forbidden 10 prohibited, proscribed
smuggler unit: 4 kilo
smuggling: 10 contraband, rum-running
smugness: 5 pride 6 vanity 7 conceit
smurf: 5 dance
Smurf: 4 toon 7 cartoon
cat: 6 Azrael
color: 4 blue
smush: 8 compress
smut: 5 filth, grime 6 fungus 8 lewdness 9 lubricity
smutch: 5 grime
Smuts, Jan: 4 Boer
smuttiness: 8 lewdness 9 bawdiness, crassness, indecency, vulgarity 10 coarseness, earthiness, indelicacy
smutty: 3 raw 4 foul, lewd, racy 5 bawdy, crude, dirty, nasty, rough 6 coarse, filthy, ribald, risqué, vulgar, X-rated 7 immoral, obscene, profane, raunchy 8 improper, indecent, off-color, unwashed 9 low-minded, salacious 10 indelicate, scurrilous
Smyrna: 4 city, port, town
locale: 5 Ionia 6 Aeolia 7 Georgia 9 Tennessee
Smyrna ___: 3 fig
Smyslov, Vasily forte: 5 chess
Smyth: 5 Patty
Smyth ___: 6 sewing
Sn: 3 tin 4 elem. 7 element
50 for ~: 4 at. no.
S.N.: 7 Behrman
snack: 3 eat, tea 4 bite, eats, gorp, grub, Ho Ho, meal, nosh, nuts, Oreo, taco 5 break, candy, chips, goody, knish, munch, nacho, piece, Smore, sweet 6 canapé, Fritos, goodie, morsel, nibble, pepita, tidbit 7 Cheetos, Doritos, falafel, goodies, munchie, peanuts, popcorn, pretzel 8 candy bar, carnitas, fast food, junk food, munchies, pick-me-up, pretzels, rice cake 9 collation, corn chips, pork rinds
like ~ dispensers: 6 coin-op
snack ___: 3 bar 5 table
snacks, like some: 5 salty, sweet
snafu: 3 err 4 goof, muff 5 boner, botch, chaos, error, hitch, mix up 6 bollix, foul-up, glitch, mishap, muddle 7 mistake, screwup 8 disorder 9 mare's nest
snag: 3 bar, bug, get, jag, nab, rip, rub, run 4 clog, curb, grab, knot, nail, stub, tear, trap 5 block, brake, catch, crimp, hitch, point, seize, stick 6 arrest, crunch, glitch, hamper, hang-up, holdup, hurdle, kicker, obtain, pickle, scrape, snatch, tangle 7 acquire, barrier, ensnare, insnare, pitfall, problem, puzzler, receive, setback 8 blockade, drawback, entangle, grab away, obstacle, tangle up 9 hindrance, roadblock, tight spot 10 bottleneck, difficulty, impediment, limitation
___ snag: 4 hit a
snail: 4 apod 5 whelk 7 dawdler, mollusc, mollusk 8 escargot, seashell, slowpoke
home: 5 shell
kin: 4 slug
snail ___: 4 bore, mail 6 darter
snail-___: 5 paced
___ snail: 3 awl, lig, sea 4 cone, land, tree 5 giant, water
snaillike: 4 poky, slow 5 slimy, tardy 6 apodal, draggy 7 apodous, gradual, halting, impeded, lagging, languid 8 crawling, creeping, dawdling, dilatory, dragging, drawn-out, hesitant, plodding, slothful, sluggish, toddling 9 leisurely, lethargic, prolonged, unhurried 10 deliberate, protracted
snail-mail alternative: 3 fax
___ snail's pace: 3 at a
snake: 3 asp, boa, cur 4 apod, coil, curl, fink, lurk, toad, turn, wind 5 adder, cobra, creep, curve, dance, knave, krait, mamba, racer, shirk, slink, snake, sneak, steal, swirl, twist, viper, weave 6 animal, bad guy, elapid, hisser, python, ramble, ratter, taipan 7 meander, rattler, reptile, schemer, serpent, sinuate, slither, wriggle 8 betrayer, cerastes, moccasin, ophidian, quisling, renegade, ringhals, rinkhals, turncoat 9 coachwhip, intriguer, slitherer 10 bushmaster, copperhead, fer-de-lance, sidewinder
African ~: 3 asp 5 cobra, mamba 8 ringhals 9 boomslang
Asian ~: 5 krait 6 dhaman, taipan
charmer's partner: 5 cobra
combining form: 4 ophi- 5 ophio-
covering: 5 scale
dancer: 4 Hopi
emulate a ~: 4 molt 5 crawl, slink 7 slither
ender: 4 bird, bite, fish, head, root, skin, weed 5 mouth, stone
in the grass: 5 knave, rogue, sneak 7 traitor 8 turncoat 9 scoundrel
like a ~: 5 scaly 6 apodal 7 apodous
mesmerize a ~: 5 charm
Mexican ~: 9 coachwhip
oil: 6 humbug
oil, supposedly: 4 cure
on Pharaoh's headdress: 3 asp
place for a ~: 5 drain
poison: 5 venom
poisonous ~: 3 asp 5 adder, cobra, krait, mamba, viper
science: 9 ophiology
shape: 3 ess
sound: 3 sss 4 hiss, siss, ssss
starter: 6 rattle
tooth: 4 fang
snake ___: 3 oil, pit 4 eyes, foot, lily, palm 5 dance, fence, plant 6 doctor, feeder 7 charmer
___ snake: 3 fox, mud, rat, sea 4 bull, corn, hoop, king, lyre, milk, pine, pipe, ring, vine, wart, whip, worm 5 black, blind, congo, coral, glass, grass, green, house, night, tiger, water 6 carpet, garter, glossy, gopher, indigo, ribbon, ringed 7 chicken, hognose, rainbow
Snake: 5 river
locale: 5 Idaho 7 Wyoming 10 Washington
snakebite plant: 5 guaco
Snake Eater actor: 5 Lamas
snake eyes: 3 two
roll ~: 4 lose
snakelike fish: 3 eel 5 moray 7 lamprey
Snake Pit, The (1948 film)
cast: Olivia de Havilland, Leo Genn, Mark Stevens
director: Anatole Litvak
Snakes and Ladders: 4 game
snaky: 3 sly 4 wavy 5 sharp 6 aspish, coiled, crafty, curved, sneaky, subtle, vipery, zigzag 7 crooked, devious, lurking, sinuous, twisted, winding 8 entwined, flexuous, guileful, indirect, slinking, tortuous, twisting, two-faced, venomous, writhing 9 deceitful, insidious, meandrous 10 convoluted, meandering, serpentine, traitorous, treasonous
character: 3 ess
shape: 4 coil
snap: 2 go 3 nip, pep, pic, pop 4 bark, bean, bite, dash, ease, easy, élan, flip, game, grab, grip, jerk, kick, vent, yank, yell, zest 5 break, catch, cinch, clack, click, crack, cushy, flare, flash, flick, go ape, grasp, growl, grunt, lurch, photo, seize, shoot, snarl, snick, split, verve, vigor 6 bite at, breeze, clutch, cookie, fasten, fillip, lose it, picnic, retort, simple, snatch 7 crackle, give way, go crazy, grumble, lash out, no sweat, panache, shatter 8 break off, card game, duck soup, fastener, fracture, go postal, kid stuff, painless, pushover, separate, vitality, vivacity, walkover, workable 9 animation, briskness, come apart, easy as pie, go bananas, go berserk, go bonkers, no problem 10 child's play, effortless, get up and go, hit the roof, photograph, resilience, unexacting
alternative: 6 button, Velcro, zipper
back: 6 bounce 7 rebound, recover
call: 3 hut 6 hut one, hut two
cold ~: 5 frost
out of it: 5 rally 6 revive 9 take heart
starter: 6 ginger
to attention: 6 salute
to it: 6 hasten
up: 3 get, nab 4 grab, take 5 seize 8 pounce on
snap ___: 3 pea 4 back, bean, link, ring, roll 6 course
snap ___ it: 5 out of
___ snap: 4 cold 6 ginger
Snap! ___! Pop!: 7 Crackle
snap-brim: 3 hat 6 fedora
snapdragon: 5 plant 6 flower
snap one's ___ off: 4 head
snapper: 4 croc, fish, jocu, sesi 5 gator 6 animal 7 reptile 9 alligator, crocodile
photo ~: 6 camera
starter: 7 whipper
trapper: 3 net 5 seine
___ snapper: 3 red 4 gray, grey 6 mutton
snappiness: 5 spice 10 impatience
snapping ___: 6 beetle, shrimp, turtle
snappish: 4 curt, edgy, sour, tart 5 huffy, moody, onery, surly, testy, upset 6 crabby, cranky, crusty, feisty, fretty, grumpy, ireful, morose, ornery, snarly, touchy 7 bearish, bilious, crabbed, fretful, grouchy, huffish, nervous, peevish, peppery, prickly, waspish 8 choleric, fretsome, growling, grumpish, petulant 9 crotchety, fractious, irascible, irritable, querulous, splenetic
Snapple: 5 drink 8 beverage 9 soft drink
snappy: 4 chic, edgy, fast, pert, racy, sour, tart 5 brisk, crisp, cross, fleet, gruff, hasty, huffy, nasty, onery, quick, rapid, sharp, short, smart, spicy, swank, swift, terse, testy 6 abrupt, classy, crabby, dapper, fretty, gnomic, lively, modish, ornery, speedy, spicey, sudden, swanky, touchy, trendy

7 dashing, grouchy, huffish, instant, peevish, peppery, stylish, voguish 8 petulant, spirited 9 breakneck, energetic, fractious, immediate, irascible, irritable, on-the-spot, querulous, sprightly 10 harefooted
make it ~: 3 hie 4 rush
snapshot: 3 pic 5 photo, print 6 candid 7 picture 8 portrait 10 photograph
collection: 5 album
snap the —: 4 whip
snare: 3 bag, gin, nab, net, web 4 bait, drum, hook, land, lure, mire, trap 5 catch, decoy, noose, seize, tempt, trick 6 arrest, cobweb, come-on, corral, dupery, enmesh, entice, entrap, immesh, inmesh, pilfer, pull in 7 capture, involve, pitfall, round up 8 entangle, interest 9 booby trap, deception, quicksand 10 allurement, enticement, entrapment, temptation
snare —: 4 drum
snarl: 3 jam, web 4 bark, gnar, knot, maze, mesh, mess, muck, snap 5 bully, chaos, gnarl, growl, gum up, jam-up, swarm, tie-up, twist 6 enmesh, immesh, inmesh, jumble, jungle, knot up, mess up, morass, muddle, mutter, tangle 7 clutter, confuse, embroil, ensnare, entwine, grumble, insnare, intwine, mistake, perplex, problem, quarrel, thunder 8 disarray, disorder, entangle, mishmash, obstacle, threaten 9 confusion, labyrinth 10 complexity, complicate, congestion, difficulty, traffic jam
up: 3 err 6 jumble, muddle, tousle, touzle 7 confuse 8 dishevel, disorder, scramble 10 complicate
snarleyyow: 3 dog 6 canine
snarly: 5 onery, surly 6 crusty, ornery 7 bearish 8 snappish 9 irritable, splenetic 10 out of sorts
snatch: 3 bit, nab, win 4 gain, grab, grip, jerk, jump, loot, nail, pull, snag, snap, take, tear, yank 5 catch, clasp, grasp, piece, pinch, pluck, seize, spell, steal, theft, wrest 6 abduct, assume, clutch, collar, jump at, kidnap, pilfer, pounce, rescue, wrench 7 capture, grapple, oddment, plunder, seizure, snippet 8 fragment, grab away, jerk away, thievery 10 commandeer, run off with, smattering, spirit away
Snatch (2000 film)
cast: Benicio Del Toro, Dennis Farina, Brad Pitt
director: Guy Ritchie
snazziness: 5 style
snazzy: 5 dandy, jazzy, natty, plush, ritzy, showy, sleek, swank 6 classy, dapper, flashy, jaunty, rakish, spiffy, sporty, swanky 7 refined, stylish 10 flamboyant
Snead, Sam: 6 golfer
milieu: 5 links 6 course
org.: 3 PGA
sneak: 3 cur, pad, sly 4 case, heel, hide, lurk, shoe, slip, toad, worm 5 cower, crawl, creep, evade, glide, louse, mooch, prowl, sculk, shirk, sidle, skulk, skunk, slide, slink, snake, steal, swipe 6 ambush, delude, rascal, weasel, wretch 7 cheater, deceive, gumshoe, slither, smuggle, traitor 8 informer, stealthy 9 con artist, miscreant, pussyfoot, scoundrel 10 ambushment, nose around
along: 5 sidle
a look: 3 pry, see, spy 4 peek, peep, peer 5 snoop 6 glance 7 glimpse
alternative: 3 moc
around: 5 steal
attack: 6 ambush 10 ambushment
away: 7 abscond
by: 4 pass 6 elapse
in: 5 crash, enter 10 infiltrate
off: 5 elope 6 desert 8 slip away
peek: 6 prevue 7 preview
up on: 8 surprise
sneak —: 5 a peek, thief 6 attack 7 preview
sneaker: 4 shoe 7 gym shoe, high top 8 footwear
brand: 4 Avia, Keds, Nike, Puma 6 Adidas, Reebok
in Britain: 8 plimsoll
part: 3 toe 4 lace, sole 6 eyelet
Sneakers (1992 film)
cast: Dan Aykroyd, Ben Kingsley, Mary McDonnell, Robert Redford
director: Phil Alden Robinson
sneakily: 8 on the sly
sneaky: 3 low, sly 4 base, mean, wily 5 nasty, snaky, snide 6 covert, feline, shifty, tricky 7 devious, furtive, knavish 8 guileful, indirect, slippery, stealthy, thieving, thievish 9 deceitful, deceptive, dishonest, insidious, malicious, secretive, underhand, unethical 10 unfaithful, unreliable
maneuver: 4 ploy
sneaky —: 4 pete
snee: 4 dirk 5 knife 6 dagger
sneer: 4 dump, gibe, grin, jeer, jest, jibe, leer, mock, slam, twit 5 crack, decry, fleer, flout, scoff, scorn, smirk, spurn, swipe, taunt 6 deride, insult, jibe at, slight 7 affront, burlesk, condemn, contemn, detract, disdain, grimace, lampoon, put down, slander, snicker, sniff at, snigger 8 belittle, ridicule, satirize, sneeze at 9 burlesque, dirty look, disparage 10 caricature, expression, look down on
sneering: 5 snide 7 cynical 8 derision, sardonic 9 sarcastic
sneeze
at: 4 mock 5 scorn, sneer, spurn 6 ignore 7 dismiss 8 brush off, laugh off, ridicule, shrug off 9 disregard
ender: 4 weed, wort
response: 8 bless you
sound: 5 achoo 6 ahchoo, hachoo 7 kerchoo
Sneezy: 5 dwarf
colleague: 3 Doc 5 Dopey, Happy 6 Grumpy, Sleepy 7 Bashful
Sneffels: 4 peak 5 mount 8 mountain
locale: 7 Rockies 8 Colorado
Snellen —: 4 test 5 chart
Snell, George: 8 Nobelist
Snell's —: 3 law
Snerd partner: 6 Bergen 7 Klinker
Sneva, Tom: 5 racer 9 auto racer
milieu: 5 track
Snezka: 4 peak 5 mount 8 mountain
locale: 6 Europe, Poland
— S. Ngor: 5 Haing
snick: 3 cut 4 snap 5 click
snick-—: 5 a-snee
snick and —: 4 snee
snicker: 5 laugh, smirk, sneer, te-hee 6 giggle, guffaw, hee-haw, heehee, teehee, titter 7 chortle, chuckle 8 laughter
derisive ~: 3 heh
ender: 4 snee
snickering: 8 giggling, laughing
Snickers: 3 bar 4 nosh 5 candy, snack 9 chocolate
alternative: 4 Mars, Twix 5 Clark, Heath 6 Kit Kat, Mounds, PayDay, Reese's, Zagnut 7 Krackel, Oh Henry 8 Baby Ruth, Hershey's, Milky Way 9 Almond Joy, Mr. Goodbar 10 NutRageous
snide: 4 base, mean 5 catty, nasty 6 sneaky, unkind 7 caustic, hateful, hurtful 8 derisive, scoffing, scornful, sneering, spiteful 9 insulting, malicious, sarcastic 10 derogatory, evil-minded
remark: 4 barb 5 crack 6 zinger
Snider: 3 Dee 4 Duke
Snider, Duke: 6 Dodger 10 outfielder
teammate: 3 Roe 5 Reese 6 Hodges 7 Erskine, Furillo 8 Newcombe, Robinson
sniff: 4 odor 5 aroma, scent, smell, whiff 6 detect, inhale 7 inspire, snuffle 9 breathe in 10 inhalation
around: 3 pry 4 nose
at: 5 scorn, sneer 7 contemn, disdain 10 look down on
out: 4 seek 6 detect, locate 9 track down
sniffle: 10 inhalation
sniffles: 4 cold
have the ~: 3 ail
sniffy: 7 haughty
snifter: 5 glass 6 goblet
contents: 6 brandy, cognac
snig: 3 eel
sniggler: 5 eeler
snare: 6 eelpot
spot: 6 eelery
snip: 3 bit, cut, nip 4 brat, clip, crop, minx, mite, nick, trim 5 crumb, fleck, prune, shave, shred, speck, touch 6 cut off, delete, hoiden, hoyden, morsel, remove, sliver, trifle 7 abridge, cut back, cut into, cutting, remnant, scissor, shorten, smidgen, smidgin 8 clipping, fragment, smidgeon 10 thimbleful
and tuck: 5 alter
off: 5 prune, shave, shear
snipe: 4 bird, fowl, jeer 5 wader 9 criticize, sandpiper
(at): 4 fire
relative: 5 poult, quail 6 avocet, chukar, godwit, grouse, peahen, turkey 7 peacock, peafowl 8 curassow, moorfowl, pheasant, woodcock 9 partridge 10 guinea fowl, jungle fowl, wild turkey
Sniper, The (1952 film)
cast: Arthur Franz, Adolphe Menjou, Marie Windsor
director: Edward Dmytryk
Snipes, Wesley: 5 actor
film: The Art of War (2000)
Blade (1998)
Demolition Man (1993)
Down in the Delta (1998)
The Fan (1996)
Jungle Fever (1991)
Mo' Better Blues (1990)
Murder at 1600 (1997)
Passenger 57 (1992)
Rising Sun (1993)
U.S. Marshals (1998)
The Waterdance (1992)
White Men Can't Jump (1992)
snippet: 3 bit 4 wisp 5 scrap, shred, trace 6 little, sliver, snatch 7 oddment 8 clipping 9 sound bite
snippy: 4 curt, flip, pert, rude, tart 5 brusk, fresh, gruff, nervy, sassy, saucy, short 6 abrupt, awless, brazen, cheeky 7 aweless, brusque, uncivil 8 churlish, flippant, impolite, impudent, insolent 9 irascible, irritable, out of line
snit: 4 huff, stew 5 pique, tizzy 6 lather, temper 7 tantrum 8 hissy fit 9 huffiness, surliness
in a ~: 3 mad 4 sore 5 cross, huffy, irate, upset, vexed
put in a ~: 3 irk 4 miff, rile 5 anger, peeve, upset
snitch: 3 rat, rob 4 blab, fink, lift, loot, nark, sing, take, tell 5 filch, rat on, steal, swipe 6 squeal, tattle 7 ratfink, tattler, traitor 8 fat mouth 10 taleteller, tattletale
in British ~: 4 nark
on: 4 name 6 turn in
snivel: 3 cry, sob 4 bawl, mewl, pule, wail, weep 5 whine 6 boohoo 7 blubber, grumble, whimper 8 languish
sniveling: 5 weepy 7 tearful, wet-eyed
SNL: Saturday Night Live
Sno-—: 3 Cat 4 Caps, Cone
snob: 5 snoot 6 egoist 7 Brahmin, elitist, high-hat, upstart 8 braggart, highbrow 9 swellhead 10 downlooker, narcissist
put-on: 4 airs
snob —: 6 appeal
snobbery: 4 airs 5 pride 10 narcissism, pretension
snobbish: 4 smug, vain 5 aloof, cocky, proud 6 la-de-da, la-di-da, lordly, remote, snooty, stuffy, uppity 7 fustian, haughty, high-hat, pompous, stuck-up 8 arrogant, boastful, lah-di-dah, superior 9 big-headed, conceited, egotistic, exclusive, hubristic 10 hoity-toity
set: 6 clique
snobbishness: 7 hauteur
Snobol: 8 language
alternative: 3 ADA, APL, SQL 4 Alef, html, Icon, Java, LISP, Logo, Orca, Perl 5 Algol, Basic, Cecil, COBOL, Dylan, SISAL 6 Delphi, Eiffel, Erlang, Oberon, Pascal, Prolog, Sather, Scheme 7 Fortran
Sno-Caps: 4 nosh 5 candy, snack
Snodgress: 6 Carrie
snood: 3 net 7 hairnet 8 headband
snook: 4 fish
snooker: 3 con 4 game, pool 5 trick
need: 3 cue 5 table
snookums: 2 jo 3 hon, pet 4 baby, dear, jill, love 5 amour, angel, chéri, cooky, cutey, cutie, deary, ducky, flame, honey, leman, lover, lovey, novia, novio, sugar, sweet 6 bon ami, chérie, cookie, dautie, dearie, steady, sweets 7 beloved, dearest, dear one, pigsney, schatzi, squeeze, sweetie, tootsie 8 chou-chou, cutie pie, dowsabel, dulcinea, ladylove, lovebird, macushla, paramour, precious, sugar pie, sweetums, truelove 9 bonne amie, boyfriend, dreamboat, inamorata, inamorato, petit chou, valentine 10 girlfriend, heartthrob, honeybunch, mavourneen, sweetheart, sweetie pie, turtledove
Snooky: 6 Lanson
snoop: 3 pry, spy 4 lurk, peek, peep, peer, poke 5 noser, prier, pryer, scout, spy on 6 butt in, ferret, gossip, meddle, search, shamus, sleuth 7 gumshoe, intrude, meddler 8 busybody, quidnunc 9 detective, eavesdrop, interfere 10 nose around, poke around, sneak a look
prone to ~: 4 nosy 5 nosey
Snoop Doggy Dogg: 6 rapper
born: Calvin Broadus
rival: 5 Dr. Dre
song: Come and Get With Me (1998)
Dre Day (1993)
Gin & Juice (1994)
Nuthin' But a 'G' Thang (1993)
What's My Name? (1993)
snoopiness: 6 prying 8 interest, meddling, nosiness 9 curiosity
snoopy: 4 busy, nosy 5 nosey 7 curious, ferrety, peering 8 invasive 10 meddlesome
one: 5 prier, pryer
Snoopy: 3 dog 6 beatle

brother: 4 Olaf
enemy: 8 Red Baron
sister: 5 Belle
Snoopy, Come Home (1972 film) director: Bill Melendez
Snoopy vs. the Red Baron (1966 song) artist: Royal Guardsmen
snoot: 4 beak, nose, snob 6 beezer, schnoz 7 grimace, high-hat, schnozz 8 highbrow 9 proboscis, schnozzle 10 high-hatter, schnozzola
snootiness: 4 airs
snooty: 5 aloof, lofty, proud 6 la-de-da, la-di-da, uppity 7 haughty 8 arrogant, boastful, cavalier, lah-di-dah, snobbish 9 hubristic 10 disdainful
one: 4 snob
snooze: 3 nap 4 doze, rest, yawn 5 sleep 6 catnap, drowse, nod off, siesta 7 drop off, saw logs, slumber 10 fall asleep, forty winks
end one's ~: 4 wake
sound: 3 zzz
snoozing: 4 abed 6 asleep 7 dormant 9 sacked out, somnolent, unmindful 10 sawing logs
snoozy: 4 lazy 6 drowsy, sleepy 7 languid 9 lethargic, soporific
Snopes: 4 Flem
Snoqualmie ___: 5 Falls
snore: 5 sleep 6 wheeze 7 saw logs, saw wood, snuffle 8 rhonchus
sound: 3 zzz
snorkel: 4 tube
alternative: 5 scuba
snorkeler
site: 6 lagoon
view: 5 coral
Snorkel, Sergeant bulldog: 4 Otto
Snorri Sturluson
work: Edda
Olaf's Saga
snort: 3 nip 4 belt, huff, pant, swig 5 drink, laugh, whiff 6 inhale 8 laughter 9 jiggerful 10 inhalation
of disgust: 3 hah, ugh 5 humph
snorting starter: 3 rip
snout: 4 beak, nose 5 trunk 6 muzzle, schnoz 7 schnozz 9 proboscis, schnozzle 10 schnozzola
combining form: 6 rhynch- 7 rhyncho-
snow: 3 lie 4 bilk, dupe, fool, hoax, sell 5 bluff, cheat, outdo, storm, trick, white 6 delude, powder, puzzle, take in 7 beguile, deceive, mislead, two-time, wheedle 8 bewilder, blizzard, fast-talk, flurries, hoodwink, inundate, inveigle, pettifog 9 bamboozle, disinform, four-flush, influence, overwhelm, victimize 10 run a game on
bump in ~: 5 mogul
combining form: 4 chio- 5 chion- 6 chiono-
creation: 4 fort
crystal: 5 flake
ender: 3 cap, man 4 ball, bell, bird, bush, drop, fall, melt, plow, shoe, suit 5 berry, blink, board, bound, brush, drift, flake, storm 6 capped, mobile
glider: 4 luge, sled 8 toboggan
goose: 4 fowl
granular ~: 4 firn, névé
job: 3 lie 4 hoax, ruse, sham 5 cheat, feint, fraud 6 deceit, dupery, humbug 7 swindle 8 artifice, trickery 9 deception, imposture 10 persuasion, subterfuge
light ~: 6 flurry
like ~: 4 cold, pure 5 white
lover: 5 skier
melter: 4 NaCl, salt 6 halite
melting ~: 5 slush
move ~: 4 blow, plow 5 sweep 6 shovel
navigate on ~: 3 ski 4 skee
pertaining to ~: 5 nival
relative: 4 bone, milk 5 cream, ivory, milky 6 argent, oyster, silver 8 eggshell
sign of ~: 6 nimbus
skier's ~: 4 corn
under: 5 swamp 6 deluge, engulf, ingulf 8 inundate 9 overwhelm
snow ___: 3 day, ice, job, pea 4 cone, crab, crop, lily, line, mold, pear, ring, tire 5 apple, board, cover, crust, fence, gauge, goose, guard, plant, train, under 6 banner, blower, flurry, grains 7 bunting, crystal, leopard, pellets, pudding, thrower
snow-___: 4 clad 5 broth, white 6 capped
___ snow: 3 red 4 corn 6 powder, spring 7 tapioca
...snow, ___ rain...: 3 nor
Snow: 2 C.P. 4 Hank 6 Phoebe
Snow ___: 4 Belt
Snow ___, The: 5 Queen 6 Maiden, Walker 7 Leopard
snowball: 4 grow 5 plant, raise, shrub 6 flower 7 burgeon, dessert, enlarge 8 bourgeon, ice cream, increase
alternative: 6 gelati, gelato, sundae 7 parfait, spumone, spumoni, tortoni
impact sound: 5 splat
relative: 5 elder 6 abelia
sometimes: 4 ammo
snowbank: 5 drift
snowberry: 5 plant 6 flower
snowbird: 5 junco
Snowbird (1970 song) artist: Anne Murray
snowboarding: 5 sport
Snow-Bound: 4 poem
author: 8 Whittier
snowbush: 5 shrub
snowcapped: 8 towering
Snow, C.P.: 6 writer 7 British
work: Corridors of Power
The New Men
The Search
Strangers and Brothers
snowdrop: 5 plant 6 flower
snowfield: 4 firn
snowflake-like: 4 lacy
snow leopard: 3 cat, fur 5 felid 6 feline
relative: 4 eyra, lion, lynx, puma 5 chita, liger, tiger, tigon 6 bobcat, cheeta, chetah, cougar, jaguar, margay, ocelot, serval, tiglon 7 bay lynx, caracal, cheetah, panther 9 catamount 10 jaguarundi
Snow Leopard, The author: Peter Matthiessen
Snow Maiden, The: 5 opera
composer: Rimsky-Korsakov
snowman
abominable ~: 4 yeti
nose: 6 carrot
wear: 3 hat 4 pipe 5 scarf
Snowmass: 6 resort 9 ski resort
locale: 8 Colorado
snowmobiler: 5 rider
snowmobiling: 5 sport
snow mold: 6 fungus
Snow, Phoebe song: Poetry Man (1975)
snowplow target: 5 drift
Snow Queen, The author: Hans Christian Andersen
snowshoe
alternative: 3 ski 4 skee
snowshoe ___: 4 hare 6 rabbit
snowslide: 9 avalanche
Snows of Kilimanjaro, The (1952 film)
cast: Ava Gardner, Susan Hayward, Gregory Peck
director: Henry King
Snows of Kilimanjaro, The author: Ernest Hemingway
snowstorm: 8 blizzard
Snow-Storm, The: 4 poem
author: 7 Emerson
Snow Walker, The author: Farley Mowat
Snow White
and her friends: 5 octad, octet
friend: 3 Doc 5 Dopey, dwarf, Happy 6 Grumpy, Sleepy, Sneezy 7 Bashful
snowy: 3 wet 4 cold, pure 5 clean, white 6 washed, wintry 7 niveous, wintery 8 spotless, unsoiled 9 laundered 10 immaculate
month: 3 Dec., Feb., Jan. 7 January 8 December, February
snowy ___: 3 owl 5 egret 6 plover
Snowy: 6 bleach
alternative: 5 Purex, Vivid 6 Clorox 8 Borateem
snub: 3 cut, dig 4 barb, duck, gibe, go by, jeer, jibe, mock, shun, slam, slap, slur 5 abuse, decry, libel, scold, scorn, spurn, taunt 6 defame, deride, dump on, heckle, humble, ignore, impugn, insult, little, malign, offend, pass up, rebuff, rebuke, slight, vilify 7 affront, asperse, boycott, calumny, catcall, censure, contemn, degrade, disdain, high-hat, mockery, neglect, obloquy, offense, putdown, rank out, repulse, scratch, slander, traduce, upstage 8 belittle, brushoff, contempt, denounce, derision, pass over, ridicule, skip over, vilipend 9 aspersion, blackball, contumely, denigrate, discredit, disparage, disregard, humiliate, indignity, ostracize 10 calumniate, defamation, disrespect, opprobrium
snub-___: 5 nosed
snuck: 5 crept 7 prowled, skulked
snuff: 5 douse, dowse, smell 10 extinguish
bring up to ~: 5 rehab 6 repair
ender: 3 box
out: 5 douse, dowse 6 quench 7 blow out 8 suppress 10 extinguish
up to ~: 3 fit 4 able, good 5 sound 7 capable 9 competent, qualified 10 acceptable
___ snuff: 4 up to
snug: 4 cosy, cozy, firm, homy, safe, soft, taut, tidy, trim, warm 5 close, comfy, cozey, cozie, cushy, homey, rigid, stiff, tight 6 nestle 7 compact, livable, restful, tighten 8 homelike, intimate, liveable, tucked in 9 cuddled up, sheltered 10 convenient
bug locale: 3 rug
make ~: 4 tuck 6 nestle
spot: 3 den 4 nest 6 hearth
snug ___ bug...: 3 as a
snuggle: 3 hug 4 neck 5 spoon 6 bundle, burrow, caress, cozy up, cuddle, curl up, huddle, nestle, nuzzle 8 ensconce, huddle up
Snuggle alternative: 5 Downy 6 Bounce 9 Cling Free 10 Final Touch
snuggly: 4 soft 6 cuddly 7 lovable 8 huggable, loveable 10 cuddlesome
snugness: 4 ease 7 comfort 8 coziness
Snyder: 3 Tom 4 Gary, Liza
Snyder, Gary: 4 poet
work: The Back Country
Regarding Wave
Turtle Island
so: 4 a lot, lots, then, thus, true, very 5 hence, quite 6 actual, indeed 7 correct, factual, for real, that way 8 accurate, likewise, truthful 9 certainly, in this way, therefore 10 definitely, positively, unimagined, unmistaken
in Latin: 3 sic 4 ergo
much as: 4 even
so ___: 3 far 4 as to, long, much, that, what 5 far as
so ___ and yet...: 4 near
so ___ as: 3 far 4 long, much
so ___ I know: 5 far as
so ___ me: 4 help
so ___ so good: 3 far
so-___: 5 and-so 6 called
___ so: 3 how 4 ever
___ so!: 5 T'aint
___ so?: 3 How
___-so: 3 say
...so ___ as a day in June?: 4 rare
So ___: 3 Bad, Big, Sad 4 be it, Fine, Rare 5 Alive
So ___!: 4 long 5 I lied, sue me, there
So ___ in Love: 4 Much
So ___ Is Paris: 4 This
So ___ to you, Fuzzy-Wuzzy: 4 'eres
So!: 3 aha
Soacha: 4 city, town
locale: 8 Colombia
soak: 3 dip, sog, wet 4 dunk, seep, wash 5 bathe, clean, douse, dowse, flood, rinse, souse, steep, toper, water 6 absorb, dampen, drench, embrue, imbrue, infuse, pour on, rain on, rip off, seethe, soften, splash, take in 7 exploit, immerge, immerse, moisten 8 infusion, irrigate, marinate, permeate, pour into, saturate, submerge, waterlog 9 four-flush, penetrate, percolate 10 impregnate, infiltrate, overcharge
again: 5 rewet
fibers: 3 ret
in: 6 absorb 9 penetrate
up: 3 mop, sop 5 drink, learn 6 absorb, draw in, gather, ingest, osmose, take in 7 drink in, swallow 10 assimilate
up some sun: 3 tan 4 bask
soaked: 3 wet 5 adrip, soggy, soppy 6 sodden, sweaty 8 drenched 10 bedraggled
soaking: 3 dip, wet 4 bath 5 soggy 7 dunking 8 bibulous
site: 6 hot tub
so-and-so: 5 rogue, scamp 8 somebody 9 reprobate, scoundrel
soap: 3 Lux 4 Dial, Dove, Lava, suds, Tone, wash, Zest 5 Camay, clean, Coast, Ivory 6 Boraxo, Caress, lather, Shield 7 bubbles 8 cleanser, Lifebuoy 9 detergent, Palmolive, Safeguard 11 Irish Spring
acid: 5 oleic
bubbles: 4 foam 6 lather
ender: 3 box 4 bark, suds, wort 5 berry, stone
ingredient: 3 lye 4 aloe 6 alkali
like a ~: 7 maudlin
opera: 5 drama, story 6 serial, series 9 imbroglio
plant: 5 amole
remove ~: 5 rinse
soft ~: 7 coaxing, palaver 8 cajolery, nonsense 9 wheedling 10 persuasion
target: 4 dirt 5 grime
unit: 3 bar 4 cake
work with ~: 5 carve
soap ___: 3 pad 4 dish 5 chips, opera, plant 6 bubble, flakes, powder
___ soap: 4 soft 5 green 6 invert, saddle, toilet 7 Castile, shaving
Soap (ABC sitcom)
cast: Jimmy Baio (Billy Tate)
Diana Canova (Corrine Tate)
Billy Crystal (Jodie Dallas)
Cathryn Damon (Mary Campbell)

Robert Guillaume (Benson)
Katherine Helmond (Jessica Tate)
Robert Mandan (Chester Tate)
Richard Mulligan (Burt Campbell)
Jennifer Salt (Eunice Tate)
Robert Urich (Peter Campbell)
Sal Viscuso (Father Timothy Flotsky)
Ted Wass (Danny Dallas)
spin-off: 6 Benson
soapbark: 4 tree
soapberry: 4 akee, tree 5 genip 6 lichee, litchi, longan, lungan 7 genipap, leechee
soapbox: 5 stump 6 podium 7 lecture, oration 8 platform
get on a ~: 5 orate 6 preach 7 address, declaim, lecture 8 harangue, proclaim
Soap Box Derby site: 5 Akron
Soapdish (1991 film)
cast: Robert Downey Jr., Sally Field, Carrie Fisher, Whoopi Goldberg, Kevin Kline, Cathy Moriarty, Elisabeth Shue
SoapNet: 7 channel
alternative: 3 BET, CMT, MTV, PAX, TBS, TLC, TNN, TNT, USA 4 ESPN, HGTV 5 A and E, C-SPAN, Style 6 Noggin, Tech TV, TV Land 7 Court TV, Ovation 8 Lifetime
soapstone: 4 talc 7 mineral
soapy: 5 foamy, slick, sudsy 6 frothy 7 foaming, lathery 8 lathered, slippery, unrinsed 9 lubricous
soar: 3 fly 4 go up, leap, lift, rise, sail, skim 5 arise, climb, glide, shoot, tower, vault 6 ascend, aspire, move up, rocket 7 fly high, shoot up, take off 8 escalate, take wing 9 hang glide, skyrocket
above: 8 overlook
soaring: 4 high, tall 5 aloft, lofty, surge 6 flight, flying 8 elevated, towering, uplifted 9 on the wing
soave: 4 wine 5 white 7 Italian
like ~: 3 sec
sob: 3 cry 4 bawl, howl, mewl, moan, pule, sigh, wail, weep 5 mourn, whine 6 boohoo, lament, snivel 7 blubber, whimper 9 break down, cry a river, shed tears 10 take it hard
sob __: 5 story 6 sister
__ so bad: 3 not
__ So Bad: 4 Hurt 5 I Feel
So Bad (1984 song) artist: Paul McCartney
sobbing: 5 tears, weepy 6 lament 7 in tears, tearful 9 sniveling 10 lachrymose, waterworks
So be it: 4 amen
sober: 4 calm, cool, dark, dull, sane, soft 5 grave, lucid, plain, quiet, solid, sound, staid, stoic 6 demure, dreary, low-key, sedate, serene, severe, solemn, somber, steady 7 ascetic, austere, careful, deadpan, pensive, serious, stoical, subdued 8 coherent, composed, forgoing, moderate, rational, reserved, sensible 9 abstinent, clear-eyed, collected, continent, eschewing, humorless, impartial, judicious, practical, pragmatic, provident, realistic, temperate, toned down, unamusing, unexcited, unextreme, unruffled, unslanted 10 abnegating, abstaining, abstemious, controlled, cool-headed, hard-bitten, no-nonsense, on the wagon, reasonable, restrained, thoughtful, unagitated, unhumorous
ender: 5 sides
sober __ judge: 3 as a
sober-__: 5 sided 6 headed, minded
Sobieski: 4 John 6 Leelee
So Big: 4 film 5 novel
author: Edna Ferber
cast: Sterling Hayden, Nancy Olson, Jane Wyman
director: Robert Wise
sobresaut: 4 leap
sobriety: 8 eschewal 10 abstinence, moderation, temperance
sobriquet: 3 tag 4 name 5 title 6 handle 7 agnomen, epithet, moniker 8 cognomen, monicker, nickname
soca: 5 dance, music
kin: 7 calypso
so-called: 4 mock, sham 5 quasi 7 alleged, nominal 8 supposed 9 allegedly, pretended, professed, purported, self-named 10 ostensible, self-styled
in French: 9 soi-disant
soccer: 5 sport
former ~ org.: 4 NASL
game fraction: 4 half
goal: 3 net
in Britain: 8 football
kick: 4 punt
position: 3 LFB, RFB 4 wing 6 goalie
score: 4 goal
shoe feature: 5 cleat
shot: 4 kick 6 header
star: 4 Pelé
stat: 6 assist
team: 6 eleven
soccer __: 3 mom
sociable: 4 easy, kind, warm 5 close, suave 6 chummy, clubby, genial, jovial, kindly, polite 7 affable, amiable, cordial 8 amicable, familiar, fireside, friendly, gracious, intimate, likeable, outgoing 9 congenial, convivial, expansive 10 accessible, benevolent, buddy-buddy, gregarious, hospitable, neighborly, personable, solicitous
be ~: 3 mix 6 hobnob, mingle
social: 3 bee 4 nice 5 civil, mixer, party 6 common, polite, public 7 cordial 8 communal, familiar, fireside, friendly, luncheon, mannerly, pleasant, polished 9 community, congenial, convivial, organized 10 collective, gregarious, hospitable, neighborly
activity: 3 bee, tea 5 dance, doing, party 6 affair, soiree 8 function
asset: 4 tact 7 manners 9 propriety
blunder: 5 gaffe
call: 5 visit
climber: 4 snob 7 elitist, upstart
dud: 4 geek, nerd, nurd 5 dweeb
elite: 5 A-list 6 jet set
ender: 3 ism, ist, ite
engagement: 4 date
graces: group: 3 set 4 clan, club
insect: 3 ant, bee
lack of ~ grace: 9 gaucherie
lack of ~ standards: 5 anomy 6 anomie
science: 7 history 9 economics
starter: 4 anti
stratum: 5 caste, class, elite 6 sphere
social __: 3 bee 4 evil, unit, wasp, work 5 class 6 action, gospel, worker 7 climber, compact, control, dancing, process, realism, science, service, statics, studies, welfare
__ social: 3 box
Social Contract, The author: Jean Jacques Rousseau
socialist: 4 left 7 leftist 8 populist
Socialist: 5 party
five-time ~ candidate: 4 Debs
Socialist __ party: 5 Labor
socialite: 9 jet setter
teen: 3 deb
socialize: 3 mix 4 join 5 go out 6 hobnob, mingle 7 consort, hang out 8 chum with 9 associate, entertain, get around, pal around 10 fraternize
social-page word: 3 née
Social Register: 4 list
folk: 5 A-list, cream, elite
word: 3 née
__ Socials: 3 Box
societal: 6 public 7 popular 8 national
attitudes: 5 mores
breakdown: 5 anomy 6 anomie
unit: 4 clan
society: 4 clan, club, gang, gild, ring 5 elite, group, guild, order, tie-in, union, world 6 circle, clique, gentry, jet set, jungle, league, nation, outfit, people, public 7 company, culture, network, rat race, who's who 8 alliance, folkways, humanity, sodality 9 beau monde, community, humankind, institute, syndicate, top drawer 10 fellowship, friendship, haute monde, membership, upper class, upper crust
column word: 3 née
dictates of ~: 5 mores 8 protocol
dregs of ~: 6 rabble 8 riffraff 9 hoi polloi
event: 5 debut 9 cotillion
girl: 3 deb
high ~: 5 elite 6 bon ton, jet set 8 nobility 9 beau monde
honor ~ letter: 3 phi 4 beta 5 kappa
secret ~: 4 tong 5 cabal
__ society: 4 book, café, folk, high, mass 5 honor, tract 6 Dorcas, humane, secret 7 benefit, learned
__ Society: 4 High 5 Amana, Bible, Great, Royal 6 Fabian 7 Audubon
Society Island: 6 Mooréa, Tahiti 8 Bora Bora
Society of __: 5 Jesus 7 Friends
Society's Child singer: 3 Ian
sociology: 7 science
__ sociology: 5 rural, urban
sock: 3 bop, hit, pop, pow 4 bang, beat, belt, blow, chop, clip, cuff, ding, nail, slap, slug, swat, wham 5 clout, flail, paste, punch, smack, smash, smite, swipe, whack, whang 6 anklet, argyle, buffet, strike, wallop 7 hosiery 8 haymaker, knee-high, uppercut
away: 4 hide, save 5 hoard, store 7 deposit 8 conserve
dealer: 6 hosier
ender: 4 eroo
fix a ~: 4 darn, mend
holder: 6 drawer
hop: 5 dance
Japanese ~: 4 tabi
kin: 6 bootee, bootie
like an old ~: 5 holey
part: 3 toe 4 foot, heel
starter: 4 wind
support: 6 garter
unit: 4 pair
sock __: 3 hop 4 away 6 lining
__ sock: 3 air 4 crew, knee, tube 7 slipper
Sock __ me!: 4 it to
sockdolager: 4 lulu, oner
socked in: 5 foggy, misty
socket: 4 slot 6 cavity, recess
nautical ~: 7 gudgeon
socket __: 3 set 6 wrench
__ socket: 3 eye 4 rope, wall 7 bayonet
sockeye: 4 fish 6 salmon
Sock it to me! sayer: 5 Carne
socko: 5 boffo 7 boffola 8 terrific 10 impressive, successful
socks: 4 hose 7 hosiery
knock one's ~ off: 3 awe, wow 4 stun 5 amaze 6 thrill
sort ~: 5 match
__ socks: 4 knee 5 bobby, sweat
Socks: 3 cat
__ Socks: 5 Fox in
socle: 4 base, foot 6 plinth
Socony today: 5 Mobil
Socorro: 4 city, town
locale: 5 Texas
Socrate composer: 5 Satie
Socrates: 5 Greek 11 philosopher
friend of ~: 5 Crito
pupil of ~: 5 Plato
wife of ~: 5 shrew 9 Xanthippe
Socratic __: 5 irony 6 method
sod: 4 land, lawn, turf 5 divot, earth, field, grass, sward 6 ground, meadow, swarth 7 pasture 9 grassland 10 greensward, native land
ender: 6 buster
grass: 5 Bahia
home: 5 hogan
like ~: 5 rooty
__ Sod: 3 Old
soda: 3 pop 4 Coke, cola, fizz, Jolt, Nehi 5 cream, drink, mixer, Pepsi, tonic 6 bubbly, cherry, Fresca, leaven, orange 7 seltzer 8 beverage 9 soft drink
accessory: 5 straw
bottle unit: 3 can 4 case 5 liter, ounce
club ~: 4 fizz 5 mixer
high-caffeine ~: 4 Jolt
make ~ water: 6 aerate
open a ~ bottle: 5 uncap
without club ~: 4 neat
soda __: 3 ash, pop 4 jerk, lime 5 bread, niter, water 7 biscuit, cracker
__ soda: 3 sal 4 club, diet 5 cream 6 baking, celery 7 caustic, washing
soda fountain
in New England: 3 spa
order: 4 cola, malt 5 float, shake
seat: 5 stool
worker: 4 jerk
sodality: 5 order, union 6 league 7 society 10 fellowship, friendship, trade union
sodden: 3 wet 4 damp 5 muddy, soggy, soppy, steep, undry 6 drench, soaked, torpid, watery 7 wettish 8 dripping 9 saturated 10 bedraggled
Soddy, Frederick: 7 chemist 8 Nobelist
So Dear to My Heart (1949 film)
cast: Beulah Bondi, Bobby Driscoll, Burl Ives
Söderberg, Hjalmar: 6 writer 7 Swedish 10 playwright
Soderbergh, Steven: 8 director
film: Erin Brockovich (2000)
King of the Hill (1993)
The Limey (1999)
Ocean's Eleven (2001)
Out of Sight (1998)
sex, lies, and videotape (1989)
Traffic (2000, AA)
Söderblom, Nathan: 8 Nobelist
sodium: 5 metal 7 element
chloride: 4 NaCl, salt
combining form: 4 natr- 5 natro-
compound: 5 niter 6 alkali
form of ~ carbonate: 5 trona
hydroxide: 3 lye 4 NaOH
sodium __: 4 lamp, pump 5 amide, oxide 6 borate, iodide 7 bromide, citrate, cyanide, lactate, nitrate, nitrite, sulfate, sulfide, sulfite
sodium-__ lamp: 5 vapor
Sodom: 4 city, town
escapee: 3 Lot
neighbor: 8 Gomorrah
__ So Easy: 3 It's
So Emotional (1987 song) artist: Whitney Houston
So Ends Our Night (1941 film)
cast: Frances Dee, Fredric March, Margaret Sullavan

soeur: 6 French, sister
soever starter: 3 how, who 4 what, when, whom 5 where, which 6 whence 7 whither
So Evil My Love (1948 film)
cast: Geraldine Fitzgerald, Ray Milland, Ann Todd
sofa: 4 seat 5 couch, divan 6 canapé, daybed, lounge, settee 7 seating, vis-à-vis 8 love seat 9 davenport, furniture, sectional, tête-à-tête
bed: 5 futon
part: 3 arm, leg 4 back 7 cushion
sofa —: 3 bed 5 table
— sofa: 4 club 5 sleep 6 tuxedo
So far — can tell...: 3 as I
So Far Away (1971 song) artist: Carole King
so far so —: 4 good
— so fast!: 3 Not
— So Few: 5 Never
so few, to Churchill: 3 RAF
— Soffel: 3 Mrs.
soffit location: 4 eave
Sofia: 4 city, town 7 capital, Coppola
locale: 8 Bulgaria
So Fine (1981 film)
cast: Ryan O'Neal, Jack Warden
director: Andrew Bergman
— So Fine: 3 He's 4 Feel
soft: 3 dim, fat, lax, low 4 cosy, cozy, daft, dull, easy, fine, hazy, kind, limp, meek, mild, pale, snug, weak 5 bland, comfy, cozey, cozie, cushy, downy, dusky, faint, fluid, furry, light, loose, mealy, mushy, muted, nappy, pappy, piano, pithy, plush, pulpy, quiet, rusty, sheer, silky, silly, slack, sober, soggy, sweet, timid 6 benign, creamy, cuddly, docile, doughy, dulcet, flabby, fleecy, fleshy, flimsy, fluffy, gentle, kindly, liquid, low-key, mellow, padded, pallid, pastel, satiny, silken, simple, smooth, spongy, supple, tender 7 amiable, clement, diffuse, ductile, elastic, fatuous, flaccid, flowing, foolish, lenient, plastic, pliable, ruthful, snuggly, sparing, squashy, squishy, subdued, untoned, velvety, witless 8 bendable, cushiony, delicate, feathery, flexible, formless, laid-back, lenitive, merciful, moderate, moldable, murmured, overripe, pampered, placable, pleasant, sibilant, silklike, soothing, tolerant, twilight, unstrict, yielding 9 assuasive, caressing, compliant, courteous, cushioned, easygoing, forgiving, indulgent, malleable, melodious, sensitive, spineless, temperate, toned down, untrained, whispered 10 cuddlesome, effortless, forbearing, gelatinous, gone to seed, manageable, namby-pamby, out of shape, permissive, pianissimo, squeezable, starchless, unexacting, unhardened
combining form: 5 malac- 6 malaco-
ender: 4 ball, head, ware, wood 5 bound, cover 6 headed 7 hearted
go ~: 4 melt, thaw 6 loosen, relent, warm up 7 defrost 8 languish, unfreeze 10 deliquesce
in French: 3 bas
in music: 5 piano
palate: 5 velum
soap: 7 coaxing, palaver 8 cajolery, nonsense 9 wheedling 10 persuasion
sound: 3 coo 5 whish
spot: 4 love 6 liking 8 fondness, velleity, weakness
touch: 6 pigeon, sucker, victim 8 pushover
soft —: 3 roe, rot 4 clam, coal, copy, hail, lens, line, news, rock, sell, sign, soap, spot, tick 5 armor, drink, focus, goods, money, paste, pedal, scale, steel, touch, water, wheat 6 energy, ground, hyphen, palate, solder 7 landing, science
soft-—: 3 top 4 bill, land, shoe 5 cover, pedal, shell 6 finned, headed 7 hearted
soft-— clam: 5 shell
soft-— crab: 5 shell
soft-— egg: 6 boiled
Soft —: 4 Cell 5 Scrub
Soft and Dri: 9 deodorant
alternative: 3 Ban 4 Sure 5 Arrid, Tussy 6 Degree, Secret 7 Dry Idea, Mitchum 10 Right Guard, Speed Stick
softball: 4 game 5 sport
path: 3 arc
softcover: 4 book
soft drink: 3 TAB 4 Coke, Nehi 5 Fanta, Pepsi, Slice 6 Fresca, Nestea, Sprite 7 Snapple 8 beverage, Coca-Cola, Diet Rite, Dr. Brown's, Dr. Pepper, Gatorade 9 Canada Dry, Pepsi-Cola, Schweppes 10 Mello Yello, Royal Crown 11 Mountain Dew
unit: 4 case 6 carton
soften: 3 sag, sap 4 bend, calm, ease, flag, mash, melt, mute, soak, tame, thaw, tire, wane 5 abate, allay, blunt, break, knead, lower, mince, quell, quiet, relax, still, yield 6 deaden, defuse, defuze, impair, lessen, mellow, modify, muffle, obtund, reduce, relent, shrink, smooth, soothe, subdue, temper, weaken 7 appease, assuage, commute, deplete, exhaust, fatigue, lighten, moisten, mollify, qualify, relieve 8 diminish, dissolve, enervate, enfeeble, humanize, mitigate, moderate, modulate, palliate, play down, slack off, tone down, turn down, unfreeze 9 alleviate, attenuate, lighten up, tenderize, undermine, water down 10 come around, debilitate, devitalize, liberalize, smooth over
— softener: 5 water 6 fabric
softening: 6 relief 7 anodyne 9 abatement 10 comforting
agent: 4 aloe
softer in music: 3 dim. 7 decresc. 10 diminuendo
softhearted: 3 lax 4 easy, kind, mild, soft, warm 5 loose 6 gentle, kindly, tender 7 clement, lenient, ruthful, sparing 8 flexible, laid-back, merciful, placable, tolerant 9 assuasive, compliant, easygoing, forgiving, indulgent 10 forbearing, permissive, unexacting
become ~: 4 melt, thaw
softheartedness: 5 mercy 8 clemency
softie: 4 dupe, wimp 6 sucker 8 weakling
like a ~: 7 lenient
softly in music: 3 ppp. 9 sotto voce
— Softly to Me: 4 Come
Soft 'N —: 3 Dri
softness: 4 woof 5 sound 6 lenity 7 texture 8 lenience
soft-pedal: 4 calm, lull, mute 5 quiet, relax 6 lessen, pacify, temper 8 minimize, moderate, play down, tone down 9 alleviate, whitewash 10 understate
Soft Scrub: 8 cleanser
alternative: 4 Ajax, Bab-O 5 Comet 6 Bon Ami
soft-sell: 4 coax 5 lobby 6 low-key
soft-shell: 4 clam, crab 7 lenient
soft-shoe: 5 dance
— soft shoe, the: 3 old
softsoap: 3 lie 4 coax 5 lobby 6 cajole 7 flatter, lay it on, wheedle 8 blandish
soft solder: 5 alloy
component: 3 tin 4 lead
soft-spoken: 5 suave 6 humble 8 reserved 9 courteous
software
bundled ~: 5 suite
company: 5 Lotus, Roxio 6 Intuit 9 Microsoft
convenience: 5 macro
fix ~: 5 debug
former statistical ~: 5 Dbase
medium: 5 CD-ROM
Microsoft ~: 4 Word 5 Excel 6 Access 10 PowerPoint
option list: 4 menu
problem: 3 bug
purchaser: 4 user
release: 7 version
runner: 2 PC 3 Mac
test: 4 beta
tycoon: 5 Gates
user: 6 hacker
Web ~: 7 browser
write ~: 4 code 7 program
— software: 7 systems
Soft Weve: 6 tissue
alternative: 5 Scott 6 Marcal 7 Charmin 8 Northern 10 Cottonelle, White Cloud
softwood: 4 tree
softy
see softie
sog: 4 soak 6 drench 7 moisten
sogginess: 3 dew 5 vapor 7 wetness 8 dampness, humidity, moisture
soggy: 3 wet 4 damp, dank, soft 5 humid, moist, mucky, muddy, muggy, mushy, soppy, undry 6 clammy, soaked, sodden, spongy, steamy, sticky, stuffy, sultry, watery 7 soaking, sopping, wettish 8 drenched, dripping 9 saturated 10 bedraggled, sopping wet
ground: 3 bog, mud
mixture: 4 glop
Soglow: 4 Otto
— so good: 5 so far
— So Good: 4 Feel 5 Feels, Hurts
So good...it's gone food: 4 Spam
So help me!: 6 honest, really
Soho —: 6 Square
Soho locale: 3 NYC 6 London 7 England, New York 9 Manhattan
So I —!: 4 lied
Soichiro: 5 Honda
soi-disant: 7 wannabe 8 so-called 10 self-styled
soil: 3 mar, tar 4 blot, clay, dirt, dust, foul, home, land, loam, mess, muck, soot, spot, turf 5 crumb, dirty, earth, grime, humus, loess, muddy, shame, smear, spoil, stain, sully, taint 6 bedaub, befoul, bemire, crud up, debase, defile, embrue, ground, imbrue, malign, mess up, muck up, muss up, region, smudge, spread 7 begrime, besmear, blacken, corrupt, country, degrade, dry land, pollute, seedbed, spatter, tarnish, topsoil 8 besmirch, discolor, disgrace, farmland, homeland 9 bedraggle, homestead 10 terra firma
additive: 4 lime, peat 5 mulch
aerator: 4 root, worm
combining form: 3 ped-, -sol 4 agro-, pedo-
component: 4 clay 5 humus 6 alkali
cultivated ~: 5 tilth
embankment: 4 berm 5 berme
farm ~: 4 dirt, land 5 earth
kind of ~: 4 clay, loam 5 humus
layer: 5 solum
like some ~: 5 loamy 6 acidic, clayey
science of ~: 8 agrology
soggy ~: 3 mud
starter: 3 top
turn the ~: 6 aerate
windborne ~: 5 loess
soil —: 3 rot 4 bank, pipe 5 creep, group, stack 6 binder 7 profile, science
— soil: 3 ABC 4 acid 5 night 6 alkali 7 potting, prairie
soil agriculture science: 9 geoponics
soiled: 5 dirty, grimy, muddy, sooty 6 filthy, grubby, grungy 7 squalid, unclean 8 befouled, begrimed, maculate, slovenly, unwashed, vitiated 9 blackened 10 bedraggled, besmirched, germ-ridden, unsanitary
—-Soiler: 4 Free
So in Love composer: 6 Porter
soir: 6 French 7 evening
soiree: 4 fete, gala 5 party, salon 6 affair 9 festivity, reception
snack: 6 canapé
Soirées de Médan author: Emile Zola
Soissons: 4 city, town
locale: 6 France
— soit qui...: 4 Honi
sojourn: 4 bide, nest, rest, stay, stop 5 abide, dwell, lodge, perch, roost, squat, tarry, visit 6 linger, remain, reside 7 inhabit, layover 8 stay over, stopover, vacation 9 residence, tarriance 10 pilgrimage, stay a while
sojourner: 5 guest, rover 8 runagate 9 journeyer 10 vacationer
Sojourner: 5 Truth
Soka: 4 city, town
locale: 5 Japan
Sokolov: 4 Ivan
sol: 4 coin, note 5 money
preceder: 2 fa
successor: 2 la
Sol: 3 sun 4 star 5 Hurok 7 Phoebus
equivalent: 6 Helios
sister of ~: 3 Eos 6 Aurora
—-Sol: 4 Pine
sola: 5 plant, shrub
solace: 4 balm 5 allay, cheer, peace 6 relief, soothe, succor 7 assuage, cheer up, comfort, compose, condole, console, hearten, relieve 8 mitigate, sympathy 9 alleviate, disburden, encourage, untrouble 10 condolence
sought ~ from: 5 ran to
solan: 4 bird 5 diver, goose 6 gannet
solano: 4 wind
solar
cycle: 4 year
gap between ~ and lunar year: 5 epact
output: 4 heat 5 light
ring: 6 corona
wind particle: 3 ion
wind phenomenon: 6 aurora
solar —: 3 day 4 apex, cell, home, mass, pond, sail, ship, wind, year 5 cycle, flare, house, month, panel, power, still 6 energy, plexus, radius, system 7 battery, chariot, eclipse, furnace, heating
solar-—: 4 heat
Solara: 3 car 4 auto 6 Toyota
Solar Barque author: Anaïs Nin
Solari: 4 Rudy
Solaris author: 3 Lem
sold
on, as a cause: 5 wed to
out: 4 bare, gone 5 empty 7 crowded 8 depleted
Soldati: 5 Mario
solder: 4 fuse, join, weld 5 alloy, braze, metal, stick 6 cement, fasten
flux: 5 borax
material: 3 tin
tool: 4 iron
— solder: 4 hard, soft
soldered: 4 firm
soldering —: 4 iron

soldier: **2** GI **5** cadet, guard, scout **6** gunner, gyrene, knight, marine **7** draftee, fighter, officer, private, recruit, trooper, veteran, warrior **8** commando, guerilla, infantry, selectee **9** combatant, conscript, guerrilla, legionary, mercenary, musketeer, volunteer, warmonger **10** Green Beret
absent ~: **4** AWOL
address: **3** APO, FPO
assignment: **4** duty, post
break: **5** leave, R and R **8** furlough
burden: **6** kitbag
camp: **5** étape
career ~: **5** lifer
cavalry ~: **6** hussar
Civil War ~: **3** reb **4** gray, grey
distaff ~: **4** WAAC
down under: **5** Anzac
fare: **4** Spam
French ~: **5** poilu
group: **3** USO, VFW **5** Amvet
horse ~: **6** lancer
I.D.: **6** dogtag
Korean ~: **3** ROK
lodging: **4** base **6** billet, casern **7** caserne **8** barracks
Moslem ~: **5** ghazi
mounted ~: **7** dragoon
Nepalese ~: **6** Gurkha
of fortune: **4** merc **9** mercenary **10** adventurer
onetime ~ of India: **5** Sepoy
rank: **2** BG, lt. **3** col., cpl., gen., maj., NCO, PFC, sgt. **4** capt. **5** lieut., lt. col., lt. gen., major **6** maj. gen. **7** captain, colonel, general, private **8** corporal, sergeant **10** lieutenant
retired ~: **3** vet **7** veteran
Tatar ~: **4** ulan **5** uhlan
tin ~: **3** toy
toy ~: **5** GI Joe
tune: **5** march
Turkish ~: **5** Nizam
uniform: **3** ODs **4** camo, drab **5** khaki, olive
U.S. ~: **4** Yank **5** GI Joe **8** doughboy
WWI ~: **5** Anzac, poilu
WWII ~: **3** WAC **5** GI Joe
see also military
__ soldier: **3** tin **4** foot **5** wagon **7** buffalo
__ Soldier: **7** Unknown
Soldier Boy (1962 song) artist: Shirelles
Soldier Field: **5** arena **7** stadium
locale: **7** Chicago **8** Illinois
Soldier in the Rain (1963 film)
cast: Jackie Gleason, Steve McQueen, Tuesday Weld
soldierly: **7** martial, warlike **8** military
soldier of __: **7** fortune
Soldier of Fortune (1955 film)
cast: Clark Gable, Susan Hayward, Michael Rennie
director: Edward Dmytryk
Soldier of Love (1989 song) artist: Donny Osmond
soldiers: **4** army **5** force, troop **6** grunts **7** cavalry **8** infantry
ten Roman ~: **6** decade
Soldiers __: **5** Three
Soldier's Daughter Never Cries (1998 film)
cast: Jesse Bradford, Barbara Hershey, Kris Kristofferson, Leelee Sobieski
director: James Ivory
soldiers of fortune group: **5** A-Team
Soldier's Pay author: William Faulkner
Soldier's Story, A (1984 film)
cast: Adolph Caesar, Dennis Lipscomb, Howard Rollins
director: Norman Jewison
Soldiers Three (1951 film)
cast: Stewart Granger, David Niven, Walter Pidgeon
director: Tay Garnett
soldo: **4** coin **5** money
sole: **3** ace, odd, one **4** fish, lone, only **5** alone **6** cobble, entrée, single, unique **7** halibut, holibut, seafood **8** flatfish, flounder, isolated, separate, singular, unshared **9** exclusive, matchless, nonpareil, remaining, unequaled, unmarried **10** individual, one and only, particular
attachment: **5** cleat
combining form: **4** pedi- **5** pedio-
ender: **5** plate, print
of the ~: **5** volar
part: **5** tread
plow ~: **5** slade
protector: **3** tap
starter: **4** turn **5** inner
sole-__: **6** source
__ sole: **4** feme, half **5** Dover, lemon **6** tongue **7** English
__-sole: **4** half
solecism: **5** error, gaffe **6** misuse **7** mistake
popular ~: **4** ain't
solecistic: **10** illiterate
__-soled: **3** lug **5** thick
Soledad: **4** city, town
locale: **6** Mexico **8** Colombia
Soleil __ Frye: **4** Moon
__ Soleil: **5** Le Roi
solely: **3** all, but **4** only **5** alone, per se **6** merely, purely, simply, singly, wholly **7** totally **8** entirely **10** completely, nothing but, separately, singularly
solemn: **4** glum, holy **5** grand, grave, heavy, sober, staid **6** august, divine, formal, ritual, sacred, somber **7** austere, deadpan, intense, learned, serious, stately, subdued, weighty **8** brooding, downbeat, hallowed, imposing, majestic **9** awestruck, dignified, humorless, momentous, religious, unamusing, venerable **10** ceremonial, devotional, impressive, liturgical, majestical, no-nonsense, portentous, reflective, sanctified, unhumorous
word: **3** vow **4** oath
Solemn __ Mass: **4** High
__ Solemnis: **5** Missa
solemnity: **4** pomp, rite **6** ritual **7** dignity **8** splendor **9** austerity, formality
solemnize: **4** keep **7** observe **9** celebrate
solemnness: **9** formality
__ Solennelle: **5** Messe
solenoid __: **6** switch
__ Solent: **4** Wolf
Sole Survivor author: Dean Koontz
soleus: **6** muscle
locale: **4** calf
solfeggio syllable: **2** do, fa, la, mi, re, ti, ut **3** sol
solicit: **3** ask, beg, bum, sue, woo **4** call, hawk, pray, seek, tout, urge **5** crave, exact, hit on, hit up, lobby, mooch, plead, query, steer **6** appeal, ask for, demand, desire, drum up, hustle, invoke, peddle, resort, sponge, sue for **7** beseech, canvass, enquire, entreat, implore, inquire, procure, promote, request **8** approach, campaign, come on to, petition, plead for, question **9** impetrate, importune, panhandle, postulate **10** pass the hat, supplicate, whistle for
solicitant: **9** candidate
solicitation: **4** call, care, plea **6** appeal **7** request
solicitor: **5** asker **6** lawyer, legist **7** counsel **9** barrister, counselor
solicitor __: **7** general
solicitous: **4** avid, keen, kind **5** close, eager **6** ardent, caring, chummy, clubby, genial, kindly, loving, polite, tender, uneasy **7** affable, amiable, anxious, careful, cordial, devoted, earnest, fearful, heedful, mindful, nervous, thirsty, worried, zealous **8** amicable, friendly, intimate, outgoing, sociable, troubled **9** attentive, brotherly, concerned, convivial, impatient, regardful **10** benevolent, buddy-buddy, neighborly, protective
be ~: **4** mind **5** hover
one: **5** carer
phrase: **5** I care, try me
solicitude: **3** TLC **4** care, heed **5** qualm, worry **6** regard, unease **7** anxiety, concern, scruple, thought **8** disquiet, kindness **9** affection, attention, eagerness **10** discretion
solid: **3** set **4** cube, firm, good, hard, hunk, lump, pure, real, rock, sure **5** beefy, block, cubic, dense, fixed, hardy, heavy, hefty, husky, rigid, rocky, sober, sound, stiff, stony, stout, thick, tight, valid **6** cogent, decent, intact, massed, potent, rooted, rugged, secure, stable, steady, steely, stocky, stoney, strong, sturdy, trusty, united, unmixt, worthy **7** compact, durable, genuine, learned, logical, serious, solvent, telling, unmixed, upright **8** accurate, complete, concrete, constant, material, palpable, physical, powerful, reliable, rocklike, sensible, stalwart, tangible, unbroken, well-made **9** compacted, condensed, continued, estimable, excellent, like a rock, nonporous, practical, steadfast, touchable, unalloyed, unanimous, undivided, unfailing, well-built **10** compressed, continuous, convincing, dependable, hard-packed, impervious, law-abiding, satisfying, set in stone, unshakable, unwavering, unyielding, upstanding
combining form: **5** stere- **6** stereo-
geometric ~: **4** cube **5** prism, torus **6** sphere **7** pyramid
geometry calculation: **6** volume
gold: **7** optimum **8** peerless, splendid **9** marvelous
in physics: **5** state
on ~ ground: **6** ashore
rock: **5** loyal **6** honest, stable, steely, trusty **7** certain, ethical, staunch **8** faithful, reliable, surefire **9** honorable, steadfast, unfailing **10** consistent, dependable, infallible
semirigid ~: **3** gel
solid __ rock: **3** as a
solid-__: **5** state **7** looking
Solid __: **5** South
Solid (1985 song) artist: Ashford and Simpson
solidarity: **5** unity **6** accord **7** concord, oneness **9** coherence, unanimity **10** friendship
Solidarity: **5** union
city: **6** Gdansk
Solid Gold Cadillac, The: **4** film, play
author: George S. Kaufman
cast: Fred Clark, Paul Douglas, Judy Holliday
director: Richard Quine
Solid Gold host: **4** Dees **5** McCoo
solidified: **4** hard **5** stiff, thick **7** jellied
solidify: **3** fix, gel, set **4** cake, clot, jell **5** unite **6** cake up, firm up, freeze, gelate, harden **7** congeal, encrust, stiffen, thicken **8** condense **9** coagulate **10** gelatinize
solidifying agent: **4** agar **8** agar-agar
solidity: **4** pith **7** reality **8** firmness **9** stability
lose ~: **4** melt, thaw
symbol of ~: **4** rock
solidly built: **5** beefy, stout **6** strong
solids: **8** sediment
solidus: **4** coin **5** money
soliloquist, like a: **5** alone
soliloquize: **5** orate **6** recite
soliloquy: **4** talk **7** monolog **9** monologue
phrase: **4** to be **5** or not
sung ~: **4** aria
woeful ~: **6** lament
Solimana: **4** peak **5** mount **8** mountain
locale: **4** Peru
Solingen: **4** city, town
locale: **7** Germany
solipsist: **6** egoist **7** egotist
preoccupation: **4** self
solitaire: **4** game **5** jewel **7** jewelry, recluse **8** card game
how ~ is played: **5** alone
variety: **8** canfield, patience
__ solitaire: **6** double
Solitaire (song) artist: Carpenters, Laura Branigan
solitarian: **6** hermit
solitarily: **5** alone, per se
solitary: **3** odd, one **4** lone, monk, only, stag **5** alone, aloof, stark, unwed **6** hermit, lonely, remote, single, unique **7** distant, eremite, oddball, private, recluse **8** anchoret, deserted, desolate, eremitic, forsaken, hermitic, isolated, lonesome, reserved, secluded, separate, singular, unsocial **9** anchorite, reclusive, withdrawn **10** antisocial, cloistered, friendless, hermitical, individual, unattended, unsociable
combining form: **4** erem-, soli- **5** eremo-
one: **5** loner **6** hermit
Solitary Man (1970 song) artist: Neil Diamond
Solitary Reaper, The author: William Wordsworth
__ solita storia: **3** E La
solitude: **7** privacy, retreat, secrecy **9** aloneness, emptiness, isolation, seclusion **10** desolation, detachment, loneliness, quarantine, withdrawal
seeker: **5** loner **6** hermit
__ Solitude: **5** Ode on
Solitude author: Alexander Pope
sollicker: **3** def, rad **4** aces, A-one, boss, braw, cool, dece, fine, gear, keen, neat, nice, phat, tuff **5** dandy, ducky, grand, great, marvy, neato, nobby, prime, slick, super, swell **6** bang on, bang-up, bonzer, bosker, choice, divine, dreamy, far-out, gnarly, groovy, lovely, peachy, slap-up, spot on, superb, terrif, tiptop, unreal, whizzo, wicked **7** amazing, awesome, capital, corking, perfect, ripping, skookum, stellar, sublime **8** dazzling, especial, eximious, fabulous, four-star, frabjous, glorious, heavenly, jim-dandy, slam-bang, smashing, splendid, standout, sterling, stickout, superior, terrific, top-level, topnotch, very good, wondrous **9** bodacious, Endsville, excellent, exemplary, exquisite, first-rate, high-grade, hunky-dory, marvelous, top-flight, wonderful **10** first-class, hotsy-totsy, jack-a-dandy, out of sight, peachy-keen, phenomenal, remarkable, stupendous, super-duper
solo: **4** aria, lone **5** alone **6** single, unique **7** unaided **8** singular **9** by oneself **10** one-man band, unassisted, unescorted
passage in music: **7** cadenza
performer: **4** diva

vocal ~: 4 aria 5 scena 6 arioso
Solo: 3 Han 4 peak 5 agent, mount 8 mountain, Napoleon
locale: 5 Andes 9 Argentina
Sologub, Fyodor: 4 poet 7 Russian
Solo, Han: 4 hero
ally: 4 Leia, Luke 6 Obi-Wan
foe: 5 Darth, Vader
portrayer: Harrison Ford
soloist: 6 player, singer 8 musician
Solomon: 4 king, sage
daughter of ~: 7 Taphath
like ~: 4 wise
parent of ~: 5 David 9 Bathsheba
queen: 5 Sheba
son of ~: 8 Rehoboam
Solomon and Sheba (1959 film)
cast: Yul Brynner, Gina Lollobrigida, George Sanders
director: King Vidor
Solomon composer: 6 Handel
Solomonic: 4 sage, wise
Solomon Islands: 6 nation 7 country
capital: 7 Honiara
money: 4 cent 6 dollar
one of the ~: 4 Buka, Savo 7 Malaita 8 Choiseul
__ Solomon's Mines: 4 King
solon: 6 pundit 8 lawmaker
Solon: 4 city, poet, sage, town
locale: 4 Ohio
Solo, Napoleon: 3 spy 5 agent
employer: 5 UNCLE
Solondz: 4 Todd
So long!: 3 bye 4 ciao, ta-ta 5 adieu, adios, aloha, I'm off, later 6 bye-bye, shalom 7 goodbye 8 sayonara
in French: 5 adieu
in Hawaiian: 5 aloha
in Italian: 4 ciao
in Latin: 3 ave 4 vale
in Spanish: 5 adios
So Long at the Fair (1950 film)
cast: Dirk Bogarde, Jean Simmons
Solothurn river: 3 Aar 4 Aare
Solow, Robert: 8 Nobelist 9 economist
solstice: 6 height
__ solstice: 6 summer, winter
Solstice author: Joyce Carol Oates
Solstices author: Louis MacNeice
Solti, Georg: 9 conductor
soluble: 10 explicable
soluble __: 3 RNA 5 glass
__-soluble: 3 fat 5 water
solum: 4 soil
solus: 5 alone
solution: 3 key, mix 5 blend, fluid, juice 6 answer, elixir, liquid, remedy, result, ticket 7 extract, mixture, pay dirt, solvent 8 compound, emulsion, quick fix
alcohol ~: 8 tincture
caustic ~: 6 alkali
corrosive ~: 4 acid 5 oleum
darkroom ~: 5 fixer, toner
high-pH ~: 6 alkali
hydroxide ~: 3 lye
inelegant ~: 5 kluge 6 kludge
low-pH ~: 4 acid
salt ~: 5 brine
__ solution: 5 Gram's, solid, stock 6 buffer, saline 7 ammonia, Dobell's, general, Ringer's
Solvay, Ernest: 7 chemist
solve: 2 do 3 fix, get, hit 4 have, lick, work 5 crack, plumb 6 answer, decide, decode, fathom, pan out, reason, settle, unlock 7 achieve, clarify, clear up, explain, expound, find out, hit upon, iron out, make out, unravel, work out 8 construe, deal with, decipher, get right, think out, untangle 9 determine, elucidate, enlighten, figure out, interpret, puzzle out 10 account for, illuminate
hard to ~: 5 nasty, tough 6 knotty
solvent: 5 solid, sound 6 acetal, afloat, eluant, hexane, hexone, liquid, liquor 7 acetone 8 cleanser, solution 10 in the black, turpentine
alcohol ~: 6 acetal
financially ~: 6 afloat
glycerol-based ~: 6 acetin
perfumery ~: 5 aldol 9 acetaldol
use a ~: 5 elute
solver: 7 puzzler
need: 6 eraser
quest: 6 answer
shout: 3 aha
Solway Firth: 5 inlet
locale: 7 England 8 Irish Sea, Scotland
tributary: 3 Esk 4 Eden
Solzhenitsyn, Aleksandr: 6 author, writer 7 Russian 8 Nobelist
formerly: 5 exile
work: Cancer Ward
The First Circle
The Gulag Archipelago
Som.
see Somalia
soma: 4 body
Somali: 3 cat 5 felid 6 feline 7 Current 8 language
home: 5 Kenya 6 Africa, Jibuti 7 Somalia 8 Djibouti, Ethiopia
Somalia: 6 nation 7 country
capital: 9 Mogadishu
group: 10 Arab League
gulf: 4 Aden
locale: 6 Africa
money: 4 cent 8 shilling
neighbor: 5 Kenya 8 Djibouti, Ethiopia
__ Somaliland: 6 French 7 British, Italian
So Many Ways (1959 song) artist: Brook Benton
__ so many words: 5 not in
somatic: 6 bodily 8 corporal, physical
somber: 3 dim, sad 4 blue, dark, dire, down, drab, dull, glum, gray, grey, grim 5 black, bleak, dingy, dusky, grave, mirky, murky, shady, sober, staid, woful 6 cloudy, dismal, dreary, gloomy, morbid, morose, sedate, solemn, sullen, woeful 7 deadpan, doleful, elegiac, hurting, joyless, obscure, serious, shadowy, unhappy, weighty 8 darkened, dejected, desolate, downcast, funereal, mournful, overcast, sourpuss, troubled 9 bummed out, cheerless, heartsick, humorless, miserable, saddening, saturnine, sorrowful, tenebrous, unamusing, woebegone 10 chapfallen, depressing, depressive, dispirited, lackluster, lugubrious, melancholy, nononsense, oppressive, sepulchral, tenebrific, unhumorous
in a ~ way: 5 sadly
music: 5 dirge
sombrero: 3 hat 7 Mexican
some: 3 any 4 a bit, a few, part 6 rather 7 a little, handful, portion, pronoun, several 8 a good bit 9 a number of 10 moderately
ender: 3 day, how, one, way 4 body, time, ways, what 5 place, thing, times, where
in French: 3 des
starter: 3 awe, irk, two, win 4 fear, four, game, glad, glee, hand, lone, long, tire, toil 5 light, three, tooth, whole 6 bother, frolic, meddle 7 trouble, venture 9 adventure
Some __ meat and canna eat: 3 hae
somebody: 3 one, VIP 4 name, star 5 nabob 6 anyone, person 7 notable, so-and-so, whoever 8 luminary 9 celebrity, dignitary, personage, superstar
Somebody __ de bay: 5 bet on
Somebody __ Me: 5 Loves
Somebody __ Moon: 5 Else's
Somebody __ My Gal: 5 Stole
Somebody in Boots author: Nelson Algren
Somebody Loves Me composer: 8 Gershwin
Somebody's Baby (1982 song) artist: Jackson Browne
Somebody's Darling author: Larry McMurtry
Somebody to Love (song) artist: Jefferson Airplane, Queen
Somebody Up There Likes Me (1956 film)
cast: Pier Angeli, Paul Newman, Everett Sloane
director: Robert Wise
Some Came Running: 4 film 5 novel
author: James Jones
cast: Shirley MacLaine, Dean Martin, Frank Sinatra
director: Vincente Minnelli
Some Can Whistle author: Larry McMurtry
someday: 3 yet 4 anon, soon, then 5 after 6 in a bit, in time 7 anytime, by and by, later on 8 in a while 9 afterward, hereafter 10 before long, eventually, ultimately
Some Day My __ Will Come: 6 Prince
Someday (song) artist: Glass Tiger, Mariah Carey, Sugar Ray
Someday We'll Be Together (1969 song) artist: Supremes
Some Enchanted Evening
composer: 7 Rodgers 11 Hammerstein
singer: 5 Emile
Some Guys Have All the Luck (1984 song) artist: Rod Stewart
somehow: 6 anyway, in a way
somehow or __: 5 other
Some Kind of Wonderful (1987 film)
cast: Mary Stuart Masterson, Craig Sheffer, Eric Stoltz, Lea Thompson
director: Howard Deutch
Some Kind of Wonderful (1974 song) artist: Grand Funk
Some Like It Hot (1959 film)
cast: Joe E. Brown, Tony Curtis, Jack Lemmon, Marilyn Monroe, George Raft
director: Billy Wilder
role: 4 Kane 5 Sugar
__ Some Lovin': 5 Gimme
Some of __ Days: 5 These
someone: 6 entity, person
Someone (1997 song)
artist: Puff Daddy, SWV
__ Someone Happy: 4 Make
Someone Saved My Life Tonight (1975 song) artist: Elton John
Someone to Call My Lover (2001 song) artist: Janet Jackson
Someone to Watch Over Me: 4 song
composer: 8 Gershwin
Someone to Watch Over Me (1987 film)
cast: Tom Berenger, Lorraine Bracco, Mimi Rogers
director: Ridley Scott
__ some rays: 4 grab 5 catch
Somers: 5 Brett 6 Joanie 7 Suzanne
somersault: 4 flip, roll 6 tumble
somersaulter: 7 gymnast
Somers, Brett spouse: Jack Klugman
Somerset: 3 car 4 auto, city, town 5 Buick 6 county 10 automobile
locale: 6 Exmoor 7 England 9 New Jersey
Somersetshire river: 3 Exe
Somers, Joanie song: Johnny Get Angry (1962)
Somerville: 4 city, town
locale: 4 Mass.
Some Tame Gazelle author: Barbara Pym
something: 3 tip 5 being 6 entity, object, rather, tipoff 7 article 9 commodity, substance 10 individual
something __: 3 new, old 4 blue, else 8 borrowed
__ something: 4 up to 5 start
Something (1969 song) artist: Beatles
Something for the Boys: 7 musical
songwriter: 6 Porter
Something Happened author: Joseph Heller
Something Happened on the Way to Heaven (1990 song) artist: Phil Collins
__ something I said?: 4 Is it 5 Was it
Something of Value: 4 film 5 novel
author: Robert Ruark
cast: Rock Hudson, Sidney Poitier, Dana Wynter
__ something over on: 3 put 4 slip
Something's Burning (1970 song)
artist: Kenny Rogers
Something's Gotta Give (1955 song)
artist: McGuire Sisters, Sammy Davis Jr.
__ Something to Me: 5 You Do
Something to Shout About (1943 film)
cast: Don Ameche, Janet Blair, Jack Oakie
composer: 6 Porter
Something to Talk About (1991 song)
artist: Bonnie Raitt
Something Unspoken author: Tennessee Williams
Something Wicked This Way Comes
author: Ray Bradbury
Somethin' Stupid (1967 song)
artist: Frank Sinatra, Nancy Sinatra
sometime: 3 old, yet 4 anon, ever, late, once, soon, then 5 after 6 any day, in a bit, in time, one day 7 by and by, later on 8 in a while, previous 9 afterward, hereafter 10 before long, eventually, on occasion, ultimately
sometimes: 6 seldom 7 usually 8 off and on 10 frequently, now and then, on occasion
Sometimes __ We Touch: 4 When
Sometimes a Great Notion author: Ken Kesey
Sometimes Love Just Isn't Enough (1992 song) artist: Don Henley
Sometimes you feel like __: 4 a nut
somewhat: 4 a bit 5 a mite, quite, sorta 6 fairly, in part, kind of, little, partly, pretty, rather, sort of 7 a little, not much 8 bearably, slightly 9 partially, to a degree, tolerably 10 moderately, more or less, relatively
prefix: 4 semi-
suffix: 3 -ish
somewhere: 5 about 6 around 9 scattered 10 ultimately
else: 3 out 4 away 6 absent
get ~: 6 arrive
Somewhere in the Night (song) artist: Barry Manilow, Helen Reddy
Somewhere in Time (1980 film)
cast: Christopher Plummer, Christopher Reeve, Jane Seymour, Teresa Wright
director: Jeannot Szwarc
Somewhere, My Love (1966 song)
artist: Ray Conniff
dedicatee: 4 Lara
Somewhere Out There (1987 song)
artist: James Ingram, Linda Ronstadt

Somewhere Tomorrow (1983 film)
cast: Nancy Addison, Sarah Jessica Parker, Tom Shea
Some Words With a Mummy author: Edgar Allan Poe
__ some Z's: 5 catch
Sominex: 8 sleep aid
alternative: 5 Nytol **6** Compoz, Unisom
Somme: 5 river **6** battle
city on the ~: 6 Amiens
locale: 6 France
sommelier: 6 server, waiter **7** steward
concern: 4 wine **6** cellar
cooler: 3 ice
Sommer: 4 Elke **5** Jaime, Josef
Sommer, Elke: 7 actress
film: The Prize (1963)
A Shot in the Dark (1964)
The Wrecking Crew (1969)
Zeppelin (1971)
Sommersby (1993 film)
cast: Jodie Foster, Richard Gere, James Earl Jones, Bill Pullman
director: Jon Amiel
Sommers, Jamie bionic implant: 3 ear
somniferous: 6 sleepy **8** hypnotic **9** soporific
somnolent: 4 dozy, lazy **5** yawny **6** asleep, dozing, drowsy, groggy, sleepy, torpid **7** dormant, napping **8** dreaming, inactive, snoozing **9** heavy-eyed, lethargic, sacked out, soporific **10** half-asleep, slumbering, slumberous
Somnus, father of: 3 Nyx
...so much __ by so many to so few: 4 owed
so much in music: 5 tanto
so much the better in French: 9 tant mieux
so much the worse in French: 7 tant pis
son: 3 boy, kid, lad **4** cion, male **5** child, scion **6** junior, laddie **7** dauphin, kinsman **8** relative, young man **10** descendant
in Gaelic: 3 Mac
Jr.'s ~ perhaps: 3 III
starter: 3 god **4** step **5** grand
son __ gun: 3 of a
son-__: 5 in-law
__ son: 6 foster, native
Son __: 5 of God, of Man
__ Son: 6 Native **7** Seventh
sonant: 6 spoken
sonar
kin: 5 radar
pulse: 4 ping
signal: 4 echo
use ~: 6 locate
sonata: 4 solo **5** music, piece
ender: 4 coda
movement: 4 trio **5** rondo
Sonata: 3 car **4** auto **7** Hyundai
__ Sonata: 6 Autumn, Spring
sonata da __: 6 camera, chiesa
Sondergaard, Gale: 7 actress
film: Anna and the King of Siam (1946)
Anthony Adverse (1936, AA)
The Climax (1944)
The Life of Emile Zola (1937)
My Favorite Blonde (1942)
The Spider Woman (1944)
Sondheim, Stephen: 8 composer
collaborator: 5 Styne **7** Rodgers **9** Bernstein
musical: Company
Do I Hear a Waltz?
Follies
A Funny Thing Happened on the Way to the Forum
Gypsy
Into the Woods
A Little Night Music
Pacific Overtures
Passion
Sunday in the Park With George
Sweeney Todd
West Side Story
Sondra: 5 Locke
son et __: 7 lumière
song: 3 air **4** aria, glee, hymn, lied, noel, oldy, pean, poem, tune **5** carol, chant, ditty, lyric, music, oldie, opera, paean, piece, psalm, verse, vocal **6** anthem, ballad, chanty, chorus, melody, number, shanty, strain **7** ballade, chanson, chantey, chorale, lullaby, refrain, shantey **8** birdcall, canticle **9** barcarole **10** plainchant
classic ~: 4 oldy **5** oldie
combining form: 4 melo-
eighteenth-century ~: 4 glee
ender: 4 bird, fest **5** smith **6** writer
German art ~: 4 lied
in music: 5 canto
name meaning ~: 6 Carmen
starter: 4 even, folk, sing **5** plain **6** cradle
syncopated ~: 3 rag
song __: 5 cycle **6** thrush **7** sparrow
__ song: 3 art **4** folk, for a, part, swan, work **5** siren, theme, torch **6** patter **7** popular
__-song: 4 part, sing
Song __, The: 5 Is You, of Los
__ Song: 4 Goat, Last, Love, Lute, No-no, Your **5** Sing a **6** Annie's, Cradle, Danny's, Valley
__ Song, A: 6 Summer
song-and-dance
show: 5 revue **6** review
Song author: Edgar Allan Poe
__ Song Before I Go: 5 Just a
songbird: 3 jay, tit **4** chat, lark, wren **5** finch, junco, mavis, pipit, robin, serin, vireo **6** bulbul, canary, linnet, oriole, parula, phoebe, singer, thrush, tityra, tomtit **7** babbler, bunting, cotinga, creeper, skylark, sparrow, swallow, tanager, wagtail, waxwing **8** bellbird, blackcap, bobolink, cardinal, nuthatch, redstart, thrasher, titmouse, whinchat, white-eye, woodlark **9** bullfinch, chaffinch, chickadee, crossbill, currawong, frogmouth, goldfinch, pardalote **10** chiffchaff, flycatcher, honeyeater
Songbird (1987 song) artist: Kenny G
songbook, church: 6 hymnal
Songcatcher (2001 film)
cast: Jane Adams, Pat Carroll, Janet McTeer, Aidan Quinn
Songea: 4 city, town
locale: 8 Tanzania
Song Flung up to Heaven, A author: Maya Angelou
Song for Mama, A (1997 song) artist: Boyz II Men
songful: 5 lyric **6** in tune **7** lilting, lyrical, musical
__ Song Go...: 5 I Let a
Songhai home: 4 Mali **5** Niger **6** Africa
Songhua: 5 river
locale: 5 China
__ Song in My Heart: 5 With a
Song Is __, The: 3 You **5** Ended
Song Is Ended, The composer: 6 Berlin
Song Is You, The composer: 4 Kern
songlike: 5 lyric **6** arioso, poetic **7** lyrical **8** poetical
Song of __: 5 Songs **7** Solomon
Song of Bernadette, The: 4 film **5** novel
author: Franz Werfel
cast: Charles Bickford, William Eythe, Jennifer Jones
director: Henry King
Song of Hiawatha, The: 4 poem
author: 10 Longfellow
tribe: 6 Ojibwa **7** Ojibway **8** Chippewa
Song of India actor: 4 Sabu
Song of Los, The author: William Blake
Song of Myself: 4 poem
author: Walt Whitman
Song of Old Hawaii, A accompaniment: 3 uke **7** ukulele
Song of Roland, The: 4 epic, poem **6** French
character: 4 Aude, Emir, Ives, Ivor **5** Ogier, Othon **6** Anseis, Oliver
Song of Rosemary author: Ira Levin
__ song of sixpence...: 5 Sing a
Song of Solomon follower: 6 Isaiah
Song of the Chattahoochee, The author: Sidney Lanier
Song of the Golden Calf: 4 aria
Song of the Islands (1942 film)
cast: Betty Grable, Victor Mature, Jack Oakie
director: Walter Lang
Song of the Lark, The author: Willa Cather
Song of the Open Road: 4 poem
author: Walt Whitman
Song of the South (1946 film)
cast: James Baskett, Bobby Driscoll, Ruth Warrick
role: 5 Remus
song: Zip-a-Dee-Doo-Dah
title: 4 Br'er
__ Songs: 3 Sad **4** Love
Songs and Sonnets author: John Donne
Songs for a Summer Day author: Archibald MacLeish
__ Songs for Me: 5 No Sad
songsmith: 8 composer, lyricist
Songs of the Sierras author: Joaquin Miller
__ Songs, The: 3 Old **5** Dream
Song Sung Blue (1972 song) artist: Neil Diamond
Songs Without Words composer: 11 Mendelssohn
__ Song Trilogy: 5 Torch
songwriter: 8 composer, lyricist
org.: 3 BMI **5** ASCAP
Sonia: 5 Braga
sonic
rebound: 4 echo
starter: 5 ultra
sonic __: 4 boom, mine **7** barrier
sonic __ finder: 5 depth
sonic boom source: 3 SST
Sonics: 4 five, team
home: 7 Seattle
org.: 3 NBA
Sonic the Hedgehog maker: 4 Sega
Sonja: 5 Henie
sonly: 6 filial
Sonnenfeld, Barry: 8 director
film: The Addams Family (1991)
Addams Family Values (1993)
Big Trouble (2002)
Get Shorty (1995)
Men in Black (1997)
Men in Black II (2002)
Wild Wild West (1999)
sonnet: 4 poem, rime **5** rhyme, verse
cousin: 3 ode
like a ~: 5 lyric
measure: 4 iamb
stanza: 5 octet **7** octette
__ sonnet: 7 English, Italian
sonneteer: 4 bard, poet **9** rhymester
Sonnets From the Portuguese author: Elizabeth Barrett Browning
Sonnets to __: 5 Delia
Sonnets to Orpheus, The author: Rainer Maria Rilke
Sonnet–To Science author: Edgar Allan Poe
sonny: 3 boy, kid **4** male
Sonny: 4 Bono **5** James, Tufts **6** Liston **7** Rollins **8** Corleone **9** Jurgensen
Sonny __: 3 Boy
Sonny and Cher: 3 duo **4** team
song: All I Ever Need Is You (1971)
Baby Don't Go (1965)
The Beat Goes On (1967)
A Cowboys Work Is Never Done (1972)
I Got You Babe (1965)
Laugh at Me (1965)
Sonny Boy (1928 song) artist: Al Jolson
son of __: 4 Adam, a gun
Son of __: 3 God, Man
Son of __ Baba: 3 Ali
Sonofagun!: 4 darn, rats **6** darn it, phooey
Son-of-a Preacher Man (1968 song) artist: Dusty Springfield
Son of a Sailor (1933 film)
cast: Joe E. Brown, Jean Muir, Thelma Todd
director: Lloyd Bacon
Son of Dracula (1943 film)
cast: Louise Allbritton, Lon Chaney Jr., Robert Paige
son of exhortation, name meaning: 7 Barnaby
Son of Flubber (1963 film)
cast: Tommy Kirk, Fred MacMurray, Nancy Olson, Keenan Wynn
director: Robert Stevenson
Son of Frankenstein (1939 film)
cast: Boris Karloff, Bela Lugosi, Basil Rathbone
director: Rowland Lee, Rowland V. Lee
role: 4 Ygor
Son of Fury (1942 film)
cast: Tyrone Power, George Sanders, Gene Tierney
son of in Arabic: 3 ibn
Son of Kong, The (1933 film)
cast: Robert Armstrong, Helen Mack
Son of Monte Cristo, The (1940 film)
cast: Joan Bennett, Louis Hayward, George Sanders
director: Rowland V. Lee
Son of Paleface (1952 film)
cast: Bob Hope, Roy Rogers, Jane Russell
director: Frank Tashlin
Son of Rosemary author: 5 Levin
Son of the Circus, A author: John Irving
son of the right, name meaning: 8 Benjamin
Son of the Sheik (1926 film)
cast: Agnes Ayres, Vilma Banky, Rudolph Valentino
Son of the Sun: 4 Inca
Sonoma: 4 city, town
firm: 5 Gallo
locale: 10 California
neighbor: 4 Napa
Sonora: 4 city, town **5** state
city: 4 Kino **5** Yaquí **6** La Doce **7** Caborca, Cananea, Empalme, Guaymas, Navajoa, Nogales, Obregón **8** Nacozari **9** Esperanza **10** Hermosillo, Huatabampo
Indian: 4 Seri
locale: 6 Mexico **10** California
Sonoran: 6 desert
locale: 6 Mexico **7** Arizona **10** California
sonority: 4 tone
sonorous: 4 deep, full, loud, rich **5** forte, noisy, sweet **6** dulcet, in tune **7** blaring, booming, jarring, lyrical, melodic, orotund, pealing, pompous, rackety,

raucous, reboant, roaring, stilted, tuneful, vibrant **8** crashing, piercing, plangent, resonant, rumbling, strident, turned up **9** big-voiced, clamorous, deafening, deep-toned, melodious **10** boisterous, euphonious, harmonious, resounding, rhetorical, stentorian, strepitous, thundering, thunderous, uproarious, vociferous
sons: **5** issue **7** kinfolk, progeny **8** kinfolks, kinsfolk
Sons __ Pioneers: **5** of the
__ Sons: **4** Four **5** All My
Sons and Lovers: **4** film **5** novel
author: D.H. Lawrence
cast: Wendy Hiller, Trevor Howard, Dean Stockwell, Mary Ure
director: Jack Cardiff
role: **5** Clara, Dawes, Edgar, Morel **6** Agatha
Sons author: Pearl S. Buck
Sons of __: **7** Liberty
Sons of Katie Elder, The (1965 film): **5** oater **7** western
cast: Martha Hyer, Dean Martin, John Wayne
director: Henry Hathaway
Sons of the Desert (1933 film)
cast: Charley Chase, Oliver Hardy, Stan Laurel
director: William A. Seiter
Sontag, Susan: **6** writer **8** essayist
work: The Benefactor
Death Kit
I, Etcetera
Illness as Metaphor
Sony: **2** TV **3** VCR **5** TV set **10** television
acquisition: **5** Loew's
alternative: **3** JVC, NEC, RCA **5** Sanyo **6** Quasar, Zenith **7** Emerson, Hitachi, ProScan, Toshiba **8** Magnavox, Sylvania **9** Panasonic
Soo: **4** Jack
Soo __: **5** Locks **6** Canals
sooey: **7** hog call
__ so often: **5** every
Sooke: **4** city, town
locale: **6** Canada
soon: **4** anon, nigh, then **5** after **6** any day, in a bit, in a sec, in time, pronto **7** betimes, by and by, erelong, fleetly, hastily, in a wink, later on, quickly, rapidly, shortly, someday **8** directly, hereupon, in a jiffy, in a while, promptly, sometime, speedily **9** afterward, any day now, any minute, any second, forthwith, hereafter, in a minute, in a moment, in a second, in due time, instantly, posthaste, presently, right away **10** any time now, before long, eventually, in good time
as ~ as: **4** once
just as ~: **6** gladly, rather **7** instead **10** preferably
sooner than ~: **6** at once
(to): **5** about
too ~: **5** early **9** premature
Soon composer: **8** Gershwin
sooner: **6** prefer, rather **10** beforehand, preferably
or later: **3** yet **4** anon **5** after **6** at last, in a bit, in time **7** by and by, finally, later on, someday **8** in a while, in the end, sometime **9** afterward, hereafter **10** before long, eventually, inevitably
than expected: **5** early **9** in advance, premature
Sooner: **9** Oklahoman
sooner or __: **5** later
soot: **4** dirt, soil **5** grime **9** lampblack
collector: **4** flue
particle: **4** smut
soothe: **3** pat **4** balm, calm, ease, help, hush, lick, love, lull **5** allay, cheer, quell, quiet, salve, still **6** becalm, defuse, defuze, gentle, make up, pacify, remedy, settle, soften, solace, stroke, subdue, temper **7** appease, assuage, compose, console, cool off, mollify, placate, relieve, sweeten **8** butter up, calm down, mitigate, palliate, play up to, unburden **9** alleviate, pour oil on, untrouble **10** conciliate, make nice to, smooth over
sooth ender: **3** say **5** sayer
soother: **4** balm **6** balsam, lotion **9** analgesic
baby ~: **4** talc
muscle ~: **6** hot tub
skin ~: **4** aloe **5** salve
sprain ~: **6** ice bag **7** ice pack
stomach ~: **5** Bromo **6** bicarb
throat ~: **6** hot tea
soothing: **4** calm, mild, soft **5** balmy, bland, sweet **6** dreamy, dulcet, smooth **7** anodyne **8** lenitive, tranquil **9** demulcent, emollient, soporific
plant: **4** aloe
word: **5** there
soothsay: **7** predict **8** foretell, prophesy
soothsayer: **4** seer **5** augur, sibyl **6** oracle, wizard **7** aruspex, diviner, prophet, psychic **8** haruspex **9** predictor **10** forecaster
observance: **4** omen
of a ~: **5** vatic **7** vatical
sooty: **4** dark **5** black, dirty, grimy, smoky **6** filthy, fouled, grubby, grungy, soiled **7** dirtied, smeared, smudged, stained, tainted, unclean **8** befouled, begrimed, maculate, polluted, slovenly, smirched **9** besmeared, blackened, tarnished **10** besmirched, fuliginous, unsanitary
relative: **3** jet **4** inky, onyx **5** ebony, raven, sable
sooty __: **4** mold, tern **6** blotch, grouse
sooty mold: **6** fungus
sop: **3** wet **4** blot, dunk **5** bribe, souse, steep **6** absorb, drench, grease, payola, soak up, splash **7** moisten **8** pacifier, saturate **10** concession
starter: **4** milk, sour **5** sweet
up: **6** absorb, draw in, gather, ingest, osmose, take in **7** drink in, swallow **10** assimilate
sopaipilla: **6** pastry **7** Mexican
soph
see sophomore
sopher: **7** copyist
Sophia: **5** Loren
in Russian: **5** Sonia
sophic: **4** wise
Sophie: **6** Tucker **7** Germain, Marceau
__-Sophie Mutter: **4** Anne
Sophie's Choice: **4** film **5** novel
author: William Styron
cast: Kevin Kline, Peter MacNicol, Meryl Streep
director: Alan J. Pakula
sophism: **6** dupery **7** fallacy, quibble **9** deception **10** invalidity
sophist: **8** logician, reasoner
sophistic: **6** faulty, flawed **7** invalid, unsound **8** specious **9** illogical **10** fallacious, irrational
sophisticated: **3** hep, hip **4** chic, cool, into, nice, wise **5** blasé, couth, sharp, slick, suave **6** jet-set, mature, modern, smooth, subtle, uptown, urbane, with it **7** complex, elegant, genteel, knowing, refined, studied, wised up, worldly **8** advanced, citified, cultured, delicate, involved, polished, schooled, seasoned, tolerant, well-bred **9** elaborate, high-toned, in the know, intricate, practiced, skeptical **10** cultivated
gathering: **5** salon
miss: **3** deb
quality: **5** class, style
Sophisticated __: **4** Lady
sophistication: **4** tact **5** class, poise, style **6** wisdom **7** culture, finesse, manners **8** elegance, judgment, maturity **9** composure
lacking ~: **4** naif **5** naive
showy ~: **5** glitz
sophistry: **7** fallacy **9** casuistry, chicanery
Sophocles: **5** Greek **10** playwright
forte: **5** drama
work: Ajax
Antigone
Electra
Oedipus at Colonus
Oedipus Rex
sophomore: **4** year **5** pupil **7** student **9** collegian, undergrad
future ~: **5** frosh
past ~: **6** junior
team: **6** jayvee
sophomoric: **4** naif **5** brash, naive, young **6** callow **7** asinine, foolish, puerile **8** immature, reckless, youthful **9** half-baked
sopor: **8** lethargy
soporific: **4** dopy, dozy, dull **5** balmy, dopey **6** drowsy, opiate, sleepy, snoozy **7** calming, nodding, numbing, tedious **8** hypnotic, sedative, soothing **9** deadening, somnolent **10** anesthetic, dullsville, enervating, monotonous
soppiness: **5** slush
sopping: **3** wet **4** damp **5** soggy, undry **7** wettish
soppy: **3** wet **5** mushy, soggy **6** soaked, sodden **7** maudlin, mawkish **8** drenched, romantic **9** saturated **10** bedraggled
soprano: **4** Alda, Bori, high, Lind, Pons, Popp **5** Calvé, Eames, Freni, Horne, Melba, Mills, Moffo, Moore, Patti, Price, Raisa, range, Sills, voice **6** Battle, Berger, Callas, Farrar, Garden, Kanawa, Norman, Peters, singer, Steber, Upshaw **7** Crespin, Farrell, Fleming, Lehmann, Nilsson, Tebaldi, Traubel **8** Albanese, Flagstad, Ponselle, vocalist **10** Galli-Curci, Sutherland, Tetrazzini
Australian ~: **5** Melba **10** Sutherland
Austrian ~: **4** Popp
between ~ and tenor: **4** alto
British ~: **6** Garden
Catfish Row ~: **4** Bess
certain ~: **5** mezzo
French ~: **4** Pons **5** Calvé **7** Crespin
German ~: **6** Berger **7** Lehmann
Italian ~: **5** Freni, Patti **7** Tebaldi **8** Albanese **10** Galli-Curci, Tetrazzini
New Zealand ~: **4** Alda
Norwegian ~: **8** Flagstad
note: **5** high C
Polish ~: **5** Raisa
Spanish ~: **4** Bori
specialty: **5** trill
Swedish ~: **4** Lind **7** Nilsson
soprano __: **3** sax **4** clef
__-soprano: **5** mezzo
Sopranos, The (HBO drama)
cast: Lorraine Bracco (Dr. Jennifer Melfi)
Edie Falco (Carmela Soprano)
James Gandolfini (Tony Soprano)
Nancy Marchand (Livia Soprano)
matriarch: **5** Livia
So Proudly We Hail! (1943 film)
cast: Claudette Colbert, Paulette Goddard, Veronica Lake
director: Mark Sandrich
__ sop to Cerberus: **5** give a
Sopwith __: **5** Camel
Sor __ Cruz: **5** Juana
sora: **4** bird, rail
milieu: **5** marsh
So Rare (1957 song) artist: Jimmy Dorsey
sorb: **4** tree **5** fruit
sorbet: **3** ice **7** dessert
sorbic __: **4** acid
Sorbo: **5** Kevin
Sorbonne site: **5** Paris **6** France
sorcerer: **4** mage **5** magus, witch **6** wizard **7** charmer, diviner, prophet, warlock **8** conjurer, conjuror, magician **9** enchanter
African ~ of fiction: **3** She
assistant: **7** famulus
of Greek myth: **5** Medea
Sorcerer's Apprentice, The composer: **5** Dukas
Sorcerer, The composer: **7** Gilbert **8** Sullivan
sorcery: **3** hex, obi **4** jinx **5** magic, obeah, spell, vodun **6** voodoo **7** alchemy, devilry, evil eye **8** black art, deviltry, witchery, witching, wizardry **10** black magic, divination, hocus-pocus, mumbo-jumbo, necromancy, witchcraft
Sordello author: Robert Browning
sordid: **3** bad, low **4** base, foul, mean, poor, slum, ugly, vile **5** cheap, dirty, dowdy, grimy, mangy, nasty, seamy, seedy, sorry, venal **6** abject, filthy, grubby, impure, mangey, scurvy, shabby, sleazy, vulgar **7** bestial, corrupt, ignoble, low-down, selfish, squalid, unclean, vicious **8** covetous, degraded, shameful, slovenly, wretched **9** corrupted, low-minded, mercenary, miserable, repellant, repellent **10** avaricious, degenerate, despicable, ungenerous
sordidness: **6** misery **7** squalor
sordino: **4** mute
__ sordino: **3** con
sore: **3** hot, mad, raw **4** achy, hurt, ired, lame **5** acute, angry, blain, cross, huffy, irate, irked, livid, riled, sharp, stung, upset, vexed, wroth **6** aching, bitter, chafed, fuming, in a pet, injury, ireful, lesion, miffed, pained, peeved, piqued, raging, raving, red-hot, severe, tender **7** annoyed, blister, bruised, burning, enraged, furious, grieved, hurting, in a snit, irksome, painful, ranting, steamed, teed off **8** abrasion, annoying, burned up, choleric, grieving, incensed, inflamed, maddened, offended, outraged, pressing, reddened, smarting, swelling, troubled, wrathful **9** afflicted, affronted, aggrieved, indignant, irritated, resentful, seeing red, sensitive, splenetic, ticked off **10** freaked out, hopping mad, infuriated, unpleasant
be a ~ loser: **4** mope, sulk
ender: **4** head
feel ~: **4** ache, hurt **6** resent
make ~: **3** ire, irk **4** rile **5** anger, peeve, upset **6** injure
point: **5** nerve **8** weakness
spot: **4** ache **8** irritant
starter: **3** eye **4** foot
sore __: **5** loser, point **6** throat
__ sore: **6** saddle
sorehead: **5** grump **6** grouch
Sorel: **4** city, town **7** Georges
locale: **6** Canada, Quebec
Sorel, Georges: **6** French **11** philosopher
sorely: **5** badly **9** seriously

soreness: 4 ache, hurt, kink, pain 10 discomfort
Sorensen, Soren: 6 Danish 7 chemist
Sorenstam, Annika: 6 golfer 7 Swedish
milieu: 5 links 6 course
org.: 4 LPGA
Sorento: 3 Kia, SUV
sorghum: 5 grain 6 fodder
grain ~: 4 milo 5 doura, durra, kafir 6 dourah, hegari
product: 5 sirup, syrup
structure: 4 silo
__ sorghum: 5 grain, grass, sugar, sweet
__ So Right: 4 Love
Sor Juana __: 4 Cruz
Sorkin: 5 Aaron 6 Arleen
Sorocaba: 4 city, town
locale: 6 Brazil
sorority: 4 club 5 order 7 coterie, society
gathering: 5 mixer
letter: 2 mu, nu, pi, xi 3 chi, eta, phi, psi, rho, tau 4 beta, iota, zeta 5 alpha, delta, gamma, kappa, omega, sigma, theta 6 lambda 7 epsilon, omicron, upsilon
member: 4 coed 6 sister
opposite: 4 frat 10 fraternity
seek a ~: 4 rush
sorority __: 5 house
sorrel: 4 roan, tree 5 brown, color, horse 6 equine 7 reddish
family: 5 heath
relative: 3 bay, dun, tan 4 bole, ecru, fawn, foxy, nude, seal 5 amber, beige, camel, cocoa, erica, hazel, khaki, mocha, sepia, tawny, umber 6 auburn, bister, bistre, bronze, coffee, copper, ginger, russet, sienna, suntan, walnut 7 arbutus, biscuit, caramel, dogwood, madrone 8 chestnut, cinnamon, mahogany 9 butternut, chocolate
soup: 5 schav
wood ~: 3 oca, oka 6 oxalis
Sorrell: 5 Booke
Sorrento: 4 city, port, town
locale: 5 Italy
sorrow: 3 woe 4 ache, moan, pain, pity, sigh 5 agony, blues, dolor, gloom, grief, groan, mourn, tears, trial, worry 6 bemoan, bewail, grieve, lament, misery, regret 7 agonize, anguish, bad news, carry on, deplore, despair, emotion, grieved, remorse, sadness, trouble, weeping 8 distress, grieving, hardship, languish, mourning, the blues 9 dejection, heartache, lamenting, penitence, suffering 10 affliction, depression, desolation, heartbreak, heavy heart, infelicity, melancholy, misfortune, repentance, woefulness
exclamation: 4 alas 5 alack 8 lackaday, welladay, wellaway
express ~: 3 sob 4 weep 5 mourn 6 grieve
express ~ for: 4 pity 6 bemoan, bewail
in music: 6 dolore
sign of ~: 4 tear
with ~: 5 sadly
sorrowful: 3 sad 4 blue, dark, glum 5 heavy, woful 6 broody, dismal, dreary, gloomy, in pain, morose, somber, tragic, woeful 7 doleful, elegiac, hangdog, hurting, joyless, painful, piteous, tearful, unhappy 8 dejected, dolorous, downcast, grieving, grievous, mournful, poignant, tragical, troubled, wretched 9 affecting, afflicted, bummed out, cheerless, depressed, heartsick, miserable, plaintive, regretful, saturnine, sniveling, woebegone 10 chapfallen, despondent, dispirited, lamentable, lugubrious, melancholy
in a ~ way: 5 sadly
one: 4 ruer
sound: 4 moan, sigh 5 groan
words: 4 ah me
sorrowfully in music: 8 doloroso
sorrows, name meaning: 7 Dolores
sorry: 3 bad, sad 4 base, dire, grim, oops, poor, ugly, vile 5 bleak, needy, small, woful 6 abject, dismal, gloomy, paltry, rotten, scummy, shabby, shamed, shoddy, sordid, tragic, woeful 7 apology, ashamed, grieved, hapless, ill-done, joyless, pitiful, ruinous, scruffy, unhappy, unlucky 8 beggarly, contrite, dejected, downcast, excuse me, grievous, indigent, inferior, luckless, mea culpa, mournful, pathetic, penitent, saddened, shameful, sheepish, touching, tragical, trifling, unusable, wretched 9 chastened, depressed, destitute, miserable, plaintive, regretful, repentant, worthless 10 apologetic, deplorable, depressing, despicable, despisable, despondent, detestable, distressed, inadequate, melancholy, pathetical, remorseful, shamefaced
be ~: 3 rue 6 regret, repent
Sorry: 4 game 9 board game
Sorry!: 4 oops 8 excuse me
__ Sorry Now: 4 Who's
Sorry Seems to Be the Hardest Word (1976 song) artist: Elton John
Sorry, Wrong Number (1948 film)
cast: Burt Lancaster, Ann Richards, Barbara Stanwyck
director: Anatole Litvak
sort: 3 ilk, lot, peg, set, tab 4 body, comb, cull, file, form, kind, make, mold, pick, race, rank, sift, type 5 array, batch, brand, breed, class, genre, genus, grade, group, index, order, stamp, style, suite 6 assort, choose, clutch, divide, family, kidney, manner, nature, number, parcel, person, screen, select, size up, stripe, winnow 7 arrange, bracket, catalog, collate, fashion, quality, species, variety 8 category, classify, graduate, organize, separate, specimen, typecast 9 catalogue, character, deficient 10 categorize, distribute, pigeonhole
sort __: 3 out
__ sort: 3 of a
sorta: 4 a bit 5 kinda 6 in a way, kind of, rather 8 somewhat 10 more or less, not exactly
sortie: 4 raid 5 foray, sally 6 attack, battle, charge 7 assault, mission 9 irruption, offensive, onslaught
sort of
suffix: 3 -ish
sorts
be out of ~: 3 ail 4 pout, sulk
out of ~: 3 ill, low, sad 4 blue, curt, dour, down, glum, grim, mean, mopy, sick, sour, ugly 5 angry, balky, bleak, cross, fed up, fussy, gruff, huffy, moody, mopey, nasty, onery, riled, sharp, short, sulky, surly, testy, tired, upset, vexed, whiny 6 ailing, bitter, broody, bummed, crabby, cranky, crusty, dismal, droopy, feisty, fretty, gloomy, grumpy, moping, mopish, morose, ornery, peaked, peeved, piqued, poorly, put out, snarly, snippy, stewed, sullen, touchy, unwell, woeful 7 annoyed, bearish, bilious, carping, crabbed, doleful, forlorn, fretful, griping, grouchy, huffish, in a funk, joyless, let down, nettled, not well, peevish, pensive, pouting, prickly, subdued, uncivil, unhappy, waspish, whining, worried 8 below par, brooding, cast down, caviling, choleric, churlish, contrary, critical, dejected, desolate, downcast, fretsome, growling, grumpish, hopeless, incensed, liverish, negative, offended, perverse, petulant, provoked, snappish, snarling, wretched 9 aggrieved, bummed-out, cheerless, crotchety, depressed, disgusted, dyspeptic, fractious, grumbling, impatient, in the pits, irascible, irritable, long-faced, miserable, querulous, resentful, splenetic, truculent, woebegone 10 censorious, chapfallen, despondent, dispirited, displeased, ill-humored, ill-natured, indisposed, in the dumps, lugubrious, melancholy, ungracious, unpleasant
Sorvino: 4 Mira, Paul
Sorvino, Mira: 7 actress
father: 4 Paul
film: At First Sight (1998)
Mighty Aphrodite (1995, AA)
Quiz Show (1994)
The Replacement Killers (1998)
Oscar: Mighty Aphrodite
Sorvino, Paul: 5 actor
daughter: 4 Mira
film: Bulworth (1998)
GoodFellas (1990)
Made for Each Other (1971)
Nixon (1995)
Oh, God! (1977)
Reds (1981)
A Touch of Class (1973)
SOS: 4 help 6 signal 7 soap pad, warning
motorist's ~: 5 flare
receiver: 4 USCG
response: 3 aid
rival: 6 Brillo
SOS (1975 song) artist: ABBA
So Sad (1960 song) artist: Everly Brothers
Sosa, Sammy sport: 8 baseball
__ So Shy: 3 He's
so-so: 2 OK 3 avg. 4 blah, fair, okay 5 ho-hum 6 medium, modest, not bad, rather 7 average 8 adequate, lukewarm, mediocre, middling, moderate, not great, ordinary, passable, passably 9 not too bad, tolerable, tolerably, unnotable 10 acceptable, adequately, fairly good, mezza-mezza, moderately, pedestrian, pretty good
sostenuto: 5 pedal
__ So Stories: 4 Just
So's your old man: 6 retort
sot: 4 lush, wino 5 souse, toper 6 barfly, bibber 7 guzzler, tippler, tosspot 9 inebriate
Sot-__ Factor, The: 4 Weed
Soter: 4 pope 7 pontiff
So that's it!: 3 aha, oho 4 I see
Sotheby's: 10 auctioneer
patron: 6 bidder
signal at ~: 3 nod
So there!: 3 hah, see
Sothern, Ann: 7 actress
film: Brother Orchid (1940)
Crazy Mama (1975)
Folies Bergère (1935)
Hooray for Love (1935)
Kid Millions (1934)
Lady Be Cool (1941)
Lady in a Cage (1964)
A Letter to Three Wives (1949)
Shadow on the Wall (1950)
Super Sleuth (1937)
The Whales of August (1987)
TV: My Mother the Car, Private Secretary
Sothis: 6 Sirius 7 Dog Star
So This Is __: 5 Paris
So This Is New York (1948 film)
cast: Henry Morgan, Rudy Vallee
Sotho: 8 language
home: 6 Africa 7 Lesotho 8 Botswana
so to __: 5 speak
Soto __: 3 Zen
__ so to bed: 3 and
Soto, Talisa: 7 actress
spouse: Benjamin Bratt
sotto voce: 6 softly 9 whispered
remark: 5 aside
Sot-Weed Factor, The author: John Barth
sou: 4 coin 5 money 8 pittance
without a ~: 4 poor 5 needy
souari: 3 nut
soubise: 5 sauce
ingredient: 5 onion
soubrette: 4 maid
souchong: 3 tea 8 beverage
__ souci: 4 sans
Soudan to Fuzzy-Wuzzy: 3 'ome
Souez: 3 Ina
soufflé, like a: 4 airy, eggy 5 light
sough: 4 rush, sigh 6 murmur, rustle 7 rushing, sighing 8 rustling 9 murmuring
sought-after: 3 hot 7 popular
souk: 4 mart 5 bazar 6 bazaar, market
shopper: 4 Arab
soul: 3 ego 4 body, life, mind, root, self 5 anima, ardor, being, bosom, cause, force, ghost, heart, human, music, sense, stuff, umbra 6 bottom, energy, fantom, fervor, genius, marrow, mortal, person, pneuma, psyche, reason, shadow, spirit 7 courage, essence, feeling, phantom, rapport, thought 8 creature, interior, nobility, vitality, vivacity 9 animation, character, élan vital, intellect, life force, personage, principle, substance 10 conscience, human being, individual
combining form: 4 thym- 5 psych-, thymo- 6 psycho-
heart and ~: 4 pith 6 wholly 8 entirely 10 completely, thoroughly
in French: 3 âme
in Hinduism: 4 atma 5 atman
in Spanish: 4 alma
living ~: 5 being, human 6 mortal, person 10 human being, individual
mate: 3 bud, pal 4 body 5 buddy 6 friend 8 alter ego
not a ~: 4 none 5 no one 6 nobody
soul __: 4 cake, food, mate 5 music 6 sister 7 brother
__ soul: 5 nary a, world
Soul: 5 David, Jimmy
Soul __: 3 Man 5 on Ice, Train 6 Asylum
Soul and Inspiration (1966 song)
artist: Righteous Brothers
Soule: 4 Olan
soulful: 5 funky 6 moving 7 intense, lyrical 9 emotional 10 expressive
Soulful Strut (1968 song) artist: Young-Holt Unlimited
Soul, Jimmy song: If You Wanna Be Happy (1963)
__ soul man: 3 I'm a
Soul Man (1967 song) artist: Sam and Dave
__ Soul Music: 5 Sweet
__ Soul Picnic: 6 Stoned
Souls at Sea (1937 film)
cast: Gary Cooper, Frances Dee, George Raft
director: Henry Hathaway
__ Souls' Day: 3 All
Souls on Fire author: Elie Wiesel

sound: **3** din, fit, hum, jar **4** bang, bark, blow, boom, buzz, clap, cool, deep, echo, emit, fair, firm, good, gulf, hale, just, look, moan, note, ping, play, ring, roar, safe, sane, seem, sing, slam, spry, thud, tone, toot, true, well, wise, word **5** audio, blare, burst, clack, clang, clank, clink, crash, creak, drone, exact, hardy, legal, legit, licit, loyal, lucid, music, noise, pitch, plumb, right, shout, smash, sober, solid, speak, tenor, thump, tight, total, valid, vital, voice, whine, whole **6** babble, cackle, cogent, entire, hearty, intact, jabber, jangle, kasher, kosher, melody, murmur, patter, proper, proven, racket, rattle, report, robust, rugged, rumble, secure, shriek, shrill, squawk, squeak, stable, static, strong, sturdy, tinkle, unhurt, up to it **7** channel, chatter, clatter, correct, durable, ethical, explode, harmony, healthy, learned, logical, measure, perfect, precise, prudent, ransack, reflect, ringing, solvent, telling, tenable, thunder, trumpet, upright, vibrant, vibrate, whisper **8** accepted, accurate, all there, analytic, coherent, complete, credible, detonate, faithful, flawless, language, laughter, luculent, methodic, orthodox, profound, rational, received, reliable, resonate, sensible, softness, thorough, together, tonality, unbroken, unflawed, unharmed, unmarked, vigorous, virtuous, well-made **9** advisable, canonical, competent, effective, effectual, faultless, holding up, honorable, in the pink, judicious, plausible, practical, pragmatic, realistic, recovered, reputable, resonance, undamaged, undecayed, uninjured, unscathed, untouched, up to snuff, vibration, well-built, wholesome **10** analytical, clattering, consequent, consistent, convincing, defensible, dependable, impeccable, intonation, legitimate, modulation, reasonable, recognized, sanctioned, satisfying, standing up, undeniable, unimpaired, unmistaken
  bite: **4** clip
  booster: **3** amp
  combining form: **3** son- **4** phon-, soni-, sono- **5** audio-, -phone, phono-, -phony
  ender: **3** man, men **5** board, proof, stage, track
  quality in music: **6** timbre
  science of ~: **9** acoustics
  stage: **3** set
  unit: **3** bel **7** decibel
sound __: **3** bow, law, man, off, out **4** bite, film, gate, head, hole, wave **5** block, stage, title, truck **6** camera, effect **7** barrier, ranging
sound __ bell: **3** as a
sound __ dollar: **3** as a
__ sound: **5** white **6** Motown, speech **7** optical
__ Sound: **4** Hobe **5** Puget **6** Kalmar, Norton **7** McMurdo, Pamlico
sound-and-__ show: **5** light
Sound and the Fury, The author: William Faulkner
sounded: **4** oral **9** vocalized
__ sounder: **5** depth
Sounder (1972 film)
  cast: Kevin Hooks, Cicely Tyson, Paul Winfield
  director: Martin Ritt
sounding __: **4** lead, line **5** board **6** rocket **7** balloon, machine
  take a ~: **5** plumb
soundless: **3** mum **4** calm **5** quiet, still **6** hushed, silent **8** nonvocal **9** inaudible, noiseless
  communication: **3** ASL
soundlessness: **5** quiet
soundly: **4** well
soundness: **4** wits **5** vigor **6** health, reason, sanity **8** strength, validity **9** integrity, stability **10** legitimacy
Sound of Music, The (1965 film)
  cast: Julie Andrews, Richard Haydn, Eleanor Parker, Christopher Plummer, Peggy Wood
  character: **3** Max **4** Elsa, Kurt, Rolf **5** Georg, Gretl, Liesl, Maria, Marta **6** Abbess, Berthe, Gruber, Louisa, Mother, Rainer, Sister, Sophia, Ursula **7** Schmidt **8** Brigitta, von Trapp **9** Detweiler, Friedrich, Schraeder **10** Margaretta
  composer: **7** Rodgers **11** Hammerstein
  director: Robert Wise
  extra: **3** nun
  setting: **4** Alps **7** Austria
  song: **5** Maria **6** Do-Re-Mi
Sound of Waves, The author: Yukio Mishima
soundproof: **6** deaden
soundproofing unit: **5** sabin
sounds
  harmonious ~: **5** music
  making ~: **5** vocal
Sounds of Silence, The (1965 song)
  artist: Simon and Garfunkel
sound system
  component: **5** phono **6** stereo **9** turntable
soundtrack
  component: **5** vocal
  prepare a ~: **3** dub, mix
soup: **3** fog, mix **4** bisk, miso, mist **5** broth, dashi, fumet, gumbo, nitro, purée, ramen, schav **6** bisque, borsch, course, menudo, oxtail, potage, tomato, turtle, won ton **7** borscht, borshch, cholent, chowder, egg drop, mixture, pottage **8** alphabet, bouillon, callaloo, consommé, gazpacho, julienne, mulligan, split pea **9** beef broth, bird's nest, madrilène, mazto ball, pepper pot, shark's fin, vegetable **10** avgolemono, hot and sour, minestrone, mock turtle
  alphabet ~ letter: **6** noodle
  base: **5** stock
  beet ~: **6** borsch **7** borscht
  chilled ~: **5** schav **8** gazpacho **9** madrilène
  Chinese ~: **6** won ton **7** egg drop **9** bird's-nest **10** hot and sour
  crabmeat ~: **8** callaloo
  duck ~: **4** snap **5** cinch, cushy **6** picnic, simple **7** no sweat **8** easy task, painless, pushover, workable **9** uncomplex **10** child's play, effortless, elementary, unexacting
  eat ~ loudly: **5** slurp
  ender: **5** spoon
  flavoring: **4** miso
  follower: **6** entrée
  herb: **4** dill
  holder: **3** can, cup **4** bowl
  Indian: **3** dal
  ingredient: **3** pea **4** bean, beet, corn, leek, lima, ocra, okra, okro **5** onion **6** barley, lentil
  in the ~: **9** desperate **10** despairing
  Italian ~: **10** minestrone
  Japanese ~: **4** miso **5** dashi, ramen **6** larmen
  okra ~: **5** gumbo
  pea ~: **3** fog
  safecracker ~: **5** nitro
  sorrel ~: **5** schav
  Spanish ~: **6** menudo
  staple: **4** bone
  sushi-bar ~: **4** miso
  thick ~: **5** purée **6** bisque
  thin ~: **5** broth
  to nuts: **4** A to Z **6** all-out **7** in-depth **8** complete, from A to Z, sweeping, thorough **9** extensive **10** exhaustive, meticulous
  up: **9** reinforce
  utensil: **5** ladle, spoon
  warmer: **6** hot pot
soup __: **5** plate, spoon **7** kitchen
__ soup: **3** pea **4** duck **5** in the
__ Soup: **4** Duck
soup-and-fish: **5** tails
Soupault, Philippe: **4** poet **6** French
soupçon: **3** dab, nip **4** dash, hint **5** pinch, taste, tinge, touch, trace, whiff **6** breath, little, morsel, nibble, tidbit, trifle **7** minimum, whisper **8** spoonful
soup du __: **4** jour
souped-up
  auto: **5** racer **6** hot rod
  sound: **5** vroom **6** varoom
__-souper: **3** pea
soupfin __: **5** shark
__ soup fog: **3** pea
soup-to-__: **4** nuts
soupy: **4** thin **5** misty, runny **6** watery
Soupy: **5** Sales
__ soup yet?: **4** Is it
sour: **3** bad, off **4** acid, dour, keen, mean, rank, tart, turn **5** acerb, acrid, musty, sharp, spoil, tarty, taste, testy **6** acetic, acidic, biting, bitter, crabby, curdle, lemony, morose, off-key, on edge, rancid, rotten, snappy, sullen, turned, unripe **7** acerbic, acetose, acetous, acidify, caustic, curdled, cutting, cynical, envenom, gone bad, grouchy, off-tune, peevish, peppery, piquant, pungent, unhappy, waspish **8** alienate, churlish, embitter, grudging, imbitter, inedible, liverish, snappish, stinging, unsavory, vinegary **9** acidulate, acidulous, clabbered, fermented, irascible, irritable, jaundiced, querulous **10** astringent, bad-tasting, disenchant, embittered, exacerbate, ill-natured, unfriendly; ungenerous, unpleasant
  compound: **4** acid
  ender: **3** sop **4** ball, puss, wood **5** dough
  expression: **5** scowl, sneer
  go ~: **4** ruin, turn **5** addle, spoil, taint **6** curdle, mildew **7** acidify
  grapes: **6** excuse, reason **9** rationale
  hit a ~ note: **5** clash **6** jangle, rattle
  make ~: **8** acerbate
  note: **5** clash **6** jangle, off-key **7** discord **9** cacophony **10** disharmony
sour __: **3** gum **4** dock, mash, note, salt **5** cream, gourd **6** cherry, grapes, orange
__ sour: **4** flat **6** whisky **7** whiskey
sourball: **4** crab **5** candy, crank, grump **6** grouch **8** grumbler **10** curmudgeon
source: **4** font, fund, germ, head, mine, rise, root, seed, text, well **5** basis, birth, cause, onset, start **6** author, expert, father, matrix, mother, origin, parent, quarry, rising, spring, supply **7** dawning, opening **8** begetter, fountain, gold mine **9** authority, beginning, etymology, inception, informant, paternity, reference, reservoir **10** antecedent, authorship, birthplace, connection, derivation, originator, provenance, specialist, wellspring
  idea ~: **4** seed **5** spark **6** kernel
source __: **4** book, code
__-source: **4** sole
Sources of Strength author: Jimmy Carter
Source, The author: James A. Michener
sour cream: **3** dip **5** dairy
  companion: **5** blini, bliny
  partner: **5** chive
  serving: **6** dollop
sourdine: **4** mute
sourdough: **5** bread, miner
  be a ~: **8** prospect
  gear: **3** pan
  mix: **5** dough
  quest: **3** ore **4** gold **5** claim
soured: **6** rancid
sour grapes coiner: **4** Esop **5** Aesop
Souris: **5** river
  locale: **6** Canada
sourness: **6** flavor **7** acidity **8** acerbity
sourpuss: **4** crab, mope **5** crank, grump **6** grouch, kvetch, somber **7** killjoy **9** pessimist, worrywart
  like a ~: **4** dour **5** surly
  look: **5** scowl, sneer
soursop: **4** tree
  family: **6** annona
  relative: **5** papaw **6** pawpaw
sour-tasting: **4** tart **5** acerb
sous-__: **4** chef
Sousa, John Philip: **8** composer **10** bandleader
  work: The Beau Ideal
    The Bride Elect
    El Capitan
    The Fairest of the Fair
    The Free Lance
    The Gallant Seventh
    The Gladiator
    Globe and Eagle
    The Glory of the Yankee Navy
    Golden Jubilee
    Hands Across the Sea
    The High School Cadets
    The Invincible Eagle
    Jack Tar
    King Cotton
    The Liberty Bell
    Manhattan Beach
    Marching Along
    The Rifle Regiment
    Sabre and Spurs
    Semper Fidelis
    The Stars and Stripes Forever
    The Thunderer
    The Washington Post
sousaphone: **4** horn, tuba, wind **5** brass
__ Sousatzka: **6** Madame
souse: **3** dip, sop, sot, wet **4** dunk, lush, soak, wino **5** brine, douse, dowse, drown, steep, toper, water **6** deluge, drench, embrue, imbrue, pickle, seethe **7** dunking, guzzler, immerse, tippler **8** marinate, preserve, saturate, submerge, submerse, waterlog **9** inebriate **10** impregnate, intoxicate
souslik: **6** animal, mammal, rodent
sous-sous: **4** leap
Souster, Raymond: **4** poet **8** Canadian
soutenu: **9** sustained
south: **5** point **9** direction
  combining form: **5** austr- **6** austro-
  ender: **3** ern, paw **4** east, land, ward **5** bound, wards **6** lander, wester **7** eastern, western **8** eastward, westerly, westward
  go ~: **4** bolt, flee, quit **5** split **6** beat it, decamp, defect, escape **7** abscond, make off, pull out, skip out, vamoose **9** cut and run, disappear, skedaddle, steal away **10** fly the coop, hightail it, make a break
  in Spanish: **3** sur
  of: **5** below
South: **3** Joe **5** Dixie

South __: 4 Asia, Bend, Park, Pole, Seas, Side 5 Asian, Downs, Korea, Yemen 6 Arabia, Island, Riding, Street 7 America, Georgia, Holland, Pacific, Shields, Vietnam
South __ Islands: 3 Sea 6 Orkney
South __ Ocean: 7 Pacific
South __ Sea: 5 China
South __ Zone: 6 Frigid
South-__ Africa: 4 West
__ South: 3 Old 4 Deep, Goin' 5 Solid
South Africa: 6 nation 7 country
 bishop: 4 Tutu
 bovine: 4 Tuli 8 Bonsmara
 capital: 8 Cape Town, Pretoria
 city: 6 Benoni, Durban, Soweto 8 Cape Town, Pretoria
 encampment: 5 lager 6 laager
 golfer: 3 Els 5 Price 6 Player 8 Ernie Els 9 Nick Price 10 Gary Player
 grazing area: 4 veld 5 veldt
 hill: 3 kop 5 kopje 6 koppie
 iris: 4 ixia
 language: 4 Taal, Xosa, Zulu 5 Sotho, Swazi, Xhosa 7 Ndebele 9 Afrikaans
 lowland: 4 vlei
 money: 4 cent, rand
 national park: 6 Kruger
 neighbor: 7 Lesotho, Namibia 8 Botswana, Zimbabwe 9 Swaziland 10 Mozambique
 Nobelist in Chemistry: 4 Klug
 Nobelist in Literature: 8 Gordimer
 Nobelist in Peace: 4 Tutu 5 Klerk 6 Lutuli 7 Mandela
 people: 4 Xosa 5 Sotho, Swazi, Xhosa 6 Basuto, Tswana 7 Ndebele 8 Khoekhoe, Khoikhoi, Matabele
 plateau: 6 Karroo
 poet: 6 Brutus, Plomer
 port: 6 Durban 8 Cape Town
 province: 5 Natal
 ravine: 5 kloof
 region: 6 Ciskei
 river: 4 Vaal 6 Orange
 sheep: 6 dorper
 shrub: 6 narras
 territory: 5 Venda
 village: 4 stad 5 craal, kraal
 waterfall: 6 Tugela
 weasel: 8 muishond
 wind: 4 berg
 writer: 4 Head 5 Paton 6 Cloete, Fugard, Plomer 7 Coetzee 8 Abrahams, Gordimer, Jacobson 9 Schreiner 10 Van der Post
South African Dutch: 4 Taal
South America: 9 continent
 airline: 5 Varig
 bird: 4 guan, rhea 5 potoo 6 quezal 7 finfoot, hoatzin, quetzal, tinamou 8 caracara, curassow, guacharo, hoactzin, ovenbird, screamer, troupial
 bovine: 4 nata
 brandy: 5 pisco
 camel: 5 llama 6 alpaca, vicuna 7 guanaco
 cape: 4 Horn
 capital: 4 Lima 5 La Paz, Quito, Sucre 6 Bogotá 7 Caracas, Cayenne 8 Asunción, Brasília, Santiago 10 Montevideo, Paramaribo 11 Buenos Aires
 cowboy: 6 gaucho
 current: 6 El Niño
 dance: 5 tango
 deer: 4 pudu 6 guemal, huemul 7 brocket
 desert: 7 Atacama, Sechura 10 Patagonian
 explorer: 5 Cabot 8 Vespucci
 farm: 5 finca
 feline: 4 puma 6 cougar, margay, ocelot 7 panther
 fish: 6 aimara 7 piranha, scalare 8 bloodfin, characin
 gulf: 9 Guayaquil
 Indian: 4 Inca, Moxo, Tama 5 Carib 6 Arawak, Aymara, Galibi, Jivaro, Kechua, Lengua, Yahgan 7 Chibcha, Guarani, Kechuan, Quechua, Quichua 8 Caingang, Quechuan 9 Tehuelche 10 Araucanian
 island: 6 Chiloe
 language: 4 Tupi 7 Spanish
 mat: 4 yapa
 monkey: 3 sai 4 titi 6 howler
 mountain: 4 Solo, Toro 5 Cachi, Chani, Cusco, Cuzco, Galan, Laudo, Negro, Pular, Quela 6 Ampato, Bonete, Juncal, Pissis, Sajama 7 Huandoy, Illampu, Palermo, San Juan 8 Ancohuma, Coropuna, El Condor, El Muerto, Famatina, Illimani, Polleras, Solimana, Tortolas, Yerupaja 9 Aconcagua, Antofalla, Condoriri, Huascarán, Incahuasi, Marmolejo, Pumasillo, Salcantay, Tupungato 10 Chimborazo, Mercedario, Nacimiento, Parinacota, Tres Cruces
 mountains: 5 Andes
 nation: 4 Peru 5 Chile 6 Brazil, Guyana 7 Bolivia, Ecuador, Uruguay 8 Colombia, Paraguay, Suriname 9 Argentina, Venezuela
 opossum: 5 yapok
 parrot: 5 macaw 6 Amazon
 plain: 5 pampa
 port: 3 Rio
 prairie: 5 pampa
 primate: 4 saki, titi 6 uakari 7 tamarin 8 capuchin, marmoset
 region: 6 Guiana
 reptile: 5 aboma
 river: 3 Apa 4 Arno, Beni, Juru, Napo 5 Apure, Cauca, Japur, Negro, Paran, Purús, Santa, Xingú 6 Amazon, Bio-Bio, Cuiabá, Javari, Javary, Mamoré 7 Berbice, Bermejo, Guaporé, Iguassú, Madeira, Mantaro, Marañón, Orinoco, Taoajós, Ucayali 8 Araguaya, Demerara, Paraguay, Parnaiba, Putumayo 9 Magdalena, Roosevelt
 rodent: 4 cavy, mara, paca 5 coypu 6 agouti 7 rice rat, visacha 8 capibara, capybara, spiny rat, tuco-tuco 9 guinea pig 10 chinchilla
 shrub: 6 feijoa 7 guarana, rhatany 9 jaborandi
 skirt: 7 pollera
 strongman: 4 jefe
 tanager: 4 yeni 5 lindo
 tree: 4 ombu 6 carapa, rubber 7 wallaba 8 andiroba, crabwood, piassava
 unit of length: 4 vara
 volcano: 4 Ruiz 6 Láscar, Puracé, Sangay 7 El Misti, Galeras 8 Cotopaxi
 weasel: 5 tayra
 wind: 5 zonda
__ South America: 6 Inside
South American: 6 Andean, Latina, Latino
Southampton: 4 city, earl, port, town
 locale: 7 England 9 Hampshire
South Atlantic: 5 ocean 7 current
 island: 8 St. Helena 9 Ascension
South Australia capital: 8 Adelaide
Southaven: 4 city, town
 locale: 4 Miss.
__ South Bay: 5 Great
South Bend: 4 city, town
 locale: 7 Indiana
 sch.: 3 NDU
south by __: 4 east, west
South Carolina: 5 state
 capital: 8 Columbia
 city: 5 Aiken 6 Easley, Sumter 7 Taylors 8 Anderson, Columbia, Florence, Rock Hill 9 Greenwood, St. Andrews 10 Charleston, Goose Creek, Greenville
 conference: 3 SEC
 island: 6 Parris
 neighbor: 7 Georgia
 port: 10 Charleston
 school: 7 Citadel, Clemson
 state amphibian: 10 salamander
 state beverage: 4 milk
 state bird: 4 wren
 state dance: 4 shag
 state flower: 9 jessamine
 state fruit: 5 peach
 state game bird: 10 wild turkey
 state gemstone: 8 amethyst
 state hospitality beverage: 3 tea
 state insect: 6 mantid
 state stone: 7 granite
 state tree: 8 palmetto
 word in ~ motto: 5 spero
South China Sea
 bay: 6 Brunei
 city on the ~: 6 Danang
 gulf: 4 Siam 6 Tonkin 8 Thailand
 inlet: 5 Subic
 island: 6 Hainan, Taiwan 7 Formosa 8 Hong Kong 9 Singapore
 locale: 5 China 6 Taiwan 7 Vietnam
 old ~ kingdom: 4 Anam 5 Annam
 river to the ~: 6 Mekong 7 Xi Jiang
South Dakota: 5 state
 capital: 6 Pierre
 city: 4 Lead 5 Huron, Onida 6 Custer, Pierre 8 Aberdeen, Deadwood 9 Rapid City, Watertown 10 Sioux Falls
 county: 5 Lyman
 Indian: 10 Miniconjou
 mountain: 6 Harney
 national park: 8 Badlands, Wind Cave
 neighbor: 3 Neb., Wyo. 4 Iowa, Minn., Mont., Nebr. 7 Montana, Wyoming 8 Nebraska 9 Minnesota
Southdown: 5 sheep
Southeast Asian: 3 Lao, Tai 4 Thai
 Buddhism: 9 Theravada
 fruit: 6 durian 8 rambutan 9 carambola
 gulf: 4 Siam 6 Tonkin 8 Thailand
 language: 3 Tai, Yao 4 Miao 5 Malay
 nation: 4 Laos 5 Burma 7 Myanmar, Vietnam 8 Malaysia, Thailand
 people: 5 Hmong
 wild ox: 4 gaur
southeaster: 4 wind
Southeastern Conference
 school: 3 LSU 4 Miss. 6 Auburn 7 Alabama, Florida, Georgia 8 Arkansas, Kentucky 9 Tennessee 10 Vanderbilt
southerly: 4 wind
southern __: 4 cane, toad 6 lights 7 cypress
Southern __: 3 Cal 4 Alps, blot, Fish, Mail 5 belle, Cross, Crown, Piute, Slavs, Yemen 6 Nights, Paiute 7 Baptist
Southern Alps: 3 mts. 4 mtns. 5 range 9 mountains
 locale: 10 New Zealand
Southern California
 see USC
Southern Comfort: 5 drink 8 beverage
Southerner, The (1945 film)
 cast: Beulah Bondi, Betty Field, J. Carrol Naish, Zachary Scott
 director: Jean Renoir
Southern Mail author: Antoine de Saint-Exupéry
Southern Methodist University
 see SMU
Southern Nights (1977 song) artist: Glen Campbell
Southern, Terry: 6 author, writer
Southern Yankee, A (1948 film)
 cast: Arlene Dahl, Brian Donlevy, Red Skelton
Southey, Robert: 4 poet 7 British
 group: Lake Poets
 work: The Battle of Blenheim
Southfield: 4 city, town
 locale: 8 Michigan
South Florida
 athletes: 5 Bulls
 locale: 5 Tampa
Southfork: 5 ranch
 matriarch: 5 Ellie
South Frigid __: 4 Zone
Southgate: 4 city, town
 locale: 8 Michigan
South Gate: 4 city, town
 locale: 8 Maryland 10 California
Southglenn: 4 city, town
 locale: 8 Colorado
South Hill: 4 city, town
 locale: 10 Washington
South Holland: 4 city, town
 locale: 8 Illinois
South, Joe
 song: Games People Play (1969) Walk a Mile in My Shoes (1970)
South Jordan: 4 city, town
 locale: 4 Utah
South Korea: 6 nation 7 country
 capital: 5 Seoul
 city: 4 Tegu 5 Ansan, Cheju, Seoul, Ulsan 6 Chonju, Inchon 7 Kwangju
 legislature: 6 Kukhoe
 money: 3 won 4 chon, jeon
 Nobelist in Peace: 10 Kim Dae Jung
 port: 5 Pusan
 sea: 9 East China
Southlake: 4 city, town
 locale: 5 Texas
south-of-the-border
 see Mexico
South Orange: 4 city, town
 athletes: 7 Pirates
 locale: 9 New Jersey
 school: 9 Seton Hall
South Orkney __: 7 Islands
South Pacific
 cairn: 3 ahu
 capital: 4 Apia, Suva 5 Agana 6 Majuro, Manila, Nouméa, Tarawa 7 Honiara, Papeete 8 Funafuti, Pago Pago, Port-Vila 9 Nuku'alofa
 cloth: 4 tapa
 explorer: 4 Cook 5 Davys 6 Tasman 7 Dampier, Johnson 9 Heyerdahl, Vancouver
 feature: 4 isle 5 atoll
 garment: 5 pareo, pareu
 island: 3 Aru 4 Aroe, Arru, Bali, Cook, Fiji, Niue, Reao, Savo 5 atoll, Samar, Samoa, Tonga, Upolu 6 Easter 7 Oceania, Society, Vanuatu 9 Australia, Marquesas, New Guinea 10 New Zealand
 islander: 6 kanaka
 nation: 4 Fiji 5 Tonga
 port: 4 Apia
 shrub: 8 snowbush
 spot: 6 lagoon
 staple: 4 taro
South Pacific (1958 film): 7 musical
 cast: Rossano Brazzi, Mitzi Gaynor, Ray Walston

character: 4 Liat 5 Abner, Cable, Emile, Ngana 6 Billis, Jerome, Joseph, Luther, Nellie 7 Forbush, Stewpot 8 de Becque 10 Bloody Mary
composer: 7 Rodgers 11 Hammerstein
director: Joshua Logan
South Pacific __: 5 Ocean 7 Current
South Park
cat: 5 Kitty
character: 4 chef
dog: 6 Sparky
puppet: 5 Mr. Hat
southpaw: 5 lefty 6 leftie 7 pitcher 9 portsider
South Platte: 5 river
city on the: 6 Denver
locale: 8 Colorado, Nebraska
South Pole
bird: 6 Adélie 7 penguin
explorer: 5 Scott 8 Amundsen
South Riding (1938 film)
cast: Edna Best, Ralph Richardson
South Street (1963 song) artist: Orlons
South Temperate __: 4 Zone
South Valley: 4 city, town
locale: 9 New Mexico
South Vietnam
former ~ rebel org.: 3 NLF
__ South Wales: 3 New
Southwell, Robert: 4 poet 7 British
Southwest: 7 airline
alternative: 5 Delta 6 United 7 Jet Blue 8 American 11 America West, Continental
Southwest Conference team: 3 SMU
southwester: 4 wind
Southwestern
barbecue: 5 asado
copse: 4 mott 5 motte
dwelling: 5 adobe
lizard: 3 uta
painter: 7 O'Keeffe
plant: 5 yucca
predator: 4 puma
school: 4 UTEP
sight: 4 mesa 6 cactus, desert
state: 5 Texas 6 Nevada 7 Arizona 9 New Mexico
tree: 5 alamo, pinon
souvenir: 4 gift 5 curio, relic, token 7 memento, vestige 8 keepsake, landmark, reminder
souvenir __: 5 sheet
Souvenir: 4 font 8 typeface
souvlaki ingredient: 4 lamb
sou'wester: 3 hat 4 coat, wind 6 jacket 8 raincoat
__ So Vain: 5 You're
sovereign: 4 best, coin, czar, king, quid, tops, tsar, tzar 5 chief, crown, lofty, money, queen, regal, royal, ruler 6 gerent, leader, master, prince, ruling, top dog, utmost 7 emperor, empress, guiding, highest, majesty, monarch, regnant, supreme, viceroy 8 absolute, autocrat, dominant, imperial, majestic, powerful, princess, reigning 9 ascendant, directing, effective, excellent, monarchal, paramount, potentate, prevalent, principal, unlimited 10 autonomous, commanding, majestical
sovereignty: 4 rule, sway 5 power, reign, state 6 empire, nation 7 command, liberty, primacy 8 dominion, kingship 9 ascendant, dominance, supremacy
emblem of ~: 3 orb
Soviet: 3 Red
cosmonaut: 7 Gagarin
first lady: 5 Raisa
first ~ premier: 5 Lenin
plane: 3 MiG
political division: 3 SSR
press arm: 4 Tass
secret org.: 3 KGB 4 OGPU
spacecraft: 3 Mir 4 Luna 5 Lunik, Soyuz 7 Sputnik
workers' group: 5 artel
see also Russia, USSR
Soviet __: 5 Union 6 Russia
__ Soviet: 7 Supreme
Sovine: 3 Red
sow: 3 hog, pig, she 4 grow, seed, till, toss 5 fling, plant, raise, strew, swine 6 animal, female, spread 7 bestrew, implant, scatter 9 broadcast, propagate 10 promulgate
chow: 4 slop 5 swill
dissension: 6 divide
ender: 5 belly, bread
fit to ~: 6 arable
home: 3 pen, sty 6 pigpen, pigsty
mate: 4 boar
offspring: 4 gilt 6 farrow
opposite: 4 reap
syllable: 4 oink
the seeds of: 6 arouse
time to ~: 6 spring
wild oats: 3 err, sin 5 act up, cut up, stray 7 carry on, go wrong 8 go astray 9 misbehave 10 fool around
__ so weiter: 3 und
So Well Remembered (1947 film)
cast: John Mills, Patricia Roc, Martha Scott
director: Edward Dmytryk
sower: 6 farmer, seeder 7 planter
Soweto: 4 city, town
locale: South Africa
So what __ is new?: 4 else
sown: 4 semé 6 seeded 9 broadcast, dispersed, implanted, scattered, spread out 10 propagated
sow one's __ oats: 4 wild
so written: 3 sic
...sow's __: 3 ear
__ sow, so shall...: 4 As ye
Sox
see Red Sox, White Sox
__ Sox to Stockings: 5 Bobby
__ Soxx: 4 Bob B.
soy: 6 legume, veggie 9 vegetable
ender: 4 bean, milk
sauce fungus: 4 koji
soy __: 3 oil 4 milk 5 flour, sauce
Soyapango: 4 city, town
locale: 10 El Salvador
soybean: 6 legume, veggie 9 vegetable
product: 3 oil 4 miso, tofu
Soyinka, Wole: 4 poet 6 writer 8 essayist, Nigerian, Nobelist 10 playwright
Soylent __: 5 Green
Soyuz launcher: 4 USSR
Sp.
see Spanish
SP: Shore Patrol
employer: 3 USN
quarry: 4 AWOL
spa: 3 Ems, gym 4 bath, Enna, well 5 Baden, Epsom, Evian, Ischl, Troon, Vichy 6 Bad Ems, hot tub, resort, spring 7 Jacuzzi 9 hot spring, Marienbad, whirlpool, Wiesbaden 10 Baden-Baden, health club, Hot Springs, Lake Placid
British ~: 4 Bath
feature: 5 sauna
French ~: 5 Evian
German ~: 3 Ems 5 Baden 6 Bad Ems
Hungarian ~: 4 Eger
Sicilian: 4 Enna
__ spa: 3 day 6 health
space: 3 bit, gap, way 4 area, hole, play, room, slot, span, spot, term, time, turf, void, zone 5 arena, blank, field, lapse, range, reach, scope, spell, tract, while 6 extent, hiatus, lacuna, leeway, length, margin, period, radius, recess, schism, season, sphere, spread, vacuum, volume 7 breadth, expanse, headway, opening, stretch, vacancy, vacuity 8 aperture, capacity, distance, duration, headroom, infinity, interval, latitude, location, omission 9 elbowroom, expansion, interlude, largeness, territory 10 interstice, separation
breathing ~: 4 lull, pore 5 pause 8 vacation
chimp: 4 Enos
combining form: 6 spatio-
empty ~: 6 vacuum 7 vacancy
ender: 4 port, ship, sick, ward 5 borne, craft, farer 6 bridge
first American woman in ~: 4 Ride
free ~: 4 play, room 6 leeway 8 headroom 9 clearance, elbowroom
join up in ~: 4 dock, link
like outer ~: 4 vast
open ~: 5 glade 8 clearing, headroom 9 clearance, elbowroom
org.: 4 NASA
out: 6 forget 8 daydream 10 woolgather
outer ~: 3 sky 6 vacuum
program: 6 Apollo, Gemini 7 Mercury
starter: 3 air, sun 4 aero, back, head, work 5 crawl
station supply: 3 air
telescope: 6 Hubble
to a poet: 5 ether 6 aether
two-dimensional ~: 4 area
visitor from ~: 2 ET 5 alien, comet
space __: 3 bar, law 4 mark, rate 5 cadet, group, opera, probe, stage 6 charge, flight, heater, travel, writer 7 biology, capsule, carrier, lattice, science, shuttle, station
space-__: 6 saving
space-__ continuum: 4 time
__ space: 3 air 4 deep, dual, free, hair, line, open 5 crawl, outer, phase, Riesz, white 6 Banach, linear, metric, normed, sample, vector 7 Crookes, Hilbert, parking
__-space: 4 null 6 double, single, triple
Space __: 3 Age 4 Camp, Race 7 Cowboys
__-Space: 4 Outa
Space author: James A. Michener
Spaceballs (1987 film)
cast: Mel Brooks, John Candy, Rick Moranis, Bill Pullman
character: 5 Vespa
director: Mel Brooks
Space Cowboys (2000 film)
cast: Clint Eastwood, James Garner, Tommy Lee Jones, Donald Sutherland
director: Clint Eastwood
spacecraft: 4 ship 5 probe
alien ~: 3 UFO
compartment: 3 pod
frame: 6 gantry
spaced-out: 6 in a fog, sparse 8 confused, mindless 10 disjointed
spaceflight
combining form: 4 astr- 5 astro-
Space Flight Center
locale: 7 Alabama, Florida
Space Invaders producer: 5 Atari
Spacek, Sissy: 7 actress
film: 3 Women (1977)
Affliction (1998)
Blast From the Past (1999)
Carrie (1976)
Coal Miner's Daughter (1980, AA)
Crimes of the Heart (1986)
The Grass Harp (1996)
In the Bedroom (2001)
JFK (1991)
The Long Walk Home (1990)
Marie (1985)
Missing (1982)
Raggedy Man (1981)
The Straight Story (1999)
role: 4 Lynn 7 Loretta
Space Merchants, The author: 4 Pohl
Space Race (1973 song) artist: Billy Preston
space shuttle
assent: 3 A-OK
org.: 4 NASA
space station
org.: 4 NASA
Russian ~: 3 Mir
__ Space Telescope: 6 Hubble
Space, the __ frontier: 5 final
spacewalk: 3 EVA
spacey: 3 odd 5 dazed 7 unaware 8 confused 9 slaphappy
Spacey, Kevin: 5 actor
film: American Beauty (1999, AA)
The Big Kahuna (2000)
Glengarry Glen Ross (1992)
L.A. Confidential (1997)
Midnight in the Garden of Good and Evil (1997)
The Negotiator (1998)
Outbreak (1995)
Pay It Forward (2000)
Se7en (1995)
The Shipping News (2001)
A Time to Kill (1996)
The Usual Suspects (1995, AA)
film (voice): a bug's life (1998)
S. Pacific
see South Pacific
spacious: 3 big 4 airy, huge, open, vast, wide 5 ample, broad, great, large, roomy 7 immense, sizable 8 enormous, far-flung, generous, infinite, sizeable, sweeping 9 boundless, capacious, cavernous, expansive, extensive, limitless, uncrowded 10 commodious, voluminous, widespread
spaciousness: 4 room 6 extent, length 9 amplitude
spackle: 7 plaster
spad: 4 nail
Spad: 5 plane 7 biplane 8 airplane
foe: 6 Fokker
spade: 4 tool 5 scoop
calling a ~ a spade: 6 candor 9 outspoken
ender: 4 fish, work
use a ~: 3 dig
Spade: 3 Sam 5 David
spadefoot: 4 toad
spadelike tool: 4 spud
Spader, James: 5 actor
film: sex, lies, and videotape (1989)
Stargate (1994)
White Palace (1990)
Wolf (1994)
spades: 4 suit
at times: 5 trump
in ~: 9 decidedly
Spade, Sam: 2 PI 3 tec 6 shamus, sleuth 7 gumshoe 9 detective
partner: 6 Archer
work: 4 case 5 caper
spaghetti: 5 pasta 7 noodles
alternative: 4 orzo, ziti 5 penne 7 lasagna, lasagne, pastina, ravioli 8 bucatini, couscous, farfalle, linguine, linguini, macaroni, rigatoni 9 agnolotti, angelhair, cavatelli, manicotti 10 cannelloni, fettuccini, tortellini, vermicelli
drainer: 5 sieve
sauce: 4 Ragu 5 Prego 6 Prince 8 Classico 10 Newman's Own
topping: 5 pesto, sauce 8 marinara

spaghetti __: **5** sauce, strap **6** squash **7** Western
spaghettini: **5** pasta **7** noodles
alternative: **4** orzo, ziti **5** penne **7** lasagna, lasagne, pastina, ravioli **8** bucatini, couscous, farfalle, linguine, linguini, macaroni, rigatoni **9** agnolotti, angelhair, cavatelli, manicotti **10** cannelloni, fettuccini, tortellini, vermicelli
Spahn, Warren: **5** Brave **6** hurler **7** pitcher
Spain: **6** España, nation **7** country
art gallery: **5** Prado
bay: **4** Vigo **6** Biscay
bovine: **7** Alberes, Cachena, Retinta
capital: **6** Madrid
castles in ~: **6** revery **7** reverie
cellist: **6** Casals
city: **4** Leon, Lugo, Reus, Vigo **5** Avila, Elche, Gijón, Palma, Palos **6** Bilbao, Madrid, Málaga, Murcia, Toledo **7** Alacant, Córdoba, Granada, Sevilla, Seville **8** Valencia, Zaragoza **9** Barcelona, Las Palmas
combining form: **7** Hispano-
conductor: **6** Iturbi
dance: **4** jota **6** bolero **7** alegras, bourrée **8** chaconne, fandango **9** malaguena, paso doble, zapateado **10** seguidilla
explorer: **6** Balboa, Cortés **7** Pizarro **8** Coronado **11** Ponce de León
golfer: **6** Garcia **11** Ballesteros
guitarist: **5** Charo **7** Segovia
gulf: **5** Cádiz
gypsy: **6** gitano
hero: **5** El Cid
invader of ~: **4** Moor
island: **6** Canary
jacket: **7** zamarra
kettledrum: **6** atabal
king: **10** Juan Carlos
language: **6** Basque **9** Castilian
legislature: **6** Cortes
linear measure: **4** vara
locale: **6** Europe, Iberia
maize grinding stone: **4** mano
money: **3** bit **4** duro, real **5** dobla **6** doblon, escudo, peseta **7** centimo, pistole **8** doubloon **9** pistareen
mountain: **5** Aneto, Teide **6** Estats, Posets **8** Pyrenees
neighbor: **6** France **7** Andorra, Morocco **8** Portugal **9** Gibraltar
Nobelist in Literature: **4** Cela **7** Jiménez **9** Benavente, Echegaray **10** Aleixandre
Nobelist in Medicine: **11** Ramón y Cajal
org.: **4** NATO
painter: **4** Dali, Goya, Gris, Miró, Sert **7** El Greco, Picasso, Pisarro **9** Velázquez
philosopher: **6** Marías **7** Unamuno
pianist: **6** Iturbi **8** Larrocha
playwright: **4** Vega **6** Encina, Mihura, Sastre **7** Alberti **8** Calderón **9** Benavente
poet: **4** Mena, Ruiz, Vega **6** Berceo, Boscán, Encina **7** Alberti, Bousoño, Góngora, Guillén, Herrera, Jiménez, Salinas **8** Manrique **11** Altoaquirre
port: **4** Adra, Vigo **5** Cadiz **6** Bilbao **8** Alicante, La Coruña **9** Algeciras, Barcelona, Cartagena
princess: **5** Elena
queen: **3** Ena
railway: **5** Renfe
region: **4** Jaén, León, Lugo **5** Alava, Avila, Cádiz, Ceuta, Soria **6** Aragon, Burgos, Cuenca, Gerona, Huelva, Huesca, Lérida, Málaga, Murcia, Orense, Teruel, Toledo, Zamora **7** Almería, Badajoz, Cáceres, Córdoba, Galicia, Granada, La Rioja, Melilla, Navarre, Segovia, Sevilla, Vizcaya **8** Albacete, Alicante, Asturias, Baleares, Castilla, La Mancha, Palencia, Valencia, Zaragoza **9** Andalusia, Barcelona, Cantabria, Castellón, Catalonia, Las Palmas, Salamanca, Tarragona **10** Pontevedra
river: **4** Ebro **5** Douro, Tinto
saint: **6** Teresa **7** Dominic, Isidore, Vincent **8** Ignatius
sculptor: **7** Picasso, Pisarro
sheep: **6** merino
stately ~ dance: **8** saraband **9** sarabande
stewpot: **4** olla
surrealist: **4** Dali, Miró
tenor: **7** Domingo **8** Carreras
weight unit: **6** arroba
wine: **4** Cava **5** rioja, tinto **6** Malaga **8** Albariño, Montilla
with, in ~: **3** con
writer: **3** Aub **4** Cela **5** Benet **6** Alemán, Chacel, Marías, Matute **7** Alarcón, Arrabal **8** Marquina **9** Cervantes, Gironella **11** Pérez Galdós **13** Ortega y Gasset
see also Spanish
__ Spain: **3** New
__ Spake Zarathustra: **4** Thus
Spalding: **2** Al **4** Gray **6** Albert
competitor: **4** Voit
spall: **4** chip **5** galet, stone **6** gallet, garret **8** break off, split off
spalpeen: **5** rogue, scamp **6** bad guy **8** scalawag **9** scallawag, scallywag **10** scapegrace
spam: **5** e-mail
like ~: **8** unwanted
Spam: **4** meat
eater: **2** GI
ingredient: **3** ham
maker: **6** Hormel
span: **3** age **4** arch, ford, hand, life, link, pair, team, term, time **5** cover, cross, range, reach, scope, space, spell, sweep, vault, width **6** amount, bridge, extent, length, period, radius, spread **7** breadth, connect, measure, stretch, twosome, viaduct **8** bestride, comprise, distance, duration, go across, interval, latitude, pass over, straddle, traverse **9** cross over, encompass, extension, longevity **10** generation, transverse, wingspread
life ~: **4** time **8** lifetime
of existence: **4** days, life **5** years **6** course, period
spic and ~: **5** clean
starter: **4** wing
__ span: **4** life **6** anchor
Span.
see Spanish
spanakopita: **6** pastry
Spanaway: **4** city, town
locale: **10** Washington
Spandau __: **6** Ballet
Spandau, last prisoner at: **4** Hess
spandex: **6** fabric **8** material
brand: **5** Lycra
spang: **5** right **7** exactly **8** directly, squarely **9** precisely
spangle: **4** trim **5** fleck **6** bauble, sequin **7** glitter, shimmer **10** decoration
__-Spangled Banner, The: **4** Star
__-Spangled Girl, The: **4** Star
__ Spangled Rhythm: **4** Star
spaniel: **3** dog **5** canid **6** canine, yes man
__ spaniel: **5** field, water **6** cocker, Sussex **7** clumber, Tibetan
Spanish: **8** language
start of many ~ place names: **3** San **5** Santa, Santo
see also Spain
Spanish __: **4** Eyes, Flea, foot, heel, iris, lime, Main, moss, plum, rice **5** broom, cedar, onion, Steps, topaz **6** Arabic, Armada, burton, button, dagger, Guinea, guitar, Harlem, omelet, Sahara **7** America, bayonet, jacinth, jasmine, Morocco, needles, paprika, trefoil **8** omelette
Spanish __ War: **5** Civil
Spanish Eyes (1965 song) artist: Al Martino
Spanish Flea (1966 song) artist: Herb Alpert and the Tijuana Brass
Spanish Guitar Player artist: **5** Manet
Spanish Harlem (song) artist: Aretha Franklin, Ben E. King
Spanish Main: **9** Caribbean
cargo: **3** oro
chest: **4** arca
coin: **4** real
Spanish Prisoner, The (1998 film)
cast: Ben Gazzara, Steve Martin, Rebecca Pidgeon, Campbell Scott
director: David Mamet
Spanish Smile, The author: **5** O'Dell
Spanish Steps locale: **4** Rome
Spanish Town: **4** city
locale: **7** Jamaica
Spanish Tragedy, The author: Thomas Kyd
__ Spanish Trail: **3** Old
Spanish words
adverb: **3** más, que **4** nada
all: **4** todo
among: **5** entre
another: **4** otra, otro
are: **5** están, estás
article: **3** las, los, una, uno
aunt: **3** tía
be: **3** ser
bear: **3** oso
beast: **5** tigre
between: **5** entre
boss: **3** amo
bull: **4** toro
but: **3** más **4** pero
chamber: **4** sala
cheer: **3** olé **4** viva
child: **4** niña, niño
conjunction: **3** más **4** pero
day: **5** lunes **6** jueves, martes, sábado **7** domingo, viernes **9** miércoles
definitely: **4** sí sí
diminutive suffix: **3** -ita, -ito
direction: **3** sur **4** este **5** norte, oeste
east: **4** este
eight: **4** ocho
everything: **4** toda, todo
exclamation: **5** salud **6** arriba
face: **4** cara
farewell: **5** adiós
father: **5** padre
female: **4** ella
fingernail: **3** una
friend: **5** amiga, amigo
fruit: **4** piña
gentleman: **3** don **5** señor **6** Latino
gold: **3** oro
hall: **4** sala
Helen: **5** Elena
home: **4** casa
honorific: **4** doña
hour: **4** hora
I love you: **5** te amo
interrogative: **3** qué **4** cómo
is: **4** está
January: **5** enero
kid: **4** niña, niño
king: **3** rey
lady: **3** sra. **4** dama, doña **6** Latina, señora **8** señorita
letter: **3** uve
love: **4** amor
marking: **5** tilde
meat: **5** carne
miss: **4** srta. **8** señorita
mister: **5** señor
month: **4** mayo **5** abril, enero, julio, junio, marzo **6** agosto **7** febrero, octubre **9** diciembre, noviembre **10** septiembre
more: **3** más
Mr.: **5** señor
Mrs.: **3** sra. **6** señora
Ms.: **4** srta. **8** señorita
nickname: **4** mote
nil: **4** nada
number: **3** dos, uno **4** diez, ocho, seis, tres **5** cinco, nueve, siete **6** cuatro
nun: **5** monja
one: **3** una, uno
other: **4** otra, otro
ourselves: **3** nos
parent: **5** madre, padre
plus: **3** más
potato: **4** papa
preposition: **3** por **5** entre
priest: **5** padre
pronoun: **4** ella, esta, este, todo **5** quien
queen: **5** reina
question: **3** qué
river: **3** río
room: **4** sala
route: **3** vía
saint: **5** santo
she: **4** ella
soul: **4** alma
south: **3** sur
sun: **3** sol
this: **4** esta, este
three: **4** tres
toast: **5** salud
to be: **3** ser
tot: **4** niña, niño
two: **3** dos
uncle: **3** tío
us: **3** nos
walk: **4** anda
water: **4** agua
wave: **3** ola
way: **3** vía
will be: **4** será
with: **3** con
year: **3** año
yes: **2** sí
spank: **3** box, hie, tan, zip **4** beat, belt, cane, cuff, dart, dash, flog, hide, hurt, lash, lick, race, slap, trim, welt, whip, whup, zoom **5** clout, scoot, smack, whack **6** buffet, hustle, larrup, paddle, punish, scurry, sprint, thrash, thwack, wallop **7** clobber **8** chastise **9** skedaddle **10** get a move on, make tracks, paddywhack
spanker: **4** mast, sail
relative: **3** jib
spanking: **3** new **4** fast, fine **5** swift **7** licking **10** punishment
spanking __: **3** new
Spanky: **9** McFarland
dog: **4** Pete **5** Petey
friend: **5** Darla, Porky **7** Alfalfa **9** Buckwheat
Spanky and Our Gang
song: Like to Get to Know You (1968) Sunday Will Never Be the Same (1967)
spanner: **6** wrench
spanning: **6** across
Spano, Vincent: **5** actor
film: Alive (1993)
Baby It's You (1982)
City of Hope (1991)

Creator (1985)
spar: **3** box **4** beam, boom, gaff, mast, pole, tilt **5** fight, joust **6** bicker **7** dispute, mineral, quarrel, quibble, wrangle **8** bowsprit **9** shadowbox
heavy ~: **6** barite **7** barytes
long ~: **4** yard
nautical ~: **4** boom, gaff **5** sprit **8** bowsprit
sparassis: **6** fungus
SPAR counterpart: **3** WAC
spare: **3** odd **4** bare, bony, free, give, lank, lean, more, pity, poor, save, slim, thin, tire, wiry **5** allow, avoid, boney, extra, forgo, gaunt, grant, lanky, leave, let be, let go, mince, other, pinch, put by, scant, short, skimp, stick, stilt, stint **6** afford, backup, bestow, dainty, excuse, exempt, forego, frugal, gangly, give up, let off, meager, modest, option, pardon, relent, scanty, scrape, scrimp, shadow, skimpy, skinny, slight, slinky, sparse, stingy, supply, svelte, twiggy, unused **7** absolve, bail out, forbear, forgive, forsake, gracile, haggard, in store, provide, release, relieve, reserve, respect, scraggy, scrawny, slender, spidery, surplus, willowy **8** dispense, exiguous, gangling, go easy on, in excess, leftover, part with, rawboned, salt away, save from, unwanted **9** do without, emergency, in reserve, sylph-like **10** additional, economical, fifth wheel, relinquish, substitute, unoccupied
difficult ~: **5** split
from: **6** exempt
get a ~: **4** bowl
the expense of: **5** grant, offer **6** afford, bestow, impart, render **7** furnish, provide
tire: **4** flab **5** belly **6** paunch **7** stomach
tire locale: **5** trunk, waist
to ~: **5** ample **6** galore
unit: **3** pin
with room to ~: **4** vast, wide **5** broad **7** sizable **8** spacious **9** capacious, expansive **10** voluminous
with time to ~: **5** early
spare __: **4** part, time, tire
Spare the ___: **3** rod
sparing: **3** lax **4** easy, kind, mild, soft, wary **5** chary, close, loose, scant, tight **6** decent, frugal, gentle, humane, kindly, saving, scanty, stingy, tender **7** careful, clement, lenient, prudent, ruthful, thrifty **8** flexible, gracious, laid-back, merciful, placable, taciturn, tolerant, ungiving **9** assuasive, compliant, easygoing, indulgent, provident **10** abstemious, altruistic, avaricious, benevolent, economical, forbearing, permissive, unexacting, unwasteful
be ~: **5** skimp, stint **9** economize
spark: **3** arc, jot, ray, vim, woo **4** beam, fire, germ, glow, hint, idea, kick, lead, life, love, prod, seed, spur, stir, zest, zing **5** court, flare, flash, gleam, glint, grain, light, liven, punch, scrap, start, trace, verve, vigor **6** arouse, excite, foster, ignite, incite, kindle, propel, pursue, spirit, stir up **7** animate, enliven, flicker, glitter, inspire, minimum, nucleus, provoke, shimmer, trigger, vestige **8** activate, engender, enkindle, motivate, touch off, vitality, vivacity **9** animation, galvanize, impassion, inamorato, life force, originate, pretty boy, scintilla, stimulate **10** bring about, enthusiasm, exuberance, friskiness, jack-a-dandy, liveliness
plug: **6** dynamo **8** catalyst
vital ~: **3** vim, zip **4** brio, dash, élan, fire, soul, zest, zing **5** being, gusto, heart, nerve, oomph, pluck, verve, vigor **6** animus, bounce, energy, esprit, psyche, spirit **7** essence, passion **8** vitality **9** animation, life force **10** enthusiasm, excitement, exuberance, get-up-and-go, liveliness
spark __: **3** gap **4** coil, plug **7** chamber
sparkle: **3** vim, wit, zap, zip **4** beam, dash, fizz, glow, kick, life, show, wink **5** blink, dance, flash, gleam, glint, glitz, light, shine **6** bubble, dazzle, esprit, fizzle, gaiety, gayety, glance, luster, quiver, spirit **7** flicker, glimmer, glisten, glitter, panache, shimmer, twinkle **8** radiance, radiancy, vitality, vivacity **9** animation, coruscate, élan vital, freshness, irradiate **10** brilliance, effervesce, effulgence, incandesce, liveliness
sparkler: **3** gem, ice **4** ring **5** jewel, tiara **7** jewelry, trinket **8** firework
sparkling: **3** lit **4** racy **5** aglow, clean, fresh, peppy, shiny, witty **6** ablaze, agleam, bright, flashy, glinty, lively, washed **7** beaming, fulgent, lambent, piquant, radiant, vibrant **8** dazzling, luminous, lustrous, spirited, unsoiled **9** brilliant, exuberant, refulgent, vivacious
make ~: **6** aerate
sparkling __: **4** wine **5** water
Spark, Muriel: **4** poet **6** author, writer **8** Scottish
work: Memento Mori
The Prime of Miss Jean Brodie
Sparks: **3** Ned **4** city, town **5** Jared **8** radioman
agreement: **5** roger
city west of ~: **4** Reno
locale: **6** Nevada
post: **5** radio
Sparks, Jared: **6** author, writer **9** historian
Sparky: **4** Lyle **8** Anderson
sparling: **4** fish **5** smelt
sparring __: **4** mate **7** partner
sparrow: **4** bird **5** finch
ender: **5** grass
sparrow __: **4** hawk
__ sparrow: **3** fox **4** Java, lark, sage, song, tree **5** dusky, field, hedge, house, swamp **6** vesper **7** English, seaside
sparse: **3** low **4** lean, poor, rare, thin **5** light, scant, short, spare **6** little, meager, scanty, scarce, skimpy, slight **7** scrimpy **8** exiguous, far apart, sporadic **9** dispersed, scattered, uncrowded **10** inadequate, infrequent, occasional, sporadical
sparsity: **4** lack, need, want **6** dearth **7** absence, paucity, poverty **8** exiguity, scarcity, shortage **9** scantness **10** deficiency, inadequacy, meagerness
Sparta: **4** city, town **5** polis
ally: **4** Elis
locale: **6** Greece
magistrate: **5** ephor
rival: **5** Argos **6** Athens
river: **3** Iri
Spartacus: **4** film **5** novel, slave
author: Howard Fast
cast: Tony Curtis, Kirk Douglas, Nina Foch, John Gavin, Charles Laughton, Laurence Olivier, Jean Simmons, Peter Ustinov
director: Stanley Kubrick
setting: **4** Rome **5** arena
Spartan: **4** firm, font, hard **5** apple, bossy, cruel, Greek, harsh, picky, plain, rigid, rough, stark, stern, tough **6** barren, severe, simple, strict **7** ascetic, austere **8** despotic, exacting, hard-line, rigorous, typeface **9** barebones, demanding, draconian, primitive, stringent, unadorned, unbending, unsparing **10** despotical, inflexible, iron-fisted, no-nonsense, oppressive, tyrannical
relative: **4** crab, Gala, Lodi, Rome **5** Mutsu **6** Empire, Ida Red, medlar, Pippin, russet **7** Baldwin, Bramley, costard, Freedom, Liberty, Wealthy, Winesap **8** Cortland, Jonathan, McIntosh **10** Rome Beauty
theater: **5** odeon
worker: **5** helot
Sparv: **7** Camilla
spasibo: **5** danke, merci **6** thanks **7** gracias **8** thank you
spasm: **3** fit, tic **4** ache, jerk, kink, pain, pang **5** burst, cramp, crick, spell, start, throe **6** frenzy, hiccup, quiver, twinge, twitch **8** hiccough, outburst, paroxysm **10** convulsion
spasmodic: **5** jerky, shaky **6** choppy, fitful, random, spotty, uneven **7** erratic, snatchy **8** far apart, on-and-off, periodic, sporadic, variable **9** irregular, momentary, twitching **10** changeable, convulsive, disjointed, hysterical, infrequent, sporadical, unfrequent
Spassky, Boris forte: **5** chess
spat: **3** ado, row **4** flap, fuss, slap, tiff, to-do **5** argue, clash, scrap, set-to, smack **6** barney, dustup, gaiter, rumpus, strife **7** dispute, gambado, legging, mix it up, quarrel, quibble, wrangle **8** argument, brouhaha, catfight, disagree, skirmish, squabble **9** altercate, bickering, have words, imbroglio **10** difference, falling-out
public ~: **5** scene
spot: **5** ankle
suffix: **3** ula
spate: **3** fit, sea **4** flow, gush, rain, rash, rush, tide **5** burst, flood, river, spirt, spurt **6** deluge, stream **7** freshet, torrent **8** downpour, overflow **10** flash flood, inundation
of activity: **5** spasm
spathe: **5** bract
spatter: **3** dot, wet **4** daub, slop, slur, soil, spit, spot **5** dirty, douse, dowse, plash, smear, spray, stain, strew **6** mottle, shower, smudge, splash, squirt **7** asperse, dribble, scatter, speckle, stipple **8** disperse, sprinkle **9** broadcast, discharge **10** calumniate
ender: **4** dock
spatterdash: **6** gaiter
__ S. Patton: **6** George
spatula, use a: **4** flip
spawn: **4** make, seed, sire **5** beget, breed, brood, hatch, issue **6** create, father, parent **7** produce, progeny **8** engender, generate, multiply **9** offspring, originate, reproduce **10** bring forth, give rise to
spawner
salt-water ~: **3** eel
upstream ~: **4** shad **6** salmon
Spawn of the North (1938 film)
cast: Henry Fonda, Dorothy Lamour, George Raft
director: Henry Hathaway
spay: **3** fix **5** alter **6** neuter
SPCA: Society for the Prevention of Cruelty to Animals
speak: **3** air, gab, gas, jaw, lip, rap, say, yak **4** bark, blab, chat, pipe, talk, tell **5** mouth, orate, pitch, plead, shout, sound, spiel, spout, state, stump, utter, voice **6** assert, confer, convey, intone, mumble, murmur, mutter, parley, pipe up, recite, remark, yammer **7** address, chatter, declaim, declare, deliver, dictate, express, lecture, testify, whisper **8** converse, modulate, ramble on, set forth, vocalize **9** discourse, enunciate, expatiate, get across, hold forth, make known, pronounce, sermonize, touch base, verbalize **10** articulate, chew the fat, make public, yakkety-yak
against: **6** oppose **7** gainsay
at length: **3** jaw, yak **4** rant **5** run on, spout **6** expand, preach, rattle **7** address, amplify, declaim, descant, enlarge, lecture, maunder **8** harangue, perorate, sound off **9** discourse, elaborate, expatiate, explicate, hold forth, sermonize, speechify **10** dissertate
doth ~: **5** saith
ender: **4** easy
excitedly: **6** burble, gibber
for: **4** laud **6** back up, defend, esteem, foster, praise, uphold **7** bespeak, commend, endorse, espouse, indorse, promote, support, sustain **8** advocate, champion **9** recommend, represent, vindicate **10** compliment
haltingly: **3** haw, hem **5** drawl **6** mumble **7** sputter, stumble
highly of: **4** hail, laud, tout **5** exalt, extol, honor **6** extoll, praise **7** acclaim, applaud, approve, commend, endorse, indorse **8** hand it to **9** recommend **10** compliment
highly of oneself: **4** brag, crow **5** boast
ill of: **3** pan **4** slur **5** abase, knock, smear **6** defame, deride, impugn, malign, smirch, vilify **7** asperse, put down, rip into, run down, slander **8** backbite, badmouth, belittle, besmirch, tear down, throw mud **9** criticize, denigrate, deprecate, disparage, fling dirt **10** calumniate, depreciate, villainize
imperfectly: **4** lisp, slur **7** stutter
in a monotone: **5** drone
irritably: **4** bark, snap
lovingly: **3** coo
of: **4** name **5** refer, touch **7** discuss, mention, refer to, touch on **9** touch upon
out: **4** avow, yell **6** assert, insist **7** declare **8** sound off **9** make plain **10** stand up for
publicly: **5** orate
right to ~: **5** floor
roughly: **4** rasp **5** croak
rudely: **4** sass
so to ~: **4** as if **8** as it were, in effect **10** implicitly
starter: **3** new **6** double
suddenly: **5** blurt
to: **7** contact **8** approach **10** get a hold of
up: **6** assert, insist **7** declare **8** sound off **9** make plain
wildly: **4** rage, rant, rave, roar, yell **5** storm
with forked tongue: **3** fib **4** dupe **5** bluff, fudge, guile **6** delude **7** deceive, falsify, mislead **8** misspeak **9** dissemble, misinform
with one's hands: **4** sign
without notes: **5** ad-lib
speak __: **3** for, out
speak __ to: **4** down
__ speak: **4** so to
Speak Easily (1932 film)
cast: Jimmy Durante, Buster Keaton, Ruth Selwyn
speakeasy: **5** joint **6** saloon, tavern **7** barroom **9** nightclub

offering: 5 booze 10 bathtub gin
speaker: 5 sayer 6 lector, orator 8 lecturer
asset: 3 wit
ender: 4 ship 5 phone
like a cheap ~: 5 tinny
need: 4 mike 5 intro 10 microphone
part: 3 amp 6 woofer 7 tweeter
pause: 2 er, uh, um
request: 5 floor
spot: 4 dais 6 podium
starter: 4 loud
system: 4 hi-fi 6 stereo
__ speaker: 7 keynote
Speaker, Tris: 6 Indian 10 outfielder
speaking: 9 utterance 10 recitation
ability: 5 oracy
generally ~: 7 overall
manner of ~: 4 tone 5 idiom, usage
not ~ to: 5 mad at
plain ~: 5 prose
speaking __: 4 part, role, tube, type
__ speaking: 6 choral, public
__ Speaks: 4 Seth 5 Harpo
spear: 4 spit, stab 5 kebab, lance, spike, stick 6 empale, impale, pierce, skewer, weapon 7 assagai, assegai, harpoon, javelin, missile, trident 9 lancinate
bearer, name meaning ~: 4 Gary 5 Garry
carrier: 4 supe 5 extra
combining form: 4 dory-
ender: 3 man, men 4 fish, head, mint, wort
fish ~: 3 gig
god, name meaning: 5 Oscar
handle: 5 shaft
name meaning ~: 5 Barry
Roman ~: 5 pilum
rule, name meaning: 6 Gerald
strength, name meaning: 8 Gertrude
thrower: 6 atlatl
tip: 4 pike
spear __: 3 gun 4 side 5 grass 7 carrier
spear-__: 7 carrier, thrower
spearhead: 4 lead, spur 7 go first, pioneer
spearmint: 4 herb
Spears: 7 Britney
spec: 6 detail 8 standard
special: 3 pet, set 4 best, gala, main, meal, rare, sale 5 chief, major 6 choice, festal, marked, proper, select, unique 7 certain, defined, express, festive, limited, primary, private, several, unalike, unusual 8 definite, isolated, peculiar, personal, singular, smashing, uncommon 9 different, earmarked, exclusive, important, memorable, momentous, recherché, red-letter 10 designated, individual, occasional, particular, privileged, restricted
ender: 3 ist
interest group: 3 org., soc. 4 assn., bloc 5 assoc., lobby 6 caucus
issue: 5 extra 6 annual
nothing ~: 5 plain, usual 7 average, routine, typical 8 ordinary, standard
Saturday night ~: 3 gun
something ~: 4 oner
treat as ~: 5 favor
special __: 3 act 4 area, jury, plea, rule, team, term 5 agent, staff 6 orders 7 effects, library, partner, session
special __ of relativity: 6 theory
Special: 3 car 4 auto 5 Buick 10 automobile
Special __: 4 Lady 6 Forces
Special Delivery (1976 film)
cast: Michael Gwynne, Cybill Shepherd, Bo Svenson
director: Paul Wendkos
Special Delivery author: Danielle Steel
Special Forces
cap: 5 beret
unit: 5 A-Team
weapon: 3 Uzi
specialist: 3 ace, pro 4 guru, sage 5 adept, maven, mavin 6 doctor, expert, old pro, pundit, savant, source 7 devotee, old hand, scholar, veteran 8 virtuoso 9 authority, physician
suffix: 5 -arian, -ician
__ specialist: 7 mission, payload
Specialist, The (1994 film)
cast: Sylvester Stallone, Rod Steiger, Sharon Stone, James Woods
cat: 5 Timer
director: Luis Llosa
spécialité __ maison: 4 de la
specialized: 9 technical
special K: 5 dance
Special K: 6 cereal
competitor: 3 Kix 4 Life, Trix 5 Kashi, Quisp, Total 6 Kaboom, Muesli, Oreo O's, Pablum, Smacks 7 All-Bran, Crispix, Harmony, Hunny B's, Mueslix, Oat Bran, Pokemon 8 Boo Berry, Cheerios, Corn Chex, Corn Pops, Fiber One, Rice Chex, Uncle Sam, Wheaties 9 Alpha Bits, Apple Zaps, Grape Nuts, Honey Comb, Just Right, Wheat Chex 10 Apple Jacks, Bran Flakes, Cap'n Crunch, Cocoa Puffs, Froot Loops, Mini-Wheats, Nutri-Grain, Puffed Rice, Quaker Oats, Smart Start 11 Cocoa Blasts, Cookie Crisp, Golden Crisp, Lucky Charms, Puffed Wheat, Sweet Crunch, Waffle Crisp
special laurel __ go, A: 4 ere I
__ Special Love Song: 5 A Very
specially: 8 uniquely 9 expressly
specialty: 3 bag, job 4 area, game, work 5 field, forte, hobby, major, niche, thing 6 career, domain, métier, number, racket 7 feature, pursuit 8 cup of tea, practice, vocation, weakness 9 commodity 10 department, discipline, magnum opus, occupation, profession
specie: 3 oof 4 cash, gelt, jack, kail, kale, loot, peag, pelf 5 bills, bread, bucks, dough, franc, funds, lucre, money, moola, mopus, pesos, rhino, sewan 6 dinero, do-re-mi, mammon, mazuma, moolah, seawan, silver, wampum, wealth 7 cabbage, capital, dollars, lettuce, ooftish, scratch, shekels 8 bankroll, cold cash, currency, hard cash, smackers 9 banknotes, frogskins, long green, simoleons 10 greenbacks, green stuff
species: 3 lot 4 kind, race, sort, type 5 breed, class, group, likes, order, taxon 6 nature, number, strain 7 variety 8 category, division 10 collection
category above ~: 5 genus
division: 3 sex
Species (1995 film)
cast: Natasha Henstridge, Ben Kingsley, Michael Madsen, Forest Whitaker
director: Roger Donaldson
specific: 3 set 4 item, such 5 exact, fixed 6 dead-on, detail, finite, proper, single, unique 7 certain, express, flat-out, limited, precise, right on, several 8 bull's-eye, clear-cut, concrete, definite, detailed, distinct, explicit, on target, outright, peculiar, positive, reserved 9 definable, different, downright, drawn fine 10 definitive, individual, occasional, particular, restricted
be ~: 4 name 6 define
specific __: 4 heat 6 charge, volume 7 gravity, impulse
__-specific: 4 site 6 gender 7 species
specifically: 5 to wit 6 as such, namely 7 clearly, exactly 8 in detail, minutely 9 expressly, pointedly, precisely, specially
specification: 4 code, term 6 clause, detail 7 proviso 8 standard 9 blueprint, condition, provision, requisite
specified: 3 set 5 given 9 necessary
those not ~: 6 others
specify: 3 fix, peg, set, tab, tag 4 cite, list, name, slot 5 label, limit, state 6 assign, define, detail, finger, lay out, set out, settle 7 itemize, mention, pin down, precise, provide, put down, refer to 8 describe, indicate, nominate, point out, spell out 9 blueprint, condition, designate, determine, elaborate, enumerate, establish, preordain, prescribe, stipulate 10 button down
specimen: 3 bit 4 case, copy, part, sort, type, unit 5 model, piece, proof 6 person, sample, swatch 7 example, exhibit, pattern, variety 8 exemplar, instance, landmark, sampling 10 embodiment, individual
specious: 4 vain 5 false, inane, silly, wacky, wrong 6 absurd, faulty, made-up, screwy, untrue, whacky 7 fatuous, in error, inexact, seeming, unsound 8 captious, cockeyed, delusive, spurious 9 beguiling, deceptive, erroneous, illogical, incorrect, plausible, senseless, sophistic, untenable 10 artificial, fallacious, flattering, groundless, inaccurate, misleading, ostensible, presumable, ungrounded
speck: 3 bit, dab, dot, jot, tad 4 atom, blot, drop, flaw, iota, lick, mark, mite, snip, spot, whit 5 crumb, fault, fleck, grain, pinch, point, scrap, shred, stain, touch, trace 6 defect, little, tittle, trifle 7 blemish, freckle, glimmer, granule, lentigo, minimum, modicum, smidgen, smidgin, splotch 8 molecule, particle, pinpoint, smidgeon 9 scintilla
starter: 3 fly
speckle: 4 spot 5 fleck 7 spatter 8 sprinkle
specklebelly: 5 goose
speckled: 6 dotted, flaked, mosaic, motley, patchy, spotty 7 dappled, flecked, mottled, spotted, studded 8 brindled, freckled, peppered, stippled 9 sprinkled 10 variegated
specs: 6 frames 7 details, glasses 8 cheaters 10 directions, eyeglasses
see also spectacles
spectacle: 4 play, show, view 5 drama, event, movie, scene, sight 6 circus, comedy, marvel, parade, wonder 7 display, pageant, picture, scenery, tableau 8 splendor 9 cavalcade, curiosity 10 exhibition, exposition, phenomenon, production
combining form: 4 -cade 5 -orama
make a ~ of: 7 show off
spectacles: 6 frames 7 glasses, lorgnon 8 cheaters, horn-rims, wire-rims 9 lorgnette 10 eyeglasses
big name in ~: 4 Lomb 6 Bausch, Pearle
piece: 4 lens
support: 3 ear 4 nose
Spectacles, The author: Edgar Allan Poe
spectacular: 3 def, rad 4 aces, A-one, boss, braw, cool, dece, epic, fine, gear, keen, neat, nice, phat, tuff 5 dandy, ducky, grand, great, marvy, neato, nobby, prime, slick, super, swell 6 bang on, bang-up, bonzer, bosker, choice, daring, divine, dreamy, far-out, gnarly, groovy, lovely, marked, peachy, scenic, slap-up, spot on, superb, terrif, tiptop, unreal, whizzo, wicked 7 amazing, awesome, capital, corking, perfect, ripping, skookum, stellar, sublime 8 dazzling, dramatic, especial, eximious, fabulous, five-star, four-star, frabjous, glorious, heavenly, jim-dandy, meteoric, scenical, slam-bang, smashing, splendid, standout, sterling, stickout, striking, stunning, superior, terrific, top-level, topnotch, very good, wondrous 9 bodacious, Endsville, excellent, exemplary, exquisite, fantastic, first-rate, high-grade, hunky-dory, marvelous, sollicker, thrilling, top-flight, wonderful 10 first-class, hotsy-totsy, jack-a-dandy, out of sight, peachy-keen, phenomenal, remarkable, stupendous, super-duper
spectator: 3 fan 4 eyer, seer 5 gazer 6 looker, viewer 7 watcher, witness 8 beholder, looker-on, observer, onlooker, playgoer, showgoer 9 bystander, moviegoer, perceiver, stander-by 10 eyewitness
spectator __: 4 pump, shoe 5 sport
spectators: 5 crowd 7 gallery 8 audience 9 listeners 10 attendance
Spectator, The writer: 6 Steele
specter: 5 ghost, shade, spook 6 fantom, shadow, spirit, wraith 7 bugbear, phantom 8 presence, revenant 10 apparition
Specter: 5 Arlen
Specter of the Rose (1946 film)
cast: Judith Anderson, Michael Chekhov, Ivan Kirov
director: Ben Hecht
Spector: 4 Phil
Spectra: 3 car, Kia 4 auto 10 automobile
spectral: 4 eery 5 eerie 7 ghostly 9 ghostlike, imaginary, unearthly 10 immaterial
type: 5 N star, O star, S star
spectral __: 4 line, type 6 series
spectre
see specter
__ spectrograph: 4 mass 5 sound
__ spectrometer: 4 mass 5 prism
spectrophobe fear: 6 ghosts
spectrum: 5 gamut, range, scale
band: 3 red 4 blue 5 green 6 indigo, orange, violet, yellow
displayer: 5 prism 7 rainbow
__ spectrum: 3 arc 4 band, line, mass 5 flash, radio, spark 7 visible
__-spectrum: 5 broad
Spectrum: 5 arena
locale: Philadelphia
speculate: 3 bet 4 dare, muse, risk 5 guess, infer, think, wager, weigh 6 assume, call it, figure, gamble, hazard, ponder, reason, review, scheme, size up, wonder 7 presume, reflect, suppose, surmise, suspect, venture, wildcat 8 chew over, cogitate, consider, give odds, make book, question, ruminate, theorize 9 figure out, pipe-dream, postulate 10 brainstorm, conjecture, deliberate, excogitate, experiment, generalize, have a hunch, kick around, take a fling
speculation: 3 bet 4 game, look, risk, shot, stab 5 guess, hunch, wager 6 belief, chance, gamble, hazard, plunge, reason, review, theory 7 backing, opinion, surmise, thought, venture 8 card game, gambling, studying, thinking 9 brainwork, guesswork
speculative: 5 risky 6 chancy 8 academic 9 tentative, uncertain, visionary
venture: 5 flier, flyer
speculator: 3 arb 6 risker 7 gambler 9 financier 10 adventurer

speculum metal: 5 alloy
component: 3 tin 4 lead, zinc 6 silver
__ Spee: 4 Graf
speech: 4 talk, word 5 idiom, lingo, pitch, prose, spiel, stump, voice 6 accent, appeal, debate, dialog, eulogy, homily, jargon, medium, parley, sermon, tirade, tongue 7 address, bombast, dialect, diction, keynote, lecture, monolog, oration, oratory, pep talk, prattle, remarks, voicing 8 dialogue, diatribe, harangue, language, parlance, rhetoric 9 chalk talk, discourse, elocution, monologue, utterance 10 allocution, apostrophe, commentary, discussion, expressing, expression, filibuster, invocation, recitation, salutation, vernacular, vocalizing
colloquial ~: 5 slang 10 vernacular
combining form: 3 log- 4 lalo-, -laly, logo- 5 gloss-, -lalia 6 glosso-, glotto-
ender: 5 maker 6 writer
figure of ~: 5 image, trope 7 imagery, similar 8 metaphor
free ~: 7 liberty
hesitation: 2 er, uh, um
instructive ~: 6 sermon
like some ~: 5 nasal
long ~: 8 rhetoric
loss of ~: 6 alogia
of ~: 4 oral
of a ~ sound: 6 apical
part of ~: 4 noun, verb 6 adverb 7 pronoun 9 adjective 11 conjunction, preposition 12 interjection
pattern: 6 accent
raucous ~: 4 yaup, yawp
regional ~: 6 patois
slow ~: 5 drawl
sound: 4 lene
source: 6 larynx
specialized ~: 5 lingo
violent ~: 4 rant
speech __: 3 act 4 form 5 organ, sound 6 island
__ speech: 4 cued, free 5 King's, stump 6 maiden, Queen's 7 curtain, keynote, visible
speechify: 5 orate 8 perorate
speechless: 3 mum 4 awed, cool, mute 5 blank, dazed, quiet 6 aghast, amazed, silent 7 aphonic, shocked 8 nonvocal, overcome, taciturn, wordless 9 astounded, clammed up, noiseless, voiceless 10 bewildered, tongue-tied, unspeaking
one: 4 mime 5 mimer
render ~: 3 awe, wow 4 stun 5 amaze, floor 9 overwhelm
Speechless (1994 film)
cast: Bonnie Bedelia, Geena Davis, Michael Keaton, Christopher Reeve
director: Ron Underwood
speed: 3 aid, fly, hie, rip, run, zip 4 belt, bomb, clip, dart, dash, flit, gait, hare, help, lick, pace, pelt, race, rate, rush, sail, tear, whiz, zoom 5 boost, flash, haste, hurry, impel, scoot, shoot, steam, tempo, whisk 6 barrel, breeze, career, course, gallop, gear up, hasten, hurtle, hustle, move it, rocket, rustle, scurry, spring, step up, streak 7 advance, agility, floor it, forward, further, headway, hop to it, press on, promote, quicken, scamper, take off, tear off, urgency 8 alacrity, celerity, cut along, dispatch, expedite, fastness, go all out, hightail, make time, momentum, rapidity, step on it, velocity 9 briskness, eagerness, fast-track, fleetness, get moving, hotfoot it, make haste, quickness, rapidness, readiness, shake a leg, skedaddle, swiftness 10 burn rubber, double-time, expedition, facilitate, get a move on, hightail it, liveliness
at a fast ~: 5 apace 7 rapidly 9 sprinting
combining form: 4 drom- 5 dromo-, tacho-
contest: 4 race
demon: 5 racer 6 hot rod
ender: 3 way 4 boat, ster, well 6 writer
inhibitor: 4 bump
lose ~: 3 lag 4 slow 5 brake, check, choke, delay, let up, relax, stall, unlax 6 ease up, go easy, loiter, reduce, unwind, weaken 7 bog down, lay back, sit back 8 moderate, slack off, slow down, wind down 9 soft-pedal 10 decelerate, settle back, simmer down
LP ~: 3 rpm
measure ~: 4 time 5 clock
no ~ demon: 5 sloth, snail 8 slowpoke
rate of ~: 4 clip, pace 8 velocity
resume ~ in music: 6 a tempo
spurt: 5 burst
starter: 3 God 6 ground
unit: 3 kph, mph
up: 4 push, rise, rush 6 hasten 7 quicken 8 expedite, get going 9 get moving, shake a leg 10 accelerate, facilitate, get a move on
up to ~: 7 capable 9 competent, qualified 10 proficient
speed __: 4 bump, gear, shop, trap 5 brake, chess, demon, light, limit, metal, skate 7 skating
speed-__: 4 read
__ speed: 3 air 4 film, full, good, up to, warp 5 flank 7 shutter
__-speed: 3 ten 4 high
Speed (1994 film)
cast: Sandra Bullock, Jeff Daniels, Dennis Hopper, Keanu Reeves
director: Jan De Bont
vehicle: 3 bus
Speed __: 5 Racer
__ speed ahead: 4 full
speedball: 4 game
__-speed bike: 3 ten 5 three
speeder: 5 racer
nemesis: 3 cop 5 radar
speedily: 3 PDQ 4 fast, soon 5 apace, madly 6 presto 7 fleetly, hastily, in a rush, in haste, quickly, rapidly, readily, swiftly 8 in a flash, in a hurry, in a jiffy, in no time, on the fly, on the run, pell-mell, promptly 9 forthwith, hurriedly, instantly, like a shot, posthaste, summarily 10 in high gear
speediness: 5 hurry 8 celerity, rapidity 9 fleetness
Speedo material: 5 latex
speedometer: 4 dial 5 gauge
part: 6 needle
reading: 3 kph, mph 8 velocity
__-speed pitch: 3 off
speed-read: 4 scan
speed skater: 4 Enke 5 Blair 6 Heiden
speed skating: 5 sport
Speed Stick: 9 deodorant
alternative: 3 Ban 4 Sure 5 Arrid, Tussy 6 Degree, Secret 7 Dry Idea, Mitchum 10 Right Guard, Soft and Dri
Speed-the-__: 4 Plow
__-speed transmission: 4 five, four
__ Speedwagon: 3 REO
speedway: 9 race track
area: 3 pit
letters: 4 IROC, NHRA 6 NASCAR
Speedway (1968 film)
cast: Bill Bixby, Gale Gordon, Elvis Presley, Nancy Sinatra
director: Norman Taurog
speedy: 4 fast 5 agile, brisk, fleet, hasty, quick, rapid, ready, swift 6 active, flying, lively, nimble, prompt, racing, snappy, winged 7 express, hurried, instant 8 headlong, meteoric 9 breakneck, galloping, immediate, lightning, posthaste, quick-fire, rapid-fire, whirlwind 10 double-time, harefooted, hypersonic, supersonic, ultrasonic
Speedy Gonzales: 4 toon 5 mouse
Speedy Gonzales (1962 song) artist: Pat Boone
Speke, John: 8 explorer
river explored by: 4 Nile
speleology topic: 4 cave
spell: 3 bit, fit, hex, jag, run 4 bout, free, jinx, mean, span, term, time, tour, turn 5 allow, charm, hitch, imply, lie by, magic, patch, shift, space, spasm, stint, throe, trick, vodun, while 6 allure, amulet, attack, course, denote, glamor, herald, hexing, import, intend, lay off, period, relief, rotate, season, snatch, streak, trance, voodoo, whammy 7 add up to, cantrip, connote, express, glamour, illness, point to, portend, promise, rapture, release, relieve, replace, signify, sorcery, stretch, suggest 8 amount to, exorcism, foretell, indicate, interval, take over, talisman, witchery 9 hypnotism, interlude, mesmerism 10 bewitching, enchanting, hocus-pocus, mumbo-jumbo, tour of duty, witchcraft
breathing ~: 4 lull, rest 5 pause 6 recess 7 respite 8 reprieve
cold ~: 4 snap
dry ~: 5 slump 6 drouth 7 drought
ender: 4 bind, down 6 binder 7 binding
for a ~: 6 awhile
out: 4 cite, mean, show 6 define, detail 7 clarify, explain, expound, itemize, specify 8 construe, simplify 9 elucidate, enumerate, interpret, put across, stipulate, translate
put a ~ on: 3 hex, zap 4 jinx, mojo 5 charm, curse 7 bewitch, conjure, enchant
under a ~: 5 hexed 9 possessed
spell __: 3 out 7 checker
spell-__: 5 check
__ spell: 3 dry 4 cold 7 sinking
spellbind: 4 grip 5 charm, rivet 6 ravish 7 bewitch, enchant, enthral, inthral 8 enthrall, entrance, inthrall, transfix 9 captivate, enrapture, fascinate, hypnotize, mesmerize, transport
spellbinder: 6 orator 8 magician
Spellbinder author: Harold Robbins
spellbinding: 5 magic, siren 7 magical 8 hypnotic
spellbound: 4 held, lost, rapt 5 agape, in awe 6 amazed, enrapt, hooked 7 bemused, charmed, far gone, gripped 8 caught up, held fast, immersed, ravished 9 bewitched, enchanted, petrified, possessed 10 fascinated, infatuated
hold ~: 5 charm 7 enchant 8 enthrall, entrance, transfix 9 captivate, fascinate, hypnotize
Spellbound (1945 film)
cast: Ingrid Bergman, Leo G. Carroll, Gregory Peck
director: Alfred Hitchcock
spelldown: 3 bee
spelled out: 5 clear, plain, vivid 6 cogent 7 evident, express, obvious 8 apparent, distinct, explicit, manifest, palpable 9 graspable
speller: 4 book, text 8 textbook
spelling
alternative ~: 7 variant
contest: 3 bee
error: 4 typo 7 erratum
game: 5 ghost
spelling __: 3 bee 4 book 6 reform
Spelling: 4 Tori 5 Aaron
Spelling, Aaron spouse: Carolyn Jones
Spelling, Tori father: 5 Aaron
__ spell on: 5 cast a
spelunker: 5 caver
hat attachment: 4 lamp
Spemann, Hans: 8 Nobelist
Spence, Michael: 8 Nobelist 9 economist
spencer: 4 coat, sail 6 jacket
Spencer: 4 John 5 Diana, Tracy 6 Tracie 7 Herbert
Spencer, Herbert: 6 writer 7 British 11 philosopher
Spencerville author: Nelson Demille
spend: 3 buy, pay, use 4 blow, drop, fill, give, idle, kill, laze, pass 5 apply, drain, drift, empty, exert, pay up, put in, use up, waste 6 ante up, bestow, confer, defray, devote, donate, employ, expend, finish, invest, lavish, lay out, misuse, occupy, outlay, pay out, settle 7 consume, cough up, deplete, exhaust, fork out, fritter, hand out, let pass, pay down, play out 8 allocate, cast away, disburse, dispense, shell out, squander 9 dissipate, go through, liquidate, spring for, throw away, while away 10 come across, contribute, run through
as time: 5 put in
ender: 6 thrift
freely: 4 blow 6 lavish 7 splurge 8 squander
place to ~ the night: 3 inn 5 B and B, hotel, motel 8 motor inn 10 campground, motor lodge
prepare to ~ the night: 6 encamp
reluctant to ~: 5 cheap, tight 6 frugal 10 skinflinty
spender: 5 sport 7 wastrel 8 prodigal 10 high roller
phrase: 4 on me
Spender, Stephen: 3 Sir 4 poet 7 British
spending: 5 outgo 6 outlay 8 dazzling
expedition: 5 spree
govt. ~ watchdog: 3 GAO, OMB
limit: 3 cap
plan: 6 budget
some Congressional ~: 4 pork
spending __: 4 orgy 5 money
__ spending: 7 deficit
__-spending: 4 free
spendthrift: 6 waster 7 wastrel 8 prodigal, wasteful 9 imprudent 10 squanderer
spendthrift __: 5 trust
Spengler, Oswald: 6 German, writer 11 philosopher
Spenser: __ Hire: 3 For
Spenser, Edmund: 4 poet 7 British
heroine: 3 Una
work: Astrophel
The Faerie Queene
Spenser: For Hire (ABC drama)
cast: Avery Brooks (Hawk)
Robert Urich (Spenser)
Spenserian __: 6 sonnet, stanza
spent: 4 dead, done, gone, limp, lost, shot, used, weak, worn 5 blown, had it, tired, weary, wiped 6 bleary, bushed, dished, done in, effete, pooped, used up, wasted 7 all gone, drained, far-gone, wearied, worn out 8 burnt-out, consumed, depleted, dog-tired, expended, fatigued, finished, lifeless, tired out, washed-up, weakened 9 disbursed, enervated, exhausted, played-out, prostrate, shattered 10 dissipated, knocked out, on the ropes, thrown away

___-spent: 3 ill
___ Spent My Summer Vacation: 4 How I
spermatophyte: 5 plant
Sperry: 5 Elmer, Roger
partner: 4 Rand
successor: 6 Unisys
Sperry, Roger: 8 Nobelist
spet: 4 fish 9 barracuda
spew: 3 jet 4 emit, gush, pour, spit 5 belch, egest, eject, erupt, expel, exude, flood, heave, issue, spirt, spume, spurt 6 spit up, spread, spritz, squirt 7 bring up, cascade, cast out, diffuse, emanate, give off, pour out, radiate, scatter, spit out 8 disgorge, throw off 9 cast forth, discharge, flow forth, send forth 10 break forth, shoot forth
sphagnum: 4 moss, peat
sphalerite: 3 ore 7 mineral
Spheeris: 8 Penelope
sphenoid: 4 bone
locale: 5 skull 7 cranium 9 braincase
sphere: 3 job, orb, sun 4 area, ball, rank, turf, zone 5 ambit, apple, arena, bourn, class, Earth, field, globe, orbit, plane, range, realm, round, scope, space, world 6 circle, domain, ground, jungle, locale, marble, milieu, planet, region 7 compass, element, globule, grounds, purview, section, station, stratum, terrain 8 baseball, capacity, dominion, function, locality, position, precinct, province 9 bailiwick, situation, territory 10 basketball, department, discipline, employment, profession, walk of life
curve: 5 rhumb
of conflict: 5 arena
of influence: 4 area 5 orbit 6 domain
shaped like a ~: 5 orbed
starter: 3 bio, eco 4 hemi, meso 5 tropo
tiny ~: 4 bead
Sphere: 4 film 5 novel
author: Michael Crichton
cast: Peter Coyote, Dustin Hoffman, Samuel L. Jackson, Sharon Stone
director: Barry Levinson
spherical: 5 orbed, orbic, round 6 global 7 globate, globoid, globose, rounded 8 globated, globular
spherical ___: 5 angle 7 polygon, sailing
spheroid: 3 pea 7 globule
spherule: 4 bead, blob 7 globule
sphinx: 6 enigma
sphinx ___: 4 moth
Sphinx
answer to ~'s riddle: 3 man
in part: 4 lion
locale: 4 Giza 5 Egypt
parent of ~: 6 Orthus 7 Echidna
Sphinx author: Robin Cook
Sphinx, The author: Edgar Allan Poe
Sphynx: 3 cat 5 felid 6 feline
spica: 3 ear 8 dressing
Spica: 4 star
constellation: 5 Virgo
spic and span: 5 clean 8 spotless
spic and span: 4 mint, neat, tidy, trim 7 orderly
spice: 3 pep, zip 4 bite, guts, kick, mace, tang, zest 5 anise, aroma, basil, clove, color, cumin, gusto, liven, punch, savor 6 cassia, cloves, fennel, flavor, garlic, ginger, nutmeg, pepper, relish, season, spirit 7 cayenne, enliven, mustard, paprika, pimento, saffron 8 allspice, cardamom, cardamon, cinnamon, jalapeño, pimiento, piquancy, pleasure, pungency, rosemary, turmeric 9 condiment, coriander, fenugreek, flavoring, fragrance, hot pepper, poppy seed, red pepper, seasoning, sharpness 10 black cumin, excitement, liveliness, snappiness
early source of ~: 6 Orient
ender: 4 bush 5 berry
holder: 4 rack
starter: 3 all
up: 5 add to 6 pepper, season 7 enhance, enliven, improve 8 heighten 9 interlard
without ~: 5 bland 9 tasteless
Spice ___: 5 Girls 7 Islands
___ Spice: 3 Old
Spice Girls
members: Victoria Adams (Posh), Melanie Brown (Scary), Emma Bunton (Baby), Melanie Chisholm (Sporty), Geri Haliwell (Ginger)
song: 2 Become 1 (1997)
Goodbye (1998)
Say You'll Be There (1997)
Stop (1998)
Too Much (1998)
Wannabe (1997)
Spice Islands: 8 Moluccas
spiciness: 4 tang 6 flavor 8 pungency
Spic & Span: 7 cleaner
alternative: 5 Brite, Lysol 6 Top Job 7 Lestoil, Mr. Clean, Pine Sol 9 Fantastik, Step Saver
spiculate: 5 spiny
spicy: 3 hot 4 blue, keen, racy, rich 5 fiery, juicy, tasty, zesty, zippy 6 erotic, red hot, ribald, risqué, savory, snappy, strong, vulgar, wicked, X-rated 7 gingery, peppery, piquant, pungent, zestful 8 aromatic, fragrant, off-color, perfumed, poignant, redolent, seasoned, spirited, unseemly 9 flavorful 10 appetizing, flavorsome, indelicate, scandalous
spider: 6 frypan 8 arachnid
combining form: 6 arachn- 7 arachno-
creation: 3 web 6 cobweb
defense: 5 venom
emulate a ~: 4 spin 5 weave
like a ~ web: 4 lacy
nest: 5 nidus
web: 3 net
web victim: 3 fly
spider ___: 3 bug, fly, web 4 band, crab, lily, mite, wasp 5 plant 6 monkey
___ spider: 3 red, sea, sun 4 crab, wolf 6 banana, violin 7 jumping, red-back
Spider: 3 car 4 auto 9 Alfa Romeo
Spider-Man (2002 film)
cast: Willem Dafoe, Kirsten Dunst, James Franco, Tobey Maguire
director: Sam Raimi
Spiders & Snakes (1973 song) artist: Jim Stafford
Spider Woman, The (1944 film)
cast: Nigel Bruce, Basil Rathbone, Gale Sondergaard
director: Roy William Neill
spidery: 4 lank, lean, slim, thin, wiry 5 lanky, spare 6 dainty, gangly, skinny, slight, slinky, svelte, twiggy 7 gracile, scraggy, scrawny, slender, willowy 8 gangling 9 sylphlike
Spiegel: 3 Sam
___ Spiegel: 3 Der
spiel: 3 say 4 line, rant, sell, tale, talk 5 pitch, speak, spout, state, story 6 patter, speech 7 address, lecture, oration, routine 8 harangue, hard sell 9 utterance 10 sales pitch, vocalizing
ad ~: 4 hype
give a carnival ~: 4 bark
starter: 4 sing
Spielberg, Steven: 8 director
film: 1941 (1979)
AI: Artificial Intelligence (2001)
Always (1989)
Amistad (1997)
Close Encounters of the Third Kind (1977)
The Color Purple (1985)
Empire of the Sun (1987)
E.T. The Extra-Terrestrial (1982)
Hook (1991)
Indiana Jones and the Last Crusade (1989)
Indiana Jones and the Temple of Doom (1984)
Jaws (1975)
Jurassic Park (1993)
The Lost World: Jurassic Park (1997)
Minority Report (2002)
Raiders of the Lost Ark (1981)
Saving Private Ryan (1998, AA)
Schindler's List (1993, AA)
The Sugarland Express (1974)
spouse: Kate Capshaw, Amy Irving
spier: 7 spotter, watcher
Spies author: Michael Frayn
Spies Like Us (1985 film)
cast: Dan Aykroyd, Chevy Chase, Steve Forrest
director: John Landis
Spies Like Us (1985 song) artist: Paul McCartney
spiff: 5 bonus
up: 5 groom, primp, prink 6 spruce 7 garnish, smarten 8 brighten 9 embellish
spiffy: 5 dandy, fancy, natty, sleek, swank 6 classy, dapper, jaunty, rakish, snazzy, sporty, spruce, swanky 7 refined 9 gussied up
spigot: 3 tap 5 valve 6 faucet
tree ~: 5 spile
spike: 3 ear, pin, rod, tap 4 barb, lace, nail, shoe, spit 5 cleat, lance, piton, point, prick, spear, stake, stalk, stick, thorn 6 empale, impale, pierce, skewer, tamper 8 footwear, high heel, prohibit, transfix 9 intensify 10 adulterate
birch ~: 5 ament 6 catkin
game: 10 volleyball
grain ~: 3 awn, ear
volleyball ~: 4 kill
spike ___: 4 heel, moss 5 heath
Spike: 3 Lee 4 Owen 5 Jones, Jonze 8 Milligan
spiked: 5 sharp, spiny 6 jagged 7 pointed
spikedace: 4 fish
spike heel: 4 shoe 8 footwear
spikelet part: 6 arista
spikenard: 5 plant 6 aralia
spiky: 4 acid 5 sharp 6 peaked, thorny 7 acerbic, peevish, pointed, prickly 8 abrasive
hair style: 4 punk
spile: 5 spout 6 spigot
fluid: 3 sap
spill: 3 run, tip 4 blab, blow, drip, drop, emit, fall, leak, lose, pour, shed, slop, tell 5 empty, let on, slide, slosh, spirt, spout, spray, spurt, upset 6 betray, header, inform, relate, reveal, run out, splash, squeal, squirt, stream, tattle, tumble 7 divulge, dribble, dump out, let slip, overrun, pour out, run over, scatter, tip over 8 disclose, disgorge, flow over, give away, overfill, overflow, overpour, overturn, slop over, splatter, sprinkle, throw off, well over 9 discharge, knock over
clean a ~: 5 mop up, sop up 6 wipe up
consequence: 5 stain
ender: 3 age, way 4 back, over
oil ~: 5 slick
over: 4 brim, gush 5 slosh
take a ~: 4 fall, slip, trip
the beans: 3 rat 4 blab, blat, leak, sing, talk, tell 5 blurt, let on 6 tattle 7 confess
___ spill: 3 oil
Spillane, Mickey: 6 author, writer
sleuth: Mike Hammer
work: The Delta Factor
The Girl Hunters
I, the Jury
Kiss Me, Deadly
Survival: Zero
Tomorrow I Die
The Twisted Thing
spillikins: 4 game
spill one's ___: 4 guts
spill the ___: 5 beans
spillway: 5 flume
spin: 3 run 4 jink, reel, ride, roll, turn 5 crank, drive, pivot, swirl, twirl, twist, weave, wheel, whirl 6 gyrate, outing, rotate, spiral, swivel 7 joyride, revolve 8 go around, gyration, rotation 9 oscillate, pirouette 10 revolution
a yarn: 4 tell 6 relate 7 narrate
doctor: 5 PR man
doctor concern: 5 image
ender: 3 off, out 5 drift
go for a ~: 4 ride 5 drive
imparter: 5 wrist
in ballet: 7 fouetté
out: 7 prolong, stretch 8 lengthen, protract
skater ~: 5 camel
starter: 3 top 4 back, down, side, tail
the bottle: 4 game
spin ___: 3 off, out 6 doctor 7 control, fishing
spin ___ top: 5 like a
spin-___: 3 dry, off
___ spin: 3 sit 5 camel
Spin ___: 4 City 7 Doctors
spinach: 6 veggie 9 vegetable
like ~: 5 leafy
spinach ___: 3 pie 4 dock 5 aphid
spinachlike plant: 5 orach 6 orache
spinal ___: 4 cord 5 canal, nerve 6 column
spinal column part: 6 sacrum
spinal cord
combining form: 4 myel- 5 myelo-
lining: 6 endyma
terminus: 5 brain
Spin City (ABC sitcom)
cast: Barry Bostwick (Randall Winston)
Connie Britton (Nikki Faber)
Michael J. Fox (Michael Flaherty)
Richard Kind (Paul Lassiter)
Alan Ruck (Stuart Bondek)
dog: 4 Rags
spindle: 4 axis, axle 6 empale, impale 8 baluster
combining form: 4 fusi-
spindly: 4 lank, thin, weak 5 lanky, leggy, rangy, weedy 6 gangly 7 stringy 14 gangling. skinny
spindrift: 4 surf 5 spray, spume
spine: 4 back, grit, guts 5 briar, chine, moxie, pluck, point, quill, ridge, thorn 6 mettle, rachis 7 bramble, courage, hogback, rhachis 8 backbone, decision, gumption 9 fortitude, stiffness, vertebrae, willpower 10 moral fiber, projection
combining form: 5 rachi- 6 acanth-, rachio-, rhachi- 7 acantho-, rhachio-, vertebr-
item: 5 title 6 author
part: 6 coccyx
where the ~ starts: 4 nape
spinel: 3 gem 4 ruby 5 balas 7 mineral 8 gemstone
spineless: 4 meek, soft, weak 5 timid 6 feeble, yellow 7 fawning, fearful,

gutless 8 cowardly, pithless, recreant 9 forceless, nerveless, squeamish, weak-kneed 10 amoebalike, frightened, inadequate, irresolute, namby-pamby, spiritless, submissive, weak-willed
one: 4 wimp, worm 5 sissy
spinelle: 3 gem 8 gemstone
Spiner, Brent: 5 actor
film: Out to Sea (1997)
Star Trek: Insurrection (1998)
role: 4 Data
TV: Star Trek: The Next Generation
spinet: 5 organ, piano 8 keyboard
spine-tingling: 4 eery 5 eerie, scary 6 spooky 8 exciting
Spingarn, Joel E.: 6 critic, writer
Spingarn Medal awarder: 5 NAACP
Spinks: 4 Leon 7 Michael
Spinks, Leon: 5 boxer
defeater: 3 Ali
milieu: 4 ring
Spinks, Michael: 5 boxer
milieu: 4 ring
spin like __: 4 a top
spinnaker: 4 sail
support: 4 mast
spinner: 2 DJ 3 top 4 lure 6 deejay
spinneret: 3 cup 5 organ, plate
Spinners
song: Could It Be I'm Falling in Love (1973)
Cupid (1980)
I'll Be Around (1972)
I'm Coming Home (1974)
One of a Kind (1973)
The Rubberband Man (1976)
Then Came You (1974)
'They Just Can't Stop It' the (Games People Play) (1975)
Working My Way Back to You (1980)
spinning: 6 awhirl, rotary 8 gyration
one's wheels: 6 in a rut
sound: 4 whir 5 whirr
spinning __: 3 box, rod 4 mule, reel, ring 5 frame, jenny, wheel
Spinning Wheel (1969 song) artist: Blood, Sweat & Tears
spinoff: 6 sequel 7 product, variant 9 byproduct, outgrowth 10 derivative
Spinone Italiano: 3 dog 5 canid 6 canine
spin one's __: 6 wheels
Spinout (1966 film)
cast: Shelley Fabares, Diane McBain, Elvis Presley, Deborah Walley
director: Norman Taurog
Spinoza, Baruch: 5 Dutch 6 writer 11 philosopher
spins, part that: 5 rotor
spin the __: 5 plate 6 bottle 7 platter
spin the bottle: 4 game
spinule: 5 thorn
spiny: 5 sharp 6 barbed, briery, hispid, spiked, thorny 7 bristly, pointed, prickly, pronged, thistly 9 acanthoid, spiculate
spiny __: 3 rat 6 lizard 7 dogfish, lobster
spiral: 4 coil, curl, loop, rise, spin, turn, wind 5 curve, helix, screw, twist, whorl 6 coiled, curled, volute 7 curling, entwine, helical, intwine, sinuate, whorled, winding 8 circling, circular, cochlear, curlicue, curlycue, flourish, gyration, scrolled 9 arabesque, corkscrew, sinuosity 10 tendrillar
combining form: 3 gyr- 4 gyro- 5 helic- 6 helico-
molecule: 3 DNA
motion: 8 gyration
spiral __: 3 arm 4 gear 6 casing, galaxy, nebula, spring 7 binding
spiral-__: 5 bound
spirals: 5 pasta 7 noodles
alternative: 4 orzo, ziti 5 penne 6 shells 7 lasagna, lasagne, pastina, ravioli 8 bucatini, couscous, farfalle, linguine, linguini, macaroni, rigatoni 9 angelhair, cavatelli, manicotti, spaghetti 10 cannelloni, fettuccini, tortellini, vermicelli
Spiral Staircase, The (1946 film)
cast: Ethel Barrymore, George Brent, Dorothy McGuire
spire: 3 tip, top 4 acme, apex, peak 5 crest, crown, point, shoot, stalk, tower 6 apogee, belfry, flèche, sprout, summit, turret, vertex 7 steeple 8 pinnacle
ornament: 6 finial
spirea: 5 plant, shrub 6 flower
family: 4 rose
relative: 4 sloe 6 kerria 7 bramble, jetbead 8 hardhack, ninebark, photinia 9 firethorn, raspberry
spiring: 5 lofty
spirit: 3 air, pep, vim, zip 4 dash, élan, fire, gist, grit, guts, jazz, life, mood, soul, tone, vein, will, zeal, zest 5 ardor, force, genie, ghost, gusto, heart, humor, moxie, nerve, oomph, pluck, sense, shade, spark, spice, spook, spunk, style, umbra, valor, verve, vigor 6 action, animus, brandy, energy, esprit, fantom, flavor, genius, intent, kelpie, liquor, mettle, morale, psyche, shadow, sprite, temper, vision, warmth, wraith 7 bravery, courage, essence, fantasm, feeling, incubus, meaning, outlook, passion, phantom, purport, purpose, resolve, sparkle, specter 8 attitude, backbone, boldness, fervency, phantasm, presence, strength, vitality 9 animation, character, élan vital, fortitude, intention, life force, substance, willpower 10 apparition, atmosphere, enterprise, enthusiasm, exuberance, liveliness, moral fiber, motivation, resolution
African ~: 4 ngai
antithesis: 5 flesh
away: 5 seize, sneak, steal 6 abduct, kidnap, snatch 10 run off with
Chinese ~: 5 hsien
combining form: 4 thym- 5 psych-, thymo- 6 pneumo-, psycho- 7 pneumat- 8 pneumato-
evil ~: 5 demon, ghoul 6 daemon, daimon
free ~: 8 bohemian
guardian ~: 5 angel 6 daemon, genius
household ~: 3 Lar
imbue with ~: 6 ensoul, insoul
in French: 3 âme
in music: 4 brio
Irish ~: 5 Pooka
Islamic ~: 3 jin 4 djin, jinn 5 djinn, genie, jinni 6 djinni
lose ~: 6 weaken
of a culture: 5 ethos
show team ~: 3 rah 4 root
water ~: 5 kelpy 6 kelpie
spirit __: 3 gum 4 lamp 5 level 7 compass, varnish
__ spirit: 3 tin 4 evil, free, wood 5 proof, world
Spirit: 3 AMC, car 4 auto 5 Dodge
Spirit __: 4 Cave, Lake
__ Spirit: 4 Holy 5 Great 6 Blithe
Spirit and the Flesh, The author: Pearl S. Buck
spirited: 3 hot 4 avid, bold, game, keen, pert, spry 5 alert, alive, brave, crisp, eager, fiery, gutsy, jazzy, lit up, lusty, nervy, peppy, perky, proud, quick, sharp, smart, spicy, vital, zesty, zingy, zippy 6 active, ardent, bouncy, bright, feisty, frisky, gritty, gung-ho, lively, plucky, snappy, spicey, spunky 7 animate, burning, coltish, dashing, gingery, peppery, piquant, playful, rocking, romping, rousing, vibrant, zealous, zinging 8 animated, fearless, intrepid, resolute, vigorous 9 audacious, dauntless, energetic, exuberant, sparkling, sprightly, strenuous, unfearing, vivacious 10 courageous, expressive, hot-blooded, mettlesome, passionate, rollicking
__-spirited: 3 low 4 high, mean, poor 6 public
spiritedness: 4 zest 8 buoyance, buoyancy
Spirit in the Sky (1970 song) artist: Norman Greenbaum
spiritless: 3 low 4 arid, blah, blue, down, dull, flat, limp, meek, tame 5 leady, tepid, timid, vapid 6 broken, draggy, drippy, droopy, jejune, leaden, torpid 7 languid, subdued, unmoved 8 cast down, dejected, downcast, lifeless, listless 9 apathetic, bloodless, depressed, enervated, exanimate, impassive, inanimate, lethargic, spineless
__ spirito: 3 con
Spirit of Goodyear: 5 blimp 8 zeppelin
Spirit of '76, The instrument: 4 drum, fife
Spirit of St. Louis builder: 4 Ryan
Spirit of St. Louis, The: 4 book, film
author: Charles Lindbergh
cast: Murray Hamilton, Patricia Smith, James Stewart
director: Billy Wilder
Spirit of the Border, The author: Zane Grey
spirits: 4 grog 5 booze, drink, hooch 6 fettle, hootch, liquor, whisky 7 alcohol, liqueur, whiskey 9 aqua vitae, firewater, hard stuff, moonshine 10 intoxicant
be in high ~: 4 crow 5 exult 6 bubble 7 enthuse, rejoice 9 make merry 10 effervesce, jump for joy
dampen the ~ of: 6 sadden 10 discourage
good ~: 3 joy, pep 4 élan, glee, life, mood 5 cheer, mirth 6 gaiety, gayety, levity 7 elation, jollity, rapture 8 buoyance, buoyancy, euphoria, felicity, gladness, hilarity 9 happiness, joviality, merriment, well-being 10 enthusiasm, exuberance, joyfulness
guardian ~: 5 Lares
in high ~: 3 gay 5 happy, jolly, riant 6 cheery, elated 7 chipper 8 cheerful, exultant, sanguine
in low ~: 3 sad 4 blue, down, glum 6 gloomy
lift the ~ of: 5 elate 7 hearten
low ~: 4 mood 5 blues 7 sadness 8 glumness 10 depression, woefulness
raise one's ~: 4 buoy 5 cheer, elate 6 buck up, buoy up, solace 7 cheer up, comfort, console, enliven, gladden 8 brighten 9 encourage
with low ~: 5 sadly
see also liqueur, liquor
__ spirits: 4 high 6 animal, ardent 7 mineral, neutral
spirits of __: 4 wine
Spirits of the Dead author: Edgar Allan Poe
Spirits that __ on mortal thoughts: 4 tend
spiritual: 4 airy, holy, hymn, pure, song 5 inner 6 divine, mystic, sacred 7 ghostly, psychic, refined 8 bodiless, ethereal, mystical, platonic, rarefied 9 celestial, ineffable, religious, unearthly, unworldly 10 devotional, immaterial, intangible, mysterious, unphysical
being: 4 soul
discipline: 4 yoga
formula: 5 credo
teacher: 4 guru, lama, yogi 5 rabbi, rebbe
word in a ~: 4 amen
spiritualist: 4 seer 7 psychic
board: 5 Ouija
spirituality: 8 religion
Spiro: 5 Agnew
spirogyra: 4 alga 5 algae
__ spiro, spero: 3 dum
spiry: 6 coiled 7 helical
spit: 3 rod 4 hiss, rain, spew, spue 5 drool, spear, spike, water 6 saliva, sizzle, squirt 7 dribble, slobber, spatter, sputter 8 splutter, sprinkle, transfix 9 brochette, discharge 10 promontory
ender: 4 ball, fire
out: 4 spew, spue, tell 5 eject
partner: 6 polish
put on a ~: 6 empale, impale
starter: 4 turn
upon: 5 scorn
spit __: 4 curl
spit __ ocean: 5 in the
spit-__: 5 shine
spit and __: 6 polish
spitball: 5 pitch
spitchcock: 3 eel
spite: 3 vex 4 crab, gall, harm, hate, hurt 5 annoy, beset, peeve, venom, wrong 6 enmity, grudge, hang up, harass, hatred, injure, malice, needle, nettle, offend, put out, rancor, spleen 7 cruelty, get even, ill will, louse up, provoke, revenge, umbrage 8 acrimony, bad blood, begrudge, contempt, defiance, meanness 9 animosity, antipathy, discomfit, hostility, nastiness, persecute, vengeance 10 grumpiness, resentment, unkindness
in ~ of: 3 tho, yet 5 altho 6 though 8 although, ignoring 10 even though
in ~ of that: 6 even so
spiteful: 4 evil, mean, ugly 5 angry, catty, cruel, dirty, nasty, onery, snide, surly 6 barbed, malign, ornery, unkind, wicked 7 hateful, hostile, hurtful, vicious 8 inimical, vengeful, venomous, virulent 9 bellicose, malicious, malignant, rancorous, splenetic 10 derogatory, ill-natured, malevolent, minimizing, pugnacious, unfriendly, vindictive
one: 5 hater, meany, viper 6 meanie
spitefulness: 5 venom 6 malice, rancor
spitfire: 5 hussy, shrew, vixen 6 chider, virago 9 henpecker, termagant
Spitfire: 5 plane 7 fighter 8 airplane
org.: 3 RAF
Spitfire (1942 film)
cast: Leslie Howard, David Niven
director: Leslie Howard
__ Spitfire: 7 Mexican
Spitsbergen: 3 isl. 4 isle 6 island
locale: 6 Arctic
Spitteler, Carl: 4 poet 5 Swiss 8 Nobelist
spitting
exclamation: 4 ptui 6 ptooey
image: 4 copy, twin 5 clone, match 6 double 7 picture 8 likeness 9 duplicate, look-alike 10 dead ringer
spitting __: 5 cobra, image
spittlebug: 6 insect
spitz: 3 dog 5 canid 6 canine 7 Samoyed 8 chow chow 10 Pomeranian

Spitz, Mark: 7 swimmer
splash: 3 lap, sop, wet 4 blob, dash, pour, show, slop, soak, spot, stir, wade 5 bathe, burst, douse, dowse, drown, flair, lobby, slosh, spill, spray, strew 6 dabble, drench, effect, gurgle, paddle, shower, spread, squirt, wallow 7 display, moisten, spatter, splurge, triumph 8 splatter, sprinkle 9 broadcast, sensation 10 spattering
ender: 4 down 5 board, guard
splash __: 3 dam 4 down 5 guard 7 erosion
Splash (1984 film)
cast: John Candy, Tom Hanks, Daryl Hannah
director: Ron Howard
__ Splash: 6 Splish
splashboard: 6 fender
splashdown: 7 landing
splashy: 5 gaudy, showy, swank 6 ornate, sloppy, swanky 8 splendid 9 grandiose, well-known 10 flamboyant
splat: 5 strip
Splat! cousin: 4 plop
splatter: 4 slop 5 spill, throw 6 splash 7 moisten
safeguard: 3 bib 5 apron 6 napkin
splay: 5 flare, slant, slope, squat 6 expand, spread
spleen: 3 ire 4 hate, rage 5 anger, gland, organ, spite, venom, wrath 6 enmity, hatred, malice, rancor 8 acrimony 9 hostility, petulance, testiness 10 crabbiness, grumpiness, irritation, touchiness, unkindness
combining form: 5 splen- 6 spleno-
vent one's ~: 4 boil, fume, rant, rave, yell 5 erupt, steam, wrath 6 blow up, rail at, scream, seethe 7 explode, rampage, run riot, run wild 8 boil over, have a fit, outburst, paroxysm, run amuck, violence 9 blow a fuse, fulminate, go berserk 10 hit the roof, kick up a row
spleenful: 8 liverish
spleenwort: 4 fern
splendid: 3 def, fab, fat, rad 4 aces, A-one, boss, braw, cool, dece, fine, gear, good, keen, luxe, neat, nice, okay, phat, posh, rare, rich, tuff 5 dandy, ducky, grand, great, legit, marvy, moral, neato, nobby, noble, plush, prime, proud, regal, royal, slick, super, swell 6 bang on, bang-up, bonzer, bosker, bright, choice, costly, deluxe, divine, dreamy, far-out, gnarly, groovy, lavish, lordly, lovely, ornate, peachy, proper, slap-up, spot on, superb, swanky, terrif, tiptop, unreal, whizzo, wicked 7 amazing, awesome, beaming, capital, corking, elegant, eminent, ethical, gallant, glowing, perfect, premium, radiant, ripping, skookum, splashy, stellar, sublime, supreme 8 all right, dazzling, especial, eximious, fabulous, five-star, four-star, frabjous, glorious, gorgeous, heavenly, imperial, jim-dandy, laudable, lustrous, majestic, palatial, peerless, pleasant, pleasing, princely, renowned, slam-bang, smashing, standout, sterling, stickout, superior, terrific, top-level, topnotch, very good, wondrous 9 admirable, agreeable, beautiful, bodacious, brilliant, Endsville, excellent, exemplary, expensive, exquisite, fantastic, first-rate, grandiose, high-grade, hunky-dory, luxurious, magnifico, marvelous, matchless, refulgent, reputable, solid gold, sol-licker, sumptuous, topflight, unrivaled, wonderful, wunderbar 10 acceptable, beneficial, celebrated, creditable, first-class, flamboyant, glittering, hotsy-totsy, impressive, jack-a-dandy, majestical, out of sight, peachy-keen, phenomenal, remarkable, stupendous, super-duper, unrivalled
splendidly: 7 rightly 8 laudably, worthily
Splendid Splinter, The: 8 Williams
splendiferous: 5 showy
splendor: 4 luxe, pomp, show 5 éclat, glory, light 6 dazzle, luster, luxury, renown 7 display, glitter, majesty, pageant 8 ceremony, elegance, grandeur, heraldry, radiance, radiancy, richness 9 solemnity, spectacle 10 brightness, brilliance, effulgence, kingliness, luminosity
Splendor (1999 film)
cast: Matt Keeslar, Kelly Macdonald, Kathleen Robertson, Johnathon Schaech
director: Gregg Anaki
Splendor in the Grass: 4 film, play
author: William Inge
cast: Warren Beatty, Pat Hingle, Natalie Wood
director: Elia Kazan
splenetic: 3 hot, mad 4 acid, ired, sore 5 angry, cross, huffy, irate, livid, moody, onery, riled, surly, testy, wroth 6 crabby, cranky, crusty, feisty, fuming, grumpy, ireful, morose, ornery, peeved, raging, raving, red-hot, snarly, touchy 7 bearish, bilious, crabbed, enraged, fretful, furious, grouchy, peevish, ranting, waspish 8 choleric, fretsome, grumpish, incensed, inflamed, maddened, outraged, petulant, snappish, spiteful, vengeful, venomous, virulent, wrathful 9 crotchety, fractious, indignant, irascible, irritable, irritated, malicious, querulous, rancorous, resentful 10 freaked out, ill-humored, infuriated, out of sorts, vindictive
splice: 3 tie, wed 4 join, knit, link, mate, mesh, yoke 5 braid, graft, hitch, joint, marry, plait, unite, weave 7 entwine, intwine 8 junction, juncture 9 interlace, interlink 10 interweave
film: 4 edit
thing to ~: 4 gene
__ splice: 3 eye 4 long 5 comma, short 6 square 7 squared
__ splicing: 4 gene
__ splint: 3 air 4 shin 6 Stader
splinter: 3 jag 4 chip, part 5 burst, crack, flake, piece, smash, split, stave 6 needle, paring, shiver, sliver 7 flinder, shatter, shaving 8 fracture, fragment
group: 4 bloc, cult, sect 7 faction
ore ~: 5 spall
splintery: 5 sharp 9 breakable
Splish Splash (1958 song) artist: Bobby Darin
activity: 4 bath
split: 2 go 3 gap, lam, rip 4 blow, bolt, exit, flee, fork, gape, gone, gulf, hack, left, open, part, rend, rent, rift, rive, slit, snap, tear, torn, went 5 allot, apart, be off, break, burst, chasm, chink, cleft, crack, divvy, forky, halve, in two, leave, riven, scram, sever, share, slash, slice 6 beat it, begone, bisect, branch, breach, broken, cleave, cloven, cut off, cut out, damage, decamp, depart, desert, detach, divide, forked, get out, go away, profit, run off, schism, secede, spread, sunder, unlink 7 abscond, asunder, break up, carve up, cracked, crack-up, crevice, deviate, disband, discord, disjoin, diverge, divided, divorce, divvy up, faction, fissure, get lost, give way, go forth, go south, head out, incised, isolate, make off, mete out, opening, portion, pull out, radiate, revenue, ride off, rupture, section, shatter, slice up, take off, walk out 8 allocate, bisected, break off, check out, cleavage, detached, dissever, disunion, disunite, division, divorced, fracture, fragment, fugitate, hightail, laminate, proceeds, run for it, separate, set apart, shove off, splinter, sundered, uncouple 9 apportion, bifurcate, bundle off, come apart, dichotomy, disengage, disunited, lacerated, parcel out, partition, pull apart, segregate, subdivide, take leave 10 alienation, come undone, difference, disconnect, disruption, dissension, distribute, divergence, go fly a kite, interspace, percentage, poles apart, put asunder, separation
combining form: 5 schiz- 6 schizo- 7 schisto-
component: 3 pin
hairs: 5 cavil 6 niggle 7 nitpick, quibble 8 pettifog
it may be ~: 4 atom
off: 5 spall
old-style: 5 reave
one's sides: 4 roar 5 laugh 6 guffaw
second: 4 jiff, wink 5 flash, jiffy, trice 6 minute, moment 7 instant
they may be ~: 4 ends
up: 4 part, rend 5 apart, break, halve, sever, share 6 bisect, divide, parcel, sunder 7 disjoin, scatter 8 fragment, separate 9 apportion, partition, pull apart, segregate
split __: 3 end, off, run 4 ends, flap, page, rail, roll 5 hairs, shift 6 screen, second, ticket 7 spindle
split-__: 4 time 5 level, phase
split-__ soup: 3 pea
__ split: 4 baby, dodo 6 banana
__-split: 7 lickety
Split: 4 city, town
locale: 7 Croatia
Split Image (1982 film)
cast: Karen Allen, Peter Fonda, Michael O'Keefe
director: Ted Kotcheff
split-level: 5 house
splitter: 5 pitch
__-splitter: 4 rail
splitter's
log ~ aid: 3 ram 4 froe, frow 5 chock, wedge
splitting: 7 fission
starter: 3 ear 4 side
splitting __: 3 adz 4 adze 5 field, hairs
__-splitting: 3 fee
split-up: 7 parting, rupture 10 detachment, separation
splotch: 4 blob, mark, spot 5 speck, stain
splotchy: 4 pied 7 mottled
splurge: 4 shop 5 binge, fling, spree, waste 6 splash 7 rampage 9 celebrate
splutter: 4 rave, spit 7 spatter, stutter
Spock, Benjamin: 2 MD 6 doctor
specialty: 10 pediatrics
Spock, Mr.: 5 alien 6 Vulcan
colleague: 4 Kirk, Sulu 5 McCoy, Scott, Uhura 7 Chekhov
father: 5 Sarek
mother: 6 Amanda
successor: 4 Data
Spode: 5 china 6 Josiah
competitor: 5 Lenox 6 Mikasa 9 Rosenthal
spodumene: 7 kunzite 9 hiddenite
spoil: 3 mar, pet, rot 4 baby, blot, harm, hurt, ruin, sack, sink, soil, sour, turn, undo 5 addle, botch, decay, favor, go bad, go off, gum up, humor, queer, smash, sully, taint, trash, upset, waste, wreck 6 befoul, coddle, crud up, curdle, damage, dampen, dandle, debase, deface, defile, dote on, go sour, impair, infect, injure, mangle, mess up, mildew, molder, muck up, oblige, pamper, ravage, squash 7 acidify, blemish, cater to, corrupt, crumble, destroy, go to pot, indulge, pillage, plunder, pollute, ransack, screw up, tarnish, turn bad, vitiate 8 demolish, desolate, disgrace, dote upon, freeboot, give in to 9 break down, decompose, depredate, desecrate, devastate, disfigure, prejudice, spoon-feed, take apart 10 overpamper
ender: 3 age 5 sport
for: 4 want, wish
rotten: 4 baby 6 pamper
spoilage: 4 ruin 5 decay
spoiled: 3 bad, off 4 gamy 5 gamey, moldy, musty, stale 6 bratty, rotten 8 inedible
child: 4 brat
spoiled __: 4 brat
spoiler: 5 doter, louse
spoilfive: 4 game 8 card game
spoils: 3 cut 4 gain, loot, make, pelf, prey, swag, take 5 booty, goods, graft, prize 6 trophy 7 pillage, plunder, squeeze 8 pickings
spoils __: 6 system
Spoils of Poynton, The author: Henry James
Spokane: 4 city, town
athlete: 3 Zag
event of 1974: 4 Expo 10 World's Fair
locale: 10 Washington
school: 7 Gonzaga
spoke: 3 bar, ray, rod 4 rung 6 radius 8 baluster
intersection: 3 hub
place: 5 wheel
umbrella ~: 3 rib
spoken: 4 oral, said, told 5 aloud, vocal 6 phonic, sonant, verbal, voiced 7 lingual, uttered 8 narrated, phonetic 9 announced, expressed, mentioned, recounted, unwritten, vocalized 10 articulate
for: 5 in use, taken 6 chosen 7 engaged 8 reserved
in French: 3 dit
not ~ of: 4 tabu 5 taboo
statement: 5 parol
__-spoken: 4 fair, free, well 5 plain, rough, short 6 smooth
spokesperson: 5 agent, mouth, sayer 6 deputy, talker 7 prophet, speaker, stand-in 8 advocate, champion, delegate, mediator 9 proponent 10 mouthpiece
spoliate: 3 rob 4 raid, ruin, sack 5 waste, wreck 6 maraud, ravage 7 despoil, destroy, pillage, plunder, ransack 8 demolish, desolate 9 desecrate, devastate
spoliation: 5 decay 9 pollution
spondee: 4 foot
relative: 4 iamb 6 dactyl 7 anapest, pyrrhic, trochee
spondulicks: 3 oof 4 cash, gelt, jack, kail, kale, loot, peag, pelf 5 bills, bread, bucks, dough, funds, lucre, money, moola, mopus, pesos, rhino, sewan 6 dinero, do-re-mi, mammon, mazuma, moolah, seawan, silver, specie, wampum, wealth 7 cabbage, capital, dollars, lettuce, ooftish, scratch, shekels 8 bankroll, cold cash, currency, hard cash, smackers 9 banknotes, frogskins, long green, simoleons 10 greenbacks, green stuff

sponge: 3 dry, mop 4 bath, cake, wash, wipe 5 cadge, clean, leech, loofa, luffa, mooch 6 cadger, loofah 7 moocher, solicit 8 deadbeat, freeload, hanger-on, parasite, scrounge 10 freeloader
gourd: 5 loofa, luffa 6 loofah
like a ~: 6 porous 9 permeable
on: 3 beg 5 cadge, mooch 8 freeload
out: 5 erase 6 efface 7 expunge 10 obliterate
target: 5 spill
up: 6 absorb
use a ~: 3 sop 4 wipe 5 sop up
sponge __: 3 bag 4 bath, cake, iron, tree 5 cloth 6 rubber
__ sponge: 4 bath, iron, wool 5 grass
sponger: 3 bum 5 drone, leech, mooch 6 cadger, loafer 7 moocher 8 hanger-on, parasite 10 freeloader
sponge-toy brand: 4 Nerf
spongy: 4 soft 5 light, mushy, pulpy, soggy 6 leachy, porous 7 elastic, rubbery, springy, squishy 8 bibulous, cushiony, flexible, yielding 9 absorbent, resilient
rubber: 4 foam
wet and ~: 5 muddy 6 swampy
wet ~ area: 3 bog, fen 5 marsh, swamp
sponsor: 4 back, fund, help 5 angel, endow, stake 6 backer, foster, patron, surety 7 finance, promote, support 8 adherent, advocate, bankroll, financer, guardian, mainstay, promoter, vouch for 9 answer for, financier, godparent, grubstake, guarantee, guarantor, patronize, subsidize, supporter, sustainer 10 benefactor, connection, grubstaker, underwrite
message: 2 ad 5 a word
sponsored child: 6 godson 11 goddaughter
sponsorship: 4 egis 5 aegis, start 8 auspices 9 patronage
spontaneity: 4 élan 7 abandon
spontaneous: 4 free, naif 5 ad-lib, naive, unbid 6 casual, simple 7 natural, offhand, up-front, willing 8 informal, unartful, unbidden, unforced 9 automatic, impetuous, impromptu, impulsive, unguarded, unplanned, unstudied, voluntary
spontaneously: 5 ad lib 9 extempore, naturally
spontoon: 7 javelin
spoof: 4 fake, fool, game, hoax, jest, joke, mock, quip, sell, sham, skit 5 bluff, cheat, phony, prank, put on, trick 6 deceit, parody, phoney, satire, send-up 7 burlesk, deceive, imitate, lampoon, mockery, take off 8 parodize, travesty, trickery 9 burlesque, deception, imposture, wisecrack 10 caricature
spoofing: 7 jesting, satiric 9 satirical
spook: 3 spy 4 stir 5 alarm, ghost, haunt, scare, upset 6 fantom, goblin, spirit, wraith 7 fantasm, fluster, petrify, phantom, specter, startle, terrify, trouble, unnerve 8 distress, frighten, phantasm, psych out, threaten, unsettle 9 give a turn, terrorize 10 intimidate, scare stiff
spooked: 5 jumpy, timid 6 afraid, scared, trepid 7 anxious, chicken, fearful, jittery, nervous, panicky 8 cowardly, fearsome, hesitant, timorous
spooky: 4 eery 5 eerie, scary, weird 6 creepy 7 eidolic, ghostly, macaber, macabre, ominous, uncanny 8 haunting 9 frightful, unearthly 10 mysterious
sound: 4 moan 5 creak
spool: 4 reel, roll, wind 6 bobbin, unwind
in Britain: 4 pirn
toy: 4 yo-yo
spoon: 3 woo 4 club, iron, lure, wood 5 court, ladle, scoop 6 cuddle, smooch 7 snuggle, stirrer, utensil 8 golf club, pitch woo 9 three wood 10 bill and coo
companion, in rhyme: 4 dish
ender: 4 bill 5 drift
greasy ~: 4 café 5 diner 6 eatery 10 restaurant
out: 5 ladle
starter: 3 tea 4 soup 5 table 7 dessert
spoon __: 3 bow 4 bait, hook, nail 5 bread
spoon-__: 3 fed 4 feed
spoon-__ chair: 4 back
__ spoon: 4 mote, salt, soup 5 acorn, berry, caddy, punch, sugar 6 coffee, greasy, silver 7 Apostle, Puritan, slotted 8 runcible
spoonbill: 4 bird
relative: 4 ibis 5 stork
spoonerism: 8 wordplay
spoon-feed: 4 baby 5 spoil 7 cater to, indulge
spoonful: 3 sip 4 bite 5 taste 6 dollop
starter: 3 tea 5 table
__ Spoonful: 5 Lovin'
spoon-playing locale: 4 knee
Spoon River Anthology author: Edgar Lee Masters
spoony, make: 6 enamor
spoor: 5 piste, scent, trace, track, trail 9 footprint 10 impression
sporadic: 3 odd 4 rare 6 broken, random, scarce, seldom, sparse, spotty 7 erratic 8 far apart, isolated, on and off, periodic, uncommon 9 hit-or-miss, irregular, scattered, spasmodic 10 flickering, infrequent, nonuniform, occasional, unfrequent
sporadically: 6 hardly, seldom 8 fitfully
spore: 4 cell, seed
case: 5 theca
case cluster: 6 telium
combining form: 4 coni- 5 conio-
fern ~ cluster: 5 sorus
fungus ~: 6 oidium
fungus ~ sac: 5 ascus 6 aecium
mark: 5 hilum
mold ~ sac: 5 ascus
producer: 4 fern
starter: 4 endo
__ spore: 4 mold
sporran: 5 purse
it's worn with a ~: 4 kilt
sporter: 4 Scot
sport: 3 don, fun, toy 4 butt, chap, crew, épée, game, golf, jest, judo, luge, mock, play, polo, pool, show, sumo, wear 5 darts, fight, games, kendo, mirth, model, prank, rodeo, rugby 6 action, aikido, antics, boxing, diving, frolic, gaiety, gambol, gayety, have on, hiking, hockey, joking, karate, kung fu, pelota, racing, riding, rowing, shinny, skiing, soccer, squash, tennis, tubing 7 archery, birling, bowling, buffoon, camping, contest, cricket, croquet, curling, cycling, display, disport, exhibit, fencing, fishing, gambler, hunting, hurling, jai alai, jesting, jollity, jujitsu, kidding, mockery, pastime, rafting, running, sailing, show off, skating, skylark, surfing, teasing, tenpins 8 aerobics, baseball, canoeing, derision, dressage, duelling, escapade, exercise, falconry, football, handball, high-jump, interest, jousting, lacrosse, laughter, long-jump, ninepins, Ping-Pong, pleasure, pole-jump, raillery, rounders, sculling, softball, swimming, trifling, tumbling, yachting 9 amusement, athletics, badminton, bicycling, billiards, broad-jump, decathlon, diversion, dog racing, enjoyment, horseplay, ice hockey, merriment, plaything, pole vault, sky-diving, sprinting, water polo, wrestling 10 acrobatics, auto-racing, ballooning, basketball, big spender, deck tennis, fly-casting, fly fishing, gymnastics, horseshoes, iceboating, ice dancing, ice fishing, ice-skating, kickboxing, lawn tennis, liveliness, pentathlon, recreation, ski jumping, skin diving, tomfoolery, volleyball 11 backpacking, bobsledding, hang-gliding, horse racing, parachuting, racquetball, scuba diving, shot-putting, table tennis, tobogganing, water skiing, windsurfing
be a ~: 3 pay 5 treat
make ~ of: 3 kid 4 jape
starter: 5 spoil
sport __: 3 car 4 fish 5 shirt
sport-__: 3 ute
__ sport: 3 be a, bud 5 blood 7 contact
__ Sport: 5 Blood
Sportage: 3 Kia, SUV
Sport Fury: 3 car 4 auto 8 Plymouth
sporting: 3 gay 4 fair, game, wild 5 antic, merry 6 frisky, impish, jaunty, joyous, lively 7 larkish, playful, roguish 8 athletic, generous 9 full of fun, sprightly 10 frolicsome, rollicking
event: 4 game, meet, race 5 match
sporting __: 3 dog 6 chance
__-sporting dog: 3 non
sporting-goods name: 4 Voit 8 Spalding
__ Sporting Life: 4 This
Sporting Life friend: 4 Bess
sportive: 3 gay 4 game, wild 5 antic, jolly, merry 6 frisky, impish, jaunty, joyous, lively 7 coltish, jocular, larkish, playful, roguish 8 generous 9 full of fun, gamboling, sprightly, vivacious 10 frolicsome, rollicking
sportiveness: 8 jocosity, mischief
sports: 9 athletics 10 recreation
award: 3 MVP
center: 3 gym 5 arena 7 stadium 9 gymnasium
championship: 5 title
college ~ org.: 3 AAU 4 NCAA
commentator's patter: 5 color
deal: 5 trade
ender: 3 man, men 4 cast, wear 5 woman, women 6 caster, writer
enthusiast: 3 fan
event: 4 bowl, game, meet, race
extra period in ~: 2 OT 8 overtime
fan: 9 spectator
group: 4 team 6 league 10 conference
legend: 5 great
network: 4 ESPN
official: 3 ref, ump 5 judge, timer 6 umpire 7 referee
page item: 4 stat 5 recap, score
position: 5 coach 7 manager, trainer
rig, as a ~ event: 3 fix
schedule word: 4 away, home
shoe attachment: 5 cleat
show feature: 5 slo-mo 6 replay
surprise: 5 upset
tally: 5 point
team: 5 squad
unguarded, in ~: 4 open
violation: 4 foul
sports __: 3 bar, car 6 jacket
Sports __: 6 Afield
Sports Arena team: 3 USC
sports car: 3 GTI, GTO, Jag 4 auto 5 Miata, 'Vette 6 Camaro, Jaguar 7 Mustang 8 Corvette 10 automobile
noseguard: 3 bra
org.: 4 IMSA
sportscaster
hockey ~ cry: 5 score
need: 4 mike
shout: 3 yes
SportsCenter network: 4 ESPN
Sports Challenge: 8 game show
host: Dick Enberg
sportsman: 6 hunter
sportsmanly: 4 fair 5 clean
sportsmanship: 7 honesty 8 courtesy, fairness, fair play, goodwill 9 integrity
Sportsman's Sketches, A author: Ivan Turgenev
sports medicine: 7 science
sportswear: 7 clothes
label: 4 Izod
Sportwagon: 3 car 4 auto 5 Buick
sporty: 5 natty, sleek, swank 6 dapper, jaunty, rakish, snazzy, spiffy, swanky 7 dashing, raffish
spot: 2 ad 3 dab, dot, fix, jam, job, jot, nip, pad, see, spy 4 blob, blot, blur, daub, drop, espy, find, flaw, hole, iota, look, lump, mark, mess, post, seat, site, slot, soil, view 5 berth, catch, dirty, drink, fleck, joint, light, lobby, locus, odium, patch, pinch, place, point, scene, sight, space, speck, stain, sully, taint, trace, track, where 6 billet, blotch, cavern, crud up, dapple, descry, detect, dollop, little, locale, locate, lounge, notice, pepper, pickle, plight, random, scrape, sector, smudge, splash, stigma, streak, stripe, turn up 7 blemish, dilemma, discern, freckle, glimpse, hangout, lentigo, look out, make out, observe, pick out, quarter, section, smidgen, smidgin, spatter, speckle, splotch, station, stipple, tarnish, trouble 8 besmirch, diagnose, discover, flyspeck, identify, locality, location, meet with, molecule, particle, perceive, pinpoint, point out, position, quandary, smidgeon, sprinkle 9 bespatter, encounter, ferret out, lay eyes on, light upon, little bit, nightclub, recognize, situation 10 connection, difficulty, imputation
combining form: 5 macul- 6 maculi-, maculo-
ender: 3 lit 5 light
starter: 3 eye, hot, sun 5 night
spot __: 4 card, line, news, pass, test 5 check, meter, of tea, plate, price 6 height, market 7 welding
spot-__: 4 weld 5 check
__ spot: 3 hot, in a, pin 4 baby, cold, dead, leaf, ring, soft, warm 5 black, blind, brown, on the, sweet, tight 6 beauty, copper, pepper 7 trouble
Spot: 3 dog
owner: 4 Dick, Jane
__ Spot: 3 Red 5 Blind, Tight
spotless: 4 neat, pure 5 blank, clean, snowy 6 chaste, decent, modest, virgin, washed 7 shining 8 flawless, gleaming, hygienic, innocent, pristine, sanitary, unsoiled, virginal, virtuous 9 blameless, faultless, guiltless, laundered, lily-white, stainless, undefiled, unspoiled, unstained, unsullied, untouched 10 immaculate, inculcable, unpolluted
spotlight: 4 fame 5 stage 6 accent, play up, stress 7 feature, point up 8 interest 9 attention, emphasize, notoriety, public eye, publicity, publicize, punctuate, underline 10 accentuate, illuminate, illustrate, underscore
filter: 3 gel
in the ~: 5 famed, noted 6 famous 7 eminent
__ Spot run: 3 See
spots
fix some bare ~: 5 resod
hit the high ~: 4 skim 5 recap 8 simplify 9 summarize

hit the low ~: 4 slum
mark with ~: 6 dapple
spotted: 4 pied 5 dirty 6 calico, flecky 7 flecked, mottled, unclean 8 brindled, maculate, speckled
animal: 4 fawn, paca 5 civet, genet, ounce 6 jaguar, ocelot
horse: 5 paint, pinto
spotted __: 3 owl 4 cavy, deer 5 adder, hyena, skunk 7 cowbane, hemlock, sunfish
spotter: 3 spy 5 scout, spier 7 lookout
Spottiswoode, Roger: 8 director
film: The 6th Day (2000)
Air America (1990)
The Best of Times (1986)
Terror Train (1980)
Tomorrow Never Dies (1997)
Turner & Hooch (1989)
Under Fire (1983)
spotty: 4 thin 5 scant 6 patchy, pimply, random, scanty, skimpy, uneven 7 blotchy, erratic, unequal 8 on-and-off, periodic, speckled, sporadic 9 desultory, irregular, piecemeal, scattered, spasmodic, vagarious 10 flickering, sporadical, unfrequent
spousal: 6 bridal, wedded 7 marital, nuptial
spouse: 3 man 4 male, mate, wife 5 bride, groom, hubby, woman 6 missis, missus, mister 7 consort, husband, partner 8 helpmate 9 companion 10 better half, bridegroom
family member: 5 in-law
former ~: 2 ex
spouseless: 5 unwed 6 single 9 unmarried 10 unattached
spouse-to-be: 6 fiancé 7 fiancée
spout: 3 jet, lip, run, tap, yak 4 brag, emit, go on, gush, pipe, pour, rant, talk, vent, yell 5 boast, eject, erupt, expel, exude, orate, speak, spiel, spile, spill, spirt, spray, spurt, surge 6 effuse, nozzle, outlet, patter, ramble, squirt, stream 7 cascade, chatter, conduit, declaim, lecture, opening 8 bloviate, fountain, harangue, overflow, proclaim, ramble on, water jet 9 discharge, expatiate, go on and on, hold forth, sermonize, waterfall
as a whale: 4 blow
geothermal ~: 6 geyser
starter: 4 down, rain 5 water
spout __: 3 cup, off
__ spout: 4 eave 5 eaves
spouted vessel: 3 jug 7 pitcher
spouting: 5 agush 8 harangue
spr.
see spring
__ Sprach Zarathustra: 4 Also
Spradlin: 2 G.D.
sprag: 4 pole 5 brake 6 timber
sprain: 4 pull, turn 5 twist 6 injury, strain, wrench
site: 5 ankle, wrist
soother: 3 ice 6 arnica, ice bag 7 ice pack
sprat: 4 fish 7 herring, sardine 8 brisling
Sprat, Jack
diet: 4 lean
no-no: 3 fat
Sprat, Mrs.
diet: 3 fat
no-no: 4 lean
sprawl: 3 lie, sit 4 flop, loll, trip 5 drape, plump, slump 6 extend, lounge, ramble, slouch, spread, tumble 7 recline, stretch 8 straddle, straggle 9 spread out
__ sprawl: 5 urban
sprawling: 9 recumbent
spray: 3 fog, wet 4 dust, foam, limb, mist, slop 5 froth, smear, spill, spout, sprig, spume, throw, water 6 dampen, shower, splash, spread, spritz, squirt 7 aerosol, atomize, bouquet, corsage, diffuse, drizzle, moisten, scatter, spatter 8 atomizer, dispense, droplets, hose down, irrigate, sprinkle 9 spindrift, sprinkler, vaporizer 10 sprinkling
banned ~: 3 DDT 4 Alar
defensive ~: 4 mace
fine ~: 4 mist
garden ~: 6 fogger
ocean ~: 4 foam, surf, wave 5 froth, spume 8 breakers 9 spindrift
plane ~: 6 deicer
small ~: 5 sprig
starter: 4 hair
spray __: 3 can, gun 4 tank 5 paint 6 millet
__ spray: 4 hair, rock 5 nasal 7 aerosol
__-spray: 3 air
Spray __: 5 'N Wash
__ Spray: 5 Ocean
__-sprayed: 4 sand
__ sprayer: 3 air
spread: 3 jam, lay, lie, rub, run, sow, wax 4 cast, coat, daub, farm, flow, grow, luau, meal, oleo, open, part, show, size, soil, span, spew, spue 5 array, bloat, cover, feast, flare, jelly, level, lunch, quilt, ranch, range, reach, relay, rub on, scale, scope, smear, space, splay, split, spray, strew, sweep, table, tract, widen, width 6 branch, butter, dilate, estate, expand, extend, extent, fan out, layout, lekvar, period, ramble, regale, splash, sprawl, uncoil, unfold, unfurl, unroll, unwind 7 arrange, banquet, bestrew, blanket, blowout, breadth, broaden, burgeon, compass, develop, deviate, diffuse, display, diverge, enlarge, even out, expanse, flatten, open out, overlay, pervade, publish, radiate, roll out, scatter, slather, stretch, suffuse, untwist 8 bedcover, bourgeon, covering, dilation, disperse, distance, escalate, heighten, increase, latitude, lengthen, multiply, mushroom, overgrow, proclaim, separate, smooth on, straggle, transmit, widening 9 advertise, bifurcate, branch off, broadcast, circulate, collation, comforter, diffusion, dispersal, expansion, extension, largeness, make known, margarine, marmalade, preserves, profusion, propagate, publicity, publicize, radiation, suffusion 10 dispersion, distribute, escalation, make public, outstretch, plantation, popularize, promulgate, tablecloth
around: 5 share, strew
bread ~: 3 jam 4 mayo, oleo 5 jelly 6 butter 7 ketchup, mustard
cracker ~: 4 Brie, pâté
ender: 5 sheet
fancy ~: 3 roe 6 caviar 7 caviare
for drying: 3 ted
lie ~ out: 4 flop, loll 5 slump 6 lounge, slouch, sprawl 7 stretch
like wildfire: 7 overrun
nondairy ~: 4 oleo
on: 5 apply
out: 3 fan 4 open, sown 5 add to, flare, roomy, widen 6 effuse, expand, extend, open up, sprawl, uncoil, uncurl, unfold, unfurl 7 augment, broaden, diffuse, enlarge, flatten, radiate, stretch 8 extended, rambling 9 diversify
over: 5 cover, smear 7 blanket, overrun, swaddle
quickly: 8 mushroom
rumors: 3 pan 4 blab, slam, slur, talk 5 libel, smear, sully, taint 6 defame, gossip, malign, tattle, vilify 7 asperse, slander, tarnish, traduce 8 backbite, badmouth, besmirch 9 denigrate, discredit, disparage 10 calumniate, scandalize, stigmatize, throw mud at, vituperate
starter: 3 bed 4 wide, wing
thickly: 7 plaster, slather
thin: 6 sparse
through: 7 pervade 8 permeate
spread __: 3 end 5 eagle 6 option
__ spread: 5 photo, point 6 center, cheese, double 7 picture
__ Spread: 6 Shedd's
spread-eagle: 8 boastful, rambling 9 bombastic
lie ~: 6 sprawl
__ spreader: 4 salt 6 butter
spreading: 5 viral 7 rampant 8 rambling 9 epizootic 10 contagious, infectious
tree: 6 banian, banyan 8 chestnut
spread oneself __: 4 thin
spread-out: 4 vast, wide
spreadsheet
abbr.: 3 YTD
material: 4 data 6 number
pro: 3 CPA
shortcut: 5 macro
software: 5 Excel, Lotus
unit: 3 row 4 cell 6 column
Sprechen __ deutsch?: 3 sie
spree: 3 jag, rip 4 ball, bash, bust, lark, romp, tear 5 binge, caper, fling, party, revel 6 bender, frolic, gambol, junket 7 blowout, rampage, revelry, splurge 8 field day, jamboree, wild time, wingding 9 carousing, high jinks
go on a ~: 5 revel, spend 7 carouse
Spree, city on the: 6 Berlin
sprig: 3 boy, kid, lad 4 cion, heir, limb, twig, wand 5 scion, shoot, spray, youth 6 branch 7 cutting 8 half-pint, juvenile 9 youngster
ender: 4 tail
sprightliness: 4 dash, élan, jazz 6 energy, esprit, spirit 8 vitality, vivacity 9 animation, briskness 10 get up and go
sprightly: 3 fun, gay 4 airy, busy, good, keen, pert, racy, spry 5 agile, alert, alive, astir, brisk, elfin, fresh, hyper, jolly, light, peppy, perky, quick, saucy, smart, zappy, zingy, zippy 6 active, blithe, bouncy, breezy, bright, cheery, chirpy, clever, dapper, jaunty, joyous, lively, nimble, snappy 7 animate, chipper, dashing, dynamic, playful, working, zinging 8 animated, bustling, cheerful, grooving, spirited, sporting, sportive 9 assiduous, energetic, exuberant, facetious, fairylike, vivacious 10 frolicsome, keen-witted, rollicking
sprigtail: 4 bird, duck, fowl
relative: 4 smew, teal 5 eider, Pekin, Rouen, scaup 6 Cayuga, scoter 7 gadwall, mallard, pintail, pochard, redhead, sea duck, widgeon 8 garganey, gray duck, mandarin, musk duck, oldsquaw, shoveler, surf duck, wood duck 9 black duck, broadbill, goldeneye, goosander, greenhead, merganser, ruddy duck 10 bufflehead, canvasback, surf scoter, tufted duck
spring: 3 fly, hop, jog, lop, spa 4 bolt, buck, coil, come, flow, free, grow, gush, jump, leap, limb, rise, root, save, skip, stem, tide, trip, well 5 arise, begin, birth, bound, cause, hatch, issue, let go, lunge, pop up, prime, shoot, speed, start, vault 6 appear, arrive, bounce, derive, emerge, gambol, geyser, hurdle, motive, origin, pardon, pounce, prance, reason, recoil, rescue, season, source, sprout, whence 7 absolve, budding, budtime, burgeon, come out, descend, develop, emanate, genesis, impetus, proceed, rebound, release, shoot up, skitter 8 bourgeon, buoyance, buoyancy, commence, flow from, fountain, mushroom, seedtime 9 beginning, flowering, originate, reservoir 10 bounciness, elasticity, hippety hop, resilience
acrobatic ~: 5 nip-up
back: 6 bounce, recoil 7 rebound
chicken: 5 youth
combining form: 4 cren- 5 creno-
ender: 4 buck, halt, hare, head, tail, tide, time, wood 5 board, house
for: 5 spend, treat 8 squander 9 entertain 10 recompense
(for): 3 pay
(from): 4 come, rise 5 arise 6 result 7 proceed
from a ~: 6 fontal
harbinger: 5 robin
having ~ fever: 6 draggy 7 languid 8 sluggish 9 lethargic
hot ~: 3 spa 6 geyser, resort
like ~ flowers: 6 abloom
month: 3 May 4 June 5 April, March
nymph: 5 naiad
observance: 4 Lent 5 Pasch, seder 6 Easter 8 Passover
opposite: 4 fall, neap 6 autumn
ready to ~: 6 coiled
sign: 3 bud 4 thaw 5 Aries 6 Gemini, Taurus
something on: 7 startle 8 surprise
sound: 5 boing
starter: 3 bed, off 4 hair, hand, head, main, well 5 inner
to mind: 5 occur
up: 5 arise, shoot 6 appear, emerge 8 mushroom, take root
spring __: 3 for 4 lamb, line, roll, snow, tide 5 a leak, break, catch, fever, vetch 6 beauty, binder, peeper 7 chicken, equinox, molding
spring-__: 6 loaded
__ spring: 3 air, box, hot 4 coil, leaf, warm 6 spiral, sulfur, volute 7 balance, mineral, thermal
Spring: 4 city, town 8 Byington
locale: 5 Texas
Spring __: 6 Parade, Sonata 7 Forward
Spring __; fall back: 5 ahead 7 forward
__ Spring: 6 Silent 7 Pierian
spring-ahead setting: 3 DST
Spring and Port Wine (1970 film)
cast: Susan George, James Mason
springboard, use a: 4 dive 5 vault
springbok: 6 animal 8 antelope
relative: 3 gnu, kob 4 guib, kudu, oryx, puku, topi 5 addax, bongo, chiru, eland, goral, korin, nyala, oribi, saiga, serow 6 chammy, dik-dik, duiker, impala, koodoo, lechwe, nilgai, rhebok, shammy, shamoy 7 blaubok, blesbok, chamois, defassa, gazelle, gemsbok, gerenuk, grysbok, nylghai, nylghau, sassaby 8 blesbuck, bontebok, bushbuck, gemsbuck, reedbuck, steenbok, steinbok 9 blackbuck, pronghorn, sitatunga, waterbuck 10 hartebeest, wildebeest
spring-break time: 6 Easter
Spring Collection author: Judith Krantz
Springdale: 4 city, town
locale: 8 Arkansas
springe: 4 trap
springer: 3 dog 5 canid 6 canine 7 spaniel
Springer: 5 Jerry
Springfield: 4 city, Rick, town 5 Dusty, rifle
county: 8 Sangamon

locale: 4 Ohio 6 Oregon 8 Illinois, Missouri, Virginia
river: 8 Sangamon
___ Springfield: 7 Buffalo
Springfield, Dusty
song: I Only Want to Be With You (1964)
Son-of-a Preacher Man (1968)
What Have I Done to Deserve This? (1987)
Wishin' and Hopin' (1964)
You Don't Have to Say You Love Me (1966)
Springfield, Rick
song: Affair of the Heart (1983)
Don't Talk to Strangers (1982)
I've Done Everything for You (1981)
Jessie's Girl (1981)
Love Somebody (1984)
Spring Forward (2000 film)
cast: Ned Beatty, Ian Hart, Liev Schreiber, Campbell Scott
director: Tom Gilroy
Spring Hill: 4 city, town
locale: 7 Florida
springiness, show: 4 flex, give
Spring Is Here: 7 musical
songwriter: 4 Hart 7 Rodgers
Spring is like a perhaps hand: 4 poem
author: e.e. cummings
springlike: 4 mild 5 leafy
name meaning ~: 6 Vernon
Spring Parade (1940 film)
cast: Mischa Auer, Robert Cummings, Deanna Durbin
director: Henry Koster
___ Springs: 4 Palm 5 Alice, Coral 6 Tarpon
___ springs eternal: 4 Hope
___ Springs National Park: 3 Hot
Spring Sonata composer: 9 Beethoven
Springsteen, Bruce
nickname: The Boss
song: Better Days (1992)
Born in the U.S.A. (1984)
Born to Run (1975)
Brilliant Disguise (1987)
Cover Me (1984)
Dancing in the Dark (1984)
Fade Away (1981)
Glory Days (1985)
Human Touch (1992)
Hungry Heart (1980)
I'm Goin' Down (1985)
I'm on Fire (1985)
My Hometown (1985)
One Step Up (1988)
Prove It All Night (1978)
Secret Garden (1997)
Streets of Philadelphia (1994)
Tunnel of Love (1987)
War (1986)
spouse: Julianne Phillips
springs, warm: 7 thermae
Spring Symphony composer: 7 Britten
Springtime in the Rockies (1942 film)
cast: Betty Grable, Carmen Miranda, John Payne
spring training locale: 7 Arizona, Florida
Spring Valley: 4 city, town
locale: 6 Nevada 7 New York 10 California
Springville: 4 city, town
locale: 4 Utah
springy: 5 agile 6 bouncy, limber, lissom, spongy, supple 7 buoyant, elastic, lissome, pliable 8 flexible, stretchy, yielding 9 resilient
sprinkle: 3 dot, wet 4 dash, drip, dust, mist, rain, shed, spit, spot, stud 5 bedew, shake, spill, spray, strew, throw, water 6 dampen, dragée, dredge, pepper, powder, shower, splash, spritz, squirt 7 asperse, baptize, bestrew, drizzle, moisten, radiate, scatter, spatter, speckle 8 christen, humidify, irrigate 9 punctuate
with: 5 admix
sprinkled: 8 speckled
in heraldry: 4 semé
sprinkler: 5 spray
sprinkler ___: 6 system
sprinkling: 3 bit, few 4 dash, dust, hint 5 spray, taste, tinge, touch, trace 6 strain 7 dusting, handful, mixture, several 8 spoonful 9 admixture, powdering
sprinkling ___: 3 can
sprint: 3 run 4 dart, dash, race, rush, tear, whiz 5 scoot, spank 6 gallop, hasten, scurry, streak 7 scamper
sprint ___: 6 medley
___ sprint: 4 wind
Sprint: 3 car, Geo 4 auto 10 automobile
competitor: 3 MCI
sprinter: 4 Tyus 5 Flo-Jo, Hayes, Lewis, loper, Owens, racer 6 Devers, runner 7 Ashford, Rudolph 8 Bob Hayes 9 Carl Lewis 10 Gail Devers, Jesse Owens, Wyomia Tyus
event: 4 dash
goal: 4 tape
need: 5 speed
path: 4 lane
problem: 3 mud
prop: 5 block
sprinting: 5 sport
sprit: 4 pole, spar
ender: 4 sail
starter: 3 bow
sprite: 3 elf, fay, imp, Mab, nix 4 nixy, peri, pixy, Puck 5 Ariel, faery, fairy, gnome, nisse, nixie, nymph, pixie, pooka, sylph 6 faerie, goblin, kelpie, kobold, Oberon, spirit 7 brownie, gremlin, Titania 9 hobgoblin 10 leprechaun, Tinker Bell
___ sprite: 5 water
Sprite: 9 soft drink
alternative: 3 TAB 4 Nehi 5 Fanta 6 Fresca 8 Diet Rite, Dr Pepper 9 Canada Dry 10 Mello Yello, Royal Crown 11 Mountain Dew
spritelike: 5 elfin
spritely: 6 elfish, elvish
spritz: 4 spew, spue 5 spirt, spray, spurt 6 squirt 8 sprinkle, water jet
spritzer: 5 drink 8 beverage
ingredient: 4 soda, wine
sprocket: 4 gear 5 tooth
sprocket ___: 4 hole 5 wheel
sprout: 3 boy, bud 4 cion, grow, push 5 bloom, plant, scion, shoot, spear, spire 6 emerge, spring 7 burgeon, develop, shoot up 8 bourgeon, mushroom, offshoot, take root, vegetate 9 germinate 10 effloresce
combining form: 4 clad- 5 -blast, clado- 6 blasto-
sprouting: 5 green 6 growth
___ sprouts: 4 bean
spruce: 4 neat, tidy, tree, trim 5 clean, color, crisp, dandy, kempt, natty, nifty, smart 6 classy, dapper, neaten, spiffy 7 elegant, groomed, orderly, stylish 8 well-kept 9 evergreen, refurbish, shipshape 10 fastidious, neat as a pin, rejuvenate
family: 4 pine
genus: 5 picea
in Britain: 4 trig
relative: 3 fir 7 hemlock 8 tamarack
up: 3 fix 4 tidy, trim, wash 5 adorn, brush, clean, groom, primp, prink, renew, sleek, slick, spiff 6 better, enrich, neaten, polish, reform 7 arrange, deck out, enhance, freshen, furbish, garnish, sharpen, smarten 8 decorate, emblazon, ornament, renovate 9 embellish, meliorate, refurbish 10 ameliorate, rejuvenate
spruce ___: 4 beer, pine 6 beetle, grouse, sawfly 7 budworm
___ spruce: 3 red 4 blue 5 black, Sitka, white 6 Norway 7 Douglas, hemlock
spruce budworm: 3 bug 6 insect
spruced up: 4 neat
Spruce Goose: 5 plane 8 airplane
builder: Howard Hughes
sprung: 5 let go 6 arisen
spry: 4 busy, pert, wiry 5 agile, alert, alive, astir, brisk, fleet, fresh, lithe, peppy, perky, quick, ready, sound, zippy 6 active, adroit, dapper, frisky, limber, lively, nimble, prompt, robust, supple 7 chipper, dynamic, healthy, on the go, rocking, working 8 animated, bustling, spirited, vigorous 9 assiduous, energetic, lightsome, lithesome, sprightly, vivacious 10 frolicsome, full of life
spud: 4 pipe 5 Idaho, tater, tuber 6 potato
bud: 3 eye
covering: 4 skin
state: 5 Idaho
spumante: 4 wine 7 Italian
___ spumante: 4 Asti
spume: 4 foam, spew, spue, surf 5 froth, spray 6 lather 7 sea foam 9 spindrift 10 effervesce
spumoni: 7 dessert 8 ice cream
alternative: 6 gelati, gelato, sundae 7 parfait, tortoni 8 snowball
spumy: 5 barmy
spun
out: 4 long
starter: 4 home
wool: 4 yarn
spun ___: 4 silk, yarn 5 glass, rayon, sugar
___-spun: 4 fine, hard
spunk: 4 élan, grit, guts, push 5 drive, heart, moxie, nerve, pluck, valor 6 daring, hutzpa, mettle, spirit 7 bravado, bravery, chutzpa, courage, hutzpah, panache, prowess 8 audacity, backbone, chutzpah, gameness, gumption, tenacity, true grit, vitality 9 derring-do, endurance, fortitude, gutsiness, toughness 10 confidence, doggedness, feistiness, initiative, moral fiber, pluckiness, resolution
spunky: 4 bold, game 5 gutsy, nervy 6 awless, daring, feisty, gritty, heroic, plucky 7 aweless, defiant, doughty, gallant, staunch, valiant 8 fearless, heroical, intrepid, resolute, spirited, stalwart, unafraid, valorous 9 audacious, dauntless, dreadless, undaunted, unfearful 10 courageous, mettlesome, undismayed, unflagging
spur: 4 abet, barb, goad, limb, prod, push, stir, urge 5 drive, egg on, favor, goose, hop up, impel, key up, liven, pique, press, prick, prong, rally, rouse, spark 6 arouse, awaken, exhort, fillip, fire up, foment, incite, induce, motive, needle, prompt, propel, siding, stir up, turn on, urge on, whip up, work up 7 actuate, animate, impetus, impulse, inspire, provoke, put up to, quicken, trigger 8 catalyst, embolden, excitant, imbolden, motivate, offshoot, stimulus 9 actuation, encourage, galvanize, impassion, incentive, instigate, spearhead, stimulate 10 activation, incitement, inducement, motivation, projection, prominence
attachment: 5 rowel
on the ~ of the moment: 5 ad-lib 6 rashly 7 brashly, hastily 8 abruptly, headlong, pell-mell, suddenly 9 headfirst
rocky ~: 5 arete
sporter: 4 boot
starter: 4 lark, long, sand
spur ___: 4 gear 5 track, wheel 6 blight 7 gearing
spur-___-moment: 5 of-the
spurge tree: 9 candlenut
spurious: 3 bum 4 bent, fake, mock, sham 5 bogus, dummy, faked, false, phony, put-on 6 ersatz, forged, framed, phoney, pirate, pseudo, unreal, untrue 7 assumed, feigned, pretend 8 affected, delusive, specious 9 contrived, deceitful, deceptive, erroneous, imitation, pretended, simulated, synthetic, unfounded, ungenuine 10 apocryphal, artificial, fabricated, fallacious, fictitious, fraudulent, mendacious, misleading, substitute, unverified
combining form: 4 noth- 5 notho-
spurn: 3 cut, nix 4 defy, drop, dump, gibe, jeer, jibe, jilt, mock, shun, slam, slur, snub, veto 5 abuse, decry, flout, flush, libel, repel, scoff, scorn, sneer, taunt 6 bounce, defame, deride, dump on, heckle, ignore, impugn, loathe, malign, offend, pass by, pass on, pass up, rebuff, refuse, reject, slight, vilify 7 abstain, affront, asperse, blow off, boycott, contemn, decline, degrade, despise, disdain, dismiss, exclude, forsake, let go of, neglect, put down, rank out, repulse, slander, sneer at, traduce 8 belittle, brush off, denounce, disallow, forswear, keep from, renounce, ridicule, sneeze at, turn away, turn back, turn down, vilipend 9 blackball, cast aside, denigrate, discredit, disparage, disregard, foreswear, humiliate, rejection, reprobate, repudiate 10 calumniate, contravene, disapprove, disrespect, look down on, steer clear
spur-of-the-moment: 5 ad-lib 7 offhand
Spur rival: 3 Cav, Mav, Net, Sun 4 Buck, Bull, Hawk, Heat, Jazz, King 5 Knick, Laker, Magic, Pacer, Sixer, Sonic 6 Celtic, Hornet, Nugget, Piston, Raptor, Rocket, Wizard 7 Clipper, Grizzly, Warrior 8 Cavalier, Maverick 10 SuperSonic, Timberwolf
Spurs: 4 five, team
former org.: 3 ABA
home: 10 San Antonio
org.: 3 NBA
sport: 10 basketball
spurt: 3 fit, jet, run 4 boom, flow, gush, jump, ooze, rush, spew, spue, wash 5 erupt, issue, shoot, spasm, spate, spill, spout, surge 6 access, effuse, emerge, flurry, geyser, spritz, squirt, stream 7 flow out, outpour, pour out 8 effusion, eruption, fountain, outburst, overflow, shoot out 9 commotion, discharge, explosion 10 accelerate, outpouring
speed ~: 5 burst
___ Spur, The: 5 Naked
Sputnik actor: 4 Auer
sputter: 4 spit 6 fizzle, mutter, sizzle 7 stammer, stutter
Spuyten ___ Creek: 6 Duyvil
spy: 3 pry, see 4 Berg, Bond, Hale, Helm, look, mole, peek, peep, peer, Solo, spot, tail, view 5 agent, plant, recon, scout, snoop, trail, watch 6 detect, meddle, notice, patrol, peeper, Philby, regard, search,

shadow, sleuth, Smiley, take in **7** examine, eyeball, fish out, glimpse, Harriet, look for, lookout, Moe Berg, observe, ransack, sleeper, spotter, watcher **8** CIA agent, come upon, discover, emissary, informer, Mata Hari, Matt Helm, observer, smell out, stake out, take note **9** detective, eavesdrop, James Bond, lay eyes on, operative, set eyes on **10** get a load of, Nick Carter, scrutinize, sneak a look
device: **3** bug
disguise: **5** cover
ender: **5** glass **6** master
fictional ~: **4** Bond, Helm, Solo **6** Smiley **8** Matt Helm **9** James Bond
first name in ~ stories: **3** Ian
in the sky: **5** AWACS
Japanese ~: **5** ninja
kind of ~: **4** mole **5** ninja, plant
name: **4** Hari, Mata
on: **3** bug **4** case, tail **5** snoop, trail, watch **6** follow, shadow **7** observe, surveil **8** check out, stake out
org.: **3** CIA, KGB, NSA, ONI
Revolutionary War ~: **4** Hale **5** André
starter: **7** counter
upon: **5** watch
work: **5** recon
writing: **4** code **10** cryptogram
Spy __: **4** Hard, Kids
__ Spy, A: **7** Perfect
Spybey: **4** Dina
Spyder: **3** car **4** auto **6** Toyota
spyglass part: **4** lens
Spy Hard (1996 film)
cast: Charles Durning, Marcia Gay Harden, Leslie Nielsen, Nicollette Sheridan
Spy in Black, The (1939 film)
cast: Valerie Hobson, Sebastian Shaw, Conrad Veidt
spying: **9** espionage **10** undercover
Spy in the House of Love, A author: Anaïs Nin
Spy Kids (2001 film)
cast: Antonio Banderas, Carla Gugino, Daryl Sabara, Alexa Vega
director: Robert Rodriguez
Spyri, Johanna: **5** Swiss **6** author, writer
work: Heidi
Spyro __: **4** Gyra
Spy, The author: James Fenimore Cooper
Spy vs. Spy mag: **3** MAD
Spy Who Came in From the Cold, The: **4** film **5** novel
author: John le Carré
cast: Claire Bloom, Richard Burton, Oskar Werner
director: Martin Ritt
Spy Who Loved Me, The: **4** film **5** novel
author: Ian Fleming
cast: Barbara Bach, Curt Jurgens, Richard Kiel, Roger Moore
director: Lewis Gilbert
role: **4** Anya
SQL: **8** language
alternative: **3** ADA, APL **4** Alef, html, Icon, Java, LISP, Logo, Orca, Perl **5** Algol, Basic, Cecil, COBOL, Dylan, SISAL **6** Delphi, Eiffel, Erlang, Oberon, Pascal, Prolog, Sather, Scheme, Snobol **7** Fortran
squab: **4** bird **6** pigeon **7** hassock
__ squab: **3** sea
squabble: **3** ado, row **4** feud, flap, fuss, rift, spat, tiff **5** argue, brawl, clash, fight, scene, scrap, set-to, words **6** barney, bicker, dustup, fracas, hassle, niggle, racket, rumpus, strife **7** dispute, fall out, quarrel, quibble, wrangle **8** argument, disagree, skirmish **9** bickering, encounter, have words, imbroglio **10** contention, difference
squad: **4** army, band, crew, gang, team, unit **5** corps, force, group, hands, party, troop **6** detail, outfit, troupe **7** brigade, company, platoon **8** division, regiment **9** battalion **10** detachment
squad __: **3** car **4** room
__ squad: **4** bomb, goon, riot, taxi **6** flying
squad car device: **5** siren
squadron: **4** unit **5** corps, force **6** patrol **7** platoon
__ Squad, The: **3** Mod
squalid: **3** low **4** base, foul, mean, poor, ugly **5** dingy, dirty, fetid, grimy, mangy, nasty, seamy, seedy **6** filthy, foetid, horrid, impure, mangey, shabby, shoddy, sleazy, sloppy, soiled, sordid **7** decayed, ignoble, odorous, reeking, run-down, unclean, unkempt **8** gruesome, horrible, slovenly, untended, wretched **9** miserable, offensive, repellent, repulsive **10** abominable, broken-down, despicable, disgusting, disheveled, ramshackle
area: **3** sty **4** dump, slum **5** hovel **6** pigsty **8** cesspool, pesthole
squall: **4** gale, gust, wail, weep, wind, yowl **5** blast, furor, noser, storm **6** racket, tumult **7** tempest, turmoil **9** commotion, windstorm **10** hurly-burly, turbulence
starter: **4** rain
squall __: **4** line
__ Squall: **5** White
squalor: **6** misery **7** poverty **10** sordidness
Squamish: **6** Indian **7** Amerind
squamous: **5** scaly
squander: **3** eat, sap **4** blow, burn, lose **5** drain, spend, trash, use up, waste **6** burn up, expend, frivol, lavish, misuse, put out, trifle **7** cash out, consume, deplete, exhaust, play out, scatter **8** fool away, misspend **9** dissipate, go through, spring for, throw away, while away **10** frivol away, gamble away, run through
squandered: **4** gone **7** all gone
squanderer: **7** wastrel **8** prodigal
Squanto: A Warrior's Tale (1994 film)
cast: Adam Beach, Michael Gambon, Mandy Patinkin
director: Xavier Koller
square: **3** fit, fix, rig **4** area, boxy, even, fair, gybe, jibe, just, knot, nerd, nurd, park, true, unit **5** adapt, agree, align, aline, block, clear, court, dated, equal, frank, legit, level, match, moral, nerdy, pay up, plaza, power, right, shape, sharp, tally, unhip **6** accord, adjust, buy off, cohere, common, decent, even up, honest, isogon, pay off, reckon, settle, stuffy, trusty **7** balance, boxlike, clear up, comport, conform, ethical, factual, rectify, redress, satisfy, sincere, upright **8** balanced, check out, clear off, coincide, credible, equalize, multiply, orthodox, outdated, out-front, quadrate, regulate, straight, truthful, unbiased **9** do justice, equitable, four-sided, harmonize, impartial, ingenuous, liquidate, make sense, objective, out-of-date, outspoken, quadratic, reconcile, reimburse, uncolored, unfeigned, unslanted, veracious **10** aboveboard, button-down, correspond, equal-sided, evenhanded, forthright, fuddy-duddy, on-the-level, quadrangle, recompense, scrupulous
accounts: **5** repay **6** avenge
away: **5** ready **6** get set, settle **7** prepare **8** get ready
ceramic ~: **4** tile
coin: **6** klippe
column: **4** anta
footage: **4** area
from ~ one: **4** anew, over **5** again **6** afresh
game-board ~: **5** start
off: **3** war **4** feud, tilt **5** clash, fight, scrap, set-to **6** action, battle, combat, tussle **7** contend, contest, dispute **8** conflict, disagree, struggle **9** lock horns **10** engagement
off against: **4** face
one: **4** nerd, nurd **5** getgo, start **6** origin **9** beginning
setting: **4** town
starter: **4** four
town ~: **5** plaza **7** commons
up: **3** pay **5** repay **6** pay off, settle **7** pay back, satisfy **8** equalize, make good **9** reimburse
(with): **5** agree **7** conform
square __: **3** leg, off, one, rod, set **4** away, deal, foot, inch, knot, meal, mile, root, sail, wave, yard **5** dance, meter, piano, serif, shake **6** matrix, number, splice **7** bracket, dancing, measure, shooter
square __ a round hole: **5** peg in
square-__: **3** law **4** toes **6** rigged
__ square: **3** cut, try **4** word **5** bevel, Latin, magic, miter, on the, out of, steel **7** framing, perfect
__-square: **3** chi **5** three **6** pocket
__ Square: **3** Red **4** Soho **5** Times
squared __: **4** ring **5** paper **6** circle, splice
__-squared: **3** pi r
square dance: **7** hoedown
attire: **6** dirndl
call: **3** gee **6** do-si-do **7** dos-à-dos
dancer tie: **4** bolo
for 4 couples: **9** quadrille
group: **5** octad, octet **7** octette
instrument: **6** fiddle
official: **6** caller
partner: **3** gal, guy
site: **4** barn
Square Egg, The author: Saki
squarely: **4** just **5** flush, right, sharp, smack, spang **9** precisely
Square Root of Wonderful, The
author: Carson McCullers
squares
one of three ~: **4** meal
set of ~: **4** grid
__ squares: **5** least
square-shooting: **6** candid, honest
squaretail: **4** fish
__-square test: **3** chi
squaring the __: **6** circle
squash: **3** jam **4** cram, game, kill, mash, pepo, pulp, push **5** crowd, crush, lie on, pound, press, quell, quiet, sit on, smash, spoil, sport, tread **6** bruise, cushaw, humble, stifle, veggie **7** deflate, depress, distort, flatten, put down, scrunch, squeeze, squelch, stamp on, trample, wedge in **8** compress, macerate, shut down, suppress **9** humiliate, vegetable **10** annihilate, extinguish
coat: **4** rind
court feature: **4** wall
kin: **5** gourd
shot: **5** carom **6** carrom
squash __: **3** bug **6** tennis **7** racquet
__ squash: **5** acorn, lemon **6** marrow, summer, turban, winter **7** Hubbard, scallop
squashy: **4** soft **5** mushy
squat: **3** low, nil, sit, zip **4** boxy, nada, wide **5** broad, dumpy, heavy, hunch, lodge, perch, pudgy, roost, short, splay, stoop, thick, tubby, zilch **6** chunky, crouch, hunker, lie low, locate, naught, nought, remain, reside, settle, stocky, stubby **7** nothing, sojourn **8** entrench, heavyset, thickset **9** crouching **10** hunker down
__-squat: **6** diddly, doodly
squatness: **5** width
squatter: **7** pioneer **8** resident
squatter's __: **5** right
squatty: **3** low **5** short
squawbush: **5** sumac **6** sumach
squawk: **3** caw, cry, yap **4** beef, crow, hoot, yaup, yell, yelp **5** croak, gripe, groan, noise, shout, sound, whine, whoop **6** cackle, grouse, holler, plaint, repine, shriek, squeal, yammer **7** grumble, protest, screech **8** complain **9** bellyache, complaint, grievance, make a fuss, raise Cain
squawk __: **3** box
squawking: **7** raucous **8** strident
Squaw Man, The (1931 film)
cast: Warner Baxter, Eleanor Boardman, Lupe Velez
director: Cecil B. DeMille
squeak: **3** cry **4** pipe, talk, time, yelp **5** cheep, creak, sound, whine **6** shrill, squeal **7** screech
by: **6** scrape **7** nose out
fix a ~: **3** oil **6** grease **9** lubricate
past, in sports: **4** edge
squeak __: **7** through
squeaker: **3** rat **5** hinge, mouse
squeaky clean: **4** pure **6** chaste, honest **9** righteous
squeal: **3** rat, yip **4** blab, howl, rasp, talk, tell, wail, yell, yelp, yowl **5** bleat, cheep, creak, rat on, shout, spill **6** betray, holler, scream, shriek, shrill, snitch, squawk, squeak, tattle **7** protest, screech **8** complain, inform on **9** make a fuss **10** tattletale
comic-book ~: **3** eek
on: **6** turn in **7** sell out
squealer: **3** pig **4** fink, nark **6** ratter **7** tattler **8** fat mouth, turncoat **10** taleteller, tattletale
squeamish: **4** prim, sick **5** dizzy, fussy, shaky, upset **6** prissy, queasy, queazy, sickly **7** finicky, mincing, prudish **8** delicate, finiking, finnicky, qualmish **9** disgusted, spineless, unsettled **10** fastidious, particular, scrupulous
squeegee: **3** mop **5** wiper
use a ~: **4** wipe
squeezable: **4** soft
squeeze: **2** jo **3** hug, jam, nip, pet, ram **4** baby, clip, cram, dear, grip, hold, jill, love, mash, milk, pack, push, vise **5** amour, angel, bleed, chéri, choke, clasp, cooky, crowd, crush, cutey, cutie, deary, ducky, flame, force, honey, leman, lover, lovey, novia, novio, pinch, press, quash, sqush, stuff, sugar, sweet, wedge, wring **6** bon ami, chérie, clinch, clutch, cookie, crunch, cuddle, dautie, dearie, eke out, enfold, extort, infold, insert, jostle, justle, lean on, pucker, racket, spoils, squash, squish, squush, steady, strait, sweets, thrust, wrench **7** beloved, dearest, dear one, embrace, extract, oppress, pigsney, problem, schatzi, scrunch, squoosh, sweetie, tighten, tootsie, wedge in **8** chou-chou, compress, contract, cutie pie, dowsabel, dulcinea, ladylove, lovebird, macushla, paramour, precious, pressure, snookums, sugar pie, sweetums, throttle, truelove **9** bonne amie, boyfriend, constrict, dreamboat, extortion, handclasp, hold tight,

inamorata, inamorato, influence, overcrowd, petit chou, restraint, shake down, valentine **10** congestion, girlfriend, heartthrob, honeybunch, mavourneen, pressurize, sweetheart, sweetie pie, turtledove
by: **3** eke **4** edge
dry: **5** wring
ender: **3** box
in: **3** jam **4** tuck **7** bunch up **9** interject, overcrowd
out liquid: **6** squirt
put the ~ on: **5** force **6** coerce **7** oppress **8** pressure
together: **7** bunch up
squeeze ___: **3** off **4** play **5** joint **6** bottle **7** through
___ squeeze: **5** tight **6** credit, profit, safety
squeezebox: **8** keyboard **9** accordion
Squeeze Box (1976 song) artist: Who
squeezed: **6** juiced **7** crammed, crowded **9** compacted, condensed, jam-packed **10** compressed
___ squeeze play: **7** suicide
squeezer: **3** boa **6** python
squeezings: **5** juice
squelch: **3** gag, nix **4** halt, kill, stop **5** crush, quash, quiet, shush, sit on **6** censor, hush up, muffle, quench, refute, settle, squash, stifle, subdue, thwart **7** abolish, censure, oppress, repress, silence, smother **8** black out, restrain, stamp out, strangle, suppress **9** keep quiet **10** extinguish, keep in line
squib: **7** lampoon, lighter **9** promotion
news ~: **4** item
squid: **7** calamar, mollusc, mollusk **8** calamari
cousin: **7** octopus
weapon: **3** ink
___ squid: **5** giant
Squier: **5** Billy
squiffed: **5** tipsy **6** blotto
squiggle: **4** curl, mark **6** scrawl, squirm
in a series: **5** comma
señor's ~: **5** tilde
squiggly: **4** wavy
squinch: **4** wink
squint: **4** leer, look, peek, peep, peer, skew, view, wink **6** glance **7** glimpse **8** lopsided
squint-___: **4** eyed
squire: **4** beau, date, gent, lead, rank **5** owner, serve **6** assist, attend, escort **7** step out **8** chaperon, courtier, landlord **9** accompany, chaperone, companion, landowner
Squire: **3** car **4** auto, Ford **10** automobile
squires: **6** gentry
squirm: **4** skew, toss, wind, worm **5** shift, twist **6** fidget, thrash, twitch, wiggle, writhe **7** agonize, wriggle **8** flounder, squiggle
squirrel: **5** xerus **6** animal, mammal, rodent, suslik **7** souslik **9** chickaree
abode: **4** tree
African ~: **5** xerus
away: **4** hide, save **5** amass, cache, hoard, put by, stash, store **6** pile up **7** deposit, harvest, reserve **8** conserve, put aside, set apart, set aside
ender: **4** fish
female: **3** doe
food: **3** nut **5** acorn
fur: **4** vair
ground ~: **6** gopher
male: **4** buck
relative: **3** rat **4** cavy, degu, jird, paca, vole **5** coypu, gundi, mouse, xerus **6** agouti, beaver, gerbil, gopher, jerboa, marmot, murine **7** hamster, lemming, muskrat, visacha **8** chipmunk, cricetid, dormouse, tuco-tuco **9** groundhog, guinea pig, porcupine, woodchuck **10** chinchilla, prairie dog
young: **3** pup **6** kitten
squirrel ___: **4** cage, corn **6** monkey
___ squirrel: **3** cat, fox, red **4** gray, grey, rock, tree **5** black **6** flying, ground, kaibab **7** striped
squirrely: **4** daft
squirt: **3** boy, jet **4** emit, flow, spew, spit, spue **5** child, eject, kiddy, spill, spirt, spout, spray, spurt, twerp, twirp **6** nobody, splash, spritz, stream **7** moisten, spatter **8** sprinkle, water jet **9** nonentity
gun: **3** toy
squirt ___: **3** can, gun
___ squirt: **3** sea
squish: **3** jam **4** mash **5** crowd, crush, press, quash, smash **7** squeeze, wedge in
squishy: **3** wet **4** oozy, soft **5** downy, furry, mushy, nappy, plush **6** fleecy, fluffy, spongy **7** velvety **8** cushiony, yielding
toy: **4** Nerf
Sr: **4** elem. **7** element **9** strontium
38 for ~: **4** at. no.
Sri Lanka: **3** isl. **4** isle **6** Ceylon, island, nation **7** country
capital: **7** Colombo
deer: **4** axis **6** chital, sambar, sambur **7** sambhar, sambhur
export: **3** tea **5** pekoe
fish: **5** danio
language: **5** Tamil **10** Singhalese
money: **4** cent **5** rupee
neighbor: **5** India
people: **5** Tamil, Vedda **6** Veddah
port: **5** Galle **7** Colombo
primate: **4** lori **5** lemur, loris
temple city: **5** Kandy
wood: **5** ebony
SRO: **7** crowded **9** chock-full
show: **3** hit **5** smash
SS: **3** pos.
he plays behind the ~: **2** LF
see also shortstop
S.S.: **7** McClure, Van Dine
SSA part: **3** Sec., Soc. **5** Admin. **6** Social **8** Security
SSE: **3** dir., hdg.
opposite: **3** NNW
SSgt.: **3** NCO **7** officer
employer: **4** USAF
s-shaped: **5** curvy, snaky **6** curved, curvey
curve: **4** ogee
SSN: **2** ID
part: **3** Soc. **6** Number, Social **8** Security
SSR
former ~: **6** Latvia **7** Estonia, Ukraine **9** Lithuania
part of ~: **6** Soviet **8** Republic **9** Socialist
SSS
classification: **4** one A
concern: **5** draft
part: **3** Sys. **4** Syst. **6** System **7** Service **9** Selective
SSSSSSS (1973 film)
cast: Dirk Benedict, Strother Martin, Heather Menzies
SST: **3** jet **7** Tupolev **8** aircraft, Concorde
crossing: **3** Atl. **8** Atlantic
go by ~: **3** fly **6** aviate
part of ~: **5** sonic, super **9** transport
term: **4** Mach
S.S. Van ___: **4** Dine
SSW: **3** dir., hdg.
opposite: **3** NNE
st.
see street
St.
see Saint
St. ___: **4** Ives, Paul **5** Croix
St. ___ and Miquelon: **6** Pierre
St. ___ Blues: **5** Louis
St. ___-bread: **5** John's
St. ___ cherry: **5** Lucie
St. ___ College: **4** Olaf
St. ___ cross: **7** Andrew's
St. ___ Day: **5** John's
St. ___ Eve: **5** John's
St. ___ fire: **5** Elmo's
St. ___ Island: **6** Simons
St. ___-l'École: **3** Cyr
St. ___ Mountains: **5** Elias
St. ___-Nevis: **5** Kitts
St. ___ Night: **5** John's
St. ___ Palace: **6** James's
St. ___ Square: **6** Peter's
St.-___: **4** Malo
St.-___ Perse: **4** John
sta.
see station
Sta-___: **3** Flo, Puf
stab: **3** cut, jab, ram, try **4** ache, blow, chop, clip, gash, gore, hurt, pang, plow, poke, shot, sink **5** brand, carve, crack, drive, fling, guess, knife, lance, lunge, prick, saber, shank, slice, spear, stick, whack, whirl, wound **6** chance, cleave, effort, empale, gamble, impale, injure, open up, pierce, plunge, skewer, thrust, twinge **7** attempt, bayonet, venture **8** endeavor, incision, lacerate, piercing, puncture **9** penetrate, perforate, wild guess **10** laceration
in the back: **4** sell **5** cross **6** betray **7** sell out **9** duplicity, treachery
starter: **4** back
take a ~ at: **3** try **5** essay, guess **7** attempt, venture **8** theorize **10** conjecture
Stabat ___: **5** Mater
stabber: **5** prong
___ Stabbers: **4** Back
stabbing: **5** sharp **8** piercing
stabile: **5** fixed **6** steady **10** unchanging
coiner: **3** Arp
Stabile: **2** Ed
stability: **5** poise **6** aplomb, fixity, sanity, wisdom **7** balance, support **8** backbone, cohesion, firmness, maturity, security, solidity, strength **9** adherence, assurance, composure, constancy, endurance, equipoise, fixedness, integrity, solidness, soundness, toughness **10** continuity, durability, permanence, perpetuity, sedateness, steadiness
period of ~: **3** pax
stabilization ___: **4** fund **5** print **7** process
stabilize: **3** fix, set **4** bolt, even, firm, prop, trim **5** brace, poise **6** anchor, fasten, firm up, fixate, freeze, ossify, secure, settle, steady, uphold **7** balance, stiffen, support, sustain **8** buttress, equalize, maintain, preserve **9** establish
___-stabilized: **4** rent
stabilizer: **4** gyro
combining form: **4** -stat
food ~: **4** agar **8** agar-agar
nautical ~: **7** ballast
plane ~: **3** fin
sailboat ~: **4** keel
surfboard ~: **4** skeg
stabilizer ___: **3** bar
stable: **3** set **4** calm, even, fast, firm, good, sure **5** fixed, level, quiet, solid, sound, stout, tight **6** manger, nailed, poised, rooted, secure, smooth, static, steady, strong, sturdy **7** abiding, durable, equable, lasting, settled, staunch, uniform **8** anchored, balanced, constant, definite, enduring, ironclad, long-term, rational, reliable, resolute, stalwart, together **9** immutable, permanent, resistant, steadfast, temperate, unvarying, well-built **10** deep-rooted, dependable, invariable, motionless, stationary, staying put, unchanging, unwavering
area: **4** mews
baby: **4** colt, foal **5** filly
bed: **5** straw
hand: **5** groom, shoer
noise: **4** clop **5** neigh, snort
parent: **3** dam **4** mare, sire
sustenance: **4** feed, oats
unit: **5** stall
worker of India: **4** sice, syce **5** saice
see also horse
___ stable: **6** livery
stableboy: **5** groom **6** lackey **7** lacquey
play about a ~: **5** Equus
Stabler, Ken: **2** QB **5** Snake
___ stables: **6** Augean
staccato: **8** detached
mark: **3** dot
not ~: **6** legato
Stacey: **4** Dash
stack: **3** lot **4** bank, heap, hill, keep, load, mass, pack, pile **5** amass, bunch, drift, hoard, mound, sheaf **6** bank up, bundle, heap up, pileup **7** chimney, pyramid **8** hold on to, mountain **9** great deal, multitude, profusion, stockpile **10** accumulate, collection, cumulation
blow one's ~: **4** rant **6** seethe **7** flare up, flip out
material: **3** hay
starter: **3** hay **5** smoke
the deck: **5** cheat **9** victimize
up: **4** rise, test **5** total **6** gather **7** compare **10** accumulate
up against: **5** equal, weigh
stacked ___: **4** deck, heel
Stack, Robert: **5** actor
film: Airplane! (1980)
Bullfighter and the Lady (1951)
The Caretakers (1963)
First Love (1939)
Good Morning, Miss Dove (1955)
The High and the Mighty (1954)
Joe Versus the Volcano (1990)
The Last Voyage (1960)
The Tarnished Angels (1958)
To Be or Not to Be (1942)
Written on the Wind (1956)
role: **4** Ness
TV: The Name of the Game, The Untouchables
stacks: **3** lot **4** lots **5** reams **6** myriad, plenty
frequent the ~: **4** read
stack-up: **8** accident
Stacy: **5** Keach **6** Hollis **8** Lattisaw
Stacy, Hollis: **6** golfer
milieu: **5** links **6** course
org.: **4** LPGA
stad: **5** craal, kraal
Stade, Frederica von: **5** mezzo **6** singer **7** soprano
specialty: **5** opera
stadium: **4** bowl, park, ring **5** arena, field, venue **7** diamond **8** coliseum, gridiron **9** colosseum, gymnasium
cry: **3** rah, yay **6** charge
display: **4** wave
employee: **5** usher
feature: **4** dome, gate, loge, ramp, tier **5** level
football ~: **4** bowl
gofer: **6** bat boy
habitué: **3** fan
hoverer: **5** blimp
instrument: **5** organ
sound: **3** boo, rah **4** hiss, roar **5** chant, cheer **6** hoorah, hooray, hurrah, hurray

stadium __: 4 coat 6 jacket
Stadler, Craig: 6 golfer, Walrus
stadt: 7 München 8 Nürnberg
Staël, Madame de: 6 author, French, writer
work: Corinne
Delphine
staff: 3 man, rod 4 cane, cast, club, crew, help, hire, mace, pole, prop, team, wand 5 aides, baton, cadre, court, crook, force, hands, stave, stick 6 agents, fasces 7 crosier, crozier, employe, faculty, scepter, support, workers 8 caduceus, deputies, employee, flagpole, legation, officers, servants, teachers 9 employees, entourage, personnel, retainers, truncheon, work force 10 alpenstock, assistants, operatives, shillelagh
ceremonial ~: 4 mace
cut: 3 RIF 6 layoff
figure: 4 clef, note 5 C clef, F clef, G clef
notation: 4 flat 5 sharp
officer: 4 aide 8 adjutant
of life: 5 bread 7 aliment
opening: 3 job 4 slot
shepherd ~: 5 crook
starter: 3 tip 4 flag, pike, wait 7 quarter
staff __: 7 captain, officer, section
__ staff: 4 back, bass, jack, poop 6 ensign, Jacob's, treble 7 balance, general, special
staffer: 4 aide 8 employee
nonpermanent ~: 4 temp
staff of __: 4 life
Stafford: 2 Jo 3 Jim 4 Jean, Repp 5 Terry 7 William
Stafford, Jean: 6 author, writer
work: The Catherine Wheel
A Winter's Tale
Stafford, Jim: 6 singer
song: Spiders & Snakes (1973)
Wildwood Weed (1974)
Staffordshire: 6 county
city: 7 Cannock
locale: 7 England
Stafford, William: 4 poet
Staffs: 6 county
locale: 7 England
stag: 3 roe 4 buck, deer, hart, lone 5 alone, party 6 animal 8 dateless, solitary 10 unescorted
attendee: 2 he 3 man 4 male
ender: 5 hound
feature: 6 antler
mate: 3 doe 4 hind
stag __: 4 line 6 beetle
Stag at __, The: 3 Eve
stage: 3 lap, leg, set 4 give, node, pass, play, rung, show, step, stop, time 5 arena, coach, drama, enact, frame, grade, level, mount, notch, phase, point, put on, round, scene, stand, venue 6 boards, degree, length, locale, moment, period, podium, status 7 arrange, execute, footing, landing, perform, plateau, present, process, produce, rostrum, scenery, setting, show biz, theater, theatre 8 bring out, Broadway, division, engineer, juncture, landmark, locality, organize, platform 9 gradation, limelight, situation, spotlight 10 footlights
alone on ~: 4 sola 5 solus
area: 3 pit 5 apron, riser, wings
award: 4 Obie, Tony
beginning: 4 Act I
center ~: 9 spotlight
curtain: 5 arras, scrim
direction: 4 exit 5 enter 6 exeunt
door symbol: 4 star
ender: 4 hand 5 coach, craft
extra: 4 supe
fill time on ~: 4 vamp
gear: 3 mic, set 4 mike, prop 5 decor
get ~ fright: 6 freeze
get off the ~: 4 exit
go on ~: 3 act 5 enter 7 perform
name: 5 alias
org.: 4 ANTA
represent on ~: 5 enact
seats near the ~: 4 row A, row B, row C
set the ~: 5 dress
setting: 5 scene
show: 4 play 5 drama, revue 6 review 10 production
signal: 3 cue
starter: 3 off 4 back, down 5 sound
success: 3 hit 5 smash
whisper: 5 aside 6 murmur
stage __: 3 set 4 door, left, wait 5 brace, right, screw 6 effect, fright, pocket 7 manager, setting, whisper
stage-__: 6 driver, manage
stage-__ Johnny: 4 door
__ stage: 4 left 5 right, sound, space 6 thrust 7 landing, perfect
Stagecoach (1939 film): 5 oater
cast: John Carradine, Andy Devine, Thomas Mitchell, Claire Trevor, John Wayne
director: John Ford
stagecoach puller: 4 team 5 horse
stagecraft: 6 acting
staged: 9 unnatural
Stage Door: 4 film, play
author: 6 Ferber 7 Kaufman
cast: Katharine Hepburn, Adolphe Menjou, Ginger Rogers
director: Gregory La Cava
stagehand: 4 crew, grip 6 flyman
concern: 3 set 4 prop
stage light: 4 spot 5 klieg
covering: 3 gel
__ stager: 3 old
stages, in: 9 gradually 10 step by step
Stage to Mesa City: 5 oater
Stagg: 4 Amos
stagger: 3 wow 4 jolt, reel, rock, stun, sway 5 amaze, floor, lurch, pitch, shake, shock, stump, waver 6 boggle, careen, dither, falter, linger, puzzle, teeter, topple, totter, wabble, wobble, zigzag 7 astound, founder, nonplus, overlap, perplex, shatter, stammer, startle, stumble, stupefy 8 astonish, bewilder, bowl over, confound, hesitate, surprise, unstring 9 alternate, devastate, dumbfound, overpower, overwhelm, take aback, vacillate
staggering: 3 big 4 vast 5 dizzy 6 untold 8 striking 9 marvelous, wonderful 10 formidable
Stagger Lee (1959 song) artist: Lloyd Price
staghorn __: 4 fern 5 coral, sumac
staging: 5 stand 10 production
staging __: 4 area, post
stagnant: 4 dull, foul, idle 5 dirty, inert, quiet, slack, stale, still 6 filthy, halted, in a rut, static, stuffy 7 odorous, passive 8 brackish, immobile, inactive, lifeless, listless, moribund, sluggish, unmoving 10 motionless, stationary
stagnate: 3 rot 4 drag, idle, rust 5 decay, stall 6 fester, stifle 7 decline, go stale 8 go to seed, languish, vegetate 9 hibernate, lie fallow 10 stand still
stagnation: 5 sloth, slump 6 acedia, torpor 7 inertia, languor 8 doldrums, idleness, laziness, otiosity 9 faineance, indolence, recession, torpidity 10 depression
sign of ~: 5 algae
__ St. Agnes, The: 5 Eve of
stagy: 5 hammy 8 affected, overdone 9 overacted, unnatural 10 histrionic, theatrical
Stahl: 4 John, Nick 6 Lesley
Stahl, John M.: 8 director
film: Back Street (1932)
The Eve of St. Mark (1944)
Holy Matrimony (1943)
The Keys of the Kingdom (1944)
Leave Her to Heaven (1945)
Magnificent Obsession (1935)
Only Yesterday (1933)
staid: 3 set 4 calm, cool 5 fixed, grave, sober, stoic 6 at ease, demure, formal, low-key, mellow, placid, sedate, serene, solemn, somber, steady, stodgy, stuffy 7 at peace, deadpan, earnest, relaxed, serious, settled, stoical, weighty 8 carefree, composed, decorous, laid-back, priggish, reserved, tranquil 9 collected, dignified, humorless, impassive, temperate, unamusing, unexcited, unruffled 10 nonchalant, no-nonsense, unagitated, unhumorous, untroubled
stain: 3 dye, mar, tar 4 blot, blur, daub, foul, mark, slur, soil, spot, tint, woad 5 brand, color, dirty, odium, paint, shade, shame, smear, speck, sully, taint, tinct, tinge 6 bedaub, befoul, blotch, crud up, damage, debase, defect, defile, embrue, finish, imbrue, malign, mottle, smirch, smudge, stigma 7 begrime, besmear, blacken, blemish, corrupt, debauch, deprave, pigment, pollute, spatter, splotch, tarnish, varnish 8 besmirch, black eye, coloring, discolor, disgrace, dishonor, impurity, infusion, maculate, reproach, tincture 10 demoralize, imputation, stigmatize
common ~: 3 ink 4 food 5 grass
driveway ~: 3 oil
escutcheon ~: 4 blot
lab ~: 5 eosin 6 eosine
starter: 4 tear 5 blood 7 counter
stained: 5 dirty, grimy, sooty 6 filthy, grubby, grungy 7 unclean 8 maculate, slovenly, vitiated 10 unsanitary
stained __: 5 glass
__-stained: 4 tear
Staines: 4 city, town
locale: 6 Surrey 7 England
stainless: 4 pure 5 clean 6 chaste, washed 8 innocent, pristine, rustless, spotless, unsoiled 9 blameless, faultless, undefiled, unspoiled, unsullied 10 immaculate, impeccable, unpolluted
stainless steel: 5 alloy
component: 4 iron 8 chromium
stair: 4 step
alternative: 4 ramp 8 elevator 9 escalator
ender: 3 way 4 case, well
part: 4 rail, step 5 riser
post: 5 newel
starter: 4 back
__ staircase: 6 moving, spiral
stairs
like some ~: 6 creaky
starter: 4 back, down
take the ~: 4 walk 5 climb
__ Stairsteps: 4 Five
__ Stair, The: 7 Winding
stairway: 6 flight
entrance ~: 5 stoop
moving ~: 9 escalator
section: 7 landing
__ stairway: 6 moving
Stairway to Heaven (1946 film)
cast: Kim Hunter, Raymond Massey, David Niven
director: Michael Powell, Emeric Pressburger
Stairway to Heaven (song) artist: Led Zeppelin, Neil Sedaka
Stairway to the __: 5 Stars
stake: 3 bet, pot, rod, set 4 ante, back, fund, game, lend, loan, pale, play, pole, post, risk 5 award, claim, kitty, means, peril, prize, purse, put on, put up, share, spike, stave, stick, wager 6 chance, gamble, hazard, invest, paling, picket, pledge, supply, timber 7 concern, finance, funding, imperil, present, provide, savings, sponsor, support, venture 8 bankroll, interest, make book 9 subsidize 10 capitalize, investment, jeopardize, underwrite
at ~: 6 risked 7 gambled, in peril 8 invested, involved 9 concerned, on the line 10 endangered, in jeopardy
ender: 3 out 6 holder
like a ~: 5 palar
out: 3 spy 4 mark 5 claim, spy on, watch 6 survey 7 surveil
put on a ~: 6 empale, impale
something to ~: 5 claim
starter: 4 grub
stake __: 3 out 4 boat, body, race 5 horse, truck
__ stake: 5 grape, table
stakeout: 5 vigil, watch
Stakeout (1987 film)
cast: Richard Dreyfuss, Emilio Estevez, Aidan Quinn, Madeleine Stowe
director: John Badham
stakes: 4 pool 7 jackpot
pull up ~: 6 decamp
starter: 5 sweep
stakes __: 4 race
__ Stakes: 4 High 7 Belmont
staking starter: 4 pain
stalactite
form a ~: 4 drip
shape: 6 icicle
site: 4 cave 6 cavern
stalag
resident: 3 POW
Stalag 17 (1953 film)
cast: William Holden, Otto Preminger, Don Taylor
director: Billy Wilder
role: 3 POW 6 Animal
stalagmite
form a ~: 4 drip
site: 4 cave 6 cavern
St. Albert: 4 city, town
locale: 6 Canada 7 Alberta
stale: 3 dry, old 4 arid, drab, dull, flat, hard, rank, weak, worn 5 banal, corny, dated, dried, faded, fetid, fuggy, fusty, hokey, musty, passé, rusty, tired, trite, vapid 6 cliché, common, foetid, frowsy, frowzy, jejune, old hat, rancid, smelly, spoilt, stuffy, watery 7 clichéd, decayed, fatuous, fogyish, humdrum, insipid, parched, prosaic, reeking, shrivel, spoiled, worn-out 8 bromidic, dried out, obsolete, outdated, outmoded, overused, shopworn, stagnant, stinking, timeworn, well-used, well-worn, zestless 9 hackneyed, out-of-date, played out, prosaical, tasteless 10 antiquated, dullsville, malodorous, threadbare, uninspired, unoriginal, yesterday's
ender: 4 mate
go ~: 3 rot 4 mold, rust, tire 5 decay 7 crumble 8 stagnate
stalemate: 3 tie 4 draw, game 5 delay, pause 6 arrest 7 impasse 8 deadlock, gridlock, standoff, tarrying 10 standstill
Stalin: 3 Red 6 Joseph 7 Russian
predecessor: 5 Lenin
realm: 4 USSR
Stalingrad: 4 city, town
locale: 6 Russia

stalk: **3** dog **4** axis, halm, hunt, pace, reed, stem, tail, walk **5** chase, haulm, haunt, hound, march, prowl, shaft, spike, spire, stick, straw, trace, track, trail, trunk **6** ambush, follow, pester, pursue, shadow, stride **7** bird-dog, pedicel, pedicle, support **8** approach, flush out **9** creep up on, track down
combining form: **4** caul- **5** cauli-, caulo-
crunchy ~: **6** celery
food: **4** corn
grass ~: **4** reed
of bananas: **4** hand, stem
plant ~: **5** scape, stipe
remove a ~: **6** destem
starter: **3** eye **4** bean, corn, foot, leaf, root
___ stalk: **4** corn, yolk **6** celery
stalker: **6** hunter
starter: **4** deer
Stalker author: Faye Kellerman
stalking-___: **5** horse
___ Stalkings: **4** Silk
stalks: **6** fodder
left after reaping: **4** halm **5** haulm
stalky: **4** slim **7** slender
stall: **3** die, lag **4** crib, halt, idle, laze, loaf, mart, slow, stay, stop, wait **5** amble, block, booth, brake, check, dally, delay, hedge, kiosk, mosey, stand, still, stimy, stymy, tarry **6** arrest, becalm, dawdle, hamper, hinder, linger, loiter, market, put off, retard, stymie **7** buy time, cubicle, hold off, prolong, quibble, saunter, suspend **8** footdrag, kill time, lollygag, obstruct, postpone, pretense, shut down, slow down, stagnate, stand off, straggle **9** accessory, hem and haw, interrupt, stonewall, waste time **10** accomplice, dillydally, equivocate, filibuster, stand still
starter: **4** book, foot, head, whip
___ stall: **3** box **6** shower
stalled: **3** out **6** static **10** gridlocked, motionless
stalling, stop: **3** act **6** decide
stallion: **4** male, sire **5** horse, mount **6** equine
future ~: **4** colt
mate: **4** mare
sound: **5** snort
stopper: **4** whoa
___ Stallion, The: **5** Black
Stallion, The author: Harold Robbins
Stallone: **5** Frank **9** Sylvester
Stallone, Sylvester: **5** actor
film: Assassins (1995)
Cliffhanger (1993)
Cop Land (1997)
Demolition Man (1993)
First Blood (1982)
F.I.S.T. (1978)
Get Carter (2000)
The Lords of Flatbush (1974)
Nighthawks (1981)
Rambo: First Blood Part II (1985)
Rambo III (1988)
Rocky (1976)
Rocky II (1979)
The Specialist (1994)
film (voice): Antz (1998)
nickname: **3** Sly
spouse: Brigitte Nielsen
Stallworth, John sport: **8** football
stalwart: **3** big, fit **4** bold, game, hale, iron, wiry **5** beefy, bound, brave, burly, gutsy, hardy, hefty, hunky, husky, lusty, nervy, solid, stout, tough **6** awless, brawny, daring, gritty, hearty, heroic, mighty, plucky, potent, robust, rugged, sinewy, spunky, stable, steely, stocky, strong, sturdy, virile **7** aweless, dead set, defiant, doughty, gallant, staunch, valiant **8** athletic, fearless, forceful, heroical, indurate, intrepid, muscular, powerful, puissant, resolute, unafraid, valorous, vigorous **9** Atlantean, audacious, dauntless, dreadless, Herculean, strapping, tenacious, undaunted, unfearful, unfearing, well-built **10** able-bodied, courageous, dependable, powerhouse, purposeful, red-blooded, undismayed
stalwartness: **4** grit, guts **5** valor **7** bravery
stamen: **5** organ
part: **6** anther
site: **6** flower
Stamford: **4** city, town
locale: **4** Conn.
stamin: **6** fabric **8** material
stamina: **3** vim, zip **4** dint, grit, guts, legs, thew **5** brawn, force, heart, might, moxie, power, thews, vigor **6** energy, mettle, muscle, starch **7** fitness, muscles, potence, potency, prowess **8** backbone, strength, vitality **9** beefiness, endurance, fortitude, gutsiness, hardiness, huskiness, lustiness, puissance, stoutness, tolerance, toughness **10** brawniness, brute force, continuity, durability, mightiness, resilience, robustness, ruggedness, sturdiness
stammer: **2** er, uh, um **4** halt, stop **5** lurch **6** falter, jabber, mumble, repeat, wabble, wobble **7** sputter, stagger, stumble, stutter **8** hesitate **9** hem and haw
stammering: **10** hesitation, incoherent
Stamos, John: **5** actor
spouse: Rebecca Romijn
stamp: **3** cut, fix, ilk, lot **4** beat, cast, etch, form, mark, mint, mold, seal, sort, type **5** brand, clomp, crush, drive, label, pound, print, punch, shape, tramp **6** emblem, enseal, hammer, incuse, makeup, offset, step on, symbol **7** approve, earmark, engrave, fashion, impress, imprint, sticker, trample **8** hallmark **9** signature **10** impression
agcy.: **4** USPS
album sticker: **5** hinge
apparatus: **5** inker
backing: **3** gum **4** glue
bank ~: **3** NSF
coin ~: **3** die
dampen a ~: **4** lick
down: **5** tromp
give a ~ of approval: **2** OK **4** okay, pass **5** bless **6** ratify **7** approve, certify, confirm, consent, endorse, license **8** sanction, validate **9** authorize, sign off on
holder: **5** album
library ~: **5** dater
of approval: **2** OK **4** okay **8** blessing, sanction
office: **3** rcd. **4** recd. **8** received
office ~: **4** paid, recd
on: **5** tread **6** squash
ornamental ~: **4** seal
out: **3** end, rid **5** crush, erase, quash, quell **6** ravage, scotch **7** abolish, destroy, put down, repress, smother, squelch **8** get rid of, suppress **9** close down, eliminate, eradicate **10** extinguish, obliterate, put an end to
passport ~: **4** visa
place in a ~ album: **5** mount
P.O. ~: **8** postmark
purchase: **4** coil, pane **5** sheet **7** booklet
rubber ~: **6** ratify
stamp ___: **3** pad, tax **4** mill **5** album
___ stamp: **3** tax **4** date, food, time **5** green, local **6** rubber **7** postage, revenue, trading
___-stamp: **5** blind
Stamp ___: **3** Act
stampede: **3** run **4** dash, rout, tear **5** chase, crash, hurry, panic, smash **6** charge, flight, onrush **7** mad rush **10** scattering
group: **4** herd
___ Stampede: **7** Calgary
stamping: **10** impression
ground: **4** turf
machine: **3** die
need: **3** pad
Stamp, Terence: **5** actor
film: The Collector (1965)
Far From the Madding Crowd (1967)
The Limey (1999)
The Mind of Mr. Soames (1970)
Stan: **3** Lee **4** Getz, Shaw **5** Drake, Smith **6** Kenton, Lathan, Laurel, Mikita, Musial **7** Barstow, Dragoti, Freberg **9** Coveleski **10** Berenstain
and Ollie foul-up: **4** mess
cohort: **5** Ollie
stance: **4** pose, side **5** slant, stand **7** bearing, conduct, posture **8** attitude, carriage, position **9** viewpoint **10** deportment, standpoint
belligerent ~: **6** akimbo
political ~: **8** platform
starter: **6** happen
___ stance: **4** open **6** closed
stanch: **4** stem, stop **6** arrest
stanchion: **4** beam, pile, prop, stay **5** brace **6** picket, pillar **7** support **8** buttress
stand: **2** go **3** put, set **4** base, bear, cope, hold, lump, pose, prop, rack, rank, rest, rise, shop, side, stay, take, view **5** abide, allow, angle, arise, booth, brook, easel, erect, frame, get up, grove, kiosk, mount, pause, place, reach, slant, stage, stall, state, stick, table, treat **6** accept, belief, endure, handle, hang on, jump up, linger, locate, notion, obtain, occupy, remain, settle, stance, submit, suffer, take up **7** bracket, counter, dispose, lectern, opinion, prevail, staging, station, stomach, support, sustain, undergo, weather **8** attitude, bear with, carriage, continue, live with, platform, position, tolerate **9** encounter, put up with, viewpoint **10** contention, engagement, experience, resistance
apart: **6** differ
around: **4** idle, loaf
art ~: **5** easel
aside: **4** quit **6** resign **8** withdraw
before: **4** face
behind: **4** avow, back **7** endorse, espouse, indorse, support, warrant **8** attest to, champion
by: **3** aid **4** help, wait **5** await, tarry **6** attest, cleave, hold on, uphold **7** support, sustain **8** attest to, lose time, maintain **9** recommend **10** rally round
(by): **4** hang
can't ~: **4** hate **5** abhor **6** detest, loathe **7** dislike
down: **4** quit **5** leave **8** withdraw **9** step aside **10** relinquish
ender: **3** off, out **4** down, pipe **5** point, still **6** offish, patter
firm: **6** insist **7** persist **9** persevere
flip-chart ~: **5** easel
for: **3** let **4** back, cope, hold, mean, okay, rest, stay, take, wear **5** abide, admit, adopt, allow, brook, favor, imply **6** accept, assent, comply, denote, embody, endure, handle, hang on, imbody, permit, submit, suffer, take up, typify **7** betoken, condone, include, signify, stomach, suggest, support, sustain, swallow, undergo, weather, welcome **8** advocate, champion, hold dear, indicate, live with, overlook, sanction, tolerate **9** approve of, epitomize, exemplify, personify, put up with, recognize, represent, sign off on, symbolize, withstand **10** concur with, experience, give the nod, illustrate
in: **3** sub **8** pinch-hit **10** substitute
in for: **5** cover, spell **7** relieve
in line: **4** wait **5** await
in the way: **3** bar **4** clog **6** hinder, impede **9** foreclose
let it ~: **4** stet
make a ~: **4** dare, defy **5** claim, fight, query, rally **6** accost, object, take on, threat **7** contest, dispute, protest, vie with **8** confront, denounce, face down, question **9** challenge, discredit, stimulate, vindicate **10** contradict, controvert, insist upon
open-mouthed: **4** gape, gawk, ogle **5** stare **6** goggle
out: **3** jut **4** bulk, loom, poke **5** bulge, excel, shine **6** beetle, emerge **7** project **8** overhang, protrude **9** prominent
over: **8** bestride
pat: **4** stay
place to ~: **8** foothold
starter: **3** cab, ink **4** band, book, hand, hard, head, kick, news, wash, with **5** grand, night
still: **5** stall **6** freeze **8** stagnate
take a ~: **3** opt **4** vote **5** judge **6** choose, decide, oppose **9** determine
the gaff: **4** cope, last **5** brook **6** endure, hang on, keep on, stay on **7** carry on, hold out, outlast, survive, weather **9** put up with **10** get through, stick it out
the test of time: **4** last **6** endure **7** survive
three-legged ~: **5** easel
together: **5** unite **6** club up
two-legged ~: **5** bipod
up: **4** jilt, rise, wear **5** arise **6** verify **7** survive **9** volunteer
up for: **6** defend **7** endorse, espouse, indorse, support, testify **9** guarantee **10** rally round
up to: **4** defy, face, meet **5** brave **6** oppose, resist **7** sustain **8** confront **9** challenge, withstand
vehicle: **3** cab **4** taxi **7** taxicab
way to ~: **3** pat **4** tall **5** in awe, on end **6** akimbo
stand ___: **3** for, off, oil, out, pat **4** down, over, tall, up to **5** guard, up for
stand ___ by: **4** idly
stand ___ of: **5** in awe
stand-___: **5** alone
___ stand: **4** home, taxi, test **5** altar, music, take a **6** missal, muffin **7** witness
Stand ___: **4** Back, by Me, Tall
Stand! (1969 song) artist: Sly and the Family Stone
Stand (1989 song) artist: R.E.M.
stand a ___: **6** chance
stand-alone: **4** unit
Stand and Deliver (1987 film)
cast: Rosanna DeSoto, Edward James Olmos, Lou Diamond Phillips
director: Ramon Menendez

standard: **3** law, par, set **4** code, flag, mean, norm, rule, test **5** axiom, basic, canon, ethic, gauge, grade, ideal, level, model, stock, typic, usual, value **6** banner, belief, common, emblem, ensign, ethics, figure, ideals, median, medium, morals, normal, rating, sample, staple, symbol, wonted **7** average, classic, correct, example, measure, paragon, pattern, pennant, popular, regular, routine, typical, vanilla **8** accepted, approved, everyday, exemplar, habitual, mediocre, official, ordinary, orthodox, paradigm, streamer **9** archetype, banderole, barometer, benchmark, canonical, criterion, customary, guideline, principle, prototype, yardstick **10** acceptable, definitive, prevailing, recognized, regulation, stereotype, touchstone, uneventful
below ~: **4** poor
deviation symbol: **5** sigma
ender: **4** bred
not ~: **7** variant
standard __: **4** cell, coin, cost, time **5** error, gauge, money, score **6** dollar, lining
standard-__: **4** bred **6** bearer
__ standard: **4** gold **6** double, living, silver, single
Standard __ Number: **4** Book
Standard and __: **5** Poor's
standardization: **8** sameness
standardize: **4** type **5** order **6** reform **9** normalize
standardized: **7** regular
standard of __: **6** living
Standard Oil
of California: **7** Chevron
of Indiana: **5** Amoco
of New Jersey: **4** Esso **5** Exxon
of New York, today: **5** Mobil
standards: **5** ethos, mores **6** morals, values **8** morality
lacking ~: **6** amoral
lack of social ~: **5** anomy **6** anomie
org.: **4** ANSI
Standards and Practices employee: **6** censor
__ Standard Time: **5** Yukon **6** Alaska, Bering, Hawaii **7** Central, Eastern, Pacific
__ Standard Version: **7** Revised
Stand Back (1983 song) artist: Stevie Nicks
Stand by Me (1986 film)
cast: Corey Feldman, River Phoenix, Wil Wheaton
director: Rob Reiner
Stand by Me (song) artist: Ben E. King, John Lennon
stand by one's __: **4** guns
standby troops: **4** USAR, USNR **5** USAFR
__ Stand by You: **3** I'll
Stand By Your Man (1968 song) artist: Tammy Wynette
standee lack: **3** lap
stander-by: **9** spectator
Stander, Lionel: **5** actor
film: Cul-de-Sac (1966)
The Last Good Time (1994)
New York, New York (1977)
Pulp (1972)
TV: Hart to Hart
stand in __ of: **3** awe
stand-in: **3** sub **4** temp **5** agent, proxy **6** backup, double, player **8** delegate **9** alternate, look-alike, surrogate **10** substitute, understudy
Stand-In (1937 film)
cast: Joan Blondell, Humphrey Bogart, Leslie Howard
director: Tay Garnett
standing: **4** mark, rank, slot, term **5** caste, class, clout, erect, fixed, level, light, on end, place, scene, state, terms **6** cachet, credit, repute, status **7** dignity, footing, quality, station, stature, stratum, upright **8** capacity, eminence, existing, good name, position, prestige, repeated **9** character, condition, permanent, perpetual, seniority, situation **10** continuing, estimation, prominence, reputation, stationary
around: **4** idle
financial ~: **5** worth **8** net worth
have ~: **4** rank, rate
high ~: **4** note **5** glory, honor **6** esteem, renown **7** acclaim, dignity **8** eminence, prestige **9** celebrity, greatness, magnitude, reverence **10** importance, prominence
of long ~: **3** old **5** early, hoary **6** age-old, senior **7** ancient, lasting, vintage **8** enduring **9** perennial, venerable **10** immemorial
of longer ~: **5** older **6** senior
one's ground: **9** unbending
out: **7** obvious
pat: **6** static **9** unbending
room only: **3** SRO **4** full **5** close, tight **6** filled, jammed, packed **7** crammed, cramped, crowded, sold out, stuffed **8** brimming, thronged **9** chock-full, congested, jam-packed **10** wall-to-wall
social ~: **5** caste **6** estate
starter: **4** free, with
tall: **4** bold, game **5** brave, gutsy, nervy, tough **6** gritty, heroic, plucky, strong **7** assured, doughty, valiant **8** fearless, heroical, resolute, unafraid, valorous **9** confident, dauntless, undaunted **10** courageous, mettlesome, red-blooded
the one left ~: **5** champ
standing __: **3** cup **4** army, crop, wave **5** order, water **7** cypress, rigging
standing __ foot: **5** on one
standing __ jump: **5** broad
standing __ only: **4** room
standing __ roast: **3** rib
__ standing: **6** credit
Standing in the Shadows of Love (1966 song) artist: Four Tops
Standing on the Corner (1956 song) artist: Four Lads
stand in good __: **5** stead
Standing Room Only author: Alan Ayckbourn
standings column: **3** won **4** lost, ties, wins **6** losses
Standish: **5** Miles, Myles
stand-in: **5** Alden
Stand like Druids of __..: **3** eld
standoff: **3** tie **4** draw **7** impasse **8** deadlock **9** stalemate
like a ~: **5** tense
__ standoff: **7** Mexican
standoffish: **3** icy, shy **4** cold, cool **5** aloof, stiff **6** chilly, frigid, modest, remote **7** bashful, distant, glacial, haughty, hostile, recluse **8** eremitic, inimical, reserved, reticent, retiring, solitary **9** diffident, reclusive, withdrawn
one: **4** snob **5** snoot
stand one's __: **6** ground
standout: **3** def, rad **4** aces, A-one, boss, braw, cool, dece, fine, gear, keen, neat, nice, oner, phat, tuff **5** dandy, doozy, ducky, grand, great, marvy, neato, nobby, prime, slick, super, swell **6** bang on, bang-up, bonzer, bosker, choice, divine, doozie, dreamy, gnarly, groovy, lovely, peachy, slap-up, spot on, superb, terrif, tiptop, unique, unreal, whizzo, wicked **7** amazing, awesome, capital, corking, perfect, ripping, skookum, stellar, sublime **8** dazzling, especial, eximious, fabulous, five-star, four-star, frabjous, glorious, heavenly, jim-dandy, slam-bang, smashing, splendid, sterling, superior, terrific, top-level, topnotch, very good, wondrous **9** bodacious, Endsville, excellent, exemplary, exquisite, first-rate, high-grade, hunky-dory, marvelous, sollicker, top-flight, wonderful **10** first-class, hotsy-totsy, jack-a-dandy, peachy-keen, phenomenal, remarkable, stupendous, super-duper
standpoint: **4** side, view **5** angle, slant **6** stance, vision **7** mind-set, opinion, outlook, posture **8** attitude, position **9** direction, situation
St. Andrews: **4** city, port, town **10** golf course
locale: **8** Scotland
St. Andrew's cross in heraldry: **7** saltire
stands: **9** bleachers
__ stands: **4** as it
standstill: **4** halt, hole, rest, stay, stop, wait **5** check, delay, pause **6** corner **7** dead end, impasse **8** deadlock, dead stop, gridlock, inaction, stoppage **9** cessation, checkmate, stalemate
at a ~: **4** calm **6** hung up, static
bring to a ~: **4** stem, stop **5** cease **6** arrest, becalm
__ standstill: **3** at a
Stand, The author: Stephen King
dog: **5** Kojak
stand to __: **6** reason
stand up __: **3** for
stand-up: **5** comic **8** comedian
bit: **3** gag **4** joke **7** monolog **8** one-liner **9** monologue
need: **4** mike **5** stool, water **10** microphone
Stanford: **5** Moore, White **6** Leland, school
athletes: **8** Cardinal
conference: **6** Pac-Ten
locale: **10** California
rival: **4** UCLA
Stanford-__ test: **5** Binet
Stanislavsky: **10** Konstantin
Stanislavsky __: **6** Method, System
Stanislaw, Lem: **6** author, writer
Stanky: **5** Eddie
Stanley: **3** Kim **5** Adams, Baker, Cohen, Donen, Elkin, Jaffe, Tucci **6** Jordan, Kramer, Kunitz **7** Baldwin, Kubrick, Wendell **8** Holloway, Kowalski, Prusiner **10** Livingston
__ Stanley: **6** Morgan
Stanley and Livingstone (1939 film)
cast: Richard Greene, Nancy Kelly, Spencer Tracy
director: Henry King
Stanley and the Women author: Kingsley Amis
Stanley Cup: **5** award, prize **6** trophy
org.: **3** NHL
__ Stanley Gardner: **4** Erle
Stanley, Henry Morton: **3** Sir **7** British **8** explorer
concern: **6** Africa
Stanley & Iris (1990 film)
cast: Robert De Niro, Jane Fonda, Swoosie Kurtz, Martha Plimpton
director: Martin Ritt
__ Stanley Range: **4** Owen
Stanley Steamer: **3** car **4** auto
contemporary: **3** Reo
Stanley, Wendell: **7** chemist **8** Nobelist
stannic __: **4** acid **5** oxide **7** sulfide
stannite: **3** ore **7** mineral
stannum: **3** tin
Stanovoi: **3** mts. **4** mtns. **5** range **9** mountains
locale: **4** Asia **6** Russia
Stansfield: **4** Lisa
Stan the Man teammate: **4** Enos
St. Anthony's __: **5** cross
Stanton: **4** city, town
locale: **10** California
Stanton, Elizabeth Cady: **8** feminist
colleague: **4** Mott
Stanton, Harry Dean: **5** actor
film: The Black Marble (1979)
Cockfighter (1974)
Death Watch (1980)
One Magic Christmas (1985)
Repo Man (1984)
The Rose (1979)
The Straight Story (1999)
Straight Time (1978)
Stanwyck, Barbara: **7** actress
film: Annie Oakley (1935)
Ball of Fire (1941)
Banjo on My Knee (1936)
The Bitter Tea of General Yen (1933)
Christmas in Connecticut (1945)
Clash by Night (1952)
Double Indemnity (1944)
Executive Suite (1954)
Flesh and Fantasy (1943)
The Lady Eve (1941)
The Lady Gambles (1949)
Lady of Burlesque (1943)
The Man With a Cloak (1951)
Meet John Doe (1941)
A Message to Garcia (1936)
The Miracle Woman (1931)
My Reputation (1946)
Night Nurse (1931)
The Night Walker (1964)
Remember the Night (1940)
Roustabout (1964)
Sorry, Wrong Number (1948)
Stella Dallas (1937)
The Strange Loves of Martha Ivers (1946)
This Is My Affair (1937)
Titanic (1953)
Union Pacific (1939)
Witness to Murder (1954)
spouse: Robert Taylor
TV: The Big Valley
stanza: **4** text **5** verse
concluding ~: **5** envoi
Greek ~: **5** epode
sonnet ~: **5** octet **7** octette
__ stanza: **6** ballad, heroic, hymnal **7** elegiac
Stanza: **3** car **4** auto **6** Nissan
stapes: **4** bone
locale: **3** ear
staph: **3** bug **8** pathogen
staple: **3** key **4** main, tack **5** affix, basic, chief **6** attach, fasten **7** bracket, popular, primary **8** standard **9** essential, important, necessary, principal
staple __: **3** gun **7** remover
__ staple: **3** box
Staple __: **7** Singers
Stapledon, Olaf: **6** writer **7** British **8** essayist **11** philosopher
work: Odd John
Staples Center player: **5** Laker
Staple Singers
one of the ~: **4** Cleo
song: If You're Ready (1973)
I'll Take You There (1972)
Let's Do It Again (1975)
Stapleton: **4** Jean **7** Maureen
Stapleton, Maureen: **7** actress
film: Bye Bye Birdie (1963)
Cocoon (1985)

The Last Good Time (1994)
The Money Pit (1986)
Nuts (1987)
Plaza Suite (1971)
Reds (1981, AA)
Sweet Lorraine (1987)

star: 3 ace, sun 4 draw, hero, idol, lead, main, name, role 5 actor, chief, great, light, major 6 bigwig, famous, player, top dog 7 actress, capital, feature, heroine, leading, top draw 8 dominant, favorite, headline, luminary, pentacle, red dwarf, red giant, renowned, somebody, topliner, twinkler, virtuoso 9 brilliant, celebrity, dignitary, headliner, paramount, principal, prominent, supernova, top banana, well-known 10 celebrated, leading man, preeminent, white dwarf 11 leading lady
attribute: 4 fame
binary ~: 6 Sirius
blazing ~: 5 plant 6 flower
combining form: 4 astr- 5 -aster, astro-, sider- 6 -astero, sidero-
constellation's brightest ~: 5 alpha 6 lucida
Dog ~: 6 Sirius
Earth's ~: 3 Sol, sun
ender: 3 dom, lit 4 doms, dust, fish, gaze, ship, wort 5 board, burst, gazer, light 6 flower, gazing, struck
evening ~: 5 Venus 6 Hesper, planet, Vesper 8 Hesperus
followers: 4 fans, Magi 6 fandom
giver: 5 rater 6 critic
gold ~: 5 award, prize 6 trophy 7 laurels
hitch it to a ~: 5 wagon
in Andromeda: 6 Almach, Mirach
in Aquila: 6 Altair 7 Alshain, Tarazed
in Aries: 5 Hamal 8 Sheratan
in Auriga: 5 Al Kab 6 Almaaz 7 Capella
in Bootes: 4 Izar 6 Nekkar 7 Muphrid, Seginus 8 Arcturus
in Cancer: 6 Al Tarf 7 Acubens
in Canes Venatici: 5 Chara
in Canis Major: 5 Wezen 6 Adhara, Aludra, Mirzam, Sirius 7 Gomeisa
in Canis Minor: 7 Procyon
in Capricorn: 5 Dabih 6 Algedi 7 Nashira
in Carina: 5 Avior 7 Canopus
in Cassiopeia: 5 Segin 6 Achird, Shedar 7 Ruchbah
in Centaurus: 5 Hadar 7 Menkent
in Cepheus: 6 Alfirk
in Cetus: 4 Mira 6 Menkar
in Columba: 5 Phact
in Coma Berenices: 6 Diadem
in Corona Borealis: 5 Gemma 7 Nusakan 8 Alphecca
in Corvus: 7 Alchiba, Algorab
in Crater: 5 Alkes
in Crux: 6 Mimosa
in Cygnus: 4 Sadr 5 Deneb 7 Albireo
in Delphinus: 7 Rotanev 8 Sualocin
in Draco: 4 Adib 6 Thuban 7 Eltanin, Giausar 8 Rastaban
in Eridanus: 4 Beid, Keid 5 Cursa 6 Acamar
in Gemini: 5 Tejat, Wasat 6 Alhena, Castor, Pollux, Propus 7 Mekbuda
in Grus: 6 Al Nair
in Hydra: 7 Alphard
in Leo: 5 Zosma 7 Algieba, Rasalas, Regulus 8 Algenubi, Denebola
in Lepus: 5 Arneb, Nihal
in Lupus: 6 Kakkab
in Lyra: 4 Vega 7 Sheliak, Sulafat
in Ophiuchus: 5 Sabik 8 Cebalrai
in Orion: 5 Rigel, Saiph 7 Alnilam, Alnitak, Mintaka 9 Bellatrix 10 Betelgeuse
in Pegasus: 4 Enif 6 Markab, Scheat 7 Algenib
in Perseus: 5 Algol 6 Menkib, Mirfak
in Phoenix: 5 Ankaa
in Pisces: 8 Alrescha
in Puppis: 4 Naos 6 Tureis
in Sagitta: 4 Sham
in Sagittarius: 5 Nunki 6 Alnasl, Rukbat
in Scorpio: 6 Girtab, Lesath, Shaula 7 Al Niyat, Antares 8 Dschubba, Graffias
in Serpens: 4 Alya
in Taurus: 3 Ain 4 Maia 5 Atlas 6 Elnath, Merope 7 Alcyone, Pleione 9 Aldebaran
in Ursa Major: 5 Alcor, Dubhe, Merak, Mizar 6 Alioth, Alkaid, Phecda 7 Muscida, Talitha
in Ursa Minor: 6 Kochab, Yildun 7 Pherkad, Polaris
in Vela: 5 Regor 6 Suhail
in Virgo: 4 Awwa 5 Spica 6 Zaniah 7 Porrima
in Vulpecula: 5 Anser
K ~: 8 Arcturus 9 Aldebaran
look like a ~: 5 shine
M ~: 7 Antares 10 Betelgeuse
male ~: 4 hero, hunk
N ~: 3 sun
name meaning ~: 6 Stella 7 Estella, Estelle
place: 3 sky 5 space
quality: 5 charm 6 glamor 7 charism, glamour 8 charisma
rising ~: 5 comer
starter: 3 all, day 4 load, lode, pole 5 earth, super
system: 6 galaxy
type of ~: 5 dwarf
utilize a falling ~: 4 wish
variable ~: 4 Mira, nova

star __: 3 cut, map 4 lily, turn 5 anise, apple, chart, cloud, drill, facet, fruit, grass, route, shell 6 cactus, system 7 chamber, cluster, jasmine, network
star-__: 6 struck 7 crossed, studded
__ star: 3 red, sea, sun 4 dark, gold, x-ray 5 dwarf, fixed, flare, giant, guest, radio, shell 6 basket, battle, binary, carbon, double 7 blazing, brittle, evening, falling, feather, leather, Mexican, morning, neutron, runaway, serpent
__-star: 3 all, one, two 4 five, four 5 three
Star: 5 paper, Scout 6 skater 8 puckster 9 newspaper
locale: 7 Toronto 10 Kansas City
rival: 4 Blue, King, Wild 5 Bruin, Devil, Flame, Flyer, Oiler, Sabre, Shark 6 Canuck, Coyote, Ranger 7 Capital, Panther, Penguin, Red Wing, Senator 8 Canadien, Islander, Predator, Thrasher 9 Avalanche, Blackhawk, Hurricane, Lightning, Maple Leaf 10 Blue Jacket, Mighty Duck
Star __: 4 Carr, Trek, Wars 6 Search 7 Chamber, Witness
Star __: Deep Space Nine: 4 Trek
Star __ Generations: 4 Trek
Star __: Insurrection: 4 Trek
Star __: The Next Generation: 4 Trek
Star __: Voyager: 4 Trek
Star! (1968 film)
cast: Julie Andrews, Richard Crenna
director: Robert Wise
Star-__ tuna: 4 Kist
__ Star: 3 All, Dog, Tin 4 Rock 5 Demon, Lucky, North, Polar 6 Bronze, Little, Silver 7 Evening, Flaming, Shining
Stara Zagora: 4 city, town
locale: 8 Bulgaria
Starbuck: 4 mate
captain: 4 Ahab
Starbucks: 6 coffee
order: 5 latte, mocha 6 au lait
Star-Bulletin: 5 paper 9 newspaper
locale: 8 Honolulu
Starburst: 4 nosh 5 candy, snack
starch: 3 pep 4 grit, guts 5 nerve, pluck, valor, vigor 6 energy, farina, mettle 7 bravery, courage, prowess, stamina, stiffen 8 boldness, ceremony, gumption, patience, rigidity, tenacity, vitality 9 formality, fortitude, stiffness 10 get up and go
combining form: 4 amyl- 5 amylo-
medium: 5 spray
source: 4 corn, taro
Star Chief: 3 car 4 auto 7 Pontiac
starchy: 4 prim 5 rigid, stiff 6 formal 7 prudish 9 impliable 10 inflexible
compound: 4 amyl
food: 4 carb
foodstuff: 4 sago 5 salep
root: 4 taro
vegetable: 3 yam 4 spud 5 tater, tuber 6 potato
Starcraft: 3 GMC, van
star-crossed: 5 curst 6 cursed, doomed, jinxed 7 accurst, hapless, unblest, unlucky 8 accursed, ill-fated, luckless 9 unblessed, unfavored 10 ill-starred
stardom: 4 fame 6 renown 9 celebrity
achieve ~: 6 arrive
Stardust Memories (1980 film)
cast: Woody Allen, Jessica Harper, Charlotte Rampling
director: Woody Allen
stare: 3 eye, fix, pry, see 4 beam, bore, gape, gaup, gawk, gawp, gaze, leer, look, ogle, peer, view 5 focus, glare, rivet, watch 6 glower, goggle, marvel, regard, take in, wonder 7 eyeball 8 eagle eye 10 give the eye, rubberneck
stare __: 4 down 7 decisis
stares, like some: 3 icy 5 stony
__ Starfighter, The: 4 Last
__ Star Final: 4 Five
Starfire: 3 car 4 auto, Olds 10 Oldsmobile
starfish part: 3 arm, ray
__-Star Game: 3 All
Stargate (1994 film)
cast: Jaye Davidson, Viveca Lindfors, Kurt Russell, James Spader
director: Roland Emmerich
stargazer: 9 visionary
science: 9 astronomy
sight: 4 nova
time: 5 night
stargazers, Biblical: 4 Magi
Stargell, Willie: 6 Pirate 10 outfielder
__-star general: 3 one, two 4 five, four 5 three
staring: 5 agape, agaze 6 aglare
Starion: 3 car 4 auto 10 Mitsubishi
Star Is Born, A (1937 film)
cast: Janet Gaynor, Fredric March, Adolphe Menjou
director: William Wellman
Star Is Born, A (1954 film)
cast: Charles Bickford, Judy Garland, James Mason
director: George Cukor
Star Is Born, A (1976 film)
cast: Gary Busey, Kris Kristofferson, Barbra Streisand
director: Frank Pierson
stark: 3 raw 4 bald, bare, cold, grim, pure, rank 5 bleak, blunt, clear, gross, harsh, naked, plain, quite, sheer, stiff, utter 6 barren, chaste, dreary, patent, severe, simple, strong, unclad 7 austere, blasted, Spartan, utterly 8 absolute, desolate, forsaken, glabrous, infernal, outright, palpable, solitary, stripped, undraped 9 barebones, cheerless, downright, glaringly, out-and-out, unadorned, unalloyed, unclothed, uncovered 10 absolutely, altogether, completely, consummate, depressing, thoroughly
stark-__: 5 naked
Stark: 6 Willie 8 Johannes
Starker, Janos: 7 cellist 9 Hungarian
starkers: 4 bare, nude 5 naked 9 unattired
Star-Kist: 4 tuna
alternative: 9 Bumble Bee
Stark, Johannes: 8 Nobelist 9 physicist
starkness: 9 austerity
Starkville: 4 city, town
athletes: 8 Bulldogs
locale: 4 Miss.
school: 3 MSU
Starland Vocal Band song: Afternoon Delight (1976)
Star-Ledger: 5 paper 9 newspaper
locale: 6 Newark
starless: 4 dark 5 black
starlet: 7 actress
quest: 4 fame, role
Starlight Express: 7 musical
composer: 11 Lloyd Webber
footwear: 5 skate
starlike: 6 astral
flower: 5 aster
starling: 4 bird 8 oxpecker
relative: 4 mina, myna 5 minah, mynah
Starling: 7 Clarice
Starman star: 7 Bridges
Star of __: 5 David 9 Bethlehem
__-Star Pictures: 3 Tri
__ Star Program: 6 Energy
Starr: 3 Kay, Ken 4 Bart 5 Belle, Edwin, Ringo 6 Brenda 7 Kenneth
Starr, Bart: 2 QB
sport: 8 football
__-starred: 3 ill
__-star review: 4 four
starring __: 4 role
starring, also: 4 with
Starr, Kay
song: My Heart Reminds Me (1957)
Rock and Roll Waltz (1956)
Starr, Ringo: 7 drummer
born: Richard Starkey
group: The Beatles
song: Back Off Boogaloo (1972)
It Don't Come Easy (1971)
No No Song (1975)
Oh My My (1974)
Only You (1974)
Photograph (1973)
You're Sixteen (1973)
spouse: Barbara Bach
starry: 6 astral
Starry __, The: 5 Night
starry-eyed: 4 owly 6 enrapt 8 romantic, youthful 9 idealized, visionary
Starry Night: 3 oil 8 painting
artist: 7 Van Gogh
stars
check out the ~: 4 gaze
give ~ to: 3 peg 4 rate 5 scale, set at, weigh 6 size up 8 classify, evaluate
in the ~: 5 fated
science: 9 astronomy
worth no ~: 5 awful
stars (with constellations)
Acamar: Eridanus
Achird: Cassiopeia
Acubens: Cancer
Adhara: Canis Major
Adib: Draco
Ain: Taurus
Albireo: Cygnus
Alchiba: Corvus

Alcor: Ursa Major
Alcyone: Taurus
Aldebaran: Taurus
Alfirk: Cepheus
Algedi: Capricorn
Algenib: Pegasus
Algenubi: Leo
Algieba: Leo
Algol: Perseus
Algorab: Corvus
Alhena: Gemini
Alioth: Ursa Major
Al Kab: Auriga
Alkaid: Ursa Major
Alkes: Crater
Almaaz: Auriga
Almach: Andromeda
Al Nair: Grus
Alnasl: Sagittarius
Alnilam: Orion
Alnitak: Orion
Al Niyat: Scorpio
Alphard: Hydra
Alphecca: Corona Borealis
Alrescha: Pisces
Alshain: Aquila
Altair: Aquila
Al Tarf: Cancer
Aludra: Canis Major
Alya: Serpens
Ankaa: Phoenix
Anser: Vulpecula
Antares: Scorpio
Arcturus: Bootes
Arneb: Lepus
Atlas: Taurus
Avior: Carina
Awwa: Virgo
Beid: Eridanus
Bellatrix: Orion
Betelgeuse: Orion
Canopus: Carina
Capella: Auriga
Caph: Cassiopeia
Castor: Gemini
Cebalrai: Ophiuchus
Chara: Canes Venatici
Cursa: Eridanus
Dabih: Capricorn
Deneb: Cygnus
Denebola: Leo
Diadem: Coma Berenices
Dschubba: Scorpio
Dubhe: Ursa Major
Elnath: Taurus
Eltanin: Draco
Enif: Pegasus
Gemma: Corona Borealis
Giausar: Draco
Girtab: Scorpio
Gomeisa: Canis Minor
Graffias: Scorpio
Hadar: Centaurus
Hamal: Aries
Izar: Bootes
Kakkab: Lupus
Keid: Eridanus
Kochab: Ursa Minor
Lesath: Scorpio
Maia: Taurus
Markab: Pegasus
Mebsuta: Gemini
Megrez: Ursa Major
Meissa: Orion
Mekbuda: Gemini
Menkar: Cetus
Menkent: Centaurus
Menkib: Perseus
Merak: Ursa Major
Merope: Taurus
Mimosa: Crux
Mintaka: Orion
Mira: Cetus
Mirach: Andromeda
Mirfak: Perseus
Mirzam: Canis Major
Mizar: Ursa Major
Muphrid: Bootes
Muscida: Ursa Major
Naos: Puppis
Nashira: Capricorn
Nekkar: Bootes
Nihal: Lepus
Nunki: Sagittarius
Nusakan: Corona Borealis
Phact: Columba
Phecda: Ursa Major
Pherkad: Ursa Minor
Pleione: Taurus
Polaris: Ursa Minor
Pollux: Gemini
Porrima: Virgo
Procyon: Canis Minor
Propus: Gemini
Rasalas: Leo
Rastaban: Draco
Regor: Vela
Regulus: Leo
Rigel: Orion
Rotanev: Delphinus
Ruchbah: Cassiopeia
Rukbat: Sagittarius
Sabik: Ophiuchus
Sadr: Cygnus
Saiph: Orion
Scheat: Pegasus
Segin: Cassiopeia
Seginus: Bootes
Sham: Sagitta
Shaula: Scorpio
Shedar: Cassiopeia
Sheliak: Lyra
Sheratan: Aries
Sirius: Canis Major
Spica: Virgo
Sualocin: Delphinus
Suhail: Vela
Sulafat: Lyra
Talitha: Ursa Major
Tarazed: Aquila
Tejat: Gemini
Thuban: Draco
Tureis: Puppis
Vega: Lyra
Wasat: Gemini
Wezen: Canis Major
Yildun: Ursa Minor
Zaniah: Virgo
Zosma: Leo
__ stars: 3 see
Stars: 3 six 4 team
home: 6 Dallas
milieu: 3 ice 4 rink
org.: 3 NHL
sport: 6 hockey
Stars __ Down, The: 4 Look 5 Shine
Stars above!: 6 dear me
Stars and __: 4 Bars 7 Stripes
Stars and Bars: 4 flag
inits.: 3 CSA
Stars and Stripes: 4 flag 8 Old Glory
Stars and Stripes Forever, The: 5 march
composer: 5 Sousa
Starship
aka: Jefferson Airplane, Jefferson Starship
song: It's Not Over (1987)
Nothing's Gonna Stop Us Now (1987)
Sara (1986)
We Built This City (1985)
starship letters: 3 NCC
Stars in My Crown (1950 film)
cast: Ellen Drew, Joel McCrea, Dean Stockwell
Starsky and Hutch actor: 4 Soul
Stars Like Dust, The author: Isaac Asimov
Stars Look Down, The (1939 film)
cast: Margaret Lockwood, Michael Redgrave, Edward Rigby
director: Carol Reed
Star-Spangled Banner: 4 flag 8 Old Glory
Star-Spangled Banner, The: 6 anthem
contraction: 3 o'er
opener: 4 O say
writer: 3 Key
Star-Spangled Girl, The author: Neil Simon
Star Spangled Rhythm (1942 film)
cast: Bing Crosby, Bob Hope, Ray Milland
director: George Marshall
Stars Shine Down, The author: Sidney Sheldon
__ Star State: 4 Lone
start: 3 jar, shy 4 bolt, buck, dart, dawn, draw, edge, jerk, jump, lead, leap, open, rise, seed, step, wade 5 arise, begin, birth, bound, break, bulge, crank, enrol, found, get-go, git-go, issue, leave, light, onset, prime, quail, react, rouse, scare, set in, set up, shock, shoot, spark, spasm, wince 6 advent, arouse, blanch, blench, bounce, create, day one, depart, dive in, embark, enroll, fire up, flinch, go to it, ignite, jump in, launch, let rip, origin, outset, recoil, ring in, set off, set out, shrink, source, spring, take up, tee off, turn on, twitch, whip up 7 aggress, dawning, develop, genesis, go ahead, infancy, jump off, kickoff, leadoff, opening, pioneer, power up, prelude, proceed, provoke, push off, sendoff, takeoff, trigger, usher in, vantage 8 activate, approach, blastoff, commence, draw back, entrance, exordium, get going, initiate, set about, set forth, surprise, touch off 9 advantage, allowance, beginning, countdown, enter upon, establish, first step, get moving, get to work, inception, instigate, institute, introduce, originate, square one, strike out 10 conception, convulsion, envisaging, foundation, hit the road, inaugurate, incipience, initiation, jump the gun, sally forth
start __ under: 5 a fire
__ start: 4 head 5 false 6 flying 7 housing, running
__-start: 4 jump, kick 5 boost
started
get ~: 4 move 5 crank 7 proceed, take off 8 turn over
Star-Telegram: 5 paper 9 newspaper
locale: 7 Ft. Worth
__ starter: 4 kick
__-starter: 4 self
__ starters: 3 for
Star, The (1952 film)
cast: Bette Davis, Sterling Hayden, Natalie Wood
__ Star, The: 3 Tin 7 Evening
starting: 4 from 8 original 10 initiatory
from: 4 as of
point: 4 base 5 basis, gitgo 6 origin, source 9 beginning, threshold
up: 3 new 8 brand-new
starting __: 4 gate, line, over 5 block 6 handle
Starting Over (1979 film)
cast: Candice Bergen, Jill Clayburgh, Burt Reynolds
director: Alan J. Pakula
startle: 3 awe, jar 4 bolt, jolt, jump, rock, stun 5 alarm, amaze, floor, rouse, scare, shake, shock, spook 6 fright 7 agitate, astound, shake up, stagger, terrify 8 affright, astonish, frighten, surprise 9 galvanize, give a turn, take aback, terrorize 10 scare stiff
startled: 5 agasp 6 afraid, scared 10 dumbstruck
cry: 4 yipe 5 yikes, yipes 7 omigosh
startling: 8 dramatic, striking, uncommon 9 different, wonderful 10 prodigious, unexpected, unforeseen
Start Me Up (1981 song) artist: Rolling Stones
Start Movin' (1957 song) artist: Sal Mineo
Start playing!: 5 hit it
Star Trek (NBC sci-fi)
cast: Majel Barrett (Nurse Christine Chapel)
James Doohan (Lt. Cmdr. Scott)
DeForest Kelley (Dr. Leonard McCoy)
Walter Koenig (Ens. Pavel Chekov)
Nichelle Nichols (Lt. Uhura)
Leonard Nimoy (Cmdr. Spock)
William Shatner (Capt. James Kirk)
George Takei (Lt. Sulu)
extra: 5 alien
setting: 5 space
speed: 4 warp
weapon: 6 phaser
weapon setting: 4 stun
Star Trek - Deep Space Nine (TV sci-fi)
cast: Rene Auberjonois (Odo)
Avery Brooks (Cmdr. Benjamin Sisko)
Terry Farrell (Jadzia Dax)
Colm Meaney (Miles O'Brien)
Alexander Siddig (Dr. Julian Bashir)
Nana Visitor (Major Kira Nerys)
Star Trek Generations (1994 film)
cast: Malcolm McDowell, William Shatner, Patrick Stewart
director: David Carson
Star Trek III: The Search for Spock (1984 film)
cast: James Doohan, DeForest Kelley, William Shatner
director: Leonard Nimoy
Star Trek II: The Wrath of Khan (1982 film)
cast: DeForest Kelley, Ricardo Montalban, Leonard Nimoy, William Shatner
director: Nicholas Meyer
Star Trek: Insurrection (1998 film)
cast: LeVar Burton, Jonathan Frakes, Brent Spiner, Patrick Stewart
director: Patrick Stewart
Star Trek IV: The Voyage Home (1986 film)
cast: Catherine Hicks, DeForest Kelley, Leonard Nimoy, William Shatner
director: Leonard Nimoy
Star Trek-The Motion Picture (1979 film)
cast: Stephen Collins, DeForest Kelley, Leonard Nimoy, William Shatner
director: Robert Wise
Star Trek: The Next Generation (TV sci-fi)
cast: LeVar Burton (Lt. Geordi La Forge)
Denise Crosby (Lt. Tasha Yar)
Michael Dorn (Lt. Worf)
Jonathan Frakes (Cmdr. Will Riker)
Whoopi Goldberg (Guinan)
Gates McFadden (Dr. Beverly Crusher)
Colm Meaney (Miles O'Brien)
Marina Sirtis (Deanna Troi)
Brent Spiner (Lt. Cmdr. Data)
Patrick Stewart (Capt. Jean-Luc Picard)
Wil Wheaton (Wesley Crusher)

cat: 4 Spot
foe: Borg
Star Trek VI: The Undiscovered Country (1991 film)
cast: DeForest Kelley, Leonard Nimoy, William Shatner
director: Nicholas Meyer
Star Trek: Voyager (UPN sci-fi)
cast: Robert Beltran (Chakotay)
Roxann Biggs-Dawson (B'Elanna Torres)
Jennifer Lien (Kes)
Robert McNeill (Lt. Tom Paris)
Kate Mulgrew (Capt. Kathryn Janeway)
Ethan Phillips (Neelix)
Robert Picardo (The Doctor)
Tim Russ (Tuvok)
Jeri Ryan (Seven of Nine)
Garrett Wang (Ens. Harry Kim)
Star Tribune: 5 paper 9 newspaper
locale: 6 St. Paul
Start the Revolution Without Me (1970 film)
cast: Hugh Griffith, Donald Sutherland, Gene Wilder
director: Bud Yorkin
starvation ___: 5 wages
starved: 4 thin 5 drawn, empty, faint, unfed 6 hungry, peaked, skinny 7 craving, haggard, peckish, pinched 8 edacious, esurient, famished, ravenous, underfed, weakened 9 emaciated, hungering, insatiate, voracious 10 gluttonous
starving: 4 thin 5 drawn, empty, faint, unfed 6 hungry, skinny 7 craving, haggard, pinched 8 famished, ravenous, underfed, weakened 9 emaciated, hungering, insatiate, voracious
Star Wars (1977 film)
cast: Peter Cushing, Carrie Fisher, Harrison Ford, Alec Guinness, Mark Hamill
director: George Lucas
foe: 6 Empire
knight: 4 Jedi
music: John Williams
planet: 5 Endor
role: 3 Han 4 Leia, Luke, Solo 5 Darth, Vader 6 Kenobi, Obi-Wan 9 Skywalker 10 Artoo Detoo
weapon: 5 laser
Star Wars, aka: 3 SDI
Star Wars Episode 1: The Phantom Menace (1999 film)
cast: Jake Lloyd, Ewan McGregor, Liam Neeson, Natalie Portman
director: George Lucas
music: John Williams
role: 3 Ani
starwort: 5 aster
Starz: 7 channel
alternative: 3 AMC, HBO, IFC, SHO, TMC 4 Flix 5 Bravo 6 Encore 7 Cinemax 8 Showtime, Sundance
stash: 4 bury, hide, save, stow 5 cache, hoard, put by, store, trove 6 pileup 7 conceal, deposit, harvest, lay away, put away, reserve, secrete 8 conserve, ensconce, hide away, salt away, stow away
stasis: 5 poise 7 balance 8 stoppage 9 equipoise 10 inactivity, quiescence
stat: 3 avg., CPI, ERA, GNP, GPA, now, PDQ, RBI, TDs, THI 4 ASAP 5 datum, hurry, net wt., repro 6 at bats, at once, pronto 7 assists, quickly 8 chop-chop 9 duplicate, facsimile, photocopy, posthaste, right away 10 this minute
starter: 4 aero, rheo 5 photo
state: 3 air, put, say 4 avow, case, form, land, mode, mood, pass, pomp, rank, tell, time, trim, vent 5 event, glory, phase, pitch, realm, shape, speak, spiel, stand, style, union, utter, voice 6 affirm, allege, assert, cachet, depone, fettle, lather, nation, nature, pickle, plight, public, recite, relate, remark, report, temper 7 chances, chime in, country, declare, dignity, display, element, enounce, explain, expound, express, footing, majesty, mention, narrate, observe, outlook, posture, present, proviso, quality, recount, specify, testify, welfare 8 announce, attitude, bring out, capacity, category, ceremony, describe, dominion, grandeur, juncture, maintain, occasion, position, prestige, proclaim, propound, rehearse, republic, set forth, standing, throw out 9 character, community, condition, elucidate, enumerate, enunciate, expound on, interpret, make clear, pronounce, situation, stipulate, territory, verbalize 10 articulate, ceremonial, federation, government, imperative, limitation, occurrence, reputation
combining form: 6 -phoria
ender: 4 room, side, wide 5 craft, house
in French: 4 état
solemnly ~: 5 swear
starter: 4 down 5 inter
suffix: 3 -age, -dom, -ism 4 -ence, -ness, -ship
U.S. ~: 3 Ala., Ark., Cal., Del., Fla., Haw., Ida., Ill., Ind., Kan., Ken., Neb., Nev., Ore., Tex., Wis., W. Va., Wyo. 4 Alas., Ariz., Colo., Conn., Iowa, Mass., Mich., Minn., Miss., Mont., N. Car., N. Dak., Nebr., N. Mex., Ohio, Okla., Penn., S. Car., S. Dak., Tenn., Utah, Wash., Wisc. 5 Calif., Idaho, Maine, Penna., Texas 6 Alaska, Hawaii, Kansas, Nevada, Oregon 7 Alabama, Arizona, Florida, Georgia, Indiana, Montana, New York, Vermont, Wyoming 8 Arkansas, Colorado, Delaware, Illinois, Kentucky, Maryland, Michigan, Missouri, Nebraska, Oklahoma, Virginia 9 Louisiana, Minnesota, New Jersey, New Mexico, Tennessee, Wisconsin 10 California, Washington 11 Connecticut, Mississippi, North Dakota, Rhode Island, South Dakota 12 New Hampshire, Pennsylvania, West Virginia 13 Massachusetts, North Carolina, South Carolina
state ___: 3 aid 4 bank, bird, tree 5 of war, visit 6 church, flower, police, prison, secret 7 chamber, trooper
state ___ art: 5 of the
___ state: 3 in a 6 buffer, client, ground, police 7 altered, excited, nascent, quantum, welfare
___-state: 4 city 5 out-of, solid 6 nation
State ___: 4 Fair 6 Secret
State ___ Union address: 5 of the
___ State: 3 Bay, Gem 4 Ball, Kent, Penn 5 Aloha 7 Buckeye
___-State: 3 all
State and Main (2000 film)
cast: Alec Baldwin, Philip Seymour Hoffman, William H. Macy, Sarah Jessica Parker
director: David Mamet
State College: 4 city, town
locale: 4 Penn.
statecraft: 8 politics 9 diplomacy 10 government
stated: 3 set 5 given 6 verbal 7 nominal, regular
State Fair (1933 film)
cast: Lew Ayres, Janet Gaynor, Will Rogers
character: 4 Abel 5 Emily, Frake, Margy 7 Eleanor, Melissa
director: Henry King
state: 4 Iowa
State Fair (1945 film): 7 musical
cast: Dana Andrews, Jeanne Crain, Dick Haymes
composer: 7 Rodgers 11 Hammerstein
director: Walter Lang
State Fair (1962 film)
cast: Ann-Margret, Pat Boone, Bobby Darin, Pamela Tiffin
director: José Ferrer
State Farm rival: 5 Aetna
stateliness: 8 grandeur, nobility, splendor
stately: 4 high 5 grand, large, lofty, noble, proud, regal, royal, stiff 6 august, formal, kingly, lordly, portly, proper, ritual, solemn, superb 7 courtly, elegant, gallant, haughty, massive, opulent, pompous, queenly, sublime 8 decorous, elevated, gracious, highbrow, imperial, imposing, majestic, measured, palatial, towering 9 dignified, grandiose, luxurious, sumptuous, venerable 10 ceremonial, high-minded, impressive, majestical, monumental, statuesque
home: 5 manor
Stately Wayne ___: 5 Manor
statement: 3 tab 4 bill, news, word 5 input, voice 6 avowal, budget, charge, dictum, record, remark, report 7 account, comment, invoice, mention, picture, recital, theorem 8 relation 9 admission, affidavit, assertion, assurance, manifesto, narrative, reckoning, testimony, utterance 10 allegation, communiqué, confession, exposition, expression, indictment, profession, recitation
brief ~: 4 note 9 sound bite
confidential ~: 5 aside
detailed ~: 6 report
entry: 5 asset, debit 6 credit 8 net worth 9 liability
false ~: 3 lie 4 tale
formal ~: 5 edict 6 dictum
itemized ~: 4 bill 7 invoice
make a ~: 3 say 4 aver, talk 5 speak
___ statement: 4 bank 5 basic, make a, proxy, sworn 6 income 7 fashion
Staten Island: 3 bor. 7 borough
locale: 3 NYC
transport: 5 ferry
state of ___: 3 war 5 grace 7 affairs
___ state of affairs: 4 a sad
State of Grace (1990 film)
cast: Ed Harris, Gary Oldman, Sean Penn, Robin Wright
director: Phil Joanou
State of Shock (1984 song) artist: Jackson 5
State of Siege author: Albert Camus
State of the ___ address: 5 Union
state-of-the-art: 3 new 6 modern, superb 7 current 8 advanced, up-to-date
State of the Union (1948 film)
cast: Katharine Hepburn, Angela Lansbury, Spencer Tracy
director: Frank Capra
State of the World (1991 song) artist: Janet Jackson
stater: 4 coin 5 money
stateroom: 5 cabin 8 quarters
state-run game: 5 lotto
states' ___: 6 rights
___ States: 4 Gulf 5 Assam, Malay, Papal 6 Balkan, Baltic, Border, Madras, Middle, Native, Punjab 7 Altered, Barbary, Gujarat, Trucial
State's Attorney (1932 film)
cast: John Barrymore, William Boyd, Helen Twelvetrees
Statesboro: 4 city, town
locale: 7 Georgia
State Secret (1950 film)
cast: Douglas Fairbanks Jr., Glynis Johns, Herbert Lom
director: Sidney Gilliat
state's evidence
turn ~: 4 sing 7 testify
___ statesman: 5 elder
Statesman: 3 car 4 auto, Nash
statesmanship: 4 tact 5 poise 7 finesse 8 delicacy, politics 9 diplomacy
___ States of America: 6 United
___ States of Brazil: 6 United
___ States of Indonesia: 6 United
statesperson: 8 lawmaker 10 politician
States, The: 3 USA 5 US of A 7 America
Statesville: 4 city, town
locale: 4 N. Car.
___ State Warriors: 6 Golden
static: 4 firm 5 fixed, inert, rigid, sound, still, stuck 6 halted, rooted, stable, sticky, strife 7 passive, settled, stalled, stopped, uniform 8 constant, definite, immobile, inactive, ironclad, lifeless, stagnant, unmoving 9 immovable, permanent, unvarying 10 changeless, contention, deadlocked, gridlocked, invariable, motionless, stationary, unchanging
not ~: 6 moving 7 kinetic 8 in motion
problem: 5 cling
static ___: 4 line, tube 5 cling, water
station: 3 CRT, job, put, VDT 4 base, duty, park, post, rank, seat, site, spot, stop 5 allot, caste, class, depot, grade, house, level, locus, lodge, order, pitch, place, plant, stand 6 assign, deploy, estate, instal, locate, office, sphere 7 appoint, footing, install, lookout, quality, quarter, service, stratum 8 entrench, garrison, location, position, quarters, standing, terminal 9 character, crow's nest, establish, situation 10 commission, department, employment, occupation, walk of life
abbr.: 3 arr., dep., ETA, ETD
bus ~: 4 stop 5 depot
ender: 5 house 6 master
live beneath one's ~: 4 slum
posting: 4 sked 8 schedule
pull into the ~: 6 arrive
starter: 4 work
wagon: 3 car 4 auto
work ~: 3 CRT, VDT 4 desk 6 office 7 cubicle
station ___: 5 agent, break, house, wagon
___ station: 3 aid, air, bus, gas, ice, key, pay, way 4 base, fire, flag, hill, work 5 earth, pilot, power, radio, space, train 6 battle, ground, police 7 coaling, comfort, docking, filling, service, weather
___ Station: 4 Penn 5 Power, Union 7 Savage's 8 Victoria
stationary: 3 pat 4 firm, idle 5 fixed, inert 6 at rest, moored, parked, rooted, stable, static 8 anchored, immobile, stagnant, standing, unmoving 9 immovable, permanent, quiescent, sedentary 10 stock-still
be ~ at sea: 5 lie to
stationary ___: 4 wave 5 front, orbit, state 6 engine 7 bicycle
stationer: 8 merchant, retailer
supply: 3 pen 5 paper 6 eraser, pencil
stationery: 5 paper 8 envelope
amount: 4 ream 5 quire
brand: 5 Eaton

station-house ritual: **6** lineup
Station West (1948 film)
cast: Jane Greer, Dick Powell
__ Station Zebra: **3** Ice
statistic: **3** avg. **4** mean, mode **5** datum, index **6** median, number **7** average, per cent
statistical
significance measure: **5** t-test
statistician no-no: **4** bias
statistics: **3** nos. **4** data **5** table **7** numbers **10** tabulation
vital ~: **5** story **6** résumé **7** profile
__ statistics: **5** Fermi, vital **7** quantum
Statler Brothers song: Flowers on the Wall (1965)
stator partner: **5** rotor
statue: **4** bust, icon, ikon **5** eikon, model, piece **6** bronze, effigy, figure, marble, trophy **8** likeness, memorial, monument **9** sculpture
armless ~: **5** Venus
base: **5** socle
headless ~: **5** torso
leaf: **3** fig
of a god: **4** idol
place: **4** apse **5** niche
play ~: **6** freeze
support: **4** base
Statue of Liberty
feature: **5** crown, torch **6** tablet
inscription starter: **4** give
ship that brought the ~: **5** Isère
skin: **6** copper
statues, island of large: **6** Easter
statuesque: **4** tall, trim **5** grand, regal **7** stately **8** graceful, imposing, majestic **9** beautiful **10** curvaceous, majestical
statuette: **4** Emmy, Obie, Tony **5** model, Oscar **8** figurine
stature: **4** rank, size **5** merit, value, worth **6** cachet, growth, height, virtue **7** ability, caliber, dignity, quality **8** capacity, eminence, position, prestige, standing **9** elevation **10** competence, importance, prominence, reputation
gain ~: **4** grow
status: **3** job **4** mode, rank, role **5** caste, class, grade, level, merit, place, stage **6** cachet, credit, degree, estate, league, rating, renown **7** caliber, dignity, footing, quality, ranking **8** capacity, eminence, position, prestige, standing **9** character, condition, situation **10** importance, prominence
have ~: **4** rank, rate
raise in ~: **5** exalt
suffix: **4** -ship
status __: **3** quo **5** group **6** symbol
statute: **3** act, law **4** bill, rule **5** bylaw, canon, edict **6** decree **7** measure, precept **9** enactment, ordinance **10** regulation
statute __: **3** law **4** book, mile
__ statute: **6** public
statutory: **5** jural, legal, licit **6** lawful, vested **7** enacted **9** canonical **10** legitimate
statutory __: **3** law **5** crime **7** offense
Staubach, Roger: **2** QB
sport: **8** football
Staub, Rusty sport: **8** baseball
Staudinger, Hermann: **7** chemist **8** Nobelist
St. Augustine author: Rebecca West
staunch: **4** bold, fast, firm, game, stem, stop, sure, true **5** gutsy, hardy, liege, loyal, nervy, stiff, stout, tough **6** ardent, awless, daring, gritty, heroic, plucky, secure, spunky, stable, steady, strong, sturdy, trusty **7** aweless, defiant, devoted, doughty, dutiful, gallant, valiant **8** constant, faithful, fearless, heroical, intrepid, reliable, resolute, stalwart, true-blue, unafraid, untiring, valorous **9** allegiant, audacious, dauntless, dedicated, dreadless, rock solid, steadfast, tenacious, undaunted, unfailing, unfearful **10** courageous, dependable, inflexible, iron-willed, purposeful, undeterred, unflagging, unwavering, unyielding
staunchness: **4** grit **5** nerve, valor **7** loyalty **8** fidelity, tenacity
Staunton: **4** city, town
locale: **8** Virginia
staurolite: **3** gem **8** gemstone
Stautner: **5** Ernie
Stavanger: **4** city, port, town
locale: **6** Norway
stave: **3** rod **4** cane, pale, pole, post, rung, slab **5** crush, smash, staff, stake, stick, verse **6** paling, picket **7** fend off, support **8** splinter
in: **4** cave, push **5** pound, press
off: **5** avert, deter, parry, repel **6** defend, rebuff **7** obviate, prevent, repulse, rule out **8** forefend, hold back, preclude, turn back **9** hold at bay
stave __: **3** off
Stavros rival: **3** Ari
stay: **3** lag **4** bide, bunk, curb, halt, hang, hold, last, live, nest, prop, rest, stem, stop, wait **5** abide, brace, break, check, dally, defer, delay, dwell, exist, lodge, pause, perch, put up, roost, stall, stand, stick, tarry, truce, visit, waive **6** arrest, column, detain, endure, hang in, hinder, inhere, insert, intern, linger, loiter, occupy, put off, remain, reside, resist, settle, shelve **7** adjourn, hang out, holiday, layover, prevent, respite, sojourn, support, suspend, ward off **8** buttress, continue, hold back, intermit, lateness, obstruct, postpone, prohibit, reprieve, sit tight, stand for, stand pat, stopover, stopping, vacation **9** cessation, deferment, hang about, remission, stanchion, take a room **10** brave it out, hang around, standstill, stick it out, suspension, wait around
away from: **4** duck, miss, shun **5** avoid, dodge, evade, shirk **6** bypass, eschew **7** abstain **10** circumvent
a while: **5** abide, dwell **6** hold on, linger, remain **7** sojourn **8** continue
didn't ~: **4** left, went
ender: **4** sail
for: **5** await
invite to ~: **5** ask in
on: **4** last **5** stick **6** endure
over: **4** bunk **5** lodge **7** sojourn
place to ~: **3** inn **5** B and B, hotel, lodge, motel **8** motor inn **10** motor lodge
put: **3** fix **4** hold **5** stick
starter: **3** bob **4** back, jack, main
the course: **5** stand **7** persist **9** persevere
stay __: **3** put **5** loose
stay-__: **5** press
__ stay: **4** lace **6** collar
stay-at-home: **5** loner **6** hermit
Stay Away, Joe (1968 film)
cast: Joan Blondell, Katy Jurado, Burgess Meredith, Elvis Presley
Stay Hungry (1976 film)
cast: Jeff Bridges, Sally Field, Arnold Schwarzenegger
director: Bob Rafelson
Stayin' Alive (1977 song) artist: Bee Gees
staying
power: **5** might, vigor **7** stamina **8** patience **9** tolerance
put: **6** stable
staying __: **5** power
Stay of Execution author: **5** Alsop
Stay (song) artist: Four Seasons, Maurice Williams and the Zodiacs
stay the __: **6** course
__ Stay Together: **4** Let's
St. Bartholomew: **3** isl. **4** isle **6** island
St. Catharines: **4** city, town
locale: **6** Canada **7** Ontario
school: **5** Brock
St. Charles: **4** city, town
locale: **8** Illinois, Maryland, Missouri
St. Clair: **5** river
River locale: **7** Ontario **8** Michigan
St. Clair Shores: **4** city, town
locale: **8** Michigan
St. Cloud: **4** city, town
locale: **7** Florida **9** Minnesota
St.-Constant: **4** city, town
locale: **6** Canada, Québec
St. Crispin's __: **3** Day
St. Croix: **3** isl. **4** isle **5** river **6** island
locale: **9** Minnesota, Wisconsin **10** West Indies
St. Cyr: **4** Lily
St. Cyr-__: **6** l'École
std.
see standard
St.-Denis: **4** city, town
locale: **6** France
Ste-__-Eglise: **4** Mère
Ste.-__-des-Plaines: **4** Anne
Ste.-__, Quebec: **3** Foy
stead: **4** lieu **5** place **8** bed frame, location, position
ender: **4** fast
starter: **3** bed **4** farm, home, road
Stead, Christina: **6** author, writer **10** Australian
work: The Man Who Loved Children
steadfast: **3** set **4** firm, sure, true **5** fixed, liege, loyal, rigid, solid **6** ardent, gritty, intent, stable, steady, strong, sturdy, trusty **7** abiding, adamant, devoted, dutiful, hard-set, intense, staunch **8** constant, enduring, faithful, hellbent, immobile, implicit, reliable, resolute, stubborn, tireless, true-blue **9** allegiant, dedicated, immovable, immutable, obstinate, permanent, rock solid, tenacious, unbending, undaunted, unfailing, unmovable **10** changeless, dependable, determined, foursquare, hard-bitten, inflexible, iron-willed, persistent, purposeful, relentless, unflagging, unswerving, unwavering, unyielding
name meaning ~: **7** Eustace
steadfastness: **4** grit **5** nerve, valor **7** loyalty, purpose, resolve **8** backbone, fidelity, tenacity **9** stability, tolerance **10** resolution
symbol of ~: **4** rock
steadily: **7** fixedly **8** intently
steadiness: **5** poise **6** aplomb **8** calmness, strength **9** certainty, constancy, fixedness, stability, tolerance **10** equanimity
Steadman: **6** Alison
steady: **2** jo **3** pet **4** baby, beau, calm, cool, dear, even, fast, firm, jill, love, safe, sane, sure, true **5** amour, angel, brace, chéri, cooky, cutey, cutie, deary, ducky, fixed, flame, honey, leman, level, liege, lover, lovey, loyal, novia, novio, paced, rocky, sober, solid, staid, sugar, sweet, tight, wooer **6** ardent, bon ami, chérie, cookie, dautie, dearie, poised, secure, sedate, serene, smooth, stable, strong, sweets **7** abiding, balance, beloved, certain, dearest, dear one, durable, endless, equable, eternal, gradual, intense, nonstop, patient, pigsney, regular, schatzi, settled, squeeze, stabile, staunch, stiffen, sweetie, tootsie, uniform **8** chou-chou, constant, cutie pie, dowsabel, dulcinea, enduring, faithful, habitual, ladylove, lovebird, macushla, paramour, precious, punctual, reliable, reserved, resolute, rhythmic, sensible, snookums, sugar pie, sweetums, truelove, unbroken, unending, unshaken, untiring, unwaning **9** allegiant, bonne amie, boyfriend, ceaseless, continual, dreamboat, immovable, inamorata, inamorato, incessant, patterned, perennial, perpetual, petit chou, stabilize, steadfast, temperate, undivided, unextreme, unvarying, valentine **10** changeless, consistent, continuous, dependable, girlfriend, heartthrob, honeybunch, mavourneen, persistent, phlegmatic, purposeful, set in stone, sweetheart, sweetie pie, true to type, turtledove, unaffected, unagitated, unchanging, undeterred, unflagging, unswerving, untroubled, unwavering
go ~: **3** pin, see, woo **4** date
keep ~: **3** fix, set **4** prop **6** freeze, secure, steady **7** balance, support **8** maintain, preserve **9** stabilize
succession: **6** stream
steady-__: **5** going **6** handed
__ steady: **4** rock
Steady __ goes!: **5** as she
Steady Eddie: **5** Lopat
steady-going: **5** loyal
steak: **4** loin, meat, rump **5** chuck, filet, flank, round, T-bone **6** entrée, rib-eye **7** red meat, sirloin
ender: **5** house
grade: **5** prime **6** choice
like overcooked ~: **5** tough
like prime ~: **4** aged
on the hoof: **5** steer
order: **4** rare, well **6** medium **8** well-done
prepare ~: **4** sear **5** broil **8** barbecue
so to speak: **4** turf
starter: **4** beef
tenderize ~: **4** cube **5** pound
steak __: **3** set **5** Diane, knife **7** tartare
__ steak: **3** rib **4** club, cube **5** cubed, round, shell, skirt, strip, Swiss, T-bone **6** cheese, minute, pepper, rib-eye, tartar **7** Chicago, chopped, Hamburg
steak au __: **6** poivre
steakhouse: **6** eatery **10** restaurant
steak tartare, like: **3** raw
steal: **3** buy, rob **4** copy, flit, glom, lift, loot, lurk, sack, slip, take **5** cheat, creep, glide, heist, pinch, poach, prowl, rifle, slide, slink, snake, sneak, strip, swipe, theft **6** abduct, burgle, divert, hijack, hold up, kidnap, pilfer, pirate, pocket, rip off, snatch, snitch, thieve, tiptoe **7** bargain, break in, defraud, despoil, larceny, pillage, plunder, purloin, ransack, slither, stick up, swindle **8** carry off, embezzle, good deal, highjack, liberate, peculate, purchase, shoplift, simulate, thievery, withdraw **9** great deal, pussyfoot **10** burglarize, plagiarize, run off with, spirit away
a march on: **5** one-up
a scene: **5** emote **7** overact
away: **2** go **3** fly **5** elope **6** escape **7** abscond, go south
(away): **4** slip
cattle: **6** rustle
from: **3** mug, rob **9** knock over
old-style: **3** nim

__ steal: 6 double
steal a __ on: 5 march
__ Steal a Million: 5 How to
Steal Away (1980 song) artist: Robbie Dupree
stealer: 5 thief 6 robber 7 burglar, rustler
scene ~: 3 ham
stealing: 5 theft 7 larceny 8 burglary, thievery 10 plagiarism
combining form: 5 klept- 6 klepto-
Stealing __: 4 Home 6 Beauty
Stealing Beauty (1996 film)
cast: Sinead Cusack, Joseph Fiennes, Jeremy Irons, Liv Tyler
director: Bernardo Bertolucci
Stealing Home (1988 film)
cast: Will Aldis, Jodie Foster, Mark Harmon
director: Steven Kampmann
steal one's __: 5 heart 7 thunder
Stealth: 3 car 4 auto 5 Dodge
steal the __: 4 show
stealthily: 8 on the sly, secretly
stealth warrior: 5 ninja
stealthy: 3 sly 4 wily 5 catty, quiet, sneak 6 covert, crafty, feline, secret, shifty, silent, sneaky 7 catlike, cunning, furtive 8 hush-hush, skulking, slinking, sneaking, thieving, thievish 9 deceitful, enigmatic, insidious, noiseless, secretive, underhand 10 undercover, under wraps
steam: 3 gas, irk, vim 4 boil, cook, fume, mist, rage, reek 5 anger, might, peeve, power, press, speed, sweat, upset, vapor, vigor 6 blanch, energy, enrage, muscle, tee off 7 moisten, smolder, tick off 8 have a fit, smoulder, strength, vitality 10 exhalation
bath: 5 sauna
blow off ~: 4 rant, rave, vent, yell 6 holler, scream
combining form: 5 atmid- 6 atmido-
conveyor: 4 pipe
cook with ~: 5 scald
ender: 4 boat, roll, ship 6 fitter, roller
give off ~: 4 reek
head of ~: 5 force
like ~: 7 gaseous
lose ~: 4 slow
sound: 4 hiss
source: 6 boiler, geyser 7 furnace
turn on the ~: 5 hurry 7 speed up
up: 3 fog 4 mist, rile 5 anger, befog 6 enrage, madden 7 enflame, inflame 9 instigate, stimulate
steam __: 3 box, fog 4 bath, beer, coal, heat, iron, room 5 chest, organ, point, table 6 boiler, engine, fitter, hammer, jacket, shovel 7 heating, turbine
Steam __: 4 Heat
Steamboat __: 6 Gothic 7 Springs
Steamboat 'Round the Bend (1935 film)
cast: Irvin S. Cobb, Will Rogers, Anne Shirley
director: John Ford
steamed: 4 sore 5 angry, het up, irate, upset, wroth 6 fuming, galled 7 furious 8 incensed, volcanic
get ~ up: 4 boil, burn, fume, stew 5 froth 6 see red, seethe, simmer 7 bristle, smolder
steam engine developer: 4 Watt
steamer: 3 wok 4 boat, clam 5 liner 6 vessel
steamer __: 3 rug 4 clam 5 chair, trunk 6 basket
__ steamer: 5 tramp 6 paddle
steaminess: 8 humidity
steaming: 3 hot 5 aboil, at sea, irate, upset 10 equatorial
steamroll: 4 push 5 forge 6 defeat
steamroller: 4 whip 6 hector 8 stalwart 9 overwhelm
Steamroller Blues (1973 song) artist: Elvis Presley
steamroom site: 3 spa
steamship: 4 boat 5 liner
steamy: 3 hot, wet 4 damp, dank, hazy 5 humid, misty, moist, muggy, soggy, undry 6 clammy, erotic, fogged, sticky, stuffy, sultry, sweaty, torrid 7 boiling, wettish 8 roasting, tropical 10 oppressive, passionate, sweltering
get ~: 5 fog up
Ste.-Anne-__-Plaines: 3 des
stearate: 4 salt 5 ester
stearic __: 4 acid
stearin: 5 ester
__ Stearns: 4 Bear
Stearns, Turkey: 10 outfielder
steatite: 4 talc
Steber, Eleanor: 6 singer 7 soprano
role: 4 Elsa
specialty: 5 opera
Stedman: 6 Edmund, Graham
Stedman, Edmund: 4 poet
steed: 4 Arab, mare 5 bronc, horse, mount, pacer 6 bronco, equine 7 Arabian, broncho, charger, courser 8 war-horse 10 Bucephalus
Cockney ~: 4 'orse
stopper: 4 whoa
see also horse
Steed, John: 7 Avenger
partner: 4 Emma, Gale, King, Peel, Tara
steel: 4 gird, tone 5 alloy, brace, build, metal, nerve, rally, ready, shore 6 anneal, beef up, buck up, harden, prop up, temper, tone up 7 bolster, brace up, build up, burgeon, develop, empower, enhance, fortify, hearten, resolve, shore up, stiffen, toughen 8 bourgeon, buttress, embolden, energize, imbolden, indurate, vitalize 9 encourage, intensify, reinforce 10 invigorate, strengthen
additive: 5 boron 6 cobalt 8 chromium
base: 4 iron 6 carbon
beam: 4 I-bar, L bar 5 H-beam, I-beam 6 girder
by-product: 4 slag
city: 3 Pgh. 4 Gary 10 Pittsburgh
ender: 4 head, work, yard 5 works 6 worker
factory: 4 mill
fine ~: 6 Toledo
German ~ center: 4 Ruhr 5 Essen
like ~ wool: 4 wove 5 woven
man of ~: 5 robot
oneself: 7 prepare
plow inventor: 5 Deere
reinforcement rod: 5 rebar
structural column: 5 lally
use ~ wool: 5 scour, scrub
what stainless ~ doesn't do: 4 rust
steel __: 4 band, blue, drum, gray, grey, mill, trap, wool 6 guitar, lumber, square
__ steel: 4 AISI, cast, cold, mild, plow, soft, tool 5 alloy, basic 6 carbon, cement, chrome, damask, nickel, rimmed 7 blister, machine
Steel: 4 Dawn 8 Danielle
Steel __: 4 Pier
__ Steel: 5 Man of
steel-belted buy: 4 tire
Steel, Danielle: 6 author, writer
work: Accident
Answered Prayers
Bittersweet
The Cottage
Daddy
Five Days in Paris
The Ghost
The Gift
Granny Dan
Heartbeat
The House on Hope Street
Irresistible Forces
Jewels
Journey
The Kiss
The Klone and I
Leap of Faith
Lightning
Lone Eagle
The Long Road Home
Malice
Message from Nam
Mirror Image
Mixed Blessings
No Greater Love
Once in a Lifetime
The Ranch
Silent Honor
Special Delivery
Sunset in Saint Tropez
Vanished
The Wedding
Wings
Steele: 4 peak 5 mount, Tommy 7 Richard 8 mountain
locale: 5 Yukon 6 Canada
Steele, Richard: 3 Sir 6 author, writer 7 British 8 essayist 10 playwright
partner: 7 Addison
publication: 6 Tatler 7 Tattler 9 Spectator
Steeler rival: 3 Jet, Ram 4 Bear, Bill, Colt, Lion 5 Brown, Chief, Eagle, Giant, Niner, Raven, Saint, Texan, Titan 6 Bengal, Bronco, Cowboy, Falcon, Jaguar, Packer, Raider, Viking 7 Charger, Dolphin, Panther, Patriot, Redskin, Seahawk 8 Cardinal 9 Buccaneer
Steelers: 4 team 6 eleven
home: 10 Pittsburgh
org.: 3 AFC, NFL
sport: 8 football
steelhead: 4 fish 5 trout
steelie alternative: 5 agate
Steel Magnolias (1989 film)
cast: Olympia Dukakis, Sally Field, Daryl Hannah, Shirley MacLaine, Dolly Parton, Julia Roberts, Sam Shepard, Tom Skerritt
director: Herbert Ross
dog: 5 Rhett
steelworkers
former ~ union chief: 4 Abel
steely: 3 icy 4 firm, hale, hard, iron, wiry 5 beefy, burly, hardy, hefty, hunky, husky, lusty, rigid, rocky, solid, stern, stiff, stony, stout, tough 6 brawny, flinty, hearty, mighty, potent, robust, rugged, sinewy, stocky, stoney, strong, sturdy, virile 7 adamant, doughty, ferrous, hard-set 8 athletic, blue-gray, concrete, forceful, hardened, indurate, intrepid, muscular, powerful, puissant, resolute, stalwart, vigorous 9 Atlantean, Herculean, impliable, strapping, unbending, undaunted, well-built 10 able-bodied, adamantine, determined, inflexible, iron-willed, red-blooded, unyielding
Steelyard Blues (1973 film)
cast: Peter Boyle, Jane Fonda, Donald Sutherland
Steely Dan
song: Do It Again (1972)
Hey Nineteen (1980)
Reeling in the Years (1973)
Rikki Don't Lose That Number (1974)
Steen: 3 Jan
steenbok: 6 animal 8 antelope
relative: 3 gnu, kob 4 guib, kudu, oryx, puku, topi 5 addax, bongo, chiru, eland, goral, korin, nyala, oribi, saiga, serow 6 chammy, dik-dik, duiker, impala, koodoo, lechwe, nilgai, rhebok, shammy, shamoy 7 blaubok, blesbok, chamois, defassa, gazelle, gemsbok, gerenuk, grysbok, nylghai, nylghau, sassaby 8 blesbuck, bontebok, bushbuck, gemsbuck, reedbuck 9 blackbuck, pronghorn, sitatunga, springbok, waterbuck 10 hartebeest, wildebeest
Steenburgen, Mary: 7 actress
film: Back to the Future Part III (1990)
Cross Creek (1983)
Dead of Winter (1987)
Goin' South (1978)
Melvin and Howard (1980, AA)
A Midsummer Night's Sex Comedy (1982)
Miss Firecracker (1989)
Nixon (1995)
One Magic Christmas (1985)
Parenthood (1989)
Philadelphia (1993)
Ragtime (1981)
Time After Time (1979)
role in Back to the Future III: 5 Clara
spouse: Ted Danson, Malcolm McDowell
TV: Ink
Steen, Jan: 5 Dutch 6 artist 7 painter
steep: 3 sop 4 boil, brew, cook, damp, dear, fill, high, soak, tall 5 bathe, erect, imbue, lofty, pricy, sharp, sheer, souse, stiff 6 costly, drench, infuse, invest, pickle, pricey, raised, sodden 7 arduous, engrain, extreme, immerse, ingrain, moisten, pervade, suffuse 8 dizzying, marinade, marinate, permeate, saturate, submerge, towering, vertical, waterlog 9 breakneck, excessive, expensive 10 exorbitant, high-priced, immoderate, impregnate, inordinate, outrageous, overpriced, straight-up
descent: 6 escarp
in brine: 5 souse
place: 5 cliff
rock: 3 tor 4 crag 5 arête, bluff, cliff, scarp 8 overhang, pinnacle 9 precipice 10 escarpment, prominence
slope: 5 chute, scarp
steeper, get: 4 rise
steeple: 3 tip 5 spire, tower 6 belfry, flèche, turret 8 pinnacle 9 bell tower, campanile
adornment: 3 epi
ender: 4 bush, jack 5 chase
feature: 4 bell
Gothic ~: 6 flèche
part: 6 belfry
steeplechase: 4 race 5 sport 9 horse race
obstacle: 5 fence 6 hurdle
steeply pitched: 6 gabled
steepness: 5 pitch, slope
Steep Trails author: 4 Muir
steer: 3 run, tip 4 helm, herd, land, lead, male, show 5 Angus, drive, guide, pilot, point, route, usher 6 advice, bovine, Brahma, cattle, direct, escort, govern, handle, jockey, manage, tipoff 7 captain, conduct, control, counsel, operate, skipper, solicit, suggest 8 longhorn, maneuver, navigate, shepherd, take over 9 influence, recommend 10 manipulate, take charge
as a ship: 4 conn
clear of: 4 duck, omit, shun 5 avoid, dodge, elude, evade, shirk, skirt, spurn 6 beware, bypass, eschew, lay off 7 abstain, shy from 8 flee

from, sidestep **10** circumvent
easy to ~: **3** yar **4** yare
enclosure: **6** corral
(for): **3** aim, try
handler: **5** roper **6** cowboy
mark on a ~: **5** brand
throw a ~: **4** rope
towards: **7** head for
wrong: **8** misguide **9** misinform
steer __ of: **5** clear
__ steer: **3** bum
steering: **10** navigation
adjustment: **5** toe-in
apparatus: **4** helm
steering __: **4** gear **5** wheel **6** column
__ steering: **5** power
steersman: **3** cox
Stefan: **5** Zweig **6** Edberg, George
Stefanie: **6** Powers
Steffens: **7** Lincoln
Steffi: **4** Graf
Ste.-Foy: **4** city, town
locale: **6** Canada, Québec
Stegner, Wallace: **6** author, writer
stegodon: **8** elephant
Steichen: **6** Edward
Steiger, Rod: **5** actor
film: Al Capone (1959)
Cattle Annie and Little Britches (1980)
The Chosen (1981)
Cry Terror (1958)
Doctor Zhivago (1965)
F.I.S.T. (1978)
Hands Over the City (1963)
Happy Birthday, Wanda June (1971)
The Harder They Fall (1956)
In the Heat of the Night (1967, AA)
Jubal (1956)
The Longest Day (1962)
No Way to Treat a Lady (1968)
Oklahoma! (1955)
On the Waterfront (1954)
The Pawnbroker (1965)
Seven Thieves (1960)
The Specialist (1994)
W.C. Fields and Me (1976)
spouse: Claire Bloom
stein: **3** mug **4** dish **6** beaker, holder, vessel **7** tankard **9** container **10** receptacle
contents: **3** ale **4** beer **5** lager
Stein: **3** Ben **7** William **8** Gertrude
part of a ~ quote: **3** is a **4** rose **5** a rose
Steinbeck, John: **6** author, writer **8** Nobelist
work: Cannery Row
East of Eden
The Grapes of Wrath
In Dubious Battle
Of Mice and Men
The Pearl
The Red Pony
Sweet Thursday
Tortilla Flat
Travels with Charley
The Wayward Bus
The Winter of Our Discontent
Steinberger, Jack: **8** Nobelist **9** physicist
Steinberg, William: **9** conductor
steinbok: **8** antelope
relative: **3** gnu, kob **4** guib, kudu, oryx, puku, topi **5** addax, bongo, chiru, eland, goral, korin, nyala, oribi, saiga, serow **6** chammy, dik-dik, duiker, impala, koodoo, lechwe, nilgai, rhebok, shammy, shamoy **7** blaubok, blesbok, chamois, defassa, gazelle, gemsbok, gerenuk, grysbok, nylghai, nylghau, sassaby **8** blesbuck, bontebok, bushbuck, gemsbuck, reedbuck **9** blackbuck, pronghorn, sitatunga, springbok, waterbuck **10** hartebeest, wildebeest
Steinbrenner: **6** George **7** The Boss
Steinem: **6** Gloria
Steiner: **3** Max **4** Fred **6** Rudolf
Steiner, Max: **8** composer
film score: The Big Sleep
The Caine Mutiny
Casablanca
Dark Victory
Gone With the Wind
Intermezzo
Key Largo
King Kong
Marjorie Morningstar
Mildred Pierce
Now, Voyager
Sergeant York
A Summer Place
The Treasure of the Sierra Madre
White Heat
Steiner, Rudolf: **11** philosopher
steinful: **3** ale
Stein, Gertrude: **6** author, writer
work: The Autobiography of Alice B. Toklas
Three Lives
Steinitz, William forte: **5** chess
Stein, Jean book: **4** Edie
Steinmetz: **3** Sol **7** Charles
Stein Song
state: **5** Maine
town: **5** Orono
Steinway: **5** grand, piano
Stein, William: **7** chemist **8** Nobelist
Ste.-Julie: **4** city, town
locale: **6** Canada, Québec
stela
see stele
stele: **4** slab **6** column, marker **8** memorial, monument
St. Elias: **2** mt. **3** mtn. **4** peak **5** mount, range **8** mountain
locale: **6** Canada
Stella: **5** Adler **7** Stevens **8** Kowalski
Stella __: **4** d'Oro **5** Maris **6** Dallas **7** Polaris
Stella Dallas (1937 film)
cast: John Boles, Anne Shirley, Barbara Stanwyck
director: King Vidor
stellar: **3** def, rad **4** aces, A-one, boss, braw, cool, dece, fine, gear, keen, main, neat, nice, phat, tuff **5** dandy, ducky, grand, great, marvy, neato, nobby, prime, slick, super, swell **6** astral, bang on, bang-up, banner, bonzer, bosker, choice, divine, dreamy, far-out, gnarly, groovy, lovely, peachy, slap-up, spot on, superb, terrif, tiptop, unreal, whizzo, wicked **7** amazing, awesome, capital, corking, leading, perfect, ripping, skookum, sublime **8** dazzling, especial, eximious, fabulous, five-star, four-star, frabjous, glorious, heavenly, jim-dandy, laudable, slam-bang, smashing, splendid, standout, sterling, stickout, superior, terrific, top-level, topnotch, very good, wondrous **9** bodacious, Endsville, excellent, exemplary, exquisite, first-rate, high-grade, hunky-dory, marvelous, principal, sollicker, topflight, universal, unrivaled, wonderful, wunderbar **10** first-class, hotsy-totsy, jack-a-dandy, out of sight, peachy-keen, phenomenal, preeminent, remarkable, stupendous, super-duper, unrivalled
prefix: **5** astro-
stellar __: **4** wind
St. Elmo's __: **4** fire **5** light
St. Elmo's Fire (1985 film)
cast: Emilio Estevez, Rob Lowe, Andrew McCarthy, Demi Moore, Judd Nelson, Ally Sheedy
director: Joel Schumacher
St. Elmo's Fire (1985 song) artist: John Parr
St. Elsewhere (NBC drama)
area: **2** ER **3** ICU
cast: Bonnie Bartlett (Ellen Craig)
Ed Begley Jr. (Dr. Victor Ehrlich)
William Daniels (Dr. Mark Craig)
Ed Flanders (Dr. Donald Westphall)
Stephen Furst (Dr. Elliot Axelrod)
Mark Harmon (Dr. Robert Caldwell)
Howie Mandel (Dr. Wayne Fiscus)
Kavi Raz (Dr. V.J. Kochar)
Denzel Washington (Dr. Phillip Chandler)
producer: MTM
setting: **6** Boston
stem: **3** bow, dam **4** axis, curb, flow, head, limb, prow, rise, root, stay, stop, twig **5** arise, block, check, issue, jam up, shoot, stick, stock, straw, trunk **6** arrest, branch, cut off, derive, hinder, oppose, resist, result, spring, stanch, stop up **7** control, curtail, develop, emanate, pedicel, pedicle, prevent, proceed, shut off, staunch **8** come from, hold back, peduncle, restrain **9** originate, withstand **10** keep in line
angle: **4** axil
berry ~: **4** cane
bulb-like ~: **4** corm
center: **4** pith
combining form: **4** caul-, corm- **5** cauli-, caulo-, cormo-, scapi-
ender: **4** ware
(from): **4** come **5** arise **6** derive
hops ~: **4** bine
joint: **4** node **8** juncture, swelling
main ~: **5** trunk
mushroom ~: **5** stipe
opposite: **5** stern
pipe ~: **5** shank
plant ~: **5** stalk
stem __: **3** rot **4** cell, rust, turn **5** duchy **7** cabbage
stem-__: **6** winder
__ stem: **4** blue, main, slip **5** black, brain, valve
__ Ste. Marie: **5** Sault
__-stemmed rose: **4** long
stempost: **6** timber
stemson: **6** timber
stem the __: **4** tide
__ stem to stern: **4** from
stem-to-stern timber: **4** keel
stemware: **5** glass **6** goblet **7** glasses
Sten: **3** gun **4** Anna
Sten, Anna: **7** actress
role: **4** Nana
stench: **4** funk, odor, reek **5** odour, smell, stink **7** malodor **9** effluvium, fetidness, redolence
stencil: **7** pattern
copy from a ~: **5** mimeo
cutter: **6** stylus
Stendhal: **6** author, French, writer
work: The Charterhouse of Parma
The Red and the Black
Stenerud, Jan sport: **8** football
Stengel, Casey: **7** manager
Mrs. ~: **4** Edna
sport: **8** baseball
stenographer: **5** clerk **6** writer **10** amanuensis
item: **3** pad
slip: **4** typo
stat.: **3** wpm
work: **6** letter
stentorian: **4** loud **5** forte, noisy, vocal **7** blaring, booming, jarring, pealing, rackety, raucous, reboant, roaring **8** crashing, piercing, plangent, resonant, rumbling, sonorous, strident, turned up **9** big-voiced, clamorous, deafening **10** boisterous, resounding, strepitous, thundering, thunderous, uproarious, vociferant, vociferous
step: **3** act, run **4** gait, hoof, move, pace, rank, rung, trip, trot, walk **5** dance, grade, level, means, notch, phase, point, print, riser, rumba, samba, stage, stair, start, stoop, trace, track, trail, tread, troop **6** action, canter, degree, gallop, motion, prance, rhumba, rundle, shimmy, stride, tiptoe, trapes, trudge **7** advance, descend, measure, process, traipse **8** ambulate, footfall, maneuver, saraband **9** footprint, gradation, increment, procedure, sarabande **10** proceeding
all over: **9** trample on, tyrannize
aside: **4** move **9** stand down
back: **6** recoil
ballet ~: **3** pas **5** coupé, pique, tombé **7** déboîté, emboîté, pas alle **8** glissade **9** pas marché
by step: **8** bit by bit, in stages **9** gradually, piecemeal
dance ~: **5** rumba, samba, waltz **6** cha cha, chassé, do-si-do, rhumba **7** dos-à-dos, fox trot
down: **4** quit **5** leave, light **6** reduce, resign **8** abdicate, decrease
ender: **3** son **4** wise **5** child **6** family, father, ladder, mother, parent, sister **7** brother, sibling **8** children, daughter
false ~: **4** trip **7** mistake
forward: **7** advance **8** progress **9** volunteer
front ~: **5** stoop
heavily: **5** stomp, tromp
in: **5** enter **7** mediate **9** intercede, interfere, interpose, intervene, lend a hand, negotiate, take a hand **10** take action
in ~: **8** together **9** consonant **10** conforming, going along, harmonious
in French: **3** pas
keep a ~ ahead of: **5** one-up, outdo
keep in ~: **4** obey **6** comply, follow **7** abide by, agree to, conform **10** toe the line
long ~: **6** stride
measured ~: **4** pace
miss a ~: **6** falter
off: **6** alight
on: **5** stamp, tread **7** trample
on it: **2** go **3** fly, hie, rev, rip, run, zip **4** bolt, dart, dash, flit, race, rush, tear, zoom **5** hurry, scoot, speed **6** barrel, gallop, hasten, hustle, rocket, scurry **7** quicken, scamper, speed up **9** shake a leg, skedaddle **10** accelerate, burn rubber, get hopping
out with: **3** see, woo **4** date **5** court **6** escort, squire
over: **8** bestride
part: **5** riser
quick ~: **4** trot
request to take a giant ~: **4** may I
starter: **4** door, foot, lock, over, side **5** quick
take the first ~: **5** start
up: **4** bump, grow, lift **5** add to, boost, build, hurry, raise, speed, stair **6** hasten **7** augment, fortify, improve, magnify, quicken **8** escalate, expedite, increase **9** increment, intensify **10** accelerate, strengthen, supplement
up or down: **4** rung
walk in ~: **5** march

watching one's ~: **4** wary **5** canny, chary, leery **7** careful, guarded, heedful, prudent **8** cautious, vigilant, watchful **9** judicious **10** deliberate, scrupulous
watch one's ~: **6** behave, beware **7** look out **10** toe the line
step __: **3** cut, off, out **4** down, on it, turn **5** aside **6** rocket
step __ gas: **5** on the
step __ rear: **5** to the
step __ the bar: **4** up to
step-__ transformer: **4** down
__ step: **4** baby, half, side **5** dance, false, goose, out of, whole **7** curtail, hanging
__-step: **3** one, two **4** high **6** corbie
Step __: **5** Saver **6** Lively
Step __!: **4** on it
Step __ crack...: **3** on a
__ step at a time: **3** one
Step by Step (song) artist: Eddie Rabbitt
artist: New Kids on the Block
Stepfanie: **6** Kramer
Stepford Wives, The: **4** film **5** novel
author: Ira Levin
cast: Peter Masterson, Paula Prentiss, Katharine Ross
director: Bryan Forbes
Stephane: **8** Mallarmé
Stephanie: **5** Mills **6** Faracy, Miller **7** Beacham **9** Zimbalist
Stephen: **3** Fry, Rea **4** Boyd, King, pope **5** Crane, Dorff, Furst, Herek, saint **6** Austin, Bishop, Breyer, Dobyns, Foster, Frears, Leslie, Stills **7** Baldwin, Collins, Douglas, Hawking, Langton, Leacock, McNally, pontiff, Spender **8** Sondheim **10** Gyllenhaal
in French: **7** Etienne
in German: **6** Stefan
in Italian: **7** Stefano
in Spanish: **7** Estéban
Stephen __ Benet: **7** Vincent
Stephen __ Gould: **3** Jay
Stephen J. __: **7** Cannell
Stephen Jay __: **5** Gould
Stephen, King mother: **5** Adela
Stephen, Leslie: **3** Sir **6** author, writer **7** British
Stephen of __: **5** Blois
Stephens: **6** Darrin, Robert **8** Samantha **9** Alexander
Stephenson: **6** George
Stephens, Robert: **3** Sir **5** actor
film: The Asphyx (1972)
The Prime of Miss Jean Brodie (1969)
The Private Life of Sherlock Holmes (1970)
A Taste of Honey (1961)
Stephen Vincent __: **5** Benet
Stepin: **7** Fetchit
Step Lively (1944 film)
cast: Adolphe Menjou, George Murphy, Frank Sinatra
Step on it!: **5** hurry **6** faster
step on one's __: **4** toes
step on the __: **3** gas
steppe: **4** moor **5** plain, plane **6** meadow **7** lowland
antelope: **5** saiga
cousin: **5** llano
horse: **6** tarpan
Steppenwolf
song: Born to Be Wild (1968)
Magic Carpet Ride (1968)
Rock Me (1969)
Steppenwolf author: Hermann Hesse
Steppin' __: **3** Out **5** Stone
Steppin' __ With My Baby: **3** Out
stepping
ender: **5** stone
place: **4** rung
stepping-__ place: **3** off
Stepping Stones: **7** musical
songwriter: **4** Kern
Steppin' Out (song) artist: Tony Orlando & Dawn
artist: Joe Jackson
Steppin' Out With My Baby composer: Irving Berlin
Steppin' Stone (1966 song) artist: Monkees
Step right in!: **5** enter
steps: **3** way **4** path **5** route **6** course **8** movement
over a fence: **5** stile
retrace one's ~: **6** return **8** turn back
riverbank ~ in India: **4** ghat **5** ghaut
series of ~: **5** stair **6** gradin **7** gradine
take ~: **3** act **4** pace, walk **7** get busy
__ steps: **5** giant **7** library
__ Steps: **7** Spanish
Steps author: Jerzy Kosinski
Step Saver: **7** cleaner
alternative: **5** Brite, Lysol **6** Top Job **7** Lestoil, Mr. Clean, Pine Sol **9** Fantastik
step to the __: **4** rear
step-up: **4** rise **5** raise **8** increase
-ster cousin: **3** -ist, -ite
stere: **10** cubic meter
stereo: **4** hi-fi **5** phono **7** boombox, Walkman **8** binaural, two-track, Victrola **10** phonograph
ancestor: **4** hi-fi
component: **5** tuner **7** speaker **9** turntable
control: **4** bass **5** fader **6** treble, volume
erstwhile relative: **4** quad
input: **4** tape **8** cassette
run the ~: **4** play
Stereoskopia: **8** asteroid
stereotype: **3** dub **4** type **5** label **6** cliché, custom, define **7** average, catalog, example, fashion, formula, pattern **8** regulate, standard **9** catalogue, formality, normalize
stereotyped: **5** stale, stock, trite **7** clichéd **8** ordinary, overused **9** hackneyed, played out
stereotypes, use: **5** label
Sterile Cuckoo, The (1969 film)
cast: Wendell Burton, Tim McIntire, Liza Minnelli
director: Alan J. Pakula
sterilize: **5** clean **6** degerm, purify **7** cleanse **8** fumigate, sanitize **9** autoclave, disinfect **10** pasteurize
sterilized: **4** pure **5** clean **10** antiseptic
sterilizer: **10** antiseptic
sterlet: **4** fish **8** sturgeon
sterling: **3** def, rad **4** aces, A-one, boss, braw, cool, dece, fine, gear, good, keen, neat, nice, phat, tuff **5** dandy, ducky, grand, great, marvy, neato, nobby, prime, slick, super, swell **6** bang on, bang-up, bonzer, bosker, choice, divine, dreamy, far-out, gnarly, groovy, lovely, peachy, silver, slap-up, spot on, superb, terrif, tiptop, unreal, whizzo, wicked **7** amazing, awesome, capital, corking, perfect, ripping, skookum, stellar, sublime **8** dazzling, especial, eximious, fabulous, five-star, four-star, frabjous, glorious, heavenly, jim-dandy, slam-bang, smashing, splendid, standout, stickout, superior, terrific, top-level, topnotch, very good, wondrous **9** bodacious, Endsville, excellent, exemplary, exquisite, first-rate, high-grade, honorable, hunky-dory, marvelous, sollicker, topflight, unrivaled, wonderful **10** first-class, hotsy-totsy, jack-a-dandy, out of sight, peachy-keen, phenomenal, remarkable, stupendous, super-duper, unrivalled
fractions: **5** pence
starter: **5** pound
sterling __: **4** area, bloc **6** silver
__ sterling: **5** pound
Sterling: **3** Jan **5** Brown, Tisha **6** Hayden, Robert **8** Holloway
Sterling Heights: **4** city, town
locale: **8** Michigan
Sterling, Jan: **7** actress
film: 1984 (1956)
The Big Carnival (1951)
The Harder They Fall (1956)
Pony Express (1953)
Rhubarb (1951)
Slaughter on Tenth Avenue (1957)
stern: **3** aft **4** back, firm, grim, hard, rear **5** bossy, cruel, harsh, picky, rigid, rough, tough **6** bitter, crusty, flinty, severe, steely, strict **7** ascetic, austere, hard-set, prudish, serious, Spartan **8** coercive, despotic, exacting, frowning, hard-core, hard-line, resolute, rigorous, ruthless, stubborn **9** by the book, demanding, draconian, hang-tough, hard-nosed, hard-shell, imperious, impliable, mortified, stringent, unbending, unpitying, unsparing **10** adamantine, astringent, autocratic, bullheaded, despotical, forbidding, hard-bitten, hard-boiled, hardheaded, implacable, inexorable, inflexible, iron-fisted, ironhanded, iron-willed, no-nonsense, oppressive, relentless, tyrannical, unmerciful, unyielding
ender: **3** way **4** most, post, ward **5** wards **8** foremost
not ~: **3** lax **4** easy **7** lenient
opposite: **4** stem
toward the ~: **3** aft **5** abaft
stern-__: **5** wheel
Stern: **4** Emil, Otto **5** Isaac **6** Daniel, Howard
__ Stern: **3** Der
Stern author: Bruce Jay Friedman
Sternberg, Josef von: **8** director
film: Blonde Venus (1932)
The Blue Angel (1930)
Crime and Punishment (1935)
The Devil Is a Woman (1935)
The Docks of New York (1928)
The King Steps Out (1936)
The Last Command (1928)
Morocco (1930)
The Scarlet Empress (1934)
Shanghai Express (1932)
Stern, Daniel: **5** actor
film: Breaking Away (1979)
City Slickers (1991)
Diner (1982)
Get Crazy (1983)
Hannah and Her Sisters (1986)
Home Alone (1990)
Home Alone 2: Lost in New York (1992)
Key Exchange (1985)
Rookie of the Year (1993)
Sterne, Laurence: **6** author, writer **7** British
work: A Sentimental Journey
Tristram Shandy
Sternhagen: **7** Frances
Stern, Isaac: **9** violinist
need: **3** bow **5** resin
sternness: **5** rigor **8** iron hand **9** austerity
Stern, Otto: **8** Nobelist **9** physicist, scientist
sternum: **4** bone **10** breastbone
sternward: **3** aft **5** abaft
sternwheeler: **4** boat
steroid: **5** lipid **6** lipide
stertorous: **7** raucous **8** strident **10** breathless
stet: **7** leave in
opposite: **4** dele
Ste.-Thérèse: **4** city, town
locale: **6** Canada, Québec
stethoscope sound: **5** thump
St.-Étienne: **4** city, town
city near ~: **4** Lyon **5** Lyons
locale: **6** France
Stetson: **3** hat **10** university
athletes: **7** Hatters
locale: **6** DeLand **7** Florida
wearer: **5** Texan
Stettin river: **4** Oder, Odra
Steuben __: **5** glass
Steubenville: **4** city, town
locale: **4** Ohio
St.-Eustache: **4** city, town
locale: **6** Canada, Québec
Steve: **3** Sax **4** Biko, Owen, Zahn **5** Allen, Earle, James, Kroft, Miner, Ovett, Perry **6** Barron, Binder, Brodie, Canyon, Carver, Forbes, Garvey, Gatlin, Harris, Kanaly, Martin, Miller, Sekely **7** Buscemi, Carlton, Cauthen, Cochran, Forrest, Largent, Mandell, Marriot, McQueen, Winwood, Wozniak, Yzerman **8** Lawrence, Lukather **9** Bedrosian, Railsback **10** Guttenberg
Steve Allen Show regular: **3** Nye
stevedore: **5** lader **6** loader
concern: **5** cargo
org.: **3** ILA
__-steven: **4** even
Steven: **3** Chu **4** Culp, Hill, Jobs **5** Bauer, Weber **6** Bochco, Seagal **8** Runciman, Weinberg **9** Spielberg **10** Soderbergh
in French: **7** Etienne
in German: **6** Stefan
in Italian: **7** Stefano
in Spanish: **7** Estéban
Stevens: **3** Art, Cat, Ray **4** Mark, Risë **5** April, Craig, Inger **6** Andrew, Connie, George, Stella **7** Wallace
Stevens, Andrew spouse: Kate Jackson
Stevens, Cat
song: Another Saturday Night (1974)
Moon Shadow (1971)
Morning Has Broken (1972)
Oh Very Young (1974)
Peace Train (1971)
Wild World (1971)
Stevens, Connie
song: Kookie, Kookie (Lend Me Your Comb) (1959)
Sixteen Reasons (1960)
spouse: Eddie Fisher
Stevens, Craig spouse: Alexis Smith
Stevens, George: **8** director
film: Alice Adams (1935)
Annie Oakley (1935)
A Damsel in Distress (1937)
The Diary of Anne Frank (1959)
Giant (1956, AA)
Gunga Din (1939)
I Remember Mama (1948)
Kentucky Kernels (1934)
The More the Merrier (1943)
The Nitwits (1935)
The Only Game in Town (1970)
Penny Serenade (1941)
A Place in the Sun (1951, AA)
Quality Street (1937)
Shane (1953)
Swing Time (1936)
The Talk of the Town (1942)
Vigil in the Night (1940)
Vivacious Lady (1938)
Woman of the Year (1942)
Stevens, Inger: **7** actress
film: Cry Terror (1958)
A Dream of Kings (1969)
A Guide for the Married Man (1967)

Hang 'em High (1968)
TV: The Farmer's Daughter
Stevenson: 2 B.W. **3** Jan **5** Adlai **6** McLean, Parker, Robert
Stevenson, Jan: 6 golfer
milieu: 5 links **6** course
org.: 4 LPGA
Stevenson, Parker spouse: Kirstie Alley
Stevenson, Robert: 8 director
film: The Absent-Minded Professor (1961)
Back Street (1941)
Bedknobs and Broomsticks (1971)
Darby O'Gill & the Little People (1959)
The Gnome-Mobile (1967)
Jane Eyre (1944)
Joan of Paris (1942)
Johnny Tremain (1957)
The Love Bug (1969)
Mary Poppins (1964)
Old Yeller (1957)
The Shaggy D. A. (1976)
Son of Flubber (1963)
That Darn Cat! (1965)
To the Ends of the Earth (1948)
Walk Softly, Stranger (1950)
Stevenson, Robert Louis: 4 poet **6** author, writer **8** Scottish
home: 5 Samoa
work: The Body Snatcher
A Child's Garden of Verses
Kidnapped
The Master of Ballantrae
The Strange Case of Dr. Jekyll and Mr. Hyde
Treasure Island
Stevens Point: 4 city, town
locale: 9 Wisconsin
Stevens, Ray
song: Ahab, the Arab (1962)
Everything Is Beautiful (1970)
Gitarzan (1969)
The Streak (1974)
Stevens, Risë: 5 mezzo **6** singer **7** soprano
specialty: 5 opera
Stevens, Stella: 7 actress
film: The Ballad of Cable Hogue (1970)
The Courtship of Eddie's Father (1963)
Girls! Girls! Girls! (1962)
The Nutty Professor (1963)
The Poseidon Adventure (1972)
The Silencers (1966)
Stevens, Wallace: 4 poet
work: The Emperor of Ice Cream
The Man with the Blue Guitar
Owl's Clover
Peter Quince at the Clavier
Sunday Morning
Steverino: 5 Allen
__, Steverino!: 4 Hi-ho
__ Steve, The: 5 Tao of
Stevie: 5 Nicks, Smith **6** Wonder
Stevie __ Vaughan: 3 Ray
stew: 3 mix **4** boil, brew, cook, dahl, flap, fret, fume, fuss, hash, huff, olla, snit **5** adobo, bigos, blaff, brood, chafe, daube, gumbo, sweat, think, tizzy, worry **6** braise, burgoo, crisis, dither, fuming, hot pot, jumble, lather, medley, ragout, scouse, seethe, simmer, tumult **7** agonize, ferment, goulash, haricot, mélange, mixture, reflect, swelter, tsimmes, turmoil, tzimmes **8** cioppino, couscous, étouffée, fretting, matelote, mishmash, mixed bag, mulligan, pot-au-feu **9** Brunswick, casserole, cassoulet, commotion, confusion, inebriate, lobscouse, pepper pot, potpourri, succotash **10** blanquette, carbonnade, intoxicate, miscellany, salmagundi, turbulence
beef ~: 5 daube **10** carbonnade
Belgian ~: 10 carbonnade
British ~: 6 hot pot
Cajun ~: 8 étouffée
cooker: 5 crock
corn ~: 9 succotash
crayfish ~: 8 étouffée
East Indian ~: 4 dahl
fish ~: 8 cioppino, matelote
in a ~: 6 pacing, peeved **9** concerned **10** distressed
lamb ~: 7 haricot **10** blanquette
lentil ~: 4 dahl
mutton ~: 7 haricot
North African ~: 8 couscous
okra ~: 5 gumbo
(over): 5 brood **7** agonize
Philippine ~: 5 adobo
pod: 4 ocra, okra, okro
Polish ~: 5 bigos
sailor's ~: 6 scouse **9** lobscouse
spicy ~: 4 olla **5** salmi **6** salmis
veal ~: 10 blanquette
vegetable: 5 onion **6** carrot
vegetable ~: 7 tsimmes, tzimmes
West Indian ~: 5 blaff **9** pepper pot
white-bean ~: 9 cassoulet
__ stew: 3 in a **5** Irish **9** Brunswick
steward: 5 agent **6** factor, keeper, lackey **7** curator, lacquey **8** watchdog **9** custodian **10** manservant
ender: 3 ess
__ steward: 4 shop, wine
Stewart: 2 Al **3** J.I.M., Jon, Rod **4** Amii, Dave, John, Mary **5** Alsop, James, Payne **6** Dugald, Elaine, French, Jackie, Martha **7** Douglas, Granger, Patrick **8** Copeland
Stewart __: 6 Island
__ Stewart: 4 Fort
Stewart, Al
song: Time Passages (1978)
Year of the Cat (1977)
Stewart, Douglas: 4 poet **10** Australian, playwright
Stewart, Jackie: 5 racer **8** Scottish **9** auto racer
Stewart, James: 5 actor
film: After the Thin Man (1936)
Airport '77 (1977)
Anatomy of a Murder (1959)
Bandolero! (1968)
Bell, Book and Candle (1958)
Bend of the River (1952)
Born to Dance (1936)
Broken Arrow (1950)
Call Northside 777 (1948)
Carbine Williams (1952)
The Cheyenne Social Club (1970)
Come Live With Me (1941)
Destry Rides Again (1939)
The Far Country (1955)
The FBI Story (1959)
Flight of the Phoenix (1966)
The Glenn Miller Story (1954)
The Greatest Show on Earth (1952)
Harvey (1950)
How the West Was Won (1962)
It's a Wonderful Life (1946)
It's a Wonderful World (1939)
The Last Gangster (1937)
Made for Each Other (1939)
Magic Town (1947)
The Man From Laramie (1955)
The Man Who Knew Too Much (1956)
The Man Who Shot Liberty Valance (1962)
The Mortal Storm (1940)
Mr. Smith Goes to Washington (1939)
The Naked Spur (1953)
Next Time We Love (1936)
Night Passage (1957)
No Highway in the Sky (1951)
The Philadelphia Story (1940, AA)
Rear Window (1954)
Rope (1948)
Shenandoah (1965)
The Shootist (1976)
The Shop Around the Corner (1940)
The Shopworn Angel (1938)
The Spirit of St. Louis (1957)
The Stratton Story (1949)
Thunder Bay (1953)
Vertigo (1958)
Vivacious Lady (1938)
Winchester '73 (1950)
You Can't Take It With You (1938)
Ziegfeld Girl (1941)
Stewart, J.I.M.: 6 author, writer **8** Scottish
Stewart, Mary: 6 author, writer **7** British
work: Airs Above the Ground
The Crystal Cave
The Gabriel Hounds
The Hollow Hills
The Ivy Tree
The Last Enchantment
Madam, Will You Talk?
Touch Not the Cat
The Wicked Day
Stewart, Patrick: 5 actor
film: Conspiracy Theory (1997)
Star Trek Generations (1994)
Star Trek: Insurrection (1998)
X-Men (2000)
TV: Star Trek: The Next Generation
Stewart, Payne: 6 golfer
milieu: 5 links **6** course
org.: 3 PGA
Stewart, Rod
homeland: England
song: All for Love (1993)
Baby Jane (1983)
Crazy About Her (1989)
Da Ya Think I'm Sexy? (1978)
Downtown Train (1989)
Forever Young (1988)
Have I Told You Lately (1993)
Hot Legs (1978)
I'm Losing You (1971)
Infatuation (1984)
Lost in You (1988)
Love Touch (1986)
Maggie May (1971)
The Motown Song (1991)
My Heart Can't Tell You No (1989)
Passion (1980)
Reason to Believe (1993)
Rhythm of My Heart (1991)
Some Guys Have All the Luck (1984)
This Old Heart of Mine (1990)
Tonight's the Night (1976)
Young Turks (1981)
You're in My Heart (1977)
You Wear It Well (1972)
spouse: Rachel Hunter
stewed: 5 huffy, tight, tipsy **6** blotto **9** irrigated
fruit: 5 sauce
fruit dessert: 5 grunt
stew in one's __ juice: 3 own
stewpot, Spanish: 4 olla
St. George: 4 city, town
locale: 4 Utah **7** Bermuda
St. George's: 3 isl. **4** city, isle, town **6** island **7** capital
locale: 7 Bermuda, Grenada
St.-Georges: 4 city, town
locale: 6 Canada, Québec
St. Gotthard: 3 mts. **4** mtns. **5** range **9** mountains
locale: 4 Alps **6** Europe **11** Switzerland
St. Helena: 3 isl. **4** isle **6** island
capital: 9 Jamestown
St. Helens: 2 mt. **3** mtn. **4** peak **5** mount **7** volcano **8** mountain
locale: 8 Cascades **10** Washington
St. Helier: 4 city, port, town
locale: 6 Jersey **7** England
Stheno sister: 6 Medusa
St.-Hubert: 4 city, town
locale: 6 Canada, Québec
St.-Hyacinthe: 4 city, town
locale: 6 Canada, Québec
stibnite: 3 ore **7** mineral
stich: 5 verse
starter: 4 hemi
Stich: 7 Michael
stick: 3 bar, bat, dig, jab, jam, lay, pin, put, ram, rod, run, set **4** bear, bind, bond, cane, clog, club, fuse, glue, gore, join, last, mast, poke, pole, prod, push, rule, sink, slab, slim, snag, stab, stay, stem, twig, wand, weld **5** abide, affix, baton, catch, clasp, cling, drive, jam up, lodge, paste, place, plant, plunk, ruler, spare, spear, spike, staff, stake, stalk, stand, stave, strip, stuff, swish, unite, wedge **6** adhere, attach, baffle, billet, branch, cement, cleave, cohere, cudgel, empale, endure, fasten, hold on, impale, insert, instal, linger, pierce, plunge, recoil, remain, slight, solder, stay on, suffer, switch, take it, thrust, timber **7** install, persist, slender, stay put, support, weather **8** beanpole, bludgeon, freeze to, hold fast, position, puncture, tolerate, transfix **9** billy club, penetrate, put up with, slap ender, truncheon, withstand **10** see through
alternative: 6 carrot
around: 4 bide, last, stay, wait **5** abide, tarry **6** linger, remain
billiards ~: 3 cue
bobby's ~: 4 cosh
by: 3 aid **6** uphold **7** support **10** go to bat for
conductor's ~: 5 baton
cotton on a ~: 4 Q-Tip
ender: 3 pin, ups **4** ball, seed, tail, weed **5** tight **6** handle **7** handler
game: 6 hockey **8** lacrosse
in one's craw: 4 rile
into: 6 pierce
it out: 4 last, stay, take **6** endure, hang on, remain **7** subsist, weather **9** challenge
it to: 5 blame **6** impugn **7** revenge
lick and ~: 4 seal
make ~: 5 prove **6** attach
meat on a ~: 5 cabob, kabab, kabob, kebab, kebob
night ~: 5 baton **9** billy club
on: 3 add **5** affix **6** attach, empale, fixate, impale
one's neck out: 5 crane **6** gamble **7** venture **9** speculate
one's nose in: 6 meddle
on the ~: 5 alert, awake, aware **7** heads-up
out: 3 jut **4** poke, pout, push, show **5** bulge, pouch **6** extend **7** extrude, obtrude, project **8** overhang, protrude
out a hand to: 3 aid **4** abet, help **6** assist
pointed ~: 4 goad
riding ~: 4 crop
starter: 3 big, dip, joy, lip, non **4** chop, crab, drum, flag, mall, maul, slap, yard **5** broom, match, night **6** candle, single
to: 4 obey **5** cling **6** keep at **7** abide by **8** continue **9** accompany
together: 4 bond, glue, join, tape **5** clump, unite **6** cement, cleave, cohere

to one's guns: 6 insist 7 persist 9 persevere
up: 3 mug, rob 4 loot 5 steal
up for: 3 aid 4 back, help 6 defend, uphold 7 support, sustain 10 rally round, speak up for
walking ~: 3 bug 4 cane 5 staff 6 insect
stick ___: 3 out 4 it to 5 shift, up for 6 around, figure, insect 7 drawing
stick ___ in the water: 4 a toe
stick-___-ive: 4 to-it
stick-___-mud: 5 in-the
___ stick: 3 big, bud, cue, job 4 buff, coup, fish, gold, joss, pogo, salt 5 night 6 hockey, orange, rhythm 7 control, digging, gambrel, swagger, swizzle, walking
___ Stick: 4 Chap
stickball
locale: 6 street
marker: 5 sewer
stick by one's ___: 4 guns
Stick 'em up!: 5 reach
sticker: 3 bur, pin, tab, tag 4 seal 5 decal, label, point, price, stamp, thorn 6 ticket
sticker ___: 5 price, shock
___ sticker: 3 pot 4 frog 6 bumper
sticker-shock site: 6 car lot
stickiness: 8 humidity
sticking: 8 cohesion 9 adherence
out: 9 obtrusive
point: 3 rub 4 beef 5 thorn
to one's guns: 3 set 4 firm 5 dug in 6 dogged, steely, strong 7 adamant, decided, do-or-die 8 hard-line, locked in, resolute 9 iron-jawed, steadfast, tenacious, unbending 10 unswayable, unyielding
sticking ___: 5 place, point 7 plaster
stick-in-the-mud: 4 fogy 5 fogey 6 fossil, square 7 diehard, old fogy
stickler: 6 ramrod 7 fusspot 8 martinet 9 nitpicker 10 fussbudget
stick-on: 5 label
stick one's ___: 5 oar in
stick one's ___ out: 4 neck
stickout: 3 def, rad 4 aces, A-one, boss, braw, cool, dece, fine, gear, keen, neat, nice, phat, tuff 5 dandy, ducky, grand, great, marvy, neato, nobby, prime, slick, super, swell 6 bang on, bang-up, bonzer, bosker, choice, divine, dreamy, gnarly, groovy, lovely, peachy, slap-up, spot on, superb, terrif, tiptop, unreal, whizzo, wicked 7 amazing, awesome, capital, corking, perfect, ripping, skookum, stellar, sublime 8 dazzling, especial, eximious, fabulous, five-star, four-star, frabjous, glorious, heavenly, jim-dandy, slam-bang, smashing, splendid, sterling, superior, terrific, top-level, topnotch, very good, wondrous 9 bodacious, Endsville, excellent, exemplary, exquisite, first-rate, high-grade, hunky-dory, marvelous, sol-licker, top-flight, wonderful 10 first-class, hotsy-totsy, jack-a-dandy, peachy-keen, phenomenal, remarkable, stupendous, super-duper
stickpin: 7 jewelry
sticks: 5 wilds 6 claves, Podunk 7 boonies 8 frontier 9 backwoods, boondocks, outskirts 10 wilderness
it comes in ~: 3 gum
one from the ~: 4 rube 5 yokel 7 hayseed
starter: 6 fiddle
Sticks and Bones author: David Rabe
stickshift selection: 3 low 4 gear, park 5 first, third 6 second 7 reverse
stick-to-itiveness: 4 grit, zeal 8 tenacity
stick to one's ___: 4 guns, ribs
stickum: 4 bond, glue 5 paste 6 cement 8 adhesive, fixative, mucilage
stickup: 3 job 5 heist, theft 6 holdup 7 robbery 8 thievery
stick up ___: 3 for
Stick-Ups alternative: 5 Glade 6 Wizard 7 Airwick, Renuzit
sticky: 4 damp, dank, icky 5 close, gluey, gooey, gummy, gunky, hairy, humid, mucky, muggy, nasty, rough, sappy, soggy, tacky, tight 6 clammy, clayey, knotty, rugged, sirupy, static, steamy, stuffy, sultry, sweaty, syrupy, thorny, tricky 7 awkward, clayish, painful, viscose, viscous 8 adhesive, clinging, delicate, tropical 9 difficult, glutinous, laborious, strenuous, tenacious 10 formidable, oppressive, sweltering, unpleasant
combining form: 5 gloeo-, gloio-
place: 4 mire
situation: 4 bind
stuff: 3 goo, gum 4 glue, goop, gunk 5 sirup, syrup
sweet: 3 bun 5 honey
sticky ___: 3 bun, end 6 wicket 7 fingers
Sticky ___: 4 Note
sticky-fingered: 8 thieving, thievish
Stieglitz: 6 Alfred
need: 4 lens 6 camera
Stieglitz, Alfred
spouse: Georgia O'Keeffe
stiff: 3 set 4 cold, dear, firm, hard, high, lame, prim, snug, taut, wiry 5 aloof, brisk, cruel, exact, fixed, great, harsh, heavy, rigid, rusty, sharp, solid, stark, steep, stony, tense, thick, tight, tough, undue 6 creaky, forced, formal, frigid, frozen, jelled, numbed, potent, severe, steely, stoney, strict, strong, trying, wooden, worker 7 arduous, austere, bookish, brittle, chilled, default, distant, drastic, extreme, hard-set, jellied, labored, pompous, starchy, stately, staunch, stilted, swindle, uptight 8 annealed, cemented, exacting, grueling, hardened, immobile, mannered, ossified, pitiless, powerful, priggish, rigorous, starched, strained, stubborn, towering, ungainly, unlimber, vigorous 9 congealed, difficult, excessive, expensive, fatiguing, graceless, hidebound, impliable, laborious, obstinate, petrified, resistant, strenuous, stringent, thickened, unbending, unnatural, unpliable, victimize 10 artificial, contracted, exorbitant, formidable, hardheaded, headstrong, high-priced, inexorable, inflexible, insociable, mechanical, oppressive, out of shape, relentless, solidified, unamenable, unbendable, ungraceful, unyielding
bindle ~: 3 bum 4 hobo 5 tramp
having a ~ upper lip: 5 stoic
in the joints: 4 achy
keep a ~ lower lip: 4 fume, mope, sulk 5 brood, frown 6 glower
keep a ~ upper lip: 4 cope 6 bear up, endure, hang in
working ~: 6 worker 7 laborer
stiff ___ board: 3 as a
stiff ___ lip: 5 upper
stiff-___: 3 arm 6 necked
___ stiff: 5 bored 6 bindle 7 working
stiffen: 3 fix, gel, set 4 clot, firm, gird, jell, prop, tone 5 brace, build, chill, shore, steel, tense 6 anneal, beef up, cement, curdle, freeze, gelate, harden, ossify, prop up, starch, steady, temper, tone up 7 bolster, brace up, build up, burgeon, congeal, develop, empower, enhance, fortify, inflate, petrify, shore up, support, thicken, tighten, toughen 8 bourgeon, buttress, condense, energize, indurate, solidify, vitalize 9 coagulate, intensify, reinforce, stabilize 10 gelatinize, inspissate, invigorate, strengthen
stiff-necked: 3 set 4 prim 5 stern 6 wilful 7 willful 8 stubborn 9 pigheaded
stiffness: 4 kink 5 cramp, spine 6 starch 7 tension, texture 8 distance, hardness 9 austerity
lose ~: 3 sag 4 wilt 5 droop
___ stiff upper lip: 5 keep a
stifle: 3 gag 4 cork, curb, hush, stop 5 check, choke, quell, sit on 6 clam up, dampen, deaden, hush up, keep in, muffle, muzzle, quench, shut up, squash 7 contain, cover up, prevent, repress, silence, smother, squelch, torpedo 8 black out, restrain, stagnate, strangle, suppress, throttle 9 choke back, clamp down, constrain, crack down, keep quiet, keep still 10 extinguish, hold it down, keep a lid on, keep in line
stifled: 4 weak 6 pent-up 8 reined in
stifling: 5 close 6 stuffy, sultry, torrid 8 tropical 10 equatorial, oppressive, sweltering
Stifter, Adalbert: 6 author, writer 8 Austrian
Stigler, George: 8 Nobelist 9 economist
Stiglitz, Joseph: 8 Nobelist 9 economist
stigma: 4 blot, mark, scar, slur, spot 5 blame, brand, odium, shame, stain, taint 6 blotch 7 blemish 8 disgrace, dishonor, reproach 9 black mark, disrepute 10 imputation
stigmatize: 5 brand, shame, smear, stain, sully, taint 6 defame 7 asperse 8 denounce, disgrace, throw mud 9 discredit, implicate 10 calumniate
stile: 7 ingress
starter: 4 turn
Stiles: 4 Ryan 5 Julia
stiletto: 5 knife, point 6 bodkin, dagger 7 poniard, sidearm
use a ~: 4 stab
stiletto ___: 4 heel
Stiletto author: Harold Robbins
still: 3 lay, tho, yet 4 calm, ease, even, hush, idle, lull, stop 5 as yet, inert, photo, quell, quiet, stall 6 and yet, at rest, but yet, even so, halted, muffle, muzzle, placid, serene, settle, shut up, silent, soften, soothe, static, though 7 alembic, assuage, dormant, even now, however, put down, silence 8 calmness, even then, immobile, inactive, in repose, overcome, peaceful, stagnant, unmoving, until now 9 in any case, noiseless, peaceable, quiescent, soundless, to this day, voiceless 10 all the same, at this time, in any event, motionless, regardless, untroubled
and all: 3 yet 6 though
be ~: 5 relax 8 calm down
in the game: 4 live 5 alive
keep ~: 3 gag 4 hush 5 choke, quiet, shush 6 muzzle, shut up, stifle 7 silence 8 pipe down
life: 6 canvas 8 painting
not ~: 5 antsy, hyper, jumpy, noisy 6 moving, on edge 7 fidgety, jittery 8 restless
product: 5 hooch 6 hootch 9 moonshine
sit ~ for: 3 let 5 abide, allow 6 accept 8 tolerate
stand ~: 5 stall 6 freeze 8 stagnate
standing ~: 6 static
still ___: 4 hunt, life, pack, wine 5 alarm, water 7 trailer
___-still: 5 stock
Still (song)
artist: Bill Anderson, Commodores
Still ___: 4 Life 5 I Rise
still and ___: 3 all
Still Breathing (1998 film)
cast: Brendan Fraser, Joanna Going, Celeste Holm, Ann Magnuson
Still Crazy star: 3 Rea
Stille ___: 5 Nacht
stilled: 5 quiet 6 silent 8 hushed up
Stiller, Ben: 5 actor 8 director
film: The Cable Guy (1996)
Keeping the Faith (2000)
Meet the Parents (2000)
Permanent Midnight (1998)
Reality Bites (1994)
The Royal Tenenbaums (2001)
There's Something About Mary (1998)
Zero Effect (1998)
Zoolander (2001)
parent: Anne Meara, Jerry Stiller
Stiller, Jerry: 5 actor 8 comedian
film: The Independent (2001)
Seize the Day (1986)
spouse: Anne Meara
TV: Seinfeld
Still Falls the Rain author: Edith Sitwell
___ Still Felt: 5 In Joy
Still I Rise author: Maya Angelou
Still Life author: A.S. Byatt
still life subject: 4 ewer, pear 5 fruit 6 banana
Still Life with Coffee artist: 4 Miró
Still Me author: 5 Reeve
stillness: 4 calm, hush, lull, rest 5 peace, quiet 6 repose 7 silence 8 calmness, serenity
Stillness at Appomattox, A author: Bruce Catton
___ Still of the Night: 5 In the
Stillson ___: 6 wrench
Stills, Stephen
member: Crosby, Stills & Nash
song: Love the One You're With (1970)
___ Still the One: 5 You're
Still the One (1976 song) artist: Orleans
Still the Same (1978 song) artist: Bob Seger
Stillwatch author: Mary Higgins Clark
Stillwater: 4 city, town
athletes: 7 Cowboys
locale: 8 Oklahoma
school: 3 OSU
stilt: 4 bird, pole, post 5 lanky, spare 7 support 9 elongator, shorebird
cousin: 5 egret, stork 6 avocet
stilted: 4 prim 5 stiff 6 forced, formal, stuffy, turgid, wooden 7 bookish, flowery, genteel, labored, pompous, prudish 8 affected, decorous, inflated, mannered, pedantic, sonorous 9 bombastic, high-flown, overblown, ponderous, unnatural 10 artificial, pedantical, rhetorical, theatrical
Stilton: 6 cheese
Stimpy: 3 cat 4 toon
pal: 3 Ren
stimulant: 4 whet 5 tonic 6 bracer, coffee 8 pick-me-up 9 analeptic, energizer, incentive
stimulate: 3 jog 4 abet, goad, grab, help, hook, prod, send, spur, stir, urge, wake, whet 5 drive, evoke, hop up, impel, juice, key up, liven, pep up, pique, rouse, spark, waken 6 arouse, bestir, excite, fillip, fire up, foment, incite, kindle, perk up, prompt, pump up, stir up, thrill, tickle, turn on, vivify, wake up, work up 7 actuate, animate,

enflame, enliven, inflame, inspire, juice up, liven up, massage, nurture, promote, provoke, quicken, refresh, steam up, trigger 8 activate, energize, engender, enspirit, inspirit, interest, motivate, vitalize 9 challenge, electrify, entertain, fascinate, galvanize, impassion, instigate, titillate 10 accelerate, exhilarate, invigorate, predispose
stimulating: 5 brisk, crisp, fresh 6 lively, strong 7 bracing, healthy, piquant 8 readable 9 evocative
hardly ~: 4 blah 5 vapid 6 boring 8 tiresome
stimulation: 4 kick 5 spice
stimulus: 4 fuel, goad, kick, push, spur, urge 5 force, tonic 6 bracer 7 impetus, impulse 8 catalyst, pick-me-up 9 incentive 10 incitement, inducement, propellant
respond to a ~: 5 react
Stine: 2 R.L.
sting: 3 con 4 bilk, bite, burn, gull, hoax, hurt, pain, pang, rook, scam, trap 5 fraud, pique, prick, setup, smart, wound 6 con job, dupery, entrap, humbug, injury, needle, offend, tingle 7 con game, prickle, swindle 8 irritate, pungency, trickery 9 deception, victimize 10 overcharge, run a game on
artist: 6 conman
ender: 3 ray
FBI ~: 6 Abscam
get in a ~: 6 entrap
react to a ~: 5 wince
take the ~ out: 4 lull 5 allay 6 lessen, smooth, soothe, temper 7 mollify
target: 4 mark 5 patsy 6 pigeon, victim
winkle: 5 shell 8 seashell
Sting
born: Gordon Sumner
song: All for Love (1993)
All This Time (1991)
Fortress Around Your Heart (1985)
If You Love Somebody Set Them Free (1985)
We'll Be Together (1987)
stinger: 3 bee 4 barb, wasp 5 drink 6 hornet 8 beverage, cocktail
flying ~: 3 bee 4 wasp 6 hornet
ingredient: 6 brandy
jellyfish ~: 5 cnida
part of an insect's ~: 5 oopod
stinginess: 6 thrift 9 frugality, parsimony
stinging: 4 acid, cold, sour 5 itchy, sharp 6 biting, bitter 7 caustic, cutting, intense, painful, peppery, piquant, pungent, satiric 8 scathing 9 sarcastic, satirical, vitriolic
comment: 4 barb
insect: 3 bee 4 wasp 6 hornet
Sting like a bee boxer: 3 Ali
stingo: 4 beer
stingray: 4 fish
Sting Ray: 3 car 4 auto 5 Chevy 8 Corvette 9 Chevrolet, sports car 10 automobile
Sting, The (1973 film)
cast: Paul Newman, Robert Redford, Robert Shaw
director: George Roy Hill
game: 5 poker
stingy: 4 mean 5 chary, cheap, close, petty, spare, tight 6 frugal, greedy, meager, measly, paltry, saving, scurvy, shabby, skimpy 7 chintzy, miserly, selfish, sparing, thrifty 8 churlish, grasping, grudging, skimping, ungiving 9 illiberal, mercenary, pennywise, penurious, scrimping 10 avaricious, economical, inadequate, pinchpenny, skinflinty, ungenerous
be ~: 5 skimp, stint
one: 5 miser, piker 10 cheapskate
stink: 4 fuss, odor, reek, to-do 5 fetor, furor, odour, smell 6 foetor, stench, uproar 7 malodor, scandal 8 brouhaha, fetidity, foulness 9 commotion, complaint, fetidness, grievance, hue and cry
ender: 3 bug, pot 4 aroo, ball, eroo, horn, weed, wood 5 stone
make a ~: 7 protest
social ~: 4 flap
stink __: 3 bug 4 bomb
__ stink: 5 make a
stinkbug: 6 insect
stinker: 3 cur 4 toad 5 knave, louse, rogue, scamp, skunk 6 bad egg, bad guy 10 holy terror
stinkhorn: 6 fungus
stinking: 3 bad 4 base, foul, grim, olid, poor, rank, vile 5 awful, fetid, funky, lousy, nasty, reeky, stale, woful 6 crumby, crummy, dismal, foetid, frowsy, frowzy, horrid, odious, rancid, rotten, smelly, strong, sweaty, woeful 7 accurst, baleful, baneful, beastly, doleful, ghastly, noisome, noxious, odorous, pungent, reeking, unclean 8 accursed, dreadful, God-awful, grievous, horrible, inferior, mephitic, shameful, terrible, unsavory, wretched 9 abhorrent, appalling, atrocious, defective, execrable, frightful, insidious, loathsome, miserable, offensive, revolting 10 abominable, deplorable, despicable, detestable, disastrous, disgusting, horrendous, lamentable, malodorous
stinkpot: 6 animal 7 reptile
__ Stinks: 4 Love
stinky
see stinking
stint: 3 bit, job 4 bird, curb, duty, lack, role, save, task, term, time, tour, turn, work 5 chore, hitch, limit, shift, spare, spell 6 grudge, scrape, scrimp 7 inhibit, skimp on, stretch 8 begrudge, hold back, restrict, withhold 9 constrain, economize, sandpiper 10 assignment, constraint, cut corners, engagement, penny-pinch, tour of duty
stinted: 6 meager 10 inadequate
stipe: 5 stalk 7 petiole
Stipe: 7 Michael
stipend: 3 fee, pay 4 take, wage 5 grant, wages 6 salary 7 pension 8 benefice, gratuity, largesse 9 allowance, emolument
stipple: 3 dot 4 spot 5 fleck, paint 7 spatter, speckle
stipulate: 3 set 4 name 5 agree, posit, state 6 detail, impose, pledge 7 bargain, lay down, promise, provide, require, specify 8 contract, spell out 9 condition, designate, guarantee, prescribe 10 insist upon, provide for
stipulated: 3 set 9 customary
stipulation: 4 term 5 order 6 clause, string 7 promise, proviso 8 contract, covenant 9 agreement, condition, fine print, provision, requisite
stir: 3 ado, din, get, jog, mix, pen, row 4 beat, fire, flap, fuss, jail, move, poke, poky, rile, rout, send, spur, to-do, toss, wake, whet, whip 5 awake, blend, budge, clink, furor, get up, hoo-ha, hop up, jails, joint, pique, pokey, psych, rally, rouse, roust, shift, spark, spook, waken, whisk 6 action, affect, arouse, awaken, buck up, bustle, come to, cooler, excite, fidget, flurry, hoopla, hubbub, incite, kindle, lockup, muddle, pother, prison, prompt, quiver, racket, recall, ruckus, rustle, splash, thrill, tumult, uproar, wake up, whip up, work up 7 agitate, enflame, ferment, flutter, hearten, hoosgow, inflame, inspire, provoke, quicken, slammer, smolder, swizzle, tremble, trigger, turmoil 8 activate, big house, brouhaha, disorder, disquiet, embolden, energize, enspirit, hoosegow, imbolden, inspirit, interest, motivate, psyche up, smoulder 9 calaboose, commotion, electrify, encourage, enhearten, galvanize, get moving, impassion, make waves, move about, recollect, sensation, shake a leg, stimulate, transport 10 excitement, get a move on, invigorate
add, then ~: 5 mix in
cause a ~: 5 act up
in: 3 add
the air: 3 fan
up: 3 get 4 brew, fire, goad, prod, rile, roil, spur, urge, wake 5 anger, churn, egg on, impel, liven, raise, rally, rouse, roust, shake, spark, stoke, waken 6 arouse, awaken, excite, foment, incite, jostle, justle 7 ferment, fluster, provoke, trouble 8 motivate 9 impassion, instigate, stimulate
stir-__: 3 fry 5 crazy, fried
Stir __: 4 It Up 5 Crazy
Stir Crazy (1980 film)
cast: Georg Sanford Brown, Richard Pryor, Gene Wilder
director: Sidney Poitier
stir-fry pan: 3 wok
Stir It Up (1973 song) artist: Johnny Nash
Stirling: 4 city, Moss, town
locale: 8 Scotland
Stir of Echoes (1999 film)
cast: Kevin Bacon, Illeana Douglas, Kevin Dunn, Kathryn Erbe
director: David Koepp
stirps: 5 stock 7 lineage
stirred: 7 touched
up: 4 agog 9 turbulent 10 disordered
stirrer: 5 spoon
__ stirreth up strifes: 6 Hatred
stirring: 5 about, afoot, alive, astir, awake 6 lively, motion, moving 7 graphic 8 electric, eloquent, imposing, in motion, movement, touching 9 emotional, evocative, graphical, thrilling 10 expressive, impressive, intoxicant, passionate
stirrup: 4 bone
and hammer partner: 5 anvil
bone: 6 stapes
locale: 3 ear
stirrup __: 3 cup, jar 4 bone, pump, vase 5 strap 7 leather
stitch: 3 sew 4 knit, mend, pain, pang, purl, tack 5 baste, cable, patch, run up, sew up, shred 6 misery, repair, suture, twinge 7 crochet 8 particle 9 embroider
hidden ~: 6 inseam
loosely: 5 baste
sewing ~: 4 purl
starter: 3 hem, top 4 back, slip, whip 7 feather
without a ~: 4 bare, nude 5 naked
__ stitch: 4 knot, lock, loop, purl, rope, slip, tent 5 cable, catch, chain, close, flame, picot, satin 6 garter, kettle, ladder, saddle 7 blanket, running
__-stitch: 4 slip, wire 5 cross 7 blanket, machine
stitches
be in ~: 5 laugh
line of ~: 4 seam
stiver: 4 coin 5 money
...St. Ives, __ a man...: 4 I met
St. Jacques, Raymond: 5 actor
film: Cotton Comes to Harlem (1970)
Lost in the Stars (1974)
Up Tight (1968)
St. James's __: 6 Palace
St.-Jérôme: 4 city, town
locale: 6 Canada, Québec
St. John: 4 city, Jill, town 5 Betta, river
locale: 5 Maine 6 Canada
St.-John: 5 Perse
St. John, Jill
spouse: Jack Jones, Robert Wagner
St. Johns: 5 river
locale: 7 Florida
St. John's: 4 city, town 7 capital 10 university
conference: 7 Big East
locale: 6 Canada 7 Antigua
school: 8 Memorial
school locale: 6 Queens 7 Jamaica, New York
St. John's __: 3 Day, Eve 5 Night
St. John's-__: 5 bread
St. John's Night author: Henrik Ibsen
St. Joseph: 4 city, town 7 aspirin
alternative: 3 APF 4 Cope 5 Advil, Aleve, Bayer 6 Anacin, Datril, Motrin 7 Ecotrin, Tylenol 8 Bufferin, Excedrin, Vanquish 9 Ascriptin
locale: 8 Missouri
stk.
see stock
St. Kitts and Nevis: 4 isls. 5 isles 6 nation 7 country, islands
capital: 10 Basseterre
locale: 10 West Indies
St.-Lambert: 4 city, town
locale: 6 Canada, Québec
St. Laurent: 4 Yves
St.-Laurent: 4 city, town
locale: 6 Canada, Québec
St. Lawrence: 4 gulf 5 river 6 seaway
city on the ~: 8 Montreal
explorer: 7 Cartier
river to the ~: 6 Ottawa 8 Saguenay 9 Richelieu
St.-Léonard: 4 city, town
locale: 6 Canada, Québec
St.-Lô: 4 city, town
locale: 6 France, Manche
St. Louis: 4 city, port, town
locale: 8 Missouri
pro team: 4 Rams 5 Blues 9 Cardinals
river: 11 Mississippi
St. Louis Blues (1939 film)
cast: Tito Guizar, Dorothy Lamour, Lloyd Nolan
director: Raoul Walsh
St. Louis Blues composer: 5 Handy
St. Lucia: 3 isl. 4 isle 6 island, nation 7 country
capital: 8 Castries
St. Malo: 4 city, gulf, port, town
locale: 6 France
river: 5 Rance
__ St. Mark, The: 5 Eve of
St. Martin: 3 isl. 4 isle 6 island
locale: 10 West Indies
St. Marys: 5 river
locale: 8 Michigan
stoa: 5 Greek 6 arcade 7 portico
Stoa of __: 7 Hadrian
stoat: 6 ermine, weasel
relative: 4 mink 5 fitch, otter, ratel, sable, skunk, tayra 6 badger, ferret, marten 7 foumart, polecat 8 carcajou, foulmart, kolinsky, muishond 9 wolverine
stock: 3 kin 4 clan, cows, fill, folk, fund, have, herd, hogs, keep, line, mdse., mine, pigs, save, stem 5 amass, array, asset, banal, basic, breed, broth, cache, carry, count, equip, faith, flock, goods, hoard, lay in, paper, plant, sheep, store, swine, tribe, trite, trust, typic, uplay, usual, wares 6 assets, beasts, cattle, common, cravat, deal

in, family, flower, gather, handle, horses, liquor, load up, normal, origin, outfit, shares, strain, supply **7** animals, backlog, capital, descent, furnish, kindred, lineage, popular, produce, progeny, provide, regular, reserve, routine, typical, variety, worn-out **8** ancestry, bouillon, everyday, gold mine, judgment, material, ordinary, overused, pedigree, reliance, standard, stow away, supplies **9** blue chips, customary, forebears, hackneyed, inebriant, inventory, parentage, posterity, provision, repertory, replenish, reservoir, selection **10** background, collection, confidence, dependance, dependence, estimation, evaluation, extraction, investment, threadbare, uninspired
acquisition pgm.: 4 ESOP
buy ~: 6 invest
counterpart: 4 bond
diet: 3 hay
ender: 3 ade, age, man, men, pot **4** fish, pile, room, yard **5** owner **6** broker, holder, jobber, piling, taking **7** breeder, holding **8** breeding **9** brokerage
have in ~: 4 keep, sell **5** carry **6** handle
holder: 6 corral
in ~: 4 here **9** available **10** obtainable
in trade: 5 asset
lock, ~ and barrel: 5 whole **6** in toto, wholly
of goods: 4 line
product: 4 soup
starter: 3 bit, die, gun, pen **4** feed, head, live, root, tail **5** drill **6** rudder **8** laughing
take ~: 10 scrutinize
take ~ in: 6 accept **7** believe
take ~ of: 4 note **5** audit **6** assess, survey
ticker inventor: 6 Edison
ticker output: 4 tape
see also stock market
stock __: 3 boy, car **4** book, dove, farm, shot **5** clerk, guard, horse, power **6** broker, ledger, market, option, record, saddle, ticker **7** buyback, company, footage, raising
stock-__: 5 route, still
stock-__ race: 3 car
__ stock: 3 sea **4** open, seed, take **5** joint, no-par, out of, penny, white **6** common, equity, letter, summer **7** capital, glamour, phantom, rolling
__ Stock: 6 Summer
stockade: 4 brig, jail, wall **5** fence **6** corral, prison **8** imprison **9** enclosure
stockade __: 5 fence
stockaded village: 5 craal, kraal
__, stock and barrel: 4 lock
Stockard: 8 Channing
stock-car racing: 5 sport
Stockhausen: 9 Karlheinz
stockholder: 8 investor
distribution: 8 dividend
vote: 5 proxy
Stockholm: 4 city, port, town **7** capital
airline to ~: 3 SAS
lake: 5 Malar
locale: 6 Sweden
prize: 5 Nobel
stock in __: 5 trade
__ stock in: 3 put **4** take
stocking: 7 hosiery
cap: 5 toque, tuque
filler: 3 leg
in French: 3 bas
material: 4 mesh, silk **5** lisle
no longer ~: 5 out of
part: 3 toe **4** foot
run in Britain: 6 ladder
shade: 4 ecru
snag: 3 run
starter: 4 blue
stuffer: 3 toy **4** coal, gift
stocking __: 3 cap **4** mask **6** stitch **7** stuffer
__ stocking: 4 body
__-stocking: 4 silk
stockings: 4 hose **6** nylons **7** hosiery, legwear
make ~: 4 knit
stockings __ hung..., The: 4 were
__ Stockings: 4 Silk
__-Stocking Tales: 7 Leather
stockman: 6 cowboy **7** cowpoke **8** wrangler
stock market: 3 OTC **4** AMEX, mart, NYSE **6** bourse, NASDAQ **10** Wall Street
figure: 3 low **4** high **6** volume
gamble: 5 flier, flyer
holding: 3 lot
listing: 5 quote
membership: 4 seat
new ~ entry: 3 IPO
option: 3 put **4** call
phrase: 5 at par
remove from the ~: 6 delist
statistic: 5 yield
unit: 5 share
volatility measurement: 4 beta
stockpile: 4 heap, mass, pile, save **5** amass, cache, hoard, put by, store, trove **6** garner, gather, load up, supply **7** arsenal, backlog, buildup, collect, lay away, put away, reserve **8** gather up, hold on to, put aside, salt away **9** gathering, inventory, reservoir, warehouse **10** accumulate, collection, cumulation
Stockport: 4 city, town
locale: 7 England
stockroom: 9 warehouse
need: 6 ladder
stocks and __: 5 bonds
stock-still: 5 inert **6** frozen **8** immobile, unmoving **10** motionless, stationary
Stockton: 4 city, John, town
locale: 10 California
Stockton-on-__: 4 Tees
Stockwell, Dean: 5 actor
film: Air Force One (1997)
Backtrack (1989)
The Boy With the Green Hair (1948)
Compulsion (1959)
Down to the Sea in Ships (1949)
The Happy Years (1950)
Kim (1950)
Long Day's Journey Into Night (1962)
Married to the Mob (1988)
Mr. Wrong (1996)
The Secret Garden (1949)
Sons and Lovers (1960)
Stars in My Crown (1950)
TV: Quantum Leap
stocky: 4 hale, iron, wiry **5** beefy, burly, fubsy, hardy, hefty, hunky, husky, lusty, obese, plump, pudgy, pursy, short, solid, squat, stout, thick, tough **6** brawny, chubby, chunky, fleshy, hearty, mighty, portly, potent, pyknic, robust, rotund, rugged, sinewy, steely, stubby, sturdy, virile, zaftig, zoftig **7** adipose, doughty, paunchy **8** athletic, forceful, heavyset, indurate, muscular, powerful, puissant, roly-poly, stalwart, thickset, vigorous **9** Atlantean, corpulent, filled-out, Herculean, strapping, well-built **10** able-bodied, overweight, red-blooded, well-padded
stockyard group: 4 herd
stodgy: 4 dull **5** dowdy, heavy, staid, unfun **6** boring, formal, stuffy **7** labored, tedious **8** pedantic, plodding **9** ponderous **10** enervating, monotonous, pedantical, pedestrian, unexciting
one: 4 fogy **5** fogey **7** old fogy **8** old fogey
stogie: 4 boot, shoe **5** cigar, smoke **8** footwear
cousin: 5 claro
stoic: 4 calm, cool **5** aloof, sober, staid **6** at ease, low-key, mellow, placid, sedate, serene, stolid **7** at peace, austere, patient, relaxed, unmoved **8** carefree, composed, detached, enduring, laid-back, resigned, tranquil **9** apathetic, collected, impassive, temperate, unexcited, unruffled **10** nonchalant, phlegmatic, poker-faced, unagitated, untroubled
one: 6 iceman
stoical
see stoic
stoicism: 8 patience **9** austerity
practice ~: 5 enure, inure
Stoic, The author: Theodore Dreiser
Stojko: 5 Elvis
stoke: 4 feed, fuel **6** stir up
ender: 4 hold, hole
Stokely: 10 Carmichael
Stoke-on-Trent: 4 city, town
locale: 7 England
Stoker, Bram: 6 author, writer
work: Dracula
Stokes, George: 9 physicist
Stokowski, Leopold: 9 conductor
STOL: 5 plane
stola: 4 gown, robe **5** tunic
stole: 3 boa, fur **4** wrap **5** amice, scarf, shawl **7** garment, orarion, orarium **8** fur piece
material: 4 mink **5** sable **10** chinchilla
stolen: 3 hot
goods: 4 loot, swag **5** booty
goods outlet: 5 fence
Stolen Blessings author: Lawrence Sanders
Stolen Kisses (1968 film) director: François Truffaut
Stolen Summer (2002 film)
cast: Bonnie Hunt, Kevin Pollak, Aidan Quinn
director: Pete Jones
Stoli: 5 vodka
rival: 5 Popov **8** Smirnoff
stolid: 4 cool, dull, dumb, slow **5** dense, heavy, inert, stoic **6** bovine, obtuse, wooden **7** lumpish, passive, stoical **8** lubberly **9** apathetic, impassive, lethargic, unruffled **10** phlegmatic, unagitated, unreactive
stolidity: 7 laxness **8** laziness
Stolle, Fred: 7 netster **9** tennis pro
milieu: 5 court
stollen: 4 cake
Stoller: 4 Mike **5** Ilona
Stoloff: 3 Ben **6** Morris
Stoloff, Morris song: Moonglow (1956)
stolon: 5 shoot
Stoltz, Eric: 5 actor
film: Fluke (1995)
Lionheart (1987)
Mask (1985)
Mr. Jealousy (1998)
Some Kind of Wonderful (1987)
The Waterdance (1992)
Stolze: 4 Lena
stoma: 4 pore
stomach: 3 gut, maw, pot, tum **4** bear, craw, lump, take **5** abide, belly, brook, stand, stick, taste, tummy, valor **6** accept, endure, liking, omasum, paunch, relish, suffer **7** abdomen, gizzard, prowess, sustain, swallow **8** appetite, bear with, overlook, potbelly, stand for, tolerate **9** put up with, spare tire
animal ~: 3 maw **4** craw
butterflies in the ~: 6 nerves
combining form: 4 celi- **5** celio-, coeli-, gastr-, ventr- **6** coelio-, gaster-, gastro-, ventri-, ventro- **7** gastero-
complaint: 5 growl **6** rumble
cow ~: 5 rumen **6** omasum
ender: 4 ache
have no ~ for: 4 hate **5** abhor **6** detest, loathe **7** dislike
muscles: 3 abs
on one's ~: 5 prone
part of the ~: 6 cardia
problem: 3 gas **4** acid **5** agita
soother: 5 Bromo **6** bicarb
tightener: 5 sit up
turn one's ~: 6 revolt, sicken
stomach __: 4 acid
stomp: 4 step **5** clump, crush, dance, pound, storm, tramp **6** stride **7** clobber, trample, trounce
around: 4 rage
__ Stomp: 7 Bristol
Stompin' __ Savoy: 5 at the
stomping ground: 4 turf **5** haunt **6** domain, locale, region, sphere **7** hangout, quarter **8** locality **9** territory
stone: 3 gem, ore, pit **4** crag, pelt, rock, slab **5** flint, grain, jewel, throw **6** gravel, jasper, pebble **7** boulder, bowlder, crystal, jewelry, mineral, trinket **8** landmark, monument **9** inebriate **10** intoxicate
altar ~: 5 mensa
ancient ~ implement: 6 amgarn
artifact: 6 eolith
basin: 6 lavabo
cherry ~: 3 pit
chip: 5 galet, spall **6** gallet, garret
combining form: 4 -lith, petr- **5** litho-, petri-, petro-
ender: 3 cat, fly **4** chat, crop, fish, wall, ware, wash, work, wort **5** mason **6** cutter, roller, worker **7** cutting, hearted, masonry
face with ~: 5 revet
grinding ~: 4 mano
hollow ~: 5 geode
launcher: 5 sling **9** slingshot
leave no ~ unturned: 4 seek **5** scour **6** search, strive **7** persist, ransack, rummage **9** persevere
lily: 6 fossil
marker: 4 carn **5** cairn
masonry ~: 6 ashlar, ashler
monument: 5 stela, stele
paving ~: 4 sett **5** favus **6** cobble
piece: 4 slab
precious ~: 3 gem **4** ruby **5** jewel **7** emerald
prehistoric ~ tower: 6 chulpa **7** chullpa
rolling ~: 5 rover **7** drifter, vagrant **8** wanderer
Roman vase ~: 5 murra **6** murrha
set in ~: 5 solid **6** steady **7** adamant **9** immovable, unbending **10** inexorable
starter: 3 cap, gem, key, mud, oil, pot, sun, tin **4** blue, brim, burr, cope, curb, drip, fire, flag, flow, foot, free, gall, gold, hail, holy, iron, jack, lime, load, lode, marl, mile, mill, moon, pipe, sand, silt, soap, toad, turn, vein, whet **5** birth, blood, brown, chalk, cling, field, green, grind, pitch, rhine, snake, stink, touch **6** cherry, cobble, corner, hearth, rotten **7** pudding, thunder **8** stepping
turn to ~: 6 freeze **7** petrify

stone __: **4** bass, crab, lily, mint, pine **5** china, fruit, plant **6** curlew, fungus, marten **7** lantern, parsley
stone-__: **5** broke, faced
stone-__ wheat: **6** ground
__ stone: **3** ayr, bed, cut, egg, pad **4** Caen, cast, clay, lich, ring **5** altar, Coade, Druid, fairy, logan, set in **6** Amazon, fungus, living, loggan, pumice **7** Blarney, colored, curling, logging, pudding, rocking, Rosetta, through
__-stone: **4** rune
Stone: **3** Sid, Sly **4** Ezra, Lucy, Matt **5** Lewis, river **6** Irving, Jagger, Norman, Oliver, Sharon **7** Milburn, Richard **8** Phillips
  locale: **9** Tennessee
Stone __: **3** Age **4** Kiss, Love
Stone __, GA: **8** Mountain
Stone __ Pilots: **6** Temple
__ Stone: **7** Moabite, Rolling, Steppin'
Stone Age relic: **6** eolith
Stone Boy, The (1984 film)
  cast: Glenn Close, Robert Duvall, Jason Presson
  director: Christopher Cain
stone-broke: **4** poor **8** strapped **9** destitute
stonechat: **4** bird
stonecrop: **5** orpin, sedum
stonecutter tool: **6** chisel
Stoned Love (1970 song) artist: Supremes
Stoned Soul Picnic (1968 song)
  artist: Fifth Dimension
  composer: **4** Nyro
stone field, name meaning: **7** Stanley
Stone for Danny Fisher, A author: Harold Robbins
...stone gathers no __: **4** moss
stone-ground __: **5** wheat
Stoneham: **4** city, town
  locale: **4** Mass.
Stonehenge: **8** monument
  builder: **4** Celt **5** druid
  river near ~: **4** Avon
Stone, Irving: **6** author, writer
  work: Adversary in the House
    The Agony and the Ecstasy
    Depths of Glory
    Love Is Eternal
    Lust for Life
    The Origin
    Sailor on Horseback
Stone Kiss author: Faye Kellerman
Stone, Lewis: **5** actor
  film: Life Begins for Andy Hardy (1941)
    Love Finds Andy Hardy (1938)
    The Mystery of Mr. X (1934)
    The Sin of Madelon Claudet (1931)
    Three Godfathers (1936)
    Treasure Island (1934)
    A Woman of Affairs (1928)
stonelike: **4** hard **7** lithoid **9** lithoidal
Stone Love (1987 song) artist: Kool and the Gang
stonemason, name meaning: **5** Dyker
Stone of __: **5** Scone
stone of help, name meaning: **8** Ebenezer
Stone, Oliver: **8** director
  film: Any Given Sunday (1999)
    Born on the Fourth of July (1989, AA)
    The Doors (1991)
    JFK (1991)
    Nixon (1995)
    Platoon (1986, AA)
    Talk Radio (1988)
    U Turn (1997)
    Wall Street (1987)
Stone, Richard: **8** Nobelist **9** economist
stones
  companions: **6** sticks
  skip ~: **3** dap
  throw ~ at: **3** pan, rap **4** pelt, slam **5** blame, decry, knock, sneer **6** malign, vilify **7** censure, condemn, put down, run down, slander, traduce **8** backbite, badmouth, belittle, denounce, derogate **9** criticize, denigrate, disparage, reprehend **10** calumniate
__ Stones: **7** Rolling
Stone, Sharon: **7** actress
  film: Above the Law (1988)
    Basic Instinct (1992)
    Casino (1995)
    He Said, She Said (1991)
    The Mighty (1998)
    The Muse (1999)
    The Quick and the Dead (1995)
    Sliver (1993)
    The Specialist (1994)
    Sphere (1998)
    Total Recall (1990)
  film (voice): Antz (1998)
Stones of Venice, The author: John Ruskin
stone's throw away, a: **4** near **5** close **6** nearby
stonewall: **5** block, evade, hedge, stall, stimy, stymy **6** hold up, impede, resist, shield, stymie **7** cover up **8** obstruct **9** dissemble **10** equivocate
Stonewall: **7** Jackson
stoneware: **6** jasper **7** pottery **8** ceramics
stone-wash: **6** abrade
stonewashed
  fabric: **5** denim
  garment: **5** jeans
stoneworker: **5** mason
stonewort: **4** alga
Stoney Creek: **4** city, town
  locale: **6** Canada **7** Ontario
Stoney End (1970 song)
  artist: Barbra Streisand
  composer: **4** Nyro
stony: **3** icy **4** cold, firm, hard **5** blank, chill, cruel, rigid, rocky, rough, solid, stiff **6** chilly, flinty, jouncy, lithic, rugged, steely **7** adamant, callous, deadpan, hostile, ice-cold **8** concrete, gravelly, hardened, indurate, obdurate, pitiless, ruthless, stubborn, uncaring **9** heartless, impassive, impliable, merciless, unbending, unfeeling, unpitying, unsmiling **10** hard-bitten, inexorable, inflexible, poker-faced, unwavering
stony-__: **5** faced **7** hearted
Stood Up (1957 song) artist: Ricky Nelson
stooge: **4** dupe, fool, pawn, tool **5** patsy, toady **6** jackal, lackey, puppet, victim **7** lacquey **8** henchman, kowtower, pushover **9** underling
Stooge: **3** Moe **5** Curly, Larry, Shemp **8** Curly Joe
  count: **5** three
Stooge, The (1953 film)
  cast: Polly Bergen, Jerry Lewis, Dean Martin
  director: Norman Taurog
Stookey, Paul: **6** singer
  member of: Peter, Paul & Mary
  song: Wedding Song (There Is Love) (1971)
stool: **4** seat **5** perch **7** ottoman **8** footrest **9** furniture
  part: **3** leg
  starter: **3** bar **4** camp, foot, step, toad
  user: **5** comic **8** comedian
__ stool: **5** cutty, joint **7** cucking, ducking, milking
stoolie
  see stool pigeon
stool pigeon: **3** rat **4** fink, nark, tool **5** namer **6** canary, ratter **7** tattler, traitor **8** informer, turncoat **9** informant **10** tattletale
stoop: **3** sag **4** bend, duck, flex, lean, orch, sink, step **5** deign, droop, hunch, kneel, kotow, lower, porch, slump, squat, swoop **6** crouch, hunker, kowtow, oblige, slouch **7** bow down **8** bend down, lose face, resort to **9** patronize **10** condescend, double over
  ender: **4** ball
stoopball: **4** game
stooped: **4** bent **6** droopy
__ Stoops to Conquer: **3** She
stop: **3** bar, end, fix, gag, nip, tab, tie **4** clog, cork, drop, foil, halt, hush, kill, lift, lull, park, plug, quit, rest, seal, stay, stem, veto **5** avast, belay, block, brake, break, cease, check, close, delay, depot, leave, letup, light, lodge, pause, quash, quell, quiet, scrub, stage, stall, still, stump, stunt, tarry, tie up, visit **6** arrest, becalm, cool it, cutoff, cut out, desist, draw up, ending, expire, finish, forbid, freeze, give up, hamper, hinder, hold it, impede, lay off, linger, muzzle, outlaw, period, pull up, recess, rein in, run out, stifle, tackle, thwart, wait up, wind up, wrap up **7** adjourn, back off, closure, congest, disrupt, embargo, fetch up, f-number, inhibit, layover, occlude, prevent, put down, refrain, repress, sign off, silence, sojourn, squelch, stammer, station, staunch, suspend, turn off, ward off **8** blockade, blockage, break off, choke off, conclude, cut short, guard cry, hang it up, hold back, knock off, leave off, obstruct, peter out, prohibit, restrain, shut down, suppress, surcease, terminus **9** barricade, cessation, close down, forestall, frustrate, hesitancy, intercept, interdict, interrupt, roadblock, terminate **10** call it a day, cold-turkey, conclusion, disruption, do away with, knock it off, put an end to, standstill
  as a ship: **5** lay to
  brief ~: **5** pause **6** recess
  by: **4** call **5** pop in, visit **6** drop in
  don't ~: **4** go on **5** run on **6** keep at **8** continue
  ender: **3** gap **4** cock, over **5** light, watch
  for: **6** pick up
  legally: **5** embar
  rest ~: **5** B and B, hotel, lodge, motel **6** hostel **7** auberge, lodging **8** hostelry **9** roadhouse **10** motor court, motor lodge
  starter: **3** non **4** back, door **5** short
  try to ~: **5** deter **10** discourage
  up: **3** dam **4** bolt, clog, cork, lock, plug, seal, shut, stem **5** block, close, latch, stuff **6** impede, secure **7** occlude, seal off, shutter **8** blockade, obstruct
  with: **5** end at
  worrying: **5** relax **6** unwind **7** cool off, lay back **8** calm down, loosen up **9** hang loose **10** settle down, simmer down
stop __: **3** off, out **4** bath, bead, knob, over, sign **5** order, price **6** clause, motion, number, street, volley **7** payment
stop __ dime: **3** on a
stop-__: **5** and-go
stop-__ order: **4** loss **5** limit
stop-__ photography: **6** action
__ stop: **3** bit, pit **4** flue, form, full, reed, rest **5** bench, click, field, truck **6** double **7** glottal, rolling, suction, whistle
__-stop: **7** whistle
Stop __!: **5** thief
Stop!: **4** halt, whoa **5** avast **6** enough, hold it, quit it
__ Stop: **3** Bus **4** Can't, Don't
Stop (1998 song) artist: Spice Girls
Stop and Smell the Roses (1974 song) artist: Mac Davis
stop at __: **7** nothing
stopcock: **3** tap **6** faucet
Stop Draggin' My Heart Around (1981 song)
  artist: Stevie Nicks, Tom Petty
stopgap: **5** shift **6** ersatz, fill-in, refuge **7** Band-Aid, interim, measure **9** contrived, emergency, expedient, impromptu, makeshift, practical, temporary **10** improvised, jury-rigged, pro tempore, substitute
Stop! In the the Name of Love (1965 song) artist: Supremes
stoplight
  color: **3** red **5** amber, green **6** yellow
  heed a ~: **5** brake
stop-listen link: **4** look
__ Stop Loving You: **5** I Can't
Stop Making Sense (1984 film) director: Jonathan Demme
stopover: **3** inn **4** camp, stay **5** B and B, hotel, lodge, motel, oasis, visit **6** hostel **7** auberge, layover, lodging, sojourn **8** hostelry **9** roadhouse **10** motor court, motor lodge
stoppage: **3** jam **4** halt **5** block, check, delay, tie-up **6** arrest, cutoff, holdup, layoff, stasis **7** closure, lockout, sitdown, walkout **8** abeyance, blockade, blockage, downtime, gridlock, shutdown, tarrying **9** abatement, cessation, interlude, occlusion **10** standstill, suspension
  combining form: **5** stasi-
__ stoppage: **4** work
Stoppard, Tom: **3** Sir **7** British **10** playwright
  work: Enter a Free Man
    Every Good Boy Deserves Favour
    Jumpers
    The Real Inspector Hound
    The Real Thing
    Rosencrantz and Guildenstern Are Dead
stopped: **5** let up **6** frozen, static **10** gridlocked
  up: **5** tight
stopper: **3** top **4** cork, plug, seal **5** block **7** closure, occlude
__-stopper: **3** gob **4** show
stopping
  device: **5** brake
  point: **5** limit
Stopping by Woods on a Snowy Evening: **4** poem
  author: Robert Frost
stopple
  see stopper
Stop pouring!: **4** when
__ stops here, the: **4** buck
__ stops here, The: **4** buck
__-stop shopping: **3** one
stop-sign sides: **5** eight
Stop Stop Stop (1966 song) artist: Hollies
Stop talking!: **3** shh **4** hush **5** bag it, can it **6** shut up
__ Stop the Rain: **5** Who'll
Stop the World I Want To Get Off character: **4** Evie
stopwatch: **5** timer
  button: **5** reset
storage
  area: **3** bin **4** crib, hold, loft, shed, silo **5** attic, chest, depot, hutch, shelf,

trunk, vault 6 armory, cellar, closet, garage, locker, recess 7 cabinet 8 basement, cupboard, landfill, magazine, wardrobe 9 warehouse 10 depository, repository
food ~ area: 5 hutch, shelf 6 closet, pantry 7 cabinet 8 cupboard
storage __: 4 cell, life, ring, wall 5 organ 7 battery
__ storage: 4 cold, dead, main, real 5 cache 7 virtual, working
storax: 4 tree 5 shrub
Storch: 5 Larry
store: 3 can, lot 4 bank, deli, fund, hide, hold, keep, load, lode, mart, mine, pile, save, shop, stow, well 5 amass, cache, depot, fount, hoard, lay up, place, put by, stash, stock, super, uplay, vault, wares 6 bakery, freeze, garner, larder, load up, market, outlet, pantry, pile up, ration, regard, retain, save up, supply, wealth 7 arsenal, backlog, deposit, harvest, husband, lay away, nest egg, put away, reserve, savings, Staples 8 boutique, business, cumulate, emporium, fountain, gold mine, hang onto, hide away, hold onto, lock away, lodgment, magazine, maintain, mothball, pack away, pharmacy, preserve, put aside, quantity, salt away, set apart, set aside, showroom, sock away, treasury 9 abundance, inventory, provision, repertory, reservoir, stockpile, superette, warehouse 10 accumulate, collection, cumulation, five-and-ten, keep on hand, repository
be in ~: 4 loom
be in ~ for: 4 look, wait 5 await 10 anticipate
ender: 4 room, wide 5 front, house, owner 6 keeper
enjoy a ~: 4 shop 6 browse
event: 4 sale
factory ~: 6 outlet
group: 5 chain
in ~: 5 on tap, spare 6 at hand, coming 8 destined, imminent 9 impending, ready to go
information: 4 file 5 enter 6 record 7 archive, catalog 8 document, preserve, tabulate
makeshift ~: 5 stand
offering: 5 goods
owner: 10 proprietor
set ~ by: 5 prize, value 6 accept, bank on, esteem, rely on 7 count on, respect, swear by, trust in 8 depend on, hold with 9 count upon
sign: 4 open 6 closed
starter: 4 book, drug
up: 5 amass, lay by, lay in, put by 6 garner 7 recruit, reserve 8 conserve, hold on to, salt away, set apart, set aside 10 accumulate
worker: 5 clerk 7 cashier
store __: 4 card 5 brand 6 cheese
store-__: 6 bought
__ store: 3 box 4 cold, dime, men's 5 chain, combo, ship's 6 anchor 7 company, country, general, grocery, package, ten-cent, variety
__ store by: 3 set 5 set no
storefront feature: 4 neon 6 awning, canopy
storehouse: 4 fund 5 cache, depot, trove 6 museum 7 arsenal 8 magazine, treasury 10 depository
__-store Indian: 5 cigar
storekeeper: 6 grocer, seller, trader 8 merchant
storer: 7 pack rat
storeroom: 5 attic
stores: 8 supplies 10 provisions
__ stores: 3 sea 5 naval, ship's, small
__ Store, The: 3 Big
Storey, David: 6 author, writer 7 British 10 playwright
storied: 5 famed 6 fabled, famous 7 eminent, honored 8 mythical, renowned 9 legendary, well-known 10 celebrated
stories
body of legendary ~: 6 mythos
handed-down ~: 4 lore
__ Stories, The: 6 Berlin
stork: 4 bird 5 wader 6 argala, jabiru 7 marabou 8 marabout 9 flinthead
cousin: 4 ibis 5 crane, egret, heron
like a ~: 5 leggy
visit: 5 birth
storm: 3 row 4 blow, boil, door, fray, fury, fuss, gale, gust, hail, howl, pour, rage, raid, rain, rant, rave, roar, rush, snow, tear, to-do, wind 5 beset, blast, blitz, burst, foray, furor, melee, onset, siege, sleet, stomp 6 assail, attack, charge, invade, lather, outcry, precip, racket, seethe, squall, temper, tumult, volley 7 assault, barrage, besiege, bluster, bombard, cyclone, ferment, monsoon, outrage, passion, rampage, run amok, tantrum, tempest, thunder, tornado, turmoil, twister 8 blizzard, downpour, have a fit, hysteria, invasion, outbreak, outburst, upheaval, violence 9 blow a fuse, broadside, cannonade, commotion, discharge, fusillade, hurricane, hysterics, intrude on, onslaught, whirlwind 10 cloudburst, convulsion, free-for-all, hit the roof, revolution
center: 3 eye
dust ~: 4 wind
electromagnetic ~: 6 aurora
ender: 5 bound
eye of the ~: 4 calm, lull
look like a ~: 5 lower
out of: 7 abandon
pellets: 4 hail 5 sleet
posting: 5 alert
preceder: 4 calm
refuge: 6 cellar
sci-fi ~ material: 3 ion
sewer: 5 drain
starter: 4 barn, fire, hail, rain, sand, snow, wind 5 brain 7 thunder
take by ~: 4 rush 6 attack
up a ~: 10 vigorously
storm __: 3 out, pit 4 boat, coat, door, sash 5 drain, house, sewer, surge, track, watch 6 cellar, center, petrel, signal, window 7 warning
storm __ teacup: 3 in a
__ storm: 3 ice 4 dust, line 7 violent
Storm: 3 car, Geo 4 auto, gale 7 Theodor
__ Storm: 6 Desert, Summer
Storm and __: 6 Stress
Störmer, Horst: 8 Nobelist 9 physicist
Storm Fear author: Robert Frost
Storm, Gale: 6 singer 7 actress
song: Dark Moon (1957)
I Hear You Knocking (1955)
Ivory Tower (1956)
Memories Are Made of This (1955)
Teen Age Prayer (1955)
Why Do Fools Fall in Love (1956)
Storm in a Teacup (1937 film)
cast: Rex Harrison, Vivien Leigh
storminess: 8 violence 10 turbulence
storming: 8 wrathful 10 infuriated
stormless: 4 calm
Storm Operation author: Maxwell Anderson
__ Storm, The: 3 Ice 6 Mortal, Secret 7 Perfect
Storm, Theodor: 4 poet 6 German
stormy: 3 hot, wet 4 cold, foul, wild 5 angry, gusty, irate, rainy, rough, windy, wroth 6 fierce, heated, raging, raving 7 furious, howling, pouring, ranting, violent 8 blustery, menacing, vehement, wrathful 9 inclement, turbulent 10 coming down, passionate, riproaring, tumultuous
stormy __: 6 petrel
Stormy __: 6 Monday 7 Weather
Stormy Monday (1988 film)
cast: Melanie Griffith, Tommy Lee Jones, Sting
director: Mike Figgis
Stormy Weather: 4 song
composer: 5 Arlen 7 Koehler
singer: 5 Horne
Stormy Weather (1943 film): 7 musical
cast: Cab Calloway, Lena Horne, Bill Robinson
director: Andrew L. Stone
Storni, Alfonsina: 4 poet 9 Argentine
Storrs: 4 city, town
athletes: 7 Huskies
school: 5 U. Conn.
Storting: 10 parliament
locale: 4 Oslo 6 Norway
story: 3 bio, fib, lie 4 book, epic, myth, news, plea, plot, saga, tale, tier, yarn 5 alibi, drama, fable, floor, level, novel, prose, rumor, scoop, spiel 6 canard, comedy, excuse, exposé, gossip, legend, memoir, record, report, script, sequel, serial 7 account, article, baloney, boloney, episode, feature, fiction, history, mystery, parable, recital, release, romance, tragedy, untruth, version, writing 8 allegory, anecdote, folktale, libretto, news item, strategy, tall tale, teleplay, thriller, white lie, whodunit 9 adventure, biography, chronicle, dime novel, fairy tale, falsehood, narration, narrative, potboiler, rationale, recountal, soap opera 10 allegation, confession, literature
animal ~: 5 fable
cover ~: 7 pretext
credit: 6 byline
ender: 4 book 5 board 6 teller, writer
end of ~: 6 period
fairy ~: 4 lore, myth, tale 5 fable 6 legend 7 fantasy, fiction 8 allegory, delusion, folktale 9 falsehood, invention
false ~: 3 lie 6 canard
fish ~: 3 fib 4 tale, yarn 7 fiction
folk ~: 4 myth, tale 5 fable 6 legend 9 tradition
funny ~: 4 joke
heroic ~: 4 epic, gest 5 geste
in Britain: 4 rede
inconsistency: 4 hole
inside ~: 4 dope 5 scoop, truth 7 lowdown
life ~: 3 bio 4 biog. 6 memoir 7 memoirs 9 biography
line: 4 plot 8 scenario
long ~: 4 epic, saga 5 novel
made-up ~: 5 novel 7 fiction
old ~: 4 myth 6 legend
sensational ~: 6 exposé
suppress a ~: 4 kill
suspect's ~: 5 alibi
tall ~: 3 lie 4 tale, yarn 9 invention
tell a ~: 7 narrate, recount
upper ~: 4 loft 5 attic
with a lesson: 4 myth 5 fable 7 parable 8 allegory, apologue
story __: 4 line
__ story: 3 sob, war 4 dope, fish, folk, half, lead, news, tall 5 cover, fairy, ghost, photo, short 6 horror, inside, second 7 bedtime, feature, running, success
__-story: 4 back
__ Story: 3 Toy 4 Love 5 Tokyo 6 Orrie's, Police 7 Bedtime
storybook: 6 unreal
__-story man: 6 second
Story of __ H, The: 5 Adele
Story of Alexander Graham Bell, The (1939 film)
cast: Don Ameche, Henry Fonda, Loretta Young
Story of an African Farm, The author: Olive Schreiner
Story of a Novel, The author: Thomas Wolfe
Story of Civilization, The author: Will Durant
Story of G.I. Joe, The (1945 film)
cast: Burgess Meredith, Robert Mitchum, Freddie Steele
director: William Wellman
Story of Louis Pasteur, The (1936 film)
cast: Josephine Hutchinson, Anita Louise, Paul Muni
Story of Mary Marlin, The: 9 radio show
Story of Philosophy, The author: Will Durant
Story of Robin Hood and His Merrie Men, The (1952 film)
cast: Peter Finch, Joan Rice, Richard Todd
director: Ken Annakin
Story of Three Loves, The (1953 film)
cast: Pier Angeli, Gottfried Reinhardt, Moira Shearer
director: Vincente Minnelli
Story of Vernon & Irene Castle, The (1939 film): 7 musical
cast: Fred Astaire, Edna May Oliver, Ginger Rogers
director: H.C. Potter
Story of Will Rogers, The (1952 film)
cast: Carl Benton Reid, Will Rogers Jr., Jane Wyman
director: Michael Curtiz
Story on Page One, The (1959 film)
cast: Tony Franciosa, Rita Hayworth, Gig Young
director: Clifford Odets
storyteller: 4 liar 6 fibber 8 fabulist, narrator, novelist 9 raconteur
ancient ~: 4 Esop 5 Aesop
Storyteller, The author: Harold Robbins
storytelling: 9 narration
dance: 4 hula
__ Story, The: 3 FBI, Zoo 4 Nun's 6 Jolson 7 Colditz
stotinka: 5 money
stotinki
100: 3 lev
Stouffville: 4 city, town
locale: 6 Canada 7 Ontario
stout: 3 big 4 bold, brew, hale, iron, wiry 5 ample, beefy, brave, bulky, burly, drink, fubsy, hardy, heavy, hefty, hunky, husky, loyal, lusty, nervy, obese, plump, pudgy, pursy, solid, tough, tubby 6 brawny, chubby, chunky, fleshy, hearty, heroic, mighty, plucky, portly, potent, pyknic, robust, rotund, rugged, sinewy, stable, steely, stocky, strong, stubby, sturdy, virile, zaftig, zoftig 7 adipose, doughty, hulking, impavid, paunchy, porcine, staunch, valiant, weighty 8 athletic, beverage, fearless, forceful, heroical, indurate, intrepid, muscular, powerful, puissant, resolute, roly-poly, sedulous, stalwart, thickset, valorous, vigorous 9 Atlantean, corpulent, dauntless, filled-out, Herculean, strapping, tenacious, undaunted, unfearing, well-built 10 able-bodied, courageous, determined, invincible, overweight, red-blooded, undismayed, well-padded
cousin: 3 ale 4 beer
ingredient: 4 malt

make ~: 6 fatten
vessel: 3 mug 4 toby 5 stein
stout-hearted: 4 bold, game 5 brave, gutsy, nervy 6 awless, daring, gritty, heroic, plucky, spunky, sturdy 7 aweless, defiant, doughty, gallant, staunch, valiant 8 fearless, heroical, intrepid, resolute, stalwart, unafraid, valorous 9 audacious, dauntless, dreadless, undaunted, unfearful 10 courageous
one: 4 hero
Stouthearted __: 3 Men
stoutness: 3 vim 4 dint, thew 5 brawn, force, might, power, thews, vigor 6 energy, muscle 7 fitness, muscles, potence, potency, stamina 8 strength, vitality 9 endurance, fortitude, puissance 10 brute force, fleshiness
Stout, Rex: 6 author, writer
sleuth: Nero Wolfe
work: The Doorbell Rang
Fer-de-Lance
stove: 4 kiln, oven 5 forge, range 6 heater 7 furnace 9 fireplace
accessory: 5 timer
ender: 3 top 4 pipe
part: 4 oven 6 burner, gas jet
right off the ~: 3 hot
__ stove: 4 camp 6 Primus 7 cookery
Stove __ Stuffing: 3 Top
__-stove league: 3 hot
stovepipe: 3 hat, lid
connection: 4 flue
like a ~: 5 sooty
stovetop item: 3 pan, pot 6 boiler 7 skillet
stow: 4 bury, hide, load, pack, save 5 amass, cache, hoard, lay in, place, put by, stash, stock, store, stuff 6 bundle, closet, garner, pile up 7 conceal, deposit, harvest, put away, reserve, secrete 8 ensconce, pack away, put aside 9 store away, warehouse
on board: 4 lade
Stow: 4 city, town 8 Randolph
locale: 4 Ohio
stowaway: 5 hider
Stowe: 4 city, town 9 ski resort
activity: 6 skiing
equipment: 3 ski 4 skee
locale: 7 Vermont
sight: 3 tow 4 snow, T-bar 5 slope
Stowe, Harriet Beecher: 6 author, writer
character: 3 Eva, Tom
work: Dred
The Minister's Wooing
Oldtown Folks
Uncle Tom's Cabin
Stowe, Madeleine: 7 actress
film: The General's Daughter (1999)
The Last of the Mohicans (1992)
Revenge (1990)
Stakeout (1987)
Twelve Monkeys (1995)
The Two Jakes (1990)
Unlawful Entry (1992)
We Were Soldiers (2002)
spouse: Brian Benben
Stow, Randolph: 4 poet 6 author, writer 10 Australian
St. Paul: 4 city, town
county: 6 Ramsey
locale: 9 Minnesota
river: Mississippi
St. Paul composer: 11 Mendelssohn
STP competitor: 4 Fram
St. Peters: 4 city, town
locale: 8 Missouri
St. Peter's __: 6 Square
St. Petersburg: 4 city, port, town
county: 8 Pinellas
locale: 6 Russia 7 Florida
newspaper: 5 Times
Strabo: 5 Greek 9 historian 10 geographer
Strachey, Lytton: 6 author, writer 7 British 9 historian 10 biographer
Strad: 6 violin
relative: 5 Amati
substance for a ~: 5 rosin
straddle: 4 span 5 mount 6 ramble, sprawl 8 bestride, fence-sit 9 vacillate
straddle __: 5 truck 7 carrier
straddle the __: 5 fence
straddling: 4 atop 6 across
the fence: 6 middle
Stradivari: 7 Antonio
teacher: 5 Amati
strafe: 4 raid 6 fire at
straggle: 3 lag 4 drag, idle, laze, loaf, poke, roam, rove, tail 5 amble, dally, drift, mosey, range, stall, stray, tarry, trail 6 dawdle, linger, loiter, ramble, sprawl, spread, wander 7 meander, saunter, shuffle 8 lollygag, scramble 9 limp along, string out, waste time 10 dillydally
straggler: 7 laggard 8 lingerer, wanderer
straight: 3 due 4 even, fair, hand, just, neat, pure, tidy, true 5 blunt, erect, exact, frank, legal, legit, level, moral, plain, plumb, right, sheer 6 candid, decent, direct, honest, in a row, in line, linear, openly, proper, square, strong, trusty, unbent, unmixt 7 aligned, correct, ethical, exactly, factual, frankly, in order, nonstop, orderly, regular, running, summary, unbowed, unmixed, upright 8 accurate, candidly, credible, directly, orthodox, out-front, outright, reliable, truthful, unbiased, unbroken, uncurled, vertical, virtuous 9 authentic, downright, equitable, honorable, out-and-out, undiluted, unfailing, veracious 10 aboveboard, continuous, evenhanded, forthright, from the hip, horizontal, inflexible, invariable, law-abiding, on the level, point-blank, scrupulous, successive, unmediated, unrelieved, unswerving
be ~: 5 level
combining form: 4 orth-, rect- 5 ortho-, recti-
don't keep ~: 4 bend, warp 5 curve, slant 6 buckle, deform 7 contort, distort
ender: 3 way 4 away, edge 5 arrow, edged 6 jacket 7 forward
go ~: 6 reform 7 shape up
in a ~ line: 8 directly
like a ~ line: 4 one-D
line: 3 row
make ~ lines: 4 rule
man: 4 foil 6 feeder, stooge
not ~: 3 wry 4 wavy 5 askew, atilt, curly 6 angled, aslant, aslope 7 crooked
off the ~ and narrow: 4 awry, lost 5 amiss 6 adrift, afield 7 missing, roaming 9 wandering
set ~: 3 fix 5 right 7 correct 8 disabuse 9 reconcile
topper: 5 flush
up: 4 neat, over
up and down: 5 plumb
with a ~ face: 9 seriously, sincerely
straight __: 3 man, off, pin 4 away, face, time 5 angle, arrow, chair, flush, poker, razor, stall 6 matter, ticket, whisky 7 shooter, whiskey
straight __ arrow: 4 as an
straight __ the heart: 4 from
straight-__: 3 arm, out 4 edge, line 5 ahead, chain, faced, laced
straight-__-the-shoulder: 4 from
__ straight: 3 set 4 skip 5 Dutch, shoot 6 inside
Straight: 8 Beatrice
__ Straight: 5 Billy
straight-A __: 7 student
straight and __: 6 narrow
straight-arrow: 6 honest 8 orthodox 9 veracious
Straight author: Dick Francis
straightaway: 3 now, PDQ 4 anon, ASAP, soon 5 apace, today 6 at once, presto, pronto 7 fleetly, hastily, quickly, rapidly, readily, swiftly 8 directly, in a flash, in a jiffy, in no time, pell-mell, promptly, right now, right off, speedily 9 at present, forthwith, hurriedly, instantly, like a shot, posthaste, presently, right away 10 at this time, here and now, this minute
Straight, Beatrice Oscar: Network
Straight Dope, The columnist: 5 Adams
straightedge: 5 ruler
straighten: 3 fix 4 even, tidy, true 5 align, aline, level 6 adjust, line up, neaten, unbend, uncoil, uncurl, unfold 7 compose, correct, rectify, untwist
out: 3 aid 5 right 6 settle 7 correct, improve, rectify 8 organize, untangle 9 seriously
up: 4 rise, tidy 5 clean 7 rectify
__ straight face: 5 keep a
straightforward: 4 easy, just, open 5 blunt, brusk, clear, frank, legit, level, plain, right, vivid 6 abrupt, candid, cogent, direct, honest, patent, simple, square 7 brusque, evident, express, factual, genuine, obvious, right-on, routine, sincere, up-front, upright 8 apparent, clear-cut, credible, definite, distinct, explicit, impolite, like it is, manifest, palpable, readable, tactless, truthful 9 barefaced, graspable, guileless, honorable, outspoken, unfeigned, unguarded, veracious 10 forthright, free-spoken, indelicate, on the level, scrupulous, spelled out
be ~: 5 level
not ~: 3 sly 4 foxy, wily 5 false, shady 6 artful, crafty, shifty, sneaky, subtle, tricky 7 crooked, cunning, devious, evasive, oblique 8 guileful, indirect, scheming, slippery 9 deceitful, designing, dishonest, insidious, insincere, underhand 10 circuitous, misleading, roundabout
straightforwardly: 4 true 6 simply
straightforwardness: 6 candor 7 honesty 9 sincerity
straight-laced
see strait-laced
straightness: 6 candor 7 honesty 9 sincerity
symbol of ~: 5 arrow
straight-out: 6 direct, flatly 8 specific, thorough
straight-shooting: 6 candid, honest 7 sincere
Straight Story, The (1999 film)
cast: Richard Farnsworth, Jane Galloway, Sissy Spacek, Harry Dean Stanton
director: David Lynch
Straight Time (1978 film)
cast: Dustin Hoffman, Theresa Russell, Harry Dean Stanton
director: Ulu Grosbard
straight-up: 5 steep 8 vertical
Straight Up (1988 song) artist: Paula Abdul
strain: 3 air, tax, try, tug 4 ache, care, moil, ooze, pain, pull, push, rack, sift, song, tear, tire, toil, toll, tone, tune, turn, vein, work 5 blood, breed, brunt, drive, exert, labor, leach, music, press, reach, sieve, stock, sweat, tinge, touch, trace, twist, unmix 6 burden, effort, family, filter, injure, injury, melody, nerves, purify, refine, screen, sprain, streak, stress, strive, temper, trauma, warble, weaken, weight, wrench 7 anxiety, descant, descent, discant, distort, fatigue, lineage, measure, overtax, peg away, refrain, species, stretch, tension, tighten, trouble, variety 8 ancestry, bear down, distress, endeavor, exertion, go all out, overload, overwork, pedigree, pressure, separate, struggle, tautness 9 leitmotif, lixiviate, overexert, percolate, suspicion, tightness, weigh down 10 bear down on, difficulty, extraction, go for broke, sprinkling, suggestion
starter: 3 eye
under a ~: 5 tense
strain __ gnat: 3 at a
strained: 4 taut 5 false, stiff, tense, tight, wired 6 forced, uneasy 7 awkward, hard-put, intense, labored, refined, uptight 9 contrived, difficult, laborious, miserable, pretended, strung out, unnatural, unrelaxed 10 far-fetched
strainer: 5 sieve 6 sifter 8 colander
strait: 4 bind, mess, neck, pass 5 pinch 6 crisis, plight 7 channel, dilemma, narrows, passage, squeeze 8 distress, hardship 9 deep water, emergency, extremity 10 difficulty, passageway 17 perplexity. euripus
ender: 6 jacket
opposite: 7 isthmus
turbulent ~: 7 euripus
strait-__: 5 laced
Strait: 6 George
Australia: 6 Torres
Gulf of Aqaba ~: 5 Tiran
Persian Gulf ~: 5 Ormuz 6 Hormuz
Red Sea ~: 5 Tiran
__ Strait: 3 Rae 4 Bass, Cook, Rion 5 Cabot, Davis, Korea, Menai, Sunda, Tiran 6 Bering, Hainan, Hudson, Taiwan, Torres 7 Denmark, Florida, Formosa, Makasar
straiten: 4 curb, ruin 5 break, limit 6 hamper, hinder, impede 7 confine 8 bankrupt, restrain, restrict 9 pauperize 10 impoverish, keep in line
straitened: 4 poor 5 broke, needy 6 bad off, hard up, ill off, in debt, in need, in want 7 pinched 8 badly off, bankrupt, beggarly, deprived, indigent, strapped, wiped out 9 destitute, insolvent, moneyless, penniless, penurious 10 down and out, pauperized
Strait Is the Gate author: André Gide
straitjacket: 8 restrain 9 restraint
strait-laced: 4 firm, hard, prim 5 bossy, cruel, picky, rigid, staid, stern, stiff, tough 6 narrow, prissy, proper, severe, square, strict 7 austere, prudish, puritan, Spartan 8 despotic, exacting, hard-line, priggish, rigorous 9 demanding, draconian, squeamish, stringent, unbending, unsparing 10 despotical, inflexible, iron-fisted, no-nonsense, oppressive, tyrannical
one: 5 priss, prude
Strait of __: 5 Canso, Dover, Ormuz 6 Hormuz, Melaka 7 Malacca, Otranto 8 Magellan 9 Belle Isle 10 Juan de Fuca
Strait of Malacca island: 6 Penang
straits: 6 plight 8 position, pressure 9 emergency, indigence 10 insolvency
dire ~: 6 crisis, penury 7 trouble
in dire ~: 5 needy 6 hard-up
__ straits: 4 dire
strand: 3 ply 4 hair, lock, rope, wisp, yarn 5 beach, cable, coast, fiber, tress,

twine **6** desert, enisle, length, maroon, string, thread **7** abandon, cowlick, forsake, isolate, let down **8** cast away, filament, littoral, seacoast, seashore
at an airport: **5** ice in
stranded: **6** ashore **7** aground, beached, wrecked **8** castaway, deserted, grounded, helpless, homeless, marooned, passed up **9** abandoned, foundered, penniless, sidelined **10** high and dry, on the rocks, run aground
Stranded sculptor: **4** Erté
Strand, Mark: **4** poet **6** author, writer
strange: **3** fey, new, odd, off **4** eery, lost, rare **5** alien, apart, crazy, eerie, funny, novel, queer, weird **6** atypic, exotic, far-out, freaky, quaint, quirky, remote, unique, way-out **7** awkward, bizarre, curious, deviant, erratic, faraway, foreign, oddball, offbeat, unalike, uncanny, uncouth, unknown, untried, unusual **8** aberrant, abnormal, atypical, freakish, isolated, peculiar, singular, uncommon **9** anomalous, different, divergent, eccentric, fantastic, grotesque, irregular, marvelous, unearthly, unheard of, unnatural, unrelated, wonderful **10** astounding, irrelevant, miraculous, mysterious, mystifying, newfangled, outlandish, out of place, perplexing, remarkable, unexplored, unfamiliar, unorthodox, unseasoned
combining form: **3** xen- **4** xeno-
in a ~ way: **5** oddly
strange ___: **5** quark
strange ___ may seem: **4** as it
Strange ___: **5** Cargo, Fruit **7** Victory
Strange Affair of Uncle Harry, The (1945 film)
cast: Geraldine Fitzgerald, Ella Raines, George Sanders
Strange Cargo (1940 film)
cast: Joan Crawford, Clark Gable, Ian Hunter
director: Frank Borzage
Strange Case of Dr. Jekyll and Mr. Hyde, The author: Robert Louis Stevenson
Strange, Curtis: **6** golfer
Strange Fruit author: Lillian Smith
Strange Impersonation (1946 film)
cast: Hillary Brooke, William Gargan, Brenda Marshall
director: Anthony Mann
Strange Interlude: **4** film, play
author: Eugene O'Neill
cast: Clark Gable, May Robson, Norma Shearer
character: **3** Ned **4** Nina **5** Leeds
director: Robert Z. Leonard
Strangelove: **2** Dr.
Strange Loves of Martha Ivers, The (1946 film)
cast: Kirk Douglas, Lizabeth Scott, Barbara Stanwyck
director: Lewis Milestone
Strange Magic artist: **3** ELO
strangeness: **6** oddity
Strange One, The (1957 film)
cast: Ben Gazzara, Pat Hingle, George Peppard
stranger: **5** alien **7** drifter, incomer, migrant, tourist, unknown, visitor **8** intruder, newcomer, outsider, squatter, wanderer **9** foreigner, immigrant, itinerant, outlander, transient **10** interloper
Stranger ___ Paradise: **4** Than
Stranger ___ Shore: **5** on the
___ Stranger: **5** Hello **7** Welcome
Stranger From the Tonto author: Zane Grey
___ Stranger Here Myself: **3** I'm a
Stranger in Between (1952 film)
cast: Dirk Bogarde, Elizabeth Sellars
director: Charles Crichton
Stranger in the Mirror author: Sidney Sheldon
Stranger Is Watching, A author: Mary Higgins Clark
Stranger's ___, The: **4** Hand **6** Return
___ Strangers: **5** Three **6** Deadly **7** Perfect
Strangers and Brothers author: C.P. Snow
Strangers author: Dean Koontz
Stranger's Hand, The (1954 film)
cast: Trevor Howard, Alida Valli
Strangers in Good Company director: **5** Scott
Strangers in the Night (1966 song)
artist: Frank Sinatra
___ Strangers Marry: **4** When
Strangers on a Train: **4** film **5** novel
author: Patricia Highsmith
cast: Farley Granger, Ruth Roman, Robert Walker
composer: **7** Tiomkin
director: Alfred Hitchcock
Stranger's Return, The (1933 film)
cast: Lionel Barrymore, Miriam Hopkins, Franchot Tone
director: King Vidor
Stranger, The (1946 film)
cast: Edward G. Robinson, Orson Welles, Loretta Young
director: Orson Welles
Stranger, The author: Albert Camus
Strange Victory author: Sara Teasdale
Strangler, The (1964 film)
cast: Victor Buono, Ellen Corby, David McLean
strap: **3** tie **4** band, belt, lace, lash, rein, whip, yoke **5** hitch, leash, thong **6** handle **7** binding, harness **8** seat belt **9** watchband
closure: **5** dring
decorative ~: **5** patte
ender: **4** hang **6** hanger
starter: **4** boot **5** black
___ strap: **4** chin **5** cheek **7** stirrup
straphanger: **5** rider **8** commuter
purchase: **5** token
strapless: **5** dress
top: **4** tube
strapped: **4** poor **5** broke, needy, short **6** bad off, hard up, ill off, in a fix, in a jam, in deep, in need, in want **7** pinched **8** badly off, bankrupt, beggarly, deprived, dirt poor, indigent **9** destitute, insolvent, moneyless, penniless, penurious **10** down and out, pauperized, stone-broke, straitened
for time: **4** late **5** tardy
strapping: **3** big, fit **4** hale, iron, wiry **5** beefy, burly, hardy, hefty, hunky, husky, lusty, stout, tough **6** brawny, hearty, mighty, potent, robust, rugged, sinewy, steely, stocky, strong, sturdy, virile **7** doughty, hulking, sizable **8** athletic, forceful, indurate, muscular, powerful, puissant, sizeable, stalwart, vigorous **9** Atlantean, Herculean, well-built **10** able-bodied, red-blooded
Strasberg: **3** Lee **5** Susan
subject: **6** acting
Strasbourg: **4** city, town
locale: **6** France
river: **3** Ill
Strassman, Marcia: **7** actress
film: Honey, I Blew Up the Kid (1992) Honey, I Shrunk the Kids (1989)
TV: MASH, Welcome Back, Kotter
stratagem: **4** move, plot, ploy, ruse, trap, wile **5** craft, dodge, trick **6** device, dupery, gambit, scheme, tactic **7** finesse, gimmick, knavery, measure, sleight, tactics **8** artifice, intrigue, maneuver **9** chicanery, deception, expedient, imposture **10** subterfuge
Stratas: **6** Teresa
strategic: **3** key **5** vital **6** clever, tricky **7** crucial, cunning, planned, politic **8** cardinal, critical, decisive **9** dishonest, important, necessary **10** calculated, deliberate, diplomatic, imperative
Strategic ___ Command: **3** Air
Strategic ___ Initiative: **7** Defense
strategist: **9** tactician
strategize: **4** plan
strategy: **4** game, plan, ploy **5** angle, craft, dodge, scene, setup, slant, story **6** design, gambit, method, policy, scheme, system **7** cunning, gimmick, program, project, tactics **8** approach, artifice, game plan, scenario, time line **9** blueprint, expedient, procedure, treatment **10** expediency
fallback ~: **5** plan B
game: **4** Risk
original ~: **5** plan A
session: **6** huddle
Strategy of Peace, The author: John F. Kennedy
Stratemeyer, Edward L.: **6** author, writer
book series: Hardy Boys, Nancy Drew, Rover Boys, Tom Swift
Stratford: **4** city, town
locale: **4** Conn. **6** Canada **7** Ontario
river: **4** Avon
Stratford-___-Avon: **4** upon
Strathairn, David: **5** actor
film: Bad Manners (1998)
Eight Men Out (1988)
Limbo (1999)
Losing Isaiah (1995)
Lost in Yonkers (1993)
A Map of the World (1999)
Passion Fish (1992)
The River Wild (1994)
With Friends Like These ... (1999)
Strathcona: **4** city, town
locale: **6** Canada **7** Alberta
strathspey: **5** dance
stratify: **8** laminate
Stratocaster: **6** guitar
play a: **5** strum
stratocumulus: **5** cloud
stratosphere, in the: **4** high **6** high up
Stratton Story, The (1949 film)
cast: June Allyson, Frank Morgan, James Stewart
director: Sam Wood
stratum: **3** bed **4** seam, tier, vein **5** caste, class, grade, layer, level, plane, sheet **6** lamina, sector, sphere, streak **7** station **8** standing
social ~: **5** caste, class, elite **6** sphere **7** station **8** standing
stratus: **5** cloud
Stratus: **3** car **4** auto **5** Dodge **10** automobile
Straub: **5** Peter
Strauss: **4** Levi **5** Peter **6** Johann **7** Richard
Strauss, Johann: **8** Austrian, composer
work: Blue Danube Waltz
Die Fledermaus
Emperor Waltz
Tales from the Vienna Woods
Strauss, Richard: **6** German **8** composer
genre: **5** opera
work: Also Sprach Zarathustra
Der Rosenkavalier
Don Quixote
Salome
Till Eulenspiegel
Stravinsky, Igor: **7** Russian **8** composer
work: Agon
The Firebird
Petrushka
Rite of Spring
Symphony of Psalms
straw: **3** hay, jot **4** feed, iota, stem, tube **5** blade, chaff, color, stalk **6** fodder, silage, sipper, trifle, yellow **7** padding **8** least bit
bit of ~: **4** wisp
boss: **6** gerent **7** manager **8** overseer **10** figurehead, supervisor
covering: **5** mulch
ender: **4** worm **5** berry, board **6** flower
in the wind: **4** omen, sign **5** token **6** augury, herald, signal **7** portent, presage, warning **9** foretoken, harbinger, indicator **10** indication
last ~: **5** limit
like a ~: **5** tubal
man: **6** effigy
pile: **4** rick
product: **3** hat, mat
relative: **4** buff, corn, gold, lime, rust, sand **5** blond, brass, coral, cream, flaxy, lemon, maize, ocher, ochre, peach, rusty **6** blonde, canary, chammy, citron, crocus, flaxen, shammy, shamoy **7** apricot, chamois, citrine, jasmine, mustard, nankeen, old gold, saffron, xanthic **8** daffodil, primrose **9** champagne, goldenrod, jessamine
starter: **3** bed **4** jack
unit: **4** bale **5** sheaf
use a ~: **3** sip **4** suck
vote: **4** poll
straw ___: **3** hat, man **4** boss, mite, poll, vote, wine **5** color **6** yellow
straw ___ wind: **5** in the
___ straw: **4** last **5** man of
___ Strawberries: **4** Wild
strawberry: **3** pie, red **5** fruit **6** flavor **8** ice cream
alternative: **5** lemon, mocha, peach **6** banana, coffee, Jamoca, toffee **7** caramel, coconut, vanilla **8** cinnamon, hazelnut **9** bubblegum, chocolate, pineapple, pistachio, raspberry, rocky road, rum raisin **10** blackberry, cheesecake, Neapolitan, peppermint
relative: **4** rose, ruby, rust, wine **5** brick, coral, grape, poppy, rusty, sandy **6** cerise, cherry, claret, garnet, maroon **7** carmine, crimson, fuchsia, magenta, pimento, scarlet, sultana, vermeil **8** amaranth, cardinal, dubonnet, geranium, rubicund **9** carnation, cranberry, vermilion
strawberry ___: **4** bass, bush, dish, roan, tree **5** blite, blond, guava **6** blonde, tomato
___ strawberry: **4** mock **6** barren, Indian
___-strawberry: **4** cran
Strawberry: **6** Darryl
once: **3** Met
Strawberry Alarm Clock song: Incense and Peppermints (1967)
Strawberry Blonde, The (1941 film)
cast: James Cagney, Olivia de Havilland, Rita Hayworth
director: Raoul Walsh
Strawberry Fields Forever (1967 song)
artist: Beatles
straw-colored: **5** flaxy **6** flaxen
Straw Dogs (1971 film)
cast: Susan George, Dustin Hoffman, Peter Vaughan
director: Sam Peckinpah
strawflower: **5** plant **6** flower
straw in the ___: **4** wind

straws
catch at ~: 5 argue, cavil 7 quibble
draw ~: 6 choose
stray: 3 cur, err, sin 4 dogy, lost, roam, rove, waif 5 dogey, dogie, drift, range 6 animal, depart, errant, orphan, ramble, random, wander 7 deviate, digress, diverge, do wrong, go wrong, maunder, meander, mongrel, vagrant 8 alley cat, divagate, homeless, isolated, maverick, renegade, straggle, wanderer 9 abandoned, foundling, gallivant 10 incidental, occasional, unattached
animal: 4 dogy, waif 5 dogey, rogue 6 doggie
dog: 3 mut 4 mutt
home for a ~: 5 pound
Stray __ Strut: 3 Cat
Stray Dog (1949 film)
cast: Keiko Awaji, Toshiro Mifune, Takashi Shimura
director: Akira Kurosawa
Strayhorn, Billy: 7 pianist 8 composer
genre: 4 jazz
straying: 6 afield, errant 7 veering 9 departure 10 digression, discursion
streak: 3 bar, ray, run 4 band, beam, dash, daub, hint, line, mark, rush, spot, tear, vein, welt, zoom 5 layer, scoot, shoot, slash, smear, spell, stria, strip, tinge, touch, trace 6 marble, period, pocket, series, sprint, strain, stripe 7 element, stratum 8 sequence 9 suspicion 10 suggestion
like a blue ~: 4 fast 5 quick, rapid
losing ~: 3 dip, sag 5 panic, slide, slump 6 plunge 7 decline, falloff, reverse 8 bad times, downturn, dry spell, slowdown 9 downslide, downswing, downtrend, hard times, recession
on a ~: 3 hot 5 blest, lucky 7 blessed, charmed, favored 9 fortunate 10 auspicious, felicitous, fortuitous
talk a blue ~: 3 yak 5 run on 6 yammer
winning ~: 3 run 4 roll
__ streak: 3 on a 4 blue 6 yellow
__ Streak: 6 Silver
streaked: 4 liny, rowy 5 liney 7 mottled 8 brindled
streaking: 3 fad
streaks, full of: 4 liny 5 liney
Streak, The (1974 song) artist: Ray Stevens
Streaky: 3 cat
stream: 3 jet, run 4 emit, flow, gush, kill, pour, race, rain, rill, roll, rush, tide 5 bourn, brook, creek, drift, flood, glide, issue, rille, river, slide, spate, spill, spirt, spout, spurt, surge, swarm 6 bourne, branch, course, emerge, influx, motion, onrush, parade, runlet, runnel, sluice, squirt 7 cascade, current, freshet, rivulet, torrent, trickle 8 continue, fountain 9 tributary 10 air current, inundation, outpouring
combining form: 4 rheo- 5 fluvi- 6 fluvio-
cross a ~: 4 ford
ender: 3 bed 4 line, side
fast-flowing ~: 3 jet 4 kill
flow like a ~: 4 purl
gentle ~ of poetry: 5 Afton
movement: 6 inflow 7 outflow
starter: 3 mid 4 down, main, mill, slip 5 blood
__ stream: 3 air, jet, mud 5 third 6 pirate
__ Stream: 4 Gulf 5 Black, Japan
streamer: 4 flag 5 title 6 banner, ensign 7 pennant 8 standard
Streamers: 4 film, play
author: David Rabe
cast: Mitchell Lichtenstein, Matthew Modine, Michael Wright
director: Robert Altman
streaming: 6 active
streamlet: 3 run 4 race, rill 5 bourn, brook, creek, rille 6 runlet, runnel 7 rivulet 9 tributary
streamline: 5 shape 7 improve 8 simplify 9 modernize 10 centralize
streamlined: 4 trim 5 sleek
Streamliner: 3 car 4 auto 7 Pontiac
Streamwood: 4 city, town
locale: 8 Illinois
Streep, Meryl: 7 actress
film: Adaptation (2002)
Before and After (1996)
The Bridges of Madison County (1995)
A Cry in the Dark (1988)
Death Becomes Her (1992)
The Deer Hunter (1978)
Defending Your Life (1991)
Falling in Love (1984)
The French Lieutenant's Woman (1981)
Heartburn (1986)
The Hours (2002)
Ironweed (1987)
Kramer vs. Kramer (1979, AA)
Manhattan (1979)
Music of the Heart (1999)
One True Thing (1998)
Out of Africa (1985)
Postcards From the Edge (1990)
The River Wild (1994)
The Seduction of Joe Tynan (1979)
She-Devil (1989)
Silkwood (1983)
Sophie's Choice (1982, AA)
street: 3 way 4 drag, lane, road 5 byway, court, drive, place, route 6 artery, avenue 7 ingress, parkway, passage, roadway, terrace 8 pavement 9 back alley, boulevard, concourse, territory
across the ~: 4 near 5 close 6 nearby
art: 5 mural
band: 4 gang
border: 4 curb
common ~ name: 3 Elm 4 Main 5 Maple
crosser: 6 avenue 10 pedestrian
ender: 3 car 4 wise 5 light, scape
eyesore: 6 litter
French ~ name starter: 5 rue de
in French: 3 rue
in Italian: 3 via
in Spanish: 5 calle
kid: 4 waif 5 gamin, stray 6 gamine, orphan, urchin 9 foundling 10 ragamuffin
language: 5 slang
maneuver: 5 U-turn
man in the ~: 6 people
noise: 5 siren
on easy ~: 4 rich 7 wealthy, well-off 8 well-to-do 10 in the chips, prosperous
on the other side of the ~: 8 opposite
performer: 4 mime 5 mimer 6 busker
person: 7 vagrant
posting: 4 sign
prohibiting cars: 4 mall
short ~: 4 lane 5 alley, court, place
show: 5 raree
sign: 4 slow, stop 5 arrow, yield
talk: 5 slang
street __: 3 rod 4 name 5 money 6 hockey, smarts 7 cleaner, fighter, orderly, railway, theater, theatre
street-__: 5 smart
__ street: 4 back, easy, side, stop 5 cross, on the 6 one-way, two-way 7 through
Street: 5 Della 6 Picabo
Street __: 5 Angel, Scene 6 Dreams
__ Street: 4 Back, Easy, Grub, Lime, Main, Side, Wall 5 Baker, Fleet, South 6 Harley, Hester, Lonely, Sesame 7 Downing, Lombard, Quality, Scarlet
Street Angel (1928 film)
cast: Charles Farrell, Janet Gaynor
director: Frank Borzage
__ Street Blues: 4 Hill 5 Basin, Beale
streetcar: 4 tram
building: 4 barn
charge: 4 fare
Streetcar Named Desire, A: 4 film, play
author: Tennessee Williams
cast: Marlon Brando, Kim Hunter, Vivien Leigh, Karl Malden
character: 4 Stan 5 Mitch, Pablo 6 DuBois, Eunice, Stella 7 Blanche, Stanley 8 Kowalski
director: Elia Kazan
setting: 9 Louisiana 10 New Orleans
street-corner call: 4 taxi
street-corner sign: 4 walk 8 don't walk
Street, Della
boss: 5 Mason
portrayer: 4 Hale
Street Dreams (1996 song) artist: Nas
__ Streeter: 4 Wall
Street of Dreams (1991 song) artist: Nia Peeples
Street, Picabo: 5 skier
streets
like some ~: 4 thru 6 gaslit
where ~ meet: 6 corner
__ Streets: 4 City, Mean
Street Scene: 4 film, play
author: Elmer Rice
cast: William Collier Jr., David Landau, Sylvia Sidney
character: 3 Abe, Sam 4 Anna, Rose 6 Kaplan
director: King Vidor
street-smart
see streetwise
Streets of __: 4 Fire 6 Laredo
Streets of Fire (1984 film)
cast: Diane Lane, Rick Moranis, Michael Paré
director: Walter Hill
Streets of Laredo author: Larry McMurtry
Streets of Philadelphia (1994 song) artist: Bruce Springsteen
Streets of San Francisco, The (ABC drama)
cast: Michael Douglas (Insp. Steve Keller)
Karl Malden (Det. Lt. Mike Stone)
__ Street, USA: 4 Main
__ Street Where You Live: 5 On the
streetwise: 4 onto 5 canny, savvy, slick 6 crafty, shrewd
Street With No Name, The (1948 film)
cast: Lloyd Nolan, Mark Stevens, Richard Widmark
St. Regis: 3 car 4 auto 5 Dodge 10 automobile, Studebaker
Streisand, Barbra: 6 singer 7 actress
film: All Night Long (1981)
For Pete's Sake (1974)
Funny Girl (1968, AA)
Hello, Dolly! (1969)
The Mirror Has Two Faces (1996)
Nuts (1987)
On a Clear Day You Can See Forever (1970)
The Owl and the Pussycat (1970)
The Prince of Tides (1991)
A Star Is Born (1976)
Up the Sandbox (1972)
The Way We Were (1973)
What's Up, Doc? (1972)
Yentl (1983)
song: Guilty (1980)
I Finally Found Someone (1996)
Love Theme from A Star Is Born (Evergreen) (1977)
The Main Event/Fight (1979)
My Heart Belongs to Me (1977)
No More Tears (1979)
People (1964)
Stoney End (1970)
The Way We Were (1973)
What Kind of Fool (1981)
Woman in Love (1980)
You Don't Bring Me Flowers (1978)
spouse: James Brolin, Elliott Gould
strength: 3 vim, zip 4 beef, dint, guts, kick, pull 5 asset, brawn, clout, depth, fiber, force, forte, juice, might, nerve, power, sinew, steam, thews, vigor 6 degree, energy, fervor, health, muscle, spirit, virtue, volume, weight 7 ability, bravery, cogency, courage, fitness, potence, potency, prowess, stamina 8 efficacy, firmness, mainstay, momentum, pressure, security, tenacity, validity, vitality 9 fortitude, hardiness, intensity, magnitude, soundness, stability, stoutness, substance, tolerance, toughness, vehemence, willpower 10 brawniness, brute force, durability, resolution, robustness, ruggedness, steadiness, sturdiness
lose ~: 3 lag 4 fade, fail, wilt
name meaning ~: 5 Ethan
of mind: 4 will 5 spine 7 resolve 8 backbone, decision, firmness, tenacity 9 fortitude, will power 10 resolution
regain ~: 5 rally 7 recover
sap the ~ of: 4 tire 5 drain 6 weaken 7 exhaust, wear out 8 enervate, enfeeble, paralyse, paralyze 9 attenuate, prostrate, undermine 10 debilitate, demoralize, devitalize
source of ~: 5 unity
test for ~: 6 stress
tower of ~: 6 pillar 7 bastion 9 supporter
__ strength: 3 wet 5 bench, brute, field, green, yield 7 dynamic, tensile
strengthen: 3 wax 4 back, feed, gird, prop 5 add to, brace, build, cheer, mount, raise, rally, ready, renew, shore, steel 6 anneal, beef up, deepen, extend, firm up, harden, step up, temper, thrive, tone up, uphold 7 animate, augment, bear out, bolster, build up, burgeon, confirm, develop, empower, enhance, enlarge, enliven, fortify, hearten, justify, nourish, nurture, prepare, prosper, quicken, recruit, refresh, restore, shore up, stiffen, support, sustain, toughen 8 bourgeon, buttress, embolden, enspirit, flourish, heighten, imbolden, increase, indurate, inspirit, multiply 9 encourage, establish, intensify, reinforce, undergird, vulcanize 10 accentuate, contribute, invigorate
__ strength of: 5 on the
strenuous: 4 hard 5 eager, heavy, lusty, rough, stiff, tough 6 active, ardent, rugged, severe, sticky, strong, taxing, thorny, trying, uphill 7 arduous, dynamic, earnest, labored, onerous, operose, serious, zealous 8 grueling, resolute, spirited, tireless, tiresome, toilsome, vigorous 9 ambitious, combative, demanding, difficult, effortful, energetic, herculean, laborious, murderous 10 aggressive, determined, exhausting, formidable, oppressive
strenuously: 4 hard 8 mightily
strep __: 6 throat
strepitous: 5 forte, noisy 7 blaring,

booming, jarring, pealing, rackety, raucous, reboant, roaring 8 crashing, piercing, plangent, rumbling, sonorous, strident, turned up 9 big-voiced, clamorous, deafening 10 boisterous, resounding, stentorian, thundering, uproarious, vociferous

Stresemann, Gustav: 8 Nobelist

stress: 3 tax 4 beat, care, fear, heat, rack 5 dread, force, labor, press, rub in, worry 6 accent, burden, crunch, harp on, hassle, import, nerves, overdo, play up, repeat, rhythm, strain, trauma, weight 7 anxiety, belabor, dwell on, feature, iterate, measure, point up, stretch, tension, trouble, urgency 8 emphasis, headline, pressure, reaffirm, reassert 9 dwell upon, emphasize, go on about, highlight, intensify, italicize, punctuate, reinforce, spotlight, tightness, underline 10 accentuate, importance, insistence, make much of, oppression, overextend, traumatize, underscore

feeling no ~: 6 at ease 7 content, relaxed 8 carefree, composed, tranquil

lack of ~: 6 atonia

result: 5 agita, ulcer

stress ___: 4 mark, test

___-stress analyzer: 5 voice

stressed: 4 taut 5 drawn, tense 8 emphatic 10 high-strung

stress-free: 4 calm 6 sedate, serene

stressful: 5 tense 6 jangly, taxing, trying 10 enervating

event: 6 crisis

stressless sound: 4 shwa 5 schwa

stretch: 3 eke, leg, run, way 4 area, grow, land, pull, rack, size, span, term, time, tour 5 cover, crane, patch, range, reach, scope, sheet, skimp, space, spell, stint, sweep, swell, tract, while, widen 6 blow up, bridge, dilate, expand, extend, extent, length, overdo, period, region, sprawl, spread, strain, stress, tauten, unfold, unroll 7 broaden, drag out, draw out, enlarge, expanse, inflate, overlap, prolong, recline, spin out, tighten 8 distance, duration, elongate, lengthen, misquote, overplay, protract 9 overstate, spread out, string out 10 exaggerate

fabric: 5 Lycra 7 spandex

out: 3 lie 4 rest 6 extend, repose, unfold 7 project, prolong, recline 8 protract

over: 4 span

starter: 4 back, home

the truth: 3 fib 10 exaggerate

stretch ___: 3 out 4 mill 6 runner

stretch a ___: 5 point

stretchable: 7 elastic, springy

stretched: 4 taut, thin 5 tight

combining form: 4 tany-

in ballet: 5 tendu 7 allongé

stretcher: 6 gurney, litter

stretching: 9 expansive, extension

combining form: 4 tono-

stretch one's ___: 4 legs

stretchy: 6 lissom, supple 7 elastic, lissome, springy 9 lethargic, resilient

cord: 6 bungee

streusel: 7 dessert, topping

strew: 3 sow 4 cast 5 throw 6 litter, splash, spread 7 diffuse, radiate, scatter, spatter 8 disperse, sprinkle 9 broadcast, cast about, circulate, toss about 10 distribute, promulgate

strewn: 7 diffuse 8 rambling

in heraldry: 4 semé

stria: 4 vein 5 ridge 6 streak 7 channel, fluting

striation: 4 vein 6 stripe

___-stricken: 3 awe 5 grief, panic 6 terror, wonder 7 poverty

strict: 3 set 4 firm, grim, hard 5 close, exact, harsh, rigid, stern, stiff, total, tough, utter 6 formal, severe, stuffy 7 austere, hard-set, literal, perfect, precise, prudish, Spartan, uptight 8 absolute, complete, despotic, exacting, rigorous 9 demanding, draconian, stringent, unbending 10 despotical, forbidding, inflexible, ironfisted, meticulous, no-nonsense, oppressive, particular, relentless, scrupulous

strictly: 5 truly 8 severely 9 literally

strictness: 5 rigor 8 hardness, iron hand 9 austerity, exactness 10 discipline

stricture: 4 slur, tabu 5 taboo 9 criticism 10 impediment, limitation, reflection

stride: 4 gait, pace, step, walk 5 march, stalk, stomp, tramp, tread, tromp 6 length, trapes 7 traipse 8 footstep

break ~: 6 falter

easy ~: 4 lope

stride ___: 5 piano

Stride ___: 4 Rite

stridency: 5 noise 9 cacophony

strident: 4 loud 5 forte, harsh, noisy, rough, vocal 6 brassy, off-key, shrill 7 blaring, blatant, booming, clarion, grating, jarring, pealing, rackety, rasping, raucous, reboant, roaring, squawky 8 clashing, crashing, jangling, piercing, plangent, rumbling, sonorous, turned up 9 big-voiced, clamorous, deafening, dissonant, outspoken, unmusical 10 boisterous, discordant, resounding, screeching, stentorian, stertorous, strepitous, thundering, uproarious, vociferant, vociferous

sound: 3 din 5 blare, noise

strides, make: 4 move 7 improve 8 progress

Stride Toward Freedom author: 4 King

stridulent: 7 grating

stridulous: 5 noisy

strife: 3 war 4 feud, fuss, riot, spat 5 brawl, clash, fight, words 6 affray, battle, blowup, combat, hassle, static, tumult, unrest, uproar 7 contest, discord, dispute, dissent, faction, quarrel, rivalry, trouble, warfare 8 argument, conflict, disunity, fighting, friction, squabble, struggle, tug of war, variance 9 animosity, bickering, wrangling 10 contention, difference, difficulty, disharmony, dissension, dissidence, dissonance, revolution

personification of ~: 4 Eris

starter: 5 loose

strigine youngster: 5 owlet

strike: 3 box, hit, rap, tap, wap 4 bang, bash, beat, blow, boff, bonk, cane, club, conk, cuff, find, flog, lash, lick, peck, pelt, quit, raid, seem, slam, slap, slug, sock, swat, sway, whap, whop, x out 5 blitz, clash, clout, crash, drive, erase, flail, knock, lunge, occur, pound, punch, reach, sit in, smack, smite, swipe, thump, touch, whack, whang 6 assail, attack, batter, buffet, delete, fillip, hammer, harrow, impact, invade, locate, picket, pommel, pummel, punish, resist, thwack, wallop 7 assault, bombard, boycott, clobber, collide, impress, inspire, lambast, occur to, protest, rear-end, run into, sit down, uncover, unearth, walkout 8 bludgeon, bump into, chastise, discover, fall upon, fire upon, interest, lambaste, register, slowdown 9 arbitrate, deal a blow, discovery, haul off on, intrude on, smash into 10 chance upon, come across, come to mind, happen upon

back: 6 resist 9 retaliate

caller: 3 ump 5 union 6 umpire

down: 4 fell 5 smite

end a ~: 6 settle

ender: 3 out 4 over 5 bound 7 breaker

go on ~: 5 rebel 6 picket, resist, revolt 7 protest, walk out

ignorer: 4 scab

issue: 5 wages 6 demand, salary 8 benefits

monitoring agcy.: 4 NLRB

on ~: 3 out

out: 3 fan, nix 4 bomb, bust, dele, fail, flop, lose, slip, trip 5 begin, elide, erase, flunk, start, whiff 6 blow it, cancel, censor, delete, falter 7 blunder, expunge, founder, go under, go wrong, misstep, stumble 8 fall flat, flounder, lay an egg 9 red-pencil

ready to ~: 6 coiled

try for a ~: 4 bowl

strike ___: 3 oil, out, pay 4 camp, down, fund, home, slip, zone 5 a pose, fault, force, hands, plate 7 benefit

strike ___ for liberty: 5 a blow

strike ___ the iron is hot: 5 while

___ strike: 3 air 4 rent 5 first, Roman 6 called, outlaw 7 general, sit-down, wildcat

___-strike: 3 ten

Strike ___: 4 It Up

strike a ___: 4 pose

strikebreaker: 4 scab

strike it ___: 4 rich

strike or spare in bowling: 4 mark

strikeout: 5 whiff

all-time ~ king: 4 Ryan

striker: 6 picket

strikes

three ~: 3 out

unable to throw ~: 4 wild

___ Strikes Back, The: 5 Saint 6 Empire

___-strikes law: 5 three

___ Strikes Out: 4 Fear

Strike up the band!: 5 hit it

Strike Up the Band: 7 musical

composer: 8 Gershwin

song: 4 Soon

striking: 4 cute 5 bonny, jazzy, lofty, showy, vivid 6 bonnie, cogent, comely, lovely, marked, pretty, scenic, signal 7 awesome, bizarre, graphic, salient, telling, unusual, visible, winsome 8 alluring, charming, dazzling, dramatic, dynamite, emphatic, fabulous, flagrant, forceful, forcible, gorgeous, handsome, imposing, powerful, scenical, singular, stunning, wondrous 9 arresting, beautiful, graphical, marvelous, memorable, prominent, ravishing, startling, wonderful 10 attractive, commanding, compelling, expressive, impressive, noteworthy, noticeable, prodigious, pronounced, remarkable, staggering, surprising

be ~: 8 stand out

striking ___: 5 price, train

strikingly: 7 greatly 8 markedly 9 eminently, extremely 10 especially, incredibly

Strindberg, August: 6 author, writer 7 Swedish 10 playwright

work: The Dance of Death
Miss Julie
The Red Room

string: 3 kit, oud, row, run, saz, tie, uke, uti 4 bass, bean, biwa, ch'in, cord, file, harp, kora, koto, lace, line, lira, lute, lyre, mvet, pipa, rank, rope, ruan, team, tier, vina, viol, yarn 5 banjo, bolon, cello, chain, chang, cobza, crwth, Dobro, fidla, kerar, ko-kiu, nguru, qanun, quena, queue, rebab, rebec, sitar, suite, train, twine, veena, viola 6 bagana, buzuki, chakay, fiddle, guitar, kissar, lacing, lirica, ramkie, rebeck, santir, series, strand, valiha, violin, zither 7 bandore, baryton, cithara, cittern, gittern, kantele, kithara, machete, mandola, obukano, pandora, quinton, samisen, tambura, theorbo, ukelele, ukulele 8 archlute, autoharp, bass viol, bousouki, bouzouki, clarsach, cymbalom, dulcimer, filament, harp lute, mandolin, psaltery, sequence, surbahar, yang chin 9 balalaika, long fiber 10 instrument, procession, succession

along: 3 lie, toy 4 dupe, fool 5 dally 6 follow, lead on, trifle 7 deceive, promise 8 play with 9 misinform

clean with ~: 5 floss

fastening: 4 knot

holder: 5 kiter

in music: 5 corda

out: 6 extend, line up 7 prolong, stretch 8 elongate, lengthen, protract, straggle

piece on a ~: 4 bead

player: 3 cat 6 kitten, lyrist 7 bassist, cellist, violist 9 violinist

quartet member: 5 cello, viola 6 violin

starter: 3 bow, ham 4 draw, shoe 5 heart, latch

strong ~: 6 catgut

together: 4 link 6 extend 7 stretch

string ___: 3 bag, tie 4 bass, bean, line 5 along 6 player, theory 7 quartet, trimmer

___ string: 3 on a 4 open 5 apron, drill 6 housed, second 7 pigging

String Along (1963 song) artist: Ricky Nelson

string bean: 5 scrag 6 legume, veggie 9 vegetable

like a: 4 lank, thin 5 lanky 6 skinny, svelte

stringency: 5 rigor 9 austerity

stringent: 3 set 4 firm, hard 5 bossy, cruel, harsh, picky, rigid, rough, stern, stiff, tight 6 forced, severe, strict 7 austere, binding, precise, Spartan 8 despotic, exacting, forceful, hard-line, rigorous 9 by the book, demanding, draconian, unbending, unsparing 10 compelling, despotical, inflexible, ironfisted, no-nonsense, oppressive, relentless, tyrannical

stringer: 8 reporter 10 journalist

___-string guitar: 6 twelve

strings: 5 power, terms 7 proviso 9 fine print, provision 10 conditions, provisions

in music: 5 corde

no ~: 9 boundless, limitless, unlimited

pull ~: 5 lobby, order, pluck 8 maneuver 10 manipulate

pull the ~: 6 govern

___ strings: 4 pull 5 purse 7 leading

stringy: 4 lank, lean, long, ropy, thin, wiry 5 lanky, ropey, tough 6 gangly, sinewy 7 fibrous, gristly, spindly 8 gangling

strip: 3 bar, gut, rob 4 band, bare, belt, flay, hull, husk, lath, peel, sack, shed, skin, slab, slip, tape 5 board, empty, harry, layer, patch, rifle, scale, shave, shred, shuck, slice, steal, stick, thong 6 denude, divest, expose, fillet, ravage, remove, ribbon, runway, streak, tongue 7 bereave, deprive, despoil, disrobe, lay bare, peel off, pillage, plunder, ransack, section, segment, take off, uncover, undress 8 displace, freeboot, get out of,

unclothe 9 depredate, dismantle, excoriate, slip out of
leather ~: 4 rein 5 thong
off: 4 flay 6 flench, flense 9 excoriate
of wood: 4 lath, slat
panel ~: 5 splat
raised ~: 5 ridge
reinforcing ~: 6 batten
starter: 3 air 4 film 5 field
suffix: 4 ling
thin ~: 4 shim
wooden ~: 4 lath
strip __: 3 map 4 bond, city, farm, mall 5 steak 6 mining 7 farming
strip-__: 4 mine
__ strip: 4 cant, drag, taxi, tear 5 comic, panel 6 flight, ledger, medial, median, medium, Möbius, ribbon, rumble 7 backing, breaker, gallery, landing, nailing, parking, parting, weather
__ Strip: 4 Gaza 7 Caprivi
Strip city: 5 Vegas 8 Las Vegas
stripe: 3 bar, ilk 4 band, line, sort, spot, vein, welt 5 class, layer, order 6 border, makeup, nature, ribbon, streak 7 variety 9 striation 10 decoration
of the same ~: 5 alike
raised ~: 4 welt
starter: 3 pin
zoologist's ~: 5 vitta
__ stripe: 5 candy, chalk 6 barley, pencil 7 hickory, service
striped: 4 liny 5 liney, tabby
animal: 4 kudu 5 bongo, skunk, tiger, zebra 6 koodoo
fabric: 7 gingham 8 bayadere
name meaning ~: 5 Rajiv
striped __: 4 bass 5 hyena, maple, skunk 6 gopher, marlin
__ striper: 5 candy
__-striper: 4 four
stripes: 7 uniform
person in ~: 3 ref 5 zebra 7 referee
remove ~ from: 6 demote
Stripes (1981 film)
cast: John Candy, Bill Murray, Warren Oates, Harold Ramis, Sean Young
director: Ivan Reitman
stripling: 3 boy, kid, lad 4 baby, teen 5 child, minor, youth 6 teener 7 preteen 8 half-pint, juvenile, teenager, young man 9 schoolboy, young lady, youngster 10 adolescent, schoolgirl
stripped: 4 bare 5 naked, plain, stark 8 in the raw 9 in the buff, in the nude
be ~ of: 7 forfeit
stripped-__: 4 down
Stripper, The (1962 song) artist: David Rose
__ stripping: 7 weather
strips: 7 funnies
cut into ~: 6 flitch
make ~: 4 tear
Stritch: 6 Elaine
strive: 3 aim, try, vie 4 moil, push, seek, toil, work 5 aim to, essay, exert, fight, labor, sweat 6 aspire, jockey, strain, tackle, take on 7 attempt, compete, contend, go after, quarrel, wrestle 8 bear down, endeavor, go all out, scramble, shoot for, struggle 10 go for broke, go the limit
for: 5 aim at 6 pursue
striving: 6 effort 8 endeavor, exertion
towards a goal: 5 nisus
strobe-light gas: 5 xenon
strobilus: 4 cone 8 pine cone
stroganoff: 6 entrée 9 casserole
__ stroganoff: 4 beef
Stroheim, Erich von: 8 director
film: Crimson Romance (1934)
Foolish Wives (1922)
Grand Illusion (1937)
Greed (1925)
The Merry Widow (1925)
Queen Kelly (1928)
Sunset Blvd. (1950)
The Wedding March (1928)
Stroh's: 4 beer
rival: 3 Bud 5 Becks, Coors, Kirin, Pabst 6 Amstel, Corona, Miller 7 Schlitz 8 Heineken, Michelob 9 Budweiser, Lowenbrau
stroke: 3 hit, pat, pet, rub 4 blow, coup, feat, laud, lick, love, luck, lull, tick 5 brush, shock, spell, touch 6 caress, pacify, praise, smooth, soothe, tickle 7 comfort, flatter 8 fawn over, flourish, inveigle, kowtow to, movement 9 reinforce, untrouble
along: 4 swim
light ~: 3 dab, pat
of genius: 4 coup, feat 7 exploit, triumph
of luck: 5 break, fluke 7 godsend 8 blessing, windfall
starter: 3 key 4 back, side 6 breast, ground, master
__ stroke: 4 butt, chop, hair 5 cross 6 ground, master 7 penalty, trudgen
stroking: 7 coaxing 8 cajolery, flattery 9 wheedling
stroll: 4 hike, turn, walk 5 amble, dance, jaunt, mosey, paseo, tramp 6 airing, foot it, junket, linger, loiter, ramble, trapes, wander 7 meander, saunter, traipse 8 ambulate 9 promenade
stroller: 4 pram 8 wanderer 10 pedestrian
occupant: 3 tot
Stroll in the Air, A author: Eugène Ionesco
Strom: 8 Thurmond
Stromboli: 3 isl. 4 isle 6 island 7 volcano
locale: 5 Italy 6 Europe
strong: 3 big, fit, hot 4 able, bold, deep, fast, firm, hale, hard, high, keen, loud, pure, rank, rich, sure, well, wiry 5 acute, beefy, brave, brute, burly, eager, fetid, fixed, great, gutsy, hardy, heady, hefty, husky, lusty, macho, nervy, pushy, sharp, solid, sound, spicy, stark, stiff, stout, tight, tough, vivid 6 active, biting, brawny, bright, cogent, fervid, fierce, foetid, hearty, living, marked, mighty, plucky, potent, rancid, robust, rotten, rugged, secure, severe, sinewy, smelly, spicey, stable, steady, steely, sturdy, unmixt, virile 7 capable, drastic, durable, extreme, fervent, glaring, handful, healthy, intense, noisome, odorous, orotund, piquant, pungent, staunch, telling, unmixed, violent, weighty 8 athletic, clear-cut, dazzling, distinct, emphatic, enduring, forceful, forcible, indurate, leathery, muscular, powerful, resolute, rocklike, stalwart, stinking, straight, untiring, vehement, vigorous, well-made 9 brilliant, dedicated, effective, energetic, hard-nosed, heavy-duty, herculean, resilient, sagacious, steadfast, strapping, strenuous, tenacious, trenchant, unbending, undiluted, well-built 10 able-bodied, aggressive, compelling, convincing, courageous, determined, formidable, full-bodied, iron-willed, malodorous, passionate, persuasive, pronounced, reinforced, unyielding
combining form: 6 trachy-
coming on ~: 4 bold 7 zealous 9 undaunted
ender: 3 box, man 4 hold
going ~: 5 palmy 7 booming, healthy, roaring, rolling 8 thriving 9 advancing 10 prospering, prosperous, successful
grow ~: 5 train 7 work out 8 exercise, pump iron
inclination: 3 yen 4 itch, urge 7 craving, impulse, passion 8 appetite, yearning 9 hankering
interest: 4 zeal, zest 5 ardor, mania 6 fervor, thirst 7 craving 8 devotion 9 intensity, obsession 10 dedication, enthusiasm
name meaning ~: 7 Valerie
not ~: 4 puny, weak 5 frail, tinny 6 feeble, flimsy
point: 5 asset, forte
starter: 4 head
strong __: 4 gale, side, suit 5 force, point 6 breeze, safety
strong __ ox: 4 as an
strong __ type: 6 silent
strong-__: 3 arm 6 minded, willed
strong-arm: 3 cow, mug, rob 4 push 5 bleed, bully, force, forge, shove 6 coerce, compel, hector, menace, prey on 8 pressure, prey upon 9 force upon, terrorize 10 intimidate
tactics: 6 duress 7 tyranny 8 coercion, violence 9 extortion 10 oppression
strongbox: 4 safe 5 chest, vault 6 coffer 7 lockbox 8 treasury
ancient ~: 4 arca
Strong Enough (1995 song) artist: Sheryl Crow
stronger: 6 better
grow ~: 5 rally 6 arouse, perk up, pick up, revive 7 get well, improve, rebound, recover, shape up 8 come back 9 get better 10 bounce back, come around, recuperate, rejuvenate, turn around
make ~: 6 beef up
stronger than dirt cleaner: 4 Ajax
strongest: 4 best
stronghold: 4 fort, keep 5 tower 6 castle, refuge 7 bastion, bulwark, citadel, defense, rampart, redoubt 8 fastness, fortress, garrison, presidio
castle ~: 4 keep
mountain ~: 4 aery, eyry 5 aerie, eyrie
Old Irish ~: 4 rath
strongly: 4 hard, well 6 keenly 8 forcibly, mightily, urgently 10 powerfully
strongman: 4 jefe 8 dictator
mythical ~: 5 Atlas 8 Heracles, Hercules
rule: 5 junta
Strong Man, The director: 5 Capra
strong-minded: 4 firm 6 all-out 7 decided 8 decisive, emphatic, forceful, resolute 9 obstinate 10 conclusive, unswerving, unwavering
Strong Poison author: Dorothy Sayers
strong-smelling: 4 olid, rank 5 sharp 6 rancid
Strongsville: 4 city, town
locale: 4 Ohio
strong-willed: 8 hellbent, resolute 9 masterful, tenacious 10 purposeful
strong work, name meaning: 9 Millicent
strontianite: 3 ore
strontium: 5 metal 7 element
ore: 9 celestite
strop: 4 edge, hone, whet 7 sharpen
stropped item: 5 razor
Strother: 6 Martin
Stroud: 4 city, town 6 Robert
locale: 7 England
Strouse, Charles
musical: Annie
Applause
Bye Bye Birdie
Golden Boy
struck: 4 hurt
down, old-style: 4 smit
out: 3 x'ed
starter: 3 awe 4 dumb, moon, star 7 thunder
structural: 5 modal 7 organic
frame: 5 truss
member: 4 I-bar 5 H-beam, I-beam
steel ~ column: 5 lally
suffix: 4 -plex
structural __: 4 gene, iron, shop 5 steel 7 formula, geology
structure: 4 cage, form, make 5 build, frame, house, order, setup, shape, shell 6 design, fabric, figure, format, makeup, nature, system 7 anatomy, complex, edifice, grammar, lattice, network 8 building, organism, skeleton 9 apparatus, fabricate, framework, machinery 10 morphology, skyscraper
combining form: 5 -morph 6 morpho-
crude ~: 5 shack 6 lean-to
science: 7 anatomy 10 morphology
sentence ~: 7 grammar
__ structure: 4 deep, fine 5 power 6 atomic, phrase, social 7 capital, surface
structured: 8 methodic
strudel: 4 cake 6 pastry 7 dessert
__ strudel: 5 apple
struggle: 3 row, try, vie, war 4 agon, bout, buck, cope, plod, tilt, toil, work 5 agony, brawl, brush, clash, essay, fight, grind, labor, pains, scrap, set-to, slave, sweat, trial 6 battle, combat, effort, hassle, hustle, strain, strife, strive, tackle, take on, tussle, writhe 7 attempt, compete, contend, contest, grapple, quarrel, scuffle, trouble, vie with, warfare, wrangle, wrestle 8 conflict, endeavor, exertion, flounder, long haul, plug away, scramble, skirmish, violence 9 bump heads, encounter, lock horns, square off 10 contention, difficulty, free-for-all, resistance
against: 6 resist 9 withstand
Greek hero's ~: 4 agon
long ~: 5 siege
__ struggle: 5 class, power
Strug, Kerri: 7 gymnast
strum: 5 plink, pluck, thrum
Struma: 5 river
locale: 6 Greece 8 Bulgaria
__ S Truman: 5 Harry
__-strung: 4 high
strung-out: 4 long, taut 5 tense 6 jangly 8 fluttery, restless, strained 10 distressed, protracted
strut: 4 beam, pose, prop, step, walk 5 dance, march, mince, pride, swank, sweep 6 flaunt, parade, prance, sashay 7 flounce, peacock, show off, support, swagger 8 auto part 9 put on airs 10 grandstand
__ strut: 4 oleo
__ Strut: 7 Soulful
Strut (1984 song) artist: Sheena Easton
Struthers: 5 Sally
strut one's __: 5 stuff
Strutt, John: 8 Nobelist 9 physicist
St. Swithin's __: 3 Day
St. Thomas: 3 isl. 4 city, isle, town 6 island
locale: 6 Canada 7 Ontario 10 West Indies
Stu: 5 Erwin 7 Gilliam, Jackson 9 Sutcliffe, Symington
Stuart: 3 J.E.B., Mel 4 Chad, city, Mary, town 5 Erwin 6 Cloete, Gloria, Gordon 7 Gilbert, Heisler, Whitman 8 Horowitz, Margolin 9 Rosenberg
last ~ monarch: 4 Anne
locale: 7 Florida
Stuart __ Flexner: 4 Berg

Stuart, Gilbert: **6** artist **7** painter
Stuart, Gloria: **7** actress
film: Gold Diggers of 1935 (1935)
The Invisible Man (1933)
The Prisoner of Shark Island (1936)
Roman Scandals (1933)
Sweepings (1933)
Titanic (1997)
The Whistler (1945)
Stuart, J.E.B.: **3** reb **7** general
Stuart Little: **4** book, film
author: E.B. White
cast: Geena Davis, Michael J. Fox, Jeffrey Jones, Nathan Lane, Hugh Laurie, Jonathan Lipnicki, Chazz Palminteri, Jennifer Tilly
director: Rob Minkoff
___ Stuart Masterson: **4** Mary
Stuart, Mel: **8** director
film: If It's Tuesday, This Must Be Belgium (1969)
One Is a Lonely Number (1972)
Wattstax (1973)
Willy Wonka and the Chocolate Factory (1971)
___ Stuart Mill: **4** John
stub: **3** end, tag, tip **4** butt, root, snag, tail **5** stump **6** tag end, ticket, tipoff **7** receipt, remnant, tail end **8** short end **9** rain check, remainder
one's toe: **3** err
stub ___: **4** a toe, nail **5** track
___ stub: **5** check
stubble: **5** beard **7** bristle
clear ~: **5** shave
remover: **5** razor
site: **4** chin
stubbly: **5** nubby, rough **7** bristly
stubborn: **3** set **4** firm, hard, iron **5** balky, fixed, onery, rigid, stern, stiff, stony, tough **6** cussed, dogged, feisty, mulish, ornery, stoney, unruly, wilful **7** adamant, defiant, hard-set, naughty, piggish, restive, wayward, willful **8** contrary, factious, hellbent, indocile, indurate, obdurate, perverse, resolute, untoward **9** fractious, hard-nosed, immovable, impliable, obstinate, pigheaded, steadfast, tenacious, unbending **10** bullheaded, determined, hard-bitten, hardheaded, headstrong, inexorable, inflexible, iron-willed, persistent, rebellious, refractory, relentless, self-willed, unshakable, unyielding
be ~: **6** resist **7** persist **9** persevere
one: **3** ass **4** cuss, mule **6** balker **7** baulker, holdout
stubborn ___ mule: **3** as a
Stubborn Hope poet: **6** Brutus
stubbornness: **4** will **8** tenacity
Stubbs: **4** Levi **6** George
stubby: **5** short, squat, stout, thick **6** little, stocky, stumpy **8** heavyset, thickset
Stubby: **4** Kaye
stucco: **7** encrust, incrust, plaster
site: **4** wall
stuck: **5** mired **6** caught, in a fix, in a jam, in a rut, static **7** adhered, at a loss, baffled, in a bind, puzzled, trapped **8** confused **9** buffaloed, immovable **10** gridlocked
be ~ on: **4** like, love **5** adore
get ~: **4** mire **5** lodge **6** wallow
in place: **3** set
it may be ~ out: **4** neck
on: **6** fond of
on oneself: **4** smug, vain
stuck ___ rut: **3** in a
Stuckenberg, Viggo: **4** poet **6** Danish
Stuck on You (song) artist: Elvis Presley, Lionel Richie
stuck-up: **4** smug, vain **5** aloof, cocky, proud **6** remote, stuffy **7** fustian, haughty, pompous **8** arrogant, boastful, snobbish, superior **9** big-headed, conceited, hubristic **10** big-talking
person: **4** snob **5** snoot
Stuck With You (1986 song) artist: Huey Lewis and the News
stud: **4** beam, bolt, boss, game, hunk, male, pole, post **5** he-man, poker **7** earring, tie tack **8** card game, cufflink, fastener, lothario, sprinkle **9** scantling
challenge: **5** I call
ender: **4** book, fish, work **5** horse
progeny: **4** colt, foal **5** filly
site: **3** ear **4** lobe
stud ___: **4** bolt **5** poker
studded: **5** beset **6** inlaid **8** speckled
studded ___: **4** tire
___-studded: **4** star
Studebaker: **3** car **4** auto **6** Avanti **10** automobile
model: **4** Hawk, Lark **5** Regal **6** Avanti, Pelham **7** Daytona, Sky Hawk, St. Regis **8** Champion, Dictator, Scotsman **9** Broadmoor, Commander, President **10** Challenger
student: **4** coed, grad **5** pupil, tutee, youth **6** intern, junior, novice **7** interne, learner, scholar **8** academic, disciple, freshman, graduate, observer **9** sophomore, undergrad, youngster **10** apprentice
award: **5** grant
become a ~: **5** enrol **6** enroll **8** register
book: **4** text
center: **4** quad **6** campus
eager ~ plea: **4** me me
first-year ~: **5** frosh **8** freshman
former ~: **4** alum, grad **6** alumna **7** alumnus **8** graduate
in French: **5** élève
last-year: **2** sr. **3** snr. **6** senior
ordeal: **4** exam, test **5** essay, final **7** midterm
place: **4** desk, dorm **6** school **7** college **9** dormitory **10** university
sack a ~: **5** expel
second-year ~: **4** soph **9** sophomore
stat: **3** GPA
third-year: **2** jr. **6** junior
unpopular ~: **4** geek, nerd, nurd
vehicle: **3** bus
student ___: **4** body, lamp **5** nurse, union **7** council, teacher
___ student: **3** day **6** pre-law, pre-med
Student Prince in Old Heidelberg, The (1927 film)
cast: Jean Hersholt, Ramon Novarro, Norma Shearer
director: Ernst Lubitsch
Student's ___: **5** t-test
studied: **6** wilful **7** labored, learned, planned, plotted, willful **8** affected, designed, gone into **9** conscious, unnatural **10** calculated, deliberate, purposeful
___ studies: **5** black **6** social, women's
studio: **4** loft **7** atelier
feature: **3** set **5** easel **6** camera
film ~: **3** lot
former ~: **3** RKO **6** Desilu
movie ~: **3** Fox, MGM **6** Disney **7** Miramax, New Line **8** Columbia **9** Paramount, Universal **10** Dreamworks, Warner Bros.
studio ___: **5** couch, glass
studious: **4** busy **5** eager **6** intent **7** bookish, careful, earnest, learned, serious **8** academic, diligent, highbrow, sedulous, well-read **9** assiduous, attentive, motivated, scholarly **10** meditative, reflective, thoughtful
studiously: **4** hard **10** designedly
studly: **5** macho
Studs: **6** Terkel
Studs Lonigan author: James T. Farrell
study: **3** con, den, dig, eye **4** case, cram, heed, look, mull, muse, plug, pore, read, room, scan **5** assay, grind, learn, paper, probe, think, train, weigh **6** bone up, debate, digest, go over, lesson, master, peruse, ponder, reason, revery, review, search, survey, take up **7** analyze, canvass, dissect, enquiry, examine, inquiry, inspect, library, observe, perusal, profile, reading, reflect, reverie, thought **8** analysis, check out, consider, learning, likeness, look into, meditate, mull over, polish up, pore over, practice, read up on, rehearse, research, scrutiny **9** attention, brood over, criticize, education, enter into, get to know, grind away, lucubrate, pick apart, sweat over, think over **10** crack a book, deliberate, experiment, reflection, rumination, scrutinize
brown ~: **4** muse **6** revery, trance **7** reverie **10** detachment
course of ~: **5** major **9** specialty
hard: **4** cram, pore
session: **6** lesson
study ___: **4** hall **5** group
___ study: **4** area, case, home, time **5** brown, quick **6** motion, nature
___-study: **4** self
Study in Scarlet, A author: Arthur Conan Doyle
Study of History, A author: Arnold Toynbee
___-study program: **4** work
stuff: **3** gas, jam, kit, pad, ram, rot, wad **4** blah, bosh, bull, bunk, cram, fill, gear, glut, guff, jazz, jive, junk, load, pack, pooh, push, sate, soul, stow, tosh **5** bilge, cloth, crowd, fudge, goods, gorge, hokum, hooey, items, prate, press, ram in, sense, shove, skill, stick, trash, tripe, wedge **6** bunkum, bushwa, drivel, fabric, fatten, footle, gabble, gammon, gibber, gobble, havers, hot air, humbug, jabber, jargon, kibosh, matter, piffle, stop up, tackle, things **7** baloney, blarney, blather, blether, boloney, bushwah, compact, congest, effects, engorge, eyewash, flannel, flubdub, fustian, garbage, hogwash, inanity, luggage, malarky, objects, overeat, rubbish, satiate, shove in, squeeze, twaddle **8** buncombe, claptrap, compress, falderal, falderol, flimflam, flummery, folderal, folderol, malarkey, material, movables, nonsense, property, slam-dunk, slipslop, tommyrot, trumpery **9** banana oil, equipment, gibberish, kidstakes, moonshine, overcrowd, poppycock, rigmarole, substance, trappings **10** applesauce, balderdash, belongings, bilge water, codswallop, double-talk, empty words, flapdoodle, galimatias, gormandize, Jabberwock, mumbo jumbo, rigamarole, taradiddle
starter: **3** dye **4** feed, food **5** bread
___ stuff: **3** hot, kid, red **4** hard **5** green, right, rough, small **7** ratline
___ Stuff: **3** Hot **5** Mr. Big
stuffed: **4** full, rife **5** close, laden, thick **6** loaded, packed **7** compact, fraught, replete, teeming **8** brimming **9** chockfull, condensed, congested, jam-packed, stoppered **10** compressed, gridlocked, obstructed, overfilled
delicacy: **5** derma **6** kishke, kiskha
in cookery: **5** farci
shirt: **4** prig, snob **5** snoot **7** elitist
stuffed ___: **5** derma, shirt **7** cabbage, peppers
Stuffed Shirts author: Clare Boothe Luce
stuffiness: **3** ego **6** egoism **7** conceit, egotism **8** humidity
stuffing: **3** pad **6** filler **7** filling, padding **8** dressing
flavoring: **4** sage
stuff one's ___: **4** face
___ Stuff, The: **5** Right
stuffy: **4** blah, damp, dank, dull, prim, smug **5** bland, close, heavy, ho-hum, humid, muggy, musty, rigid, soggy, staid, stale, thick, unfun **6** boring, clammy, formal, prissy, proper, square, steamy, sticky, stodgy, strict, sultry **7** airless, blocked, bookish, clogged, haughty, high-hat, pompous, prudish, stilted, stuck-up, tedious **8** priggish, puffed up, snobbish, stagnant, stifling, tiresome **9** conceited, humorless, ponderous, Victorian **10** big-talking, egocentric, oppressive, sweltering
Stuka: **5** plane **6** bomber **8** airplane
stull: **6** timber
stultify: **6** thwart **7** nullify, vitiate **9** frustrate, hamstring
stumble: **3** dud, err **4** bomb, bust, fall, flop, halt, lose, loss, muff, reel, slip, trip **5** error, fluff, flunk, lurch, waver **6** blow it, bumble, defeat, falter, fiasco, header, mishap, teeter, topple, totter, trudge, turkey, wabble, wobble **7** blunder, debacle, founder, go under, go wrong, misstep, shuffle, stagger, stammer, stutter, washout **8** downfall, fall flat, flounder, hesitate, lay an egg **9** indecorum, strike out **10** chance upon, come across, happen upon
across: **5** hit on **6** strike
ender: **3** bum
on: **4** find **5** learn **6** detect, locate **7** run into, uncover, unearth **8** bump into, chance on, discover **9** run across **10** chance upon
verbal ~: **2** er, uh, um
stumblebum: **2** ox **3** oaf **4** lout **5** klutz, looby **6** lubber
stumbling: **5** gawky **6** clumsy, klutzy, oafish **7** awkward, gawkish, halting, unadept **8** bungling, ungainly **9** all thumbs, graceless, maladroit, unskilled **10** hesitation, unskillful
block: **3** bar, rub **4** snag **5** catch, hitch **6** hurdle, kicker **7** barrier, pitfall, problem, setback **8** drawback, handicap, obstacle **9** hindrance **10** impediment
Stumblin' In (1979 song) artist: Suzi Quatro
stump: **3** end, leg, nub, run, vex **4** butt, foil, fool, knub, plod, stop, stub, talk, tour, walk **5** clomp, clump, floor, speak, stamp, stimy, stomp, stymy, tramp **6** baffle, lumber, nubbin, outwit, podium, puzzle, speech, stymie, trudge **7** buffalo, confuse, galumph, mystify, nonplus, perplex, stagger, tail end **8** bewilder, campaign, confound, hustings, platform **9** dumbfound, frustrate
for: **4** help **6** assist **7** endorse, indorse, support **8** advocate
source: **4** tree
take the ~: **5** orate, speak **7** address
___ stump: **3** off, up a **6** middle
stumped: **4** asea **5** at sea **7** at a loss, puzzled **8** confused
stumper: **4** koan **5** poser **6** enigma, riddle **7** problem, toughie
___ Stumper: **8** Saturday
stumpy: **5** thick **6** stubby

stun: 2 KO 3 awe, jar, wow 4 daze, faze, jolt, kayo, numb, rock 5 amaze, appal, floor, shock 6 appall, baffle, bedaze, bemuse, benumb, deaden, lay out 7 astound, confuse, flummox, nonplus, petrify, shake up, stagger, startle, stupefy, terrify 8 astonish, bedazzle, bewilder, blow away, bowl over, confound, knock out, overcome, paralyse, paralyze, surprise, transfix 9 dumbfound, overpower, overwhelm, take aback 10 discompose, scare stiff
gun: 5 taser
with sound: 6 deafen
stung: 4 sore 5 burnt 6 burned 7 injured
be ~ by conscience: 3 rue 5 atone 6 regret
__ Stung: 4 I Got
stunned: 4 agog 5 agasp, in awe, shook 6 aghast, jolted 8 overcome 9 awestruck 10 dumbstruck
appear ~: 4 gape
stunner: 6 beauty, eyeful, looker, marvel, vision 7 miracle, prodigy 8 knockout 9 sensation
stunning: 4 cute 5 bonny 6 bonnie, comely, lovely, pretty, superb 7 amazing, awesome, winsome 8 adorable, alluring, dazzling, fetching, gorgeous, handsome, heavenly, pleasing, smashing, striking 9 arresting, beautiful, brilliant, marvelous, number one, ravishing 10 attractive, impressive, prodigious, remarkable, stupendous
stunt: 3 act 4 deed, feat, ruse, slow, stop 5 caper, dwarf, thing, trick 6 hinder, impede 7 exploit, gimmick 8 activity, pretense 10 shenanigan
performer: 5 clown 7 acrobat 9 daredevil
stunted: 3 low 4 puny, tiny 5 runty, scrub, short, small 6 bantam, little, peewee 7 dwarfed 9 pint-sized, undersize 10 diminutive, undersized
animal: 4 runt
tree: 5 scrub
Stunt Man, The (1980 film)
cast: Barbara Hershey, Peter O'Toole, Steve Railsback
director: Richard Bush
stupa: 4 tope 8 monument
stupe: 3 ass, nit, oaf, sap 4 boob, clod, dodo, dolt, dope, fool, gowk, zany 5 chump, clown, cluck, dummy, dunce, goose, joker, klutz, looby, ninny, patsy 6 cuckoo, dimwit, doofus, lubber, lummox, nitwit, sucker, turkey 7 buffoon, dingbat, dullard, fathead, half-wit, jackass, pinhead, saphead 8 bonehead, dumbbell, lunkhead, meathead, numskull 9 birdbrain, blockhead, greenhorn, harebrain, lamebrain, numbskull, simpleton 10 dunderhead, nincompoop
stupefaction: 3 awe 4 daze 5 shock 8 hypnosis
stupefied: 4 logy 5 agape 9 lethargic 10 bewildered
stupefy: 4 daze, drug, numb, rock, stun, zonk 5 addle, amaze, besot, floor, shock 6 bemuse, benumb, boggle, dazzle, muddle 7 astound, confuse, petrify, shake up, stagger, terrify 8 astonish, bewilder, blow away, bowl over, confound, knock out, paralyse, paralyze, surprise 9 dumbfound, inebriate, overwhelm 10 intoxicate, scare stiff
stupendous: 3 big, def, rad 4 aces, A-one, boss, braw, cool, dece, fine, gear, huge, keen, neat, nice, phat, tuff, vast 5 dandy, ducky, giant, grand, great, jumbo, large, marvy, neato, nobby, prime, slick, super, swell 6 bang on, bang-up, bonzer, bosker, choice, cosmic, divine, dreamy, far-out, gnarly, groovy, lovely, mighty, peachy, slap-up, spot on, superb, terrif, tiptop, unreal, whizzo, wicked 7 amazing, awesome, capital, corking, hulking, immense, mammoth, massive, perfect, radical, ripping, sizable, skookum, stellar, sublime, titanic, too much 8 colossal, cosmical, dazzling, dynamite, enormous, especial, eximious, fabulous, five-star, four-star, frabjous, gigantic, glorious, heavenly, jim-dandy, king-size, oversize, sizeable, slam-bang, smashing, splendid, standout, sterling, stickout, stunning, superior, terrific, top-level, topnotch, towering, very good, whapping, whopping, wondrous 9 bodacious, Endsville, excellent, exemplary, exquisite, fantastic, first-rate, Herculean, high-grade, humongous, hunky-dory, marvelous, monstrous, overlarge, sollicker, top-flight, unrivaled, wonderful 10 first-class, gargantuan, hotsy-totsy, jack-a-dandy, monumental, out of sight, peachy-keen, phenomenal, prodigious, remarkable, super-duper, tremendous, unrivalled
Stupid __ Tricks: 3 Pet
Stupid Cupid (1958 song) artist: Connie Francis
stupor: 4 daze 5 shock, swoon 6 apathy, torpor, trance 7 inertia, languor, slumber 8 dullness, hypnosis, lethargy, loginess, numbness 9 indolence, lassitude 10 somnolence
sturdiness: 3 vim 4 dint, thew 5 brawn, force, might, power, thews, vigor 6 energy, muscle 7 fitness, muscles, potence, potency, stamina 8 strength, vitality 9 endurance, fortitude, puissance 10 brute force
sturdy: 4 firm, hale, iron, wiry 5 beefy, burly, hardy, hefty, hunky, husky, lusty, solid, sound, stout, tight, tough 6 brawny, hearty, mighty, potent, robust, rugged, secure, sinewy, stable, steely, stocky, strong, virile 7 doughty, durable, healthy, hulking, staunch 8 athletic, forceful, indurate, muscular, powerful, puissant, resolute, stalwart, vigorous, well-made 9 Atlantean, fortified, Herculean, steadfast, strapping, tenacious, well-built 10 able-bodied, determined, red-blooded, reinforced
sturgeon: 4 fish 6 beluga 7 sterlet
product: 3 roe 6 caviar 7 caviare
__ sturgeon: 4 lake 5 white 7 Pacific
Sturgeon, Theodore: 6 author, writer
genre: 5 sci-fi
Sturges: 4 John 7 Preston
Sturges, John: 8 director
film: Bad Day at Black Rock (1955)
The Capture (1950)
The Eagle Has Landed (1977)
Escape From Fort Bravo (1953)
The Great Escape (1963)
Gunfight at the O.K. Corral (1957)
Ice Station Zebra (1968)
Kind Lady (1951)
Last Train From Gun Hill (1959)
The Law and Jake Wade (1958)
The Magnificent Seven (1960)
The Magnificent Yankee (1950)
McQ (1974)
The Old Man and the Sea (1958)
The Satan Bug (1965)
The Walking Hills (1949)
Sturges, Preston: 8 director
film: Christmas in July (1940)
The Great McGinty (1940)
Hail the Conquering Hero (1944)
The Lady Eve (1941)
The Miracle of Morgan's Creek (1944)
The Palm Beach Story (1942)
Sullivan's Travels (1941)
Unfaithfully Yours (1948)
Sturgis: 4 city, town
locale: 4 S. Dak. 10 Black Hills
Sturm und Drang: 5 drama 6 tumult 7 turmoil 8 upheaval
stutter: 4 slur 6 falter, mumble 7 sputter, stammer, stumble 8 hesitate, splutter
Stuttgart: 4 city, town
locale: 7 Germany
river: 6 Neckar
Stutz Bearcat: 3 car 4 auto 10 automobile
contemporary: 3 Reo 5 Essex
Stuyvesant: 5 Peter
St. Vincent and the Grenadines: 6 nation 7 country
capital: 9 Kingstown
locale: 10 West Indies
__ St. Vincent Millay: 4 Edna
sty: 3 pen 4 dump, slum 5 hovel, sewer 6 pigpen 7 piggery 8 cesspool, pesthole 9 enclosure, hordeolum
baby: 4 gilt 5 shoat, shote, shott 6 piglet
comment: 4 oink 5 grunt
dweller: 3 hog, pig, sow 5 swine
fare: 4 slop 5 swill
free from the ~: 5 unpen
starter: 3 pig
Stygian: 3 dim 4 dark, evil 6 nether 9 lightless
style: 3 air, cut, dub, fad, tag, way 4 call, coif, dash, ease, élan, form, kind, mode, name, rage, sort, term, tone, type, vein 5 class, craze, decor, flair, genre, genus, grace, label, model, state, taste, tenor, thing, title, trend, vogue 6 aplomb, beauty, bon ton, custom, design, flavor, format, glamor, Gothic, luxury, manner, method, nature, pizazz, polish, rococo, spirit, tailor, temper 7 baroque, bearing, comfort, costume, diction, fashion, glamour, Moorish, panache, pattern, suavity, wording 8 approach, artistry, delicacy, elegance, grandeur, language, phrasing, Sheraton, urbanity 9 character, classical, designate, nattiness, ritziness, suaveness, technique, treatment 10 art nouveau, complexion, dapperness, denominate, flashiness, modishness, refinement, Romanesque, snazziness, swankiness
cramp one's ~: 5 spite 8 obstruct
in ~: 3 hip, mod 4 tony 5 natty, sharp, swank, toney 6 chi-chi, classy, dapper, dressy, modish, trendy 7 à la mode, current, dashing, elegant, popular, voguish 10 all the rage, prevailing
in the ~ of: 3 à la
no longer in ~: 3 old, out 4 past 5 dated, dowdy, dusty, fusty, passé 6 bygone, old hat, quaint 7 ancient, archaic, fogyish 8 decrepit, long gone, medieval, obsolete, timeworn 10 antiquated, superseded
starter: 4 free, life
style __: 5 sheet
__ style: 3 old 4 hair, high, type 5 grass, out of 6 family 7 Chicago
__-style: 4 home 5 boxer 6 French
Style: 7 channel
alternative: 3 BET, CMT, MTV, PAX, TBS, TLC, TNN, TNT, USA 4 ESPN, HGTV 5 A and E, C-SPAN 6 Noggin, Tech TV, TV Land 7 Court TV, Ovation, SoapNet 8 Lifetime
__-styled: 4 self
styling goo: 3 gel 5 gelee
stylish: 3 hip, mod, now 4 chic, neat, tony 5 class, faddy, funky, haute, jazzy, natty, nifty, ritzy, sharp, slick, smart, swank, swell, swish, toney 6 chichi, classy, dapper, dressy, flossy, modern, modish, snappy, snazzy, spruce, swanky, trendy, uptown 7 à la mode, current, dashing, elegant, genteel, in vogue, popular, voguish 8 artistic, handsome, polished, up-to-date 9 exclusive, high-class, in fashion 10 all the rage, artistical
too ~: 4 arty 5 artsy
stylishness: 3 ton 4 chic 5 vogue
stylist: 6 barber
activity: 3 cut, dye 8 makeover
challenge: 3 mop
creation: 4 coif 6 hairdo
supply: 3 gel 4 comb 5 spray 9 hairspray
Stylistics
hometown: Philadelphia
song: Betcha By Golly, Wow (1972)
Break Up to Make Up (1973)
I'm Stone in Love With You (1972)
You Are Everything (1971)
You Make Me Feel Brand New (1974)
stylograph: 3 pen
stylus: 3 pen
holder: 3 arm 7 tonearm
target: 6 groove
Stylus: 3 car 4 auto 5 Isuzu 10 automobile
stymie: 4 balk, foil, tree, undo 5 baulk, block, cramp, crimp, stall, stump 6 baffle, corner, defeat, hamper, hang up, hinder, impede, thwart 7 dead-end, inhibit, nonplus, prevent, ward off 8 confound, obstruct, prohibit 9 frustrate, stonewall
stymied: 5 stuck 6 in a fix, in a jam
Styne, Jule: 8 composer
collaborator: 4 Cahn 7 Merrill 8 Sondheim
musical: Bells Are Ringing
Do Re Mi
Funny Girl
Gentlemen Prefer Blondes
Gypsy
Hallelujah, Baby!
High Button Shoes
Lorelei
Sugar
song: Diamonds Are a Girl's Best Friend
Don't Rain on My Parade
Everything's Coming Up Roses
Five Minutes More
I Don't Want to Walk Without You, Baby
It's Been a Long, Long Time
It's Magic
I've Heard That Song Before
Just in Time
Let Me Entertain You
Make Someone Happy
The Party's Over
People
Saturday Night Is the Loneliest Night of the Week
Small World
Three Coins in the Fountain
styptic: 4 alum 7 binding 10 astringent
pencil coverup: 4 nick
Styr: 5 river
locale: 7 Ukraine
Styrofoam: 7 padding, plastic
Styron, William: 6 author, writer
work: The Confessions of Nat Turner
In the Clap Shack

Lie Down in Darkness
The Long March
The Quiet Dust
Set This House on Fire
Sophie's Choice
Styx: 5 river
daughter: 4 Nike
locale: 5 Hades
tributary: 5 Lethe 6 Aornis 7 Acheron, Cocytus 10 Phlegethon
Styx (rock group)
hometown: Chicago
song: Babe (1979)
The Best of Times (1981)
Come Sail Away (1977)
Don't Let It End (1983)
Lady (1975)
Lorelei (1976)
Mr. Roboto (1983)
Show Me the Way (1981)
Too Much Time on My Hands (1981)
suave: 4 cool, glib, oily 5 bland, civil 6 genial, poised, polite, smooth, urbane 7 affable, cordial, courtly, gallant, politic, refined, tactful, worldly 8 charming, cultured, debonair, finished, gracious, obliging, pleasant, pleasing, polished, sociable, unctuous, well-bred 9 agreeable, civilized, courteous, debonaire, high-toned 10 cultivated, debonnaire, diplomatic, soft-spoken
Suave: 7 shampoo
competitor: 4 Flex, Pert 5 Prell, Wella 7 Finesse, Pantene
suaveness: 4 tact 5 couth, style 6 polish 8 courtesy 11 savoir faire
sub: 4 hero, temp 5 hoagy, proxy, U-boat, under 6 backup, deputy, fill in, hoagie 7 replace, stand-in 8 pinch-hit, sandwich 9 alternate, fill in for, surrogate 10 understudy
concern: 5 depth
detector: 5 asdic, sonar
device: 5 scope 7 torpedo 9 periscope
door: 5 hatch
hazard: 4 mine 6 ashcan
locale: 3 sea 4 deep 5 ocean
on sonar: 3 pip 4 blip
outlet: 4 deli
sub __: 4 rosa, voce 5 verbo 6 judice
sub-__: 4 zero 5 level 7 Saharan
subaltern: 4 rank 7 officer
Subaru: 3 car 4 auto 6 import 10 automobile
competitor: 5 Honda, Isuzu 6 Toyota
model: 3 SVX, WRX 5 Justy, Leone 6 Legacy, Loyale 7 Impreza, Outback 8 Forester
subatomic particle: 2 xi 4 kaon, muon, pion 5 boson, gluon, meson, quark 6 baryon, hadron, lepton, photon 7 fermion, hyperon, neutron, tachyon 8 deuteron, electron, graviton, neutrino, positron
subcompact: 3 car 4 auto 10 automobile
subconscious: 4 mind 5 inner 6 hidden, inmost, latent, psyche 9 intuitive 10 archetypal
subculture: 6 hip-hop
subdeacon: 6 cleric
subdivide: 5 halve, slice, split 9 partition
minutely: 4 cube, dice 5 mince
subdivision: 3 arm 4 part 5 class, group, split, tract 6 branch, sector 7 element, section, segment 9 community
subdue: 3 cow 4 beat, curb, lull, mute, tame 5 abate, break, crush, quash, quell, quiet, worst 6 bridle, deaden, defeat, gentle, govern, humble, mellow, muffle, pacify, reduce, soften, soothe, temper 7 appease, conquer, control, oppress, put down, repress, silence, squelch, trample, triumph 8 keep down, mitigate, moderate, overcome, restrain, strangle, suppress, surmount, tone down, vanquish 9 humiliate, overpower, quiet down, subjugate 10 keep in line
subdued: 3 dim, low, sad 4 meek, mild, soft, tame 5 bated, faint, grave, muted, piano, quiet, sober, yoked 6 broken, broody, docile, gentle, hushed, lowkey, mellow, pliant, solemn, subtle 7 neutral, serious, trained 8 dejected, delicate, downcast, lamblike, murmured, obedient, resigned, tasteful 9 chastened, compliant, repentant, repressed, toned down, tractable, whispered 10 manageable, restrained, spiritless, submissive
color: 3 ash, tan 4 gray, grey, navy 5 beige, brown, mauve, ocher, ochre, umber
Subic __: 3 Bay
subito: 8 suddenly
subjacent: 5 lower 6 lesser
subject: 3 apt 4 item, noun, serf, text 5 class, issue, liege, model, motif, prone, ruled, theme, thing, topic, under 6 client, course, liable, likely, vassal 7 captive, exposed, inflict, patient, servile, villein 8 enslaved, governed, inferior, obedient 9 dependant, dependent, guinea pig, leitmotif, secondary, tentative 10 answerable, contingent, controlled, discipline, vulnerable
subject __: 6 matter
subjection: 7 loyalty 9 captivity, liability 10 domination
subjective: 6 biased, mental 8 illusive, illusory, personal 9 arbitrary, emotional, intuitive
subjectivity: 4 bias 9 prejudice 10 favoritism, preference
Subject Was Roses, The (1968 film)
cast: Jack Albertson, Patricia Neal, Martin Sheen
director: Ulu Grosbard
subjoin: 3 add 5 affix
subjugate: 4 tame 5 crush, quell 6 defeat, prey on, reduce, subdue 7 conquer, enslave, enthral, inthral, oppress, put down, triumph 8 bring low, dominate, enthrall, inthrall, keep down, overcome, prey upon, suppress, vanquish 9 overpower
subjugation: 6 defeat 7 slavery, victory 9 servitude
subjugator: 4 hero 6 master, victor, winner 8 champion 9 conqueror 10 vanquisher
sublet: 4 rent 5 lease
sublimate: 6 purify 7 ennoble
sublime: 3 def, rad 4 aces, A-one, boss, braw, cool, dece, fine, gear, high, keen, neat, nice, phat, tuff 5 dandy, ducky, grand, great, lofty, marvy, neato, nobby, noble, prime, proud, slick, super, swell 6 bang on, bang-up, bonzer, bosker, choice, divine, dreamy, far-out, gnarly, groovy, lovely, peachy, slap-up, spot on, superb, terrif, tiptop, unreal, whizzo, wicked 7 amazing, awesome, capital, corking, exalted, perfect, refined, ripping, skookum, stately, stellar 8 dazzling, dynamite, elevated, empyreal, empyrean, especial, ethereal, eximious, fabulous, five-star, four-star, frabjous, glorious, gorgeous, heavenly, imposing, jim-dandy, majestic, rarefied, slam-bang, smashing, splendid, standout, sterling, stickout, superior, terrific, top-level, topnotch, towering, ultimate, very good, wondrous 9 beautiful, bodacious, celestial, Endsville, excellent, exemplary, exquisite, first-rate, high-grade, hunky-dory, marvelous, sollicker, top-flight, unrivaled, wonderful 10 first-class, hotsy-totsy, jack-a-dandy, majestical, out of sight, peachy-keen, phenomenal, remarkable, stupendous, super-duper, unrivalled
subliminal: 6 mental 9 intuitive
sublimity: 5 glory 8 grandeur, nobility 9 elevation, greatness 10 perfection
submachine gun: 3 Uzi
submarine
see sub
__ Submarine: 6 Yellow
submerge: 3 dip 4 duck, dunk, sink, soak 5 douse, dowse, drown, flood, lower, souse, steep, swamp 6 deluge, drench, engulf, ingulf, plunge 7 descend, founder, go under, immerse 8 inundate, overflow 9 hit bottom, overwhelm
submerged: 4 sunk 6 sunken 8 immersed, scuttled 9 engrossed 10 underwater
submerse: 3 dip 4 sink 5 bathe, souse, swamp
submission: 3 bid 6 assent 7 loyalty 8 docility, humility, meekness, yielding 9 deference, endurance, obedience, orthodoxy, passivity, servility, surrender 10 compliance, conformity
contest ~: 5 entry
editorial: 5 draft 10 manuscript
submissive: 4 easy, meek, mild, tame 5 lowly, timid 6 abject, broken, docile, humble, pliant 7 dutiful, orderly, passive, pliable, servile, slavish, subdued, trained, willing 8 amenable, gracious, lamblike, obedient, resigned, yielding 9 agreeable, compliant, groveling, malleable, prostrate, spineless, tractable 10 governable, manageable
submit: 3 bid, bow, put 4 bend, cave, fold, obey, pose 5 defer, kotow, offer, refer, stand, yield 6 assert, buckle, comply, endure, give in, hand in, kowtow, suffer, tender, turn in 7 advance, contend, present, proffer, propose, succumb, suggest, truckle 8 nominate, propound, put forth, say uncle, stand for 9 acquiesce, prostrate, reconcile, surrender 10 capitulate, come around, put forward, toe the line
subnormal: 7 lacking 9 defective, deficient
subordinate: 4 aide, asst., less, side 5 gofer, lower, lowly, minor, slave, under 6 deputy, flunky, gopher, helper, junior, lesser, second 7 flunkey, servant 8 adjuvant, henchman, inferior 9 accessory, ancillary, assistant, attendant, auxiliary, dependant, dependent, gal Friday, man Friday, overwhelm, satellite, secondary, subaltern, tributary, underling 10 girl Friday
subordinate __: 6 clause
subordinates: 5 staff
subordination: 4 sway 5 might 7 control, mastery 9 supremacy, upper hand 10 domination, occupation, oppression
suborn: 5 bribe 7 corrupt, falsify
suborned: 5 false 7 corrupt 9 on the take
Subotica: 4 city, town
locale: 6 Serbia
subpar hole: 3 ace 5 eagle 6 birdie
subpoena: 4 call, cite, writ 5 paper 6 summon 7 process, summons, warrant
sub rosa: 6 secret 7 furtive, illegal 8 hush-hush, on the sly, secretly 9 entre nous, furtively, privately, underhand 10 undercover
subscribe: 3 buy 4 back, give, sign 5 agree, bless, boost, enrol, favor, grant, put up 6 ante up, chip in, donate, enroll, pledge, second, sign up 7 approve, endorse, indorse, pitch in, promise, support 8 advocate, register, sanction 9 acquiesce, autograph, get behind 10 contribute, underwrite
subscriber: 6 patron, reader 9 proponent, supporter 10 benefactor
subscribing, keep: 5 renew 6 extend, update 7 prolong 8 continue
subscription
card: 6 insert
unit: 5 issue
subsequent: 4 next 5 after, later 6 coming, future, second 7 ensuing 8 eventual, upcoming 9 following, posterior, proximate, resulting, secondary 10 consequent, succeeding
subsequently: 4 anon, next 5 after, hence, later, since 6 behind 7 ensuing, finally, someday 8 in back of, in the end 9 afterward, following 10 succeeding
subservience: 4 fear 8 docility, humility, meekness 9 cowardice, servility
subservient: 4 meek, mild 5 slave, under 6 abject, docile, menial, useful 7 fawning, ignoble, servile, slavish 8 cowering, cringing, resigned 9 prostrate
be ~: 4 fawn 5 cower 6 cringe, grovel, kowtow 8 bootlick
subside: 3 die, ebb, set 4 ease, fall, lull, sink, wane 5 abate, lapse, let up, lower 6 go down, lessen, recede, relent, settle 7 decline, die down, dwindle, quieten, slacken, tail off 8 blow over, collapse, contract, decrease, diminish, head away, level off, moderate, peter out, slack off, taper off 9 lighten up, retrocede 10 de-escalate
subsidence: 5 lysis 9 abatement, remission
subsidiary: 4 side 5 minor, under 6 backup, branch, lesser 9 ancillary, auxiliary, secondary 10 collateral, incidental
subsidiary __: 6 rights 7 company
subsidize: 3 aid 4 abet, back, fund, help 5 endow, juice, set up, stake 7 finance, promote, sponsor, support 8 bankroll 9 encourage, grubstake 10 capitalize, contribute, supplement, underwrite
subsidy: 3 aid 4 gift 5 bonus, grant 6 bounty, reward 7 alimony, backing, bequest, payment, pension, premium, support 8 donation, largesse 9 allowance, endowment, patronage 10 assistance, fellowship, honorarium
subsist: 4 last, live 5 exist 6 endure, hang on, manage 7 breathe, ride out, survive 8 continue, get along, scrape by 9 keep going, stay alive 10 stick it out
subsistence: 4 life 5 means, wages 6 income, living, salary, upkeep 7 aliment, capital, support 8 earnings 9 provision, resources 10 livelihood
subsistence __: 7 farming
subsoil: 4 dirt 5 earth
substance: 3 nub 4 body, core, gist, guts, heft, knub, meat, pith, root, size, soul 5 drift, fiber, focus, force, heart, means, sense, stuff, tenor, theme, thing, value, worth 6 burden, import, kernel, marrow, matter, moment, riches, spirit, thrust, upshot, wealth 7 content, essence, keynote, meaning, purport, reality 8 contents, material, property, strength, sum total, validity 9 actuality, affluence, essential, lifeblood, something 10 importance

full of ~: 4 rich 5 meaty, pithy 7 weighty 8 profound
in ~: 6 nearly 9 virtually
lacking ~: 4 thin 5 inane 8 ethereal
sum and ~: 3 nub 4 core, gist 5 heart, theme 6 kernel
Substance of Fire, The writer: 5 Baitz
substandard: 3 bad, low, off 4 poor, weak 7 wanting 8 inferior
substantial: 3 big, key 4 firm, good, much, real, rich, tidy, true, vast 5 ample, beefy, bulky, hardy, heavy, hefty, large, meaty, solid, sound, stout, thick, valid 6 actual, goodly, hearty, rugged, stable, steady, strong, sturdy 7 durable, for real, gainful, massive, serious, sizable, visible, wealthy, weighty, well-off 8 abundant, concrete, definite, explicit, generous, material, physical, positive, sizeable, stalwart, tangible, valuable, well-made, well-to-do 9 corporeal, important, momentous, objective, well-built
substantiality: 4 size 7 reality 9 stability
substantially: 4 well 6 mainly 7 heavily, largely 9 in essence, in the main
substantiate: 4 test 5 prove, vouch 6 affirm, attest, ratify, verify 7 bear out, certify, confirm, justify, support 8 attest to, check out, evidence, flesh out, validate 9 establish, vindicate
substantiation: 5 proof 8 acid test, evidence 9 testimony
substitute: 4 mock, sham, swap, swop, temp 5 agent, cover, false, ghost, other, proxy, shift, sit-in, spare, vicar 6 act for, backup, change, deputy, ersatz, fill in, relief, second, switch 7 another, plastic, relieve, replace, reserve, stand-in, stopgap 8 cover for, displace, exchange, pinch-hit, spurious 9 alternate, assistant, auxiliary, expedient, fill in for, makeshift, surrogate, temporary 10 artificial, equivalent, pro tempore, quid pro quo, understudy
name meaning ~: 4 Seth
substitution: 6 change 8 exchange
substratum: 3 bed 4 base 5 layer 7 support 10 foundation, groundwork
substructure: 5 basis 7 support
subsume: 4 have 7 contain, include
subsumed: 5 under
subterfuge: 3 lie 4 hoax, ploy, ruse, sham, trap, wile 5 blind, bluff, craft, dodge, feint, fraud, shift, trick 6 deceit, device, dupery, humbug, scheme 7 evasion, knavery, pretext, sleight, snow job, swindle 8 artifice, maneuver, pretense 9 chicanery, deception, expedient, fourberie, imposture, stratagem 10 hanky-panky
subterranean: 4 deep 5 below 6 buried, hidden 7 abysmal 9 cavernous
area: 4 mine 5 crypt 6 cavern, cellar, grotto 8 basement
creature: 3 bat 4 mole 5 gnome, troll
lockup: 6 donjon 7 dungeon
passageway: 6 dromos
subtle: 3 sly 4 deep, fine, keen, nice 5 faint, snaky 6 artful, astute, clever, low-key, polite, slight, tricky 7 devious, implied, logical, politic, refined, subdued, tactful, tenuous 8 abstruse, delicate, discreet, finespun, guileful, illusive, indirect, inferred, profound, scheming 9 astucious, courteous, designing, exquisite, ingenious, insidious, judicious, sensitive 10 diplomatic, intriguing, perceptive, suggestive, thoughtful
indication: 4 clue, hint 5 trace 10 suggestion
not ~: 5 broad 7 obvious
signal: 3 nod 4 wink 7 gesture
subtlety: 4 tact 5 craft 6 nicety, nuance 7 finesse, mystery 8 delicacy, quiddity 9 diplomacy 10 refinement
subtract: 4 take 6 deduct, remove 7 compute, detract 8 decrease, diminish, discount, knock off, take away, withhold 9 calculate
subtraction: 9 lessening, reduction
result: 10 difference
word: 4 less 5 minus
suburb: 4 town 6 hamlet 7 village
suburban: 8 outlying
resident: 8 commuter
status symbol: 4 pool 6 hot tub
tool: 5 mower
Suburban: 3 car, GMC, SUV 4 auto 5 Chevy, Dodge 8 Plymouth 9 Chevrolet 10 automobile
subversion: 4 ruin 7 undoing 8 betrayal, sabotage
subversive: 5 rebel 7 harmful, traitor 8 disloyal, frondeur, quisling, saboteur 9 insurgent, seditious 10 incendiary, rebellious
subvert: 4 oust, ruin, undo 5 upset, wreck 6 debase, depose, poison, topple, tumble, unseat 7 abolish, conquer, corrupt, deprave, destroy, vitiate 8 demolish, overturn, pull down, sabotage, undercut, vanquish 9 discredit, overthrow, undermine
subway: 4 tube 5 metro 6 tunnel 8 railroad
access: 5 stair, stile 9 escalator
alternative: 2 el 3 bus, car 4 auto, taxi 7 car pool
artwork: 5 mural 8 graffiti
fare: 5 token
NYC ~: 3 BMT, IRT, MTA
of song: 6 A Train
power source: 4 rail
station: 4 stop
take the ~: 7 commute
succeed: 2 go 3 win 4 boom, pass, rise, take, work 5 avail, bloom, click, ensue, go far, score, trail, worst 6 accede, arrive, assume, follow, fulfil, go next, go well, hack it, make it, manage, pan out, pay off, result, rotate, secure, thrive 7 achieve, acquire, blossom, come off, conquer, fulfill, go after, inherit, make out, prevail, prosper, pull off, realize, replace, triumph, turn out, work out 8 carry off, come into, displace, flourish, go places, hit it big, make a hit, make good, overcome, postdate, supplant, surmount, take over 9 come after, supersede 10 accomplish, do the trick
don't ~: 4 fail, flop 6 fizzle 9 strike out
one likely to ~: 5 comer
__ Succeed in Business...: 5 How to
succeeding: 4 next 5 after, later 6 behind, second, serial 7 ensuing 8 in back of 9 following, posterior 10 attainment, subsequent
succès __: 3 fou 7 d'estime
success: 3 hit, win 4 fame, luck, palm 5 éclat, smash 6 big hit, growth 7 fortune, triumph, victory, welfare 8 eminence, fruition, progress, walkover 9 grand slam, happiness, well-being 10 ascendance, ascendancy, ascendence, ascendency, attainment, gold record, gravy train, prosperity
achieve ~: 6 arrive
assure ~: 3 ice
exclamation: 4 ta-da 5 voilà 6 I did it
path to ~: 5 rungs 6 ladder
sign of ~: 3 SRO
success __: 5 story
Success: 4 rice
alternative: 6 Minute 8 Carolina 9 Uncle Ben's
Success at Any Price (1934 film)
cast: Douglas Fairbanks Jr., Frank Morgan, Genevieve Tobin
director: J. Walter Ruben
Success author: Martin Amis
successful: 4 huge 5 happy, lucky, on top, palmy, socko 6 banner, paying 7 booming, notable, ongoing, on track, roaring, wealthy, well-off, winning 8 at the top, blooming, fruitful, thriving, unbeaten 9 effectual, favorable, fortunate, lucrative, rewarding 10 flying high, prosperous, victorious
be ~: 3 win 6 thrive 7 prevail 8 flourish, get ahead, make good
successfully: 4 well 10 swimmingly
succession: 3 row, run 4 line, rash, turn 5 chain, cycle, order, queue, round, suite, train 6 course, series, string 7 lineage 8 kingship, sequence 9 accession, gradation 10 continuity, procession
in ~: 6 lineal 7 running
rapid ~: 6 flurry
steady ~: 6 stream
successive: 4 next 6 in a row, in turn, serial 7 ensuing, regular 8 straight, unbroken 9 following 10 consequent
successor: 4 cion, heir 5 scion 7 heiress 8 follower 10 descendant
succinct: 4 curt 5 blunt, brief, brusk, crisp, pithy, short, terse, tight 7 brusque, compact, concise, laconic, summary 9 condensed 10 boiled down, synopsized, to the point
succor: 3 aid 4 help, lift 6 assist, relief, solace, uphold 7 comfort, help out, relieve, support 8 kindness, minister 9 encourage 10 assistance
succotash: 4 stew
ingredient: 4 corn, lima 8 lima bean
Succoth celebrator: 3 Jew
succulent: 4 aloe, good, lush, nice, rich 5 agave, juicy, moist, sedum, tasty, undry, yummy 6 cactus, divine, liquid, mellow, toothy 8 heavenly, luscious 9 delicious, kalanchoe, nectarous 10 appetizing
succumb: 3 bow 4 cave, fall, fold, lose, quit, sink, wilt 5 yield 6 buckle, give in, submit 7 founder, give way, go under 8 collapse 9 break down, surrender 10 capitulate
such: 4 akin, like, very 5 alike 6 on a par 7 similar 8 parallel, specific 9 analogous, uniformly 10 comparable, equivalent, especially
as: 4 like 5 to wit 6 namely 10 for example
as ~: 5 per se 8 in itself
at ~ time as: 4 when
in ~ a way: 4 as if, so as, thus
in prescriptions: 3 tal.
starter: 4 none
(Such an) Easy Question (1965 song)
artist: Elvis Presley
Such a Night (1964 song) artist: Elvis Presley
__ Such As I: 5 A Fool
Such Good Friends (1971 film)
cast: Dyan Cannon, James Coco, Jennifer O'Neill
director: Otto Preminger
suck: 6 draw in, inhale
dry: 3 sap 5 drain 7 exhaust 8 enervate
in: 4 dupe, fool, lure, nick, sway, trap 5 decoy, shill, trick 6 absorb, entrap, inhale 7 deceive, defraud, ensnare, mislead 8 hoodwink 9 bamboozle, prevail on
up: 6 absorb, draw in, gather, gobble, ingest, inhale, osmose, take in 7 drink in, swallow 10 assimilate
up to: 4 fawn 5 toady 6 cajole, pander 7 flatter 8 bootlick
sucker: 3 ass, oaf, sap 4 boob, butt, clod, dolt, dupe, fish, fool, gull, lamb, pawn, prey, sham, tool 5 candy, cheat, chump, clown, cluck, dummy, dunce, joker, ninny, patsy, softy 6 delude, dimwit, lummox, nitwit, pigeon, remora, softie, turkey, victim 7 buffoon, dingbat, dullard, fall guy, fathead, half-wit, jackass, pinhead, pretend, saphead, schnook, swindle, two-time 8 bonehead, dumbbell, easy mark, meathead, numskull, pushover 9 birdbrain, blockhead, disinform, lamebrain, numbskull, scapegoat, simpleton, soft touch, victimize 10 dunderhead
eat a ~: 3 lap 4 lick
in: 4 dupe, fool, lure, nick, sway, trap 5 decoy, shill, trick 6 absorb, entrap 7 deceive, defraud, ensnare, mislead 8 hoodwink 9 bamboozle
on a stick: 5 lolly 8 lollipop
play for a ~: 3 use 7 exploit
starter: 4 goat, seer 5 blood
sucker __: 5 punch
__ sucker: 3 hog 5 apple, black 6 all-day
Suckling, John: 4 poet 7 British
sucre: 5 money
Sucre: 4 city, town 7 capital
locale: 7 Bolivia
sucrose: 5 sugar
suction: 6 intake 8 leverage
fish with a ~ disk: 4 goby
prefix: 4 lipo
suction __: 3 cup 4 pump
Sudafed alternative: 5 Afrin 6 Contac, Nyquil, Tavist 7 Actifed, Comtrex, Dayquil, Dristan, Sinutab 8 Benadryl, Dimetapp, Drixoral, TheraFlu 9 Coricidin, Triaminic 10 Robitussin
Sudan: 6 nation 7 country
capital: 8 Khartoum
desert: 6 Libyan, Nubian 7 Arabian
language: 7 Shilluk
money: 7 piaster, piastre 8 millieme
most of ~: 6 Sahara
neighbor: 4 Chad 5 Congo, Egypt, Kenya, Libya 6 Uganda 7 Eritrea 8 Ethiopia
old name for ~: 4 Kush
people: 4 Beja, Nuer 5 Dinka, Zande 6 Azande, Nubian 7 Shilluk, Turkana
region: 6 Darfur, Gezira
river: 4 Nile
__ Sudan: 6 French
sudatorium: 5 sauna 9 steam bath
Sudbury: 4 city, town
locale: 6 Canada 7 Ontario
sudden: 4 fast, rash 5 acute, fleet, hasty, quick, rapid, sharp, short, swift 6 abrupt, snappy 7 hurried 8 headlong, meteoric 9 immediate, impetuous, impromptu, impulsive 10 unexpected, unforeseen
all of a ~: 3 bam 8 abruptly
attack: 4 raid 5 blitz, foray 6 ambush
happening: 5 burst 7 flare-up 8 outbreak 9 explosion
impact: 3 jar 4 jolt 5 shock 9 collision
rise: 5 spike, surge 6 upturn 7 upsurge
sudden-__ overtime: 5 death
Sudden __: 4 Fear 6 Impact
Sudden Fear (1952 film)
cast: Joan Crawford, Gloria Grahame, Jack Palance
Sudden Impact (1983 film)
cast: Bradford Dillman, Clint Eastwood, Pat Hingle, Sondra Locke
director: Clint Eastwood
dog: 8 Meathead

suddenly: **4** bang, then **5** bingo, sharp, short **6** astart **7** briefly, quickly, swiftly, unaware **8** abruptly, unawares **9** all at once, thereupon
in music: **6** subito
Suddenly (1954 film)
cast: James Gleason, Sterling Hayden, Frank Sinatra
Suddenly, Last Summer (1959 film)
author: Tennessee Williams
cast: Montgomery Clift, Katharine Hepburn, Elizabeth Taylor
director: Joseph L. Mankiewicz
Suddenly Last Summer (1983 song)
artist: Motels
Suddenly (song) artist: Billy Ocean, Olivia Newton-John
Suddenly Susan (NBC sitcom)
cast: Judd Nelson (Jack Richmond) Brooke Shields (Susan Keane)
Suddenly There's a Valley (1955 song)
artist: Gogi Grant
Sudermann, Hermann: **6** German **10** playwright
Sudeten: **3** mts. **4** mtns. **5** range **9** mountains
locale: **6** Europe
Sudra: **5** caste, Hindu **6** Hindoo
suds: **3** ale **4** beer, brew, foam, head, soap **5** froth **6** lather **7** brewski, bubbles **8** cleanser **10** malt liquor
get rid of the ~: **5** rinse
place: **3** bar, mug, pub **5** stein **6** tavern, washer **8** alehouse, schooner **10** Laundromat
starter: **4** soap
sudsy: **7** foaming **8** unrinsed
sue: **3** beg, bid **4** pray, urge **5** plead, press **6** accuse, appeal, demand, indict, pursue **7** apply to, beseech, contest, entreat, implore, request, solicit **8** appeal to, litigate, petition, plead for **9** fight over, importune, prosecute **10** supplicate
Sue: **4** Lyon **6** Eugène **7** Grafton **8** Thompson
Sue __ Ewing: **5** Ellen
Sue __ honey: **3** Bee
Sue __ Langdon: **3** Ane
__ Sue: **5** Peggy
__ Sue Anderson: **7** Melissa
suede: **3** kid **7** leather **8** goatskin
feature: **3** nap
__ Suede: **6** Johnny
__ Suede Shoes: **4** Blue
Sue, Eugène: **6** author, French, writer
work: The Mysteries of Paris
__ Sue Got Married: **5** Peggy
__ Sue, Just You: **5** Sweet
__ Sue Martin: **6** Pamela
suer: **8** litigant **9** plaintiff **10** petitioner
__ Sue Robinson: **5** Vicki
Sues: **4** Alan
suet: **6** tallow **7** pudding
cousin: **4** lard
Suetonius: **5** Roman **6** author, writer **9** historian
__ suey: **4** chop
Suez: **4** city, gulf, port, town **5** canal **7** isthmus
locale: **5** Egypt
Suez (1938 film)
cast: Annabella, Tyrone Power, Loretta Young
director: Allan Dwan
Suez Canal
fueling station: **4** Aden
opera for the opening of the ~: **4** Aïda
suffer: **2** go **3** ail, bow, let **4** ache, bear, cope, have, hurt, lump, take **5** abide, allow, bleed, brave, droop, leave, smart, stand, stick, yield **6** accept, endure, grieve, permit, resist, submit, take it, writhe **7** agonize, license, receive, stomach, support, survive, sustain, swallow, undergo, wait out **8** bear with, languish, live with, meet with, sanction, stand for, tolerate **9** acquiesce, go through, put up with, withstand **10** experience
defeat: **4** fail, fall, lose **5** yield **6** go down
from: **5** catch
the consequences: **3** pay
sufferer: **6** victim **7** patient **8** casualty
suffering: **3** woe **4** ache, hell, hurt, pain, sick **5** agony, dolor, grief, trial **6** misery, ordeal, sorrow, trauma **7** anguish, passion, pitiful, torment, torture, travail, trouble **8** distress, hard luck, hardship **9** adversity, endurance, heartache, miserable **10** affliction, difficulty, discomfort, heartbreak, misfortune, oppression
combining form: **5** patho-, -pathy **6** -pathic
__-suffering: **4** long
__ suffer the slings...: **4** or to
suffice: **2** do **4** pass, suit **5** avail, get by, serve **6** answer, fulfil **7** content, fulfill, qualify, satisfy **10** hit the spot
Suffice __ say...: **4** it to
sufficient: **3** due **4** full **5** ample **6** decent, enough, plenty, up to it **8** adequate, all right **9** competent, plentiful, tolerable, up to grade **10** acceptable
nonstandardly: **4** enuf, 'nuff
to a poet: **4** enow
__-sufficient: **4** self
suffixes (by meaning)
advocate: **5** -arian
aggregate: **3** -age
art: **3** -ery
attendee: **4** -goer
believer: **5** -arian
capable: **4** -able, -ible
capacity: **7** -ability, -ibility
collection: **3** -age, -ana, -ery **4** -iana
condition: **3** -dom
deserving: **6** -worthy
direction: **3** -ern
doer: **4** -ator
drink: **3** -ade
enzyme: **3** -ase
expert: **7** -meister
fit for: **6** -worthy
fitness: **7** -ability, -ibility
garden: **4** -etum
imitation: **3** -een **4** -ette
jurisdiction: **3** -dom
lacking: **4** -free
language: **3** -ese
like: **4** -eous **5** -esque
long-running: **5** -athon
nationality: **3** -ese, -ish
occupation: **3** -eer, -eur **4** -euse, -ster
office: **3** -dom
place: **3** -ery **5** -arium
practice: **3** -ery
process: **3** -age
procession: **4** -cade
producer: **5** -arian
product: **3** -ade
realm: **3** -dom
resembling: **4** -eous
resident: **3** -ese
resistant: **5** -proof
scenery: **5** -scape
skill: **7** -manship
somewhat: **3** -ish
specialist: **5** -ician
spectacle: **4** -cade
state: **3** -age, -dom
study: **5** -ology
times: **4** -fold
trade: **3** -ery
typical: **3** -ish
vehicle: **6** -mobile
view: **5** -scape
worthy: **4** -able, -ible
see also combining forms
suffixes (by root)
-ability: **7** fitness **8** capacity
-able: **6** worthy **7** capable
-ade: **5** drink **7** product
-age: **5** state **7** process **9** aggregate **10** collection
-ana: **10** collection
-arian: **8** advocate, believer, producer
-arium: **5** place
-ase: **6** enzyme
-athon: **4** long
-ator: **4** doer
-cade: **9** spectacle **10** procession
-dom: **5** realm, state **6** office **9** condition
-een: **9** imitation
-eer: **10** occupation
-eous: **4** like **10** resembling
-ern: **9** direction
-ery: **3** art **5** place, trade **8** practice **10** collection
-ese: **8** language, resident
-esque: **4** like
-ette: **9** imitation
-etum: **6** garden
-eur: **10** occupation
-euse: **10** occupation
-fold: **5** times
-free: **7** lacking
-goer: **8** attendee
-iana: **10** collection
-ibility: **7** fitness **8** capacity
-ible: **6** worthy **7** capable
-ician: **10** specialist
-ish: **7** typical **8** somewhat
-manship: **5** skill
-meister: **6** expert
-mobile: **7** vehicle
-ology: **5** study
-proof: **9** resistant
-scape: **4** view **7** scenery
-ster: **10** occupation
-worthy: **6** fit for **9** deserving
suffocating: **5** close **6** stuffy, sultry **10** sweltering
Suffolk: **3** pig **4** city, town **5** swine **6** county **10** sheep breed
city: **7** Ipswich
locale: **7** England **8** Virginia
suffrage: **4** vote **5** voice **7** liberty **9** franchise
letters: **3** SBA
suffuse: **3** mix **5** cover, imbue, steep, tinge **6** embrue, imbrue, redden, spread **7** pervade **8** permeate, saturate **9** penetrate **10** overspread
sugar: **2** jo **3** hon, pet **4** baby, dear, jill, love **5** amour, angel, chéri, cooky, cubes, cutey, cutie, deary, ducky, flame, honey, leman, lover, lovey, lumps, novia, novio, sweet **6** bon ami, chérie, cookie, dautie, dearie, hexose, steady, sweets **7** beloved, darling, dearest, dear one, glucose, lactose, maltose, pigsney, schatzi, squeeze, sucrose, sweeten, sweetie, tootsie **8** babydoll, chou-chou, cutie pie, dextrose, dollface, dowsabel, dulcinea, fructose, ladylove, levulose, lovebird, macushla, paramour, precious, snookums, sweetums, truelove **9** bonne amie, boyfriend, dreamboat, inamorata, inamorato, muscovado, petit chou, sweetener, valentine **10** girlfriend, heartthrob, honeybunch, mavourneen, sweetheart, sweetie pie, turtledove
add ~: **7** sweeten
combining form: **4** gluc-, glyc-, sucr- **5** gluco-, glyco-, sucro- **7** sacchar- **8** sacchari-, saccharo-
ender: **4** coat, plum
in woody tissue: **5** xylan
metabolism chemical: **3** ATP
portion: **3** cup **4** cube, loaf, lump **6** cupful **8** spoonful, teaspoon **10** tablespoon
source: **4** beet, cane, carb **5** maple
suffix: **3** -ose
syrup: **5** glaze
sugar __: **3** pea, pie **4** beet, bowl, camp, cane, cone, corn, palm, pine, tree **5** apple, basin, candy, grove, maple, spoon, tongs **6** glider, sifter **7** orchard, sorghum
__ sugar: **4** beet, cane, corn, malt, milk, palm, spun, wood **5** acorn, blood, brown, fruit, grape, maple, table **6** barley, castor, double, invert, simple
Sugar: **7** musical
songwriter: **5** Styne
Sugar __: **3** Act, Ray **4** Moon, Town **5** Blues, Daddy, Shack, Walls
Sugar __ Leonard: **3** Ray
Sugar __ Mountain: **4** Loaf
Sugar __ Robinson: **3** Ray
sugarbush: **5** grove, shrub **7** orchard **9** evergreen
family: **6** cashew
product: **3** sap **5** sugar, syrup
relative: **5** sumac **6** sumach
tap a ~: **5** spile
unit: **4** tree **5** maple
sugarcane
cutter: **4** bolo
eater: **6** agouti
exporter: **4** Maui **7** Jamaica **10** West Indies
product: **3** rum **5** sugar **8** molasses
sugarcoat: **4** ease **5** glaze **7** sweeten **9** whitewash
sugar-coated: **5** glacé, sweet, tasty **6** glazed **7** candied **9** palatable
Sugarfoot (ABC western)
cast: Will Hutchins (Tom Brewster)
sugar-free: **4** lite **5** no-cal
Sugar Land: **4** city, town
locale: **5** Texas
Sugarland Express, The (1974 film)
cast: William Atherton, Goldie Hawn, Ben Johnson, Michael Sacks
director: Steven Spielberg
Sugar Lips artist: Al Hirt
Sugar Loaf Mountain locale: **3** Rio
Sugar Moon (1958 song) artist: Pat Boone
sugarplum: **5** candy, sweet
Sugar Ray: **5** boxer **7** Leonard **8** Robinson
Sugar Shack (1963 song) artist: Fireballs
Sugar, Sugar (1969 song) artist: Archies
Sugartime (1958 song) artist: McGuire Sisters
Sugar Town (1966 song) artist: Nancy Sinatra
sugary: **5** mushy, sweet **6** honied **7** candied, honeyed **9** sweetened **10** saccharine
suggest: **3** put, say, tip **4** hint, mean, move, pose, seem, warn **5** argue, evoke, get at, imply, infer, let on, offer, opine, point, posit, refer, spell, steer **6** advert, advise, allude, broach, denote, hint at, prompt, remind, submit, tip off, typify **7** advance, commend, connote, counsel, make out, mention, point to, proffer, propose, purport, signify, smack of **8** advocate, allude to, indicate, intimate, lead up to, motivate, nominate, propound, rough out, stand for, theorize, throw out **9** adumbrate, insinuate, introduce,

predicate, recommend, represent, symbolize, volunteer **10** conjecture, put forward
itself: **5** occur
strongly: **4** urge **8** armtwist, pressure
suggested: **5** tacit **7** implied **9** advisable
suggestible: **5** naive **8** gullible **9** receptive
suggestion: **3** tip **4** aura, clew, clue, hint, idea, lead, lick, plan, sign, tint, wind **5** pitch, rumor, shade, smack, taste, tinge, touch, trace **6** advice, breath, feeler, motion, notion, scheme, shadow, strain, streak, tipoff, trifle **7** glimmer, inkling, pointer, warning, whisper **8** allusion, innuendo, overtone, proposal, reminder **9** amendment, reference, suspicion, undertone **10** hypothesis, indication, intimation, invitation
formal ~: **6** motion
starter: **4** auto
suggestions: **5** input
open to ~: **8** amenable **9** receptive
suggestive: **6** subtle **8** symbolic **9** evocative, remindful **10** expressive, indicative, meaningful
Suggs, Louise: **6** golfer
milieu: **5** links **6** course
org.: **4** LPGA
Suhail: **4** star
sui __: **5** juris **7** generis
Suicide __: **5** Kings **6** Blonde
Suicide Blonde (1990 song) artist: INXS
Suicide Kings (1998 film)
cast: Sean Patrick Flanery, Denis Leary, Henry Thomas, Christopher Walken
director: Peter O'Fallon
sui generis: **4** rare **6** unique **10** unexampled
suint: **6** grease
Suisse range: **5** Alpes
Suisun City: **4** town
locale: **10** California
suit: **2** do **3** fit **4** case, exec, gear, plea **5** adapt, befit, cause, clubs, getup, match, serve, trial, yuppy **6** action, adjust, answer, appeal, attire, become, belong, beseem, gerent, hearts, livery, modify, outfit, please, prayer, revise, series, spades, tailor, tuxedo, wooing, yuppie **7** conform, costume, flatter, garment, lawsuit, manager, qualify, request, satisfy, suffice, threads, uniform **8** clothing, diamonds, ensemble, entreaty, petition, proposal, readjust **9** agree with, courtship, executive, reconcile **10** litigation, pass muster, proceeding
accessory: **3** tie **6** cravat
award: **7** damages
change to ~: **5** adapt, alter, slant **6** tailor
ender: **4** case
fabric: **4** wool **5** serge, tweed, twill
feature: **4** vent **5** lapel **6** crease
file ~: **3** sue **8** litigate
follow ~: **3** ape **4** copy, echo **6** parrot **7** imitate
grounds for a ~: **4** tort **5** abuse, crime, libel, smear, wrong **6** attack **7** calumny, slander **10** defamation
legal ~: **4** case
maker: **6** tailor
measurement: **5** chest, waist **6** inseam, sleeve
monkey ~: **3** tux **5** tails **6** tuxedo
neaten a ~: **5** brush, press, steam
one of a ~: **3** ace, six, ten, two **4** club, five, four, jack, king, nine **5** deuce, eight, heart, queen, seven, spade, three **7** diamond
piece: **4** vest **5** pants **6** jacket **8** trousers
pocket item: **4** keys **5** hanky **6** change, hankie, wallet
power ~: **5** trump
press one's ~: **3** woo **5** court, spark **7** propose
starter: **3** law **4** jump, pant, play, snow, swim **7** counter
strong ~: **5** armor, forte
two-piece ~: **6** bikini
up: **4** garb, wear **5** array, dress **6** attire
suit __ tee: **3** to a
__ suit: **3** cat, dry, gym, Mao, ski, wet **4** body, flak, long, sack, side, tank, zoot **5** anti-G, civil, dress, major, minor, pants, plain, scrub, slack, sweat, track, union **6** boiler, diving, flight, follow, lounge, monkey, safari, strong **7** bathing, jogging, leisure, trouser
Suita: **4** city, town
locale: **5** Japan
suitable: **2** OK **3** apt, due, fit, pat **4** good, just, meet, okay, ripe **5** happy, right **6** decent, fitted, proper, seemly, timely, up to it, useful **7** apropos, condign, correct, fitting, germane, helpful, perfect, politic **8** adequate, apposite, becoming, decorous, deserved, feasible, pleasing, relevant, rightful **9** advisable, allowable, befitting, competent, expedient, favorable, in keeping, opportune, pertinent, up to grade **10** acceptable, applicable, compatible, convenient, propitious, reasonable, seasonable
absolutely ~: **5** ideal **7** perfect
make ~: **5** adapt **6** change, modify, tailor
position: **5** niche
suitableness: **6** accord, parity **7** concord, fitness, harmony **9** agreement, coherence, congruity, propriety **10** accordance, conformity, consonance, proportion, similarity
suitably: **7** rightly **8** laudably, worthily
suitcase: **3** bag **4** grip **5** trunk **6** valise **7** baggage, luggage
fill a ~: **4** pack
suite: **4** flat **5** condo, group, rooms, train **6** office, rental, series, string **7** battery, cortege, retinue **8** sequence **9** apartment, entourage, hangers-on, retainers **10** attendants, succession
musical ~ ender: **5** gigue
__ Suite: **5** Czech, Plaza **6** London, Petite **7** Holberg
__-suited: **3** ill **4** well
Suite: Judy Blue Eyes (1969 song)
artist: Crosby, Stills & Nash
__-suiter: **3** one, two **5** three **6** single
__ Suites: **6** French **7** English
Suitland: **4** city, town
locale: **8** Maryland
suitor: **3** man **4** beau, date, love **5** Romeo, swain, woman, wooer **6** fellow **7** admirer **8** cavalier, courtier, litigant, lover boy, paramour **9** boyfriend, inamorato **10** girlfriend, supplicant, sweetheart
what a ~ pitches: **3** woo
Suits me!: **3** yes **4** fine, okay **5** swell **8** very well
suit to a __: **3** tee
suk: **5** bazar **6** bazaar
Sukiyaki (song) artist: A Taste of Honey, Kyu Sakamoto
Sukuka: **4** city, town
locale: **5** Japan
Sukuma home: **6** Africa **8** Tanzania
Sula author: Toni Morrison
Sulafat: **4** star
Sulawesi: **4** isle **6** island **7** Celebes
locale: **9** Indonesia
neighbor: **6** Borneo
sulcus: **6** furrow
sulfa drug: **10** antibiotic
__ sulfate: **4** iron, zinc **6** barium, copper, cupric, methyl, sodium **7** cadmium, ferrous
__ sulfide: **4** amyl, zinc **5** allyl, ethyl **6** barium, diamyl, sodium **7** cadmium, calcium, diallyl, ferrous, mercury, stannic
sulfur: **7** element **8** nonmetal
combining form: **3** thi- **4** thia-, thio- **5** thion- **6** thiono-
sulk: **4** fume, moon, mope, pout, tiff **5** brood, frown, gripe, grump, lower, scowl **6** glower, grouse **7** bad mood, silence
in Britain: **4** mump
sulky: **3** rig **4** cart, dour, glum, grim, mopy **5** huffy, moody, mopey, surly **6** crabby, gloomy, grouty, grumpy, in a pet, morose, sullen **7** grouchy, peevish, pouting **8** grumpish, liverish, petulant **9** saturnine **10** ill-natured
Sulla: **5** Roman **7** general **8** dictator
opponent: **6** Marius
Sullavan, Margaret: **7** actress
film: Back Street (1941)
Cry Havoc (1943)
The Good Fairy (1935)
Little Man, What Now? (1934)
The Mortal Storm (1940)
Next Time We Love (1936)
No Sad Songs for Me (1950)
Only Yesterday (1933)
The Shop Around the Corner (1940)
The Shopworn Angel (1938)
So Ends Our Night (1941)
Three Comrades (1938)
spouse: Henry Fonda, Leland Hayward
sullen: **4** dark, dour, dull, glum, grim, mopy, sour, ugly **5** cross, gruff, heavy, huffy, moody, mopey, onery, pouty, surly, testy, upset **6** bitter, cloudy, crabby, dismal, gloomy, grumpy, morose, ornery, silent, somber **7** hostile, peevish, pouting, sulking, uptight, vicious **8** brooding, churlish, darkened, frowning, grumpish, liverish, lowering, perverse, petulant, sluggish **9** cheerless, glowering, irritable, obstinate, querulous, saturnine, truculent **10** ill-humored, ill-natured, out of sorts, unsociable
look: **5** frown, scowl **7** grimace
look ~: **4** lour, mope, pout, sulk **5** brood
sullied: **4** foul **5** dirty **6** impure **7** unclean **8** maculate, vitiated **10** bedraggled
Sullivan: **2** Ed **3** Pat **4** Anne **5** Barry, Frank, Louis, Susan **6** Arthur **8** Kathleen
Sullivan, Arthur: **3** Sir **7** British **8** composer
collaborator: **7** Gilbert
work: The Gondoliers
The Grand Duke
HMS Pinafore
Iolanthe
The Mikado
Patience
The Pirates of Penzance
Princess Ida
Ruddigore
The Sorcerer
Trial by Jury
Utopia, Ltd.
The Yeoman of the Guard
Sullivan, Barry: **5** actor
film: Cause for Alarm (1951)
The Gangster (1947)
Payment on Demand (1951)
Queen Bee (1955)
Smart Woman (1948)
The Woman of the Town (1943)
Sullivan, Ed: **2** MC **4** host **5** emcee
network: **3** CBS **5** CBS-TV
Sullivan, Frank: **6** writer **8** humorist **9** columnist
Sullivan, Pat cat: **5** Felix
Sullivan's __: **5** Sting **7** Travels
Sullivan's Sting author: Lawrence Sanders
Sullivans, The (1944 film)
cast: Anne Baxter, Thomas Mitchell, Selena Royle
director: Lloyd Bacon
Sullivan's Travels (1941 film)
cast: Veronica Lake, Joel McCrea, Robert Warwick
director: Preston Sturges
Sullivan Trophy org.: **3** AAU
sully: **3** mar **4** blot, blur, foul, soil, spot **5** dirty, smear, spoil, stain, taint **6** befoul, crud up, deface, defame, defile, embrue, imbrue, malign, revile, smudge, vilify **7** asperse, begrime, besmear, blacken, blemish, pollute, slander, tarnish **8** backbite, besmirch, discolor, disgrace, dishonor, maculate, throw mud **9** denigrate **10** adulterate, calumniate, stigmatize, villainize
Sully: **9** Prudhomme
sulphur: **7** element
Sulphur: **4** city, town
locale: **9** Louisiana
Sulston, John: **8** Nobelist
sultan: **5** ruler **6** gerent **7** emperor
cousin: **4** amir, emir **5** ameer, emeer
decree: **5** irade
Ottoman ~: **5** Selim
pride: **5** haram, harem, harim, wives **6** hareem
sultana: **3** red **5** queen, ruler **6** raisin **8** purplish
sultanate
Gulf ~: **4** Oman
Malay ~: **6** Brunei
old Arabian ~: **4** Nejd
Sultan of Sulu, The author: George Ade
Sultan of Swat: Babe Ruth
sultriness: **4** heat **6** allure **8** humidity
sultry: **3** hot **4** damp, dank **5** close, heavy, humid, lurid, muggy, soggy **6** baking, clammy, erotic, red-hot, steamy, sticky, stuffy, toasty, torrid **7** boiling, summery **8** broiling, ovenlike, sizzling, stifling, tropical **9** scorching **10** equatorial, oppressive, passionate, sweltering
weather: **7** dog days
Sulu: **3** sea
locale: **6** Borneo
Sulu Archipelago island: **4** Jolo **6** Sibutu **7** Basilan
sum: **3** add, all **4** body, bulk **5** add up, count, gross, score, tally, total, tot up, value, whole, works **6** amount, number, reckon **7** compute, epitome, essence, payment, tally up **8** entirety, integral, quantity, totality **9** aggregate, calculate, keep score, reckoning **10** bottom line
and substance: **3** nub **4** core, gist **5** heart, tenor, theme
component: **6** addend, augend
double-check a ~: **5** readd
in Latin: **3** I am
of the parts: **5** whole
to ~ up: **4** last **6** lastly **7** finally
trifling ~: **3** sou **5** groat
up: **3** add **5** close, count, recap, tally, total **6** digest, figure, review, typify **7** examine, outline **8** conclude, condense, estimate **9** calculate, enu-

merate, epitomize, keep score, synopsize
up to: 5 equal, total
sum __: 5 total
__ sum: 3 dim 4 lump, tidy 6 direct, vector 7 Boolean, capital, logical, partial
sumac: 4 tree 5 shrub 9 squawbush
family: 6 cashew
genus: 4 rhus
relative: 5 mango 6 fustet, mastic 9 pistachio, sugarbush
Sumac: 3 Yma
Sumatra: 3 isl. 4 isle 6 island
animal: 5 rhino
city: 5 Medan 6 Padang 9 Palembang
island off ~: 4 Nias 5 Banka 6 Bangka
locale: 4 Asia 9 Indonesia
people: 5 Batak
port: 6 Padang
primate: 5 orang 7 siamang 9 orang-utan 10 orangutang
volcano: 7 Kerinci
Sumerian city: 4 Kish, Uruk 5 Eridu 6 Lagash
sum, es, __: 3 est
__-sum game: 4 zero
sum grano __: 5 salis
Sumida: 5 river
city on the ~: 5 Tokio, Tokyo
locale: 5 Japan
summa cum __: 5 laude
summarily: 7 readily, swiftly 8 promptly, speedily 9 forthwith, on the spot
summarize: 4 trim 5 brief, prune, recap 6 digest, rehash, review, survey 7 abridge, compile, cut down, outline, run down, run over, shorten 8 abstract, boil down, compress, condense 9 capsulize, inventory, synopsize, telescope 10 abbreviate
summary: 4 core, curt, gist 5 brief, pithy, recap, sense, short, table, terse 6 aperçu, digest, gnomic, précis, rehash, report, résumé, review, sketch, survey, wrap-up 7 epitome, essence, extract, outline, pandect, roundup, rundown, version 8 abstract, analysis, recapped, scenario, skeleton, straight, succinct, syllabus, synopsis 9 inventory, momentary, reduction, temporary 10 abridgment, compendium, highlights, literature, prospectus, tabulation, to the point
career ~: 4 vita 6 résumé
news ~: 5 recap 6 review 8 synopsis
summation: 6 ending, wrap-up 8 addition 9 reckoning
summer: 5 adder 6 season 7 dog days
appliance: 2 AC 3 fan
attire: 3 tee 6 Capris, halter, shades, shorts 7 cut-offs 8 swimsuit 10 sunglasses
clock setting: 3 CDT, CST, DST, EDT, EST, MDT, MST, PDT, PST
cooler: 3 ade, fan, ice, pop 4 pool, soda 6 breeze, ice tea 7 iced tea, limeade 8 lemonade
dessert: 4 cone 6 malted, sundae 7 Sno-cone 8 ice cream 9 milkshake
ender: 4 time 5 house
escape: 4 camp, lake, pool 5 cabin 8 vacation
fabric: 4 poly 5 linen, nylon, voile 6 cotton 7 acrylic, chiffon 9 polyester
feature: 4 heat 8 humidity
follower: 4 fall
forecast: 3 hot 4 rain, warm 5 humid, muggy, sunny
in French: 3 été
month: 3 Aug., Jul., Jun., Sep. 4 July, June, Sept. 6 August 9 September
pest: 3 ant, fly 4 gnat 5 midge 8 horse fly, mosquito
preceder: 6 spring
retreat: 5 shade
shade: 3 tan
shoe: 5 thong 6 sandal 8 flip-flop
sign: 3 Leo 5 Virgo 6 Cancer
TV fare: 5 rerun
summer __: 4 camp, sale 5 stock 6 savory, school, squash 7 kitchen, sausage
__ summer: 6 Indian
Summer: 5 Donna 7 Phoenix
Summer __: 4 Rain, Wind 5 Brave, Games, Girls, Stock, Storm 6 Breeze, Nights 7 Sisters
Summer __, A: 4 Song 5 Place
__ Summer: 4 Last 5 Cruel 6 Indian, Stolen 7 Firefly
Summerall: 3 Pat
Summer and Smoke: 4 film, play
author: Tennessee Williams
cast: Laurence Harvey, Una Merkel, Geraldine Page
director: Peter Glenville
heroine: 4 Alma
Summer Brave author: William Inge
Summer Breeze (1972 song) artist: Seals and Crofts
summer camp
do a ~ activity: 3 row 4 hike, swim
Summer, Donna: 6 singer
nickname: Queen of Disco
song: Bad Girls (1979)
Dim All the Lights (1979)
Heaven Knows (1979)
Hot Stuff (1979)
I Feel Love (1977)
Last Dance (1978)
Love Is in Control (1982)
Love to Love You Baby (1975)
MacArthur Park (1978)
No More Tears (1979)
On the Radio (1980)
She Works Hard for the Money (1983)
This Time I Know It's for Real (1989)
The Wanderer (1980)
Summer Games
see Olympics
Summer Girls (1999 song) artist: LFO
summerhouse: 6 gazebo 8 pavilion
Summer House, The (1993 film)
cast: Jeanne Moreau, Joan Plowright
director: Waris Hussein
Summer in the City (1966 song) artist: Lovin' Spoonful
Summer Knowledge author: Delmore Schwartz
__ Summer Long: 3 All
__ Summer Night: 3 One
Summer Nights (1978 song)
artist: John Travolta, Olivia Newton-John
Summer of __, The: 5 Katya
Summer of '42 (1971 film)
cast: Gary Grimes, Jerry Houser, Jennifer O'Neill
director: Robert Mulligan
Summer of '42 Theme (1971 song)
artist: Peter Nero
Summer of '42 pianist: 4 Nero
Summer of '49 author: David Halberstam
Summer Place, A: 4 film 5 novel
author: Sloan Wilson
cast: Sandra Dee, Troy Donahue, Richard Egan, Dorothy McGuire
director: Delmer Daves
music: Max Steiner
Summers: 4 Marc
Summer Sisters author: Judy Blume
Summer Song, A (1964 song) artist: Chad & Jeremy
Summer Stock (1950 film)
cast: Eddie Bracken, Judy Garland, Gene Kelly
director: Charles Walters
Summer Storm (1944 film)
cast: Linda Darnell, Edward Everett Horton, George Sanders
director: Douglas Sirk
__ Summer, The: 7 Endless
Summertime: 4 aria, song
composer: 8 Gershwin
Summertime (1955 film)
cast: Rossano Brazzi, Katharine Hepburn, Isa Miranda
director: David Lean
__ Summertime: 5 In the
Summertime and the __ is easy: 5 livin'
Summertime Blues (1958 song) artist: Eddie Cochran
Summer Wishes, Winter Dreams (1973 film)
cast: Martin Balsam, Sylvia Sidney, Joanne Woodward
director: Gilbert Cates
summery: 3 hot 4 warm 5 balmy, humid, muggy, sunny 6 sultry, toasty 7 boiling 8 broiling, ovenlike, sizzling, tropical 10 sweltering
summit: 3 tip, top 4 acme, apex, head, peak, roof 5 crest, crown, point, spire 6 apogee, climax, height, tipoff, vertex, zenith 7 maximum 8 capstone, meridian, pinnacle 9 crescendo, high point 10 prominence
approach the ~: 5 climb, mount 6 ascend
attendee: 2 P.M. 6 leader 8 diplomat 9 president
combining form: 5 apico-
summit __: 7 meeting
Summit: 4 city, town
locale: 9 New Jersey
summon: 3 bid 4 beep, call, cite, hail, levy, page, ring, tell 5 draft, evoke, order, rally 6 ask for, beckon, call to, gather, invite, invoke, muster, recall 7 command, convene, convoke, pluck up, request, send for 8 assemble, mobilize, muster up, subpoena 9 call forth, prosecute, recollect
up: 6 recall, relive
summoner: 5 pager 6 beeper
summons: 4 writ 5 paper 7 process, warrant 8 citation, subpoena
Sumner, James: 7 chemist 8 Nobelist
sumo: 5 sport 9 wrestling
home: 5 Japan
like ~ wrestlers: 5 obese
Sum of All Fears, The (2002 film)
cast: Ben Affleck, James Cromwell, Morgan Freeman, Liev Schreiber
director: Phil Alden Robinson
sump: 4 well 5 drain 7 cistern 8 cesspool 10 catch basin
sump __: 4 pump
__-sum payment: 4 lump
sumptuous: 4 dear, lush, luxe, posh, rich 5 fancy, grand, plush, ritzy, showy, swank, swish, ultra 6 costly, deluxe, flashy, frilly, glitzy, lavish, lordly, ornate, swanky 7 elegant, opulent, profuse, stately 8 gorgeous, imposing, luscious, palatial, princely, prodigal, splendid 9 decorated, elaborate, expensive, luxuriant, luxurious 10 impressive, ornamented
meal: 4 feed 5 feast 6 spread 7 banquet
sumptuousness: 4 luxe 6 luxury, wealth 7 glamour 8 elegance, grandeur, splendor
sums, do: 3 add 4 tote 5 total 6 figure
__ Sumter: 4 Fort
sun: 3 orb, Sol, tan 4 ager, bask, star 5 light 6 figure, sphere 7 daystar 8 daylight, fireball, luminary
Babylonian ~ god: 3 Utu
block: 5 cloud, shade, smaze 6 lotion, shades 10 sunglasses
combining form: 4 heli-, soli- 5 helio-
cool ~: 5 K star
dancer: 3 Ute 6 Dakota
disk: 4 Aten, Aton
dry in the ~: 4 bake
Egyptian ~ god: 4 Aten, Aton
emulate the ~: 5 shine
ender: 3 dog, lit, set, tan 4 bath, beam, bird, burn, dial, down, fish, less, rise, roof, room, spot, ward 5 baked, bathe, burnt, burst, dress, light, scald, shade, shine, shiny, space, stone, wards 6 bather, bonnet, downer, flower, screen, tanned 7 bathing, glasses
Greek ~ god: 6 Apollo, Helios
hang in the ~: 3 air, dry
hat: 4 topi 5 topee
in French: 6 soleil
in Latin: 3 sol
in Spanish: 3 sol
lie in the ~: 3 tan 4 bask, laze, loll 5 relax 6 lounge 9 luxuriate
of the ~: 5 solar
once around the ~: 4 year
orbiter: 5 comet 6 planet 8 asteroid
red ~: 5 N star
Roman ~ god: 3 Sol
screen: 5 visor, vizor 6 lotion
spot: 6 facula
toward the rising ~: 4 east
toward the setting ~: 4 west
sun __: 3 god 4 bear, deck, disk, lamp, sign 5 block, dance, porch, visor 6 parlor 7 glasses
sun-__: 5 cured, dried
Sun: 5 paper 9 newspaper
ender: 3 day
locale: 6 Ottawa 7 Calgary, Toronto 8 Edmonton, Las Vegas 9 Baltimore, Vancouver
rival: 3 Cav, Mav, Net 4 Buck, Bull, Hawk, Heat, Jazz, King, Spur 5 Knick, Laker, Magic, Pacer, Sixer, Sonic 6 Celtic, Hornet, Nugget, Piston, Raptor, Rocket, Wizard 7 Clipper, Grizzly, Warrior 8 Cavalier, Maverick 10 SuperSonic, Timberwolf
Sun __: 4 Belt, City, King 6 Devils, Valley
Sun __ Moon: 5 Myung
Sun __-sen: 3 Yat
__ Sun: 6 Rising
Sun Also Rises, The: 4 film 5 novel
author: Ernest Hemingway
cast: Mel Ferrer, Ava Gardner, Tyrone Power
character: 4 Bill, Cohn, Jake 5 Brett, Pedro 6 Ashley, Barnes, Gorton, Robert, Romero 7 Michael, Montoya 8 Campbell 10 Bill Gorton, Jake Barnes, Robert Cohn
director: Henry King
sunbathe: 3 tan 4 bask
to excess: 4 burn 7 blister
sunbather: 6 basker, tanner
need: 5 towel 6 lotion 7 glasses
seat: 6 chaise
sunbeam: 3 ray 5 light
Sunbird: 3 car 4 auto 7 Pontiac
sunblock: 6 lotion
apply ~: 3 dab, pat, rub 5 rub on 6 smooth
ingredient: 4 aloe, PABA
it's blocked by ~: 2 UV
letters: 3 SPF
sunbonnet: 3 hat 4 poke
Sun Bowl site: 6 El Paso
sunburned: 3 red 4 pink 7 flaking, peeling
sunburn remedy: 4 aloe 5 cream 6 lotion 7 Noxzema

Sunbury: 4 city, town
locale: 6 Surrey 7 England
Sun City: 4 town
locale: 7 Arizona
Sunda ___: 6 Strait 7 Islands
sundae: 5 treat 7 dessert
alternative: 4 cone 7 parfait 8 snowball
ingredient: 7 berries 8 ice cream
sauce: 5 fudge
topping: 4 nuts 6 cherry 8 hot fudge
Sundance: 3 car 4 auto 8 Plymouth
Sundance Film Festival locale: 4 Utah
Sundance Kid: 5 alias 6 outlaw
girlfriend: 4 Etta 5 Place
sidekick: 5 Butch 7 Cassidy
Sunday: 5 Billy
best: 4 duds, garb, gear, rags, togs, wear 5 array, dress, frock, getup, mufti 6 attire, civies, finery, livery, outfit, things 7 apparel, civvies, clothes, costume, raiment, regalia, threads 8 ensemble, frippery, garments, wardrobe 9 trappings 10 habiliment
book: 6 hymnal
closing: 4 amen
excursion: 5 drive
section: 6 comics 7 funnies 8 magazine
service: 4 Mass
Sunday ___: 4 best 5 punch 6 driver, school 7 clothes
Sunday-___-meeting: 4 go-to
___ Sunday: 3 Low 4 Palm 5 Black, Great, My Gal, On Any, Super 6 Advent, Easter, Shrove 7 Laetare, Mid-Lent, Passion, Trinity
___ Sunday Afternoon: 3 On a, One
Sunday, Bloody Sunday (1971 film)
cast: Peter Finch, Glenda Jackson
director: John Schlesinger
Sunday Dinner for a Soldier (1944 film)
cast: Anne Baxter, John Hodiak, Charles Winninger
director: Lloyd Bacon
Sunday in New York (1963 film)
cast: Jane Fonda, Cliff Robertson, Rod Taylor
Sunday in the Park With George: 7 musical
songwriter: 8 Sondheim
Sunday Morning: 4 poem
author: Wallace Stevens
Sunday Will Never Be the Same (1967 song) artist: Spanky and Our Gang
sunder: 4 part, rend, rive, tear 5 break, crack, sever, slice, split 6 breach, cleave, divide 7 disjoin, divorce, rupture, split up 8 fracture, separate
sundered: 3 cut 4 rent, slit, torn 5 apart, cleft, riven, split 6 broken, parted 7 cracked 8 separate 9 separated
Sunderland: 4 city, town
locale: 7 England
Sun Devils
home: 5 Tempe
school: 3 ASU
sundial: 9 timepiece 10 timekeeper
numeral: 3 III, VII, XII 4 VIII
part: 6 gnomon
Sun Dial, The author: Don Marquis
sundown: 4 dusk 5 night 7 evening 8 twilight 9 nightfall
Sundown (1974 song) artist: Gordon Lightfoot
sundowner: 4 hobo 5 drink, tramp 8 libation
Sundowners, The (1960 film)
cast: Deborah Kerr, Robert Mitchum, Peter Ustinov
director: Fred Zinnemann
sundries case: 4 etui 5 etwee
sundry: 3 odd 4 many 6 divers, legion, varied 7 diverse, oddball, unalike, various 8 assorted, manifold, multiple 9 different
Sunfire: 3 car 4 auto 7 Pontiac
sunfish: 5 bream, roach 7 crappie 8 bluegill
ocean ~: 4 mola
___ sunfish: 5 ocean 6 redear 7 spotted
Sunfish: 5 skiff
sunflower: 5 plant
center: 4 disc, disk
family member: 5 aster
product: 3 oil 4 seed
support: 4 stem 5 stalk
Sunflowers: 3 oil 8 painting
artist: 7 Van Gogh
setting: 5 Arles
Sunflower State: 3 Kan. 6 Kansas
sung: 5 vocal 6 choral
correctly ~: 5 on key
___ Sung Blue: 4 Song
sunglare, respond to: 5 blink 6 squint 7 squinch
sunk: 5 kaput 6 doomed, ruined 7 done for 8 washed-up 9 submerged 10 humiliated
sunken: 3 low 6 hollow 7 concave 8 immersed, scuttled 9 depressed, submerged, submersed 10 underwater
fence: 4 ha-ha
ship explorer: 5 diver
sunken ___: 6 garden
Sun King's number: 3 XIV
sunless: 4 dark, gray, grey, hazy 5 foggy 6 cloudy 8 darkened, overcast 9 tenebrous, unlighted
Sunlight: 9 detergent
competitor: 3 Joy 4 Ajax, Dawn 7 Cascade 9 Palmolive 10 Electrasol
Sunliner: 3 car 4 auto, Ford 10 automobile
sunlit: 6 bright
Sun Myung ___: 4 Moon
sunn: 5 shrub
Sunne Rising, The: 4 poem
author: John Donne
Sunni: 4 sect 6 Moslem
faith: 5 Islam
sunny: 3 gay 4 fair, fine, mild, warm 5 clear, happy, jolly, light, merry, perky, shiny 6 blithe, bright, cheery, chirpy, daylit, genial, jovial, joyful, joyous 7 beaming, buoyant, clement, glowing, radiant, shining, smiling, summery, well-lit 8 carefree, cheerful, jubilant, laughing, mirthful, pleasant 9 brilliant, cloudless, ebullient, unclouded 10 bright-eyed, flying high, optimistic
color: 6 canary, golden, orange, yellow 8 daffodil
side: 5 south
Sunny: 7 musical
songwriter: 4 Kern
Sunny ___ Home: 4 Came
Sunny (1966 song) artist: Bobby Hebb
sunny-side up: 5 light
item: 3 egg
Sunnyvale: 4 city, town
locale: 10 California
Sunny von ___: 5 Bülow
Sunoco: 3 gas 8 gasoline
rival: 4 Arco, Hess 5 Exxon, Getty, Mobil, Shell 7 Chevron
Sun Prairie: 4 city, town
locale: 9 Wisconsin
sun protection ___: 6 factor
sunrise: 4 dawn, morn 5 light, prime 6 aurora 7 morning 8 cockcrow, daybreak, daylight
color: 4 pink
goddess: 3 Eos 6 Aurora
locale: 4 east
time before ~: 5 night
to sunset: 3 day
Sunrise: 4 city, town
locale: 7 Florida
___ Sunrise: 7 Tequila
Sunrise at Campobello (1960 film)
cast: Ralph Bellamy, Hume Cronyn, Greer Garson
Sunrise Manor: 4 city, town
locale: 6 Nevada
Sunrise Serenade composer: 5 Carle
Sunrise Sunset: 4 song, tune 5 waltz
composer: 4 Bock 7 Harnick
Suns: 4 five, team
home: 7 Phoenix
org.: 3 NBA
sport: 10 basketball
sunscreen: 6 lotion
abbr.: 3 SPF
ingredient: 4 aloe, PABA
Sun-Sentinel: 5 paper 9 newspaper
locale: 7 Florida
sunset: 3 eve 4 dusk 5 night 7 evening 8 eventide, twilight 9 nightfall
direction: 4 west
hue: 3 red
sunrise to ~: 3 day
time after ~: 5 night
Sunset: 4 city, town
locale: 7 Florida
Sunset (1988 film)
cast: James Garner, Mariel Hemingway, Malcolm McDowell, Bruce Willis
director: Blake Edwards
Sunset Blvd. (1950 film)
cast: William Holden, Erich von Stroheim, Gloria Swanson
director: Billy Wilder
Sunset Boulevard: 7 musical
songwriter: 11 Lloyd Webber
Sunset in Saint Tropez author: Danielle Steel
Sunset Limited: 5 train
Sunset Pass author: Zane Grey
___ Sunset, The: 4 Last
sunshade: 3 cap, hat 5 visor, vizor 6 awning, canopy 7 parasol 8 umbrella
sunshine: 5 light 8 daylight
line: 6 isohel
sunshine ___: 3 act, law
Sunshine: 6 cookie
competitor: 7 Archway, Keebler, Nabisco 9 Mrs. Fields 10 Famous Amos, Peak Freans
Sunshine and Snow artist: 5 Monet
Sunshine Boys, The: 4 film, play
author: Neil Simon
cast: Richard Benjamin, George Burns, Walter Matthau
director: Herbert Ross
Sunshine of Your Love (1968 song) artist: Cream
Sunshine on My Shoulders (1974 song) artist: John Denver
Sun Shines Bright, The (1953 film)
cast: Lord John Russell, Arleen Whelan, Charles Winninger
director: John Ford
Sunshine State: 7 Florida
Sunshine Superman (1966 song) artist: Donovan
sunshiny: 4 fair 9 cloudless, unclouded
sunspot ___: 5 cycle
sunspot center: 5 umbra
___ sunt: 3 ubi
suntan ___: 3 oil 6 lotion
suntan lotion ingredient: 4 aloe, PABA
letters: 3 SPF
___ Sun, The: 5 Naked
Sun-Times: 5 paper 9 newspaper
locale: 7 Chicago
sunup: 4 dawn, morn 5 early, prime 7 morning 8 daybreak, daylight 10 first light
direction: 4 east
Sun Valley: 4 city, town
enjoy ~: 3 ski 4 skee
locale: 3 Ida. 5 Idaho
Sun Valley Serenade (1941 film)
cast: Sonja Henie, John Payne
Sun Yat-___: 3 sen
suo ___: 4 jure, loco
sup: 3 eat 4 dine 8 chow down 9 have a bite 10 break bread
___ Supastar: 6 Ghetto
super: 3 ace, big, def, fab, rad 4 aces, A-one, boss, braw, cool, dece, fine, gear, keen, neat, nice, phat, role, tops, tuff 5 crack, dandy, ducky, grand, great, large, marvy, neato, nifty, nobby, prime, slick, store, swell 6 bang on, bang-up, bonzer, bosker, choice, divine, dreamy, far-out, gnarly, groovy, lovely, peachy, slap-up, spot on, terrif, tiptop, unreal, whizzo, wicked 7 amazing, awesome, capital, corking, immense, perfect, ripping, skookum, stellar, sublime 8 dazzling, director, especial, eximious, fabulous, five-star, four-star, frabjous, glorious, heavenly, jim-dandy, slam-bang, smashing, splendid, standout, sterling, stickout, terrific, top-level, topnotch, very good, watchdog, wondrous 9 admirable, bodacious, caretaker, custodian, Endsville, excellent, exemplary, exquisite, extremely, fantastic, first-rate, high-grade, hunky-dory, marvelous, organizer, sollicker, top-drawer, topflight, unrivaled, wonderful, wunderbar 10 first-class, hotsy-totsy, jack-a-dandy, out of sight, peachy-keen, phenomenal, remarkable, stupendous, tremendous, unrivalled, world-class
Super ___: 3 Mex 4 Bowl, Glue 6 Sleuth, Sunday 7 Tuesday
Super ___ Bros.: 5 Mario
Super ___, The: 4 Cops
superabundance: 4 glut, much 5 ocean 6 excess 9 amplitude
superabundant: 4 rich 6 plenty 8 prodigal 9 luxuriant, plentiful
superannuated: 3 old 4 aged 5 aging 6 ageing 7 ancient, elderly, wizened 8 grizzled, obsolete, outmoded 9 geriatric, getting on, senescent, up in years
superannuation: 7 pension
superb: 3 ace 4 A-one, best, fine, rare 5 first, grand, great, lofty, noble, prime, proud, royal 6 choice 7 capital, elegant, exalted, optimal, perfect, stately, sublime, supreme 8 elevated, fabulous, glorious, majestic, peerless, splendid, stunning, terrific 9 admirable, beautiful, brilliant, excellent, exquisite, fantastic, first-rate, marvelous, matchless, topflight, unrivaled, virtuosic, wonderful, wunderbar 10 consummate, impressive, majestical, stupendous, unrivalled
Superba: 3 car 4 auto 7 Checker
Super Bowl: 5 event
org.: 3 NFL
sight: 5 blimp 7 airship 9 dirigible
Superboy
girlfriend: 4 Lana, Lang
supercharger: 5 turbo
Super Chief: 3 car 4 auto 5 train 7 Pontiac 10 automobile
supercilious: 4 smug, vain 5 cocky, lofty, proud 6 snobby, uppity 7 fustian, haughty, pompous, stuck-up 8 arrogant, boastful, cavalier, egoistic, scornful, snobbish, superior 9 bigheaded, egotistic, imperious, quizzical

Super Cops, The (1974 film)
cast: Sheila Frazier, Ron Leibman, David Selby
director: Gordon Parks
super-duper
see super
Super 8: 5 motel
alternative: 7 Days Inn **9** Ramada Inn **10** Comfort Inn, Econo Lodge, Hampton Inn, Holiday Inn, Quality Inn, Red Roof Inn, Travelodge **11** Best Western
superego: 6 ethics **8** scruples **10** conscience
supererogatory: 7 unasked **9** excessive
superficial: 4 glib, side, weak **5** empty, hasty, light, outer, rough, slick, vague **6** casual, flimsy, hollow, slight **7** cursory, hurried, outward, partial, passing, seeming, shallow, sketchy, summary, surface, trivial, vacuous **8** affected, apparent, cosmetic, exterior, external, skin-deep **9** depthless, desultory, frivolous **10** uncritical
superfluity: 4 glut **6** excess, frills **7** surplus **8** overflow, plethora
superfluous: 4 over **5** extra, spare **6** de trop, excess, lavish **7** profuse, surplus, useless **8** left over, needless, overmuch, residual, unneeded, unwanted **9** abounding, excessive, overblown, redundant, remaining
Superfly (1972 film)
cast: Sheila Frazier, Carl Lee, Ron O'Neal
director: Gordon Parks
Superfly (1972 song) artist: Curtis Mayfield
Superfortress: 5 plane **6** bomber **8** airplane, warplane
Superfudge author: Judy Blume
supergiant: 4 star **5** Rigel **7** Antares **10** Betelgeuse
super giant __: 6 slalom
Supergirl
cat: 7 Streaky
home: 4 Argo
superintend: 3 run **4** boss, mind **5** watch **6** direct, govern, manage **7** command, oversee **8** regulate **9** officiate
superintendent: 4 boss, head **5** chief, super **6** keeper, leader, master, warden **7** curator, manager **8** director, governor, guardian, overseer **9** caretaker, conductor, custodian, inspector, principal, straw boss, zookeeper **10** headmaster
superior: 3 ace, CEO, def, rad, VIP **4** aces, A-one, boss, braw, cool, dece, exec, fine, gear, head, jefe, keen, neat, nice, over, phat, smug, tops, tuff **5** above, bossy, brass, chief, cocky, crack, dandy, ducky, elder, finer, grand, great, hirer, legit, lofty, marvy, moral, neato, nobby, noble, on top, prime, proud, ruler, slick, swell, upper **6** bang on, bang-up, better, bonzer, bosker, choice, deluxe, divine, dreamy, expert, far-out, gnarly, goodly, groovy, honcho, leader, lovely, peachy, proper, select, senior, slap-up, spot on, terrif, tiptop, top dog, unreal, uppity, whizzo, wicked **7** amazing, awesome, capital, corking, elegant, eminent, ethical, exalted, foreman, grander, greater, haughty, high-hat, leading, manager, perfect, premium, primary, ripping, skookum, stellar, stuck-up, sublime, vintage **8** all right, arrogant, brass hat, cavalier, champion, dazzling, director, dominant, enviable, especial, eximious, fabulous, five-star, four-star, frabjous, glorious, heavenly, higher-up, in charge, insolent, jim-dandy, laudable, peerless, pleasant, pleasing, slam-bang, smashing, snobbish, splendid, standout, sterling, stickout, terrific, top-level, topnotch, towering, uncommon, very good, wondrous **9** a cut above, admirable, agreeable, bodacious, chieftain, Endsville, exceeding, excellent, executive, exemplary, exquisite, first-rate, high-class, high-grade, hunky-dory, marvelous, matchless, overlying, paramount, preferred, principal, reputable, sollicker, topflight, unrivaled, wonderful **10** acceptable, beneficial, commanding, creditable, disdainful, first-class, hotsy-totsy, jack-a-dandy, noteworthy, out of sight, peachy-keen, phenomenal, preeminent, preferable, prevailing, remarkable, stupendous, surpassing, unrivalled, world-class
__ superior: 6 mother
Superior: 4 city, lake, town
locale: 6 Canada **9** Minnesota, Wisconsin
superiority: 4 edge, lead, pull, rank **5** power, value **7** vantage **8** eminence, goodness, position, prestige, priority, whip hand **9** advantage, authority, dominance, influence, landslide, seniority, supremacy, upper hand
superiority __: 7 complex
superlative: 4 A-one, best, rare, tops **5** crack, great, prime **6** divine, superb **7** all-time, capital, highest, optimum, perfect, stellar, supreme **8** gilt-edge, greatest, peerless, splendid, sterling, ultimate **9** excellent, masterful, matchless, unequaled, unrivaled **10** unrivalled
superliner: 5 train
Superman: 4 hero
alias: Clark Kent
attire: 4 cape
cover: 8 reporter
dog: 6 Krypto
foe: Lex Luthor
girlfriend: Lois Lane
home: 10 Metropolis
newspaper: 6 Planet
parent: 4 Lara **5** Jor-El
portrayer: 4 Alyn, Cain **5** Reeve **6** Reeves
symbol: 3 ess
Superman (1978 film)
cast: Ned Beatty, Marlon Brando, Jackie Cooper, Gene Hackman, Margot Kidder, Valerie Perrine, Christopher Reeve, Susannah York
director: Richard Donner
role: 4 Otis
Superman (1979 song) artist: Herbie Mann
Superman II (1980 film)
cast: Ned Beatty, Gene Hackman, Margot Kidder, Christopher Reeve
director: Richard Lester
villain: 3 Zod **4** Ursa
supermarket: 5 store **7** grocery **8** emporium
employee: 5 clerk **6** bagger **7** cashier, stocker
feature: 4 cart, line
freebie: 3 bag **4** sack
saver: 6 coupon
section: 5 aisle, dairy
tabloid: 5 Globe
work at the ~: 3 bag
see also grocery
supermodel, single-name: 4 Iman
supernal: 6 divine **7** angelic **8** ethereal, heavenly **9** ambrosial, angelical, celestial
supernatural: 4 dark, eery **5** eerie, weird **6** fantom, hidden, mystic, occult, secret, spooky **7** ghostly, phantom, psychic, uncanny, unknown **8** heavenly, mystical, numinous, spectral **9** invisible, marvelous, unearthly, unnatural
being: 5 ghost, haunt, spook **6** spirit **7** phantom, specter
occurrence: 6 séance **7** miracle
power: 5 magic **6** occult, voodoo **8** wizardry **10** witchcraft
Supernatural Thing (1975 song) artist: Ben E. King
supernova: 4 star
supernumerary: 5 extra **9** excessive
Super Password host: 5 Convy
superpower, former: 4 USSR
supersede: 6 follow **7** abolish, discard, outmode, replace, succeed **8** displace, override, overrule, set aside, supplant **9** antiquate, discharge
superseded: 5 passé **8** obsolete, outmoded, unusable
supersensory: 7 psychic
Supersition (1972 song) artist: Stevie Wonder
Super Six: 3 car **4** auto **6** Hudson
Super Sleuth (1937 film)
cast: Edgar Kennedy, Jack Oakie, Ann Sothern
supersonic: 4 fast **5** brisk, fleet, hasty, quick, rapid, swift **6** flying, racing, speedy **7** express, hurried, instant **9** breakneck **10** double-time
speed unit: 4 Mach
transport: 3 jet, SST **5** plane **7** Tupolev **8** Concorde
SuperSonic rival: 3 Cav, Mav, Net, Sun **4** Buck, Bull, Hawk, Heat, Jazz, King, Spur **5** Knick, Laker, Magic, Pacer, Sixer **6** Celtic, Hornet, Nugget, Piston, Raptor, Rocket, Wizard **7** Clipper, Grizzly, Warrior **8** Cavalier, Maverick **10** Timberwolf
SuperSonics: 4 five, team
home: 7 Seattle
org.: 3 NBA
sport: 10 basketball
superstar: 4 hero, idol, name **5** celeb, great **8** luminary, renowned, somebody, virtuoso **9** celebrity, headliner, personage, well-known
Superstar (1971 song) artist: Carpenters
superstition: 4 fear, lore, tabu **5** magic, taboo **6** notion
supervene: 5 ensue **6** follow
supervise: 3 run **4** boss, head, lead, mind, tend **5** chair, guard, watch **6** direct, govern, handle, manage **7** command, conduct, control, inspect, monitor, oversee, preside **8** chaperon, overlook, regulate **9** chaperone, check up on, look after **10** administer, ride herd on, run the show
supervision: 4 care, rule **5** trust **6** charge **7** command, conduct, control, custody, running **8** auspices, guidance, handling, tutelage **9** direction, oversight
supervisor: 4 boss, head **5** chief, hirer **6** gerent, keeper, master, top dog **7** curator, foreman, headman, manager, monitor **8** brass hat, director, employer, governor, guardian, higher-up, overseer, watchdog **9** caretaker, conductor, custodian, executive, inspector, organizer, straw boss, zookeeper
supine: 4 flat, lazy **5** slack **6** face-up **7** languid **8** listless **9** lethargic, prostrate, recumbent
opposite: 5 prone
supper: 4 feed, meal **6** buffet, dinner, spread **7** banquet, potluck **9** reception
club: 6 bistro **7** cabaret **10** restaurant
ender: 4 time
fix ~: 5 eat in
have ~: 3 eat **4** dine
__ Supper: 4 Last **5** Lord's
Supper Club radio host: 4 Como
supplant: 4 oust **5** usurp **6** change, follow, unseat **7** cast out, replace, succeed **8** displace, force out **9** supersede
supplanter, name meaning: 5 Jacob
supple: 4 limp, soft, spry, wiry **5** agile, lithe **6** limber, lissom, pliant, svelte **7** ductile, elastic, lissome, plastic, pliable, rubbery, sinuous, springy, willowy **8** flexible, graceful, stretchy, yielding **9** adaptable, lightsome, lithesome, malleable, resilient
supplement: 3 add, eke, pad **4** grow, rise **5** add-on, add to, annex, build, extra, rider **6** append, beef up, eke out, enrich, extend, insert, jazz up, option, step up **7** adjunct, augment, broaden, build up, codicil, enhance, fill out, fortify **8** addendum, addition, additive, appendix, buttress, complete, escalate, increase, round off, round out **9** accessory, accompany, amendment, appendage, extension, increment, reinforce, subsidize **10** attachment, complement, contribute, elongation, postscript
dietary ~: 4 iron **7** mineral, vitamin
__ supplement: 6 Sunday
supplementary: 3 new **4** more **5** added, extra, fresh, other, spare **7** adjunct, further **9** ancillary, auxiliary, secondary **10** additional, subsidiary
Suppliant Women, The author: Aeschylus
supplicant: 5 lover **6** beggar, pauper, suitor
supplicate: 3 beg, sue **4** pray **5** plead, press **6** adjure, appeal, demand **7** beseech, entreat, implore, request, solicit **8** petition **9** importune
supplication: 4 plea, suit **6** appeal, demand, litany, prayer **7** request **8** entreaty, petition
supplier: 6 jobber, seller, vendor **8** retailer **10** wholesaler
supplies: 3 kit **4** food **5** items, stock **6** outfit, stores **7** rations **9** equipment, inventory, materials **10** provisions
supply: 3 arm, rig **4** drop, feed, fill, find, fund, give, lend, mine **5** bring, cache, cater, endow, equip, fix up, grant, hoard, put up, serve, spare, stake, stock, store, yield **6** afford, amount, fulfil, kick in, load up, outfit, pony up, purvey, ration, render, source, vittle **7** appoint, backlog, deliver, fulfill, furnish, prepare, produce, provide, recruit, reserve, satisfy, service, surplus, sustain, victual **8** accouter, accoutre, dispense, hand over, material, minister, quantity, turn over **9** inventory, provision, repertory, replenish, reservoir, stockpile **10** administer, come up with, contribute
anew: 5 refit **10** replenish
depot: 5 étape **6** armory **9** warehouse
full ~: 7 satiety, surfeit **8** plethora **9** plenitude **10** saturation
hidden ~: 5 cache, hoard, stash
in short ~: 4 rare **5** scant **6** exotic, scanty, scarce, sparse **8** uncommon
rich ~: 4 mine, vein
supply-__ economics: 4 side
__ Supply: 3 Air
supply and __: 6 demand
support: 3 aid, fan, job, leg **4** abet, back,

base, bear, earn, egis, feed, food, fund, gird, hand, help, hold, keep, lift, pier, post, prop, rest, rock, stay **5** aegis, allow, boost, brace, carry, cheer, endow, favor, found, guard, guide, means, money, nurse, pylon, raise, shore, staff, stake, stalk, stand, stave, stick, stilt, strut **6** assist, back up, bottom, buoy up, column, cradle, crutch, defend, foster, ground, handle, hold up, living, pay for, pillar, prop up, relief, second, succor, suffer, timber, uphold, upkeep, verify **7** advance, alimony, approve, backing, bolster, bracket, care for, comfort, endorse, espouse, finance, footing, fortify, forward, further, help out, indorse, justify, lectern, loyalty, nourish, nurture, payment, pension, promote, protect, provide, pull for, rampart, relieve, shore up, sponsor, stand by, stick by, stiffen, subsidy, sustain **8** abutment, advocacy, advocate, approval, auspices, banister, bankroll, blessing, buttress, champion, chaperon, espousal, exponent, foothold, mainstay, maintain, platform, plead for, plump for, sanction, shoulder, side with, skeleton, speak for, stand for **9** agree with, allowance, chaperone, encourage, establish, flotation, get behind, insurance, patronage, patronize, provision, reinforce, stability, stabilize, stanchion, subscribe, subsidize, testimony, undergird, underside, vindicate **10** assistance, foundation, friendship, go to bat for, groundwork, livelihood, perpetuate, protection, provide for, put forward, rally round, speak up for, stand up for, stick up for, strengthen, substratum, sustenance, underwrite
obtain, as ~: **5** draft **6** muster **7** recruit **8** mobilize
support ___: **4** hose **5** group **7** mission
___ support: **4** arch, tech **5** child, moral, price
supporter: **3** aye, fan **4** ally **5** angel, giver, urger **6** backer, cohort, friend, helper, patron, rooter, votary **7** admirer, apostle, devotee, grantor, sponsor **8** adherent, advocate, believer, champion, defender, disciple, endorser, espouser, exponent, financer, follower, henchman, mainstay, partisan, upholder **9** apologist, assistant, auxiliary, comforter, expounder, proponent **10** benefactor, enthusiast, subscriber, well-wisher
combining form: **4** -crat **5** -ocrat
___-supporting: **4** self
supporting factor: **4** crux, root **5** cause **6** motive, reason **7** footing, grounds, premise, pretext **8** evidence **9** criterion, principle **10** assumption, foundation
supportive: **3** for **7** helpful **8** fatherly, motherly, parental **9** favorable **10** reassuring
Support Your Local Gunfighter (1971 film)
cast: Jack Elam, James Garner, Suzanne Pleshette
Support Your Local Sheriff (1969 film)
cast: Walter Brennan, James Garner, Joan Hackett
supposable: **6** likely **10** believable, imaginable
suppose: **4** deem, feel, take **5** fancy, grant, guess, infer, opine, think, trust **6** assume, expect, figure, gather, reason, reckon, regard, what if **7** believe, daresay, imagine, presume, pretend, surmise, suspect **8** conceive, conclude, consider, estimate, theorize **9** postulate, speculate **10** conjecture, understand
old-style: **4** trow, ween
supposed: **7** nominal, reputed, seeming **8** apparent, putative, reported, so-called, unproved **9** imaginary, pretended **10** ostensible
supposedly: **4** as if **5** quasi **9** doubtless **10** apparently
supposing: **9** given that, providing
even ~: **6** though
that: **8** as long as
supposition: **4** idea **5** doubt, given, guess, hunch, rumor **6** belief, notion, theory, thesis **7** concept, opinion, premise, surmise, thought **9** condition, guesswork, suspicion
suppress: **3** gag, nix **4** bury, curb, hide, hush, kill, stop, tame **5** check, crush, elide, leash, quash, quell, shush, sit on **6** arrest, bottle, bridle, censor, cut off, deaden, defeat, hold in, hush up, muffle, muzzle, quench, squash, stifle, subdue **7** abolish, conceal, conquer, contain, cover up, inhibit, oppress, put down, repress, silence, smother, squelch **8** beat down, hold back, hold down, keep down, overcome, restrain, snuff out, stamp out, throttle **9** keep quiet, overpower, overthrow, put a lid on, subjugate **10** annihilate, extinguish, keep a lid on, keep in line, keep secret, put an end to
suppressed: **6** latent, pent-up, untold **9** forgotten **10** unrecalled
suppressor ___: **5** T cell
supra: **9** preceding
opposite: **5** infra
___ supra: **3** ubi **4** vide
Supra: **3** car **4** auto **6** Toyota
___ supra citato: **4** loco
supranormal: **7** psychic, uncanny **10** paranormal
supremacy: **4** lead, rule, sway **5** power, reign **6** empire **7** command, control, primacy, victory **8** dominion, hegemony, kingship, priority **9** advantage, authority, dominance, influence **10** ascendance, ascendancy, ascendence, ascendency, domination, excellence, government, leadership, perfection
___ Supremacy, The: **6** Bourne
supreme: **3** top **4** best, head, last, main **5** chief, final, first, grand, ideal, noble, prime, royal **6** all-out, divine, master, ruling, utmost **7** dessert, highest, in front, leading, maximum, perfect, regnant, topmost **8** absolute, almighty, cardinal, crowning, dominant, foremost, greatest, headmost, peerless, powerful, splendid, towering, ultimate **9** excellent, first-rate, high-class, marvelous, matchless, nonpareil, paramount, principal, sovereign, topflight, unequaled, unmatched, unrivaled, uppermost, virtuosic, worthiest **10** consummate, first-class, inimitable, overriding, preeminent, prevailing, surpassing, unrivalled
Supreme ___: **5** Being, Court **6** Soviet **7** Council
Supreme Court: **6** ennead
complement: **4** nine
position: **4** seat
work: **6** appeal, ruling **7** hearing
supremely: **4** very **7** greatly **8** above all **9** perfectly **10** especially
Supremes
hometown: Detroit
members: Ross, Wilson, Ballard, Birdsong
song: Baby Love (1964)
Back in My Arms Again (1965)
Come See About Me (1964)
Floy Joy (1972)
The Happening (1967)
I Hear a Symphony (1965)
I'm Gonna Make You Love Me (1968)
I'm Livin' in Shame (1969)
In and Out of Love (1967)
Love Child (1968)
Love Is Here and Now You're Gone (1967)
Love Is Like an Itching in My Heart (1966)
My World Is Empty Without You (1966)
Nothing But Heartaches (1965)
Reflections (1967)
Someday We'll Be Together (1969)
Stoned Love (1970)
Stop! In the the Name of Love (1965)
Up the Ladder to the Roof (1970)
Where Did Our Love Go (1964)
You Can't Hurry Love (1966)
You Keep Me Hangin' On (1966)
Suquamish: **6** Indian **7** Amerind **8** language
___ Sur: **3** Big
sura: **7** chapter
compilation: **5** Koran, Quran
Surabaya: **4** city, town
locale: **9** Indonesia
surah: **4** silk **6** fabric **8** material
surbahar: **4** lute **6** string
origin: **5** India
surcease: **3** end **4** halt, stop **5** close, delay **6** desist, ending, finish, wind up **8** break off, complete, conclude, leave off, wind down **9** finish off, terminate **10** conclusion
surcharge: **3** fee, tax **5** add-on **6** excise
surcingle: **4** belt
surcoat: **6** jacket
surdo: **4** drum
origin: **6** Brazil
sure: **3** aye, oui, set, yea, yep, yes, yup **4** fast, fine, firm, okay, real, safe, true, yeah **5** bound, clear, fixed, good-o, natch, quite, right, roger, solid, uh-huh, valid **6** agreed, gladly, good-oh, indeed, just so, rather, righto, secure, stable, steady, strong, you bet, yowzah **7** assured, certain, cinched, decided, exactly, genuine, go ahead, indeedy, mais oui, quite so, settled, staunch, ten-four **8** absolute, all right, as you say, clinched, composed, constant, definite, enduring, fail-safe, for a fact, inerrant, in the bag, of course, positive, reliable, resolved, sanguine, thumbs up, unerring, unshaken, very well **9** assertive, be my guest, certainly, certified, confident, convinced, darn right, doubtless, downright, foolproof, goofproof, naturally, persuaded, precisely, satisfied, steadfast, unfailing, unvarying, you betcha, you said it **10** absolutely, by all means, conclusive, definitely, dependable, determined, documented, guaranteed, inevitable, infallible, legitimate, optimistic, positively, that's right, unarguable, unchanging, undeniable, undisputed, undoubtful, unshakable, unwavering
as hell: **5** truly **9** certainly, doubtless **10** absolutely, definitely, positively, undeniably
ender: **6** footed
feel ~ of: **4** rely **5** bet on, trust **6** bank on **7** believe
for ~: **3** yes **5** natch, quite, truly **6** indeed, rather, you bet **7** certain, exactly, quite so **8** definite, manifest, of course **9** certainly, darn right, naturally, you betcha **10** absolutely, by all means, conclusive, definitely, guaranteed, positively, that's right, unarguable, undeniable
make ~: **5** check **6** affirm, verify **7** confirm **9** ascertain, guarantee
make ~ of: **3** ice **5** sew up
victory: **5** cinch **9** certainty
yeah, ~: **4** as if, I bet
Sure: **9** deodorant
competitor: **3** Ban **5** Arrid, Tussy **6** Degree, Secret **7** Dry Idea, Mitchum **10** Right Guard, Soft and Dri, Speed Stick
sure as ___: **7** shootin'
surefire: **9** foolproof, rock solid **10** guaranteed
surefooted: **5** agile **6** nimble
Sure Gonna Miss Her (1966 song)
artist: Gary Lewis and the Playboys
surely: **2** OK **3** aye, yes **4** okay, okeh, okey **6** and how, easily, indeed, really **7** clearly, for real, plainly **8** for a fact, of course **9** certainly, decidedly, doubtless, no mistake **10** absolutely, by all means, definitely, far and away, for certain, inevitably, inexorably, infallibly, invariably, manifestly, positively, presumably
Surely you ___!: **4** jest
sureness: **5** trust **8** accuracy, optimism **10** confidence, conviction
...sure plays ___ pinball: **5** a mean
surety: **4** bail, egis, gage **6** pledge **7** hostage, sponsor **8** security, warranty **9** certainty, guarantee, safeguard **10** collateral, conviction
agreement: **4** bond
poster: **6** bailor
surf: **4** foam, wave **5** froth, spume, surge, swell, waves **7** hang ten **8** breakers, hang five, sea spray **9** spindrift **10** catch a wave
and turf: **3** duo **6** entree
droplets: **4** mist **5** spray, spume **6** mizzle **7** drizzle
ender: **5** board
get ready to ~: **5** log in, log on
like the ~: **5** aroar, foamy **6** frothy **7** foaming, roaring **8** frothing **10** thundering
motion: **4** tide, wave **5** swell **6** roller
murmur: **4** rote
place to ~: **3** Net, Web **8** Internet
starter: **4** body, wind
surf ___: **4** boat, clam, duck **5** music, smelt **6** scoter **7** casting
surf-___: **5** 'n 'turf
___-surf: **7** channel
Surf: **9** detergent
competitor: **3** All, Biz, Era, Fab, Yes **4** Bold, Dash, Gain, Tide, Wisk **5** Cheer, Dreft, Purex **6** Calgon, Dynamo, Oxydol **7** Octagon **9** Ivory Snow
Surf ___: **4** City
surface: **3** nap, top **4** area, face, pave, peel, rind, side, skin, wall **5** arise, cover, level, outer, plane, sheet, shell **6** appear, come up, crop up, emerge, facade, finish, loom up, move up, veneer **7** expanse, flare up, outside, outward, shallow, texture **8** apparent, cosmetic, covering, exterior, external **9** periphery **10** peripheral
beneath the ~: **5** inner **6** latent
flat ~: **5** plane
measurement: **4** area
on the ~: **7** outward **9** outwardly
surface-to-___: **3** air
surf and ___: **4** turf
Surfaris song: Wipe Out (1963)
surfboard
application: **3** wax

stabilizer: 4 skeg
use a ~: 4 ride 7 hang ten 8 hang five
Surf City (1963 song) artist: Jan & Dean
surfeit: 4 cloy, cram, fill, glut, jade, load, orgy, pall, sate 5 gorge 6 excess 7 nimiety, satiate, satiety, satisfy 8 bellyful, overfeed, overfill, overflow, overkill, plethora, saturate 9 profusion, repletion 10 gormandize, oversupply
surfeited: 5 blasé, jaded 10 world-weary
surfer
challenge: 5 crest, swell 6 comber
hangout: 3 net, Web 5 beach 8 Internet
Internet ~: 4 user
need: 5 board, modem 8 computer
shopping place: 3 Net, Web 4 eBay 8 Internet
wannabe: 5 ho-dad
worry: 5 shark
Surfer Girl (1963 song) artist: Beach Boys
Surfin' __: 3 USA 4 Bird 6 Safari
Surfin' Safari (1962 song) artist: Beach Boys
Surfin' U.S.A. (1963 song) artist: Beach Boys
surf scoter: 4 duck, fowl
relative: 4 smew, teal 5 eider, Pekin, Rouen, scaup 6 Cayuga 7 gadwall, mallard, pintail, pochard, redhead, sea duck, widgeon 8 garganey, gray duck, mandarin, musk duck, oldsquaw, shoveler, wood duck 9 black duck, broadbill, goldeneye, goosander, greenhead, merganser, ruddy duck, sprigtail 10 bufflehead, canvasback, tufted duck
surge: 3 jet 4 eddy, flow, gush, jump, leap, pour, rise, roll, rush, surf, wash, wave, zoom 5 arise, climb, drive, flood, heave, lunge, mount, rally, spirt, spout, spurt, swash, swell, swirl 6 billow, deluge, growth, influx, onrush, pounce, ripple, roller, seethe, sluice, stream, upturn, well up 7 barrage, breaker, overrun, soaring, upswing 8 effusion, increase, outbreak, outburst, overflow, swelling, undulate, upgrowth 9 crescendo, upwelling, well forth 10 move upward, outpouring
estuary ~: 5 eager, eagre
ocean ~: 4 tide, wave 5 swell 6 comber
__ surge: 5 storm
surgeon: 2 dr., MD 6 doctor 9 physician
attire: 4 gown 6 scrubs
dressing: 5 gauze
glove: 5 latex
prefix: 5 neuro
procedure: 9 operation
surname: 4 Mayo
tool: 5 clamp, laser, probe 6 lancet 7 forceps, scalpel
word: 4 stat
surgeon __: 7 general
__ surgeon: 4 oral, tree 5 house 6 flight
surgery: 9 operation, treatment
before ~: 5 pre-op
locale: 2 OR 8 hospital
perform ~: 7 operate
prepare for ~: 5 scrub
starter: 5 micro
__ surgery: 5 laser 7 plastic
Surinam: 6 nation 7 country
capital: 10 Paramaribo
language: 6 Arawak
money: 6 gilder, gulden 7 guilder
neighbor: 6 Brazil, Guyana
org.: 3 OAS
Sur la plage artist: 5 Degas
surliness: 9 short fuse
surly: 4 cold, cool, dark, dour, glum, mean, rude, ugly 5 brusk, cross, gruff, huffy, irate, nasty, onery, rough, sulky, testy 6 chilly, crabby, cranky, crusty, dismal, feisty, fretty, gloomy, grouty, grumpy, ireful, morose, ornery, sullen 7 bearish, bilious, brusque, glacial, grouchy, hateful, hostile, peevish, uncivil, vicious 8 choleric, churlish, contrary, frowning, growling, grumpish, inimical, inurbane, liverish, lowering, perverse, snappish, snarling, spiteful 9 bellicose, cheerless, crotchety, fractious, irascible, irritable, malicious, saturnine, splenetic, ungallant 10 ill-humored, ill-natured, malevolent, out of sorts, pugnacious, unfriendly, ungracious
__-sur-Marne: 7 Châlons
surmise: 4 deem, feel, idea 5 fancy, guess, hunch, infer, opine, think, trust 6 assume, deduce, expect, gather, notion, reckon, regard, take it, theory, thesis 7 imagine, opinion, predict, presume, suppose, suspect, thought, venture 8 conclude, consider, estimate, theorize 9 deduction, guesswork, inference, prognosis, speculate, suspicion 10 assumption, conclusion, conjecture, hypothesis, understand
surmount: 3 cap, top 4 best, lick, pass, rise 5 clear, scale, tower, vault 6 better, defeat, exceed, hurdle, subdue 7 conquer, prevail, succeed, weather 8 overcome, vanquish 9 negotiate, rise above, transcend
surname: 4 name 6 handle 8 cognomen 10 patronymic
common ~: 5 Jones, Smith
follower: 3 née
surpass: 3 cap, top 4 beat, best, lead, lick, pass 5 break, excel, outdo, tower, trump 6 better, exceed, outrun 7 eclipse, outpace, outrank, outstep, overrun, run over 8 go beyond, outclass, outmatch, outshine, outstrip, outweigh, overstep 9 transcend 10 outperform, overshadow, put to shame, tower above
surpassing: 5 above 6 beyond 7 ahead of, supreme 8 superior, towering, ultimate 9 unequaled, unrivaled 10 unrivalled
surplice: 5 cotta
surplus: 3 odd 4 glut, over, rest 5 extra, flood, spare 6 de trop, excess, margin, profit, supply, unused 7 balance, nimiety, overage, overrun, remnant, residue 8 leftover, overflow, plethora, residual 9 overstock, profusion, redundant, remainder 10 inordinate, lavishness, oversupply, unconsumed
__ surplus: 3 war 6 earned, paid-in 7 capital
surprise: 3 awe, jar, nab 4 daze, jolt, rock, stun, trap, turn 5 alarm, amaze, catch, floor, shock, start, treat, upset 6 ambush, dazzle, dismay, lay for, marvel, waylay, whammy, wonder 7 astound, capture, confuse, godsend, miracle, nonplus, perplex, shake up, stagger, startle, stupefy 8 astonish, blow away, bowl over, confound, discover, drop in on, unsettle 9 amazement, bombshell, burst in on, bushwhack, curveball, dumbfound, electrify, eyeopener, lie in wait, overwhelm, sensation, sneak up on, take aback 10 come down on, disconcert, revelation, unexpected, unforeseen, wonderment
attack: 4 raid 5 foray 6 ambush 10 ambushment
by ~: 5 aback, short 8 unawares
ending: 5 twist
nice ~: 5 bonus, treat
win: 5 upset
surprise __: 5 party 6 ending
Surprise: 4 city, town
locale: 7 Arizona
surprised: 4 numb 5 agape 7 in shock, stunned 10 taken aback
Surprise Symphony composer: 5 Haydn
surreal: 5 weird 6 far-out 7 bizarre 8 freakish 9 fantastic, grotesque 10 incredible
Surrealist: 6 artist
French ~: 6 Tanguy
German ~: 5 Ernst
predecessor: 4 Dada
Spanish ~: 4 Dali, Miró, Varo
Swiss ~: 4 Klee
surrender: 3 bow 4 cave, cede, drop, dump, fall, fold, give, lose, quit, sell, shed 5 chuck, ditch, forgo, leave, let go, waive, yield 6 fess up, forego, fork up, give in, give up, go down, resign, submit, toss in, unhand 7 abandon, concede, consign, entrust, forfeit, forsake, intrust, lay down, release, sell out, succumb 8 abdicate, forswear, get rid of, hand over, jettison, part with, renounce, roll over, say uncle, sign away, throw out, turn over 9 cast aside, deliver up, dispose of, extradite, foreswear, sacrifice, throw away, white flag 10 abdication, abnegation, capitulate, concession, relinquish, submission
cry of ~: 5 I quit, uncle
flag color: 5 white
Surrender (1987 film)
cast: Peter Boyle, Michael Caine, Sally Field, Steve Guttenberg
director: Jerry Belson
__ Surrender: 5 Never, Sweet
Surrender (1961 song) artist: Elvis Presley
surreptitious: 3 sly 6 covert, hidden, masked, secret, sneaky, unseen, veiled 7 cloaked, devious, furtive, on the QT, private 8 hush-hush, obscured, on the sly, secluded, shrouded, sneaking, stealthy 9 concealed, disguised, underhand 10 undercover, under wraps
surreptitiously: 7 sub rosa 8 on the sly, secretly 9 furtively, in private, underhand 10 undercover
surrey: 5 buggy
puller: 5 horse 6 equine
trim: 6 fringe
Surrey: 4 city, town 5 shire 6 county
city: 5 Egham 7 Staines 12 Sunbury. Epsom
locale: 6 Canada 7 England
Surrey With the Fringe on Top, The
composer: 7 Rodgers 11 Hammerstein
surrogate: 3 sub 5 agent, proxy, vicar 6 acting, backup, deputy, fill-in 7 stand-in 8 delegate 9 alternate, appointee, vicarious 10 substitute
surround: 3 mob, rim 4 edge, gird, hoop, ring, wrap 5 bathe, beset, bound, bower, boxin, embay, fence, hedge, hem in, skirt, verge 6 begird, border, circle, cordon, encase, enfold, engird, engulf, enlace, enwrap, fringe, girdle, incase, infold, ingulf, inlace, inwrap 7 besiege, compass, confine, embrace, enclave, enclose, envelop, environ, fence in, inclose, shelter, smother 8 blockade, cincture, encircle, neighbor 9 beleaguer, close in on, encompass 10 circumvent, lay siege to
prefix: 6 circum-
surrounded: 3 mid 4 amid 5 among 6 amidst, mongst 7 amongst, between
surroundings: 4 area 6 medium, milieu 7 climate, habitat, scenery, setting 8 ambiance, ambience, environs, location, position, purlieus, vicinity
__-sur-Saône: 7 Châlons
__-sur-Seine: 4 Ivry 7 Neuilly
Surtees, Robert Smith: 6 author, writer 7 British
surtout: 4 coat 6 jacket
Suruga: 3 bay
locale: 5 Japan 6 Honshu
surveillance: 3 bug 4 look, tail 5 recon, vigil, watch 6 spying 7 lookout, wiretap 8 eagle eye, scrutiny, security, stakeout 9 vigilance
device: 3 bug 4 mike 5 radar, sonar 6 camera 7 wiretap 9 satellite 10 microphone
engage in ~: 3 spy
keep under ~: 4 tail 5 guard, trace, watch 6 follow, patrol, police, shadow 7 baby-sit, observe, protect 9 chaperone, safeguard
outfit: 3 CIA, FBI, NSA
survey: 3 eye, map, see 4 case, look, plot, poll, rate, read, scan, view 5 assay, audit, cover, scope, scout, study 6 assess, census, digest, look at, précis, review, sample, search, size up, sketch, voting 7 canvass, enquiry, examine, explore, inquiry, inspect, legwork, measure, monitor, observe, outline, oversee, perusal, profile, summary, valuate 8 analysis, appraise, critique, estimate, evaluate, look over, look upon, overlook, overview, prospect, research, scrutiny, stake out 9 check over, range over, summarize 10 compendium, inspection, scrutinize
instrument: 6 alidad 7 compass, transit
survival __: 3 kit
survival of the __: 7 fittest
Survival: Zero author: Mickey Spillane
survive: 4 bear, last, live 5 cut it, exist, get by 6 endure, handle, linger, live on, make do, manage, remain, revive, suffer 7 carry on, hold out, make out, outlast, outlive, outwear, persist, recover, ride out, stand up, subsist, sustain, wait out, weather 8 continue, live down, overcome 9 persevere, withstand 10 get through, keep afloat, make the cut, see through, tough it out
__ Survive: 5 I Will
surviving: 5 alive 6 extant, with us 9 remaining
__ survivor: 4 sole
Survivor (CBS)
shelter: 3 hut
team: 5 tribe
Survivor (rock group)
hometown: Chicago
song: Burning Heart (1985)
Eye of the Tiger (1982)
High on You (1985)
Is This Love (1986)
The Search Is Over (1985)
Survivor (2001 song) artist: Destiny's Child
__ Survivors: 4 Soul
Susan: 3 Dey 4 Rook 5 Anton, Clark, Lucci, Olsen 6 Faludi, George, Oliver, Powter, Ruttan, Sontag 7 Anspach, Blakely, Hayward, Tyrrell 8 Glaspell, Sarandon, Sullivan 9 Hampshire, Seidelman, Strasberg
black-eyed ~: 5 plant 6 flower 9 perennial 10 wildflower
lazy ~: 4 tray 6 server
Susan __ James: 5 Saint
__ Susan: 4 lazy

Susanin: **4** Ivan
Susann: **10** Jacqueline
Susanna: **5** Hoffs **6** Moodie
Susanna composer: **6** Handel
Susannah: **4** York
Susanne: **6** Langer
Susan Saint ___: **5** James
___ Susan Williams: **4** Stop
susceptible: **4** easy, naif, open, soft **5** naive, prone **6** liable, swayed **7** exposed, given to, pliable, psychic, subject, taken in, tending, touched **8** affected, gullable, gullible, inclined, wide open **9** receptive, sensitive
not ~: **6** immune
sushi: **4** fish **5** snack **9** appetizer
bar soup: **4** miso
ingredient: **3** eel, egg **4** fish, rice, tuna **7** octopus, seaweed
like ~: **3** raw
source: **5** Japan
Susie ___: **6** Darlin'
suslik: **6** animal, mammal, rodent
relative: **3** rat **4** cavy, degu, jird, paca, vole **5** coypu, gundi, mouse, xerus **6** agouti, beaver, gerbil, gopher, jerboa, marmot, murine **7** hamster, lemming, muskrat, visacha **8** chipmunk, cricetid, dormouse, squirrel, tuco-tuco **9** chickaree, groundhog, guinea pig, porcupine, woodchuck **10** chinchilla, prairie dog
suspect: **4** fear, feel, hold, moot, open, take **5** doubt, fishy, guess, query, shady, shaky, smell, think **6** assume, expect, gather, louche, pseudo, reckon, unsure, wonder **7** believe, dubious, imagine, presume, suppose, surmise, unclear **8** conclude, consider, distrust, doubtful, mistrust, question, theorize, unlikely **9** smell a rat, speculate, uncertain **10** conjecture, disbelieve, have a hunch, incredible, ridiculous, understand
check a ~: **5** frisk **7** pat down
need: **5** alibi
___ suspect: **5** prime
Suspect (1987 film)
cast: Cher, Liam Neeson, Dennis Quaid
director: Peter Yates
___ Suspects, The: **5** Usual
Suspect, The (1944 film)
cast: Charles Laughton, Ella Raines
suspend: **3** bar **4** file, halt, hang, pend, quit, stay, stop **5** break, cease, check, debar, defer, delay, poise, sling, stall, swing, table, waive **6** arrest, dangle, depend, freeze, hold up, lay off, put off, recall, retard, shelve **7** adjourn, break up, hold off, neglect **8** cut short, intermit, lay aside, postpone, protract, put on ice, shut down **9** interrupt **10** inactivate, pigeonhole
suspended: **5** slung **6** frozen **7** abeyant, dormant, hanging **10** up in the air
hang ~: **5** float, hover
suspenders: **6** braces
alternative: **4** belt
suspense: **4** plot **5** doubt **7** anxiety, tension **10** expectancy
suspenseful: **8** dramatic
suspension: **4** halt, stay **5** break, delay, letup, pause, truce **6** arrest, cutoff, freeze, recess **7** latency, respite, timeout **8** abeyance, breather, dormancy, downtime, lateness, reprieve, solution, stoppage **9** armistice, cessation, deferment, dismissal, exclusion, expulsion, remission
suspension ___: **5** point **6** bridge, system
suspicion: **4** clew, clue, hint, idea **5** doubt, guess, hunch, qualm, shade, smell, tinge, touch, trace, whiff **6** belief, notion, shadow, strain, streak, trifle **7** feeling, glimmer, inkling, opinion, surmise, vestige, whisper **8** bad vibes, cynicism, distrust, jealousy, mistrust, question, wariness **9** chariness, guesswork, leeriness, misgiving, nonbelief **10** assumption, conjecture, gut feeling, impression, intimation, skepticism, suggestion
above ~: **5** clean **8** innocent **9** blameless, guiltless **10** inculpable, in the clear
Suspicion (1941 film)
cast: Joan Fontaine, Cary Grant, Cedric Hardwicke
director: Alfred Hitchcock
___ Suspicion: **5** Above
Suspicions (1979 song) artist: Eddie Rabbitt
suspicious: **4** cagy, wary **5** cagey, chary, fishy, funny, leery, phony, queer, shady, shaky **6** louche, phoney, unsure **7** careful, cynical, dubious, guarded, jealous, unusual, uptight **8** cautious, doubtful, doubting, hesitant, peculiar, watchful **9** diffident, equivocal, green-eyed, ill at ease, irregular, jaundiced, out of line, quizzical, skeptical, uncertain, wondering **10** far-fetched
Suspicious Minds (1969 song) artist: Elvis Presley
suspire: **4** sigh **6** exhale
Susquehanna: **5** river, tribe
city on the ~: **5** Owego **10** Harrisburg
locale: **4** Penn. **7** New York **8** Maryland
suss (out): **6** figure
Sussex: **3** cow **4** bull, fowl **6** bovine, cattle, county **7** chicken
city: **7** Bexhill, Crawley **8** Brighton, Hastings **10** Eastbourne
locale: **7** England
relative: **6** Bantam, Brahma, Houdan **7** Cornish, Dorking, Leghorn **8** Araucana, Langshan, Shanghai **9** Dominique, Orpington, Wyandotte
Susskind, David: **2** MC **4** host **5** emcee
Sussudio (1985 song) artist: Phil Collins
sustain: **3** aid **4** back, bear, buoy, feed, help, hold, keep, prop, save **5** abide, brace, brook, carry, nurse, prove, shore, stand **6** afford, assist, convey, defend, endure, foster, hang in, ratify, suffer, supply, uphold, verify **7** approve, bolster, comfort, confirm, endorse, fortify, indorse, justify, nourish, nurture, prolong, provide, receive, relieve, ride out, shore up, stand by, stomach, support, survive, undergo **8** bankroll, bear with, befriend, buttress, continue, preserve, protract, stand for, tolerate, validate **9** keep alive, keep going, lend a hand, put up with, reinforce, stabilize, stand up to, withstand **10** experience, perpetuate, provide for, speak up for, stick up for, strengthen
sustained: **7** chronic **8** constant **9** chronical, perennial, unabating **10** relentless
in ballet: **7** soutenu
in music: **6** tenuto
sustaining: **7** ongoing **10** alimentary, comforting, continuing, nutritious
sustenance: **3** aid, job **4** diet, fare, food, fuel, grub, keep, meat **5** bacon, bread **6** living, ration, relief, upkeep, viands **7** aliment, edibles, support, victual **8** eatables, victuals **9** nutrition, provender **10** assistance, livelihood, provisions
spiritual ~: **5** manna **6** prayer
take ~: **3** eat, sup **4** dine
sustineo ___: **4** alas
Susumu, Tonegawa: **8** Nobelist **9** biologist
susurrus: **6** murmur **7** whisper
Sutcliffe: **3** Stu
Sutherland: **4** Earl, Joan **6** Donald, Kiefer
Sutherland, Donald: **5** actor
film: The Act of the Heart (1970)
Backdraft (1991)
Bethune (1977)
Buffy the Vampire Slayer (1992)
The Day of the Locust (1975)
The Dirty Dozen (1967)
Disclosure (1994)
Don't Look Now (1973)
The Eagle Has Landed (1977)
Eye of the Needle (1981)
The Great Train Robbery (1979)
Heaven Help Us (1985)
Instinct (1999)
Invasion of the Body Snatchers (1978)
JFK (1991)
Kelly's Heroes (1970)
Klute (1971)
MASH (1970)
Max Dugan Returns (1983)
National Lampoon's Animal House (1978)
Ordinary People (1980)
Panic (2000)
Six Degrees of Separation (1993)
Space Cowboys (2000)
Start the Revolution Without Me (1970)
Steelyard Blues (1973)
Without Limits (1998)
son: **6** Keifer
Sutherland, Earl: **8** Nobelist
Sutherland, Joan: **4** Dame, diva **6** singer **7** soprano **10** prima donna
milieu: **5** opera
solo: **4** aria
Sutherland, Kiefer: **5** actor
father: **6** Donald
film: Bright Lights, Big City (1988)
Crazy Moon (1986)
Dark City (1998)
A Few Good Men (1992)
Flatliners (1990)
Freeway (1996)
The Three Musketeers (1993)
Young Guns (1988)
Sutlej: **5** river
feeder: **6** Chenab
locale: **5** India, Tibet **6** Thibet, Xizang **7** Sitsang **8** Pakistan
___ Sutra: **4** Kama **5** Heart, Lotus **7** Diamond
Sutter: **4** John
Sutter's ___: **4** Mill
Sutton: **3** Don, Hal **4** John **5** Frank **6** Willie
Sutton ___: **3** Hoo **5** Place
Sutton, Don: **6** Dodger, hurler **7** pitcher
Sutton, Hal: **6** golfer
milieu: **5** links **6** course
org.: **3** PGA
Sutton, Willie, emulate: **3** rob **5** steal
suture: **3** sew **4** seam **6** stitch
combining form: **6** -rhaphy **7** -rrhaphy
material: **4** silk **6** catgut
Suu Kyi, Aung San: **8** Nobelist
SUV: **3** ute **7** vehicle
Suva: **4** city, town **7** capital
locale: **4** Fiji
Suvari: **4** Mena
Suwannee: **5** river
locale: **7** Florida, Georgia
Suzanne: **4** Vega **6** Somers **7** Farrell **9** Pleshette
Suzanne composer: **5** Cohen
suzerain: **4** lord **5** ruler **6** gerent
suzerainty: **4** rule
___ suzette: **5** crêpe
Suzi: **6** Quatro
Suzuki: **3** car **4** auto **6** Ichiro, import **10** automobile
model: **5** Aerio, Swift **6** Esteem, Vitara **7** Samurai **8** Sidekick
Suzuki, Ichiro sport: **8** baseball
Suzy: **4** Amis **6** Parker **7** Chaffee
Svedberg, Theodor: **7** chemist **8** Nobelist
svelte: **4** lank, lean, slim, thin, trim, wiry **5** lanky, lithe, spare **6** dainty, gangly, lissom, skinny, slight, slinky, supple, twiggy **7** gracile, scraggy, scrawny, slender, spidery, willowy **8** gangling, graceful **9** lithesome, sylphlike
Sven: **5** Hedin
Svengali (1931 film)
cast: John Barrymore, Donald Crisp, Marian Marsh
director: Archie Mayo
Svenson: **2** Bo
Sverdrup ___: **7** Islands
Sverige neighbor: **5** Norge
Svevo, Italo: **6** author, writer **7** Italian
svgs. ___: **4** acct.
SVX: **3** car **4** auto **6** Subaru **10** automobile
swab: **3** gob, mop, tar **4** Q-Tip, salt, wash, wipe **5** clean, mop up **6** sailor **7** cleanse, jack tar, mariner **10** applicator
salutation: **4** ahoy **5** avast
target: **3** wax **6** earwax
swabbie: **3** gob, tar **4** salt **6** seaman **7** jack tar
swaddle: **3** lap **4** tuck, wrap **5** cover **6** enwrap, inwrap
swaddling ___: **5** bands **7** clothes
swag: **4** tilt **5** booty, prize **6** boodle, spoils **7** festoon, garland, jobbery, plunder **9** valuables
Aussie's ~: **5** bluey
Swaggart: **5** Jimmy
swagger: **4** brag, crow **5** boast, bully, gloat, pride, strut, swank, swash **6** hector, parade, prance **7** bluster, conceit, peacock, rub it in, show off, triumph **8** brandish, domineer, flourish **9** arrogance, put on airs **10** grandstand, lord it over
stick: **4** cane
swagger ___: **4** coat **5** stick
swaggerer: **5** bully **6** gascon **7** showoff **8** blowhard, braggart
swaggering: **4** vain **6** jaunty **8** arrogant, boastful, cocksure
swagman: **6** Aussie
Swahili: **5** Bantu **8** language
freedom, in ~: **5** uhuru
honorific: **5** bwana
swain: **3** lad **4** beau, love, male **5** adore, flame, lover, Romeo, wooer **6** adorer, suitor **7** admirer, gallant **8** lover boy **9** boyfriend, inamorato **10** sweetheart
offering: **4** rose **5** candy **10** chocolates
starter: **3** cox **4** boat
Swain: **9** Dominique
SWAK
part of ~: **4** kiss, with **6** sealed
site: **6** letter **8** envelope **10** billet-doux, love letter
swale: **5** swamp **6** valley **7** lowland
swallow: **3** buy, eat, nip, sip **4** belt, bird, bolt, down, drop, gulp, lump, swig, take, toss, wolf **5** abide, drink, quaff, slurp, sop up, swill, taste **6** absorb, accept, devour, digest, draw in, endure, engulf, gather, gobble, guzzle, herald, imbibe, ingest, ingulf, inhale, martin, osmose, soak up, suck up, suffer, take in **7** believe, consume,

dispose, drink in, fall for, put away, repress, stomach **8** chug-a-lug, dispatch, spoonful, stand for, tolerate, wash down **9** put up with **10** assimilate
don't ~: **5** doubt **6** reject **7** laugh at **8** pooh-pooh **10** disbelieve
ender: **4** tail
home: **4** nest
lookalike: **4** gull **5** swift
nervous ~: **4** gulp
prepare to ~: **4** chew **9** masticate
sea ~: **4** bird, tern
__ swallow: **3** sea **4** bank, barn, tree **5** cliff **7** chimney
swallowtail: **4** coat **9** butterfly
swami: **4** guru, seer **5** Hindu **6** Hindoo, master, pundit
swamp: **3** bog, fen, mud **4** load, mire, moor, quag, rout, sink, wash **5** bayou, beset, crowd, drown, flood, marsh, swale, waste **6** defeat, deluge, drench, engulf, ingulf, morass, muskeg, slough **7** besiege, bottoms, lowland, overrun, peat bog, trounce **8** inundate, overflow, overload, quagmire, submerge, submerse, waterlog, wetlands **9** backwater, marshland, overcrowd, overpower, overwhelm, snow under **10** everglades, overburden
Australian ~ monster: **6** bunyip
denizen: **4** croc, frog **5** crane, egret, gator, heron, snake **6** caiman, cayman **9** alligator, crocodile
grass: **5** sedge
hazard: **4** croc **5** gator, snake **6** caiman, cayman **7** reptile **9** alligator, crocodile, quicksand
pink: **5** plant **6** flower
sound: **5** croak
tree: **6** tupelo **7** live oak
swamp __: **3** gas **4** pink, rose **5** buggy **6** azalea, locust, mallow, rabbit **7** cabbage, cypress, sparrow
__ Swamp: **6** Dismal
swamped: **4** busy **5** awash **7** deluged **10** overworked
swampy: **3** low, wet **4** miry **5** boggy, fenny, muddy **6** marshy, quaggy **7** paludal **8** low-lying
__ Swampy: **4** Camp
swan: **4** bird
female ~: **3** pen
genus: **4** olor
male ~: **3** cob
song: **3** end **4** last **6** ending
young ~: **6** cygnet
swan __: **4** dive, song **6** maiden
__ swan: **4** mute **6** tundra **7** Bewick's, whooper **9** trumpeter
Swan: **5** Billy
city on the ~: **5** Perth
constellation: **6** Cygnus
Swan, Billy song: I Can Help (1974)
Swanee (1920 song) artist: Al Jolson
composer: **6** Caesar **8** Gershwin
swank: **4** chic, posh, rich, tony **5** dandy, fancy, grand, haute, natty, plush, ritzy, sharp, showy, sleek, smart, strut, style, swank, swish, toney **6** chichi, classy, dapper, deluxe, dressy, flashy, jaunty, lavish, lordly, modish, rakish, snappy, snazzy, spiffy, sporty, trendy, with-it **7** dashing, elegant, opulent, refined, splashy, stylish, swagger, voguish **8** palatial, peacocky, princely, splendid **9** exclusive, expensive, glamorous, luxurious, nattiness, sumptuous **10** flamboyant
up: **5** preen, primp
Swank, Hilary: **7** actress
Oscar: Boys Don't Cry
spouse: Chad Lowe
swanky
see swank
Swan Lake: **6** ballet
composer: Tchaikovsky
role: **5** Odile
Swann, Lynn sport: **8** football
__ swans a-swimming...: **5** seven
__ Swans at Coole, The: **4** Wild
Swansea: **4** city, port, town
locale: **5** Wales
Swanson: **6** Gloria, Kristy, Robert
Swanson, Gloria: **7** actress
film: The Loves of Sunya (1927)
Music in the Air (1934)
Queen Kelly (1928)
Sadie Thompson (1928)
Sunset Blvd. (1950)
role: **5** Norma, Sadie
spouse: Wallace Beery
Swan, The (1956 film)
cast: Alec Guinness, Louis Jourdan, Grace Kelly
director: Charles Vidor
__ Swan, The: **5** Black
swap: **4** deal **5** bandy, trade, truck **6** barter, change, switch **7** bargain **8** exchange **9** negotiate, transpose **10** horse-trade, quid pro quo, substitute
swap __: **4** meet, shop
sward: **3** lea, ley, sod **4** lawn, turf **5** field, grass **6** meadow **9** grassland
starter: **5** green
swarm: **3** jam, mob **4** army, bevy, herd, host, mass, pack, pour, teem **5** bunch, covey, crawl, crowd, crush, drove, flock, flood, horde, press, snarl, troop **6** abound, legion, myriad, school, stream, throng **7** cluster, numbers, overrun **9** gathering, multitude **10** congregate
home: **4** hive **7** beehive, bee tree
swarming: **4** busy, rife **5** alive, dense, thick **6** active, packed **7** crowded, teeming **8** infested, thronged
swarms: **4** lots **6** flocks **7** legions
Swarm, The menace: **4** bees
swarth
see sward
swarthy: **3** tan **4** dark **5** black, dusky, swart, tawny
far from ~: **4** fair, pale **5** light
swash: **4** rush **5** boast, surge **6** onrush, parade **7** bluster, bravado, swagger
ender: **7** buckler **8** buckling
swashbuckle: **5** boast **7** bluster, swagger
swashbuckler: **5** Athos **6** Aramis **7** Porthos **9** D'Artagnan
weapon: **5** sword
swashbuckling: **4** bold **5** brave **6** daring, rakish **7** dashing, gallant, raffish **8** colorful, fearless, spirited **9** impetuous **10** flamboyant
actor: Errol Flynn
swat: **3** box, hit, zap **4** beat, belt, biff, blow, cuff, ding, slam, slap, slug, sock **5** clout, knock, smack, smash, swipe, whack, whang **6** buffet, larrup, strike, wallop **7** clobber **9** haul off on
SWAT __: **4** team
swatch: **4** snip **6** sample
Swatch competitor: **4** Ebel, Rado **5** Casio, Elgin, Lorus, Omega, Rolex, Seiko, Timex **6** Bulova, Fossil, Movado, Pulsar **7** Citizen **8** Longines, Tag Heuer, Tourneau
swath: **3** row **4** belt, path
swathe: **3** lap **4** tape, wrap **5** dress **6** enfold, infold **7** bandage **8** muffle up
__ swatter: **3** fly
S.W.A.T. Theme (1976 song) artist: Rhythm Heritage
sway: **3** get, run, wag, win **4** bend, bias, keel, lean, move, push, reel, rock, roll, rule, tilt, toss, turn, wave, yo-yo **5** budge, carry, clout, dance, lobby, lurch, might, power, range, reach, reign, scope, shake, slope, sweep, swing, waver, weave **6** affect, careen, dangle, empire, govern, induce, regime, strike, suck in, teeter, totter, wabble, waddle, waffle, wobble **7** control, convert, deviate, impress, incline, inspire, potence, potency, stagger, vibrate, win over **8** dominate, dominion, hegemony, impact on, kingship, motivate, persuade, pressure, prestige, undulate **9** authority, brainwash, fluctuate, hem and haw, influence, oscillate, prejudice, prevail on, supremacy **10** domination, leadership, predispose
hold ~: **4** head, rule **5** reign **6** direct, govern, manage **7** command, control, prevail **8** dominate, overrule **9** influence
sway __: **3** bar
__-sway bar: **4** anti
swayed: **9** influence
easily ~: **4** meek, soft, weak **5** naive, timid **7** pliable **10** indecisive, irresolute
Swayin' to the Music (1977 song)
artist: Johnny Rivers
Swayze, Patrick: **5** actor
film: Dirty Dancing (1987)
Ghost (1990)
Grandview, U.S.A. (1984)
Point Break (1991)
song: She's Like the Wind (1988)
Swaziland: **6** nation **7** country
bovine: **5** Nguni
capital: **7** Mbabane
city: **7** Manzini, Mbabane
locale: **6** Africa
money: **9** lilangeni
neighbor: **10** Mozambique
Swe.
see Sweden
swear: **3** vow **4** aver, avow, cuss **5** curse, vouch **6** affirm, assert, assure, attest, pledge **7** certify, declare, profane, promise, testify, warrant **8** maintain **9** blaspheme, guarantee **10** asseverate
by: **4** rely **5** trust **6** bank on, rely on **7** believe, count on **8** depend on **9** believe in, count upon
ender: **4** word
falsely: **3** lie **7** perjure
in: **6** adjure, induct **7** instate
off: **4** quit **5** forgo **6** abjure, eschew, forego, reform **7** forsake **8** renounce
word: **4** oath **5** curse **9** expletive
swearing: **4** vice **7** cursing, cussing **9** blasphemy, profanity
Swearin' to God (1975 song) artist: Frankie Valli
swearword: **4** oath **5** curse **9** expletive, profanity
sweat: **3** job **4** care, drip, fret, glow, moil, ooze, plod, seep, stew, toil, wilt, work **5** chafe, exert, exude, grind, labor, steam, worry **6** effort, egesta, lather, strain, strive **7** agonize, excrete, secrete, swelter, work out **8** drudgery, exertion, moisture, perspire, struggle **9** give a darn, percolate
bit of ~: **4** bead, drop
combining form: **4** hidr- **5** hidro-
ender: **3** box **4** band, shop **5** house, pants, shirt
it out: **4** wait **5** worry **6** endure
no ~: **4** easy, snap **5** cinch **6** simple **8** duck soup **9** easy as pie **10** child's play, effortless
over: **4** mull **5** study, think, weigh **6** debate, ponder **7** revolve **8** cogitate, ruminate **9** cerebrate **10** deliberate, kick around
source: **4** pore **5** gland
sweat __: **3** bee, out **4** suit **5** blood, gland, it out, socks **6** equity **7** bullets
__ sweat: **4** cold
Sweat: **5** Keith
sweatband site: **5** wrist
sweater: **4** wrap **5** V-neck, wooly **6** jersey, woolly **7** kashmir **8** cardigan, cashmere, cowlneck, crew neck, pullover, slipover **10** protection, turtleneck
fabric: **4** poly, wool **5** Orlon **6** angora, cotton, mohair
letter: **2** mu, nu, pi, xi **3** chi, eta, phi, psi, rho, tau **4** beta, iota, zeta **5** alpha, delta, gamma, kappa, omega, sigma, theta **6** lambda **7** epsilon, omicron, upsilon
make a ~: **4** knit
needing a ~: **4** cold, cool **5** nippy, windy **6** chilly, drafty
part: **3** arm **4** neck
size: **2** sm., XL **3** lge., med. **5** large, small **6** medium
sweat of one's __: **4** brow
sweatshirt part, maybe: **4** hood **5** pouch
__, Sweat & Tears: **5** Blood
sweaty: **3** hot, wet **4** damp, warm **5** moist, undry **6** clammy, soaked, steamy, sticky, stinky **7** glowing, wettish **8** drenched, dripping **10** perspiring, sweltering
Sweden: **6** nation **7** country
astronomer: **7** Celsius **8** Ångström
bath: **5** sauna
botanist: **8** Linnaeus
bovine: **5** Fjall
canal: **4** gota
capital: **9** Stockholm
car: **4** Saab **5** Volvo
chemist: **5** Nobel **7** Scheele **8** Svedberg, Tiselius **9** Arrhenius, Berzelius
city: **4** Lund, Umea **5** Gavle, Luleå, Malmö, Ystad **6** Kalmar, Upsala **7** Uppsala **8** Göteborg, Halmstad **9** Stockholm
district: **3** lan
economist: **5** Ohlin **6** Myrdal
explorer: **5** Hedin **12** Nordenskjold
furniture chain: **4** Ikea
geographer: **5** Hedin
golfer: **9** Sorenstam
island: **5** Oland **7** Gotland
lake of ~: **5** Malar
legislature: **7** Riksdag
money: **3** ore **5** krona
mountain: **6** Kjölen
native: **4** Lapp
neighbor: **6** Norway **7** Denmark, Finland
Nobelist in Chemistry: **8** Svedberg, Tiselius **9** Arrhenius **15** von Euler-Chelpin
Nobelist in economics: **5** Ohlin **6** Myrdal
Nobelist in Literature: **5** Sachs **7** Johnson **8** Lagerlöf **9** Karlfeldt, Martinson **10** Lagerkvist **13** von Heidenstam
Nobelist in Medicine: **6** Granit **8** Carlsson, Theorell, von Euler **9** Bergström **10** Gullstrand, Samuelsson
Nobelist in Peace: **6** Myrdal **8** Branting **9** Arnoldson, Söderblom **12** Hammarskjöld
Nobelist in Physics: **5** Dalén **6** Alfvén **8** Siegbahn
philosopher: **10** Swedenborg
physicist: **5** Dalén **6** Alfvén **8** Ångström **9** Arrhenius
playwright: **9** Söderberg **10** Strindberg

poet: 6 Ekelöf 7 Bellman, Fröding 9 Karlfeldt 10 Gustafsson, Strindberg
port: 5 Gavle, Luleå, Malmö, Ystad 6 Kalmar 8 Göteborg, Halmstad 9 Stockholm
river: 3 Dal, Ume 4 Gota 5 Torne
rock group: 4 ABBA
rug: 3 rya
sea: 6 Baltic
soprano: 4 Lind 7 Nilsson
tennis pro: 4 Borg
toast: 5 skoal
waterfall: 6 Handol, Skykje
writer: 5 Weiss 6 Bremer, Moberg, Myrdal, Wägner, Wahlöö 7 Bergman, Johnson, Sjöwall 8 Almqvist, Lagerlöf, Matinson 9 Söderberg 10 Lagerkvist
Swedenborg, Emanuel: 6 writer 7 Swedish 11 philosopher
Swede neighbor: 4 Dane, Finn 9 Norwegian
Swedish: 8 language
Swedish __: 3 ivy 6 turnip 7 massage
Swedish Nightingale, The: 4 Lind
Swee' __: 3 Pea
Sweeney: 2 D.B. 5 Julia
Sweeney, D.B.: 5 actor
film: The Book of Stars (2000) A Day in October (1990) Eight Men Out (1988) Gardens of Stone (1987)
film (voice): Dinosaur (2000)
Sweeney Todd: 7 musical
composer: 8 Sondheim
prop: 5 razor
sweep: 3 arc, fly, mop, pan 4 area, bend, comb, flit, lick, play, raid, rake, sail, scan, scud, skim, span, sway, wing, zoom 5 ambit, broom, brush, clean, clear, curve, gamut, glide, orbit, range, reach, realm, scope, strut, swing, vista, whisk 6 career, course, extent, glance, length, radius, remove, spread, tidy up, vacuum 7 breadth, clean up, clear up, compass, expanse, flounce, purview, stretch, triumph 8 clear out, confines, flourish, latitude, panorama, progress 9 extension, full range, landslide, ranginess 10 boundaries, clean house
away: 4 toss 6 ravage, ravish 7 destroy, discard, enchant 9 overwhelm
clean ~: 7 triumph, victory 9 landslide
ender: 4 back 6 stakes
off one's feet: 5 besot, charm, tempt 6 allure, entice, rope in 7 attract, beguile, bewitch, enchant 8 entrance 9 captivate, fascinate, infatuate
upward: 4 rise, soar 5 climb 6 ascend
__ sweep: 5 clean 7 chimney
sweeper: 4 fish, maid 5 broom 7 janitor
starter: 4 mine
__ sweeper: 6 carpet, vacuum
sweeping: 3 big 4 epic, vast, wide 5 broad, chore, large, roomy, total 6 all-out, global 7 blanket, general, overall, plenary, radical 8 extended, far-flung, spacious, thorough, whole-hog 9 all-around, capacious, expansive, extensive, full-dress, housework, inclusive, universal, wholesale 10 exhaustive, large-scale, soup-to-nuts, unspecific, widespread
sweepings: 4 dust, junk 5 trash, waste 6 litter, refuse 7 garbage, rejects, residue, rubbish 8 residuum
Sweepings (1933 film)
cast: Lionel Barrymore, William Gargan, Gloria Stuart
sweep one off one's __: 4 feet
sweep-second __: 4 hand
sweepstakes: 6 raffle 7 contest, lottery
__ Sweepstakes: 5 Irish
sweet: 3 jam, new, pet 4 cake, dear, kind, mild, pure, rich, soft 5 balmy, candy, clean, fresh, lolly, mushy, snack, taste, treat 6 bonbon, dainty, dulcet, gentle, goodie, honied, in tune, kindly, lovely, loving, mellow, pastry, sirupy, smooth, sugary, syrupy, taking, tender, washed 7 amiable, angelic, beloved, candied, cloying, darling, dearest, dessert, honeyed, likable, lovable, melodic, musical, pudding, scented, sugared, treacly, tuneful, winning, winsome 8 amicable, aromatic, charming, engaging, euphonic, fragrant, friendly, generous, gumdrops, heavenly, junk food, ladylove, loveable, luscious, nectared, perfumed, pleasant, pleasing, precious, redolent, sonorous, soothing 9 agreeable, ambrosial, angelical, appealing, beautiful, cherished, chocolate, courteous, delicious, enjoyable, lucrative, melodious, nectarous, preserves, sugarplum, toothsome, treasured, unselfish, wholesome 10 attractive, confection, delectable, delightful, euphonical, euphonious, gratifying, harmonious, profitable, reasonable, saccharine, thoughtful, unhardened
be ~ on: 4 like, love 5 adore 6 admire 7 care for
ender: 3 sop 4 meat, shop 5 bread, briar, brier, heart
food: 3 bar, jam, pie 4 cake, tart 5 candy, honey, jelly 6 bonbon, cookie, mousse, pastry 7 brownie 8 ice cream 9 marmalade, preserves 10 confection
girl of song: 3 Sue
on: 6 fond of, keen on 8 mad about
science: 6 boxing
shop: 6 bakery 10 patisserie
starter: 4 semi 6 bitter, meadow
suffix: 3 -ose
talk: 4 sell 7 blarney, coaxing, palaver 8 cajolery, flattery 9 wheedling 10 endearment, inducement, persuasion
too ~: 4 icky 6 cutesy 7 cutesie, gushing, mawkish
sweet __: 3 bay, gum, oil, pea 4 corn, flag, gale, roll, spot, talk 5 basil, birch, cider, grass, shrub, spire, tooth 6 acacia, almond, cherry, cicely, clover, fennel, marten, orange, pepper, potato, violet 7 alyssum, calamus, cassava, sorghum, william
Sweet: 5 Dolph 7 Blanche
Sweet __: 3 Pea 4 Lady, Love, Mary 5 Afton, Thing 6 Dreams 7 Adeline, Charity, Freedom, Liberty, Nothin's, Seasons
Sweet __ Brown: 7 Georgia
Sweet __, Just You: 3 Sue
Sweet __ Music: 4 Soul
Sweet __ O'Grady: 5 Rosie
Sweet __ Woman: 4 City
Sweet Adeline: 7 musical
songwriter: 4 Kern
Sweet Afton author: Robert Burns
sweet-and-__: 4 sour
...sweet and __ you: 5 so are
Sweet and Innocent (1971 song) artist: Donny Osmond
Sweet and Lowdown (1999 film)
cast: Brian Markinson, Samantha Morton, Sean Penn, Uma Thurman
director: Woody Allen
Sweet and Low-Down composer: 8 Gershwin
Sweet are the __ of adversity: 4 uses
Sweet as apple cider girl: 3 Ida
Sweet Bird of Youth: 4 film, play
author: Tennessee Williams
cast: Shirley Knight, Paul Newman, Geraldine Page
director: Richard Brooks
sweetbrier: 4 rose 5 plant 6 flower
Sweet Caroline (1969 song) artist: Neil Diamond
Sweet Charity: 4 film, play 7 musical
author: Neil Simon
cast: Shirley MacLaine, John McMartin, Ricardo Montalban
director: Bob Fosse
Sweet Cherry Wine (1969 song) artist: Tommy James and the Shondells
Sweet Child o' Mine (1988 song) artist: Guns N' Roses
Sweet Crunch: 6 cereal
competitor: 3 Kix 4 Life, Trix 5 Kashi, Quisp, Total 6 Kaboom, Muesli, Oreo O's, Pablum, Smacks 7 All-Bran, Crispix, Harmony, Hunny B's, Mueslix, Oat Bran, Pokemon 8 Boo Berry, Cheerios, Corn Chex, Corn Pops, Fiber One, Rice Chex, Special K, Uncle Sam, Wheaties 9 Alpha Bits, Apple Zaps, Grape Nuts, Honey Comb, Just Right, Wheat Chex 10 Apple Jacks, Bran Flakes, Cap'n Crunch, Cocoa Puffs, Froot Loops, Mini-Wheats, Nutri-Grain, Puffed Rice, Quaker Oats, Smart Start 11 Cocoa Blasts, Cookie Crisp, Golden Crisp, Lucky Charms, Puffed Wheat, Waffle Crisp
__ Sweet Day: 3 One
Sweet Dreams (1985 film)
cast: Ed Harris, Jessica Lange, Ann Wedgeworth
director: Karel Reisz
subject: Patsy Cline
Sweet Dreams author: Michael Frayn
Sweet Dreams (song) artist: Air Supply, Eurythmics
sweeten: 3 pay 4 mull 5 sugar 6 enrich, pacify, soothe 7 appease, assuage, mollify, placate 8 soften up 9 alleviate, candy-coat, deodorize, sugar-coat 10 conciliate, propitiate
sweetened: 5 tasty 6 sugary 10 appetizing
sweetener: 3 tip 4 lure 5 Equal, honey, sirup, sugar, syrup 6 reward 8 gratuity, largesse, molasses 9 saccharin 10 enticement
natural ~: 5 honey 8 cinnamon
sweeten the __: 3 pot
__ Sweeter Than Wine: 6 Kisses
Sweeter Than You (1959 song) artist: Ricky Nelson
Sweetest __, The: 5 Taboo, Thing 6 Sounds
Sweetest Sounds, The composer: 7 Rodgers
Sweetest Taboo, The (1985 song) artist: Sade
Sweetest Thing, The (2002 film)
cast: Christina Applegate, Selma Blair, Cameron Diaz
director: Roger Kumble
Sweetest Thing, The (1981 song) artist: Juice Newton
sweetheart: 2 jo 3 hon, luv, pet 4 baby, beau, dear, doll, jill, love, wife 5 amour, angel, chéri, cooky, cutey, cutie, deary, ducky, flame, honey, leman, lover, lovey, novia, novio, sugar, swain 6 bon ami, chérie, cookie, dautie, dearie, steady, suitor 7 admirer, beloved, darling, dearest, dear one, pigsney, schatzi, squeeze, tootsie 8 chou-chou, cutie pie, dowsabel, dulcinea, ladylove, lovebird, macushla, paramour, precious, snookums, sugar pie, treasure, truelove 9 bonne amie, boyfriend, companion, dreamboat, inamorata, inamorato, petit chou, valentine 10 girlfriend, heartthrob, honeybunch, mavourneen, turtledove
of yore: 5 leman
sweetheart __: 4 deal, neck
Sweetheart of Sigma __, The: 3 Chi
Sweet Hearts Dance (1988 film)
cast: Jeff Daniels, Don Johnson, Elizabeth Perkins, Susan Sarandon
Sweet Hitch-Hiker (1971 song) artist: Creedence Clearwater Revival
Sweet Home Alabama (2002 film)
cast: Candice Bergen, Patrick Dempsey, Josh Lucas, Mary Kay Place, Reese Witherspoon
director: Andy Tennant
Sweet Home Alabama (1974 song) artist: Lynyrd Skynyrd
sweetie
see sweatheart
__ sweet it is!: 3 How
Sweet Liberty (1986 film)
cast: Alan Alda, Michael Caine, Bob Hoskins, Michelle Pfeiffer
director: Alan Alda
Sweet Little Sixteen (1958 song) artist: Chuck Berry
Sweet Lorraine (1987 film)
cast: Trini Alvarado, Lee Richardson, Maureen Stapleton
director: Steve Gomer
Sweet Love (song) artist: Anita Baker, Commodores
sweetly in music: 5 dolce
sweetmeat: 5 candy, fudge, lolly, taffy, toffy 6 bonbon, dainty, nougat, toffee 7 caramel 8 lollipop 9 chocolate, sugar plum 10 confection, peppermint
sweet-natured: 4 kind, nice 6 genial, polite 7 helpful, likable 8 friendly 10 thoughtful
sweetness and __: 5 light
Sweet 'N Low rival: 5 Equal
sweet nothings
whisper ~: 3 coo, woo
Sweet Nothin's (1960 song) artist: Brenda Lee
Sweet November (2001 film)
cast: Greg Germann, Jason Isaacs, Keanu Reeves, Charlize Theron
director: Pat O'Connor
Sweet Old Fashioned Girl, A (1956 song) artist: Teresa Brewer
Sweet Pea (1966 song) artist: Tommy Roe
sweet potato: 3 yam 6 veggie 7 ocarina 9 vegetable
sweet potato __: 3 pie
Sweet Seasons (1972 song) artist: Carole King
Sweet Sixteen org.: 4 NCAA
sweet-smelling: 5 balmy 7 scented 8 aromatic, fragrant, perfumed, redolent 9 ambrosial
Sweet Smell of Success: 4 film, play
author: Clifford Odets
cast: Tony Curtis, Burt Lancaster, Martin Milner
sweetsop: 4 tree 5 fruit, shrub
hybrid: 7 atemoya
sweet-sounding: 4 soft 6 dulcet 7 lyrical, melodic, musical 9 melodious
Sweet Swan of __: 4 Avon
__ Sweet Symphony: 6 Bitter
sweet-talk: 3 con 4 coax 5 lobby, tempt 6 cajole, enamor, entice, induce 7 flatter, wheedle 8 blandish, inveigle, persuade
Sweet Talkin' Guy (1966 song) artist: Chiffons
Sweet Thing (1976 song) artist: Chaka Khan

Sweet Thursday author: John Steinbeck
swell: 3 def, fab, fop, rad, sea, wax 4 aces, A-one, boss, braw, chic, cool, dece, fine, flow, gear, grow, gush, keen, neat, nice, phat, posh, pout, puff, rise, surf, tuff, wash, wave 5 add to, belly, bloat, bulge, dandy, ducky, grand, great, heave, marvy, mount, neato, nifty, nobby, plump, plush, pouch, prime, ritzy, slick, smart, super, surge, swish, widen 6 abound, bang on, bang-up, beef up, billow, blow up, bonzer, bosker, choice, deluxe, dilate, divine, dreamy, expand, extend, far-out, fatten, gather, gnarly, groovy, growth, lovely, modish, peachy, puff up, pump up, ripple, slap-up, spot on, superb, terrif, tiptop, unreal, uprise, well up, whizzo, wicked 7 amazing, amplify, augment, awesome, balloon, broaden, burgeon, capital, corking, coxcomb, distend, elegant, enlarge, fill out, inflate, magnify, perfect, ripping, skookum, stellar, stretch, stylish, sublime, thicken, voguish 8 bloating, bourgeon, dazzling, escalate, especial, eximious, fabulous, fancy Dan, five-star, four-star, frabjous, gay blade, glorious, heavenly, heighten, increase, jim-dandy, lengthen, mushroom, protrude, round out, slam-bang, smashing, splendid, standout, sterling, stickout, superior, terrific, top-level, topnotch, undulate, very good, wondrous 9 agreeable, bodacious, crescendo, desirable, Endsville, excellent, exemplary, exquisite, first-rate, high-grade, hunky-dory, intensify, intumesce, luxurious, marvelous, pretty boy, sollicker, top-flight, upwelling, wonderful 10 accumulate, first-class, hotsy-totsy, jack-a-dandy, out of sight, peachy-keen, phenomenal, remarkable, stupendous, super-duper, undulation
  as the sea: 5 heave
  at sea: 4 surf, tide, wave 6 roller
  British ~: 4 toff
  ender: 4 fish, head
  in space: 3 A-OK
  person: 4 dear 5 peach 7 sweetie 10 sweetheart
  starter: 6 ground
  time: 3 gas 5 blast
__ Swell: 4 Thou
swelled head: 3 ego 5 pride, quirk 6 egoism, vanity 7 conceit, egotism, hauteur, swagger 8 self-love, smugness 9 arrogance, immodesty, vainglory 10 pretension, stuffiness
swelling: 4 bump, corn, knob, lump, node, nurl, sore, wale, welt 5 blain, bulge, edema, gnarl, knurl, ridge, surge 6 bruise, bunion, injury, nodule, oedema 7 blister 8 dilation, increase 9 contusion, expansion, inflation, puffiness 10 distention, prominence
  reducer: 3 ice 6 ice bag 7 ice pack
swell with __: 5 pride
swelter: 4 bake, boil, cook, heat, wilt 5 broil, roast, sweat 6 scorch 8 humidity, perspire
sweltering: 3 hot 4 warm 5 close, fiery, humid 6 baking, red-hot, steamy, sticky, stuffy, sultry, sweaty, toasty, torrid 7 airless, burning, stewing, summery 8 broiling, ovenlike, sizzling, stifling, tropical 9 scorching 10 equatorial
Swenson: 3 May 4 Inga
Swenson, May: 4 poet
swept: 4 neat, tidy 5 clean 7 in order
  starter: 4 back, wind
Swept Away ... (1975 film) director: Lina Wertmuller
Swept Away (1984 song) artist: Diana Ross
swerve: 3 dip, yaw, zag, zig 4 bend, duck, skew, skid, slew, slue, tack, turn, vary, veer, wind 5 lurch, sheer, shift, slant, swing, waver, wince 6 careen, divert, recoil, slough 7 deflect, deviate, diverge 8 sheer off, sideslip, sidestep 9 turn aside
swift: 4 bird, fast 5 apace, brief, brisk, fleet, hasty, quick, rapid 6 abrupt, clever, flying, nimble, prompt, pronto, racing, snappy, speedy, sudden, winged 7 cursory, express, flat-out, hurried, instant 8 cracking, full tilt, headlong, meteoric, spanking 9 breakneck, galloping, lightning, posthaste, rapid-fire, whirlwind 10 double-time, hypersonic, short-lived, supersonic, ultrasonic, unexpected
  combining form: 5 tachy-
  ender: 4 ness
__ swift: 4 tree 7 chimney, crested
Swift: 3 car, Kay, Tom 4 auto 5 David 6 Suzuki 8 Jonathan 10 automobile
Swift, David: 8 director
  film: Good Neighbor Sam (1964)
    How to Succeed in Business
      Without Really Trying (1967)
    The Interns (1962)
    The Parent Trap (1961)
    Pollyanna (1960)
    Under the Yum Yum Tree (1963)
swift horse, name meaning: 6 Roscoe
Swift, Jonathan: 6 author, writer 7 British 8 satirist
  colleague: 4 Pope 6 Steele
  creature: 5 Yahoo
  work: Drapier's Letters
    Gulliver's Travels
    A Modest Proposal
    The Tale of a Tub
swiftly: 3 PDQ 4 ASAP, fast, stat 5 apace 6 presto, pronto 7 briefly, flat out, fleetly, hastily, in a rush, in haste, quickly, rapidly 8 full tilt, in a flash, in a hurry, in a jiffy, in no time, on the fly, on the run, pell-mell, promptly, right now, right off, speedily, suddenly 9 forthwith, hurriedly, instantly, like a shot, posthaste, right away, summarily 10 in high gear
swiftness: 4 pace 5 haste, hurry, speed 8 alacrity, celerity, dispatch, rapidity, velocity 9 fleetness, quickness 10 expedition
Swifty: 5 Lazar
swig: 4 belt, chug, gulp, slug 5 draft, drink, quaff, snort 6 guzzle, imbibe 7 swallow 8 mouthful
  quick ~: 4 belt 5 snort
  small ~: 3 sip, tot 4 dram
swill: 4 chug, gulp, slop, swig 5 dregs, offal, quaff, waste 6 guzzle, liquid, refuse 7 garbage, hogwash, rubbish, swallow
  eater: 3 hog, pig, sow 4 boar
swim: 3 dip 4 dive 5 bathe, crawl, float 6 paddle 8 skin-dive, take a dip 9 dog paddle, freestyle, scuba-dive 10 backstroke, keep afloat, sidestroke
  alternative: 4 sink
  brief ~: 3 dip
  competition: 4 meet
  ender: 4 suit, wear
  make one's head ~: 5 amaze 6 dazzle 7 impress
  place to ~: 3 gym, sea 4 lake, pond, pool, the Y, YMCA, YWCA 5 beach, ocean, river 6 lagoon, stream 8 seashore
  with the tide: 4 cope 5 adapt 6 adjust
swim __: 3 fin 4 mask
__ swim: 5 in the
swim against the __: 4 tide
swimmer: 4 Otto 5 Dyken, Ender, Evans, Gould, Spitz 6 Biondi, Crabbe, Fraser
  Australian ~: 5 Gould 6 Fraser
  German ~: 4 Otto 5 Ender
  playful ~: 4 seal 5 otter
  see also fish
Swimmer, The (1968 film)
  cast: Burt Lancaster, Janice Rule
swimming: 5 sport 6 afloat, natant
  combining form: 4 nect- 5 necto-
  convenience: 6 cabana
  gear: 3 fin 4 mask 5 wings 7 goggles 10 water wings
  go ~: 5 bathe
  hazard: 5 cramp, shark 9 jellyfish
  in it: 4 rich 5 flush 7 wealthy 8 affluent 9 well-fixed 10 well-heeled
  motion: 5 crawl 10 backstroke
  spot: 4 hole, lake, pond, pool 5 beach, river 6 stream 8 seashore
  unit: 3 lap
swimming __: 4 bath, hole, pool
swimmingly: 4 fine, well 5 great 6 easily 7 handily, happily, quickly, readily 8 adroitly, laudably, smoothly, very well 9 as planned, favorably, hands down 10 skillfully
swimming pool
  problem: 5 algae
  site: 3 gym, spa 4 the Y, YMCA, YWCA 6 resort
  sound: 5 plash 6 splash
Swimming Pool, The author: Mary Roberts Rinehart
__ Swimmin' Hole, The: 3 Old
swim wear: 6 bikini, trunks 7 maillot 8 one-piece, two-piece
  part: 3 bra
Swinburne, Algernon: 4 poet 7 British
  work: Astrophel
    Atalanta in Calydon
    Hymn to Proserpine
swindle: 2 do 3 con, gyp, job, rob 4 bilk, burn, clip, dupe, flam, flay, fool, gull, have, hoax, nick, rook, ruse, scam, sham, skin, take, trim, work 5 bunco, cheat, cozen, feint, fraud, gouge, mulct, pluck, set up, shaft, steal, stiff, sting, theft, trick 6 chisel, chouse, con job, deceit, diddle, dupery, euchre, extort, fleece, humbug, hustle, outwit, racket, rip off, sucker, take in 7 deceive, defraud, fast one, finagle, sandbag, snow job 8 artifice, flimflam, hoodwink, outsmart, thievery 9 bamboozle, deception, dirty pool, extortion, four-flush, imposture, shakedown, shell game, victimize 10 illegality, run a game on, subterfuge
swindler: 4 rook 5 cheat, crook, fraud, ganef, gonef, gonif, knave, quack, rogue, shark, sharp, thief 6 bad guy, conman, dodger, forger, goniff, gouger, rascal, rip-off, robber 7 grifter, hustler, sharper, sharpie 8 chiseler, imposter, impostor, operator 9 absconder, charlatan, con artist, defrauder, inveigler, scoundrel, trickster 10 mountebank
  take: 5 grift
Swindon: 4 city, town
  locale: 7 England 9 Wiltshire
swine: 3 cad, cur, hog, pig, sow 4 boar, boor, Kele, lout, toad 5 Bazna, beast, brute, Duroc, Hezuo, louse, piggy, shoat, shote, shott, stock, Welsh 6 animal, barrow, Jinhua, Minzhu, Mukota, oinker, piggie, piglet, porker, savage, tusker 7 bounder, grunter, Iberian, Lacombe, lowlife, Meishan, Mong Cai, peccary, Suffolk 8 babirusa, blighter, Hereford, Landrace, Pietrain, Potbelly, Tamworth 9 Berkshire, Hampshire, razorback, scoundrel, Yorkshire
  combining form: 3 hyo-
  ender: 3 pox 4 herd
  food: 4 slop 5 swill
  little ~: 3 pig 4 gilt 5 shoat, shote, shott 6 piggie, piglet
  place: 3 pen, sty 4 farm 6 pigpen, pigsty
swine __: 3 flu
swing: 3 wag 4 beat, flap, hang, jazz, keel, lilt, reel, rock, sway, toss, tour, trip, turn, vary, veer, wave 5 curve, dance, guide, lunge, lurch, meter, music, pivot, reach, shake, shift, sling, sweep, tempo, twirl, wheel, whirl 6 change, dangle, direct, leeway, manage, rhythm, rotate, swerve, swivel, travel, wabble, waggle, wangle, wobble 7 cadence, cadency, librate, measure, revolve, suspend, vibrate, work out 8 flourish, free hand, latitude, undulate 9 fluctuate, influence, negotiate, oscillate, vacillate 10 ebb and flow, equivocate
  around: 4 slew, slue, spin, turn 5 avert, pivot, whirl 6 slough, swivel
  by: 4 call 5 visit 6 stop in
  ersatz ~: 4 tire
  half a ~: 3 fro
  loose: 4 flap, hang 6 dangle
  music: 4 jive
  partner: 4 sway
  place for a ~: 4 lawn, limb, park, tree, yard 5 bough, porch 10 playground
  ready to ~: 5 at bat
swing __: 3 leg 4 door, loan 5 music, shift
Swing __: 4 Time 5 My Way
Swing __, Sweet Chariot: 3 Low
Swing and sway bandleader: 4 Kaye
swinger: 4 roué 5 flirt, Romeo 6 golfer, hepcat 7 Don Juan 8 Lothario 9 jet-setter, libertine 10 profligate
Swinger: 3 car 4 auto 5 Dodge
swinging: 5 loose 6 lively 9 pendulous
swinging __: 4 door
Swinging on a Star
  beast: 3 pig 4 fish, mule 6 monkey
  composer: 5 Burke 9 Van Heusen
Swingin' Safari, A (1962 song) artist: Billy Vaughan
Swingin' School (1960 song) artist: Bobby Rydell
__ Swings: 7 England
Swing Time (1936 film): 7 musical
  cast: Fred Astaire, Eric Blore, Helen Broderick, Betty Furness, Victor Moore, Ginger Rogers
  director: George Stevens
  music: 4 Kern 6 Fields
  studio: 3 RKO
swinish: 6 greedy 7 hoggish, loutish
  remark: 4 oink
Swinton: 5 Tilda
swipe: 3 cop, hit, nab, rap, rob 4 bash, blow, clip, cuff, gibe, glom, hook, jibe, lick, lift, loot, nick, slam, slap, sock, swat, take, wipe 5 clout, filch, heist, knock, lunge, pinch, smack, sneak, sneer, steal, taunt 6 assume, pilfer, pocket, rip off, snitch, strike, thieve, wallop 7 lash out, purloin 8 liberate, shoplift, uppercut 10 run off with
  starter: 4 side
  take a ~ at: 3 dis 4 swat 5 decry 6 impugn, insult, malign 7 lash out, put down
swirl: 4 boil, coil, curl, eddy, reel, roil, roll, turn, wash, wave 5 churn, crimp, snake, surge, twirl, whirl, whorl 6 bustle, swoosh, tumult, unrest

7 agitate, sinuate, tempest, turmoil 8 disorder, gyration 9 circulate, confusion, maelstrom, whirlpool 10 spin around
swirling: 6 roiled 9 turbulent
swish: 3 lap, rod 4 posh, tony, wash, whiz 5 grand, plush, ritzy, smart, sound, stick, swank, swell, toney, whisk, woosh 6 classy, deluxe, rustle, sizzle, trendy, whoosh, with-it 7 elegant, stylish 8 flourish, rustling, sibilate 9 exclusive, sumptuous, whooshing 10 sibilation
Swiss: 4 font 5 steak 6 alpine, cheese 8 typeface
like ~ cheese: 5 holey
partner: 3 ham, rye
see also Switzerland
Swiss __: 4 Alps 5 chard, Guard, lapis, steak 6 cheese, muslin
Swiss army __: 5 knife
Swiss Family Robinson: 4 book
author: 4 Wyss
character: 5 Emily, Fritz 6 Ernest
dog: 4 Duke, Turk
Swiss Family Robinson (1940 film)
cast: Freddie Bartholomew, Edna Best, Thomas Mitchell
Swiss Family Robinson (1960 film)
cast: James MacArthur, Dorothy McGuire, John Mills
director: Ken Annakin
Swit: 7 Loretta
costar: 4 Alda, Farr
role: 5 nurse 7 Hot Lips 8 Houlihan
sitcom: 4 MASH
switch: 3 rod, wag 4 limb, ruse, swap, swop, tack, turn, veer, whip 5 shift, shunt, stick, trade 6 button, change, cudgel, divert, ferule, punish, rotate, toggle 7 convert, replace, reverse 8 exchange, modulate, reversal, variance 9 about-face, alternate, change off, inversion, oscillate, rearrange, take turns, transpose, turnabout 10 alteration, flagellate, substitute
activator: 4 clap
asleep at the ~: 3 lax 5 slack 6 remiss 9 negligent
bait and ~: 4 scam 7 con game
electric ~: 5 relay 6 dimmer
ender: 4 back, eroo 5 blade, board
hit the ~: 4 kill, stop 5 douse, light 6 kindle, turn on 7 turn off 8 activate
position: 2 on 3 off
sides: 6 defect
switch __: 3 box, off 5 gears 6 engine, hitter
__ switch: 6 dimmer, toggle
Switch (CBS drama)
cast: Eddie Albert (Frank McBride) Charlie Callas (Malcolm Argos) Sharon Gless (Maggie) Robert Wagner (Pete Ryan)
switchback: 4 road 5 curve
shape: 3 ess
switchblade: 4 shiv 5 knife
switchboard
employee: 8 operator
letters: 3 ext.
switcheroo: 6 change 8 reversal
pull a ~: 9 back-pedal
Switching Channels (1988 film)
cast: Ned Beatty, Christopher Reeve, Burt Reynolds, Kathleen Turner
director: Ted Kotcheff
Swithin: 5 saint
Switzerland: 6 nation 7 country
Alp: 4 Jura, Zupo 5 Eiger 6 Castor 7 Bernina 8 Jungfrau 9 Mont Blanc, Monte Rosa 10 Matterhorn, St. Gotthard
archeological site: 4 Biel
artist: 4 Klee
bovine: 6 Herens 9 Simmental
cabin: 6 chalet
canton: 3 Uri, Zug 4 Bern, Jura, Vaud 5 Berne 6 Aargau, Geneva, Glarus, Schwyz, Ticino, Valais, Zurich 7 Lucerne, Thurgau 8 Fribourg, Obwalden 9 Neuchâtel, Nidwalden, Saint Gall, Solothurn
capital: 4 Bern 5 Berne
cheese: 7 Gruyère, sapsago 8 Emmental 9 Emmenthal, Jarlsberg 10 Emmentaler
chocolatier: 5 Lindt
city: 3 Zug 4 Sion 5 Basel, Basle, Vevey 6 Geneva, Genève, Zurich 8 Lausanne
conductor: 8 Ansermet
educator: 6 Piaget
export: 5 clock, watch 6 cheese 9 chocolate
lake: 3 Zug 4 Biel, Thun 6 Bienne, Brienz, Geneva, Lugano, Zurich 7 Lucerne 8 Maggiore 9 Neuchâtel
language: 6 French, German 7 Italian
legendary hero: 4 Tell
mathematician: 5 Euler
money: 5 franc, rappe 7 centime
mountain: 3 alp
natural historian: 6 Gesner
neighbor: 5 Italy 6 France 7 Austria, Germany
Nobelist in Chemistry: 5 Ernst 6 Karrer, Werner 7 Ruzicka 8 Wüthrich
Nobelist in Literature: 9 Spitteler
Nobelist in Medicine: 4 Hess 5 Arber 6 Kocher, Müller 10 Reichstein 11 Zinkernagel
Nobelist in Peace: 5 Gobat 6 Dunant 8 Ducommun
Nobelist in Physics: 6 Müller, Rohrer
physicist: 6 Müller, Rohrer 7 Piccard
pianist: 6 Cortot 7 Fischer
poet: 6 Keller 9 Spitteler
province: 6 canton
psychologist: 3 Neo 6 Piaget
river: 3 Aar 4 Aare 5 Reuss, Rhone
ski resort: 5 Davos 6 Gstaad
state: 6 canton
strain: 5 yodel, yodle
waterfall: 6 Simmen
writer: 5 Meyer, Ramuz, Spyri 6 Frisch, Piaget
swivel: 3 pan 4 jink, look, roll, spin, turn, veer 5 hinge, joint, pivot, swing, twist, wheel, whirl 6 rotate 7 librate, revolve 9 oscillate, pirouette
swivel __: 3 gun 5 chair
swizzle: 4 stir
ingredient: 3 rum
swizzle __: 5 stick
Swoboda: 3 Ron
swollen: 5 puffy, tumid 7 bloated, bulging 8 enlarged, inflamed, inflated 9 distended, tumescent
combining form: 4 phys- 5 physo-
'S Wonderful composer: 8 Gershwin
swoon: 5 faint, plotz 6 go limp 7 crumple, pass out, syncope 8 black out, fall over, keel over
swoop: 3 dip, fly 4 dive, drop, fall, raid, rush, sink 5 slide, stoop 6 go down, plunge, pounce 7 descend, descent, plummet 8 downrush, nosedive
down on: 4 dive 6 ambush, pounce, snap up, waylay
up: 4 grab 5 scoop, seize 6 snatch
swoosh: 5 swirl
Nike ~: 4 logo
Swoosie: 5 Kurtz
swop
see swap
__ Swope: 6 Putney
sword: 4 épée, fern, foil 5 blade, knife, point, saber, sabre 6 anlace, cutlas, rapier, Toledo 7 anelace, bayonet, cutlass, simitar 8 claymore, scimitar, scimiter 9 cold steel, Excalibur
combining form: 4 xiph- 5 xiphi-, xipho-
ender: 4 bill, fish, play, tail
fencing ~: 4 épée, foil 5 saber 6 rapier
fight: 4 duel, epée 7 fencing
handle: 4 haft, hilt
medieval ~: 5 estoc
name meaning ~: 6 Brenda
short ~: 6 dagger
Turkish ~: 5 kilij
wield a ~: 5 lunge, parry, slash 6 pierce
sword __: 4 bean, belt, cane, fern, knot, lily 5 dance, grass
Sword and the Rose, The (1953 film)
cast: Glynis Johns, James Robertson Justice, Richard Todd
director: Ken Annakin
Sword Blades and Poppy Seed
author: Amy Lowell
swordfish: 6 entrée
constellation: 6 Dorado
Swordfish (2001 film)
cast: Halle Berry, Don Cheadle, Hugh Jackman, John Travolta
director: Dominic Sena
Sword in the Stone, The
author: T.H. White
bird: 3 owl
dog: 5 Tiger 6 Talbot
swords
cross ~: 4 buck, defy, duel, spar, tilt 5 argue, clash, fight 6 attack, battle, bicker, combat, debate, engage, oppose, resist, tussle 7 contend, contest, dispute, quarrel, wrangle 8 conflict, confront, disagree, do battle, struggle 9 duke it out, have it out, lock horns, slug it out
sword-shaped: 6 ensate
swordsman: 5 blade 6 fencer
swordsmanship: 4 épée 5 kendo 7 fencing
swordtail: 4 fish
sworn: 6 avowed 7 pledged
statement: 3 vow 4 oath
sworn __: 5 enemy
sybarite: 4 roué 7 playboy 8 hedonist, rakehell 9 bon vivant, libertine 10 voluptuary
delight: 4 ease 8 pleasure
sybaritic: 9 dissolute, epicurean, luxurious
sybaritism: 6 excess 7 license, revelry 8 hedonism 9 decadence, depravity 10 indulgence
Sybil: 4 Leek 7 Danning 9 Thorndike
sycamore: 4 tree
sycee: 5 money
Sychaeus, wife of: 4 Dido
sycophancy: 6 praise 8 flattery 9 adulation, servility
sycophant: 3 fan 5 leech, slave, toady 6 fawner, flunky, lackey, minion, puppet, yes man 7 doormat, flunkey, groupie, lacquey 8 adulator, courtier, groveler, hanger-on, kowtower, parasite, servitor 9 flatterer 10 bootlicker, handshaker, politician
answer: 3 yes
sycophantic: 6 menial 7 fawning, slavish 8 toadying, unctuous 9 groveling
sycophants: 6 claque 7 fan club 9 entourage, following
Sycorax: 4 moon
planet: 6 Uranus
Syd: 4 Hoff 7 Barrett, Chaplin
Sydney: 4 city, port, town 5 Penny, Smith 7 Brenner, Chaplin, Pollack
locale: 3 NSW 9 Australia
__ Sydow: 6 Max von
Sykes: 5 Peter
Sylk-E. __: 4 Fyne
syllabub: 7 dessert
ingredient: 4 wine 5 cider, cream
syllabus: 4 list, plan, text 6 précis, sketch 7 program, summary 10 prospectus
Syllabus of __: 6 Errors
syllogism: 5 logic 9 reasoning
word: 4 ergo
words: 4 is to
syllogistics: 5 logic
syllogize: 6 reason
sylph: 5 nymph 6 sprite
__ Sylphides: 3 Les
sylphlike: 4 slim 5 light 6 slight 7 gracile, slender, willowy 8 graceful
sylva: 8 woodland
Sylva: 7 Koscina
sylvan: 5 bosky, rural, woody 6 rustic, wooded, woodsy 8 arboreal, forested, pastoral 9 arboreous
area: 5 glade, grove, trees, woods 6 forest
deity: 3 Pan 4 faun 5 satyr
Sylvan historian, to Keats: 3 urn
Sylvania: 2 TV 5 TV set 10 television
competitor: 3 JVC, NEC, RCA 4 Sony 6 Quasar, Zenith 7 Emerson, Hitachi, ProScan, Toshiba 8 Magnavox 9 Panasonic
sylvanite: 3 ore 7 mineral
Sylvester: 3 cat 4 pope 7 pontiff 8 Stallone
to Tweety: 3 tat 8 puddy tat
Sylvester and the Magic Pebble
author: 5 Steig
Sylvia: 4 Syms 5 Miles, Plath 6 ballet, Porter, Sidney, Warner 7 Delibes
Sylvia Ashton-__: 6 Warner
Sylvia Scarlett (1935 film)
cast: Brian Aherne, Cary Grant, Katharine Hepburn
director: George Cukor
Sylvia's Mother (1972 song) artist: Dr. Hook
Sylvie and Bruno author: Lewis Carroll
sylvite: 3 ore 7 mineral
__ Sylvius: 6 Aeneas
Symaethis, son of: 4 Acis
symbiosis: 5 union 7 benefit 10 dependence
symbol: 4 icon, ikon, logo, mark, note, sign 5 badge, crest, eikon, image, index, model, motif, stamp, token, totem 6 design, device, emblem, figure, letter 7 imprint, insigne, numeral, pattern, regalia 8 colophon, hallmark, heraldry, ideogram, insignia, metaphor, standard 9 attribute, character, indicator, trademark 10 denotation, embodiment, indication
__ symbol: 3 UPC 5 peace 6 status
symbolic: 5 token 7 nominal 10 denotative, emblematic, figurative, indicatory, suggestive
symbolize: 4 mean, show 6 denote, embody, imbody, mirror 7 betoken, connote, express, signify, suggest 8 indicate, stand for 9 adumbrate, epitomize, exemplify, personify, represent 10 illustrate
Symington: 3 Stu 6 Stuart
Symmachus: 4 pope 7 pontiff
symmetrical: 4 trim 5 equal 7 regular, shapely, uniform 8 balanced
not ~: 4 alop, awry 7 crooked 9 irregular, out of line 10 unbalanced
symmetry: 4 form 5 order, shape 6 rhythm 7 balance, harmony 8 equality, evenness, neatness 9 agreement, equipoise 10 conformity, proportion,

regularity
Symons, Julian: **4** poet **7** British
sympathetic: **4** easy, kind, open, soft, warm **5** close, noble, sweet **6** benign, caring, chummy, clubby, decent, genial, gentle, humane, kindly, loving, polite, tender **7** affable, amiable, clement, cordial, helpful, lenient, likable, sparing, tactful, tuned in **8** all heart, amenable, amicable, friendly, gracious, intimate, merciful, outgoing, pleasant, sociable, tolerant **9** agreeable, concerned, congenial, convivial, fraternal, receptive, sensitive, simpatico, vicarious **10** altruistic, benevolent, buddy-buddy, neighborly, responsive, solicitous, supportive
be ~: **4** care **6** listen **9** empathize
not ~: **4** cold **5** stony **6** stoney **8** uncaring **9** impatient
sympathetic ___: **3** ink **5** magic
sympathize: **4** pity **5** agree **7** ache for, comfort, console, feel for **8** bleed for, relate to, side with **9** empathize **10** understand
sympathizer: **6** backer, patron **8** partisan **9** supporter **10** benefactor
sympathy: **3** aid **4** pity **5** heart, mercy, unity **6** accord, lenity, liking, pathos, regard, solace, warmth **7** comfort, emotion, rapport, thought **8** affinity, feelings, kindness, lenience **9** agreement, tolerance **10** compassion, connection
words of ~: **5** I care
sympathy ___: **6** strike
symphonic: **7** lyrical **10** harmonious, orchestral
movement: **5** largo, rondo **7** prelude
symphonic ___: **4** band, poem
Symphonic Ode composer: **7** Copland
Symphonie Espagnole composer: **4** Lalo
Symphonie Fantastique composer: **7** Berlioz
symphony: **4** opus, work **5** music, piece **9** orchestra
___ Symphony: **3** Toy **4** Linz **5** Clock, Dante, Faust, Paris, Short **6** Choral, Eroica, Prague, Simple, Spring, Tragic **7** Haffner, Italian, Jupiter, Kaddish, Manfred, October, Unbegun
Symphony in Black artist: **4** Erté
Symphony of a Thousand composer: **6** Mahler
Symphony of Psalms composer: **10** Stravinsky
Symphony, The author: Sidney Lanier
symposium: **4** talk **5** forum **7** meeting **8** assembly **10** conference, discussion, round table
Symposium, subject of Plato's: **4** Eros
symptom: **4** hint, mark, sign **5** token **7** warning **8** evidence **9** precursor **10** indication
symptomatic: **10** indicative, suggestive
Syms, Sylvia: **7** actress
film: Asylum (1972)
Conspiracy of Hearts (1960)
Desert Attack (1960)
The Quare Fellow (1962)
Victim (1961)
Woman in a Dressing Gown (1957)
synagogue: **4** shul **5** schul **6** temple
attender: **3** Jew
container: **3** ark
language: **6** Hebrew
official: **5** rabbi, rebbe **6** cantor, chazan
platform: **4** bema
platforms: **6** bemata
prayer: **5** shema
scroll: **4** Tora **5** Torah
vestment: **5** ephod
sync: **6** kilter **7** harmony **9** agreement
be in ~: **4** jibe **5** agree **6** accord **8** coincide
get in ~: **5** adapt **6** adjust, attune **10** coordinate
in ~: **4** same **7** fitting, matched **8** suitable, together **9** accordant, agreeable, congruent, consonant, simpatico **10** coinciding, compatible, concurrent, consistent, harmonious, like-minded
out of ~: **3** off
___-sync: **3** lip **5** out-of
synch: **6** accord **7** harmony **9** harmonize **10** coordinate
___-synch: **3** lip **5** out-of
synchronal: **9** concerted, confluent **10** coexistent, coexisting, coincident, coinciding, collateral, compatible, concurrent, consistent, convergent, converging, harmonious, incidental, like-minded
Synchronicity II (1983 song) artist: Police
synchronous ___: **5** motor, orbit, speed **7** machine
Syncopated Clock, The composer: Leroy Anderson
syncopation: **6** rhythm
syncope: **5** faint, swoon
syndicate: **3** mob **4** bloc, gang, ring **5** board, chain, group, merge, trust, union **6** cartel **7** combine, company, council, society **8** megacorp, monopoly **9** gangsters **10** federation, monopolize, underworld
crime ~ head: **3** don **4** capo **9** godfather
syndicated prose: **6** column
syndication, air in: **5** rerun
Syndor: **4** font **8** typeface
syndrome: **6** malady **7** ailment, complex **8** disorder, sickness **9** complaint, condition, infirmity
___ Syndrome, The: **5** China
syne: **3** ago
synecdoche: **5** trope
synergize: **8** interact **9** cooperate
Synge, John: **5** Irish **10** playwright
work: Playboy of the Western World
Riders to the Sea
Synge, Richard: **7** chemist **8** Nobelist
Syngman: **4** Rhee
synod: **7** council **8** assembly, conclave, ecclesia
synonymist: **5** Roget
synonym opposite: **3** ant. **7** antonym
synonymous: **4** like, same **5** alike, equal **9** identical **10** equivalent, two of a kind
synopsis: **5** brief, recap, table **6** digest, précis, résumé, review, sketch **7** capsule, epitome, outline, pandect, rundown, summary **8** abstract **10** abridgment, compendium, highlights, prospectus, tabulation
synopsize: **5** recap, sum up **6** digest, sketch **7** outline **8** abstract, boil down, condense **9** capsulize, summarize, telescope
synopsized: **3** cut **4** firm **5** dense, short, solid, terse, thick **6** cut off, gnomic, packed **7** capsule, compact, concise, crammed, cutback, cut down, reduced, stuffed **8** abridged, cut short, digested, squeezed, succinct **9** compacted, condensed, curtailed, shortened **10** abstracted, compressed, summarized
syntax: **7** grammar
unit: **4** word **5** morph **6** phrase **8** sentence **9** paragraph
Syntax: **4** font **8** typeface
synthesis: **5** blend, union, unity **6** fusion **7** amalgam **8** compound, pastiche **9** composite, formation, immixture
antithesis and ~: **5** logic
synthesize: **4** fuse, join, make **5** blend, merge, unify, unite **7** combine **8** coalesce **9** integrate **10** amalgamate
___ synthesizer: **4** Moog
___ synthetase: **3** RNA
synthetic: **4** fake, mock, sham **5** bogus, false, phony, quasi **6** ersatz, phoney, pseudo **7** plastic **8** rational, spurious **9** imitation, simulated, unnatural **10** artificial, fabricated
fabric: **4** poly **5** Arnel, Dynel, Kodel, Lycra, nylon, Orlon, rayon **6** Ban-Lon, Dacron, Kevlar **7** Gore-Tex, spandex **9** polyester
synthetic ___: **5** fiber **6** rubber
Syr.
see Syria
Syracuse: **4** city, town
athletes: **9** Orangemen
city near ~: **5** Utica **6** Oneida
conference: **7** Big East
lake near ~: **6** Oneida
locale: **7** New York
team color: **6** orange
to Buffalo dir.: **3** WSW
Syr Darya: **5** river
locale: **10** Kazakhstan, Kyrgyzstan
Syria: **6** nation **7** country
ancient ~: **4** Aram
ancient city in ~: **4** Ebla
ancient kingdom in ~: **4** Moab
bovine: **6** Baladi, Jaulan
capital: **8** Damascus
city: **4** Hama, Homs **6** Aleppo **8** Damascus
leader: **5** Assad
money: **7** piaster, piastre
mountain: **6** Hermon
neighbor: **4** Irak, Iraq **5** Egypt **6** Israel, Jordan, Turkey **7** Lebanon
resident: **4** Arab **5** Druse, Druze
shrub: **5** retem
Syrian ___: **6** Desert **7** hamster
Syrian ___ Republic: **4** Arab
syringa: **4** tree **5** shrub
family: **9** saxifrage
syringe: **4** hypo
syrinx: **4** wind **7** panpipe
syrup: **7** topping
alternative: **5** honey
brand: **4** Karo **8** Log Cabin
flavoring: **5** maple
source: **3** sap **4** corn **5** sorgo **6** sorgho
sugar ~: **5** glaze
___ syrup: **3** bar **4** corn **5** cough, gomme, maple **6** golden, simple, starch **7** sorghum
syrupy: **5** mushy, sweet, thick **6** sticky **7** maudlin, mawkish, viscose, viscous **8** romantic **9** oversweet **10** saccharine
system: **3** ism, way **4** form, mode, plan, rule, unit **5** means, order, setup **6** custom, hookup, manner, method, policy, regime, scheme, theory **7** complex, machine, network, pattern, process, red tape, routine **8** ideology, practice, strategy, totality **9** machinery, mechanism, operation, procedure, structure, technique **10** philosophy
starter: **3** eco
___ system: **3** ABO, air **4** case, farm, open, root, star, wall, zone **5** block, Boehm, buddy, honor, merit, point, quota, solar, touch, track, truck, T-stop, vowel, water **6** Bedaux, binary, closed, crypto, dyadic, expert, feudal, French, immune, limbic, metric, portal, spoils **7** crystal, decimal, English, exhaust, fixed-do, Hepburn, lateral, nervous, support, Torrens, turnkey, voucher, weapons
systematic: **4** neat, tidy **6** formal **7** logical, orderly, precise, regular **8** accurate, coherent, habitual, methodic **9** efficient, organized
systematize: **4** plan, sort **5** array, group, order **6** codify **7** arrange, dispose **8** classify, organize, regulate, tabulate **9** establish, institute, methodize
systems ___: **7** analyst **10** programmer
systems go, all: **3** A-OK **5** ready **8** prepared
S.Z.: **6** Sakall
Szczecin: **4** port
locale: **6** Poland
river: **4** Oder
Szechuan pan: **3** wok
Szeged: **4** city, town
locale: **7** Hungary
Szell, George: **9** conductor
Szent-Györgyi, Albert von: **8** Nobelist
Szigeti, Joseph: **9** Hungarian, violinist
Szilard: **3** Leo
Szwarc: **7** Jeannot
Szymborska, Wislawa: **6** writer **8** Nobelist

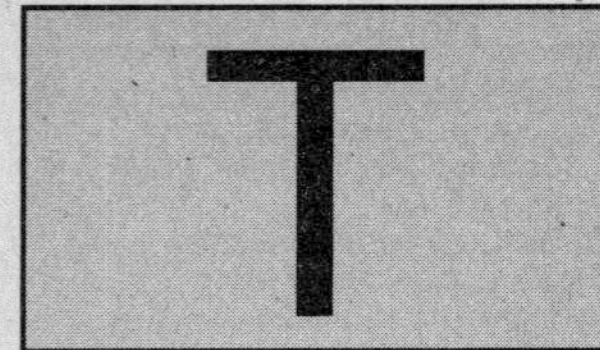

2
mult. by ~: 3 dbl.
wks. off: 3 vac.
x 4: 5 board
2%: 4 milk
#2: 4 veep 6 veepee
2 Become 1 (1997 song) artist: Spice Girls
2 Legit 2 Quit (1991 song) artist: M.C. Hammer
2-pointer, easy: 4 dunk
$2 window action: 5 wager
3:10 to Yuma (1957 film)
cast: Felicia Farr, Glenn Ford, Van Heflin
director: Delmer Daves
3 A.M. Eternal (1991 song) artist: KLF
3 Bad Men (1926 film)
cast: J. Farrell MacDonald, George O'Brien, Lou Tellegen
director: John Ford
3Com Park player: 5 Niner
3-D
exam: 3 MRI
graph line: 5 z-axis
quality: 5 depth
__-3 fatty acid: 5 omega
3 Godfathers (1948 film)
cast: Pedro Armendariz, Harry Carey Jr., John Wayne
director: John Ford
3-in-__ Oil: 3 One
3 Men and a Baby (1987 film)
cast: Ted Danson, Steve Guttenberg, Tom Selleck, Nancy Travis
director: Leonard Nimoy
3M's
one of ~ M's: 3 mfg. 4 Minn.
3 Musketeers: 5 candy 9 chocolate
alternative: 4 Mars, Twix 5 Clark, Heath 6 Kit Kat, Mounds, PayDay, Reese's, Zagnut 7 Krackel, Oh Henry 8 Baby Ruth, Hershey's, Milky Way, Snickers 9 Almond Joy, Mr. Goodbar 10 NutRageous
3 Penny Opera (1931 film), The
cast: Rudolph Forster, Lotte Lenya
director: G.W. Pabst
3 P.M. in a monastery: 5 nones
3rd Rock from the Sun (NBC sitcom)
cast: Jane Curtin (Dr. Mary Albright) Kristen Johnston (Sally Solomon) John Lithgow (Dick Solomon) French Stewart (Harry Solomon)
3 Women (1977 film)
cast: Shelley Duvall, Janice Rule, Sissy Spacek
director: Robert Altman
3 Worlds of Gulliver (1960 film), The
cast: Kerwin Mathews, Jo Morrow
director: Jack Sher
10: 7 sawbuck
10 (1979 film)
cast: Julie Andrews, Bo Derek, Dudley Moore, Robert Webber
director: Blake Edwards
theme: 6 Bolero
10 __ or less: 5 items
__-10: 3 Pac
10cc
homeland: England
song: I'm Not in Love (1975) The Things We Do for Love (1977)
10-cent
former ~ coin: 5 disme
10K: 4 race
10 Lb. Penalty author: Dick Francis
10 Rillington Place (1971 film)
cast: Sir Richard Attenborough, Judy Geeson
director: Richard Fleischer
10 Things I Hate About You (1999 film)
cast: Joseph Gordon-Levitt, Heath Ledger, Larisa Oleynik, Julia Stiles
director: Gil Junger
10-year-old: 5 'tween
12: 7 boxcars
dozen: 3 gro. 5 gross
every ~ months: 4 yrly. 6 yearly
__ 12: 4 Adam
__-12: 6 carbon
12 Angry Men (1957 film)
cast: Martin Balsam, Ed Begley, Lee J. Cobb, Henry Fonda, Jack Klugman, E.G. Marshall, Jack Warden
director: Sidney Lumet
12-pack: 6 carton
12-year-old: 5 'tween
13 __ Madeleine: 3 Rue
__ 13: 6 Apollo
__-13: 6 carbon
13 Days to Glory subject: 5 Alamo
13th Warrior (1999 film), The
cast: Antonio Banderas, Vladmir Kulich, Dennis Storhoi, Diane Venora
director: John McTiernan
20%: 5 fifth
20/20 (ABC news)
host: Hugh Downs
20 Million Miles to Earth (1957 film)
cast: William Hopper, Frank Puglia, Joan Taylor
director: Nathan Juran
20-mule team load: 5 borax
21
exceed: 4 bust
over ~: 5 of age
__ 21: 4 Over 7 Century
23 __: 6 Skidoo
23 Paces to Baker Street (1956 film)
cast: Van Johnson, Vera Miles, Cecil Parker
director: Henry Hathaway
24
every ~ hours: 4 a day 5 daily
horas: 3 día
sheets: 5 quire
24/7 (1999 song) artist: Kevon Edmonds
24-carat: 4 pure 7 optimum
24-hour __: 3 flu
24-pack: 6 carton
25 or 6 to 4 (1970 song) artist: Chicago
26 Miles (1958 song) artist: Four Preps
28 Days (2000 film)
cast: Sandra Bullock, Diane Ladd, Viggo Mortensen, Dominic West
director: Betty Thomas
28 Up (1985 film) director: Michael Apted
30 Manhattan East author: Hillary Waugh
35mm: 6 camera
setting: 5 f-stop
35 Up (1991 film) director: Michael Apted
38 Special
lead singer: Donnie Van Zant
song: Caught Up in You (1982) Second Chance (1989)
38th-parallel land: 5 Korea
39+ inches, in Britain: 5 metre
39 Steps (1935 film), The
cast: Madeleine Carroll, Robert Donat, Lucie Mannheim
director: Alfred Hitchcock
__ 200: 5 Dutch
__ 222: 4 Room
227 (NBC sitcom)
cast: Marla Gibbs (Mary Jenkins) Jackée Harry (Sandra Clark) Alaina Reed-Hall (Rose Lee Holloway) Hal Williams (Lester Jenkins)
__ 235: 7 uranium
237 milliliters: 3 cup
__ 238: 7 uranium
__ 239: 7 uranium
1040: 4 form
completer: 5 filer
data: 6 income
figure: 3 net
form ~ deduction: 4 dues
form ~ ID: 3 SSN
imprinter: 3 GPO
submitter: 5 filer
1066 conqueror: 6 Norman
1300: 5 one p.m.
2001: A Space Odyssey (1968 film)
beast: 3 ape
cast: Keir Dullea, Gary Lockwood, William Sylvester
computer: 3 Hal
director: Stanley Kubrick
studio: 3 MGM
2010 (1984 film)
cast: John Lithgow, Helen Mirren, Roy Scheider
director: Peter Hyams
2200
about ~ pounds: 5 tonne
3000 Miles to Graceland (2001 film)
cast: Kevin Costner, Courteney Cox, Kurt Russell, Christian Slater
director: Demian Lichtenstein
3280.8 ft.: 3 kil.
10,000 Maniacs
song: Because the Night (1993) More Than This (1997)
vocalists: Natalie Merchant, Mary Ramsey
10,000 meters, for short: 4 ten K
$10,000/25,000 Pyramid, The
host: Dick Clark, Bill Cullen, Donny Osmond
genre: game show
20,000 Leagues Under the Sea (1954 film)
captain: 4 Nemo
cast: Kirk Douglas, Paul Lukas, James Mason
director: Richard Fleischer
seal: 4 Esme
20,000 Years in Sing Sing (1933 film)
cast: Bette Davis, Spencer Tracy
director: Michael Curtiz
T: 5 shirt 6 letter
followers: 3 UVW 4 UVWX 5 UVWXY
in phonetic alphabet: 5 Tango
model ~: 4 Ford
preceders: 3 QRS 4 PQRS 5 OPQRS
to a ~: 4 well 6 just so 7 exactly 8 laudably, very well, worthily 9 correctly, just right, on the nose, perfectly, precisely 10 accurately, flawlessly
to Morse: 3 dah 4 dash
use a ~ square: 5 aline
T __: 4 and E, cell 5 hinge 6 number, square
T __ Tom: 4 as in
T-__: 3 bar, Man 4 bill, bone
T-__ lift: 3 bar
T-__ steak: 4 bone
T. __ Pickens: 5 Boone
T. __ Price: 4 Rowe
__ T: 3 to a
__-T: 3 Ice
Ta: 4 elem. 7 element 8 tantalum
73 for ~: 4 at. no.
Ta-__-Boom-De-Ré: 4 Ra-Ra
TA: 4 aide, asst.
superior: 4 prof 9 professor
Taal: 4 lake 7 volcano 8 language 9 Afrikaans
locale: 4 Asia 5 Luzon
Taanith __: 6 Esther
tab: 3 IOU, tag 4 bill, chit, cost, flag, flap, list, name, rank, rate, sort, stop 5 check, label, price, score, title 6 amount, charge, choose, credit, marker, outlay, select, tariff, ticket 7 account, bar bill, earmark, invoice, specify, sticker 8 bookmark, identify, indicate, nominate 9 appendage, liability, reckoning, recognize, statement 10 projection
pick up the ~: 4 foot 5 treat 6 defray 9 subsidize
put on one's ~: 3 owe 6 charge 8 purchase
settle the ~: 3 pay 5 pay up
use the ~ key: 6 indent
tab __: 3 key
__-tab: 4 pull
Tab: 3 key 5 drink 6 Hunter 9 soft drink
alternative: 4 Nehi 5 Fanta 6 Fresca, Sprite 8 Diet Rite, Dr Pepper 9 Canada Dry 10 Mello Yello, Royal Crown 11 Mountain Dew
neighbor: 5 Shift
tabard: 4 cape, coat 6 jacket
Tabard Inn serving: 3 ale
tabaret: 6 fabric 8 material
tabasco __: 6 pepper
Tabasco: 5 sauce, state 7 Mexican
city: 5 Jalpa, Teapa 7 Paraíso 8 Balancán, Cárdenas, Frontera, Parrilla 9 Macuspana, Tenosique 10 Comalcalco
quality: 4 zest 5 spice
see also Spanish
tabbouleh: 5 salad
tabby: 3 cat, pet 4 puss 5 felid 6 feline 7 striped 8 brindled 9 grimalkin
sound: 3 mew, pur 4 meow, purr 5 miaou, miaow, miaul
__ Ta Be My Girl: 3 Use
Taber: 4 city, town
locale: 6 Canada 7 Alberta
tabernacle: 5 abbey 6 chapel, church, shrine, temple 8 basilica 9 cathedral, sanctuary
singer: 4 alto, bass 5 choir, tenor 7 soprano
tabernacle __: 5 frame 6 mirror
tabi: 4 sock 7 hosiery
tabinet: 6 fabric 8 material
Tabitha's brother: 4 Adam
tabla: 4 drum
origin: 5 India
table: 3 bar 4 dais, desk, food, list, meal, menu, mesa, roll, slab 5 bench, board, defer, delay, graph, index, stand, waive 6 agenda, buffet, legend, pulpit, put off, record, shelve, spread, upland 7 console, cuisine, desk top, diagram, dresser, lectern, plateau, summary, suspend 8 appendix, file away, flatland, lay aside, postpone, put aside, put on ice, register, schedule, set aside, synopsis, victuals 9 furniture, inventory, sideboard, tableland, visual aid 10 bill of fare, compendium, gastronomy, pigeonhole, reschedule, statistics
accessory: 4 lamp
at the ~: 6 eating, gaming
cover: 5 cloth, scarf
decoration: 5 doily 6 doyley
d'hôte: 4 fare, food, meal 6 dinner
ender: 3 top 4 land, mate, side, ware 5 cloth, spoon 8 spoonful
follower: 5 spoon

insert: 4 leaf
makeshift ~: 5 spool
material: 3 oak 4 data 8 mahogany
part: 3 leg
place at the ~: 4 seat
prepare the ~: 3 lay, set
put one's cards on the ~: 6 reveal
remove dishes from the ~: 3 bus
round ~: 6 parley, powwow 9 symposium 10 conference
scrap: 3 ort
staple: 4 salt 5 sugar 6 pepper
starter: 4 time, turn, work 5 round
talk: 3 gab, rap 5 prate 6 banter, gabble, gibber, gossip 7 chatter, palaver 8 chin-chin, chitchat, repartee
tea ~: 4 cart
tennis: 4 game 5 sport
TV dinner ~: 4 tray
with folding leaves: 5 tip up
writing ~: 7 rolltop 9 secretary
table __: 3 cut, saw 4 corn, lamp, salt, talk, wine 5 board, d'hôte, linen, stake, sugar 6 tennis, tripod 7 manners
table-__: 3 hop
__ table: 3 bag, bed, end, tax, tea 4 card, draw, drop, drum, head, high, hunt, pier, pool, rent, sand, side, sofa, tide, tier, tray 5 bench, brace, chair, Essex, light, Lord's, night, on the, plain, plane, poker, range, round, snack, stack, steam, tip-up, toddy, truth, water 6 basset, bridge, coffee, corbel, corner, dining, dinner, gaming, picnic, sewing, tavern 7 butler's, capstan, Carlton, console, counter, cricket, drawing, draw-out, folding, gateleg, glacier, library, nesting, Parsons, sawbuck, tilt-top, trestle
tableau: 4 view 5 scene 7 picture 8 panorama 9 depiction, spectacle
tableau __: 6 vivant 7 curtain
__-table book: 6 coffee
tablecloth: 6 spread
material: 5 linen 6 damask
tabled: 6 put off 7 abeyant, shelved 8 deferred, set aside 9 postponed, suspended
Table for Five (1983 film)
cast: Marie-Christine Barrault, Richard Crenna, Jon Voight
table-hop: 3 mix 6 hobnob, mingle 7 consort, hang out 9 socialize 10 fraternize
tableland: 4 mesa 5 table 7 plateau
African ~: 5 karoo
tables
attend ~: 5 serve
turn the ~: 5 shift 6 oppose 7 revenge, reverse 9 retaliate
__ tables: 4 dive, wait
tablespoons, sixteen: 3 cup
tablet: 3 pad 4 dose, pill 5 slate 6 sheets, troche 7 capsule, lozenge, memo pad, notepad 8 medicine, memorial, monument, notebook 10 medication, scratch pad
combining form: 4 plac- 5 pinac-, pinak-, placo- 6 pinaco-
tablet __: 5 chair
__ tablet: 3 wax 5 waxed
table tennis: 4 game 5 sport
see also Ping-Pong
tablets, two: 4 dose 6 dosage
tableware: 4 dish, fork 5 china, forks, glass, knife, spoon 6 dishes, knives, spoons 7 glasses, utensil 8 utensils
tabloid: 3 rag 4 pulp 5 paper 7 journal 9 newspaper
boss: 6 editor
like some ~ headlines: 4 racy 5 lurid 6 risqué 7 graphic 8 shocking 9 low-minded
pages: 3 ads
topic: 3 UFO 5 alien, celeb 6 exposé, gossip
taboo: 3 ban, bar, law 4 don't, no-no, veto 5 magic 6 banned, forbid, outlaw, vetoed 7 exclude, illegal, illicit, keep out, rule out, shut out 8 anathema, criminal, disallow, improper, leave out, outlawed, prohibit, sanction, unlawful, verboten, wrongful 9 blackball, exclusion, felonious, forbidden, frowned on, interdict, off-limits, ostracize, proscribe, restraint, stricture, unallowed 10 limitation, not allowed, prohibited, proscribed, regulation
tabor: 4 drum
Tabor: 4 city, peak, town 8 mountain
ancient site near Mt. ~: 5 Endor
from ~: 5 Czech
peak locale: 6 Israel
Tabora: 4 city, town
locale: 8 Tanzania
taboret: 7 hassock
Tabriz: 4 city, town
locale: 4 Iran
town near ~: 4 Ahar
tabs
keep ~: 5 gauge, judge 6 assess, figure, notice 7 account, compute, measure 8 appraise, evaluate, watch out 9 calculate
keep ~ on: 4 tend 5 check, track, watch
tabu
see taboo
tabula __: 4 rasa
tabulate: 3 add 4 list 5 chart, index, order 6 assort, codify, figure, record 7 arrange, catalog 8 classify 9 catalogue, enumerate, formulate, keep count 10 categorize
tabulation: 4 list 5 index, tally 6 record, roster 7 catalog, summary 8 counting, register
__ tac: 3 tie
Tacan: 7 volcano
locale: 9 Guatemala
__ Tac Dough: 3 Tic
tach reading: 3 rpm 4 revs
tachyon: 8 particle
tacit: 4 mute 6 silent, unsaid 7 assumed, implied, virtual 8 hinted at, implicit, indirect, inferred, unspoken, unstated, unvoiced, wordless 9 alluded to, intimated, suggested, unwritten 10 undeclared, understood
taciturn: 3 mum 4 cold, curt, dour, mute 5 aloof, close, quiet 6 morose, silent 7 distant, laconic, sparing 8 brooding, reserved, reticent 9 impassive, secretive, withdrawn 10 antisocial, speechless
one: 4 clam
taciturnity: 7 silence
Tacitus: 5 Roman 6 writer 9 historian
work: Annales
Germania
Historiae
tack: 3 add, fix, hem, sew, tag, yaw 4 bend, brad, glue, line, nail, path, turn, veer, yoke 5 affix, annex, baste, paste, shift 6 append, attach, course, fasten, method, secure, staple, stitch, swerve, switch, zigzag 7 heading, routine, tangent 8 approach 9 direction
kin: 3 pin 7 pushpin
like a ~: 5 sharp
material: 5 brass
on: 3 add 4 link 5 affix, annex 6 append, attach
starter: 4 hard, tick 5 thumb
up a hem: 3 sew 5 baste 6 stitch
tack __: 4 claw, room 6 hammer
__ tack: 3 bar, tie 6 carpet
tackle: 3 kit, rig, tie, try 4 gear, grab, halt, hook, line, nail, sack, stop, wade 5 begin, block, goods, hoist, seize, stuff, throw, tools, upset 6 accept, attack, have at, launch, lifter, outfit, pursue, strive, take on, work on 7 athlete, attempt, get busy, go about, go for it, grapple, pitch in, rigging 8 confront, deal with, engage in, material, materiel, set about, struggle 9 apparatus, bring down, equipment, intercept, machinery, pitch into, trappings, undertake 10 embark upon, implements, make a run at
block and ~: 4 lift 5 hoist 6 lifter, pulley 10 dumbwaiter
teammate: 3 end 4 back 5 guard 6 center, tackle 8 fullback, halfback 11 quarterback
the quarterback: 4 sack
see also football
__ tackle: 3 cat, gun 4 fish, luff 6 double, flying, ground
__-tackle: 5 touch
tackle box item: 4 hook, line, lure, reel 5 float, snell
tacks
brass ~: 5 facts 7 reality 9 actuality, essential 10 foundation
down to brass ~: 5 pithy
get down to brass ~: 6 detail 7 account, itemize, specify 9 make clear, stipulate
__-tack-toe: 4 tick
tacky: 5 cheap, crass, crude, dingy, dowdy, faded, gaudy, gluey, gooey, messy, ratty, seedy 6 coarse, flashy, frumpy, garish, grubby, ragged, shabby, shoddy, sleazy, sloppy, sticky, tawdry, vulgar 7 chintzy, kitschy, rundown, scruffy, uncouth 8 adhesive, outmoded, schlocky, slipshod, slovenly 9 inelegant, out-of-date, shameless, tasteless, unstylish 10 broken-down, second-rate, threadbare, unbecoming, unsuitable
not ~: 5 smart 6 classy, modish, urbane 7 elegant, refined, stylish, voguish 8 esthetic, polished, tasteful 9 dignified, exquisite, glamorous
stuff: 4 glue, goop
__-tacky: 5 ticky
Tacloban's island: 5 Leyte
Tacna: 4 city, town
locale: 4 Peru
taco: 7 Mexican
chip brand: 7 Doritos
ingredient: 4 beef 5 salsa 6 cheese
Taco Bell dog: 5 Dinky
Tacoma: 4 city, port, town
locale: 4 Wash. 10 Washington
taconite: 3 ore 7 mineral
tact: 5 asset, poise, sense, skill 6 comity, policy 7 aptness, control, finesse, suavity 8 civility, courtesy, delicacy, judgment, subtlety, urbanity 9 diplomacy, gallantry, good taste, suaveness 10 discretion, perception, politeness, refinement, smoothness
ender: 3 ics, ile
lack of ~: 5 gaffe 7 faux pas 9 gaucherie
tactful: 4 kind, wise 5 aware, civil, suave 6 gentle, kindly, poised, polite, subtle, urbane 7 gallant, heedful, mindful, politic, prudent, skilled 8 delicate, discreet, gracious, obliging, polished 9 courteous, judicious, observant, sensitive, unselfish 10 diplomatic, perceptive, thoughtful
tactfully: 7 lightly 9 carefully 10 cautiously, delicately, gracefully, skillfully
tactic: 4 ploy, ruse 5 means 8 artifice, maneuver 9 expedient, stratagem 10 expediency
tactical __: 4 unit, wire
Tactical __ Command: 3 Air
tactician: 7 planner 10 mastermind, strategist
tactics: 4 plan, ploy 5 means, trick 6 course, method, policy, scheme 7 defense 8 approach, campaign, channels, strategy 9 stratagem, technique
strong-arm ~: 6 duress 7 tyranny 8 coercion, violence 9 extortion 10 oppression
__ tactics: 5 scare
tactile: 7 sensory, sensual 9 sensorial
tactless: 4 rude 5 blunt, brash, brusk, crude, frank, gruff, harsh, hasty, inept, nervy, rough, sharp 6 abrupt, candid, clumsy, gauche, stupid, unkind, vulgar 7 awkward, boorish, brusque, selfish, unadept, uncivil 8 bungling, heedless, impolite, inurbane, unsubtle 9 impolitic, imprudent, maladroit, outspoken, tasteless, unfeeling, ungallant, untactful 10 blundering, indelicate, indiscreet, ungracious, unpolished, unthinking
__-tac-toe: 3 tic
tad: 3 bit, boy, jot 4 iota, mite, tike, tyke 5 child, skosh, speck 7 smidgen, smidgin 8 small fry, smidgeon 9 little bit, little boy, youngster
ender: 4 pole
__ tad: 5 just a
Tad: 5 Mosel 7 Lincoln
father of ~: 3 Abe
ta-da: 5 there, voilà 6 I did it
Tadeusz: 8 Borowski, Konwicki, Rózewicz
tadpole: 4 frog, toad 5 larva 9 amphibian
cousin: 3 eft
Tadzhikistan
see Tajikistan
Taegu: 4 city, town
locale: 10 South Korea
tae kwon do relative: 4 judo 6 karate
tael: 5 liang, money
TAE part: 4 Alva, Thos. 6 Edison, Thomas
__ Tae Woo: 3 Roh
__ Tafari: 3 Ras
Taff: 5 river
city on the ~: 7 Cardiff
locale: 5 Wales
taffeta: 5 weave 6 fabric, faille
sound: 5 swish
taffrail, toward the: 3 aft
taffy: 5 candy, treat 9 sweetmeat
like ~: 5 chewy, gooey 6 sticky
taffy __: 4 pull 5 apple
__ taffy: 7 Turkish
tafia: 3 rum
source: 5 Haiti
__ Taft Benson: 4 Ezra
Taft-Hartley __: 3 Act
Taft, William Howard: 9 president
alma mater: 4 Yale
former occupation: 6 lawyer
home: 4 Ohio
opponent: 4 Debs 5 Bryan
state: 4 Ohio
V.P.: 7 Sherman
wife: 5 Helen
tag: 2 ID 3 add, dog, dub, pin, tab, tap 4 call, card, flap, game, heel, logo, mark, name, note, pick, rate, slip, stub, tack, tail, term 5 affix, badge, chase, label, style, title, touch, trail 6 append, attend, button, emblem, fasten, follow, marker, pursue, select, shadow, ticket 7 earmark, specify,

sticker, voucher **8** christen, identify, indicate, nickname, subtitle **9** accompany, designate, recognize, sobriquet, track down, trademark
along: 4 come, link **5** trail
attach, as a name ~: 5 pin on
cry: 5 not it
end: 4 tail
ender: 4 line **5** along
ID ~: 5 badge, label
on: 3 add **4** link **5** affix **6** append **8** vinculum
price ~: 3 tab **4** cost **5** total, value **6** amount, charge, outlay
red ~ event: 4 sale
starter: 3 rag **4** hang, name
up: 9 touch base
words: 4 as is
tag __: 3 day, end **4** boat, line, sale, team **5** along
tag __ with: 5 along
__ tag: 3 dog, ear, red **5** phone, price **7** Chinese
__ tag!: 5 Guten
Tag, __ it!: 5 you're
__ Tag: 5 Lazer
Tagalog: 8 language
tagalong's cry: 5 ditto, me too
Taganrog: 4 gulf
locale: 6 Europe **7** Ukraine
Taggard, Genevieve: 4 poet
__-taggle: 6 raggle
Tag Heuer: 5 watch **10** wristwatch
alternative: 4 Ebel, Rado **5** Casio, Elgin, Lorus, Omega, Rolex, Seiko, Timex **6** Bulova, Fossil, Movado, Pulsar, Swatch **7** Citizen **8** Longines, Tourneau
Tagliabue, Paul org.: 3 NFL
tagliarini: 5 pasta **7** noodles
tag-on abbr.: 3 etc.
Tagore, Rabindranath: 3 Sir **4** poet **6** Indian, writer **8** Nobelist
work: Chitra
The Crescent Moon
Fireflies
The Golden Boat
One Hundred Poems of Kabir
Red Oleanders
tagrag and __: 7 bobtail
tag-renewal org.: 3 DMV
__-tag sale: 3 red
Tagus: 5 river
city on the ~: 6 Lisbon, Toledo
locale: 5 Spain **6** Iberia **8** Portugal
tahini base: 6 sesame
Tahiti: 3 île, isl. **4** isle **6** island
dish: 4 taro
garment: 5 pareo, pareu
Island near ~: 7 Raiatea **8** Pitcairn
novel set in ~: 4 Omoo
port: 7 Papeete
see also French
Tahnee: 5 Welch
mother of ~: 6 Raquel
Tahoe: 3 SUV **4** lake **5** Chevy **6** resort **9** Chevrolet
locale: 6 Nevada **10** California
visitor: 5 skier
Tahoma: 4 font **8** typeface
Tahoua: 4 city, town
locale: 5 Niger
tahr: 4 goat
relative: 4 geep, ibex **6** Angora **7** markhor **8** markhoor
tai: 4 fish
tai __: 3 chi
tai __ ch'uan: 3 chi
__ tai: 3 mai, red
__-tai: 3 mao
Tai: 7 Siamese **8** language **9** Babilonia
language: 3 Lao **4** Shan
Tai Hu: 4 lake

locale: 5 China
taiko: 4 drum
origin: 5 Japan
tail: 3 dog, end, eye, lag, spy, tag **4** rear, rump, scut, stub **5** hound, spy on, stalk, track, trail, train **6** behind, follow, pursue, shadow, tag end, wagger **8** follower, run after, straggle **9** appendage, extremity, posterior, track down **10** conclusion
combining form: 2 ur- **3** uro- **4** caud-, cerc- **5** caudi-, caudo-, cerco-
end: 4 back, rear, stub **5** stump
ender: 3 fin **4** back, bone, coat, gate, pipe, race, skid, spin, wind **5** board, gater, light, piece, stock **6** gating
in two shakes of a lamb's ~: 3 now **4** soon **6** at once, in a sec, pronto **7** hastily, quickly, rapidly, shortly **8** directly, promptly, right now, speedily **9** forthwith, in a minute, in a second, right away **10** this moment
lacking a ~: 5 anury **7** acaudal
of a ~: 6 caudal
off: 3 ebb **4** drop, ease, fade, fall, pale, sink, wane **5** abate, let up, lower, remit, slump **6** lessen, recede, weaken **7** decline, die down, dwindle, lighten, slacken, subside, thin out **8** decrease, diminish, head away, moderate, peter out, roll back, slow down **9** retrocede
shake a ~: 4 lose
starter: 3 bob, cat, cur, fan, fox, pig, pin, rat, wag **4** bang, coat, dove, duck, fish, high, horn, pony, ring, whip **5** broad, horse, shirt, sprig, stick, sword, white **6** cotton, spring, square, triple, yellow **7** bristle, flicker, scissor, swallow
turn ~: 3 run **4** bolt, flee **6** escape **7** retreat, run away, take off **8** fugitate, run for it **9** cut and run, skedaddle
two shakes of a lamb's ~: 4 jiff **5** jiffy, trice **6** moment, second
tail __: 3 end, fan, fin, off **4** coat, cone, lamp, skid, wind **5** plane **6** covert
__ tail: 3 fee **4** boat, turn **5** horse, lamb's **6** burro's, horse's, monkey **7** donkey's, dragon's, rooster
__-tail: 5 mare's **6** wiggle **7** lizard's
tailbone: 6 coccyx
__-tail cactus: 3 rat
tailed __: 4 frog, toad
__-tailed: 3 fan, pin **4** ring **5** bushy **6** double
__-tailed deer: 5 black, white
tailless
cat: 4 Manx
primate: 3 ape **4** lori **5** chimp, orang **7** gorilla **9** orangutan **10** chimpanzee
tailor: 3 fit **4** gear, suit **5** adapt, alter, shape, style **6** adjust, attune, fitter, hemmer, modify **7** alterer, arrange, fashion, measure **8** clothier, readjust **9** couturier, outfitter **10** custom-make, dressmaker
anew: 5 refit
don at the ~: 5 try on
do ~ work: 3 fit, hem **5** alter, plait, pleat, rehem, resew
measure: 6 inseam
name meaning ~: 6 Snyder **9** Schneider
need: 3 pin **4** iron, tape **5** chalk, cloth **6** needle, shears **8** scissors
of song: 3 Sam
work: 3 hem **4** seam **5** plait, pleat

tailor-__: 4 made
__-tailor: 4 hand **6** custom
tailored, not custom: 3 RTW
tailor-made: 6 fitted
Tailor of Panama, The (2001 film)
cast: Pierce Brosnan, Jamie Lee Curtis, Geoffrey Rush
director: John Boorman
__, Tailor, Soldier, Spy: 6 Tinker
tails: 4 coat **6** jacket **10** monkey suit
accompaniment: 3 tie
make heads or ~ of: 3 see **6** fathom, follow, pick up **9** figure out **10** comprehend, understand
tailspin: 5 slump **7** descent **8** nosedive **9** rough time
tailward: 3 aft **6** astern
Tainan: 4 city, port, town
locale: 6 Taiwan **7** Formosa
Taine, Hippolyte: 6 French, writer **9** historian **11** philosopher
specialty: 10 positivism
Taino: 6 Indian **7** Amerind
taint: 3 mar, rot, tar **4** blot, blur, foul, ruin, soil, spot, tint, turn **5** abuse, brand, decay, dirty, muddy, smear, spoil, stain, sully **6** befoul, blight, crud up, debase, defame, defect, defile, doctor, embrue, go sour, imbrue, infect, malign, poison, smudge, stigma **7** asperse, begrime, blacken, blemish, corrupt, pollute, tarnish, vitiate **8** besmirch, discolor, disgrace, dishonor, impurity, throw mud **9** discredit, disrepute, pollution **10** adulterate, defilement, imputation, stigmatize, villainize
tainted: 3 off **4** foul, gamy, rank **5** gamey, grimy, sooty **6** filthy, grubby, grungy, impure, rancid, rotten **7** corrupt, unclean **8** inedible, maculate, slovenly, vitiated **10** germ-ridden, malodorous, unsanitary
taintless: 4 pure **5** clean **6** chaste **7** ethical, sterile **8** germfree, hygienic, innocent, pristine, sanitary, spotless, unsoiled, virtuous **9** exemplary, honorable, incorrupt, stainless, undefiled, unspoiled, unspotted, unsullied, untouched, wholesome **10** immaculate, impeccable, inculpable, sterilized
'tain't opposite: 3 'tis
taipan: 5 snake **6** animal **7** reptile
relative: 3 asp, boa **5** aboma, adder, cobra, krait, mamba, racer, viper **6** dhaman, python **7** markhor, rattler **8** anaconda, moccasin, ringhals **9** boomslang, coachwhip **10** bushmaster, copperhead, sidewinder
Tai-Pan author: James Clavell
Taipei: 4 city, town **7** capital
locale: 6 Taiwan **7** Formosa
Taiwan: 3 isl. **4** isle **6** island, nation, strait **7** country
capital: 6 Taipei
city: 6 Taibei, Tainan, Taipei
computer company: 4 Acer
ender: 3 ese
island: 4 Mazu **5** Matsu **7** Formosa
island near ~: 3 Lan
money: 4 cent **6** dollar
port: 6 Tainan **7** Chilung, Keelung **9** Kaohsiung
sea: 9 East China **10** South China
Taiwanese: 5 Asian
Taiwan Strait island: 4 Amoy **6** Jinmen, Kinmen, Quemoy **7** Chinmen **10** Pescadores
Ta'izz: 4 city, town
locale: 5 Yemen
taj: 3 cap **9** headdress
wearer: 6 Moslem, Muslem, Muslim
Tajiki: 8 language
Tajikistan: 6 nation **7** country
capital: 8 Dushanbe

mountain: 9 Lenin Peak, Trans Alai
neighbor: 5 China **10** Kyrgyzstan, Uzbekistan
once: 3 SSR
region: 5 Pamir **6** Pamirs
Taj Mahal: 4 tomb
feature: 4 dome
locale: 4 Agra **5** India
Tajo: 5 Italo
taka: 4 coin **5** money
takahe: 4 bird **8** notornis
Takaoka: 4 city, town
locale: 5 Japan
take: 2 go **3** bag, buy, con, cut, eat, get, lug, nab, opt, rob, use, win **4** bear, beat, bilk, book, cart, cull, deem, down, dupe, earn, gate, grab, grip, gull, hack, haul, have, hire, hold, lead, lift, loot, lump, nail, need, pack, pick, reap, rent, tote, trap, verb **5** abide, admit, adopt, booty, bring, brook, carry, catch, charm, cheat, clasp, drink, drive, elect, ferry, fetch, filch, grasp, guide, lease, lucre, marry, pilot, pinch, pluck, react, see as, seize, share, stand, steal, swipe, trick, truck, usher, yield **6** abduct, accept, arrest, assume, borrow, choose, clutch, collar, convey, deduct, demand, derive, devour, endure, entrap, escort, fleece, go with, handle, hang in, haul in, hijack, imbibe, ingest, inhale, obtain, opt for, output, pay for, pick up, pilfer, pocket, prefer, profit, reckon, regard, relish, remove, rip off, salary, secure, select, snap up, snatch, snitch, spoils, suffer **7** acquire, bewitch, call for, capture, charter, collect, conduct, contain, deceive, defraud, deliver, enchant, ensnare, extract, imagine, impound, include, insnare, lighten, opinion, plunder, preempt, presume, procure, profits, purloin, receive, require, reserve, returns, revenue, ride out, salvage, stipend, stomach, succeed, suppose, suspect, swallow, swindle, two-time, utilize, weather, welcome **8** arrogate, bear with, carry off, carve out, decide on, flimflam, gather up, handpick, highjack, hoodwink, liberate, live with, look upon, proceeds, purchase, reaction, receipts, shoulder, stand for, submit to, subtract, tolerate, transmit **9** accompany, apprehend, bamboozle, captivate, fascinate, four-flush, hang tough, intercept, lay hold of, piggyback, put up with, single out, transport, withstand **10** commandeer, confiscate, settle upon, stick it out
aback: 4 faze, stun **5** shake **7** astound, nonplus, stagger, startle **8** astonish, bowl over, surprise **9** discomfit, dumbfound, give a turn **10** disconcert
a break: 4 rest **5** pause, relax **6** lay off, recess, rest up, unwind **8** intermit, loosen up
account of: 6 reckon **7** measure
a chance: 4 bite, dare, risk **5** wager **6** gamble, hazard **7** venture **9** speculate
a crack at: 3 try **7** venture
action: 4 move **6** step in **7** proceed
action against: 3 sue
a dim view of: 5 knock, scorn **7** censure, deplore, put down, run down **8** belittle, derogate, disfavor **9** deprecate, disesteem, disparage, poormouth **10** disapprove
advantage of: 3 use **4** have, milk **5** abuse, cozen, wrong **6** impose, play on, prey on **7** deceive, exploit, utilize **8** hoodwink, play upon **9** victimize
advantage (of): 5 avail

advice: 4 heed, obey 5 adopt 6 accept, attend, follow, harken, listen, regard 7 abide by, hear out, observe 8 adhere to, consider, pick up on 9 entertain 10 bear in mind
a fling: 4 risk 6 gamble, hazard 7 venture
a flyer: 6 gamble 7 venture
after: 6 follow 7 emulate, reflect 8 resemble
a gander: 3 eye 4 look, peer, scan, view
a hand: 6 butt in, step in 7 barge in, mediate 9 intercede
a header: 4 fall, risk, trip 6 topple, tumble
a hike: 2 go 4 blow, exit, part, quit, scat 5 leave, scram 6 begone, get out 8 light out, withdraw 10 go fly a kite
a holiday: 4 loaf, rest, slow 5 break, pause, relax 6 unwind 8 recreate, slack off, slow down, vacation
a load off: 3 sit 5 relax 6 unload 7 lighten
along: 4 lead, tote 5 bring, guide, usher 6 convey, escort 7 conduct 9 transport
a look at: 3 eye, see 4 case 5 assay, gauge, probe, scout, try on 6 assess, size up, verify 7 confirm, examine, inspect, qualify 8 appraise, check out, evaluate, follow up
a loss: 7 devalue 8 give up on
amiss: 6 resent
a nap: 7 saw logs
another look: 5 audit, check, weigh 6 assess, go over, rehash, survey 7 analyze, examine, inspect, revisit 8 appraise, critique, evaluate, reassess 9 reexamine, think over 10 reconsider, reevaluate, run through, scrutinize
apart: 4 ruin, undo 5 level, spoil, unrig, unrip, wreck 6 detach, tinker 7 destroy, dissect 8 demolish, tear down 9 devastate, dismantle, knock down 10 demoralize, disconnect
a powder: 2 go 3 lam 4 blow, bolt, exit, flee, scat 5 leave, scram 6 escape 7 abandon
a quick look: 4 leaf, skim 5 check 6 browse, riffle, size up, survey 7 monitor 8 look over 10 glance over, run through
a risk: 4 dare, defy 6 gamble, hazard 7 presume, venture 9 challenge, speculate
a room: 4 stay 7 sojourn 8 stop over
as fact: 6 accept 7 believe, suppose, surmise 9 postulate
as gospel: 3 buy 6 accept, credit, rely on 7 swallow, swear by
as one's own: 5 adopt, co-opt 6 accept 7 espouse
a stand: 3 opt 4 vote 5 judge 6 choose, decide, oppose 9 determine
at face value: 4 rely 5 bet on 6 accept, assume, bank on, commit, credit, expect, lean on, look to, rely on 7 believe, consign, count on, entrust, presume, suppose, swear by 8 depend on, rely upon
away: 4 less, wipe 5 minus 6 abduct, deduct, reduce, remove 7 ransack 8 decrease, diminish, discount, subtract, withdraw
a wrong turn: 3 err 5 stray 6 slip up 8 go astray, trespass 10 transgress
back: 5 rewin, unsay 6 recall, recant, regain, return, revoke 7 disavow, forgive, reclaim, recover, retract 8 disclaim, exchange, withdraw 9 recapture, repossess, repudiate
bets: 8 give odds
by the hand: 5 guide, steer, usher 6 assist, direct, escort 7 bolster, conduct 9 encourage
can't ~: 4 hate 5 abhor 6 detest, loathe 7 despise 8 execrate 9 abominate
care of: 3 pay 4 feed, mall, maul, tend 5 act on, nurse, see to, watch 6 advert, attend, foster, handle, reward 7 address, baby-sit, execute, nurture, protect, provide, shelter, sit with 8 attend to, cope with, deal with, maintain, minister, see about, transact 9 cultivate, do justice, look after, overpower, watch over 10 accomplish, compensate, consummate
care of a tot: 4 mind 5 watch 7 oversee 9 look after
charge: 4 lead, rule 5 steer 6 head up 7 command
cover: 3 den 4 hide, wait 6 hole up, lie low 7 shelter
don't ~ no for an answer: 7 persist, protest 8 speak out 9 stand firm
down: 3 jot 4 land, note, rase, raze, ruin, undo 5 abase, level, lower, shame, wreck, write 6 debase, demean, humble, record, topple 7 deflate, degrade, destroy, devalue, mortify 8 belittle, bulldoze, demolish, disgrace, inscribe, register 9 deprecate, devaluate, devastate, discredit, dismantle, disparage, humiliate 10 journalize, transcribe
down a peg: 5 abase, lower, shame 6 demean, demote, humble, reduce 7 degrade, mortify 8 belittle 9 downgrade
effect: 4 tell, work 5 enure, inure, set in 6 happen
ender: 3 off, out 4 away, down, over
everything: 7 possess 10 monopolize
exception: 5 demur 6 differ 7 protest, quarrel
exception to: 4 mind 5 cavil, demur 6 object, oppose, resent 7 dissent 8 question 9 challenge, deprecate
five: 4 rest 5 break, pause, relax 6 recess, rest up 8 intermit
flight: 2 go 3 lam, run 4 bolt, flee, wing 5 scram, split 6 depart, escape 8 fugitate 9 disappear
for a ride: 3 con, gyp 4 bilk, dupe, gull, hoax, scam 5 cheat, cozen, trick 6 fleece 7 deceive, defraud, mislead, swindle 8 flimflam, hoodwink 9 bamboozle
for a time: 6 borrow
forcibly: 5 seize, wrest
forever: 4 drag 5 dally, stall, tarry 10 dillydally
for granted: 5 posit 6 assume 7 believe, presume, suppose 9 postulate
form: 3 gel 4 jell 5 shape 8 incubate
for oneself: 3 hog 7 possess 10 monopolize
give and ~: 4 swap, swop 5 bandy, share, trade 8 exchange
hard to ~: 5 nasty, rough 7 galling 8 abrasive, annoying, grinding 10 irritating, unpleasant
heed: 4 mind 5 watch 6 beware 7 hearken
heed of: 4 mind 6 notice 7 observe 8 listen to
heist ~: 4 loot 5 booty 7 plunder
hold: 3 fix
hold of: 3 bag, nab 4 bust, grab, grip, nail, snag 5 catch, grasp, pinch, snare 6 abduct, arrest, collar, detain, hijack, obtain, secure, snap up, snatch, tackle 7 capture, impound, overrun, procure, receive 8 carry off 9 apprehend, overwhelm 10 commandeer, confiscate
home: 3 net 4 earn 5 clear 8 pull down
how much to ~: 4 dose 6 dosage
in: 3 con, eat, eye, lie, see, spy 4 bilk, dupe, earn, fool, gull, have, hear, hoax, make, nick, note, reap, sell, snow, soak, view 5 admit, adopt, bluff, board, catch, cheat, cover, grasp, gross, hocus, house, learn, lodge, put up, sense, sop up, stare, trick, visit 6 absorb, attend, betray, billet, delude, devour, digest, follow, gather, incept, ingest, notice, osmose, outwit, pick up, redeem, soak up, suck up 7 beguile, contain, deceive, defraud, embrace, glimpse, include, mislead, observe, quarter, realize, receive, recruit, shelter, swallow, swindle, two-time 8 comprise, contract, flimflam, hoodwink, outsmart, perceive 9 apprehend, bamboozle, disinform, encompass, four-flush 10 assimilate, comprehend, understand
in a guest: 5 greet 6 invite 7 welcome
in law: 5 seise
into account: 4 heed, note 5 cover 6 regard 7 respect 8 consider
into custody: 3 nab 4 book, nail 5 pinch, run in, seize 6 arrest 9 apprehend
issue: 5 argue, clash 6 differ, oppose 7 quarrel, quibble 8 conflict, disagree
it: 5 abide, infer, stick 6 deduce, gather, reckon, suffer 7 imagine, presume, surmise 9 withstand 10 understand
it easy: 3 sit 4 idle, laze, loaf, lull, rest 5 coast, relax, slide, unlax 6 lounge, repose, rest up, unwind 8 loosen up 9 luxuriate
it hard: 3 cry, sob 4 bawl, howl, keen, moan, mope, wail, weep 5 brood, mourn 6 bemoan, bewail, grieve, lament
it on the lam: 3 fly, run 4 flee 6 escape
lodgings: 3 let 4 rent 5 lease 8 sublease
no note of: 6 ignore 7 neglect 8 brush off, skip over 9 disregard
notice: 4 heed 5 sit up, watch 6 listen
nourishment: 3 sup 4 dine, nosh 5 feast, graze 6 ingest 7 consume, partake 9 have a bite, have a meal 10 gormandize
off: 2 go 3 fly, hie, run 4 blow, bolt, dash, doff, exit, flee, move, part, quit, shed, soar 5 begin, climb, elope, leave, mimic, scram, speed, split, strip 6 ascend, aviate, beat it, decamp, deduct, depart, desert, divest, embark, get out, let rip, remove, retire, set out 7 abscond, disrobe, head out, lampoon, pull out, undress, vamoose 8 clear out, get out of, hightail, light out, turn tail, withdraw 9 disappear, slip out of 10 go fly a kite, hit the road
off after: 4 hunt, tail 5 chase, stalk 6 follow, pursue, shadow 7 hunt for
off weight: 4 diet, slim, thin 6 shrink 7 lighten 8 slim down
on: 2 do 3 add, pit, vie 4 face, hire 5 adopt, annex, fight, match, worry 6 accept, affect, assume, attach, employ, engage, enlist, join in, oppose, retain, strive, tackle 7 acquire, attempt, compete, contend, embrace, espouse, grapple, quarrel, recruit, venture, vie with 8 deal with, endeavor, shoulder, struggle 9 agree to do, challenge, have a go at, pitch into
one's breath away: 3 awe, wow 5 amaze 6 boggle, excite, thrill 7 astound, stagger 8 astonish
one's leave: 2 go 4 exit 5 split 6 beat it, depart, go away, move on, retire 7 make off, pull out, push off 8 blast off, hightail, light out, set forth, shove off, slip away, withdraw
one's time: 5 dally, delay, mosey, relax, stall, tarry 6 dawdle, linger, loiter 7 goof off 8 lollygag 10 dillydally
on faith: 5 trust 6 accept, assume 7 believe
on the ~: 5 venal 7 corrupt 8 suborned 9 dissolute
out: 3 see 4 date, dele 5 court, erase, pluck, treat 6 deduct, delete, murder, remove, wallop 7 expunge, release 8 diminish, sabotage 9 eliminate, overpower
over: 4 grab, rule 5 adopt, co-opt, seize, spell, steer, usurp 6 assume, manage, occupy 7 inherit, preempt, succeed 10 commandeer, fall heir to, monopolize
over for: 5 cover 6 fill in, follow 7 relieve, replace, succeed 8 supplant
part: 4 join 6 accept, assist, engage, join in 8 deal with 9 cooperate
part in: 4 join 5 enter, share
partner: 4 give
place: 4 fall 5 occur 6 befall, betide, happen 9 come about, eventuate, transpire 10 come to pass
pleasure: 4 live 5 revel 6 wallow
pleasure in: 5 eat up, enjoy
prepare to ~ off: 4 taxi
responsibility: 6 fess up 7 confess
root: 6 settle, sprout 7 develop 8 spring up 9 germinate
shape: 3 gel 4 form, jell, loom
sides: 6 choose, prefer
steps: 7 get busy
stock of: 4 note 5 audit 6 assess, survey
ten: 4 rest 5 break, pause, relax 6 recess, rest up 8 intermit
the ~: 4 gate 8 proceeds, receipts
the bit in one's teeth: 4 defy 5 rebel 6 revolt 7 disobey 9 break away
the edge off: 5 blunt 6 lessen, pacify, smooth, soothe, temper 8 mitigate, tone down
the elevator: 4 rise 5 climb 6 ascend
the floor: 4 talk 5 orate, speak, spout 6 recite 7 lecture 9 hold forth, sermonize, speechify
the heat off: 5 allay, let up, relax 6 lessen, relent 7 lighten, slacken 8 mitigate, moderate 9 alleviate, disburden
the lead: 4 head, rule 5 exact, order, reign 6 direct, enjoin, govern, handle, manage 7 command, control, dictate, mandate, oversee 8 dominate, instruct 9 officiate, supervise
the liberty: 4 dare 6 impose 8 be so bold 9 go so far as
the plunge: 3 wed 4 dare 5 marry, start 7 venture
the sting out: 4 lull 5 allay 6 lessen, smooth, soothe, temper
the wheel: 4 helm 5 drive, pilot 8 navigate

the wind out of: 6 defeat, hamper, hinder, hogtie, hold up, impede, stymie 8 obstruct 9 frustrate, hamstring, undermine
the wraps off: 4 bare 6 expose, reveal 7 lay bare, uncover
the wrong road: 4 flub, goof, muff, slip 5 lapse, stray 6 boo-boo, bungle, foul up, fumble, mess up, slip up, wander 7 blunder, deviate, louse up, stumble 8 go astray 10 transgress
thief ~: 4 cash, jack 5 bills, booty, dough, graft, lucre, money 6 dinero, moolah, snatch 7 plunder, scratch 8 bankroll
to: 4 like 7 care for 10 fall back on
to heart: 4 obey 6 follow 7 abide by, observe, respect
to mean: 4 draw, make 5 glean, guess, infer, think 6 assume, decode, deduce, derive, gather 7 imagine, surmise 8 conclude, construe 10 understand
to task: 3 rag 5 blame, decry, scold 6 berate, punish, rebuke 7 censure, contemn, reprove, tell off 8 denounce, reproach 9 inculpate, reprehend, reprimand 10 denunciate
to the cleaners: 3 gyp 4 bilk 6 fleece 7 deceive, defraud, swindle 8 hoodwink
turns: 4 vary 5 spell 6 rotate, switch 8 exchange, trade off 9 alternate, change off
umbrage: 6 object, resent
up: 4 lift 5 adopt, alter, renew, scoop, stand, start, study 6 assume, attack, choose, occupy, resume 7 address, embrace, espouse, proceed 8 commence, consider, continue, engage in, initiate, set about, stand for 10 monopolize, recommence
up quarters: 4 live, stay 5 abide, lodge, roost 6 occupy, reside, settle 7 inhabit, sojourn
up with: 4 join 8 befriend 9 associate
up (with): 7 consort
take __: 3 for, off, out, ten 4 a dip, a hit, a nap, a vow, back, care, down, five, hold, part, root, wing 5 a bath, a dive, after, a hike, apart, a peek, a rest, a risk, a seat, a stab, a trip, a walk, cover, heart, issue, place, shape, sides, steps, stock, turns 6 charge, effect, flight
take __ account: 4 into
take __ after: 3 off, out
take __ an answer: 5 no for
take __ a peg: 4 down
take __ at: 5 a shot, a stab
take __ breath: 5 a deep
take __ check: 5 a rain
take __ cleaners: 5 to the
take __ down: 5 lying
take __ for the worse: 5 a turn
take __ from: 4 a cue, away
take __ grain of salt: 5 with a
take __ granted: 3 for 5 it for
take __ in: 5 stock
take __ in the dark: 5 a shot
take __ leave it: 4 it or
take __ of: 4 care 6 notice 7 account
take __ off: 5 a load
take __ on: 4 pity 5 a toll, it out
take __ peg: 5 down a
take __ ride: 4 for a
take __ slack: 5 up the
take __ stride: 4 it in
take __ the chin: 4 it on
take __ the garden path: 4 down
take __ the lam: 4 it on
take __ the waist: 4 in at
take __ to: 6 kindly
take __ toll: 3 its
take __ view: 4 a dim
take-__: 5 along 6 alongs, charge
take-__ pay: 4 home
__ take: 5 on the 6 double
Take __: 4 a Bow, Down, Five, on Me, That
Take __!: 4 care, that 5 a seat
Take __ a compliment!: 4 it as
Take __ Care of My Baby: 4 Good
Take __ from me!: 4 a tip
Take __ leave it!: 4 it or
Take __ on the Reading: 5 a Ride
Take __ out of crime!: 5 a bite
Take __, She's Mine: 3 Her
Take __ song and make it better: 4 a sad
Take __ the Limit: 4 It to
Take __ to the Ball Game: 5 Me Out
Take __ Train: 4 The A
Take __ your leader: 4 me to
take a __: 4 bath, dive, hike, seat, walk 5 stand 6 powder
take a __ at: 4 shot, stab 5 whack
take a __ on: 4 toll
take a __ to: 5 shine
take a __ view: 3 dim
Take a Bow (1994 song) artist: Madonna
Take a Chance on Me (1978 song) artist: ABBA
take a crack __: 4 at it
take a dim __: 4 view
Take a Girl Like You author: Kingsley Amis
Take a hike!: 4 scat 5 scram 6 beat it 7 amscray, get lost 8 scramola
Take a Letter, Darling (1942 film)
cast: Fred MacMurray, Constance Moore, Rosalind Russell
director: Mitchell Leisen
Take a Letter Maria (1969 song) artist: R.B. Greaves
__ take all: 6 winner
__ Take an Old-Fashioned Walk: 4 Let's
...__ take arms...: 4 or to
take at one's __: 4 word
take by __: 5 storm 8 surprise
take-charge: 8 forceful
takedown: 7 lampoon
take down __: 4 a peg
Take Down (1978 film)
cast: Edward Herrmann, Lorenzo Lamas, Kathleen Lloyd
take down the __ path: 6 garden
Take Five (1961 song) artist: Dave Brubeck
take for __: 5 a ride 7 granted
Take Good Care of Her (1961 song) artist: Adam Wade
Take Good Care of My Baby (1961 song) artist: Bobby Vee
Take Good Care of My Baby singer: 3 Vee
Take Her, __ Mine: 4 She's
take-home: 3 net, pay 4 wage 5 wages
Takei, George role: 4 Sulu
take in __: 6 stride
take into __: 7 account
take it __: 5 out on
take it __ chin: 5 on the
take it __ lam: 5 on the
take it __ man: 5 like a
take it __ oneself: 4 upon
Take It Away (1982 song) artist: Paul McCartney
Take it easy!: 3 bye 4 ta-ta 5 adios, aloha, later, see ya 6 bye-bye, shalom, so long 7 goodbye 8 au revoir, sayonara
take it in __: 6 stride
take it like __: 4 a man
take it on the __: 3 lam 4 chin
Take It on the Run (1981 song) artist: REO Speedwagon
take it or leave it: 4 as is
take its __: 4 toll
Take It to the Limit (1976 song) artist: Eagles
Takelma: 6 Indian 7 Amerind
take lying __: 4 down
__ Take Manhattan: 3 I'll
Take Me __: 5 Along
Take Me __ Am: 3 as I
Take Me Home, Country Roads (1971 song) artist: John Denver
Take Me Home (song) artist: Cher, Phil Collins
Take Me Home Tonight (1986 song) artist: Eddie Money
Take Me Out to the Ball Game: 5 waltz
Take Me Out to the Ball Game (1949 film)
cast: Gene Kelly, Frank Sinatra, Esther Williams
director: Busby Berkeley
Take Me There (1998 song) artist: Mase, Mya
Take me to your __: 6 leader
Take my __, please!: 4 wife
taken: 3 occ. 4 rapt 5 burnt, in use 6 burned 8 occupied, reserved 9 preferred, spoken for
aback: 5 agape, fazed 6 shamed 7 abashed, ashamed, at a loss, fuddled, puzzled 9 astounded, befuddled, chagrined, flustered, in a dither, mortified, mystified, perplexed, staggered, stupefied, surprised 10 astonished, bewildered, bowled over, confounded, dumbstruck, speechless
advantage of: 4 used 7 put upon 9 exploited
alone: 5 per se
care of: 4 done 8 finished
down: 3 low, sad 4 blue, glum, mopy 5 moody, mopey 6 gloomy, morose 7 forlorn, unhappy 8 dejected, desolate, liverish, wretched 9 aggrieved, bummed-out, cheerless, depressed, in the pits, miserable, sorrowful, woebegone 10 despairing, despondent, dispirited, in the dumps, lugubrious, melancholy, out of sorts, spiritless
easily ~ in: 4 naif 5 naive 6 unwary 8 gullible, ignorant, lamblike, trustful, trusting, wide-eyed
for granted: 5 given, tacit 6 unsaid 7 assumed 8 implicit, unspoken, unstated, unvoiced 9 axiomatic 10 understood
not ~ care of: 5 unmet
not ~ in by: 4 onto
old-style: 4 taen
with: 4 into 8 obsessed, turned on 9 wild about
taken __: 4 with 5 aback
taken-back item: 4 repo
take notice in Latin: 8 nota bene
takeoff: 5 spoof, start 6 ascent, comedy, parody, satire, send-up 7 burlesk, lampoon, mockery 8 ridicule, travesty 9 beginning, burlesque, departure, imitation 10 caricature, impression
artist: 4 aper 5 mimic
do a ~: 3 ape 4 mime 5 mimic 8 simulate 9 duplicate
hr.: 3 ETD
vertical ~: 4 jato
take off __: 5 after
Take one!: 5 try it
take one's __: 4 part, time 5 leave
take one's __ away: 6 breath
take one's __ off to: 3 hat
Take on Me (1985 song) artist: A-HA
takeout
call for ~: 5 eat in, order 7 order in
counter call: 4 next
for ~: 4 to go
shop: 4 deli 8 pizzeria
take out __: 5 after, a loan
takeover: 3 LBO 4 coup 6 buyout, merger 7 triumph 9 coup d'état 10 assumption, occupation, usurpation
taker: 5 buyer, donee 6 better, bettor 8 acceptor, customer 9 con artist 10 pickpocket, plagiarist
odds ~: 6 player 7 gambler, wagerer 8 gamester
starter: 4 care, poll
__ taker: 6 census
__ Take Romance: 3 I'll
__ takers?: 3 Any
takes
what it ~: 5 drive, knack, savvy, skill 6 talent 7 ability, faculty, know-how, prowess 8 aptitude, capacity, facility, gumption 9 expertise, potential 10 capability, initiative, right stuff
__ Takes a Chance: 5 A Lady
__ Takes a Wife, The: 6 Doctor, Farmer
__ Takes Command: 5 Grant
__ Takes Time: 4 Love
take the __: 3 hit, rap 4 cake, fall, heat, road 5 bench, count, field, Fifth, floor, stand 6 plunge
take the __ by the horns: 4 bull
Take the High Ground (1953 film)
cast: Karl Malden, Elaine Stewart, Richard Widmark
director: Richard Brooks
Take the Money and Run (1969 film)
cast: Woody Allen, Janet Margolin
director: Woody Allen
Take the Money and Run (1976 song) artist: Steve Miller Band
Take These Chains From My Heart (1963 song) artist: Ray Charles
Take this!: 4 here
take to __: 4 task 5 heart
take to one's __: 5 heels
take to the __: 6 bricks
take up __: 4 with
take-up __: 4 reel
take up the __: 5 slack
take with a __ of salt: 5 grain
Take your time!: 6 no rush
takin: 5 bovid 6 bovine
relative: 3 yak 4 anoa, arna, gaur, urus, zebu 5 bison, gayal 6 mithan, muskox 7 aurochs, banteng, banting, beefalo, buffalo, carabao, cattalo, kouprey, tamarao, tamarau, timarau
taking: 5 sweet 7 receipt, winning, winsome 8 receipts 10 assumption
after: 3 à la
it easy: 5 still 8 inactive, unmoving 10 motionless
one's time: 3 lax 4 easy, lazy, slow 5 slack 6 calmly, casual, gentle, lazily, slowly 7 relaxed 8 casually, laid-back 9 gradually, languidly, unhurried 10 composedly, deliberate, indolently
out the garbage: 3 job 4 duty, task 5 chore 9 housework
__ taking: 6 profit
__-taking: 5 leave
Taking __ of Business: 4 Care
Taking Off (1971 film)
cast: Lynn Carlin, Buck Henry
director: Milos Forman
Taking of Pelham One Two Three, The (1974 film)
cast: Martin Balsam, Walter Matthau,

Robert Shaw
takings: 5 booty, yield 6 profit
Taklamakan: 6 desert
locale: 4 Asia 5 China
Tal: 7 Mikhail
tala: 5 money
Tala: 4 city, town
locale: 6 Mexico 7 Jalisco
talamba: 4 drum
origin: 10 Yugoslavia
talapoin: 7 primate
relative: 3 ape 4 saki, titi 5 chimp, drill, jocko, lemur, loris, magot, orang, potto, shrew 6 aye-aye, baboon, Bandar, galago, gelada, gibbon, grivet, guenon, howler, langur, macaco, monkey, rhesus, uakari, vervet 7 colobus, gorilla, guereza, hoolock, macaque, sapajou, siamang, tamarin, tarsier 8 bush baby, capuchin, mandrill, mangabey, marmoset 9 orangutan 10 Barbary ape, chimpanzee, orangutang
talar: 4 robe
talaria: 5 wings 7 sandals
like ~: 4 alar 5 alary
Talbot: 4 Lyle, Nita
Talbot Odyssey, The author: Nelson Demille
talc: 6 powder 7 mineral 8 steatite 9 soapstone 10 bath powder
to Mohs: 3 one
Talca: 4 city, town
locale: 5 Chile
Talcahuano: 4 city, town
locale: 5 Chile
talcum __: 6 powder
Talcum is walcum poet: 4 Nash
tale: 3 fib, lie 4 epic, myth, saga, yarn 5 fable, novel, rumor, spiel, story 6 canard, excuse, legend, report 7 account, evasion, fiction, megilla, parable, recital, romance, scandal, slander, untruth, version, western, whapper, whopper 8 anecdote, chestnut, relation, sob story, whodunit 9 chronicle, deception, dime novel, falsehood, fish story, folk story, invention, mendacity, moonshine, narration, narrative, recountal, rigmarole, tall story 10 concoction, fairy story, inaccuracy, short story, taradiddle
ancient ~: 4 myth 5 fable
contrived a ~: 4 wove
ender: 6 bearer, teller 7 bearing
epigrammatic ~: 4 myth, tale, yarn 5 story 6 legend 7 parable 8 allegory
fairy ~: 4 yarn 5 story 7 romance
fairy ~ villain: 5 giant 7 monster
heroic ~: 4 edda, epic, gest, saga 5 conte, geste
in Britain: 4 rede
malicious ~: 5 rumor 6 canard 7 untruth 9 falsehood
starter: 4 folk, tell 6 tattle
tall ~: 4 yarn 5 story 9 invention
tell a ~: 4 spin 7 narrate
teller: 4 liar 7 tattler
tale __: 5 of woe
__ tale: 3 old 4 folk, tall 5 fairy
Tale __ Cities, A: 5 of Two
Tale __ Tub: 3 of a
__ Tale, A: 5 Bronx 7 Winter's
__-Tale Heart, The: 4 Tell
Talence: 4 city, town
locale: 6 France
talent: 3 ace 4 bent, gift, head, nose, turn, whiz 5 craft, flair, forte, knack, money, power, skill, touch 6 artist, genius 7 ability, faculty, know-how, prodigy, promise, prowess 8 aptitude, artistry, capacity, facility 9 endowment, ingenuity 10 capability, green thumb, right stuff
have no ~: 5 stink
having ~: 4 able
scout: 3 rep 5 agent 8 promoter 9 middleman
seeker: 5 scout
show device: 4 gong
talent __: 4 show 5 scout
talented: 3 ace 4 deft, good 5 adept, crack 6 adroit, clever, gifted 7 capable 8 artistic, masterly, skillful 9 ingenious, masterful, promising, qualified, versatile 10 artistical, precocious, proficient
be ~: 3 top 4 lead 5 excel, outdo, shine 7 surpass 8 outclass, outshine, outstrip 10 overshadow
Talented Mr. Ripley, The: 4 film 5 novel
author: Patricia Highsmith
cast: Cate Blanchett, Matt Damon, Jude Law, Gwyneth Paltrow
director: Anthony Minghella
tale of __: 3 woe
Tale of __ Saltan, The: 4 Tsar
Tale of a Tub, The author: Jonathan Swift
Tale of Benjamin Bunny, The author: Beatrix Potter
Tale of Genji, The author: Murasaki Shikibu
Tale of Jerusalem, A author: Edgar Allan Poe
Tale of Peter Rabbit, The author: Beatrix Potter
Tale of the Body Thief, The author: Anne Rice
Tale of the Ragged Mounains, A author: Edgar Allan Poe
Tale of the Tape measure: 5 reach 6 weight
Tale of Tom Kitten, The author: Beatrix Potter
Tale of Two Cities, A: 4 film 5 novel
author: Charles Dickens
cast: Elizabeth Allan, Ronald Colman, Edna May Oliver
character: 3 Cly 5 Lorry, Lucie, Pross, Roger 6 Carton, Darnay, Ernest, Jarvis, Sydney 7 Charles, Defarge, Gaspard, Manette, Stryver, Thérèse 8 Roger Cly 9 Alexander
director: Jack Conway
setting: 5 Paris 6 France, London 7 England
tales: 4 lore 7 legends
tell ~: 3 gab, yak 4 blab, dish 6 gossip, tattle 8 schmooze
Tales __ Jazz Age: 5 of the
Tales __ South Pacific: 5 of the
Tales __ the Hood: 4 From
Tales __ Wayside Inn: 3 of a
__ tale's best for winter: 4 A sad
Talese. Gay: 6 author, writer
work: Fame and Obscurity
Honor Thy Father
The Kingdom and the Power
Thy Neighbor's Wife
Unto the Sons
Tales from Shakespeare author: 4 Elia, Lamb
Tales From the Crypt
like ~: 4 eery 5 eerie
Tales From the Hood (1995 film)
cast: Lamont Bentley, Corbin Bernsen, De'Aundre Bonds
director: Rusty Cundieff
Tales from the Vienna Woods composer: 7 Strauss
Tales of Adventure author: Jack London
Tales of a Wayside Inn: 4 poem
author: 10 Longfellow
town: 4 Atri
Tales of Hoffman: 5 opera
character: 6 Andrès, Luther, Stella 7 Antonia, Hermann, Lindorf, Olympia 9 Coppélius, Giulietta, Nathaniel 10 Nicklausse
composer: 9 Offenbach
setting: 5 Italy 6 Munich, Venice 7 Germany 9 Nuremberg
Tales of Manhattan (1942 film)
cast: Charles Boyer, Henry Fonda, Rita Hayworth
Tales of Terror (1962 film)
cast: Peter Lorre, Vincent Price, Basil Rathbone
director: Roger Corman
Tales of the Jazz Age author: F. Scott Fitzgerald
Tales of the South Pacific author: James A. Michener
Tales of the Wolf author: Lawrence Sanders
Tales of Wells Fargo (NBC western)
cast: Dale Robertson (Jim Hardie)
__ Tale, The: 6 Reeve's 7 Winter's
tale told by an __, A: 5 idiot
tali: 10 ankle bones
Talia: 5 Shire
talinka: 4 wind 5 flute
origin: 6 Europe
__ talionis: 3 lex
talipot: 4 palm, tree
Talisa: 4 Soto
talisman: 4 mojo 5 charm, spell 6 amulet, scarab 7 periapt
Talisman, The author: Stephen King, Walter Scott
Talitha: 4 star
talk: 3 gab, jaw, lip, rap, rot, say, yak 4 bunk, buzz, cant, chat, hint, jive, sing, vent, word, yack, yarn 5 argot, argue, drawl, drone, forum, lingo, noise, orate, pitch, prate, prose, rumor, run on, slang, speak, spiel, spout, stump, utter, visit, voice, words 6 accost, babble, banter, broach, confab, confer, dialog, earful, gabble, gossip, homily, hot air, huddle, inform, intone, jabber, jargon, mumble, parley, patois, patter, powwow, preach, racket, reason, relate, report, reveal, rumble, rumors, screed, sermon, speech, squeak, squeal, tattle 7 address, blather, blether, bombast, buzzing, canvass, chatter, chime in, commune, confess, confide, consult, contact, declaim, descant, dialect, dictate, discant, discuss, divulge, express, hearsay, lecture, meeting, monolog, network, oration, palaver, prattle, rubbish, scandal, seminar, tell all 8 badinage, causerie, chitchat, colloquy, converse, dialogue, exchange, harangue, innuendo, interact, language, locution, nonsense, parlance, persuade, raillery, rattle on, reach out, verbiage, vocalize 9 comment on, discourse, grapevine, hold forth, interface, interview, monologue, negotiate, pronounce, soliloquy, symposium, tête-à-tête, thrash out, touch base, utterance, verbalize 10 articulate, chew the fat, chew the rag, discussion, groupthink, peroration, persiflage, prelection, recitation, rhapsodize, vocalizing
about: 5 state 7 clarify, comment, discuss, mention 8 report on, set forth, spell out 9 interpret
amorously: 3 coo
baby ~: 3 goo, mom 4 lisp, mama, papa 5 mamma 6 goo-goo
back: 4 sass 5 react 6 answer 7 respond 8 get fresh, mouth off
back ~: 3 jaw, lip 4 echo, guff, sass 5 cheek, mouth, reply, sauce 8 defiance, reaction, response 9 impudence, insolence, wisemouth 10 smartmouth
big: 4 brag, crow 5 boast, vaunt 6 overdo 7 bluster, lay it on 9 gasconade
big ~: 9 hyperbole 10 pretension
chalk ~: 6 lesson, speech 7 address, lecture, oration 8 training
don't ~: 6 clam up
down: 3 pan 5 knock 8 belittle, derogate, minimize 9 criticize, disparage, underplay 10 depreciate
down to: 5 agree, deign, lower, stoop, yield 9 acquiesce, patronize, vouchsafe 10 condescend
effusively: 4 gush, rave 9 pour forth
empty ~: 3 gas, pap 4 wind 5 prate 6 humbug
ender: 4 back, fest
fast ~: 4 bull, bunk 5 prate 6 banter, hot air, humbug, patter 7 baloney, blarney, blather 8 malarkey 9 banana oil 10 applesauce, balderdash
foolish ~: 3 rot, yap 4 bosh, bull, bunk, guff, jazz, jive, pooh, tosh, yaup, yawp 5 bilge, fudge, hokum, hooey, prate, stuff, trash, tripe 6 bunkum, bushwa, drivel, footle, gabble, gammon, gibber, havers, hot air, humbug, jabber, jargon, kibosh, piffle 7 baloney, blarney, blather, blether, boloney, bushwah, eyewash, flannel, flubdub, fustian, garbage, hogwash, inanity, rubbish, twaddle 8 buncombe, claptrap, falderal, falderol, flimflam, flummery, folderal, folderol, nonsense, slipslop, tommyrot, trumpery 9 banana oil, gibberish, kidstakes, moonshine, poppycock, rigmarole 10 applesauce, balderdash, bilge water, codswallop, flapdoodle, galimatias, Jabberwock, mumbo jumbo, rigamarole
formal ~: 6 speech 7 oration
fresh ~: 3 lip 4 guff, sass 5 cheek, sauce 9 impudence, insolence, sauciness
full of back ~: 5 lippy
give a ~: 5 orate, speak 6 preach 7 address, declaim, deliver, expound, lecture 9 discourse, hold forth
give a pep ~: 4 urge 6 charge 8 admonish 9 encourage
have a ~ with: 3 see
hoarsely: 4 rasp
idle ~: 3 gab, gas, yap 4 wind 5 mouth, prate 6 babble, cackle, gossip 8 babbling, chitchat 9 loquacity
idly: 5 prate 6 babble, gibber 7 blather, blether
insider ~: 5 argot, idiom, lingo 6 jargon, patois
insincere ~: 4 cant, jive 6 bunkum 8 buncombe
into: 3 con 4 coax, goad 6 reason 7 win over 8 convince, persuade 9 prevail on
jive ~: 5 argot, lingo, slang 6 patois 8 parlance 10 vernacular
like: 3 ape 4 echo, mock 5 mimic 6 follow, mirror, parrot 7 copycat, imitate, portray 8 resemble, ridicule 9 make fun of
like a child: 4 lisp
local ~: 5 lingo 6 patois
loose ~: 6 gossip 7 hearsay

low: 7 whisper
monotonously: 5 drone, whine
nonsense: 4 jive 5 prate 6 footle, gabble, ramble, wander 7 blather, blether
out of: 5 deter 6 reason 8 dissuade 10 discourage
over: 6 air out 7 discuss, hash out 9 bat around 10 deliberate, kick around
over again: 6 rehash
pep ~: 6 speech 7 address, lecture, oration
playful ~: 5 humor 6 banter, joking 7 jesting, joshing, kidding, ribbing, teasing 8 badinage, chitchat, raillery, repartee 10 persiflage
rhythmically: 3 rap
session: 5 forum 8 assembly, colloquy 9 symposium 10 conference
slowly: 5 drawl
small ~: 4 chat 6 banter, gossip 7 palaver 8 babbling, chitchat
starter: 4 shop 5 cross
straight: 5 level
street ~: 5 slang
sweet ~: 4 sell 7 blarney, coaxing, palaver 8 cajolery 9 wheedling 10 endearment, inducement, persuasion
table ~: 3 gab, rap 5 prate 6 banter, gabble, gibber, gossip 7 chatter, palaver 8 chin-chin, chitchat, repartee
tech ~: 5 lingo 6 jargon
the talk: 4 brag 5 boast 6 flaunt, parade 7 show off, swagger 10 grandstand
to: 7 contact 8 approach 9 interview 10 get a hold of
too much: 3 gab, gas, jaw, yak, yap 5 drone, run on 6 ramble, rattle 7 drone on
unclearly: 4 slur 6 babble
up: 4 hype, plug, push, tout 7 promote, push for 8 ballyhoo 9 get behind, publicize
wildly: 4 rant, rave
worthless ~: 3 gas, rot 4 blah, bosh, bull, bunk, guff, jazz, jive, pooh, tosh 5 bilge, fudge, hokum, hooey, prate, stuff, trash 6 bunkum, bushwa, drivel, footle, gabble, gammon, gibber, havers, hot air, humbug, jabber, jargon, kibosh, piffle 7 baloney, blarney, blather, bushwah, eyewash, flannel, flubdub, fustian, garbage, hogwash, inanity, rubbish, twaddle 8 buncombe, claptrap, falderal, flimflam, flummery, folderal, nonsense, slipslop, tommyrot, trumpery 9 banana oil, gibberish, kidstakes, moonshine, poppycock, rigmarole 10 applesauce, balderdash, bilge water, codswallop, double-talk, empty words, flapdoodle, galimatias, Jabberwock, mumbo jumbo, rigamarole, taradiddle

talk __: 3 big, out 4 back, down, into, over, shop, show 5 radio, sense 6 around, turkey
__ talk: 3 big, pep 4 baby, back, girl, town 5 chalk, cross, sales, small, sweet, table 6 pillow
__ talk?: 5 Can we
__-talk: 4 fast 6 double, smooth
Talk __ Town, The: 5 of the
__ Talk: 4 Baby 5 Happy 6 Pillow
talkathon: 7 gabfest 10 filibuster
talkative: 4 glib, long 5 gabby, slick, vocal, windy, wordy 6 chatty, fluent, mouthy, prolix, smooth 7 diffuse, gossipy, lengthy, unterse, verbose, voluble 8 effusive, eloquent, rambling, rattling 9 bombastic, expansive, garrulous 10 articulate, bigmouthed, chattering, discursive, long-winded, loquacious, palaverous
less ~: 5 muter
one: 6 gasbag, gossip, magpie, yakker 8 prattler 10 chatterbox
talkativeness: 9 garrulity, loquacity, prolixity, verbosity, wordiness
talked: 5 spoke
at length: 5 ran on
impolitely: 5 swore
old-style: 5 spake
talker: 6 orator 7 speaker 8 lecturer
excessive ~: 6 gossip, magpie, yakker 8 prattler
proverbial ~: 5 money
__ talker: 5 shelf
talkie: 4 film, show 5 flick, movie 7 picture
attraction: 5 sound
__-talkie: 6 walkie
__ Talkin': 4 Jive
talking
not ~: 3 mum 4 mute 5 quiet 6 silent 8 nonvocal, taciturn 9 voiceless 10 speechless
stop ~: 6 shut up 8 pipe down
talking __: 4 book, down, head 5 chief, point 7 machine, picture
__-talking: 5 trash
Talking __: 5 Heads
Talking Peace author: 6 Carter
talking-to: 6 rebuke 7 lecture 8 reproval, scolding 9 reprimand 10 upbraiding
Talking Trees, The author: Sean O'Faolain
__ Talkin' Guy: 5 Sweet
Talk is __: 5 cheap
talk it __: 4 over
Talk of Angels (1998 film)
cast: Frances McDormand, Franco Nero, Vincent Perez, Polly Walker
director: Nick Hamm
Talk of the Town, The (1942 film)
cast: Jean Arthur, Ronald Colman, Cary Grant
director: George Stevens
Talk Radio (1988 film)
cast: Alec Baldwin, Eric Bogosian, Ellen Greene
director: Oliver Stone
__ Talks: 5 Garbo
talk show
host: 4 Leno, Paar 5 Allen, Dinah, Oprah, Rosie, Shore 6 Carson 7 Winfrey 8 O'Donnell 9 Letterman
partner: 6 cohost
radio ~ participant: 6 caller
talk through one's __: 3 hat
Talk to Me (1985 song) artist: Stevie Nicks
__ Talk to Strangers: 4 Don't
talky: 5 wordy 6 chatty 7 verbose, voluble 9 garrulous 10 bigmouthed, long-winded, loquacious
tall: 3 big 4 high, lank, long, size 5 giant, great, lanky, lathy, leggy, lofty, rangy, steep 6 absurd, alpine, gangly 7 sizable, sky-high, soaring, willowy 8 elevated, gangling, sizeable, towering, uplifted 9 overblown 10 exorbitant, far-fetched, improbable, long-legged, statuesque
in Spanish: 4 alto
stand ~: 5 tower
standing ~: 4 bold, game 5 brave, gutsy, nervy, tough 6 gritty, heroic, plucky, strong 7 assured, doughty, valiant 8 fearless, heroical, resolute, unafraid, valorous 9 confident, dauntless, undaunted 10 courageous, mettlesome, redblooded
tale: 3 lie 4 yarn 5 story 9 invention
tall __: 3 oil, one 4 tale 5 drink, order, story
tall, __, and handsome: 4 dark
__ tall: 5 stand 7 walking
Tallahassee: 4 city, town 7 capital
athletes: 9 Seminoles
county: 4 Leon
locale: 3 Fla. 7 Florida
school: 3 FSU
Tallahassee Lassie (1959 song) artist: Freddy Cannon
Tallchief, Maria: 6 dancer 8 danseuse 9 ballerina
taller, get: 4 grow
Talley's Folly author: Lanford Wilson
Tallinn: 4 city, port, town 7 capital
locale: 7 Estonia
native: 4 Esth
Tall in the Saddle (1944 film): 5 oater
cast: Ward Bond, Ella Raines, John Wayne
director: Edwin L. Marin
tallith feature: 6 fringe
tallness: 5 reach 6 height, length 7 stature 8 altitude 9 elevation
tallow: 4 lard, suet 6 grease 9 lubricate
acid in ~: 5 oleic
combining form: 5 steat- 6 steato-
product: 4 soap 6 candle
Tall Paul (1959 song) artist: Annette Funicello
__ Tall Sally: 4 Long
Tall Target, The (1951 film)
cast: Adolphe Menjou, Dick Powell, Paula Raymond
director: Anthony Mann
Tall T, The (1957 film)
cast: Richard Boone, Maureen O'Sullivan, Randolph Scott
Tallulah: 8 Bankhead
tally: 3 add, sum 4 gybe, jibe, list, poll, tell 5 add up, agree, chalk, count, gauge, score, sum up, total, tot up 6 census, figure, notate, number, reckon, record, square, voting 7 account, catalog, chalk up, compute, conform, itemize 8 check out, coincide, mark down, numerate, register 9 calculate, catalogue, enumerate, head count, inventory, keep count, keep score, reckoning 10 bottom line, correspond, count heads
mark: 5 notch
tally __: 4 card 5 sheet
Talmadge: 5 Norma
Talmadge Girls, The author: Anita Loos
Talman: 7 William
Tal, Mikhail forte: 5 chess
Talmud
follower: 3 Jew
language: 6 Hebrew
scholar: 4 gaon 5 rabbi, rebbe
section: 6 Gemara
Talmud __: 5 Torah
talon: 4 claw 6 ungual, unguis
Taltos author: Anne Rice
talus: 4 bone 5 ankle, scree
decoration: 6 anklet
tam: 3 cap, hat, lid 8 balmoral
cousin: 5 beret
wearer: 4 Scot
Tama: 4 city, town 8 Janowitz
locale: 5 Japan
__ tamale: 3 hot
Tamale: 4 city, town
locale: 5 Ghana
Tamar
brother of ~: 7 Absalom
father of ~: 5 David 7 Absalom
Tamara: 7 Jenkins 9 Karsavina
Tamarac: 4 city, town
locale: 7 Florida
tamarack: 4 tree 5 larch
relative: 3 fir 4 pine 6 spruce 7 hemlock
tamarau: 5 bovid 6 bovine
relative: 3 yak 4 anoa, arna, gaur, urus, zebu 5 bison, gayal, takin 6 mithan, muskox 7 aurochs, banteng, banting, beefalo, buffalo, carabao, cattalo, kouprey
tamarin: 6 animal 7 primate
relative: 3 ape 4 saki, titi 5 chimp, drill, jocko, lemur, loris, magot, orang, potto, shrew 6 aye-aye, baboon, Bandar, galago, gelada, gibbon, grivet, guenon, howler, langur, macaco, monkey, rhesus, uakari, vervet 7 colobus, gorilla, guereza, hoolock, macaque, sapajou, siamang, tarsier 8 bush baby, capuchin, mandrill, mangabey, marmoset, talapoin 9 orangutan 10 Barbary ape, chimpanzee, orangutang
tamarind: 4 tree 5 fruit 6 veggie 9 vegetable
family: 6 legume
relative: 3 koa 5 carob 6 cassia, cercis, locust, padauk, padouk, redbud 7 araroba, mesquit 8 mesquite 9 poinciana
Tamarind Seed, The (1974 film)
cast: Julie Andrews, Anthony Quayle, Omar Sharif, Sylvia Syms
director: Blake Edwards
tamarisk: 4 atle, tree 5 plant, shrub 6 flower
Tamaulipas: 5 state 7 Mexican
city: 6 Aldama, Madero 7 El Mante, Miramar, Reynosa, Tampico 8 Altamira, Río Bravo, Victoria 9 Matamoros
tambac: 5 alloy
component: 4 zinc 6 copper
tambala: 5 money
Tamblyn: 4 Russ
Tambor: 7 Jeffrey
tambour: 4 drum
tambourin: 5 dance
tambourine: 3 riq 4 drum 6 chimta 8 pandéiro
__ Tambourine: 5 Green
tambura: 4 lute 6 string
origin: 5 India 10 Yugoslavia
Tamburlaine the Great author: Christopher Marlowe
tame: 4 bust, curb, dull, flat, meek, mild, slow, weak 5 bland, break, check, train, unfun, vapid, yoked 6 boring, bridle, broken, busted, docile, feeble, gentle, govern, jejune, pacify, placid, pliant, soften, subdue, temper 7 conquer, diluted, enslave, harness, humdrum, insipid, muzzled, prosaic, repress, routine, subdued, tedious, trained 8 amenable, biddable, domestic, harmless, lamblike, obedient, restrain, sheepish, suppress, tone down, unafraid, unlively 9 civilized, colorless, compliant, dry-as-dust, harnessed, prosaical, subjugate, tractable, wearisome 10 cultivated, dullsville, manageable, monotonous, spiritless, submissive, unexciting, white-bread
tamed: 6 broken 7 crushed, subdued 10 spiritless
tamer: 6 catman 9 Petruchio 10 roughrider
need: 4 hoop, whip
place: 6 circus
Tamerlane: 5 Timur
Tamerlane author: Edgar Allan Poe

Tam Glen author: Robert Burns
Tamiami: 4 city, town
locale: 7 Florida
Tamiami __: 5 Trail
__ Tamid: 3 Ner
Tamil: 5 Asian 8 language
Tamil Nadu capital: 6 Madras
Taming of the Shrew, The: 4 film, play
author: William Shakespeare
cast: Richard Burton, Elizabeth Taylor
character: 3 Sly 6 Bianca, Curtis, Gremio, Grumio, Tranio 8 Baptista, Lucentio 9 Biondello, Hortensio, Katharina, Petruchio, Vincentio 11 Christopher
director: Franco Zeffirelli
setting: 5 Italy, Padua
Tamiroff, Akim: 5 actor
film: Anastasia (1956)
The Corsican Brothers (1941)
Five Graves to Cairo (1943)
For Whom the Bell Tolls (1943)
The General Died at Dawn (1936)
The Great McGinty (1940)
The Jungle Princess (1936)
Pardon My Past (1945)
Thieves' Holiday (1946)
T.A.M.I. Show, The (1964 film)
cast: Chuck Berry, James Brown, Rolling Stones
director: Steve Binder
Tammany Hall foe: 4 Nast
Tammi: 7 Terrell
tammie: 6 fabric 8 material
Tamm, Igor: 8 Nobelist 9 physicist
Tammuz: 5 month 6 Hebrew
predecessor: 5 Sivan
successor: 2 Av
tammy: 6 fabric 8 material
Tammy: 6 Grimes 7 Wynette
Tammy (1957 song)
artist: Ames Brothers, Debbie Reynolds
Tammy __ Bakker: 4 Faye
Tammy and the Bachelor (1957 film)
cast: Walter Brennan, Leslie Nielsen, Debbie Reynolds
tam-o'-shanter: 3 cap, hat
Tam O'Shanter author: Robert Burns
tamp: 3 jam, ram 4 cram, pack 7 pat down 8 pack down, push down 9 pound down
Tampa: 3 bay 4 city, port, town
athletes: 5 Bulls
city near ~: 5 Largo 6 St. Pete
clock setting: 3 EDT, EST
locale: 3 Fla. 7 Florida
newspaper: 4 Trib 7 Tribune
pro team: 9 Devil Rays, Lightning 10 Buccaneers
school: 3 USF
tamper: 3 cut, fix, rig 4 cook 5 alter, bribe, get to, plant, reach, spike 6 butt in, change, doctor, fiddle, horn in, meddle, tinker 7 corrupt, intrude, phony up 8 mess with 9 interfere, interlope, muck about 10 fiddle with, manipulate
don't ~ with: 5 let be 7 leave be 8 let alone 10 deregulate
with: 3 fix, rig 5 fudge 6 change, damage, doctor, juggle, monkey
(with): 6 fiddle, monkey
Tampere: 4 city, town
locale: 7 Finland
Tampico: 4 city, port, town
locale: 6 Mexico 10 Tamaulipas
see also Spanish
Tampico __: 4 hemp 5 fiber
tam-tam: 4 bell, gong 5 chime 10 percussion
TAMU
conference: 9 Big Twelve
see also Texas A&M
Tamuín: 4 city, town
locale: 6 Mexico
Tamworth: 3 pig 5 swine
tan: 3 sun 4 buff, drab, drub, flog, lick, sand, whip 5 brown, color, cream, flail, olive, spank, taupe 6 almond, bronze, darken, defeat, larrup, saddle, swarth, thrash, thwack, wallop 7 bronzed, natural, neutral, scourge, swarthy 8 brownish, sunbathe 9 yellowish 10 light brown, olive-brown
a hide: 6 punish
get a ~: 3 sun 4 bask 8 sunbathe
leather: 4 cure
relative: 3 bay, dun 4 bole, ecru, fawn, foxy, nude, seal 5 amber, beige, camel, cocoa, hazel, khaki, mocha, sepia, tawny, umber 6 auburn, bister, bistre, bronze, coffee, copper, ginger, russet, sienna, sorrel, walnut 7 biscuit, caramel, dogwood 8 chestnut, cinnamon, mahogany 9 butternut, chocolate
starter: 3 sun
tan __: 3 oak
__ tan: 3 arc 7 mayfair
__-tan: 3 fan
Tana: 4 lake 5 river
locale: 5 Kenya 8 Ethiopia
tanager: 4 bird, yeni 5 lindo
__ tanager: 6 summer 7 scarlet, western
Tanaina: 6 Indian 7 Amerind
Tanaka, Koichi: 7 chemist 8 Nobelist
Tan, Amy: 6 author, writer
work: The Bonesetter's Daughter
The Hundred Secret Senses
The Joy Luck Club
The Kitchen God's Wife
Moon Lady
The Opposite of Fate
Sagwa, the Chinese Siamese Cat
Tanana: 5 Frank, river 6 Indian 7 Amerind
locale: 6 Alaska
Tanana, Frank sport: 8 baseball
Tanaro, city on the: 4 Asti
Tancredi composer: 7 Rossini
tandan: 4 fish
tandem __: 4 bike 7 bicycle, trailer
tandoor: 4 oven
tandoori-baked bread: 3 nan
__ T. and the MGs: 6 Booker
Tandy, Jessica: 7 actress
film: The Birds (1963)
Butley (1974)
Cocoon (1985)
The Desert Fox (1951)
Driving Miss Daisy (1989, AA)
Fried Green Tomatoes (1991)
Nobody's Fool (1994)
A Woman's Vengeance (1947)
spouse: Hume Cronyn, Jack Hawkins
Tandy product: 2 PC 8 computer
tang: 3 nip, zip 4 bite, hint, kick, odor, zest 5 aroma, drink, punch, sapor, savor, scent, smack, smell, spice, taste 6 flavor, relish 8 piquancy, pungency 9 sharpness, spiciness 10 aftertaste
lacking ~: 5 bland, vapid
T'ang: 7 Chinese, dynasty
capital: 4 Sian
follower ~: 4 Liao
Tanga: 4 city, town
locale: 8 Tanzania
Tanganyika: 4 lake
locale: 5 Zaire 6 Africa 8 Tanzania
tangelo: 4 tree, ugli 5 fruit 6 citrus
relative: 4 lime 5 lemon, navel 6 orange, pomelo, tangor 7 kumquat, satsuma, Seville 8 bergamot, mandarin, shaddock, Valencia 9 tangerine 10 calamondin, grapefruit
tangent: 4 tack 5 ratio
cousin: 4 sine 6 cosine, secant
go off on a ~: 5 stray 6 ramble, wander 7 digress
Tangent Factor, The author: Lawrence Sanders
tangential: 4 side 6 beside 7 close by 8 touching 9 alongside, bordering, excursive, proximate 10 digressive, side-by-side
remark: 5 aside 10 digression
to: 4 near
Tangent Objective, The author: Lawrence Sanders
tangerine: 4 tree 5 color, fruit 6 citrus, orange 7 reddish, satsuma
relative: 4 lime, Ugli 5 flame, henna, lemon, navel 6 orange, pomelo, tangor 7 kumquat, pumpkin, saffron, satsuma, Seville, tangelo 8 bergamot, hyacinth, mandarin, shaddock, Valencia 10 calamondin, grapefruit, terra cotta
tangibility: 7 reality
tangible: 4 real 5 solid 6 actual 7 evident, obvious, visible 8 concrete, definite, embodied, explicit, manifest, material, palpable, physical 9 corporeal, objective, touchable 10 detectable, observable, unimagined, verifiable
Tangier: 4 city, port, town
locale: 7 Morocco
tanginess: 4 zest, zing 6 flavor
tangle: 3 mat, mix, mop, web 4 coil, foul, kink, knot, maze, mesh, mess, muss, snag, trap 5 mix up, skein, snarl, twist 6 enlace, enmesh, entrap, immesh, inmesh, jumble, jungle, morass, muddle, ruffle, rumple, tousle, touzle 7 clutter, embroil, ensnare, insnare, mistake, quarrel, sinuate 8 dishevel, entangle 9 confusion, implicate, labyrinth, patchwork 10 disarrange, intertwine, interweave
with: 3 box, vie 4 feud, spar 5 argue, brawl, clash, fight 6 attack, bicker, combat, defend, go at it, hassle, oppose, resist, rumble, take on 7 contend, dispute, grapple, lay into, mix it up, protest, quarrel, scuffle, wage war, wrangle 8 do battle, squabble 9 altercate, challenge, scrimmage, square off 10 put up a fuss
tangled: 5 afoul, kinky 6 knotty, matted, thorny 7 chaotic, complex, jumbled, knotted, mixed up, tousled 8 involved, pell-mell 9 difficult, intricate 10 disorderly, topsy-turvy
get ~: 3 mat 4 knot 5 snarl, twist
Tanglewood Festival locale: 4 Mass. 5 Lenox
tango: 5 dance, music
feature: 3 dip
requirement: 3 duo, two 4 pair 6 couple 7 twosome
__ Tango: 4 Blue
Tango and __: 4 Cash
Tango author: Slawomir Mrozek
__ Tango in Bayreuth: 4 Last
__ Tango in Paris: 4 Last
tangor: 5 fruit 6 citrus
relative: 4 lime, ugli 5 lemon, navel 6 orange, pomelo 7 kumquat, satsuma, Seville, tangelo 8 bergamot, mandarin, shaddock, Valencia 9 tangerine 10 calamondin, grapefruit
Tanguay: 3 Eva
Tanguy, Yves: 6 artist 7 painter
homeland: 6 France
tangy: 4 tart 5 minty, salty, zesty, zippy 6 acetic, biting, lemony, savory 7 piquant, pungent 9 flavorful
tania: 4 taro
tank: 3 vat 4 pool 6 panzer 7 cistern, Sherman, vehicle 8 aquarium 9 container, reservoir
closer: 6 gas cap
filler: 3 gas 4 fuel 8 gasoline
fill the ~: 4 fuel 5 gas up
level: 4 full 5 empty
starter: 4 anti
think ~ output: 6 notion, theory 7 concept 8 proposal 10 brainstorm
top: 5 shirt
when ~ warfare began: 3 WWI
tank __: 3 car, top 4 farm, suit, town 5 truck 7 farming, fighter, trailer
__ tank: 3 gas 5 glass, scuba, spray, think 6 septic 7 heeling, holding, Sherman, whippet
tanka: 4 poem 8 Japanese
kin: 5 haiku
tankard: 3 mug, pot 5 stein
contents: 3 ale 4 beer 5 stout 6 porter
tanker: 4 boat, ship 5 oiler 6 vessel
cargo: 3 oil 5 crude 8 crude oil
insignia, once: 4 Esso
leak: 5 spill
__ tanker: 3 oil, ore 6 aerial, parcel
tankful: 3 gas
Tank Girl actor: 4 Ice-T
tanned: 5 brown 6 bronze, bronzy
not ~: 4 pale
starter: 3 sun
tannenbaum: 3 fir
tanner, name meaning: 6 Barker, Garver, Gerber 7 Currier
Tanners' houseguest: 3 Alf
Tannhäuser: 5 opera
composer: 6 Wagner
role: 5 Venus 7 Hermann, Wolfram 9 Elisabeth
setting: 7 Germany 9 Thuringia
song: 4 aria
tannic __: 4 acid
tanning: 7 licking 8 flailing, flogging, whipping
bark for ~: 5 sumac 6 sumach
need: 3 sun 4 hide
solution: 4 bate
tanning __: 3 bed 6 parlor
tanning-lotion letters: 3 SPF 4 PABA
tannin source: 5 sumac 6 sumach
tan one's __: 4 hide
tantalite: 3 ore
tantalize: 4 bait 5 charm, taunt, tease, worry 6 entice, lead on 7 provoke, torment 8 interest 9 fascinate, frustrate, titillate
tantalizing: 5 juicy, siren 8 tempting
tantalum: 5 metal 7 element
Tantalus
daughter of ~: 5 Niobe
father of ~: 4 Zeus
son of ~: 6 Pelops 7 Broteas
wife of ~: 12 Clytemnestra
tantamount: 4 like, same 5 equal 6 as good, on a par 9 duplicate, identical 10 comparable, coordinate, equivalent
tantara: 5 blare 7 fanfare 8 flourish
tante: 4 aunt 6 French
possession: 5 plume
spouse: 5 oncle
tanto: 6 so much 7 too much
tantrum: 3 fit 4 rage, snit, tiff 5 scene, storm 6 blowup, temper 7 flare-up, rampage 8 outburst, paroxysm 9 explosion, hysterics 10 conniption
throw a ~: 4 rant
thrower: 3 imp 4 brat 5 child 9 youngster
__ tantrum: 6 temper
Tanya: 6 Tucker 7 Roberts
Tanzania: 6 nation 7 country

capital: 6 Dodoma
city: 5 Mbeya, Moshi, Tanga, Ujiji 6 Dodoma, Iringa, Kigoma, Mtwara, Musoma, Mwanza, Songea, Tabora 8 Morogoro, Zanzibar
island: 5 Pemba 8 Zanzibar
lake: 5 Nyasa 6 Malawi 8 Victoria 10 Tanganyika
language: 5 Masai 6 Maasai
locale: 3 Afr. 6 Africa
money: 4 cent 5 senti 8 shilling
mountain: 4 Meru
neighbor: 5 Kenya 6 Malawi, Rwanda, Uganda, Zambia 7 Burundi 10 Mozambique
people: 3 Yao 5 Chaga, Makua, Masai, Ngoni, Nguni 6 Chagga, Dorobo, Maasai, Sukuma 7 Makonde 8 Nyamwezi 9 Wandorobo
region: 5 Tanga
tanzanite: 3 gem 8 gemstone
Tao
homophone: 3 Dow
literally: 3 way
Taoajós: 5 river
locale: 6 Brazil
Taoism: 3 rel. 9 religiion
power in ~: 3 teh
Tao of Pooh, The author: 4 Hoff
Taormina mount: 4 Etna 5 Aetna
Taos: 4 city, town 6 Indian 7 Amerind
locale: 4 N. Mex. 9 New Mexico
Tao Te Ching author: Lao-tzu
tap: 3 bug, dab, pat, rap, tag, use 4 draw, drum, milk, name, open, peck, tick 5 draft, drain, flick, knock, spike, spile, spout, thrum, thump, touch, valve 6 assign, broach, choose, draw on, faucet, fillip, lounge, nozzle, patter, select, siphon, spigot, strike, syphon, unplug 7 appoint, bibcock, exploit, hydrant, petcock, utilize 8 draw upon, keep time, nominate, stopcock 9 designate, eavesdrop, siphon off, unstopper 10 settle upon
choice: 3 ale 4 beer 5 draft, stout 6 porter
ender: 4 room, root
on ~: 4 open 5 ready 7 in store 9 available, in reserve, ready to go, scheduled 10 at the ready, convenient, obtainable, time-saving
problem: 4 drip, leak 5 crack 7 dribble, trickle
starter: 4 heel, wire
word: 3 hot 4 cold
tap __: 3 off 4 bell, bolt, into 5 dance, pants, water 6 dancer
Tap (1989 film)
cast: Sammy Davis Jr., Suzzanne Douglas, Gregory Hines
director: Nick Castle
tapa: 4 bark 5 cloth 8 mulberry
Tapachula: 4 city, town
locale: 6 Mexico 7 Chiapas
tapan: 4 drum
origin: 6 Turkey
tapas: 9 appetizer 10 finger food
tap-dance: 6 hoof it
tape: 4 band, bind, bond, line, mend, seal, wrap 5 strip, truss, video 6 edging, fasten, record, ribbon, secure, swathe, wrap up 7 bandage 8 cassette 9 prerecord 10 finish line, transcribe, transcript
beginning: 6 leader
clear a ~: 5 erase 6 delete
ender: 4 line, worm
format: 3 VHS 4 Beta
half: 5 side A, side B
linen ~: 5 inkle
machine: 3 VCR
measure: 5 ruler
player: 7 boombox
put on ~: 6 record
recorder measure: 3 ips
red ~: 4 maze 5 delay 6 policy, system 8 protocol 9 paperwork, procedure, rigmarole 10 impediment
reel: 5 spool
sample ~: 4 demo
starter: 5 audio, video
wrap in red ~: 5 delay, sit on
tape __: 4 deck 5 drive, grass 6 player 7 editing, machine, measure
tape-__: 6 record
__ tape: 3 mag, red 4 duct, name 5 blank, metal, paper, pilot 6 barbed, double, Scotch, single, ticker 7 masking, tracing
Tape (2001 film)
cast: Ethan Hawke, Robert Sean Leonard, Uma Thurman
director: Richard Linklater
__-tape parade: 6 ticker
taper: 5 abate, light, slack 6 candle, lessen, narrow, recede, reduce 7 sharpen, slacken 8 diminish
off: 4 fade, flag, wane 5 abate, close, drain 6 lessen, narrow, recede, reduce 7 die away, dwindle, subside, thin out 8 decrease, diminish, peter out, wind down 9 retrocede
part: 4 wick
taper __: 3 off 4 jack
tape recorder
attachment: 3 mic 10 microphone
button: 3 fwd, rec, rew 4 play 5 pause 6 record, rewind 7 forward
tapered: 5 sharp 6 fusate, narrow, pointy 7 pointed
tapestry: 5 arras 6 carpet 7 drapery
fiber: 5 ramee, ramie
make a ~: 5 weave
motif: 6 bocage
Norman Conquest ~: 6 Bayeux
spot ~: 4 wall
thread: 4 weft
tapestry __: 4 moth
taphouse: 3 bar, pub 6 saloon, tavern
tap-in: 5 gimme
tapioca: 6 junket
source: 6 casava
tapir: 6 animal, mammal
cousin: 5 rhino
feature: 5 snout
Tappan __ Bridge: 3 Zee
Tappan alternative: 5 Amana, Norge 6 Bendix, Maytag 7 Admiral, Jenn-Air, Kenmore 8 Hotpoint 9 Magic Chef, Whirlpool 10 Frigidaire, Kelvinator, KitchenAid
tapped: 7 abroach
item: 3 keg 5 maple 9 maple tree
out: 5 broke 8 bankrupt, depleted, strapped 9 insolvent, penniless
tapper: 5 gavel
starter: 4 wire
vein ~: 5 miner
taproom: 3 bar, pub 4 dive 6 lounge, saloon, tavern
taps
like some ~: 5 leaky 6 drippy
Taps: 4 tune 9 bugle call
instrument: 5 bugle
time, at times: 3 ten 5 ten p.m.
tar: 3 gob 4 drum, goop, pave, salt, soil, swab, swob 5 pitch, smear, stain, taint 6 crud up, impugn, larrup, sailor, sea dog, seaman, thrash 7 asphalt, bitumen, crewman, encrust, incrust, mariner, matelot, matelow, swabbie, tarnish 8 deckhand, seafarer 10 bluejacket
coal ~ extract: 6 cresol
ender: 3 mac 4 weed 5 paper
in Spanish: 4 brea 6 la brea
jack ~: 4 bo's'n, hand, salt, swab 5 bosun, middy 6 pirate, sea dog, seaman 7 boatman, captain, crewman, mariner, matelot, old salt, recruit, skipper 8 coxswain, deck hand, helmsman, salty dog, seafarer, water dog 9 boatswain, first mate, yachtsman 10 midshipman
juniper ~: 4 cade
pits locale: 6 La Brea 10 Los Angeles
source: 4 coal, pine
whale the ~ out of: 3 tan 4 rout 6 defeat, ravage 9 overpower
see also sailor
tar __: 4 baby, ball, sand
__ tar: 4 coal, pine, wood 5 jacky 6 jackie 7 juniper, mineral
Tar __: 4 Baby, Heel
__ Tar: 4 Jack
Tara: 4 Kemp 6 estate 8 Lipinski 10 Fitzgerald
family name: 5 O'Hara
land of ~: 4 Eire, Erin 7 Ireland
locale: 7 Atlanta, Georgia
taradiddle: 3 fib, gas, rot 4 blah, bosh, bull, bunk, guff, jazz, jive, pooh, tale, tosh 5 bilge, fudge, hokum, hooey, prate, stuff, trash, tripe 6 bunkum, bushwa, drivel, footle, gabble, gammon, gibber, havers, hot air, humbug, jabber, jargon, kibosh, piffle 7 baloney, blarney, blather, blether, boloney, bushwah, eyewash, flannel, flubdub, fustian, garbage, hogwash, inanity, rubbish, twaddle 8 buncombe, claptrap, falderal, falderol, flimflam, flummery, folderal, folderol, nonsense, slipslop, tommyrot, trumpery 9 banana oil, gibberish, goofiness, kidstakes, moonshine, poppycock, rigmarole 10 applesauce, balderdash, bilge water, codswallop, double-talk, flapdoodle, galimatias, Jabberwock, mumbo jumbo, rigamarole
taradiddler: 4 liar
Tarahumara: 6 Indian 7 Amerind 8 language
tar and __: 7 feather
tarantella: 5 dance
Tarantino: 7 Quentin
Taranto: 4 city, gulf, town
locale: 5 Italy
tarantula: 3 bug 6 insect
leg count: 5 eight
like a ~: 5 fuzzy, hairy
toxin: 5 venom
Tarantula (1955 film)
cast: John Agar, Leo G. Carroll, Mara Corday
Ta-Ra-Ra-Boom-__: 4 De-Ré
Tara Road author: Maeve Binchy
Taras Bulba author: Nikolai Gogol
Tarascan: 6 Indian 7 Amerind
tarata: 4 tree
Tarawa: 4 city, town 7 capital
locale: 8 Kiribati
Tarazed: 4 star
Tar Baby author: Toni Morrison
Tar-Baby, The author: Joel Chandler Harris
Tarbell, Ida: 6 author, writer 9 muckraker
work: History of the Standard Oil Company
Tarbes: 4 city, town
locale: 6 France
tarboosh cousin: 3 fez
tarde: 7 Spanish 9 afternoon
activity: 6 siesta
tardy: 4 late, lazy, poky, slow 5 slack 6 behind, held up, hung up 7 belated, delayed, languid, overdue, past due, unready 8 dawdling, detained, dilatory, slothful 9 laggardly, leisurely, lethargic, snaillike 10 behindhand, behind time, delinquent, unpunctual
be ~: 3 lag 4 idle 5 dally, delay, mosey, tarry, trail 6 dawdle, linger, loiter 10 dillydally
make ~: 5 laten
somewhat ~: 6 latish
tare: 4 weed 5 vetch
Targa: 3 car 4 auto 7 Porsche 9 sports car 10 automobile
target: 3 aim, end 4 butt, goal, goat, gull, mark, prey 5 aim at, focus, patsy 6 intent, object, pigeon, quarry, reason, victim 7 purpose 8 ambition, bull's-eye 9 intention, objective, scapegoat 10 ground zero
face the ~: 3 aim
on ~: 3 apt 7 apropos
target __: 4 date 5 rifle
__ target: 5 water 6 moving
target practice game: 5 skeet
Targets (1968 film)
cast: Nancy Hsueh, Boris Karloff, Tim O'Kelly
director: Peter Bogdanovich
Tar Heel State: 4 N. Car.
school: 3 UNC 4 Elon
tariff: 3 fee, tab, tax 4 cost, duty, fare, levy, rate, toll 5 price 6 charge, excise, impost, towage 7 expense 8 exaction 10 assessment
pact: 4 GATT 5 NAFTA
Tarija: 4 city, town
locale: 7 Bolivia
Tarim: 5 river
locale: 5 China
Tarimoro: 4 city, town
locale: 6 Mexico 10 Guanajuato
Tarkanian: 5 Jerry
Tarkenton, Fran: 2 QB
sport: 8 football
Tarkington, Booth: 6 author, writer
work: Alice Adams
The Gentleman From Indiana
The Magnificent Ambersons
Monsieur Beaucaire
Penrod
Seventeen
tarlatan: 6 fabric 8 material
tarmac
area: 5 apron
lay down ~: 4 pave
reached the ~: 4 alit
roll on the ~: 4 taxi
tarn: 4 lake, pond, pool 5 lough 9 reservoir
tarnish: 3 dim, mar, tar 4 blot, dull, foul, rust, soil, spot 5 dirty, oxide, smear, spoil, stain, sully, taint 6 befoul, damage, darken, deface, defame, defile, malign, smudge 7 begrime, blacken, blemish, corrode, oxidize, pollute, slander 8 besmirch, discolor, disgrace, throw mud 10 imputation
tarnished: 5 dirty, grimy, sooty 6 filthy, grubby, grungy 7 unclean 8 maculate, slovenly, vitiated 10 unsanitary
Tarnished Angels, The (1958 film)
cast: Rock Hudson, Dorothy Malone, Robert Stack
director: Douglas Sirk
taro: 5 aroid, tania, tuber 6 veggie 9 rootstock, vegetable
product: 3 poi
root: 4 eddo
tuber: 4 corm
tarok: 4 game 8 card game
tarot card: 3 Sun 4 Fool, King, Moon, Page, Star 5 Death, Devil, Queen, Tower, World 6 Hermit, Knight, Lovers 7 Chariot, Emperor, Empress, Justice 8 Magician, Strength 9 Hanged Man, Judgement 10 Hierophant, Temperance

group: 6 arcana
reader: 4 seer 7 prophet, psychic
reading: 10 prediction
suit: 4 cups 5 wands 6 swords 9 pentacles
tarp
see tarpaulin
tarpan: 5 horse 6 equine
tarpaulin: 5 sheet 6 canvas 8 covering 10 protection
tarpon: 4 fish
Tarpon Springs: 4 city, town
locale: 7 Florida
tarragon: 4 herb
tarry: 3 lag 4 bide, drag, idle, laze, loaf, poke, stay, stop, wait 5 abide, amble, dally, delay, mosey, pause, stall, trail, visit 6 dawdle, linger, loiter, remain 7 saunter, sojourn, stand by 8 footdrag, hold back, lollygag, stop over, straggle 9 temporize, waste time 10 dillydally, filibuster, goof around, hang around, wait around
tarsal
see tarsus
tarsier: 7 primate
relative: 3 ape 4 saki, titi 5 chimp, drill, jocko, lemur, loris, magot, orang, potto, shrew 6 aye-aye, baboon, Bandar, galago, gelada, gibbon, grivet, guenon, howler, langur, macaco, monkey, rhesus, uakari, vervet 7 colobus, gorilla, guereza, hoolock, macaque, sapajou, siamang, tamarin 8 bush baby, capuchin, mandrill, mangabey, marmoset, talapoin 9 orangutan 10 Barbary ape, chimpanzee, orangutang
tarsus: 4 bone
adornment: 6 anklet
locale: 4 foot 5 ankle
starter: 4 meta
tart: 3 pie 4 acid, cake, sour 5 acerb, acrid, salty, sharp, tangy, testy, zingy 6 acidic, biting, bitter, crabby, lemony, pastry, snappy, snippy 7 acerbic, caustic, cutting, dessert, piquant, popover, pungent, zinging 8 snappish, snippety, vinegary 9 acidulous, trenchant 10 astringent
fruit: 4 sloe 5 berry, lemon
ingredient: 5 dough, flour, fruit, sugar
substance: 4 acid
thief of fiction: 5 knave
tartan: 4 kilt, sett 5 plaid 6 fabric
trousers: 5 trews
wearer: 4 clan, Scot
tartar: 5 sauce
grape ~: 5 argal, argol
sauce ingredient: 5 caper
tartar ___: 5 sauce, steak
___ tartare: 5 steak
Tartarian ___: 5 aster
tartaric ___: 4 acid
tartness: 6 flavor 7 acidity 8 acerbity, acrimony 10 bitterness
with ~: 6 acidly
tartrate: 4 salt 5 ester
___-Tarts: 3 Pop
tart-tongued: 4 mean 5 catty, nasty 7 hateful, vicious 8 spiteful, venomous 9 rancorous 10 backbiting, ill-natured
Tartu: 4 city, town
locale: 7 Estonia
resident: 4 Esth
Tartuffe: 4 play 6 comedy
author: 7 Molière
character: 5 Damis, Orgon 6 Dorine, Elmire, Valère 7 Cléante, Mariane
tarty: 4 sour
tar with the ___ brush: 4 same
Tarzan: 4 hero 5 he-man 6 ape man
companion: 3 ape 5 chimp
home: 6 jungle
lion: 4 Numa 5 simba
love: 4 Jane
mother: 5 Alice
portrayer: 3 Ely 4 Brix 5 Henry, Scott 6 Barker, O'Keefe, Ron Ely 7 Lambert, Lincoln 9 Lex Barker, Mike Henry 10 Herman Brix 11 Gordon Scott, Miles O'Keefe, Weissmuller
son: 3 Boy
transport: 4 vine 5 liana, liane
Tarzan (1999 film)
voice cast: Glenn Close, Minnie Driver, Tony Goldwyn, Rosie O'Donnell
Tarzan (NBC/CBS adventure)
cast: Ron Ely (Tarzan) Manuel Padilla Jr. (Jai)
Tarzana: 4 city, town
locale: 10 California
Tarzan and His Mate (1934 film)
cast: Neil Hamilton, Maureen O'Sullivan, Johnny Weissmuller
Tarzan Escapes (1936 film)
cast: Maureen O'Sullivan, Johnny Weissmuller
Tarzan Finds a Son! (1939 film)
cast: Maureen O'Sullivan, Johnny Sheffield, Johnny Weissmuller
Tarzan, the Ape Man (1932 film)
cast: Maureen O'Sullivan, Johnny Weissmuller
director: W.S. Van Dyke
Tarzan Triumphs (1943 film)
cast: Frances Gifford, Johnny Sheffield, Johnny Weissmuller
Taschhorn: 3 Alp
taser: 3 gun 7 stun gun
Tashi Lama: 6 cleric
Tashkent: 4 city, town 7 capital
city near ~: 3 Osh
language: 5 Usbeg, Usbek, Uzbeg, Uzbek
locale: 4 Asia 10 Uzbekistan
Tashlin, Frank: 8 director
film: Artists and Models (1955)
The Disorderly Orderly (1964)
The Glass Bottom Boat (1966)
It'$ Only Money (1962)
Rock-a-Bye Baby (1958)
Son of Paleface (1952)
Will Success Spoil Rock Hunter? (1957)
task: 3 job 4 duty, onus, part, role, toil, work 5 chore, grind, labor, stint, thing 6 burden, charge, errand, lesson 7 mission, project 8 activity, business, function, headache, homework, overload 9 millstone 10 assignment, enterprise, obligation
simple ~: 4 snap 6 breeze
unpleasant ~: 4 onus
task ___: 5 force
taskmaster: 5 taxer 6 ramrod 8 martinet
Tasman: 3 sea 4 Abel
locale: 9 Australia 10 New Zealand
Tasman, Abel Janszoon: 5 Dutch 8 explorer
Tasmania: 3 isl. 4 isle 6 island
capital: 6 Hobart
fish: 6 inanga
mountain: 4 Ossa
pine: 4 huon
river: 5 Tamar
Tasmanian ___: 4 wolf 5 devil, tiger
Tasmanian devil: 9 marsupial
relative: 4 euro 5 bilbi, bilby, koala 6 numbat, wombat 7 bettong, dasyure, opossum, wallaby 8 kangaroo, wallaroo 9 bandicoot, phalanger
Tasmanian wolf: 9 marsupial
relative: 4 euro 5 bilbi, bilby, koala 6 numbat, wombat 7 bettong, dasyure, opossum, wallaby 8 kangaroo, wallaroo 9 bandicoot, phalanger
___-Tass: 4 Itar
tasse: 3 cup 6 French
contents: 3 thé 4 café
starter: 4 demi
tassel: 4 tuft
combining form: 6 thysan- 7 thysano-
corn ~: 4 silk
tasseled
cap: 3 fez, tam
hem: 6 fringe
Tasso, Torquato: 4 poet 7 Italian
patron: 4 Este
work: Aminta
Jerusalem Delivered
Rinaldo
taste: 3 bit, eat, nip, sip, try, zip 4 bite, chew, dash, drop, hint, kick, know, lick, sour, tang, test, zest, zing 5 enjoy, fancy, flair, gusto, punch, salty, sapor, savor, sense, share, smack, style, sweet, tinge, touch 6 bitter, canapé, flavor, ginger, liking, little, morsel, nibble, palate, polish, relish, sample, tidbit, trifle 7 culture, decorum, leaning, portion, soupçon, stomach, swallow 8 appetite, delicacy, elegance, fondness, judgment, mouthful, penchant, piquancy, sapidity, spoonful, weakness 9 encounter, partake of, restraint 10 excellence, experience, partiality, preference, proclivity, propensity, refinement, savoriness, sprinkling, suggestion
again: 5 retry
bad ~: 9 crassness, indecorum, vulgarity 10 coarseness, indelicacy
ender: 5 maker
get a ~ of: 3 try 6 sample
good ~: 4 tact 5 taste 7 culture
have no ~ for: 4 hate 5 abhor 6 detest 7 despise, dislike 9 abominate
having a ~ for: 6 fond of 9 partial to
like: 7 smack of
like a ~ bud: 5 ovoid
small ~: 3 nip, sip 4 bite, lick 6 sample
starter: 5 after
stimulus: 5 aroma
tease the ~ buds: 4 whet
taste ___: 3 bud 4 test
tasteful: 4 fine, nice 5 quiet 6 classy, pretty 7 elegant, refined, subdued 8 artistic, charming, cultured, esthetic, graceful, handsome, pleasing, polished 9 ambrosial, beautiful, exquisite 10 artistical, cultivated, gratifying, harmonious, restrained
tastefulness: 5 charm, class, grace, style, taste 6 beauty, luxury, polish 7 dignity 8 elegance 9 gentility 10 refinement
tasteless: 4 blah, dull, flat, loud, mild, rude, thin, weak 5 bland, cheap, crass, crude, gaudy, gross, plain, rough, showy, stale, tacky, vapid 6 boring, coarse, flashy, garish, ornate, tawdry, vulgar, watery 7 insipid, raffish, raunchy, uncouth, vanilla 8 improper, off-color, tactless, unlovely, unsalted, unsavory, unseemly, unsubtle 9 graceless, inelegant, savorless, unrefined 10 flavorless, indecorous, indelicate, outlandish, unbecoming, unpolished, unseasoned
Taste of Honey, A (1961 film)
cast: Dora Bryan, Robert Stephens, Rita Tushingham
director: Tony Richardson
Taste of Honey, A (1965 song) artist: Herb Alpert and the Tijuana Brass
Taster's Choice: 6 coffee
alternative: 5 Sanka, Yuban 7 Folgers, Melitta, Nescafe, Savarin 9 Hills Bros.
taster's need: 4 fork 5 spoon
tasty: 4 good, nice, rich 5 sapid, spicy, yummy, zesty 6 dainty, delish, divine, mellow, savory, spicey, toothy 7 piquant, zestful 8 heavenly, luscious, noshable 9 ambrosial, delicious, flavorful, nectarous, palatable, succulent, sweetened, toothsome, with a kick 10 appetizing, delectable, flavorsome
tat
give tit for ~: 5 spite 6 avenge 7 get even, pay back, revenge 9 retaliate
tit for ~: 7 revenge 8 exchange, reprisal 9 interplay, vengeance
___-tat: 4 rat-a
ta-ta: 3 bye 5 later, see ya 6 goodby, so long 7 goodbye 8 farewell
in French: 5 adieu 8 au revoir
in Hawaiian: 5 aloha
in Italian: 4 ciao
in Latin: 3 ave 4 vale
in Spanish: 5 adios
tatami: 3 mat 8 Japanese
material: 5 straw
Tatar: 7 Crimean
chief: 4 khan
soldier: 4 ulan 5 uhlan
Tatar Strait, river into the: 4 Amur
Tate: 5 Allen, Laura, Nahum 6 Sharon
Tate, Allen: 4 poet 6 writer
work: Ode to the Confederate Dead
Tate Gallery display: 3 art
Tate, Nahum: 4 poet 7 British
tater: 4 spud 5 tuber 9 vegetable
see also potato
Tater ___: 4 Tots
Tate, Sharon spouse: Roman Polanski
Tati: 7 Jacques
Tatiana: 8 Troyanos
Tatis, Fernando sport: 8 baseball
Tatler, The essayist: 6 Steele 7 Addison
tatou: 9 armadillo
Tatra: 5 range 9 mountains
locale: 6 Europe, Poland 8 Slovakia
___-tat-tat: 4 rat-a
tatter: 3 rag 4 rent, tear 5 shred
tatterdemalion: 4 waif 6 urchin 10 ragamuffin
tattered: 4 worn 5 mangy, ratty, seedy 6 in rags, mangey, ragged, shabby 7 in holes, run-down, scruffy, worn-out 8 slipshod, untended 9 ungroomed 10 threadbare
Tattered Tom author: Horatio Alger
tattersall: 6 fabric 8 material
tatters, in: 4 shot, torn 6 ragged
tatting: 4 lace
tattle: 3 rat 4 blab, chat, fink, leak, sing, talk 5 prate, rat on, rumor, spill 6 babble, gossip, jabber, report, snitch, squeal, tell on 7 chatter, hearsay, prattle 8 informer, telltale 9 informant
ender: 4 tale
on: 6 give up, turn in 8 give away
___-tattle: 6 tittle
tattler: 3 rat 4 bird, fink, nark 5 namer 6 canary, gossip, ratter, snitch, squeal 7 ratfink, traitor 8 bigmouth, busybody, fat mouth, informer, squealer, telltale, turncoat 9 informant 10 talebearer, taleteller
tattletale
see tattler
tattletale ___: 4 gray, grey
Tattletales: 8 game show
host: Bert Convy

tattoo: 4 call 6 design, signal 9 bugle call
place: 3 arm
popular ~: 3 Mom
__ Tattoo, The: 4 Rose
tatty: 4 worn 5 cheap 6 frayed, ragged, shabby 8 decrepit, ill-kempt 9 moth-eaten
Tatum: 3 Art 5 Goose, O'Neal 6 Edward
dad: 4 Ryan
Tatum, Art: 7 pianist
genre: 4 jazz
Tatum, Edward: 8 Nobelist
Tatyana: 3 Ali
tau: 5 Greek 6 letter
predecessor: 5 sigma
successor: 7 upsilon
tau __: 5 cross 6 lepton
Taubaté: 4 city, town
locale: 6 Brazil
Taube, Henry: 7 chemist 8 Nobelist
taught: 4 wise 5 shown 8 educated, well-bred
be ~: 5 learn, study 6 absorb, master, soak up 7 major in, minor in 9 brush up on 10 get down pat
information ~: 6 lesson
__-taught: 4 self
taunt: 3 cut, dig, egg, guy, jab, rag, rib, vex 4 barb, gibe, goad, haze, jape, jeer, jest, jibe, mock, razz, ride, slam, slap, slur, snub, twit 5 abuse, chaff, crack, decry, get on, libel, roast, scorn, sneer, spurn, swipe, tease 6 banter, bother, defame, deride, dump on, harass, heckle, impugn, insult, jeer at, jibe at, malign, needle, noodge, offend, rebuff, slight, vilify 7 affront, asperse, calumny, catcall, degrade, disdain, laugh at, mockery, obloquy, offense, provoke, put down, rank out, sarcasm, scoff at, slander, snigger, torment, traduce 8 belittle, contempt, denounce, derision, ridicule, vilipend 9 aspersion, cheap shot, contumely, denigrate, discredit, disparage, humiliate, make fun of, poke fun at, tantalize 10 calumniate, defamation, disrespect, make game of, opprobrium
taunting: 7 jeering, satiric 8 derisive 9 annoyance, sarcastic, satirical
exclamation: 3 oho
one: 5 darer
Taunton: 4 city, town
locale: 4 Mass.
taupe: 3 tan 4 gray, grey 5 color 8 brownish
relative: 3 ash 4 dove, drab 5 beige, dusty, merle, pearl, putty, slate 6 silver 7 grizzly 8 charcoal, gun-metal, platinum
Taupin: 6 Bernie
Taurog, Norman: 8 director
film: The Beginning or the End (1947)
Blue Hawaii (1961)
Boys Town (1938)
Broadway Melody of 1940 (1940)
Don't Give Up the Ship (1959)
Double Trouble (1967)
G.I. Blues (1960)
Girl Crazy (1943)
Girls! Girls! Girls! (1962)
It Happened at the World's Fair (1963)
Live a Little, Love a Little (1968)
Living It Up (1954)
Mad About Music (1938)
Mrs. Wiggs of the Cabbage Patch (1934)
Room for One More (1952)
Skippy (1931, AA)
Speedway (1968)
Spinout (1966)
The Stooge (1953)
Tickle Me (1965)
The Way to Love (1933)
We're Not Dressing (1934)
You Can't Have Everything (1937)
Young Tom Edison (1940)
You're Never Too Young (1955)
Taurus: 3 car 4 auto, Ford, sign 5 range 9 mountains 10 automobile
locale: 4 Asia 6 Turkey
month: 3 Apr., May 5 April
nebula in ~: 4 crab
neighbor: 5 Orion
predecessor: 5 Aries
ruler of ~ in astrology: 5 Venus
successor: 6 Gemini
taut: 4 firm, snug, trim 5 drawn, rigid, stiff, tense, tight 7 nervous, wound up 8 fluttery, strained, stressed 9 ship-shape, stretched, unrelaxed 10 high-strung, inflexible, unyielding
not ~: 5 loose, slack
tauten: 4 tidy 7 stretch, tighten 9 constrict
tautness: 6 strain 7 tension 9 tightness
lose ~: 3 sag
tautog: 4 fish 9 blackfish
tautological: 7 verbose 9 redundant
tautology: 8 verbiage 10 repetition
tautomeric compound: 4 enol
tav: 6 Hebrew, letter
predecessor: 4 shin
Tavel: 4 pink, rosé, wine
origin: 6 France
tavern: 3 bar, inn, pub 4 dive 5 hotel, joint, lodge 6 bistro, lounge, saloon 7 barroom, gin mill, taproom 8 ale-house, grog shop, hostelry, lodgment, taphouse 9 honky-tonk, nightspot, roadhouse, speakeasy
old-style: 4 inne
supply: 3 ale 4 beer, grog 5 lager, stout 6 liquor
visit ~ s: 6 barhop
see also bar
tavern __: 4 nuts 5 table
__ Tavern: 6 Duffy's 7 Mermaid
Taverny: 4 city, town
locale: 6 France
Tavist alternative: 5 Afrin 6 Contac, Nyquil 7 Actifed, Comtrex, Dayquil, Dristan, Sinutab, Sudafed 8 Benadryl, Dimetapp, Drixoral, TheraFlu 9 Coricidin, Triaminic 10 Robitussin
taw: 5 aggie 6 Hebrew, letter
predecessor: 4 shin
...taw a __ tat!: 5 puddy
tawdry: 4 loud, mean 5 cheap, crude, gaudy, jazzy, junky, showy, tacky 6 brazen, common, flashy, garish, glitzy, ornate, shoddy, sleazy, tinsel, vulgar 7 blatant, chintzy, raffish 8 gimcrack, schlocky 9 tasteless 10 glittering, second-rate
things: 6 kitsch
tawn: 5 flaxy 6 flaxen
tawny: 3 tan 5 blond, brown, color 6 blonde, golden, swarth, yellow 7 old gold, saffron, swarthy 8 brindled 9 yellowish
animal: 3 owl 4 lion
combining form: 5 fusco-, pyrrh-, pyrro- 6 pyrhho-
relative: 3 bay, dun, tan 4 bole, ecru, fawn, foxy, nude, seal 5 amber, beige, camel, cocoa, hazel, khaki, mocha, sepia, umber 6 auburn, bister, bistre, bronze, coffee, copper, ginger, russet, sienna, sorrel, suntan, walnut 7 biscuit, caramel, dogwood 8 chestnut, cinnamon, mahogany 9 butternut, chocolate
Tawny: 6 Kitaen
tax: 3 sap, try 4 bite, dues, duty, fine, lade, levy, load, rate, tire, toll, wear 5 blame, enact, exact, tithe, weary 6 accuse, assess, burden, charge, cumber, custom, demand, excise, impose, impost, impugn, impute, indict, lumber, prey on, saddle, strain, stress, tariff, towage, weaken 7 arraign, censure, exhaust, expense, extract, impeach, oppress, reprove, tribute, wear out 8 encumber, exaction, overload, overtask, overwork, reproach 9 inculpate, surcharge, weigh down 10 assessment, imposition, overburden
basis: 5 ratal
determine a ~: 4 rate 5 gauge, value 6 assess 8 appraise, evaluate
do a ~ calculation: 6 deduct
ender: 3 man, men 5 payer 6 paying
expert: 3 acc., CPA 4 acct. 10 accountant
form: 4 W two
form part: 5 line A
import ~: 4 duty, levy 6 charge, excise, impost, tariff 10 assessment
month: 3 Apr. 5 April
of old: 4 geld, sess
org.: 3 IRS
shelter: 3 IRA 5 Keogh 7 Roth IRA 8 Roth plan
tax __: 4 code, deed, lien, rate, sale 5 exile, haven, stamp, table, title 6 return 7 evasion, sharing, shelter
tax-__: 4 free 6 exempt
__ tax: 3 gas, sin, use 4 exit, gift, head, poll 5 nanny, sales, stamp 6 border, direct, estate, excise, hidden, income, luxury, single 7 cabaret, payroll
__-tax: 5 after
taxable __: 6 income
Taxation without representation coiner: 4 Otis
tax-bracket __: 5 creep
Taxco: 4 city, town
locale: 6 Mexico 8 Guerrero
see also Spanish
tax-deferred __: 7 annuity
taxed: 5 laden, weary 7 fraught 10 encumbered
taxes
before ~: 5 gross
earn after ~: 3 net 4 make 5 clear
evade ~: 4 duck 5 cheat, dodge 6 scheme
__ taxes: 5 No new
taxi: 3 cab, car 4 auto, hack, ride 5 sedan 7 vehicle 8 transfer 9 transport 10 automobile
Asian ~: 5 cyclo
device: 5 meter
driver: 4 hack 5 cabby 6 cabbie, hackie
drop-off point: 4 curb
ender: 3 cab, way 5 meter
fee: 4 fare
forerunner: 6 hansom
go by ~: 4 ride
passenger: 4 fare
summon a ~: 4 flag, hail 8 flag down
water ~: 4 boat 5 ferry 6 launch 7 gondola
taxi __: 5 squad, stand, strip 6 dancer, driver
__ taxi: 3 air 5 radio, water
Taxi (ABC/NBC sitcom)
cast: Tony Danza (Tony Banta)
Danny DeVito (Louie De Palma)
Marilu Henner (Elaine Nardo)
Judd Hirsch (Alex Rieger)
Carol Kane (Simka Gravas)
Andy Kaufman (Latka Gravas)
dog: 5 Buddy
__ Taxi: 7 Tijuana
Taxi (1972 song) artist: Harry Chapin
Taxi Driver (1976 film)
cast: Peter Boyle, Robert De Niro, Jodie Foster, Harvey Keitel, Cybill Shepherd
director: Martin Scorsese
taxing: 5 heavy, hefty, tough 6 leaden, rugged, severe, tiring, trying, uphill 7 arduous, onerous, operose, tedious, wearing, weighty 8 exacting, grievous, grueling 9 demanding, ponderous, strenuous, stressful, wearisome 10 burdensome, enervating, oppressive
taxol source: 3 yew
taxon: 5 class, genus, order 6 phylum 7 species 8 category
taxonomic
division: 5 class, genus, order 6 family, phylum 7 kingdom, species
divisions: 5 phyla
suffix: 3 -ota, -ote 4 -ella
taxonomy: 7 science
taxpayer: 5 filer, voter 6 earner 7 citizen
fear: 5 audit 8 scrutiny 10 inspection
ID: 3 SSN
Tay: 5 river 7 Garnett
city on the ~: 5 Perth
Firth of ~ port: 6 Dundee
locale: 8 Scotland
Tayback: 3 Vic
Taye: 5 Diggs
__ Tayloe Ross: 6 Nellie
Taylor: 3 Don, Dub, Jim, Rip, Rod, Sam 4 Lili 5 Dayne, Deems, James, Renee 6 Joseph, Robert 7 Johnnie, Richard, Zachary 8 Caldwell, Hackford, Lawrence 9 Elizabeth
Taylor, Andy: 8 Griffith
aunt: 3 Bee
son: 4 Opie
__ Taylor Bradford: 7 Barbara
__ Taylor Coleridge: 6 Samuel
Taylor, Don: 8 director
film: Escape From the Planet of the Apes (1971)
The Final Countdown (1980)
The Island of Dr. Moreau (1977)
The Naked City (1948)
Stalag 17 (1953)
Tom Sawyer (1973)
Taylor, Elizabeth: 4 Dame 7 actress
film: Beau Brummel (1954)
Butterfield 8 (1960, AA)
Cat on a Hot Tin Roof (1958)
Cleopatra (1963)
Father of the Bride (1950)
Father's Little Dividend (1951)
Giant (1956)
Ivanhoe (1952)
The (1954) Last Time I Saw Paris
Life With Father (1947)
The Mirror Crack'd (1980)
National Velvet (1944)
The Only Game in Town (1970)
A Place in the Sun (1951)
Raintree County (1957)
The Sandpiper (1965)
Secret Ceremony (1968)
Suddenly, Last Summer (1959)
The Taming of the Shrew (1967)
The V.I.P.s (1963)
Who's Afraid of Virginia Woolf? (1966, AA)
spouse: Richard Burton, Eddie Fisher, Mike Todd, John Warner, Michael Wilding
Taylor, James
song: Fire and Rain (1970)
Handy Man (1977)
Her Town Too (1981)
How Sweet It Is (1975)
Mockingbird (1974)
You've Got a Friend (1971)
spouse: Carly Simon

Taylor, Johnnie
song: Disco Lady (1976)
I Believe in You (1973)
Who's Making Love (1968)
Taylor, Joseph: 8 Nobelist **9** physicist
Taylor, Lawrence sport: 8 football
Taylor, Lili: 7 actress
film: The Addiction (1995)
Dogfight (1991)
Household Saints (1993)
The Imposters (1998)
Mystic Pizza (1988)
Say Anything ... (1989)
Taylor, Renee: 7 actress
film: Last of the Red Hot Lovers (1972)
Made for Each Other (1971)
spouse: Joseph Bologna
TV: The Nanny
Taylor, Richard: 8 Nobelist **9** physicist
Taylor, Robert: 5 actor
film: Above and Beyond (1952)
Bataan (1943)
Broadway Melody of 1936 (1935)
Camille (1937)
D-Day the Sixth of June (1956)
The Devil's Doorway (1950)
Escape (1940)
High Wall (1947)
Ivanhoe (1952)
Johnny Eager (1941)
The Law and Jake Wade (1958)
Magnificent Obsession (1935)
The Night Walker (1964)
Party Girl (1958)
Quo Vadis? (1951)
Rogue Cop (1954)
Saddle the Wind (1958)
Small Town Girl (1936)
This Is My Affair (1937)
Three Comrades (1938)
Tip on a Dead Jockey (1957)
Waterloo Bridge (1940)
Westward the Women (1951)
A Yank at Oxford (1938)
spouse: Barbara Stanwyck
Taylor, Rod: 5 actor
film: The Birds (1963)
Dark of the Sun (1968)
A Gathering of Eagles (1963)
The Glass Bottom Boat (1966)
Open Season (1996)
Sunday in New York (1963)
The Time Machine (1960)
Young Cassidy (1965)
Taylorsville: 4 city, town
locale: 4 Utah
__ Taylor Thomas: 8 Jonathan
Taylor-Young: 5 Leigh
Taylor, Zachary: 9 president
former occupation: 7 soldier
opponent: 4 Cass
V.P.: 8 Fillmore
wife: 8 Margaret
tayra: 6 weasel
relative: 4 mink **5** fitch, otter, ratel, sable, skunk, stoat **6** badger, ermine, ferret, marten **7** foumart, polecat **8** carcajou, foulmart, kolinsky, muishond **9** wolverine
Tb: 4 elem. **7** element, terbium
65 for ~: 4 at. no.
T-bar: 4 bolt, lift **6** ski tow **7** ski lift
terrain: 5 slope
user: 5 skier
Tbilisi: 4 city, town **7** capital
locale: 7 Georgia
T-Bird: 3 car **4** auto, Ford **10** automobile
rival: 5 'Vette
T-bone: 4 meat **5** steak
source: 4 loin
T-Bone: 6 Walker
T. Boone __: 7 Pickens
TBS alternative: 3 BET, CMT, MTV, PAX, TLC, TNN, TNT, USA **4** ESPN, HGTV **5** A and E, C-SPAN, Style **6** Noggin, Tech TV, TV Land **7** Court TV, Ovation, SoapNet **8** Lifetime
tbsp.: 3 amt. **4** meas.
fraction: 3 tsp. **4** fl. oz.
Tc: 4 elem. **7** element **10** technetium
43 for ~: 4 at. no.
Tchaikovsky, Peter: 7 Russian **8** composer
work: 1812 Overture
Eugene Onegin
Manfred Symphony
Marche Slave
The Nutcracker
Pathétique Symphony
Romeo and Juliet
Sleeping Beauty
Swan Lake
tchr.: 4 prof. **5** instr.
deg.: 3 Ed.B., Ed.D., MSE **7** Ed.M. MSEd.
org.: 3 AFT, NEA, UFT
place: 3 sch.
see also teacher
TCU rival: 3 SMU
TD: 4 stat
passer: 2 QB
scorer: 2 HB
six, for a ~: 3 pts.
te __: 3 amo
te-__: 3 hee
Te: 4 elem. **7** element **9** tellurium
52 for ~: 4 at. no.
Te __: 4 Deum
T.E.: 8 Lawrence
tea: 4 brew, meal **5** bohea, congo, cuppa, drink, fluid, hyson, party, pekoe, snack **6** congou, Lipton, Nestea, oolong, Salada, Tetley **7** Bigelow, cambric, lapsang, Red Rose **8** beverage, camomile, Earl Grey, souchong, Twinings **9** chamomile, elevenses, gunpowder, reception, yerba maté **10** Darjeeling
additive: 4 herb, milk, mint **5** honey, sugar
Arabian ~: 3 qat
black ~: 5 bohea, congo, oopak **6** congou, oopack
brewer: 3 urn **7** samovar
ceremony need: 4 raku
Chinese ~: 3 cha **5** bohea, congo **6** congou
cup of ~: 3 bag **5** field **7** leaning **9** specialty **10** preference
ender: 3 cup, pot **4** cake, cart, cher, room, shop, time **5** berry, house, spoon **6** cupful, kettle **8** spoonful
follower: 5 spoon
genus: 4 thea
have ~: 5 drink
high ~: 4 meal
holder: 3 bag, cup **4** cozy **5** caddy
Indian ~ source: 5 Assam
in French: 3 thé
leaf reader: 7 psychic
leaves: 4 lees **5** dregs **8** sediment
make ~: 4 brew **5** steep
medicinal ~: 5 tansy
party: 5 salon
quantity: 3 cup **4** spot
serve ~: 4 pour
time: 3 aft. **4** four **6** four p.m. **9** afternoon
tea __: 3 bag, set **4** ball, cozy, gown, rose, shop, tray, tree **5** break, caddy, dance, maker, money, party, table, towel, wagon **6** basket, garden **7** biscuit, service
__ tea: 3 hot **4** beef, herb, high, iced, meat, pink **5** black, cup of, green, Texas **6** herbal, hybrid, Oswego, shower **7** cambric, crystal, jasmine, kitchen, Mexican
Tea __ Two: 3 for
Téa: 5 Leoni
Tea and Sympathy: 4 film, play
author: Robert Anderson
cast: Leif Erickson, Deborah Kerr, John Kerr
director: Vincente Minnelli
teaberry: 5 fruit
teacake: 5 scone
teacart: 5 wagon
teach: 4 form, rear, show **5** brief, coach, drill, edify, guide, imbue, train, tutor **6** advise, direct, ground, impart, inform, instil, school **7** break in, educate, engrain, explain, expound, implant, ingrain, instill, lecture, nurture, prepare, profess **8** exercise, initiate, instruct, polish up **9** brainwash, catechize, cultivate, enlighten, inculcate, interpret, irradiate, pound into, sermonize **10** discipline, evangelize, illustrate, promulgate
a lesson to: 6 punish
easy to ~: 3 apt **5** quick
teacher: 4 guru, prof **5** coach, guide, instr., tutor **6** lector, master, mentor, pundit **7** adviser, advisor, pedagog, scholar, trainer **8** educator, lecturer **9** abecedary, assistant, counselor, pedagogue, preceptor, professor **10** instructor, missionary
charge: 5 class
college ~: 4 prof **6** docent, lector **8** lecturer **9** professor **10** instructor
country ~: 4 marm **10** schoolmarm
degree: 3 Ed.B., Ed.D., Ed.M., M.Ed., MSE **4** MSEd
figuratively: 4 lamp
Hindu ~: 4 guru **5** swami, swamy
Islamic ~: 5 mulla **6** mullah
name meaning ~: 5 Enoch **6** Lehrer
need: 3 map, pen **4** desk **5** chalk, paper, ruler **6** eraser
note from the ~: 5 see me
org.: 3 AFT, NEA, UFT
place: 3 sch. **4** acad., coll., univ. **6** school **7** academy, college **10** high school, university
private ~: 5 tutor
religious ~: 3 nun **5** rabbi, rebbe
roster: 4 roll
starter: 6 school
student ~: 6 intern, novice **7** interne, trainee **10** apprentice
__ teacher: 7 student
__-Teacher Association: 6 Parent
teachers: 5 staff **7** faculty **9** lecturers
teacher's __: 3 pet
Teachers (1984 film)
cast: Judd Hirsch, Ralph Macchio, Nick Nolte, JoBeth Williams
director: Arthur Hiller
Teacher's Pet (1958 film)
cast: Doris Day, Clark Gable, Gig Young
director: George Seaton
teaching: 4 lore **5** drill, tenet **6** homily, lesson **7** tuition **8** doctrine, pedagogy, training **9** education, paedagogy, principle **10** profession
teaching __: 3 aid **5** elder **6** fellow **7** machine
teachings: 5 creed, dogma, tenet **6** belief **7** precept **8** doctrine
Teach Your Children (1970 song)
artist: Crosby, Stills & Nash
TEAC rival: 4 Bose
teacup
like a ~: 5 eared
part: 3 ear, lip **4** brim **6** handle
Tea for Two: 4 duet, song
composer: 6 Caesar **7** Youmans
Teagarden, Jack: 10 trombonist
genre: 4 jazz
Teague: 5 Lewis
teahouse: 10 restaurant
hostess: 6 geisha
Teahouse of the August Moon, The (1956 film)
cast: Marlon Brando, Glenn Ford, Machiko Kyo
director: Daniel Mann
teak: 4 tree, wood **5** color **8** hardwood
family: 7 verbena
teakettle
part: 5 spout
sound: 3 sss **4** hiss, ssss
teal: 4 bird, blue, duck, fowl **5** color **8** greenish
faux ~: 5 decoy
relative: 4 anil, cyan, navy, Nile, smew **5** Alice, azure, eider, Pekin, Rouen, scaup, slate **6** Cayuga, cobalt, indigo, raisin, scoter, violet, wigeon **7** gadwall, mallard, peacock, pintail, pochard, redhead, sea duck, widgeon **8** cerulean, garganey, gray duck, mandarin, musk duck, oldsquaw, sapphire, shoveler, surf duck, wood duck **9** black duck, broadbill, goldeneye, goosander, greenhead, merganser, ruddy duck, sprigtail, turquoise **10** aquamarine, bufflehead, canvasback, periwinkle, surf scoter, tufted duck
team: 3 duo, rig, set **4** band, body, club, crew, gang, pair, side, span, trio, unit, yoke **5** bunch, cadre, corps, group, hands, party, squad, staff, troop **6** lineup, outfit, string, troupe **7** company, coterie, faction, platoon, varsity, workers **8** athletic, ball club, foursome, partners **10** contingent
B ~: 6 scrubs
be on a ~: 4 play
drop from the ~: 3 cut
ender: 4 mate, ster, work
goal: 3 win
leader: 3 mgr. **5** coach **7** manager
member: 5 horse **6** player **10** contestant
show ~ spirit: 4 root **5** cheer **7** cheer on
the other ~: 3 foe **4** them **5** enemy
up: 3 wed **4** bond, join, link, pair **5** marry, merge, unite **6** couple, hook up **7** combine, conjoin, connect, pair off **8** side with, tag along **9** affiliate, interface, tie in with **10** amalgamate, assist with, go partners
team __: 6 player
__ team: 3 tag **4** farm, SWAT **5** delta, dream, drill **6** combat **7** special
__, team!: 3 Yay, Yea
__-team: 6 double
__-Team: 4 The A
teammate: 7 partner **8** co-worker **9** colleague
Te Amo: 5 cigar
team player, not a: 5 loner, rebel
Teamster: 6 hauler **7** trucker
unit: 4 semi **5** local
Teamsters: 5 union
team-supporting word: 3 rah
teamwork obstacles: 4 egos
Teaneck: 4 city, town
athletes: 7 Knights
locale: 9 New Jersey
Teapa: 4 city, town
locale: 6 Mexico **7** Tabasco
tea party
attendee: 5 Alice
host a ~: 4 pour
__ Tea Party: 6 Boston
teapot: 6 kettle

cover: 4 cozy
feature: 5 spout
tempest in a ~: 3 ado 4 fuss
Teapot Dome victim: 4 Fall
teapoy: 5 table
tear: 3 cut, fly, hie, rip, run, zip 4 bolt, bust, claw, dart, dash, flit, fray, gash, grab, hole, hurt, part, pull, race, rack, rage, rend, rent, rift, rive, rush, slit, snag, weep, yank, zoom 5 binge, break, crack, hurry, pluck, scoot, seize, sever, shoot, shred, slash, speed, split, spree, storm, whisk, wrest 6 barrel, bender, breach, careen, career, cleave, crying, damage, divide, gallop, hasten, hurtle, hustle, impair, injure, mangle, move it, plunge, rocket, scurry, snatch, sprint, strain, streak, sunder, tatter, wrench 7 divulse, droplet, fissure, floor it, frazzle, globule, hop to it, opening, quicken, rampage, rip open, rupture, scamper, scratch 8 carousal, jerk away, lacerate, moisture, mutilate, separate, stampede, step on it, teardrop, zip along 9 come apart, fulgurate, hotfoot it, pull apart, shake a leg, skedaddle 10 come undone, get a move on, get hopping, hightail it, laceration, make tracks
apart: 3 cut, hew, rip 4 chop, part, rend, rive 5 rip up, sever, slash, split 6 avulse, cleave, divide, rebuke 7 disjoin 8 dissever, disunite, separate
channel: 4 duct
combining form: 5 dacry- 6 dacryo-
down: 4 rase, raze, ruin, slur 5 level, libel, smash, wreck 6 malign, refute, topple, vilify 7 degrade, destroy, slander, unbuild 8 badmouth, belittle, bulldoze, demolish, diminish, disprove 9 denigrate, devastate, discredit, dismantle, take apart 10 calumniate
dryer: 5 hanky 6 hankie
ender: 4 down, drop 5 stain 6 jerker
go on a ~: 4 rage 5 storm
holder: 3 sac
into: 4 lash 5 roast, scold 6 assail, attack, have at, oppugn, vilify 9 excoriate 10 vituperate
(into): 4 lace
mend a ~: 5 resew
off: 3 hie, lop, run 4 race 5 sever, speed 6 detach, loosen, remove 7 disjoin 8 separate, unfasten 10 disconnect
old-style: 5 reave
on a ~: 4 wild 5 rowdy 6 unruly 7 lawless, raucous 9 fractious 10 boisterous, disorderly, disruptive, rebellious
out: 5 pluck 6 remove, uproot 9 extirpate
out a seam: 5 unrip
partner: 4 wear
small ~: 4 slit
try to ~: 5 rip at
up the road: 4 zoom 5 spank
wear and ~: 3 use 6 damage 8 breakage 9 shrinkage 10 impairment
tear ___: 3 gas, off, out 4 away, bomb, down, into 5 sheet, shell, strip 7 grenade
tear-___: 6 jerker 7 jerking, stained
___ tear: 3 hot, on a
___ Teardrops: 6 Lonely
Tear Fell, A (1956 song) artist: Teresa Brewer
tearful: 3 sad 5 moist, upset, weepy, woful 6 crying, woeful 7 bawling, maudlin, sobbing, weeping, wet-eyed 8 blubbery, dolorous, mournful, pathetic, poignant 9 lamenting, sniveling, sorrowful 10 blubbering, distressed, lachrymose, lamentable, pathetical, whimpering
tearjerker: 4 play 5 drama, flick, movie, story 7 romance
kitchen ~: 5 onion
quality: 6 pathos
tear-jerking: 3 sad 5 mushy 7 maudlin, mawkish 8 romantic, touching 9 sorrowful
tear one's ___ out: 4 hair
tearoom cousin: 4 café 6 bistro 10 restaurant
tears: 5 drops 6 crying, egesta, lament, sorrow 7 sobbing, wailing, weeping 8 distress, grieving, moisture 10 blubbering, waterworks, whimpering
antibody in ~: 3 IGA
combining form: 7 lacrimo-
dim with ~: 4 blur 5 blear, cloud
in ~: 5 weepy 7 bawling, sobbing, weeping 8 broken up 9 sniveling
like ~: 5 salty
move to ~: 3 get 5 upset 6 affect
near ~: 5 misty
shed ~: 3 cry, sob 4 bawl, mewl, pule, wail, weep 6 boohoo, snivel 7 blubber, whimper
___ tears: 5 baby's, Pele's 9 crocodile
___-tears: 4 baby, Job's 7 maiden's
Tears and Roses (1964 song) artist: Al Martino
Tears for Fears
song: Everybody Wants to Rule the World (1985)
Head Over Heels (1985)
Shout (1985)
Sowing the Seeds of Love (1989)
Tears, Idle Tears author: Alfred Tennyson
Tears in Heaven (1992 song) artist: Eric Clapton
Tears of a Clown, The (1970 song) artist: Miracles
Tears on My Pillow (1958 song) artist: Little Anthony and the Imperials
teary: 3 sad, wet 5 blear, moist, weepy 6 crying 7 bawling, maudlin, mawkish, sobbing, unhappy 8 broken up, choked up 9 emotional, misty-eyed, sniveling 10 blubbering, lachrymose
Teasdale: 4 Sara 6 Verree
Teasdale, Sara: 4 poet
work: Dark of the Moon
Flame and Shadow
Love Songs
Rivers to the Sea
Strange Victory
tease: 3 dog, kid, rag, rib, toy, vex 4 bait, be at, comb, gibe, gnaw, goad, guye, jest, jibe, jive, joke, josh, mock, pest, razz, ride, twit 5 annoy, chaff, devil, flirt, harry, nudge, put on, rag on, roast, taunt, tweak, worry 6 badger, banter, bother, harass, heckle, hector, kidder, lead on, needle, pester, pick on, plague 7 bedevil, disturb, fluff up, provoke, put down, torment, toy with 8 backcomb, bullyrag, coquette, ridicule 9 aggravate, beleaguer, importune, make fun of, persecute, poke fun at, tantalize, titillate 10 make eyes at
teasel: 5 plant 6 flower
teaser: 4 bait, pest 5 poser, promo, vexer 6 enigma 7 problem, stumper 9 conundrum, promotion
starter: 5 brain
teasing: 5 sport 6 banter 7 naughty, playful 8 badinage 9 annoyance, quizzical, vexatious 10 allurement
teasingly: 5 in fun
teaspoon, use a: 4 stir
Teatro ___ Scala: 4 alla
Tebaldi, Renata: 4 diva 6 singer 7 soprano
role: 5 Tosca
specialty: 5 opera
tec: 2 PI 6 Holmes, shamus, sleuth 7 Columbo, gumshoe 8 hawkshaw, Sherlock 10 Mike Hammer, private eye
Tecámac: 4 city, town
locale: 6 Mexico
Tecate: 4 city, town
locale: 6 Mexico
tech: 4 geek, guru, nerd, nurd
starter: 3 bio
talk: 5 argot, lingo 6 jargon
tech. ___: 3 sgt.
___-tech: 3 low, sci 4 high
___ Tech: 3 Cal 5 Texas 7 Georgia
techie: 4 geek, guru, nerd, nurd
___ Te Ching: 3 Tao
technetium: 7 element
technical: 8 abstruse, detailed 9 scholarly 10 industrial, mechanical, restricted, scientific, vocational
word: 4 term
technical ___: 4 foul 6 school
technicality: 5 point 6 detail, nicety 7 minutia 8 loophole 9 fine point, punctilio
technician: 4 guru 6 expert 8 mechanic, repairer 9 authority 10 specialist
___ technician: 4 x-ray 6 dental
technique: 3 art, way 4 mode 5 craft, knack, means, skill, style, trick 6 manner, method, recipe, system 7 know-how, process, routine, science, tactics 8 approach, artistry, facility, hang of it 9 execution, procedure
combining form: 4 -urgy
technology: 3 sci. 7 science 9 procedure
___ technology: 3 low 4 high
Tech TV alternative: 3 BET, CMT, MTV, PAX, TBS, TLC, TNN, TNT, USA 4 ESPN, HGTV 5 A and E, C-SPAN, Style 6 Noggin 7 Ovation, SoapNet 8 Lifetime
Tecomán: 4 city, town
locale: 6 Colima, Mexico
Tecpan: 4 city, town
locale: 6 Mexico 8 Guerrero
___ tectonics: 5 plate 6 global
tectonics event: 5 quake, seism 6 tremor
tectrix: 5 plume
Tecuala: 4 city, town
locale: 6 Mexico 7 Nayarit
___ Tecumseh Sherman: 7 William
Ted: 3 Key 4 Mack, Post, Ross, Wass 5 Demme, Lange, Lewis, Raimi, Shawn, Weems, Wilde 6 Baxter, Berman, Danson, Hughes, Husing, Knight, Koppel, Nugent, Turner 7 Bessell, Cassidy, Kennedy, Lindsay 8 Kotcheff, McGinley, Nicolaou, Tetzlaff, Williams 10 Kluszewski
Caroline, to ~: 5 niece
Maria, to ~: 5 niece
TED defeater: 3 FDR, HST
teddy ___: 4 bear
Teddy: 7 Kennedy 9 Roosevelt
Eleanor, to ~: 5 niece
mom: 4 Rose
1904 opponent: 5 Alton
Teddy Bears song: To Know Him, Is to Love Him (1958)
tedious: 3 dry 4 arid, drab, dull, flat, poky, slow, tame 5 banal, bland, dusty, heavy, ho-hum, prosy, unfun, vapid, wordy, yawny 6 boring, dreary, jejune, stodgy, stuffy, taxing, tiring 7 endless, humdrum, insipid, irksome, lengthy, operose, painful, prosaic, routine, verbose 8 annoying, dragging, drudging, lifeless, tiresome 9 fatiguing, laborious, ponderous, prosaical, soporific, wearisome 10 dullsville, enervating, exhausting, monotonous, uneventful, unexciting
account: 6 litany 10 recitation
be ~: 4 bore, pall
one: 4 bore, drag, drip, pain, pest, pill 5 creep 8 nuisance 10 wet blanket
routine: 3 rut 5 grind 8 drudgery
tediousness: 6 tedium 8 monotony 9 heaviness
tedium: 5 ennui, grind 7 boredom, routine 8 banality, doldrums, drabness, dullness, flatness, monotony, sameness 9 weariness 10 dreariness, melancholy
sign of ~: 4 yawn
___ & Ted's Excellent Adventure: 4 Bill
tee: 3 peg 5 joint, shirt 8 pullover 10 undershirt
ender: 5 total
off: 3 irk 4 miff, rile, roil 5 anger, annoy, drive, peeve, start, steam, upset 6 enrage 7 pitch in 9 infuriate 10 exasperate
(off): 4 tick
partner: 5 jeans
preceder: 3 ess
to a ~: 8 very well 9 on the nose, precisely 10 positively
up: 5 start
user: 6 golfer
tee ___: 3 off 4 time 5 shirt
tee-___: 3 hee
___ tee: 3 air, to a 4 drop, golf, wind 7 landing
teed off: 3 mad 4 sore 5 angry, irate, upset 9 disgusted, resentful
tee-hee: 6 giggle, titter 7 snicker, snigger
teel: 6 sesame
teem: 4 brim, pour, swim 5 crawl, crowd, swarm 6 abound, bustle, deluge, wallow 7 bristle, overrun 8 overflow 9 pullulate
teeming: 3 wet 4 full, lush, many, rife 5 alive, dense, laden, thick 6 aswarm, fecund, filled, imbued, jammed, loaded, packed 7 brimful, crammed, crowded, fertile, profuse, replete, stuffed 8 abundant, brimfull, bursting, fruitful, infested, numerous, populous, prodigal, prolific, swarming, thronged 9 bristling, chock-full, exuberant, luxuriant, plentiful
teen: 3 kid 4 girl 5 child, minor, youth 6 Archie 8 juvenile 9 childhood, stripling, youngster 10 adolescent, bobbysoxer
activist org.: 4 SADD
big day: 4 prom 10 graduation
channel: 3 MTV 5 Spike
concern: 6 curfew
culture: 6 hip-hop
desire: 3 car 4 auto 6 wheels 10 automobile
ender: 3 age 4 aged, ager
exclamation: 3 rad
former ~: 5 adult 7 grownup
hangout: 4 mall 6 arcade
mustache: 4 wisp
outcast: 4 geek, nerd, nurd
punishment, perhaps: 4 no TV
room, often: 4 mess 5 chaos, wreck 7 clutter, eyesore 8 disarray, shambles
sentence ender: 6 and all
socialite: 3 deb
starter: 3 six, ump 4 four, nine 5 seven
woe: 3 zit 4 acne

teen ___: **4** idol
___-teen: **3** mid
Teen: **6** Harold
Teen ___: **4** Beat, Wolf **5** Angel
Teena: **5** Marie
teenage: **5** young **8** juvenile **10** adolescent
Teen-Age Crush (1957 song) artist: Tommy Sands
Teen Age Idol (1962 song) artist: Ricky Nelson
Teenage Mutant ___ Turtles: **5** Ninja
Teen Age Prayer (1955 song) artist: Gale Storm
teenager: **3** kid **4** girl **5** child, minor, youth **8** juvenile **9** stripling, youngster **10** adolescent
see also teen
Teenager in Love, A (1959 song) artist: Dion and the Belmonts
Teenager's Romance, A (1957 song) artist: Ricky Nelson
___ Teen-age Werewolf: **5** I Was a
Teena Marie
real name: Mary Christine Brokert
song: Lovergirl (1985)
Teen Angel (1960 song) artist: Mark Dinning
teenie-___: **6** weenie
teensy-___: **6** weensy
Teen Wolf (1985 film)
cast: Michael J. Fox, James Hampton
teeny-___: **5** weeny **6** bopper
teenybopper: **4** girl, miss **10** adolescent, schoolgirl
teeny-weeny: **3** wee **4** baby, itsy, puny, tiny **5** bitsy, bitty, teeny, weeny **6** atomic, bantam, little, minute, peewee, petite, teensy **8** atomical, atomlike **9** itsy-bitsy, itty-bitty, miniature, pint-sized, undersize **10** diminutive, vest-pocket
Tees: **5** river
locale: **7** England
teeter: **4** reel, rock, sway **5** lurch, pivot, waver, weave **6** falter, jiggle, quiver, seesaw, topple, totter, wabble, wobble **7** balance, flutter, stagger, stumble, tremble, whiffle **9** fluctuate, oscillate, vacillate
ender: **5** board **6** totter
teetering: **5** shaky **6** jiggly, unfirm, wabbly, wobbly **8** unstable, unsteady
teeter-totter: **6** seesaw **9** oscillate
teeth: **5** vigor
bare one's ~: **4** dare **5** snarl
by the skin of one's ~: **4** just **6** barely **8** narrowly, scarcely
device with ~: **3** saw **4** comb, gear, rake
enough to sink one's ~ into: **5** meaty
grit one's ~: **5** gnarl, gnash, steel **6** clench
kick in the ~: **4** slur **6** rebuff, rebuke **7** repulse **9** rejection
like some ~: **6** capped
of ~: **6** dental
science of ~: **9** dentistry
straighteners: **6** braces
take the bit in one's ~: **4** defy **5** rebel **6** revolt **7** disobey **9** break away
to the ~: **5** fully **8** entirely **10** completely
use one's ~: **3** nip **4** bite, chew, gnaw
see also tooth
___ teeth: **4** baby **5** false, to the
teething ___: **4** ring
teetotaler: **3** dry **9** abstainer **10** nondrinker
grp.: **4** WCTU
Teflon company: **6** DuPont
teg: **5** sheep
Tegucigalpa: **4** city, town **7** capital
locale: **8** Honduras
Tegus, city on the: **6** Toledo
Tehachapi: **5** range **9** mountains
locale: **10** California
te-hee: **6** giggle, titter **7** snicker, snigger
Teheran: **4** city, town **7** capital
city near ~: **3** Qom, Qum
language: **5** Farsi
locale: **4** Iran
VIP: **4** imam **5** imaum
Tehuacán: **4** city, town **6** valley
locale: **6** Mexico, Puebla
Tehuantepec: **4** city, town
locale: **6** Mexico, Oaxaca
Tehuelche: **6** Indian **7** Amerind
Teicher, Louis: **7** pianist
partner: **8** Ferrante
Teide: **4** peak **5** mount **8** mountain
locale: **5** Spain **6** Europe
teiid: **6** animal **7** reptile
teil: **4** tree **6** linden
Teilhard de Chardin, Pierre: **6** French, writer **10** theologian **11** philosopher
specialty: **9** mysticism
work: The Divine Milieu
The Phenomenon of Man
Tejat: **4** star
Tejo, city on the: **6** Toledo
Tejupilco: **4** city, town
locale: **6** Mexico
Te Kanawa, Kiri: **4** Dame, diva **5** Maori **6** Aussie, singer **7** soprano
solo: **4** aria
specialty: **5** opera
Tekax: **4** city, town
locale: **6** Mexico **7** Yucatán
Tel ___: **4** Aviv **6** Amarna
telamon: **5** atlas
Telamon: **8** Argonaut
father of ~: **6** Aeacus
son of ~: **4** Aias, Ajax
Tel Aviv: **4** city, town
airport: **3** Lod
locale: **3** Isr. **6** Israel
port near ~: **4** Gaza **5** Haifa
telecast: **4** news, on TV, show **7** program
like some ~ s: **4** live
signal: **5** audio, video
telecom letters: **3** GTE, ITT, MCI
telecommuter workplace: **4** home **6** at home
telecopy: **3** fax
tele ender: **4** gram, path, play, port, thon, type, vise **5** graph, metry, pathy, phone, photo, scope **7** commute **9** marketing **10** conference
Telefon (1977 film)
cast: Charles Bronson, Tyne Daly, Patrick Magee, Donald Pleasence, Lee Remick
director: Don Siegel
Telefone (1983 song) artist: Sheena Easton
telegram: **4** news, wire **5** cable, flash, telex **6** report **7** message **8** teletype **9** cablegram, radiogram
sender: **5** wirer
word: **4** stop
telegraph: **4** wire
datum: **3** dah, dit, dot **4** dash
inventor: **5** Morse
operator: **5** coder
part: **3** key **5** relay
receiver: **5** inker
sound: **5** clack
starter: **5** radio
telekinetic: **7** psychic
Telemachus parent: **8** Odysseus, Penelope
Telemann, Georg: **6** German **8** composer
telemarketer: **6** caller
device: **6** dialer
telemetry: **7** science
telepathic: **6** mental **7** psychic
telepathist: **4** seer
telepathy: **3** ESP, psi **10** sixth sense
___ telepathy: **6** mental
Telephassa child: **6** Cadmus, Europa
telephone: **4** buzz, call, dial, horn, ring **5** phone **6** blower, notify, report, ring up **7** contact **9** broadcast, touch base **10** get a hold of
button: **3** ABC, DEF, GHI, JKL, MNO, PRS, TUV, WXY **4** OPER, star **9** pound sign
charge: **4** toll
company: **4** util. **7** utility
device: **4** jack **5** modem **6** dialer **7** headset
exclamation: **8** greeting **10** salutation
greeting: **5** hello
line: **4** cord **5** trunk
number part: **3** ext. **8** area code, exchange **9** extension
part: **4** cord, wire **6** cradle **8** receiver
starter: **5** radio
user: **5** party **6** caller
wait on the ~: **4** hold
see also phone
telephone ___: **3** tag **4** bank, book, pole **5** booth
___ telephone: **6** French, mobile
Telephone Line (1977 song) artist: ELO
telephoto ___: **4** lens
teleplay: **5** story **6** script
TelePromp___: **3** Ter
telescope: **3** cut **6** Hubble, reduce **7** abridge, shorten **8** abstract, boil down, compress, condense, cut short, truncate **9** capsulize, summarize, synopsize **10** abbreviate
adjust a ~: **5** focus
part: **4** lens **5** optic **8** eyepiece **9** magnifier
view: **4** moon **6** cosmos, galaxy, planet **8** Milky Way
___ telescope: **4** Hale **5** coudé, radar, radio **6** Kepler, zenith **7** Schmidt
Telescopium neighbor: **3** Ara
Telesphorus: **4** pope **7** pontiff
telesterion: **6** temple
telesthesia: **3** ESP **9** intuition, telepathy
Telesto: **4** moon
planet: **6** Saturn
telethon: **6** appeal **7** benefit **10** fundraiser
Teletubby: **2** Po **5** Dipsy **6** Laa-Laa **10** Tinky Winky
fan: **3** kid, tot
televise: **3** air **4** send **8** transmit **9** broadcast
television: **3** box, JVC, NEC, RCA, set **4** Sony, tube **5** media, telly **6** Quasar, Zenith **7** Emerson, Hitachi, monitor, ProScan, Toshiba **8** boob tube, idiot box, Magnavox, Sylvania **9** goggle box, Panasonic
fare: **4** news, show, talk **5** drama **6** series, sitcom **8** game show, talk show
former ~ brand: **6** Dumont
letters on a ~: **3** UHF, VHF
like early ~: **4** live
signal component: **5** audio, video
tube gas: **4** neon
tuner: **4** dial
see also TV
television ___: **7** station
___ television: **3** pay **5** cable **6** public **7** console
Television, Mr.: **5** Berle
Telford: **4** city, town
locale: **7** England **10** Shropshire
tell: **3** air, bid, rat, say, see **4** blab, know, leak, warn **5** learn, let on, level, order, speak, spill, state, tally, utter, voice, weigh **6** advise, clinch, clue in, convey, deduce, depict, detail, direct, divine, enjoin, fill in, impart, inform, notify, number, open up, recite, reckon, relate, report, reveal, set out, snitch, squeal, summon, tip off, unveil **7** apprise, apprize, breathe, bring up, command, compute, confess, declare, discern, divulge, explain, express, find out, give out, lay bare, lay open, let in on, let know, let slip, make out, mention, narrate, portray, recount, reel off, require, signify, spit out, uncover, whisper **8** acquaint, announce, call upon, describe, disclose, discover, identify, instruct, let it out, militate, numerate, perceive, proclaim, register, rehearse, set forth, throw out **9** ascertain, authorize, calculate, chronicle, determine, enumerate, expound on, leave word, make known, put before, recognize, represent **10** comprehend, keep posted, take effect, understand
again: **5** resay
all: **3** air **4** bare, blab, sing, talk **6** fess up **8** unburden **9** name names
ender: **4** tale
hear ~: **5** learn **6** listen
of: **5** cover **7** bespeak, narrate, recount **9** adumbrate
off: **4** lash, rail **5** chide, scold **6** berate, rebuff, rebuke, revile **7** censure, lecture, reprove, upbraid **8** admonish, reproach **9** lash out at, reprimand **10** take to task
on: **3** rat **6** give up, report, tattle, turn in
partner: **4** kiss, show
tales: **3** gab, yak **4** blab, dish **6** gossip, tattle **8** schmooze
the judge: **3** sue **5** argue **6** appeal **7** declare **8** petition
tell ___: **3** off **4** a fib, a lie
tell ___ glance: **3** at a
tell-___ book: **3** all
___ tell!: **4** Pray
Tell: **7** Wilhelm, William
Tell ___: **3** Him **5** Her No, Me Why
Tell ___ About It: **3** Her
Tell ___ I Love Her: **5** Laura
Tell ___ My Heart: **4** It to
Tell ___ Sweeney!: **4** it to
Tell ___ the judge!: **4** it to
Tell ___ the Marines!: **4** it to
Tell-___ Heart, The: **4** Tale
tell-all: **4** book **6** exposé
teller: **5** clerk **7** cashier **9** paymaster
cry: **4** next
fish story ~: **6** fibber **8** deceiver
place: **4** bank, cage **5** booth, S and L
starter: **4** tale **5** story **7** fortune
whopper ~: **4** liar **6** fibber **8** deceiver
Teller: **6** Edward
partner: **4** Penn **8** Jillette
Tell Her About It (1983 song) artist: Billy Joel
Tell Her No (1965 song) artist: Zombies
telling: **5** solid, sound, valid **6** cogent, marked, potent, strong **7** graphic, logical, pointed, pungent, recital **8** decisive, forceful, forcible, material, powerful, striking **9** effective, effectual, graphical, trenchant **10** conclusive, convincing, expressive, impressive, persuasive, recitation, unarguable
it like it is: **5** blunt, frank **6** candid, candor, direct, honest **7** honesty, up-front **8** straight, veracity **9** outspoken **10** aboveboard, forthright, free-spoken, from the hip, point-blank, unreserved

off: **6** rebuke, tirade **7** reproof **8** harangue, scolding **9** reprimand, talking-to
__ telling me!: **5** You're
telling-off: **6** earful, rebuke
Tell it __ Marines!: **5** to the
tell it like __: **4** it is
Tell It Like It Is (song) artist: Aaron Neville, Heart
Tell It to My Heart (1987 song) artist: Taylor Dayne
Tell It to the Rain (1966 song) artist: Four Seasons
Tell Laura I Love Her (1960 song) artist: Ray Peterson
__ tell me!: **4** Don't
Tell Me How Long the Train's Been Gone author: James Baldwin
Tell me more!: **4** Go on
Tell Me Something Good (1974 song) artist: Chaka Khan
Tell Me That You Love Me, Junie Moon (1970 film)
cast: Ken Howard, Liza Minnelli, Robert Moore
director: Otto Preminger
__ Tell Me True: **5** Tammy
Tell Me Why (song) artist: Elvis Presley, Exposé
Tell Me Your Dreams author: Sidney Sheldon
__ Tells Me So, The: **5** Bible
telltale: **6** tattle **7** tattler **9** revealing **10** meaningful
sign: **4** odor
Tell-Tale Heart, The author: **3** Poe
Tell Them Willie Boy Is Here (1969 film)
cast: Robert Blake, Robert Redford, Katharine Ross
Telluride: **4** city, town
enjoy ~: **3** ski **4** skee
locale: **8** Colorado
tellurium: **5** metal **7** element
Tell, William: **6** archer, bowman
home: **3** Uri **11** Switzerland
target: **5** apple
weapon: **3** bow **5** arrow
telly: **2** TV **3** set **4** tube **5** TV set **10** television
network: **3** BBC
Telly: **7** Savalas
Telma: **7** Hopkins
Telstar (1962 song) artist: Tornadoes
Telugu: **8** language
tema: **5** motif
Tema: **4** city, town
locale: **5** Ghana
temblor: **5** quake, seism **6** tremor **8** upheaval **10** earthquake
Temecula: **4** city, town
locale: **10** California
temerarious: **8** reckless
temerity: **4** gall **5** brass, cheek, nerve, pluck **6** daring **7** courage, license **8** audacity, boldness, chutzpah, defiance, rudeness **9** impudence **10** effrontery
Temin, Howard: **8** Nobelist
Temixco: **4** city, town
locale: **6** Mexico **7** Morelos
temp: **3** sub **6** fill-in, helper **7** stand-in **9** assistant, fill in for, makeshift **10** substitute
employer: **4** firm **6** agency, office **7** company
temp.
scale: **3** Fah. **4** Fahr
unit: **3** deg.
Tempe: **4** city, town
athletes: **9** Sun Devils
locale: **4** Ariz. **7** Arizona
river: **4** Salt
school: **3** ASU
temper: **3** ire **4** bile, calm, cool, curb, ease, fury, gird, heat, lull, mood, rage, snit, tame, tiff, tone, vein **5** allay, anger, build, humor, Irish, poise, shore, state, steel, storm, style, trend, wrath **6** animus, anneal, beef up, choler, dampen, dander, esprit, harden, lessen, makeup, modify, nature, pacify, prop up, refine, season, soften, soothe, spirit, strain, subdue, tone up, weaken **7** assuage, bad mood, bolster, brace up, build up, burgeon, develop, empower, enhance, fortify, leaning, mollify, passion, qualify, relieve, shore up, stiffen, tantrum, toughen **8** bourgeon, buttress, calmness, energize, humanize, ill humor, indurate, mitigate, moderate, modulate, outburst, palliate, regulate, restrain, restrict, slow burn, tone down, vitalize **9** character, composure, huffiness, intensify, petulance, pugnacity, reinforce, short fuse, softpedal, surliness **10** equanimity, grumpiness, impatience, invigorate, keep in line, resentment, strengthen, sullenness, touchiness
even ~: **8** patience **9** composure **10** sedateness
fit of ~: **3** pet **4** rage, snit **5** blast, blaze, flash, scene, storm, surge **6** access, attack, flurry, frenzy, outcry, tirade **7** flare-up, tantrum, torrent **8** eruption, outbreak, outburst, paroxysm, upheaval **9** discharge, explosion, hysterics **10** conniption, outpouring
ill ~: **4** fury, rage **5** anger, wrath **6** enmity, rancor **7** sarcasm, umbrage **8** acerbity, acrimony, rudeness, sourness, tartness **9** surliness **10** bitterness
lose one's ~: **4** rage, rant, roar, yell **6** blow up
temper __: **5** color **7** tantrum
__ temper: **3** ill
tempera: **5** paint
temperament: **4** bent, cast, mood, soul, vein **5** humor, stamp **6** makeup, mettle, nature, spirit **7** outlook **8** attitude **9** character, mentality **10** complexion
temperamental: **3** hot **5** fiery, hyper, moody, onery **6** cussed, fickle, ornery, touchy, wilful **7** erratic, froward, waspish, willful **8** petulant, ticklish, unstable, variable, volatile **9** emotional, excitable, explosive, hotheaded, impatient, irritable, mercurial, sensitive, uncertain
temperance: **6** virtue **8** eschewal, sobriety **9** austerity, restraint **10** abnegation, abstinence, moderation
advocate: **3** dry **4** WCTU
temperate: **4** calm, cool, easy, even, fair, kind, mild, soft, warm, zone **5** balmy, quiet, sober, staid, stoic, tepid **6** at ease, benign, gentle, lowkey, medium, mellow, modest, placid, sedate, serene, stable, steady **7** amiable, at peace, clement, equable, pacific, relaxed, stoical, unmoved, warmish **8** amicable, carefree, composed, discreet, laid-back, moderate, peaceful, pleasant, sensible, tranquil **9** abstinent, agreeable, collected, continent, easy-going, impassive, quiescent, unexcited, unextreme, unruffled **10** abstemious, nonchalant, phlegmatic, reasonable, restrained, unagitated, untroubled
Temperate __: **4** Zone
__ Temperate Zone: **5** North, South
temperature: **4** heat **5** fever **6** warmth **7** climate, degrees, pyrexia **8** body heat
extreme: **3** low **4** high
freezing ~: **5** teens
high ~: **4** heat **5** fever
measure: **6** degree, Kelvin **7** Celsius **10** Centigrade, Fahrenheit
__ temperature: **4** mean, room, run a **5** color, Curie
temperature-humidity __: **5** index
__-tempered: **3** bad, hot, ill **4** even, good **5** quick, short, sweet
__-Tempered Clavier, The: **4** Well **5** Short
tempering: **9** abatement, reduction **10** diminution, mitigation, moderation, palliation, subsidence
tempest: **4** blow, gale, wind **5** blast, furor, storm, swirl **6** squall, tumult, uproar **7** bluster, cyclone, rampage, tornado, typhoon **8** blizzard, upheaval **9** hurricane, windstorm **10** convulsion
in a teapot: **3** ado **4** fuss
tempest-__: **4** tost **6** tossed
Tempest: **3** car **4** auto **5** Marie **7** Pontiac **10** automobile
tempest in a __: **6** teacup, teapot
Tempestt: **7** Bledsoe
Tempest, The: **4** play **6** comedy
author: Shakespeare
role: **5** Ariel **6** Alonso **7** Antonio, Caliban, Gonzalo, Miranda **8** Prospero, Stephano, Trinculo **9** Ferdinand, Sebastian
tempestuous: **4** wild **5** fiery, rough **6** fierce, heated, raging, stormy **7** excited, furious, intense, lawless, violent **8** agitated, feverish **9** emotional, turbulent, unbridled **10** tumultuous
tempestuousness: **4** fire, fury **7** passion **8** savagery **9** intensity **10** turbulence
__ Templar: **7** Knights
Templar, Simon: The Saint
portrayer: Val Kilmer, Roger Moore
template: **7** pattern
temple: **4** fane, shul **5** abbey, schul, zendo **6** chapel, church, mosque, pagoda, shrine, temple **7** synagog **8** pantheon, sacellum **9** cathedral, sanctuary, synagogue **10** tabernacle
ancient Greek ~: **4** naos **6** hieron
Buddhist ~: **3** wat
chamber: **4** naos **5** cella **6** adytum
combining form: **7** temporo-
of India: **4** rath **5** ratha
table: **5** altar
teacher: **5** rabbi, rebbe
tongue: **6** Hebrew
worshiper: **3** Jew
temple __: **6** orange
Temple: **4** city, town **7** Shirley
athletes: **4** Owls
locale: **4** Penn. **5** Phila., Texas
__ Temple Black: **7** Shirley
Temple City: **4** town
locale: **10** California
Temple of __: **4** Ares **7** Artemis
Temple of the Golden Pavilion, The author: Yukio Mishima
__ Temple Pilots: **5** Stone
temples: **4** naoi
Temple, Shirley: **7** actress
costar: **5** Ebsen **8** Robinson
film: The Bachelor and the Bobby-Soxer (1947)
Fort Apache (1948)
The Little Colonel (1935)
Little Miss Marker (1934)
The Little Princess (1939)
The Littlest Rebel (1935)
Poor Little Rich Girl (1936)
Wee Willie Winkie (1937)
spouse: John Agar
Temple, The author: Jerome Weidman
Templeton: **4** Alec
tempo: **4** beat, pace, rate, time **5** grave, largo, lento, meter, pulse, speed, swing **6** adagio, presto, rhythm, vivace **7** allegro, andante, cadence, cadency, measure **8** downbeat, moderato, momentum, velocity
a ~: **6** in time
modified ~: **6** rubato
Tempo: **3** car **4** auto, Ford, Nino **10** automobile
Tempoal: **4** city, town
locale: **6** Mexico **8** Veracruz
Tempo and April Stevens, Nino song: Deep Purple (1963)
temporal: **3** lay **4** laic **5** civil **6** laical, mortal **7** earthly, mundane, passing, profane, secular, worldly **8** banausic, fleeting, fugitive, material, physical **9** ephemeral, momentary, transient **10** evanescent, short-lived, transitory, unhallowed
temporal __: **4** bone, hour, lobe
temporarily: **6** for now **7** briefly **8** meantime **9** meanwhile
temporary: **5** ad hoc, brief, short **6** acting, make-do, pro tem **7** interim, migrant, passing, stopgap, summary **8** fleeting, flitting, fugitive, slapdash **9** alternate, ephemeral, makeshift, migratory, momentary, overnight, provisory, revocable, transient **10** changeable, evanescent, jury-rigged, perishable, short-lived, substitute, transitory, unenduring
resident: **6** lodger, roomer **7** boarder
__ tempore: **3** pro
temporize: **4** duck **5** dally, delay, dodge, evade, hedge, skirt, stall, tarry, waver **6** put off, waffle **8** hesitate, postpone, sidestep **9** hem and haw, pussyfoot **10** equivocate
__-temps: **5** entre
tempt: **3** oil, woo **4** bait, coax, dare, draw, hook, lure, urge, whet **5** charm, decoy, rouse, shill, snare **6** allure, appeal, beckon, cajole, entice, entrap, incite, induce, invite, lead on, pull in **7** attract, beguile, bewitch, mislead, promote, provoke **8** appeal to, butter up, interest, inveigle, motivate, persuade, play up to **9** captivate, fascinate, influence, mousetrap, sweet-talk
fate: **4** dare
temptation: **4** bait, lure, trap, urge **5** decoy, snare **6** allure, carrot, come-on **9** incentive **10** attraction, enticement, inducement, invitation
lead into ~: **4** hook, lure, trap **5** snare, trick **6** entice, entrap, lead on, reel in, rope in, suck in **7** deceive
Temptations
song: Ain't Too Proud to Beg (1966)
All I Need (1967)
Ball of Confusion (1970)
Beauty Is Only Skin Deep (1966)
Cloud Nine (1968)
I Can't Get Next to You (1969)
I'm Gonna Make You Love Me (1968)
I'm Losing You (1966)
I Wish It Would Rain (1968)
Just My Imagination (1971)
Masterpiece (1973)
The Motown Song (1991)
My Girl (1965)
Papa Was a Rollin' Stone (1972)
Psychedelic Shack (1970)
Run Away Child, Running Wild (1969)
The Way You Do the Things You Do (1964)
You're My Everything (1967)

temptation walk: 5 dance
Temp, The (1993 film)
cast: Lara Flynn Boyle, Faye Dunaway, Timothy Hutton
director: Tom Holland
tempting: 5 siren, yummy 6 savory 8 alluring, charming, enticing, fetching, inviting 9 palatable 10 appetizing, intriguing
one: 5 lurer 7 enticer
temptress: 4 vamp 5 lurer, siren
tempura mix: 6 batter
tempus fugit: 9 time flies
Temuco: 4 city, town
locale: 5 Chile
ten: 5 decad 6 decade, number 7 perfect, respite, sawbuck 9 honor card
combining form: 3 dec-, dek- 4 deca-, deka- 5 decem-
in French: 3 dix
in German: 4 zehn
in Italian: 5 dieci
in Portuguese: 3 dez
in Spanish: 4 diez
take ~: 4 rest 5 break, pause, relax 6 recess, rest up 8 intermit
to Mohs: 7 diamond
to one: 4 odds
ten __: 5 to one
ten-__: 4 four, spot 5 speed 6 strike
ten-__ bike: 5 speed
ten-__ hat: 6 gallon
ten-__ shotgun: 5 gauge
ten-__ store: 4 cent
__ ten: 3 top 4 hang, take 5 one to
Ten __ a Dance: 5 Cents
Ten __ a-leaping: 5 lords
Ten __ Frederick: 5 North
Ten __ scholar: 6 o'clock
Ten __ That Shook the World: 4 Days
Ten __ War: 5 Years'
tenable: 5 sound 6 cogent, viable 7 logical 8 analytic, arguable, coherent, credible, methodic, rational, sensible 9 excusable, plausible, pragmatic 10 analytical, believable, condonable, consistent, defensible, reasonable, vindicable
tenacious: 3 set 5 fixed, hardy, nervy, stout, tight, tough 6 clingy, dogged, gritty, mulish, sticky, strong, sturdy 7 adamant, durable, staunch 8 clinging, hellbent, obdurate, resolute, stalwart, stubborn, untiring 9 obstinate, retentive, steadfast, unbending 10 courageous, determined, hard-bitten, iron-willed, persistent, possessive, purposeful, relentless, undeterred, unflagging, unshakable, unswerving, unyielding
tenacity: 4 grit, guts 5 moxie, nerve, pluck, spunk 6 starch 7 courage, purpose, resolve 8 backbone, chutzpah, firmness, strength 9 assiduity, diligence, endurance, gutsiness, hardiness, obstinacy 10 confidence, doggedness, moral fiber, resolution
Tenafly: 4 city, town
locale: 9 New Jersey
Tenancingo: 4 city, town
locale: 6 Mexico
tenancy: 9 occupancy, ownership 10 occupation, possession
__ tenancy: 5 joint
tenancy in __: 6 common
tenant: 5 guest, liver 6 holder, leaser, lessee, lodger, occupy, renter, reside, roomer 7 boarder, dweller, inhabit 8 occupant, resident 9 addressee, possessor 10 inhabitant
awaiting a ~: 5 unlet
find a ~: 4 rent
find a new ~: 5 relet
organization: 4 co-op
pact: 5 lease
tenant __: 6 farmer
tenantless: 5 to let 6 vacant
Tenant of Wildfell Hall, The author: Anne Brontë
Tenants, The author: Bernard Malamud
Tenant, The (1976 film)
cast: Isabelle Adjani, Roman Polanski
director: Roman Polanski
ten-armed animal: 5 squid
ten-cent __: 5 store
Ten Cents a Dance composer: 4 Hart 7 Rodgers
tench: 4 fish
Ten Commandments
recipient: 5 Moses
repository: 3 ark
word: 3 not, thy 5 shalt
Ten Commandments, The (1923 film): 4 epic
director: Cecil B. DeMille
Ten Commandments, The (1956 film): 4 epic
cast: Judith Anderson, Anne Baxter, Yul Brynner, John Carradine, Yvonne De Carlo, John Derek, Nina Foch, Cedric Hardwicke, Charlton Heston, Debra Paget, Vincent Price, Edward G. Robinson, Martha Scott
director: Cecil B. DeMille
role: 4 Seti 5 Aaron, Moses 6 Dathan 7 Pharaoh, Rameses
__ Ten Conference: 3 Big, Pac
tend: 4 bear, feed, head, keep, lead, lean, look, mind, till 5 do for, drift, groom, guard, labor, nurse, point, see to, serve, trend, verge, watch 6 foster, handle, manage, shield, wait on 7 baby-sit, care for, cater to, conduce, dispose, incline, nurture, oversee, protect, redound, sit with, verge on 8 maintain, minister, result in, see after, shepherd, wait upon 9 cultivate, gravitate, look after, safeguard, supervise, watch over 10 administer, keep tabs on, minister to, move toward, ride herd on, take care of
a fire: 5 stoke
a horse: 5 brush
an orchard: 3 lop, mow, top 4 clip, crop, snip, trim 5 shear
to: 4 mind 5 nurse, serve 6 wait on 8 see about, wait upon 9 look after
towards: 5 favor
(towards): 4 lean
Ten Days That Shook the World
author: John Reed
tendency: 3 way 4 bent, bias, tide, wont 5 drift, habit, trend 6 course, liking 7 bearing, current, heading, impulse, leaning, mindset 8 penchant, velleity, weakness 9 appetence, direction, liability, proneness, readiness 10 likelihood, partiality, proclivity, propensity
combining form: 6 -phoria
suffix: 3 -ive
__ tendency: 7 central
tendentious: 6 biased 7 partial
tender: 3 bid, put, raw 4 boat, fond, give, hand, hurt, kind, lush, mild, pose, ship, soft, sore, warm, weak 5 frail, green, mushy, offer, quote, silky, sweet, yield, young 6 accord, aching, callow, caring, decent, feeble, gentle, hand in, humane, kindly, loving, moving, render, submit, turn in, vernal 7 amatory, amorous, bruised, clement, commend, cordial, fragile, hugging, kissing, lenient, lighter, painful, present, proffer, propose, sparing 8 all heart, delicate, gracious, immature, inflamed, maternal, merciful, nominate, overture, parental, poignant, proposal, reddened, romantic, tolerant, touching, yielding, youthful 9 amatorial, childlike, emotional, forgiving, irritated, quotation, sensitive, volunteer 10 administer, altruistic, benevolent, contribute, lovey-dovey, responsive, solicitous, unhardened, vulnerable
age: 5 teens, youth 6 cradle 7 infancy, puberty 8 minority 9 childhood, juniority 10 immaturity, juvenility, schooldays
an offer: 3 ask, bid 5 quote 6 invite, submit 7 proffer, propose 10 make a pitch
become ~: 6 soften
ender: 4 foot, loin 7 hearted
feeling: 4 pity 5 heart, mercy 6 lenity 7 charity, empathy, quarter 8 clemency, kindness, lenience, sympathy 9 sentiment, tolerance 10 compassion, condolence, humaneness
legal ~: 3 oof 4 cash, coin, gelt, jack, kail, kale, loot, peag, pelf 5 bills, bread, bucks, dough, funds, lucre, money, moola, mopus, pesos, rhino, sewan 6 dinero, do-re-mi, mammon, mazuma, moolah, seawan, silver, specie, wampum, wealth 7 cabbage, capital, dollars, lettuce, ooftish, scratch, shekels 8 bankroll, cold cash, currency, hard cash, smackers 9 banknotes, frogskins, long green, simoleons 10 greenbacks, green stuff
loving care: 7 concern
starter: 3 bar 4 goal
tender __: 5 offer
tender-__: 6 minded 7 hearted
__ tender: 5 legal
Tender __: 4 Love 7 Mercies, Vittles
tenderfoot: 4 dude, tiro, tyro 5 newie, pupil, young 6 greeny, intern, novice, rookie 7 entrant, interne, learner, new hand, recruit, trainee 8 beginner, initiate, neophyte, newcomer 9 fledgling, greenhorn 10 apprentice, dilettante, first-timer, uninitiate
Tenderfoot: 5 Scout 8 Boy Scout
org.: 3 BSA
tender-hearted: 4 kind, soft 6 caring, kindly 8 merciful 9 concerned
one: 5 softy 6 softie
tender-heartedness: 5 mercy 6 lenity 8 clemency, humanity, kindness, mildness, patience, softness, sympathy 10 compassion, generosity, gentleness, indulgence, moderation, toleration
Tender Is the Night
author: F. Scott Fitzgerald
character: 3 Abe 4 Beth, Clay, Hoyt 5 Diver, Elsie 6 Barban, Collis, Kaethe, Nicole, Speers
tenderize: 6 soften
tenderloin: 4 meat 5 filet
tenderly: 6 gently, softly 7 lightly
in music: 7 pietoso
treat ~: 4 baby, love 6 coddle, cosset, dote on, pamper 7 cater to, indulge
Tender Mercies (1983 film)
cast: Robert Duvall, Tess Harper, Allan Hubbard
director: Bruce Beresford
tenderness: 4 love, pain, pity 5 heart, mercy 8 lenience 9 affection 10 attachment, compassion
Tender Trap, The: 4 film, song
artist: Frank Sinatra
cast: Celeste Holm, Debbie Reynolds, Frank Sinatra
composer: 4 Cahn 9 Van Heusen
director: Charles Walters
tending: 3 apt 5 prone 6 liable, likely 8 inclined
(to): 8 disposed
to (suffix): 3 -ish
tendon: 5 chord, sinew 6 muscle
combining form: 4 teno-
tendon-bone connector: 5 bursa
tendril: 4 hair 5 fiber 6 strand 8 filament
tenebrific: 4 dark, drab, dull 5 black, bleak, mirky, murky 6 dismal, dreary, gloomy, somber 7 austere 9 cheerless 10 depressing, oppressive
tenebrous: 3 dim 4 dark 5 dusky, mirky, murky, unlit, vague 6 dismal, gloomy, opaque, somber 7 obscure, shadowy, sunless 8 lowering 9 ambiguous, equivocal, unlighted
tenement locale: 4 slum
__ Tenenbaums, The: 5 Royal
__ tenens: 5 locum
Tenerife: 3 isl. 4 isle 6 island
locale: 8 Canaries
tenet: 3 ism 4 rule, view 5 bylaw, canon, credo, creed, dogma, ethos, faith 6 belief, policy, thesis 7 precept 8 doctrine, ideology, platform, teaching 9 principle, teachings 10 conviction
tenfold: 6 denary
ten-four: 3 aye, oui, yea, yep, yup 4 fine, okay, sure, yeah 5 good-o, natch, quite, right, roger, uh-huh 6 agreed, gladly, good-oh, indeed, just so, rather, righto, surely, you bet, yowzah 7 exactly, go ahead, indeedy, mais oui, quite so 8 all right, as you say, of course, thumbs up, very well 9 be my guest, certainly, darn right, naturally, precisely, sure thing, you betcha, you said it 10 absolutely, by all means, definitely, positively, sure enough, that's right
buddy: 4 CBer
ten-gallon __: 3 hat
Ten Gentlemen From West Point (1942 film)
cast: George Montgomery, Maureen O'Hara, John Sutton
director: Henry Hathaway
Ten-hut! opposite: 6 at ease
Tenley: 8 Albright
__ Ten List: 3 Top
Tennant: 4 Andy, Emma 8 Victoria
Tennant, Andy: 8 director
film: Anna and the King (1999)
Ever After (1998)
Sweet Home Alabama (2002)
Tennant, Victoria spouse: Steve Martin
tenner: 4 bill 8 banknote
half a ~: 3 fin
Tennessee: 5 river, state 8 Williams
athlete: 3 Vol
capital: 9 Nashville
city: 5 Alcoa 6 Smyrna 7 Bristol, Jackson, Lebanon, Memphis 8 Bartlett, Columbia, Franklin, Gallatin, Oak Ridge 9 Brentwood, Cleveland, East Ridge, Kingsport, Knoxville, Maryville, Nashville 10 Cookeville, Germantown, Morristown
conference: 3 SEC
neighbor: 7 Alabama, Georgia 8 Arkansas, Kentucky, Missouri, Virginia
pro team: 6 Titans
River locale: 7 Alabama 8 Kentucky
River tributary: 3 Elk
school: 10 Vanderbilt
state flower: 4 iris
state gem: 5 pearl
state reptile: 9 box turtle
state wild animal: 7 raccoon

Tennessee __: 7 warbler
Tennessee __ Authority: 6 Valley
Tennessee __ Ford: 5 Ernie
Tennessee __ horse: 7 walking
Tennesseean: 5 paper 9 newspaper
locale: 9 Nashville
Tennessee Waltz beginning: 4 I was
Tenney: 3 Jon
Tennille: 4 Toni
partner: 6 Dragon 7 Captain
tennis: 4 game 5 sport
area: 5 court 8 baseline
Argentine ~ pro: 5 Vilas
Australian ~ pro: 4 Hoad 5 Court, Laver 6 Fraser, Rafter, Stolle 7 Emerson, Lew Hoad 8 Newcombe, Rod Laver, Rosewall 9 Goolagong 10 Fred Stolle, Roy Emerson
Brazilian ~ pro: 5 Bueno 10 Maria Bueno
call: 3 let 4 long 5 fault
cup: 5 Davis
Czech ~ pro: 5 Kodes, Lendl 8 Jan Kodes 9 Ivan Lendl 10 Mandlikova 11 Navratilova
Ecuadorean ~ pro: 6 Segura
edge: 4 ad in 5 ad out
exchange: 5 rally 6 volley
French ~ pro: 7 Lacoste
need: 3 net 4 ball 5 court 6 racket
official: 3 ref, ump 6 umpire 7 referee
org.: 4 USTA 5 USLTA
pro: 4 Ashe, Borg, Hoad, King, Wade 5 Budge, Bueno, Court, Evert, Kodes, Laver, Lendl, Moody, Riggs, Seles, Smith, Vilas 6 Agassi, Austin, Casals, Fraser, Gibson, Hingis, Kramer, Marble, Rafter, Segura, Stolle, Tilden 7 Connors, Emerson, Lacoste, Lew Hoad, McEnroe, Nastase, Ralston, Sampras, Trabert 8 Capriati, Connolly, Don Budge, Gonzales, Jan Kodes, Newcombe, Rod Laver, Rosewall, Williams 9 Bjorn Borg, Davenport, Goolagong, Ivan Lendl, Stan Smith 10 Arthur Ashe, Bill Tilden, Bobby Riggs, Chris Evert, Jack Kramer, Kournikova, Mandlikova 11 Navratilova
Romanian ~ pro: 7 Nastase
Russian ~ pro: 10 Kournikova
score: 3 ace 4 love 5 forty 6 thirty 7 fifteen
shot: 3 lob 4 chop, dink 5 slice, smash 6 volley 8 backhand, forehand
six games in ~: 3 set
Slovakian ~ pro: 6 Hingis
start a ~ game: 5 serve
status: 3 bye 4 seed
surface: 4 lawn 5 grass
Swedish ~ pro: 4 Borg 9 Bjorn Borg
teacher: 3 pro
term: 3 ace, all, bye, let, lob, net, ref, set, ump 4 ad in, game, love, seed 5 ad out, court, deuce, fault, match, point, serve, smash 6 do-over, racket, rubber, umpire, volley 7 doubles, referee, service, singles, topspin 8 backhand, baseline, forehand, overspin
tie: 5 deuce
tourney: 6 U.S. Open 9 Wimbledon 10 French Open
unit: 3 set 4 game 5 match
wear: 6 anklet, shorts, sneaks 8 headband, sneakers 9 wristband
Yugoslavian ~ pro: 5 Seles
tennis __: 4 ball, shoe 5 elbow
__ tennis: 4 deck, lawn 5 court, royal, table 6 paddle, squash
Tennis, __?: 6 anyone
tennis elbow site: 4 ulna
Tenn. neighbor: 3 Ala., Ark., Ken. 4 Miss, N. Car., Virg.
see also Tennessee
Ten North Frederick: 4 film 5 novel
author: John O'Hara
cast: Gary Cooper, Suzy Parker, Diane Varsi
director: Philip Dunne
Tennyson, Alfred: 4 Lord, poet 7 British
character: 3 Ida 4 Enid 6 Elaine
work: Charge of the Light Brigade
Crossing the Bar
Enoch Arden
Idylls of the King
In Memoriam
The Lady of Shalott
Locksley Hall
The Lotus-Eaters
Mariana
Maud
Oenone
Tears, Idle Tears
Tenochtitlán resident: 5 Aztec
tenon: 6 insert 8 dovetail
tenor: 4 clef, gist, male, mood, pith, tone, vein 5 drift, Lanza, Pears, range, sense, sound, style, theme, trend, voice 6 burden, Caruso, intent, Peerce, singer, Tucker 7 caroler, Corelli, current, Domingo, essence, meaning, purport, Vickers 8 Carreras, Melchior, vocalist 9 chorister, direction, Jan Peerce, Pavarotti, substance 10 Mario Lanza, Peter Pears
British ~: 5 Pears 10 Peter Pears
colleague: 4 alto, bass 5 mezzo 7 soprano 8 baritone 9 contralto
Danish ~: 8 Melchior
Italian ~: 6 Caruso 7 Corelli 9 Pavarotti
Spanish ~: 7 Domingo 8 Carreras
starter: 7 counter
tenor __: 3 cor, sax 4 clef, horn
Tenosique: 4 city, town
locale: 6 Mexico 7 Tabasco
ten-pack: 6 carton
tenpenny __: 4 nail
ten-percenter: 3 agt., rep 5 agent
tenpins: 4 game 5 sport 7 bowling
participant: 6 kegler 7 kegeler
ten-point type: 5 elite
tenrec: 6 animal, mammal
ten's __: 5 place
tense: 4 edgy, shot, taut 5 antsy, drawn, hyper, itchy, jumpy, key up, rigid, shaky, stiff, tight, wired 6 jangly, on edge, uneasy 7 anxious, excited, fidgety, fretful, harried, in knots, jittery, keyed up, nervous, restive, stiffen, tighten, uptight, worried, wound up 8 agitated, distress, fluttery, fretsome, in a tizzy, preterit, restless, skittish, strained, troubled, unnerved, worked up 9 concerned, excitable, ill at ease, knotted up, pressured, stressful, strung out, unbending, unsettled, up the wall 10 distressed, highstrung, overstrung
be ~: 5 worry 6 simmer
vb. ~: 3 fut. 4 impf., pres., pret. 6 imperf.
__ tense: 4 past 6 future 7 present 8 preterit 9 imperfect
tenseness: 6 nerves, strain, stress 7 anxiety
__, tens, hundreds: 5 units
tension: 5 drama, worry 6 nerves, shakes, strain, stress, unease, unrest 7 anxiety, jitters 8 disquiet, edginess, pressure, suspense, tautness 9 hostility, intensity, stiffness, tightness 10 uneasiness
combining form: 4 tono-
lose ~: 3 sag
treatment: 3 rub 7 massage
__ tension: 5 vapor 7 surface
__-tension: 3 low 4 high
ten-speed: 4 bike 5 cycle, racer 7 bicycle
part: 4 gear
rider: 5 biker
ten-spot, half a: 5 fiver
tent: 4 camp, tipi, yurt 5 dress, tepee 6 big top, teepee, wigwam 7 camp out, shelter 8 barracks, covering, pavilion, quarters
Asian ~: 4 yurt
dismantle a ~: 5 unpeg
dweller: 5 nomad
fabric: 4 duck 6 canvas
flap: 3 fly
holder: 3 peg 5 stake
pitch a ~: 7 rough it
set up a ~: 4 camp, stay 5 abide, pitch 6 encamp
set up a ~ again: 5 repeg
show: 4 fair 6 big top, circus 8 carnival
tent __: 3 bed, fly 4 show 5 dress 6 circus, stitch 7 meeting, trailer
__ tent: 3 pup 4 wall 6 circus 7 shelter
tentacle: 3 arm 5 organ 6 feeler
tentative: 4 iffy 5 shaky, trial 6 acting, unfirm, unsure, wabbly, wobbly 7 halting, interim, subject 8 cautious, doubtful, hesitant, unproved 9 dependant, dependent, faltering, provisory, reluctant, uncertain, undecided, unsettled 10 contingent, indecisive, indefinite, irresolute, unfinished
tenterhook: 4 nail
tenterhooks
be on ~: 5 sweat, worry
on ~: 4 edgy 5 antsy, itchy, jumpy, tense 6 on edge, queasy, queazy, uneasy 7 alarmed, anxious, jittery, keyed up, nervous, restive, uptight, worried 8 agitated, qualmish, restless, skittish, troubled 9 concerned, excitable, ill at ease 10 high-strung
tenth: 5 tithe 6 decile
combining form: 4 deci-
Tenth Commandment, The author: Lawrence Sanders
Tenth Man, The author: Paddy Chayefsky
ten thousand combining form: 5 myria-
tenth's __: 5 place
Tentmaker: 4 Omar 7 Kháyyam
Tent Peak: 5 mount 8 mountain
locale: 4 Asia 5 Nepal 9 Himalayas
tenuous: 4 slim, thin, weak 5 faint, frail, light, shaky 6 flimsy, slight, subtle, unfirm 7 dubious, sketchy, slender 8 doubtful, ethereal, exiguous, gossamer, nebulous, rarefied
fragment: 4 wisp
tenure: 3 job 4 hold, term 5 reign 6 regime 7 holding 8 duration, security 9 longevity, occupancy, ownership, residence 10 incumbency, occupation, possession
tenure-__: 5 track
tenuto: 9 sustained
Ten Years' __: 3 War
Tenzing: 6 Norgay
colleague: 6 Edmund
Teodoro in English: 8 Theodore
Teoloyucan: 4 city, town
locale: 6 Mexico
Teotihuacán: 4 city, town
locale: 6 Mexico
Tepeaca: 4 city, town
locale: 6 Mexico, Puebla
tepee: 4 tent 5 abode 6 wikiup 7 wickiup, wickyup
like a ~: 5 conic 7 conical
Tepeji: 4 city, town
locale: 6 Mexico 7 Hidalgo
Tepic: 4 city, town
locale: 6 Mexico 7 Nayarit
tepid: 4 cool, mild, warm 7 languid, warmish 8 lifeless, lukewarm, milkwarm, moderate, not so hot 9 apathetic, temperate, unextreme 10 spiritless, unagitated
tequila: 5 drink 8 beverage
source: 5 agave
Tequila: 4 city, town
locale: 6 Mexico 7 Jalisco
Tequila (1958 song) artist: Champs
Tequila Sunrise (1988 film)
cast: Mel Gibson, Raul Julia, Michelle Pfeiffer, Kurt Russell
director: Robert Towne
terai: 3 hat 6 helmet, sun hat
teratoid: 8 aberrant, freakish 9 monstrous
terbang: 4 drum
origin: 4 Java
terbium: 5 metal 7 element
Ter Borch, Gerard: 6 artist 7 painter
homeland: 7 Holland 11 Netherlands
terce: 4 hour
tercel: 4 bird, hawk, male 6 falcon
Tercel: 3 car 4 auto 6 Toyota 10 automobile
teredo: 4 worm
Terence: 5 Roman, Stamp, Young 6 Fisher 10 playwright
Terence __ D'Arby: 5 Trent
Teresa: 5 saint 6 Brewer, Mother, Wright 7 Stratas
Teresa of __: 5 Avila
Teresina: 4 city, town
locale: 6 Brazil
tergiversate: 5 fence, hedge, waver 6 seesaw, waffle 8 flip-flop, hesitate 9 vacillate 10 equivocate
tergiversator: 9 chameleon
Terhune: 6 Albert
canine: 3 Lad
Teri: 4 Garr, Polo 6 Austin, Copley 7 DeSario, Hatcher
teriyaki: 4 meat
ingredient: 4 soya 6 ginger
Terkel, Studs: 6 author, writer
book: 7 Working
term: 3 dub, tag 4 call, name, span, time, tour, word 5 hitch, label, limit, phase, space, spell, stint, style, title 6 course, length, period, phrase, season, tenure 7 baptize, caption, quarter, session, stretch 8 christen, confines, describe, duration, interval, nominate, semester, sentence, standing, subtitle 9 condition, designate, occupancy, provision 10 denominate, expression
term __: 3 day 5 paper 6 limits, policy
term.
marking: 3 neg., pos.
__ term: 5 major, minor 6 middle 7 inkhorn, special
__-term: 4 full, long, near 5 short
termagant: 4 crab 5 harpy, scold, shrew, vixen 6 chider, virago 7 needler, rebuker 8 grumbler, harridan, spitfire 9 henpecker, Xanthippe 10 disorderly
terminable: 7 bounded, limited 10 dissoluble, measurable
terminal: 3 CRT, end, sta., stn., VDT 4 base, last 5 anode, depot, final 6 distal, screen 7 cathode, display, extreme, monitor, station 8 eventual, ultimate 10 concluding
approach the ~: 4 taxi
battery ~: 3 neg., pos. 5 anode 7 cathode 8 negative, positive

info: **3** arr., ETA, ETD
of a ~: **6** anodal
terminal ___: **5** leave **6** market **7** moraine
___ terminal: **5** video **6** dial-up
Terminal author: Robin Cook
Terminal Man, The: **4** film **5** novel
author: Michael Crichton
cast: Richard Dysart, Joan Hackett, George Segal
director: Mike Hodges
Terminal Velocity (1994 film)
cast: James Gandolfini, Nastassja Kinski, Charlie Sheen
director: Deran Sarafian
terminate: **2** ax **3** axe, can, end **4** boot, drop, fire, halt, lift, oust, quit, sack, stop **5** abort, annul, cease, close, lapse, let go, limit, scrub, sever **6** bounce, cancel, cut off, expire, finish, lay off, recess, resign, result, run out, wind up, wrap up **7** abolish, adjourn, break up, cashier, dismiss, drum out, release, scratch **8** complete, conclude, cut short, dissolve, furlough, get rid of, intermit, obstruct, pack it in, pink-slip, prorogue, round off, round out, surcease, wind down **9** culminate, discharge, eliminate, eventuate, liquidate **10** call it a day, consummate, extinguish
terminated: **3** out **4** done, over **6** lapsed **7** all over, through **8** done with
terminating ___: **7** decimal
termination: **3** end **4** halt **5** close, limit **6** cut-off, demise, ending, expiry, finale, finish, period, result, windup, wrap-up **7** closure, outcome, passing **8** curtains, surcease **9** abatement, cessation **10** conclusion
Terminator 2 - Judgment Day (1991 film)
cast: Edward Furlong, Linda Hamilton, Arnold Schwarzenegger
director: James Cameron
dog: **3** Max
Terminator, The (1984 film)
cast: Michael Biehn, Linda Hamilton, Arnold Schwarzenegger
director: James Cameron
role: **5** Sarah
terminer's partner: **4** oyer
terminology: **5** argot, lingo **6** jargon **7** lexicon, wording **8** language, locution, phrasing
terminus: **3** end **4** pole, stop **5** close **6** ending, finale, finish, windup, wrap-up **10** conclusion, denouement, resolution
terminus ___: **4** a quo
terminus ad ___: **4** quem
termitarium: **4** nest
termite: **3** bug **5** borer **6** insect
group: **5** swarm
home: **4** nest
kin: **3** ant
meal: **4** wood
___-term memory: **4** long **5** short
term paper
abbr.: **4** et al., ibid. **5** op. cit. **6** loc. cit.
terms: **4** rate **5** truce **6** points, treaty **7** details, footing, payment, premise, proviso, strings **8** position, proposal, standing **9** agreement, fine print, provision, relations, requisite **10** conditions, small print
be on good ~ with: **4** know
bring to ~: **7** mediate **9** negotiate, reconcile
come to ~: **5** agree, level, yield **6** make up, settle **7** bargain, work out **10** capitulate
on good ~: **4** kind **5** close, thick **6** chummy, clubby, genial, kindly **7** affable, amiable, cordial **8** amicable, friendly, intimate, outgoing, peaceful, sociable **9** convivial **10** benevolent, buddy-buddy, neighborly, solicitous
Terms of Endearment: **4** film **5** novel
author: Larry McMurtry
cast: Jeff Daniels, Danny DeVito, John Lithgow, Shirley MacLaine, Jack Nicholson, Debra Winger
director: James L. Brooks
tern: **4** bird **5** noddy **7** seabird **9** shorebird **10** sea swallow
in England: **5** starn
relative: **4** gull
___ tern: **5** sooty **6** arctic, common
terne metal: **5** alloy
component: **3** tin **4** lead
ternion: **4** trio **6** triple
Terpsichore: **4** Muse
colleague: **4** Clio **5** Erato **6** Thalia, Urania **7** Euterpe **8** Calliope **9** Melpomene **10** Polyhymnia
parent of ~: **4** Zeus **9** Mnemosyne
terpsichorean: **6** dancer, hoofer **8** coryphée, Rockette **9** ballerina, chorus boy **10** chorus girl
work: **5** dance **6** ballet
terra ___: **4** alba **5** cotta, firma, mater, verde
Terra ___: **5** Mater
terrace: **4** yard **6** street **7** balcony **8** platform
Terrace at Le Havre painter: **5** Monet
terra cotta: **4** clay **6** orange **7** pottery **8** brownish, clayware, crockery
relative: **5** flame, henna **7** pumpkin, saffron **8** hyacinth **9** tangerine
Terra, daughter of: **4** Thea
terra firma: **4** land, soil **5** earth, shore **6** ground
on ~: **6** ashore
terrain: **4** area, land, turf **5** field **6** domain, ground, region, sphere **7** contour, country, grounds, habitat, scenery **8** confines, dominion **9** landscape, territory **10** topography
terra incognita: **6** enigma **7** mystery
___-terrain vehicle: **3** all
Terraplane: **3** car **4** auto **5** Essex **6** Hudson **10** automobile
___-terre: **5** pied-à
___-Terre: **5** Basse
Terre author: Emile Zola
Terrebonne: **4** city, town
locale: **6** Canada, Québec
Terre Haute: **4** city, town
locale: **3** Ind. **7** Indiana
sch.: **3** ISU
Terrell, Tammi: **6** singer
song: Ain't No Mountain High Enough (1967)
Ain't Nothing Like the Real Thing (1968)
If I Could Build My Whole World Around You (1967)
You're All I Need to Get By (1968)
Your Precious Love (1967)
Terrence: **6** Malick **7** McNally **8** Rattigan
terrene: **7** earthly, worldly **8** material
terrestrial: **6** global **7** earthly, terrene **8** telluric **9** earthlike
terrestrial ___: **5** globe **6** planet
Terri: **5** Clark, Gibbs, Treas
terrible: **3** bad **4** base, dire, foul, grim, hard, poor, ugly, vile **5** awful, dread, gross, lousy, woful **6** crumby, crummy, dismal, grisly, horrid, mortal, odious, putrid, rotten, severe, tragic, wicked, woeful **7** accurst, awesome, baleful, baneful, beastly, doleful, dreaded, extreme, fearful, ghastly, hateful, hellish, hideous, ill-done, painful, serious, ungodly, violent **8** accursed, dreadful, God-awful, grievous, gruesome, horrible, inferior, shameful, shocking, stinking, terrific, tragical, wretched **9** abhorrent, appalling, atrocious, dangerous, defective, desperate, execrable, frightful, harrowing, ill-omened, insidious, loathsome, miserable, monstrous, obnoxious, offensive, repellant, repulsive, revolting, unnerving, unsightly **10** abominable, deplorable, despicable, detestable, disastrous, disturbing, formidable, horrendous, horrifying, petrifying, tremendous, unpleasant
be ~: **5** stink
combining form: **3** din- **4** dein-, dino- **5** deino-
enfant ~: **4** brat **5** devil, scamp
feeling ~: **3** ill, low **4** hurt, sick **6** ailing, infirm, queasy, unwell **7** laid low **8** below par **9** in a bad way, miserable **10** out of sorts
terrible ___: **4** twos
___ terrible: **6** enfant
Terrible Swift Sword author: Bruce Catton
...___ terrible thing to waste: **3** is a
terribly: **4** much, very **5** badly **6** highly **7** awfully, gravely, greatly **8** horribly, markedly **9** decidedly, extremely, fearfully, in a big way, intensely, seriously, unhappily, unusually **10** dreadfully, remarkably, thoroughly
terrier: **3** dog, pet **5** canid, pooch **6** canine
fictional ~: **4** Asta
like a ~ coat: **4** wiry
___ terrier: **3** fox, rat **4** bull, Skye **5** Cairn, Irish, silky, Welsh **6** Border, Boston, Scotch **7** Norfolk, Norwich, Tibetan, wheaten **8** Airedale
terrific: **3** def, fab, rad **4** aces, A-one, boss, braw, cool, dece, fine, gear, huge, keen, neat, nice, phat, tuff **5** awful, dandy, ducky, grand, great, harsh, marvy, neato, nifty, nobby, prime, slick, socko, super, swell **6** bang on, bang-up, bonzer, bosker, choice, divine, dreamy, far-out, fierce, gnarly, groovy, lovely, peachy, severe, slap-up, spot on, superb, tiptop, unreal, whizzo, wicked **7** amazing, awesome, capital, corking, extreme, fearful, immense, intense, perfect, ripping, skookum, stellar, sublime **8** dazzling, dreadful, enormous, especial, eximious, fabulous, five-star, four-star, frabjous, gigantic, glorious, heavenly, horrible, horrific, jim-dandy, laudable, shocking, slam-bang, smashing, splendid, standout, sterling, stickout, superior, terrible, top-level, topnotch, very good, wondrous **9** appalling, bodacious, deafening, Endsville, excellent, excessive, exemplary, exquisite, fantastic, first-rate, frightful, high-grade, hunky-dory, marvelous, monstrous, sollicker, top-flight, unrivaled, wonderful, wunderbar **10** first-class, formidable, hotsy-totsy, jack-a-dandy, out of sight, peachy-keen, phenomenal, remarkable, stupendous, super-duper, thunderous, tremendous, unrivalled
time: **4** ball, gala **5** blast, party, spree
Terrific!: **3** wow **4** fine **5** great, super **9** marvelous, wonderful
terrified: **5** ashen, funky, timid **6** afraid, aghast, scared, trepid **7** anxious, chicken, fearful, nervous, panicky **8** cowardly, fearsome, hesitant, timorous **10** frightened
terrify: **3** awe **4** stun **5** alarm, appal, chill, daunt, haunt, scare, shock, spook **6** adread, appall, dismay, freeze, menace **7** horrify, petrify, startle, stupefy **8** frighten, paralyse, paralyze **9** terrorize **10** intimidate, scare stiff
terrifying: **5** dread, scary **6** creepy, grisly **7** dreaded, ghastly, hideous **8** gruesome, horrible **9** appalling, harrowing **10** formidable
combining form: **4** dino-
territorial: **8** colonial, regional
territorial ___: **5** court **6** system, waters
territory: **4** area, belt, land, turf, walk, ward, zone **5** arena, block, field, range, realm, space, state, tract **6** colony, domain, empire, extent, locale, nation, parish, region, sector, sphere, street **7** country, enclave, expanse, grounds, habitat, mandate, purview, quarter, section **8** boundary, confines, district, dominion, locality, province, vicinity **9** community **10** boundaries, possession
___ territory: **4** fair, foul **5** trust
___ Territory: **5** Yukon **6** Dakota, Indian **7** Badman's
terror: **3** awe **4** fear, funk **5** alarm, dread, panic, shock **6** dismay, fright, horror, phobia **7** anxiety, scourge **9** trepidity
cry of ~: **4** oh no **5** oh God
holy ~: **3** cad, cur, imp, rat **4** brat, toad **5** churl, demon, knave, louse, rogue, scamp **6** bad boy, rascal, urchin **7** bounder, dastard, hellion, lowlife, ruffian, stinker **8** blighter, picaroon, scalawag, spalpeen **9** miscreant, prankster, reprobate, scoundrel **10** blackguard, malefactor, ne'er-do-well, scapegrace
reign of ~: **5** purge **7** tyranny **9** despotism **10** oppression
terrorist: **4** thug **5** enemy **9** anarchist, ill-wisher
'70s ~ org.: **3** SLA
terrorize: **3** awe, cow **5** alarm, appal, bully, haunt, panic, scare, shock, spook **6** appall, coerce, dismay, fright, hector, menace, prey on **7** dragoon, horrify, oppress, petrify, scourge, startle, terrify **8** bludgeon, browbeat, bulldoze, frighten, prey upon, threaten **9** strong-arm **10** intimidate, scare stiff
Terror, The author: Edgar Wallace
Terror Train (1980 film)
cast: Hart Bochner, Jamie Lee Curtis, Ben Johnson
director: Roger Spottiswoode
terry: **5** cloth **6** fabric **8** material
product: **4** robe **5** towel **9** washcloth
Terry: **3** Eli **4** Bill **5** Ellen, Jacks, Moore **6** Carter **7** Farrell, Gilliam, Sawchuk **8** Bradshaw, McMillan, Southern, Stafford **9** Pendleton
Terry-___: **6** Thomas
Terry, Bill: **5** Giant
Terry-Thomas
film: Blue Murder at St. Trinian's (1957)
How to Murder Your Wife (1965)
School for Scoundrels (1960)
Your Past Is Showing (1957)
Terrytown: **4** city
locale: **9** Louisiana
terse: **4** curt, lean **5** blunt, brief, brusk, close, crisp, pithy, short, tight **6** abrupt, gnomic, snappy **7** brusque, clipped, compact, concise, cryptic, laconic, pointed, summary **8** clear-cut, incisive, succinct **9** axiomatic, condensed, cryptical, trenchant **10** aphoristic, boiled down, elliptical, synopsized, to the point
terseness: **7** brevity **8** laconism

tertiary __: 5 color
Tertiary Period epoch: 6 Eocene
terza __: 4 rima
Teseo composer: 6 Handel
Tesh, John: 7 pianist
  former colleague: 4 Hart
  genre: 6 New Age
  spouse: Connie Sellecca
Tesistán: 4 city, town
  locale: 6 Mexico 7 Jalisco
Tesla __: 4 coil
Tesla, Nikola: 9 physicist, scientist
  rival: 6 Edison
Tess: 6 Harper 9 Trueheart
Tess (1979 film)
  cast: Peter Firth, Nastassja Kinski
  director: Roman Polanski
Tess __ d'Urbervilles: 5 of the
tessellate: 5 inlay
tessellated: 6 inlaid
Tess of the d'Urbervilles author: Thomas Hardy
  character: 3 Izz 4 Alec, Hope, Jack, Joan 5 Angel, Chant, Clare, Crick, Farmy, Felix, Groby, Huett, James, Mercy, Nancy, Retty 6 Liza-Lu, Marian, Sorrow 7 Abraham, Dark Car, Modesty, Richard 8 Car Darch, Cuthbert, Izz Huett, Tringham 10 Angel Clare, Christiana, Farmy Groby, Mercy Chant
test: 2 go 3 sip, try 4 comp, exam, oral, quiz 5 assay, check, essay, final, gauge, grill, probe, proof, prove, taste, trial, try on 6 assess, dry run, enduro, handle, lesson, ordeal, sample, tryout, verify 7 analyze, confirm, examine, match up, midterm, midyear, pop quiz, stack up 8 analysis, audition, blue book, check out, crucible, gauntlet, rehearse, scrutiny, standard, trial run, validate 9 catechism, challenge, countdown, criterion, give it a go, probation, shake down, true-false, yardstick 10 evaluation, experiment, inspection, run-through, touchstone, ultrasound
  acid ~: 5 proof, trial
  British ~: 6 A level
  coll. student: 3 GRE 4 GMAT, LSAT, MCAT
  command to ~ takers: 4 open 5 begin, start
  comparison ~ item: 6 Brand X
  HS proficiency ~: 3 GED
  kind of ~ question: 5 essay 9 true-false
  medical ~: 3 ECG, EEG, EKG, MRI 4 X-ray
  one's endurance again: 5 retax
  response: 3 ans. 4 true 5 false 6 answer
  stand the ~ of time: 4 last 6 endure
  the waters: 4 poll 5 query 6 survey
  venue: 3 lab 5 class 9 classroom
  version: 4 beta
test __: 3 act, ban 4 case, tube 5 blank, drive, match, paper, pilot, stand 6 flight 7 pattern
test-__: 3 fly 5 drive 6 market
test-__ treaty: 3 ban
__ test: 3 DNA 4 acid, Ames, bead, beta, Dick, oral, pour, road, root, skin, spot 5 alpha, bench, Binet, blood, essay, Marsh, means, patch, ratio, taste 6 breath, litmus, Marsh's, Schick, screen, stress 7 analogy, Babcock, inkblot, scratch, Snellen 9 true-false
__-test: 3 low 4 high 5 field, shock 6 flight
testa: 8 seed coat
  cousin: 4 aril
testament: 4 will 5 proof 8 covenant 9 guarantee 10 instrument
Testament (1983 film)
  cast: Jane Alexander, William Devane
__ Testament: 3 New, Old
testamentary __: 5 trust
Testament, The author: Elie Wiesel
testar: 4 fish
Testarossa: 3 car 4 auto 7 Ferrari 10 automobile
testator's bequest: 6 estate
testatrix: 5 woman
Testaverde, Vinny: 2 QB
  sport: 8 football
test-ban __: 6 treaty
__ Test Dummies: 5 Crash
tested: 5 tried, valid 9 qualified
  they may be ~: 5 wills
__-tested: 4 time
tester: 4 coin, vial 5 money 6 bottle 8 examiner 9 inspector
  output: 5 scent 7 perfume
testify: 4 show, sing 5 argue, prove, speak, state, swear, vouch 6 affirm, allege, assert, avouch, depone, depose 7 bespeak, certify, declare, swear to, warrant, witness 8 vouch for 10 stand up for
  prepare to ~: 5 swear
testimonial: 5 honor, medal, salvo 6 homage, salute 7 ovation, tribute, warrant, witness 8 citation, memorial, monument 9 reference
testimony: 5 proof 6 avowal, record 7 grounds, support, witness 8 evidence 9 admission, affidavit, statement 10 deposition, indication, profession
  disparage ~: 5 rebut
  give ~: 5 swear, vouch 6 assert, depone, depose 7 certify, declare, warrant, witness
  give false ~: 7 perjure
  hearer: 4 jury 5 judge, juror
  preceder: 4 oath
testiness: 6 spleen, temper 10 irritation
test of __: 4 time 5 wills 8 strength
Test Pilot (1938 film)
  cast: Clark Gable, Myrna Loy, Spencer Tracy
  director: Victor Fleming
test tube: 4 vial 5 phial
  glass: 5 Pyrex
testy: 4 edgy, mean, sour, tart 5 cross, huffy, moody, onery, raspy, short, surly 6 crabby, cranky, crusty, fretty, grouty, grumpy, in a pet, ireful, morose, on edge, ornery, snappy, sullen, touchy 7 annoyed, bearish, crabbed, fretful, grouchy, huffish, peevish, peppery, uptight, waspish 8 captious, choleric, fretsome, growling, grumpish, liverish, petulant, snappish 9 crotchety, excitable, fractious, impatient, irascible, irritable, querulous, splenetic 10 out of sorts
  mood: 4 snit
tet: 6 Hebrew, letter
  predecessor: 4 heth 5 cheth
  successor: 3 yod 4 yodh
__ tet: 6 carbon
tetard: 4 fish
tetched: 3 mad 7 bananas, lunatic
tetchy: 7 peevish
tête-__: 5 bêche
__ tête: 5 mal de
tête-à-tête: 3 rap 4 chat, sofa, talk, word 5 couch, tryst 6 confab, dialog 7 schmoos 8 causerie, dialogue, schmoose, schmooze 9 interview 10 discussion, rendezvous
tête de __: 4 pont
teth: 6 Hebrew, letter
  predecessor: 4 heth 5 cheth
  successor: 3 yod 4 yodh
tether: 3 tie 4 bind, cord, know, lead, moor, rein, rope 5 chain, hitch, leash, tie up 6 fasten, halter, hobble, hopple, lariat, picket, secure 7 harness 8 restrain, restrict 9 restraint 10 keep in line
tetherball: 4 game
Tethys: 4 moon 5 giant, Titan
  daughter of ~: 5 Argia, Metis
  husband of ~: 7 Oceanus
  parent of ~: 4 Gaea 6 Uranus
  planet: 6 Saturn
Tetla: 4 city, town
  locale: 6 Mexico 8 Tlaxcala
Tetley: 3 tea
  alternative: 6 Lipton, Nestea, Salada 7 Bigelow, Red Rose 8 Twinings
Tet locale: 3 Nam 7 Vietnam
Teton: 5 range, tribe 6 Indian, Lakota 7 Amerind, Lakhota
  range locale: 5 Idaho 7 Wyoming
__ Teton National Park: 5 Grand
tetra: 3 pet 4 fish
tetra-: 4 four
  plus one: 5 penta-
  predecessor: 3 tri-
  twice ~: 4 octa-, octo-
__ tetra: 4 neon
__ tetrachloride: 3 tin 6 carbon 7 silicon
tetrad: 8 foursome
  half a ~: 4 dyad
__ tetraethyl: 4 lead
tetrahedrite: 3 ore
tetrarch: 4 king
__ tetrazzini: 7 chicken
Tetrazzini, Luisa: 6 singer 7 soprano
  specialty: 5 opera
Tetris: 4 game 9 video game
tetr- successor: 4 pent-
Tetzlaff: 3 Ted
Teut.: 3 Ger.
Teuton, early: 4 Goth
Teutonic
  combining form: 7 Germano-
  god: 3 Tiu
  goddess: 4 Erda, Norn
  see also German
Tevere, city on the: 4 Roma
Tevet: 5 month 6 Hebrew
  predecessor: 6 Kislev
  successor: 6 Shevat
Tevin: 8 Campbell
Tevye: 7 Russian
  portrayer: 4 Zero 5 Topol 6 Mostel 10 Zero Mostel
  wife: 5 Golde
Tewa: 6 Indian 7 Amerind
Tewes: 6 Lauren
Tewksbury: 5 Peter
Tex: 3 Joe 5 Avery 6 Beneke, Ritter 7 McCrary
Tex (1982 film)
  cast: Matt Dillon, Meg Tilly
Tex-__: 3 Mex
Tex.
  neighbor: 3 Ark., Mex. 4 N. Mex., Okla.
  see also Texas
__-Tex: 4 Gore
Texaco: 8 gasoline
  former ~ rival: 4 Esso 7 Flying A 8 Sinclair
  rival: 4 Gulf, Hess 5 Amoco, Exxon, Getty, Mobil 7 Chevron
Texaco Star Theater star: 5 Berle
Texan rival: 3 Jet, Ram 4 Bear, Bill, Colt, Lion 5 Brown, Chief, Eagle, Giant, Niner, Raven, Saint, Titan 6 Bengal, Bronco, Cowboy, Falcon, Jaguar, Packer, Raider, Viking 7 Charger, Dolphin, Panther, Patriot, Redskin, Seahawk, Steeler 8 Cardinal 9 Buccaneer
Texans
  home: 7 Houston
  org.: 3 AFC, NFL
  sport: 8 football
Texarkana: 4 city, town
  locale: 5 Texas 8 Arkansas
Texas: 5 novel, state 6 Guinan
  author: James A. Michener
  bay: 9 Galveston
  capital: 6 Austin
  city: 4 Eola, Waco 5 Alice, Allen, Alvin, Bryan, Cisco, Ennis, Hurst, Olney, Pampa, Paris, Pharr, Plano, Tioga, Tyler 6 Austin, Conroe, Dallas, Del Rio, Denton, DeSoto, El Paso, Euless, Frisco, Irving, Keller, Laredo, Lufkin, Odessa, Orange, Seguin, Spring, Temple, Uvalde 7 Abilene, Baytown, Bedford, Coppell, Denison, Garland, Houston, Killeen, La Porte, Lubbock, Midland, Mission, Rowlett, San Juan, Sherman, Socorro, Watauga, Weslaco 8 Amarillo, Beaumont, Benbrook, Burleson, Cleburne, Deer Park, Edinburg, Fort Hood, Longview, MacAllen, Marshall, Mesquite, Pasadena, Pearland, Victoria 9 Arlington, Big Spring, Cedar Hill, Cedar Park, Corsicana, Eagle Pass, Fort Worth, Galveston, Grapevine, Harlingen, Kerrville, Lancaster, MacKinney, Mansfield, Plainview, Rosenberg, Round Rock, San Angelo, San Benito, San Marcos, Southlake, Sugar Land, Texarkana, The Colony 10 Atascocita, Carrollton, Cloverleaf, Georgetown, Greenville, Haltom City, Huntsville, Kingsville, League City, Lewisville, Port Arthur, Richardson, San Antonio, Waxahachie
  collegian: 5 Aggie, Miner
  conference: 9 Big Twelve
  county: 4 Cass, Coke, Frio, Hays, Kerr, Rusk, Webb 5 Bexar, Comal, Crane, Duval, Ector, Erath, Foard, Garza, Gregg, Irion, Llano, Milam, Nolan, Pecos, Starr, Titus 6 Brazos, Castro, Concho, DeWitt, Dimmit, Donley, Karnes, Kenedy, Kimble, Lavaca, Loving, Medina, Menard, Motley, Nueces, Oldham, Panola, Scurry, Shelby, Upshur, Uvalde, Yoakum, Zapata, Zavala 7 Aransas, Briscoe, Coryell, Hidalgo, Jim Hogg, Kleberg, Live Oak, Navarro, Refugio, San Saba, Swisher, Tarrant, Willacy 8 Atascosa, Comanche, Crockett, Hansford, Jim Wells, Maverick, Presidio, Tom Green, Val Verde, Van Zandt 9 Deaf Smith, Jeff Davis, Matagorda, Palo Pinto
  desert: 10 Chihuahuan
  dish: 5 chile, chili 6 chilli
  Indian: 9 Karankawa
  leaguer: 3 fly
  national park: 7 Big Bend
  neighbor: 4 Gulf 6 Mexico 8 Arkansas, Oklahoma 9 Louisiana, New Mexico
  port: 7 Houston 9 Galveston
  pro team: 4 Mavs 5 Spurs, Stars 6 Astros, Texans 7 Cowboys, Rangers 9 Mavericks
  river: 5 Pecos 6 Brazos, Nueces 9 Rio Grande 10 Pedernales
  school: 3 SMU, TCU 4 Rice, UTEP 5 Lamar 6 Baylor
  state dish: 5 chili
  state fiber: 6 cotton

state fish: 4 bass
state flower: 10 bluebonnet
state gem: 5 topaz
state large mammal: 8 longhorn
state musical instrument: 6 guitar
state pepper: 8 jalapeno
state shell: 5 whelk
state small mammal: 9 armadillo
state sport: 5 rodeo
state tree: 5 pecan
state vegetable: 10 sweet onion
tourist site: 5 Alamo
University of ~ locale: 6 Austin
Texas (1941 film)
cast: Glenn Ford, William Holden, Claire Trevor
director: George Marshall
Texas __: 3 tea 4 sage, Tech 5 A and M, tower 6 Ranger 7 leaguer
Texas __ M: 4 A and
Texas Across the River (1966 film)
cast: Joey Bishop, Alain Delon, Dean Martin
Texas A&M
athletes: 6 Aggies
conference: 9 Big Twelve
rival: 3 SMU
Texas Chain Saw Massacre, The (1974 film)
cast: Marilyn Burns, Gunner Hansen, Ed Neal
director: Tobe Hooper
Texas Christian locale: 9 Fort Worth
Texas-El Paso conference: 3 WAC
Texas Longhorn: 3 cow 4 bull 6 bovine, cattle
__, Texas Ranger: 6 Walker
Texas Rangers, The (1936 film)
cast: Fred MacMurray, Jack Oakie, Jean Parker
director: King Vidor
Texas tea: 3 oil
Texas Tech
athletes: 10 Red Raiders
conference: 9 Big Twelve
locale: 7 Lubbock
Texas Troubadour, The: Ernest Tubb
Texas two-step: 5 dance
Texasville: 4 film 5 novel
author: Larry McMurtry
cast: Timothy Bottoms, Jeff Bridges, Annie Potts, Cybill Shepherd
director: Peter Bogdanovich
Texcoco: 4 city, town
locale: 6 Mexico
Tex, Joe
song: Hold What You've Got (1965)
I Gotcha (1972)
Skinny Legs and All (1967)
Texmelucan: 4 city, town
locale: 6 Mexico, Puebla
Tex-Mex
item: 4 taco 5 chile, chili, nacho, salsa 6 chilli, fajita 7 burrito
prepare ~ beans: 5 refry
text: 4 book, copy, idea, line 5 issue, point, prose, theme, topic, verse, words 6 manual, matter, primer, reader, script, source, stanza, thesis 7 content, extract, passage, speller, subject, wording 8 argument, contents, document, handbook, libretto, main body, material, sentence, syllabus, workbook 9 paragraph, quotation, reference 10 assignment, schoolbook, transcript
addendum: 5 index
authoritative ~: 4 book 5 Bible 6 manual 8 handbook 9 guidebook, scripture, vade mecum
change ~: 3 fix 4 edit 5 alter, emend 6 doctor, polish, refine, revise 7 correct, improve, rewrite, touch up 8 rephrase 10 blue-pencil
ender: 4 book
mistakes: 6 errata
preliminary ~: 4 plot 5 draft 7 outline
reviewer: 6 editor 8 compiler, redactor
starter: 5 plain
work on ~ together: 6 coedit
text __: 4 hand 6 editor 7 edition
__ text: 5 clear, cover 6 church 7 running
textbook: 4 tome 5 guide 6 manual, primer, reader, volume 10 compendium
category: 4 elhi
division: 4 quiz, test, unit 5 drill 6 lesson 7 reading 8 exercise
textile: 5 cloth 6 fabric 8 material
component: 4 noil, yarn 5 fiber 6 strand, thread
dye: 5 eosin 6 eosine
lubricant: 5 olein 6 oleine
machine: 4 loom
texture: 4 wale, woof
unit: 6 dye lot
worker: 4 dyer
see also fabric
textiles: 5 cloth
texture: 3 nap 4 feel, warp, woof 5 grain, touch, weave 6 makeup 7 essence, feeling, quality, surface 8 fineness, softness 9 character, roughness, stiffness 10 coarseness, smoothness
Tey, Josephine: 6 writer 8 Scottish
work: The Daughter of Time
The Franchise Affair
Miss Pym Disposes
Tezontepec: 4 city, town
locale: 6 Mexico 7 Hidalgo
__ T. Farrell: 5 James
__ T. Firefly: 5 Rufus
__ T Ford: 5 model
T.G.I. __: 7 Friday's
TGIF
part of ~: 3 Fri., God, It's 5 Thank 6 Friday
sayer: 6 worker
Th: 4 elem. 7 element, thorium
90 for ~: 4 at. no.
T.H.: 5 White
Thackeray, William Makepeace: 6 author, writer 7 English
work: The Book of Snobs
Henry Esmond
Pendennis
The Ring and the Rose
Vanity Fair
The Virginians
Thai: 5 Asian 7 Siamese 8 language
ender: 4 land
Thailand: 4 gulf 6 nation 7 country
capital: 7 Bangkok
cat: 5 korat
dance: 4 khon
export: 4 teak
language: 3 Lao 5 Hmong
money: 3 att 4 baht 5 tical
native: 3 Lao 4 Miao
neighbor: 4 Laos 7 Myanmar 8 Cambodia, Malaysia
old name for ~: 4 Siam
org. for ~: 5 ASEAN
royal name: 4 Rama
temple: 3 wat
Thaïs: 5 opera
composer: 8 Massenet
role: 6 Albine, Nicias 7 Crobyle, Myrtale, Palemon 8 Athanaël
setting: 5 Egypt 10 Alexandria
Thaïs author: Anatole France
Thal: 4 Eric
Thalassa: 4 moon
planet: 7 Neptune
thalassic: 5 naval 6 marine 7 aquatic 8 maritime, nautical
thalassophobe fear: 3 sea
Thalberg, Irving spouse: Norma Shearer
thaler: 5 money
Thales: 5 Greek 11 philosopher
Thalia: 4 Muse 5 Grace
colleague: 4 Clio 5 Erato 6 Aglaia, Urania 7 Euterpe 8 Calliope 9 Melpomene 10 Euphrosyne, Polyhymnia 11 Terpsichore
parent of ~: 4 Zeus 9 Mnemosyne
__ T. Hall: 3 Tom
thallium: 5 metal 7 element
Thalmus: 8 Rasulala
Thames: 5 river
city on the ~: 6 London
county on the ~: 5 Essex
craft: 4 punt
locale: 7 England
school on the ~: 4 Eton
tributary: 3 Wey
thamin: 4 deer 6 mammal
relative: 3 elk, roe 4 axis, pudu, shou, sika 5 moose 6 chital, guemal, hangul, huemul, sambar, sambur, wapiti 7 brocket, caribou, muntjac, muntjak, sambhar, sambhur 8 reindeer 9 barasingh
__ than: 4 less 5 other
__ than a breadbox: 6 bigger
__ Than a Feeling: 4 More
__-than-air: 7 heavier, lighter
Thanatopsis author: 6 Bryant
Thanatos Syndrome, The author: Walker Percy
Thandie: 6 Newton
thane: 4 lord 5 title 8 nobleman
group: 4 clan
Thanet: 4 isle
locale: 7 England
__ than ever: 4 more
thank: 5 blame, bless 6 credit, praise 9 bow down to, recognize 10 appreciate
thank __: 3 you 6 heaven 7 heavens 8 goodness
thank-__ card: 3 you
Thank __ for Little Girls: 6 Heaven
Thank __ Lucky Stars: 4 Your
thankful: 7 content, pleased 8 beholden, grateful, indebted, relieved 9 gratified, satisfied
Thank God I Found You (2000 song) artist: Mariah Carey
Thank God I'm a Country Boy (1975 song) artist: John Denver
Thank Heaven for Little Girls composer: 5 Loewe 6 Lerner
show: 4 Gigi
thankless: 4 vain 6 futile 7 useless 8 wretched 9 fruitless, miserable, unwelcome 10 ungracious, ungrateful, unpleasant, unreturned
thanks: 5 danke, merci 6 credit, grazie, praise 7 gracias, spasibo 8 blessing 9 gratitude
give ~: 6 praise 10 appreciate
give ~ to: 4 laud 5 bless, exalt, extol, honor 7 glorify
Londoner's ~: 3 tas
to: 7 because, through 10 by virtue of
__ thanks: 4 many
Thanks __ the Memory: 3 for
Thanks a __!: 3 lot 4 heap 7 million
Thanks a Million (1935 film)
cast: Fred Allen, Ann Dvorak, Dick Powell
director: Roy Del Ruth
Thanksgiving
day: 4 Thur. 5 Thurs.
month: 3 Nov. 8 November
offering: 3 yam 4 bird, corn 5 feast, maize 6 turkey
parade producer: 5 Macy's
parade sight: 5 float, Santa 10 Santa Claus
VIP: 6 carver
where ~ is in October: 6 Canada
Thanksgiving __: 3 Day 6 cactus
Thanks, I __ that!: 6 needed
thanks to God in Latin: 10 Deo gratias
Thank U (1998 song) artist: Alanis Morissette
thank-you __: 4 card, note
Thank You... (1970 song) artist: Sly and the Family Stone
Thank You All Very Much (1969 film)
cast: Sandy Dennis, Ian McKellen
director: Waris Hussein
thank-you card
subject: 4 gift 5 award, favor 7 present 8 donation
Thank You, Mr. Moto (1938 film)
cast: Sidney Blackmer, Pauline Frederick, Peter Lorre
director: Norman Foster
Thank Your Lucky Stars (1943 film)
cast: Eddie Cantor, Joan Leslie, Dennis Morgan
__-than-life: 6 bigger, larger
__ than meets the eye: 4 more
__ Than Springtime: 7 Younger
__-than-thou: 6 holier
__ Than You Know: 4 More
thar: 4 goat 6 yonder
relative: 4 geep, ibex 6 Angora 7 markhor 8 markhoor
Thar: 6 desert
locale: 5 India 8 Pakistan
Thar __ blows!: 3 she
Tharp: 5 Twyla
that: 4 as if 7 pronoun
after ~: 4 next, then 5 since 10 thereafter
at ~: 7 besides 10 all the same, as it stands, in addition
at ~ place: 3 yon 5 there 6 yonder
at ~ time: 4 then 9 thereupon
be ~ as it may: 6 anyhow, anyway, even so 7 however
being ~: 3 for 5 since 7 because, whereas
being the case: 4 ergo, if so, then, thus 5 hence 9 therefore
by ~ time: 7 already
failing ~: 4 else
following ~: 4 next 5 later 9 thereupon 10 afterwards
for all ~: 6 though 7 however 10 regardless
given ~: 3 tho 6 though 8 although, assuming, provided 9 providing, subject to, supposing 10 in the event
in spite of ~: 6 even so
is: 5 id est
is to say: 3 viz. 5 to wit 6 namely
it follows ~: 4 ergo, then, thus 9 therefore
kind of: 7 similar
not ~: 4 this
on ~ occasion: 4 when 9 thereupon
provided ~: 4 so as 6 in case 8 as long as
this and ~: 4 both 10 miscellany
this or ~: 6 either
that __ say: 4 is to
that __ you do!: 5 thing
__ that!: 5 Fancy 7 Imagine
...that __ men's souls: 3 try
That __: 4 Girl 5 is all
That __ Black Magic: 3 Old
That __ Cat!: 4 Darn
That __ Feeling: 7 Certain
That __ Gang of Mine: 3 Old
That __ hay!: 4 ain't
That __ is, so was he made: 4 as he

That __ it!: 4 does 5 tears
That __ it all!: 4 says
That __ lady...: 5 was no
That __ Then, This Is Now: 3 Was
__ that a dainty dish...: 5 Wasn't
__ that again?: 4 How's
That ain't __!: 3 hay
That Ain't Love (1987 song) artist: REO Speedwagon
__ That a Shame: 4 Ain't
__ that be: 6 powers
That Certain Feeling composer: 8 Gershwin
thatch: 3 mop 5 cogon, reeds, straw 6 leaves, rushes
palm ~: 4 atap, nipa
Thatcher: 5 Torin 8 Margaret
Thatcher, Margaret: 2 P.M. 4 Tory 7 British
predecessor: 9 Callaghan
successor: 5 Major
__ That Could Happen: 5 Worst
That Darn Cat! (1965 film)
cast: Dean Jones, Hayley Mills, Dorothy Provine
director: Robert Stevenson
That Don't Impress Me Much (1999 song) artist: Shania Twain
__ That Dream: 4 Darn 6 Follow
__ That Failed, The: 5 Light
That feels good!: 3 aah
__ That Ghost: 4 Hold
That Girl (ABC sitcom)
cast: Ted Bessell (Don Hollinger) Marlo Thomas (Ann Marie)
__ That Girl: 4 Who's
That Girl (song) artist: Maxi Priest, Stevie Wonder
__ that glitters...: 3 All
__ that got away, the: 3 one
__ That Got Away, The: 3 Man
That Hamilton Woman (1941 film)
cast: Vivien Leigh, Alan Mowbray, Laurence Olivier
director: Alexander Korda
__ that has gits: 4 Them
__ That Heaven Allows: 3 All
That hurts!: 2 ow 3 oof, yow 4 ouch, yeow
__ That I Marry, The: 4 Girl
that is __: 5 to say
That is...: 5 I mean
that is in Latin: 5 id est
__ That Jack Built, The: 5 House
__ That Jazz: 3 All
That Kind of Woman (1959 film)
cast: Tab Hunter, Sophia Loren, George Sanders
director: Sidney Lumet
That Lady (1973 song) artist: Isley Brothers
That'll Be the Day (1974 film)
cast: David Essex, Ringo Starr
That'll Be the Day (song) artist: Buddy Holly and the Crickets, Linda Ronstadt
That makes sense!: 3 aha 6 I get it
...that married dear old __: 3 Dad
__ that matter: 3 for
__ that men do..., The: 4 evil
That old black magic ___...: 5 has me
That Old Black Magic (1958 song) artist: Louis Prima and Keely Smith
That Old Black Magic composer: 5 Arlen 6 Mercer
That rings __!: 5 a bell
__ That Roared, The: 5 Mouse
That's __: 4 Life 5 Amore
That's __!: 3 all 4 a gas, a lie 5 a wrap
That's __, folks!: 3 all
That's __ for you to say: 4 easy
That's __ how-do-you-do!: 5 a fine
That's __ off my mind!: 5 a load
That's __ she wrote: 3 all
That's a __!: 4 no-no, wrap
That's a joke, __!: 3 son
That's a laugh!: 3 hah 4 ha-ha
That's a lie!: 5 not so
That's all __ wrote: 3 she
That's All! (1983 song) artist: Genesis
That's all, folks! voice: Mel Blanc
That's All I Want from You (1954 song) artist: Jaye P. Morgan
That's all there __ it!: 4 is to
That's All You Gotta Do (1960 song) artist: Brenda Lee
That's amazing!: 3 gee, wow 5 golly
That's Amore composer: 6 Brooks, Warren
That's a pity: 3 tsk 4 alas 5 alack 6 tsk tsk
That's a relief!: 4 phew
That's a riot!: 4 ha-ha
That's a surprise!: 5 hello
That's cheating!: 6 no fair
That's enough for me: 6 I'm good
That's Entertainment! (1974 film)
director: Jack Haley Jr.
hosts: Fred Astaire, Bing Crosby, Gene Kelly, Peter Lawford, Liza Minnelli, Donald O'Connor, Debbie Reynolds, Mickey Rooney, Frank Sinatra, James Stewart, Elizabeth Taylor
studio: 3 MGM
That's hilarious!: 4 ha-ha 6 hee-hee
That's it!: 3 aha 5 bingo
That's Life! (1986 film)
cast: Julie Andrews, Sally Kellerman, Jack Lemmon
director: Blake Edwards
That's Life (1966 song) artist: Frank Sinatra
that's life in French: 9 c'est la vie
That's My Desire singer: 5 Laine
That's no lie!: 6 really
That's not __ idea!: 4 a bad
That's not the __ of it: 4 half
That's obvious!: 3 duh
That's okay: 6 no prob
That's Old Fashioned (1962 song) artist: Everly Brothers
That's one small step for ___...: 4 a man
__ that special?: 4 Isn't
that's right: 3 oui, yea, yep, yes, yup 4 amen, okay, sure, yeah 5 natch, uh-huh 6 indeed, verily 7 exactly, for sure, granted, ten-four, totally 8 for a fact, of course, thumbs up, to be sure 9 assuredly, naturally, obviously, perfectly, precisely, sure thing 10 absolutely, by all means, definitely, positively, sure enough, undeniably
That's Rock 'N' Roll (1977 song) artist: Shaun Cassidy
That's the __!: 6 ticket
That's the last __!: 5 straw
That's the truth!: 6 honest
That's the Way (1975 song) artist: KC and the Sunshine Band
That's the Way It Is (1999 song) artist: Celine Dion
That's the Way I've Always Heard It Should Be (1971 song) artist: Carly Simon
That's the Way Love Goes (1993 song) artist: Janet Jackson
That's the Way Love Is (1969 song) artist: Marvin Gaye
That's What Friends Are For (1985 song)
artist: Dionne Warwick, Elton John, Gladys Knight, Stevie Wonder
That's What Love Is for (1991 song) artist: Amy Grant
That's what you think!: 3 hah
that thing you do! (1996 film)
cast: Tom Hanks, Johnathon Schaech, Tom Everett Scott, Liv Tyler
director: Tom Hanks
setting: 4 Erie, Penn.
__ That Time Forgot, The: 4 Land
That Touch of __: 4 Mink
__ That Tune: 4 Name
That Uncertain Feeling (1941 film)
cast: Melvyn Douglas, Burgess Meredith, Merle Oberon
director: Ernst Lubitsch
That Uncertain Feeling author: Kingsley Amis
That was close!: 4 phew, whew
That was no ___: 4 lady
That Was Then, This Is Now (1986 song) artist: Monkees
That will do!: 6 enough
__ that you can be: 5 Be all
thaumaturge: 6 wizard 8 magician, sorcerer
thaumaturgic: 5 magic 7 magical, uncanny 8 mystical, wizardly 10 bewitching, enchanting, miraculous
thaumaturgy: 5 magic 7 sorcery
thaw: 3 run 4 flow, flux, fuse, melt, warm 6 ice out, loosen, open up, soften, unbend, warm up 7 defrost, détente, liquefy, liquify, melting 8 dissolve, fluidize, melt away, unfreeze 10 deliquesce
out: 5 deice 7 defrost 8 unfreeze
Th.D.: 3 deg.
curriculum: 3 rel. 5 relig.
the: 7 article
in French: 3 les
in German: 3 das, der, die
in Spanish: 3 las, los
thé: 3 tea 6 French
holder: 5 tasse
thé __: 7 dansant
The __, OR: 6 Dalles
Thea
daughter of ~: 4 Arne
father of ~: 6 Chiron 7 Cheiron
__ the above: 5 all of 6 none of
__ the act: 4 in on
__ the air: 4 up in 5 clear
__-the-air: 4 over
__ the Americas: 5 Ave. of
__ the ancient yuletide carol: 5 Troll
__ the Angels Sing: 3 And
__, the Ape Man: 6 Tarzan
__ the Apostle: 4 John
__ the Arab: 4 Ahab
__ the arm on: 3 put
theater: 3 art 4 barn, hall, site 5 arena, drama, movie, odeon, odeum, scene, stage 6 boards, cinema, kabuki, locale, lyceum 7 drive-in 8 coliseum, locality 9 colosseum, playhouse 10 auditorium, footlights, hippodrome, movie house, opera house
abbr.: 3 SRO
area: 4 loge, tier 5 foyer, lobby 6 lounge 7 balcony 9 box office, orchestra 13 orch. Mezzanine
attendees: 5 house 8 audience
award: 4 Obie, Tony
buy: 3 tix, tkt. 5 ducat 6 ticket
chain: 5 Loews
cheer: 5 brava, bravo 6 hurrah, huzzah
company: 3 rep 4 cast 6 troupe 9 repertory
drop: 5 scrim 7 curtain
ender: 4 goer 5 going
funder: 3 NEA
Greek ~: 5 odeon, odeum
in French: 4 cine
Japanese ~: 3 noh 6 kabuki
light: 4 neon
local ~: 4 nabe
location: 4 row A
name: 4 Roxy 5 Bijou 6 Lyceum
offering: 4 film, play, show 5 drama, farce, movie, revue 6 comedy, review 7 musical 10 production
org.: 4 ANTA
passage: 5 aisle
platform: 5 stage
seating: 3 box, row
sign: 4 Exit
sound system: 5 Dolby
souvenir: 4 stub 7 program 8 Playbill
success: 3 hit 4 boff 5 boffo, smash 7 boffola
summer ~ often: 4 barn
walk-on, for short: 4 supe
warning: 3 shh 4 hush 5 quiet
work in a ~: 3 ush 5 usher
see also Broadway
theater __: 5 of war
theater-__-round: 5 in-the
__ theater: 3 art 4 IMAX 5 arena, movie 6 dinner, little, shadow, street, summer
__ Theater: 5 Ford's
theatergoer: 9 spectator
__ the 'A' Train: 4 Take
theatre
see theater
__ Theatre: 5 Abbey, Globe 6 Habima
Theatre of Blood (1973 film)
cast: Vincent Price, Diana Rigg
Theatre of the absurd writer: 5 Genet
theatrical: 4 camp 5 campy, hammy, showy, stagy 6 flashy, stagey 7 stilted 8 affected, dramatic, mannered, operatic 9 grandiose, unnatural 10 artificial, flamboyant, histrionic
bit: 3 act 4 skit
overly ~: 4 arty 5 artsy
see also theater
__ the back: 5 pat on
__, the Bad, and the Ugly, The: 4 Good
__ the bag: 4 hold
__ the bag!: 5 It's in
__ the ball: 5 carry
__ the Ball Is Over: 5 After
__ the ball rolling: 4 keep
__ the Band Played On: 3 And
__ the Baptist: 4 John
__ the Barbarian: 5 Conan
__ the bat: 3 off
Thebe: 4 moon
planet: 7 Jupiter
__ the beans: 5 spill
__ the Bear: 4 Jack
__ the Beasts and Children: 5 Bless
__ the Beat Around: 4 Turn
__ the Beat Goes On: 3 And
__ the beef?: 6 Where's
__ the Beguine: 5 Begin
__, the Beloved Country: 3 Cry
__ the belt: 5 below
__ the bench: 4 take, warm
__ the bend: 6 around
Thebes: 4 city 5 ruins
ancient city near ~: 6 Abydos
land: 5 Egypt
river: 4 Nile
site of ancient ~: 5 Luxor
__ the best: 3 for
__ the best for last: 4 save
__ the best of: 3 get 4 have
__ the bill: 4 fill, foot
__ the birdie: 5 watch
__ the birds: 3 for
__ the Bismarck!: 4 Sink
__ the bite on: 3 put
__ the Blame on Mame: 3 Put
__ the block: 5 put on
__ the blue: 5 out of
__ the Blue Horizon: 6 Beyond
__ the blues: 4 sing

__ the board: 4 go by
__-the-board: 6 across
__ the boards: 5 tread
__ the Boardwalk: 5 Under
__ the boat: 4 miss, rock
__ the Body Electric!: 5 I Sing
__ the book at: 5 throw
__ the books: 3 hit 4 cook
__-the-books: 3 off
__ the boom: 5 lower
__ the Boss?: 4 Who's
__ the bottle: 4 spin
__ the bough breaks...: 4 When
__ the Boys: 3 For 6 Follow
__ the Boys Are: 5 Where
__ the breeze: 5 shoot
__ the bridge: 5 under
__ the Bruce: 6 Robert
__ the buck: 4 pass
__ the bud: 5 nip in
__ the bull by the horns: 4 grab, take
__ the bullet: 4 bite
__ the bushes: 4 beat
theca: 3 sac
contents: 5 spore 6 pollen
__ the cake: 3 cut 4 take
__ the calmly gathered thought: 4 unto
__ the candle at both ends: 4 burn
__ the cat: 4 bell
__ the cat out of the bag: 3 let
__ the ceiling: 3 hit
__ the Champions: 5 We Are
__ the chase: 5 cut to
__ the Children: 4 Save
__ the chutes: 5 shoot
__ the circumstances: 5 under
__ the Circus, A: 5 Son of
__ the city: 5 key to
__ the clear blue sky: 5 out of
__-the-clock: 5 round 6 around
__ the Clock: 4 Beat
__ the cloth: 5 man of
__ the Clouds Roll By: 4 Till
__ the cold: 5 out in
__ the compass: 3 box
__ the Confessor: 6 Edward
__ the Conquering Hero: 4 Hail
__ the Conqueror: 5 Pelle, Robur 7 William
__ the coop: 3 fly 4 blow
__ the corner: 4 turn
__-the-counter: 4 over 5 under
__ the course: 4 stay
__ the Covenant: 5 Ark of
__ the Cow: 5 Elsie
__ the cows come home: 4 till
__ the crack of dawn: 4 up at
__ the Craziest Dream: 4 I Had
__ the cud: 4 chew
__-the-cuff: 3 off
Theda: 4 Bara
colleague: 4 Pola
__ the Dark, A: 5 Cry in
__ the day: 3 rue, win 5 carry, seize
__ the Deal, The: 5 Art of
__ the deck: 3 hit 5 clear, stack
__ the deep end: 3 off 5 go off
__ the Defiant!: 4 Damn
__ the devil: 5 raise
__ the Devil: 4 Beat 7 Memnoch
__ the devil his due: 4 give
__ the dice: 4 load
__ the difference: 5 split
__ the dirt: 4 dish
__, the doctor!: 5 My son
__ the dog: 5 put on
__ the Dog: 3 Wag 7 Walking
__ the dogs: 4 go to
__ the door: 4 show
__ the door on: 4 shut 5 close
__ the door open: 5 leave
__-the-dots: 7 connect
__ the Dragon: 5 Enter
__ the drain: 4 down
__ the drop on: 3 get 4 have
__ the drum: 4 beat
__ the Drum Slowly: 4 Bang
__ the dust: 4 bite
thee: 7 pronoun
belonging to ~: 5 thine
__ the Earth Move: 5 I Feel
__ the Earth Stood Still, The: 3 Day
__ the east, and Juliet...: 4 It is
__ the edge: 4 over
__ the eight ball: 6 behind
__ the elbows: 4 up to 5 out at
__ the Elder: 5 Pliny
__ the end of my rope!: 4 I'm at
__ the end of Rico?: 6 Is this
__ the End of Time: 4 Till
__ the envelope: 4 push
__-thee-well: 4 fare
__ the eye: 4 give
__ the eye can see: 5 far as
__ the face of: 5 fly in
__ the Fair: 6 Philip
__ the faith: 4 keep
__ the fall: 4 take
__ the Fall: 5 After
__ the Family: 5 All in
__ the Fanatic: 3 Eli
__ the Farmer: 7 Isidore
__ the fat: 4 chew
__ the feedbag: 5 put on
__ the field: 4 play, take
__ the fields we go...: 3 O'er
__ the Fifth: 4 take
__, the final frontier: 5 Space
__ the finish: 4 in at
__ the fire?: 6 Where's
__ the first stone: 4 cast
__ the Fleet: 6 Follow
__ the flesh: 5 press
__ the floor: 4 take
__ the floor with: 3 mop 4 wipe
__ the fool: 3 act 4 play
__ the Force be with you!: 3 May
__ the fort: 4 hold
__ the Fox: 7 Reynard
__ the Frog: 6 Kermit
__ the Frost Is on the Punkin': 4 When
theft: 3 job 5 caper, crime, fraud, heist, pinch, score, steal 6 felony, holdup, piracy, racket, ripoff, snatch 7 break-in, larceny, lifting, looting, mugging, plunder, robbery, robbing, stickup, swindle, swiping 8 banditry, burglary, filching, fleecing, poaching, rustling, stealing, thievery 9 extortion, pilferage, pilfering, swindling 10 illegality, peculation, plagiarism, plundering, purloining
combining form: 5 klept- 6 klepto-
__ theft: 5 grand, petty
Theft, A author: Saul Bellow
__ Theft Auto: 5 Grand
__ the Fugue, The: 5 Art of
__ the fur fly: 4 make
__ the game: 4 play
__ the games begin: 3 Let
__ the gate: 3 get
__ the Giant: 5 André
__ the Giant Killer: 4 Jack
__ the gold: 5 go for
__ the good: 5 all to
__ the good life: 4 live
__ the Good Times: 3 For
__ the Good Times Roll: 3 Let
__ the grade: 4 make
__ the Gray Flannel Suit, The: 5 Man in
__ the Great: 4 Ivan 5 Elmer, Herod, James, Peter 6 Alfred, Darius, Norval, Pompey 7 Charles 9 Alexander, Catherine, Frederick 10 Theodosius
__ the greatest!: 5 You're
__ the Great Pumpkin, Charlie Brown: 3 It's
__ the Greek: 4 Nick 5 Jimmy, Zorba
__ the green: 5 rub of
__ the Grinch Stole Christmas: 3 How
__ the Grouch: 5 Oscar
__ the ground: 3 off 5 ear to, run to
__ the ground running: 3 hit
__ the ground up: 4 from
__ the gun: 4 jump 5 under
__ the habit: 4 kick
__ the half of it: 3 not
__ the hat: 4 pass
__ the hatch: 4 down
__ the hatchet: 4 bury
__ the Hat, The: 5 Cat in
__ the hay: 3 hit
__ the head of the class: 4 go to
__ the heart: 4 from
__ the heat: 4 take
__ the heck: 4 what
__ the heck of it: 3 for
__ the heels: 5 out at
__! The Herald Angels Sing: 4 Hark
__ the high spots: 3 hit
__-the-hill: 4 over
__ the hills: 5 old as
__ the hilt: 4 up to
__ the hit: 4 take
__ the Hittite: 5 Uriah
__ the hole: 5 ace in
__ the Hood: 5 Boyz N
__ the hook: 3 get, off
__ the Hoople: 4 Mott
__ the Horrible: 5 Hägar
__ the horses: 4 play
__ the hour: 5 man of
__ the house: 5 man of
__ the hump: 4 over
__ the Hutt: 5 Jabba
__ the ice: 5 break
__ the iceberg: 5 tip of
Theiler, Max: 8 Nobelist
their: 4 pron. 7 pronoun
like ~: 4 poss. 10 possessive
not ~: 3 our 4 your
Their __ Hour: 6 Finest
Their Eyes Were Watching God
author: Zora Neale Hurston
Their Finest Hour author: Winston Churchill
__ the Iron Mask, The: 5 Man in
theirs: 4 pron. 6 others 7 pronoun
like ~: 4 poss. 10 possessive
not ~: 4 ours 5 yours
Theirs __ to reason why...: 3 not
theistic: 6 divine 9 religious
__ the Jackal, The: 5 Day of
__ the jackpot: 3 hit
__ the jump on: 3 get 4 have
__ the jungle: 5 law of
__ the Kid: 5 Billy
__, The Killer Whale: 4 Namu
__ the King's Men: 3 All
__ the kitty: 4 feed
__ the Knife: 4 Mack
__ the knot: 3 tie
__ the land: 5 law of, lay of
__ the land of the free: 3 o'er
__ the land, the: 5 fat of
__ the Last Dance for Me: 4 Save
__ the Last Rose of Summer: 3 'Tis
__ the law: 5 above
__ the leader: 6 follow
__ the lead out: 3 get
__ the least: 5 not in, to say
__ the Liar: 5 Jakob
__ the lid off: 4 blow
__ the lie to: 4 give
__ the Life, A: 5 Day in
__ the lifeboats!: 3 Man
__ the light: 3 see
__ the light fantastic: 4 trip
__ the lily: 4 gild
__ the limit!, The: 4 sky's
__ the line: 3 toe 4 down, draw, hold 5 above, below, end of
__-the-line: 5 top-of
__ the Line: 5 I Walk
__ the lines: 7 between
__ the lion: 5 beard
__ the Lion-Hearted: 7 Richard
__ the Little Girl Dance: 3 Let
Thelma: 4 Todd 6 Ritter 7 Houston
Thelma & Louise (1991 film)
cast: Geena Davis, Harvey Keitel, Michael Madsen, Susan Sarandon
director: Ridley Scott
__ the Locust, The: 5 Day of
__ the loneliest number: 5 One is
__ the Lonely: 4 Only
Thelonious: 4 Monk
__ the Look: 4 U Got
__ the Looking-Glass: 7 Through
__ the Lovin': 5 After
them: 4 side 5 those 6 others 7 pronoun
author: Joyce Carol Oates
belonging to ~: 5 their
ender: 6 selves
to us: 3 foe 5 enemy
...them __ hills!: 4 thar
Them __ Eyes: 5 There
Them! (1954 film)
cast: Edmund Gwenn, Joan Weldon, James Whitmore
creature: 3 ant
director: Gordon Douglas
thema: 6 thesis
__ the Magic Dragon: 4 Puff
__ the Magnificent: 8 Suleiman
__ the Man: 4 Stan
__ the manger: 5 dog in
__ the map: 5 put on
__ the mark: 3 toe 5 shy of 6 beside
__ the market: 4 play
__ the mat: 4 go to
__ the matter?: 5 What's
__ the mayo!: 4 Hold
theme: 4 gist, idea, text 5 essay, motif, paper, tenor, topic 6 melody, report, thesis 7 keynote, message, subject, writing 8 argument, exercise 9 discourse, leitmotif, substance, term paper 10 exposition, literature
park feature: 4 maze, ride
theme __: 4 park, song
__ Theme: 5 Lara's, Love's, Tara's 6 Nadia's
__ the Menace: 6 Dennis
__ the merrier!, The: 4 more
__ the message: 3 get
__ the midnight oil: 4 burn
__ the mill: 7 through
__-the-mill: 5 run-of
__-the-minute: 4 up-to
Themis: 5 giant, Titan
daughter of ~: 5 Irene 6 Clotho 7 Atropos 8 Lachesis
parent of ~: 4 Gaea 6 Uranus
__ the Money and Run: 4 Take
__ the Moocher: 6 Minnie
__ the Mood for Love: 4 I'm in
__ the moon: 5 man in
__ the Moon: 4 I See 5 Lasso, Man on, Shoot
__ the morning!: 4 Top o'
__ the Morning, No: 5 But in
__ the most of: 4 make
__ the most part: 3 for
__ the music: 4 face
__ the music!: 4 Stop
__ the mustard: 3 cut
then: 4 anon, ergo, if so, next, soon, thus, when 5 after, again, hence, later 6 in a bit, in time, just as, not now 7 by and by, further, later on, someday 8 formerly, in a while, sometime, suddenly, years ago 9 after that, after-

ward, all at once, following, hereafter, in the past, therefore, thereupon 10 afterwards, at that time, back in time, before long, eventually, in that case, previously
as of ~: 5 until
back ~: 4 once, past
between ~ and now: 5 since
by ~: 7 already
even ~: 5 still
now and ~: 6 rarely, seldom 7 at times 9 sometimes 10 on occasion
or ~: 9 otherwise
Then __ will guide the planets...: 5 peace
Then __ You: 4 Came
Then Again, Maybe I Won't author: Judy Blume
__ the nail on the head: 3 hit
then and __: 5 there
__ then and there: 5 right
thenar: 4 palm
__ the Nation: 4 Face
__ the Navigator: 5 Henry
Then Came You (1974 song)
artist: Dionne Warwick, Spinners
thence: 9 from there, therefrom
ender: 5 forth 7 forward
__ the Needle: 5 Eye of
__ the nerve!: 5 Of all
__ the news today...: 5 I read
Then He Kissed Me (1963 song)
artist: Crystals
__ the Night: 4 Into 5 Seize 7 Because
__ the Night Away: 7 Twistin'
__ the night before Christmas...: 4 'Twas
__ the Nightlife: 5 I Love
__ then I wrote...: 3 And
Then punctual as __...: 5 a star
__ Then There Were None: 3 And
Then You Can Tell Me Goodbye (1967 song) artist: Casinos
Theo: 5 Kojak 7 van Gogh 8 Huxtable
__ & Theo: 7 Vincent
__ the Obscure: 4 Jude
theocratical: 5 papal 8 churchly, clerical, pastoral, priestly 9 apostolic, religious 10 pontifical, rabbinical
Theocritus: 4 poet 5 Greek
theodolite: 7 transit
Theodor: 5 Herzl, Storm 6 Geisel 7 Fontane, Mommsen, Schwann 8 Svedberg
Theodor __ Geisel: 5 Seuss
Theodora composer: 6 Handel
Theodora Goes Wild (1936 film)
cast: Melvyn Douglas, Irene Dunne, Thomas Mitchell
Theodore: 4 pope 5 Bikel 7 Dreiser, pontiff, Roethke, Schultz 8 chipmunk, Richards, Rousseau, Sturgeon 9 Roosevelt
brother of ~: 5 Alvin, Simon
Eleanor, to ~: 5 niece
in Italian: 7 Teodoro
in Russian: 6 Feodor, Fyodor
Theodore H. __: 5 White
Theodore Roosevelt Award giver: 4 NCAA
Theodoric: 4 pope 7 pontiff
__ the ointment: 5 fly in
__ Theologica: 5 Summa
theological: 6 divine 7 deistic 8 churchly, theistic 9 canonical, doctrinal, religious
doctrine: 7 kenosis
theology: 3 rel. 5 faith, relig. 8 religion
__ theology: 3 new 5 moral 6 crisis 7 natural, process
__ the One: 4 I Was, She's 5 Still, You're
Theophilus North author: Thornton Wilder
Theophrastus: 5 Greek 11 philosopher
theorbo: 4 lute 6 string
origin: 6 Europe
Theorell, Axel: 8 Nobelist
theorem: 3 law 4 rule 5 axiom, truth 6 dictum, thesis 7 formula, opinion 9 deduction, postulate, principle, statement 10 assumption, principium
auxiliary ~: 5 lemma
initials: 3 QED
__ theorem: 3 CPT, PCT, TCP 5 Bayes' 6 Green's, Larmor, Rolle's 7 Carnot's, Fermat's, Morera's, Pascal's
theoretical: 4 moot, pure 5 ideal 6 unreal 7 assumed, logical, nominal, on-paper 8 abstract, academic, pedantic, presumed, supposed, unproved 9 tentative 10 pedantical
theoretically: 7 ideally
theorist: 5 muser 7 idea man, thinker 9 visionary
theorize: 4 feel 5 guess, infer, think 6 assume, expect, ideate, reckon, wonder 7 believe, imagine, predict, presume, project, suggest, suppose, surmise, suspect 8 estimate, propound 9 formulate, postulate, speculate, take a shot, take a stab 10 anticipate, conjecture
theory: 3 ism 4 idea, view 5 basis, guess, hunch 6 belief, system, thesis 7 concept, feeling, opinion, premise, surmise, thought 8 argument, doctrine, position 9 inference, postulate, rationale, suspicion 10 assumption, conception, conjecture, hypothesis, philosophy, principium
combining form: 4 -logy
in ~: 7 ideally
__ theory: 3 BCS, set 4 Bohr, cell, game, gate, germ, wave 5 field, graph, group 6 atomic, auteur, domino, Galois, hormic, number, Oxford, string 7 quantum, queuing
__ theory of relativity: 7 general, special
Theory of Semiotics, A author: Umberto Eco
theos: 3 god
__ the other: 5 one or
__ the other cheek: 4 turn
__ the Other Half Lives: 3 How
__ the other shoe: 4 drop
__ the pace: 3 set
__ the pale: 6 beyond
__ the pants: 4 wear
__ the Parents: 4 Meet
__ the pavement: 5 pound
__ the peace: 4 keep
__ the Perverse, The: 5 Imp of
__ the phone: 4 hold
__ the picture!: 4 I get
__ the Pinhead: 5 Zippy
__ the piper: 3 pay
__ the pity!: 5 More's
__ the plank: 4 walk
__ the plug on: 4 pull
__ the plunge: 4 take
__ the point: 3 get 6 beside
__ the ponies: 4 play
__ the Pooh: 6 Winnie
__ the pot: 7 sweeten
__ the present: 3 for
__ the President's Men: 3 All
__ the Press: 4 Meet
__ the pump: 5 prime
__ the punch: 6 beat to
__ the question: 3 pop 5 out of
__ the quick: 5 cut to
Thera: 3 isl. 4 isle 6 island 9 Santorini
locale: 6 Greece 8 Cyclades
__ the races!: 5 Off to
__ the Races, A: 5 Day at
__-the-rack: 3 off
TheraFlu alternative: 5 Afrin 6 Contac, Nyquil, Tavist 7 Actifed, Comtrex, Dayquil, Dristan, Sinutab, Sudafed 8 Benadryl, Dimetapp, Drixoral 9 Coricidin, Triaminic 10 Robitussin
__ the rag: 4 chew
__ the rage: 3 all
__ the Rainbow: 4 Over
__ The Rain Must Fall: 4 Baby
__ the ramparts...: 3 O'er
__ the rap: 4 beat, take
therapeutic: 7 healing, medical 8 curative, remedial, salutary 9 analeptic 10 beneficial
datum: 4 dose 6 dosage
__ the rapids: 5 shoot
therapist: 6 doctor, healer, shrink 7 analyst
degree: 3 MSW
org.: 3 APA
therapy: 4 cure 5 rehab 6 remedy 7 healing 8 analysis, medicine 9 treatment
starter: 4 sero 5 aroma
__ the raven...: 5 Quoth
there: 3 yon 4 here, yond 5 voilà 6 on hand, yonder 7 present, pronoun, thither 10 over yonder
all ~: 4 sane 5 lucid, quick, right, sound 6 intact 8 rational, sensible 10 reasonable
almost ~: 4 near 5 close
always ~: 6 trusty 9 unfailing
ender: 3 for 4 fore, from, unto, upon, with 5 about, after, under 6 abouts, withal 7 against
for the ride: 5 along
from ~ on: 4 then 6 thence
get ~: 4 be at, come, go to, land 5 enter, light, pop in, pop up, reach 6 alight, appear, arrive, attend, blow in, make it, pull in, roll in, show up, sign in, turn up 7 check in, clock in, fetch up, hit town 8 breeze in 9 disembark, touch down 10 drop anchor
get ~ fast: 3 run 4 dash, rush, tear, whiz, zoom 5 hurry, speed, whisk 6 hasten, scurry 7 scamper
go here and ~: 3 gad 4 roam, rove, trek 5 drift, range 6 ramble, travel, wander 7 explore, journey, meander, traipse 9 bat around, bum around, gallivant, run around 10 knock about
hang in ~: 3 try 6 endure 9 withstand
here and ~: 5 about 6 around 7 in spots 8 rambling 9 irregular, sometimes, somewhere
it's neither here nor ~: 7 nowhere
means of getting ~: 4 belt, lane, path, pike, road, ship 5 guide, route, trail 6 access, artery, avenue, detour, street 7 channel, freeway, highway, parkway, passage, roadway, thruway, viaduct 8 short cut, turnpike 9 boulevard, itinerary 10 expressway, throughway
not ~: 3 off, out 4 away, AWOL, gone, here 6 absent 7 missing 9 elsewhere
over ~: 3 yon 4 afar, yond 6 yonder
partner: 4 here, then
the one ~: 4 that
the ones ~: 5 those
way out ~: 5 eerie, weird 7 strange
__ there: 3 all, get
__ there?: 4 Who's
There __ atheists...: 5 are no
There __ bad boys: 5 are no
There __ be a law!: 6 oughta
There __ crooked man...: 4 was a
There __ Frigate...: 4 is no
There __ My Baby: 4 Goes
There __ tavern...: 3 is a
There __ tide...: 3 is a
There!: 5 voilà
There! __ Said It Again: 3 I've
__ There: 3 Hey 4 Over 5 Being, I'll Be
thereabouts: 4 or so
thereafter: 4 next 5 later 9 after that, following
there and __: 4 then
There are __ that make us happy: 6 smiles
Thereby hangs __: 5 a tale
__-the-record: 3 off
__ the Red: 4 Eric, Erik
__ there, done that: 4 been
__ There Eyes: 4 Them
therefore: 2 so 4 ergo, then, thus 5 and so, hence, since 6 whence 9 as a result, to that end 10 inasmuch as
__ There for You: 5 I'll Be
therefrom: 6 thence
There Goes My Baby (1994 film)
cast: Dermot Mulroney, Rick Schroder, Kelli Williams
director: Floyd Mutrux
There Goes My Baby (1959 song)
artist: Drifters
There Goes My Heart (1938 film)
cast: Virginia Bruce, Patsy Kelly, Fredric March
director: Norman Z. McLeod
There is __!: 4 a God
There is __ in the affairs...: 5 a tide
There is no Frigate like __: 5 a book
There Is Nothin' Like a Dame composer: 7 Rodgers 11 Hammerstein
There! I've Said It Again (1963 song)
artist: Bobby Vinton
There'll be __ time...: 4 a hot
There'll Be Sad Songs (1986 song)
artist: Billy Ocean
__ There Lonely Girl: 3 Hey
theremin: 8 keyboard 10 instrument
There oughta be __!: 4 a law
There's __ every crowd!: 5 one in
There's __ here but...: 5 no one
There's __ in my soup!: 4 a fly
There's __ in My Soup: 5 a Girl
There's __ of Hush: 5 a Kind
There's __ Out Tonight: 5 a Moon
Theresa: 5 Maria 7 Russell, Saldana
of Avila: 3 nun 5 saint
__ Theresa: 5 Maria
There's a fly __ soup!: 4 in my
There's a Girl in My Soup (1970 film)
cast: Goldie Hawn, Peter Sellers
There's a Kind of Hush (song) artist: Carpenters, Herman's Hermits
There's Always a Woman (1938 film)
cast: Mary Astor, Joan Blondell, Melvyn Douglas
director: Alexander Hall
There's a Moon Out Tonight (1961 song) artist: Capris
There's a place __: 5 for us
There's a Rainbow Round My Shoulder (1928 song) artist: Al Jolson
There's a Small Hotel composer: 4 Hart 7 Rodgers
There's a Wocket in My Pocket! author: Dr. Seuss
Thérèse: 3 Ste. 6 sainte
see also French
__ Thérèse, Que.: 3 Ste.
Thérèse Raquin author: Emile Zola
There Shall Be No Night author: Robert E. Sherwood
__ there's life ...: 5 Where
There's many __ 'twixt...: 5 a slip
There's never __ around...: 4 a cop
There's no __ like home: 5 place

There's No Business Like Show Business composer: Irving Berlin
There's no future __: 4 in it
(There's) No Gettin' Over Me (1981 song) artist: Ronnie Milsap
There's no I in __: 4 team
There's Only One of You (1958 song) artist: Four Lads
There's Something About Mary (1998 film)
cast: Cameron Diaz, Matt Dillon, Ben Stiller
director: Bobby Farrelly, Peter Farrelly
dog: 5 Puffy
There, there!: 5 it's OK
thereupon: 4 then
__ the Revolution Without Me: 5 Start
There was __ woman...: 5 an old
There Was a Crooked Man ... (1970 film)
cast: Hume Cronyn, Kirk Douglas, Henry Fonda
director: Joseph L. Mankiewicz
__ There Was You: 4 Till
__ there yet?: 5 Are we
There you __!: 3 are
__ the Right Moves: 3 All
__ the Ring: 7 Closing
__ the riot act: 4 read
__ the ritz: 5 put on
__ the Riveter: 5 Rosie
thermae: 4 spas 5 baths, sauna 10 hot springs
thermal: 3 hot 4 warm 6 heated
starter: 3 geo
thermal __: 4 unit 5 noise 6 spring 7 barrier, neutron, printer
__ thermal unit: 7 British
__ thermidor: 7 lobster
thermionics: 7 science
thermochemistry: 7 science
study: 4 heat
thermodynamics: 7 science
study: 4 heat 6 energy
__ thermodynamics: 5 law of
thermometer: 5 gauge 10 instrument
marking: 5 notch 6 degree 9 gradation
part: 4 bulb, merc. 5 glass 7 mercury
scale: 6 Kelvin 7 Celsius 10 Centigrade, Fahrenheit
__ thermometer: 3 gas 4 oral 7 dry-bulb, maximum, minimum, wet-bulb
thermonuclear: 6 atomic 8 atomical
reaction: 6 fusion 7 fission
Thermopylae: 6 battle
locale: 6 Greece
thermos: 5 flask 6 bottle 7 canteen 9 container
__ the road: 3 hit 4 down 5 end of
__-the-road: 4 over
__ the Road Jack: 3 Hit
Theron, Charlize: 7 actress
film: Cider House Rules (1999)
The Curse of the Jade Scorpion (2001)
The Devil's Advocate (1997)
The Legend of Bagger Vance (2000)
Men of Honor (2000)
Mighty Joe Young (1998)
Sweet November (2001)
Trial and Error (1997)
__ the roof: 3 hit 5 raise
__ the Roof: 4 Up on
__ the roost: 4 rule
__ the ropes: 4 know
theropod: 5 biped 8 dinosaur
__ the Rose: 5 So Red
__ the Roses, The: 5 War of
__ the rounds: 4 make
Theroux, Paul: 6 author, writer
work: The Family Arsenal
The Great Railway Bazaar
The Mosquito Coast
The Old Patagonian Express
O-Zone
__ the rug out: 4 pull
__ the running: 5 out of
__ the sack: 3 hit
__ the Sailor: 6 Popeye, Sinbad 7 Sindbad
__ the same: 3 all 4 just
__ the Same Old Song: 3 It's
thesaurus: 4 book, list 5 lexis 7 lexicon 9 reference 10 vocabulary
compiler: 5 Roget
detail: 3 syn. 7 synonym
__ the scale: 3 tip
__ the scene: 4 make
__-the-scenes: 6 behind
__ the score: 4 even, know
these: 7 pronoun
not ~: 5 those 6 others
These __ Things: 7 Foolish
__ the Sea: 5 Under 6 Beyond
These are the __...: 5 times
__ the season...: 3 'Tis
__ the seas run dry...: 3 'til
These Boots Are Made for Walkin' (1966 song) artist: Nancy Sinatra
__ these days...: 5 One of
These Eyes (1969 song) artist: Guess Who
These Thousand Hills (1959 film)
cast: Richard Egan, Don Murray, Lee Remick
director: Richard Fleischer
These Three (1936 film)
cast: Miriam Hopkins, Joel McCrea, Merle Oberon
director: William Wyler
Theseus
friend of ~: 8 Aphidnus
lover of ~: 5 Helen 7 Ariadne
parent of ~: 6 Aegeus, Aethra 8 Poseidon
son of ~: 6 Acamas 8 Demophon 10 Hippolytus
stepmother of ~: 5 Medea
victim of ~: 8 Minotaur
__ the seven seas: 4 sail
__ the Sham: 3 Sam
__ the Sheik, The: 5 Son of
__-the-shelf: 3 off
__ the Sheriff: 5 I Shot
__ the Short: 5 Pepin
__ the shots: 4 call
__ the show: 3 run 5 steal
__ the show on the road: 3 get
__ the side of caution: 5 err on
thesis: 4 idea, text, view 5 essay, logic, paper, posit, prose, tenet, thema, theme, topic 6 belief, theory 7 opinion, premise, surmise, theorem, writing 8 argument, downbeat, position, proposal, treatise 9 discourse, monograph, postulate, term paper 10 contention, exposition
starter: 3 syn 4 meta
__ the Sixth Happiness: 5 Inn of
__ the skids on: 3 put
__ the sky: 5 pie in
__ the slip: 4 give
__ the Snowman: 6 Frosty
__ the socks off: 5 knock
thespian: 5 actor, mimic 6 player 7 actress, trouper 9 performer 10 histrionic
org.: 3 AEA, SAG 5 AFTRA
quest: 4 part, role
signal: 3 cue 6 prompt
work: 6 acting
workplace: 5 stage
Thespis: 4 poet 5 Greek
__ the spot: 3 hit
__ the squeeze on: 3 put
Thessalonians: 4 book
follower: 7 Timothy
preceder: 10 Colossians
Thessaloniki: 4 city, port, town
locale: 6 Greece
Thessaly, mountain in: 4 Ossa
__ the stage for: 3 set
__ the stakes: 5 raise
__ the stand: 4 take
__ the Stars Get in My Eyes: 4 I Let
__ the stick: 5 get on
__ the Stoic: 4 Zeno
__ the storm: 7 weather
__ the street: 5 man in, man on
__ the Strong Survive: 4 Only
__ the sun: 5 under
__ the Sun in the Morning: 4 I Got
__ the 13th: 6 Friday
theta: 5 Greek 6 letter
predecessor: 3 eta
successor: 4 iota
theta __: 4 wave 6 rhythm
__-the-table: 5 under
__ the tables: 4 turn
__ the tail on the donkey: 3 pin
__, the Tattooed Lady: 5 Lydia
__ the Teenage Witch: 7 Sabrina
__ the teeth of: 5 fly in
__ the Terrible: 4 Ivan
__ the test: 5 put to
__ the Things You Are: 3 All
__ the thought: 6 perish
__ the ticket!: 5 That's
__ the tide: 4 stem, turn
__ the Tiger: 4 Save 5 Eye of
__ the time: 4 pass 5 all of
__ the time being: 3 for
__ the time for all...: 5 Now is
__ the time of day: 4 pass
__ the times: 6 behind
__ the Times: 5 Sign o'
__ the Time To Fall In Love: 4 Now's
__ the Toiler: 6 Tillie
__ the top: 4 over
__ the Top: 5 You're
__ the top of one's head: 3 off
__ the torch: 4 pass
__ the torpedoes...: 4 Damn
__ the town red: 5 paint
__ the track: 3 off
__ the trail: 5 hot on
__ the transom: 4 over
__ the trick: 4 turn
__ the Triffids, The: 5 Day of
__ the tubes: 4 down
__ the tune: 4 call
__ the Turtle: 6 Yertle
__ the twain shall meet: 4 ne'er 5 never
__ the Two of Us: 4 Just
theurgist: 4 seer
__ the use!: 5 What's
__ the valley of death...: 4 Into
__ the Vampire Slayer: 5 Buffy
__ & the Vandellas: 6 Martha
thew: 3 vim 4 dint 5 brawn, force, might, power, sinew, vigor 6 energy, muscle 7 fitness, muscles, potence, potency, stamina 8 vitality 9 beefiness, endurance, fortitude, hardiness, huskiness, puissance, stoutness, toughness 10 browniness, brute force, mightiness, robustness, sturdiness
__ the wagons: 6 circle
__ the wall: 3 hit, off 4 go to
__-the-wall: 3 off
__ the walls: 5 climb
__ the Walrus: 3 I am
__ the way: 3 all 4 lead, pave 5 out of
__ the way it is: 5 That's
__ the wayside: 4 go by
__ the Way You Are: 4 Just
__ the weather: 5 under
__ the West Was Won: 3 How
__ the West Wind: 5 Ode to
__ the wheel: 6 behind
__ the whip: 4 snap 5 crack
__ the whistle: 4 blow
...__ the whole thing!: 4 I ate
__ the Wild Wind: 4 Reap
__ the Wind: 6 Saddle 7 Against, Inherit
__ the window: 5 go out
__ the wire: 5 under
__-the-wisp: 5 will-o'
Thewlis, David: 5 actor
film: Black Beauty (1994)
Dragonheart (1996)
Restoration (1995)
__ the wolf from the door: 4 keep
__ the woods: 5 out of
__ the Woods: 4 Into
__ the woodwork: 5 out of
__ the word!: 4 Mum's
__ the works: 5 gum up, shoot
__ the world: 5 man of, way of
__ the World: 5 End of, Joy to, Top of, We Are 6 Around, Change
__ the World Go Away: 4 Make
__ the World in Eighty Days: 6 Around
__ the World Needs Now: 4 What
__ the world of: 5 think
__ the world on fire: 3 set
__ the Worlds, The: 5 War of
__ the worst of it: 3 get 4 have
__ the wrong horse: 4 back
__ the wrong way: 3 rub
thews: 5 brawn, might, power, sinew, vigor 6 muscle 8 strength
thewy: 5 beefy, hefty, tough 6 brawny, robust, sinewy, strong, virile 7 hulking 8 athletic, muscular, pumped up 9 herculean, well-built 10 able-bodied
they: 4 pron. 5 those 6 others, people 7 pronoun
in Italian: 4 esse, esso
what ~ say: 4 buzz, talk 6 gossip 7 hearsay 9 grapevine
They __ Be Giants: 5 Might
They __ Believe Me: 4 Won't 5 Didn't
They __ Expendable: 4 Were
They __ Have Music: 5 Shall
They __ Horses, Don't They?: 5 Shoot
They __ It's Wonderful: 3 Say
They __ Laughed: 3 All
They __ serve...: 4 also
They __ the Wind Maria: 4 Call
They All Laughed (1981 film)
cast: Ben Gazzara, Audrey Hepburn, John Ritter
director: Peter Bogdanovich
They All Laughed composer: 8 Gershwin
__ They Are A-Changin', The: 5 Times
They called her frivolous __: 3 Sal
They Call the Wind Maria composer: 5 Loewe 6 Lerner
They Can't Take That Away From Me composer: 8 Gershwin
They Didn't Believe Me composer: 4 Kern
They Died With Their Boots On (1941 film)
cast: Olivia de Havilland, Errol Flynn, Arthur Kennedy
director: Raoul Walsh
They Don't Know (song) artist: Jon B, Tracey Ullman
They Drive by Night (1940 film)
cast: Humphrey Bogart, Ida Lupino, George Raft, Ann Sheridan
director: Raoul Walsh
__ the year: 5 man of
__ They Fall, The: 6 Harder
They Knew What They Wanted: 4 film, play
author: Sidney Howard
cast: William Gargan, Charles Laughton, Carole Lombard

director: Garson Kanin
They laughed when ___...: 4 I sat
They Learned About Women (1930 film)
cast: Bessie Love, Joseph T. Schenck, Gus Van
director: Jack Conway, Sam Wood
They Live by Night (1949 film)
cast: Howard da Silva, Farley Granger, Cathy O'Donnell
director: Nicholas Ray
They'll ___ Every Time: 4 Do It
They Might Be Giants (1971 film)
cast: Jack Gilford, George C. Scott, Joanne Woodward
___ the Younger: 5 Pliny
They're ___!: 3 off
They're ___ Our Song: 7 Playing
They're Biting painter: 4 Klee
They're Coming to Take Me Away, Ha-Haaa! (1966 song) artist: Napoleon XIV
They're Playing Our Song author: Neil Simon
...___ they say: 4 or so
They Say It's Wonderful composer: Irving Berlin
...they shall ___ the whirlwind: 4 reap
They Shall Have Music (1939 film)
cast: Jascha Heifetz, Andrea Leeds, Joel McCrea
director: Archie Mayo
They Shoot Horses, Don't They? (1969 film)
cast: Jane Fonda, Michael Sarrazin, Susannah York, Gig Young
director: Sydney Pollack
___ the Yum Yum Tree: 5 Under
They Were Expendable (1945 film)
cast: Robert Montgomery, Donna Reed, John Wayne
director: John Ford
They Won't Believe Me (1947 film)
cast: Jane Greer, Susan Hayward, Robert Young
They Won't Forget (1937 film)
cast: Gloria Dickson, Otto Kruger, Claude Rains
director: Mervyn LeRoy
They worshipped from ___: 4 afar
THI: 4 stat.
part: 4 temp. 5 index 8 humidity
Thia: 5 giant, Titan
brother of ~: 8 Hyperion
daughter of ~: 3 Eos 6 Selene
parent of ~: 4 Gaea 6 Uranus
son of ~: 6 Helios
thiamine: 3 vit. 7 vitamin 8 B vitamin
thick: 3 dim, fat 4 deep, dopy, dull, full, hard, logy, rank, ropy, slow, wide 5 broad, bulky, burly, bushy, caked, close, dense, dopey, foggy, gooey, gummy, gunky, heavy, husky, midst, mirky, muddy, murky, obese, pudgy, ropey, smoky, solid, squat, stiff, tight 6 chummy, chunky, clotty, clubby, gloppy, heaped, jammed, jelled, middle, obtuse, opaque, packed, simple, sirupy, stocky, stubby, stuffy, stumpy, stupid, syrupy, turbid, viscid 7 bulbous, clotted, compact, crammed, crowded, curdled, devoted, jellied, massive, obscure, profuse, raucous, replete, stuffed, teeming, viscose, viscous 8 abundant, familiar, friendly, ignorant, intimate, lubberly, numerous, populous, sisterly, swarming, thickset, thronged 9 abounding, bristling, brotherly, clabbered, condensed, congealed, dim-witted, jam-packed, jellylike, populated, thickened 10 boneheaded, buddy-buddy, coagulated, compressed, dull-witted, gelatinous, half-witted, hard-packed, impervious, palsy-walsy, slow-witted, solidified
be ~ with: 4 know, teem 5 swarm 6 abound, infest
combining form: 4 pycn- 5 pachy-, pycno-
in the ~ of: 3 mid 4 amid 5 among 6 amidst, mongst 7 amongst
lay it on ~: 8 overplay
piece: 4 hunk, slab 5 block, chunk, wedge
thick-___: 4 knee 5 soled 6 witted 7 skinned, skulled
thick and ___: 4 thin
thick as a ___: 5 brick, plank
thick-bodied: 5 squat, stout
Thicke: 4 Alan
thicken: 3 add, gel, set 4 cake, clot, curd, jell 5 swell, widen 6 curdle, deepen, expand, fatten, freeze, gelate, harden 7 acidify, clabber, clobber, congeal, enlarge, stiffen 8 buttress, condense, solidify 9 coagulate 10 gelatinize, inspissate
thickened: 5 stiff, thick 7 jellied
thickening agent: 4 agar, guar 5 algin 7 guar gum 8 agar-agar
___ thickens, The: 4 plot
Thicker Than Water (1977 song)
artist: Andy Gibb
thicket: 4 bosk, bush, wood 5 brush, clump, copse, hedge, scrub, woods 6 jungle 7 coppice
thickhead: 2 ox 3 oaf, sap 4 boor, clod, dolt, fool, lout 5 chump, clown, dunce 6 dimwit, lummox 7 bungler, jackass 9 blockhead, simpleton
thickheaded: 4 daft, dopy, slow 5 dense, dopey 6 obtuse 7 doltish, foolish, lumpish, witless 8 mindless 9 dim-witted
thickness: 3 ply 5 depth, layer, width
thickset: 4 boxy 5 beefy, burly, dense, husky, obese, pudgy, squat, stout, thick 6 brawny, chunky, stocky, stubby
thick-skinned: 4 hard, numb 5 tough 7 callous 8 hardened, obdurate 9 unfeeling 10 hard-boiled
thick-witted: 3 dim 4 dopy, dull, dumb, slow 5 crass, dense, dopey 6 bovine, oafish, obtuse, simple, stolid, stupid 7 boorish, doltish, fatuous, loutish, lumpish 9 pigheaded
Thidwick: The Big-Hearted Moose
author: Dr. Seuss
thief: 4 punk, yegg 5 cheat, crook, felon, ganef, gonef, gonif 6 bandit, goniff, klepto, lifter, mugger, outlaw, pirate, rip-off, robber, vandal 7 brigand, burglar, filcher, footpad, heister, prowler, rustler, stealer 8 criminal, cutpurse, hijacker, marauder, picklock, pilferer, swindler 9 embezzler, hold-up man, larcenist, peculator, plunderer, privateer, purloiner, scoundrel, scrounger 10 bushranger, cat burglar, highwayman, pickpocket, plagiarist, shoplifter
be a ~: 3 rob 4 loot, sack 5 steal, strip
customer: 5 fence
jewel ~: 6 iceman
job: 5 heist 7 robbery
take: 4 cash, jack, loot, swag 5 bills, booty, dough, graft, lucre, money 6 dinero, moolah, snatch 7 plunder, scratch 8 bankroll
___ thief: 5 horse, panel, sneak
Thief (1981 film)
cast: James Caan, Willie Nelson, Tuesday Weld
director: Michael Mann
Thief of Bad Gags, The: 5 Berle
Thief of Bagdad, The (1924 film)
cast: Douglas Fairbanks Sr., Anna May Wong
director: Raoul Walsh
Thief of Bagdad, The (1940 film)
cast: June Duprez, John Justin, Sabu
Thief of Paris, The (1967 film)
cast: Jean-Paul Belmondo, Genevieve Bujold, Marie Dubois
director: Louis Malle
Thief River Falls: 4 city, town
locale: 9 Minnesota
___ Thief, The: 5 King's 7 Bicycle
___-Thierry: 7 Château
Thiès: 4 city, town
locale: 7 Senegal
thieve: 3 nip, rob 4 lift, loot 5 boost, filch, heist, pinch, steal, swipe 6 burgle, pilfer, rip off 7 purloin, ransack 8 embezzle, shoplift 10 burglarize, run off with
thievery: 3 job 5 heist 7 larceny, robbery 8 burglary, stealing 9 pilfering 10 illegality, purloining
___ thieves: 5 den of
Thieves' Carnival author: Jean Anouilh
Thieves' Highway (1949 film)
cast: Lee J. Cobb, Richard Conte, Valentina Cortese
director: Jules Dassin
Thieves' Holiday (1946 film)
cast: Signe Hasso, Carole Landis, George Sanders, Akim Tamiroff
director: Douglas Sirk
Thieves in the Temple (1990 song)
artist: Prince
Thieves Like Us (1974 film)
cast: Keith Carradine, Shelley Duvall, John Schuck
director: Robert Altman
thievish: 6 sneaky 7 crooked, cunning, piratic 8 stealthy 9 dishonest, larcenous, pilfering, predatory, rapacious, secretive 10 fraudulent
thigh: 6 haunch
combining form: 3 mer- 4 mero-
ender: 4 bone
it's above the ~: 3 hip
muscle: 4 quad 6 biceps, rectus, vastus
muscles: 5 recti, vasti
site: 3 leg
terminus: 5 groin
thigh-___: 7 slapper
thighbone: 5 femur
thighbones: 6 femora
thigh-highs: 4 hose 7 hosiery
thigh-rotation
muscle: 5 psoas
muscles: 5 psoae, psoai
thimble ender: 3 rig 4 weed 5 berry
thimbleful: 3 sip 4 snip
Thimble Theatre
name: 3 Oyl 5 Bluto, Olive, Wimpy 6 Popeye 7 Swee' Pea 8 Olive Oyl
Thimphu: 4 city, town 7 capital
locale: 6 Bhutan
thin: 3 wan 4 bony, edit, fade, fine, lacy, lame, lank, lean, poor, puny, rare, slim, trim, weak, wiry 5 boney, filmy, gaunt, gauzy, gawky, lanky, lathy, light, lousy, prune, rangy, reedy, runny, scant, shave, sheer, soupy, spare, tinny, water, weedy, wispy 6 dainty, dilute, faulty, feeble, flimsy, gangly, lessen, limpid, liquid, meager, narrow, peaked, reduce, refine, scanty, scarce, skimpy, skinny, slight, slinky, sparse, spotty, svelte, twiggy, wasted, watery, weaken 7 cut back, diffuse, diluted, fragile, gawkish, gracile, haggard, lacking, lighten, pinched, refined, rickety, scraggy, scrawny, sketchy, slender, spidery, spindly, starved, stringy, tenuous, vitiate, weed out, willowy, wispish, wizened 8 decrease, delicate, disperse, exiguous, gangling, gossamer, raillike, rarefied, rawboned, skeletal, starving, twiglike, wisplike 9 attenuate, cut back on, dispersed, emaciated, permeable, scattered, shriveled, stretched, sylphlike, tasteless, uncrowded, untenable, waferlike, water down 10 adulterate, attenuated, diaphanous, improbable, inadequate, indistinct, see-through, threadlike
combining form: 4 lept- 5 lepto-
covering: 7 coating
limb: 4 wand 5 sprig, stick
not ~: 5 broad, bulky, heavy, husky, obese, plump, pudgy, squat, thick 6 brawny, chubby, chunky, stocky 8 thickset
one: 5 scrag 8 beanpole 10 string bean
on ~ ice: 5 risky 6 unsafe 8 perilous 9 uncertain 10 precarious
out: 4 bald 5 prune 7 tail off 8 taper off
piece: 5 slice 8 splinter
thin-___: 7 skinned
___ thin: 4 wear
___-thin: 5 paper, wafer
thin as ___: 5 a rail, a reed
thine: 5 yours
not ~: 4 mine
Thine ___ kingdom...: 5 is the
Thine alabaster ___ gleam: 6 cities
...thine own self be ___: 4 true
thing: 3 bag, fad, job 4 duty, fact, feat, form, gear, idea, item, noun, task, tool, work 5 craze, dodad, event, facet, forte, gizmo, mania, means, point, quirk, shape, stunt, style, trait, trend 6 affair, aspect, detail, device, dingus, doodad, entity, factor, fetich, fetish, figure, gadget, hang-up, matter, notion, object, phobia, widget 7 article, concept, episode, feature, machine, quality, subject, thought 8 attitude, business, creature, fixation, idée fixe, incident, material, occasion, property, vocation 9 apparatus, commodity, doohickey, equipment, happening, implement, mechanism, obsession, situation, specialty, substance 10 individual, instrument, livelihood, occurrence, particular, phenomenon, proceeding
harmful ~: 5 curse 6 blight, plague, poison 7 scourge 8 calamity 9 detriment
improper ~: 5 taboo
in ~: 3 fad 4 mode, rage 5 craze, trend, vogue 7 fashion 8 last word
indispensable ~: 4 need 9 essential, necessity, requisite 10 imperative, obligation, sine qua non
in Latin: 3 res
living ~: 5 beast, being 6 animal, person 8 creature, organism
not a ~: 3 nil, zip 4 nada, none, zero 5 aught, zilch 6 naught, nought 7 nothing
one's ~: 5 skill 9 specialty
starter: 3 any 4 play, some 5 every
too much of a good ~: 4 glut 5 flood 7 surfeit, surplus 8 overload 10 indulgence, oversupply
wicked ~: 4 evil, vice 5 crime 7 misdeed, offense 8 atrocity, iniquity, trespass 9 sacrilege 10 misconduct
___ thing: 3 new 4 sure 5 first, young
Thing
Addams Family's ~: 4 hand
___ Thing: 4 Good, Wild
thingamajig: 5 dodad, gismo, gizmo 6 device, dingus, doodad, gadget, whosis, widget

__ thing at a time: 3 one
__ Thing Called Love: 4 This
thing of beauty..., A writer: 5 Keats
thing of beauty is __ forever, A: 4 a joy
__ **Thing on My Mind, The:** 4 Last
things: 4 duds 5 goods, stuff 6 attire 7 apparel, baggage, clothes, effects, garment, luggage, raiment 8 chattels, clothing 9 trappings 10 belongings
all living ~: 5 world 6 nature 8 universe
how ~ are: 6 status 7 reality 9 situation
in philosophy: 5 entia
one of those ~: 4 that
work ~ out: 6 manage
__ **things:** 3 see 6 seeing
Things __ for Love, The: 4 We Do
__ **Things:** 4 Last, Wild 7 Needful
Things (1962 song) artist: Bobby Darin
Things could be __!: 5 worse
__ **Things Mean a Lot:** 6 Little
Things of This World author: Richard Wilbur
Things to Come (1936 film)
cast: Cedric Hardwicke, Raymond Massey
director: William Cameron Menzies
__ **things up:** 5 patch
Things You Can Tell Just by Looking at Her (2001 film)
cast: Kathy Baker, Glenn Close, Cameron Diaz, Calista Flockhart
director: Rodrigo Garcia
thingy: 5 dodad, gismo, gizmo 6 device, dingus, doodad, gadget, whosis, widget
__ **thing you do!:** 4 that
think: 3 see 4 deem, feel, hold, muse, stew 5 brood, fancy, guess, infer, judge, sense, study, weigh 6 assume, deduce, esteem, expect, gather, ideate, ponder, reason, recall, reckon, regard, wonder 7 analyze, believe, daresay, examine, feature, foresee, imagine, presume, project, realize, reflect, resolve, revolve, sort out, suppose, surmise, suspect 8 appraise, cogitate, conceive, conclude, consider, envisage, envision, estimate, evaluate, look upon, meditate, mull over, perceive, remember, ruminate, theorize, turn over 9 cerebrate, determine, figure out, recollect, reminisce, speculate, sweat over, visualize 10 call to mind, comprehend, conjecture, deliberate, have in mind, understand
about: 4 view 5 study 6 ponder 7 reflect, revolve 8 consider, mull over, turn over
alike: 4 jibe, mesh 5 agree 6 accord, concur 9 harmonize
back: 6 recall, relive 8 remember 9 reminisce
better of: 3 rue 6 regret
hard: 5 focus 6 fixate
highly of: 4 love 5 adore, favor, value 6 admire, esteem, revere 7 idolize, respect 8 look up to, venerate 9 reverence
I ~ not: 3 nah, naw, nay, nix, non 4 nein, nope, nyet, uh-uh 5 ixnay, never, no how, no way 6 no deal, noways, nowise 8 forget it, negative, negatory 9 by no means, fat chance 10 count me out, thumbs down
little of: 4 skip, snub 5 let go, scorn, spurn 6 forget, ignore, rebuff, slight 7 disdain, dismiss, let pass, tune out 8 discount, laugh off, let slide, pass over, shrug off 9 disregard, gloss over, pay no mind 10 brush aside
no more of: 6 forget, ignore 8 discount, overlook, pass over 9 disregard
of: 5 hit on 6 recall, reckon 7 imagine
of as: 6 look on
old-style: 4 trow
out: 4 plan 5 solve 6 reason 7 analyze
over: 4 mull, muse 5 study, weigh 6 digest, review 8 consider, meditate, ruminate 9 entertain 10 reconsider
(over): 4 chew, pore
piece: 4 Op-Ed 5 essay, paper, theme, tract 7 article 8 critique, treatise 10 exposition
similar: 6 equate
starter: 5 group 6 double
the worst of: 4 hate 5 abhor 6 detest, loathe 7 despise, dislike 8 execrate 9 abominate
too much of: 8 overrate
twice: 5 pause 7 scruple 8 reassess 10 reconsider
up: 5 fancy, hatch 6 create, design, devise, invent 7 concoct, devises, imagine 8 conceive, contrive 9 formulate, improvise, originate 10 mastermind
(up): 4 make 5 dream
think __: 4 tank 5 aloud, piece, twice 7 factory, through
think __ about: 5 twice
think __ of: 4 much 6 better, little 7 nothing
Think (1968 song) artist: Aretha Franklin
thinkable: 6 likely 8 feasible, possible, probable 9 potential 10 believable, imaginable
Think company: 3 IBM, NCR
thinker: 3 ace 4 sage, whiz 5 brain 6 pundit, savant 7 egghead, idea man, prodigy, scholar 8 Einstein, highbrow, theorist, virtuoso 9 intellect 10 mastermind
pause: 2 er, uh, um
Thinker, The: 6 statue
creator: 5 Rodin
Think Fast, Mr. Moto (1937 film)
cast: Virginia Field, Peter Lorre, Sig Ruman
director: Norman Foster
Think I'm in Love (1982 song) artist: Eddie Money
thinking: 6 mental, motive 7 logical, pensive, thought 8 analytic, cerebral, rational 10 analytical, philosophy, reflection, reflective, thoughtful
clear ~: 5 logic, sense 6 reason, sanity, thesis, wisdom 9 coherence, deduction, dialectic, good sense, induction, inference, rationale, reasoning, syllogism 10 philosophy
not ~ straight: 5 woozy 8 confused
twice: 7 prudent
way of ~: 4 mind, view 9 mentality, sentiment, viewpoint
thinking __: 3 cap 7 machine
__ **thinking:** 7 magical, wishful
__**-thinking:** 5 right 7 forward
Thinking Eye, The artist: 4 Klee
Thinking Reed, The author: Rebecca West
Think nothing __!: 4 of it
Think of Laura (1983 song) artist: Christopher Cross
ThinkPad producer: 3 IBM
think tank
name: 4 Rand
output: 4 idea 6 notion, theory 7 concept 8 proposal 10 brainstorm
think the __ of: 5 world
Thin Man Goes Home, The (1944 film)
cast: Myrna Loy, William Powell, Lucile Watson
director: Richard Thorpe
Thin Man, The: 4 film 5 novel
author: Dashiell Hammett,
cast: Myrna Loy, Maureen O'Sullivan, William Powell
character: 4 Mimi, Nick, Nora, Shep 5 Clyde 6 Wynant 7 Charles
director: W.S. Van Dyke
dog: 4 Asta
Thinnes: 3 Roy
thinness symbol: 4 dime, rail, reed 5 razor, wafer
Thin red line of __: 5 'eroes
Thin Red Line, The: 4 film 5 novel
author: James Jones
cast: Adrien Brody, Jim Caviezel, Ben Chaplin, Sean Penn
director: Terrence Malik
__ **Thins:** 5 Wheat
thin-skinned: 5 testy 6 feisty, tender, touchy 8 choleric, liverish, petulant 9 fractious, humorless, irritable, querulous, sensitive
thin-voiced: 5 reedy
third: 8 fraction
combining form: 4 trit- 5 trito-
degree: 3 Ph.D. 5 probe 7 torture 8 question
finish ~: 4 lose, show
give the ~ degree: 4 pump, quiz 5 grill 8 question
section: 5 part C
to the ~ power: 5 cubed, cubic
third __: 3 ear, eye, man 4 base, gear, mate, rail 5 class, force, house, party 6 degree, estate, eyelid, finger, person, sector, stream 7 baseman, officer, reading
third-__: 4 rate 5 class
Third __: 5 Order, World 7 Worlder
Third __ Blind: 3 Eye
Third __, The: 3 Key, Man 5 Night, Voice 7 Miracle
third baseman, Hall of Fame: 5 Brett 7 Johnson, Mathews, Schmidt, Traynor 8 Robinson 9 Dandridge, Ed Mathews 10 Pie Traynor
third-class __: 4 mail
Third Deadly Sin, The author: Lawrence Sanders
Third Man on the Mountain (1959 film)
cast: James MacArthur, Janet Munro, Michael Rennie
director: Ken Annakin
Third Man, The: 4 film 5 novel
author: Graham Greene
cast: Joseph Cotten, Alida Valli, Orson Welles
director: Carol Reed
role: 4 Lime 5 Harry
Third Miracle, The (1999 film)
cast: Ed Harris, Anne Heche, Armin Mueller-Stahl, Michael Rispoli
director: Agnieszka Holland
Third Night, The author: Thomas Wolfe
third-place award: 6 bronze
third-rate: 3 bad 4 poor 5 cheap, lousy 6 cheesy, crumby, crummy 7 ill-done 8 inferior, pathetic 9 miserable 10 pathetical
third-stringer: 5 scrub
Third Voice, The (1960 film)
cast: Laraine Day, Julie London, Edmond O'Brien
Third World area: 6 Africa
thirst: 3 yen 4 long, lust, need, pant, pine, sigh, want, wish 5 yearn 6 desire, drouth, hunger 7 craving, drought, dryness, longing, passion 8 appetite, keenness, yearning 9 appetence, eagerness, esurience, hankering
for: 4 want 5 covet, crave 6 desire
(for): 4 long, lust, pant, pine
quencher: 3 ade, ale, tea 4 beer, cola, soda 5 drink, juice, water
satisfy ~: 5 slake 6 quench
thirst-quenching sound: 4 glug
thirsty: 3 dry 4 arid, avid, keen 5 eager, unwet 6 greedy, hungry 7 bone-dry, craving, parched, wishful 8 desirous, droughty, yearning 9 absorbent, waterless 10 dehydrated, solicitous
(for): 4 wild
make ~: 5 parch
Thirteen Clocks, The author: James Thurber
Thirteen Conversations About One Thing (2001 film)
cast: Alan Arkin, Matthew McConaughey, John Turturro
director: Jill Sprecher
Thirteen Days (2000 film)
cast: Dylan Baker, Kevin Costner, Steven Culp, Bruce Greenwood
thirteenth-century traveler: 4 Polo
Thirty days __ September...: 4 hath
thirty-eight: 3 gun 6 pistol, weapon 7 firearm 8 revolver
Thirty Seconds Over Tokyo (1944 film)
cast: Van Johnson, Spencer Tracy, Robert Walker
director: Mervyn LeRoy
thirtysomething (ABC drama)
cast: Timothy Busfield (Elliot Weston)
Polly Draper (Ellyn)
Mel Harris (Hope Steadman)
Peter Horton (Gary Shepherd)
Melanie Mayron (Melissa Steadman)
Ken Olin (Michael Steadman)
Patricia Wettig (Nancy Weston)
dog: 7 Grendel
Thirty Years' __: 3 War
this: 5 hence 7 pronoun
after ~: 5 hence, later 9 from now on, hereafter 10 henceforth
and that: 4 both 10 miscellany
at ~ juncture: 3 now 4 here 5 as yet, today 8 promptly, right now, right off 9 forthwith, presently, right away 10 here and now
at ~ time: 3 now 8 until now 9 presently
before ~: 5 prior 8 hitherto, until now
can't be: 4 oh no
concerning ~: 6 hereof
for ~ reason: 4 ergo, then, thus 6 hereat
found at ~ place: 6 herein
from ~ point: 6 hereon 8 evermore
from ~ time forward: 6 always 9 endlessly, eternally 10 henceforth
in ~ fashion: 4 thus 6 like so, thusly 7 that way
in Latin: 3 hic
in ~ place: 4 here 6 herein
in Spanish: 4 esta, esto
instant: 3 now, PDQ 4 anon, ASAP, soon 5 today 6 at once 7 quickly 8 in no time, promptly, right now, right off 9 at present, forthwith, instantly, posthaste, presently, right away 10 here and now
in ~ way: 4 thus 6 hereby
like ~ in prescriptions: 3 tal.
not ~: 4 that
or that: 6 either
out of ~ world: 3 def, rad 4 aces, A-one, boss, braw, cool, dece, eery, fine, gear, keen, neat, nice, phat, tuff 5 alien, dandy, ducky, eerie,

grand, great, marvy, neato, nobby, prime, slick, super, swell 6 bang on, bang-up, bonzer, bosker, choice, divine, dreamy, far-out, gnarly, groovy, lovely, peachy, slap-up, spot on, superb, terrif, tip-top, unreal, whizzo, wicked 7 amazing, awesome, capital, corking, perfect, ripping, skookum, stellar, sublime 8 dazzling, especial, eximious, fabulous, five-star, four-star, frabjous, glorious, heavenly, jim-dandy, slam-bang, smashing, splendid, standout, sterling, stick-out, stunning, superior, terrific, top-level, topnotch, very good, wondrous 9 bodacious, Endsville, excellent, exemplary, exquisite, fantastic, first-rate, high-grade, hunky-dory, marvelous, sollicker, sumptuous, top-flight, wonderful 10 first-class, hotsy-totsy, incredible, jack-a-dandy, peachy-keen, phenomenal, remarkable, stupendous, super-duper
regarding ~: 6 hereto 8 hereunto
to ~ day: 5 still 8 until now
to ~ point: 3 yet 4 here 5 so far 6 hither
up to ~ time: 3 yet 6 ere now, of late 7 thus far 8 until now 10 heretofore, previously
way: 4 thus 6 like so
with ~ action: 6 hereby
this __ and age: 3 day
this __ of: 4 side
this __ of tears: 4 vale
This __: 4 Is It, Kiss, Time 5 House
This __ Army: 5 Is the
This __ Army, Mr. Jones: 5 Is the
This __ be!: 4 can't
This __ Be: 4 Will
This __ Be Love: 4 Can't
This __ Country: 4 Is My
This __ Earth: 6 Island
This __ Feeling: 5 Happy
This __ fine how-do-you-do!: 3 is a
This __ for Hire: 3 Gun
This __ Heart of Mine: 3 Old
This __ I Ask: 5 Is All
This __ in Love with You: 4 Guy's
This __ joke!: 4 is no
This __ Kisses: 5 Year's
This __ man, he played...: 3 old
This __ Moment: 5 Magic
This __ of Paradise: 4 Side
This __ on me!: 4 one's
This __ outrage!: 4 is an
This __ recording: 3 is a
This __ Song: 4 Is My
This __ stickup!: 3 is a
This __ sudden!: 4 is so
This __ test: 3 is a
This __ the Dream's on Me: 4 Time
This __ Up: 3 End 4 Side
This Above All (1942 film)
cast: Joan Fontaine, Thomas Mitchell, Tyrone Power
director: Anatole Litvak
__ This a Lovely Day: 4 Isn't
this and __: 4 that
__ This and Heaven Too: 3 All
Thisbe's love: 7 Pyramus
This Boy's Life (1993 film)
cast: Ellen Barkin, Robert De Niro, Leonardo DiCaprio
director: Michael Caton-Jones
This Brunette Prefers Work author: Anita Loos
This can't be!: 4 oh no
This Can't Be Love composer: 4 Hart 7 Rodgers
__ this corner...: 5 And in

This Day and Age (1933 film)
cast: Judith Allen, Charles Bickford, Richard Cromwell
director: Cecil B. DeMille
This Diamond Ring (1965 song) artist: Gary Lewis and the Playboys
This early?: 6 so soon
__ This Earth: 5 Not of
This Girl Is a Woman Now (1969 song) artist: Gary Puckett and the Union Gap
This Girl's in Love With You (1969 song) artist: Dionne Warwick
This Gun for Hire: 4 film 5 novel
author: Graham Greene
cast: Alan Ladd, Veronica Lake, Robert Preston
director: Frank Tuttle
This Guy's in Love With You (1968 song) artist: Herb Alpert
This Happy Breed (1944 film)
cast: Celia Johnson, John Mills, Robert Newton
director: David Lean
This Happy Feeling (1958 film)
cast: Curt Jurgens, Debbie Reynolds, John Saxon
director: Blake Edwards
This I Remember author: Eleanor Roosevelt
This is __: 5 a test
This is __-brainer!: 3 a no
This Is __ Ask: 4 All I
This Is __ Life: 4 Your
This Is __ Tap: 6 Spinal
This Is for the Lover in You (1996 song) artist: Babyface, Jody Watley, LL Cool J
This Is It (1979 song) artist: Kenny Loggins
This Is Just to Say author: William Carlos Williams
This Island __: 5 Earth
This Is My Affair (1937 film)
cast: Victor McLaglen, Barbara Stanwyck, Robert Taylor
director: William A. Seiter
__ This Is My Beloved: 3 And
This Is My Song (1967 song) artist: Petula Clark
This Is My Story author: Eleanor Roosevelt
This is only __: 5 a test
This Is Spinal Tap (1984 film)
cast: Christopher Guest, Michael McKean, Rob Reiner, Harry Shearer
director: Rob Reiner
This Is the Army (1943 film): 7 musical
cast: Joan Leslie, George Murphy, Ronald Reagan
composer: Irving Berlin
director: Michael Curtiz
This is the thanks __?: 4 I get
This Is Your __: 4 Life
This Kiss (1998 song) artist: Faith Hill
This little __ went to market...: 6 piggie
This Magic Moment (1969 song) artist: Jay and the Americans
This Man's Navy (1945 film)
cast: Wallace Beery, Tom Drake, James Gleason
director: William Wellman
This Masquerade (song) artist: Carpenters, George Benson
This means __!: 3 war
This minute!: 3 now, PDQ 4 ASAP 6 pronto 9 right away
__ This Moment On: 4 From
This must weigh __!: 4 a ton
This Old Heart of Mine (1990 song) artist: Rod Stewart

This Old House
host: Bob Vila
network: 3 PBS
This Ole House (1954 song) artist: Rosemary Clooney
This one __ me!: 4 is on
this one in Spanish: 4 esta, esto
This one's __!: 4 on me
This One's for the Children (1989 song) artist: New Kids on the Block
This One's for You (1976 song) artist: Barry Manilow
This Perfect Day author: Ira Levin
__ this ring...: 4 With
...this sceptred __: 4 isle
This Side of Paradise author: F. Scott Fitzgerald
This Sporting Life (1963 film)
cast: Richard Harris, Rachel Roberts
director: Lindsay Anderson
sport: 5 rugby
This Thing Called Love (1941 film)
cast: Binnie Barnes, Melvyn Douglas, Rosalind Russell
director: Alexander Hall
This Time for Keeps (1947 film)
cast: Jimmy Durante, Lauritz Melchior, Esther Williams
director: Richard Thorpe
This Time I Know It's for Real (1989 song) artist: Donna Summer
This Time the Dream's on Me composer: 5 Arlen 6 Mercer
thistle: 4 burr, weed 5 plant 6 flower 7 bramble
down: 5 pappi 6 pappus
relative: 6 arnica
__ thistle: 3 sow 4 blue, bull, holy, milk, musk 5 globe 6 Canada, cotton, golden, Scotch 7 Russian
thistly: 5 spiny 6 thorny
This Used to Be My Playground (1992 song) artist: Madonna
this vale of __: 5 tears
This was their __ hour: 6 finest
__ this way...: 4 Come, Walk
This weighs __!: 4 a ton
This Will Be (1975 song) artist: Natalie Cole
This won't hurt __!: 4 a bit
__ this world: 5 out of
This Year's Kisses composer: 6 Berlin
thither: 4 yond 5 there 6 yonder
move hither and ~: 3 gad 4 roam, rove 5 range 6 ramble, wander 7 meander, traipse 8 ambulate, nomadize 9 bum around, gallivant, globe-trot
thither and __: 3 yon
thith, thpeak like: 4 lisp 8 sibilate
Thjórs: 5 river
locale: 7 Iceland
__ Tho: 5 Le Duc
thole: 3 pin 7 oarlock
insert: 3 oar
Tho, Le Duc: 8 diplomat, Nobelist 10 Vietnamese
Thom: 4 Gunn, Mc An
Thomas: 2 B.J. 3 Cal, Ira, Kid, Kyd 4 Arne, Cech, Cole, Dave, Debi, Gray, Hood, Ince, Irma, Mann, More, Nast, Reid, Seth 5 Betty, Carew, Chong, Danny, Dewey, Dolby, Dylan, Foley, Frank, Hardy, Helen, Henry, Isiah, Marlo, Moore, Nashe, Paine, Ralph, Rufus, saint, Timmy, Tryon, Wolfe, Wyatt, Young 6 Berger, Browne, Dekker, Eakins, Edison, Gibson, Hobbes, Huxley, Malory, Merton, Morgan, Starzl, Warton, Weller, Wolsey 7 à Becket, à Kempis, Aquinas, Beecham, Calabro, Campion, Carlyle, Costain, Cranmer, Donnall, Erastus, Heather, Heywood, Malthus, Noguchi, Parnell, Peacock, Pynchon, Richard 8 Bernhard, Bulfinch, Campbell, Clarence, Keneally, Kinsella, Lawrence, Macaulay, Mitchell, Overbury, Shadwell 9 De Quincey, Gallaudet, Jefferson, Middleton, Sackville, Schippers 10 Chatterton, Haliburton
doubting ~: 7 sceptic, skeptic
in Italian: 7 Tommaso
in Spanish: 5 Tomás
Thomas __ Benton: 4 Hart
__-Thomas: 5 Terry
Thomas, B.J.
song: Another Somebody Done Somebody Wrong Song (1975)
Hooked on a Feeling (1968)
I Just Can't Help Believing (1970)
I'm So Lonesome I Could Cry (1966)
Raindrops Keep Fallin' on My Head (1969)
Thomas Crown Affair, The (1968 film)
cast: Paul Burke, Faye Dunaway, Steve McQueen
director: Norman Jewison
Thomas Crown Affair, The (1999 film)
cast: Pierce Brosnan, Ben Gazzara, Denis Leary, Rene Russo
director: John McTiernan
Thomas, Debi: 6 skater
maneuver: 4 axel, lutz
milieu: 3 ice 4 rink
rival: 4 Witt
Thomas, Donnall: 8 Nobelist
Thomas, Dylan: 4 poet 5 Welsh
work: Do not go gentle into that good night...
Under Milk Wood
Thomas E. __: 5 Dewey
Thomas, Frank sport: 8 baseball
Thomas Hart __: 6 Benton
Thomas, Henry: 5 actor
film: All the Pretty Horses (2000)
Cloak & Dagger (1984)
E.T. The Extra Terrestrial (1982)
Fever (2001)
Suicide Kings (1998)
Thomasina: 3 cat
Thomas, Isiah: 8 hoopster
milieu: 5 court
org.: 3 NBA
sport: 10 basketball
Thomas, Kristin Scott: 7 actress
film: Angels & Insects (1995)
Four Weddings and a Funeral (1994)
Gosford Park (2001)
The Horse Whisperer (1998)
Life as a House (2001)
Thomas, Lowell milieu: 5 radio
Thomas, Marlo spouse: Phil Donahue
Thomas, Michael Tilson: 9 conductor
Thomas, Richard: 5 actor
film: Last Summer (1969)
Red Sky at Morning (1970)
Winning (1969)
TV: The Waltons
Thomas Stearns __: 5 Eliot
Thomasville: 4 city, town
locale: 4 N. Car.
Thompson: 3 Kay, Lea, Sue 4 Emma, Gina, Jack, J. Lee, Sada 5 David, Sadie 6 Ernest 7 Francis
Thompson, Emma: 7 actress
film: Carrington (1995)
Howards End (1992, AA)
In the Name of the Father (1993)
Judas Kiss (1999)
Junior (1994)
Much Ado About Nothing (1993)
Peter's Friends (1992)
Primary Colors (1998)
The Remains of the Day (1993)
Sense and Sensibility (1995)
spouse: Kenneth Branagh

Thompson, Francis: **4** poet
Thompson, Jack: **5** actor
film: 'Breaker' Morant (1979)
Burke and Wills (1986)
The Club (1980)
Midnight in the Garden of Good and Evil (1997)
Thompson, J. Lee: **8** director
film: The Ambassador (1984)
Brotherly Love (1969)
Cape Fear (1962)
Desert Attack (1960)
Flame Over India (1959)
The Guns of Navarone (1961)
I Aim at the Stars (1960)
Return From the Ashes (1965)
Tiger Bay (1959)
What a Way to Go! (1964)
Woman in a Dressing Gown (1957)
Thompson, Lea: **7** actress
film: All the Right Moves (1983)
Back to the Future (1985)
Back to the Future Part II (1989)
Back to the Future Part III (1990)
Some Kind of Wonderful (1987)
TV: Caroline in the City
Thompson seedless: **5** grape
Thompson submachine __: **3** gun
Thompson Twins: **4** trio
song: Doctor! Doctor! (1984)
Hold Me Now (1984)
King for a Day (1986)
Lay Your Hands on Me (1985)
Thomson: **5** Bobby **6** George, Joseph, Virgil **7** William
Thomson, George: **8** Nobelist **9** physicist
Thomson, Joseph: **8** Nobelist **9** physicist, scientist
Thomson, Virgil: **8** composer
work: Four Saints in Three Acts
The Mother of Us All
thong: **4** lace, shoe, whip **5** strap, strip **6** lacing **7** leather **8** flip-flop, footwear
oxhide ~: **4** riem
thon starter: **4** tele **5** radio, walka
't Hooft: **8** Gerardus
Thor: **3** god **5** Norse **9** Heyerdahl
brother of ~: **3** Tiu
father of ~: **4** Odin **5** Othin
son of ~: **3** Ull
wife of ~: **3** Sif
Thora: **5** Birch
thoracic __: **4** duct **6** artery
thorax: **5** chest, trunk
Thoreau, Henry David: **6** author, writer
work: Civil Disobedience
Walden
thorite: **3** ore **7** mineral
thorium: **5** metal **7** element
isotope: **6** ionium
thorn: **3** bur **4** barb, burr **5** briar, brier, point, prick, spike, spine, trial **6** sliver **7** barbule, bramble, bristle, prickle, spicule, spinule, sticker **8** apiculus, irritant **9** annoyance **10** impediment
be a ~: **3** irk **4** rile **5** annoy **6** pester
in the side: **4** bane, pain, pest **6** bother, gadfly, hassle **7** bugbear **8** irritant, nuisance **9** annoyance
like a ~: **5** spiny
mishap: **5** prick
starter: **3** box, haw **4** buck **5** black
Thorn Birds, The: **5** novel **10** miniseries
author: Colleen McCullough
network: **3** ABC
setting: **9** Australia
star: **4** Ward **8** Stanwyck **11** Chamberlain
Thornburgh predecessor: **5** Meese
Thorndike, Sybil: **4** Dame **7** actress
Thorne: **5** Smith
Thorne-Smith: **8** Courtney
Thornfield governess: **4** Eyre
thorn in one's __: **4** side
Thornton: **4** city, town **6** Wilder
locale: **8** Colorado
Thornton, Billy Bob: **5** actor
film: All the Pretty Horses (2000)
The Apostle (1997)
Armageddon (1998)
Bandits (2001)
Homegrown (1998)
The Man Who Wasn't There (2001)
Monster's Ball (2001)
One False Move (1992)
Pushing Tin (1999)
A Simple Plan (1998)
spouse: Angelina Jolie
thorny: **4** hard **5** risky, rough, sharp, spiky, spiny, tough **6** barbed, knotty, sticky, tricky, trying, uphill **7** arduous, awkward, brambly, bristly, complex, hard-won, irksome, onerous, prickly, tangled, thistly **8** baffling, grueling, ticklish, toilsome, worrying **9** dangerous, demanding, difficult, laborious, strenuous, vexatious **10** bothersome, formidable, irritating, nettlesome, oppressive, perplexing
plant: **4** rose **5** briar, brier **7** bramble
thorough: **4** full, pure, rank **5** clean, exact, fussy, sheer, sound, total, uncut, utter, whole **6** all-out, arrant, entire, minute **7** careful, finicky, in-depth, orderly, overall, perfect, plenary, prudent, radical **8** absolute, cautious, complete, detailed, exacting, finiking, finished, finnicky, from A to Z, itemized, outright, profound, rigorous, sweeping, whole-hog **9** assiduous, attentive, downright, efficient, elaborate, expansive, extensive, full-dress, intensive, judicious, observant, out-and-out, searching, undivided, unreduced **10** blow-by-blow, consummate, exhaustive, fastidious, meticulous, particular, scrupulous, soup-to-nuts, unabridged
thoroughbred: **4** pure **5** horse **6** equine, unmixt **7** unmixed **8** pedigree **9** blue-blood, pedigreed, racehorse **10** aristocrat
mother: **3** dam **4** mare **5** filly **6** equine
no ~: **3** nag
thoroughfare: **2** av., rd., st. **3** ave., way **4** blvd., drag, lane, pike, road **5** paseo, route **6** artery, avenue, street **7** freeway, highway, parkway, passage, roadway **8** causeway, toll road, turnpike **9** boulevard, concourse **10** expressway, interstate
thoroughgoing: **4** full, pure, rank **5** exact, sheer, total, utter, whole **6** all-out, arrant, entire, minute, plenty **7** careful, in-depth, perfect, radical **8** absolute, complete, detailed, from A to Z, itemized, outright, profound, straight, sweeping, whole-hog **9** assiduous, downright, efficient, intensive, out-and-out
thoroughly: **4** hard, very, well **5** fully, plumb, quite, stark **6** au fond, highly, hugely, wholly **7** but good, flat out, in depth, notably, totally, utterly **8** entirely, from A to Z, in detail, laudably, terribly, very well, whole hog, worthily **9** carefully, downright, earnestly, every inch, extremely, inside out, intensely, like a book, perfectly, to the full, up-and-down **10** absolutely, altogether, completely, to the limit
prefix: **3** per-
Thoroughly Modern Millie (1967 film)
cast: Julie Andrews, Carol Channing, James Fox, Mary Tyler Moore
composer: **4** Cahn **9** Van Heusen
director: George Roy Hill
thoroughness: **5** rigor
thorp: **4** town **6** hamlet **7** village **9** community **10** settlement
Thorpe: **3** Jim **7** Richard
Thorpe, Jim: **10** decathlete
sport: **8** football
Thorpe, Richard: **8** director
film: Above Suspicion (1943)
Black Hand (1950)
Carbine Williams (1952)
Cry 'Havoc' (1943)
Double Wedding (1937)
Fun in Acapulco (1963)
The Great Caruso (1951)
Huckleberry Finn (1939)
Ivanhoe (1952)
Jailhouse Rock (1957)
Night Must Fall (1937)
On an Island With You (1948)
Tarzan Escapes (1936)
Tarzan Finds a Son! (1939)
The Thin Man Goes Home (1944)
This Time for Keeps (1947)
Three Little Words (1950)
Tip on a Dead Jockey (1957)
The Truth About Spring (1965)
Two Girls and a Sailor (1944)
Thorson: **5** Linda
those: **4** them, they **7** pronoun
not ~: **5** these
not these or ~: **6** others
one of ~ things: **4** that
Those __ But Goodies: **6** Oldies
Those __ the Days: **4** Were
Those Calloways (1965 film)
cast: Brandon de Wilde, Brian Keith, Vera Miles
director: Norman Tokar
Those Lazy-Hazy-Crazy Days of Summer (1963 song) artist: Nat King Cole
Those Lips, Those Eyes (1980 film)
cast: Tom Hulce, Frank Langella, Glynnis O'Connor
director: Michael Pressman
Those Magnificent Men in Their Flying Machines (1965 film)
cast: James Fox, Sarah Miles, Stuart Whitman
director: Ken Annakin
Those Oldies But Goodies (1961 song) artist: Little Caesar and the Romans
Those the River Keeps author: David Rabe
Those Were the Days (1968 song)
artist: Mary Hopkin
__ Those Years Ago: **3** All
thou: **3** gee, you **4** one G **5** G-note, grand **7** pronoun
objectively: **4** thee
Thou __: **5** Swell
Thou __ not be false...: **5** canst
Thou Art the Man author: Edgar Allan Poe
though: **3** but, yet **5** altho, still, while **6** albeit, even if, much as, whilst **7** despite, granted, however, whereas **8** after all, allowing **10** all the same, for all that
though __ and thin: **5** thick
__, though I walk...: **3** Yea
thought: **3** aim **4** care, heed, hope, idea, plan, soul, view **5** drift, fancy, guess, image, logic, study, thing **6** albeit, belief, caring, design, musing, notion, regard, revery, theory **7** concept, concern, feeling, knowing, opinion, premise, purpose, reputed, reverie, surmise **8** judgment, kindness, scrutiny, sympathy, thinking **9** attention, brainwork, deduction, inference, intention, intuition, knowledge, reasoning, sentiment **10** aspiration, assumption, brainchild, brainstorm, cogitation, conception, conclusion, conjecture, conviction, discerning, estimation, hypothesis, impression, meditation, perception, philosophy, reflection, rumination, solicitude
be lost in ~: **4** muse **5** dream **8** daydream **9** fantasize
capricious ~: **4** whim
combining form: **4** ideo-, -noia
course of ~: **5** logic, tenor, train
have a ~: **6** ideate
lose one's train of ~: **6** wander
lost in ~: **4** rapt **5** taken **6** intent **7** bemused, gripped **8** absorbed, immersed, involved **9** engrossed, oblivious **10** fascinated
on second ~: **6** rather **7** instead
provoker: **4** Muse
second ~: **5** qualm **7** scruple **10** retrospect
sound of deep ~: **3** hmm
starter: **5** afore, after, merry
train of ~: **5** logic **9** reasoning
venture a ~: **3** say **5** guess **7** comment, suppose, surmise
well ~ out: **4** sane **7** logical **8** sensible
without ~: **4** idly
__ thought: **4** free **5** law of **6** second
thoughtful: **4** deep, keen, kind, rapt, sane, wise **5** aware, canny, civil, sober, sweet **6** astute, brainy, caring, decent, intent, kindly, loving, musing, polite, subtle **7** careful, gallant, heedful, helpful, logical, mindful, pensive, politic, prudent, serious, tactful, wistful **8** absorbed, discreet, generous, gracious, obliging, profound, rational, studious, thinking, well-bred **9** astucious, attentive, concerned, courteous, engrossed, judicious, observant, pondering, provident, reasoning, regardful, sensitive, unselfish **10** charitable, deliberate, diplomatic, expressive, forbearing, reasonable, reflective
one: **5** carer, muser
thoughtfulness: **4** care, tact **6** effort, regard **7** concern **8** interest, prudence **9** alertness, assiduity, attention, diligence **10** discretion, precaution
though thick and __: **4** thin
thoughtless: **4** rash, rude **5** blind, brash, crass, hasty, inane, nervy, short, silly **6** madcap, remiss, shabby, stupid, unkind, unwary, unwise **7** boorish, flighty, foolish, selfish, vacuous, witless **8** careless, headlong, heedless, impolite, listless, mindless, reckless, slapdash, tactless, uncaring **9** hot-headed, imprudent, negligent, senseless, unadvised, unguarded, unheeding, unmindful **10** ungracious, unthinking
thoughtlessly: **7** lightly **8** absently, pell-mell
thoughtlessness: **5** folly **7** abandon, neglect **8** omission **9** disregard, frivolity, looseness, oversight, stupidity **10** negligence, wantonness
__-thought-of: **4** well
__ Thought of You, The: **4** Very
thought-out: **10** considered, deliberate, reasonable, well-chosen
__-thought-out: **4** well
thought-provoking: **4** deep **5** heavy, meaty, pithy **7** complex, intense, serious, weighty **8** profound **10** mysterious
thoughts
have second ~: **4** balk **5** baulk **6** falter, regret **8** question
offer for one's ~: **5** penny
offer one's ~: **3** say **5** opine **7** com-

ment, observe, suppose, surmise
one with second ~: 4 ruer
__ Thou Now O Soul: 6 Darest
thousand
and one: 4 a lot, gobs, lots, many, tons 5 heaps, piles, scads 6 myriad, oodles, scores, untold 7 copious, profuse, teeming, umpteen 8 manifold, numerous 9 abundance, countless, multitude
combining form: 4 kilo- 5 chilo-, milli-
dollar bill: 3 gee 5 G-note 6 big one
grams: 4 kilo
G's: 3 mil 7 million
Thousand __: 4 Oaks 7 Islands
Thousand __, A: 5 Acres, Stars 6 Clowns
thousand and one __, A: 4 uses
Thousand and One Nights, A (1945 film)
cast: Evelyn Keyes, Phil Silvers, Cornel Wilde
Thousand-and-Second Tale of Scheherazade, The author: Edgar Allan Poe
Thousand Clowns, A (1965 film)
cast: Martin Balsam, Barbara Harris, Jason Robards
director: Fred Coe
Thousand Days queen: 4 Anne
Thousand Island: 7 Russian 8 dressing
alternative: 5 ranch 6 French 7 Italian 10 bleu cheese
Thousand Oaks: 4 city, town
locale: 10 California
thousand's __: 5 place
thousandth combining form: 5 milli-
thousandth's __: 5 place
...... thousand times...: 3 no a
__ thou slain the Jabberwock?: 4 Hast
Thou Swell composer: 4 Hart 7 Rodgers
...thou vain world, __: 5 adieu
thpeak like thith: 4 lisp 8 sibilate
Thracian: 8 language
thrall: 4 esne, peon, serf 5 slave 7 chattel, slavery 9 servitude
thralldom: 7 bondage, slavery 9 captivity, servitude, vassalage 10 internment
thrash: 3 hit, tan, tar, zap 4 beat, belt, bury, cane, drub, flap, flog, jerk, lash, lick, mall, maul, pelt, rout, rush, toss, trim, whip 5 baste, birch, crush, flail, knock, paste, pitch, pound, punch, smite, spank, thump, trash, whack, worst 6 batter, beat up, buffet, defeat, hammer, larrup, paddle, pommel, pummel, punish, squirm, thrash, thresh, wallop, writhe 7 chasten, clobber, lambast, overrun, scourge, trounce, wriggle 8 chastise, lambaste, work over 9 castigate, overwhelm, slaughter
out: 4 talk 5 argue 6 debate 7 discuss
thrash __: 3 out
thrasher: 4 bird 10 sicklebill
Thrasher rival: 4 Blue, King, Star, Wild 5 Bruin, Devil, Flame, Flyer, Oiler, Sabre, Shark 6 Canuck, Coyote, Ranger 7 Capital, Panther, Penguin, Red Wing, Senator 8 Canadien, Islander, Predator 9 Avalanche, Blackhawk, Hurricane, Lightning, Maple Leaf 10 Blue Jacket, Mighty Duck
Thrashers
home: 7 Atlanta, Georgia
org.: 3 NHL
sport: 6 hockey
thrashing: 4 rout 6 defeat, hiding 7 licking 8 flogging
thread: 4 lace, line, plot, poil, vein, wisp, yarn 5 fiber, filum, twine 6 enlace, inlace, strand 8 filament
ball: 4 clew
bits: 4 fuzz, lint
combining form: 3 mit-, nem- 4 fili-, mito-, nema-, nemo- 5 nemat- 6 nemato-
cotton ~: 5 lisle
embroidery ~: 5 floss
ender: 3 fin 4 bare, worm
hanging by a ~: 5 risky 6 unsafe 9 uncertain
holder: 5 spool
knot: 4 burl, node
weight unit: 6 denier
thread __: 4 mark, rope, silk 6 blight
__ thread: 5 lisle, screw 6 sacred
threadbare: 3 old 4 dull, poor, worn 5 banal, dingy, musty, ratty, seedy, stale, stock, tacky, tired, trite 6 beat-up, frayed, ragged, shabby, used-up 7 clichéd, in holes, run-down, scruffy, worn-out 8 bathetic, decrepit, dog-eared, overused, shopworn, tattered, timeworn, well-used, well-worn 9 hackneyed, imitative, moth-eaten, ungroomed 10 bedraggled
become ~: 4 fray, tear, wear 5 shred
threadfin: 4 fish
threadlike: 4 ropy, slim, thin 5 filar, ropey 6 narrow 7 slender
threads: 4 fila, garb, gear, suit, togs 5 array, dress 6 attire, livery 7 apparel, clothes, raiment 8 garments, wardrobe 10 Sunday best
fabric ~: 4 weft, woof
provide with ~: 5 cover 6 attire, clothe, outfit, tog out 7 costume, furnish 8 accouter
threadwork: 4 lace
threat: 4 omen, risk 5 bluff, peril 6 danger, hazard, menace 7 portent, presage, warning 9 blackmail, challenge 10 foreboding
ender: 4 else 6 or else
urban ~: 3 mob 4 pack, ring
__ threat: 5 empty 6 triple
threaten: 3 cow 4 loom, warn 5 augur, bully, scare, scowl, snarl, spook 6 coerce, impend, loom up, menace 7 advance, imperil, portend, presage 8 admonish, approach, browbeat, endanger, forebode, forewarn, frighten, hang over, overhang, pressure 9 blackmail, terrorize, undermine 10 foreshadow, intimidate, jeopardize, push around
threatening: 4 dire, grim, ugly 5 black, close, loury, scary 6 at hand, lowery, stormy, unsafe 7 baleful, baneful, fateful, looming, ominous, serious, warning 8 alarming, bullying, imminent, lowering, menacing, minatory, overcast, perilous, scowling, sinister 9 dangerous, ill-boding, impending 10 pugnacious
three: 4 trey, trio 5 triad 6 number, triple
ender: 4 some 5 pence, penny, score
in French: 5 trois
in German: 4 drei
in Italian: 3 tre
in Japanese: 3 san
in Portuguese: 4 tres
in Spanish: 4 tres
it had ~ parts: 4 Gaul
or four: 3 few 4 a few 7 several
prefix: 3 ter-, tri-
proverbially: 5 crowd
R's org.: 3 AFT, NEA, UFT
squared: 4 nine
to Mohs: 7 calcite
three __ kind: 3 of a
three __ match: 3 on a
three-__: 3 ply 4 a-cat, peat, spot 5 birds, phase 6 bagger, decker, gaited, handed, master, square, suiter, valued 7 pointer, quarter, wheeler
three-__ bike: 5 speed
three-__ bulb: 3 way
three-__ circus: 4 ring
three-__ fire: 5 alarm
three-__ general: 4 star
three-__ hit: 4 base
three-__ landing: 5 point
three-__ length: 7 quarter
three-__ limit: 4 mile
three-__ monte: 4 card
three-__ race: 6 legged
three-__ sloth: 4 toed
three-__ suit: 5 piece
three-__ time: 7 quarter
Three __: 4 Ages 5 Fires, Hours, Kings, Lives 7 Degrees, Seasons, Secrets, Sisters
Three __!: 6 Amigos
Three __ a Horse: 5 Men on
Three __ a Lady: 5 Times
Three __ Fishies: 6 Little
Three __ Girls: 5 Smart
Three __ in the Fountain: 5 Coins
Three __ Island: 4 Mile
Three __ Night: 3 Dog
Three __ of Eve, The: 5 Faces
Three __ of the Condor: 4 Days
Three __ on a Horse: 3 Men
Three __ Words: 6 Little
Three Amigos! (1986 film)
cast: Chevy Chase, Steve Martin, Martin Short
director: John Landis
three-base __: 3 hit
Three Bears
one of the ~: 4 Baby, Mama, Papa
Three Blind __: 4 Mice
Three Came Home (1950 film)
cast: Claudette Colbert, Florence Desmond, Patric Knowles
director: Jean Negulesco
three-card monte: 3 con 4 game, scam 8 card game
Three Coins in the Fountain (1954 film)
cast: Dorothy McGuire, Jean Peters, Clifton Webb
composer: 4 Cahn 5 Styne
director: Jean Negulesco
locale: 4 Rome 5 Italy, Trevi
title song: Frank Sinatra
Three Comrades (1938 film)
cast: Margaret Sullavan, Robert Taylor, Franchot Tone, Robert Young
director: Frank Borzage
Three-Cornered Hat, The: 6 ballet
composer: 5 Falla
Three-Cornered Moon (1933 film)
cast: Richard Arlen, Mary Boland, Claudette Colbert
Three Days of the Condor (1975 film)
cast: Faye Dunaway, Robert Redford, Cliff Robertson, Max von Sydow
director: Sydney Pollack
Three Degrees
song: TSOP (1974)
When Will I See You Again (1974)
three-dimensional: 5 cubic, solid
figure: 3 sph. 4 cube 5 globe, prism 6 sphere 7 pyramid
three-dog
night: 3 raw 6 chilly, frigid 8 freezing
Three Dog Night
members: Hutton, Wells, Negron
song: Black & White (1972)
Celebrate (1970)
Easy to Be Hard (1969)
Eli's Coming (1969)
Joy to the World (1971)
Liar (1971)
Mama Told Me (1970)
Never Been to Spain (1972)
An Old Fashioned Love Song (1971)
One (1969)
Pieces of April (1972)
Shambala (1973)
The Show Must Go On (1974)
Try a Little Tenderness (1969)
three-dollar bill
like a ~: 4 fake 5 phony
Three Faces of Eve, The (1957 film)
cast: Lee J. Cobb, David Wayne, Joanne Woodward
director: Nunnally Johnson
threefold: 5 trine 6 triple
Three Godfathers (1936 film)
cast: Walter Brennan, Chester Morris, Lewis Stone
Three Hours to Kill (1954 film)
cast: Dana Andrews, Dianne Foster, Donna Reed
director: Alfred Werker
Three Kings (1999 film)
cast: George Clooney, Ice Cube, Spike Jonze, Mark Wahlberg
director: David O. Russell
three-legged __: 4 race
Three Little Girls in Blue (1946 film)
cast: Vivian Blaine, June Haver, George Montgomery
Three Little Words: 4 song, tune
composer: 4 Ruby 6 Kalmar
one of the: 3 you 4 love
Three Little Words (1950 film): 7 musical
cast: Fred Astaire, Red Skelton, Vera-Ellen
director: Richard Thorpe
__ Three Lives: 4 I Led
Three Lives author: Gertrude Stein
Three Lives of Thomasina, The (1964 film)
cast: Karen Dotrice, Susan Hampshire, Patrick McGoohan
director: Don Chaffey
three men __ tub: 3 in a
Three Men on a Horse (1936 film)
cast: Joan Blondell, Sam Levene, Frank McHugh
director: Mervyn LeRoy
three-mile __: 5 limit
Three Mile __: 6 Island
three-minute __: 3 egg
Three Musketeers, The
author: Alexandre Dumas (père)
character: 5 Athos 6 Aramis, Milady 7 Porthos 9 D'Artagnan
Three Musketeers, The (1939 film)
cast: Don Ameche, Lionel Atwill, Ritz Brothers
director: Allan Dwan
Three Musketeers, The (1974 film)
cast: Richard Chamberlain, Oliver Reed, Raquel Welch
director: Richard Lester
Three Musketeers, The (1993 film)
cast: Chris O'Donnell, Charlie Sheen, Kiefer Sutherland
director: Stephen Herek
three of __: 5 a kind, clubs 6 hearts, spades 8 diamonds
Three of a Kind author: James M. Cain
Three on a Match (1932 film)
cast: Joan Blondell, Bette Davis, Warren William
director: Mervyn LeRoy
three-peat coiner: Pat Riley
threepence: 4 coin 5 money
Threepenny Opera, The: 7 musical
author: Bertolt Brecht
composer: Kurt Weill
three-piece __: 4 suit
three-point __: 4 line, play 7 landing
three-quarter __: 4 time 5 armor

6 length, nelson 7 binding
three-ring ___: 6 binder, circus
Three's Company (ABC sitcom)
cast: Priscilla Barnes (Terri Alden) Joyce DeWitt (Janet Wood) Norman Fell (Stanley Roper) Richard Kline (Larry Dallas) Don Knotts (Ralph Furley) Audra Lindley (Helen Roper) John Ritter (Jack Tripper) Suzanne Somers (Chrissy Snow)
threescore: 5 sixty
three-seater: 4 sofa
Three Secrets (1950 film)
cast: Patricia Neal, Eleanor Parker, Ruth Roman
director: Robert Wise
Three Sisters: 4 film, play
author: Anton Chekhov
cast: Alan Bates, Laurence Olivier, Joan Plowright
director: Laurence Olivier
role: 4 Ivan, Olga 5 Irina, Masha 6 Andrey, Fyodor 7 Natasha
Three Smart Girls (1936 film)
cast: Binnie Barnes, Alice Brady, Deanna Durbin
director: Henry Koster
Three Smart Girls Grow Up (1939 film)
cast: Deanna Durbin, Nan Grey, Charles Winninger
director: Henry Koster
Three Soldiers author: John Dos Passos
threesome: 4 trin, trio 5 trine 6 triple
Threesome (1994 film)
cast: Stephen Baldwin, Lara Flynn Boyle, Josh Charles
director: Andrew Fleming
three-speed ___: 4 bike
three-spot: 4 trey
three-star ___: 7 general
three-star off.: 3 gen. 5 lt. gen.
Three Stars Will Shine Tonight (1962 song) artist: Richard Chamberlain
three-step: 6 cha-cha
Three Stooges
laugh: 4 nyuk
one of the ~: 3 Joe, Moe 4 Fine 5 Curly, Larry, Shemp 6 Besser, De Rita, Howard 8 Curly Joe
Three Strangers (1946 film)
cast: Geraldine Fitzgerald, Sydney Greenstreet, Peter Lorre
director: Jean Negulesco
three-striper: 3 NCO, sgt. 8 sergeant
Three Sundays in a Week author: Edgar Allan Poe
Three Tall Women author: Edward Albee
Three Teeny Preludes composer: PDQ Bach
___ Three Times: 5 Knock
Three Times a Lady (1978 song)
artist: Commodores
three-toed ___: 5 sloth
three-way ___: 4 bulb
three-way circuit: 3 wye
Three Weeks author: 4 Glyn
three-wheeled taxi: 5 cyclo
three-wheeler: 5 trike 8 tricycle
three-year-old: 3 kid, tot 4 tike, tyke
threnody: 5 dirge, elegy 6 lament 7 keening
thresher ___: 5 shark
threshing: 7 farming, reaping 10 harvesting
aid: 5 flail 6 scythe
refuse: 4 husk 5 chaff, waste 7 remains
threshold: 3 eve 4 dawn, door, edge, gate, line, sill 5 brink, entry, point, verge 6 border, origin, outset, portal 7 doorway, ingress, opening 8 doorstep, entrance 9 beginning, inception
cross the ~: 4 go in 5 enter, pop in 6 blow in, come in, step in 8 breeze in
opposite: 6 lintel
psychological ~: 5 limen
thrice
combining form: 3 ter-
in prescriptions: 3 ter
thrift: 5 plant 6 flower, saving 7 economy 8 prudence 9 austerity, frugality, parsimony 10 stinginess
starter: 5 spend
thriftless: 6 lavish 8 wasteful
thrift shop: 5 store
transaction: 6 resale
thrifty: 4 mean 5 canny, chary, cheap, close, tight 6 frugal, on sale, stingy 7 careful, prudent, sparing 8 ungiving 9 provident 10 economical, unwasteful
be ~: 4 save
one: 5 saver
Thrifty: 9 car rental 10 auto rental
alternative: 4 Avis 5 Alamo, Hertz 6 Budget, Dollar 8 National 10 Enterprise
thrill: 3 fun, wow 4 bang, glow, kick, move, rush, send, stir 5 blast, cheer, elate, flash, juice, key up, kicks, rouse, score, throb 6 arouse, charge, excite, fire up, please, quiver, tickle, tingle, turn on 7 animate, delight, emotion, enchant, enthuse, flutter, gladden, gratify, happify, hearten, impress, inspire, quicken, tremble, vibrate 8 blow away, entrance, pleasure 9 adventure, electrify, enjoyment, fascinate, fireworks, galvanize, go over big, inebriate, sensation, stimulate, titillate, transport 10 exhilarate, intoxicate
seeker: 8 hedonist, sybarite 9 bon vivant, libertine 10 sensualist
to: 4 love 5 adore, eat up, enjoy, go for 6 dote on 7 revel in 8 flip over 9 delight in, get high on 10 appreciate, experience
Thrilla in Manila: 4 bout 5 fight, match
boxer: 3 Ali 7 Frazier
thrilled: 4 agog, glad 5 happy, merry 6 blithe, cheery, jovial, joyful, joyous, upbeat 7 gleeful 8 blissful, cheerful, ecstatic, euphoric, exultant, jubilant, mirthful, ravished 9 delirious, overjoyed, rapturous, rejoicing, rhapsodic 10 flying high
thriller: 4 book 5 novel, story 7 mystery 9 narrative
___-thriller: 6 techno
Thriller (1984 song) artist: Michael Jackson
Thriller sequel: 3 Bad
thrilling: 3 fab 4 boss, wild 5 heady, kicky 7 rousing 8 dramatic, electric, exciting, fabulous, gripping, riveting, stirring, wondrous 9 emotional, exquisite, trembling 10 delightful, enchanting, impressive, intoxicant, miraculous, passionate, rip-roaring
not ~: 4 blah, drab, dull, flat 5 banal, bland, ho-hum, vapid 6 boring 7 humdrum 8 lifeless 9 wearisome 10 dullsville, lackluster, monotonous, pedestrian, spiritless
Thrill of It All, The (1963 film)
cast: Doris Day, Arlene Francis, James Garner
director: Norman Jewison
thrive: 2 go 3 wax, win 4 boom, grow, live 5 bloom, get on 6 abound, arrive, batten, do well, hack it, make it, pan out, profit 7 advance, blossom, burgeon, develop, luck out, make out, prevail, prosper, shoot up, succeed, triumph, work out 8 bourgeon, flourish, get ahead, go places, grow rich, increase, make good, mushroom, progress 9 bear fruit, luxuriate 10 strengthen
thriving: 4 rich, well 5 palmy 6 robust 7 booming, cooking, growing, healthy, roaring, rolling, wealthy, well-off 8 affluent, blooming, home free, prolific, well-to-do 9 advancing, doing well, luxuriant 10 burgeoning, developing, prospering, prosperity, prosperous, successful, well-heeled
throat: 3 maw 4 neck 6 gullet
armor: 6 gorget
bird's ~: 6 gorget
bug: 5 staph, strep
clearer: 4 ahem
combining form: 3 der- 4 dero- 6 bronch- 7 broncho-, pharyng- 8 pharyngo-
feature: 6 dewlap
frog in one's ~: 4 rasp 7 scratch 10 hoarseness
infection: 5 strep
jump down one's ~: 5 blame, chide, scold 6 berate, lean on, rebuke 7 bawl out, chew out, go after, lay into, lecture, reprove, rip into, tell off, upbraid 8 admonish, lambaste 9 dress down, reprimand, tear apart 10 take to task
of the ~: 5 gular
problem: 4 frog, lump
projection: 5 uvula
rinse one's ~: 6 gargle
soother: 6 hot tea
starter: 3 cut
upper ~: 4 gula
___ throat: 4 sore 5 strep
throaty: 5 gruff, husky, raspy, velar 6 froggy, hoarse 8 gravelly, guttural 10 laryngitic
throb: 4 ache, beat, hurt, pain, pang, thud, tick 5 pound, pulse, smart, thump 6 quiver, rhythm, thrill, tingle, twinge 7 flutter, pitapat, pulsate, tremble, vibrate 8 resonate 9 heartbeat, palpitate, pulsation, vibration
starter: 5 heart
throbbing: 4 ache, achy, beat 7 painful, vibrant 8 resonant 9 vibration
throe: 3 fit 4 ache, pain, pang 5 spasm, spell 6 misery, twinge 7 seizure 8 paroxysm, upheaval
thrombus: 4 clot
throne: 4 seat 5 chair
cover: 6 canopy, dosser
locale: 4 dais 6 castle, palace
name meaning ~: 5 Cyrus
put on the ~: 6 enseat
seize the ~: 5 usurp
sit on the ~: 4 rule 5 reign 6 govern
sitter: 4 czar, king 5 queen, ruler 7 monarch, pharaoh
take the ~: 6 accede, ascend
throne ___: 4 room
Throne: 7 Malachi
Throneberry: 4 Marv
Throne of Blood (1957 film)
cast: Toshiro Mifune, Takashi Shimura, Isuzu Yamada
director: Akira Kurosawa
Throne of Saturn, The author: Allen Drury
throng: 3 jam, mob 4 army, bevy, herd, host, many, mass, pack, pour 5 bunch, crowd, crush, drove, flock, group, horde, press, swarm, troop 6 gather, huddle, legion, muster, rabble 7 company, numbers, sellout, turnout 8 assembly 9 concourse, gathering, multitude 10 assemblage, concursion
throngs: 4 lots 6 flocks, hoards, scores 7 legions
___ Thro' the Rye: 5 Comin'
throttle: 3 gag 5 seize, wring 6 muzzle, stifle 7 inhibit, occlude, silence, squeeze 8 obstruct, suppress
open up the ~: 4 race 5 speed
throttle ___: 5 lever, valve
through: 3 for, per, via 4 done, fini, free, over, past, with 5 clear, ended, finis, using 6 during, within 7 between, by way of, nonstop, wound up 8 complete, finished, in and out, washed-up 9 as a result, because of, by means of, concluded, wrapped up 10 by virtue of, terminated
ender: 3 out, put, way
prefix: 3 dia-, per- 5 trans-
starter: 4 feed 5 break, where 6 follow
through ___: 4 bass 5 stone 6 street
through ___-colored glasses: 4 rose
___ through: 3 get, put, run, see 4 come, fall, look, walk, work 5 break, carry, think 6 follow, muddle, squeak 7 squeeze
___-through: 3 see 4 pass, read, rust, show 5 drive, floor
Through a Glass, Darkly (1962 film)
cast: Harriet Andersson, Gunnar Bjornstrand, Max von Sydow
director: Ingmar Bergman
___ through hoops: 4 jump
___ through one's fingers: 4 slip
___ through one's hat: 4 talk
___ through one's teeth: 3 lie
throughout: 6 during 7 all over, overall 8 every bit, to the end 9 up-and-down 10 everywhere
combining form: 4 -wide
through the ___: 4 mill
___ through the cracks: 4 fall
Through the Looking-Glass author: Lewis Carroll
___ Through the Night: 3 All
___ through the nose: 3 pay
throughway: 4 road 5 route
throw: 3 boa, fit, lob, peg, shy 4 buck, cast, dash, dump, flip, hurl, lick, pass, pelt, roll, shot, toss 5 addle, bandy, chuck, flick, fling, floor, heave, impel, let go, mix up, pitch, scarf, shawl, shoot, sling, spray, stone, strew, upset 6 afghan, baffle, launch, let fly, pepper, propel, puzzle, rattle, shower, tackle, unseat 7 blanket, bombard, confuse, deliver, disturb, fluster, muffler, mystify, nonplus, project, scatter, unhorse, unnerve 8 astonish, befuddle, bewilder, catapult, confound, coverlet, coverlid, mantilla, splatter, sprinkle, unsettle 9 dumbfound, give a turn 10 disconcert
a ~: 4 each
a curve to: 4 stun 6 delude 7 stupefy 8 misquote, surprise
a fit: 4 rage, rant, rave, yell 5 go ape 10 hit the roof
a monkey wrench into: 5 block 6 hamper, hinder 7 disrupt 8 obstruct 9 frustrate, undermine
around: 5 spray, strew 7 scatter
a stone's ~ away: 4 near 5 close 6 nearby
away: 3 rid 4 blow, drop, dump, junk, lose, shed 5 chuck, ditch, scrap, shuck, spend, waste 6 reject 7 abandon, cast off, discard, fritter, let go of 8 get rid of, jettison, squander, throw out 9 dispose of, dissipate 10 run through

back: **6** revert **7** reflect, regress
cold water on: **5** deter **6** sadden **8** dispirit
dice ~: **3** six, ten, two **4** five, four, nine **5** eight, seven, three **6** eleven, twelve **7** boxcars **9** snake eyes
down the gauntlet: **4** defy **9** challenge **10** make a stand
ender: **4** away, back
for a loop: **4** faze, stun **5** addle, upset **6** baffle **7** fluster, stagger **9** take aback
in: **3** add **6** donate **9** interject, introduce
in one's hand: **4** fold, quit **5** yield **6** submit **7** concede **9** surrender
in the towel: **4** give, quit **5** yield **6** resign **7** concede, succumb **9** surrender
into a panic: **5** scare, spook **8** frighten
in together: **3** mix, wed **4** band, join, link, pool, yoke **5** admix, blend, group, marry, merge, unite **6** league, mingle, team up **7** bunch up, combine **9** affiliate, aggregate, commingle, integrate, syndicate **10** amalgamate
in with: **4** join, link **5** unite **7** support
in (with): **9** affiliate
light on: **4** show **5** solve **6** answer, unfold **7** clarify, explain, expound **8** illumine, simplify, spell out **9** bring home, elaborate, elucidate, interpret, make plain, translate **10** illuminate, illustrate
like a bad ~: **4** wide, wild **6** errant
mud at: **4** slam, slur **5** knock, libel, smear, sully, taint, wrong **6** defame, malign, vilify **7** asperse, blacken, run down, slander, tarnish, traduce **8** backbite, badmouth, besmirch, dishonor **9** denigrate, discredit, disparage **10** calumniate, stigmatize, vituperate
off: **4** beam, emit, lose, shed, spew, spue, trip **5** eject, elude, evade, expel, exude, issue, shake, spill, trick **6** delude, escape, outrun **7** cast out, confuse, deceive, diffuse, emanate, excrete, mislead, radiate, unnerve **8** confound, unburden, unsettle **9** disinform, exfoliate, misdirect, send forth, take aback
off guard: **4** stun **5** shake **7** astound, nonplus, stagger **8** astonish, bowl over, surprise **9** discomfit, dumbfound **10** disconcert
oneself into: **6** attack, have at, take up **7** address, focus on **8** engage in **9** have a go at, undertake **10** plug away at, take care of
one's lot in with: **3** wed **4** join **5** marry **6** go with, hook up
one's weight around: **5** bully **6** hector **7** oppress **8** browbeat, domineer **9** tyrannize **10** intimidate
on the pile: **3** add
open: **6** turn on **8** activate
out: **2** ax **3** axe, ban, say **4** boot, cast, drop, dump, emit, junk, nail, oust, shed, spew, spue, tell, veto, void **5** chuck, ditch, eject, evict, expel, forgo, scrap, state, utter, waste **6** depose, forego, give up, reject, remove **7** abandon, bring up, chime in, comment, exclude, forsake, lighten, mention, radiate, suggest **8** forswear, get rid of, jettison, part with, relegate, turn down **9** cast aside, dispose of, eliminate, foreswear, ostracize **10** relinquish
out of whack: **4** skew **7** distort
over: **4** drop, dump, jilt, quit **5** leave, sling, upset **6** desert **7** abandon, forsake **9** eighty-six, walk out on **10** finish with, go away from
overboard: **4** dump, hurl, junk **5** chuck, ditch, eject, heave, scrap **6** unload **7** abandon, cast off, deep-six, discard, lighten **8** jettison
stones at: **3** pan, rap **4** pelt, slam **5** blame, decry, knock, sneer **6** malign, vilify **7** censure, condemn, put down, run down, slander, traduce **8** backbite, badmouth, belittle, denounce, derogate **9** criticize, denigrate, disparage, reprehend **10** calumniate
the book at: **6** punish **7** condemn, convict **8** sentence
together: **4** make **5** build, hatch **6** devise
underhand ~: **4** toss **5** pitch
water on: **6** drench, splash **8** saturate **10** extinguish
throw ___: **3** off, out, rug **4** a fit, away, back, over **6** pillow, weight
throw ___ loop: **4** for a
throw ___ on: **5** light
throw ___ the gauntlet: **4** down
___ throw: **4** free **6** hammer, stone's **7** javelin
throw a ___: **3** fit
throwaway: **6** dodger **7** handout, offhand **8** handbill, pamphlet **10** disposable
throwaways: **5** lagan, ligan **6** jetsam, jetsom
throwback: **6** legacy **7** atavism **8** archaism **10** archaicism
of a ~: **6** atavic
throw down the ___: **8** gauntlet
thrower
tantrum ~: **3** imp **5** child **9** youngster
___ thrower: **4** snow
throw for ___: **5** a loop, a loss
Throwing It All Away (1986 song)
artist: Genesis
throw in the ___: **5** towel
___-throw line: **4** free
Throw Momma From the Train (1987 film)
cast: Billy Crystal, Danny DeVito, Anne Ramsey
director: Danny DeVito
role: **4** Owen
throw one's ___ around: **6** weight
throw one's ___ in the ring: **3** hat
throw the ___ at: **4** book
throw up one's ___: **5** hands
thru: **3** o'er, via
ender: **3** way
___-thru: **3** see **5** drive
thrum: **3** tap **5** drone, pluck, pulse, strum **7** pulsate
thrush: **4** bird, chat **5** mavis, shama, veery **7** redwing **8** redstart, wheatear, whinchat **9** blackbird, fieldfare, stonechat
Hawaiian ~: **4** omao
home: **4** nest
relative: **5** ousel, ouzel, robin **6** dipper
___ thrush: **4** rock, song, wood **5** brown, water **6** hermit, missel, mistle, varied **7** Wilson's
thrust: **3** jab, jam, ram **4** butt, core, crux, gist, jerk, meat, pith, poke, prod, push, sink, stab, tilt **5** blitz, boost, drive, elbow, embed, force, forge, heave, imbed, impel, lunge, nudge, point, press, punch, sense, shove, slide, stick **6** effect, empale, impale, import, jostle, justle, pierce, plunge, propel, upshot **7** impetus, meaning, purport, squeeze **8** momentum, pressure, transfix **9** impulsion, interject, onslaught, penetrate, substance **10** incitement, propulsion
forward: **5** sally
in: **5** embed, imbed
out: **6** exsert
thwart a ~: **5** parry
upon: **3** tax **4** heap, pour **5** exact, foist, force, order **6** bestow, compel, decree, deluge, demand, enjoin, impose, lavish, shower **7** dictate, inflict **9** institute, stipulate
thrusting weapon: **4** épée **5** estoc, spear
thruway: **4** road **5** route **8** turnpike
entrance: **4** ramp
warning: **3** SLO
Thu.: **3** day
Thuban: **4** star
thud: **3** bam, jar **4** bang, fall **5** clonk, clump, clunk, knock, noise, pound, pulse, smack, sound, throb, thump, thunk, whomp
thug: **4** goon, hood **5** rowdy, tough **6** bandit, gunsel, menace, mugger, outlaw, robber **7** brigand, gorilla, hoodlum, ruffian, torpedo **8** criminal, gangster, hard case, hired gun, hooligan, plugugly, tough guy **9** desperado, racketeer, roughneck, terrorist **10** highwayman, triggerman
group: **3** mob **4** gang **5** cabal **9** syndicate **10** Cosa Nostra, underworld
knife: **4** shiv
thuja: **4** tree **9** evergreen **10** arborvitae
thulium: **5** metal **7** element **9** rare earth
thumb: **4** leaf **5** digit **6** finger, pollex
a ride: **5** hitch **9** hitchhike
bird's ~: **5** alula
ender: **3** nut **4** hole, nail, tack **5** print, screw
fleshy part of a ~: **4** soft
green ~: **3** art **4** gift **5** flair, knack, touch **6** genius, talent **7** faculty, know-how **8** aptitude, facility, instinct **9** expertise
one's nose at: **4** defy, mock **5** flout, rebel, scoff, spurn **6** deride
rule of ~: **4** norm **8** standard
site: **4** fist, hand, mitt
through: **4** scan **6** browse
(through): **3** run **4** leaf, page, read, scan, skim
under one's ~: **4** weak **7** subject **8** helpless **9** dependant, dependent, powerless **10** vulnerable
thumb ___: **5** a ride, glass, index, piano
___ thumb: **5** green
___ Thumb: **3** Tom
thumbnail: **3** bio **5** brief, short, small **7** concise, outline, profile
thumb one's ___ at: **4** nose
thumbprint feature: **5** whorl
thumbs
all ~: **5** gawky, inept, unapt **6** cloddy, clumsy, klutzy, oafish **7** awkward, gawkish, unadept **8** bumbling, bungling, fumbling, ungainly **9** graceless, lumbering, maladroit, stumbling, unskilled **10** unskillful
be all ~: **4** flub, slip **5** botch **6** bungle, fumble, goof up, mess up **7** blunder, louse up, screw up
birds' ~: **6** alulae
twiddle one's ~: **4** idle, laze **5** shirk **6** lounge **7** goof off, sit back **8** malinger, mark time, slack off **9** do nothing
___ thumbs: **3** all
thumbs down: **2** no **3** nah, naw, nay, nix, non **4** nein, nope, nyet, uh-uh, veto **5** I won't, ixnay, never, no how, no way **6** no deal, noways, nowise, rebuff **7** I refuse, refusal **8** forget it, I will not, negative, negatory **9** blacklist, by no means, fat chance, I think not, rejection **10** count me out, not a chance
give a ~ to: **3** nix, pan **4** deny, rate, veto **6** refuse, refute, reject
vocal ~: **3** boo **4** hiss, jeer **7** catcall **8** ridicule **9** sibilance **10** sibilation
voter: **4** anti
worth two ~: **3** bad **5** awful, gross, lousy **7** beastly, ghastly, ungodly **8** dreadful, horrible, horrific, terrible **9** appalling, atrocious, frightful, revolting **10** abominable, deplorable, disgusting, horrendous
thumbs up: **2** ay, da, ja, sí **3** aye, oui, yea, yep, yup **4** fine, okay, sure, yeah **5** good-o, natch, quite, right, roger, uh-huh **6** agreed, assent, gladly, good-oh, indeed, just so, rather, righto, surely, you bet, yowzah **7** exactly, go ahead, indeedy, mais oui, quite so, ten-four **8** all right, as you say, of course, very well **9** be my guest, certainly, darn right, naturally, precisely, sure thing, you betcha, you said it **10** absolutely, by all means, definitely, positively, sure enough, that's right
critic: **5** Ebert **10** Roger Ebert
give a ~ to: **2** OK **4** okay, rate **6** accept, assent, permit **7** approve **9** recommend
Thummim's Biblical partner: **4** Urim
thump: **3** hit, jar, rap, tap, wap **4** bang, bash, beat, blow, cuff, drum, fall, plop, slam, slap, slug, thud, tick, whap, whop **5** clonk, clout, clump, clunk, knock, lobby, pound, pulse, punch, smack, sound, throb, thunk, whack **6** batter, beat up, buffet, impact, pommel, pummel, strike, thwack, wallop **7** pulsate **8** pounding **9** fisticuff, haul off on
for: **4** back **6** foster **7** endorse, espouse, further, indorse, promote, support **8** advocate, champion
thumping: **3** big **5** hefty, large
Thun: **4** lake, town **7** commune
locale: Switzerland
river: **3** Aar **4** Aare
thunder: **3** din **4** boom, clap, drum, echo, peal, rail, rave, roar, roll, yell **5** blast, crack, crash, growl, pound, shout, snarl, sound, storm **6** bellow, deafen, go boom, rumble **7** declaim, explode, resound **8** bloviate, detonate **9** cannonade, discharge, fulminate
ender: **4** bird, bolt, clap, head **5** cloud, stone, storm **6** shower, struck
god: **4** Thor
sound: **4** boom, clap, peal, roar **5** blast, crash **9** cannonade, explosion
unit: **4** bolt, peal
Thunder ___: **3** Bay **4** Road, Rock **6** Island
Thunder Alley star: Ed Asner
Thunderball: **4** film **5** novel
author: Ian Fleming
cast: Claudine Auger, Adolfo Celi, Sean Connery
director: Terence Young
role: **5** Fiona, Largo **6** Emilio
theme singer: Tom Jones
Thunder Bay: **4** city, port, town
locale: **3** Ont. **6** Canada **7** Ontario
school: **8** Lakehead
Thunder Bay (1953 film)
cast: Joanne Dru, Gilbert Roland, James Stewart
director: Anthony Mann
Thunderbird: **3** car **4** auto, Ford **10** automobile
thunderbolt: **4** jolt, roar **6** boomer

7 thunder 8 surprise
Thunderbolt and Lightfoot (1974 film)
cast: Jeff Bridges, Clint Eastwood, George Kennedy
director: Michael Cimino
thunderclap: 4 roar 6 boomer
Thunderer, The: 5 march
composer: 5 Sousa
thunderhead: 5 cloud 7 cumulus
Thunderhead's mother: 6 Flicka
Thunderheart (1992 film)
cast: Graham Greene, Val Kilmer, Sam Shepard
director: Michael Apted
thundering: 3 big 4 loud 5 aroar, forte, noisy 7 blaring, booming, jarring, pealing, rackety, raucous, reboant, roaring 8 crashing, piercing, plangent, resonant, rumbling, sonorous, strident, turned up 9 big-voiced, clamorous, deafening 10 boisterous, resounding, stentorian, strepitous, uproarious, vociferous
Thundering Herd, The author: Zane Grey
Thunder In Paradise star: 3 Alt
Thunder on the Hill (1951 film)
cast: Ann Blyth, Claudette Colbert, Robert Douglas
director: Douglas Sirk
thunderous: 8 resonant, sonorous, terrific 9 deafening 10 stentorian
Thunder Out of China author: Theodore H. White
Thunder Road (1958 film)
cast: Gene Barry, Robert Mitchum
director: Arthur Ripley
thundershower: 4 rain
thunderstone: 7 mineral
thunderstorm product: 4 rain 5 ozone
thunderstruck: 4 awed 5 agape, dazed, in awe 6 aghast, amazed 7 floored, shocked, stunned 9 astounded 10 astonished, bowled over, speechless, taken aback
reaction: 3 awe 5 shock 6 dazzle, terror, wonder 8 surprise 9 amazement, reverence
thunk: 4 thud 5 thump
Thurber, James: 6 author, writer
work: Alarms and Diversions
Fables for Our Time
The Male Animal
The Middle-Aged Man on the Flying Trapeze
The Seal in the Bedroom
The Secret Life of Walter Mitty
The Thirteen Clocks
Thurgood, Marshall: 5 judge 7 justice
thurible: 6 censer
use a ~: 5 cense
Thüringen: 5 state 6 German
city: 5 Gotha 6 Weimar
Thuringian __: 6 Forest
thurm: 3 cut 5 carve, shape 6 chisel, incise, sculpt 7 engrave
Thurman: 3 Uma 6 Munson
Thurman, Uma: 7 actress
film: The Avengers (1998)
Batman & Robin (1997)
Dangerous Liaisons (1988)
Final Analysis (1992)
Gattaca (1997)
The Golden Bowl (2001)
Henry & June (1990)
Les Misérables (1998)
Mad Dog and Glory (1993)
Pulp Fiction (1994)
Sweet and Lowdown (1999)
Tape (2001)
The Truth About Cats and Dogs (1996)
spouse: Ethan Hawke, Gary Oldman
Thurmond: 4 Nate 5 Strom
Thurmond, Nate
milieu: 5 court
org.: 3 NBA
sport: 10 basketball
Thurmond, Strom: 3 sen. 7 senator
Thurs.: 3 day
follower: 3 Fri.
preceder: 3 Wed.
__ Thursday: 4 Holy 5 Sweet 6 Maundy
Thursday eponym: 4 Thor
Thurston: 6 Harris, Howell
thus: 3 sic 4 ergo, then 5 hence 6 hereby, in kind, like so 9 as follows, therefore 10 for example, in such a way
far: 3 yet 5 as yet 8 until now
in Latin: 3 sic
thus __: 3 far
Thus __ Zarathustra: 5 Spake
Thus Spake Zarathustra author: Friedrich Nietzsche
thwack: 3 hit, jab, tan 4 bash, beat, belt, blow, cane, conk, slam, slap 5 crown, flail, knock, paste, pound, punch, smite, spank, thump, whack, whang, whomp 6 batter, buffet, pommel, pummel, strike, wallop 7 lambast, lay into 8 lace into, lambaste, uppercut
thwart: 3 nip 4 balk, beat, curb, dash, defy, foil, halt, mock, stop 5 avert, baulk, block, cheat, check, cramp, crimp, cross, elude, queer, stimy, stymy, upset 6 baffle, defeat, hamper, hinder, hogtie, hold up, impede, oppose, outwit, resist, scotch, stymie 7 buffalo, counter, nonplus, prevent, repulse, squelch, trammel, ward off 8 handcuff, obstruct, outflank, override, overrule, preclude, restrain, turn back 9 discomfit, forestall, frustrate, hamstring, undermine 10 circumvent, contravene, counteract, disappoint
THX 1138 (1978 film)
cast: Robert Duvall,, Donald Pleasance
director: George Lucas
thy: 4 your
Thy kingdom __...: 4 come
thyme: 4 herb
__ thyme: 4 wild 5 basil
thymus: 5 gland
Thy Neighbor's Wife author: 6 Talese
thyroid: 5 gland
Thyrsis author: Matthew Arnold
Thy word is __ unto...: 5 a lamp
ti: 4 note
follower: 2 do
preceder: 2 la 4 so la
Ti: 4 elem. 7 element 8 titanium
22 for ~: 4 at. no.
Tia: 5 Mowry 7 Carrere
Tia __: 5 Juana, Maria
Tia Maria: 5 drink 8 beverage
Tiananmen __: 6 Square
Tianjin: 4 city, town
locale: 5 China
Tian Shan: 5 range
locale: 4 Asia 5 China 10 Kyrgyzstan
Tiant, Luis: 6 hurler 7 pitcher
tiara: 5 crown 6 diadem 7 coronet, jewelry
inset: 3 gem 5 bijou, jewel, stone 8 gemstone
Tiatia: 7 volcano
locale: 4 Asia 6 Russia
Tibbets, Col. mom: 5 Enola
Tibbett, Lawrence: 6 singer 8 baritone, barytone
specialty: 5 opera
Tibbs: 6 Virgil
Tiber: 5 river
feeder: 4 Nera
locale: 4 Rome 5 Italy
Tiberius: 5 Roman 6 Caesar
mother of ~: 5 Livia
see also Latin
Tibet
beast: 5 panda
bovine: 3 yak
Buddhism: 6 Tantra 9 Vajrayana
capital: 4 Lasa 5 Lassa, Lhasa
creature: 4 yeti
deer: 4 shou
equine: 5 kiang
explorer: 5 Hedin 6 Norgay 9 David-Neel
gazelle: 3 goa
icon: 5 tanka
language: 4 Naga
locale: 4 Asia
monastery: 5 gompa
monk: 4 lama
mountain: 5 Kamet 6 Cho Oyu, Kangto, Lhotse, Makalu 7 Everest 8 Changtzu, Pauhunri 9 Himalayas 10 Chomo Lhari
mysticism: 8 dzogchen
neighbor: 5 India, Nepal
Nobelist in Peace: 9 Dalai Lama
people: 4 Nosu
river rising in ~: 5 Indus
sheep: 6 bharal 7 burrhel
Tibetan: 5 Asian 8 language
ocean, in ~: 5 Dalai
Tibetan __: 7 spaniel, terrier
tibia: 4 bone, shin 8 shinbone
connectors: 5 tarsi
locale: 3 leg
neighbor: 5 ankle, talus 6 fibula, tarsus
Tibullus, Albius: 4 poet 5 Roman
Tiburon: 3 car 4 auto 7 Hyundai 10 automobile
tic: 3 fit 4 jerk 5 spasm 6 oddity, quiver, twinge, twitch 9 mannerism
tic-__-toe: 3 tac
Tic __ Dough: 3 Tac
Tic-__: 3 Tac
tical: 5 money
tick: 3 bug, rap, run, tap 4 beat, blow, dash, line, mark, pest, wink 5 check, clack, click, cross, flash, flick, pulse, shake, throb, thump 6 acarid, insect, minute, moment, second, stroke 7 instant, operate, pulsate, tapping 8 clicking 9 checkmark, pulsation, twinkling 10 indication
away: 2 go 4 pass 6 elapse, roll on
ender: 4 bird, seed, tack
maker: 5 clock, watch 10 wristwatch
off: 3 ire, irk, vex 4 list, miff, rile, roil 5 anger, annoy, count, peeve, steam, upset 6 enrage, number, rebuke, reckon 8 distress 9 enumerate
(off): 3 tee
tick __: 3 off 4 bird 7 trefoil
tick-__-toe: 4 tack
__ tick: 3 dog 4 hard, plus, seed, soft, wood 5 minus 6 cattle 7 harvest
__-tick: 5 ricky
Tick __: 4 Tock
tickbird: 3 ani
animal followed by a ~: 5 rhino
ticked off: 3 mad 4 sore 5 angry, irate, upset 6 galled 9 resentful
ticker: 5 clock, heart, watch
ticker __: 4 tape
__ ticker: 5 stock
ticker-tape __: 6 parade
ticket: 3 key, tab, tag 4 card, chit, cite, list, mark, note, pass, slip, stub 5 badge, board, check, ducat, label, paper, price, token 6 coupon, docket, entrée, invite, marker, notice, permit, record 7 license, passage, receipt, sticker, voucher 8 citation, document, passport, password, solution 9 admission, raincheck 10 credential, open sesame
abbr.: 4 orch.
again: 5 retag
choose a ~: 4 vote
endorser: 5 voter
free ~: 4 comp, pass
leftover: 4 stub
office sign: 3 SRO
punishment: 4 fine
risk a ~: 5 speed
word on a ~: 3 row 4 seat 5 admit
word on a track ~: 3 win 4 show 5 place
writer: 5 citer 7 officer, trooper 9 meter maid, policeman
ticket __: 5 agent 6 agency, office 7 puncher, scalper
__ ticket: 3 job 4 lift, meal, pawn 5 split 6 return, season, single 7 mileage, walking
__-ticket: 3 big, low 4 hard, high
ticketholder, season: 6 abonne
__-ticket item: 3 big
tickets, overcharge for: 5 scalp
Ticket to Ride (1965 song) artist: Beatles
Ticket to the Moon artist: 3 ELO
Ticket to Tomahawk, A (1950 film)
cast: Anne Baxter, Rory Calhoun, Dan Dailey
director: Richard Sale
ticking: 5 alive 6 fabric, living
tickle: 3 pat, pet 4 itch, play 5 amuse, brush, charm, cheer, elate, goose, touch 6 caress, divert, excite, please, stroke, thrill, tingle, turn on 7 beguile, delight, enchant, gratify 8 convulse, interest 9 entertain, make laugh, stimulate, titillate, vellicate
response: 5 te-hee 6 giggle
tickle __: 4 pink
tickled: 4 glad 5 happy, merry 6 blithe, cheery, jovial, joyful, joyous, upbeat 7 content, gleeful, pleased 8 blissful, cheerful, ecstatic, euphoric, exultant, jubilant, mirthful 9 delighted, overjoyed, rejoicing 10 flying high
feeling: 4 glee
it may be ~: 3 rib 5 fancy
Tickle Me (1965 film)
cast: Julie Adams, Jocelyn Lane, Elvis Presley
director: Norman Taurog
Tickle Me __: 4 Elmo
tickler: 4 list, memo, note 7 jotting 8 reminder 10 memorandum
rib ~: 3 pun 4 jest, joke 5 antic, farce, laugh 6 banter 8 drollery
tickler __: 4 coil, file
tickle the __: 7 ivories
__-tickling: 3 rib
ticklish: 4 nice 5 dicey, goosy, itchy, risky, rocky, tight 6 chancy, fickle, goosey, thorny, touchy, tricky, trying, unsafe 7 awkward, prickly 8 critical, delicate, perilous, unstable, unsteady, variable, volatile 9 dangerous, difficult, mercurial, sensitive, uncertain 10 capricious, changeable, inconstant, precarious, touch-and-go
situation: 5 pinch 6 plight
tick-tack-toe: 4 game
Tick Tock author: Dean Koontz
ticky-__: 5 tacky
Tico: 10 Costa Rican
Ticonderoga: 4 Fort
Ticotin: 6 Rachel
tic-tac-__: 3 toe
Tic Tac alternative: 5 Certs 6 Binaca, Mentos 7 Altoids, Clorets, Dentyne
Tic Tac Dough: game show
host: Gene Barry, Wink Martindale
tic-tac-toe: 4 game
nonwinner: 3 OOX, OXO, OXX, XOO, XOX, XXO

result: 3 tie 4 draw 8 standoff 9 stalemate
side: 3 Xes
win: 3 OOO, XXX
Ticul: 4 city, town
locale: 6 Mexico 7 Yucatán
tidal
bore: 5 eager, eagre
motion: 3 ebb 4 flow 6 waning 7 outflow
wave: 4 bore 6 tumult 7 tempest, tsunami, turmoil 8 disaster, upheaval 9 cataclysm
tidal __: 3 air 4 bore, flat, pool, wave 5 basin, datum, light
tidbit: 4 bite 5 crumb, goody, snack, taste, treat 6 goodie, morsel, nibble 7 soupçon 8 delicacy, mouthful, spoonful 9 collation
juicy ~: 4 buzz, dirt, talk, word 5 rumor 6 report 7 hearsay, scandal
tiddlywinks: 4 game
tide: 3 ebb, rip, run 4 drag, eddy, flow, flux, neap, race, rush, time, wave 5 drift, flood, ocean, spate, trend 6 assist, billow, course, sluice, spring, stream, vortex 7 current, torrent 8 movement, tendency, undertow 9 direction, whirlpool 10 inundation
cause: 4 moon
double ~ phenomenon: 5 agger
ender: 3 rip, way 4 land, mark 5 water 6 waiter
lapped by the ~: 5 awash
low ~: 3 ebb
over: 3 aid 4 help 6 assist 7 satisfy 9 help along 10 see through
ride the ~: 4 surf 7 hang ten
starter: 3 rip 4 even, noon, Yule 5 flood 6 Easter, spring 7 Passion 9 Christmas
swim with the ~: 4 cope 5 adapt 6 adjust
tide __: 4 gate, lock, mill, over, pool 5 gauge, table
__ tide: 3 ebb, lee, low, red, rip 4 half, high, neap 5 flood 6 double, spring 7 weather
Tide: 9 detergent
alternative: 3 All, Biz, Era, Fab, Yes 4 Bold, Dash, Gain, Surf, Wisk 5 Cheer, Dreft, Purex 6 Calgon, Dynamo, Oxydol 7 Octagon 9 Ivory Snow
__ Tide: 3 Ebb 7 Crimson
Tide Is High, The (1980 song) artist: Blondie
Tidewater Tales, The author: John Barth
tidiness: 5 order
tidings: 4 dirt, info, news, word 6 advice, report 7 message 8 bulletin 9 greetings
tidy: 4 fair, good, neat, nice, prim, snug, trig, trim, vast 5 ample, clean, crisp, fix up, frame, groom, kempt, large, order, sleek 6 decent, goodly, neaten, police, spruce, tauten 7 chipper, cleanly, groomed, healthy, in order, largish, ordered, orderly, shape up, sizable 8 adequate, generous, handsome, methodic, passable, readable, sizeable, spruce up, straight, to rights, well-kept 9 good-sized, organized, shipshape, smarten up, tolerable 10 acceptable, fastidious, methodical, neat as a pin, pretty good, straighten, systematic
not ~: 5 messy 7 in a mess, jumbled 8 messed up, slovenly 9 cluttered, jumbled up 10 disheveled, disorderly, in disarray, out of order, topsy-turvy
up: 4 dust 5 clean, groom, sweep 6 neaten 7 arrange 8 organize
tidytips: 5 plant 6 flower
tie: 3 fix, gag, wed 4 band, bind, bond, clog, cord, curb, do up, draw, duty, gird, hold, join, knot, know, lace, lash, link, meet, moor, push, rope, stop, yoke 5 ascot, brace, cinch, delay, deuce, equal, hitch, joint, leash, level, limit, marry, match, nexus, rival, rivet, strap, touch, truss, unite 6 anchor, attach, batten, begird, bundle, clinch, couple, cravat, enlace, even up, fasten, fetter, hamper, hinder, hook on, hookup, inlace, lace up, lacing, ligate, lock up, outfit, secure, splice, string, tackle, tether, zipper 7 balance, bandage, bracket, confine, conjoin, connect, foulard, kinship, liaison, loyalty, network, shackle, tighten, trammel 8 alliance, dead heat, deadlock, fastener, ligament, ligation, ligature, make fast, neckwear, obstruct, parallel, restrain, restrict, standoff, vinculum 9 break even, entrammel, fastening, indenture, interlace, measure up, stalemate 10 allegiance, attachment, commitment, connection, four-in-hand, keep up with, obligation
a horse: 6 tether
black ~: 6 tuxedo 10 monkey suit
department: 4 men's
down: 4 lash 6 fasten, pinion, secure 8 restrain
fabric: 3 rep 4 repp, silk 7 charvet, Mogador
feature: 4 knot
holder: 3 pin, tac 4 stud 5 clasp
in: 4 link 5 merge 6 belong, mingle, relate 7 connect 8 catenate 9 correlate 10 connection, coordinate
in a ~: 4 even 5 drawn
like some ~ s: 4 loud 5 gaudy 6 clip-on, flashy
off: 6 ligate
on: 5 affix 6 attach 7 connect
place: 4 neck
starter: 3 hog 4 neck 5 cross
tack: 4 stud 7 jewelry
the knot: 3 wed 4 mate 5 marry 10 get hitched
tightly: 5 truss
together: 4 join, loop, yoke 7 conjoin
up: 4 bind, clog, curb, dock, halt, hold, join, knot, moor, stop, wrap 5 delay, leash, limit, match, truss 6 engage, fasten, fetter, hamper, hinder, impede, ligate, occupy, pinion, secure, tether 7 confine, shackle, trammel 8 deadlock, encumber, finalize, handicap, keep busy, obstruct, prohibit, restrain, restrict, slow down 9 entrammel 10 traffic jam
up loose ends: 6 finish 8 complete, finalize
up the phone: 3 gab, rap, yak 4 chat, talk
Western ~: 4 bola, bolo
tie __: 3 bar, rod, tac 4 beam, clip, down, line, plug, tack 5 clasp, one on, plate
tie __ on: 3 one
tie-__: 3 dye
__ tie: 3 bow 4 bola, bolo 5 black, power, twist, white 6 clip-on, cotton, Oxford, school, string 7 paisley, Windsor
__-tie: 3 hog 6 tongue
Tie a Yellow Ribbon... (1973 song)
artist: Tony Orlando & Dawn
tree: 3 oak
tiebreaker: 2 OT 8 overtime
tied: 4 even 5 equal, tight 6 even up, liable 7 at deuce
fit to be ~: 3 mad 4 wild 5 angry, irate, livid, riled, vexed 6 fuming, heated, piqued, raging, red-hot 7 boiling, enraged, furious, intense, steamed, violent 8 incensed, up in arms, wrathful 9 bummed-out, indignant 10 hysterical, infuriated
in: 6 united 8 in league, relevant
not ~ down: 4 free 5 loose 7 unbound 8 cut loose, detached 9 footloose, unchained, unengaged, unimpeded 10 autonomous, disengaged, unattached, unconfined, unhampered, unhindered, unshackled
up: 4 busy 5 tight 7 engaged, in knots, related 8 immersed, obsessed, occupied
with hands ~: 5 at bay 8 helpless
__-tied: 6 tongue
tie-dyed fabric: 4 ikat 5 batik 6 battik
Tiegs: 6 Cheryl
tie-in: 7 society 8 junction, juncture 9 relevance 10 connection
tieless: 6 casual
Tie Me Kangaroo Down, Sport (1963 song) artist: Rolf Harris
Tien Shan: 5 range
locale: 4 Asia 5 China 10 Kyrgyzstan
Tientsin: 4 city, port, town 7 seaport
locale: 5 China
tiepin: 7 jewelry
Tiepolo: 4 font 8 Giovanni, typeface
Tiepolo, Giovanni: 6 artist 7 Italian, painter
tier: 3 row 4 bank, deck, file, line, rank 5 class, grade, group, lacer, layer, level, order, queue, range, story 6 course, league, rating, series, string 7 echelon, gallery, section, stratum 8 category, grouping 9 mezzanine 10 pigeonhole
fly ~: 9 fisherman
__-tier: 3 two
tierce: 4 hour
Tierney: 4 Gene 5 Maura
Tierney, Gene: 7 actress
film: A Bell for Adano (1945)
Close to My Heart (1951)
The Ghost and Mrs. Muir (1947)
Heaven Can Wait (1943)
The Iron Curtain (1948)
Laura (1944)
Leave Her to Heaven (1945)
The Left Hand of God (1955)
The Mating Season (1951)
On the Riviera (1951)
The Razor's Edge (1946)
The Return of Frank James (1940)
Son of Fury (1942)
Where the Sidewalk Ends (1950)
Whirlpool (1949)
spouse: Oleg Cassini
Tierra Blanca: 4 city, town
locale: 6 Mexico 8 Veracruz
Tierra del Fuego: 4 isle 6 island
co-owner: 3 Arg. 5 Chile 9 Argentina
native: 3 Ona 6 Yahgan
range: 5 Andes
tiers __: 4 état
__ Ties: 6 Family, School
Tietê, city on the: 8 Sao Paulo
tie the __: 4 knot
tie-up: 3 jam 4 link 5 delay, snarl 6 logjam 8 blockage, slowdown, stoppage 10 bottleneck, congestion, traffic jam
tiff: 3 ado, fit, pet, row 4 huff, miff, spat, sulk 5 argue, clash, fight, pique, run-in, scrap, set-to, words 6 barney, bicker, dustup, rumpus, temper 7 bad mood, dispute, quarrel, tantrum, wrangle 8 argument, skirmish, squabble 9 altercate, bickering 10 difference, falling-out, irritation
tiffany: 6 fabric 8 material
Tiffany: 4 Chin, font 5 Louis 7 Bolling 8 typeface
Tiffany (singer)
last name: Darwish
song: All This Time (1988)
Could've Been (1987)
I Saw Him Standing There (1988)
I Think We're Alone Now (1987)
Tiffany __: 4 lamp 5 glass 7 setting
Tiffin: 6 Pamela
tiffin, take: 3 eat, sup 4 dine
Tigard: 4 city, town
locale: 6 Oregon
Tige: 3 dog 7 Andrews
tiger: 3 cat 4 Tony 5 beast, felid 6 animal, big cat, feline, mammal 8 go-getter 9 Shere Khan 10 sabertooth
by the tail: 9 obsession
home: 3 zoo
like a ~: 4 wild 7 striped
prehistoric ~: 8 smilodon
relative: 4 eyra, lion, lynx, puma 5 chita, liger, ounce, tigon 6 bobcat, cheeta, chetah, cougar, jaguar, margay, ocelot, serval, tiglon 7 bay lynx, caracal, cheetah, leopard, panther 9 catamount 10 jaguarundi
swallowtail: 3 bug 6 insect
tooth: 4 fang
young: 3 cub
tiger __: 3 cat 4 lily, moth 5 shark, snake 6 beetle, lizard
__ tiger: 4 sand 5 blind, paper, water 6 Bengal 7 clouded
Tiger: 5 Woods 10 baseballer
Hall of Famer: 4 Cobb 6 Kaline, Ty Cobb 8 Al Kaline 9 Greenberg, Newhouser
org.: 3 PGA
rival: 3 Cub, Met, Red 4 Expo, Twin 5 Angel, Astro, Brave, Giant, Padre, Rocky, Royal 6 Brewer, Dodger, Indian, Marlin, Oriole, Philly, Pirate, Ranger, Red Sox, Yankee 7 Blue Jay, Mariner 8 Athletic, Cardinal, Devil Ray, White Sox
Tiger __: 3 Bay, Rag 4 Beat, Eyes 5 Shark 6 Lilies
Tiger (1959 song) artist: Fabian
Tiger Bay (1959 film)
cast: Horst Buchholz, Hayley Mills, John Mills
director: J. Lee Thompson
Tiger Beat reader: 4 teen
Tiger Eyes author: Judy Blume
Tiger in your tank company: 4 Esso
tigerish: 4 wild 5 feral 6 fierce, savage 7 furious, intense, vicious 8 menacing 9 barbarous, ferocious, merciless, predatory, rapacious, voracious 10 passionate
Tigerland (2000 film)
cast: Clifton Collins Jr., Matthew Davis, Colin Farrell, Thomas Guiry
director: Joel Schumacher
Tiger Lilies author: Sidney Lanier
Tigers: 3 ten 4 team 6 Auburn 7 Clemson 9 Grambling, Princeton
home: 7 Detroit
org.: 3 ALC, MLB
sport: 8 baseball
__ Tigers: 6 Flying
Tigers are Better-Looking author: Jean Rhys
tiger's-eye: 3 gem 6 quartz 8 gemstone
Tiger Shark (1932 film)
cast: Richard Arlen, Zita Johann, Edward G. Robinson
director: Howard Hawks
Tiger Walks, A star: 4 Sabu
Tigger
creator: A.A. Milne
pal: 3 Owl, Roo 4 Pooh 6 Eeyore

Tigger Comes to the Forest author: A.A. Milne
Tighe: **5** Kevin
tight: **3** set **4** fast, firm, high, mean, near, shut, snug, taut, tied **5** blind, boozy, bound, cheap, close, dense, drawn, fixed, proof, quick, rigid, rough, scant, short, solid, sound, stiff, tense, terse, thick, tipsy, tough **6** bolted, buzzed, firmly, frugal, gnomic, greedy, loaded, locked, nailed, narrow, scanty, sealed, secure, skimpy, stable, steady, stewed, sticky, stingy, stoned, strong, sturdy, tied up, tricky, trying **7** arduous, blocked, choking, clasped, clumped, compact, concise, cramped, crowded, cutting, laconic, miserly, pickled, plugged, selfish, slammed, smashed, snapped, sparing, thrifty **8** clear-cut, cramping, critical, crushing, enduring, exacting, fastened, grasping, hermetic, intimate, ironclad, perilous, pinching, shrunken, strained, succinct, ticklish, ungiving **9** compacted, dangerous, difficult, hazardous, hidebound, leakproof, nonporous, padlocked, penurious, plastered, punishing, stopped up, stretched, stringent, tenacious, unbending, upsetting, worrisome **10** avaricious, compressed, contracted, disturbing, hard-packed, impervious, inebriated, inflexible, nip and tuck, obstructed, precarious, skinflinty, smothering, to the point, unyielding, waterproof, watertight
ender: **3** wad **4** rope
grip: **4** lock **6** clinch, clutch **7** squeeze
hold ~: **5** clasp, cling **6** clench **7** squeeze
not ~: **3** lax **4** free **5** baggy, loose, slack **6** limber, sloppy, undone **7** relaxed **8** loosened, rambling, slipshod, unhooked **10** disjointed, unbuttoned, unfastened
not ~ in Britain: **5** lowse
pack ~: **3** jam, ram **4** cram, fill, load, tamp, tuck **5** crowd, crush, press, stuff **6** squash **7** squeeze **8** compress, overfill **9** overcrowd
sit ~: **4** stay, wait
spot: **3** fix, jam, rub **4** bind, snag **5** pinch **6** corner, crunch, hassle, pickle, plight, scrape
starter: **3** air, gas **4** skin **5** stick, water
tight __: **3** end **4** shot, spot
tight __ drum: **3** as a
tight-__: **4** knit **6** fisted, lipped **7** mouthed
__ tight: **3** sit **4** hand
__ tight budget: **3** on a
tighten: **3** fix, tie **4** bind, edit, grip, snug **5** cinch, close, cramp, crush, pinch, purse, screw, tense **6** batten, clench, fasten, harden, hold in, lace up, narrow, pull in, redact, secure, strain, tauten **7** congeal, squeeze, stiffen, stretch, toughen **8** compress, condense, contract, pressure, rigidify, strangle **9** constrict
a lid: **5** twist
one's belt: **5** skimp **9** economize
up: **4** edit **6** redact
tightened: **4** firm
tightening, belt: **6** layoff **7** cutback **8** decrease **9** lessening, reduction **10** diminution
tight-fisted: **4** mean **5** cheap **6** greedy, skimpy, stingy **7** chintzy, miserly, sparing **8** grasping, stinting **9** penurious **10** skinflinty
one: **5** miser, piker
tight-fitting: **4** snug
tight-laced: **6** prissy
tight-lipped: **3** mum **4** mute **5** quiet **6** silent **8** reticent, taciturn **9** secretive, voiceless **10** speechless
tightly: **9** immovably
tightness: **7** tension **8** shortage
Tight Rope (1972 song) artist: Leon Russell
tightrope, walk a: **4** dare
tights: **4** hose **7** leotard **8** leggings
wearer: **6** dancer **9** ballerina
__ tight ship: **4** run a
Tight Spot (1955 film)
cast: Brian Keith, Edward G. Robinson, Ginger Rogers
tightwad: **5** miser, piker **7** Scrooge **9** skinflint **10** cheapskate, pinchpenny
tigon: **3** cat **5** felid **6** feline, hybrid
relative: **4** eyra, lion, lynx, puma **5** chita, liger, ounce, tiger **6** bobcat, cheeta, chetah, cougar, jaguar, margay, ocelot, serval **7** bay lynx, caracal, cheetah, leopard, panther **9** catamount **10** jaguarundi
Tigra: **3** car **4** auto, Opel **10** automobile
Tigran: **9** Petrosian
Tigré home: **6** Africa **8** Ethiopia
Tigris: **4** boat, ship **5** river
ancient city near the ~: **6** Arbela
city on the ~: **5** Amara, Mosul **7** Baghdad
locale: **4** Irak, Iraq **6** Turkey
river to the ~: **7** Karkheh
Tijuana: **4** city, town
locale: **4** Baja **6** Mexico
see also Spanish
Tijuana Taxi (1966 song) artist: Herb Alpert and the Tijuana Brass
__ Tikes: **6** Little
tiki: **4** idol **8** figurine
Tiki: **6** Barber
__-Tiki: **3** Kon
__-tikki-tavi: **5** Rikki
til: **6** sesame
'Til __: **7** Tuesday
tilapia: **4** fish
Tilburg: **4** city, town
locale: **7** Holland **11** Netherlands
Tilda: **7** Swinton
tilde: **4** mark
topper: **3** ESC
Tilden, Bill: **7** netster **9** tennis pro
milieu: **5** court
tile: **4** pave **5** inlay **6** domino **7** encrust, incrust
convex ~: **6** imbrex
dotted ~: **6** domino
install ~: **3** lay, set
__ tile: **4** book **6** carpet, hollow, quarry **7** bleeder, ceiling, ceramic, parquet
tiled: **6** inlaid
tiler
job: **4** roof **5** floor **7** kitchen
need: **5** grout, putty
till: **3** box, dig, hoe, sow, yet **4** farm, grow, plow, safe, tend, tray, turn, work **5** dress, kitty, labor, mulch, plant, vault **6** before, drawer, garden, harrow **7** cash box, prepare **8** money box, register, treasury, turn over **9** cultivate, meanwhile
co.: **3** NCR
ender: **3** age
fit to ~: **6** arable **7** fertile **8** farmable, plowable **10** cultivable
now: **5** as yet, so far, still
slot: **4** ones, tens **5** fives **8** twenties
Till: **4** Eric
Till __ Was You: **5** There
tillage: **4** land **5** field **7** farming
Tillamook __: **3** Bay
tiller: **4** helm **5** reins, wheel **6** farmer, handle **7** control
locale: **3** aft **4** rear **6** astern
tool: **3** hoe
__-tiller: **4** roto
Till Eulenspiegel composer: **7** Strauss
Tilley: **7** Eustace
Tillich, Paul: **11** philosopher
specialty: **8** theology
Tillie and Gus (1933 film)
cast: W.C. Fields, Baby LeRoy, Alison Skipworth
Tillie the __: **6** Toiler
Tillis: **3** Mel, Pam
Tillotson: **6** Johnny
Tillstrom: **4** Burr
till the __ come home: **4** cows
Till the Clouds Roll By composer: **4** Kern **6** Bolton **9** Wodehouse
Till the Day I Die author: Clifford Odets
Till the End of Time (1946 film)
cast: Guy Madison, Dorothy McGuire, Robert Mitchum
director: Edward Dmytryk
Till the End of Time (1945 song)
artist: Perry Como
Till We Meet Again author: Judith Krantz
Till We Meet Again songwriter: **4** Egan
Tilly: **3** Meg **8** Jennifer
Tilly, Meg: **7** actress
film: Agnes of God (1985)
The Big Chill (1983)
Masquerade (1988)
Tex (1982)
The Two Jakes (1990)
Tilsit: **6** cheese
__ Tilson Thomas: **7** Michael
tilt: **3** dip, tip, yaw **4** bend, bias, bout, cant, drop, duel, fall, heel, lean, list, meet, rake, skew, spar, swag, sway, turn **5** angle, bevel, break, clash, fight, grade, joust, lurch, pitch, set-to, shift, slant, slide, slope, upset **6** attack, careen, charge, combat, fracas, seesaw, slouch, thrust, tussle **7** contend, contest, incline, leaning, recline, scuffle, tourney **8** conflict, gradient, skirmish, struggle **9** collision, encounter, overthrow, scrimmage **10** declension, tournament
at full ~: **5** amain **8** pell-mell
competitor: **6** knight **7** warrior **8** horseman
full ~: **4** fast **5** swift **7** rapidly, swiftly
toward: **5** favor **6** prefer
tilt __: **5** board **6** hammer
tilt-__ table: **3** top
__ tilt: **4** full
Tilt-a-Whirl: **4** ride
tilted: **4** alop **5** alist, bevel, leant **6** aslant, aslope
tilth: **4** farm, land, soil **5** acres, earth, field, tract **6** ground **7** acreage, tillage
__ 'Til the Sun Shines, Nellie: **4** Wait
tilting: **5** alist **8** lopsided
tilting __: **5** board, chest
Tilton: **8** Charlene
'Til Tuesday
lead singer: Aimee Mann
song: Voices Carry (1985)
__ 'Til You Drop: **4** Shop
Tim: **4** Holt, Hunt, Mara, Reid, Rice, Roth, Russ, Tiny **5** Allen, Curry, Keefe **6** Burton, Conway, Hunter, McGraw, Raines, Whelan **7** Meadows, Robbins **8** Cratchit, Matheson, McCarver, McIntire **9** Considine **10** Kazurinsky
__ Tim: **4** Tiny
timarau: **5** bovid **6** bovine
relative: **3** yak **4** anoa, arna, gaur, urus, zebu **5** bison, gayal, takin **6** mithan, muskox **7** aurochs, banteng, banting, beefalo, buffalo, carabao, cattalo, kouprey
timbale: **4** drum **6** pastry
timber: **3** log, rib **4** balk, beam, boom, club, mast, pole, tree, wood **5** board, frame, grove, joist, plank, stake, stick, trees, woods **6** forest, girder, lumber, rafter **7** support **8** hardwood, woodland
ender: **4** head, land, line, work
foundation ~: **4** sill
made of ~: **6** wooden
mine ~: **5** brace, sprag, stull
problem: **4** knot **5** gnarl **6** dryrot
ship: **3** sny **4** bibb, keel, mast **6** inwale, poppet **7** cathead, futtock, stemson **8** stempost
tool: **3** axe, saw **4** adze
use ~ for support: **5** shore
wolf: **4** lobo
timber __: **4** mill, wolf **5** hitch, right **6** beetle **7** cruiser
__ timber: **3** top **4** horn **6** breast
timberland: **4** wood **5** woods **6** forest **8** wildwood **9** backwoods
__ Timberlane: **4** Cass
timberline, above the: **6** alpine
__ Timbers: **6** Fallen
Timberwolf rival: **3** Cav, Mav, Net, Sun **4** Buck, Bull, Hawk, Heat, Jazz, King, Spur **5** Knick, Laker, Magic, Pacer, Sixer, Sonic **6** Celtic, Hornet, Nugget, Piston, Raptor, Rocket, Wizard **7** Clipper, Grizzly, Warrior **8** Cavalier, Maverick **10** SuperSonic
Timberwolves: **4** five, team
home: **9** Minnesota
org.: **3** NBA
sport: **10** basketball
timbre: **4** tone **5** pitch **6** accent **10** inflection
Timbuktu: **4** town
locale: **4** Mali
river near ~: **5** Niger
time: **3** age, bit, day, era **4** ager, bout, date, hour, life, pace, past, peak, rate, shot, show, slot, span, term, tide, tour, turn, week, year **5** break, clock, epoch, month, point, shift, space, spell, stage, state, stint, tempo, while **6** chance, extent, future, heyday, heydey, length, look-in, moment, period, rhythm, season, second, squeak **7** instant, leisure, measure, opening, present, stretch **8** duration, eternity, infinity, instance, interval, juncture, lifespan, occasion, regulate, sentence **9** allotment **10** chronology, generation
ahead of ~: **5** early **9** in advance **10** beforehand
ahead of its ~: **3** new **8** advanced **10** innovative
allowance: **5** grace
ancient ~: **4** yore **9** antiquity
and again: **3** oft **4** a lot, much **5** often **9** quite a bit, regularly, routinely **10** frequently, habitually
another ~: **4** anew, anon, over, soon, then **5** after, again **6** in a bit **7** by and by, later on, someday **8** in a while, sometime **9** afterward, hereafter **10** before long, eventually
appointed ~: **4** date, hour **5** H-Hour **8** zero hour
a second ~: **4** anew, over **5** again
a short ~ ago: **5** newly **6** lately **7** just now **8** latterly, recently
a single ~: **4** once
at a future ~: **3** yet **5** later **10** eventually, ultimately
at a later ~: **9** following **10** afterwards, before long, subsequent
at any ~: **3** e'er **4** ever **8** even once
at no ~: **4** ne'er **5** never **7** not ever
at one ~: **8** back when, formerly, hitherto, together **9** a while ago, in the past **10** heretofore, previously
at such ~ as: **4** when
at that ~: **4** then **9** thereupon

at the present ~: 3 now 5 today
at the right ~: 3 apt 5 on cue 6 prompt 7 fitting 8 apposite, punctual 9 expedient 10 auspicious, convenient, felicitous
at the same ~: 5 along 6 in sync 8 together 9 meanwhile
at the same ~ as: 5 while 6 during, whilst
at the same ~ (prefix): 3 syn-
at this ~: 3 now 4 here 5 still, today 8 promptly, right now, right off, until now 9 forthwith, presently, right away 10 here and now
at what ~: 4 when
back in ~: 3 ago
behind ~: 4 late 5 tardy 7 overdue 8 detained
being: 5 nonce 7 present
bide one's ~: 4 wait 5 delay, tarry 6 lie low 7 stand by
by that ~: 7 already
call ~: 5 pause 6 recess
can do it: 4 heal, mend
combining form: 5 chron- 6 chrono-
correct the ~: 5 reset
current ~: 3 now 7 present
delay: 3 lag
display: 3 LCD, LED
earlier in ~: 5 prior 10 previously
ender: 4 card, less, work, worn 5 piece, saver, table 6 keeper, saving, server, worker 7 keeping
extra ~: 5 slack, space 6 leeway, margin 8 latitude
fool away ~: 4 idle, laze, loll 5 dally, dream, shirk, stall 6 dawdle, loiter, lounge 7 hang out 8 malinger, slack off 9 goldbrick 10 dillydally, fool around, knock about
for a ~: 6 awhile
for all ~: 3 e'er 4 ever 7 finally
for the ~ being: 3 now 9 meanwhile, temporary
free ~: 4 ease 6 recess, repose 7 holiday, leisure, liberty 8 vacation 10 recreation, relaxation, sabbatical
from that ~: 4 then
from this ~ forward: 6 always 8 evermore 9 endlessly, eternally 10 henceforth
from time to ~: 10 now and then
further in ~: 4 anon 5 after 8 eventual 9 afterward 10 thereafter
galactic ~ period: 3 age
gap: 4 stay 5 delay, hitch, pause, stall 6 holdup 7 respite, setback 8 interval, reprieve, slowdown, stoppage 9 deferment, extension, interlude 10 standstill, suspension
get on, as ~: 5 laten
give a hard ~: 3 irk, nag, vex 5 annoy, tease, upset 6 harass 7 torment
gone by: 4 past
good ~: 3 fun, gas 4 ball, lark, romp 5 blast 6 laughs
hard ~: 4 bind 5 trial 6 crisis, crunch, hassle, rebuff, rebuke 7 squeeze, trouble 8 distress 9 adversity, emergency, rejection 10 misfortune, upbraiding
have a bad ~: 6 suffer
have a good ~: 5 enjoy, party 6 cavort 7 carouse, skylark 8 cut loose, live it up 9 celebrate, make merry, whoop it up
have a good ~ with: 5 enjoy
high ~: 4 noon 5 spree
high old ~: 5 caper, fling, revel, spree 6 frolic, gambol, picnic 7 rollick
hit the big ~: 6 arrive, make it, thrive 7 prosper, succeed 8 make good
important ~: 3 age, era 5 epoch
in ~: 4 anon, soon, then 5 after, later 6 a tempo, not now 7 by and by, later on, someday 8 bit by bit 9 afterward, hereafter 10 before long, eventually, ultimately
infinite ~: 7 forever 8 eternity
in good ~: 4 anon, soon 6 prompt 7 by and by, erelong, shortly 8 punctual 9 presently 10 beforehand, before long
in ~ in music: 6 a tempo
in no ~: 3 PDQ 4 fast 5 apace 6 presto 7 fleetly, hastily, quickly, rapidly, readily, swiftly 8 pell-mell, speedily 9 forthwith, hurriedly, instantly, like a shot, posthaste
in the ~ left: 4 till 5 still
in the nick of ~: 9 opportune 10 felicitous
it's about ~: 5 enfin 6 at last 7 finally
keep ~ manually: 4 clap
kill ~: 5 stall 8 lallygag
length of ~: 4 span 5 sweep
limit: 6 curfew
limited ~: 4 span, term, tour 5 hitch, phase 6 period, tenure 7 stretch 8 duration, interval, semester, sentence
line: 4 plan 6 agenda 7 outline 8 game plan, scenario, schedule, strategy 9 blueprint, framework 10 big picture
long ~: 3 age, eon 4 aeon, ages 5 years 7 century, decades, forever
lose no ~: 3 fly, hie, run 4 dash, race, rush, tear 5 hurry, scoot, speed 6 hasten 10 get hopping
make ~ with: 3 woo 4 date 5 court 6 pursue 7 take out
mark ~: 4 drag, idle, laze, loaf, tick, wait 5 abide, stall 6 loiter, lounge 8 vegetate
most of the ~: 6 mainly 7 as a rule, overall, usually 8 as a whole 9 generally, in general 10 by and large, on the whole
not give the ~ of day: 3 cut 4 shun, snub 5 spurn 6 ignore, rebuff, slight 8 brush off
occupy ~ and space: 4 last, live 7 breathe 8 continue
of ~: 8 temporal
of a ~: 4 eral
of day: 4 dawn, dusk, hour, morn, noon 5 sunup 6 sunset 7 evening, morning, sunrise 9 afternoon
off: 4 rest 5 leave, R and R 6 recess 7 holiday, leisure 8 furlough, vacation
of one's life: 4 ball 5 blast
of ~ past: 5 olden
on ~: 5 sharp 6 prompt 8 promptly, punctual 10 punctually
once upon a ~: 6 before, erenow 9 in the past
one at a ~: 6 singly 9 piecemeal
opportune ~: 4 shot 6 chance 8 occasion
out: 5 break, pause 7 respite
palindromic ~: 3 eve 4 noon
partner: 4 tide
pass, as ~: 5 spend, while
play for ~: 5 dally, delay, stall 6 put off 8 postpone 9 temporize
pleasant ~: 4 idyl 5 idyll
point in ~: 4 date, hour 5 point, stage 6 moment
rough ~: 6 downer 8 dry spell, tailspin
science of ~: 8 horology
short ~: 3 bit, sec 4 jiff, msec. 5 jiffy, trice 6 minute, moment 10 nanosecond
some ~ ago: 4 once 6 before 7 earlier 8 formerly 9 in the past 10 heretofore, originally, previously
spare ~: 4 ease, rest 7 freedom, holiday, leisure, liberty, respite 8 vacation 10 recreation, sabbatical
spend, as ~: 5 put in
stand the test of ~: 4 last 6 endure, hold up
starter: 3 air, any, bed, big, day, nap, rag, tea, war 4 down, flex, half, life, long, meal, mean, noon, over, seed, show, some, zone 5 afore, after, lunch, night, peace, small 6 before, dinner, spring, summer, supper, winter 9 Christmas
take ~ off: 4 rest 5 pause, relax
take one's ~: 5 dally, delay, mosey, relax, stall, tarry 6 dawdle, linger, loiter 7 goof off 8 lollygag 10 dillydally
taking one's ~: 3 lax 4 easy, lazy, slow 5 slack 6 calmly, casual, gentle, lazily, slowly 7 relaxed 8 casually, laid-back 9 gradually, languidly, leisurely, unhurried 10 composedly, deliberate, indolently
teller: 4 dial 5 clock, watch 10 wristwatch
terrific ~: 4 gala 5 blast, party, spree
to reflect: 4 lull, rest 5 break 6 hiatus 7 respite 8 breather
to the end of ~: 3 e'er 4 ever 7 forever 8 evermore
unit: 2 hr., mo. 3 day, eon, era, min., sec. 4 aeon, half, hour, span, term, week, year 5 epoch, month, space, spell 6 decade, minute, moment, period, second 7 century, quarter 10 millennium
up to this ~: 3 yet 5 as yet 6 ere now, of late 7 thus far 8 hitherto, until now 10 heretofore, previously
vacation ~: 3 Aug., Jul. 4 July 6 August, summer 7 dog days
very long ~: 3 age 4 ages 7 century 9 centuries, millennia 10 millennium
was: 4 once 10 previously
waste ~: 3 lag 4 futz, idle, kill, laze, loaf, moon, mope 5 amble, dally, mosey, stall, tarry 6 dawdle, diddle, linger, loiter, lounge, trifle 7 saunter 8 lollygag, straggle 10 dillydally, fool around
wild ~: 5 spree
working ~: 5 stint
zone abbr.: 3 CDT, CST, EDT, EST, MDT, MST, PDT, PST
time __: 3 lag, was 4 bill, bomb, copy, lamp, line, loan, lock, note, warp, zone 5 chart, clock, draft, frame, limit, money, of day, sheet, stamp, study 6 killer, series, signal 7 capsule, deposit, machine
time __ half: 4 and a
time __ mind: 5 out of
time __ time: 5 after
time-__: 3 lag, out 5 lapse, share 6 tested 7 binding, honored, release, sharing
time-__ photography: 5 lapse
__ time: 3 air, big, buy, cut, tee 4 at no, comp, dead, face, fast, full, gain, good, hang, hard, high, in no, keep, kill, lead, lose, make, mark, peak, post, real, sack, slow, true, word, zone 5 at one, buy on, decay, drive, duple, equal, local, many a, press, prime, quick, quiet, short, spare, waltz, Yukon 6 access, Alaska, at this, bottom, common, crunch, double, family, Hawaii, simple, travel, triple 7 braking, Central, connect, curtain, driving, Eastern, elapsed, Pacific, quality, release, running, two-part
__-time: 3 all, old, one 4 lead, long, part 5 first, small, split, whole 6 double
Time: 3 mag 8 magazine
contents: 4 news
founder: 4 Luce 6 Hadden
onetime ~ film critic: 4 Agee
staffer: 6 editor 8 reporter
Time __, A: 5 To Die
Time __ Bottle: 3 in a
Time __ Let Me: 4 Won't
Time __ Life: 4 of My
Time __ My Side: 4 Is on
Time __ Season: 5 of the
Time __ the essence: 4 is of
__ Time: 3 Bad, Big, Our 4 Play, Pony, This 5 Magic, One Mo', Swing 6 Bering, Crying, Father, Kissin' 7 Another, Closing, Killing
Time (1983 song) artist: Culture Club
Time After Time (1979 film)
cast: Malcolm McDowell, Mary Steenburgen, David Warner
director: Nicholas Meyer
Time After Time (song) artist: Cyndi Lauper, Inoj
time and __: 4 tide 5 again, a half
Time and Time Again author: Alan Ayckbourn
__ Time Around, The: 6 Second
__ Time at All: 3 Any
Time Bandits (1981 film)
cast: John Cleese, Sean Connery, Shelley Duvall, Katherine Helmond
director: Terry Gilliam
Time Bomb author: Jonathan Kellerman
time-capsule event: 6 burial
__-time Charlie: 4 good
Timecode (2000 film)
cast: Saffron Burrows, Salma Hayek, Stellan Skarsgård, Jeanne Tripplehorn
director: Mike Figgis
time-consuming: 4 long, slow 7 lengthy, spun-out 8 drawn-out, unending 10 long-winded, protracted
__-time continuum: 5 space
Timecop (1994 film)
cast: Mia Sara, Jean-Claude Van Damme
director: Peter Hyams
timed-__: 7 release
__-timed: 3 ill 4 well 6 stress
timed, perfectly: 5 on cue
__ Time Gal: 6 Sleepy
time-honored: 3 old 4 trad. 6 age-old 7 classic, regular
__ Time I Get to Phoenix: 5 By the
Time in a Bottle (1973 song) artist: Jim Croce
__ Time I Saw Paris, The: 4 Last
Time is money: 3 saw 5 adage, maxim
Time Is on My Side (1964 song) artist: Rolling Stones
Time Is Ripe, The author: Clifford Odets
Time Is Tight (1969 song) artist: Booker T. and the MGs
timekeeper: 5 alarm, clock, watch 6 ticker 7 sundial 9 hourglass 10 alarm clock, wristwatch
timeless: 6 eterne 7 abiding, eternal, undying 8 enduring, immortal, unending 9 deathless, perennial, perpetual, unceasing
Time Limit (1957 film)
cast: Richard Basehart, Dolores Michaels, Richard Widmark
director: Karl Malden
Timeline author: Michael Crichton
Time Lost and Time Remembered (1966 film)
cast: Cyril Cusack, Sarah Miles
Time, Love and Tenderness (1991 song) artist: Michael Bolton

timely: 3 apt, fit, now, pat 4 meet, ripe 5 happy, lucky 6 likely, modern, prompt, proper, with it 7 apropos, fitting, germane, helpful, hopeful 8 apposite, punctual, relevant, suitable, towardly, up-to-date 9 expedient, favorable, judicious, opportune, pertinent, promising 10 auspicious, convenient, felicitous, propitious, prosperous, seasonable
in a ~ fashion: 5 on cue
time-machine destination: 4 past 6 future
Time Machine, The (1960 film)
cast: Yvette Mimieux, Rod Taylor, Alan Young
character: 4 Eloi 5 Weena 7 Morlock
director: George Pal
Time Machine, The (2002 film)
cast: Orlando Jones, Samantha Mumba, Guy Pearce
director: Simon Wells
Time Machine, The author: H.G. Wells
__ Time, Next Year: 4 Same
__ time no see!: 4 long
time of __: 3 day
Time of My Life author: Alan Ayckbourn
Time of My Life, The (1987 song)
artist: Bill Medley, Jennifer Warnes
time of one's __: 4 life
Time of Their Lives, The (1946 film)
cast: Bud Abbott, Lou Costello, Marjorie Reynolds
director: Charles Barton
Time of the Season (1969 song)
artist: Zombies
Time of Your Life, The author: William Saroyan
time on one's __: 5 hands
time-out: 3 nap 4 lull 5 pause 6 recess, siesta 7 interim 8 interval 9 cessation 10 suspension
time out of __: 4 mind
Time out of Mind singer: 5 Dylan
timepiece: 5 clock, watch 7 sundial 9 hourglass
sound: 4 tick, tock
timer: 5 clock, watch 6 gadget 9 hourglass, stopwatch
place: 7 kitchen
__ timer: 3 egg 6 pigeon
__-timer: 3 big, old 4 full, part 5 clock, first
Time Regained (1999 film)
cast: Emmanuelle Béart, Catherine Deneuve, Marcello Mazzarella, Vincent Perez
director: Raul Ruiz
times
abreast of the ~: 7 current 8 up-to-date
a number of ~: 9 regularly 10 frequently, repeatedly
at ~: 3 occ. 9 not always 10 now and then, on occasion
at all ~: 4 ever 6 always 10 unendingly
at various ~: 6 cyclic 8 cyclical, frequent, repeated, seasonal, sporadic 9 recurrent, recurring, spasmodic 10 occasional
bad ~: 5 slump 9 recession 10 depression
behind the ~: 3 out 5 dated, fusty 6 square 8 outdated, outmoded 9 out-of-date
good ~: 3 fun 6 laughs 10 prosperity
hard ~: 5 slump 9 adversity, recession 10 depression, woefulness
in ~ past: 4 once 7 earlier 8 formerly, hitherto, until now 10 heretofore, previously
in these ~: 3 now 5 today 9 at present
keep up with the ~: 5 adapt, alter 6 adjust, change, modify, revise 7 conform, convert, remodel 8 accustom 9 acclimate 10 assimilate, come around
many ~: 3 oft 5 often 6 mostly 10 frequently, repeatedly
most ~: 7 as a rule, largely, usually 9 generally, in general 10 by and large, frequently, on the whole
olden ~: 4 past, yore 5 antiq. 9 antiquity, yesterday
seven ~ a week: 7 diurnal
starter: 3 oft 4 some 5 often 7 between
suffix: 4 -fold
these ~: 8 today. now
Times: 4 font 5 paper 9 newspaper
locale: 7 New York 10 Los Angeles
Times __: 5 Roman 6 Square
__ Times: 3 Old 4 Good, Hard 6 Modern
__ Times a Lady: 5 Three
Time's Arrow author: Martin Amis
__ Times at Ridgemont High: 4 Fast
timesaver: 4 tool 6 gadget
time-saving: 5 handy, on tap, ready 6 nearby 7 close by, helpful, in reach 9 expedient, immediate, opportune 10 convenient, economical
Times-Dispatch: 5 paper 9 newspaper
locale: 8 Richmond
time-share: 5 lease 6 sublet 7 rent out 8 sublease
time-shifting device: 3 VCR
time-slot abbr.: 3 TBA
Times of Glory (1960 film)
cast: Alec Guinness, John Mills, Susannah York
director: Ronald Neame
Times of Your Life (1975 song) artist: Paul Anka
Times-Picayune: 5 paper 9 newspaper
locale: 10 New Orleans
Times Roman: 4 font 8 typeface
__ Times Seven: 5 Woman
Times Square
light: 4 neon
locale: 3 NYC 7 New York 9 Manhattan
timetable: 4 card, list, sked 5 sched. 6 agenda, docket 7 program 8 schedule
abbr.: 3 arr., ETA, ETD
time-tested: 3 old 5 tried
__ Time, The: 4 Last 5 First 6 Monkey 7 Longest
__ Time the Dream's on Me: 4 This
Time to Kill, A (1996 film)
cast: Sandra Bullock, Samuel L. Jackson, Matthew McConaughey, Kevin Spacey
director: Joel Schumacher
Time to leave!: 4 c'mon 6 let's go
Time to Love and a Time to Die, A: 4 film 5 novel
author: Erich Maria Remarque
cast: John Gavin, Jock Mahoney
director: Douglas Sirk
__ time to time: 4 from
time-wasting: 3 lax 4 lazy, slow, vain 5 slack, tardy 6 remiss 8 dallying, delaying, dilatory, tarrying 9 snaillike, unhurried
Time Without Pity (1956 film)
cast: Alec McCowen, Michael Redgrave
director: Joseph Losey
Time Won't Let Me (1966 song) artist: Outsiders
timeworn: 3 old 5 dated, dusty, hoary, passé, stale, trite 6 eroded, old-hat, shabby 7 archaic, run-down 8 decrepit, obsolete, out of use 9 crumbling, hackneyed, out-of-date, weathered 10 antiquated, broken-down, ramshackle, threadbare
time-worn: 8 well-used
Time wounds all __: 5 heels
Timex: 5 watch 10 wristwatch
alternative: 4 Ebel, Rado 5 Casio, Elgin, Lorus, Omega, Rolex, Seiko 6 Bulova, Fossil, Movado, Pulsar, Swatch 7 Citizen 8 Longines, Tag Heuer, Tourneau
timid: 3 coy, shy 4 meek, soft, weak 5 cowed, mousy, pavid, shaky 6 afraid, craven, demure, feeble, gentle, gun-shy, humble, modest, mousey, scared, trepid, yellow 7 abashed, alarmed, anxious, bashful, bullied, chicken, daunted, fearful, nervous, panicky, prudish, spooked, wimpish 8 badgered, blushing, cowardly, cowering, fearsome, hesitant, recreant, retiring, sheepish, skittish, unnerved, wavering 9 dastardly, diffident, flinching, nerveless, petrified, shrinking, spineless, terrified, trembling, tremulous, unassured, withdrawn 10 ambivalent, browbeaten, capricious, frightened, indecisive, irresolute, namby-pamby, spiritless, submissive, uneffusive, unsociable
not ~: 4 bold, pert 5 brash, brave, fresh, gutsy, nervy, pushy, saucy 6 brassy, brazen, cheeky, daring, flashy, heroic, plucky, spunky 7 dashing, defiant, forward, gallant, valiant 8 fearless, forceful, immodest, impudent, intrepid, resolute, spirited, unafraid, valorous 9 audacious, confident, dauntless, shameless, undaunted, unfearing 10 courageous, incautious, unreserved
one: 4 wimp 5 sissy 6 coward 7 chicken
timidity: 4 fear 7 modesty 8 cold feet, humility 9 cowardice, weak knees 10 constraint, diffidence, faint heart, insecurity
timidly: 5 shyly 7 charily, lightly
timidness: 7 modesty, reserve, shyness 8 meekness 9 hesitancy, mousiness 10 constraint, diffidence, insecurity, reluctance
timing __: 4 belt 5 chain
__-timing: 3 two
Timmins: 4 city, town
locale: 6 Canada 7 Ontario
Timon of Athens author: William Shakespeare
Timor: 3 isl., sea 4 isle 6 island
island group near ~: 4 Leti 5 Letti
locale: 5 Malay
Nobelist in Peace: 4 Belo 10 Ramos-Horta
sea near ~: 4 Savu, Sawu
__ Timor: 4 East
timorous: 4 weak 5 faint, jumpy, mousy 6 afraid, craven, mousey, scared, trepid 7 abashed, alarmed, anxious, bashful, chicken, daunted, fearful, nervous, panicky, spooked, wimpish 8 cowardly, fearsome, hesitant, retiring 9 petrified, terrified 10 frightened
timothy: 3 hay 5 grass
Timothy: 4 Daly 5 Aluko, Leary, saint 6 Dalton, Dwight, Hutton 7 Bottoms, Findley 8 Busfield
follower: 5 Titus
mother of ~: 6 Eunice
Timothy Files, The author: Lawrence Sanders
Timothy Mouse, friend of: 5 Dumbo
Timothy's Game author: Lawrence Sanders
tin: 3 can 5 metal 6 canful 7 element, package, stannum 8 preserve 9 baking pan, container
alloy: 6 bronze, oreide, oroide, pewter 8 calamine, gunmetal 9 barberite, bell metal, type metal 10 gold bronze, soft solder, terne metal, Wood's metal
anniversary: 5 tenth
can eater: 4 goat
combining form: 5 stann- 6 stanno- 7 stannic-
ear: 6 asonia
ender: 4 horn, type, work 5 smith, stone 7 selling
lizzie: 3 car 4 auto 10 automobile
ore: 8 stannite
organ: 3 ear
plate: 4 tain
remove from a ~: 5 uncan
tin __: 3 ash, can, ear, god, hat 4 fish, foil, pest 5 pants, plate 6 lizzie, pyrite, spirit 7 soldier
tin-__: 3 pan, pot 5 white
__ tin: 3 pie 5 block 6 baking
Tin __: 3 Cup, Man, Men
Tin __ Alley: 3 Pan
Tin __, The: 4 Drum, Star 5 Flute
Tina: 4 Cole 5 Brown 6 Louise, Turner 7 Sinatra, Yothers 8 Majorino, Weymouth
Tina Marie (1955 song) artist: Perry Como
tinamou: 4 bird
Tinbergen: 3 Jan 8 Nikolaas
Tinbergen, Jan: 8 Nobelist 9 economist
Tinbergen, Nikolaas: 8 Nobelist
Tin Can Tree author: Anne Tyler
tinct: 3 dye, hue 4 tone 5 color, shade, stain, tinge 7 colored, pigment 8 coloring, flavored
tincture: 3 dye, hue 4 odor, tint 5 color, stain, tinge, trace 7 pigment 8 infusion, medicine 10 medication
Tin Cup (1996 film)
cast: Kevin Costner, Don Johnson, Cheech Marin, Rene Russo
director: Ron Shelton
tinder: 5 twigs 6 amadou 8 kindling
ender: 3 box
Tinderbox, The author: Hans Christian Andersen
Tin Drum, The author: Günter Grass
tine: 3 bug 5 point, prong 6 insect
tool with ~ s: 4 fork 5 spork 7 trident 9 pitchfork
tinea: 6 insect 8 ringworm
tined: 5 forky, sharp 6 forked
tineid: 4 moth
Tin Flute, The author: Gabrielle Roy
ting-__: 5 a-ling
tinge: 3 bit, dye, hue, nib 4 cast, dash, drop, hint, lick, tint, tone, wash 5 color, imbue, pinch, savor, shade, smack, stain, taste, tinct, touch, trace 6 nuance, shadow, strain, streak 7 modicum, pigment, soupçon, suffuse, whisper 8 colorant, coloring, dyestuff, infusion, jaundice, saturate, tincture 9 suspicion, undertone 10 coloration, complexion, impregnate, infiltrate, intimation, smattering, sprinkling, suggestion
with: 5 admix
tingle: 4 itch 5 creep, itchy, sting, throb 6 shiver, thrill, tickle, tinkle 7 prickle, twitter 9 sensation
tingling: 4 itch, numb 5 itchy
__-tingling: 5 spine
tingly: 4 numb 5 itchy
Ting, Samuel: 8 Nobelist 9 physicist
tinhorn: 4 punk 5 cheap, minor 7 gambler 9 small-time

tiniest: 5 least 7 minimum
tinker: 3 fix, toy 4 mess, play 6 dabble, doodle, fiddle, monkey, puddle, putter, repair, tamper 8 fool with, mess with 9 muck about, take apart 10 fiddle with, mess around, play around, trifle with
with: 6 adjust
Tinker Bell: 5 fairy 6 sprite
Tinker, Grant spouse: Mary Tyler Moore
tinker's __: 3 dam 4 damn, weed
Tinker, Tailor, Soldier, Spy author: John le Carré
Tinker to __ to Chance: 5 Evers
Tinkertoy alternative: 4 Lego
tinkle: 4 ding, ring, ting 5 chime, chink, clink, plink, sound 6 jangle, jingle, murmur, tingle
Tinky Winky: 9 Teletubby
Tinley Park: 4 city, town
locale: 8 Illinois
Tin Man
need: 3 oil 5 heart
portrayer: Jack Haley
tool: 3 axe
Tin Man (1974 song) artist: America
Tin Men (1987 film)
cast: Danny DeVito, Richard Dreyfuss, Barbara Hershey, John Mahoney
director: Barry Levinson
tinny: 4 thin 5 cheap 6 flimsy, shoddy
not ~: 6 strong 7 durable
sound: 4 ping
tiñosa: 4 fish
Tin Pan Alley
org.: 3 BMI 5 ASCAP
product: 4 song, tune
Tin Pan Alley (1940 film)
cast: Alice Faye, Betty Grable, Jack Oakie
director: Walter Lang
tinsel: 5 gaudy, showy 6 bauble, flashy, garish, tawdry 7 glitter 10 decoration
strand: 6 icicle
time: 4 Noel, yule 8 December, yuletide 9 Christmas
use ~: 6 bedeck
Tinseltown
see Hollywood, Los Angeles
Tin Star, The (1957 film)
cast: Henry Fonda, Betsy Palmer, Anthony Perkins
director: Anthony Mann
tint: 3 dye, hue 4 cast, dash, glow, hint, tone, wash 5 color, flush, paint, rinse, shade, stain, taint, tinge, touch, trace 6 affect, chroma, redden 7 pigment, shading 8 coloring, jaundice, tincture 9 influence 10 coloration, complexion, luminosity, suggestion
starter: 4 aqua
see also color, dye
Tintagel Head: 4 cape
locale: 7 England 8 Cornwall
tinted windows reduce it: 5 glare
Tintern Abbey author: William Wordsworth
Tintern Abbey's river: 3 Wye
__ Tin Tin: 3 Rin
tintinnabulate: 4 peal, ring 5 chime 6 tinkle
tintinnabulation: 4 ding, peal, ring 5 knell 8 ding-dong
Tintoretto, Jacopo: 6 artist 7 Italian, painter
tintype: 5 photo 7 picture 10 photograph
color: 5 sepia
tinware: 4 tole
Tin Woodman
see Tin Man
tiny: 3 wee 4 baby, itsy, mini, puny 5 bitsy, bitty, dinky, dwarf, eensy, light, small, teeny, weeny 6 atomic, bantam, little, midget, minute, peewee, petite, pocket, slight, teensy 7 cramped, minikin, minimum 8 atomical, atomlike, trifling 9 fairylike, itsy-bitsy, itty-bitty, miniature, minuscule, pint-sized, undersize 10 diminutive, minuscular, negligible, pocket-size, teeny-weeny, vest-pocket
amount: 3 bit, dab, jot, ppm, sip 4 atom, drib, iota, mote, whit 5 crumb, grain, ounce, pinch, shred, speck, touch 6 morsel, sliver, tidbit
bug: 3 ant 4 gnat, mite 5 midge
mark: 3 dot 5 fleck 6 tittle
Tiny __: 3 Tim 5 Alice
Tiny Alice author: Edward Albee
Tiny Bubbles singer: 5 Don Ho
Tiny Tim
born: Herbert Khaury
instrument: 3 uke 7 ukulele
song: Tip-Toe Thru' the Tulips With Me (1968)
Tioga: 4 city, town
locale: 5 Texas
Tiomkin, Dimitri: 7 Russian 8 composer
film score: The Alamo
Dial M for Murder
Friendly Persuasion
Giant
The Guns of Navarone
The High and the Mighty
High Noon
It's a Wonderful Life
Meet John Doe
Mr. Smith Goes to Washington
The Old Man and the Sea
Rio Bravo
Strangers on a Train
Town Without Pity
tip: 3 bug, cap, cue, end, fee, nib, nip, top 4 apex, bang, bend, butt, buzz, cant, cash, clew, clue, cusp, dope, dump, edge, gift, give, head, heel, hint, info, lead, lean, list, news, peak, perc, perk, pour, stub, tilt, warn, word 5 bonus, crown, empty, money, point, shift, slant, slope, spill, spire, steer, upend, upset 6 advice, advise, careen, dollar, height, one-way, prompt, reward, summit, topple, unload, upturn, vertex 7 capsize, caution, handout, hot lead, incline, inkling, lookout, overset, pointer, recline, steeple, suggest, warning, whisper 8 forecast, forewarn, gratuity, heel over, mnemonic, overturn, turn over 9 extremity, knock over, knowledge, lagniappe, pourboire, something, sweetener 10 honorarium, perquisite, prediction, recompense, suggestion, topple over
ender: 3 toe, top 4 cart, ster 5 staff
give a ~ to: 4 tell, warn 5 alert, brief, edify, teach 6 advise, clue in, fill in, impart, inform, notify, reward 7 apprise, caution, counsel, educate, let in on, let know 8 acquaint, forewarn
leave no ~ to: 5 stiff
off: 4 tell, tout, warn 5 alert 6 advise, clue in, inform, notify 7 apprise, apprize, caution, let in on, let know, prewarn, suggest 8 forewarn, intimate
of the ~: 6 apical
one's hand: 4 show, tell 6 expose, reveal 7 divulge, lay bare, lay open, uncover 8 disclose 9 make known
one's hat to: 4 hail 5 cheer, greet, honor 6 praise, salute 7 applaud, commend 10 compliment
one's topper: 4 doff 5 unhat
over: 4 cant, fall 5 spill, upend, upset 6 topple 7 capsize 8 overturn
(over): 4 keel 6 topple
seller: 4 tout
starter: 4 wing 6 finger, silver
to one side: 3 sag 4 lean, list, rock, sway, tilt 5 lurch, slant, slope 6 careen, totter, wobble 7 incline, stagger
tip __: 5 sheet
__ tip: 4 foul, wing
Tip: 6 O'Neill
Tip-__: 4 Toes
tip-off: 3 cue 4 dope, hint, news, word 6 notice 7 inkling, warning, whisper 8 forecast 9 knowledge 10 prediction, suggestion
__ tip of one's tongue: 5 on the
tip of the __: 7 iceberg
Tip on a Dead Jockey (1957 film)
cast: Dorothy Malone, Gia Scala, Robert Taylor
director: Richard Thorpe
tip one's __: 3 cap, hat 4 hand
Tippecanoe: 5 river
locale: 7 Indiana
__-tip pen: 4 felt
Tipper: 4 Gore
Tipperary locale: 4 Eire, Erin 7 Ireland
tippet: 4 cape, wrap 5 scarf
Tippi: 6 Hedren
daughter: 7 Melanie
tipple: 5 drink 6 guzzle, imbibe
tippler: 3 sot 4 lush, wino 5 souse, toper 6 barfly, bibber 7 guzzler, tosspot
debt: 6 bar tab
tippy: 6 wabbly, wobbly 8 unstable, unsteady
tippy-__: 3 toe
tips: 6 income 9 emolument
tip-sheet buyer: 6 bettor 7 wagerer
tipster: 4 fink, tout 8 informer 9 informant
tipsy: 3 lit 4 high 5 dazed, dizzy, drunk, happy, merry, oiled, tight, woozy 6 addled, loaded, mellow, stewed 7 fuddled, reeling 8 besotted, unsteady 9 irrigated 10 inebriated, in one's cups
tip the __: 5 scale 6 scales
tiptoe: 4 skip, step 5 steal 9 pussyfoot 10 walk on eggs
move on ~: 5 creep, slink
Tip-Toes: 7 musical
songwriter: 8 Gershwin
Tip-Toe Thru' the Tulips With Me (1968 song) artist: Tiny Tim
tiptop: 3 ace, def, rad 4 aces, acme, A-one, apex, best, boss, braw, cool, dece, fine, gear, keen, neat, nice, peak, phat, tuff 5 dandy, ducky, elite, grand, great, marvy, neato, nobby, prime, slick, super, swell 6 apogee, bang on, bang-up, bonzer, bosker, choice, divine, dreamy, far-out, gnarly, groovy, height, lovely, peachy, slap-up, spot on, superb, terrif, unreal, whizzo, wicked, zenith 7 amazing, awesome, capital, corking, perfect, ripping, skookum, stellar, sublime 8 champion, dazzling, especial, eximious, fabulous, five-star, four-star, frabjous, glorious, heavenly, jim-dandy, slam-bang, smashing, splendid, standout, sterling, stickout, superior, terrific, very good, wondrous 9 bodacious, Endsville, excellent, exemplary, exquisite, first-rate, high-grade, hunky-dory, marvelous, sollicker, wonderful 10 first-class, hotsy-totsy, jack-a-dandy, out of sight, peachy-keen, phenomenal, remarkable, stupendous, super-duper
tirade: 4 rant 5 abuse, anger 6 screed, sermon, speech 7 censure, dispute, lecture, ranting 8 berating, diatribe, harangue, jeremiad, outburst 9 invective, philippic 10 revilement, upbraiding, vocalizing
deliver a ~: 4 rage, rant, rave, yell 5 storm
tiramisu: 4 cake 7 dessert, Italian
Tirana: 4 city, town 7 capital
locale: 7 Albania
Tirane: 4 city, town 7 capital
locale: 7 Albania
tire: 3 irk, sag, sap, tax, try, vex 4 bore, bush, drop, fade, fail, flag, fold, jade, pain, pall, poop, sink, wane, wear, wilt, yawn 5 annoy, blunt, crawl, drain, droop, faint, recap, spare, weary, wheel, worry 6 deject, harass, impair, radial, soften, strain, weaken 7 bias-ply, burn out, deplete, depress, disgust, exhaust, fatigue, give out, go stale, overtax, poop out, retread, slacken, vitiate, wear out 8 collapse, dispirit, distress, enervate, enfeeble, irritate, overwork, peter out, slow down, wear down 9 attenuate, displease, prostrate, undermine, whitewall 10 debilitate, devitalize, dishearten, exasperate, overburden, overstrain, put to sleep
attachment: 3 lug, rim 5 valve 6 hubcap, lug nut
bicycle ~ feature: 5 spoke
brand: 5 Kelly 6 Cooper, Dunlop 7 General, Pirelli 8 Goodrich, Goodyear, Michelin, Uniroyal 9 Firestone 11 Bridgestone
contents: 3 air
do a ~ job: 5 align, aline
ender: 4 some
extra ~: 5 spare
fixed-up ~: 5 recap
leaky ~ sound: 3 sss 4 ssss
like an old ~: 4 bald
out: 5 drain, weary 7 exhaust, fatigue, frazzle 8 enervate, enfeeble
(out): 4 poop 5 peter 6 tucker
part: 4 belt, tube 5 tread
place for a ~ swing: 4 limb
pressure meas.: 3 psi
spare ~: 4 flab 5 belly 6 paunch 7 stomach 9 bay window
tool: 4 jack, pump
town: 5 Akron
track: 3 rut
trouble: 4 flat 8 puncture
tire __: 4 iron 5 chain
__ tire: 4 flat, snow 5 spare 6 belted, radial 7 balloon, bias-ply, studded
tired: 3 old 4 beat, dull, lazy, limp, sick, worn 5 all in, bored, corny, empty, faint, fed up, irked, jaded, musty, seedy, spent, stale, trite, weary, wiped 6 asleep, bleary, bushed, dished, done in, droopy, drowsy, pooped, shabby, sleepy, wasted 7 annoyed, done for, drained, haggard, insipid, run-down, worn out 8 careworn, consumed, dog-tired, drooping, fatigued, finished, flagging, outdated, outmoded, wiped out 9 burned out, enervated, exhausted, hackneyed, irritated, out-of-date, overtaxed, played out, prostrate 10 broken-down, collapsing, distressed, dullsville, half-asleep, knocked out, on the ropes, overworked, petered out, prostrated, threadbare, warmed-over
appear ~: 4 yawn
get ~: 4 fade, flag, jade 5 droop, weary 8 languish, peter out, slow down

(of): 4 sick
partner: 4 sick
___-tired: 3 dog
___ Tired: 4 I'm So
tiredness: 6 anemia 7 anaemia, fatigue, languor 9 lassitude 10 exhaustion
Tired of Waiting for You (1965 song)
artist: Kinks
tireless: 5 eager, grind, hyper, perky 6 active 7 jumping, on the go 8 diligent, resolute, sedulous, vigorous 9 energetic, incessant, laborious, steadfast, strenuous, unwearied 10 determined, persistent, undeterred, unflagging, unwearying
Tiresias: 4 seer 5 Greek
tiresome: 4 drag, dull, flat, hard, yawn 5 heavy, hefty, ho-hum, tough, unfun, vapid, yawny 6 boring, dreary, jading, jejune, stuffy, trying, uncool 7 arduous, humdrum, irksome, lengthy, nowhere, onerous, operose, tedious, too much, wearing 8 a bit much, annoying, boresome, dragging, drudging, exacting, wearying 9 demanding, difficult, fatiguing, laborious, strenuous, vexatious, wearisome 10 burdensome, dullsville, enervating, enervative, exhausting, irritating, monotonous, oppressive, unrelieved
become ~: 4 bore, pall, wear
one: 4 bore, drag, pest, pill
tiresomeness: 3 rut 5 ennui 6 tedium 7 boredom 8 monotony 10 dreariness, insipidity, uniformity
Tiriac: 3 Ion
Tirich Mir: 4 peak 5 mount 8 mountain
locale: 4 Asia 8 Pakistan
tiring: 4 hard 6 taxing 7 onerous, tedious 10 enervating, exhausting
tiro: 3 cub 4 naif, pleb 5 newie, plebe, pupil 6 newbie, novice, rookie 7 amateur, dabbler, learner, new hand, recruit, trainee 8 beginner, initiate, neophyte, newcomer, putterer 9 fledgling, greenhorn, new member, novitiate 10 apprentice, catechumen, dilettante, tenderfoot
Tirtoff, Romain de: 4 Erté 6 artist 7 Russian
'tis
answer: 5 'taint
in the past: 4 'twas
Tisa: 6 Farrow
sister: 3 Mia
tisane: 3 tea 7 herb tea 8 beverage 9 herbal tea
'Tis a pity!: 4 alas 5 alack 6 too bad
Tisdale: 4 city, town
locale: 4 Sask. 6 Canada
Tiselius, Arne: 7 chemist 8 Nobelist
'Tis good to keep ___ egg: 5 a nest
Tisha: 8 Campbell, Sterling
Tishah ___: 3 b'Av
Tish author: Mary Roberts Rinehart
Tishri: 5 month 6 Hebrew
predecessor: 4 Elul
successor: 7 Heshvan
Tisiphone: 4 Fury
sister: 6 Alecto 7 Megaera
...'tis of ___: 4 thee
Tissot, James: 6 artist, French 7 painter
tissue: 3 web 4 tela 5 paper, telae 6 muscle 8 gift wrap, membrane
additive: 4 aloe
body ~: 4 tela 5 flesh, telae
build new ~: 4 heal
combining form: 4 hist- 5 histi-, histo-, -plasm 6 histio-
connective ~: 6 fascia
connector: 6 areola, areole
fluid: 5 lymph
of ~: 5 telar
plant ~: 5 xylem 6 cambia
separators: 5 septa
soft ~: 4 flab
target: 4 tear 5 tears
tissue ___: 5 paper 7 culture
___ tissue: 6 carbon, facial 7 adipose, elastic, primary
tissuelike: 4 soft, thin 5 filmy, gauzy, light, sheer 8 delicate, finespun, gossamer
Tisza: 5 river
locale: 7 Hungary 10 Yugoslavia
tit: 4 bird
ender: 3 bit 4 lark, mice 5 mouse
for tat: 7 revenge 8 exchange, reprisal 9 interplay, vengeance
give ~ for tat: 5 spite 6 avenge 7 get even, pay back, revenge 9 retaliate
starter: 3 tom
tit ___ tat: 3 for
titan: 5 giant, whale 8 colossus 9 leviathan
Titan: 4 ICBM, moon, Rhea, Thia 5 Atlas, Coeus, Crius, Dione 6 Cronus, Phoebe, Tethys, Themis 7 Eurybia, Iapetus, missile, Oceanus 8 Hyperion 9 Menoetius, Mnemosyne 10 Epimetheus, footballer, Prometheus
locale: 4 silo
parent of ~: 4 Gaea 6 Uranus
planet: 6 Saturn
rival: 3 Jet, Ram 4 Bear, Bill, Colt, Lion 5 Brown, Chief, Eagle, Giant, Niner, Raven, Saint, Texan 6 Bengal, Bronco, Cowboy, Falcon, Jaguar, Packer, Raider, Viking 7 Charger, Dolphin, Panther, Patriot, Redskin, Seahawk, Steeler 8 Cardinal 9 Buccaneer
rocket stage: 5 Agena
titania: 3 gem 8 gemstone
Titania: 4 moon 6 sprite
planet: 6 Uranus
spouse: 6 Oberon
titanic: 3 big 4 huge, vast 5 giant, great, jumbo, large 6 mighty 7 hulking, immense, mammoth, massive, sizable 8 colossal, enormous, gigantic, king-size, oversize, sizeable, towering, whapping, whopping 9 herculean, humongous, monstrous, overlarge 10 gargantuan, monumental, prodigious, stupendous, tremendous
Titanic: 4 boat, ship 5 liner
undoing: 4 berg 7 iceberg
Titanic (1953 film)
cast: Barbara Stanwyck, Robert Wagner, Clifton Webb
director: Jean Negulesco
Titanic (1997 film)
cast: Kathy Bates, Leonardo DiCaprio, Frances Fisher, Bill Paxton, David Warner, Kate Winslet, Billy Zane
director: James Cameron
titanium: 5 metal 7 element
alloy: 7 nitinol
ore: 8 ilmenite
titanium ___: 5 oxide, white 7 dioxide
titanothere: 10 rhinoceros
Titans
home: 9 Tennessee
org.: 3 AFC, NFL
sport: 8 football
Titans, The author: André Maurois
Titan, The author: Theodore Dreiser
tit-for-tat: 6 in kind
tithe: 3 tax 4 levy 5 tenth 6 donate 8 offering
titi: 5 shrub 7 primate
relative: 3 ape 4 saki 5 chimp, drill, jocko, lemur, loris, magot, orang, potto, shrew 6 aye-aye, baboon, Bandar, galago, gelada, gibbon, grivet, guenon, howler, langur, macaco, monkey, rhesus, uakari, vervet 7 colobus, gorilla, guereza, hoolock, macaque, sapajou, siamang, tamarin, tarsier 8 bush baby, capuchin, mandrill, mangabey, marmoset, talapoin 9 orangutan 10 Barbary ape, chimpanzee, orangutang
titian: 3 red 5 color 6 orange
Titian: 6 artist 7 Italian, painter
work: 3 art
Titicaca: 4 lago, lake
locale: 4 Peru 7 Bolivia
titillate: 4 grab, hook, send 5 amuse, tease 6 arouse, excite, please, thrill, tickle, turn on 7 grapple, palpate, provoke 8 interest, intrigue, switch on 9 entertain, fascinate, stimulate, tantalize 10 tickle pink
titillation: 8 pleasure
titivate: 5 preen, primp
titlark: 4 bird
title: 3 dub, due, tab, tag 4 call, dame, deed, dibs, duke, earl, head, miss, name, role, sign, term 5 baron, brand, claim, close, count, crest, crown, label, medal, merit, nomen, power, prize, proof, right, style 6 banner, degree, desert, handle, header, laurel, legend, ribbon, rights, rubric 7 address, baptize, caption, dauphin, duchess, epithet, heading, holding, license, moniker 8 baroness, christen, cognomen, countess, document, headline, monicker, pretense, property, streamer, subtitle 9 authority, designate, honorific, occupancy, ownership, privilege, pseudonym, sobriquet 10 commission, decoration, denominate, nom de plume, possession, pretension, salutation
ender: 6 holder
proof of ~: 4 deed
title ___: 4 bout, deed, page, role 5 entry 6 lining 7 catalog 9 catalogue
___ title: 3 tax 4 good, half 5 short, sound 7 running, working
titled: 5 elite, lofty, noble 8 elevated, imperial, well-born 9 honorable, patrician 10 upper-class
man: 4 duke, earl, lord, peer 5 baron 7 marquis 8 marquess, viscount
woman: 4 dame 7 duchess 8 baroness, countess
titleholder: 5 champ, owner 6 victor, winner 8 champion
titleless one: 4 pleb 7 peasant 8 commoner, plebeian
titmouse: 4 bird
home: 4 nest
relative: 9 chickadee
___ titmouse: 6 tufted
Tito: 4 Broz 6 Puente 7 Jackson
titter: 4 ha-ha 5 laugh, te-hee 6 cackle, giggle, guffaw, hee-hee 7 break up, chortle, chuckle, crack up, snicker, snigger 8 laughter
tittle: 3 dot, jot 4 iota, mite 5 grain, speck
tittle-___: 6 tattle
Tittle, Y.A.: 2 QB 5 Giant
sport: 8 football
titular: 7 nominal 8 honorary 10 in name only
Titus: 4 book 5 Roman, saint 6 Caesar
follower: 8 Philemon
preceder: 7 Timothy
Titus (1999 film)
cast: Alan Cumming, Anthony Hopkins, Jessica Lange, Jonathan Rhys Meyers
director: Julie Traynor
Titus Andronicus: 4 play
author: 11 Shakespeare
role: 5 Aaron 6 Chiron, Lucius, Mutius, Tamora 7 Alarbus, Lavinia, Martius, Publius, Quintus 8 Aemilius 9 Bassianus, Demetrius
Titusville: 4 city, town
locale: 7 Florida
tityra: 4 bird
titzu: 4 wind 5 flute
origin: 5 China
Tiu worshiper: 4 Celt 6 Celtic
Tiverton's river: 3 Exe
Tiv home: 6 Africa 7 Nigeria
Tiwa: 6 Indian 7 Amerind
tix: 6 ducats, passes
Tixtla: 4 city, town
locale: 6 Mexico 8 Guerrero
Tizayuca: 4 city, town
locale: 6 Mexico 7 Hidalgo
Tizimín: 4 city, town
locale: 6 Mexico 7 Yucatán
tizzy: 4 flap, huff, snit, stew 5 hoo-ha, upset 6 dither, frenzy, lather 9 agitation
in a ~: 4 agog 5 het up, manic, tense, upset 6 jangly 7 abashed, anxious, excited, frantic 8 fluttery, frenetic, frenzied 9 perturbed 10 distressed, infuriated
___ tizzy: 3 in a
T.J. ___: 6 Hooker
T.J. Hooker (ABC/CBS drama)
cast: James Darren (Off. Jim Corrigan)
Heather Locklear (Off. Stacy Sheridan)
William Shatner (Sgt. T.J. Hooker)
Adrian Zmed (Off. Vince Romano)
TKO caller: 3 ref 7 referee
Tl: 4 elem. 7 element 8 thallium
81 for ~: 4 at. no.
Tlapa: 4 city, town
locale: 6 Mexico 8 Guerrero
Tlaxcala: 4 city, town 5 state
city: 5 Tetla 6 Contla, Tlaxco 7 Apizaco, Panotla 8 Xaloztoc 9 Huamantla, Zacatelco
locale: 6 Mexico
Tlaxco: 4 city, town
locale: 6 Mexico 8 Tlaxcala
Tlaxiaco: 4 city, town
locale: 6 Mexico, Oaxaca
TLC: 7 channel, concern 9 attention 10 solicitude
alternative: 3 BET, CMT, MTV, PAX, TBS, TNN, TNT, USA 4 ESPN, HGTV 5 A and E, C-SPAN, Style 6 Noggin, Tech TV, TV Land 7 Court TV, Ovation, SoapNet 8 Lifetime
dispenser: 2 RN 3 LPN 5 carer, doter, nurse
part: 4 care 6 loving, tender
TLC (rock group)
members: Watkins, Lopes, Thomas
song: Ain't 2 Proud 2 Beg (1992)
Baby-Baby-Baby (1992)
Creep (1994)
Diggin' on You (1995)
No Scrubs (1999)
Red Light Special (1995)
Unpretty (1999)
Waterfalls (1995)
What About Your Friends (1992)
Tlingit: 5 tribe 6 Indian 7 Amerind 8 language
home: 6 Alaska
Tm: 4 elem. 7 element, thulium
69 for ~: 4 at. no.
T-man: 3 agt., Fed 5 agent 8 revenuer
TMC: 7 channel
alternative: 3 AMC, HBO, IFC, SHO 4 Flix 5 Bravo, Starz 6 Encore 7 Cinemax 8 Showtime, Sundance

T-Men (1947 film)
cast: June Lockhart, Dennis O'Keefe, Alfred Ryder
director: Anthony Mann
TM, where to register a: 3 PTO
TN
see Tennessee
__ T. Nelson: 5 Craig
T-note relative: 2 CD
tnpk.: 2 rd. 3 hwy., rte.
TNT: 7 channel 9 explosive
alternative: 3 BET, CMT, MTV, PAX, TBS, TLC, TNN, USA 4 ESPN, HGTV 5 A and E, C-SPAN, Style 6 Noggin, Tech TV, TV Land 7 Court TV, Ovation, SoapNet 8 Lifetime
ingredient: 5 niter
mixture: 6 amatol
part: 3 tri 5 nitro 7 toluene
use ~: 5 blast, wreck 7 explode 8 demolish, dynamite
to: 5 until
in Scottish: 3 tae
to __: 3 wit 4 a man, a tee, boot, date 5 a turn, blame, spare
to __ and to hold: 4 have
to __ intents and purposes: 3 all
to __ nothing of: 3 say
to __ of: 5 speak
to __ phrase: 5 coin a
to __ purpose: 4 good 6 little
to __ the band: 4 beat
to __ the least: 3 say
to __ with: 5 start
__ to: 3 due, get, has, hop, lay, lie, put, see, set 4 come, fall, look, next, so as, take, turn 5 add up, alive, bring, cater, ought, owing, prior, privy, put it, refer, stand 6 amount, lead up, thanks
__-to: 3 set 4 lean 7 talking
...to __ few: 5 name a
To __: 3 F.S.O., M.L.S. 4 Asra 5 Celia, Helen, Homer, Sleep, Zante 6 Autumn 7 Isadore
To __ a Mockingbird: 4 Kill
To __ and a bone...: 4 a rag
To __ and Back: 4 Hell
To __ and Have Not: 4 Have
To __ a Thief: 5 Catch
To __ breeze unfurled: 6 April's
To __ For: 3 Die
To __, From Prison: 6 Althea
To __ go where no man...: 6 boldly
To __ His Own: 4 Each
To __ is human: 3 err
To __ it may concern: 4 whom
To __ Mockingbird: 5 Kill a
To __ not to...: 4 be or
To __ own self...: 5 thine
To __ their golden eyes: 3 ope
To __ the Truth: 4 Tell
To __, With Love: 3 Sir
to a __: 3 man, tee 4 turn 5 fault, woman 6 degree
to a __-thee-well: 4 fare
__ to Abelard: 6 Eloisa
__ to account: 4 call
__ to a crisp: 5 burnt 6 burned
__ to a customer: 3 one
toad: 3 cad, cur, rat 4 heel, worm 5 knave, rogue, scamp, skunk, snake, sneak, swine 6 anuran, bad guy, hopper, wretch 7 lowlife, paddock, stinker, tadpole 9 amphibian, scoundrel, spadefoot 10 blackguard, natterjack
combining form: 7 batrach- 8 batracho-
ender: 4 fish, flax 5 eater, stone, stool
feature: 4 wart
group: 4 knot
home: 4 pond
like a ~: 5 warty
relative: 4 frog
__ toad: 4 bell, tree, true 6 horned, ribbed, tailed 7 Fowler's, midwife, Surinam
toadeater: 5 sheep 6 fawner, flunky, jackal, lackey, minion, stooge, yes man 7 Babbitt, doormat, flunkey, lacquey 8 adulator, assenter, bootlick, courtier, emulator, groveler, kowtower, parasite, servitor, truckler, yeasayer 9 applauder, flatterer, sycophant 10 bootlicker, conformist, handshaker
toadflax: 4 weed
toadies: 6 claque
toadstool: 5 plant 6 fungus
unlike a ~: 6 edible
toady: 3 bow 4 fawn 5 cower, crawl, kneel, kotow, sheep 6 fawner, flunky, grovel, jackal, kowtow, lackey, minion, stooge, submit, yes man 7 Babbitt, doormat, flatter, flunkey, lacquey 8 adulator, assenter, bootlick, courtier, emulator, fawn over, groveler, kowtower, kowtow to, parasite, servitor, truckler, yeasayer 9 applauder, flatterer, sycophant 10 bootlicker, conformist, handshaker
act the ~: 5 kotow 6 kowtow
like a ~: 7 servile
to a fare-__-well: 4 thee
__ to a halt: 5 bring, grind
__ to a head: 4 come
__-to-air: 6 ground 7 surface
__ to a Kill: 5 A View
__ to a Kiss: 7 Prelude
__ to Alaska: 5 North
to all __ and purposes: 7 intents
To All the Girls I've Loved Before (1984 song)
artist: Julio Iglesias, Willie Nelson
To a Louse author: Robert Burns
To Althea from Prison author: Richard Lovelace
__ to America: 6 Coming
To a Mountain Daisy: 3 ode 4 poem
author: Robert Burns
To a Mouse: 3 ode 4 poem
author: Robert Burns
To an Athlete Dying Young author: A.E. Housman
to and __: 3 fro
__ to a Nightingale: 3 Ode
To a Poor Old Woman: 4 poem
author: William Carlos Williams
__ to arms: 4 call
To a Skylark: 3 ode 4 poem
author: 7 Shelley
__ to a Small Planet: 5 Visit
To Asra author: 9 Coleridge
toast: 3 dry 4 burn, cook, heat, rusk, warm 5 bread, brown, crisp, drink, grill, honor, parch, prost, roast, salud, salut, skoal 6 cheers, pledge, prosit, salute 7 drink to, l'chayim, lehayim, tribute 8 ceremony, here's how, lechayim, libation, proposal 9 happy days, sentiment 10 compliment, here's to you
Cockney ~ start: 4 'eres
edge: 5 crust
ender: 6 master 8 mistress
finish the ~: 5 drink
French ~ word: 5 santé 6 votree
in French: 5 salut
In German: 5 prost
in Hebrew: 6 l'chaim
in Portuguese: 5 saude
in Scandinavia: 5 skoal
in Spanish: 5 salud
like ~: 5 brown, crisp 6 crusty 7 crumbly, crunchy
necessity: 5 drink, glass 6 goblet
of the town: 3 VIP 4 hero 5 celeb 6 big gun 7 big name 8 luminary 9 celebrity
Scandinavian ~: 5 skoal
sound of a ~: 5 clink
topper: 3 jam 4 oleo 5 jelly 6 butter
where ~ s are proposed: 4 dais
word: 3 mud 6 health
__ toast: 4 milk 5 Melba 6 French
To a Steam Roller poet: 5 Moore
Toasted Oatmeal: 6 cereal
competitor: 3 Kix 4 Life, Trix 5 Kashi, Quisp, Total 6 Kaboom, Muesli, Oreo O's, Pablum, Smacks 7 All-Bran, Crispix, Harmony, Hunny B's, Mueslix, Oat Bran, Pokemon 8 Boo Berry, Cheerios, Corn Chex, Corn Pops, Fiber One, Rice Chex, Special K, Uncle Sam, Wheaties 9 Alpha Bits, Apple Zaps, Grape Nuts, Honey Comb, Just Right, Wheat Chex 10 Apple Jacks, Bran Flakes, Cap'n Crunch, Cocoa Puffs, Froot Loops, Mini-Wheats, Nutri-Grain, Puffed Rice, Quaker Oats, Smart Start 11 Cocoa Blasts, Cookie Crisp, Golden Crisp, Lucky Charms, Puffed Wheat, Sweet Crunch, Waffle Crisp
toaster __: 4 oven 6 pastry
toastmaster: 2 MC 4 host 5 emcee 7 hostess 10 introducer
Toast of New York, The (1937 film)
cast: Edward Arnold, Frances Farmer, Cary Grant
director: Rowland V. Lee
Toast of New York, The director: 3 Lee
toasty: 3 hot 4 cosy, cozy, warm 6 sultry 7 boiling, summery 8 broiling, ovenlike, sizzling, tropical 10 sweltering
__ to a T: 3 fit 4 suit
__ to a turn: 4 done
__ to Autumn: 3 Ode
To Autumn: 3 ode 4 poem
author: 5 Keats
To a Waterfowl: 3 ode 4 poem
author: 6 Bryant
tobacco: 4 shag 6 burley
dryer: 4 oast
Tobacco Road author: Erskine Caldwell
character: 3 Ada, Lov 4 Dude 6 Bensey, Bessie, Jeeter, Lester
Toback: 5 James
Tobago: 3 isl. 4 isle 6 island
neighbor: 4 Trin. 8 Trinidad
__ to Bali: 4 Road
__-to-basics: 4 back
__ to Bataan: 4 Back
to be
in French: 4 être
in Italian: 3 ser
in Latin: 4 esse
in Spanish: 3 ser 5 estar
like ~: 3 irr. 5 irreg. 9 irregular
part of ~: 3 are, was 4 been, were
to be __: 4 fair, sure
Tobe: 6 Hooper
To be __...: 5 or not
To Be a Lover (1986 song) artist: Billy Idol
__ to bear: 5 bring
to beat the __: 4 band
__ to Beauty: 3 Ode
__ to be born...: 5 A time
__ to bed: 3 put 5 And so
__ to Be Happy: 5 I Want
__ to Be Hard: 4 Easy
__ to Be in Love: 5 I Need
__ to Believe: 6 Reason
To Be or Not to Be (1942 film)
cast: Jack Benny, Carole Lombard, Robert Stack
director: Ernst Lubitsch
To Be or Not to Be (1983 film): 6 remake
cast: Anne Bancroft, Mel Brooks, Charles Durning, Jose Ferrer
director: Mel Brooks
dog: 5 Mutki
__ to Berlin: 7 Goodbye
Tobermory author: 4 Saki
__ to be seen: 7 remains
__ to Be There: 3 Got
__ to be tied: 3 fit
__ to Be Wild: 4 Born
__ to Be With You: 4 Born, Nice
To Be with You (1992 song) artist: Mr. Big
Tobey: 7 Maguire
__ to Be You: 5 It Had
To Be Young, Gifted and Black
author: Lorraine Hansberry
Tobias: 5 Asser 6 Andrew, George 8 Smollett
Tobias, George: 5 actor
film: Objective, Burma! (1945) The Set-Up (1949) The Seven Little Foys (1955)
__ to Billie Joe: 3 Ode
__ to Billy Joe: 3 Ode
Tobin, James: 8 Nobelist 9 economist
tobira: 5 shrub
__ to black: 4 fade
Toblerone: 5 candy, Swiss 9 chocolate
__ to blows: 4 come
toboggan: 4 sled 5 slide 6 bobcat
area: 5 chute 6 ice run
cousin: 4 luge
go by ~: 5 slide
tobogganing: 5 sport
Tobol: 5 river
locale: 6 Russia 10 Kazakhstan
__-to book: 3 how
__ to Bountiful, The: 4 Trip
Tobruk: 4 city, town
locale: 5 Libya
...to buy __ hog: 4 a fat
...to buy __ pig: 4 a fat
toby: 3 jug, mug 5 stein
contents: 3 ale 4 beer, brew 5 stout 6 porter
Toby: 5 Keith, Tyler 6 Harrah
Toby author: Sidney Sheldon
__ to Byzantium: 7 Sailing
To Catch a Thief (1955 film)
cast: Cary Grant, Grace Kelly, Jessie Royce Landis
director: Alfred Hitchcock
toccata: 5 music
Toccata Festiva composer: 6 Barber
Toce: 5 falls 9 waterfall
locale: 5 Italy 8 Piedmont
To Celia author: Ben Jonson
__ to Come: 6 Things
__ to Cook Book, The: 5 I Hate
__-tocopherol: 5 alpha
__ to Creation: 3 Ode
tocsin: 4 bell 5 alarm, alert 6 signal 7 warning
tod: 3 ivy 4 mass 5 clump 6 weight 7 measure
Tod: 8 Browning
__ Tod: 4 Ase's
Toda: 4 city, town
locale: 5 Japan
__ to Dance: 4 Born
today: 3 now 6 at once, modern, recent 7 present 8 promptly, right now, right off, up-to-date 9 at present, currently, forthwith, in this era, presently, right away 10 at this time, aujourd'hui, here and now, the present, this minute
__ today: 4 as of
Today __ a man!: 3 I am
__ Today: 3 USA
__ today, gone...: 4 Here
__ today, hot tamale: 5 Chili
Today's Children: 9 radio show

Today Show, The
chimp: 5 Beebe, Muggs
host: 5 Lauer 6 Gumbel, Pauley 8 Garroway
rival: 3 GMA
weatherman: 5 Roker
Todd: 3 Ann 4 Mike, Tony 6 Duncan, Haynes, Thelma 7 Bridges, Richard, Solondz, Sweeney 8 Rundgren 9 Alexander
Todd, Alexander: 7 chemist 8 Nobelist
toddle: 4 walk 6 waddle 7 saunter
toddler: 3 tot 4 baby, tike, tyke 5 child 6 infant, rug rat 8 juvenile
glassful: 4 wawa
mishap: 5 spill
perch: 3 lap 4 knee
question: 3 why
ritual: 3 nap
school: 4 pre-K
vehicle: 5 trike
watch a ~: 3 sit
wear: 6 diaper
words to a ~: 3 nos 4 noes
__ Todd Lincoln: 4 Mary
toddling: 4 poky 6 draggy 7 gradual, halting, impeded, lagging, languid 8 dilatory, drawn-out, hesitant, plodding, slothful, sluggish 9 leisurely, lethargic, prolonged, snaillike, unhurried 10 deliberate, protracted
Todd, Mary man: 3 Abe 7 Abraham, Lincoln
Todd, Mike spouse: Joan Blondell, Elizabeth Taylor
Todd, Richard: 5 actor
film: The Bohemian Girl (1936)
The Boys (1961)
Chase a Crooked Shadow (1958)
The Dam Busters (1955)
D-Day the Sixth of June (1956)
The Devil's Brother (1933)
Horse Feathers (1932)
A Man Called Peter (1955)
Monkey Business (1931)
Son of a Sailor (1933)
The Story of Robin Hood and His Merrie Men (1952)
The Sword and the Rose (1953)
The Virgin Queen (1955)
Todd, Thelma: 7 actress
Todd, Sweeney street: 5 Fleet
toddy: 4 palm 5 drink 8 beverage
hot ~ spice: 5 clove
toddy __: 4 palm 5 table
__ toddy: 3 hot
To Die For (1995 film)
cast: Matt Dillon, Illeana Douglas, Nicole Kidman, Joaquin Phoenix
director: Gus Van Sant
dog: 6 Walter
__ to differ!: 4 I beg
to-do: 3 row 4 flap, fuss, riot, spat, stir 5 fight, furor, hoo-ha, mania, melee, run-in, scene, stink, storm, whirl 6 bother, bustle, clamor, flurry, fracas, frenzy, hassle, hoopla, hubbub, matter, pother, racket, ruckus, rumpus, tumult, unrest, uproar 7 ferment, quarrel, ruction, trouble, turmoil 8 activity, brouhaha, busyness, disorder, disquiet, foofaraw, rowdydow 9 agitation, commotion 10 difficulty, donnybrook, excitement, hullabaloo, hurly-burly
list: 6 agenda
list entry: 3 job 4 item, task 5 chore 6 errand 7 project
to-do __: 4 list
__-to-do: 4 well
__ to Duty: 3 Ode
tody: 4 bird
toe: 5 digit 6 dactyl, hallux, member 7 minimus 9 appendage, extremity
combining form: 6 dactyl- 7 dactylo-
ender: 3 cap 4 hold, nail
hurt one's ~: 4 stub
in the water: 4 test
starter: 3 tip
stubber's cry: 2 ow 3 yow 4 ouch, yeow
the line: 4 heed, mind, obey 5 agree, bow to, defer, yield 6 accept, adhere, behave, bend to, comply, follow, fulfil, listen, submit 7 conform, consent, fulfill, observe, respect 8 carry out 10 keep in step
topper: 4 nail 6 enamel, polish
tot's ~: 5 piggy 6 piggie
woe: 4 corn, gout 6 agnail, bunion
toe __: 3 box 4 clip, loop, pick 5 crack, dance
__ toe: 3 big 5 great, knurl 6 little
__-toe: 5 tippy
To Each His Own (1946 film)
cast: Mary Anderson, Olivia de Havilland, John Lund
director: Mitchell Leisen
To Each His Own (1960 song) artist: Platters
__ to earth: 3 run
__-to-earth: 4 down
To Earthward: 4 poem
author: 5 Frost
__-toed: 3 web 6 pigeon
toed combining form: 9 -dactylous
__ to Eden: 4 Exit
__-toed sloth: 3 two 5 three
toehold: 5 ledge, niche, way in 6 access
toe-in: 6 camber
toeing the line: 5 loyal 8 obedient
toe loop: 4 jump
where to do a ~: 3 ice 4 rink
toenail: 6 unguis
To err is __: 5 human
toes
on one's ~: 4 atip, wary 5 alert, awake, ready 7 heads-up, heedful, mindful 8 cautious, vigilant, watchful 9 attentive, observant, wide-awake
tread on one's ~: 3 bug, get, irk, try, vex 4 gall, miff, rile 5 annoy, grate, peeve, pique 6 bother, enrage, nettle, offend, ruffle 7 affront, agitate, disturb, incense, inflame, outrage, provoke 8 distress, irritate 9 infuriate 10 antagonize, exasperate
__-Toes: 3 Tip
To E.T. author: Robert Frost
toe the __: 4 line, mark
Toe, The: Lou Groza
toe-to-toe, go: 5 fight 6 battle
__ to Exhale: 7 Waiting
__ to Extremes: 3 I Go
...to fetch __ of water: 5 a pail
toff: 4 dude 5 dandy 9 pretty boy 10 jack-a-dandy
toffee: 5 candy 8 ice cream 9 sweetmeat
alternative: 5 lemon, mocha, peach 6 banana, coffee, Jamoca 7 caramel, coconut, vanilla 8 cinnamon, hazelnut 9 bubblegum, chocolate, pineapple, pistachio, raspberry, rocky road, rum raisin 10 blackberry, cheesecake, Neapolitan, peppermint, strawberry
like ~: 5 chewy 7 crunchy
Toffler: 5 Alvin
To Find a Man (1972 film)
cast: Pamela Sue Martin, Darren O'Connor
director: Buzz Kulik
__-to-five: 4 nine
__-to-fiver: 4 nine
To form __ perfect Union...: 5 a More
To F.S.O. author: Edgar Allan Poe
tofu: 6 legume 8 bean curd
base: 3 soy 4 soya
tog: 4 coat 5 dress 6 clothe, outfit 7 garment
out: 4 deck, garb 5 array, dress 6 attire, clothe 7 bedrape
toga: 7 garment
alternative: 5 tunic
venue: 4 frat, Rome 5 Forum 10 fraternity
__ to Garcia, A: 7 Message
__ to get: 4 hard
together: 3 one 4 calm, cool, sane 5 as one, at one, lucid, sound, whole 6 at once, in step, in sync, intact, stable 7 en masse, en suite, jointly 8 as a group, combined, commonly, composed, in unison, mutually, rational, sensible, unitedly 9 all at once, at one time, collected, in concert 10 conjointly, hand in hand, phlegmatic, reasonable, side by side, unagitated
in music: 4 a due
prefix: 3 col-, com-, con-, sym-, syn-
__ together: 3 get, put 4 hang, pull 6 cobble
__-together: 3 get
__ Together: 3 Get 4 Come 5 Get It, Happy
Together (1961 song) artist: Connie Francis
Together Again (1944 film)
cast: Charles Boyer, Charles Coburn, Irene Dunne
director: Charles Vidor
Together Again (1997 song) artist: Janet Jackson
Together Forever (1988 song) artist: Rick Astley
togetherness: 5 synch, unity 7 rapport 9 proximity
__ to get ready...: 5 three
toggery: 4 garb 6 attire 7 clothes
toggle __: 4 bolt, iron, rail 5 joint 6 switch
To Gillian on Her 37th Birthday (1996 film)
cast: Claire Danes, Peter Gallagher, Michelle Pfeiffer
director: Michael Pressman
__ to Give It Up: 3 Got
Tognazzi: 3 Ugo
__ to go: 5 rarin' 6 raring
__ to go!: 3 Way
Togo: 6 nation 7 country
capital: 4 Lomé
language: 3 Ewe, Gbe
locale: 3 Afr. 6 Africa
money: 5 franc
neighbor: 5 Benin, Ghana
people: 3 Ewe 6 Yoruba
__-to-God: 6 honest
to go. like: 3 irr. 5 irreg. 9 irregular
__-to-goodness: 6 honest
to-go order: 3 BLT 5 pizza 6 burger, hot dog 8 sandwich 9 hamburger
__ to grief: 4 come
__ to grips with: 4 come
__-to-ground: 3 air
__ to grow on: 3 one
togs: 4 duds, gear 5 dress, getup, jeans 6 attire, outfit 7 apparel, clothes, jerseys, raiment, threads 8 clothing, ensemble, garments, glad rags, wardrobe 9 jumpsuits 10 Sunday best
to have __ hold: 5 and to
To Have and Have Not: 4 film 5 novel
author: Ernest Hemingway
cast: Lauren Bacall, Humphrey Bogart, Walter Brennan, Hoagy Carmichael
director: Howard Hawks
__ to heart: 4 take
__ to Heaven: 3 Cry 5 Hands 7 Highway
To Helen author: Edgar Allan Poe
To Hell and Back (1955 film)
cast: Charles Drake, Audie Murphy, Marshall Thompson
director: Jesse Hibbs
toheroa: 4 clam 7 bivalve
__ to Him: 3 Run
To His Coy Mistress: 4 poem
author: Andrew Marvell
__ to Hold Your Hand: 5 I Want
__ to home: 5 close
To Homer: 3 ode 4 poem
author: John Keats
__ to Hong Kong, The: 4 Road
to-ho shouter: 6 hunter
toil: 3 job 4 grub, moil, plod, plug, slog, task, wade, work 5 grind, labor, pains, serve, slave, sweat 6 drudge, effort, strain, strive 7 peg away, slavery, travail 8 drudgery, endeavor, exercise, exertion, hardship, industry, struggle 9 grind away, grunt work, hard labor, lucubrate, slave away 10 nine-to-five
ender: 4 some
toil and __: 7 trouble
toile: 6 fabric 8 material
toiler: 5 labor, slave 6 drudge, worker
toilet: 2 WC 3 lav, loo 4 john 7 latrine 8 bathroom, lavatory, rest room
water: 5 scent 7 cologne, perfume 9 fragrance
toilet __: 3 set 4 soap 5 water
toiletries case: 4 etui 5 etwee 6 kitbag
__ toilette: 5 eau de
toilet water: 5 scent
toilful: 4 hard
toiling away: 4 at it, busy
toils: 3 web 4 mesh
toilsome: 4 hard 5 heavy, rough, tough 6 severe, thorny, trying, uphill 7 arduous, hard-won, labored, onerous, operose 8 grueling 9 demanding, difficult, herculean, laborious, strenuous 10 formidable, oppressive
__ to Innocence: 6 Return
To Isadore author: Edgar Allan Poe
__ to it: 3 get, hop, see
__-to-it-ive: 5 stick
__-toity: 5 hoity
Toiyabe National Forest locale: 3 Nev. 6 Nevada
To Jerusalem and Back author: Saul Bellow
__ to Joy: 3 Ode
Tokar: 6 Norman
tokay: 5 gecko 6 lizard
Tokay: 4 wine 5 grape, white
origin: 7 Hungary
relative: 5 Gamay, pinot 6 Merlot 7 Catawba, Concord, Niagara 8 Cabernet, malvasia, muscatel 9 muscadine, Sauvignon, zinfandel 10 Chardonnay
toke: 3 tip
token: 4 coin, gage, gift, hint, mark, note, omen, pawn, sign 5 badge, favor, index, proof, relic, trace 6 emblem, herald, pledge, sample, signal, symbol, ticket 7 earnest, memento, minimal, nominal, presage, promise, symptom, vestige, warning 8 evidence, gratuity, indicium, keepsake, reminder, security, souvenir 10 expression, indication
by the same ~: 3 and, yet 4 also 6 as well 7 besides, further 8 moreover
taker: 4 slot
user: 4 fare 5 rider 9 passenger
token __: 4 coin 7 economy, payment
Tokens song: The Lion Sleeps Tonight (1961)
__ to Kill: 4 Born, Hard 5 A Time 7 Dressed, Licence

To Kill a Mockingbird: 4 film 5 novel
author: Harper Lee
cast: Philip Alford, Mary Badham, Robert Duvall, John Megna, Gregory Peck, Brock Peters
character: 3 Boo, Jem 4 Dill 5 Ewell, Finch, Scout 6 Radley 7 Atticus 9 Boo Radley
director: Robert Mulligan
screenwriter: 5 Foote
Toklas: 5 Alice 6 Alice B.
friend: 5 Stein
__-to-know: 5 right
__-to-know basis: 4 need
To Know Him, Is to Love Him (1958 song) artist: Teddy Bears
__ to Know You: 7 Getting
Toko-Ri structure: 6 bridge
Tokugawa: 6 Ieyasu
shogunate capital: 3 Edo 4 Yedo 5 Yeddo
Tokushima: 4 city, port, town
locale: 5 Japan
Tokuyama: 4 city, town
locale: 5 Japan
Tokyo: 4 city, port, town 7 capital
area: 5 Ginza
destroyer: 5 Rodan
former name: 3 Edo 4 Yedo 5 Yeddo
locale: 5 Hondo, Japan 6 Honshu
river: 6 Sumida
town near ~: 5 Nagai, Urawa
Tokyo __: 3 Bay 4 Rose, Woes 5 Story
Tokyo Woes author: Bruce Jay Friedman
Tolbachik: 7 volcano
locale: 4 Asia 6 Russia
told: 4 oral 6 spoken, verbal
be ~: 4 hear 5 catch, learn 6 pick up 7 find out, receive 8 discover 9 ascertain, get wind of 10 understand
do as ~: 4 mind, obey 6 behave, comply, listen 7 abide by, respect 8 take heed 10 toe the line
I ~ you so: 3 see
__ told: 3 all
__-told: 5 twice
__ told by an idiot: 5 a tale
Told by an Idiot author: Rose Macaulay
__ Told Ev'ry Little Star: 3 I've
__ Told Me: 4 Mama 6 Nobody
__-Told Tales: 5 Twice
tole: 9 metalware 10 enamelware
material: 3 tin
__ to leap tall buildings...: 4 Able
Toledo: 4 city, town
athletes: 7 Rockets
conference: 3 MAC
county: 5 Lucas
lake: 4 Erie
locale: 4 Ohio 5 Spain 6 España
newspaper: 5 Blade
product: 5 steel
river: 4 Tejo 5 Tegus
see also Spanish
Toler: 6 Sidney
role: 4 Chan
tolerable: 2 OK 4 fair, okay, so-so, tidy 6 decent, medium, not bad, venial 7 average, livable 8 adequate, all right, bearable, liveable, mediocre, middling, moderate, ordinary, passable 9 endurable, unnotable 10 acceptable, admissible, forgivable, good enough, reasonable, sufficient
tolerably: 4 so-so 6 rather 8 somewhat 10 adequately, moderately
tolerance: 5 grace, mercy 6 leeway 7 charity, freedom, license, stamina 8 altruism, clemency, goodwill, humanity, kindness, lenience, leniency, patience, strength, sympathy 9 endurance, fortitude, hardiness 10 compassion, indulgence, resilience, resistance, steadiness
tolerant: 3 big, lax 4 easy, fair, just, kind, meek, mild, soft, wide 5 broad, loose, noble 6 gentle, humane, kindly, tender 7 clement, lenient, liberal, patient, ruthful, sparing 8 catholic, flexible, laid-back, merciful, moderate, placable, unstrict 9 assuasive, compliant, condoning, easygoing, forgiving, indulgent, receptive 10 benevolent, charitable, forbearing, open-minded, permissive, reasonable, unexacting, unhardened
tolerate: 3 let 4 bear, bide, have, lump, take 5 abide, allow, brook, humor, stand, stick 6 accept, endure, excuse, permit, suffer, wink at 7 blink at, condone, indulge, let ride, stomach, sustain, swallow, undergo 8 accede to, assent to, bear with, live with, sanction, stand for, tough out 9 approve of, authorize, consent to, put up with, withstand 10 understand
can't ~: 4 hate 5 abhor 6 detest, loathe 7 despise
toleration: 6 lenity 9 allowance, endurance 10 indulgence
__ to Liberty: 3 Ode
__ to life: 4 come, true 5 bring
__ to light: 4 come 5 bring
to little __: 7 purpose
__ to Live: 5 A Rage
__ to Live!: 5 I Want
To Live and Die __: 4 in L.A.
Tolkien, J.R.R.: 6 author, writer 7 British
creature: 3 Ent, orc 6 hobbit
work: The Fellowship of the Ring
The Hobbit
The Lord of the Rings
The Return of the King
The Silmarillion
The Two Towers
toll: 3 fee, tax 4 bong, cost, duty, fare, gong, levy, peal, rate, ring 5 chime, clang, knell, price 6 charge, damage, impost, losses, strain, tariff, towage 7 penalty, ring out, tribute 8 exaction 10 assessment
ender: 4 gate 5 booth, house
road: 3 tpk. 4 pike, tnpk. 5 route 7 highway 8 turnpike
stop: 5 stile
take a ~ on: 3 tax 6 strain
toll __: 3 bar 4 call, line, road 6 bridge
Toll __ cookies: 5 House
Tollbooth (1994 film)
cast: Fairuza Balk, Will Patton, Lenny von Dohlen
director: Salome Breziner
tollbooth site: 5 plaza
toll collector, name meaning: 7 Travers
toll-free __: 4 call
tollhouse: 6 cookie
__ toll on: 5 take a
Tolomeo composer: 6 Handel
__ to Look At: 6 Lovely
__ to Love: 4 Easy 7 Goodbye, Someone
Tolstoy, Leo: 6 author, writer 7 Russian
work: Anna Karenina
The Cossacks
The Death of Ivan Ilyich
War and Peace
Toltec: 5 Nahua 6 Indian 7 Amerind
city: 4 Tula
tolu: 5 resin 6 balsam
Toluca: 4 city, town 7 volcano
locale: 6 Mexico
To Lucasta, Going to the Wars
author: Richard Lovelace
__ to lunch: 3 out
tom: 3 cat 4 male 6 turkey 7 gobbler
ender: 3 boy, cat, cod, tit 4 fool 7 foolery
mate: 3 hen
Tom: 3 cat, Mix 4 Bell, Gola, Joad, kite 5 Brown, Conti, Dewey, Drake, Ewell, Foley, Gries, Hanks, Hulce, Jones, Kalin, Mboya, Petty, Ridge, Sneva, Swift, Tryon, uncle, Waits, Wolfe, Wopat 6 Arnold, Bosley, Brokaw, Clancy, Conway, Cruise, Harkin, Harmon, Hayden, Landry, Lehrer, Lester, Noonan, Parker, Poston, Sawyer, Seaver, Snyder, Watson 7 Bradley, DiCillo, Glavine, Holland, Johnson, Kennedy, Robbins, Selleck, Shadyac, Shipley, Welling 8 Berenger, Cochrane, Heinsohn, Laughlin, Sizemore, Skerritt, Smothers, Stoppard 9 Courtenay
Tom & __: 3 Viv
Tom __: 5 Thumb 6 Dooley 7 Collins
Tom, __ and Harry: 4 Dick
tomahawk: 2 ax 3 axe 7 hatchet
Tom and Jerry: 5 drink 8 beverage, cocktail
bulldog: 5 Spike
cat: 3 Tom
dog: 5 Jerry
ingredient: 3 egg, rum 4 eggs, milk
__ to Marry a Millionaire: 3 How
Tomás: 10 Torquemada
in English: 6 Thomas
tomatillo: 5 fruit 6 veggie 9 vegetable
tomato: 4 Roma, soup 5 fruit, sauce 6 Big Boy, cherry, veggie 9 beefsteak, Better Boy, Early Girl, love apple, Quick Pick, vegetable
container: 3 can
impact sound: 5 splat
pest: 5 aphid
plant support: 5 stake
product: 5 aspic, paste, purée, sauce
sauce ingredient: 5 basil, purée
__ tomato: 4 husk, plum, tree 6 cherry, creole 7 currant
__ to maturity: 5 yield
Tomba, Alberto: 5 skier 7 Italian
tombac: 5 alloy
component: 4 zinc 6 copper
Tombaugh, Clyde: 10 astronomer
discovery: 5 Pluto
tombé: 4 step
tomboy: 6 hoiden, hoyden
Tomb Raider heroine: 4 Lara 5 Croft
Tombstone: 4 town 5 pizza
alternative: 5 Jeno's, Tony's 6 Ellio's 7 Celeste, Totino's 8 DiGiorno 10 Freschetta
locale: 4 Ariz. 7 Arizona
marshal: 4 Earp
newspaper: 7 Epitaph
Tombstone (1993 film)
cast: Michael Biehn, Powers Boothe, Val Kilmer, Kurt Russell
director: George P. Cosmatos
tomcat: 3 gib 4 male, puss 6 feline
tomcod: 4 fish
Tom Collins ingredient: 3 gin 4 lime, soda 5 lemon
Tom Corbett, Space Cadet role: 5 Astro
Tom, Dick and Harry: 4 trio 5 males
Tom, Dick and Harry (1941 film)
cast: George Murphy, Ginger Rogers
director: Garson Kanin
Tom, Dick, or Harry: 4 male
Tom Dooley (1958 song) artist: Kingston Trio
tome: 2 bk. 3 vol 4 book, opus 6 volume 7 classic, writing 9 great work 10 magnum opus
home: 5 shelf 9 bookshelf
__ to Me: 3 Bad 4 Come, Mean, Roll, Talk 6 Return
__ Tomé and Principe: 3 Sao
__-to-measure: 4 made
Tomei: 6 Marisa 8 Concetta
Tomei, Marisa: 7 actress
film: In the Bedroom (2001)
My Cousin Vinny (1992, AA)
Only You (1994)
The Paper (1994)
Slums of Beverly Hills (1998)
What Women Want (2000)
__ to mention: 3 not
__ to Me Only With Thine Eyes: 5 Drink
__ to Methuselah: 4 Back
tomfool: 3 lug, mad, oaf 4 boor, clod, daft, dolt, dope, goof, jerk, lout, mutt, rube, yo-yo 5 batty, chump, daffy, dunce, flaky, goofy, inane, nutty, silly, wacky 6 absurd, dimwit, freaky, galoot, lummox, nitwit, screwy 7 asinine, bumbler, bumpkin, dingbat, fathead, fumbler, half-wit, jackass, jughead, palooka, pinhead 8 bonehead, dumbbell, dummkopf, goofball, lunkhead, meathead, numskull 9 birdbrain, blockhead, ding-a-ling, harebrain, ignoramus, illogical, lamebrain, laughable, ludicrous, senseless, simpleton 10 dunderhead, muttonhead, off-the-wall, ridiculous, stumblebum
tomfoolery: 3 fun 4 jape, jest 5 antic, caper, humor, prank, sport, trick 6 antics, capers, pranks 7 inanity 8 mischief 9 escapades, funniness, goofiness 10 friskiness, hanky-panky, impishness, jocoseness
__ to Michael: 7 Message
__ to middling: 4 fair
__ to mind: 4 come 5 bring
Tom Jones: 4 film 5 novel
author: Henry Fielding
cast: Albert Finney, Hugh Griffith, Susannah York
character: 6 Blifil, Sophia
director: Tony Richardson
Tomlin, Lily: 7 actress 10 comedienne
film: All of Me (1984)
The Beverly Hillbillies (1993)
Big Business (1988)
The Late Show (1977)
Nashville (1975)
Nine to Five (1980)
The Search for Signs of Intelligent Life in the Universe (1991)
TV: Rowan & Martin's Laugh-In
Tomlinson, David: 5 actor
film: Bedknobs and Broomsticks (1971)
Mary Poppins (1964)
The Wooden Horse (1950)
To M.L.S. author: Edgar Allan Poe
Tommaso in English: 6 Thomas
Tommie: 4 Agee 5 Aaron
Tommy: 3 Lee, Moe, Roe 4 Bolt, John, Kirk, Page, Tune 5 Aaron, Boyce, Chong, James, opera, Sands 6 Armour, Dorsey, Norden, Rettig, Steele 7 Edwards, Henrich, Lasorda, soldier 8 Hilfiger, Smothers
ally: 5 poilu
band: 6 The Who
Tommy (1975 film)
cast: Ann-Margret, Roger Daltrey
director: Ken Russell
Tommy __: 3 gun 6 Atkins
Tommy __ Jones: 3 Lee
tommycod: 4 fish
tommy ender: 3 rot
Tommy gun: 4 Sten
Tommyknockers, The author: Stephen King
tommyrot: 3 gas 4 blah, bosh, bull,

bunk, guff, jazz, jive, pooh, tosh **5** bilge, fudge, hokum, hooey, prate, stuff, trash, tripe **6** bunkum, bushwa, drivel, footle, gabble, gammon, gibber, havers, hot air, humbug, jabber, jargon, kibosh, piffle **7** baloney, blarney, blather, blether, boloney, bushwah, eyewash, flannel, flubdub, fustian, garbage, hogwash, inanity, malarky, rubbish, twaddle **8** buncombe, claptrap, falderal, falderol, flimflam, flummery, folderal, folderol, malarkey, nonsense, slipslop, trumpery **9** banana oil, gibberish, goofiness, kidstakes, moonshine, poppycock, rigmarole **10** applesauce, balderdash, bilge water, codswallop, double-talk, flapdoodle, galimatias, Jabberwock, mumbo jumbo, rigamarole, taradiddle

Tomonaga, Sin-Itiro: 8 Nobelist **9** physicist

___ to Morocco: 4 Road

tomorrow: 6 future, mañana
 preceder: 5 today

Tomorrow: 4 song, tune
 composer: 7 Charnin, Strouse
 musical: 5 Annie

Tomorrow File, The author: Lawrence Sanders

Tomorrow I Die author: Mickey Spillane

Tomorrow Is Forever (1946 film)
 cast: George Brent, Claudette Colbert, Orson Welles

Tomorrow Never Dies (1997 film)
 cast: Pierce Brosnan, Judi Dench, Teri Hatcher, Jonathan Pryce, Michelle Yeoh
 director: Roger Spottiswoode

Tomorrow the World (1944 film)
 cast: Betty Field, Fredric March, Agnes Moorehead
 director: Leslie Fenton

___-to-mouth: 4 hand

Tom Sawyer: 4 film **5** novel
 author: Mark Twain
 cast: Celeste Holm, Warren Oates, Johnnie Whitaker
 character: 3 Joe, Sid **4** Finn, Mary, Muff **5** Becky, Polly **8** Injun Joe, Thatcher **9** Aunt Polly, Joe Harper **10** Muff Potter **11** Huckleberry
 director: Don Taylor

___ Tom's Cabin: 5 Uncle

Toms, David: 6 golfer
 milieu: 5 links **6** course
 org.: 3 PGA

Tom's Diner (1990 song) artist: Suzanne Vega

Tom's of Maine: 10 toothpaste
 alternative: 3 Aim **5** Crest, Gleem, Topol **7** Close-Up, Colgate, Viadent **9** Aquafresh, Mentadent, Pepsodent, Rembrandt, Sensodyne **10** Pearl Drops, Ultra Brite

Toms River: 4 city, town
 locale: 9 New Jersey

Tom T. ___: 4 Hall

Tom Terrific dog: 7 Manfred

tom thumb (1958 film)
 cast: Peter Sellers, Russ Tamblyn, June Thorburn
 director: George Pal

Tom Thumb author: Henry Fielding

tomtit: 4 bird

tom-tom: 4 drum

Tom, Tom, the Piper's ___: 3 Son

Tom & Viv (1994 film)
 cast: Willem Dafoe, Rosemary Harris, Miranda Richardson
 director: Brian Gilbert

___ to My Lou: 4 Skip

To My Mother author: Edgar Allan Poe

Tomy product: 3 toy

ton: 4 chic, lots, raft **5** bunch, ocean, scads, style, vogue **6** oodles **8** mountain **9** profusion
 bon ~: 4 chic, dash **5** class, style, vogue
 fraction: 2 lb. **3** cwt. **5** pound
 hit like a ~ of bricks: 3 jar **4** jolt, kayo, stun **5** shock **6** bedaze **7** astound, flummox, horrify, nonplus, outrage, stagger, stupefy, terrify **8** astonish, bewilder, blow away, bowl over, confound, knock out, paralyze, surprise, unsettle **9** dumbfound, overpower, overwhelm, take aback **10** discompose
 starter: 4 mega **6** double

___ ton: 3 bon, net **4** long **5** assay, gross, short **6** metric **7** freight

___-ton: 4 foot

tonal: 5 on key **7** melodic, musical **8** harmonic
 combination: 5 chord, triad

Tonalá: 4 city, town
 locale: 6 Mexico **7** Chiapas, Jalisco

tonality: 5 sound **6** accent **10** inflection

Tonawanda: 4 city, town
 locale: 7 New York

tone: 3 air, hue **4** aura, beep, cast, feel, gird, mood, note, tint, vein **5** blend, build, chime, color, drift, humor, pitch, shade, shore, sound, steel, style, tenor, tinct, tinge, trend, voice **6** accent, anneal, beef up, firm up, flavor, harden, manner, prop up, spirit, strain, temper, timbre **7** bolster, brace up, build up, burgeon, cadence, cadency, develop, empower, enhance, fortify, quality, shore up, stiffen, toughen **8** ambiance, ambience, attitude, bourgeon, buttress, coloring, emphasis, energize, indurate, sonority, vitalize **9** character, condition, intensify, reinforce, resonance **10** elasticity, inflection, intonation, invigorate, modulation, resiliency
 down: 3 dim **4** fade, mute, tame **5** lower, mince, quiet, relax, shade **6** dampen, darken, deaden, lessen, modify, muffle, obtund, reduce, soften, subdue, temper **7** let up on **8** mitigate, moderate, modulate, restrain, slack off **9** soft-pedal **10** keep in line
 earth ~: 5 beige, brown, ocher, ochre, umber
 emotional ~: 3 air **4** aura, mood **5** humor, state, tenor **6** nature, spirit, temper **7** climate, feeling **8** attitude **9** character
 hushed ~: 6 murmur
 prefix for ~: 4 mono
 skin ~: 4 look **5** flesh **6** aspect **8** coloring **10** appearance, complexion
 up: 4 firm **7** work out **8** exercise **9** condition **10** strengthen

tone ___: 3 arm, row **4** down, poem **5** color **7** cluster, control, dialing

tone-___: 4 deaf

___ tone: 4 cold, dial, fuzz, half, head, warm **5** earth **7** leading, partial, passing, quarter

___-tone: 3 two **5** touch

Tone: 4 soap **8** Franchot
 alternative: 3 Lux **4** Dial, Dove, Lava, Zest **5** Camay, Coast, Ivory, Lever **6** Boraxo, Caress, Shield **8** Lifebuoy **9** Palmolive, Safeguard **11** Irish Spring

toned: 3 fit **4** hale, trim **5** agile, burly, hardy, tough **6** brawny, robust, strong **7** healthy **8** athletic, muscular **9** strapping **10** able-bodied
 down: 3 dim, low **4** soft **5** faint, piano, quiet, sober **6** low-key **7** subdued

___-toned: 4 high **6** copper

Tone, Franchot: 5 actor
 film: Dancing Lady (1933)
  Dangerous (1935)
  Five Graves to Cairo (1943)
  Gabriel Over the White House (1933)
  The Girl From Missouri (1934)
  Here Comes the Groom (1951)
  I Love Trouble (1948)
  The King Steps Out (1936)
  The Lives of a Bengal Lancer (1935)
  The Man on the Eiffel Tower (1949)
  Midnight Mary (1933)
  Mutiny on the Bounty (1935)
  Nice Girl? (1941)
  Phantom Lady (1944)
  Quality Street (1937)
  Sadie McKee (1934)
  The Stranger's Return (1933)
  Three Comrades (1938)
  True to Life (1943)
 spouse: Joan Crawford

Tonegawa, Susumu: 8 Nobelist

toneless: 4 weak **5** unfit **6** flabby **7** droning, flaccid, uniform **8** sing-song **9** unvarying **10** monotonous, out of shape

Tone Loc: 6 rapper
 born: Anthony Smith
 song: Funky Cold Medina (1989)
  Wild Thing (1988)

tone of ___: 5 voice

___-tone phone: 5 touch

toner: 6 dry ink, imager **9** skin cream

tonette: 4 wind **5** flute **10** instrument

Tong: 6 Sammee

Tonga: 3 isl. **4** isle **6** island, nation **7** country
 capital: 9 Nuku'alofa
 neighbor: 4 Fiji, Niue

tongs: 7 forceps

___ tongs: 3 ice **4** lazy **5** sugar **7** curling

tongue: 5 argot, idiom, lingo, organ, shaft, strip, voice **6** glossa, lingua, patois, speech **7** clapper, dialect **8** language, parlance **10** vernacular
 bone: 5 hyoid
 clicking sound: 3 tsk **6** tsk tsk
 combining form: 4 -glot **5** gloss- **6** glosso-, glotto-
 covering: 4 coat
 hinged ~: 4 pawl
 hold one's ~: 6 clam up, shut up **7** silence
 in cheek: 7 as a joke **8** jokingly **9** jestingly, kiddingly
 mollusk's ~: 6 radula
 neighbor: 5 uvula
 one with a forked ~: 4 liar
 part: 6 frenum **7** fraenum
 partner: 6 groove
 part of a dog's ~: 5 lytta
 sharp of ~: 4 tart **5** acerb **6** bitter **7** caustic **9** sarcastic
 slip of the ~: 5 gaffe **7** blunder, faux pas, mistake
 speak with forked ~: 3 fib, lie **4** dupe **5** bluff, fudge, guile **6** delude **7** deceive, falsify, mislead **8** misspeak **9** dissemble, misinform
 see also language

tongue ___: 4 sole **5** cover **7** twister

tongue-___: 3 tie **4** lash, tied **7** lashing

___ tongue: 3 ice **4** acid, bull **5** calf's, earth, lamb's, shawl **6** kiltie, mother **7** painted

___-tongue: 5 beard, deer's, hart's **6** adder's, devil's, double, hound's, triple

tongue-and-___ joint: 6 groove

tongue-burning: 6 bitter

___-tongued: 4 acid, long **5** loose, sharp **6** silver, smooth

tongue-in-cheek: 7 jesting, playful

tongue-lash: 3 jaw, nag, rag **4** carp, harp, lash, rail, whip **5** scold **6** berate **7** upbraid **9** castigate, dress down, reprehend

tongue-lashing: 5 abuse **6** rebuke, tirade **9** reprimand
 give a ~: 3 rag **5** blame, decry, scold **6** berate, punish, rebuke **7** censure, contemn, reprove, tell off **8** denounce, reproach **9** inculpate, reprehend, reprimand **10** denunciate

tonguelike part: 6 ligula

tongues do it: 3 wag **4** lash

tongue-tie: 3 gag **7** silence

tongue-tied: 3 mum **4** mute **6** silent **7** at a loss **8** choked up, nonvocal, wordless **9** voiceless **10** dumbstruck, incoherent, speechless, unspeaking

tongue-wagging: 6 drivel, patter **7** chatter, palaver, prattle **8** chitchat

Toni: 5 Basil **6** Fisher **7** Bambara, Braxton, Colette **8** Morrison, Tennille

tonic: 4 drug, soda **5** drink **6** bracer, elixir, fillip, pickup, potion **7** cordial, healthy **8** curative, medicine, pick-me-up, sanative, stimulus **9** stimulant **10** invigorant, medication
 amount: 4 dose **6** dosage
 companion: 3 gin
 ingredient: 7 bitters
 starter: 3 iso
 water: 4 fizz, soda **5** mixer **7** seltzer **8** club soda

tonic ___: 5 sol-fa, water **6** accent

Tonight and Every Night (1945 film)
 cast: Janet Blair, Lee Bowman, Rita Hayworth

Tonight, I Celebrate My Love (1983 song)
 artist: Peabo Bryson, Roberta Flack

Tonight She Comes (1985 song)
 artist: Cars

Tonight Show
 bandleader: 5 Melis **10** Severinsen
 host: 4 Leno, Paar **5** Allen **6** Carson
 regular: 3 Nye **7** McMahon
 theme composer: 4 Anka

Tonight (song) artist: Ferrante & Teicher, New Kids on the Block

Tonight's the Night (1954 film)
 cast: Yvonne De Carlo, Barry Fitzgerald, David Niven

Tonight's the Night (1976 song) artist: Rod Stewart

Tonight, Tonight, Tonight (1987 song)
 artist: Genesis

Tonight You Belong to Me (1956 song) artist: Patience & Prudence

toning target: 4 flab **6** muscle

Tonio Kroger author: Thomas Mann

___-tonk: 5 honky

tonka bean: 4 tree **6** legume

Tonka product: 3 toy **5** Gobot, truck

Tonkin: 4 gulf
 locale: 3 Nam **5** Hanoi **7** Vietnam

Tonkinese: 3 cat **5** felid **6** feline

Tonle Sap: 4 lake
 locale: 8 Cambodia

tonnage: 4 size **5** cargo **6** weight

to no ___: 5 avail **7** purpose

Tono-___: 6 Bungay

___ to none: 4 slim

tons: 4 a lot, lots, many, much, scad **5** loads, ocean **6** hoards, oodles, plenty, scores **7** legions **10** inundation

___ Tons: 7 Sixteen

tonsil
 combining form: 7 amygdal- **8** amygdalo-
 neighbor: 5 uvula

tonsorial
artist: 6 barber, shaver
challenge: 3 mop
item: 4 comb 5 razor, strop
procedure: 3 cut 4 clip, trim 5 shave
___ ton soup: 3 won
tonsure: 5 shave
tonsured: 5 shorn
tontine: 4 pact 6 pledge
Tonto: 3 cat 4 hero 6 Indian
friend: 8 Kemo Sabe 10 Long Ranger
horse: 5 Scout
___-to-nuts: 4 soup
tony: 3 mod 5 ritzy, swank, swish 6 chichi, classy, modish, swanky, trendy 7 à la mode, current, in style, popular, stylish, upscale, voguish 9 high-toned, in fashion 10 all the rage
Tony: 3 Dow 4 Bill, Lema, Peña, Rome, Todd, Zale 5 award, Blair, Danza, Gwynn, horse, Kubek, Oliva, Perez, Scott, tiger 6 Curtis, equine, Martin 7 Bennett, Dorsett, Goldwyn, Kushner, La Russa, Lazzeri, Musante, Orlando, Perkins, Randall, Roberts, Soprano, Trabert 8 Lo Bianco, Luraschi, Shalhoub 9 Franciosa 10 Richardson
daughter of ~: 5 Jamie 8 Jamie Lee
of cereal fame: 5 tiger
relative: 4 Obie 5 Oscar
rider: Tom Mix
Tonya: 7 Harding
Tony Rome (1967 film)
cast: Richard Conte, Sue Lyon, Frank Sinatra, Jill St. John
Tony's: 5 pizza
alternative: 5 Jeno's 6 Ellio's 7 Celeste, Totino's 8 DiGiorno 9 Tombstone 10 Freschetta
Tony the Tiger favorite word: 5 great
too: 3 yet 4 also, ever, more, most, over, plus, very 5 along 6 adverb, as well, beyond, either, overly, to boot, unduly 7 awfully, besides, further 8 likewise, moreover, overmuch 9 extremely 10 improperly, in addition
familiar: 4 dull, flat 5 banal, corny, hokey, stale, tired, vapid 6 common, jejune, old hat 7 clichéd, insipid, prosaic, routine 8 bromidic, ordinary, shopworn, timeworn 9 hackneyed 10 pedestrian, uninspired, unoriginal, warmed-over
fast: 4 rash 5 brash 6 abrupt, madcap 8 careless, headlong, heedless, pell-mell, reckless, slapdash 9 foolhardy, impetuous, impulsive
feed ~ well: 4 cloy, glut 5 gorge, stuff 7 surfeit 8 overfill 10 gormandize
frank: 9 impolitic 10 indiscreet
frugal: 4 mean, near 5 cheap 6 greedy, stingy 7 miserly 9 penurious
get ~ excited over: 4 gush 7 enthuse
get ~ personal: 3 spy 5 snoop, stare 6 butt in, horn in, meddle 7 intrude, obtrude, wiretap 8 question 9 interfere
give ~ much: 4 cloy, glut 5 gorge 7 surfeit
go ~ far: 4 hype 6 pile on 7 belabor, lay it on, stretch 8 overplay 9 overstate 10 exaggerate
go ~ fast: 4 tear, whiz, zoom 6 barrel
little too late: 9 deficient, half-baked, shortfall 10 inadequate
me ~: 5 ditto
much: 5 ultra, undue 6 de trop, excess, overly 8 tiresome, to a fault 9 excessive, overblown 10 inordinate, outrageous, stupendous, unbearable, untempered
much (French): 6 de trop
much of a good thing: 4 glut 5 flood 7 surfeit, surplus 8 overload 10 indulgence, oversupply
only ~: 4 very 6 highly, overly 7 greatly 9 extremely, intensely, unusually 10 strikingly, uncommonly
prefix: 4 over-
too ___ by half: 6 clever
too ___ for comfort: 5 close
too ___ for one's britches: 3 big
too ___ to be true: 4 good
too ___ to handle: 3 hot
too ___ to pop: 6 pooped
Too ___: 3 Hot, Shy 4 Much 5 Close, Funky, Young
Too ___ cooks...: 4 many
Too ___ Hot: 4 Darn
Too ___ the Phalarope: 4 Late
Too ___, Too Little, Too Late: 4 Much
___ too bad: 3 not
Too bad!: 3 tsk 4 alas, pity 5 alack 6 tsk tsk
Too Busy Thinking About My Baby (1969 song) artist: Marvin Gaye
too clever by ___: 4 half
Too Close for Comfort (ABC sitcom)
cast: Lydia Cornell (Sara Rush) Nancy Dussault (Muriel Rush) Ted Knight (Henry Rush) Deborah Van Valkenburgh (Jackie Rush)
Too Darn Hot composer: 6 Porter
Toodle-oo!: 3 bye 4 ciao, ta-ta 5 adieu, adios, I'm off, later 6 bye-bye, so long 7 goodbye 8 farewell
Toody, Gunther: 3 cop
portrayer: 4 Ross
uncle: 4 Igor
Tooele: 4 city, town
locale: 4 Utah
Too Far to Go author: John Updike
Too Funky (1992 song) artist: George Michael
too good ___ true: 4 to be
Too Hot (1980 song) artist: Kool and the Gang
Too Hot to Handle (1938 film)
cast: Clark Gable, Myrna Loy, Walter Pidgeon
director: Jack Conway
tool: 3 awl, axe, bit, hoe, lag, saw, zax 4 adze, dupe, file, froe, frow, jack, mark, pawn, pick, rake, rasp, vise 5 agent, anvil, auger, burin, chump, clamp, drill, edger, gizmo, gouge, knife, lathe, lever, means, organ, patsy, plane, poker, punch, snake, spade, thing 6 chisel, device, dibble, engine, flunky, gadget, gimlet, hammer, harrow, jackal, lackey, linger, mallet, medium, minion, pliers, puppet, router, shovel, sickle, stooge, sucker, trowel, victim, wrench 7 cat's-paw, flunkey, hacksaw, hatchet, hayfork, ice pick, lacquey, machine, mattock, nail set, scalpel, utensil, vehicle 8 clippers, easy mark, forceps, hireling 9 accessory, apparatus, appliance, greenhorn, implement, machinery, mechanism, timesaver 10 accomplice, figurehead, instrument, jackhammer
along: 3 zip 4 ride 5 drive, motor, steer 7 advance, journey
boring ~: 10 jackhammer
building: 4 shed
carpentry ~: 3 adz, saw 4 adze, vise 5 bevel, clamp, drill, level, plane 6 chisel, hammer, jigsaw, pliers
chef's ~: 4 mill 5 corer, dicer, parer, ricer, whisk 6 beater, slicer
cutting ~: 3 axe, saw 4 adze 5 blade, knife 6 bowsaw, stylus 7 scalpel
ender: 3 box 5 maker
forester's ~: 7 hatchet
garden ~: 3 hoe 4 hose, rake 5 edger, spade 6 dibble
handle: 4 haft 5 helve
orthopedist's ~: 4 x-ray 10 radiograph
partner: 3 die
point: 3 nib
prehistoric ~: 3 axe 4 adze 6 eolith
rotary ~: 5 auger
yard ~: 4 rake 5 edger, mower
tool ___: 3 kit 4 post 5 steel 7 subject
___ tool: 4 edge, hand 5 flake, power 6 facing, McLeod 7 machine
tool and ___: 3 die
___ Too Late: 3 It's 4 Born
Too Late for Goodbyes (1985 song)
artist: Julian Lennon
Too Late the Hero (1970 film)
cast: Michael Caine, Henry Fonda, Cliff Robertson
director: Robert Aldrich
Too Late the Phalarope author: 5 Paton
Too Late to Say Goodbye (1990 song)
artist: Richard Marx
toolbox item: 3 nut 4 bolt, nail, T-nut 5 screw
toolhouse: 4 shed
toolmaking: 5 skill
tools: 3 kit 4 gear 6 tackle 8 hardware 9 equipment
good with ~: 4 able, deft 5 adept, handy 6 adroit 7 skilled 8 skillful 9 dexterous
Too Many ___ in the Sea: 4 Fish
Too many cooks...: 3 saw 5 adage, maxim
Too Many Girls (1940 film): 7 musical
cast: Lucille Ball, Eddie Bracken, Richard Carlson
director: George Abbott
songwriter: 4 Hart 7 Rodgers
Too Many Husbands (1940 film)
cast: Jean Arthur, Melvyn Douglas, Fred MacMurray
director: Wesley Ruggles
Too Many Rivers (1965 song) artist: Brenda Lee
Toomey: 4 Bill 5 Regis
Toomey, Bill: 10 decathlete
Too Much Heaven (1978 song) artist: Bee Gees
too much in music: 5 tanto 6 troppo
Too Much (song) artist: Elvis Presley, Spice Girls
Too Much Time on My Hands (1981 song) artist: Styx
Too Much, Too Little, Too Late (1978 song)
artist: Deniece Williams, Johnny Mathis
toon: 4 tree 9 character
art: 3 cel 4 cell
Toonces: 3 cat
___ to One, A: 7 Million
To One in Paradise author: Edgar Allan Poe
Toonerville ___: 7 Trolley
to one's ___: 4 face, name 5 taste
to one's ___ content: 6 heart's
___ to oneself: 4 keep
___ to one's guns: 5 stick
___ to one's heart: 5 close
___ to one's heels: 4 take
___ to one's knees: 5 bring
___ to one's knitting: 5 stick
___ to one's ribs: 5 stick
___ to one's word: 4 true
too pooped ___: 5 to pop
___ Too Proud to Beg: 4 Ain't
Too-Ra-___...: 5 Loo-ra
___ to order: 4 call
___-to-order: 4 made
___ too shabby!: 3 Not
toot: 4 beep, blow, honk, pipe 5 binge, blast, fling, sound 6 bender 10 inhalation
one's own horn: 4 brag, crow 5 boast, vaunt 7 talk big
___ toot: 3 on a
tooter: 5 piper
tooth: 3 cog 4 fang, tusk 5 molar 6 canine, cuspid, liking 7 grinder, incisor 8 sprocket 10 projection
and nail: 5 madly 6 wildly 8 fiercely, savagely 9 violently
cleaner: 5 brush, floss 7 dentist
combining form: 4 dent- 5 denti-, dento-, odont- 6 odonto-
doctor's degree: 3 DDS, DMD
doctor's org.: 3 ADA
ender: 4 ache, pick, some, wort 5 brush, paste 6 powder
extract a ~: 4 yank
filling: 5 inlay 7 amalgam
fix a ~: 4 fill
for a tooth: 7 revenge
gear ~: 3 cog
holder: 3 jaw 4 gums 5 mouth
long in the ~: 4 aged 5 aging, hoary 6 ageing 7 ancient, elderly, wizened 8 grizzled 9 geriatric, getting on, senescent, up in years
of a ~: 6 dental
part: 4 cusp, pulp, root 5 crown 6 dentin, enamel 7 dentine
partner: 4 nail
starter: 3 dog, eye 4 buck
sweet ~: 4 urge 6 desire, hunger 9 addiction
taker: 5 fairy
topper: 3 cap 5 crown
trouble: 4 ache 5 decay 6 caries, cavity
tooth ___: 5 decay, fairy, shell 6 chisel, fungus, powder
___ tooth: 3 dog, egg 4 baby, milk 5 cheek, molar, pivot, raker, sweet 6 canine, wisdom 7 cleaner, primary
tooth and ___: 4 nail
toothbrush brand: 3 Tek 5 Oral B, Reach 7 Colgate
___-tooth check: 6 hound's
___-tooth comb: 4 fine
toothed: 8 serrated
bar: 5 ratch
device: 3 saw 4 comb, gear, rake
___-toothed: 3 gap, gat, saw
Tooth Fairy: 4 myth
toothpaste: 3 Aim 5 Crest, Gleem, Topol 7 Close-Up, Colgate, Viadent 9 Aquafresh, Mentadent, Pepsodent, Rembrandt, Sensodyne 10 Pearl Drops, Ultra Brite 11 Tom's of Maine
approving org.: 3 ADA
kind of ~: 3 gel
1950s ~: 5 Ipana
open, as ~: 5 uncap
unit: 4 tube
toothpicks, like some: 5 minty
toothpick, treat on a: 6 canapé
toothsome: 5 sapid, sweet, tasty, yummy 6 edible, savory 8 luscious 9 ambrosial, delicious, flavorful, nectarous, palatable 10 appetizing, delectable
make ~: 7 sweeten
___-tooth tiger: 5 saber
tootle: 4 beep, blow, honk 5 blare
toot one's own ___: 4 horn
too-too: 5 artsy, ultra 6 la-de-da, la-di-da, overly 7 mincing 8 lah-di-dah
Toots: 4 Shor
tootsie: 2 jo 3 dog, hon, pet 4 baby, dear, foot, jill, love 5 amour, angel,

chéri, cooky, cutey, cutie, deary, ducky, flame, honey, leman, lover, lovey, novia, novio, sugar, sweet **6** bon ami, chérie, cookie, dautie, dearie, steady, sweets **7** beloved, dearest, dear one, pigsney, schatzi, squeeze, sweetie **8** chou-chou, cutie pie, dowsabel, dulcinea, ladylove, lovebird, macushla, paramour, precious, snookums, sugar pie, sweetums, truelove **9** bonne amie, boyfriend, dreamboat, inamorata, inamorato, petit chou, valentine **10** girlfriend, heartthrob, honeybunch, mavourneen, sweetheart, sweetie pie, turtledove

Tootsie (1982 film)
  cast: Dabney Coleman, Geena Davis, Charles Durning, Teri Garr, Dustin Hoffman, Jessica Lange, Bill Murray, Sydney Pollack
  director: Sydney Pollack

Tootsie Roll: **5** candy, snack, sweet

tootsy: **4** foot

tootsy-__: **6** wootsy

Toot Toot Tootsie (1922 song) artist: Al Jolson

Too Young (1972 song) artist: Donny Osmond

top: **3** ace, cap, end, fox, ice, lid, rim, tip **4** acme, A-one, apex, beat, best, boss, cork, cusp, dock, fine, head, lead, lick, peak, roof, skim, trim, whip **5** break, chief, climb, cover, cream, crest, crown, elite, excel, limit, major, one up, outdo, prize, prune, scale, shirt, spire, tower, upper **6** apogee, better, blouse, bodice, choice, cut off, defeat, exceed, finest, finial, height, lop off, outfox, outwit, refute, select, summit, utmost, vertex, zenith **7** ceiling, dreidel, eclipse, garnish, highest, leading, maximum, overrun, primary, shut out, spinner, stopper, supreme, surface, surpass **8** covering, dominant, five-star, foremost, go beyond, greatest, lingerie, loftiest, outclass, outshine, outsmart, outstrip, outweigh, pinnacle, round off, surmount, truncate **9** beginning, excellent, first-rate, high point, number one, paramount, plaything, principal, prominent, uppermost **10** first-class, preeminent, tower above, upper limit
  again: **5** reice
  at ~ speed: **4** fast **5** apace **7** hastily, quickly, rapidly, swiftly **8** in no time, speedily **9** hurriedly, posthaste
  at the ~: **5** aloft **6** apical **8** unbeaten **10** successful
  banana: **4** boss **5** brass, ruler **6** honcho, kahuna, leader **7** kingpin, skipper **8** kingfish **9** big cheese, big kahuna, commander **10** head honcho
  be on ~: **4** rule
  big ~: **4** show, tent **6** circus **9** spectacle
  blow one's ~: **4** rage, rant, rave **5** erupt, freak **7** flare up, flip out
  brass: **5** chief, mogul **8** kingfish, official **9** commander **10** management
  come out on ~: **3** ace, win **7** prevail, triumph **8** overcome
  dog: **4** boss, head, jefe, king, star **5** champ, chief, first, Mr. Big, ruler **6** bigwig, gerent, honcho, leader, master, winner **7** captain, headman, manager, premier **8** big wheel, brass hat, cardinal, champion, director, foremost, governor, higher-up, kingfish, official, overseer, superior **9** authority, big cheese, commander, executive, number one, personage, president, principal, sovereign **10** supervisor
  draw: **4** star
  ender: **4** coat, knot, mast, most, sail, side, soil, spin **5** lofty, notch **6** minnow, stitch **7** gallant
  floor: **4** loft **6** garret
  from the ~: **4** anew, over **6** afresh, de novo
  from ~ to bottom: **5** thoro **8** complete, thorough
  get ~ billing: **4** star
  go at ~ speed: **3** run **4** dash, race, rush, tear, whiz **5** scoot **6** gallop, scurry, sprint, streak **7** scamper
  group: **4** best **5** A-list, elite **6** choice, gentry, jet set, select **7** in crowd, society **8** literati, nobility, old money **9** exclusive, high-class **10** blue bloods, glitterati, privileged, upper class, upper crust
  jar ~: **3** cap **5** cover
  level: **4** acme, apex, head, peak, roof **5** crest, crown **6** apogee, heyday, summit, zenith **7** maximum **8** mountain, pinnacle
  off: **3** cap, end **4** fill **5** crown **8** round out **9** culminate, replenish **10** complement
  off the ~ of one's head: **5** ad-lib **7** offhand **9** extempore, impromptu, unplanned **10** improvised, off-the-cuff, unprepared
  on ~: **5** above, ahead **7** winning **8** dominant, reigning, superior, unbeaten **9** in command, in the lead **10** successful, triumphant, victorious
  on ~ of: **3** o'er **4** over, upon **5** above **6** shrewd **7** besides
  on ~ of the world: **4** glad **5** happy, merry **6** blithe, cheery, elated, jovial, joyful, joyous, upbeat **7** gleeful, pleased, tickled **8** blissful, cheerful, ecstatic, euphoric, exultant, jubilant, mirthful, thrilled **9** delighted, overjoyed, rejoicing
  out: **4** peak
  over the ~: **7** bonkers
  put the ~ on: **3** cap **4** cork, seal **5** close, cover **7** stopper
  rating: **3** ten **4** A-one **5** A plus
  reach the ~: **4** rise **5** climb **6** arrive, ascend **7** prosper, succeed, triumph **8** flourish, get ahead, surmount
  room at the ~: **4** loft **5** attic **6** garret
  spot: **4** lead **5** first **9** front rank, title role **10** first place
  starter: **3** car, lap, rag, red, tip **4** desk, flat, hard, hill, main, roof, tree **5** black, house, stove, table **6** bubble **7** counter **8** mountain
  take it from the ~: **4** redo
  take off the ~: **4** skim
  to bottom: **7** totally **10** thoroughly

top __: **3** dog, gun, hat, off, ten **4** boot, kick, tier **5** brass, quark, round, yeast **6** banana, dollar, loader, timber **7** billing, echelon, slicing

top-__: **4** down, hole **5** heavy, level **6** drawer, flight, secret

top-__-line: **5** of-the

__ top: **3** big, box, peg, pop **4** buff, dish, dome, draw, roll, slab, slip, tank, tube **5** anvil, crazy, curly **6** bonnet, bubble, cotton, halter, hooded

__-top: **3** pop **4** pull, soft **5** screw **6** carrot

Top __: **3** Cat, Gun, Hat **6** Banana

Top __ mornin'!: **4** o the

Top __, White Tie and Tails: **3** Hat

Top __ World: **5** of the

Top-__: **5** Sider

__ to pass: **4** come **5** bring

__ to pay: **4** hell

__ to pay, the: **5** devil

topaz: **3** gem **5** color, jewel **7** citrine, mineral **8** gemstone
  month: **3** Nov. **8** November
  to Mohs: **5** eight

__ topaz: **5** false, smoky **6** common **7** Madeira, Spanish

Topaz: **3** car **4** auto, film **5** novel **7** Mercury **10** automobile
  author: Leon Uris
  cast: John Forsythe, Dany Robin, Frederick Stafford
  director: Alfred Hitchcock

Topaze (1933 film)
  cast: John Barrymore, Myrna Loy

Top Banana (1954 film)
  cast: Rose Marie, Danny Scholl, Phil Silvers
  director: Alfred E. Green

top-billed one: **4** star

topcoat: **6** jacket, ulster **10** mackintosh

__-top desk: **4** roll **5** slant

top-drawer: **3** AAA, ace, top **4** A-one, best, fine, one A **5** adept, elite, great, prime, slick, super **6** choice, finest, goodly, worthy **7** exalted **8** champion, fabulous **9** important, memorable

tope: **4** fish **5** stupa **6** bibble, guzzle, imbibe **9** hoist a few

topee: **6** helmet, sun hat **10** pith helmet

Topeka: **4** city, town
  county: **7** Shawnee
  locale: **3** Kan. **6** Kansas
  river: **6** Kansas

toper: **3** sot **4** lush, soak, wino **5** rummy, souse **6** barfly, bibber **7** guzzler, tippler, tosspot **10** bar crawler
  bill: **6** bar tab

__ to Perdition: **4** Road

topflight: **3** AAA, ace **4** A-one, best, fine, one A **5** adept, crack, dandy, elite, great, prime, primo, super **6** expert, famous, finest, grade A, superb **7** eminent, optimal, premier, stellar, supreme **8** choicest, five-star, foremost, four-star, greatest, peerless, renowned, selected, splendid, sterling, superior, ultimate **9** excellent, exemplary, first-rate, high-class, matchless, nonpareil, paramount, prominent, unequaled, unrivaled, wonderful **10** celebrated, first-class, preeminent, unrivalled, world-class

Top Gun (1986 film)
  cast: Tom Cruise, Anthony Edwards, Val Kilmer, Kelly McGillis
  director: Tony Scott

Top Hat (1935 film): **7** musical
  cast: Fred Astaire, Edward Everett Horton, Ginger Rogers
  composer: **6** Berlin
  director: Mark Sandrich
  studio: **3** RKO

Top Hat, White Tie and Tails composer: Irving Berlin

top-heavy: **7** leaning, tilting **8** lopsided, one-sided, unsteady **10** off-balance, unbalanced

topi: **3** hat **6** helmet **8** antelope
  material: **4** pith
  relative: **3** gnu, kob **4** guib, kudu, oryx, puku **5** addax, bongo, chiru, eland, goral, korin, nyala, oribi, saiga, serow **6** chammy, dik-dik, duiker, impala, koodoo, lechwe, nilgai, rhebok, shammy, shamoy **7** blaubok, blesbok, chamois, defassa, gazelle, gemsbok, gerenuk, grysbok, nylghai, nylghau, sassaby **8** blesbuck, bontebok, bushbuck, gemsbuck, reedbuck, steenbok, steinbok **9** blackbuck, pronghorn, sitatunga, springbok, waterbuck **10** hartebeest, wildebeest

topic: **4** case, subj., text **5** field, issue, motif, thema, theme **6** affair, matter, thesis **7** problem, subject **8** argument, business, question
  hot ~: **5** issue **7** problem **8** argument **10** contention
  list: **6** agenda

topical: **3** new **4** live **5** local, newsy **6** modern **7** current, insular, limited, popular **8** regional **9** parochial **10** newsworthy, particular, restricted

__ to pick: **4** bone

__ to pieces: **4** pick

__ to Pieces: **3** I Go **5** I Fall

Top Job: **7** cleaner
  alternative: **5** Brite, Lysol **7** Lestoil, Mr. Clean, Pine Sol **9** Fantastik, Step Saver

Topkapi (1964 film)
  cast: Melina Mercouri, Robert Morley, Maximilian Schell, Peter Ustinov
  director: Jules Dassin

topknot: **4** coif, tuft **5** crest **6** hairdo **8** coiffure

__ to play: **4** come

__ to please!: **5** We aim

topless towers of __, The: **5** Ilium

topliner: **4** star

topminnow: **4** fish **5** guppy

topmost: **3** top **4** head **5** upper **6** apical **7** highest, maximal, maximum, supreme **8** greatest **9** paramount

topnotch: **3** def, rad **4** aces, A-one, best, boss, braw, cool, dece, fine, gear, keen, neat, nice, phat, tuff **5** adept, dandy, ducky, elite, first, grand, great, marvy, neato, nobby, prime, primo, prize, slick, super, swell **6** bang on, bang-up, bonzer, bosker, choice, divine, dreamy, far-out, gnarly, goodly, grade A, groovy, lovely, peachy, select, slap-up, spot on, superb, terrif, unreal, whizzo, wicked, worthy **7** amazing, awesome, capital, corking, perfect, ripping, skookum, stellar, sublime **8** champion, dazzling, especial, eximious, fabulous, five-star, four-star, frabjous, glorious, heavenly, jim-dandy, slam-bang, smashing, splendid, standout, sterling, stickout, superior, terrific, very good, wondrous **9** bodacious, Endsville, excellent, exemplary, exquisite, first-rate, high-grade, hunky-dory, marvelous, sollicker, unrivaled, wonderful, wunderbar **10** first-class, hotsy-totsy, jack-a-dandy, out of sight, peachy-keen, phenomenal, remarkable, stupendous, super-duper, unrivalled

Topo __: **5** Gigio

top-of-the-line: **4** aces, A-one, best, fine, posh **5** elite, first, great, plush, prime, primo, ritzy, super, swank, swish **6** choice, costly, deluxe, finest, select, superb, swanky **7** highest, leading, optimum, opulent, premier, ranking **8** choicest, five-star, foremost, superior, very good **9** excellent, expensive, first-rate, high-class, high-grade, luxurious, matchless, nonpareil, number one, numero uno, sumptuous, unequaled, unrivaled **10** consummate, first-class, out of sight, perfection, super-duper, unrivalled

Top of the World (1973 song) artist: Carpenters

topog.: **3** sci.

topographic
  feature: **2** mt. **3** mtn. **4** cape, gulf, lake, spit **6** valley **8** mountain
  map info: **4** elev. **9** elevation

topography: **6** layout **7** science, terrain
Topol: **10** toothpaste
alternative: **3** Aim **5** Crest, Gleem **7** Close-Up, Colgate, Viadent **9** Aquafresh, Mentadent, Pepsodent, Rembrandt, Sensodyne **10** Pearl Drops, Ultra Brite **11** Tom's of Maine
Topol (actor)
film: Fiddler on the Roof (1971)
Flash Gordon (1980)
For Your Eyes Only (1981)
topper: **3** cap, hat, lid **6** capper **8** headgear, headwear
kitchen ~: **3** cap **5** cover
tooth ~: **5** crown
see also hat
Topper (1937 film)
cast: Constance Bennett, Cary Grant, Roland Young
director: Norman Z. McLeod
Topper (TV sitcom)
cast: Leo G. Carroll (Cosmo Topper)
Anne Jeffreys (Marion Kerby)
Robert Sterling (George Kerby)
dog: Neil
Topper Returns (1941 film)
cast: Joan Blondell, Carole Landis, Roland Young
director: Roy Del Ruth
Topper Takes a Trip (1939 film)
cast: Constance Bennett, Billie Burke, Roland Young
director: Norman Z. McLeod
topping: **5** above, icing **8** frosting
toppings, minus: **5** plain
topple: **3** tip **4** fall, flop, oust, rase, raze, ruin, trip **5** crash, level, pitch, slump, smash, upend, upset, wreck **6** depose, falter, go down, plunge, teeter, totter, tumble, unseat **7** capsize, destroy, founder, stagger, stumble, subvert, tip over, unhorse **8** bulldoze, collapse, demolish, keel over, overturn, take down, tear down, turn over **9** bring down, devastate, dismantle, knock down, knock over, overthrow, take apart **10** hit the dirt
top-priority: **6** urgent
Topps rival: **5** Fleer
top-rated: **3** AAA **4** A-one, best, fine, one A **5** first, great, primo
top round: **4** beef, meat
tops: **4** best **5** crack, first, great, limit, prime, primo, super **6** choice, select, wizard **7** capital, highest, in front, perfect **8** fabulous, foremost, four-star, greatest, peerless, superior **9** excellent, first-rate, high-grade, number one, paramount, sovereign, unequaled **10** first-class, preeminent, super-duper, unexcelled
high ~: **6** sneaks **8** sneakers
what ~ do: **4** spin
__ Tops: **3** Box **4** Four
top-secret org.: **3** NSA
top-shelf: **4** posh **5** fancy, grand, plush, ritzy **6** choice, deluxe, select, swanky **7** opulent **8** palatial, splendid, superior **9** exclusive, high-class **10** first-class
Top-Sider: **4** shoe **8** footwear
topsmelt: **4** fish
__-top sneakers: **4** high
topsoil: **4** dirt, loam, soil **5** earth **6** ground
layer: **5** solum
__ Top Stuffing: **5** Stove
__ to Psyche: **3** Ode
Topsy friend: **3** Eva
Topsy II (1958 song) artist: Cozy Cole
topsy-turvy: **5** askew, messy, mussy, on end **6** unneat, untidy **7** chaotic, jumbled, mixed-up, muddled, riotous, tangled, upended **8** confused, inverted, littered, pell-mell, slovenly **9** cluttered, inside-out **10** disorderly
turn ~: **5** upend, upset **6** invert, jumble, muss up **7** derange **8** disarray, unsettle
Topsy-Turvy (2000 film)
cast: Jim Broadbent, Allan Corduner, Eleanor David, Lesley Manville
director: Mike Leigh
Top Ten, Letterman's: **4** list
toque: **3** hat
feature: **5** plume
material: **6** velvet
wearer: **5** woman
tor: **4** crag, hill **8** mountain, pinnacle **10** prominence, rocky ledge
tora: **8** antelope **10** hartebeest
relative: **3** gnu, kob **4** guib, kudu, oryx, puku, topi **5** addax, bongo, chiru, eland, goral, korin, nyala, oribi, saiga, serow **6** chammy, dikdik, duiker, impala, koodoo, lechwe, nilgai, rhebok, shammy, shamoy **7** blaubok, blesbok, chamois, defassa, gazelle, gemsbok, gerenuk, grysbok, nylghai, nylghau, sassaby **8** blesbuck, bontebok, bushbuck, gemsbuck, reedbuck, steenbok, steinbok **9** blackbuck, pronghorn, sitatunga, springbok, waterbuck **10** wildebeest
Torah: **10** Pentateuch
authority: **5** rabbi, rebbe
medieval ~ commentary: **5** zohar
place: **3** ark **4** shul **5** schul **9** synagogue
place marker: **3** yad
__ Torah: **5** Sefer **6** Sepher, Simhat, Talmud **7** Simchas, Simhath
Tora! Tora! Tora! (1970 film)
cast: Martin Balsam, Kinji Fukasuku, Toshio Masuda
character: **4** Tojo
director: Richard Fleischer
torch: **4** burn **5** flare, light **6** ignite **7** firebug, lantern **8** arsonist, flambeau **10** incinerate, pyromaniac
carry a ~: **4** pine **5** adore **6** suffer
crime: **5** arson **9** pyromania
in America: **10** flashlight
starter: **4** blow
use an acetylene ~: **4** weld
torch __: **4** lily, song **6** singer
Torch __ Trilogy: **4** Song
Torch-Bearers, The author: Alfred Noyes
torched: **3** lit
toreador: **7** matador
toreador __: **5** pants
Toreador Song: **4** aria
composer: **5** Bizet
opera: **6** Carmen
__ to reason: **5** stand
__ to Rebecca, The: **3** Key
__ to Remember: **3** Try
__ to Remember, A: **4** Walk **5** Night
__ to Remember, An: **6** Affair
Toren: **5** Marta
torero: **7** matador
cape color: **4** rojo
Torero Saluting painter: **5** Manet
__ to rest: **3** lay, put
tori: **5** rings
Tori: **4** Amos **8** Spelling
father: **5** Aaron
role: **5** Donna
__ to ribbons: **3** cut
__ to riches: **4** rags
__ to Ride: **6** Ticket
__ to rights: **4** dead
torii: **4** gate **7** gateway
Torin: **8** Thatcher
Torino: **3** car **4** auto, city, Ford, town **5** Turin **10** automobile
locale: **5** Italy **6** Italia
river: **5** the Po
__ to Rio: **3** I Go **4** Road
Tork, Peter: **6** Monkee
colleague: **5** Jones **6** Dolenz **7** Nesmith
Torme, Mel: **6** singer
technique: **4** scat
torment: **3** nag, rag, try, vex **4** bait, fret, gall, haze, hell, hurt, pain, rack, ride **5** abuse, agony, angst, annoy, bully, curse, devil, grind, harry, haunt, hound, press, smite, taunt, tease, worry, wound **6** badger, bother, harass, harrow, heckle, menace, misery, noodge, ordeal, pester, pick on, plague, punish, put out, rankle **7** afflict, agonize, anguish, bedevil, depress, henpeck, oppress, provoke, scourge, torture, travail, trouble **8** aggrieve, distress, irritate, lacerate, mistreat **9** heartache, martyrdom, persecute, suffering, tantalize **10** affliction, excruciate, heartbreak, infliction, oppression
tormented: **7** worried **8** obsessed **9** miserable **10** distraught, distressed
tormenting: **5** abuse **9** agonizing, harrowing
tormentor: **4** pest **5** bully **6** tyrant **10** browbeater, persecutor
torn: **4** rent, slit **5** burst, cleft, ratty, riven, seedy, split **6** broken, gashed, ragged, ripped, shabby, sliced, unsure **7** asunder, cracked, cut open, damaged, divided, mangled, severed, slashed, snapped **8** impaired, in shreds, ruptured, sundered, wavering, wrenched **9** fractured, in tatters, lacerated, uncertain, undecided **10** irresolute, of two minds
all ~ up: **3** low, sad **4** glum **5** tense, upset **6** gloomy, morose **7** anxious, doleful, forlorn, frantic, in a funk, unhappy, worried **8** dejected, downcast, grieving, wretched **9** bummed-out, cheerless, depressed, exercised, in despair, miserable, sorrowful, strung out, tormented, woebegone **10** despairing, despondent, dispirited, distraught, distressed, melancholy
apart, old-style: **4** reft
tornado: **4** wind **5** storm **7** cyclone, tempest, twister **9** hurricane, whirlwind, windstorm
part: **6** funnel
refuge: **6** cellar **7** shelter **8** basement
tornado __: **4** belt **5** cloud
Tornadoes song: Telstar (1962)
Tornami a dir che m'ami: **4** duet
Torn Between Two Lovers (1967 song) artist: Mary MacGregor
Torn Curtain (1966 film)
cast: Julie Andrews, Lila Kedrova, Paul Newman, David Opatoshu
director: Alfred Hitchcock
Torngat: **5** range
locale: **6** Canada **8** Labrador
Torn, Rip: **5** actor
film: Beach Red (1967)
Birch Interval (1977)
Cross Creek (1983)
Defending Your Life (1991)
Heartland (1979)
The Man Who Fell to Earth (1976)
Men in Black (1997)
Nadine (1987)
Payday (1973)
Pork Chop Hill (1959)
The Seduction of Joe Tynan (1979)
Trial and Error (1997)
Tropic of Cancer (1970)
spouse: Geraldine Page
toro: **4** bull **7** Spanish
at times: **5** gorer
opponent: **7** matador, picador
target: **4** capa
Toro: **4** peak **5** mount **8** mountain
locale: **5** Chile
Toronado: **3** car **4** auto, Olds **10** automobile, Oldsmobile
Toronto: **4** city, port, town
former name: **4** York
locale: **3** Ont. **6** Canada **7** Ontario
newspaper: **3** Sun **4** Star
pro team: **7** Raptors **8** Blue Jays **10** Maple Leafs
school: **4** York **7** Ryerson
Toronto Argonauts' org.: **3** CFL
torpedo: **4** bomb, fish, hero, raid, rout, thug **5** blast, shoot, wreck **6** cancel, stifle **7** destroy, shatter **8** abrogate, demolish, sabotage, undercut **9** overpower, undermine
WWII ~ vessel: **5** E-boat
Torpedo: **3** car **4** auto **7** Pontiac **10** automobile
torpedoes: **4** ammo **9** munitions **10** ammunition
torpid: **3** lax **4** dopy, dull, idle, lazy, logy, numb, slow **5** dopey, heavy, inert **6** asleep, draggy, drowsy, latent, leaden, sleepy, sodden **7** dormant, languid, passive **8** benumbed, comatose, fainéant, inactive, indolent, lifeless, listless, slothful, sluggish **9** apathetic, lethargic, paralyzed, sedentary, somnolent, unhurried **10** disengaged, languorous, motionless, slow-moving, spiritless, unreactive
torpidity: **5** sleep, sloth **6** acedia **7** inertia, languor **8** hebetude, idleness, laziness, lethargy **9** faineance, indolence, inertness **10** stagnation
torpor: **4** coma **5** sleep, sloth **6** acedia, apathy **7** inertia, languor, latency, slumber, vacuity **8** doldrums, dormancy, hebetude, idleness, laziness, lethargy, loginess, otiosity **9** faineance, inanition, indolence, inertness, lassitude **10** inactivity, stagnation
Torquato: **5** Tasso
torque __: **6** wrench
Torquemada: **5** Tomás
Torrance: **4** city, town
locale: **10** California
Torre: **3** Joe **5** Frank
torrefy: **4** heat **5** parch, singe
Torre, Joe sport: **8** baseball
Torrence: **4** Dean **6** Ernest
Torrens: **4** lake
city on the ~: **8** Adelaide
locale: **9** Australia
torrent: **4** flux, gush, hail, pour, rain, rash, rush, tide **5** blaze, burst, flood, spate **6** deluge, onrush, stream **7** cascade, niagara **8** cataract, downpour, effusion, outburst, overflow **9** avalanche, cataclysm, waterfall **10** cloudburst, inundation, outpouring
Torreón: **4** city, town
locale: **6** Mexico **8** Coahuila
Torres __: **6** Strait
Torrey __: **4** pine
Torrey, John: **8** botanist
Torricelli, Evangelista: **7** Italian **9** physicist
Torricelli's __: **3** law
torrid: **3** dry, hot **4** arid **5** fiery **6** ardent, erotic, heated, red-hot, steamy, sultry **7** blazing, boiling, burning, fervent, flaming, intense, parched **8** broiling, parching, scalding, scorched, sizzling, stifling, tropical, white-hot **9** scorching **10** blistering, equatorial, hot-blooded, oppressive, passionate, sweltering

torridity: **4** heat **8** warmness
Torrid Zone (1940 film)
 cast: James Cagney, Pat O'Brien, Ann Sheridan
Torrijos: **4** Omar
Torrington: **4** city, town
 locale: **4** Conn.
Tórshavn: **4** city, town
 locale: **6** Faroes **7** Faeroes
torsion: **5** twist
torsion __: **3** bar **5** group **7** balance, modulus
torsk: **3** cod **4** cusk, fish
torso: **3** bod **4** body, form **5** trunk **6** figure **8** physique
tort: **5** crime, libel, wrong **8** trespass
 ender: **3** oni
torte: **4** cake **6** pastry **7** dessert **10** confection
 like a ~: **4** rich
 part: **4** nuts **5** layer
 shop: **6** bakery
__ torte: **6** Linzer, Sacher
tortellini: **5** pasta **7** noodles
 alternative: **4** orzo, ziti **5** penne **7** lasagna, lasagne, pastina, ravioli **8** bucatini, couscous, farfalle, linguine, linguini, macaroni, rigatoni **9** agnolotti, angelhair, cavatelli, manicotti, spaghetti **10** cannelloni, fettuccini, vermicelli
 topping: **5** pesto, sauce **8** marinara
tortilla: **7** Mexican
 chip: **4** nosh **5** nacho, snack
 dish: **4** taco **6** fajita, flauta
 flour: **4** masa **8** cornmeal
 like a ~: **4** flat
 topper: **5** salsa
Tortilla Flat: **4** film **5** novel
 author: John Steinbeck
 cast: John Garfield, Hedy Lamarr, Spencer Tracy
 director: Victor Fleming
 dog: **4** Alec **5** Fluff **7** Enrique, Rudolph **8** Pajarito
 role: **4** Tito **5** Pablo, Pilon **6** Sweets **7** Dolores
tortoise: **6** animal **7** reptile
 feature: **5** shell
 like a ~: **4** poky, slow **6** draggy **7** halting, lagging, languid **8** crawling, creeping, dawdling, dilatory, dragging, drawn-out, plodding, slothful, sluggish, toddling **9** leisurely, lethargic, snaillike, unhurried **10** deliberate, protracted
 opponent: **4** hare
tortoise __: **5** plant **6** beetle, brooch
__ tortoise: **3** box **5** giant **6** gopher
Tortoise and the Hare, The: **5** fable
 source: **4** Esop **5** Aesop
tortoiseshell __: **3** cat **6** turtle
Tortolas: **4** peak **5** mount **8** mountain
 locale: **5** Andes, Chile **9** Argentina
tortoni: **7** dessert **8** ice cream
 alternative: **6** gelati, gelato, sundae **7** parfait, spumone, spumoni **8** snowball
__ Tortugas: **3** Dry
tortuous: **4** bent, mazy, wavy **5** snaky **6** skewed, zigzag **7** bending, complex, crooked, curving, devious, sinuous, snaking, twisted, verbose, winding **8** indirect, involved, twisting **9** ambiguous, entangled, intricate **10** circuitous, convoluted, meandering, roundabout, serpentine
tortured: **5** woful **6** woeful **9** miserable
torturous: **4** hard **5** harsh **6** brutal, severe, taxing, trying **7** onerous **8** crushing, grueling **9** demanding, difficult, harrowing, herculean, punishing, strenuous **10** enervating, exhausting
__ to ruin, the: **4** road
torula: **6** fungus
__ to Run: **4** Born **7** Nowhere
torus: **4** ring **5** donut **8** doughnut **9** inner tube
Torvill partner: **4** Dean
Tory: **5** Major **8** loyalist
 opponent: **4** Whig
__ to Save Your Own Life: **3** How
to say __ of: **7** nothing
__ to say...: **5** I mean
to say the __: **5** least
Tosca: **5** opera
 composer: **7** Puccini
 piece: **4** aria
 role: **5** Mario **6** Cesare **7** Scarpia **8** Spoletta
 setting: **4** Rome **5** Italy
 trio: **4** acts
Toscanini, Arturo: **7** Italian **9** conductor
__ to School: **4** Back
__ to Sea: **3** Out
__ to seed: **3** run
to see, like: **3** irr. **5** irreg. **9** irregular
__ to sell: **6** priced
__ to Sender: **6** Return
tosh: **3** gas, rot **4** blah, bosh, bull, bunk, guff, jazz, jive, pooh **5** bilge, fudge, hokum, hooey, prate, stuff, trash, tripe **6** bunkum, bushwa, drivel, footle, gabble, gammon, gibber, havers, hot air, humbug, jabber, jargon, kibosh, piffle **7** baloney, blarney, blather, blether, boloney, bushwah, eyewash, flannel, flubdub, fustian, garbage, hogwash, inanity, rubbish, twaddle **8** buncombe, claptrap, falderal, falderol, flimflam, flummery, folderal, folderol, nonsense, slipslop, tommyrot, trumpery **9** banana oil, gibberish, kidstakes, moonshine, poppycock, rigmarole **10** applesauce, balderdash, bilge water, codswallop, double-talk, flapdoodle, galimatias, Jabberwock, mumbo jumbo, rigamarole, taradiddle
__ to shame: **3** put
Toshiba: **2** TV **5** TV set **10** television
 alternative: **3** JVC, NEC, RCA **4** Sony **6** Quasar, Zenith **7** Emerson, Hitachi, ProScan **8** Magnavox, Sylvania **9** Panasonic
Toshiro: **6** Mifune
__-to-shore: **4** ship
__ to Silence: **3** Ode
__ to Singapore: **4** Road
To Sir, With Love (1967 film)
 cast: Judy Geeson, Sidney Poitier, Christian Roberts
 director: James Clavell
 theme singer: Lulu
...to skin __: **4** a cat
To Sleep author: John Keats
To Sleep With Anger (1990 film)
 cast: Mary Alice, Paul Butler, Danny Glover
 director: Charles Burnett
__ to Smoochy: **5** Death
__ to sow...: **5** A time
__ to spare: **4** room
toss: **3** bob, lob, sip, sow **4** cast, flip, hurl, jolt, keel, rock, roll, stir, sway **5** bandy, chuck, fling, heave, lurch, pitch, quaff, shake, sling, strew, swing, throw **6** buffet, jiggle, joggle, launch, let fly, plunge, propel, seesaw, squirm, thrash **7** agitate, discard, flounce, flutter, project, swallow **8** flounder, get rid of **9** dispose of, eighty-six
 about: **5** bandy, strew **7** flutter
 and turn: **4** fret **5** brood, worry **7** agonize
 around: **6** debate **7** discuss **8** consider
 back: **4** down, gulp, swig, tope **5** drink, quaff **6** guzzle, imbibe **7** put away
 dice ~: **3** six, ten, two **4** five, four, nine, roll **5** eight, seven, three **6** eleven, twelve **7** boxcars **9** snake eyes
 down: **3** eat, use **4** bolt, gulp, ruin, wolf **5** drain, drink, eat up, empty, erode, gorge, put in, scarf, spend, use up **6** absorb, devour, digest, engulf, expend, feed on, finish, guzzle, imbibe, ingest, ingulf, inhale, nosh on, obsess, prey on, ravage **7** consume, corrode, deplete, destroy, engross, exhaust, partake, play out, put away, scarf up, smolder, snack on, swallow, utilize, wear out **8** gobble up, nibble on, smoulder, squander **9** devastate, dissipate, go through, polish off, preoccupy **10** lay waste to, monopolize, run through
 ender: **3** pot
 it in: **4** quit **6** give up **9** surrender
 out: **3** rid **4** drop, junk **5** eject, evict, scrap **6** depose, reject **7** let go of
toss __: **3** off **6** around
toss and __: **4** turn
tossed __: **5** salad
__-tossed: **7** tempest
tossed-off: **5** ad-lib **6** casual **9** extempore, impromptu, whipped-up **10** improvised, unscripted
Tossin' and Turnin' (1961 song)
 artist: Bobby Lewis
tossing and turning: **5** awake **8** restless
tosspot: **3** sot **4** lush, wino **5** toper **7** tippler
__-tost: **7** tempest
tostada cousin: **4** taco
__ to Steal a Million: **3** How
__ to stern: **4** stem
__ to suggestions: **4** open
tot: **3** add, cub, kid **4** babe, baby, dram, tike, tyke **5** child, kiddy **6** infant, jigger, kiddie, moppet, reckon, rug rat **7** crawler, creeper, toddler **8** juvenile, small fry **9** youngster
 cry: **5** Mommy
 first word: **4** dada, mama
 in Spanish: **4** niña, niño
 place: **3** lap **4** crib **7** nursery, playpen **8** bassinet **9** high chair
 query: **3** why
 refresher: **4** wawa
 take care of a ~: **4** mind **5** watch **7** baby-sit, oversee **9** look after
 time-out: **3** nap
 toe: **5** piggy **6** piggie
 tool: **6** crayon
 toy: **4** doll **5** Legos
 up: **3** add, sum **5** count, tally **6** figure, number, reckon **9** keep score
 vehicle: **4** sled **5** trike, wagon **6** go-cart, go-kart **8** tricycle
 watcher: **4** nana **5** nanny **6** nannie, sitter **10** babysitter
 wear: **3** bib **6** diaper
 see also baby
total: **3** add, all, sum **4** body, bulk, full, mass, rank, rase, raze, rout, ruin, tote **5** add up, clean, count, crash, crush, equal, gross, reach, run to, score, sheer, sound, sum up, tally, uncut, utter, whole, wreck, yield **6** all-out, amount, budget, come to, entire, figure, global, number, pile up, ravage, reckon, result, ring up, strict, volume **7** balance, compute, destroy, flat-out, full-out, general, in-depth, jackpot, mount up, overall, perfect, plenary, rear-end, run into, shatter, stack up, trounce **8** absolute, amount to, complete, comprise, demolish, entirety, finished, implicit, integral, livelong, outright, profound, quantity, sweeping, the works, thorough **9** aggregate, calculate, devastate, downright, enumerate, full-dress, inclusive, keep score, out-and-out, overpower, overwhelm, undivided, universal, unlimited, unreduced, wholesale **10** bottom line, consummate, count heads, exhaustive, final score, unabridged
 again: **5** readd
 as a ~: **5** in all
 component: **6** addend
 starter: **3** tee
total __: **4** heat, loss **5** bases **6** recall **7** eclipse, impulse
__ total: **3** sum
Total: **6** cereal
 competitor: **3** Kix **4** Life, Trix **5** Kashi, Quisp **6** Kaboom, Muesli, Oreo O's, Pablum, Smacks **7** All-Bran, Crispix, Harmony, Hunny B's, Mueslix, Oat Bran, Pokemon **8** Boo Berry, Cheerios, Corn Chex, Corn Pops, Fiber One, Rice Chex, Special K, Uncle Sam, Wheaties **9** Alpha Bits, Apple Zaps, Grape Nuts, Honey Comb, Just Right, Wheat Chex **10** Apple Jacks, Bran Flakes, Cap'n Crunch, Cocoa Puffs, Froot Loops, Mini-Wheats, Nutri-Grain, Puffed Rice, Quaker Oats, Smart Start **11** Cocoa Blasts, Cookie Crisp, Golden Crisp, Lucky Charms, Puffed Wheat, Sweet Crunch, Waffle Crisp
Total Eclipse of the Heart (song)
 artist: Bonnie Tyler, Nicki French
totaled: **4** beat **5** kaput, ran to **7** done for, wrecked **8** finished, wiped out **10** demolished
totalitarian: **8** absolute, despotic, dictator, one-party **9** fascistic **10** despotical
totalitarianism: **7** tyranny
totality: **3** sum **5** gross, unity, whole **6** system **8** ensemble, entirety **9** aggregate, integrity
totalizer numbers: **4** odds
totally: **3** all **4** only **5** fully, plumb, quite, right, sheer **6** bodily, in full, purely, simply, solely, wholly **7** flat out, utterly **8** all in all, entirely, whole hog **9** every inch, full blast, inside out, perfectly, to the hilt **10** absolutely, altogether, completely, thoroughly, to the limit
Total Recall (1990 film)
 cast: Arnold Schwarzenegger, Sharon Stone, Rachel Ticotin
 director: Paul Verhoeven
 setting: **4** Mars
__ to task: **4** call, take **5** bring
tote: **3** lug **4** bear, cart, haul, pack, take **5** add up, bring, carry, ferry, fetch, purse, shlep, total **6** convey, reckon, schlep, shlepp **7** handbag, portage **8** carryall, transfer **9** transport **10** bring along, count heads, pocketbook
 board numbers: **4** odds
 easy to ~: **5** light
 up: **3** add, sum **5** count, tally, total **6** figure, reckon **7** compute **9** calculate, enumerate **10** count heads
tote __: **3** bag, box **4** road **5** board
__ to tears: **4** bore
To Tell the Truth: **8** game show
 contestant: **4** liar
 host: Bud Collyer, Garry Moore, Bill Cullen
 regular: **4** Bean, Cass **9** Orson Bean, Peggy Cass

totem: 3 xat 6 column, emblem, symbol
make a ~: 5 carve
material: 4 tree, wood 5 trunk
totem __: 4 pole
Totem __ Tabu: 3 und
Totem and Taboo author: Sigmund Freud
__ to ten: 3 one
Totentanz composer: 5 Liszt
toter: 6 bearer, hauler, porter, skycap 7 carrier 9 schlepper 10 backpacker
__ to terms: 4 come 5 bring
__ to that!: 4 Amen
to the __: 3 max, sky 4 fore, good, hilt 5 gills, nines, point, skies, teeth 6 letter 7 fullest
to the __ born: 6 manner
to the __ degree: 3 nth
to the __ of: 4 tune
to the __ of the earth: 4 ends
__ to the Beach: 4 Back
__ to the Bottom of the Sea: 6 Voyage
__ to the chase: 3 cut
__ to the Chief: 4 Hail
__ to the Church on Time: 5 Get Me
__ to the cleaners: 4 take
__ to the core: 6 rotten
__ to the draw: 4 beat
To the Ends of the Earth (1948 film)
cast: Ludwig Donath, Signe Hasso, Dick Powell
director: Robert Stevenson
__ to the Future: 4 Back 5 North
__ to the Galatians: 7 Epistle
__ to the good: 3 all
__ to the ground: 3 run
To the Hilt author: Dick Francis
__ to the last drop: 4 Good
To the Last Man author: Zane Grey
To the Lighthouse author: Virginia Woolf
to the manner __: 4 born
__ to the Marines!: 6 Tell it
__ to the Mob: 7 Married
__ to the Moon: 5 Fly Me
__ to the Music: 5 Dance 6 Listen, Swayin'
__ to the nines: 7 dressed
to the nth __: 6 degree
__ to the occasion: 4 rise
__ to the People: 5 Power
to the point (French): 7 à propos
__ to the punch: 4 beat
__ to the purple: 4 born
__ to the quick: 3 cut
__ to the rear: 4 step
__ to the Sea: 6 Riders
__ to the Sea in Ships: 4 Down
__ to the teeth: 5 armed
__ to the Territory: 5 Going
__ to the test: 3 put
__ to the throne: 4 heir
__ to the Trees: 5 I Talk
To the Virgins to Make Much of Time: 4 poem
author: 7 Herrick
__ to the wall: 4 push
__ to the West Wind: 3 Ode
__ to the wire: 4 down
__ to the wise...: 5 A word
__ to the World: 3 Joy
To thine own __ be true: 4 self
__ to think of it: 4 come
to this extent in Latin: 8 quoad hoc
__ to Three Wives, A: 6 Letter
Totie: 6 Fields
Totino's: 5 pizza
alternative: 5 Jeno's, Tony's 6 Ellio's 7 Celeste 8 DiGiorno 9 Tombstone 10 Freschetta
Toto
song: Africa (1982)
Hold the Line (1978)
I Won't Hold You Back (1983)
Rosanna (1982)
vocalist: Bobby Kimball
__ to toe: 4 head
toto, in: 3 all 5 fully, quite 6 wholly 8 as a whole, entirely, from A to Z 9 competely 10 altogether, completely, to the limit
Tototlán: 4 city, town
locale: 6 Mexico 7 Jalisco
__ to Treat a Lady: 5 No Way
__ to trot: 3 hot
__ Tots: 5 Tater
__-totsy: 5 hotsy
totter: 4 limp, reel, rock, roll, slip, sway, trip 5 lurch, quake, shake, waver, weave 6 careen, dodder, falter, linger, quiver, seesaw, shimmy, teeter, topple, wabble, waddle, weaken, wobble 7 blunder, stagger, stumble, tremble, whiffle 8 flounder, hesitate 9 oscillate
__-totter: 6 teeter
Totter: 6 Audrey
tottering: 4 sick 5 shaky 6 unfirm, wabbly, wobbly 7 rickety, unsound 9 doddering 10 ramshackle
Tottori: 4 city, town
locale: 5 Japan
Toubkal: 4 peak 5 mount 8 mountain
locale: 6 Africa 7 Morocco
toucan: 3 pet 4 bird, toco
feature: 3 neb, nib 4 beak, bill
touch: 3 bit, dab, eat, hit, hug, jot, pat, paw, pet, rub, sip, tag, tap, tie 4 abut, dash, drop, feel, hint, join, kiss, lick, loan, meet, melt, move, peck, snip, tint 5 brush, cover, drink, equal, flair, frisk, graze, grope, knack, nudge, probe, reach, rival, sense, shade, shave, skill, smack, speck, taste, tinge, trace, verge, whiff 6 adjoin, affect, allude, bedaub, border, breath, butt on, caress, cuddle, detail, excite, finger, fondle, handle, impact, little, shadow, smooth, strain, streak, strike, stroke, talent, tickle, trifle 7 ability, concern, contact, discuss, disturb, embrace, examine, faculty, impress, inkling, inspect, inspire, involve, larceny, massage, mastery, mention, modicum, palpate, quicken, refer to, request, soupçon, speak of, texture, verge on, whisper 8 artistry, bear upon, border on, come up to, converge, deftness, facility, interest, neighbor, osculate, spoonful 9 keep close, measure up, partake of, pertain to, scintilla, suspicion, undertone 10 green thumb, intimation, manipulate, smattering, sprinkling, suggestion, virtuosity
and go: 5 hairy, risky 6 tricky, unsafe, unsure, urgent 7 parlous 8 perilous, ticklish 9 dangerous, debatable, hazardous, uncertain 10 precarious
barely ~: 4 kiss 5 graze 6 glance 9 glance off
don't ~: 4 duck, shun, skip 5 avoid, elude, evade, forgo 6 eschew, give up 7 abstain, boycott 8 forswear, renounce, swear off 10 circumvent
down: 4 land 5 light, perch 6 alight, arrive, settle 8 get there
easy ~: 3 pat, tap 4 lick 5 flick, softy 6 caress, pigeon, softie, sucker, victim 8 pushover
ender: 4 back, down, hole, line, tone, wood 5 stone
gentle ~: 3 hug, pat, pet 6 cuddle, stroke 7 embrace, snuggle
get in ~: 5 reply 7 respond
keep in ~: 4 call, meet 5 phone, reach, write 6 roll in, show up 7 check in, contact 9 get hold of, telephone 10 get a hold of
loving ~: 3 hug, pat, pet 6 cuddle, stroke 7 embrace
off: 4 fire 5 begin, spark, start 6 ignite, kindle 7 actuate, trigger 8 detonate, initiate, motivate 9 instigate
on: 4 abut 5 cover, refer, treat 6 go into, review, talk of 7 mention, pertain, refer to, speak of 8 allude to, deal with, point out
out of ~: 4 away 5 apart 6 cut off, lonely, remote 7 distant 8 detached, isolated
put in ~: 5 refer
science of ~: 7 haptics
up: 3 fix 4 edit 5 amend, emend, gloss, paint, patch, renew 6 better, doctor, modify, polish, redact, repair, revamp, revise 7 correct, enhance, improve, perfect, restore 8 renovate 9 refurbish
up against: 4 abut, join, meet 6 adjoin 8 border on, neighbor
upon: 4 note 5 cover, treat 6 advert, allude, go into, review, talk of 7 mention, refer to, speak of 8 allude to, deal with, point out 9 appertain
touch __: 3 off 4 base, down, upon 5 and go, paper, plate 6 system
touch __ with: 4 base
touch-__: 4 tone, type 5 me-not 6 tackle
touch-__ phone: 4 tone
__ touch: 4 soft 5 Midas 6 common
Touch __ the Cat: 3 Not
Touch __ the Morning: 4 Me in
__ Touch: 4 Love 5 Final, Human, Out of
touchdown: 4 goal 7 landing
make a ~: 5 score
Touché cryer: 6 fencer
touched: 4 daft 5 batty, dotty 6 cuckoo, swayed 7 bonkers, fanatic, grabbed, stirred 8 affected, obsessed, peculiar, softened 9 eccentric, impressed, pixilated
down: 3 lit 4 alit
Touched by an Angel (CBS fantasy)
cast: Valerie Bertinelli (Gloria)
Roma Downey (Monica)
John Dye (Andrew)
Della Reese (Tess)
touchiness: 6 spleen, temper 9 surliness
touching: 3 sad 4 near, next 5 sorry 6 moving, tender 7 contact, emotive, piteous, pitiful, wistful 8 adjacent, eloquent, pathetic, poignant, stirring 9 affecting, emotional, resting on 10 contiguity, contiguous, expressive, impressive, juxtaposed, pathetical
touch-me-__: 3 not
Touch Me in the Morning (1973 song)
artist: Diana Ross
Touch Me (song) artist: Cathy Dennis, Doors, Samantha Fox
Touch Not the Cat author: Mary Stewart
Touch of Class, A (1973 film)
cast: Glenda Jackson, George Segal, Paul Sorvino
director: Melvin Frank
Touch of Evil (1958 film)
cast: Charlton Heston, Janet Leigh, Orson Welles
director: Orson Welles
Touch of Grey (1987 song) artist: Grateful Dead
Touch of Larceny, A (1959 film)
cast: James Mason, George Sanders
director: Guy Hamilton
__ Touch of Mink: 4 That
Touch of the __, A: 4 Poet
__ Touch of Venus: 3 One
touchstone: 4 norm, test 5 gauge, ideal, model 7 measure, pattern 8 exemplar, paradigm, standard 9 archetype, benchmark, criterion, yardstick
Touch the Wind, song subtitled: 6 Eres Tu
__ Touch This: 5 U Can't
touch-tone: 5 phone 9 telephone
touchy: 3 hot 4 edgy 5 cross, dicey, hairy, huffy, jumpy, moody, onery, risky, testy, wired 6 chancy, cranky, crusty, feisty, fretty, grumpy, ireful, ornery, snappy, tricky, unsafe 7 bearish, bristly, crabbed, fretful, grouchy, huffish, peevish, peppery, prickly 8 choleric, churlish, fretsome, growling, grumpish, liverish, perilous, petulant, snappish, ticklish 9 excitable, fractious, hotheaded, irascible, irritable, querulous, sensitive, splenetic 10 easily hurt, ill-natured, out of sorts, precarious
touchy-feely: 9 sensitive
tough: 3 fit 4 firm, goon, hale, hard, hood, iron, mean, punk, ropy, thug, wiry 5 beefy, bossy, bully, burly, chewy, cruel, hairy, hardy, harsh, heavy, hefty, hunky, husky, lusty, macho, picky, rigid, ropey, rough, rowdy, stern, stiff, stout, tight 6 brawny, feisty, flinty, gritty, gunsel, hearty, knotty, mighty, potent, rascal, robust, rugged, savage, severe, sinewy, steely, stocky, strict, strong, sturdy, taxing, thorny, trying, uphill, virile 7 adamant, arduous, austere, callous, doughty, durable, fibrous, gristly, hard-set, hard-won, hoodlum, onerous, ruffian, serious, Spartan, staunch, steeled, stringy, vicious, villain 8 athletic, baffling, cohesive, despotic, exacting, forceful, gangster, grievous, grueling, hardened, hardline, hooligan, indurate, leathery, muscular, obdurate, overdone, powerful, puissant, puzzling, resolute, rigorous, ruthless, seasoned, stalwart, stubborn, tiresome, toilsome, unsavory, vigorous 9 Atlantean, confirmed, demanding, difficult, draconian, hard-nosed, herculean, laborious, merciless, obstinate, resilient, resistant, roughneck, strapping, strenuous, stringent, tenacious, two-fisted, unbending, unsparing, well-built 10 able-bodied, courageous, despotical, exhausting, forbidding, formidable, hard-bitten, hardboiled, headstrong, inflexible, iron-fisted, no-nonsense, oppressive, perplexing, pugnacious, red-blooded, refractory, reinforced, tyrannical, unyielding
get ~: 5 adapt 6 harden, punish 8 accustom 9 acclimate, condition, crack down, habituate
guy: 4 goon, thug 5 he-man 6 outlaw, Samson, Tarzan 7 brigand, bruiser, Goliath, ruffian 8 gangster, Hercules, hooligan 10 powerhouse
hang ~: 6 endure, take it 7 persist 8 tolerate 9 persevere, withstand
hanging ~: 3 set 7 adamant 8 stalwart
luck: 3 woe 6 mishap 9 adversity 10 hard knocks, misfortune
not ~: 3 lax 4 easy, soft 5 slack 7 lenient 8 yielding 9 easygoing 10 permissive
nut to crack: 5 poser 6 enigma 7 mystery, stumper
situation: 3 fix, jam 4 bind, mess 5 pinch 6 plight 7 dilemma
street ~: 4 punk

to outwit: 3 hip, sly 4 foxy, keen, wily, wise 5 acute, canny, quick, ready, savvy, sharp, smart 6 brainy, bright, clever, crafty, shrewd 7 cunning, knowing 8 sensible 9 farseeing, judicious, on the ball, realistic, sagacious 10 discerning, insightful, perceptive, thoughtful
tough __: 4 love, luck 5 break, it out, pitch
tough __ to crack: 3 nut
tough __ to hoe: 3 row
__ tough: 3 get 4 hang
Tough!: 5 sue me 6 too bad
__-Tough: 4 Semi
tough as __: 5 nails
toughen: 4 gird, tone 5 build, enure, inure, shore, steel 6 anneal, beef up, harden, prop up, season, temper, tone up 7 bolster, brace up, build up, burgeon, coarsen, develop, empower, enhance, fortify, shore up, stiffen, tighten 8 bourgeon, buttress, energize, indurate, vitalize 9 acclimate, climatize, intensify, reinforce 10 invigorate, strengthen
up: 5 adapt, build, enure, inure 8 accustom 9 condition, habituate
Tough Guys (1986 film)
cast: Kirk Douglas, Charles Durning, Burt Lancaster, Alexis Smith
director: Jeff Kanew
Tough Guys Don't Dance author: Norman Mailer
toughie: 5 poser 6 enigma, puzzle, riddle 7 mystery, stumper
toughness: 3 vim 4 dint, grit, thew 5 brawn, force, might, power, sinew, spunk, thews, vigor 6 energy, muscle 7 fitness, muscles, potence, potency, stamina 8 backbone, hardness, strength, vitality 9 beefiness, endurance, fortitude, puissance, stability 10 brute force, moral fiber
tough nut to __: 5 crack
toujours __: 3 gai 7 perdrix
Toulon: 4 city, port, town
locale: 3 Var 6 France
Toulouse: 4 city, town
city near ~: 4 Albi
locale: 6 France
river: 7 Garonne
Toulouse-Lautrec, Henri de: 6 artist, French 7 painter
__ to understand...: 3 Am I
toupee: 3 rug, wig 4 hair 6 carpet, peruke 9 hairpiece
tour: 2 do 3 hop, job, run 4 term, time, trek, trip, turn, walk 5 drive, hitch, jaunt, shift, spell, stint, stump, swing, visit 6 cruise, junket, outing, ramble, safari, travel, voyage 7 circuit, explore, getaway, holiday, journey, stretch, weekend 8 conquest, go abroad, sightsee, vacation 9 barnstorm, excursion, globe-trot, overnight, round trip 10 expedition, hit the road, knock about
again: 5 resee
date: 3 gig 7 booking 10 engagement
de force: 4 coup, feat 5 stunt 7 classic, exploit, triumph
go for another ~: 4 reup
guide: 3 map
leader: 5 guide 6 docent, escort
of duty: 5 hitch, spell, stint
participant: 3 pro 6 bowler, golfer
planning org.: 3 AAA
segment: 3 leg 4 stop
vehicle: 3 bus 5 coach 9 transport
tour __: 4 jeté 5 group
__ tour: 5 Cook's, grand 7 package
touraco: 4 bird
Tourane today: 6 Da Nang
tourbillion: 4 wind
Tour de France: 4 race 8 bike race
participant: 5 racer
tour en __: 4 l'air
touring: 4 away 6 abroad 9 on the road 10 on vacation
touring __: 3 car
__ touring: 3 ski
tourist: 7 pilgrim, visitor, voyager 8 stranger, traveler, vagabond, wayfarer 9 jet-setter, journeyer, sightseer 10 day-tripper, vacationer
attraction: 4 cave 5 sight 6 cavern
magnet: 5 Mecca
need: 3 map 4 visa 6 camera
stop: 3 inn, spa 5 B and B, hotel, motel 6 resort 10 motor court, motor lodge
tourist __: 3 car 4 home, trap 5 class, court
tourmaline: 3 gem 7 mineral 8 gemstone 9 rubellite
tournament: 4 game, meet, tilt 5 event, fight, joust, match 7 contest, tourney
attire: 5 armor
compete in a ~: 5 joust
kind of ~: 4 open 5 pro-am
pass: 3 bye
round: 5 semis 6 finals
Tourneau: 5 watch 10 wristwatch
alternative: 4 Ebel, Rado 5 Casio, Elgin, Lorus, Omega, Rolex, Seiko, Timex 6 Bulova, Fossil, Movado, Pulsar, Swatch 7 Citizen 8 Longines, Tag Heuer
Tourneur, Jacques: 8 director
film: Berlin Express (1948)
Canyon Passage (1946)
Cat People (1942)
The Comedy of Terrors (1964)
Curse of the Demon (1957)
Easy Living (1949)
The Flame and the Arrow (1950)
I Walked With a Zombie (1943)
Nightfall (1956)
Out of the Past (1947)
Stars in My Crown (1950)
tour of __: 4 duty
Tour of the Moon, A author: Jules Verne
Tours: 4 city, town
locale: 6 France
river: 5 Loire
__ to use: 3 put
tousle: 4 muss 6 muss up, ruffle, rumple, tangle 7 snarl up
tousled: 5 messy, mussy 6 blowsy, blowzy, matted, mussed, unneat, untidy 7 blowsed, blowzed, ruffled, rumpled, tangled, unkempt 8 messed up, mussed up, uncombed 10 disheveled, disordered
Toussaint: 9 L'Overture
tout: 4 hype, plug, push 5 boost, extol, shill 6 advise, extoll, herald, hype up, praise, talk up, tip off 7 acclaim, boast of, glorify, lionize, promote, show off, solicit, tipster 8 advocate, ballyhoo 9 advertise, brag about, publicize, recommend 10 make much of
British ~: 4 spiv
hangout: 3 OTB 5 track 9 racetrack
offering: 3 tip 6 hot tip
talk: 5 spiel
topic: 4 odds
tout __: 5 à fait, à vous
__ tout: 5 pas du
tout de suite: 3 now, PDQ 4 anon, soon 6 at once, pronto 7 rapidly 8 in a flash, in a jiffy, promptly, right now 9 forthwith, instantly, on the spot, right away 10 here and now, this moment
tout le monde: 3 all 6 French 8 everyone
__ to Utopia: 4 Road
__ tov: 3 yom 5 mazal, mazel
Tovah: 8 Feldshuh
Tovarich (1937 film)
cast: Charles Boyer, Claudette Colbert, Basil Rathbone
director: Anatole Litvak
toves did, what the slithy: 4 gyre
tow: 3 lug, tug 4 drag, draw, haul, pull, yank 5 ferry, flaxy, trail, trawl 6 convey, flaxen, propel 7 wrecker 8 haul away 9 drag along, pull along, transport
ender: 3 age 4 boat, head, line, path 6 headed
ski ~: 4 J-bar, T-bar
tow __: 3 bar, bug, car 5 truck
tow-__ zone: 4 away
__ tow: 3 ski 4 rope
toward: 4 in re 5 about 6 almost, facing, nearly 7 apropos, vis-à-vis 8 fronting, not quite 9 headed for, regarding 10 concerning
prefix: 4 pros-
Toward Freedom author: 5 Nehru
towardly: 6 timely
towards: 3 via 4 in re 5 about 6 almost, facing, nearly 7 apropos, vis-à-vis 8 fronting, not quite 9 as regards, headed for, regarding 10 concerning
move ~: 5 aim at, favor 6 orient 7 head for
__ to Watch Over Me: 7 Someone
tow-away __: 4 zone
__-to-wear: 5 ready
__ to Wed: 4 Easy
towel: 3 dry 4 wipe 5 linen
again: 5 redry
fabric: 5 crash, terry
feature: 3 nap 4 fuzz
holder: 3 rod
off: 3 dry, mop 4 wipe
starter: 4 dish
target: 5 spill
throw in the ~: 4 give, quit 5 yield 6 give up, resign 7 concede, succumb 8 say uncle 9 surrender
word: 3 his 4 hers
towel __: 4 rack
__ towel: 3 cup, tea 4 bath, face, jack 5 guest 6 roller 7 Turkish
__ to Wellville, The: 4 Road
tower: 3 top 4 hulk, keep, loom, mast, rear, rise, soar 5 mount, pylon, spire 6 belfry, castle, column, exceed, pillar, prison, turret 7 citadel, lookout, minaret, obelisk, shelter, steeple, surpass, zikurat 8 dominate, fastness, fortress, high-rise, monolith, monument, pinnacle, surmount, ziggurat, zikkurat 9 campanile, rise above, stand tall 10 lighthouse, skyscraper, stronghold
above: 3 top 5 dwarf, excel 6 exceed 7 eclipse, surpass 8 bestride, dominate, outclass, outshine, outstrip, overhang, overlook 9 transcend 10 outperform, overshadow, put to shame
bell ~: 5 spire 6 belfry 7 steeple 8 pinnacle
ivory ~: 4 lair 5 haven 6 asylum, escape 7 hideout, retreat 8 hideaway 9 sanctuary
of strength: 6 pillar 7 bastion 9 supporter
Old Testament ~: 5 Babel
prehistoric stone ~: 6 chulpa 7 chullpa
ringers: 5 bells 6 chimes
rural ~: 4 silo
starter: 5 watch
TV ~: 4 mast
tower __: 4 bolt 5 block, wagon
__ tower: 4 fire, shot 5 drill, ivory, Texas, water 7 conning, control, cooling, mooring
__ Tower: 4 Coit 5 Ivory, Sears 6 Eiffel
Tower Bridge river: 6 Thames
towering: 4 high, huge, tall, vast 5 giant, great, jumbo, large, lofty, steep, stiff 6 alpine, high up, mighty 7 hulking, immense, mammoth, massive, sizable, soaring, stately, sublime, supreme, titanic 8 colossal, elevated, enormous, gigantic, imposing, king-size, oversize, sizeable, superior, ultimate, uplifted, whapping, whopping 9 Herculean, humongous, monstrous, overlarge, paramount, unequaled 10 cloud-swept, gargantuan, impressive, monumental, preeminent, prodigious, snowcapped, stupendous, surpassing, tremendous
Towering Inferno, The (1974 film)
cast: Fred Astaire, Susan Blakely, Richard Chamberlain, Faye Dunaway, William Holden, Jennifer Jones, Steve McQueen, Paul Newman, Robert Vaughn, Robert Wagner
cat: 4 Elke
director: Irwin Allen, John Guillermin
tower of __: 7 silence 8 strength
Tower of __: 5 Babel, Hanoi 6 London
Tower of Ivory author: Archibald MacLeish
Tower of London, once: 4 gaol
__ Tower of Pisa: 7 Leaning
Tower of Pisa, like the: 5 atilt
Tower of Strength (1961 song) artist: Gene McDaniels
Towers, Constance: 7 actress
film: The Naked Kiss (1964)
Sergeant Rutledge (1960)
Shock Corridor (1963)
Towers of Trezibond, The author: Rose Macaulay
__ Tower, The: 4 Dark 5 Ebony 7 Leaning
tow-headed: 4 fair 5 blond, light, sandy 6 blonde
towhee: 4 bird
cousin: 5 serin
To whom __ concern...: 5 it may
__ to Witch Mountain: 6 Escape
town: 4 burg, city, seat 5 place, urban 6 hamlet, Podunk 7 borough, village 9 boondocks, community, municipal 10 metropolis, settlement
ender: 5 house, scape
starter: 4 down, home 5 cross 6 shanty
town __: 3 car 4 hall, talk 5 clerk, crier, house 7 manager, meeting
__ town: 3 cow, new 4 boom, go to, skip, tank 5 ghost, Hansa, on the 6 market 7 company
__-town: 5 out-of, small
__ Town: 3 Our 4 Bean, Boom, Boys, Cape 5 Funky, Magic, On the, Small, Sugar 7 Abilene
Town Beyond the Wall, The author: Elie Wiesel
Town Car: 3 car 4 auto, Linc 7 Lincoln 10 automobile
Town & Country: 3 car 4 auto 8 Chrysler 10 automobile
Towne, Robert: 8 director
film: Personal Best (1982)
Tequila Sunrise (1988)
Without Limits (1998)
__-Towners, The: 5 Out-of
Townes, Charles: 8 Nobelist 9 physicist
townhouse: 4 home 5 condo 9 residence
townie: 5 local 8 resident 10 inhabitant
Town Like Alice, A author: Nevil Shute

Town Sedan: 3 car 4 auto, Ford 10 automobile
Townsend: 6 Robert
towns ender: 3 man, men 4 folk 5 woman, women 6 people
Townshend __: 4 Acts
Townshend, Pete
group: The Who
song: Let My Love Open the Door (1980)
townsman: 5 local 7 citizen 8 resident
Townsman: 3 car 4 auto 5 Chevy 9 Chevrolet 10 automobile
town-square structure: 6 gazebo
Townsville: 4 city, town
locale: 9 Australia
Town, The author: Conrad Richter
__ Town Too: 3 Her
Town Without Pity (1961 film)
cast: Kirk Douglas, E.G. Marshall
composer: 7 Tiomkin
director: Gottfried Reinhardt
theme singer: Gene Pitney
To Wong __, Thanks...: 3 Foo
__-to-work law: 5 right
__ to worry!: 3 Not
towpath: 5 track, trail
Towson: 4 city, town
locale: 8 Maryland
toxic: 6 malign, poison, septic 7 adverse, baleful, baneful, harmful, hurtful, noxious, ruinous 8 damaging, negative, venomous, virulent 9 dangerous, injurious, poisonous 10 calamitous, disastrous, pernicious
chemical: 3 PCB 5 venom 6 dioxin
condition: 6 sepsis
gas: 5 radon
org. overseeing ~ cleanups: 3 EPA
toxin: 5 ricin, venin, venom 6 curara, curare, poison, venene, venine 7 botulin, hemlock, henbane 8 pathogen 9 wolfsbane 10 belladonna
starter: 4 anti 5 neuro
Toxin author: Robin Cook
toxiphobe fear: 6 poison
toxophilite: 6 archer, bowman
famous ~: 4 Tell
weapon: 3 bow 5 arrow
toy: 3 top 4 ball, doll, game, hoop, jest, kite, play, sled, yo-yo 5 block, dally, flirt, GI Joe, kazoo, Legos, small, sport, tease, train, truck 6 bauble, cap gun, coquet, fiddle, geegaw, gewgaw, glider, kewpie, lead on, little, popgun, puppet, rattle, Slinky, stilts, tinker, trifle 7 balloon, fribble, Frisbee, trinket 8 Hula Hoop, jump rope, pinwheel, water gun 9 bagatelle, miniature, paper doll, play games, plaything, pogo stick, squirt gun 10 mess around, peashooter, tin soldier, trifle with
ball: 4 Nerf
bathtub ~: 4 boat, duck
beach ~: 4 pail
holder: 3 box 5 chest, trunk
maker: 3 elf 4 Lego, Tomy 5 Ideal 6 Hasbro, Mattel
'90s ~ disk: 3 pog
with: 3 rag, use 5 flirt, tease 6 finger, lead on, trifle
(with): 4 fool 6 fiddle
toy __: 3 dog 4 line, with 5 chest
Toyama: 4 city, town
locale: 5 Japan
toyer: 5 flirt 7 dallier, trifler
Toyland visitor: 4 babe
toy-mouse stuffing: 6 catnip
Toynbee, Arnold: 6 author, writer 7 English 9 historian
work: A Study of History
toyon: 5 shrub
Toyonaka: 4 city, town
locale: 5 Japan
Toyota: 3 car 4 auto, city, town 10 automobile
competitor: 5 Mazda 6 Nissan
locale: 5 Japan
model: 3 RAV 4 Echo 5 Camry, Paseo, Supra 6 Avalon, Celica, Matrix, Previa, Sienna, Solara, Spyder, Tercel 7 Corolla, Sequoia 8 Cressida 10 Highlander 11 Landcruiser
__ to you!: 5 Here's
__ to You: 3 Run 4 So in 5 Close, It's Up, I Turn 7 Devoted
__ to you, New York...: 5 It's up
To your health!: 5 salud, skoal, toast 6 cheers, prosit
Toys __: 3 R Us
Toys for __: 4 Tots
Toys in the Attic author: Lillian Hellman
character: 3 Gus 4 Anna, Lily 5 Prine 6 Carrie, Julian
Toy Soldiers (1989 song) artist: Martika
Toy Soldiers star: 5 Astin
Toys song: A Lover's Concerto (1965)
Toy Story (1995 film)
director: John Lasseter
dog: 4 Scud
voice cast: Tim Allen, Tom Hanks, Don Rickles, Jim Varney
Toy Symphony composer: 5 Haydn
__ to Z: 5 from A
To Zante author: Edgar Allan Poe
__ to Zanzibar: 4 Road
tpk.: 3 hwy., rte.
tra-__: 4 la-la
Trabert, Tony: 7 netster 9 tennis pro
milieu: 5 court
trace: 3 bit, dab, jot, map, ray 4 atom, clew, clue, copy, dash, draw, drop, find, hint, hunt, iota, lick, mark, seek, sign, spot, step, tint, whit, wisp 5 crumb, grain, infer, pinch, proof, relic, scrap, shade, shred, smell, spark, speck, spoor, stalk, tinge, token, touch, track, trail, whiff 6 breath, deduce, derive, detect, follow, little, nuance, pursue, record, shadow, sketch, strain, streak, trifle 7 glimmer, outline, remains, remnant, run down, smidgen, smidgin, snippet, soupçon, unearth, vestige, whisper 8 chalk out, discover, evidence, fragment, landmark, particle, smell out, smidgeon, tincture 9 adumbrate, attribute, delineate, duplicate, ferret out, footprint, reproduce, scintilla, search for, suspicion, track down, undertone 10 indication, intimation, sprinkling, suggestion
leave no ~ of: 3 end 4 doom, raze, ruin 5 blast, crush, total, wreck 7 despoil, destroy, scourge, scuttle, wipe out 8 bulldoze, clean out, decimate, demolish, lay waste 9 devastate 10 annihilate, obliterate
trace __: 6 fossil 7 element
__ trace: 4 edit 6 memory
__ Trace: 7 Natchez
tracer __: 6 bullet
__ tracer: 4 skip
Tracer: 3 car 4 auto 7 Mercury 10 automobile
tracer, medical: 6 iodine
Tracer of Lost Persons: Mr. Keen
tracery: 3 web 7 lattice, network 8 filigree
traces
kick over the ~: 4 riot 5 rebel 6 mutiny, revolt 7 run amok, run riot
Tracey: 4 Gold 6 Ullman
trachea: 4 tube
neighbor: 6 larynx
Traci: 5 Lords 7 Bingham
Trac II alternative: 4 Atra
tracing: 4 copy, line 6 ectype 7 drawing, outline
tracing __: 4 tape 5 paper
track: 3 dog, pan, rut, way 4 hunt, lane, line, mark, path, rail, road, sign, spot, step, tail, wake, walk 5 alley, chase, orbit, rails, route, scent, spoor, stalk, trace, trail, tread 6 artery, course, follow, groove, pursue 7 channel, circuit, heading, imprint, monitor, pathway, railway, recount, towpath 8 bearings, footpath 9 direction, footprint 10 beaten path, footprints, impression, indication, keep tabs on, passageway, trajectory
advisor: 4 tout
alternative: 3 OTB
and field need: 4 shot 6 hammer, hurdle 7 javelin
animal ~: 5 spoor
athlete: 5 miler, racer 6 runner 7 hurdler 10 high jumper
bet: 5 wager 6 exacta 8 perfecta, quinella 9 quiniella
circuit: 3 lap 4 loop 6 course
combining form: 4 ichn- 5 ichno-
distance: 4 mile
down: 3 dog, tag 4 find, hunt, seek, tail 5 catch, chase, scour, stalk, trace, trail 6 detect, follow, locate, look up, pursue, search, shadow, turn up 7 bird-dog, capture, go after, run down, scout up, unearth 8 discover, scout out, smell out, sniff out 9 apprehend, ferret out
event: 3 run 4 dash, meet 5 event, relay 6 discus, sprint 7 hurdles, javelin, shot put
figures: 4 odds
framework: 6 gantry
get off the ~: 5 stray 6 derail
hit the ~: 3 jog, run 4 trot 8 exercise
in Spanish: 3 vía
keep ~ of: 5 watch 6 follow 7 monitor, oversee
lose ~ of: 6 mislay 7 misfile 8 misplace
official: 5 timer 7 referee, starter
off the ~: 4 asea, lost 5 at sea 6 afield, astray, errant 8 mistaken 10 digressing, on a tangent
off the beaten ~: 6 afield, lonely 8 isolated, secluded
on ~: 7 correct, working 10 successful
path: 4 lane
patron: 6 better, bettor 7 gambler, wagerer
racer: 3 car 4 auto, cart, kart 5 horse 6 go-cart, go-kart, runner 8 sprinter
shape: 4 oval
side ~: 4 spur
starter: 4 back, race, side 5 sound
surface: 4 turf
tear up the ~: 4 zoom
tire ~: 3 rut
trial: 3 mud 4 heat 8 humidity
unit: 4 yard 5 meter
winnings: 5 purse
word on a ~ ticket: 3 win 4 show 5 place
track __: 4 down, meet, shoe, shot, suit 5 brake, event, spike 6 record, system
__ track: 4 body, fast, lead, slab, spur, stub 5 laugh, mommy, storm 6 cinder, ground, inside, ladder 7 optical, warning
__-track: 3 one, two 5 trick 6 single, tenure
track and __: 5 field
trackball relative: 5 mouse
__-track betting: 3 off
tracker: 5 loran, NORAD, radar, sonar 6 hunter
Tracker: 3 Geo, SUV 5 Chevy 9 Chevrolet
tracking __: 4 poll, shot 6 system 7 station
__-track mind: 3 one
__ track of: 4 keep, lose
tracks: 8 railroad
cover another's ~: 4 abet 7 collude
make ~: 3 hie, run 4 bolt, flee, race, rush, tear 5 hurry, scoot, scram, spank 6 depart, hasten 8 fugitate 10 accelerate, get hopping
stop in one's ~: 4 halt 5 pause 6 arrest, freeze, hold up 7 suspend, terrify 8 paralyze, prohibit 10 scare stiff
wrong side of the ~: 4 slum
__ tracks: 3 hen 4 make 7 sorting
Tracks of My Tears (song), The artist: Johnny Rivers, Miracles
__-track tape: 5 eight
tract: 3 lot 4 area, belt, land, plat, plot, zone 5 essay, field, patch, space 6 extent, locale, parcel, region, sector, spread 7 booklet, expanse, grounds, leaflet, quarter, section, stretch, writing 8 brochure, circular, district, freehold, locality, location, pamphlet, property 9 territory 10 exposition, literature
tract __: 5 house 7 housing, society
__ tract: 6 census 7 feather
tractable: 4 easy, meek, tame 6 broken, docile, gentle, pliant 7 dutiful, passive, plastic, pliable, subdued, trained, willing 8 amenable, biddable, flexible, gracious, lamblike, obedient, resigned, yielding 9 adaptable, agreeable, compliant, malleable 10 governable, manageable, submissive
traction: 4 drag, grip, pull 8 friction 9 adherence 10 resistance
lose ~: 4 skid, slip 5 coast, skate, slide 7 slither
tractor
adjunct: 5 baler, mower 7 trailer
home: 4 barn, farm
maker: 5 Deere
owner: 5 sower 6 farmer, grower, plower, reaper, tiller 7 planter 9 harvester 10 agronomist, cultivator
tractor __: 4 feed, pull
tractor-trailer: 2 tk. 3 rig 4 semi 5 truck
Tracy: 3 Lee 4 city, Dick, town 6 Austin, Pollan 7 Chapman, Spencer 8 Caulkins, Lawrence, Scoggins
locale: 10 California
to Hepburn: 6 costar
Tracy and Hepburn author: 5 Kanin
Tracy, Dick: 3 cop 9 detective
drawer: 5 Gould
foe: 5 Itchy 7 Flat Top, Mumbles 9 Prune Face
wife: 4 Tess
Tracy, Spencer: 5 actor
film: 20,000 Years in Sing Sing (1933)
Adam's Rib (1949)
Bad Day at Black Rock (1955)
Boom Town (1940)
Boys Town (1938, AA)
Broken Lance (1954)
Captains Courageous (1937, AA)
Desk Set (1957)
Dr. Jekyll and Mr. Hyde (1941)
Edison, the Man (1940)
Father of the Bride (1950)
Father's Little Dividend (1951)
Fury (1936)
Guess Who's Coming to Dinner (1967)
Inherit the Wind (1960)

It's a Mad Mad Mad Mad World (1963)
Judgment at Nuremberg (1961)
Keeper of the Flame (1943)
The Last Hurrah (1958)
Libeled Lady (1936)
Man's Castle (1933)
Me and My Gal (1932)
The Murder Man (1935)
Northwest Passage (1940)
The Old Man and the Sea (1958)
Pat and Mike (1952)
The Power and the Glory (1933)
San Francisco (1936)
The Seventh Cross (1944)
Stanley and Livingstone (1939)
State of the Union (1948)
Test Pilot (1938)
Thirty Seconds Over Tokyo (1944)
Tortilla Flat (1942)
Without Love (1945)
Woman of the Year (1942)

trade: 3 biz, job 4 deal, game, line, sell, shop, swap, swop, wind, work 5 bandy, craft, sales, skill, truck 6 barter, change, handle, market, métier, peddle, switch 7 calling, traffic 8 business, commerce, dealings, exchange, industry, regulars, vocation 9 carpentry, clientele, customers, newspaper, patronage, situation, traffic in 10 buy and sell, employment, enterprise, line of work, livelihood, merchantry, occupation, profession, quid pro quo
abroad: 4 ship 6 export, import 7 smuggle
agreement: 4 GATT 5 NAFTA
carriage ~: 5 elite
carry on a ~: 3 ply 4 work
ender: 3 off 4 mark 5 craft
horse ~: 4 deal 5 argue 6 barter 7 bargain 8 exchange 9 negotiate 10 compromise, do business
in: 4 deal, sell 5 carry, stock 6 handle, redeem, retail
journal: 5 organ 6 review 8 magazine 10 instrument, periodical
medieval ~ union: 4 club, gild 5 guild
off: 6 rotate 7 mediate 9 take turns 10 compromise
org.: 4 assn. 5 assoc.
place: 3 mkt, OTC 4 AMEX, exch., mart, NYSE 6 market, NASDAQ
regulating org.: 3 ICC
show presentation: 4 demo
suffix: 3 -ery, -ier
union: 5 guild, local 8 sodality 9 coalition 10 federation
with: 9 patronize
trade ___: 3 rat 4 book, name, show, wind 5 guild, paper, route, union 6 dollar, places, school, secret 7 balance, barrier, council, deficit, edition
trade-___: 3 off
___ trade: 3 rag 4 fair, free 5 block, horse
___-trade law: 4 fair
trademark: 3 tag 4 logo, mark 5 brand, label 6 emblem, patent, slogan, symbol 7 imprint
trader: 3 arb 4 boat 6 argosy, dealer, seller, vender, vendor 8 merchant, retailer 10 shopkeeper
order: 3 buy 4 sell
___ trader: 4 sole 5 floor, horse
___-trader: 3 day
Trader ___: 3 Vic 4 Horn
Trader Horn (1931 film)
cast: Edwina Booth, Harry Carey, Duncan Renaldo
director: W.S. Van Dyke
tradesperson: 5 plier, plyer 6 worker 8 merchant
Trade Winds (1938 film)
cast: Ralph Bellamy, Joan Bennett, Fredric March
director: Tay Garnett
___-trade zone: 4 free 7 foreign
Tradiciones Peruanas author: Ricardo Palma
trading ___: 4 card, post 5 stamp
___ trading: 7 insider, program
___-trading: 5 horse
Trading Places (1983 film)
cast: Don Ameche, Dan Aykroyd, Ralph Bellamy, Jamie Lee Curtis, Denholm Elliott, Eddie Murphy
director: John Landis
tradition: 4 form, lore 5 ethic, mores, usage 6 belief, legacy, legend, mythos, ritual 7 culture, customs 8 folkways, habitude, heritage, localism, practice 9 formality, mythology 10 background, convention, observance
___ tradition: 4 oral
traditional: 3 old 4 folk 5 right, stock, typic, usual 6 age-old, common, normal, rooted, spoken, wonted 7 popular, regular, routine, typical 8 everyday, habitual, historic, ordinary, orthodox, standard 9 ancestral, customary, legendary, unwritten 10 accustomed, prevailing
traditionalistic: 5 rigid 7 diehard, old-line 8 orthodox
traditions: 4 lore 8 folklore
of ~: 5 loral
traduce: 4 gibe, jeer, jibe, mock, slam, slur, snub 5 abuse, decry, libel, scorn, smear, spurn, taunt 6 defame, deride, dump on, heckle, impugn, injure, malign, offend, rebuff, slight, vilify 7 affront, asperse, blacken, degrade, disdain, put down, rank out, slander 8 backbite, badmouth, belittle, denounce, lie about, ridicule, vilipend 9 blaspheme, denigrate, discredit, disparage, humiliate 10 calumniate, disrespect
traducement: 3 dig 4 barb, gibe, jibe, slam, slap, slur, snub 5 abuse, libel, scorn, taunt 6 rebuff, slight 7 affront, calumny, catcall, disdain, mockery, obloquy, offense, put-down, slander 8 contempt, derision, ridicule 9 aspersion, cheap shot, contumely 10 defamation, disrespect, opprobrium
Trafalgar: 4 cape 6 battle, square
locale: 5 Spain 6 London 7 England
traffic: 3 jam 4 deal, sell 5 trade, truck 6 barter, deal in, handle, influx, logjam 7 bargain, bootleg, cartage, freight 8 business, commerce, dealings, gridlock, vehicles 9 move goods, patronage 10 buy and sell, passengers
be rude in ~: 5 cut in 6 cut off
circle: 6 rotary
controller: 4 cone 5 light, pylon
director: 3 cop 5 arrow
in: 5 trade 6 handle 10 buy and sell
jam unit: 3 car, van 4 auto 5 truck 10 automobile
noise: 4 beep, honk, horn 5 blare
reporter's transport: 6 copter
report source: 5 radio
sign: 3 Slo 4 Slow, Stop 5 Merge, Yield
signal: 3 red 5 amber, green, light 6 yellow
sign shape: 5 arrow 7 octagon 8 triangle
slower: 4 bump 9 speed bump
time: 8 rush hour
trouble: 3 jam 4 clog 5 snarl, tie-up 6 logjam 7 squeeze 8 blockage, clogging, crowding, gridlock, overflow 9 profusion 10 bottleneck, congestion
traffic ___: 3 cop, jam 4 cone 5 court, light 6 circle, island, signal 7 manager, pattern
___ traffic: 3 air 4 thru
Traffic (1972 film)
cast: Jacques Tati
director: Jacques Tati
Traffic (2000 film)
cast: Don Cheadle, Benicio Del Toro, Michael Douglas, Catherine Zeta-Jones
director: Steven Soderbergh
___-traffic control: 3 air
___ tragacanth: 3 gum
tragedies, like some: 5 Greek
tragedy: 3 lot, woe 4 blow, doom, play 5 drama, genre, shock, story, wreck 6 mishap 7 bad luck, failure, setback 8 accident, calamity, disaster, hardship, reversal 9 adversity, cataclysm, mischance 10 misfortune
Tragedy of Korosko, The author: Arthur Conan Doyle
Tragedy of Nan, The author: John Masefield
Tragedy (song) artist: Bee Gees, Fleetwoods
tragic: 3 sad 4 dire, grim 5 awful, fatal, sorry, woful 6 deadly, woeful 7 adverse, doleful, fateful, forlorn, hapless, painful, pitiful, ruinous, unhappy 8 crushing, dreadful, grievous, hopeless, ill-fated, mournful, pathetic, pitiable, shocking, terrible, wretched 9 anguished, appalling, harrowing, ill-omened, miserable, sorrowful 10 calamitous, deplorable, disastrous, ill-starred, lamentable, pathetical, petrifying
fate: 4 doom, ruin 7 undoing 8 downfall 9 cataclysm, ruination
tragic ___: 4 flaw 5 irony
Tragical History of Dr. Faustus, The author: Christopher Marlowe
Tragic Muse, The author: Henry James
Tragic Overture composer: 6 Brahms
Tragic Symphony composer: 8 Schubert
tragopan: 4 bird 8 pheasant
tragus site: 3 ear
trail: 3 dog, lag, rut, spy, tag, tow, way 4 drag, draw, flag, haul, hunt, mark, path, plod, pull, road, slog, step, tail, wake, walk 5 byway, chase, dally, delay, droop, ensue, piste, route, scent, smell, spoor, spy on, stalk, tarry, trace, track 6 course, dangle, dawdle, follow, groove, linger, loiter, pursue, ramble, shadow, ski run 7 draggle, footway, go after, nose out, pathway, pugmark, pursuit, shuffle, succeed, towpath 8 drop back, footpath, hang back, hang down, straggle, tag along 9 come after, lag behind, poke along, track down 10 bridle path, drop behind, fall behind, footprints
boat's ~: 4 wake
boss: 6 drover
ender: 4 head, side 6 blazer 7 blazing, breaker
hit the ~: 3 run 4 tour 5 start 6 depart, set off, set out 7 take off 8 campaign, set forth
hound ~: 4 odor 5 scent, spoor, track
leave the ~: 5 stray
like many a ~: 4 cold
mark a ~: 4 lead 5 blaze, guide 7 pioneer
mix: 4 gorp
off: 4 fade 6 lessen 7 fade out 9 fizzle out
off the ~: 4 lost 6 afield, astray
paper ~: 5 proof 6 record
resolutely: 3 bug, dog 4 tail 5 harry, haunt, hound 6 harass, plague, pursue 7 bird-dog
secondary ~: 5 byway 6 bypath
ski ~: 5 piste
the field: 3 lag 4 lose 8 slip away 9 fall short
user: 5 hiker
trail ___: 3 man, mix 4 bike, boss, herd, rope
___ trail: 5 audit, paper, vapor 6 nature 7 exhaust, sawdust
___ Trail: 6 Oregon 7 Santa Fe, Tamiami 8 Chisholm, Overland
trailblaze: 4 lead 5 guide 7 go first, pioneer
trailblazer: 7 pioneer 8 explorer, vagabond 10 pathfinder
Trailblazer: 3 SUV 5 Chevy 9 Chevrolet
Trail Blazer rival: 3 Cav, Mav, Net, Sun 4 Buck, Bull, Hawk, Heat, Jazz, King, Spur 5 Knick, Laker, Magic, Pacer, Sixer, Sonic 6 Celtic, Hornet, Nugget, Piston, Raptor, Rocket, Wizard 7 Clipper, Grizzly, Warrior 8 Cavalier, Maverick 10 SuperSonic, Timberwolf
Trail Blazers: 4 five, team
org.: 3 NBA
sport: 10 basketball
Trail Driver, The author: Zane Grey
trailer: 3 van 4 clip, semi 5 promo
brand of ~: 5 Ryder, U-Haul
trailer ___: 3 car 4 camp, park 5 court, truck
___ trailer: 4 full, open, tank, tent 5 house, still, truck 6 tandem, travel 7 flatbed
___-trailer: 7 tractor
trailing: 4 last 5 in tow 6 behind, in back, losing 7 lagging 8 rambling
trailing ___: 4 edge 5 phlox 7 arbutus, fuchsia
Trail of the Lonesome Pine, The (1936 film)
cast: Henry Fonda, Fred MacMurray, Sylvia Sidney
director: Henry Hathaway
___ Trail, The: 3 Big 4 Last 6 Oregon 7 Rainbow
train: 2 el 3 row, toy 4 beam, file, form, hone, mold, rear, tail, tame, wake 5 aim at, coach, drill, enure, equip, focus, groom, guide, inure, level, nurse, point, prime, queue, study, suite, teach, tutor 6 column, convoy, course, direct, escort, ground, harden, school, season, series, string, update, warm up, zero in 7 break in, caravan, cortege, develop, educate, engrain, express, implant, ingrain, limited, nurture, prepare, qualify, railway, retinue, vehicle, work out 8 accustom, drum into, espalier, exercise, indurate, initiate, instruct, limber up, practice, rehearse, sequence 9 catechize, condition, cultivate, draw a bead, enlighten, entourage, habituate, make ready, retainers, transport 10 cannonball, continuity, discipline, evangelize, housebreak, procession, specialize, succession, superliner
Amtrak's bullet ~: 5 Acela
away from: 4 wean
bed on a ~: 5 berth
bullet ~ locale: 5 Japan
ender: 3 man, men 4 band, load 6 bearer
express ~: 3 ltd. 7 limited
freight ~: 6 coaler
fuel: 4 coal
in Spanish: 4 tren
line: 2 RR, ry. 3 rwy. 7 railway 8 railroad

lose one's ~: 6 forget, wander
mail locale: 3 RPO
NYC: 3 BMT, IRT
of thought: 5 logic 9 reasoning
on a ~: 6 aboard 7 en route 8 embarked 9 in transit, traveling
part: 3 car 5 diner 6 bar car, boxcar, engine, smoker 7 caboose 10 locomotive
patron: 5 rider 9 passenger
rush-hour: 3 exp. 7 express
shift a ~: 5 shunt
sound: 4 whoo 8 choo choo
stop: 3 sta., stn. 5 depot 7 station
take the ~: 4 ride 5 board 6 travel 7 commute
wheel sound: 5 clack
train __: 3 oil 7 station
__ train: 3 air, sky 4 boat, dial, gear, hop a, milk, mule, pack, pool, snow, unit, wave, work 5 drive, going, goods, gravy, local, power, wagon 6 bullet 7 express, freight
__-train: 3 cat 4 road 5 cross
__ Train: 4 Love, Mule 5 Crewe, Peace, Wagon 6 Terror 7 Freight, Morning, Mystery, Runaway
trained: 4 able, deft, tame 5 slick 6 adroit, au fait, broken, docile, expert, nimble, pliant, versed 7 capable, skilled, subdued 8 dextrous, graceful, lamblike, masterly, obedient, seasoned, skillful, well-bred 9 competent, compliant, dexterous, efficient, masterful, qualified, tractable 10 accustomed, manageable, proficient, submissive
get ~: 5 learn
__-trained: 4 well
trainee: 4 tiro, tyro 5 newie, pupil 6 greeny, intern, novice 7 interne, learner, recruit 8 beginner, neophyte 9 fledgling 10 first-timer, tenderfoot
trainer: 5 coach, tutor 6 mentor 7 pedagog, teacher 8 educator 9 abecedary, pedagogue 10 instructor
place: 3 gym, spa 9 health spa
training: 5 drill 6 basics, tune-up 7 buildup, culture, tuition, workout 8 coaching, exercise, guidance, learning, pedagogy, practice, teaching, tutelage 9 chalk talk, education, grounding, paedagogy, schooling 10 background, discipline, experience, foundation, groundwork, upbringing
exercise: 6 lesson 8 maneuver
govt. ~ program: 4 CETA
manual ~ system: 5 sloid, slojd, sloyd
room complaint: 4 ache
training __: 3 aid 4 ship, wall 5 table 6 school, wheels 7 college
__ training: 5 basic 6 manual, spring, weight
Training Day (2001 film)
cast: Tom Berenger, Scott Glenn, Ethan Hawke, Denzel Washington
director: Antoine Fuqua
__ Train Lane: 5 Night
__ Train Robbery, The: 5 Great
Trains and Boats And __: 6 Planes
Train, The (1965 film)
cast: Burt Lancaster, Jeanne Moreau, Paul Scofield
director: John Frankenheimer
__ Train to Clarksville: 4 Last
traipse: 4 roam, step, trek, walk 5 range, tramp 6 linger, loiter, ramble, stride, stroll, trudge, wander 7 meander, saunter 9 gallivant 10 knock about
trait: 3 way 4 bent, cast, mark 5 habit, quirk, thing 6 detail, oddity 7 earmark, feature, quality 8 hallmark, property 9 attribute, mannerism
carrier: 3 DNA 4 gene
desirable ~: 4 plus 5 asset 6 virtue 8 resource, strength 9 advantage
heroic ~: 4 grit, guts, will 5 moxie, pluck, valor 6 daring, mettle 7 bravery, courage 8 audacity, backbone, boldness, gumption, strength, tenacity 9 brashness, fortitude, gallantry 10 confidence
traitor: 3 rat 4 fink, nark 5 enemy, Judas, knave, rebel, sneak, viper 6 ratter, snitch 7 ratfink, serpent 8 apostate, betrayer, deceiver, defector, deserter, forsaker, informer, mutineer, quisling, renegade, turncoat, two-timer 9 ill-wisher 10 subversive, tattletale, treasonist
traitorous: 4 base, evil 5 false, snaky 6 untrue 7 lawless, unloyal 8 disloyal, recreant, two-faced 9 dishonest, faithless, insidious, two-timing 10 inconstant, perfidious, rebellious
act ~: 6 betray
traits: 4 ways 6 makeup, nature 9 character 10 ins and outs
good character ~: 5 arete
Trajan: 5 Roman 6 Caesar
see also Latin
trajectile: 4 dart 5 arrow 6 bullet, pellet 7 missile
trajectory: 3 arc 4 line 5 curve, orbit, track 6 course 7 heading 9 direction
in a ~: 5 arced
Tralee: 4 city, town
locale: 4 Eire, Erin 5 Kerry 7 Ireland
tram: 3 car 7 coal car 8 cable car
cargo: 3 ore
ender: 3 car, way 4 line
in America: 9 streetcar
trammel: 3 tie 4 curb, rein, trap 5 deter, tie up 6 fetter, halter, hamper, hinder, hobble, impede, thwart 7 enchain, inhibit 8 hold back, obstacle, obstruct, restrain, restrict 9 constrain, deterrent, hindrance, restraint 10 constraint, impediment, inhibition
Trammell, Alan sport: 8 baseball
trammels: 5 bonds, gyves 6 chains 7 bilboes, bondage, fetters, slavery 8 manacles, shackles 9 handcuffs, restraint
tramp: 3 bum 4 hike, hobo, plod, roam, rove, slog, trek, walk 5 march, pound, range, stamp, stomp, stump, tread 6 beggar, ramble, rascal, stride, stroll, trapes, trudge, wander 7 drifter, floater, migrant, outcast, traipse, vagrant 8 derelict, long haul, traveler, vagabond, wanderer 9 gallivant, rail rider 10 hitchhiker, knock about, panhandler, ragamuffin
tramp __: 3 art 7 steamer
trample: 4 hurt, mall, maul 5 crush, stamp, stomp, tread, tromp, worst 6 defeat, injure, ravage, squash, step on, subdue 7 flatten, oppress, run over 8 infringe, override, overrule, vanquish
on: 5 bully 7 oppress, violate 8 browbeat, domineer, keep down 9 dictate to, tyrannize 10 boss around, intimidate, lord it over
trampoline
like a ~: 4 taut
surface: 3 bed
tramp steamer: 4 boat
__, Tramps & Thieves: 6 Gypsys
__ tramway: 5 cable 6 aerial
trance: 4 coma, daze, muse 5 dream, sleep, spell 6 revery, vision 7 ecstasy, rapture, reverie 8 daydream, hypnosis 10 brown study
come out of a ~: 4 wake 5 awake, waken 6 awaken, come to
__ trance: 3 in a
trance-inducing: 8 hypnotic, mesmeric
Trancers (1985 film)
cast: Helen Hunt, Art La Fleur, Tim Thomerson
director: Charles Band
Trancoso: 4 city, town
locale: 6 Mexico 9 Zacatecas
Trane alternative: 5 Rheem 6 Lennox 7 Carrier, Fedders 9 Friedrich
tranmontane: 4 wind
tranquil: 4 calm, cool, easy, even, mild 5 quiet, staid, stoic 6 at ease, gentle, hushed, irenic, low-key, mellow, placid, poised, sedate, serene, smooth 7 amiable, at peace, easeful, equable, halcyon, orderly, pacific, relaxed, restful, stoical, unmoved 8 amicable, carefree, composed, irenical, laid-back, pastoral, peaceful, soothing 9 collected, easy-going, impassive, nerveless, peaceable, quiescent, temperate, unexcited, unruffled, unworried 10 nonchalant, rippleless, unagitated, untroubled
be ~: 4 rest 5 relax
in music: 7 placido
tranquilize: 4 calm, lull 5 quiet, relax, still 6 settle, soothe 7 compose, quieten 8 mitigate, unruffle
__ Tranquillitatis: 4 Mare
tranquillity: 4 calm, ease, hush, lull, rest 5 order, peace, quiet 6 repose, temper 7 concord, harmony 8 calmness, coolness, serenity 9 composure, stillness
__ Tranquillity: 5 Sea of
Trans __ Range: 4 Alai
Trans-__ Pipeline: 6 Alaska
transact: 2 do 3 buy 4 sell 5 close, enact, sew up 6 clinch, finish, handle, manage, settle, wrap up 7 carry on, conduct, execute, operate, perform 8 carry out, practice 9 discharge, negotiate 10 do business, effectuate, take care of
transaction: 4 coup, deal, sale 5 trade 6 affair, matter 7 bargain 8 business, contract, covenant, exchange, purchase 9 agreement, execution
cashless ~: 4 swap, swop 5 trade 6 barter
transactions: 7 traffic
Trans Alai: 5 range 9 mountains
locale: 4 Asia 10 Kyrgyzstan, Tajikistan
Transalpine __: 4 Gaul
Trans Am: 3 car 4 auto 7 Pontiac 10 automobile
rival: 6 Camaro
transatlantic: 7 oversea 8 overseas
transceiver: 3 set 5 radio
button: 3 vol. 4 send 6 volume 7 squelch
user: 4 CBer
transcend: 3 cap 4 lead, pass 5 excel, outdo 6 better, exceed 7 eclipse, surpass 8 go beyond, outrival, outshine, outstrip, outweigh, surmount 9 cut across, rise above 10 overshadow, tower above
transcendent: 5 whole 6 entire, innate 7 eternal, perfect, sublime, supreme 8 absolute, abstract, infinite, platonic, splendid, superior, towering, ultimate 9 boundless, exceeding, masterful, unequaled
transcendental: 6 innate, mystic 7 eternal, perfect, sublime, supreme 8 absolute, infinite, mystical, peerless, superior, ultimate 9 boundless, exceeding, intuitive, matchless, spiritual, unworldly
transcendental __: 3 ego 5 logic 6 number
Transcendental Blues singer: 5 Earle
transcending prefix: 5 ultra-
transcribe: 4 copy, tape, type 5 write 6 record, render 7 put down 8 take down, write out 9 audiotape, duplicate, reproduce, write down
transcriber: 7 copyist 9 scrivener, secretary 10 amanuensis
transcript: 4 copy, tape, text 6 ectype, record 9 audiotape, duplicate, facsimile, recording
datum: 3 GPA 5 grade
transcription: 6 record 9 rendition
transdermal __: 5 patch
transfer: 3 lug 4 bear, cart, cede, deed, give, haul, mail, move, pass, post, sell, send, ship, taxi, tote 5 bring, carry, ferry, relay, shift 6 assign, change, convey, depute, pass on, remove 7 consign, convert, deliver, forward, removal 8 delegate, delivery, dispatch, hand over, make over, movement, relegate, relocate, sign over, transmit, turn over 10 abdication, assignment, reposition
art: 5 decal, rub-on
illegal goods: 4 push 7 bootleg
transfer __: 3 RNA 5 agent, orbit 6 factor 7 company, molding, payment, station
__ transfer: 3 dye 4 gene, wire 7 passive
transference: 5 shift
thought ~: 9 telepathy
transferred employee benefit: 4 relo
transfigure: 6 change, modify
transfix: 3 awe 4 hold, nail, spit, stun 5 rivet, spike, stick 6 arrest, empale, impale, pierce, skewer, thrust 7 bewitch, enchant, engross, petrify 8 paralyse, paralyze 9 captivate, fascinate, hypnotize, mesmerize, penetrate, spellbind
transfixed: 4 rapt 6 enrapt 10 fascinated
transform: 4 turn, vary 5 act on, alter, morph, renew 6 affect, change, modify, mutate, reform, revamp 7 act upon, commute, convert, process, remodel, reshape, restyle 8 innovate, make over
into: 6 become
transformation: 5 shift 6 change, switch 7 renewal 8 flip-flop, mutation 9 about-face
transformer
part: 4 core
unit: 4 watt
__ transformer: 5 Tesla
transfuse: 3 mix 5 endue, indue 6 infuse, inject 7 diffuse, instill 8 permeate 9 percolate
transfusion: 7 mixture
liquids: 4 sera
transgress: 3 err, sin 5 break 6 offend 7 infract, violate 9 misbehave 10 contravene
transgression: 3 sin 4 slip, vice 5 crime, error, fault, guilt, lapse, wrong 6 breach 7 misdeed, offense 8 iniquity, trespass 9 violation
transgressor: 4 thug 5 crook, felon, thief 6 bandit, outlaw, sinner 7 brigand, convict, culprit, hoodlum, mobster, villain 8 criminal, evildoer, fugitive, hooligan, murderer, offender, prisoner, scofflaw 9 desperado, miscreant, racketeer, wrongdoer 10 delinquent, lawbreaker, trespasser
transient: 4 hobo 5 brief, guest, rover, short 7 drifter, migrant, passing, ranging, vagrant, visitor 8 fleeting, flitting,

fugitive, gadabout, meteoric, runagate, stranger, temporal, vagabond, volatile 9 ephemeral, journeyer, migratory, momentary, short-term, temporary 10 changeable, evanescent, fly-by-night, short-lived, unenduring

transistor

part: 5 diode

predecessor: 4 tube

transistor ___: 5 radio

transit: 6 motion, travel 7 osmosis, passage, portage 8 carriage, crossing, movement 10 conveyance, theodolite

in ~: 6 aboard, coming 7 en route 8 embarked, on the way

transit ___: 4 shed 6 circle, lounge, number

___ transit: 4 mass 5 rapid

___ transit gloria mundi: 3 sic

transition: 4 flux 5 segue, shift 6 change, growth 7 passage, passing 8 movement, progress, upheaval 9 evolution

logician ~: 4 then, thus 5 hence 9 therefore

make a slow ~: 6 ease in

sudden ~: 4 leap 5 surge 7 upsurge, upswing

transitive ___: 4 verb

transitory: 5 brief 7 passing 8 fleeting, flitting, fugitive, temporal, volatile 9 ephemeral, momentary, short-term, temporary 10 pro tempore, short-lived, unenduring

translate: 3 put 4 read 5 alter, gloss 6 change, decode, recast, render, reword 7 clarify, commute, convert, explain 8 construe, decipher, rephrase, simplify, spell out 9 elucidate, explicate, interpret, make clear 10 paraphrase

translating device: 5 coder

translation: 3 key 4 crib 5 gloss 7 reading, version 9 rendering, rendition, rewording

translocation: 5 shift

translucent: 4 thin 5 clear, lucid, sheer 6 glassy, limpid 8 knowable, luminous, pellucid

transmission: 3 fax 6 spread 8 delivery

choice: 3 low 4 gear, park 5 drive, first 6 manual, second 7 reverse 9 automatic

understand a ~: 4 read

transmission ___: 4 line

transmit: 3 fax 4 beam, mail, pass, pipe, send, ship, take 5 carry, issue, radio, relay, remit, route 6 convey, funnel, hand on, impart, instil, pass on, siphon, spread, syphon 7 channel, conduct, consign, deliver, diffuse, forward, instill, project, radiate 8 bequeath, dispatch, hand down, televise 9 broadcast, propagate

transmittable: 8 catching 10 contagious, infectious

transmittal: 7 mailing, passage 8 delivery, dispatch, shipment

transmitter: 3 sdr., set 6 sender

neural ~: 4 axon 5 axone

prefix for ~: 5 micro, neuro

transmogrify: 6 change, modify, mutate

transmundane: 6 occult 7 psychic

transmutation: 4 flux 5 shift 6 change 8 make-over 10 alteration, conversion, revolution

transmute: 5 alter 6 change, modify

transoceanic: 7 oversea 8 overseas

transoceanic flight

pioneer: 4 Post 7 Earhart, Markham 9 Lindbergh, Wiley Post

transom ___: 5 light 6 window

transpacific: 7 oversea 8 overseas

___ transparency: 5 color

transparent: 4 lacy, open, pure, thin 5 clear, filmy, gauzy, lucid, plain, sheer, white 6 candid, flimsy, glassy, hyalin, limpid, patent, simple 7 artless, crystal, evident, hyaline, obvious 8 apparent, clear-cut, gossamer, knowable, luminous, manifest, peekaboo, pellucid 9 guileless, ingenuous 10 diaphanous, see-through

combining form: 7 diaphan- 8 diaphano-

transpicuous: 5 clear, lucid, sheer 6 limpid 10 see-through

transpire: 2 go 4 pass 5 arise, break, ensue, occur 6 befall, betide, elapse, emerge, happen, result, turn up 7 come out, develop 9 come about, eventuate, take place 10 come to pass

transplant: 4 move 5 graft, plant, repot 6 remove, uproot 8 displace, emigrate, relocate, resettle 9 immigrate

participant: 5 donee, donor

transport: 2 RV 3 ATV, bus, cab, car, jet, lug, run, SST, SUV, tow, van, wow 4 auto, bear, bike, boat, cart, hack, haul, jeep, lift, limo, move, oust, pack, raft, rail, ride, semi, send, ship, stir, take, taxi, tote, tram 5 barge, bring, canoe, carry, charm, exile, ferry, fetch, kayak, liner, lorry, moped, plane, stage, train, trike, truck, umiak, wagon 6 banish, big rig, convey, copter, deport, excite, go-cart, go-kart, jitney, ravish, remove, thrill 7 beatify, bewitch, bicycle, carrier, conduct, delight, deliver, elevate, enthral, forward, inthral, passage, passion, rapture, taxicab, vehicle 8 airplane, carriage, displace, enthrall, entrance, haul away, inthrall, railroad, relegate, rickshaw, shipping, tricycle 9 ambulance, captivate, carry away, electrify, enrapture, fascinate, freighter, limousine, motor home, order to go, spellbind 10 automobile, conveyance, enthusiasm, exaltation, expatriate, exultation, helicopter, stagecoach

transportation: 4 lift, ride 7 traffic

system: 4 line 8 railroad

Transportation Dept. div: 3 FAA

transported: 4 rapt 5 borne 6 enrapt 9 overjoyed 10 spellbound

transporter: 5 dolly 6 bearer 7 carrier, vehicle 8 conveyor 9 consignee

transpose: 3 put 4 move, swap, swop 5 alter, shift 6 change, invert, switch 7 reorder, reverse 8 exchange, flip-flop, relocate 9 rearrange

transposition: 8 exchange

Trans-Siberian Railroad city: 4 Omsk 6 Moscow 7 Irkutsk 11 Vladivostok

transude: 4 ooze, seep

Transvaal resident: 4 Boer

transverse: 4 span 5 cross 6 skewed, zigzag 8 diagonal

to: 6 across

transverse ___: 4 axis, wave 7 process, section

transversely: 4 over 6 across 7 athwart

Transylvania, from: 6 Balkan 8 Romanian, Rumanian

trap: 3 bag, get, gin, nab, net, web, yap 4 bait, door, dupe, fool, grab, hook, land, lure, nail, plot, ploy, ruse, snag, take, wile 5 bazoo, box in, catch, decoy, feint, lasso, mouth, noose, prank, seize, setup, snare, trick 6 ambush, bunker, collar, come-on, corner, corral, device, dupery, enmesh, entrap, gambit, gotcha, immesh, inmesh, rope in, suck in, tangle, trip up 7 beguile, capture, deceive, dragnet, ensnare, insnare, mineral, pitfall, springe, trammel 8 accouter, accoutre, artifice, entangle, intrigue, inveigle, maneuver, overtake, quagmire, surprise 9 ambuscade, bushwhack, deception, quicksand, stratagem 10 ambushment, bring to bay, circumvent, conspiracy, enticement, lobster pot, subterfuge, temptation

booby ~: 4 mine, ruse, trap 5 snare 7 pitfall 8 obstacle 9 explosive

elephant ~: 5 kheda 6 keddah, khedah

ender: 5 light 7 shooter 8 shooting

filler: 4 sand

fish ~: 3 net, pot 4 weir 5 seine 6 eelpot

fly ~: 3 web 5 mouth 6 cobweb

fodder: 4 bait 6 cheese

like some ~ s: 6 baited

sand ~: 6 bunker, hazard

set a ~: 4 bait, draw, hook, lure 5 decoy, snare, tempt, trick 6 allure, entice, induce, lead on, rope in, suck in 7 attract, capture, ensnare, mislead

shut one's ~: 6 clam up

starter: 3 fly, rat 4 clap, fire 5 mouse 6 rattle

trap ___: 3 car, cut 4 door, play, shot

___ trap: 3 air 4 lint, sand, set a, wave 5 booby, radar, speed, steel, water 7 lobster, tourist

Trapani: 4 city, port, town

locale: 5 Italy 6 Sicily

trapdoor: 4 drop 5 hatch 6 device

locale: 5 floor

Trapeze (1956 film)

cast: Tony Curtis, Burt Lancaster, Gina Lollobrigida

director: Carol Reed

trapeze artist: 7 acrobat

like a ~: 5 agile, gutsy 6 daring 8 fearless, intrepid 9 unfearing

need: 3 net

often: 5 flier, flyer

Trapeze, The artist: 4 Erté

trapezium: 4 bone

locale: 5 wrist

trapezoid: 4 bone 5 shape

trapped: 5 at bay, stuck 6 in a box, in a fix, in a jam 7 in a mess, up a tree 9 on the spot 10 in hot water, on the ropes

trapped like ___: 4 a rat

trapper: 6 hunter

bundle: 3 kip

commodity: 4 hide, pelt

Trapper John, M.D. (CBS drama)

cast: Gregory Harrison (Dr. George Gonzo Gates)
Brian Mitchell (Dr. Justin "Jackpot" Jackson)
Christopher Norris (Nurse Gloria Brancusi)
Pernell Roberts (Dr. John McIntyre)
Charles Siebert (Dr, Stanley Riverside)

trappings: 4 garb, gear 5 dress, getup, goods, robes, stuff 6 attire, finery, livery, outfit, tackle, things 7 apparel, clothes, costume, effects, garment, panoply, raiment, rigging 8 clothing 9 caparison, equipment, ornaments, trimmings 10 adornments, Sunday best

Trappist: 4 monk

home: 5 abbey

Trappist ___: 4 monk 6 cheese

traps game: 4 golf 5 skeet

trapshooting: 5 skeet

shout: 4 pull

Trap, The (1966 film)

cast: Oliver Reed, Rita Tushingham

___ Trap, The: 6 Parent, Tender

trash: 3 gas, rot, sap 4 blah, bosh, bull, bunk, guff, jazz, jive, junk, pooh, rout, scum, tosh, whip 5 abuse, bilge, chaff, drain, dregs, dross, filth, fudge, hokum, hooey, offal, outdo, prate, quash, scorn, scrap, smash, spoil, stuff, tripe, waste, wreck 6 bunkum, burn up, bushwa, debris, deface, defeat, defile, drivel, footle, gabble, gammon, gibber, grunge, havers, hot air, humbug, impugn, jabber, jargon, kibosh, litter, piffle, ravage, refuse, review, rubble, scraps, shards 7 baloney, blarney, blather, blether, boloney, bushwah, deplete, destroy, eyewash, flannel, flubdub, fustian, garbage, hogwash, inanity, malarky, profane, residue, rubbish, trounce, twaddle 8 buncombe, claptrap, demolish, falderal, falderol, flimflam, flummery, folderal, folderol, fool away, leavings, leftover, malarkey, mistreat, nonsense, oddments, sediment, shavings, slipslop, squander, tommyrot, trumpery 9 banana oil, criticize, devastate, dissipate, eradicate, gibberish, kidstakes, moonshine, overpower, pick apart, poppycock, rigmarole, scourings, sweepings, vandalize 10 applesauce, balderdash, bilge water, codswallop, double-talk, flapdoodle, galimatias, Jabberwock, mumbo jumbo, rigamarole, taradiddle

collector: 5 sanit. 6 ashman 10 sanitation

collector in Britain: 7 dustman

compactor part: 6 basket

hauler: 4 scow

holder: 4 dump 6 ashcan 8 Dumpster, landfill

ignore the ~ can: 5 strew 6 litter 7 clutter, scatter 9 make a mess

trash ___: 3 bin, can 4 fish, rack

trashing: 6 defeat

trashy: 4 base, junk, punk 5 cheap 6 grungy, shoddy, sleazy 7 raffish 8 unusable 9 worthless

Trasimeno: 4 lake

locale: 5 Italy

Trask: 3 Cal 4 Adam, Aron

trattoria: 6 eatery 7 Italian 10 ristorante

dessert: 6 gelati, gelato 7 spumoni, tortoni 8 tiramisu

device: 6 grater

order: 4 orzo, vino, ziti 5 pasta, penne, pesce, pollo, squid, zitti, zuppa 7 lasagna, lasagne, pastina, ravioli 8 bucatini, calamari, farfalle, linguine, linguini, macaroni, rigatoni 9 agnolotti, angelhair, cavatelli, manicotti, scungilli, spaghetti 10 cannelloni, fettuccini, tortellini, vermicelli

topping: 5 pesto 8 marinara

Traubel, Helen: 6 singer 7 soprano

specialty: 5 opera

trauma: 4 blow, hurt, jolt, pain 5 agony, shock, upset, wound 6 damage, injury, ordeal, strain, stress 7 anguish, torture 8 collapse, upheaval 9 confusion, suffering

aftermath: 4 scar

site: 2 ER

traumatic: 6 tragic 7 painful 8 chilling, grievous 9 harrowing, torturous 10 disturbing, petrifying, terrifying, tormenting

traumatize: 4 hurt, scar 5 shock, wound 6 stress

traumatophobe fear: 6 injury

travail: 3 ado, woe 4 pain, toil, work 5 agony, grind, labor 6 misery

7 anguish, despair, torment 8 distress, drudgery, exertion, hardship 9 adversity, grunt work, suffering 10 hard knocks, infelicity
Travail author: Emile Zola
travel: 2 go 3 fly, gad, jet 4 move, ride, roam, rove, sail, tour, trek, trip, waft, walk, wend 5 drive, jaunt, motor, range, swing, visit 6 biking, cruise, flying, junket, motion, ramble, repair, set out, voyage, wander 7 commute, explore, go to see, journey, migrate, passage, proceed, transit, weekend 8 ambulate, go abroad, movement, progress, set forth, sightsee, vacation 9 adventure, circulate, excursion, overnight, range over, round trip, seafaring, take a trip, wayfaring 10 expedition, knock about, locomotion, navigation, wanderlust
abbr.: 3 arr., ETA, ETD
account: 3 log
across: 4 span 5 cover 7 stretch 8 traverse
agent offering: 4 tour 6 cruise 8 vacation
aimlessly: 3 gad 4 roam, rove 6 ramble
bag: 4 grip 5 trunk 8 suitcase
brief ~: 7 sojourn
document: 4 visa 8 passport
fast: 3 fly 4 zoom
guide: 8 Baedeker, handbook, tour book
guide name: 5 Fodor 7 Frommer
in: 2 do
in neutral: 5 coast, glide 6 cruise
mode of ~: 3 bus, cab, car, jet 4 auto, boat, foot, rail, ship 5 liner, plane, train 10 cruise ship
org.: 3 AAA
plan: 5 route 8 schedule 9 itinerary
prepare to ~: 4 pack
reference: 3 map 4 plan 5 atlas, chart, globe
to work: 4 ride 5 drive 7 commute
watchdog: 4 NTSB
travel __: 4 shot, time 5 agent 6 agency 7 trailer
__ travel: 5 space
__-traveled: 4 well
traveler: 4 goer, hobo 5 farer, gypsy, nomad, rover, tramp 6 roamer, sailor, vender, vendor 7 drifter, migrant, pilgrim, rambler, tourist, trekker, trouper, vagrant, voyager 8 commuter, explorer, gadabout, seafarer, vagabond, wanderer, wayfarer 9 itinerant, jet-setter, journeyer, navigator, passenger, sightseer 10 adventurer, hitchhiker, vacationer
bane: 4 duty, wait 5 delay 6 jet lag
choice: 3 bus, car, jet 4 auto, boat, ship 5 liner, plane, route, train
fast ~: 7 bad news
need: 3 bag, inn, map 4 visa 5 hotel, motel 7 lodging, luggage 8 passport
world ~: 5 nomad, rover 7 voyager 8 gadabout, vagabond, wanderer, wayfarer 10 adventurer
__ traveler: 6 fellow
Traveler: 3 car 4 auto 6 Hudson 10 automobile
traveler's __: 5 check
Travelin' Band (1970 song) artist: Creedence Clearwater Revival
traveling: 4 gone 6 aboard, abroad, errant, mobile 7 en route, nomadic, on the go 8 embarked, underway 9 itinerant, migratory, on the move, on the road, peregrine, wayfaring 10 locomotion, navigation
group: 4 band 6 convoy, safari 7 caravan, cortege 9 cavalcade 10 expedition, procession
traveling __: 3 bag 5 block
traveling salesman, name meaning: 6 Tinker
Travelin' Man (1961 song) artist: Ricky Nelson
Traveller: 4 mare 5 horse, steed 6 equine
rider: Robert E. Lee
Travelodge: 5 motel
alternative: 7 Days Inn 9 Ramada Inn 10 Comfort Inn, Econo Lodge, Hampton Inn, Holiday Inn, Quality Inn, Red Roof Inn 11 Best Western
travelogue: 5 short
Travels with Charley author: John Steinbeck
Travels With My __: 4 Aunt
Travers: 2 P.L. 4 Bill, Mary 5 Henry
traversal: 4 xing 6 bridge 8 crossing, junction, overpass 10 cloverleaf
traverse: 4 move, rove, span, walk 5 cover, cross, range 6 bridge, go over 7 explore, viaduct 8 go across, overpass 9 cut across, intersect, negotiate, range over 10 crisscross
traverse __: 3 rod 4 jury
Travers, Henry: 5 actor
film: The Bells of St. Mary's (1945)
Madame Curie (1943)
The Moon Is Down (1943)
None Shall Escape (1944)
traversing: 6 across
Travers, P.L.: 6 author, writer 10 Australian
Travers, P.L. work: Mary Poppins
travertine: 7 mineral 9 limestone
travesty: 4 mock, sham 5 farce, roast, spoof 6 parody, satire, send-up 7 burlesk, lampoon, mockery, takeoff 9 burlesque, imitation 10 caricature, distortion
Travis: 4 Bill 5 Nancy, Randy, Tritt 7 William
Travis, Nancy: 7 actress
film: 3 Men and a Baby (1987)
Air America (1990)
Fluke (1995)
Travolta, John: 5 actor
film: Blow Out (1981)
Broken Arrow (1996)
Carrie (1976)
A Civil Action (1998)
Domestic Disturbance (2001)
Face/Off (1997)
The General's Daughter (1999)
Get Shorty (1995)
Grease (1978)
Look Who's Talking (1989)
Lucky Numbers (2000)
Michael (1996)
Perfect (1985)
Phenomenon (1996)
Primary Colors (1998)
Pulp Fiction (1994)
Saturday Night Fever (1977)
Swordfish (2001)
Urban Cowboy (1980)
song: Let Her In (1976)
Summer Nights (1978)
You're the One That I Want (1978)
spouse: Kelly Preston
TV: Welcome Back, Kotter
trawl: 3 net, tow 4 drag, fish 7 dragnet, fish net
trawl __: 3 net 4 line
trawler: 4 boat 6 angler 9 fisherman
equipment: 3 net 5 seine
tray: 3 hod 4 till 5 plate 6 salver, server 7 platter 9 container, lazy Susan
starter: 3 ash
tray __: 5 table
__ tray: 3 bed, tea 6 cheese 7 butler's
Traynor, Pie: 6 Pirate 9 infielder
tre: 5 three 7 Italian
follower: 7 quattro
preceder: 3 due
tre __: 5 corde
Treacher: 6 Arthur
treacherous: 3 icy, sly 4 evil, ugly 5 false, hairy, lying, Punic, risky, slick, snaky 6 chancy, feline, rotten, shifty, tricky, unsafe, untrue, wicked 7 corrupt, crooked, devious, knavish, ominous 8 disloyal, menacing, perilous, slippery, two-faced 9 betraying, dangerous, deceitful, deceptive, faithless, hazardous, insidious, nefarious, two-timing, underhand, unhealthy
one: 5 viper
treachery: 5 fraud, guile 6 deceit, dupery 7 falsity, perfidy, sellout, treason 8 bad faith, betrayal, sabotage 9 deception, desertion, dirty work, duplicity, fourberie, two-timing 10 conspiracy, dishonesty, disloyalty, infidelity, untrueness
treacly: 5 sweet
tread: 3 pad 4 gait, pace, plod, rung, slog, step, walk 5 clomp, crush, march, track, tramp 6 squash, step on, stride, trudge 7 oppress, stamp on, trample 8 ambulate, footstep
ender: 4 mill
heavily: 5 stomp, tromp
on one's toes: 3 bug, get, irk, try, vex 4 gall, miff, rile 5 anger, annoy, grate, peeve, pique, upset 6 bother, enrage, nettle, offend, ruffle 7 affront, agitate, disturb, incense, inflame, outrage, provoke 8 distress, irritate 9 infuriate 10 antagonize, exasperate
on the heels of: 4 tail 5 trail
riser plus ~: 5 stair
the boards: 3 act 4 play 7 perform
warily: 9 pussyfoot
tread __: 5 water
treadless: 4 bald
treadmill: 3 rut 7 routine 10 monotonous
use a ~: 3 run
tread the __: 6 boards
treas.: 4 exec.
treason: 5 crime 6 felony, mutiny, revolt 7 perfidy 8 betrayal, sedition 9 duplicity, treachery 10 disloyalty, untrueness
commit ~: 6 betray, desert 7 sell out
in French: 11 lèse majesté
__ treason: 4 high
treasonous: 3 bad 7 corrupt 8 disloyal 9 seditious
treasure: 3 gem, pet 4 find, gold, like, love, pile, save 5 adore, angel, cache, catch, go for, guard, hoard, jewel, money, pearl, prize, trove, value 6 esteem, revere, riches, wealth 7 care for, cherish, fortune, idolize, jewelry, paragon, worship 8 enshrine, hold dear, inshrine, remember, richness, valuable 9 care about, nonpareil, reverence 10 appreciate, sweetheart
guarder: 5 gnome
hide ~: 4 bury 5 cache, inter, stash
holder: 4 safe 5 chest 6 coffer
hunter gear: 3 map 5 scuba, sonar
map features: 3 xes 4 exes
trove: 4 mine 7 bonanza
treasure __: 4 hunt 5 chest, house
treasure-__: 5 trove
treasured: 4 dear 5 sweet 7 beloved, darling 8 precious, valuable 9 priceless
Treasure Island: 4 film 5 novel
author: Robert Louis Stevenson
cast: Wallace Beery, Jackie Cooper, Lewis Stone
character: 3 Jim, Pew 4 Bill 5 Bones, Hands 6 Israel, pirate, Silver 7 Ben Gunn, Hawkins, Livesey 8 Black Dog, Long John, Smollett 9 Bill Bones, Trelawney 10 Jim Hawkins
director: Victor Fleming
prop: 3 map
topic: 6 piracy
Treasure of Love (1956 song) artist: Clyde McPhatter
Treasure of the Sierra Madre, The (1948 film)
cast: Humphrey Bogart, Tim Holt, Walter Huston
composer: 7 Steiner
director: John Huston
treasurer: 3 CFO 4 fisc 6 banker, bursar, purser 8 official
treasures: 9 valuables
Treasure State capital: 6 Helena
treasury: 4 bank, fisc, fund, mine, safe, till 5 hoard, purse, store, vault 6 coffer, museum 7 archive 8 exchange, Fort Knox, money box, war chest 9 anthology, exchequer, strongbox 10 collection, compendium, cumulation, depository, repository, storehouse
Treasury
agent: 4 T-man
Dept. agcy.: 3 ATF, IRS
offering: 4 bill, bond, note 5 E bond, T-bill, T-bond, T-note
treat: 4 blow, cure, dose, gift, heal, verb 5 dress, goody, nurse, party, stand, sweet, taffy, toffy 6 buy for, dainty, doctor, employ, go into, goodie, handle, look on, luxury, morsel, pay for, regale, regard, sundae, tidbit, toffee 7 discuss, indulge, operate, process, provide, take out, touch on 8 deal with, delicacy, lollipop, look upon, medicate, minister, play host, pleasure, surprise 9 act toward, amusement, entertain, interpret, prescribe, spring for, touch upon 10 minister to, reckon with, speak about, write about
as inferior: 5 deign, stoop 7 stoop to 10 condescend, look down on, talk down to
badly: 4 snub 5 abuse, cheat, shaft, spurn, wrong 6 demean, deride, ill-use, slight 7 swindle 8 mistreat
ender: 3 ise
glass: 6 temper 7 toughen
tenderly: 4 baby 6 cosset, dote on, pamper 7 cater to, indulge
__ treat: 5 Dutch
__-treat: 3 ill 4 heat
Treat: 8 Williams
__-treated: 4 well
treater's phrase: 4 on me
treating, he's: 5 payer
treatise: 5 essay, paper 6 thesis, volume 7 descant, discant, writing 9 discourse, monograph 10 commentary, exposition, literature
Treatise of Human Nature, A author: 4 Hume
Treatise on Money author: 6 Keynes
Treat Me Nice (1957 song) artist: Elvis Presley
treatment: 3 use 4 cure, diet 5 style, usage 6 design, method, remedy 7 conduct, healing, reading, regimen, surgery, therapy 8 analysis, approach, behavior, handling, medicine, practice, strategy 9 attention, doctoring, execution, operation, reception 10 management, medication
bad ~: 4 harm 5 abuse 6 attack, injury, insult, misuse 7 affront, assault, beating, mauling, slander, torment, torture 8 derision, inequity 9 injustice, invective 10 backbiting,

defamation, disrespect, imputation, oppression, revilement, upbraiding
favored ~: 4 bias 9 advantage, privilege, seniority 10 preference
__ treatment: 5 water 6 silent, window
treaty: 4 bond, pact 5 peace, terms, truce 6 accord, cartel, league 7 charter, compact, concord, entente 8 alliance, contract, covenant, protocol 9 agreement, armistice, concordat 10 convention, settlement
initials: 4 SALT 5 SEATO
modern ~ subject: 5 A-test
party to a ~: 4 ally 9 signatory
signer: 5 inker
subject: 6 border 8 boundary, frontier 9 perimeter
1629 ~ city: 5 Nîmes
1814 ~ site: 5 Ghent
1993 ~: 5 NAFTA
__ treaty: 5 peace 7 private, test-ban
Treaty of __: 5 Ghent, Paris
Treaty of Nanking port: 4 Amoy
Trebbia: 5 river
locale: 5 Italy
Trebek: 4 Alex, host 5 emcee
answer ~: 3 ask 5 query 7 inquire
treble: 4 clef, high 6 shrill 8 piercing
clef lines: 5 EGBDF
staff marking: 5 G clef
Tredia: 3 car 4 auto 10 automobile, Mitsubishi
tree: 3 apa, ash, bay, bel, elm, fig, fir, koa, oak, ule, yew 4 acle, agba, akee, bael, baum, cork, hebe, ilex, ipil, itea, kaki, karo, kola, lime, neem, ombu, palm, pear, pich, pili, pine, plum, poon, pulp, shea, sloe, sorb, teak, trap, upas 5 abele, alder, algum, almon, almug, apple, arbre, areca, aspen, athel, babul, balsa, beech, birch, bodhi, boldo, cacao, carob, cedar, ceiba, cirio, ebony, elder, erica, ficus, genip, guava, hakea, hazel, henna, holly, ixora, karri, kauri, kiawe, kukui, larch, lehua, lemon, limba, mahoe, mahua, mahwa, mango, maple, mohwa, mowra, mulga, olive, osier, papal, papaw, peach, pecan, plant, ramon, rowan, shrub, smoke, stimy, stymy, sumac, thuja, thuya, wahoo, yapon, yulan 6 acacia, acajou, alerce, almond, amugis, anatto, annona, antiar, balata, balche, banana, banian, banyan, baobab, bonduc, boojum, calaba, carapa, cashew, cassia, cercis, cherry, citron, cobnut, coffee, cornel, corner, deodar, durian, fatsia, fustet, fustic, gaboon, gingko, ginkgo, hognut, jarrah, jujube, kapuka, kowhai, laurel, lebbek, lichee, linden, litchi, locust, longan, loquat, lungan, mammee, mastic, mayten, medlar, mimosa, mowrah, nutmeg, obeche, orange, padauk, padouk, papaya, pawpaw, pignut, pituri, pomelo, poplar, pumelo, quince, redbud, rubber, sapele, sapota, sorrel, spruce, storax, stymie, sumach, tarata, timber, tupelo, walnut, wandoo, willow, yaupon 7 acerola, almique, ambatch, annatto, apricot, araroba, arbutus, assagai, assegai, avocado, avodire, banksia, boxwood, buckeye, cajeput, camphor, canella, catalpa, champac, cypress, deodara, dogwood, filbert, geebung, genipap, hemlock, hickory, juniper, karanda, leechee, logwood, madrone, mesquit, morello, plumcot, pommelo, pummelo, quassia, redwood, sapling, sequoia, seringa, soursop, syringa, tangelo, wallaba, yohimbe, zelkova 8 alamiqui, albizzia, allspice, andiroba, barbasco, basswood, bauhinia, bayberry, beefwood, bergamot, bluewood, calabash, caragana, carnauba, champaca, chestnut, cinchona, cinnamon, coat rack, cockspur, cocobolo, coolabah, crabwood, divi-divi, gardenia, hardwood, hawthorn, hibiscus, hornbeam, jelutong, landmark, limequat, magnolia, mahogany, mandarin, mangrove, mesquite, milkwood, mulberry, oiticica, oleaster, palmetto, photinia, piassava, rosewood, sandarac, seedling, shaddock, shagbark, softwood, sycamore, tamarack, tamarind, tamarisk 9 ailanthus, bloodwood, buckthorn, butternut, candlenut, hackberry, jacaranda, nectarine, persimmon, pistachio, poinciana, sapodilla, sassafras, tangerine 10 arborvitae, blackthorn, breadfruit, bring to bay, buttonwood, cottonwood, eucalyptus, grapefruit, vegetation
Africa: 4 kola, shea 5 babul, limba 6 balata, baobab, gaboon, obeche, padauk, padouk, sapele 7 almique, ambatch, assagai, assegai, avodire, yohimbe 8 alamiqui, sandarac 9 bloodwood
anchor: 4 root 7 rootage
aromatic ~: 3 fir 4 pine 5 cedar 8 bayberry, rosewood
Asia: 4 toon, upas 5 henna 6 cassia, durian, lichee, litchi, padauk, padouk 7 champac, leechee, zelkova 8 caragana, champaca 9 candlenut, carambola
Australia: 5 hakea, karri, mulga 6 jarrah, pituri, wandoo 7 banksia, cajeput, geebung 8 beefwood, coolabah 10 eucalyptus
banned ~ spray: 4 Alar
barking up the wrong ~: 5 wrong 6 all wet, misled, way off 7 deluded, off-base 8 deceived, mistaken 9 misguided 10 ill-advised
bark up the wrong ~: 3 err 7 blunder
branch: 4 limb, rame
branches: 5 shade 6 canopy 8 overhang
bump: 4 burl, knar, knot, knur 5 gnarl
Canada: 5 maple
China: 5 yulan 6 gingko, ginkgo, lichee, litchi, longan, lungan 7 leechee 14 mandarin. loquat
Christmas ~: 3 fir 4 pine 6 balsam
citrus ~: 3 bel 4 bael, lime 5 lemon 6 orange, pomelo, pumelo 7 pommelo, pummelo, tangelo 8 bergamot, mandarin, shaddock 9 tangerine 10 grapefruit
combining form: 3 dry- 4 dryo- 5 dendr- 6 dendri-, dendro- 7 -dendron
covering: 4 bark
cut down a ~: 3 axe, hew, log, saw 4 fell 5 clear 6 lumber
decorate the ~: 4 trim
end: 5 stump
ender: 3 top 4 nail 6 hopper
Europe: 4 sorb 5 larch, rowan
evergreen ~: 3 yew 4 pine 5 athel, boldo, cacao, erica, hakea, olive, thuja, thuya 6 alerce, laurel, longan, loquat, lungan, spruce 7 arbutus, cypress, juniper 8 gardenia 9 sapodilla 10 arborvitae
fallen ~: 3 log
family ~: 5 roots 8 pedigree 9 forebears
feller: 3 axe, saw 5 axman 6 axeman
graft a ~ branch: 6 inarch
graft site: 4 node
group: 4 mott 5 copse, grove, motte, stand, woods 6 forest 7 coppice, orchard
growth: 4 leaf 5 frond 6 needle 7 foliage
hardwood ~: 3 ash, oak 4 poon, teak 5 ebony, larch, lehua 6 jarrah, locust, wandoo 7 wallaba 8 mahogany
Hawaii: 3 koa 4 ohia 5 kukui, lehua
hybrid ~: 7 plumcot 8 limequat
India: 3 bel 4 bael, pich, poon, teak 5 bodhi, ebony, mahua, mahwa, mohwa, mowra, papal, pipal, rohan 6 banian, banyan, deodar, mowrah, nutmeg, peepul 7 deodara, karanda, soursop 8 cinnamon
Japan: 4 kaki 6 bonsai, loquat
juice: 3 sap
like a summer ~: 6 in leaf
like ground around a ~: 5 rooty
like some ~ barks: 5 mossy
like some ~ trunks: 6 gnarly
locale: 5 woods
malady: 6 dry rot
Mediterranean: 4 cork 5 carob 6 mastic
Mexico: 5 cirio 6 boojum, sapota
name meaning ~: 4 Baum
New Zealand: 4 hebe, karo, rimu 5 kauri, mapau 6 kapuka, kowhai, tarata
nymph: 5 dryad
ornament: 4 star 5 angel
palm ~: 4 sago 5 areca 8 carnauba, piassava
part: 5 bough, trunk 6 branch
part of a family ~: 3 son 4 aunt 5 niece, uncle 6 cousin, father, mother, nephew 8 daughter
Philippines: 3 tua 4 acle, ipil, pili 5 almon, lauan 6 amugis
product: 4 pulp, wood 5 resin 6 lumber
rings: 6 annuli
science: 8 forestry
shade ~: 3 ash, elm, oak 5 beech, maple 6 linden
shoot: 4 twig
small ~: 5 shrub
South America: 4 ombu 5 boldo, maqui 6 alerce, carapa, mayten, rubber 7 araroba, seringa, wallaba 8 andiroba, carnauba, cinchona, crabwood, oiticica, piassava
Southwest: 5 alamo, pinon
spigot: 5 spile
sprite: 5 nymph
stunted ~: 5 scrub
tissue: 5 xylem 6 phloem
trim a ~: 3 lop 5 prune
tropical ~: 3 apa, fig 4 agba, akee, kola, neem, palm, upas 5 balsa, cacao, ficus, genip, guava, ixora, kiawe, mahoe, mango, ramon 6 anatto, annona, antiar, balata, banana, baobab, bonduc, calaba, cashew, coffee, fustic, jujube, lebbek, mammee, mimosa, obeche, padauk, padouk, papaya, pawpaw 7 acerola, annatto, avocado, genipap, quassia, yohimbe 8 albizzia, allspice, barbasco, bauhinia, calabash, cocobolo, divi-divi, mahogany, mangrove, tamarind, tamarisk 9 jacaranda, poinciana, sapodilla 10 breadfruit, grapefruit
trunk: 4 bole
trunk, in Britain: 4 stam
up a ~: 6 in a fix, in a jam 7 trapped 10 in hot water, on the ropes
West Indies: 4 pich 7 canella 8 milkwood
tree __: 3 ear 4 crab, farm, fern, frog, lawn, line, post, ring, toad 5 aster, heath, house, hyrax, peony, poppy, shrew, snail, swift, yucca 6 lupine, tomato 7 creeper, cricket, diagram, sparrow, surgeon, swallow
tree-__: 6 hugger
__ tree: 3 bay, bee, big, gum, hat, hau, may, pea, sad, tea, up a 4 bead, bean, boot, coat, cork, crab, hall, hemp, lead, lime, ming, neem, rain, salt, shea, silk 5 athel, bodhi, bully, China, coral, devil, fever, flame, fruit, grass, Jesse, Judas, kapok, money, plane, shade, smoke, state, sugar, tulip 6 banian, banyan, boojum, bottle, bullet, butter, chaste, coffee, dragon, family, fringe, Joshua, lebbek, orchid, ordeal, pagoda, pepper, planer, rubber, sorrel, sponge, tallow 7 cabbage, camphor, clothes, empress, incense, lacquer, liberty, sandbox, sausage, service, tung-oil, varnish
__ Tree: 5 Lemon
Tree at My Window author: Robert Frost
treecreeper: 4 bird
treed: 5 at bay 7 trapped 8 cornered 10 out on a limb
__ tree falls...: 3 If a
Tree Grows in Brooklyn, A: 4 film 5 novel
author: Betty Smith
cast: Joan Blondell, James Dunn, Dorothy McGuire
director: Elia Kazan
treehopper: 6 insect
treehouse support: 4 limb 6 branch
treeless area: 5 llano, marsh, pampa
treelike: 6 sylvan 8 arboreal
tree-lined: 5 shady
road: 4 pkwy. 5 paseo 7 parkway
__ Tree National Park: 6 Joshua
tree of __: 4 life 5 Jesse 6 heaven 7 sadness
tree of life location: 4 Eden
Tree of Man, The author: Patrick White
Tree Planters State: 3 Neb. 4 Nebr. 8 Nebraska
trees: 4 wood 5 silva, sylva, woods 6 timber
Trees author: Joyce Kilmer
Trees, The author: Conrad Richter
tree-to-be: 4 seed 5 acorn
tref, not: 6 kasher, kosher
trefoil: 5 plant 6 flower
__ Treize: 5 Louis
trek: 4 hadj, hike, plod, roam, rove, slog, tour, trip, walk 5 jaunt, march, range, tramp 6 foot it, junket, outing, safari, trapes, travel, trudge, wander 7 journey, migrate, odyssey, passage, traipse 8 ambulate 9 migration 10 emigration, expedition, knock about, pilgrimage
__ Trek: 4 Star
trekker: 5 hiker 8 traveler, vagabond, wayfarer 9 journeyer
trellis: 3 web 5 arbor 7 lattice
ender: 4 work
piece: 4 lath
plant: 3 ivy 5 grape
Tremain: 6 Johnny
Tremayne: 3 Les
tremble: 3 jar 4 lick, rock, stir 5 cower, pulse, quail, quake, shake, throb 6 cringe, dodder, jitter, quaver, quiver, recoil, shiver, teeter, thrill, totter, twitch, wabble, weaken, wobble 7 flutter, pulsate, shudder, vibrate 9 oscillate, palpitate
trembler: 4 bird 5 quake 10 earthquake
trembling: 5 jumpy, quaky, shaky, timid 6 ashake, tremor 7 jittery, vibrant 9 doddering, thrilling, vibration
Tremeloes song: Silence is Golden (1967)

tremendous: **3** big **4** huge, vast **5** awful, giant, great, hefty, jumbo, large, marvy, massy, super **6** mighty **7** amazing, awesome, fearful, hulking, immense, mammoth, massive, sizable, titanic **8** colossal, enormous, fabulous, gigantic, king-size, oversize, sizeable, terrible, terrific, towering, whapping, whopping **9** boundless, deafening, excellent, fantastic, Herculean, humongous, marvelous, monstrous, overlarge, wonderful **10** formidable, gargantuan, monumental, prodigious, stupendous
tremendousness: **5** range, reach **6** import **7** breadth, expanse **8** enormity, grandeur **9** amplitude, magnitude **10** dimensions, importance
tremor: **4** vibe **5** L wave, quake, seism, shake, shock **6** quaver, quiver, ripple, shiver, wabble, wobble **7** flutter, shudder, tremble **8** upheaval **9** trembling, vibration **10** aftershock, earthquake
Tremor Christ (1994 song) artist: Pearl Jam
tremorous: **5** shaky
tremula, populus: **5** aspen
tremulous: **4** edgy, wavy **5** jumpy, shaky, timid **6** afraid, ashake, craven, on edge, scared, yellow **7** fearful, jittery, nervous, panicky, quivery, shaking **8** cowardly, shuddery, skittish **9** quivering **10** frightened, shuddering
trench: **3** cut, pit, rut **4** dike, foss, hole, moat **5** canal, ditch, fosse, gouge, gulch, gully **6** dugout, furrow, groove, gullet, gulley, gutter, trough **7** channel, foxhole **9** earthwork **10** depression, excavation
moon ~: **5** rille
ocean ~: **4** deep
trench __: **4** coat **5** knife **6** mortar **7** warfare
__ Trench: **4** Java **7** Mariana
trenchant: **4** acid, keen, tart **5** blunt, clear, crisp, edged, pithy, sharp, terse **6** biting, gnomic, ireful, strong **7** acerbic, caustic, cutting, driving, graphic, mordant, peppery, piquant, pointed, pungent, salient, telling **8** clear-cut, critical, distinct, emphatic, forceful, incisive, poignant, powerful, sardonic, scathing **9** corrosive, effective, graphical, unsparing **10** razor-sharp, to the point
trencher: **5** plate
ender: **3** man, men
trencherman: **5** diner, eater **7** epicure, glutton **8** consumer, devourer, gourmand
trend: **3** fad, run **4** bent, bias, flow, look, mode, rage, tend, tide, tone, turn **5** craze, drift, style, tenor, thing, vogue **6** course, temper **7** current, fashion, in-thing, leaning **8** movement, tendency **9** direction, gravitate **10** likelihood
ender: **6** setter **7** setting
hot ~: **3** fad **4** rage **5** craze, mania, vogue **7** in thing
starter: **4** down
__ Trend: **5** Motor
trendy: **3** hip, hot, mod, new, now, out **4** chic, posh, tony **5** faddy, fresh, novel, sharp, smart, swank, swish, toney, vogue **6** chichi, latest, modish, snappy, swanky, unique **7** à la mode, current, in style, in vogue, popular, stylish, voguish **8** brand-new, last word, original, up-to-date **9** different, in fashion **10** all the rage, avant-garde, futuristic, innovative
group: **5** elite **6** jet set **7** in-crowd, society **8** well-to-do **9** beau monde **10** upper crust
no longer ~: **3** old **4** worn **5** dated, dusty, hoary, passé, stale, trite **6** old-hat **7** archaic, run-down, worn-out **8** obsolete, out of use, timeworn **9** hackneyed, out-of-date **10** antiquated
Trent: **4** city, Lott, town **5** river **6** Reznor **7** Barbara
city locale: **5** Italy
river: **5** Adige
River locale: **7** England
__ Trent D'Arby: **7** Terence
Trento: **4** city, town
locale: **5** Italy
river: **5** Adige
Trenton: **4** city, town **7** capital
county: **6** Mercer
locale: **8** Michigan **9** New Jersey
river: **8** Delaware
Trent's __ Case: **4** Last
Trent's Last Case author: E.C. Bentley
Trent University
location: **6** Canada **7** Ontario
trepak: **5** dance **9** Ukrainian
trepid: **5** timid **6** afeard, afraid, scared **7** abashed, afeared, alarmed, anxious, chicken, daunted, fearful, nervous, panicky, spooked **8** cowardly, fearsome, hesitant, timorous **9** petrified, terrified **10** frightened
not ~: **4** bold, pert **5** brash, brave, fresh, gutsy, macho, nervy, pushy, saucy **6** brassy, brazen, cheeky, daring, flashy, heroic, plucky, spunky **7** dashing, defiant, forward, gallant, valiant **8** fearless, forceful, immodest, impudent, resolute, spirited, unafraid, valorous **9** audacious, confident, dauntless, shameless, undaunted, unfearing **10** courageous, incautious, unreserved
trepidation: **4** fear **5** alarm, angst, dread, panic, qualm, shock, worry **6** creeps, dismay, fright, horror, stress, terror **7** anxiety, jitters **8** blue funk, cold feet, disquiet **9** cold sweat **10** uneasiness
tres: **5** three **7** Spanish
follower: **6** cuatro
preceder: **3** dos
Trés __!: **4** bien
Tres Cruces: **4** peak **5** mount **8** mountain
locale: **5** Andes, Chile **9** Argentina
trespass: **3** sin **4** tort **5** crime, error, fault, lapse, poach **6** breach, butt in, horn in, inroad, invade, meddle, nose in, offend **7** break in, intrude, misdeed, obtrude, offense, pillage, violate **8** encroach, infringe, invasion, muscle in, overstep **9** interlope, intrude on, intrusion, misbehave, obtrusion, penetrate, violation **10** encroach on, infraction, wrongdoing
Trespass (1992 film)
cast: Ice Cube, Ice-T, Bill Paxton, William Sadler
director: Walter Hill
trespasser: **7** invader **8** criminal, intruder **10** interloper
Trespasser, The author: D.H. Lawrence
trespassing: **6** inroad **7** ingress **9** violation
tress: **4** curl, hair, lock **5** braid, plait **6** strand **7** ringlet
tresses: **3** mop **4** hair **8** coiffure
trestle: **4** beam, rack **6** bridge
trevally: **4** fish
Trevayne author: Robert Ludlum
Trevi Fountain
locale: **4** Rome **5** Italy
money: **4** euro, lira, lire
Trevino, Lee: **6** golfer
milieu: **5** links **6** course
org.: **3** PGA
Trevor: **4** Nunn **6** Claire, Howard **7** Berbick **9** Griffiths
Trevor, Claire: **7** actress
film: The Adventures of Martin Eden (1942)
Allegheny Uprising (1939)
The Amazing Doctor Clitterhouse (1938)
Born to Kill (1947)
Crack-Up (1946)
Crossroads (1942)
Dark Command (1940)
The High and the Mighty (1954)
Johnny Angel (1945)
Key Largo (1948, AA)
The Man Without a Star (1955)
Marjorie Morningstar (1958)
Murder, My Sweet (1944)
Raw Deal (1948)
Stagecoach (1939)
Texas (1941)
The Woman of the Town (1943)
trews: **5** pants
T-rex: **5** biped **8** dinosaur
trey: **4** card, trio **6** triple **9** three-spot
card before ~: **5** deuce
topper: **4** four
Trey: **6** Parker, Wilson
Tri-__ Pictures: **4** Star
__ Tri: **5** Quang
triacetate fiber: **5** Arnel
triad: **4** trin, trio **5** chord, trine **6** triple, troika
triage site: **2** ER
trial: **3** woe **4** bane, care, case, drag, gage, load, loss, pain, pest, pill, suit, test **5** assay, check, essay, fight, fling, grief, pilot, proof, thorn, worry **6** action, burden, dry run, hassle, misery, ordeal, sorrow, tryout **7** attempt, contest, hearing, lawsuit, process, test run, trouble **8** acid test, analysis, audition, crucible, distress, endeavor, gauntlet, hardship, irritant, nuisance, struggle, tribunal, vexation **9** adversity, nightmare, probation, suffering, tentative **10** affliction, difficulty, experiment, heartbreak, indictment, irritation, litigation, misfortune, visitation
balloon: **4** test **6** feeler **7** enquiry, inquiry
bring to ~: **6** charge, indict **7** arraign **9** prosecute
companion: **5** error
evidence: **3** DNA
figure: **2** DA **5** judge, juror **6** lawyer **7** bailiff **9** barrister
precursor: **3** nab **4** bust, raid **6** arrest, collar **7** capture, hearing **9** detention
ritual: **4** oath, plea
run: **4** test **5** trial, whirl **10** experiment
scene: **5** venue
session: **6** assize
trial __: **3** run **4** jury **5** court, horse **6** docket, lawyer **7** balance, balloon
Trial (1955 film)
cast: Glenn Ford, John Hodiak, Dorothy McGuire
director: Mark Robson
__ Trial: **6** Monkey, Scopes
trial and __: **5** error
Trial and Error (1997 film)
cast: Jeff Daniels, Michael Richards, Charlize Theron, Rip Torn
director: Jonathan Lynn
__ trial basis: **3** on a
trial by __: **4** fire, jury
Trial by Jury
composer: **7** Gilbert **8** Sullivan
Trial of a Poet author: Karl Shapiro
Trial Run author: Dick Francis
trials: **3** woe **10** infelicity
Trials of Oscar Wilde, The (1960 film)
cast: Peter Finch, Yvonne Mitchell
director: Ken Hughes
Trial, The author: Franz Kafka
Triaminic alternative: **5** Afrin **6** Contac, Nyquil, Tavist **7** Actifed, Comtrex, Dayquil, Dristan, Sinutab, Sudafed **8** Benadryl, Dimetapp, Drixoral, TheraFlu **9** Coricidin **10** Robitussin
triangle: **4** trio **5** shape, slice **6** triple **10** percussion
in heraldry: **5** gyron
kind of ~: **5** acute, right **6** obtuse **7** scalene **8** isoceles
part: **3** leg **4** base, side
ratio: **4** sine **6** cosine, secant **7** tangent
sound: **4** ting
tip: **4** apex **6** vertex
__ Triangle: **6** Devil's, Golden **7** Bermuda
triangular: **7** deltoid
heraldic charge: **5** gyron
insert: **6** gusset
letter: **5** delta
sail: **3** jib **5** raffe **6** lateen, raffee, raffie
sign: **5** Yield
support: **6** A-frame
wall: **5** gable
triathlete need: **4** bike
triathlon: **4** meet **5** event **7** contest
event: **3** run **4** swim **8** bike race
__ Triathlon: **7** Ironman
tribal: **6** racial
division: **4** clan **6** family
leader: **4** head **5** chief, elder **6** senior **9** matriarch, patriarch
Tribal-Love Rock Musical, The: **4** Hair
tribe: **3** Fox, Han, Kaw, Oto, Ree, Sac, Ute **4** clan, Coos, Cree, Crow, Cuna, Erie, Eyak, Hopi, Inca, Iowa, Levi, Maya, Otoe, Pima, Pomo, race, Sauk, Seri, Tama, Taos, Tewa, Tiwa, Tupi, Yana, Yuma, Zuni **5** Ahtna, Bantu, Brulé, Caddo, Carib, Creek, Haida, horde, Huron, Inuit, Kansa, Kaska, Kiowa, Lenca, Lipan, Maidu, Makah, Miami, Miwok, Modoc, ocean, Omaha, Osage, Otomi, Piute, Ponca, Sioux, stock, Taino, Teton, Unami, Washo, Wintu, Yaqui **6** Abnaki, Ahtena, Apache, Arawak, Aymara, Cayuga, Cayuse, Dakota, Galibi, Innuit, Inupik, Jivaro, Kechua, Laguna, Lakota, Lengua, Lumbee, Mandan, Micmac, Mohave, Mohawk, Mojave, Munsee, nation, Navaho, Navajo, Nootka, Oglala, Ojibwa, Oneida, Ottawa, Paiute, Papago, Patwin, Pawnee, people, Pequot, Piegan, Plains, Pueblo, Quapaw, Salish, Santee, Seneca, Shasta, Skagit, Tanana, Toltec, Washoe, Wintun, Yahgan, Yakima, Yokuts **7** Abenaki, Arapaho, Arikara, Atakapa, Bannock, Chibcha, Chilcat, Chilkat, Chinook, Choctaw, Chumash, Guarani, Huastec, Kechuan, kindred, Klamath, Koyukon, Kutchin, Kutenai, Lakhota, lineage, Mahican, Mazatec, Miskito, Mohegan, Mohican, Naskapi, Nipmuck, Ojibway, Quechua, Quichua, San Blas, Shawnee, Takelma, Tanaina, Tlingit, Washita, Wichita, Wyandot, Yankton, Yavapai, Yucatec, Zapotec **8** Arapahoe, Cahuilla, Caingang, Cherokee, Cheyenne, Chippewa, Comanche, Delaware, Flathead, Hunkpapa,

Illinois, Iroquois, Kickapoo, Kwakiutl, Malecite, Maricopa, Mikasuki, Missouri, Muskogee, Nez Percé, Onondaga, Ouachita, Powhatan, Puyallup, Quechuan, Sahaptin, Seminole, Shoshone, Squamish, Tarascan, Wabanaki, Wahpeton **9** Blackfoot, Chickasaw, Havasupai, Jicarilla, Karankawa, Menominee, Mescalero, Nanticoke, Penobscot, Saulteaux, Suquamish, Tehuelche, Tsimshian, Tuscarora, Wahpekute, Wampanoag, Winnebago, Wyandotte **10** Adirondack, Araucanian, Assiniboin, Athabaskan, Bellabella, Bellacoola, Chiricahua, Gros Ventre, Miniconjou, Potawatomi, Tarahumara
combining form: 4 phyl- **5** phylo-
see also Indian
tribes
father of twelve ~: 5 Jacob
tribulation: 3 woe **4** care, pain **5** agony, curse, grief, trial, worry **6** burden, hassle, misery, ordeal, sorrow **7** bad luck, bad time, despair, reverse, sadness, trouble **8** distress, hard luck, hardship, hard time, headache, rainy day **9** adversity, heartache, suffering **10** hard knocks, misfortune
tribunal: 4 jury **5** court, forum, trial
Tribune: 5 paper **9** newspaper
locale: 5 Tampa **7** Chicago, Oakland
Tribune-Review: 5 paper **9** newspaper
locale: 10 Pittsburgh
tributary: 4 fork **5** creek, river **6** branch, feeder, inflow, stream **8** waterway **9** confluent, secondary, streamlet **10** collateral
tribute: 3 tax **4** geld, hand, kudo, toll **5** award, honor, kudos, salvo, toast **6** bounty, esteem, eulogy, heriot, homage, impost, praise, salute **7** acclaim, mention, ovation, plaudit, respect **8** accolade, applause, citation, encomium, flattery, good word, libation, memorial, monument, offering **9** extolment, laudation, panegyric, reference **10** compliment, exaltation
pay ~ to: 4 hail **5** exalt, extol, honor **6** extoll, praise, salute **8** eulogize
Tribute: 3 SUV **5** Mazda
Tribute to a Bad Man (1956 film)
cast: James Cagney, Don Dubbins, Stephen McNally
director: Robert Wise
trice: 3 sec **4** jiff **5** jiffy **6** moment, second **7** eyewink, instant **9** twinkling
triceps locale: 3 arm
triceratops: 8 dinosaur
Tricia's mom: 3 Pat
trick: 2 do **3** art, con, fox, gag, use, way **4** bilk, dupe, fool, game, gull, have, hoax, lark, lure, nick, plot, ploy, rook, ruse, sham, snow, take, trap, verb, wile **5** antic, blind, bluff, caper, catch, cheat, cozen, decoy, dodge, feint, fraud, hocus, knack, lying, phony, prank, put on, quirk, set up, shift, shill, skill, snare, spell, spoof, stunt **6** ambush, befool, deceit, delude, device, dupery, entrap, gambit, humbug, lead on, method, outwit, phoney, racket, rip off, scheme, secret, take in **7** beguile, deceive, defraud, ensnare, evasion, exploit, fake out, finagle, finesse, gimmick, insnare, knavery, know-how, mislead, sleight, snooker, snow job, swindle, tactics, two-time **8** artifice, disguise, flimflam, hang of it, hoodwink, illusion, maneuver, outsmart, pettifog, practice, pretense, sucker in, throw off **9** bamboozle, deception, disinform, expedient, four-flush, imposture, stratagem, technique, victimize **10** ambushment, hocus-pocus, imposition, shenanigan, subterfuge, tomfoolery
alternative: 5 treat
dirty ~: 5 cheat **8** mischief **9** duplicity
do the ~: 4 work **7** satisfy, succeed **10** accomplish
ender: 4 ster
not missing a ~: 8 watchful **9** observant
trick __: 4 knee **6** ending
__ trick: 3 hat, odd **4** card **5** do the, honor, quick **7** lobster, playing, quitted
Trick (1999 film)
cast: Christian Campbell, Steve Hayes, John Paul Pitoc, Tori Spelling
director: Jim Fall
__ Trick: 5 Cheap
trickery: 3 art **4** hoax, scam **5** craft, dodge, fraud, guile, spoof, sting **6** deceit, dupery **7** con game, evasion, knavery, snow job **8** artifice, cheating, flimflam, intrigue, jugglery, pretense **9** chicanery, deception, fourberie, imposture, shell game, swindling **10** dishonesty
get by ~: 4 gull **5** cheat, mulct **6** extort, fleece **7** defraud, swindle
__ trick in the book!, The: 6 oldest
trickle: 3 bit **4** drip, drop, flow, leak, ooze, seep, weep **5** exude, issue **6** filter, murmur, stream **7** distill, dribble **9** percolate
trickle __: 6 charge
trickle-__ theory: 4 down
Trick of It, The author: Michael Frayn
Trick or __!: 5 treat
__-Trick Pony: 3 One
tricks: 5 magic
bag of ~: 7 arsenal
bid to take no ~: 5 nullo
like dirty ~: 6 covert
__ tricks: 5 bag of, dirty
__ tricks?: 4 How's
tricks of the __: 5 trade
trickster: 4 liar **5** cheat, rogue **6** rascal **8** swindler
Trick to Catch the Old One, A author: Thomas Middleton
trick-winning feat: 4 slam
tricky: 3 sly **4** cagy, deep, foxy, wily **5** cagey, dicey, false, lying, risky, rocky, shady, sharp, slick, tight **6** artful, chancy, crafty, knotty, quirky, shifty, shrewd, smooth, sneaky, sticky, subtle, thorny, touchy **7** complex, crooked, cunning, devious, elusive, elusory, evasive, furtive, knavish, prickly **8** delicate, delusive, guileful, involved, scheming, slippery, ticklish **9** deceitful, deceptive, designing, difficult, dishonest, insidious, insincere, intricate, sensitive, strategic, underhand **10** mendacious, misleading, perplexing, precarious, serpentine, touch-and-go, unreliable, untruthful
problem: 5 poser **7** dilemma
tricolor: 4 flag
tricorne: 3 hat
tricot: 6 fabric **8** material
tricycle: 6 wheels
user: 3 kid, tot **9** youngster
trident: 5 spear
like a ~: 5 forky, tined **6** forked
part: 4 tine
Trident: 10 chewing gum
alternative: 5 Extra, Orbit **7** Dentyne **8** Carefree, Chiclets, Freedent **10** Doublemint, Juicy Fruit
tried and true: 4 safe, sure **5** liege, loyal, sound **6** proven, tested, trusty **7** staunch **8** approved, reliable **9** certified, qualified, reputable, steadfast, unfailing, venerable **10** dependable, time-tested
triens: 4 coin
trier: 5 judge **10** prosecutor
Trier: 4 city, town
locale: 7 Germany
Trieste: 4 city, gulf, port, town
city near ~: 5 Udine
locale: 5 Italy **6** Istria
trifecta: 3 bet **5** wager **6** gamble
trifle: 3 bit, jot, toy **4** cake, dash, drop, hint, laze, play, snip, whit **5** curio, dally, flirt, pinch, shade, smack, speck, straw, taste, touch, trace **6** bauble, bêtise, coquet, dabble, dawdle, diddly, doodle, frivol, geegaw, gewgaw, lead on, linger, little, misuse, monkey, palter, potter, putter **7** bibelot, dessert, fribble, fritter, modicum, novelty, soupçon, toy with, trinket **8** fraction, lollygag, nicknack, particle, picayune, spoonful, squander **9** bagatelle, bric-a-brac, no big deal, play games, plaything, suspicion **10** dillydally, fool around, knickknack, mess around, play around, suggestion, triviality
away: 5 drain, waste **8** misspend, squander **9** dissipate
with: 5 tease **6** lead on
(with): 3 toy **5** flirt **6** monkey, tinker
trifler: 5 flirt, toyer **7** dawdler
trifles: 6 trivia **8** minutiae
trifling: 3 low **4** lazy, mere, poor, puny, tiny, vain **5** banal, dinky, extra, light, minor, petty, silly, small, sorry, sport, teeny **6** little, measly, minute, paltry, slight, teensy, yeasty **7** nominal, shallow, trivial **8** needless, niggling, nugatory, optional, picayune, piddling, uncostly, unneeded **9** frivolity, frivolous, minuscule, redundant, worthless **10** negligible
amount: 3 fig **8** pittance
trifocals: 5 specs **6** frames **7** glasses **10** spectacles
trig: 4 math, neat, tidy
cousin: 3 alg. **7** algebra **8** calculus, geometry
function: 3 cos, cot., sin, tan **4** cosh, sine, sinh, tanh **5** cosec. **6** arcsin, arctan, cosine, secant **7** tangent **8** cosecant
trigger: 4 spur, stir **5** cause, rouse, spark, start **6** elicit, ignite, incite, prompt, set off **7** inspire, produce, provoke **8** activate, generate, initiate, motivate, touch off **9** stimulate **10** bring about, give rise to, lead the way
like some ~ fingers: 5 itchy
mechanism: 5 timer
pull the ~: 4 fire **5** shell, shoot
quick on the ~: 5 sharp **6** astute
trigger __: 6 finger
trigger-__: 5 happy
__ trigger: 4 hair
Trigger: 5 horse, steed **6** equine
rider: Roy Rogers
Triglov: 4 peak **5** mount **8** mountain
locale: 6 Europe **7** Croatia
triglyceride: 5 ester
__ trigonometry: 5 plane
trike: 5 cycle
part: 5 wheel
rider: 3 kid, tot **9** youngster
Trikora: 4 peak **5** mount **8** mountain
locale: 4 Asia **9** New Guinea
trilby: 3 hat
material: 4 felt
Trilby author: George du Maurier
trill: 4 pipe, roll, sing **5** chirr, churr **6** chirre, quaver, warble **7** chirrup, vibrato
Trillin, Calvin piece: 5 essay
Trilling: 6 Lionel
trillion combining form: 4 tera-, treg- **5** trega-
trillions: 4 lots **6** scores **7** legions
trillionth combining form: 4 pico-
trillium: 5 plant **6** flower
Trillo: 5 Manny
trilobite: 6 fossil
trilogy: 4 trio **6** triple
first of a ~: 5 part I
trim: 3 bob, cut, fit, lop, mow, top, wax **4** beat, clip, crop, deck, dock, drub, edge, edit, form, hale, lace, lean, lick, neat, nice, pare, skin, slim, snip, snug, taut, thin, tidy, whip **5** adorn, array, clean, dress, erase, frame, frill, kempt, level, order, plane, prank, prink, prune, shape, shave, shear, sleek, slick, smart, spank, state, whack **6** barber, bedeck, border, comely, cut off, cut out, dapper, defeat, delete, digest, edging, even up, excise, fettle, fringe, health, kilter, neaten, piping, reduce, repair, spruce, svelte, thrash, wallop **7** abridge, clobber, compact, curtail, cut away, cut back, cut down, dress up, festoon, fitness, garnish, gilding, healthy, lambast, orderly, overrun, scissor, shapely, shorten, slender, smother, spangle, swindle, trounce, whittle, willowy **8** beautify, beribbon, boil down, clean-cut, condense, decorate, downsize, emblazon, graceful, lambaste, neatness, ornament, pare down, pretty up, slice off, spruce up, to rights, trimming, truncate, well-kept **9** adornment, beautiful, condition, cut back on, embellish, embroider, reprehend, scale down, shipshape, situation, smarten up, stabilize, summarize **10** abbreviate, blue-pencil, commission, decoration, fastidious, neat as a pin, statuesque
again: 5 recut, remow
a tree: 5 prune
in fighting ~: 5 tough **6** strong
trim __: 3 die, tab **4** rail, size
__ trim: 5 out of
trimaran: 4 boat
Trimble, David: 8 Nobelist
__-Trimeton: 5 Chlor
trimmed: 5 level **7** fringed
it's often ~: 4 hair, sail
Trimmed Lamp, The author: O. Henry
trimmer: 5 edger, razor
__ trimmer: 4 lamp, line **6** string
trimming: 4 edge, lace, trim **5** frame, frill **6** fringe **7** garnish **8** ornament **9** adornment **10** decoration
trimmings: 7 fixings **9** trappings
trim one's __: 5 sails
trin: 4 trio **5** triad **7** triplet **9** threesome
trine: 4 trio **5** triad **6** triple **7** triplet **9** threefold, threesome
Trini: 5 Lopez **8** Alvarado
Trinidad: 3 isl. **4** isle **6** island
Trinidad and Tobago: 4 isls. **5** isles **6** nation **7** country, islands
money: 4 cent **6** dollar
org.: 3 OAS
writer: 6 Selvon
Trinitron maker: 4 Sony
trinity: 4 trio **6** triple
Trinity: 5 river
city on the ~: 6 Dallas **9** Fort Worth
Trinity __: 6 Sunday
__ Trinity: 4 Holy **7** Blessed
Trinity author: Leon Uris
Trinity Western University
location: 6 Canada **7** Langley
trinket: 3 toy **4** bead, gaud, junk, rock **5** bijou, charm, curio, dodad, glass,

jewel, stone **6** bangle, bauble, doodad, gadget, geegaw, gewgaw, trifle **7** bibelot, fribble, jewelry, nothing, novelty, whatnot **8** bracelet, gimcrack, hardware, nicknack, ornament, reminder, sparkler, wristlet **9** bagatelle, objet d'art, plaything **10** decoration, knickknack

trio: 4 Magi, team, trey, trin **5** leash, three, triad, trine **6** triune, troika **7** ternion, trilogy, trinity, triplet **8** ensemble, triangle, triptych **9** threesome **10** triplicate
maybe: 4 band **5** combo
times three: 5 nonet
times two: 6 sextet

__ Triomphe: 5 Arc de

trip: 3 err, hop, run **4** bomb, buck, bust, fall, flop, hadj, hike, lope, lose, miss, play, skip, slip, step, tour, trek **5** drive, error, flunk, foray, jaunt, lapse, lurch, pitch, slide, swing **6** blow it, bungle, canter, cruise, errand, falter, flight, frolic, header, junket, outing, plunge, ramble, slip on, slip up, sprawl, spring, topple, totter, travel, tumble, vision, voyage **7** blunder, confuse, faux pas, founder, go under, go wrong, journey, misstep, mistake, odyssey, passage, stumble, wash out, weekend **8** fall flat, fall over, flounder, lay an egg, long haul, pratfall, throw off, unsettle **9** excursion, false move, false step, overnight, strike out **10** disconcert, expedition, pilgrimage
boat ~: 4 sail **6** cruise, voyage
delayer: 4 flat
ego ~: 5 pride **6** vanity
end a ~: 4 dock, land **6** arrive
ender: 4 wire **6** hammer
head ~: 6 vision **7** reverie
long ~: 4 trek **7** journey, sojourn **10** pilgrimage
motor ~: 4 spin
pleasure ~: 5 jaunt **6** junket, outing
prepare for a ~: 4 pack
record: 3 log **5** diary **7** journal, logbook
round ~: 4 tour **5** jaunt **6** junket, travel **7** circuit, journey **9** excursion
segment: 3 leg
short ~: 4 spin **5** jaunt, whirl **6** dayhop, errand, outing
souvenir: 5 photo **6** magnet, T-shirt
take a ~: 5 motor **6** travel
taker: 7 tourist **8** traveler **10** vacationer
the light fantastic: 4 step **5** dance, party, rumba, tango, waltz **6** cha-cha, rhumba **7** cut a rug
up: 4 trap **6** ascent
(up): 4 foul

__ trip: 3 ego **4** head, road, side **5** field, guilt, power, round, take a **6** return **7** fishing

__-trip: 3 day

tripe: 3 gas, rot **4** blah, bosh, bull, bunk, guff, jazz, jive, meat, pooh, tosh **5** bilge, fudge, hokum, hooey, prate, stuff, trash **6** bunkum, bushwa, drivel, footle, gabble, gammon, gibber, havers, hot air, humbug, jabber, jargon, kibosh, piffle **7** baloney, blarney, blather, blether, boloney, bushwah, eyewash, flannel, flubdub, fustian, garbage, hogwash, inanity, rubbish, twaddle **8** buncombe, claptrap, falderal, falderol, flimflam, flummery, folderal, folderol, nonsense, slipslop, tommyrot, trumpery **9** banana oil, gibberish, goofiness, kidstakes, moonshine, poppycock, rigmarole **10** applesauce, balderdash, bilge water, codswallop, double-talk, empty words, flapdoodle, galimatias, Jabberwock, mumbo jumbo, rigamarole, taradiddle

triphosphate: 5 ester

triple: 3 hit **4** trey **5** leash, triad, trine **6** triune, troika **7** ternion, trilogy, trinity **8** triangle **9** threesome

triple __: 3 sec **4** axel, bond, jump, play, time **5** bogey, cream, crème, fugue, point, rhyme, voile **6** rhythm, threat **7** dresser, measure

triple-__: 5 digit, space **6** decker, double, header, nerved, tongue

Triple __: 5 Crown **7** Entente

Triple Alliance country: Austria-Hungary, Germany, Italy

Triple Crown: 5 award
event: 4 race **5** Derby **7** Belmont **9** Preakness
horse: 5 Omaha **7** Assault **8** Affirmed, Citation **9** Sir Barton, Whirlaway **10** Count Fleet, Gallant Fox, War Admiral **11** Seattle Slew, Secretariat
jockey: 5 Sande **6** Arcaro, Loftus **7** Cauthen, Cruguet, Longden **8** Mehrtens, Saunders, Turcotte **9** Earl Sande **10** Kurtsinger

tripled combining form: 4 tris-

triple-decker: 4 club **8** sandwich

Triple Fool, The author: John Donne

triplet: 4 trin, trio **5** trine

triple witching __: 4 hour

triplicate: 4 trio

tripmeter setting: 3 OOO

tripod: 5 easel, stand
part: 3 leg

Tripoli: 4 city, port, town **7** capital
locale: 5 Libya **6** Africa **7** Lebanon, Mideast
native: 6 Libyan **8** Lebanese
old ~ governor: 3 dey

tripondius: 5 money

__-tripper: 3 ego

__ Tripper: 3 Day

trippet: 3 cam

Trippin' (1998 song)
artist: Missy Elliott, Total

tripping: 4 foul

Tripplehorn, Jeanne: 7 actress
film: Basic Instinct (1992)
The Firm (1993)
Sliding Doors (1998)
Timecode (2000)
Waterworld (1995)

trip-routing org.: 3 AAA

trip the __ fantastic: 5 light

Triptik org.: 3 AAA

Trip to Bountiful, The (1985 film)
cast: Carlin Glynn, John Heard, Geraldine Page
director: Peter Masterson

triptych: 4 trio
image: 5 icons
panel: 5 volet

trireme: 4 boat **6** galley
complement: 4 crew
tool: 3 oar
weapon: 3 ram

Tris: 7 Speaker

Triscuit: 7 cracker
alternative: 4 Ritz **5** Zesta **6** Krispy **7** Cheez-It **10** Cheese Nips, Wheat Thins

trisection part: 5 third

Trish: 9 Van Devere

Trisha: 8 Yearwood

triskaidekaphobe fear: 8 thirteen

Tristan: 6 knight
love: 6 Iseult, Isolde
Mark to: 5 uncle

Tristan da Cunha: 3 isl. **4** isle **6** island

Tristan und Isolde: 5 opera
composer: 6 Wagner
role: 4 Mark **5** Melot **8** Brangäne, King Mark, Kurwenal
setting: 6 France **7** England **8** Brittany, Cornwall

triste: 3 sad **6** French

__ Triste: 5 Valse

__ Tristesse: 7 Bonjour

Tristia writer: 4 Ovid

Tristram: 4 poem **6** Coffin, Shandy
author: Edward Arlington Robinson

Tristram Shandy author: Laurence Sterne

Trisul: 4 peak **5** mount **8** mountain
locale: 4 Asia **5** India **9** Himalayas

trite: 3 set **4** dull, flat, worn **5** banal, chain, corny, hokey, musty, passé, silly, stale, stock, tired, vapid **6** common, jejune, old hat, used-up **7** clichéd, drained, fatuous, humdrum, insipid, prosaic, routine, trivial, worn-out **8** bathetic, bromidic, cornball, mildewed, ordinary, outdated, outmoded, overused, shopworn, time-worn, well-worn **9** exhausted, hackneyed, moth-eaten, played-out, prosaical, ready-made **10** dullsville, overworked, pedestrian, threadbare, uninspired, unoriginal, warmed-over
not as ~: 5 newer
remark: 6 cliché, saying **7** bromide **8** chestnut **9** platitude

triton: 4 newt **5** shell **8** seashell

Triton: 3 god **4** moon
daughter of ~: 6 Pallas
parent of ~: 8 Poseidon **10** Amphitrite
planet: 7 Neptune
sister of ~: 5 Rhode

Tritt: 6 Travis

triturate: 5 grind, pound **6** powder **7** crumble **9** granulate, pulverize

triumph: 3 hit, joy, win **4** best, coup, crow, feat, gain, luck, palm, riot, sell, sink **5** cinch, exult, gloat, glory, homer, pride, revel, score, sweep **6** big hit, big win, make it, pan out, shoo-in, splash, subdue, thrive, winner, win out **7** achieve, conquer, delight, elation, jubilee, luck out, make out, prevail, prosper, rejoice, succeed, success, sure bet, swagger, trounce, victory, work out **8** blow away, conquest, dominate, flourish, get ahead, go places, hit it big, jubilate, make good, overcome, pushover, reveling, smash hit, takeover, vanquish, walkover **9** celebrate, checkmate, exultance, festivity, grand slam, jubilance, landslide, merriment, overwhelm, rejoicing, sensation, subjugate, sure thing **10** ascendance, ascendancy, ascendence, ascendency, attainment, clean sweep, exultation, gold record, jubilation, jump for joy
again: 5 rewin
exclamation: 3 aah, aha, hah, oho, olé, yay **4** I win, ta-da **5** hoo-ha, tadah, voilà **6** eureka, gotcha, hoohah, hoorah, hooray, hurrah, hurray, I did it, yippee **7** whoopee, whoopie

triumphal __: 4 arch

Triumph and Tragedy author: Winston Churchill

triumphant: 5 happy, lucky, on top, proud **6** elated, joyful, joyous **7** gleeful, winning, winsome **8** boastful, champion, dominant, exultant, glorious, jubilant, out front, unbeaten **9** fortunate, rejoicing, triumphal **10** flying high, victorious
be ~: 4 brag, crow **5** exult, revel **7** rejoice **9** celebrate **10** effervesce, jump for joy

Triumph of the Egg, The author: Sherwood Anderson

Triumph of the Spirit (1989 film)
cast: Willem Dafoe, Robert Loggia, Edward James Olmos
director: Robert M. Young

Triumph of the Will (1935 film) director: Leni Riefenstahl

triumvirate: 4 trio **6** triple

triune: 4 trio **6** triple

trivia: 7 details, trifles **8** minutiae **10** fine points
category: 5 music **6** movies, sports **10** television
collection: 3 ana

trivial: 4 idle, mean, puny **5** empty, least, light, minor, petty, small, trite **6** atomic, flimsy, little, meager, minute, paltry, scanty, slight, stupid, yeasty **7** nominal, puerile, shallow **8** atomical, everyday, ill-spent, needless, nugatory, picayune, piddling, skin-deep, trifling, unneeded **9** frivolous, momentary, secondary, senseless, valueless, vanishing, worthless **10** diminutive, evanescent, immaterial, incidental, irrelevant, negligible, nonserious, unprofound
detail: 3 nit
most ~: 5 least

Trivial Breath author: Elinor Wylie

trivialites: 7 details **8** minutiae, niceties

triviality: 6 trifle **9** frivolity

Trivial Pursuit: 4 game **9** board game
maker: 6 Hasbro
need: 4 dice **5** cards **6** wedges **9** questions

Trix: 6 cereal
competitor: 3 Kix **4** Life **5** Kashi, Quisp, Total **6** Kaboom, Muesli, Oreo O's, Pablum, Smacks **7** All-Bran, Crispix, Harmony, Hunny B's, Mueslix, Oat Bran, Pokemon **8** Boo Berry, Cheerios, Corn Chex, Corn Pops, Fiber One, Rice Chex, Special K, Uncle Sam, Wheaties **9** Alpha Bits, Apple Zaps, Grape Nuts, Honey Comb, Just Right, Wheat Chex **10** Apple Jacks, Bran Flakes, Cap'n Crunch, Cocoa Puffs, Froot Loops, Mini-Wheats, Nutri-Grain, Puffed Rice, Quaker Oats, Smart Start **11** Cocoa Blasts, Cookie Crisp, Golden Crisp, Lucky Charms, Puffed Wheat, Sweet Crunch, Waffle Crisp

-trix cousin: 3 -ess

Trixie: 6 Norton
friend: 5 Alice

trk. agency: 3 ICC

Trobriand: 4 isls. **5** isles **7** islands

troche: 4 pill **6** pastil, tablet **7** lozenge **8** pastille

Troche: 4 rose

trochee: 4 foot
relative: 4 iamb **6** dactyl **7** anapest, pyrrhic, spondee

trodden starter: 4 down

Troggs
song: Love Is All Around (1968)
Wild Thing (1966)

troglodyte: 7 recluse **8** anchoret **9** anchorite, barbarian

troglodytic: 6 lonely **8** solitary, unsocial **9** reclusive, withdrawn

trogon: 4 bird

Troia: 5 Ilium

Troi, friend of: 4 Worf **5** Riker

troika: 4 sled, trio **5** triad **6** triple

Troilus
brother of ~: 5 Paris **6** Hector
parent of ~: 5 Priam **6** Hecuba **7** Priamus
sister of ~: 9 Cassandra
slayer of ~: 8 Achilles

Troilus and Cressida: 4 play
author: Shakespeare
role: 4 Ajax 5 Helen, Paris, Priam 6 Aeneas, Hector, Nestor 7 Antenor, Calchas, Helenus, Ulysses 8 Achilles, Diomedes, Menelaus, Pandarus 9 Agamemnon, Cassandra, Deiphobus, Patroclus, Thersites 10 Andromache
setting: 4 Troy
Troilus and Criseyde: 4 poem
author: 7 Chaucer
___ trois: 5 pas de
___ Trois Mousquetaires: 3 Les
Trois-Rivières: 4 city, port, town
locale: 6 Canada, Québec
Trojan: 5 Paris 6 Dardan
ally: 4 Ares
like the ~ horse: 5 false 9 deceitful
opponent: 5 UCLAn
work like a ~: 4 toil 5 slave
Trojan ___: 3 War 5 group, horse
Trojan horse: 4 ruse 10 subterfuge
like the ~: 6 hollow
Trojans: 3 USC 9 Troy State
Trojans, The composer: 7 Berlioz
Trojan War
cause: 5 Helen
epic: 5 Iliad
instigator: 4 Eris
lure: 5 apple
Trojan Women, The author: Euripides
troll: 4 doll, fish, ogre, pull 5 angle, carol, gnome
concern: 6 bridge
whence the word ~: 5 Norse
___ Troll: 4 Atta
troller: 6 angler 7 trawler 9 fisherman
hook: 5 drail
need: 3 net
trolley
in America: 4 cart
line: 8 railroad
passage: 4 fare
sound: 5 clang
take the ~: 4 ride
trolley ___: 3 bus, car 4 line 5 coach
Trolley Song, The word: 5 clang
Troll Garden, The author: Willa Cather
Trollope, Anthony: 6 author, writer 7 British
work: Barchester Towers
The Claverings
Phineas Finn
Phineas Redux
trombone: 4 horn, wind 5 brass 7 sackbut 10 instrument
accessory: 4 mute
effect: 4 wawa
part: 5 slide, valve
___ trombone: 5 slide, valve
trombonist: 3 Ory 6 Dorsey, Kid Ory, Miller 9 Teagarden
tromp: 4 hike, plod 5 stamp 6 stride 7 clobber, shellac 8 shellack
trompe ___: 5 l'oeil
Tromsö: 4 city, port, town
locale: 6 Norway
Trondheim: 4 city, port, town 5 fiord, fjord
locale: 6 Norway
Troon: 3 spa 4 town
locale: 8 Scotland
troop: 3 mob 4 army, band, body, crew, gang, herd, host, mass, pack, ring, step, team, unit, walk 5 bunch, corps, crowd, drove, flock, force, group, hands, horde, march, party, squad, swarm 6 clique, detail, gather, legion, muster, number, outfit, parade, throng 7 brigade, company, crowd in, numbers, platoon 8 assemble, assembly, regiment, soldiers 9 gathering, multitude, personnel 10 collection, contingent, detachment
deployment: 6 tactic 8 maneuver, movement 9 operation
ender: 4 ship
group: 3 BSA, rgt. 4 regt., unit 5 corps, force, squad 8 division, regiment 9 battalion
lodging: 4 bunk, post 6 billet 8 barracks, quarters
mover: 3 APC, LST 6 amtrac 7 amtrack
stopover: 4 camp 5 étape 7 bivouac
troupe: 3 USO
Troop Beverly Hills (1989 film)
cast: Mary Gross, Shelley Long, Craig T. Nelson, Betty Thomas
director: Jeff Kanew
trooper: 3 cop 5 horse 6 equine 7 charger, dragoon, officer, soldier 8 war-horse 9 legionary, policeman
bulletin: 3 APB
concern: 3 mph 5 radar 8 speeding
like a ~: 9 earnestly, zealously
starter: 4 para
___ trooper: 5 state
Trooper: 3 SUV 5 Isuzu
troops: 4 army 7 cavalry 8 military, presence 9 personnel
call for ~: 5 rally
disband ~: 5 demob
supply fresh ~ to: 5 reman
supply ~ to: 3 man 6 deploy
___ troops: 3 ski 5 shock
troopship: 4 boat
trop, de: 7 surplus, too much 9 redundant
trope: 5 irony 8 metaphor, metonymy 9 hyperbole 10 synecdoche
___-Tropez: 5 Saint
trophy: 3 cup 4 Emmy, Obie, Tony 5 award, booty, crown, grail, honor, medal, Oscar, prize 6 reward, ribbon, spoils, statue 7 guerdon, laurels, memento 8 citation, gold star, reminder 10 blue ribbon, decoration
room: 3 den
take home a ~: 3 win
winner: 5 champ 6 victor
trophy ___: 4 room
tropical: 3 hot 4 lush, rank, warm 5 balmy, fiery, humid 6 baking, steamy, sticky, sultry, toasty, torrid 7 blazing, boiling, burning, searing, summery 8 broiling, ovenlike, parching, roasting, sizzling, steaming, stifling 9 scorching 10 equatorial, sweltering
fish: 4 mola 5 manta, moray, tetra 6 louvar
fruit: 4 akee 5 guava, mango 6 banana
shrub: 3 bay 5 aalii, ficus, guava, ixora, urena 6 annona, cleome, coffee, mimosa, papaya, pawpaw 7 quassia 8 abutilon, barbasco, bayberry, bignonia, columnea, dividivi, guaiacum, huisache, mangrove 9 bouvardia, monacillo 10 frangipani
spot: 3 isl. 4 isle, reef 5 atoll 6 island
tree: 3 apa, fig 4 agba, akee, kola, neem, palm, upas 5 balsa, cacao, ficus, genip, guava, ixora, kiawe, mahoe, mango, ramon 6 anatto, annona, antiar, balata, banana, baobab, bonduc, calaba, cashew, coffee, fustic, jujube, lebbek, mammee, mimosa, obeche, padauk, padouk, papaya, pawpaw 7 acerola, annatto, avocado, genipap, quassia, yohimbe 8 albizzia, allspice, barbasco, bauhinia, calabash, cocobolo, divi-divi, mahogany, mangrove, tamarind, tamarisk 9 jacaranda, poinciana, sapodilla 10 breadfruit, grapefruit
tropical ___: 4 fish, year 5 storm 7 cyclone
Tropicana product: 2 OJ
tropic of ___: 6 Cancer 9 Capricorn
Tropic of Cancer: 4 film 5 novel
author: Henry Miller
cast: Ellen Burstyn, James Callahan, Rip Torn
director: Joseph Strick
Tropic of Capricorn author: Henry Miller
tropophyte: 4 tree 5 plant
troppo: 7 too much
___ troppo: 3 non
trot: 3 hie, jog, pad, run 4 crib, gait, lope, move, pony, ride, step 5 hurry 6 canter 7 scamper 10 cheat sheet
ender: 4 line
hot to ~: 4 avid 5 eager 6 gung ho 7 anxious, excited 10 raring to go
out: 4 show 6 flaunt, parade 7 display, exhibit, present, show off 8 brandish 10 wave around
relative: 6 canter, gallop
starter: 5 globe
trot ___: 3 out
___ trot: 3 fox, jog 5 hot to 6 turkey
troth: 3 vow 6 pledge, verity 7 loyalty, promise 8 espousal, fidelity 10 engagement
plight one's ~: 3 wed 4 mate 5 marry, unite 10 get hitched, settle down, tie the knot
Trotsky: 3 Red 4 Leon
foe: 5 Lenin
trotter: 4 foot 5 horse, pacer, racer 6 equine
burden: 5 sulky 6 driver
Trottier, Bryan
milieu: 3 ice 4 rink 5 arena
org.: 3 NHL
Trotwood: 4 city, town
locale: 4 Ohio
troubadour: 6 singer
prop: 4 lute
song: 4 alba 6 ballad
trouble: 3 ado, ail, bug, ill, irk, row, vex, woe 4 care, fret, fuss, gall, hurt, loss, mess, pain, spot, to-do, work 5 annoy, beset, curse, exert, get to, grief, grind, harry, haunt, hitch, mix up, pains, peeve, press, spook, trial, upset, visit, worry 6 bother, burden, crisis, crunch, danger, effort, grieve, harass, hassle, hazard, holdup, malady, matter, mayhem, misery, mishap, ordeal, pester, pickle, plague, plight, pother, prey on, put out, puzzle, sadden, scrape, sorrow, stir up, strain, stress, strife, tsuris, tumult, unrest 7 afflict, agitate, bad news, concern, dilemma, discord, disturb, illness, perplex, perturb, problem, setback, shake up, torment, tsouris 8 aggrieve, disorder, disquiet, distress, exercise, exertion, friction, hard luck, hardship, headache, hot water, impose on, irritate, jeopardy, mischief, nuisance, pressure, quandary, struggle, unsettle, vexation 9 adversity, annoyance, commotion, complaint, deep water, heartache, incommode, make a fuss, make waves, suffering, take pains, weigh down 10 affliction, difficulty, discomfort, disconcert, hard knocks, infliction, misfortune
amount of ~: 4 heap, peck
borrow ~: 5 worry
ender: 4 shot, some 5 maker, shoot 7 shooter 8 shooting
exclamation: 4 help, oh-oh, uh-oh, yipe 5 yikes, yipes
make ~: 4 abet 5 rouse 6 foment, incite, stir up, work up 7 agitate, inflame, provoke 9 instigate, misbehave
no ~: 4 easy 6 picnic
partner: 4 toil
without ~: 6 easily 7 handily 9 hands down 10 swimmingly
trouble ___: 3 man 4 spot
trouble-___: 7 shooter
___ trouble: 6 borrow
___ Trouble: 3 Big, Car 5 I Love, Shark 6 Double, Monkey
troubled: 3 sad 4 blue, down, glum, sore 5 antsy, beset, itchy, jumpy, tense, upset, woful 6 gloomy, in a fix, in a jam, morose, queasy, queazy, somber, uneasy, woeful 7 anxious, doleful, jittery, joyless, keyed up, nervous, restive, unhappy, uptight, worried 8 downcast, obsessed, restless, skittish 9 cheerless, concerned, excitable, heartsick, ill at ease, miserable, sorrowful, woebegone 10 chapfallen, high-strung, melancholy, solicitous, unbalanced
not ~: 6 at ease 7 content, relaxed 8 carefree, composed, tranquil
troubled ___: 6 waters
Trouble for Two (1936 film)
cast: Robert Montgomery, Frank Morgan, Rosalind Russell
Trouble in July author: Erskine Caldwell
Trouble in Paradise (1932 film)
cast: Kay Francis, Miriam Hopkins, Herbert Marshall
director: Ernst Lubitsch
troubleless: 4 easy 6 picnic, simple, smooth 7 no sweat 8 carefree, no bother, pushover 9 no problem 10 child's play, elementary, manageable
troublemaker: 3 imp 4 punk 5 rogue, rowdy, scamp, snake 6 bad egg, gadfly, gossip, heller, menace, rascal, weasel 7 gremlin, hellion 8 agitator, hooligan, nuisance 9 firebrand 10 instigator
troublemakers: 6 bad lot
Trouble Man (1972 song) artist: Marvin Gaye
troubles: 5 grief 6 misery, sorrow 7 travail 8 hardship 9 suffering 10 affliction, infelicity
___ troubles: 5 sea of
troubleshoot: 3 fix 5 debug 7 correct, rectify
troubleshooter: 5 fixer 8 mediator 9 gobetween 10 arbitrator
T-R-O-U-B-L-E singer: 5 Tritt
troublesome: 4 hard, ugly 5 heavy, pesky, pesty, rough, spiny, tight, tough 6 feisty, knotty, taxing, thorny, tricky, trying, unruly, uphill 7 arduous, awkward, irksome, onerous, painful, prickly, weighty 8 alarming, annoying, tiresome 9 dangerous, demanding, difficult, laborious, pestilent, upsetting, vexatious, wearisome, worrisome 10 bothersome
Trouble With Girls, The (1969 film)
cast: Marlyn Mason, Sheree North, Elvis Presley
Trouble With Harry, The (1955 film)
cast: John Forsythe, Edmund Gwenn, Shirley MacLaine
director: Alfred Hitchcock
troubling: 3 bad 8 annoying 9 dangerous 10 bothersome
troublous: 6 stormy 9 turbulent
trou-de-___: 4 loup
trough: 3 cup, hod 4 duct, moat 5 canal, ditch, flume, gully, slump

6 feeder, furrow, gulley, gutter, manger, trench, valley 7 channel 8 low point 10 depression
combining form: 5 bothr- 6 bothro-
contents: 4 feed
diner: 3 hog, pig 5 horse, swine
trounce: 3 wax, win, zap 4 bash, beat, bury, drub, dust, flog, lick, mall, maul, rout, trim, whip, whup 5 baste, crush, paste, pound, stomp, swamp, total, trash, waste, whomp, worst 6 defeat, hammer, pommel, pummel, thrash, wallop 7 clobber, lambast, put away, triumph 8 lambaste, overcome, walk over 9 checkmate, overpower, overwhelm
trouncing: 4 rout 6 defeat 7 beating, debacle
Troup, Bobby spouse: Julie London
troupe: 4 band, bevy, cast, crew, gang, ring, team 5 party, squad 6 muster, outfit 7 company 8 ensemble
trouper: 5 actor 6 player 7 actress, veteran 8 thespian, traveler 9 performer
troupial: 4 bird
trousers: 4 slax 5 cords, jeans, Levi's, pants 6 Capris, chinos, denims, khakis, slacks 7 gauchos 8 breeches, britches, flannels, knickers, overalls 9 corduroys, dungarees, plus fours 10 hiphuggers
like some ~: 4 wide 5 baggy, loose 7 sagging
material: 5 chino, denim, twill
measure: 4 lgth. 5 waist 6 inseam, length
part: 3 leg 4 cuff, knee, loop, seat 6 crease, pocket
partner: 5 shirt
tartan ~: 5 trews
see also pants
trousseau: 8 wardrobe
collector: 5 bride 7 fiancée
trout: 4 char, fish, pogy 9 cutthroat, namaycush, steelhead
home: 5 river
__ trout: 3 sea 4 bull, gray, grey, lake 5 brook, brown 6 salmon, silver 7 rainbow
__ Trout: 5 Paris
Trout Quintet composer: 8 Schubert
__ trouvé: 5 objet
Trouville-sur-__: 3 Mer
trove: 5 booty, cache, hoard 8 treasure 9 discovery, stockpile 10 collection, storehouse
treasure ~: 4 mine 7 bonanza
T. Rowe __: 5 Price
trowel: 4 tool 5 scoop
troy __: 6 weight
Troy: 4 city, town 5 Ilium 6 Aikman 7 Donahue 8 Shondell
locale: 4 Ohio 7 Alabama, New York 8 Michigan
peak of ancient ~: 5 Mt. Ida
school: 3 RPI, TSU
Troyanos, Tatiana: 5 mezzo 6 singer 7 soprano
specialty: 5 opera
Troyer: 5 Verne
Troyes: 4 city, town
locale: 6 France
Troy State
athletes: 7 Trojans
locale: 7 Alabama
Tru
star: 5 Morse
subject: 6 Capote
truancy: 5 hooky 6 no-show 7 absence
truant: 5 idler 6 loafer 7 at large, runaway, shirker, slacker 8 absentee, layabout, loiterer, sluggard 9 do-nothing, goldbrick, lazybones 10 malingerer
soldier: 4 AWOL 8 deserter
truant __: 7 officer
truce: 4 halt, lull, rest, stay 5 letup, pause, peace, terms 6 accord, treaty 7 amnesty, détente, respite 8 breather, reprieve 9 agreement, armistice, cease-fire, cessation, white flag 10 cooling off, moratorium, suspension
flag color: 5 white
Trucial __: 4 Oman 5 Coast 6 States
Trucial States: 3 UAE
truck: 3 GMC, rig, ute, van 4 haul, jeep, Mack, pull, semi, swap, swop, take 5 bring, carry, crate, dolly, lorry, trade, U-Haul 6 camion, convey, dumper, hauler, pickup, wheels 7 deliver, traffic, vehicle 8 leavings 9 transport 10 do business
agency: 3 ICC
attachment: 4 plow
bring by ~: 4 haul, ship 6 cart in
British ~: 5 lorry
ender: 3 age 4 load, stop
filler: 4 load 5 cargo 7 freight
fuel: 6 diesel 8 gasoline
group: 5 fleet 6 convoy
hand ~: 4 cart 5 dolly 6 barrow
how a ~ goes uphill: 5 in low
maker: 3 GMC 4 Mack
military ~: 6 camion
part: 3 bed, cab 4 axle 7 tractor, trailer
radio: 2 CB
rental name: 5 Ryder, U-Haul
stop: 5 diner 6 eatery 10 restaurant
stop sign: 3 gas 4 eats, food
unit: 3 ton
truck __: 4 crop, farm, stop 6 camper, garden, jobber, system 7 bolster, tractor, trailer
__ truck: 3 tow 4 dump, fire, fork, hand, lift, tank 5 crash, motor, panel, sound, stake 6 camper, double, ladder, pickup 7 flatbed, trailer
Truckee: 5 river
city on the ~: 4 Reno
locale: 6 Nevada 10 California
trucker: 6 hauler
choice: 4 gear
often: 4 CBer
truckle: 3 woo 4 bend 5 court, cower, crawl 6 comply, kowtow, stroke, submit 7 adulate, conform, flatter 8 butter up, kowtow to 9 prostrate 10 toe the line
to: 4 obey 6 submit 8 fawn over
truckle __: 3 bed
truckler: 5 toady 6 fawner, flunky, minion, yes man 7 flunkey 8 adulator
truckload: 4 gobs, lots, many, tons 5 cargo, goods, heaps, piles, scads 6 oceans, oodles, plenty, stacks 7 freight 8 good deal, shipment 9 multitude
truculent: 4 mean, rude, ugly 5 cross, gruff, harsh, nasty, onery 6 animal, brutal, feisty, fierce, grumpy, ornery, savage, sullen, unkind, wanton 7 abusive, beastly, callous, defiant, hateful, hostile, hurtful, scrappy, vicious 8 barbaric, bullying, fiendish, grumpish, inhumane, militant, pitiless, ruthless, sadistic, scathing, vengeful 9 barbarous, combative, cutthroat, ferocious, merciless, monstrous 10 aggressive, pugnacious, vindictive
Trudeau: 5 Garry 6 Pierre
Trudeau, Garry spouse: Jane Pauley
Trudeau, Pierre: 2 P.M. 8 Canadian
party: 3 Lib. 7 Liberal
predecessor: 5 Clark 7 Pearson
successor: 5 Clark 6 Turner
trudge: 3 lag 4 hike, plod, slog, step, trek, wade, walk 5 clomp, clump, march, shlep, stump, tramp, tread 6 linger, lumber, schlep, trapes 7 schlepp, stumble, traipse 9 plug along
in muck: 5 slosh
(on): 5 press
true: 3 yes 4 fast, firm, real, sure 5 aline, exact, level, loyal, no lie, plumb, right, sound, valid 6 actual, adjust, ardent, direct, honest, likely, proper, spot on, square, steady, worthy 7 certain, correct, devoted, dutiful, factual, for real, genuine, literal, natural, precise, sincere, staunch, upfront, upright 8 accurate, bona fide, candidly, constant, definite, faithful, knightly, obedient, official, on target, orthodox, regulate, reliable, resolute, rightful, straight, unerring, verified, yeomanly 9 allegiant, authentic, axiomatic, confirmed, dedicated, fraternal, heartfelt, honorable, intrinsic, on the mark, patriotic, realistic, sincerely, steadfast, undoubted, unfailing, unfeigned, veracious, veritable 10 aboveboard, dependable, infallible, inviolable, legitimate, on the level, scrupulous, straighten, unaffected, undeniable, unimagined, unmistaken, unswerving, upstanding, verifiable
at times: 3 ans. 6 answer
be ~: 6 adhere, cleave 7 abide by, stand by 8 hold fast
come ~: 5 ensue, occur 6 betide, happen, pan out, result 7 develop 9 eventuate, take place, transpire
ender: 4 born, love 5 penny
it can't be ~: 4 oh no
name that means ~: 4 Vera
not ~: 4 fake, sham 5 bogus, false, lying, wrong 6 made-up, unreal 7 inexact 8 cooked-up, disloyal, mistaken, specious 9 concocted, deceptive, dishonest, erroneous, imaginary, incorrect, synthetic, trumped-up 10 fabricated, fallacious, fictitious, fraudulent, groundless, inaccurate, mendacious, misleading, perfidious, unfaithful
old-style: 5 sooth
prefix: 4 docu-
regard as ~: 3 buy 4 avow, hold 5 adopt, agree, trust 6 accept, affirm, assent, assume, credit 7 believe, concede, embrace, respect, swallow 10 understand
say is ~: 4 aver, avow 6 affirm, attest
show to be ~: 5 prove
to type: 4 even, firm, like, same 5 level 6 steady 7 equable, logical, regular, uniform 8 coherent, constant, of a piece, rational 9 accordant, agreeable, congenial, congruent, congruous, consonant, unanimous, unfailing, unvarying 10 compatible, concurrent, consistent, dependable, harmonious, homogenous, invariable, legitimate, persistent, reasonable, unchanging
tried and ~: 4 safe, sure 5 liege, loyal, sound 6 proven, tested, trusty 7 staunch 8 approved, reliable 9 certified, qualified, reputable, steadfast, unfailing, venerable 10 dependable, time-tested
up: 4 even 5 align, aline 6 adjust 10 straighten
true __: 3 bug, fly, rib 4 bill, blue, frog, seal, time, toad 5 fruit, level, north, rhyme 6 course, fresco 7 anomaly
true-__: 4 blue, life
true-__ test: 5 false
__ true: 4 come, ring
True __: 4 Blue, Grit, Lies, Love 5 Crime 6 Colors 7 Romance
True Believer (1989 film)
cast: Robert Downey Jr., Yuji Okumoto, James Woods
director: Joseph Ruben
true-blue: 5 loyal, moral 7 devoted, dutiful, sincere, staunch 8 constant, faithful, reliable, virtuous, yeomanly 9 allegiant, dedicated, steadfast 10 inviolable
True Blue (1986 song) artist: Madonna
True Colors (1986 song) artist: Cyndi Lauper
True Confessions: 4 film 5 novel
author: John Gregory Dunne
cast: Robert De Niro, Charles Durning, Robert Duvall, Ed Flanders
director: Ulu Grosbard
True Crime (1999 film)
cast: Clint Eastwood, Lisa Gay Hamilton, Denis Leary, Diane Venora, Isaiah Washington
director: Clint Eastwood
true-false __: 4 exam, test
True Grit (1969 film): 5 oater 7 western
cast: Glen Campbell, Kim Darby, John Wayne
director: Henry Hathaway
Trueheart: 4 Tess
trueheartedness: 5 ardor, faith 7 honesty, loyalty 8 devotion, fidelity 9 integrity, sincerity 10 allegiance, attachment, dedication, resolution
True Lies (1994 film)
cast: Tom Arnold, Jamie Lee Curtis, Arnold Schwarzenegger
dance: 5 tango
director: James Cameron
truelove: 2 jo 3 pet 4 baby, dear, jill, love 5 amour, angel, chéri, cooky, cutey, cutie, deary, ducky, flame, honey, leman, novia, novio, sugar, sweet 6 bon ami, chérie, cookie, dautie, dearie, steady, sweets 7 darling, dearest, dear one, pigsney, schatzi, squeeze, sweetie, tootsie 8 chouchou, cutie pie, dowsabel, dulcinea, macushla, paramour, precious, snookums, sugar pie, sweetums 9 bonne amie, boyfriend, dreamboat, inamorata, inamorato, petit chou, valentine 10 girlfriend, heartthrob, honeybunch, mavourneen, sweetheart, sweetie pie, turtledove
True Love: 4 song 5 waltz
artist: Bing Crosby
composer: Cole Porter
True Love (1989 film)
cast: Ron Eldard, Annabella Sciorra, Aida Turturro
director: Nancy Savoca
__ True Love: 5 My Own
True Romance (1993 film)
cast: Patricia Arquette, Dennis Hopper, Gary Oldman, Christian Slater
director: Tony Scott
__ True Thing: 3 One
true-to-life: 4 real 6 actual 7 factual, genuine 9 authentic, realistic 10 historical, realistic
True to Life (1943 film)
cast: Mary Martin, Dick Powell, Franchot Tone
director: George Marshall
true to one's __: 4 word
__ True to You in My Fashion: 6 Always
__ True What They Say About Dixie?: 4 Is it
Truex: 6 Ernest
Truffaut, François: 5 actor 6 French 8 director

film: The Bride Wore Black (1968)
Close Encounters of the Third Kind (1977)
Day for Night (1973)
Fahrenheit 451 (1967)
The Four Hundred Blows (1959)
Jules and Jim (1961)
Shoot the Piano Player (1960)
Small Change (1976)
Stolen Kisses (1968)
The Story of Adele H (1975)
Truly (1982 song) artist: Lionel Richie
truffle: 6 fungus 8 mushroom
spore sac: 5 ascus
truism: 3 saw 4 fact, rule 5 adage, axiom, maxim, moral, motto 6 dictum, gospel, phrase, saying 7 proverb 8 aphorism 9 platitude 10 folk wisdom
Trujillo: 4 city, town
locale: 4 Peru
Truk: 4 isls. 5 isles 7 islands
truly: 3 aye, yea 4 amen, just, very 5 quite, right 6 aright, indeed, in fact, it is so, justly, really, so be it, verily 7 at heart, de facto, exactly, for sure, frankly, no doubt, validly 8 actually, candidly, honestly, in effect, lawfully, of course, strictly 9 assuredly, certainly, decidedly, factually, in reality, literally, no mistake, sincerely 10 absolutely, definitely, far and away, rightfully, sure as hell, unerringly, verifiably
__ truly: 5 yours
Truly __ Deeply: 5 Madly
Truman: 4 Bess 5 Harry 6 Capote 8 Margaret
Truman, Harry S: 9 president
birthplace: 5 Lamar
child: 8 Margaret
home: 8 Missouri
opponent: 5 Dewey 7 Wallace 8 Thurmond
V.P.: 7 Barkley
wife: 4 Bess
Truman Show, The (1998 film)
cast: Jim Carrey, Noah Emmerich, Ed Harris, Laura Linney
director: Peter Weir
dog: 5 Pluto
Trumbull: 4 city, town 7 Douglas
locale: 4 Conn.
trump: 4 beat, best, suit 5 excel, one-up, outdo 6 better, defeat, outwit 7 surpass 10 outperform
high ~: 3 ace
play a ~ card: 4 ruff
up: 3 rig 4 fake, make 5 hatch 6 cook up, create, devise, invent, scheme 7 concoct 8 conceive, contrive, misquote 9 fabricate
trump __: 4 card
__-trump: 5 one no, two no
Trump: 5 Ivana 6 Donald, Ivanka
rival: 5 Icahn
Trump __: 5 Plaza, Tower 6 Castle
Trump Castle: 6 casino
employee: 6 dealer 7 pit boss 8 croupier
Trump, Donald
spouse: Marla Maples, Ivana Trump
trumped-up: 5 false 9 imaginary, unfounded 10 fictitious
story: 4 tale 6 canard
trumpery: 3 gas, rot 4 blah, bosh, bull, bunk, guff, jazz, jive, pooh, tosh 5 bilge, fudge, hokum, hooey, prate, stuff, trash, tripe 6 bunkum, bushwa, drivel, footle, gabble, gammon, gibber, havers, hot air, humbug, jabber, jargon, kibosh, piffle 7 baloney, blarney, blather, blether, boloney, bushwah, eyewash, flannel, flubdub, fustian, garbage, hogwash, inanity, rubbish, twaddle 8 buncombe, claptrap, falderal, falderol, flimflam, flummery, folderal, folderol, nonsense, slipslop, tommyrot 9 banana oil, gibberish, kidstakes, moonshine, poppycock, rigmarole 10 applesauce, balderdash, bilge water, codswallop, double-talk, flapdoodle, galimatias, Jabberwock, mumbo jumbo, rigamarole, taradiddle
trumpet: 4 horn, hype, roar, wind 5 boast, brass, bugle, sound 6 carnyx, herald, lituus, report 7 buisine, clarion, promote, salpinx 8 announce, proclaim 9 pronounce, publicize 10 instrument, promulgate
accessory: 4 mute
cousin: 4 horn 5 bugle 6 cornet
creeper: 5 plant 6 flower
play a ~: 4 blow
sound: 4 blat, wail, wawa 5 blare, blast, tusch 6 wah-wah 7 fanfare 8 flourish
trumpet __: 3 leg 4 vine 5 shell 6 flower, marine 7 creeper
__ trumpet: 3 ear 4 Bach 6 angel's
__ Trumpet: 7 Gideon's
trumpeter: 4 bird, swan 5 Davis, James 6 Alpert 7 Nichols 8 Cheatham, Eldridge, Ferguson, Mangione, Marsalis 9 Armstrong, Gillespie 10 Herb Alpert, Miles Davis, Red Nichols 11 Beiderbecke
trumpeter __: 4 swan
Trumpeter's Lullaby, A composer: Leroy Anderson
Trumpet Overture composer: 11 Mendelssohn
trumpets
Roman ~: 5 tubae
truncate: 3 cut, lop, top 4 chop, clip, crop, pare, trim 5 prune, shear 6 lessen, reduce 7 abridge, curtail, shorten 9 telescope 10 abbreviate
truncated: 5 brief, short 6 little, stubby
truncheon: 3 bat, rod 4 cane, club, cosh, mace 5 baton, billy, flail, staff, stick 6 cudgel, ferule 7 war club 8 bludgeon 9 bastinado, blackjack 10 nightstick, shillelagh
trundle: 3 bed, cot 4 roll 5 wheel 6 lumber
trunk: 3 box, log 4 body, bole, case, main, stem 5 aorta, chest, snout, stalk, torso 6 coffer, locker, thorax 7 baggage, luggage 8 suitcase, wardrobe 9 container, proboscis 10 footlocker, travel case
chambers: 5 atria
combining form: 4 corm- 5 cormo-
feature: 4 bark, knar, knot
fill a ~: 4 pack
in Britain: 4 boot
item: 4 jack, tire 5 spare 9 spare tire
of a ~: 6 aortal, aortic
of the lower ~: 5 iliac
palm ~: 6 caudex
place: 4 tree
tree ~ in Britain: 4 stam
upper ~: 6 thorax
trunk __: 4 call, hose, line 5 cabin 6 engine, piston
__ trunk: 5 nerve 7 steamer
trunks: 6 shorts 8 swimwear
like some tree ~: 6 gnarly
Truro: 4 city, town
locale: 4 Mass. 6 Canada 10 Nova Scotia
truss: 3 tie 4 bind, lash, tape 5 tie up 6 begird, bind up, fasten, wrap up 7 bandage 8 make fast 10 cantilever
up: 4 bind 6 hobble, hogtie 7 shackle 9 constrain, hamstring
truss __: 3 rod 4 hoop 6 bridge
__ truss: 4 jack, king, pony 5 queen 6 arched
trust: 3 let 4 care, lean, lend, loan, rely 5 bet on, faith, stock 6 accept, assume, bank on, belief, cartel, charge, commit, confer, credit, expect, lean on, look to, office, rely on 7 advance, believe, build on, combine, consign, count on, custody, entrust, intrust, keeping, mission, presume, suppose, surmise, swear by 8 covenant, credence, delegate, depend on, gamble on, megacorp, monopoly, optimism, reliance, rely upon, sign over, sureness, wardship 9 believe in, build upon, certitude, confide in, count upon, patronize, syndicate 10 commission, confidence, conviction, dependance, dependence, obligation
brain ~: 5 board, panel 7 cabinet, council 8 advisors 9 syndicate 10 counselors
ender: 6 buster, worthy 7 busting
hold in ~: 6 escrow
in: 7 believe 10 set store by
trust __: 4 deed, fund 7 account, company
__ trust: 4 unit 5 blind, brain, fixed 6 living, public, Totten 7 private
__ Trust: 6 Brains
trustbuster concern: 6 cartel 8 monopoly
trusted
not to be ~: 3 sly 4 cagy, foxy, wily 5 cagey, false, lying, shady, slick 6 artful, crafty, shifty, shrewd, smooth, sneaky, tricky 7 crooked, cunning, devious, elusive, elusory, evasive, furtive, knavish 8 delusive, guileful, scheming, slippery 9 deceitful, deceptive, designing, dishonest, insidious, insincere 10 mendacious, misleading, serpentine, unreliable, untruthful
to be ~: 4 fair 5 moral 6 honest, square, worthy 7 ethical, genuine, sincere, upright 8 bona fide, credible, reliable, truthful, virtuous 9 heartfelt, honorable, reputable, righteous, veracious 10 aboveboard, evenhanded, high-minded, law-abiding, legitimate, on the level, reasonable, scrupulous, upstanding
trustee: 5 agent 8 director, executor, guardian, watchdog 9 custodian, executive
watchdog: 8 executor, guardian
trustees: 5 board, panel 7 council 9 committee, syndicate 10 commission, management
trusteeship: 4 care, egis 5 aegis 6 charge 7 custody, keeping 8 auspices 10 protection
trustiness: 7 honesty, loyalty 9 constancy, fixedness
trusting: 4 easy, naif 5 naive 6 simple 7 hopeful 8 gullable, gullible, lamblike, unartful 9 childlike, credulous, ingenuous, unworldly 10 falling for, optimistic
trustworthiness: 5 honor 6 virtue 7 honesty, loyalty, probity 8 fidelity, veracity 9 sincerity
trustworthy: 4 fair, good, just, open, safe, true 5 loyal, moral, solid, sound, tried, valid 6 decent, honest, mature, secure, square 7 ethical, genuine, sincere, staunch, tenable, up-front, upright 8 accurate, constant, credible, harmless, reliable, straight, true-blue, truthful, unerring 9 authentic, honorable, plausible, realistic, reputable, righteous, rock-solid, steadfast, unfailing, veracious
trusty: 4 naif, open 5 loyal, naive, solid 6 honest, mature, square 7 ethical, staunch, up-front, upright 8 accurate, constant, faithful, jailbird, reliable, sensible, straight, truthful 9 authentic, honorable, righteous, rock-solid, steadfast, unfailing, veracious 10 dependable, inviolable, on the level, principled
name meaning ~: 4 Drew
truth: 3 law 4 fact 5 axiom, facts, maxim, right, scoop, score 6 candor, factum, gospel, verity 7 epigram, lowdown, loyalty, precept, proverb, reality, theorem 8 accuracy, aphorism, validity, veracity 9 actuality, certainty, good faith, integrity, platitude, precision, principle, sincerity 10 exactitude, factuality, honestness, legitimacy, principium
alternative: 4 dare
in ~: 3 nay, yea 5 quite 6 indeed, really 8 actually
moment of ~: 4 test 8 showdown, zero hour
name meaning ~: 4 Vera
old-style: 5 sooth
presumed ~: 5 given
stretch the ~: 3 lie 5 fudge 6 invent
tell the ~: 5 level, own up
twister: 4 liar
twist the ~: 3 con, fib 4 bull, dupe, fake, hoax, sham, snow 5 bluff, fudge, libel, put on 6 delude, invent, malign 7 deceive, distort, falsify, mislead, perjure, slander 8 misguide, misstate 9 disinform, dissemble, misinform 10 equivocate, exaggerate
truth __: 5 claim, quark, serum, table
__ truth: 4 home 5 naked 6 gospel
__-truth: 4 half
Truth: 9 Sojourner
Truth About Cats and Dogs, The (1996 film)
cast: Ben Chaplin, Jamie Foxx, Janeane Garofalo, Uma Thurman
director: Michael Lehmann
Truth About Spring, The (1965 film)
cast: Hayley Mills, John Mills
director: Richard Thorpe
Truth author: Emile Zola
truthful: 4 open 5 exact, frank, legit, moral, right 6 actual, candid, honest, infelt, square, trusty 7 correct, factual, literal, precise, sincere 8 accurate, out-front, reliable, straight, verified 9 guileless, honorable, ingenuous, outspoken, realistic, unfeigned, veracious 10 aboveboard, forthright, from the hip, on the level, point-blank, scrupulous
Truthful James creator: 5 Harte
truthfully: 6 as it is 8 like it is 9 sincerely 10 point-blank
truthfulness: 5 honor 7 honesty, loyalty, probity 8 accuracy, veracity 9 sincerity
truth-in-lending
org.: 3 FTC
stat.: 3 APR
Truth or Consequences: 4 city, town 8 game show
host: Bob Barker
locale: 9 New Mexico
Truth or Dare artist: 7 Madonna
__ Truth, The: 5 Awful, Naked
try: 2 go 3 aim, bid, irk, pop, tax, vex 4 hear, push, rack, risk, seek, shot, stab, test, tire, turn 5 annoy, check, crack, essay, fling, judge, prove, taste, weary, weigh, whack, whirl 6 aspire, effort, handle, harass, plague, sample, strain, strive, tackle,

verify 7 afflict, attempt, compete, examine, go for it, have a go, inspect, referee, torment, venture 8 audition, bear down, check out, distress, drive for, endeavor, evaluate, exercise, go all out, irritate, make a bid, shoot for, struggle 9 challenge, give it a go, have a go at, prosecute, take a shot, take a stab, undertake 10 adjudicate, chip away at, enterprise, experiment
again: 4 redo
ender: 3 out 4 sail
for: 6 pursue 8 aspire to
(for): 3 aim, vie 5 angle, steer
hard: 4 push 5 apply, exert, sweat 6 strain 8 put forth
on: 3 fit 4 test, wear 8 check out
one's patience: 3 irk 4 rile 5 weary 7 provoke
out: 4 test 5 assay, prove 7 inspect 8 audition, evaluate, rehearse 10 experiment
ready to ~: 4 game
to find: 4 seek 5 trace, track, trail 6 gun for, pursue 7 fish for, go after, hunt for, look for, scout up 8 quest for, run after, scout out, sniff out 9 track down
to get answers: 4 pump, quiz 5 grill, query 7 canvass, consult, inquire, request
to learn: 4 cram, quiz, read 5 probe, query, train 6 bone up, digest, go over, take up 7 analyze, dissect, inquire 8 look into, read up on, research 10 experiment
try __: 3 out 6 square
try __ size: 5 on for
__ try: 7 college
Try __ might...: 3 as I
Try __ see: 5 it and
Try Again (2000 song) artist: Aaliyah
Try a Little Tenderness (1969 song) artist: Three Dog Night
Trygve: 3 Lie 8 Haavelmo
successor: 3 Dag
trying: 4 hard 5 rough, stiff, tight, tough 6 rugged, severe, taxing, thorny, uphill, vexing 7 arduous, awkward, hard-won, irksome, onerous, painful, prickly 8 annoying, exacting, grueling, no picnic, rigorous, ticklish, tiresome, toilsome, worrying 9 demanding, difficult, fatiguing, laborious, strenuous, stressful, upsetting, vexatious, wearisome 10 bothersome, enervating, formidable, irritating, oppressive, unamenable
time: 4 bind 5 trial 6 crisis, crunch 7 squeeze, trouble 9 adversity, emergency 10 misfortune
Trying to Save Piggy Sneed author: John Irving
Tryin' to Get the Feeling Again (1976 song) artist: Barry Manilow
Tryin' to Live My Life Without You (1981 song) artist: Bob Seger
Tryon: 3 Tom 6 Thomas
try one's __: 4 hand, luck
try on for __: 4 size
Tryon, Thomas: 5 actor 6 author, writer
work: All That Glitters
Crowned Heads
Harvest Home
In the Fire of Spring
Lady
Nigh of the Moonbow
Night Magic
The Other
The Wings of the Morning
tryout: 4 test 5 essay 7 attempt, hearing 8 audition 9 probation, rehearsal 10 experiment
tryst: 4 date 7 meeting, vis-à-vis 9 tête-à-tête 10 engagement, rendezvous
Try to Remember: 4 song 5 waltz
T.S.: 5 Eliot
tsade: 6 Hebrew, letter
predecessor: 2 pe 3 peh
successor: 4 koph, qoph
Tsana: 4 lake
locale: 6 Africa 8 Ethiopia
tsar: 4 czar, Ivan, male, Paul, tzar 5 Boris, Fedor, mogul, Peter 6 Alexis, despot, Fyodor, tyrant 7 emperor, kingpin, Mikhail, monarch 8 autocrat, dictator, Nicholas 9 Alexander, oppressor, potentate
see also czar
Tsar's Bride, The composer: Rimsky-Korsakov
__-tse: 3 Lao
tsetse: 3 fly
territory: 6 Africa
Tse-tung: 3 Mao
TSgt. employer: 4 USAF
T-shirt: 3 top
like a: 6 casual
material: 6 cotton
size: 2 lg., XL 3 lge., med., sml. 5 large, small 6 medium
tsimmes: 4 stew 6 uproar
Tsimshian: 6 Indian 7 Amerind
Tsk!: 3 tut 4 alas, pity 5 shame 6 tut-tut 8 for shame
Tsotsi author: Athol Fugard
tsp.: 3 amt. 4 meas.
tsps., three: 4 tbsp.
T-square: 5 ruler
Tsu: 4 city, town
locale: 5 Japan
Tsui, Daniel: 8 Nobelist 9 physicist
Tsukuba: 4 city, town
locale: 5 Japan
TSU locale: 5 Texas 7 Houston
tsunami: 4 wave 9 tidal wave
tsuris: 3 woe 6 hassle 7 trouble
Tsushima __: 6 Strait 7 Current
tsuzumi: 4 drum
origin: 5 Japan
Tswana: 3 cow 4 bull 6 bovine, cattle
home: 6 Africa 8 Botswana
TSX: 3 car 4 auto 5 Acura 10 automobile
TT manufacturer: 4 Audi
t-top: 4 roof
TTU conference: 9 Big Twelve
tu-__ tu-whoo: 4 whit
__ tu: 3 eri
__ Tu: 4 Eres
Tualatin: 4 city, town
locale: 6 Oregon
Tuareg home: 4 Mali 5 Libya, Niger 6 Africa 7 Algeria
tub: 3 keg, vat 4 boat, cask 5 basin 6 barrel, firkin, vessel 8 hogshead, puncheon 9 container
hot ~: 3 spa 5 sauna 7 Jacuzzi 9 whirlpool
Japanese ~: 4 furo
old ~: 4 scow
ritual: 4 bath
starter: 4 bath, wash
toy: 4 boat, duck 6 duckie 10 rubber duck
use the ~: 3 wet 4 lave, soak, wash 5 bathe, clean 6 splash
wooden ~ of yore: 3 soe
tub-__: 7 thumper
__ tub: 3 hot
tuba: 4 horn, wind 5 brass 7 helicon, saxhorn 9 euphonium 10 sousaphone
Tubac: 4 city, town
locale: 7 Arizona
Tubb: 6 Ernest
Tubbs beat: 5 Miami
tubby: 5 obese, plump, pudgy, round, squat, stout 6 chubby 8 roly-poly 9 filled-out 10 abdominous
Tubby girlfriend: 4 Lulu
Tubby the Tuba author: 5 Tripp
tube: 2 IV, TV 4 duct, flue, hose, pipe, vial 5 diode, phial, pipet, stent, straw, telly, TV set 6 subway, tunnel 7 conduit, pipette, snorkel, trachea 8 cylinder, idiot box, railroad, windpipe 10 television
boob ~: 2 TV 5 TV set 10 television
cathode ray ~: 8 terminal
combining form: 4 styl- 5 solen-, stylo- 6 siphon-, soleno-, syring- 7 siphoni-, siphono-, syringo-
in America: 6 subway
light in a ~: 4 neon
put on the ~: 3 air 9 broadcast
trophy: 4 Emmy
see also television, TV
tube __: 3 pan, top 4 foot, sock 7 railway
__ tube: 3 gas 4 boob, test, x-ray 5 acorn, draft, drift, flash, image, inner, Pitot, radio, sieve 6 camera, Lenard, neural, pastry, pickup, pollen, static, vacuum, zenith 7 Crookes, mailing, picture, thistle, torpedo, venturi
tubeless __: 4 tire
tubenose: 4 fish
tuber: 3 oca, oka, yam 4 apio, coco, corm, eddo, root, spud, taro 5 ahipa, baddo, tater 6 jicama, manioc, potato, tanier, tannia, turnip, yautia 7 cassava, cocoyam, dasheen, malanga, sunroot, tannier 8 girasole 9 arracacha, arrowhead, arrowroot, yucca root
Andes ~: 3 oca, oka
like a ~: 5 rooty
Polynesian ~: 4 corm, eddo, taro
tuberculin __: 4 test
tuberose: 5 plant 6 flower
tubes
down the ~: 4 gone, lost, no-go 5 kaput
go down the ~: 4 fail
tubesnout: 4 fish
tubing: 4 hose, pipe
Tubman: 7 Harriet
Tubular Bells (1974 song) artist: Mike Oldfield
Tucci, Stanley: 5 actor
film: Big Trouble (2002)
The Imposters (1998)
In Too Deep (1999)
Joe Gould's Secret (2000)
A Midsummer Night's Dream (1999)
Sidewalks of New York (2001)
tuck: 3 hem 4 cram, fold, seam, wrap 5 plait, pleat, shove 6 gather, insert, pucker, ruffle 7 crinkle, swaddle 8 contract, fold over 9 squeeze in
away: 3 eat, sup 4 bury, dine, hide, nosh 5 cache, feast, gorge, munch, stash 6 devour, ingest, inhale, pig out 7 conceal, consume, partake, protect, scarf up, snack on 8 chow down, ensconce, gobble up, take food, withhold, wolf down 9 have a bite, have a meal, polish off, scarf down 10 gormandize, keep secret
nip and ~: 5 close, tight
partner: 3 nip
tuck __: 4 away
__ tuck: 5 tummy
__ Tuck: 5 Friar
tuckahoe: 5 plant
Tuckahoe: 4 city, town
locale: 8 Virginia
tucked
away: 4 dark 5 blind, perdu, privy 6 covert, hidden, inside, latent, occult, perdue, secret, unseen 7 private, unknown 8 secluded, ulterior 9 concealed, covered up, incognito, invisible, nonpublic, out of view, potential, recondite, underhand, unexposed 10 enshrouded, undercover, underlying, under wraps, undetected, unviewable
in: 4 abed, cosy, cozy, safe, snug, warm 5 comfy, cozey, cozie 6 secure 7 nestled 9 cuddled up, sheltered
it may be ~ in: 5 shirt
tucker
bib and ~: 4 duds, garb, rags, togs 5 getup 6 attire, finery, outfit 7 apparel, clothes, raiment, threads 8 wardrobe 10 Sunday best
out: 4 jade, tire 5 weary 7 exhaust, fatigue, frazzle 9 prostrate
Tucker: 3 car 4 auto, city, town 5 Chris, Tanya 6 Sophie 7 Forrest, Michael, Preston, Richard 10 automobile
locale: 7 Georgia
tuckered out: 4 beat, worn 5 all in, spent, tired, weary 8 fatigued 9 exhausted
__ tuckered out: 5 plumb
Tucker, Forrest: 5 actor
film: Auntie Mame (1958)
Flaming Feather (1951)
TV: F Troop
Tucker, Michael spouse: Jill Eikenberry
Tucker, Richard: 5 tenor 6 singer
specialty: 5 opera
Tucker: The Man and His Dream (1988 film)
cast: Joan Allen, Jeff Bridges, Martin Landau
director: Francis Ford Coppola
Tuck, Friar quaff: 3 ale
tuco-tuco: 6 animal, mammal, rodent
relative: 3 rat 4 cavy, degu, jird, paca, vole 5 coypu, gundi, mouse, xerus 6 agouti, beaver, gerbil, gopher, jerboa, marmot, murine 7 hamster, lemming, muskrat, visacha 8 chipmunk, cricetid, dormouse, squirrel 9 chickaree, groundhog, guinea pig, porcupine, woodchuck 10 chinchilla, prairie dog
Tucson: 4 city, town
athletes: 8 Wildcats
county: 4 Pima
locale: 4 Ariz. 7 Arizona
river: 9 Santa Cruz
Tucson-to-Flagstaff dir.: 3 NNW
Tudor: 3 car 4 auto, Ford, Mary 5 house 8 Henry VII 9 Henry VIII 10 automobile
Tues.: 3 day
follower: 3 Wed.
Mon., to ~: 4 yest.
preceder: 3 Mon.
Tuesday: 4 Weld
was named for him: 3 Tiu
__ Tuesday: 3 Fat, 'Til 4 Ruby 5 Black, Super 6 Shrove
__ Tuesday, This Must Be Belgium: 5 If It's
tufa: 4 rock 9 limestone
like ~: 6 porous
tuff: 3 def, rad 4 aces, A-one, boss, braw, cool, dece, fine, gear, keen, neat, nice, phat, rock 5 dandy, ducky, grand, great, marvy, neato, nobby, prime, slick, super, swell 6 bang on, bang-up, bonzer, bosker, choice, divine, dreamy, far-out, gnarly, groovy, lovely, peachy, slap-up, spot on, superb, terrif, tiptop, unreal, whizzo, wicked 7 amazing, awesome, capital, corking, mineral, perfect, ripping,

skookum, stellar, sublime **8** dazzling, especial, eximious, fabulous, five-star, four-star, frabjous, glorious, heavenly, jim-dandy, slam-bang, smashing, splendid, standout, sterling, stickout, superior, terrific, top-level, topnotch, very good, wondrous **9** bodacious, Endsville, excellent, exemplary, exquisite, first-rate, high-grade, hunky-dory, marvelous, sollicker, top-flight, wonderful **10** first-class, hotsy-totsy, jack-a-dandy, out of sight, peachy-keen, phenomenal, remarkable, stupendous, super-duper
Tuff __: 5 Enuff
tuft: 3 wad **4** floc, knot, wisp **5** clump, shock **6** goatee, tassel **7** cluster, cowlick, plumage, topknot, tussock **8** feathers
combining form: 4 loph- **5** lophi-, lopho- **6** lophio-
starter: 5 candy
tufted: 5 rough **6** comate
tufted duck: 4 fowl
relative: 4 smew, teal **5** eider, Pekin, Rouen, scaup **6** Cayuga, scoter **7** gadwall, mallard, pintail, pochard, redhead, widgeon **8** garganey, mandarin, oldsquaw, shoveler **9** broadbill, goldeneye, goosander, greenhead, merganser, sprigtail **10** bufflehead, canvasback, surf scoter
tuft-hunter: 4 snob **5** snoot
Tuft of Flowers, The author: Robert Frost
Tufts: 5 Sonny **10** university
locale: 4 Mass.
Tu Fu, contemporary: 4 Li Po
tug: 3 lug, tow **4** boat, drag, draw, haul, jerk, pull, ship, yank **5** heave, hitch, pluck, wrest **6** pull on, strain, wrench **7** jerk out
at the heart: 4 move **5** touch **6** affect
ender: 4 boat
of war: 4 game **5** fight **6** strife **7** contest **8** conflict
tow: 5 barge
tug __: 5 of war
Tug: 6 McGraw
Tugboat __: 5 Annie
tugboat sound: 4 toot
Tugela: 5 falls **9** waterfall
locale: 5 Natal **11** South Africa
tugrik: 5 money
tui: 4 bird
Tuileries, Jardin des: 4 parc
locale: 5 Paris **6** France
tuille: 5 armor **6** tasset **10** protection
tuition: 3 fee **4** cost **5** price **6** charge **7** lessons **8** learning, teaching, training **9** education, schooling
recipient: 6 bursar **9** treasurer **10** controller
Tula: 4 city, town
locale: 6 Mexico, Russia
resident: 6 Toltec
Tulancingo: 4 city, town
locale: 6 Mexico **7** Hidalgo
Tulane: 6 school **10** university
athletes: 9 Green Wave
locale: 9 Louisiana **10** New Orleans
Tulare: 4 city, town
locale: 10 California
tule: 7 bulrush
Tuli: 3 cow **4** bull **6** bovine, cattle
tulip: 4 bulb **5** plant **6** flower
part: 5 tepal
tulip __: 4 tree **5** chair **6** poplar
__ tulip: 4 lady **6** Darwin, parrot **7** cottage
__ Tulip, The: 5 Black
Tull: 6 Jethro
tulle: 4 silk **6** fabric
garment: 4 tutu
Tulle: 4 city, town
locale: 6 France
Tully: 5 falls **9** waterfall
locale: 9 Australia **10** Queensland
__ Tully Hall: 5 Alice
Tulsa: 4 city, town
city near ~: 3 Ada **4** Enid
conference: 3 WAC
locale: 4 Okla. **8** Oklahoma
newspaper: 5 World
river: 8 Arkansas
school: 3 ORU
Tulsa (1949 film)
cast: Pedro Armendariz, Susan Hayward, Robert Preston
director: Stuart Heisler
Tulsidas: 4 poet **6** Indian
Tultepec: 4 city, town
locale: 6 Mexico
Tuluá: 4 city, town
locale: 8 Colombia
tum: 3 gut **5** belly, tease **6** middle **7** midriff, stomach **10** midsection
tumble: 3 dip, sag **4** dive, drop, fall, flip, flop, roll, slip, trip **5** crash, learn, pitch, slide, slump, smash, spill, upset, whirl **6** jumble, plunge, sprawl, topple **7** descend, descent, give way, plummet, stumble, subvert **8** disorder, overturn **9** cartwheel **10** disarrange, somersault
ender: 3 bug, set **4** weed
out: 4 wake **5** awake, waken **6** awaken
take a ~: 4 fall, trip
tumble __: 4 cart, home
tumble-__: 3 dry **4** down
Tumblebrutus: 3 cat
tumbledown: 6 flimsy, unfirm **7** rickety, run-down **8** decrepit, untended **9** crumbling **10** ramshackle
structure: 3 hut **5** shack **6** lean-to, shanty
__ Tumble 4 Ya: 3 I'll
tumbler: 3 cup **5** glass **7** acrobat, gymnast, vaulter
contents: 3 ice **4** soda **5** water
movement: 5 split
pad: 3 mat **7** cushion
place: 3 gym **4** lock
turner: 3 key
Tumbleweed author: Janwillem van de Wetering
Tumbleweeds cartoonist: 4 Ryan
tumbling: 5 sport **10** gymnastics
Tumbling Dice (1972 song) artist: Rolling Stones
Tumbling Tumbleweeds singer: 5 Autry
tumbrel: 4 cart **5** wagon
Tumen: 5 river
locale: 5 China **6** Russia **10** North Korea
tumid: 6 turgid **7** bloated, fustian, orotund, pompous, swollen **8** enlarged, inflated, puffed up **9** bombastic, distended, overblown, puffed out **10** rhetorical
tummy: 3 gut **5** belly **6** middle, paunch **7** abdomen, midriff, stomach **10** midsection
butterflies in the ~: 6 nerves
exercise: 5 sit up
noise: 5 growl **6** rumble **7** grumble
soother: 6 bicarb
trouble: 4 ache
tummy __: 4 tuck
Tum, Rigoberta: 8 Nobelist
Tums: 7 antacid
alternative: 6 Maalox, Pepcid, Riopan, Zantac **7** Gelusil, Lactaid, Mylanta, Rolaids **8** Gaviscon **11** Alka-Seltzer, Pepto-Bismol
target: 3 gas **4** acid
tumult: 3 ado, din, row **4** flap, fuss, mess, riot, stew, stir, to-do **5** babel, brawl, chaos, fight, furor, hoo-ha, noise, shout, storm, swirl **6** affray, bedlam, clamor, dither, émeute, flurry, fracas, hassle, hubbub, jangle, lather, mayhem, outcry, pother, racket, rumpus, squall, strife, unrest, uproar **7** anarchy, clangor, ferment, quarrel, rampage, ruction, tempest, trouble, turmoil **8** disarray, disorder, outbreak, paroxysm, seething, upheaval, wildness **9** agitation, commotion, confusion, maelstrom **10** convulsion, excitement, hullabaloo, hurly-burly, turbulence
tumultuous: 4 wild **5** aroar, noisy, rough, rowdy **6** fierce, hectic, raging, stormy, unruly **7** chaotic, rampant, raucous, riotous, violent **8** anarchic **9** clamorous, turbulent **10** anarchical, boisterous, disorderly, in an uproar
tumulus: 5 mound **6** barrow
tun: 3 vat **4** cask **9** container
tuna: 4 fish **5** tunny **6** bonito, cactus **7** bluefin, Charlie **8** albacore, food fish, skipjack, Star Kist **9** Bumble Bee, yellowfin
anagram: 4 aunt
catcher: 3 net **4** hook **5** seine **7** netting
Hawaiian ~: 3 ahi
holder: 3 can, tin
how ~ is packed: 5 in oil **7** in water
salad ingredient: 4 mayo **6** celery
tuna __: 4 fish, melt **5** on rye, salad **9** casserole
Tuna __: 6 Helper
Tuna-Fishing artist: 4 Dali
Tunbridge Wells: 3 spa **4** town
locale: 4 Kent **7** England
tundra: 4 moor **5** plain, waste **7** lowland
animal: 3 elk **4** loon, tern **5** raven **6** falcon, musk ox, rabbit **7** caribou, lemming, penguin **8** squirrel **9** polar bear
__ tundra: 6 alpine
tune: 3 air, fix, lay, set **4** aria, dial, lied, lilt, pean, sing, song **5** adapt, carol, chant, ditty, music, paean, piece, price **6** adjust, chorus, jingle, melody, number, outlay, strain **7** ariette, conform, euphony, harmony, refrain **8** modulate, readjust, regulate **9** harmonize, reconcile **10** conformity
ender: 5 smith
in ~: 5 on key, sweet **7** melodic **8** sonorous **9** consonant, melodious **10** euphonious, harmonious
like some ~ s: 6 catchy
tune __: 3 out
__-tune: 4 fine
Tune: 5 Tommy
__ Tune: 6 Elmer's
tuned
in: 3 hep, hip **4** wise **5** aware, savvy **6** versed, wise to, with it **7** knowing, mindful **8** apprised, informed, skillful **9** cognizant, sensitive **10** perceptive
out: 4 cold, numb **6** deaf to, inured **7** blind to, callous **8** hardened, uncaring **9** apathetic, insensate, unfeeling
tuneful: 5 in key, lyric, sweet **6** ariose, arioso, dulcet **7** lyrical, melodic, musical **8** sonorous **9** melodious **10** euphonious, harmonious
tunefulness: 7 harmony
__ tune of: 5 to the
__ tuner: 5 piano
__ Tunes: 6 Looney
Tune, Tommy musical: 4 Nine
tune-up: 8 practice, training
need: 4 plug **5** point **9** condenser, spark plug
Tune Weavers song: Happy, Happy Birthday Baby (1957)
tung: 3 oil
tunga: 4 flea
tungsten: 5 metal **7** element, wolfram
ore: 9 scheelite
tungsten __: 4 lamp **5** oxide, steel **6** rating **7** carbide
tunic: 3 alb **4** coat, robe **5** cotta, shirt, stola **6** blouse, chiton, jacket
eye ~: 4 uvea
Vietnamese ~: 5 aodai
tunicate, marine: 4 salp **5** salpa
tuning: 10 regulation
tuning __: 4 fork, pipe
Tunis: 4 city, town **7** capital
locale: 3 Afr. **6** Africa **7** Tunisia
Tunisia: 6 nation **7** country
capital: 5 Tunis
city: 4 Sfax **5** Susah, Tunis **6** Ariana
desert: 6 Sahara
gulf: 5 Gabès
island off ~: 6 Djerba
it's n. of ~: 5 Medit.
language: 6 Arabic, Berber
money: 5 dinar
mountain range: 5 Atlas
neighbor: 5 Libya **7** Algeria
ruler: 3 bey
Tunja: 4 city, town
locale: 8 Colombia
tunnel: 3 dig, pit **4** adit, bore, hole, mine, tube **5** gouge, shaft **6** burrow, escape, subway **7** channel, passage **8** catacomb, crawlway, crosscut, excavate **9** penetrate, undermine, underpass **10** passageway
builder: 3 ant **4** mole **5** emmet, miner **6** gopher
make a ~: 3 dig **4** bore, mine, root **6** burrow **8** excavate, scoop out **9** hollow out
tunnel __: 5 vault **6** effect, vision
__ tunnel: 4 wind
Tunnel of Love (1987 song) artist: Bruce Springsteen
Tunnel of Love, The (1958 film)
cast: Doris Day, Richard Widmark, Gig Young
director: Gene Kelly
__ tunnel syndrome: 6 carpal
Tunney, Gene: 5 boxer
milieu: 4 ring
tunny: 4 fish, tuna **7** bluefin **8** albacore
Tupac: 6 Shakur
song: California Love (1996)
Dear Mama (1995)
How Do U Want It (1996)
I Get Around (1993)
Keep Ya Head Up (1993)
Smile (1997)
tupan: 4 drum
origin: 6 Turkey
tupelo: 4 tree
Tupelo: 4 city, town
locale: 4 Miss.
singer from ~: 5 Elvis **7** Presley
Tupi: 6 Indian **7** Amerind **8** language
Tupolev: 3 SST **5** plane **7** Russian **8** airplane
tuppence: 4 coin **5** money
Tupper: 4 Amos
Tupungato: 4 peak **5** mount **8** mountain
locale: 5 Andes, Chile **9** Argentina
turaco: 4 bird
Turandot: 5 opera
composer: 7 Puccini
librettist: 5 Adami
role: 3 Liù, Tiu **4** Pang, Ping, Pong **5** Calaf, Timur **8** Pu-tin-Pao
setting: 5 China **6** Peking **7** Beijing
tune: 4 aria

turban: 3 hat 8 headgear 9 headdress
material: 6 Madras
poolside ~: 5 towel
wearer: 4 Sikh 5 Hindu, swami, swamy
turban __: 6 squash
turbid: 5 mirky, muddy, murky, roily, thick 6 cloudy, opaque 7 clouded, muddied, muddled, unclear 8 darkened
turbine: 5 motor 6 diesel, engine 9 generator
part: 4 vane 5 rotor
__ turbine: 3 air, gas 4 wind 5 steam, water 7 impulse
turbo-__ engine: 6 ramjet
Turbo: 3 car 4 auto 7 Bentley 10 automobile
turbofan: 6 engine
turbojet: 5 plane 6 engine 8 airplane
turboprop: 5 plane 6 engine 8 airplane
turboshaft: 6 engine
turbot: 4 bret, fish 5 brill
TurboTax company: 6 Intuit
turbulence: 4 fury, rage, stew 5 chaos, noise 6 bedlam, lather, racket, squall, tumult, unrest, uproar 7 anarchy, discord, ferment 8 disarray, disorder 9 commotion, confusion 10 disharmony, storminess
turbulent: 4 wild 5 bumpy, noisy, roily, rough, rowdy, wroth 6 choppy, fierce, hectic, jouncy, raging, stormy, unruly 7 chaotic, foaming, furious, howling, lawless, moiling, rampant, raucous, riotous, roaring, ruffled, untamed, violent 8 agitated, blustery, restless, swirling 9 disturbed, inclement, stirred up, unsettled 10 blustering, boisterous, disordered, disorderly, in an uproar, rebellious, tumultuous, unpeaceful
Turcotte, Ron: 6 jockey
milieu: 5 track
tureen: 4 bowl 5 crock 6 vessel 9 container
accessory: 5 ladle
contents: 4 soup
Tureis: 4 star
turf: 3 sod 4 area, home, lawn, soil 5 earth, grass, realm, space, sward 6 domain, ground, locale, region, sphere, swarth 7 habitat, quarter, terrain 8 locality, location, vicinity 9 bailiwick, community, home field, racetrack, territory 10 greensward
add more ~: 5 resod
grabber: 5 cleat
loose ~: 5 divot
material: 4 peat
starter: 5 Astro
surf and ~: 4 meal 6 dinner, entrée
warriors: 4 band, gang, pack
__-turf: 5 surf-'n'
Turgenev, Ivan: 6 author, writer 7 Russian
birthplace: 4 Orel
character: 5 Elena
work: Fathers and Sons
A Month in the Country
A Sportsman's Sketches
turgid: 5 tumid, windy, wordy 7 pompous, stilted, unterse 8 inflated 9 distended, overblown 10 rhetorical
Turhan: 3 Bey
Turia, city on the: 8 Valencia
Turin: 4 city, town 5 Adela
city near ~: 4 Asti
locale: 5 Italy
river: 5 the Po
Shroud of ~: 5 relic
Turing: 4 Alan
__ Turismo Omologato: 4 Gran
Turk: 5 Asian 6 Othman 7 Ottoman, upstart 9 Anatolian
neighbor: 5 Greek, Irani, Iraqi 6 Syrian 8 Georgian 9 Bulgarian
__ Turk: 5 Grand, Young
Turkana: 4 lake
locale: 3 Afr. 5 Kenya 6 Africa
Turkel: 3 Ann
turkey: 3 ass, dud, oaf, sap 4 bird, bomb, boob, bust, clod, dolt, flop, fool, fowl, jerk, loss, meat, play 5 chump, clown, cluck, dummy, dunce, joker, lemon, ninny, patsy 6 defeat, dimwit, fiasco, lummox, mishap, nitwit, sucker 7 blunder, buffoon, debacle, dingbat, dullard, failure, fathead, gobbler, halfwit, jackass, misstep, pinhead, poultry, saphead, stumble, washout 8 bonehead, downfall, dumbbell, meathead, numskull 9 birdbrain, blockhead, jellyfish, lamebrain, numbskull, simpleton 10 dunderhead, nonsuccess
baster: 4 chef, cook 5 pipet
do the ~: 5 baste, carve, stuff, truss
female ~: 3 hen
go cold ~: 4 quit
like some ~ s: 5 plump 6 basted
like some ~ stuffing: 4 sagy
male ~: 3 tom 7 gobbler
meat choice: 3 leg 4 dark 5 thigh, white 6 breast 9 drumstick
relative: 5 poult, quail, snipe 6 chukar, grouse, peahen 7 peacock, peafowl 8 curassow, moorfowl, pheasant, woodcock 9 partridge 10 guinea fowl, jungle fowl
roaster: 4 oven
talking ~: 4 open 9 outspoken
topper: 5 gravy
walk like a ~: 5 strut
young ~: 5 poult
turkey __: 3 oak, red 4 cock, trot 5 shoot 7 buzzard, vulture
__ turkey: 4 cold, talk, wild 5 brush, water
Turkey: 6 nation 7 country, Stearns
ancient city: 5 Adana 6 Edessa, Sestos
ancient region: 6 Aeolia
bovine: 5 Kurdi
candy: 5 halva 6 halvah 7 halavah
capital: 6 Ankara
çavalryman: 5 spahi 6 spahee
chamber: 3 oda 4 odah
city: 4 Urfa 5 Adana, Brusa, Bursa, İzmir, Konya, Maras 6 Angora, Ankara, Edirne, Elâzig 8 Istanbul
coffee: 5 mocha
combining form: 5 Turco-
decree: 5 irade
garment: 6 caftan, kaftan
government of old: 5 porte
gulf: 5 Izmir
highest point: 6 Ararat
inn: 5 serai 6 imaret
island near ~: 5 Samos 6 Cyprus, Rhodes, Rhodos
lake: 3 Van
language: 6 Othman 7 Ottoman
liquor: 4 raki 5 rakee
locale: 4 Asia 6 Europe
money: 4 lira 5 asper, kurus 6 sequin 7 piaster, piastre
mountain: 3 Ida 6 Ararat, Pontic, Taurus, Zagros 7 Ala Dagh
mountain dweller: 4 Kurd
neighbor: 4 Irak, Iran, Iraq 5 Syria 6 Greece 7 Armenia, Georgia 8 Bulgaria 10 Azerbaijan
org.: 4 NATO
poet: 6 Hikmet
port: 5 Izmir 6 Smyrna 8 Istanbul
region: 6 Levant
river: 4 Aras, Kura 5 Murat 6 Tigris
robe: 6 dolman
scholars: 5 ulema
sea: 5 Egean 6 Aegean 7 Marmara
soldier: 5 Nizam
staple: 6 sesame
sword: 5 kilij
title: 3 aga, bey 4 agha, amir, emir 5 ameer, emeer, pacha, pasha
topper: 3 fez
weight: 3 oka
Turkey Hill: 8 ice cream
alternative: 4 Edy's 7 Breyer's 9 Friendly's, Good Humor 10 Dairy Queen, Haagen Dazs
Turkey in the __: 5 Straw
turkey trot: 5 dance
Turki: 8 language
Turkic
language: 5 Tatar, Yakut
tent: 4 yurt
Turkish: 8 language
see also Turkey
Turkish __: 3 rug 4 bath, knot 5 paste, pound, taffy, towel 6 carpet, coffee, Empire 7 delight, Letters
Turkish Angora: 3 cat 5 felid 6 feline
Turkish bath: 5 sauna
like a ~: 3 hot 5 humid 6 steamy
need: 5 towel
Turkish delight: 5 candy
Turkish Letters author: Mary Wortley Montagu
Turkish Van: 3 cat 5 felid 6 feline
__-Turkish War: 5 Italo
Turkmenistan: 6 nation 7 country
capital: 9 Ashkhabad
desert: 7 Kara Kum
neighbor: 4 Iran 10 Kazakhstan, Uzbekistan
once: 3 SSR
river: 4 Oxus
Turkoman: 3 rug 6 Afghan, carpet 7 Afghani
Turks and Caicos: 4 isls. 5 isles 7 islands
Turk's-head: 4 knot 6 cactus
Turku: 4 city, town
locale: 7 Finland
to a Swede: 3 Åbo
Turlock: 4 city, town
locale: 10 California
Turman: 5 Glynn
turmeric: 5 spice 9 condiment
turmoil: 3 ado 4 flap, fuss, mess, riot, stew, stir, to-do 5 chaos, furor, hoo-ha, mix-up, storm, swirl, upset, whirl 6 action, bedlam, clamor, flurry, frenzy, hassle, hubbub, lather, mayhem, pother, racket, squall, tumult, unrest, uproar 7 anarchy, anxiety, ferment, mad rush, rampage, rioting 8 disarray, disorder, disquiet, distress, madhouse, upheaval 9 agitation, confusion, maelstrom, mobocracy 10 donnybrook, excitement, hullabaloo
in ~: 6 uneasy
inner ~: 3 woe 5 angst, dread, worry 7 anxiety, malaise 8 disquiet 10 inquietude, uneasiness
turn: 2 go 3 arc, lap, rat, rot, try, use, yaw 4 bend, bent, curl, deed, eddy, fork, gift, head, hook, lean, loop, mold, move, play, roll, shot, sour, spin, sway, tack, till, tilt, time, tour, veer, vein, walk, wind 5 alter, at bat, crank, curve, cycle, decay, drift, favor, flair, go bad, jaunt, knack, level, orbit, pivot, point, quirk, round, scare, screw, shape, sheer, shift, shunt, snake, spell, spoil, stint, swing, swirl, taint, trend, twirl, twist, whack, wheel, whirl 6 attack, become, circle, curdle, defect, detour, direct, divert, employ, go back, go sour, gyrate, invert, modify, molder, mutate, orient, outing, ramble, recoil, renege, revert, revolt, rotate, spiral, sprain, strain, stroll, swerve, switch, swivel, talent, wrench, zigzag 7 acidify, capsize, convert, deviate, digress, diverge, flexure, incline, meander, retract, reverse, revolve, seizure, service, shy away, subvert, utilize, veer off, winding 8 aptitude, go around, persuade, renounce, resort to, rotation, surprise 9 about-face, alternate, backslide, circulate, decompose, excursion, hang a left, influence, oscillate, pirouette, promenade, sidetrack, sinuosity, transform, transmute, volte-face 10 come around, double back, hang a right, propensity, revolution, right-about, succession
a blind eye to: 8 overlook
about: 4 slew, slue 6 slough
a deaf ear to: 4 deny 5 scorn 6 refuse, slight
against: 5 rebel 6 betray, revolt 7 sell out
around: 5 rally, shift 6 invert 7 correct, redress, reverse
aside: 4 skew, veer 5 avert, parry, repel, shunt 6 divert, swerve 7 deflect, prevent, ward off 10 discourage
away: 4 shun 5 avert, spurn 6 ignore, rebuff, recoil, refuse 7 repulse 8 alienate
back: 5 repel, spurn 6 rebuff, thwart 7 regress, relapse, repulse 8 stave off
bad: 3 rot 5 spoil
combining form: 4 trop- 5 tropo-
do a ~: 4 solo 7 perform
down: 3 dim, nix 4 deny, mute, shun, veto 5 say no, scorn, spurn, waive 6 bounce, pass on, rebuff, reduce, refuse, reject, resist, soften 7 decline, disdain, dismiss, exclude, ward off 8 disallow, throw out 9 blackball, cast aside, frown upon, repudiate 10 disapprove
ender: 3 key, off, out 4 coat, down, over, pike, sole, spit 5 about, stile, stone, table 6 around, buckle
for the better: 5 rally
full ~: 5 orbit 10 revolution
give a ~: 5 alarm, scare, shake, shock, spook, throw 6 dismay, rattle 7 fluster, startle, unnerve 8 affright, frighten, surprise, unsettle 9 take aback 10 disconcert, intimidate
good ~: 5 favor 8 courtesy, kindness 10 kindliness
green over: 4 envy 5 covet 8 begrudge
half a ~: 3 zag, zig
in: 3 lie, nap 4 flop, rest, sing 5 rat on, sleep, spill 6 betray, expose, finger, fink on, give up, retire, squeal, submit, tell on, tender 7 deliver, go to bed, lie down, sack out, saw logs, sell out 8 give away, hand over, inform on, snitch on, squeal on, tattle on 9 deliver up, go to sleep, hit the hay 10 call it a day, hit the sack, put forward
in ~: 8 one by one
inside out: 4 comb, sack 5 evert, probe, rifle, scour 6 forage, invert, ravage, ravish, search 7 examine, inspect, pillage, ransack, rummage 8 overhaul 9 go through 10 scrutinize
into: 5 end up 6 become, evolve, modify 8 emerge as
left: 3 haw

loose: **5** let go **6** unbind **7** manumit, release
180-degree ~: **3** uey
off: **3** vex **4** bore, kill, sour, stop **5** close, douse, dowse, repel **6** offend, revolt, sadden, sicken, unplug **7** disgust, repulse **8** alienate, shut down **9** displease **10** disenchant, extinguish
of phrase: **5** idiom **7** wording **10** expression
on: **4** open, send, spur **5** elate, impel, light, liven, pep up, start **6** arouse, enable, excite, ignite, kindle, please, pump up, thrill, tickle, vivify, work up **7** actuate, animate, delight, enchant, enliven, gladden, inspire, juice up, liven up, power up, start up **8** activate, energize, enspirit, inspirit, interest, vitalize **9** captivate, instigate, stimulate, throw open, titillate **10** invigorate
one's back on: **4** shun **5** avoid, scorn **6** desert, disown, ignore, refuse, reject **7** abandon, forsake, neglect **8** overlook, renounce **9** disregard, repudiate **10** leave alone
one's nose up at: **5** scorn, sneer, spurn **7** disdain **10** look down on
out: **2** ax, go **3** axe, can, rig **4** come, fare, fire, form, make, oust, rise, show, wake **5** arise, eject, end up, enter, equip, evict, exile, expel, get up, occur, pop in, prove, waken, write, yield **6** appear, arrive, attend, betide, blow in, drop in, go well, happen, invent, result, roll in, show up **7** appoint, cashier, dismiss, furnish, produce, release, succeed **8** accouter, accoutre, assemble, breeze in **9** arise from, caparison, eventuate, fabricate
out badly: **3** die, sag **4** bomb, fail, flop, fold, lose, miss, sink **6** fizzle **7** founder, go under, let down **8** backfire, collapse, fall flat, go astray, languish **9** fall short **10** go bankrupt, go downhill
outward: **5** flare
over: **3** tip **4** give, mull, muse, plow, roll, till **5** crank, refer, relay, think, upend, yield **6** assign, commit, fork up, hand in, invert, pass on, ponder, render, rotate, supply, topple **7** capsize, commend, consign, deliver, entrust, intrust, lay down, provide, reverse, revolve **8** consider, delegate, meditate, mull over, relegate, ruminate, transfer **9** reflect on, surrender **10** deliberate, get started, relinquish, think about
over a new leaf: **6** change, reform **7** redress, shape up **10** go straight
partner: **4** toss **5** twist
right: **3** gee
sharp ~: **3** jog, zag, zig **4** jink **6** dogleg
signal: **5** arrow
single ~: **10** revolution
starter: **4** down
suddenly: **4** veer **6** careen
tail: **3** run **4** bolt, flee **6** escape **7** retreat, run away, take off **8** fugitate, run for it **9** cut and run, skedaddle
take a wrong ~: **3** err **5** stray **6** slip up **8** go astray, trespass **9** misbehave **10** transgress
the key: **6** fasten, secure
the other cheek: **5** spare **6** pardon **7** forgive, let it go, let pass **8** bear with, overlook
the tables: **5** shift **6** oppose **7** revenge, reverse **9** retaliate
things around: **5** rally **7** rectify, redress
to: **3** ask, see **7** consult
(to): **5** refer **6** resort
to a ~: **9** perfectly
topsy-turvy: **5** upend, upset **6** invert, jumble, muss up **7** derange **8** disarray, unsettle
toss and ~: **5** brood, worry **7** agonize
toward: **4** face, meet **6** engage **7** eyeball **8** confront
up: **4** come, find, show, spot **5** learn, occur, pop in, reach **6** appear, arrive, attend, blow in, detect, locate, report, reveal **7** hit upon, punch in, uncover, unearth, weigh in **8** discover, get there **9** get to know, track down, transpire **10** come to pass
up one's nose: **5** sneer
upside-down: **4** comb, flip **6** invert **7** ransack, reverse, rummage, shake up **8** overturn
turn __: **3** off, out, pro **4** away, back, down, over, tail **5** a hair, loose **6** button, signal, turtle
turn __ ear: **5** a deaf
turn __ evidence: **6** state's
turn __ new leaf: **5** over a
__ turn: **3** bat, to a **4** jump, kick, star, stem, step **5** out of, round **7** Buggin's
__-turn: **4** half **6** ampere
Turn __, Look at Me: **6** Around
Turn __ Screw, The: **5** of the
__ Turn: **5** It's My, Rose's
__-Turn: **3** No U
turn a __: **4** hair **6** corner, profit
turn a __ ear: **4** deaf
turn a __ eye: **5** blind
turnabout: **6** switch **7** reverse **8** apostasy, flip-flop, reversal **9** inversion, one-eighty
(French): **9** volte-face
turnaround: **6** change **8** flip-flop, upheaval
Turn Around, Look at Me (1968 song) artist: Vogues
Turn Back the Clock (1933 film)
cast: Mae Clarke, Otto Kruger, Lee Tracy
director: Edgar Selwyn
Turn Back the Hands of Time (1970 song) artist: Tyrone Davis
turncoat: **3** rat **4** fink, nark **5** Judas, rebel, snake, viper **6** ratter **7** ratfink, stoolie, tattler, traitor **8** apostate, betrayer, forsaker, quisling, recreant, renegade, squealer, two-timer
turndown: **2** no **3** nay **4** veto **6** denial, rebuff **7** refusal, regrets **9** rejection **10** nonconsent
emphatic ~: **5** never, no sir, no way
slangy ~: **3** nah **4** nope, uh-uh
turned: **4** rank, sour **5** swung **6** rancid **7** gone bad **8** inedible
back on: **5** relit
be ~ off by: **4** hate **5** abhor **6** detest, loathe
combining form: **7** -tropous
down: **3** low **5** faint, piano, quiet
off: **8** outraged **9** disgusted, squeamish **10** displeased, grossed out
on: **3** lit **4** into **6** enrapt **8** obsessed
up: **4** loud **5** forte, noisy **7** blaring, booming, jarring, pealing, rackety, raucous, reboant, roaring **8** crashing, piercing, plangent, rumbling, sonorous, strident **9** big-voiced, clamorous, deafening **10** boisterous, resounding, stentorian, strepitous, thundering, vociferous
well ~ out: **4** chic, neat, trim **5** dandy, natty, sharp, sleek, smart, swank **6** chichi, classy, dapper, jaunty, snappy, snazzy, spiffy, sporty, spruce, swanky **7** dashing, stylish **8** handsome
turned toward combining form: **6** -tropic
turner: **7** gymnast, tumbler
device: **5** lathe
starter: **4** wood
__-turner: **4** page
Turner: **3** Ike, J.M.W., Joe, Nat, Ted **4** John, Lana, Tina **5** Sammy **6** Big Joe, Janine, Odessa **8** Kathleen
network: **3** CNN, TBS, TNT
Turner & __: **5** Hooch
Turner Field site: **7** Atlanta
Turner & Hooch (1989 film)
cast: Tom Hanks, Craig T. Nelson, Reginald VelJohnson, Mare Winningham
director: Roger Spottiswoode
Turner, Ike and Tina song: Proud Mary (1971)
Turner, John: **2** P.M. **8** Canadian
predecessor: **7** Trudeau
successor: **8** Mulroney
Turner, Kathleen: **7** actress
film: The Accidental Tourist (1988)
Body Heat (1981)
The Jewel of the Nile (1985)
The Man With Two Brains (1983)
Moonlight and Valentino (1995)
Peggy Sue Got Married (1986)
Prizzi's Honor (1985)
Romancing the Stone (1984)
Serial Mom (1994)
Switching Channels (1988)
The Virgin Suicides (2000)
The War of the Roses (1989)
Turner, Lana: **7** actress
film: The Bad and the Beautiful (1952)
Dr. Jekyll and Mr. Hyde (1941)
Imitation of Life (1959)
Johnny Eager (1941)
Marriage Is a Private Affair (1944)
Peyton Place (1957)
The Postman Always Rings Twice (1946)
Weekend at the Waldorf (1945)
Ziegfeld Girl (1941)
spouse: Lex Barker
Turner, Nat: **5** rebel, slave
__-Turner Overdrive: **7** Bachman
Turner, Ted spouse: Jane Fonda
Turner, Tina
born: Anna Mae Bullock
song: Better Be Good to Me (1984)
I Don't Wanna Fight (1993)
It's Only Love (1985)
Private Dancer (1985)
Typical Male (1986)
We Don't Need Another Hero (1985)
What's Love Got to Do With It (1984)
spouse: Ike Turner
turning: **6** aswirl, rotary **7** sinuous, winding **8** gyration **9** diversion **10** divergence
combining form: **6** stroph- **7** stropho-
point: **3** hub **4** axis, axle, crux **5** hinge, pivot, rally **6** climax, crisis **8** juncture, landmark, zero hour **9** milestone
starter: **4** wood
tool: **5** lathe
tossing and ~: **5** awake **8** restless
turning __: **5** piece, point **6** chisel
__ turning: **4** ball, wood **6** bamboo, bobbin, bottle, engine **7** sausage
Turning Point author: **6** Carter
Turning Point, The (1977 film)
cast: Anne Bancroft, Mikhail Baryshnikov, Leslie Browne, Shirley MacLaine
director: Herbert Ross
Turning to Stone director: **4** Till
turnip: **4** root **5** tuber **6** veggie **9** vegetable
Scottish ~: **4** neep
__ turnip: **5** white **6** Indian **7** Italian, prairie, Swedish
Turn It Up (1998 song) artist: Busta Rhymes
turnkey: **6** gaoler, jailer **10** doorkeeper
domain: **4** jail
Turn Me Loose (1959 song) artist: Fabian
turnoff: **4** exit
Turn of the Screw, The author: Henry James
character: **5** Flora, Grose, Miles, Quint
turn-on: **6** thrill **8** pleasure
turn one's __: **4** head
turn one's __ on: **4** back
turn one's __ to: **4** hand
turnout: **3** rig **4** gate **5** crowd, getup, yield **6** output, throng **7** meeting **8** assembly, audience **9** gathering, listeners, multitude **10** attendance, production
turnover: **5** knish, upset **6** change, pastry, resale **8** movement
turn over __ leaf: **4** a new
turnpike: **4** road **5** route **7** highway, thruway **10** expressway
access: **4** ramp
like a ~: **5** laned
maneuver: **5** merge
stop: **5** motel, plaza
tariff: **4** toll
turns: **10** ins and outs
take ~: **4** vary **5** spell **6** rotate, switch **8** exchange, trade off **9** alternate, change off
turnstile: **4** exit, gate **5** entry **6** entrée, portal **7** ingress **8** entrance, entryway **10** admittance
cheater: **4** slug
drop-in: **5** token
opening: **4** slot
turnstone: **4** bird
turntable
abbr.: **3** rpm
extension: **3** arm **7** tonearm
topper: **2** LP **5** album **6** record
turn the __: **4** tide **5** trick **6** corner, tables
Turn the Beat Around (1976 song) artist: Vicki Sue Robinson
turn the other __: **5** cheek
__ Turn to Cry: **5** Judy's
Turn to Stone artist: **3** ELO
turn toward combining form: **5** -trope
Turn! Turn! Turn! (1965 song) artist: Byrds
turn up one's __ at: **4** nose
Turn Your Love Around (1981 song) artist: George Benson
Turow, Scott: **6** author, writer
work: The Burden of Proof
The Laws of Our Fathers
One L
Personal Injuries
Pleading Guilty
Presumed Innocent
Reversible Errors
turpentine: **5** pitch
source: **4** pine
__ turpentine: **4** wood **5** Chian, oil of **6** Canada
Turpin: **3** Ben **4** Dick
Turpin, Dick horse: **9** Black Bess
turpitude: **4** evil, vice **5** wrong **10** corruption
turquoise: **3** gem **4** aqua, blue **5** color, green **6** bluish **7** blueish, mineral

8 gemstone, greenish
like ~: 6 bluish 7 blueish
month: 3 Dec. 8 December
relative: 3 pea 4 anil, cyan, jade, navy, Nile, sage, teal 5 Alice, azure, beryl, breen, olive, slate, virid 6 cobalt, indigo, myrtle, raisin, reseda, violet 7 avocado, celadon, emerald, peacock, verdant 8 cerulean, sapphire 9 pistachio 10 aquamarine, chartreuse, periwinkle
__ turquoise: 4 bone 6 fossil
turret: 5 spire, tower 7 steeple
turret __: 5 lathe
Turteltaub: 3 Jon
turtle: 3 pet 4 soup 6 animal, cooter, ridley 7 reptile, snapper 8 stinkpot 9 hawksbill 10 loggerhead
about to turn ~: 5 alist
ender: 4 back, dove, head, neck
genus: 4 emys
group: 4 bale
home: 4 pond 5 shell
plate: 5 scute
plates: 5 scuta
toon ~: 5 ninja
__ turtle: 3 bog, box, map, mud, sea 4 musk, turn 5 green 6 gopher 7 chicken, painted
__ Turtle: 4 Mock
Turtle Diary (1985 film)
cast: Glenda Jackson, Richard Johnson, Ben Kingsley
turtledove: 2 jo 3 pet 4 baby, bird, dear, jill, love 5 amour, angel, chéri, cooky, cutey, cutie, deary, ducky, flame, honey, leman, lover, lovey, novia, novio, sugar, sweet 6 bon ami, chérie, cookie, dautie, dearie, steady, sweets 7 beloved, dearest, dear one, pigsney, schatzi, squeeze, sweetie, tootsie 8 chou-chou, cutie pie, dowsabel, dulcinea, ladylove, lovebird, macushla, paramour, precious, snookums, sugar pie, sweetums, truelove 9 bonne amie, boyfriend, dreamboat, inamorata, inamorato, petit chou, valentine 10 girlfriend, heartthrob, honeybunch, mavourneen, sweetheart, sweetie pie
...__ turtledoves...: 3 two
Turtle Island author: Gary Snyder
turtleneck: 6 blouse 7 sweater 8 pullover
material: 4 wool
what a ~ hides: 4 nape
Turtles
song: Elenore (1968)
Happy Together (1967)
It Ain't Me Babe (1965)
She'd Rather Be With Me (1967)
You Showed Me (1969)
__ turtle soup: 4 mock
Turturro: 4 Aida, John
Turturro, John: 5 actor
film: Barton Fink (1991)
Clockers (1995)
Five Corners (1988)
Mac (1992)
O Brother, Where Art Thou? (2000)
Quiz Show (1994)
Rounders (1998)
Thirteen Conversations About One Thing (2001)
__-turvy: 5 topsy
Tuscaloosa: 4 city, town
locale: 3 Ala. 7 Alabama
Tuscan: 5 order, Pisan 8 language
Tuscany
city: 4 Pisa 5 Massa, Prato, Siena 7 Firenze, Leghorn, Livorno 8 Florence
locale: 5 Italy
river: 4 Arno
Tuscarora: 6 Indian 7 Amerind
ally: 6 Cayuga, Mohawk, Oneida, Seneca 8 Onondaga
Tush (1975 song) artist: ZZ Top
Tushingham, Rita: 7 actress
film: The Knack, and How to Get It (1965)
A Taste of Honey (1961)
The Trap (1966)
Tusi home: 6 Africa, Rwanda 7 Burundi
tusk: 5 ivory, tooth
Tusk (1979 song) artist: Fleetwood Mac
tusker: 3 hog 4 boar 5 swine 6 walrus
tussah: 3 bug 6 fabric, insect
__ Tussaud's Wax Museum: 3 Mme.
Tussi home: 6 Africa, Rwanda 7 Burundi
tussle: 4 bout, fray, tilt 5 brawl, brush, clash, fight, melee, mix-up, run-in, set-to 6 barney, battle, go at it, hassle 7 grapple, mix it up, scuffle, wrestle 8 conflict, do battle, scramble, skirmish, struggle 9 fistfight, square off 10 donnybrook, free-for-all
tussock: 4 tuft
Tussy: 9 deodorant
alternative: 3 Ban 4 Sure 5 Arrid 6 Degree, Secret 7 Dry Idea, Mitchum 10 Right Guard, Soft and Dri, Speed Stick
Tustin: 4 city, town
locale: 10 California
tut: 3 tsk 6 tsk tsk 8 for shame
__ Tut: 4 King
tutee: 5 pupil 7 learner, student
tutelage: 4 care 7 keeping 8 guidance, training, wardship 9 oversight, schooling 10 protection
tutelary deity: 3 Lar
tutor: 4 guru 5 coach, drill, edify, groom, guide, ready, teach, train 6 direct, ground, master, mentor, school 7 adviser, advisor, educate, lecture, teacher, trainer 8 academic, educator, instruct, lecturer 9 abecedary, governess, preceptor 10 instructor
charge: 5 pupil
Oxford ~: 3 don
tutorial: 6 lesson 7 session 9 pedagogic
Tutsi
foe: 4 Hutu
home: 6 Africa, Rwanda 7 Burundi
Tutte le feste: 4 aria
tutti: 3 all
tutti-frutti: 8 ice cream
alternative: 5 lemon, mocha, peach 6 banana, coffee, Jamoca, toffee 7 caramel, coconut, vanilla 8 cinnamon, hazelnut 9 bubblegum, chocolate, pineapple, pistachio, raspberry, rocky road, rum raisin 10 blackberry, cheesecake, Neapolitan, peppermint, strawberry
Tutti-Frutti (1956 song) artist: Little Richard
Tuttle: 5 Frank 6 Lurene
Tuttle, Frank: 8 director
film: The Big Broadcast (1932)
The Glass Key (1935)
Roman Scandals (1933)
This Gun for Hire (1942)
Waikiki Wedding (1937)
Tuttles of Tahiti, The (1942 film)
cast: Peggy Drake, Jon Hall, Charles Laughton
director: Charles Vidor
Tuttlingen: 4 city, town
locale: 7 Germany
river: 6 Danube
Tut-tut!: 3 tsk 6 tsk tsk
tutu: 5 skirt 7 costume
event: 6 ballet
fabric: 5 tulle
Tutu, Desmond: 8 Nobelist 11 archibishop
Tuvalu: 6 nation 7 country
city: 8 Funafuti
formerly: 6 Ellice
money: 4 cent 6 dollar
TUV neighbor: 3 JKL, PRS, WXY 4 oper.
tu-whit tu-__: 4 whoo
tuxedo: 4 coat, suit 6 formal, jacket 8 black tie 10 formal wear, monkey suit
accessory: 6 bowtie 10 cummerbund
junction: 4 seam
occasion: 4 prom 7 wedding
wearer: 5 groom
tuxedo __: 4 sofa 5 couch
Tuxpam: 4 city, town
locale: 6 Mexico 8 Veracruz
Tuxpan: 4 city, town
locale: 6 Mexico 7 Jalisco, Nayarit
Tuxtepec: 4 city, town
locale: 6 Mexico, Oaxaca
Tuxtla: 4 city, town
locale: 6 Mexico 8 Veracruz
Tuzla: 4 city, town
locale: 6 Bosnia
TV: 3 set 4 tube 5 telly 7 console, monitor 8 boob tube, idiot box 9 goggle box
adjunct: 3 VCR 4 dish 5 cable 6 aerial 7 antenna 9 DVD player 10 rabbit ears
band: 3 UHF, VHF
big week in ~: 6 sweeps
cartoon: 6 kidcom
children's ~: 6 kidvid
commercial: 2 ad 4 advt., spot
fare: 4 film, news, soap, talk 5 drama, movie 6 series, sitcom 7 cartoon 8 game show 9 soap opera
feature: 6 stereo
former ~ network: 6 Dumont
free ~ ad: 3 PSA
knob: 3 hor., vol. 4 dial, tint, vert 5 tuner 8 vertical 10 horizontal
listing abbr.: 3 TBA
monitoring device: 5 V-chip
network: 3 ABC, CBC, CBS, Fox, NBC, PBS, UPN
networks: 5 media
news hour: 3 six, ten 5 six p.m., ten p.m. 6 eleven 8 eleven p.m.
not edited for ~: 5 uncut
nuisance: 4 snow
on ~: 6 airing 7 running 8 telecast 9 broadcast
on-the-spot ~ report: 4 nemo
overseer: 3 FCC
part: 3 CRT 4 tube 5 diode, tuner 6 screen
part of ~: 4 tele 6 vision
part of a ~ broadcast: 5 audio, video
pay ~: 5 cable
premiere season: 4 fall
put on ~: 3 air 9 broadcast
record label in ~ ads: 4 K-Tel
remote control: 4 nemo
remote-control button: 4 mute 6 volume 7 channel
reporter: 6 anchor
room: 3 den
show on ~ again: 5 reair
signal receiver: 4 dish
statuette: 4 Emmy
studio need: 4 mike 6 camera 10 microphone
studio sign: 5 on air
summer ~ fare: 5 rerun
tower: 4 mast
tube filler: 5 xenon
watch, as a ~ show: 6 have on
TV __: 5 print, table 6 dinner
__ TV: 4 spot 5 cable, Court 7 console
__-TV: 3 pay
TVA
part of ~: 4 Auth., Tenn. 6 Valley 9 Authority, Tennessee
product: 3 pwr. 4 elec. 5 power 11 electricity
project: 3 dam
TV-14: 6 rating
TV-G: 6 rating
TV Guide: 3 mag 8 magazine
abbr.: 3 TBA
onetime ~ reviewer: 5 Amory
span: 4 week
TV Land alternative: 3 BET, CMT, MTV, PAX, TBS, TLC, TNN, TNT, USA 4 ESPN 5 A and E, C-SPAN, Style 6 Noggin 7 Ovation, SoapNet 8 Lifetime 11 Nickelodeon
TV-M: 6 rating
TV-PG: 6 rating
TV-Y: 6 rating
twa: 3 two 8 Scottish
preceder: 3 ane
TWA: 7 airline
airline bought by ~: 5 Ozark
airline that bought ~: 8 American
part of ~: 5 Trans, World 8 Airlines
twaddle: 3 gas, pap, rot, yak 4 blah, bosh, bull, bunk, guff, jazz, jive, pooh, tosh 5 bilge, fudge, hokum, hooey, prate, stuff, trash, tripe 6 bunkum, bushwa, drivel, footle, gabble, gammon, gibber, havers, hot air, humbug, jabber, jargon, kibosh, piffle 7 baloney, blarney, blather, blether, boloney, bushwah, chatter, eyewash, flannel, flubdub, fustian, garbage, hogwash, inanity, malarky, prattle, rubbish 8 buncombe, claptrap, falderal, falderol, flimflam, flummery, folderal, folderol, malarkey, nonsense, slipslop, tommyrot, trumpery 9 banana oil, gibberish, goofiness, kidstakes, moonshine, poppycock, rigmarole 10 applesauce, balderdash, bilge water, codswallop, double-talk, flapdoodle, galimatias, Jabberwock, mumbo jumbo, rigamarole, taradiddle
twain: 3 duo, two 4 both, pair 6 couple
Twain: 4 Mark 6 Shania
Twain, Mark: 6 author, writer 8 humorist
work: The Celebrated Jumping Frog of Calaveras County
A Connecticut Yankee in King Arthur's Court
Following the Equator
Huckleberry Finn
The Innocents Abroad
The Prince and the Pauper
Pudd'nhead Wilson
Roughing It
Tom Sawyer
Twain, Shania: 6 singer
born: Eileen Edwards
homeland: Canada
song: From This Moment On (1998)
That Don't Impress Me Much (1999)
You're Still the One (1998)
twang: 5 drawl, pluck, plunk 6 accent 8 localism, nasality
twangy: 5 nasal
__ T. Washington: 6 Booker
'Twas the __ before Christmas...: 5 night
tweak: 3 nip, rag 4 pull, twit 5 annoy, pinch, pluck, tease, twist 6 adjust, modify 7 jerk out 8 fine-tune 10 adjustment
target: 4 nose 7 schnozz 10 schnozzola
twee: 8 bird call
tweed: 6 fabric 8 material

like ~: 5 nubby 6 coarse
wearer: 6 preppy 7 preppie
__ tweed: 5 Irish 6 Harris 7 Donegal
Tweed: 4 Boss 5 river 7 Shannon, William
locale: 7 England 8 Scotland
nemesis: 4 Nast
river to the ~: 6 Yarrow
Tweedle Dee (1955 song) artist: Georgia Gibbs
Tweedlee Dee (1955 song) artist: LaVern Baker
tweeds: 5 pants
'tween: 5 'twixt 7 amongst 9 youngster
tweet: 4 call, peep, pipe, sing 5 cheep, chirp 7 chitter, twitter 8 bird call
Tweety: 4 bird
home: 4 cage
Twelfth __: 3 Day 5 Night
Twelfth Night author: William Shakespeare
character: 4 Toby 5 Belch, Feste, Maria, Viola 6 Olivia, Orsino 9 Toby Belch
Twelfth of Never (song), The artist: Donny Osmond, Johnny Mathis
twelve: 4 noon 5 dozen 6 midday 8 high noon, meridian, midnight, noontime
combining form: 5 dodec- 6 dodeca-
dozen: 5 gross
every ~ months: 4 yrly. 6 yearly
months: 4 year
one of ~: 5 juror, month
twelve-__ guitar: 6 string
twelve-__ limit: 4 mile
Twelve __: 4 Oaks
Twelve Chairs, The (1970 film)
cast: Dom DeLuise, Frank Langella, Ron Moody
director: Mel Brooks
Twelve Days of Christmas gift: 5 birds, lords, maids, rings, swans 6 ladies, pipers 8 drummers, pear tree 9 gold rings, partridge 10 French hens 11 turtledoves 12 calling birds
Twelve Little Preludes composer: 4 Bach
Twelve Monkeys (1995 film)
cast: Brad Pitt, Christopher Plummer, Madeleine Stowe, Bruce Willis
director: Terry Gilliam
twelvemonth: 4 year
Twelve Oaks neighbor: 4 Tara
Twelve O'Clock High (1949 film)
cast: Hugh Marlowe, Gary Merrill, Gregory Peck
director: Henry King
org.: 4 USAF
twelve-string __: 6 guitar
Twelve Thirty (1967 song) artist: Mamas & the Papas
Twelvetrees: 5 Helen
__ Twenties: 7 Roaring
Twentieth Century (1934 film)
cast: John Barrymore, Walter Connolly, Carole Lombard
director: Howard Hawks
twenty: 5 score
change for a ~: 4 ones, tens 5 fives
combining form: 4 icos- 5 eicos-, icosa-, icosi- 6 eicosa-
give ~ lashes: 4 cane, drub, whip 5 flail 6 larrup 7 scourge 10 flagellate
twenty-__ seven: 4 four
twenty-first century: 3 new 5 fresh, novel 6 latest, modern, modish, recent, timely, with-it 7 current, topical 8 up-to-date 10 avant-garde, modernized, present-day
twenty-four
carat: 4 pure 7 sincere 8 rightful
one of ~: 4 hour
Twenty Four Hours from Tulsa (1963 song) artist: Gene Pitney
twenty lashes with __ noodle: 4 a wet
Twenty-Mule __ Borax: 4 Team
twenty-one: 4 game 7 pontoon 8 card game 9 blackjack, vingt-et-un
words: 5 hit me
Twenty Questions
category: 6 animal 7 mineral 9 vegetable
reply: 2 no 3 yes
twenty-six, all: 4 A to Z
Twenty Thousand Leagues Under the Sea: 5 novel
author: Jules Verne
character: 3 Ned 4 Land, Nemo 6 Pierre 7 Aronnax, Conseil, Ned Land
twenty-twenty __: 6 vision
Twenty Years After author: Alexandre Dumas (père)
Twenty Years on Broadway autobiographer: 5 Cohan
't weren't nothin': 6 shucks
twerp: 4 jerk, nerd, nurd, pest, punk, wimp 5 creep, dweeb 6 nudnik, squirt 7 nebbish 9 pipsqueak
twi-__ doubleheader: 5 night
Twi: 8 language
twice: 3 bis 5 again 6 doubly
combining form: 2 bi-
halved: 4 once
in music: 3 bis
think ~: 5 pause 7 scruple 8 reassess 10 reconsider
thinking ~: 7 careful, prudent
twice-__: 4 born, laid, told
__ twice: 5 think
Twice in a Lifetime (1985 film)
cast: Ann-Margret, Ellen Burstyn, Gene Hackman
director: Bud Yorkin
Twice Shy author: Dick Francis
twice-told: 3 old
Twice-Told Tales: 4 book, film
author: Nathaniel Hawthorne
cast: Sebastian Cabot, Vincent Price
twiddle one's thumbs: 4 idle, laze 5 shirk 6 lounge 7 goof off, sit back 8 malinger, mark time, slack off 9 do nothing
twig: 4 limb, stem, wand 5 shoot, sprig, stick 8 offshoot
broom: 5 besom
willow ~: 5 withe
twiggy: 4 lank, lean, slim, thin, wiry 5 lanky, spare 6 dainty, gangly, skinny, slight, slinky, svelte 7 gracile, scraggy, scrawny, slender, spidery, willowy 8 gangling 9 sylphlike
Twiggy: 5 model 6 Lawson
emulate ~: 3 sit 4 pose 5 model
real name: Lesley Hornby
twiglike
see twiggy
twigs: 4 wood 6 tinder 8 firewood, kindling
twilight: 3 ebb, e'en, end 4 dusk, soft 5 gloam, night 6 sunset 7 decline, evening, sundown 8 eventide, gloaming 9 afterglow, nightfall, nighttime
like ~: 5 dusky
turn to ~: 6 darken
twilight __: 4 glow, zone 5 sleep
Twilight (1998 film)
cast: Gene Hackman, Paul Newman, Susan Sarandon, Reese Witherspoon
director: Robert Benton
Twilight __: 4 Eyes, Time, Zone
Twilight __ Gods, The: 5 of the
Twilight band: 3 ELO
Twilight Eyes author: Dean Koontz
Twilight in Italy author: D.H. Lawrence
Twilight Time (1958 song) artist: Platters
Twilight Zone (song) artist: Golden Earring, Manhattan Transfer
Twilight Zone, The (CBS sci-fi)
host: Rod Serling
like ~: 4 eery 5 eerie
twilit: 3 dim 4 dark, gray 5 dusky, murky 7 shadowy 9 unlighted
twill fabric: 5 chino, denim, serge 6 coburg, coutil, oxford 7 Cheviot, estamin, foulard, hickory, nankeen, silesia, Viyella 8 canotier, casimere, casimire, moleskin, prunella, prunelle, prunello, shalloon, Venetian 9 bombazeen, bombazine, cassimere, gabardine, henrietta, paramatta, sharkskin 10 broadcloth
twin: 3 bed 4 dual, mate, same 5 clone, match, sosie 6 double, duplex, ringer, second 7 brother, similar, twofold 8 matching, selfsame 9 duplicate, facsimile, identical, look-alike 10 dead ringer
Biblical ~: 4 Esau 5 Jacob
identical ~: 5 sosie
mythical: 5 Remus 7 Romulus
name meaning ~: 6 Thomas
twin __: 3 bed 4 bill, room 7 killing
twin-__: 4 size
twin-__ camera: 4 lens
twin-__ plane: 6 engine
__ twin: 7 Siamese
Twin
Hall of Famer: 5 Carew 7 Puckett 8 Rod Carew 9 Killebrew
rival: 3 Cub, Met, Red 4 Expo 5 Angel, Astro, Brave, Giant, Padre, Rocky, Royal, Tiger 6 Brewer, Dodger, Indian, Marlin, Oriole, Philly, Pirate, Ranger, Red Sox, Yankee 7 Blue Jay, Mariner 8 Athletic, Cardinal, Devil Ray, White Sox
Twin __: 5 Peaks 6 Cities
Twin City: 6 St. Paul 11 Minneapolis
suburb: 5 Eagan, Edina
twine: 4 bend, coil, cord, curl, lace, loop, rope, wind, wrap, yarn 5 dance, twist, weave 6 enlace, enmesh, immesh, inlace, inmesh, lacing, strand, string, thread 7 cordage, meander, sinuate, wreathe 8 encircle, entangle, filament, undulate 9 corkscrew, interlace, interwind 10 interweave
material: 4 jute 5 ramee, ramie, sisal
nautical ~: 7 marline
twin-engine: 5 plane 8 airplane
Twin Falls: 4 city, town
locale: 5 Idaho
twinge: 3 tic 4 ache, kink, pain, pang, stab 5 cramp, crick, pinch, prick, qualm, smart, spasm, throb, throe 6 injury, misery, stitch, twitch 7 scruple
twining plant: 4 bine 5 vetch
Twinings: 3 tea
alternative: 6 Lipton, Nestea, Salada, Tetley 7 Bigelow, Red Rose
twinkle: 4 glow, wink 5 blink, flash, gleam, glint, shine 6 glance 7 flicker, glimmer, glisten, glitter, light up, shimmer, sparkle 9 coruscate
it may ~: 3 eye
twinkler: 4 star
twinkle-toed: 4 spry 5 agile 6 nimble
Twinkle, Twinkle, Little __: 4 Star
twinkling: 4 jiff, tick, wink 5 jiffy, trice 6 minute, moment, second 7 instant
in the ~ of an eye: 7 quickly
twin-lens __: 6 camera
Twin Peaks: 4 soap 9 soap opera
character: 4 Dale, Pete 5 Harry, Josie, Laura, Sarah 6 Cooper, Leland, Palmer, Truman 7 Packard
creator: David Lynch
network: 3 ABC
setting: 5 Idaho
twins: 3 duo 4 pair
__ twins: 7 Bobbsey
Twins: 3 ten 4 sign, team 6 Gemini
home: 4 Minn. 9 Minnesota
month: 3 Jun., May 4 June
org.: 3 ALC, MLB
predecessor: 4 Bull
sport: 8 baseball
successor: 4 Crab
Twins (1988 film)
cast: Danny DeVito, Kelly Preston, Arnold Schwarzenegger
cat: 6 Julius
director: Ivan Reitman
twin-size __: 3 bed
Twin Sombreros author: Zane Grey
twiny: 6 clingy 10 meandering
twirl: 4 coil, curl, loop, reel, roll, spin, turn, wave, wind 5 pivot, swing, twist, wheel 6 gyrate, rotate 7 revolve, sinuate 8 gyration 9 pirouette
__ twirler: 5 baton
twirling: 8 gyration, rotation 10 revolution
twirp: 4 jerk, nerd, nurd, pest, punk, wimp 5 dweeb 6 nudnik, squirt 7 nebbish 9 pipsqueak
twist: 3 arc, ply 4 bend, bias, coif, coil, curl, hank, jerk, jink, kink, knot, loaf, loop, pull, roll, ruse, skew, spin, turn, veer, warp, wind, wisp, yank, yarn 5 braid, color, curve, dance, helix, knead, mix-up, quirk, screw, slant, snake, snarl, tweak, twine, twirl, weave, whirl, wring 6 deform, enlace, garble, hairdo, inlace, oddity, pastry, ramble, rotate, scheme, spiral, sprain, squirm, strain, swivel, tangle, volute, wiggle, wrench, writhe, zigzag 7 contort, distort, entwine, falsify, intwine, meander, revolve, sinuate, torsion, wreathe, wriggle, wrinkle 8 coiffure, curlicue, curlycue, jaundice, misquote, misstate 9 corkscrew, sinuosity, variation 10 intertwine, interweave, wrap around
around one's little finger: 3 use 6 misuse 7 control 10 manipulate
in the wind: 4 hang 6 dangle 7 draggle
of fate: 4 luck 5 fluke, quirk 8 fortuity
one's arm: 4 make 5 force 6 coerce, compel, lean on 8 browbeat, bulldoze, pressure 10 bear down on
relative: 4 frug
the truth: 3 con, fib, lie 4 bull, dupe, fake, hoax, sham, snow 5 bluff, fudge, libel, put on 6 delude, invent, malign 7 deceive, distort, falsify, mislead, perjure, slander 8 misguide, misstate 9 disinform, dissemble, misinform 10 equivocate, exaggerate
violently: 3 pry 5 wrest, wring 6 snatch, wrench
__ twist: 3 air 4 full, half 6 French
__-twist: 3 arm
Twist: 6 Oliver
__ Twist Again: 4 Let's
Twist and Shout (1964 song) artist: Beatles
twisted: 3 wry 4 awry, bent, vile, wove 5 askew, bandy, curly, kinky, snaky, wound, wrung 6 gnarly, matted, skewed, zigzag 7 crooked, knotted 8 depraved, tortuous 9 malformed
combining form: 5 plect- 6 plecto-, strept- 7 strepsi-, strepto-
Twisted Thing, The author: Mickey Spillane

twister: 4 wind 5 storm 7 cyclone, tornado 9 hurricane, whirlwind
__ twister: 3 arm 6 tongue
Twister (1996 film)
  cast: Cary Elwes, Helen Hunt, Bill Paxton
  director: Jan De Bont
  dog: 4 Toby 5 Moose
twisting: 4 wavy 5 snaky 6 aswirl, zigzag 7 crooked, sinuous, winding 8 flexuous, tortuous 10 serpentine
  arm ~: 8 coercion, pressure
  combining form: 6 stroph- 7 stropho-
Twistin' the Night Away (1962 song)
  artist: Sam Cooke
twist of __: 4 fate
twist-off __: 3 cap
__ Twist of Faith, A: 6 Simple
Twist of Fate (1983 song) artist: Olivia Newton-John
Twist, Oliver request: 4 more
twist one's __: 3 arm
twists: 10 ins and outs
Twist, The (1960 song) artist: Chubby Checker
twit: 3 ass, guy, rag, rib 4 bait, dolt, fool, gibe, hoot, jeer, jibe, mock, razz 5 roast, scorn, sneer, taunt, tease, tweak 6 berate, deride, dimwit, gibe at, needle, nudnik, rebuke 7 burlesk, catcall, censure, contemn, lampoon, upbraid 8 brickbat, reproach, ridicule, satirize 9 birdbrain, burlesque, make fun of, poke fun at, raspberry 10 nincompoop
twitch: 3 tic, wag 4 jerk, jump, kick, pain, pull, yank 5 blink, spasm, start 6 jiggle, quaver, quiver, shiver, squirm, twinge, wiggle 7 flutter, shudder, tremble, wriggle 9 vellicate
twitchy: 4 edgy 5 itchy, jumpy, tense 6 on edge, pacing, uneasy 7 anxious, fidgety, jittery, nervous, ruffled 8 agitated, fluttery, restless 9 excitable, flustered, irritable, tremulous 10 hysterical
twite: 4 bird 5 finch
Twits, The author: Roald Dahl
twitter: 4 flap, peep, pipe 5 cheep, chirp 6 lather, tingle 7 shudder 8 bird call
Twittering Machine, The artist: 4 Klee
Twitty, Conway
  born: Harold Jenkins
  song: Danny Boy (1959)
    It's Only Make Believe (1958)
    Lonely Blue Boy (1960)
Twix: 5 candy 9 chocolate
  alternative: 4 Mars 5 Clark, Heath 6 Kit Kat, Mounds, PayDay, Reese's, Zagnut 7 Krackel, Oh Henry 8 Baby Ruth, Hershey's, Milky Way, Snickers 9 Almond Joy, Mr. Goodbar 10 NutRageous
'twixt: 3 'mid 4 amid 5 among, 'tween 6 amidst, mongst 7 amongst, between
  partner: 5 'tween
  something ~ cup and lip: 4 slip
Twizzlers: 5 candy 8 licorice
two: 3 duo 4 duad, duet, dyad, pair 5 brace, deuce, twain 6 couple, number 7 couplet, doublet, wee hour
  bits: 7 quarter
  break in ~: 5 halve, sever 6 bisect 8 separate 9 intersect
  cents' worth: 3 tip 4 view 6 advice, tipoff 7 comment 9 viewpoint
  combining form: 2 bi- 3 bin-, bis-, duo-, dyo-, twi-
  cubed: 5 eight
  divisible by ~: 4 even
  easy ~ points: 5 lay-up
  ender: 3 fer 4 some 5 pence, penny
  for ~: 4 dual 5 a deux
  for ~ musically: 4 a due
  halves: 4 buck 5 whole 6 dollar, single 7 one-spot, smacker 8 simoleon
  in ~: 5 apart, cleft, split 6 halved 7 asunder, divided 9 separated
  in French: 4 deux
  in German: 4 zwei
  in Italian: 3 due
  in Portuguese: 4 dois
  in Scottish: 3 twa
  in ~ shakes of a lamb's tail: 3 now 4 soon 6 at once, in a sec, pronto 7 hastily, quickly, rapidly, shortly 8 directly, promptly, right now, speedily 9 forthwith, in a minute, in a second, right away 10 this moment
  in Spanish: 3 dos
  it takes ~: 5 tango
  not divisible by ~: 3 odd
  number ~: 2 VP 4 veep 6 veepee
  of a kind: 4 pair, same 5 alike 9 identical 10 synonymous
  of ~ minds: 4 torn 8 wavering 9 undecided 10 ambivalent, indecisive, on the fence
  one of ~: 6 either
  one or ~: 3 few 4 a few 5 scant 6 meager, paltry 7 handful, limited 9 hardly any
  put one's ~ cents in: 3 pry 4 poke 6 butt in, horn in, kibitz, meddle, worm in 7 barge in, break in, chime in, intrude, obtrude 9 interfere
  put two and ~ together: 3 add 5 solve 9 figure out, puzzle out
  second of ~: 6 latter
  song for ~: 4 duet
  the ~: 4 both
  times: 3 dbl. 5 twice 6 double
  to Mohs: 6 gypsum
  turn ~ into eight: 4 cube
  worth ~ thumbs down: 3 bad 5 gross, lousy 7 beastly, ghastly, ungodly 8 dreadful, horrible, horrific, terrible 9 appalling, atrocious, frightful, revolting 10 abominable, deplorable, disgusting, horrendous
two __: 4 bits, o' cat, pair
two __ kind: 3 of a
two __ of a lamb's tail: 6 shakes
two __ time: 3 at a
two __ worth: 5 cents
two-__: 3 bit, ply 4 a-cat, beat, fold, shot, spot, step, tier, tone 5 color, cycle, edged, faced, phase, sided, track 6 bagger, fisted, handed, master, seater, suiter, timing 7 wheeler
two-__ conversion: 5 point
two-__ general: 4 star
two-__ hit: 4 base
two-__ house: 6 family
two-__ paper towels: 3 ply
two-__ sloth: 4 toed
two-__ street: 3 way
two-__ suit: 5 piece
two-__ system: 5 party
two-__ warning: 6 minute
Two __: 3 Men 5 Ninas, Women 6 Hearts, Lovers 7 Princes, Sisters
Two __ Before the Mast: 5 Years
Two __ for Sister Sara: 5 Mules
Two __ People: 6 Sleepy
Two __ Souls: 4 Lost
Two __, The: 5 Jakes 7 Thieves
Two __ the Road: 3 for
Two __ the Seesaw: 3 for
Two-__ Woman: 5 Faced
__ Two: 7 Chapter
__ two and two together: 3 put
Two Arabian Knights (1927 film)
  cast: Mary Astor, William Boyd, Louis Wolheim
  director: Lewis Milestone
__ two aspirin...: 4 Take
two at __: 5 a time
two-bagger: 3 dbl. 6 double
two-base __: 3 hit
two-bit: 4 puny 5 cheap, lousy, minor, petty 8 inferior, picayune
__, two, buckle my shoe: 3 One
two-by-four: 4 beam
two-by-twelve: 5 plank
Two by Two: 7 musical
  composer: 7 Rodgers
  role: 4 Noah
  star: Danny Kaye
two-by-two vessel: 3 ark
two cents __: 5 worth
two-dimensional: 4 flat 5 plane 6 planar
  measure: 4 area
  not ~: 5 solid
  of ~ space: 5 areal
Two Doors Down (1978 song) artist: Dolly Parton
Two Duchesses author: Emile Zola
two-face: 9 hypocrite
two-faced: 5 false, lying, snaky 6 rotten, untrue 7 corrupt, unloyal 8 disloyal, recreant 9 deceitful, deceptive, faithless, insincere, underhand, unethical 10 traitorous, unfaithful
Two-Faced Woman (1941 film)
  cast: Constance Bennett, Melvyn Douglas, Greta Garbo, Roland Young
  director: George Cukor
Two-Face foe: 6 Batman
Two Faces Have I (1963 song) artist: Lou Christie
two-family __: 5 house
two-finger sign: 3 vee
two-fisted: 5 macho, tough
two fives for __: 4 a ten
twofold: 4 dual, twin 5 binal, duple 6 binary, binate, double, doubly, duplex 9 duplicate
two-footer: 5 biped
Two for the Road (1967 film)
  cast: Albert Finney, Audrey Hepburn
  director: Stanley Donen
Two for the Seesaw (1962 film)
  cast: Shirley MacLaine, Robert Mitchum, Edmond Ryan
  director: Robert Wise
Two Gentlemen of Verona: 4 play 6 comedy
  author: William Shakespeare
  character: 5 Julia, Speed 6 Launce, Silvia, Thurio 7 Antonio, Lucetta, Proteus 8 Eglamour, Panthino 9 Valentine
  dog: 4 Crab
  setting: 5 Italy
Two Girls and a Sailor (1944 film)
  cast: June Allyson, Gloria De Haven, Van Johnson
  director: Richard Thorpe
__ two hats: 4 wear
Two Hearts (1988 song) artist: Phil Collins
Two hearts that beat __: 5 as one
Two Hundred Motels director: 5 Zappa
...two if __: 5 by sea
Two Jakes, The (1990 film)
  cast: Harvey Keitel, Jack Nicholson, Madeleine Stowe, Meg Tilly
  director: Jack Nicholson
two-l ___, The: 5 llama
Two-Lane Blacktop (1971 film)
  cast: Laurie Bird, Warren Oates, James Taylor
two left __: 4 feet
two-letter sequence: 6 digram
Two Lost Souls (1955 song) artist: Jaye P. Morgan
two-masted vessel: 4 brig, yawl 5 ketch
Two Men author: Edward Arlington Robinson
two mints in one: 5 Certs
two-minute __: 7 warning
Two Mules for Sister Sara (1970 film): 5 oater
  cast: Clint Eastwood, Shirley MacLaine
  director: Don Siegel
Two Ninas (2001 film)
  cast: Cara Buono, Ron Livingston, Amanda Peet, Bray Poor
  director: Neil Turitz
__ & Two Noughts: 4 A Zed
two of __: 5 a kind
Two Out of Three Ain't Bad (1978 song) artist: Meat Loaf
Two owls and ___...: 4 a hen
two-page ad: 6 spread
two-pair, high: 6 aces up
two-part: 4 dual 6 binary, double
  combining form: 5 dicho-
two-party __: 6 system
twopence: 4 coin 5 money 8 currency
two-percent: 4 milk
  alternative: 4 skim
two-person: 4 dual 6 double, paired
two-piece __: 4 suit
two-pointer: 4 hoop 5 score 6 basket
  easy ~: 5 tap-in 10 tip-in. lay-up
__-two punch: 3 one
two-quark particle: 4 pion 7 pi meson
two-reeler: 5 short
two-rod: 6 dipole
two-run homer requirement: 5 one on
twoscore: 5 forty
two-seater: 3 car 4 auto 10 automobile
two shakes __ lamb's tail: 3 of a
two-shilling piece: 6 florin
two-shoes
  goody ~: 4 prig 7 puritan 9 nice Nelly
two-sided: 4 dual 6 duplex 9 bilateral
Two Sisters author: Gore Vidal
Two Sisters From Boston (1946 film)
  cast: June Allyson, Kathryn Grayson, Lauritz Melchior
  director: Henry Koster
twosome: 2 pr. 3 duo 4 duad, duet, dyad, pair, span 5 brace 6 adjoin, couple, daters 7 doublet 9 newlyweds
two-spot: 5 deuce
two-star __: 7 general
two-step: 5 dance, music
two-striper: 3 NCO, PFC
Two Thieves, The author: T.F. Powys
__, Two, Three: 3 One
__, two, three, four: 3 Hup
Two Tickets to Paradise (1978 song)
  artist: Eddie Money
two-time: 4 burn, dupe, fool, have, nick, snow, take 5 cheat, cozen, shaft, trick, wrong 6 delude, sucker, take in 7 beguile, cheat on, deceive, mislead 8 hoodwink 9 bamboozle, victimize 10 double-deal
two-timer: 3 cad 7 traitor 8 turncoat 9 hypocrite
two-timing: 5 false, lying 6 deceit 7 knavish, unloyal 8 disloyal, forsworn, recreant 9 dishonest, faithless, treachery, underhand, unethical 10 inconstant, infidelity, perfidious, traitorous, unfaithful
two-toed sloth: 4 unau
Two-ton __ Galento: 4 Tony
two to one: 4 odds 5 ratio
two-track: 6 stereo
Two Treatises on Government author: John Locke
two-unit: 6 duplex
two-way __: 6 mirror, street
Two Way Stretch (1960 film)
  cast: Wilfrid Hyde-White, Peter Sellers

Two Way Stretch director: 3 Day
Two Weeks in Another Town (1962 film)
cast: Cyd Charisse, Kirk Douglas, Edward G. Robinson
director: Vincente Minnelli
two-wheeled vehicle: 4 cart, dray 5 dolly 6 barrow 8 rickshaw
two-wheeler: 4 bike 5 cycle 7 bicycle
Two Women: 4 film 5 novel
author: Albert Moravia
cast: Jean-Paul Belmondo, Eleanora Brown, Sophia Loren, Raf Vallone
director: Vittorio De Sica
two-year-old: 3 kid, tot 4 tike, tyke
Two Years Before the Mast author: Richard Henry Dana
Twyla: 5 Tharp
Twyman, Jack
milieu: 5 court
org.: 3 NBA
sport: 10 basketball
TX
see Texas
Ty: 4 Cobb 6 Hardin
contemporary: 4 Babe, Tris
Tybee Island: 4 city, town
locale: 7 Georgia
Tycho: 5 Brahe 6 crater
tycoon: 4 boss, king 5 baron, mogul, nabob, nawab 6 fat cat 7 big shot, magnate 8 big wheel, director 9 executive, financier 10 capitalist
home: 5 manor 6 estate 7 mansion
Tycoon author: Harold Robbins
__ Tycoon, The: 4 Last
Ty-D-__: 3 Bol
tye: 4 rope 5 chain
Tyger, The author: William Blake
tyke: 3 imp, tad, tot 5 child, wee 'un, youth 6 moppet 7 toddler 9 little boy, youngster
Tylenol: 9 analgesic, ibuprofen 10 painkiller
alternative: 3 APF 4 Cope 5 Advil, Aleve, Bayer 6 Anacin, Datril, Motrin 7 Ecotrin 8 Bufferin, Excedrin, St. Joseph, Vanquish 9 Ascriptin
target: 4 ache
unit: 5 table 6 caplet
Tyler: 3 Liv 4 Anne, city, John, Judy, town 6 Bonnie 7 Collins
locale: 5 Texas
Tyler, Anne: 6 author, writer
work: The Accidental Tourist
Back When We Were Grownups
Breathing Lessons
Celestial Navigation
The Clock Winder
Dinner at the Homesick Restaurant
Earthly Possessions
If Morning Ever Comes
Ladder of Years
Morgan's Passing
Patchwork Planet
Saint Maybe
Searching for Caleb
A Slipping-Down Life
Tin Can Tree
Tyler, Bonnie
homeland: Wales
song: Holding Out for a Hero (1984)
It's a Heartache (1978)
Total Eclipse of the Heart (1983)
Tyler, John: 9 president
home: 8 Virginia
predecessor: 8 Harrison
successor: 4 Polk
wife: 5 Julia 7 Letitia
Tyler, Liv: 7 actress
film: Armageddon (1998)
Cookie's Fortune (1999)
Heavy (1996)
The Lord of the Rings: The Fellowship of The Ring (2001)
One Night at McCool's (2001)
Stealing Beauty (1996)
that thing you do! (1996)
__ Tyler Moore: 4 Mary
Tylo: 6 Hunter
tympanic __: 4 bone
tympanum: 4 drum
Tynan, Joe portrayer: Alan Alda
Tyndall: 4 John, peak 5 mount 8 mountain
locale: 10 California
Tyndall, John: 9 physicist, scientist
Tyndareus' wife: 4 Leda
Tyne: 4 Daly 5 river
ender: 5 mouth
locale: 7 England 8 Scotland
Tynemouth: 4 city, port, town
locale: 7 England
type: 3 ilk, peg 4 cast, copy, font, form, kind, mold, norm, rank, sign, sort 5 brand, breed, class, genre, genus, group, input, likes, model, order, print, stamp, style 6 assort, kidney, letter, manner, nature 7 dash off, epitome, italics, pattern, put down, species, variety 8 category, classify, exemplar, paradigm, printing, specimen 9 character 10 persuasion, pigeonhole, transcribe
assortment: 4 font
ender: 3 set 4 cast, face 5 style, write 6 script, setter, writer
starter: 3 tin 4 logo, tele 6 stereo
style: 5 agate 6 Italic 7 Italics
typewriter ~: 4 pica 5 elite 7 courier
widths: 3 ems, ens
type __: 5 genus, metal, style 7 founder, section, species
type-__: 4 cast, high, site, word 6 caster
__ type: 3 hot 4 body, cold, wild 5 blood, ideal, not my 7 display, foundry, movable, primary
__-type: 5 large, touch
typecast: 4 sort, type 10 categorize
Typee author: Herman Melville
sequel: 4 Omoo
typeface: 4 City, Elan, font, Pica, Saga, Skia, Zeal 5 Abadi, Aldus, Arial, Basel, Bembo, Boton, Dante, Delta, Devin, Didot, Dutch, Elite, Emona, Gamma, Goudy, Imago, Kabel, Kalix, Norma, print, Romic, Sabon, Savoy, Swiss, Weiss, Wilke 6 Aldine, Amasis, Apollo, Auriol, Avenir, Batang, Bodoni, Bulmer, Caslon, Catull, Caxton, Cerigo, Cooper, Corona, Cosmos, Delima, Dialog, Esprit, Fenice, Futura, Gareth, Geneva, Glypha, Gothic, Guardi, Joanna, Legacy, Lucida, Maxima, Melior, Minion, Modern, Monaca, Myriad, Nofret, Odense, Optima, Orator, Praxis, Quorum, Romana, Serifa, Syndor, Syntax, Tahoma, Utopia, Zurich 7 Amerigo, Barmeno, Bauhaus, Bergamo, Berling, Bookman, Calisto, Candida, Centaur, Century, Courier, Cremona, Cushing, Diotima, Electra, Formata, Korinna, Leawood, Matisse, Memphis, Origami, Pacella, Panache, Peignot, Photina, Plantin, Poetica, Present, Sassoon, Shannon, Spartan, Tiepolo, Tiffany, Univers, Vectora, Verdana, Walbaum 8 Broadway, Caecilia, Cantoria, Carniola, Compacta, Concorde, Fournier, Frutiger, Galliard, Garamond, Giovanni, Hadriano, Meridien, Minister, Novarese, Palatino, Perpetua, Rockwell, Slimbach, Souvenir 9 Helvetica 10 Avant Garde, Times Roman
detail: 5 serif
option: 4 bold 7 Italics 9 underline
type metal: 5 alloy
component: 3 tin 4 lead 8 antimony
typesetter: 10 compositor
boo-boos: 6 errata
line: 6 em dash, en dash
org.: 3 ITU
short last line: 5 widow
typewriter
accessory: 6 eraser
key: 3 Tab 5 Shift 8 Caps Lock
name: 5 Smith 6 Corona
part: 3 key 5 spool 6 ribbon
sound: 5 clack, click
symbol: 5 brace, colon, comma, paren., slash 6 equals 7 bracket, percent, virgule 8 asterisk 9 ampersand, pound sign, semicolon 10 equals sign 11 parenthesis
type: 4 pica 5 elite
Typewriter, The composer: 8 Anderson
Typhoid __: 4 Mary
typhon: 4 horn
typhoon: 4 blow, wind 7 tempest 9 hurricane
Typhoon author: Joseph Conrad
typic: 7 regular 8 symbolic 10 emblematic, figurative, indicative
typical: 3 avg. 5 ideal, model, stock, usual 6 common, normal, wonted 7 average, classic, general, natural, regular, routine 8 everyday, expected, habitual, ordinary, orthodox, standard 9 customary, essential, prevalent 10 accustomed, emblematic, legitimate, prevailing
preceder: 5 proto
suffix: 3 -ish
typically: 5 about 6 mainly, mostly 7 as a rule, largely, roughly, usually 8 by nature 9 generally, naturally, on average, primarily, regularly 10 on the whole, ordinarily
Typical Male (1986 song) artist: Tina Turner
typification: 5 ideal, model 7 epitome, essence, paragon 8 exemplar 9 archetype 10 apotheosis, embodiment
typify: 5 sum up 6 embody, imbody, mirror 7 suggest 8 stand for 9 adumbrate, epitomize, exemplify, personify, represent 10 illustrate
typist: 9 secretary
colleague: 5 clerk, steno
need: 6 eraser
output: 3 wds. 4 memo 5 words
stat.: 3 wpm
typo: 4 flaw, slip 5 error 7 erratum, mistake 8 misprint 10 inaccuracy
typographic flourish: 5 serif
typos: 6 errata
check for ~: 5 proof
make some ~: 3 err
Tyr
son: 4 Odin
Tyra: 5 Banks
tyrannical: 4 firm, hard 5 bossy, cruel, picky, rigid, stern, tough 6 severe 7 austere, Spartan 8 absolute, despotic, dogmatic, exacting, hard-line, imperial, rigorous 9 arbitrary, demanding, draconian, imperious, inclement, stringent, unbending, unsparing 10 autocratic, despotical, dogmatical, inflexible, iron-fisted, iron-handed, no-nonsense, oppressive, peremptory
tyrannically: 4 hard
tyrannize: 4 ride 5 bully, grind 6 hector 7 oppress 8 browbeat, dominate, domineer, keep down 9 dictate to, persecute, trample on 10 boss around, intimidate, lord it over, ride herd on
tyranno ending: 4 saur
Tyrannosaurus __: 3 Rex
tyranny: 7 cruelty, fascism 8 coercion, iron hand, severity 9 autocracy, despotism, oligarchy 10 absolutism, domination, oppression
tyrant: 4 czar, ogre, tsar, tzar 5 bully 6 despot, ramrod 8 autocrat, dictator, martinet 9 oppressor 10 inquisitor
get rid of a ~: 4 oust 5 eject 6 depose, unseat 7 boot out, kick out 8 dethrone 9 overthrow
Tyre: 4 city, port, town
king of ~: 5 Hiram
locale: 7 Lebanon 9 Phoenicia
queen of ~: 5 Elise
Tyree: 4 peak 5 mount 8 mountain
locale: 10 Antarctica
tyro: 3 cub 4 naif, pleb 5 newie, plebe, pupil 6 newbie, novice, rookie 7 amateur, dabbler, learner, new hand, recruit, trainee 8 beginner, initiate, neophyte, newcomer, putterer 9 fledgling, greenhorn, novitiate 10 apprentice, catechumen, dilettante, tenderfoot
like a ~: 3 new 5 green 9 untrained
Tyrol
capital: 9 Innsbruck
garb: 6 dirndl
locale: 4 Alps 7 Austria
river: 4 Isar
song: 5 yodel, yodle
Tyrone: 5 Davis, Power 7 Guthrie
Tyrrhenian Sea
gulf: 5 Gaeta
island: 3 Sar. 6 Lipari 8 Sardinia 9 Stromboli
locale: 5 Italy
port: 6 Naples
river to the ~: 8 Volturno
__ Tyrrhenum: 4 Mare
Tyson: 4 Mike 6 Cicely
Tyson, Cicely: 7 actress
film: Bustin' Loose (1981)
The River Niger (1976)
Sounder (1972)
spouse: Miles Davis
Tyson, Mike: 5 boxer
Holyfield, to ~: 5 rival
milieu: 4 ring
spouse: Robin Givens
Tyus, Wyomia: 6 runner 8 sprinter
Tzara, Tristan movement: 4 Dada
__-tze: 3 Lao
tzetze __: 3 fly
Tzigane composer: 5 Ravel
tzimmes: 4 stew 6 uproar
__-tzu: 3 Lao

u ___: 5 quark
u.: 3 sch. 4 coll., inst.
___-u: 6 double
ü
dots: 6 umlaut
U: 4 elem. 5 ritzy, Thant, vowel 6 letter 7 element, uranium
followers: 3 VWX 4 VWXY 5 VWXYZ
in phonetic alphabet: 7 Uniform
92 for ~: 4 at. no.
preceders: 3 RST 4 QRST 5 PQRST
U ___: 2 Nu 4 bolt, Turn 5 Thant
U ___ Touch This: 4 Can't
U ___ uncle: 4 as in
U-___: 4 boat, Haul, turn
___ U: 5 I Hate, Thank
___-U: 3 non
U2
song: Desire (1988)
Discothèque (1997)
I Still Haven't Found What I'm Looking For (1987)
Mysterious Ways (1991)
One (1992)
Theme From Mission: Impossible (1996)
Where the Streets Have No Names (1987)
With or Without You (1987)
U-571 (2000 film)
cast: Jon Bon Jovi, Harvey Keitel, Matthew McConaughey, Bill Paxton
UAE
group: 4 OPEC 10 Arab League
honcho: 4 amir, emir, Zaid 5 ameer, emeer, sheik 6 shaikh, sheikh
money: 4 fils 6 dirham
neighbor: 4 Oman
part: 4 Arab 5 Dibai, Dubai 6 United 8 Abu Dhabi, Emirates
see also United Arab Emirates
uakari: 6 monkey 7 primate
relative: 3 ape 4 saki, titi 5 chimp, drill, jocko, lemur, loris, magot, orang, potto, shrew 6 aye-aye, baboon, Bandar, galago, gelada, gibbon, grivet, guenon, howler, langur, macaco, rhesus, vervet 7 colobus, gorilla, guereza, hoolock, macaque, sapajou, siamang, tamarin, tarsier 8 bush baby, capuchin, mandrill, mangabey, marmoset, talapoin 9 orangutan 10 Barbary ape, chimpanzee, orangutang
UAL
destination: 3 JFK, LAX, LGA, ORD, SFO
former ~ rival: 3 TWA
see also United
UAR part: 4 Arab 5 Egypt, Syria 6 United 8 Republic
UAW: 5 union
locale: 6 Motown 7 Detroit 8 Michigan
members: 5 labor
product: 3 car, SUV 4 auto 5 coupe, sedan, truck
UB40
song: Can't Help Falling in Love (1993)
Here I Am (1991)
Red Red Wine (1988)
The Way You Do the Things You Do (1990)
Ubangi: 5 river
feeder: 4 Uele
outlet: 5 Congo
Ube: 4 city, town
locale: 5 Hondo, Japan 6 Honshu
Uberaba: 4 city, town
locale: 6 Brazil
Uberto in English: 6 Hubert
ubi ___: 4 sunt 5 supra
ubiety: 8 presence
___ ubique: 5 hic et
ubiquitous: 4 rife 5 broad 7 all-over, popular 9 pervasive, prevalent, universal, worldwide 10 everywhere
ubiquity: 8 presence 9 existence
U-boat: 3 sub 6 vessel
sinker: 6 ashcan 7 torpedo
U-bolt place: 4 door, hasp 5 latch
U-Boot, danger for a: 3 eis
U Can't Touch This (1990 song) artist: M.C. Hammer
Ucayali: 5 river
locale: 4 Peru
UCB conference: 6 Pac-Ten
Uccello: 5 Paolo
UCLA: 3 sch.
athlete: 5 Bruin
group: 4 NCAA 6 Pac-Ten
part of ~: 3 Cal., Los 4 Univ. 7 Angeles
rival: 3 USC
stat: 3 GPA
U. Conn: 3 sch. 4 coll.
conference: 7 Big East
locale: 6 Storrs
Udall, Nicholas school: 4 Eton
udder output: 4 milk
___ Ude: 4 Ulan
Udine: 4 city, town
locale: 5 Italy
udu: 4 drum
origin: 6 Africa
Ueberroth: 5 Peter
Uecker: 3 Bob
Ueda: 4 city, town
locale: 5 Japan
Uele: 5 river
locale: 5 Congo
river to the ~: 4 Bomu 5 Mbomu
U2
members: Bono, Hewson, Evans, Clayton, Mullen
Ufa: 4 city, town
locale: 6 Russia 7 Bashkir
Uffizi contents: 3 art 4 arte
UFO: 8 aircraft
dossier: 5 X file
movies: 5 sci-fi
occupant: 2 ET 3 ETI 5 alien 7 Martian
shape: 4 disk 6 saucer
UFT
member: 4 tchr. 7 teacher
rival: 3 NEA
Uganda: 6 nation 7 country
capital: 7 Kampala
city: 4 Gulu 5 Jinja, Mbale 6 Masaka 7 Entebbe, Kampala
exile: 3 Idi 4 Amin
lake: 5 Kioga, Kyoga 6 Albert, Mobuto 8 Victoria
money: 4 cent 8 shilling
mountain: 5 Elgon
neighbor: 5 Congo, Kenya, Sudan 6 Rwanda 8 Tanzania
people: 7 Turkana
river from ~: 4 Nile
Uggams, Leslie: 6 singer 7 actress
film: Black Girl (1972)
TV: Roots, Sing Along With Mitch
Ugh!: 3 ick 4 yuck 5 gross
ugli: 5 fruit 6 citrus 7 tangelo
relative: 4 lime 5 lemon, navel 6 orange, pomelo, tangor 7 kumquat, satsuma, Seville 8 bergamot, mandarin, shaddock, Valencia 9 tangerine 10 calamondin, grapefruit
ugly: 3 low 4 base, dark, dour, evil, fell, foul, glum, mean, vile 5 angry, awful, black, dirty, grave, gross, major, messy, nasty, pesky, pesty, rough, sorry, surly 6 brutal, crabby, filthy, gloomy, grisly, horrid, morose, odious, sordid, sullen, wicked 7 beastly, crabbed, hideous, ignoble, low-down, noisome, ominous, peevish, serious, servile, squalid, vicious, violent 8 depraved, grievous, horrible, menacing, scowling, shocking, sinister, spiteful, terrible, unseemly, wretched 9 appalling, bellicose, dangerous, execrable, frightful, grotesque, loathsome, monstrous, obnoxious, offensive, repellent, repelling, repugnant, repulsive, revolting, saturnine, troublous, truculent, unsightly, vexatious 10 despicable, disgusting, forbidding, formidable, ill-favored, malevolent, pugnacious, scandalous, uninviting, unpleasant
___ Ugly: 6 Coyote
ugly duckling: 4 swan
Ugly Duckling, The author: Hans Christian Andersen
Ugo: 5 Betti 7 Foscolo 8 Tognazzi
in English: 4 Hugh
U Got the Look (1987 song) artist: Prince
___-Ugrian: 5 Finno
Ugric: 8 language
uh-___: 3 huh
U-Haul: 3 van 5 truck
rival: 5 Ryder
uh cousin: 2 er, um 4 ahem
UHF ___: 7 antenna, channel, station
UHF part: 4 freq., high 5 ultra 9 frequency
uh-huh: 2 ay, da, ja, OK, sí 3 aye, oui, yea, yeh, yep, yes, yup 4 fine, I see, okay, sure, yeah 5 good-o, natch, quite, right, roger 6 agreed, gladly, good-oh, indeed, just so, rather, righto, surely, you bet, yowzah 7 exactly, for sure, go ahead, indeedy, mais oui, quite so, ten-four 8 all right, as you say, of course, thumbs up, very well 9 be my guest, certainly, darn right, naturally, precisely, sure thing, you betcha, you said it 10 absolutely, by all means, definitely, positively, sure enough, that's right
uhlan: 6 lancer 7 dragoon, soldier
Uhland, Johann Ludwig: 4 poet
Uhnak: 7 Dorothy
uh-oh: 4 my-my, oh my, oops, yipe 5 yikes, yipes 6 my oh my, oh dear
uh-uh: 2 no 3 nah, naw, nay, nix, non 4 nein, nope, nyet 5 I won't, ixnay, never, no how, noway 6 no deal, noways, nowise 7 I refuse 8 forget it, I will not, negative, negatory 9 by no means, fat chance, I think not 10 count me out, not a chance, thumbs down
Highlander's ~: 3 nae
Uhuru author: 5 Ruark
Uigur: 4 Turk 8 language
Uinta: 5 range
locale: 4 Utah
mountain: 9 Kings Peak
Uji: 4 city, town
locale: 5 Japan
UK: 7 England
award: 3 GBE, MBE, OBE
carrier of old: 4 BOAC
city: 4 Lond.
clock setting: 3 GMT
defenders: 3 RAF
fast way to the ~: 3 SST
half of the ~: 4 Gr. Br., Gt.Br.
inc. in the ~: 3 ltd.
money, once: 3 LSD, stg.
network: 3 BBC
part of the ~: 3 Eng., Ire. 4 Scot.
party: 3 Lib.
recording company: 3 EMI
religion: 4 Angl.
ruling body: 4 Parl.
S.S. in the ~: 3 HMS
territory: 3 Gib.
title: 3 esq.
VIP: 2 p.m. 4 QE II
see also England, United Kingdom
ukase: 4 fiat, word 5 edict, irade, order 6 decree, ruling 9 directive, ordinance
Ukraine: 6 nation 7 country
city: 4 Kiev, Lvov 5 Lutsk, Odesa, Yalta 6 Odessa 7 Donetsk, Kharkov, Poltava
dance: 5 gopak, hopak 6 trepak
figure skater: 5 Baiul
legislature: 4 Rada
money: 5 ruble 6 rouble
neighbor: 6 Poland, Russia 7 Belarus, Hungary, Moldova, Romania 8 Slovakia
once: 3 SSR
peninsula: 6 Crimea
river: 4 Prut, Seim, Seym 5 Seret, Siret, Tisza 7 Dnieper
Ukrainian: 4 Slav 7 Cossack 8 language
ukulele: 6 string
cousin: 5 banjo 6 guitar
feature: 4 fret, neck
play a ~: 5 pluck, strum, thrum
Ukulele ___: 3 Ike
ula: 4 gums
Ulalume: 4 poem
author: 3 Poe
like the skies in ~: 5 ashen
monogram: 3 EAP
Ulan ___: 3 Ude 5 Bator
Ulan Bator: 4 city, town 7 capital
formerly: 4 Urga
locale: 8 Mongolia
Ulanov: 4 Igor
Ulanova, Galina: 6 dancer 7 Russian 8 danseuse 9 ballerina
Ulan-Ude: 4 city, town
locale: 6 Russia
Ulawun: 7 volcano
locale: 4 Asia
ule: 4 tree 6 caucho, rubber 10 rubber tree
-ule: 3 -kin 4 tiny 5 small, teeny 6 teensy
Ulee's Gold (1997 film)
cast: Jessica Biel, Peter Fonda, Patricia Richardson
ulex: 5 gorse
Ulf: 7 Nilsson 8 von Euler
___ U Like Me Now: 3 How
Ulla: 9 Jacobsson
Ullman: 4 Norm 6 Tracey
Ullmann, Liv: 7 actress 9 Norwegian
film: Autumn Sonata (1978)
Cries and Whispers (1972)
Faithless (2000)
Gaby-A True Story (1987)
The Passion of Anna (1969)
Persona (1966)
Scenes From a Marriage (1973)
Shame (1968)
Ullman, Tracey: 7 actress
film: Household Saints (1993)
Panic (2000)
Small Time Crooks (2000)
song: They Don't Know (1984)
Ullsten: 3 Ola
Ulm: 4 city, town
locale: 7 Germany
river: 6 Danube
ulna: 4 bone
locale: 3 arm 7 forearm
neighbor: 6 radius

ulnar: 5 nerve
ulp: 4 gasp
Ulrich: 5 Skeet
ulster: 4 coat 6 jacket 7 topcoat 8 overcoat 9 outerwear
ulterior: 4 dark 6 buried, covert, future, hidden, secret, unsaid, unseen 7 cryptic, obscure, selfish 8 obscured, personal, shrouded 9 concealed, cryptical, enigmatic, equivocal, invisible, secondary 10 undercover, under wraps, undivulged, unrevealed
  motive: 4 plan, wile 6 agenda, design, reason, scheme
ultima ___: 5 Thule
ultimate: 3 end, max, nth 4 best, last, most 5 basic, final, ideal, limit, prime 6 far-out, height, latest, utmost 7 capping, closing, extreme, highest, maximum, paragon, primary, radical, sublime, supreme 8 absolute, crowning, decisive, empyreal, empyrean, eventual, farthest, furthest, greatest, terminal, towering 9 elemental, paramount, unequaled, unmatched, worthiest 10 concluding, conclusive, consummate, definitive, lattermost, overriding, preeminent, surpassing
  objective: 3 aim 4 goal 5 be-all 6 payoff, reason, target 7 mission, outcome, purpose 8 terminus 10 aspiration, conclusion
  purpose: 3 aim 4 goal 6 end-all, end use, object, target
ultimately: 3 yet 4 last 6 at last, lastly 7 by and by, finally, for good, someday 8 after all, in future, in the end, sometime 9 basically, hereafter, in due time, presently, somewhere 10 completely, eventually
Ultimate Reality, Buddhist symbol of: 5 lotus
ultima Thule: 4 isle 6 island 7 highest 8 farthest, furthest
ultimatum: 6 demand, or else, threat 7 dictate 9 challenge
  ending: 4 else
___ Ultimatum, The: 6 Bourne
ultra: 4 very 5 rabid 6 all-out, far-out, too-too 7 extreme, radical, too much 9 excessive, extremist, fanatical 10 immoderate, outlandish
Ultra Brite: 10 toothpaste
  alternative: 3 Aim 5 Crest, Gleem, Topol 7 Close-Up, Colgate, Viadent 9 Aquafresh, Mentadent, Pepsodent, Rembrandt, Sensodyne 10 Pearl Drops 11 Tom's of Maine
ultraconservative: 4 fogy 5 fogey 7 diehard 8 far right, rightist 9 hidebound
ultraist: 5 rebel 7 fanatic, liberal, radical 8 maverick, nihilist, pacifist, reformer 9 anarchist, extremist, firebrand 10 immoderate, left-winger
ultramarine: 4 blue 5 color
  relative: 4 anil, cyan, navy, Nile, teal 5 Alice, azure, slate 6 cobalt, indigo, raisin, violet 7 peacock 8 cerulean, sapphire 9 turquoise 10 aquamarine, periwinkle
ultramodern: 3 neo, new 5 novel, style 10 avant-garde
ultrasonic: 4 fast 5 quick, rapid, swift 6 speedy
ultrasound: 4 exam, test
  image: 8 sonogram
ultraviolet ___: 3 ray 4 lamp 5 light 6 filter
ultraviolet-blocking chemical: 4 PABA
ulu: 5 knife
Ulu: 8 Grosbard
ulua: 4 fish
Ulúa: 5 river
  River locale: 8 Honduras
Ulugh Muztagh: 4 peak 5 mount 8 mountain
  locale: 4 Asia 5 Tibet 6 Thibet, Xizang 7 Sitsang
ululate: 3 bay 4 bawl, howl, keen, wail, weep, yell, yowl 6 holler 10 vociferate
ululation: 3 bay 4 wail 6 lament
Ulupalakua locale: 4 Maui 6 Hawaii
ulva: 10 sea lettuce
Ulyanov: 5 Lenin 8 Vladimir
Ulysses
  author: James Joyce
  character: 4 Buck 5 Bloom, Molly 7 Dedalus, Leopold, Stephen 8 Mulligan 10 Molly Bloom
  dog: 5 Athos
  last word of ~: 3 yes
  rival: 4 Aias, Ajax
  see also Odysseus
___ Ulysses Grant: 5 Hiram
Ulysses S. ___: 5 Grant
Ulzana's Raid (1972 film)
  cast: Bruce Davison, Burt Lancaster
  director: Robert Aldrich
um: 2 er 7 stammer, stutter 8 hesitate 9 hem and haw
___-um: 5 no-see
Uma: 7 Thurman
Umán: 4 city, town
  locale: 6 Mexico 7 Yucatán
U Mass location: 6 Boston
umber: 5 brown, color 7 reddish 9 earth tone
  relative: 3 bay, dun, tan 4 bole, ecru, fawn, foxy, nude, rust, seal 5 amber, beige, camel, cocoa, hazel, khaki, mocha, sepia, tawny 6 auburn, bister, bistre, bronze, coffee, copper, ginger, russet, sienna, sorrel, suntan, walnut 7 biscuit, caramel, dogwood 8 chestnut, cinnamon, mahogany, red-brown 9 butternut, chocolate
___ umber: 3 raw 5 burnt
Umberto: 3 Eco 6 Nobile
  see also Italian
Umberto D (1952 film) director: Vittorio De Sica
umbilical ___: 4 cord
umbilicus: 5 navel 8 omphalos
umble ___: 3 pie
'umble character: 4 Heep 5 Uriah
umbo: 4 boss, knob
umbra: 4 soul 5 ghost, shade 6 fantom, shadow, spirit 7 phantom
umbrage: 3 ire 4 fury, huff, rage 5 anger, pique, shade, spite, wrath 6 grudge, injury, malice, rancor, shadow 7 chagrin, offense 8 vexation 9 annoyance 10 ill feeling, irritation, resentment
  take ~ at: 4 mind 6 object, resent
umbrageous: 5 leafy, shady 6 touchy 9 sensitive
umbrella: 4 egis, gamp, palm, tree 5 aegis 6 brolly, screen 7 overall, parasol, shelter 8 sunshade 9 inclusive 10 protection
  in Britain: 6 brolly
  of song: 5 smile
  picnic ~: 4 tree
  -shaped tree: 6 acacia
  spoke: 3 rib
umbrella ___: 4 bird, palm, pine, step, tent, tree 5 plant, skirt, stand
___ umbrella: 4 golf 5 beach 6 shower
Umbrella, The author: Guy de Maupassant
umbrette relative: 5 heron
Umbria
  city: 4 Todi 6 Assisi 7 Perugia
  locale: 5 Italy
  province: 5 Terni
Umbrian: 8 language
___-Umbrian: 4 Osco
Umbriel: 4 moon
  planet: 6 Uranus
Ume: 5 river
  locale: 6 Sweden
Umeki, Miyoshi Oscar: Sayonara
umiak: 4 boat 6 vessel 10 watercraft
  builder: 5 Inuit 6 Eskimo, Innuit, Inupik
  home: 6 Alaska
  kin: 5 canoe, kayak
umlaut, half an: 3 dot
Umm: 7 Kulthum
___-ump: 5 umpty
ump ender: 3 ire 4 teen
umpire: 3 ref 5 judge 7 arbiter, mediate, referee 8 mediator, moderate 9 interpose, moderator, officiate 10 adjudicate, arbitrator, negotiator, peacemaker
  call: 3 out 4 balk, fair, foul, safe
  need: 4 mask 5 whisk
  purview: 4 base 5 plate
  ride the ~: 3 boo 4 jeer, razz
umpteen: 4 many 6 a lot of, divers, gobs of, lots of, myriad, tons of, untold 7 a host of, a slew of, copious, heaps of, loads of, no end of, piles of, profuse, scads of 8 a bunch of, abundant, an army of, manifold, numerous, oodles of, scores of 9 a passel of, bountiful, countless, quite a few 10 innumerous, jillions of, zillions of
umpty-___: 3 ump 5 umpth
UMW: 5 union
  member: 5 miner
  opening: 4 adit
'un
  young ~: 4 tike, tyke 6 infant
Un ___ in Maschera: 5 Ballo
Un-___ My Heart: 5 Break
UN
  agcy.: 3 FAO, ILO, IMF, WHO 6 UNICEF
  arm of the ~: 4 agcy.
  Day mo.: 3 Oct.
  delegate: 3 amb.
  license plate abbr.: 3 DPL
  like the ~: 4 intl.
  locale: 3 NYC 7 New York 8 East Side 9 Manhattan
  member: 3 Alb., Alg., Arg., Col., Den., Eng., Eth., Fin., Ger., Ind., Ire., Isr., Lat., Nor., Pan., Pol., Rom., RSA, Rus., Swe., Syr., Tun., USA 4 Chad, Cuba, Ital., Laos, Mali, Peru, Port., Togo 5 Haiti
  name in ~ history: 3 Dag, Lie 4 Kofi 5 Annan 6 Trygve, U Thant
  observer grp.: 3 PLO
  onetime ~ group: 3 IRO
una ___: 4 voce 5 corda
Una: 6 Merkel 7 O'Connor
unabashed: 4 bold, open 6 at ease, brassy, brazen, daring 7 blatant 8 fearless, impudent 9 barefaced, shameless
unabating: 5 usual 6 inborn 7 abiding, chronic, lasting 8 constant, enduring, habitual 9 ceaseless, chronical, continual, incessant, ingrained, perennial, sustained 10 deep-seated, inveterate, persistent, relentless, unyielding
unabbreviated: 4 full 5 total, whole 6 entire 7 plenary 8 complete, finished, thorough 10 exhaustive
unable: 4 weak 5 inept, unfit 6 clumsy 7 hog-tied, not up to 8 helpless, unfitted 9 incapable, powerless, sidelined, unskilled 10 impuissant, inadequate, unequipped
  is ~ to: 4 can't 6 cannot
  to say no: 3 lax 5 timid 6 docile 7 lenient, servile, slavish 8 lamblike, yielding 9 spineless 10 obsequious, submissive
unabridged: 4 full 5 total, uncut, whole 6 entire, intact 7 plenary 8 absolute, complete, finished, thorough 10 exhaustive
  dictionary: 4 tome
unaccented: 4 weak 6 atonic
unacceptable: 3 bad, out 4 tabu 5 lousy, taboo, wrong 7 damaged 8 below par, improper, rejected, unwanted 9 half-baked, obnoxious, offensive, repugnant, unwelcome
  it's ~: 4 no-no, tabu 5 taboo
unaccommodating: 5 loath, rigid, stern 9 unwilling 10 inflexible
unaccompanied: 3 odd 4 lone, sole, solo, stag 5 alone, apart 6 single 8 deserted, detached, isolated, solitary 9 abandoned, a cappella, by oneself, on one's own 10 unescorted
unaccountable: 3 odd 5 weird 6 arcane, mystic 7 strange, unusual 8 baffling, peculiar, puzzling, uncommon, unwonted 9 unheard-of, unnatural
unaccounted for: 3 MIA 4 AWOL, lost 5 short 6 absent 7 at large, left out, mislaid, missing, omitted 9 misplaced
unaccustomed: 3 new 4 rare 5 alien, green, new to, novel 6 exotic, quaint 7 altered, bizarre, foreign, special, strange, unknown, unusual, variant 8 ignorant, imported, singular, uncommon, untaught, unwonted 9 different, eccentric, unskilled, untrained
  to: 5 new at
Unaccustomed ___ am...: 3 as I
unacknowledged: 6 secret 7 virtual 8 nameless 9 anonymous
unacquired: 6 inborn, innate, native 7 natural 10 congenital, connatural, indigenous
unactualized: 6 latent 7 dormant
una de ___: 4 gato
unadept: 5 gawky, inept 6 clumsy, gauche 7 awkward, boorish, gawkish, halting, unhandy 8 bumbling, bungling, cloddish, clownish, helpless, inexpert, tactless, unpoised 9 all thumbs, graceless, ham-handed, inelegant, maladroit, stumbling 10 blundering, left-handed, unskillful
unadmired one: 4 nerd, nurd, wimp 5 dweeb, loser, schmo
unadorned: 4 bald, bare, mere 5 naked, plain, stark 6 barren, modest, severe, simple 7 austere, factual, Spartan, unfussy 9 bare-bones
unadulterated: 4 mere, pure 5 clean, sheer 6 simple 8 pristine, spotless, straight 9 stainless 10 immaculate
unadvised: 4 rash 5 brash, hasty 6 unwary, unwise 7 foolish, unaware 8 careless, heedless, ignorant, mistaken, reckless, unwarned 9 hotheaded, imprudent, in the dark, unknowing 10 incautious, indiscreet, uninformed
unaffected: 4 calm, cool, homy, naif, true 5 aloof, frank, homey, naive, plain 6 candid, casual, direct, folksy, honest, modest, simple, steady 7 artless, callous, genuine, natural, sincere, unmoved, up-front 8 innocent, laid-back, unartful, unspoilt 9 childlike, easygoing, guileless, impassive, ingenuous, unaltered, unchanged, unexcited, unruffled, unstirred, unstudied, untouched, unworldly 10 impervious, unagitated
unaffectedness: 4 ease 10 simplicity
unaffectionate: 4 cold, cool 5 aloof 6 chilly 7 distant

unaffiliated: 3 ind. 4 neut. 7 neutral

unafraid: 4 bold, game, tame 5 brave, gutsy, nervy 6 awless, daring, gritty, heroic, plucky, spunky 7 aweless, defiant, doughty, gallant, impavid, staunch, valiant 8 fearless, heroical, intrepid, resolute, stalwart, valorous 9 audacious, confident, dauntless, dreadless, undaunted, unfearing 10 courageous, undismayed

unaggressive: 3 lax 4 meek 5 mousy, timid 6 mousey

one: 4 lamb 8 pushover, pussycat

unagi: 3 eel

unagitated: 4 calm, cold, cool, even, mild 5 aloof, quiet, sober, staid, stoic, tepid 6 at ease, casual, frigid, frosty, gentle, low-key, mellow, placid, poised, remote, sedate, serene, steady, stolid 7 amiable, assured, at peace, distant, equable, glacial, neutral, offhand, pacific, relaxed, stoical 8 amicable, carefree, composed, detached, laid-back, lukewarm, moderate, peaceful, pleasant, rational, reserved, together, tranquil 9 apathetic, collected, easygoing, impassive, incurious, nerveless, quiescent, temperate, unexcited, unextreme, unruffled, unstirred, unworried, withdrawn 10 coolheaded, impersonal, nonchalant, phlegmatic, reasonable, restrained, unaffected, untroubled

unaided: 4 solo 5 alone 9 by oneself

unaimed: 6 chance, random 9 haphazard

unal: 6 single 8 singular

unalarmed: 4 calm, cool 5 stoic 6 at ease, sedate 9 undaunted

Unalaska: 4 isle 6 island

resident: 5 Aleut 8 Aleutian

unalert: 6 dozing, unwary 7 napping, nodding 8 sleeping 10 incautious

unaligned: 6 uneven, zigzag 7 crooked, neutral 8 far apart, peaceful 9 irregular 10 achromatic, uninvolved

unalike: 3 odd 4 mixt 5 mixed, other 6 atypic, sundry, unique, varied 7 altered, changed, diverse, offbeat, special, strange, unequal, variant, various 8 aberrant, assorted, atypical, contrary, discrete, distinct, opposite, peculiar, separate 9 deviating, different, disparate, divergent, irregular, multiform, otherwise, unrelated 10 antithetic, at variance, discordant, discrepant, dissimilar, individual, mismatched, poles apart, unfamiliar

unallowed: 4 tabu 5 taboo 7 not done 8 verboten 9 forbidden

unalloyed: 4 pure 5 solid, stark 6 simple, single 7 perfect

unalterable: 4 firm, sure 5 final, fixed, rigid 6 rooted, stable, static 7 binding, settled 8 constant, definite, ironclad 9 obstinate, permanent, tenacious 10 changeless

unaltered: 4 same 6 intact 8 pristine

unambiguity: 7 clarity 8 lucidity 9 certainty, plainness, precision 10 directness, exactitude

unambiguous: 5 clear, lucid, plain, vivid 6 cogent, direct, honest, limpid 7 certain, evident, express, obvious 8 absolute, apparent, clean-cut, definite, distinct, explicit, knowable, manifest, palpable, specific 9 graspable 10 spelled out

unambitious: 4 lazy 8 slothful

one: 3 bum 5 idler, sloth 6 loafer 8 layabout

unamenable: 5 fussy, rigid, stiff 6 feisty, trying 7 prickly 8 exacting 9 demanding, difficult, fractious, obstinate 10 inflexible, refractory

Unami: 6 Indian 7 Amerind

unamicable: 3 icy 4 cold 5 aloof 6 remote 7 distant, hostile 8 reserved 10 unfriendly

Unamuno, Miguel de: 4 poet 6 writer 7 Spanish 11 philosopher

unamusing: 5 sober, staid 6 solemn, somber 7 deadpan, serious 9 humorless 10 no-nonsense

unanchored: 6 adrift 8 unmoored

unanimated: 4 calm 5 quiet 6 serene

unanimity: 5 peace, union, unity 6 accord 7 concord, harmony, oneness, rapport 9 agreement, consensus 10 solidarity

unanimous: 5 as one, at one, solid, total 6 common, shared, united 7 unified 8 accepted, agreeing, communal, in unison 9 accordant, concerted, consonant, of one mind, undivided 10 agreed upon, concordant, consensual, consistent, harmonious, like-minded, undisputed

unanimously: 5 as one, at one 6 to a man 8 together

unanswerable: 4 sure, true 5 solid, sound, valid 6 proven, tested 7 certain, factual, genuine, logical, telling 8 official, verified 9 confirmed 10 compelling, conclusive, convincing, documented, unarguable

ask an ~ question: 5 stump 6 baffle, puzzle, stymie 7 confuse, mystify, nonplus, perplex 8 bewilder, confound 9 dumbfound

question: 6 enigma, riddle 7 mystery, paradox, stumper 9 conundrum

Unanswered Question, The composer: 4 Ives

unanticipated: 3 pop 6 abrupt, sudden 8 surprise

unanxious: 4 calm, safe 6 at ease, secure 8 carefree 9 protected

unappareled: 4 bare, nude 5 naked 6 peeled, unclad 8 disrobed, in the raw, undraped 9 au naturel, in the buff, unclothed, uncovered, undressed 10 stark-naked

unapparent: 6 hidden 9 invisible 10 impalpable, intangible, unviewable

unappeasable: 4 grim, hard, mean 5 harsh, stern, stony 6 savage 7 vicious 8 ruthless 9 ferocious, heartless, merciless, unfeeling 10 implacable, ironfisted, relentless, vindictive

unappetizing: 4 blah, flat, icky 5 grody, gross, nasty, vapid, yucky 6 stinky 7 insipid 8 unsavory 9 savorless, tasteless 10 flavorless

food: 4 glop 5 gruel, swill

unappreciative: 7 selfish 9 forgetful, thankless 10 ungracious, ungrateful

unapproachable: 4 cold, cool, mean 5 aloof, nasty, onery, surly 6 chilly, frigid, ornery, remote 7 distant, glacial, hateful, hostile 8 contrary, hesitant, inimical, reserved, spiteful 9 bellicose, malicious, withdrawn 10 malevolent, pugnacious

unapproached: 5 alone 9 matchless

unapt: 4 dull, slow 5 unfit 6 clumsy, klutzy, oafish, undeft 7 awkward 8 cloddish, fumbling, improper 9 all thumbs, graceless, ill-suited, impolitic, imprudent, inapropos, incapable, lumbering, maladroit 10 inapposite, indecorous, irrelevant, malapropos, nongermane, out of order, out of place, unskillful, unsuitable

unarguable: 3 net 4 last, sure 5 clean, clear, final, valid 6 cogent 7 certain, flat-out, obvious, telling 8 absolute, accurate, critical, deciding, decisive, definite, official, positive, ultimate, verified 9 clinching, effectual, revealing 10 compelling, conclusive, convincing, definitive, undeniable, undoubtful

unarm: 6 defeat 8 overcome 10 neutralize

unarmed: 5 clean 9 powerless 10 barehanded, weaponless

combining form: 5 anopi- 6 anoplo-

Unarmed Victory author: Bertrand Russell

unartful: 4 open 5 green, naive 6 candid, simple 7 natural 8 innocent, trusting 9 childlike, guileless, ingenuous, unguarded, unstudied, unworldly 10 unaffected, unreserved, unschooled

unashamed: 4 open 6 brassy, brazen 7 forward 8 immodest

— Unashamed: 4 Cora

unasked-for: 9 causeless, unmerited, voluntary 10 gratuitous, unprovoked

unaspirated: 4 lene

unassailable: 4 safe 6 secure 8 airtight

unassertive: 3 coy, shy 4 mild 5 timid 6 demure, modest 7 bashful, passive 8 resigned, retiring 9 groveling

unassisted: 4 solo 5 alone

unassuming: 3 shy 4 meek, mild, prim 5 lowly, mousy, plain, quiet, timid 6 demure, folksy, humble, modest, mousey, simple 7 bashful 8 reserved, retiring 9 diffident

unassured: 3 shy 5 timid 9 diffident, flinching, tentative

unattached: 4 free, stag 5 alone, loose, stray, unwed 6 adrift, single, untied 7 at large, movable 8 mateless, moveable, separate, wifeless 9 at liberty, separated, unmarried 10 disjointed, friendless, spouseless

unattainable: 5 ideal 7 utopian

unattended: 4 lone 5 alone 6 lonely 7 private 8 solitary 9 abandoned, by oneself

unattested: 9 anonymous

unattired: 4 bare, nude 5 naked 6 unclad 8 disrobed, in the raw, starkers 9 au naturel, in the buff, unclothed, undressed

unattributed: 4 anon 9 anonymous

unau: 5 sloth 6 animal, mammal

unauthentic: 4 sham 5 false 8 spurious 10 fictitious 11 counterfeit

unauthorized: 4 tabu 5 shady, taboo 6 banned 7 crooked, illegal, illicit, pirated, wildcat 8 criminal, improper, outlawed, unlawful, verboten, wrongful 9 felonious, forbidden 10 prohibited

look: 4 peek, peep

unavailability: 4 lack, need, want 6 dearth 7 absence, paucity 8 sparsity 9 privation 10 deficiency

unavailable: 4 busy 5 in use, taken 6 absent 7 engaged 8 occupied

unavailing: 4 idle, null, vain 6 futile, otiose 7 inutile, of no use, useless 8 bootless, hopeless 9 for naught, fruitless, pointless, worthless

Una voce poco fa: 4 aria

unavoidable: 3 set 4 firm, sure 5 fated 7 certain, decided, settled 8 destined, ordained, required 9 impending, necessary, requisite

unaware: 5 blind 6 deaf to, spacey 7 in a daze, mooning, out cold, out of it 8 careless, heedless, ignorant, mindless, nescient, suddenly 9 forgetful, negligent, oblivious, unadvised, unknowing, unmindful, unwitting 10 insensible, out to lunch, unfamiliar, uninformed

unawares: 5 aback, short 8 abruptly, off-guard, suddenly 9 by mistake 10 by accident, by surprise

take ~: 5 catch 6 ambush, pounce 7 startle 8 surprise

unbaked: 3 raw

unbalance: 5 addle 6 madden 7 derange, shake up 8 unsettle 10 disconcert

unbalanced: 4 alop 5 shaky 6 biased, jiggly, uneven, wabbly, wobbly 7 erratic, partial, unequal, unsound 8 lopsided, one-sided, partisan, top-heavy, unstable, unsteady 9 arbitrary, eccentric, unsettled 10 immoderate, prejudiced

at sea: 5 alist

Un Ballo in Maschera composer: 5 Verdi

unbar: 4 open 5 loose 6 loosen, open up

unbarred: 4 free, open 5 loose

unbearable: 5 awful 6 enough 7 painful, too much, very bad 8 grievous 10 deplorable

Unbearable Bassington, The author: Saki

Unbearable Lightness of Being, The: 4 film 5 novel

author: Milan Kundera

cast: Juliette Binoche, Daniel Day Lewis, Lena Olin

unbeatable: 5 ideal 9 nonpareil 10 infallible, invincible

unbeaten: 5 on top 7 winning 8 at the top, dominant, out front 9 in the lead, on a streak 10 flying high, successful, triumphant, victorious

unbecoming: 3 low 5 inapt, inept, rough, tacky 6 clumsy, gauche 7 awkward, lowbred 8 improper, indecent, shameful, uncomely, unseemly, unsuited, unworthy 9 ill-suited, maladroit, offensive, salacious, tasteless, unfitting, unsightly 10 indelicate

unbefitting: 5 below 7 beneath 8 unseemly, unworthy

'Unbegun' Symphony composer: PDQ Bach

Un bel di: 4 aria

unbelievable: 4 tall, thin, weak 5 fishy, flaky, kooky, phony, thick 6 flakey, flimsy, kookie, phoney, screwy 7 amazing, awesome, dubious, surreal, suspect, too much, ungodly 8 cockeyed, doubtful, fabulous, reaching, unlikely 9 marvelous, unheard-of 10 incredible

Unbelievable!: 3 wow 5 great

Unbelievable (1991 song) artist: EMF

unbelievably: 4 oh so, very 8 terribly

unbeliever: 5 pagan 7 atheist, infidel, sceptic, skeptic

unbelieving: 5 pagan 7 cynical 9 atheistic, quizzical, skeptical

unbend: 4 thaw 5 relax 6 unfold, unwind 10 straighten

unbending: 3 set 4 firm, hard, iron 5 aloof, balky, bossy, cruel, dug in, exact, fixed, picky, rigid, stern, stiff, stony, tense, tight, tough 6 dogged, formal, mulish, severe, steely, stoney, strict, strong, wooden 7 adamant, austere, decided, distant, do-or-die, hard-set, piggish, Spartan, uptight 8 despotic, exacting, hardened, hardline, locked in, obdurate, reserved, resolute, rigorous, stubborn 9 demanding, draconian, impliable, inelastic, iron-jawed, obstinate, pigheaded, steadfast, stringent, tenacious 10 despotical, hard-bitten, implacable, inexorable, inflexible, ironfisted, no-nonsense, oppressive, relentless, set in stone, tyrannical, unswayable, unyielding

unbent: 6 in a row, linear 8 straight
unbiased: 4 cold, even, fair, just, open 5 aloof, equal, valid 6 honest, square 7 factual, liberal, neutral 8 balanced, detached, straight 9 equitable, impartial, objective, uncolored, unslanted 10 evenhanded, open-minded, reasonable
unbidden: 7 unasked 9 uninvited, voluntary
unbigoted: 4 just 7 liberal, neutral 8 catholic 9 impartial, unslanted
unbilled performer: 5 extra
unbind: 4 free, undo 5 loose 6 loosen, redeem 7 release, set free 8 let loose, liberate, set loose 9 disengage, extricate, turn loose
unbleached: 6 greige 7 natural
hue: 3 tan 4 ecru 5 beige, brown
unblemished: 4 pure 5 clean, clear, sound 6 unhurt 7 perfect 8 absolute, flawless, innocent, spotless, unflawed, unmarked, unmarred 9 faultless, snow-white, stainless, undamaged, undefiled, uninjured, unstained, unsullied, untouched
unblended: 4 neat 6 simple, single
unblessed: 5 curst 6 cursed, doomed, jinxed 7 hapless 8 ill-fated, luckless 10 ill-starred
unblock: 4 free, open 5 clear
unblocked: 4 open 8 passable 9 navigable, unstopped 10 accessible
unblurred: 5 clear, lucid 7 crystal
unblushing: 6 brassy, brazen 7 blatant 9 shameless 10 indelicate
unbolt: 4 open 5 loose 6 loosen
unbolted: 4 open 5 loose
unborn: 6 future
of an ~: 5 fetal 6 foetal
unbosoming: 5 story 6 avowal, exposé 9 admission, allowance, assenting, assertion, narration, statement, utterance 10 concession, confession, disclosure, divulgence, profession, recitation, revelation
unbothered: 4 airy, calm 6 at ease, blithe, breezy, cheery, jaunty, jovial 7 buoyant 8 carefree, cheerful, feckless, laid back, reckless 9 easygoing 10 flying high, insouciant, untroubled
unbound: 4 free 5 loose 6 untied
unbounded: 3 big 4 vast 7 endless, immense 8 infinite 9 excessive, limitless, unlimited
unbowed: 6 in a row, linear 8 straight
unbox: 4 open
unbranded cow: 4 calf 5 stray 8 maverick
unbreakable: 4 firm 5 solid, tight, tough 6 rugged, strong 7 durable, lasting 9 resistant, toughened
Un-Break My Heart (1996 song) artist: Toni Braxton
unbribed: 5 clean 6 honest 10 upstanding
unbridled: 4 rash, wild 5 feral, rabid 6 ferine 7 beastly, rampant 9 ferocious, impetuous, out of hand 10 immoderate
unbroken: 4 deep, even, fast, wild 5 feral, level, rabid, solid, sound, whole 6 direct, entire, ferine, intact, smooth, steady 7 beastly, endless, nonstop, perfect, regular, running 8 constant, flawless, profound, straight, unwaning 9 ceaseless, continual, faultless, ferocious, incessant, inviolate, perpetual, undivided 10 continuous, immaculate, relentless, successive, unimpaired
horse: 5 bronc 6 bronco
unbuckle: 4 open 5 loose 6 loosen
unbuild: 4 bomb, rase, raze 5 level, wreck 7 destroy, flatten 8 bulldoze, demolish, dynamite, pull down, tear down 9 devastate, knock down
unburden: 3 rid 4 dump, ease, free, lose, open 5 clear, empty 6 reveal, soothe, unload 7 confess, confide, divulge, lay bare, lighten, relieve, tell all, unbosom 8 disclose, get rid of, shake off, throw off 9 disburden, dispose of, untrouble
unburdensome: 4 easy, snap 5 cinch, cushy 6 breeze, picnic, simple 8 duck soup, painless, pushover 10 child's play, effortless, unexacting
unbutton: 4 undo 5 loose 6 loosen
unbuttoned: 5 loose 10 disheveled
uncaged: 4 free, open 5 loose
uncalculable: 4 vast 6 cosmic, untold 7 endless, immense 8 infinite, unending 9 boundless, countless, limitless, unbounded, unlimited 10 bottomless, numberless
uncalled-for: 5 undue, wrong 6 unfair, wanton 7 unasked, uncouth 8 improper, needless, overmuch 9 merciless, misguided 10 groundless
uncancelled: 3 new 4 mint
uncanny: 3 odd 4 eery 5 eerie, queer, scary, weird 6 creepy, secret, spooky 7 ghostly, magical, oddball, strange, unusual 8 singular 9 fantastic, unearthly, unheard-of, unnatural 10 astounding, incredible, miraculous, mysterious, mystifying, prodigious, remarkable, superhuman
uncap: 3 pop 4 open
uncarbonated: 4 flat 5 still
uncared-for: 5 alone 7 run-down 8 untended 9 neglected
uncareful: 4 rash, wild 5 brash, hasty 6 daring, madcap, unwary, unwise 8 feckless, headlong, heedless, pell-mell, reckless 9 audacious, breakneck, daredevil, desperate, foolhardy, imprudent 10 incautious
uncaring: 5 stony 6 stoney, unkind 7 callous 8 hardened, heedless 9 apathetic, heartless, insensate, unfeeling, unpitying 10 neglectful, nonchalant, unmerciful, unthinking
Uncas craft: 5 canoe
unceasing: 7 abiding, endless, eternal, lasting, undying 8 enduring, timeless, unending, untiring, unwaning 9 ceaseless, continual, deathless, incessant, perennial, perpetual 10 continuous, unflagging
unceasingly: 4 ever 5 on end 6 always
uncelebrated: 7 unknown 8 nameless
unceremonious: 4 curt, homy, rude 5 blunt, brusk, crude, frank, gruff, homey, rough, short 6 abrupt, candid, casual, coarse, folksy, vulgar 7 boorish, brusque, cursory, offhand, uncivil 8 churlish, impolite, informal, inurbane, tactless 9 outspoken 10 indelicate
dismissal: 2 ax 3 axe 4 boot, sack 7 heave-ho 9 eighty-six
unceremoniously, leave: 4 drop, dump, jilt 5 chuck, ditch 6 desert 7 abandon, forsake
uncertain: 3 dim 4 asea, hazy, iffy, moot, open, torn, wary 5 at sea, chary, dicey, fluid, hairy, leery, muddy, risky, rocky, shaky, vague 6 casual, chancy, fickle, fitful, queasy, queazy, unsafe, unsure 7 dubious, erratic, guarded, halting, mutable, protean, suspect, unclear, unfixed 8 cautious, doubtful, doubting, hesitant, insecure, lukewarm, nebulous, not final, perilous, possible, shifting, slippery, ticklish, unsteady, variable, wavering 9 ambiguous, debatable, equivocal, faltering, hazardous, irregular, mercurial, on thin ice, reluctant, skeptical, tentative, undecided, unsettled, whimsical 10 ambivalent, bewildered, borderline, changeable, contingent, disputable, improbable, inconstant, indecisive, indefinite, indistinct, inexplicit, irresolute, precarious, suspicious, touch and go, unreliable, unresolved, up for grabs, up in the air, weak-willed, wishy-washy
amount: 3 any, few 4 some
response: 4 shot, stab 5 guess, hunch, maybe 6 notion, theory 7 feeling, opinion, perhaps, surmise, venture 9 suspicion 10 conjecture, hypothesis, prediction, projection
state: 5 limbo
__ Uncertain Feeling: 4 That
__ uncertain terms: 4 in no
uncertainty: 4 risk 5 doubt, peril, qualm, query, worry 6 hazard, wonder 7 anxiety, concern, dilemma, dubiety, reserve, scruple, trouble 8 disquiet, distrust, mistrust, quandary, question, suspense 9 ambiguity, confusion, dubiosity, guesswork, hesitancy, misgiving, suspicion, vagueness 10 hesitation
show ~: 5 shrug
sound of ~: 2 er, uh, um
state of ~: 5 limbo
UNCF, part of: 4 Coll., Fund 5 Negro 6 United 7 College
unchain: 4 free, save 5 loose 6 loosen, redeem 7 release 8 liberate
unchained: 4 free 5 loose 6 untied
Unchained Melody (song)
artist: Al Hibbler, Les Baxter and his Orchestra, Righteous Brothers, Roy Hamilton
Unchain My Heart (1961 song) artist: Ray Charles
unchallenged: 5 alone
unchangeable: 4 firm 5 fixed, rigid 6 stable, steady, strong 8 constant, resolute 9 immovable, immutable, permanent, steadfast, unmovable
unchangeableness: 3 rut 6 fixity, tedium 8 dullness, evenness, flatness, monotony, sameness 10 continuity, uniformity
unchanged: 4 as is, same 10 monotonous, unaffected
unchanging: 4 even, firm, same, sure 5 fixed, level, rigid 6 rooted, stable, static, steady 7 abiding, equable, eternal, lasting, regular, settled, stabile, uniform 8 constant, definite, enduring, ironclad, unfading 9 continual, immutable, perennial, permanent, perpetual, unfailing, unvarying 10 consistent, dependable, invariable, true to type
uncharitable: 4 hard, mean 5 harsh 6 stingy, unkind 8 inhumane, spiteful, uncaring 9 heartless, unfeeling
uncharitableness: 5 spite 6 rancor
uncharted: 7 unknown
unchecked: 4 rash, wild 7 rampant 9 out of hand
spread ~: 4 rage
uncia: 5 money
uncial: 6 letter
uncinch: 4 open 5 loose 6 loosen
uncircumspect: 4 rash 6 unwary 8 careless 9 unguarded 10 headstrong
uncivil: 4 bold, curt, flip, pert, rude 5 blunt, brash, fresh, gruff, harsh, nervy, rough, sassy, saucy, short, surly 6 abrupt, awless, brazen, cheeky, coarse, snippy 7 aweless, bearish, caddish, ill-bred, uncouth 8 churlish, flippant, growling, impolite, impudent, insolent, inurbane, snippety, tactless 9 barbarian, barbarous, insulting, offensive, out of line, ungallant 10 indecorous
uncivilized: 4 rude, wild 5 crass, crude, feral, gross, pagan, rabid, rough 6 animal, brutal, coarse, ferine, Gothic, rugged, savage, unholy, vulgar, wicked 7 beastly, boorish, brutish, ill-bred, lawless, loutish, uncouth, ungodly 8 barbaric, churlish, impolite 9 barbarian, barbarous, ferocious, primitive, unrefined
one: 5 beast, brute 6 animal
place: 4 wild 6 jungle
unclad: 3 raw 4 bare, nude 5 naked, stark 9 in the buff, in the nude, unattired
unclasp: 4 open 5 loose 6 loosen
Unclay author: T.F. Powys
uncle: 3 kin, man, rel. 4 male 5 I give, I quit 6 enough 7 I give up, kinsman 8 relative
brother: 3 dad, pop 6 father
Dutch ~: 7 adviser, advisor
everybody's ~: 3 Sam
in Spanish: 3 tío
kid: 3 coz 6 cousin
mom: 4 gram, nana
say ~: 4 quit 5 yield 6 accede, fess up, give up, relent, submit 7 concede 9 acquiesce, surrender
sister: 3 mom 6 mother
starter: 5 grand
wife: 4 aunt 5 aunty 6 auntie
__ uncle: 3 cry, say 5 Dutch
__-uncle: 5 great
Uncle __: 3 Ned, Sam 4 Ben's, Buck 5 Remus, Vanya 6 Fester, Miltie
Uncle __ Cabin: 4 Tom's
Uncle __ Rice: 4 Ben's
U.N.C.L.E. agent: 4 Solo 8 Kuryakin
Uncle Albert/Admiral Halsey (1971 song) artist: Paul McCartney
unclean: 4 evil, foul, rank, vile 5 black, dirty, dusty, fetid, germy, grimy, messy, muddy, nasty, sooty 6 filthy, foetid, impure, rancid, rotten, sloppy, soiled, sordid 7 corrupt, decayed, defiled, smeared, smudged, spotted, squalid, stained, sullied, tainted, unkempt, unswept 8 befouled, polluted, profaned, shameful, slovenly, stinking, vitiated 9 tarnished 10 bedraggled, besmirched, desecrated, insanitary
uncleaned: 5 dirty, dusty 8 unwashed
uncleanness: 5 filth, taint 8 impurity 9 pollution 10 corruption, defilement
unclear: 3 dim 4 hazy 5 blear, faint, foggy, fuzzy, mirky, misty, muddy, murky, shaky, vague, wooly 6 arcane, bleary, cloudy, opaque, turbid, woolly 7 cryptic, dubious, evasive, obscure, suspect 8 abstruse, darkened, nebulous, puzzling 9 confusing, cryptical, difficult, enigmatic, equivocal, illegible, uncertain, undecided, unfocused, unsettled 10 indefinite, indistinct, perplexing, unexplicit, unreadable
make ~: 3 dim, fog 4 blur, roil, veil 5 bedim, befog 6 darken 7 becloud, confuse, mystify, obscure 8 bewilder, confound 9 obfuscate
Uncle Ben's: 4 rice
alternative: 6 Minute 7 Success 8 Carolina
Uncle Buck (1989 film)
cast: John Candy, Amy Madigan
director: John Hughes
Uncle Fester: 6 Addams

Uncle Miltie: 5 Berle
Uncle Ned composer: 6 Foster
Uncle Remus: 10 tale teller
creator: 6 Harris
epithet: 4 Br'er
Uncle Sam: 6 cereal 10 government
agent: 3 Fed
artist: 5 Flagg
competitor: 3 Kix 4 Life, Trix 5 Kashi, Quisp, Total 6 Kaboom, Muesli, Oreo O's, Pablum, Smacks 7 All-Bran, Crispix, Harmony, Hunny B's, Mueslix, Oat Bran, Pokemon 8 Boo Berry, Cheerios, Corn Chex, Corn Pops, Fiber One, Rice Chex, Special K, Wheaties 9 Alpha Bits, Apple Zaps, Grape Nuts, Honey Comb, Just Right, Wheat Chex 10 Apple Jacks, Bran Flakes, Cap'n Crunch, Cocoa Puffs, Froot Loops, Mini-Wheats, Nutri-Grain, Puffed Rice, Quaker Oats, Smart Start 11 Cocoa Blasts, Cookie Crisp, Golden Crisp, Lucky Charms, Puffed Wheat, Sweet Crunch, Waffle Crisp
feature: 3 hat 5 beard
invitation: 6 call-up 8 I Want You
Uncle Tom's Cabin
author: 5 Stowe
character: 3 Eva 5 Eliza, Simon, Topsy 6 Legree 9 Little Eva
Uncle Vanya
author: Anton Chekhov
character: 4 Ilia, Ivan 5 Marya, Sonya 6 Astrov, Helena, Marina
uncloak: 6 show up 7 lay bare, undress
uncloaked: 4 open 5 overt 8 knowable
unclog: 4 free, open 5 clear 6 unstop
unclogger, sink: 5 Drano 7 plunger
unclose: 3 ope 4 open, undo
unclosed: 4 open
unclothe: 4 bare, peel 5 strip 6 reveal 7 disrobe, uncover, undress
unclothed: 3 raw 4 bare, nude 5 naked, stark 9 in the buff, unattired
unclouded: 4 fair, pure 5 clear, light, sunny 6 bright 8 sunshiny
uncluttered: 4 neat, open, tidy, trim 5 clean, kempt 6 simple, spruce 7 orderly 8 well-kept 9 shipshape 10 fastidious
uncoerced: 4 free 9 voluntary
uncoil: 6 spread, unfold, unwind 7 untwine 9 spread out 10 straighten
uncollected: 3 due 7 payable
uncolored: 4 fair, just 6 square 8 balanced, unbiased 9 equitable, impartial, objective, unslanted 10 even-handed, impersonal
uncombed: 6 blowsy, blowzy, matted, shaggy, unneat, untidy 7 blowsed, blowzed, knotted, tousled, unkempt
uncomfortability scale: 3 THI
uncomfortable: 4 achy, hard, sore, worn 5 close, rough, stiff, tight, tired, upset, weary 6 aching, in pain, pained, queasy, queazy, thorny, uneasy 7 awkward, chafing, cramped, galling, hurting, nervous, painful, wracked 8 annoying, fatigued, restless, sheepish, smarting, strained, troubled, wretched 9 agonizing, exhausted, ill at ease, miserable, suffering, wearisome
uncommitted: 4 free, open 7 neutral 8 cut loose, floating, lukewarm, wavering 9 undecided, unpledged 10 off the hook, on the fence
uncommon: 3 odd 4 eery, rare 5 alien, eerie, novel, queer, weird 6 arcane, atypic, exotic, freaky, quirky, scanty, scarce, single, unique 7 bizarre, curious, deviant, extreme, notable, oddball, offbeat, special, strange, unusual 8 aberrant, abnormal, atypical, far apart, freakish, original, peculiar, precious, singular, sporadic, superior, unwonted 9 anomalous, different, divergent, eccentric, egregious, fantastic, irregular, recherché, startling, unheard of, wonderful 10 at a premium, hard to find, infrequent, inimitable, noteworthy, occasional, prodigious, remarkable, sporadical, surprising, unfamiliar, unfrequent, unorthodox
in French: 9 recherché
in Latin: 4 rara
sense: 3 ESP 9 intuition, telepathy
uncommonly: 4 very 5 extra, oddly 6 rarely, seldom 8 not often 9 extremely, strangely, unusually 10 especially
uncommunicative: 3 mum, shy 4 cool, curt 5 aloof, close, quiet, short 6 remote, silent 7 distant, evasive, guarded, on the QT 8 hush-hush, reserved, reticent, retiring, taciturn 9 clammed up, secretive, voiceless, withdrawn
uncompanionable: 5 aloof 6 remote 7 distant 8 reserved, solitary 9 withdrawn 10 antisocial, unsociable
uncompassionate: 5 stern, stony 6 stoney 7 callous 9 unfeeling
uncompelled: 4 free 9 voluntary
uncomplaining: 4 calm, meek, mild 5 stoic 6 dogged, gentle, serene, stolid 7 patient, stoical 8 detached, enduring, resigned, tolerant, untiring 9 apathetic, easygoing, forgiving, impassive, unruffled 10 forbearing, unflagging
uncompleted: 7 halfway, partial 10 fractional, in the works
uncomplex: 4 easy 5 basic 6 simple 8 duck soup 10 child's play, elementary
uncompliant: 4 wild 6 mulish, unruly 7 naughty, wayward, willful 8 contrary, perverse, stubborn 9 obstinate 10 delinquent, disorderly, rebellious, refractory, self-willed
uncomplicated: 4 easy 5 basic, clear, plain 6 facile, simple 8 duck soup
uncompounded: 6 simple, single
uncomprehending: 4 dull 5 dense, dopey, silly, thick, vapid 6 obtuse, vacant 7 foolish, vacuous 9 airheaded, half-baked
uncompromising: 4 firm, grim, hard, sure 5 bossy, cruel, picky, rigid, stern, tough 6 severe, strict, strong, wilful 7 adamant, austere, decided, diehard, precise, radical, Spartan, willful 8 despotic, exacting, hard-core, hardline, ironclad, locked in, obdurate, resolute, rigorous, stubborn 9 brick-wall, demanding, draconian, obstinate, pigheaded, steadfast, stringent, tenacious, unbending 10 despotical, inflexible, iron-fisted, no-nonsense, oppressive, tyrannical
response: 5 never
unconcealed: 4 bare, open 5 clear, naked, overt, plain 6 in view, patent, public 7 exposed, glaring, obvious, visible 8 apparent, clear-cut, explicit, knowable, manifest 9 barefaced 10 observable
unconcentrated: 4 thin 5 loose 6 effuse, strewn 7 diffuse, general 9 dispersed, scattered, spread out 10 discursive
unconcern: 6 laxity 7 neglect 8 lethargy 9 disregard 10 detachment, neutrality
unconcerned: 4 cold, cool, easy, lazy 5 aloof, blasé, blind, staid, stoic, stony 6 at ease, blithe, deaf to, low-key, mellow, placid, sedate, serene, stoney 7 at peace, callous, distant, languid, neutral, offhand, relaxed, stoical, unaware, unmoved 8 carefree, careless, composed, detached, feckless, hardened, heedless, laid-back, lukewarm, reserved, tranquil 9 apathetic, collected, forgetful, impassive, incurious, negligent, oblivious, temperate, unruffled, untouched, unworried, withdrawn 10 nonchalant, regardless
uncondensed: 5 total, whole 6 entire 7 plenary 8 complete, finished, thorough 10 exhaustive
unconditional: 4 flat, full, open 5 clean, total, utter 6 all-out, entire 7 assured, blanket, certain, flat-out, genuine 8 absolute, complete, outright, thorough 9 downright, no-strings, out-and-out, unlimited
unconditionally: 5 fully 6 flatly, in full, purely, wholly 7 cap-a-pie, flat out, totally, utterly 8 entirely, from A to Z 9 all the way, every inch 10 absolutely, completely, positively
unconfident: 3 shy 4 weak 5 timid 6 afraid, unsure 7 fearful, nervous 8 doubtful, hesitant 9 faltering, tentative 10 indecisive
unconfined: 4 free 5 loose 6 untied 7 at large 9 boundless, unlimited 10 on the loose
unconfirmed: 7 rumored 8 baseless 9 tentative, uncertain
uncongealed: 4 soft, thin 5 runny 6 liquid, watery
unconnected: 4 free 5 loose 6 parted 7 severed 8 detached, distinct, separate 9 disjoined, disunited, excursive, unrelated
unconquerable: 4 safe 6 secure 10 impassable, invincible
unconscionable: 5 undue 6 amoral, unfair, unholy, unjust, wanton, wicked 7 extreme, immoral, knavish, ungodly 8 criminal 9 barbarous, dishonest, excessive, unethical
unconscious: 3 out 4 numb 6 asleep, bombed, latent, zonked 7 out cold, stunned, unaware 8 benumbed, comatose, in a faint, lifeless, swooning 9 automatic, entranced, flattened, insensate, passed out, repressed, senseless, stupefied, unknowing, unmindful, unwitting 10 knocked out, suppressed
become ~: 4 doze 5 faint, sleep, swoon 6 go limp, nod off 7 pass out 8 black out, fall over, keel over
render ~: 2 KO 4 drug, kayo, stun 5 floor, punch 7 flatten 8 knock out
unconsenting: 5 balky, loath 6 averse, mulish 7 hostile, opposed 8 contrary, hesitant 9 reluctant
unconsidered: 6 random 9 unadvised, unnoticed
unconstitutional: 7 illegal 8 outlawed 10 prohibited, proscribed
unconstrained: 4 free 5 loose, merry 8 outgoing 9 unlimited, voluntary 10 licentious
unconstraint: 7 liberty, license
unconsumed: 5 extra 6 unused 7 surplus, uneaten 8 leftover, residual 9 remaining
uncontaminated: 4 pure 5 clean 8 pristine, sanitary, spotless 9 stainless 10 immaculate
uncontested: 6 united 7 unified 9 concerted, of one mind, unanimous 10 consensual, undisputed
uncontrived: 5 naïve 6 candid, honest 7 artless, genuine, natural, sincere 8 innocent 9 guileless
uncontrollable: 3 mad 4 amok, wild 5 amuck 6 bratty, fierce, strong, unruly 7 excited, frantic, freaked, furious, lawless, rampant, violent 8 obdurate, stubborn 9 fractious, insurgent, obstinate 10 licentious
circumstance: 4 fate, luck 5 karma
uncontrolled: 3 mad 4 rash, wild 5 blind 7 chaotic, rampant 10 licentious
unconventional: 3 odd 4 beat, eery 5 crazy, dotty, eerie, flaky, fresh, kinky, kooky, novel, outré, queer, weird 6 atypic, clever, far-out, flakey, freaky, kookie, quirky, unique, way-out 7 bizarre, curious, deviant, liberal, oddball, offbeat, raffish, strange, unusual 8 aberrant, atypical, bohemian, creative, freakish, informal, inspired, original, peculiar, uncommon 9 anomalous, divergent, eccentric, fantastic, ingenious, inventive, irregular 10 innovative, unorthodox
unconversant: 8 ignorant
unconvinced: 6 unsure 8 doubtful 9 skeptical
unconvincing: 4 lame, poor, thin, weak 6 flimsy 8 unlikely
uncooked: 3 raw
uncool: 5 nerdy 7 nowhere 8 tiresome 9 loathsome, malicious
one: 4 geek, nerd, nurd 5 dweeb
uncooperative: 5 balky, onery, rigid 6 mulish, ornery 7 hostile, piggish 9 pigheaded, unwilling 10 refractory
uncoordinated: 5 gawky, inept 6 clumsy, klutzy, oafish 7 awkward, doltish, gawkish, hulking 8 bumbling, bungling, cloddish 9 all thumbs, graceless, lumbering, maladroit, stumbling
uncork: 3 pop 4 open 6 broach
uncorked: 4 open 9 unstopped
uncorroborated: 8 baseless 9 tentative
uncorrupt: 4 just, pure 8 innocent 9 high-toned
uncorrupted: 4 fair, good, pure, true 5 clean 6 virgin 8 pristine, spotless, virginal 9 stainless 10 immaculate
uncostly: 3 low 6 modest, on sale 7 cut-rate, reduced 8 trifling 10 economical, marked down, reasonable, rock-bottom
uncounted: 4 many 6 myriad, untold 10 unnumbered
uncouple: 4 part 5 sever, split, unpeg 6 cut off, detach, divide 7 disjoin, split up 8 break off, disunite, separate, set apart 9 disengage 10 disconnect
uncourageous: 3 shy 5 timid 6 scared
one: 5 sissy 6 coward 7 chicken, dastard
uncourteous: 3 raw 4 loud, rude 5 crass, crude, nervy, rough 6 coarse 7 bearish, boorish, lowbred, lowbrow, uncouth 8 churlish, inurbane 9 inelegant, tasteless, unrefined
uncourtly: 5 brash, rough 7 forward 8 inurbane 9 ungallant
uncouth: 3 low, raw 4 loud, non-U, rude 5 brash, crass, crude, gawky, gross, rough, tacky 6 clumsy, coarse, gauche, oafish, rustic, unmeet, vulgar 7 awkward, bearish, boorish, caddish, forward, gawkish, ill-bred, loutish, lowbred, raffish, raunchy, strange, uncivil 8 barbaric, clownish, impolite, indecent, ungainly, unseemly 9 backwater, graceless, inelegant, low-minded, tasteless, ungallant, ungenteel, unrefined 10 indecorous, indelicate, outlandish, ungracious, unpolished
one: 3 ape, oaf 4 boor, clod

uncover: 3 ope 4 bare, find, grub, leak, open, show, tell 5 dig up, learn, shuck, strip 6 denude, detect, expose, ferret, locate, open up, reveal, strike, turn up, unfold, unmask, unveil, unwrap 7 display, divulge, exhibit, hit upon, lay bare, lay open, let slip, rout out, unearth 8 disclose, discover, disinter, give away, smell out, unclothe 9 get to know, make known, stumble on 10 make public
uncovered: 3 raw 4 bald, bare, nude, open 5 naked, stark 10 unshielded
uncovered ___: 4 call 6 option
uncovering: 6 espial, exposé 8 exposure 9 detection, discovery 10 disclosure
uncreative: 5 bland 6 boring, in a rut
uncredited: 8 nameless 9 anonymous
uncritical: 6 casual 7 cursory, offhand, shallow 8 careless, slipshod 9 credulous, easygoing, imprecise 10 falling for
uncrowded: 4 open, thin 5 broad, roomy 6 sparse 8 far apart, spacious 10 commodious
unction: 4 balm 5 salve 8 liniment, ointment 9 demulcent, emollient
extreme ~: 4 rite 9 sacrament
unctuous: 4 oily 5 slick, suave 6 greasy, smooth 7 fawning, servile 8 slippery 9 adulatory, insincere, lubricous 10 lubricated, lubricious, obsequious
uncultivable: 4 arid, poor 5 waste 6 barren, fallow 7 parched
uncultivated: 4 rude, wild 5 fresh, rough 6 coarse, fallow 7 boorish, lawless, natural, uncouth 8 plebeian
uncultured: 3 raw 4 non-U, rude, wild 5 crude, gross, rough 6 coarse, gauche 7 boorish, loutish 8 churlish, plebeian, unpoised 9 backwater, barbarian, barbarous, graceless, inelegant
one: 3 oaf 4 boor, clod, slob
uncurbed: 4 fast, open, wild 5 loose 6 rakish, wanton 8 depraved 9 dissolute, libertine, salacious 10 libidinous, licentious, lubricious, profligate
uncurl: 6 unfold 9 spread out 10 straighten
uncurled: 8 straight
uncustomary: 3 odd 8 peculiar, uncommon 9 different
uncut: 4 pure 5 rough, total, whole 6 entire, in full, intact 7 plenary 8 complete, finished, thorough 9 undivided 10 exhaustive, full-length, in one piece, in the rough, unabridged
UND
see Notre Dame
undamaged: 2 OK 4 mint, okay, okeh, okey, safe, well 5 sound, whole 6 entire, intact, secure 7 perfect 8 all right, complete, flawless 9 faultless, untouched 10 immaculate, in one piece
___ Undarum: 4 Mare
undaunted: 3 icy 4 bold, game 5 brave, gutsy, nervy, stout 6 awless, daring, gritty, heroic, plucky, spunky, steely 7 aweless, defiant, doughty, gallant, impavid, staunch, valiant 8 fearless, heroical, intrepid, resolute, stalwart, unafraid, valorous 9 audacious, confident, dreadless, steadfast, unalarmed, unfearful, unfearing 10 courageous, fire-eating, mettlesome, undeterred, undismayed
___ und Drang: 5 Sturm
Undead, The (1957 film) director: Roger Corman
undecaying: 8 enduring 9 immutable, permanent 10 changeless
undeceitful: 6 candid, honest 8 straight
undeceive: 8 disabuse 9 enlighten, unbeguile 10 disenchant
undeceptive: 4 open 6 honest, trusty 7 ethical, genuine, up-front 8 reliable, straight, truthful 9 veracious 10 aboveboard, dependable, on the level
undecided: 4 iffy, moot, open, torn 5 vague 6 unsure 7 dubious, neutral, not sure, pendant, pendent, pending, unclear 8 doubtful, hesitant, lukewarm, waffling, wavering 9 debatable, dithering, equivocal, tentative, uncertain, unsettled 10 ambivalent, borderline, indecisive, indefinite, irresolute, of two minds, on the fence, unfinished, unresolved, up in the air, wishy-washy
be ~: 4 hang, pend 5 waver
perch for the ~: 5 fence
undecipherable: 4 deep 6 knotty, thorny, tricky 7 complex 8 abstruse, involved, mazelike, tortuous 9 Byzantine, Daedalean, difficult, enigmatic, intricate 10 circuitous, convoluted, perplexing
undeclared: 5 tacit 6 unsaid 7 implied
undecorated: 4 bare 6 simple 7 Spartan
undefended: 4 open 8 wide open 9 unguarded 10 vulnerable
undefiled: 4 pure 5 clean 6 chaste, virgin 8 pristine, spotless, unsoiled, virginal 9 stainless 10 immaculate
undefined: 9 limitless, open-ended 10 indefinite
undeliverable letter: 4 nixy 5 nixie
undemanding: 4 easy, meek, snap, soft 5 cinch, cushy, light 6 breeze, picnic, simple 8 duck soup, painless, pushover 10 child's play, effortless
undemocratic rule: 5 junta
undemonstrative: 3 shy 5 aloof, staid, stoic, timid 6 demure 7 distant, languid, stoical 8 listless, reserved, retiring 9 apathetic, withdrawn
undeniability: 7 urgency 9 necessity
undeniable: 4 real, sure, true 5 clear, sound 6 actual, patent, proven, simple 7 certain, evident, for sure, obvious 8 absolute, accurate, decisive, definite, manifest, outright, positive 9 necessary, undoubted 10 conclusive, inevitable, unarguable, undoubtful, unimagined
it's ~: 4 fact 5 given, thing, truth 6 verity 7 reality 9 actuality, certainty
undeniably: 6 easily, indeed 9 hands down 10 definitely, far and away
undependable: 5 loose, shaky 6 fickle, no-good, tricky, unsafe, unsure 7 dubious, erratic, wayward 8 careless, derelict, skittish, unstable, variable 9 uncertain 10 unreliable
one: 4 kook 5 flake 6 maniac 7 lunatic
under: 3 low, sub 4 down 5 below, infra, lower, neath 6 asleep, junior, lesser, nether, pinned 7 beneath, subject 8 downward, governed, held down, included, inferior, sleeping, subsumed 9 covered by, subject to 10 hypnotized, inferior to, insentient, subjugated, subsidiary, supporting, underneath
combining form: 6 infero-
ender: 3 age 4 wear 5 world 6 ground
prefix: 3 sub- 4 hypo-
sail: 4 asea 5 at sea
starter: 4 here 5 there
the covers: 4 abed 8 sleeping
way: 5 afoot, going
under ___: 3 way 4 fire, foot, oath 5 cover, wraps 6 arrest, canvas
under ___ and key: 4 lock
under ___ of: 4 pain
___ under: 4 down, fall, plow, snow 7 knuckle
___-under: 4 over
Under ___: 4 Fire 5 Siege
Under ___ Wood: 4 Milk
underachiever: 5 loser 7 also-ran, failure
social ~: 4 nerd, nurd
underage: 5 minor, young 6 callow 7 deficit 8 immature, juvenile, youthful 9 shortfall 10 inadequacy
Under a Glass Bell author: Anaïs Nin
undercarriage: 4 body 5 frame 7 chassis 9 framework
underclassman: 5 pupil 6 rookie 7 student 8 beginner, freshman 9 collegian
undercoating prevents it: 4 rust 5 decay 6 patina 7 tarnish 9 corrosion, iron oxide, oxidation
undercooked: 3 raw, red 4 pink, rare
undercounted: 3 low 5 short
undercover: 6 covert, hidden, masked, secret, spying, unseen, veiled 7 cloaked, furtive, on the QT, private, sub rosa 8 hush-hush, obscured, on the sly, secluded, shrouded, stealthy 9 concealed, disguised, incognito, nonpublic, secretive, unexposed
agent: 3 spy 4 mole 5 plant
Cold War ~ gp.: 3 KGB
cop: 4 narc, nark 5 agent, narco
go ~: 3 spy 4 hide 6 hole up, lay low, lie low 7 sleeper
govt. ~ group: 3 CIA, NSA
officer, at times: 4 bait, lure 5 decoy, shill 6 come-on
operation: 5 sting
recognize, as an ~ cop: 4 make, name 6 finger
Undercover Angel (1977 song) artist: Alan O'Day
Undercover Man, The (1949 film) cast: Nina Foch, Glenn Ford, James Whitmore
Undercover Man, The director: 5 Lewis
Undercover of the Night (1983 song) artist: Rolling Stones
undercurrent: 4 aura, eddy, hint, pull, race, tide 5 drift, sense, tenor, tinge, trace, trend, vibes 6 flavor, murmur 7 feeling, riptide 8 overtone, tendency, undertow 9 direction, undertone, whirlpool
undercut: 5 blunt, erode 6 weaken 7 cripple, sandbag, subvert, torpedo 8 sabotage 9 attenuate, bring down, undermine
underdeveloped: 4 puny 5 runty, short 8 immature
underdevelopment: 4 lack, want 7 paucity, poverty 10 meagerness
underdog: 5 loser 8 longshot 9 dark horse
underdone: 3 raw 4 rare
underestimate: 3 err 6 slight 7 mistake, neglect, put down 8 belittle, minimize, misjudge 9 deprecate, disesteem, disparage, sell short, underrate
underestimation: 5 error 7 mistake 8 miscount, omission
underfed: 4 puny 6 meager 7 starved 8 starving 9 emaciated
Under Fire (1983 film) cast: Joanna Cassidy, Gene Hackman, Nick Nolte
___ Under Fire: 5 Grace 7 Courage
underfoot: 8 in the way
crush ~: 5 crush, stamp, stomp, worst 6 defeat 7 flatten, trample
it may be ~: 3 mat, rug 4 sole
underfunded: 5 short
undergarment: 4 slip 5 stays, teddy 6 corset, girdle 8 lingerie 10 foundation
undergird: 5 brace 6 hold up, prop up 7 shore up, support 8 buttress 9 reinforce 10 strengthen
undergo: 4 bear, feel, have 5 abide, stand, yield 6 endure, suffer 7 receive, sustain, weather 8 meet with, stand for, submit to, tolerate 9 encounter, put up with, withstand 10 experience
undergraduate: 4 soph 5 pupil 6 junior, senior 7 scholar, student 8 freshman 9 sophomore
British ~: 5 sizar, sizer
see also college
underground: 4 deep, tube 6 buried, covert, hidden, secret, subway, sunken 7 covered, on the QT, private, radical 8 hush-hush, on the sly 9 concealed, resistant, resistive
chamber: 4 cave, kiva, mine 5 vault 6 bunker, cavern, grotto
dweller of folklore: 5 gnome, troll
event: 5 A-test, H-test, N-test
explorer: 5 caver 9 spelunker
find: 3 oil, ore 7 mineral 9 petroleum
go ~: 4 hide 6 hole up, lay low, lie low
growth: 4 root 5 radix, tuber 7 radicle, rhizome
org.: 3 UMW
passage: 4 mine, pipe 5 drain, sewer 7 conduit, culvert
retreat: 3 pit 6 dugout, trench 7 foxhole 10 excavation
rodent: 4 mole 6 gopher
room: 6 bunker, cellar 8 basement
root: 5 tuber
worker: 5 miner
WWII ~ resistance movement: 3 EAM 4 ELAS 6 Maquis
underground ___: 5 movie 7 railway, trolley
Underground ___, The: 3 Man 4 City
Underground City, The author: Jules Verne
Underground Man, The author: Ross Macdonald
undergrowth: 5 brush, gorse, scrub, shrub 6 bushes 7 thicket 9 chaparral, shrubbery
underhand: 3 sly 4 wily 5 shady, sharp 6 crafty, secret, shifty, shrewd, sneaky, tricky, unfair, unjust 7 crooked, cunning, devious, furtive, oblique, on the QT, sub rosa 8 guileful, hush-hush, indirect, scheming, slippery, sneaking, stealthy, two-faced 9 concealed, deceitful, deceptive, dishonest, insidious, secretive, two-timing, unethical 10 fraudulent, undeserved
throw: 3 lob 4 toss 5 pitch
underhanded: 3 sly 4 foul, wily 5 cheap, dirty, false, shady, snaky, undue 6 covert, secret, sneaky, tricky, unfair 7 corrupt, crooked, devious, furtive, knavish 8 delusive, guileful, scheming, sneaking 9 deceitful, dishonest, insincere, unethical 10 mendacious, unreliable, untruthful
one: 5 rogue, sneak 6 con man
underhandedness: 4 hoax, ruse, sham, wile 5 craft, fraud, guile, lying 6 deceit, humbug 7 cunning, falsity, slyness, snow job, swindle 8 artifice, cheating, flimflam, pretense, trickery 9 chicanery, duplicity, imposture, treachery, two-timing 10 craftiness, dishonesty, subterfuge

underivative: 3 new 5 early, first, fresh, novel, prime 7 genuine, radical, seminal 8 creative, original, primeval, singular 9 authentic, demiurgic, formative, ingenious, inspiring, inventive, primitive 10 archetypal, avant-garde, innovative, primordial, refreshing
underline: 4 mark, rule 6 accent, legend, play up, stress 7 bracket, caption, feature, point to, point up 8 indicate 9 emphasize, highlight, italicize, punctuate, reinforce, spotlight 10 accentuate
underling: 4 aide, pawn 6 deputy, flunky, lackey, minion, stooge, yes man 7 flunkey, lacquey
underlining: 6 stress 8 emphasis
under lock and __: 3 key
underlying: 4 root 5 basal, basic, prime, vital 6 bottom, hidden, latent, veiled 7 crucial, lurking, primary, radical 8 cardinal, critical 9 concealed, elemental, essential, intrinsic, necessary, primitive 10 elementary
sentiment: 5 pulse
__-under-Lyne: 6 Ashton
Under Milk Wood author: Dylan Thomas
undermine: 3 dig, sag, sap 4 flag, foil, hurt, ruin, tire, undo, wane, wear 5 blunt, erode, wreck 6 damage, debase, impair, poison, reduce, shrink, soften, thwart, tunnel, weaken 7 corrupt, cripple, deplete, disable, eat away, exhaust, fatigue, sandbag, subvert, torpedo, unnerve, vitiate 8 enervate, enfeeble, excavate, sabotage, threaten, undercut 9 attenuate, bring down, frustrate, hollow out 10 debilitate, demoralize, devitalize
underneath: 4 down 5 below, infra, lower, neath, under 6 nether 7 covered
prefix: 5 intra-
undernourished: 4 bony, thin 5 boney 6 ill-fed, skinny 7 scrawny, starved 8 starving
under one's __: 3 hat 4 belt, nose, wing 5 thumb 6 breath
__ under one's skin: 3 get
underpaid one: 4 peon 5 slave 6 drudge
underpass: 6 tunnel 8 crossing 10 cloverleaf
in Britain: 4 tube 5 metro 6 subway
underpin: 4 hold 5 shore 6 prop up 7 shore up
underpinning: 4 base, prop, root, stay 5 basis, brace 7 footing, support 8 buttress
underplay: 5 gloze 8 discount, minimize, palliate, pooh-pooh, shrug off, talk down 9 gloss over, whitewash
__ under pressure: 5 grace
Under Pressure (1981 song) artist: Queen
underprivileged: 4 poor 5 broke, needy, sorry 6 bad off, hard up, ill off, in need, in want 7 hapless, have-not, pinched 8 badly off, bankrupt, beggarly, deprived, ill-fated, indigent, strapped 9 destitute, insolvent, moneyless, penniless, penurious 10 down and out, pauperized, straitened
underrate: 7 cry down, devalue 8 belittle, minimize, misjudge, play down, write off 9 devaluate, disparage 10 depreciate
underscore: 6 accent, play up, stress 7 feature, iterate, point up 9 emphasize, highlight, punctuate, spotlight 10 accentuate
underscoring: 6 accent 8 emphasis
undersea measure: 5 depth 6 fathom, league
undershirt: 3 tee 8 lingerie
in Britain: 4 vest 7 singlet
size: 3 med. 5 large, small 6 medium
undershoot: 4 miss
underside: 3 bed 4 base, foot 5 floor 6 bottom, ground 7 reverse, support 10 foundation
on the ~: 5 below, lower 6 nether 7 beneath 8 downward 9 covered by
Under Siege (1992 film)
cast: Gary Busey, Erika Eleniak, Tommy Lee Jones, Steven Seagal
undersize: 3 wee 4 baby, puny, tiny 5 dwarf, elfin, pigmy, pygmy, short, small, teeny, weeny 6 bantam, lesser, little, midget, minute, peewee, petite, pocket, slight, teensy 7 stunted 9 miniature 10 diminutive, teeny-weeny
underspend: 3 eke 4 save 5 skimp 6 scrape, scrimp 8 conserve, roll back, withhold 9 economize 10 cut corners
understand: 3 dig, get, ken, see 4 hear, know, note, read, tell, wake 5 catch, get it, grasp, infer, learn, savvy, sense, think, waken 6 absorb, accept, assume, decode, deduce, expect, fathom, follow, gather, intuit, master, reckon, take in, take it 7 believe, catch on, cognize, concede, discern, explain, feel for, find out, imagine, make out, presume, realize, suppose, surmise, suspect 8 conceive, conclude, consider, decipher, perceive, register, relate to, tolerate 9 apprehend, figure out, get to know, interpret, penetrate, recognize 10 appreciate, assimilate, comprehend, sympathize
easy to ~: 5 clear, lucid, plain, vivid 6 cogent, simple 7 evident, express, legible, obvious 8 apparent, coherent, distinct, explicit, knowable, luculent, luminous, manifest, palpable, readable 9 graspable 10 explicable, reasonable, spelled out
hard to ~: 4 mazy 5 tough 6 arcane, knotty, opaque, sticky, thorny, tricky 7 complex, labored, obscure, unclear 8 abstruse, baffling, puzzling 9 difficult, intricate 10 formidable, mystifying, perplexing
in sci-fi: 4 grok
slow to ~: 5 dense 6 obtuse
Understand?: 3 see 5 get it, get me
understandable: 5 clear, lucid, plain, vivid 6 cogent, simple 7 evident, express, legible, obvious 8 apparent, coherent, distinct, explicit, knowable, luculent, luminous, manifest, palpable, readable 9 graspable 10 explicable, reasonable, spelled out
make ~: 7 clarify, clear up 9 bring home, elucidate, explicate, get across 10 illuminate, illustrate
understanding: 3 ken, wit 4 deal, grip, idea, kind, nice, pact, pity, tact, view, wise, wits 5 grasp, light, savvy, sense 6 accord, acumen, belief, import, intent, kindly, lenity, notion, reason, sanity, uptake, wisdom 7 ability, compact, concord, empathy, entente, harmony, inkling, insight, knowing, liberal, mastery, meaning, message, opinion, patient, purport, purview, rapport, reading, tactful, thought 8 amicable, contract, decision, generous, judgment, keenness, kindness, lenience, sympathy, tolerant 9 accepting, awareness, forgiving, fraternal, handshake, intellect, intuition, knowledge, observant, sensitive, sharpness, tolerance, viewpoint 10 perception, perceptive, responsive, supportive
come to an ~: 4 jibe 5 agree 6 accord, settle 7 concede, consent, go along, resolve 8 cut a deal, play ball 9 acquiesce, harmonize, negotiate
exclamation of ~: 4 I see, okay 5 got it, right 6 I get it, righto
with the ~: 2 if 8 as long as, assuming, provided 9 given that, providing, subject to, supposing 10 in the event
words of ~: 3 ohs 5 I know 6 I get it
Understanding __: 5 Media
Understanding Media author: Marshall McLuhan
Understanding (song) artist: Bob Seger, Xscape
understate: 5 fudge 8 downplay, minimize, play down 9 soft-pedal
understated: 3 low 4 soft 5 faint, piano, quiet 6 low-key, subtle
understatement: 7 litotes
understood: 3 pat 4 on to 5 given, known, roger, tacit 6 unsaid, wise to 7 assumed, down pat, implied 8 accepted, implicit, inferred, presumed, unspoken, unstated, unvoiced, very well, wordless 9 axiomatic, customary, intuitive, unwritten
easily ~: 5 clear, lucid, plain, vivid 6 cogent, simple 7 evident, express, legible, logical, obvious 8 apparent, clear-cut, coherent, distinct, explicit, knowable, luculent, luminous, manifest, palpable, readable, sensible 9 graspable 10 explicable, reasonable, spelled out
not easily ~: 4 deep, mazy 5 tough 6 arcane, hidden, knotty, occult, opaque, secret, sticky, thorny, tricky 7 complex, Delphic, labored, obscure, unclear 8 abstract, abstruse, baffling, esoteric, profound, puzzling 9 difficult, intricate, recondite 10 fathomless, formidable, mysterious, mystifying, perplexing
Understood!: 4 I dig, I see 5 got it, I'm hip, roger 6 I get it
understudy: 3 sub 5 actor 6 backup, player 7 stand-in 9 alternate, attendant 10 substitute
undertake: 3 try 4 wage 5 begin, essay, start 6 assume, embark, go into, hazard, launch, pledge, set out, tackle 7 address, attempt, get into, go about, pitch in, presume, promise, propose, venture 8 approach, commence, contract, endeavor, engage in, have a try, initiate, practice, set about, shoulder 9 answer for, enter upon, guarantee, volunteer 10 bargain for, make a run at
undertaking: 3 act, job 4 deal, duty, move, task, work 5 essay, labor 6 action, affair, effort, matter 7 attempt, mission, project, pursuit, venture 8 activity, business, endeavor, movement, struggle 9 adventure, operation
easy ~: 4 snap 5 cinch 6 breeze, picnic 8 duck soup, kid stuff 9 no trouble 10 child's play
Undertaking, The author: John Donne
under the __: 3 gun, sun 4 wire 5 radar, table 7 weather
Under the __: 3 Sea
Under the Boardwalk (1964 song) artist: Drifters
__ under the bridge: 5 water
Under the Bridge (1992 song) artist: Red Hot Chili Peppers
__ under the collar: 3 hot
under-the-counter: 7 bootleg, crooked, illegal, illicit 8 improper, unlawful 10 not allowed, prohibited, unlicensed
__ Under the Elms: 6 Desire
__ under the hammer: 4 come
Under the hawthorne in the __: 4 dale
__ under the haystack...: 3 he's
Under the Mountain Wall author: Peter Matthiessen
Under the Net author: Iris Murdoch
Under the Sea-Wind author: Rachel Carson
__ Under the Sun: 4 Evil
under-the-table: 6 covert, secret 7 furtive, illegal 8 hush-hush
Under the Tonto Rim author: Zane Grey
Under the Volcano (1984 film)
cast: Anthony Andrews, Jacqueline Bisset, Albert Finney
director: John Huston
Under the Volcano author: 5 Lowry
under-the-wipers item: 5 flier, flyer 7 leaflet 8 circular 9 broadside
Under the Yum Yum Tree (1963 film)
cast: Edie Adams, Dean Jones, Jack Lemmon, Carol Lynley
undertone: 3 hum 4 hint 5 rumor, tinge, touch, trace 6 flavor, mumble, murmur, mutter 7 feeling, whisper 10 atmosphere, suggestion
undertow: 4 race, tide 9 whirlpool
Under Two Flags (1936 film)
cast: Claudette Colbert, Ronald Colman, Victor McLaglen
director: Frank Lloyd
Under Two Flags author: 5 Ouida
undervalue: 5 lower 7 cry down 8 belittle, write off 9 disparage, downgrade 10 depreciate
underwater: 4 sunk 6 sunken 9 submarine, submerged
boat: 3 sub 9 submarine
breathing apparatus: 4 gill 5 scuba
cave dweller: 3 eel
explorer: 5 Beebe 8 Cousteau
go ~: 3 dip 4 dive, sink, swim 5 drown, scuba 6 fall in 7 capsize, founder, immerse 8 submerge 9 scuba-dive, shipwreck
organism: 4 alga, kelp 5 polyp
shelf: 4 reef 5 ledge
tracker: 5 sonar
underway: 5 afoot, astir 6 moving 7 going on, ongoing 8 in motion 9 advancing, happening, occurring, on the move, traveling 10 in progress
get ~: 5 begin, start 6 set off, set out 8 set forth, shove off
underwear: 3 bra 4 BVDs, slip, stay 6 bikini, boxers, briefs, corset, shorts 7 drawers, garment, Jockeys 8 clothing, lingerie, skivvies 9 long johns
brand: 3 BVD 5 Hanes 6 Jockey
__ underwear: 4 long 7 thermal
underweight: 4 bony, lank, lean, puny, thin 5 boney 6 gangly, skinny 7 angular, scrawny, starved 8 angulose, angulous
Under Western Eyes author: Joseph Conrad
Underwood: 3 Ron 5 Blair
underworld: 3 mob 4 hell 5 abyss, Hades, Mafia, Orcus 6 Erebus, racket 7 inferno 8 riffraff 9 criminals, gangsters, syndicate
Babylonian ~: 5 Aralu 6 Arallu
Biblical ~: 5 Sheol
entrance: 6 Averno

figure: 3 don 5 devil, Satan
god: 3 Dis 5 Orcus, Pluto
lingo: 5 argot
river: 4 Styx 5 Lethe
weapon: 3 gat
woman: 4 moll
Underworld author: Don DeLillo
Underworld Story, The (1950 film)
cast: Dan Duryea, Gale Storm
underwrite: 3 pay 4 back, fund, seal, sign 5 angel, endow, float, stake 6 assure, cosign, ensure, insure, secure 7 approve, endorse, finance, indorse, promise, sponsor, support, warrant 8 bankroll, sanction 9 guarantee, subscribe, subsidize
a risk: 5 cover 6 ensure, insure, shield 7 protect, warrant 9 guarantee, indemnify
underwriter: 5 angel 6 backer, patron 7 sponsor 9 guarantor, supporter 10 benefactor, grubstaker
govt. bank ~: 4 FDIC 5 FSLIC
undeserved: 4 foul 5 undue 6 shabby, unjust 7 extreme, low-down 8 improper, needless, wrongful 9 excessive, underhand, unmerited 10 gratuitous, inordinate
charge: 5 frame 6 bad rap 7 frameup
undeserving: 3 low 4 base 5 unfit 6 no-good 7 ignoble 8 unworthy, wretched 9 no-account 10 ineligible
undesignated: 8 nameless 9 anonymous
undesigned: 9 hit or miss
undesirable: 4 icky 5 creep 7 dreaded, loathed, outcast, scorned, shunned, useless 8 annoying, disliked, rejected, unsavory, unsought, unwanted 9 defective, loathsome, obnoxious, offensive, repellent, repugnant, unhealthy, unlikable, unpopular, unwelcome
act: 4 no-no, tabu 5 taboo
undesired: 7 unasked 8 needless
undetailed: 7 general, sketchy
undetected: 6 hidden, latent, secret, unseen, veiled 7 lurking 8 shrouded 9 concealed, invisible, unexposed, unnoticed 10 out of sight, tucked away, unobserved
undetermined: 4 open 5 vague 7 pending 9 uncertain, undecided, unsettled
undeterred: 6 dogged, steady 7 devoted, staunch 8 resolute, tireless, untiring 9 dedicated, energetic, tenacious, undaunted, unwearied 10 determined, persistent, relentless, unflagging, unswerving, unwavering
un, deux, __: 5 trois
undeveloped: 4 puny 5 crude, young 6 latent, little 7 ignored 8 backward, immature, inchoate, untaught 9 embryonic, half-baked, incipient, potential, premature, primitive, shapeless, unevolved, untrained
undeviating: 4 even, firm, sure 5 fixed, level 6 direct, linear, rooted, smooth, stable, static, steady 7 literal, regular, settled, uniform 8 constant, definite, directly, ironclad, straight 9 permanent 10 dependable, foursquare
undeviatingly: 5 right 6 wholly 7 exactly, totally, utterly 8 entirely, reliably, squarely 9 honorably, literally, perfectly, precisely 10 absolutely, completely, dependably 12 scrupulously
undexterous: 5 inapt, inept, unapt
undies: 6 briefs, shorts 7 drawers 8 lingerie, skivvies
undifferentiated: 4 like, same, such 5 equal 6 on a par 7 similar, uniform 8 matching, parallel, selfsame 9 identical 10 comparable, consistent, equivalent, tantamount, true to type
undignified: 5 crude, gross 6 coarse, vulgar 8 immodest, improper, indecent, unseemly 9 inelegant 10 in bad taste, indecorous, indelicate, out of place
undiluted: 4 pure 5 sheer 6 strong 8 straight
undiminished: 5 total, whole 6 entire 7 plenary, undying 8 finished, thorough 10 exhaustive
undiplomatic: 5 brash 8 inurbane, tactless 9 maladroit, unguarded
undirected: 7 aimless, erratic 8 headless, unguided
undisciplined: 3 lax, raw 4 wild 7 coltish 10 disorderly
undisclosed: 6 hidden, secret 7 private 8 ulterior 9 potential
undiscounted: 5 at par
undiscovered: 6 unseen 7 unknown 9 unheard-of, unnoticed
undisguised: 4 bald, open 5 clear, naked, overt, plain 6 direct, honest, in view, patent, public 7 exposed, obvious, visible 8 apparent, clear-cut, explicit, knowable, manifest 10 observable
undismayed: 4 bold, game 5 brave, gutsy, nervy, stout 6 daring, gritty, heroic, plucky, spunky 7 doughty, gallant, valiant 8 fearless, intrepid, stalwart, unafraid, valorous 9 audacious, confident, dauntless, undaunted, unfearing 10 chivalrous, courageous, mettlesome
undisputable: 4 sure 5 final 7 assured, certain 8 admitted, positive, unerring 9 undoubted
undisputed: 4 sure 5 final 7 assured, certain 8 admitted, positive, unerring 9 arbitrary, unanimous, undoubted, universal 10 inarguable, undoubtful
Undisputed Truth song: Smiling Faces Sometimes (1971)
undistinguished: 4 blah, so-so 5 bland, plain 6 boring, common, humble, simple 7 average, unknown 8 mediocre, nameless, ordinary 10 pedestrian
group: 4 ruck 8 riffraff
undistorted: 4 real, true 5 right 6 honest 7 correct 8 faithful, straight
undistracted: 4 rapt 8 absorbed 9 engrossed, undivided
undisturbed: 4 calm, cool, even 5 quiet 6 in situ, low-key, mellow, placid, sedate, serene, smooth, virgin 7 amiable, at peace, easeful, equable, pacific, relaxed, stoical 8 amicable, composed, laid-back, peaceful, tranquil, unbroken, virginal 9 collected, easy-going, impassive, quiescent, temperate
undiversified: 4 same 5 alike 7 similar, uniform
undivided: 3 one 4 full, sole 5 solid, total, uncut, whole 6 entire, joined, single, steady, united 7 intense 8 absorbed, combined, complete, integral, thorough, unbroken, vigilant 9 concerted, connected, engrossed, exclusive, unanimous 10 collective, continuous, unflagging, unswerving
undivulged: 6 buried, covert, hidden, secret 7 sub rosa 8 ulterior 10 under wraps, unrevealed
undo: 4 free, open, ruin 5 annul, crimp, erase, loose, quash, queer, smash, spoil, stimy, stymy, untie, unzip, upset, wreck 6 cancel, defeat, injure, loosen, negate, offset, stymie, unbind, unfold, unlock, unwind, unwrap 7 abolish, destroy, nullify, release, restore, reverse, screw up, shatter, subvert, unclose, unravel 8 abrogate, come open, demolish, outsmart, overturn, separate, take down, unbutton, unfasten, unloosen 9 bring down, disengage, dismantle, overreach, overthrow, take apart, undermine 10 counteract, disconnect, impoverish, invalidate, lay waste to, neutralize
undocumented one, perhaps: 5 alien 7 refugee 9 foreigner, immigrant, outlander 10 noncitizen
undoing: 3 end 4 bane, blow, doom, loss, ruin 6 defeat 7 bad luck, failure 8 calamity, collapse, disgrace, downfall, reversal 9 adversity, annulment, mischance, perdition, ruination 10 affliction, misfortune, subversion, visitation
undomesticated: 4 wild 5 feral, rabid 6 ferine, savage 7 beastly 9 ferocious
undone: 5 kaput, loose 6 beaten, broken, doomed, ruined, untied 7 crushed, smashed, wrecked 8 finished, wiped out 9 destroyed, shattered 10 irremedial
come ~: 3 rip 4 fray, open, tear, wear 5 break, burst, crack, shred, split 7 frazzle, give way, rupture 8 fragment, separate 9 disengage, pull apart 10 disconnect
leave ~: 4 omit, wait 5 slack 8 overlook
remain ~: 4 hang, pend, wait 5 await, delay
wish ~: 3 rue 5 mourn 6 bemoan, bewail, grieve, lament, regret 8 repent of
undoubted: 4 true 5 right 9 veritable 10 undeniable, undisputed
undoubtedly: 2 ay, da, ja, sí 3 aye, oui, yea, yep, yes, yup 4 fine, okay, sure, yeah 5 good-o, natch, quite, right, roger, truly, uh-huh 6 agreed, easily, gladly, good-oh, indeed, just so, rather, really, righto, surely, you bet, yowzah 7 exactly, go ahead, indeedy, mais oui, quite so, ten-four 8 all right, as you say, of course, thumbs up, very well 9 assuredly, be my guest, certainly, darn right, doubtless, naturally, precisely, sure thing, you betcha, you said it 10 absolutely, by all means, definitely, positively, sure enough, that's right
undoubtful: 3 set 4 sure 5 clear, on ice, valid 7 certain, settled 8 accurate, definite, destined, fail-safe, ironclad, unerring 9 authentic, axiomatic, foolproof, unfailing 10 conclusive, inevitable, infallible, unarguable, undeniable, undisputed, verifiable
undraped: 4 bare, nude 5 naked, stark 9 in the buff, in the nude 10 unshielded
undreamed of: 6 untold
undress: 4 doff, peel, shed 5 strip 6 denude, devest, show up 7 disrobe, slip off, take off, uncloak 8 get out of, unattire, unclothe 9 dismantle, slip out of
undressed: 4 bare, nude 5 naked 9 unattired
undry: 3 wet 4 damp, dank, dewy, oozy 5 humid, juicy, misty, moist, muddy, muggy, rainy, soggy 6 clammy, drippy, oozing, sodden, steamy, sweaty, watery 7 drizzly, sopping 8 dripping 9 drizzling, saturated, succulent
Undset, Sigrid: 6 Danish, writer 8 Nobelist
und so __: 6 weiter
__ und Tabu: 5 Totem
__ und Träume: 5 Nacht
undue: 5 stiff 6 unfair, unjust 7 extreme, too much 8 improper, needless, overmuch, unseemly, untimely 9 exceeding, excessive, overblown, unfitting 10 exorbitant, gratuitous, immoderate, inordinate, undeserved
undulate: 4 beat, curl, roll, sway, wave 5 slink, surge, swell, swing, twine 6 billow, ripple 7 slither
undulating: 4 wavy 6 zigzag 7 sinuous
undulation: 4 beat, wave 5 swell 6 billow 9 arabesque 10 earthquake
unduly: 3 too 4 over, very 6 overly 8 overmuch, to a fault, unfairly, unjustly 9 extremely 10 improperly
undusted: 5 dirty 6 filthy
__ und Verklärung: 3 Tod
undying: 7 abiding, endless, eternal, lasting, unended 8 constant, enduring, immortal, infinite, timeless, unending, unfading 9 ceaseless, incessant, perennial, permanent, perpetual, unceasing 10 continuing, persistent
uneager: 3 shy 4 loth 5 loath 6 afraid, averse 8 hesitant 9 reluctant 10 indisposed, uninclined
unearned __: 3 run 6 income
unearth: 3 dig, get, see 4 find, grub, root 5 delve, dig up, learn, trace 6 dredge, exhume, expose, locate, reveal, strike, turn up, unbury 7 find out, root out, rout out, uncover 8 discover, disinter, dredge up, excavate 9 ascertain, determine, ferret out, stumble on, track down
unearthing: 9 detection, discovery 10 excavation
unearthly: 4 eery 5 eerie, scary, weird 6 absurd, divine, fantom, occult, spooky, unholy 7 ghastly, ghostly, haunted, phantom, uncanny, ungodly 8 ethereal, ghoulish, spectral 9 spiritual 10 immaterial, ridiculous, sepulchral, superhuman
unease: 4 fear 5 alarm, angst, dread, panic, qualm 6 dismay, fright, horror, phobia, terror 7 anxiety, concern, malaise, tension 9 misgiving 10 foreboding, infirmness, solicitude
uneasiness: 4 care 5 angst, qualm, worry 6 nerves, regret 7 fidgets, jitters, malaise, scruple, tension 8 disquiet, hangover 9 tightness 10 discomfort, discontent, impatience
uneasy: 4 edgy 5 antsy, chary, itchy, jumpy, queer, shaky, tense, upset 6 afraid, on edge, pacing, queasy, queazy, shaken 7 alarmed, anxious, awkward, fearful, fidgety, fretful, jittery, keyed up, nervous, restive, uptight, worried 8 agitated, bothered, dismayed, fluttery, fretsome, harassed, insecure, restless, skittish, strained, troubled 9 all nerves, concerned, disturbed, excitable, impatient, in turmoil, perturbed, unsettled 10 disquieted, high-strung, solicitous
feel ~: 4 fret 5 worry 6 jitter, regret
Uneasy Rider (1973 song) artist: Charlie Daniels
uneaten: 5 scrap 8 leftover 9 remaining, untouched 10 unconsumed
uneconomical: 6 lavish 8 wasteful
uneducated: 6 simple, unread 7 loutish, lowbrow 8 ignorant, untaught 9 benighted, inerudite, unlearned, untutored 10 illiterate, unlettered
uneffusive: 3 shy 4 wary 5 chary, leery, mousy, quiet, timid 6 demure, modest 7 bashful 8 cautious, reserved, reticent, retiring, sheepish 9 diffident, reluctant, withdrawn
unelaborate: 5 plain 6 simple
unelected group: 4 outs 5 junta
unelevated: 3 low 4 flat 5 short 8 knee-high, sea-level

unembellished: 4 bald, bare, real 5 basic, plain, stark 6 barren, common, honest, severe, simple 7 austere, Spartan 8 ordinary 9 bare-bones

unemotional: 3 dry, icy 4 blah, cold, cool, flat 5 aloof, bland, chill, quiet, stoic, stony 6 chilly, frigid, low-key, mellow, placid, remote, sedate, serene, stolid, stoney, wooden 7 amiable, at peace, callous, deadpan, equable, glacial, ice-cold, pacific, relaxed, stoical 8 amicable, composed, laid-back, listless, obdurate, peaceful, reserved, reticent, tranquil 9 apathetic, collected, easy-going, heartless, impassive, nerveless, quiescent, temperate, unfeeling

unemploy: 3 axe, can 4 fire 6 lay off

unemployed: 4 free, idle 5 fired 6 unused 7 jobless, laid off, loafing, resting 8 inactive, leisured, on layoff, workless 9 at liberty, on the dole, out of a job, out of work, unengaged

unemployment: 6 layoff 7 leisure 9 recession

unencouraging word: 3 nah, nay 4 nope

unencumbered: 3 rid 4 free 5 loose

unending: 4 ever, long 6 eterne, steady 7 abiding, abysmal, endless, eternal, lasting, nonstop, undying 8 constant, enduring, immortal, infinite, timeless, unwaning 9 boundless, ceaseless, continual, countless, incessant, limitless, perennial, perpetual, unceasing 10 continuous

unendingly: 4 ever 6 always 7 forever, for good 8 evermore, for keeps 9 eternally 10 at all times, constantly, enduringly

unendurable: 3 bad, sad 4 grim, vile 5 awful, cruel, harsh 6 rotten 7 adverse, beastly, brutish, heinous, hurtful, painful, ruinous 8 criminal, dreadful 9 appalling, atrocious, injurious, miserable, third-rate 10 abominable, detestable, inadequate, pernicious

unenduring: 5 brief, short 7 passing 8 fleeting, flitting 9 ephemeral, momentary, temporary, transient 10 evanescent, transitory

unenergetic: 4 beat, lazy, limp 5 all in, spent, tired, weary 6 done in, drowsy, pooped, sleepy 7 drained, worn out 8 careworn, dog-tired, drooping, fatigued, flagging 9 burned out, exhausted, played out, pooped out, prostrate 10 half-asleep

unengaged: 4 free 7 resting 8 on layoff 9 at liberty, on the dole, out of a job, out of work 10 unemployed

unenlightened: 3 raw 4 dark, naif 5 naive 7 out of it, unaware 8 ignorant, medieval 9 in the dark, mediaeval

unentertaining: 4 arid, blah, drab, dull, flat, limp, tame 5 bland, inane, prosy, trite, vapid 6 boring, jejune 7 humdrum, insipid, tedious 8 tiresome, zestless 9 colorless 10 dullsville, lackluster

unenthusiastic: 4 cold, cool 5 aloof, blasé, stoic, tepid, token 7 languid, stoical 8 lukewarm, negative 9 apathetic, reluctant, unwilling

unequal: 3 odd 5 other 6 spotty, uneven, unlike 7 distant, diverse, unalike, varying 8 lopsided, one-sided 9 different, differing, disparate, divergent, irregular, unmatched 10 dissimilar, ill-matched, mismatched, off-balance, poles apart, unbalanced

combining form: 5 aniso-

unequaled: 4 A-one, best, only, sole, tops 5 alone 6 unique 7 in front, supreme 8 peerless, towering, ultimate 9 matchless, nonpareil, paramount, unmatched, unrivaled 10 inimitable, preeminent, surpassing, unrivalled

unequipped: 5 unfit 6 unable 8 helpless 9 incapable, powerless, unskilled 10 inadequate, ineligible, unskillful, unsuitable

unequivocal: 4 sure 5 clear, exact, plain 6 direct, patent 7 certain, decided, evident, flat-out, obvious, precise 8 absolute, apparent, clear-cut, decisive, definite, distinct, dogmatic, emphatic, explicit, knowable, manifest, outright, palpable, positive, readable, specific, straight 9 downright, out-and-out, outspoken, trenchant 10 dogmatical, foursquare, peremptory, point-blank

response: 2 no 3 nah, naw, nay, nix, non 4 nein, nope, nyet, uh-uh 5 ixnay, never, no how, no way 6 no deal, nowise 7 not ever 8 at no time, forget it, negative, not at all 9 by no means, fat chance 10 count me out, impossible, not a chance, thumbs down

unequivocally: 5 fully 6 easily, surely, wholly 8 for keeps 10 point-blank

unequivocating: 4 open 5 bluff, blunt, frank, plain, vocal 6 candid, direct, honest 7 artless, genuine, sincere, upfront 8 straight, truthful 9 guileless, ingenuous, outspoken, veracious 10 aboveboard, forthright, foursquare, free-spoken, from the hip, point-blank

unerring: 4 sure, true 5 exact, right, valid 7 certain, correct, factual, literal, perfect, precise 8 accurate, dogmatic, fail-safe, flawless, reliable 9 errorless, faultless, foolproof, unfailing 10 dogmatical, impeccable, infallible, undisputed, undoubtful

unerringly: 5 truly 7 exactly 9 literally, precisely 10 faithfully

unescorted: 4 lone, solo, stag 5 alone

unessential: 5 extra, small 6 slight 8 needless 9 redundant 10 gratuitous

unethical: 3 bad, low 5 dirty, fishy, shady, sharp, slick, wrong 6 sneaky, unfair, wicked 7 corrupt, crooked, illegal, immoral, knavish 8 cheating, flimflam, improper, slippery, two-faced, wrongful 9 dishonest, mercenary, two-timing, underhand 10 fly-by-night

one: 5 knave, louse, rogue, scamp, sneak, swine 9 miscreant

uneven: 3 odd 4 alop 5 bumpy, erose, hilly, jerky, lumpy, ridgy, rough 6 broken, craggy, fickle, fitful, hackly, jagged, jiggly, jouncy, knobby, patchy, ragged, rugged, spotty, unfair, wabbly, wobbly 7 cragged, erratic, knurled, mutable, notched, scraggy, serrate, unequal, unlevel 8 lopsided, one-sided, unsmooth, unsteady, variable 9 differing, disparate, irregular, mercurial, spasmodic, unaligned 10 capricious, changeable, ill-matched, inconstant, off-balance, unbalanced

combining form: 5 aniso-

unevenness: 9 disparity, imbalance 10 coarseness, inequality, unjustness

uneventful: 4 blah, dull, slow 5 quiet 6 boring, dreary, normal, smooth 7 humdrum, prosaic, regular, routine, tedious 8 ordinary, standard 9 prosaical

unevolved: 4 wild 5 crude, early 7 ancient 8 primeval 9 primitive, vestigial 10 aboriginal, primordial

unexacting: 3 lax 4 easy, kind, mild, snap, soft 5 cinch, cushy, light, loose 6 breeze, gentle, kindly, picnic, simple 7 clement, ruthful, sparing 8 duck soup, flexible, laid-back, merciful, painless, placable, pushover, tolerant, untaxing 9 assuasive, compliant, easygoing, forgiving, indulgent 10 child's play, effortless, forbearing, permissive

unexaggerated: 4 real, true 5 sober 6 actual, candid 7 literal

unexampled: 4 lone, rare 6 unique 8 peerless, singular 9 matchless, nonpareil, unmatched 10 inimitable, one-of-a-kind, sui generis

unexcelled: 4 A-one, tops 5 alone

unexceptional: 4 so-so 5 typic, usual 6 common, decent, modest 7 average, regular, routine, typical 8 adequate, everyday, familiar, mediocre, middling, moderate, ordinary, standard

unexcessive: 2 OK 3 low 4 mild, sane 5 cheap, sober 6 modest 7 average, low-cost 8 moderate, sensible 9 excusable, low-priced, realistic, temperate, tolerable 10 acceptable, controlled, economical, reasonable, restrained

unexcitable: 4 even 5 quiet, stoic 6 serene, stolid 7 equable, ice-cold

unexcited: 4 calm, cool, even 5 blasé, quiet, sober, staid, stoic 6 at ease, low-key, mellow, placid, sedate, serene, stolid 7 amiable, at peace, equable, pacific, relaxed, stoical 8 amicable, carefree, composed, laid-back, peaceful, tranquil 9 collected, easy-going, impassive, quiescent, temperate, unstirred 10 nonchalant, phlegmatic, unaffected, unagitated

unexciting: 4 blah, dull, flat, tame 5 bland, ho-hum 6 stodgy 7 tedious

work: 5 McJob

unexclusive: 4 open 6 public 8 exoteric

unexpansive: 3 shy 4 meek 5 quiet, timid 6 demure, modest 7 bashful 8 reserved, reticent, retiring 9 diffident, shrinking, withdrawn 10 restrained, unassuming

unexpected: 3 odd 5 fluky, swift 6 abrupt, casual, chance, flukey, ironic, sudden 7 amazing, unusual 8 abnormal, surprise 9 haphazard, impetuous, impulsive, startling, unplanned 10 accidental, contingent

benefit: 5 bonus, gravy, treat

development: 4 snag 5 twist 7 wrinkle

movement: 3 jab 4 dash, dive, jump, leap, poke 5 bound, burst, lunge, lurch, pitch, surge, swing, swipe 6 charge, plunge, pounce, spring, strike, thrust

unexpectedly: 5 short 8 suddenly, unawares

unexplainable: 4 eery 5 eerie, weird

unexplained: 3 odd 4 dark 5 alien 6 hidden, occult, secret 7 obscure, strange, unknown 10 mysterious

sighting: 3 UFO

unexplicit: 4 hazy 5 fuzzy, muzzy, vague 7 evasive, muddled, oblique, unclear 9 ambiguous, equivocal 10 ambivalent, clear as mud, indefinite, left-handed, misleading

unexplored: 5 novel 7 foreign, strange, unknown

unexposed: 6 buried, hidden, latent, masked, unseen, veiled 7 cloaked, covered 8 screened, secluded, shrouded 9 concealed, incognito, out of view 10 tucked away, undercover, undetected, unrevealed

unexpressed: 4 mute 5 quiet, tacit 6 latent, silent, unsaid, untold 7 implied 8 implicit, ulterior

unexpressive: 4 cold 5 blank 7 deadpan 8 taciturn

unexpurgated: 3 all 4 full 5 total, uncut, whole 6 entire, intact 7 plenary 8 complete, finished, thorough 9 inviolate 10 definitive, exhaustive, unabridged

unextinguished: 4 live 7 burning

unextreme: 6 normal 9 temperate 10 reasonable, unagitated

unfaceted gem: 4 opal 5 pearl

unfacile: 5 inapt

unfaded: 3 new 5 fresh 6 bright 8 unwilted

unfading: 7 eternal, undying 9 deathless, permanent 10 unchanging

unfailing: 4 same, sure, true 5 loyal, solid 6 trusty 7 certain, endless, eternal, staunch 8 absolute, constant, diligent, faithful, reliable, straight, surefire, unerring, untiring, unwaning 9 assiduous, boundless, ceaseless, continual, counted on, perennial, perpetual, rock-solid, steadfast, unlimited 10 bottomless, consistent, continuous, delivering, dependable, infallible, invariable, persistent, true to type, unchanging, undoubtful, unflagging

unfair: 3 low 4 foul, mean 5 cruel, dirty, petty, undue, wrong 6 biased, uneven, unjust 7 bigoted, crooked, immoral, partial 8 cheating, criminal, grievous, improper, one-sided, partisan, unlawful, wrongful 9 arbitrary, dishonest, underhand, unethical 10 ill-matched, prejudiced, ungrounded, unsporting

accusation: 6 bad rap 9 cheap shot

be ~ to: 5 wrong 8 misjudge

judgment: 5 frame

unfairly: 5 badly 10 improperly

unfairness: 4 bias 6 racism 7 bigotry 8 inequity, nepotism 9 injustice, prejudice 10 favoritism, inequality

unfaithful: 5 false 6 fickle, shifty, untrue 7 corrupt, unloyal 8 cheating, disloyal, forsworn, recreant, sneaking, two-faced 9 deceitful, insincere, two-timing

Unfaithful (2002 film)

cast: Richard Gere, Diane Lane

director: Adrian Lyne

Unfaithfully Yours (1948 film)

cast: Linda Darnell, Rex Harrison, Rudy Vallee

director: Preston Sturges

unfaked: 4 true 6 candid, honest

unfaltering: 3 set 4 firm, sure 5 bound 6 bent on, steady 7 abiding, decided, nonstop 8 enduring, resolute, sedulous, tireless, untiring 9 dead set on, steadfast, tenacious, undaunted, unfailing

unfalteringly: 4 hard

unfamed: 6 no-name, unsung 7 obscure, unknown 8 nameless, ordinary 9 anonymous, unheard-of

unfamiliar: 3 new, odd 5 alien, novel, weird 6 exotic, remote 7 bizarre, curious, foreign, obscure, strange, unalike, unaware, unknown, unusual 8 ignorant, original, peculiar, uncommon, unversed 9 anomalous, different, fantastic, recondite, unheard-of, unknowing, unskilled, unwitting

with: 5 new at, new to

unfar: 4 near, nigh 5 handy 6 at hand 7 close by 8 adjacent 9 alongside, proximate

unfarmed: 6 fallow

unfashionable: 3 old, out 5 dated, dowdy, not in, passé 6 frumpy, old-hat

7 archaic **8** obsolete, outdated, outmoded **9** out-of-date **10** antiquated, out of style
one: **4** geek, nerd, nurd, wonk **7** egghead
unfasten: **4** open, undo **5** loose, untie, unzip **6** detach, loosen **7** release, tear off **9** disengage
unfastened: **4** open **5** loose **6** untied
become ~: **5** loose **6** loosen
unfastidious: **5** messy **6** untidy **7** unkempt **8** slovenly
unfathomable: **4** deep, vast **6** arcane, opaque **7** abysmal, complex, eternal, obscure **8** abstruse, baffling, esoteric, profound, puzzling **9** boundless, enigmatic, limitless, soundless, unlimited, unplumbed **10** bottomless
unfavorable: **3** bad, ill **4** poor **5** risky **7** adverse, hostile, ominous, unlucky **8** contrary, inimical, negative, sinister, untimely, untoward **10** detractive, lamentable, thumbs-down
more ~: **5** worse
review: **3** pan
unfavorably: **3** ill
unfavored: **5** curst **6** cursed, jinxed **7** accurst, hapless **8** ill-fated, luckless **10** ill-starred
unfazed: **4** calm, cool, even **6** serene
unfearful: **4** bold, game **5** brave, gutsy, nervy **6** awless, daring, gritty, heroic, plucky, spunky **7** aweless, defiant, doughty, gallant, staunch, valiant **8** heroical, intrepid, resolute, stalwart, valorous **9** audacious, dauntless, dreadless **10** courageous
unfearing: **4** bold, game **5** brave, stout **6** awless, daring, heroic, plucky **7** aweless, doughty, gallant, valiant **8** heroical, intrepid, resolute, spirited, stalwart, unafraid, valorous **9** audacious, confident, dauntless, undaunted **10** courageous, invincible, mettlesome, undismayed
unfeasible: **3** out **4** airy **6** absurd **7** utopian **8** hopeless, quixotic **9** grandiose, ludicrous, visionary **10** idealistic, impossible, unworkable
unfed: **5** empty **6** hungry **7** peckish, starved **8** edacious, esurient, famished, ravenous, starving **9** voracious
Unfederated __ States: **5** Malay
unfeeling: **3** icy **4** cold, hard, numb **5** crass, cruel, harsh, rough, stern, stony **6** brutal, severe, stoney, unkind **7** callous, ice-cold, inhuman **8** benumbed, churlish, deadened, exacting, hardened, indurate, obdurate, pitiless, ruthless, tactless, uncaring **9** apathetic, bloodless, heartless, impassive, inanimate, inclement, insensate, merciless, senseless, unpitying **10** insensible, mechanical, nonchalant, regardless, unmerciful
unfeigned: **4** real, true **5** frank **6** candid, hearty, honest, infelt, square **7** earnest, genuine, natural, sincere **8** truthful **9** childlike, heartfelt
unfermented juice: **4** must
unfertile: **3** dry **4** arid, poor, sere
unfetter: **4** free **5** let go, loose **6** redeem **7** manumit, release
unfettered: **4** free, wild **5** loose **6** single, untied **9** unlimited
unfilled: **4** open **5** blank, empty **6** hollow, hungry, vacant **7** untaken
unfilleted: **4** bony **5** boney
unfinished: **3** cut, raw **5** crude, rough **6** ragged **7** lacking, ongoing, partial, reduced, sketchy **8** abridged, cut short, formless, half-done, immature **9** condensed, curtailed, deficient, half-baked, imperfect, roughhewn, shortened, tentative, undecided **10** diminished, expurgated, incomplete
room: **4** loft **5** attic **6** garret **8** basement
work: **7** backlog
Unfinished Business director: **4** Owen
Unfinished Symphony composer: **8** Schubert
unfirm: **5** shaky **6** flimsy, wobbly **7** dubious, rickety, tenuous **8** doubtful, insecure, unstable **9** jellylike, quivering, teetering, tentative, tottering **10** indecisive, jerry-built, precarious, ramshackle, tumbledown
unfit: **4** weak **5** inapt, inept, unapt **6** feeble, flabby, unable **7** amateur, laid low, not up to, untoned **8** below par, decrepit, improper, inexpert, unsuited, unworthy **9** ill-suited, incapable, sedentary, unhealthy, unskilled **10** inadequate, inapposite, ineligible, nongermane, out of place, out of shape, unequipped, unprepared, unskillful, unsuitable
be ~ for: **10** disqualify
for consumption: **4** rank **5** moldy **6** rancid, rotten **8** inedible
for farming: **3** dry **4** arid, sere **5** dusty **6** barren, desert, torrid **7** bone-dry, parched **9** waterless
make ~: **4** lame, maim, ruin **5** lay up, wreck **6** injure **8** sabotage **9** hamstring
unfitness: **9** inability **10** disability, inadequacy
unfitting: **5** inapt, undue **8** improper **9** incorrect **10** unbecoming
unfix: **5** loose **6** detach, loosen **8** separate
unfixable: **5** kaput **9** incurable **10** inveterate, remediless
unfixed: **4** as is **8** floating, variable **9** uncertain **10** indefinite
unflagging: **4** firm **5** fixed, hardy **6** active, dogged, gritty, plucky, spunky, steady **7** dynamic, patient, scrappy, staunch **8** constant, diligent, resolute, sedulous, tireless, untiring, unwaning **9** assiduous, continual, deathless, energetic, laborious, steadfast, tenacious, unceasing, undivided, unfailing, unwearied **10** determined, persistent, relentless, undeterred, unwearying
unflappable: **3** set **4** calm, cool, easy **5** quiet, stoic **6** low-key, mellow, placid, sedate, serene **7** amiable, assured, at peace, equable, pacific, relaxed, stoical **8** amicable, composed, laid-back, peaceful, tranquil **9** collected, easy-going, impassive, quiescent, temperate, unruffled
unflattering: **4** mean **5** ideal, snide **6** unkind **7** hurtful, perfect **8** scornful, sneering, spiteful
unflawed: **5** sound **8** absolute **10** impeccable
unfledged: **4** naif **5** naive, young **7** puerile **8** juvenile **9** premature
hawk: **4** eyas
unflinching: **4** firm, game **5** brave, fixed, gutsy, stoic **6** dogged, gritty, plucky **7** staunch **8** fearless, intrepid, resolute, stalwart, untiring **9** dauntless, obstinate, steadfast, tenacious, undaunted **10** foursquare, relentless
unfluctuating: **4** even, firm **5** level **6** stable, static, steady **7** equable, uniform **8** constant **9** unvarying
unflustered: **4** calm, cool, even **5** stoic **6** serene **10** phlegmatic
unfocused: **4** hazy **5** foggy, fuzzy, muddy, muzzy, vague **6** bleary, blurry, woolly **7** blurred, unclear **10** ill-defined, indistinct
unfold: **3** fan, ope **4** dawn, grow, open, show, undo **5** widen **6** evince, evolve, expand, expose, extend, fan out, loosen, mature, reveal, spread, unbend, uncoil, uncurl, unfurl, unroll, unwind, unwrap **7** blossom, clarify, clear up, develop, display, divulge, dope out, explain, flatten, lay bare, narrate, present, produce, reel out, resolve, stretch, uncover, untwist **8** announce, describe, disclose, discover, manifest, shake out, uncrease **9** bear fruit, elaborate, elucidate, explicate, expound on, make known, spread out **10** illustrate, straighten, stretch out
unfolded: **4** open
unfolding: **6** course **7** ongoing, process **8** progress, showdown **9** evolution, expansion
unforbidden: **4** fine, okay **9** allowable
unforced: **7** natural, willing **8** optional **9** unlabored, voluntary
unforeseeable: **3** odd **5** fluky, lucky **6** chance, flukey, random, sudden **7** aimless, oddball **9** haphazard, hit-or-miss, uncertain, unplanned, unwitting **10** accidental, fortuitous, unexpected, unintended
unforeseen: **5** lucky **6** abrupt, casual, chance, sudden **8** surprise **9** startling **10** accidental, contingent, fortuitous
unforgettable: **8** enduring, haunting **9** memorable, nostalgic, obsessive
Unforgettable (song) artist: Dinah Washington, Natalie Cole, Nat King Cole
unforgivable: **5** awful **6** odious, unjust **7** heinous, ignoble **8** grievous, horrible, shameful, terrible **9** abhorrent, atrocious **10** deplorable, despicable
Unforgiven (1992 film)
cast: Clint Eastwood, Morgan Freeman, Gene Hackman, Richard Harris
director: Clint Eastwood
Unforgiven, The (1960 film)
cast: Audrey Hepburn, Burt Lancaster, Audie Murphy
director: John Huston
unforgiving: **5** stern, stony **6** stoney **8** ruthless, vengeful **9** merciless
unformed: **8** inchoate, nebulous **9** amorphous, shapeless
unforthcoming: **3** mum **6** silent **8** taciturn **9** secretive, withdrawn
unfortunate: **3** bad, ill, sad **5** broke, curst, needy, sorry, woful **6** bad off, cursed, doomed, hard up, ill off, in need, in want, jinxed, tragic, unwise, woeful, wretch **7** accurst, adverse, hapless, pinched, ruinous, unhappy, unlucky **8** accursed, badly off, bankrupt, beggarly, forsaken, hopeless, ill-fated, ill-timed, indigent, luckless, sinister, strapped, stricken, terrible, tragical, troubled, untimely, untoward, wretched **9** destitute, insolvent, moneyless, out of luck, penniless, penurious **10** disastrous, down and out, ill-starred, lamentable, pauperized, straitened
feeling for the ~: **4** pity **6** warmth **7** empathy **8** sympathy **10** compassion, kindliness, tenderness
unfortunately: **8** sad to say **10** sorry to say
Unfortunate Traveller, The author: **5** Nashe
unfouled: **4** pure **5** clean **8** unsoiled
unfounded: **4** idle **5** false **6** untrue **7** invalid **8** baseless, mistaken, spurious **9** erroneous, trumped-up **10** bottomless, fabricated, fallacious, gratuitous, groundless
report: **3** lie **4** buzz, dirt, tale, talk, word **5** bruit, rumor **6** canard, earful, gossip, tattle **7** fiction, hearsay, whisper **9** falsehood, grapevine, invention **10** suggestion
unfreeze: **4** melt, thaw **5** deice **6** soften **7** thaw out
unfrequent: **4** rare **6** seldom, spotty **8** far apart, on and off, sporadic, uncommon **9** irregular, scattered, spasmodic **10** occasional, sporadical
unfrequented: **5** quiet **6** lonely, secret **7** private **8** secluded, solitary
unfriendliness: **4** bile **5** chill, spite, venom **6** animus, enmity, grudge, hatred, malice, rancor, spleen **7** ill will **8** acrimony, bad blood **9** animosity, antipathy, harshness, hostility **10** antagonism, resentment
unfriendly: **3** icy **4** cold, cool, sour **5** aloof, chill, crisp, gruff, nasty, surly **6** chilly, unkind **7** against, distant, glacial, hostile, warlike **8** contrary, grudging, inimical, spiteful, vengeful **9** alienated, combative, estranged, jaundiced, malicious **10** antisocial, forbidding, ill-natured, impersonal, insociable, pugnacious, unamicable
one: **3** foe **5** enemy **9** ill-wisher
sound: **3** grr **5** growl, snarl
unfrocking: **7** removal **8** ejection **9** dismissal **10** deposition
unfruitful: **6** meager **7** sterile **9** infertile
unfulfilled: **7** lacking, missing, wanting **8** deprived **10** incomplete
unfun: **4** blah, dull, tame **6** boring, dreary, stodgy, stuffy **7** humdrum, tedious **8** dragging, tiresome **9** wearisome **10** dullsville, lackluster, monotonous, pedestrian
unfurl: **4** open, show **6** spread, unfold **7** display, roll out **9** spread out
unfurled: **4** open
unfurling: **9** expansion
unfurnished: **4** bare **5** empty
unfussy: **5** basic, clean, plain **6** simple **8** informal **9** unadorned
ungainly: **5** gawky, inept, stiff, weedy **6** clumsy, klutzy, oafish, wooden **7** awkward, gawkish, hulking, lumpish, uncouth **8** bumbling, bungling, cloddish, lubberly, unwieldy **9** all thumbs, graceless, lumbering, maladroit, stumbling, unwieldly
ungallant: **4** rude **5** crass, crude, surly **7** boorish, caddish, ill-bred, loutish, uncivil, uncouth **8** impolite, inurbane, tactless **9** insulting, uncourtly **10** indelicate, ungracious, unmannerly
Ungava: **3** bay
ungenerous: **4** mean, near, sour **5** close, small **6** skimpy, sordid, stingy **7** miserly, selfish **8** ungiving
one: **5** miser
ungenteel: **7** uncouth
ungentle: **5** rough **8** baseborn
ungentlemanly: **5** rough **7** caddish, ill-bred, lowbred, uncouth **8** inurbane
ungenuine: **4** fake, sham **8** spurious **10** apocryphal **11** counterfeit
Unger, Felix: **7** neatnik
actor: **6** Carney, Lemmon **7** Randall
unginned: **5** seedy
ungiving: **4** mean **5** cheap, close, tight **6** frugal, greedy, stingy **7** chintzy, miserly, selfish, sparing, thrifty **8** churlish, grasping, grudging **9** illiberal, mercenary, pennywise **10** abstemious, avaricious, economical, pinchpenny, skinflinty, ungenerous
one: **5** miser **7** hoarder, Scrooge

8 tightwad 9 skinflint 10 cheapskate, pinchpenny
unglazed clay: 7 biscuit
unglue: 5 break, shake, upset 6 rattle 7 depress, nonplus, unnerve 8 dispirit, psych out, unsettle, unstring 9 discomfit, embarrass 10 demoralize, disconcert, discourage, dishearten
unglued: 4 amok 5 upset 6 addled 7 flipped, frantic, haywire 8 frenetic, frenzied 9 unscrewed 10 disordered, unbalanced
come ~: 4 flip, rage, rail, rant, rave, yell 5 break, go ape, go mad, shout, storm 6 bellow 7 carry on, explode, flare up, give way, go crazy, lash out, run amok, thunder 8 freak out, get angry, harangue 9 come apart, go bananas, raise Cain 10 hit the roof
__ unglued: 4 come
ungodliness: 3 sin 7 impiety
ungodly: 4 vile 5 awful 6 horrid, unholy, wicked 7 corrupt, impious, profane 8 depraved, dreadful, horrible, shocking, terrible 9 appalling, atrocious, barbarous, frightful, monstrous, unearthly 10 horrendous, irreverent, outrageous, petrifying
ungovernable: 4 wild 6 unruly 7 naughty, rampant, violent, wayward 8 indocile, stubborn 9 obstinate, out of hand
ungoverned: 7 lawless 8 anarchic, headless 9 audacious 10 anarchical
ungraceful: 5 stiff 6 wooden 8 bungling 9 inelegant, maladroit
ungracious: 4 bold, curt, pert, rude 5 blunt, brash, brusk, crude, fresh, gruff, harsh, nervy, rough, sassy, saucy, sharp, short, surly 6 abrupt, brazen, coarse, vulgar 7 bearish, boorish, brusque, forward, loutish, selfish, uncouth 8 churlish, heedless, impolite, impudent, insolent, inurbane, petulant, tactless 9 thankless, ungallant 10 unthinking
be ~: 5 foist 6 demand, impose, insist, meddle 7 intrude, obtrude, presume 9 incommode
ungrateful: 6 klutzy 7 selfish 9 forgetful, thankless
ungroomed: 5 mangy, messy, mussy, rough, seedy 6 ragged, shabby, shoddy, unneat, untidy 7 scruffy, unkempt 8 slovenly, tattered 10 bedraggled, threadbare
ungrounded: 4 wide 5 false, wrong 6 afield, all wet, unfair, unjust, untrue 7 in error, invalid, unsound 8 mistaken, specious 9 erroneous, incorrect 10 fallacious, groundless, ill-advised, inaccurate, mendacious, misleading
ungrudging: 6 giving 7 liberal 8 generous 9 unselfish 10 free-handed, munificent, unstinting
ungrudgingly: 6 freely, gladly, warmly 7 happily, readily 8 cheerily, heartily, joyfully, joyously 9 naturally, willingly 10 cheerfully
ungual: 4 claw 5 talon 6 unguis 7 toenail 10 fingernail
unguarded: 4 naif, open, rash, weak 5 frank, naive 6 candid, unwary, unwise 7 artless, exposed, offhand, sincere, up-front 8 careless, heedless, unartful 9 guileless, impolitic, imprudent, impulsive, ingenuous 10 accessible, incautious, indiscreet, undefended, unthinking, unvigilant, unwatchful, vulnerable
unguent: 4 balm 5 cream, salve 6 hot oil, lotion 8 lenitive, liniment, ointment 9 emollient
apply ~: 3 oil 5 bless 6 anoint, ordain 8 sanctify 9 lubricate 10 consecrate
unguided: 7 aimless 8 headless 10 leaderless, rudderless, undirected
unguis: 4 claw, hoof, nail 5 talon 7 toenail 10 fingernail
ungulate: 5 rhino, tapir 6 hoofed
Unh: 4 elem. 7 element
106 for ~: 4 at. no.
unhackneyed: 3 new 5 fresh, novel 7 offbeat 8 brand-new, creative, original 10 avant-garde, innovative
unhallowed: 8 diabolic, temporal 10 diabolical, irreverent
unhampered: 4 free 5 clear
unhand: 4 free 5 let go, loose 6 acquit 7 release, set free 8 liberate 9 surrender
unhandled: 3 new
unhandy: 5 bulky, inapt, inept 6 clumsy 7 unadept 8 inexpert 9 maladroit 10 cumbersome
unhappily: 8 sad to say 10 sorry to say
unhappiness: 3 woe 4 care 5 blues, gloom, grief 6 misery, sorrow 7 sadness, tragedy 8 distress
exclamation of ~: 4 alas 5 alack 8 lackaday
unhappy: 3 low, sad 4 blue, down, glum, grim, hurt, sour 5 bleak, curst, sorry, teary, woful 6 booing, broody, cursed, dismal, dreary, gloomy, in pain, morose, somber, tragic, woeful 7 doleful, forlorn, griping, hurting, joyless, let-down, pouting, unlucky 8 bleeding, dejected, downbeat, downcast, grieving, ill-fated, luckless, mournful, saddened, scowling, tragical, troubled, untoward, wretched 9 afflicted, aggrieved, bummed-out, cheerless, depressed, disgusted, heartsick, long-faced, mirthless, miserable, saturnine, sorrowful, woebegone 10 chapfallen, despondent, dispirited, ill-starred, in the dumps, melancholy, oppressive, out of joint, out of sorts, unpleasant
unhardened: 4 easy, kind, mild, soft 5 sweet 6 gentle, kindly, mellow, tender 7 lenient, pliable 8 flexible, moderate, tolerant, yielding 9 easygoing, indulgent, sensitive 10 permissive
unharmed: 4 safe 5 sound, whole 6 intact, secure 7 perfect 8 unmarked 9 inviolate, unscathed, untouched
unharmonious: 5 noisy 7 raucous
unhasty: 4 poky, slow 9 leisurely
unhat: 4 doff
unhatched fish: 3 egg, roe
unhazardous: 4 safe 6 secure 8 harmless, riskless
UNHCR predecessor: 3 IRO
unhealthful: 3 bad 5 toxic 7 noisome, unclean 9 unhealthy
atmosphere: 4 smog 9 pollution
unhealthiness: 7 illness, malaise 8 debility, sickness 9 infirmity 10 feebleness
unhealthy: 3 bad, ill 4 sick, weak 5 frail, pasty, risky, unfit 6 ailing, feeble, infirm, nocent, peaked, rancid, rotten, sallow, sickly, unwell 7 baneful, harmful, invalid, laid low, noisome, noxious, parlous, unsound 8 below par, delicate, negative, perilous, perverse, virulent 9 dangerous, degrading, hazardous, injurious, nefarious, poisonous 10 corruptive, germ-ridden, jeopardous, out of shape, unsanitary
unheard: 3 mum 4 mute 6 silent
unheard-of: 3 new, odd 4 rare 5 alien, novel 6 unique, unsung 7 obscure, offbeat, strange, uncanny, unfamed, unknown, unusual 8 nameless, shocking, singular, uncommon, unlikely 9 different, wonderful 10 outlandish, phenomenal, unfamiliar, unrenowned
unhearing: 4 deaf, rash 8 heedless, reckless 10 regardless
unheavy: 4 easy 5 light 8 untaxing
unheedful: 3 lax 4 deaf 5 loose, slack 7 cursory, offhand 8 careless, mindless, reckless, slapdash, slipshod 9 forgetful, negligent 10 behindhand, headstrong, neglectful, nonchalant, unthinking
unhelped: 4 solo 5 alone
unhesitating: 4 firm 6 all-out, prompt 7 assured, decided 8 emphatic, forceful, hellbent, resolute 10 conclusive
unhesitatingly: 6 openly 7 readily 8 promptly 10 forcefully
unhidden: 4 open 5 clear, overt, plain 6 in view, patent, public 7 exposed, obvious, visible 8 apparent, clear-cut, explicit, knowable, manifest 10 observable
unhindered: 3 rid 4 free, open, safe 5 clear 7 set free
unhinge: 5 addle, freak, upset 6 flurry, madden, sicken 7 agitate, confuse, derange, fluster, unnerve 8 confound, disquiet, frighten, unsettle 9 dislocate 10 discompose
unhip: 5 geeky, nerdy 6 square, uncool 7 out of it
one: 4 geek, nerd, nurd 5 dweeb
unhitch: 5 loose 6 detach, loosen
UNH locale: 6 Durham
unholy: 4 base, evil, vile 5 awful 6 guilty, wicked 7 corrupt, heinous, immoral, impious, profane, ungodly 8 blameful, culpable, depraved, dreadful, shocking 9 appalling, barbarous, dishonest, unearthly, unnatural 10 horrendous, iniquitous, irreverent, outrageous, virtueless
mess: 5 havoc 7 debacle 8 collapse, disaster 9 cataclysm
Unholy Loves author: Joyce Carol Oates
Unholy Partners (1941 film)
cast: Edward Arnold, Laraine Day, Edward G. Robinson
director: Mervyn LeRoy
unhook: 5 loose 6 loosen 8 liberate
unhooked: 5 loose
unhoped-__: 3 for
unhopeful: 6 gloomy 8 dejected, downbeat, negative 9 cheerless, defeatist 10 dispirited
unhorse: 5 throw 6 topple, unseat
unhot: 5 tepid 8 lukewarm
unhumorous: 5 sober, staid 6 solemn, somber 7 deadpan 10 no-nonsense
unh-unh: 3 nah 4 nope
unhurried: 4 easy, lazy, poky, slow 6 draggy, otiose, torpid 7 gradual, halting, impeded, lagging, languid 8 crawling, creeping, dawdling, dilatory, dragging, drawn-out, hesitant, plodding, slothful, sluggish, toddling 9 easygoing, leisurely, lethargic, prolonged, slow-going, snaillike 10 deliberate, protracted
unhurriedly: 6 calmly, lazily, slowly 8 bit by bit, casually 9 by degrees, gradually, languidly, leisurely, piecemeal 10 composedly, inch by inch, indolently, step by step
unhurt: 2 OK 4 okay, safe 5 sound, whole 6 intact 8 unmarked 9 inviolate, unscathed, untouched
unhygienic: 5 dirty 6 filthy 7 unclean
uni-: 3 mon-, one 4 mono-
Uni-Ball: 3 pen
alternative: 3 Bic 5 Pilot 7 Sharpie 9 PaperMate
unicellular creature: 6 amoeba
unicorn: 5 money 6 animal, equine
feature: 4 horn, mane
unicorn fish: 4 unie
Unicorn, The (1968 song) artist: Irish Rovers
Unicorn, The author: Iris Murdoch
unicycle part: 5 pedal, wheel 7 ratchet
unidealistic: 9 pragmatic, realistic
unidentified: 6 secret 7 unknown, unnamed 8 nameless, unmarked 9 anonymous
plane: 5 bogey, bogie
unidentified __ object: 6 flying
unification: 5 union, unity 6 fusion, hookup, merger 7 linkage, melding 8 alliance 9 coalition, synthesis
Unification __: 6 Church
unified: 3 one 5 as one 6 allied, united 7 grouped 8 hooked up 9 unanimous 10 collective, integrated
group: 4 core 5 cadre, force, staff 9 personnel
unified __ theory: 5 field
uniflow __: 6 engine
uniform: 4 even, garb, like, same, suit 5 alike, dress, equal, fixed, habit, khaki, level, paced, plane 6 attire, livery, smooth, stable, static, steady 7 costume, equable, orderly, regalia, regular, similar, stripes 8 balanced, constant, of a piece, selfsame 9 analogous, consonant, identical, olive drab, unvarying 10 consistent, dependable, invariable, monolithic, monotonous, true to type, unchanging
Army ~: 3 ODs 5 drabs 6 khakis
make ~: 4 even, sand 5 level, plane 6 smooth
material: 5 chino, khaki
part: 4 sash 5 braid, shirt, tunic 6 lacing
(prefix): 3 iso-
WWII lady in ~: 3 WAC 4 WAAC
__ uniform: 5 dress 7 service, undress
Uniform __ Report: 5 Crime
uniformed group: 4 army, navy, team 7 marines 8 air force
uniformity: 5 order 6 parity 8 likeness, monotony, sameness 9 constancy, fixedness
uniformly: 4 even, such 5 alike 6 evenly 7 equally 9 unvarying 10 the same way
unify: 4 fuse, join, meld 5 blend, marry, merge, unite 6 center, link up 7 combine 8 coalesce, federate 9 commingle, integrate 10 amalgamate, synthesize
unilluminated: 3 dim 4 dark 5 dusky, mirky, murky 6 gloomy, somber 7 darkish, shadowy, subdued 9 tenebrous
unimaginable: 4 rare 6 unique, untold 8 doubtful, singular, uncommon, unlikely 9 fantastic, ineffable, marvelous, unheard-of
unimaginative: 3 dry 4 arid, dull, flat, tame 5 banal, corny, ho-hum, hokey, passé, prosy, stale, trite, usual, vapid 6 barren, common, jejune, old hat, square, stodgy 7 clichéd, fatuous, humdrum, insipid, prosaic, routine, tedious, vanilla 8 bromidic, lifeless, ordinary, outdated, outmoded, well-worn 9 hackneyed, prosaical 10 dullsville
unimagined: 4 live, real, true 5 right 6 actual, living 7 certain, correct, de facto, genuine, literal, sincere 8 concrete, definite, existent, existing, material, physical, tangible, verified 9 authentic, confirmed, veritable 10 definitive, historical, undeniable,

unmistaken
unimpaired: 5 clean, sound, whole 6 intact 7 healthy, perfect 8 unbroken
unimpassioned: 4 calm, cool 5 sober, staid, stoic 6 sedate, severe, somber 7 ascetic, austere, stoical, subdued 8 composed 9 collected, pragmatic 10 controlled, restrained
unimpeachable: 4 sure 7 genuine, upright 8 innocent, spotless 9 guiltless
unimpeded: 4 free, open, wild 5 clear 6 untied
unimportant: 4 idle, mere 5 extra, least, light, minor, petty, small, sorry 6 frothy, humble, little, minute, paltry, slight, yeasty 7 trivial, useless 8 needless, nugatory, optional, picayune, piddling, trifling 9 frivolous, redundant, senseless, valueless, worthless
unimpressed: 4 cold 7 unmoved
unimproved: 4 as is
uninclined: 5 loath 6 averse 7 uneager 8 hesitant 9 reluctant 10 indisposed
unindustrious: 4 lazy 6 otiose
uninfected: 5 clean 7 sterile 8 sanitary
uninformed: 4 naif 5 naive 7 out of it, unaware 8 ignorant 9 in the dark, unadvised
uninhabited: 4 wild 5 bleak, empty 6 barren, lonely, vacant 8 deserted, desolate, lifeless
uninhibited: 4 bold, free, open 5 frank, loose 6 amoral, candid, earthy 7 natural, relaxed 8 cut loose, informal, uncurbed 9 audacious, expansive, fancy-free, footloose, liberated, unbridled, unchecked
uninhibitedness: 4 élan 5 verve 7 abandon, freedom, license 8 wildness 10 exuberance
uninitiate: 7 amateur, dabbler 9 greenhorn, half-baked, unskilled 10 dilettante, half-cocked, tenderfoot
uninitiated: 4 naif 5 naive 8 ignorant
uninjured: 4 safe 5 sound, whole 6 intact 8 unmarked 9 unscathed, untouched
uninspired: 4 arid, drab, dull, flat, so-so, tame 5 banal, corny, hokey, passé, stale, stock, trite, vapid 6 common, jejune, old hat 7 clichéd, fatuous, humdrum, prosaic, sterile 8 bromidic, everyday, mediocre, ordinary, outdated, outmoded 9 hackneyed, ponderous, prosaical 10 dullsville
uninsulated: 6 chilly, drafty
unintelligent: 4 dull, slow 5 dense, silly, thick 6 obtuse, simple 7 shallow, vacuous, witless 8 mindless 9 brainless, dim-witted, senseless 10 dull-witted
one: 3 ass 4 clod, dolt 5 ninny 7 dullard
unintelligible: 6 opaque 7 garbled, jumbled, muddled, slurred, unclear 9 illegible, uncertain 10 incoherent
unintended: 6 chance, random 7 aimless 9 haphazard, undevised, unplanned, unwitting 10 accidental, fortuitous
unintentional: 5 fluky 6 casual, chance, flukey, random 7 aimless 9 haphazard, undevised, unplanned, unwitting 10 accidental, fortuitous, unexpected
unintentionally: 8 by chance, unawares
uninterested: 4 cool 5 aloof, blasé, bored, jaded 6 remote 7 distant, languid, offhand 8 detached, listless, lukewarm, negative, unbiased 9 apathetic, impassive, incurious, turned off, withdrawn
uninteresting: 3 dry 4 arid, blah, drab, dull, flat, tame 5 banal, bland, dusty, ho-hum, plain, prosy, stale, tired, trite, vapid 6 boring, common, dismal, dreary, jejune, stodgy 7 humdrum, insipid, prosaic, tedious 8 bromidic, tiresome 9 fatiguing, prosaical, soporific, tasteless, wearisome 10 dullsville
uninterrupted: 5 clean, level, solid 6 direct, smooth, steady 7 endless, nonstop 8 constant, enduring, straight, unbroken, unending 9 ceaseless, continual, incessant, perennial, perpetual, sustained, unceasing
continue ~: 3 yak, yap 4 talk 5 run on 6 rattle 7 maunder
uninterruptedly: 5 on end
uninvited: 7 unasked 8 unbidden, unsought 9 unwelcome 10 gratuitous, unprompted
guest: 6 drop-in 7 crasher
Uninvited (1998 song) artist: Alanis Morissette
Uninvited, The (1944 film)
cast: Donald Crisp, Ruth Hussey, Ray Milland
uninviting: 4 icky, ugly 5 gross, yucky 9 repellent, revolting
uninvolved: 6 simple 7 neutral 8 innocent 9 unaligned
union: 3 mix 4 bloc, bond, gild, weld 5 blend, guild, labor, local, match, state 6 accord, fusion, league, merger, nation 7 amalgam, concord, joining, melding, mixture, society, wedding 8 alliance, assembly, compound, congress, junction, juncture, marriage, sodality 9 coalition, composite, employees, matrimony, symbiosis, syndicate, synthesis, unanimity 10 confluence, connection, consortium, federation, fraternity, government, Solidarity
actors' ~: 3 SAG 5 AFTRA
bane: 4 scab
branch: 5 local
combining form: 3 gam- 4 gamo-, -gamy 6 -gamous
Detroit ~: 3 UAW
dockworkers' ~: 3 ILA
educ. ~: 3 AFT, NEA, UFT
form a ~: 3 wed 4 bond, join, yoke 5 marry, merge, unite 7 combine, make one 9 integrate 10 tie the knot
issue: 3 bid 4 call, need, plea 5 claim, order, price 6 appeal, demand 7 inquiry, proviso, request 8 petition 9 provision, ultimatum 10 injunction
largest U.S. ~: 3 NEA
letters: 6 AFL-CIO
levy: 4 dues 7 charges 10 assessment
medieval trade ~: 5 guild
orch. ~: 3 AFM
regulating agcy.: 4 NLRB
supporters: 5 labor 7 hard hat 9 work force 10 blue collar
to Greeks and Cypriots: 6 enosis
trade ~: 5 guild, local, union 8 sodality 9 coalition 10 federation
Western Union ~: 3 ITU
wirers' ~: 4 IBEW
Wobblies' ~: 3 IWW
union __: 4 card, jack, list, shop, suit 5 label, scale 6 buster, church 7 catalog
union-__: 4 made
__ union: 3 art 4 open 5 craft, labor, trade 6 closed, credit, postal 7 company, customs, student
Union: 4 city, town 6 sta. stn. 8 The North
member: 5 state
opp.: 3 CSA
Union __: 3 Day 4 Jack 5 Depot 7 Carbide, Pacific, Station
__ Union: 6 French, Soviet 7 Western
Union City: 4 town
locale: 9 New Jersey 10 California
Uniondale: 4 city, town
locale: 7 New York
Union Depot (1932 film)
cast: Joan Blondell, Douglas Fairbanks Jr., Guy Kibbee
unionize: 4 ally 5 unite 9 affiliate
Union Jack: 4 flag
holder: 4 mast
Union Label grp.: 5 ILGWU
Union of __ Africa: 5 South
Union of the Snake (1983 song) artist: Duran Duran
Union Pacific (1939 film)
cast: Joel McCrea, Robert Preston, Barbara Stanwyck
director: Cecil B. DeMille
Union Pacific terminus: 5 Omaha
Union Station client: 6 Amtrak
Union-Tribune: 5 paper 9 newspaper
locale: 8 San Diego
unique: 3 new, odd, one 4 best, lone, only, rare, sole, solo 5 alone, novel, primo 6 far-out, single 7 oddball, offbeat, onliest, special, strange, unalike, unusual 8 distinct, isolated, peculiar, peerless, separate, singular, solitary, specific, standout, uncommon 9 anomalous, different, exclusive, matchless, nonpareil, recherché, unequaled, unheard-of, unmatched, unrivaled 10 individual, inimitable, one and only, one-of-a-kind, particular, phenomenal, refreshing, remarkable, sui generis, unexampled, unrivalled
in Latin: 10 sui generis
thing: 4 oner
uniquely: 4 only 9 specially 10 especially
uniqueness: 7 novelty 8 identity 9 freshness 11 originality
uni- relative: 3 mon- 4 mono-
unisex garb: 5 jeans, pants 6 slacks, T-shirt 8 trousers
Unisom: 8 sleep aid
alternative: 5 Nytol 6 Compoz 7 Sominex
unison: 6 accord 7 concert, concord, harmony 8 sameness 9 agreement
be in ~: 4 sync 5 agree 9 harmonize
in ~: 5 as one 6 at once, in sync 7 en masse 8 as a group, combined, together 9 all at once, in concert, unanimous 10 conjointly
speak in ~: 6 chorus
Unisys competitor: 3 IBM
unit: 3 arm, one 4 gram, item, limb, link, part, team, wing 5 block, bunch, corps, digit, group, party, piece, pound, squad, troop, whole 6 degree, detail, entity, league, length, member, module, outfit, sample, square, system 7 article, brigade, chapter, element, integer, platoon, portion, section, segment 8 assembly, division, fraction, molecule, specimen, squadron, work crew 9 apartment, appliance, battalion, component 10 assemblage, complement, department, detachment, stand-alone
combining form: 4 -plex
unit __: 4 card, cell, cost, rule 5 price, train, trust 6 circle, factor, record, stress, vector 7 element, pricing
__ unit: 4 base, cost, wall 5 motor 6 Eötvös, living, mobile, second, social, volume 7 control, derived, formula, message, synchro, thermal
unitary: 6 single
Unitas, Johnny: 2 QB
sport: 8 football
unit-cost word: 3 per 4 each 6 apiece
unite: 3 mix, tie, wed 4 ally, band, bond, fuse, join, knit, knot, link, lock, meet, pool, weld, yoke 5 blend, focus, marry, merge, money, rally, stick, unify 6 adjoin, attach, cement, cleave, club up, cohere, concur, couple, embody, gather, hook up, imbody, league, link up, mingle, pair up, relate, splice, team up 7 combine, conjoin, connect, hitch on, match up, partner 8 assemble, coalesce, converge, solidify, unionize 9 affiliate, associate, commingle, cooperate, integrate, interlink 10 amalgamate, close ranks, go partners, hook up with, intertwine, join forces, synthesize
united: 3 one 4 mixt 5 as one, at one, joint, mixed, solid 6 agreed, allied, banded, joined, linked, pooled, tied in 7 federal, unified 8 combined, in accord, in league, joined up 9 assembled, concerted, corporate, in cahoots, of one mind, plugged in, unanimous, undivided 10 affiliated, agreed upon, associated, collective, concordant, integrated, like-minded
be ~: 4 jell, join 5 agree, merge 6 cleave, cohere 7 conform
group: 4 bloc, bund, ring 5 junta, party 6 cartel, clique, league 7 combine, council, entente, faction 8 alliance 9 anschluss, coalition, syndicate 10 federation
(prefix): 3 syn-
united __: 5 front
United: 5 mover 7 airline, van line
alternative: 5 Delta 6 Allied 7 Jet Blue 8 American 9 Southwest, US Airways 11 America West, Continental
former ~ rival: 3 TWA 5 Pan Am, USAir 7 Braniff, Eastern 8 National
United __: 3 Way 7 Nations
United __ College Fund: 5 Negro
United __ Day: 7 Nations
United __ Emirates: 4 Arab
United __ International: 5 Press
United __ of America: 6 States
United __ of Brazil: 6 States
United __ of Christ: 6 Church
United __ of Indonesia: 6 States
United __ Republic: 4 Arab
United __ Service: 6 Parcel
United __ States: 4 Arab
United Arab Emirates: 6 nation 7 country
capital: 8 Abu Dhabi
group: 4 OPEC 10 Arab League
honcho: 4 amir, emir, Zaid 5 ameer, emeer, sheik 6 shaikh, sheikh
money: 4 fils 6 dirham
neighbor: 4 Oman
part: 4 Arab 5 Dibai, Dubai 6 United 8 Abu Dhabi, Emirates
United Artists offering: 4 film 5 movie
United Federation of Planets member: 5 Earth 6 Vulcan
United Kingdom: 6 nation 7 country
capital: 6 London
city: 3 Ayr 4 Bath, Rhyl, Ryde, York 5 Blyth, Crewe, Derby, Dover, Egham, Leeds, Luton, Neath, Newry, Poole, Rugby 6 Antrim, Batley, Bolton, Bootle, Dudley, Dundee, Eccles, Exeter, Havant, Irvine, Jarrow, Kendal, London, Lurgan, Oldham, Ossett, Oxford, Seaham, Slough, Stroud, Widnes, Wishaw, Yeovil 7 Airdrie, Banbury, Belfast, Berwick, Bexhill, Bristol, Burnley, Cannock, Cardiff, Crawley, Falkirk, Glasgow, Ipswich, Lisburn, Margate, Newport, Norwich, Paisley, Reading, Renfrew, Staines, Sunbury, Swansea, Swindon,

Telford, Walsall, Watford 8 Aberdeen, Bearsden, Bradford, Brighton, Coventry, Dumfries, Greenock, Hastings, Hereford, Plymouth, Stirling 9 Cambridge, Edinburgh, Leicester, Liverpool, Rotherham, Sheffield, Stockport, Worcester 10 Birmingham, Bournmouth, Chelmsford, Colchester, Eastbourne, Gloucester, Manchester, Nottingham, Sunderland
money: 4 quid 5 penny, pound 8 new pence, new penny, shilling 9 sovereign
native: 4 Brit 6 Briton
org.: 4 NATO
see also England, Great Britain
United Methodist __: 6 Church
United Nations
see UN
United Nations __: 3 Day
United Parcel __: 7 Service
United States: 6 nation 7 country
money: 4 cent, dime 5 eagle, penny 6 dollar, nickel 7 quarter
neighbor: 6 Canada, Mexico
org.: 3 OAS 4 NATO
see also U.S.
United States of __: 6 Brazil 7 America
United Way request: 4 give
unit investment __: 5 trust
unit of __: 7 measure
units, __, hundreds: 4 tens
unit's __: 5 place
unity: 5 amity, peace, whole 6 accord, esprit, fusion 7 concord, harmony, oneness, rapport 8 alliance, good will, sameness, sympathy, totality 9 agreement, coherence, communion, consensus, integrity, synthesis, unanimity, wholeness 10 congruence, consonance, friendship, singleness, solidarity
Unity: 4 city, town
locale: 6 Canada
Unity of India, The author: 5 Nehru
__ Unit Zappa: 4 Moon
univ.: 3 sch. 4 coll., inst.
degree: 3 BLS, LHD, LL.B. 4 B.Lit.
discourse: 4 lect.
employee: 2 TA 4 prof. 5 instr.
grant source: 3 NSF
hotshot: 4 BMOC
major: 3 Eng., lit., mus. 4 biol., chem., hist., phys. 6 phys. ed.
offering: 2 BA, BS 3 deg.
requirement: 3 GED
senior's hurdle: 3 GRE 4 GMAT, MCAT
sports org.: 4 NCAA
see also college, school, university
UNIVAC preceder: 5 Eniac
univalve: 5 shell 8 seashell
Univers: 4 font 8 typeface
universal: 3 big 4 rife, wide 5 broad, total 6 common, cosmic, entire, global, public 7 all-over, diffuse, general, natural, stellar 8 accepted, catholic, cosmical, sweeping 9 customary, extensive, pervasive, prevalent, unlimited, worldwide 10 ecumenical, prevailing, ubiquitous, undisputed, widespread
be ~: 4 rule
donor: 5 type O
philosopher's ~: 3 Tao
prefix: 4 omni-
principle: 3 law 5 axiom
wish: 5 amity, order, peace 6 accord 7 harmony 10 friendship
universal __: 3 set 4 life, mill, time 5 chuck, class, donor, joint, motor, stage 7 grammar
Universal: 6 studio
competitor: 3 Fox, MGM 6 Disney 7 Miramax, New Line 8 Columbia 9 Paramount 10 Dreamworks, Warner Bros.
creation: 4 film 5 movie
former owner: 3 MCA
workplace: 3 lot 10 soundstage
Universal __ Code: 7 Product
Universal __ Union: 6 Postal
universally acknowledged: 5 given 7 evident, granted, obvious 8 manifest 9 axiomatic 10 understood
universe: 5 world 6 cosmos, nature 8 creation 9 macrocosm 10 everything
be part of the ~: 4 last, live 5 abide, exist 6 endure, remain 7 breathe, subsist, survive 8 continue
Buddhist symbol of the ~: 5 lotus
combining form: 4 cosm- 5 cosmo-
of the ~: 6 cosmic 8 cosmical
preceder: 5 chaos
__ universe: 6 closed, island 8 parallel
Universe, like Mr.: 5 macho, manly
université preceder: 5 lycée 6 lyceum
university: 6 campus, school 7 college 9 alma mater
award: 6 degree 7 diploma, master's 9 doctorate, sheepskin
degree: 2 AB, BA, MA, MS 3 MBA, Ph.D.
feature: 4 dorm, quad 5 court 6 campus 9 courtyard, dormitory
head: 4 prex, prez 5 prexy 9 president
keepsake: 2 yb. 8 yearbook
major: 3 art, bio., eco., Eng., geo., mus. 4 econ., hist., math 5 drama, music 6 phys. ed., speech 7 biology, English, geology, history, physics, theater 9 chemistry, economics, sociology 10 philosophy
offering: 4 term 5 class 6 course 7 program, regimen, seminar
sports org.: 4 NCAA
staffer: 4 dean 6 bursar, docent, lector 8 lecturer 9 professor, registrar 10 instructor
woman: 4 coed
see also college, school
__ university: 4 free 5 state
University __: 4 Wits
__ University: 4 Open
University City: 4 town
locale: 8 Missouri
University of Akron
athletes: 4 Zips
locale: 4 Ohio
University of Alabama
athletes: 7 Blazers
locale: 10 Birmingham, Tuscaloosa
University of Arizona
athletes: 8 Wildcats
locale: 6 Tucson
University of Arkansas athletes: 10 Razorbacks
University of British Columbia
abbr.: 3 UBC
location: 6 Canada 9 Vancouver
University of California
athletes: 6 Bruins
locale: 8 Berkeley 10 Los Angeles
University of Central Florida locale: 7 Orlando
University of Cincinnati
athletes: 8 Bearcats
locale: 4 Ohio
University of Colorado
athletes: 9 Buffaloes
locale: 7 Boulder
University of Connecticut
athletes: 7 Huskies
locale: 6 Storrs
University of Delaware
athletes: 8 Blue Hens
locale: 6 Newark
University of Florida athletes: 6 Gators
University of Georgia
athletes: 8 Bulldogs
locale: 6 Athens
University of Guelph
location: 6 Canada 7 Ontario
University of Hawaii
athletes: 8 Warriors
locale: 8 Honolulu
University of Houston
athletes: 7 Cougars
locale: 5 Texas
University of Idaho
athletes: 7 Vandals
locale: 6 Moscow
University of Illinois
athletes: 6 Illini
locale: 9 Champaign
University of Iowa athletes: 8 Hawkeyes
University of Kansas
athletes: 8 Jayhawks
locale: 8 Lawrence
University of Kentucky
athletes: 8 Wildcats
locale: 9 Lexington
University of Louisville
athletes: 9 Cardinals
locale: 8 Kentucky
University of Maine
athletes: 10 Black Bears
locale: 5 Orono
University of Maryland
athletes: 5 Terps 9 Terrapins
University of Massachusetts
athletes: 9 Minutemen
locale: 7 Amherst
University of Memphis
athletes: 6 Tigers
locale: 9 Tennessee
University of Miami athletes: 5 Canes 10 Hurricanes
University of Michigan
athletes: 10 Wolverines
locale: 8 Ann Arbor
University of Mississippi
athletes: 6 Rebels 7 Ole Miss
locale: 6 Oxford
University of Missouri
athletes: 6 Tigers
locale: 8 Columbia
University of Montana
athletes: 9 Grizzlies
locale: 8 Missoula
University of Nebraska
athlete: 6 Husker 10 Cornhusker
locale: 7 Lincoln
University of Nevada
athletes: 6 Rebels 8 Wolf Pack
locale: 4 Reno 8 Las Vegas
University of New Hampshire
athletes: 8 Wildcats
locale: 6 Durham
University of New Mexico athletes: 5 Lobos
University of North Carolina
athletes: 8 Tar Heels
locale: 10 Chapel Hill
University of Oklahoma
athletes: 7 Sooners
locale: 6 Norman
University of Oregon
athletes: 5 Ducks
locale: 6 Eugene
University of Pennsylvania athletes: 7 Quakers
University of Pittsburgh athletes: 8 Panthers
University of Rhode Island
athletes: 4 Rams
locale: 8 Kingston
University of South Carolina
athletes: 9 Gamecocks
locale: 8 Columbia
University of Tennessee
athletes: 4 Vols 10 Volunteers
locale: 9 Knoxville
University of Texas
athletes: 6 Miners 9 Longhorns
locale: 6 Austin, El Paso
University of Toledo
athletes: 7 Rockets
locale: 4 Ohio
University of Utah athletes: 4 Utes
University of Vermont
athletes: 10 Catamounts
locale: 10 Burlington
University of Virginia athletes: 9 Cavaliers
University of Washington
athletes: 7 Huskies
locale: 7 Seattle
University of Wisconsin
athletes: 7 Badgers
locale: 7 Madison
University of Wyoming
athletes: 7 Cowboys
locale: 7 Laramie
University Park: 4 city, town
locale: 5 Texas 7 Florida
school: 3 PSU 9 Penn State
University Place: 4 city, town
locale: 10 Washington
unjaded: 4 naif 5 fresh, naive 8 innocent, wide-eyed 9 ingenuous
unjam: 4 free 6 unclog
unjust: 4 foul, hard 5 undue, wrong 6 biased, shabby, unfair 7 low-down, partial 8 improper, one-sided, partisan, wrongful 9 arbitrary, injurious, underhand, unmerited 10 oppressive, prejudiced, undeserved, ungrounded
criticism: 6 bad rap 9 cheap shot
verdict: 5 frame
unjustified: 5 undue 6 unjust, wanton 8 baseless 10 groundless
unjustness: 9 prejudice 10 inequality, unevenness, unfairness
unkempt: 4 wild 5 crude, dirty, dowdy, messy, mussy, ratty, seamy, seedy 6 blowsy, blowzy, coarse, frowsy, frowzy, frumpy, grubby, grungy, ragged, shabby, shaggy, sloppy, unneat, untidy 7 blowsed, blowzed, rumpled, scruffy, squalid, tousled, unclean 8 mussed up, slipshod, slovenly, uncombed 9 neglected, ungroomed 10 bedraggled, disheveled, disorderly, unpolished
one: 4 slob 5 sight
unkeyed: 6 atonal
unkind: 4 curt, evil, hard, mean 5 catty, cruel, harsh, nasty, snide, stern 6 animal, brutal, fierce, savage, shabby, wanton 7 beastly, callous, hateful, hurtful, inhuman, vicious 8 barbaric, fiendish, inhumane, pitiless, ruthless, sadistic, spiteful, tactless, uncaring, unsubtle, vengeful 9 barbarous, bloodless, cutthroat, ferocious, heartless, inclement, malicious, merciless, monstrous, truculent, unfeeling 10 ill-natured, unfriendly, vindictive
unkindness: 4 fury 5 anger, spite, venom, wrath 6 enmity, hatred, malice, rancor, spleen 7 ill will, sarcasm 8 acerbity, acrimony, asperity, rudeness 9 animosity, antipathy, harshness 10 disservice, irritation, resentment
unknowable: 4 dark, deep, vast 6 arcane, mystic, occult 7 abysmal, obscure 8 esoteric, mystical, oracular, profound 9 recondite, unsounded 10 fathomless, mysterious
unknowing: 4 naif 5 blind, naive 7 out

of it, unaware **8** ignorant **9** in the dark, unadvised, unwitting **10** unfamiliar
unknowingly: **8** unawares
unknowledgeable: **3** raw **5** green, naive **6** gauche, simple **8** ignorant, innocent, untaught **9** untrained
unknown: **3** new **4** dark **5** alien, novel **6** exotic, far-off, hidden, humble, occult, remote, secret, unsung, untold **7** distant, faraway, foreign, obscure, strange, unfamed, unnamed, unnoted **8** desolate, nameless, stranger **9** anonymous, concealed, incognito, uncharted, unheard-of **10** indefinite, mysterious, unexplored, unfamiliar, unrevealed
author: **4** anon. **9** anonymous
hitherto ~: **5** fresh **7** offbeat **8** original **9** different **10** innovative, newfangled
legal ~: **3** Doe, Roe
parts ~: **5** about **6** around **9** scattered, somewhere
Unknown __: **7** Soldier
Unknown Soldier and his Wife, The
author: Peter Ustinov
unlabored: **6** innate, simple **7** natural **8** unforced
unlace: **4** open **5** loose **6** loosen
unlade: **4** dump **6** remove, unload **7** lighten, off-load **9** discharge
unladylike: **7** ill-bred, lowbred **8** inurbane
unlash: **5** loose **6** loosen
unlatch: **3** ope **4** open **5** loose **6** loosen
unlatched: **4** open **5** loose
unlaundered: **5** dirty **6** soiled
unlawful: **4** tabu **5** taboo, wrong **6** banned, unfair **7** bootleg, crooked, illegal, illicit **8** criminal, improper, verboten, wrongful **9** felonious, forbidden, nefarious **10** actionable, disorderly, flagitious, indictable, iniquitous, not allowed, prohibited, unlicensed
act: **4** tort **5** bribe, crime, heist, theft, wrong **6** felony, holdup, murder **7** larceny, misdeed, offense, treason **8** atrocity, burglary, delictum, thievery, trespass **9** violation **10** infraction
Unlawful Entry (1992 film)
cast: Ray Liotta, Kurt Russell, Madeleine Stowe
Unlawful Entry cat: **4** Tiny
unleaded: **3** gas **8** gasoline
unlearned: **6** innate, unread **8** ignorant **9** backwater, inerudite **10** illiterate, uneducated, unschooled
unleash: **4** free, vent **5** loose, wreak **6** loosen **7** release **9** force upon
one's anger: **4** rage, rant, rave, yell **5** erupt, freak, storm **6** blow up, rail at, scream **7** bluster, bristle, explode, rampage **8** boil over, have a fit, run amuck **9** blow a fuse, fulminate, go berserk **10** hit the roof, kick up a row
upon: **5** let at
unleashed: **5** loose **6** untied
unleavened bread: **5** matzo **6** matzah, matzoh
unled: **4** free **5** alone **9** on one's own
unless: **3** but **4** nisi, save **6** and yet, except **7** barring
unlessened: **5** whole **6** entire **8** complete
unlet: **6** vacant **7** for rent **9** available
unlettered: **9** untutored **10** illiterate, uneducated, unschooled
unlevel: **5** bumpy, rocky, rough **6** craggy, jagged, ridged, rugged, uneven **7** serrate **8** unsmooth
unlicensed: **7** illegal, illicit **8** unlawful
unlighted: **3** dim **4** dark, ebon, inky **5** black, dusky, mirky, murky **6** dismal, dreary, gloomy **7** shadowy, sunless **8** jetblack **9** tenebrous **10** pitch-black
unlike: **3** new **5** other **6** motley **7** distant, diverse, offbeat, unequal, variant, various **8** clashing, contrary, discrete, distinct, opposite, separate **9** different, disparate, dissonant, divergent, unrelated **10** atypical of, contrasted, discordant, dissimilar, mismatched, poles apart, strange for
be ~: **4** vary **5** range **6** change, depart, differ, modify, mutate **7** deviate, diverge **8** contrast **9** transform
unlikely: **4** rare **5** faint **6** absurd, remote, slight **7** dubious, outside, suspect **8** doubtful **9** unheard-of **10** improbable, incredible, infeasible
unlikeness: **9** disparity, diversity **10** difference, divergence
unlimber: **5** stiff
unlimited: **3** big **4** full, vast **5** clear, great, total **6** all-out, entire, untold **7** endless, full-out, immense, no end of, no end to **8** absolute, complete, infinite, wide open **9** boundless, countless, extensive, full-blown, full-scale, no-strings, sovereign, unbounded, unfailing, universal **10** indefinite, innumerous, numberless, unconfined, unfathomed, unfettered, unnumbered
__ Unlimited Orchestra: **4** Love
unlink: **4** part **5** sever, split **6** cut off, detach, divide **7** disjoin, split up **8** break off, disunite, separate, set apart, uncouple **10** disconnect
unlit: **4** dark **5** black **6** gloomy **9** in the dark, lightless, tenebrous **10** blacked out, pitch black
buoy: **3** nun
unlived in: **5** empty **6** vacant
unlively: **4** dull, flat, tame **6** dreary **7** insipid, prosaic **9** bloodless, colorless **10** dullsville, lackluster, monotonous
unload: **3** rid, tip **4** drop, dump, sell, vend **5** clear, drain, empty, use up **6** divest, peddle, remove, unlade **7** drop off, exhaust, let go of, lighten, pour out, recount, relieve **8** evacuate, get rid of, jettison, unburden **9** discharge, dispose of, liquidate, move goods **10** auction off
unloading: **8** emptying **9** clearance, discharge
unlock: **3** ope **4** open, undo **5** loose, solve **6** decode, loosen
unlocked: **4** open **5** loose
unlooked-__: **3** for
unloose: **4** undo **5** eject **6** rescue **7** release
unloved: **5** hated **7** loathed **8** abhorred, despised, detested, disliked, forsaken **9** unpopular
unlovely: **9** tasteless **10** unpleasant
unloyal: **5** false **6** fickle, untrue **8** cheating, forsworn, two-faced **9** deceitful, faithless, insincere, two-timing **10** capricious, changeable, inconstant, traitorous, unfaithful, unreliable
unlucky: **5** black, curst, sorry **6** cursed, doomed, jinxed **7** hapless, ominous, unhappy **8** ill-fated, luckless, sinister, untimely, untoward **9** ill-omened, out of luck **10** calamitous, disastrous, ill-starred, out of joint
UNLV: **3** sch. **4** coll.
org.: **4** NCAA
part of ~: **3** Las, Nev. **5** Vegas **6** Nevada
unmalleable: **3** set **4** hard **5** rigid, stern **6** flinty, mulish, steely **7** adamant, dead set, diehard **8** hard-line, locked in, obdurate, resolute, stubborn **9** hidebound, immovable, obstinate, pig-headed, steadfast, unbending **10** bullheaded, determined, implacable, inflexible, unamenable, unswerving, unyielding
unman: **8** dispirit, frighten **10** dishearten
unmanageable: **4** wild **5** balky, bulky, onery **6** ornery, unruly **7** defiant, naughty, problem, wayward **8** contrary, obdurate, stubborn, unwieldy **9** difficult, obstinate, out of hand, unwieldly **10** disorderly, rebellious
unmannerly: **4** rude **5** brusk, crass, gruff, rough **6** vulgar **7** brusque, caddish, ill-bred, loutish **8** churlish, impolite, impudent **9** graceless, offensive, ungallant
unmarked: **4** safe **5** blank, sound, whole **6** intact, unhurt **8** unharmed **9** uninjured, unscarred, unscathed, untouched
unmarred: **4** mint, pure **5** clean, whole **6** virgin **7** perfect **8** flawless, pristine, virginal **9** faultless, inviolate, untouched **10** immaculate
unmarried: **4** sole **5** unwed **6** single **7** widowed **8** bachelor, divorced, eligible, unwedded, wifeless **10** spouseless, unattached
one: **4** maid, miss **6** single **8** bachelor
Unmarried Woman, An (1978 film)
cast: Alan Bates, Jill Clayburgh, Michael Murphy
director: Paul Mazursky
role: **5** Erica
unmask: **4** bare, leak, show **6** detect, expose, reveal, show up **7** display, divulge, exhibit, lay bare, let slip, uncover **8** disclose, smell out **9** make known **10** make public
unmasking: **6** baring, espial, exposé **8** exposure **9** detection **10** revelation
unmatched: **3** odd **5** alone **6** unique **7** supreme, unequal **8** peerless, ultimate, unpaired **9** nonpareil, unequaled, unrivaled **10** inimitable, unexampled, unrivalled
unmechanized: **6** by hand, manual
unmediated: **5** blunt **6** candid, direct, head-on **7** express **8** outright, straight **9** downright, firsthand **10** face-to-face, forthright, point-blank, to the point
unmeet: **5** bawdy, crass, crude, gross, inapt, rough **6** coarse, common, ribald, risqué, vulgar **7** uncouth **8** improper, indecent, unseemly **10** indecorous, indelicate
unmelodic: **6** atonal **7** raucous
unmemorable: **4** dull, so-so **5** stock, trite, usual **6** common, normal, wonted **7** average, generic, humdrum, insipid, mundane, prosaic, routine, vanilla **8** everyday, familiar, mediocre, middling, ordinary, plebeian, standard, workaday **9** quotidian **10** pedestrian, second-rate, uneventful, uninspired
unmentionable: **4** tabu **5** taboo **8** anathema **9** off-limits
unmentionables: **6** undies **7** drawers **8** lingerie, skivvies **9** underwear
unmerciful: **4** hard **5** cruel, stern, stony **6** brutal, flinty, stoney **7** bestial, hurtful **8** inhumane, pitiless, ruthless, uncaring, vengeful **9** ferocious, heartless, inclement, monstrous, unfeeling, unpitying, unsparing
unmerited: **6** unjust **8** unworthy **10** gratuitous, unasked-for, undeserved
unmetamorphosed animal: **5** larva
unmethodical: **5** messy **6** patchy, random, spotty **7** chaotic, erratic, jumbled, mixed up, muddled **8** anarchic, confused, pell-mell, sporadic **9** cluttered, desultory, haphazard, irregular, piecemeal, scrambled, spasmodic **10** all mixed-up, disorderly, out-of-order, topsy-turvy, upside down
unmeticulous: **6** sloppy **8** slipshod
unmew: **7** release **8** liberate
unmindful: **3** lax **5** blind, hasty **6** remiss, sloppy **7** napping, out of it, unaware **8** careless, derelict, heedless, ignorant, sleeping, slipshod, snoozing **9** forgetful, imprudent, in the dark, negligent, oblivious **10** incautious, neglectful, nonchalant, regardless, unthinking
unmindfulness: **5** sleep **6** apathy, laxity, phlegm, stupor, torpor **7** boredom, languor, neglect **8** dullness, hebetude, lethargy **9** disregard, lassitude, unconcern **10** drowsiness, remissness, sleepiness
unmistakable: **4** sure **5** clear, naked, plain, vivid **6** cogent, patent, simple, strong **7** certain, decided, evident, express, glaring, obvious, visible **8** apparent, definite, distinct, emphatic, explicit, knowable, manifest, palpable, positive, readable **9** graspable, prominent **10** spelled out
unmistakably: **4** just **5** truly **6** indeed, in fact, really, surely, verily **7** de facto, exactly, for real, in truth, utterly **8** for a fact **9** assuredly, certainly, genuinely, in reality, precisely **10** absolutely, admittedly, definitely, positively
unmistaken: **2** OK, so **4** okay, okeh, okey, true **5** exact, right, sound **6** actual, dead-on **7** correct, factual, precise **8** accurate, official, on target **9** on the beam, veracious **10** unimagined
unmitigated: **4** pure, rank **5** sheer, stark, total, utter, whole **6** arrant, simple **7** blatant, chronic, perfect **8** absolute, clear-cut, complete, outright, positive **9** chronical, downright, out-and-out
unmitigated __: **4** gall
unmix: **4** cull, sift **6** filter, screen, strain **8** separate
unmixed: **4** neat, pure **5** sheer, solid **6** simple, single, strong **8** straight
unmoist: **3** dry **4** arid
unmoored: **6** adrift **8** castaway **10** unanchored
unmotivated: **4** idle, lazy **5** bored **6** otiose **8** indolent **9** apathetic, shiftless
unmovable: **5** fixed **9** steadfast **10** inexorable, motionless, unyielding
unmoved: **4** cool **5** blasé, quiet, stoic **6** in situ, low-key, mellow, placid, sedate, serene **7** amiable, at peace, equable, pacific, relaxed, stoical **8** amicable, composed, laid-back, peaceful, tranquil **9** apathetic, collected, easy-going, impassive, quiescent, temperate, unstirred, untouched **10** motionless, spiritless, unaffected
remain ~: **5** sit by
unmoving: **4** firm **5** inert, still **6** at rest, halted, static **8** stagnant **9** quiescent **10** motionless, stationary, stock-still
unmusical: **5** harsh **6** off-key, shrill **7** grating, jarring, raucous **8** jangling, strident **9** dissonant, out of tune **10** cacophonic, discordant, inharmonic
Unna: **4** city, town
locale: **7** Germany
Unnamable, The author: Samuel Beckett
unnatural: **3** odd **4** eery **5** false, phony, put-on, queer, stagy, stiff, weird **6** atypic, ersatz, forced, freaky, la-de-

da, la-di-da, made-up, morbid, off-key, phoney, pseudo, staged, stagey, unholy **7** assumed, bizarre, feigned, labored, mincing, stilted, strange, studied, uncanny, unusual **8** aberrant, abnormal, affected, atypical, freakish, lah-di-dah, mannered, perverse, strained **9** anomalous, contrived, divergent, eccentric, grotesque, imitation, insincere, irregular, monstrous, synthetic **10** artificial, fabricated, factitious, far-fetched, outlandish, outrageous, theatrical

unneat: 5 dowdy, messy, mussy **6** blowzy, frowzy, frumpy, grubby, grungy, shabby, shaggy, sloppy, untidy **7** chaotic, jumbled, rumpled, scruffy, tousled, unkempt **8** littered, mussed up, slovenly, uncombed **9** cluttered, ungroomed **10** bedraggled, disheveled, in disorder, topsy-turvy

unnecessary: 5 extra, undue **6** excess **7** nominal, surplus, useless **8** needless, optional, unneeded **9** avoidable, causeless, extrinsic, pointless, redundant **10** extraneous, gratuitous

make ~: 7 obviate

unneeded: 5 extra, minor, spare **7** trivial **8** optional, picayune, trifling **9** redundant

unnerve: 3 cow, sap **4** faze, ride **5** alarm, appal, chill, daunt, floor, get to, panic, shake, spook, throw, upset **6** appall, disarm, dismay, needle, rattle, unglue, weaken **7** agitate, buffalo, disturb, fluster, perturb, shake up, unhinge **8** bewilder, bowl over, confound, dispirit, distract, enervate, enfeeble, frighten, psych out, throw off, unsettle, unstring **9** give a turn, give pause, undermine **10** demoralize, disconcert, discourage, dishearten, intimidate

unnerved: 5 tense, timid **6** jangly **8** fluttery **9** unsettled **10** hysterical

unnerving: 4 eery **5** eerie, scary **8** terrible **9** appalling **10** petrifying

unnilhexium: 7 element

unnilpentium: 7 element

unnilquadium: 7 element

unnilseptium: 7 element

unnotable: 4 fair, so-so **6** not bad **7** average **8** adequate, mediocre, middling, ordinary, passable **9** tolerable

unnoticed: 5 perdu **6** hidden, perdue, secret, unseen **7** ignored **8** passed by, unheeded, winked at **9** neglected **10** overlooked, undetected, unobserved, unremarked

unnumbered: 4 vast **6** myriad, untold **7** endless **8** infinite, manifold **9** boundless, countless, limitless, uncounted, unlimited

uno: 6 numero **7** Italian, Spanish **8** card game

follower: 3 dos, due

minus uno: 4 cero, nada

numero ~: 4 boss **5** first **8** champion **10** celebrated

numero ~ place: 5 first, on top

unobjectionable: 4 safe **8** harmless, nontoxic **9** innocuous

unobliging: 5 loath **6** forced **7** evasive **8** grudging, hesitant **9** reluctant, unwilling, unwishful **10** begrudging

unobscure: 5 clear, lucid, naked **8** knowable, luminous, manifest, pellucid

unobscured: 4 open **5** light, overt

unobservant: 3 lax **5** blind, loose, slack **6** remiss **7** cursory **8** careless, heedless, mindless, reckless, slapdash, slipshod **9** incurious, negligent, oblivious **10** neglectful

unobserved: 6 unseen **8** secretly **9** unnoticed **10** undetected

unobstruct: 4 free, open **5** clear

unobstructed: 4 free, open **5** clear

unobtrusive: 4 meek **5** quiet **6** casual, humble, low-key, modest, unseen **7** subdued **8** reserved, retiring, tasteful **9** unnoticed

unobtrusiveness: 7 modesty

unoccupied: 4 free, idle, open **5** empty, spare **6** vacant **7** untaken **8** deserted, desolate, inactive **9** abandoned, available **10** up for grabs

be ~: 4 laze, loaf, loll, rest **5** relax **6** dawdle, loiter, lounge, piddle **7** hang out **8** kill time, malinger, slack off, vegetate **9** bum around, goldbrick, sit around, waste time **10** fool around, knock about, take it easy

uno, dos, __: 4 tres

uno, due, __: 3 tre

unofficial: 7 private **8** informal **9** irregular

Unofficial Rose, An author: Iris Murdoch

unona: 5 shrub

unoppressive: 3 lax **4** easy, mild, soft **5** light, loose, quiet **6** benign, casual, docile, gentle **7** amiable, clement, lenient, no sweat, relaxed **8** amenable, carefree, flexible, informal, merciful, no bother, obliging, outgoing, painless, peaceful, pleasant, tolerant, yielding **9** compliant, forgiving, indulgent, no problem, tractable **10** child's play, effortless, forbearing, manageable, permissive, submissive, unexacting

unordained: 3 lay **4** laic **6** laical

unordinary: 4 rare **8** singular

unorganized __: 7 ferment

unoriginal: 3 old **4** dull **5** corny, hokey, passé, stale, trite, vapid **6** common, jejune, old hat **7** clichéd, fatuous, humdrum, prosaic **8** bromidic, outdated, outmoded **9** hackneyed, imitative, prosaical **10** derivative

be ~: 3 ape **4** copy, echo **5** mimic **6** do like, mirror, repeat **7** emulate, imitate **8** make like, parallel, simulate **9** duplicate, reiterate, reproduce

one: 3 ape **5** mimic **6** copier

unornamented: 4 bare **5** plain **6** modest, simple **7** Spartan

unorthodox: 3 odd **4** eery **5** eerie, weird **6** atypic, errant, far-out, freaky, quirky **7** beatnik, bizarre, deviant, lawless, liberal, offbeat, strange **8** aberrant, abnormal, atypical, bohemian, freakish, peculiar **9** anomalous, different, dissident, divergent, eccentric, fantastic, heretical, irregular

opinion: 6 heresy **7** dissent **9** blasphemy, sacrilege

unostentatious: 5 plain **6** humble, modest, simple

unostentatiousness: 7 modesty

Unp: 4 elem. **7** element

105 for ~: 4 at. no.

unpackaged: 5 loose

unpaid: 3 due **4** free **5** owing **6** mature **7** donated, overdue, past due, payable **8** honorary **9** in arrears, unsettled, voluntary, volunteer **10** delinquent, gratuitous, on the house, unsalaried

bill: 4 debt **6** arrear, red ink **7** arrears, deficit **9** liability, shortfall **10** obligation

labor: 6 corvée

worker: 4 serf **5** helot, slave **6** vassal **7** bondman, chattel, villein

unpaired: 3 odd **8** mateless **9** unmatched

unpalatable: 4 blah, vile **6** bitter **7** insipid **8** unsavory **9** tasteless **10** flavorless

unparalleled: 3 ten **4** best, lone, only, rare, sole, tops **5** alone, first, prime **6** unique, utmost **7** all-time, leading, stellar, supreme, unusual **8** champion, foremost, greatest, peerless, renowned, singular, splendid, superior, towering, ultimate, uncommon **9** matchless, nonpareil, number one, paramount, solid gold, unequaled, unmatched, unrivaled **10** consummate, preeminent, unrivalled

Unparalleled Adventure of One Hans Pfaall, The author: Edgar Allan Poe

unpardonable: 4 vile **6** odious **7** heinous, ignoble **8** horrible, shameful, terrible **9** abhorrent **10** abominable

unpartnered: 4 lone, solo, stag **5** alone **6** single **8** deserted **9** by oneself, on one's own, separated

unpasteurized: 3 raw

unpatriotic: 8 disloyal, renegade **9** seditious **10** rebellious, subversive, traitorous

unpeaceful: 5 rowdy **6** fierce **7** chaotic, lawless, violent, warlike **8** mutinous **9** insurgent, turbulent **10** anarchical, disorderly, rebellious

unpeg: 4 open **6** detach, loosen **8** separate, uncouple **9** disengage **10** disconnect

unpen: 6 let out **7** release, set free **8** let loose

unperceived: 6 unseen **7** unknown **9** unnoticed

unperceptive: 8 tactless

unpermissable: 4 tabu **5** taboo

unpersevering: 4 lazy **6** otiose

unpersuasive: 4 lame, weak

unperturbed: 4 calm, cool **5** quiet, staid, stoic **6** low-key, mellow, placid, poised, sedate, serene **7** amiable, at peace, equable, pacific, relaxed, stoical **8** amicable, composed, laid-back, peaceful, tranquil **9** collected, easy-going, impassive, quiescent, temperate

unphysical: 4 airy **7** ghostly **8** bodiless, ethereal, rarefied **9** spiritual **10** immaterial, intangible

unpigmented: 6 albino

unpin: 4 free, open **5** loose **6** detach, loosen **8** let loose

unpinned: 4 free, open **5** loose

unpitying: 4 grim, hard, mean **5** cruel, harsh, stern, stony **6** brutal, fierce, flinty, savage **7** bestial, callous **8** inhumane, ruthless, uncaring, vengeful **9** barbarous, cutthroat, dog-eat-dog, ferocious, heartless, inclement, merciless, monstrous, unfeeling, unsparing **10** implacable, inexorable, ironfisted, relentless, unmerciful, unyielding

unplanned: 5 ad-lib, fluky, loose **6** casual, chance, flukey, random **7** aimless **8** rambling **9** impetuous, unwitting **10** accidental, fortuitous, unexpected, unintended

unplanted: 6 fallow **8** untilled

unpleasant: 3 bad **4** foul, grim, hard, icky, rude, sore, sour, ugly **5** awful, gross, harsh, lousy, nasty, rough, seamy, yucky **6** Augean, bitter, horrid, odious, rotten, severe, sticky **7** bad news, grating, hellish, hideous, irksome, painful, unhappy **8** abrasive, annoying, bad scene, brackish, churlish, horrible, no picnic, terrible, unlovely, unsavory, wretched **9** appalling, frightful, loathsome, monstrous, murderous, obnoxious, offensive, repellant, repulsive, revolting, thankless, unlikable, unsightly, unwelcome **10** forbidding, ill-natured

combining form: 3 cac- **4** caco-

incident: 4 drag, mess **5** run-in **6** bummer, downer

most ~: 5 worst

one: 3 nag **4** pest, pill **6** noodge

task: 4 duty, onus **6** burden **9** millstone

unpleasantry: 3 cut, dig **4** barb, slam, slap, slur, snub **5** crack, sneer, taunt **6** insult, rebuff, slight **7** affront, put-down **8** rudeness **9** aspersion, cheap shot, insolence

unpliable: 4 hard **5** fixed, rigid, rusty, stiff **6** frozen **7** brittle **8** hardened, ossified **9** petrified **10** inflexible

unplowed: 6 fallow **8** untilled

unplug: 3 tap **7** turn off **10** disconnect

__ Unplugged: 3 MTV **6** Alanis

unpointed: 4 dull

unpoised: 6 clumsy, gauche **7** awkward, boorish, ill-bred, unadept **8** inurbane **9** graceless, unrefined **10** uncultured, unpolished

unpolished: 3 raw **4** wild **5** blunt, crude, green, rough **6** coarse, gauche, rustic, vulgar **7** awkward, boorish, loutish, lowbred, uncouth, unkempt **8** homespun, tactless, unpoised, unsubtle **9** backwater, inelegant, makeshift, primitive, tasteless **10** amateurish

unpolished __: 4 rice

unpolluted: 4 pure, safe **5** clean **8** pristine, sanitary, spotless **9** stainless **10** antiseptic, immaculate

unpopular: 3 out **5** hated, lousy, nerdy, wimpy **7** avoided, scorned, shunned, unloved, wimpish **8** despised, detested, disliked, rejected, unvalued, unwanted **9** disdained, obnoxious, unwelcome **10** ostracized, out of favor, unaccepted

one: 4 geek, nerd, nurd **5** twerp, twirp

play: 4 bomb, flop **6** turkey

unpopulated: 5 bleak **8** desolate

unpowdered: 5 shiny

unpracticed: 5 fresh, green, rusty, young **8** inexpert

unprecedented: 3 new **5** first, novel **6** signal, unique **8** original, singular, uncommon **9** unheard-of, unrivaled **10** phenomenal, unrivalled

unpredictable: 4 iffy **5** dicey, fluky, wacky **6** chance, chancy, fickle, fitful, flukey, random, touchy, tricky, whacky **7** erratic, wayward **8** doubtful, slippery, unstable, unsteady **9** mercurial, uncertain, whimsical

unpredictably: 8 by chance, randomly

move ~: 3 zag, zig

unprejudiced: 4 even, fair, just, open **5** equal **6** honest, square **7** liberal, neutral **8** balanced, catholic, detached, tolerant, unbiased **9** equitable, impartial, objective, unbigoted, uncolored **10** reasonable

unpremeditated: 5 ad-lib **6** random, snappy **7** offhand **9** unguarded

unprepared: 5 ad-lib, rough, unfit **6** unwary **7** offhand **9** impromptu **10** flat-footed, improvised

catch ~: 3 jar **4** numb, rock, stun **5** abash, floor, shock **6** appall, dismay **7** astound, horrify, shake up, stagger, stupefy **8** astonish, bowl over, paralyze, surprise, unsettle **9** electrify, galvanize, overwhelm **10** scare stiff

unprescribed: 6 chosen **8** optional, unbidden **9** voluntary, volunteer **10** unprompted, volitional

unpresuming: 3 shy 4 meek, nice 5 quiet, timid 6 demure, humble, modest 7 bashful 8 reserved, retiring 9 diffident 10 unaffected
unpresumptuous: 4 nice 6 kindly, modest, polite 7 genteel, refined 8 delicate, gracious, ladylike, obliging, pleasant, well-bred 9 agreeable, courteous
unpretended: 4 real, true 6 candid, modest 7 sincere 9 heartfelt, unfeigned
unpretentious: 4 easy, homy, meek, real 5 homey, lowly, naïve, plain, quiet, small, sober 6 casual, demure, folksy, honest, humble, modest, simple 7 artless, genuine, natural, sincere, up-front 8 discreet, down home, innocent, laid-back, ordinary, reserved, retiring 9 diffident, easygoing, guileless, uncomplex, unspoiled
unpretentiously: 6 freely, simply 7 frankly, plainly, readily 8 casually, directly, honestly, modestly 9 naturally, sincerely 10 informally
unpretentiousness: 7 modesty, reserve 8 delicacy, humility, meekness 9 reticence 10 diffidence, simplicity
Unpretty (1999 song) artist: TLC
unpreventable: 4 sure 5 fated 7 certain 10 inevitable, in the cards
unprincipled: 3 sly 4 bent, evil 5 shady, venal 6 amoral, shifty, tricky, unfair, wanton, wicked 7 corrupt, crooked, devious, immoral, knavish 8 cheating, two-faced 9 cutthroat, deceitful, dishonest, dissolute, mercenary, miscreant, reprobate, shameless, two-timing, unethical 10 licentious
one: 3 cad, cur 4 boor, toad 5 knave, rogue, scamp, swine 6 rascal 9 miscreant, scoundrel 10 blackguard
unprocessed: 3 raw 5 crude, rough 6 coarse 7 natural 9 inelegant, makeshift, primitive 10 amateurish
unproductive: 4 arid, idle, lean, null, poor, sere, slow, vain 6 barren, desert, effete, fallow, futile 7 inutile, sterile, useless 8 bootless 9 for naught, fruitless, pointless, to no avail, valueless, worthless
unprofessional: 3 lax 7 amateur 8 improper 9 negligent, nonexpert, unethical, unfitting, untrained
unproficient: 5 inapt, inept 6 clumsy, gauche 7 awkward, labored, unadept 8 bumbling, bungling, fumbling, inexpert 9 all thumbs, unskilled 10 amateurish, unskillful
unprofitable: 4 vain 6 barren, futile 7 sterile, useless 8 bootless 9 pointless, thankless, valueless, worthless
unprofound: 5 empty, inane, silly 7 foolish, shallow, trivial 8 skin-deep 9 frivolous, senseless
unprogressive: 4 lazy, slow 5 slack 6 leaden, remiss 7 halting, lagging 8 backward, dawdling, dilatory, plodding, slothful, sluggish 9 backwater, ponderous, prolonged 10 protracted
unprohibited: 2 OK 5 legal, legit, licit 6 kosher, lawful 8 all right 9 allowable 10 acceptable, legitimate
unprolific: 4 idle, slow, vain 6 barren, hollow 7 sterile, useless 8 plodding 9 fruitless 10 unavailing
unpromising: 3 dim 4 dire 5 bleak 6 gloomy 7 ominous
unprompted: 6 wilful 7 offhand, unasked, willful 9 impulsive, uninvited, voluntary
unpronounced: 4 mute 6 silent
unpropitious: 7 adverse, ominous 8 sinister, untimely, untoward
unprosperous: 4 poor 5 broke, needy 8 beggarly, dirt poor, indigent 9 dead broke, destitute, on welfare, penniless, penurious 10 down-and-out, down at heel, straitened
unprotected: 4 bare, open 5 naked 7 exposed 8 helpless, insecure 9 in the open, unguarded 10 barehanded, vulnerable
unprotesting: 4 meek 5 stoic 6 docile 7 passive, patient, stoical, subdued 8 amenable, biddable, obedient, resigned, yielding 9 agreeable, compliant, peaceable, tractable 10 reconciled, submissive
unprovoked: 6 wanton 10 gratuitous, groundless, unasked-for
unpublished: 6 covert, secret 8 hush-hush 10 classified, privileged, restricted, under wraps, unrevealed
unpunctual: 4 late, slow 5 tardy 7 belated 8 detained 9 irregular
Unq: 4 elem. 7 element
104 for ~: 4 at. no.
unqualified: 4 firm, flat, open, pure, rank, weak 5 gross, sheer, total, unfit, utter 6 simple, unable 7 flat-out, not up to, perfect, plenary 8 absolute, complete, outright, positive, straight, thorough, unfitted 9 downright, incapable, out-and-out, unalloyed, unlimited, unskilled 10 consummate
unquenchable: 6 greedy 8 ravening 9 voracious 10 gluttonous, insatiable
desire: 4 ache, pang 6 regret
unquestionable: 4 sure, true 5 clear 6 actual, patent, proven 7 certain, evident, factual, genuine, obvious 8 absolute, accurate, bona fide, decisive, definite, flawless, manifest 9 authentic, axiomatic, faultless, undoubted, veritable 10 undeniable
unquestionably: 2 ay, da, ja, sí 3 aye, oui, yea, yep, yes, yup 4 fine, okay, sure, yeah 5 good-o, natch, quite, right, roger, truly, uh-huh 6 agreed, easily, gladly, good-oh, indeed, just so, rather, really, righto, surely, you bet, yowzah 7 exactly, go ahead, indeedy, mais oui, quite so, ten-four 8 all right, as you say, of course, thumbs up, very well 9 be my guest, certainly, darn right, hands down, naturally, precisely, sure thing, you betcha, you said it 10 absolutely, by all means, definitely, positively, sure enough, that's right
unquestioned: 4 sure 5 clear 9 unanimous
unquestioning: 4 naif 5 naive 6 steady 9 steadfast
unravel: 3 run 4 fray, undo 5 clear, plumb, solve 6 decode, loosen 7 clear up, comb out, dope out, resolve, unweave, work out 8 decipher, separate, untangle 9 figure out, penetrate, puzzle out
unravelling: 6 answer 8 solution
unreactive: 4 logy, slow 5 inert, quiet 6 latent, stolid, torpid 7 passive 8 listless, sluggish 9 impassive, inanimate, lethargic, quiescent 10 insentient, motionless
unread: 8 ignorant, untaught 9 unlearned, untutored 10 illiterate, uneducated
unreadable: 6 in code 7 obscure, scrawly, unclear 8 scrawled 9 illegible 10 indistinct
unready: 4 lazy 5 slack, tardy 7 laggard, lagging 8 dallying, dilatory, feckless 10 flat-footed
unreal: 3 def, rad 4 aces, A-one, boss, braw, cool, dece, eery, fake, fine, gear, keen, mock, neat, nice, phat, sham, tuff 5 bogus, dandy, ducky, eerie, false, grand, great, ideal, marvy, neato, nobby, phony, prime, put-on, slick, super, swell 6 bang on, bang-up, bonzer, bosker, choice, divine, dreamy, ersatz, fabled, far-out, forged, gnarly, groovy, lovely, made-up, peachy, phoney, pseudo, slap-up, spot on, superb, terrif, tiptop, whizzo, wicked 7 amazing, assumed, awesome, capital, corking, feigned, perfect, ripping, skookum, stellar, sublime 8 abstract, chimeric, dazzling, delusive, especial, eximious, fabulous, fanciful, five-star, four-star, frabjous, glorious, heavenly, illusive, illusory, imagined, invented, jim-dandy, mistaken, mythical, notional, slam-bang, smashing, splendid, spurious, standout, sterling, stickout, superior, terrific, top-level, topnotch, very good, wondrous 9 bodacious, dreamlike, Endsville, excellent, exemplary, exquisite, fantastic, first-rate, high-grade, hunky-dory, imaginary, imitation, insincere, legendary, marvelous, pretended, simulated, sollicker, storybook, synthetic, top-flight, visionary, wonderful 10 artificial, chimerical, fabricated, fictitious, first-class, fraudulent, hotsy-totsy, incredible, intangible, jack-a-dandy, misleading, out of sight, peachy-keen, phenomenal, remarkable, stupendous, super-duper
combining form: 5 pseud- 6 pseudo-
unrealistic: 4 wild 5 crazy, silly 6 absurd 7 asinine, blue-sky, foolish, utopian 8 fanciful, illusive, illusory, quixotic, romantic 9 half-baked, illogical, visionary 10 chimerical, idealistic, improbable, quixotical, starry-eyed
unreality: 7 fantasy 8 ideality, illusion 9 dreamland, fairyland
unrealized: 6 future, latent 7 budding, dormant 8 inactive, sleeping 9 potential 10 in abeyance, smoldering
unreasonable: 3 mad 4 dear, wild 5 pricy, silly, steep, undue 6 absurd, all wet, biased, far-out, lavish, pricey, stupid, too-too, unfair, unholy, unjust 7 extreme, foolish, invalid, ungodly 8 improper, overmuch, stubborn 9 arbitrary, excessive, illogical, misguided, senseless, unearthly 10 exorbitant, far-fetched
unreasoned: 7 invalid 9 illogical 10 fallacious, ill-founded, irrational
unrecalled: 9 forgotten, repressed 10 suppressed
unrecognized: 7 unknown 9 anonymous, thankless, unnoticed
unreconstructed: 4 firm 5 rigid 7 diehard, fogyish, old-line 8 loyalist, mossback, orthodox, partisan 9 immovable 10 inflexible
unreduced: 5 total, whole 6 entire 7 plenary 8 complete, finished, thorough 10 exhaustive
unreel: 6 unwind 7 untwine
unrefined: 3 raw 4 rude, wild 5 crass, crude, gross, rough, wooly 6 coarse, earthy, grainy, impure, risqué, vulgar, woolly 7 boorish, loutish, natural, raffish, uncouth 8 impolite, plebeian, unpoised, unseemly 9 backwater, inelegant, makeshift, primitive, tasteless 10 amateurish, indecorous
unregulated: 4 free
unrehearsed: 5 ad-lib 7 offhand 9 extempore, impromptu 10 improvised, off-the-cuff
unrelated: 5 other 6 unlike 7 strange, unalike 8 discrete, distinct, separate 9 different, inapropos 10 dissimilar, extraneous, irrelevant
unrelaxed: 4 taut 5 antsy, jumpy 7 nervous 8 strained 9 ill at ease
unrelenting: 3 set 4 grim, hard 5 cruel, harsh, rigid, stern, stiff, stony, tough 6 mortal, savage, severe, steady, stoney 7 adamant, dead set, endless 8 constant, diligent, pitiless, ruthless, sedulous, unabated, unbroken 9 ceaseless, continual, incessant, merciless, perpetual, tenacious, unbending, unfailing, unsparing
unreliable: 3 bad 4 fake, weak 5 false, flaky, lying, risky, shaky 6 errant, fickle, flakey, hollow, shifty, sneaky, tricky, unsafe, unsure 7 dubious, erratic, furtive, unloyal, unsound 8 delusive, derelict, fallible, mistaken, skittish, slippery, unstable, wavering 9 deceitful, deceptive, erroneous, faithless, incorrect, irregular, makeshift, shiftless, uncertain 10 capricious, changeable, fly-by-night, inaccurate, precarious
source: 4 liar 5 rumor
unreligious: 4 laic 6 laical 7 secular 8 temporal 9 atheistic
unremarkable: 5 usual 6 normal 8 middling, ordinary, standard
unremarked: 9 unnoticed
unremembered: 4 lost, past 6 bygone 7 faraway, ignored 8 passed by 9 forgotten, neglected, unnoticed 10 overlooked
unremitting: 4 hard 5 stern 6 all-out, steady 7 endless, lasting, nonstop 8 constant, enduring, sedulous, unbroken, unending, untiring 9 ceaseless, incessant, perennial, perpetual
unremunerative: 8 bootless 9 for naught, worthless 10 profitless
unrenowned: 6 unsung 7 obscure 8 nameless, ordinary 9 unheard-of
unrepeatable: 4 lone, rare, sole 6 unique 7 curious, oddball, special, strange, uncanny, unusual 8 atypical, peculiar, singular, unwonted 9 exclusive, marvelous, unheard-of 10 phenomenal, prodigious
unrepentant: 3 bad, set 4 evil, mean 5 cruel, rigid, stony 6 flinty, no good, sinful, steely, wicked 7 baleful, corrupt, crooked, hateful, immoral, lawless, satanic, vicious 8 depraved, devilish, diabolic, fiendish, hardened, indurate, infamous, obdurate, stubborn 9 execrable, malicious, monstrous, nefarious, obstinate, rancorous 10 adamantine, iniquitous, malevolent, perfidious, villainous
unrequired: 7 useless 8 needless, optional 10 expendable
unrequited love, avenger of: 7 Anteros, Anterus
unreserved: 4 bold, free, open 5 blunt, frank 6 candid, direct, hearty, simple 7 gushing, up-front 8 effusive, outgoing, unartful 9 expansive, ingenuous, outspoken 10 forthright, free-spoken, from the hip, unreticent
unreservedness: 4 ease
unresisting: 4 meek 7 passive, servile 8 lamblike, resigned, yielding
unresolved: 4 iffy, moot, open 6 chancy 7 pending 8 doubtful, hesitant, lukewarm, unsolved, waffling 9 ambiguous, insoluble, uncertain, undecided, unsettled 10 ambivalent, indefinite, up for grabs, up in the air
unrespectable: 3 low 4 base 5 shady 6 shifty, shoddy, tricky 7 corrupt, crooked, devious, dubious, suspect

8 shameful, slippery, unsavory 9 dishonest, notorious, underhand, unethical 10 fly-by-night, scandalous, suspicious

unresponsive: 3 shy 4 cold, cool, slow 5 aloof, inert, stony 6 stoney 7 ice-cold 8 lukewarm, sluggish

unrest: 3 war 4 flux, fuss, mess, riot, to-do 5 chaos, swirl 6 bedlam, crisis, mayhem, strife, tumult, uproar 7 anarchy, anxiety, discord, ferment, fidgets, protest, tension, trouble, turmoil 8 disarray, disorder, disquiet, movement, sedition, upheaval 9 agitation, confusion, rebellion 10 discontent, dissension, inquietude, turbulence

unrestrained: 4 free, rash, wild 5 loose 6 adrift, all-out, hearty, lavish, savage, wanton 7 gushing, lawless, rampant, violent 8 effusive, informal, outgoing 9 unlimited

unrestraint: 5 haste 6 excess 7 abandon, freedom, license

unrestricted: 4 free, open 5 clean, loose 6 freely, public 8 absolute 9 boundless, limitless, open-ended, universal, unlimited

unrestrictedness: 4 play, span 5 range, reach, scope, space 6 leeway, margin 7 breadth, compass, freedom, liberty, license 8 free hand, latitude 9 elbow room

unreticent: 4 free, open 5 bluff, blunt, frank, vocal 6 candid, direct 7 up-front 9 outspoken 10 forthright, point-blank, unreserved

unrevealed: 6 hidden, occult, secret 7 unknown 8 ulterior 9 out of view, unexposed 10 undivulged

unrewarding: 3 off 6 barren 9 thankless

unrig: 9 dismantle, take apart 10 disconnect

unrighteous: 4 evil 5 wrong 6 unjust

unrigorous: 5 loose

unrinsed: 5 foamy, soapy, sudsy 7 lathery

unrip: 6 reveal 8 disclose, tear open 9 take apart

unripe: 4 sour 6 latent 8 immature, juvenile 9 premature

unrivaled: 4 aces, A-one, best, boss, only, rare 5 alone, grand, great, prime, super 6 choice, deluxe, divine, expert, far-out, select, single, superb, unique 7 amazing, awesome, corking, exalted, in front, leading, perfect, premium, ripping, stellar, sublime, supreme, vintage 8 dazzling, dominant, fabulous, five-star, four-star, frabjous, glorious, heavenly, peerless, smashing, splendid, sterling, superior, terrific, topnotch, very good 9 a cut above, Endsville, excellent, exemplary, exquisite, first-rate, marvelous, matchless, nonpareil, top-flight, unequaled, unmatched 10 consummate, first-class, inimitable, out of sight, phenomenal, preeminent, remarkable, stupendous, super-duper, surpassing, world-class

unrobed: 4 bare, nude 5 naked

unroll: 4 open 6 spread, unfold, unwind 7 display, stretch

unromantic: 6 earthy 8 sensible 9 practical, pragmatic, realistic 10 hard-bitten, hard-boiled

unruffled: 4 calm, cool, even 5 quiet, sober, staid, stoic 6 at ease, low-key, mellow, placid, poised, sedate, serene, smooth, stolid 7 amiable, at peace, easeful, equable, pacific, patient, relaxed, stoical 8 amicable, carefree, composed, laid-back, peaceful, tranquil 9 collected, easy-going, impassive, quiescent, temperate, unstirred, unworried 10 nonchalant, phlegmatic, unaffected, unagitated, untroubled

unruliness: 5 chaos 7 license 8 disorder 9 mobocracy

unruly: 3 bad 4 wild 5 balky, onery, rowdy 6 bratty, feisty, hoiden, hoyden, ornery, wilful 7 coltish, defiant, forward, lawless, naughty, playful, problem, rampant, raucous, restive, wayward, willful 8 contrary, factious, heedless, indocile, mutinous, perverse, stubborn 9 fractious, out of hand, out of line, turbulent 10 boisterous, disorderly, headstrong, ill-behaved, licentious, rebellious, refractory, tumultuous

__-uns: 3 you 5 young

Uns: 4 elem. 7 element

107 for ~: 4 at. no.

unsafe: 3 mad 4 weak 5 hairy, risky, shaky 6 chancy, touchy 7 harmful, parlous, unsound 8 alarming, fearsome, insecure, perilous, slippery, ticklish, unstable 9 dangerous, explosive, hazardous, on thin ice, uncertain 10 precarious, ramshackle, touch and go, unreliable, vulnerable

Unsafe at Any Speed author: 5 Nader

unsafety: 4 risk 5 peril 6 danger, hazard 8 jeopardy 10 insecurity

unsaid: 5 tacit 6 silent 7 implied 8 implicit, inferred, ulterior, unspoken, unstated, unvoiced, wordless 9 intimated, unuttered, unwritten 10 undeclared, understood

unsalaried: 6 unpaid 8 honorary 9 volunteer

unsalted: 4 blah, flat 5 bland, plain 9 tasteless 10 flavorless

unsanctioned: 4 null, void 7 invalid, negated 9 cancelled, rescinded 10 unratified

unsanitary: 5 dirty, grimy, sooty 6 filthy, fouled, grubby, grungy, soiled 7 smudged, stained, tainted 8 befouled, begrimed, maculate, polluted, slovenly 9 blackened, tarnished, unhealthy 10 besmirched, germ-ridden

unsatisfactorily: 3 ill 5 badly 9 adversely

unsatisfactory: 3 bad, off 4 lame, poor, thin, weak 5 amiss, inept 6 futile, no good, rotten 7 lacking, limited 8 below par, mediocre, schlocky, unworthy 9 deficient 10 inadequate, lamentable

most ~: 5 worst

unsatisfied: 3 due 5 eager, empty, itchy, owing 6 greedy, hungry, unpaid 7 longing, overdue, payable, starved, thirsty, wishful 8 covetous, desirous, edacious, esurient, famished, ravenous, starving, unfilled 9 hankering, in arrears, insatiate, unsettled, voracious

unsatisfying: 4 blah, lame, poor, thin 6 faulty 10 inadequate

unsavory: 4 dull, foul, icky, rank, sour 5 bland, gross, nasty, seamy, shady, tough 6 rancid 7 insipid, odorous 8 stinking 9 offensive, repugnant, tasteless 10 bad-tasting, flavorless, unpleasant

sort: 5 rogue 6 bad egg 9 scoundrel

unsay: 6 recall, recant 7 retract 8 take back, withdraw 9 back-pedal

unscathed: 4 safe 5 sound, whole 6 intact, unhurt 8 unharmed, unmarked 9 uninjured, unscarred, untouched 10 in one piece

unscheduled: 3 TBA 4 open

unschooled: 3 raw 4 naif 5 naive 6 simple 8 ignorant, inexpert, unartful 9 inerudite, ingenuous 10 illiterate, unlettered

unscientific: 6 untrue 7 invalid, unsound 9 illogical, unfounded 10 unreasoned

unscramble: 6 decode 8 decipher, simplify, untangle 9 puzzle out

unscrew: 4 open 5 loose 6 loosen

unscripted: 5 ad-lib 9 extempore, impromptu, tossed-off, whipped up 10 improvised, off-the-cuff

unscrupulous: 3 sly 4 base, foul 5 dirty, false, shady, sharp, venal 6 amoral, crafty, shifty, sneaky, unfair 7 corrupt, crooked, devious, illegal, immoral, knavish, low-down, selfish 8 degraded, ruthless, scheming, slippery, two-faced, wrongful 9 deceitful, degrading, dishonest, mercenary, shameless, underhand, unethical

one: 4 vamp 6 con man

plan: 3 con 4 scam

unseal: 3 ope 4 open

unsealed: 4 open 9 unstopped

unseasoned: 3 new, raw 4 naif 5 green, naive, plain, young 7 strange 8 immature, inexpert 9 tasteless

unseat: 4 buck, oust 5 throw 6 depose, remove, topple 7 dismiss, kick out, subvert, unhorse 8 dethrone, supplant 9 overthrow

unsecured: 5 loose

unseeded: 6 fallow 8 untilled

unseemly: 4 rude, ugly 5 crude, gross, inapt, nasty, spicy, undue 6 coarse, spicey, unmeet, vulgar 7 lowbred, raffish, uncouth 8 immodest, improper, indecent, untimely, untoward 9 inelegant, low-minded, tasteless, unrefined 10 in bad taste, indecorous, indelicate, malapropos, out of place, suggestive, unbecoming, unsuitable

unseen: 4 dark 6 hidden, latent, masked, occult, secret, veiled 7 cloaked, furtive, lurking, obscure, private 8 hush-hush, imagined, obscured, secluded, shrouded, ulterior 9 concealed, disguised, invisible, out of view, unexposed, unnoticed 10 out of sight, tucked away, undercover, under wraps, undetected, unobserved, unviewable

__ unseen: 5 sight

Unseld, Wes

milieu: 5 court

org.: 3 NBA

sport: 10 basketball

unselfish: 4 kind 5 noble, sweet 6 giving, humane, kindly, loving, polite 7 devoted, gallant, heedful, helpful, liberal, mindful, tactful 8 generous, gracious, obliging 9 sensitive 10 altruistic, benevolent, charitable, chivalrous, free-handed, humanistic, open-handed, thoughtful, ungrudging

unsentimental: 5 stony 6 stoney 9 pragmatic, realistic 10 hard-bitten

unseparated: 3 one 5 whole 6 united

Unser: 2 Al 5 Bobby, racer 8 car racer 9 auto racer

milieu: 5 track

rival: 4 Foyt

unset: 5 runny 9 tentative 10 up in the air

unsettle: 4 trip 5 get to, shake, shock, spook, throw, upset, worry 6 bother, flurry, jumble, rattle, ruffle, sicken, unglue 7 agitate, confuse, derange, disrupt, disturb, fluster, perturb, shake up, trouble, unhinge, unnerve 8 befuddle, confound, convulse, disarray, disorder, displace, disquiet, psych out, surprise, throw off, unstring 9 discomfit, give a turn, unbalance 10 demoralize, disarrange, discommode, discompose, disconcert

unsettled: 3 due 4 edgy, iffy, live, moot, open 5 antsy, fluid, owing, shaky, tense, upset 6 chancy, cloudy, mobile, on edge, shaken, thrown, uneasy, unpaid 7 anxious, dubious, fidgety, hanging, migrant, mutable, overdue, payable, pending, rattled, restive, shook up, unclear, unquiet 8 agitated, changing, confused, darkened, doubtful, floating, fluttery, immature, insecure, restless, shifting, unnerved, unstable, variable, volatile, waffling, wavering, wobbling 9 ambiguous, debatable, delirious, disturbed, explosive, flustered, ill at ease, in arrears, itinerant, migratory, perturbed, squeamish, tentative, turbulent, uncertain, undecided 10 borderline, changeable, disordered, disorderly, inconstant, indecisive, indefinite, irresolute, on the fence, unbalanced, unresolved, up for grabs, up in the air

unsettling: 6 creepy 8 involved, puzzling 9 confusing, difficult, obscuring, upsetting 10 disruptive, disturbing, embroiling, misleading, perplexing

unshackle: 4 free, save 6 loosen 7 deliver, manumit, release 8 liberate 9 discharge 10 emancipate

unshackled: 4 free, wild 5 loose 6 untied

unshakable: 4 firm, sure 5 solid 7 adamant 8 implicit, resolute, stubborn 9 immovable, tenacious 10 hard-bitten

unshaken: 4 sure 6 steady 8 resolute 10 determined, unwavering

unshaped: 8 inchoate 9 amorphous

unshared: 4 sole 6 single 9 exclusive

unsharpened: 4 dull 5 blunt 8 edgeless

unshaven: 5 hairy, rough 7 bearded, bristly, hirsute, unshorn

unsheltered: 4 open 7 exposed 9 in the open 10 vulnerable

unshielded: 4 bare, nude, open 5 naked 7 exposed 8 undraped 9 in the open, uncovered 10 vulnerable

unshod: 8 barefoot, shoeless

unshorn: 5 bushy, furry, fuzzy, hairy 6 shaggy 7 bearded, bristly, hirsute 8 unshaven 9 whiskered 10 long-haired

unshortened: 3 all 4 A to Z, full 5 uncut, whole 6 entire, intact 8 complete 10 exhaustive, unabridged

unshrinking: 4 bold, game 5 brash, brave, crass, gutsy, nervy, pushy, stout 6 brassy, brazen, cheeky, daring, heroic, plucky, spunky, steely 7 doughty, forward, gallant, staunch, valiant 8 fearless, intrepid, resolute, stalwart, unafraid 9 audacious, dauntless, steadfast, tenacious, unalarmed, undaunted, unfearing 10 courageous, fire-eating, mettlesome, undeterred, undismayed

unshrouded: 4 open 5 clear, overt, plain 6 in view, patent, public 7 obvious, visible 8 apparent, clear-cut, explicit, manifest 10 observable

unshut: 4 open 9 unstopped

unshy: 5 brash 6 brassy 7 forward

unsightly: 4 ugly 5 awful, gross, plain 6 horrid 7 hideous 8 terrible, wretched 9 appalling, frightful, loathsome, monstrous, offensive, repellant, revolting 10 lackluster, unbecoming, unpleasant

unsimilar: 9 different, disparate, divergent 10 dissimilar

unsimulated: 6 honest 7 artless, genuine, sincere 9 guileless, heartfelt, ingenuous, unfeigned

Unsinkable Molly Brown, The (1964 film)
cast: Ed Begley, Harve Presnell, Debbie Reynolds
unskilled: 3 new, raw **5** fresh, gawky, inapt, inept, unfit **6** clumsy, klutzy, oafish, unable **7** awkward, gawkish **8** bumbling, bungling, inexpert **9** all thumbs, graceless, incapable, lumbering, maladroit, stumbling **10** dilettante, unequipped, unfamiliar, uninitiate
in: 5 bad at
one: 3 cub **4** tyro **6** novice **7** amateur, learner, recruit, trainee **8** beginner, freshman, initiate, neophyte, newcomer **9** fledgling, greenhorn **10** apprentice, tenderfoot
sailor: 6 lubber **10** landlubber
worker: 4 peon **5** prole **7** laborer
writer: 4 hack **6** drudge
unskillful: 5 crude, green, inept, unapt, unfit **6** clumsy, gauche, klutzy, oafish **7** awkward, unadept **8** bumbling, bungling, cloddish, fumbling, inexpert **9** all thumbs, incapable, maladroit **10** amateurish, unequipped
Unskinny Bop (1990 song) artist: Poison
unslanted: 4 fair, just **5** sober **6** candid, honest, square **7** neutral **8** detached, moderate, rational, unbiased **9** equitable, impartial, objective, unbigoted, uncolored **10** evenhanded, fair-minded, impersonal, open-minded
unsleeping: 5 alert, awake, aware **7** wakeful **8** vigilant, watchful
unsmiling: 4 dour **5** grave, stony **6** severe, stoney **7** serious **8** lowering
unsmooth: 5 bumpy, lumpy **6** jagged, uneven **7** unlevel
unsmudged: 5 clean **8** unsoiled
unsnap: 4 open **5** loose **6** loosen
unsnarl: 8 untangle
unsociable: 3 shy **4** cold, cool **5** aloof, timid **6** crabby, silent, sullen **7** distant, hostile, recluse **8** brooding, reserved, retiring, solitary **9** reclusive, secretive, withdrawn **10** antisocial
unsoiled: 4 pure **5** clean, fresh, snowy, white **6** chaste, washed **8** dirtless, germfree, hygienic, innocent, pristine, sanitary, spotless, unfouled **9** blameless, guiltless, honorable, laundered, lily-white, sparkling, stainless, undefiled, unsmudged, unspotted, unstained, unsullied, untainted, untouched **10** immaculate, impeccable
unsolicited: 4 free **6** gratis **7** offered **8** unsought **9** undesired, uninvited, unwelcome, voluntary **10** gratuitous
manuscripts: 5 slush
Unsolved Mysteries (NBC/CBS) host: Robert Stack
unsophisticate: 4 babe, lamb **5** yokel
unsophisticated: 4 hick, homy, naif, pure **5** corny, crass, crude, green, homey, naive, rough, rural **6** callow, earthy, folksy, gauche, honest, rustic, simple **7** artless, genuine, natural, sincere **8** homespun, innocent, lamblike, wide-eyed **9** backwater, childlike, guileless, ingenuous, unworldly **10** unaffected
unsound: 3 bad, ill **4** daft, idle, sick, weak **5** false, frail, inane, risky, shaky, silly, wacky, wrong **6** absurd, ailing, broken, faulty, flawed, flimsy, infirm, laid up, marred, screwy, sickly, unsafe, untrue, unwell, unwise, whacky **7** damaged, fatuous, fragile, in error, inexact, invalid, parlous, rickety, shallow **8** cockeyed, decrepit, delicate, fallible, ill-spent, impaired, insecure, mistaken, perilous, specious, unbacked, unhinged, unstable, unsteady **9** afflicted, bedridden, breakable, dangerous, defective, erroneous, frangible, hazardous, illogical, imperfect, incorrect, senseless, sophistic, tottering, unhealthy **10** fallacious, groundless, ill-founded, inaccurate, indisposed, irrational, jerry-built, unbalanced, ungrounded, unreliable
unsounded: 4 mute **5** tacit **10** bottomless, fathomless, unknowable
unsparing: 4 firm, free, hard **5** ample, bossy, cruel, harsh, picky, rigid, stern, tough **6** lavish, severe **7** austere, copious, liberal, profuse, Spartan **8** abundant, despotic, exacting, generous, handsome, hard-line, rigorous **9** bountiful, demanding, draconian, merciless, plentiful, stringent, trenchant, unpitying **10** altruistic, charitable, despotical, inflexible, iron-fisted, munificent, no-nonsense, oppressive, tyrannical, unmerciful
unspeakable: 4 dire **5** awful **6** horrid, odious **7** beastly, fearful, heinous **8** dreadful, horrible, nameless, shocking **9** appalling, atrocious, execrable, frightful, ineffable, loathsome, monstrous, obnoxious, offensive, repellent, repugnant, repulsive, revolting
unspeaking: 3 mum **4** mute **5** close, muted, quiet **6** silent **7** muzzled, quieted, stilled **8** hushed up **9** clammed up, secretive, voiceless **10** buttoned up, restrained, speechless, tongue-tied
unspecific: 4 hazy **5** broad, fuzzy, loose, vague **7** diffuse, general, inexact **8** nebulous, sweeping **9** ambiguous, imprecise **10** indefinite, undetailed
unspecified: 4 hazy **5** fuzzy, loose, muddy, murky, vague **6** unsure **7** general, obscure, sketchy, unclear **8** nebulous **9** enigmatic, imprecise, uncertain, undecided **10** ill-defined, indefinite
amount: 3 any, few **4** some
individual: 3 one **6** anyone **7** someone
unspiritual: 3 lay **4** laic **6** laical **7** earthly, mundane, profane, secular, terrene, worldly **8** material, temporal
unspoiled: 3 new **4** good **5** fresh **6** virgin **7** like new, perfect **8** pristine, spotless, virginal **9** good as new, stainless **10** immaculate
unspoken: 5 tacit **6** silent, unsaid **7** assumed, implied **8** implicit, unvoiced **9** intimated **10** understood
unspontaneous: 5 phony **6** forced, phoney **7** labored **8** affected, overdone, strained **9** contrived, rehearsed, unnatural **10** artificial
unsportsmanlike: 5 dirty **6** unfair
conduct: 7 low blow **9** cheap shot **10** defamation
unspotted: 5 clean **6** chaste **8** unsoiled **9** blameless, faultless
unstable: 4 weak **5** dizzy, fluid, giddy, shaky, tippy **6** fickle, fitful, jiggly, mobile, unfirm, unsafe, wabbly, wiggly, wobbly **7** dubious, erratic, mutable, parlous, protean, rickety, unsound, weaving **8** doubtful, insecure, shifting, slippery, ticklish, unsteady, variable, volatile, wavering **9** dangerous, mercurial, sensitive, teetering, uncertain, unsettled, vagarious **10** borderline, capricious, changeable, inconstant, irrational, precarious, unbalanced, unreliable
socially ~: 6 anomic
unstained: 5 clean **6** chaste **8** pristine, spotless, unsoiled **9** untouched
unstamped enclosure: 3 env., SAE
unstated: 5 tacit **6** unsaid **8** unvoiced **9** intimated **10** understood
unsteady: 4 wavy **5** dizzy, rocky, shaky, slack, tippy, tipsy **6** fickle, fitful, infirm, jiggly, uneven, wabbly, wobbly **7** erratic, halting, mutable, rickety, unsound, weaving **8** lopsided, slippery, ticklish, unstable, variable, volatile, wavering **9** irregular, mercurial, teetering, uncertain **10** capricious, changeable, inconstant, nonuniform, precarious, ramshackle, unbalanced
unstick: 4 open **5** loose **6** loosen
unstinting: 6 lavish **7** liberal, profuse **8** generous, princely **10** altruistic, charitable, free-handed, ungrudging
unstirred: 4 calm, cool **5** aloof **7** callous, unmoved **9** impassive, unexcited, unruffled **10** impervious, unaffected, unagitated, untroubled
unstop: 3 ope **4** open **5** clear **6** unclog
unstopped: 4 open **6** unshut **8** draining, uncorked, unsealed **9** unblocked, unclogged
unstrap: 4 open **5** loose **6** loosen
unstressed: 4 weak **6** at ease, atonic
unstrict: 3 lax **4** easy, soft **5** broad, loose, slack **6** casual **7** lenient **8** tolerant, yielding **9** easygoing **10** permissive
unstring: 4 jolt, rock **5** alarm, daunt, shake, upset, worry **6** dismay, rattle, unglue **7** agitate, disturb, horrify, perturb, stagger, unnerve **8** disquiet, distress, frighten, unsettle **9** discomfit **10** demoralize, discompose, disconcert, intimidate
unstructured: 6 blobby **8** formless, inchoate, nebulous, unformed, unshaped **9** amorphous, shapeless
unstrung: 5 fazed, upset **6** shaken **7** nervous **8** agitated **9** flustered **10** confounded
unstudied: 6 simple **7** natural, offhand **8** unartful **9** guileless, ingenuous **10** improvised, unaffected
unstylish: 3 out **5** dowdy, tacky **6** frumpy **8** outmoded
unsubstantial: 4 aery, less, limp, null, thin **5** empty, frail, light, wrong **6** dreamy, flimsy **7** fragile, rickety, unsound **8** delicate, ethereal **9** breakable, frangible
unsubstantiated: 4 idle **5** false **6** flimsy, untrue **7** invalid **8** baseless, fanciful, mistaken, spurious **9** erroneous, trumped-up, unfounded **10** fabricated, fallacious, gratuitous, groundless
unsubtle: 5 blunt, gross, overt, plain **6** gauche, patent **7** blatant, glaring, obvious **8** explicit, flagrant, tactless **9** barefaced **10** in-your-face
unsuccessful: 4 vain **6** futile, in vain **7** failing, unlucky, useless **9** fruitless
be ~: 4 fail, lose **8** fall flat
venture: 3 dog, dud **4** bomb, bust, flop **5** lemon, loser **6** fiasco, fizzle **7** debacle, failure, washout **8** disaster
unsuccinct: 4 long **5** gabby, windy, wordy **6** chatty, prolix, turgid **7** gushing, lengthy, unterse, verbose, voluble **8** babbling, inflated, rambling **9** bombastic, garrulous, jabbering, talkative **10** bigmouthed, blathering, discursive, long-winded, loquacious, rhetorical
unsuitable: 4 lame **5** inapt, tacky, unapt, unfit, wrong **8** improper, unseemly, untimely **9** incorrect **10** ineligible, irrelevant, unequipped
unsuitably: 4 awry **5** amiss **7** wrongly **10** improperly
unsuited: 5 unfit **10** inapposite, unbecoming
unsullied: 4 pure **5** clean **6** chaste, virgin **8** flawless, innocent, pristine, sanitary, spotless, unsoiled, virginal, virtuous **9** blameless, faultless, guiltless, stainless **10** immaculate
unsung: 7 obscure, unfamed, unknown **8** nameless **9** anonymous, unheard-of **10** unrenowned
unsupported: 5 shaky **8** baseless **10** groundless
unsuppressed: 4 wild **6** wanton
unsure: 4 asea, iffy, lost, torn, wary, weak **5** at sea, chary, leery, shaky, vague, wimpy **6** chancy **7** dubious, guarded, suspect, wimpish **8** cautious, doubtful, doubting, hesitant, untrusty, wavering **9** ambiguous, faltering, skeptical, tentative, unassured, uncertain, undecided **10** indecisive, indefinite, irresolute, precarious, suspicious, touch and go, unreliable, up for grabs, up in the air
response: 5 maybe **6** I guess **7** it may be, perhaps **9** it could be
unsurpassable: 5 ideal, prime **6** superb **7** leading, perfect, sublime, supreme **8** crowning, foremost, greatest, peerless, ultimate **9** excellent, first-rate, matchless, nonpareil, paramount, sovereign, unequaled, unmatched **10** consummate, inimitable, preeminent
unsurpassed: 4 A-one, best, tops **5** alone, first, prime **6** finest **7** highest, supreme **8** greatest, peerless, splendid **9** matchless, nonpareil, unequaled **10** preeminent
unsusceptible: 6 immune
unsuspecting: 4 easy, naif **5** naive **6** unwary **7** taken in, unaware **8** gullable, gullible, innocent, off-guard, trustful, trusting **9** confiding, credulous, ingenuous, unadvised, unwitting
one: 4 babe, lamb, naif **9** greenhorn
unsuspicious: 4 naif **5** naive **6** unwary
unsustained: 5 brief, short **7** cursory **8** fleeting **9** ephemeral, momentary **10** short-lived, transitory
unswayable: 4 firm, iron **7** adamant **9** unbending **10** inflexible
unswept: 4 foul **5** dirty, dusty, grimy, messy **6** filthy, grubby, grungy, untidy **7** unclean **8** begrimed, slovenly
unswerving: 4 firm, true **5** loyal, rigid **6** all-out, direct, in a row, linear, steady **7** adamant **8** directly, emphatic, forceful, resolute, straight, untiring **9** religious, steadfast, tenacious, undivided **10** conclusive, undeterred
unswervingly: 4 hard **8** candidly, directly, honestly, promptly, straight **9** precisely
unsymmetrical: 4 alop **6** uneven **8** lopsided, one-sided **10** off-balance
unsympathetic: 3 icy **4** cold, cool, hard **5** aloof, harsh, nasty, stony **6** flinty, frigid, stoney, unkind **7** callous, unmoved **8** lukewarm, tactless **9** apathetic, heartless, merciless, repellent, unfeeling, unpitying **10** hard-boiled, unfriendly
unsystematic: 5 messy **6** random, spotty **7** aimless, chaotic, jumbled, mixed up, muddled **8** confused, slipshod **9** haphazard, illogical **10** disordered, disorderly, in disarray
untactful: 5 brash **6** clumsy **7** forward **8** unsubtle **9** maladroit **10** indelicate, unthinking
untainted: 4 good, pure **5** clean, fresh **6** chaste **7** sinless **8** innocent, pristine, unsoiled, virtuous **9** guiltless
untaken: 4 free, open **5** empty, to let

6 unused, vacant **8** unfilled **9** available **10** unoccupied

untamed: **4** wild **5** feral, rabid **6** animal, ferine, fierce, savage **7** beastly, coltish, lawless **9** ferocious, primitive, turbulent

land: **4** wild

Untamed (1955 film)

cast: Susan Hayward, Agnes Moorehead, Tyrone Power

director: Henry King

untangle: **4** comb **5** ravel, solve **6** decode, unwind **7** clear up, explain, unravel, unsnarl, untwine, untwist, unweave **8** decipher **9** extricate **10** disembroil, unscramble

untanned: **4** pale **5** white **6** pallid

untapped: **3** new **6** latent, virgin **8** virginal

untarnished: **4** pure **5** clean **6** bright, chaste **7** perfect, shining, sinless **8** absolute, flawless, innocent, pristine, spotless, virtuous **9** faultless, guiltless, stainless **10** immaculate

untaught: **4** naif **5** crude, naive **6** unread **8** ignorant **10** uneducated, unschooled

untaxing: **4** easy, soft **5** cushy, light **6** casual, frothy, gentle, simple, smooth **7** unheavy **8** carefree **10** effortless, manageable, unexacting

untempered: **6** wanton **7** extreme, too much **8** a bit much **9** excessive **10** immoderate, inordinate

untenable: **4** thin, weak **5** inane, silly, wacky **6** absurd, faulty, flawed, screwy, whacky **7** fatuous **8** baseless, cockeyed, specious **9** illogical, senseless **10** groundless, incredible

untended: **5** seedy **6** grungy, shabby, shoddy **7** rickety, run-down, scruffy, squalid **8** decrepit, derelict, forsaken, tattered **9** abandoned, crumbling, neglected **10** in bad shape, ramshackle, tumbledown, uncared-for

Untermeyer, Louis: **6** writer

work: Burning Bush

Modern American Poetry

unter opposite: **4** über

unterse: **4** long **5** gabby, windy, wordy **6** chatty, prolix, turgid **7** gushing, lengthy, verbose, voluble **8** babbling, inflated, rambling **9** bombastic, garrulous, jabbering, talkative **10** bigmouthed, blathering, discursive, longwinded, loquacious, rhetorical, unsuccinct

Unterseeboot: **3** sub **5** U-boat

untested: **3** new, raw **5** green **6** callow **8** immature

unthinkable: **6** absurd **8** hopeless **10** infeasible, out of reach

unthinking: **3** lax **4** rash, rude **5** brash, hasty, nervy **6** blithe, remiss, sloppy, stupid, unwise, vacant **7** boorish, foolish, selfish, shallow, witless **8** careless, feckless, heedless, impolite, knee-jerk, mindless, off-guard, slapdash, slipshod, tactless, uncaring **9** automatic, haphazard, impetuous, imprudent, impulsive, negligent, oblivious, senseless, unguarded, unheedful, unheeding, unmindful, untactful, unwitting **10** incautious, irrational, nonchalant

unthinkingly, say: **5** blurt **8** blurt out

unthorough: **6** remiss, sloppy **7** botched **8** careless, slapdash, slipshod **9** haphazard, hit-or-miss, negligent **10** jerry-built

unthought-of: **3** new **5** novel **8** original

unthreatened: **2** OK **4** safe **6** secure **8** home-free **9** protected **10** impervious

unthreatening: **4** meek, mild, tame, weak **6** docile, gentle **8** biddable, harmless, lamblike, obedient **9** compliant, tractable **10** spiritless, submissive

unthrifty: **6** lavish **7** liberal **8** prodigal, wasteful **10** immoderate, profligate

untidiness: **4** mess, muss **6** litter **7** clutter **8** disarray, disorder **9** confusion

untidy: **4** wild **5** a mess, dirty, dowdy, messy, mussy **6** blowsy, blowzy, frowsy, frowzy, sloppy, unneat **7** blowsed, blowzed, chaotic, jumbled, rumpled, scruffy, tousled, unkempt, unswept **8** littered, slapdash, slipshod, slovenly, uncombed **9** cluttered, ungroomed **10** bedraggled, disarrange, disarrayed, disheveled, disordered, disorderly, in disorder, topsy-turvy

make ~: **4** muss **6** jumble, mess up, ruffle, rumple, tangle, tousle **7** clutter, crumple, disturb, rummage, wrinkle **8** dishevel **10** disarrange

one: **4** slob

untie: **4** free, open, undo **5** let go, loose **6** loosen **7** disjoin, release, set free **8** disunite, let loose, liberate, separate, set loose **9** disengage, extricate **10** disconnect

the knot: **4** free, part **5** sever **6** loosen **7** break up, divorce, split up **10** put asunder

untied: **4** free **5** let go, loose **6** undone **7** at large, rescued, unbound **8** cut loose, detached, let loose, released, set loose **9** at liberty, unchained, unimpeded, unleashed **10** disengaged, on the loose, unattached, unconfined, unfastened, unfettered, unshackled

untighten: **4** ease, open **5** loose, relax, unzip **6** loosen

until: **4** as of, till, up to **6** before, down to **7** as far as, pending, prior to **9** meanwhile

now: **3** yet **5** since, so far

__ Until Dark: **4** Wait

Until It Sleeps (1996 song) artist: Metallica

untilled: **4** idle **6** fallow, unused **8** unplowed, unseeded **9** unplanted

Until You Come Back to Me (1973 song) artist: Aretha Franklin

untimely: **5** inapt, undue **7** awkward, too late, unlucky **8** improper, mistimed, oversoon, too early, unseemly, untoward **9** ill-suited, premature **10** irrelevant, malapropos, unsuitable

untiring: **5** perky **6** dogged, steady, strong **7** devoted, patient, staunch **8** constant, resolute, sedulous, tireless, unwaning **9** ceaseless, continual, continued, dedicated, energetic, tenacious, unceasing, unfailing, unstinted, unwearied **10** continuing, determined, persistent, relentless, undeterred, unflagging, unswerving, unwavering, unwearying

untiringly: **4** hard

untitled: **6** common **7** lowborn **8** baseborn, nameless

__ unto Caesar...: **6** render

__ unto itself: **4** a law

untold: **4** many, vast **6** a lot of, divers, gobs of, hidden, lots of, myriad, umteen **7** a host of, a slew of, copious, endless, heaping, heaps of, no end of, piles of, private, profuse, scads of, umpteen, unknown **8** a bunch of, abundant, an army of, infinite, manifold, numerous, oodles of, scores of, umpsteen, very many **9** a passel of, boundless, bountiful, countless, limitless, quite a few, uncounted, unlimited **10** innumerous, numberless, staggering, suppressed, unnumbered, zillions of

years: **3** eon **4** aeon

untoned: **4** soft **5** slack, unfit **6** flabby **7** flaccid **10** out of shape

unto starter: **4** here **5** there, where

untouchable: **4** tabu **7** outcast **9** inviolate **10** sacrosanct

Untouchable: **4** Ness, T-man

untouchables: **4** rank **5** caste **6** status

Untouchables, The (1987 film)

cast: Sean Connery, Kevin Costner, Robert De Niro, Andy Garcia, Charles Martin Smith

director: Brian De Palma

Untouchables, The (ABC drama)

cast: Robert Stack (Eliot Ness)

narrator: Walter Winchell

untouched: **3** new **4** pure **5** blank, fresh, sound, whole **6** entire, intact, secure, unhurt, virgin **7** perfect, uneaten, unmoved **8** flawless, leftover, sanitary, spotless, unharmed, unmarked, unmarred, unsoiled, virginal **9** apathetic, incorrupt, undamaged, uninjured, unscathed, unstained **10** immaculate, unaffected

Unto us __ is given: **4** a son

untoward: **7** adverse, unhappy, unlucky **8** contrary, improper, perverse, stubborn, unseemly, untimely **10** disastrous, disturbing, out of place

untraditional, musically: **6** atonal

untrained: **3** new, raw **4** soft, weak **5** crude, fresh, green, messy, rough **6** callow **7** amateur **8** ignorant, inexpert **10** disorderly

untried: **3** new **5** fresh, green, young **6** virgin **7** strange **8** original, virginal

untrodden: **3** new **5** fresh

untrouble: **4** ease, lull **5** allay, cheer, salve **6** pacify, solace, soothe, stroke **7** appease, assuage, compose, console, mollify, placate, relieve **8** calm down, unburden **9** alleviate, pour oil on **10** conciliate, smooth over

untroubled: **4** calm, cool, easy **5** clear, quiet, staid, still, stoic **6** at ease, blithe, hushed, low-key, mellow, placid, sedate, serene, smooth, steady **7** amiable, at peace, easeful, equable, halcyon, pacific, relaxed, stoical **8** amicable, carefree, composed, laid-back, peaceful, tranquil **9** collected, easy-going, impassive, quiescent, temperate, unruffled, unstirred, unworried **10** insouciant, nonchalant, unagitated, unbothered

untroublesome: **4** easy **5** light **6** facile, simple **9** no problem

untrue: **3** not, off **4** sham **5** false, lying, not so, wrong **6** faulty, hollow, made-up **7** in error, inexact, invalid, unloyal, unsound **8** delusive, disloyal, forsworn, libelous, mistaken, perjured, recreant, specious, spurious, two-faced **9** deceptive, dishonest, distorted, erroneous, faithless, imprecise, incorrect, insincere, out of line, unfounded **10** apocryphal, fallacious, fictitious, inaccurate, inconstant, mendacious, misleading, perfidious, traitorous, unfaithful, ungrounded

declare ~: **4** deny **5** rebut **6** negate, recant, reject **7** disavow, dispute, gainsay **8** disclaim **9** repudiate **10** contradict

untrueness: **7** perfidy, treason **9** perfidity, treachery **10** disloyalty, infidelity

untrustworthy: **5** false, shady, sharp, snaky **6** fickle, rotten, shifty, sneaky, tricky, unsafe, unsure, untrue **7** corrupt, crooked, devious, dubious **8** derelict, disloyal, fallible, guileful, slippery, two-faced, unsteady, untrusty **9** conniving, deceitful, dishonest, faithless, two-timing, unassured

sort: **4** liar **5** rogue, scamp, sneak

untruth: **3** fib, lie **4** tale **5** story **6** canard, dupery **7** calumny, fallacy, falsity, fiction **9** deception, falsehood, invention, mendacity **10** imputation, inveracity

untruthful: **5** false, lying **6** shifty, tricky **7** crooked, devious, fibbing **8** delusive, guileful **9** deceitful, dishonest, faithless, insincere **10** mendacious

be ~: **3** con, fib, lie **4** dupe, fake, hoax, snow **5** bluff, couch, fudge **6** delude, invent, take in **7** concoct, deceive, distort, falsify, mislead, perjure **8** misguide, misquote, misstate, simulate, soft-soap **9** disinform, dissemble, four-flush, misinform **10** equivocate, exaggerate

be ~ with: **5** lie to **7** deceive

one: **4** liar **5** cheat, phony **6** fibber **7** deluder **8** deceiver, perjurer **9** con artist, falsifier, trickster **10** fabricator

unturned, leave no stone: **4** seek **5** scour **6** search, strive **7** persist, ransack, rummage **9** persevere

untutored: **3** raw **5** rough **6** unread **8** inexpert, untaught **10** illiterate, uneducated, unlettered, unschooled

untwine: **4** free **5** loose, ravel **6** uncoil, unreel, unwind **7** untwist **8** untangle

untwist: **5** ravel **6** spread, unfold, unwind **7** untwine **8** untangle **10** straighten

a rope, nautically: **5** feaze, feeze

untypical: **7** strange **8** isolated **9** anomalous, divergent

unum: **3** one **5** Latin

unusable: **4** junk **5** passé, sorry **6** crummy, no-good, trashy **7** inutile **8** bootless, obsolete, outmoded, pathetic, wretched **9** no-account, worthless **10** antiquated, superseded

become ~: **3** rot **4** mold, rust, sour, turn **5** decay, go bad, spoil, taint **6** molder **7** corrode, crumble **9** break down

unused: **3** new **4** free, idle, mint, over **5** blank, extra, fresh, spare **6** fallow, vacant, virgin **7** sitting, surplus, untaken **8** leftover, pristine, residual, untilled, virginal **10** on the shelf, unconsumed, unemployed

go ~: **3** sit **5** lie by **6** remain

unusual: **3** new, odd **4** eery, rare **5** alien, eerie, freak, fresh, funny, novel, outré, queer, weird **6** atypic, clever, exotic, freaky, quaint, quirky, scarce, unique, way-out **7** amazing, awesome, bizarre, curious, deviant, oddball, offbeat, special, strange, uncanny **8** aberrant, abnormal, atypical, creative, far apart, freakish, inspired, isolated, original, peculiar, singular, striking, uncommon, unwonted **9** anomalous, arresting, different, divergent, eccentric, fantastic, ingenious, inventive, irregular, laughable, marvelous, memorable, recherché, unheard-of, unnatural **10** individual, infrequent, innovative, noteworthy, occasional, outlandish, phenomenal, prodigious, remarkable, surprising, suspicious, unexpected, unfamiliar

article: **5** curio, relic **7** bibelot, whatnot **9** objet d'art **10** knickknack

combining form: **4** anom- **5** anomo-

in Latin: **4** rara

person: **4** oner

unusually: **4** very **5** extra, oddly

6 mighty, rarely 7 awfully 8 terribly 9 curiously, extremely, strangely 10 especially, peculiarly, remarkably, uncommonly
unuttered: 5 quiet, tacit 6 unsaid 7 implied 8 implicit, unvoiced
unvaried: 4 same 6 boring 9 wearisome 10 monotonous
unvarnished: 3 raw 4 bare, open, pure, real 5 frank, naked, plain, stark 6 candid, honest, simple 7 genuine, literal 9 unadorned
unvarnished __: 5 truth
unvarying: 4 even, same, sure 5 rigid 6 smooth, stable, static, steady 7 equable, regular, routine, uniform 8 constant 9 continual, uniformly 10 consistent, homogenous, monotonous, true to type, unchanging
unveil: 3 ope 4 bare, leak, open, show, tell 6 expose, reveal 7 display, divulge, exhibit, lay bare, lay open, let slip, uncover 8 disclose, discover 9 make known 10 make public
unveiled: 4 open 5 clear, naked, overt, plain, shown 6 in view, patent, public 7 obvious, visible 8 apparent, clear-cut, explicit, knowable, manifest 10 observable
unveiling: 6 exposé 10 appearance, disclosure, revelation
cry of ~: 4 ta-da 5 ta-dah
unventilated: 4 shut 5 close, stale, thick 6 stuffy 8 confined 9 sealed off 10 oppressive
unveracious: 5 false, lying 7 devious 8 two-faced 9 deceitful, dishonest, insincere 10 mendacious, perfidious, untruthful
unverified: 8 spurious 9 equivocal 10 apocryphal
unversed: 3 raw 4 naif 5 fresh, green, naive, young 10 unfamiliar
one: 4 lamb, naif 6 rookie
unviewable: 5 perdu 6 covert, hidden, latent, minute, unseen 8 obscured 9 concealed, invisible 10 intangible, not in sight, out of sight, tucked away, unapparent
unvigilant: 6 unwary 7 napping 8 sleeping 9 unguarded 10 incautious
unvoiced: 4 mute 5 tacit 6 silent, unsaid 7 implied 8 implicit, inferred, unspoken, wordless 9 intimated, unuttered 10 understood
unwaning: 6 steady 7 chronic, endless, eternal, lasting, regular 8 constant, enduring, frequent, habitual, unbroken, unending, untiring 9 ceaseless, chronical, continual, incessant, perennial, permanent, perpetual, recurrent, unceasing, unfailing 10 persistent, persisting, relentless, repetitive, unflagging
unwanted: 5 spare 7 unasked 8 leftover, loveless, needless 9 unpopular, unwelcome
give ~ advice: 6 butt in, meddle
guest: 3 ant, bug, fly, nag 4 bore, drag, drip, flea, gnat, pain, pest, pill 5 creep, mouse 6 insect 7 termite 8 headache, housefly, mosquito, nuisance 9 cockroach
layer: 4 dust
plant: 4 weed
pounds: 4 flab
unwarranted: 5 unapt, undue, wrong 6 unfair, unjust 8 baseless, improper, mistaken 9 misguided, unfounded 10 bottomless, groundless
unwary: 4 naif, rash 5 brash, hasty, naive 7 unalert 8 careless, heedless, off-guard, reckless, sleeping 9 credulous, impetuous, imprudent, unadvised, uncareful, unguarded 10 falling for, ill-advised, incautious, indiscreet, unprepared, unvigilant, unwatchful
unwashed: 4 foul 5 dirty, dusty, grimy, muddy 6 filthy, grubby, grungy, smutty, soiled 7 smudged 8 begrimed 9 uncleaned 10 insanitary
great ~: 5 plebs 6 masses, people 8 riffraff 9 hoi polloi
unwasteful: 6 frugal 7 sparing, thrifty 10 economical
unwatchful: 3 lax 6 unwary 7 napping 9 unguarded 10 incautious
unwavering: 3 set 4 even, fast, firm, sure 5 fixed, loyal, solid, stony 6 all-out, stable, steady, stoney 7 abiding, dead set, decided, intense, staunch 8 constant, emphatic, enduring, faithful, forceful, hellbent, ironclad, resolute, unshaken, untiring 9 dedicated, immovable, iron-jawed, steadfast 10 conclusive, determined, foursquare, invariable, undeterred, unswerving
unwaxed: 4 dull, flat 10 lusterless
unweaned: 8 juvenile
unwearied: 5 fresh 8 tireless, untiring 10 undeterred, unflagging
unwearying: 5 hyper 8 diligent, resolute, tireless, untiring 9 energetic 10 persistent, unflagging
unweave: 5 ravel 7 unravel 8 untangle 9 come apart
unwed: 5 alone 6 single 8 bachelor, divorced, eligible, solitary, wifeless 9 by oneself, on one's own, unmarried 10 spouseless, unattached
unwelcome: 5 lousy, pesky, pesty 7 shut out, unasked 8 excluded, rejected, unsought, unwanted 9 obnoxious, thankless, uninvited, unpopular 10 ill-favored, unpleasant
unwelcoming: 3 icy 4 cold, cool 6 chilly 10 unfriendly
unwell: 3 bad, ill, low 4 sick, weak 6 ailing, infirm, laid up, poorly, queasy, queazy, sickly 7 unsound 8 diseased 9 afflicted, bedridden, unhealthy 10 indisposed, out of sorts
unwellness: 6 malady 7 ailment, disease, illness, malaise 8 debility, disorder, sickness 9 complaint, fragility, frailness, infirmity 10 affliction
unwet: 3 dry 4 arid, sere 7 drained, parched, thirsty 8 rainless 9 anhydrous, shriveled, waterless 10 dehydrated, desiccated
unwheeled vehicle: 4 sled 6 glider, sleigh 8 toboggan
unwholesome: 4 gamy, sour 5 gamey 6 impure, morbid, sickly 7 noisome 8 virulent 9 unhealthy
unwieldy: 5 bulky, gross, heavy, hefty 6 clumsy, clunky 7 awkward, hulking, massive, weighty 8 ungainly 9 lumbering, ponderous 10 burdensome, cumbersome
unwilling: 3 coy, shy 4 loth 5 loath 6 afraid, averse, forced 7 evasive, opposed 8 grudging, hesitant, negative 9 compelled, demurring, reluctant, resistant, shrinking, unwishful 10 begrudging, indisposed, intolerant, unobliging
be ~: 4 balk 5 demur, hedge, tarry, waver 6 boggle, object, recoil, refuse, regret, resist, seesaw, shrink, waffle 7 decline, hold off, protest, scruple, shy away 8 complain, disagree, hang back, hesitate, hold back, pull back, question 9 hem and haw, make a fuss, pussyfoot, vacillate 10 disapprove, equivocate, think twice
be ~ to: 4 hate 5 abhor, scorn 6 detest, loathe 7 despise, disdain, dislike 9 abominate 10 flinch from, recoil from
to move: 4 iron 5 rigid 6 flinty, intent 7 adamant, diehard 8 hardened, hard-line, hellbent, obdurate, resolute, stubborn 9 immovable, immutable, obstinate, steadfast 10 inflexible
unwillingness: 7 refusal 8 aversion 10 hesitation
to work: 5 sloth 7 languor 8 idleness, laziness, lethargy, otiosity 9 fainéance, indolence, passivity, slackness 10 torpidness
unwilted: 4 dewy 5 crisp, fresh, green 7 unfaded, verdant
unwind: 4 free, reel, rest, undo 5 loose, ravel, relax, spool 6 loosen, spread, unbend, uncoil, unfold, unreel, unroll, unwrap 7 cool off, ease off, recline, sit back, slacken, untwine, untwist 8 calm down, loosen up, recreate, separate, slow down, untangle, wind down 9 quiet down 10 take a break, take it easy
unwise: 4 naif, rash 5 inane, inept, naive, silly 7 foolish, unsound 8 childish, immature, reckless 9 foolhardy, impolitic, imprudent, misguided, senseless, unadvised, uncareful, unguarded 10 ill-advised, indiscreet, irrational, unthinking
act: 4 no-no, tabu 5 taboo
in an ~ way: 4 illy
unwished-for: 8 rejected, unsought, unwanted 9 thankless, uninvited, unpopular, unwelcome 10 unpleasant
unwitting: 6 chance 7 unaware, unmeant 8 innocent 9 forgetful, unknowing, unplanned 10 accidental, unfamiliar, unintended, unthinking
victim: 4 pawn 5 patsy
unwittingly: 8 by chance, casually, unawares 9 by mistake 10 by accident
unwonted: 4 rare 7 unusual 8 singular, uncommon
unworkable: 7 of no use, useless, utopian 9 idealized, visionary 10 impossible, unfeasible
unworldly: 4 naif 5 green, naive 6 astral, dreamy 7 artless, corn-fed 8 ethereal, innocent, lamblike, trusting, unartful, wide-eyed 9 celestial, ingenuous, spiritual, visionary 10 idealistic, unaffected
unworried: 4 calm, cool, easy 6 placid, serene 8 carefree, composed, tranquil 9 unruffled 10 insouciant, nonchalant, unagitated, untroubled
unworthy: 3 low 4 base, vile 5 unfit 6 no-good, shabby 7 ignoble 8 shameful, wretched 9 degrading, no-account, unmerited, valueless 10 ineligible, inglorious, out of place, unbecoming
of: 5 below 7 beneath 10 inferior to, too good for
unwrap: 3 ope 4 open, undo 6 unfold, unwind 7 uncover
unwrinkle: 4 iron 5 press 6 smooth
unwritten: 4 oral 5 tacit, vocal 6 spoken, unsaid, verbal 8 accepted, narrated 9 customary 10 understood, unrecorded
on: 5 blank, clean, empty 8 unmarked
rule: 4 wont 5 usage 6 custom, policy 7 folkway 8 practice 9 etiquette, precedent, tradition 10 convention, observance
unwritten __: 3 law
unwrought: 5 crude, rough
unyielding: 3 set 4 deaf, firm, grim, hard, iron, taut 5 fixed, rigid, rocky, solid, stern, stiff, tight, tough 6 flinty, mulish, steely, strong, wilful 7 adamant, chronic, decided, hard-set, staunch, willful 8 hard-core, hard-line, locked in, obdurate, resolute, ruthless, stubborn 9 chronical, dead set on, difficult, hard-nosed, immovable, impliable, insistent, iron-jawed, merciless, obstinate, pigheaded, steadfast, tenacious, unbending, unmovable, unpitying 10 foursquare, headstrong, implacable, inexorable, inflexible, invincible
one: 4 mule 7 diehard, holdout
Unzen: 7 volcano
locale: 4 Asia 5 Japan 6 Kyushu
unzip: 4 ease, open, undo 6 loosen 7 disjoin 8 unfasten 9 disengage, untighten
Unzipped (1995 film) director: Douglas Keeve
up: 4 hike, lift, over 5 alert, aloft, astir, awake, aware, boost, happy, light, on end, raise, risen 6 arisen, elated, uphill 8 cheerful, increase, vigilant, watchful 9 attentive, conscious
neither ~ nor down: 4 even
prefix: 3 ano-
up __: 5 a tree, quark, to now, to par 6 in arms 7 against
up __ air: 5 in the
up __ elbows: 5 to the
up __ good: 4 to no
up __ grabs: 3 for
up __ hilt: 5 to the
up __ point: 3 to a
up __ the wall: 7 against
up-__: 3 bow 5 close, front, phase, tempo 6 anchor, to-date
up-__-minute: 5 to-the
__ up: 3 act, add, ate, buy, cry, cut, dig, dry, eat, fed, fix, gas, get, gum, het, ice, jam, key, lap, lay, let, mix, mop, one, own, pay, pep, pin, pop, put, rev, run, set, sew, sit, sop, sum, tee, tie, tog, use 4 a leg, ante, back, ball, bang, bear, beef, blow, bone, buck, bulk, burn, call, chat, chin, clam, come, cook, crop, curl, doll, draw, drum, ease, fair, fess, fill, fold, foul, free, gear, give, goof, grow, hang, hard, haul, heat, hoke, hold, hole, hook, jack, jazz, keep, kick, lace, lash, line, look, make, mark, mess, move, muck, open, pass, pent, perk, pick, pile, pipe, play, pony, prop, pull, pump, rack, rake, ramp, rile, ring, roll, root, send, show, shut, sign, size, slip, slow, snap, soak, soup, step, stir, suit, take, talk, tank, team, tear, tidy, tied, tone, tool, trip, tune, turn, warm, wash, whip, wind, wise, work, wrap 5 brace, break, bring, brush, buddy, build, catch, chalk, choke, clean, clear, climb, cough, cover, crack, crank, cross, dream, dress, duked, dummy, fetch, flare, goose, gussy, ham it, hurry, juice, light, liven, louse, match, mix it, patch, phony, piled, rough, round, scare, scarf, screw, scrub, shake, shape, shoot, shore, sober, speak, speed, spiff, split, stack, stand, start, stick, think, touch, trump, write 6 buckle, butter, button, cooped, double, follow, freeze, geared, gummed, loosen, messed, polish, rustle, spruce, square, strike, thumbs, washed 7 measure, ponying, ratchet, wrought
__ up!: 3 Get 4 Shut 5 Heads, Put 'em, Surf's
__-up: 3 fly, jam, lay, nip, one, pop, put,

sit, tie **4** bang, beat, chin, foul, hang, high, made, mock, pile, pull, push, send, slip, tune, warm, wrap **5** close, heads, hyped, smash, start, stuck, write **6** backer, bottom, change, follow, higher, runner, washed
Up __: **5** Tight **7** Country
Up __ & Personal: **5** Close
Up __ Roof: **5** on the
Up __ the Bend: **6** Around
Up __ We Belong: **5** Where
__ Up: **4** Word **5** Rip It, Stood **6** Coming, Ending **7** Hanging, Tighten
U.P.: **2** RR
up a __: **4** tree **5** stump
__ up against: **4** come
up against the __: **4** wall
up and __: **5** about **6** around
up-and-__: **4** down **5** comer **6** coming
Up and __!: **4** at 'em
up and around: **5** about **8** stirring
up-and-coming: **3** apt **4** able **6** bright, gifted, likely, odds-on **7** budding **8** talented **9** ambitious, promising
one: **4** doer **6** dynamo **7** hustler **8** achiever, go-getter, live wire, operator
up-and-down: **8** vertical, volatile, whole hog **9** irregular, mercurial **10** capricious, thoroughly, throughout
__ Up and Dream: **4** Wake
__-up-and-go: **3** get
up-and-up
on the ~: **4** fair **5** legit, licit **6** kosher
Upanishads studier: **5** Hindu **6** Hindoo
__-up apartment: **4** walk
Up Around the Bend (1970 song)
artist: Creedence Clearwater Revival
upas: **4** tree **6** antiar
relative: **3** fig **5** ficus, ramon **6** antiar, fustic **8** mulberry **10** breadfruit
upbeat: **4** glad, rosy **5** alive, arsis, happy, light, merry **6** blithe, cheery, genial, jovial, joyful, joyous **7** buoyant, gleeful, hopeful, pleased, tickled **8** blissful, cheerful, ecstatic, euphoric, exultant, jubilant, mirthful, positive, sanguine, thrilled **9** confident, delighted, overjoyed, promising, rejoicing, vivacious **10** flying high, heartening, optimistic
upbraid: **3** jaw, nag, rag **4** lash, rail, rate, twit **5** abuse, blame, chide, scold **6** berate, rebuke **7** bawl out, censure, chew out, condemn, lambast, reprove, tell off **8** admonish, chastise, denounce, lambaste, reproach **9** castigate, criticize, dress down, excoriate, fulminate, reprehend, reprimand **10** denunciate, tongue-lash, vituperate
upbraiding: **5** abuse **6** earful, rebuke, tirade **7** lecture, reproof **8** berating, hard time, scolding **9** going-over, reprimand, talking-to **10** admonition, bawling-out, chewing-out, correction, impugnment
upbringing: **7** history **8** training **9** education, framework, grounding, schooling **10** background, experience
__-up call: **4** wake
upclimb: **4** rise
Up Close & Personal (1996 film)
cast: Stockard Channing, Michelle Pfeiffer, Robert Redford
director: Jon Avnet
upcoming: **6** future **7** by and by, looming, nearing **8** eventual, expected, imminent, oncoming **9** impending, onrushing, potential **10** subsequent
upcountry: **6** inland
Up Country author: Nelson Demille
UPC, part of: **3** Bar **4** Code **9** Universal
site: **4** mdse.
update: **4** post, redo **5** amend, brief, emend, renew, reset, train **6** inform, revise **7** freshen, improve, refresh, restore **8** renovate, revision **9** modernize, refurbish **10** rejuvenate
updated: **3** new **5** added, fresh **6** modern **7** current **8** brand-new, improved **9** au courant **10** redesigned
__-up demand: **4** pent
Updike, John: **6** author, writer
work: Bech Is Back
Pigeon Feathers
Rabbit at Rest
Rabbit Is Rich
Rabbit Redux
Rabbit, Run
Too Far to Go
updo: **4** coif **9** hairstyle
__ Up, Doc?: **5** What's
upend: **3** tip **5** raise **6** defeat, invert, topple **7** capsize, reverse, tip over **8** flip over, overturn, turn over
upended: **7** upright **8** inverted, vertical **9** inside-out **10** topsy-turvy
up for __: **5** grabs
__ up for: **4** make **5** stand, stick
up-front: **4** open, true **5** frank **6** candid, honest, trusty **7** genuine, natural, sincere, upright **9** ingenuous, outspoken, unguarded, veracious **10** aboveboard, forthright, from the hip, point-blank, unaffected, unreserved, unreticent
be ~: **5** level **9** come clean
upgo: **4** rise **6** ascend, ascent
upgrade: **4** bump, hill, lift, rise **5** boost, emend, raise **6** ascent, better, enrich, glacis, polish, reform **7** advance, elevate, enhance, improve, promote, sharpen **8** increase, progress **9** acclivity, meliorate, refurbish **10** ameliorate
upgrading: **9** elevation **10** betterment, exaltation
upgrowth: **4** rise **5** surge
upheaval: **4** mess, riot **5** chaos, quake, storm, throe **6** bedlam, blowup, mayhem, trauma, tremor, tumult, unrest, uproar **7** anarchy, ferment, new deal, temblor, tempest, turmoil **8** disarray, disaster, eruption, outburst, shakeout, uprising **9** agitation, cataclysm, confusion, explosion, tidal wave **10** disruption, earthquake, hurly-burly, revolution, transition, turnaround
primeval ~: **5** chaos
upheave: **4** lift, rear **5** hoist, raise **7** elevate **9** bear aloft
uphill: **4** hard **5** rough, tough **6** rising, taxing, thorny, trying **7** arduous, hardwon, labored, onerous, operose, skyward, sloping **8** climbing, grueling, toilsome **9** acclivous, ascending, demanding, difficult, effortful, laborious, punishing, strenuous **10** enervating, exhausting, formidable, oppressive
uphold: **3** aid **4** back, bear, help, lift, obey, prop **5** boost, brace, carry, hoist, honor, prove, raise, shore, vouch **6** affirm, assist, attest, defend, ratify, second **7** approve, bolster, confirm, elevate, endorse, indorse, justify, promote, respect, stand by, stick by, support, sustain **8** advocate, buttress, champion, maintain, preserve, side with **9** encourage, recommend, stabilize, vindicate **10** strengthen
upholder: **8** believer, mainstay **9** proponent, supporter
upholding: **9** consoling, succoring **10** comforting, reassuring, sustaining
upholster: **3** pad
upholstery
fabric: **5** frise, vinyl **6** damask, velour **7** tabaret, velours **8** moquette **9** horsehair, Naugahyde
lace for ~: **5** orris
tool: **3** awl
UPI: **4** wire **8** news wire
former ~ equipment: **3** TTY
part of ~: **4** Intl. **5** Press **6** United
up in __: **4** arms **5** smoke
__ up in: **7** wrapped
__ Up in New Guinea: **7** Growing
Up in Smoke (1978 film)
cast: Tommy Chong, Stacy Keach, Cheech Marin
up in the __: **3** air
Up in the Cellar (1970 film)
cast: Joan Collins, Larry Hagman, Wes Stern
director: Theodore J. Flicker
__-up job: **4** bang
upkeep: **5** costs, price **6** budget, outlay **7** repairs, support **8** expenses, overhead **10** sustenance
upland: **4** hill **5** ridge, table **7** plateau
plain: **4** moor, wold
upland __: **6** cotton, plover
Upland: **4** city, town
locale: **10** California
uplay: **5** stock, store
uplift: **4** buoy **5** cheer, edify, exalt, hoist, raise **6** reform, uphold **7** advance, elevate **10** exhilarate, regenerate
seismic ~: **5** horst
uplifted: **4** tall **5** lofty **7** soaring **8** towering
uplifting: **7** refined **8** artistic, cultural **9** enriching, nurturing **10** artistical, broadening, civilizing, exaltation
__ Up Little Susie: **4** Wake
__-upmanship: **3** one
UPN: **7** network
rival: **3** ABC, CBS, Fox, NBC **5** ABC-TV, CBS-TV, NBC-TV, The WB
Upolu: **4** isle **6** island
port: **4** Apia
upon: **2** on **4** atop, onto **7** on top of
in French: **3** sur
prefix: **3** epi-, sur-
starter: **4** here **5** there, where
upon __: **7** request
__ upon: **3** hit, put, set, sit **4** call, come, fall, look **5** build, count, enter, foist, pitch, smile, touch **6** chance, happen
__ up on: **4** bone, gang, keep, pick, read **5** brush, check
__-upon: **3** put
__ upon a time: **4** once
up one's __: **5** alley **6** sleeve
__ up one's act: **5** clean
__ up one's hands: **5** throw
__ up one's heels: **4** kick
__ up one's mind: **4** make
__ up one's nose at: **4** turn
__ up one's sleeve: **4** card **5** laugh
upon my __: **4** word
Up on the Roof (1962 song) artist: Drifters
__-upon-Trent: **6** Burton
__-upon-Tweed: **7** Berwick
__ up or shut up: **3** put
upper: **3** top **4** high **5** above, berth, elite **6** higher **7** eminent, loftier, topmost **8** overhead, superior
atmosphere: **3** sky **5** ether **6** aether
boot ~: **4** vamp
case: **7** capital
chamber: **4** loft **5** attic **6** dormer, garret, Senate
crust: **4** rich **5** elite **6** gentry, jet set **7** society **8** nobility **9** exclusive, gentility **10** haute monde
ender: **3** cut **4** case, most
garment: **4** vest **6** jerkin **9** waistcoat
get the ~ hand: **4** beat, bury, drub, rout, stun **5** cream, crush, drown, quell, smash, total, trash, upset, waste **6** defeat, subdue **7** clobber, conquer, oppress, put away, stagger, take out, torpedo, trounce **8** bear down, blow away, bulldoze, overcome, roll over, shellack, suppress, vanquish **9** overpower, overthrow, subjugate **10** take care of
hand: **4** edge **7** control, victory **9** advantage, authority, dominance
have the ~ hand: **4** boss, head, lead, rule **5** reign **6** direct, govern, manage **7** command, control, dictate, prevail, shellac, triumph **8** dominate, overrule **9** subjugate, tyrannize **10** monopolize, run the show
keep a stiff ~ lip: **4** cope **6** bear up, hang in, manage **8** face up to
limit: **3** cap, lid, max, top **7** ceiling, maximum **8** pinnacle
part: **3** cap, lid, tip, top **4** apex, peak, roof **5** cover, crest, crown, spire **6** finial, summit, vertex **7** ceiling **8** pinnacle
prefix: **3** ano-
trunk: **5** chest **6** thorax
upper __: **3** air, arm **4** case, deck, hand **5** berth, bound, class, crust, house **6** school **7** chamber
__-upper: **5** fixer **6** pepper, picker, warmer **7** cheerer
Upper __: **5** Egypt, Volta **6** Canada **7** Austria, Chinook, Silesia
Upper __ Side: **4** East, West
Upper Arlington: **4** city, town
locale: **4** Ohio
__ upper bound: **5** least
upper-class: **4** posh **5** elite, noble **6** aristo **7** moneyed **8** affluent, highborn **9** important, patrician
upperclassman: **2** sr. **3** snr. **6** senior
upper-crust: **6** aristo **8** literati, well-bred **9** exclusive, highbrows, patrician **10** haute monde, illuminati
uppercut: **3** hit, jab **4** bash, belt, biff, blow, clip, jolt, slam, slug, sock **5** clout, punch, smack, smash, swipe, whack, whomp **6** thwack, wallop **8** haymaker **10** roundhouse
target: **4** chin
Upper Egypt: **4** Cush
upper house member: **3** sen. **7** senator
Upper Klamath: **4** lake
locale: **6** Oregon
__ upper lip: **5** stiff
uppermost: **3** top **4** main **5** chief, prime **6** apical **7** highest, leading, primary, supreme **8** dominant, greatest, loftiest **9** paramount, principal **10** overriding, preeminent
upper right in heraldry: **6** canton
uppers, on one's: **5** broke, needy **6** bad off, hard up, ill off, in need, in want **7** pinched **8** badly off, bankrupt, beggarly, indigent, strapped **9** destitute, insolvent, moneyless, penniless, penurious **10** down and out, pauperized, straitened
Upperworld (1934 film)
cast: Mary Astor, Ginger Rogers, Warren William
director: Roy Del Ruth
uppity: **6** remote **8** snobbish, superior **10** hoity-toity
act ~: **4** snap **5** deign
one: **4** snip, snob **5** snoot
Uppsala: **4** city, town
locale: **6** Sweden
upraise: **4** lift **5** boost, cheer, erect, hoist **7** console, elevate, lighten **8** heighten
upraised: **4** high **5** above, aloft **8** elevated
uprear: **4** lift **5** erect, hoist
upright: **3** leg **4** fair, good, jamb, just, pier, pile, post, prim, pure, true, vert.

5 clean, erect, frank, jambe, legit, moral, noble, on end, piano, plumb, proud, pylon, shaft, sheer, solid, sound 6 candid, column, decent, honest, picket, pillar, raised, square, trusty, worthy 7 endways, ethical, factual, upended 8 baluster, credible, innocent, keyboard, reliable, standing, straight, vertical, virtuous 9 blameless, exemplary, honorable, reputable, righteous, veracious 10 aboveboard, evenhanded, forthright, high-minded, inculcable, law-abiding, on the level, principled, scrupulous, vertically
relative: 5 grand 6 spinet
uprightly: 9 honorably
uprightness: 5 honor 6 virtue 7 honesty, loyalty, probity 8 morality, nobility, veracity 10 principles
uprise: 5 rebel, swell 7 elevate
uprising: 4 riot 6 émeute, mutiny, revolt 7 ferment 8 civil war, outbreak, upheaval 9 rebellion 10 insurgence, insurgency, revolution
upriver: 6 inland
uproar: 3 ado, cry, din, row 4 flap, fuss, mess, rage, riot, stir, to-do 5 babel, brawl, chaos, furor, hoo-ha, mania, melee, mix-up, noise, stink, storm 6 babble, bedlam, bustle, clamor, fracas, furore, hassle, hoo-hah, hubbub, jangle, mayhem, outcry, pother, racket, ruckus, rumpus, strife, tumult, unrest 7 anarchy, clangor, clatter, dispute, ferment, rampage, ruction, tempest, turmoil 8 big scene, brouhaha, disarray, disorder, hangover, madhouse, violence 9 commotion, confusion, hue and cry, maelstrom, mobocracy 10 donnybrook, hubba-hubba, hullabaloo, hurly-burly, turbulence
in an ~: 4 busy, wild 6 heated, hectic, woolly 7 chaotic, excited, frantic, furious, hurried 8 confused, exciting, feverish, frenetic, frenzied 9 turbulent 10 boisterous, disordered, tumultuous
uproarious: 4 loud, wild 5 a riot, forte, funny, merry, noisy 7 blaring, booming, jarring, pealing, rackety, raucous, reboant 8 crashing, piercing, plangent, rumbling, sonorous, strident, turned up 9 big-voiced, clamorous, deafening, hilarious 10 boisterous, gut-busting, hysterical, resounding, stentorian, strepitous, thundering, vociferous
uproariousness: 3 din 5 noise
uproot: 3 rid 4 grub, move, pull, weed 5 exile, pluck, purge 6 remove, rip out 7 destroy, extract, jerk out, tear out, weed out, wipe out 8 demolish, dislodge, displace 9 eliminate, eradicate, extirpate 10 annihilate, do away with, transplant
uprooting: 7 pulling, removal 9 taking out 10 extraction
__ up roses: 4 come
__-ups: 3 lay, mix 4 mock, send 5 close, cover, grown 6 higher
UPS
competitor: 3 DHL 5 FedEx
delivery: 3 ctn., pak., pkg.
part: 4 Serv. 6 Parcel, United 7 Service
units: 3 lbs.
upsa-__: 5 daisy
ups and __: 5 downs
upscale: 4 nice, posh, rich, tony 5 ritzy, swank, toney 6 swanky 7 moneyed, wealthy 8 affluent 9 expensive, luxurious
upset: 3 ail, bug, get, ire, irk, mad, tip, vex, win 4 beat, gall, hurt, jolt, miff, pain, rile, rout, sick, sore, tilt, undo 5 agita, alarm, angry, annoy, cross, fazed, floor, get to, harry, huffy, jumpy, key up, livid, messy, mix up, peeve, pique, psych, riled, scare, shake, shock, spill, spilt, spoil, spook, steam, teary, throw, tizzy, vexed, worry 6 affect, bother, defeat, dismay, enrage, excite, flurry, fuming, grieve, harass, hassle, heated, in a pet, invert, jumble, madden, mess up, muddle, nettle, offend, peeved, pick on, piqued, pother, put out, queasy, queazy, raging, rankle, rattle, raving, ruffle, shaken, sicken, sorrow, stir up, sullen, tackle, tee off, thrown, thwart, topple, trauma, tumble, uneasy, unglue, work up 7 agitate, annoyed, beat out, capsize, chagrin, conquer, depress, derange, disrupt, disturb, excited, fluster, frantic, furious, illness, in a huff, in a snit, jittery, licking, make ill, muddled, nervous, nettled, outplay, peevish, perturb, pouting, provoke, ranting, rattled, reverse, ruffled, rummage, screw-up, shake up, shatter, shocked, shook up, spilled, steamed, stewing, subvert, tearful, teed off, tick off, tip over, toppled, trouble, turmoil, unglued, unhinge, unnerve, victory, worried 8 agitated, bothered, bowl over, burned up, capsized, confound, confused, convulse, dismayed, disorder, disquiet, distract, distress, embitter, exercise, freak out, fretting, imbitter, in a tizzy, incensed, irritate, outraged, overcome, override, overrule, overturn, provoked, snappish, steaming, surprise, troubled, unsettle, unstring, unstrung, worked up 9 aggravate, agitation, bellicose, bristling, bummed-out, concerned, discomfit, dislocate, displease, disturbed, indignant, indispose, knock over, make waves, overpower, overthrow, overwhelm, perturbed, seeing red, sniveling, sorrowful, squeamish, throw over, ticked off, unsettled 10 demoralize, disarrange, discomfort, discompose, disconcert, disgruntle, disheveled, disordered, displeased, disquieted, disruption, distraught, distressed, exasperate, freaked out, hysterical, in disarray, infuriated, make a scene, overturned, psyched out, queasiness, revolution, run afoul of, tipped over, upside-down
be ~ about: 3 rue 4 care, moan, mope 5 worry 6 bemoan, bewail, lament, regret, repent, repine 7 cry over, deplore, scruple 8 look back, weep over 9 apologize 10 be sorry for, disapprove
get ~: 4 burn, pout, stew 6 blow up, seethe, simmer 7 bristle, smolder
political ~: 4 coup 5 purge 6 revolt, stroke 10 revolution
state: 3 pet 4 huff, snit, stew 5 pique 6 temper
with: 5 mad at
upset __: 5 price
upsetting: 3 sad 5 tight 6 trying 7 hurtful 8 grievous 9 confusing, saddening 10 depressing, disruptive, lamentable, unsettling
upsetting __: 5 lever 6 moment
Upshaw: 4 Dawn, Gene
Upshaw, Dawn: 6 singer 7 soprano
specialty: 5 opera
__ up shop: 3 set
__ up short: 4 come
upshot: 3 end 4 core, gist, meat, pith 5 issue, sense 6 burden, effect, ending, payoff, result, thrust 7 meaning, outcome, product, purport 8 key point 9 aftermath, outgrowth, substance 10 conclusion, denouement, resolution
upside-__ cake: 4 down
upside-down: 4 cake 5 upset 7 haywire, in chaos, jumbled, mixed-up 8 backward, bottom up, confused, inverted, reversed 10 disorderly
sleeper: 5 sloth
smile: 5 frown, scowl
turn ~: 4 comb, flip 6 invert 7 ransack, reverse, rummage, shake up 8 overturn
Upside Down (1980 song) artist: Diana Ross
__ up sides: 6 choose
upsilon: 5 Greek 6 letter
follower: 3 phi
preceder: 3 tau
upslope: 4 rise
upstager: 3 ham
upstairs: 4 over 5 above 10 management
kick ~: 4 bump 5 boost, favor, raise 6 better, move up 7 advance, elevate, endorse, further, promote
Upstairs, Downstairs role: 4 maid
__ up stakes: 4 pull
upstanding: 4 good, just, true 5 clean, erect, moral, solid 6 decent, honest 7 ethical, upright 8 elevated 9 honorable 10 law-abiding, scrupulous
upstart: 4 snob, Turk 5 yahoo 6 nobody 7 parvenu, wannabe 9 arriviste, latecomer, nonentity, pretender, vulgarian, young Turk 10 jackanapes
__-up-sticks: 4 pick
upsurge: 4 boom, jump, leap, rise, wave 6 expand 7 enlarge 8 increase 9 crescendo
upsweep: 3 bun 4 coif, puff 6 hairdo 7 beehive, chignon 8 coiffure 9 pompadour
upswing: 4 boom, leap, rise 5 boost, rally, surge 8 increase
__ upswing: 4 on an
upsy-__: 5 daisy
uptake
quick on the ~: 3 apt 4 keen 5 alert, quick, sharp, smart 6 adroit, astute, bright 9 astucious, receptive
slow on the ~: 3 dim 5 dense 6 obtuse
__-up terminal: 4 dial
up the __: 4 ante, wall 5 creek, river
Up the __ Staircase: 4 Down
__ Up the Band: 6 Strike
__ up the curtain: 4 ring
Up the Down Staircase (1967 film)
cast: Patrick Bedford, Sandy Dennis, Eileen Heckart
director: Robert Mulligan
Up the Ladder to the Roof (1970 song) artist: Supremes
__ up the pieces: 4 pick
__ up the rear: 5 bring
__ up the road: 4 burn
Up the Sandbox (1972 film)
cast: David Selby, Barbra Streisand
director: Irvin Kershner
__ up the slack: 4 take
__ up the works: 3 gum
__ up the wrong tree: 4 bark
__ Up, Tiger Lily?: 5 What's
uptight: 4 edgy, prim 5 antsy, itchy, jumpy, stiff, tense, testy 6 jangly, on edge, strict, sullen, uneasy 7 anxious, fearful, jittery, nervous, prudish, restive, worried 8 agitated, choleric, fluttery, restless, skittish, strained, troubled 9 concerned, excitable, ill at ease, irascible, querulous, unbending, withdrawn 10 distressed, frightened, high-strung, restrained, suspicious
Uptight (Everything's Alright) (1966 song) artist: Stevie Wonder
up to __: 3 now, par 4 date 5 snuff, speed 7 scratch
__ up to: 3 add, own, put 4 face, feel, lead, live, look, play 5 stand
__ up to be: 7 cracked
up-to-date: 2 in 3 hot, mod, new, now 4 chic 5 faddy, fresh, in use, today 6 extant, latest, modern, modish, newest, recent, red-hot, timely, trendy, with it 7 abreast, à la mode, current, faddish, in-thing, in vogue, popular, present, stylish, voguish 8 advanced, brand-new, neoteric 9 au courant, in fashion 10 all the rage, avant-garde, newfangled
in French: 9 au courant
make ~: 3 fix 5 fix up, refit, renew 6 extend, resume 7 freshen, furbish, remodel, restore 8 overhaul, renovate 9 modernize, refurbish 10 revitalize
__ Up to Make Up: 5 Break
Upton: 4 Camp 8 Sinclair
up to no __: 4 good
up to one's __: 4 ears, neck 6 elbows
up to one's __ tricks: 3 old
up to the __: 4 hilt 6 elbows
up-to-the-__: 6 minute
__ up to the bar: 4 step
up-to-the-minute: 3 hip, hot, mod, new 4 chic 5 vogue 6 modern, modish, snappy, timely, trendy 7 in style, in vogue, stylish
uptown: 4 posh, rich 5 ritzy, swank 6 swanky 7 moneyed, stylish, worldly
Uptown Girl (1983 song) artist: Billy Joel
Uptown Hoedown composer: 4 Bach 7 PDQ Bach
Uptown New York star: 5 Oakie
__ Up to You: 3 It's
U.P. Trail, The author: Zane Grey
uptrend: 4 rise
upturn: 3 tip 4 boom, jump, rise 5 boost, rally, surge 6 invert 8 increase
brief ~: 3 pip 4 blip 5 spike
market ~: 5 rally 6 uptick 8 recovery 10 turnaround
upturned: 5 on end
Upturned Glass, The (1947 film) cast: James Mason, Pamela Mason
Up, Up and Away (1967 song) artist: Fifth Dimension
Up Up and Away composer: 4 Webb
__-up visor: 4 flip
upward: 4 atop, over 5 above, aloft 7 hanging 8 in the sky, overhead, vertical
combining form: 3 ano- 6 sursum-
extension: 4 rise
move ~: 4 lift, rise 5 arise, climb, hoist, raise, surge 6 ascend 7 surface
movement: 4 rise 6 ascent
prefix: 3 ana-, ano-
shove: 4 lift, push 5 boost, heave, hoist 6 assist, thrust
slope: 4 bank, hill, rise 5 grade 6 ascent, glacis 7 hillock, incline 8 gradient, hillside 9 acclivity, elevation
slope ~: 4 rise 5 climb 6 ascend
upwardly mobile professional, young: 4 suit 5 yuppy 6 yuppie
upwards of: 4 over 5 above 6 nearly 8 more than
upwelling: 4 gush, rise 5 surge, swell 6 influx, onrush
Up Where We Belong (1982 song): 4 duet
artist: Jennifer Warnes, Joe Cocker

__ up with: 3 put 4 come, take
__ up with the Joneses: 4 keep
__ Up Your Overcoat: 6 Button
__ Up Your Shakespeare: 5 Brush
Ur: 4 city, town
locale: 4 Irak, Iraq 5 Sumer
uraeus: 3 asp 5 snake 7 reptile
Ural: 5 range, river
city on the ~: 4 Orsk 6 Guryev
locale: 6 Russia
Urals: 4 mtns. 5 range 9 mountains
area east of the ~: 4 Asia
area west of the ~: 3 Eur. 6 Europe
locale: 6 Russia
metropolis: 3 Ufa
Urania: 4 Muse
lover of ~: 6 Apollo
parent of ~: 4 Zeus 9 Mnemosyne
sister: 4 Clio 5 Erato 6 Thalia 7 Euterpe 8 Calliope 9 Melpomene 10 Polyhymnia 11 Terpsichore
uranium: 5 metal 7 element
mineral: 6 curite
uranium __: 5 oxide 6 dating 7 dioxide
uranology: 9 astronomy
Uranus: 3 orb 6 planet
child of ~: 5 Titan
daughter of ~: 4 Rhea, Thea, Thia 5 Aetna 6 Phoebe, Tethys, Themis 9 Mnemosyne
moon: 4 Puck 5 Ariel 6 Bianca, Juliet, Oberon, Portia 7 Belinda, Caliban, Miranda, Ophelia, Sycorax, Titania, Umbriel 8 Cordelia, Cressida, Rosalind 9 Desdemona
mother of ~: 4 Gaea
son of ~: 4 Anax 6 Cronos, Cronus 7 Iapetus, Oceanus 8 Hyperion
wife of ~: 4 Gaea
Urawa: 4 city, town
locale: 5 Japan
urb: 4 city 8 downtown 9 inner city
urban: 3 mun. 4 city, town 5 civic, metro 6 public 7 built-up, central, village 8 citified, downtown, non-rural 9 inner-city, municipal
area: 4 park, slum, ward 5 block 6 ghetto
blight: 4 slum, smog 5 smaze 6 litter
combining form: 5 metro-
dwelling: 4 flat, loft 5 condo 6 duplex 9 apartment
employee: 8 commuter
executive: 5 mayor
greenery: 4 lawn, park 6 common, square 7 reserve 8 preserve
noise: 4 beep, honk, toot 5 blare, blast, siren
oasis: 4 park 6 common 8 preserve 10 playground
opposite: 5 rural 6 rustic, sylvan 7 bucolic 8 agrarian, Arcadian, pastoral 9 backwoods 10 provincial
planner, at times: 5 zoner
porch: 5 stoop
professional: 5 yuppy 6 yuppie
route: 2 av., st. 3 ave. 4 blvd. 6 avenue, street 9 boulevard
tawdrily ~: 4 neon
threat: 3 mob 4 gang, pack, ring
transport: 3 bus, cab, els 4 hack, taxi, tram 5 moped
walker: 3 ped. 10 pedestrian
urban __: 4 myth 6 blight, legend, sprawl 7 renewal
Urban: 4 pope 7 pontiff
Urban __: 6 Cowboy 7 Horrors
Urbana: 4 city, town
locale: 8 Illinois
team: 6 Illini
Urban Cowboy (1980 film)
cast: Scott Glenn, John Travolta, Debra Winger
director: James Bridges
Urbandale: 4 city, town
locale: 4 Iowa
urbane: 4 chic 5 bland, civil, ritzy, slick, suave 6 poised, polite, smooth 7 affable, courtly, elegant, gallant, genteel, politic, refined, tactful, worldly 8 cultured, debonair, finished, gracious, mannerly, obliging, pleasant, polished, well-bred 9 civilized, courteous, debonaire, high-toned 10 cultivated, debonnaire
Urban Horrors author: Ray Bradbury
urbanity: 4 tact 5 charm, class, couth, grace, style 6 polish 7 culture, finesse, manners 8 breeding, civility, courtesy 9 gallantry 10 refinement
urbanize: 6 citify
Urban Prospect, The author: Lewis Mumford
urbia: 6 cities
urbi et __: 4 orbi
__ urbis conditae: 4 anno
urchin: 3 imp, pup 4 brat, waif 5 gamin, scamp 6 gamine 9 young punk 10 holy terror, ragamuffin
sea ~: 7 echinus
sea ~ feature: 5 spine
street ~: 3 imp 4 waif 5 gamin, stray 6 orphan 9 foundling 10 ragamuffin
__ urchin: 3 sea 5 heart 6 street
Urdu: 5 Indic 8 language
poet: 6 Ghalib
Ure: 4 Mary 6 Andrew
Urea: 5 nymph
father of ~: 8 Poseidon
lover of ~: 6 Apollo
uredo: 5 hives
Ure, Mary: 7 actress, British
film: The Luck of Ginger Coffey (1964)
Sons and Lovers (1960)
Where Eagles Dare (1969)
Windom's Way (1957)
urena: 5 shrub
relative: 4 ocra, okra, okro 6 mallow 8 abutilon
urethane: 5 ester
Urey, Harold: 7 chemist 8 Nobelist
Urfa: 4 city, town
locale: 6 Turkey
once: 6 Edessa
urge: 2 id 3 ask, beg, egg, get, yen 4 coax, goad, itch, lust, move, pray, prod, push, spur, warn, whim, will, wish 5 drive, egg on, fancy, impel, lobby, plead, press, rally, tempt 6 adjure, advise, cajole, charge, demand, desire, enjoin, exhort, incite, induce, insist, prompt, propel, reason, whip up, work on 7 beseech, cheer on, counsel, craving, entreat, impetus, implore, impulse, inspire, longing, passion, promote, propose, push for, put up to, quicken, request, solicit, wanting, wheedle 8 advocate, appeal to, appetite, argue for, insist on, instinct, maneuver, motivate, persuade, petition, press for, pressure, stimulus, weakness, yearning 9 encourage, hankering, importune, influence, instigate, recommend, stimulate 10 compulsion, incitement, inducement, motivation, persuasion, sweet tooth, temptation
have an ~ for: 4 ache, itch, long, lust, miss, pine, seek, want, wish 5 covet, crave, fancy, yearn 6 demand, desire, hanker, hunger, thirst 8 feel like
not to: 4 warn 5 deter 7 caution 8 dissuade 9 talk out of 10 discourage
on: 3 egg 4 abet, goad, move, poke, prod, push, spur 5 drive, impel, press, shove 6 compel, incite, induce, prompt, propel, thrust, turn on 7 inspire, quicken 8 mobilize, motivate, persuade, pressure, railroad 9 instigate
urgency: 4 need, rush, zeal 5 haste, hurry, press, speed 6 crisis, stress 7 gravity 8 exigence, exigency, pressure, priority 9 immediacy, necessity
without ~: 4 idly 6 slowly
urgent: 4 dire, rush 5 acute, grave, vital 6 crying 7 burning, crucial, driving, earnest, exigent, hurry-up, instant, intense, primary, serious, weighty 8 critical, exigeant, foremost, pressing, required 9 called-for, demanding, desperate, essential, immediate, impelling, important, insistent, momentous, necessary, paramount 10 compelling, imperative, passionate, touch and go
appeal: 4 plea, suit 6 demand, orison, prayer 8 entreaty, petition
letters: 3 PDQ, SOS 4 ASAP
situation: 4 emer. 9 emergency
Urgent (1981 song) artist: Foreigner
urgently: 4 hard 5 madly 6 keenly 7 acutely 8 intently, severely, strongly 9 earnestly, intensely, seriously
urger: 6 patron 7 apostle, booster 8 advocate, espouser, exponent, lobbyist 9 apologist, proponent, supporter
urging: 6 behest 7 coaxing 8 advocacy 9 wheedling 10 insistence
Uri: 6 canton, Geller
Uriah: 4 Heep 7 Hittite
urial: 5 sheep
relative: 4 geep 5 argal 6 aoudad, argali, bharal, merino 7 bighorn, burrhel, mouflon 8 cimarron, moufflon
Urich, Robert: 5 actor
TV: Soap, Spenser: For Hire, Vega$
Uriel: 5 angel
Urim and __: 7 Thummim
Uris, Leon: 6 author, writer
character: 3 Ari
work: Armageddon
Battle Cry
Exodus
A God in Ruins
The Haj
Mila 18
Mitla Pass
O'Hara's Choice
QB VII
Redemption
Topaz
Trinity
URL: 7 address 10 Web address
ender: 3 com, edu, net, org
part: 3 www
Urmia: 4 lake
locale: 4 Iran
urn: 4 bowl, vase 6 brewer, holder, vessel 7 amphora, samovar 9 container 10 jardiniere
homophone for ~: 3 ern 4 earn, erne
protuberance: 3 ear
urne contents: 4 café
Urquhart: 6 Thomas
Ursae __: 7 Majoris, Minoris
Ursa Major: 4 bear
constellation near ~: 5 Draco
star in ~: 5 Mizar
Ursa Minor: 4 bear
ursid: 4 bear 6 Kodiak 7 grizzly
noise: 5 growl
Ursinus: 4 pope 7 pontiff
Ursula: 5 saint 6 Le Guin 7 Andress
Ursuline: 9 religious
Uru.
locale: 5 S. Amer.
neighbor: 3 Arg. 4 Braz.
org.: 3 OAS
urua: 4 wind 8 clarinet
origin: 6 Brazil
Uruapan: 4 city, town
locale: 6 Mexico 9 Michoacán
Uruguay: 6 nation 7 country
capital: 10 Montevideo
city: 4 Melo 5 Salto 10 Montevideo
money: 4 peso 9 centesimo
neighbor: 6 Brazil 9 Argentina
org.: 3 OAS
writer: 6 Reyles 7 Sánchez 9 Benedetti
see also Spanish
__-Urundi: 6 Ruanda
urus: 5 bovid 6 bovine 7 aurochs
relative: 3 yak 4 anoa, arna, gaur, zebu 5 bison, gayal, takin 6 mithan, muskox 7 banteng, banting, beefalo, buffalo, carabao, cattalo, kouprey, tamarao, tamarau, timarau
us: 4 pron. 7 pronoun
according to Pogo: 5 enemy
belonging to ~: 3 our
between ~: 7 sub rosa 8 secretly 9 entre nous, privately
how others see ~: 5 image 9 depiction 10 appearance, conception, impression, perception, projection
in German: 3 uns
in Spanish: 3 nos
not ~: 4 rest, them 6 others
them or ~: 4 side
them, to ~: 3 foe 5 enemy
with ~: 4 here, left 5 alive 6 extant, living, on hand 7 current, on board, ongoing, present 9 attending, remaining, surviving
Us: 3 mag 8 magazine
__ Us: 5 One of, Toys R
U.S.: 7 America 9 the States
alliance: 3 OAS 4 NATO
ally: 3 Eng. 5 the U.K.
business competitor: 3 Jpn.
citizen: 4 Amer.
coin word: 4 unum 5 trust
financial capital: 3 NYC
former capital: 3 NYC
language: 7 English
leader: 4 pres. 9 president
money: 3 dol. 4 buck, cent, dime, half 5 penny 6 dollar, nickel 7 quarter 10 half dollar
national flower: 4 rose
neighbor: 3 Mex. 6 Canada, Mexico
of the ~: 4 Amer., natl.
region: 4 N. Eng.
soldier: 4 Yank
southernmost ~ city: 4 Hilo
state: 3 Ala., Ark., Cal., Del., Fla., Ida., Kan., Ken., Neb., Nev., Ore., Tex., Wis., W. Va., Wyo. 4 Ariz., Colo., Conn., Mass., Mich., Minn., Miss., Mont., N. Car., N. Dak., Nebr., N. Mex., Ohio, Okla., Penn., S. Car., S. Dak., Tenn., Utah, Wash., Wisc. 5 Calif., Idaho, Maine, Penna., Texas 6 Alaska, Hawaii, Kansas, Nevada, Oregon 7 Alabama, Arizona, Florida, Georgia, Montana, New York, Vermont, Wyoming 8 Arkansas, Colorado, Delaware, Kentucky, Maryland, Michigan, Missouri, Nebraska, Oklahoma 9 Louisiana, Minnesota, New Jersey, New Mexico, Tennessee, Wisconsin 10 California, Washington 11 Connecticut, Mississippi, North Dakota, Rhode Island, South Dakota 12 New Hampshire, Pennsylvania, West Virginia 13 Massachusetts, North Carolina, South Carolina

territory: 4 Guam
trading partner: 3 EEC
U.S. ___: 4 Army, Male, Navy, Open 5 Acres
U.S. ___ Corps: 6 Marine
U.S. ___ Force: 3 Air
U.S. ___ Guard: 5 Coast
U.S. ___ Service: 6 Postal, Secret 7 Customs
USA: 4 army, serv., svce. 7 channel, network 9 the States
alternative: 3 BET, CMT, MTV, PAX, TBS, TLC, TNN, TNT 4 ESPN, HGTV 5 A and E, C-SPAN, Style 6 Noggin, Tech TV, TV Land 7 Court TV, Ovation, SoapNet 8 Lifetime
see also army, U.S.
USA ___: 5 Today
USA ___ Africa: 3 for
___ U.S.A.: 6 Inside, Surfin'
U.S.A. author: John Dos Passos
usable: 3 fit 4 open 5 ready, utile 6 at hand, liquid 7 helpful, in order, running, working 8 valuable, workable 9 adaptable, available, operative, practical 10 accessible, applicable, employable, functional, utilizable
make ~: 3 fit 5 adapt, alter 6 adjust, change, modify, revise, tailor 7 remodel 8 regulate
make ~ again: 5 refit, renew 9 refurbish
___ us a child...: 4 Unto
USAF: 3 svc. 4 serv., svce.
decoration: 3 DFC
part: 3 Air, SAC 5 Force
plane: 4 VTOL
rank: 2 lt. 3 amn., gen. 4 capt., genl., Ssgt., TSgt.
weapon: 3 ABM
see also Air Force
USAFA: 3 sch. 4 acad., coll. 7 academy
grad: 2 lt. 5 lieut.
home: 4 Colo.
USA for Africa song: We Are the World (1985)
usage: 3 way 4 form, mode, rule, wont, word 5 habit 6 custom, manner, method, praxis 7 diction, fashion, formula, lexicon, routine, wording 8 currency, habitude, handling, phrasing, practice 9 operation, procedure, tradition, treatment 10 acceptance, convention, employment, management
fee: 3 tax 4 duty, levy, toll 6 charge, impost, tariff, towage 10 assessment
informal ~: 4 cant 5 argot, lingo, slang 6 jargon, patois, pidgin 7 dialect 10 street talk, vernacular
US Airways
former ~ rival: 3 TWA 5 Pan Am 7 Braniff, Eastern 8 National
rival: 3 UAL 5 Delta 6 United 7 Jet Blue 8 American 9 Southwest 11 America West, Continental
USAR, part of: 3 Air, Res. 7 Reserve
___ us a son is given: 4 unto
___ U.S. Bonds: 4 Gary
USC: 3 sch. 6 school
group: 6 Pac-Ten
locale: 2 L.A. 3 Cal.
rival: 3 Cal. 4 UCLA
student's rival: 5 UCLAn
U.S. Capitol architect: 7 Latrobe 8 Bulfinch
USCG
part of ~: 5 Coast, Guard
rank: 3 ens. 4 capt. 5 lt com.
signal: 3 SOS
USCGA locale: 4 Conn. 9 New London
U.S. Coast ___: 5 Guard
U.S. Customs ___: 7 Service
USDA
part of ~: 3 Agr. 4 Dept. 10 Department
rating: 5 Prime 6 Choice
use: 3 end, ply, run, tap 4 good, help, milk, need, take, turn, wear 5 adopt, apply, avail, eat up, enjoy, point, put in, sense, spend, trick, usage, value, waste, wield, worth 6 accept, behoof, custom, do with, draw on, employ, engage, expend, handle, invoke, manage, milage, moment, occupy, play on, praxis, profit, reason, resort, rip off 7 benefit, break in, consume, control, deplete, exhaust, exploit, harness, meaning, mileage, operate, purpose, service, toy with, utility, utilize 8 call upon, exercise, function, gobble up, handling, occasion, practice, put forth, work with 9 advantage, implement, occupancy, operation, partake of, patronize, put to work, relevance, treatment, usability, victimize 10 administer, capitalize, employment, fall back on, make do with, manipulate, run through, usefulness
a gimlet: 4 ream 5 drill, gouge 6 pierce 8 puncture
a hammock: 3 lie 4 bask, idle, loaf, loll, rest 5 relax 6 dawdle, lounge, repose 7 goof off 10 take it easy
a keyboard: 6 sign on 9 make music, typewrite
a knife: 3 cut, lop 4 chop, cube, dice, dock, gash, hack, nick, pare, peel, skin, slit, snip, trim 5 carve, gouge, lance, mince, notch, prune, score, sever, shave, shred, slash, slice 6 bisect, cleave, cut off, incise, open up, scrape, sunder 7 cut away, cut back, cut down, scratch, whittle 8 lacerate 9 split open
a Nautilus: 5 train 7 work out 8 exercise
be of ~: 3 aid 4 help 5 avail, serve 6 assist, profit, wait on 7 benefit, suffice
deny ~: 3 ban, bar 5 debar, expel 6 censor, forbid, outlaw 7 boycott, exclude, rule out 8 disallow, prohibit 9 blackball, ostracize, proscribe
don't ~: 4 shun 5 avoid, forgo 6 eschew, give up 7 abstain, boycott, refrain 8 renounce, swear off
easy to ~: 5 handy 6 nearby, wieldy 7 close by 8 portable 10 accessible, convenient, time-saving
effectively: 5 wield
elbow grease: 4 buff 5 scour, sweat 6 polish, strain
entirely: 5 eat up 7 exhaust 9 polish off
for a while: 6 borrow
hard to ~: 7 awkward 8 affected, unwieldy 9 ponderous 10 cumbersome
have ~ for: 4 need 7 require
have no ~ for: 4 hate 5 abhor 6 detest, loathe 7 despise
in ~: 4 busy 5 taken 6 extant, living, modern 7 current, engaged, present 8 employed, occupied, up-to-date 9 prevalent, spoken for
let ~: 4 lend, loan, pool 5 allot, share 6 assign, oblige
make ~ of: 5 apply, avail, exert, wield 6 employ, look to, resort 7 utilize 10 fall back on, profit from
make ready for ~ again: 5 refit
no ~: 6 futile 8 hopeless 9 pointless
no longer in ~: 3 out 4 gone 5 dated, dusty, moldy, musty, passé, stale 6 old-hat 7 archaic, outworn 8 obsolete, outdated, outmoded, timeworn 9 discarded, moth-eaten, out-of-date 10 antiquated, superseded
not in ~: 4 free, idle 6 fallow, vacant 7 untaken 8 untilled
of ~: 5 handy 6 useful 7 helpful 8 valuable 9 practical 10 beneficial, convenient, worthwhile
of no ~: 4 vain 6 futile, hollow 7 inutile, useless, worn-out 8 bootless, hopeless, pathetic 9 pointless, worthless 10 profitless, unavailing, unworkable
one's hands: 4 mime, wave 6 beckon, signal 9 pantomime
one's head: 6 reason 8 cogitate 9 cerebrate
one's noodle: 6 ideate, reason 7 analyze 8 cogitate 9 cerebrate, figure out
out of ~: 3 old 5 dated, fusty, hoary, passé 6 bygone 7 archaic, outworn 8 obsolete, timeworn 9 forgotten, moss-grown 10 antiquated, superseded
pay for the ~ of: 4 hire, rent 5 lease 6 engage 7 charter 8 sublease
poor judgment: 4 flub, goof, muff 5 botch 6 bungle, foul up, mess up, slip up 7 blunder, go wrong, louse up, snarl up, stumble 9 mishandle, mismanage
ready for ~: 9 available 10 disposable
save for future ~: 5 set by 7 lay away
show ~: 4 fade, fray, wear 5 decay, erode, scuff 6 abrade, weaken 7 corrode, crumble, wear out, weather 8 wear down
skillfully: 3 ply 5 wield
sparingly: 3 eke 4 keep, save 5 hoard, lay by, lay up, skimp, stash, stint 6 ration, scrimp 7 cut back, protect, store up 8 conserve, maintain, preserve, scrimp on, sock away 9 cut back on, economize, preserves, safeguard
temporarily: 4 loan 6 borrow
unnecessarily: 5 drain, waste 6 burn up 7 fribble, splurge 8 squander 9 dissipate, overspend, throw away 10 gamble away, run through, trifle away
up: 3 eat 4 blow, lose 5 drain, empty, put in, spend, waste 6 expend, finish, run out 7 consume, deplete, exhaust, play out, wipe out 8 run out of, squander 9 dissipate, finish off, go through, polish off 10 fail to keep, run through
weasel words: 5 dodge, evade, fudge, skirt, waver 6 waffle 8 flip-flop, sidestep 9 hem and haw, pussyfoot, stonewall, vacillate 10 equivocate
use ___: 3 tax
use ___ as directed: 4 only
___ use: 3 end 4 good 5 put to
___-use: 3 ill
Use ___ My Girl: 4 Ta Be
used: 3 old 4 worn 5 spent, tired 7 worn-out 8 pre-owned, recycled 9 hackneyed, moth-eaten 10 hand-me-down, secondhand, threadbare
get ~ to: 6 grow on 7 break in 8 accustom, grow upon 9 acclimate, reconcile
get ~ (to): 5 adapt, enure, inure 6 attune 9 habituate
much ~: 4 flat 5 banal, corny, stale, stock, tired, trite 6 common, jejune 7 clichéd, insipid, worn-out 8 bathetic, bromidic, cornball, ordinary, shopworn, timeworn, well-worn 9 hackneyed, moth-eaten, played out 10 pedestrian, uninspired, unoriginal, warmed-over
never ~ , in coin-collecting: 3 unc.
no longer ~: 3 obs., old, out 5 dated, passé 6 bygone, old hat, square 7 archaic, outworn 8 obsolete, outdated, outmoded, timeworn 10 antiquated, out of style
one: 4 dupe, mark, pawn, tool 5 patsy 6 flunky, lackey, minion, pigeon, puppet, stooge, sucker, victim 7 cat's-paw, flunkey 8 creature, henchman 10 instrument
seldom ~: 5 dusty
to: 3 did 5 would 6 at home 10 accustomed
(to): 4 wont 5 prone
to be: 3 was 4 were
up: 3 out 4 bare, gone, shot, worn 5 spent, trite 6 barren, vacant 7 run-down, worn-out 10 threadbare
Used Cars (1980 film)
cast: Gerrit Graham, Kurt Russell, Jack Warden
director: Robert Zemeckis
useful: 3 fit 4 good 5 handy, utile 6 aidful, benign 7 gainful, helpful, working 8 fruitful, positive, remedial, salutary, suitable, valuable 9 covetable, desirable, effective, effectual, efficient, expedient, favorable, of service, practical, pragmatic 10 all-purpose, applicable, beneficial, convenient, functional, mechanical, productive, profitable, worthwhile
be ~: 2 do 3 pay 5 serve 6 assist
item: 3 aid 5 asset
more ~: 6 better 8 improved, superior 10 preferable
prove ~: 3 aid 4 help 5 avail
usefulness: 4 good, wear 5 avail, value, worth 7 service, utility 9 handiness 10 importance
useless: 4 idle, null, vain, weak, worn 5 inept, no-win, scrap 6 barren, futile, hollow, no good, otiose 7 inutile, worn-out 8 abortive, bootless, feckless, hopeless, needless, pathetic 9 desperate, for naught, fruitless, pointless, thankless, valueless, worthless 10 expendable, for nothing, impossible, pathetical, profitless, unavailing, unrequired, unworkable
become ~: 3 rot 4 ruin, sour, turn 5 decay, go bad, spoil, taint 6 mildew, molder 7 crumble 9 decompose
uselessly: 6 vainly 8 futilely 9 to no avail 10 for nothing
Use Me (1972 song) artist: Bill Withers
Usenet protocol: 4 http
Use No ___: 5 Hooks
___ use of: 4 make
user: 5 buyer, eater 6 client, hacker, patron 7 habitué, shopper 8 consumer, customer, operator 9 purchaser
annoyance: 4 spam 8 down time
user ___: 3 fee 5 group
___ user: 3 end
user-friendly: 5 handy 6 simple 9 foolproof, practical
feature: 4 icon
username, enter one's: 5 log in
Use Ta Be My Girl (1978 song) artist: O'Jays
USGA
part of ~: 4 Golf 5 Assoc.
ush: 4 seat 6 escort
u-shaped bend: 5 oxbow
usher: 3 see, sit 4 lead, page, seat, take 5 bring, guide, see in, steer 6 convoy, escort, herald, launch, lead

in, show in **7** bring in, conduct, go first, marshal, precede, preface, show out **9** accompany, attendant, introduce **10** doorkeeper, gatekeeper, inaugurate, pave the way, show around
ender: 4 ette
in: 5 begin, greet, set up, start **6** herald, launch **7** receive, welcome **8** antecede, initiate **9** institute, introduce, originate **10** inaugurate, lead the way
(in): 3 see **4** ring, show
offering: 3 arm **4** wing
route: 5 aisle
USIA div.: 3 VOA
__ Us If You Can: 5 Catch
U.S. Information __: 6 Agency
using: 3 via **7** by way of, through **9** by means of **10** by virtue of
refrain from ~: 5 avoid, spurn **6** eschew **7** boycott
Usk: 5 river
locale: 5 Wales **7** England
USLTA
part of ~: 4 Lawn **5** Assoc. **6** Tennis
USMA grad: 2 lt. **5** lieut.
see also Army, West Point
U.S. Male (1968 song) artist: Presley
U.S. Marine __: 5 Corps
U.S. Marshals (1998 film)
cast: Robert Downey Jr., Tommy Lee Jones, Kate Nelligan, Wesley Snipes
USMC: 4 serv., svce.
part of ~: 5 Corps **6** Marine
rank: 3 maj., PFC
rookie: 3 pvt., rct.
vessel: 3 LST
see also Marines, military
U.S. Merchant __ Academy: 6 Marine
U.S. Military __: 7 Academy
USN: 3 svc. **4** Navy, serv., svce.
branch: 3 ONI
cops: 2 SP
member: 3 CNO
offense: 4 AWOL
outpost: 3 NAS
rank: 2 lt. **3** adm., cdr., CPO, CWO, ens., yeo. **4** capt., RAdm, VAdm. **5** comdr.
rookie: 3 rct.
see also military, navy
USNA: 3 sch. **4** coll. **9** Annapolis
freshman: 4 pleb **5** plebe
part of ~: 3 Nav. **4** Acad. **5** Naval **7** Academy
student: 3 mid **5** middy
__ Us Now Praise Famous Men: 3 Let
USO
attendee: 2 GI **3** NCO, PFC
show introducer: 2 MC **5** emcee
stalwart: 4 Hope **7** Bob Hope
U.S. Open
org.: 3 PGA
stadium: 4 Ashe
U.S. Open golf champs:
2004 - Retief Goosen
2003 - Jim Furyk
2002 - Tiger Woods
2001 - Retief Goosen
2000 - Tiger Woods
1999 - Payne Stewart
1998 - Lee Janzen
1997 - Ernie Els
1996 - Steve Jones
1995 - Corey Pavin
1994 - Ernie Els
1993 - Lee Janzen
1992 - Tom Kite
1991 - Payne Stewart
1990 - Hale Irwin
1989 - Curtis Strange
1988 - Curtis Strange
1987 - Scott Simpson
1986 - Ray Floyd
1985 - Andy North
1984 - Fuzzy Zoeller
1983 - Larry Nelson
1982 - Tom Watson
1981 - David Graham
1980 - Jack Nicklaus
1979 - Hale Irwin
1978 - Andy North
1977 - Hubert Green
1976 - Jerry Pate
1975 - Lou Graham
1974 - Hale Irwin
1973 - Johnny Miller
1972 - Jack Nicklaus
1971 - Lee Trevino
1970 - Tony Jacklin
1969 - Orville Moody
1968 - Lee Trevino
1967 - Jack Nicklaus
1966 - Billy Casper
1965 - Gary Player
1964 - Ken Venturi
1963 - Julius Boros
1962 - Jack Nicklaus
1961 - Gene Littler
1960 - Arnold Palmer
1959 - Billy Casper
1958 - Tommy Bolt
1957 - Dick Mayer
1956 - Cary Middlecoff
1955 - Jack Fleck
1954 - Ed Furgol
1953 - Ben Hogan
1952 - Julius Boros
1951 - Ben Hogan
1950 - Ben Hogan
1949 - Cary Middlecoff
1948 - Ben Hogan
1947 - Lew Worsham
1946 - Lloyd Mangrum
1942–45 - no tournament
1941 - Craig Wood
1940 - Lawson Little
1939 - Byron Nelson
1938 - Ralph Guldahl
1937 - Ralph Guldahl
1936 - Tony Manero
1935 - Sam Parks Jr
1934 - Olin Dutra
1933 - Johnny Goodman
1932 - Gene Sarazen
1931 - Billy Burke
1930 - Bobby Jones
1929 - Bobby Jones
1928 - Johnny Farrell
1927 - Tommy Armour
1926 - Bobby Jones
1925 - Willie Macfarlane
1924 - Cyril Walker
1923 - Bobby Jones
1922 - Gene Sarazen
1921 - Jim Barnes
1920 - Ted Ray
1919 - Walter Hagen
1917–18 - no tournament
1916 - Chick Evans
1915 - John Travers
1914 - Walter Hagen
1913 - Francis Ouimet
1912 - John McDermott
1911 - John McDermott
1910 - Alex Smith
1909 - George Sargent
1908 - Fred McLeod
1907 - Alec Ross
1906 - Alex Smith
1905 - Willie Anderson
1904 - Willie Anderson
1903 - Willie Anderson
1902 - Laurie Auchterlonie
1901 - Willie Anderson
1900 - Harry Vardon
1899 - Willie Smith
1898 - Fred Herd
1897 - Joe Lloyd
1896 - James Foulis
1895 - Horace Rawlins
U.S. Open tennis champs:
2003 - Andy Roddick, Justine Hedin-Hardenne
2002 - Pete Sampras, Serena Williams
2001 - Lleyton Hewitt, Venus Williams
2000 - Marat Safin, Venus Williams
1999 - Andre Agassi, Serena Williams
1998 - Patrick Rafter, Lindsay Davenport
1997 - Patrick Rafter, Martina Hingis
1996 - Pete Sampras, Steffi Graf
1995 - Pete Sampras, Steffi Graf
1994 - Andre Agassi, Arantxa Sanchez Vicario
1993 - Pete Sampras, Steffi Graf
1992 - Stefan Edberg, Monica Seles
1991 - Stefan Edberg, Monica Seles
1990 - Pete Sampras, Gabriela Sabatini
1989 - Boris Becker, Steffi Graf
1988 - Mats Wilander, Steffi Graf
1987 - Ivan Lendl, Martina Navratilova
1986 - Ivan Lendl, Martina Navratilova
1985 - Ivan Lendl, Hana Mandlikova
1984 - John McEnroe, Martina Navratilova
1983 - Jimmy Connors, Martina Navratilova
1982 - Jimmy Connors, Chris Evert Lloyd
1981 - John McEnroe, Tracy Austin
1980 - John McEnroe, Chris Evert Lloyd
1979 - John McEnroe, Tracy Austin
1978 - Jimmy Connors, Chris Evert
1977 - Guillermo Vilas, Chris Evert
1976 - Jimmy Connors, Chris Evert
1975 - Manuel Orantes, Chris Evert
1974 - Jimmy Connors, Billie Jean King
1973 - John Newcombe, Margaret Court
1972 - Ilie Nastase, Billie Jean King
1971 - Stan Smith, Billie Jean King
1970 - Ken Rosewall, Margaret Court
1969 - Rod Laver, Margaret Court
1968 - Arthur Ashe, Virginia Wade
1967 - John Newcombe, Billie Jean King
1966 - Fred Stolle, Maria Bueno
1965 - Manuel Santana, Margaret Smith
1964 - Roy Emerson, Maria Bueno
1963 - Rafael Osuna, Maria Bueno
1962 - Rod Laver, Margaret Smith
1961 - Roy Emerson, Darlene Hard
1960 - Neale Fraser, Darlene Hard
1959 - Neale Fraser, Maria Bueno
1958 - Ashley Cooper, Althea Gibson
1957 - Mal Anderson, Althea Gibson
1956 - Ken Rosewall, Shirley Fry
1955 - Tony Trabert, Doris Hart
1954 - Vic Seixas, Doris Hart
1953 - Tony Trabert, Maureen Connolly
1952 - Frank Sedgman, Maureen Connolly
1951 - Frank Sedgman, Maureen Connolly
1950 - Art Larsen, Margaret duPont
1949 - Pancho Gonzales, Margaret duPont
1948 - Pancho Gonzales, Margaret duPont
1947 - Jack Kramer, Louise Brough
1946 - Jack Kramer, Pauline Betz
1945 - Frank Parker, Sarah Cooke
1944 - Frank Parker, Pauline Betz
1943 - Joe Hunt, Pauline Betz
1942 - Fred Schroeder, Pauline Betz
1941 - Bobby Riggs, Sarah Cooke
1940 - Don McNeill, Alice Marble
1939 - Bobby Riggs, Alice Marble
1938 - Don Budge, Alice Marble
1937 - Don Budge, Anita Lizana
1936 - Fred Perry, Alice Marble
1935 - Wilmer Allison, Helen Jacobs
1934 - Fred Perry, Helen Jacobs
1933 - Fred Perry, Helen Jacobs
1932 - Ellsworth Vines, Helen Jacobs
1931 - Ellsworth Vines, Helen Moody
1930 - John Doeg, Betty Nuthall
1929 - Bill Tilden, Helen Wills
1928 - Henri Cochet, Helen Wills
1927 - Rene Lacoste, Helen Wills
1926 - Rene Lacoste, Molla Mallory
1925 - Bill Tilden, Helen Wills
1924 - Bill Tilden, Helen Wills
1923 - Bill Tilden, Helen Wills
1922 - Bill Tilden, Molla Mallory
1921 - Bill Tilden, Molla Mallory
1920 - Bill Tilden, Molla Mallory
1919 - William Johnston, Hazel Wightman
1918 - R.L. Murray, Molla Bjurstedt
1917 - R.L. Murray, Molla Bjurstedt
1916 - Dick Williams, Molla Bjurstedt
1915 - William Johnston, Molla Bjurstedt
1914 - Richard Williams, Mary Browne
1913 - Maurice McLoughlin, Mary Browne
1912 - Maurice McLoughlin, Mary Browne
1911 - Bill Larned, Hazel Hotchkiss
1910 - Bill Larned, Hazel Hotchkiss
1909 - Bill Larned, Hazel Hotchkiss
1908 - Bill Larned, Maud Wallach
1907 - Bill Larned, Evelyn Sears
1906 - William Clothier, Helen Homans
1905 - Beals Wright, Elisabeth Moore
1904 - Holcombe Ward, May Sutton
1903 - Laurie Doherty, Elisabeth Moore
1902 - Bill Larned, Marion Jones
1901 - Bill Larned, Elisabeth Moore
1900 - Malcolm Whitman, Myrtle McAteer
1899 - Malcolm Whitman, Marion Jones
1898 - Malcolm Whitman, Juliette Atkinson
1897 - Robert Wrenn, Juliette Atkinson
1896 - Robert Wrenn, Elisabeth Moore
1895 - Fred Hovey, Juliette Atkinson
1894 - Robert Wrenn, Helen Hellwig
1893 - Robert Wrenn, Aline Terry
1892 - Oliver Campbell, Mabel Cahill
1891 - Oliver Campbell, Mabel Cahill
1890 - Oliver Campbell, Ellen Roosevelt
1889 - Henry Slocum Jr., Bertha Townsend
1888 - Henry Slocum Jr., Bertha Townsend
1887 - Richard Sears, Ellen Hansell
1886 - Richard Sears
1885 - Richard Sears
1884 - Richard Sears
1883 - Richard Sears
1882 - Richard Sears
1881 - Richard Sears
Uspallata __: 4 Pass
__ U.S. Patent Off.: 3 Reg.
U.S. Postal __: 7 Service
__ us pray: 3 Let
USPS
alternative: 3 fax **5** e-mail

circuit: 3 rte.
item: 3 ltr. 4 mail 6 stamps
letters: 3 RFD
limbo: 3 DLO
part of ~: 3 Svc. 4 Svce. 6 Postal 7 Service
units: 3 lbs., ozs.
VIP: 3 PMG
see also mail, post office
__ usque ad aras: 6 amicus
U.S. Secret __: 7 Service
USS Enterprise officer: 3 cdr.
USSR
aircraft: 3 MiG
neighbor: 3 Afg.
part of ~: 3 Rus., Sov., Ukr.
secret police: 3 KGB 4 NKVD, OGPU
successor: 3 CIS
see also Russia
Ussuri: 5 river
locale: 6 Russia 9 Manchuria
USTA
see tennis
Ustinov, Peter: 3 Sir 5 actor 6 author 7 British
film: Beau Brummel (1954)
Billy Budd (1962)
Lorenzo's Oil (1992)
Quo Vadis? (1951)
Romanoff and Juliet (1961)
Spartacus (1960, AA)
The Sundowners (1960)
Topkapi (1964, AA)
Vice Versa (1948)
work: The Love of Four Colonels
Romanoff and Juliet
The Unknown Soldier and his Wife
Usu: 7 volcano
locale: 4 Asia 5 Japan 8 Hokkaido
USU
see Utah State
usual: 3 par, set, typ. 4 norm 5 fixed, grind, plain, stock, typic 6 common, normal, proper, wonted 7 average, chronic, current, general, generic, natural, regular, routine, typical 8 accepted, constant, everyday, expected, familiar, frequent, habitual, ordinary, orthodox, standard, workaday 9 chronical, customary, generical, prevalent, quotidian 10 accustomed, legitimate, mainstream, prevailing, white-bread, widespread
as ~: 8 normally
combining form: 5 normo-
procedure: 4 wont 5 habit, usage 6 custom, policy, system 7 routine 8 practice 9 tradition 10 observance
usually: 3 oft 5 often 6 mainly, mostly 7 as a rule 8 commonly, normally 9 generally, in general, in the main, most often, regularly, routinely, sometimes 10 by and large, frequently, habitually, on the whole, ordinarily
Usual Suspects, The (1995 film)
cast: Stephen Baldwin, Gabriel Byrne, Chazz Palminteri, Kevin Pollak, Kevin Spacey
usurer: 5 shark 6 lender 7 Shylock 8 creditor 9 loan shark
interest, to a ~: 3 vig 8 vigorish
usurp: 4 grab 5 annex, co-opt, seize, wrest 6 assume, borrow, cut out, hijack, pirate 7 preempt 8 arrogate, displace, highjack, move in on, muscle in, supplant, take over 9 lay hold of 10 commandeer, dispossess, encroach on, infringe on, plagiarize
usurpation: 4 coup, grab 7 seizure 8 takeover 10 arrogation, assumption
U.S. Virgin Islands: 3 ter. 4 terr.
USX product: 5 steel
ut __: 4 dict. 5 infra, supra
UT
see Utah
U2
homeland: Ireland
U-235: 7 isotope
device: 5 A bomb
regulator: 3 AEC, NRC
uta: 6 animal 7 reptile
Uta: 5 Hagen 6 Pippig
Utah: 5 state
canyon: 5 Bryce
city: 3 Roy 4 Alta, Lehi, Moab, Orem 5 Kanab, Logan, Magna, Ogden, Provo, Sandy 6 Draper, Kearns, Layton, Murray, Tooele 7 Midvale 8 Riverton, St. George 9 Bountiful, Cedar City, Kaysville, Millcreek 10 Clearfield, West Jordan
county: 4 Juab 5 Piute 6 Tooele, Uintah 8 Salt Lake
grp.: 3 LDS
Indian: 3 Ute 5 Piute 6 Paiute
inst.: 3 BYU
lake: 9 Great Salt
mountain: 5 Lasal, Uinta 7 Wasatch 9 Kings Peak
national forest: 5 Uinta
national park: 4 Zion 6 Arches
neighbor: 5 Idaho 6 Nevada 7 Arizona, Wyoming 8 Colorado 9 New Mexico
pro team: 4 Jazz
resort: 4 Alta
state animal: 3 elk
state bird: 7 sea gull
state cooking pot: 9 Dutch oven
state fish: 5 trout
state flower: 4 sego 8 sego lily
state fossil: 10 allosaurus
state fruit: 6 cherry
state gem: 5 topaz
state insect: 8 honeybee
state mineral: 6 copper
state rock: 4 coal
state tree: 10 blue spruce
Utah State
athletes: 6 Aggies
locale: 5 Logan
ute: 7 vehicle
cousin: 3 ATV
__-ute: 5 sport
Ute: 5 tribe 6 Indian, Siouan 7 Amerind 8 language, Shoshone
language family: 5 Numic
Ute __: 4 Pass
utensil: 3 pan 4 fork, tool 5 knife, ladle, scoop, spoon 6 device, gadget, vessel 7 cutlery 9 implement, tableware 10 instrument, silverware
coating: 5 glaze 6 enamel
eating ~: 4 fork 5 knife, spoon, spork
kitchen ~: 3 pan, pot, wok 5 knife, ladle, parer, ricer, sieve 6 baster, boiler, cooker
kitchen ~ brand: 3 Oxo 4 Ekco
maker: 6 cutler
point: 4 tine
utensils: 3 kit 4 gear 7 cutlery 9 equipment
UTEP
athlete: 5 Miner
conference: 3 WAC
part of ~: 4 Paso 5 Texas
rival: 3 BYU
uti: 4 lute 6 string
origin: 10 Yugoslavia
Utica: 4 city, town
locale: 7 New York
util: 3 tel. 4 elec.
utile: 5 handy 6 usable, useful 7 helpful, useable 8 availing, feasible 9 practical 10 applicable, beneficial, functional
utilitarian: 6 useful 7 helpful 8 sensible 9 efficient, practical, pragmatic, realistic
utility: 3 gas, use 4 help, wear 5 avail, power, value, water, worth 6 profit 7 benefit, fitness, purpose, service 8 adequacy, efficacy, function 9 relevance 10 expediency, usefulness
bill abbr.: 3 kwh
building: 4 shed 6 lean-to
device: 5 gauge, meter 9 indicator
regulating agcy.: 3 PSC
vehicle: 3 rig, van 4 jeep, semi 5 dolly, lorry, truck, U-Haul 6 pickup
utility __: 3 man 4 pole, room 6 closet 7 program
__ utility: 6 public 8 marginal
utility room
feature: 5 drier, dryer 6 washer
__-utility vehicle: 5 sport
utilization: 8 exercise 10 employment
utilize: 3 ply, tap, use 4 take, turn 5 apply, exert, put in, wield 6 draw on, employ, handle, occupy, resort 7 consume, exploit, harness 8 exercise, profit by, put to use, resort to 9 make use of
Utley: 7 Garrick
utmost: 3 nth, top, ult. 4 full, last, main 5 chief, final, first, ideal, limit, major, prime 6 all-out 7 capital, extreme, highest, leading, maximal, maximum, supreme 8 absolute, cardinal, farthest, greatest, ultimate 9 paramount, sovereign 10 preeminent
do one's ~: 3 aim, try, vie 4 moil, push, toil 5 essay, fight, labor, sweat 6 strain, strive, tackle, take on 7 attempt, compete, contend 8 bear down, endeavor, go all out, scramble, shoot for, struggle 10 go for broke, go the limit
Uto-__: 7 Aztecan
utopia: 4 Eden 5 bliss 6 Avalon, heaven 7 Arcadia, Erewhon 8 paradise 9 happiness, Shangri-la
Utopia: 4 font 5 essay 8 typeface
author: Thomas More
Utopia, Ltd.: 8 operetta
composer: 7 Gilbert 8 Sullivan
utopian: 4 airy 5 dream, ideal, lofty 6 dreamy, edenic 7 perfect 8 idealist, platonic, quixotic, romantic 9 grandiose, idealized, just right, visionary 10 idealistic, impossible, optimistic, quixotical, unfeasible, unworkable
Utrecht: 4 city, town
city near ~: 3 Ede 5 Zeist 6 Arnhem
locale: 7 Holland 11 Netherlands
Utrillo, Maurice: 6 artist, French 7 painter
contemporary: 5 Monet
__ ut supra: 4 vide
Uttar Pradesh
city: 4 Agra 6 Jhansi, Kanpur
locale: 5 India
utter: 3 air, cry, jaw, put, say 4 chin, give, main, mere, pure, rank, talk, tell, vent 5 blurt, chant, couch, gross, mouth, right, sheer, shout, speak, stark, state, thoro, total, voice, whole 6 affirm, all-out, arrant, assert, entire, intone, mumble, mutter, recite, reveal, strict 7 breathe, chime in, declaim, declare, deliver, dictate, divulge, exclaim, express, extreme, flat-out, glaring, perfect, whisper 8 absolute, announce, bring out, complete, disclose, flagrant, outright, proclaim, profound, shocking, thorough, throw out, vocalize 9 downright, egregious, ejaculate, enunciate, make known, out-and-out, pronounce, verbalize, wholesale 10 articulate, asseverate, consummate
ender: 4 most
loudly: 3 baa, cry 4 blat, bray, honk, hoot, wail, yell 5 bleat, neigh 6 bellow, holler, scream, whinny
sharply: 3 rap 4 bark, snap
softly: 3 hum 4 sigh 5 drone 6 mumble, murmur, mutter 7 whisper
suddenly: 4 blab 5 blurt 7 exclaim, let slip 8 blurt out
utterance: 4 rant, talk, word 5 parol, reply, spiel, voice, words 6 phrase, remark, saying, speech 7 opinion, oration 8 delivery, language, response, sentence, speaking 9 assertion, discourse, elocution, statement 10 confession, expression, peroration, recitation, revelation, vocalizing
uttered: 4 oral 5 spake, spoke, vocal 6 spoken 9 vocalized
utterly: 3 all 4 just, only 5 fully, quite, right, stark 6 purely, simply, wholly 7 totally 8 entirely 9 every inch, extremely, perfectly, to the core 10 absolutely, altogether, completely, thoroughly, to the limit
uttermost: 4 last, most 5 first, major, prime 7 capital, highest, maximum 8 cardinal, farthest, furthest, greatest
U-turn: 8 flip-flop, reversal 9 about-face, one-eighty
U Turn (1997 film)
cast: Powers Boothe, Jennifer Lopez, Nick Nolte, Sean Penn
director: Oliver Stone
UV __: 4 rays 6 filter
Uvalde: 4 city, town
locale: 5 Texas
uvula combining form: 4 clon- 5 clono- 8 staphylo-
Uwe: 7 Johnson
Uxmal resident: 5 Mayan
uxor's husband: 3 vir
Uzbek: 8 language
Uzbekistan: 6 nation 7 country
capital: 8 Tashkent
desert: 8 Kyzyl Kum
neighbor: 10 Kazakhstan, Kyrgyzstan, Tajikistan
once: 3 SSR
river: 4 Oxus
Uzi: 3 gun 7 firearm, Israeli 9 automatic

V: **4** elem., five **6** letter **7** element **8** vanadium
followers: **3** WXY **4** WXYZ
inverted ~: **5** caret
preceders: **3** STU **4** RSTU **5** QRSTU
23 for ~: **4** at. no.
V __: **4** neck, sign **5** block, joint **6** region
V __ Victor: **4** as in
V-__: **4** chip, neck **6** shaped
V-__ engine: **3** six **4** type **5** eight
V.: **5** novel
author: Thomas Pynchon
V. __: **3** Adm., Rev.
__ V: **5** Henry
Va.
neighbor: **3** Ken., W. Va. **4** N. Car.
training base: **5** Ft. Lee
see also Virginia
__-Vac: **4** Mini, Ray-o
vaca catcher: **5** reata **6** gaucho
vacancy: **3** gap **4** post, room, slot, void **5** house, space **6** rental **7** absence, opening **8** position **9** apartment, emptiness, situation **10** job opening
sign: **5** to let **9** available
vacant: **4** bare, free, open, void **5** blank, clear, empty, inane, to let, unlet, vapid **6** absent, barren, dreamy, glassy, hollow, unused, used up, wooden **7** deadpan, drained, untaken, vacuous **8** depleted, deserted, desolate, dreaming, listless, unfilled **9** abandoned, available, evacuated, exhausted, unlived in **10** abstracted, glassy-eyed, tenantless, unoccupied, unthinking
hour: **6** recess **7** leisure **8** free time **9** idle hours, spare time **10** recreation, relaxation
vacate: **2** go **4** exit, quit **5** clear, empty, leave **6** depart, give up, go away, resign **7** abandon, abolish, move out, nullify, retreat **8** abdicate, abrogate, evacuate, part with, withdraw **9** disappear, discharge, move out of **10** relinquish
vacated: **4** bare, left, open, went **5** empty **6** barren **9** available
vacation: **4** rest, stay, tour **5** break, leave, R and R, visit **6** cruise, outing, recess, travel **7** holiday, leisure, liberty, respite, sojourn, time off **8** furlough, go abroad **10** recreation, sabbatical
ender: **4** land
home: **2** RV **5** cabin, lodge, motel, villa **6** A-frame, camper **8** bungalow
military ~: **5** leave **8** furlough
month: **3** Aug., Jul. **4** July **6** August
on ~: **3** far, off, out **4** away, gone **6** absent **9** elsewhere
option: **4** tour, trip **5** jaunt **6** cruise, flight, junket, safari, voyage **9** excursion **10** expedition
prepare for a ~: **4** load, pack **8** get ready
souvenir: **5** photo **6** T-shirt **8** postcard **10** photograph
spot: **4** cape, lake **5** shore **6** resort
time: **6** summer **7** dog days
vehicle: **2** RV **9** Winnebago **10** mobile home
__ vacation: **4** long **7** two-week
Vacation __ School: **5** Bible
vacationer: **5** guest **6** lodger, renter, roomer **7** tourist, visitor, voyager **8** traveler, wayfarer **9** sightseer, sojourner **10** day-tripper
goal: **3** tan **4** rest **5** break, peace, quiet **6** suntan **7** holiday, respite **8** breather, calmness, downtime, quietude **10** inactivity, recreation, relaxation
winter ~: **5** skier
Vacation From Marriage (1945 film)
cast: Robert Donat, Deborah Kerr
director: Alexander Korda
vacationing: **4** away **6** abroad, far-off **9** elsewhere, not at home
Vacation (song) artist: Connie Francis, Go-Go's
Vacaville: **4** city, town
locale: **10** California
vaccinate: **6** inject **7** protect **8** immunize **9** inoculate
vaccine: **4** hypo, oral, shot **5** serum **8** medicine **9** antitoxin **10** medication
container: **4** vial **5** ampul, phial **6** ampule **7** ampoule
place to get a ~: **3** arm
polio ~ developer: **4** Salk **5** Sabin
__ vaccine: **4** oral, Salk **5** Sabin
Vachel: **7** Lindsay
vacillate: **3** wag **4** halt, lick, yo-yo **5** hedge, hover, pause, shift, swing, waver **6** change, dither, falter, linger, seesaw, teeter, wabble, waffle, wobble **7** stagger, whiffle **8** fence-sit, hesitate, straddle **9** alternate, fluctuate, hem and haw, oscillate, pussyfoot
vacillating: **4** torn, weak **5** shaky, timid **6** fickle, infirm, unsure **7** halting **8** hesitant, unstable, unsteady, variable **9** uncertain, undecided, unsettled **10** ambivalent, capricious, indecisive, irresolute, of two minds, on the fence, weak-willed, wishy-washy
vacillation: **4** bend, rock, sway, tilt **5** delay, doubt, pause, qualm, swing **6** teeter, totter **8** wavering **10** averseness, hesitation, indecision, reluctance
Václav: **5** Havel
V.A. concern: **3** POW
vacuity: **3** gap **4** gulf, hole, void **5** abyss, space **6** cavity, hollow, torpor **7** absence, languor, opening **8** lethargy, nihility **9** blankness, emptiness, inanition
vacuole former: **6** amoeba
vacuous: **4** bare, dull, idle, null, void **5** blank, clear, empty, inane, silly, vapid **6** absent, inept, stupid, vacant **7** drained, foolish, shallow **9** airheaded, half-baked **10** weak-minded
vacuum: **3** gap **4** void **5** clean, space, sweep **8** nihility **9** emptiness **10** outer space
brand: **5** Kirby, Oreck **6** Hoover **10** Electrolux
like a ~: **5** blank, empty **6** barren, hollow **7** airless **8** deserted, desolate, lifeless
part: **3** bag **4** hose, wand **5** brush
target: **4** crud, dirt, gunk, soil **5** grime
tube gas: **5** argon
tube type: **5** diode
use a ~: **4** suck
vacuum __: **3** pan **4** pump, tube **5** gauge **6** bottle **7** cleaner, sweeper
vacuum __ maker: **6** coffee
vacuum-__: **4** pack **6** packed
__ vacuum: **7** partial
vacuuming: **5** chore **9** housework
vacuum-tube part: **6** dynode
vade mecum: **5** bible, guide **8** handbook
Vader, Darth: **7** villain
foe: **4** Leia, Luke, Solo
like ~: **4** evil
Vadim, Roger: **6** French **8** director
spouse: Brigitte Bardot, Jane Fonda
__ Vadis?: **3** Quo
VAdm. employer: **3** USN
Vaduz: **4** city, town **7** capital
locale: Liechtenstein
vagabond: **3** bum **4** hobo, idle, roam **5** farer, gypsy, nomad, rover, tramp **6** beggar, errant, roving **7** aimless, drifter, migrant, nomadic, outcast, rambler, roaming, tourist, trekker **8** derelict, drifting, explorer, gadabout, homeless, prodigal, rambling, rootless, traveler, wanderer, wayfarer **9** footloose, itinerant, itinerate, journeyer, transient, wandering, wayfaring **10** hitchhiker, journeying, pathfinder, ragamuffin
Vagabond King, The composer: **5** Friml
Vagabond Lover, The: **6** Vallee
vagarious: **6** chancy, fickle, quirky, spotty **7** erratic, flighty **8** careless, fanciful, rambling, unstable, variable **9** arbitrary, eccentric, fluctuant, haphazard, impulsive, irregular, mercurial, wandering, whimsical **10** capricious
vagary: **4** whim **5** fancy, quirk **6** notion, whimsy **7** caprice, impulse, whimsey **8** crotchet
vagrant: **3** bum **4** hobo **5** stray, tramp **6** beggar **7** drifter, floater, nomadic, outcast, sinuous **8** derelict, homeless, traveler, wanderer **9** itinerant, transient, wayfaring **10** ragamuffin
vague: **3** dim, lax **4** dark, hazy **5** exact, faint, foggy, fuzzy, loose, mirky, misty, muddy, murky, rough, shady **6** arcane, bleary, cloudy, dreamy, unsure **7** blurred, cryptic, dubious, evasive, general, obscure, shadowy, sketchy, unclear **8** abstruse, doubtful, nebulous, oracular, puzzling **9** ambiguous, amorphous, confusing, cryptical, dreamlike, enigmatic, equivocal, hard to see, imprecise, shapeless, tenebrous, uncertain, undecided, unfocused **10** clear as mud, ill-defined, indefinite, indistinct, inexplicit, perplexing, unexplicit, unspecific
amount: **4** some
form: **4** blob, glob, lump, mass, spot **5** smear **6** smudge **7** splotch
idea: **4** clew, clue **6** notion
make ~: **3** fog **4** blur, daze, mist **5** befog, blear, cloud, muddy, smear **6** smudge **7** becloud, obscure
Vague: **4** Vera
vagueness: **4** haze **9** ambiguity, fogginess, fuzziness, ignorance
vagus __: **5** nerve
Vail: **4** city, town
conveyor: **3** tow **4** T-bar
enjoy ~: **3** ski **4** skee
like ~ in winter: **5** snowy, white
locale: **8** Colorado
vain: **4** idle, null, puny, smug **5** cocky, empty, no-win, petty, proud **6** barren, futile, hollow **7** fustian, haughty, inutile, pompous, shallow, sterile, stuck-up, useless **8** abortive, arrogant, boastful, bootless, cocksure, egoistic, hopeless, inflated, nugatory, puffed up, snobbish, specious, trifling **9** bigheaded, conceited, desperate, for naught, frivolous, fruitless, hubristic, pointless, senseless, thankless, to no avail, worthless **10** big-talking, egocentric, egoistical, for nothing, profitless, swaggering, unavailing
be in ~: **3** die **4** bust, fail, flop, lose **7** founder **9** fall short
claim: **5** boast
ender: **5** glory **8** glorious
in ~: **6** futile **9** fruitless, to no avail
male: **3** fop **4** dude **5** dandy **9** pretty boy
walk: **5** mince, strut **6** prance, sashay **7** flounce, peacock, swagger
vainglorious: **4** smug **5** proud **7** fustian, haughty, pompous **8** arrogant, boastful **9** conceited
vainglory: **4** pomp **5** pride **7** conceit **10** narcissism, pretension
vainly: **8** futilely **9** to no avail, uselessly **10** for nothing
act ~: **5** groom, preen, primp **7** deck out, dress up, spiff up
vair: **3** fur **7** minever, miniver
Val: **5** Avery, Guest **6** Kilmer
Val __: **4** lace **6** d'Isère
Valachi Papers, The
author: Peter Maas
Valais, capital of: **4** Sion
Val-Belair: **4** city, town
locale: **6** Canada, Québec
Valcour: **3** isl. **4** isle **6** island
Val d'__: **4** Arno
Valdai Hills, river that starts in the: **5** Volga
Valdez: **4** city, Juan, Luis, town
locale: **6** Alaska
product: **3** oil
__ Valdez: **5** Exxon
Valdivia: **4** city, town
locale: **5** Chile
Val-d'Or: **4** city, town
locale: **6** Canada, Québec
Valdosta: **4** city, town
locale: **7** Georgia
vale: **4** glen **6** hollow
Vale: **5** Jerry, Vicki
valediction: **5** leave **7** goodbye, parting, sendoff **8** farewell **9** departure **10** separation
Valediction, A author: John Donne
valedictorian's pride: **3** GPA
valedictory: **6** speech **7** goodbye, parting **8** farewell **9** departing
valence
atom with a ~ of one: **5** monad
Valence: **4** city, town
locale: **6** France
Valencia: **4** city, port, town
locale: **5** Spain
river: **5** Turia
Valenciennes: **4** lace
Valene: **5** Ewing
Valens, Ritchie
song: Donna (1958)
La Bamba (1959)
valentine: **2** jo **3** pet **4** baby, dear, jill, love **5** amour, angel, chéri, cooky, cutey, cutie, deary, ducky, flame, heart, honey, leman, lover, lovey, novia, novio, sugar, sweet **6** bon ami, chérie, cookie, dautie, dearie, steady, sweets **7** beloved, dearest, dear one, pigsney, schatzi, squeeze, sweetie, tootsie **8** chou-chou, cutie pie, dowsabel, dulcinea, ladylove, lovebird, macushla, paramour, precious, snookums, sugar pie, sweetums, truelove **9** bonne amie, boyfriend, dreamboat, inamorata, inamorato, petit chou **10** girlfriend, heartthrob, honeybunch, mavourneen, sweetheart, sweetie pie, turtledove
color: **3** red
decor: **5** Cupid, heart **6** cherub
message: **6** be mine
month: **3** Feb. **8** February
purchase: **4** rose **9** chocolate
words: **5** I love **7** love you **8** I love you
words on a Spanish ~: **5** te amo
Valentine: **4** pope **5** Karen, saint **7** pontiff
__ Valentine: **4** Be my **7** Shirley
Valentine, A author: Edgar Allan Poe

Valentine author: George Sand
__ Valentine's Day: 5 Saint
Valentine's Day figure: 4 Amor, Eros 5 Cupid 8 Dan Cupid
Valentino, Rudolph: 5 actor
costar: 5 Banky, Naldi
film: The Eagle (1925)
The Four Horsemen... (1921)
The Sheik (1921)
Son of the Sheik (1926)
__ vale of tears: 4 this
__ Valera: 7 Eamon De
Valeria: 6 Golino
__ valerian: 3 red 5 Greek
Valerian: 5 Roman
Valerie: 6 Harper, Hobson 7 Perrine, Simpson 10 Bertinelli
Valerie (1987 song) artist: Winwood
Valery: 7 Bryusov
Valéry __ D'Estaing: 7 Giscard
Valéry, Paul: 4 poet 6 French
valet: 6 butler, flunky, Jeeves 7 flunkey, footman, man's man, servant 9 launderer 10 manservant
valet __: 7 parking
valet de __: 7 chambre
Valhalla: 4 Eden, hall 6 heaven 7 Elysium, Nirvana, rapture 8 paradise 9 Shangri-la
dweller: 4 Odin, Thor 5 Othin
locale: 6 Asgard
valiance: 4 grit, guts 5 nerve 7 bravery, heroism 9 fortitude, gallantry
valiant: 4 bold, game 5 brave, gutsy, nervy, noble, stout 6 awless, daring, gritty, heroic, plucky, spunky 7 aweless, defiant, doughty, gallant, impavid, staunch 8 fearless, heroical, intrepid, resolute, stalwart, unafraid 9 audacious, confident, dauntless, dreadless, herculean, undaunted, unfearful, unfearing 10 chivalrous, courageous, mettlesome, undismayed
Valiant
see Prince Valiant
valid: 2 OK 4 good, okay, real, sure, true 5 exact, jural, legal, legit, licit, right, solid, sound 6 cogent, kasher, kosher, lawful, proven, tested 7 binding, certain, correct, factual, genuine, in force, logical, precise, telling 8 accurate, attested, bona fide, credible, flawless, in effect, official, original, rightful, unbiased, unerring, verified 9 authentic, certified, confirmed, effective, errorless, pertinent, veracious, veritable 10 acceptable, accredited, applicable, compelling, conclusive, convincing, defendable, defensible, documented, legitimate, meaningful, on the level, reasonable, sanctioned, unarguable, undoubtful
be ~: 4 deem, have, hold, keep 5 allow, apply, claim, favor, judge, stand 6 accept, defend, embody, endure, permit 7 condone, signify, support, sustain 8 indicate, maintain, sanction, stand for, underpin 9 approve of, epitomize, put up with, represent, symbolize, withstand 10 illustrate
reasoning: 5 logic, sense 6 reason, sanity 7 thought 9 coherence, deduction, good sense, induction, inference, rationale, reasoning, syllogism
validate: 2 OK 3 vet 4 okay, okeh, okey, seal, test 5 prove 6 affirm, attest, ratify, verify 7 approve, bear out, certify, confirm, endorse, indorse, justify, sustain 8 legalize, sanction, vouch for 9 authorize, establish, sign off on 10 constitute, legitimize
validation: 2 OK 4 okay 5 proof 9 collation 10 comparison
__-validation: 5 cross
validity: 5 force, punch, right, truth 6 weight 7 cogency, grounds, reality 8 efficacy, legality, strength 9 authority, soundness, substance 10 foundation, lawfulness, legitimacy
valiha: 6 string, zither
origin: 6 Africa
Valinda: 4 city, town
locale: 10 California
valise: 3 bag 4 case, grip 7 carry-on, luggage 8 suitcase 9 briefcase
Valkyries
lord: 4 Odin 5 Othin
mother: 4 Erda
Valladolid: 4 city, town
locale: 6 Mexico 7 Yucatán
__ Vallarta: 6 Puerto
Valle __: 6 d'Aosta
Valledupar: 4 city, town
locale: 8 Colombia
Vallee, Rudy: 5 actor 6 singer
film: How to Succeed in Business Without Really Trying (1967)
Live a Little, Love a Little (1968)
The Palm Beach Story (1942)
So This Is New York (1948)
Unfaithfully Yours (1948)
Valle Hermoso: 4 city, town
locale: 6 Mexico 10 Tamaulipas
Vallejo: 4 city
city near ~: 4 Napa
locale: 10 California
Valleri (1968 song) artist: Monkees
Valletta: 4 city 7 capital
locale: 5 Malta
valley: 4 dale, dell, glen 5 basin, cañon, gorge, notch, plain, swale 6 arroyo, bottom, canyon, coulee, dingle, hollow, ravine, trough 7 channel, lowland 10 depression
ancient Greek ~: 5 Nemea
broad ~: 4 glen, lawn, park 5 field, green, plaza 6 common, meadow, valley
Canadian ~: 5 droke
European river ~: 4 Saar
German ~: 4 Ruhr 5 Mosel
Golden State ~: 4 Napa
lily of the ~: 5 plant 6 flower
lunar ~: 4 rill 5 rille
narrow ~: 5 combe, coomb 6 coombe
Peloponnesian ~: 5 Nemea
side of a ~: 6 coteau
wine ~: 4 Napa 5 Loire, Rhine
__ valley: 4 rift 5 ridge 7 drowned, hanging
Valley __: 4 Girl, Song 5 Forge
Valley __ Dolls: 5 of the
__ Valley: 3 Sun 4 Deep, Napa 5 Death, Loire 7 Central, Raritan, Silicon
__ Valley, CA: 4 Napa, Simi 5 Squaw
__ valley civilization: 5 Indus
__ Valley Days: 5 Death
Valley Forge: 4 city, town
locale: 4 Penn.
Valley Forge author: Maxwell Anderson
Valley Girl (1983 film)
cast: Nicolas Cage, Colleen Camp, Deborah Foreman, Frederic Forrest
director: Martha Coolidge
exclamation: 5 oh wow
Valley Girl (1982 song) artist: Zappa
__ Valley, ID: 3 Sun
Valley Island: 4 Maui
Valley of Decision, The (1945 film)
cast: Donald Crisp, Greer Garson, Gregory Peck
Valley of Fear, The author: Doyle
Valley of Horses, The author: Jean Auel
Valley of Tears (1957 song) artist: Fats Domino
Valley of the __: 3 Sun 5 Kings
Valley of the Dolls (1968 song) artist: Dionne Warwick
Valley of the Dolls character: 5 Neely
Valley of the Kings
locale: 5 Egypt
town near the ~: 5 Luxor
Valley of the Moon, The author: Jack London
Valley of the Sun (1942 film)
cast: Lucille Ball, Sir Cedric Hardwicke, Dean Jagger
Valley of Unrest, The author: Poe
Valley of Wild Horses author: Grey
__ Valley, OH: 4 Enon
__ Valley P.T.A.: 6 Harper
__ Valley Ranch: 6 Hidden
Valley Road, The (1988 song) artist: Bruce Hornsby and the Range
__ Valley Serenade: 3 Sun
Valley Song author: Athol Fugard
Valley Station: 4 city, town
locale: 8 Kentucky
Valley Stream: 4 city, town
locale: 7 New York
__ Valley, The: 3 Big
Valli: 4 June 5 Alida 7 Frankie
Valli, Frankie
song: Can't Take My Eyes... (1967)
Grease (1978)
My Eyes Adored You (1975)
Our Day Will Come (1975)
Swearin' to God (1975)
Vallone: 3 Raf
Valmiki: 4 poet 5 Hindu
Valo, Elmer sport: 8 baseball
Valona: 3 bay
locale: 6 Europe 7 Albania
valor: 4 grit, guts, sand 5 fight, heart, moxie, nerve, pluck, spunk 6 daring, mettle, spirit, starch 7 bravery, courage, heroism, prowess, stomach 8 audacity, backbone, boldness, firmness 9 derring-do, fortitude, gallantry, hardihood, hardiness 10 knighthood, resolution
valorous: 4 bold, game 5 brave, gutsy, nervy, stout 6 awless, daring, gritty, heroic, plucky, spunky 7 aweless, defiant, doughty, gallant, impavid, staunch 8 fearless, heroical, intrepid, resolute, stalwart, unafraid 9 audacious, dauntless, dreadless, undaunted, unfearful, unfearing 10 chivalrous, courageous, undismayed
valorousness: 4 grit 7 heroism, prowess
Valotte (1984 song) artist: Julian Lennon
Valova: 5 Elena
Valparaiso: 4 city, port, town
locale: 5 Chile 7 Indiana
see also Spanish
valse: 5 dance, waltz 6 French
Valse __: 6 Triste
valuable: 3 gem, hot 4 dear, gold, plum, rich 5 asset, jewel, of use 6 costly, golden, nugget, prized, scarce, silver, usable, useful, worthy 7 antique, helpful, useable 8 esteemed, heirloom, held dear, in demand, precious, relevant, salutary, treasure 9 cherished, commodity, expensive, important, priceless, rewarding, treasured 10 beneficial, high-priced, invaluable, productive, profitable, worthwhile
extra: 4 perk 5 bonus, gravy, lucre 6 reward 8 dividend
least ~ part: 4 lees 5 chaff, dregs, trash, waste 6 refuse 7 garbage, residue 8 sediment 9 remainder
more ~: 5 finer 6 better 7 greater 8 souped up, stronger, superior, worthier 9 healthier, improving, sharpened 10 preferable
pass as ~: 5 foist 6 fob off, impose 9 insinuate
valuables: 4 swag 7 jewelry 8 treasure
place for ~: 4 safe 5 vault 6 coffer
valuate: 6 assess, survey 8 appraise
valuation: 3 est. 5 price, worth 6 rating 8 estimate 9 appraisal 10 assessment, estimation, evaluation
value: 3 buy, sum, use 4 cost, rate 5 asset, gauge, merit, price, prize, sense, worth 6 amount, assess, beauty, esteem, import, moment, profit, regard, repute, revere, virtue, weight 7 bargain, benefit, caliber, care for, cherish, content, expense, meaning, premium, quality, respect, service, stature, utility 8 appraise, estimate, hold dear, standard, treasure 9 appraisal, care about, recommend, reverence, substance 10 assessment, excellence, importance, set store by, usefulness
add ~ to: 6 better, enrich 7 build up, elevate, enhance, fortify 8 decorate 9 embellish 10 supplement
be of ~: 5 count, weigh 6 cut ice, matter, regard 8 interest 10 have weight
for face ~: 5 at par
get extra ~ from: 5 reuse
having practical ~: 5 handy, utile 6 usable, useful
high ~: 7 premium
highly: 4 love, rate 5 award, honor, prize 6 admire, esteem, regard, revere 7 cherish, idolize, premium 8 accolade, hold dear, hold high, look up to, treasure, venerate 9 care about, recommend 10 appreciate
item of ~: 5 asset 6 virtue 8 resource, strength 9 commodity
judgment: 4 idea, view 5 slant, stand 6 belief, notion 7 concept, feeling, opinion, outlook, thought 8 attitude, position 9 sentiment, viewpoint 10 assessment, conception, conviction, impression, persuasion, philosophy, standpoint
lacking ~: 9 worthless
lacking face ~: 5 no par
lessen the ~ of: 5 abase 6 derate
lose ~: 4 sink 5 lower 6 reduce 7 decline, deflate 8 decrease 10 depreciate
making no ~ judgments: 6 amoral
of little ~: 6 crumby, crummy, paltry
put a ~ on: 3 tag 4 deem, rank, rate 5 gauge, grade, guess, judge, quote, scale, weigh 6 assess, charge, esteem, figure, regard, size up, survey 7 measure 8 appraise, classify, estimate 9 determine
reduced in ~: 7 debased 8 degraded 9 worthless
system: 5 ethic 6 morals 9 principle
take at face ~: 4 rely 5 bet on, trust 6 accept, assume, bank on, commit, credit, expect, lean on, look to 7 believe, consign, count on, entrust, presume, suppose, swear by 8 depend on, rely upon
too highly: 6 exceed 8 misjudge, overrate 9 overprize 10 exaggerate, overassess, overesteem, overpraise
value-__ tax: 5 added
__ value: 3 par 4 acid, book, cash, face, loan, mean 5 added, truth 6 market, proper, resale 7 nominal, surplus
Value __: 4 Line

valued: **4** dear **7** beloved, darling **8** esteemed, precious **9** priceless
valueless: **3** nil **4** idle, null **5** empty, petty **6** futile **7** trivial, useless **8** ill-spent, unworthy **9** worthless
values: **5** ethic, ethos, mores **6** ethics, ideals, morals **7** culture **8** folkways **9** standards **10** principles
  lack of ~: **5** anomy **6** anomie
__ values: **6** family
__ value theorem: **4** mean **7** maximum
valuing: **4** fond, love **5** honor **6** caring, doting, esteem, liking, loving, regard **7** adoring, concern, devoted, fervent, opinion, prizing, respect, worship **8** admiring, approval, devotion, enamored, fondness, interest **9** affection, deference, reverence **10** admiration, cherishing, estimation, observance, passionate, respecting, veneration
valve: **3** tap **4** cock, flap, gate **6** faucet, spigot **7** hydrant, shutoff
  air ~: **6** intake
  butterfly ~: **6** damper
  device with a ~: **4** pump **5** heart
  exhaust ~: **6** cutout
  Fleming ~: **5** diode
  nautical ~: **7** seacock
  part: **4** stem
  safety ~: **4** duct, vent **5** spout **6** nozzle, outlet **7** channel
valve __: **4** gear, stem **6** lifter
__ valve: **3** air, EGR, PCV **4** ball, drop, flap, flux **5** check, clack, float, globe, light, slide **6** aortic, intake, mitral, mixing, needle, poppet, relief, rotary, safety, sleeve **7** bleeder, Fleming, orchard, rocking
valveless
  instrument: **4** horn **5** bugle **7** trumpet
vamoose: **2** go **3** fly, git, lam, run **4** flee, scat, shoo **5** leave, leg it, scram **6** beat it, begone, decamp, get out **7** abscond, get lost, go south, head out, make off, take off **8** hightail, shove off **9** bundle off, disappear **10** hightail it
vamp: **3** fix **4** Bara, mend, minx, riff **5** ad-lib, charm, fix up, flirt, intro, patch, siren **6** repair **7** beguile, enticer, Jezebel, patch up **8** beguiler, coquette **9** captivate, hypnotize, improvise, temptress
vamped: **5** ad-lib **6** casual **9** extempore, impromptu **10** improvised, off-the-cuff, unscripted
__ Vamp From East Broadway: **3** I'm a
vampire: **7** Dracula **9** Nosferatu
  bane: **5** cross, stake **6** garlic
  craving: **4** bite **5** blood
  female ~: **5** lamia
  like ~ movies: **4** gory **5** lurid **6** bloody
  portrayer: **6** Cruise, Lugosi
  time: **5** night
  trademark: **4** fang
vampire __: **3** bat
Vampire Armand, The author: Rice
Vampire Chronicles, The author: Rice
Vampire Lestat, The author: Rice
van: **5** front, truck, U-Haul **7** fourgon, trailer, vehicle **9** forefront
  ender: **4** load, pool **5** guard
  in the ~: **5** ahead, first **7** leading
  line: **5** fleet, mover
  starter: **4** mini
van __: **7** pooling
van __ Waals forces: **3** der
__ van: **5** motor **6** moving
Van: **4** lake **5** Bobby, McCoy **6** Heflin **7** Cliburn, Johnson **8** Morrison
  locale: **6** Turkey
Van __: **4** Dine, Gogh **5** Halen **6** Heusen
Van __ belt: **5** Allen
Van __, CA: **4** Nuys
Van __ Mungo: **6** Lingle
Van __ Parks: **4** Dyke
Van __'s Land: **6** Diemen
__ Van: **5** Chevy
vanadinite: **3** ore **7** mineral
vanadium: **5** metal, steel **7** element
  ore: **10** vanadinite
Van Allen __: **4** belt
Van Allen, James: **9** physicist, scientist
Van Ark: **4** Joan
Vanatu: **6** nation **7** country
van Beethoven: **6** Ludwig
Van Brocklin: **4** Norm
Van Buren: **6** Martin **7** Abigail
  sister: **7** Landers
Van Buren, Martin: **9** president
  former occupation: **6** lawyer
  home: **7** New York **10** Kinderhook
  opponent: **5** White **7** Webster **8** Harrison
  V.P.: **7** Johnson
  wife: **6** Hannah
Vance: **5** Cyrus, Dazzy, Philo **6** Colvig, Palmer, Vivian **7** Packard
Vance AFB, home of: **4** Enid, Okla.
Vance, Dazzy: **6** Dodger **7** pitcher
Van Cleef: **3** Lee
Vancouver: **4** city, isle, peak, port, town **5** mount **6** George, island **8** mountain
  locale: **6** Canada **10** Washington
  newspaper: **3** Sun **8** Province
  pro team: **7** Canucks
Vancouver, George: **7** British **8** explorer
vandal: **3** Hun **5** rowdy, thief **6** looter, pirate **7** brigand, defacer, hoodlum, invader, ravager **8** pillager **9** barbarian, despoiler, destroyer, plunderer
vandalism: **4** evil, harm **5** prank **6** damage **7** knavery, roguery, trouble **8** mischief, sabotage **9** high jinks, rascality, treachery **10** demolition, dirty trick, impishness, misconduct, wrongdoing
vandalize: **3** mar **4** harm **5** trash, wreck **6** damage, deface **7** despoil **8** sabotage
Van Damme: **10** Jean-Claude
Van de __ generator: **6** Graaff
Vandenberg AFB, city near: **6** Lompoc
van der __ forces: **5** Waals
Van Der Beek: **5** James
Vanderbilt: **3** Amy **6** Gloria **9** Cornelius
  athletes: **10** Commodores
  conference: **3** SEC
  locale: **9** Nashville, Tennessee
Vanderbilt, Gloria: **8** designer
  logo: **4** swan
  spouse: Sidney Lumet
Vander Meer: **6** hurler, Johnny **7** pitcher
van der Meer, Simon: **5** Dutch **8** Nobelist **9** physicist
Van der Post, Laurens: **6** author, writer **12** South African
  work: The Dark Eye in Africa
    A Far-Off Place
    The Heart of the Hunter
    The Lost World of the Kalahari
    Venture to the Interior
Vander Pyl: **4** Jean
__ van der Rohe: **4** Mies
van der Waals, Johannes: **5** Dutch **8** Nobelist **9** physicist
Van Devere, Trish: **5** actor **7** actress
  spouse: George C. Scott
van de Wetering, Janwillem: **5** Dutch **6** author, writer
  work: The Blond Baboon
    The Japanese Corpse
    The Mind Murders
    Outsider in Amsterdam
    Tumbleweed
Van Diemen's Land today: **8** Tasmania
Van Dien: **6** Caspar
Van Dine, S.S.: **5** alias
Van Doren: **4** Carl, Mark **5** Mamie **7** Charles
Van Doren, Mark: **4** poet
Vandross, Luther
  song: The Best Things in Life... (1992)
    Don't Want to Be a Fool (1991)
    Endless Love (1994)
    Here and Now (1990)
    Power of Love/Love Power (1991)
Vandura: **3** GMC, van
Van Duyn, Mona: **4** poet
van Dyck, Anthony: **6** artist **7** painter
  home: **8** Flanders
Vandyke __: **5** beard, brown **6** collar
Van Dyke: **2** W.S. **4** Dick **5** Jerry, Leroy, Parks
Van Dyke, Dick: **5** actor
  film: Bye Bye Birdie (1963)
    Cold Turkey (1971)
    Divorce American Style (1967)
    Mary Poppins (1964)
  TV: Diagnosis Murder, The Dick Van Dyke Show
Van Dyken: **3** Amy
Vandyke site: **4** chin
vane
  direction: **4** east, west **5** north, south
  part: **4** cock **5** arrow **7** rooster
  starter: **7** weather
  support: **6** cupola
  turner: **4** wind
__ vane: **4** wind **7** weather
Vane, John: **8** Nobelist
Vänern: **4** lake
  locale: **6** Europe, Sweden
Vanessa: **5** Angel **6** Marcil **8** Huxtable, Redgrave, Williams
  sister: **4** Lynn
Vanessa composer: **6** Barber
van Eyck, Jan: **6** artist **7** painter
  homeland: **8** Flanders
Van Fleet: **2** Jo
vang: **4** rope
Vangelis
  homeland: Greece
  song: Chariots of Fire (1982)
Van Gogh in __: **5** Arles
van Gogh, Vincent: **6** artist **7** painter
  brother: **4** Theo
  homeland: **7** Holland
  locale: **5** Arles
  medium: **3** oil
  painting: **6** Irises **10** Sunflowers
vanguard: **4** head **5** front, scout **7** new wave **9** forefront, precursor **10** avant-garde
Van Halen: **4** Alex **5** Eddie
  members: **4** Roth **5** Hagar **7** Anthony
  song: Dance the Night Away (1979)
    Finish What Ya Started (1988)
    I'll Wait (1984)
    Jump (1984)
    Panama (1984)
    When It's Love (1988)
    Why Can't This Be Love (1986)
Van Heusen, James: **8** composer
  collaborator: **4** Cahn
  song: All the Way
    Call Me Irresponsible
    High Hopes
    Love and Marriage
    Moonlight Becomes You
    My Kind of Town
    Personality
    Pocketful of Miracles
    The Road to Morocco
    The Second Time Around
    Swinging on a Star
    The Tender Trap
    Thoroughly Modern Millie
vanilla: **4** bean, mild **5** plain, plant **6** flavor, flower **7** prosaic **8** ice cream, mediocre, ordinary, standard **9** prosaical, tasteless **10** lackluster
  alternative: **5** lemon, mocha, peach **6** banana, coffee, Jamoca, toffee **7** caramel, coconut **8** cinnamon, hazelnut **9** bubblegum, chocolate, pineapple, pistachio, raspberry, rocky road, rum raisin **10** blackberry, cheesecake, Neapolitan, peppermint, strawberry
vanilla __: **4** bean, leaf **5** plant **7** extract
__ vanilla: **4** wild **5** plain
Vanilla __: **3** Ice, Sky **5** Fudge
vanilla bean: **5** spice **6** legume
Vanilla Fudge song: You Keep Me Hangin' On (1968)
Vanilla Ice
  song: Ice Ice Baby (1990)
    Play That Funky Music (1990)
vanilla-like bean: **5** tonka
Vanilla Sky (2001 film)
  cast: Tom Cruise, Penélope Cruz, Cameron Diaz, Kurt Russell
  director: Cameron Crowe
__ Vanilli: **5** Milli
vanish: **2** go **3** die **4** fade, lift, melt **5** leave **6** die out, escape, go away, perish **7** abscond **8** dissolve, evanesce, fade away, vaporize **9** disappear, dissipate, evaporate
  make ~: **6** dispel
vanish __ thin air: **4** into
vanished: **4** gone, lost **6** absent, bygone **7** extinct, missing **9** elsewhere
Vanished author: Danielle Steel
Vanished Diamond, The author: Verne
__ Vanishes, The: **4** Lady
vanishing: **3** off **7** trivial **9** momentary
  sound: **4** poof
vanishing __: **5** cream, point
Vanishing Prairie, The (1954 film)
  director: James Algar
Vanishing Virginian, The (1942 film)
  cast: Spring Byington, Kathryn Grayson, Frank Morgan
vanity: **3** ego **4** airs, show **5** pride **6** egoism, hubris, hybris **7** conceit, egotism, ego trip, hauteur **8** self-love, smugness **9** arrogance, vainglory **10** narcissism, pretension
  verbalize ~: **4** brag, crow **5** boast **6** flaunt, parade **7** lay it on, show off, talk big **10** grandstand
vanity __: **3** bag, box **4** case **5** plate, press **9** publisher
Vanity Fair
  author: William Makepeace Thackeray
  character: **4** Pitt, Smee, Wirt **5** Becky, Sharp **6** Amelia, Dobbin, George, Rawdon, Sedley, Steyne **7** Crawley, Osborne, William
Vanity Fare song: Hitchin' a Ride (1970)
van Leeuwenhoek: **5** Anton
Van Lingle: **5** Mungo
Van Lustbader: **4** Eric
Vanna: **4** host **5** White
  boss: **4** Merv
  cohost: **3** Pat
  turnover: **3** an a, an e, an i, an o
Vannelli, Gino
  song: I Just Wanna Stop (1978)
    Living Inside Myself (1981)
Vannes: **4** city, town
  locale: **6** France
Van Nuys: **4** city, town
  locale: **10** California
  town near ~: **6** Encino
Vanocur: **6** Sander
Van Patten: **4** Dick, Nels **5** Joyce
Van Peebles: **5** Mario **6** Melvin
vanquish: **3** zap **4** beat, best, lick, rout, sink, slay **5** break, crush, quell, repel,

smash, worst **6** defeat, humble, reduce, subdue, wallop **7** conquer, put down, repress, subvert, trample, triumph **8** overcome, overturn, surmount **9** checkmate, overpower, overthrow, overwhelm, subjugate
Vanquish alternative: **3** APF **4** Cope **5** Advil, Aleve, Bayer **6** Anacin, Datril, Motrin **7** Ecotrin, Tylenol **8** Bufferin, Excedrin, St. Joseph **9** Ascriptin
vanquisher: **6** victor, winner **9** conqueror
vanquishment: **6** defeat **7** beating, debacle, triumph **8** conquest
Van Sant, Gus: **8** director
film: Drugstore Cowboy (1989)
Finding Forrester (2000)
Good Will Hunting (1997)
My Own Private Idaho (1991)
To Die For (1995)
Van Shelton: **5** Ricky
Van Slyke: **4** Andy **5** Helen
Vantaa: **4** city, town
locale: **7** Finland
vantage point: **5** light, perch, venue **8** landmark, position
van't Hoff, Jacobus: **5** Dutch **7** chemist **8** Nobelist
van Tilburg Clark: **6** Walter
Vanua __: **4** Levu
Vanuatu: **4** isls. **5** isles **6** nation **7** islands
capital: **8** Port-Vila
formerly: **4** N. Heb.
volcano: **4** Gaua **5** Yasur **6** Ambrym, Lopevi
Van Valkenburgh: **7** Deborah
Vanves: **4** city, town
locale: **6** France
van Vleck, John: **8** Nobelist **9** physicist
Vanwarmer, Randy song: Just When I Needed You Most (1979)
Van Winkle: **3** Rip
emulate ~: **3** nap **5** sleep
__ Vanya: **5** Uncle
Vanya in English: **6** Johnny
Vanya on 42nd Street (1994 film)
cast: Phoebe Brand, George Gaynes, Julianne Moore, Wallace Shawn
director: Louis Malle
Van Zant: **6** Ronnie
Vanzetti colleague: **5** Sacco
vapid: **4** arid, blah, drab, dull, flat, limp, mild, tame, weak **5** bland, corny, empty, hokey, inane, passé, prosy, stale, trite **6** barren, boring, common, jejune, old hat, vacant **7** clichéd, fatuous, humdrum, insipid, mundane, prosaic, puerile, tedious, vacuous **8** bromidic, lifeless, outdated, outmoded, tiresome, zestless **9** colorless, driveling, hackneyed, pointless, prosaical, tasteless, wearisome **10** dullsville, flavorless, lackluster, spiritless, uninspired, unoriginal, wishy-washy
vapor: **3** dew, fog, gas **4** fume, haze, mist, smog **5** fumes, miasm, smoke, steam **6** breath, miasma **8** dampness, moisture **9** effluvium, sogginess **10** exhalation
assimilate ~: **6** adsorb
combining form: **3** atm- **4** atmo-, mano- **5** atmid- **6** atmido-
ender: **4** ware
mine ~: **4** damp
vapor __: **4** lock **5** trail **7** barrier, tension
__ vapor: **5** water
vaporize: **6** aerify, finish, gasify, vanish **7** distill **8** evanesce **9** disappear
vaporizer: **4** mist **5** spray **6** shower, spritz, squirt **7** aerosol **8** atomizer, droplets **9** sprinkler **10** sprinkling
__-vapor lamp: **6** sodium **7** mercury
vaporous: **4** fumy **5** gassy, misty, smoky **6** asteam **8** volatile
VapoRub maker: **5** Vicks
__ Vaporum: **4** Mare
vaquero: **6** cowboy, gaucho **7** cowpoke **8** wrangler
gear: **4** bola **5** reata
var.: **4** misc.
Varanasi today: **7** Benares
Vardalos: **3** Nia
Vardar: **5** river
locale: **6** Greece **9** Macedonia
__ Varden trout: **5** Dolly
Vardon Trophy awarder: **3** PGA
Varens: **5** Adele
Varèse, Edgard: **6** French **8** composer
__ Vargas Llosa: **5** Mario
vargueno: **4** desk
variable: **4** iffy **5** fluid **6** fickle, fitful, myriad, patchy, uneven **7** erratic, mutable, protean, wayward **8** changing, floating, shifting, slippery, ticklish, unstable, unsteady, volatile, wavering **9** irregular, mercurial, parameter, spasmodic, uncertain, unsettled, vagarious **10** capricious, changeable, inconstant
star: **4** Mira, nova
variable __: **4** cost, life, star **5** pitch **6** region **7** annuity
variable-__ mortgage: **4** rate
__ variable: **4** free, Mira, real **5** bound **6** random **7** Cepheid, cluster, complex
variable-interest loan: **3** ARM
variance: **5** clash **6** breach, change, permit, rancor, strife, switch **7** discord, dispute, dissent **8** argument, conflict, disunity, division, flip-flop **9** about-face, departure, deviation, disaccord, diversity **10** alteration, difference, dissension, dissidence, divergence
at ~: **7** unalike **9** different, disparate, dissonant **10** discrepant
variant: **5** other **6** byform, unlike **7** deviant, diverse, spinoff, unalike, version **8** discrete, distinct, modified, separate **9** different, differing, divergent, exception
variation: **5** range, shade, shift, twist **6** change **8** contrast, mutation **9** departure, deviation, disparity, diversion, diversity, exception, gradation **10** aberration, adaptation, alteration, difference, digression, divergence, inequality, inflection, innovation
cause of hereditary ~: **6** allele
color ~: **3** hue **4** tint, tone **5** blend, shade, tinct, tinge
molecular ~: **6** isomer
rug color ~: **6** abrash
__ variation: **3** bud **4** free, grid
__ Variations: **6** Enigma
varicolored: **4** pied **6** motley **7** brindle, dappled, mottled, piebald **8** brindled, speckled **9** multihued **10** variegated
flower: **4** glad, rose **5** canna, pansy, phlox, stock, viola **6** azalea, dahlia, oxalis, zinnia **7** anemone, comfrey, lobelia, petunia, verbena **8** clematis, gladiola, gloxinia, hibiscus, rain lily, sweet pea **9** carnation, cineraria, fairy lily, gladiolus, impatiens, portulaca, pyrethrum **10** floribunda, frangipani, snapdragon, zephyr lily
varied: **3** odd **4** many, mixt **5** mixed **6** divers, motley, sundry **7** diverse, unalike **8** assorted, discrete, manifold, multiple, separate **9** different, disparate
varied(abbr.): **4** misc.
variegated: **4** pied **6** dapple, motley **7** dappled, diverse **8** brindled, speckled **9** checkered, different
stone: **5** agate
variegation: **5** prism **7** rainbow
variety: **3** ilk, mix **4** form, kind, make, sort, type **5** array, brand, breed, class, combo, genre, genus, grade, order, range, stock **6** change, kidney, manner, medley, strain, stripe **7** mélange, mixture, pattern, quality, species **8** category, mishmash, mixed bag, quantity, specimen **9** diversity, potpourri **10** assortment, collection, cumulation, difference, divergency, miscellany
variety __: **4** meat, show **5** store
__-variety: **6** garden
variety show segment: **3** act **4** skit
Varig stop: **3** Rio
various: **3** odd **4** many, mixt **5** mixed **6** divers, legion, motley, sundry, unlike **7** certain, diverse, several, unalike **8** assorted, discrete, distinct, manifold, multiple, numerous, separate **9** different, disparate, divergent **10** dissimilar, individual
at ~ times: **6** cyclic **8** cyclical, frequent, periodic, repeated, seasonal, sporadic **9** recurrent, recurring, spasmodic **10** occasional
combining form: **5** parti-, party- **6** poecil-, poikil- **7** poecilo-, poikilo-
varlet: **3** cad **5** knave **9** reprobate, scoundrel
varmint: **5** beast, rogue **6** animal, rascal **9** scoundrel
Varmus, Harold: **8** Nobelist
Varna: **4** city, port, town
locale: **8** Bulgaria
Varner: **4** Eula
Varney, Jim persona: **6** Ernest **7** Worrell
varnish: **4** coat, gild **5** adorn, cover, glaze, gloss, japan, paint, stain **6** enamel, finish, luster, polish, smooth **7** coating, encrust, incrust, lacquer, shellac **8** decorate, palliate, shellack **9** embellish
apply, as ~: **5** apply, lay on
ingredient: **3** lac **5** elemi, resin, rosin
oil: **4** tung
resin: **5** anime, copal, damar **6** dammar
__ varnish: **3** oil **4** nail, spar **6** desert, spirit **7** natural
Varrick: **7** Charley
Varsi: **5** Diane
varsity: **4** team **5** A-team
award: **6** letter
__ varsity: **6** junior, senior
Varsity __, The: **4** Drag
Varsity Show (1937 film)
cast: Priscilla Lane, Dick Powell, Fred Waring
vary: **3** run **4** yo-yo **5** alter, range, shift, swing, waver **6** assort, change, depart, differ, modify, mutate, swerve **7** deviate, digress, dissent, diverge, inflect, qualify **8** contrast, disagree, displace, modulate, separate **9** alternate, change off, diversify, fluctuate, hem and haw, oscillate, permutate, take turns, transform
__ Vary: **7** Karlovy
varying: **6** patchy **7** diverse, mutable, unequal, variant
Vasco: **6** da Gama
Vasco __ de Balboa: **5** Núñez
vascular __: **3** ray **5** plant **6** bundle, tissue
vascular channel: **4** vein
vase: **3** jar, urn **6** bowpot, holder **8** boughpot **9** container **10** jardiniere, receptacle
occupant: **3** bud, mum **4** posy **7** bouquet, nosegay
Roman ~ stone: **5** murra **6** murrha
__ vase: **4** Ming **7** stirrup
__ Vashem: **3** Yad
Vasily: **7** Rozanov, Smyslov **8** Aksyonov **9** Kandinsky, Zhukovsky
in English: **5** Basil
see also Russian
Vaslav: **8** Nijinsky
vassal: **4** leud, serf **5** liege, slave **7** subject, villein
of a ~: **6** feudal
place: **4** fief **5** manor
shogun ~: **6** daimio, daimyo
vassalage: **7** slavery **9** captivity, servitude
Vassar: **6** school **7** college
most ~ grads: **5** women
vast: **3** big **4** huge, tidy, wide **5** ample, broad, enorm, giant, great, jumbo, large **6** cosmic, gaping, mighty, untold **7** endless, eternal, hulking, immense, mammoth, massive, sizable, titanic **8** colossal, cosmical, detailed, enormous, expanded, far-flung, gigantic, infinite, king-size, oversize, sizeable, spacious, sweeping, towering, whapping, whopping **9** boundless, capacious, cavernous, expansive, extensive, Herculean, humongous, limitless, monstrous, overlarge, prolonged, spread-out, unbounded, unlimited, very large **10** fathomless, gargantuan, large-scale, monumental, prodigious, staggering, stupendous, tremendous, unknowable, unnumbered, voluminous, widespread
amount: **3** sea **4** lots, slew, tons **5** array, ocean
holdings: **5** realm **6** empire **7** kingdom **8** dominion **9** territory
vastly: **3** far **4** a lot, lots, many, much, tons, very **5** amply, loads, no end, quite, scads, truly **6** a bunch, deeply, highly, hugely, plenty, rather, really **7** acutely, aplenty, greatly, largely, notably **8** famously, markedly, very many, very much **9** copiously, decidedly, extremely, glaringly, immensely, in a big way, intensely, like crazy, supremely **10** abundantly, enormously, especially, incredibly, profoundly, remarkably, strikingly, thoroughly, uncommonly
vastness: **4** room, size **7** breadth **8** enormity **9** amplitude, immensity, largeness, magnitude **10** infinitude
symbol of ~: **3** sea **5** ocean
vat: **3** tub, tun **4** cask, keir, kier, tank **6** barrel, kettle, vessel **7** caldron, cistern **8** cauldron **9** container **10** receptacle
worker: **4** dyer
__ Vat: **6** Angkor
vat-dye ingredient: **6** isatin
vatic: **8** Delphian, divining, oracular **9** prophetic **10** portending
Vatican City
head: **4** pope **7** pontiff **10** Holy Father
money: **4** lira, lire
name: **3** Leo **4** John, Paul, Pius **5** Urban **6** Adrian, Sixtus, Victor **7** Clement, Gregory, Stephen **8** Benedict, Boniface, Innocent, John Paul **9** Alexander, Celestine
neighbor: **4** Rome **5** Italy
of ~: **5** papal
ruling body: **5** curia
staffer: **6** legate
treasure: **5** Pietà
wear: **5** orale
vaticinal: **8** Delphian, oracular, sibyllic **9** prescient, prophetic **10** prognostic
vaticinate: **7** predict, presage **8** foreshow, prophesy

vaticinator: **4** seer **5** augur, sibyl **6** medium, oracle **7** diviner, palmist, prophet, psychic **9** Cassandra, predictor, visionary **10** forecaster, foreteller, mind reader, palm reader, soothsayer
VAT, part of: **3** tax **5** added, value
Vättern: **4** lake
vaudeville: **4** show **7** burlesk **9** bawdy show, burlesque **10** lampoonery
routine: **3** act **4** olio, skit, solo
show: **4** perf. **5** revue **6** review
vaudevillian: **5** comic **6** dancer, hoofer
prop: **4** cane **8** straw hat
Vaughan: **4** Arky, city, town **5** Billy, Sarah
locale: **6** Canada **7** Ontario
Vaughan, Arky: **6** Pirate **9** shortstop
Vaughan, Henry: **4** poet
Vaughan, Sarah
nickname: **5** Sassy **9** Divine One
song: Broken-Hearted Melody (1959)
C'est La Vie (1955)
Make Yourself Comfortable (1954)
Mr. Wonderful (1956)
Whatever Lola Wants (1955)
Vaughan Williams, Ralph: **7** British **8** composer
Vaughn: **5** Billy, Hippo, Vince **6** Monroe, Robert
Vaughn, Robert: **5** actor
film: The Bridge at Remagen (1969)
Bullitt (1968)
The Magnificent Seven (1960)
The Mind of Mr. Soames (1970)
The Towering Inferno (1974)
role: **4** Solo **8** Napoleon
TV: The Man From U.N.C.L.E.
Vaughn, Vince: **5** actor
film: The Cell (2000)
Clay Pigeons (1998)
A Cool, Dry Place (1999)
Domestic Disturbance (2001)
Made (2001)
Return to Paradise (1998)
vault: **3** pit **4** arch, dome, jump, leap, room, safe, soar, span, till, tomb **5** bound, clear, crypt, mount, store **6** bounce, cavern, hurdle, prance, spring **7** dungeon, lockbox **8** catacomb, jump over, leapfrog, overleap, surmount, treasury **9** negotiate, strongbox **10** depository, repository
architectural ~ feature: **5** groin
cracker: **4** yegg **5** thief **7** burglar
of heaven: **3** sky **8** empyrean
rib: **5** ogive **6** lierne
__ vault: **3** fan, rib **4** pole **5** coved, wagon, Welsh **6** corbel, cradle, ribbed, tunnel
vaulted alcove: **4** apse **6** recess
vaulter: **7** acrobat, gymnast, tumbler **9** aerialist
vaulting __: **5** horse
vaunt: **4** brag, crow **5** boast, pride **6** parade **7** big talk, boast of, talk big **8** flourish **9** brag about, crow about
vav: **6** Hebrew, letter
predecessor: **2** he **3** heh
successor: **5** zayin
Va-va-__!: **4** voom
vaw: **6** Hebrew, letter
predecessor: **2** he **3** heh
successor: **5** zayin
Vaya con __: **4** Dios
vb.
form: **3** inf. **5** infin.
modifier: **3** adv.
tense: **3** fut. **4** pres., pret. **6** imperf.
type: **3** int., irr. **4** intr. **5** irreg., trans.
vbs., like some: **5** irreg.
VCR: **3** VHS **4** Beta **7** Betamax
accessory: **3** mic
button: **3** fwd., rec, rew **4** play, stop **5** eject, pause, reset
feature: **5** timer
function: **5** erase **6** delete
input: **4** tape **9** videotape
maker: **3** JVC, RCA **5** Sanyo **9** Panasonic
need: **2** TV **5** TV set **6** remote **10** television
part: **5** video **8** cassette, recorder
place for a ~: **3** den **6** TV room
sound adjuster: **3** AVC
speed setting: **3** SLP
__ V. Debs: **6** Eugene
VDT: **6** screen **8** terminal
V-E __: **3** Day
V8 juice: **4** beet **6** carrot, celery, tomato **7** lettuce, parsley, spinach **10** watercress
V-8 unit: **3** cyl. **8** cylinder
veal: **4** meat **6** course, entree
in French: **4** veau
serving: **4** chop **6** cutlet **7** piccata
source: **4** calf
__ Vecchio: **5** Ponte
vector __: **3** sum **5** field, space **7** product
__ vector: **3** row **4** line, unit, zero **6** column, radius **7** sliding
Vectora: **4** font **8** typeface
Vector author: Robin Cook
Vectra: **3** car **4** auto, Opel **10** automobile
Ved: **5** Mehta
__-Veda: **3** Rig **7** Atharva
Veda believer: **5** Hindu **6** Hindoo
Veda language: **3** Skr., Skt. **4** Skrt. **8** Sanskrit
V-E Day
conflict: **4** WWII
month: **3** May
Vedder: **5** Eddie
Vedic
god: **4** Agni, Kama, Siva, Soma, Yama **5** Indra, Shiva, Surya **6** Brahma, Varuna, Vishnu **7** Ganesha, Hanuman, Krishna
goddess: **4** Devi, Kali, Usha **5** Durga, Ushas **7** Lakshmi, Parvati **9** Sarasvati
Vee, Bobby
song: Come Back When You Grow Up (1967)
Devil or Angel (1960)
The Night Has a Thousand Eyes (1962)
Rubber Ball (1960)
Run to Him (1961)
Take Good Care of My Baby (1961)
Veeck: **4** Bill, Mike
veejay
cousin: **4** host **5** emcee
employer: **3** MTV
veep: **4** exec **9** number two
boss: **4** prex, prez **5** prexy
veer: **3** yaw, zag, zig **4** bend, lean, skew, skid, slew, slue, tack, turn **5** avert, curve, dodge, drift, pivot, shift, slant, slide, swing, twist, wheel **6** careen, change, divert, slough, swerve, switch, swivel, wander **7** deflect, deviate **8** angle off, sheer off, sideslip **9** turn aside
veering: **5** dodge, shift, swing **6** change, swerve, switch **8** maneuver, movement, straying, variance **9** avoidance, departure, deviation, diversion, variation **10** aberration, alteration, deflection, digression, divergence, separation
veery: **4** bird **6** thrush
vee starter: **3** jay
veg: **3** bum **4** laze **5** idler **6** loafer **7** goof-off, slacker **8** indolent, sluggard **9** do nothing, goldbrick, lazybones **10** ne'er-do-well
Vega: **3** car **4** auto, star **5** Chevy **7** Suzanne **9** Chevrolet **10** automobile
constellation: **4** Lyra
Vega$ (ABC drama)
cast: Bart Braverman (Binzer)
Tony Curtis (Philip Roth)
Robert Urich (Dan Tanna)
Vega, Lope de: **4** poet **7** Spanish **10** playwright
vegan taboo: **4** meat
Vegas
action: **3** bet **4** ante, play **5** wager
alternative: **4** Reno **5** Tahoe
area: **5** strip
cube: **3** die
cubes: **4** dice
game: **4** faro, keno **5** craps, poker, slots **8** baccarat, roulette **9** blackjack, twenty-one
headliner: **4** Anka **6** Newton
lighting: **4** neon
natural: **5** seven **6** eleven
posting: **4** odds
worker: **6** dealer **7** pit boss **8** croupier
see also Las Vegas
__ Vegas: **3** Las
vegetable: **3** cos, pea, yam **4** bean, beet, Bibb, cole, corn, cuke, herb, kail, kale, leek, lime, ocra, okra, okro, pepo, root, soup, taro **5** chard, chive, cress, cubeb, gourd, green, olive, onion, plant, pulse, savoy, tater **6** carrot, celery, cushaw, edible, endive, greens, jicama, legume, lentil, peanut, pepper, pickle, potato, radish, russet, squash, tomato, turnip **7** arugula, avocado, bok choy, cabbage, cardoon, gherkin, haricot, lettuce, parsley, parsnip, produce, pumpkin, salsify, shallot, spinach, wax bean **8** broccoli, celeriac, chickpea, collards, cucumber, earthnut, eggplant, kohlrabi, scallion, soya bean, tamarind, zucchini **9** artichoke, asparagus, aubergine, broad bean, crookneck, green bean, groundnut, red pepper, sweetcorn, tomatillo **10** bell pepper, cos lettuce, kidney bean, red cabbage, runner bean, string bean, Swiss chard, watercress
cooker: **3** wok
Creole ~: **4** ocra, okra, okro
green ~: **3** pea **7** cabbage, lettuce
holder: **3** can, tin **7** package **9** container
Japanese ~: **3** udo
leafy ~: **4** kail, kale **5** chard **7** lettuce
matter: **4** pulp **9** cellulose
processor: **5** dicer, ricer **6** slicer
starchy ~: **3** yam **5** tuber **6** potato
tray item: **3** dip **5** olive **6** carrot, celery
vegetable __: **3** oil, wax **4** gold, pear, silk, wool **5** ivory **6** butter, cellar, marrow, oyster, sponge, tallow **7** kingdom, tanning
__ vegetable: **5** green
vegetable-oil ingredient: **5** olein **6** oleine
__, vegetable, or mineral: **6** animal
vegetables: **4** crop **5** yield **7** harvest, produce
big name in ~: **5** Libby **6** Libby's **8** Birdseye, Del Monte **10** Green Giant
like some ~: **5** green, leafy **7** verdant
old-style: **5** pease
prepare ~: **4** dice **5** cream, slice, steam **7** stir-fry
preserve ~: **3** can **6** freeze **9** freeze-dry
__-vegetarian: **3** ovo
vegetarian no-no: **4** meat
vegetate: **3** bud **4** grow, idle, loaf **5** bloom **6** sprout **7** blossom, burgeon, go to pot **8** bourgeon, go to seed, languish, pass time, stagnate **9** germinate
vegetation: **4** tree **5** flora, grass, plant, scrub **6** plants, shrubs **7** foliage, herbage **9** shrubbery
lacking ~: **3** dry **4** arid **6** barren, fallow **7** parched, sterile **8** deserted, desolate, infecund, lifeless **9** fruitless
rife with ~: **4** lush, rich, wild **5** dense, green **6** lavish **7** fertile, teeming, verdant **8** abundant, tropical **9** plentiful, succulent
study of ~: **6** botany
veggie
see vegetable
vehemence: **4** fury, heat, rage, zeal **5** anger, furor **6** frenzy **7** emotion, passion **8** strength, wildness **9** eagerness, fieriness, intensity **10** enthusiasm, impatience
with ~: **4** hard **5** hotly **6** loudly, wildly **7** angrily, like mad **8** fiercely **9** furiously, violently **10** vigorously
vehement: **3** hot, mad **4** ired, loud, warm **5** angry, eager, fiery, hyper, rabid **6** ablaze, ardent, fervid, fierce, hearty, heated, stormy, strong **7** burning, earnest, fervent, frantic, furious, intense, rampant, violent, zealous **8** emphatic, forceful, hopped up, inflamed **9** desperate, ferocious **10** hysterical, passionate, pronounced, vociferant, vociferous
vehicle: **3** bus, cab, car, LST, SUV, ute, van, way **4** auto, bike, boat, cart, dray, hack, jeep, limo, pram, raft, shay, ship, sled, tank, taxi, tool **5** agent, buggy, canoe, coach, craft, crate, liner, means, moped, organ, plane, train, trike, truck, U-Haul, wagon **6** agency, jalopy, medium, wheels **7** bicycle, carrier, channel, chariot, machine, phaeton **8** tricycle **9** expedient, implement, machinery, mechanism, transport **10** automobile, conveyance, instrument, motorcycle
all-purpose ~: **3** ute
British ~: **4** pram **5** lorry
city ~: **3** bus, cab **4** hack, taxi
combining form: **6** -mobile
commuter ~: **3** bus **5** train
construction-site ~: **5** dozer
defective ~: **3** dud **4** heap **5** crate, lemon, wreck **6** jalopy, junker **7** clunker **10** hunk of junk
emergency ~: **4** raft **9** ambulance
family ~: **3** car, van **4** auto **5** sedan
gravity-powered ~: **4** luge, pung, sled **6** sleigh **8** toboggan
horse-pulled ~: **4** cart, dray **5** buggy, wagon **8** carriage
kid's ~: **5** trike, wagon
moving ~: **3** van **5** truck, U-Haul
off-road ~: **3** ATV **4** jeep **6** Hummer, Humvee
one-wheeled ~: **6** barrow
recreational ~: **3** ATV **5** canoe
replacement ~: **6** loaner
rescue ~: **6** copter **7** chopper
sticker: **5** decal
suffix: **6** -mobile
two-wheeled ~: **4** cart **5** dolly **6** barrow **8** rickshaw
utility ~: **3** rig, van **4** jeep, semi **5** dolly, lorry, truck, U-Haul **6** pickup
vacation ~: **2** RV **6** camper **9** Winnebago **10** mobile home
WWII ~: **3** LCT, LST **4** jeep
__ vehicle: **5** motor **6** launch **7** off-road, reentry
vehicles: **7** traffic

Veidt: 6 Conrad
veil: 3 dim 4 film, hide, mask, pall, wrap 5 cache, cloak, cloud, couch, cover, drape, guise, purda, shade 6 enfold, infold, mantle, pardah, purdah, screen, shadow, shield, shroud 7 becloud, blanket, conceal, cover up, curtain, eclipse, enclose, envelop, inclose, obscure, pretext, protect, secrete, shut off, shut out, yashmac, yashmak 8 disguise, enshroud, mantilla, pretense 9 adumbrate, semblance 10 camouflage, keep secret
  fabric: 3 net 5 tulle 6 barege
___ veil: 6 bridal 7 humeral
veiled: 4 dark 6 covert, hidden, latent, occult, secret, unseen 7 furtive, private 8 hush-hush 9 innermost, unexposed 10 mysterious, undercover, underlying, under wraps, undetected
___ Veil Falls: 6 Bridal
Veil of ___: 4 Isis
___ Veil, The: 4 Blue 7 Seventh
vein: 3 rib, way 4 bent, duct, line, lode, mine, mode, mood, note, seam, tone, turn 5 humor, layer, metal, stria, style, tenor 6 manner, nature, pocket, spirit, strain, streak, stripe, temper, thread 7 fashion, stratum 8 attitude, vena cava 9 capillary, character, striation 10 complexion, mother lode
  combining form: 3 ven- 4 veni-, veno- 5 phleb- 6 phlebo-
  leaf ~: 3 rib
  material: 3 ore 4 gold, lode
  opposite: 6 artery
  place: 4 mine 8 gold mine
___ vein: 5 renal 6 portal 7 basilic, jugular
___-veined: 3 net 7 feather
vel.: 3 spd.
  measure: 3 MPH
velar: 3 low 5 gruff, husky 6 hoarse 7 grating, rasping, throaty 8 gravelly, guttural
Velázquez, Diego: 6 artist 7 painter
  homeland: 5 Spain
Velcro: 4 hook 8 fastener 10 attachment
  alternative: 4 band, cord, lace, rope, snap 5 strap 6 string, thread 8 fastener, shoelace
  emulate ~: 5 cling, stick 6 adhere, cleave
Velcro Fly (1986 song) artist: ZZ Top
veldt: 3 lea, sod 5 campo, field, green, llano 6 meadow, pampas 7 pasture, savanna 8 savannah 9 grassland
  beast: 3 gnu 4 lion 5 eland, hyena, oribi 6 hyaena, impala
Velez: 4 Lupe 6 Lauren
VelJohnson: 8 Reginald
velleity: 4 bent, will, wish 6 desire, liking 7 leaning, passion 8 affinity, penchant, soft spot, tendency 10 attraction, favoritism, partiality
vellicate: 3 pet 6 caress, stroke, tickle, tingle 8 convulse 9 stimulate, titillate
vellum: 5 paper
velocipede: 4 bike 5 trike 7 bicycle, vehicle 8 tricycle
  need: 4 gear, tire
velociraptor: 8 dinosaur
velocity: 3 spd. 4 pace, rate 5 haste, hurry, speed, tempo 8 alacrity, celerity, dispatch, movement, rapidity 9 fleetness, quickness, swiftness 10 expedition, promptness
  abbr.: 3 mph
  cockpit ~ reading: 3 IAS
  decrease the ~ of: 4 slow 5 brake 6 retard, slow up 8 slow down 10 decelerate
___ velocity: 5 areal, group, phase 6 escape, muzzle, radial, volume 7 angular, exhaust, orbital
velocity of ___: 5 money
velour: 6 fabric 8 material
velouté: 5 sauce
Veltman, Martinus: 8 Nobelist 9 physicist
velum: 6 palate
___ Velva: 4 Aqua
Velveeta maker: 5 Kraft
velvet: 5 panne 6 fabric 7 jobbery
  ender: 3 een 4 leaf
  hat: 5 toque
velvet ___: 3 ant 4 bean, bent 5 glove, plant 6 carpet
___ velvet: 3 cut 5 black 7 crushed
___ Velvet: 4 Blue 5 Black
velveteen: 6 fabric 8 material
Velvet Fog, The: 3 Mel 5 Torme
velvetlike fabric: 6 velour 7 mockado, velours 8 moquette
velvety: 4 soft 5 downy, furry, nappy, plush, silky 6 creamy, fleecy, flossy, fluffy, smooth 7 squishy 8 cushiony
  surface: 3 nap 4 down 6 fleece
Venable: 6 Evelyn
vena cava: 4 vein 9 capillary
  counterpart: 5 aorta
venal: 6 sordid 7 corrupt 8 bribable, hireling 9 mercenary, on the take, rapacious
venality: 4 vice 5 graft, greed 6 payoff, payola 7 bribery, jobbery 8 baseness 9 extortion, looseness, shadiness 10 corruption, dishonesty, immorality
___ Venatici: 5 Canes
vend: 4 hawk, sell 6 market, peddle, retail, unload 7 publish 9 dispose of, liquidate 10 auction off
vended: 3 sld. 4 sold
vendee: 5 buyer 6 emptor, patron 8 consumer, customer
vendetta: 4 feud 7 quarrel, rivalry
  undertake a ~: 6 avenge 7 revenge
vendible: 4 ware 7 salable 9 commodity 10 marketable
vendibles: 4 line 5 goods, wares
vending machine
  buy: 4 Coke, nosh, soda 5 candy, Pepsi, snack 6 coffee 8 candy bar 9 chocolate
  fooler: 4 slug
  part: 4 slot 7 plunger 10 coin return
vendition: 4 sale 7 auction
vendor: 5 crier 6 dealer, grocer, hawker, pedlar, pedler, seller, trader 7 peddler, pitcher 8 huckster, merchant
  area: 4 cart 5 booth, kiosk
  street ~ offering: 4 nosh, pita 5 frank, snack 6 hot dog 7 pretzel 8 ice cream
veneer: 4 coat, face, mask 5 cloak, cover, front, gloss, inlay, layer, paint, sheet, shell 6 enamel, facade, facing, finish, lamina 7 coating, encrust, incrust, lacquer, outside, overlay, surface 8 covering, exterior, laminate, pretense 9 semblance 10 appearance
  cover with ~: 4 coat 5 layer 7 overlay 8 laminate
venerable: 3 old 4 aged, sage, wise 5 hoary, noble 6 age-old, august, sacred, solemn 7 ancient, elderly, honored, revered, stately, vintage 8 esteemed, glorious 9 dignified, estimable, graybeard, honorable, respected 10 gray-haired
  one: 5 elder 6 senior 8 superior 9 matriarch, patriarch
Venerable ___: 4 Bede
venerate: 4 laud, love 5 adore, deify, honor 6 admire, esteem, hallow, revere 7 beatify, cherish, glorify, idolize, observe, respect, worship 8 look up to
venerated: 7 beloved 8 esteemed
veneration: 3 awe 5 honor, piety 6 esteem, regard 7 respect, worship 9 adoration, deference, reverence 10 admiration, estimation
  object of ~: 4 icon, idol, ikon 5 eikon
Venetian: 6 fabric 7 Italian
  see also Venice
Venetian ___: 3 red 4 ball, blue, door 5 cloth, glass, sumac 6 dentil, school, window
Venetian Alps city: 5 Udine
venetian blind
  component: 4 slat
  wood: 4 teak
___ Veneto: 3 Via
Venezia: 4 city, town
  locale: 5 Italy 6 Italia
  see also Venice
Venez. locale: 5 S. Amer.
Venezuela: 6 nation 7 country
  capital: 7 Caracas
  city: 6 Cumana 7 Cabimas, Caracas 8 La Guaira 9 Maracaibo
  dance: 6 joropo
  falls: 5 Angel
  gulf: 5 Paria 9 Maracaibo
  Indian: 5 Carib
  island near ~: 5 Aruba 6 Tobago 7 Curaçao 8 Trinidad
  lake: 9 Maracaibo
  money: 7 centimo
  neighbor: 6 Brazil, Guyana 8 Colombia
  org.: 3 OAS 4 OPEC
  river: 3 Aro 5 Apure
  writer: 5 Bello 8 Gallegos
  see also Spanish
vengeance: 5 spite 6 rancor 7 payback, redress, revenge 8 reprisal, requital 9 repayment, tit for tat
  obtain, as ~: 5 exact, force, wreak 6 demand, direct 7 call for, command, inflict
  take ~: 3 fix, get 6 avenge 7 get even 9 retaliate
  with a ~: 6 wildly 7 like mad 8 fiercely 9 furiously, violently
___ vengeance: 5 with a
Vengeance is ___...: 4 mine
vengeful: 4 mean 5 cruel, harsh, nasty 6 animal, brutal, fierce, savage, unkind, wanton 7 beastly, callous, hurtful, vicious 8 barbaric, fiendish, inhumane, pitiless, punitive, ruthless, sadistic, spiteful 9 cutthroat, ferocious, malicious, merciless, monstrous, rancorous, splenetic, truculent, unpitying 10 implacable, malevolent, unfriendly, unmerciful, vindictive
vengefulness: 5 spite 6 malice, rancor, spleen
veni: 5 I came, Latin
  follower: 4 vidi
venial: 9 allowable, excusable, tolerable 10 forgivable, pardonable
veniality: 3 sin 4 evil, vice 5 crime, error 7 misdeed, offense 8 atrocity, iniquity, trespass 9 blasphemy, evildoing, sacrilege, violation 10 immorality, infraction, misconduct, peccadillo, transgress, wickedness, wrongdoing
Venice: 4 city, gulf, port, town
  beach: 4 Lido
  city near ~: 5 Padua, Udine
  explorer: 4 Polo
  feature: 5 canal
  locale: 5 Italy
  money: 6 sequin
  old ruler of ~: 4 doge
  symbol of ~: 4 lion
  transporter: 5 poler 7 gondola
  villain of ~: 4 Iago
Venice of Japan, The: 5 Osaka
venire ___: 6 facias
veniremen: 4 jury 5 panel
venison: 4 deer, game, meat
  cut: 4 rump, side 5 flank, thigh 6 haunch
  like ~: 4 gamy 5 gamey
veni, vidi, ___: 4 vici
Venlo: 4 city, town
  locale: 7 Holland 11 Netherlands
Venn ___: 7 diagram
Venner: 5 Elsie
venom: 4 bile, gall, hate 5 anger, spite, toxin 6 enmity, grudge, hatred, malice, poison, rancor, spleen 7 cruelty, ill will 8 acrimony, bad blood 9 animosity, hostility, nastiness 10 bitterness, grumpiness, resentment, unkindness
  conveyor: 4 fang
  extract ~ from: 4 milk
  with ~: 6 acidly 10 spitefully
venomous: 4 mean 5 catty, snaky, toxic 6 aspish, deadly, fierce, ireful, lethal 7 baleful, baneful, hateful, hostile, vicious, waspish 8 spiteful, viperous, virulent 9 malicious, poisonous, rancorous, splenetic 10 malevolent, pernicious, vindictive
  snake: 3 asp 5 krait, mamba
Venora: 5 Diane
vent: 3 air, gap 4 duct, emit, exit, flue, hole, open, pipe, slit, snap, talk 5 drain, eject, empty, erupt, expel, issue, spout, state, utter, voice, wreak 6 air out, airway, crater, let out, louver, louvre, outgas, outlet, window 7 air duct, air hole, chimney, express, fissure, opening, orifice, pour out, release, relieve, unleash 8 aperture, blowhole, fumarole, proclaim, vocalize 9 cast forth, discharge, force upon, ventilate
  dermal ~: 4 pore 5 stoma 10 sweat gland
  fireplace ~: 4 flue, vent 6 airway 7 chimney 10 smokeshaft
  like a clogged dryer ~: 5 fuzzy, linty
  one's spleen: 4 boil, fume, rage, rant, rave, yell 5 erupt, steam, wrath 6 blow up, rail at, scream, seethe 7 explode, rampage, run riot, run wild 8 boil over, have a fit, outburst, run amuck 9 blow a fuse, fulminate, go berserk 10 hit the roof, kick up a row
  with frenzy: 5 wreak 7 unleash
vent ___: 4 pipe 6 window
___-vent: 5 vol-au
vented, not: 6 pent-up
ventilate: 3 air 6 aerate, air out 7 freshen 9 circulate
ventilated: 4 airy, open 5 windy 6 breezy
  poorly ~: 5 heavy, muggy, musty, stale, thick 6 stuffy, sultry 7 airless, clogged 8 stagnant, stifling 10 oppressive, sweltering
ventilation: 3 air 4 puff, vent, wind 5 draft 6 breeze, oxygen 10 exhalation
  channel: 4 duct, pipe
  system: 4 flue 6 airway
ventilator: 3 fan 6 blower 7 air-cool 9 propeller
venting: 5 vocal 8 emission, harangue
Ventnor: 3 ave. 6 avenue
vent one's ___: 6 spleen
ventral ___: 3 fin 4 root
ventre à ___: 5 terre
ventricle neighbor: 5 aorta 6 atrium
ventriloquist dummy's home: 5 trunk
Ventura: 3 Ace, car 4 auto 5 Jesse, Robin 7 Pontiac 10 automobile
Ventura Highway (1972 song) artist: America

Ventura, Robin sport: **8** baseball
venture: **3** bet, bid, job, try **4** dare, risk, shot, sink, spec, stab **5** assay, brave, essay, fling, foray, guess, put up, stake, wager **6** chance, effort, gamble, hazard, plunge, take on **7** attempt, daresay, presume, project, pursuit, surmise **8** activity, endeavor **9** adventure, speculate, take a risk, undertake, volunteer **10** enterprise, experiment, investment, pet project, take a flyer
a thought: **3** say **5** guess, opine **7** comment, suppose, surmise
ender: **4** some
(forth): **5** sally
joint ~: **4** co-op
like ~ capital investments: **5** dicey, risky **6** chancy, daring, unsafe **9** uncertain **10** precarious
speculative ~: **5** flier, flyer
unsuccessful ~: **3** dog, dud **4** bomb, bust, flop **5** lemon, loser **6** fiasco, fizzle **7** debacle, failure, washout **8** disaster
venture __: **7** capital
__ venture: **5** joint
Venture: **3** van **5** Chevy **9** Chevrolet
Ventures
song: Hawaii Five-O (1969) Walk-Don't Run (1960)
venturesome: **4** bold, game, rash **5** brave, gutsy, nervy, risky, stout **6** awless, daring, gritty, heroic, plucky, spunky, sturdy **7** aweless, defiant, doughty, gallant, staunch, valiant **8** fearless, heroical, intrepid, overbold, reckless, resolute, spirited, stalwart, unafraid, valorous **9** audacious, daredevil, dauntless, dreadless, foolhardy, undaunted, unfearful **10** courageous
one: **5** darer
Venture to the Interior author: Laurens Van der Post
Venturi, Ken: **6** golfer
milieu: **5** links **6** course
org.: **3** PGA
venturous: **5** brave **6** daring **8** reckless **9** foolhardy **10** courageous
venue: **4** site **5** locus, place, scene **6** ground, locale **7** setting **8** locality, location **9** nightclub
Venus: **3** dea, orb **6** beauty, planet, sphere **8** Williams
equivalent: **9** Aphrodite
father of ~: **7** Jupiter
part of ~ atmosphere: **4** neon
son of ~: **4** Amor, Eros **5** Cupid
where ~ was found: **4** Milo **5** Melos, Milos
Venus __: **6** de Milo, figure **7** flytrap
Venus Among the Fishes author: **5** O'Dell
Venus and Adonis painter: **6** Rubens
Venus artist: **4** Erté
Venus d'__: **5** Arles
Venus de Milo: **6** statue
lack: **4** arms
site: **6** Louvre
Venus flytrap: **5** plant **6** flower
feature: **5** hinge
Venusian: **2** ET **5** alien
Venus of __: **5** Melos
Venus of the Counting House author: Emile Zola
Venus of Urbino: **4** nude
Venus's-hair: **4** fern
Venus (song) artist: Bananarama, Frankie Avalon, Shocking Blue
Vep: **4** Irma
__ Ver.: **3** Com., Rev. **4** Auth.
__ vera: **4** aloe **5** cutis
Vera: **4** Lynn **5** Billy, Miles, Vague **6** Panova, Zorina **7** Caspary **8** Brittain
Vera __: **4** Cruz
Vera-__: **5** Ellen
veracious: **4** just, open, real, true **5** exact, frank, legit, right, valid **6** honest, square, trusty **7** correct, ethical, factual, genuine, up-front, upright **8** accurate, credible, like it is, reliable, straight, truthful, verified **9** righteous **10** aboveboard, dependable, forthright, on the level, scrupulous
veracity: **5** honor, right, truth **6** candor **7** honesty, probity **8** accuracy, like it is, openness **9** exactness, frankness, integrity, precision, rectitude, sincerity **10** exactitude, factuality, honestness
Veracruz: **4** city, port, town **5** state
ancient ~ Indian: **5** Olmec
capital of ~: **6** Jalapa
city: **4** Isla **5** Alamo, Clara, Lerdo, Oluta **6** Cabada, Fortín, Jalapa, La Poza, Pánuco, Perote, Sayula, Tuxpam, Tuxtla **7** Allende, Anáhuac, Córdoba, El Tejar, Mendoza, Nogales, Orizaba, Oteapan, Palmira, Tempoal **8** Acayucan, Alvarado, Carrillo, Catemaco, Coatepec, Huatusco, Jáltipan, Maltrata, Martínez, Misantla, Naranjos, Papantla, Poza Rica **9** Agua Dulce, Cerro Azul, Nanchital, Tantoyuca **10** Alto Lucero, Coatzintla, Las Choapas, Minatitlán, Tlapacoyan
locale: **6** Mexico
see also Spanish
Vera Cruz (1954 film)
cast: Gary Cooper, Denise Darcel, Burt Lancaster
Vera Cruz Indian, ancient: **5** Olmec
Vera-Ellen: **7** actress
film: The Kid From Brooklyn (1946) On the Town (1949) Three Little Words (1950) White Christmas (1954) Wonder Man (1945)
veranda: **5** lanai, porch **6** piazza **7** balcony
verb
ender: **3** ose
poetic ~: **3** ope
suffix: **3** -ate, -eth, -ify, -ize **4** -esce
tense: **3** fut. **4** past, pres. **6** future **7** perfect, present **8** preterit
type: **3** int., irr., reg. **7** regular **9** irregular **10** transitive
verb __: **6** phrase
__ verb: **4** main **6** finite **7** helping, linking, phrasal, two-word
verbal: **4** oral, said, told **5** parol, vocal **6** spoken, stated **7** lingual **8** narrated **9** expressed, unwritten, vocalized
attack: **3** rap **4** bash, belt, flak, lash, slam, slur **5** abuse, flack, salvo, smear **6** insult, outcry **7** barrage, potshot, slander **8** outburst, reproach **9** criticism **10** defamation
departure: **5** aside **10** digression
exchange: **4** quip, talk **6** banter **7** jesting, joshing, kidding, ribbing, teasing **8** chitchat, repartee **9** small talk, table talk
fanfare: **4** ta-da **5** ta-dah
fight: **4** spat **5** fight, set-to **6** debate **7** dispute, polemic, quarrel, rhubarb **8** argument, polemics, squabble **9** bickering, encounter **10** war of words
give a ~ account: **4** tell **6** recite
noun: **6** gerund
sigh: **4** alas
significance: **6** action
stumble: **2** er, uh, um
verbal __: **4** noun
verbalization: **6** speech **8** language **9** statement, utterance
verbalize: **3** say **4** talk **5** speak, state, utter, voice **6** mumble, murmur, phrase, relate **7** dictate, express, recount **8** set forth, vocalize **9** pronounce **10** articulate
verbalized: **4** oral **5** vocal
verbally: **5** aloud, parol **8** viva voce
fight ~: **5** argue, claim, plead **6** appeal, bicker, debate, dicker, haggle, oppose, reason **7** contend, dispute, dissent, protest, quarrel, quibble, wrangle **8** disagree, hash over, squabble **9** lock horns **10** controvert, deliberate
verbatim: **3** sic **5** exact **7** exactly, literal **8** directly **9** literally, precisely **10** accurately
repeat ~: **4** cite **5** quote **6** parrot, recite, repeat, retell **7** excerpt, extract
verbena: **5** plant **6** flower
tree: **4** teak
verbiage: **4** talk **7** diction, wording **8** parlance, phrasing, pleonasm **9** elocution, floridity, loquacity, prolixity, tautology, verbosity, wordiness **10** redundancy, vocabulary
verbose: **4** glib, long **5** gabby, talky, windy, wordy **6** prolix **7** diffuse, flowery, fustian, gushing, lengthy, tedious, unterse, voluble **8** inflated, involved, rambling, tortuous **9** bombastic, garrulous, overblown, ponderous, redundant, talkative **10** bigmouthed, discursive, long-winded, loquacious, palaverous, pleonastic, repetitive, rhetorical
verbosity: **4** wind **8** rhetoric, verbiage **9** garrulity, loquacity, wordiness
verboten: **4** tabu **5** taboo **6** banned **7** illegal, illicit **8** criminal, improper, outlawed, unlawful, wrongful **9** felonious, forbidden **10** prohibited
item: **4** nono, tabu **5** taboo
Verdana: **4** font **8** typeface
verdant: **4** lush **5** fresh, green, leafy, virid **6** floral, grassy **8** blooming, unwilted
relative: **3** pea **4** cyan, jade, sage **5** beryl, breen, olive, virid **6** myrtle, reseda **7** avocado, celadon, emerald **9** pistachio, turquoise **10** aquamarine, chartreuse
__ verde: **4** palo **5** chile, chili, terra **6** chilli
__ Verde: **4** Cape, Mesa
verdict: **6** answer, decree, guilty, ruling **7** finding, opinion **8** decision, judgment, sentence **10** conclusion, conviction, resolution
follower: **6** appeal
giver: **4** jury **5** juror, panel, peers **8** tribunal **9** veniremen
unjust ~: **5** frame **6** bum rap
Verdict, The (1982 film)
cast: James Mason, Paul Newman, Milo O'Shea, Charlotte Rampling, Jack Warden
director: Sidney Lumet
Verdi, Giuseppe: **7** Italian **8** composer
aria: **5** eri tu
baritone: **4** Iago
highlight: **4** aria
milieu: **5** opera
work: Aïda
Alzira
Araldo
Attila
Don Carlos
Ernani
Falstaff
Il Trovatore
La Forza del Destino
La Traviata
Luisa Miller
Macbeth
Nabucco
Oberto
Otello
Rigoletto
Un Ballo in Maschera
verdin: **4** bird
Verdon, Gwen: **6** dancer **7** actress
role: **4** Lola
spouse: Bob Fosse
Verdugo: **5** Elena
Verdun: **4** city, town **6** battle
fighter: **5** poilu
locale: **6** Canada, France, Québec
river: **4** Maas **5** Meuse
village near ~: **5** Ornes
see also French
verdure: **3** lea, ley **5** grass **6** meadow **7** foliage, herbage, pasture **8** greenery **9** grassland, greenness, pasturage
Vere, Aubrey Thomas De: **4** poet
Vereen: **3** Ben
verge: **3** eve, hem, lip, rim **4** abut, brim, edge, join, line, side, tend **5** brink, limit, skirt, touch **6** adjoin, border, bounds, fringe, limits, margin **7** extreme, incline, selvage **8** approach, boundary, come near, neighbor, selvedge, surround **9** extremity, juxtapose, perimeter, periphery, threshold **10** lean toward
on: **4** near, tend **5** touch
on the ~ of: **4** near **6** at hand, likely
upon: **4** meet, near **5** reach, verge **6** come at, gain on **7** advance **8** approach **9** catch up to, close in on **10** draw near to, move toward
Vergil: **4** poet **5** Roman
contemporary: **6** Horace
work: **6** Aeneid
Verhoeven, Paul: **8** director
film: Basic Instinct (1992) RoboCop (1987) Total Recall (1990)
veridical: **4** just, true **6** honest **7** correct
verifiable: **4** real, true **7** certain **8** tangible **10** historical, legitimate, undoubtful
verification: **4** test **5** audit, check, proof **8** acid test **9** collation
verified: **4** real, true **5** legit, valid **6** actual, proven **7** certain, factual, genuine **8** accurate, bona fide, definite, official, positive, truthful **9** authentic, confirmed, pertinent **10** conclusive, defendable, definitive, documented, legitimate, sanctioned, unarguable, unimagined
verify: **3** peg, try **4** test **5** audit, check, probe, prove, vouch **6** attest, hold up, settle, size up **7** bear out, certify, collate, confirm, eyeball, find out, stand up, support, sustain **8** check out, document, make sure, validate, vouch for **9** ascertain, check up on, determine, establish, recognize
verily: **4** amen **5** truly **6** indeed, it is so, really **8** in effect
old-style: **5** pardi, pardy **6** pardie, perdie
Verily!: **3** yea **4** amen
verisimilar: **4** true **6** liable, likely **8** apparent, credible, probable, rational **9** doubtless, inferable, plausible **10** believable, imaginable, presumable, prima facie, reasonable, supposable
verisimilitude: **4** show **7** realism, reality **8** likeness **9** semblance
veritable: **4** real, true **5** legit, right, valid **6** actual, kasher, kosher **7** factual, genuine **8** bona fide, verified **9** authentic, undoubted **10** unimagined

__ **vérité:** **5** video **6** cinéma
verity: **4** fact **5** troth, truth **6** gospel **7** reality **8** accuracy **9** actuality
Verizon
ancestor: **5** NYNEX
competitor: **3** MCI
employee: **5** wirer **8** operator
Verlaine, Paul: **4** poet **6** French
Vermeer, Jan: **6** artist **7** painter
contemporary: **5** Steen
homeland: **7** Holland **11** Netherlands
vermeil: **3** red **5** color
relative: **4** rose, ruby, rust, wine **5** brick, coral, grape, poppy, rusty, sandy **6** cerise, cherry, claret, garnet, maroon **7** carmine, crimson, fuchsia, magenta, pimento, scarlet, sultana **8** amaranth, cardinal, dubonnet, geranium, rubicund **9** carnation, cranberry, vermilion **10** strawberry
vermicelli: **5** pasta **7** noodles **9** spaghetti
alternative: **4** orzo, ziti **5** penne **6** noodle **7** lasagna, lasagne, pastina, ravioli **8** bucatini, couscous, farfalle, linguine, linguini, macaroni, rigatoni **9** agnolotti, angelhair, cavatelli, manicotti **10** cannelloni, fettuccini, tortellini
vermilion: **3** red **5** color
relative: **4** rose, ruby, rust, wine **5** brick, coral, grape, poppy, rusty, sandy **6** cerise, cherry, claret, garnet, maroon **7** carmine, crimson, fuchsia, magenta, pimento, scarlet, sultana, vermeil **8** amaranth, burgundy, cardinal, dubonnet, geranium, rubicund **9** carnation, cranberry **10** strawberry
__ **vermilion:** **7** Chinese
Vermillion sch.: **3** USD
vermin: **3** bug, rat **4** flea, scum **5** mouse **6** insect
Vermont: **5** state
capital: **10** Montpelier
city: **5** Barre **7** Rutland **10** Burlington, Montpelier
harvest: **3** sap
lake: **9** Champlain
mountains: **5** Green
neighbor: **6** Canada, Quebec **7** New York
product: **5** sirup, syrup
ski area: **5** Okemo, Stowe
state bird: **6** thrush
state butterfly: **7** monarch
state cold water fish: **10** brook trout
state insect: **8** honeybee
state mineral: **4** talc **6** garnet
state tree: **10** sugar maple
state warm water fish: **7** walleye
tree: **5** maple
vermouth: **4** wine **5** booze, drink, white **6** liquor **7** alcohol, potable **8** beverage, cocktail, libation
ingredient: **7** martini
vermouth __: **6** cassis
Verna: **5** Bloom
vernacular: **4** cant **5** argot, idiom, lingo, slang **6** jargon, patois, patter, speech, tongue, vulgar **7** dialect **8** jive talk, language, parlance **9** idiomatic **10** colloquial
vernal: **5** fresh, young **6** tender **8** juvenile, youthful **10** springlike
season: **6** spring
vernal __: **5** point **7** equinox
Verne: **5** Jules, Larry **6** Troyer
Verne, Jules: **6** author, French, writer
captain: **4** Nemo
work: 800 Leagues on the Amazon
Among the Cannibals
Around the World in Eighty Days
The Blockade Runners
Caesar Cascabel
The Castaways of the Flag
The Castle of the Carpathians
The Chase of the Golden Meteor
The Desert of Ice
The English at the North Pole
Facing the Flag
The Field of Ice
Five Weeks in a Balloon
A Floating City
From the Earth to the Moon
Giant Raft
The Green Ray
Hector Servadac
In Search of the Castaways
Invasion of the Sea
Journey to the Center of the Earth
Magellania
The Master of the World
Michael Strogoff
The Mighty Orinoco
The Mysterious Island
Off on a Comet
Paris in the Twentieth Century
Robur the Conqueror
A Tour of the Moon
Twenty Thousand Leagues...
The Underground City
The Vanished Diamond
A Voyage to the Center of the Earth
vernier __: **5** scale **6** engine **7** caliper, compass
Vernon: **4** city, Duke, John, town **5** Smith **6** Castle
locale: **6** Canada
Vero Beach: **4** city, town
locale: **7** Florida
Verona: **4** city, town
locale: **5** Italy
river: **5** Adige
Veronese: **5** Paolo
veronia: **5** plant **6** flower
Veronica: **4** Lake, pase **5** Hamel, saint **10** Cartwright
rival: **5** Betty
Veronica's Closet: **6** sitcom
dog: **5** Buddy
star: **5** Alley
Verrazano-__ Bridge: **7** Narrows
verruca: **4** wart
verrucose: **5** warty
vers __: **5** libre
__ **versa:** **4** vice
Versace: **6** Gianni
Versailles: **3** car **4** auto **7** Lincoln
attraction: **6** palace, palais
see also French
versant: **4** able, deft **5** adept, aware, crack, handy, privy **6** adroit, artful, expert, wise to **7** abreast, capable, knowing, learned, trained **8** familiar, informed, seasoned, skillful, talented **9** cognizant, competent, efficient, masterful, practiced, qualified **10** proficient
versatile: **4** able **5** handy **6** adroit, gifted, mobile **7** protean, skilled **8** flexible, talented **9** adaptable, all-around, many-sided **10** adjustable, all-purpose, changeable
transport: **3** ATV, ute
worker: **5** do-all **8** handyman
versatility: **4** sway **5** array, gamut, range, reach, scale, scope, sweep, width **6** extent, leeway, sphere **7** breadth, expanse, purview, variety **8** latitude, spectrum **9** diversity **10** assortment, parameters
verse: **3** lay, ode **4** epic, idyl, poem, rime, rune, song, text **5** canto, epode, haiku, idyll, lyric, poesy, psalm, rhyme, stave, stich **6** ballad, jingle, poetry, school, sonnet, stanza **7** couplet, passage, refrain **8** clerihew, doggerel, limerick, quatrain, rondelet
alternative: **5** prose
analyze ~: **4** scan
ancient Greek ~ form: **4** epos
chapter and ~: **6** detail
honorer in ~: **4** poet **5** odist
Japanese ~: **5** haiku
part: **4** line **5** stave, stich **6** stanza
quote chapter and ~: **4** list, tell **6** detail, relate, report **7** account, analyze, itemize, narrate, recount, specify **8** describe **9** elaborate, enumerate, expound on, make clear
reciter: **4** bard, poet **8** poetizer **9** sonneteer, versifier
short syllable, in ~: **4** mora
syllable: **4** foot, iamb **6** dactyl **7** spondee, trochee
title starter: **5** ode to
writer: **4** bard, poet **5** odist **6** author, rhymer **9** balladist
see also poet, poetry
__ **verse:** **4** free **5** blank, light **6** heroic, linked, memory **7** catalog, leonine, society
versed: **3** hep, hip **4** up on, wise **5** savvy **6** au fait, expert, posted, up to it, wise to, with it **7** abreast, knowing, learned, mindful, skilled, trained, tuned in **8** apprised, educated, familiar, informed, literate, polished, schooled, skillful, well-read **9** abreast of, au courant, cognizant, competent, in the know, plugged in, practiced, qualified **10** acquainted, proficient
become ~: **3** see **5** grasp, learn **6** absorb, master, pick up, soak up, take in **7** find out **8** discover **9** catch on to **10** apprentice, get down pat
be ~ in: **3** get **4** know **5** grasp, sense **6** fathom **7** realize **10** comprehend, understand
versifier: **4** bard, poet **5** rimer
versify: **4** rime **5** rhyme
version: **4** side, tale **5** model, story **6** report, sketch **7** account, edition, reading, summary, variant **9** chronicle, narrative, portrayal, rendering, rendition, rewording **10** adaptation, paraphrase
abbreviated ~: **4** mini **6** digest
first ~: **4** plan, plot **5** draft **6** design, layout, sketch **7** outline **9** blueprint
new ~: **6** change, update **7** redraft, rewrite **8** overhaul, revision **9** amendment, redaction **10** adjustment, alteration, correction, emendation
__ **Version:** **5** Douay **7** Revised
verso: **4** leaf, page **5** folio, recto, sheet **7** reverse
opposite: **5** recto
versus: **6** contra **7** against, athwart **8** opposing **9** counter to, opposed to **10** contrary to
__ **Versus the Volcano:** **3** Joe
vert: **5** color, green **6** French
vert.
not ~: **3** hor.
vertebra: **4** bone **5** spine **6** lumbar, sacrum **8** backbone
combining form: **7** spondyl- **8** spondylo-
head-supporting ~: **5** atlas
neighbor: **4** disc, disk
vertebral __: **5** canal **6** column
vertex: **3** cap, tip, top **4** acme, apex, head, node, peak **5** crest, crown, spire **6** apogee, corner, height, summit, tipoff, zenith **8** pinnacle
vertical: **5** erect, on end, plumb, sheer, steep **6** upward **7** upended, upright, upwards **8** baluster, straight **9** up-and-down **10** lengthways, lengthwise, straight-up
at sea: **5** apeak, apeek
be ~: **5** stand
face: **4** crag, hill **5** bluff, cliff **8** mountain **9** precipice
line: **5** y-axis
lineup: **4** heap, mass, pile **5** mound, stack
nearly ~: **5** erect, steep **8** towering
passageway: **3** rod **4** axis, beam, pole, post **5** pylon, shaft, stalk **6** column, pillar
post: **4** beam, jamb **5** jambe **8** doorpost **9** doorframe
vertical __: **4** file **5** angle, union **6** circle
vertically: **5** on end **7** upright **8** vertical
vertiginous: **5** dizzy, faint **7** rolling **8** gyrating, spinning, whirling
Vertigo (1958 film)
cast: Barbara Bel Geddes, Kim Novak, James Stewart
composer: **8** Herrmann
director: Alfred Hitchcock
Vertou: **4** city, town
locale: **6** France
verve: **2** go **3** pep, vim, zip **4** brio, dash, élan, fire, kick, life, snap, zeal, zest, zing **5** ardor, flair, gusto, moxie, oomph, punch, savor, spark, vigor **6** bounce, energy, esprit, fervor, pizazz, spirit **7** abandon, panache, pizzazz **8** flourish, vitality, vivacity **9** animation **10** enthusiasm, exuberance, liveliness
sans ~: **4** blah, drab, dull, flat **5** banal, bland, ho-hum, vapid **6** boring, jejune **7** humdrum, languid **8** lifeless **9** apathetic, lethargic, wearisome **10** dullsville, flavorless, lackluster, monotonous, pedestrian, spiritless
vervet: **6** monkey **7** primate
relative: **3** ape **4** saki, titi **5** chimp, drill, jocko, lemur, loris, magot, orang, potto, shrew **6** aye-aye, baboon, Bandar, galago, gelada, gibbon, grivet, guenon, howler, langur, macaco, rhesus, uakari **7** colobus, gorilla, guereza, hoolock, macaque, sapajou, siamang, tamarin, tarsier **8** bush baby, capuchin, mandrill, mangabey, marmoset, talapoin **9** orangutan **10** Barbary ape, chimpanzee, orangutang
very: **3** far, too **4** mere, most, much, oh so, such **5** amply, mucho, quite, right, truly, ultra **6** actual, adverb, damned, danged, darned, deeply, ever so, highly, hugely, rather, really, unduly, vastly **7** acutely, awfully, but good, greatly, largely, only too, rabidly **8** selfsame, terribly **9** certainly, decidedly, downright, extremely, seriously, supremely, unusually, zealously **10** absolutely, enormously, especially, incredibly, profoundly, remarkably, sure-enough, thoroughly, uncommonly
in French: **4** tres
in music: **5** assai, molto
in Spanish: **5** mucha, mucho
very __ frequency: **3** low **4** high
very __!, The: **4** idea
very __ yours: **5** truly
Very __ Array: **5** Large
Very __ for May: **4** Warm
very foolish fond old man, Shakespeare's: **4** Lear
Very funny!: **4** ha-ha **6** ha ha ha
very little brain, bear of: **4** Pooh
Very Private Eye, A author: Barbara Pym

Very Thought __, The: 5 of You
Very Warm for May: 7 musical
songwriter: 4 Kern 11 Hammerstein
Very well: 6 so be it
vesicle: 3 sac 4 cyst 5 bursa, pouch 7 blister
__ vesicle: 3 air 4 otic
Vesle
city on the ~: 5 Reims 6 Rheims
Vesoul: 4 city, town
locale: 6 France
vespa: 4 wasp
Vespasian: 5 Roman 6 Caesar
son of ~: 5 Titus
vesper __: 4 bell 5 mouse 7 sparrow
vespers: 4 hour 7 worship 8 evensong
preceder: 5 nones
vespertilian: 3 bat 6 mammal
vespiary: 4 hive, nest 6 apiary
animal: 4 wasp
Vespucci, Amerigo: 7 Italian 8 explorer
vessel: 3 ark, can, dau, dow, jar, jug, LCT, LST, mug, pan, pot, tub, urn, vat, wok 4 bark, boat, bowl, brig, dhow, dory, ewer, pail, ship, vase, yawl 5 barge, basin, canoe, craft, crock, cruet, ferry, flask, ketch, laker, liner, oiler, shell, skiff, sloop, stein, U-boat, umiak, yacht 6 barque, bateau, beaker, bireme, bottle, bucket, caique, dinghy, kettle, tanker, wherry 7 amphora, galleon, pitcher, rowboat, samovar, steamer, trireme, tumbler, utensil 8 crucible, decanter, sailboat, test tube 9 catamaran, container, freighter, hydrofoil, outrigger, tube. kayak 10 cruise ship, hydroplane, ice-breaker, ocean liner, receptacle
anatomical ~: 3 vas
Arab ~: 3 dau, dow 4 dhow
beaked ~: 5 cruet 6 beaker, carafe 7 alembic
blood ~: 4 vein 5 aorta 6 artery
combining form: 3 vas- 4 vaso- 5 angio-
cook's ~: 3 pan, pot, wok 6 kettle, teapot, vessel 7 dishpan, roaster, skillet 8 saucepan
dispatch ~: 5 aviso
doctor's ~: 5 ampul 6 ampule 7 ampoule
drinking ~: 3 cup, mug 5 flask, glass 6 goblet 7 tumbler
earthenware ~: 3 jug, pot 4 ewer 6 bottle, carafe
expensive ~: 5 yacht
glass ~: 5 ampul 6 ampule 7 ampoule
harbor ~: 3 tow 4 boat 5 barge, ferry
heating ~: 4 etna
lab ~: 5 ampul, flask 6 ampule, beaker, retort 7 ampoule 8 test tube
large ~: 3 vat
Mediterranean ~: 4 saic 6 caique
ocean ~: 4 boat, ship 5 liner
pear-shaped ~: 6 aludel
river ~: 4 boat 5 canoe, craft, kayak 6 vessel 7 rowboat 9 outrigger
Roman ~: 6 bireme 7 trireme
sailing ~: 4 boat, ship, yawl 5 craft, sloop 6 barque
small ~: 4 boat 5 canoe, kayak, skiff 6 dinghy 8 sailboat 9 catamaran
spouted ~: 3 jug 4 ewer 7 pitcher
stout ~: 3 mug 4 toby 5 stein
two-masted ~: 4 boat, brig 5 ketch, yacht 8 sailboat
wrecked ~: 4 hulk
WWI ~: 5 U-boat
WWII ~: 3 LCT, LST 5 E-boat
see also boat, ship
__ vessel: 3 war 4 food, keel, seed 5 blood, Dewar
vest: 4 robe 5 array, dicky, endow 6 belong, bestow, confer, dickey, dickie, jerkin, weskit 7 apparel, deck out, empower, entrust, garment, intrust 9 authorize, waistcoat 10 flak jacket
fitted ~: 6 bodice
in America: 10 undershirt
vest-__: 6 pocket
__ vest: 4 flak, life
vesta: 5 match 7 lighter
Vesta: 8 asteroid
brother of ~: 5 Pluto 7 Jupiter, Neptune
equivalent: 6 Hestia
parent of ~: 3 Ops 6 Saturn
sister of ~: 4 Juno 5 Ceres
vestal: 6 chaste, virgin 8 virginal 9 religious
Vestavia Hills: 4 city, town
locale: 7 Alabama
vested: 3 due 5 legal, privy 6 lawful, proper, select 7 decreed, favored 8 eligible, enjoined, entitled, licensed, official, rightful 9 empowered, legalized, statutory 10 admissible, authorized, privileged
be ~ in: 6 relate 8 belong to
vestibule: 4 hall 5 entry, foyer, lobby 7 hallway, ingress, passage 8 anteroom, corridor, entrance, entryway 10 passageway
vestige: 3 ash 4 dreg, hint, sign 5 relic, scrap, shred, spark, token, trace 6 shadow 7 glimmer, memento, remains, remnant 8 landmark, souvenir 9 suspicion 10 indication
leave no ~ of: 4 doom, raze, ruin, sack 5 crush, level, total, wreck 6 blow up, ravage 7 destroy, flatten, pillage, wipe out 8 bankrupt, bulldoze, clean out, decimate, demolish 9 bring down, devastate 10 annihilate, obliterate
vestigial: 3 old 5 basic 6 simple 7 ancient, austere, natural, surplus 8 earliest, enduring, leftover, residual 9 lingering, primitive, remaining, unevolved 10 aboriginal, elementary, indigenous
Vesti la giubba: 4 aria
singer: 5 Canio
vestment: 4 garb, robe 5 dress, habit 6 attire
church ~: 3 alb 4 cope 5 amice, fanon, orale
synagogue ~: 5 ephod
vest-pocket: 3 wee 4 baby, puny, tiny 5 bitty, small, teeny 6 bantam, little, minute, peewee, petite, pocket, teensy 9 itsy-bitsy, itty-bitty, miniature, pint-sized 10 diminutive, teeny-weeny
Vesuvius: 7 volcano
city near ~: 6 Naples
locale: 5 Italy 6 Europe
output: 4 lava
vet: 3 doc, DVM 4 ex-GI 7 examine, inspect, old hand 8 check out, evaluate, old-timer, skillful, validate
case for a ~: 4 lice
do a ~ job: 4 spay 6 declaw, deflea, neuter
patient: 3 cat, cow, dog, ewe, hog, kid, pet, ram, sow 4 calf, goat, lamb, mare, mule 5 horse 6 canine, equine, feline
theater: 3 Nam 7 Vietnam
see also veteran
vet. __: 3 med., sci.
vetch: 3 ers 4 crop, tare 5 ervil, plant 6 axseed, flower, forage
__ vetch: 3 cow 4 milk 5 crown, hairy 6 bitter, kidney, spring, winter
veteran: 2 GI 3 old, pro 5 adept 6 expert, old pro 7 old hand, soldier, trouper, warrior 8 long-time, old guard, old-timer, seasoned, skillful, warhorse 9 exercised, practiced, qualified, shellback 10 specialist
abbreviation for a ~: 3 ret.
benefit: 6 GI Bill
not a ~: 3 neo 4 tiro, tyro 6 rookie 8 beginner, newcomer 9 greenhorn 10 tenderfoot
org.: 3 DAV, VFW
Veterans Day mo.: 3 Nov.
Veterans of __ Wars: 7 Foreign
veterinary medicine: 7 science
study: 7 animals
vetiver: 5 grass
veto: 2 no 3 ban, bar, nay, nix 4 deny, kill, nyet, shun, stop, tabu 5 debar, quash, spurn 6 abjure, bounce, defeat, denial, forbid, negate, outlaw, pass on, rebuff, reject 7 decline, disdain, dismiss, embargo, exclude, put down, refusal, rule out 8 disallow, negation, override, overrule, preclude, prohibit, throw out, turn down, vote down 9 blackball, cast aside, frown upon, interdict, proscribe, rejection, repudiate, shoot down 10 disapprove, nonconsent, thumbs down
veto __: 5 power 7 message
__ veto: 4 item 6 pocket 7 liberum
vetoed: 4 tabu 9 forbidden 10 prohibited
vets, theater for some: 3 Nam
'Vette alternative: 3 Jag 5 T-bird
vex: 3 bug, get, ire, irk, nag, try 4 faze, fret, gall, hurt, miff, pain, ride, rile, roil, tire, wear 5 anger, annoy, chafe, chivy, eat at, grate, harry, haunt, hound, peeve, pique, press, spite, stump, taunt, tease, upset, weary, worry 6 badger, bother, chivvy, fester, harass, hassle, hector, madden, needle, nettle, noodge, offend, pester, plague, pother, put out, rankle, ruffle 7 afflict, agitate, bedevil, disturb, enflame, grate on, inflame, perturb, provoke, tick off, torment, trouble, turn off 8 aggrieve, confound, disquiet, distress, exercise, irritate 9 aggravate, displease, embarrass 10 antagonize, discompose, exasperate
vexation: 4 care, pain, pest 5 anger, grief, pique, trial, upset, worry, wrath 6 bother, hassle 7 affront, trouble, umbrage 8 headache, irritant, nuisance 9 abashment, annoyance 10 irritation, resentment
exclamation of ~: 3 tch, tsk
vexatious: 4 mean, ugly 5 pesky, pesty 6 thorny, trying 7 irksome, nagging, onerous, painful, teasing 8 annoying, tiresome, worrying 9 worrisome 10 bothersome, disturbing, in one's hair, irritating
vexed: 3 mad 4 ired, sore 5 angry, cross, fed up, huffy, irate, upset 6 galled, ireful, peeved 7 furious, in a snit 9 irritated 10 hopping mad, up in the air
be ~: 4 mind 6 resent, see red 7 dislike 8 object to
vexer: 5 poser 6 enigma, puzzle, riddle, teaser 7 mystery, problem, stumper, toughie 9 conundrum 10 puzzlement
vexing: 6 trying 7 galling, irksome 8 tiresome, worrying 9 annoyance, difficult 10 bothersome, irritating
__ vez: 4 otra
Vezina Trophy org.: 3 NHL
VFW
celebration: 7 Flag Day
hall subj.: 4 WWII
member: 3 vet 4 ex-GI
VHF part: 4 freq., high, very 9 frequency
VH-1: 7 network
alternative: 3 MTV
viewing: 5 video
VHS: 3 VCR 4 tape 9 videotape
alternative: 4 Beta 7 Betamax
__ VI: 5 Henry
via: 3 per 4 thru 5 along, using 7 by way of, through, towards 9 by means of 10 by virtue of
ender: 4 duct
via __: 5 media
Via __: 5 Appia 6 Lactea, Veneto
Via __ Corso: 3 del
Via Appia terminus: 4 Rome
viability: 4 life
viable: 5 alive 6 doable, likely 7 tenable, working 8 credible, feasible, possible, workable 9 plausible, potential, practical 10 achievable, applicable, attainable, imaginable, reasonable
Viadent: 10 toothpaste
alternative: 3 Aim 5 Crest, Gleem, Topol 7 Close-Up, Colgate 9 Aquafresh, Mentadent, Pepsodent, Rembrandt, Sensodyne 10 Pearl Drops, Ultra Brite 11 Tom's of Maine
viaduct: 4 link, road, span 6 bridge 8 crossing, overpass, traverse 10 connection
vial: 5 ampul, flask 6 ampule, bottle 7 ampoule 8 test tube 9 container
Via Lactea: 8 Milky Way
units: 5 astra
viand: 4 dish, food 8 delicacy
viands: 4 diet, food 7 aliment, edibles 8 eatables, victuals 9 foodstuff, nutriment, provender 10 delicacies, provisions, sustenance
anagram: 6 divans
Vianney, John: 5 saint
vibe: 4 aura 6 tremor 9 intuition, resonance, sensation
Vibe: 3 car 4 auto 7 Pontiac
vibes: 4 aura 5 karma 7 portent 8 reaction, response 9 sensation 10 instrument, percussion
bad ~: 4 omen 5 doubt, qualm, smell 6 augury, signal, threat 7 warning 8 distrust, mistrust, wariness 9 chariness, harbinger, misgiving, suspicion 10 foreboding, gut feeling, indication, prediction
get ~: 4 feel, know, mind, read 5 grasp, sense, smell 6 absorb, divine, intuit, notice, pick up, reason, take in 7 believe, catch on, discern, observe, realize 8 perceive 9 apprehend 10 anticipate, have a hunch, understand
good ~: 4 bond 5 unity 6 accord 7 concord, empathy, harmony, rapport 8 affinity 9 agreement, communion 10 friendship
have ~: 5 react, sense 6 intuit
__ vibes: 3 bad 4 good
vibraharp: 10 instrument, percussion
vibrant: 4 rich 5 alive, peppy, sound, vital, vivid, zesty, zippy 6 lively, virile 7 aquiver, dynamic, glowing, pulsing, ringing 8 animated, colorful, resonant, sonorous, spirited, vigorous 9 brilliant, energetic, pulsating, sparkling, throbbing, trembling, vivacious 10 responsive, shimmering
vibraphone: 10 instrument, percussion
vibraphonist: 5 Norvo 7 Hampton
vibrate: 3 hum 4 beat, echo, lick, ring, rock, sway, whir 5 pulse, quake, shake, sound, swing, throb, whirr 6 judder, quiver, rattle, ripple, shimmy, shiver, thrill 7 flutter, pulsate, resound, tremble 8 resonate 9 fluctuate, oscillate
vibrating: 4 wavy 5 snaky 7 rippled, shaking, sinuous 8 rippling 10 serpen-

tine, undulating
vibration: 4 beat 5 drone, pulse, quake, seism, sound, throb 6 quiver, tremor 7 shaking 9 pulsation, quivering, resonance, throbbing, trembling
__ Vibrations: 4 Good
vibrations, good: 7 rapport
vibrato: 5 trill 7 tremolo
viburnum: 5 plant 6 flower
Vic: 4 Dana 6 Damone, Morrow 7 Tayback
__ Vic: 3 Old
Vic and Sade: 9 radio show
vicar: 5 envoy, proxy 6 cleric, deputy, pastor 8 delegate, minister, preacher 9 churchman, clergyman, surrogate 10 substitute
assistant: 6 curate
residence: 5 manse 7 rectory 9 parsonage
vicar-__: 7 general
__ vicar: 3 lay 5 clerk 7 secular
vicarious: 7 by proxy, deputed, done for 8 imagined, indirect 9 delegated, pretended, secondary, surrogate 10 empathetic, on behalf of, secondhand
Vicar of __: 6 Christ
Vicar of Wakefield, The: 5 novel
author: Oliver Goldsmith
character: 4 Livy 5 Sophy 6 George, Olivia, Sophia, Wilmot 7 Charles, Deborah 8 Arabella, Burchell, Primrose 9 Thornhill
vice: 3 sin 4 evil, flaw, lust 5 crime, fault, wrong 6 defect, deputy, foible 7 cussing, devilry, failing, frailty 8 bad habit, deviltry, drinking, gambling, iniquity, swearing, venality, weakness 9 depravity, evildoing, looseness, lubricity, turpitude, veniality, weak point 10 corruption, immorality, profligacy, wickedness
squad: 5 bunco
versa: 9 about-face, in reverse, inversely 10 conversely, oppositely
vice __: 4 pres. 5 squad, versa
vice-__: 6 consul, regent 7 admiral
__ Vice: 5 Miami
__ vice-marshal: 3 air
__ Vicente, Brazil: 3 Sao
vice president: 4 veep
first ~: 5 Adams
viceroy: 3 bug 4 king 5 chief, royal, ruler 6 gerent, insect, leader 7 emperor, monarch 8 overlord 9 sovereign
vice squad action: 4 raid
vichy __: 5 water
Vichy: 3 spa 4 city, town
locale: 6 France
river: 6 Allier
vichyssoise: 4 soup
ingredient: 4 leek
vici
preceder: 4 vidi
vicinage: 4 area 8 purlieus
vicinity: 4 area, hood, turf 5 place, range 6 locale, region, sector 7 section 8 ballpark, district, environs, locality, nearness, precinct, premises, purlieus 9 immediacy, local area, outskirts, proximity, territory
covering the ~: 5 areal
immediate ~: 5 midst 8 nearness, presence 9 closeness, proximity
in the ~: 4 near 5 about, anear, close 6 around 7 close by
vicious: 3 bad 4 evil, foul, mean, ugly, vile, wild 5 catty, cruel, feral, harsh, lousy, nasty, rough, surly, tough 6 animal, brutal, fierce, horrid, malign, rotten, savage, sordid, sullen, unkind, wanton, wicked 7 beastly, callous, hateful, heinous, hellish, hurtful, immoral, inhuman, intense, parlous, violent 8 barbaric, churlish, depraved, diabolic, fiendish, infamous, inhumane, perverse, pitiless, ruthless, sadistic, spiteful, vengeful, venomous, virulent 9 abhorrent, atrocious, barbarian, barbarous, cutthroat, dangerous, ferocious, frightful, malicious, merciless, miscreant, monstrous, nefarious, poisonous, truculent 10 backbiting, defamatory, diabolical, ill-humored, ill-natured, malevolent, profligate, slanderous, villainous, vindictive, virtueless
in a ~ circle: 4 vain 5 inane 6 absurd, futile, stupid 7 insipid 9 for naught, frivolous, pointless, worthless 10 ridiculous
vicious __: 6 circle
Vicious: 3 Sid
viciously: 4 hard 5 madly 7 cruelly, harshly, sternly 8 ardently, bitterly, brutally, doggedly, fiercely, intently, savagely, severely, strongly, terribly 9 callously, furiously, intensely, zealously 10 gruelingly, pitilessly, ruthlessly, vehemently, vigorously
viciousness: 4 evil 6 malice 7 cruelty 8 enormity, ferocity
vicissitude: 5 trial 6 change, switch 7 reverse 8 flip-flop, mutation, obstacle, reversal 9 about-face
vicissitudes: 4 life
Vickers: 3 Ann, Jon 6 Martha
Vickers, Jon: 5 tenor 6 singer
specialty: 5 opera
Vicki: 4 Baum, Vale 8 Lawrence
Vicki __ Robinson: 3 Sue
Vickrey: 7 William
Vicksburg: 4 city, town 6 battle
event: 5 siege
locale: 4 Miss. 11 Mississippi
victim: 4 butt, dupe, gull, mark, pawn, prey, tool 5 clown, patsy, slave 6 hunted, pigeon, puppet, quarry, stooge, sucker, target, wretch 8 casualty, easy mark, fatality, innocent, pushover, sufferer 9 sacrifice, scapegoat, soft touch
Victim (1961 film)
cast: Dirk Bogarde, Sylvia Syms
victimize: 3 con, use 4 burn, clip, dupe, fool, gull, have, hoax, nick, snow 5 abuse, cheat, cozen, gouge, set up, stiff, sting, trick 6 chisel, fleece, pick on, prey on, rope in, sucker 7 deceive, defraud, exploit, mislead, swindle, two-time 8 flimflam, hoodwink, prey upon 9 bamboozle, persecute
Victim of the Aurora author: Keneally
Victims of Duty author: Eugène Ionesco
Victim, The author: Saul Bellow
__ victis: 3 vae
victor: 4 hero, king 5 champ, first, queen 6 master, winner 8 champion, defeater, medalist 9 conqueror 10 subjugator, vanquisher
prize: 5 medal 6 laurel, spoils
shout: 4 I win, I won 5 we win, we won
Victor: 4 Hess, Hugo, Jory, Kiam, pope 5 Borge, Buono, Lasky, Moore, Young 6 French, Mature 7 Fleming, Herbert, pontiff, Saville, Sen Yung 8 Grignard, McLaglen, Seastrom
in Italian: 8 Vittorio
__ Victor: 3 RCA
Victoria: 3 car, cat, sta. 4 auto, city, Ford, Holt, isle, lake, town 5 Falls, queen, ruler, state 6 desert, island 7 capital, Jackson, station, Tennant 9 Principal, waterfall 10 automobile
capital: 9 Melbourne
city: 7 Geelong 9 Melbourne
granddaughter of ~: 3 Ena
in Italian: 8 Vittoria
Lake ~ locale: 6 Africa
locale: 5 Kenya, Texas 6 Canada, Mexico, Uganda 8 Hong Kong, Tanzania 9 Australia 10 Seychelles, Tamaulipas
prime minister: 4 Peel
to Albert: 6 cousin
to William IV: 5 niece
Victoria __: 3 Day 4 Land 5 Cross, Falls 6 Desert, Island, Nyanza, Regina
Victoria __ Angeles: 5 de los
__ Victoria: 5 Crown
Victoria Cross: 5 medal
Victorian: 3 Age, Era 4 prig, prim 5 prude, style 6 prissy, quaint, stuffy 7 prudish 9 bourgeois
garden feature: 4 maze
garment: 6 bustle, corset, girdle
like ~ houses: 6 gaslit
Victorian __: 3 box, Era
Victoria's Secret purchase: 3 bra 5 teddy, thong 7 nightie 8 negligee
Victoriaville: 4 city, town
locale: 6 Canada, Québec
Victorien: 6 Sardou
victorious: 5 on top 7 arrived, winning, winsome 8 unbeaten 9 fortunate 10 successful, triumphant
be ~: 3 win 4 beat, best, lick, stun 5 outdo, upset 6 defeat 7 conquer, prevail, succeed, triumph 8 overcome 9 overpower, overwhelm, rise above
be ~ again: 5 rewin
__ Victorious: 6 Purlie
Victor Rosales
locale: 9 Zacatecas
Victors, The (1963 film)
cast: Vince Edwards, George Hamilton, George Peppard
Victor/Victoria (1982 film)
cast: Julie Andrews, James Garner, Alex Karras, Robert Preston, Lesley Ann Warren
composer: 7 Mancini
director: Blake Edwards
Victorville: 4 city, town
locale: 10 California
victory: 3 hit, win 4 feat, luck, palm 5 upset 6 big hit, winner 7 laurels, success, triumph 8 conquest, dominion 9 checkmate, grand slam, supremacy, upper hand 10 ascendance, ascendancy, ascendence, ascendency
complete ~: 5 sweep 7 triumph 9 landslide 10 clean sweep
easy ~: 4 rout 5 waltz 7 debacle, pasting, shutout, washout 8 conquest, disaster, drubbing, stampede, walkover 9 landslide, thrashing, trouncing
emblem of ~: 5 title 6 laurel, wreath 10 blue ribbon
gain a ~: 3 win 4 beat, earn, sway, take 5 score, upset 6 defeat 7 achieve, conquer, edge out, prevail, realize, succeed, triumph, trounce 8 overcome 9 overwhelm
goddess of ~: 4 Nike
insure a ~: 5 sew up 6 clinch
margin of ~: 4 neck, nose
name meaning ~: 6 Sigrid 7 Sigmund
noughts-and-crosses ~: 3 OOO, XXX
opposite: 4 loss 6 defeat, losing, mishap 7 failure
overly relish ~: 4 brag, crow 5 gloat 7 rub it in, swagger 9 whoop it up
shout: 4 hoot, howl, yell 5 bingo, cheer, whoop 6 holler, hurrah, scream
sign: 3 vee
sure ~: 4 lock 5 cinch 9 certainty
victory __: 6 garden
__ victory: 7 Cadmean, Pyrrhic
__ victory!: 4 On to
Victory (1940 film)
cast: Betty Field, Sir Cedric Hardwicke, Fredric March
Victory (song)
artist: Notorious B.I.G., Puff Daddy
Victory __: 4 ship 5 at Sea, Medal
__ Victory: 4 Dark 6 Bright, Winged 7 Strange, Unarmed
Victory author: Joseph Conrad
victory people
name meaning ~: 6 Nicole 8 Nicholas
Victory (song) artist: Kool and the Gang
Victrola: 10 phonograph
descendant: 4 hi-fi 6 stereo 7 boombox 8 CD player
maker: 3 RCA
part: 4 horn 5 crank 6 needle, stylus
victual: 4 chow, fare, feed, food, grub, meat 6 supply 7 aliment, edibles 9 foodstuff, nutriment 10 comestible, provisions, sustenance
victuals: 4 chow, diet, eats, fare, food, grub, meal 5 board, table 6 repast, viands 7 aliment, edibles, rations 8 eatables 9 foodstuff, nutriment, provender 10 provisions, sustenance
vicuna: 4 wool 6 animal, fabric, mammal
home: 5 Andes
relative: 5 camel, llama 6 alpaca 7 guanaco 8 Bactrian 9 dromedary
__-vid: 3 kid
Vida: 4 Blue
Vidal: 4 Gore 7 Sassoon
Vidal, Gore: 6 author, writer
pseudonym: Edgar Box
work: The Best Man
Burr
Empire
An Evening with Richard Nixon
Kalki
Myra Breckinridge
Rocking the Boat
Two Sisters
Visit to a Small Planet
Vidalia __: 5 onion
vide __: 4 ante, post 5 infra, supra
videlicet: 5 to wit 6 namely
video: 4 clip, film, tape 6 record 8 news clip
arcade patron: 5 gamer
award: 3 Ava
companion: 5 audio
display: 6 screen 7 monitor 8 terminal
ender: 4 disc, disk, tape, text 5 phone 6 taping 8 cassette 10 conference
make a ~: 4 tape 6 record
room: 3 den
screen dot: 5 pixel
what ~ means: 4 I see
video __: 3 art 4 game 5 drama 6 camera, jockey, screen, vérité
video __ terminal: 7 display
video-__: 4 text 6 record
__ video: 4 home 5 music 7 reverse
__ Video: 7 Captain
videocassette contents: 4 film, show, tape 5 flick, movie 7 picture
video game: 4 Myst, Pong 6 Pacman, Tetris 10 Donkey Kong
center: 6 arcade
game maker: 3 NES 4 Sega 5 Atari
hero: 5 Mario, Sonic
Microsoft ~ console: 4 Xbox

Video Killed the Radio Star (1979 song) artist: Buggles
videos, network with: 3 MTV
video-store section: 5 drama **6** action, comedy, horror **7** mystery
videotape: 4 tape **5** movie **6** record
borrow a ~: 4 rent
material: 5 Mylar
speed meas.: 3 ips
vidi: 4 I saw **5** Latin
follower: 4 vici
preceder: 4 veni
Vidor: 4 King **7** Charles
Vidor, King: 8 director
film: The Big Parade (1925)
The Champ (1931)
The Citadel (1938)
The Crowd (1928)
Duel in the Sun (1946)
Hallelujah (1929)
H.M. Pulham, Esq. (1941)
La Bohème (1926)
The Man Without a Star (1955)
Northwest Passage (1940)
Show People (1928)
Solomon and Sheba (1959)
Stella Dallas (1937)
The Stranger's Return (1933)
Street Scene (1931)
The Texas Rangers (1936)
vie: 3 pit **4** play **5** fight, match, rival **6** oppose, strive, take on **7** compete, contend, contest **8** scramble, struggle **9** challenge
(for): 2 go **3** try **5** fight
for office: 3 run
with: 5 rival **6** take on
__ vie: 5 eau de
Vieira: 8 Meredith
viejo: 3 old **7** Spanish
opposite: 5 nuevo
Vieni __ Mar: 3 Sul
Vienna: 4 city, town, Wien **7** capital
dance: 5 waltz
locale: 3 Aus. **4** Aust. **7** Austria **8** Virginia
river: 5 Donau **6** Danube
see also Austrian, German
Vienna __: 7 Fingers, sausage
Vienne, city on the: 7 Limoges
Viennese __: 5 table
Vientiane: 4 city, town **7** capital
locale: 4 Laos
vier: 4 four **5** rival **9** combatant, contender **10** competitor, contestant
doubled: 4 acht
follower: 4 finf
preceder: 4 drei
Vierzon: 4 city, town
locale: 6 France
Viet __: 3 Nam **4** Cong, Minh **7** Journal
Vietcong grp.: 3 NLF
Viet Journal author: James Jones
Vietnam: 6 nation **7** country
Buddhism of ~: 8 Mahayana
capital: 5 Hanoi
city: 3 Hue **5** Hanoi, My Lai **6** Can Tho, Da Nang **7** Bien Hoa, Qui Nhon **8** Haiphong, Nha Trang
ender: 3 ese
farming area: 5 paddy
festival: 3 Tet
former president: 4 Diem
language: 5 Hmong
money: 2 xu **3** hao **4** dong
neighbor: 4 Laos **5** China **8** Cambodia
Nobelist in Peace: 3 Tho
people of ~: 4 Miao
region of ~: 4 Anam **5** Annam
sea: 10 South China
tunic: 5 aodai
Vietnam __: 3 War
__ Vietnam: 5 North, South
Vietnamese: 5 Asian **8** language
Vietnam Veterans Memorial architect: Maya Lin
Vieux __: 5 Carré
view: 3 eye, see, spy **4** deem, espy, gaze, hold, idea, look, mark, mind, read, scan, show, side, spot **5** audit, judge, scape, scene, scope, sight, slant, stand, stare, tenet, vista, watch **6** advert, aspect, behold, belief, eyeful, gander, gape at, glance, look at, notice, notion, peek at, peer at, reckon, regard, squint, survey, take in, thesis, vision **7** believe, close-up, concept, discern, examine, explore, eyeball, eyeshot, feeling, glimpse, inspect, lookout, look-see, observe, opening, opinion, outlook, picture, scenery, tableau, thought, witness **8** analysis, attitude, check out, consider, judgment, look upon, overlook, panorama, perceive, position, prospect, seascape, theorize **9** check over, cityscape, landscape, lay eyes on, sentiment, spectacle, viewpoint **10** appearance, assessment, conception, conjecture, contention, conviction, eyewitness, get a load of, impression, inspection, persuasion, philosophy, reflection, rubberneck, scrutinize, standpoint, think about
a computer file: 6 access
aerial ~ provider: 5 blimp **7** airship, balloon **8** aircraft, zeppelin **9** dirigible
again: 5 resee
combining form: 5 -scape
come into ~: 4 loom, rise **5** heave **6** appear, emerge
command a ~: 4 face, look, view **6** survey **7** lookout **8** overlook, prospect **9** look out on
dim ~: 5 gloom **7** despair, sadness **8** cynicism, dark side, glumness **9** dejection, pessimism **10** depression, gloominess, melancholy, woefulness
ender: 4 data **5** point **6** finder
express a ~: 5 opine
follower: 5 point
grand ~: 5 sight, sweep, vista **7** horizon, scenery **8** panorama, prospect **9** landscape
have in ~: 3 aim **4** plan **6** aspire, design, expect, intend **7** resolve **10** have in mind
hold another ~: 6 differ **7** dissent **8** disagree
hold in ~: 3 eye, spy **4** espy, spot **5** watch **7** discern **8** perceive **10** get a load of
in ~: 4 open **5** clear, plain **6** patent, public **7** exposed, obvious, visible **8** apparent, clear-cut, explicit, imminent, manifest, unhidden, unveiled **10** observable, unshrouded
in full ~: 4 open, seen **6** openly
in ~ of: 6 herein **7** because
mind's-eye ~: 5 image **7** concept **10** appearance, envisaging, impression, perception, projection
out of ~: 6 buried, hidden, latent, unseen **7** cloaked, covered, obscure, on the QT **8** abstruse, eclipsed, secluded, shrouded **9** concealed, disguised, incognito, innermost, in the dark, unexposed **10** cloistered, tucked away, unrevealed
point of ~: 4 mind, side, view **5** angle, light, slant **6** aspect, vision **7** feeling, opinion, outlook, posture
put on ~: 3 air **4** bare, show **6** expose, flaunt, lay out, parade, reveal **7** display, exhibit, present, show off, trot out **8** showcase **10** illustrate
quick ~: 3 see **4** gaze, look, peek **6** gander, glance **7** eyeshot, glimpse, look-see
range of ~: 3 ken **6** vision **8** eyesight
screen from ~: 4 hide **6** enisle **7** conceal, confine, isolate, seclude **8** cloister, separate **9** keep apart, segregate, sequester **10** quarantine
share a ~: 5 agree, match **6** accord, concur **7** conform **9** harmonize **10** go together
side ~: 7 contour, profile **10** silhouette
starter: 5 world
suffix: 5 -scape
take a dim ~ of: 5 knock, scorn **7** censure, deplore, put down, run down **8** bad-mouth, belittle, derogate, disfavor **9** deprecate, disesteem, disparage, poor-mouth **10** disapprove
with alarm: 4 fear **5** dread, panic **6** dismay **10** foreboding
within ~: 4 near, nigh **5** close, handy **6** around, nearby **7** close by, close to, looming **8** imminent, next door, proximal **9** alongside, bordering **10** accessible, near-at-hand
View __ Kill, A: 3 to a
View __ the Bridge, A: 4 From
viewable: 7 in sight, visible
viewer: 4 eyer, seer **7** witness **8** attendee, beholder, observer, onlooker, playgoer, showgoer **9** moviegoer, spectator **10** eyewitness
combining form: 5 -scope
gem ~: 5 loupe
viewers: 8 assembly, audience
View from the Bridge, A author: Miller
View from the Fortieth Floor, The author: Theodore H. White
viewing: 4 look **5** sight
combining form: 5 -scopy **6** -scopic
viewpoint: 4 idea, side **5** angle, light, slant, stand **6** aspect, stance **7** horizon, opinion, outlook, posture **8** attitude, position, two cents **9** direction **10** estimation, philosophy
views, old-style: 5 seest
View to a Kill, A: 4 film, song **5** novel
artist: Duran Duran
author: Ian Fleming
cast: Grace Jones, Roger Moore, Tanya Roberts, Christopher Walken
director: John Glen
Viggo: 9 Mortensen
vigil: 4 wake **5** watch **7** lookout **8** eagle eye, sharp eye, stakeout **10** weather eye
light: 5 taper **6** candle, shames **7** shammes **9** luminaria
vigilance: 4 care, heed **5** watch **6** acuity **7** caution, lookout **9** alertness, attention **10** discretion
vigilant: 2 up **4** keen, live, wary **5** acute, alert, awake, aware, sharp **6** prompt **7** all ears, careful, guarded, heads-up, heedful, mindful, on alert, on guard, prudent, wakeful **8** cautious, keen-eyed, on the job, open-eyed, watchful **9** attentive, conscious, observant, on the ball, provident, receptive, undivided, wide-awake **10** on one's toes, perceptive, protective, unsleeping
be ~: 5 watch
one: 5 guard **6** heeder, sentry
Vigil in the Night (1940 film)
cast: Brian Aherne, Carole Lombard
director: George Stevens
Vigilius: 4 pope **7** pontiff
vignette: 6 sketch **7** profile **8** portrait
Vigny, Alfred Victor de: 4 poet **6** author, French **10** playwright
Vigo: 3 bay **4** city, town
locale: 5 Spain
Vigoda: 3 Abe
vigor: 3 pep, vim, zip **4** brio, dash, dint, élan, fire, kick, life, push, snap, thew, zeal, zing **5** brawn, drive, force, juice, might, moxie, oomph, power, prime, punch, sinew, spark, steam, teeth, thews, verve **6** action, bounce, energy, esprit, fervor, health, muscle, spirit, starch **7** fitness, muscles, pizzazz, potence, potency, prowess, stamina **8** ambition, dynamism, industry, strength, vitality **9** animation, beefiness, briskness, diligence, endurance, fortitude, freshness, hardiness, huskiness, intensity, lustiness, puissance, soundness, stoutness, toughness, well-being **10** brawniness, brute force, enterprise, enthusiasm, exuberance, get up and go, heartiness, initiative, liveliness, mightiness, robustness, sturdiness
ending: 3 ous
full of ~: 4 hale **5** alert, lusty, peppy, perky, zippy **6** active, bubbly, feisty, lively, potent, robust, strong, sturdy, virile **7** dashing, dynamic, healthy, vibrant, zestful **8** animated, muscular, powerful, spirited **9** energetic, sprightly, strenuous, vivacious
in music: 4 brio
lacking ~: 4 weak, worn **6** effete, feeble **7** worn-out
lack of ~: 6 anemia, anergy **7** anaemia
lose ~: 4 fade, fail, wilt **5** droop
name meaning ~: 6 Ernest
with fresh ~: 4 anew **5** newly **6** afresh **7** freshly
__ vigor: 6 hybrid
Vigor: 3 car **4** auto **5** Acura **10** automobile
vigorish: 3 fee **5** usury **8** interest
collector: 4 bank **6** bookie, lender, usurer **8** creditor **9** bookmaker, loan shark **10** pawnbroker
vigorlessness: 6 anemia **7** anaemia **10** enervation, exhaustion, feebleness
vigorous: 3 fit **4** hale, hard, iron, live, racy, spry, well, wiry **5** alive, beefy, brisk, burly, fresh, hardy, hefty, hunky, husky, lusty, nervy, peppy, pithy, sharp, smart, sound, stiff, stout, tough, vital, zippy **6** active, ardent, brawny, hearty, lively, living, mighty, potent, robust, rugged, sinewy, steely, stocky, strong, sturdy, virile **7** bracing, doughty, driving, dynamic, healthy, intense, rousing, vibrant, zestful **8** athletic, bouncing, emphatic, forceful, indurate, muscular, powerful, puissant, spirited, stalwart, tireless, youthful **9** Atlantean, energetic, exuberant, Herculean, in the pink, strapping, strenuous, well-built **10** able-bodied, fortifying, red-blooded
activity: 4 push **7** workout **8** exercise
vigorously: 4 hard **5** amain **7** like mad **8** mightily, up a storm **9** seriously **10** vehemently
VII: 5 seven **6** septet
VIII: 4 octo **5** eight, octet
Vijay: 5 Singh **8** Amritraj
Viking: 5 probe **7** brigand, corsair **8** Norseman **9** buccaneer **10** freebooter
headgear: 6 helmet
maybe: 4 fair **5** blond, light **6** blonde, golden **10** fair-haired
poet: 5 scald, skald
reading: 4 edda
rival: 3 Jet, Ram **4** Bear, Bill, Colt,

Lion **5** Brown, Chief, Eagle, Giant, Niner, Raven, Saint, Texan, Titan **6** Bengal, Bronco, Cowboy, Falcon, Jaguar, Packer, Raider **7** Charger, Dolphin, Panther, Patriot, Redskin, Seahawk, Steeler **8** Cardinal **9** Buccaneer
touchdown site: 4 Mars
weapon: 3 axe
Vikings: 4 team **5** Norse **6** eleven
home: 9 Minnesota
org.: 3 NFC, NFL
sport: 8 football
__-Vikings: 4 Dell
Vikings at Helgeland author: Ibsen
Vikki: 4 Carr
Vila: 3 Bob **4** city, town **7** capital
locale: 6 Vanatu
Vilas, Guillermo: 6 netman **7** netster **9** tennis pro
milieu: 5 court
Vila Velha: 4 city, town
locale: 6 Brazil
vile: 3 bad, low **4** base, dark, evil, foul, mean, ugly **5** dirty, lousy, nasty, slimy, sorry **6** abased, coarse, filthy, grungy, horrid, impure, odious, rotten, sleazy, sordid, unholy, vulgar, wicked **7** accurst, beastly, bestial, corrupt, debased, demonic, hateful, ignoble, immoral, noisome, noxious, pitiful, satanic, twisted, unclean, ungodly, vicious **8** accursed, daemonic, degraded, depraved, diabolic, gruesome, horrible, indecent, infamous, shameful, shocking, sinister, stinking, terrible, unworthy, wretched **9** appalling, dastardly, demonical, execrable, loathsome, miserable, monstrous, nefarious, obnoxious, offensive, repellant, repellent, repugnant, repulsive, revolting, satanical, worthless **10** abominable, despicable, diabolical, disgusting, flagitious, indecorous, indelicate, inexpiable, iniquitous, loathesome, malodorous, petrifying, villainous, virtueless
remark: 5 rumor **6** canard **7** untruth
Vile Bodies author: Evelyn Waugh
vileness: 4 evil **8** enormity **9** indecency
Vilhelm: 6 Moberg **8** Bjerknes
vilification: 3 dig **4** barb, gibe, jibe, slam, slap, slur, snub **5** abuse, libel, scorn, taunt **6** attack, insult, rebuff, slight **7** affront, calumny, catcall, disdain, mockery, obloquy, offense, putdown, slander **8** contempt, derision, ridicule **9** aspersion, cheap shot, contumely **10** defamation, disrespect, opprobrium
vilifier: 6 censor, critic **7** defamer, reviler **8** asperser, attacker, impugner, maligner **9** belittler, derogater, detractor, muckraker **10** denigrator, deprecator, disparager
vilify: 3 dis, pan, rap **4** cuss, damn, gibe, jeer, jibe, mock, slam, slur, snub **5** abuse, curse, decry, knock, libel, rip up, roast, scorn, smear, spurn, sully, taunt **6** assail, attack, berate, debase, defame, deride, dump on, heckle, impugn, injure, insult, malign, offend, rebuff, revile, scorch, slight **7** affront, asperse, blacken, blister, censure, degrade, disdain, put down, rank out, rip into, run down, slander, traduce **8** backbite, bad-mouth, belittle, call down, denounce, mudsling, ridicule, tear down, tear into, throw mud **9** blaspheme, denigrate, discredit, disparage, dress down, excoriate, fulminate, humiliate, skin alive **10** blackguard, calumniate, disrespect, speak ill of, villainize, vituperate
vilifying: 8 libelous **9** invidious
10 defamatory, derogatory
vilipend: 4 gibe, jeer, jibe, mock, slam, slur, snub **5** abuse, decry, libel, scorn, spurn, taunt **6** defame, deride, dump on, heckle, impugn, malign, offend, rebuff, slight **7** affront, asperse, degrade, disdain, put down, rank out, slander, traduce **8** belittle, denounce, ridicule **9** denigrate, discredit, disparage, disregard, humiliate **10** calumniate, disrespect
villa: 4 casa, home **5** lodge **6** estate **7** mansion **9** residence
boundary: 4 wall
features: 5 atria
Russian ~: 5 dacha **6** datcha
Villa: 6 Pancho
Villa __, GA: 4 Rica
__ Villa!: 4 Viva
Villa d' __: 4 Este
Villaflores: 4 city, town
locale: 6 Mexico **7** Chiapas
village: 2 tp. **3** twp. **4** burg, dorp, town **5** exurb, place, thorp, urban **6** center, hamlet, suburb, thorpe **8** township **10** crossroads
center: 5 green
green: 4 park **5** plaza **6** common, square
Hindu ~ chief: 5 patel
Japanese ~: 4 mura
medieval ~: 5 bourg
not chartered, as a ~ (abbr.): 5 uninc.
oldest continuously inhabited US ~: 5 Acoma
Russian ~: 3 mir
South African ~: 5 craal, kraal
__ village: 6 global, police
Village __: 4 Tale **5** Voice **6** People
Village Blacksmith, The author: Henry Wadsworth Longfellow
Village of the Damned, The author: John Wyndham
Village People
song: In the Navy (1979)
Macho Man (1978)
Y.M.C.A. (1978)
Villager: 3 car, van **4** auto **5** Edsel **7** Mercury **10** automobile
Village Voice award: 4 Obie
Village Wedding artist: 5 Steen
Villagrán: 4 city, town
locale: 6 Mexico **10** Guanajuato
Villahermosa: 4 city, town
locale: 6 Mexico **7** Tabasco
villain: 3 cad, cur **4** heel, ogre, part **5** baddy, brute, creep, demon, devil, enemy, fiend, heavy, rogue, tough **6** baddie, bad egg, bad guy, bad man, daemon, daimon, rascal, wretch **7** caitiff, lowlife, monster **8** antihero, criminal, evildoer, offender **9** archfiend, ill-wisher, libertine, miscreant, reprobate, scoundrel **10** blackguard, malefactor, profligate
fairy tale ~: 4 ogre **5** giant, troll **7** monster
foe: 4 hero
greeting for the ~: 3 boo **4** hiss, siss
greet the ~: 3 boo **4** jeer **8** sibilate
heroine's answer to a ~: 5 never
lament: 6 curses, foiled
laugh: 3 hah, heh
opera ~ often: 4 alto, bass **5** basso
thwart the ~: 4 foil **6** thwart
visage: 4 leer **5** scoff, smirk, sneer
villainize: 4 slam, slur **5** decry, libel, smear, sully, taint **6** accuse, assail, defame, insult, malign, revile, vilify **7** rip into, slander **8** badmouth, besmirch, mudsling **9** denigrate, deprecate, disparage **10** speak ill of
villainous: 3 bad **4** base, evil, foul, vile **5** black, nasty **6** rotten, sinful, wicked **7** heinous, ignoble, immoral, knavish, satanic, vicious **8** depraved, devilish, diabolic, grievous, infamous, shameful, sinister **9** atrocious, dishonest, miscreant, monstrous, nefarious, notorious, satanical **10** diabolical, iniquitous, maleficent, virtueless
expression: 4 leer **5** scowl, smirk, sneer **7** snicker
sort: 4 ogre **5** meany **6** meanie
stare: 3 eye **4** leer, ogle **5** sneer
villains: 6 bad lot
villainy: 4 evil **5** wrong **6** infamy **7** knavery, misdeed **10** wickedness
Villa Madero: 4 city, town
locale: 6 Mexico **8** Coahuila
villanella: 5 dance
villanelle: 4 poem
Villanova: 6 school **10** university
athletes: 8 Wildcats
conference: 7 Big East
locale: 4 Penn.
Villa, Pancho: 6 bandit **7** Mexican
emulate ~: 4 raid
see also Spanish
Villa Park: 4 city, town
locale: 8 Illinois
Villavicencio: 4 city, town
locale: 8 Colombia
Villechaize: 5 Hervé
villein: 4 serf **5** helot, slave **6** vassal, worker **7** chattel, servant, subject
Villella, Edward: 6 dancer **7** danseur
specialty: 6 ballet
Villette author: Charlotte Brontë
Villon, François: 4 poet **6** French
Vilma: 5 Banky
Vilnius: 4 city, town **7** capital
locale: 9 Lithuania
vim: 3 pep, zip **4** brio, dash, dint, élan, thew, zeal, zest, zing **5** brawn, force, gusto, might, oomph, power, spark, steam, thews, verve, vigor **6** action, bounce, energy, esprit, muscle, pizazz, spirit **7** fitness, muscles, pizzazz, potence, potency, sparkle, stamina **8** strength, vitality **9** animation, beefiness, endurance, fortitude, hardiness, huskiness, puissance, stoutness, toughness **10** brawniness, brute force, enthusiasm, get up and go, liveliness, mightiness, robustness, sturdiness
full of ~: 5 alert, brisk, peppy, perky, vital, zesty, zingy, zippy **6** active, bright, bubbly, feisty, frisky, lively **7** dashing, dynamic, piquant, vibrant, zestful **8** animated, skittish, spirited, vigorous **9** energetic, sparkling, sprightly, vivacious
vim and __: 5 vigor
Vimy locale: 6 France
vin: 4 wine **5** blanc, Médoc, pinot, rouge **7** Chablis **8** Bordeaux, Burgundy **9** Champagne, Sauternes **10** Beaujolais, Chardonnay
__ vin: 5 coq au
Vin: 6 Diesel, Scully
vina: 6 string, zither
origin: 5 India
Viña del Mar: 4 city, town
locale: 5 Chile
vinaigrette: 5 sauce **8** dressing
__ vinaigrette: 4 herb
vinca: 10 periwinkle
Vince: 4 Gill, Neil **6** Vaughn **7** Edwards **8** DiMaggio, Guaraldi, Lombardi
Vince Lombardi Trophy awarder: 3 NFL
Vincent: 4 Gene **5** Canby, d'Indy, Perez, Price, Spano **6** Hamlin **7** Sherman, van Gogh, Youmans **8** Bugliosi, D'Onofrio, Gardenia, McEveety **10** Jan-Michael
brother: 4 Theo
in Italian: 8 Vincenzo
Vincent & __: 4 Theo
Vincent __: 6 de Paul
Vincent (1972 song) artist: Don McLean
__ Vincent Benét: 7 Stephen
Vincent de Paul: 5 saint
Vincente: 6 Ibañez **8** Minnelli
daughter: 4 Liza
wife: 4 Judy
Vincent of Saragossa: 5 saint
__ Vincent Peale: 6 Norman
Vincent & Theo (1990 film)
cast: Paul Rhys, Tim Roth
director: Robert Altman
Vincenzo: 7 Bellini
in English: 7 Vincent
vincible: 5 prone **6** liable **8** beatable, in danger **9** sensitive **10** assailable, attackable, penetrable, vulnerable
vincit __ veritas: 5 omnia
__ vincit amor: 5 omnia
__ vincit omnia: 4 amor
vinculum: 3 tie **4** bond, link, lock, seam, yoke **5** annex, joint, nexus, tag on **6** bridge, hookup, joiner **7** coupler **8** ligament **9** fastening **10** attachment, connection, connective
vin de __: 4 pays
Vindho: 4 city, town
locale: 6 Mexico **7** Hidalgo
Vindhya __: 5 Hills, Range
vindicable: 6 proper, venial **7** tenable **9** excusable **10** condonable, defensible, pardonable
vindicate: 5 clear, right **6** acquit, avenge, defend, excuse, refute, uphold **7** absolve, justify, redress, revenge, support **8** champion, disprove, maintain, plead for **9** challenge, do justice, exculpate, exonerate, whitewash **10** disculpate, speak up for
vindicated: 4 free **6** exempt **7** cleared **9** acquitted **10** exonerated, off the hook
name meaning ~: 4 Dina **5** Dinah
vindication: 4 plea **6** pardon, reason
vindictive: 4 mean **5** cruel, harsh, nasty **6** animal, bitter, brutal, fierce, savage, unkind, wanton **7** beastly, callous, hateful, hurtful, vicious **8** avenging, barbaric, fiendish, grudging, inhumane, pitiless, punitive, ruthless, sadistic, spiteful, vengeful, venomous, virulent **9** cutthroat, ferocious, malicious, merciless, monstrous, rancorous, resentful, splenetic, truculent **10** implacable
feeling: 3 ire **4** bile, fury, hate, rage **5** anger, wrath **6** rancor, spleen **7** outrage, umbrage **8** acrimony, vexation
vindictiveness: 5 spite **6** malice, rancor, spleen **9** vengeance
vine: 3 ivy **5** haoma, kudzu, liana, liane, plant, vetch **6** briony, bryony **7** creeper, jasmine **8** clematis, wistaria, wisteria **9** jessamine
combining form: 4 viti-
die on the ~: 3 ebb, rot, sag **4** fade, wilt **5** decay, lapse **6** go soft, worsen **7** decline, dwindle **8** languish, vegetate **9** fizzle out, waste away **10** degenerate, retrogress
emulate a ~: 5 climb
ender: 4 yard **7** dresser
Hawaiian: 5 maile
like a ~: 5 twiny
place for a ~: 5 arbor
product: 5 berry, grape, melon
starter: 5 grape
wax ~: 4 hoya

vine __: 5 maple, snake 6 cactus
__ vine: 3 ivy 4 love, pipe, tara, wire 5 coral, kudzu, lemon 6 potato, silver 7 balloon, cypress, trumpet
__-vine: 5 cross 6 fleece
vine-covered: 5 ivied
vinegar: 4 acid 6 acetum 10 acetic acid
combining form: 4 acet- 5 aceto-
flavorer: 6 balsam
full of ~: 4 flip, pert 5 sassy
holder: 3 jar, jug 5 cruet, flask 6 bottle, carafe 8 decanter
like ~: 4 sour 6 acidic 7 acerbic
malt ~: 6 alegar
partner: 3 oil
radical: 6 acetyl
source: 4 wine 5 cider
vinegar __: 3 eel, fly 4 worm
__ vinegar: 4 rice, wine, wood 5 cider
Vinegar __ Mizell: 4 Bend
vinegary: 4 acid, sour, tart 5 acerb, sharp 6 acetal, acetic, acidic, bitter, crusty 7 gone bad, pungent 9 crotchety
Vineland: 4 city, town
locale: 9 New Jersey
__ Vines Have Tender Grapes: 3 Our
vineyard: 5 field 8 cropland
French ~: 3 cru 5 Médoc
pick of the ~: 5 grape
valley: 4 Napa
__ Vineyard: 7 Martha's
Ving: 6 Rhames
Vingt ans après character: 5 Athos
vingt-et-un: 4 game 8 card game
alias: 7 pontoon 9 blackjack, twenty-one
Vinny: 10 Testaverde
vino: 4 wine 6 blanco 7 Chianti
like ~ tinto: 4 rojo
region: 4 Asti
variety: 5 soave
vinous: 4 winy 5 winey
vins, like some: 5 blanc, rouge
Vinson Massif: 4 peak 5 mount
locale: 10 Antarctica
vintage: 3 era, old 4 best, crop, rare, wine, year 5 epoch, prime 6 choice, mature, select 7 classic 8 outdated, outmoded, superior 9 excellent, out-of-date, unrivaled, venerable 10 back-number, unrivalled
vintage __: 4 wine, year
vintner: 9 winemaker
need: 3 vat 7 cistern 8 cauldron
prefix: 3 oen- 4 oeno-
Vinton, Bobby
nickname: Polish Prince
song: Blue on Blue (1963)
Blue Velvet (1963)
I Love How You Love Me (1968)
Mr. Lonely (1964)
My Heart Belongs to Only You (1964)
My Melody of Love (1974)
Please Love Me Forever (1967)
Rose Are Red (1962)
There! I've Said It Again (1963)
vinyl: 2 EP, LP 6 fabric, record 8 material
fabric: 9 Naugahyde
vinyl __: 5 ether, resin 7 acetate, alcohol, polymer, radical
viol: 6 string 7 quinton 10 instrument
feature: 4 fret
__ viol: 4 bass
viola: 5 plant 6 flower, string
cousin: 4 bass 5 cello
viola __: 4 clef 6 d'amore
viola da __: 5 gamba 7 braccio
Viola's love: 6 Orsino
violate: 4 defy 5 abuse, break, flout, force, rebel 6 breach, ignore, invade, oppose, resist, revolt 7 assault, disobey, disrupt, infract, profane, sell out 8 encroach, infringe, trespass 9 desecrate, disregard, trample on 10 contravene, transgress
violation: 3 sin 4 foul 5 abuse, break, crime, lapse, wrong 6 breach 7 assault, misdeed, offense 8 dishonor, invasion, trespass 9 blasphemy, injustice, sacrilege, veniality 10 defilement, disloyalty, illegality, infraction
__ violation: 6 moving
violence: 4 fury, heat, rage, riot 5 might, power, storm 6 attack, duress, émeute, mayhem, rumble, uproar 7 assault, battery, cruelty, passion, rampage 8 coercion, disorder, ferocity, fighting, foul play, savagery, severity, struggle, wildness 9 brutality, harshness, intensity, onslaught, roughness, terrorism 10 brute force, compulsion, fierceness, inhumanity, revolution, storminess, wrongdoing
wanton ~: 4 fury 5 abuse, anger, crime, wrath 7 offense, outrage 9 barbarism, evildoing
violent: 3 hot, mad 4 gory, ugly, wild 5 acute, cruel, fiery, irate, lurid, rabid, rough, sharp, wroth 6 brutal, fierce, heated, mighty, potent, raging, savage, severe, stormy, strong 7 aroused, berserk, enraged, furious, intense, lawless, radical, rampant, vicious 8 coercive, demoniac, forceful, forcible, inflamed, maddened, maniacal, powerful, terrible, vehement, volcanic, wild-eyed 9 ferocious, gale-force, hotheaded, turbulent 10 immoderate, infuriated, passionate, tumultuous, unpeaceful
downfall: 4 ruin 5 wrack
episode: 4 rant 5 quake, seism 10 earthquake
struggle: 3 fit 5 agony, spasm, throe 7 seizure 8 paroxysm
weather: 4 gale, gust, hail, snow 5 blast, sleet, storm 6 precip, squall 7 cyclone, monsoon, tempest, thunder, tornado, twister 8 blizzard, downpour 9 hurricane, windstorm 10 cloudburst
Violent Bear It Away, The author: Flannery O'Connor
violently: 4 bang, hard 5 madly, rough 7 like mad 8 insanely 9 extremely 10 vehemently
aggressive type: 5 Rambo
angry one: 5 rager
force ~: 6 wrench
issue ~: 5 eruct
shake ~: 5 upset 6 quiver 7 agitate, disturb 8 convulse, unsettle 10 discompose
twist ~: 3 pry 5 wrest, wring 6 snatch, wrench
Violent Saturday (1955 film)
cast: Richard Egan, Victor Mature
violet: 4 blue 5 color, mauve, plant 6 dahlia, flower, grapee, purple
like a shrinking ~: 3 coy, shy 5 timid 6 demure, modest 7 bashful 8 blushing, reserved
mineral: 6 iolite
relative: 4 anil, cyan, navy, Nile, teal 5 Alice, azure, pansy, slate 6 cobalt, indigo, raisin 7 peacock 8 cerulean, sapphire 9 turquoise 10 aquamarine, periwinkle
-scented compound: 5 irone
starter: 5 ultra
sweet ~: 5 parma
__ violet: 4 Mars 5 dame's, Parma, sweet 6 bishop 7 African, crystal, gentian, Persian
violin: 4 lira 5 ko-kiu 6 fiddle, lirica, string
ancestor: 5 rebec 6 rebeck
attachment: 4 mute
bow part: 4 frog
cousin: 4 bass 5 cello
ender: 5 maker 6 making
fine ~: 5 Amati, Strad
material: 6 catgut
part: 3 peg 4 neck 5 f hole, waist
relative: 5 rebab, viola
stroke: 5 upbow
violin __: 4 clef 6 spider
Violin author: Anne Rice
violinist: 4 Auer, Bull, Hahn 5 Elman, Fodor, Stern, Tatum, Ysaye 6 Enesco, Midori, Morini, Mutter 7 Heifetz, Joachim, Kubelik, Menuhin, Ole Bull, Perlman, Szigeti 8 Kreisler, Milstein, Oistrakh, Zukerman 9 Zimbalist 10 Isaac Stern, Mischa Auer
Austrian ~: 8 Kreisler
Belgian ~: 5 Ysaye
Czech ~: 7 Kubelik
direction: 4 arco
German ~: 6 Mutter
Hungarian ~: 4 Auer 7 Joachim, Szigeti
Israeli ~: 7 Perlman 8 Zukerman
Japanese ~: 6 Midori
jazz ~: 5 Tatum
need: 3 bow 5 resin, rosin
Norwegian ~: 4 Bull
Romanian ~: 6 Enesco
Russian ~: 5 Elman 8 Milstein, Oistrakh 9 Zimbalist
Viorst: 6 Judith
VIP: 4 BMOC, exec., lion 5 biggy, celeb, mogul, mover, Mr. Big, nabob 6 biggie, bigwig, cheese, honcho, kahuna, shaker 7 bigshot, hotshot, magnate, notable 8 luminary, somebody, superior 9 big cheese, celebrity, dignitary, key player, muck-a-muck, personage
part of ~: 4 very 6 person 9 important
viper: 3 asp 5 adder, cobra, snake 6 animal, gaboon 7 reptile, serpent, traitor 8 betrayer, quisling, turncoat 9 no-goodnik, puff adder, scoundrel 10 blackguard, fer-de-lance
ender: 4 fish
group: 4 nest
like a ~: 6 hooded
relative: 3 boa 5 aboma, adder, krait, mamba, racer 6 dhaman, python, taipan 7 markhor, rattler 8 anaconda, moccasin, ringhals 9 boomslang, coachwhip 10 bushmaster, copperhead, sidewinder
weapon: 4 fang 5 venom
__ viper: 3 pit 4 sand 6 gaboon, horned
Viper: 3 car 4 auto 5 Dodge 10 automobile
viperous: 6 aspish 7 hostile 8 venomous 9 poisonous
Vipers' Tangle author: François Mauriac
V.I.P.s, The (1963 film)
cast: Richard Burton, Louis Jourdan, Margaret Rutherford, Elizabeth Taylor
vir: 3 man 5 Latin
wife: 4 uxor
virago: 3 nag 5 harpy, scold, shrew 6 beldam, chider, noodge 7 beldame, needler 8 fishwife, harridan, spitfire 9 henpecker, termagant, Xanthippe
viral: 8 catching, virulent 9 spreading 10 contagious, infectious
vireo: 4 bird
Virgil: 4 Earp, poet 5 Roman, Tibbs 7 Thomson
brother of ~: 5 Wyatt 6 Morgan
described its eruption: 4 Etna 5 Aetna
genre: 4 epos, idyl 5 idyll
see also Latin
virgin: 3 new 4 mint, pure 5 first, fresh 6 intact, unused, vestal 7 initial, untried 8 brand-new, innocent, original, primeval, pristine, spotless, unmarred, untapped 9 primaeval, unspoiled, unsullied, untouched 10 immaculate
virgin __: 4 wool 5 metal 8 olive oil
Virgin: 4 sign 5 Virgo 6 August 9 September
predecessor: 4 Lion
successor: 6 Scales 7 Balance
the ~: 4 sign
Virgin __: 4 Mary 5 Queen 7 Islands
__ Virgin: 5 Like a 7 Blessed
virginal: 3 new 4 pure 5 first, fresh, piano 6 intact, modest, unused, vestal 7 initial, untried 8 brand-new, innocent, keyboard, original, primeval, pristine, spotless, unmarred, untapped 9 lily-white, primaeval, unspoiled, unsullied, untouched 10 immaculate
Virginia: 4 Dare, Grey, Mayo, Wade 5 Apgar, Bruce, state, Woolf 6 Madsen 7 McKenna
bay: 10 Chesapeake
capital: 8 Richmond
caverns: 5 Luray
city: 5 Burke, Salem 6 Oakton, Reston, Vienna 7 Fairfax, Hampton, Herndon, MacLean, Norfolk, Roanoke, Suffolk 8 Dale City, Danville, Groveton, Hopewell, Leesburg, Manassas, Quantico, Richmond, Staunton, Tuckahoe 9 Annandale, Arlington, Chantilly, Franconia, Jefferson, Lake Ridge, Lynchburg, Newington 10 Alexandria, Appomattox, Blacksburg, Cave Spring, Chesapeake, Petersburg, Portsmouth, Waynesboro, Winchester, Woodbridge
conference: 3 ACC
explorer: 7 Raleigh
famous family of ~: 4 Lees
mountain: 6 Rogers 8 Catoctin
national park: 10 Shenandoah
neighbor: 8 Kentucky, Maryland 9 Tennessee
once: 6 colony 10 settlement
school: 3 ODU, VMI
state beverage: 4 milk
state bird: 8 cardinal
state dog: 8 foxhound
state fish: 10 brook trout
state flower: 7 dogwood
state shell: 6 oyster
state tree: 7 dogwood
Virginia __: 3 ham 4 deer, pine, plan, rail, reel 5 fence, stock 6 willow 7 cowslip, creeper
__, Virginia,...: 3 Yes
Virginia Beach: 4 city, town 6 resort
Virginia City neighbor: 4 Reno
Virginia ham: 4 meat
Virginian-Pilot: 5 paper 9 newspaper
locale: 7 Norfolk
Virginians, The author: Thackeray
Virginian, The (NBC western)
cast: Lee J. Cobb (Judge Henry Garth)
Janes Drury (The Virginian)
Doug McClure (Trampas)
Virginia reel: 5 dance
Virginia Tech: 3 VPI
athletes: 6 Hokies 8 Gobblers
conference: 7 Big East
locale: 10 Blacksburg
...Virginia Woolf author: 5 Albee
Virgin in a Tree artist: 4 Klee

Virgin Islander, certain: 6 Cruzan
Virgin Islands
clock setting: 3 AST
island: 7 St.Croix 8 St. Thomas
urbanite: 6 Cruzan
__ Virgin Islands: 6 Danish 7 British
__-virgin olive oil: 5 extra
Virgin Queen, The (1955 film)
cast: Joan Collins, Bette Davis, Richard Todd
Virgin Suicides, The (2000 film)
cast: Kirsten Dunst, Hannah Hall, Kathleen Turner, James Woods
director: Sofia Coppola
Virgin with the Monkey artist: 5 Durer
Virgo: 4 sign 6 Virgin
constellation near ~: 5 Libra 6 Corvus
follower: 5 Libra
month: 3 Aug. 4 Sept. 6 August 9 September
preceder: 3 Leo
star in ~: 5 Spica
virgule: 5 slash
virid: 4 jade, lime 5 green 7 emerald
relative: 3 pea 4 cyan, sage 5 beryl, breen, olive 6 myrtle, reseda 7 avocado, celadon, verdant 9 pistachio, turquoise 10 aquamarine, chartreuse
virile: 4 bold, hale, iron, male, sexy, wiry 5 beefy, burly, hardy, hefty, hunky, husky, lusty, macho, manly, stout, tough, vital 6 brawny, hearty, mighty, potent, robust, rugged, sinewy, steely, stocky, strong, sturdy 7 doughty, healthy, vibrant 8 athletic, forceful, indurate, muscular, powerful, puissant, stalwart, vigorous 9 Atlantean, energetic, Herculean, masculine, masterful, strapping, well-built 10 able-bodied, red-blooded
type: 4 hunk 5 Atlas, he-man, Rambo 6 Samson, Tarzan 7 Goliath 8 Hercules, macho man, tough guy
virility, deprive of: 5 unman
Virna: 4 Lisi
Virtanen, Artturi: 7 chemist, Finnish 8 Nobelist
virtu: 6 curios 10 objets d'art
virtual: 5 quasi, tacit 7 implied 8 implicit, indirect
virtual __: 3 tie 5 image 6 memory 7 machine, reality, storage
virtually: 4 nigh 6 almost, nearly 8 as good as, in effect 9 basically, in essence
virtue: 4 boon, good, hope, love, plus 5 asset, faith, honor, merit, power, right, value, worth 6 ethics, purity 7 benefit, charity, dignity, feature, honesty, justice, modesty, probity, quality, stature 8 chastity, fineness, goodness, kindness, morality, nobility, prudence, strength 9 advantage, character, fortitude, good point, innocence, integrity, rectitude 10 excellence, generosity, honestness, temperance, worthiness
Buddhist ~: 8 paramita
by ~ of: 3 via 5 due to, using 7 because, owing to, through 8 thanks to
cardinal ~: 4 hope 5 faith 7 charity, justice 8 prudence 9 fortitude 10 temperance
cite the ~ of: 4 laud 5 exalt, extol 6 esteem, extoll, praise 7 acclaim, commend, worship 8 eulogize 9 brag about 10 compliment
model of ~: 5 saint
religious ~: 4 zeal 5 faith, piety 8 devotion 9 reverence 10 devoutness, veneration
symbol of ~: 4 halo
Virtue is __ own reward: 3 its
virtueless: 3 bad, low 4 evil, vile 5 cruel 6 no good, unholy 7 corrupt, crooked, heinous, immoral, vicious 8 depraved, diabolic, ignominy, sinister 9 execrable, loathsome, malicious, monstrous, nefarious, repugnant, revolting 10 malevolent, villainous
Virtue of Selfishness, The author: 4 Rand
Virtues of Aging, The author: 6 Carter
virtuosity: 3 art 5 craft, skill, touch 7 mastery, prowess 8 artistry, wizardry 9 expertise 10 brilliance
virtuoso: 3 ace 4 star, whiz 5 adept, brain, maven, mavin 6 artist, expert, genius, master, player, wizard 7 artiste, egghead, hotshot, old hand, prodigy, thinker 8 Einstein, highbrow, musician 9 performer, superstar 10 mastermind, specialist
performance: 5 éclat
virtuous: 4 good, just, nice, pure 5 clean, moral, noble, pious, right, sound 6 chaste, decent, honest, worthy 7 ethical, saintly, upright 8 celibate, elevated, faithful, innocent, spotless, straight, true-blue 9 blameless, exemplary, guiltless, honorable, righteous, unsullied, untainted, wholesome 10 goody-goody, high-minded, immaculate, inculpable, inviolable, moralistic, principled
one: 5 angel, model, saint
path of ~ conduct: 3 Tao
virtuousness: 5 grace, honor, merit 6 esteem, renown 7 decency, dignity, honesty, loyalty, probity 8 eminence, fairness, goodness, morality, nobility, veracity 9 adoration, character, gallantry, greatness, integrity, rectitude, reverence, sincerity 10 admiration
virtute et __: 5 armis
virulence: 6 rancor 8 acrimony 9 animosity, hostility 10 bitterness
virulent: 5 fatal, sharp, toxic, viral 6 bitter, deadly, ireful, lethal, malign, septic 7 baneful, cutting, harmful, hateful, hostile, vicious 8 scathing, spiteful, venomous 9 corrosive, infective, injurious, malicious, poisonous, rancorous, resentful, splenetic, unhealthy, vitriolic 10 infectious, malevolent, pernicious, vindictive
__ virumque cano: 4 Arma
virus: 3 bug 4 germ 6 grippe 7 illness, microbe 9 infection, influenza
antibacterial ~: 5 phage
computer ~: 4 worm
starter: 4 echo
target: 2 PC 3 CPU 8 computer
__ virus: 3 DNA, RNA
visa: 4 pass 6 papers, permit 7 passage
Visa: 10 credit card
charge: 4 debt 7 arrears 9 arrearage, liability
rival: 8 Discover 10 Diner's Club, MasterCard
use ~: 3 buy 6 charge 8 purchase
visacha: 6 animal, mammal, rodent
relative: 3 rat 4 cavy, degu, jird, paca, vole 5 coypu, gundi, mouse, xerus 6 agouti, beaver, gerbil, gopher, jerboa, marmot, murine 7 hamster, lemming, muskrat 8 chipmunk, cricetid, dormouse, squirrel, tuco-tuco 9 chickaree, groundhog, guinea pig, porcupine, woodchuck 10 chinchilla, prairie dog
visage: 3 mug 4 cast, face, look, puss 6 aspect 8 features 10 expression
villain ~: 4 leer 5 scoff, smirk, sneer
Visalia: 4 city, town
locale: 10 California
vis-à-vis: 4 sofa 5 tryst 6 direct, toward 7 against, towards 8 opposite 10 compared to, face-to-face
Visayan: 8 language
Visayan Islands, one of the: 5 Samar
viscera: 4 guts 5 heart 7 innards
combining form: 9 splanchno-
visceral: 3 gut 5 inner 8 physical 9 emotional, innermost, intuitive
visceral __: 4 arch 5 cleft 6 groove
viscid: 4 icky, ropy 5 gluey, gooey, gummy, ropey, thick 9 glutinous
substance: 3 goo 4 ooze 5 slime
Visconti: 7 Luchino
viscosity __: 5 index
viscount: 4 lord, peer, rank 5 noble, title 8 nobleman
superior: 4 earl
viscountess: 4 lady, peer, rank 5 noble, title
viscous: 4 ropy 5 gluey, gooey, goopy, gummy, ropey, slimy, thick 6 clammy, glairy, liquid, sirupy, sticky, syrupy, viscid 8 adhesive 9 glutinous, jellylike 10 gelatinous
liquid: 3 oil 4 lard 5 pitch 6 grease 9 lubricant, petroleum
substance: 3 tar 4 goop 5 slime
Viscuso: 3 Sal
vise: 4 grip, hold, tool 5 clamp, press 6 C-clamp 7 gripper
part: 3 jaw
Vishnu: 9 Preserver
avatar of ~: 4 Rama
companion: 4 Siva 5 Shiva 6 Brahma
worshiper: 5 Hindu 6 Hindoo
visibility: 4 look, show 5 scene, sight 6 glance, seeing 7 display, exhibit, eyeshot, glimpse, observe, viewing 9 spectacle 10 appearance, exhibition, perception
improve ~: 5 defog, deice
problem: 3 fog 4 haze, mist 5 smaze
zero: 3 fog 4 haze, smog
visible: 4 bold, open, seen 5 clear, overt, plain 6 in view, marked, patent, public 7 evident, exposed, glaring, in sight, obvious, outward 8 apparent, clear-cut, definite, explicit, external, manifest, palpable, revealed, striking, tangible, unhidden, unveiled, viewable 9 big as life, obtrusive 10 detectable, noticeable, observable, pronounced, unshrouded
barely ~: 3 dim 4 dull, hazy, pale 5 faded, faint, fuzzy, vague, woozy 6 subtle 7 obscure, unclear
be ~: 3 see 4 come, show, view 5 pop up, shine 6 appear, arrive, attend, expose, flaunt, lay out, mirror, parade, report, reveal, show up, turn up, unfold, unfurl, unveil 7 exhibit, trot out, turn out, uncover 8 bring out, discover, indicate, manifest, stick out 9 make known, spectacle
become ~: 4 loom 6 appear, emerge
combining form: 6 phaner- 7 phanero-
make ~: 5 flare, flash, light, shine 6 ignite, illume, kindle, turn on 7 inflame, lighten 8 brighten, enkindle, illumine 9 highlight, set fire to, set on fire, spotlight 10 illuminate
visible __: 5 light 6 speech 7 horizon
Visigoth foe: 3 Hun
vision: 3 eye 4 idea, trip, view 5 angel, dream, ideal, image, scope, sight 6 beauty, eyeful, fantom, looker, mirage, optics, oracle, seeing, spirit, trance 7 concept, dazzler, fantasy, insight, outlook, phantom, realize, stunner 8 daydream, eyesight, head trip, illusion, keenness, knockout, prophecy 9 foresight, intuition, nightmare, pipe dream 10 appearance, astuteness, conception, envisaging, perception, prescience, revelation, standpoint
beatific ~: 8 afflatus
combining form: 4 -opia, opto- 5 -opsia
field of ~: 3 ken 4 view 5 range, reach, scope, sight, vista 7 compass, horizon, purview
frightening ~: 8 bad dream 9 nightmare
good ~: 6 acuity 8 keenness
of ~: 5 optic 6 visual
starter: 4 Pana, tele 5 cable
vision __: 5 cloth, quest
__ vision: 4 X-ray 5 dream 6 double, mosaic, tunnel 7 machine
visionary: 3 fey 4 airy, seer 5 lofty 6 dreamy, mystic, unreal, zealot 7 utopian 8 creative, delusory, fanciful, illusive, illusory, mystical, mythical, quixotic, romantic, theorist 9 ambitious, idealized, imaginary, prophetic, stargazer, unworldly 10 Don Quixote, idealistic, impossible, quixotical, starry-eyed, unfeasible, unworkable
of old: 4 aery
Vision of Love (1990 song) artist: Mariah Carey
Vision of Sir Launfal, The author: James Russell Lowell
visions, having: 6 adream
Visions of Cody author: Jack Kerouac
Vision, The author: Dean Koontz
visit: 2 do 3 see 4 call, chat, come, go to, stay, stop, talk, tour 5 go see, haunt, pop by, pop in, run in, smite, tarry, wreak 6 arrive, attend, befall, call on, come by, come to, drop by, drop in, look up, remain, show up, stop by, stop in, take in, travel 7 afflict, go to see, holiday, inflict, sit in on, sojourn, stop off, swing by, trouble 8 call upon, converse, drop over, frequent, look in on, pay a call, stay with, stopover, vacation 9 force upon, get around, hang out at, interview, touch base 10 come around, pay a call on, social call
anew: 5 resee
hotel ~: 4 rest, stay 7 holiday, respite, sojourn 8 stopover, vacation
nautical ~: 3 gam
often: 5 haunt 7 hang out 8 frequent 9 hang out at 10 hang around
__ visit: 5 state
Visit __ Small Planet: 3 to a
visitation: 5 trial 6 mishap, ordeal 7 undoing
Visit From St. Nicholas, A: 4 poem
opener: 4 'twas
writer: 5 Moore
visiting: 4 here 6 in town
visiting __: 4 card 5 hours, nurse 7 fireman, teacher 9 professor
visitor: 5 guest 6 caller, drop-in 7 company, habitué, invitee, tourist 8 stranger 9 foreigner, sightseer, transient 10 vacationer
annual ~: 5 Santa
from space: 2 ET 5 alien, comet
receive a ~: 3 see 4 host, mark, view 5 greet, lodge, pop in, put up 6 attend, behold 7 receive 9 entertain, recognize 10 anticipate
room: 5 salon 6 parlor 7 gallery
Visitor: 4 Nana
visitors: 4 team 5 party 7 company, society 8 assembly 9 gathering
accepting ~: 6 at home

Visit to a Small Planet
author: Gore Vidal
cat: **10** Clementine
dog: 3 Red
visor: **4** bill, brim, mask **8** eyeshade, sunshade
__ visor: **3** sun **6** flip-up
visored headgear: **4** kepi **5** armet
Vissi d'arte: **4** aria
opera: **5** Tosca
vista: **4** view **5** scape, scene, sight, sweep **7** horizon, outlook, scenery **8** panorama, prospect **9** landscape
Vista: **4** city, town
locale: **10** California
__ Vista: **4** Alta **5** Buena, Chula
VISTA part: **4** Amer., Serv. **7** America, Service **10** Volunteers
Vistula: **5** river
city on the ~: **6** Cracow, Krakow, Warsaw
locale: **6** Poland
river to the ~: **3** Bug, San
visual: **4** seen **5** optic **6** beheld, imaged, ocular **7** graphic, optical, seeable, sensory **8** viewable **9** graphical, sensorial
aid: **3** map **4** grid, plan, plot **5** chart, graph, table **6** sketch **7** diagram **9** blueprint, floor plan
enhancers: **5** specs **7** glasses **8** contacts
examination: **4** gaze, look, peek, scan **5** sight, study **6** gander, glance, review, survey **7** glimpse, look-see, viewing **8** once-over, scrutiny **10** inspection
signal: **3** bat **4** wink **5** blink, flick **6** squint **7** flutter, twinkle **8** high sign
starter: **5** audio
visual __: **3** aid **4** arts **5** field, range **6** acuity, binary, cortex, purple
visual __ terminal: **7** display
__-visual: **5** audio
visualization: **7** imagery **9** imagining, picturing
visualize: **3** see **5** fancy, think **6** call up **7** dream up, imagine, picture, project, realize, think up **8** envisage, envision **9** conjure up **10** anticipate, call to mind, conceive of
visually, examine: **4** look
vita: **6** résumé **7** profile **9** biography
__ vita: **5** dolce **7** durante
vitae
aqua ~: **5** booze, drink, sauce **6** liquor **7** alcohol, liqueur, potable, spirits, whiskey **9** firewater, inebriant, moonshine **10** intoxicant
curriculum ~: **3** bio **6** digest, précis, record, résumé **7** outline, summary **8** synopsis
lignum ~: **4** tree
starter: **5** arbor
__ vitae: **4** aqua **5** arbor **6** lignum
vital: **3** key, nec., req. **4** live, main, must **5** acute, alive, basic, fresh, lusty, major, peppy, sound **6** lively, living, needed, urgent, virile **7** central, crucial, dynamic, organic, pivotal, primary, radical, vibrant, zestful **8** cardinal, critical, decisive, integral, pressing, required, spirited, vigorous **9** energetic, essential, important, mandatory, momentous, necessary, paramount, requisite, right-hand, strategic, vivacious **10** bottom-line, imperative, meaningful, portentous, underlined, underlying
élan ~: **4** life, soul **6** psyche, spirit
fluid: **3** sap **5** blood, serum
force: **4** soul **5** anima, being **6** energy, psyche **8** vivacity
moment: **4** D-day **5** H-hour **6** crisis **8** juncture, zero hour **9** crossroad, emergency
part: **3** cog **9** essential, necessity
remove ~ parts: **3** gut **4** sack **5** rifle **6** ravage **7** destroy, pillage, plunder, ransack **8** clean out, decimate
sign: **5** pulse
something ~: **4** must, need **5** vital **9** essential, necessity, requisite **10** imperative, obligation, sine qua non
spark: **3** vim, zip **4** brio, dash, élan, fire, life, soul, zest, zing **5** being, gusto, heart, nerve, oomph, pluck, verve, vigor **6** animus, bounce, energy, esprit, psyche, spirit **7** essence, passion **9** animation, life force **10** enthusiasm, excitement, exuberance, get-up-and-go, liveliness
stat: **3** age, DOB **6** height, weight
stats: **3** bio **5** story **6** résumé **7** profile
vital __: **5** force, signs **10** statistics
__ vital: **4** élan
Vitale: **4** Dick
Vitalian: **4** pope **7** pontiff
vitality: **2** go **3** pep, vim, zip **4** dint, élan, guts, kick, life, push, snap, soul, thew, zest, zing **5** ardor, brawn, drive, force, juice, might, oomph, power, prime, punch, spark, spunk, steam, thews, verve, vigor **6** action, bounce, energy, fervor, muscle, pizazz, spirit, starch **7** fitness, muscles, pizzazz, potence, potency, sparkle, stamina **8** presence, strength, vivacity **9** animation, beefiness, endurance, fortitude, hardiness, huskiness, lustiness, puissance, stoutness, toughness **10** brawniness, brute force, ebullience, exuberance, get up and go, liveliness, mightiness, robustness, sturdiness
have ~: **4** live **5** exist **7** breathe, prosper **8** flourish
lack of ~: **6** anemia, anergy **7** anaemia
vitalize: **4** gird, tone **5** build, liven, pep up, shore, steel **6** anneal, arouse, beef up, harden, prop up, pump up, temper, tone up, turn on, vivify **7** animate, bolster, brace up, build up, burgeon, develop, empower, enhance, enliven, fortify, juice up, liven up, quicken, shore up, stiffen, toughen **8** activate, bourgeon, buttress, energize, enspirit, indurate, inspirit **9** impassion, intensify, reinforce, stimulate **10** invigorate, rejuvenate
Vitallium: **5** alloy
component: **6** cobalt **8** chromium **10** molybdenum
Vital Parts author: Thomas Berger
vitals: **6** inside, organs **7** filling, innards **8** contents
Vital Signs author: Robin Cook
vitamin
A source: **4** kail, kale **6** carrot
B ~: **6** biotin, folate
C: **4** acid
chain: **3** GNC
C source: **3** ade **4** lime **6** citrus, orange
D source: **4** milk
monitor: **3** FDA
P: **5** rutin
quantity: **2** IU **3** RDA **4** dose, pill **5** bolus **6** pellet, tablet **7** capsule
starter: **4** mega **5** multi
vitamin B __: **7** complex
__ vitamins: **7** One-a-Day
vitamins, add: **6** enrich
like ~: **3** OTC
Vitara: **3** SUV **6** Suzuki
Vitas: **10** Gerulaitis
vitiate: **3** mar, sap **4** harm, hurt, jade, thin, tire **5** abase, quash, spoil, taint, weary **6** damage, debase, defile, dilute, impair, infect, injure, negate, weaken **7** abolish, corrupt, degrade, deprave, exhaust, fatigue, pollute, subvert, tire out, wear out **8** abrogate, enervate, enfeeble **9** attenuate, undermine, water down **10** adulterate, debilitate, devitalize, emasculate, invalidate
vitiated: **6** coarse, filthy, impure, soiled **7** corrupt, dirtied, stained, sullied, tainted, unclean **8** maculate, polluted, unchaste **9** tarnished, unrefined **10** unsanitary
vitiation: **8** baseness **9** annulment, depravity **10** corruption, debasement, degeneracy
Viti Levu: **3** isl. **4** isle **6** island
locale: **4** Fiji
Vito: **6** Scotti **8** Corleone
Vitoria: **4** city, town
locale: **6** Brazil
vitreous: **5** clear, lucid **6** glassy **7** crystal **10** reflective
vitreous __: **5** humor
vitrify: **4** jell **6** anneal, harden **7** calcify, congeal **8** indurate, solidify
vitriol: **4** acid
__ vitriol: **4** blue, iron **5** green, oil of, white
vitriolic: **4** acid **5** acrid, sharp **6** bitter **7** hostile, mocking **8** derisive, scathing, scornful, stinging, virulent **10** disdainful
vittles: **4** chow, eats, fare, feed, food, grub **7** aliment, edibles **9** provender **10** provisions
have ~: **3** eat **4** dine, nosh **5** feast, gorge, graze, munch, scarf, snack **6** devour, ingest, nibble, pig out, take in **7** consume, put away, scarf up **8** chow down, gobble up, take food, wolf down **9** have a bite, have a meal, polish off, scarf down **10** break bread
__ Vittles: **6** Tender
Vittorio: **6** De Seta, De Sica **7** Alfieri, Gassman
in English: **6** Victor
Vittorio the Vampire author: Anne Rice
vituperate: **3** jaw **4** lash, rail, slur **5** abuse, blame, curse, growl, scold **6** accuse, bark at, berate, defame, injure, insult, malign, revile, vilify, yell at **7** bawl out, censure, chew out, condemn, lambast, rip into, run down, upbraid **8** denounce, lace into, lambaste, tear into **9** blaspheme, castigate, find fault, fulminate **10** blackguard
vituperation: **5** abuse **6** insult, tirade **7** censure **8** diatribe, scolding
vituperator: **3** nag **5** scold, shrew **6** chider, grouch, kvetch, virago, whiner **7** caviler, rebuker, reviler **8** grumbler **9** henpecker, termagant, Xanthippe **10** castigator, complainer
Vitus: **5** saint **6** Bering
__ & Viv: **3** Tom
viva: **5** huzza **6** hoorah, hooray, hurrah, hurray, huzzah **8** long live
voce: **4** oral **5** aloud, vocal **6** loudly, orally **7** out loud **8** verbally
viva __: **4** voce
Viva: **10** paper towel
alternative: **5** Scott **6** Bounty, Brawny
Viva __!: **5** Villa **6** Zapata
Viva __ Vegas: **3** Las
ViVa author: e.e. cummings
vivace: **5** speed, tempo **8** velocity
vivacious: **3** gay **4** pert, spry **5** alert, alive, brash, brisk, happy, jazzy, jolly, merry, peppy, perky, vital, zesty **6** active, bouncy, breezy, bright, hearty, jaunty, lively, upbeat **7** animate, dashing, jumping, playful, rocking, vibrant, zestful **8** animated, bubbling, cheerful, spirited, sportive, swinging **9** convivial, ebullient, energetic, exuberant, sparkling, sprightly **10** frolicsome, full of life
Vivacious Lady (1938 film)
cast: James Ellison, Ginger Rogers, James Stewart
director: George Stevens
vivaciousness: **3** vim **4** brio, élan, life, zest **5** flair, oomph, spunk, vigor **6** energy, spirit **7** abandon, panache **8** flourish, vitality **10** enthusiasm, exuberance, liveliness
vivacity: **2** go **3** pep, zip **4** brio, dash, élan, fire, jazz, life, snap, soul **5** spark, verve **6** action, bounce, energy, esprit, gaiety, gayety, pizazz **7** pizzazz, sparkle **8** keenness, vitality **9** animation **10** ebullience, enthusiasm, get up and go, liveliness, vital force
Viva Las Vegas (1964 film)
cast: Ann-Margret, Cesare Danova, Elvis Presley
Vivaldi, Antonio: **7** Italian **8** composer
work: The Four Seasons
__ vivant: **3** bon **7** tableau
vivant, bon: **7** gourmet **8** hedonist, sybarite **9** epicurean **10** voluptuary
Vivarin alternative: **5** No-Doz
Viva Villa! (1934 film)
cast: Wallace Beery, Leo Carrillo, Fay Wray
Viva Zapata! (1952 film)
cast: Marlon Brando, Arnold Moss, Jean Peters, Anthony Quinn, Joseph Wiseman
director: Elia Kazan
vive: **5** huzza **6** hoorah, hooray, hurrah, hurray, huzzah
on the qui ~: **4** wary **5** alert **6** uneasy **7** heads-up, heedful, wakeful **8** keen-eyed, vigilant, watchful
__ vive: **3** qui
Vive __!: **5** le roi
Viveca: **8** Lindfors
__ vivendi: **5** modus
Vivian: **5** Vance **6** Blaine
Vivica A. __: **3** Fox
vivid: **3** gay **4** bold, live, loud, rich **5** clear, gaudy, juicy, light, lucid, lurid, plain, sharp, showy **6** bright, cogent, lively, strong **7** evident, express, glowing, graphic, intense, obvious, shining, vibrant **8** animated, apparent, colorful, definite, distinct, dramatic, eloquent, explicit, luminous, manifest, palpable, powerful, striking **9** brilliant, graphical, graspable, memorable **10** expressive, flamboyant, spelled out
display: **4** riot
quality: **5** color **10** brightness
Vivid: **6** bleach
alternative: **5** Purex, Snowy **6** Clorox **8** Borateem
Vivien: **5** Leigh **8** Merchant
vivify: **5** hop up, liven, pep up, rouse **6** bestir, pump up, turn on **7** animate, enliven, inspire, juice up, liven up, quicken, refresh **8** activate, energize, enspirit, inspirit, vitalize **9** stimulate **10** invigorate
Vivitar: **6** camera
alternative: **4** Fuji **5** Canon, Kodak, Leica, Nikon **6** Konica, Pentax, Rollei **7** Minolta, Olympus, Yashica **8** Polaroid
__-vivre: **6** savoir

vivre, joie de: **4** zest **6** gaiety, gayety **8** pleasure
vixen: **3** fox **5** flirt, harpy, shrew, siren **6** animal, chider **8** spitfire **9** termagant, Xanthippe
home: **3** den
offspring: **3** kit
Vixen: **8** reindeer
colleague: **5** Comet, Cupid **6** Dancer, Dasher, Donder **7** Blitzen, Prancer
Viyella: **6** fabric **7** flannel
viz.: **2** i.e. **5** id est, to wit **6** namely **10** for example
__ vizier: **5** grand
vizier superior: **3** aga **4** agha
Vizsla: **3** dog **5** canid **6** canine
V-J Day ended it: **4** WWII
VJ employer: **3** MTV
Vladimir: **5** Lenin, Putin, saint **6** Prelog **7** Kramnik, Nabokov **8** Horowitz, Sloukhin, Zworykin **9** Ashkenazy **10** Mayakovsky
see also Russian
Vladivostok: **4** city, port, town
locale: **6** Russia **7** Siberia
Vlasic ad animal: **5** stork
__ Vleck: **7** John van
V-Letter and Other Poems author: Karl Shapiro
Vlissingen: **4** city, port
locale: **7** Holland **11** Netherlands
Vltava: **5** river
VMD patient: **3** cat, cur, dog, pet, pup **4** mutt **5** hound, kitty, pooch, puppy, tabby **6** canine, feline, kitten **7** mongrel
see also vet
VMI: **3** sch. **4** coll.
locale: **8** Virginia **9** Lexington
student: **5** cadet **6** Keydet **7** soldier
V-neck: **5** shirt **6** blouse **7** sweater
vo-__: **4** tech
VOA agcy.: **4** USIA
__ vobiscum: **3** pax **4** deus **7** Dominus
vocab.: **3** lex., wds.
vocabulary: **4** cant, list **5** lexis, lingo, words **6** jargon **7** lexicon **8** glossary, language, verbiage **9** thesaurus **10** dictionary
special ~: **5** argot, idiom, lingo, slang **6** jargon, patois
unit: **4** word **5** idiom, sound **6** lexeme, phrase **8** morpheme **9** utterance
vocal: **4** glib, loud, oral, said, song, sung **5** blunt, frank, lyric, noisy **6** choral, facile, fluent, phonic, spoken, verbal, voiced **7** out loud, uttered, venting **8** eloquent, narrated, operatic, phonetic, strident, viva voce **9** clamorous, expressed, intonated, outspoken, talkative, unwritten **10** articulate, bigmouthed, expressive, forthright, free-spoken, pronounced, stentorian, unreticent
composition: **4** aria **5** motet **6** arioso
effect: **5** trill **7** vibrato
ender: **3** ist
expression: **6** speech
fanfare: **4** ta-da **5** ta-dah
gaffe: **4** flub, gaff, goof, slip **5** error, gaffe, lapse **7** blooper, misstep
group: **4** trio **5** choir, octet **6** chorus **7** octette **8** ensemble
of a ~ sound: **5** tonal
preceder: **4** vamp **5** intro
range: **4** alto, bass **5** tenor **7** soprano
space between ~ cords: **7** glottis
vocal __: **5** cords, folds
vocalist: **4** alto, bass, diva **5** mezzo, tenor **6** canary, singer **7** caroler, chanter, crooner, soprano, warbler **8** baritone, barytone, choir boy, musician **9** chanteuse, choir girl, chorister, contralto **10** coloratura, prima donna
vocalists: **5** choir **6** chorus **7** chorale **8** ensemble, glee club
vocalization: **6** speech **8** language **9** statement, utterance
vocalize: **3** rap, say **4** moan, sing, talk, vent **5** argue, chant, chirp, croon, groan, shout, speak, utter, voice, yodel, yodle **6** convey, impart, intone, mumble, murmur, warble **7** belt out, discuss, express, inflect **8** set forth, sound off **9** enunciate, pronounce, verbalize
displeasure: **3** boo **4** jeer **5** scoff, whoop **6** deride **7** catcall **8** ridicule
vocalized: **4** oral, said **6** spoken, verbal, voiced **7** sounded, uttered **8** narrated, viva voce **9** recounted
pause: **2** er, uh, um
vocalizing: **4** talk **5** pitch, spiel **6** homily, sermon, speech, tirade **7** bombast, lecture, oration, oratory, prattle **8** dialogue, diatribe, harangue, rhetoric **9** discourse, elocution, monologue, utterance **10** expressing, filibuster, recitation
vocally: **5** aloud **7** out loud **8** viva voce
vocation: **3** job **4** game, line, post, walk, work **5** craft, field, niche, thing, trade **6** career, métier, office, racket **7** calling, mission, pursuit **8** business, lifework, practice **9** specialty **10** department, employment, livelihood, nine-to-five, occupation, profession, walk of life
vocational __: **6** school
voce
sotto ~: **6** softly
sotto ~ remark: **5** aside
viva ~: **4** oral **5** aloud, vocal **6** loudly, orally **7** out loud **8** verbally
__ voce: **3** sub, una **4** viva **5** mezza, sotto
__ voce poco fa: **3** una
vociferant: **4** loud, wild **5** brash, noisy, rowdy, vocal **6** brassy, flashy, strong, unruly **7** blaring, booming, intense, raucous, riotous, roaring **8** emphatic, piercing, strident, vehement **9** clamorous, deafening **10** boisterous, disorderly, loud-voiced, resounding, stentorian, tumultuous, uproarious
vociferate: **3** cry **4** bawl, call, hoot, howl, roar, wail, yell **5** shout, whoop **6** bellow, holler, scream, shriek **7** screech, ululate **8** shout out
vociferation: **3** din **5** shout **6** racket **9** utterance
vociferous: **4** loud **5** forte, noisy **6** shrill **7** blaring, booming, jarring, pealing, rackety, ranting, raucous, reboant, roaring **8** crashing, piercing, plangent, rumbling, shouting, sonorous, strident, turned up, vehement **9** big-voiced, clamorous, deafening, insistent **10** boisterous, resounding, stentorian, strepitous, thundering, uproarious
vocoder: **8** keyboard **10** instrument
vodka: **5** drink **8** beverage
brand: **5** Popov, Stoli **7** Smirnov
cousin: **3** gin
drink: **6** gimlet **8** salty dog **10** bloody Mary, Moscow mule **11** screwdriver
vodun: **3** hex **5** magic, spell **6** voodoo **7** sorcery **10** witchcraft
VO5 rival: **4** Pert **5** Prell
__ Vogler: **3** Abt
vogue: **3** fad, mod, now, ton **4** chic, mode, rage **5** craze, dance, favor, style, trend **6** custom, latest, modish, trendy, with it **7** fashion, in thing, popular **8** last word **9** nattiness **10** acceptance, dernier cri, modishness, popularity
in ~: **3** hip, hot, now **4** chic **5** faddy **6** classy, latest, modish, trendy **7** current, popular, stylish **8** accepted, up-to-date **10** newfangled
no longer in ~: **3** out **5** dated, passé
Vogue (1990 song) artist: Madonna
Vogues
song: Five O'Clock World (1965)
My Special Angel (1968)
Turn Around, Look at Me (1968)
You're the One (1965)
voguish: **3** hip, mod **4** chic, tony **5** haute, natty, nifty, sharp, smart, swank, swell, toney **6** chi-chi, classy, dapper, dressy, flossy, modish, snappy, trendy **7** à la mode, current, dashing, elegant, in style, popular, stylish **8** up-to-date **9** high-class, in fashion **10** all the rage
voice: **3** air, cry, put, say **4** alto, bass, call, part, roar, talk, tell, tone, vent, vote, yell **5** opine, organ, say-so, shout, sound, speak, state, tenor, utter, words **6** active, assert, choice, intone, mumble, murmur, mutter, option, phrase, speech, tongue **7** declare, divulge, express, mention, opinion, passive, present, recount, soprano **8** announce, baritone, barytone, decision, language, proclaim, put forth, set forth, sound off, suffrage, vocalize **9** comment on, contralto, elocution, emphasize, enunciate, make known, pronounce, statement, utterance, verbalize, vox populi **10** articulate, coloratura, inflection, intonation, preference
an objection: **5** argue, demur, groan
box: **6** larynx
combining form: **4** phon- **5** phono-
ender: **4** over **5** print
give ~ to: **5** speak, utter
gravelly ~: **4** rasp **5** grate **7** scratch
in full ~: **5** aroar
inner ~: **8** scruples, superego **10** conscience, principles
let one's ~ be heard: **6** assert, insist **7** declare, speak up **8** sound off, speak out **10** stand up for
lift up one's ~: **4** sing **5** chant, croon **6** intone, warble **7** belt out, perform **8** melodize, vocalize **10** carry a tune
low ~: **3** hum **4** deep **6** breath, mumble, murmur, mutter **7** whisper
of ~ pitch: **5** tonal
quality: **4** tone **5** twang **6** accent
raise one's ~: **4** roar, yell **5** shout **6** bellow, holler, scream
range: **4** alto, bass **5** mezzo, tenor **7** soprano **8** baritone
small ~: **4** soul **8** scruples, superego **10** conscience, moral sense
transmitter: **4** mike **9** megaphone
vote: **3** aye, nay, yea
with one ~: **5** as one, whole **6** in sync, united **7** en masse, jointly, unified **8** as a group, combined, communal, in unison, mutually, together, unitedly **9** accordant, all at once, in concert, unanimous **10** agreed upon, conjointly, harmonious, like-minded
voice __: **3** box **4** coil, mail, part, vote
voice-__ analyzer: **6** stress
Voice __ Turtle, The: **5** of the
voice box
combining form: **6** laryng- **7** laryngo-
voiced: **4** oral **5** aloud, vocal **6** spoken **9** vocalized
__-voiced: **4** deep **5** rough
voiceless: **3** mum **4** hush, mute **5** quiet, still **6** silent **9** noiseless **10** speechless, tongue-tied
consonant: **4** surd
voicemail, check: **6** call in
Voice of America org.: **4** USIA
Voice of Israel author: **4** Eban
Voice of the Night, The author: Dean Koontz
voiceover: **6** review **7** remarks **8** analysis, exegesis **9** discourse, narration **10** commentary, exposition, expression
do a ~: **3** dub **4** tape **6** record
edit a ~: **5** redub
voices
eight ~: **5** octet **7** octette
five ~: **7** quintet
for ~: **5** lyric, vocal **6** choral **7** lyrical, musical
four ~: **7** quartet
six ~: **6** sextet **8** sextette
three ~: **4** trio
Voices __ Night: **5** of the
Voices of the Night author: Henry Wadsworth Longfellow
Voice, The (1981 song) artist: Moody Blues
void: **3** gap, nix **4** bare, dump, emit, gulf, hole, lack, null, zero **5** abysm, abyss, annul, blank, clear, drain, eject, empty, quash, space, waste **6** barren, cancel, cavity, glassy, hollow, negate, recant, repeal, revoke, vacant, vacuum **7** abolish, absence, deflate, deplete, drained, emptied, invalid, negated, nullify, opening, rescind, reverse, vacancy, vacuity, vacuous **8** abrogate, dissolve, evacuate, nihility, overturn, throw out **9** blankness, cancelled, discharge, emptiness, repudiate **10** blue-pencil, invalidate, unratified
become ~: **3** end **5** cease, lapse **6** breach, expire, weaken **7** default, misstep, regress, relapse **9** terminate
declare ~: **5** quash **6** repeal, revoke **7** rescind **8** override, overrule **9** discharge, repudiate
partner: **4** null
voided serve: **3** let
Voight, Jon: **5** actor
daughter: Angelina Jolie
film: Ali (2001)
Catch-22 (1970)
Coming Home (1978, AA)
Conrack (1974)
Deliverance (1972)
Desert Bloom (1986)
Enemy of the State (1998)
Heat (1995)
Lara Croft: Tomb Raider (2001)
Midnight Cowboy (1969)
Mission: Impossible (1996)
The Odessa File (1974)
Pearl Harbor (2001)
The Rainmaker (1997)
The Revolutionary (1970)
Runaway Train (1985)
Table for Five (1983)
voilà: **4** ta-da **5** ta-dah, there **6** behold
voile: **5** ninon **6** fabric **7** chiffon
Voina i __: **3** mir
voir __: **4** dire
Voiron: **4** city, town
locale: **6** France
vol.: **2** bk.
measure: **2** cc., ml. **4** cu. ft., cu. in, cu. yd.
Vol: **10** Tennessean
Volans neighbor: **5** Mensa
volant: **6** aerial, flying **8** airborne, in the air
Volare: **3** car **4** auto **8** Plymouth
Volare (song) artist: Bobby Rydell, Dean Martin
Volare word: **3** blu, nel **7** dipinto

volary: **6** aviary **8** birdcage, dovecote **9** birdhouse
volatile: **4** fumy **5** gassy, irate, saucy **6** fickle **7** erratic, flighty, nervous **8** fugitive, skittish, ticklish, unstable, unsteady, variable **9** ephemeral, excitable, explosive, fugacious, hotheaded, mercurial, momentary, transient, unsettled, up-and-down, whimsical **10** capricious, changeable, inconstant, short-lived, transitory
liquid: **5** nitro
volatility: **5** folly **6** whimsy **8** dallying, zaniness **9** flippancy, frivolity, giddiness, lightness, sauciness, silliness
measure, on Wall Street: **4** beta
volcanic: **5** angry, irate **6** fuming, heated, ireful, raging, red-hot **7** enraged, igneous, steamed, violent **8** inflamed, volatile, wrathful **10** hysterical
crater: **4** maar
emission: **3** ash **4** fume **6** ejecta
formation: **4** cone
in appearance: **5** conic **7** conical
rock: **4** lava, slag, tuff **5** magma **6** basalt, pumice **8** obsidian
volcanic __: **3** ash **4** bomb, cone, neck, tuff **5** glass
volcano: **3** Aso, Oku, Usu **4** Akan, cone, Etna, Fogo, Fuji, Gaua, Nasu, peak, Póas, Popo, Ruiz, Taal **5** Alaid, Asama, Azuma, Fuego, Hekla, Irazú, Kelut, Manam, Mayon, mound, Pelee, Raung, Tacan, Unzen, Yasur **6** Ambrym, Arenal, Bagana, Bandai, Chokai, Colima, Dukono, Erebus, Krafla, Láscar, Lassen, Lopevi, Masaya, Merapi, Ontake, Oshima, Pacaya, Pavlof, Puracé, Rabaul, Sangay, Semeru, Slamet, Tiatia, Toluca, Ulawun **7** Adatara, Bulusan, Canlaon, El Misti, Erta-Ale, Galeras, Gareloi, Iliamna, Kerinci, Kilauea, Langila, Orizaba, Redoubt, Ruapehu **8** Cotopaxi, Gamalama, Karthala, Karymsky, Mauna Loa, mountain, Pinatubo, St. Helens, Vesuvius, Wrangell **9** Momotombo, Santorini, Stromboli, Tolbachik **10** Nyiragongo
Africa: **3** Oku **4** Fogo **7** Erta-Ale **8** Karthala **10** Nyiragongo
Alaska: **6** Katmai, Pavlof **7** Gareloi, Iliamna, Redoubt **8** Wrangell
Antarctic: **6** Erebus
Asia: **3** Aso, Usu **4** Akan, Fuji, Gaua, Nasu, Taal **5** Alaid, Asama, Azuma, Kelut, Manam, Mayon, Raung, Unzen, Yasur **6** Ambrym, Bagana, Bandai, Chokai, Dukono, Lopevi, Merapi, Ontake, Oshima, Rabaul, Semeru, Slamet, Tiatia, Ulawun **7** Adatara, Bulusan, Canlaon, Kerinci, Langila **8** Gamalama, Karymsky, Pinatubo **9** Tolbachik
California: **6** Lassen
Cameroon: **3** Oku
Cape Verde Islands: **4** Fogo
Caribbean: **5** Pelee
cavity: **3** pit **6** crater
Central America: **4** Póas **5** Fuego, Irazú, Tacan **6** Arenal, Masaya, Pacaya **9** Momotombo
Chile: **6** Láscar
Colombia: **4** Ruiz **5** Huila, Pasto **6** Puracé **7** Galeras
Comoros: **8** Karthala
Congo: **10** Nyiragongo
Costa Rica ~: **4** Póas **5** Irazu **6** Arenal
crack: **4** vent
Ecuador: **6** Sangay **8** Cotopaxi
emulate a ~: **4** blow, spew, spue **5** erupt
Ethiopia: **7** Erta-Ale
Europe: **4** Etna **8** Vesuvius **9** Santorini, Stromboli
extinct Caucasus ~: **6** Kazbek
goddess: **4** Pele
Greece: **9** Santorini
Guatemala: **5** Fuego, Tacan **6** Pacaya
Hawaii: **7** Kilauea **8** Mauna Loa
Hokkaido: **3** Usu **4** Akan **6** Oshima
Honshu: **5** Azuma **6** Bandai, Chokai, Ontake **7** Adatara
Iceland: **5** Hekla **6** Krafla
Indonesia: **5** Kelut, Raung **6** Dukono, Merapi, Semeru, Slamet **7** Kerinci **8** Gamalama
Italy: **4** Etna **8** Vesuvius **9** Stromboli
Japan: **3** Aso, Usu **4** Akan, Fuji, Nasu **5** Asama, Azuma, Oyama, Unzen **6** Asosan, Bandai, Chokai, Ontake, Oshima **7** Adatara
Java: **5** Kelut, Raung **6** Merapi, Semeru, Slamet
Kyushu: **5** Unzen
Luzon: **4** Taal **5** Mayon **7** Bulusan **8** Pinatubo
Martinique: **5** Pelee
Mexico: **4** Popo **6** Colima, Toluca **7** Orizaba
mud ~: **5** salse
New Zealand: **7** Ruapehu
Nicaragua: **6** Masaya **9** Momotombo
opening: **5** Mauna
output: **3** ash **4** lava
Papua New Guinea: **5** Manam **6** Bagana, Rabaul, Ulawun **7** Langila
Peru: **7** El Misti
Philippines: **3** Apo **4** Taal **5** Mayon **7** Bulusan, Canlaon **8** Pinatubo
residue: **3** ash **5** ember **6** cinder
Russia: **5** Alaid **6** Tiatia **8** Karymsky **9** Tolbachik
shape: **4** cone
Sicily: **4** Etna **5** Aetna
South America: **4** Ruiz **6** Láscar, Puracé, Sangay **7** El Misti, Galeras **8** Cotopaxi
Sumatra: **7** Kerinci
Vanuatu: **4** Gaua **5** Yasur **6** Ambrym, Lopevi
Washington: **8** St. Helens
__ volcano: **3** mud **6** active **7** dormant
Volcano (1997 film)
cast: Anne Heche, Tommy Lee Jones
dog: **3** Max
Volcano Island: **7** Iwo Jima
volcanology: **7** science
vole: **5** mouse **6** animal, mammal, rodent **10** field mouse
relative: **3** rat **4** cavy, degu, jird, paca **5** coypu, gundi, xerus **6** agouti, beaver, gerbil, gopher, jerboa, marmot, murine **7** hamster, lemming, muskrat, visacha **8** chipmunk, cricetid, dormouse, squirrel, tucotuco **9** chickaree, groundhog, guinea pig, porcupine, woodchuck **10** chinchilla, prairie dog
__ volens: **6** nolens
__ volente: **3** deo
Volga: **5** river
city on the ~: **5** Gorki
denizen: **5** Tatar
locale: **6** Russia
river to the ~: **3** Oka **4** Kama
Volga Boatman ingredient: **5** vodka
Volgograd: **4** city, town
locale: **6** Russia
volitate: **3** fly **4** flit **5** drift, glide, hover **7** flutter
volitation: **4** flit, trip **5** glide **6** aviate, flight, voyage **7** flutter, getaway, journey **8** aviation, hovering **9** departure
volition: **4** will, wish **6** choice, desire, intent, option **8** free will **9** intention **10** discretion, preference, resolution
do on one's own ~: **5** offer **6** enlist, sign up **7** pitch in, proffer, recruit, stand up, venture **9** undertake, volunteer **10** put forward
volitional: **5** meant **6** wilful **7** planned, willful **8** intended **9** voluntary **10** preplanned, purposeful
Volkswagen: **3** car **4** auto **10** automobile
model: **3** Bug, Fox, GTI **4** Golf **5** Jetta **6** Beetle, Cabrio, Passat, Rabbit **7** Eurovan **8** Scirocco
rival: **4** Audi, Opel
volley: **4** fire, rain **5** blast, burst, salvo, storm **6** attack **7** barrage, battery **8** enfilade, outbreak, shelling **9** broadside, cannonade, discharge, fusillade
ender: **4** ball
__ volley: **4** half, stop
volleyball: **4** game **5** sport
need: **3** net
shot: **4** dink, kill **5** spike
where ~ was first played: **4** YMCA
__ volleyball: **5** beach
volplane: **3** fly **4** soar **5** coast, float, glide
Volpone: **4** play **6** comedy
author: Ben Jonson
character: **5** Celia, Mosca **7** Bonario, Corvino, Voltore
Volstead Act
opponent: **3** Wet
supporter: **3** Dry
Volsunga Saga king: **4** Atli
Volta: **5** river **10** Alessandro
locale: **5** Ghana **6** Africa
__ Volta: **5** Black, Upper, White
Volta, Alessandro: **7** Italian **9** physicist
voltage: **5** force, power **6** energy, muscle **7** stamina **8** dynamism, momentum, strength **9** magnetism, supremacy
jump: **5** surge
measure: **3** EMF
reduction: **6** dim out
regulator: **5** zener
voltaic: **8** electric **10** electrical
voltaic __: **4** cell, pile **6** couple **7** battery
voltaic cell part: **5** anode
Voltaire: **6** French, writer **11** philosopher
love: **6** Émilie
real name: **6** Arouet
work: Candide
volte-face: **4** turn **7** reverse **9** turnabout
volt ender: **3** age **5** meter **7** ammeter
Volturno: **5** river
locale: **5** Italy
volubility: **8** glibness **9** eloquence, garrulity, gift of gab, readiness
voluble: **4** glib, long **5** gabby, talky, windy, wordy **6** prolix **7** diffuse, lengthy, unterse, verbose **8** rambling **9** bombastic, garrulous, talkative **10** bigmouthed, discursive, long-winded, loquacious, palaverous, rhetorical
volume: **4** book, bulk, mass, much, room, size, tome **5** album, space, total **6** amount, cubage, degree, extent, number **7** edition, writing **8** capacity, contents, loudness, quantity, strength, treatise **9** amplitude, dimension, intensity, largeness, magnitude
control: **4** knob **5** fader
decrease the ~: **3** gag **4** calm, hush, lull, mute **5** quiet, shush **6** deaden, muffle, muzzle, shut up, stifle, subdue **7** be quiet, silence **8** pipe down, suppress **9** quiet down **10** extinguish, keep it down
increase the ~: **3** amp **5** amp up, blare
lacking ~: **4** bony, lank, lean, puny, slim, thin, trim **5** gaunt, lanky, reedy, wispy **6** flimsy, meager, skimpy, skinny, slight, slinky, sparse, wasted **7** haggard, scrawny, slender **8** skeletal, twiglike, wisplike **9** emaciated, paper-thin, wafer-thin
setting: **3** low **4** bass, high
unit: **2** cc **3** cup **4** cu. ft., cu. in., cu. yd., gill, peck, sone **5** liter, minim, quart, stere **6** bushel, gallon **8** hogshead **9** board foot, cubic foot, cubic yard **10** cubic meter, fluid ounce
__ volume: **4** mole **5** molar **6** atomic
volumes: **4** a lot, much **6** plenty
voluminous: **3** big **4** full, much, vast, wide **5** ample, broad, bulky, great, large, roomy **6** legion **7** copious, massive, sizable **8** abundant, sizeable, spacious **9** billowing, capacious, cavernous, expansive, extensive
voluminousness: **7** bigness, fulness **8** hugeness, wideness **9** abundance, amplitude, broadness, immensity, largeness, magnitude, plenitude
voluntarily: **5** unbid **6** freely **8** by choice **9** on one's own, willingly
voluntary: **4** free **5** meant, unbid **6** chosen, freely, unpaid, wilful, willed, wished **7** elected, planned, unasked, willful, witting **8** intended, optional, unbidden, unforced **10** autonomous, considered, deliberate, gratuitous, purposeful, unprompted, volitional
voluntary __: **6** muscle
volunteer: **4** bite **5** offer **6** chip in, enlist, helper, sign up, tender, unpaid **7** advance, pitch in, proffer, recruit, soldier, stand up, suggest, venture **9** undertake **10** put forward, unsalaried
firefighter: **4** vamp
literacy ~: **5** coach, tutor **6** master, mentor **7** teacher **8** educator, lecturer **9** professor **10** instructor
words: **4** I can **5** I will **7** I'll do it
volunteer __: **4** army
Volunteer author: **4** Agee
Volunteers (1985 film)
cast: John Candy, Tom Hanks, Rita Wilson
director: Nicholas Meyer
Volunteers?: **6** Anyone
Volunteers of __: **7** America
Volunteer State: **4** Tenn. **9** Tennessee
Volupta
daughter of ~: **6** Psyche
father of ~: **4** Eros
voluptuary: **4** roué **7** playboy **8** hedonist, sybarite **9** bon vivant, libertine
volute: **4** coil **5** helix, shell, twist, whorl **6** spiral **8** seashell **9** corkscrew
imperial ~: **5** shell **8** seashell
Volvo: **3** car **4** auto **10** automobile
competitor: **4** Saab
like a ~: **7** Swedish
vomer: **4** bone
locale: **4** nose **5** skull
__ vomica: **3** nux
Von __ Express: **5** Ryan's
von Baeyer, Adolf: **7** chemist **8** Nobelist
von Behring, Emil: **8** Nobelist
von Békésy, Georg: **8** Nobelist
von Bismarck: **4** Otto
von Braun: **7** Wernher **9** rocketeer
contemporary: **3** Ley
von Bülow: **4** Hans **5** Claus, Sunny
portrayer: **5** Close, Irons
von Clausewitz: **4** Carl
Vonda: **7** Shepard **8** McIntyre
von Euler-Chelpin, Hans: **7** chemist **8** Nobelist

von Euler, Ulf: 8 Nobelist
von Frisch, Karl: 8 Nobelist
von Fürstenberg: 4 Egon 5 Diane
von Hayek, Friedrich: 8 Nobelist 9 economist
von Heidenstam, Verner: 6 author 7 Swedish 8 Nobelist
von Hindenburg: 4 Paul
von Karajan, Herbert: 8 Austrian 9 conductor
Von Kempelen and His Discovery
author: Edgar Allan Poe
von Klitzing, Klaus: 8 Nobelist 9 physicist
von Laue, Max: 8 Nobelist 9 physicist
von Leibnitz: 7 Wilhelm
von Lenard, Philipp: 8 Nobelist 9 physicist
Vonnegut Jr., Kurt: 6 author, writer
work: Bluebeard
Breakfast of Champions
Cat's Cradle
Deadeye Dick
Galápagos
Happy Birthday, Wanda June
Hocus Pocus
Jailbird
Mother Night
Player Piano
The Sirens of Titan
Slapstick
Slaughterhouse-Five
von Ossietzky, Carl: 8 Nobelist
von Richthofen: 3 ace 5 baron 6 German 7 Manfred 8 Red Baron
Von Ryan's Express (1965 film)
cast: Trevor Howard, Frank Sinatra
von Schiller: 9 Friedrich
von Stade: 9 Frederica
von Stroheim: 5 Erich
von Suttner, Bertha: 8 Nobelist
von Sydow, Max: 5 actor 7 Swedish
film: The Best Intentions (1992)
Dreamscape (1984)
The Exorcist (1973)
Hannah and Her Sisters (1986)
Hawaii (1966)
Minority Report (2002)
Never Say Never Again (1983)
The Passion of Anna (1969)
Pelle the Conqueror (1988)
The Quiller Memorandum (1966)
The Seventh Seal (1957)
Shame (1968)
Three Days of the Condor (1975)
Through a Glass, Darkly (1962)
Voyage of the Damned (1976)
What Dreams May Come (1998)
von Trapp: 5 Maria
von Weber: 4 Carl 5 Maria
von Webern: 5 Anton
Von Zell: 5 Harry
Von Zeppelin: 9 Ferdinand
voodoo: 3 hex, obi 5 magic, obeah, spell, vodun 7 sorcery 10 witchcraft
amulet: 4 mojo
country: 5 Haiti
___-voom!: 4 Va-va
voracious: 4 avid 5 eager, piggy, unfed 6 greedy, hungry, piggie 7 gorging, lustful, peckish, piggish, starved 8 edacious, esurient, famished, grasping, ravening, ravenous, starving 9 devouring, dog-hungry, ferocious, insatiate, predatory, rapacious, vulturous 10 gluttonous, insatiable, omnivorous, prodigious
appetite: 3 maw
voracity: 5 greed 6 desire, hunger 7 edacity 8 appetite, cupidity, gluttony, yearning 9 eagerness
vortex: 4 eddy, gyre, tide, wind 9 maelstrom, whirlpool
Vosges: 3 cow 4 bull 5 range 6 bovine, cattle
capital: 6 Épinal
region: 6 Alsace
___ vos jeux: 6 faites
Vos Savant: 7 Marilyn
Voss locale: 6 Norway
___ vostra salute!: 4 Alla
votary: 6 backer, patron 7 booster 8 advocate, defender, partisan 9 proponent, religious, supporter 10 enthusiast
vote: 2 ay, no 3 aye, nay, opt, yea, yes 4 poll 5 elect, enact, voice 6 ballot, choice, choose, decide 8 decide on, majority, suffrage 9 determine, franchise 10 plebiscite, referendum, settle upon
against: 2 no 3 con, nay 4 veto
for: 2 ay 3 aye, yea, yes 5 elect 6 assent, choose
in: 4 pass, pick 5 elect
one too young to ~: 4 baby 5 child, minor, youth 6 infant, junior 8 juvenile, underage 9 schoolboy, youngster 10 adolescent, schoolgirl
right to ~: 6 ballot 9 franchise
seeker: 3 pol 9 candidate
solicit a ~: 4 urge 5 lobby 8 campaign
stockholder's ~: 5 proxy
straw ~: 4 poll 6 survey
___ vote: 5 straw, voice 6 silent 7 casting, popular, protest, write-in
voted: 3 x'ed
voter: 6 native 7 citizen, denizen 8 resident, taxpayer 10 inhabitant
no ~: 8 opponent
type of ~: 3 Dem., Ind., Lib., Rep. 7 Liberal 8 Democrat 10 Republican
___ voter law: 5 motor
voters: 6 public 7 country 8 citizens, populace 9 citizenry 10 electorate
voting: 4 poll 5 count, tally 6 ballot, option, sample, survey 7 canvass 8 choosing, election 9 balloting, franchise 10 referendum
age: 8 majority 9 adulthood
booth closer: 3 bar 5 lever
district: 4 ward 8 precinct
group: 4 bloc 5 party 7 council, faction 8 alliance 9 coalition 10 federation
power: 5 agent, proxy 8 delegate
voting ___: 5 booth, paper 7 machine
votive ___: 4 Mass
___ votre permission: 4 avec
...votre santé: 5 toast 6 French
vouch: 4 avow, back 5 swear 6 affirm, assert, assure, attest, pledge, uphold, verify 7 certify, confirm, declare, profess, promise, swear to, testify, warrant, witness 8 attest to, maintain 9 guarantee 10 asseverate
ender: 4 safe
for: 6 affirm, assure, attest, depone, verify 7 certify, confirm, endorse, indorse, sponsor, testify, warrant, witness 8 accredit, attest to, sanction, validate 9 guarantee, recommend, testify to
voucher: 3 tag 4 chit, rcpt. 5 alibi, paper 6 coupon, credit, ticket 7 receipt 9 indenture
voucher ___: 4 plan 6 system
___ voucher: 4 gift 6 travel
vouchsafe: 4 give 5 deign, grant 6 accord, bestow 10 condescend
vous ___: 4 etes
___-vous français?: 6 Parlez
___ vous plaît: 3 s'il
Vouvray: 4 wine 5 white
origin: 6 France
vow: 4 aver, oath, word 5 swear, troth 6 affirm, assert, assure, pledge, plight 7 declare, promise, warrant 8 affiance, covenant 9 assurance, guarantee 10 commitment, engagement
giver: 4 mate, monk 5 bride, groom
marriage ~: 3 I do
take a ~: 3 wed 5 marry 10 get hitched
venue: 5 altar 6 chapel
___ vow: 6 simple, solemn
vowel: 6 letter
disappearance: 7 aphesis
French ~ sound: 5 nasal
Greek ~: 3 eta 4 iota 5 alpha, omega 7 epsilon, omicron
group: 5 AEIOU
mark: 5 breve 6 macron, umlaut
sometime ~: 3 wye
sound: 4 shwa 5 schwa
vowel ___: 5 point, rhyme 6 system 7 harmony
___ Vowel Shift: 5 Great
vox ___: 3 Dei, pop. 6 humana, populi 7 barbara
Vox Pop: 9 radio show
voyage: 4 sail, tour, trip 5 jaunt, quest 6 cruise, flight, junket, travel 7 journey, passage 8 crossing, navigate 10 expedition
on a ~: 4 asea 5 at sea
___ voyage: 3 bon 6 maiden
___ Voyage Home, The: 4 Long
Voyage of the Damned (1976 film)
cast: Faye Dunaway, Max von Sydow, Oskar Werner
voyager: 5 farer, rover 7 tourist 8 traveler, wanderer, wayfarer 9 journeyer, passenger 10 adventurer, vacationer
Voyager: 3 car, van 4 auto 5 probe 7 Mercury 8 Plymouth 10 spacecraft
___, Voyager: 3 Now
Voyager org.: 4 NASA
Voyage to the Bottom of the Sea (1961 film)
cast: Joan Fontaine, Walter Pidgeon, Robert Sterling
director: Irwin Allen
Voyage to the Bottom of the Sea (ABC sci-fi)
cast: Richard Basehart (Adm. Harriman Nelson)
David Hedison (Capt. Lee Crane)
producer: Irwin Allen
Voyage to the Center of the Earth, A
author: Jules Verne
Voyageurs: 4 park
locale: 9 Minnesota
voyaging: 4 asea 5 at sea 9 wayfaring 10 navigation
Voyna i ___: 3 mir
V.P.
part of: 4 vice 9 president
'70s ~: 3 GRF, NAR, STA
Vries, Hugo De: 5 Dutch 8 botanist
Vronsky girl: 4 Anna
vroom maker: 5 motor 6 engine 7 turbine
vs.: 3 opp. 7 against 8 opposite
V.S.: 7 Naipaul 9 Pritchett
Vsevolod: 6 Ivanov
v-shaped: 7 angular, notched 8 angulose, angulous
___ vs. the Red Baron: 6 Snoopy
___ vs. Wade: 3 Roe
Vt.
clock setting: 3 EDT, EST
neighbor: 3 Que. 4 Mass.
region: 4 N. Eng.
see also Vermont
VTOL: 5 plane
user: 4 USAF
___ vu: 4 déjà
Vue: 3 SUV 6 Saturn
Vulcan: 3 god 5 Sarek, Spock
equivalent: 10 Hephaestus
forge: 4 Etna 5 Aetna
mother of ~: 4 Juno
son of ~: 8 Caeculus
wife of ~: 4 Maia
vulcanize: 6 harden 8 indurate 10 strengthen
vulcanized ___: 5 fiber 6 rubber
vulcanologist concern: 4 lava, rock 5 magma
vulgar: 3 bad, low, raw 4 base, blue, foul, lewd, loud, racy, rude, vile 5 bawdy, cheap, crass, crude, dirty, gaudy, gross, nasty, rough, spicy, tacky 6 brassy, coarse, common, filthy, flashy, garish, little, native, public, ribald, risqué, smutty, sordid, spicey, tawdry, unmeet, X-rated 7 bearish, beastly, boorish, ignoble, loutish, lowbred, naughty, obscene, profane, raffish, uncouth 8 barbaric, baseborn, degraded, everyday, familiar, improper, impudent, indecent, off-color, ordinary, plebeian, shameful, tactless, unseemly 9 barbarian, barbarous, idiomatic, inelegant, low-minded, lubricous, offensive, tasteless, unrefined 10 colloquial, disgusting, indecorous, indelicate, scurrilous, ungracious, unmannerly, unpolished, vernacular
Vulgar ___: 5 Latin
vulgarian: 3 cad, cur 4 boor, heel, lout, worm 5 brute, churl, knave, rogue, scamp 6 rascal 7 parvenu, peasant, upstart 9 arriviste, miscreant, reprobate, scoundrel 10 blackguard
vulgarity: 5 filth 7 crudity 8 lewdness 9 barbarity, grossness, indecency 10 coarseness, corruption, smuttiness
Vulgate: 5 Bible
vulnerability: 5 peril 8 jeopardy, weakness 9 liability
vulnerable: 4 open, puny, weak 5 frail, naked, wimpy 6 anemic, atonic, effete, feeble, flabby, flimsy, liable, tender, unsafe 7 anaemic, exposed, fragile, parlous, subject, wimpish 8 delicate, helpless, pervious, pithless, vincible, wide open 9 dangerous, dependant, dependent, faltering, on the spot, powerless, sensitive, unguarded 10 barehanded, undefended, unshielded
vulpine: 3 sly 4 foxy 6 crafty 8 guileful
vulture: 4 bird 6 condor 7 buzzard 9 ossifrage
___ vulture: 4 king 5 black 6 turkey 7 bearded, culture
vulturous: 8 ravaging 9 ferocious, on the hunt, pillaging, predatory, rapacious, voracious 10 plundering, predacious
v.v. part: 4 vice 5 versa
VW: 3 Bug, GTI 4 Golf 5 Jetta 6 Beetle, Cabrio, Passat, Rabbit 7 Eurovan 8 Scirocco
follower: 3 XYZ
preceder: 3 STU 4 RSTU 5 QRSTU
___ v. Wade: 3 Roe

W: 3 dir., mag **4** elem., west **6** letter **7** wolfram **8** magazine, tungsten **9** direction
  follower: 3 XYZ
  in phonetic alphabet: 7 Whiskey
  preceder: 3 TUV **4** STUV **5** RSTUV
  74 for ~: 4 at. no.
  sometimes: 5 vowel
W ___ wall: 4 as in
W. ___ Maugham: 8 Somerset
___ W: 4 C and
WA
  clock setting: 3 PDT, PST
  see also Washington
WAAC part: 3 Aux. **5** Corps
Waal: 5 river
  locale: 7 Holland **11** Netherlands
___ Waart: 5 Edo de
Wabanaki: 6 Indian **7** Amerind
Wabash: 5 river **6** avenue
  locale: 3 Ill., Ind. **4** Ohio **7** Chicago, Indiana **8** Illinois
  river to the ~: 10 Tippecanoe
Wabasha: 4 city, town
  locale: 9 Minnesota
Wabash Avenue (1950 film)
  cast: Betty Grable, Phil Harris, Victor Mature
  director: Henry Koster
Wabash Cannonball: 5 train
WAC: 2 GI **6** GI Jane **10** conference
  colleague: 3 WAF **4** Wave
  school: 3 BYU, SMU **4** Rice, UTEP **5** Tulsa **6** Hawaii, Nevada **10** Boise State **11** Fresno State
Wace: 4 poet **6** Norman
  work: Roman de Brut
wacke: 7 mineral
Wackiest Ship in the Army, The (1960 film)
  cast: Jack Lemmon, John Lund, Ricky Nelson
wacky: 3 odd **4** bats, daft, loco, wild, zany **5** balmy, daffy, flaky, goofy, inane, nutty, silly **6** absurd, flakey, screwy **7** comical, erratic, fatuous, foolish, unsound **8** cockeyed, peculiar, specious **9** eccentric, illogical, off-center, senseless, untenable **10** groundless, irrational, off-the-wall, ridiculous
Waco: 4 city, town
  athletes: 5 Bears
  locale: 5 Texas
  river: 6 Brazos
  school: 6 Baylor
wad: 3 gob, pad **4** ball, chaw, chew, glob, heap, hunk, lump, mass, mint, pile, plug, ream, roll, slew, tuft **5** bunch, chunk, clump, money, stuff **6** boodle, bundle, moolah, packet **7** fortune, tobacco **8** bankroll, compress
  starter: 5 tight
  unit: 3 fin, one, ten **4** five **5** C-note, fiver **7** sawbuck
  up: 5 crush **7** crumple
Waddell, Rube: 6 hurler **7** pitcher
wadding: 3 pad **4** fill **7** filling, padding
waddle: 4 limp, plod, roll, sway **6** lumber, toddle, totter, wabble, wobble **7** shuffle
wade: 4 ford, plod, slog, toil **5** bathe, labor, slosh **6** drudge, paddle, splash, tackle, trudge **9** light into
  in: 5 begin, start
  through: 4 read, slog **5** learn, study **6** peruse **8** pore over
wade ___: 4 into
Wade: 4 Adam, peak **5** Boggs, mount **8** mountain, Virginia
  locale: 10 Antarctica
  opponent: 3 Roe
Wade-___ system: 5 Giles
___ Wade: 4 Roe v. **5** Roe vs.
Wade, Adam
  song: As If I Didn't Know (1961)
    Take Good Care of Her (1961)
    The Writing on the Wall (1961)
wader: 4 boot, ibis, rail, shoe **5** crane, egret, heron, snipe, stilt, stork **6** avocet, jacana, plover **8** footwear, overshoe **9** shorebird
Wade, Virginia: 7 netster **9** tennis pro
  milieu: 5 court
wadi: 5 gulch, gully **6** arroyo, gulley, ravine
wading ___: 4 bird, pool
wading bird: 4 ibis, rail **5** crane, egret, heron, snipe, stilt, stork **6** avocet, jacena, plover **9** shorebird
Wadkins, Lanny: 6 golfer
  milieu: 5 links **6** course
  org.: 3 PGA
wadmal: 6 fabric **8** material
wads: 4 lots **5** scads **6** oodles, scores
___ Wadsworth Longfellow: 5 Henry
WAF: 5 flier, flyer
wafer: 4 disc, disk **5** cooky, snack **6** cookie **7** biscuit
wafer-___: 4 thin
waferlike: 4 thin **6** narrow **7** slender
___ Wafers: 5 Nilla
waffle: 4 cake, Eggo, sway **5** bread, hedge, shift, waver **6** weasel **7** quibble **8** hesitate **9** hem and haw, vacillate **10** equivocate
  topper: 4 oleo **5** sirup, syrup **6** butter
waffle ___: 3 cut **4** iron, slab **5** cloth, weave
Waffle Crisp: 6 cereal
  competitor: 3 Kix **4** Life, Trix **5** Kashi, Quisp, Total **6** Kaboom, Muesli, Oreo O's, Pablum, Smacks **7** All-Bran, Crispix, Harmony, Hunny B's, Mueslix, Oat Bran, Pokemon **8** Boo Berry, Cheerios, Corn Chex, Corn Pops, Fiber One, Rice Chex, Special K, Uncle Sam, Wheaties **9** Alpha Bits, Apple Zaps, Grape Nuts, Honey Comb, Just Right, Wheat Chex **10** Apple Jacks, Bran Flakes, Cap'n Crunch, Cocoa Puffs, Froot Loops, Mini-Wheats, Nutri-Grain, Puffed Rice, Quaker Oats, Smart Start **11** Cocoa Blasts, Cookie Crisp, Golden Crisp, Lucky Charms, Puffed Wheat, Sweet Crunch
waffling: 9 undecided, unsettled **10** indecisive, unresolved
waft: 4 bear, blow, gust, puff, ride **5** carry, drift, float, glide, whiff **6** convey
wag: 3 bob, nod, wit **4** card, flap, lash, rock, sway, wave, zany **5** clown, comic, cutup, joker, shake, swing **6** gossip, jester, kidder, quiver, switch, twitch, wiggle **7** buffoon, farceur, flutter, punster, wise guy **8** banterer, comedian, fish-tail, humorist, jokester, kibitzer, quipster **9** oscillate, pendulate, prankster, vacillate
  ender: 4 tail
  remark: 3 gag, pun **4** barb, joke, quip **6** zinger
  starter: 3 wig
wage: 2 do **3** cut, fee, pay **4** make **5** bacon, bread, money, share **6** income, pursue, return, reward, salary **7** carry on, conduct, payment, stipend **8** earnings, engage in, receipts, take-home **9** emolument, prosecute, undertake **10** recompense
  earner: 5 prole **6** worker **7** employe **8** employee
  earner cry: 4 TGIF
  ender: 6 worker
  war: 5 fight **6** battle
wage ___: 5 scale, slave **6** earner
___ wage: 4 base **5** basic **6** annual, living **7** minimum
wager: 3 bet, lay, pot **4** ante, game, play, risk **5** flyer, hedge, put up, stake **6** chance, exacta, gamble, hazard, parlay, pledge, plunge **7** quinela, venture **8** long shot, make book, perfecta, quinella, quiniela, trifecta **9** challenge, speculate
  maker: 6 bettor **7** gambler
  minimum ~: 4 chip
  spot for a ~: 3 OTB **5** track
___ wager: 4 lay a
wages: 3 cut, fee, pay **5** bacon, bread, price, share **6** income, return, reward, salary **7** payment, revenue, stipend **8** earnings, receipts, take-home **9** emolument **10** recompense
  collect ~: 4 earn
  like some ~: 6 hourly
  old-style: 4 meed
  slave ~: 7 peanuts **8** pittance
  withhold ~: 4 dock
___ wages: 4 real **7** nominal
wages of ___, The: 5 sin is
Wages of Sin author: Andrew Greeley
Wagga Wagga resident: 6 Aussie
wagger: 4 tail
waggery: 4 jape **8** drollery, jocosity, wordplay, zaniness **10** jocularity
waggish: 4 arch **5** droll, funny, silly, witty **6** impish, jocose **7** amusing, comical, jesting, jocular, knavish, playful **8** farcical, humorous **9** facetious, whimsical
waggle: 4 wave **5** shake, swing **9** oscillate
waggling: 5 snaky **6** zigzag **7** crooked, erratic **8** tortuous
Waggoner: 4 Lyle
Wagner: 4 Jack **5** Honus **6** Robert **7** Lindsay, Richard
Wagner Act org.: 4 NLRB
Wägner, Elin: 6 writer **7** Swedish
Wagner, Honus: 6 Pirate **9** shortstop
  like a ~ baseball card: 4 rare
Wagner-Jauregg, Julius: 8 Nobelist
Wagner, Lindsay: 7 actress
  film: Nighthawks (1981)
    The Paper Chase (1973)
  TV: The Bionic Woman
Wagner, Richard
  cycle: 4 Ring
  father-in-law: 5 Liszt
  genre: 5 opera
  role: 3 Eva **4** Elsa, Erda, Norn **5** Senta
  wife: 5 Minna
  work: Die Meistersinger
    Die Walküre
    The Flying Dutchman
    Götterdämmerung
    Lohengrin
    Parsifal
    Rienzi
    Siegfried
    Tannhäuser
    Tristan and Isolde
Wagner, Robert: 5 actor
  film: Austin Powers: The Spy Who Shagged Me (1999)
    Banning (1967)
    Beneath the 12 Mile Reef (1953)
    Broken Lance (1954)
    Dragon: The Bruce Lee Story (1993)
    A Kiss Before Dying (1956)
    Titanic (1953)
    The Towering Inferno (1974)
  spouse: Jill St. John, Natalie Wood
  TV: Hart to Hart, It Takes a Thief, Switch
  TV role: 4 Hart
wagon: 4 cart, dray, wain **5** buggy **7** teacart, tumbrel, tumbril, vehicle **8** carriage, pushcart **10** Radio Flyer
  chuck ~: 7 canteen
  ender: 4 load
  fall off the ~: 5 drink, lapse **6** revert **7** regress, relapse **9** backslide
  farm ~: 4 dray, wain
  fix one's ~: 6 avenge **7** get back, revenge
  go on the ~: 4 quit **7** abstain, refrain
  horse and ~: 3 rig
  load: 3 hay
  on the ~: 5 sober
  part: 4 axle, neap **5** sprag
  starter: 4 band **6** battle
  station ~: 3 car **4** auto **10** automobile
  wheels: 5 pasta **8** macaroni
wagon ___: 4 boss, roof, seat **5** train, vault **6** jobber, master **7** soldier
wagon-___: 3 lit **6** headed
___ wagon: 3 sag, tea **5** chuck, goods, paddy, tower, water **6** battle, patrol, police **7** covered, station
Wagon ___: 5 Train **6** Master
___ Wagon: 7 Welcome
Wagoneer: 3 SUV **4** Jeep
Wagoner: 6 Porter
wagon-lit: 3 car
wagonload: 5 cargo, goods **6** weight **7** freight **8** shipment
wagonmaker, name meaning: 5 Wayne **10** Wainwright
Wagon Master (1950 film)
  cast: Harry Carey Jr., Joanne Dru, Ben Johnson
  director: John Ford
___ Wagon, The: 3 War **4** Band, Last
wagon train
  direction: 4 west
  puller: 4 mule, team
Wagon Train (NBC/ABC western)
  cast: Ward Bond (Seth Adams)
    Robert Horton (Flint McCullough)
wagtail: 4 bird
Wag the Dog (1997 film)
  cast: Robert De Niro, Anne Heche, Dustin Hoffman, Denis Leary
  director: Barry Levinson
Wagyu: 3 cow **4** bull **6** bovine, cattle
Wah ___, The: 6 Watusi
___ Wah Diddy: 3 Doo
wahine: 4 girl, lady **5** woman **8** Hawaiian
  dance: 4 hula
  feast: 4 luau
  instrument: 3 uke
  welcome: 3 lei **5** aloha
Wahl: 3 Ken
Wahlberg: 4 Mark **6** Donnie
Wahlberg, Mark: 5 actor
  film: The Big Hit (1998)
    Boogie Nights (1997)
    The Perfect Storm (2000)
    Planet of the Apes (2001)
    Rock Star (2001)
    Three Kings (1999)
wahoo: 3 cry **4** fish, peto, tree, yell **6** yippee **8** mackerel
Wahoo: 4 city, town
  locale: 8 Nebraska
Wahpekute: 6 Indian **7** Amerind
Wahpeton: 6 Indian **7** Amerind
___ wahr: 5 nicht
Wah Watusi, The (1962 song) artist: Orlons
waif: 3 kid **4** calf, dogy **5** dogey, dogie, gamin, stray **6** orphan, urchin

9 foundling 10 ragamuffin, street Arab
Waikiki
feast: 4 luau
locale: 4 Oahu 6 Hawaii 8 Honolulu
music maker: 3 uke
ride: 4 wave
welcome: 3 lei 5 aloha
Waikiki Wedding (1937 film)
cast: Bing Crosby, Martha Raye, Shirley Ross
wail: 3 bay, cry, sob 4 bawl, bray, fuss, howl, keen, kick, mewl, moan, pule, weep, yell, yowl 5 mourn, whine 6 bellow, bemoan, bewail, boohoo, grieve, holler, lament, repine, scream, shriek, snivel, squall, squeal 7 blubber, carry on, deplore, ululate, whimper 8 complain 9 caterwaul, make a fuss, shed tears, ululation 10 vociferate
wailer: 5 siren 7 banshee
wailing: 5 noisy, tears 6 lament 8 mourning 9 querulous 10 waterworks
Waimalu: 4 city, town
locale: 6 Hawaii
wain: 4 cart 5 wagon
ender: 4 scot 6 wright
Wain: 3 Bea 4 John
Wain, John: 4 poet 6 author, writer 7 British
work: Hurry on Down
wainscot: 5 panel
wainscot ___: 5 chair
Wainwright: 5 James, Rufus 6 Loudon
battleground: 6 Bataan
Waipahu: 4 city, town
locale: 6 Hawaii
waist: 6 bodice, middle 8 beltline 10 midsection
ender: 4 band, coat, line 5 cloth
pincher: 6 corset
size: 4 girt 5 girth
starter: 5 shirt
waist-___: 4 deep, high
___ waist: 4 wasp 7 dropped
waistband: 4 belt, sash 6 girdle
waistcoat: 4 vest
waistline reducer: 4 diet 6 corset
wait: 3 sit 4 bide, halt, hang, lurk, rest, stay 5 abide, await, dally, delay, hover, pause, poise, stall, tarry, watch 6 cool it, expect, hold on, holdup, hole up, lie low, linger, loiter, remain 7 interim, look for, stand by, sweat it 8 downtime, hesitate, interval, mark time, sit tight, sweat out 9 interlude 10 anticipate, hang around, standstill
after a ~: 6 at last 7 finally
around: 4 loll, stay 5 abide, hover, tarry 6 dawdle, linger, loiter, remain 7 hang out, sojourn
don't ~: 3 act 5 cut in
ender: 5 staff 6 people, person
for: 6 expect, plan on 7 count on 10 anticipate
in line: 5 stand
lie in ~: 4 lurk 5 sculk, skulk 6 waylay 8 surprise
on: 4 help, tend 5 nurse, serve 6 assist, attend, tend to 7 care for, cater to, deliver, service 8 attend to, minister 10 minister to
on the phone: 4 hold
out: 5 abide 6 endure, suffer 7 stomach, survive 8 stand for 9 withstand
partner: 3 see
wait ___: 6 tables
___ wait: 5 lie in, stage
Wait ___ the Sun Shines, Nellie: 3 'Til
___ Wait: 3 I'll 5 I Can't
wait a ___: 3 bit, sec 6 minute, moment
Wait a minute!: 3 hey 4 stop
wait and ___: 3 see
Waite: 4 Hoyt, John 5 Ralph
waiter: 4 mozo 6 carhop, garçon, server
aide: 6 busboy
at times: 5 adder
burden: 4 tray 5 order, plate
help a ~: 3 bus
inattentive ~ reward: 5 no tip
injunction: 5 enjoy
offering: 4 menu
one way to call a ~: 4 ahem
reward: 3 tip
starter: 4 dumb, head
waiting: 5 on tap, ready 6 in line 7 abeyant 8 abeyance 9 expectant
area: 5 depot, lobby, queue 6 lounge 7 ingress
in the wings: 5 ready 9 available
waiting ___: 4 game, list, room 6 period
___ waiting: 4 call
Waiting for Godot: 4 play
author: Samuel Beckett
character: 4 Didi, Gogo 5 Pozzo 8 Estragon, Vladimir
star: 4 Lahr
Waiting for Lefty: 4 play 8 one-acter
author: Clifford Odets
Waiting for the Robert ___: 4 E. Lee
Waiting for Tonight (1999 song)
artist: Jennifer Lopez
Waiting on a Friend (1981 song)
artist: Rolling Stones
waiting room
cry: 4 next
reading: 3 mag 8 magazine
Waiting, The (1981 song) artist: Tom Petty and the Heartbreakers
Waiting to Exhale (1995 film)
cast: Angela Bassett, Loretta Devine, Whitney Houston, Lela Rochon
director: Forest Whitaker
waitperson: 9 attendant
Waits: 3 Tom
waits for no one, it: 4 time
Wait 'Til the Sun Shines, Nellie (1952 film)
cast: Hugh Marlowe, Jean Peters, David Wayne
director: Henry King
Wait Until Dark (1967 film)
cast: Alan Arkin, Richard Crenna, Audrey Hepburn
composer: 7 Mancini
director: Terence Young
Waitz, Grete: 6 runner 9 Norwegian 10 marathoner
waive: 4 cede, stay 5 defer, delay, forgo, grant, let go, remit, table, yield 6 forego, give up, hold up, pass up, put off, resign, shelve 7 abandon, decline, suspend 8 disclaim, hand over, overlook, postpone, prorogue, renounce, set aside, sign away, turn down 9 disregard, surrender 10 relinquish
waiver: 9 dismissal 10 abdication, disclaimer
Wajda, Andrzej: 8 director
film: Danton (1982)
Man of Iron (1980)
Man of Marble (1977)
wake: 3 see 4 call, prod, rise, stir, wash 5 arise, get up, liven, nudge, pep up, rally, renew, rouse, shake, track, trail, train, vigil, waves 6 arouse, bestir, come to, excite, fire up, kindle, revive, stir up 7 enliven, freshen, quicken, ripples, roll out, turn out 8 backwash 9 aftermath, galvanize, obsequies, stimulate, tumble out 10 understand
in the ~ of: 5 after, due to 6 astern 7 owing to 9 following
one up: 8 disabuse, set right
Wake ___: 6 Forest, Island
Wake ___ Dream: 5 Up and
Wakefield: 4 city, town
cleric: 5 vicar
locale: 7 England 9 Yorkshire
Wake Forest conference: 3 ACC
wakeful: 4 wary 5 alert, alive, astir 7 careful, heedful, on guard 8 open-eyed, restless, vigilant, watchful, wide-eyed 9 attentive, insomniac, observant, sleepless, wide-awake 10 on the alert, unsleeping
Wake Island (1942 film)
cast: Macdonald Carey, Brian Donlevy, Robert Preston
director: John Farrow
Wake Me Up Before You Go-Go (1984 song) artist: George Michael
Wake Me When It's Over (1960 film)
cast: Ernie Kovacs, Dick Shawn
director: Mervyn LeRoy
waken: 3 see 4 call, prod, rise, stir 5 arise, get up, liven, nudge, pep up, rally, renew, rouse, roust, shake 6 arouse, bestir, come to, excite, fire up, kindle, recall, revive, stir up, wake up 7 enliven, freshen, provoke, quicken, roll out, turn out 9 galvanize, recollect, stimulate, tumble out 10 understand
___ wake of: 5 in the
waker-upper: 4 java 5 alarm, latte 6 coffee
wake-up
call: 5 alarm
time: 2 a.m. 7 morning
Wake Up and Dream: 7 musical
songwriter: 6 Porter
Wake Up and Live (1937 film)
cast: Ben Bernie, Alice Faye, Walter Winchell
Wake Up Everybody (1975 song)
artist: Harold Melvin and the Blue Notes
Wake Up Little Susie (1957 song)
artist: Everly Brothers
Waking ___ Devine: 3 Ned
waking dream, a: 4 hope
Waking, The author: Theodore Roethke
Waking the Dead (2000 film)
cast: Jennifer Connelly, Billy Crudup, Hal Holbrook
waking up: 5 astir
Waksman, Selman: 8 Nobelist
Wal-___: 4 Mart
Walbaum: 4 font 8 typeface
Walbrook, Anton: 5 actor
film: Dangerous Moonlight (1941)
Gaslight (1940)
La Ronde (1950)
The Red Shoes (1948)
Sixty Glorious Years (1938)
Victoria the Great (1937)
Walburga: 5 saint
Walcott: 3 Joe 5 boxer, Derek 9 Jersey Joe
Walcott, Derek: 6 writer 8 Nobelist 10 West Indian
Walcott, Jersey Joe: 5 boxer
milieu: 4 ring
opponent: 7 Charles
Wald: 5 Jerry 6 George
Walden: 4 pond 6 Robert
Walden author: Henry David Thoreau
Wald, George: 8 Nobelist
Waldheim: 4 Kurt
Waldo: 5 Janet
uncle: 5 Magoo 6 Quincy
___ Waldo?: 6 Where's
___ Waldo Emerson: 5 Ralph
___ Waldo Pepper, The: 5 Great
Waldorf: 4 city, town 5 salad
ingredient: 4 mayo, nuts 5 apple 6 celery
locale: 8 Maryland
Waldorf-Astoria: 5 hotel
Waldstein Sonata composer: 9 Beethoven
wale: 3 rib 4 welt 5 ridge 8 swelling
Wales
bay: 8 Cardigan
capital: 7 Cardiff
cheese: 10 caerphilly
city: 4 Rhyl 5 Neath 7 Cardiff, Newport, Swansea 8 Holyhead, Llanelly
dog: 5 corgi
golfer: 7 Woosnam
historian: 7 Nennius
John, in ~: 4 Evan
land west of ~: 4 Eire
language: 6 Celtic
meter: 6 cywydd
natives: 5 Cymry, Kymry
poet: 7 Herbert
product: 4 coal
river: 3 Dee, Usk, Wye
saint: 5 David
symbol: 4 leek
waterfall: 7 Rhaiadr
writer: 3 Map 4 Abse 6 Thomas 7 Nennius 8 Williams
Walesa, Lech: 4 Pole 8 Nobelist
Walfish: 3 bay
locale: 7 Namibia
Walgreen rival: 3 CVS 4 Osco 6 Eckerd 7 Rite-Aid
walk: 3 pad, way 4 file, gait, hike, lane, mall, move, pace, path, pier, plod, road, roam, rove, slog, step, tour, trek, turn, wend, work 5 aisle, alley, amble, byway, court, dance, field, jaunt, leg it, march, mosey, paseo, scuff, slink, stalk, strut, stump, track, trail, tramp, tread, troop 6 by-path, canter, career, escort, foot it, go free, hoof it, junket, lumber, parade, patrol, prance, ramble, region, stride, stroll, toddle, trapes, travel, trudge, wander 7 advance, calling, circuit, gangway, meander, passage, pathway, saunter, schlepp, shamble, shuffle, swagger, traipse 8 ambulate, carriage, cloister, crossing, exercise, footpath, pavement, platform, traverse, vocation 9 esplanade, promenade, territory 10 beat the rap, discipline, hit the road, knock about, profession
a beat: 5 guard 6 patrol
all over: 5 abuse 6 berate, dump on 7 rough up 8 belittle, ill-treat, mistreat 9 deprecate, disparage, victimize 10 disrespect
a tightrope: 4 dare
destination: 5 first
down the aisle: 3 wed 5 marry 10 tie the knot
ender: 3 out, way 4 away, over 5 about
heavily: 4 plod, slog 5 clomp, clump, pound, stomp, tramp, tromp 6 lumber
in: 5 enter 6 arrive
in Spanish: 4 anda
in water: 4 wade 5 slosh
like a duck: 6 waddle
off with: 5 filch, steal 6 pilfer, thieve
of life: 4 turf, work 5 field, orbit, realm 6 career, métier, milieu, sphere 7 calling, purview, station 8 province, vocation 9 bailiwick 10 occupation, profession
on air: 5 exult
on eggs: 6 tiptoe 9 pussyfoot
on tiptoe: 5 creep, sneak
out: 4 exit, quit 5 leave, split 6 picket, resign, strike
out on: 4 quit 6 desert 7 abandon, forsake 8 forswear 9 foreswear, throw over

over: 7 trounce 10 kick around
ready to ~: 5 fed up
sidewise: 4 crab
starter: 3 cat, jay, sky 4 cake, moon, rope, side 5 board, cross, sleep
take a ~: 2 go 4 quit 5 leave
the line: 4 heed, obey 6 listen, submit
through: 8 practice, rehearse
tiredly: 4 plod, slog 6 lumber, trudge
unsteadily: 4 limp, reel 6 teeter, totter 7 stagger
walk __: 3 out 4 over 5 on air, out on 6 on eggs, shorts 7 through
walk __ from: 4 away
walk __ on: 3 out
walk __ with: 3 off
__ walk: 4 bird 5 take a 6 Castle, nature, random, widow's 7 Lambeth
__-walk: 4 duck, hand, race
Walk __: 4 On By
Walk __ a Man: 4 Like
Walk __ In: 5 Right
Walk __ in My Shoes: 5 a Mile
Walk __ Man: 5 Like a
Walk __ Moon, A: 5 on the
Walk __ Renee: 4 Away
Walk __ way: 4 this
Walk __ Wild Side: 5 on the
Walk, __ Run: 4 Don't
__ Walk: 4 Don't 5 A Late, Sleep 7 Gunman's
Walk a Mile in My Shoes (1970 song)
artist: Joe South
walk away __: 4 from
Walk Away Renee (1966 song) artist: Left Banke
Walk, Don't Run (1966 film)
cast: Samantha Eggar, Cary Grant, Jim Hutton
director: Charles Walters
setting: 5 Japan
Walk–Don't Run (1960 song) artist: Ventures
__ Walked In: 4 Love
__ Walked Into My Life: 4 If He
Walken, Christopher: 5 actor
film: The Addiction (1995)
At Close Range (1986)
Batman Returns (1992)
Biloxi Blues (1988)
Blast From the Past (1999)
Brainstorm (1983)
The Dead Zone (1983)
The Deer Hunter (1978, AA)
The Dogs of War (1980)
Pennies From Heaven (1981)
Scotland, Pa. (2002)
Suicide Kings (1998)
A View to a Kill (1985)
walker: 3 ped. 10 pedestrian
starter: 3 jay 4 wire 5 floor, track
Walker: 3 Hal 4 Ally, Doak, John, Mort, town 5 Alice, Clint, Evans, Larry, Marcy, Nancy, Percy, T-Bone 6 Jimmie, Junior, Robert 8 Herschel, Margaret
Walker __: 3 Cup 5 hound
Walker, Alice: 6 author, writer
work: The Color Purple
Meridian
Walker, Clint: 5 actor
TV: Cheyenne
Walker, John: 7 chemist 8 Nobelist
Walker, Larry sport: 8 baseball
Walker, Margaret: 6 writer
work: Jubilee
Walker, Robert: 5 actor
Walker, Texas Ranger (CBS western)
cast: Clarence Gilyard (Jimmy Trivette)
Chuck Norris (Cord Walker)
Noble Willingham (C.D. Parker)
Sheree J. Wilson (Alex Cahill)

__ Walker, The: 4 Snow 5 Night
Walker Through Walls, The author: 4 Ayme
Walk Hand in Hand (1956 song) artist: Tony Martin
__ Walk Home, The: 4 Long
walkie-talkie: 5 radio
word: 4 over 5 roger
walk-in __: 6 closet
Walkin' After Midnight (1957 song)
artist: Patsy Cline
walking
combining form: 5 -grade
in heraldry: 7 passant
leaf: 3 bug 4 fern 6 insect
manner of ~: 4 gait, pace, step
on air: 4 glad, high 5 happy, merry 6 blithe, cheery, elated, jovial, joyful, joyous, upbeat 7 gleeful, pleased, tickled 8 blissful, cheerful, ecstatic, euphoric, exultant, jubilant, mirthful, thrilled 9 delighted, overjoyed, rapturous, rejoicing, rhapsodic
on eggs: 8 cautious
papers: 5 the ax 8 pink slip
shoe: 4 flat
starter: 3 jay 5 sleep
stealthily: 4 atip
stick: 3 bug 4 cane 5 staff 6 insect
walking __: 4 bass, beam, fern, fish, leaf, line, tall 5 horse, on air, stick 6 papers, shorts, ticket 7 catfish
walking-__ money: 6 around
Walking __ Orleans: 5 to New
Walking __, The: 4 Dead 5 Hills
Walking Dead, The (1936 film)
cast: Marguerite Churchill, Edmund Gwenn, Boris Karloff
director: Michael Curtiz
Walking Hills, The (1949 film)
cast: Ella Raines, Randolph Scott
director: John Sturges
__ Walking in the Rain: 4 Just
Walking Man, The: Eddie Yost
Walking My Baby Back Home (1953 film)
cast: Buddy Hackett, Janet Leigh, Donald O'Connor
director: Lloyd Bacon
walking on __: 3 air 4 eggs
walking-on-air feeling: 3 joy 5 bliss 7 ecstasy, elation, rapture 8 euphoria, gladness 9 happiness
Walking on a Thin Line (1984 song)
artist: Huey Lewis and the News
Walking on Broken Glass (1992 song)
artist: Annie Lennox
Walking on Sunshine (1985 song)
artist: Katrina and the Waves
Walking on Thin Ice singer: 3 Ono
Walking to New Orleans (1960 song)
artist: Fats Domino
Walkin' in the Rain... (1972 song)
artist: Love Unlimited
Walk in the __, A: 3 Sun 6 Clouds
Walk in the Clouds, A (1995 film)
cast: Anthony Quinn, Keanu Reeves
director: Alfonso Arau
Walkin' the Floor Over You singer: 4 Tubb
Walk in the Sun, A (1945 film)
cast: Dana Andrews, Richard Conte, Sterling Holloway
director: Lewis Milestone
Walk Like a Man (1963 song) artist: Four Seasons
Walk Like an Egyptian (1986 song)
artist: Bangles
Walkman: 4 Sony 5 radio 6 stereo
walk of __: 4 life
walk off __: 4 with
Walk of Fame embedment: 4 star

Walk of Life (1985 song) artist: Dire Straits
walk on __: 3 air 4 eggs
walk-on: 4 part, role, supe 5 cameo, extra 6 player
Walk On By (song) artist: Dionne Warwick, Leroy Van Dyke
Walk on the Moon, A (1999 film)
cast: Diane Lane, Viggo Mortensen, Anna Paquin, Liev Schreiber
director: Tony Goldwyn
Walk on the Wild Side (1973 song)
artist: Lou Reed
Walk on the Wild Side, A author: Nelson Algren
Walk on Water (1988 song) artist: Eddie Money
walkout: 6 strike 8 stoppage 9 departure, job action
walkover: 4 rout, snap 6 picnic, simple 7 success, triumph
Walk Right Back (1961 song) artist: Everly Brothers
Walk Right In (1963 song) artist: Rooftop Singers
__ walks in beauty...: 3 She
Walk Softly, Stranger (1950 film)
cast: Spring Byington, Joseph Cotten, Alida Valli
director: Robert Stevenson
walk the __: 4 line 5 plank
walk the dog toy: 4 yo-yo
Walk the Proud Land (1956 film)
cast: Anne Bancroft, Pat Crowley, Audie Murphy
Walk This Way (song) artist: Aerosmith, Run-D.M.C.
walk-through: 9 rehearsal
Walk to Remember, A (2002 film)
cast: Peter Coyote, Daryl Hannah, Mandy Moore, Shane West
walk-up: 3 apt 4 flat 9 apartment
__ Walküre: 3 Die
walkway: 4 hall, lane, path, ramp 5 aisle, alley 7 ingress 8 footpath 9 esplanade
covered ~: 4 stoa 6 arcade
wall: 3 dam 4 dike, side 5 fence, hem in, levee, panel 6 facade, screen, septum 7 barrier, bastion, bulwark, defense, divider, enclose, inclose, parapet, rampart, surface 8 bulkhead, membrane, obstacle, palisade, paneling, retainer, stockade 9 barricade, hindrance, partition, roadblock 10 battlement, embankment, impediment
Biblical ~ word: 4 mene 5 tekel
classroom ~ hanging: 3 map
climber: 4 vine
column: 4 anta
covering: 4 tile 5 paint, panel 6 stucco
decoration: 4 dado 5 arras 7 drapery
defensive ~: 6 bailey 7 ballium 9 barricade
display: 3 art 5 arras, mural, op art 7 picture 8 painting
dividing ~: 6 septum
drive up the ~: 3 bug, irk, nag 4 rile 5 annoy, peeve 6 enrage, harass, pester 7 torment, trouble
ender: 3 eye 4 eyed, less 5 board, paper 6 flower 8 papering
fixture: 4 rack, safe
hanging: 3 art 5 arras, litho, photo, pin-up, shelf, tapis 6 cobweb, sconce 7 diploma, picture 8 painting
in: 6 immure 7 enclose, inclose
in jai alai: 6 rebote
like some ~ s: 4 viny 5 ivied
off: 4 shut 6 screen, seal up 7 confine 8 imprison 9 partition
off the ~: 5 daffy, hyper, weird 7 strange

recess: 5 niche 6 alcove
sea ~: 4 dike 5 levee 10 breakwater
starter: 3 dry, sea 4 fire, foot, side 5 flood, stone
to wall: 9 extensive
triangular ~: 5 gable
up against the ~: 7 trapped
writing on the ~: 4 omen, sign 7 portent, warning 8 graffiti
wall __: 3 box, rue 4 fern, plug, rock, tent, unit 5 plate 6 socket, system 7 creeper, hanging, molding
__ wall: 3 dry, sea 4 cell, fire, pack, rock 5 blank, flood, gable, party, up the 6 breast, cavity, fourth, Trombe 7 bearing, curtain, hanging, storage
Wall: 2 St. 3 Art 6 Street
__ Wall: 4 High 6 Berlin 7 Chinese, Mending, Western
wallaba: 4 tree 8 hardwood
wallaby: 3 'roo 6 animal, mammal 9 marsupial
female: 4 jill
male: 4 jack
relative: 4 euro 5 bilbi, bilby, koala 6 numbat, wombat 7 bettong, dasyure, opossum 8 kangaroo, wallaroo 9 bandicoot, phalanger
young: 4 joey
Wallace: 3 Dee, Lew 4 Ford, Mike 5 Beery, Edgar, Jerry, Shawn 6 Dewitt, George, Irving, Marcia 7 Langham, Richard, Stegner, Stevens, William 9 Carothers
colleague: 5 Kroft, Safer, Stahl 6 Rooney 7 Bradley
specialty: 4 list
Wallace, Dee: 7 actress
film: Cujo (1983)
E.T. The Extra-Terrestrial (1982)
The Howling (1981)
Wallace, Edgar: 6 author, writer
work: King Kong
The Terror
Wallace, Jerry song: Primrose Lane (1959)
Wallace, Lew: 6 author, writer
work: Ben-Hur
Wallace, Richard: 8 director
film: Bombardier (1943)
It's in the Bag! (1945)
The Little Minister (1934)
A Night to Remember (1943)
Sinbad the Sailor (1947)
The Young in Heart (1938)
Wallach, Eli: 5 actor
film: Baby Doll (1956)
Cinderella Liberty (1973)
Girlfriends (1978)
The Godfather Part III (1990)
The Good, the Bad, and the Ugly (1966)
How the West Was Won (1962)
Keeping the Faith (2000)
Lord Jim (1965)
The Magnificent Seven (1960)
The Misfits (1961)
Movie Movie (1978)
Nuts (1987)
spouse: Anne Jackson
Wallach, Otto: 7 chemist 8 Nobelist
wallaroo: 4 euro 6 animal, mammal 9 marsupial
relative: 5 bilbi, bilby, koala 6 numbat, wombat 7 bettong, dasyure, opossum, wallaby 8 kangaroo 9 bandicoot, phalanger
Walla Walla: 4 city, town
locale: 10 Washington
__ Wallbanger: 6 Harvey
Wallenda: 4 Karl 7 aerobat 9 aerialist
walkway: 4 wire 8 high wire
Waller, Edmund: 4 poet 7 British
work: Go, Lovely Rose
Waller, Fats: 7 pianist 8 composer

genre: 4 jazz
real first name: 6 Thomas
wallet: 8 billfold
item: 2 ID 3 one, ten 4 bill, five 6 dollar
lifter: 3 dip 10 pickpocket
Walley: 7 Deborah
walleye: 4 dory, fish, pike 7 pollock 8 John Dory
wallflower: 4 herb 5 loner, plant 9 introvert
like a ~: 3 shy 5 timid 8 reticent, retiring, unsocial 9 withdrawn 10 unsociable
not a ~: 5 mixer
Wallflowers
member: Jakob Dylan
song: One Headlight (1997)
Wallis: 3 Hal 5 Shani 7 Simpson 8 Warfield
Wallis and __ Islands: 6 Futuna
__ Wall of China: 5 Great
wallop: 3 bam, bop, hit, jar, tan, zap 4 bang, bash, beat, belt, best, blow, boff, clip, deck, drub, jolt, kick, lick, pelt, rout, slam, slap, slog, slug, sock, swat, trim, wham, whip 5 baste, blast, clout, crush, knock, paste, pound, punch, shock, smack, smash, smite, spank, swipe, thump, whack, whang, whomp 6 attack, batter, buffet, defeat, hammer, impact, pommel, pummel, strike, thrash, thwack 7 clobber, lambast, shellac, take out, trounce 8 haymaker, lambaste, shellack, vanquish
packing a ~: 5 harsh 6 potent 8 powerful
__-walloper: 3 pot 4 dock
walloping: 3 big 4 huge 7 massive
wallow: 4 bask, loll, roll, slop 5 enjoy, glory, lie in, lurch, pitch, revel 6 relish, roll in, splash 7 delight, immerse 8 flounder 9 luxuriate
in: 4 brag, crow, teem 5 gloat 6 abound 7 swagger
Wallowa: 3 mts. 4 mtns. 5 range 9 mountains
locale: 6 Oregon
wallpaper
put up ~: 4 hang 5 paste
unit: 4 bolt, roll
wall rue: 4 fern
__ Walls: 4 Four 5 Hello 7 Between
walls have __, the: 4 ears
Wall St. Lays __: 5 an Egg
Wall Street: 6 market
arena: 4 AMEX, NYSE
asset: 3 stk. 4 bond 5 stock
concern: 3 yld. 5 yield 6 growth
decline: 3 dip 5 slide 7 falloff
dread: 5 crash, panic
good news on ~: 5 rally, runup
initials: 3 IPO, LBO, OTC 4 DJIA
locale: 3 NYC 7 New York 9 Manhattan
membership: 4 seat
name: 3 Dow, Dun
optimist: 4 bull
option: 3 put 4 call
order: 3 buy 4 sell
pessimist: 4 bear
phrase: 5 at par, no par
publication: 6 Forbes 7 Barron's, Fortune
unit: 3 shr. 5 share
volatility measure: 4 beta
watchdog: 3 SEC
worker: 3 arb, MBA 6 broker 7 analyst
Wall Street (1987 film)
cast: Michael Douglas, Daryl Hannah, Hal Holbrook, Charlie Sheen, Martin Sheen
director: Oliver Stone
theme: 5 greed
Wall, The author: John Hersey
wall-to-wall: 6 carpet, loaded, packed 7 crowded 9 extensive, inclusive
Wally: 3 Cox 4 Amos 7 Cleaver, Schirra 8 Westmore
Wal-Mart rival: 5 Kohl's, Sears 6 Penney
Walmsley: 3 Jon
walnut: 4 tree, wood 5 brown 7 hickory, reddish
innards: 4 meat
relative: 3 bay, dun, tan 4 bole, ecru, fawn, foxy, nude, seal 5 amber, beige, camel, cocoa, hazel, khaki, mocha, sepia, tawny, umber 6 auburn, bister, bistre, bronze, coffee, copper, ginger, russet, sienna, sorrel, suntan 7 biscuit, caramel, dogwood 8 chestnut, cinnamon, mahogany 9 butternut, chocolate
__ walnut: 3 sea 5 black, maple, white 7 English, Persian
Walnut Creek: 4 city, town
locale: 10 California
Walpole: 4 earl, Hugh 6 Horace, Robert
Walpole, Horace: 6 author, writer 7 British 9 historian
work: The Castle of Otranto
Walpole, Hugh: 3 Sir 6 author, writer 7 British
work: Mr. Perrin and Mr. Traill
Walpurgis __: 5 Night
walrus: 6 animal, mammal
feature: 4 musk, tusk
female: 3 cow
kin: 4 seal 7 sea lion
male: 4 bull
young: 3 pup
Walser, Martin: 6 German, writer
Walsh: 2 Ed, J.T. 3 Joe, Kay 4 Bill, peak 5 mount, Raoul 8 mountain
locale: 5 Yukon 6 Canada
Walsh, Raoul: 8 director
film: Background to Danger (1943)
Battle Cry (1955)
The Big Trail (1930)
The Bowery (1933)
Captain Horatio Hornblower (1951)
College Swing (1938)
Colorado Territory (1949)
Dark Command (1940)
Desperate Journey (1942)
Gentleman Jim (1942)
Going Hollywood (1933)
High Sierra (1941)
The Horn Blows at Midnight (1945)
In Old Arizona (1929)
Klondike Annie (1936)
The Lawless Breed (1952)
The Man I Love (1946)
Manpower (1941)
Me and My Gal (1932)
The Naked and the Dead (1958)
Objective, Burma! (1945)
Pursued (1947)
Regeneration (1915)
The Roaring Twenties (1939)
Sadie Thompson (1928)
Sailor's Luck (1933)
Salty O'Rourke (1945)
St. Louis Blues (1939)
The Strawberry Blonde (1941)
They Died With Their Boots On (1941)
They Drive by Night (1940)
The Thief of Bagdad (1924)
What Price Glory? (1926)
White Heat (1949)
The World in His Arms (1952)
The Yellow Ticket (1931)
Walston, Ray: 5 actor
film: Convicts 4 (1962)
Damn Yankees (1958)
Kiss Me, Stupid (1964)
Paint Your Wagon (1969)
Popeye (1980)
South Pacific (1958)
TV: My Favorite Martian, Picket Fences
__-walsy: 5 palsy
Walt: 4 Kuhn 5 Kelly 6 Disney 7 Bellamy, Frazier, Whitman
Walt __ World: 6 Disney
Walter: 3 Map 4 Abel, Camp, Egan, Hess, Hill, Hunt, Kerr, Kohn, Lang, Reed 5 Bruno, Hagen, Lantz, Mitty, Pater, Scott 6 Alston, Carlos, Farley, Huston, Koenig, Murphy, Payton, Piston, Slezak, Wanger 7 Brennan, Catlett, Gilbert, Gropius, Haworth, Jessica, Johnson, Matthau, Mirisch, Mondale, Pidgeon, Raleigh 8 Brattain, Chrysler, Connolly, Cronkite, Damrosch, Lippmann, Winchell 9 Annenberg
successor: 3 Dan
Walter __ Army Medical Center: 4 Reed
Walter __ Disney: 5 Elias
Walter __ Mare: 4 de la
Walter, Bruno: 7 maestro 9 conductor
Walter, Jessica spouse: Ron Leibman
Walters: 5 Bucky, Julie 7 Barbara, Charles
Walters, Barbara
network: 3 ABC 5 ABC-TV
Walters, Charles: 8 director
film: Ask Any Girl (1959)
The Barkleys of Broadway (1949)
Billy Rose's Jumbo (1962)
Dangerous When Wet (1953)
Easter Parade (1948)
Easy to Love (1953)
Good News (1947)
High Society (1956)
Lili (1953)
Please Don't Eat the Daisies (1960)
Summer Stock (1950)
The Tender Trap (1955)
The Unsinkable Molly Brown (1964)
Walk, Don't Run (1966)
Walters, Julie: 7 actress
film: Billy Elliot (2000)
Car Trouble (1985)
Educating Rita (1983)
The Wedding Gift (1993)
Waltham: 4 city, town
locale: 4 Mass.
Walther: 5 Bothe 6 Nernst
Walton: 3 Sam 4 Bill 5 Izaak 6 Ernest
Walton, Bill: 5 cager
milieu: 5 court
org.: 3 NBA
sport: 10 basketball
Walton, Ernest: 8 Nobelist 9 physicist
Walton, Izaak: 6 writer 7 British 9 fisherman
need: 3 rod
work: The Compleat Angler
Waltons, The (CBS drama)
cast: Joe Conley (Ike Godsey)
Ellen Corby (Esther Walton)
Will Geer (Zeb Walton)
David W. Harper (Jim Bob Walton)
Kami Kotler (Elizabeth Walton)
Michael Learned (Olivia Walton)
Mary McDonough (Erin Walton)
Judy Norton-Taylor (Mary Ellen Walton)
Eric Scott (Ben Walton)
Richard Thomas (John Boy Walton)
Ralph Waite (John Walton)
Jon Walmsley (Jason Walton)
dog: 8 Reckless
narrator: Earl Hamner Jr.
waltz: 5 dance, glide, music, valse 6 prance
predecessor: 7 ländler
through: 3 ace
variation: 6 Boston
waltz __: 4 time
__ Waltz: 6 Devil's, Minute 7 Emperor
Waltzing Cat, The composer: Leroy Anderson
Waltz of the Toreadors (1962 film)
cast: Dany Robin, Peter Sellers
director: John Guillermin
Wambaugh, Joseph: 5 ex-cop 6 author, writer
work: The Blooding
The Delta Star
Echoes in the Darkness
Finnegan's Week
Floaters
Fugitive Nights
The Glitter Dome
The Golden Orange
Lines and Shadows
The New Centurions
The Onion Field
WAM, composer taught by: 3 LvB
wammus: 4 coat 6 jacket
Wampanoag: 6 Indian 7 Amerind
wampum: 3 oof 4 cash, gelt, jack, kail, kale, loot, peag, pelf 5 beads, bills, bread, bucks, dough, funds, lucre, money, moola, mopus, pesos, rhino, sewan 6 dinero, do-re-mi, mammon, mazuma, moolah, silver, specie, wealth 7 cabbage, capital, dollars, lettuce, ooftish, scratch, shekels 8 bankroll, cold cash, currency, hard cash, smackers 9 banknotes, frogskins, long green, simoleons 10 greenbacks, green stuff
wampus: 4 coat, lout 6 jacket
wamus: 4 coat 6 jacket
wan: 4 ashy, pale, thin, weak, worn 5 ashen, faint, livid, pasty, waxen, white 6 anemic, blanch, chalky, feeble, pallid, peaked, sallow, sickly 7 anaemic, bilious, ghastly, haggard, languid 8 bleached, liverish 9 albescent, bloodless, colorless, ghostlike, lily-white, washed-out, whey-faced 10 pasty-faced
Wanamaker: 3 Sam, Zöe 4 John
contemporary: 4 Macy
wand: 3 rod 4 twig 5 baton, sprig, staff, stick 7 scepter, sceptre 8 caduceus
combining form: 6 rhabdo-
magic ~ owner: 5 fairy 6 wizard 8 magician, sorcerer
wand __: 6 reader
__ wand: 5 fairy, magic
Wanda: 9 Landowska
wander: 3 err, gad, sin 4 hike, mill, rave, roam, rove, trek, veer, walk 5 amble, drift, float, jaunt, mosey, prowl, range, stray, tramp 6 cruise, ramble, stroll, trapes, travel 7 deviate, digress, diverge, get lost, journey, maunder, meander, migrate, saunter, traipse 8 go astray, straggle 9 bat around, circulate, expatiate, gallivant, globe-trot, hopscotch
let one's mind ~: 3 nod 4 miss 8 daydream
wanderer: 3 bum, gad 4 hobo, waif 5 gipsy, gypsy, nomad, stray, tramp 6 estray 7 pilgrim, vagrant, voyager 8 explorer, gadabout, stranger, vagabond, wayfarer 9 itinerant 10 adventurer
Wanderer (song), The artist: Dion, Donna Summer
Wanderers, The (1979 film)
cast: Karen Allen, Ken Wahl
director: Philip Kaufman
__ Wanderer, The: 5 Happy
wandering: 4 lost 6 astray, errant

7 aimless, erratic, journey, migrant, nomadic 8 vagabond 9 delirious, departure, excursion, excursive, itinerant, migratory, peregrine, wayfaring 10 aberration, digression, discursion, incoherent
Wandering __: 3 Jew
wanderlust
indulge ~: 4 roam, rove 5 range 6 travel
wandoo: 4 tree 8 hardwood
Wandorobo home: 5 Kenya 6 Africa 8 Tanzania
wane: 3 die, dim, ebb, lag, sag, sap 4 fade, fail, fall, flag, lull, sink, tire 5 abate, blunt, decay, let up, slack 6 go down, impair, lessen, recede, reduce, relent, shrink, soften, weaken, wither 7 decline, deplete, die away, drop off, dwindle, ease off, exhaust, fatigue, slacken, subside, tail off, thin out 8 blow over, contract, decrease, diminish, enervate, enfeeble, fade away, moderate, peter out, slack off, taper off, wind down 9 attenuate, disappear, undermine, waste away 10 debilitate, devitalize, falling off
__ wane: 5 on the
Waner, Lloyd: 6 Pirate 10 outfielder
Waner, Paul: 6 Pirate 10 outfielder
Wang: 3 Wei 4 Lung 5 Chung, Wayne 7 Garrett
Wanger, Walter: 8 producer
wangle: 3 fix, get 4 coax, plot 5 swing 6 manage, obtain 7 acquire, arrange, connive, finagle, finesse, procure, pull off 8 bring off, conspire, maneuver 9 machinate
Wang Lung wife: 4 O-Lan
Wang, Wayne: 8 director
film: The Center of the World (2001)
Chan Is Missing (1982)
Dim Sum: a Little Bit of Heart (1984)
Eat a Bowl of Tea (1989)
The Joy Luck Club (1993)
Smoke (1995)
Wang Wei: 4 poet 7 Chinese
waning: 3 ebb 7 decline 8 decrease 9 abatement, remission
Wankel: 6 engine
engine part: 5 rotor
__-Wan Kenobi: 3 Obi
wannabe: 5 yahoo 7 parvenu, upstart 9 arriviste, pretender, soi-disant, vulgarian 10 self-styled
Wannabe (1997 song) artist: Spice Girls
Wanna Be Startin' Somethin' (1983 song) artist: Michael Jackson
Wanna bet?: 6 oh yeah
Wanna buy __?: 5 a duck
__ Wanna Cry: 5 I Don't
__ Wanna Do: 4 All I
Wanna make __?: 4 a bet
wanness: 6 anemia, pallor 7 anaemia
want: 3 aim, yen 4 ache, lack, like, long, lust, miss, need, pine, seek, will, wish 5 covet, crave, fancy, yearn 6 aspire, choose, dearth, demand, desire, famine, hanker, hunger, misery, penury, please, prefer, thirst 7 absence, burn for, call for, craving, hope for, itch for, longing, paucity, poverty, require, sigh for, wish for 8 exigence, exigency, feel like, scarcity, shortage, sparsity, spoil for, yearn for, yearning 9 appetence, go without, hanker for, hankering, indigence, neediness, privation, starve for 10 deficiency, desiderate, have need of, meagerness, scantiness, skimpiness
ad abbr.: 3 EEO
answer a ~ ad: 5 apply
be in ~: 4 need
in ~: 4 poor 5 broke, needy 6 bad off, hard up, ill off 7 pinched 8 badly off, bankrupt, beggarly, indigent, strapped 9 destitute, insolvent, moneyless, penniless, penurious 10 down and out, pauperized, straitened
want __: 3 ads 4 list
wanted: 7 at large, welcome 10 on the loose
one: 7 escapee, runaway
poster word: 5 alias, alive, armed 6 reward
Wanted Dead or Alive (1987 song) artist: Bon Jovi
Wanted: Dead or Alive (CBS western) cast: Steve McQueen (Josh Randall)
__ wanted list: 4 most
__ want for Christmas...: 4 All I
wanting: 4 less, slim 5 minus, scant, short, shy of 6 absent, devoid, faulty, in need, meager, scanty, skimpy 7 lacking, missing, slender 8 deprived, inferior 9 defective, deficient, destitute, half-baked, imperfect 10 inadequate, incomplete
__ want is a room somewhere: 4 All I
want-it-all type: 3 hog, pig 7 glutton
__ Want Me: 5 Do You
wanton: 4 lewd, mean, rake, rash, wild 5 cruel, harsh, loose, nasty, undue 6 animal, brutal, fierce, lavish, rakish, savage, unkind, wicked, wilful 7 beastly, callous, drastic, extreme, hurtful, lustful, naughty, rampant, vicious, wayward, willful 8 barbaric, careless, depraved, fiendish, heedless, inhumane, mindless, needless, perverse, pitiless, prodigal, reckless, ruthless, sadistic, vengeful, wasteful 9 cutthroat, dissolute, egregious, excessive, fanatical, ferocious, libertine, lubricous, luxuriate, malicious, merciless, monstrous, senseless, shameless, truculent, unbridled 10 deliberate, groundless, immoderate, inordinate, malevolent, motiveless, outrageous, profligate, unprovoked, vindictive
wantonness: 4 evil 7 abandon, license 8 lewdness
__ Want to Be Right: 5 I Don't
__ Want to Dance?: 5 Do You
__ Want to Know a Secret?: 5 Do You
__ Want to Set the World on Fire: 5 I Don't
__ Want to Walk Without You: 5 I Don't
wapiti: 3 elk 4 deer 6 animal, mammal
relative: 3 roe 4 axis, pudu, shou, sika 5 moose 6 chital, guemal, hangul, huemul, sambar, sambur, thamin 7 brocket, caribou, muntjac, muntjak, sambhar, sambhur 8 reindeer 9 barasingh
Wapner, Joseph: 5 judge
Wapshot Chronicle, The author: John Cheever
war: 4 game 5 fight, jehad, jihad 6 attack, battle, combat, enmity, strife 7 contend, crusade, quarrel 8 card game, conflict, fighting, struggle 9 bloodshed, hostility 10 contention, take up arms
1850s ~ zone: 6 Crimea
1960s ~ zone: 3 Nam
advocate: 4 hawk
at ~: 8 battling, fighting
cause of an 1840s ~: 5 opium
chest: 4 fund 6 coffer 8 treasury 9 exchequer
civil ~: 6 revolt 7 anarchy 8 sedition, uprising 9 rebellion 10 revolution
club: 4 mace 6 cudgel 9 truncheon
cry: 5 alarm, motto, whoop 6 slogan
ender: 4 fare, head, lock, lord, path, time, V-day 5 horse, plane, ships, truce 6 monger
games: 4 test 5 drill 9 maneuvers
god: 4 Ares, Mars, Odin 5 Othin
goddess: 6 Athena, Athene
hero: 3 ace 5 flier, flyer, pilot 7 aviator
of words: 6 debate 8 argument
partner: 4 ally
prepare for ~: 3 arm 5 rearm 8 embattle
reward: 5 booty 6 spoils
wage ~: 5 fight 6 invade 9 prosecute
war __: 3 cry, hat 4 game, hawk, nose, room, zone 5 bride, chest, cloud, dance, games, paint, party, story, whoop 6 bonnet, hammer, powers, vessel 7 surplus
__ war: 3 air, hot 4 cold, holy 5 act of, civil, class, dirty, law of, price, tug of, world 7 declare, limited
War
song: The Cisco Kid (1973)
Gypsy Man (1973)
Low Rider (1975)
Spill the Wine (1970)
Summer (1976)
Why Can't We Be Friends? (1975)
The World Is a Ghetto (1972)
War __: 7 Requiem
War __ Peace: 3 and
War __ Roses, The: 5 of the
War __, The: 4 Game, Lord, Room 5 Wagon
War __ Worlds, The: 5 of the
__ War: 3 Tek 4 Boer, Cold, Gulf, Man o' 5 Creek, Great, Hart's, Opium, Sioux 6 Balkan, Korean, Pequot, Six-Day, Social, Trojan 7 Crimean, Gordon's, Mexican, Murphy's, Vietnam
War and Peace: 4 epic 5 novel
author: Leo Tolstoy
character: 4 Berg, Ilya, Vera 5 Boris, Julie, Marya, Sonya 6 Hélène, Rostov
game: 4 faro
War Between the __, The: 5 Tates 6 States
War Between the Tates, The author: Alison Lurie
warble: 4 call, pipe, sing 5 croon, trill, yodel, yodle 6 intone, strain 8 vocalize
warbler: 4 bird, lark, wren 6 singer 8 vocalist
__ warbler: 4 leaf, palm, pine, reed, wood 6 golden, hooded, myrtle, parula, willow, yellow 7 prairie, Wilson's
Warbucks, Daddy
like ~: 4 rich
underling: 3 Asp 6 Punjab, The Asp
ward: 5 Annie
Warburg, Otto: 8 Nobelist
ward: 4 area, zone 5 child, minor 6 canton, charge, orphan, parish, region 7 adoptee, lookout, protege, quarter 8 district, division, godchild, precinct 9 dependent, foundling, pensioner, territory 10 department, protection
ender: 4 robe, room
heeler: 3 pol 10 politician
off: 4 fend, foil, halt, stay, stop 5 avert, avoid, block, check, deter, guard, parry, rebut, repel, stimy, stymy 6 defend, divert, rebuff, shield, stymie, thwart 7 deflect, obviate, prevent, repulse, rule out 8 preclude, turn down 9 forestall, frustrate, keep at bay, turn aside, withstand
starter: 3 lee, man, sea, sky, sun, way 4 east, home, land, left, side, west, wind 5 coast, front, north, right, river, shore, south, space, stern 6 heaven, hither 7 thither 9 northeast, northwest, southeast, southwest
ward __: 3 off 5 eight 6 heeler
Ward: 3 Jay 4 Bond, Burt, Fred, Sela 5 Anita, Baker, Simon 6 Rachel 7 Artemus, Cleaver 10 Montgomery
June, to ~: 4 wife
to the Beaver: 3 Dad
Ward, Anita song: Ring My Bell (1979)
Ward, Artemus: 6 author, writer
birthplace: 5 Maine
__ Ward Beecher: 5 Henry
ward eight: 5 drink 8 beverage, cocktail
ingredient: 4 soda 7 whiskey 9 grenadine 10 lemon juice
warden: 5 guard 6 deacon, jailer, keeper, ranger 7 manager, officer 8 governor, overseer, watchdog 9 caretaker, custodian 10 doorkeeper, gamekeeper
African game ~: 6 askari
starter: 6 church
__ warden: 3 dog 4 fish, game 6 animal 7 air-raid
Warden, Jack: 5 actor
film: 12 Angry Men (1957)
All the President's Men (1976)
... And Justice for All (1979)
The Apprenticeship of Duddy Kravitz (1974)
Being There (1979)
Bulworth (1998)
Edge of the City (1957)
Heaven Can Wait (1978)
Run Silent, Run Deep (1958)
So Fine (1981)
Used Cars (1980)
The Verdict (1982)
Ward, Fred: 5 actor
film: Big Business (1988)
Henry & June (1990)
The Player (1992)
The Right Stuff (1983)
__ Ward Howe: 5 Julia
wardrobe: 4 duds, rags, togs 5 dress, suits, trunk 6 attire, closet, locker, outfit 7 apparel, clothes, outfits, threads 8 clothing, costumes, cupboard, garments 9 ensembles, furniture, trousseau, vestments 10 chiffonier, Sunday best
wardship: 4 care 5 trust 7 custody, keeping 8 auspices, tutelage
wards starter: 3 man, sea, sky, sun 4 east, home, land, side, west 5 coast, front, north, river, shore, south, stern 6 heaven, hither 9 northeast, northwest, southeast, southwest
ware: 4 delf 5 delft, goods 7 article, pottery, product 8 ceramics, vendible 9 commodity
ender: 4 room 5 house
starter: 3 bar, sea 4 cook, dish, firm, flat, gift, hard, iron, oven, slip, soft, stem 5 brass, china, glass, stone, table, vapor 6 copper, course, dinner, enamel, hollow, jasper, luster, silver, willow, wooden 7 crackle, earthen, granite, kitchen
__ ware: 5 cameo, delft, Imari, Mocha 6 bamboo, Fiesta, jasper, Jesuit, Parian, queen's, Samian, Sèvres 7 Belleek, biscuit, Dresden, lacquer, Limoges, Nanking, Satsuma, sponged
warehouse: 4 stow 5 depot, étape, store 6 bodega 8 magazine 9 stockpile, stockroom 10 depository, repository
charge: 4 stor. 7 storage
Chinese ~: 4 hong 6 godown

renovated ~ space: 4 loft
stamp: 4 recd.
unit: 3 bin, box, ton 4 skid 5 crate
wares: 4 line, mdse. 5 goods, stock, store 7 produce 8 articles, material, products 9 vendibles
warfare: 6 battle, combat, strife 7 discord 8 campaign, conflict, fighting, struggle 10 opposition
combining form: 5 -machy
__ warfare: 5 class 6 trench
Warfield: 4 Paul 6 Marsha, Wallis
WarGames (1983 film)
cast: Matthew Broderick, Dabney Coleman, Ally Sheedy
director: John Badham
dog: 4 Beau
org.: 5 NORAD
warhead
carrier: 4 ICBM
remove the ~: 6 disarm
Warhol, Andy: 6 artist 9 pop artist
film: 5 Trash
subject: 3 can, Mao 6 Monroe 7 Marilyn, soup can
war-horse: 5 steed 7 charger, palfrey, trooper, veteran 8 destrier
War in a Time of Peace author: David Halberstam
wariness: 5 doubt, qualm 8 distrust, mistrust 9 chariness, leeriness, misgiving, suspicion 10 insecurity, precaution, skepticism
Waring: 4 Fred 7 blender
competitor: 5 Oster
War is __: 4 hell
War Is Kind author: Stephen Crane
Warks: 6 county
locale: 7 England
warlike: 7 hawkish, hostile, lawless, martial 8 fighting, inimical, militant, military, ructious 9 bellicose, combative, soldierly 10 aggressive, pugnacious, unfriendly
name meaning ~: 6 Marcia, Marsha
warlock: 4 male 5 witch 6 wizard 8 magician, sorcerer
circle: 5 coven
Warlock (1959 film)
cast: Henry Fonda, Anthony Quinn, Richard Widmark
director: Edward Dmytryk
War Lord, The (1965 film)
cast: Richard Boone, Charlton Heston
director: Franklin Schaffner
warm: 3 hot 4 bake, cook, cosy, cozy, fond, heat, homy, kind, melt, mild, nice, rich, snug, thaw 5 aglow, angry, balmy, chafe, close, cozey, cozie, happy, homey, human, riled, sunny, tepid, toast 6 ardent, fervid, genial, gung-ho, hearty, heated, heat up, kindly, living, loving, simmer, sweaty, tender, toasty 7 affable, amiable, amorous, clement, cordial, earnest, excited, fervent, flushed, glowing, intense, melting, prepare, sincere, summery, thermal 8 animated, cheerful, effusive, friendly, gracious, intimate, maternal, moderate, outgoing, parental, pleasant, roasting, sizzling, sociable, sweating, tropical, tucked in, vehement 9 congenial, emotional, heartfelt, microwave, scorching, temperate, unextreme 10 empathetic, hospitable, passionate, personable, perspiring, responsive, sweltering
getting ~: 4 near 5 close 7 close by
hello: 3 hug 4 kiss 7 embrace
in the pocket: 4 rich 5 flush 6 loaded 7 wealthy 8 well-to-do
sensation: 4 glow
spot: 5 ingle 6 hearth 9 fireplace
spring: 3 spa 4 bath
springs: 7 thermae
up: 4 heat, melt, thaw 5 ready, train 7 prepare 8 practice, rehearse, unfreeze
warm __: 4 spot, tone 5 front 6 sector, spring
warm-__: 7 blooded, hearted
warmed-over: 4 flat 5 banal, tired, trite
Warmed Over __: 6 Kisses
warmer
bench ~: 3 sub 5 scrub 9 alternate 10 substitute
starter: 3 leg
winter ~: 3 tea 4 coat, muff 5 cocoa, glove, quilt, scarf, toddy 6 hot tea 8 hot toddy
warmer-__: 5 upper
__ warmer: 3 leg 4 foot 5 bench, chair
__ Warm for May: 4 Very
warmhearted: 4 kind 6 decent, genial, gentle, humane, kindly, loving, tender 7 clement, lenient, sparing 8 gracious, merciful 10 altruistic, benevolent
warmheartedness: 6 regard 7 empathy 8 kindness, sympathy 10 compassion
warming __: 3 pan
__ warming: 6 global
warming starter: 5 heart, house
warmness: 4 heat 8 calidity 9 torridity 10 caloricity
warmonger: 4 hawk 7 soldier 9 guerrilla, mercenary
Warm Springs: 3 spa 6 resort
locale: 7 Georgia
warmth: 4 heat, pity, zeal 5 ardor, heart 6 fervor, spirit 7 emotion, passion 8 lyricism, radiance, radiancy, sympathy 9 geniality, sincerity 10 cordiality, friendship, kindliness, liveliness
source: 3 sun 4 oven 5 stove 6 burner, heater 9 fireplace
without ~: 3 icy 4 cold 5 icily, stony 6 coldly, stoney 7 stonily
warm the __: 5 bench
warm-up: 4 prep 5 drill 7 workout 9 rehearsal
gear: 6 sweats
warn: 3 tip 4 hint, post, tell, urge 5 alert, guide, order 6 advise, clue in, enjoin, exhort, fill in, forbid, inform, notify, prompt, remind, signal, tip off 7 apprise, apprize, caution, counsel, cry wolf, forearm, predict, prepare, presage, reprove, suggest 8 acquaint, admonish, dissuade, foreshow, foretell, forewarn, prophesy, threaten 9 adumbrate 10 give notice
of: 4 bode 5 augur 6 herald 7 bespeak, portend 8 forebode, prophesy 10 foreshadow
Warner: 3 Abe, Pop, Rex 4 Jack, John, Saem 5 David, Harry, Julie, Oland 6 Baxter, Sylvia
Warner Bros.: 3 Abe, Sam 4 Jack 5 Harry 6 studio
competitor: 3 Fox, MGM 6 Disney 7 Miramax, New Line 8 Columbia 9 Paramount, Universal 10 Dreamworks
creation: 4 film 5 movie
toon: 3 Taz 4 Bugs, Fudd, Pepe 5 Daffy, Elmer, Porky, Wile E. 6 Coyote 8 Porky Pig 9 Bugs Bunny, Daffy Duck, Elmer Fudd, Pepe Le Pew, Sylvester 10 Road Runner
Warner, David: 5 actor
film: The Ballad of Cable Hogue (1970)
The Bofors Gun (1968)
The Man With Two Brains (1983)
Morgan! (1966)
Time After Time (1979)
Titanic (1997)
Warner, John spouse: Elizabeth Taylor
Warner, Rex: 6 author, writer 7 British
Warner Robins: 4 city, town
locale: 7 Georgia
Warner, Sylvia: 4 poet 6 author, writer 7 British
work: The Corner That Held Them
Lolly Willowes
Warnes, Jennifer
song: Right Time of the Night (1977)
The Time of My Life (1987)
Up Where We Belong (1982)
warning: 3 SOS, tip 4 hint, omen, sign 5 alarm, alert, siren, token 6 advice, alarum, augury, beacon, beware, caveat, lesson, Mayday, notice, signal, threat, tipoff, tocsin 7 caution, example, heads up, ominous, pointer, portent, presage, symptom 8 guidance, reminder 9 foretaste, foretoken, indicator 10 admonition, admonitory, cautionary, foreboding, indication, injunction, intimation, prediction, suggestion
canine: 3 grr 4 gnar 5 gnarl, gnarr, growl, snarl
device: 4 horn 5 alarm, flare, fusee, fuzee, siren 6 beacon, claxon, klaxon 7 monitor
early ~ system: 5 NORAD 7 DEW line
exclamation: 2 no 3 grr, nix, shh 4 ahem, fore, no no, oh-oh, uh-oh 6 beware 7 gangway
without ~: 5 short 7 swiftly 8 suddenly, unawares
word of ~: 4 don't 6 beware, danger
warning __: 4 shot 5 track
__ warning: 3 act 4 gale 5 early, flood, storm
Warning Shot (1967 film)
cast: Ed Begley, David Janssen, Keenan Wynn
director: Buzz Kulik
war of __: 6 nerves 9 attrition
War of 1812
hero: 7 Jackson
issue: 6 Canada
treaty site: 5 Ghent
War of the __: 5 Roses 6 Worlds
War of the Roses, The (1989 film)
cast: Danny DeVito, Michael Douglas, Kathleen Turner
director: Danny DeVito
War of the Saints, The author: Jorge Amado
War of the Worlds: 4 film 5 novel 9 radio show
author: H.G. Wells
cast: Gene Barry, Ann Robinson, Les Tremayne
foe: 4 Mars
name: 5 Orson 6 Welles
warp: 3 mar 4 bend, bias 5 color, curve, screw, slant, twist 6 buckle, change, debase, deform, garble, poison, wrench 7 contort, corrupt, deflect, deprave, distort, texture 8 jaundice, misquote, misshape 9 brutalize 10 aberration
count: 4 sley
opposite: 4 weft, woof
work with ~: 5 weave
warp __: 4 beam, ikat, knit, roll 5 speed
__ warp: 4 time
warpath
be on the ~: 4 fume, rage, stew 5 storm 6 see red, seethe 7 flame up
on the ~: 6 raging 7 furious 8 incensed, wrathful
warped: 4 bent 6 skewed 7 crooked 8 lopsided 9 malformed
warplane: 3 MiG 6 bomber
warrant: 3 let, vow 4 back, bail, earn, word, writ 5 basis, merit, paper, proof, prove, swear, vouch 6 assert, assure, attest, depone, ensure, excuse, permit, pledge, reason 7 bear out, call for, certify, declare, deserve, empower, endorse, entitle, go-ahead, indorse, intitle, justify, license, mandate, passage, promise, summons, testify 8 attest to, guaranty, occasion, sanction, security, subpoena, vouch for 9 authorize, guarantee, indemnify, indemnity 10 green light, permission, underwrite
officer: 4 bo's'n, rank 5 bosun
__ warrant: 5 bench 6 arrest, search
warrantable: 6 lawful 7 tenable 9 allowable
warranted: 5 legal, licit 6 lawful 10 admissible, guaranteed, legitimate
warranty: 4 bail, bond 6 pledge, surety 7 promise 8 contract, covenant, guaranty 9 assurance, guarantee
without a ~: 4 as is
word: 6 defect
__ warranty: 7 express, implied
Warren: 4 city, Earl, Moon, town 5 Giles, Harry, Oates, Spahn, Zevon 6 Beatty, Burger 7 Buffett, Harding, Leonard, Michael, William 8 Jennifer
locale: 4 Ohio 8 Michigan
veep: 3 Cal 6 Calvin
warren dweller: 6 rabbit
Warren, Harry: 8 composer
song: About a Quarter to Nine
Boulevard of Broken Dreams
Chattanooga Choo Choo
Cheerful Little Earful
Forty-Second Street
Go Into Your Dance
I Only Have Eyes for You
I've Got a Gal in Kalamazoo
Jeepers Creepers
Lullaby of Broadway
Lulu's Back in Town
The More I See You
Shuffle Off to Buffalo
That's Amore
We're in the Money
You'll Never Know
You Must Have Been a Beautiful Baby
You're Getting to Be a Habit With Me
Warren, Leonard: 6 singer 8 baritone, barytone
specialty: 5 opera
Warren, Lesley Ann spouse: Jon Peters
Warren, Mrs. creator: 3 GBS 4 Shaw
Warren, Robert Penn: 4 poet 6 writer
work: All the King's Men
At Heaven's Gate
World Enough and Time
__ Warren's Profession: 3 Mrs.
War Requiem composer: 7 Britten
Warrick, Ruth: 7 actress
film: The Corsican Brothers (1941)
Perilous Holiday (1946)
Song of the South (1946)
Warrington: 4 city, town
locale: 7 Florida
warrior: 2 GI 4 hero 5 ninja 6 archer, bowman, knight 7 fighter, soldier, veteran 9 combatant, conscript, legionary, mercenary 10 campaigner, contestant
Old West ~: 5 brave 6 Apache
__ warrior: 4 cold, road 5 happy 6 Indian 7 weekend
__ Warrior: 4 Road
__: Warrior Princess: 4 Xena
Warrior rival: 3 Cav, Mav, Net, Sun 4 Buck, Bull, Hawk, Heat, Jazz, King,

Spur 5 Knick, Laker, Magic, Pacer, Sonic 6 Celtic, Hornet, Nugget, Piston, Raptor, Rocket, Wizard 7 Clipper, Grizzly 8 Cavalier, Maverick 10 SuperSonic, Timberwolf
Warriors: 4 five, team
org.: 3 NBA
sport: 10 basketball
Warrior's Barrow, The author: Henrik Ibsen
Warrior, The (1984 song) artist: Patty Smyth
war-room fixture: 3 map 5 radar 7 hot line
__ Wars: 4 Star 5 Punic 6 Gallic
Warsaw: 4 city, pact, town 7 capital
city near ~: 4 Lodz
locale: 6 Poland
river: 7 Vistula
Warsaw Pact
member: 3 GDR 4 USSR 6 Poland, Russia 7 Hungary, Romania 8 Bulgaria 11 East Germany
opposite: 4 NATO
War Scenes composer: 5 Rorem
warship: 4 boat 5 razee 6 PT boat 7 flattop, frigate, galleon, gunboat, monitor 8 corvette, ironclad, man-of-war 9 destroyer, minelayer 10 patrol boat
initials: 3 USS
warships: 5 fleet 6 armada
Wars of the __: 5 Roses
War (song) artist: Bruce Springsteen, Edwin Starr
Warszawa instrumentalist: 3 Eno
wart: 4 flaw 5 fault 6 defect 7 blemish, failing, verruca
ender: 3 hog
starter: 5 worry
Warta: 5 river
locale: 6 Poland
__ War, The: 4 Holy 5 Art of
warthog: 5 beast 6 animal, mammal 7 critter
tooth: 4 tusk
Warton, Thomas: 4 poet 6 writer 7 British
warts and all: 4 as is 6 openly 7 frankly, plainly 8 candidly, honestly
warty: 5 bumpy 6 knobby 9 verrucose
critter: 4 frog, toad
War Wagon, The (1967 film): 5 oater 7 western
cast: Kirk Douglas, Howard Keel, John Wayne
Warwick, Dionne
cousin: Whitney Houston
song: Alfie (1967)
Anyone Who Had a Heart (1964)
Don't Make Me Over (1963)
Do You Know the Way to San José (1968)
Heartbreaker (1982)
I'll Never Fall in Love Again (1970)
I'll Never Love This Way Again (1979)
I Say a Little Prayer (1967)
Love Power (1987)
Message to Michael (1966)
That's What Friends Are For (1985)
Then Came You (1974)
This Girl's in Love With You (1969)
Valley of the Dolls (1968)
Walk On By (1964)
Warwickshire: 6 county
locale: 7 England
river: 4 Avon
town: 5 Rugby
War With the Newts, The author: Karel Capek
wary: 3 shy 4 cagy, safe, wise 5 alert, cagey, canny, chary, leery 6 unsure 7 careful, dubious, guarded, heads-up, heedful, mindful, on guard, prudent, sparing, wakeful 8 cautious, discreet, doubtful, doubting, hesitant, keen-eyed, vigilant, watchful 9 attentive, defensive, eagle-eyed, reluctant, sharp-eyed, skeptical, uncertain, wide-awake 10 on one's toes, suspicious
be ~: 4 mind 5 doubt, watch 7 look out, suspect 8 distrust, mistrust 10 disbelieve
was: 4 verb 5 lived 7 existed, had been
at: 6 went to 8 attended
not what it ~: 5 rusty 9 neglected 10 out of shape
__ was: 4 time
wasabi: 9 condiment
__ was a crooked man...: 5 There
__ was a cunning hunter: 4 Esau
__ was a lad...: 5 When I
__ Was a Lady: 5 Eadie, Nelly 7 DuBarry
__ was a man!: 4 This
__ Was a Rolling Stone: 4 Papa
Wasat: 4 star
Wasatch: 5 range
locale: 4 Utah 5 Idaho
ski resort: 4 Alta
Was blind but now __: 4 I see
Wasco: 4 city, town
locale: 10 California
__ was going to St. Ives: 3 As I
wash: 3 dip, lap, mop, wet 4 bath, coat, eddy, film, flow, gush, lave, lick, soak, soap, swab, swob, tint, wipe 5 bathe, clean, douse, dowse, float, flush, groom, heave, paint, rinse, scour, scrub, slosh, spirt, spurt, surge, swamp, swell, swirl, swish, tinge 6 drench, lather, lotion, murmur, neaten, purify, ravine, shower, sponge 7 cleanse, coating, deterge, dunking, freshen, immerse, launder, laundry, moisten, overlay, scrub up, shampoo 8 ablution, hose down, irrigate, lavation, prove out, spruce up 9 deodorize, disinfect, freshen up, hold water, take a bath 10 ebb and flow
against: 3 lap 4 lick 5 lap at
away: 4 wear 5 erode, leach, purge
cycle: 4 soak, spin 5 rinse
down: 4 hose 7 swallow
ender: 3 day, out, rag, tub 4 able, bowl, room 5 basin, board, cloth, stand, woman, women
get ruined in the ~: 3 run
off: 5 clean, rinse
one's hands of: 6 disown 7 abandon, bail out, disavow, forsake 8 forswear, renounce 9 foreswear, repudiate
out: 4 bomb, bust, fade, fail, lose, slip, trip 5 elute, erode, flunk 6 bleach, blow it, falter 7 blunder, founder, go under, go wrong, misstep, stumble 8 backfire, etiolate, fall flat, flounder, lay an egg
starter: 3 eye, hog 4 back 5 black, brain, mouth, stone, white
wash __: 3 out 4 down, sale 5 goods 7 drawing
__ wash: 3 car, dry, jet, wet 4 mold, prop 5 brain
__-wash: 4 hand, wish 5 belly 7 machine
Wash __: 4 'n Dri
Wash.
airport: 4 Natl.
neighbor: 3 Can., Ida., Ore. 4 Oreg.
Sq. campus: 3 NYU
see also Washington
__-washable: 7 machine
wash-and-wear material: 5 nylon 6 Dacron 9 synthetic
washbasin user: 5 laver
washboard __: 3 abs
washboard, use a: 5 scrub
Washbourne: 4 Mona
washbowl: 4 sink 5 basin 6 lavabo
washcloth: 5 linen
in Britain: 7 flannel
washday
brand: 3 All, Biz, Era, Fab, Yes 4 Bold, Dash, Gain, Surf, Tide, Wisk 5 Cheer, Dreft, Purex 6 Calgon, Clorox, Dynamo, Oxydol 7 Octagon 9 Ivory Snow
challenge: 3 tar 4 soil 5 paint, stain 6 collar 7 splotch
washed: 4 neat, pure, tidy 5 clean, snowy, sweet, white 6 bathed, bright, decent, spruce 7 refined, shining 8 dirtless, germfree, hygienic, pristine, purified, sanitary, spotless, unfouled, unsoiled 9 laundered, sparkling, stainless, unsmudged, unspotted, unstained 10 immaculate, impeccable
__-washed: 4 acid
washed-out: 3 wan 4 drab, dull, pale 5 faded 8 bleached, fatigued 9 colorless, enervated, etiolated, exhausted 10 lackluster
washed-up: 4 shot, sunk 5 kaput, spent 7 done for, through 8 finished
__ was here: 6 Kilroy
washer starter: 4 dish
washing: 6 lavabo, lavage 7 laundry 8 ablution 9 housework
washing __: 4 soda 7 machine
washing machine: 6 Bendix, Maytag 9 appliance, Whirlpool
companion: 5 drier, dryer
contents: 4 load, suds 6 bundle 7 laundry
phase: 4 soak, spin 5 cycle, rinse
Washington: 3 mtn., Ned 4 lake, peak 5 Dinah, Mount, state 6 Denzel, George, Irving, Martha 8 mountain 10 government
Washington (state)
cape: 5 Alava
capital: 7 Olympia
city: 4 Kent 5 Lacey, Pasco 6 Auburn, Burien, Renton, Tacoma, Yakima 7 Bothell, Cascade, Edmonds, Everett, Olympia, Pullman, Redmond, Seattle, Spokane 8 Bellevue, East Hill, Fairwood, Finn Hill, Kirkland, Lakewood, Longview, Lynnwood, Meridian, Parkland, Puyallup, Richland, Spanaway 9 Bremerton, Des Moines, Fort Lewis, Inglewood, Kennewick, Oak Harbor, Sammamish, Shoreline, South Hill, Vancouver, Wenatchee 10 Bellingham, Federal Way, Marysville, North Creek, Paine Field, Silver Firs, Walla Walla
conference: 6 Pac-Ten
Indian: 5 Makah 6 Nootka, Yakima 8 Puyallup, Sahaptin 9 Suquamish
mountain: 5 Adams 7 Rainier 8 St. Helens
national park: 7 Olympic
neighbor: 5 Idaho 6 Canada, Oregon
pro team: 6 Sonics 8 Mariners, Seahawks 11 SuperSonics
school: 7 Gonzaga
state bird: 9 goldfinch
state fish: 5 trout
state fossil: 7 mammoth
state fruit: 5 apple
state insect: 9 dragonfly
state tree: 7 hemlock
volcano: 8 St. Helens
waterfall: 8 Sluiskin
waterway: 5 Puget
Washington __: 3 pie 4 clam, lily 5 State, thorn 6 Square
Washington __ here: 5 Slept
Washington and __: 3 Lee
Washington, D.C.: 4 city, town 7 capital
airport: 6 Dulles, Reagan 8 National
athletes: 5 Bison, Hoyas
bank: 5 Riggs
court in ~: 5 lobby
helper: 4 aide, page
hostess: 5 Mesta
hundred: 6 Senate
newspaper: 4 Post 5 Times
onetime ~ ballplayer: 3 Nat 7 Senator
river: 7 Potomac 9 Anacostia
school: 6 Howard 10 Georgetown
stadium: 3 RFK
suburb: 5 Olney 8 Bethesda 9 Arlington
subway: 5 Metro
team: 7 Wizards 8 Capitals, Redskins
Washington, Denzel: 5 actor
film: The Bone Collector (1999)
Courage Under Fire (1996)
Crimson Tide (1995)
Cry Freedom (1987)
Devil in a Blue Dress (1995)
Glory (1989, AA)
He Got Game (1998)
The Hurricane (1999)
John Q (2002)
Malcolm X (1992)
Mo' Better Blues (1990)
Much Ado About Nothing (1993)
The Pelican Brief (1993)
Philadelphia (1993)
The Preacher's Wife (1996)
Remember the Titans (2000)
The Siege (1998)
Training Day (2001, AA)
TV: St. Elsewhere
Washington, Dinah
song: Baby (You've Got What It Takes) (1960)
A Rockin' Good Way (1970)
Unforgettable (1959)
What a Diff'rence a Day Makes (1959)
Washington, George: 7 general 9 president
bill: 3 one
former occupation: 7 soldier 8 surveyor
home: 8 Virginia
no-no: 3 lie
opponent: 4 Howe 8 Burgoyne 10 Cornwallis
portraitist: 5 Peale 6 Stuart
signature part: 3 Geo.
successor: 5 Adams
V.P.: 5 Adams
wife: 6 Martha
Washington Jr., Grover song: Just the Two of Us (1981)
Washington Post, The composer: 5 Sousa
Washington Square author: Henry James
Washington State
athletes: 7 Cougars
conference: 6 Pac-Ten
locale: 7 Pullman
Washita: 6 Indian 7 Amerind
Wash 'n __: 3 Dri
Washoe: 5 tribe 6 Indian 7 Amerind
wash one's __ of: 5 hands
washout: 3 dud 4 bust, flop, loss, rout 6 defeat, fiasco, mishap, turkey 7 blunder, debacle, failure, letdown, misstep, stumble 8 disaster, downfall
washroom: 2 W.C. 3 lav., loo 4 bath 8 lavatory
washstand item: 4 ewer 5 basin

Wash tributary: 4 Ouse
___-washy: 5 wishy
Wasilla: 4 city, town
  locale: 6 Alaska
___ was in the beginning...: 4 as it
___ was I to know?: 3 How
___ was no lady...: 4 That
wasn't it: 3 hid
___ Was One-and-Twenty: 5 When I
___ was only a bird...: 3 She
wasp: 3 bug 4 pest 6 hornet, insect
  colony: 4 nest
  genus: 5 vespa
  like a ~: 6 winged
  prey: 3 ant
wasp ___: 5 waist
___ wasp: 3 fig, mud, sea 4 gall, sand 5 mason, paper 6 cuckoo, digger, potter, social, spider
Wasp: 3 car 4 auto 6 Hudson
waspish: 4 mean, sour 5 cross, huffy, onery, testy 6 crabby, cranky, crusty, feisty, grumpy, ornery 7 grouchy, huffish, peevish, prickly 8 grumpish, petulant, snappish, venomous 9 crotchety, fractious, irascible, irritable, querulous, splenetic 10 ill-humored, malevolent, out of sorts
waspishness: 5 spite 6 enmity, rancor, spleen 8 acrimony, ill humor 9 hostility, petulance
Wass: 3 Ted
wassail: 5 drink
  ingredient: 4 wine 5 clove
wassailer: 7 reveler 9 bacchanal 10 merrymaker
  quaff: 3 nog 4 grog 6 eggnog
  song: 4 noel 5 carol
___ was saying...: 3 As I
wasser: 5 water 6 German
  frozen: 3 eis
Wassermann, Jakob: 6 writer 8 Austrian
  work: The World's Illusion
Wasserstein, Wendy: 10 playwright
  work: An American Daughter
    The Heidi Chronicles
    The Sisters Rosensweig
Wassily: 8 Leontief 9 Kandinsky
Wasson, Craig: 5 actor
  film: Body Double (1984)
    Four Friends (1981)
    Go Tell the Spartans (1978)
    The Outsider (1979)
waste: 3 eat, sap, use 4 blow, fade, junk, kill, lose, loss, moor, orts, rase, raze, ruin, sack, scum, sink, slay, slop, void, wilt 5 chaff, decay, drain, dregs, dross, havoc, level, offal, scrap, spend, spoil, swamp, swill, trash, use up, wilds 6 barren, burn up, debris, desert, excess, lavish, litter, misuse, murder, ravage, refuse, rubble, scraps, shrink, tundra, wither 7 aridity, atrophy, deplete, despoil, destroy, eat away, fribble, garbage, pillage, play out, rubbish, rummage, splurge, trounce 8 badlands, dust bowl, enfeeble, languish, leavings, lifeless, misapply, misspend, quagmire, sediment, spoliate, squander, throw out 9 devastate, dissipate, leftovers, marshland, misemploy, overpower, overspend, ruination, sweepings, throw away, while away 10 gamble away, run through, trifle away, wilderness, wreak havoc
  allowance: 4 tret
  as time: 4 kill
  away: 4 melt, wane 6 shrink, wither 8 emaciate, languish
  don't ~: 5 reuse
  ender: 4 land 5 paper, water 6 basket
  holder: 6 ashcan 8 Dumpster, landfill, trash can
  lay ~ to: 3 aid 4 ruin, sack, undo 5 harry, smash, smite, wreck 6 ravage 7 consume, destroy, pillage, plunder, ransack 8 desolate, freeboot 9 depredate
  maker: 5 haste
  matter: 5 dross, trash 6 refuse 7 garbage
  no time: 3 hie, run 4 dash, race 5 speed
  time: 3 lag 4 futz, idle, laze, loaf, moon, mope 5 amble, dally, mosey, stall, tarry 6 dawdle, diddle, linger, loiter, lounge, trifle 7 saunter 8 lollygag, straggle 10 dillydally, fool around
waste ___: 4 gate, pipe, well
___ waste: 3 lay 4 go to
wastebasket: 3 can 8 trash can 10 receptacle
wasted: 4 lean, lost, thin 5 spent, tired 8 fatigued, misspent
Wasted Days and Wasted Nights (1975 song) artist: Freddy Fender
Wasted on the Way (1982 song)
  artist: Crosby, Stills & Nash
wasteful: 4 wild 6 lavish, wanton 7 liberal, ruinous 8 careless, cavalier, overdone, prodigal 9 unthrifty 10 immoderate, inordinate, profligate, thriftless
  be ~: 5 use up 6 frivol, lavish, misuse 7 deplete 8 misspend, squander 9 dissipate, throw away 10 run through
wasteland: 4 moor, wild 5 heath, waste 6 desert, jungle
  like a ~: 4 arid 5 bleak, stark 6 barren 8 desolate
Waste Lands, The author: Stephen King
Waste Land, The: 4 poem
  author: T.S. Eliot, TSE
  subject: 3 Apr. 5 April 6 lilacs
Waste not, want not: 3 saw 5 adage, maxim 6 saying
waste one's ___: 6 breath
___ was the sky so deep a hue: 4 ne'er
wastrel: 5 knave, rogue 6 loafer, rascal 7 spender 8 prodigal 10 ne'er-do-well, profligate
  no ~: 5 saver
wat: 6 temple
___ Wat: 6 Angkor
Watauga: 4 city, town
  locale: 5 Texas
watch: 3 eye, see, spy 4 case, duty, Ebel, espy, gaze, heed, look, mark, mind, note, peer, Rado, scan, tend, view, wait 5 Casio, clock, Elgin, guard, Lorus, Omega, Rolex, scout, Seiko, spy on, stare, timer, Timex, vigil 6 advert, attend, Bulova, follow, Fossil, gape at, gaze at, gaze on, listen, look at, Movado, notice, patrol, picket, police, Pulsar, regard, sentry, shadow, Swatch, ticker 7 baby-sit, care for, Citizen, glimpse, look for, lookout, monitor, observe, oversee, protect, spy upon, stare at, witness 8 chaperon, eagle eye, glance at, Longines, look in on, scope out, scrutiny, see after, sentinel, stake out, Tag Heuer, take heed, Tourneau 9 chaperone, look after, oversight, safeguard, supervise, timepiece, vigilance 10 eyewitness, get a load of, keep tabs on, monitoring, rubberneck, scrutinize, stand guard, take care of, take notice, timekeeper, weather eye
  brand: 4 Ebel, Rado 5 Casio, Elgin, Lorus, Omega, Rolex, Seiko, Timex 6 Bulova, Fossil, Movado, Pulsar, Swatch 7 Citizen 8 Longines, Tag Heuer, Tourneau
  display: 3 LCD, LED
  ender: 3 dog, eye, man, men 4 band, case, word 5 maker, tower
  feature: 5 alarm, timer
  for: 5 await 6 expect 7 count on 8 reckon on 9 count upon 10 anticipate
  holder: 3 fob 4 band 5 chain, wrist
  intently: 3 eye 4 gawk, gaze, ogle 5 stare 6 take in 7 eyeball
  keep ~: 4 look 6 patrol
  numeral: 3 III, VII, XII 4 VIII
  one's step: 6 behave, beware 7 look out 8 watch out 10 toe the line
  out: 6 beware 7 heads up
  out for: 4 heed, mind 8 beware of
  over: 3 sit 4 keep, mind, tend 5 cover 6 cradle, defend, manage 7 protect, shelter, sit with 8 chaperon, shepherd 9 chaperone, safeguard 10 take care of
  part: 4 band, case, dial, face, hand, stem 5 bezel, crown, jewel 6 detent 7 crystal 8 movement
  secretly ~: 3 spy 4 tail 5 spy on
  something to ~: 4 step 5 mouth
  sound: 4 beep, tick 5 alarm
  starter: 3 dog 4 stop 5 wrist
  tend to a ~: 3 set 4 wind 5 reset
watch ___: 3 cap, fob, out 4 fire, list, over 5 chain, guard, night 6 pocket 7 meeting
___ watch: 3 dog 4 deck 5 clock, night, storm, Swiss, wrist 6 analog, anchor, middle, quartz 7 digital, evening, hunting, morning, sunrise
Watch ___ Rhine: 5 on the
Watch ___ step!: 4 your
watchband: 5 strap
watchdog: 5 super 6 keeper, warden 7 curator, janitor, manager, monitor, steward 8 executor, guardian, overseer 9 attendant, bodyguard, caretaker, concierge, custodian, protector 10 baby sitter, doorkeeper, supervisor
  breed: 5 Akita, boxer 8 doberman, shepherd 10 Rottweiler
watcher: 3 fan, spy 4 eyer, nana 5 guard, nanny, spier 6 nannie 7 lookout, witness 8 beholder, onlooker 9 governess, spectator 10 eyewitness
  weight ~ bane: 4 nosh 5 snack, sweet 7 munchie
  weight ~ concern: 3 fat 8 calories
___ watcher: 4 bird, poll 5 clock
___ Watchers: 6 Weight
Watchers author: Dean Koontz
watchful: 4 keen, wary 5 alert, awake, aware, canny, chary, glued, ready 6 intent, prompt 7 all ears, careful, guarded, heads-up, heedful, mindful, on guard, wakeful 8 cautious, keen-eyed, on the job, open-eyed, parental, prepared, vigilant 9 attentive, conscious, defensive, expectant, farseeing, observant, on the ball, regardful, wide-awake 10 longheaded, on one's toes, protective, suspicious, unsleeping
  eye: 5 vigil 7 lookout 8 guidance, tutelage, wardship 9 oversight
  name meaning ~: 3 Ira 7 Gregory
watchfulness: 4 care, heed 7 caution 9 vigilance
watching
  closely: 7 all eyes
  one's step: 4 wary 5 canny, chary, leery 7 careful, guarded, heedful, prudent 8 cautious, vigilant, watchful 9 judicious 10 deliberate, scrupulous
Watching Scotty Grow (1971 song)
  artist: Bobby Goldsboro
Watching the Wheels (1981 song)
  artist: John Lennon
Watch it!: 3 hey 7 look out 9 be careful
Watch It (1993 film)
  cast: Suzy Amis, Peter Gallagher, John C. McGinley
  director: Tom Flynn
watchkeeper: 3 spy 5 guard, scout 6 patrol, picket, ranger, sentry, warden 7 curator, flagger, lookout, spotter 8 observer, sentinel 9 caretaker, custodian, detective, signaller
watchmaker: 7 jeweler 10 horologist
  art: 5 horol. 8 horology
  length unit: 5 ligne
  lens: 5 loupe
watchman: 5 guard 8 defender, sentinel 9 bodyguard, protector
___ watchman: 5 night
Watch Mr. Wizard (NBC) host: Don Herbert
watch one's ___ Q's: 5 P's and
Watch on the Rhine: 4 film, play
  author: Lillian Hellman
  cast: Bette Davis, Geraldine Fitzgerald, Paul Lukas
watch the ___: 6 birdie
watchtower: 4 beam 6 beacon 7 lookout 10 lighthouse
watchword: 5 motto 6 phrase, slogan
watch your ___: 4 step
water: 3 dew, wet 4 aqua, hose, need, rain, soak, spit, tear, thin 5 douse, dowse, drink, drool, fluid, oxide, souse, spray 6 dampen, dilute, drench, liquid, weaken 7 logical, moisten, utility 8 Adam's ale, beverage, inundate, irrigate, moisture, saturate, sprinkle
  add ~ to: 4 thin 6 dilute, weaken
  away from ~: 6 inland
  barrier: 3 dam 4 dike, weir 5 levee 10 embankment
  beach ~: 4 surf
  bird: 4 coot, ibis 5 egret, heron
  blow out of the ~: 4 beat, best, rout, stun 5 cream, crush, outdo 6 dazzle, defeat, thrash 7 astound, conquer, overrun, stagger, stupefy, trounce 8 astonish, bowl over, vanquish 9 devastate, dumbfound, overpower, overwhelm
  boatman: 3 bug 6 insect
  body of ~: 3 sea 4 lake, pond, pool, tarn 5 creek, ocean, river, sound 6 lagoon, strait, stream
  border: 4 bank 5 beach, coast, shore 7 seaside 8 littoral, seaboard, seashore 9 shoreline
  bottled: 4 Naya 5 Evian 7 Perrier 8 Aquafina 9 Arrowhead
  bounce on ~: 3 dap
  cannon target: 3 mob 5 crowd
  carrier: 3 rut 4 duct, hose, line, pail, pipe, race 5 canal, ditch, drain, flume, gulch, gully 6 arroyo, furrow, gulley, gutter, outlet, siphon, strait, syphon, trench, trough 7 channel, conduit, culvert, passage 8 aqueduct
  chestnut: 5 tuber
  closet: 2 WC 3 lav, loo 7 latrine 8 bathroom, lavatory
  collector: 4 sump
  color: 4 aqua
  combining form: 4 aqua-, aqui-, hydr- 5 hydat-, hydro- 6 hydato-
  company: 4 util. 7 utility
  container: 3 cup, pan, pot, urn, vat 4 ewer, olla, pail, tank, vase 5 glass 6 goglet, guglet 7 cistern, gurglet 9 reservoir
  container of India: 4 lota 5 lotah
  containing ~: 7 hydrous

convey over ~: 5 ferry
cook in ~: 4 boil
cooler: 3 ice
covered with ~: 5 awash, soggy, soppy 6 soaked, sodden 7 sopping 8 drenched, dripping 9 saturated
craft: 3 dau, dow 4 boat, dhow, ship 5 canoe, liner, shell, sloop 6 jetski
deep ~: 3 fix, jam 4 bind, mess 5 pinch 6 crisis, pickle, plight, scrape, strait 7 dilemma, problem, trouble 8 quandary 9 adversity 10 difficulty
dog: 3 gob, tar 6 sailor
down: 3 cut, wet 4 thin 5 blunt 6 dilute, rarefy, rarify, soften, weaken 7 vitiate 10 adulterate
draw ~: 4 pump
droplets: 3 dew 4 mist 5 vapor 8 dampness, moisture
empty of ~: 4 bail
ender: 3 bed, bus, log, man, men, way 4 buck, fall, fowl, leaf, mark, shed, side, weed 5 borne, color, craft, cress, front, melon, power, proof, scape, spout, tight, works 6 course, finder, logged, marked 8 colorist, proofing
fish out of ~: 6 misfit 7 oddball 8 maverick
flounder in ~: 5 slosh 6 splash
form: 3 ice 5 steam, vapor
free from ~: 5 wring
frozen ~: 3 ice 6 icicle
get ~ from a well: 4 draw
glide on ~: 3 ski 4 skee
go by ~: 4 sail
heater: 6 boiler
hold ~: 4 wash 6 cohere 9 make sense
holder: 3 cup, pan, pot 4 ewer, olla, pail, tube, vase 5 basin, glass 6 bottle 7 canteen
holding ~: 4 sane 5 sound 7 logical
hole: 4 pond, well
hot ~: 3 fix 4 bind 6 pickle 7 problem, trouble 9 deep water 10 difficulty
in French: 3 eau
in hot ~: 7 trapped
in Latin: 4 aqua
in Spanish: 4 agua
it doesn't hold ~: 3 net 5 sieve 8 colander
jet: 5 spirt, spurt
keep one's head above ~: 5 tread
leave the ~: 6 emerge 7 surface
let the ~ out: 3 tap 4 vent 5 drain 6 siphon 7 draw off
low ~: 3 ebb
main: 4 line, pipe
make soda ~: 6 aerate
moccasin: 5 snake 7 serpent
moisten with ~: 4 soak, wash 5 bathe, douse, flush 6 drench, shower 7 immerse
mover: 3 oar
name meaning ~: 3 Ava
of flowing ~: 5 lotic
of still ~: 6 lentic 7 lenitic
on the ~: 4 asea 5 at sea 6 afloat
organism: 4 alga
out of the ~: 6 ashore, on land
pipe: 4 main 5 hooka 6 hookah
pistol: 3 toy
pitcher: 4 ewer
plant: 4 alga
platform by the ~: 4 dock, pier, quay, slip 5 berth, jetty, wharf
play in the ~: 4 swim, wade 5 slosh
power: 5 hydro
power org.: 3 TVA
prefix: 4 aqua- 5 hydro-
rat: 6 animal, mammal, rodent
receptacle: 4 sink 5 basin
regulator: 3 tap 5 valve 6 faucet, spigot 7 hydrant
remove ~: 4 bail, pump 5 wring
ring of ~: 4 moat
running, as ~: 5 aflow
salt ~: 3 bay, sea 5 brine, ocean
science of ~: 9 hydrology
search in ~: 6 dredge
seek ~: 5 dowse 6 divine
slide: 5 chute, flume
soapy ~: 4 suds 6 lather
softener: 5 borax
sound: 6 babble, gurgle, murmur, ripple, splash
source: 3 tap 4 well 6 faucet 7 aquifer
spend like ~: 5 waste 6 lavish 8 squander
sport: 4 polo 6 diving 8 swimming
sprite: 4 nixy 5 kelpy, nixie, nymph 6 kelpie
starter: 3 cut, sea 4 back, dish, fair, fire, head, jerk, lime, rain, salt, tide 5 break, flood, fresh, shear, under, waste, White 6 ground
stay above ~: 5 float
step through ~: 4 wade
surround with ~: 6 enisle
take on ~: 4 leak
tester: 3 toe
test the ~: 4 poll 5 query 6 survey 7 canvass
thoroughly: 4 soak 6 drench 8 saturate
throw cold ~ on: 5 deter 6 sadden 8 dispirit
throw ~ on: 5 douse, dowse 6 drench, splash 8 saturate 10 extinguish
toilet ~: 5 scent 7 cologne, perfume 9 fragrance
tonic ~: 4 fizz 5 mixer
tread ~: 4 swim
treat sea ~: 6 desalt 10 desalinate, desalinize
wheel: 5 noria
white ~: 6 rapids
without ~: 3 dry 4 arid, neat, sere
water ___: 3 boy, bug, dog, elm, gap, gas, gum, gun, hen, ice, oak, rat, ski 4 arum, back, bath, bear, bird, boat, bomb, cure, down, flag, flea, gate, hole, jump, leaf, lily, line, loss, main, mill, mold, oats, pipe, plug, polo, rail, rice, sign, taxi, trap, wave 5 bench, clock, gauge, glass, lemon, level, meter, motor, nymph, ousel, ouzel, paint, pipit, plant, poppy, power, right, slide, snail, snake, table, tiger, tower, vapor, wagon, wings, witch 6 ballet, beetle, bouget, budget, cannon, closet, clover, cooler, hammer, heater, jacket, locust, meadow, pistol, pocket, shield, sprite, sprout, supply, system, target, thrush, turkey, willow 7 biscuit, boatman, buffalo, carrier, curtain, feather, hemlock, lettuce, milfoil, opossum, parting, platter, spaniel, strider, turbine
water ___ the bridge: 5 under
water-___: 3 bus 4 cool, fast, inch, laid, soak 6 harden 7 soluble
___ water: 3 hot, ice, low, tap 4 bath, cold, dead, hard, high, hold, holy, rose, salt, soda, soft 5 above, bilge, first, fresh, heavy, in hot, Javel, light, slack, still, tonic, tread, vichy, white 6 barley, baryta, branch, broken, ground, lithia, static, toilet 7 ammonia, bottled, Cologne, Javelle, mineral, quinine, seltzer
___-water: 4 blue, deep
Water ___: 3 Rat 5 Music 6 Bearer
Water-___: 3 Pik
___ Water: 3 Hot 5 Afton, Black, Muddy
water-balloon sound: 5 splat
Water Bearer: 4 sign 8 Aquarius
month: 3 Feb., Jan. 7 January 8 February
predecessor: 4 Goat
successor: 4 Fish
waterborne: 4 asea 5 at sea 6 afloat
___-water bottle: 3 hot
Waterboy, The (1998 film)
cast: Fairuza Balk, Kathy Bates, Adam Sandler, Henry Winkler
director: Frank Coraci
waterbuck: 8 antelope
relative: 3 gnu, kob 4 guib, kudu, oryx, puku, topi 5 addax, bongo, chiru, eland, goral, korin, nyala, oribi, saiga, serow 6 chammy, dikdik, duiker, impala, koodoo, lechwe, nilgai, rhebok, shammy, shamoy 7 blaubok, blesbok, chamois, defassa, gazelle, gemsbok, gerenuk, grysbok, nylghai, nylghau, sassaby 8 blesbuck, bontebok, bushbuck, gemsbuck, reedbuck, steenbok, steinbok 9 blackbuck, pronghorn, sitatunga, springbok 10 hartebeest, wildebeest
Waterbury: 4 city, town
locale: 4 Conn.
water clover: 4 fern 5 plant
watercolor: 3 art 5 paint 6 canvas, fresco, medium 7 picture 8 painting
watercolorist: 6 artist 7 painter
watercourse: 4 duct 5 canal, creek, drain, gully, river 6 gulley, gutter, stream 7 channel, conduit, culvert
dry ~: 4 wadi, wady
watercraft: 3 dau, dow 4 boat, dhow, ship 5 canoe, liner, shell, sloop 6 jetski
watercress: 6 veggie 9 vegetable
unit: 5 sprig
Waterdance, The (1992 film)
cast: Helen Hunt, Wesley Snipes, Eric Stoltz
watered-down: 3 cut 4 tame, thin, weak 9 tasteless
ideas: 3 pap
Wateree: 5 river
locale: 4 S. Car.
waterfall: 5 chute, sault, spout 7 cascade, torrent
Africa ~: 8 Victoria
Alberta ~: 7 Panther
Argentina ~: 6 Iguaçu 7 Iguassú
Australia ~: 5 Tully
Austria ~: 7 Gastein 8 Krimmler
Brazil ~: 6 Iguaçu 7 Iguassú
British Columbia ~: 5 Della
California ~: 7 Feather
Canada ~: 5 Della 7 Niagara, Panther
effect: 5 spray
Ethiopia ~: 6 Fincha
France ~: 8 Gavarnie
Guyana ~: 8 Kaieteur
Hawaii ~: 5 Akaka
Idaho ~: 8 Shoshone
Italy ~: 4 Toce
Japan ~: 5 Kegon
Nevada ~: 6 Ribbon
New York ~: 7 Niagara
New Zealand ~: 6 Helena
Ontario ~: 7 Niagara
Scottish ~: 3 lin 4 linn
South Africa ~: 6 Tugela
Sweden ~: 6 Handol, Skykje
Switzerland ~: 6 Simmen
U.S. ~: 5 Akaka 6 Ribbon 7 Feather, Niagara 8 Shoshone, Sluiskin
Venezuela ~: 5 Angel
Wales ~: 7 Rhaiadr
Washington ~: 8 Sluiskin
Zambia ~: 8 Victoria
Zimbabwe ~: 8 Victoria
___ Waterfall: 3 By a, To a
Waterfalls (1995 song) artist: TLC
___-water flat: 4 cold
Waterford: 4 city, port, town
locale: 7 Ireland 8 Michigan
worker: 6 etcher
Waterford ___: 5 glass 7 crystal
waterfowl: 4 duck
___ Waterfowl: 3 To a
waterfront: 4 dock, port 5 beach, shore
city with a ~: 4 port
inn: 5 botel 6 boatel
org.: 3 ILA
sight: 4 pier, quay 5 wharf 6 marina
___ Waterfront: 5 On the
Watergate: 5 hotel
acronym: 5 CREEP
record: 4 tape
witness: 4 Dean
___ Waterhouse: 5 Price
watering
can alternative: 4 hose
hole: 3 bar, pub 4 pond, well 5 haunt, oasis 6 bar car, bistro, lounge, saloon, tavern
place: 4 well 5 river 6 spring
watering ___: 3 can 4 hole, spot 5 place
___-watering: 5 mouth
water-insoluble substance: 5 lipid, olein 6 lipide, oleine
Waterland (1992 film)
cast: Sinead Cusack, Jeremy Irons
director: Stephen Gyllenhaal
waterless: 3 dry 4 arid, sere 7 parched, thirsty 8 droughty 10 dehydrated
combining form: 6 anhydr- 7 anhydro-
Water Lilies painter: 5 Monet
waterlog: 4 soak 5 souse, steep, swamp 7 moisten 8 saturate
waterlogged: 3 wet 5 soggy 6 sodden
Waterloo: 4 city, ruin, town 6 battle, defeat 8 downfall
locale: 4 Iowa 6 Canada 7 Belgium, Ontario
Waterloo ___: 4 Road 6 Bridge 7 Station
Waterloo (1974 song) artist: ABBA
Waterloo Bridge (1940 film)
cast: Vivien Leigh, Robert Taylor
director: Mervyn LeRoy
Waterloo Bridge painter: 5 Monet
Waterloo Road (1944 film)
cast: Stewart Granger, John Mills
Waterman
filler: 3 ink
invention: 3 pen
one end of a ~: 3 nib
___-water mark: 3 low 4 high
Watermark singer: 4 Enya
watermelon: 4 pepo 5 fruit
covering: 4 rind
like ~: 5 seedy
shape: 4 oval
watermelon crawl: 5 dance
Water-Method Man, The author: John Irving
Water Music composer: 6 Handel
Water of Kronos, The author: Conrad Richter
water park feature: 5 flume, slide
water polo: 5 sport
waterproof: 4 seal 5 tight 10 impervious
coat: 5 loden
fabric: 5 loden 7 Gore-Tex, oilskin 8 oilcloth
waterproofing: 5 grout
Water Runs Dry (1995 song) artist: Boyz II Men
Waters: 4 John, Matt 5 Alice, Ethel, Muddy 7 Crystal
Waters, Ethel: 6 singer 7 actress
film: Cabin in the Sky (1943)
The Member of the Wedding (1952)
Pinky (1949)

song: 5 Dinah
TV: Beulah
water shamrock: 4 fern 5 plant
waters, healing: 3 spa
watershed: 5 basin 8 landmark
dividing line: 5 ridge
Watership Down: 5 novel
author: 5 Adams
dog: 3 Bob
waterside: 5 shore
accommodations: 5 botel 6 boatel
Waters, John: 8 director
film: Cry-Baby (1990)
Hairspray (1988)
Serial Mom (1994)
water skiing: 5 sport
Waterston, Sam: 5 actor
film: Hopscotch (1980)
The Killing Fields (1984)
The Man in the Moon (1991)
Rancho Deluxe (1975)
Serial Mom (1994)
TV: I'll Fly Away, Law & Order
__ water taffy: 4 salt
watertight: 5 right, tight 10 impervious
make ~: 4 calk 5 caulk 6 batten
water-to-wine town: 4 Cana
Watertown: 4 city
locale: 7 New York 9 Wisconsin
water under the __: 6 bridge
waterway: 5 canal, river 6 stream
waterways, like some: 6 inland
waterwheel: 5 noria, sakia
waterwitch: 5 dowse
waterworks: 5 tears 6 crying 7 sobbing, wailing, weeping
turn on the ~: 3 cry, sob 7 blubber
Waterworks, The author: E.L. Doctorow
Waterworld (1995 film)
cast: Kevin Costner, Dennis Hopper, Jeanne Tripplehorn
role: 5 Enola
watery: 3 wet 4 damp, pale, thin, weak 5 fluid, moist, runny, soggy, soupy, stale 6 dilute, liquid, marshy, sodden 7 aqueous, diluted, hydrous, wettish 9 tasteless 10 flavorless
expanse: 3 sea 5 ocean
sound: 4 glug 5 swash
Watford: 4 city, town
locale: 7 England
Watkins: 5 Peter
Watkins __, NY: 4 Glen
Watley, Jody
hometown: Chicago
song: Don't You Want Me (1987)
Everything (1989)
Friends (1989)
Looking for a New Love (1987)
Real Love (1989)
Some Kind of Lover (1988)
This Is for the Lover in You (1996)
Watling __: 6 Island
Watson: 2 MD 3 Bob, Tom 4 John 5 James 6 Lucile
colleague: 4 Bell 5 Crick 6 Holmes
Watson, James: 8 Nobelist 10 geneticist
concern: 3 DNA
Watson, Tom: 6 golfer
milieu: 5 links 6 course
org.: 3 PGA
Watsonville: 4 city, town
locale: 10 California
WATS, part of: 3 Tel. 4 Area, Serv., Wide 7 Service 9 Telephone
watt: 4 unit 7 measure
ender: 3 age 5 meter
measure: 5 power
relative: 3 amp, ohm 6 ampere
starter: 4 kilo, mega
watt-__: 4 hour 6 second
Watt: 5 James
Watt author: Samuel Beckett

Watterson: 4 Bill
wattle: 4 jowl 6 dewlap, lappet
__ wattle: 5 black 6 golden, silver
wattlebird: 3 iao
Watts: 5 André, Isaac 7 Charlie, Rolonda
Watts, André: 7 pianist
Watts, Charlie: 7 drummer
genre: 4 rock
Watts, Isaac: 6 writer 7 British
work: Horae Lyricae
Wattstax (1973 film)
cast: Isaac Hayes, Luther Ingram, Staple Singers
director: Mel Stuart
Watusi: 5 dance
home: 6 Africa, Rwanda 7 Burundi
__ Watusi, The: 3 Wah
Waugh: 4 Alec 6 Evelyn 7 Auburon, Hillary
Waugh, Auburon: 6 writer 7 British
work: A Bed of Flowers
Consider the Lilies
The Foxglove Saga
Path of Dalliance
Waugh, Evelyn: 6 writer 7 British
work: Black Mischief
Brideshead Revisited
Decline and Fall
The End of the Battle
A Handful of Dust
A Little Order
The Loved One
Men at Arms
Officers and Gentlemen
The Ordeal of Gilbert Pinfold
Scoop
Vile Bodies
Waugh, Hillary
work: 30 Manhattan East
Last Seen Wearing
Madman at My Door
Waukegan: 4 city, town
locale: 8 Illinois
native: Jack Benny
Waukesha: 4 city, town
locale: 9 Wisconsin
Wausau: 4 city, town
locale: 9 Wisconsin
Wauwatosa: 4 city, town
locale: 9 Wisconsin
wave: 3 set, wag 4 curl, flap, foam, perm, rash, sign, surf, sway, tide 5 crest, crimp, heave, pulse, shake, surge, swell, swing, swirl, twirl 6 beckon, billow, comber, dangle, hairdo, influx, motion, onrush, ripple, roller, ruffle, salute, signal, waggle, wigwag 7 breaker, flutter, gesture, pulsate, shudder, tsunami, upsurge 8 brandish, flourish, indicate, outbreak, undulate, whitecap 9 oscillate 10 inundation, outpouring
amplifier: 5 laser, maser
a red flag: 6 enrage 7 caution 8 forewarn
around: 4 show 6 flaunt, parade 7 display, exhibit, show off, trot out 8 brandish
away: 4 shoo
barrier: 4 mole 5 jetty, levee, wharf 7 sea wall 10 breakwater
big ~: 3 sea
combining form: 3 cym-, kym- 4 cymo-, kymo-
cutter: 4 prow
destination: 5 beach, coast, shore
down: 4 flag, hail 6 call to, signal, yell to 7 yell for
ender: 4 band, form 6 length
heraldic ~: 4 undé 5 undée
in Spanish: 3 ola
new ~: 5 novel 6 exotic, modern 8 vanguard 9 inventive 10 avant-garde, innovative

part: 5 crest, spume 6 billow
phenomenon: 4 chop
rise on a ~: 5 scend
starter: 3 air 5 micro, short
tidal ~: 6 tumult 7 tempest, tsunami, turmoil 8 disaster, upheaval 9 cataclysm
to: 4 hail 5 greet 7 welcome 9 recognize
wave __: 4 band, drag, trap 5 front, train 6 number, scroll, theory 7 cyclone
wave __ future: 5 of the
wave-__: 4 form 5 guide
__ wave: 3 bow, lee, new, sky 4 beta, body, cold, edge, heat, long, sine, slow 5 alpha, blast, brain, crime, delta, earth, radio, shock, sound, theta, tidal, water 6 Alfvén, finger, ground, guided, matter, square 7 carrier, elastic, gravity, primary
__ Wave: 4 Heat
WAVE counterpart: 3 WAF 4 WAAC
wavelength
be on the same ~: 5 agree, click 8 hit it off
on the same ~: 5 alike 6 in sync
waveless: 4 calm
wavelike pattern: 5 moiré
wave of the __: 6 future
waver: 4 halt, lick, reel, sway, vary, yo-yo 5 hedge, pause 6 boggle, change, dither, falter, palter, recoil, seesaw, swerve, teeter, totter, wabble, waffle, wobble 7 flicker, flutter, stagger, stumble, whiffle 8 flip-flop, flounder, hesitate 9 fluctuate, hem and haw, oscillate, pussyfoot, vacillate 10 deliberate, dillydally, equivocate
flag ~: 4 gale, wind 7 patriot
wavering: 4 torn, weak 5 fluid, shaky, timid 6 fickle, unsure 7 erratic, halting, mutable, protean 8 hesitant, shifting, unstable, unsteady, variable 9 faltering, mercurial, uncertain, undecided, unsettled 10 ambivalent, changeable, hesitation, indecisive, irresolute, of two minds, unreliable, weak-willed, wishy-washy
Waverley author: Walter Scott
waves: 3 sea 4 surf, wake
braving the ~: 4 asea 5 at sea 6 afloat 7 sailing
don't make ~: 4 obey 6 accept, comply
make ~: 4 stir 5 rebel, shake, upset 6 revolt 7 trouble 9 instigate 10 complicate, exasperate
rise in ~: 5 heave, pitch, surge, swell 6 billow
sound of ~: 4 roar
starter: 3 air
Waves: 10 Pepperdine
__ waves of grain: 5 amber
Waves, The author: Virginia Woolf
wavy: 5 curly, curvy, snaky 6 curvey, gyrose, permed 7 curling, curving, rippled, sinuous, winding 8 rippling, squiggly, tortuous, twisting 9 tremulous, vibrating 10 serpentine, undulating
in heraldry: 4 onde, undé 5 undéé
make ~: 4 curl 5 crimp, frizz, swirl
waw: 6 Hebrew, letter
predecessor: 2 he 3 heh
successor: 5 zayin
__ Wawa: 4 Baba
wawa device: 4 mute
wax: 4 grow, rise, trim 5 build, lipid, mount, sheen, shine, swell, widen 6 dilate, expand, finish, gather, lipide, lipoid, polish, record, spread, thrive 7 amplify, augment, broaden, build up, cerumen, develop, enlarge, fill out, magnify, Simoniz, trounce 8 heighten, increase, lipoidal, paraffin 9 lubricant, lubricate 10 strengthen
apply ~ to: 4 seal
car ~: 7 Simoniz
cleaner: 4 Q-tip
closure: 4 seal
combining form: 3 cer- 4 cero-
ender: 4 bill, wing, work 5 berry
insert: 4 wick
maker: 3 bee, ear
opposite: 4 wane
pencil: 6 crayon
product: 4 seal 6 candle
starter: 3 ear 4 bees
target: 3 car 4 auto 5 floor, table 9 furniture
vine: 4 hoya
whole ball of ~: 3 all 5 total 8 entirety, sum total 9 aggregate 10 everything
wrap in ~: 4 cere
wax __: 4 bean, jack, moth, palm 5 gourd, light, paper, plant, wroth 6 flower, insect, museum, myrtle, tablet
__ wax: 5 Japan, sumac, white 6 insect, montan 7 Chinese, lignite, mineral, sealing
Waxahachie: 4 city, town
locale: 5 Texas
waxbill: 4 bird 8 amadavat, avadavat
waxed
cheese: 4 Edam 5 Gouda
it's often ~: 5 floor, floss
waxed __: 5 paper 6 tablet
waxen: 3 wan 4 pale 5 livid, pasty, white 6 pallid 7 pliable 8 lustrous 9 colorless
starter: 4 woad, wood
waxing: 6 growth 8 blooming, increase
Waxman: 2 Al 5 Franz
waxwing: 4 bird
waxy: 4 oily 5 slick 6 sallow 8 lustrous, slippery 9 ceraceous, lubricous
way: 4 gate, lane, line, mode, path, plan, plot, road, room, vein, walk 5 alley, entry, habit, knack, means, orbit, route, space, steps, style, track, trail, trait, trick, usage 6 access, artery, avenue, course, custom, living, manner, method, nature, policy, scheme, street, system 7 bearing, channel, conduct, fashion, ingress, passage, process, routine, stretch, vehicle 8 approach, behavior, distance, entrance, practice, tendency 9 boulevard, direction, elbowroom, mannerism, procedure, technique 10 instrument
about one: 3 air 5 style 6 aspect, manner 7 bearing 8 carriage, demeanor, presence 9 character, mannerism 10 appearance, deportment
across the ~ from: 3 opp. 8 opposite
all the ~: 5 fully 6 wholly 9 to the hilt 10 completely, to the limit
a long ~: 3 far 4 afar 6 far cry
any old ~: 5 about 6 remiss 8 reckless 9 haphazard 10 incautious
back when: 4 once, past, yore 8 formerly
be on your ~: 2 go 3 run 4 exit 5 leave
by ~ of: 3 via 4 thro, thru 7 through
by the ~: 9 in passing
combining form: 3 -ode
covered ~: 4 stoa 6 arcade 7 gallery, portico 9 colonnade
down: 3 bad, low 4 base, deep 6 gloomy, nether, sunken, woeful 7 forlorn 9 depressed, in the pits 10 dispirited, rock-bottom

ender: **3** lay **4** bill, laid, side, ward, worn **5** farer, point **6** faring
every which ~: **5** messy, mussy **6** hectic, untidy **7** chaotic, haywire, jumbled, lawless, riotous, tangled **8** anarchic, confused, pell-mell **10** anarchical, disjointed, disordered, disorderly, topsy-turvy, tumultuous
feel one's ~: **5** grope **6** fumble **8** flounder **9** cast about
find a ~: **4** cope, lead **6** manage
from ~ back: **5** of old **6** age-old **7** veteran
get in the ~ of: **4** clog **5** deter **6** hamper, hinder, impair, impede, impose **8** handicap, obstruct
get out of the ~: **4** duck **5** dodge, evade **8** sidestep
get the hard ~: **3** pry **5** wrest, wring **6** extort, wrench
get the old-fashioned ~: **4** earn
get under ~: **4** sail, send **5** begin, speed, start **7** proceed **9** strike out
give ~: **3** sag **4** fall, move, snap **5** budge, burst, split, yield **6** buckle, cave in, relent, retire, tumble, weaken **7** crumble, crumple, succumb **8** collapse, fall down, withdraw
give ~ (to): **5** defer
go all the ~: **4** last **6** endure, hold on, linger **7** carry on, persist, survive **8** continue, plug away **9** hang tough, keep going, persevere, stand firm **10** tough it out
go out of one's ~: **6** bother
having a ~ with words: **8** eloquent
in: **4** door, gate **5** entry **6** entrée, portal **8** entrance
in a ~: **5** kinda, sorta **6** kind of, sort of **7** somehow **8** as it were, possibly
in a bad ~: **3** ill **4** illy, sick
in a big ~: **4** a lot, lots, much, tons **5** loads, no end **6** galore, highly, hugely, oodles **7** aplenty, grandly, greatly, largely **8** beaucoup, lavishly, terribly **9** copiously, extremely, immensely, liberally, profusely **10** abundantly, a great deal, enormously, prodigally
in any ~: **5** at all
in Italian: **3** via
in Latin: **4** iter
in one ~ or another: **7** somehow
in Spanish: **3** vía
in such a ~: **4** as if, so as, thus
in that ~: **4** ergo, then, thus
in the same ~: **3** too **4** also **6** as well **8** likewise **9** similarly
in the worst ~: **3** bad **5** badly
in this ~: **4** thus **6** hereby
in what ~: **3** how **5** how so
lead the ~: **5** guide **7** conduct, pioneer, trigger, usher in **8** initiate **9** instigate
long ~ around: **6** bypass, detour
look the other ~: **6** ignore **7** neglect **8** overlook
lose one's ~: **3** err **5** drift, stray **6** ramble **7** digress, diverge, meander **9** wander off
make one's ~: **4** wend **6** stroll, travel
no ~: **3** nah, naw, nay, nix, non **4** nein, nope, nyet, uh-uh **5** I won't, ixnay, my eye, never **7** I refuse **8** forget it, I will not, negative, negatory **9** fat chance, I think not, rejection **10** count me out, impossible, not a chance, thumbs down
not in any ~: **5** nohow
numbered: **3** rte. **5** route **10** interstate
off: **3** far, yon **4** afar, ramp **8** mistaken **9** incorrect **10** inaccurate
on: **4** ramp **6** access
one ~ or another: **7** somehow
on the ~: **3** off **6** coming **7** en route **8** imminent **9** in the wind
on the ~ out: **5** dated, hoary, passé, stale **6** old hat **9** hackneyed
other ~ around: **9** vice versa
out: **4** door, exit, gate **5** weird **6** egress, escape, outlet, refuge **7** bizarre, radical **8** creative, loophole, recourse
out of harm's ~: **4** alee, safe **6** secure
out of the ~: **3** far **4** awry **6** afield, astray
paper deliverer's ~: **5** route
partner: **4** will
pave the ~: **4** ease **5** ready, usher **6** smooth **9** introduce
point the ~: **4** lead **5** spark, steer, teach, train, tutor, usher **6** direct, orient **7** conduct **8** instruct **9** spearhead
put another ~: **5** resay **8** rephrase
right of ~: **8** priority
rubbing the wrong ~: **5** nasty **7** caustic **10** unpleasant
rub the wrong ~: **3** get, ire, irk, vex **4** miff, rile, roil **5** annoy, chafe, grate, peeve **6** abrade, offend
set on its ~: **4** send **6** convey, propel **8** dispatch
show the ~: **4** lead **5** guide, point **6** direct, lead in, lead on **7** pioneer
since ~ back when: **6** in ages **9** for a while
smooth the ~: **4** ease **5** set up **6** loosen **7** further, lighten, prepare **8** expedite, mitigate, moderate, simplify
stand in the ~: **3** bar **6** hinder, impede **9** foreclose
starter: **3** air, any, fly, key, lee, mid, run, sea, sky, sub **4** arch, area, belt, bike, door, fair, folk, foot, free, gang, gate, half, hall, head, high, park, path, race, rail, road, roll, ship, side, slip, some, taxi, thru, tide, tram, walk **5** alley, cable, cause, cross, drive, entry, green, hatch, motor, speed, spill, stair, stern, water **6** breeze, sluice **7** passage, through **8** entrance, steerage, straight **9** companion
that ~: **4** thus **6** like so, thusly
the ~: **3** how
the same ~: **5** alike **9** similarly, uniformly **10** comparably
things are: **6** status
to go: **5** huzza, route **6** hoorah, hooray, hurrah, hurray, huzzah
to put it another ~: **5** I mean
under ~: **8** in motion **9** on the move **10** in progress
up: **4** rise **5** slope, stair **6** ascent **7** incline
up the slope: **3** tow **4** T-bar
with words: **4** tact **9** diplomacy
wrong ~: **8** backward **9** backwards **10** upside-down
way __: **3** car **5** point **7** station
way __ world: **5** of the
way-__: **3** out
__ way: **3** in a **4** atta, give, make **5** by the, harm's, in the, on the, under
Way __ Flesh, The: **5** of All
Way __ Look Tonight, The: **3** You
Way __, The: **4** It Is, West **5** Ahead
Way __ West: **3** Out
Way __ Yonder in New Orleans: **4** Down
__ Way: **3** His **5** Milky **6** Appian, United **7** Windom's
Way Ahead, The (1944 film)
cast: Stanley Holloway, David Niven
director: Carol Reed
Wayans: **3** Kim **5** Damon **6** Keenen
__-way bulb: **5** three
__-way chili: **4** five
Way cool!: **3** rad
__ Way Corrigan: **5** Wrong
Way Down (1977 song) artist: Elvis Presley
Way Down East (1920 film)
cast: Richard Barthelmess, Lillian Gish
director: D.W. Griffith
Way Down Yonder in New Orleans (1959 song) artist: Freddy Cannon
wayfarer: **5** nomad, rover **6** roamer **7** pilgrim, tourist, trekker, voyager **8** gadabout, traveler, vagabond, wanderer **9** journeyer, meanderer, passenger **10** adventurer
refuge: **3** inn **5** hotel, lodge, motel **6** hostel **9** roadhouse
Wayfarer: **3** car **4** auto **5** Dodge
wayfaring: **6** roving, travel **7** journey, nomadic, on the go, roaming, vagrant, walking **8** drifting, gadabout, rambling, vagabond, voyaging **9** itinerant, itinerate, on the move, traveling, wandering **10** jet-setting, journeying
Way It Is, The (1986 song) artist: Bruce Hornsby and the Range
Way I Want to Touch You, The (1975 song) artist: Captain & Tennille
Wayland: **7** Flowers
waylay: **4** jump, lurk **5** prowl **6** accost, ambush, assail, attack, hold up, kidnap, lay for **7** set upon **8** pounce on, surprise **9** bushwhack, intercept
Waylon: **8** Jennings
Wayne: **4** city, Dyer, John, town, Wang **5** Bruce, David, Morse **6** Knight, Morris, Newton, Rogers **7** Anthony, Gretzky, Millner
locale: **9** New Jersey
Wayne, Bruce: **6** Batman
dog: **3** Ace
home: **5** manor
Wayne, David: **5** actor
film: Adam's Rib (1949)
The Last Angry Man (1959)
The Three Faces of Eve (1957)
Wait 'Til the Sun Shines, Nellie (1952)
__ Wayne, IN: **4** Fort
Wayne, John: **5** actor
birthplace: **4** Iowa
film: 3 Godfathers (1948)
The Alamo (1960)
Allegheny Uprising (1939)
Angel and the Badman (1947)
Back to Bataan (1945)
The Big Trail (1930)
The Comancheros (1961)
Dark Command (1940)
Donovan's Reef (1963)
El Dorado (1967)
The Fighting Seabees (1944)
The Flying Leathernecks (1951)
Flying Tigers (1942)
Fort Apache (1948)
Hatari! (1962)
The High and the Mighty (1954)
Hondo (1953)
How the West Was Won (1962)
A Lady Takes a Chance (1943)
The Longest Day (1962)
The Long Voyage Home (1940)
The Man Who Shot Liberty Valance (1962)
McLintock! (1963)
McQ (1974)
North to Alaska (1960)
Operation Pacific (1951)
The Quiet Man (1952)
Reap the Wild Wind (1942)
Red River (1948)
Rio Bravo (1959)
Rio Grande (1950)
Rio Lobo (1970)
Rooster Cogburn (1975)
Sands of Iwo Jima (1949)
The Searchers (1956)
Shepherd of the Hills (1941)
She Wore a Yellow Ribbon (1949)
The Shootist (1976)
The Sons of Katie Elder (1965)
Stagecoach (1939)
Tall in the Saddle (1944)
They Were Expendable (1945)
True Grit (1969, AA)
The War Wagon (1967)
Without Reservations (1946)
real name: Marion Morrison
Waynesboro: **4** city, town
locale: **8** Virginia
Wayne's World (1992 film)
cast: Lara Flynn Boyle, Tia Carrere, Dana Carvey, Rob Lowe, Mike Myers
catchword: **3** not
director: Penelope Spheeris
setting: **6** Aurora **9** Illlinois
Way of All Flesh, The (1927 film)
cast: Belle Bennett, Emil Jannings
director: Victor Fleming
Way of All Flesh, The author: Samuel Butler
way of a man with __, the: **5** a maid
Way of Love, The (1972 song) artist: Cher
way of the __: **5** cross, world
way of the gods, literally: **6** Shinto
__ way or the other: **3** one
way-out: **3** odd **5** weird **6** freaky **7** bizarre, offbeat, strange, unusual **8** aberrant, abnormal, freakish, peculiar **9** irregular **10** off-the-wall
Way Out West (1937 film)
cast: Oliver Hardy, Stan Laurel
director: James Horne
waypost: **6** marker **8** landmark **9** milestone
ways: **6** habits, traits **7** customs **8** patterns **10** ins and outs
and means: **7** capital, revenue **9** resources
change one's ~: **4** mend **6** reform **7** shape up **10** make amends
go different ~: **4** part **5** split **8** separate
see the error of one's ~: **6** repent
set in one's ~: **4** firm, iron **5** balky, fixed, rigid, stern, stiff, stony **6** dogged, mulish, ornery **7** adamant, piggish, willful **8** contrary, indurate, obdurate, perverse, resolute, stubborn **9** fractious, hardnosed, immovable, obstinate, pigheaded, tenacious, unbending **10** bullheaded, hard-bitten, hardheaded, headstrong, inflexible, refractory, unshakable, unyielding
starter: **4** side
__ Ways: **4** Evil
__ ways about it: **5** no two
ways and __: **5** means
__-way street: **3** one, two
Way That You Love Me, The (1989 song) artist: Paula Abdul
__ Way, The: **4** Hard **5** Milky **6** Family
way to __ heart..., The: **5** a man's
__ way to go!: **4** Atta
__ Way to Go!: **5** What a
Way to Love, The (1933 film)
cast: Maurice Chevalier, Ann Dvorak, Edward Everett Horton
director: Norman Taurog
Way to Natural Beauty, The author: **5** Tiegs

__ Way to Pay Old Debts: 4 A New
Way to the Stars, The (1945 film)
  cast: John Mills, Michael Redgrave
  director: Anthony Asquith
Way Upstream author: Alan Ayckbourn
wayward: 4 lost, wild 5 onery 6 errant, feisty, fickle, mulish, ornery, unruly, wanton, wicked, wilful 7 aimless, defiant, deviant, erratic, flighty, impious, naughty, willful 8 contrary, factious, obdurate, perverse, stubborn, variable 9 dissolute, obstinate, whimsical 10 capricious, changeable, delinquent, disorderly, headstrong, inconstant, rebellious, refractory, self-willed
Wayward Bus, The author: John Steinbeck
waywardness: 8 mischief 10 misconduct
Wayward Wind, The (1956 song)
  artist: Gogi Grant
Way West, The: 4 film 5 novel
  actor: 4 Elam, Kaye 7 Douglas, Mitchum, Widmark
  author: A.B. Guthrie
Way We Were, The: 4 film, song
  artist: Barbra Streisand
  cast: Bradford Dillman, Robert Redford, Barbra Streisand
  director: Sydney Pollack
Way You Do the Things You Do, The (1964 song) artist: Temptations
Way You Look Tonight, The (1961 song) artist: Lettermen
Way You Look Tonight, The composer: 4 Kern 6 Fields
Way You Make Me Feel, The (1987 song) artist: Michael Jackson
__ way you slice it: 3 any
WB: 7 network
  competitor: 3 ABC, CBS, Fox, NBC, UPN 5 ABC-TV, CBS-TV, NBC-TV
  mascot: 4 frog 8 Michigan
WBA
  area: 4 ring 5 arena
  athlete: 3 pug 5 boxer
  part: 4 Assn. 5 Assoc., World 6 Boxing
  result: 2 KO 3 TKO
WBC
  area: 4 ring 5 arena
  athlete: 3 pug 5 boxer
  part: 5 World 6 Boxing
__ W. Bush: 6 George
W.C.: 3 lav, loo 4 bath, john 5 Handy 6 Fields 8 bathroom, lavatory
W.C. Fields and Me (1976 film)
  cast: John Marley, Valerie Perrine, Rod Steiger
  director: Arthur Hiller
WCTU
  member: 3 Dry
  target: 3 alc., wet 6 saloon
wd.
  component: 3 ltr., syl. 4 syll.
  connecting ~: 4 conj.
  descriptive ~: 3 adj., adv.
  ender: 4 suff.
  group: 3 phr.
  shortened ~: 4 abbr.
  source: 4 etym. 5 deriv.
  starter: 4 pref.
  stock: 5 vocab.
  see also word
WD40: 9 lubricant
__ we: 5 royal
__ we?: 5 Shall
We __ Family: 3 Are
We __ Harder: 3 Try
We __ Kings of Orient Are: 5 Three
We __ Little Christmas: 5 Need a
We __ Love: 3 Got 5 Are in
We __ Not Alone: 3 Are
We __ not amused: 3 are
We __ Overcome: 5 Shall
We __ please: 5 aim to
We __ robbed!: 3 was, wuz
We __ Start the Fire: 5 Didn't
We __ the Champions: 3 Are
We __ the World: 3 Are
We __ Work It Out: 3 Can
__ We?: 5 Didn't
We Accuse author: 5 Alsop
weak: 3 dim, low, wan 4 lame, limp, meek, mild, pale, poor, puny, sick, slim, soft, tame, thin 5 faded, faint, frail, inept, light, lousy, reedy, runny, rusty, shaky, slack, spent, stale, timid, unfit, vapid, wimpy 6 ailing, anemic, atonic, craven, dilute, effete, fading, faulty, feeble, flabby, flimsy, infirm, mortal, sickly, skimpy, slight, tender, unable, unsafe, unsure, unwell, wabbly, watery, wobbly, yellow 7 anaemic, diluted, failing, flaccid, fragile, insipid, lacking, languid, limited, maudlin, muffled, nervous, puerile, rickety, rundown, shallow, slender, spindly, stifled, tenuous, unsound, useless, wimpish, worn out 8 cowardly, decrepit, delicate, flagging, helpless, hesitant, immature, insecure, pathetic, sluggish, timorous, unstable, wavering 9 deficient, dependant, dependent, enervated, exhausted, faltering, frangible, inaudible, nerveless, powerless, prostrate, spineless, tasteless, unguarded, unhealthy, untenable, untrained, whispered 10 improbable, inadequate, indecisive, irresolute, pathetical, unaccented, unreliable, unstressed, vulnerable, wishy-washy
  combining form: 4 lept- 5 lepto- 6 asthen- 7 astheno-
  ender: 4 ling
  in phonetics: 5 lenis
  in the knees: 5 dazed, dizzy, faint, giddy, shaky, woozy 6 wobbly 7 reeling 8 unsteady
  knees: 4 fear 8 cold feet, timidity 9 cowardice 10 faint heart
  one: 4 prey 6 victim
  point: 4 vice 5 minus 6 defect, foible
weak __: 4 side 5 force 6 ending, safety, sister
weak-__: 5 kneed 6 headed, minded, willed
Weak (1993 song) artist: SWV
weaken: 3 cut, sap, tax 4 fade, fail, flag, jade, sink, thin, tire, wane, wear, wilt 5 abate, blunt, break, decay, droop, erode, faint, lapse, lower, mince, relax, shake, water, weary 6 damage, debase, defuse, defuze, dilute, ease up, enerve, falter, impair, lessen, reduce, relent, soften, strain, temper, totter 7 break up, crumble, decline, degrade, deplete, dwindle, exhaust, fatigue, give way, qualify, relapse, tail off, tire out, tremble, unnerve, vitiate, wear out 8 decrease, diminish, enervate, enfeeble, languish, minimize, mitigate, moderate, paralyse, paralyze, peter out, slow down 9 attenuate, indispose, undermine, water down 10 adulterate, debilitate, devitalize, dishearten, emasculate
weakened: 5 spent 6 feeble 7 haggard, injured, starved 8 starving
weakening: 7 decline 9 abatement, attrition 10 diminution
Weakest Link, The: 8 game show
  host: Anne Robinson
weak-kneed: 6 craven 7 fearful, wimpish 9 spineless 10 indecisive, irresolute, wishy-washy
weakling: 3 sap 4 baby, wimp, wuss 5 sissy, softy 6 coward, softie 7 chicken, crybaby, quitter 8 mama's boy, pushover 9 cream puff, jellyfish
  like a ~: 4 puny
  no ~: 5 he-man
weak-minded: 4 daft 5 daffy, dizzy, dopey, goofy, inane, sappy, silly 6 absurd 7 asinine, doltish, fatuous, foolish, vacuous, witless 9 dim-witted, half-baked, senseless 10 addlepated, boneheaded, cockamamie, half-witted, ill-advised
weakness: 3 gap 4 flaw, need, urge, vice 5 fault, lapse, minus, taste 6 anemia, defect, foible, hurdle, liking 7 anaemia, barrier, blemish, failing, fatigue, frailty, languor, malaise, passion 8 appetite, debility, delicacy, drawback, fondness, handicap, obstacle, penchant, shortage, soft spot, tendency 9 detriment, fragility, frailness, hindrance, infirmity, lassitude, liability, proneness, sore point, specialty 10 deficiency, feebleness, impairment, impediment, inadequacy, incapacity, indecision, insecurity, insipidity, invalidity, partiality, proclivity, propensity
  cause: 6 anemia 7 anaemia
  minor ~: 4 vice 6 foible
  muscle ~: 5 atony 6 atonia
weak-willed: 6 fickle 8 hesitant, wavering 9 faltering, spineless, uncertain 10 ambivalent, irresolute, wishy-washy
  one: 3 sop
weal: 4 luck, welt 9 happiness
__ weal: 6 common
weald: 4 wood 5 woods
__ We All?: 5 Aren't
wealth: 3 oof 4 cash, gelt, gold, jack, kail, kale, loot, luck, mine, peag, pelf, pile 5 asset, bills, bread, bucks, dough, funds, goods, hoard, lucre, means, money, moola, mopus, pesos, rhino, sewan, store 6 assets, bounty, clover, dinero, do-re-mi, estate, luxury, mammon, mazuma, moolah, plenty, riches, seawan, silver, specie, wampum 7 cabbage, capital, dollars, fortune, lettuce, ooftish, revenue, scratch, shekels 8 bankroll, cold cash, currency, hard cash, holdings, opulence, opulency, property, richness, security, smackers, treasure 9 abundance, affluence, banknotes, frogskins, long green, plenitude, profusion, resources, simoleons, substance 10 belongings, cornucopia, greenbacks, green stuff, luxuriance, prosperity
  combining form: 4 plut- 5 pluto-
  ill-gotten ~: 4 pelf 5 booty, lucre
  starter: 6 common
Wealth of Nations, The author: Adam Smith
wealthy: 4 rich 5 flush 6 loaded, monied 7 booming, moneyed, opulent, upscale, well-off 8 affluent, in clover, thriving, well-to-do 9 fortunate, pecunious, well-fixed 10 in the dough, in the money, privileged, propertied, prosperous, successful, well-heeled
  become ~: 6 do well, make it, thrive 7 make out, prosper, succeed 8 fare well, flourish, go places, grow rich, hit it big, make good 9 make money
  make ~: 6 enrich
  name meaning ~: 4 Otto
  one: 4 have 5 nabob, nawab 6 fat cat
Wealthy: 5 apple
  relative: 4 crab, Gala, Lodi, Rome 5 Mutsu 6 Empire, Ida Red, medlar, Pippin, russet 7 Baldwin, Bramley, costard, Freedom, Liberty, Spartan, Winesap 8 Cortland, Jonathan, McIntosh 10 Rome Beauty
wean: 6 cut off 8 break off, separate 9 ablactate, break away, disengage
weapon: 3 arm, bow, gat, gun, rod 4 bomb, épée, mine 5 arrow, lance, spear, sword 6 cudgel 7 firearm, grenade, missile 8 catapult
__ Weapon: 6 Lethal
weaponless: 5 clean 7 unarmed 10 barehanded
weaponry: 4 arms, guns 6 rifles, sabers, swords 7 cannons, pistols 8 bayonets, bazookas, matériel, ordnance, shotguns 9 artillery, firepower, munitions
weapons: 4 arms 7 battery 8 materiel, ordnance 9 artillery, munitions
  cross ~ with: 4 face 6 attack, battle, engage, take on
  depot: 6 armory
  equip with ~: 3 arm 5 enarm 7 fortify 8 embattle
  strip of ~: 5 unarm 6 disarm
weapons __: 6 system 7 carrier
wear: 3 don, irk, rub, tax, use, vex 4 fade, fray, gall, garb, gear, jade, last, tire 5 chafe, decay, erode, get on, graze, grind, model, put on, scuff, sport, try on 6 abrade, attire, fit out, have on, hold up, milage, pester, scrape, slip on, suit up, weaken 7 apparel, clothes, corrode, crumble, display, dress in, erosion, exhaust, exhibit, fatigue, inroads, mileage, overuse, service, show off, stand up, utility, weather 8 abrasion, clothing, friction, garments, stand for, wash away 9 attrition, corrosion, undermine 10 exasperate, impairment, usefulness
  starter: 3 day, eye, ski 4 foot, head, knit, mens, neck, play, rain, skee, swim 5 beach, dance, inner, night, outer, sleep 6 formal, lounge, sports 7 evening, leather, leisure
wear __: 3 off, out 4 down, thin
wear __ hats: 3 two
wear __ one's welcome: 3 out
__ wear: 4 men's 6 active, women's 7 wash and
wear and __: 4 tear
__ Wear Daily: 6 Women's
We are __ amused: 3 not
We Are Family (1979 song) artist: Sister Sledge
We Are the Champions (1977 song) artist: Queen
We Are the World (1985 song) artist: USA for Africa
wearied: 4 beat, limp 5 spent 6 dished 9 prostrate
weariness: 5 ennui 6 tedium 7 boredom, fatigue, languor 8 lethargy 9 lassitude 10 enervation, exhaustion
  exclamation: 5 ho-hum 7 heigh-ho
wearing: 4 hard 6 clad in, taxing 7 erosion, erosive 8 tiresome 9 laborious 10 enervating
wearing __: 7 apparel
wearisome: 4 arid, blah, dull, tame 5 bland, heavy, ho-hum, vapid 6 boring, dreary, taxing, trying 7 humdrum, insipid, lengthy, tedious 8 dragging, tiresome, unvaried 9 difficult, laborious 10 cumbersome, enervating, monotonous
  become ~: 4 cloy, jade, pall
  task: 5 chore, grind 6 burden
wearisomeness: 3 rut 5 ennui 6 tedium 7 boredom 8 banality, monotony
Wear My Ring Around Your Neck (1958 song) artist: Elvis Presley

wear the __: 5 pants
wear two __: 4 hats
weary: 3 irk, sag, sap, tax, try, vex 4 beat, bore, cloy, fade, flag, glut, jade, lazy, pall, sick, tire, worn 5 all in, annoy, blasé, bored, drain, fed up, had it, jaded, spent, taxed, tired 6 burden, bushed, done in, drowsy, harass, pooped, punchy, sicken, sleepy, weaken, zonked 7 depress, disgust, drained, exhaust, fatigue, languid, oppress, run-down, tire out, vitiate, worn out 8 careworn, dog-tired, drooping, enervate, enfeeble, fatigued, flagging, listless, out of gas, overwork, peter out, wiped out, worn-down 9 bone-tired, burned out, dead-tired, disgusted, enervated, exhausted, grow tired, impatient, lethargic, overtired, played out, prostrate, tucker out 10 debilitate, devitalize, dishearten, exasperate, knocked out, overworked
grow ~: 3 sag 4 fade, flag, jade, tire 7 fatigue, tire out 8 pêter out 9 tucker out
looking ~: 5 drawn
make ~: 4 bore
name meaning ~: 4 Leah
sound: 4 sigh
__-weary: 3 war 4 wing 5 world
wearying
see wearisome
weasel: 4 fink, mink 5 fitch, otter, pekan, ratel, sable, skunk, sneak, stoat, tayra 6 animal, badger, ermine, ferret, marten, waffle 7 foumart, polecat 8 carcajou, foulmart, kolinsky, muishond 9 pussyfoot, scoundrel, wolverine
Africa: 5 ratel 8 muishond
Asia: 5 ratel 8 kolinsky
cousin: 4 mink 5 otter, pekan, sable, skunk
Europe: 5 fitch, sable 6 ermine 7 foumart, polecat 8 foulmart
North America: 4 mink 5 skunk 6 badger, marten 7 polecat 8 carcajou 9 wolverine
out: 6 recant, renege 9 disengage
out of: 4 duck 5 avoid, dodge, evade, get by, shirk 7 disavow 8 go back on 9 get around
South America: 5 tayra 6 grison
use ~ words: 5 dodge, evade, fudge, hedge, skirt, waver 6 waffle 8 flip-flop, sidestep 9 hem and haw, pussyfoot, stonewall, vacillate 10 equivocate
word: 3 pop 5 maybe
weasel __: 3 out 4 word 5 out of
weather: 3 dry 4 last, take, wear 5 brave, clime, stand, stick 6 bear up, endure, expose, make it, resist, season 7 climate, ride out, survive, undergo 8 elements, overcome, stand for, surmount 9 rise above, withstand 10 get through, stick it out
away from the ~: 4 alee
bad ~: 4 gale, hail, rain, snow 5 sleet, storm 7 tornado 8 blizzard 9 hurricane
cause of extreme ~: 6 El Niño
combining form: 6 meteor-
device: 4 vane 9 barometer, rain gauge
ender: 4 cast, cock, vane, worn 5 board, glass, proof 6 caster
eye: 5 vigil, watch 7 lookout 8 scrutiny
factor: 5 chill
feel under the ~: 3 ail
forecast: 3 dry, hot, wet 4 cold, cool, damp, fair, gale, hail, mild, rain, snow, warm 5 clear, crisp, foggy, gusty, humid, muggy, sleet, storm, sunny 6 cloudy, frigid, stormy 7 drizzle
hot ~: 6 dog day
info: 4 rept. 6 report
line: 5 front
permitting: 5 maybe
phenomenon: 4 haze 5 storm 6 fogdog 7 rainbow
probe: 5 sonde
satellite: 4 ESSA 5 Tiros
science of ~: 11 meteorology
stat.: 3 THI, WCF
system: 3 low 4 high 5 front
under the ~: 3 ill 4 achy, sick 6 ailing, infirm, laid up, peaked, queasy, queazy, sickly, unwell 7 run-down, unsound 8 diseased 9 afflicted, bedridden 10 indisposed, out of sorts
wet ~: 4 rain, snow 5 sleet 7 drizzle
winter ~: 4 snow 5 sleet 8 blizzard
with a ~ eye open: 8 vigilant
weather __: 3 eye, map 4 deck, ship, tide, vane 5 gauge, joint, radar, strip 6 report, signal 7 balloon, station
weather-__: 4 wise 5 bound 6 beaten
__-weather: 3 all
Weather __: 6 Bureau
__ Weather: 6 Stormy
weather-beaten: 3 old 4 aged, worn 5 erose 6 rugged, shabby 7 rickety, run-down 8 decrepit, timeworn 10 bedraggled, ramshackle, tumble-down
weathercock: 4 vane
weathered: 5 hardy, hoary 6 brawny, robust, rugged, shabby, strong, sturdy 7 run-down 8 decrepit, timeworn 9 crumbling, well-built 10 able-bodied, broken-down, ramshackle, threadbare
__ weather eye open: 5 keep a
__-weather friend: 4 fair
weather-map feature: 5 ridge 6 isobar, isohel
Weathers, Carl: 5 actor
film: Predator (1987)
Rocky (1976)
Rocky II (1979)
weather the __: 5 storm
weathervane holder: 4 roof 6 cupola
Weatherwax: 3 Ken 4 Rudd
weatherworn: 5 erose 6 beaten
weave: 4 join, knit, reel, spin, sway, wind 5 blend, braid, lurch, plait, snake, twine, twist 6 careen, dodder, splice, teeter, totter, zigzag 7 entwine, intwine, meander, texture 8 contrive 9 fabricate, interfold, interlace 10 crisscross, intertwine
a chair seat: 4 cane
fabric ~: 3 net 5 satin, twill 6 Madras
having an open ~: 5 meshy
mate: 3 bob
starter: 4 hair
__ weave: 4 leno 5 dobby, gauze, plain, satin, twill 6 basket, waffle 7 chevron, taffeta
weaver
device: 4 loom 5 frame
ender: 4 bird
frame: 4 sley
hitch: 4 knot
name meaning ~: 5 Weber 7 Webster 8 Penelope
Weaver: 4 Earl 5 Fritz 6 Dennis 7 Charley 9 Sigourney
__ Weaver: 5 Dream
weaverbird: 6 bishop, whidah, whydah
Weaver, Dennis: 5 actor
colleague: 5 Blake 6 Arness
film: The Gallant Hours (1960)
Gentle Giant (1967)
What's the Matter With Helen? (1971)
TV: Gentle Ben, Gunsmoke, McCloud
weaver's __: 4 knot 5 hitch
Weaver, Sigourney: 7 actress
film: Alien (1979)
Aliens (1986)
Copycat (1995)
Dave (1993)
Death and the Maiden (1994)
Galaxy Quest (1999)
Ghostbusters (1984)
Ghostbusters II (1989)
Gorillas in the Mist (1988)
Heartbreakers (2001)
The Ice Storm (1997)
A Map of the World (1999)
Working Girl (1988)
The Year of Living Dangerously (1983)
weaving: 4 mesh 5 craft 8 unstable, unsteady
term: 4 weft
__ weaving: 6 lappet, swivel
web: 3 net 4 maze, mesh, trap 5 snare, snarl, toils 6 morass, tangle, tissue 7 complex, lattice, netting, network, pitfall, trellis 8 filagree, filigree, gossamer, membrane 9 fillagree, labyrinth 10 wickerwork
ender: 4 feet, foot, worm
like a ~: 4 lacy 5 filmy, wispy
make a ~: 4 spin 5 weave
starter: 3 cob, orb
victim: 3 fly
web __: 4 foot 5 frame, press 6 member 7 spinner
web-__: 4 toed 6 footed
__ web: 4 food 6 spider
Web: 8 Internet 10 cyberspace
access the ~: 5 log on
ad: 6 banner
address: 3 URL
address start: 4 http
address suffix: 3 com, edu, gov, net
auction site: 4 eBay
communiqué: 2 IM
company: 6 dot-com
connector: 5 modem
ender: 4 cast
explore the ~: 4 surf
language: 4 html, Java
leave the ~: 6 log off
locale: 3 URL 7 address
page access: 4 link
service: 3 AOL
site info: 3 FAQ
software: 6 applet 7 browser
worker: 5 sysop
see also Internet
Web __: 4 page, site 6 portal
W.E.B.: 6 Du Bois
Web and the Rock, The author: Thomas Wolfe
Webb: 4 Jack 5 Chick, Chloe, Jimmy 6 Karrie, Pierce 7 Clifton 8 Beatrice
Webb, Chick: 7 drummer
genre: 4 jazz
Webb, Clifton: 5 actor
film: Cheaper by the Dozen (1950)
The Dark Corner (1946)
Dreamboat (1952)
Laura (1944)
Mister Scoutmaster (1953)
Sitting Pretty (1948)
Three Coins in the Fountain (1954)
Titanic (1953)
Woman's World (1954)
Webber: 6 Robert
__ Webber: 5 Paine
Webb, Jack spouse: Julie London
Webb, Karrie: 6 golfer
milieu: 5 links 6 course
org.: 4 LPGA
__ We Be Friends?: 4 Can't
We Belong (1984 song) artist: Pat Benatar
Weber: 3 Max 4 Dick, Joan, Pete 6 Steven
opera: 6 Oberon
Weber, Dick: 3 PBA 6 bowler
milieu: 4 lane 5 alley
Weber, Joan song: Let Me Go Lover (1954)
Weber, Steven: 5 actor
film: At First Sight (1998)
Single White Female (1992)
Sour Grapes (1998)
TV: Wings
web-footed
bird: 3 auk 4 duck, loon, nene, swan 5 goose, solan
mammal: 4 mink 5 coypu, otter 6 beaver
weblike: 4 lacy 5 meshy
Webster: 4 John, Noah 6 Daniel 8 Nicholas
Webster (ABC sitcom)
cast: Susan Clark (Katherine Papadapolis)
Alex Karras (George Papadapolis)
Emmanuel Lewis (Webster Long)
Webster, Daniel: 6 orator
Webster Groves: 4 city, town
locale: 8 Missouri
Webster, John: 7 British 10 playwright
work: The Duchess of Malfi
The White Devil
Webster, Noah: 6 writer 13 lexicographer
alma mater: 4 Yale
Web, The (1947 film)
cast: William Bendix, Edmond O'Brien, Ella Raines
__ Web, The: 5 Glass
We Built This City (1985 song) artist: Starship
webzine: 4 e-mag
We Can Work It Out (song) artist: Beatles, Stevie Wonder
wed: 3 tie 4 bind, bond, fuse, join, link, mate, tied, yoke 5 blend, bound, elope, fused, marry, mated, merge, unite, yoked 6 allied, couple, eloped, joined, linked, merged, splice, united 7 blended, combine, conjoin, connect, coupled, espouse, married, spliced 8 coalesce, combined, espoused 9 coalesced, commingle, conjoined, connected, dedicated, integrate 10 commingled, get hitched, got hitched, integrated, tie the knot
ender: 4 lock
pledge to ~: 5 troth 10 engagement
starter: 5 newly
Wed.: 3 day
follower: 3 Thu. 4 Thur. 5 Thurs.
preceder: 3 Tue. 4 Tues.
to Thurs.: 4 yest.
__ We Dance: 5 Shall
wedded: 5 joint 7 marital, nuptial, spousal 8 conjugal 9 connubial
Weddell: 3 sea
locale: 10 Antarctica
wedding: 5 union 6 bridal 8 espousal, marriage, nuptials 9 matrimony
announcement word: 3 née
avoid a big ~: 5 elope
band: 4 ring
cake feature: 4 tier
conveyance: 4 limo 9 limousine
dessert: 4 cake
gift: 5 dowry 6 dowery
keepsake: 5 album
official: 2 JP 5 rabbi 8 minister
old-fashioned ~ word: 4 obey
party member: 3 kin 5 bride, groom, in-law, niece, usher 7 best man
party members: 6 family 7 kinfolk

ring holder: 6 bearer
route: 5 aisle
site: 5 altar 6 chapel
throw: 6 garter 7 bouquet
tradition: 5 toast
wear: 3 tux 4 gown, lace, tuck, veil 5 dress, satin, tiara 6 tuxedo
words: 3 I do, vow
worker: 2 DJ 6 deejay
wedding __: 3 day 4 band, cake, ring 5 chest, march
__ wedding: 4 June 6 golden, silver
Wedding __, The: 4 Gift 5 March 6 Singer 7 Planner
__ Wedding: 5 Delta, Royal 6 Betsy's, Double, Polish, Silver 7 Muriel's, Waikiki
wedding anniversaries:
1st - Paper
2nd - Cotton
3rd - Leather
4th - Linen, Silk
5th - Wood
6th - Iron
7th - Wool, Copper
8th - Bronze
9th - Pottery, China
10th - Tin, Aluminum
11th - Steel
12th - Silk
13th - Lace
14th - Ivory
15th - Crystal
20th - China
25th - Silver
30th - Pearl
35th - Coral, Jade
40th - Ruby
45th - Sapphire
50th - Gold
55th - Emerald
60th - Diamond
Wedding Bell Blues (1969 song)
artist: Fifth Dimension
composer: 4 Nyro
Wedding Gift, The (1993 film)
cast: Jim Broadbent, Thora Hird, Julie Walters
Wedding March, The (1928 film)
cast: ZaSu Pitts, Erich von Stroheim, Fay Wray
director: Erich von Stroheim
Wedding Night, The star: 4 Sten
Wedding Planner, The (2001 film)
cast: Jennifer Lopez, Matthew McConaughey
director: Adam Shankman
Wedding Singer, The (1998 film)
cast: Drew Barrymore, Allen Covert, Angela Featherstone, Adam Sandler
director: Frank Coraci
Wedding Song (1971 song) artist: Paul Stookey
Wedding, The author: Danielle Steel
Wedekind, Frank: 6 author, German, writer
wedel: 4 turn
perform a ~: 3 ski 4 skee
__ we devils?: 5 Aren't
wedge: 3 ram 4 club, cram, cusp, hunk, iron, lump, pack, plug, push, shim, slab 5 block, chock, chunk, cleat, coign, jam in, quoin, slice, stick, stuff 6 coigne, cotter 7 segment, squeeze, stuff in 8 doorstop, golf club, keystone
combining form: 5 embol-, sphen- 6 emboli-, embolo-, spheno-
in: 3 jam 5 block 6 hinder, impede, squash, squish 7 squeeze 8 obstruct 9 insinuate, interpose 10 infiltrate
in heraldry: 4 pile
machinist's ~: 3 gib
shaped: 6 cuneal
splitting ~: 4 froe, frow
use a ~: 4 golf, loft
wooden ~: 4 shim
__ wedge: 7 foxtail, optical
wedged, become: 5 lodge
Wedgeworth: 3 Ann
wedgie: 4 shoe 8 footwear
Wedgwood: 4 blue 5 china 6 Josiah
competitor: 5 Lenox 6 Mikasa
style: 6 jasper
We Didn't Start the Fire (1989 song)
artist: Billy Joel
wedlock: 8 marriage 9 matrimony
Wednesday: 6 Addams
__ Wednesday: 3 Any, Ash
We Don't Need Another Hero (1985 song) artist: Tina Turner
We Don't Talk Anymore (1979 song)
artist: Cliff Richard
We Do Our Part org.: 3 NRA
wee: 3 sma 4 baby, itsy, puny, tiny 5 bitsy, bitty, early, light, pigmy, pygmy, short, small, teeny, weeny 6 atomic, bantam, little, minute, pee-wee, petite, pocket, teensy 8 atomical, atomlike 9 itsy-bitsy, itty-bitty, miniature, minuscule, pint-sized, undersize 10 diminutive, teeny-weeny, vest-pocket
bit: 4 dram, iota
enter the ~ hours: 5 laten
hour: 3 one, two 4 four 5 one a.m., three, two a.m. 6 four a.m. 7 three a.m.
hours: 4 late 5 night 7 morning
one: 3 tot 4 tike, tyke 6 infant, sprite 10 homunculus
Wee __ Hours: 5 Small
Wee __ Winkie: 6 Willie
Weeb: 6 Ewbank
weed: 4 pest, pull, rake, tare 5 plant 6 arnica, garden, henbit, jimson, joe-pye, nettle, uproot 7 burdock, pussley, thistle 8 plantain, purslane, toadflax 9 crab grass, dandelion, dog fennel, groundsel 10 goatsbeard, nightshade, pennycress, quack grass
Biblical ~: 4 tare
out: 4 cull, thin 6 select, uproot, winnow 7 extract 9 eradicate
rooter: 3 hoe 6 harrow
starter: 3 hog, may, pig, pin, rag, sea, tar 4 bind, blue, duck, fire, gout, gulf, hawk, iron, knap, knot, loco, milk, poke, pond, rich, rock, silk 5 bugle, chick, clear, crazy, fever, ghost, horse, jewel, river, rosin, skunk, smart, snake, stick, stink, water 6 beetle, butter, carpet, cotton, silver, sneeze, tumble, yellow 7 camphor, thimble 8 pickerel
weed __: 3 out 6 burner, cutter
__ weed: 4 deer, loco 6 jimson, joe-pye 7 jimpson, Klamath, mermaid, tinker's
__-weed: 5 dyer's, ghost 7 bishop's
Weed-__: 4 B-Gon
__-Weed Factor, The: 3 Sot
weedy: 5 lanky, rangy 7 scrawny, spindly 8 ungainly 9 overgrown
__-wee Herman: 3 Pee
week: 4 time 6 period 8 hebdomad
component: 3 day
ender: 3 day, end 5 night
seven times a ~: 5 daily 7 diurnal
starter: 3 mid 4 work
Week __ Glance: 3 at a
__ Week: 3 One 4 Holy, Whit 5 Great 7 Passion
weekday abbr.: 3 Fri., Mon., Thu., Tue., Wed. 4 Thur., Tues. 5 Thurs.
weekend __: 3 bag 7 warrior
__ Weekend: 3 USA
Weekend at the Waldorf (1945 film)
cast: Walter Pidgeon, Ginger Rogers, Lana Turner
director: Robert Z. Leonard
Weekend Edition network: 3 NPR
Week-end in Havana (1941 film)
cast: Alice Faye, Carmen Miranda, John Payne
director: Walter Lang
Weekend in New England (1976 song)
artist: Barry Manilow
__ Weekend, The: 4 Lost
Weekend Update show: 3 SNL
__ Wee King: 3 Pee
weekly: 5 paper 8 magazine, periodic 9 newspaper 10 periodical
starter: 4 news
weeks, 52: 4 year
Weems: 3 Ted 5 Mason 6 Parson
weenie: 5 frank 6 hot dog 7 sausage
holder: 3 bun
__-weenie: 5 eenie 6 teenie
__-weensie: 6 eensie 7 teensie
__-weensy: 5 eensy 6 teensy
__-weentsy: 6 eentsy 7 teentsy
weeny: 4 nerd, nurd, tiny 5 frank, sissy, small, teeny 6 hot dog, little, teensy 9 itty-bitty, pipsqueak, undersize
no ~: 5 he-man
__-weeny: 5 teeny
weep: 3 cry, sob 4 bawl, drip, howl, keen, mewl, moan, ooze, pule, seep, tear, wail, yell, yowl 5 let go, mourn 6 bemoan, bewail, boohoo, grieve, lament, regret, snivel, squall 7 blubber, deplore, trickle, ululate, whimper 8 complain 9 break down, make a fuss, percolate, shed tears
for: 4 pity 6 bemoan, lament
(for): 4 feel
over: 6 bewail, regret, repent
ready to ~: 5 misty
...__ weepers: 6 losers
__ Weep for Me: 6 Willow
weeping: 5 tears 6 lament, sorrow 7 in tears, tearful 8 mourning 9 sniveling 10 waterworks
weeping __: 3 fig 5 myall 6 willow
Weep No More, My Lady author: Mary Higgins Clark
weepy: 5 mushy, teary 6 crying 7 maudlin, sobbing, tearful, wet-eyed 9 sniveling, teary-eyed 10 blubbering, lachrymose
__ Wee Reese: 3 Pee
weever: 4 fish
weevil: 3 bug 4 pest 6 insect
food: 4 boll 6 cotton
__ weevil: 3 nut, pea 4 bean, boll, rice, rose, seed 7 alfalfa, granary
Wee Willie Winkie (1937 film)
cast: Victor McLaglen, Shirley Temple
director: John Ford
__ we forget: 4 lest
weft: 4 woof 7 filling
having warp and ~: 5 woven
Wegener: 6 Alfred
We Got a Love Thing (1992 song)
artist: Ce Ce Peniston
__ We Got Fun: 4 Ain't
We Got Love (1959 song) artist: Bobby Rydell
We Got the Beat (1982 song) artist: Go-Go's
We have met the enemy and he __: 4 is us 6 is ours
__! We Have No Bananas: 3 Yes
__ we having fun yet?: 3 Are
We hold __ truths...: 5 these
Weidman, Jerome: 6 writer 10 playwright
work: Counselors-at-Law
A Family Fortune
Fiorello!
I Can Get It for You Wholesale
Other People's Money
Praying for Rain
The Temple
What's In It for Me?
weigh: 3 see, try 4 heft, mull, muse, rate, tell 5 gauge, study, think 6 assess, burden, cumber, lumber, matter, muse on, ponder, rehash, review 7 analyze, balance, compare, examine, measure, reflect, signify, sort out 8 appraise, consider, estimate, evaluate, factor in, militate, mull over, ruminate 9 speculate, sweat over, think over 10 deliberate, meditate on, scrutinize
anchor: 4 sail 7 cast off 8 shove off 9 cast loose
down: 3 tax 4 load 5 press, worry 6 burden, cumber, hamper, sadden, saddle, strain 7 depress, oppress, overtax, trouble 8 encumber, obstruct, overload 10 overburden
in: 5 opine 6 arrive, report, show up, turn up 8 register
on: 3 tax 5 haunt 7 oppress 8 distress
(upon): 4 bear
weigh __: 4 down
weighed down: 4 full 5 heavy, laden 7 replete
weigh-station stopper: 3 van 4 semi 5 truck
weight: 4 bulk, heft, load, mass, onus, pull 5 clout, power, slant, value, worth 6 accent, burden, import, lading, moment, sinker, strain, stress 7 ballast, density, G-factor, gravity, tonnage, tunnage 8 emphasis, leverage, plumb bob, poundage, pressure, prestige, strength, validity 9 authority, heaviness, heftiness, influence, magnitude, millstone 10 difficulty, importance, prominence
allowance: 4 tare, tret
Asian ~: 4 tael 5 catty, liang, picul
attach ~ to: 6 accept 7 believe, presume
carry ~: 4 tell 5 count 6 matter 7 signify
check the ~: 4 heft, lift 5 hoist
combining form: 3 bar- 4 baro-
dead ~: 4 load, onus 10 impediment
ender: 6 lifter 7 lifting
extra ~: 4 flab
fabric ~ unit: 6 denier
freight ~: 3 ton
gain ~: 4 grow 5 put on, swell, widen 6 expand, spread 7 broaden, enlarge, fill out, thicken
Greek ~: 5 oboli 6 obolus
Indian ~: 3 ser 4 tola
lose ~: 4 diet, slim 6 reduce
metric ~: 3 ton 4 gram 5 tonne
Mideast ~: 4 rotl 5 artal
packing some ~: 5 heavy, hefty, laden
pharmacist's ~: 4 dram, gram
plan: 4 diet 7 regimen
starter: 3 fly 4 make, over 5 heavy, light, paper, penny 6 bantam, middle, welter 7 cruiser, feather, hundred
system: 4 Troy
take off ~: 4 diet, slim, thin 6 reduce, shrink 7 lighten 8 slim down
throw one's ~ around: 5 bully 7 oppress 8 browbeat, domineer 9 tyrannize 10 intimidate, lord it over
unit: 2 kg., lb. 3 cwt, keg, mol, ton 4 dram, gram, kilo, pint 5 carat, grain, ounce, point, pound 6 denier 7 megaton 8 kilogram 9 centigram, metric ton, milligram
weight __: 4 belt 7 density

__ weight: 4 curb, dead, draw, free, lose, sash, troy 5 basic, basis, gross, legal, put on, throw 6 atomic 7 formula
weight-and-fortune cost, once: 4 cent 5 penny
weighted __: 4 mean 7 average
weightiness: 4 heft 6 moment 9 heaviness, magnitude
weightless: 5 light, wispy 6 dainty, slight 7 wispish 8 feathery
weightlifter
bane: 3 fat 4 flab
pride: 3 abs, bod 5 torso 6 biceps 7 muscles 8 physique
routine: 4 curl, jerk, reps 5 squat
sound: 5 grunt
unit: 3 rep
weightlifting: 5 sport
weights and measures agcy.: 3 NBS
weighty: 3 big 4 deep 5 bulky, dense, grave, gross, heavy, hefty, major, meaty, obese, staid, stout 6 cogent, fleshy, leaden, portly, severe, solemn, somber, strong, taxing, urgent 7 big-deal, crucial, earnest, hulking, massive, onerous, porcine, salient, serious 8 critical, crushing, exacting, grievous, powerful, profound, unwieldy 9 difficult, important, momentous, ponderous, unwieldly 10 burdensome, cumbersome, meaningful, oppressive, persuasive, portentous
Weihai: 4 port
locale: 5 China
Weill: 4 Kurt 5 Sandy 7 Sanford
Weill, Kurt: 8 composer
collaborator: 6 Brecht
musical: Knickerbocker Holiday
Lady in the Dark
Lost in the Stars
One Touch of Venus
The Threepenny Opera
spouse: Lotte Lenya
Weil, Simone: 6 French, mystic, writer
Weimar
see German
Weimaraner: 3 dog 5 canid 6 canine
Weinberg, Steven: 8 Nobelist 9 physicist
weir: 3 dam 4 dike 5 levee 7 barrier 9 barricade 10 embankment
Weir: 3 Bob 4 Mike 5 Peter
weird: 3 odd 4 camp, eery, zany 5 awful, crazy, dippy, eerie, flaky, funky, funny, kooky, outré 6 atypic, creepy, far-out, flakey, freaky, kookie, occult, quirky, spooky, way-out 7 bizarre, curious, deviant, erratic, fearful, ghastly, ghostly, macaber, macabre, magical, nerdish, oddball, offbeat, strange, surreal, uncanny, unusual 8 aberrant, abnormal, atypical, eldritch, freakish, haunting, horrific, peculiar, uncommon 9 anomalous, divergent, eccentric, fantastic, grotesque, irregular, unearthly, unnatural 10 Kafkaesque, mysterious, off the wall, outlandish, unorthodox
Weird Al: 8 Yankovic
weirdo: 4 geek, kook, zany 7 oddball 8 original 9 character, eccentric
Weird Science (1985 film)
cast: Anthony Michael Hall, Kelly LeBrock, Ilan Mitchell-Smith, Bill Paxton
director: John Hughes
Weir, Mike: 6 golfer
Weir, Peter: 8 director
film: The Cars That Ate Paris (1974)
Dead Poets Society (1989)
Fearless (1993)
Gallipoli (1981)
Green Card (1990)
The Mosquito Coast (1986)
The Truman Show (1998)
Witness (1985)
The Year of Living Dangerously (1983)
Weirton: 4 city, town
locale: 3 W. Va.
Weis: 2 Al 3 Don
Weismann, August: 9 biologist
Weiss: 4 font 5 Peter 8 typeface
Weisshorn: 3 alp
Weissmuller, Johnny: 5 actor
film: Tarzan and His Mate (1934)
Tarzan Escapes (1936)
Tarzan Finds a Son! (1939)
Tarzan, the Ape Man (1932)
Tarzan Triumphs (1943)
Weiss, Peter: 6 author, German, writer
work: Marat/Sade
Weisz: 6 Rachel
Welby: 2 dr., GP, MD 6 doctor, Marcus
org.: 3 AMA
Welch: 3 Bob 5 Lenny 6 Raquel, Tahnee
Welch, Raquel: 7 actress
daughter: 6 Tahnee
film: Bandolero! (1968)
Fantastic Voyage (1966)
Fathom (1967)
The Four Musketeers (1975)
The Last of Sheila (1973)
Mother, Jugs & Speed (1976)
Myra Breckinridge (1970)
One Million Years B.C. (1966)
The Three Musketeers (1974)
Welch's: 5 jelly
alternative: 5 Kraft 6 Knott's 7 Polaner 8 Smucker's
welcome: 3 ave, hug 4 good, hail, meet, nice, okay, take 5 admit, adopt, allow, go for, greet, hello, howdy, let in, see in 6 accept, assent, comply, entrée, invite, lead in, listen, ring in, salute, show in, wanted 7 desired, embrace, honored, include, invited, ovation, receive, usher in 8 accepted, befriend, greeting, pleasant, pleasing, stand for 9 agreeable, cherished, desirable, enjoyable, entertain, favorable, handshake, put up with, reception, recognize, red carpet, sign off on 10 appreciate, concur with, give the nod, gratifying, refreshing, salutation, satisfying
make ~: 5 ask in, greet, put up 7 receive
uncivilly: 3 boo 4 hiss, jeer
warm ~: 3 hug 4 kiss 7 embrace
welcome __: 3 mat
__ welcome: 5 hero's
Welcome __: 3 Ode 4 Back 5 Wagon
Welcome!: 2 Hi 5 Enter, Hello, Howdy 6 Come in 9 Greetings
Welcome Back (1976 song) artist: John Sebastian
Welcome Back, Kotter (ABC sitcom)
cast: Robert Hegyes (Juan Epstein)
Lawrence-Hilton Jacobs (Freddie Boom Boom Washington)
Gabe Kaplan (Gabe Kotter)
Ron Palillo (Arnold Horshack)
Marcia Strassman (Julie Kotter)
John Travolta (Vinnie Barbarino)
Welcome Ode composer: 7 Britten
Welcome Stranger (1947 film)
cast: Joan Caulfield, Bing Crosby, Barry Fitzgerald
Welcome to Hard Times: 4 film 5 novel
author: E.L. Doctorow
cast: Henry Fonda, Janice Rule, Keenan Wynn
Welcome to Our City author: Thomas Wolfe
Welcome to the Jungle (1988 song) artist: Guns N' Roses
welcoming: 4 open 7 cordial 8 friendly 9 favorable, receptive 10 hospitable
weld: 3 arc, fix 4 bind, bond, fuse, join, link 5 braze, stick, unite 6 cement, fasten, solder 8 junction, juncture
__-weld: 4 cold, spot, tack
Weld: 7 Tuesday, William
welded: 4 firm
__ welding: 3 arc 4 skip, spot 5 flash, forge
Weldon: 3 Fay
__ Weldon Johnson: 5 James
Weld, Tuesday: 7 actress
film: Author! Author! (1982)
Looking for Mr. Goodbar (1977)
Lord Love a Duck (1966)
Once Upon a Time in America (1984)
Pretty Poison (1968)
Serial (1980)
Soldier in the Rain (1963)
Thief (1981)
Who'll Stop the Rain (1978)
Wild in the Country (1961)
spouse: Dudley Moore, Pinchas Zukerman
TV: The Many Loves of Dobie Gillis
welfare: 3 aid 4 dole, good, sake 5 state 6 health, profit 7 benefit, success 8 interest 9 happiness 10 prosperity
on ~: 4 poor 5 needy 8 indigent 9 destitute, penurious 10 down-and-out, down at heel, straitened
welfare __: 4 fund, work 5 state
__ welfare: 5 child 6 social
Welk, Lawrence: 10 bandleader
intro: 4 A one
song: Calcutta (1960)
well: 3 fit, pit, spa 4 ably, bore, fine, good, hale, hole, ooze, pool, root, sane, sump, to a T 5 abyss, amply, fount, fully, happy, hardy, husky, lucky, quite, right, shaft, sound, store, whole 6 aright, easily, hearty, highly, nicely, origin, proper, rather, really, robust, source, spring, strong, wholly 7 adeptly, capably, chipper, clearly, closely, fitting, greatly, happily, healthy, rightly, soundly, up to par 8 blooming, entirely, expertly, famously, flow over, fountain, heartily, laudably, properly, smoothly, strongly, suitably, thriving, very much, vigorous, worthily 9 admirably, advisable, carefully, correctly, extremely, favorably, fittingly, fortunate, inside out, in the pink, perfectly, reservoir, undamaged, water hole 10 able-bodied, abundantly, accurately, adequately, becomingly, completely, intimately, pleasantly, profoundly, skillfully, splendidly, swimmingly, thoroughly
act ~: 6 behave
as ~: 3 too, yet 4 also, more 5 along 6 either, to boot 7 besides 8 likewise, moreover 10 in addition
as ~ as: 3 and 6 beyond 9 including
combining form: 4 bene-
contents: 3 ink, oil 5 water
do ~: 3 ace 5 excel, shine 6 make it, thrive 7 prosper 8 flourish, make good
do ~ enough: 4 cope 6 manage 7 make out
doing ~: 4 rich 7 booming 8 affluent, thriving 10 prospering, prosperous, successful
done: 10 impressive
ender: 4 away, born, head 6 spring
enough: 9 tolerably 10 acceptably, adequately
feed too ~: 4 cloy, glut, sate 5 gorge, stuff 7 surfeit 8 overfill
functioning ~: 5 sound
get ~: 4 heal, mend 5 rally 6 recoup 7 rebound, recover 10 recuperate
go ~: 6 pan out 7 succeed, work out
go together ~: 4 mesh 5 blend, click
less ~: 5 worse
look ~ on: 4 suit 6 become 7 enhance, flatter
make ~: 4 cure, heal 6 recoup
mechanism: 4 pump
not ~ done: 5 messy 6 shabby, shoddy, sloppy, untidy 7 unkempt 8 careless, fouled-up, slapdash, slipshod 9 haphazard, hit-or-miss, neglected
not sit ~: 3 irk, vex 4 gall, rile 5 anger, annoy, chafe, grate 6 bother, nettle, pester, rankle 8 irritate 10 exasperate
oil ~: 6 gusher
over: 4 brim, gush 5 spill
partner: 4 good 5 alive
put: 3 apt 6 cogent, timely 8 relevant, suitable 10 to the point
speak ~ of: 4 laud 6 esteem, praise 7 commend 9 recommend 10 compliment
starter: 3 dry, ink 4 fare 5 speed, stair
think ~ of: 5 favor 6 admire, esteem 8 look up to
thought-out: 4 sane
turned out: 4 chic, neat, trim 5 dandy, natty, sharp, sleek, smart, swank 6 chichi, classy, dapper, jaunty, snappy, snazzy, spiffy, sporty, spruce, swanky 7 dashing, stylish 8 handsome
up: 4 rise 5 heave, surge, swell 6 billow 8 escalate
very ~: 2 ay, da, ja, sí 3 aye, oui, yea, yep, yes, yup 4 fine, okay, sure, yeah 5 good-o, natch, quite, right, roger, uh-huh 6 agreed, gladly, good-oh, indeed, just so, rather, righto, surely, you bet, yowzah 7 exactly, go ahead, indeedy, mais oui, quite so, ten-four 8 all right, as you say, of course, thumbs up 9 be my guest, certainly, darn right, naturally, precisely, sure thing, you betcha, you said it 10 absolutely, by all means, definitely, positively, sure enough, swimmingly, that's right
wear ~: 4 last 6 endure
well: 4 my my, oh my 5 golly
work ~: 5 click
well-__: 3 fed, off, put 4 bred, done, kept, made, nigh, paid, read, to-do, worn 5 aimed, armed, aware, being, built, known, liked, timed 6 chosen, earned, heeled, rested, served, spoken, suited, versed, wisher 7 advised, behaved, defined, dressed, founded, groomed, meaning, rounded, trained, treated, written
__ well: 3 air, dry, gas, hot, oil 4 dust, mean, salt 5 bilge, waste 6 shut-in 7 wishing
__ well!: 4 All's, Very
Well!: 6 I never
Well, __!: 5 I'll be
Well, __ You Evah!: 3 Did
Wella: 7 shampoo
alternative: 4 Flex, Pert 5 Prell, Suave 7 Finesse, Pantene
well-adapted: 8 apposite
well-adjusted: 4 sane 5 sound 6 stable 8 composed, rational, sensible, together 10 reasonable
well-advised: 5 sound 7 prudent 8 rational 10 reasonable
Welland: 4 city, port, town 5 canal
locale: 6 Canada 7 Ontario

Welland Canal terminus: **4** Erie
well-appointed: **4** lush, posh **5** fancy, grand, plush, ritzy, swank **6** deluxe, lavish, ornate, swanky **7** elegant, opulent, stately **8** imposing, palatial, splendid **9** elaborate, luxurious, sumptuous
Wellaway!: **4** alas **5** alack
  modern ~: **6** oh dear
well-balanced: **4** calm, cool, even, fair, just, trim **6** serene, smooth, stable, steady **7** equable, uniform **8** composed, peaceful, tranquil **9** equitable, impartial, temperate, unruffled **10** consistent, unagitated, unwavering
well-balanced ___: **4** diet
well-behaved: **4** good, ruly **6** polite **7** orderly **8** decorous, mannerly
  kid: **4** doll **5** angel
well-being: **4** ease, good, sake **5** vigor **6** health, luxury, profit **7** benefit, comfort, rapture, success **8** felicity, interest **9** affluence, happiness **10** prosperity
We'll Be Together (1987 song) artist: Sting
wellborn: **5** noble **6** titled **8** ladylike **9** patrician
  name meaning ~: **6** Eugene **7** Eugenia
  people: **5** elite **6** gentry **7** society **8** nobility **10** upper crust
well-bred: **4** nice **5** civil, noble, suave **6** gentle, polite, taught, urbane **7** courtly, gallant, genteel, refined, trained **8** cultured, ladylike, mannerly, polished **9** courteous, patrician **10** cultivated, thoughtful, upper-crust
well-built: **3** big **4** hale, iron, wiry **5** beefy, burly, hardy, hefty, hunky, husky, lusty, solid, sound, stout, tough **6** brawny, hearty, mighty, potent, robust, rugged, sinewy, stable, steely, stocky, strong, sturdy, virile **7** doughty **8** athletic, forceful, indurate, muscular, powerful, puissant, stalwart, vigorous **9** Atlantean, Herculean, strapping **10** able-bodied, red-blooded
___-well card: **3** get
WellCare: **3** HMO
well-cared-for: **4** tidy **5** sleek **6** smooth **8** polished
well-chosen: **6** wilful **7** advised, express, reputed, willful **8** moderate **9** designful, judicious, voluntary **10** considered, deliberate, felicitous, thought-out
well-considered: **4** sane **5** lucid, sober, sound **7** careful, planned, serious, studied **8** rational, sensible **9** conscious, practical, pragmatic, provident, realistic **10** calculated, deliberate, purposeful, reasonable, thoughtful
well-constructed: **5** sound
well-coordinated: **4** deft, spry **5** agile **6** limber, nimble **8** athletic, graceful **9** dexterous
well-defined: **5** clear, plain, sharp, vivid **6** cogent **7** evident, express, obvious, precise, salient **8** apparent, clean-cut, clear-cut, definite, distinct, explicit, manifest, palpable **9** graspable, trenchant, unblurred **10** spelled out
well-deserved: **4** fair, just, meet **5** right **6** lawful, proper **7** condign, fitting **8** rightful, suitable
well-designed: **4** neat
Well, Did You Evah! composer: **6** Porter
well-disposed: **7** willing **8** amenable **9** agreeable, favorable, receptive, tractable **10** hospitable, open-minded
___ well done: **4** a job
Well done!: **4** nice **5** bravo
well-done, not: **4** pink, rare **6** medium
well-dressed: **5** natty, sleek, smart, swank **6** dapper, jaunty, rakish, snazzy, spiffy, sporty, swanky **8** handsome
well-educated: **5** smart **6** brainy **7** erudite, learned **8** literate **9** scholarly
___ well enough alone: **5** leave
Weller: **5** Peter **6** Thomas
Weller, Thomas: **8** Nobelist
Wellesley: **4** city, town
  grad: **5** woman **6** alumna
  locale: **4** Mass.
  student: **4** coed
Welles, Orson: **5** actor **8** director
  film: Butterfly (1981)
    Casino Royale (1967)
    Catch-22 (1970)
    Chimes at Midnight (1967)
    Citizen Kane (1941)
    Compulsion (1959)
    Crack in the Mirror (1960)
    Follow the Boys (1944)
    I'll Never Forget What's 'is Name (1967)
    Jane Eyre (1944)
    Journey Into Fear (1942)
    The Lady From Shanghai (1948)
    Macbeth (1948)
    The Magnificent Ambersons (1942)
    A Man for All Seasons (1966)
    Othello (1952)
    The Stranger (1946)
    The Third Man (1949)
    Tomorrow Is Forever (1946)
    Touch of Evil (1958)
    The Trial (1962)
  role: **4** Kane, Lime
  spouse: Rita Hayworth
well-expressed: **4** glib **5** vivid **6** moving **8** eloquent, stirring, touching **10** articulate, persuasive
well-favored: **5** bonny **6** comely, lovely, pretty **8** charming, fetching, handsome **9** appealing, beautiful **10** attractive
well-fixed: **5** flush **6** loaded, monied **7** moneyed, wealthy **8** affluent, in clover **10** in the dough, in the money, privileged, propertied, prosperous
well-flavored: **5** sharp, spicy, tangy, tasty, zesty **6** savory **7** peppery, piquant, pungent
well-formed: **6** comely **8** gorgeous, handsome, pleasing, splendid, striking, stunning **9** appealing, beautiful, exquisite **10** attractive
well-founded: **4** good, just, sane **5** solid, sound, valid **6** secure, stable, strong **8** luculent
We'll go to ___, and eat bologna...: **5** Coney
well-groomed: **4** neat, tidy, trim **5** clean, crisp, kempt, natty, sleek, smart, swank **6** combed, dapper, jaunty, rakish, snazzy, spiffy, sporty, spruce, swanky **7** duded up **8** clean-cut **9** spruced up **10** fastidious
well-grounded: **4** just **5** sober, sound, valid **6** cogent, versed **7** learned
well-handled: **4** deft **5** adept, slick **6** adroit, clever, facile, nimble **7** skilled **8** masterly, skillful **9** dexterous, ingenious, masterful, practiced
wellhead: **4** font **8** fountain
well-heeled: **4** rich **5** flush **6** loaded, monied **7** moneyed, opulent, wealthy **8** affluent, in clover, thriving **10** in the dough, in the money, privileged, propertied, prosperous
Well, I ___!: **5** never
Well, I'll be!: **3** gee **4** gosh **5** golly
well-informed: **4** up on, wise **6** at home, versed **7** knowing, learned **8** educated
Wellington: **4** boot, city, shoe, town **7** capital **8** footwear
  alma mater: **4** Eton
  horse: **10** Copenhagen
  locale: **7** Florida **10** New Zealand
  to Napoleon: **3** foe **5** enemy
Wellington ___: **4** boot
___ Wellington: **4** beef, half **6** Duke of
Wellington's Victory composer: **9** Beethoven
well-intentioned: **4** kind **6** do-good
___ well it were done quickly: **5** 'Twere
well-kept: **4** neat, tidy, trim **5** clean **6** spruce **7** orderly **9** shipshape **10** fastidious
well-known: **3** big, VIP **4** star **5** known, large, noted **6** common, famous, public **7** eminent, leading, notable, popular, splashy, storied **8** familiar, glorious, historic, infamous, renowned **9** acclaimed, important, legendary, notorious, prominent, reputable, superstar **10** celebrated, proverbial, recognized
  become ~: **6** emerge
well-liked: **7** popular
well-lit: **5** shiny, sunny **6** bright, lucent **7** shining **11** illuminated
well-made: **5** solid, sound **6** rugged, strong, sturdy
well-maintained: **4** neat
well-mannered: **4** good, nice **5** couth **6** polite, urbane **7** orderly, refined **8** gracious, mannerly, pleasing
  behavior: **4** tact **7** decorum **8** breeding, civility, courtesy, protocol, urbanity **9** etiquette, gallantry, gentility **10** politeness, refinement
Wellman, William: **8** director
  film: Battleground (1949)
    Beau Geste (1939)
    The Call of the Wild (1935)
    The Happy Years (1950)
    Heroes for Sale (1933)
    The High and the Mighty (1954)
    The Iron Curtain (1948)
    Lady of Burlesque (1943)
    The Light That Failed (1939)
    Magic Town (1947)
    Midnight Mary (1933)
    Night Nurse (1931)
    Nothing Sacred (1937)
    The Ox-Bow Incident (1943)
    The Public Enemy (1931)
    Small Town Girl (1936)
    A Star Is Born (1937)
    Star Witness (1931)
    The Story of G.I. Joe (1945)
    This Man's Navy (1945)
    Westward the Women (1951)
    Wild Boys of the Road (1933)
    Wings (1927)
    Yellow Sky (1948)
well-marked: **5** plain, sharp **7** express, obvious, precise **8** definite, distinct, explicit
well-meaning: **4** kind
We'll Meet Again author: Mary Higgins Clark
wellness: **6** fettle, health **7** fitness **9** salubrity
  grp.: **3** HMO, NIH, PPO
We'll Never Have to Say Goodbye Again (1978 song) artist: England Dan and John Ford Coley
well-nigh: **4** most **5** about **6** almost
well-off: **4** rich **5** flush, lucky **6** loaded, monied **7** moneyed, opulent, wealthy **8** affluent, in clover, thriving **9** fortunate **10** in the dough, in the money, privileged, propertied, prosperous, successful
well-ordered: **4** neat, tidy **6** spruce
well-organized: **4** neat, tidy **5** sound **6** cogent **7** logical, tenable **8** analytic, coherent, methodic, rational, sensible, together **9** pragmatic **10** analytical, consistent
well-outlined: **4** neat, trim **5** clear, crisp **7** regular **8** clean-cut, distinct
well-padded: **5** bulky, burly, heavy, hefty, husky, large, obese, plump, stout **6** chubby, fleshy, portly, rotund, stocky **9** corpulent, ponderous **10** abdominous, embonpoint, overweight
well-paying: **7** gainful **9** lucrative **10** profitable
well-planned: **4** neat **6** clever, superb **7** orderly **8** methodic, skillful, terrific **9** dexterous, effective, efficient, excellent, exemplary **10** methodical
well-pleased: **5** cocky, proud **7** haughty, pompous, stuck-up **8** arrogant, egoistic, puffed up **9** conceited **10** hoity-toity
well-practiced: **5** adept
well-prepared: **4** ripe **5** ready **7** careful, prudent **8** seasoned **9** provident **10** farsighted, thoughtful
well-proportioned: **3** fit **4** trim **5** sleek **6** comely **9** beautiful
well-protected: **4** safe **6** secure **7** guarded
well-provided: **4** rife **5** laden **6** jammed, lavish, loaded, packed **7** crammed, crowded, fraught, glutted, replete, teeming **8** abundant, brimming, swarming **9** abounding, chock-full, jam-packed, plenteous, plentiful
well-put: **3** apt **6** clever **7** apropos, germane **8** apposite, skillful
well-read: **4** wise **5** smart **6** versed **7** erudite, learned **8** literary, studious **9** scholarly
well-reasoned: **4** sage, sane, wise **5** lucid, smart, sober, solid, sound **6** astute, shrewd **7** logical, politic, prudent, sapient **8** balanced, rational, sensible **9** judicious, practical, pragmatic, realistic, sagacious **10** reasonable, thoughtful
well-received: **7** in favor, likable, popular, voguish **8** accepted, approved **10** celebrated
well-recognized: **5** known **6** famous **7** popular **10** celebrated
well-regulated: **4** neat **7** careful, ordered, orderly, precise **8** methodic **9** by the book, efficient, organized **10** meticulous, scrupulous, structured, systematic
well-rehearsed: **3** set **5** ready **6** all set, primed **8** geared up, prepared
well-rounded: **4** sage **5** plump **6** versed **7** learned **8** cultured, educated
Wells: **2** H.G. **3** Ida **4** Dawn, Mary **5** Kitty
Wells ___: **5** Fargo
well-schooled: **5** canny, smart **6** brainy **7** erudite, learned **8** masterly, skillful
Wells Fargo (1937 film)
  cast: Frances Dee, Joel McCrea
  director: Frank Lloyd
Wells Fargo transport: **5** stage
Wells, H.G.: **6** author, writer **7** British
  race: **4** Eloi **8** Morlocks
  work: Experiment in Autobiography
    The History of Mr. Polly
    The Invisible Man
    The Island of Dr. Moreau
    Mankind in the Making
    Men Like Gods
    Mind at the End of Its Tether
    A Modern Utopia
    The New Machiavelli
    The Open Conspiracy
    Outline of History

A Short History of the World
The Time Machine
The War of the Worlds
The World of William Clissold
We'll Sing in the Sunshine (1964 song) artist: Gale Garnett
Wells, Mary
song: My Guy (1974)
The One Who Really Loves You (1962)
Two Lovers (1962)
You Beat Me to the Punch (1962)
well-spent: 8 fruitful **9** rewarding **10** beneficial, worthwhile
well-spoken: 5 slick **6** fluent **8** ladylike **9** courteous **10** articulate
wellspring: 4 font, mine **5** fount **6** origin, source **8** fountain **10** derivation
well-stocked: 4 full, rife **5** laden **6** filled, jammed, loaded, packed **7** crammed, crowded, replete, stuffed, teeming **8** brimming
well-stuffed: 4 full **5** beefy, burly, obese, plump, pudgy, pursy, stout, tubby **6** chubby, chunky, fleshy, portly, rotund, stocky **9** corpulent **10** abdominous
well-suited: 3 fit **8** apposite **9** congenial
well-supplied: 4 rich **6** lavish **8** abundant, affluent **9** abounding, bounteous, bountiful, luxurious, plentiful, sumptuous
be ~: 4 teem **5** swarm **6** abound **8** overflow
We'll tak __ o' kindness yet: 4 a cup
Well-Tempered Clavier, The composer: 4 Bach
__ Well That...: 4 All's
well-thought-of: 6 prized, valued **7** admired, exalted, honored, revered **8** esteemed **9** acclaimed, honorable, reputable, respected, venerable, venerated
well-thought-out: 4 sane **5** sound **8** sensible
well-timed: 5 happy **6** timely **7** apropos, hopeful **9** favorable, opportune **10** auspicious, felicitous, propitious
well-to-do: 4 rich **5** flush **6** jet set, loaded, monied **7** moneyed, opulent, wealthy, well-off **8** affluent, in clover, thriving **9** fortunate **10** in the dough, in the money, privileged, propertied, prosperous
well-trained: 6 versed **7** skilled **8** educated, polished, skillful **9** competent, practiced
one: 3 ace **5** adept **6** expert, master, wizard **10** specialist
well-tuned: 7 lyrical, melodic **10** euphonious, harmonious
well-turned: 6 comely **7** shapely **9** beautiful
well-used: 3 old **5** dated, hoary, passé, stale **8** decrepit, outdated, outmoded, time-worn **9** hackneyed **10** threadbare, unoriginal
well-versed: 4 ripe **5** adept **6** at home, au fait, expert, fluent **8** lettered, skillful **9** practiced
in French: 6 au fait
well-wisher: 3 pal **4** ally, chum **5** amigo, buddy, crony **6** backer, cohort, friend, patron **7** comrade **8** sidekick **9** associate, colleague, confidant, supporter **10** benefactor, compatriot
gesture: 5 toast
well-worn: 5 stale, trite **10** threadbare
well-written: 5 clear **7** flowing, legible **8** coherent, eloquent, readable
Welsh: 3 pig **5** swine **6** Cymric, Kymric **8** language
rabbit ingredient: 6 cheese
Welsh __: 4 pony **5** corgi, poppy, vault **6** rabbit **7** dresser, rarebit, terrier
Welsh black: 3 cow **4** bull **6** bovine, cattle
Welsh corgi: 3 dog **5** canid **6** canine
Welshman: 4 Celt
name meaning ~: 7 Wallace
welt: 4 blow, scar, seam, wale, weal **5** mouse, ridge, smash, spank, wheal, wound **6** bruise, injury, streak, stripe **8** swelling **9** contusion
welter: 5 parch, pitch **7** shrivel **9** dehydrate, desiccate
ender: 6 weight
welterweight: 5 boxer **7** fighter
weapon: 4 fist
Welty, Eudora: 6 author, writer
work: A Curtain of Green
Delta Wedding
The Golden Apples
The Optimist's Daughter
The Ponder Heart
The Wide Net
Welu, Billy: 3 PBA **6** bowler
milieu: 4 lane **5** alley
__ We Meet Again: 4 Till
__ we met?: 6 Haven't
wen: 3 sac **4** bleb, bump, cyst **7** blister
Wenatchee: 4 city, town
locale: 10 Washington
__ Wences: 5 Señor
Wenceslaus: 5 saint
wend: 4 walk **6** travel **7** proceed
Wendell: 5 Berry, Corey **7** Stanley, Willkie
__ Wendell Holmes: 6 Oliver
Wenders: 3 Wim
Wendie: 6 Malick
Wendie Jo: 7 Sperber
Wendt, George: 5 actor
film: Guilty by Suspicion (1991)
Gung Ho (1986)
Outside Providence (1999)
TV: Cheers
Wendy: 6 Barrie, Carlos, Hiller **8** Williams
Wendy's, go to: 3 eat **6** eat out
Wensleydale: 6 cheese
went: 5 split **7** buckled, took off **8** departed, sashayed, traveled, withdrew **9** collapsed, shoved off **10** hit the road
after: 5 set at
down: 4 fell
for: 3 bit, OK'd
up: 4 rose **5** arose
__ Went Over the Mountain, The: 4 Bear
__ went thataway!: 4 They
__! Went the Strings of My Heart: 4 Zing
Went to Coney Island... (2000 film)
cast: Rafael Baez, Jon Cryer, Ione Skye, Rick Stear
__ Went to Haiti: 5 Katie
were: 7 existed, had been
as it ~: 6 in a way **7** so to say **9** so to speak **10** in some sort
ender: 4 wolf
if it ~ not for: 6 except **7** besides, without **8** omitting **9** apart from, aside from, excluding
__ were: 4 as it **5** as you
Were __ That Special Face: 5 Thine
We're __ Dressing: 3 Not
We're __ Money: 5 in the
We're __ See the Wizard: 5 Off to
We're __ we're out of the money: 4 in or
__ Were a Bell: 3 If I
__ Were a Carpenter: 3 If I
We're All Alone (1977 song) artist: Rita Coolidge
We're an American Band (1973 song) artist: Grand Funk
__ Were a Rich Man: 3 If I
__ Were Expendable: 4 They
We're having __ wave: 5 a heat
We're in the Money composer: 5 Dubin **6** Warren
__ Were King of the Forest: 3 If I
__ Were Never Lovelier: 3 You
We're Not Dressing (1934 film)
cast: George Burns, Bing Crosby, Carole Lombard
director: Norman Taurog
We're Not Married (1952 film)
cast: Fred Allen, Victor Moore, Ginger Rogers
director: Edmund Goulding
We're number __!: 3 one
We're Off to See the Wizard composer: 5 Arlen **7** Harburg
We're Ready (1986 song) artist: Boston
__ Were, The: 5 Way We
__ Were the Days: 5 Those
werewolf: 7 monster
feature: 4 fang, hair
Werewolves of London (1978 song) artist: Warren Zevon
__ were you...: 3 If I
Werfel, Franz: 6 author, writer **8** Austrian
work: Goat Song
The Song of Bernadette
Werner: 5 Arber, Oskar, Peter **6** Alfred, Erhard, Herzog **9** Forssmann, Klemperer **10** Heisenberg
see also German
Werner, Alfred: 7 chemist **8** Nobelist
__ Werner Fassbinder: 6 Rainer
Werner, Oskar: 5 actor
film: Decision Before Dawn (1952)
Fahrenheit 451 (1967)
Jules and Jim (1961)
Ship of Fools (1965)
The Spy Who Came in From the Cold (1965)
Voyage of the Damned (1976)
Wernher: 8 von Braun
Werther composer: 8 Massenet
Wertmuller: 4 Lina
Wes: 6 Craven, Unseld **9** Covington **10** Montgomery
Wes Craven's New Nightmare (1994 film)
cast: Robert Englund, Heather Langenkamp
director: Wes Craven
Weser: 5 river
city on the ~: 6 Bremen
locale: 7 Germany
Wesker, Arnold: 7 British **10** playwright
weskit: 4 vest
Weslaco: 4 city, town
locale: 5 Texas
Wesley: 4 John **6** Snipes **7** Charles, Ruggles
...__ we speak: 6 even as
Wesson: 3 oil
alternative: 6 Crisco, Mazola **7** Puritan
partner: 5 Smith
west: 2 pt. **3** way **5** point **6** course **7** bearing, heading **9** direction
ender: 3 ern **4** ward **5** bound, wards
on a map: 4 left
sink in the ~: 3 set
starter: 3 mid **5** north, south
way ~: 5 trail
wind: 8 favonian
West: 3 key, Mae **4** Adam **5** Jerry **6** Dottie, Morris **7** Anthony, Rebecca **8** Benjamin, Jessamyn, Occident **9** Nathanael
from the ~: 3 occ. **10** occidental
the ~ had one: 4 code
West __: 3 End **4** Bank, Goth, Side **5** Coast, Haven, Point, Saxon **6** Africa, Bengal, Berlin, German, Indies, Orange, Sussex **7** Germany, Prussia
West __ Beach: 4 Palm
West __, CT: 5 Haven
West __ Story: 4 Side
West, __ and You, The: 5 a Nest
__ West: 3 Far, Key, Old **4** Wild **6** Middle **7** Station
West, Adam role: 6 Batman
__ West Africa: 6 French **7** British
West Allis: 4 city, town
locale: 9 Wisconsin
West Babylon: 4 city, town
locale: 7 New York **10** Long Island
West Bank
city: 6 Hebron
grp.: 3 PLO
West Bend: 4 city, town
locale: 9 Wisconsin
West Bloomfield: 4 city, town
locale: 8 Michigan
Westbrook: 6 Pegler
west by __: 5 north, south
Westchester: 4 city, town
locale: 7 Florida
West Coast
airport: 3 LAX, SEA, SFO
campus: 3 USC **4** UCLA
clock setting: 3 PDT, PST
st.: 3 Cal., Ore. **4** Oreg., Wash. **5** Calif.
West Covina: 4 city, town
locale: 10 California
West End Girls (1986 song) artist: Pet Shop Boys
westerly: 4 wind
starter: 5 north, south
Westerly: 4 town
locale: Rhode Island
western __: 4 wool **5** frame **6** omelet **7** hemlock, juniper, tanager **8** omelette
Western: 4 tale **5** novel, oater
alliance: 3 OAS **4** NATO
Athletic Conference player: 3 Ute
author: 4 Grey **5** Harte **6** L'Amour
backdrop: 4 mesa **5** butte, cañon **6** canyon
beast: 5 bison
capital: 5 Boise, Salem **6** Denver, Helena **7** Olympia, Phoenix **10** Sacramento
character: 6 cowboy, outlaw **7** marshal, sheriff
exclamation: 5 wahoo
half a ~ city: 5 Walla
hero: 4 Earp
horse: 10 Indian pony
howler: 6 coyote
Indian: 3 Ute **4** Crow, Hopi **5** Piute **6** Apache, Navaho, Navajo, Paiute **8** Shoshone
lizard: 3 uta
painter: 9 Remington
plot element: 6 ambush
reptile: 3 uta
sch.: 3 USC **4** UCLA
setting: 4 fort
show: 5 oater, rodeo
state: 3 Ida., Ore. **4** Ariz., Colo., Mont., Oreg., Utah, Wash. **5** Idaho **6** Oregon **7** Arizona, Montana **8** Colorado **10** California, Washington
tie: 4 bola, bolo
wear: 4 boot, spur, vest
Western __: 3 Han **4** blot, Wall **5** Ghats, Hindi, Ocean, Samoa, Slavs, Union **6** Church, Empire, Europe, Movies, saddle, Sahara, Thrace **7** Islands, Reserve
Western Athletic Conference school:

3 SMU 4 Rice, UTEP 5 Tulsa 6 Hawaii, Nevada 10 Boise State 11 Fresno State
Western Australia capital: 5 Perth
Westerner, The (1940 film)
cast: Walter Brennan, Gary Cooper, Fred Stone
director: William Wyler
Western Hemisphere: 4 Amer. 8 Americas
former alliance: 3 PAU
pact: 3 OAS 5 NAFTA
Western Michigan
athletes: 7 Broncos
conference: 3 MAC
locale: 9 Kalamazoo
western omelet
ingredient: 3 egg, ham 5 onion
__ Western Reserve: 4 Case
Western Sahara
neighbor: 7 Algeria, Morocco 10 Mauritania
Western Samoa: 4 isls. 5 isles 6 nation 7 country, islands
capital: 4 Apia
island: 5 Upolu
money: 4 sene, tala
Western Star poet: 5 Benét
Western Union
message: 4 wire 5 cable, teleg., telex 8 telegram
union: 3 ITU
Western Union (1941 film)
cast: Dean Jagger, Randolph Scott, Robert Young
director: Fritz Lang
Western Union (1967 song) artist: Five Americans
wester starter: 3 nor, sou 5 north, south
Westerville: 4 city, town
locale: 4 Ohio
Westfield: 4 city, town
locale: 9 New Jersey
__ West, FL: 3 Key
West Flanders city: 5 Ypres
West Haven: 4 city, town
locale: 4 Conn.
Westheimer: 4 Ruth 6 Dr. Ruth
Westin: 5 hotel
alternative: 4 Omni 5 Hyatt 6 Hilton 7 Wyndham 8 Marriott, Radisson, Sheraton 10 DoubleTree 11 Crowne Plaza, Four Seasons
__ West India Company: 5 Dutch
West Indies: 5 isles 7 islands
bird: 4 tody
city: 6 Havana
dance: 5 limbo
explorer: 7 Hawkins 8 Columbus
fish: 6 bigeye
fruit: 5 mamey 6 annona 7 acerola
Indian: 5 Carib, Taino
island: 3 cay, key 4 Cuba, Saba 5 Aruba, Haiti 7 Bahamas, Jamaica 8 Antilles, Barbados, Windward 10 Hispaniola, Martinique, Puerto Rico
magic: 3 obi 5 obeah 6 voodoo
music: 3 ska
native: 5 Carib, Cuban 6 Aruban, Creole 7 Haitian 8 Bahamian, Jamaican 9 Barbadian
Nobelist in Literature: 7 Walcott
republic: 5 Haiti
rodent: 6 agouti
sea: 8 Sargasso 9 Caribbean
shrub: 4 anil, pich
stew: 5 blaff 9 pepper pot
tree: 4 pich 7 canella
witchcraft: 3 obi 5 obeah 6 voodoo
writer: 7 Naipaul, Walcott
__ West Indies: 5 Dutch 6 Danish, French 7 British
Westinghouse: 6 George 9 appliance
alternative: 5 Amana, Norge 6 Bendix, Maytag, Tappan 7 Admiral, Jenn-Air, Kenmore 8 Hotpoint 9 Magic Chef, Whirlpool 10 Frigidaire, Kelvinator, KitchenAid
Westinghouse __: 5 brake
West Islip: 4 city, town
locale: 7 New York 10 Long Island
West, Jerry: 5 cager
milieu: 5 court
org.: 3 NBA
sport: 10 basketball
West Jordan: 4 city, town
locale: 4 Utah
West Lafayette: 4 city, town
locale: 7 Indiana
school: 6 Purdue
Westlake: 4 city, town 6 Donald
locale: 4 Ohio
Westland: 4 city, town
locale: 8 Michigan
West Lealman: 4 city, town
locale: 7 Florida
West Linn: 4 city, town
locale: 6 Oregon
West, Mae: 7 actress
feathers: 3 boa
film: Belle of the Nineties (1934)
Every Day's A Holiday (1937)
Goin' to Town (1935)
Go West, Young Man (1936)
I'm No Angel (1933)
Klondike Annie (1936)
My Little Chickadee (1940)
Myra Breckinridge (1970)
She Done Him Wrong (1933)
role: 3 Lil
West Memphis: 4 city, town
locale: 8 Arkansas
West Mifflin: 4 town
locale: 4 Penn.
Westminster: 4 city, town 5 abbey
district: 4 Soho
locale: 8 Colorado 10 California
Westmont: 4 city, town
locale: 8 Illinois 10 California
Westmore: 3 Bud, Ern 4 Perc 5 Frank, Monty, Wally 6 George
Westmoreland: 7 general, William
Westmorland: 6 county
locale: 7 England
West, Morris: 6 author, writer 10 Australian
work: The Devil's Advocate
The Shoes of the Fisherman
Westmount: 4 city, town
locale: 6 Canada, Québec
West, Nathanael: 6 author, writer
work: A Cool Million
The Day of the Locust
Miss Lonelyhearts
West New York: 4 city, town
locale: 9 New Jersey
West of the Pecos author: Zane Grey
West of Zanzibar (1928 film)
cast: Lionel Barrymore, Lon Chaney, Mary Nolan
director: Tod Browning
Weston: 4 city, Jack, town 5 Celia
locale: 7 Florida
Weston, Jack: 5 actor
film: Cactus Flower (1969)
Cuba (1979)
The Four Seasons (1981)
A New Leaf (1971)
West Orange: 4 city, town
locale: 9 New Jersey
West Palm Beach: 4 city, town
locale: 7 Florida
Westphalia
city: 5 Essen 6 Bochum
locale: 7 Germany
once: 5 duchy
Westphalian __: 3 ham
West Point: 4 Army, USMA
byword: 4 duty 5 honor 7 country
freshman: 4 pleb 5 plebe
grad: 2 lt. 5 lieut. 10 lieutenant
mascot: 4 mule
meal: 4 mess
student: 5 cadet
subject: 3 war
Westport: 4 city, town
locale: 4 Conn.
West, Rebecca: 4 Dame 5 alias 6 author, writer 7 British
work: The Bird Falls Down
The Fountain Overflows
Henry James
The Judge
St. Augustine
The Thinking Reed
__-West relations: 4 East
West Seneca: 4 city, town
locale: 7 New York
__ West show: 4 Wild
West Side Story (1961 film): 7 musical
cast: Richard Beymer, George Chakiris, Rita Moreno, Russ Tamblyn, Natalie Wood
character: 3 Doc 4 A-rab, Luis, Pepe, Riff, Tony, Toro 5 Anita, Chino, Indio, Juano, Maria, Moose, Tiger, Velma 6 Action, Diesel, Gee-Tar, Krupke, Minnie 7 Anxious, Big Deal, Clarice, Estella, Nibbles, Pauline, Rosalia, Schrank, Snowboy 8 Baby John, Bernardo, Consuelo, Glad Hand, Teresita 9 Francisca, Graziella, Margarita 10 Mouthpiece
composer: 8 Sondheim 9 Bernstein
director: Jerome Robbins, Robert Wise
dustup: 6 rumble
gang: 4 Jets 6 Sharks
song: 5 Maria 7 Tonight
West Springfield: 4 city, town
locale: 8 Virginia
__ West, The: 3 Way
West Valley City: 4 town
locale: 4 Utah
West Virginia: 5 state
capital: 10 Charleston
city: 7 Weirton 8 Fairmont, Wheeling 10 Charleston, Huntington, Morgantown
conference: 7 Big East
neighbor: 4 Ohio 8 Kentucky, Maryland, Virginia
resource: 4 coal
state animal: 9 black bear
state bird: 8 cardinal
state butterfly: 7 monarch
state fish: 10 brook trout
state fruit: 5 apple
state state fossil: 5 coral
state tree: 10 sugar maple
West Virginia University locale: 10 Morgantown
Westward the Women (1951 film)
cast: Denise Darcel, Robert Taylor
director: William Wellman
West With the Night author: 7 Markham
Westworld (1973 film)
cast: Richard Benjamin, James Brolin, Yul Brynner
director: Michael Crichton
wet: 3 dip, sop 4 damp, dank, dewy, lick, soak, wash 5 bathe, bedew, douse, dowse, drown, foggy, humid, juicy, misty, moist, muggy, rainy, rinse, slimy, snowy, soggy, soppy, souse, spray, teary, water 6 clammy, dampen, drench, liquid, slushy, soaked, sodden, soused, splash, steamy, stormy, sweaty, watery 7 aqueous, drizzle, moisten, pouring, raining, showery, soaking, sopping, spatter, squishy, teeming 8 dampness, drenched, dripping, hose down, irrigate, moisture, saturate, slippery, sprinkle 9 drizzling, saturated, water down
all ~: 5 wrong 7 in error, off-base 8 cockeyed, mistaken 9 erroneous 10 inaccurate
and spongy: 5 boggy, muddy 6 swampy
behind the ears: 3 new 4 naif 5 green, naive, young 6 callow, tender 8 immature
blanket: 4 bore, drag, drip 9 pessimist, worrywart
combining form: 5 hygro-
down: 4 hose, soak 5 douse, dowse, rinse, spray, water 6 dampen 7 moisten 8 irrigate, saturate, sprinkle 10 besprinkle
ender: 4 land 5 lands
expanse: 3 sea 5 ocean
get one's feet ~: 4 wade 5 begin 6 splash
one's whistle: 4 swig 5 drink 6 imbibe, tipple 7 swallow
very ~: 5 adrip, soggy, soppy 10 bedraggled
weather: 4 rain 5 storm 6 shower
wet __: 3 bar, fly, mop 4 cell, dock, suit, wash 7 blanket, compass, contact, machine
wet __ the ears: 6 behind
__ wet: 3 all 7 soaking, sopping
__ we talk?: 3 Can
wet-eyed: 5 teary, weepy 7 tearful 9 sniveling
We the Living author: Ayn Rand
We, the People author: Elmer Rice
__ we there yet?: 3 Are
Wethersfield: 4 town
locale: 4 Conn.
We Think the World of You (1988 film)
cast: Alan Bates, Gary Oldman
director: Colin Gregg
Wet Hot American Summer (2001 film)
cast: Janeane Garofalo, David Hyde Pierce, Michael Showalter
director: David Wain
wetland: 3 bog, fen 5 marsh, swamp 7 lowland
vegetation: 5 sedge
wetness: 8 dampness, humidity, moisture 9 sogginess
exemplar of ~: 3 mop
wet-noodle stroke: 4 lash
wet one's __: 7 whistle
__ We Trust: 5 In God
We try harder company: 4 Avis
wet-suit
material: 5 latex
wearer: 5 diver
Wettig, Patricia: 7 actress
film: City Slickers (1991)
Guilty by Suspicion (1991)
spouse: Ken Olin
TV: thirtysomething
wettish: 4 damp, dank, dewy, oozy 5 humid, misty, moist, muddy, muggy, soggy 6 clammy, drippy, liquid, sodden, steamy, sweaty, watery 7 drizzly, sopping 9 saturated
__, we various passions find: 5 In men
We've Got Tonight (1983 song)
artist: Kenny Rogers, Sheena Easton
We've Got Tonite (1978 song) artist: Bob Seger
We've Only Just Begun (1970 song)
artist: Carpenters

We want __!: 4 a hit
We Were Soldiers (2002 film)
cast: Sam Elliott, Mel Gibson, Greg Kinnear, Madeleine Stowe
We Were Strangers (1949 film)
cast: Pedro Armendariz, John Garfield, Jennifer Jones
director: John Huston
__ We Were, The: 3 Way
We will __ undersold!: 5 not be
Wexford: 4 city, town
locale: 7 Ireland
Wexler: 4 peak 5 mount 8 mountain
locale: 10 Antarctica
Weyburn: 4 city, town
locale: 6 Canada
Weymouth: 4 city, port, Tina, town
locale: 4 Mass.
Wezen: 4 star
WFU
see Wake Forest
wgt., small: 2 mg., oz. 3 mcg.
W.H.: 5 Auden 6 Hudson
whack: 2 go 3 bat, box, hit, pop, pow, rap, try 4 bang, bash, beat, belt, biff, blow, clip, club, cuff, ding, flog, hurt, nail, shot, slam, slap, slug, sock, stab, swat, trim, turn, wham 5 clout, crack, fling, knock, pound, smack, smash, smite, spank, thump, whang, whirl 6 buffet, defeat, hammer, strike, thrash, wallop 7 attempt, clobber, lambast 8 lambaste 9 fisticuff
out of ~: 4 awry 5 atilt 7 damaged, haywire 10 broken-down
starter: 4 bush
take a ~: 3 try 5 swing
throw out of ~: 4 skew 7 distort
__ whack: 5 out of
__ whack at: 5 have a, take a
whacker, weed: 3 hoe
whale: 3 sei 4 lash, whip 5 giant, minke, titan 6 animal, beluga, mammal 7 finback, monster, Monstro, scourge 8 cetacean, colossus, humpback, Moby Dick, narwhale 9 leviathan
combining form: 3 cet- 4 ceto-
constellation: 5 Cetus
ender: 4 back, boat, bone
female: 3 cow
food: 4 brit 5 krill
group: 3 gam, pod
have a baby ~: 5 calve
home: 3 sea 5 ocean 8 high seas
hunter of fiction: 4 Ahab
killer ~: 3 orc 4 orca 7 grampus
male: 4 bull
on a ~ watch, perhaps: 4 asea 5 at sea
relative: 3 orc 6 narwal 7 cowfish, dolphin, finback, grampus, narwhal, rorqual 8 narwhale, porpoise
tail: 5 fluke
the tar out of: 3 tan 4 rout 5 cream 6 defeat, ravage 9 overpower
young: 4 calf
whale __: 3 oil 5 shark
__ whale: 3 fin, sei 4 blue, gray, grey 5 black, minke, pilot, right, white 6 baleen, beaked, killer 7 finback, toothed
whalebone: 6 baleen
garment: 6 corset
Whale, James: 8 director
film: Bride of Frankenstein (1935)
Frankenstein (1931)
The Great Garrick (1937)
The Invisible Man (1933)
The Man in the Iron Mask (1939)
The Old Dark House (1932)
One More River (1934)
Show Boat (1936)
whalelike: 3 big 5 bulky 7 hulking, immense, massive 8 enormous, gigantic, whopping
whaler: 4 boat, ship
does a ~ job: 6 flench, flense
sunk by a whale: 5 Essex
word: 4 thar 5 blows
Whales: 3 bay
locale: 10 Antarctica
Whales of August, The (1987 film)
cast: Bette Davis, Lillian Gish, Vincent Price, Ann Sothern
Whalley, Joanne spouse: Val Kilmer
wham: 3 hit, pow 4 bang, boom, slam, slap, slug, sock 5 blast, crash, kapow, noise, smack, smash, sound, whack 6 larrup, wallop 8 abruptly
whammy: 3 hex 4 jinx 5 curse, shock, spell 8 surprise
put the ~ on: 3 hex 4 damn, jinx 5 curse 7 bedevil, bewitch, condemn 9 imprecate
whang: 3 hit 4 bash, beat, belt, drub, flog, sock, swat 5 knock, noise, pound, punch, smack, thump, whack 6 batter, buffet, larrup, strike, thrash, thwack, wallop 7 clobber
whapuku: 4 fish
wharf: 4 dock, pier, port, quay, slip 5 berth, jetty, levee 6 harbor, marina 7 harbour, landing 9 anchorage 10 breakwater
workers' org.: 3 ILA
wharf __: 3 rat 4 shed
Wharton: 6 school
degree: 3 MBA
locale: 4 Penn.
subj.: 4 econ. 7 finance
Wharton, Edith: 6 author, writer
work: The Age of Innocence
A Backward Glance
Ethan Frome
The House of Mirth
Old New York
what: 3 huh, yes
at ~ time: 4 when
come ~ may: 6 surely 7 somehow 10 in any event
do ~ one can: 3 try 6 strive 7 attempt, have a go, venture 9 have a go at, have a shot, have a stab 10 have a whack
ender: 3 not 4 ever 6 soever
for: 3 why 9 reprimand
give ~ for: 3 rag 4 rail 5 chide, scold 6 berate, rail at, rebuke, vilify 7 bawl out, censure, chasten, chew out, lecture, reprove, tell off, upbraid 8 admonish, chastise, denounce, lace into, lambaste, reproach, sail into, tear into 9 castigate, criticize, dress down, light into, reprehend, reprimand 10 denunciate, tongue-lash
have I done: 4 oh no
have we here: 3 oho
in ~ place: 5 where
in ~ way: 3 how 5 how so
it takes: 5 knack, savvy, skill 6 talent 7 ability, faculty, know-how, prowess 8 aptitude, capacity, facility 9 expertise, potential 10 capability, right stuff
no matter ~: 6 anyhow, anyway 9 at any rate 10 in any event, regardless
not ~ it was: 5 rusty 9 neglected 10 out of shape
say ~: 3 ask 7 inquire
starter: 4 some
they say: 4 buzz, talk 5 rumor 6 gossip 9 grapevine
what's ~: 5 truth 7 reality 10 bottom line, brass tacks
what __: 3 for
what __ you: 4 have
what-__: 3 not
__ what: 5 what's
__ what?: 3 Now, Say
What __!: 4 a gas 5 a deal, a drag, a dump
What __?: 3 now 4 is it, of it, to do
What __, a mind reader?: 3 am I
What __ Believes: 5 a Fool
What __ Beneath: 4 Lies
What __ bid?: 3 am I
What __ Bob?: 5 About
What __ boy am I!: 5 a good
What __ can I say?: 4 else, more
What __, chopped liver?: 3 am I
What __ do for you?: 4 can I
What __ doing here?: 3 am I
What __ done?: 5 have I
What __ for Love: 4 I Did
What __ Glory?: 5 Price
What __ God wrought?: 4 hath
What __ Happened to Baby Jane?: 4 Ever
What __ mind reader?: 4 am I a
What __ mood I'm in: 5 a rare
What __ My Love: 3 Now
What __ of baloney!: 4 a lot
What __ of Fool Am I: 4 Kind
What __ rare...?: 4 is so
What __ Sammy Run?: 5 Makes
What __ say?: 4 can I
What __ Scared Of?: 4 Was I
What __ to Go!: 4 a Way
What __ Want: 3 You 5 Women
What __ Wants: 5 a Girl
What __ Woman Knows: 5 Every
What __ wrong?: 4 went
What a __!: 4 dump 5 world
What About Bob? (1991 film)
cast: Richard Dreyfuss, Julie Hagerty, Bill Murray
director: Frank Oz
What About Us? (2002 song) artist: Brandy
What About Your Friends (1992 song) artist: TLC
What a Diff'rence a Day Makes (1959 song) artist: Dinah Washington
What a Fool Believes (1970 song) artist: Doobie Brothers
What a Girl Wants (1999 song) artist: Christina Aguilera
What a good boy __!: 3 am I
What am __?: 4 I bid
What Am I Going to Do With You (1975 song) artist: Barry White
What a piece of work __: 5 is man
What a pity!: 4 alas 5 alack 6 too bad
What a rare mood __: 4 I'm in
What a relief __: 4 it is
What a relief!: 4 phew, whew
What a Way to Go! (1964 film)
cast: Shirley MacLaine, Robert Mitchum, Paul Newman
director: J. Lee Thompson
What a Wonderful World (1988 song) artist: Louis Armstrong
What Becomes of the Brokenhearted (1977 song) artist: Jimmy Ruffin
Whatcha Gonna Do? (1977 song) artist: Pablo Cruise
whatchamacallit: 4 tool 5 dodad, gismo, gizmo, thing 6 doodad, gadget, widget
Whatcha See Is Whatcha Get (1971 song) artist: Dramatics
What color is an __?: 6 orange
__ What Comes Natur'lly: 4 Doin'
...what course __ may take...: 6 others
What did I tell you?: 3 see
What Did You Do in the War, Daddy? (1966 film)
cast: James Coburn, Dick Shawn
director: Blake Edwards
What'd I Say (song) artist: Elvis Presley, Ray Charles
What Does It Take (1969 song) artist: Junior Walker and the All Stars
What Dreams May Come (1998 film)
cast: Cuba Gooding Jr., Annabella Sciorra, Max von Sydow, Robin Williams
dog: 6 Ginger
What else?: 3 and
whatever: 3 any 8 anything
anything ~: 5 aught, ought
in ~ place: 8 anywhere
person: 5 whoso
Whatever Gets You Thru the Night (1974 song) artist: John Lennon
Whatever Happened to Aunt Alice? (1969 film)
cast: Rosemary Forsyth, Ruth Gordon, Geraldine Page
director: Lee H. Katzin
What Ever Happened to Baby Jane? (1962 film)
cast: Victor Buono, Joan Crawford, Bette Davis
director: Robert Aldrich
Whatever Happened to Jacy Farrow? author: Larry McMurtry
Whatever Lola Wants: 4 song 5 tango
composer: 4 Ross 5 Adler
Whatever Lola Wants (1955 song) artist: Dinah Shore, Sarah Vaughan
Whatever you want!: 4 okay 6 name it
What Every Woman Knows: 4 film, play
author: James M. Barrie
cast: Brian Aherne, Madge Evans, Helen Hayes
director: Gregory La Cava
whatfor: 6 reason 9 rationale
__ what friends are for: 5 That's
What happened ___...: 3 was
What happened __?: 4 next, then
What has four wheels and __?: 5 flies
What hath God wrought sender: 5 Morse
what have __: 3 you
What have I done!: 4 oh no
What Have I Done to Deserve This? (1987 song)
artist: Dusty Springfield, Pet Shop Boys
What have we here?: 3 aha, oho 5 hello
What have you been __?: 4 up to
What Have You Done for Me Lately (1986 song) artist: Janet Jackson
What I Am (1989 song) artist: Edie Brickell and the New Bohemians
what-if feeling: 6 regret
What in __ Hill...?: 3 Sam
What Is Life (1971 song) artist: George Harrison
What is so ___...: 4 rare
What Is This Thing Called Love composer: 6 Porter
what it __: 5 takes
__ what it's worth: 3 for
What It Takes (1990 song) artist: Aerosmith
What Kind of Fool Am I (1962 song) artist: Sammy Davis Jr.
What Kind of Fool (song) artist: Barbra Streisand, Tams
What Kind of Man Would I Be? (1989 song) artist: Chicago
What Lies Beneath (2000 film)
cast: Harrison Ford, Miranda Otto, Michelle Pfeiffer, Diana Scarwid
director: Robert Zemeckis
dog: 6 Cooper
What'll __?: 3 I do 4 it be
What'll I Do composer: Irving Berlin
What Maisie Knew author: Henry James

What Makes Sammy Run? author: Budd Schulberg
__ what may: 4 come
What, me worry? mag: 3 MAD
whatnot: 5 curio 7 trinket 8 nicknack 10 knickknack
What Planet Are You From? (2000 film)
  cast: Annette Bening, Ben Kingsley, Greg Kinnear, Garry Shandling
  director: Mike Nichols
What Price Glory?: 4 film, play
  author: Maxwell Anderson
  cast: Dolores Del Rio, Edmund Lowe, Victor McLaglen
  director: Raoul Walsh
What Price Hollywood? (1932 film)
  cast: Constance Bennett, Neil Hamilton
  director: George Cukor
what's-__-name: 3 her, his
What's __?: 2 up 3 new
What's __ for me?: 4 in It
What's __ Got to Do With It: 4 Love
What's __ like?: 5 not to
What's __ name?: 3 in a
What's __ on?: 5 going
What's __ pleasure?: 4 your
What's __ Pussycat?: 3 New
What's __ you?: 6 eating
What's Going On (song) artist: Cyndi Lauper, Marvin Gaye
What's Hecuba to him __ to Hecuba: 4 or he
what's-his-name: 6 whosis
What's in __?: 5 a name
What's in it __?: 5 for me
What's in It for Me? author: Jerome Weidman
whatsis: 5 do-dad, gismo, gizmo 6 doo-dad, gadget
What's it all about, __?: 5 Alfie
What's It All About? author: 5 Caine
What's It Gonna Be (song) artist: Busta Rhymes, Janet Jackson
What's Love Got to Do With It: 4 film, song
  artist: Tina Turner
  cast: Angela Bassett, Laurence Fishburne
  director: Brian Gibson
What's Missing? artist: 4 Klee
what's more: 3 and 4 also 7 besides
What's My Line?: 8 game show
  group: 5 panel
  host: 4 Daly 6 Blyden, Bruner
  regular: 4 Cerf 6 Arlene 7 Bennett, Dorothy, Francis 9 Kilgallen
What's My Name? (1993 song) artist: Snoop Doggy Dogg
What's New Pussycat? (1965 song)
  artist: Tom Jones
What's O'Clock author: Amy Lowell
whatsoever: 5 at all
What's the __?: 3 dif, use 4 rush
What's the __ of Wond'rin'?: 3 Use
What's the __ word?: 4 good
What's the big idea?: 3 hey
What's the Frequency, Kenneth? (1994 song) artist: R.E.M.
What's the Matter With Helen? (1971 film)
  cast: Debbie Reynolds, Dennis Weaver, Shelley Winters
What's the Worst That Could Happen? (2001 film)
  cast: Danny DeVito, Glenne Headly, Martin Lawrence, John Leguizamo
  director: Sam Weisman
__ What's Up: 5 U Know
What's Up, Doc? (1972 film)
  cast: Madeline Kahn, Kenneth Mars, Ryan O'Neal, Barbra Streisand
  director: Peter Bogdanovich
What's up, Doc? voice: 5 Blanc
What's Up, Tiger Lily? (1966 film)
  director: Woody Allen
What's your __?: 4 name, sign 7 problem
What's Your Name (song) artist: Don & Juan, Lynyrd Skynyrd
Whatta Man (1994 song)
  artist: En Vogue, Salt-n-Pepa
what the __: 3 hey 4 heck, hell
What the Butler Saw author: Joe Orton
What the hey: 6 oh well
What the World Needs Now Is Love (1965 song) artist: Jackie DeShannon
What this country __...: 5 needs
What thou __, write: 5 seest
What time __?: 4 is it
What was __ do?: 3 I to
What Was I Scared Of? author: Dr. Seuss
What will __ think of next?: 4 they
What Will Mary Say (1963 song)
  artist: Johnny Mathis
What Women Want (2000 film)
  cast: Mark Feuerstein, Mel Gibson, Helen Hunt, Marisa Tomei
  director: Nancy Meyers
__ What You Did: 4 I Saw
What You Don't Know (1989 song)
  artist: Exposé
What You Need (1986 song) artist: INXS
__ what you think!: 5 That's
What You Want (1998 song)
  artist: Mase, Total
wheal: 4 welt
wheat: 5 durum, emmer, grain, spelt 6 bulgur, cereal, golden 8 semolina
  bundle: 5 sheaf
  cracked ~: 6 bulgur, groats
  ender: 3 ear 4 worm
  feature: 3 awn 4 bran, germ 5 spica, stalk
  grow ~: 4 farm
  like ~: 5 awned
  product: 5 bread, flour, pasta 6 farina
  protein: 6 gluten
  rust: 6 fungus
  starter: 4 buck
wheat __: 4 cake, germ, rust 5 berry, bread
__ wheat: 4 club, hard, soft 5 durum, India, river 6 Polish, winter 7 cracked, poulard
__-wheat: 5 whole
Wheat: 4 Zack
Wheat __: 4 Chex 5 Thins
Wheat Chex: 6 cereal
  competitor: 3 Kix 4 Life, Trix 5 Kashi, Quisp, Total 6 Kaboom, Muesli, Oreo O's, Pablum, Smacks 7 All-Bran, Crispix, Harmony, Hunny B's, Mueslix, Oat Bran, Pokemon 8 Boo Berry, Cheerios, Corn Chex, Corn Pops, Fiber One, Rice Chex, Special K, Uncle Sam 9 Alpha Bits, Apple Zaps, Grape Nuts, Honey Comb, Just Right 10 Apple Jacks, Bran Flakes, Cap'n Crunch, Cocoa Puffs, Froot Loops, Mini-Wheats, Nutri-Grain, Puffed Rice, Quaker Oats, Smart Start 11 Cocoa Blasts, Cookie Crisp, Golden Crisp, Lucky Charms, Sweet Crunch, Waffle Crisp
wheatear: 4 bird
wheat flakes: 6 cereal
Wheaties: 6 cereal
  competitor: 3 Kix 4 Life, Trix 5 Kashi, Quisp, Total 6 Kaboom, Muesli, Oreo O's, Pablum, Smacks 7 All-Bran, Crispix, Harmony, Hunny B's, Mueslix, Oat Bran, Pokemon 8 Boo Berry, Cheerios, Corn Chex, Corn Pops, Fiber One, Rice Chex, Special K, Uncle Sam 9 Alpha Bits, Apple Zaps, Grape Nuts, Honey Comb, Just Right 10 Apple Jacks, Bran Flakes, Cap'n Crunch, Cocoa Puffs, Froot Loops, Mini-Wheats, Nutri-Grain, Puffed Rice, Quaker Oats, Smart Start 11 Cocoa Blasts, Cookie Crisp, Golden Crisp, Lucky Charms, Sweet Crunch, Waffle Crisp
Wheatley, Phillis: 4 poet
Wheaton: 3 Wil 4 city, town
  locale: 8 Illinois, Maryland
Wheat Ridge: 4 city, town
  locale: 8 Colorado
Wheat Thins: 7 cracker
  alternative: 4 Ritz 5 Zesta 6 Krispy 7 Cheez-It 8 Triscuit 10 Cheese Nips
Wheat, Zack: 6 Dodger 10 outfielder
whee: 5 oh boy
wheedle: 3 con, get, oil, ply 4 coax, prod, snow, urge, worm 5 charm, court, kotow 6 cajole, entice, induce, kowtow, work on 7 beguile, finagle, flatter, lay it on 8 blandish, butter up, freeload, inveigle, persuade, play up to, scrounge, softsoap 9 sweet-talk 10 spread it on
wheedling: 4 oily 5 charm, guile 6 urging 7 blarney, coaxing 8 cajolery, entreaty, flattery, humoring, jollying, soft soap, stroking 9 sweet talk 10 persuasion
wheel: 4 bike, disk, drum, gyre, helm, hoop, limb, reel, ring, roll, spin, tire, turn, veer 5 cycle, mogul, orbit, pivot, round, swing, twirl, whirl 6 caster, circle, gyrate, honcho, pulley, roller, rotate, swivel 7 bicycle, big shot, circuit, ratchet, revolve, trundle 8 auto part, tricycle 9 pirouette 10 velocipede
  alignment measure: 5 toe in 6 camber
  around: 4 spin, turn 5 pivot
  big ~: 4 head, king, name 5 chief, mogul, nabob 6 top dog, tycoon 7 notable 9 executive
  combining form: 5 troch- 6 trocho-
  cover: 3 mag 6 fender, hubcap
  ender: 3 man, men 4 base, work 5 chair, house, works 6 barrow, wright
  fifth ~: 5 spare
  furniture ~: 6 caster
  hub: 4 nave
  of fortune: 4 fate 5 karma
  part: 3 hub, rim 4 gear 5 spoke 6 flange
  partner: 4 deal
  play the ~: 3 bet 5 wager 6 gamble
  projection: 3 cam
  rim: 6 flange
  rod: 4 axle 5 spoke
  shaft ~: 3 cam
  sharp-toothed ~: 5 rowel
  ship's ~: 4 helm 6 tiller
  starter: 3 cog, fly, pin 4 cart, free, gear
  take the ~: 4 helm 5 drive, pilot, steer 8 navigate
  toothed ~: 4 gear, pawl
  tooth on a ~: 3 cog
  train ~ sound: 5 clack
  water ~: 5 noria
wheel __: 3 bug 4 lock 5 horse 6 static, window
__ wheel: 3 big, cam, mag, sun 4 buff, bull, disk, fish, idle, jury, mill, spur, wire, worm 5 at the, brake, color, crown, daisy, emery, fifth, great, print, scape 6 breast, center, escape, Ferris, paddle, Pelton, planet, prayer, salmon 7 balance, buffing, casting, chimney, driving, flutter, lantern, potter's, ratchet
__-wheel: 4 side 5 stern
wheel and __: 4 axle, deal
wheel-back: 5 chair
wheelbarrow: 4 cart
wheelbarrow __: 4 race
__-wheel drive: 3 all 4 four 5 front
wheeler-__: 6 dealer
__ wheeler: 6 paddle
__-wheeler: 3 six, two 4 side 5 three 8 eighteen
Wheeler: 4 Anne, Bert, peak 5 mount 8 mountain
  locale: 9 New Mexico
wheeler-dealer: 4 doer 5 Mr. Big
Wheeler Dealers, The (1963 film)
  cast: Jim Backus, James Garner, Lee Remick
  director: Arthur Hiller
__ Wheeler Wilcox: 4 Ella
wheeling: 4 roll, spin 5 swirl, twirl, whirl 8 rotation
Wheeling: 4 city, town
  locale: 3 W. Va. 8 Illinois
  river: 4 Ohio
wheel of __: 4 life 7 fortune
Wheel of Fortune: 8 game show
  buy: 3 an A, an E, an I, an O 5 vowel
  category: 5 event, place, thing, title 6 phrase
  host: 5 Sajak, White 7 Woolery 8 Stafford
  prize: 3 car 4 cash, trip
  turn: 4 spin
Wheel of Fortune, The singer: 5 Starr
wheels: 3 car 4 auto 5 crate, truck 7 vehicle 10 automobile
  adjust the ~: 5 align, aline
  expensive ~: 3 BMW 4 limo 5 Caddy, Rolls
  grease the ~: 4 ease 6 assist
  home on ~: 2 RV 6 camper 9 motor home
  kid's ~: 4 bike 5 trike, wagon
  off-road ~: 3 ATV
  on ~: 6 mobile 7 movable 8 moveable, portable
  one on two ~: 5 biker 7 cyclist
  spinning one's ~: 5 stuck 6 in a rut
  temporary ~: 6 loaner
  wagon ~: 8 macaroni
  see also automobile, car
__ wheels: 3 mag
__ Wheels: 3 Hot 4 Wild 5 Helen, Steel
wheeze: 4 gasp, hiss, pant, puff, rasp, sigh 5 cough, snore 6 breath, sizzle 7 breathe, whistle
  cause: 6 asthma
Whelan: 3 Tim 4 Jill
Whelchel: 4 Lisa
whelk: 5 shell 8 seashell
whelm: 6 engulf, ingulf 8 overcome
whelp: 3 dog, pup 4 seal 5 puppy, youth
when: 4 then 5 while 6 during, just as, whilst
  back ~: 4 once, past, yore 8 formerly 9 at one time 10 previously
  ender: 4 ever 6 soever
  from way back ~: 6 age-old
  in Spanish: 6 cuando
  since way back ~: 6 in ages 9 for a while
when __ comes to shove: 4 push
__ when: 3 say 5 if and
__ when?: 5 Since
When __ a lad,...: 4 I was
When __ Be Loved: 5 Will I
When __ Collide: 6 Worlds
When __ Comes Marching Home: 6 Johnny

When __ door not...: 3 is a
When __ eat?: 4 do we
When __ Eyes Are Smiling: 5 Irish
When __ Fears: 5 I Have
When __ in Love: 5 I Fall
When __ Married: 5 We Get
When __ Marries: 5 a Girl
When __ Met Sally ...: 5 Harry
When __ One-and-Twenty: 4 I Was
When __ said and done...: 5 all is
When __ See You Again: 5 Will I
When __ seventeen...: 4 I was
When __ Sleepy Time Down South: 3 It's
When __ Smiling: 5 You're
When __ to Old to Dream: 5 I Grow
When __ Up: 5 I Grow
When __ Wish Upon a Star: 3 You
When __ You: 5 I Lost, I Need
When!: 4 stop 6 enough, no more
When a Girl Marries: 9 radio show
When a Man Loves a Woman (1994 film)
  cast: Ellen Burstyn, Andy Garcia, Meg Ryan
When a Man Loves a Woman (song)
  artist: Michael Bolton, Percy Sledge
whence: 6 spring 9 therefore
  ender: 6 soever
When donkeys fly!: 5 never, no how, no way 8 forget it 9 fat chance 10 impossible, not a chance
When Doves Cry (1984 song) artist: Prince
whenever: 6 at will
Whenever I Call You Friend (1978 song) artist: Kenny Loggins
When Harry Met Sally... (1989 film)
  cast: Billy Crystal, Carrie Fisher, Meg Ryan
  director: Rob Reiner
When I __ my lips...: 3 ope
When I Fall in Love (1961 song) artist: Lettermen
When I Grow Too __ Dream: 5 Old to
When I Grow Up (1951 film)
  cast: Bobby Driscoll, Robert Preston, Martha Scott
  director: Michael Kanin
When I Grow Up (1964 song) artist: Beach Boys
When I Have Fears author: John Keats
__ When I Laugh: 4 Only
When I Looked at Him (1989 song)
  artist: Exposé
When I Lost You composer: 6 Berlin
When I'm Back on My Feet Again (1990 song) artist: Michael Bolton
When I Need You (1977 song) artist: Leo Sayer
When in Rome, __...: 4 do as
When in the course of human __...: 6 events
When Irish Eyes are Smiling: 5 waltz
When I Take My Sugar __: 5 to Tea
When I Think of You (1986 song)
  artist: Janet Jackson
When It's Love (1988 song) artist: Van Halen
When I Wanted You (1980 song)
  artist: Barry Manilow
When I was a __...: 3 lad
When I Was One-and-Twenty author: A.E. Housman
When Ladies Meet (1933 film)
  cast: Ann Harding, Myrna Loy, Robert Montgomery
When Lilacs Last... author: Walt Whitman
When My Baby Smiles __: 4 at Me
When My Blue Moon... (1956 song)
  artist: Elvis Presley
when one's __ comes in: 4 ship
When pigs fly!: 5 never, nohow, no way 8 forget it 9 fat chance 10 impossible, not a chance
when push __ to shove: 5 comes
When She Was Good author: Philip Roth
When Strangers Marry (1944 film)
  cast: Kim Hunter, Dean Jagger, Robert Mitchum
when the __ are down: 5 chips
When the Bough Breaks author: Jonathan Kellerman
When the Boy in Your Arms (1961 song) artist: Connie Francis
When the Daltons Rode (1940 film)
  cast: Brian Donlevy, Kay Francis, Randolph Scott
  director: George Marshall
When the Frost Is on the Punkin author: James Whitcomb Riley
When the Going Gets Tough... (1985 song) artist: Billy Ocean
When the Legends Die (1972 film)
  cast: Luana Anders, Frederic Forrest, Richard Widmark
  director: Stuart Millar
When the moon __ the seventh house: 4 is in
When the moon hits your eye: 5 amore
When there's __...: 5 a will
When We Dead Awaken author: Henrik Ibsen
When We Get Married (1961 song)
  artist: Dreamlovers
When We Were Kings subject: 3 Ali
When We Were Very Young author: A.A. Milne
When Will I Be Loved (song) artist: Everly Brothers
  artist: Linda Ronstadt
When Will I See You Again (1974 song) artist: Three Degrees
When Worlds Collide: 4 film 5 novel
  author: 5 Wylie 6 Balmer
  cast: Richard Derr, Peter Hanson, Barbara Rush
  director: Rudolph Maté
  planet: 4 Zyra
When You're Hot... (1971 song) artist: Jerry Reed
When You're in Love... (1979 song)
  artist: Dr. Hook
When You Wish Upon __: 5 a Star
where: 4 site, spot 5 place, point 7 whither 8 location, position
  ender: 4 fore, from, into, unto, upon, with 6 soever, withal 7 through
  starter: 3 any 4 else, ever, some 5 every
where __: 5 it's at
Where __?: 3 am I 4 was I
Where __ All the Flowers Gone: 4 Have
Where __ Dare: 6 Eagles
Where __ I?: 3 was
Where __ Life ...: 6 There's
Where __ Love: 5 Is the
Where __ Our Love Go: 3 Did
Where __ smoke...: 6 there's
whereabouts: 4 loca, loci 5 place 6 locale 8 bearings, location, position, presence 9 situation
  forget the ~: 4 lose 6 mislay 7 misfile 8 misplace
Where America's day begins: 4 Guam
Where Are the Children? author: Mary Higgins Clark
whereas: 3 for 5 since, while 6 though, whilst 7 because 10 seeing that
Where did __ wrong?: 3 I go
Where Did Our Love Go (1964 song)
  artist: Supremes
Where Do __?: 3 I Go
Where Do Broken Hearts Go (1988 song) artist: Whitney Houston
Where Does My Heart Beat Now (1991 song) artist: Celine Dion
Where Eagles Dare (1969 film)
  cast: Richard Burton, Clint Eastwood, Mary Ure
  director: Brian G. Hutton
  gun: 4 Sten
wherefore: 6 motive, reason 7 grounds, purpose 9 rationale
  partner: 3 why
Wherefore art thou __?: 5 Romeo
Where Have All the Cowboys Gone? (1997 song) artist: Paula Cole
Where I Live author: Tennessee Williams
Where Is Love? musical: 6 Oliver!
Where Is the Life That Late __?: 4 I Led
Where Is the Love (1972 song)
  artist: Donny Hathaway, Roberta Flack
Where Love Has Gone author: Harold Robbins
Where or When: 4 song, tune
  composer: 4 Hart 7 Rodgers
__ where prohibited: 4 void
Where's __?: 5 Daddy, Poppa, Waldo 7 Charley
Where's Charley? (1952 film): 7 musical
  cast: Ray Bolger, Allyn Ann McLerie, Robert Shackleton
  composer: 7 Loesser
  role: 3 Amy
Where's Daddy? author: William Inge
Where's Poppa? star: 5 Segal 6 Gordon
Where's the __?: 4 beef, fire
Where's the Rest __?: 4 of Me
Where the __ meet to eat: 5 elite
Where the Boys Are (1961 song)
  artist: Connie Francis
...where the buffalo __: 4 roam
__ where the heart...: 6 Home is
Where the Red Fern Grows (1974 film)
  cast: Beverly Garland, Jack Ging, James Whitmore
  director: Norman Tokar
Where there's __...: 4 life 5 a will
Where There's Life ... (1947 film)
  cast: William Bendix, Signe Hasso, Bob Hope
  director: Sidney Lanfield
Where the Sidewalk Ends (1950 film)
  cast: Dana Andrews, Gary Merrill, Gene Tierney
  director: Otto Preminger
Where the Spies Are (1965 film)
  cast: Françoise Dorléac, David Niven
  director: Val Guest
wherever: 4 site, spot 5 place 6 locale 7 whither 8 locality, position
  you are: 4 here
Wherever He __: 4 Ain't
wherewithal: 3 oof 4 cash, gelt, jack, kail, kale, loot, peag, pelf 5 bills, bread, bucks, dough, funds, lucre, means, money, moola, mopus, pesos, purse, rhino, sewan 6 assets, dinero, do-re-mi, mammon, mazuma, moolah, seawan, silver, specie, wampum, wealth 7 ability, cabbage, capital, dollars, lettuce, ooftish, scratch, shekels 8 bankroll, cold cash, currency, hard cash, smackers 9 banknotes, frogskins, long green, potential, resources, simoleons 10 greenbacks, green stuff
  has the ~: 3 can
  having the ~: 4 able
  lacks the ~: 6 cannot
wherry: 4 boat 5 craft 6 vessel
  implement: 3 oar 6 paddle
whet: 4 edge, file, hone, stir 5 grind, pique, raise, rally, rouse, strop, tempt 6 arouse, awaken, excite, kindle 7 quicken, sharpen 8 increase, motivate 9 acuminate, appetizer, intensify, stimulant, stimulate
  ender: 5 stone
whether __: 4 or no 5 or not
Whether __ nobler...: 3 'tis
whetstone: 4 hone
  use a ~: 5 grind 7 sharpen
whetted: 4 keen 5 sharp 6 pointy 9 acuminate
Whew!: 6 I'm beat
  feeling: 6 relief
whey: 4 sera 5 dairy, serum
  partner: 4 curd
whey-faced: 3 wan 4 ashy 5 ashen
which
  at ~ time: 4 when
  besides ~: 3 and 4 also, plus 8 moreover
  ender: 4 ever 6 soever
  every ~ way: 5 about, messy, mussy 6 hectic, remiss, untidy 7 chaotic, haywire, jumbled, lawless, riotous, tangled 8 anarchic, confused, pell-mell, reckless 10 anarchical, disjointed, disordered, disorderly, topsy-turvy, tumultuous
  in ~ case: 4 then
  person: 3 who 4 whom
  person's: 5 whose
which __ the wind blows: 3 way
Which came first?
  choice: 3 egg 7 chicken
whichever: 3 any 6 either
Which nobody can __: 4 deny
__ which way: 3 any 5 every
__ Which Way But Loose: 5 Every
which way the __ blows: 4 wind
__ Which Way You Can: 3 Any
Which Way You Goin' Billy? (1970 song) artist: Poppy Family
__ which will live in infamy: 5 a date
whidah: 4 bird
whiff: 3 air, fan 4 dash, gust, hint, lick, odor, puff, waft 5 aroma, scent, smell, sniff, snort, touch, trace 6 breath, inhale 7 draught, soupçon, whisper 9 strike out, suspicion
Whiffenpoof: 3 Eli 5 Yalie 7 Bulldog
  word: 3 baa
whiffle: 4 yo-yo 5 hedge, waver 6 dither, seesaw, teeter, totter 8 fence-sit, flip-flop, hesitate 9 hem and haw, pussyfoot, vacillate 10 dilly-dally, equivocate
Whigs: 5 party
while: 4 laze, pass, time, when 5 altho, space, spell 6 during, moment, much as, period, though 7 interim, stretch, whereas 8 although, as long as, meantime 10 even though
  a ~ ago: 4 once 6 before 7 earlier 9 at one time, in the past 10 beforehand, previously
  all the ~: 6 during 10 throughout
  a short ~ ago: 6 lately, of late 8 recently 9 yesterday
  away: 3 use 5 spend, use up, waste 6 expend, misuse 7 deplete, fritter 8 squander 9 dissipate
  away hours: 4 idle, laze, loaf, loll 5 dally 6 dawdle, loiter 8 kill time, malinger, slack off 9 bum around, goldbrick, sit around, waste time 10 dillydally, fool around, knock about, take it easy
  in a ~: 3 yet 4 anon, soon, then 5 after, later 7 by and by, later on, shortly, someday 8 directly, sometime 9 afterward, hereafter

10 before long, eventually
long ~: 4 ages, days, eons 5 years
once in a ~: 3 occ. 6 rarely, seldom 7 at times 8 scarcely 9 sometimes 10 hardly ever
prefix for ~: 4 erst
short ~: 3 bit 4 jiff 5 jiffy 7 instant
starter: 3 ere 4 erst, mean 5 worth
stay a ~: 5 abide, dwell 6 hold on, linger, remain 7 sojourn 8 continue
stop for a ~: 4 rest 5 break, pause 7 breathe, suspend
use for a ~: 6 borrow
___ while: 3 in a
While My Pretty One Sleeps author: Mary Higgins Clark
While the City Sleeps (1956 film)
cast: Dana Andrews, Rhonda Fleming, Ida Lupino
director: Fritz Lang
___ while the iron is hot: 6 strike
While the Sun Shines author: Terrence Rattigan
While You See a Chance (1981 song) artist: Steve Winwood
while-you-wait: 4 fast 5 quick, rapid 6 prompt, snappy 7 instant 9 immediate, on-the-spot
While You Were Sleeping (1995 film)
cast: Peter Boyle, Sandra Bullock, Peter Gallagher, Bill Pullman
director: Jon Turteltaub
___ While You Work: 7 Whistle
whillikers: 3 gee 4 gosh 5 golly
whilom: 4 erst, once 6 former 7 onetime, quondam
whim: 4 lark, urge, wish 5 fancy, quirk 6 desire, notion, vagary 7 caprice, impulse 8 crotchet
___ whim: 3 on a
whimbrel: 4 bird
whimper: 3 cry, sob 4 bawl, fuss, mewl, moan, pule, wail, weep 5 bleat, whine 6 boohoo, snivel 7 blubber 8 complain 9 make a fuss, shed tears
alternative: 4 bang
go out with a ~: 6 fizzle
whimpering: 5 tears 7 tearful 9 querulous, sniveling
whimsical: 3 fey, odd 5 droll, funny, light, silly, witty 6 dreamy, fickle, jocose, quaint 7 amusing, comical, curious, erratic, jocular, playful, waggish, wayward 8 fanciful, farcical, humorous, peculiar, skittish, volatile 9 arbitrary, eccentric, facetious, fantastic, frivolous, grotesque, imaginary, quizzical, uncertain 10 capricious, changeable, outlandish
whimsy: 5 humor, quirk 6 vagary 9 frivolity
whin: 5 gorse, shrub
whinchat: 4 bird
whine: 3 cry, sob 4 carp, fuss, howl, kick, mewl, moan, pule, sigh, sing, wail, yowl 5 bleat, cavil, drone, gripe, groan, sound 6 grouch, grouse, kvetch, murmur, repine, snivel, squawk, squeak, yammer 7 grumble, nitpick, quibble, whimper 8 complain 9 bellyache, complaint, criticism, criticize, make a fuss
whiner: 5 grump, shrew 6 grouch, kvetch, moaner 7 crybaby
whinny: 4 bray 5 bleat, neigh
companion: 5 snort
whiny: 6 cranky 7 fretful, peevish 8 fretsome, petulant 9 querulous
whip: 3 mix, rod, tan, tar, top 4 beat, belt, best, cane, crop, drub, flay, flog, hide, hurt, jerk, lash, lick, race, rout, stir, trim 5 birch, blend, knout, mop up, shake, spank, strap, thong, trash, whale, whisk, whomp, worst 6 berate, defeat, ferule, hammer, larrup, lather, punish, switch, thrash, wallop 7 bawl out, chew out, clobber, conquer, lambast, lay into, overrun, rawhide, scamper, scourge, shellac, trounce 8 bludgeon, chastise, give it to, lambaste, shellack 9 castigate, dress down, horsewhip, overwhelm 10 discipline, tongue-lash
ender: 3 saw 4 cord, lash, tail, worm 5 sawed, stall 6 stitch
into shape: 4 tidy 5 train 7 arrange 8 organize 9 supervise
mark: 4 weal, welt
riding ~: 4 crop 5 quirt
sound: 5 crack
starter: 4 bull 5 horse
together: 3 mix 4 meld, stir 5 blend, merge 7 combine 8 intermix 9 integrate 10 amalgamate
up: 3 fix, set 4 brew, goad, make, prod, spur, stir, urge 5 drive, hatch, prick, start 6 arouse, create, devise, excite, foment, incite, kindle 7 agitate, disturb, enflame, inflame, provoke 8 contrive, generate 9 fabricate, instigate
whip ___: 3 off 4 hand, roll 5 graft, snake
whip ___ shape: 4 into
___ whip: 3 sea 5 party 6 double, single
___ Whip: 4 Cool 5 Let It 7 Miracle
Whip Hand author: Dick Francis
Whip It artist: 4 Devo
Whiplash, Snidely, like: 4 evil
whipped-cream portion: 4 glob 6 dollop
whipped-up: 5 ad-lib 7 offhand 9 extempore, impromptu, tossed-off 10 improvised, off-the-cuff, unscripted
whippersnapper: 3 boy, lad, pup 4 brat, punk 5 minor, whelp, youth 6 urchin 9 stripling
whippet: 3 dog 5 pooch 6 canine
whipping ___: 3 boy 5 cream
whipping boy: 3 sap 4 dupe, fool, goat, lamb 5 chump, patsy 6 pigeon, sucker, victim 7 cat's-paw, doormat 8 pushover 9 scapegoat
Whipple, George: 8 Nobelist
whippoorwill: 4 bird
relative: 9 nighthawk
whir
see whirr
whirl: 2 go 3 try 4 daze, eddy, reel, ride, roll, rush, shot, spin, stab, to-do, turn, zoom 5 crack, fling, pivot, round, swing, swirl, twirl, twist, whack, wheel 6 circle, flurry, gyrate, hassle, hubbub, rotate, swivel, tumble 7 attempt, revolve, turmoil 8 gyration, trial run 9 pirouette 10 hullabaloo, spin around
ender: 4 pool, wind
give it a ~: 3 try 6 tackle 7 attempt
___ whirl: 3 in a 4 dust
___-Whirl: 5 Tilt-a
whirling: 5 aspin, dizzy 6 rotary 8 gyration
whirling ___: 7 dervish
whirlpool: 3 spa 4 eddy, tide 5 swirl 6 hot tub, vortex 8 undertow 9 maelstrom
combining form: 4 dino-
whirlpool ___: 4 bath
Whirlpool: 9 appliance
alternative: 5 Amana, Norge 6 Bendix, Maytag, Tappan 7 Admiral, Jenn-Air, Kenmore 8 Hotpoint 9 Magic Chef 10 Frigidaire, Kelvinator, KitchenAid
Whirlpool (1949 film)
cast: Richard Conte, José Ferrer, Gene Tierney
director: Otto Preminger
whirlwind: 2 oe 4 rash, wind 5 hasty, quick, rapid, storm, swift 6 speedy, vortex 7 cyclone, tornado, twister 8 headlong 9 breakneck, dust devil, impetuous, impulsive 10 waterspout
Whirlwind author: James Clavell
whirlybird: 4 giro 6 copter 7 chopper 8 autogiro 10 helicopter
blade: 5 rotor
Whirly Girl (1983 song) artist: OXO
whirr: 3 hum 4 birr, buzz, roll, whiz 5 churr, drone, noise, skirr 6 bustle 7 vibrate
whish: 5 sound, zip by
whisk: 3 fly, zip 4 dart, dash, flit, race, rush, stir, tear, whip, whiz 5 broom, brush, flick, hurry, mixer, shoot, speed, sweep, swish 6 beater, hasten, scurry 8 brush off
ender: 5 broom
user: 3 ump 6 umpire
whisk ___: 5 broom
Whiskas: 7 cat food
alternative: 5 Amore 6 Figaro, Purina 8 Friskies 10 Chef's Blend, Fancy Feast
whisker: 3 awn 6 barbel 7 bristle
by a ~: 6 barely 8 narrowly
whisker ___: 4 boom, pole
___ whisker: 3 by a, cat 4 cat's
whiskered: 5 hairy 7 bearded, bristly, hirsute
whiskers: 4 fuzz, hair 5 beard 6 goatee
creature with ~: 3 cat 6 walrus
like ~: 5 bushy
where ~ grow: 4 chin, face, neck 5 cheek
whiskey: 3 rye 5 booze, drink, hooch, sauce 6 chaser, hootch, liquor, redeye, rotgut, Scotch 7 alcohol, bourbon, spirits 8 beverage 9 firewater, hard stuff, moonshine
a way to drink ~: 4 neat 10 on the rocks
bottle: 4 pint 5 fifth
holder: 4 cask 5 flask
measure: 4 dram, shot 5 proof 6 jigger
source: 3 rye 4 corn, mash
whiskey ___: 4 jack, sour
___ whiskey: 3 rye 4 corn, malt 5 Irish 6 bonded, Scotch 7 blended, bourbon
Whiskey Rebellion suppressor: 3 Lee
whiskey sour: 5 drink 8 beverage, cocktail
ingredient: 10 lemon juice
whisper: 3 hum, pst, tip 4 buzz, hint, hiss, psst, sigh, tell, wind, word 5 rumor, sound, speak, tinge, touch, trace, utter, whiff 6 breath, gossip, intone, mumble, murmur, mutter, report, rustle, shadow, sizzle, tipoff 7 breathe, confide, soupçon 8 innuendo, intimate, sibilate 9 insinuate, suspicion, susurrate, undertone 10 suggestion
___ whisper: 5 stage
whispered: 3 low 4 soft, weak 5 bated, faint, muted, piano, quiet 6 hushed 7 muffled, subdued 8 dampened, deadened 9 toned down 10 turned down
whisperer's request: 6 closer
___ Whisperer, The: 5 Horse
whispering: 5 rumor 6 canard, gossip, report 7 hearsay 9 grapevine
Whispering Bells (1957 song) artist: Dell-Vikings
Whispers author: Dean Koontz
whist: 4 game 8 card game
relative: 6 bridge, écarté
variety: 6 Boston
whistle: 4 blow, hiss, pipe, sign 5 blast, siren 6 signal, wheeze
after the ~: 4 late
blow the ~: 4 sing, tell 6 accuse, inform
blow the ~ on: 4 halt 5 blame 6 betray, charge, expose, give up, turn in 7 sell out
for: 7 solicit
sound: 4 toot
starter: 5 penny
stop: 4 town
time: 4 noon
wet one's ~: 4 swig 5 drink 6 imbibe, tipple 7 swallow
whistle ___: 3 pig 4 stop 5 Dixie
whistle-___: 4 stop 6 blower
___ whistle: 5 organ, penny
Whistle ___ You Work: 5 While
whistle-blower: 4 fink 7 tattler, traitor 10 tattletale
Whistle Blower, The (1986 film)
cast: Michael Caine, James Fox, Nigel Havers
Whistle Down the Wind (1961 film)
cast: Alan Bates, Bernard Lee, Hayley Mills
director: Bryan Forbes
whistle in the ___: 4 dark
whistler: 4 bird, wolf 9 thickhead
Whistler, James McNeill: 6 artist 7 painter
Whistler's mother's wear: 5 shawl
whistle-stop: 4 tour
whistles, with all the bells and: 6 deluxe
Whistle While You Work singer: 3 Doc 5 dwarf, Happy 6 Grumpy, Sleepy, Sneezy 7 Bashful
whistling ___: 4 buoy, duck, swan
Whistling in Dixie (1942 film)
cast: George Bancroft, Ann Rutherford, Red Skelton
Whistling in the Dark (1941 film)
cast: Virginia Grey, Ann Rutherford, Red Skelton
whit: 3 bit, fig, jot 4 atom, dash, drop, iota, mite, mote 5 crumb, grain, pinch, scrap, shred, speck, trace 6 little, trifle 7 minimum, modicum, smidgen, smidgin, tiny bit 8 fragment, least bit, particle, smidgeon 9 scintilla
not a ~: 3 nil, zip 4 nada, none, zero 5 zilch 6 naught, nought 7 nothing
Whit: 7 Bissell
Whit ___: 4 Week
Whitaker: 4 Jack 6 Forest 7 Johnnie
Whitaker, Forest: 5 actor
film: Bird (1988)
The Crying Game (1992)
Diary of a Hitman (1992)
Good Morning, Vietnam (1987)
Hope Floats (1998)
Light It Up (1999)
Panic Room (2002)
Phenomenon (1996)
Platoon (1986)
Species (1995)
Waiting to Exhale (1995)
Whitby: 4 city, town
locale: 6 Canada 7 Ontario
Whitchurch: 4 city, town
locale: 6 Canada 7 Ontario
Whitcomb: 3 Ian
___ Whitcomb Riley: 5 James
white: 3 wan 4 fair, pale, pure, wine 5 Anglo, ashen, bread, clean, clear, color, hoary, ivory, light, Mâcon, milky, pasty, Pinot, snowy, soave, Tokay, waxen, Yquem 6 Arneis, chalky, creamy, pallid, peaked, pearly, silver, washed 7 aligoté, cabinet, Catawba, Chablis, frosted, heurige, Madeira, Moselle, neutral, niveous, Orvieto, silvery, Vouvray 8 Albariño, blanched, bleached, Frascati, Muscadet, Riesling, Sancerre, Sauterne,

Sylvaner, vermouth **9** alabaster, albescent, bloodless, Caucasian, colombard, colorless, Meursault **10** achromatic, Chardonnay, immaculate, Montrachet
alternative: **3** rye **5** wheat
and yellow flower: **7** calypso **8** camomile **9** calla lily, chamomile
as a sheet: **3** wan **4** ashy, pale **5** ashen
black plus ~: **4** gray, grey
black, to ~: **3** opp. **8** opposite
cliffs locale: **5** Dover
cloud: **3** pet **4** fish
collar: **6** worker
color: **4** bone, milk, snow **5** cream, ivory, milky **6** argent, oyster, silver **8** eggshell **9** alabaster
combining form: **3** alb- **4** albo-, leuc-, leuk- **5** leuco-, leuko-
complement: **4** yolk
egg ~: **5** glair **6** glaire
ender: **3** cap, fly, out **4** bait, face, fish, tail, wash, wood **5** print, smith **6** throat, washed **7** washing
flag: **5** truce **9** surrender
flower: **3** mum **4** flag, iris, lily **5** calla, camas, daisy, lilac, lotus, peony, poppy, tulip, yucca **6** camass, crocus, lupine, mallow, maypop, myrtle, spirea, thrift, violet, yarrow **7** aconite, arbutus, catalpa, dog rose, dogwood, freesia, hogweed, jasmine, jonquil, rambler, saguaro, spiraea **8** aconitum, ageratum, arum lily, asphodel, boltonia, camellia, erigeron, gardenia, hawthorn, hepatica, hyacinth, larkspur, magnolia, oleander, rockrose, snowball, snowdrop, tamarisk, trillium, tuberose, viburnum, wistaria, wisteria **9** arrowhead, bloodroot, calla lily, candytuft, colicroot, edelweiss, horehound, hydrangea, jessamine, mayflower, narcissus, pussy-toes, water lily **10** bluebottle, buttonbush, cornflower, delphinium, Easter lily, fleur-de-lis, goatsbeard, Indian pipe, marguerite, mock orange, poinsettia, ranunculus, spider lily
gem: **4** opal **5** pearl
grayish ~: **6** oyster, silver
in black and ~: **5** clear, plain **8** explicit
in heraldry: **6** argent
lie: **3** fib **4** tale **5** story
lightning: **5** booze, hooch **6** hootch
mineral: **5** chalk
name meaning ~: **5** Weiss **6** Bianca **7** Blanche **9** Guinevere, Gwendolyn
out: **5** erase, scrub **6** delete, efface, remove **7** expunge
pages: **8** listings **9** directory
paper: **3** rpt. **6** report
sale buy: **5** linen, sheet, towel
starter: **3** bob **4** lint
stuff: **4** snow
turn ~: **4** pale **6** blanch **8** etiolate
water: **6** rapids
wine: **3** kir **5** Mâcon, Mosel, pinot, Rhine, soave, Tokay, Yquem **7** Catawba, Chablis, Madeira, Moselle, Orvieto, Vouvray **8** Albariño, Frascati, Muscadet, Riesling, Sancerre, Sauterne, Sylvaner **10** Chardonnay, Montrachet
with shock: **3** wan **4** ashy, pale **5** ashen
woman in ~: **5** bride, nurse
yellowish ~: **4** bone **5** cream, ivory **8** eggshell

white __: **3** ant, ash, fir, fox, gum, hat, lie, oak, rat, rot, tie, wax **4** bass, bear, belt, book, cell, chip, coal, crab, flag, gold, hake, heat, hole, hope, iron, lead, line, list, meat, mule, pine, rose, rust, sage, sale, wine, work **5** alder, alert, aspen, bacon, birch, bread, bucks, cedar, cloud, daisy, dwarf, frost, goods, gourd, horse, light, lotus, magic, metal, noise, pages, paper, perch, sauce, shark, sound, space, stock, stork, water, wavey, whale **6** alkali, clover, ensign, ginger, hunter, kerria, knight, liquor, lupine, market, marlin, matter, pepper, poplar, potato, salmon, sapote, spruce, squall, turnip, walnut **7** admiral, campion, croaker, eardrop, feather, leather, melilot, mustard, rainbow, truffle, vitriol
white __ cell: **5** blood
white __ ghost: **3** as a
white __ lily: **5** globe, water **7** trumpet
white __ sheet: **3** as a
white-__: **3** eye, hot **4** shoe **5** faced, glove, robed **6** collar, ground, haired, headed **7** knuckle, livered
white-__ deer: **6** tailed
__ white: **3** egg **4** lead, zinc **5** clown, flake **6** oyster, pearly **7** Chinese
__-white: **3** off, tin **4** milk, snow **5** ivory
White: **2** E.B., T.H. **3** sea **5** Barry, Betty, Byron, David, Karyn, Perry, range, river, Vanna **6** Jaleel **7** Patrick **8** Stanford
colleague: **5** Sajak
river: **4** Nile
river locale: **8** Arkansas
sea locale: **6** Russia
White __: **3** Sea, Sox **4** Fang, Heat, Lion, Nile, Pass, Room **5** Friar, House, Noise, Sands, Smoke, Volta **6** Castle, Nights, Palace, Rabbit, Russia, Squall, Zombie
White __ Can't Jump: **3** Men
White __, NM: **5** Sands
White __ of Dover: **6** Cliffs
White __, The: **5** Album, Devil **7** Company, Goddess, Peacock
__ White: **4** Snow **5** Great, Men in **7** Chester, Tony Joe
White Album, The author: Joan Didion
White April poet: **5** Reese
white as __: **5** chalk **6** a ghost, a sheet
white as a __: **5** ghost, sheet
whitebait: **4** fish
White, Barry
song: Can't Get Enough... (1974)
I'm Gonna Love You... (1973)
It's Ecstasy... (1977)
Never, Never Gonna Give Ya Up (1973)
Practice What You Preach (1994)
What Am I Going to Do With You (1975)
You're the First... (1974)
White Bear Lake: **4** city, town
locale: **9** Minnesota
White, Betty spouse: Allen Ludden
whiteboard need: **6** eraser, marker
white-bread: **4** tame **5** usual **8** ordinary
white bucks: **4** shoe **8** footwear
white buck shoes singer: **5** Boone
white cabbage: **6** veggie **9** vegetable
whitecap: **4** foam, wave **6** billow
White Christmas: **4** film, song
artist: Bing Crosby
cast: Rosemary Clooney, Bing Crosby, Danny Kaye, Vera-Ellen
composer: Irving Berlin
director: Michael Curtiz
record label: **5** Decca
White Cliffs of Dover, The (1944 film)
cast: Irene Dunne, Van Johnson

White Cloud: **10** paper towel
alternative: **5** Scott **6** Marcal **7** Charmin **8** Northern, Soft Weve **10** Cottonelle
white-collar __: **5** crime **6** worker
white-collar worker: **5** clerk, yuppy **6** yuppie **7** cashier, employe **8** employee **10** amanuensis, bookkeeper
White Company, The author: Arthur Conan Doyle
White Devil, The author: John Webster
White, E.B.: **6** author, writer
work: Charlotte's Web
The Elements of Style
Stuart Little
white-eye: **4** bird
whiteface
one in ~: **4** mime **5** mimer
white-faced: **3** wan **4** ashy, pale **5** ashen
White Fang: **4** film **5** novel
author: Jack London
cast: Klaus Maria Brandauer, Ethan Hawke
director: Randal Kleiser
White Fang creator: Soupy Sales
whitefish: **4** chub **5** cisco **6** pollan
__ whitefish: **4** lake **5** round
Whitefish __: **3** Bay
White Goddess, The author: Robert Graves
white gold: **5** alloy
component: **4** zinc **6** nickel **8** platinum **9** palladium
Whitehall: **4** city, town **6** palace
locale: **4** Ohio
white hat wearer: **2** RN **4** chef, hero **5** nurse
Whitehead, Alfred North: **7** British **11** philosopher
work: Principia Mathematica
Science and the Modern World
Whitehead, William: **4** poet
White Heat (1949 film)
cast: James Cagney, Virginia Mayo, Edmond O'Brien
composer: **7** Steiner
director: Raoul Walsh
__ White Hope, The: **5** Great
Whitehorse: **4** city, town
locale: **5** Yukon **6** Canada
river: **5** Yukon
white-hot: **3** mad **5** angry, fiery, irate, livid, rabid, riled, wroth **6** crazed, fuming, ireful, raging, raving, torrid **7** boiling, burning, enraged, frantic, furious, ranting **8** frenzied, in a tizzy, incensed, inflamed, sizzling, wrathful **10** blistering, infuriated
White House
architect: **5** Hoban
area: **4** lawn
dog: **3** Her, Him **4** Fala **5** Buddy
dweller: **4** prez **9** first lady, president
French ~: **6** Elysée
group: **3** NSC, OMB **7** cabinet
initials: **3** DDE, FDR, HST, JFK, LBJ, RMN
nickname: **3** Abe, Cal, Ike **4** Bill
room: **4** East
section: **4** wing
staffer: **4** aide
turndown: **4** veto
Web site suffix: **3** gov
'70s ~ daughter: **3** Amy **5** Susan
see also president
White Hunter, Black Heart (1990 film)
cast: George Dzundza, Clint Eastwood, Jeff Fahey
director: Clint Eastwood
white-knuckled: **4** taut **5** jumpy, tense **6** on edge **7** anxious, excited, fretful, jittery, keyed up, nervous, restive, uptight, worried **9** strung out **10** distressed

__ White Lies: **6** Little
White Line Fever (1975 film)
cast: Kay Lenz, Slim Pickens, Jan-Michael Vincent
director: Jonathan Kaplan
Whiteman: **4** Paul
White Men Can't Jump (1992 film)
cast: Woody Harrelson, Rosie Perez, Wesley Snipes
director: Ron Shelton
White Mischief (1988 film)
cast: John Hurt, Sarah Miles, Greta Scacchi
director: Michael Radford
whiten: **4** fade, pale **5** chalk, frost **6** blanch, bleach, blench, silver **7** decolor, grizzle, lighten **8** etiolate **9** whitewash **10** decolorize
White Nile people: **4** Nuer
White Noise author: Don DeLillo
__ white oak: **5** swamp
White Oak: **4** city, town
locale: **8** Maryland
White of the Eye (1987 film)
cast: David Keith, Cathy Moriarty
White Oleander (2002 film)
cast: Robin Wright Penn, Michelle Pfeiffer, Noah Wyle, Renée Zellweger
White Palace (1990 film)
cast: Jason Alexander, Susan Sarandon, James Spader
White, Patrick: **6** author, writer **8** Nobelist **10** Australian
work: The Tree of Man
White Peacock, The author: D.H. Lawrence
White, Perry: **4** boss **6** editor
White Plains: **4** city, town
locale: **7** New York
White Rabbit
associate: **5** Alice
like the ~: **4** late
White Rabbit (1967 song) artist: Jefferson Airplane
White Room (1968 song) artist: Cream
Whiter Shade of Pale, A (1967 song)
artist: Procol Harum
__ whites: **6** pearly
White Sands (1992 film)
cast: Willem Dafoe, Samuel L. Jackson, Mary Elizabeth Mastrantonio, Mickey Rourke
White Sands county: **5** Otero
White Sea
bay: **5** Dvina, Onega
river to the ~: **5** Dvina
__ White Season: **4** A Dry
__ white shark: **5** great
White Silver Sands (song) artist: Bill Black Combo, Don Rondo
White Smoke author: Andrew Greeley
White Sox: **3** ten **4** team
Hall of Famer: **7** Appling
home: **7** Chicago
org.: **3** ALC, MLB
rival: **3** Cub, Met, Red **4** Expo, Twin **5** Angel, Astro, Brave, Giant, Padre, Rocky, Royal, Tiger **6** Brewer, Dodger, Indian, Marlin, Oriole, Philly, Pirate, Ranger, Red Sox, Yankee **7** Blue Jay, Mariner **8** Athletic, Cardinal, Devil Ray
sport: **8** baseball
White Sport Coat, A (1957 song)
artist: Marty Robbins
White Squall (1996 film)
cast: Jeff Bridges, Caroline Goodall, John Savage
director: Ridley Scott
White, Stanford: **9** architect
whitetail: **4** deer
White, T.H.: **6** writer **7** British
work: The Age of Scandal
The Book of Merlyn

The Candle in the Wind
The Ill-Made Knight
The Once and Future King
The Sword in the Stone
White, Theodore H.: 6 author, writer 10 journalist
work: Breach of Faith
Fire in the Ashes
The Making of the President
Thunder Out of China
The View from the Fortieth Floor
whitethroat: 4 bird
white tornado cleaner: 4 Ajax
White, Vanna: 4 host
colleague: Pat Sajak
whitewall: 4 tire, tyre 5 wheel
whitewash: 4 coat, hide 5 chalk, gloss, mince, paint 6 deceit, dupery, excuse, whiten 7 absolve, conceal, cover up, encrust, incrust, justify, pretend 8 downplay, minimize, overlook, palliate, play down 9 collusion, deception, dissemble, exonerate, gloss over, soft-pedal, sugarcoat, vindicate
ingredient: 4 lime
white water: 6 rapids
craft: 4 raft 5 canoe
site: 5 cañon 6 canyon
white-water rafting: 5 sport
__ White Way: 5 Great
White Wedding singer: 4 Idol
Whitey: 4 Ford 6 Herzog
White Zombie (1932 film)
cast: Madge Bellamy, Bela Lugosi
whither: 5 where 8 wherever
ender: 6 soever
Whither thou ___...: 5 goest
whiting: 4 fish, hake
Whiting: 4 John 7 Richard 8 Margaret
Whiting, John: 7 British 10 playwright
Whiting, Richard: 8 composer
song: Ain't We Got Fun
Beyond the Blue Horizon
Hooray for Hollywood
On the Good Ship Lollipop
Sleepy Time Gal
Too Marvelous for Words
whitish: 4 ashy, pale 5 ashen, milky 6 chalky, pearly 7 opaline 8 blanched 10 opalescent
color: 6 silver
stone: 4 opal
Whitley: 8 Strieber
whitlow: 6 agnail
Whitman: 3 Mae 4 Mayo, poet, Slim, Walt 6 Stuart
Whitman, Stuart: 5 actor
film: The Comancheros (1961)
Convicts 4 (1962)
Crazy Mama (1975)
Hound-Dog Man (1959)
Murder, Inc. (1960)
Rio Conchos (1964)
Those Magnificent Men in Their Flying Machines (1965)
Whitman, Walt: 4 poet
work: Crossing Brooklyn Ferry
I Hear America Singing
I Sing the Body Electic
Leaves of Grass
O Captain! My Captain!
Out of the Cradle Endlessly Rocking
Song of Myself
Song of the Open Road
When Lilacs Last in the Dooryard Bloom'd
Whitmore, James: 5 actor
film: Above and Beyond (1952)
Black Like Me (1964)
Face of Fire (1959)
Give 'Em Hell, Harry! (1975)
The McConnell Story (1955)
Oklahoma! (1955)
Them! (1954)
The Undercover Man (1949)
Where the Red Fern Grows (1974)
Whitney: 3 Eli 4 peak 5 Blake, mount 7 Houston 8 mountain
invention: 3 gin
locale: 10 California
partner: 5 Pratt
__ Whitney Payson: 4 Joan
Whittaker: 5 Roger 8 Chambers
Whittier: 4 city, John, poet, town
locale: 10 California
Whittier, John Greenleaf: 4 poet
work: Barbara Frietchie
The Barefoot Boy
Ichabod
Maud Muller
Snow-Bound
whittle: 4 chip, mold, pare, trim 5 carve, model, shape, shave, slash 6 lessen, reduce, sculpt 7 curtail 8 decrease, diminish, wear away 9 sculpture
down: 4 pare, trim 5 erode 9 undermine
whittling material: 4 pine, wood 5 balsa
Whitty, May: 4 Dame 7 actress
film: Lassie Come Home (1943)
Mrs. Miniver (1942)
My Name Is Julia Ross (1945)
Night Must Fall (1937)
Whitworth: 5 Kathy 6 golfer
milieu: 5 links 6 course
org.: 4 LPGA
whiz: 3 ace, fly, hum, pro, run, zip 4 buzz, dart, flit, hiss, race, rush, whir, zoom 5 adept, brain, hurry, maven, mavin, smart, speed, swish, whirr, whisk, woosh 6 artist, expert, genius, hurtle, marvel, master, sizzle, sprint, whoosh 7 egghead, hotshot, old hand, prodigy, thinker 8 Einstein, highbrow, skillful, virtuoso 10 mastermind
at: 5 adept 6 adroit 7 skilled 8 skillful, talented 9 dexterous 10 proficient
gee ~: 4 gosh 5 golly
kid: 5 brain 6 dynamo, wizard 7 prodigy
no ~ kid: 5 dunce
whiz __: 3 kid
whiz-__: 4 bang
__ whiz!: 3 Gee
__ Whiz: 5 Cheez
whizzo: 3 def, rad 4 aces, A-one, boss, braw, cool, dece, fine, gear, keen, neat, nice, phat, tuff 5 dandy, ducky, grand, great, marvy, neato, nobby, prime, slick, super, swell 6 bang on, bang-up, bonzer, bosker, choice, divine, dreamy, far-out, gnarly, groovy, lovely, peachy, slap-up, spot on, superb, terrif, tiptop, unreal, wicked 7 amazing, awesome, capital, corking, perfect, ripping, skookum, stellar, sublime 8 dazzling, especial, eximious, fabulous, five-star, four-star, frabjous, glorious, heavenly, jim-dandy, slam-bang, smashing, splendid, standout, sterling, stickout, superior, terrific, top-level, topnotch, very good, wondrous 9 bodacious, Endsville, excellent, exemplary, exquisite, first-rate, high-grade, hunky-dory, marvelous, sollicker, top-flight, wonderful 10 first-class, hotsy-totsy, jack-a-dandy, out of sight, peachy-keen, phenomenal, remarkable, stupendous, super-duper
who: 7 pronoun
ender: 4 ever 6 soever
one ~ (suffix): 3 -ist
sayer: 3 owl
who's ~: 5 elite 7 society 8 register 9 directory
__ who?: 3 Sez 4 Says 5 Guess
Who __?: 4 is it 5 Cares
Who __ it?: 5 needs
Who __ I Turn To: 3 Can
Who __ kidding?: 3 am I
Who __ my purse...: 6 steals
Who __ Roger Rabbit: 6 Framed
Who __ that masked man?: 3 was
Who __ the Bomp: 3 Put
Who __ there?: 4 goes
Who __ to say?: 3 am I
Who __ Trust?: 5 Do You
Who __ Turn To: 4 Can I
Who __ You: 3 Are 5 Loves, Needs
Whoa!: 4 halt, stop
Whoa, __!: 6 Nellie
Who am __ say?: 3 I to
__ Who Came In..., The: 3 Spy
__ Who Came to Dinner, The: 3 Man
Who Can It Be Now? (1982 song)
artist: Men at Work
Who Can I Turn To (1964 song) artist: Tony Bennett
Who cares!: 6 so what 7 big deal
Who Cares composer: 8 Gershwin
Who composer: 4 Kern
Who Dat (1999 song)
artist: JT Money, Solé
Who Done It? (1942 film)
cast: Bud Abbott, Lou Costello
director: Erle C. Kenton
Who Do You Trust?: 8 game show
host: Johnny Carson
whodunit: 4 book, tale 5 genre, novel, prose, story 7 mystery 9 narrative
award: 5 Edgar
board game: 4 Clue
character: 6 butler
item: 4 body, clew, clue, plot 5 alibi, crime, twist 6 murder
name: 3 Rex 4 Erle 5 Queen, Stout 6 Agatha, Ellery 7 Gardner 8 Christie
whoever: 6 anyone, person 8 somebody
__ Who Fell to Earth, The: 3 Man
Who Framed Roger Rabbit (1988 film)
cast: Joanna Cassidy, Charles Fleischer, Bob Hoskins, Stubby Kaye, Christopher Lloyd
director: Robert Zemeckis
Who goes there?
asker: 5 guard 6 sentry
preceder: 4 halt
__! Who goes there?: 4 Halt
__ Who Had a Heart: 6 Anyone
Who Is Killing the Great Chefs of Europe? (1978 film)
cast: Jacqueline Bisset, Robert Morley, George Segal
director: Ted Kotcheff
Who Killed __ Robin?: 4 Cock
__ Who Knew Too Much, The: 3 Man
Who knows what ___...: 4 evil
whole: 3 all, lot, one, sum 4 A to Z, bulk, full, hale, mint, unit, well 5 every, gross, round, sound, total, uncut, unity, utter 6 corpus, entire, entity, intact, unhurt 7 healthy, jackpot, oneness, perfect, plenary 8 absolute, assembly, complete, entirety, finished, fullness, integral, livelong, organism, sum total, thorough, together, totality, unbroken, unharmed, unmarred 9 aggregate, inviolate, recovered, undamaged, undivided, uninjured, unreduced, unscathed, untouched 10 able-bodied, big picture, collective, everything, exhaustive, in one piece, opera omnia, unabridged, unimpaired, unlessened
alternative: 4 skim
as a ~: 6 en bloc, in full, in toto 7 en masse 9 in general 10 altogether
ball of wax: 3 all 5 total 8 entirety, sum total 9 aggregate 10 everything
bunch: 3 lot, ton 4 bevy, lots, many, raft, scad, slew 6 legion, myriad, oodles, umteen, untold 7 umpteen 8 umpsteen 9 countless
combining form: 3 hol-, pan- 4 holo-, pano-, pant-, toti- 5 panta-, panto- 7 integri-
ender: 4 sale, some 7 hearted
hog: 4 full 5 fully 7 flat out, in depth, totally 8 complete, entirely, from A to Z, in detail, thorough 9 extensive, inside out, up-and-down 10 completely, exhaustive, meticulous
make ~: 4 cure, heal, mend 5 right, treat 6 remedy, repair 7 correct, relieve, restore 8 medicate
nine yards: 4 A to Z 5 whole 8 entirety
on the ~: 5 in all 6 mainly, mostly 7 as a rule, at large, overall, usually 9 generally, in general, primarily 10 altogether, by and large
part of the ~: 4 item, unit 5 piece 6 member, sample 7 portion, section, segment 8 fraction
whole __: 3 hog 4 gale, milk, note, rest, step 5 blood, snipe 6 number, sister 7 brother
whole __ ball game: 3 new
whole __ yards, the: 4 nine
whole-__: 3 hog 4 time 5 grain, wheat 6 length, souled
__ whole: 3 as a 5 on the
Whole __ Loving: 5 Lotta
Whole __ World, A: 3 New
__ whole cloth: 5 out of
whole-grain: 5 bread
feature: 5 fiber
wholehearted: 4 real, true, warm 5 total 6 all-out, ardent, steady 7 devoted, earnest, fervent, genuine, serious, sincere 8 implicit 9 committed, dedicated, heartfelt, steadfast, undivided, unfeigned
wholeheartedness: 6 candor 7 honesty, probity 8 openness 9 frankness, integrity, sincerity
Whole Lot of Shakin' Going On (1957 song) artist: Jerry Lee Lewis
Whole Lotta Love (1969 song) artist: Led Zeppelin
Whole Lotta Loving (1958 song)
artist: Fats Domino
wholeness: 5 unity 9 integrity 10 perfection
whole new __ game: 4 ball
Whole New World, A (1993 song)
artist: Peabo Bryson, Regina Belle
Whole Nine Yards, The (2000 film)
cast: Rosanna Arquette, Michael Clarke Duncan, Natasha Henstridge, Matthew Perry, Bruce Willis
director: Jonathan Lynn
wholesale: 4 mass, sell 5 broad, price, total, utter 6 at cost, in bulk, market 7 overall 8 complete, outright, sweeping 9 extensive 10 commercial, in quantity, large-scale, widespread
quantity: 5 crate, gross 6 job lot
wholesaler: 6 dealer, jobber 8 merchant
wholesome: 3 fit 4 good, pure, safe 5 clean, moral, sound, sweet 6 chaste, decent, edible 7 ethical, healthy 8 clean-cut, edifying, hygienic, innocent, salutary, sanitary, virtuous 9 exemplary, favorable, healthful, righteous 10 beneficial, nourishing, nutritious, salubrious
name meaning ~: 6 Althea

Whole Town's Talking, The (1935 film)
cast: Jean Arthur, Wallace Ford, Edward G. Robinson
director: John Ford
Who let the ___ out?: 4 dogs
whole-wheat: 5 bread
...who lived in ___: 5 a shoe
Who'll Stop the Rain (1978 film)
cast: Michael Moriarty, Nick Nolte, Tuesday Weld
director: Karel Reisz
wholly: 3 all 4 only, well 5 fully, quite, right 6 bodily, flatly, in full, in toto, purely, simply, solely 7 cap-a-pie, en masse, totally, utterly 8 entirely, from A to Z 9 all the way, downright, every inch, expressly, like a book, out-and-out, perfectly, plenarily, to the hilt 10 absolutely, altogether, completely, positively, thoroughly, to the limit
Who Lost an American? author: Nelson Algren
___ Who Loved Cat Dancing, The: 3 Man
___ Who Loved Me, The: 3 Spy
Who loves ya, ___?: 4 baby
Who Loves You (1975 song) artist: Four Seasons
whom: 7 pronoun
ender: 4 ever 6 soever
Who, me?: 3 moi
whomp: 3 hit 4 blow, flog, rout, thud, whip 5 baste, pound, punch, smite, worst 6 defeat, hammer, larrup, thwack, wallop 7 trounce
___ Whom the Bell Tolls: 3 For
Who Needs You (1957 song) artist: Four Lads
whoop: 3 boo, cry 4 hoot, howl, jeer, yell 5 cheer, laugh, shout, yahoo 6 bellow, cry out, holler, hoorah, hooray, hurrah, hurray, outcry, scream, shriek, squawk, war cry 7 exclaim 9 battle cry 10 vociferate
it up: 4 riot, romp 5 caper, gloat, party, revel 6 frolic, gambol 7 carouse
whoop-___: 4 de-do 5 de-doo
___ whoop: 3 war
whoop-de-do: 3 ado 5 furor 7 revelry
whoopee: 3 yay 5 oh boy, wahoo 6 hooray, hot dog
make ~: 4 romp 5 revel 6 frolic, gambol 7 carouse
whoopee ___: 7 cushion
Whoopee! (1930 film)
cast: Eddie Cantor, Eleanor Hunt
___ Whoopee: 5 Makin'
whooper: 4 swan 5 crane
Whoopi: 8 Goldberg
disguise: 3 nun
whooping it up: 4 wild 5 noisy 7 raucous, riotous 9 clamorous 10 boisterous, disorderly, tumultuous, uproarious
Whoops!: 4 uh-oh, yipe 5 yikes, yipes 6 pardon 8 excuse me, pardon me
whoosh: 3 run 4 dart, rush, whiz 5 swish 6 hurtle 8 rustling
whop: 5 punch, thump 6 strike
whopper: 3 lie 4 lulu, tale 6 canard 9 falsehood, humdinger, mendacity
teller: 4 liar 6 fibber 7 deluder 8 deceiver
Whopper: 9 hamburger
part: 3 bun 4 mayo 5 patty, sauce 6 burger, pattie, pickle, tomato 7 ketchup, lettuce
rival: 6 Big Mac
whopping: 3 big 4 huge, vast 5 giant, great, hefty, jumbo, large 6 mighty 7 hulking, immense, mammoth, massive, sizable, titanic 8 colossal, enormous, gigantic, king-size, oversize, sizeable, towering 9 Herculean, humongous, monstrous, overlarge, whalelike 10 gargantuan, monumental, prodigious, stupendous, tremendous
Who Put the Bomp (1961 song) artist: Barry Mann
whorl: 4 coil, curl, eddy, loop 5 curve, helix, swirl 6 spiral 7 sinuate 9 corkscrew, sinuosity
combining form: 7 spondyl- 8 spondylo- 9 verticill-
whorled: 6 spiral 7 helical, sinuate 8 circular
whortleberry: 5 fruit
Who's ___ eating my porridge?: 4 been
Who's ___ Girl: 4 That
Who's ___ Now: 5 Sorry
Who's ___ of Virginia Woolf?: 6 Afraid
Who's ___ the Mint?: 7 Minding
Who's ___ Who: 6 Zoomin'
Who's Afraid of Virginia Woolf?: 4 film, play
author: Edward Albee
cast: Richard Burton, Sandy Dennis, George Segal, Elizabeth Taylor
director: Mike Nichols
___ Who's Coming to Dinner: 5 Guess
Whose ___ Is It Anyway?: 4 Life, Line
Whose Body? author: Dorothy Sayers
Whose Life Is It Anyway? (1981 film)
cast: John Cassavetes, Richard Dreyfuss, Christine Lahti
director: John Badham
Whose Line Is It Anyway? (ABC comedy) host: Drew Carey
whosever: 7 anyone's 8 anybody's
Whose woods these ___ think I know: 4 are I
Who's Holding Donna Now (1985 song) artist: DeBarge
Who Shot J.R.? series: 6 Dallas
___ Who Shot Liberty Valance, The: 3 Man
whosis: 5 do-dad, gismo, gizmo 6 doodad, gadget
Who's Johnny (1986 song) artist: DeBarge
Who Slew Auntie ___?: 3 Roo
Who's minding the ___?: 5 store
Who's Minding the Mint? (1967 film)
cast: Milton Berle, Jim Hutton, Dorothy Provine
director: Howard Morris
whoso: 6 anyone 7 anybody
whosoever: 6 anyone 7 anybody
Who's on ___?: 5 first
Who's Sorry Now (1958 song) artist: Connie Francis
___ Who's Talking: 4 Look
Who's That Girl (1987 song) artist: Madonna
Who's That Knocking at My Door? (1968 film)
cast: Zina Bethune, Anne Collette, Harvey Keitel
director: Martin Scorsese
Who's the Boss? (ABC sitcom)
cast: Tony Danza (Tony Micelli)
Katherine Helmond (Mona Robinson)
Judith Light (Angela Bower)
Alyssa Milano (Samantha Micelli)
Danny Pintauro (Jonathan Bower)
Who's there? reply: 5 It's me
who's who: 5 elite 7 society 8 register 9 directory
Who's Who entry: 3 bio
Who's Zoomin' Who (1985 song)
artist: Aretha Franklin
Who, The
members: Daltrey, Townshend, Entwistle, Moon
rock opera: Tommy, Quadrophenia
song: Happy Jack (1967)
I Can See for Miles (1967)
I'm Free (1969)
Magic Bus (1968)
Pinball Wizard (1969)
See Me, Feel Me (1970)
Squeeze Box (1976)
Who Are You (1978)
Won't Get Fooled Again (1971)
You Better You Bet (1981)
Who Wants to Be a Millionaire
host: 5 Regis 6 Vieira 7 Philbin
network: 3 ABC 5 ABC-TV
___ Who Wasn't There, The: 3 Man
Who was that ___ man?: 6 masked
Who Was That Lady? (1960 film)
cast: Tony Curtis, Janet Leigh, Dean Martin
director: George Sidney
Who Will You Run To (1987 song)
artist: Heart
___ Who Would Be King, The: 3 Man
whse. contents: 3 gds. 4 ctns., mdse.
box: 3 ctn.
whup: 4 beat, flog, lick 5 paste, spank 7 trounce
why: 5 query 6 motive, reason 7 grounds, purpose 9 rationale
cousin of ~: 3 how, who 4 what, when 5 where
Why ___ fall in love...: 5 can't I
Why ___ Love You?: 3 Do I
Why ___ thou forsaken me?: 4 hast
Why ___ We Be Friends?: 4 Can't
Why ___ woman be more like a man?: 5 can't a
Why Baby Why (1957 song) artist: Pat Boone
Why Can't I Touch You (1970 song)
artist: Ronnie Dyson
Why Can't This Be Love (1986 song)
artist: Van Halen
Why Can't We Be Friends? (1975 song) artist: War
whydah: 4 bird
Why Do Fools Fall in Love (song)
artist: Diana Ross, Frankie Lymon and the Teenagers, Gale Storm
Why Do I Love You? composer: 4 Kern
Why England Slept author: 3 JFK 7 Kennedy
whyfor: 6 motive, reason 9 rationale
Why Is There Air? comic: 5 Cosby
Why not?: 3 yes 4 let's, okay, sure
Why Not the Best? author: 6 Carter
why, oh, why ___?: 5 can't I
Why Shoot the Teacher? (1977 film)
cast: Bud Cort, Samantha Eggar
Why (song) artist: Frankie Avalon
artist: Donny Osmond
___ Why the Caged Bird Sings: 5 I Know
Why, the very ___!: 4 idea
WI
see Wisconsin
wicca: 5 magic 7 sorcery 10 white magic, witchcraft
Wichita: 4 city, town 5 tribe 6 Indian 7 Amerind
athletes: 8 Shockers
county: 8 Sedgwick
locale: 3 Kan. 6 Kansas
school: 3 WSU
town near ~: 4 Iola
Wichita Falls: 4 city, town
locale: 5 Texas
town near ~: 5 Olney
Wichita Lineman (1968 song) artist: Glen Campbell
composer: 4 Webb
Wichita State
athletes: 8 Shockers
locale: 6 Kansas
wick: 4 cord, fuse 7 draw off 8 draw away
surroundings: 3 wax 5 taper 6 candle 8 paraffin
wicked: 3 bad, def, ill, rad 4 aces, A-one, base, blue, boss, braw, cool, dark, dece, evil, fine, foul, gear, keen, mean, neat, nice, phat, tuff, ugly, vile 5 awful, cruel, dandy, ducky, grand, great, marvy, nasty, neato, nobby, prime, slick, spicy, super, swell, wrong 6 amoral, bang on, bang-up, bonzer, bosker, choice, divine, dreamy, far-out, gnarly, groovy, guilty, impish, little, lovely, malign, peachy, rotten, severe, slap-up, spicey, spot on, superb, terrif, tiptop, unholy, unreal, wanton, whizzo 7 amazing, awesome, capital, corking, corrupt, debased, demonic, heinous, hellish, immoral, low-down, naughty, parlous, perfect, profane, ripping, satanic, skookum, stellar, sublime, ungodly, vicious, wayward 8 daemonic, dazzling, depraved, devilish, diabolic, dreadful, especial, eximious, fabulous, fiendish, five-star, four-star, frabjous, glorious, heavenly, indecent, infamous, infernal, jim-dandy, perilous, shameful, slam-bang, smashing, spiteful, splendid, standout, sterling, stickout, superior, terrible, terrific, top-level, top-notch, very good, wondrous, wrongful 9 abandoned, atrocious, bodacious, dangerous, demonical, dissolute, egregious, Endsville, excellent, exemplary, exquisite, first-rate, hazardous, heartless, high-grade, hunky-dory, laborious, malicious, marvelous, miscreant, nefarious, satanical, shameless, sollicker, top-flight, unethical, wonderful 10 abominable, diabolical, first-class, hotsy-totsy, indelicate, inexpiable, iniquitous, jack-a-dandy, maleficent, malevolent, out of sight, outrageous, peachy-keen, pernicious, phenomenal, profligate, remarkable, scandalous, stupendous, super-duper, villainous
one: 5 beast, brute, demon, devil, fiend, knave 6 savage 7 dastard 9 barbarian
thing: 3 sin 4 evil, vice 5 crime 7 misdeed, offense 8 atrocity, iniquity, trespass 9 sacrilege 10 misconduct
Wicked ___ of the West: 5 Witch
Wicked Day, The author: Mary Stewart
Wicked Game (1991 song) artist: Chris Isaak
wickedness: 3 ill, sin 4 evil, vice 5 wrong 6 infamy 7 devilry, impiety, perfidy 8 atrocity, deviltry, ignominy, iniquity, villainy 9 depravity 10 corruption
Wicked Wasp of Twickenham: 4 Pope
wicker: 4 twig 5 osier 6 willow
ender: 4 work
expert: 5 caner
like ~: 4 wove 5 woven
product: 3 web 5 creel
Wicker: 3 Tom
Wicker Man, The (1973 film)
cast: Britt Ekland, Christopher Lee, Edward Woodward
director: Robin Hardy
wicket: 4 gate, hoop 7 ingress
cricket ~: 3 end
croquet ~: 4 hoop
ender: 6 keeper
material: 4 wire
topper: 4 bail
___ wicket: 6 double, single, sticky

Wickford Point author: J.P. Marquand
wickiup: 3 hut 4 tipi 5 tepee 6 teepee, wigwam
__ Widder Brown: 5 Young
wide: 3 big 4 full, open, vast 5 ample, baggy, beamy, broad, hippy, large, loose, roomy, squat, thick, wrong 6 astray, gaping 7 dilated, general 8 catholic, extended, far-flung, spacious, sweeping, tolerant 9 boundless, capacious, cavernous, expansive, extensive, inclusive, off-course, outspread, spread-out, universal 10 commodious, inaccurate, indefinite, large-scale, off the mark, voluminous
all wool and a yard ~: 4 real, true 6 trusty 7 genuine, sincere 8 constant, faithful, true-blue
berth: 4 room 6 leeway 7 license
combining form: 4 eury-
divergence: 3 gap 4 gulf 5 abyss
ender: 6 spread
far and ~: 6 afield 7 broadly, largely 10 everywhere
give a ~ berth: 4 shun 5 avoid, scorn 6 eschew 10 shrink from
look far and ~: 4 hunt 5 scour
make half as ~: 4 fold
of the mark: 3 off 5 amiss, wrong 6 faulty 7 in error, inexact 8 mistaken 9 erroneous, imprecise, off-target 10 inaccurate
open: 5 agape 6 gaping 9 unlimited 10 undefended, vulnerable
open ~: 4 gape, yawn
partner: 3 far
shoe: 2 EE 3 EEE 4 EEEE, six E, ten E 5 five E, nine E 6 eight E, seven E 7 eleven E, twelve E
starter: 4 city 5 state, store, world 6 county, double, nation, single 7 country 8 district
street: 3 ave. 4 blvd. 6 avenue 9 boulevard
wide __: 5 awake, world
wide __ mark: 5 of the
wide __ spaces: 4 open
wide-__: 4 eyed, open 5 awake 6 screen 7 ranging
wide-__ lens: 5 angle
wide-__ plane: 4 body
wide-awake: 4 wary 5 alert, aware 6 prompt 7 heads-up, wakeful 8 keen-eyed, on the job, vigilant, watchful 9 attentive, observant, on the ball 10 on one's toes
Wide Awake (1998 film)
cast: Joseph Cross, Dana Delany, Denis Leary
director: M. Night Shyamalan
__ wide berth to: 5 give a
wide-eyed: 4 agog, naif 5 agape, alert, naive 7 wakeful 9 unworldly
remark: 3 gee, wow 5 golly
Widefield: 4 city, town
locale: 8 Colorado
widen: 3 wax 4 grow, ream 5 add to, bloat, flare, swell 6 beef up, dilate, expand, extend, let out, open up, spread, unfold 7 augment, broaden, burgeon, develop, distend, enlarge, inflate, open out, ream out, stretch, thicken 8 bourgeon, escalate, heighten, increase, lengthen 9 branch out, spread out 10 liberalize
a hole: 4 ream
widened at the top: 5 evase
wideness: 5 scope 7 breadth 9 amplitude
__ wide net: 5 cast a
Wide Net, The author: Eudora Welty
widening: 6 growth, spread 8 increase 9 extension
wide of the __: 4 mark
wide-open: 5 agape, naked, risky 7 yawning 9 limitless
wide-ranging: 3 big 5 broad 7 blanket 8 far-flung
Wide Sargasso Sea author: Jean Rhys
__ Wide Shut: 4 Eyes
widespread: 3 big 4 rife, vast 5 broad, roomy, usual 6 common, public, ruling 7 current, diffuse, general, generic, popular, rampant, routine 8 epidemic, everyday, far-flung, frequent, ordinary, pandemic, spacious, sweeping 9 boundless, capacious, expansive, extensive, generical, pervasive, prevalent, universal, wholesale 10 epidemical
be ~: 5 reign 6 abound 7 prevail 8 dominate
__ wide swath: 4 cut a
wide vertical band in heraldry: 4 pale
__ Wide Web: 5 World
Wide World of Sports host: 5 McKay
widgeon: 4 bird, duck, fowl
relative: 4 smew, teal 5 eider, Pekin, Rouen, scaup 6 Cayuga, scoter 7 gadwall, mallard, pintail, pochard, redhead, sea duck 8 garganey, gray duck, mandarin, musk duck, oldsquaw, shoveler, surf duck, wood duck 9 black duck, broadbill, goldeneye, goosander, greenhead, merganser, ruddy duck, sprigtail 10 bufflehead, canvasback, surf scoter, tufted duck
widget: 5 do-dad, gismo, gizmo, thing 6 device, dingus, doodad, gadget 7 machine 9 doohickey
Widmark, Richard: 5 actor
film: The Alamo (1960)
The Bedford Incident (1965)
Cheyenne Autumn (1964)
Down to the Sea in Ships (1949)
The Frogmen (1951)
How the West Was Won (1962)
Judgment at Nuremberg (1961)
The Last Wagon (1956)
The Law and Jake Wade (1958)
Madigan (1968)
Murder on the Orient Express (1974)
No Way Out (1950)
Panic in the Streets (1950)
Pickup on South Street (1953)
A Prize of Gold (1955)
Run for the Sun (1956)
The Street With No Name (1948)
Take the High Ground (1953)
Time Limit (1957)
The Tunnel of Love (1958)
Warlock (1959)
When the Legends Die (1972)
Yellow Sky (1948)
Widnes: 4 city, town
locale: 7 England 8 Cheshire
__ widow: 4 golf 5 black
Widowers' Houses author: George Bernard Shaw
Widow for One Year, A author: John Irving
widow's __: 4 mite, peak, walk 5 cruse
__ Widow, The: 5 Merry 7 College
width: 2 AA, EE 3 AAA, EEE 4 EEEE, girt, size, span 5 girth, range, reach, scope 6 extent, length, spread 7 breadth, compass, expanse, measure 8 diameter, distance, latitude 9 amplitude, broadness, dimension, immensity, largeness, squatness, thickness 10 wiggle room
ender: 4 wise
having no ~: 4 one-D
length and ~: 4 area, size 5 scope, space 6 extent
length times ~: 4 area
shoe: 2 EE 3 AAA, EEE 4 AAAA, EEEE, six A, six B, six C, six D, six E, ten A, ten B, ten C, ten D, ten E 5 five A, five B, five C, five D, five E, nine A, nine B, nine C, nine D, nine E, six EE, ten EE 6 eight A, eight B, eight C, eight D, eight E, five EE, nine EE, seven A, seven B, seven C, seven D, seven E, six EEE, ten EEE 7 eight EE, eleven A, eleven B, eleven C, eleven D, eleven E, five EEE, nine EEE, seven EE, twelve A, twelve B, twelve C, twelve D, twelve E 8 eight EEE, eleven EE, seven EEE, twelve EE 9 eleven EEE, twelve EEE
starter: 4 band
typesetter: 2 em, en
wie __: 5 geht's
Wiebe, Rudy: 6 writer 8 Canadian
work: The Mad Trapper
Wiedersehen, auf: 3 bye 4 ciao, ta ta 5 adios, later 7 goodbye 8 farewell
Wieland, Christopher Martin: 6 German, writer
Wieland, Heinrich: 7 chemist 8 Nobelist
wield: 3 ply, use 4 have, hold, work 5 apply, exert 6 employ, handle 7 control, operate, possess, utilize 8 brandish, exercise, flourish, put to use 9 make use of 10 manipulate
wieldy: 5 handy, utile 6 useful 9 easy to use, practical 10 convenient, functional
Wieman, Carl: 8 Nobelist 9 physicist
Wien: 4 city, town 6 Vienna 7 Wilhelm
locale: 7 Austria
see also German
wiener: 4 meat 5 frank 6 hot dog
ender: 5 wurst
roast: 6 picnic 7 cookout 8 barbecue
topping: 5 kraut 10 sauerkraut
unit: 4 link
wrapping: 4 skin 6 casing
Wiener schnitzel base: 4 veal
Wienerwald: 3 mts. 4 Alps, mtns. 5 range
locale: 7 Austria
Wien, Wilhelm: 8 Nobelist 9 physicist
Wiesbaden: 3 spa 4 city, town
locale: 5 Hesse 7 Germany
Wieschaus, Eric: 8 Nobelist
Wiesel, Elie: 6 author, writer 8 Nobelist
work: The Accident
The Fifth Son
The Gates fo the Forest
Legends of Our Time
Night
One Generation After
Souls on Fire
The Testament
The Town Beyond the Wall
Wiesel, Torsten: 8 Nobelist
Wiesenthal: 5 Simon
Wiest, Dianne: 7 actress
film: the birdcage (1995)
Bullets Over Broadway (1994, AA)
Cookie (1989)
Edward Scissorhands (1990)
Footloose (1984)
Hannah and Her Sisters (1986, AA)
The Horse Whisperer (1998)
I Am Sam (2001)
Little Man Tate (1991)
Parenthood (1989)
The Purple Rose of Cairo (1985)
wife: 4 lady, mate 5 bride, woman 6 matron, missis, missus, spouse, the Mrs. 7 consort, partner 8 helpmate, helpmeet 9 companion, other half 10 better half, monogamist
former: 2 ex 8 divorcée
partner: 4 mate 5 hubby 7 husband
starter: 3 ale 4 fish, good 5 house
wear: 4 ring
__ wife had seven sacks...: 4 Each
Wife, Husband and Friend (1939 film)
cast: Binnie Barnes, Warner Baxter, Loretta Young
director: Gregory Ratoff
wifeless: 5 unwed 6 single 8 eligible, unwedded 9 unmarried 10 unattached
Wife of __: 4 Bath
__ Wife, The: 4 Hill 7 Bishop's, Country
wife-to-be: 7 fiancée 9 betrothed
Wifey author: Judy Blume
wig: 3 rug 4 hair 6 peruke, toupee 9 hairpiece, headpiece
cousin: 4 fall
ender: 3 wag
flip one's ~: 4 rage 5 freak 8 freak out
starter: 3 big, ear 4 peri
wearer: 5 clown 9 barrister
__ wig: 4 buzz 6 fright 7 scratch
wigan: 6 fabric 8 material
wigeon: 4 bird
__ Wiggily: 5 Uncle
wiggle: 3 wag 4 jerk, push, worm 5 slink, twist 6 jiggle, shimmy, squirm, twitch, writhe, zigzag
room: 4 play 5 space, width 6 leeway 7 freedom 8 latitude
wiggle __: 4 nail, room
Wigglesworth, Michael: 6 writer
work: The Day of Doom
wiggly: 6 fickle 7 mutable 8 slippery, unstable, unsteady, wavering 9 mercurial
__ Wiggs of the Cabbage Patch: 3 Mrs.
wiggy: 3 odd 5 flaky 8 crackers 9 eccentric
wight: 5 being, human 10 human being
Wight: 3 isl. 4 isle 6 island
resort: 5 Cowes
Wigner, Eugene: 8 Nobelist 9 physicist
wigwag: 4 wave 6 signal
wigwam: 4 tent 7 shelter
cousin: 4 tipi 5 tepee 6 teepee
like a ~: 5 conic 7 conical
Wil: 7 Shriner, Wheaton
Wilander: 4 Mats 5 Swede 7 netster 9 tennis pro
milieu: 5 court
Wilbert: 8 Harrison, Robinson
Wilbur: 4 Post 6 Wright 7 Richard
Wilbur, Richard: 4 poet
work: Things of This World
Wilby Conspiracy, The (1975 film)
cast: Michael Caine, Sidney Poitier, Nicol Williamson
director: Ralph Nelson
__ wilco: 5 roger
Wilcox: 4 Fred 5 Larry 7 Herbert
Wilcox, Fred M.: 8 director
film: Forbidden Planet (1956)
The Hills of Home (1948)
Lassie Come Home (1943)
The Secret Garden (1949)
Wilcoxon: 5 Henry
wild: 3 mad, rad 4 avid, camp, free, lush, nuts, rank, rash, rude, zany 5 crazy, eager, feral, giddy, manic, messy, noisy, rabid, rough, rowdy, wacky, windy 6 animal, choppy, crazed, far-out, fierce, hectic, hoiden, hoyden, lavish, madcap, native, raging, rakish, raving, remote, rugged, savage, stormy, unruly, untidy, wanton, whacky 7 berserk, bizarre, brutish, chaotic, coltish, escaped, flighty, foolish, frantic, furious, howling, intense, lawless, natural, overrun, raffish, rampant, riotous, runaway, unkempt, untamed, vicious, violent, wayward 8 barbaric, blustery, desert-

ed, desolate, ecstatic, freakish, frenzied, in a furor, maniacal, reckless, romantic, rowdyish, sporting, sportive, unbroken, uncurbed, unhinged, wasteful **9** barbarian, barbarous, delirious, dissolute, disturbed, fanatical, ferocious, foolhardy, grotesque, hot-headed, impetuous, imprudent, in a dither, inclement, last-ditch, luxuriant, neglected, overgrown, primitive, thrilling, turbulent, unbridled, unchecked, unimpeded, unrefined, wasteland, wrought-up **10** blustering, boisterous, disheveled, disordered, disorderly, distracted, hysterical, immoderate, incautious, indigenous, irrational, outlandish, outrageous, passionate, profligate, rebellious, self-willed, tumultuous, uncultured, unfettered, unpolished, unshackled, uproarious
about: **4** into **5** hot on **7** taken by
be ~ for: **4** like, love **5** adore **6** admire, revere **7** cherish, idolize, worship **8** hold dear, treasure
blue yonder: **3** sky **5** ether **6** aether
bunch: **3** mob **4** pack **5** horde
canine: **3** fox **4** wolf **5** dhole, dingo **6** coyote, jackal
card: **5** deuce, joker
cat: **4** eyra, lion, lynx, puma **5** civet, tiger **6** cougar, jaguar, ocelot **7** panther
combining form: **5** agrio-
ender: **3** cat **4** fire, fowl, life, wood **6** flower
equine: **3** ass **5** bronc, kiang **6** bronco, brumby, ladino **7** broncho
go ~: **4** flip **7** run amok **8** run amuck
make less ~: **4** tame **5** break **6** soften **7** harness **8** tone down
one: **4** brat **5** beast, raver, yahoo **6** animal
on the ~ side: **4** lewd, racy **5** bawdy, lurid **6** risqué, vulgar **8** immodest, off-color **10** indelicate
party: **5** blast **6** bustup **7** blowout
run ~: **4** rage, riot **7** rampage **8** cut loose **9** go berserk
running ~: **4** amok **5** amuck **7** haywire
sheep: **4** dall **5** argal, urial **6** argali
sow ~ oats: **3** sin **5** act up **7** carry on **9** misbehave
time: **4** toot **5** binge, spree **6** bender
wild __: **3** fig, man, oat, rye, yam **4** bean, boar, card, date, leek, oats, rice, rose, silk, type **5** brier, calla, goose, guess, olive, pansy, pitch, senna, thyme **6** carrot, celery, cherry, fennel, ginger, indigo, madder, orange, potato, rubber, turkey **7** apricot, lettuce, mustard, parsley, pumpkin, spinach, vanilla
wild-__: **4** eyed **6** headed
wild-__ chase: **5** goose
__ wild: **3** run **6** deuces **7** running
__-wild: **3** hog
Wild: **4** Earl
home: **9** Minnesota
org.: **3** NHL
rival: **4** Blue, King, Star **5** Bruin, Devil, Flame, Flyer, Oiler, Sabre, Shark **6** Canuck, Coyote, Ranger **7** Capital, Panther, Penguin, Red Wing, Senator **8** Canadien, Islander, Predator, Thrasher **9** Avalanche, Blackhawk, Hurricane, Lightning, Maple Leaf **10** Blue Jacket, Mighty Duck
sport: **6** hockey
Wild __: **3** One **4** Hunt, West **5** Night, River, Thing, World **6** Cherry, Horses, Rovers, Things, Weasel, Wheels **7** Kingdom, Weekend
Wild __ at Coole, The: **5** Swans
Wild __ Hickok: **4** Bill
Wild __ show: **4** West
Wild __, The: **3** One **4** Boys, Duck, Seed **5** Bunch, Geese, Swans
wild-and-__: **6** woolly
Wild Animals I Have Known author: **5** Seton
Wild Bill: **6** Hickok
wild blue yonder org.: **4** USAF
wild boar, name meaning: **6** Wilbur
Wild Boys, The (1984 song) artist: Duran Duran
Wild Bunch, The (1969 film)
cast: Ernest Borgnine, William Holden, Warren Oates, Edmond O'Brien, Robert Ryan
director: Sam Peckinpah
wildcat: **4** eyra, lynx **6** animal, ocelot **7** illegal **9** speculate **10** prohibited
concern: **3** oil **4** well
wildcat __: **4** bank **6** strike
Wildcat: **3** car **4** auto **5** Buick
Wildcats: **3** KSU **9** Villanova
Wildcats (1986 film)
cast: Goldie Hawn, Swoosie Kurtz, Nipsey Russell
director: Michael Ritchie
Wild Cherry song: Play That Funky Music (1976)
Wild Duck, The author: **5** Ibsen
Wilde: **3** Kim, Ted **5** Oscar **6** Cornel
Wild, Earl: **7** pianist
wildebeest: **3** gnu **6** animal **8** antelope
hunter: **4** lion
relative: **3** kob **4** guib, kudu, oryx, puku, topi **5** addax, bongo, chiru, eland, goral, korin, nyala, oribi, saiga, serow **6** chammy, dik-dik, duiker, impala, koodoo, lechwe, nilgai, rhebok, shammy, shamoy **7** blaubok, blesbok, chamois, defassa, gazelle, gemsbok, gerenuk, grysbok, nylghai, nylghau, sassaby **8** blesbuck, bontebok, bushbuck, gemsbuck, reedbuck, steenbok, steinbok **9** blackbuck, pronghorn, sitatunga, springbok, waterbuck **10** hartebeest
Wilde, Cornel: **5** actor
film: Beach Red (1967)
The Big Combo (1955)
Forever Amber (1947)
The Greatest Show on Earth (1952)
Leave Her to Heaven (1945)
Life Begins at Eight-Thirty (1942)
The Naked Prey (1966)
Road House (1948)
Shockproof (1949)
A Thousand and One Nights (1945)
Wilde, Oscar: **3** wit **5** Irish **6** author **10** playwright
work: The Ballad of Reading Gaol
De Profundis
The Happy Prince and Other Tales
An Ideal Husband
The Importance of Being Earnest
Lady Windermere's Fan
The Picture of Dorian Gray
Salomé
A Woman of No Importance
Wilder: **4** Alec, Gene **5** Billy **6** Robert **7** Matthew **8** Thornton
Wilder, Billy: **8** director
film: The Apartment (1960, AA)
Avanti! (1972)
The Big Carnival (1951)
Buddy Buddy (1981)
Double Indemnity (1944)
Five Graves to Cairo (1943)
A Foreign Affair (1948)
The Fortune Cookie (1966)
The Front Page (1974)
Irma la Douce (1963)
Kiss Me, Stupid (1964)
The Lost Weekend (1945, AA)
Love in the Afternoon (1957)
The Major and the Minor (1942)
One, Two, Three (1961)
The Private Life of Sherlock Holmes (1970)
Sabrina (1954)
The Seven Year Itch (1955)
Some Like It Hot (1959)
The Spirit of St. Louis (1957)
Stalag 17 (1953)
Sunset Blvd. (1950)
Witness for the Prosecution (1957)
Wilder, Gene: **5** actor
film: Blazing Saddles (1974)
The Frisco Kid (1979)
The Producers (1968)
Quackser Fortune ... (1970)
Silver Streak (1976)
Start the Revolution Without Me (1970)
Stir Crazy (1980)
Willy Wonka... (1971)
The Woman in Red (1984)
Young Frankenstein (1974)
spouse: Gilda Radner
wilderness: **4** bush **5** waste, woods **6** desert, forest, jungle, sticks **7** barrens, outback **8** badlands **9** boondocks, confusion
home: **4** camp
outing: **4** hike, trek
path: **5** trace, trail
wilderness __: **4** area
Wilderness Road blazer: **5** Boone
Wilderness were Paradise __!: **4** enow
Wilder, Thornton: **6** author, writer **10** playwright
work: The Bridge of San Luis Rey
The Eighth Day
The Ides of March
The Matchmaker
Our Town
The Skin of Our Teeth
Theophilus North
wild-eyed: **3** mad **4** avid, keen **5** eager, manic, rabid **6** ardent, crazed, fervid, gung-ho, raging **7** devoted, fervent, intense, violent, zealous **8** frenetic, frenzied, maniacal, spirited **9** ambitious, delirious, fanatical **10** hysterical, infuriated, passionate
wildfire: **5** blaze **6** flames
like ~: **3** PDQ **4** fast **5** apace **6** presto **7** fleetly, hastily, quickly, rapidly, swiftly **8** in a flash, in a jiffy, in no time, pell-mell, speedily **9** forthwith, hurriedly, instantly, posthaste
Wildfire (1975 song) artist: Michael Murphey
Wildfire author: Zane Grey
wildflower: **5** bluet, daisy **6** lupine
site: **3** lea, ley **6** meadow
Wildflowers (1999 film)
cast: Tomas Arana, Clea DuVall, Daryl Hannah, Eric Roberts
Wild Geese, The author: Mori Ögai
wild-goose __: **5** chase
Wild Hearts Can't Be Broken (1991 film)
cast: Gabrielle Anwar, Cliff Robertson
director: Steve Miner
Wild Horse Mesa author: Zane Grey
Wild Horses (1971 song) artist: Rolling Stones
Wild Horses author: Dick Francis
wilding: **5** plant
Wilding, Michael spouse: Elizabeth Taylor
Wild in the Country (1961 film)
cast: Hope Lange, Millie Perkins, Elvis Presley, Tuesday Weld
director: Philip Dunne
Wild Kingdom (NBC) host: Marlin Perkins
wildlife: **5** fauna **6** beasts **7** animals
home: **4** nest **9** sanctuary
wildly: **4** amok **5** amuck, madly **7** like mad **8** insanely **9** fervently, like crazy
wildness: **6** tumult **7** abandon, license **8** ferocity, violence **9** looseness, vehemence
consequence of ~: **4** walk
Wild Night (song) artist: John Cougar Mellencamp, Van Morrison
__ wild oats: **3** sow
Wild One (1960 song) artist: Bobby Rydell
Wild One, The (1954 film)
cast: Marlon Brando, Robert Keith, Mary Murphy
director: Laslo Benedek
Wild River (1960 film)
cast: Montgomery Clift, Lee Remick, Jo Van Fleet
director: Elia Kazan
__ Wild Rose: **3** To a
Wild Rovers (1971 film)
cast: William Holden, Karl Malden, Ryan O'Neal
director: Blake Edwards
wilds: **4** bush **5** waste **6** desert, forest, jungle, sticks **7** barrens, outback **8** badlands **9** backwater, boondocks **10** hinterland
Wildside (1991 song) artist: Marky Mark and the Funky Bunch
Wildspitze's region: **5** Tirol, Tyrol
Wild Strawberries (1957 film)
cast: Bibi Andersson, Victor Sjostrom, Ingrid Thulin
director: Ingmar Bergman
Wild Swans at Coole, The author: William Butler Yeats
wild sweet __: **6** potato **7** william
wild-tasting: **4** gamy **5** gamey
__ Wild, The: **5** River **6** Joker's
Wild Things (1998 film)
cast: Kevin Bacon, Neve Campbell, Matt Dillon, Theresa Russell
director: John McNaughton
Wild Thing (song) artist: Troggs
artist: Tone Loc
wild turkey: **4** fowl
relative: **5** poult, quail, snipe **6** chukar, grouse, peahen **7** peacock, peafowl **8** curassow, moorfowl, pheasant, woodcock **9** partridge **10** guinea fowl, jungle fowl
Wild West show: **5** rodeo
Wild Wild West (1999 film)
cast: Kenneth Branagh, Salma Hayek, Kevin Kline, Will Smith
director: Barry Sonnenfeld
Wild Wild West, The (CBS western)
cast: Robert Conrad (James West)
Michael Dunn (Miguelito Loveless)
Ross Martin (Artemus Gordon)
wildwood: **6** forest **10** timberland
Wildwood: **4** city, town
locale: **8** Missouri **9** New Jersey
Wildwood Weed (1974 song) artist: Jim Stafford
wile: **3** art **4** coax, lure, ploy, ruse, trap **5** dodge, feint, shift, trick **6** cajole, deceit, device, dupery, entice, gambit **7** beguile, finesse, gimmick **8** artifice, intrigue, maneuver, pretense **9** chicanery, deception, duplicity, imposture, stratagem **10** subterfuge
Wile E. __: **6** Coyote
wiles: **3** art **5** craft, guile **7** cunning, knavery, slyness **8** foxiness **9** chicanery **10** artfulness, shrewdness
Wiley: **4** Post **6** Harvey
Wilford: **7** Brimley

Wilfred: 4 Owen 7 Jackson
Wilfrid: 5 Blunt, Sheed 9 Hyde-White, Pelletier
Wilhelm: 4 Hoyt, Wien 5 Grimm, Raabe, Wundt 6 Heinse 7 Ostwald, Röntgen, Von Opel 8 Leibnitz, Roentgen
in English: 7 William
Wilhelm ___: 4 Tell 7 Meister
Wilhelm, Hoyt: 6 hurler 7 pitcher
Wilhelmshaven: 4 port
locale: 6 Saxony 7 Germany
Wilhelm Tell author: Friedrich von Schiller
wiliness: 3 art 5 craft, guile
Wilke: 4 font 8 typeface
Wilkens, Lenny
milieu: 5 court
org.: 3 NBA
sport: 10 basketball
Wilkes-Barre: 4 city, town
locale: 4 Penn.
___ Wilkes Booth: 4 John
Wilkie: 7 Collins
Wilkins: 3 Roy 7 Maurice 8 Micawber
Wilkinsburg: 4 city, town
locale: 4 Penn.
Wilkins, Maurice: 8 Nobelist
Wilkinson, Geoffrey: 7 chemist 8 Nobelist
will: 3 aim, opt 4 give, urge, want, wish, word 5 crave, drive, endow, fancy, heart, leave, moxie, nerve, paper, pluck, shall 6 animus, choose, decree, demand, desire, intend, intent, legacy, liking, ordain, pass on, please, spirit 7 bequest, craving, longing, passion, probate, purpose, resolve 8 ambition, appetite, backbone, bequeath, bestowal, decision, firmness, hand down, pleasure, volition, yearning 9 endurance, hankering, hardiness, intention, testament 10 discipline, insistence, preference, resolution
against one's ~: 8 forcibly
at ~: 6 freely 7 anytime 8 whenever
bend to one's ~: 8 dominate, override, overrule
combining form: 5 -bulia
create good ~: 6 endear
divine ~: 4 fate 5 karma 6 kismet
ender: 5 power
exert one's ~: 3 opt 6 choose, select
free ~: 6 choice, option 8 volition
good ~: 5 asset, unity 7 harmony 8 kindness 9 readiness, tolerance 10 friendship
ill ~: 4 hate 5 odium, spite, venom 6 animus, enmity, grudge, hatred, malice, rancor 8 acrimony, aversion, bad blood 9 animosity, antipathy, hostility 10 antagonism, resentment
I ~ not: 3 nah, naw, nay, nix, non 4 nein, nope, nyet, uh-uh 5 ixnay, never, no how, no way 6 no deal, noways, nowise 8 forget it, negative, negatory 9 by no means, fat chance 10 count me out, thumbs down
partner: 3 way
power: 5 force, spine 6 desire 8 decision
starter: 4 free, good
subject: 4 heir 6 estate, legacy 7 bequest
(to): 5 leave 8 bequeath
to win: 6 fervor 8 ambition 9 obsession
will-___-wisp: 4 o'-the
___ will: 3 ill 4 free
___-will: 4 poor, self
Will: 4 Geer, Hays, Weng 5 Cuppy, Smith 6 Durant, George, Patton, Rogers, Shortz 7 Kellogg, Sampson 8 Hutchins
wife: 4 Anne
Will ___ Love Me Tomorrow: 3 You
Willa: 6 Cather
Willamette: 5 river
city on the ~: 5 Salem 6 Eugene 8 Portland
locale: 6 Oregon
University site: 5 Salem
Willard: 3 rat 4 Emma, Espy, Jess 5 Libby, Scott 6 Motley 7 Frances
sequel: 3 Ben
Willard, Jess: 3 pug 5 boxer
milieu: 4 ring
___ Will Be: 4 This
___ will be done: 3 thy
will be in Spanish: 4 será
___ will dwell...: 4 and I
___-willed: 4 weak 6 strong
Willem: 5 Dafoe 7 Barents 8 de Sitter 9 de Kooning, Einthoven
willemite: 3 ore 7 mineral
Willemstad: 4 port
locale: 7 Curaçao
willet: 4 bird
___ Will Find a Way: 4 Love
willful: 5 meant, onery 6 dogged, mulish, ornery, unruly, wanton 7 adamant, froward, naughty, piggish, planned, studied, wayward, witting 8 indocile, intended, obdurate, perverse, stubborn 9 arbitrary, conscious, fractious, hard-nosed, obstinate, pigheaded, voluntary 10 bullheaded, considered, deliberate, determined, headstrong, inflexible, persistent, preplanned, purposeful, refractory, unprompted, unyielding, volitional
willfulness: 4 grit, guts 5 moxie, pluck, spunk 7 courage, resolve 8 tenacity 9 assiduity, endurance 10 confidence, doggedness
Will & Grace (NBC sitcom)
cast: Sean Hayes (Jack McFarland)
Eric McCormack (Will Truman)
Debra Messing (Grace Adler)
Megan Mullally (Karen Walker)
___ Will Hunting: 4 Good
___ william: 5 sweet
William: 4 Boyd, Hurt, Inge, Katt, Kidd, Mayo, Penn, Pitt, Roth, Tell 5 Beebe, Blake, Bligh, Bragg, Casey, Clark, Eythe, Hanna, James, Marcy, Paley, Parry, saint, Simms, Stein, Wyler, Yeats 6 Baffin, Bendix, Boeing, Bolcom, Castle, Conrad, Cowper, Cremer, Devane, Dunbar, Empson, Farnum, Fowler, Gaddis, Gaines, Gargan, Gaxton, Gibson, Halsey, Harris, Harvey, Henley, Hickey, Holden, Hopper, Jenney, Kapell, Kelvin, Levitt, Morris, Morton, Murphy, Perkin, Plomer, Powell, Ramsay, Rowley, Safire, Sansom, Seward, Sharpe, Shirer, Styron, Talman, Warren 7 Baldwin, Brennan, Buckley, Cobbett, Collins, Crookes, Dampier, Daniels, Douglas, Frawley, Giauque, Golding, Goldman, Hazlitt, Hewlett, Hogarth, Huggins, Kennedy, Lederer, Painter, Saroyan, Shatner, Sherman, Thomson, Vickrey, Wellman, Wrigley 8 Atherton, Bradford, Brewster, Carleton, Congreve, Demarest, DeVaughn, Dieterle, Faulkner, Friedkin, Herschel, Keighley, Kunstler, Lipscomb, McKinley, Phillips, Proxmire, Ragsdale, Shockley, Stafford, Steinitz 9 Gladstone, Rehnquist, Steinberg, Thackeray, Whitehead, Wycherley 10 Blackstone, Manchester, Wordsworth
in French: 9 Guillaume
in German: 7 Wilhelm
in Irish: 4 Liam
in Italian: 9 Guglielmo
in Spanish: 9 Guillermo
of Orange foe: 6 De Witt
sweet ~: 4 pink 5 plant 6 flower
to Charles: 3 son
William ___: 4 Tell 6 of Sens, Wilson
William ___ Benét: 4 Rose
William ___ Blatty: 5 Peter
William ___ Bryan: 8 Jennings
William ___ Bryant: 6 Cullen
William ___ Garrison: 5 Lloyd
William ___ Gladstone: 5 Ewart
William ___ Harrison: 5 Henry
William ___ Hearst: 8 Randolph
William ___ Howells: 4 Dean
William ___ Sherman: 8 Tecumseh
William ___ Taft: 6 Howard
William ___ Thackeray: 9 Makepeace
William ___ Williams: 6 Carlos
William ___ Yeats: 6 Butler
___ William: 5 sweet
William and ___: 4 Mary
William Butler ___: 5 Yeats
William Carlos ___: 8 Williams
William Cullen ___: 6 Bryant
William Dean ___: 7 Howells
William F. ___: 4 Cody
William F. ___ Jr.: 7 Buckley
William H. ___: 4 Gass, Macy
William Henry ___: 8 Harrison
William Howard ___: 4 Taft
William III: 4 king
house: 6 Orange
successor: 4 Anne
William IV, to Victoria: 5 uncle
William Jennings ___: 5 Bryan
William L. ___: 6 Shirer
William Lloyd ___: 8 Garrison
William Makepeace ___: 9 Thackeray
William O. ___: 7 Douglas
William of ___: 4 Sens 5 Occam 6 Ockham, Orange 10 Malmesbury
William of Baskerville creator: 3 Eco
William of Malmesbury: 6 writer 7 British
work: Chronicles of the Kings of England
William Peter ___: 6 Blatty
William Randolph ___: 6 Hearst
William Ratcliff composer: 3 Cui
William Rose ___: 5 Benét
Williams: 3 Don, Guy, Hal, Joe, Ted 4 Amir, Andy, Cara, Hank, Jody, John, Otis, Paul, Remo 5 Anson, Barry, Betty, Billy, Brian, Cindy, Cynda, Danny, Emlyn, Grant, Kelli, Mason, Robin, Roger, Treat, Venus 6 Ashley, Bernie, Cootie, Esther, JoBeth, Montel, Serena 7 Charles, Deniece, Maurice, Vanessa 8 Kimberly, Michelle 9 Tennessee
ender: 4 burg, port
___ Williams: 4 Remo 7 Carbine
___-Williams: 7 Sherwin
William S. ___: 4 Hart 7 Gilbert, Knowles 9 Burroughs
Williams and the Zodiacs, Maurice
song: Stay (1960)
Williams, Andy
song: Are You Sincere (1958)
Butterfly (1957)
Canadian Sunset (1956)
Can't Get Used to Losing You (1963)
Days of Wine and Roses (1963)
Dear Heart (1964)
The Hawaiian Wedding Song (Ke Kali Nei Au) (1959)
I Like Your Kind of Love (1956)
Lonely Street (1959)
Love Story (1971)
On the Street Where You Live (1964)
The Village of St. Bernadette (1959)
Williams, Bernie sport: 8 baseball
Williams, Betty: 8 Nobelist
Williams, Billy: 3 Cub 10 outfielder
Williams, Billy Dee: 5 actor
film: The Bingo Long Traveling All-Stars & Motor Kings (1976)
The Empire Strikes Back (1980)
Hit! (1973)
Lady Sings the Blues (1972)
Nighthawks (1981)
Return of the Jedi (1983)
The Visit (2000)
Williams, Charles: 6 writer 7 British
work: All Hallows' Eve
Descent into Hell
Williams, Cindy: 7 actress
film: American Graffiti (1973)
Gas-s-s-s (1970)
TV: Laverne & Shirley
Williams, Deniece
song: It's Gonna Take a Miracle (1982)
Let's Hear It for the Boy (1984)
Too Much, Too Little, Too Late (1978)
Williams, Emlyn: 5 Welsh 6 author, writer
work: The Corn Is Green
Williams, Esther: 7 actress, swimmer
film: Bathing Beauty (1944)
Dangerous When Wet (1953)
Easy to Love (1953)
Easy to Wed (1946)
Jupiter's Darling (1955)
Million Dollar Mermaid (1952)
Neptune's Daughter (1949)
On an Island With You (1948)
Take Me Out to the Ball Game (1949)
This Time for Keeps (1947)
spouse: Fernando Lamas
___ Williams III: 8 Clarence
Williams, JoBeth: 7 actress
film: The Big Chill (1983)
Desert Bloom (1986)
Memories of Me (1988)
Poltergeist (1982)
Teachers (1984)
Williams, Jody: 8 Nobelist
Williams, John: 6 writer 8 composer 9 conductor
film score: The Accidental Tourist
Amistad
Born on the Fourth of July
Close Encounters of the Third Kind
The Empire Strikes Back
E.T. The Extra-Terrestrial
Harry Potter and the Sorcerer's Stone
Home Alone
Jaws
Jurassic Park
Raiders of the Lost Ark
Return of the Jedi
Saving Private Ryan
Schindler's List
Star Wars
Superman
The Witches of Eastwick
Williams, Mason song: Classical Gas (1968)
Williams, Michelle: 7 actress
film: Dick (1999)
Halloween H20: 20 Years Later (1998)
TV: Dawson's Creek
Williamson: 4 Jack, peak 5 Kevin, mount, Nicol 8 mountain
locale: 10 California
Williamson, Nicol: 5 actor
film: Black Widow (1987)

The Bofors Gun (1968)
Excalibur (1981)
The Seven-Per-Cent Solution (1976)
The Wilby Conspiracy (1975)
__ William Sound: 6 Prince
Williamsport: 4 city, town
locale: 4 Penn. 5 Penna.
Williams, Robin: 5 actor 8 comedian
film: Awakenings (1990)
The Best of Times (1986)
Bicentennial Man (1999)
The birdcage (1995)
Cadillac Man (1990)
Dead Poets Society (1989)
Death to Smoochy (2002)
The Fisher King (1991)
Good Morning, Vietnam (1987)
Good Will Hunting (1997, AA)
Hook (1991)
Insomnia (2002)
Jack (1996)
Jakob the Liar (1999)
Jumanji (1995)
Moscow on the Hudson (1984)
Mrs. Doubtfire (1993)
One Hour Photo (2002)
Patch Adams (1998)
Popeye (1980)
Seize the Day (1986)
Toys (1992)
What Dreams May Come (1998)
The World According to Garp (1982)
film voice: Aladdin (1992)
forte: 5 ad-lib
role: 5 genie
TV: Mork & Mindy
Williams, Roger: 7 pianist
song: Autumn Leaves (1955)
Born Free (1966)
Near You (1958)
Williams, Serena: 7 netster 9 tennis pro
milieu: 5 court
sister: 5 Venus
Williams, Ted: 6 Red Sox 10 outfielder
Williams, Tennessee: 10 playwright
work: Battle of Angels
Camino Real
Cat on a Hot Tin Roof
Clothes for a Summer Hotel
The Eccentricities of a Nightingale
Eight Mortal Ladies Possessed
The Glass Menagerie
Hard Candy
In the Bar of a Tokyo Hotel
The Knightly Quest
A Lovely Day for Creve Coeur
The Milk Train Doesn't Stop Here Anymore
The Night of the Iguana
Orpheus Descending
Period of Adjustment
The Roman Spring of Mrs. Stone
The Rose Tattoo
The Seven Descents of Myrtle
Small Craft Warnings
Something Unspoken
A Streetcar Named Desire
Suddenly Last Summer
Summer and Smoke
Sweet Bird of Youth
Where I Live
Williams, Vanessa: 6 singer 7 actress
film: The Adventures of Elmo in Grouchland (1999)
Dance With Me (1998)
Eraser (1996)
Shaft (2000)
song: Colors of the Wind (1995)
Dreamin' (1989)
Love Is (1993)
Save the Best for Last (1992)
Williams, Venus: 7 netster 9 tennis pro
milieu: 5 court
sister: 6 Serena
__ William's War: 4 King
Williams, William Carlos: 4 poet
work: Between Walls
Paterson
Queen-Anne's-Lace
The Red Wheelbarrow
Smell!
This Is Just to Say
To a Poor Old Woman
Young Sycamore
William Tecumseh __: 7 Sherman
William Tell: 5 opera
composer: 7 Rossini
song: 4 aria
William the Conqueror: 4 king 6 Norman
daughter of ~: 5 Adela
son of ~: 6 Henry I
William, Warren: 5 actor
film: Cleopatra (1934)
Employees' Entrance (1933)
Go West, Young Man (1936)
Lady for a Day (1933)
The Lone Wolf Spy Hunt (1939)
The Man in the Iron Mask (1939)
The Mouthpiece (1932)
Skyscraper Souls (1932)
Three on a Match (1932)
Upperworld (1934)
William Wilson author: Edgar Allan Poe
__ Will I Be Loved: 4 When
Willie: 2 GI 3 Pep 4 Mays 5 Aames, McGee, Stark 6 Keeler, Lanier, Morris, Nelson, Sutton 7 McCovey 8 Stargell 9 Shoemaker
Willie and Phil (1980 film)
cast: Margot Kidder, Michael Ontkean, Ray Sharkey
director: Paul Mazursky
willies: 4 fear 6 shakes 7 anxiety, fidgets, jitters, shivers
__ Willie Winkie: 3 Wee
__ Will I Know: 3 How
willing: 4 game, glad, life 5 can-do, eager, prone, ready 6 prompt 7 content, dutiful, pleased 8 amenable, cheerful, desirous, disposed, gracious, inclined, obedient, prepared, reliable, unforced, yielding 9 agreeable, compliant, energetic, in the mood, tractable 10 consenting, submissive
is ~ to: 5 would
more than ~: 4 avid, keen 5 eager
one: 5 taker
partner: 4 able 5 ready
to listen: 4 fair, open 8 amenable, flexible 9 receptive
__ willing, and able: 5 ready
Willingboro: 4 city, town
locale: 9 New Jersey
Willingham: 5 Noble 6 Calder
Willingham, Calder: 6 writer
work: Eternal Fire
Willingham, Noble: 5 actor
film: City Slickers (1991)
The Last Boy Scout (1991)
TV: Walker, Texas Ranger
willingly: 3 yes 4 lief 5 lieve 6 gladly, openly, rather 7 happily, readily 8 by choice 9 agreeably, favorably
Willis: 4 Bill, Lamb, Reed 5 Bruce, Chuck
Willis, Bruce: 5 actor
film: Armageddon (1998)
Bandits (2001)
Billy Bathgate (1991)
The Bonfire of the Vanities (1990)
Death Becomes Her (1992)
Die Hard (1988)
Die Hard 2 (1990)
Die Hard With a Vengeance (1995)
The Fifth Element (1997)
Hart's War (2002)
In Country (1989)
The Jackal (1997)
The Last Boy Scout (1991)
Mercury Rising (1998)
Nobody's Fool (1994)
The Siege (1998)
The Sixth Sense (1999)
Sunset (1988)
Twelve Monkeys (1995)
The Whole Nine Yards (2000)
spouse: Demi Moore
TV: Moonlighting
Willis, Chuck
song: C.C. Rider (1957)
What Am I Living For (1958)
Will It Go Round in Circles (1973 song) artist: Billy Preston
Will it play in __?: 6 Peoria
williwaw: 4 wind
Willkie: 7 Wendell
will-o'-the-wisp: 5 plant
locale: 3 fen 5 marsh, swamp
Willoughby: 4 city, town
locale: 4 Ohio
willow: 4 itea, tree 5 osier, shrub
flower: 5 ament 6 catkin
tree: 4 itea 5 osier 6 poplar
twig: 5 withe
willow __: 3 oak 4 herb 7 pattern, warbler
__ willow: 5 pussy, water 7 diamond, weeping
Willow (1988 film)
cast: Warwick Davis, Val Kilmer, Joanne Whalley
director: Ron Howard
Willow __ for Me: 4 Weep
Willowbrook: 4 city, town
locale: 10 California
__ Willowes: 5 Lolly
Willow Tree artist: 4 Erté
willowy: 4 lank, lean, slim, tall, thin, trim, wiry 5 lanky, leggy, lithe, spare 6 dainty, gangly, limber, lissom, skinny, slight, slinky, supple, svelte, twiggy 7 gracile, lissome, scraggy, scrawny, slender, spidery, sylphic 8 gangling, graceful 9 lithesome, sylphlike 10 long-legged
Will Penny (1968 film)
cast: Joan Hackett, Charlton Heston, Donald Pleasence
director: Tom Gries
willpower: 4 grit 5 drive, spine 6 spirit 7 resolve 8 backbone, firmness, strength 10 discipline, resolution
Will Rogers Follies prop: 5 lasso 6 lariat
Wills: 3 Bob 4 Mark 5 Chill, Helen, Maury
__ Will Say We're in Love: 6 People
__ Wills Moody: 5 Helen
Willson, Meredith: 8 composer
score: The Music Man, The Unsinkable Molly Brown
Willstötter, Richard: 7 chemist 8 Nobelist
Will Success Spoil Rock Hunter? (1957 film)
cast: Betsy Drake, Jayne Mansfield, Tony Randall
director: Frank Tashlin
Will, The author: James M. Barrie
willy-__: 5 nilly
Willy: 4 orca 5 Loman, whale, Wonka 6 Brandt
son: 4 Biff
__ Willy: 4 Free 6 Little
willy-nilly: 6 random 7 aimless, erratic, offhand 8 pell-mell, reckless, slapdash, slipshod 9 arbitrary, desultory, haphazard, hit-or-miss, irregular
Will You Be There (1993 song) artist: Michael Jackson
Will You Love Me Tomorrow (1960 song) artist: Shirelles
Will You Still Love Me? (1986 song) artist: Chicago
Willys: 3 car 4 auto 10 automobile
model: 3 Ace 4 Aero 6 Knight 7 Bermuda 8 Aero-Lark, Americar, Overland 10 Aero-Falcon
Willys-Knight contemporary: 3 Reo
Willy Wonka... (1971 film)
cast: Jack Albertson, Peter Ostrum, Gene Wilder
director: Mel Stuart
Wilma: 7 Rudolph 10 Flintstone
husband: 4 Fred
Wilmette: 4 city, town
locale: 8 Illinois
Wilmington: 4 city, town
locale: 8 Delaware
Wilmut: 3 Ian
Wilshire 5000: 5 index
Wilson: 2 Al 3 Ann, Don 4 Bill, Carl, city, Earl, Flip, Hack, Hugh, Luke, Mara, Mary, Owen, peak, Peta, Pete, Rita, town, Trey 5 Angus, Brian, Cindy, Colin, Ethel, Gahan, Larry, Marie, mount, Nancy, Scott, Sloan 6 August, Demond, Dennis, Dooley, Edmund, Harold, Harris, Jackie, Mizner, Mookie, Robert 7 Charles, Kenneth, Lanford, Pickett, Woodrow 8 mountain
locale: 7 Rockies 8 Colorado 10 California
Wilson (1944 film)
cast: Charles Coburn, Geraldine Fitzgerald, Cedric Hardwicke, Alexander Knox, Thomas Mitchell, Vincent Price
director: Henry King
Wilson, Angus: 6 author, writer 7 British
work: The Mulberry Bush
Wilson, Ann
lead singer of: Heart
song: Almost Paradise... (1984)
Surrender to Me (1989)
Wilson, Charles: 8 Nobelist 9 physicist
Wilson, Colin: 6 critic, writer 7 British
work: Anti-Sartre
Existential Essays
The Occult
The Outsider
Wilson, Edmund: 6 writer
cat: 4 Lulu
work: Axel's Castle
Patriotic Gore
A Piece of My Mind
The Wound and the Bow
Wilson, Ethel: 6 writer 8 Canadian
Wilson, Hack: 3 Cub 7 slugger 10 outfielder
Wilson, Harold
predecessor: 5 Heath 11 Douglas-Home
successor: 5 Heath 9 Callaghan
Wilson, Hugh: 8 director
film: Blast From the Past (1999)
Dudley Do-Right (1999)
The First Wives Club (1996)
Guarding Tess (1994)
Wilson, Jackie
lead singer of: Dominoes
song: Alone at Last (1960)
Baby Workout (1963)
Higher and Higher (1967)
Lonely Teardrops (1958)
My Empty Arms (1961)
Night (1960)
Wilson, Kenneth: 8 Nobelist 9 physicist
Wilson, Lanford: 10 playwright

work: The Hot l Baltimore
Talley's Folly
Wilson, Marie TV role: 4 Irma
Wilson, Owen: 5 actor
film: Behind Enemy Lines (2001)
The Minus Man (1999)
Permanent Midnight (1998)
Shanghai Noon (2000)
Zoolander (2001)
Wilson Phillips
members: Carnie Wilson, Wendy Wilson, Chynna Phillips
song: The Dream Is Still Alive (1991)
Hold On (1990)
Impulsive (1990)
Release Me (1990)
You're in Love (1991)
Wilson, Rita spouse: Tom Hanks
Wilson, Robert: 8 Nobelist **9** physicist
Wilson, Scott: 5 actor
film: G.I. Jane (1997)
The Grissom Gang (1971)
In Cold Blood (1967)
The Ninth Configuration (1980)
Wilson, Sloan: 6 author, writer
work: All the Best People
Ice Brothers
The Man in the Gray Flannel Suit
Small Town
A Summer Place
Wilson, Woodrow: 8 Nobelist **9** president
alma mater: 9 Princeton
birthplace: 8 Staunton, Virginia
film portrayer: 4 Knox
former occupation: 7 teacher
home: 9 New Jersey
opponent: 4 Debs, Taft **6** Hughes **9** Roosevelt
predecessor: 4 Taft
real first name: 6 Thomas
successor: 7 Harding
V.P.: 8 Marshall
wife: 5 Edith, Ellen
wilt: 3 ebb, sag **4** drop, fade, fail, flag, sink, tire **5** droop, dry up, faint, slump, sweat, waste, wizen **6** cave in, dry out, go limp, slouch, weaken, wither **7** decline, dwindle, give out, shrivel, succumb, swelter **8** collapse, languish **9** break down
__ wilt: 6 branch
wilted: 4 limp **6** droopy **8** flagging
Wilton: 4 city, town
locale: 4 Conn.
Wilton __: 3 rug **6** carpet
Wilts: 6 county
locale: 7 England
Wiltshire: 6 cheese, county **10** sheep breed
city: 7 Swindon
locale: 7 England
Wilt the __: 5 Stilt
wily: 3 sly **4** arch, cagy, foxy **5** cagey, canny, sharp, slick **6** artful, astute, clever, crafty, feline, shifty, shrewd, smooth, sneaky, tricky **7** crooked, cunning, devious, furtive, knavish, knowing **8** guileful, scheming, slippery, stealthy **9** astucious, deceitful, deceptive, designing, insidious, underhand **10** contriving, intriguing, serpentine
in a ~ way: 5 slyly
Wim: 7 Wenders
Wimbledon
call: 3 let, out **5** deuce, fault
division: 4 men's **6** women's **7** doubles
game: 6 tennis
need: 3 net
rating: 4 seed
shot: 3 ace, lob **5** serve, smash
surface: 4 lawn **5** grass
Wimbledon winners:
2003 - Roger Federer, Serena Williams
2002 - Lleyton Hewitt, Serena Williams
2001 - Goran Ivanisevic, Venus Williams
2000 - Pete Sampras, Venus Williams
1999 - Pete Sampras, Lindsay Davenport
1998 - Pete Sampras, Jana Novotna
1997 - Pete Sampras, Martina Hingis
1996 - Richard Krajicek, Steffi Graf
1995 - Pete Sampras, Steffi Graf
1994 - Pete Sampras, Conchita Martinez
1993 - Pete Sampras, Steffi Graf
1992 - Andre Agassi, Steffi Graf
1991 - Michael Stich, Steffi Graf
1990 - Stefan Edberg, Martina Navratilova
1989 - Boris Becker, Steffi Graf
1988 - Stefan Edberg, Steffi Graf
1987 - Pat Cash, Martina Navratilova
1986 - Boris Becker, Martina Navratilova
1985 - Boris Becker, Martina Navratilova
1984 - John McEnroe, Martina Navratilova
1983 - John McEnroe, Martina Navratilova
1982 - Jimmy Connors, Martina Navratilova
1981 - John McEnroe, Chris Evert Lloyd
1980 - Bjorn Borg, Evonne Cawley
1979 - Bjorn Borg, Martina Navratilova
1978 - Bjorn Borg, Martina Navratilova
1977 - Bjorn Borg, Virginia Wade
1976 - Bjorn Borg, Chris Evert
1975 - Arthur Ashe, Billie Jean King
1974 - Jimmy Connors, Chris Evert
1973 - Jan Kodes, Billie Jean King
1972 - Stan Smith, Billie Jean King
1971 - John Newcombe, Evonne Goolagong
1970 - John Newcombe, Margaret Court
1969 - Rod Laver, Ann Jones
1968 - Rod Laver, Billie Jean King
1967 - John Newcombe, Billie Jean King
1966 - Manuel Santana, Billie Jean King
1965 - Roy Emerson, Margaret Smith
1964 - Roy Emerson, Maria Bueno
1963 - Chuck McKinley, Margaret Smith
1962 - Rod Laver, Karen Susman
1961 - Rod Laver, Angela Mortimer
1960 - Neale Fraser, Maria Bueno
1959 - Alex Olmedo, Maria Bueno
1958 - Ashley Cooper, Althea Gibson
1957 - Lew Hoad, Althea Gibson
1956 - Lew Hoad, Shirley Fry
1955 - Tony Trabert, Louise Brough
1954 - Jaroslav Drobny, Maureen Connolly
1953 - Vic Seixas, Maureen Connolly
1952 - Frank Sedgman, Maureen Connolly
1951 - Dick Savitt, Doris Hart
1950 - Budge Patty, Louise Brough
1949 - Ted Schroeder, Louise Brough
1948 - Bob Falkenburg, Louise Brough
1947 - Jack Kramer, Margaret Osborne
1946 - Yvon Petra, Pauline Betz
1940–45 - no tournament
1939 - Bobby Riggs, Alice Marble
1938 - Don Budge, Helen Wills Moody
1937 - Don Budge, Dorothy Round
1936 - Fred Perry, Helen Jacobs
1935 - Fred Perry, Helen Moody
1934 - Fred Perry, Dorothy Round
1933 - Jack Crawford, Helen Moody
1932 - Ellsworth Vines, Helen Moody
1931 - Sidney Wood, Cilly Aussem
1930 - Bill Tilden, Helen Moody
1929 - Henri Cochet, Helen Wills
1928 - Rene Lacoste, Helen Wills
1927 - Henri Cochet, Helen Wills
1926 - Jean Borotra, Kathleen Godfree
1925 - Rene Lacoste, Suzanne Lenglen
1924 - Jean Borotra, Kathleen McKane
1923 - Bill Johnston, Suzanne Lenglen
1922 - Gerald Patterson, Suzanne Lenglen
1921 - Bill Tilden, Suzanne Lenglen
1920 - Bill Tilden, Suzanne Lenglen
Wimmer: 2 Al **5** Brian
wimp: 4 nerd, nurd, wuss **5** dweeb, loser, sissy, softy, twerp, twirp **6** coward, craven, moaner, nobody, softie **7** chicken, crybaby, dastard, milksop, quitter **8** mama's boy, poltroon, pushover, weakling **9** cream puff, fraidy cat, jellyfish, nonentity
no ~: 4 hunk **5** he-man **6** Samson **7** bruiser **8** Hercules, tough guy **10** powerhouse
(out): 7 chicken
word: 4 can't
wimpish: 5 timid **6** craven, scared, yellow **7** chicken, fearful, gutless, servile **8** cowardly, recreant, timorous **9** dastardly, fraidy-cat, weak-kneed **10** scaredy-cat
wimple: 5 scarf **6** gorget
wearer: 3 nun **6** sister **8** prioress
wimpy: 4 mild, puny, weak **5** frail, nerdy **6** anemic, atonic, craven, effete, feeble, flabby, flimsy, unsure **7** anaemic, fragile, languid **8** delicate, helpless, pithless **9** faltering, lethargic, powerless, unpopular **10** vulnerable
Wimpy's payback time: 3 Tue. **4** Tues. **7** Tuesday
Wimsey, Peter: 4 lord
alma mater: 4 Eton
work for ~: 4 case
win: 3 bag, get, hit **4** beat, earn, gain, land, lead, luck, sway, take **5** carry, reach, score, upset **6** attain, better, big hit, come by, disarm, gammon, garner, make it, master, obtain, pan out, pick up, rack up, secure, snatch, thrive **7** achieve, acquire, capture, conquer, convert, edge out, luck out, make out, prevail, procure, prosper, pull off, realize, receive, shut out, succeed, success, triumph, trounce, victory, work out **8** come into, conquest, convince, flourish, get ahead, go places, make good, outscore, overcome, persuade **9** checkmate, landslide, overwhelm **10** accomplish
against: 4 beat, best, drub, rout **5** crush, outdo, upset, worst **6** better, defeat, outrun, outwit, subdue, thrash **7** conquer, nose out, outplay, trounce **8** knock out, outscore, outshine **9** overpower, overwhelm
back: 6 recoup, redeem, regain **7** recover, restore **8** retrieve
barely: 4 edge **7** edge out, nose out
don't ~: 4 fail, fall, lose
ender: 4 some
every game: 5 sweep
lopsided ~: 4 romp, rout **7** laugher
over: 3 get, wow **4** draw, hook, sell, sway **5** carry, charm **6** allure, defeat, disarm, endear, induce, reason **7** convert, recruit, satisfy **8** convince, persuade, talk into **9** argue into, influence, prevail on, reconcile **10** conciliate
seek to ~: 3 woo **5** chase, court, spark **6** pursue **10** bill and coo
surprise ~: 5 upset
will to ~: 6 desire, fervor **8** ambition **9** obsession
win __: 3 out
Win, __ or Draw: 4 Lose
__ Win: 5 Eat to
Win Ben Stein's Money: 8 game show
win by __: 5 a neck, a nose
wince: 3 shy **4** duck, jump **5** cower, dodge, quail, start **6** blanch, blench, cringe, flinch, recoil, shrink, swerve, writhe **7** back off, grimace **8** draw back **9** make a face
Wincer, Simon: 8 director
film: Free Willy (1993)
Phar Lap (1983)
Quigley Down Under (1990)
winch: 5 crank **6** lifter **8** windlass
Winchell: 4 Paul **6** Walter
Winchester: 4 city, town **5** rifle **8** asteroid
locale: 6 Nevada **8** Virginia
Winchester __: 4 disk **5** rifle **6** bushel
Winchester '73 (1950 film)
cast: Dan Duryea, James Stewart, Shelley Winters
director: Anthony Mann
Winchester Cathedral (1966 song)
artist: New Vaudeville Band
wind: 3 air, jug **4** berg, bise, blow, bora, coil, curl, fife, furl, gale, gust, hint, loop, oboe, pipe, puff, puna, reel, roll, tuba, turn, urua, waft, wrap, zobo **5** aulos, blast, bugle, bumpa, crook, curve, draft, flute, foehn, gazoo, hooey, kazoo, rumor, screw, shawm, snake, spool, storm, titzu, trade, twine, twirl, twist, weave, zonda **6** alboka, arctic, biniou, boreal, boreas, breath, breeze, carnyx, coil up, cornet, encoil, fujara, ghibli, lituus, notice, ramble, samiel, shofar, simoom, solano, spiral, squall, squirm, swerve, syrinx, vortex, zephyr, zigzag **7** arghool, austral, bagpipe, baloney, bassoon, boloney, buisine, chinook, clarion, current, cyclone, draught, entwine, hautboy, helicon, hogwash, inkling, intwine, khamsin, lyricon, meander, mistral, monsoon, musette, norther, ocarina, onshore, pampero, panpipe, piccolo, sackbut, salpinx, saxhorn, saxtuba, shiwaya, shophar, sinuate, sirocco, slither, talinka, tempest, tonette, tornado, trumpet, twister, typhoon, whisper, wreathe **8** altohorn, anabatic, boasting, claptrap, clarinet, encircle, favonian, hornpipe, levanter, mirliton, nonsense, offshore, post horn, recorder, Santa Ana, scirocco, trombone, westerly, williwaw **9** alpenhorn, corkscrew, dust devil, dust storm, empty talk, euphonium, gibberish, harmattan, harmonica, hurricane, jet stream, nor'easter, northerly, nor'wester, sandstorm, saxophone, sou'easter, southerly, sou'wester, whirlwind **10** balderdash, contrabass, cor Anglais, flugelhorn, instrument, intimation, sousaphone, suggestion
about: 4 coil, furl, gird, loop, ring, turn **5** curve, twine **6** circle, engird **7** envelop **8** go around, surround **9** encompass

Africa: 4 berg 6 ghibli, samiel 9 harmattan
Aleutians: 8 williwaw
Alps: 4 bise
ancient ~ instrument: 5 aulos
Argentina: 7 pampero
away from the ~: 4 alee
be in the ~: 4 loom 6 impend
burst of ~: 4 gust
California: 8 Santa Ana
catcher: 4 sail
cold ~: 4 bise, bora, puna 7 mistral, pampero 8 williwaw
combining form: 4 anem- 5 anemo-, venti-, vento-
cyclonic storm ~: 9 hurricane
danger: 5 shear
deprive of ~: 5 stall 6 becalm
dir.: 3 ENE, ESE, NNE, NNW, SSE, SSW, WNW, WSW
down: 4 slow, wane 5 close, relax 6 lessen, reduce 7 thin out 8 slack off, surcease, taper off 9 terminate
dry ~: 4 berg, bise 5 foehn 6 samiel, simoom 7 chinook, mistral 8 Santa Ana
dusty ~: 9 harmattan
east ~: 6 solano 8 levanter
Egypt: 7 khamsin
ender: 3 age, bag, row 4 burn, fall, flaw, lass, mill, pipe, sock, surf, ward 5 blast, blown, break, burnt, shake, storm, swept 6 burned, flower, jammer, screen, shield, sucker 7 sailing, surfing
equipped with a ~ indicator: 5 vaned
Europe: 4 bise, bora, fohn 5 foehn
France: 7 mistral
gentle westerly ~: 6 zephyr
get a second ~: 5 rally 8 come back
get ~ of: 4 hear 5 scent, smell 8 discover
god: 5 Eurus, Njord
goddess: 4 Aura
go like the ~: 3 fly, hie, run 4 dash, race, whiz 5 speed 6 hurtle
Hawaii: 4 kona
hot ~: 6 ghibli, samiel, simoom, solano 7 khamsin, sirocco 8 Santa Ana
humid ~: 5 zonda
Indian Ocean: 7 monsoon
indicator: 4 sock, vane
instrument: 3 sax 4 horn, oboe, tuba 5 flute 6 cornet 7 ocarina, trumpet 8 trombone
in the ~: 4 near, nigh 6 coming 7 brewing, looming, pending 8 imminent, on the way 9 impending, proximate
Mediterranean: 6 solano 7 sirocco 8 levanter
mountain ~: 9 katabatic
mountainside ~: 5 foehn
move like the ~: 4 blow
night ~: 9 katabatic
north ~: 4 bora 6 arctic, boreal, boreas
off the ocean ~: 9 sea breeze
of the ~: 5 eolic
Peru: 4 puna
rainy ~ direction: 4 east
resistance: 4 drag
ride the ~: 3 fly 4 luff, scud, soar 5 glide
rising ~: 8 anabatic
Rocky Mountains: 7 chinook
run before the ~: 4 gybe, jibe
Sahara: 6 simoom
seasonal ~: 7 monsoon
solar ~ phenomenon: 6 aurora
south ~: 7 austral
South America: 5 zonda
starter: 4 down, head, tail, wood 5 cross, whirl
stiff ~: 5 noser, storm 6 squall 7 cyclone, tempest
straw in the ~: 4 omen, sign 5 token 6 augury, herald, signal 7 portent, presage, warning 9 foretoken, harbinger, indicator 10 indication
250 mph ~: 9 jet stream
take the ~ out of: 6 defeat, hamper, hinder, hogtie, hold up, impede, stymie, thwart 8 obstruct 9 frustrate, hamstring, undermine
toward the ~: 8 aweather
toward the equator: 5 trade
twist in the ~: 4 hang 6 dangle 7 draggle
up: 3 end 4 halt, land, quit, stop 5 cease, crank 6 finish, run out, settle, wrap up 7 achieve, adjourn, break up, play out 8 complete, conclude, finalize, pack it in, surcease 9 close down, culminate, terminate 10 call it a day, completion, consummate, put through
up at: 4 go to 5 get to, reach 6 come to, land on 8 amount to 9 set foot in
violent ~: 6 squall
warm ~: 4 berg 5 foehn, zonda 7 chinook
west ~: 8 favonian
wind __: 3 gap, tee 4 cone, down, harp, pump, rose, sail, ship, vane 5 chill, gauge, plant, poppy, power, scale, shaft, shake, shear, shelf 6 chimes, energy, sleeve, sprint, tunnel 7 erosion, turbine
wind __ factor: 5 chill
wind-__: 4 bell 5 borne, swept 6 screen, shaken
__ wind: 3 ill 4 beam, berg, fall, head, land, plow, tail 5 bag of, brass, cross, in the, local, solar, trade 6 canyon, cayuse, second, valley 7 gravity, leading, stellar
Wind __ National Park: 4 Cave
Wind __ Willows, The: 5 in the
__ Wind: 6 Second, Summer
__, Wind and Fire: 5 Earth
Windaus, Adolf: 7 chemist 8 Nobelist
windbag: 4 bore 6 magpie 9 loudmouth
like a ~: 5 gassy
words: 3 gas 5 boast 6 hot air
Wind Beneath My Wings (1989 song)
artist: Bette Midler
windborne: 5 eolic 6 eolian
Windbreaker: 4 coat, wrap 5 shell 6 anorak, jacket 7 slicker 9 outerwear
close a ~: 5 zip up 6 zipper
Wind Cave: 4 park
locale: 4 S. Dak.
windcheater: 4 coat 6 jacket
wind chill __: 6 factor
winded: 9 exhausted 10 breathless
be ~: 4 huff, pant, puff
become ~: 4 drop, fade, tire 5 droop, weary 6 weaken 7 fatigue, give out, poop out, wear out 8 peter out, wear down 9 grow weary
__-winded: 4 long 5 short
__-winder: 4 stem
Windermere: 4 lake
locale: 7 England
__ Windermere's Fan: 4 Lady
winder starter: 4 side
Windex alternative: 9 Glass Plus
windfall: 4 boon, luck, plum 5 manna, melon, prize 7 bonanza, godsend, jackpot 8 blessing
Windhoek: 4 city, town
locale: 6 Africa 7 Namibia
windigo: 5 giant
winding: 4 bent, mazy, turn, wavy 5 bowed, curly, curvy, snaky 6 curvey, spiral, zigzag 7 angular, bending, crooked, curving, sinuous, turning 8 angulose, angulous, cockeyed, tortuous, twisting 9 spiraling 10 circuitous, convoluted, meandering, roundabout, serpentine
device: 4 stem
shape: 3 ess
winding __: 4 road 5 frame, sheet 6 number
__-winding: 4 self
Winding: 3 Kai
Winding Stair, The author: William Butler Yeats
Wind in the Willows, The
author: Kenneth Grahame
character: 4 Mole, Toad 5 Otter 6 Badger 8 Sea-Farer, Water Rat
windjammer: 4 boat 6 vessel 8 sailboat
windlass: 3 gin 4 crab 5 crank, winch 6 grouch, lifter 7 capstan
windless: 4 calm
windmill blade: 4 vane
Windmills of the Gods author: Sidney Sheldon
Windmills of Your __, The: 4 Mind
__ wind of: 3 get 5 catch
Windom's Way (1957 film)
cast: Peter Finch, Mary Ure
director: Ronald Neame
window: 5 light, oriel 6 lancet 7 opening 8 casement, fenestra, porthole
attic ~: 6 dormer
bay ~: 5 belly, oriel 6 paunch
covering: 5 blind, drape, glass, grill, shade 6 grille, screen 7 curtain, drapery
dressing: 4 mask 5 front 6 facade, veneer
ender: 4 pane, sill
install a ~: 5 glaze
installer: 7 glazier
it may have a ~: 3 env. 8 envelope
opening: 6 louver, louvre
out the ~: 4 away, gone, lost 6 missed, ruined, wasted 8 departed, vanished
part: 4 jamb, pane, sash 5 frame, jambe, ledge 6 casing, lintel
shopper: 4 eyer 7 browser
small ~: 4 vent 5 oxeye
sticker: 5 decal
$2 ~ action: 3 bet 5 wager 6 exacta 8 perfecta, quinella, trifecta 9 quiniella
window __: 3 box 4 back, sash, seat, sill 5 blind, board, shade 7 dresser
window-__: 4 shop
__ window: 3 bay, bow, fan 4 drop, loop, oval, rose, show, vent 5 front, gable, Jesse, opera, radio, round, storm, wheel 6 awning, dormer, French, hopper, lancet, launch, ribbon 7 Chicago, cottage, lowside, picture, transom
__ Window: 3 At a 4 Rear 7 Bedroom
windowpane adhesive: 5 putty
Windows
owner: 4 user
precursor: 3 DOS 5 MS-DOS
runner: 2 PC 8 computer
window-shop: 3 gad 4 roam 6 browse 7 saunter
Window, The (1949 film)
cast: Bobby Driscoll, Barbara Hale, Arthur Kennedy
director: Ted Tetzlaff
windpipe: 4 tube 6 airway 7 trachea
combining form: 7 tracheo-
Wind River __: 5 Range
__ winds: 5 trade
Wind, Sand and Stars author: Antoine de Saint-Exupéry
windshield
adjunct: 4 tint 5 visor, vizor
annoyance: 3 ice 5 frost, sleet
attachment: 5 decal
clear a ~: 4 wipe 5 defog, deice 7 defrost
material: 5 glass
Winds of War, The author: Herman Wouk
Windsor: 3 car 4 auto, city, town 8 Chrysler 10 automobile
locale: 3 Ont. 6 Canada 7 Ontario 10 California
merry ones: 5 wives
racetrack near ~: 5 Ascot
Windsor __: 3 tie 4 knot 5 bench, chair 6 Castle, settee
Windsor Beauties, The painter: 4 Lely
Windsor Castle
river near ~: 6 Thames
school near ~: 4 Eton
Windsor Forest poet: 4 Pope
Windstar: 3 SUV, van 4 Ford
windstorm: 4 gale 6 squall 7 cyclone, tempest, tornado
windsurfer mecca: 4 Maui 6 Hawaii
windsurfing: 5 sport
__ Wind, The: 7 Wayward
windup: 3 end 4 wrap 5 close, finis 6 ending, finale, finish 7 last act, outcome 8 curtains, terminus 10 completion, conclusion, denouement, resolution
Windward __: 7 Islands, Passage
Windward Island: 7 Grenada, St. Lucia 8 Dominica 9 St. George's 10 Grenadines
windward, not: 4 alee
wind-worn: 5 erose 6 eroded
windy: 3 raw 4 airy, wild 5 brisk, fresh, gusty, sharp, wordy 6 breezy, drafty, prolix, stormy, turgid 7 blowing, gusting, lengthy, pompous, verbose, voluble 8 blustery, boastful, inflated, rambling 9 bombastic, garrulous, overblown, redundant, talkative, windswept 10 bigmouthed, blustering, long-winded, loquacious, meandering, palaverous, rhetorical
Windy (1967 song) artist: Association
Windy City: 3 Chi. 7 Chicago
el train initials: 3 CTA
windy-day
hobbyist: 5 kiter
wear: 5 parka
wine: 3 kir, red, zin 4 Cava, hock, port, rosé, sake, saki, Sekt 5 blush, color, corvo, drink, Gamay, Mâcon, Médoc, Pinot, Rhine, Rioja, soave, Tavel, Tokay, Yquem 6 Arneis, Barolo, claret, Graves, Malaga, purple 7 aligoté, Amarone, Auslese, Barbera, cabinet, Catawba, Chablis, Chianti, Concord, heurige, Madeira, malmsey, Marsala, Moselle, Musigny, Orvieto, Pommard, retsina, vintage, Vouvray 8 Albariño, beverage, Bordeaux, burgundy, Cabernet, cold duck, Dolcetto, Dubonnet, Frascati, Montilla, Muscadet, muscatel, Riesling, Sancerre, Sauterne, spumante, Sylvaner, vermouth 9 Bardolino, Champagne, colombard, dandelion, lambrusco, Meursault, Zinfandel 10 Beaujolais, Chambertin, Chardonnay, Hochheimer, Montrachet
additive: 4 stum
and dine: 3 woo 4 feed, fete 5 treat 9 entertain
Austria: 7 heurige
bouquet: 4 nose 5 aroma, scent 9 fragrance
byproduct: 5 argal, argol
California ~ valley: 4 Napa
color kin: 4 rose, ruby, rust 5 brick,

coral, grape, poppy, rusty, sandy 6 cerise, cherry, claret, garnet, maroon 7 carmine, crimson, fuchsia, magenta, pimento, scarlet, sultana, vermeil 8 amaranth, cardinal, dubonnet, geranium, rubicund 9 carnation, cranberry, vermilion 10 strawberry
combining form: 2 en- 3 eno-, oen-, vin- 4 oeno-, vini-, vino-
container: 3 tun, vat 4 cask, skin 6 barrel, foudre
cooler base: 3 ade
designation: 3 cru, dry, red, sec 4 aged, brut, rosé, seco, year 5 blush, sweet, white 7 vintage
drink: 5 negus 6 bishop 7 sangria
dry ~: 5 gamay, soave
ender: 4 skin 5 glass, maker, press 6 bibber, grower, making 7 tasting
France: 4 Moët 5 Gamay, Mâcon, Médoc, tavel, Yquem 6 claret, Graves 7 aligoté, Chablis, Musigny, Pommard, Vouvray 8 Bordeaux, Cabernet, Muscadet, Sancerre 9 Bourdeaux, Champagne, Meursault 10 Beaujolais, Chambertin, Montrachet
France ~ region: 5 Loire, Médoc, Rhone
Germany: 4 hock, Sekt 7 Auslese, cabinet, Moselle 8 cold duck 10 Hochheimer
Germany ~ region: 5 Mainz, Rhine
good ~ quality: 4 body
Greece: 7 malmsey, retsina
Greek ~ pitcher: 4 olpe
holder: 6 bottle, carafe, flagon 8 decanter
honey: 7 oenomel
hot spiced ~: 5 glogg, negus
Hungary: 5 Tokay
Hungary ~ city: 4 Eger
Iberian ~ center: 5 Porto
improve, as ~: 3 age
impurity: 6 ketone
inferior ~ in Britain: 5 plonk
In Portuguese: 5 vinho
Italy: 5 corvo, soave 6 Arneis, Barolo 7 Amarone, Barbera, Chianti, Marsala, Orvieto 8 Dolcetto, Frascati, spumante 9 Bardolino, lambrusco
Italy ~ measure: 4 orna
Italy ~ region: 4 Asti
Japan: 4 sake, saki
like ~: 6 fruity
make hot spiced ~: 4 mull
name: 4 Remy 5 Gallo
new ~: 4 must
of ~: 5 vinic
off-tasting, as ~: 5 corky
partner: 4 dine 6 cheese
place: 6 cellar
Portugal: 4 port 7 Madeira, malmsey
prepare grapes for ~: 5 stomp
product: 6 brandy
purchase: 3 jug 6 bottle, carafe
quality: 4 nose
red ~: 4 port 5 gamay, Médoc, pinot, tavel 6 barolo, claret
Rhine ~: 4 hock
rice ~: 4 sake, saki
Roman ~ pitcher: 4 olpe
sediment: 4 lees 5 dregs 7 residue 9 settlings
serve ~: 4 pour 6 decant
shop: 6 bodega
Sicily: 5 corvo 7 Marsala
source: 5 elder, grape
Spain: 4 Cava 5 rioja, tinto 6 Malaga 8 Albariño, Montilla
sparkling ~: 4 Asti
stopper: 4 cork
white ~: 3 kir 5 Mosel, pinot, Rhine, soave 7 Chablis
wine ___: 3 bag, bar 4 list, palm 5 press 6 cellar, cooler, gallon 7 steward
___ wine: 3 jug, low, May, pop, red 4 high, palm, rice 5 altar, blush, Rhine, Rhone, still, straw, table, white 7 cabinet, château, dessert, vintage
wine and ___: 4 dine 6 cheese
wine-colored: 6 vinous
wineglass: 5 flute 6 goblet
feature: 4 stem
___ wine in old bottles: 3 new
winemaking device: 5 press
winery: 7 château
Winesap: 5 apple
relative: 4 crab, Gala, Lodi, Rome 5 Mutsu 6 Empire, Ida Red, medlar, Pippin, russet 7 Baldwin, Bramley, costard, Freedom, Liberty, Spartan, Wealthy 8 Cortland, Jonathan, McIntosh 10 Rome Beauty
Winesburg, Ohio author: Sherwood Anderson
wineskin: 4 bota
Winfield: 4 Dave, Paul 5 Scott
Winfield, Dave: 10 outfielder
Winfield, Paul: 5 actor
film: Conrack (1974)
Gordon's War (1973)
Sounder (1972)
Winfrey: 5 Oprah
wing: 3 ala, arm, ell, fly 4 limb, sect, unit 5 annex, graze, organ, pinna, sweep 6 branch, member, pinion 7 aileron, airfoil, chapter, faction, section 8 addition, division, forelimb 9 appendage, extension 10 finger food, take flight
build a ~: 3 add 5 add on, annex 6 adjoin, append, tack on
building ~: 3 ell 5 annex 6 alette
combining form: 4 pter- 5 ptero- 6 pteryg- 7 pterygo-
ender: 3 bow, man, men, tip 4 back, ding, over, span 5 chair 6 spread
in America: 6 fender
it: 3 fly 4 soar, vamp 5 ad-lib 6 make up 9 improvise
left ~: 7 liberal
of a ~: 4 alar 5 alary, alate 6 alated
one on the ~: 4 bird 5 flier, flyer
on the ~: 5 aloft 6 flying 7 soaring 8 in flight
political ~: 4 left 5 right
shape: 5 delta
spurious ~: 5 alula
starter: 3 lap, red, wax 4 bite, gull, lace 5 clear, swept
take ~: 3 fly 4 soar 6 aviate
take under one's ~: 4 help 6 shield 7 protect
under one's ~: 4 safe 5 in tow
wing ___: 3 bar, bit, bow, dam, nut, tip 4 bolt, case, flat, shot, skid 5 chair 6 collar 7 coverts, formula, loading
wing-___: 4 ding 5 weary 6 footed
___ wing: 4 hind, take 5 delta, on the 6 canard, double, flying, rotary, single
___-wing: 4 gull, left 5 fixed, right
Wing and a Prayer (1944 film)
cast: Don Ameche, Dana Andrews, William Eythe
director: Henry Hathaway
wing-ding: 4 bash, fete, gala 5 party, spree 7 jubilee, rampage 8 jamboree 9 festivity
winged: 4 alar 5 alary, alate, quick, rapid, swift 6 alated, speedy 9 impromptu
child: 4 Amor, Eros 5 Cupid 6 cherub
combining form: 7 -pterous
nuisance: 3 fly 4 gnat, wasp 5 midge
one: 5 angel 6 cherub
walker: 3 emu 4 emeu
woman: 3 WAF
winged ___: 3 elm, pea 4 bean
Winged ___: 5 Horse 7 Victory
Winged Victory: 4 Nike
Winger, Debra: 7 actress
film: Big Bad Love (2002)
Black Widow (1987)
Cannery Row (1982)
Forget Paris (1995)
Leap of Faith (1992)
Legal Eagles (1986)
An Officer and a Gentleman (1982)
Shadowlands (1993)
Terms of Endearment (1983)
Urban Cowboy (1980)
spouse: Arliss Howard, Timothy Hutton
wingless stage: 5 larva
winglike: 4 alar 5 alary, alate 6 alated
Wingrave: 4 Owen
wings
beat, as ~: 4 bate, flap 7 flutter
clear the ~: 5 deice
earn one's ~: 4 pass 5 cut it, train 6 make it 7 qualify 9 measure up 10 pass muster
in Latin: 4 alae
waiting in the ~: 5 on tap, ready 9 available
___ wings: 5 in the, water 7 buffalo
Wings: 6 Hauser
Wings (1927 film)
cast: Richard Arlen, Clara Bow, Buddy Rogers
director: William Wellman
Wings (NBC sitcom)
cast: Crystal Bernard (Helen Chappel)
Timothy Daly (Joe Hackett)
Steven Weber (Brian Hackett)
Wings author: Danielle Steel
Wings of the Dove, The author: Henry James
Wings of the Morning, The author: Thomas Tryon
wingspread: 4 span
___ Wing, The: 4 West
wingtip: 4 shoe 8 footgear, footwear
Winifred: 5 saint
win in ___: 5 a rout, a walk
wink: 3 bat 4 jiff, sign, tick 5 blink, flash, flick, flirt, gleam, jiffy, shake 6 minute, moment, second, signal, squint 7 flicker, flutter, gesture, glad eye, glimmer, glitter, instant, nictate, signify, sparkle, squinch, twinkle 8 high sign 9 nictitate, twinkling
at: 6 excuse, ignore, permit 7 absolve, condone, forgive, let pass, let ride 8 let slide, overlook, shrug off, tolerate 9 disregard, put up with
catch a ~: 3 nod 4 doze 5 sleep 6 nod off
double ~: 5 blink
in a ~: 4 anon, soon 7 quickly
like a ~: 3 coy
of the eye: 4 jiff 5 jiffy, trice 6 moment 7 instant
starter: 3 eye 4 hood
wink ___: 3 out
Wink: 10 Martindale
winker: 6 eyelid
winkle: 5 shell 8 seashell
sting ~: 5 shell 8 seashell
Winkler: 5 Henry, Irwin
Winkler, Henry: 5 actor
film: The Lords of Flatbush (1974)
Memories of Me (1988)
Night Shift (1982)
The Waterboy (1998)
TV: Happy Days
winks, forty: 3 nap 4 doze, rest 5 sleep 6 catnap, snooze 7 slumber
taking forty ~: 5 adoze 6 asleep
Winky Dink and You dog: 6 Woofer
Win, Lose or Draw: 8 game show
host: Vicki Lawrence, Bert Convy
Winn-___: 5 Dixie
Winnebago: 2 RV 4 lake 5 tribe 6 camper, Indian 7 Amerind 8 language
locale: 9 Wisconsin
winner: 3 hit 4 hero 5 champ, smash 6 big hit, select, top dog, victor 7 triumph, victory 8 champion, medalist 9 conqueror, number one 10 subjugator, vanquisher
Derby ~ flower: 4 rose
starter: 5 bread, prize
winner ___ all: 4 take
Winner, Michael: 8 director
film: Death Wish (1974)
I'll Never Forget What's 'Isname (1967)
Lawman (1971)
You Must Be Joking! (1965)
winner's ___: 6 circle
Winner Takes It All, The (1980 song)
artist: ABBA
Winnie: 7 Mandela
Winnie ___: 3 Mae
Winnie ___ Pu: 4 Ille
Winnie the Pooh: 4 book
author: A.A. Milne
character: 3 owl, Roo 5 Kanga 6 Eeyore
winning: 4 cute, nice 5 ahead, on top, sweet 6 lovely, taking 7 likable, lovable 8 adorable, alluring, charming, engaging, fetching, inviting, loveable, pleasing 9 disarming, endearing 10 attractive, bewitching, enchanting, personable, successful, triumphant, victorious
barely ~: 5 one up, up one
gesture: 5 V sign
margin: 4 neck, nose 5 a neck, a nose
streak: 3 run
winning ___: 4 post 6 hazard, streak 7 gallery, opening
Winning (1969 film)
cast: Paul Newman, Richard Thomas, Joanne Woodward
director: James Goldstone
Winning ___ everything!: 4 isn't
Winninger, Charles: 5 actor
film: Destry Rides Again (1939)
Hard to Get (1938)
A Lady Takes a Chance (1943)
Sunday Dinner for a Soldier (1944)
The Sun Shines Bright (1953)
Three Smart Girls Grow Up (1939)
Winningham: 4 Mare
winnings: 3 pot 4 gain, loot 5 prize, purse 6 profit
in horse racing: 5 purse
Winnipeg: 4 city, lake, town
hockey player: 3 Jet
locale: 6 Canada 8 Manitoba
newspaper: 9 Free Press
Winnipesaukee: 4 lake
winnow: 4 cull, pick, sift, sort 5 glean 6 choose, filter, screen 7 examine, sort out, weed out 8 separate
wino: 3 sot 4 lush 5 souse, toper 7 tippler, tosspot
affliction: 3 D.T.'s
Winona: 4 city, town 5 Ryder
locale: 9 Minnesota
Win one for the ___: 6 Gipper
Winooski, city on the: 10 Montpelier
Winslet, Kate: 7 actress
film: Enigma (2001)
Iris (2001)
Quills (2000)

Sense and Sensibility (1995)
Titanic (1997)
spouse: Sam Mendes
Winslow: 3 Ola 4 city, town 5 Homer
locale: 4 Ariz. 7 Arizona
Winslow Boy, The (1948 film)
cast: Richard Donat, Cedric Hardwicke, Margaret Leighton
director: Anthony Asquith
Winslow Boy, The (1999 film)
cast: Nigel Hawthorne, Gemma Jones, Jeremy Northam, Rebecca Pidgeon
director: David Mamet
Winslow Boy, The author: Terrence Rattigan
winsome: 4 cute, nice 5 bonny, sweet 6 bonnie, comely, lovely, pretty, taking 7 darling, likable, lovable 8 adorable, alluring, charming, engaging, fetching, gorgeous, handsome, inviting, loveable, pleasing, striking, stunning 9 beautiful, disarming, endearing, ravishing 10 attractive, bewitching, delightful, enchanting, triumphant, victorious
winsomeness: 5 charm 6 allure, appeal, beauty, glamor 7 glamour 8 elegance, radiance 9 good looks 10 attraction
Winsor: 5 McCay 8 Kathleen
heroine: 5 Amber
Winston: 3 Ron 5 Smith 9 Churchill
Winston-__, NC: 5 Salem
Winston Cup
entry: 3 car 4 auto 5 racer
Winston-Salem: 4 city, town
locale: 4 N. Car.
school: 3 WFU 10 Wake Forest
winter: 4 cold 6 season 9 Jack Frost
aid: 4 plow 6 deicer
ailment: 3 flu 4 ague, cold 5 strep
air: 4 noel 5 carol
coating: 3 ice 4 hoar, snow
do ~ airport work: 5 deice
ender: 4 time 5 berry, green
enjoy a ~ sport: 3 ski 4 skee, sled 5 skate
exclamation ~: 3 brr
festival: 4 yule
follower: 3 spr. 6 spring
forecast: 3 icy 4 cold, snow 5 frost, nippy, sleet, snowy 6 chilly 8 blizzard
month: 3 Dec., Feb., Jan., Mar. 5 March 7 January 8 December, February
month, in Spanish: 5 enero, marzo 7 febrero 9 diciembre
prefix: 3 mid
quarters: 3 den
runner: 3 ski 4 skee 5 skate
sight: 6 breath
sign: 6 Pisces 8 Aquarius 9 Capricorn
sign of ~: 3 ice 4 snow 5 sleet, slush 6 icicle
sound: 5 achoo 6 ahchoo, hachoo 7 kerchoo
transportation: 3 tow 4 luge, sled, T-bar 8 toboggan
vacationer: 5 skier
warmer: 3 fur, nog 4 coat, grog 5 cocoa, quilt, toddy 6 eggnog, hot tea 8 hot toddy 9 comforter
wear: 4 coat, muff 5 glove, loden, parka, scarf 6 anorak 8 earmuffs
weather: 4 snow 5 sleet 8 blizzard
woe: 3 flu 4 ague
winter __: 4 oats, rose, wren 5 apple, break, cress, melon, vetch, wheat 6 barley, cherry, garden, savory, squash 7 aconite, jasmine 8 aconitum
Winter: 4 Alex 5 Edgar 6 Johnny
Winter __: 4 Moon 5 Games 6 Palace
Winter __ Discontent, The: 5 of Our
Winter __, FL: 5 Haven
Winter __ too long in country towns...: 4 lies
__ Winterbourne: 3 Mrs.
Winter Games org.: 3 IOC
wintergreen: 5 fruit
fruit: 8 teaberry
__ wintergreen: 5 oil of 7 spotted
Wintergreen for President composer: 8 Gershwin
__ Winter Group: 5 Edgar
Winterhalter, Hugo song: Canadian Sunset (1956)
Winter Haven: 4 city, town
locale: 7 Florida
Winter Moon author: Dean Koontz
Winter of Artifice author: Anaïs Nin
Winter of Our Discontent, The
author: John Steinbeck
character: 4 Joey 5 Alfio, Allen, Ellen, Ethan
Winter Olympics
see Olympics
Winter on Majorca, A author: George Sand
Winter Palace
resident: 4 czar, tsar, tzar
river: 4 Neva
Winter Park: 4 city, town
locale: 7 Florida
Winters: 4 Yvor 7 Shelley 8 Jonathan
Winter's __: 4 bark 5 Tales
Winterset author: Maxwell Anderson
character: 3 Mio 4 Carr, Piny 5 Garth, Lucia, Trock 6 Esdras
Winters, Jonathan: 5 actor 8 comedian
film: It's a Mad Mad Mad Mad World (1963)
The Loved Ones (1965)
Moon Over Parador (1988)
TV: Mork & Mindy
Winter Springs: 4 city, town
locale: 7 Florida
Winters, Shelley: 7 actress
film: Alfie (1966)
The Big Knife (1955)
The Diary of Anne Frank (1959, AA)
Harper (1966)
Heavy (1996)
I Am a Camera (1955)
Let No Man Write My Epitaph (1960)
Lolita (1962)
Next Stop, Greenwich Village (1976)
The Night of the Hunter (1955)
Odds Against Tomorrow (1959)
A Patch of Blue (1965, AA)
Phone Call From a Stranger (1952)
A Place in the Sun (1951)
The Poseidon Adventure (1972)
What's the Matter With Helen? (1971)
Winchester '73 (1950)
spouse: Tony Franciosa, Vittorio Gassman
Winter's Tale, A author: Jean Stafford
Winter's Tales author: Isak Dinesen
Winter's Tale, The author: William Shakespeare
Winters, Yvor: 4 poet
win the __: 3 day
Winthrop: 4 desk, John
wintry: 3 icy, raw 4 cold, cool 5 bleak, chill, crisp, gelid, harsh, nippy, polar, snowy 6 arctic, biting, brumal, chilly, frigid, frosty, frozen, hiemal 7 glacial, ice-cold, numbing, shivery 8 freezing, hibernal 9 inclement
see also winter
Wintu: 6 Indian 7 Amerind
Winwood, Steve
group: Spencer Davis Group, Blind Faith, Traffic
song: Back in the High Life Again (1987)
Don't You Know What the Night Can Do? (1988)
The Finer Things (1987)
Higher Love (1986)
Holding On (1988)
Roll With It (1988)
Valerie (1987)
While You See a Chance (1981)
winy: 6 vinous
winze: 5 shaft
__ Wip: 5 Reddi
wipe: 3 dab, dry, mop, rub 4 buff, dust, swab, swob, wash 5 brush, clean, clear, erase, towel 6 dry off, remove, rub off, sponge 8 take away 10 obliterate
off the books: 5 annul, erase 6 cancel 7 rescind, scratch 8 dissolve 10 invalidate
off the map: 4 rase, raze, ruin, sack, undo 5 blast, crush, level, smash, total, trash, waste, wreck 6 defeat, ravage, uproot 7 despoil, destroy, flatten, shatter, torpedo 8 bulldoze, decimate, demolish, desolate, spoliate 9 depredate, devastate, eradicate, extirpate, overwhelm, pulverize, take apart 10 annihilate, obliterate
out: 4 bomb, rase, raze, rout, ruin, slay 5 erase, purge, use up 6 cancel, defeat, delete, efface, finish, remove, rub off, uproot 7 abolish, destroy, expunge, pluck up, trounce 8 decimate, get rid of 9 eliminate, eradicate, extirpate, liquidate 10 annihilate, extinguish, obliterate
the slate clean: 6 pardon 7 absolve, forgive, release 8 overlook
wipe __: 3 off, out
wipe __ the map: 3 off
wiped: 5 tired 8 dog-tired 9 exhausted
not ~ out: 5 alive 6 extant, living 9 surviving
out: 4 lost, worn 5 all in, kaput, weary 6 undone 7 drained 8 deprived 9 destitute, insolvent 10 straitened
Wipe Out (1963 song) artist: Surfaris
wiper: 3 rag 6 eraser 8 squeegee
foot ~: 3 mat
__-Wipes: 5 Handi
wipe the __ with: 5 floor
wire: 4 line, send 5 cable, teleg., telex 6 report 7 message 8 telegram 9 electrify, telegraph 10 finish line
bacteriologist's ~: 4 oese
bender: 6 pliers
chicken ~: 4 mesh
electrical ~: 4 cord
enclosure: 4 cage
ender: 3 man, men, tap 4 draw, hair, work, worm 5 drawn, grass 6 haired, puller, tapper, walker 7 pulling, tapping
feature: 6 ground
high-tension ~ support: 5 pylon
inside ~: 3 tip 6 tipoff
live ~: 4 doer, grig 6 dynamo 7 busy bee, hustler 8 fireball, go-getter 9 workhorse 10 powerhouse
measure: 3 mil
mesh: 5 sieve
problem: 5 short
sender of old: 3 TTY 8 teletype
service: 3 UPI
services: 5 media
starter: 3 hay 4 hard, news, trip
wire __: 4 rope, side, vine 5 brush, cloth, gauge, gauze, glass, grass, house, wheel 6 agency, cutter 7 netting, service
wire-__: 4 wove 6 stitch
wire-__ terrier: 6 haired
__ wire: 3 bob 4 high, jump, litz, live 5 piano, razor 6 barbed, ground 7 chicken, gallery
__-wire: 3 hot 5 fly-by
__-wire act: 4 high
wired: 4 edgy 5 eager, hyper, jumpy, manic, ready, tense 6 aflame, touchy 7 anxious, excited, fired up, frantic, nervous 8 fluttery, frenetic, frenzied, juiced up, prepared, strained 10 distressed, high-strung
__-wired: 4 hard
wirehair of film: 4 Asta
wireless: 5 radio
wirer: 7 lineman
wire-rims: 5 specs 7 glasses 10 spectacles
wirers' union: 4 IBEW
wiretap: 3 bug, pry 9 eavesdrop
wiry: 4 hale, iron, lank, lean, slim, spry, thin 5 agile, beefy, burly, hardy, hefty, hunky, husky, kinky, lanky, light, lusty, rangy, spare, stiff, stout, tough 6 brawny, dainty, gangly, hearty, limber, lissom, mighty, potent, robust, rugged, sinewy, skinny, slight, slinky, steely, stocky, strong, sturdy, supple, svelte, twiggy, virile 7 bristly, doughty, gracile, lissome, scraggy, scrawny, slender, spidery, stringy, willowy 8 athletic, forceful, gangling, indurate, muscular, powerful, puissant, stalwart, vigorous 9 Atlantean, Herculean, strapping, sylphlike, well-built 10 able-bodied, red-blooded
Wisc. neighbor: 3 Ill. 4 Iowa, Mich., Minn.
Wisconsin: 5 river, state
athlete: 6 Badger
bay: 5 Green
capital: 7 Madison
city: 5 Ripon 6 Beloit, De Pere, Mequon, Neenah, Racine, Wausau 7 Kenosha, Madison, Muskego, Oshkosh 8 Franklin, Green Bay, La Crosse, Oak Creek, Superior, Waukesha, West Bend 9 Caledonia, Eau Claire, Fitchburg, Fond du Lac, Manitowoc, Milwaukee, New Berlin, Sheboygan, Watertown, Wauwatosa, West Allis 10 Brookfield, Greenfield, Janesville, Sun Prairie
conference: 6 Big Ten
Indian: 9 Menominee, Winnebago 10 Potawatomi
lake: 9 Winnebago
native language: 3 Fox, Sac 4 Sauk 9 Winnebago
neighbor: 4 Iowa 8 Illinois, Michigan 9 Minnesota
product: 6 cheese
school: 5 Ripon 6 Beloit 9 Marquette
state animal: 6 badger
state beverage: 4 milk
state bird: 5 robin
state dance: 5 polka
state domestic animal: 8 dairy cow
state flower: 6 violet
state fossil: 9 trilobite
state grain: 4 corn
state insect: 8 honeybee
state mineral: 6 galena
state stone: 7 granite
state tree: 10 sugar maple
wisdom: 3 wit 4 info, mind, wits 5 depth, savvy, sense 6 acumen, brains, genius, reason, sanity 7 balance, insight, know-how 8 judgment, keenness, learning, maturity, pru-

dence, sagacity, sageness, sapience **9** erudition, foresight, knowledge, stability **10** astuteness, experience, horse sense, philosophy, profundity, shrewdness
combining form: **5** -sophy
Egyptian god of ~: **5** Thoth
folk ~: **3** saw **5** adage, gnome, maxim, moral **6** byword, dictum, saying, slogan, truism **7** epigram, proverb **8** aphorism, apothegm **9** platitude
Greek goddess of ~: **6** Athena, Athene
lacking ~: **4** naif **5** naive
morsel of ~: **5** pearl
name meaning ~: **6** Sophia
tooth: **5** molar
words of ~: **3** saw **5** adage, motto
wisdom __: **5** tooth
Wisdom: **6** Norman
Wisdom of __: **5** Jesus **7** Solomon
Wisdom of Eve, The author: **3** Orr
wise: **3** hep, hip **4** just, mode, onto, sage, sane, wary **5** alert, aware, canny, fresh, nervy, privy, right, savvy, sharp, slick, smart, sound **6** astute, clever, manner, method, shrewd, sophic, taught, versed, with it **7** careful, erudite, knowing, logical, mindful, owllike, politic, process, prudent, sapient, tactful, tuned in **8** apprised, discreet, educated, impudent, informed, insolent, oracular, profound, rational, sensible, well-read **9** advisable, astucious, cognizant, farseeing, in the know, intuitive, judicious, pansophic, plugged in, provident, sagacious, scholarly, Solomonic, venerable **10** all-knowing, diplomatic, discerning, farsighted, insightful, longheaded, omniscient, perceptive, reasonable, reflective, thoughtful
about: **4** on to **5** hep to
become ~: **6** evolve, grow up, mature, mellow **8** maturate
bird: **3** owl
crack ~: **4** jeer, jest, joke
ender: **4** acre **5** crack **7** cracker
get ~: **9** smarten up
goddess: **6** Athena, Athene
guy: **3** wag **4** guru, mage, sage **5** magus **9** know-it-all **10** jackanapes
men: **4** Magi
starter: **3** any, end, man **4** crab, edge, flat, like, long, side, step **5** clock, coast, cross, least, other, penny, slant, width **6** corner, length, street **7** breadth
to: **3** hep, hip **4** in on, up on **5** aware, privy, savvy **6** versed, with it **7** knowing, mindful, tuned in **8** familiar, informed, sensible **9** au courant, cognizant, conscious, in the know, observant, on the beam, plugged in, sensitive **10** acquainted, conversant, perceptive, understood
up: **5** edify, ready **6** get hep **9** enlighten
wise __: **3** guy
wise __ owl: **4** as an
__ wise: **3** get **5** crack
__-wise: **5** penny **7** weather, worldly
wiseacre: **5** joker **6** smarty **7** smartie **9** know-it-all **10** jackanapes, smart aleck
Wise Blood: **4** film **5** novel
author: Flannery O'Connor
cast: Brad Dourif, Daniel Shor, Amy Wright
director: John Huston
__ wise child...: **4** It's a
wisecrack: **3** dig, gag, mot, pun **4** jape, jest, joke, quip **5** humor, reply, spoof **6** gasser, remark **7** comment, observe, sarcasm **8** reaction, response **9** rejoinder, witticism
wisecracker: **3** wag, wit **4** zany **5** clown, comic, joker **8** comedian
wisecracking: **5** humor **6** comedy, joking, send-up **7** jesting, takeoff **8** drollery
__ wise guy, eh?: **3** Oh a
Wiseman: **5** Adele **6** Joseph
Wise Men gift: **4** gold **5** myrrh **12** frankincense
wisent: **5** bison
wiser, maybe: **5** older
Wise, Robert: **8** director
film: Blood on the Moon (1948)
The Body Snatcher (1945)
Born to Kill (1947)
Curse of the Cat People (1944)
The Day the Earth Stood Still (1951)
The Desert Rats (1953)
Executive Suite (1954)
The Haunting (1963)
I Want to Live! (1958)
Odds Against Tomorrow (1959)
Run Silent, Run Deep (1958)
The Sand Pebbles (1966)
The Set-Up (1949)
So Big (1953)
Somebody Up There Likes Me (1956)
The Sound of Music (1965, AA)
Star! (1968)
Star Trek -The Motion Picture (1979)
Three Secrets (1950)
Tribute to a Bad Man (1956)
Two for the Seesaw (1962)
West Side Story (1961, AA)
wish: **3** aim, bid, yen **4** envy, hope, itch, long, miss, pine, pray, urge, want, whim, will **5** covet, crave, dream, fancy, order, yearn **6** aspire, desire, hanker, hunger, intent, please, thirst **7** command, longing, require **8** ambition, daydream, pleasure, volition, yearning **9** appetence, hankering, intention **10** aspiration, desiderate
ender: **4** bone
for: **4** need, want **5** covet, fancy **6** desire
(for): **4** hope, long, pant, pine, sigh **5** spoil, yearn
granter: **5** genie
joy to: **4** fete **5** bless, honor, toast **10** compliment, felicitate
something to ~ on: **4** star **5** a star
(to): **6** aspire
undone: **3** rue **6** bemoan, regret
universal ~: **5** peace
wish __: **4** list
wish __ were here: **3** you
Wish __, wish...: **4** I may
__ Wish: **5** Death
Wishaw: **4** city, town
locale: **8** Scotland
Wish-Bone: **8** dressing
alternative: **9** Seven Seas **11** Good Seasons
__-wisher: **3** ill **4** well
wishes
as one ~: **6** at will
best ~: **7** regards **8** blessing, respects
last ~: **4** will **9** testament
Wishin' and Hopin' (1964 song) artist: Dusty Springfield
wishing: **4** avid **5** eager, itchy **6** hungry **7** athirst, hopeful, jealous, longing, thirsty, wistful **8** aspiring, covetous, desirous, grasping, yearning **9** ambitious
wishing __: **4** well
Wishing Well (1988 song) artist: Terence Trent D'Arby
...wishing will make __: **4** it so
Wishing You Were Here (1974 song) artist: Chicago
Wish me __!: **4** luck
wishy-__: **5** washy
Wish you were __: **4** here
Wish You Were Here (1987 film)
cast: Tom Bell, Emily Lloyd
director: David Leland
wishy-washy: **4** weak **5** vapid **6** fickle, jejune **7** insipid **8** hesitant, lukewarm, wavering **9** faltering, uncertain, undecided, weak-kneed **10** ambivalent, indecisive, irresolute, weak-willed
reply: **5** maybe **7** perhaps **8** possibly **9** it could be, it might be, perchance
Wisk: **9** detergent
alternative: **3** All, Biz, Era, Fab, Yes **4** Bold, Dash, Gain, Surf, Tide **5** Cheer, Dreft, Purex **6** Calgon, Dynamo, Oxydol **7** Octagon **9** Ivory Snow
wisp: **3** bit **4** hint, puff, tuft **5** shock, shred, trace, twist **6** bundle, strand, streak, thread **7** smidgen, smidgin, snippet **8** fragment, smidgeon
wispy: **4** thin **5** faint, filmy **6** dainty, skinny, slight **7** slender **8** feathery **10** weightless
wistaria
see wisteria
Wister: **4** Owen
wisteria: **4** vine **5** plant, shrub **6** flower
wistful: **3** sad **6** dreamy, musing **7** forlorn, longing, pensive, wishful **8** desirous, mournful, touching, yearning **9** nostalgic, plaintive **10** meditative, melancholy, reflective, thoughtful
exclamation: **4** ah me, alas **5** oh gee
one: **4** ruer **5** piner
sound: **4** sigh
Wistful Widow of Wagon Gap, The (1947 film)
cast: Bud Abbott, Lou Costello, Marjorie Main
director: Charles Barton
wit: **3** wag **4** card, mind **5** comic, grasp, humor, irony, joker, sally, sense **6** acuity, acumen, banter, brains, esprit, jester, levity, reason, sanity, satire, wisdom **7** farceur, insight, marbles, punster, sparkle **8** badinage, comedian, drollery, humorist, jocosity, jokester, judgment, keenness, lucidity, quipster, raillery, repartee, sagacity, saneness, sapience, wordplay **9** acuteness, awareness, ingenuity, jokesmith, mentality **10** astuteness, braininess, brainpower, brilliance, cleverness, jocularity, perception, pleasantry, shrewdness
bit of ~: **3** gag, pun **4** jest, joke, quip **5** crack **6** bon mot, zinger **7** epigram **8** one-liner **9** wisecrack
lacking ~: **4** dull **5** prosy, vapid **7** humdrum, prosaic, tedious
like some ~: **3** dry **4** acid **5** sharp **6** biting
starter: **3** dim, nit
to ~: **3** viz. **4** scil. **6** namely, such as **9** videlicet **10** explicitly, for example
__ wit: **5** attic **6** mother
__-wit: **4** half
witch: **3** hag **5** crone **6** beldam **7** beldame, warlock **8** conjurer, sorcerer **9** sorceress
conveyance: **5** broom
creation: **3** hex **4** brew **5** curse
ender: **5** craft
familiar: **3** cat **9** grimalkin
feature: **4** wart
group: **5** coven, esbat
hunt: **5** purge **6** search
hunt locale: **5** Salem
laugh: **6** cackle
repellent: **6** amulet
witch __: **4** ball, hunt, moth **5** alder, grass, hazel **6** doctor, hobble
__ witch: **5** black, water, white
witchcraft: **5** magic, spell, wicca **6** hoodoo, occult, voodoo **7** sorcery **8** black art, wizardry **9** conjuring **10** black magic
Witchcraft (1958 song) artist: Frank Sinatra
Witch Doctor (1958 song) artist: David Seville and the Chipmunks
witches' brew need: **4** frog, newt
Witches of Eastwick, The (1987 film)
cast: Cher, Jack Nicholson, Michelle Pfeiffer, Susan Sarandon
composer: **8** Williams
Witches, The (1990 film)
cast: Anjelica Huston, Mai Zetterling
director: Nicolas Roeg
witching __: **4** hour
Witching Hour, The author: Anne Rice
Witch of __: **5** Endor
Witch of Coos, The author: Robert Frost
Witch of the Low Tide, The author: **4** Carr
__ Witch of the West: **6** Wicked
__ Witch Project, The: **5** Blair
witch's __: **4** brew, mark
Witchy Woman (1972 song) artist: Eagles
with: **5** among **6** dating, mongst, near to, next to **7** amongst, through **9** alongside, escorting, including **10** attached to, supporting
ender: **3** out **4** draw, drew, held, hold **5** drawn, stand, stood
in French: **4** avec
in German: **3** mit
in music: **3** con
in Spanish: **3** con
it: **3** hep, hip **4** chic
prefix: **3** col-, com-, con-, sym-, syn-
starter: **4** here **5** forth, there, where
with __: **5** child **6** reason
with __ and main: **5** might
with __ arms: **4** open
with __ colors: **6** flying
with __ gloves: **3** kid
with __ grace: **3** bad **4** good
with __ on: **5** bells
with __ one's heart: **3** all
with __ to: **5** an eye **6** regard
with __ voice: **3** one
__ with: **3** toy **4** deal, go in, hold, live, make, over, part, side **5** alive, go out, plead, put up, taken **6** reckon
...with __ bodkin: **5** a bare
...with __-foot pole!: **4** a ten
With __ Born Again: **5** You I'm
With __ in My Heart: **5** a Song
With __ My Heart Is Laden: **3** Rue
With __ of thousands!: **5** a cast
With __ ring...: **4** this
With __ toward none...: **6** malice
With __ You Get Eggroll: **3** Six
with a __: **5** nod to
with a __ of salt: **5** grain
...with a __ on my knee: **5** banjo
With a __ in My Heart: **4** Song
...with a cherry __: **5** on top
__ with a grain of salt: **4** take
__ With a Kiss: **6** Sealed
withal: **3** yet **7** however **8** likewise
starter: **5** there, where
With a Little Bit of Luck composer: **5** Loewe **6** Lerner
With a Little Luck (1978 song) artist: Paul McCartney
with all one's __: **5** heart

with an __ to: 3 eye
With a Song in My Heart: 4 song, tune
  composer: 4 Hart 7 Rodgers
With a Song in My Heart (1952 film)
  cast: Rory Calhoun, Susan Hayward
  director: Walter Lang
__ With a View: 5 A Room
__ With a Z: 4 Liza
__ With Bob Costas: 5 Later
__ with care: 6 handle
__ With Charley: 7 Travels
__ With Dick and Jane: 3 Fun
__ With Dirty Faces: 6 Angels
withdraw: 2 go 3 ebb 4 exit, flee, move, part, quit 5 demit, leave, steal, unsay 6 abjure, bow out, depart, flinch, get out, recall, recant, recede, recoil, refuse, remove, renege, repeal, retire, revoke, secede, shrink, vacate 7 abandon, back off, back out, bail out, disavow, drop out, ease out, get away, get lost, give way, make off, pull out, retract, retreat, scratch, seclude, take off 8 abdicate, check out, disclaim, fall back, forswear, phase out, pull back, take away, take back 9 back-pedal, disappear, disengage, foreswear, sequester, stand down, take a hike 10 give ground
  from: 4 wean 5 avoid
withdrawal: 3 ebb 4 exit 5 leave 6 egress, exodus, recall 7 leaving, parting, pullout, removal, retreat 8 apostasy, reaction, solitude 9 abolition, deduction, defection, departure, desertion, secession, seclusion, sundering 10 alienation, evacuation, extraction, retraction, revocation
withdrawn: 3 shy 4 cold, cool, gone 5 aloof, timid 6 chilly, lonely, modest, remote, silent 7 bashful, distant, glacial, private, recluse, removed, retired, uptight 8 departed, detached, isolated, reserved, reticent, retiring, secluded, shielded, solitary, taciturn 9 diffident, flinching, inhibited, reclusive, retreated, secretive, shrinking 10 antisocial, cloistered, restrained, unagitated, unsociable
withe: 4 twig 6 willow
__ with envy: 5 green
wither: 3 dry, rot 4 fade, rust, sear, wane, wilt 5 decay, droop, dry up, parch, waste 6 blight, scorch, shrink 7 atrophy, shrivel 8 decrease, emaciate, languish 9 desiccate
withered: 3 dry 4 sere 7 parched, wizened
withering: 3 rot 4 wane 5 decay 6 biting, fading 7 atrophy, decline 8 decrease 9 crumbling
witherite, metal in: 6 barium
Withers, Bill
  song: Ain't No Sunshine (1971)
    Just the Two of Us (1981)
    Lean on Me (1972)
    Use Me (1972)
Witherspoon: 4 Cora 5 Reese
Witherspoon, Reese: 7 actress
  film: Best Laid Plans (1999)
    Election (1999)
    A Far Off Place (1993)
    Freeway (1996)
    Legally Blonde (2001)
    Sweet Home Alabama (2002)
    Twilight (1998)
  spouse: Ryan Phillippe
With Every Beat of My Heart (1989 song) artist: Taylor Dayne
__ with faint praise: 4 damn
__ With Father: 4 Life
__ with fire: 4 play
__ With Flowers: 5 Say It
with flying __: 6 colors
With Friends Like These... (1999 film)
  cast: Adam Arkin, Amy Madigan, David Strathairn
with full authority in Latin: 9 pleno jure
__ with gas: 7 cooking
__ With Harry, The: 7 Trouble
withhold: 4 deny, hide, keep, save 5 check, sit on, skimp, stint 6 bridle, clam up, deduct, refuse, retain 7 abstain, conceal, forbear, refrain, reserve 8 decrease, diminish, hold back, keep back, subtract
withholding: 6 rebuff, rebuke 7 refusal 8 defiance
withholding __: 3 tax
within: 7 between, through
  combining form: 3 end-, ent- 4 endo-, ento-
  prefix: 5 infra-, inter-, intra-, intro-
within __: 4 hail 5 reach 6 reason
within an __ of: 3 ace 4 inch
Within the Gates author: Sean O'Casey
within the walls in Latin: 10 intra muros
with-it: 3 hip 5 faddy, swank, swish 6 modern, modish, slangy, swanky
__ with it!: 3 Get 4 Deal 5 Get on
__ With Judy: 5 A Date
with kid __: 6 gloves
__ with kindness: 4 kill
__ With Love: 5 To Sir
With malice toward __...: 4 none
__ With Me: 4 Come, Here, Stay 5 Abide, Dance
__ With Me Henry: 5 Dance
with might and __: 4 main
__ With Music: 5 Say It
__ with Nineveh and Tyre: 5 is one
__ With No Name, A: 5 Horse
with one __: 5 voice
with one's __ closed: 4 eyes
with one's __ down: 5 pants
with one's eyes __: 4 open 6 closed
__ with one's feet: 4 vote
with open __: 4 arms
without: 3 bar, out 4 less, sans 5 minus, outer 6 absent, beyond, devoid, except 7 lacking, outside 8 devoid of, outdoors
  delay: 4 ASAP, stat 5 apace
  in French: 4 sans
  in Latin: 4 sine
  in music: 5 senza
  suffix: 4 -less
without __: 4 a fee, a sou, fail 5 a cent, a clue, merit 6 number
without __ ado: 7 further
without __ a hair: 7 turning
without __ to stand on: 4 a leg
Without __: 3 You 4 Love 5 a Song 6 Limits
without a __: 3 sou 5 doubt, hitch 6 stitch
without a __ stand on: 5 leg to
__ Without a Cause: 5 Rebel
Without a doubt!: 3 yes
__ Without a Face, The: 3 Man
__ without a net: 4 work
__ without end: 5 world
without further __: 3 ado
without honor, name meaning: 7 Ichabod
__ without leave: 6 absent
Without Limits (1998 film)
  cast: Billy Crudup, Monica Potter, Jeremy Sisto, Donald Sutherland
  director: Robert Towne
Without Love (1945 film)
  cast: Lucille Ball, Katharine Hepburn, Spencer Tracy
Without Love (1970 song) artist: Tom Jones
without missing __: 5 a beat
__ Without Pity: 4 Time, Town
Without Reservations (1946 film)
  cast: Claudette Colbert, Don DeFore, John Wayne
  director: Mervyn LeRoy
without turning __: 5 a hair
Without You (song) artist: Johnny Tillotson, Mariah Carey, Mötley Crüe, Nilsson
__ with pride: 5 swell
With Reagan: The Inside Story
  author: 5 Meese
with respect to, in math: 6 modulo
With Rue My Heart Is Laden author: A.E. Housman
With silver __ and cockle...: 5 bells
With Six You Get Eggroll (1968 film)
  cast: Doris Day, Brian Keith
  dog: 5 Taffy 6 Calico
withstand: 4 bear, buck, cope, defy, face, lump, stem, take 5 abide, brace, brave, brook, enure, inure, repel, stick 6 combat, endure, oppose, resist, suffer, take it, win out 7 hold out, ride out, survive, sustain, undergo, wait out, ward off, weather 8 confront, stand for, tolerate 9 go through, hang tough, stand up to
__ With the Blue Dress On: 5 Devil
__ With the Golden Arm, The: 3 Man
__ With the Golden Gun, The: 3 Man
...with the greatest of __: 4 ease
With the jawbone of __: 5 an ass
__ With the Light Brown Hair: 6 Jeanie
__ With the Moon: 6 Racing
__ with the punches: 4 roll
__ with the same brush: 3 tar
with the stroke of __: 4 a pen
__ With the Wind: 4 Gone
With this ring, __ wed: 5 I thee
With This Ring (1967 song) artist: Platters
__ With Two Brains, The: 3 Man
__ With Wolves: 6 Dances
__ With You: 4 Rock 5 Being, Stuck
With You I'm Born Again (1980 song)
  artist: Billy Preston
witigo: 5 giant
witless: 4 daft, dopy, dull, soft 5 dense, dopey, inane, silly 6 obtuse, simple, stupid 7 doltish, fatuous, foolish 8 headless, mindless 9 half-baked, insensate 10 unthinking, weak-minded
witness: 3 see 4 espy, eyer, mark, note, seer, sign, view 5 proof, prove, vouch, watch 6 attend, attest, behold, depone, depose, looker, look on, record, regard, signer, viewer 7 bear out, certify, confirm, endorse, eyeball, indorse, observe, testify, watcher 8 attest to, beholder, evidence, looker-on, look upon, observer, onlooker, vouch for 9 bystander, signatory, spectator, testimony 10 get a load of
  bear ~: 4 aver 5 swear, vouch 6 attest, depose 7 testify 8 attest to
  bear false ~: 3 lie 5 libel 7 perjure 9 dissemble
  starter: 3 eye
  statement: 3 I do 4 oath 9 testimony
witness __: 5 stand 6 corner
__ witness: 4 star 6 expert
Witness (1985 film)
  cast: Harrison Ford, Lukas Haas, Kelly McGillis
  director: Peter Weir
  group: 5 Amish
witnesses: 7 gallery 8 assembly, audience 10 attendance
Witness for the Prosecution: 4 film, play
  author: Agatha Christie
  cast: Marlene Dietrich, Elsa Lanchester, Charles Laughton, Tyrone Power
  director: Billy Wilder
Witness to Murder (1954 film)
  cast: Gary Merrill, George Sanders, Barbara Stanwyck
wits: 4 mind 5 grasp, sense 6 acumen, brains, reason, sanity, wisdom 7 balance, insight, marbles 8 judgment, keenness, lucidity, presence, prudence, sagacity, sageness, saneness, sapience 9 acuteness, awareness, ingenuity, intellect, mentality, smartness, soundness 10 astuteness, brainpower, cleverness, perception, shrewdness
wits' end, at: 7 frantic 8 frenetic, frenzied
Witt: 6 Alicia 8 Katarina
__-witted: 3 fat 4 dull, slow 5 quick, ready, sharp, thick
Witten: 4 city, town
  locale: 7 Germany
Wittenberg: 4 city, town
  locale: 7 Germany
__ Witter: 4 Dean
Wittgenstein: 6 Ludwig
witticism: 3 gag, mot, pun 4 jest, joke, quip 5 crack, humor 6 bon mot, retort, ripost, zinger 7 epigram, riposte 8 drollery, one-liner, repartee, wordplay 9 wisecrack 10 pleasantry
witticisms, exchange: 6 banter
Wittig, Georg: 7 chemist 8 Nobelist
witting: 6 wilful 7 willful 9 voluntary 10 deliberate
wittingly: 9 knowingly, on purpose, purposely, willfully 10 designedly
Witt, Katarina: 6 German, skater
  maneuver: 4 axel, spin 5 camel
  milieu: 3 ice 4 rink
witty: 3 gay 4 keen, racy 5 campy, droll, funny, light, salty 6 bright, clever, jocose, lively 7 amusing, comical, jesting, jocular, waggish 8 humorous, original, piercing 9 brilliant, diverting, facetious, laughable, sparkling, whimsical
  one: 3 wag 4 card
  remark: 3 mot 5 sally, squib 6 banter, bon mot
__ Wives Club, The: 5 First
__ Wives of Windsor, The: 5 Merry
__ wives' tale: 3 old
wives' tale, old: 4 lore, myth 6 legend
wiz
  see wizard
wizard: 3 ace, pro 4 mage, seer, tops 5 adept, magus, shark 6 expert, genius, master, pundit, shaman 7 charmer, diviner, hotshot, old hand, prodigy, prophet, warlock 8 conjurer, conjuror, magician, sorcerer, virtuoso 9 authority, enchanter 10 soothsayer
  assistant: 7 famulus
  weapon: 3 hex 5 curse, spell
Wizard
  alternative: 5 Glade 7 Airwick, Renuzit 8 Stick-Ups
  rival: 3 Cav, Mav, Net, Sun 4 Buck, Bull, Hawk, Heat, Jazz, King, Spur 5 Knick, Laker, Magic, Pacer 6 Celtic, Hornet, Nugget, Piston, Raptor, Rocket 7 Clipper, Grizzly, Warrior 8 Cavalier, Maverick 10 SuperSonic, Timberwolf
Wizard __, The: 4 of Id, of Oz
Wizard, Mr. subject: 3 sci. 7 science
Wizard of __ Park: 5 Menlo
Wizard of Oz, The (1939 film)
  cast: Ray Bolger, Billie Burke, Judy Garland, Jack Haley, Margaret Hamilton, Bert Lahr, Frank Morgan

character: **4** Gale, Lion, Zeke **5** Henry, Witch **6** Aunt Em, Glinda, Marvel, Tin Man **7** Dorothy, Hickory **8** Munchkin **9** Scarecrow
director: Victor Fleming
dog: **4** Toto
flower: **5** poppy
last word of ~: **4** home
music: **5** Arlen **7** Harburg
producer: **5** Leroy
prop: **3** axe **5** broom **6** oilcan
setting: **3** Kan. **6** Kansas
studio: **3** MGM
tint: **5** sepia
wizardry: **5** magic **7** sorcery **10** virtuosity, witchcraft
Wizards: **4** five, team
home: **10** Washington
org.: **3** NBA
sport: **10** basketball
wizen: **3** dry **4** wilt **5** dry up **6** shrink **7** shrivel **9** desiccate
wizened: **3** dry, old **4** aged, sere, thin, worn **5** aging **6** ageing, little, shrunk **7** ancient, dried up, elderly **8** grizzled, shrunken, withered, wrinkled **9** geriatric, getting on, senescent, shriveled, up in years
Wiz, The (1978 film)
cast: Lena Horne, Michael Jackson, Mabel King, Richard Pryor, Diana Ross, Ted Ross, Nipsey Russell
composer: Charlie Smalls
director: Sidney Lumet
song: **4** Home **10** Ease on Down
WJM staffer: **3** Lou, Ted **4** Mary **5** Grant **6** Baxter, Murray, Sue Ann
wk., day of the: **3** Fri., Mon., Sat., Sun., Thu., Tue., Wed. **4** Thur., Tues. **5** Thurs.
WKRP in Cincinnati (CBS sitcom)
cast: Loni Anderson (Jennifer Marlowe)
Frank Bonner (Herb Tarlek)
Howard Hesseman (Johnny Fever)
Gordon Jump (Arthur Carlson)
Tim Reid (Gordon Sims/Venus Flytrap)
Richard Sanders (Les Nessman)
Gary Sandy (Andy Travis)
Jan Smithers (Bailey Quarters)
medium: **5** radio
producer: MTM
sign: **5** on air
wks., many: **2** mo. **3** mos.
WNBA
player: **5** woman
team: **3** Sun **4** Lynx **5** Fever, Shock, Sting, Storm **6** Comets, Sparks **7** Liberty, Mercury, Mystics, Rockers **8** Monarchs
WNW: **3** dir. **9** direction
opposite: **3** ESE
Wo-___: **3** Fat
woad: **3** dye **5** stain **7** pigment **8** colorant, tincture
wobble: **3** bob **4** reel, rock, sway **5** lurch, quake, shake, swing, waver **6** careen, falter, quaver, shimmy, teeter, totter, tremor, waddle **7** stagger, stammer, stumble, tremble **9** oscillate, vacillate
Wobblies' union: **3** IWW
wobbly: **4** sick, weak **5** dizzy, loose, rocky, shaky, tippy **6** flimsy, infirm, uneven **7** rickety **8** insecure, unstable, unsteady **9** irregular, teetering, tentative, tottering, unsettled **10** precarious, unbalanced
Wobegon: **4** lake
Woburn: **4** city, town
locale: **4** Mass.
Wodehouse, P.G.: **6** writer **7** British **8** humorist
character: **6** Bertie, Jeeves **7** Wooster
work: The Code of the Woosters
French Leave
Jeeves
The Plot That Thickened
woe: **4** care, pain **5** agony, angst, blues, dolor, gloom, grief, trial, worry **6** blight, misery, regret, sorrow, trials, tsuris **7** anguish, anxiety, despair, problem, sadness, tragedy, travail, trouble, tsouris **8** calamity, disaster, distress, hardship, mourning, the blues **9** adversity, dejection, heartache, suffering **10** affliction, depression, desolation, difficulty, heartbreak, infelicity, melancholy, misfortune
ender: **6** begone
Woe ___!: **4** is me
woebegone: **3** low, sad **4** blue, down, glum, grim, mopy **5** bleak, mopey **6** broody, dismal, dreary, gloomy, morose, somber **7** doleful, forlorn, hangdog, joyless, unhappy **8** dejected, dolorous, downcast, mournful, troubled, wretched **9** bummed-out, cheerless, depressed, heartsick, long-faced, miserable, plaintive, sorrowful **10** chapfallen, despondent, dispirited, lugubrious, melancholy
woeful: **3** bad, low, sad **4** blue, dire, down, foul, glum, grim, poor **5** awful, lousy, sorry **6** bitter, crumby, crummy, dismal, feeble, gloomy, horrid, morose, odious, racked, rotten, somber, tragic **7** accurst, baleful, baneful, beastly, doleful, ghastly, hapless, joyless, piteous, pitiful, tearful, unhappy **8** accursed, agonized, dejected, dolorous, downcast, dreadful, God-awful, grieving, grievous, hopeless, horrible, inferior, luckless, mournful, pathetic, pitiable, poignant, shameful, sinister, stinking, terrible, tortured, tragical, troubled, wretched **9** abhorrent, afflicted, aggrieved, anguished, appalling, atrocious, bummed out, cheerless, defective, execrable, frightful, heartsick, insidious, loathsome, miserable, offensive, plaintive, revolting, sniveling, sorrowful **10** abominable, calamitous, chapfallen, deplorable, despicable, detestable, disastrous, dispirited, distressed, horrendous, inadequate, lachrymose, lamentable, melancholy, pathetical
comment: **4** ah me, alas **6** lament
woefulness: **4** funk **5** blahs, blues, dolor, gloom, grief **6** misery, sorrow **7** despair, malaise, sadness **8** distress, doldrums **9** bleakness, dejection, hard times, heartache, pessimism **10** abjectness, affliction, depression, desolation, discontent, gloominess, heartbreak, low spirits, melancholy
Woe is me!: **4** alas, oh no **5** alack **6** oh dear
Wohl: **3** Ira
wok: **3** pan **6** cooker, frypan **7** steamer **9** frying pan
concoction: **6** lo mein **8** chow mein **9** fried rice
use a ~: **7** stir-fry
wold: **4** moor
Wole: **7** Soyinka
wolf: **3** eat, fur **4** bolt, cram, gulp, lobo, roué **5** bayer, canid, dig in, gorge, ogler **6** animal, canine, devour, gobble, guzzle **7** consume, engorge, swallow **8** gobble up, lothario, whistler **9** libertine, polish off
cry ~: **4** warn
down: **3** eat **4** bolt, gulp **5** scarf **6** devour, englut, gobble, guzzle, inhale **7** put away
ender: **5** berry, hound
group: **4** pack
in sheep's clothing: **4** fake **5** knave, viper **7** traitor
keep the ~ from the door: **4** toil, work **7** peg away **9** grind away
kin: **3** dog, fox **5** dhole, dingo **6** corsac, coydog, coyote, fennec, jackal
Kipling ~: **5** Akela
pack member: **5** U-boat
sea ~: **6** pirate **7** brigand, corsair **9** buccaneer
sound: **4** howl
starter: **4** were
tooth: **4** fang
young: **3** cub, pup
wolf ___: **3** cub, dog **4** call, down, note, pack **6** spider **7** herring
wolf ___ the door, The: **4** is at
___ wolf: **3** cry, red, sea **4** dire, gray, grey, lone **5** maned **6** Indian, strand, timber **7** prairie
Wolf: **5** Peter, Scott **7** Blitzer
constellation: **5** Lupus
Wolf (1994 film)
cast: Jack Nicholson, Michelle Pfeiffer, James Spader
director: Mike Nichols
Wolf ___: **3** Gal **6** number, Solent
___ Wolf: **4** Teen **6** Howlin'
wolf counsel, name meaning: **5** Ralph
Wolfe: **3** Ian, Tom **4** Nero **5** James **6** Thomas
wolf-eel: **4** fish
Wolfen (1981 film)
cast: Albert Finney, Edward James Olmos, Diane Venora
director: Michael Wadleigh
Wolfe, Nero, like: **5** obese
Wolfert: **3** Ira
Wolfe, Thomas: **6** author, writer
work: From Death to Morning
The Hills Beyond
Look Homeward, Angel
Mannerhouse
Of Time and the River
A Portrait of Bascom Hawke
The Return of Buck Gavin
The Story of a Novel
The Third Night
The Web and the Rock
Welcome to Our City
You Can't Go Home Again
Wolfe, Tom: **6** author, writer
work: The Bonfire of the Vanities
The Electric Kool-Aid Acid Test
From Bauhaus to Our House
A Man in Full
Mauve Gloves & Madmen...
Our Time
The Pump House Gang
The Purple Decades
Radical Chic
The Right Stuff
Wolfgang: **4** Paul **5** Pauli **6** Mozart **8** Borchert, Ketterle, Petersen **10** Reitherman
see also German
Wolfgang ___ Mozart: **7** Amadeus
___ Wolfgang Korngold: **5** Erich
___ Wolfgang von Goethe: **6** Johann
wolfhound: **3** dog **5** canid **6** canine
Russian ~: **6** borzoi
___ wolfhound: **5** Irish **7** Russian
wolfhound, Russian: **6** borzoi
wolf in ___ clothing: **6** sheep's
Wolf in Sheep's Clothing, The
source: **4** Esop **5** Aesop
wolflike: **6** lupine, savage **7** lustful **8** ravenous **9** ferocious, predatory
Wolfman Jack records: **3** LPs
Wolf Man, The (1941 film)
cast: Evelyn Ankers, Lon Chaney Jr., Claude Rains
___ Wolf McQuade: **4** Lone
Wolf, Peter group: J. Geils Band
wolfram: **7** element **8** tungsten
wolfsbane: **5** plant, toxin **6** flower, poison
Wolfsburg: **4** city, town
locale: **7** Germany
Wolf Solent author: J.C. Powys
___ Wolf, The: **3** Sea
___ Wolf Too: **4** Teen
Wolfville school: **6** Acadia
Wolitzer: **3** Meg
Wollaston ___: **4** Lake, wire
Wollongong: **4** city, town
locale: **9** Australia
Wolof: **8** language
home: **6** Africa **7** Senegal
Wolsey: **6** Thomas
successor: **4** More
Wolverhampton: **4** city, town
locale: **7** England
wolverine: **6** animal, weasel
relative: **4** mink **5** fitch, otter, ratel, sable, skunk, stoat, tayra **6** badger, ermine, ferret, marten **7** foumart, polecat **8** carcajou, foulmart, kolinsky, muishond
Wolverine state: **4** Mich. **8** Michigan
Wolverton Mountain (1962 song)
artist: Claude King
Wolves
see Timberwolves
Womack: **5** Bobby **6** Lee Ann
woman: **3** gal, her, Mrs., she **4** aunt, Dame, girl, lady, lass, maid, miss, wife **5** adult, bride, human, madam, niece, queen **6** Amazon, damsel, female, lassie, madame, maiden, matron, mortal, mother, person, spouse **7** colleen, dowager, duchess, fiancée, grown-up **8** aviatrix, countess, daughter, ladylove, princess **9** earthling, great-aunt **10** demoiselle, girlfriend, handmaiden, individual
bio word: **3** née
combining form: **3** gyn- **4** gyne-, gyno-, -gyny **5** gynec- **6** gyneco-, -gynous
ender: **4** kind **5** power
garment of ancient Greece: **6** peplos, peplus
hat: **5** toque **6** Breton, cloche
Muslim ~ garment: **4** izar **5** burga, burka **6** burkha, chadar, chador **7** bourkha, chaddar, chuddar
robe of old: **5** simar
starter: **3** lay, mad **4** bond, char, club, door, farm, Manx, news, oars, wash, work **5** chair, clans, dairy, Dutch, freed, horse, Irish, lines, marks, noble, sales, Scots, scrub, stunt, towns **6** anchor, camera, church, clergy, crafts, drafts, French, gentle, patrol, police, repair, select, spokes, sports, states, tribes, vestry, washer, yachts **7** Cornish, council, counter, country, English, service, working **8** assembly, business, outdoors **9** committee, newspaper
that ~: **3** her, she
title: **3** Mrs. **4** dame, lady **5** queen **7** czarina, empress **8** countess, princess
wear: **4** slip **5** dress, skirt, teddy **6** blouse, camise, halter **8** camisole
woman-___: **3** day **4** hour, year
___ woman: **3** to a **5** point, stunt **6** career **7** conjure
Woman ___ Importance, A: **4** of No

Woman __ Seven: 5 Times
Woman __ Sometime Thing, A: 3 Is a
Woman __ Year: 5 of the
__ Woman: 3 I Am, I'm a 4 Evil 5 Born a, Cobra, Devil, Gypsy, She's a, Smart 6 Little, Marked, Modern, Police, Pretty, Witchy, Wonder 7 Another
woman about __: 4 town
womanhood: 8 majority, maturity 9 adulthood
Woman in __, The: 3 Red 5 Green
Woman in a Dressing Gown (1957 film)
cast: Yvonne Mitchell, Anthony Quayle, Sylvia Syms
director: J. Lee Thompson
Woman in Green, The (1945 film)
cast: Hillary Brooke, Nigel Bruce, Basil Rathbone
director: Roy William Neill
Woman in Love (1980 song) artist: Barbra Streisand
Woman in Mind author: Alan Ayckbourn
Woman in Red, The (1984 film)
cast: Kelly LeBrock, Gilda Radner, Gene Wilder
director: Gene Wilder
Woman in the Dunes, The author: 3 Abe
Woman in the Window, The (1944 film)
cast: Joan Bennett, Dan Duryea, Edward G. Robinson
director: Fritz Lang
Woman in White: 4 film 5 novel
author: Wilkie Collins
cast: Sydney Greenstreet, Eleanor Parker, Alexis Smith
Woman Is a Sometime Thing, A composer: 8 Gershwin
womanly: 6 female 8 feminine, ladylike
__ woman never yields: 5 A wise
woman of __: 7 letters
Woman of Affairs, A (1928 film)
cast: Greta Garbo, John Gilbert, Lewis Stone
Woman of Distinction, A (1950 film)
cast: Edmund Gwenn, Ray Milland, Rosalind Russell
director: Edward Buzzell
Woman of No Importance, A author: Oscar Wilde
Woman of Paris, A (1923 film)
cast: Adolphe Menjou, Carl Miller, Edna Purviance
director: Charles Chaplin
woman of the __: 5 house, world
Woman of the Inner Sea author: Thomas Keneally
Woman of the Pharisees, A author: François Mauriac
Woman of the Town, The (1943 film)
cast: Albert Dekker, Barry Sullivan, Claire Trevor
Woman of the Year (1942 film)
cast: Fay Bainter, Katharine Hepburn, Spencer Tracy
director: George Stevens
Woman on the Run (1950 film)
cast: Robert Keith, Dennis O'Keefe, Ann Sheridan
Woman Rebels, A (1936 film)
cast: Elizabeth Allen, Katharine Hepburn, Herbert Marshall
director: Mark Sandrich
Woman's __: 3 Day 5 World
Woman's Face, A (1941 film)
cast: Joan Crawford, Melvyn Douglas, Conrad Veidt
director: George Cukor
__-woman show: 3 one
Woman (song) artist: John Lennon, Peter and Gordon
Woman's Vengeance, A (1947 film)
cast: Ann Blyth, Charles Boyer, Jessica Tandy
director: Zoltan Korda
Woman's World (1954 film)
cast: June Allyson, Van Heflin, Clifton Webb
director: Jean Negulesco
__ Woman, The: 5 Other 6 Bionic, Spider 7 Miracle
Woman Times Seven (1967 film)
cast: Rossano Brazzi, Shirley MacLaine, Peter Sellers
director: Vittorio De Sica
Woman, Woman (1967 song) artist: Gary Puckett and the Union Gap
wombat: 6 animal, mammal 9 marsupial
female: 4 jill
male: 4 jack
relative: 4 euro 5 bilbi, bilby, koala 6 numbat 7 bettong, dasyure, opossum, wallaby 8 kangaroo, wallaroo 9 bandicoot, phalanger
young: 4 joey
women
ender: 4 folk, kind
for men and ~: 4 coed 6 unisex
magazine for ~: 4 Elle, Self 5 Cosmo 6 Allure
org. for ~: 3 DAR, NOW
org. for ~ golfers: 4 LPGA
__ Women: 3 Two 5 Jake's, Smart 6 Little
...Women __ From Venus: 3 Are
Women and Love author: 4 Hite
Women Drying Their Hair artist: 5 Sloan
Women in Love: 4 film 5 novel
author: D.H. Lawrence
cast: Alan Bates, Glenda Jackson, Oliver Reed
director: Ken Russell
Women Ironing artist: 5 Degas
Women of __, The: 5 Arles
women's __: 4 wear 6 rights 7 studies
Women's __: 3 Lib
Women's __ Daily: 4 Wear
Women, The: 4 film, play
author: Clare Boothe Luce
cast: Joan Crawford, Rosalind Russell, Norma Shearer
director: George Cukor
Women Who Run With the Wolves
author: 5 Estes
won: 5 money
as good as ~: 5 on ice 7 assured 8 in the bag 10 guaranteed
homophone: 3 one
to be ~: 9 on the line
won __ soup: 3 ton
wonder: 3 awe 5 doubt, query, stare, think 6 boggle, marvel, ponder, puzzle, rarity 7 enquire, inquire, miracle, portent, prodigy, reflect, suspect 8 mistrust, question, rara avis, surprise, theorize 9 amazement, curiosity, reverence, sensation, spectacle, speculate 10 admiration, conjecture, disbelieve, phenomenon, puzzlement, skepticism
about: 4 mull 5 doubt 7 suspect 8 consider, distrust, meditate, mistrust, mull over, question, turn over 9 reflect on 10 deliberate
aloud: 3 ask 7 request
cause ~: 3 awe 5 amaze 8 surprise
combining form: 8 thaumato-
ender: 4 land, work
exclamation: 3 boy, gee, wow 4 gosh 5 golly, hello 6 jiminy, whizzo 7 jeepers, jimminy
showing ~: 5 agape, in awe
suffix: 4 -ment
word of ~: 3 gee, ooh, wow
wonder __: 3 boy 4 drug 5 child
wonder-__: 6 worker
__ wonder: 3 boy 4 girl 5 small 6 one-hit
Wonder __: 3 Man 4 Boys 5 Woman
Wonder __, The: 5 of You, Years
Wonder (1996 song) artist: Natalie Merchant
Wonder Boys (2000 film)
cast: Michael Douglas, Robert Downey Jr., Tobey Maguire, Frances McDormand
director: Curtis Hanson
wonderful: 3 aah, ace, def, fab, ooh, rad 4 aces, A-one, boss, braw, cool, dece, fine, gear, good, keen, neat, nice, okay, phat, tuff 5 dandy, ducky, grand, great, legit, marvy, moral, neato, nobby, noble, prime, slick, super, swell 6 bang on, bang-up, bonzer, bosker, choice, divine, dreamy, far-out, gnarly, groovy, lovely, peachy, proper, slap-up, spot on, superb, terrif, tiptop, unreal, whizzo, wicked 7 amazing, awesome, capital, corking, ethical, perfect, ripping, skookum, stellar, strange, sublime 8 all right, dazzling, dynamite, especial, eximious, fabulous, five-star, four-star, frabjous, glorious, heavenly, jim-dandy, laudable, pleasant, pleasing, slam-bang, smashing, splendid, standout, sterling, stickout, striking, superior, terrific, top-level, topnotch, uncommon, very good 9 admirable, agreeable, beautiful, bodacious, brilliant, Endsville, excellent, exemplary, exquisite, fantastic, first-rate, high-grade, hunky-dory, marvelous, reputable, sollicker, startling, top-flight, unheard-of 10 acceptable, astounding, beneficial, creditable, first-class, hotsy-totsy, incredible, jack-a-dandy, miraculous, out of sight, peachy-keen, phenomenal, prodigious, remarkable, staggering, stupendous, super-duper, surprising, tremendous
time: 4 idyl 5 blast, idyll
Wonderful __-Hoss Shay, The: 3 One
Wonderful __ of Oz, The: 6 Wizard
Wonderful Adventures of Nils, The
author: Selma Lagerlöf
Wonderful Guy, A composer: 7 Rodgers 11 Hammerstein
Wonderful Ice Cream Suit, The (1999 film)
cast: Joe Mantegna, Esai Morales, Edward James Olmos, Gregory Sierra
__ Wonderful Life: 4 It's a
Wonderful One-Hoss Shay, The
author: Oliver Wendell Holmes
Wonderful Time Up There, A (1958 song) artist: Pat Boone
Wonderful Wizard of Oz, The author: L. Frank Baum
Wonderful! Wonderful! (song) artist: Johnny Mathis, Tymes
__ Wonderful World: 4 It's a 5 What a
Wonderful World of the Brothers Grimm, The (1962 film)
cast: Claire Bloom, Laurence Harvey
director: Henry Levin, George Pal
Wonderful World (song) artist: Herman's Hermits
Wondering (1957 song) artist: Patti Page
Wonderland
cake phrase: 5 eat me
character: 4 dodo, hare
drink: 3 tea
girl: 5 Alice
__ Wonderland: 6 Alex in, Boogie, Winter 7 Alice in
Wonderland by Night (1960 song)
artist: Bert Kaempfert, Louis Prima and Keely Smith
Wonder Like You, A (1961 song)
artist: Ricky Nelson
Wonder Man (1945 film)
cast: Danny Kaye, Virginia Mayo, Vera-Ellen
wonderment: 3 awe 8 surprise 9 amazement 10 admiration
Wonder of You, The (1970 song)
artist: Elvis Presley
__ Wonders of the World: 5 Seven
Wonder, Stevie
hometown: Saginaw
instrument: 5 piano 9 harmonica
song: Blowin' in the Wind (1966)
Boogie On Reggae Woman (1974)
Do I Do (1982)
Ebony and Ivory (1982)
Fingertips-Pt. 2 (1963)
For Once in My Life (1968)
Go Home (1985)
Heaven Help Us All (1970)
Higher Ground (1973)
I Ain't Gonna Stand for It (1981)
If You Really Love Me (1971)
I Just Called to Say I Love You (1984)
I'm Wondering (1967)
I Was Made to Love Her (1967)
I Wish (1976)
Living for the City (1973)
Master Blaster (Jammin') (1980)
My Cherie Amour (1969)
Part-Time Lover (1985)
A Place in the Sun (1966)
Send One Your Love (1979)
Shoo-Be-Doo-Be-Doo-Da-Day (1968)
Signed, Sealed, Delivered I'm Yours (1970)
Sir Duke (1977)
Supersition (1972)
That Girl (1982)
That's What Friends Are For (1985)
Uptight (Everything's Alright) (1966)
We Can Work It Out (1971)
Yester-Me, Yester-You, Yesterday (1969)
You Are the Sunshine of My Life (1973)
You Haven't Done Nothin' (1974)
__ wonder what you are: 4 How I
Wonder Woman (ABC/CBS adventure)
cast: Lynda Carter (Diana Prince/Wonder Woman)
Lyle Waggoner (Maj. Steve Trevor)
Wonder Years, The (ABC sitcom)
cast: Olivia d'Abo (Karen Arnold)
Jason Hervey (Wayne Arnold)
Dan Lauria (Jack Arnold)
Alley Mills (Norma Arnold)
Fred Savage (Kevin Arnold)
wondrous: 8 striking 9 marvelous, thrilling 10 miraculous, phenomenal
Wong: 2 B.D. 7 Anna May
wonk: 4 geek, grub, nerd, nurd 5 brain, dweeb, grind 7 egghead 8 bookworm
Wonka creator: 4 Dahl
Wonsan: 4 port
locale: 10 North Korea
wont: 4 rule 5 habit, usage 6 custom, likely, manner, praxis 7 routine 8 habitude, inclined, penchant, practice, tendency 10 accustomed, consuetude, convention, observance, proclivity
(to): 4 used
won't: 5 shan't 7 refuses
I ~: 2 no 3 nah, naw, nay, nix, non 4 nein, nope, nyet, uh-uh 5 ixnay, never, no how, no way 6 no deal,

noways, nowise **8** forget it, negative, negatory **9** by no means, fat chance **10** count me out, not a chance, thumbs down
wonted: **5** typic, usual **6** common, normal **7** regular, routine, typical **8** everyday, habitual, ordinary, orthodox, standard **9** customary, prevalent **10** prevailing
Won't Get Fooled Again (1971 song)
artist: Who
__ Won the War: **4** How I
won ton: **4** soup **8** dumpling
Won't you __ neighbor?: **4** be my
woo: **3** beg **4** date, love, rush **5** charm, chase, court, spark, spoon, tempt **6** caress, pursue **7** address, entreat, propose, romance, solicit, step out **8** butter up, fawn over, go steady, persuade, run after **9** cultivate, importune, shine up to **10** bill and coo, chase after, curry favor
pitch ~: **4** neck **5** spoon
__ woo: **5** pitch
Woo: **4** John
wood: **3** log, oak **4** aloe, club, pine, teak **5** balsa, birch, cedar, copse, ebony, grove, maple, spoon, trees, weald **6** brassy, cherry, driver, forest, lumber, timber, walnut **7** brassey, brassie, coppice, thicket **8** golf club, kindling, mahogany **10** timberland
black ~: **5** ebony
color: **5** stain
combining form: **3** hyl-, xyl- **4** hylo-, lign-, xylo- **5** ligni-, ligno-
component: **6** lignin
cut ~: **3** axe, hew, saw
durable ~: **4** teak **5** cedar, larch
ender: **3** bin, cut, lot, man, men **4** bine, chat, cock, land, lark, note, pile, ruff, shed, wind, work, worm **5** block, borer, chuck, craft, print, waxen **6** carver, cutter, lander, pecker, turner, worker **7** carving, chopper, cutting, turning, working **8** crafting
feature: **5** grain
flaw: **4** knar, knot **8** knothole
fragrant ~: **4** aloe **5** cedar
furniture ~: **3** oak **4** acle, pine, teak **5** alder, ebony, maple **6** cherry, gaboon
hard ~: **3** ash, oak **4** teak **5** cedar, maple
holder: **4** nail **5** screw
join ~: **4** nail **6** hammer
joint: **5** tenon **7** mortise
knotty ~: **4** pine
light ~: **5** balsa
like some ~: **4** aged
louse: **6** isopod
made of ~: **5** treen
mahoganylike ~: **4** agba
measure: **4** cord
name meaning ~: **5** Horst
piece: **4** chip, lath, slab, slat **5** board **6** billet
problem: **6** dry rot
processor: **3** saw **4** mill **7** sawmill
product: **3** tar **4** slat **5** board, plank, table **6** bureau, timber **7** cabinet
rat: **6** animal, mammal, rodent
residue: **3** ash
saw ~: **5** sleep, snore
smooth ~: **4** sand **5** plane
sorrel: **3** oca, oka **6** oxalis
splitter: **4** mall, maul
stack of ~: **4** rick
starter: **3** bog, box, dog, dye, fat, gum, log, red, sap **4** bass, beef, bent, cord, cork, dead, fire, hard, iron, king, pine, pulp, rose, sass, soft, sour, teak, wild, worm **5** briar, brush, devil, drift, fruit, green, heart, lance, light, match, moose, olive, satin, stink, torch, touch, tulip, white, zebra **6** button, candle, cotton, grease, marble, orange, pepper, poison, sandal, spring, summer, yellow **7** leather
tissue: **5** xylem **6** phloem
tool: **3** adz, axe, saw **4** adze, vise **5** bevel, gouge, lathe, plane **6** chisel
tropical ~: **4** teak **5** balsa, ebony
twist in ~: **4** warp
white ~: **5** birch
wood __: **3** ear, lot, rat, ray, tar **4** coal, duck, fern, frog, ibis, lily, pulp, rose, shot, tick **5** louse, mouse, nymph, pewee, pitch, screw, stork, sugar **6** betony, grouse, hoopoe, pigeon, rabbit, sorrel, spirit, thrush **7** alcohol, anemone, cudweed, turning, vinegar, warbler
__ wood: **3** air, saw **4** late **5** early, knock, metal, olive **6** bullet, citron, gopher, violet **7** Amboina, Amboyna
Wood: **2** Ed **3** Ron, Sam **4** Lana **5** Craig, Grant, Peggy **6** Elijah, Evelyn, Lauren **7** Brenton, Natalie
__ Wood: **7** Belleau, Plastic
Woodard, Alfre: **7** actress
film: Bopha! (1993)
Crooklyn (1994)
Down in the Delta (1998)
Heart and Souls (1993)
Love and Basketball (2000)
Mumford (1999)
Passion Fish (1992)
Primal Fear (1996)
film (voice): Dinosaur (2000)
wood ash product: **3** lye
woodborer: **3** bug **6** insect
Woodbridge: **4** city, town
locale: **8** Virginia **9** New Jersey
Woodburn: **4** city, town
locale: **6** Oregon
Woodbury: **4** city, town
locale: **9** Minnesota
woodcarving: **5** craft
woodchat: **4** bird
woodchopper: **5** axman **6** axeman
woodchuck: **6** animal, mammal, rodent **9** groundhog
look-alike: **5** hyrax **6** dassie
relative: **3** rat **4** cavy, degu, jird, paca, vole **5** coypu, gundi, mouse, xerus **6** agouti, beaver, gerbil, gopher, jerboa, marmot, murine **7** hamster, lemming, muskrat, visacha **8** chipmunk, cricetid, dormouse, squirrel, tuco-tuco **9** chickaree, guinea pig, porcupine **10** chinchilla, prairie dog
...__ woodchuck could chuck wood?: **3** if a
woodcock: **4** bird, fowl
relative: **5** poult, quail, snipe **6** chukar, grouse, peahen, turkey **7** peafowl **8** curassow, moorfowl, pheasant **9** partridge **10** guinea fowl, jungle fowl, wild turkey
Woodcraft author: William Simms
Wood, Craig: **6** golfer
woodcreeper: **4** bird
woodcut: **5** plate **9** engraving
woodcutter
in a children's story: **3** Ali
name meaning ~: **6** Hacker
woodcutting: **7** logging
wood duck: **4** fowl
relative: **4** smew, teal **5** eider, Pekin, Rouen, scaup **6** Cayuga, scoter **7** gadwall, mallard, pintail, pochard, redhead, widgeon **8** garganey, mandarin, oldsquaw, shoveler **9** broadbill, goldeneye, goosander, greenhead, merganser, sprigtail **10** bufflehead, canvasback, surf scoter
wooded: **5** leafy **6** silvan, sylvan **9** arboreous
country, old-style: **5** weald
wooded island, name meaning: **6** Ramsey
Wood, Elijah: **5** actor
film: Deep Impact (1998)
The Faculty (1998)
Forever Young (1992)
The Lord of the Rings: The Fellowship of the Ring (2001)
Paradise (1991)
Radio Flyer (1992)
wooden: **4** dull **5** gawky, rigid, stiff **6** clumsy, gauche, stolid, vacant **7** awkward, deadpan, gawkish, stilted **8** bumbling, lifeless, ligneous, ungainly **9** clapboard, impassive, maladroit, ponderous, unbending **10** glassy-eyed, inflexible, poker-faced, ungraceful
boat: **5** canoe, umiak
clog: **4** geta
container: **3** box **4** case **5** crate
ender: **4** head, ware
frame: **4** rack
pin: **3** peg **4** nogg **5** dowel
post: **3** rod **5** stake **6** picket, timber
stake: **5** spile
strip: **4** lath
travel on ~ runners: **3** ski **4** skee
tub of yore: **3** soe
wedge: **4** shim
yoke: **6** cangue
wooden __: **4** shoe **6** Indian
Wooden Horse, The director: **3** Lee
Wooden, John: **5** coach
milieu: **5** court
org.: **3** NBA
sport: **10** basketball
wooden shoe: **4** clog **5** sabot
sailor: **3** Nod **6** Wynken **7** Blynken
sound: **4** clop
Wood, Grant: **6** artist **7** painter
home: **4** Iowa
Woodhouse: **4** Emma
woodland: **4** bush, park, wood **5** silva, sylva, woods **6** forest, timber
creature: **4** deer
deity: **4** faun **5** satyr
plant: **4** moss, tree
Woodland: **4** city, town
locale: **10** California
Woodlanders, The author: Thomas Hardy
woodlark: **4** bird
Woodlawn: **4** city, town **5** Holly
locale: **8** Maryland
Woodman Spare That __: **4** Tree
Wood, Natalie: **7** actress
film: Bob & Carol & Ted & Alice (1969)
Brainstorm (1983)
The Great Race (1965)
Gypsy (1962)
Inside Daisy Clover (1965)
Kings Go Forth (1958)
Love With the Proper Stranger (1963)
Marjorie Morningstar (1958)
Miracle on 34th Street (1947)
Rebel Without a Cause (1955)
Sex and the Single Girl (1964)
Splendor in the Grass (1961)
The Star (1952)
West Side Story (1961)
sister: **4** Lana
spouse: Robert Wagner
woodpecker: **4** bird
relative: **7** wryneck
tool: **3** neb
__ woodpecker: **4** Gila **5** downy, green, hairy
__ Woodpecker: **5** Woody
Wood, Peggy TV role: **4** Mama
wood-pulp product: **5** rayon
Woodridge: **4** city, town
locale: **8** Illinois
Woodrow: **6** Wilson
woods: **4** park **5** copse, grove, trees, weald **6** forest, lumber, timber **7** coppice, thicket **8** outdoors **9** backwater **10** timberland
babe in the ~: **4** fawn, lamb, naif **6** victim **9** unworldly
be out of the ~: **4** mend **5** rally **7** get well, rebound, recover **8** snap back **9** get better **10** bounce back, come around, convalesce, recuperate
carrier: **5** caddy **6** caddie
dweller: **4** deer **7** raccoon
element: **4** tree
ender: **3** man, men
home in the ~: **4** nest
like a babe in the ~: **4** naif **5** naive
like some ~: **4** piny **5** piney
name meaning ~: **3** Guy
neck of the ~: **4** area **6** locale, region, sphere **7** quarter **8** locality, location, purlieus, vicinity **9** territory
out of the ~: **4** safe **6** better, secure **8** home free **10** in the clear
small ~: **5** copse, grove **7** coppice
starter: **4** back, king
Woods: **3** Ren **4** Elle **5** James, Tiger
Wood, Sam: **8** director
film: Command Decision (1948)
A Day at the Races (1937)
The Devil and Miss Jones (1941)
For Whom the Bell Tolls (1943)
Goodbye, Mr. Chips (1939)
Hold Your Man (1933)
Kings Row (1942)
Kitty Foyle (1940)
A Night at the Opera (1935)
Our Town (1940)
Peck's Bad Boy (1921)
The Pride of the Yankees (1942)
The Stratton Story (1949)
They Learned About Women (1930)
__ Woods, CA: **4** Muir
__ Woods Conference: **7** Bretton
woodsia: **4** fern
Woods, James: **5** actor
film: Another Day in Paradise (1998)
Any Given Sunday (1999)
Casino (1995)
Contact (1997)
Ghosts of Mississippi (1996)
Immediate Family (1989)
John Q (2002)
Nixon (1995)
Once Upon a Time in America (1984)
The Onion Field (1979)
The Specialist (1994)
True Believer (1989)
The Virgin Suicides (2000)
woodsman's leaving: **5** stump
Wood's metal: **5** alloy
component: **3** tin **4** lead **7** bismuth, cadmium
wood-splitter head: **5** wedge
__ woods these are...: **5** Whose
Woods, Tiger: **6** golfer
milieu: **5** links **6** course
org.: **3** PGA
real first name: **7** Eldrick
Woodstock: **4** city, town
attendee: **5** hippy **6** hippie
locale: **6** Canada **7** New York, Ontario **8** Illinois
setting: **4** farm

Woodstock (1970 song) artist: Crosby, Stills & Nash
wood-stove receptacle: 6 ashpan
woodsy: 5 bosky 6 silvan, sylvan
area: 5 glade
home: 4 camp
Wood, The (1999 film)
cast: Trent Cameron, Taye Diggs, Omar Epps, Sean Nelson
Woodward: 3 Bob 6 Edward, Joanne, Robert
Woodward, Joanne: 7 actress
film: A Big Hand for the Little Lady (1966)
A Fine Madness (1966)
From the Terrace (1960)
The Glass Menagerie (1987)
The Long Hot Summer (1958)
Mr. & Mrs. Bridge (1990)
No Down Payment (1957)
Paris Blues (1961)
Rachel, Rachel (1968)
Summer Wishes, Winter Dreams (1973)
They Might Be Giants (1971)
The Three Faces of Eve (1957, AA)
Winning (1969)
WUSA (1970)
role: 3 Eve
spouse: Paul Newman
Woodward, Robert: 7 chemist 8 Nobelist
woodwind: 3 sax 4 oboe, reed
of old: 5 shawm
woodworker: 6 joiner 9 carpenter
woodworm: 3 bug 6 insect
woody: 5 bosky 6 silvan, sylvan
fiber: 4 bast
Woody: 5 Allen, Hayes 6 Herman, Strode 7 Guthrie 9 Harrelson 10 Woodpecker
frequent costar: 3 Mia
son: 4 Arlo
Woody Herman's Thundering ___: 4 Herd
wooer: 4 beau 5 flame, lover, swain 6 steady, suitor 7 admirer, gallant, tempter 8 loverboy, paramour 9 boyfriend, inamorato
word: 5 honey
woof: 3 arf 4 bark, weft 6 bowwow 7 texture
crosser: 4 warp
work with ~: 5 weave
woof-woof: 5 doggy 6 doggie
___-woogie: 6 boogie
Woo-Hah!!... (1996 song) artist: Busta Rhymes
wooing: 4 suit 6 dating 7 pursuit, romance 9 courtship 10 engagement
Woo, John: 8 director
film: Broken Arrow (1996)
A Bullet in the Head (1990)
Face/Off (1997)
Mission: Impossible II (2000)
wool: 3 fur 4 pelt 5 cloth 6 alpaca, angora, fabric, fleece 7 kashmir 8 cashmere
all ~ and a yard wide: 4 real, true 6 trusty 7 genuine, sincere 8 constant, faithful, true-blue
coarse ~: 3 aba 4 abba 5 tweed
coil of ~: 5 skein
combining form: 3 lan- 4 erio-, lani-, lano-
ender: 4 sack, skin 6 gather, grower 7 growing 8 gatherer 9 gathering
fabric: 3 rep 4 felt, repp 5 baize, Kasha, khaki, loden, plush, serge, tweed, voile 6 alpaca, Angora, armure, chally, damask, gloria, jersey, kersey, merino, mohair, moreen, poplin, saxony, stamin, tartan, tricot, vicuña, wadmal 7 bunting, challie, challis, Cheviot, drugget, duvetyn, flannel, grogram, paisley, tabinet, Viyella, worsted 8 algerine, homespun, marocain, shalloon, tabbinet, Venetian, whipcord 9 astrakhan, calamanco, grenadine, henrietta, paramatta 10 Irish tweed
fine ~: 6 alpaca, angora 7 kashmir 8 cashmere
foreign particle in ~: 4 moit, mote
garment: 5 shawl 7 sweater 8 mackinaw
grease: 5 suint
harvest ~: 5 shear
knot: 4 burl
like ~: 4 warm 6 fleecy, toasty
low-grade ~: 5 mungo
outerwear: 5 ruana
pull the ~ over: 5 trick 6 take in 7 mislead
raw ~: 6 fleece
source: 3 ewe, ram 5 llama, sheep 6 alpaca
spun ~: 4 yarn
substitute: 5 Orlon
tease ~: 3 tum
type of ~: 4 ragg
water-repellent ~: 5 loden
weight unit: 3 tod
wool ___: 3 fat 4 clip 6 sponge 7 stapler
___ wool: 4 rock 5 glass, lamb's, range, steel 6 Angora, Berlin, Botany, bright, cotton, grease, modock, virgin, wether 7 mineral, western
___ wool and a yard wide: 3 all
woolens: 4 hose 5 socks 7 hosiery
Woolery, Chuck spouse: Jo Ann Pflug
Wooley, Sheb song: The Purple People Eater (1958)
Woolf, Virginia: 6 author, writer 7 British
work: Between the Acts
Jacob's Room
Mrs. Dalloway
Orlando
A Room of One's Own
To the Lighthouse
The Waves
woolgather: 4 hope, moon 5 fancy 7 imagine, picture 8 daydream, space out 9 fantasize
woolgathering: 6 revery, trance 7 reverie
Woolite: 8 cleanser 9 detergent
Woollcott, Alexander: 3 wit 6 writer
Woolley: 5 Monty 7 Charles
Woolley, Monty: 5 actor
film: Holy Matrimony (1943)
Life Begins at Eight-Thirty (1942)
The Man Who Came to Dinner (1941)
Molly and Me (1945)
The Pied Piper (1942)
wool-like fabric: 7 satinet 9 satinette
woolly: 5 downy, fuzzy, rough, rowdy 6 fleecy, hectic, lanate, lanose, rugged 7 chaotic, muddled, sweater, unclear 8 confused 9 rough-hewn, unrefined
bear: 3 bug 6 insect
woolly ___: 4 bear, worm 5 aphid 6 monkey 7 mammoth
___-woolsey: 6 linsey
Woolsey: 5 James 6 Robert
Woolsey, James former org.: 3 CIA
Woolworth: 2 F.W. 5 Frank
Woolworth Building architect: 7 Gilbert
wooly
see woolly
Wooly Bully (1965 song) artist: Sam the Sham and the Pharaohs
Woonsocket: 4 city, town
locale: Rhode Island
Woosnam, Ian: 6 golfer
milieu: 5 links 6 course
org.: 3 PGA
Wooster: 4 city, town 6 Bertie
locale: 4 Ohio
___-wootsy: 6 tootsy
woozy: 5 dizzy, faint, tipsy 7 muddled
___-wop: 3 doo
Wopat: 3 Tom
Worcester: 4 city, town
athletes: 9 Crusaders
ender: 5 shire
locale: 7 England 8 Hereford
school: 9 Holy Cross
Worcester ___: 5 china
___ Worcester: 5 Royal
Worcestershire: 5 sauce 6 county
locale: 7 England
Worcs: 6 county
locale: 7 England
word: 3 put, saw, tip, vow 4 chat, name, news, oath, talk, term, will 5 couch, edict, idiom, order, rumor, say-so, sound, ukase, usage 6 adverb, advice, behest, byword, confab, decree, dictum, gossip, notice, parole, phrase, pledge, plight, remark, report, rumble, saying, signal, slogan, speech, tipoff 7 account, article, bidding, command, comment, concept, dictate, go-ahead, hearsay, mandate, message, missive, promise, proverb, tidings, warrant, whisper 8 bulletin, chitchat, colloquy, dispatch, language, locution, morpheme 9 adjective, assurance, directive, discourse, guarantee, statement, tête-à-tête, utterance 10 commitment, communiqué, discussion, expression, green light, injunction, intimation
combining form: 3 log- 4 logo-, -onym 5 gloss- 6 glosso-, glotto- 7 onomato-
ender: 3 age 4 book, less, play 5 smith 6 monger
in French: 3 mot
in Spanish: 7 palabra
starter: 3 key, mis 4 buzz, fore, head, loan, pass 5 after, backs, catch, cross, guide, swear, watch 6 broads, double
word ___: 4 game, time, wrap 5 class, order, salad 6 accent, square, stress 7 picture
word ___ word: 3 for
word-___: 4 lore 5 hoard
___ word: 3 at a, in a, key 4 code, form, full, good, last, loan 5 dirty, empty, entry, ghost, guide, nonce, smear, vogue 6 weasel 7 clipped, content, machine
wordbook: 3 lex. 4 dict., thes. 7 lexicon 9 thesaurus 10 dictionary
word-for-word: 5 exact 6 verbal 7 literal, precise 8 faithful, verbatim
wordiness: 3 gas 8 rhetoric, verbiage 9 garrulity, loquacity, prolixity, verbosity
wording: 4 text 5 style, usage, words 6 phrase 7 diction 8 language, locution, parlance, verbiage
wordless: 3 mum 4 mute 5 tacit 6 silent, unsaid 8 unvoiced 9 noiseless 10 speechless, tongue-tied, understood
word of ___: 5 honor, mouth
Word of Honor author: Nelson Demille
word-of-mouth: 4 oral 6 verbal 9 unwritten
WordPerfect headquarters: 4 Orem
wordplay: 3 pun, wit 6 banter, bon mot, ripost 7 riposte, waggery 8 badinage, drollery, repartee 9 equivoque, witticism 10 persiflage, spoonerism
given to ~: 5 punny
word processor: 7 program 8 software
alternative: 3 pen
command: 3 cut 4 edit, quit, save, sort 5 paste 6 delete
words: 3 row 4 talk, text, tiff 5 set-to, vocab., voice 6 strife 7 wording 8 squabble 9 utterance 10 vocabulary
at a loss for ~: 5 blank, dazed 7 shocked, stunned 8 overcome 9 awestruck 10 bowled over, nonplussed, speechless
bandy ~: 3 rap 4 chat, spar 5 argue
choice ~: 5 and/or, or not
contest of ~: 3 bee
eat one's ~: 6 recant 7 retract 9 back-pedal
empty ~: 3 rot 4 bunk, wind 5 prate, stuff, tripe 6 bunkum, humbug 7 blarney, bombast, fustian, hogwash, malarky, palaver 8 buncombe, claptrap, malarkey, nonsense 9 gibberish, moonshine 10 mumbo jumbo
four-letter ~: 5 oaths 7 cursing, cussing 8 swearing 9 blasphemy, profanity 10 expletives
give ~ to: 3 say 5 speak, utter, voice 6 assert 7 express 8 proclaim 9 enunciate, verbalize 10 articulate
good with ~: 4 glib 5 suave 6 facile, fluent 8 eloquent 10 articulate, loquacious
have ~: 4 spat 5 scrap 7 quarrel, wrangle 8 squabble
in other ~: 5 id est 6 namely, that is
like a play on ~: 5 punny
not mincing ~: 5 blunt, frank 6 candid 10 forthright, free-spoken, from the hip, unreserved
of few ~: 4 curt 5 brief, crisp, pithy, short, terse 6 snappy 7 brusque, clipped, concise, laconic 8 succinct 10 aphoristic, to the point
opening ~: 5 intro 6 prolog 7 prelude 8 foreword, preamble, prologue
parting ~: 5 I quit, see ya 6 so long 8 au revoir
play on ~: 3 pun 9 equivoque
put into ~: 3 say 4 limn, talk 5 speak, state, utter, vocal, voice 6 phrase, relate, spoken 7 express 8 vocalize
run ~ together: 4 slur 6 garble, mumble
stock of ~: 5 lexis 7 lexicon
to live by: 5 adage, credo, creed, motto
use four-letter ~: 4 cuss 5 curse, swear 9 blaspheme
use weasel ~: 5 dodge, evade, fudge, skirt, waver 6 waffle 8 flip-flop, sidestep 9 hem and haw, pussyfoot, stonewall, vacillate 10 equivocate
war of ~: 6 debate 8 argument
way with ~: 4 tact 9 diplomacy
___ words: 5 mince, of few
Words (1967 song) artist: Monkees
Words for the Wind author: Theodore Roethke
Words Get in the Way (1986 song) artist: Gloria Estefan
wordsmith: 6 author, editor, scribe, writer 8 essayist, novelist, reporter 9 columnist 10 journalist, librettist, playwright
Words of Love (1966 song) artist: Mamas & the Papas
___ words were never spoken: 5 truer
Wordsworth, William: 7 British
colleague: 5 Byron, Keats 7 Shelley
piece: 3 ode 4 poem
work: Elegaic Stanzas
I Wandered Lonely as a Cloud

Lines Composed a Few Miles Above Tintern Abby
Lucy Gray
Lyrical Ballads
Michael
My Heart Leaps Up
Ode: Intimations of Immortality
Ode to Duty
She Was a Phantom of Delight
The Solitary Reaper
Tintern Abbey
The World Is Too Much With Us

__ word with: 5 have a
wordy: 4 long 5 gabby, talky, windy 6 chatty, prolix, turgid 7 diffuse, gushing, lengthy, tedious, unterse, verbose, voluble 8 babbling, inflated, rambling 9 bombastic, garrulous, jabbering, redundant, talkative 10 bigmouthed, blathering, discursive, longwinded, loquacious, palaverous, pleonastic, rhetorical, roundabout, unsuccinct
wore: 5 had on 7 sported
__ Wore a Yellow Ribbon: 3 She
Worf: 5 alien 7 Klingon
portrayer: 4 Dorn
work: The Decline and Fall of the Roman Empire 2 do, go 3 dig, gig, job, ply, run 4 book, deed, duty, farm, line, moil, opus, play, push, slog, slot, task, till, toil, walk 5 chore, craft, drama, grind, knead, labor, serve, shape, skill, slave, solve, stint, sweat, thing, trade, wield, wreak 6 behave, career, create, drudge, effort, employ, handle, hustle, living, métier, muscle, oeuvre, office, output, racket, strain, strive 7 achieve, calling, carry on, come off, control, exploit, fashion, mission, operate, peg away, product, project, pursuit, scratch, service, slavery, succeed, swindle, travail, trouble, writing 8 activity, business, contract, creation, drudgery, exercise, exertion, function, industry, lifework, maneuver, painting, plug away, position, practice, progress, struggle, toil away, vocation 9 cultivate, freelance, grind away, handiwork, moonlight, salt mines, sculpture, servitude, specialty 10 accomplish, assignment, buckle down, commission, commitment, concoction, daily grind, effectuate, employment, engagement, handicraft, livelihood, magnum opus, manipulate, nine-to-five, occupation, production, profession, take effect
alone: 4 solo
around: 4 duck, shun 5 avoid, elude, evade, skirt 6 bypass, eschew, ignore 8 sidestep 10 circumvent
assignment: 4 task 5 chore, stint 6 errand 7 project 8 activity
at ~: 4 busy 5 astir 6 active, on duty 7 dynamic, engaged, in force 8 bustling, employed, in action, on the job 9 assiduous, on the move 10 in progress
averse to ~: 4 idle, lazy 6 otiose, torpid 7 laggard, languid, passive 8 indolent, slothful 9 do-nothing, lethargic, sedentary, shiftless 10 languorous
avoid ~: 4 idle, laze, loaf 5 dog it, shirk, slack 6 dawdle 7 goof off 8 lollygag, malinger, slack off 9 bum around, pussyfoot 10 featherbed, mess around
away: 3 peg, ply
back from ~: 4 home
body of ~: 5 canon 6 corpus, oeuvre
cease ~: 4 quit 5 leave 6 bow out, resign, retire 8 hang it up, step down 10 give notice
combining form: 3 erg- 4 ergo-, -ergy, -urgy
comprehensive ~: 5 summa
creative ~: 6 design 9 blueprint, invention
crew: 4 team, unit 5 corps, labor, staff 9 personnel
detail: 4 spec
dirty ~: 5 fraud 6 deceit, dupery 7 falsity, perfidy 9 chicanery, deception, duplicity, hypocrisy, treachery 10 dishonesty
ender: 3 day, man, men, out 4 boat, book, fare, flow, folk, load, room, shop, week 5 bench, force, horse, house, place, sheet, space, table, woman, women 6 people 7 station
evade ~ in Britain: 5 sculk, skulk
evader: 5 idler 6 loafer, truant 7 goof-off, shirker, slacker 8 fainéant 9 do-nothing, goldbrick, lazybones 10 ne'er-do-well
for: 4 earn, help 5 serve 6 assist 7 benefit, cater to, promote
free: 4 undo 5 loose, untie 6 loosen, unbind 7 release, unhitch, unloose 9 disengage
get to ~: 5 begin, start 6 set off, set out 7 lead off, proceed 8 commence, set about, set forth
give ~ to: 4 hire 6 employ, engage, sign on, take on 10 give a job to
great ~: 4 opus, tome 10 magnum opus
hard: 4 moil, plod, slog, toil 5 labor, slave 6 drudge, hustle, strain 8 struggle 9 persevere
hard ~: 4 moil, toil 5 grind, sweat 7 travail 8 drudgery, exertion, industry 10 punishment
hater: 5 drone, idler 6 loafer, rascal, truant 7 dawdler, laggard, shirker, slacker 8 parasite 9 do-nothing, goldbrick, lazybones 10 ne'er-do-well
history: 4 vita 6 résumé
house ~: 5 chore
in: 3 mix 9 interpose, introduce 10 specialize
in the ~ cited: 5 op. cit.
in unison: 4 sync
life's ~: 5 trade 6 career 7 calling
not ~ out: 4 fail, flop
not ~ very hard: 5 coast 7 goof off
of art: 7 drawing 8 painting, pastiche
off from ~: 4 free, idle 7 dormant, loafing, resting 8 inactive 9 loitering
on: 3 bug, nag 4 coax, urge 5 press 6 attend, cajole, pester, tackle 7 wheedle 8 pressure 9 importune
out: 2 do 3 fix, jog, win 4 plan 5 crack, educe, solve, sweat, swing, train 6 devise, evolve, figure, finish, get fit, go well, handle, happen, make it, reason, result, settle, thrive, tone up 7 achieve, arrange, develop, prevail, program, prosper, resolve, satisfy, succeed, triumph, unravel 8 bring off, conclude, contrive, exercise, finalize, flourish, get ahead, go places, make good, rehearse 9 calculate, construct, determine, elaborate, formulate, negotiate 10 accomplish, aerobicize, compromise
out of ~: 4 free, idle 7 jobless 9 at liberty 10 unemployed
over: 4 mall, maul, redo 6 bang up, thrash
overwhelm with ~: 4 snow 6 deluge 9 snow under
period: 4 week
place: 4 cube, desk 6 office 7 cubical
prepare for ~: 5 dress, shave
provider: 5 hirer 8 employer
put to ~: 3 use 4 hire 5 apply 6 employ, engage
quickly (through): 6 breeze
reason for a ~ break: 5 lunch 6 coffee
refuse to ~: 6 strike
safety agcy.: 4 OSHA
shift: 4 days 5 stint 6 nights
slowly: 4 drag, plod, slog 5 crawl 6 trudge
starter: 3 art, cut, leg, net, pin, tin, wax 4 bead, body, busy, case, duct, fire, flat, foot, form, fret, hack, hand, head, heel, home, iron, life, mesh, mill, open, over, road, rock, scut, seat, slop, stud, team, time, wire, wood 5 after, brain, brick, brush, clock, craft, earth, fancy, field, frame, frost, glass, grill, guess, house, metal, paper, patch, piece, press, quill, spade, steel, stone, wheel 6 breast, bridge, bright, crewel, donkey, drudge, ground, master, needle, rubble, school, silver, stucco, timber, wicker 7 cabinet, journey, lattice, leather, passage, plaster, trellis, trestle
stop ~: 4 halt, quit 5 relax 6 retire 8 knock off 10 call it a day
things out: 4 cope 6 manage
(through): 4 wade
to do: 6 agenda
together: 3 fit, nod 4 gybe, jibe 5 agree, unite, yield 6 accede, accord, assent, club up, concur, league 7 approve, comport, consent 8 coincide 9 acquiesce, cooperate 10 join forces
(together): 4 band
toward: 6 pursue 7 go after 8 quest for 9 cultivate, strive for
travel to ~: 4 ride 5 drive 7 commute
unexciting ~: 5 McJob
unfinished ~: 7 backlog
unit: 3 erg, job 4 task 5 joule 9 foot-pound
unwillingness to ~: 5 sloth 7 languor 8 laziness, lethargy, otiosity 9 fainéance, indolence, passivity 10 torpidness
up: 3 irk 4 move, rile, spur, stir 5 hatch, peeve, rouse, shape, upset 6 arouse, enrage, excite, foment, incite, kindle, turn on 7 agitate, develop, enflame, enthuse, ferment, fluster, improve, inflame, inspire, produce, provoke 8 generate 9 instigate, stimulate
up to: 8 grow into
well: 4 mesh, tick 5 click
with: 3 use 5 apply, wield 6 employ, engage, handle 7 operate 10 manipulate
work __: 3 off, out 4 camp, farm, into, load, over, song 5 ethic, force, of art, order, rules, sheet, train 7 station, through
work __ a net: 7 without
work __ charm: 5 like a
work __ sweat: 3 up a
work __ team: 3 as a
work-__: 4 hour 5 study 7 release
__ work: 3 dog, job 4 cape, case, desk, mill, scut 5 bench, dirty, drawn, group, grunt, out of, white 6 Bantam, donkey, motion, social 7 cut-card, welfare
__-work: 3 hot 4 book, cold, make 5 floor
__ Work: 5 Men at
workable: 4 easy, snap 5 cinch 6 breeze, doable, likely, simple, usable, viable 7 no sweat, plastic, useable 8 credible, duck soup, feasible, possible 9 malleable, operative, plausible, potential, practical 10 achievable, applicable, attainable, imaginable
workaday: 5 usual 6 common 7 mundane, prosaic, routine 8 ordinary 9 practical, prosaical
workaholic: 5 type A
work as __: 5 a team
work behind __: 5 a desk
workbench item: 3 nut 4 adze, nail, tool 5 clamp 6 pliers
workbook: 4 text 5 guide 6 manual
worked
get ~ up: 3 irk 4 rave, rile 5 anger, peeve, upset
up: 3 mad 4 agog 5 angry, irate, tense, upset 7 frantic, furious 8 frenetic, frenzied
worker: 3 ant, bee 4 doer, hand, help, serf 5 labor, slave, stiff 6 earner, jobber, toiler 7 artisan, employe, laborer, peasant 8 employee 9 hired hand, operative 10 blue collar, wage earner
cry: 4 TGIF
ID: 3 SSN
office ~: 4 asst. 5 clerk 9 assistant, secretary
perk: 4 ESOP 5 bonus
protection org.: 4 EEOC, NLRB, OSHA
starter: 4 auto, dock, head, iron, mine, time, wage, wood 5 field, house, metal, piece, steel, stone 6 wonder 7 leather
worldwide ~ grp.: 3 ILO
worker __: 3 ant, bee
__ worker: 4 case, fast, mine 5 guest 6 social 7 migrant
__-worker: 6 wonder 7 counter
workers: 4 crew, help, team 5 staff 9 personnel
group: 5 union
supply with ~: 3 man 5 staff
workers' __: 4 comp
Workers of the world __!: 5 unite
__ Worker, The: 7 Miracle
workhorse: 5 slave 6 dynamo 8 live wire
__ Work if You Can Get It: 4 Nice
working: 4 at it, busy, live, spry 5 alive, astir, going, perky 6 active, in gear, lively, usable, useful, viable 7 dynamic, engaged, in force, on track, running, useable 8 animated, bustling, employed, laboring, occupied, on the job, operable 9 assiduous, effective, energetic, in process, on the move, operation, operative, practical, reckoning, sprightly
again: 5 fixed 7 rebuilt
good ~ condition: 6 kilter
no longer ~: 3 ret. 4 retd. 7 retired
one ~ hard: 5 plier, plyer
or not: 4 as is
people: 5 labor, staff 9 personnel
person: 5 prole 7 laborer
starter: 4 lamp, wood
stop ~: 4 fail, rest 6 retire 9 break down
time: 5 shift, stint
together: 6 in sync
working __: 3 day, dog 4 face, girl, hour, rail 5 asset, class, fluid, order, stiff, title 6 papers 7 capital, drawing, storage
Working Girl (1988 film)
cast: Alec Baldwin, Joan Cusack, Harrison Ford, Melanie Griffith, Sigourney Weaver
character: 4 Tess
director: Mike Nichols

Working Man, The (1933 film)
cast: George Arliss, Bette Davis
director: John G. Adolfi
Working My Way Back to You (song)
artist: Four Seasons, Spinners
workings: 4 core 5 gears 7 innards 9 apparatus, machinery, mechanism 10 components
working without __: 4 a net
__ Work It Out: 5 We Can
work like __: 4 a dog 6 a charm
workman ender: 4 like, ship
workmanship: 3 art 5 craft, flair, skill, style 7 mastery 8 artistry 9 expertise
workmate: 4 ally 7 partner 9 associate, colleague 10 compatriot
workmen's __: 4 comp
work of __: 3 art
work on __: 4 spec
work-order detail: 4 spec
workout: 5 drill 6 warm-up 7 routine, session 8 aerobics, exercise, practice, training 9 rehearsal 10 gymnastics, isometrics
aftermath: 4 ache 5 cramp 8 soreness
attire: 6 sweats 7 leotard
facility: 3 gym, spa 8 YMCA. YWCA
routine: 4 curl 5 press, squat
target: 3 abs 4 flab, pecs 5 delts, quads 6 biceps 7 triceps
workplace: 4 desk, shop 5 store 6 office
workroom: 4 shop 6 studio 7 atelier
works: 4 goes, mill 5 opera, plant 7 insides 9 machinery, mechanism
complete ~: 5 canon 6 corpus, oeuvre 10 collection, opera omnia
gum up the ~: 3 err, jam 4 flub, mess, muff, slip 5 botch, fluff 6 boggle, bumble, bungle, fumble 7 blunder, stumble 9 mishandle, mismanage
in the ~: 5 afoot 7 pending 8 imminent 9 impending
starter: 3 gas 4 iron, salt 5 skunk, steel, water, wheel
the ~: 3 all, sum 5 total 6 entire 10 everything
__ works: 5 in the, skunk 6 public
__ Works Administration: 6 Public
__ Works Hard for the Money: 3 She
workshop: 6 clinic, studio 7 atelier
hardware: 3 nut 4 nail 5 screw
tool: 3 saw 4 file, rasp, vise 5 drill, gouge, lathe, plane 6 chisel, hammer
Works of Love, The author: Wright Morris
workstations, connected: 3 LAN
worktable: 5 bench
workweek
part: 3 Fri., Mon., Thu., Tue., Wed. 4 Thur., Tues. 5 Thurs. 6 Friday, Monday 7 Tuesday 8 Thursday 9 Wednesday
start of a French ~: 5 lundi
work without __: 4 a net
world: 3 orb 4 life 5 Earth, field, globe, realm 6 cosmos, domain, global, milieu, nature, planet, region, sphere 7 mankind, society 8 creation, everyone, humanity, province, universe 9 biosphere, everybody, humankind, human race, macrocosm, microcosm
book: 5 atlas
bring into the ~: 4 bear, have 5 beget
combining form: 4 cosm- 5 cosmo-
come up in the ~: 4 rise 5 go far 8 get ahead
ender: 4 ling, view, wide
in a perfect ~: 7 ideally
in one's own ~: 5 spacy 6 spacey
it makes the ~ go round: 4 love
most of the ~: 3 sea 5 ocean, water
natural ~: 8 creation, universe
nether ~: 4 hell 5 Hades 7 inferno
next ~: 8 paradise 9 hereafter
not of this ~: 4 eery 5 eerie 8 eldritch 9 unearthly
on top of the ~: 4 glad 5 happy, merry 6 blithe, cheery, elated, jovial, joyful, joyous, upbeat 7 gleeful, pleased, tickled 8 blissful, cheerful, ecstatic, euphoric, exultant, jubilant, mirthful, thrilled 9 delighted, overjoyed, rejoicing
out of this ~: 3 def, rad 4 aces, A-one, boss, braw, cool, dece, eery, fine, gear, keen, neat, nice, phat, tuff 5 alien, dandy, ducky, eerie, grand, great, marvy, neato, nobby, prime, slick, super, swell 6 bang on, bang-up, bonzer, bosker, choice, divine, dreamy, far-out, gnarly, groovy, lovely, peachy, slap-up, spot on, superb, terrif, tiptop, unreal, whizzo, wicked 7 amazing, awesome, capital, corking, perfect, ripping, skookum, stellar, sublime 8 dazzling, especial, eximious, fabulous, five-star, four-star, frabjous, glorious, heavenly, jim-dandy, slambang, smashing, splendid, standout, sterling, stickout, stunning, superior, terrific, top-level, topnotch, very good, wondrous 9 bodacious, Endsville, excellent, exemplary, exquisite, fantastic, first-rate, highgrade, hunky-dory, marvelous, sollicker, sumptuous, top-flight, wonderful 10 first-class, hotsy-totsy, incredible, jack-a-dandy, peachykeen, phenomenal, remarkable, stupendous, super-duper
real ~: 9 actuality, existence
show the ~: 3 air 4 bare 6 reveal
starter: 5 after, other, under 6 nether
supporter: 5 Atlas
think the ~ of: 4 love 5 adore 6 admire, esteem
traveler: 5 nomad, rover 7 voyager 8 gadabout, vagabond, wanderer, wayfarer 10 adventurer
trip around the ~: 5 orbit
world __: 3 car, war 4 beat, line, soul 5 point, power 6 spirit 7 process
world __ end: 7 without
world-__: 4 view 5 class, weary 6 famous, shaker
__ world: 4 free, real, wide 5 dream, lower, small 6 nether
World: 5 paper 9 newspaper
locale: 5 Tulsa
World __: 3 Cup 4 Bank, War I 5 Court, War II 6 Savior, Series
World __ Much With Us, The: 5 Is Too
World __ Web: 4 Wide
__ World: 3 New, Old 4 Cool, Wild 5 First, Ghost, Night, Small, Third, Young 6 Fourth, Second, Wayne's, Woman's 7 Another, Perfect
World According to Garp, The: 4 film 5 novel
author: John Irving
cast: Glenn Close, Mary Beth Hurt, John Lithgow, Robin Williams
director: George Roy Hill
dog: 7 Bonkers
World According to Me, The star: Jackie Mason
World Changes, The (1933 film)
cast: Mary Astor, Aline MacMahon, Paul Muni
director: Mervyn LeRoy
world-class: 4 A-one, best, fine 5 elite, great, prime, super 6 select 7 capital 8 champion, peerless 9 excellent
WorldCom competitor: 3 GTE
WorldCom partner: 3 MCI
World Cup
game: 6 soccer
objective: 4 goal 5 score
org.: 4 FIFA
ploy: 4 punt
World Enough and Time author: Robert Penn Warren
World Factbook compiler: 3 CIA
World-Herald: 5 paper 9 newspaper
locale: 5 Omaha
World in His Arms, The (1952 film)
cast: Ann Blyth, John McIntire, Gregory Peck
director: Raoul Walsh
World Is a Ghetto, The (1972 song)
artist: War
World Is a Wedding, The author: Delmore Schwartz
World Is Not Enough, The (1999 film)
cast: Pierce Brosnan, Robert Carlyle, Judi Dench, Sophie Marceau, Denise Richards
director: Michael Apted
World Is Not Enough, The author: Zoé Oldenbourg
World Is Too Much With Us, The author: William Wordsworth
worldly: 5 blasé, suave 6 uptown, urbane 7 earthly, knowing, mundane, profane, secular, selfish 8 material, physical, temporal 9 practical
starter: 5 other
worldly-__: 4 wise 6 minded
worldly-wise: 3 hep, hip 4 cool 5 canny 6 urbane, with it 7 knowing 9 au courant
World of Henry Orient, The (1964 film)
cast: Tom Bosley, Angela Lansbury, Paula Prentiss, Peter Sellers
director: George Roy Hill
World of Tomorrow, The director: 4 Bird
World of William Clissold, The author: H.G. Wells
__ world order: 3 new
world power, name meaning: 6 Donald
World's __: 3 End 4 Fair
__ Worlds Collide: 4 When
World's End author: Upton Sinclair
World Series: 5 event
month: 3 Oct. 7 October
prelude: 4 ALCS, NLCS
sport: 8 baseball
World Series of Golf site: 5 Akron
__ World Service: 3 BBC
World's Fair: 4 expo
1893 site: 3 USA 7 Chicago 8 Illinois
1904 site: 3 USA 7 St. Louis 8 Missouri
1933 site: 3 USA 7 Chicago 8 Illinois
1939 site: 3 USA 6 Queens 7 New York
1958 site: 7 Belgium 8 Brussels
1962 site: 3 USA 7 Seattle 10 Washington
1964 site: 3 USA 6 Queens 7 New York
1967 site: 6 Canada 8 Montreal
1970 site: 5 Japan, Osaka
1992 site: 5 Spain 7 Seville
2000 site: 7 Germany, Hanover
World's Fair author: E.L. Doctorow
World's Greatest Athlete, The (1973 film)
cast: John Amos, Tim Conway, Jan-Michael Vincent
World's Illusion, The author: Jakob Wassermann
world's mine __, The: 6 oyster
__ World Symphony: 3 New
__ World, The: 4 Lost 6 Silent
__ World Turns: 5 As the
World War I
see WWI
World War II
see WWII
world-weary: 5 blasé, bored, jaded, sated 6 cloyed 8 satiated 9 apathetic, surfeited
feeling: 5 ennui 6 apathy, tedium 7 boredom, languor 9 lassitude
sound: 4 sigh
worldwide: 3 big, int. 4 intl. 6 common, cosmic, global 7 general 8 catholic, cosmical, pandemic 9 extensive, planetary, universal 10 ecumenical, prevailing, ubiquitous
World Wide Web: 3 Net 8 Internet
World Wildlife Fund symbol: 5 panda
...world will __ path...: 5 beat a
world without __: 3 end
World Without End, __: 4 Amen
World Without Love, A (1964 song)
artist: Peter and Gordon
World Without Sun (1964 film) director: Jacques-Yves Cousteau
Worley: 6 Jo Anne
worm: 3 cur 4 bait, heel, naid, nema, push, toad 5 churl, crawl, knave, leech, rogue, scamp, sneak 6 rascal, squirm, teredo, wiggle 7 annelid, wheedle, wriggle 8 fish bait 9 insinuate, miscreant, reprobate, scoundrel, slitherer, vulgarian 10 blackguard
catcher: 4 beak, bird 5 robin
combining form: 5 vermi- 6 scolec-, -scolex 7 scoleco-
ender: 4 hole, seed, wood 5 grass
in: 5 enter 6 meddle 9 insinuate, interpose
into: 5 enter 9 penetrate 10 infiltrate
like a ~: 4 slow 6 apodal 7 apodous
measuring ~: 3 bug 6 insect
out: 6 recant, renege 8 withdraw
product: 4 silk
starter: 3 bag, bud, cut, ear, eel, lob, lug, pin, web 4 army, boll, book, clam, flat, gape, glow, hair, hook, horn, inch, lung, meal, muck, ring, root, sand, ship, silk, slow, span, tape, tube, whip, wire, wood 5 angle, blind, blood, earth, heart, joint, round, screw, straw, wheat 6 canker, pickle, thread 7 cabbage
worm __: 4 gear 5 drive, fence, grass, snake, wheel 6 lizard
__ worm: 3 dew, fan, red 5 acorn, arrow, beard 6 guinea, palolo, peanut, potato, ribbon, woolly 7 bladder, feather, fishing, peacock, vinegar
__-Worm: 4 Glow
worm's-__ view: 3 eye
Worms: 4 city, town
locale: 7 Germany
river: 5 Rhine
worms, can of: 7 problem 9 adversity
wormwood
flower: 9 santonica
gall and ~: 7 dudgeon 10 bitterness, resentment
worn: 3 old, wan 4 beat, gone, shot, used 5 all in, drawn, had it, jaded, kaput, put on, ratty, seedy, spent, stale, tatty, tired, trite, weary 6 beat-up, bushed, effete, eroded, frayed, pooped, ragged, rugged, ruined, shabby, used up 7 clichéd, damaged, decayed, drained, haggard, pinched, raggedy, run-down, useless, wizened 8 decrepit, dog-eared, dog-tired, fatigued, frazzled, out of gas, overused, tattered, timeworn, tired out, wiped out, wrung out 9 burned out, exhausted, hackneyed, moth-eaten,

overtired, played out, pooped out **10** overworked, secondhand, threadbare
become ~: **4** fray, wear **5** decay, erode **7** corrode, weather
irregularly ~: **5** erose
starter: **3** way **4** care, shop, time **7** weather
to a frazzle: **4** beat **5** all in, tense, tired **6** bushed
what's ~: **4** duds, garb, gear **5** array, dress, getup **6** attire, outfit **7** apparel, clothes, costume, raiment, threads, toggery **8** clothing, garments, wardrobe
worn-out: **3** old **4** beat, dull, gone, limp, shot, used, weak **5** bored, drawn, had it, jaded, kaput, spent, stale, stock, tired, trite, weary **6** bushed, dished, effete, frayed, pooped, ragged, ruined, shabby, used up **7** clichéd, drained, haggard, pinched, run-down, useless **8** depleted, fatigued, overused, tattered **9** enervated, exhausted, hackneyed, prostrate **10** dullsville, overworked, threadbare
phrase: **6** cliché **7** bromide **8** chestnut **9** platitude
Worrell: **6** Ernest
worried: **5** tense, upset **6** afraid, hung up, on edge, pacing, uneasy **7** anxious, fearful, fretful, nervous, uptight **8** bothered, fluttery, fretsome, restless, troubled **9** concerned, disturbed, ill-at-ease, perturbed, tormented **10** distracted, distraught, distressed, frightened, solicitous
act ~: **4** pace
worrier: **9** pessimist
risk: **5** ulcer
worrisome: **5** tight **8** annoying **9** vexatious
worry: **3** ail, bug, dog, eat, nag, vex, woe **4** bait, care, fear, fret, fuss, goad, pain, pest, stew, tire **5** angst, annoy, beset, brood, chafe, doubt, eat at, grief, harry, press, shake, sweat, tease, trial, upset **6** bother, excite, gnaw at, harass, hassle, hector, matter, misery, needle, pester, plague, pother, prey on, regret, sorrow, stress, take on **7** afflict, agonize, anguish, anxiety, anxious, bad news, bedevil, concern, depress, disturb, oppress, perturb, problem, tension, torment, trouble **8** aggrieve, disquiet, distress, exercise, headache, irritate, sweat out, unsettle, vexation **9** annoyance, beleaguer, heartache, importune, misgiving, persecute, tantalize, tightness, weigh down **10** infliction, irritation, perplexity, solicitude, uneasiness
about: **4** fret **5** dread, sweat
cause: **4** risk **5** peril
ender: **4** wart
perhaps: **4** ager
words of ~: **4** oh-oh, uh-oh
worry __: **5** beads
__ worry: **5** not to
__ Worry Be Happy: **4** Don't
worrying: **5** pesky **6** knotty, thorny, trying, vexing **7** galling, grating, irksome **8** annoying, nettling **9** vexatious **10** bothersome, irritating, nettlesome
stop ~: **5** relax **6** unwind **7** cool off, lay back **8** calm down, loosen up **9** hang loose **10** settle down, simmer down
worrywart: **7** killjoy, skeptic **8** sourpuss **9** gloomy Gus, pessimist **10** wet blanket
worse: **8** inferior
for wear: **4** worn **6** ragged **7** worn-out
worsen: **4** sink **6** impair **7** decline, fall off, relapse **8** compound, diminish **9** aggravate **10** degenerate, exacerbate, go downhill, retrogress
worsening: **3** dip, sag **4** dive **5** lapse, slide, slump **7** decline, failing **8** downturn, nosedive, slowdown **9** downslide, downswing
__ worse than...: **5** a fate
worship: **3** awe **4** laud, like, love, pray **5** adore, chant, deify, exalt, extol, go for, honor, lauds **6** admire, chapel, dote on, esteem, extoll, homage, matins, praise, prayer, pray to, regard, revere **7** adulate, care for, cherish, glorify, idolize, lionize, liturgy, magnify, respect, service, vespers **8** canonize, devotion, dote upon, hold dear, look up to, offering, sanctify, treasure, venerate **9** adoration, adulation, bow down to, care about, celebrate, genuflect, reverence **10** admiration, invocation, veneration
combining form: **5** -latry
house of ~: **4** shul **5** abbey, schul **6** bethel, chapel, church, mosque, temple **9** cathedral, synagogue **10** tabernacle
object of ~: **3** god **4** icon, idol, ikon **5** deity, eikon
supreme ~: **6** latria
__ worship: **4** hero, idol **6** nature
worshiped: **7** beloved
one: **4** hero, icon, idol, star **7** beloved, darling, pop star **8** favorite, folk hero, luminary **9** celebrity, superstar
worshiper: **3** fan **7** devotee **8** adherent, disciple, follower **10** aficionado
combining form: **5** -later
worshipers: **5** flock, laity **6** parish
worship from __: **4** afar
worshipful: **5** pious **6** devout, loving
Worsley, Gump
milieu: **3** ice **4** rink **5** arena **6** hockey
org.: **3** NHL
worst: **4** beat, best, do in, drub, lick, rout, whip **5** crush, nadir, whomp **6** defeat, outwit, subdue, thrash **7** clobber, conquer, overrun, shellac, succeed, the pits, trample, trounce **8** outsmart, overcome, shellack, vanquish **9** faultiest, polish off **10** rock bottom
in the ~ way: **3** bad **5** badly
think the ~ of: **4** hate **5** abhor **6** detest, loathe **7** despise, dislike **8** execrate **9** abominate
worst-__ scenario: **4** case
Worst __ in London, The: **4** Pies
worsted: **4** yarn **5** cloth **6** fabric **8** material
be ~: **4** fail, lose
fabric: **5** serge **6** wadmal **7** estamin, etamine **8** casimere, casimire, sanglier, Venetian **9** cassimere, gabardine, sharkskin
Worst That Could Happen (1969 song) artist: Brooklyn Bridge
__ worst way: **5** in the
wort: **4** mash
starter: **3** fan, fig, mad, rag, rib **4** bell, cole, drop, horn, lead, lung, moon, pile, salt, sand, soap, star **5** birth, fever, glass, liver, louse, money, navel, penny, quill, spear, stone, tooth, wound **6** butter, mother, pepper, sneeze, spider, spleen **7** bladder, slipper, swallow **8** thorough
worth: **3** use, val. **4** cost, note **5** avail, merit, price, ratal, sense, value **6** assets, beauty, credit, import, moment, riches, virtue, weight **7** account, benefit, caliber, dignity, meaning, quality, stature, utility **8** goodness, property **9** substance, valuation **10** estimation, excellence, expediency, importance, perfection, usefulness, worthiness
be ~: **4** cost, rate **5** price, quote, value **6** charge, come to **7** sell for **8** amount to
determine ~: **4** rate **5** assay **6** assess, size up **7** valuate **8** appraise, evaluate
ender: **5** while
net ~: **6** estate
not ~ mentioning: **5** lousy, minor, petty **7** trivial **8** trifling **9** small-time **10** incidental
of ~: **5** utile
two cents' ~: **3** tip **4** view **6** advice, tipoff **7** comment **9** viewpoint
worth __: **4** a try **5** doing
__ worth: **3** net
__-worth: **4** self
Worth: **4** Mary **5** Irene
__ worth a sou: **3** not
worthier: **6** better
worthiest: **3** top **4** best **5** prime **7** leading, optimal, supreme **8** foremost, ultimate **9** nonpareil **10** preeminent
worthily: **4** ably, fine, to a T, well **6** aright, nicely **7** adeptly, capably **8** expertly, laudably, properly, smoothly, suitably **9** admirably, inside out, perfectly **10** adequately, skillfully, splendidly, thoroughly
worthiness: **5** merit, worth **6** virtue **7** dignity **8** morality **9** greatness
worthless: **4** idle, junk, null, poor, puny, vain, vile **5** cheap, empty, inane, junky, sorry **6** abject, crumby, crummy, drossy, futile, hollow, no-good, paltry, trashy **7** inutile, invalid, pitiful, trivial, useless **8** bootless, degraded, feckless, pathetic, piddling, trifling, unusable, wretched **9** for naught, miserable, no-account, pointless **10** despicable, pathetical, profitless, unavailing
amount: **3** sou **6** diddly
matter: **4** slag **5** chaff, dregs **6** debris, refuse **7** rubbish
talk: **3** gas, rot **4** blah, bosh, bull, bunk, guff, jazz, jive, pooh, tosh **5** bilge, fudge, hokum, hooey, prate, stuff, trash, tripe **6** bunkum, bushwa, drivel, footle, gabble, gammon, gibber, havers, hot air, humbug, jabber, jargon, kibosh, piffle **7** baloney, blarney, blather, bushwah, eyewash, flannel, flubdub, fustian, garbage, hogwash, inanity, rubbish, twaddle **8** buncombe, claptrap, falderal, flimflam, flummery, folderal, nonsense, slipslop, tommyrot, trumpery **9** banana oil, gibberish, kidstakes, moonshine, poppycock, rigmarole **10** applesauce, balderdash, bilge water, codswallop, double-talk, empty words, flapdoodle, galimatias, Jabberwock, mumbo jumbo, rigamarole, taradiddle
worth one's __: **4** salt
__ Worth, TX: **4** Fort
worthwhile: **4** good **5** of use **6** aidful, benign, paying, useful **7** gainful, helpful, livable **8** fruitful, liveable, positive, readable, remedial, salutary, valuable **9** covetable, desirable, effectual, expedient, favorable, important, lucrative, rewarding, well-spent **10** beneficial, meaningful, productive, profitable
be ~: **3** pay
consider ~: **5** prize, value **6** esteem **8** hold dear **9** recommend
worthy: **3** fit **4** good, true **5** moral, noble, solid **6** choice, decent, figure, honest **7** upright **8** eligible, laudable, luminary, reliable, top-notch, valuable, virtuous **9** admirable, blameless, deserving, estimable, excellent, exemplary, first-rate, honorable, incorrupt, personage, praisable, reputable, righteous, top-drawer **10** creditable, dependable, first-class, invaluable, satisfying
be ~ of: **4** earn, rate **5** merit **6** beseem **7** deserve, warrant
of: **3** due **7** condign, merited **8** rightful, suitable
starter: **3** air, sea **4** news, note, road **5** blame, crash, thank, trust **6** credit, flight, praise
suffix: **4** -able, -ible
Wotan: **4** Odin **5** Othin
Wot's It to Ya (1987 song) artist: Robbie Nevil
Wouk, Herman: **6** author, writer
work: Aurora Dawn
The Caine Mutiny
City Boy
Don't Stop the Carnival
The Glory
The Hope
Inside, Outside
Marjorie Morningstar
This Is My God
War and Remembrance
The Winds of War
Youngblood Hawke
would: **6** used to
possibly ~: **5** might
rather: **6** prefer **10** like better
Would __ to you?: **4** I lie
would-be: **5** quasi **8** aspiring **9** potential **10** self-styled
Would I Lie to You? (1985 song) artist: Eurythmics
Wouldn't It Be Loverly composer: **5** Loewe **6** Lerner
Wouldn't It Be Nice (1966 song) artist: Beach Boys
Wouldn't Take Nothing... author: Maya Angelou
Would thou hadst __ been born: **4** ne'er
Would you like to swing on __?: **5** a star
wound: **3** cut, hit **4** bump, burn, clip, gash, harm, hurt, maim, nick, pain, scar, stab, welt **5** pique, prick, slash, slice, sting **6** boo-boo, bruise, coiled, damage, grieve, injure, injury, insult, lesion, mangle, offend, open up, pierce, scrape, trauma **7** anguish, contuse, scratch, torment, twisted **8** abrasion, distress, lacerate, mistreat **9** contusion, meandered **10** laceration, traumatize
combining form: **7** traumat- **8** traumato-
cover: **4** scab **5** gauze **7** bandage
rub salt in the ~: **3** vex **5** harry **6** harass, pester, pick on, plague **7** afflict, agonize, anguish, bedevil, oppress, torment, torture **8** distress, irritate **9** persecute
slightly: **4** wing **5** prick
up: **4** taut **5** tense **7** through **8** fluttery **9** engrossed
__ wound: **5** flesh
Wound and the Bow, The author: Edmund Wilson
wounded: **4** hurt **5** burnt **6** burned **7** injured **9** miserable
be ~: **6** suffer
cry from the ~: **5** medic
Wounded __, SD: **4** Knee
woundwort: **5** plant **6** flower
wove: **8** entwined, worked in **9** zigzagged

woven: **9** contrived **10** interlaced
material: **4** knit, mesh, wool **5** linen **6** fabric **8** barathea
starter: **4** hand
together: **4** mixt **5** mixed **6** melded, merged, united **7** blended **8** combined
wow: **3** awe, gee, man, ooh **4** gosh, stun **5** amaze, golly, oh boy, shock, smash, zowie **6** far out, jiminy, oh baby, oo-la-la, please, thrill **7** astound, attract, beguile, delight, enchant, jeepers, jimminy, stagger, win over **8** bowl over, entrance, knock out **9** dumbfound, overwhelm, sensation, transport
starter: **3** bow
__-wow: **3** bow
Wozniak: **5** Steve
company: **5** Apple
partner: **4** Jobs
Wozzeck: **5** opera
composer: **4** Berg
W.P.: **8** Kinsella
WPA
creator: **3** FDR
project: **4** road
wpm: **4** stat.
part of ~: **3** min., per, wds. **5** words **6** minute
__-wracking: **5** nerve
wrack up: **4** ruin **5** crash, total, wreck **7** destroy, rear-end, shatter
wrack-up: **8** accident
wraith: **5** ghost, shade, spook **6** fantom, spirit **7** phantom, specter **8** presence **10** apparition
wraithlike: **7** ghostly **9** invisible **10** immaterial
Wrangel: **3** isl. **4** isle **6** island
locale: **6** Arctic, Russia
Wrangell: **4** peak **5** mount, range **7** volcano **8** mountain
locale: **6** Alaska
peak: **4** Bona
wrangle: **3** row **4** earn, feud, flap, herd, spar, spat, tiff **5** argue, brawl, clash, fight, scene, scrap, set-to **6** barney, bicker, fracas, haggle, hassle, racket, ruckus, rumble, rumpus, scheme **7** connive, contest, dispute, fall out, quarrel, quibble, round up, ruction, scuffle **8** argument, brouhaha, disagree, exchange, have at it, squabble, struggle **9** brannigan, bump heads, have words, lock horns **10** contention, falling-out, tangle with
wrangler: **6** cowboy, drover, gaucho **7** cowpoke, rancher, vaquero **8** buckaroo, stockman
need: **6** lariat
Wrangler: **3** SUV **4** Jeep
Wranglers: **5** jeans, pants **9** dungarees
wrangling: **5** fight **6** strife **7** discord **8** friction, polemics **9** bellicose **10** contention, discussion
wrap: **3** boa, fur, lap **4** bind, cape, coat, do up, fold, hide, mask, pack, roll, tape, tuck, veil, wind **5** capot, cloak, cover, drape, scarf, shawl, stole, tie up, twine **6** bundle, capote, dolman, encase, enfold, ermine, finish, incase, infold, jacket, mantle, muffle, roll up, shroud, swathe **7** bandage, blanket, car coat, enclose, envelop, inclose, package, protect, sheathe, swaddle, sweater **8** bundle up, covering, encircle, enshroud, fur piece, muffle up, surround
around: **4** coil **5** twine, twist
around one's little finger: **3** use **6** misuse **7** control **10** manipulate
ender: **6** around
evening ~: **3** boa, fur **4** mink, muff **5** stole
food ~: **4** foil, Glad **5** cello, Saran **6** Baggie **7** plastic **10** cellophane
gift ~: **5** paper
Indian ~: **4** sari **5** saree
in wax: **4** cere
nautically: **4** frap
Spanish ~: **5** manta **6** sarape, serape
up: **2** do **3** cap, end **4** fold, furl, halt, quit, stop, tape **5** cease, close, enrol, truss **6** enfold, enroll, finish, infold **7** adjourn, envelop, play out **8** complete, conclude, finalize, pack it in, transact **9** terminate **10** call it a day, consummate
__ wrap: **3** ear **4** gift, word **6** bubble **7** plastic
__-wrap: **4** gift **5** plain **6** shrink
__ Wrap: **5** Saran
wrapped: **4** done
homophone: **4** rapt
in red tape: **5** sat on
up: **6** intent **7** engaged, through **8** absorbed, immersed, obsessed **9** engrossed
wrapped __: **4** up in
Wrapped Around Your Finger (1984 song) artist: Police
wrapper: **4** robe **6** casing **8** covering, envelope
still in the ~: **3** new **6** unused **8** brand-new **9** untouched
wrapping
material: **5** twine
paper: **5** kraft
wiener ~: **6** casing
wraps
keep under ~: **5** sit on **6** hush up **7** secrete
take the ~ off: **4** bare, open **6** expose, reveal, unmask **7** lay bare, uncover
under ~: **6** covert, hidden, masked, secret, unseen, veiled **7** cloaked, furtive, private **8** hush-hush, obscured, secluded, shrouded, stealthy, ulterior **9** concealed, disguised **10** tucked away
__ wraps: **5** under
wrap-up: **3** end **5** recap **6** ending, epilog, finale, finish **7** summary **8** terminus **9** summation **10** conclusion, denouement, resolution
wrasse: **4** fish **6** cunner
wrath: **3** ire, sin **4** bile, fury, hate, rage **5** anger **6** choler, dander, rancor, spleen, temper **7** dudgeon, offense, outrage, passion, umbrage **8** acrimony, asperity, vexation **10** irritation, resentment
wrathful: **3** hot, mad **4** ired, sore **5** angry, cross, huffy, irate, livid, riled, wroth **6** fuming, heated, ireful, peeved, raging, raving, red-hot, stormy **7** enraged, furious, ranting **8** choleric, incensed, inflamed, maddened, outraged, storming **9** indignant, irritated, resentful, splenetic **10** displeased, freaked out, infuriated
Wray: **3** Fay **4** Link
Wray, Fay: **7** actress
film: Bulldog Jack (1934)
The Clairvoyant (1934)
King Kong (1933)
The Most Dangerous Game (1932)
One Sunday Afternoon (1933)
The Richest Girl in the World (1934)
Viva Villa! (1934)
The Wedding March (1928)
wreak: **4** vent, work **5** visit, wreck **6** incite **7** inflict, unleash **8** carry out **9** force upon, knock down, retaliate **10** bring about, perpetrate
havoc on: **4** loot, raid, ruin, sack **5** rifle, spoil, strip, waste, wreck **6** harrow, maraud, ravage **7** despoil, destroy, pillage, plunder, ransack **9** depredate, desecrate, devastate, vandalize
vengeance: **3** fix, get **9** retaliate
wreath: **3** lei **4** haku, loop, ring **5** crown **6** anadem, diadem, laurel **7** chaplet, circlet, coronet, festoon, garland
bridal ~: **5** plant **6** flower
heraldic ~: **5** torse
laurel ~ alternative: **5** medal
ornamental: **4** cone
place for a ~: **4** brow
Wreath and a Curse, A author: Robert Anderson
wreathe: **4** coil, curl, wind **5** twine, twist **7** sinuate **10** interweave
with laurels: **5** honor
wreck: **3** mar, sap **4** bash, dash, harm, heap, hulk, hurt, mess, rase, raze, ruin, sink, undo **5** beach, blast, botch, break, crack, crash, crate, crush, level, relic, shock, smash, spoil, total, trash, wreak **6** bang up, batter, blight, damage, debris, derail, impair, jalopy, junker, mangle, pile-up, quench, ravage, topple **7** butcher, capsize, crack up, debacle, despoil, destroy, disable, failure, flatten, founder, louse up, scuttle, shatter, smash-up, subvert, torpedo, tragedy, wrack up **8** accident, bulldoze, demolish, derelict, lay waste, pull down, sabotage, spoliate, take down, tear down **9** collision, devastate, dismantle, knock down, overwhelm, pulverize, rear-ender, take apart, undermine, vandalize **10** demolition, rattletrap, run aground
ender: **3** age
starter: **4** ship
__-Wreck: **5** Rent-a
wreckage: **4** loss, ruin **5** havoc, ruins **6** debris **7** flotsam
wrecked: **4** lost **5** kaput **6** undone **8** finished, stranded
vessel: **4** hulk
wrecker: **3** tow **8** tow truck
need: **5** crane, hoist
wrecker's __: **4** ball
wrecking __: **3** bar, car **4** crew **5** crane
Wrecking Crew, The (1969 film)
cast: Nancy Kwan, Dean Martin, Elke Sommer, Sharon Tate
Wreck of the Edmund Fitzgerald, The (1976 song) artist: Gordon Lightfoot
Wreck of the Hesperus, The author: Henry Wadsworth Longfellow
Wreck of the Mary __, The: **5** Deare
wren: **4** bird **7** warbler **8** songbird
__ wren: **3** emu **4** rock **5** house, marsh, sedge **6** cactus, winter
wrench: **3** rip, tug **4** jerk, pang, pull, rack, tear, tool, turn, warp, yank **5** exact, force, screw, seize, twist, wrest, wring **6** extort, snatch, sprain, strain **7** contort, distort, spanner, squeeze **9** dislocate
monkey ~: **4** snag **5** block, crimp, hitch, snarl **7** barrier, problem, setback **8** handicap, obstacle **10** impediment
open: **4** rive
part: **3** jaw
throw a monkey ~ into: **5** block **6** hamper, hinder **7** disrupt **8** obstruct, sabotage **9** frustrate, undermine
__ wrench: **3** box, lug, pin **4** pipe **5** Allen **6** impact, monkey, socket, torque **7** spanner
__-wrenching: **3** gut
Wren, Christopher: **3** Sir **7** British **9** architect
wrest: **3** pry, tug **4** levy, pull, tear, yank **5** exact, seize, usurp, wring **6** extort, ravage, snatch, wrench **7** deprive, distort, extract **9** force away
out: **5** pluck **9** extirpate
wrestle: **4** cope **5** fight **6** battle, strive, tussle **7** contend, grapple, scuffle **8** struggle
Wrestle ender: **5** mania
wrestlers, like: **5** beefy **6** brawny
wrestling: **5** sport
defeat again, in ~: **5** repin
Japanese: **4** sumo
locale: **5** arena
maneuver: **3** pin **4** hold, lock, slam **6** nelson **7** armlock **8** headlock
match: **4** bout **5** fight, round **6** tussle **7** contest **9** encounter
official: **3** ref **5** timer **7** referee
pro ~ org.: **3** WWF
result: **3** pin **4** draw
round: **4** fall
surface: **3** mat **6** canvas
__ wrestling: **3** arm, mud **4** sumo **5** wrist **6** Indian
wretch: **3** cur **4** toad **5** sneak **6** misfit, pariah, rascal, victim **7** outcast, sad case, sad sack, villain **8** sufferer **9** miscreant, poor devil, reprobate, scoundrel **10** blackguard
wretched: **3** low, sad **4** base, foul, grim, mean, poor, ugly, vile **5** awful, gross, lousy, ratty, sorry, woful **6** abject, broody, bummed, crumby, crummy, dismal, dreary, flimsy, gloomy, grotty, grungy, horrid, humble, odious, paltry, rotten, shabby, sordid, tragic, woeful **7** accurst, baleful, baneful, beastly, crushed, doleful, forlorn, ghastly, hapless, hideous, hurting, ignoble, in a funk, low-down, piteous, pitiful, squalid, unhappy **8** accursed, beggarly, dejected, desolate, dolorous, downcast, dreadful, God-awful, grievous, hopeless, horrible, inferior, luckless, pathetic, pitiable, shameful, stinking, terrible, tragical, unworthy **9** abhorrent, afflicted, appalling, atrocious, cheerless, defective, depressed, desperate, execrable, frightful, insidious, in the pits, loathsome, miserable, monstrous, offensive, repellant, revolting, sorrowful, thankless, unsightly, woebegone, worthless **10** abominable, deplorable, despairing, despicable, despondent, detestable, disastrous, distressed, down-and-out, horrendous, lamentable, melancholy, pathetical, unpleasant
feel ~: **3** ail **6** suffer
wretchedness: **3** woe **4** pain **5** grief **6** misery, sorrow **7** despair, squalor
wriggle: **4** worm **5** crawl, creep, snake, twist **6** jiggle, squirm, thrash, twitch, wiggle, writhe
wriggler: **3** eel **5** larva
wriggly: **4** eely **7** squirmy
wright: **5** maker
starter: **4** mill, play, ship, wain **5** wheel
Wright: **3** Amy **4** Gary, town **5** Betty, Chely, James, Robin **6** Judith, Mickey, Morris, Teresa, Wilbur **7** Charles, Orville, Richard
Wright, Frank Lloyd: **9** architect
Wright, James: **4** poet
Wright, Judith: **4** poet **10** Australian
Wright, Mickey: **6** golfer
milieu: **5** links **6** course
org.: **4** LPGA
Wright-Patterson: **3** AFB
__ Wright Penn: **5** Robin

Wright, Richard: 6 author, writer
work: Native Son
Wright, Robin: 7 actress
film: Forrest Gump (1994)
Message in a Bottle (1999)
The Pledge (2001)
The Princess Bride (1987)
State of Grace (1990)
spouse: Sean Penn
Wright, Teresa: 7 actress
film: The Best Years of Our Lives (1946)
The Capture (1950)
Enchantment (1948)
The Little Foxes (1941)
The Men (1950)
Mrs. Miniver (1942, AA)
The Pride of the Yankees (1942)
Pursued (1947)
Roseland (1977)
Shadow of a Doubt (1943)
Somewhere in Time (1980)
Wrigley: 4 Bill, Phil 6 Philip 7 William
product: 3 gum 10 chewing gum
Wrigley Field: 5 arena 8 ballpark
home: 3 Chi. 7 Chicago
like ~ walls: 4 viny 5 ivied
player: 3 Cub
wring: 3 dry, pry 4 levy, milk, rack 5 choke, exact, force, screw, twist, wrest 6 coerce, dry out, extort, wrench 7 contort, extract, squeeze 8 compress, strangle, throttle
wringer
hand ~: 4 ruer
put through the ~: 5 grill 7 torment 8 question 9 challenge
wringing wet: 5 soggy, soppy 10 bedraggled
wrinkle: 4 fold, line, muss, ruck 5 crimp, crush, purse, ridge, twist 6 crease, furrow, method, pucker, ruffle, rumple, shrink 7 crinkle, crumple, scrunch, shrivel 8 compress 9 corrugate, crow's-foot
anatomical ~: 4 ruga
new ~: 4 rage 5 trend 9 departure
wrinkled: 5 seamy 6 rugged 7 wizened 8 leathery 9 roughened 10 corrugated, disheveled
wrinkle-resistant fabric: 5 Orlon 6 Dacron
wrinkles
remove ~: 4 iron 5 press 8 facelift
wrist: 5 joint
bone: 6 carpal, carpus, hamate
combining form: 5 carpo-
coverer: 6 sleeve
ender: 4 band, lock 5 watch
jewelry: 5 chain 6 bangle 8 bracelet
movement: 5 flick
neighbor: 4 hand 7 forearm
nerve: 5 ulnar
slap on the ~: 5 chide, scold 6 punish, rebuke 7 lecture, reprove, upbraid 8 admonish, reproach 9 reprehend, reprimand
wrist ___: 3 pin 5 plate, watch
wristband: 4 cuff
wristlet: 6 bangle, gewgaw 7 jewelry, trinket 8 ornament
wristwatch: 4 Rado 5 Casio, Elgin, Lorus, Omega, Rolex, Seiko, Timex 6 Bulova, Fossil, Movado, Pulsar, Swatch 7 Citizen 8 Longines, Tag Heuer, Tourneau 9 timepiece
writ: 3 law 4 mise 5 paper 6 decree, elegit 7 command, mandate, process, refusal, summons, warrant 8 document, replevin, sanction, subpoena 9 prescript 10 court order, injunction
writ ___: 5 large
___ Writ: 4 Holy 6 Sacred
write: 3 ink, jot, pen 4 copy, sign 5 draft, ghost, print 6 author, draw up, indite, notify, pencil, record, scrawl, scribe 7 bang out, compose, dash off, engross, jot down, produce, publish, put down, set down, turn out 8 inscribe, knock off, knock out, mark down, note down, scribble, set forth, take down 9 autograph, drop a line, formulate, lucubrate 10 correspond, journalize, put on paper, transcribe
able to read and ~: 8 literate
a check: 4 draw
anew: 5 repen
at length: 6 ramble 7 expound 9 expatiate 10 dissertate
back: 5 reply 6 answer 9 respond to
down: 4 list, note 6 record 7 devalue 8 register 9 devaluate 10 transcribe
hastily: 3 jot 4 dash 6 scrawl
nothing to ~ home about: 4 fair, so-so 7 average 8 mediocre, middling, ordinary, passable 9 tolerable
off: 4 drop 5 amort., lower 6 cancel, deduct, forget, pardon 7 devalue, discard 8 amortize, give up on 9 devaluate, downgrade, underrate 10 undervalue
one's name: 4 sign 9 autograph
on metal: 4 etch
on the front: 6 enface
plans for: 4 spec 7 spec out
software: 6 encode 7 program
starter: 4 type 5 ghost
to: 5 reach 7 contact 8 approach 9 check with, touch base 10 get a hold of
up: 5 cover 8 describe 9 expound on, publicize
without credit: 5 ghost
write ___: 3 off, out 4 down
write-in ___: 4 vote
write-off: 9 abatement, deduction
write one's ___ ticket: 3 own
writer: 3 Ade, Bly, Day, Lee, Nin, Poe, Tan 4 Agee, Asch, Auel, Bate, Baum, Buck, Bull, Cain, Cobb, Cook, Dana, Dick, Dove, Edel, Fast, Gale, Gass, Grau, Grey, Hall, Hart, Inge, Jong, King, Koch, Loos, Luce, Mead, Muir, Nash, poet, Pohl, Puzo, Rand, Reed, Rice, Riis, Roth, Saki, Shaw, Tate, Uris, Ward, West, Wouk 5 Adams, Aiken, Albee, Alger, Barry, Barth, Beard, Benet, Berry, Blish, Bloom, Blume, Bogan, Boyle, Brown, Busch, Cable, Chase, Child, Clark, Corso, Crane, Dodge, Drury, Dunne, Elkin, Fromm, Frost, Glück, Green, Greer, Guare, Haley, Harte, Hayne, Hearn, Hecht, Henry, Herne, Hicks, Himes, Hurst, James, Jones, Kesey, Kopit, Kumin, Levin, Lewis, Lurie, Mamet, Oates, O'Hara, Paley, Percy, Plath, Potok, Price, Purdy, Riley, Royce, Selby, Seton, Seuss, Sheed, Simms, Smith, Steel, Stein, Stone, Stout, Stowe, Tryon, Turow, Twain, Tyler, Vidal, Waugh, Welty, White, Wolfe, Wylie, Yerby 6 Alcott, Algren, Asimov, Auster, author, Baraka, Barlow, Barnes, Barzun, Bellow, Berger, Bester, Bidart, Bierce, Bowles, Brooks, Bryant, Butler, Capote, Carson, Carver, Cather, Catton, Chopin, Ciardi, Cooper, Coover, critic, Cullen, De Voto, Dickey, Didion, Dobyns, Dunbar, Duncan, Durant, Dwight, Ferber, Fisher, Forché, French, Fuller, Gaddis, Gaines, Gelber, Gibson, Gilman, Godwin, Harper, Harris, Hawkes, Hayden, Heller, Henley, Hersey, Hobson, Hoffer, Holmes, Horgan, Howard, Hughes, Hunter, Irving, Judson, Keller, Knebel, Knight, Koontz, Krantz, London, Lowell, Ludlum, Mailer, Merton, Millay, Miller, Morley, Morris, Motley, Nevins, Norris, Norton, O'Neill, Parker, Peirce, Porter, Rogers, Rosten, Runyon, Sandoz, scribe, Shirer, Snyder, Sontag, Sparks, Styron, Updike, Walker, Warner, Warren, Wiesel, Wilder, Wilson, Wright 7 Angelou, Ashbery, Baldwin, Bambara, Beattie, Beecher, Bennett, Biggers, Brodkey, Bullins, Burgess, Carruth, Cheever, Clavell, Costain, Cozzens, Creeley, DeLillo, Demille, De Vries, Diderot, Dillard, Dreiser, Ellison, Ellmann, Emerson, Erdrich, Farrell, Friedan, Gardner, Garland, Gaskell, Glasgow, Grafton, Greeley, Gregory, Gunther, Guthrie, Hammett, Hellman, Herbert, Heyward, Howells, Hurston, Ignatow, Jackson, Jansson, Jarrell, Jeffers, Johnson, Kaufman, Kennedy, Kerouac, Kinnell, La Farge, Lardner, Lazarus, Malamud, Marcuse, Marquis, Masters, McKenny, Mencken, Merrill, Mitford, Mumford, Niebuhr, O'Connor, Parkman, Pynchon, Richter, Robbins, Roberts, Rölvaag, Sanders, Saroyan, Sheldon, Skinner, Stegner, Stevens, Tarbell, Theroux, Thoreau, Thurber, Wallace, Webster, Weidman, Wescott, Wharton, Winters 8 Anderson, Bartlett, Benchley, Berenson, Berryman, Billings, Bontemps, Bradbury, Bukowski, Buntline, Caldwell, Calisher, Chandler, Clampitt, Connelly, Crichton, cummings, DeForest, Doctorow, Eberhart, essayist, Faulkner, Friedman, Ginsberg, Glaspell, Gurganus, Hoagland, Kinsella, Koestler, Kosinski, MacLeish, Marquand, McCarthy, McMurtry, Melville, Michener, Mitchell, Morrison, Nordhoff, novelist, O'Donnell, Perelman, Phillips, Pulitzer, Rawlings, reporter, Rinehart, Salinger, Sandburg, Sinclair, Southern, Spillane, Spingarn, Stafford, Steffens, Sullivan, Vonnegut, Williams, Zukofsky 9 Barthelme, Bemelmans, Bodenheim, Burroughs, Buscaglia, Chayefsky, Childress, columnist, Dos Passos, dramatist, Gernsback, Hansberry, Hawthorne, Hemingway, Highsmith, Kellerman, Lindbergh, Macdonald, McCullers, Podhoretz, Roosevelt, Santayana, Schulberg, scribbler, Steinbeck, Woollcott, wordsmith, Yourcenar 10 biographer, Bradstreet, Fitzgerald, freelancer, Halberstam, journalist, Kingsolver, librettist, playwright, Tarkington, Untermeyer, Willingham 11 Auchincloss, Matthiessen, Schlesinger, Schoolcraft, Stratemeyer
Algerian ~: 6 Djebar
Argentine ~: 6 Borges, Gálvez, Sábato 8 Cortázar 9 Güiraldes, Sarmiento 11 Bioy Casares
Australian ~: 4 Stow, West 5 Stead, White 6 Furphy, Jolley, Palmer, Porter 7 Herbert, Manning, Travers 8 Franklin, Keneally 9 Moorehead 10 McCullough
Austrian ~: 5 Broch, Freud, Kafka, Kraus, Musil, Zweig 6 Handke, Lorenz, Werfel 7 Stifter 8 Bernhard 9 Aichinger 10 Wassermann
Belgian ~: 10 Conscience
Bosnian ~: 6 Andric
Brazilian ~: 5 Amado, Ramos 7 Alencar, Queirós
British ~: 3 Pym 4 Amis, Cary, Dahl, Ford, Glyn, Hall, Lamb, Lear, More, Rhys, Ryle, Snow, Wain, West 5 Arlen, Auden, Bates, Blunt, Bowen, Byatt, Defoe, Doyle, Eliot, Frayn, Green, Hardy, James, Lewis, Locke, Mason, Menen, Milne, Moore, Murry, Noyes, Orczy, Paine, Pater, Pepys, Powys, Reade, Rolfe, Shute, Watts, Waugh, Wells, White, Woolf, Young 6 Aldiss, Ambler, Austen, Barnes, Binyon, Braine, Brontë, Brophy, Browne, Bryher, Bunyan, Burney, Butler, Clarke, Conrad, Evelyn, Fowles, Fraser, Gibbon, Graves, Greene, Hallam, Hilton, Hudson, Huxley, Milton, Morgan, Morris, Orwell, Petrie, Popper, Potter, Powell, Ruskin, Sansom, Sayers, Sterne, Storey, Symons, Walton, Warner, Warton, Wilson 7 Bennett, Bentley, Blunden, Burgess, Carroll, Chatwin, Collins, Corelli, Dickens, Douglas, Drabble, Durrell, Firbank, Fleming, Forster, Francis, Gissing, Golding, Grahame, Haggard, Hartley, Hazlitt, Johnson, Kipling, le Carré, Marryat, Marston, Maugham, Meynell, Mitford, Montagu, Painter, Peacock, Renault, Russell, Shelley, Sitwell, Spencer, Stephen, Stewart, Surtees, Tolkien, Toynbee, Ustinov, Walpole 8 Beerbohm, Brookner, Christie, Connelly, Fielding, Forester, Jhabvala, Lawrence, Macaulay, Matineau, Meredith, Mortimer, Quennell, Runciman, Sillitoe, Smollett, Strachey, Trollope, Williams 9 Blackwood, Churchill, du Maurier, Goldsmith, Isherwood, Masefield, Massinger, Mitchison, Partridge, Priestley, Pritchett, Radcliffe, Stapledon, Thackeray, Whitehead, Wodehouse 10 Bainbridge, Chesterton, Galsworthy, Muggeridge, Richardson
Bulgarian-born ~: 7 Canetti
Cameroonian ~: 4 Beti
Canadian ~: 3 Roy 5 Blais, Engel, Moore, Mowat, Munro, Wiebe 6 Atwood, Davies, Moodie, Nowlan, Parker, Wilson 7 Findley, Gallant, McLuhan, Richter 9 Callaghan 10 Haliburton, Montgomery
Chilean ~: 5 Rojas 6 Bombal, Donoso 7 Allende, Barrios, Dorfman, Edwards 9 Blest Gana
Chinese ~: 6 Lao She, Lao-tzu, Pa Chin
Colombian ~: 6 Rivera 7 Márquez
Cuban ~: 5 Martí 6 Arenas, Barnet 10 Carpentier
Czech ~: 5 Capek, Hasek, Klíma 6 Hrabal 7 Jirásek, Kundera 9 Skvorecky
Danish ~: 4 Bang, Nexö 6 Jensen 7 Dinesen, Holberg 8 Andersen, Jacobsen 9 Gjellerup
deg.: 3 BFA, MFA 4 Lit.B., Lit.M.
Dutch ~: 7 Erasmus, Spinoza 8 Couperus
Ecuadoran ~: 5 Adoum 8 Montalvo
Egyptian ~: 9 el Saadawi
Finnish ~: 4 Kivi 5 Canth 8 Haavikko 9 Sillanpää
French ~: 3 Sue 4 Aymé, Gary, Gide, Hugo, Loti, Sade, Sand, Weil, Zola 5 Butor, Camus, Dumas, Duras, Giono, Green, Hémon, Renan, Sagan, Simon, Taine, Verne 6 Aragon, Balzac, Barrès, Belloc, Boulle, Céline, Cixous, Daudet,

France, Guitry, Lesage, Marcel, Pascal, Proust, Sartre **7** Aubigné, Bergson, Bourget, Claudel, Cocteau, Colette, Duhamel, Mauriac, Maurois, Mérimée, Prévost, Queneau, Rolland, Romains, Scudéry, Simenon **8** Bataille, Beauvoir, Bernanos, Cendrars, Flaubert, Goncourt, Gringore, Huysmans, Maritain, Perrault, Proudhon, Rabelais, Rousseau, Sarraute, Stendhal, Voltaire **9** Giraudoux, Montaigne **10** La Fontaine, Maupassant, Oldenbourg **11** Montesquieu, Sainte-Beuve

German ~: 4 Benn, Böll, Mann, Marx **5** Arnim, Grass, Grimm, Hesse, Heyse, Raabe, Zweig **6** Döblin, Goethe, Heinse, Jünger, Kleist, Luther, Walser **7** Fontane, Freytag, Gutzkow, Hoffman, Johnson, Novalis, Richter, Wieland **8** Borchert, Remarque, Spengler, Wedekind **10** Schliemann

Ghanaian ~: 5 Aidoo, Armah **7** Awoonor

Greek ~: 5 Plato **6** Zoilus **8** Plotinus, Plutarch, Xenophon **11** Kazantzakis

Guadeloupean ~: 5 Condé

Guatemalan ~: 8 Asturias

Guyanese ~: 6 Harris

Hebrew ~: 5 Agnon

Hungarian ~: 6 Molnár

ID: 6 byline

Indian ~: 3 Rao **5** Anand, Desai, Mehta **6** Hosain, Tagore **7** Narayan, Rushdie **9** Premchand **10** Markandaya

Irish ~: 5 Behan, Joyce, Moore **6** Binchy, Crofts, Heaney, O'Brien **7** Beckett, Maturin, Murdoch, O'Connor **8** Carleton, Donleavy, O'Faolain **9** Edgeworth, O'Flaherty

Israeli ~: 2 Oz **7** Amichai **9** Appelfeld

Italian ~: 3 Eco **5** Svevo **6** Basile, Silone **7** Alberti, Alfieri, Aretino, Bassani, Calvino, Capuana, Cassola, Collodi, Deledda, Foscolo, Manzoni, Morante, Moravia, Rovetta **8** Ginzburg **18** Pico della Mirandola

Jamaican ~: 7 Brodber

Japanese ~: 2 Oe **7** Abe Kobo, Mishima **8** Kawabata, Mori Ogai **9** Nagai Kafu **10** Dazai Osamu **11** Endo Shusaku

jingle ~: 5 adman

Lebanese ~: 6 Gibran

Martinican ~: 8 Glissant

Mexican ~: 5 Rulfo, Yañez **6** Azuela, Guzmán **7** Fuentes

Moroccan ~: 10 Ben Jelloun

name meaning ~: 9 Schreiber

need: 3 pad, pen **5** paper **6** editor, eraser, pencil

New Zealand ~: 5 Frame, Marsh **8** Ihimaera, Sargeson **9** Mansfield

Nigerian ~: 5 Aluko, Amadi, Nwapa **6** Achebe **7** Ekwensi, Equiano, Munonye

Norwegian ~: 4 Duun **5** Bojer **6** Hamsun, Sandel **10** Falkberget

Old English ~: 7 Aelfric

org.: 3 BMI, PEN **5** ASCAP

Peruvian ~: 5 Palma **7** Alegría **8** Arguedas

Philippine ~: 5 Rizal

Polish ~: 6 Milosz, Mrozek **8** Borowski, Konwicki **10** Gombrowicz **11** Sienkiewicz

Puerto Rican ~: 5 Ferré

Roman ~: 4 Livy **5** Pliny **7** Martial, Sallust, Tacitus **9** Suetonius

Russian ~: 4 Grin **5** Babel, Gogol, Gorky **6** Daniel, Ivanov, Krylov, Kuprin, Olesha, Panova, Yashin **7** Aksakov, Amalrik, Bryusov, Fadayev, Gladkov, Katayev, Nabokov, Pushkin, Rozanov, Sologub, Tolstoy **8** Aksyonov, Andreyev, Bulgakov, Karamzin, Nekrasov, Saltykov, Sloukhin, Turgenev, Zamyatin **9** Goncharov, Sholokhov, Sinyavsky **10** Zoshchenko **11** Aleshkovsky, Dostoyevsky **12** Solzhenitsyn

Salvadoran ~: 7 Alegría

Scottish ~: 3 Tey **5** Scott, Smith, Spark **6** Buchan, Cronin **7** Boswell, Carlyle **8** Mitchell **9** Stevenson

South African ~: 4 Head **5** Paton **6** Cloete, Fugard, Plomer **7** Coetzee **8** Abrahams, Gordimer, Jacobson **9** Schreiner **10** Van der Post

Spanish ~: 3 Aub **4** Cela **5** Benet **6** Alemán, Chacel, Marías, Matute, Sender **7** Alarcón, Arrabal, Unamuno **8** Marquina **9** Cervantes, Gironella **11** Pérez Galdós

starter: 3 sky **4** copy, song, type **5** ghost, speed, story **6** screen, script, speech, sports

Swedish ~: 5 Weiss **6** Bremer, Moberg, Myrdal, Wägner, Wahlöö **7** Bergman, Johnson, Sjöwall **8** Almqvist, Lagerlöf, Matinson **9** Söderberg **10** Lagerkvist, Swedenborg

Swiss ~: 5 Meyer, Ramuz, Spyri **6** Frisch, Piaget

Trinidadian ~: 6 Selvon

unskilled ~: 4 hack

Uruguayan ~: 6 Reyles **9** Benedetti

Venezuelan ~: 8 Gallegos

Welsh ~: 3 Map **4** Abse **6** Thomas **7** Nennius **8** Williams

West Indian ~: 7 Naipaul, Walcott

Yiddish ~: 6 Singer **8** Aleichem

___ writer: 5 ghost, space

writer's ___: 5 block, cramp

write-up: 4 puff **5** story **6** report, review **7** article **9** publicity

writhe: 4 jerk **5** crawl, creep, flail, twist, wince **6** recoil, squirm, suffer, thrash, thresh, wiggle **7** agonize, contort, wriggle **8** struggle **10** twist about

writhing: 5 snaky **7** sinuous **10** serpentine

writing: 3 ode **4** book, opus, play, poem, tome, work **5** diary, essay, novel, paper, piece, print, prose, story, theme, tract **6** column, letter, medium, record, review, scrawl, script, thesis, volume **7** article, caption, journal, letters **8** document, libretto, longhand, pamphlet, scribble, treatise **9** autograph, cuneiform, discourse, editorial, reference, shorthand, signature, term paper **10** journalism, literature, manuscript, penmanship

bad ~: 4 slop **5** tripe **8** hack work

brief ~: 5 squib

collection: 4 anth. **7** omnibus **9** anthology

combining form: 4 -gram **5** -graph **6** grapho-, -graphy

comprised of quotes: 5 cento

dull, as ~: 5 prosy

manner: 4 vein

metrical ~: 3 ode **4** poem **5** verse

need: 3 ink, pen **6** marker, pencil, stylus

on the wall: 4 omen, sign **7** portent, warning **8** graffiti

piece of ~: 3 ode **4** book, memo, note, play, poem, text **5** essay, music, novel, prose, story, theme, verse **6** thesis **7** article **8** material **10** literature

put in ~: 3 log, pen **4** mark **5** enter **6** record **7** catalog, jot down, set down **8** mark down, take down **10** transcribe

secret ~: 4 code **6** cipher

starter: 3 sky **4** hand, type **5** speed **6** screen, script, speech

style: 5 genre

table: 4 desk **7** rolltop **9** secretary

writing ___: 4 desk **5** paper

writing ___ wall: 5 on the

Writing on the Wall, The (1961 song)

artist: Adam Wade

writ of ___: 5 error, right **6** extent **7** summons

written

articles may be ~ on it: 4 spec **5** paper

communication: 4 line **6** letter **7** missive

history: 6 annals, record

___ Written in a Country Churchyard: 5 Elegy

Written in the Stars (1999 song)

artist: LeAnn Rimes

Written on the Wind (1956 film)

cast: Lauren Bacall, Rock Hudson, Robert Stack

director: Douglas Sirk

Wroclaw: 4 city, town

locale: 6 Poland

river: 4 Oder, Odra

wrong: 3 bad, ill, sin **4** awry, base, evil, goof, harm, hurt, tort, vice, wide **5** abuse, amiss, askew, badly, cheat, crime, error, false, fault, funny, guilt, inapt, libel, lying, shady, spite **6** adrift, afield, all wet, amoral, astray, damage, defame, errant, erring, faulty, felony, gauche, guilty, injure, injury, insult, liable, malign, offend, rotten, slight, unfair, unjust, untrue, way off, wicked **7** affront, at fault, awkward, blunder, crooked, cruelty, erratic, faux pas, foolish, illegal, illicit, immoral, in error, inexact, invalid, inverse, misdeed, naughty, not done, off-base, offense, oppress, outrage, reverse, slander, to blame, two-time, unsound **8** aggrieve, blamable, criminal, culpable, dishonor, foul play, ill-treat, improper, indecent, inequity, iniquity, maltreat, misdoing, mistaken, mistreat, perverse, shameful, specious, unfairly, unjustly, unlawful, villainy **9** blameable, discredit, erroneous, felonious, grievance, harmfully, ill-suited, imprudent, incorrect, injustice, misguided, off-target, out of line, persecute, turpitude, unethical, violation **10** censurable, despicable, detestable, fallacious, groundless, ill-advised, immorality, impose upon, inaccurate, inapposite, infraction, in the wrong, malapropos, mendacious, misfigured, mishandled, misleading, mistakenly, oppression, out of order, out of place, ungrounded, unsuitable, wickedness

application: 6 misuse

back the ~ horse: 4 lose

be ~: 3 err **7** blunder, mistake **8** misjudge

be rubbed the ~ way: 4 mind **6** resent **8** object to

do ~: 3 err, sin **5** stray **9** misbehave

ender: 4 doer **5** doing

give the ~ idea: 4 dupe, fool, hoax, scam **5** bluff, cheat, put on, trick **6** delude, lead on, rope in, suck in, take in **7** confuse, deceive, defraud, mislead **8** hoodwink, inveigle, misguide, throw off **9** misinform **10** lead astray

go ~: 3 err **4** bomb, bust, fail, flop, lose, slip, trip **5** flunk, misdo, stray **6** blow it, falter **7** blunder, founder, misstep, stumble, wash out **8** fall flat, flounder, lay an egg **9** misbehave, strike out

have something ~: 3 ail **4** hurt **6** suffer

ignorant of right and ~: 6 amoral

in the ~: 6 guilty, liable **7** at fault, to blame **8** blamable, culpable **9** blameable

legal ~: 4 tort

marked ~: 3 x'ed

morally ~: 3 bad **4** evil **6** horrid, sinful, wicked **7** baneful, corrupt, heinous, immoral **8** depraved **9** nefarious **10** villainous

prefix: 3 mal-, mis-

prove ~: 5 parry, rebut **6** negate, oppugn, refute **7** confute, explode **8** disprove, overturn **10** contradict, controvert, invalidate

right a ~: 6 avenge **7** get even, pay back, redress, requite **9** retaliate, retribute

rubbing the ~ way: 5 nasty **7** caustic **8** abrasive **10** unpleasant

rub the ~ way: 3 get, ire, irk, vex **4** miff, rile, roil **5** anger, annoy, chafe, grate, peeve **6** abrade, offend

way: 8 backward **9** backwards **10** upside-down

wrong ___: 4 font **6** number

Wrong ___ Corrigan: 3 Way

Wrong ___, The: 3 Box, Man

Wrong Arm of the Law, The (1962 film)

cast: Lionel Jeffries, Peter Sellers

director: Cliff Owen

Wrong Box, The (1966 film)

cast: Michael Caine, John Mills, Ralph Richardson

director: Bryan Forbes

wrongdoer: 4 perp **8** criminal **9** miscreant **10** delinquent

wrongdoing: 3 sin **4** evil **5** abuse, fault **7** knavery, misdeed, offense, outrage, scandal **8** iniquity, mischief, trespass **9** improbity, injustice

aid in ~: 4 abet **7** collude

lure into ~: 5 snare, tempt, trick **6** entrap, lead on, suck in **7** beguile, ensnare **8** entangle, inveigle

___ wrong foot: 5 on the

wrongful: 4 evil, tabu **5** taboo **6** banned, unfair, unjust, wicked **7** illegal, illicit, immoral, lawless **8** criminal, improper, outlawed, unlawful, verboten **9** dishonest, felonious, forbidden, injurious, unethical **10** prohibited

act, in law: 4 tort

combining form: 3 mal-

wrong-headed: 6 unwise **9** impolitic, imprudent, misguided **10** ill-advised

Wrong Man, The (1957 film)

cast: Henry Fonda, Vera Miles, Anthony Quayle

director: Alfred Hitchcock

___, Wrong Number: 5 Sorry

wrong way

be rubbed the ~: 4 mind **6** resent **8** object to

Wrong Way ___: 8 Corrigan

wroth: 3 hot, mad **4** ired, sore **5** angry, cross, huffy, irate, livid, riled **6** fuming, ireful, peeved, raging, raving, red-hot, stormy **7** boiling, enraged, furious, ranting, steamed, violent **8** choleric, incensed, inflamed, maddened, out-

raged, seething, white-hot, wrathful 9 indignant, irritated, resentful, splenetic, turbulent 10 freaked out, infuriated
wrought: 4 done 6 worked 8 executed, rendered 9 performed
  highly ~: 5 gaudy, showy 6 ornate 7 opulent 9 elaborate, luxurious 10 ornamented
wrought __: 4 iron
wrought-up: 4 wild 5 angry, huffy, irate, manic, rabid 6 crazed, raving, roused 7 excited, furious 8 frenzied, incensed 9 indignant 10 flipped out, freaked out
WRX: 3 car 4 auto 6 Subaru
wry: 3 dry 4 awry 5 askew, droll 6 aslant, ironic, rueful, skewed 7 crooked, cynical, mocking, twisted 8 lopsided, perverse, sardonic 9 contorted, distorted, sarcastic
  look: 4 moue
wrymouth: 4 fish
wryneck: 4 bird
__ W's: 4 five
W.S.: 6 Merwin 7 Gilbert, Van Dyke
W. Somerset __: 7 Maugham
W's, one of the five: 3 who, why 4 what, when 5 where
WSU
  conference: 6 Pac-Ten
  team: 7 Cougars
WSW: 3 dir.
  opposite: 3 ENE
wt.: 2 cg., ct., gm., gr., kg., kt., lb., mg., oz. 4 avdp. 5 avoir.
W-2: 4 form
  ID: 3 SSN
wts. and meas. agency: 3 NBS
__ W. Tuchman: 7 Barbara
Wuhan: 4 city, town
  locale: 5 China
Wuhl, Robert: 5 actor
  film: Batman (1989)
    Bull Durham (1988)
    Cobb (1994)
    Open Season (1996)
  TV: Arli$$
Wuhu: 4 port
  locale: 5 China
wulfenite: 3 ore 4 rock 7 mineral
wunderbar: 4 fine, neat 5 dandy, grand, great, super 6 superb 7 awesome, stellar 8 fabulous, five-star, glorious, smashing, splendid, terrific, topnotch 9 excellent, fantastic, first-rate, marvelous 10 first-class, phenomenal
Wunderbar composer: 6 Porter
wunderkind: 5 comer 7 prodigy, whiz kid
wurst: 4 meat 7 sausage
  starter: 4 brat 5 knack, knock, liver 6 wiener
__-Württemberg: 5 Baden
Würzburg: 4 city, town
  locale: 7 Germany
__-wurzel: 6 mangel 7 mangold
WUSA (1970 film)
  cast: Paul Newman, Anthony Perkins, Joanne Woodward
wuss: 4 nerd, nurd 5 dweeb
Wuthering Heights: 4 film 5 novel
  author: Emily Brontë
  cast: David Niven, Merle Oberon, Laurence Olivier
  cat: 9 Grimalkin
  character: 4 Dean 5 Cathy, Edgar, Nelly 6 Linton 7 Hareton, Hindley 8 Earnshaw, Isabella 9 Catherine 10 Heathcliff
  director: William Wyler
  dog: 4 Juno, Wolf 7 Gnasher, Skulker
  like ~: 6 Gothic
  setting: 4 moor
Wüthrich, Kurt: 7 chemist 8 Nobelist
__-Wuzzy: 5 Fuzzy
W. Va.
  neighbor: 3 Ken. 4 Ohio, Penn.
  setting: 3 EDT, EST
  see also West Virginia
WWI
  airplane: 4 Spad
  battle: 4 Yser 5 Marne, Somme, Ypres
  leader: 4 Foch, Spee 6 Kaiser 8 Pershing
  soldier: 5 Anzac, poilu 8 doughboy
  soldiers: 3 AEF, RAF
  venue: 3 Eur.
WWII
  address: 3 APO
  agcy.: 3 OPA, OSS, OWI
  aircraft carrier: 6 Hornet
  arena: 3 ETO
  auxiliary: 4 WAAC, WAAF
  battle site: 4 Caen, St. Lô 5 Anzio 6 Bataan
  bomber: 5 Stuka
  Brit. group: 3 RAF 4 WAAF
  celebration: 5 VE Day, VJ Day
  code machine: 6 Enigma
  conference site: 5 Cairo, Yalta 6 Tehran 7 Potsdam
  craft: 3 LCI, LCT, LST 5 E-boat, U-boat 6 amtrac, PT boat 7 amtrack
  fare: 4 Spam
  female: 3 WAC 4 WAAC, Wasp, Wave
  fliers: 3 AAF, RAF, WAF
  general: 3 DDE
  gun: 4 Bren, Sten 6 ack ack, garand
  journalist: 4 Pyle
  nickname: 3 Hap, Ike
  one-third of a ~ film title: 4 Tora
  Pope: 4 Pius
  side: 4 Axis 6 Allies
  soldier: 2 GI 5 Amvet, GI Joe
  sub detector: 5 asdic, sonar
  supply base: 3 Lae
  turning point: 4 D-Day
  underground: 3 EAM 4 EDES, ELAS 6 Maquis
  vehicle: 4 jeep, tank
  weapon: 5 A bomb
WWW: 3 Net 8 Internet
  address: 3 URL
  address source: 3 ISP
  address starter: 4 http
  connector: 5 modem
  part of ~: 3 Web 4 Wide 5 World
  periodical: 5 e-zine
  see also Internet, Web
www.harvard.__: 3 edu
WXY, telephone's: 4 nine
WY
  see Wyoming
Wyandot: 5 Huron, tribe 6 Indian 7 Amerind 8 language
  cousin: 4 Erie
Wyandotte: 4 cave, city, fowl, town 7 chicken
  locale: 8 Michigan
  relative: 6 Bantam, Brahma, Houdan, Sussex 7 Cornish, Dorking, Leghorn 8 Araucana, Langshan, Shanghai 9 Dominique, Orpington
Wyatt: 4 Earp, Jane 6 Thomas
  cohort of ~: 3 Doc 6 Morgan, Virgil
Wyatt Earp (1994 film)
  cast: Kevin Costner, Jeff Fahey, Gene Hackman, Dennis Quaid
  director: Lawrence Kasdan
Wyatt, Jane: 7 actress
  film: Boomerang! (1947)
    The House by the River (1950)
    Lost Horizon (1937)
    Pitfall (1948)
  TV: Father Knows Best
Wyatt, Thomas: 4 poet 7 British
wych __: 3 elm
Wycherley, William: 7 British 10 playwright
  work: The Country Wife
    The Plain Dealer
Wyclef: 4 Jean
Wycliffe: 4 John
wye: 4 pipe 6 letter
  follower: 3 zed, zee
  preceder: 2 ex
Wye: 5 river
  locale: 5 Wales 7 England
Wyeth: 2 N.C. 5 Jamie 6 Andrew, artist 7 painter
  subject: 5 Helga
Wyle: 4 Noah
Wyler, William: 8 director
  film: Ben-Hur (1959, AA)
    The Best Years of Our Lives (1946, AA)
    The Collector (1965)
    Come and Get It (1936)
    Counsellor-at-Law (1933)
    Dead End (1937)
    The Desperate Hours (1955)
    Detective Story (1951)
    Dodsworth (1936)
    Friendly Persuasion (1956)
    Funny Girl (1968)
    The Good Fairy (1935)
    The Heiress (1949)
    How to Steal a Million (1966)
    Jezebel (1938)
    The Letter (1940)
    The Little Foxes (1941)
    Mrs. Miniver (1942, AA)
    Roman Holiday (1953)
    These Three (1936)
    The Westerner (1940)
    Wuthering Heights (1939)
Wylie: 4 Paul 6 Elinor, Philip
Wylie, Elinor: 4 poet 6 author, writer
  work: Black Armour
    Jennifer Lorn
    Nets to Catch the Wind
    Trivial Breath
Wyman: 4 Bill, Jane
Wyman, Jane: 7 actress
  film: All That Heaven Allows (1955)
    Bad Men of Missouri (1941)
    The Blue Veil (1951)
    Footlight Serenade (1942)
    Here Comes the Groom (1951)
    Johnny Belinda (1948, AA)
    Just for You (1952)
    Larceny, Inc. (1942)
    Let's Do It Again (1953)
    The Lost Weekend (1945)
    Magic Town (1947)
    Magnificent Obsession (1954)
    Pollyanna (1960)
    So Big (1953)
    The Story of Will Rogers (1952)
    The Yearling (1946)
  spouse: Ronald Reagan
  TV: Falcon Crest
Wyndham: 4 John 5 hotel, Lewis
  alternative: 4 Omni 5 Hyatt 6 Hilton, Westin 8 Marriott, Radisson, Sheraton 10 DoubleTree 11 Crowne Plaza, Four Seasons
Wyndham, John: 6 author, writer 7 British
  genre: 5 sci-fi
  work: The Day of the Triffids
    Out of the Deeps
    The Village of the Damned
Wynette, Tammy
  song: Stand By Your Man (1968)
  spouse: George Jones
Wynken, Blynken and Nod: 4 trio
  writer: 5 Field
Wynn: 2 Ed 3 Bob 5 Early, Steve 6 Keenan
Wynn, Early: 6 hurler, Indian 7 pitcher
Wynn, Ed: 5 actor 8 comedian
  film: The Absent-Minded Professor (1961)
    The Diary of Anne Frank (1959)
    The Great Man (1956)
    Marjorie Morningstar (1958)
    Mary Poppins (1964)
    Son of Flubber (1963)
Wynn, Keenan: 5 actor
  film: The Absent-Minded Professor (1961)
    Angels in the Outfield (1951)
    Bikini Beach (1964)
    Dr. Strangelove (1964)
    Easy to Wed (1946)
    The Great Man (1956)
    The Killer Inside Me (1976)
    Neptune's Daughter (1949)
    Point Blank (1967)
    See Here, Private Hargrove (1944)
    Son of Flubber (1963)
    Warning Shot (1967)
    Welcome to Hard Times (1967)
Wynonna: 4 Judd
  mother: 5 Naomi
  sister: 6 Ashley
Wynter, Dana: 7 actress
  film: D-Day the Sixth of June (1956)
    Invasion of the Body Snatchers (1956)
    The List of Adrian Messenger (1963)
    On the Double (1961)
    Shake Hands With the Devil (1959)
    Sink the Bismarck! (1960)
    Something of Value (1957)
Wynton: 8 Marsalis
Wynyard: 4 city, town 5 Diana
  locale: 6 Canada
Wynyard, Diana: 7 actress
  film: Cavalcade (1933)
    Gaslight (1940)
    One More River (1934)
    Reunion in Vienna (1933)
Wyo.
  neighbor: 3 Ida., Neb. 4 Colo., Mont., Nebr., S. Dak., Utah
  see also Wyoming
Wyomia: 4 Tyus
Wyoming: 4 city, town 5 state
  capital: 8 Cheyenne
  city: 4 Cody 6 Casper 7 Laramie 8 Cheyenne
  Indian: 7 Arapaho 8 Arapahoe 10 Miniconjou
  locale: 8 Michigan
  mountain: 6 Tetons 7 Bighorn, Laramie
  national park: 10 Grand Teton
  neighbor: 4 Utah 5 Idaho 7 Montana 8 Colorado, Nebraska
  state bird: 10 meadowlark
  state gemstone: 4 jade
  state mammal: 7 buffalo
  state tree: 10 cottonwood
Wyoming author: Zane Grey
WYSIWYG, part of: 3 Get, See, You 4 What
Wythe: 6 George

XYZ

x-___: 3 ray 4 axis, line, unit 6 height
X: 3 chi, unk., var. 4 axis, mark, spot, tick 6 delete, letter 7 mark off, unknown 8 check off, variable 10 chromosome
  file: 7 dossier
  in phonetic alphabet: 4 X-ray
  mark with an ~: 4 sign
  out: 5 erase 6 cancel, delete, excise, strike 7 expunge 8 cross off 9 eliminate 10 obliterate
  perhaps: 3 tac, tic, toe
  preceder: 3 UVW 4 TUVW 5 STUVW
  rated ~: 4 lewd, racy 5 spicy 6 erotic, risqué, sultry, torrid
X ___ the spot: 5 marks
X ___ xylophone: 4 as in
X-___: 3 Men 5 rated
X-___, The: 5 Files
X-___ vision: 3 ray
___ X: 3 Gen 5 Brand 6 Madame, planet 7 Malcolm
Xaloztoc: 4 city, town
  locale: 6 Mexico 8 Tlaxcala
Xanadu: 6 estate
  owner: 4 Kane
  river: 4 Alph
Xanadu (1980 song)
  artist: ELO, Olivia Newton-John
Xanadu band: 3 ELO
...Xanadu did ___ Khan...: 5 Kubla
Xander: 8 Berkeley
xanthan ___: 3 gum
xanthic: 6 yellow
  relative: 4 buff, corn, gold, lime, rust, sand 5 blond, brass, coral, cream, flaxy, lemon, maize, ocher, ochre, peach, rusty, straw 6 blonde, canary, chammy, citron, crocus, flaxen, shammy, shamoy 7 apricot, chamois, citrine, jasmine, mustard, nankeen, old gold, saffron 8 daffodil, primrose 9 champagne, goldenrod, jessamine
Xanthippe: 3 nag 5 harpy, scold, shrew, vixen 6 chider, noodge, virago 8 fishwife 9 henpecker, termagant
  husband of ~: 8 Socrates
Xanthippus, son of: 8 Pericles
xanthous: 5 flaxy 6 flaxen
xat: 4 pole 5 totem 9 totem pole
Xaverian ___: 7 Brother
Xavier: 5 Cugat 7 Francis, Herbert 8 McDaniel
  athletes: 10 Musketeers
  ex: 4 Abbe 5 Charo
  locale: 4 Ohio 10 Cincinnati
X-axis, like the: 3 hor. 10 horizontal
___ X. Bushman: 7 Francis
Xe: 4 elem. 5 xenon 7 element
  54 for ~: 4 at. no.
xebec: 4 boat, ship
x'ed: 5 voted 6 marked 7 deleted 9 struck out 10 crossed out, eliminated
Xena (TV adventure)
  cast: Lucy Lawless (Xena)
    Renee O'Connor (Gabrielle)
    Ted Raimi (Joxer)
    Kevin Smith (Ares)
Xenia: 4 city, town
  locale: 4 Ohio
xenon: 3 gas 7 element 8 noble gas
  discoverer: 6 Ramsay
  like ~: 5 inert 8 inactive
Xenophanes: 5 Greek 11 philosopher
xenophobe fear: 6 aliens 9 strangers 10 foreigners
Xenophon: 5 Greek 6 writer
  work: Anabasis
___-Xer: 3 Gen
Xeres product: 6 sherry
xerography powder: 5 toner
xerophyte: 5 plant 6 cactus
Xerox: 4 copy, same 5 clone, ditto 6 double, ectype 7 replica 8 knockoff, likeness 9 duplicate, imitation, photocopy, reproduce
  competitor: 4 Mita 5 Canon, Ricoh 7 Brother
  precursor: 5 ditto, mimeo
xerus: 6 animal, mammal, rodent
  relative: 3 rat 4 cavy, degu, jird, paca, vole 5 coypu, gundi, mouse 6 agouti, beaver, gerbil, gopher, jerboa, marmot, murine 7 hamster, lemming, muskrat, visacha 8 chipmunk, cricetid, dormouse, squirrel, tuco-tuco 9 chickaree, groundhog, guinea pig, porcupine, woodchuck 10 chinchilla, prairie dog
Xerxes: 4 king 7 Persian
  composer: 6 Handel
  parent of ~: 6 Atossa, Darius
  wife: 6 Esther
X-Files, The (Fox sci-fi)
  cast: Gillian Anderson (Dana Scully)
    William B. Davis (Smoking Man)
    David Duchovny (Fox Mulder)
    Annabeth Gish (Monica Reyes)
    Robert Patrick (John Doggett)
    Mitch Pileggi (Walter Skinner)
  creator: Chris Carter
  dog: 8 Queequeg
  employer: FBI
  like ~: 4 eery 5 eerie
  topic: 3 ETs, UFO 5 alien
X-Games telecaster: 4 ESPN
Xhosa: 8 language
  home: 6 Africa
xi: 5 Greek 6 letter 8 particle
  follower: 7 omicron
  preceder: 2 nu 4 mu nu
___ XI: 7 Chapter
Xiamen: 4 Amoy, city, port, town
Xian: 4 city, town
  locale: 5 China
Xiaoping: 4 Deng
Xico: 4 city, town
  locale: 6 Mexico
Xicotepec: 4 city, town
  locale: 6 Mexico, Puebla
Xi Jiang: 5 river
  locale: 5 China
___-Xing: 3 Ped
X-ing a Paragrab author: Poe
Xingú: 5 river
  locale: 6 Brazil
  the ~ flows into it: 6 Amazon
XJS: 3 car 4 auto 6 Jaguar
XKE: 3 car, Jag 4 auto 6 Jaguar
XKR: 3 car 4 auto 6 Jaguar
XL: 4 size 5 forty
  it's smaller than ~: 2 lg. 3 lge., med.
XLI Poems author: e.e. cummings
X marks the ___: 4 spot
Xmas: 4 Noel, yule 8 yuletide
  mo.: 3 Dec.
  see also Christmas
X-Men (2000 film)
  cast: Halle Berry, Hugh Jackman, Famke Janssen, James Marsden, Ian McKellen, Anna Paquin, Rebecca Romijn-Stamos, Patrick Stewart
  director: Bryan Singer
Xosa home: 6 Africa
Xoxocotlan: 4 city, town
  locale: 6 Mexico, Oaxaca
XOXOX: 4 hugs 6 kisses
X-rated: 4 lewd 5 adult, spicy 6 erotic, risqué, smutty, spicey, sultry, vulgar
  perhaps: 5 uncut
x-ray: 7 analyze 9 skiagraph 10 photograph, radiograph
  blocker: 4 lead
  descendant: 3 MRI, NMR
  dose: 3 rad, rem
  machine: 6 imager
x-ray ___: 4 star, tube 6 vision 7 burster
Xsara: 3 car 4 auto 7 Citroen
Xscape
  members: Scott, Burruss, Cottle
  song: The Arms of the One... (1998)
    Just Kickin' It (1993)
    Keep On, Keepin' On (1996)
    My Little Secret (1998)
    Understanding (1994)
    Who Can I Run To? (1995)
XT: 2 PC 3 IBM 8 computer
Xterra: 3 SUV 6 Nissan
___ XVI Gustav: 4 Carl
XXX
  drink: 3 ale
  opposite: 3 OOO
  part: 3 tac, tic, toe
XXX (2002 film)
  cast: Vin Diesel, Samuel L. Jackson
xylem: 6 tissue
  source: 4 tree, wood
xylographer: 6 etcher 8 engraver
xylophone: 7 balafon 8 amadinda
XYZ ___: 6 Affair
-y
  comparative of: 3 -ier
  equivalent: 3 -ish
  plural of: 3 -ies
Y: 4 axis, elem. 6 letter 7 element, yttrium
  having a ~ chromosome: 4 male 9 masculine
  in phonetic alphabet: 6 Yankee
  preceders: 3 VWX 4 UVWX 5 TUVWX
  sometimes: 5 vowel
  39 for ~: 4 at. no.
  wearer: 3 Eli 5 Yalie 7 Bulldog
Y ___ yellow: 4 as in
ya-___: 4 ta-ta
Ya ___ have heart: 5 gotta
Y.A.: 6 Tittle
Yabba ___ doo!: 5 dabba
yacht: 4 boat, ship, yawl 5 craft, ketch, racer, sloop 6 vessel 7 cruiser 8 sailboat
  device: 5 loran, radar
  flag: 6 burgee
  heading: 4 tack
  jib: 5 Genoa
  like a ~: 4 chic, lush, posh, tony 5 fancy, plush, ritzy, swank 6 chichi, classy, deluxe, flashy, lavish, snazzy, swanky 7 elegant, refined 8 palatial, princely 9 expensive, high-class, luxurious, sumptuous
  shelter: 5 basin
  squad: 4 crew 5 hands
  stopover: 5 botel 6 boatel
  yon ~: 3 her, she
yacht ___: 4 club 5 chair
___ yacht: 4 land, sand
yachtie: 6 boater, sailor 7 mariner
yachting: 4 asea 5 at sea, naval, sport 8 nautical 10 navigation
yachtsman: 6 boater, sailor 7 jack tar
yachtswoman: 6 boater, sailor
yack
  see yak
yackety-___: 3 yak 4 yack
yackety-yak: 3 gab, gas, rap 4 blab, chat, chin 5 prate
Yad ___: 6 Vashem
Yada yada yada...: 3 etc.
yager: 6 hunter
Yahgan: 6 Indian 7 Amerind
yahoo: 3 rah 4 boor, lout, rube 5 brute, cheer, churl, clown, rowdy, schmo, yokel 6 lummox, schmoe 7 bounder, lowbrow, lowlife, parvenu, peasant, ruffian, upstart, whoopee, whoopie 9 arriviste 10 Philistine
Yahoo: 3 ISP 7 Serious
  competitor: 3 AOL
Yahtzee need: 4 dice 8 score pad
Yahweh: 4 Lord 6 Adonai
Yaizu: 4 city, town
  locale: 5 Japan
Yajalón: 4 city, town
  locale: 6 Mexico 7 Chiapas
yak: 2 ox 3 cow, gab, gas, jaw, rap, say, yap 4 blab, bull, buzz, chat, chin, gush, talk 5 bovid, clack, noise, prate, run on, speak, spout 6 animal, babble, bovine, gabble, gibber, gossip, jabber, mammal, natter, parley, patter, rattle, yammer 7 blather, blether, chatter, maunder, palaver, prattle, twaddle 8 converse, ramble on, spout off 9 go on and on, quadruped, touch base 10 chew the fat, chew the rag
  habitat: 4 Asia 5 Tibet 6 Thibet, Xizang 7 Sitsang
  relative: 4 anoa, arna, gaur, urus, zebu 5 bison, gayal, takin 6 mithan, muskox 7 aurochs, banteng, banting, beefalo, buffalo, carabao, cattalo, kouprey, tamarao, tamarau, timarau
  young: 4 calf
___-yak: 6 yakety, yakity 7 yackety
Yakety ___: 3 Sax, Yak
Yakety Sax artist: 8 Randolph
Yakety Yak (1958 song) artist: Coasters
Yakima: 4 city, town 5 river, tribe 6 Indian 7 Amerind
  locale: 10 Washington
yakity-___: 3 yak
yakker: 6 gossip, magpie 8 prattler 10 chatterbox
yakkety-yak
  see yak
yakking: 7 chatter 8 babbling, chitchat 9 loquacity 10 loquacious
Yakov: 8 Smirnoff
  in English: 5 Jacob
yaks: 4 oxen 6 cattle
Yakut: 8 language
  people: 6 Evenki
Yakutsk: 4 city, port, town
  river: 4 Lena
Yakuza, The (1975 film)
  cast: Brian Keith, Robert Mitchum
  director: Sydney Pollack
Yale: 4 Lary, peak 5 Elihu, Linus, mount 8 mountain
  athletes: 4 Elis 8 Bulldogs
  cheer: 5 boola
  Harvard, to ~: 5 rival
  league: 3 Ivy
  locale: 4 Conn. 7 Rockies, Sawatch 8 Colorado, New Haven
  product: 4 lock
Yalie: 3 Eli 7 Bulldog 10 Ivy Leaguer
  rival: 6 Cantab
y'all: 8 everyone 9 everybody
Yalow, Rosalyn: 8 Nobelist 9 physicist
Yalta: 4 city, port, town
  locale: 6 Crimea 7 Ukraine
Yalu: 5 river
  River locale: 9 Manchuria 10 North Korea
yam: 5 tuber 6 veggie 9 vegetable
___ yam: 4 wild 7 candied
Yamagata: 4 city, town 7 Aritomo
  locale: 5 Japan
Yamaguchi, Kristi: 6 skater
  maneuver: 4 axel, spin 5 camel
  milieu: 3 ice 4 rink

Yamaha rival: 6 Harley 8 Kawasaki
Yamato: 4 city, town
locale: 5 Japan
yammer: 3 gab, gas, jaw, rap, yak, yap 4 beef, blab, chat, chin, moan 5 gripe, groan, prate, shout, speak, whine 6 squawk 7 grumble 8 complain 9 bellyache, make a fuss
Yamoussoukro: 4 city, town 7 capital
locale: 10 Ivory Coast
Yampa: 5 river
locale: 8 Colorado
Yamuna: 5 river
city on the ~: 4 Agra 5 Delhi
locale: 5 India
Yan: 4 cook 6 Martin
pan: 3 wok
Yana: 6 Indian 7 Amerind
Yanan region: 6 Shensi
Yanbian: 3 cow 4 bull 6 bovine, cattle
Yañez, Augustín: 6 writer 7 Mexican
work: The Edge of the Storm
yang: 4 honk
of the ~: 4 masc. 9 masculine
partner: 3 yin
Yang, Chen Ning: 8 Nobelist 9 physicist
yang chin: 6 string, zither
origin: 5 China
Yangon: 4 city, town 7 capital
locale: 4 Asia 5 Burma 7 Myanmar
Yangtze: 5 river
city on the ~: 5 Wuhan 6 Anqing
river to the ~: 3 Han
yank: 3 lug, rip, tow, tug 4 draw, jerk, pull, snap, tear 5 hitch, pluck, twist, wrest 6 evulse, snatch, twitch, wrench 7 extract, jerk out
out: 5 pluck, roust 9 extirpate
Yank: 5 GI Joe 7 soldier 8 American, doughboy 10 Northerner
ally: 4 Brit 5 poilu, Tommy
foe: 3 Reb
Yank __ RAF, A: 5 in the
Yank at __, A: 4 Eton 6 Oxford
Yank at Oxford, A (1938 film)
cast: Lionel Barrymore, Vivien Leigh, Maureen O'Sullivan, Robert Taylor
Yankee: 4 ALer
Hall of Famer: 4 Ford, Ruth 5 Berra, Combs, Gomez 6 Dickey, Gehrig, Mantle 7 Lazzeri, Rizzuto, Ruffing 8 Babe Ruth, DiMaggio 9 Lou Gehrig, Yogi Berra 10 Bill Dickey, Earle Combs, Lefty Gomez, Whitey Ford
manager: 4 Dent, Houk, King, Neun 5 Berra, Chase, Green, Lemon, Torre 6 Chance, Dickey, Harris, Howser, Martin, McGraw, Virdon 7 Donovan, Huggins, Merrill, Michael, Shawkey, Stengel 8 Fletcher, Griffith, McCarthy, Piniella, Robinson 9 Elberfeld, Showalter, Stallings
nickname: 4 Babe, Yogi 5 DiMag 7 Bambino, Scooter
rival: 3 Cub, Met, Red 4 Expo, Twin 5 Angel, Astro, Brave, Giant, Padre, Rocky, Royal, Tiger 6 Brewer, Dodger, Indian, Marlin, Oriole, Philly, Pirate, Ranger, Red Sox 7 Blue Jay, Mariner 8 Athletic, Cardinal, Devil Ray, White Sox
Yankee __: 4 bond 6 dollar, Doodle
Yankee __ Dandy: 6 Doodle
Yankee __ soup: 4 bean
Yankee Clipper: 5 DiMag 8 DiMaggio
brother: 3 Dom 5 Vince
Yankee Doodle Boy, The composer: 5 Cohan
__ Yankee Doodle dandy: 3 I'm a
Yankee Doodle Dandy (1942 film)
cast: James Cagney, Walter Huston, Joan Leslie
director: Michael Curtiz
Yankee Doodle's mount: 4 pony
Yankees: 3 ten 4 team
home: 3 NYC 5 Bronx 7 New York
org.: 3 ALE, MLB
sport: 8 baseball
__ Yankees: 4 Damn
Yankee Stadium surface: 5 grass
Yank in the RAF, A (1941 film)
cast: Betty Grable, Tyrone Power
Yankovic, Weird Al: 8 parodist
song: Eat It (1984)
Yanks: 9 See Yankee
Yanks (1979 film)
cast: William Devane, Lisa Eichhorn, Richard Gere, Vanessa Redgrave
director: John Schlesinger
Yankton: 6 Indian 7 Amerind
Yannick, Noah: 7 netster 9 tennis pro
Yao: 4 city, town 8 language
home: 6 Africa, Malawi 8 Tanzania 10 Mozambique
locale: 5 Japan
Yaoundé: 4 city, town 7 capital
locale: 8 Cameroon
yap: 3 gab, jaw, yak 4 bark, chat, puss, trap, yell, yelp 5 clack, mouth, prate, run on, shout 6 babble, gossip, holler, jabber, kisser, squawk, yammer 7 blather, blether, chatter, kyoodle, prattle 8 idle talk, mouth off
Yap: 4 isle 6 island
locale: 7 Pacific
Yaphet: 5 Kotto
yapon: 4 tree 5 holly, shrub
Yaqui: 5 river 6 Indian 7 Amerind 8 language
Yaquí: 4 city, town
locale: 6 Mexico, Sonora
yar: 6 lively 10 responsive
__ Yar: 4 Babi
Yarborough: 4 Cale 9 auto racer
milieu: 5 track
Yarbrough, Glenn group: Limeliters
yard: 3 lot 4 lawn 5 close, court, depot, grass, patio, plant 6 corral, garden 7 terrace 8 backyard, barnyard, clearing, outdoors 9 courtyard, enclosure 10 playground, quadrangle
bought at a ~ sale: 4 worn 10 hand-me-down, secondhand
covering: 4 lawn 5 grass
do ~ work: 3 mow, sod 4 rake 5 resod
enclosure: 5 fence, hedge
ender: 3 age, arm, man, men 5 stick 6 master
European ~: 5 meter, metre
fraction: 4 foot, inch
goods: 5 cloth, stuff 6 fabric 8 material, textiles
like some ~ s: 5 weedy
1000 ~s: 4 one K
pest: 4 mole 6 gopher
sale staple: 3 LPs 4 toys 9 bric-a-brac, glassware
starter: 4 back, barn, deer, dock, door, farm, junk, ship, tilt, vine 5 brick, court, steel, stock 6 church, lumber, school, switch
tool: 4 rake 5 mower
whole nine ~ s: 4 a to z 8 entirety
yard __: 4 sale 5 goods, of ale
__ yard: 4 back, main, navy 6 square 7 sorting
Yard: 5 Molly
yardage
first-down ~: 3 ten
football ~: 4 gain
gain ground ~: 4 rush
yardbird: 3 con 5 felon 6 inmate 7 convict 8 internee, prisoner
Yardbirds
members: Clapton, Beck, Page
song: For Your Love (1965)
Heart Full of Soul (1965)
I'm a Man (1965)
Over Under Sideways Down (1966)
Shapes of Things (1966)
yard-long: 6 legume
__ Yards: 6 Camden
yardstick: 4 norm, test 5 gauge, ruler, scale 7 measure 8 standard 9 benchmark, criterion 10 touchstone
org.: 4 ANSI
__ Yard, The: 7 Longest
yare: 5 agile 6 lively 10 responsive
Yarmuk: 5 river
River locale: 6 Jordan
yarmulke: 3 cap, hat 6 beanie
yarn: 3 lie 4 saga, tale 5 alibi, fable, fiber, story, twine 6 crewel, strand, string, thread 7 fiction, worsted 8 anecdote, tall tale 9 adventure, fairy tale, fish story, invention, narration, narrative, tall story
ball of ~: 4 clew, hank 5 skein
difficulty: 4 knot 6 tangle
flaw: 4 slub
holder: 5 spool
looped ~: 6 boucle
low-grade ~: 3 abb
make ~: 4 spin 5 weave
material: 4 ragg, wool 6 angora
measure: 6 denier
metallic ~: 5 lurex
silk ~: 4 poil
spin a ~: 3 fib, lie 6 relate
unit: 3 ply 4 hank 5 skein
__ yarn: 4 rope, spun 6 aramid, combed, crewel, rogue's, zephyr 7 genappe
Yarra: 5 river
city on the: 9 Melbourne
locale: 8 Victoria 9 Australia
yarrow: 5 plant 6 flower
Yarrow: 5 Peter, river
locale: 8 Scotland
Yarrow, Peter: 6 singer 10 folk singer
colleague: 4 Mary, Paul 7 Stookey, Travers
Yasbeck: 3 Amy
Yashica: 6 camera
alternative: 4 Fuji 5 Canon, Kodak, Leica, Nikon 6 Konica, Pentax, Rollei 7 Minolta, Olympus, Vivitar 8 Polaroid
Yashin, Alexsandr: 6 writer 7 Russian
real name: Alexsandr Popin
yashmak: 4 veil
Yasmine: 6 Bleeth
Yasmin mother: 4 Rita
Yasodhara's husband: 6 Buddha
Yasser: 6 Arafat
Yastrzemski, Carl: 10 outfielder
Yasur: 7 volcano
locale: 4 Asia 7 Vanuatu
yate: 10 eucalyptus
Yates, Peter: 8 director
film: Breaking Away (1979)
Bullitt (1968)
The Deep (1977)
The Dresser (1983)
Eleni (1985)
Eyewitness (1981)
For Pete's Sake (1974)
The Friends of Eddie Coyle (1973)
The Hot Rock (1972)
Mother, Jugs & Speed (1976)
Murphy's War (1971)
Suspect (1987)
Yat-sen: 3 Sun
yaup: 3 cry 6 squawk
yaupon: 4 tree 5 holly, shrub
Yautepec: 4 city, town
locale: 6 Mexico 7 Morelos
Yavapai: 6 Indian 7 Amerind
yaw: 4 bend, keel, roll, tack, tilt, turn, veer 5 drift, lurch, pitch 6 swerve 7 deviate 9 deviation
yawl: 4 boat, ship 5 yacht 8 sailboat 9 jolly boat
look-alike: 5 ketch
pole: 4 boom, mast, spar
yawn: 3 gap, nap 4 doze, gape, part, tire 5 sleep 6 drowse, snooze 8 oscitate, tiresome 10 catch flies
inducer: 4 bore 5 ennui 6 tedium 7 boredom 8 monotony
yawning: 4 open 5 agape 6 gaping, sleepy 7 abysmal 8 profound 9 cavernous 10 bottomless
hole: 5 abyss, chasm
yawny: 4 dull 6 boring 7 tedious 8 tiresome 9 heavy-eyed, somnolent
yawp: 4 bawl 6 bellow
yay: 3 cry, olé, rah 6 goodie 7 whoopee
Yay __!: 4 team
Yazoo: 5 river
locale: 4 Miss. 9 Vicksburg
Yb: 4 elem. 9 ytterbium
70 for ~: 4 at. no.
Ybor City: 4 city, town
locale: 7 Florida
neighbor: 5 Tampa
yclept: 5 named 6 called
yds.: 4 lgth., meas.
Ye __ Tea Shoppe: 4 Olde
yea: 2 ay 3 aye, yes 4 vote 5 goody, truly 6 assent, goodie, hoorah, hooray, hot dog, hurrah, indeed, it is so 7 in truth 8 thumbs up
opposite: 3 nay
Yeager, Chuck: 3 ace 5 flier, flyer, pilot 7 aviator
milestone: 5 Mach 1
yeah: 2 ay, da, ja, OK, sí 3 aye, oui, yep, yes, yup 4 fine, okay, okeh, okey, sure 5 good-o, natch, quite, right, roger, uh-huh 6 agreed, gladly, good-oh, indeed, just so, rather, righto, surely, you bet, yowzah 7 exactly, go ahead, indeedy, mais oui, quite so, ten-four 8 all right, as you say, of course, thumbs up, very well 9 be my guest, certainly, darn right, naturally, precisely, sure thing, you betcha, you said it 10 absolutely, by all means, definitely, positively, sure enough, that's right
opposite of ~: 3 nah 4 nope
Yeah, right!: 4 as if, I bet, sure 6 I'll bet, I'm sure, oh sure
yeanling: 4 lamb
year: 4 time 5 grade 6 junior, length, senior 7 vintage 8 freshman 9 sophomore
ender: 3 end 4 book, long
hold back a ~: 5 flunk
once a ~: 6 annual 8 annually, per annum, periodic 9 perennial, regularly
part: 3 day 4 week 5 month 7 quarter
solar-lunar ~ discrepancy: 5 epact
symbolically: 6 candle
year __ day, A: 4 and a
year-__: 3 end 5 round
__ year: 3 new, off 4 leap 5 civil, lunar, once a, solar 6 church, common, fiscal, school, Sothic 7 jubilee, perfect, regular, vintage
__-year: 3 all, man 5 light, woman 6 person
Year __ Cat: 5 of the
__ Year: 4 Holy 5 Great
yearbook: 6 annual
photo: 2 sr. 3 snr. 6 senior
Yeardley: 5 Smith
year-end
drink: 3 nog 6 eggnog
helper: 3 elf
month: 3 Dec. 8 December

reward: 5 bonus
tune: 4 Noel 5 carol
Year in Provence, A author: 5 Mayle
___ Year Itch, The: 5 Seven
yearling: 4 deer, fawn, lamb 5 sheep
Yearling, The: 4 film 5 novel
author: Marjorie Kinnan Rawlings
cast: Claude Jarman Jr., Gregory Peck, Jane Wyman
character: 3 Lem, Ora 4 Buck, Ezra, Flag, Jody 5 Hutto, Twink 6 Baxter, Oliver 9 Forrester, Weatherby
yearly: 6 annual 8 annually, per annum, periodic 9 perennial, regularly
yearn: 4 ache, burn, hope, itch, long, lust, moon, mope, pant, pine, sigh, wish 5 chafe, dream 6 hanker, hunger, thirst 8 languish
for: 4 envy, miss, need, seek, want 5 covet, crave, fancy 7 welcome
(to): 6 aspire, desire
yearning: 3 yen 4 ache, hope, itch, love, urge, want, will, wish 5 eager, fancy, itchy 6 desire, hunger, thirst 7 avidity, longing, thirsty, wishful, wistful 8 ambition, appetite, desirous, voracity 9 appetence, eagerness, hankering 10 aspiration
sound: 4 sigh
year of ___: 5 grace
Year of Living Dangerously, The (1983 film)
cast: Mel Gibson, Linda Hunt, Sigourney Weaver
director: Peter Weir
Year of the ___: 3 Gun 5 Comet, Tiger 6 Dragon
Year of the Cat (1977 song) artist: Al Stewart
Year of the Intern, The author: Cook
___-Year Plan: 4 Five
years: 3 age 4 ages 6 dotage 7 oldness 8 agedness, caducity, coon's age, lifespan, lifetime, long time 10 generation, senescence
ago: 4 once, past, then
formative ~: 5 teens, youth 7 boyhood 8 girlhood 9 childhood 10 immaturity, pubescence
from ~ past: 3 old 5 olden 6 bygone 7 archaic 8 outmoded
hundred ~: 7 century 9 centenary
in French: 3 ans
many ~: 3 eon 4 aeon, ages
ten ~: 5 decad 6 decade
up in ~: 3 old 4 aged 5 aging 6 ageing 7 ancient, elderly, wizened 8 grizzled 9 geriatric, getting on, senescent
years ___: 3 ago
___ years: 3 dog 6 golden, locust 7 donkey's
___ Years After: 6 Twenty
___ Years Before the Mast: 3 Two
___ Year's Day: 3 New
___ Year's Eve: 3 New
___ Year's Kisses: 4 This
___ Years of Our Lives, The: 4 Best
___ Years, The: 5 Happy 6 Living, Wonder
___ Years' War: 3 Ten 5 Seven 6 Thirty 7 Hundred
___ Year 2525: 5 In the
Yearwood, Trisha song: How Do I Live
yeas and ___: 4 nays
yeasayer: 5 toady 6 flunky, lackey, minion, stooge 7 flunkey 8 kowtower, servitor 9 sycophant 10 bootlicker, conformist
yeast: 4 koji 6 fungal, fungus, lather, leaven 7 ferment
brewers' ~: 4 barm
use ~: 6 leaven
work, as ~: 4 rise
___ yeast: 3 top 6 baker's, bottom 7 brewer's, surface
yeasty: 5 barmy, foamy, petty 6 bouncy, frothy, paltry 7 buoyant, fired up, trivial 8 agitated, animated, exciting, piddling, trifling, youthful 9 ebullient, energetic, exuberant, frivolous
Yeats, William Butler: 4 poet 5 Irish 6 author 8 Nobelist 10 playwright
colleague: 5 Eliot, Synge
work: Byzantium
The Countess Cathleen
Down by the Salley Gardens
The Fiddler of Dooney
The Herne's Egg
The Hour Glass
The Lake Isle of Innisfree
Leda and the Swan
Long-Legged Fly
Purgatory
Sailing to Byzantium
The Second Coming
The Wild Swans at Coole
The Winding Stair
yecch: 3 ick, ugh 5 gross 6 phooey
Yeehaw Junction: 4 city, town
locale: 7 Florida
yegg: 5 thief 7 burglar, peteman 8 peterman, picklock 11 safecracker
activity: 5 crime, heist, theft 7 break-in
target: 4 safe 5 vault 9 strongbox
ye, hear: 4 oyes, oyez
Yehudi: 7 Menuhin
Yelena in English: 5 Ellen, Helen
yell: 3 cry, rah, yap, yip 4 bark, bawl, call, hoot, howl, rage, rant, roar, snap, wail, weep, yelp, yowl 5 cheer, hallo, hillo, hullo, huzza, shout, spout, voice, wahoo, whoop 6 bellow, cry out, halloa, halloo, hallow, hilloa, holler, hoorah, hooray, hulloo, hurrah, hurray, huzzah, lament, outcry, scream, shriek, shrill, squawk, squeal 7 belt out, exclaim, screech, sing out, thunder, ululate 8 complain, let loose, speak out 9 caterwaul, make a fuss, throw a fit 10 vociferate
at: 5 abuse, curse, scold 6 berate, malign, revile, vilify 7 bawl out, censure, chew out, condemn, rip into, upbraid 8 denounce, lace into, lambaste, tear into 9 castigate 10 vituperate
for: 4 hail 5 cheer 6 praise, salute 7 applaud, approve, commend, welcome 10 compliment
___ yell: 5 rebel
___ Yeller: 3 Old
yelling: 3 din 5 noise, noisy 6 ruckus, tumult
___ Yello: 5 Mello
yellow: 3 low 4 bisk, buff, gold, sand, weak, yolk 5 amber, blond, cream, flaxy, ivory, lemon, maize, straw, tawny, timid 6 afeard, afraid, bisque, blonde, craven, fallow, flaxen, golden, scared 7 afeared, chicken, fearful, gutless, saffron, wimpish 8 cowardly, liverish, recreant 9 spineless, tremulous 10 frightened
belly: 4 wimp 5 sissy 6 coward, craven 7 chicken, dastard 8 weakling 9 fraidy cat, jellyfish
blue and ~: 5 green
brownish ~: 4 buff, sand 7 nankeen
color: 4 bisk, buff, corn, gold, lime, rust, sand 5 amber, blond, brass, coral, cream, flaxy, lemon, maize, ocher, ochre, peach, rusty, straw, tawny 6 banana, bisque, blonde, canary, chammy, citron, crocus, flaxen, shammy, shamoy 7 apricot, chamois, citrine, jasmine, mustard, nankeen, old gold, saffron, xanthic 8 daffodil, primrose 9 champagne, goldenrod, jessamine
combining form: 4 flav- 5 chrys-, flavo-, luteo-, xanth- 6 chryso-, xantho-
compound: 5 aloin
dark ~: 5 ocher, ochre
dye: 6 kamala
ender: 4 bird, cake, legs, tail, weed, wood 5 belly 6 hammer, throat
flower: 3 mum 4 flag, iris, lily 5 broom, tulip 6 acacia, arnica, cosmos, crocus, mullen, orchid, violet, yarrow 7 berseem, cowslip, day lily, freesia, jonquil, mullein, ragwort, tea rose 8 asphodel, daffodil, hyacinth, laburnum, marigold, primrose, rockrose, tidytips 9 buttercup, calendula, celandine, colicroot, corydalis, dandelion, forsythia, goldenrod, groundsel, horsemint, narcissus 10 goatsbeard, marguerite, nasturtium, ranunculus, wallflower
grayish ~: 3 dun 6 chammy, citron, shammy, shamoy 7 chamois
greenish ~: 4 lime 6 acacia, citron 7 luteous 9 champagne
jacket: 4 pest, wasp 6 insect
jacket cousin: 6 hornet
ocher: 3 sil
orangish ~: 5 ocher, ochre 6 crocus 7 saffron
pinkish ~: 5 coral, peach 7 apricot
red and ~: 6 orange
reddish ~: 4 rust, sand 5 brass, coral, ocher, ochre, rusty
vehicle: 3 cab 4 taxi
white and ~ flower: 7 calypso 8 camomile 9 calla lily, chamomile
word on a ~ sign: 5 merge
yellow ___: 3 dog, gum, pad 4 flag, jack, pine, rain, rust, sage 5 alert, avens, birch, daisy, fever, light, ocher, ochre, pages, perch 6 jacket, locust, mombin, poplar, ribbon, streak 7 gentian, jasmine, parilla, puccoon, warbler
yellow-___: 7 bellied
yellow-___ contract: 3 dog
yellow-___ sapsucker: 7 bellied
___ yellow: 4 high, Mars 5 Hansa, king's, lemon, straw 6 barium, canary, Cassel, chrome, cobalt, Indian, Naples 7 cadmium, saffron, spectra
Yellow ___: 3 Cab, Sea, Sky 4 Bird, Hats
Yellow ___ of Texas, The: 4 Rose
Yellow ___ Road: 5 Brick
Yellow ___, The: 3 Kid 4 Room 6 Ticket
___ Yellow: 5 Crome 6 Mellow
Yellowbeard (1983 film)
cast: Peter Boyle, Graham Chapman, Tommy Chong, Marty Feldman, Cheech Marin
yellow-bellied: 4 weak 5 timid 6 craven, scared 9 nerveless, spineless
yellowbelly: 6 coward 8 poltroon
Yellow Bird (1961 song) artist: Arthur Lyman Group
___ Yellow Brick Road: 7 Goodbye
Yellow Brick Road flower: 5 poppy
Yellow Cab Man, The (1950 film)
cast: Gloria De Haven, Red Skelton, Walter Slezak
yellowcake: 3 ore
yellow-fever carrier: 5 aedes 8 mosquito
yellowfin: 3 ahi 4 fish, tuna
yellow-haired: 5 blond 6 blonde, flaxen
yellowhammer: 4 bird
Yellowhammer State: 3 Ala. 7 Alabama
yellowish: 3 tan 4 eggy 5 amber, flaxy, sandy 6 flaxen, sallow
brown: 5 amber, khaki, tawny, umber
color: 3 tan 4 bone, drab, fawn, foxy, jade, nude, rust 5 amber, camel, cocoa, coral, cream, ivory, khaki, olive, putty, rusty, sandy, tawny 6 auburn, bister, bistre, ginger, russet, salmon, sienna, suntan 7 apricot, caramel, dogwood 8 cinnamon 9 alabaster 10 chartreuse
pink: 5 peach
red: 5 coral, sandy
white: 5 cream
yellow jack: 4 fish
yellow jacket: 3 bug 4 wasp 6 insect
genus: 5 vespa
Yellowknife: 4 city, town
locale: 3 NWT 6 Canada
yellowlegs: 4 bird
Yellow Newtown: 5 apple
relative: 4 crab, Gala, Lodi, Rome 5 Mutsu 6 Empire, Ida Red, medlar, Pippin, russet 7 Baldwin, Bramley, costard, Freedom, Liberty, Spartan, Wealthy, Winesap 8 Cortland, Jonathan, McIntosh 10 Rome Beauty
Yellow Pages entries: 3 ads, cos.
yellow-rayed flower: 9 coreopsis, owl's claws, rudbeckia, sunflower 10 coneflower, gaillardia
yellow-red dye: 6 anatto
___ Yellow Ribbon...: 4 Tie a
Yellow River
joiner: 3 Wei
locale: 5 China, Korea
port: 5 Jinan
Yellow Rolls-Royce, The (1964 film)
cast: Ingrid Bergman, Rex Harrison, Shirley MacLaine
Yellow Room, The author: 8 Rinehart
Yellow Rose of Texas, The (1955 song)
artist: Johnny Desmond, Mitch Miller
Yellow Sea
arm: 5 Bohai, Pohai
locale: 5 Korea
port: 6 Lüshun
river to the ~: 4 Yalu
Yellow Sky (1948 film)
cast: Anne Baxter, Gregory Peck, Richard Widmark
director: William Wellman
Yellowstone: 4 lake, park 5 falls, river
gateway: 4 Cody
locale: 5 Idaho 7 Montana, Wyoming
mgr.: 3 NPS
river to the ~: 7 Bighorn
sight: 3 elk 4 bear 5 bison, moose 6 geyser
visitor: 6 camper 7 tourist
Yellow Submarine (1966 song) artist: Beatles
Yellow Submarine (1968 film) director: George Dunning
yellowtail: 4 fish
___ Yellow Taxi: 3 Big
yellowthroat: 4 bird
Yellow Ticket, The (1931 film)
cast: Lionel Barrymore, Elissa Landi, Laurence Olivier
director: Raoul Walsh
Yellow Transparent: 5 apple
relative: 4 crab, Gala, Lodi, Rome 5 Mutsu 6 Empire, Ida Red, medlar, Pippin, russet 7 Baldwin, Bramley, costard, Freedom, Liberty, Spartan, Wealthy, Winesap 8 Cortland, Jonathan, McIntosh 10 Rome Beauty
yelp: 3 yap, yip 4 bark, howl, yell, yowl 6 bellow, holler, squawk, squeak, squeal 7 kyoodle, screech
Yeltsin: 5 Boris, Naina
aide: 5 Lebed
see also Russian
Yemana, Nick portrayer: 3 Soo

Yemen: **6** nation **7** country
capital: **4** San`a **5** Sanaa
city: **3** Ibb **4** Aden, Taiz **5** Mocha, Mukha, Taizz
group: **10** Arab League
gulf near ~: **4** Aden
locale: **6** Arabia **7** Mideast
money: **4** rial **10** dinar. riyal
neighbor: **4** Oman
of old: **5** Sheba
port: **4** Aden
Yemeni: **4** Arab
neighbor: **5** Omani, Saudi
port dweller: **5** Adeni
yen: **4** ache, coin, itch, lust, need, pine, urge, want, wish **5** fancy, money **6** desire, hunger, thirst **7** craving, impulse, itching, longing, passion **8** appetite, yearning **9** hankering **10** compulsion
for: **4** ache, long, want, wish **5** yearn **6** desire, hanker **7** dream of
fraction: **3** sen
have a ~ for: **4** long, want **5** crave, fancy, yearn
Yenan region: **6** Shensi
Yenisei: **5** river
city on the ~: **6** Abakan
locale: **6** Russia
yenta: **6** gossip **7** meddler **8** busybody, quidnunc
like a ~: **4** nosy **5** nosey
Yentl (1983 film)
cast: Amy Irving, Mandy Patinkin, Barbra Streisand
director: Barbra Streisand
Yeobright: **4** Clym
yeo. employer: **3** USN
Yeoh: **8** Michelle
Ye Olde ___: **6** Shoppe
yeoman: **4** rank **6** sailor
place: **4** navy
Yeoman: **3** car **4** auto **5** Chevy **9** Chevrolet **10** automobile
yeomanly: **4** true **5** loyal **7** devoted **8** faithful, true-blue **9** allegiant, dedicated
Yeoman of the Guard, The
composer: **7** Gilbert **8** Sullivan
role: **4** Jack, Kate **5** Elsie **6** Meryll, Phoebe **7** Fairfax, Leonard, Wilfred
yeoman's ___: **4** work **7** service
Yeovil: **4** city, town
locale: **7** England
yep: **2** ay, da, ja, OK, sí **3** aye, oui, yea, yes **4** fine, okay, okeh, okey, sure, yeah **5** good-o, natch, quite, right, roger, uh-huh **6** agreed, gladly, good-oh, indeed, just so, rather, righto, surely, you bet, yowzah **7** exactly, go ahead, indeedy, mais oui, quite so, ten-four **8** all right, as you say, of course, thumbs up, very well **9** be my guest, certainly, darn right, naturally, precisely, sure thing, you betcha, you said it **10** absolutely, by all means, definitely, positively, sure enough, that's right
opposite: **3** nah **4** nope
yerba ___: **4** maté **5** buena
yerba maté: **3** tea **8** beverage
Yerby, Frank: **6** writer
work: Devilseed
The Foxes of Harrow
Goat Song
Judas, My Brother
Mackenzie's Hundred
An Odor of Sanctity
Yer darn ___!: **6** tootin'
Yerevan: **4** city, town **7** capital
locale: **7** Armenia
Yerma author: **5** Lorca
Yerres: **4** city, town
locale: **6** France
Yertle the Turtle
creator: **5** Seuss
home: **4** pond
Yerupaja: **4** peak **5** mount **8** mountain
locale: **4** Peru **5** Andes **12** South America
yes: **2** ay, da, ja, OK, sí **3** aye, hai, I do, oui, yea, yep, yup **4** amen, fine, okay, okeh, okey, sure, true, vote, yeah **5** good-o, natch, right, roger, uh-huh **6** agreed, assent, aye aye, even so, gladly, good-oh, indeed, it is so, just so, rather, righto, so be it, surely, why not, you bet, yowzah **7** exactly, go ahead, granted, indeedy, mais oui, quite so, right on, ten-four **8** all right, as you say, for a fact, of course, thumbs up, very well **9** be my guest, certainly, darn right, naturally, precisely, sure thing, willingly, you betcha, you said it **10** by all means, definitely, green light, positively, that's right
alternative to ~: **5** maybe **7** perhaps **8** possibly, probably **9** it could be, it might be, perchance
follower: **3** sir **4** ma'am **5** siree **6** sirree
in French: **3** oui
in Japanese: **3** hai
in Scottish: **2** ay **3** aye
man: **5** sheep, toady **6** flunky, jackal, lackey, minion **7** Babbitt, flunkey, lacquey, spaniel **8** assenter, emulator, truckler **9** sycophant, underling **10** conformist, handshaker
say ~: **2** OK **3** nod **4** okay **5** agree, yield **6** accede, accept, assent, permit **7** consent, go along
silent ~: **3** nod
vote: **2** ay **3** aff., aye, yea
yes ___: **3** man **5** and no
yes-___ answer: **4** or-no
Yes: **9** detergent
alternative: **3** All, Biz, Era, Fab **4** Bold, Dash, Gain, Surf, Tide, Wisk **5** Cheer, Dreft, Purex **6** Calgon, Dynamo, Oxydol **7** Octagon **9** Ivory Snow
Yes ___?: **4** or no
Yes, ___: **4** Dear, I Can
Yes, ___!: **3** sir **4** ma'am **5** siree **6** sirree
Yes, ___, That's My Baby: **3** Sir
Yes, Dear (CBS sitcom)
cast: Anthony Clark (Greg Warner)
Jean Louisa Kelly (Kim Warner)
Mike O'Malley (Jimmy Hughes)
Liza Snyder (Christine Hughes)
yeshiva: **6** school
student: **3** Jew
teacher: **5** rabbi, rebbe
Yes, I ___: **3** Can
Yes, I'm Ready (song) artist: Barbara Mason, KC and the Sunshine Band, Teri DeSario
yes-man: **5** toady **6** echoer, fawner, flunky, lackey **7** flunkey, lacquey **8** adulator, kowtower **9** flatterer
Yes Sir, That's My Baby: **4** song, tune
lyricist: **4** Kahn
singer: **6** Cantor
yesterday: **4** past **8** recently **10** not long ago, recent past
born ~: **3** raw **4** naif **5** naive
not born ~: **5** sharp **6** astute **7** veteran **9** astucious
___ Yesterday: **4** Born, Only
Yesterday (1965 song) artist: Beatles
Yesterday Once More (1973 song) artist: Carpenters
Yesterday's Songs (1981 song) artist: Neil Diamond
Yesterday, Today and Tomorrow (1964 film)
cast: Sophia Loren, Marcello Mastroianni
director: Vittorio De Sica
Yesterday, When I Was Young (1969 song) artist: Roy Clark
Yester Lover (1968 song) artist: Miracles
Yester-Me... (1969 song) artist: Stevie Wonder
yesteryear: **3** eld **4** past, yore **9** olden days
___ Yes, The: **5** Lady's
___, Yes, The: **6** People
Yes We Can Can (1973 song) artist: Pointer Sisters
Yes, Yes, ___: **6** Yvette
yet: **3** but, now, too **4** also, even, more, till **5** along, altho, as yet, by now, so far, still **6** as well, even so, hereto, though, to boot, to date, withal **7** besides, despite, earlier, finally, further, howbeit, however, prior to, someday, thus far, up to now **8** after all, although, hitherto, likewise, moreover, sometime, until now **9** at any rate, in spite of **10** all the same, beyond this, even though, eventually, in addition, ultimately, up until now
and ~: **3** but **6** unless
as ~: **3** now, yet **5** so far, still **6** erenow, hereto, to date **7** thus far, till now **8** right now, until now **10** heretofore, up until now
didn't ~: **5** hasn't
to a poet: **3** e'en
to be decided: **4** open **9** ambiguous, debatable **10** in question, unresolved, up in the air
___ yet: **3** but, not **4** as of
yeti: **5** biped **6** legend **7** snowman, Tibetan
___ yet to be, The: **6** best is
Yevgeny in English: **6** Eugene
Yevtushenko, Yevgeny: **4** poet **7** Russian
yew: **4** tree **5** taxus **9** evergreen
name meaning ~: **4** Yves
___ yew: **5** Hicks, Irish **7** English
Yggdrasil: **4** tree
Yiddish: **8** language
humorist: **8** Aleichem
interjection: **2** oy **5** oy vey
writer: **6** Singer **8** Aleichem
yield: **3** bow, buy, net, pay, sag **4** bear, bend, cede, crop, drop, dump, earn, fail, fall, flex, fold, give, hand, lose, melt, quit, shed, take **5** agree, allow, break, bring, budge, chuck, defer, ditch, fit in, forgo, grant, let go, offer, relax, say OK, share, total, waive **6** accede, accept, accrue, afford, assent, buckle, cave in, comply, concur, desist, fess up, fold up, forego, fork up, give in, give up, income, output, permit, profit, relent, render, resign, return, say yes, soften, submit, suffer, supply, tender **7** abandon, blossom, bring in, concede, consent, crumple, forfeit, forsake, furnish, give off, give way, harvest, produce, proffer, prosper, provide, radiate, release, revenue, sell for, succumb, takings, turnout, undergo **8** abdicate, back down, collapse, earnings, forswear, generate, get rid of, give over, hand over, jettison, part with, proceeds, say uncle, throw out, turn over **9** acquiesce, cast aside, deliver up, discharge, dispose of, foreswear, reconcile, send forth, surrender, throw away **10** bring forth, capitulate, come around, condescend, relinquish, toe the line, toe the mark, vegetables
bank ~: **3** int. **8** interest
don't ~: **4** urge **5** force, press **6** be firm, demand, insist, pester **7** persist, protest, speak up **8** pressure, speak out **9** importune, stand firm
quarry ~: **3** gem, ore **4** rock **5** jewel **6** gravel **7** crystal, mineral
to: **5** act on **6** accept **7** act upon, indulge
___ yield: **7** current **9** effective
Yield: **4** sign **8** road sign **10** street sign
yielding: **3** lax **4** easy, limp, meek, soft **5** mushy, shaky **6** docile, humble, pliant, spongy, supple, tender **7** dutiful, elastic, lenient, passive, plastic, pliable, springy, squishy, willing **8** amenable, biddable, flexible, gracious, obedient, resigned, tractile, unstrict **9** agreeable, compliant, malleable, resilient, tractable **10** abdication, concession, submission, submissive, unhardened
not ~: **3** set **4** firm, hard, iron, taut **5** fixed, harsh, rigid, stern, stiff, tight **6** flinty, mulish, severe, steely, strict, wooden **7** adamant, dead set, diehard, precise, prudish **8** exacting, hard-line, immobile, indurate, ironclad, obdurate, resolute, stubborn **9** demanding, difficult, hidebound, immovable, inelastic, obstinate, pig-headed, steadfast, stringent, unbending, unvarying **10** bullheaded, determined, implacable, inexorable, inflexible, invariable, relentless, unchanging, unswerving
Yikes!: **3** eek, eep **4** egad, oh no, oh oh, uh-oh **5** egads
Yildun: **4** star
yin
of the ~: **3** fem. **8** feminine
partner: **4** yang
yip: **3** cry **4** bark, yell, yelp, yowl **6** squeal
Yip: **7** Harburg
yipe: **2** ow **3** eek, yow **4** egad, ouch, yeow **5** egads **7** holy cow
Yipes!: **3** eek, eep **4** egad, oh no, oh oh, uh-oh **5** egads
yippee: **3** yay **5** huzza, wahoo **6** hoorah, hooray, hot dog, hurrah, hurray, huzzah
yipper: **3** pup **5** puppy, whelp
___ Yisrael: **5** Eretz
Yitzhak: **5** Rabin **6** Shamir
Y Kant Tori Read artist: **4** Amos
y, letter like an inverted: **6** lambda
YM: **3** mag **8** magazine
Yma: **5** Sumac
YMCA
activity: **4** swim **7** workout
class: **3** CPR
genre: **5** disco
member: **3** boy, man
part of ~: **4** assn., Men's **5** Young **9** Christian
Y.M.C.A. (1978 song) artist: Village People
Ymir: **5** giant
yo-___-ho: **5** heave
Yo!: **3** hey **4** ahoy **6** hey you
Yo, ___!: **6** Adrian
Yoakam: **6** Dwight
yod: **6** Hebrew, letter
follower: **4** caph, kaph
preceder: **3** tet **4** teth
yodel: **4** sing **6** warble **8** vocalize
place to ~: **4** Alps **5** Tirol, Tyrol **7** Austria
yodh: **6** Hebrew, letter
follower: **4** caph, kaph
preceder: **3** tet **4** teth
Yoelson: **3** Asa **6** Jolson
yoga
point: **6** chakra
position: **5** asana, lotus

practice: 4 anga
practitioner: 5 Hindu 6 Hindoo
principle: 5 prana
type: 5 hatha
Yogi: 4 Bear 5 Berra 7 catcher
team: 5 Yanks 7 Yankees
yogurt: 5 dairy 7 dessert
base: 4 milk 7 culture
brand: 4 TCBY 6 Dannon 7 Yoplait
like some ~: 5 no fat 6 low-fat
variety: 5 plain 7 vanilla
__ yogurt: 6 frozen
yogurtlike drink: 5 kefir
__ Yo Hands: 4 Clap
yohimbe: 4 tree
Yo-ho-ho, and a bottle of __: 3 rum
yoke: 3 tie, wed 4 bind, bond, join, link, pair, tack, team 5 chain, hitch, marry, nexus, strap, unite 6 attach, burden, cohere, collar, couple, fasten, hook on, hook up, inspan, secure, splice 7 bondage, bracket, combine, conjoin, connect, coupler, harness, helotry, hitch on, peonage, serfdom, shackle, slavery 8 coupling, crossbar, ligature, vinculum 9 associate, restraint, servitude 10 oppression
combining form: 3 zyg- 4 zygo-
lace ~: 6 guimpe
locale: 4 neck
part: 5 oxbow
sharers: 4 team
together: 3 mix, tie, wed 4 ally, bind, link, yoke 5 hitch, unite 6 append, couple, league, team up 7 combine, conjoin, connect 8 coalesce, federate 9 associate, integrate
wooden ~: 6 cangue
yokel: 3 oaf 4 boor, clod, hick, rube 5 yahoo 6 lummox, rustic 7 bumpkin, hayseed, peasant, plowboy 9 hillbilly 10 clodhopper, provincial
Yoko: 3 Ono
son: 4 Sean
Yokohama: 4 city, port, town
locale: 5 Japan
Yokomitsu Riichi: 6 writer 8 Japanese
Yokosuka: 4 city, town
locale: 5 Japan
Yokum: 5 Abner, Mammy, Pansy, Pappy 7 Lucifer
creator: 4 Capp
home: 8 Dogpatch
Yokuts: 6 Indian 7 Amerind
Yolanda and the __: 5 Thief
yolk: 6 yellow
combining form: 6 lecith- 7 lecitho-
companion: 5 white
yolk __: 3 sac 5 stalk
yom __: 3 tov
Yom Kippur: 6 Jewish 7 holiday
observe ~: 4 fast 5 atone
yon: 5 there 6 way off, yonder
opposite: 6 hither
Yonago: 4 city, town
locale: 5 Japan
Yond' Cassius has __...: 5 a lean
yonder: 3 far, yon 4 afar, away 5 there 6 beyond, far off, remote 7 distant, faraway, farther, further
folks: 4 them, they
over ~: 4 thar 5 there
things: 5 those
wild blue ~: 3 sky 5 ether 6 aether
Yonkers: 4 city, town
locale: 7 New York
Yoo-hoo!: 3 hey
Yoplait competitor: 4 TCBY 6 Dannon
Yorba Linda: 4 city, town
locale: 10 California
yore: 3 eld 4 past 5 of old 7 ages ago, long ago 9 antiquity, olden days 10 yesteryear
of ~: 3 old 6 bygone
Yorick, lament for: 4 alas
York: 3 sgt. 4 cape, city, Dick, town 5 Alvin, House 7 Michael 8 Susannah
ender: 4 town 5 shire
House of ~ symbol: 9 white rose
locale: 7 England
__ York City: 3 New
Yorkie: 3 dog 6 lap dog
York Imperial: 5 apple
relative: 4 crab, Gala, Lodi, Rome 5 Mutsu 6 Empire, Ida Red, medlar, Pippin, russet 7 Baldwin, Bramley, costard, Freedom, Liberty, Spartan, Wealthy, Winesap 8 Cortland, Jonathan, McIntosh 10 Rome Beauty
Yorkin: 3 Bud
York, Michael: 5 actor
film: Austin Powers in Goldmember (2002)
Austin Powers: International Man of Mystery (1997)
Austin Powers: The Spy Who Shagged Me (1999)
Cabaret (1972)
The Four Musketeers (1974)
The Island of Dr. Moreau (1977)
Logan's Run (1976)
Murder on the Orient Express (1974)
Romeo and Juliet (1968)
The Three Musketeers (1973)
Zeppelin (1971)
Yorks: 6 county
locale: 7 England
Yorkshire: 3 pig 5 swine 6 county
city: 5 Leeds, Otley 6 Batley, Ossett 8 Bradford 9 Rotherham, Sheffield
locale: 7 England
river: 3 Ure 4 Aire, Ouse
Yorkshire __: 4 bond 5 chair 7 pudding, terrier
Yorkshire terrier: 3 dog 5 canid 6 canine
York, Susannah: 7 actress
film: Brotherly Love (1969)
Freud (1962)
Happy Birthday, Wanda June (1971)
Images (1972)
A Man for All Seasons (1966)
Sky Riders (1976)
Superman (1978)
They Shoot Horses... (1969)
Times of Glory (1960)
Tom Jones (1963)
Yorkton: 4 city, town
locale: 6 Canada
Yorktown: 6 battle
York University location: 6 Canada 7 Ontario, Toronto
Yoruba home: 4 Togo 5 Benin 6 Africa 7 Nigeria
Yosano Akiko: 4 poet 8 Japanese
Yosemite: 4 park 5 falls
locale: 10 California
mgr.: 3 NPS
peak: 4 Kuna 9 El Capitan
Yosemite __: 3 Sam 5 Falls
Yost, Eddie sport: 8 baseball
Yo te __: 3 amo
Yothers: 4 Tina
you: 4 self, thee, thou 7 pronoun
away with ~: 2 go 4 exit, move 5 be off, leave, scram 6 beat it, depart, get out, move it, vanish 7 get away, get lost, move off, move out, push off, take off, vamoose 8 run along, shove off 9 move along, take a hike 10 get a move on, hit the road, shuffle off
before ~ know it: 4 anon, soon
bet: 2 ay, da, ja, sí 3 aye, oui, yea, yep, yup 4 fine, okay, sure, yeah 5 good-o, natch, quite, right, roger, uh-huh 6 agreed, and how, gladly, good-oh, indeed, just so, rather, righto, surely, yowzah 7 exactly, go ahead, indeedy, mais oui, quite so, ten-four 8 all right, as you say, of course, thumbs up, very well 9 be my guest, certainly, darn right, naturally, precisely, sure thing 10 absolutely, by all means, definitely, positively, sure enough, that's right
between ~ and me: 7 sub rosa 8 in secret, secretly 9 entre nous, privately
how do ~ do: 2 hi 4 ciao, hail 5 aloha, hello, howdy 7 bon jour, welcome 8 greeting
I caught ~: 3 aha
in French: 4 vous
in German: 3 sie
in Spanish: 5 usted
I told ~ so: 3 see
May I help ~ ?: 3 yes
see ~ later: 3 bye 4 ciao, ta-ta 5 adios 7 goodbye 8 sayonara
you __ say that again: 3 can
you-__: 3 all, uns
__ you!: 3 Sez 4 Says 5 After, I dare
You __: 3 Are 4 and I 5 and Me, Got It, Learn
You __!: 3 bet 6 betcha
You __?: 4 rang
You __ a mouthful: 4 said
You __ Beautiful: 5 Are So
You __ Be in Pictures: 6 Oughta
You __ be joking!: 4 must
You __ Be Right: 3 May
You __ be there!: 5 had to
You __ bother!: 6 needn't
You __ Can Tell: 5 Never
You __ Change That: 4 Can't
You __ Cheat an Honest Man: 4 Can't
You __ Count on Me: 3 Can
You __ Destiny: 5 Are My
You __ for It: 5 Asked
You __ Get a Man With a Gun: 4 Can't
You __ Go Home Again: 4 Can't
You __ Have Everything: 4 Can't
You __ Have to Be So Nice: 5 Didn't
You __ heard nothin' yet!: 4 ain't
You __ here: 3 are
You __ Hurry Love: 4 Can't
You __ it!: 3 did, got 4 said
You __ It Well: 4 Wear
You __ kidding!: 5 aren't
You __ Know: 6 Oughta
You __ Know Me: 4 Don't
You __ Live Once: 4 Only
You __ Live Twice: 4 Only
You __ Love: 3 Are 5 Are My
You __ Lucky Star: 5 Are My
You __ Me: 4 Send 6 Needed, Showed
You __ Me, Al: 4 Know
You __ Meant for Me: 4 Were
You __ Me Hangin' On: 4 Keep
You __ Me Love You: 4 Made
You __ Mouthful: 5 Said a
You __ My Breath Away: 4 Take
You __ my day!: 4 made
You __ My Destiny: 3 Are
You __ My Lucky Star: 3 Are
You __ My Sunshine: 3 Are
You __ Own Me: 4 Don't
You __ rat!: 5 dirty
You __ Right: 5 May Be
You __ Say: 4 Don't
You __ See Me: 4 Won't
You __ seen nothin' yet!: 4 ain't
You __ serious?: 5 aren't
You __ Sixteen: 3 Are
You __ So Beautiful: 3 Are
You __ Sunshine: 5 Are My
You __ Take It With You: 4 Can't
You __ There: 3 Are
You __ the Sunshine of My Life: 3 Are
You __ to Me: 6 Belong
You __ Too Much: 4 Talk
You __ Up My Life: 5 Light
You __ What It Takes: 3 Got
You __ what you eat: 3 are
You __ worry!: 6 needn't
__ You: 3 For 4 I Got, I'm in, Miss, Near, Only, Over 5 All of, Bless, I Miss, I Need, I Want, Lovin', Run to 6 Kissin', Losing, Loving 7 Another, Missing, Satisfy, Without
__ You a Bromide?: 3 Are
You ain't __ nothin' yet: 4 seen 5 heard
...__ You Ain't Ma Baby?: 4 or Is
You Ain't Woman Enough singer: 4 Lynn
You and I (1982 song)
artist: Crystal Gayle, Eddie Rabbitt
__ you and me: 7 between
You and Me (1977 song) artist: Alice Cooper
You and Me Against the World (1974 song) artist: Helen Reddy
__ you any wool?: 4 Have
You Are __: 4 Here, Love 5 There
You Are (1983 song) artist: 6 Richie
You Are Everything (1971 song) artist: Stylistics
You Are Love composer: 4 Kern 11 Hammerstein
You Are My __ Star: 5 Lucky
You Are My Destiny singer: 4 Anka
You Are My Love (1955 song) artist: Joni James
You Are My Sunshine (1962 song) artist: Ray Charles
You Are Not Alone (1995 song) artist: Michael Jackson
You Are So Beautiful (1975 song) artist: Joe Cocker
You Are There (CBS drama) host: Walter Cronkite
You Are the Sunshine of My Life (1973 song) artist: Stevie Wonder
You Are the Woman (1976 song) artist: Firefall
__ you asked...: 5 Since
You Asked __ It: 3 For
__ you asleep?: 3 Are
__ You Babe: 4 I Got
You Beat Me to the Punch (1962 song) artist: Mary Wells
__ You Being Served?: 3 Are
__ You Belong to Me: 7 Tonight
You Belong to Me author: 5 Clark
You Belong to Me (song) artist: Carly Simon, Duprees
You Belong to the City (1985 song) artist: Glenn Frey
__ you be my neighbor?: 4 Won't
You bet!: 3 yep, yup 4 okay, sure, yeah 6 and how 7 for sure
You Bet __ Life: 4 Your
You Better Sit Down Kids (1967 song) artist: Cher
You Bet Your Life (game show) host: Groucho Marx
you can __ that again: 3 say
You can __ horse...: 5 lead a
You can __ man from Harvard...: 5 tell a
You can bank on it!: 6 I'm sure
you can bet __: 4 on it
You can bet __!: 4 on it
You Can Call Me Al
singer: Paul Simon
You Can Count on Me (2000 film)
cast: Matthew Broderick, Rory Culkin, Laura Linney, Mark Ruffalo
You Can Depend on Me (1961 song)
artist: Brenda Lee

You Can Do Magic (1982 song) artist: America
You can fool ___ of the people...: **4** some
You can say that again!: **4** amen
You Can't ___ Everything: **4** Have
You Can't Change That (1979 song) artist: Ray Parker Jr.
You Can't Cheat an Honest Man (1939 film)
cast: Edgar Bergen, W.C. Fields
You Can't Deny It (1990 song) artist: Lisa Stansfield
You Can't Get a Man With a Gun
composer: **6** Berlin
singer: **5** Annie **6** Oakley
You Can't Get There From Here author: **4** Nash
You Can't Go Home Again
author: Thomas Wolfe
character: **4** Else **6** Esther, McHarg, Webber
You Can't Have Everything (1937 film) cast: Don Ameche, Alice Faye, Ritz Brothers
You Can't Hurry Love (1966 song) artist: Supremes
You can't judge ___...: **5** a book
You can't make ___ purse...: **5** a silk
You Can't Sit Down (1963 song) artist: Dovells
You Can't Take It With You: **4** film, play
author: **4** Hart **7** Kaufman
cast: Jean Arthur, Lionel Barrymore, James Stewart
director: Frank Capra
You can't teach ___ dog...: **5** an old
___-you card: **5** thank
___ You Come Again: **4** Here
You Couldn't Be ___: **5** Cuter
You'd Be So Nice... composer: **6** Porter
You'd Be Surprised composer: **6** Berlin
You Decorated My Life (1979 song) artist: Kenny Rogers
You Didn't Have to ___ Nice: **4** Be So
___ you didn't know!: **4** As if
You dirty ___!: **3** rat
___ you do: **5** how do
You Don't ___ Me: **3** Own **4** Know
You Don't Bring Me Flowers: **4** duet
You Don't Bring Me Flowers (1978 song) artist: **7** Diamond **9** Streisand
You Don't Have to Be a Baby to Cry (1963 song) artist: Caravelles
You Don't Have to Say You Love Me (song) artist: Dusty Springfield, Elvis Presley
You Don't Know ___: **4** Jack **5** Paree
You Don't Know How It Feels (1994 song) artist: Tom Petty
You Don't Know Me (song) artist: Jerry Vale, Ray Charles
You Don't Mess Around With Jim (1972 song) artist: Jim Croce
You Don't Owe Me a Thing (1957 song) artist: Johnnie Ray
You Don't Own Me (1964 song) artist: Lesley Gore
You don't say!: **4** gosh **6** indeed, my word, really
You Don't Say (game show) host: Tom Kennedy
You Do Something to Me composer: **6** Porter
___ You Down: **4** Love **5** Shake **6** Follow
(You Drive Me) Crazy (1999 song) artist: Britney Spears
___ you for real?: **3** Are
You Give Good Love (1985 song) artist: Whitney Houston
You Give Love a Bad Name (1986 song) artist: Bon Jovi
___ You Glad You're You?: **5** Aren't
___ you go: **5** pay as, there
You Go ___ Head: **4** to My
You Got It All (1987 song) artist: Jets
You Got It (song) artist: Bonnie Raitt, New Kids on the Block, Roy Orbison
You Got Lucky (1982 song) artist: Tom Petty and the Heartbreakers
You Gotta Be (1994 song) artist: Des'ree
You Gotta Be a Football ___: **4** Hero
You got that right!: **6** I'll say
You Got What It Takes (1967 song) artist: Dave Clark Five
You Haven't Done Nothin (1974 song) artist: Stevie Wonder
___ you heard?: **4** Have
___ You in September: **3** See
___, You Is My Woman: **4** Bess
___ you jest!: **6** Surely
You Keep Me Hangin' On (song) artist: Kim Wilde, Supremes, Vanilla Fudge
___ you kidding?: **3** Are
___ You Kind of Glad We Did?: **5** Aren't
___ You Knocking: **5** I Hear
you-know-___: **3** who
___ you know!: **4** A lot
___ You Know: **3** Now **4** Don't
You Know I Can't Hear You... author: Robert Anderson
You Know Me, Al author: Ring Lardner
You know the ___!: **5** drill
___ you later!: **3** See
You Learn (1996 song) artist: Alanis Morissette
You Light Up My Life (1977 song) artist: Debby Boone
You Light Up My Life star: **4** Conn
You'll Accomp'ny Me (1980 song) artist: Bob Seger
You'll Lose a Good Thing (1962 song) artist: Barbara Lynn
You'll Never Find... (1976 song) artist: Lou Rawls
You'll Never Get Rich (1941 film)
cast: Fred Astaire, Rita Hayworth
music: Cole Porter
You'll Never Know composer: **6** Gordon, Warren
You'll Never Never Know (1956 song) artist: Platters
You'll Never Walk Alone composer: **7** Rodgers **11** Hammerstein
You'll See (1995 song) artist: Madonna
___ You Lonesome Tonight?: **3** Are
___ You Look Tonight, The: **3** Way
___ you loud and clear!: **5** I read
___ You Love: **5** I Wish
you love in Latin: **4** amas
___ You Love Me Tomorrow: **4** Will
___-you-ma'am: **5** thank
Youma author: Lafcadio Hearn
You Make Loving Fun (1977 song) artist: Fleetwood Mac
You Make Me Feel Brand New (1974 song) artist: Stylistics
You Make Me Feel Like Dancing (1976 song) artist: Leo Sayer
___ You Make Me Feel, The: **3** Way
You Make My Dreams (1981 song) artist: Hall and Oates
Youmans: **7** Vincent
You May Be Right (1980 song) artist: Billy Joel
You Mean the World to Me (1994 song) artist: Toni Braxton
You Might Think (1984 song) artist: Cars
You Must Have Been a Beautiful Baby composer: **6** Mercer, Warren
You Must Love Me (1996 song) artist: Madonna
You Must Love Me show: **5** Evita
You Must Remember This author: **5** Oates
You Needed Me (1978 song) artist: Anne Murray
___ You Need Is Love: **3** All
You Never Can Tell author: George Bernard Shaw
You never had ___ good!: **4** it so
young: **3** new, raw **4** baby, kids **5** brood, early, fresh, green, issue, small **6** babies, boyish, callow, calves, family, infant, junior, litter, little, modern, recent, tender, vernal **7** boylike, budding, girlish, growing, infants, kittens, newborn, progeny, puerile, teenage, untried **8** blooming, childish, girllike, ignorant, immature, juvenile, teenaged, underage, unversed, youthful **9** childlike, fledgling, half-grown, offspring, unfledged **10** adolescent, blossoming, burgeoning, developing, little ones, sophomoric, tenderfoot, unseasoned
ender: **4** ster **5** berry
young ___: **3** man, one **4** lady **5** adult, blood, hyson, thing **6** fustic
young-___: **3** uns **4** eyed
Young: **2** Cy, MC **3** Gig **4** Alan, Burt, Chic, Neil, Paul, Sean **5** Angus, Barry, Faron, Kathy **6** Andrew, Edward, Lester, Robert, Roland, Thomas **7** Brigham, Loretta, Malcolm, Terence
Young ___: **4** Bess, Girl, Guns, Love, plan, Turk **5** Blood, Italy, Turks, World **6** Lovers **7** Cassidy, Winston
Young ___ Brown: **6** Widder
Young ___, The: **5** Lions, Miner **7** Doctors, Savages
Young ___ With a Horn: **3** Man
___ Young: **3** Too **7** Forever
___ & Young: **5** Ernst
Young, Alan: **5** actor
film: Androcles and the Lion (1952)
The Time Machine (1960)
TV: Mister Ed
Young and Innocent (1937 film) director: Alfred Hitchcock
Young and the Restless, The: **4** soap
Young at Heart (1954 film)
cast: Doris Day, Frank Sinatra, Gig Young
Young Bess (1953 film)
cast: Stewart Granger, Charles Laughton, Jean Simmons
Youngblood: **4** Jack **5** Hawke
Young Blood (1957 song) artist: Coasters
Youngbloods song: Get Together (1969)
Young, Brigham territory: **4** Utah
___ Young Cannibals: **4** Fine
Young Cassidy (1965 film)
cast: Julie Christie, Maggie Smith, Rod Taylor
Young, Cy: **6** hurler **7** pitcher
Young Doctors, The (1961 film)
cast: Dick Clark, Ben Gazzara, Fredric March
Young Dr. Malone: **9** radio show
Young, Edward: **6** writer **7** English
Young Emotions (1959 song) artist: Ricky Nelson
younger: **5** minor **6** junior
Younger: **3** Bob, Jim **4** Cole, John
Younger ___: **4** Edda
Younger Than Springtime composer: **7** Rodgers **11** Hammerstein
Young, Faron song: Hello Walls (1961)
Young Frankenstein (1974 film)
cast: Peter Boyle, Marty Feldman, Teri Garr, Madeline Kahn, Cloris Leachman, Kenneth Mars, Gene Wilder
director: Mel Brooks
role: **4** Igor, Inga
___ Young, Gifted and Black: **4** To Be
Young, Gig: **5** actor
film: Air Force (1943)
City That Never Sleeps (1953)
Desk Set (1957)
Kid Galahad (1962)
Lovers and Other Strangers (1970)
Old Acquaintance (1943)
The Story on Page One (1959)
Teacher's Pet (1958)
That Touch of Mink (1962)
They Shoot Horses... (1969, AA)
The Tunnel of Love (1958)
Young at Heart (1954)
spouse: Elizabeth Montgomery
Young Girl (1968 song) artist: Gary Puckett and the Union Gap
Young Goodman Brown author: Nathaniel Hawthorne
Young Guns (1988 film)
cast: Emilio Estevez, Lou Diamond Phillips, Charlie Sheen, Kiefer Sutherland
Young-Holt Unlimited song: Soulful Strut (1968)
Young in Heart, The (1938 film)
cast: Douglas Fairbanks Jr., Janet Gaynor, Paulette Goddard
Young, John Paul song: Love Is in the Air (1978)
Young, Lester: **11** saxophonist
genre: **4** jazz
nickname: **4** Pres
youngling: **3** pup **5** youth **9** youngster
Young Lions, The: **4** film **5** novel
author: Irwin Shaw
cast: Marlon Brando, Montgomery Clift, Dean Martin
director: Edward Dmytryk
Young, Loretta: **7** actress
film: The Accused (1948)
Along Came Jones (1945)
Bedtime Story (1941)
The Bishop's Wife (1947)
The Call of the Wild (1935)
Cause for Alarm (1951)
Come to the Stable (1949)
The Crusades (1935)
The Doctor Takes a Wife (1940)
Employees' Entrance (1933)
The Farmer's Daughter (1947, AA)
Four Men and a Prayer (1938)
Heroes for Sale (1933)
House of Rothschild (1934)
It Happens Every Thursday (1953)
Kentucky (1938)
Life Begins (1932)
The Life of Jimmy Dolan (1933)
Man's Castle (1933)
Midnight Mary (1933)
A Night to Remember (1943)
Platinum Blonde (1931)
Rachel and the Stranger (1948)
The Ruling Voice (1931)
The Story of Alexander Graham Bell (1939)
The Stranger (1946)
Suez (1938)
Wife, Husband and Friend (1939)
Zoo in Budapest (1933)
Young Love (1957 song)
artist: Sonny James, Tab Hunter
___, Young Lovers: **5** Hello
Young Lovers (1963 song) artist: Paul and Paula
___ young man: **5** angry
Youngman: **5** Henny
repertoire: **4** gags **5** jokes **9** one-liners
Young Man From Atlanta, The author: **5** Foote

Young Man With a Horn (1950 film)
cast: Lauren Bacall, Doris Day, Kirk Douglas
director: Michael Curtiz
Young MC song: Bust a Move (1989)
Young Miner, The author: Horatio Alger
Young Mr. Lincoln (1939 film)
cast: Alice Brady, Henry Fonda
director: John Ford
Young, Neil song: Heart of Gold (1972)
Young Philadelphians, The (1959 film)
cast: Paul Newman, Barbara Rush, Alexis Smith
Young, Robert: 5 actor
film: The Canterville Ghost (1944)
Claudia (1943)
Claudia and David (1946)
Crossfire (1947)
Fierce Creatures (1997)
Goodbye, My Fancy (1951)
H.M. Pulham, Esq. (1941)
Journey for Margaret (1942)
The Kid From Spain (1932)
Lady Be Cool (1941)
Lady Luck (1946)
The Mortal Storm (1940)
Northwest Passage (1940)
Sitting Pretty (1948)
They Won't Believe Me (1947)
Three Comrades (1938)
Western Union (1941)
TV: Father Knows Best, Marcus Welby, M.D.
Young Savages, The (1961 film)
cast: Burt Lancaster, Dina Merrill
director: John Frankenheimer
Young, Sean: 7 actress
film: Ace Ventura: Pet Detective (1994)
Blade Runner (1982)
Cousins (1989)
Hold Me, Thrill Me, Kiss Me (1992)
No Way Out (1987)
Once Upon a Crime (1992)
Stripes (1981)
youngster: 3 boy, cub, kid, lad, pup, tad, tot **4** baby, brat, girl, lass, teen, tike, tyke **5** chick, child, kiddy, laddy, minor, pupil, sprig, 'tween, whelp, youth **6** junior, lassie, moppet **7** sapling, student **8** half-pint, juvenile, teenager **9** fledgling, stripling **10** adolescent
in Spanish: 4 niña, niño
naughty ~: 4 brat **6** urchin
query: 3 why
ride: 4 pony
Youngstown: 4 city
city near ~: 6 Girard
locale: 4 Ohio
Young Stranger, The (1957 film)
cast: James Daly, Kim Hunter, James MacArthur
director: John Frankenheimer
Young Sycamore author: William Carlos Williams
Young Tom Edison (1940 film)
cast: Fay Bainter, Mickey Rooney
Young Turk: 5 comer
Young Turks (1981 song) artist: Rod Stewart
Young Widder Brown: 9 radio show
Young Winston (1972 film)
cast: Anne Bancroft, Simon Ward
director: Sir Richard Attenborough
Young World (1962 song) artist: Ricky Nelson
__ you not!: 4 I kid
__ You Now: 5 I Need
Yount, Robin: 6 Brewer **9** shortstop
__ you one!: 4 I owe
You Only Live Once (1937 film)
cast: Henry Fonda, William Gargan, Sylvia Sidney
director: Fritz Lang
You Only Live Twice: 4 film **5** novel
author: Ian Fleming
cast: Sean Connery, Donald Pleasance
scriptwriter: Roald Dahl
You Oughta Know (1995 song) artist: Alanis Morissette
You Ought to Be With Me (1972 song)
artist: Al Green
your: 3 thy
ender: 4 self **6** selves
like ~: 4 poss. **10** possessive
not on ~ life: 3 nay **5** never
to ~ health: 5 salud, salut, skoal, toast **6** cheers, prosit **7** l'chayim **9** happy days
your __ serv.: 4 obdt.
Your __ Don't Dance: 4 Mama
Your __ Heart: 7 Cheatin'
Your __ Parade: 3 Hit
Your __ Too Big: 5 Feet's
__ your battle stations: 3 Man
__ your best shot!: 4 take
__ Your Blessings: 5 Count
__ Your Booty: 5 Shake
Your Cheatin' Heart (1964 film)
cast: Red Buttons, George Hamilton, Susan Oliver
__ your disposal!: 4 I'm at
__ Your Dog: 4 Curb
...you're __ the old ball game: 5 out at
You're __: 7 Sixteen
You're __ and don't know it: 5 a poet
You're __ Hear from Me: 5 Gonna
You're __ Need to Get By: 4 All I
You're __ Old Once!: 4 Only
You're __ talk!: 5 one to
You're __ the One: 5 Still
You're a __, Alice!: 4 riot
You're a Big Boy Now (1966 film)
cast: Elizabeth Hartman, Peter Kastner, Geraldine Page
director: Francis Ford Coppola
__ you ready yet?: 5 Aren't
You're a fine __ talk!: 5 one to
You're a Grand Old Flag composer: 5 Cohan
You're all __!: 3 wet
You're All I Need to Get By (1968 song)
artist: Marvin Gaye, Tammi Terrell
You Really Got Me (1964 song) artist: Kinks
__ You're a Rich Man: 4 Baby
You're Getting to Be a Habit With Me composer: 5 Dubin **6** Warren
You're in Love (1991 song) artist: Wilson Phillips
You're in My Heart (1977 song) artist: Rod Stewart
__, you're it!: 3 Tag
You're Makin' Me High (1996 song)
artist: Toni Braxton
You Remind Me of Something (1995 song) artist: R. Kelly
You're My Angel singer: 3 Ono
You're My Best Friend (1976 song)
artist: Queen
You're My Everything (1967 song)
artist: Temptations
You're My World (1977 song) artist: Helen Reddy
You're Never Too Young (1955 film)
cast: Jerry Lewis, Dean Martin
You're No Good (1975 song) artist: Linda Ronstadt
You're Not Alone (1989 song) artist: Chicago
__! You're on Candid Camera!: 5 Smile
You're Only Human (1985 song)
artist: Billy Joel
You're Only Old Once! author: Dr. Seuss
You're pulling my __!: 3 leg
You're putting __!: 4 me on
Your Erroneous Zones author: 4 Dyer
__ you're satisfied!: 5 I hope
You're Sixteen (song) artist: Johnny Burnette, Ringo Starr
__ You're Smiling: 4 When
You're So Vain (1972 song) artist: Carly Simon
You're Still the One (1998 song)
artist: Shania Twain
You're Telling Me (1934 film)
cast: Buster Crabbe, W.C. Fields
You're the First... (1974 song) artist: Barry White
You're the flower of my __: 5 heart
You're the Inspiration (1984 song)
artist: Chicago
You're the One (song) artist: SWV, Vogues
You're the One That I Want (1978 song)
artist: John Travolta, Olivia Newton-John
film: 6 Grease
You're the Top composer: 6 Porter
You're welcome: 6 de nada
Your excellency: 4 Sire
__ Your Eyes Only: 3 For
__ your fingers: 4 snap **5** cross
__ Your Girl: 7 Forever
Your Good Thing (1969 song) artist: Lou Rawls
__ Your Hand in the Hand: 3 Put
Your Hit Parade: 9 radio show
__ your life!: 5 Not on
__ Your Love: 3 For, It's **5** I Want, Prove, Shake
__ Your Love Tonight: 5 I Need
__ Your Lucky Stars: 5 Thank
Your Majesty: 4 Ma'am, Sire
Your Mama Don't Dance (song) artist: Loggins & Messina, Poison
Your mileage may __: 4 vary
__ Your Name: 4 Sign **5** What's
__ your old man!: 3 So's
__ your pardon!: 4 I beg
Your Past Is Showing (1957 film)
cast: Peter Sellers, Terry-Thomas
Your Precious Love (1967 song)
artist: Marvin Gaye, Tammi Terrell
yours: 5 thine
and mine: 3 our **4** ours
like ~: 4 poss. **10** possessive
not ~: 3 his **4** hers, mine **6** theirs
yours __: 5 truly
__ your seat belt: 6 fasten
__-yourself: 4 do-it
__ Yourself: 5 Enjoy **7** Express, Respect
yourself, by: 4 solo **5** alone
__ Yourself Go: 3 Let
__ Yourself Up: 4 Pick
Your Show of Shows (NBC variety)
cast: Sid Caesar
Imogene Coca
Howard Morris
Carl Reiner
producer: Max Liebman
writer: Woody Allen, Mel Brooks, Larry Gelbart, Neil Simon
Yours, Mine and Ours (1968 film)
cast: Lucille Ball, Henry Fonda, Van Johnson
Your Song (1970 song) artist: Elton John
__ Your Wagon: 5 Paint
Your Wildest Dreams (1986 song)
artist: Moody Blues
You Said a Mouthful (1932 film)
cast: Joe E. Brown, Ginger Rogers
You said it!: 3 yes **4** amen **6** and how, I agree, so true
__ you satisfied?: 3 Are
You say ___...: 6 potato
You Send Me (1957 song)
artist: Sam Cooke, Teresa Brewer
__ you serious?: 3 Are
You Shook Me All Night Long artist: 4 AC/DC
You Should Be Dancing (1976 song)
artist: Bee Gees
You Should Be Mine (song) artist: Brian McKnight & Mase, Jeffrey Osborne
You Showed Me (1969 song) artist: Turtles
__, You Sinners: 4 Sing
Youskevitch, Igor: 6 dancer **7** danseur
specialty: 6 ballet
__ you so!: 5 I told
Yousuf: 5 Karsh
__ you sure?: 3 Are
You Take My Breath Away (1979 song) artist: Rex Smith
You Talk Too Much (1960 song)
artist: Joe Jones
youth: 3 boy, cub, kid, lad, pup, tad, tot **4** baby, brat, girl, lass, male, teen, tike, tyke **5** bloom, chick, child, laddy, minor, prime, pupil, puppy, sprig, 'tween, whelp **6** junior, lassie, maiden, moppet, nonage, shaver **7** boyhood, sapling, student **8** girlhood, half-pint, juvenile, minority, small fry, teenager **9** childhood, fledgling, freshness, greenness, ignorance, innocence, puerility, salad days, schoolboy, stripling, youngster **10** adolescent, boyishness, immaturity, pubescence, schoolgirl
club for rural ~: 5 four H
magazine: 4 Teen
org.: 3 BSA **4** YMHA, YWCA, YWHA **5** GSUSA
stopover: 6 hostel
subculture: 6 hip-hop
uncool ~: 4 nerd, nurd
youth __: 5 group **6** hostel
__ you the clever one!: 5 Aren't
You there!: 3 hey **4** ahoy
Youth, Fountain of site: 6 Bimini
youthful: 3 new **5** fresh, green, young **6** active, boyish, callow, infant, tender, vernal, yeasty **7** budding, buoyant, girlish, puerile **8** childish, immature, juvenile, underage, vigorous **9** childlike **10** adolescent, bright-eyed, full of life, sophomoric, starry-eyed
youthfulness: 5 prime, youth **9** greenness **10** immaturity
__ you think you are?: 5 Who do
__ You Top This?: 3 Can
__ You to Want Me: 5 I Want
__ You Truly: 5 I Love
__ You Trust?: 5 Who Do
You Turn Me On (1975 song) artist: Ian Whitcomb
You used to come ___...: 5 at ten
__ You Use Me?: 5 Could
You've __ a Friend: 3 Got
__ You've Gone: 5 After
You've got __!: 5 a deal
You've Got a Friend __: 4 in Me
You've Got a Friend (1971 song)
artist: James Taylor
You've Got Mail (1998 film)
cast: Dabney Coleman, Tom Hanks, Greg Kinnear, Parker Posey, Meg Ryan, Steve Zahn
director: Nora Ephron
You've got mail co.: 3 AOL
(You've Got) The Magic Touch (1956 song) artist: Platters
You've Got Your Troubles (1965 song) artist: Fortunes

You've Made __ Very Happy: 4 Me So
You've Really Got __ On Me: 5 a Hold
You Want This (1994 song) artist: Janet Jackson
You Wear It Well (1972 song) artist: Rod Stewart
__ You Went Away: 5 Since
__ You Were Here: 4 Wish 7 Wishing
You Were Meant for Me (1948 film)
cast: Jeanne Crain, Dan Dailey, Oscar Levant
You Were Meant for Me (1996 song)
artist: Jewel
You Were Never Lovelier (1942 film)
cast: Fred Astaire, Rita Hayworth, Adolphe Menjou
music: Jerome Kern
You Were on My Mind (1965 song)
artist: We Five
__ You Were Sleeping: 5 While
__ You Wish Upon a Star: 4 When
You Won't See Me (1974 song) artist: Anne Murray
You wouldn't __!: 4 dare
You, You, You (1953 song) artist: Ames Brothers
Yow, Kay: 5 coach
milieu: 5 court
org.: 3 NBA
sport: 10 basketball
yowl: 3 bay, cry, yip 4 bawl, howl, long, mewl, wail, weep, yell, yelp 5 whine 6 holler, scream, squall, squeal 7 protest, screech, ululate 9 caterwaul
yowzah: 2 ay, da, ja, sí 3 aye, oui, yea, yep, yup 4 fine, okay, sure, yeah 5 good-o, natch, quite, right, roger, uh-huh 6 agreed, gladly, good-oh, indeed, just so, rather, righto, surely, you bet 7 exactly, go ahead, indeedy, mais oui, quite so, ten-four 8 all right, as you say, of course, thumbs up, very well 9 be my guest, certainly, darn right, naturally, precisely, sure thing, you betcha, you said it 10 absolutely, by all means, definitely, positively, sure enough, that's right
yo-yo: 3 oaf, toy 4 dolt, jerk, sway, vary 5 dunce, waver 6 nitwit 7 dingbat, whiffle 9 fluctuate, mercurial, vacillate 10 nincompoop
brand: 6 Duncan
part: 5 spool 6 string
Yo-Yo: 2 Ma
Yo-Yo (1971 song) artist: Osmonds
__ y Plata: 3 Oro
Ypsilanti: 4 city, town
athletes: 6 Eagles
locale: 8 Michigan
river: 5 Huron
school: 3 EMU
Yquem: 4 wine 5 white
origin: 6 France
yr.
by the ~: 5 per an.
100 ~: 3 cen.
opener: 3 Jan.
part: 2 mo. 3 spr. 4 quar.
part of an academic ~: 3 sem.
prior to ~ 1: 3 BCE
Ysaye, Eugene: 7 Belgian 9 violinist
Yser: 5 river
River locale: 6 France 7 Belgium
__ Ysidro, CA: 3 San
YSL fragrance: 5 Opium
ytterbium: 5 metal 7 element 9 rare earth
yttrium: 5 metal 7 element 9 rare earth
yuan: 5 money
Yuan: 3 Lee
Yüang-chang: 3 Chu
Yuba City: 4 city, town
locale: 10 California
Yuban: 6 coffee
alternative: 5 Sanka 7 Folgers, Melitta, Nescafé, Savarin 9 Hills Bros.
Yucaipa: 4 city, town
locale: 10 California
Yucatán: 5 state 7 Mexican
city: 4 Muná, Peto, Umán 5 Motul, Tekax, Ticul 6 Cancún, Chemax, Izamal, Mérida 7 Hunucmá, Kanasín, Maxcanú, Tizimín 8 Progreso 10 Valladolid
Indian: 4 Maya 5 Mayan
see also Spanish
Yucatec: 4 Maya 6 Indian 7 Amerind
yucca: 4 palm 5 plant 6 flower 10 Joshua tree
cousin: 4 aloe 5 agave, sotol 6 cactus
fiber: 5 istle, ixtle
root: 5 amole
yuck: 3 ick, ugh 4 joke 5 gross, laugh 7 chuckle 8 laughter
yucky: 4 icky 5 gross, nasty, slimy 6 grungy, horrid 8 inedible 9 repugnant 10 disgusting, uninviting, unpleasant
stuff: 3 goo 4 goop, gunk
Yüen: 5 river
locale: 5 China
__ Yuga: 4 Kali 5 Krita, Satya, Treta 7 Dvapara
Yugoslavia: 6 nation 7 country
bovine: 4 Busa
capital: 8 Belgrade
city: 3 Nis 5 Vrsac 7 Novi Sad 8 Belgrade
former leader: 4 Tito
former ~ republic: 6 Bosnia
gulf: 8 Quarnero
lake: 7 Scutari
money: 4 para 5 dinar
neighbor: 7 Albania, Croatia, Hungary, Romania 8 Bulgaria 9 Macedonia
Nobelist in Chemistry: 6 Prelog
Nobelist in Literature: 6 Andric
novelist: 6 Adamic
port: 6 Rijeka 9 Dubrovnik
region: 5 Banat
river: 4 Sava 5 Tisza
tennis pro: 5 Seles
yuk: 4 joke 5 laugh 7 chuckle
yukata: 4 robe
Yukawa, Hideki: 8 Nobelist 9 physicist
yukky: 5 slimy 8 inedible
Yukon: 3 GMC, SUV, ter. 4 city, terr., town 5 river 9 territory
area E. of the ~: 3 NWT
city: 4 Faro, Mayo 7 Old Crow 8 Carcross, Keno City 10 Dawson City, Mount Lorne, Whitehorse
discovery: 4 gold
dog: 5 husky
dweller: 6 Eskimo
home: 4 iglu 5 igloo
locale: 6 Canada
mountain: 4 King 5 Logan, Walsh 6 Steele 7 Lucania
native: 3 Esk. 5 Kaska 6 Eskimo
neighbor: 6 Alaska
river: 5 Liard
river to the ~: 6 Tanana 8 Klondike
vehicle: 4 sled
wear: 5 parka
Yul: 7 Brynner
yulan: 4 tree 8 magnolia
yule: 4 Noel 9 Christmas
yule __: 3 log 4 clog 5 block
yuletide: 4 Noel, Xmas 9 Christmas
aroma: 5 myrrh
beginning of ~: 6 Advent
burner: 3 log
buy: 4 tree
décor: 5 holly
display: 6 crèche
drink: 3 nog 6 eggnog
figure: 5 Santa
mo.: 3 Dec.
song: 4 Noel 5 carol
sound: 4 ho ho
tree: 3 fir
trio: 4 Magi
see also Christmas
Yulin: 6 Harris
yum: 5 goody 6 goodie 9 delicious
__ Yum: 6 Bubble
Yuma: 4 city, town 5 tribe 6 Indian 7 Amerind 8 language
locale: 7 Arizona
yummy: 4 good 5 sapid, tasty 6 edible, savory, toothy 8 heavenly, luscious, noshable, tempting 9 delicious, flavorful, good to eat, nectarous, palatable, succulent, toothsome 10 appetizing, delectable
Yummy Yummy Yummy (1968 song)
artist: Ohio Express
Yum-Yum sash: 3 obi
yup: 2 ay, da, ja, sí 3 aye, oui, yea, yes 4 fine, okay, sure, yeah 5 good-o, natch, quite, right, roger, uh-huh 6 agreed, gladly, good-oh, indeed, just so, rather, righto, surely, you bet, yowzah 7 exactly, go ahead, indeedy, mais oui, quite so, ten-four 8 all right, as you say, of course, thumbs up, very well 9 be my guest, certainly, darn right, naturally, precisely, sure thing, you betcha, you said it 10 absolutely, by all means, definitely, positively, sure enough, that's right
opposite: 3 nah
Yupik: 6 Eskimo
yuppie: 4 suit 10 button-down
abode: 4 loft 5 condo
auto: 4 Audi 6 Beamer, Beemer
couple, maybe: 4 dink
ender: 3 dom
farewell: 4 ciao
Yuri: 7 Gagarin, Zhivago 8 Andropov
in English: 6 George
love: 4 Lara
see also Russian
Yuriria: 4 city, town
locale: 6 Mexico 10 Guanajuato
Yuro, Timi song: Hurt (1961)
yurt: 4 tent 7 shelter
Yury: 6 Olesha
Yves: 5 Klein, Leroy 6 Tanguy 7 Montand 9 St. Laurent
see also French
__-Yves Cousteau: 7 Jacques
Yvette: 7 Mimieux
see also French
Yvonne: 5 Craig 7 De Carlo, Elliman, Sherman 8 Mitchell
Yvor: 7 Winters
YWCA part: 4 Assn. 5 Assoc., Young 6 Women's 9 Christian
Yzerman: 5 Steve
Z: 3 zed 4 axis, zeta 6 izzard, letter
Anglo-Saxon ~: 4 yogh
A to ~: 5 gamut, whole 6 entire 9 full-dress 10 completely, exhaustive, to the limit
from A to ~: 5 fully, gamut 6 in toto, wholly 7 in depth 8 thorough, whole hog 9 full-range, like a book 10 soup to nuts, thoroughly
in comics: 5 sleep, snore
in phonetic alphabet: 4 Zulu
0
degrees longitude setting: 3 GST
figure above ~: 5 paren.
on a telephone: 4 oper.
see also zero
0-06-057156-5: 4 ISBN
007: 3 spy
foe: 3 KGB
watch: 5 Rolex
0600: 5 six a.m.
Z (1969 film)
cast: Yves Montand, Irene Papas
director: Costa-Gavras
Z __: 5 score, twist
Z __ zebra: 4 as in
__ Z: 3 A to
Zaachila: 4 city, town
locale: 6 Mexico, Oaxaca
zabaglione: 7 dessert
ingredient: 3 egg 4 wine 5 sugar
Zabolotsky, Nikolay: 4 poet 7 Russian
zabuton: 3 pad
Zacapú: 4 city, town
locale: 6 Mexico 9 Michoacán
Zacatecas: 4 city, town 5 state
city: 5 Jalpa, Jérez 6 Loreto 8 Trancoso 9 Fresnillo, Guadalupe, Río Grande
locale: 6 Mexico
Zacatelco: 4 city, town
locale: 6 Mexico 8 Tlaxcala
Zacatepec: 4 city, town
locale: 6 Mexico 7 Morelos
Zacatlán: 4 city, town
locale: 6 Mexico, Puebla
Zach: 8 Galligan
Zachariah, daughter of: 3 Abi
Zachary: 4 pope 5 Scott 6 Taylor 7 pontiff
Zacherle, John song: Dinner With Drac (1958)
Zack: 5 Wheat
Zacoalco: 4 city, town
locale: 6 Mexico 7 Jalisco
Zadora: 3 Pia
zaftig: 5 beefy, buxom, fubsy, heavy, obese, plump, pudgy, pursy, stout 6 chubby, fleshy, portly, pyknic, rotund, stocky 7 adipose, paunchy 8 roly-poly 9 corpulent 10 overweight
zafu stuffing: 5 kapok
zag: 4 turn, veer 6 swerve
starter: 3 zig
Zager and Evans song: In the Year 2525 (1969)
Zagnut: 5 candy 8 candy bar 9 chocolate
alternative: 4 Mars, Twix 5 Clark, Heath 6 Kit Kat, Mounds, PayDay, Reese's 7 Krackel, Oh Henry 8 Baby Ruth, Hershey's, Milky Way, Snickers 9 Almond Joy, Mr. Goodbar 10 NutRageous
__ Zagora, Bulgaria: 5 Stara
Zagreb: 4 city, town 7 capital
city near ~: 5 Fiume, Sisak, Sisek
locale: 6 Europe 7 Croatia
river: 4 Sava
Zagros: 5 range 9 mountains
locale: 4 Asia, Irak, Iran, Iraq 6 Turkey
Zaharias, Babe Didrikson: 6 golfer 7 Mildred
milieu: 5 links 6 course
org.: 4 LPGA
Zahn: 5 Paula, Steve
zaire: 5 money
Zaire: 5 Congo, river 6 nation 7 country
city in ~: 4 Boma 6 Matadi
lake: 4 Kivu 5 Mweru 6 Albert, Mobuto 10 Tanganyika
language: 4 Luba
money: 5 zaire 6 likuta, makuta
people of ~: 4 Luba 5 Mongo
river: 4 Uele
Zal: 6 Roxana
Zale, Tony: 5 boxer
milieu: 4 ring
Zama: 4 city, town
locale: 5 Japan
zamarra: 4 coat 6 jacket

Zambezi: 5 river
basin people: 4 Lozi
locale: 6 Angola, Zambia 8 Zimbabwe
river to the ~: 5 Kafue
town on the ~: 4 Sena
Zambia: 6 nation 7 country
capital: 6 Lusaka
city: 5 Kabwe, Kitwe, Ndola 6 Lusaka
lake: 5 Mweru 6 Kariba 9 Bangweulu
language: 4 Lozi
money: 5 ngwee 6 kwacha
neighbor: 5 Congo 6 Angola, Malawi 7 Namibia 8 Tanzania, Zimbabwe 10 Mozambique
people: 4 Cewa, Lozi 5 Bemba, Chewa, Lunda, Ngoni, Nguni
waterfall: 8 Victoria
Zamboni: 7 machine
creation: 3 ice
where to see a ~: 4 rink
Zamora: 4 city, town
locale: 6 Mexico 9 Michoacán
Zamyatin, Yevgeny: 6 writer 7 Russian
Zandalee actor: 4 Cage
Zande home: 5 Congo, Sudan 6 Africa
zander: 4 fish
Zander: 5 Robin
Zane: 4 Grey, Lisa 5 Billy, Lasky
Zanesville: 4 city, town
author from ~: 4 Grey
locale: 4 Ohio
Zanetto composer: 8 Mascagni
Zaniah: 4 star
zaniness: 6 joking, levity 7 foolery, inanity, jesting, waggery 8 clowning, drollery 9 frivolity 10 buffoonery
Zanoni author: Edward Bulwer-Lytton
Zantac: 7 antacid
alternative: 4 Tums 6 Maalox, Pepcid, Riopan 7 Gelusil, Lactaid, Mylanta, Rolaids 8 Gaviscon 11 Alka-Seltzer, Pepto-Bismol
zany: 3 nut, wag 4 card, fool, kook, loon, luny, wack, wild 5 balmy, batty, campy, clown, comic, crazy, cutup, daffy, dizzy, flake, flaky, funny, goofy, joker, kooky, loony, nutty, sappy, silly, wacky, weird 6 flakey, jester, kookie, looney, madcap, screwy, weirdo, whacko, whacky 7 buffoon, comical, farceur, flighty, foolish, half-wit, show-off 8 clownish, comedian, humorist, humorous 9 eccentric, harlequin, ludicrous, prankster, screwball, simpleton, slapstick 10 off-the-wall, outlandish
zanza: 10 instrument, percussion
origin: 6 Africa
Zanzibar: 4 city, isle, port, town 6 island
island north of ~: 5 Pemba
locale: 8 Tanzania
zap: 4 beat, drub, jolt, nuke, rout, ruin, slay, swat, zest 5 crush, shoot, smite 6 cancel, charge, defeat, energy, finish, impugn, lay out, pommel, pummel, rebuke, rub out, thrash, wallop 7 abolish, bombard, conquer, expunge, sparkle, trounce 8 dispatch, get rid of, knock off, vanquish 9 overthrow
channel surfers ~ them: 3 ads
Zapata: 8 Emiliano 9 guerrilla
see also Spanish
___ Zapata!: 4 Viva
zapateado: 4 step 5 dance
Zapopan: 4 city, town
locale: 6 Mexico 7 Jalisco
Zapotec: 6 Indian 7 Amerind
Zappa: 5 Frank 7 Dweezil 8 Moon Unit
Zappa, Frank song: Valley Girl (1982)
___ zapper: 3 bug
zapper victim: 3 bee, bug, fly 4 gnat, moth, pest 5 aphid 6 hornet, insect 8 mosquito
zappy: 4 spry 5 agile, brisk, peppy, perky, zingy, zippy 6 active, blithe, bouncy, breezy, chirpy, jaunty, nimble, snappy 7 animate, chipper, playful 8 animated, cheerful 9 energetic, exuberant, sprightly, vivacious 10 frolicsome, rollicking
Zara composer: 4 Arne
Zaragoza: 4 city, town
locale: 5 Spain 6 Aragón, Mexico 8 Coahuila
river: 4 Ebro
zarf: 3 cup 6 finjan
Zaria: 4 city, town
locale: 7 Nigeria
Zarkov's friend: 6 Gordon
Zarqa: 4 city, town
locale: 6 Jordan
ZaSu: 5 Pitts
Zátopek: 4 Emil 5 Czech 6 runner 10 marathoner
Zaurak: 4 star
zax: 4 tool
Zayak: 6 Elaine
zayin: 6 Hebrew, letter
predecessor: 3 vav, vaw, waw
successor: 4 heth 5 cheth
Zaza composer: 11 Leoncavallo
Zazie author: Raymond Queneau
Zbigniew: 7 Herbert 10 Brzezinski
zea: 5 grass, maize
zeal: 3 vim 4 fire, push, zest 5 ardor, drive, flame, gusto, mania, oomph, piety, verve, vigor 6 energy, fervor, relish, spirit, warmth 7 emotion, loyalty, passion, urgency 8 alacrity, delirium, devotion, dispatch, fervency, industry, keenness 9 animation, assiduity, diligence, eagerness, godliness, intensity, monomania, readiness, sincerity, vehemence 10 enterprise, enthusiasm, fanaticism, fierceness, initiative, intentness, liveliness
with great ~: 5 hotly
Zeal: 4 font 8 typeface
___ Zealand: 3 New
Zealander: 4 Dane
zealot: 3 nut 5 bigot, crank, fiend, freak 6 addict 7 diehard, fanatic 8 crusader, reformer 9 extremist, sectarian, visionary 10 enthusiast
zealous: 3 hot, mad 4 avid, keen 5 afire, antsy, eager, fired, itchy, pushy, rabid, ready 6 ablaze, active, ardent, devout, fervid, gung-ho, hearty, loving, red-hot 7 burning, devoted, earnest, fanatic, fervent, flaming, glowing, intense 8 fireball, frenetic, obsessed, partisan, spirited, vehement, wild-eyed 9 ambitious, dedicated, emotional, fanatical, possessed, strenuous 10 inspirited, passionate, solicitous
zealously: 4 hard, very 6 keenly 8 heartily 9 seriously, viciously
zebra: 3 ref 6 animal, equine 7 referee
ender: 4 wood
female: 4 mare
group: 4 herd
home: 6 Africa
kin: 6 quagga
like a ~: 5 maned 7 striped
male: 8 stallion
predator: 4 lion
relative: 3 ass 5 burro, horse, kiang 6 donkey, onager, quagga 7 jackass 8 chigetai 9 dziggetai
young: 4 colt, foal
zebra ___: 5 finch, label, plant 6 mussel
zebrawood: 4 tree
zebu: 5 bovid 6 animal, bovine
feature: 4 hump
relative: 3 yak 4 anoa, arna, gaur, urus 5 bison, gayal, takin 6 mithan, muskox 7 aurochs, banteng, banting, beefalo, buffalo, carabao, cattalo, kouprey, tamarao, tamarau, timarau
Zebulon: 4 Pike
son of ~: 4 Elon
Zebulun
parent of ~: 4 Leah 5 Jacob
sibling of ~: 3 Dan, Gad 4 Levi 5 Asher, Dinah, Judah 6 Joseph, Reuben, Simeon 8 Benjamin, Issachar, Naphtali
Zechariah
follower: 7 Malachi
preceder: 6 Haggai
zed: 3 zee 6 izzard
___ zed: 3 a to
zedoary: 9 condiment
Zedong: 3 Mao
zee: 3 zed
preceder: 3 wye
___ Zee: 6 Tappan, Zuider
Zeebrugge: 4 port
locale: 7 Belgium
Zeeman, Pieter: 8 Nobelist 9 physicist
Zeena spouse: 5 Ethan
Zeffirelli, Franco: 8 director
film: Hamlet (1990)
La Traviata (1982)
Otello (1986)
Romeo and Juliet (1968)
The Taming of the Shrew (1967)
Zelda: 6 Gilroy 10 Fitzgerald
Zelda ___ Fitzgerald: 5 Sayre
Zelig (1983 film)
cast: Woody Allen, Mia Farrow
director: Woody Allen
zelkova: 4 tree
relative: 3 elm 9 hackberry
Zellweger, Renée: 7 actress
film: Bridget Jones's Diary (2001)
Chicago (2002)
Jerry Maguire (1996)
Me, Myself & Irene (2000)
Nurse Betty (2000)
One True Thing (1998)
Price Above Rubies (1998)
Zemeckis, Robert: 8 director
film: Back to the Future (1985)
Back to the Future Part II (1989)
Back to the Future Part III (1990)
Cast Away (2000)
Contact (1997)
Death Becomes Her (1992)
Forrest Gump (1994, AA)
I Wanna Hold Your Hand (1978)
Romancing the Stone (1984)
Used Cars (1980)
What Lies Beneath (2000)
Who Framed Roger Rabbit (1988)
Zen
greeting: 6 gassho
head cook: 5 tenzo
interview: 7 dokusan
master: 4 monk
master's poem: 5 haiku
meditation: 5 zazen
meditation hall: 5 zendo
origin: 5 Japan
poem: 4 waka 5 haiku
retreat: 7 sesshin
school: 4 Soto 6 Rinzai
sitting posture: 5 seiza
temple: 5 zendo
term: 4 hara, koan 5 mondo
___ Zen: 4 Soto 6 Rinzai
zenana: 5 haram, harem, harim 6 hareem
room: 3 oda 4 odah
Zener ___: 5 cards
Zenica: 4 city, town
locale: 6 Bosnia
zenith: 3 cap, top 4 acme, apex, peak, roof 5 crest, crown, prime 6 apogee, climax, height, heyday, heydey, summit, tiptop, vertex 7 maximum 8 capstone, eminence, high noon, high spot, meridian, pinnacle 9 crescendo, elevation, high point
at the ~: 4 atop
opposite: 5 nadir 6 bottom 7 the pits 10 rock bottom
Zenith: 2 TV 5 TV set 10 television
alternative: 3 JVC, NEC, RCA 4 Sony 6 Quasar 7 Emerson, Hitachi, ProScan, Toshiba 8 Magnavox, Sylvania 9 Panasonic 10 Mitsubishi
product: 3 VCR 6 remote
Zeno: 5 Greek
follower of ~: 5 Stoic
where ~ taught: 4 stoa
Zenobia husband: 5 Ethan
Zeno of ___: 4 Elea 6 Citium
Zeno's ___: 7 paradox
Zephaniah
follower: 6 Haggai
preceder: 8 Habakkuk
Zepho, grandfather of: 4 Esau
zephyr: 4 wind 6 breeze
like a ~: 4 mild, soft 5 balmy, light 6 gentle 7 pacific, subdued 8 moderate, pleasant, tranquil 9 temperate
lily: 5 plant 6 flower
zephyr ___: 4 lily, yarn 5 cloth 7 worsted
Zephyr: 3 car 4 auto 7 Lincoln, Mercury
mother: 3 Eos
Zephyrinus: 4 pope 7 pontiff
zeppelin: 5 blimp, craft 7 balloon 8 aircraft 9 dirigible
like a ~: 3 LTA 5 rigid
Zeppelin (1971 film)
cast: Elke Sommer, Michael York
___ Zeppelin: 3 Led 4 Graf
Zeppo: 4 Marx
brother: 5 Chico, Gummo, Harpo 7 Groucho
Zerah, grandfather of: 4 Esau
Zerbe: 7 Anthony
Zeresh, husband of: 5 Haman
Zermatt locale: 4 Alps
Zernike, Frits: 8 Nobelist 9 physicist
zero: 3 nil, nix, zip 4 love, meek, nada, nary, none, null, void 5 aught, blank, nadir, ought, zilch 6 bubkes, bupkis, cipher, naught, nobody, nought 7 nothing, nullity, scratch, shutout 8 goose egg, lifeless, nihility 9 nonentity 10 lackluster, rock bottom
below ~: 4 cold 6 frigid
chance: 3 nah 4 nope, uh-uh 5 never, no how 8 forget it
ground ~: 4 goal 5 focus 6 target 8 bull's-eye 9 objective
hour: 4 D-day 6 crisis 7 due date 8 deadline, exigence, exigency, juncture 9 countdown, crossroad, emergency
in: 3 aim, set 5 focus, point, train 6 fixate
in on: 5 level 6 locate 7 pin down 8 pinpoint
in tennis: 4 love
less than ~: 3 neg. 8 negative
letters above ~: 4 oper
like ~: 4 oval 5 ovate, ovoid, round 7 rounded 8 elliptic 9 egg-shaped 10 elliptical
longitude setting: 3 GMT
more than ~: 3 pos. 8 positive
put back to ~: 5 reset
through nine: 5 digit
visibility ~: 3 fog 4 haze, mist, smog
zero ___: 4 hour, in on 6 vector 7 defects, gravity, tillage
zero-___: 4 base 7 divisor
zero-___ bond: 6 coupon

zero-__ budgeting: **4** base
zero-__ game: **3** sum
__ zero: **6** ground **7** ceiling
__-zero: **3** sub **5** aleph
Zero: **5** plane **6** Mostel **8** airplane
zero-dimensional object: **5** point
Zero Effect (1998 film)
  cast: Ryan O'Neal, Bill Pullman, Ben Stiller
  director: Jake Kasdan
zero-emission __: **7** vehicle
zero population __: **6** growth
zero-star: **3** bad **4** poor **5** awful
  movie: **3** dud **4** bomb, flop **6** turkey
zest: **3** pep, vim, zap, zip **4** bite, body, brio, élan, jazz, kick, life, peel, salt, snap, tang, zeal, zing **5** ardor, charm, cheer, gusto, liven, moxie, oomph, punch, savor, spark, spice, taste, verve **6** bounce, energy, fervor, flavor, ginger, pizazz, relish, spirit **7** delight, elation, passion **8** appetite, interest, keenness, piquancy, pleasure, pungency, vitality **9** animation, eagerness, enjoyment, flavoring, seasoning, tanginess **10** ebullience, enthusiasm, exuberance, get-up-and-go, heartiness, liveliness
  add ~ to: **5** liven, pep up **6** excite, perk up, spur on, stir up, vivify **7** animate **8** energize, vitalize **10** exhilarate, invigorate
  source: **4** peel, rind **6** citrus
Zest: **4** soap
  alternative: **3** Lux **4** Dial, Dove, Lava, Tone **5** Camay, Coast, Ivory, Lever **6** Boraxo, Caress, Shield **8** Lifebuoy **9** Palmolive, Safeguard **11** Irish Spring
Zesta: **7** cracker, saltine
  alternative: **4** Ritz **6** Krispy **7** Cheez-It, Premium **8** Triscuit **10** Cheese Nips, Wheat Thins
Zest for Life author: Emile Zola
zestful: **4** racy **5** alive, eager, jazzy, kicky, peppy, spicy, tasty, vital **6** feisty, frisky, lively, spicey **7** peppery, piquant, pungent **8** animated, exciting, vigorous **9** ebullient, energetic, exuberant, vivacious **10** inspirited
zestless: **5** stale, vapid **6** boring
zesty: **3** hot **5** jazzy, peppy, spicy, tangy, tasty **6** frisky, red-hot, spicey **7** piquant, pungent, vibrant **8** spirited **9** energetic, flavorful, vivacious, with a kick
zeta: **5** Greek **6** letter
  follower: **3** eta
  preceder: **7** epsilon
Zeta-Jones, Catherine: **7** actress
  film: America's Sweethearts (2001)
    Chicago (2002, AA)
    Entrapment (1999)
    The Mask of Zorro (1998)
    Traffic (2000)
  spouse: Michael Douglas
Zetterling: **3** Mai
Zeus: **3** god **8** Olympian
  attendant of ~: **3** Bia
  brother of ~: **5** Hades **8** Poseidon
  changed her into a spring: **4** Aura
  daughter-in-law of ~: **5** Niobe
  daughter of ~: **3** Ate **4** Clio, Eris, Hebe, Muse **5** Erato, Grace, Helen, Irene **6** Athena, Athene, Pandia, Thalia, Urania **7** Artemis, Astraea, Euterpe **8** Calliope, Harmonia **9** Aphrodite, Melpomene **10** Persephone, Polyhymnia **11** Terpsichore
  epithet of ~: **5** Soter **6** Nemean **7** Cenaean, Clarius, Ctesius, Lycaeus, Patrous, Phyxius, Polieus, Teleius **8** Aphesius, Cappotas, Dodonian, Herceius, Leucaeus, Megistus, Semaleus, Sthenius, Tropaean **9** Croceatas, Hypsistus, Lecheates
  equivalent: **4** Jove **7** Jupiter
  lover of ~: **2** Io **4** Gaea, Leda, Leto, Maia **5** Danae, Dione, Elare, Lamia, Niobe, Thyia **6** Aegina, Antope, Boetis, Calyce, Europa, Hybris, Othris, Pyrrha, Selene, Semele, Themis **7** Alcmena, Asteria, Demeter, Electra, Himalia, Nemesis, Pandora, Taygete **8** Callisto, Eurynome, Lysithoe **9** Mnemosyne **10** Cassiopeia, Eurymedusa, Persephone, Protogenia
  mount where ~ was worshiped: **3** Ida
  Norse ~: **4** Odin **5** Othin
  parent of ~: **4** Rhea **6** Cronos, Cronus, Kronos
  shield: **4** egis **5** aegis
  sister of ~: **4** Hera **6** Hestia **7** Demeter
  son of ~: **3** Pan **4** Ares, Saon **5** Arcas, Argus, Cytus, Lamus, Minos **6** Aeacus, Apollo, Asopus, Castor, Clarus, Hermes, Iasion, Magnes, Pollux, Themon, Tityus, Zethus **7** Aegipan, Aetolus, Amphion, Bacchus, Colaxes, Cronius, Epaphus, Graecus, Latinus, Macedon, Megarus, Perseus, Xanthus, Zagreus **8** Aethlius, Atymnius, Crinacus, Dardanus, Dionysus, Emathion, Endymion, Heracles, Meliteus, Myrmidon, Pelasgus, Sarpedon, Tantalus **9** Corinthus, Pirithous, Spartaeus, Targitaus
  Temple of ~ locale: **5** Nemea
  wife of ~: **4** Hera
Zevon: **6** Warren
Zewail, Ahmed: **7** chemist **8** Nobelist
Zez: **7** Confrey
Zheng He landed here in 1416: **4** Aden
Zhengzhou: **4** city, town
  locale: **5** China, Henan, Honan
Zhivago: **4** Yuri **6** doctor
__ Z. Hobson: **5** Laura
Zhou __: **5** En-lai
Zhukovsky, Vasily: **4** poet **7** Russian
Zia author: **5** O'Dell
zibet: **3** cat **5** civet, felid **6** feline
Ziegfeld: **3** Flo **7** Florenz
Ziegfeld __: **4** Girl **7** Follies
Ziegfeld, Flo
  spouse: Billie Burke, Anna Held
Ziegfeld Follies: **5** revue **6** review
  designer: **4** Erté
Ziegfeld Follies (1946 film)
  cast: Fred Astaire, Lucille Ball, Fanny Brice, Judy Garland, Lena Horne, William Powell, Red Skelton
  director: Vincente Minnelli
Ziegfeld Girl (1941 film)
  cast: Judy Garland, Hedy Lamarr, James Stewart, Lana Turner
__ Ziegfeld, The: **5** Great
Ziegler: **3** Ron **4** Karl
Ziegler, Karl: **7** chemist **8** Nobelist
Ziering: **3** Ian **5** Nikki
zig: **4** dart, turn, veer **5** angle **6** swerve **8** sidestep
  ender: **3** zag
Zigeunerliebe composer: **5** Lehár
ziggurat: **5** tower
Ziggy: **4** toon **5** comic, Elman **6** Marley
  cat: **3** Sid
  creator: **6** Wilson
  dog: **4** Fuzz
  duck: **4** Wack
  fish: **6** Goldie
  parrot: **4** Josh
zigzag: **4** awry, bent, tack, turn, wind **5** askew, bowed, forky, snaky, twist, weave **6** forked, jagged, ramble, wiggle **7** angular, crooked, devious, erratic, meander, oblique, sinuous, snaking, stagger, twisted, winding **8** angulose, angulous, cockeyed, diagonal, indirect, rambling, serrated, tortuous, twisting, waggling **9** interlace, irregular, unaligned **10** meandering, nonuniform, transverse, undulating
  cut in a ~: **4** pink
zil: **6** cymbal **10** percussion
  origin: **5** Egypt
Zil: **3** car **4** auto **7** Russian **10** automobile
zilch: **3** nil, nix, zip **4** nada, none, zero **5** squat, zippo **6** cipher, cypher, naught, nought **7** nothing **8** goose egg
  in Spanish: **4** nada
  in tennis: **4** love
zillions: **4** a lot, many **5** scads **6** oceans
  of: **6** divers, myriad, umteen, untold **7** copious, profuse, umpteen **8** abundant, manifold, numerous, umpsteen **9** bountiful, countless, quite a few
Zilpah, son of: **3** Gad **5** Asher
Zima maker: **5** Coors
Zimapán: **4** city, town
  locale: **6** Mexico **7** Hidalgo
Zimbabwe: **6** nation **7** country
  bovine: **4** Tuli **7** Mashona
  capital: **6** Harare
  city: **5** Gweru **6** Harare, Kadoma, Kwekwe, Mutare
  grassland: **4** veld **5** veldt
  lake: **6** Kariba
  language: **7** Ndebele
  money: **4** cent **6** dollar
  neighbor: **6** Zambia **8** Botswana **10** Mozambique
  once: **4** Rhod. **8** Rhodesia
  people: **5** Shona **7** Mashona, Ndebele **8** Matabele
  waterfall: **8** Victoria
Zimbalist, Efrem: **5** actor **7** Russian **9** violinist
  spouse: Alma Gluck
  teacher: **4** Auer
Zimbalist Jr., Efrem: **5** actor
  daughter: **9** Stephanie
  TV: The FBI, 77 Sunset Strip
Zimmer: **3** Don
Zina: **7** Bethune
zinc: **5** metal **7** element **9** galvanize
  alloy: **5** brass **6** latten, oreide, ormolu, oroide, tambac, tombac **8** calamine, gunmetal **9** Dutch foil, Dutch gold, Dutch leaf, pinchbeck, platinoid, white gold **10** Dutch metal, gold bronze, mosaic gold
  ore: **6** blende **7** zincite **9** willemite **10** sphalerite
zinc __: **5** green, oxide, white **6** blende **7** sulfate, sulfide
zincite: **3** ore **7** mineral
Zinder: **4** city, town
  locale: **5** Niger
zine: **3** mag **4** E-mag
zinfandel: **3** red **4** wine **5** grape **6** claret
  like ~: **3** dry
  relative: **5** Gamay, pinot, Tokay **6** Merlot **7** Catawba, Concord, Niagara **8** Cabernet, malvasia, muscatel **9** muscadine, Sauvignon **10** Chardonnay
zing: **3** pep, vim, zip **4** brio, dash, élan, fire, hurt, kick, life, slur, zest **5** abuse, ardor, gusto, oomph, spark, taste, verve, vigor **6** energy, esprit, flavor, impugn, insult, offend **7** lambast, potence, potency, put down **8** lambaste, vitality **9** animation, criticize, eagerness, excoriate **10** enthusiasm, exuberance, get-up-and-go
  add ~ to: **5** spice **6** flavor, pepper
Zing a __ Zong: **6** Little
zinger: **3** mot **4** barb, quip, slur **6** ripost **7** offense, riposte **9** witticism
zingy: **4** cool, tart **8** animated, spirited **9** exuberant, sprightly **10** full of life
Zinkernagel, Rolf: **8** Nobelist **9** biologist
Zinnemann, Fred: **8** director
  film: Act of Violence (1949)
    The Day of the Jackal (1973)
    From Here to Eternity (1953, AA)
    A Hatful of Rain (1957)
    High Noon (1952)
    Julia (1977)
    Kid Glove Killer (1942)
    A Man for All Seasons (1966, AA)
    The Member of the Wedding (1952)
    The Men (1950)
    The Nun's Story (1959)
    Oklahoma! (1955)
    The Search (1948)
    The Seventh Cross (1944)
    The Sundowners (1960)
zinnia: **5** plant **6** annual, flower
Zion: **4** city, park, town **6** Israel **8** Holy Land
  locale: **4** Utah **8** Illinois
Zion National Park
  location: **4** Utah
  sight: **5** cañon **6** canyon
zip: **2** go **3** fly, hie, nil, pep, rip, run, vim **4** bite, brio, dart, dash, élan, fire, flit, life, nada, none, race, rush, tang, tear, whiz, zero, zest, zing, zoom **5** drive, flair, gusto, hurry, oomph, punch, scoot, spank, speed, spice, squat, taste, verve, vigor, whisk, zilch **6** barrel, bounce, bustle, cipher, energy, fasten, gallop, hasten, hustle, move it, naught, nought, pizazz, relish, rocket, scurry, spirit **7** floor it, hop to it, nothing, pizzazz, potence, potency, quicken, scamper, sparkle, stamina **8** goose egg, hightail, step on it, strength, vitality, vivacity **9** animation, hotfoot it, make haste, shake a leg, skedaddle **10** ebullience, enthusiasm, exuberance, get a move on, get hopping, get up and go, hightail it, liveliness
  add ~ to: **5** liven **6** flavor **7** enliven
  by: **2** go **3** fly **4** tear **5** whish
  over the surface: **4** skim **5** skate
  through: **8** look over
  (through): **6** breeze
  up: **5** close **6** fasten
zip __: **3** gun **4** code
Zip-__-Doo-Dah: **4** a-Dee
Zip Drive maker: **6** Iomega
ZIP+4 org.: **4** USPS
Zip it!: **5** quiet, shush **6** shut up
Ziploc: **3** bag
  alternative: **4** Glad **5** Hefty **8** Reynolds **9** Saran Wrap
zipper: **3** tie **8** fastener
  cover: **3** fly
zippo: **3** nil **4** nada **5** zilch **6** bubkes, bupkis **7** nothing **8** goose egg
Zippo, part of a: **4** wick
Zipporah
  husband of ~: **5** Moses
  son of ~: **7** Eliezer, Gershom
zippy: **4** go-go, spry **5** brisk, jazzy, peppy, spicy, tangy **6** frisky, lively, spicey **7** dynamic, hyped-up, vibrant **8** animated, spirited, vigorous **9** ebullient, energetic, exuberant, sprightly
zircon: **3** gem **6** ligure **7** mineral **8** gemstone

__ zirconia: 5 cubic
zirconium: 5 metal 7 element
zit: 6 pimple 7 blemish
Zitácuaro: 4 city, town
 locale: 6 Mexico 9 Michoacán
zither: 4 ch'in, koto, mvet, vina 5 fidla, qanun, veena 6 chakay, string, valiha 8 autoharp, dulcimer, psaltery, yang chin 10 instrument
 forerunner: 4 asor
 geisha's ~: 4 koto
 play the ~: 5 strum
ziti: 5 pasta 7 noodles 8 macaroni 9 maccaroni
 alternative: 4 orzo 5 penne 7 lasagna, lasagne, pastina, ravioli 8 bucatini, couscous, farfalle, linguine, linguini, rigatoni 9 agnolotti, angelhair, cavatelli, manicotti, spaghetti 10 cannelloni, fettuccini, tortellini, vermicelli
__ ziti: 5 baked
zloty: 4 coin 5 money 8 currency
 fraction: 5 grosz
 locale: 6 Poland
Zmed: 6 Adrian
Zn: 4 elem., zinc 7 element
 30 for ~: 4 at. no.
Zobeide sculptor: 4 Erté
zobo: 4 wind 5 gazoo, kazoo 8 mirliton
zodiac: 4 belt 5 chart
 animal: 3 ram 4 bull, crab, fish, goat, lion 8 scorpion
 boundary: 4 cusp
 Chinese ~ animal: 2 ox 3 dog, pig, rat 4 goat, hare 5 horse, sheep, snake, tiger 6 dragon, monkey, rabbit 7 rooster
 division: 5 house
zodiac signs:
 Aquarius - Water Bearer (Jan.-Feb.)
 Aries - Ram (Mar.-Apr.)
 Cancer - Crab (Jun.-Jul.)
 Capricorn - Goat (Dec.-Jan.)
 Gemini - Twins (May-Jun.)
 Leo - Lion (Jul.-Aug.)
 Libra - Scales (Sep.-Oct.)
 Pisces - Fish (Feb.-Mar.)
 Sagittarius - Archer (Nov.-Dec.)
 Scorpio - Scorpion (Oct.-Nov.)
 Taurus - Bull (Apr.-May)
 Virgo - Maiden (Aug.-Sep.)
Zoe: 8 Caldwell
Zoë: 5 Akins
zoea: 5 larva
Zoeller, Fuzzy: 6 golfer
 milieu: 5 links 6 course
 org.: 3 PGA
Zoilus: 5 Greek 6 writer 11 rhetorician
zoisite: 3 gem 7 mineral 8 gemstone
 transparent ~ gem: 9 tanzanite
Zola, Émile: 6 French, writer
 portraitist: 5 Manet
 portrayer: 4 Muni
 work: Albine
  Argent
  Assommoir
  Belly of Pairs
  Debacle
  Doctor Pascal
  The Dram Shop
  Dream
  Earth
  The Experimental Novel
  Germinal
  Hélène
  The Human Beast
  J'Accuse
  Joie de Vivre
  La Bête Humaine
  Labor
  La Confession de Claude
  La Curée
  The Ladies' Delight
  La Fortune des Rougons
  The Land of Darkness
  Les Rougon-Macquart
  Les Trois Villes
  Lourdes
  Madeleine Férat
  Money
  Mysteries of Marseilles
  Nana
  Pot Luck
  Quatre Evangiles
  Rêve
  Savage Paris
  Sin of Father Mouret
  Soirées de Médan
  Terre
  Thérèse Raquin
  Travail
  Truth
  Two Dutchesses
  Venus of the Counting House
  Zest for Life
Zoltán: 5 Korda 6 Kodály
zombie: 5 booze, drink 6 liquor 7 alcohol, machine, potable 8 beverage, cocktail, libation, potation 10 intoxicant
 ingredient: 3 rum 10 fruit juice
 like a ~: 6 undead
Zombie author: 5 Oates
Zombies
 song: She's Not There (1964)
  Tell Her No (1965)
  Time of the Season (1969)
Zona: 4 Gale
zonda: 4 wind
zone: 4 area, band, belt, ward 5 bourn, level, place, realm, space, tract 6 ground, locale, region, sector, sphere 7 circuit, quarter, section, segment 8 district, locality, precinct, province 9 territory
 combat ~: 5 arena, front
 demilitarized ~: 5 limbo 6 buffer
 hurricane ~: 9 shoreline
 meteorological ~: 5 clime
 time ~ abbr.: 3 AST, CDT, CST, EDT, EST, GMT, MDT, MST, PDT, PST
zone __: 4 line, time 5 plate 6 system 7 defense, melting
__ zone: 3 end, war 4 drop, free, rift, time 5 fault, in the, no-fly, shear 6 buffer, combat, impact, photic, strike 7 auroral, Benioff, comfort, neutral, support, tow-away
__ Zone: 3 End 4 Love 5 Canal 6 Arctic, Danger, Frigid, Torrid 9 Temperate
zoning unit: 4 acre
zonk: 7 stupefy 8 knock out
 out: 3 nod 4 doze 5 crash, sleep 6 drowse, nod off, snooze, turn in 7 drop off 9 hit the hay 10 hit the sack
zonked: 5 weary 9 insensate 10 insentient, knocked out
 out: 6 asleep, dozing 7 napping 8 sleeping, snoozing 9 somnolent 10 slumbering
zoo: 9 mare's nest, menagerie 10 animal park, safari park
 barrier: 4 moat
 enclosure: 4 cage 6 aviary
 ender: 6 keeper
 petting ~ beast: 4 deer, goat 5 sheep
 resident: 3 ape, bat, boa, emu, gnu 4 bear, emeu, lion, seal 5 chimp, hippo, koala, llama, macaw, orang, panda, rhino, snake, tiger, zebra 6 animal, monkey, ocelot, toucan 7 cheetah, giraffe 8 elephant
 sound: 4 roar
 staffer: 3 DVM, vet 6 keeper
__ zoo: 7 petting
zoography: 7 science
Zoo in Budapest director: 3 Lee
Zoolander (2001 film)
 cast: Ben Stiller, Christine Taylor, Owen Wilson
 director: Ben Stiller
zoological __: 6 garden
zoology: 7 science
 band of color, in ~: 5 vitta
 branch of ~: 9 zoography 10 entomology 11 herpetology, ichthyology, ornithology
 classification: 6 family
 foot: 3 pes
 stripe: 5 vitta
 study: 5 fauna 7 animals
 suffix: 4 -acea 5 -oidea
zoom: 3 fly, hie, hum, jet, rip, run, zip 4 buzz, dart, dash, dive, flit, lens, race, rush, tear, whiz 5 flash, mount, scoot, shoot, spank, speed, surge, sweep, whirl 6 barrel, gallop, hasten, hurtle, hustle, move it, rocket, scurry, streak 7 floor it, hop to it, quicken, scamper, shoot up 8 hightail, outstrip, pour it on, step on it 9 hotfoot it, shake a leg, skedaddle, skyrocket 10 get a move on, go pell-mell, hightail it
 in: 3 pan 5 focus
zoom __: 4 lens, shot
zoophilist org.: 4 SPCA
zoophobe fear: 7 animals
Zoo Story, The author: Edward Albee
zoot __: 4 suit
Zoot: 4 Sims
Zora __ Hurston: 5 Neale
Zorba the Greek: 4 film 5 novel
 author: Nikos Kazantzakis
 cast: Alan Bates, Lila Kedrova, Irene Papas, Anthony Quinn
 setting: 5 Crete
Zorilla y Moral, José: 6 writer 7 Spanish
 work: Don Juan Tenorio
Zorina: 4 Vera
Zorn's __: 5 lemma
Zoroastrian Bible: 4 Zend 6 Avesta
Zoroastrian king: 4 Yima
Zorro
 portrayer: 8 Banderas, Hamilton, Williams
 wear: 4 cape, mask
 see also Spanish
Zoshchenko, Mikhail: 6 writer 7 Russian
Zosimus: 4 pope 7 pontiff
Zosma: 4 star
zounds: 4 egad, oath 5 egads 6 my word 8 gadzooks
zowie: 3 wow 5 oh boy
zoysia: 5 grass
Zr: 4 elem. 7 element 9 zirconium
 40 for ~: 4 at. no.
z's: 3 nap 5 sleep 6 catnap, snooze
 grab some ~: 3 nap 4 doze, rest 5 sleep, snore 6 catnap, drowse, nod off, snooze, turn in 7 drop off, slumber
Zsa Zsa: 5 Gabor
 mother: 5 Jolie
 real name: 4 Sari
 secret: 3 age
 sister: 3 Eva 5 Magda
Zsigmondy, Richard: 7 chemist 8 Nobelist
Z-28: 3 car 4 auto 6 Camaro 10 automobile
Zubin: 5 Mehta
zucchetto: 3 cap
zucchini: 6 veggie 9 vegetable
Zucker: 5 David, Jerry
Zucker, Jerry: 8 director
 film: Airplane! (1980)
  First Knight (1995)
  Ghost (1990)
  Rat Race (2001)
  Ruthless People (1986)
Zuckerman Bound author: 4 Roth
Zuckerman Unbound author: 4 Roth
Zuckmayer, Carl: 6 German 10 playwright
 work: The Devil's General
Zug: 4 lake
 locale: Switzerland
Zuider Zee: 4 lake
 locale: 7 Holland 11 Netherlands
 sight: 4 dike
Zukerman, Pinchas: 7 Israeli 9 violinist
 spouse: Tuesday Weld
Zukofsky, Louis: 6 writer
Zukor: 6 Adolph
Zulu: 5 Bantu 8 language
 council: 6 indaba
 ender: 4 land
 home: 5 Natal
Zulu (1964 film)
 cast: Michael Caine, Jack Hawkins
Zulu Dawn (1979 film)
 cast: Burt Lancaster, Peter O'Toole
Zumpango: 4 city, town
 locale: 6 Mexico 8 Guerrero
Zumwalt: 4 Elmo 7 admiral
Zuni: 5 tribe 6 Indian 7 Amerind 8 language
Zuniga: 6 Daphne
Zupo: 4 peak 5 mount 8 mountain
 locale: 4 Alps 6 Europe 11 Switzerland
zuppa __: 7 di pesce, inglese
Zurich: 4 city, font, lake, town 8 typeface
 banker: 5 gnome
 city SW of ~: 4 Bern 5 Berne
 locale: 11 Switzerland
 peak: 3 alp
 river: 4 Sihl 6 Limmat
zwei: 3 two 6 German
 cubed: 4 acht
 follower: 4 drei
 preceder: 4 eins
 squared: 4 vier
 x drei: 5 sechs
Zweig: 6 Arnold, Stefan
Zweig, Arnold: 6 German, writer
 work: The Case of Sergeant Grischa
Zweig, Stefan: 6 writer 8 Austrian
Zwick: 4 Joel 6 Edward
Zwick, Edward: 8 director
 film: About Last Night ... (1986)
  Courage Under Fire (1996)
  Glory (1989)
  The Siege (1998)
zwieback: 4 rusk 5 bread 7 biscuit
Zworykin: 8 Vladimir
zygoma: 4 bone
 locale: 5 skull 7 cranium 9 braincase
zygomatic: 4 bone 5 malar
 locale: 5 skull 7 cranium 9 braincase
zygomatic __: 4 arch, bone 7 process
zygote component: 6 gamete
zymology: 7 science
 study: 7 enzymes
zymurgy: 7 science
ZZ Top
 members: Gibbons, Hill, Beard
 song: Legs (1984)
  Sleeping Bag (1985)
  Tush (1975)
  Velcro Fly (1986)
zzz: 5 sleep, snore